# NELSON'S FOUNDATIONAL BIBLE CONCORDANCE

King James Version

THOMAS NELSON
*Since 1798*

NASHVILLE DALLAS MEXICO CITY RIO DE JANEIRO

Published in Nashville, Tennessee, by Thomas Nelson. Thomas Nelson is a registered trademark of HarperCollins Christian Publishing, Inc.

Thomas Nelson titles may be purchased in bulk for educational, business, fund-raising, or sales promotional use. For information, please e-mail SpecialMarkets@ThomasNelson.com.



ISBN 978-0-5291-0631-5

Previously published as *World's Concise Bible Concordance*, ISBN 0-5291-1903-X

*Printed in the United States of America*

14 15 16 17 18 RRD 5 4 3 2 1

# PREFACE

While no concordance to the Bible lists a Scripture quotation for every use of every word in the Bible, all concordances use various methods to balance the need for both portability and completeness. In creating **Nelson's Foundational Bible Concordance** a method was developed to include the most likely places for the user to find every verse in Scripture.

Like all other concordances, the most common of words are not indexed in the body of the concordance. Words that are not distinctive or have such a vast number of occurrences as to not be useful have not been listed. Examples of such words are prepositions and extremely common modifiers. The second occurrence within a verse may be omitted in certain words that have vast numbers of entries.

The principle is to retain references to the more distinctive words within a given verse and to omit those that are obviously so common as to not be an aid in finding the passage. By removing the clutter of those entries that do not readily point to a particular reference or repeated references within a verse, we have made it quicker to find Scripture passages.

In most cases proper nouns have a suggested pronunciation shown along with a definition.

**HARARITE** (*har´-a-rite*) *Native of the hill country of Judah.*

At times there are a variety of pronunciations for a given word or there is some debate over its exact meaning. The most common has been selected. Where there are multiple people or places indicated, the references are divided to indicate which occurrence references a particular individual or place.

**HARAN** (*ha'-ran*) See Beth-Haran, Charran.
*1. A son of Terah*
Gen 11:26 and begat Abram, Nahor, and *H*
*2. A Levite*
1Chr 23:9 Shelomith, and Haziel, and *H*
*3. A son of Caleb*
1Chr 2:46 Ephah, Caleb's concubine, bare *H*
*4. A city in northern Mesopotamia*
Gen 11:31 and they came unto *H*, and dwelt

Several guiding principles have been kept in mind in preparing **Nelson's Foundational Bible Concordance**: immediacy, simplicity, thoroughness, and accuracy. The user will be able to find every passage of Scripture quickly and with ease. The most helpful tools have been included to help in pronunciation, distinguishing multiple persons or places, and to understand actual meaning.

# ABBREVIATIONS

## Old Testament

Gen ........................Genesis
Ex ........................Exodus
Lev ........................Leviticus
Num ......................Numbers
Deut ......................Deuteronomy
Josh ......................Joshua
Judg ......................Judges
Ruth ......................Ruth
1Sa ........................1 Samuel
2Sa ........................2 Samuel
1Kin ......................1 Kings
2Kin ......................2 Kings
1Chr ......................1 Chronicles
2Chr ......................2 Chronicles
Ezr ........................Ezra
Neh ........................Nehemiah
Est ........................Esther
Job ........................Job
Ps..........................Psalms
Prov ......................Proverbs
Eccl........................Ecclesiastes
Song ......................Song of Solomon
Is ..........................Isaiah
Jer ........................Jeremiah
Lam........................Lamentations
Eze ........................Ezekiel
Dan ........................Daniel
Hos ........................Hosea
Joel ........................Joel
Amos ......................Amos
Obad ......................Obadiah
Jonah ......................Jonah
Mic ........................Micah
Nah ........................Nahum
Hab ........................Habakkuk
Zeph ......................Zephaniah
Hag ........................Haggai
Zec ........................Zechariah
Mal ........................Malachi

## New Testament

Mt ........................Matthew
Mk ........................Mark
Lk ........................Luke
Jn..........................John
Acts........................Acts
Rom ......................Romans
1Cor ......................1 Corinthians
2Cor ......................2 Corinthians
Gal ........................Galatians
Eph ........................Ephesians
Phil ........................Philippians
Col ........................Colossians
1Th ........................1 Thessalonians
2Th ........................2 Thessalonians
1Ti ........................1 Timothy
2Ti ........................2 Timothy
Titus ......................Titus
Philem ..................Philemon
Heb ........................Hebrews
Jas ........................James
1Pet........................1 Peter
2Pet........................2 Peter
1Jn ........................1 John
2Jn ........................2 John
3Jn ........................3 John
Jude ......................Jude
Rev ........................Revelation

# MAIN CONCORDANCE

# A

**AARON** *(a'-ur-un)* See AARON'S, AARONITES. *First High Priest of Israel; brother of Moses.*
Ex 4:14 Is not *A* the Levite thy brother
Ex 4:27 And the LORD said to *A*, Go into
Ex 4:30 *A* spake all the words which the
Ex 5:1 *A* went in, and told Pharaoh, Thus
Ex 5:4 them, Wherefore do ye, Moses and *A*
Ex 7:2 *A* thy brother shall speak unto
Ex 7:6 *A* did as the LORD commanded them,
Ex 7:7 *A* fourscore and three years old,
Ex 8:5 LORD spake unto Moses, Say unto *A*
Ex 8:6 *A* stretched out his hand over the
Ex 11:10 *A* did all these wonders before
Ex 15:20 the prophetess, the sister of *A*
Ex 16:2 Moses and *A* in the wilderness
Ex 16:6 *A* said unto all the children of
Ex 17:12 and *A* and Hur stayed up his hands,
Ex 28:35 And it shall be upon *A* to minister
Ex 28:38 that *A* may bear the iniquity of
Ex 29:20 the tip of the right ear of *A*
Ex 29:32 And *A* and his sons shall eat the
Ex 32:35 they made the calf, which *A* made
Ex 34:30 And when *A* and all the children of
Lev 8:6 And Moses brought *A* and his sons,
Lev 8:14 and *A* and his sons laid their hands
Lev 8:30 the altar, and sprinkled it upon *A*
Lev 8:30 and sanctified *A*, and his garments,
Lev 10:1 And Nadab and Abihu, the sons of *A*
Lev 10:4 the sons of Uzziel the uncle of *A*
Lev 16:1 the death of the two sons of *A*
Lev 16:6 *A* shall offer his bullock of the
Lev 16:8 *A* shall cast lots upon the two
Lev 22:4 of the seed of *A* is a leper
Lev 22:18 Speak unto *A*, and to his sons, and
Num 3:1 also are the generations of *A*
Num 4:16 office of Eleazar the son of *A*
Num 6:23 Speak unto *A* and unto his sons,
Num 7:8 Ithamar the son of *A* the priest
Num 8:21 *A* made an atonement for them to
Num 8:22 of the congregation before *A*
Num 12:10 *A* looked upon Miriam, and, behold,
Num 12:11 *A* said unto Moses, Alas, my lord,
Num 13:26 went and came to Moses, and to *A*
Num 14:2 against Moses and against *A*
Num 14:5 *A* fell on their faces before all
Num 20:24 *A* shall be gathered unto his
Num 20:25 Take *A* and Eleazar his son, and
Num 20:26 strip *A* of his garments, and put
Num 20:28 *A* died there in the top of the
Num 20:29 congregation saw that *A* was dead
Num 20:29 they mourned for *A* thirty days
Num 33:39 *A* was an hundred and twenty and
Josh 21:19 the cities of the children of *A*
1Chr 6:50 And these are the sons of *A*
Ps 115:12 he will bless the house of *A*
Ps 118:3 Let the house of *A* now say
Ps 135:19 bless the LORD, O house of *A*
Mic 6:4 and I sent before thee Moses, *A*
Lk 1:5 wife was of the daughters of *A*
Acts 7:40 Saying unto *A*, Make us gods to go
Heb 5:4 that is called of God, as was *A*
Heb 7:11 be called after the order of *A*

**AARONITES** *(a'-ur-un-ites) Priests; Aaron's descendants.*
1Chr 12:27 Jehoiada was the leader of the *A*
1Chr 27:17 of the *A*, Zadok

**ABADDON** *(ab-ad'-dun) Angel of the Abyss.*
Rev 9:11 name in the Hebrew tongue is *A*

**ABAGTHA** *(ab-ag'-thah) Servant of King Ahaseurus.*
Est 1:10 Biztha, Harbona, Bigtha, and *A*

**ABANA** *(ab-ay'-nah) A river in Syria.*
2Kin 5:12 Are not *A* and Pharpar, rivers of

**ABARIM** *(ab'-ar-im)* See IJE-ABARIM. *A mountain range in Moab.*
Num 27:12 Get thee up into this mount *A*
Num 33:47 and pitched in the mountains of *A*
Num 33:48 departed from the mountains of *A*
Deut 32:49 Get thee up into this mountain *A*

**ABASE**
Job 40:11 every one that is proud, and *a* him
Is 31:4 nor *a* himself for the noise of
Eze 21:26 is low, and *a* him that is high
Dan 4:37 walk in pride he is able to *a*

**ABASED**
Mt 23:12 shall exalt himself shall be *a*
Lk 14:11 exalteth himself shall be *a*
Lk 18:14 that exalteth himself shall be *a*
Phil 4:12 I know both how to be *a*, and I

**ABASING**
2Cor 11:7 Have I committed an offence in *a*

**ABATED**
Gen 8:3 and fifty days the waters were *a*
Gen 8:8 to see if the waters were *a* from
Gen 8:11 waters were *a* from off the earth
Lev 27:18 it shall be *a* from thy estimation
Deut 34:7 not dim, nor his natural force *a*
Judg 8:3 Then their anger was *a* toward him

**ABBA** *(ab'-bah) Aramaic for "Father."*
Mk 14:36 And he said, *A*, Father, all things
Rom 8:15 of adoption, whereby we cry, *A*
Gal 4:6 Son into your hearts, crying, *A*

**ABDA** *(ab'-dah)*
*1. Father of Adoniram.*
1Kin 4:6 Adoniram the son of *A* was over
*2. A chief Levite after the exile.*
Neh 11:17 *A* the son of Shammua, the son of

**ABDEEL** *(ab'-de-el) Father of Shelemiah.*
Jer 36:26 Azriel, and Shelemiah the son of *A*

**ABDI** *(ab'-di)*
*1. Levite grandfather of Ethan.*
1Chr 6:44 the son of Kishi, the son of *A*
2Chr 29:12 sons of Merari, Kish the son of *A*
*2. Married a foreigner while in exile.*
Ezr 10:26 Zechariah, and Jehiel, and *A*

**ABDIEL** *(ab'-de-el) Son of Guni.*
1Chr 5:15 Ahi the son of *A*, the son of Guni

**ABDON** *(ab'-dun)*
*1. Levitical city in Asher.*
Josh 21:30 her suburbs, *A* with her suburbs,
1Chr 6:74 suburbs, and *A* with her suburbs,
*2. A judge of Israel.*
Judg 12:13 after him *A* the son of Hillel, a
Judg 12:15 And *A* the son of Hillel the
*3. A Benjamite in Jerusalem.*
1Chr 8:23 And *A*, and Zichri, and Hanan,
*4. Son of Jehiel.*
1Chr 8:30 And his firstborn son *A*, and Zur,
1Chr 9:36 And his firstborn son *A*, then Zur,
*5. Son of Micah.*
2Chr 34:20 *A* the son of Micah, and Shaphan

**ABED-NEGO** *(ab-ed'-ne-go) A companion of Daniel in captivity.*
Dan 1:7 and to Azariah, of *A*
Dan 2:49 and he set Shadrach, Meshach, and *A*
Dan 3:12 Babylon, Shadrach, Meshach, and *A*
Dan 3:16 Shadrach, Meshach, and *A*, answered
Dan 3:20 to bind Shadrach, Meshach, and *A*
Dan 3:26 Then Shadrach, Meshach, and *A*

**ABEL** *(a'-bel)*
*1. Second son of Adam.*
Gen 4:2 And she again bare his brother *A*
Gen 4:4 And the LORD had respect unto *A*
Gen 4:8 And Cain talked with *A* his brother
Gen 4:9 unto Cain, Where is *A* thy brother
Gen 4:25 me another seed instead of *A*
Mt 23:35 from the blood of righteous *A*
Lk 11:51 From the blood of *A* unto the
Heb 11:4 By faith *A* offered unto God a
Heb 12:24 better things than that of *A*
*2. Great stone near Beth-shemesh.*
1Sa 6:18 even unto the great stone of *A*
*3. A city in Naphtali.*
2Sa 20:14 all the tribes of Israel unto *A*
2Sa 20:15 besieged him in *A* of Beth-maachah
2Sa 20:18 shall surely ask counsel at *A*

**ABEL ACACIA GROVE** See ABEL-SHITTIM.

**ABEL-BETH-MAACHAH** *(a'-bel-beth-ma'-a-kah) A city in northern Israel.*
1Kin 15:20 and smote Ijon, and Dan, and *A*
2Kin 15:29 of Assyria, and took Ijon, and *A*

**ABEL-MAIM** *(a'-bel-ma'-im) Another name for Abel-beth-maachah.*
2Chr 16:4 and they smote Ijon, and Dan, and *A*

**ABEL-MEHOLAH** *(a'-bel-me-ho'-lah) A city in Issachar.*
Judg 7:22 Zererath, and to the border of *A*
1Kin 4:12 Jezreel, from Beth-shean to *A*
1Kin 19:16 Elisha the son of Shaphat of *A*

**ABEL-MIZRAIM** *(a'-bel-miz'-ra-im) A place east of the Jordan River.*
Gen 50:11 the name of it was called *A*

**ABEL-SHITTIM** *(a'-bel-shit'-tim) A place in Moab.*
Num 33:49 even unto *A* in the plains of Moab

**ABEZ** *(a'-bez) A place in Issachar.*
Josh 19:20 And Rabbith, and Kishion, and *A*

**ABHOR**
Lev 26:11 and my soul shall not *a* you
Lev 26:15 or if your soul *a* my judgments
Lev 26:30 idols, and my soul shall *a* you
Lev 26:44 them away, neither will I *a* them
Deut 7:26 it, and thou shalt utterly *a* it
Deut 23:7 Thou shalt not *a* an Edomite
1Sa 27:12 people Israel utterly to *a* him
Job 9:31 and mine own clothes shall *a* me
Job 30:10 They *a* me, they flee far from me,
Job 42:6 Wherefore I *a* myself, and repent
Ps 5:6 the LORD will *a* the bloody
Ps 119:163 I hate and *a* lying
Prov 24:24 people curse, nations shall *a* him
Jer 14:21 Do not *a* us, for thy name's sake,
Amos 5:10 gate, and they *a* him that speaketh
Amos 6:8 I *a* the excellency of Jacob, and
Mic 3:9 that *a* judgment, and pervert all
Rom 12:9 *A* that which is evil

**ABHORRED**
Ex 5:21 to be *a* in the eyes of Pharaoh
Lev 20:23 things, and therefore I *a* them
Lev 26:43 because their soul *a* my statutes
Deut 32:19 he *a* them, because of the
1Sa 2:17 for men *a* the offering of the
2Sa 16:21 that thou art *a* of thy father
1Kin 11:25 he *a* Israel, and reigned over
Job 19:19 All my inward friends *a* me
Ps 22:24 For he hath not despised nor *a*
Ps 78:59 he was wroth, and greatly *a* Israel
Ps 89:38 But thou hast cast off and *a*
Ps 106:40 insomuch that he *a* his own
Prov 22:14 he that is *a* of the LORD shall

Lam 2:7 he hath a his sanctuary, he hath
Eze 16:25 and hast made thy beauty to be a
Zec 11:8 them, and their soul also a me

**ABHORREST**
Is 7:16 the land that thou a shall be
Rom 2:22 thou that a idols, dost thou

**ABHORRETH**
Job 33:20 So that his life a bread, and his
Ps 10:3 the covetous, whom the LORD a
Ps 36:4 he a not evil
Ps 107:18 Their soul a all manner of meat
Is 49:7 to him whom the nation a

**ABHORRING**
Is 66:24 they shall be an a unto all flesh

**ABI** *(a'-bi)* See ABI-ABLON, ABI-EZER. *Mother of King Hezekiah.*
2Kin 18:2 His mother's name also was A

**ABIA** *(ab-i'-ah)* See ABIAH, ABIJAH, ABIJAM.
*1. A son of Rehoboam.*
1Chr 3:10 Rehoboam, A his son, Asa his son,
Mt 1:7 and Roboam begat A
*2. A priest.*
Lk 1:5 Zacharias, of the course of A

**ABIAH** *(ab-i'-ah)* See ABIA.
*1. A son of Samuel.*
1Sa 8:2 and the name of his second, A
1Chr 6:28 the firstborn Vashni, and A
*2. Mother of Ashur.*
1Chr 2:24 then A Hezron's wife bare him
*3. Son of Becher.*
1Chr 7:8 and Omri, and Jerimoth, and A

**ABI-ALBON** *(ab'-i-al'-bun) A "mighty man" of David.*
2Sa 23:31 A the Arbathite, Azmaveth the

**ABIASAPH** *(ab-i'-as-af)* See EBIASAPH. *A son of Korah.*
Ex 6:24 Assir, and Elkanah, and A

**ABIATHAR** *(ab-i'-uth-ur)* See ABITHAR'S. *High Priest during David's reign.*
1Sa 22:21 A shewed David that Saul had
1Sa 23:6 when A the son of Ahimelech fled
1Sa 30:7 And David said to A the priest
2Sa 8:17 Ahitub, and Ahimelech the son of A
2Sa 15:24 A went up, until all the people
2Sa 15:27 thy son, and Jonathan the son of A
2Sa 15:29 A carried the ark of God again to
2Sa 20:25 and Zadok and A were the priests
1Kin 1:7 of Zeruiah, and with A the priest
1Kin 1:19 A the priest, and Joab the captain
1Kin 1:25 of the host, and A the priest
1Kin 2:22 for A the priest, and for Joab the
1Kin 2:27 So Solomon thrust out A from
1Kin 4:4 and Zadok and A were the priests
1Chr 15:11 A the priests, and for the Levites
1Chr 18:16 Ahitub, and Abimelech the son of A
1Chr 24:6 priest, and Ahimelech the son of A
1Chr 27:34 Jehoiada the son of Benaiah, and A
Mk 2:26 in the days of A the high priest

**ABIATHAR'S** *(ab-i'-uth-urs)*
2Sa 15:36 Zadok's son, and Jonathan A son

**ABIB** *(a'-bib)* See TEL-ABIB. *First month of the Hebrew year.*
Ex 13:4 day came ye out in the month A
Ex 23:15 the time appointed of the month A
Ex 34:18 thee, in the time of the month A
Deut 16:1 Observe the month of A, and keep

**ABIDA** *(ab'-id-ah)* See ABIDAH. *A son of Midian.*
1Chr 1:33 Ephah, and Epher, and Henoch, and A

**ABIDAH** *(ab'-id-ah)* See ABIDA. *Same as Abida.*
Gen 25:4 Ephah, and Epher, and Hanoch, and A

**ABIDAN** *(ab'-id-an) Son of Gideoni.*
Num 1:11 A the son of Gideoni
Num 2:22 shall be A the son of Gideoni
Num 7:60 On the ninth day A the son of
Num 7:65 offering of A the son of Gideoni
Num 10:24 Benjamin was A the son of Gideoni

**ABIDE**
Gen 19:2 but we will a in the street all
Gen 22:5 young men, A ye here with the ass
Gen 24:55 Let the damsel a with us a few
Gen 29:19 a with me
Gen 44:33 let thy servant a instead of the
Ex 16:29 a ye every man in his place, let
Lev 8:35 Therefore shall ye a at the door
Lev 19:13 a with thee all night until the
Num 22:5 earth, and they a over against me
Num 31:19 do ye a without the camp seven
Num 31:23 Every thing that may a the fire
Num 35:25 he shall a in it unto the death
Deut 3:19 shall a in your cities which I
Josh 18:5 Judah shall a in their coast on
Ruth 2:8 but a here fast by my maidens
1Sa 1:22 the LORD, and there a for ever
1Sa 5:7 God of Israel shall not a with us
1Sa 19:2 a in a secret place, and hide
1Sa 22:5 unto David, A not in the hold
1Sa 22:23 A thou with me, fear not
1Sa 30:21 made also to a at the brook Besor
2Sa 11:11 and Israel, and Judah, a in tents
2Sa 15:19 to thy place, and a with the king
2Sa 16:18 will I be, and with him will I a
1Kin 8:13 place for thee to a in for ever
2Chr 25:19 a now at home
2Chr 32:10 that ye a in the siege in
Job 24:13 nor a in the paths thereof
Job 38:40 a in the covert to lie in wait
Job 39:9 to serve thee, or a by thy crib
Ps 15:1 who shall a in thy tabernacle
Ps 61:4 I will a in thy tabernacle for
Ps 61:7 He shall a before God for ever
Ps 91:1 shall a under the shadow of the
Prov 7:11 her feet a not in her house
Prov 19:23 he that hath it shall a satisfied
Eccl 8:15 for that shall a with him of his
Jer 10:10 not be able to a his indignation
Jer 42:10 If ye will still a in this land
Jer 49:18 the LORD, no man shall a there
Jer 49:33 there shall no man a there
Jer 50:40 so shall no man a there, neither
Hos 3:3 Thou shalt a for me many days
Hos 3:4 shall a many days without a king
Hos 11:6 the sword shall a on his cities
Joel 2:11 and who can a it
Mic 5:4 and they shall a
Nah 1:6 who can a in the fierceness of
Mal 3:2 But who may a the day of his
Mt 10:11 there a till ye go thence
Mk 6:10 there a till ye depart from that
Lk 9:4 house ye enter into, there a
Lk 19:5 for to day I must a at thy house
Lk 24:29 him, saying, A with us
Jn 12:46 on me should not a in darkness
Jn 14:16 that he may a with you for ever
Jn 15:4 A in me, and I in you
Jn 15:6 If a man a not in me, he is cast
Jn 15:7 If ye a in me, and my words a
Jn 15:10 ye shall a in my love
Acts 15:34 it pleased Silas to a there still
Acts 16:15 come into my house, and a there
Acts 20:23 that bonds and afflictions a me
Acts 27:31 Except these a in the ship
Rom 11:23 if they a not still in unbelief,
1Cor 3:14 If any man's work a which he hath
1Cor 7:8 good for them if they a even as I
1Cor 7:20 Let every man a in the same
1Cor 7:24 he is called, therein a with God
1Cor 7:40 But she is happier if she so a
1Cor 16:6 And it may be that I will a
Phil 1:24 Nevertheless to a in the flesh is
Phil 1:25 confidence, I know that I shall a
1Ti 1:3 thee to a still at Ephesus
1Jn 2:24 Let that therefore a in you
1Jn 2:27 taught you, ye shall a in him
1Jn 2:28 And now, little children, a in him

**ABIDETH**
Num 31:23 all that a not the fire ye shall
2Sa 16:3 king, Behold, he a at Jerusalem
Job 39:28 a on the rock, upon the crag of
Ps 49:12 man being in honour a not
Ps 55:19 them, even he that a of old
Ps 119:90 established the earth, and it a
Ps 125:1 cannot be removed, but a for ever
Prov 15:31 reproof of life a among the wise
Eccl 1:4 but the earth a for ever
Jer 21:9 He that a in this city shall die
Jn 3:36 but the wrath of God a on him
Jn 8:35 but the Son a ever
Jn 12:24 the ground and die, it a alone
Jn 12:34 of the law that Christ a for ever
Jn 15:5 He that a in me, and I in him, the
1Cor 13:13 now a faith, hope, charity, these
2Ti 2:13 we believe not, yet he a faithful
Heb 7:3 a a priest continually
1Pet 1:23 God, which liveth and a for ever
1Jn 2:6 He that saith he a in him ought
1Jn 2:10 loveth his brother a in the light
1Jn 2:14 and the word of God a in you
1Jn 2:17 doeth the will of God a for ever
1Jn 3:6 Whosoever a in him sinneth not
1Jn 3:14 loveth not his brother a in death
1Jn 3:24 And hereby we know that he a in us
2Jn 9 a not in the doctrine of Christ,

**ABIDING**
Num 24:2 he saw Israel a in his tents
Judg 16:9 a with her in the chamber
Judg 16:12 liers in wait a in the chamber
1Sa 26:19 driven me out this day from a in
1Chr 29:15 as a shadow, and there is none a
Lk 2:8 country shepherds a in the field
Jn 5:38 And ye have not his word a in you
Acts 16:12 were in that city a certain days
1Jn 3:15 hath eternal life a in him

**ABIEL** *(a'-be-el)*
*1. Grandfather of King Saul.*
1Sa 9:1 whose name was Kish, the son of A
1Sa 14:51 father of Abner was the son of A
*2. A "mighty man" of David.*
1Chr 11:32 brooks of Gaash, A the Arbathite,

**ABI-EZER** *(ab-i-e'-zur)* See ABIEZRITE, JE-EZER.
*1. A descendant of Manasseh.*
Judg 6:34 and A was gathered after him
Judg 8:2 better than the vintage of A

**ABIEZER**
Josh 17:2 for the children of A, and for the
2Sa 23:27 A the Anethothite, Mebunnai the
1Chr 7:18 Hammoleketh bare Ishod, and A
1Chr 11:28 the Tekoite, A the Antothite,
1Chr 27:12 ninth month was A the Anetothite

**ABI-EZRITE** *(ab-i-ez'-rite)* See ABI-EZRITES. *A descendant of Abiezer.*
Judg 6:11 that pertained unto Joash the A

**ABI-EZRITES** *(ab-i-ez'-rites)*
Judg 6:24 day it is yet in Ophrah of the A
Judg 8:32 his father, in Ophrah of the A

**ABIGAIL** *(ab'-e-gul)*
*1. A wife of David.*
1Sa 25:3 and the name of his wife A
1Sa 25:14 But one of the young men told A
1Sa 25:18 Then A made haste, and took two
1Sa 25:23 when A saw David, she hasted, and
1Sa 25:32 And David said to A, Blessed be
1Sa 25:36 And A came to Nabal
1Sa 25:39 And David sent and communed with A
1Sa 25:40 of David were come to A to Carmel
1Sa 25:42 A hasted, and arose, and rode upon
1Sa 27:3 A the Carmelitess, Nabal's wife
2Sa 2:2 A Nabal's wife the Carmelite
1Chr 3:1 Daniel, of A the Carmelitess
*2. Mother of Amosa.*
2Sa 17:25 that went in to A the daughter of
1Chr 2:16 Whose sisters were Zeruiah, and A
1Chr 2:17 And A bare Amasa

**ABIHAIL** *(ab-e-ha'-il)*
*1. Head of Levital family of Merari.*
Num 3:35 of Merari was Zuriel the son of A
*2. Wife of Abishur.*
1Chr 2:29 name of the wife of Abishur was A
*3. Chief of a family of Gad.*
1Chr 5:14 the children of A the son of Huri
*4. Descendant of Eliab.*
2Chr 11:18 A the daughter of Eliab the son
*5. Father of Esther.*
Est 2:15 the daughter of A the uncle of
Est 9:29 the queen, the daughter of A

**ABIHU** *(a-bi'-hew) A son of Aaron.*
Ex 6:23 and she bare him Nadab, and A
Ex 24:1 LORD, thou, and Aaron, Nadab, and A
Ex 24:9 up Moses, and Aaron, Nadab, and A
Ex 28:1 office, even Aaron, Nadab and A
Lev 10:1 And Nadab and A, the sons of Aaron,
Num 3:2 Nadab the firstborn, and A
Num 3:4 A died before the LORD, when they
Num 26:60 unto Aaron was born Nadab, and A
Num 26:61 A died, when they offered strange
1Chr 6:3 Nadab, and A, Eleazar, and Ithamar
1Chr 24:2 A died before their father, and

**ABIHUD** *(a-bi'-hud) A son of Bela.*
1Chr 8:3 Bela were, Addar, and Gera, and *A*

**ABIJAH** *(a-bi'-jah)* See ABIA, ABIJAM.
*1. A son of Jeroboam I.*
1Kin 14:1 At that time *A* the son of
*2. A priest during David's reign.*
1Chr 24:10 to Hakkoz, the eighth to *A*
*3. A son of Rehoboam.*
2Chr 11:20 which bare him *A*, and Attai, and
2Chr 12:16 *A* his son reigned in his stead
2Chr 13:1 began *A* to reign over Judah
2Chr 13:4 *A* stood up upon mount Zemaraim,
2Chr 13:15 Jeroboam and all Israel before *A*
2Chr 13:17 And *A* and his people slew them with
2Chr 13:21 But *A* waxed mighty, and married
2Chr 14:1 So *A* slept with his fathers, and
*4. Mother of King Hezekiah.*
2Chr 29:1 And his mother's name was *A*
*5. A priest in Nehemiah's time.*
Neh 10:7 Meshullam, *A*, Mijamin,
*6. A priest who returned from Exile under Zerubbabel.*
Neh 12:4 Iddo, Ginnetho, *A*,
Neh 12:17 Of *A*, Zichri

**ABIJAM** *(a-bi'-jum) Son and successor of King Rehoboam.*
1Kin 14:31 *A* his son reigned in his stead
1Kin 15:1 son of Nebat reigned *A* over Judah
1Kin 15:8 And *A* slept with his fathers

**ABILENE** *(ab-i-le'-ne) A Roman tetrarchy in northern Palestine.*
Lk 3:1 and Lysanias the tetrarch of *A*

**ABILITY**
Lev 27:8 according to his *a* that vowed
Ezr 2:69 They gave after their *a* unto the
Neh 5:8 We after our *a* have redeemed our
Dan 1:4 such as had *a* in them to stand in
Mt 25:15 man according to his several *a*
Acts 11:29 every man according to his *a*
1Pet 4:11 it as of the *a* which God giveth

**ABIMAEL** *(a-bim'-ah-el) A son of Joktan in Arabia.*
Gen 10:28 And Obal, and *A*, and Sheba,
1Chr 1:22 And Ebal, and *A*, and Sheba,

**ABIMELECH** *(a-bim'-e-lek)* See ABIMELECH'S.
*1. Philistine king in Abraham's time.*
Gen 20:2 *A* king of Gerar sent, and took
Gen 20:3 But God came to *A* in a dream by
Gen 20:9 Then *A* called Abraham, and said
Gen 20:10 *A* said unto Abraham, What sawest
Gen 20:14 *A* took sheep, and oxen, and
Gen 20:17 and God healed *A*, and his wife, and
Gen 20:18 all the wombs of the house of *A*
Gen 21:25 Abraham reproved *A* because of a
Gen 21:26 *A* said, I wot not who hath done
Gen 21:29 *A* said unto Abraham, What mean
Gen 21:32 then *A* rose up, and Phichol the
Gen 26:1 Isaac went unto *A* king of the
Gen 26:8 that *A* king of the Philistines
Gen 26:11 *A* charged all his people, saying,
Gen 26:16 *A* said unto Isaac, Go from us
Gen 26:26 Then *A* went to him from Gerar, and
*2. Son of Gideon.*
Judg 8:31 him a son, whose name he called *A*
Judg 9:1 *A* the son of Jerubbaal went to
Judg 9:3 their hearts inclined to follow *A*
Judg 9:4 wherewith *A* hired vain and light
Judg 9:6 of Millo, and went, and made *A* king
Judg 9:16 in that ye have made *A* king
Judg 9:19 this day, then rejoice ye in *A*
Judg 9:20 if not, let fire come out from *A*
Judg 9:22 When *A* had reigned three years
Judg 9:23 God sent an evil spirit between *A*
Judg 9:24 be laid upon *A* their brother
Judg 9:27 and did eat and drink, and cursed *A*
Judg 9:28 the son of Ebed said, Who is *A*
Judg 9:31 he sent messengers unto *A* privily
Judg 9:38 wherewith thou saidst, Who is *A*
Judg 9:39 men of Shechem, and fought with *A*
Judg 9:40 *A* chased him, and he fled before
Judg 9:41 And *A* dwelt at Arumah
Judg 9:45 *A* fought against the city all
Judg 9:48 *A* gat him up to mount Zalmon, he
Judg 9:48 *A* took an axe in his hand, and cut
Judg 9:50 Then went *A* to Thebez, and
Judg 9:52 *A* came unto the tower, and fought
Judg 9:55 men of Israel saw that *A* was dead
Judg 10:1 after *A* there arose to defend
2Sa 11:21 Who smote *A* the son of
*3. Son of Abiathar the High Priest.*
1Chr 18:16 *A* the son of Abiathar, were the
*4. Used in title of Psalm 34.*
Ps 34:*t* he changed his behaviour before *A*

**ABIMELECH'S** *(a-bim'-e-leks)*
Gen 21:25 which *A* servants had violently
Judg 9:53 piece of a millstone upon *A* head

**ABINADAB** *(a-bin'-ah-dab)*
*1. A Levite of Kirjath-jearim.*
1Sa 7:1 into the house of *A* in the hill
2Sa 6:3 the house of *A* that was in Gibeah
1Chr 13:7 a new cart out of the house of *A*
*2. A brother of David.*
1Sa 16:8 Then Jesse called *A*, and made him
1Sa 17:13 first born, and next unto him *A*
1Chr 2:13 *A* the second, and Shimma the third
*3. A son of King Saul.*
1Sa 31:2 Philistines slew Jonathan, and *A*
1Chr 8:33 Jonathan, and Malchi-shua, and *A*
1Chr 9:39 Jonathan, and Malchi-shua, and *A*
1Chr 10:2 Philistines slew Jonathan, and *A*
*4. Father of an officer of Solomon.*
1Kin 4:11 The son of *A*, in all the region

**ABINOAM** *(a-bin'-o-am) Father of Barak.*
Judg 4:6 son of *A* out of Kedesh-naphtali
Judg 4:12 of *A* was gone up to mount Tabor
Judg 5:1 and Barak the son of *A* on that day
Judg 5:12 captivity captive, thou son of *A*

**ABIRAM** *(a-bi'-rum)*
*1. A conspirator against Moses.*
Num 16:1 the son of Levi, and Dathan and *A*
Num 16:12 And Moses sent to call Dathan and *A*
Num 16:24 tabernacle of Korah, Dathan, and *A*
Num 16:27 tabernacle of Korah, Dathan, and *A*
Num 26:9 Nemuel, and Dathan, and *A*
Deut 11:6 And what he did unto Dathan and *A*
Ps 106:17 and covered the company of *A*
*2. Son of Hiel the Bethelite.*
1Kin 16:34 thereof in *A* his firstborn

**ABISHAG** *(ab'-e-shag) An attendant of David.*
1Kin 1:3 found *A* a Shunammite, and brought
1Kin 1:15 *A* the Shunammite ministered unto
1Kin 2:17 that he give me *A* the Shunammite

**ABISHAI** *(ab'-e-shahee) David's nephew.*
1Sa 26:6 to *A* the son of Zeruiah, brother
1Sa 26:8 Then said *A* to David, God hath
2Sa 2:18 sons of Zeruiah there, Joab, and *A*
2Sa 2:24 also and *A* pursued after Abner
2Sa 3:30 *A* his brother slew Abner, because
2Sa 10:10 into the hand of *A* his brother
2Sa 10:14 then fled they also before *A*
2Sa 16:9 Then said *A* the son of Zeruiah
2Sa 18:2 the hand of *A* the son of Zeruiah
2Sa 18:5 And the king commanded Joab and *A*
2Sa 18:12 the king charged thee and *A*
2Sa 19:21 But *A* the son of Zeruiah answered
2Sa 20:6 And David said to *A*, Now shall
2Sa 20:10 *A* his brother pursued after Sheba
2Sa 21:17 But *A* the son of Zeruiah
2Sa 23:18 And *A*, the brother of Joab, the
1Chr 2:16 *A*, and Joab, and Asahel, three
1Chr 11:20 *A* the brother of Joab, he was
1Chr 18:12 *A* the son Zeruiah slew of the
1Chr 19:11 unto the hand of *A* his brother

**ABISHALOM** *(a-bish'-ah-lum)* See ABSALOM. *Father of Maachah.*
1Kin 15:2 was Maachah, the daughter of *A*
1Kin 15:10 was Maachah, the daughter of *A*

**ABISHUA** *(a-bish'-u-ah)*
*1. Son of Phinehas.*
1Chr 6:4 begat Phinehas, Phinehas begat *A*
1Chr 6:50 son, Phinehas his son, *A* his son,
Ezr 7:5 The son of *A*, the son of Phinehas
1Chr 8:4 And *A*, and Naaman, and Ahoah,

**ABISHUR** *(ab'-e-shur) A son of Shammai.*
1Chr 2:28 Nadab, and *A*
1Chr 2:29 name of the wife of *A* was Abihail

**ABITAL** *(ab'-e-tal) A wife of David.*
2Sa 3:4 fifth, Shephatiah the son of *A*
1Chr 3:3 The fifth, Shephatiah of *A*

**ABITUB** *(ab'-e-tub) Son of Shahareim.*
1Chr 8:11 And of Hushim he begat *A*, and

**ABIUD** *(a-bi'-ud) A descendant of Zerubbabel; ancestor of Jesus.*
Mt 1:13 And Zorobabel begat *A*
Mt 1:13 and *A* begat Eliakim

**ABJECTS**
Ps 35:15 the *a* gathered themselves

**ABLE**
Gen 13:6 the land was not *a* to bear them
Gen 15:5 if thou be *a* to number them
Gen 33:14 me and the children be *a* to endure
Ex 10:5 one cannot be *a* to see the earth
Ex 18:18 thou art not *a* to perform it
Ex 18:21 out of all the people *a* men
Ex 18:23 then thou shalt be *a* to endure
Ex 18:25 Moses chose *a* men out of all
Ex 40:35 Moses was not *a* to enter into the
Lev 5:7 if he be not *a* to bring a lamb,
Lev 5:11 But if he be not *a* to bring two
Lev 12:8 if she be not *a* to bring a lamb,
Lev 14:22 pigeons, such as he is *a* to get
Lev 14:31 Even such as he is *a* to get
Lev 14:32 whose hand is not *a* to get that
Lev 25:26 himself be *a* to redeem it
Lev 25:28 But if he be not *a* to restore it
Lev 25:49 or if he be *a*, he may redeem
Num 1:3 all that are *a* to go forth to war
Num 1:20 all that were *a* to go forth to
Num 11:14 I am not *a* to bear all this
Num 13:30 for we are well *a* to overcome it
Num 13:31 We be not *a* to go up against the
Num 14:16 Because the LORD was not *a* to
Num 22:11 I shall be *a* to overcome them
Num 22:37 am I not *a* indeed to promote thee
Num 26:2 all that are *a* to go to war in
Deut 1:9 I am not *a* to bear you myself
Deut 7:24 no man be *a* to stand before thee
Deut 9:28 Because the LORD was not *a* to
Deut 11:25 no man be *a* to stand before you
Deut 14:24 that thou art not *a* to carry it
Deut 16:17 Every man shall give as he is *a*
Josh 1:5 There shall not any man be *a* to
Josh 14:12 then I shall be *a* to drive them
Josh 23:9 no man hath been *a* to stand
Judg 8:3 what was I *a* to do in comparison
1Sa 6:20 Who is *a* to stand before this
1Sa 17:9 If he be *a* to fight with me, and
1Sa 17:33 Thou art not *a* to go against this
1Kin 3:9 for who is *a* to judge this thy so
1Kin 9:21 were not *a* utterly to destroy
2Kin 3:21 all that were *a* to put on armour
2Kin 18:23 if thou be *a* on thy part to set
2Kin 18:29 for he shall not be *a* to deliver
1Chr 5:18 men *a* to bear buckler and sword,
1Chr 9:13 very *a* men for the work of the
1Chr 26:8 *a* men for strength for the
1Chr 29:14 that we should be *a* to offer so
2Chr 2:6 But who is *a* to build him an
2Chr 7:7 *a* to receive the burnt offerings
2Chr 20:6 so that none is *a* to withstand
2Chr 20:37 they were not *a* to go to Tarshish
2Chr 25:5 *a* to go forth to war, that could
2Chr 25:9 The LORD is *a* to give thee much
2Chr 32:13 *a* to deliver their lands out of
2Chr 32:14 that your God should be *a* to
2Chr 32:15 *a* to deliver his people out of
Ezr 10:13 we are not *a* to stand without,
Neh 4:10 we are not *a* to build the wall
Job 41:10 who then is *a* to stand before me
Ps 18:38 them that they were not *a* to rise
Ps 21:11 which they are not *a* to perform
Ps 36:12 down, and shall not be *a* to rise
Ps 40:12 me, so that I am not *a* to look up
Prov 27:4 but who is *a* to stand before envy
Eccl 8:17 yet shall he not be *a* to find it
Is 36:8 if thou be *a* on thy part to set
Is 36:14 he shall not be *a* to deliver you
Is 47:11 thou shalt not be *a* to put if off
Is 47:12 so be thou shalt be *a* to profit
Jer 10:10 not be *a* to abide his indignation
Jer 11:11 they shall not be *a* to escape
Jer 49:10 he shall not be *a* to hide himself
Lam 1:14 from whom I am not *a* to rise up
Eze 7:19 their gold shall not be *a* to
Eze 33:12 *a* to live for his righteousness
Eze 46:5 lambs as he shall be *a* to give
Eze 46:11 to the lambs as he is *a* to give
Dan 2:26 Art thou *a* to make known unto me
Dan 3:17 our God whom we serve is *a* to
Dan 4:18 not *a* to make known unto me the

Dan 4:37 walk in pride he is *a* to abase
Dan 6:20 *a* to deliver thee from the lions
Amos 7:10 the land is not *a* to bear all his
Zeph 1:18 *a* to deliver them in the day of
Mt 3:9 that God is *a* of these stones to
Mt 9:28 Believe ye that I am *a* to do this
Mt 10:28 but are not *a* to kill the soul
Mt 19:12 He that is *a* to receive it, let
Mt 20:22 Are ye *a* to drink of the cup that
Mt 22:46 no man was *a* to answer him a word
Mt 26:61 I am *a* to destroy the temple of
Mk 4:33 them, as they were *a* to hear it
Lk 1:20 not *a* to speak, until the day
Lk 3:8 That God is *a* of these stones to
Lk 12:26 If ye then be not *a* to do that
Lk 13:24 to enter in, and shall not be *a*
Lk 14:29 is not *a* to finish it, all that
Lk 14:30 to build, and was not *a* to finish
Lk 14:31 consulteth whether he be *a* with
Lk 21:15 not be *a* to gainsay nor resist
Jn 10:29 no man is *a* to pluck them out of
Jn 21:6 now they were not *a* to draw it
Acts 6:10 they were not *a* to resist the
Acts 15:10 our fathers nor we were *a* to bear
Acts 20:32 which is *a* to build you up, and to
Acts 25:5 said he, which among you are *a*
Rom 4:21 he was *a* also to perform
Rom 8:39 shall be *a* to separate us from
Rom 11:23 for God is *a* to graff them in
Rom 14:4 for God is *a* to make him stand
Rom 15:14 *a* also to admonish one another
1Cor 3:2 hitherto ye were not *a* to bear it
1Cor 6:5 not one that shall be *a* to judge
1Cor 10:13 to be tempted above that ye are *a*
2Cor 1:4 that we may be *a* to comfort them
2Cor 3:6 Who also hath made us *a* ministers
2Cor 9:8 God is *a* to make all grace abound
Eph 3:18 May be *a* to comprehend with all
Eph 3:20 Now unto him that is *a* to do
Eph 6:11 that ye may be *a* to stand against
Eph 6:13 that ye may be *a* to withstand in
Eph 6:16 wherewith ye shall be *a* to quench
Phil 3:21 to the working whereby he is *a*
2Ti 1:12 am persuaded that he is *a* to keep
2Ti 2:2 who shall be *a* to teach others
2Ti 3:7 never *a* to come to the knowledge
2Ti 3:15 which are *a* to make thee wise
Titus 1:9 that he may be *a* by sound
Heb 2:18 he is *a* to succour them that are
Heb 5:7 that was *a* to save him from death
Heb 7:25 Wherefore he is *a* also to save
Heb 11:19 that God was *a* to raise him up
Jas 1:21 which is *a* to save your souls
Jas 3:2 *a* also to bridle the whole body
Jas 4:12 who is *a* to save and to destroy
2Pet 1:15 *a* after my decease to have these
Jude 24 Now unto him that is *a* to keep
Rev 5:3 was *a* to open the book, neither
Rev 6:17 and who shall be *a* to stand
Rev 13:4 who is *a* to make war with him
Rev 15:8 no man was *a* to enter into the

**ABNER** *(ab'-nur)* See ABNER'S. *King Saul's military commander.*
1Sa 14:50 of the captain of his host was *A*
1Sa 17:55 the Philistine, he said unto *A*
1Sa 17:55 the captain of the host, *A*
1Sa 17:57 *A* took him, and brought him before
1Sa 20:25 *A* sat by Saul's side, and David's
1Sa 26:7 but *A* and the people lay round
1Sa 26:14 to *A* the son of Ner, saying,
2Sa 2:8 But *A* the son of Ner, captain of
2Sa 2:14 *A* said to Joab, Let the young men
2Sa 2:17 *A* was beaten, and the men of
2Sa 2:19 And Asahel pursued after *A*
2Sa 2:20 Then *A* looked behind him, and said
2Sa 2:24 also and Abishai pursued after *A*
2Sa 2:29 And *A* and his men walked all that
2Sa 2:30 And Joab returned from following *A*
2Sa 3:6 that *A* made himself strong for
2Sa 3:7 and Ish-bosheth said to *A*,
2Sa 3:8 Then was *A* very wroth for the
2Sa 3:11 could not answer *A* a word again
2Sa 3:12 *A* sent messengers to David on his
2Sa 3:16 Then said *A* unto him, Go, return
2Sa 3:19 *A* also spake in the ears of
2Sa 3:20 So *A* came to David to Hebron, and
2Sa 3:21 *A* said unto David, I will arise
2Sa 3:26 David, he sent messengers after *A*
2Sa 3:27 when *A* was returned to Hebron,
2Sa 3:28 the blood of *A* the son of Ner
2Sa 3:30 and Abishai his brother slew *A*
2Sa 3:32 And they buried *A* in Hebron
2Sa 3:33 and said, Died *A* as a fool dieth
2Sa 3:37 the king to slay *A* the son of Ner
2Sa 4:1 heard that *A* was dead in Hebron
2Sa 4:12 in the sepulchre of *A* in Hebron
1Kin 2:5 unto *A* the son of Ner, and unto
1Kin 2:32 *A* the son of Ner, captain of the
1Chr 26:28 *A* the son of Ner, and Joab the son
1Chr 27:21 of Benjamin, Jaasiel the son of *A*

**ABNER'S** *(ab'-nurs)*
2Sa 2:31 of A men, so that three hundred

**ABOARD**
Acts 21:2 over unto Phenicia, we went *a*

**ABODE**
Gen 29:14 he *a* with him the space of a
Gen 49:24 But his bow *a* in strength
Ex 24:16 of the LORD *a* upon mount Sinai
Ex 40:35 because the cloud *a* thereon
Num 9:17 and in the place where the cloud *a*
Num 9:18 as long as the cloud *a* upon the
Num 9:20 of the LORD they *a* in their tents
Num 9:21 when the cloud *a* from even unto
Num 9:22 of Israel *a* in their tents
Num 11:35 and *a* at Hazeroth
Num 20:1 and the people *a* in Kadesh
Num 22:8 the princes of Moab *a* with Balaam
Num 25:1 Israel *a* in Shittim, and the
Deut 1:46 So ye *a* in Kadesh many days,
Deut 1:46 unto the days that ye *a* there
Deut 3:29 So we *a* in the valley over
Deut 9:9 then I *a* in the mount forty days
Josh 2:22 *a* there three days, until the
Josh 5:8 that they *a* in their places in
Josh 8:9 *a* between Beth-el and Ai, on the
Judg 5:17 Gilead *a* beyond Jordan
Judg 11:17 and Israel *a* in Kadesh
Judg 19:4 and he *a* with him three days
Judg 20:47 *a* in the rock Rimmon four months
Judg 21:2 *a* there till even before God, and
1Sa 1:23 So the woman *a*, and gave her son
1Sa 7:2 while the ark *a* in Kirjath-jearim
1Sa 13:16 them, *a* in Gibeah of Benjamin
1Sa 22:6 (now Saul *a* in Gibeah under a
1Sa 23:14 David *a* in the wilderness in
1Sa 23:18 David *a* in the wood, and Jonathan
1Sa 23:25 *a* in the wilderness of Maon
1Sa 25:13 two hundred *a* by the stuff
1Sa 26:3 But David *a* in the wilderness, and
1Sa 30:10 for two hundred *a* behind, which
2Sa 1:1 David had *a* two days in Ziklag
2Sa 11:12 So Uriah *a* in Jerusalem that day,
2Sa 15:8 vow while I *a* at Geshur in Syria
1Kin 17:19 him up into a loft, where he *a*
2Kin 19:27 But I know thy *a*, and thy going
Ezr 8:15 there *a* we in tents three days
Ezr 8:32 Jerusalem, and *a* there three days
Is 37:28 But I know thy *a*, and thy going
Jer 38:28 So Jeremiah *a* in the court of the
Mt 17:22 And while they *a* in Galilee
Lk 1:56 Mary *a* with her about three
Lk 8:27 neither *a* in any house, but in
Lk 21:37 *a* in the mount that is called the
Jn 1:32 like a dove, and it *a* upon him
Jn 1:39 he dwelt, and *a* with him that day
Jn 4:40 and he *a* there two days
Jn 7:9 unto them, he *a* still in Galilee
Jn 8:44 *a* not in the truth, because there
Jn 10:40 and there he *a*
Jn 11:6 he *a* two days still in the same
Jn 14:23 unto him, and make our *a* with him
Acts 1:13 where *a* both Peter, and James, and
Acts 12:19 Judaea to Caesarea, and there *a*
Acts 14:3 Long time therefore *a* they
Acts 14:28 there they *a* long time with the
Acts 17:14 Silas and Timotheus *a* there still
Acts 18:3 he *a* with them, and wrought
Acts 20:3 And there *a* three months
Acts 20:6 where we *a* seven days
Acts 21:7 brethren, and *a* with them one day
Acts 21:8 of the seven; and *a* with him
Gal 1:18 Peter, and *a* with him fifteen days
2Ti 4:20 Erastus *a* at Corinth

**ABOLISHED**
Is 51:6 my righteousness shall not be *a*
Eze 6:6 cut down, and your works may be *a*
2Cor 3:13 to the end of that which is *a*
Eph 2:15 Having *a* in his flesh the enmity,
2Ti 1:10 Jesus Christ, who hath *a* death

**ABOMINABLE**
Lev 7:21 or any *a* unclean thing, and eat of
Lev 11:43 *a* with any creeping thing that
Lev 18:30 not any one of these *a* customs
Lev 19:7 at all on the third day, it is *a*
Lev 20:25 not make your souls *a* by beast
Deut 14:3 Thou shalt not eat any *a* thing
1Chr 21:6 for the king's word was *a* to Joab
2Chr 15:8 put away the *a* idols out of all
Job 15:16 How much more *a* and filthy is man,
Ps 14:1 corrupt, they have done *a* works
Ps 53:1 are they, and have done *a* iniquity
Is 14:19 out of thy grave like an *a* branch
Is 65:4 broth of *a* things is in their
Jer 16:18 of their detestable and *a* things
Jer 44:4 do not this *a* thing that I hate
Eze 4:14 neither came there *a* flesh into
Eze 8:10 *a* beasts, and all the idols of the
Eze 16:52 hast committed more *a* than they
Mic 6:10 and the scant measure that is *a*
Nah 3:6 I will cast *a* filth upon thee, and
Titus 1:16 in works they deny him, being *a*
1Pet 4:3 banquetings, and *a* idolatries
Rev 21:8 fearful, and unbelieving, and the *a*

**ABOMINATION**
Gen 43:32 for that is an *a* unto the
Gen 46:34 is an *a* unto the Egyptians
Ex 8:26 for we shall sacrifice the *a* of
Ex 8:26 shall we sacrifice the *a* of the
Lev 7:18 it shall be an *a*, and the soul
Lev 11:10 they shall be an *a* unto you
Lev 11:11 They shall be even an *a* unto you
Lev 11:12 that shall be an *a* unto you
Lev 11:13 shall have in *a* among the fowls
Lev 11:20 all four, shall be an *a* unto you
Lev 11:23 four feet, shall be an *a* unto you
Lev 11:41 upon the earth shall be an *a*
Lev 11:42 for they are an *a*
Lev 18:22 with womankind: it is *a*
Lev 20:13 both of them have committed an *a*
Deut 7:25 for it is an *a* to the LORD thy
Deut 7:26 thou bring an *a* into thine house
Deut 12:31 for every *a* to the LORD, which he
Deut 13:14 that such *a* is wrought among you
Deut 17:1 for that is an *a* unto the LORD
Deut 17:4 that such *a* is wrought in Israel
Deut 18:12 things are an *a* unto the LORD
Deut 22:5 do so are *a* unto the LORD thy God
Deut 23:18 these are *a* unto the LORD thy God
Deut 24:4 for that is *a* before the LORD
Deut 25:16 are an *a* unto the LORD thy God
Deut 27:15 an *a* unto the LORD, the work of
1Sa 13:4 was had in *a* with the Philistines
1Kin 11:5 Milcom the *a* of the Ammonites
1Kin 11:7 the *a* of Moab, in the hill that
2Kin 23:13 Ashtoreth the *a* of the Zidonians
2Kin 23:13 for Milcom the *a* of the children
Ps 88:8 thou hast made me an *a* unto them
Prov 3:32 For the froward is *a* to the LORD
Prov 6:16 yea, seven are an *a* unto him
Prov 8:7 and wickedness is an *a* to my lips
Prov 11:1 A false balance is *a* to the LORD
Prov 11:20 a froward heart are *a* to the LORD
Prov 12:22 Lying lips are *a* to the LORD
Prov 13:19 but it is *a* to fools to depart
Prov 15:8 of the wicked is an *a* to the LORD
Prov 15:9 the wicked is an *a* unto the LORD
Prov 15:26 the wicked are an *a* to the LORD
Prov 16:5 in heart is an *a* to the LORD
Prov 16:12 It is an *a* to kings to commit
Prov 17:15 even they both are *a* to the LORD
Prov 20:10 of them are alike *a* to the LORD
Prov 20:23 weights are an *a* unto the LORD
Prov 21:27 The sacrifice of the wicked is *a*
Prov 24:9 and the scorner is an *a* to men
Prov 29:27 An unjust man is an *a* to the just
Is 1:13 incense is an *a* unto me
Is 41:24 an *a* is he that chooseth you
Is 44:19 I make the residue thereof an *a*
Is 66:17 eating swine's flesh, and the *a*
Jer 2:7 land, and made mine heritage an *a*
Jer 6:15 ashamed when they had committed *a*
Jer 8:12 ashamed when they had committed *a*
Jer 32:35 mind, that they should do this *a*
Eze 16:50 haughty, and committed *a* before me
Eze 18:12 to the idols, hath committed *a*
Eze 22:11 one hath committed *a* with his

Eze 33:26 stand upon your sword, ye work *a*
Dan 11:31 place the *a* that maketh desolate
Dan 12:11 the *a* that maketh desolate set up
Mal 2:11 an *a* is committed in Israel and in
Mt 24:15 shall see the *a* of desolation
Mk 13:14 ye shall see the *a* of desolation
Lk 16:15 men is *a* in the sight of God
Rev 21:27 neither whatsoever worketh *a*

**ABOMINATIONS**

Lev 18:26 shall not commit any of these *a*
Lev 18:27 (For all these *a* have the men of
Lev 18:29 shall commit any of these *a*
Deut 18:9 do after the *a* of those nations
Deut 18:12 because of these *a* the LORD thy
Deut 20:18 you not to do after all their *a*
Deut 29:17 And ye have seen their *a*, and their
Deut 32:16 with *a* provoked they him to anger
1Kin 14:24 *a* of the nations which the LORD
2Kin 16:3 according to the *a* of the heathen
2Kin 21:2 after the *a* of the heathen, whom
2Kin 21:11 king of Judah hath done these *a*
2Kin 23:24 all the *a* that were spied in the
2Chr 28:3 after the *a* of the heathen whom
2Chr 33:2 like unto the *a* of the heathen,
2Chr 34:33 Josiah took away all the *a* out of
2Chr 36:8 his *a* which he did, and that which
2Chr 36:14 after all the *a* of the heathen
Ezr 9:1 lands, doing according to their *a*
Ezr 9:11 people of the lands, with their *a*
Ezr 9:14 with the people of these *a*
Prov 26:25 there are seven *a* in his heart
Is 66:3 their soul delighteth in their *a*
Jer 4:1 put away thine *a* out of my sight
Jer 7:10 are delivered to do all these *a*
Jer 7:30 they have set their *a* in the
Jer 13:27 thine *a* on the hills in the
Jer 32:34 But they set their *a* in the house
Jer 44:22 because of the *a* which ye have
Eze 5:9 the like, because of all thine *a*
Eze 5:11 things, and with all thine *a*
Eze 6:9 have committed in all their *a*
Eze 6:11 Alas for all the evil *a* of the
Eze 7:3 recompense upon thee all thine *a*
Eze 7:4 thine *a* shall be in the midst of
Eze 7:8 recompense thee for all thine *a*
Eze 7:9 thine *a* that are in the midst of
Eze 7:20 they made the images of their *a*
Eze 8:6 even the great *a* that the house
Eze 8:9 the wicked *a* that they do here
Eze 8:13 shalt see greater *a* that they do
Eze 8:15 shalt see greater *a* than these
Eze 8:17 the *a* which they commit here
Eze 9:4 that cry for all the *a* that be
Eze 11:18 all the *a* thereof from thence
Eze 11:21 detestable things and their *a*
Eze 12:16 *a* among the heathen whither they
Eze 14:6 away your faces from all your *a*
Eze 16:2 cause Jerusalem to know her *a*
Eze 16:22 And in all thine *a* and thy
Eze 16:36 and with all the idols of thy *a*
Eze 16:43 this lewdness above all thine *a*
Eze 16:47 ways, nor done after their *a*
Eze 16:51 multiplied thine *a* more than they
Eze 16:58 borne thy lewdness and thine *a*
Eze 18:13 he hath done all these *a*
Eze 18:24 the *a* that the wicked man doeth
Eze 20:4 to know the *a* of their fathers
Eze 20:7 away every man the *a* of his eyes
Eze 20:8 man cast away the *a* of their eyes
Eze 20:30 commit ye whoredom after their *a*
Eze 22:2 thou shalt shew her all her *a*
Eze 23:36 yea, declare unto them their *a*
Eze 33:29 their *a* which they have committed
Eze 36:31 for your iniquities and for your *a*
Eze 43:8 their *a* that they have committed
Eze 44:6 let it suffice you of all your *a*
Eze 44:7 my covenant because of all your *a*
Eze 44:13 their *a* which they have committed
Dan 9:27 for the overspreading of *a* he
Hos 9:10 their *a* were according as they
Zec 9:7 his *a* from between his teeth
Rev 17:4 golden cup in her hand full of *a*
Rev 17:5 AND *A* OF THE EARTH

**ABOUND**

Prov 28:20 man shall *a* with blessings
Mt 24:12 And because iniquity shall *a*
Rom 5:20 entered, that the offence might *a*
Rom 6:1 continue in sin, that grace may *a*
Rom 15:13 believing, that ye may *a* in hope
2Cor 1:5 the sufferings of Christ *a* in us
2Cor 8:7 as ye *a* in every thing, in faith,
2Cor 9:8 to make all grace *a* toward you
Phil 1:9 that your love may *a* yet more
Phil 4:12 to be abased, and I know how to *a*
Phil 4:17 fruit that may *a* to your account
Phil 4:18 But I have all, and *a*
1Th 3:12 *a* in love one toward another, and
1Th 4:1 to please God, so ye would *a* more
2Pet 1:8 if these things be in you, and *a*

**ABOUNDED**

Rom 3:7 *a* through my lie unto his glory
Rom 5:15 Jesus Christ, hath *a* unto many
Rom 5:20 But where sin *a*, grace did much
2Cor 8:2 their deep poverty *a* unto the
Eph 1:8 Wherein he hath *a* toward us in

**ABRAHAM** *(a'-bra-ham)* See ABRAHAM'S, ABRAM. *Father of the nation of Israel.*

Gen 17:5 Abram, but thy name shall be *A*
Gen 17:9 And God said unto *A*, Thou shalt
Gen 17:15 And God said unto *A*, As for Sarai
Gen 17:17 Then *A* fell upon his face, and
Gen 17:22 with him, and God went up from *A*
Gen 17:23 *A* took Ishmael his son, and all
Gen 17:24 *A* was ninety years old and nine,
Gen 17:26 selfsame day was *A* circumcised
Gen 18:6 *A* hastened into the tent unto
Gen 18:7 *A* ran unto the herd, and fetcht a
Gen 18:11 Now *A* and Sarah were old and well
Gen 18:22 but *A* stood yet before the LORD
Gen 18:33 as he had left communing with *A*
Gen 18:33 *A* returned unto his place
Gen 19:27 *A* gat up early in the morning to
Gen 19:29 the plain, that God remembered *A*
Gen 20:1 *A* journeyed from thence toward
Gen 20:2 *A* said of Sarah his wife, She is
Gen 20:9 Then Abimelech called *A*, and said
Gen 20:10 And Abimelech said unto *A*, What
Gen 20:11 *A* said, Because I thought, Surely
Gen 20:14 and gave them unto *A*, and restored
Gen 21:4 *A* circumcised his son Isaac being
Gen 21:5 *A* was an hundred years old, when
Gen 21:9 which she had born unto *A*
Gen 21:24 And *A* said, I will swear
Gen 21:25 *A* reproved Abimelech because of a
Gen 21:29 And Abimelech said unto *A*, What
Gen 21:33 *A* planted a grove in Beer-sheba,
Gen 21:34 *A* sojourned in the Philistines'
Gen 22:1 things, that God did tempt *A*
Gen 22:6 *A* took the wood of the burnt
Gen 22:7 And Isaac spake unto *A* his father
Gen 22:8 *A* said, My son, God will provide
Gen 22:9 *A* built an altar there, and laid
Gen 22:13 *A* lifted up his eyes, and looked,
Gen 22:13 *A* went and took the ram, and
Gen 22:14 *A* called the name of that place
Gen 22:20 these things, that it was told *A*
Gen 23:2 *A* came to mourn for Sarah, and to
Gen 23:3 *A* stood up from before his dead,
Gen 23:5 the children of Heth answered *A*
Gen 23:10 Ephron the Hittite answered *A* in
Gen 23:12 *A* bowed down himself before the
Gen 23:14 And Ephron answered *A*, saying unto
Gen 23:16 And *A* hearkened unto Ephron
Gen 23:16 *A* weighed to Ephron the silver,
Gen 23:18 Unto *A* for a possession in the
Gen 23:19 *A* buried Sarah his wife in the
Gen 24:1 *A* was old, and well stricken in
Gen 24:1 LORD had blessed *A* in all things
Gen 24:27 be the LORD God of my master *A*
Gen 24:42 said, O LORD God of my master *A*
Gen 25:1 Then again *A* took a wife, and her
Gen 25:5 *A* gave all that he had unto Isaac
Gen 25:6 of the concubines, which *A* had
Gen 25:8 Then *A* gave up the ghost, and died
Gen 25:10 The field which *A* purchased of
Gen 25:12 Sarah's handmaid, bare unto *A*
Gen 25:19 *A* begat Isaac
Gen 26:1 famine that was in the days of *A*
Gen 26:3 which I sware unto *A* thy father
Gen 26:5 Because that *A* obeyed my voice,
Gen 26:24 I am the God of *A* thy father
Gen 28:4 And give thee the blessing of *A*
Gen 31:42 God of my father, the God of *A*
Gen 31:53 The God of *A*, and the God of Nahor
Gen 32:9 Jacob said, O God of my father *A*
Gen 35:12 And the land which I gave *A*
Gen 35:27 Arbah, which is Hebron, where *A*
Gen 48:15 God, before whom my fathers *A*
Gen 49:30 which *A* bought with the field of
Gen 50:13 which *A* bought with the field for
Gen 50:24 unto the land which he sware to *A*
Ex 2:24 remembered his covenant with *A*
Ex 3:6 God of thy father, the God of *A*
Ex 6:3 And I appeared unto *A*, unto Isaac,
Ex 6:8 which I did swear to give it to *A*
Ex 32:13 Remember *A*, Isaac, and Israel, thy
Ex 33:1 the land which I sware unto *A*
Lev 26:42 covenant with *A* will I remember
Num 32:11 see the land which I sware unto *A*
Deut 1:8 LORD sware unto your fathers, *A*
Deut 6:10 he sware unto thy fathers, to *A*
Deut 9:5 LORD sware unto thy fathers, *A*
Deut 9:27 Remember thy servants, *A*, Isaac,
Deut 29:13 hath sworn unto thy fathers, to *A*
Josh 24:2 time, even Terah, the father of *A*
Josh 24:3 I took your father *A* from the
1Kin 18:36 came near, and said, LORD God of *A*
2Kin 13:23 because of his covenant with *A*
1Chr 1:27 Abram; the same is *A*
1Chr 16:16 the covenant which he made with *A*
2Chr 20:7 the seed of *A* thy friend for ever
2Chr 30:6 turn again unto the LORD God of *A*
Neh 9:7 and gavest him the name of *A*
Ps 47:9 even the people of the God of *A*
Ps 105:6 O ye seed of *A* his servant
Ps 105:42 holy promise, and *A* his servant
Is 29:22 saith the LORD, who redeemed *A*
Is 41:8 chosen, the seed of *A* my friend
Is 51:2 Look unto *A* your father, and unto
Is 63:16 though *A* be ignorant of us, and
Jer 33:26 to be rulers over the seed of *A*
Eze 33:24 *A* was one, and he inherited the
Mic 7:20 truth to Jacob, and the mercy to *A*
Mt 1:1 the son of David, the son of *A*
Mt 1:17 from *A* to David are fourteen
Mt 3:9 We have *A* to our father
Mt 8:11 and west, and shall sit down with *A*
Mt 22:32 I am the God of *A*, and the God of
Mk 12:26 him, saying, I am the God of *A*
Lk 1:55 As he spake to our fathers, to *A*
Lk 1:73 which he sware to our father *A*
Lk 3:8 We have *A* to our father
Lk 3:34 of Isaac, which was the son of *A*
Lk 13:16 this woman, being a daughter of *A*
Lk 13:28 of teeth, when ye shall see *A*
Lk 16:23 seeth *A* afar off, and Lazarus in
Lk 16:29 *A* saith unto him, They have Moses
Lk 19:9 as he also is a son of *A*
Lk 20:37 he calleth the Lord the God of *A*
Jn 8:39 and said unto him, *A* is our father
Jn 8:52 *A* is dead, and the prophets
Jn 8:56 Your father *A* rejoiced to see my
Jn 8:57 years old, and hast thou seen *A*
Acts 3:13 The God of *A*, and of Isaac, and of
Acts 3:25 with our fathers, saying unto *A*
Acts 7:2 glory appeared unto our father *A*
Acts 7:8 so *A* begat Isaac, and circumcised
Acts 7:16 laid in the sepulchre that *A*
Acts 7:17 nigh, which God had sworn to *A*
Acts 7:32 God of thy fathers, the God of *A*
Acts 13:26 children of the stock of *A*
Rom 4:1 we say then that *A* our father
Rom 4:3 *A* believed God, and it was counted
Rom 4:9 reckoned to *A* for righteousness
Rom 4:12 of that faith of our father *A*
Rom 4:16 also which is of the faith of *A*
Rom 9:7 because they are the seed of *A*
Rom 11:1 am an Israelite, of the seed of *A*
2Cor 11:22 Are they the seed of *A*
Gal 3:6 Even as *A* believed God, and it was
Gal 3:14 That the blessing of *A* might come
Gal 3:18 but God gave it to *A* by promise
Gal 4:22 that *A* had two sons, the one by a
Heb 2:16 but he took on him the seed of *A*
Heb 6:13 For when God made promise to *A*
Heb 7:1 who met *A* returning from the
Heb 7:5 they come out of the loins of *A*
Heb 7:9 tithes, payed tithes in *A*
Heb 11:8 By faith *A*, when he was called to
Heb 11:17 By faith *A*, when he was tried,
Jas 2:21 Was not *A* our father justified by
Jas 2:23 *A* believed God, and it was imputed
1Pet 3:6 Even as Sarah obeyed *A*, calling

**ABRAM** *(a'-brum)* See ABRAHAM, ABRAM'S. *Abraham's original name.*
Gen 11:26 lived seventy years, and begat *A*
Gen 12:1 Now the LORD had said unto *A*
Gen 12:4 So *A* departed, as the LORD had
Gen 12:4 *A* was seventy and five years old
Gen 12:5 *A* took Sarai his wife, and Lot his
Gen 12:6 *A* passed through the land unto
Gen 12:9 *A* journeyed, going on still
Gen 12:10 *A* went down into Egypt to sojourn
Gen 12:14 when *A* was come into Egypt, the
Gen 12:16 he entreated *A* well for her sake
Gen 12:18 And Pharaoh called *A*, and said,
Gen 13:1 *A* went up out of Egypt, he, and
Gen 13:2 *A* was very rich in cattle, in
Gen 13:5 And Lot also, which went with *A*
Gen 13:8 *A* said unto Lot, Let there be no
Gen 13:12 *A* dwelled in the land of Canaan,
Gen 13:18 Then *A* removed his tent, and came
Gen 14:13 had escaped, and told *A* the Hebrew
Gen 14:19 Blessed be *A* of the most high God
Gen 14:21 And the king of Sodom said unto *A*
Gen 14:22 *A* said to the king of Sodom, I
Gen 14:23 shouldest say, I have made *A* rich
Gen 15:1 the LORD came unto *A* in a vision
Gen 15:3 *A* said, Behold, to me thou hast
Gen 15:11 the carcases, *A* drove them away
Gen 15:18 the LORD made a covenant with *A*
Gen 16:2 And Sarai said unto *A*, Behold now,
Gen 16:3 to her husband *A* to be his wife
Gen 16:5 And Sarai said unto *A*, My wrong be
Gen 16:15 *A* called his son's name, which
Gen 16:16 *A* was fourscore and six years old,
Gen 17:3 And *A* fell on his face
Gen 17:5 thy name any more be called *A*
1Chr 1:27 *A*; the same is Abraham
Neh 9:7 LORD the God, who didst choose *A*

**ABROAD**
Gen 10:18 of the Canaanites spread *a*
Gen 11:4 lest we be scattered *a* upon the
Gen 11:8 So the LORD scattered them *a* from
Gen 11:9 did the LORD scatter them *a* upon
Gen 15:5 And he brought him forth *a*
Gen 19:17 they had brought them forth *a*
Gen 28:14 thou shalt spread *a* to the west
Ex 5:12 *a* throughout all the land of
Ex 9:29 I will spread *a* my hands unto the
Ex 9:33 spread *a* his hands unto the LORD
Ex 12:46 of the flesh *a* out of the house
Ex 21:19 walk *a* upon his staff, then shall
Ex 40:19 he spread *a* the tent over the
Lev 13:7 scab spread much *a* in the skin
Lev 13:12 a leprosy break out *a* in the skin
Lev 13:22 if it spread much *a* in the skin
Lev 13:27 it be spread much *a* in the skin
Lev 14:8 shall tarry *a* out of his tent
Lev 18:9 she be born at home, or born *a*
Num 11:32 they spread them all *a* for
Deut 23:10 shall he go *a* out of the camp
Deut 23:12 whither thou shalt go forth *a*
Deut 23:13 be, when thou wilt ease thyself *a*
Deut 24:11 Thou shalt stand *a*, and the man to
Deut 24:11 bring out the pledge *a* unto thee
Deut 32:11 her young, spreadeth *a* her wings
Judg 12:9 thirty daughters, whom he sent *a*
1Sa 9:26 out both of them, he and Samuel, *a*
1Sa 30:16 they were spread *a* upon all the
2Sa 22:43 the street, and did spread them *a*
1Kin 2:42 walkest *a* any whither, that thou
2Kin 4:3 borrow thee vessels *a* of all thy
1Chr 13:2 let us send *a* unto our brethren
1Chr 14:13 spread themselves *a* in the valley
2Chr 26:8 his name spread *a* even to the
2Chr 26:15 And his name spread far *a*
2Chr 29:16 to carry it out *a* into the brook
2Chr 31:5 as soon as the commandment came *a*
Neh 1:8 scatter you *a* among the nations
Est 1:17 queen shall come *a* unto all women
Est 3:8 is a certain people scattered *a*
Job 4:11 lion's whelps are scattered *a*
Job 15:23 He wandereth *a* for bread, saying,
Job 40:11 Cast *a* the rage of thy wrath
Ps 41:6 when he goeth *a*, he telleth it
Ps 77:17 thine arrows also went *a*
Prov 5:16 Let thy fountains be dispersed *a*
Is 24:1 scattereth *a* the inhabitants
Is 28:25 doth he not cast *a* the fitches
Is 44:24 that spreadeth *a* the earth by
Jer 6:11 pour it out upon the children *a*
Lam 1:20 *a* the sword bereaveth, at home
Eze 34:21 till ye have scattered them *a*
Zec 1:17 prosperity shall yet be spread *a*
Zec 2:6 for I have spread you *a* as the
Mt 9:26 hereof went *a* into all that land
Mt 9:31 spread *a* his fame in all that
Mt 9:36 they fainted, and were scattered *a*
Mt 12:30 not with me scattereth *a*
Mt 26:31 of the flock shall be scattered *a*
Mk 1:28 immediately his fame spread *a*
Mk 1:45 to blaze *a* the matter, insomuch
Mk 4:22 secret, but that it should come *a*
Mk 6:14 (for his name was spread *a*
Lk 1:65 all these sayings were noised *a*
Lk 2:17 they made known *a* the saying
Lk 5:15 more went there a fame *a* of him
Lk 8:17 shall not be known and come *a*
Jn 11:52 of God that were scattered *a*
Jn 21:23 this saying *a* among the brethren
Acts 2:6 Now when this was noised *a*
Acts 8:1 they were all scattered *a*
Acts 8:4 they that were scattered *a* went
Acts 11:19 Now they which were scattered *a*
Rom 5:5 *a* in our hearts by the Holy Ghost
Rom 16:19 obedience is come *a* unto all men
2Cor 9:9 is written, He hath dispersed *a*
1Th 1:8 faith to God-ward is spread *a*
Jas 1:1 tribes which are scattered *a*

**ABSALOM** *(ab'-sal-um) A son of David.*
2Sa 3:3 *A* the son of Maacah the daughter
2Sa 13:1 that *A* the son of David had a
2Sa 13:22 for *A* hated Amnon, because he had
2Sa 13:23 that *A* had sheepshearers in
2Sa 13:25 And the king said to *A*, Nay, my
2Sa 13:28 Now *A* had commanded his servants,
2Sa 13:30 *A* hath slain all the king's sons,
2Sa 13:32 for by the appointment of *A* this
2Sa 13:39 David longed to go forth unto *A*
2Sa 14:1 the king's heart was toward *A*
2Sa 14:21 bring the young man *A* again
2Sa 14:23 Geshur, and brought *A* to Jerusalem
2Sa 14:25 much praised as *A* for his beauty
2Sa 14:27 unto *A* there were born three sons
2Sa 14:28 So *A* dwelt two full years in
2Sa 14:29 Therefore *A* sent for Joab, to
2Sa 14:32 *A* answered Joab, Behold, I sent
2Sa 15:1 that *A* prepared him chariots and
2Sa 15:2 *A* rose up early, and stood beside
2Sa 15:6 so *A* stole the hearts of the men
2Sa 15:7 that *A* said unto the king, I pray
2Sa 15:10 But *A* sent spies throughout all
2Sa 15:11 with *A* went two hundred men out
2Sa 15:12 *A* sent for Ahithophel the
2Sa 15:13 of the men of Israel are after *A*
2Sa 15:14 we shall not else escape from *A*
2Sa 15:31 is among the conspirators with *A*
2Sa 15:34 return to the city, and say unto *A*
2Sa 15:37 city, and *A* came into Jerusalem
2Sa 16:15 And *A*, and all the people the men
2Sa 16:17 *A* said to Hushai, Is this thy
2Sa 16:20 Then said *A* to Ahithophel, Give
2Sa 16:21 And Ahithophel said unto *A*
2Sa 16:23 both with David and with *A*
2Sa 17:5 Then said *A*, Call now Hushai the
2Sa 17:14 the LORD might bring evil upon *A*
2Sa 17:15 and thus did Ahithophel counsel *A*
2Sa 17:18 a lad saw them, and told *A*
2Sa 17:24 *A* passed over Jordan, he and all
2Sa 17:25 *A* made Amasa captain of the host
2Sa 18:5 the captains charge concerning *A*
2Sa 18:9 *A* rode upon a mule, and the mule
2Sa 18:10 Behold, I saw *A* hanged in an oak
2Sa 18:14 them through the heart of *A*
2Sa 18:15 armour compassed about and smote *A*
2Sa 18:18 Now *A* in his lifetime had taken
2Sa 18:29 said, Is the young man *A* safe
2Sa 18:33 God I had died for thee, O *A*
2Sa 19:1 king weepeth and mourneth for *A*
2Sa 19:4 loud voice, O my son *A*, O *A*
2Sa 19:6 that if *A* had lived, and all we
2Sa 20:6 Bichri do us more harm than did *A*
1Kin 1:6 and his mother bare him after *A*
1Kin 2:7 I fled because of *A* thy brother
1Kin 2:28 though he turned not after *A*
1Chr 3:2 *A* the son of Maachah the daughter
2Chr 11:20 he took Maachah the daughter of *A*
2Chr 11:21 daughter of *A* above all his wives
Ps 3:*t* when he fled from *A* his son

**ABSENCE**
Lk 22:6 them in the *a* of the multitude
Phil 2:12 only, but now much more in my *a*

**ABSENT**
Gen 31:49 when we are *a* one from another
1Cor 5:3 as *a* in body, but present in
2Cor 5:6 the body, we are *a* from the Lord
2Cor 5:8 rather to be *a* from the body
2Cor 5:9 that, whether present or *a*
2Cor 10:1 but being *a* am bold toward you
2Cor 10:11 in word by letters when we are *a*
2Cor 13:2 being *a* now I write to them which
2Cor 13:10 I write these things being *a*
Phil 1:27 I come and see you, or else be *a*
Col 2:5 For though I be *a* in the flesh

**ABSTAIN**
Acts 15:20 that they *a* from pollutions of
Acts 15:29 That ye *a* from meats offered to
1Th 4:3 that ye should *a* from fornication
1Th 5:22 *A* from all appearance of evil
1Ti 4:3 and commanding to *a* from meats
1Pet 2:11 *a* from fleshly lusts, which war

**ABUNDANCE**
Deut 28:47 of heart, for the *a* of all things
Deut 33:19 shall suck of the *a* of the seas
1Sa 1:16 for out of the *a* of my complaint
2Sa 12:30 the spoil of the city in great *a*
1Kin 1:19 oxen and fat cattle and sheep in *a*
1Kin 1:25 oxen and fat cattle and sheep in *a*
1Kin 10:10 there came no more such *a* of
1Kin 10:27 trees that are in the vale, for *a*
1Kin 18:41 for there is a sound of *a* of rain
1Chr 22:3 David prepared iron in *a* for the
1Chr 22:4 Also cedar trees in *a*
1Chr 22:14 for it is in *a*
1Chr 22:15 there are workmen with thee in *a*
1Chr 29:2 stones, and marble stones in *a*
1Chr 29:21 sacrifices in *a* for all Israel
2Chr 1:15 trees that are in the vale for *a*
2Chr 2:9 Even to prepare me timber in *a*
2Chr 4:18 made all these vessels in great *a*
2Chr 9:1 that bare spices, and gold in *a*
2Chr 9:9 of gold, and of spices great *a*
2Chr 9:27 that are in the low plains in *a*
2Chr 11:23 and he gave them victual in *a*
2Chr 14:15 carried away sheep and camels in *a*
2Chr 15:9 fell to him out of Israel in *a*
2Chr 17:5 and he had riches and honour in *a*
2Chr 18:1 had riches and honour in *a*
2Chr 18:2 killed sheep and oxen for him in *a*
2Chr 20:25 they found among them in *a* both
2Chr 24:11 by day, and gathered money in *a*
2Chr 29:35 the burnt offerings were in *a*
2Chr 31:5 in *a* the firstfruits of corn
2Chr 32:5 and made darts and shields in *a*
2Chr 32:29 of flocks and herds in *a*
Neh 9:25 oliveyards, and fruit trees in *a*
Est 1:7 from another,) and royal wine in *a*
Job 22:11 and *a* of waters cover thee
Job 36:31 he giveth meat in *a*
Job 38:34 that *a* of waters may cover thee
Ps 37:11 themselves in the *a* of peace
Ps 52:7 trusted in the *a* of his riches
Ps 72:7 *a* of peace so long as the moon
Ps 105:30 land brought forth frogs in *a*
Eccl 5:10 he that loveth *a* with increase
Eccl 5:12 but the *a* of the rich will not
Is 7:22 for the *a* of milk that they shall
Is 15:7 Therefore the *a* they have gotten,
Is 47:9 and for the great *a* of thine
Is 60:5 because the *a* of the sea shall be
Is 66:11 delighted with the *a* of her glory
Jer 33:6 reveal unto them the *a* of peace
Eze 16:49 *a* of idleness was in her and in
Eze 26:10 By reason of the *a* of his horses
Zec 14:14 and silver, and apparel, in great *a*
Mt 12:34 for out of the *a* of the heart the
Mt 13:12 be given, and he shall have more *a*
Mt 25:29 be given, and he shall have *a*
Mk 12:44 all they did cast in of their *a*
Lk 6:45 for of the *a* of the heart his
Lk 12:15 in the *a* of the things which he
Lk 21:4 For all these have of their *a*
Rom 5:17 they which receive *a* of grace
2Cor 8:2 of affliction the *a* of their joy
2Cor 8:14 that now at this time your *a* may
2Cor 8:20 *a* which is administered by us
2Cor 12:7 through the *a* of the revelations
Rev 18:3 through the *a* of her delicacies

### ABUNDANT
Ex 34:6 and *a* in goodness and truth,
Is 56:12 be as this day, and much more *a*
Jer 51:13 *a* in treasures, thine end is come
1Cor 12:23 these we bestow more *a* honour
1Cor 12:24 having given more *a* honour to
2Cor 4:15 that the *a* grace might through
2Cor 7:15 affection is more *a* toward you
2Cor 9:12 the saints, but is *a* also by many
2Cor 11:23 in labours more *a*, in stripes
Phil 1:26 *a* in Jesus Christ for me by my
1Ti 1:14 Lord was exceeding *a* with faith
1Pet 1:3 which according to his *a* mercy

### ABUNDANTLY
Gen 1:20 Let the waters bring forth *a* the
Gen 1:21 which the waters brought forth *a*
Gen 8:17 they may breed *a* in the earth
Gen 9:7 bring forth *a* in the earth, and
Ex 1:7 were fruitful, and increased *a*
Ex 8:3 river shall bring forth frogs *a*
Num 20:11 and the water came out *a*, and the
1Chr 12:40 wine, and oil, and oxen, and sheep *a*
1Chr 22:5 David prepared *a* before his death
1Chr 22:8 saying, Thou hast shed blood *a*
2Chr 31:5 of all things brought they in *a*
Job 12:6 into whose hand God bringeth *a*
Job 36:28 do drop and distil upon man *a*
Ps 36:8 They shall be *a* satisfied with
Ps 65:10 waterest the ridges thereof *a*
Ps 132:15 I will *a* bless her provision
Ps 145:7 They shall *a* utter the memory of
Song 5:1 drink, yea, drink *a*, O beloved
Is 15:3 every one shall howl, weeping *a*
Is 35:2 It shall blossom *a*, and rejoice
Is 55:7 to our God, for he will *a* pardon
Jn 10:10 and that they might have it more *a*
1Cor 15:10 I laboured more *a* than they all
2Cor 1:12 the world, and more *a* to you-ward
2Cor 2:4 love which I have more *a* unto you
2Cor 10:15 by you according to our rule *a*
Eph 3:20 that is able to do exceeding *a*
1Th 2:17 endeavoured the more *a* to see
Titus 3:6 Which he shed on us *a* through
Heb 6:17 willing more *a* to shew unto the
2Pet 1:11 shall be ministered unto you *a*

### ABUSE
1Sa 31:4 and thrust me through, and *a* me
1Chr 10:4 these uncircumcised come and *a* me
1Cor 9:18 that I *a* not my power in the

### ABUSED
Judg 19:25 *a* her all the night until the

### ABUSERS
1Cor 6:9 nor *a* of themselves with mankind,

### ABUSING
1Cor 7:31 that use this world, as not *a* it

### ACCAD *(ak'-kad) A city of Shinar.*
Gen 10:10 kingdom was Babel, and Erech, and *A*

### ACCEPT
Gen 32:20 peradventure he will *a* of me
Ex 22:11 the owner of it shall *a* thereof
Lev 26:41 they then *a* of the punishment of
Lev 26:43 they shall *a* of the punishment of
Deut 33:11 and *a* the work of his hands
1Sa 26:19 against me, let him *a* an offering
2Sa 24:23 the king, The LORD thy God *a* thee
Job 13:8 Will ye *a* his person
Job 13:10 you, if ye do secretly *a* persons
Job 32:21 *a* any man's person, neither let
Job 42:8 for him will I *a*
Ps 20:3 and *a* thy burnt sacrifice
Ps 82:2 *a* the persons of the wicked
Ps 119:108 *A*, I beseech thee, the freewill
Prov 18:5 It is not good to *a* the person of
Jer 14:10 the LORD doth not *a* them
Jer 14:12 and an oblation, I will not *a* them
Eze 20:40 there will I *a* them, and there
Eze 20:41 I will *a* you with your sweet
Eze 43:27 and I will *a* you, saith the Lord
Amos 5:22 meat offerings, I will not *a* them
Mal 1:8 with thee, or *a* thy person
Mal 1:10 neither will I *a* an offering at
Mal 1:13 should I *a* this of your hand
Acts 24:3 We *a* it always, and in all places,

### ACCEPTABLE
Lev 22:20 for it shall not be *a* for you
Deut 33:24 let him be *a* to his brethren, and
Ps 19:14 be *a* in thy sight, O LORD, my
Ps 69:13 unto thee, O LORD, in an *a* time
Prov 10:32 of the righteous know what is *a*
Prov 21:3 judgment is more *a* to the LORD
Eccl 12:10 sought to find out *a* words
Is 49:8 In an *a* time have I heard thee,
Is 58:5 a fast, and an *a* day to the LORD
Is 61:2 To proclaim the *a* year of the
Jer 6:20 your burnt offerings are not *a*
Dan 4:27 let my counsel be *a* unto thee
Lk 4:19 To preach the *a* year of the Lord
Rom 12:1 *a* unto God, which is your
Rom 12:2 may prove what is that good, and *a*
Rom 14:18 things serveth Christ is *a* to God
Rom 15:16 up of the Gentiles might be *a*
Eph 5:10 Proving what is *a* unto the Lord
Phil 4:18 of a sweet smell, a sacrifice *a*
1Ti 2:3 *a* in the sight of God our Saviour
1Ti 5:4 for that is good and *a* before God
1Pet 2:5 *a* to God by Jesus Christ
1Pet 2:20 it patiently, this is *a* with God

### ACCEPTED
Gen 4:7 doest well, shalt thou not be *a*
Gen 19:21 I have *a* thee concerning this
Ex 28:38 they may be *a* before the LORD
Lev 1:4 it shall be *a* for him to make
Lev 7:18 the third day, it shall not be *a*
Lev 10:19 should it have been *a* in the
Lev 19:7 it shall not be *a*
Lev 22:21 it shall be perfect to be *a*
Lev 22:23 but for a vow it shall not be *a*
Lev 22:25 they shall not be *a* for you
Lev 22:27 thenceforth it shall be *a* for an
Lev 23:11 before the LORD, to be *a* for you
1Sa 18:5 he was *a* in the sight of all the
1Sa 25:35 thy voice, and have *a* thy person
Est 10:3 *a* of the multitude of his
Job 42:9 the LORD also *a* Job
Is 56:7 shall be *a* upon mine altar
Jer 37:20 I pray thee, be *a* before thee
Jer 42:2 our supplication be *a* before thee
Lk 4:24 No prophet is *a* in his own
Acts 10:35 righteousness, is *a* with him
Rom 15:31 Jerusalem may be *a* of the saints
2Cor 5:9 or absent, we may be *a* of him
2Cor 6:2 I have heard thee in a time *a*
2Cor 6:2 behold, now is the *a* time
2Cor 8:12 it is *a* according to that a man
2Cor 8:17 For indeed he *a* the exhortation
2Cor 11:4 gospel, which ye have not *a*
Eph 1:6 he hath made us *a* in the beloved

### ACCESS
Rom 5:2 By whom also we have *a* by faith
Eph 2:18 For through him we both have *a* by
Eph 3:12 *a* with confidence by the faith of

### ACCHO *(ak'-ko) A coastal city in Asher.*
Judg 1:31 drive out the inhabitants of *A*

### ACCOMPANIED
Acts 10:23 certain brethren from Joppa *a* him
Acts 11:12 these six brethren *a* me
Acts 20:4 there *a* him into Asia Sopater of
Acts 20:38 And they *a* him unto the ship

### ACCOMPANY
Heb 6:9 you, and things that *a* salvation

### ACCOMPANYING
2Sa 6:4 was at Gibeah, *a* the ark of God

### ACCOMPLISH
Lev 22:21 unto the LORD to *a* his vow
1Kin 5:9 and thou shalt *a* my desire
Job 14:6 that he may rest, till he shall *a*
Ps 64:6 they *a* a diligent search
Is 55:11 but it shall *a* that which I
Jer 44:25 ye will surely *a* your vows
Eze 6:12 thus will I *a* my fury upon them
Eze 7:8 thee, and *a* mine anger upon thee
Eze 13:15 Thus will I *a* my wrath upon the
Eze 20:8 to *a* my anger against them in the
Eze 20:21 to *a* my anger against them in the
Dan 9:2 that he would *a* seventy years in
Lk 9:31 which he should *a* at Jerusalem

### ACCOMPLISHED
2Chr 36:22 the mouth of Jeremiah might be *a*
Est 2:12 the days of their purifications *a*
Job 15:32 It shall be *a* before his time, and
Prov 13:19 The desire *a* is sweet to the soul
Is 40:2 unto her, that her warfare is *a*
Jer 25:12 to pass, when seventy years are *a*
Jer 25:34 and of your dispersions are *a*
Jer 29:10 be *a* at Babylon I will visit you
Jer 39:16 they shall be *a* in that day
Lam 4:11 The LORD hath *a* his fury
Lam 4:22 punishment of thine iniquity is *a*
Eze 4:6 And when thou hast *a* them, lie
Eze 5:13 Thus shall mine anger be *a*
Eze 5:13 when I have *a* my fury in them
Dan 11:36 prosper till the indignation be *a*
Dan 12:7 when he shall have *a* to scatter
Lk 1:23 days of his ministration were *a*
Lk 2:6 the days were *a* that she should
Lk 2:21 when eight days were *a* for the
Lk 2:22 to the law of Moses were *a*
Lk 12:50 how am I straitened till it be *a*
Lk 18:31 the Son of man shall be *a*
Lk 22:37 is written must yet be *a* in me
Jn 19:28 that all things were now *a*
Acts 21:5 And when we had *a* those days
1Pet 5:9 *a* in your brethren that are in

### ACCORD
Lev 25:5 *a* of thy harvest thou shalt not
Josh 9:2 Joshua and with Israel, with one *a*
Acts 1:14 continued with one *a* in prayer
Acts 2:1 were all with one *a* in one place
Acts 2:46 daily with one *a* in the temple
Acts 4:24 up their voice to God with one *a*
Acts 5:12 all with one *a* in Solomon's porch
Acts 7:57 ears, and ran upon him with one *a*
Acts 8:6 the people with one *a* gave heed
Acts 12:10 which opened to them of his own *a*
Acts 12:20 but they came with one *a* to him
Acts 15:25 us, being assembled with one *a*
Acts 18:12 with one *a* against Paul, and
Acts 19:29 with one *a* into the theatre
2Cor 8:17 of his own *a* he went unto you
Phil 2:2 the same love, being of one *a*

### ACCOUNT
2Kin 12:4 of every one that passeth the *a*
1Chr 27:24 was the number put in the *a* of
2Chr 26:11 to the number of their *a* by the
Job 33:13 for he giveth not *a* of any of his
Ps 144:3 of man, that thou makest *a* of him
Eccl 7:27 one by one, to find out the *a*
Mt 12:36 they shall give *a* thereof in the
Mt 18:23 would take *a* of his servants
Lk 16:2 give an *a* of thy stewardship
Acts 19:40 may give an *a* of this concourse
Rom 14:12 us shall give *a* of himself to God
1Cor 4:1 Let a man so *a* of us, as of the
Phil 4:17 fruit that may abound to your *a*
Philem 18 thee ought, put that on mine *a*
Heb 13:17 souls, as they that must give *a*
1Pet 4:5 Who shall give *a* to him that is
2Pet 3:15 *a* that the longsuffering of our

### ACCOUNTED
Deut 2:11 Which also were *a* giants, as the
Deut 2:20 (That also was *a* a land of giants
1Kin 10:21 it was nothing *a* of in the days
2Chr 9:20 it was not any thing *a* of in the
Ps 22:30 it shall be *a* to the Lord for a
Is 2:22 for wherein is he to be *a* of
Mk 10:42 are *a* to rule over the Gentiles
Lk 20:35 But they which shall be *a* worthy
Lk 21:36 that ye may be *a* worthy to escape
Lk 22:24 of them should be *a* the greatest
Rom 8:36 we are *a* as sheep for the
Gal 3:6 it was *a* to him for righteousness

### ACCURSED
Deut 21:23 for he that is hanged is *a* of God
Josh 6:17 And the city shall be *a*, even it,
Josh 6:18 keep yourselves from the *a* thing
Josh 7:1 a trespass in the *a* thing
Josh 7:11 have even taken of the *a* thing
Josh 7:12 enemies, because they were *a*
Josh 7:13 There is an *a* thing in the midst
Josh 7:15 *a* thing shall be burnt with fire
Josh 22:20 commit a trespass in the *a* thing
1Chr 2:7 who transgressed in the thing *a*
Is 65:20 an hundred years old shall be *a*
Rom 9:3 *a* from Christ for my brethren
1Cor 12:3 the Spirit of God calleth Jesus *a*
Gal 1:8 preached unto you, let him be *a*
Gal 1:9 ye have received, let him be *a*

### ACCUSATION
Ezr 4:6 wrote they unto him an *a* against
Mt 27:37 up over his head his *a* written
Mk 15:26 of his *a* was written over
Lk 6:7 they might find an *a* against him

Lk 19:8 any thing from any man by false *a*
Jn 18:29 What *a* bring ye against this man
Acts 25:18 they brought none *a* of such
1Ti 5:19 Against an elder receive not an *a*
2Pet 2:11 bring not railing *a* against them
Jude 9 not bring against him a railing *a*

**ACCUSE**
Prov 30:10 *A* not a servant unto his master,
Mt 12:10 that they might *a* him
Mk 3:2 that they might *a* him
Lk 3:14 to no man, neither *a* any falsely
Lk 11:54 his mouth, that they might *a* him
Lk 23:2 And they began to *a* him, saying,
Lk 23:14 those things whereof ye *a* him
Jn 5:45 that I will *a* you to the Father
Jn 8:6 that they might have to *a* him
Acts 24:2 forth, Tertullus began to *a* him
Acts 24:8 these things, whereof we *a* him
Acts 24:13 the things whereof they now *a* me
Acts 25:5 *a* this man, if there be any
Acts 25:11 these things whereof these *a* me
Acts 28:19 I had ought to *a* my nation of
1Pet 3:16 *a* your good conversation in

**ACCUSED**
Dan 3:8 came near, and *a* the Jews
Dan 6:24 those men which had *a* Daniel
Mt 27:12 when he was *a* of the chief
Mk 15:3 the chief priests *a* him of many
Lk 16:1 the same was *a* unto him that he
Lk 23:10 scribes stood and vehemently *a* him
Acts 22:30 wherefore he was *a* of the Jews
Acts 23:28 the cause wherefore they *a* him
Acts 23:29 Whom I perceived to be *a* of
Acts 25:16 before that he which is *a* have
Acts 26:2 things whereof I am *a* of the Jews
Acts 26:7 king Agrippa, I am *a* of the Jews
Titus 1:6 children not *a* of riot or unruly
Rev 12:10 which *a* them before our God day

**ACCUSER**
Rev 12:10 for the *a* of our brethren is cast

**ACCUSERS**
Jn 8:10 Woman, where are those thine *a*
Acts 23:30 gave commandment to his *a* also to
Acts 23:35 when thine *a* are also come
Acts 24:8 Commanding his *a* to come unto
Acts 25:16 accused have the *a* face to face
Acts 25:18 Against whom when the *a* stood up
2Ti 3:3 affection, trucebreakers, false *a*
Titus 2:3 as becometh holiness, not false *a*

**ACELDAMA** *(as-el'-dam-ah) A burial ground bought with Judas' betrayal money.*
Acts 1:19 called in their proper tongue, *A*

**ACHAIA** *(ak-ah'-yah) Roman province in Greece.*
Acts 18:12 when Gallio was the deputy of *A*
Acts 18:27 he was disposed to pass into *A*
Acts 19:21 had passed through Macedonia and *A*
Rom 15:26 *A* to make a certain contribution
Rom 16:5 the firstfruits of *A* unto Christ
1Cor 16:15 that it is the firstfruits of *A*
2Cor 1:1 all the saints which are in all *A*
2Cor 9:2 that *A* was ready a year ago
2Cor 11:10 this boasting in the regions of *A*
1Th 1:7 that believe in Macedonia and *A*
1Th 1:8 Lord not only in Macedonia and *A*

**ACHAICUS** *(ak-ah'-yah-cus) A Corinthian who visited Paul in Philippi.*
1Cor 16:17 of Stephanas and Fortunatus and *A*

**ACHAN** *(a'-kan)* See ACHAR. *Soldier under Joshua executed for disobedience.*
Josh 7:1 for *A*, the son of Carmi, the son
Josh 7:18 and *A*, the son of Carmi, the son
Josh 7:19 And Joshua said unto *A*, My son,
Josh 7:20 *A* answered Joshua, and said,
Josh 7:24 took *A* the son of Zerah, and the
Josh 22:20 Did not *A* the son of Zerah commit

**ACHAR** *(a'-kar)* See ACHAN. *A form of Achan.*
1Chr 2:7 *A*, the troubler of Israel, who

**ACHAZ** *(a'-kaz)* See AHAZ. *The Greek form of Ahaz.*
Mt 1:9 and Joatham begat *A*
Mt 1:9 and *A* begat Ezekias

**ACHBOR** *(ak'-bor)*
*1. Father of an Edomite king.*
Gen 36:38 the son of *A* reigned in his stead
Gen 36:39 And Baal-hanan the son of *A* died
1Chr 1:49 the son of *A* reigned in his stead
*2. A messenger of Josiah to Huldah.*
2Kin 22:12 *A* the son of Michaiah, and Shaphan
2Kin 22:14 the priest, and Ahikam, and *A*
*3. Father of Elnathan.*
Jer 26:22 namely, Elnathan the son of *A*
Jer 36:12 and Elnathan the son of *A*

**ACHIM** *(a'-kim) Son of Sadoc; ancestor of Jesus.*
Mt 1:14 and Sadoc begat *A*

**ACHISH** *(a'-kish)*
*1. A king of Gath who aided David.*
1Sa 21:10 went to *A* the king of Gath
1Sa 21:11 the servants of *A* said unto him
1Sa 21:12 sore afraid of *A* the king of Gath
1Sa 27:2 men that were with him unto *A*
1Sa 27:3 And David dwelt with *A* at Gath
1Sa 27:6 Then *A* gave him Ziklag that day
1Sa 27:12 *A* believed David, saying, He hath
1Sa 28:1 *A* said unto David, Know thou
1Sa 29:3 *A* said unto the princes of the
1Sa 29:6 Then *A* called David, and said unto
*2. A king of Gath during Solomon's reign.*
1Kin 2:39 of Shimei ran away unto *A* son of
1Kin 2:40 went to Gath to *A* to seek his

**ACHMETHA** *(ak'-meth-ah) A city in Media.*
Ezr 6:2 And there was found at *A*, in the

**ACHOR** *(a'-kor) A valley near Jericho.*
Josh 7:24 brought them unto the valley of *A*
Josh 7:26 place was called, The valley of *A*
Josh 15:7 toward Debir from the valley of *A*
Is 65:10 the valley of *A* a place for the
Hos 2:15 the valley of *A* for a door of

**ACHSA** *(ak'-sah)* See ACHSAH. *Daughter of Caleb.*
1Chr 2:49 and the daughter of Caleb was *A*

**ACHSAH** *(ak'-sah)* See ACHSA. *A form of Achsa.*
Josh 15:16 to him will I give *A* my daughter
Judg 1:12 to him will I give *A* my daughter

**ACHSHAPH** *(ak'-shaf) A Phoenician city in Asher.*
Josh 11:1 of Shimron, and to the king of *A*
Josh 12:20 the king of *A*, one
Josh 19:25 Helkath, and Hali, and Beten, and *A*

**ACHZIB** *(ak'-zib)* See CHEZIB.
*1. A town in western Judah.*
Josh 15:44 And Keilah, and *A*, and Mareshah
Mic 1:14 the houses of *A* shall be a lie to
*2. A coastal city in Asher.*
Josh 19:29 at the sea from the coast to *A*
Judg 1:31 of Zidon, nor of Ahlab, nor of *A*

**ACKNOWLEDGE**
Deut 21:17 But he shall *a* the son of the
Deut 33:9 neither did he *a* his brethren
Ps 51:3 For I *a* my transgressions
Prov 3:6 In all thy ways *a* him, and he
Is 33:13 and, ye that are near, *a* my might
Is 61:9 all that see them shall *a* them
Is 63:16 of us, and Israel *a* us not
Jer 3:13 Only *a* thine iniquity, that thou
Jer 14:20 We *a*, O LORD, our wickedness, and
Jer 24:5 so will I *a* them that are carried
Dan 11:39 a strange god, whom he shall *a*
Hos 5:15 till they *a* their offence, and
1Cor 14:37 let him *a* that the things that I
1Cor 16:18 therefore *a* ye them that are such
2Cor 1:13 unto you, than what ye read or *a*

**ACKNOWLEDGED**
Gen 38:26 And Judah *a* them, and said, She
Ps 32:5 I *a* my sin unto thee, and mine
2Cor 1:14 As also ye have *a* us in part

**ACKNOWLEDGING**
2Ti 2:25 repentance to the *a* of the truth
Titus 1:1 the *a* of the truth which is after
Philem 6 may become effectual by the *a* of

**ACQUAINTANCE**
2Kin 12:5 it to them, every man of his *a*
2Kin 12:7 receive no more money of your *a*
Job 19:13 mine *a* are verily estranged from
Job 42:11 that had been of his *a* before
Ps 31:11 neighbours, and a fear to mine *a*
Ps 55:13 mine equal, my guide, and mine *a*
Ps 88:8 hast put away mine *a* far from me
Ps 88:18 from me, and mine *a* into darkness
Lk 2:44 him among their kinsfolk and *a*
Lk 23:49 And all his *a*, and the women that
Acts 24:23 *a* to minister or come unto him

**ACQUIT**
Job 10:14 thou wilt not *a* me from mine
Nah 1:3 and will not at all *a* the wicked

**ACRE**
1Sa 14:14 as it were an half *a* of land

**ACRES**
Is 5:10 ten *a* of vineyard shall yield one

**ACT**
Is 28:21 to pass his *a*, his strange *a*
Is 59:6 the *a* of violence is in their
Jn 8:4 taken in adultery, in the very *a*

**ACTIONS**
1Sa 2:3 and by him *a* are weighed

**ACTIVITY**
Gen 47:6 knowest any men of *a* among them

**ACTS**
Deut 11:3 And his miracles, and his *a*
Deut 11:7 great *a* of the LORD which he did
Judg 5:11 the righteous *a* of the LORD
1Sa 12:7 all the righteous *a* of the LORD
2Sa 23:20 of Kabzeel, who had done many *a*
1Kin 10:6 I heard in mine own land of thy *a*
1Kin 11:41 And the rest of the *a* of Solomon
1Kin 14:19 And the rest of the *a* of Jeroboam
1Kin 14:29 Now the rest of the *a* of Rehoboam
1Kin 15:7 Now the rest of the *a* of Abijam
1Kin 15:23 The rest of all the *a* of Asa
1Kin 15:31 Now the rest of the *a* of Nadab
1Kin 16:5 Now the rest of the *a* of Baasha
1Kin 16:14 Now the rest of the *a* of Elah
1Kin 16:20 Now the rest of the *a* of Zimri
1Kin 16:27 Now the rest of the *a* of Omri
1Kin 22:39 Now the rest of the *a* of Ahab
1Kin 22:45 the rest of the *a* of Jehoshaphat
2Kin 1:18 Now the rest of the *a* of Ahaziah
2Kin 8:23 And the rest of the *a* of Joram
2Kin 10:34 Now the rest of the *a* of Jehu
2Kin 12:19 And the rest of the *a* of Joash
2Kin 13:8 Now the rest of the *a* of Jehoahaz
2Kin 13:12 And the rest of the *a* of Joash
2Kin 14:15 Now the rest of the *a* of Jehoash
2Kin 14:18 And the rest of the *a* of Amaziah
2Kin 14:28 Now the rest of the *a* of Jeroboam
2Kin 15:6 And the rest of the *a* of Azariah
2Kin 15:11 And the rest of the *a* of Zachariah
2Kin 15:15 And the rest of the *a* of Shallum
2Kin 15:21 And the rest of the *a* of Menahem
2Kin 15:26 And the rest of the *a* of Pekahiah
2Kin 15:31 And the rest of the *a* of Pekah
2Kin 15:36 Now the rest of the *a* of Jotham
2Kin 16:19 Now the rest of the *a* of Ahaz
2Kin 20:20 And the rest of the *a* of Hezekiah
2Kin 21:17 Now the rest of the *a* of Manasseh
2Kin 21:25 Now the rest of the *a* of Amon
2Kin 23:19 the *a* that he had done in Beth-el
2Kin 23:28 Now the rest of the *a* of Josiah
2Kin 24:5 the rest of the *a* of Jehoiakim
1Chr 11:22 of Kabzeel, who had done many *a*
1Chr 29:29 Now the *a* of David the king,
2Chr 9:5 heard in mine own land of thine *a*
2Chr 9:29 Now the rest of the *a* of Solomon
2Chr 12:15 Now the *a* of Rehoboam, first and
2Chr 13:22 And the rest of the *a* of Abijah
2Chr 16:11 the *a* of Asa, first and last, lo,
2Chr 20:34 the rest of the *a* of Jehoshaphat
2Chr 25:26 Now the rest of the *a* of Amaziah
2Chr 26:22 Now the rest of the *a* of Uzziah
2Chr 27:7 Now the rest of the *a* of Jotham
2Chr 28:26 Now the rest of his *a* and of all
2Chr 32:32 Now the rest of the *a* of Hezekiah
2Chr 33:18 Now the rest of the *a* of Manasseh
2Chr 35:26 Now the rest of the *a* of Josiah
2Chr 36:8 the rest of the *a* of Jehoiakim
Est 10:2 all the *a* of his power and of his
Ps 103:7 his *a* unto the children of Israel
Ps 106:2 utter the mighty *a* of the LORD
Ps 145:4 and shall declare thy mighty *a*
Ps 145:6 of the might of thy terrible *a*
Ps 145:12 to the sons of men his mighty *a*
Ps 150:2 Praise him for his mighty *a*

**ADADAH** *(ad'-ad-ah) A city in southern Judah.*
Josh 15:22 And Kinah, and Dimonah, and *A*

**ADAH** *(a'-dah)*
*1. A wife of Lemech.*
Gen 4:19 the name of the one was *A*
Gen 4:20 And *A* bare Jabal
Gen 4:23 And Lamech said unto his wives, *A*
*2. A wife of Esau.*
Gen 36:2 *A* the daughter of Elon the
Gen 36:4 And *A* bare to Esau Eliphaz
Gen 36:10 the son of *A* the wife of Esau
Gen 36:12 were the sons of *A* Esau's wife
Gen 36:16 these were the sons of *A*

**ADAIAH** *(ad-a-i'-yah)*
*1. Grandfather of King Josiah.*
2Kin 22:1 the daughter of *A* of Boscath
*2. A Levite descendant of Gershon.*
1Chr 6:41 the son of Zerah, the son of *A*
*3. A son of Shimhi.*
1Chr 8:21 And *A*, and Beraiah, and Shimrath,
*4. A Levite of Jerusalem.*
1Chr 9:12 *A* the son of Jeroham, the son of
*5. Father of Maaseiah.*
2Chr 23:1 of Obed, and Maaseiah the son of *A*
*6. Married a foreign wife in Exile.*
Ezr 10:29 Meshullam, Malluch, and *A*, Jashub,
*7. Married a foreign wife in Exile.*
Ezr 10:39 And Shelemiah, and Nathan, and *A*
*8. A descendant of Pharez.*
Neh 11:5 the son of Hazaiah, the son of *A*
*9. An Aaronite Levite.*
Neh 11:12 *A* the son of Jeroham, the son of

**ADALIA** *(ad-al-i'-yah) A son of Haman.*
Est 9:8 And Poratha, and *A*, and Aridatha,

**ADAM** *(ad'-um)* See ADAM'S.
*1. First man created by God.*
Gen 2:19 whatsoever *A* called every living
Gen 2:20 *A* gave names to all cattle, and to
Gen 2:21 a deep sleep to fall upon *A*
Gen 2:23 *A* said, This is now bone of my
Gen 3:8 and *A* and his wife hid themselves
Gen 3:9 And the LORD God called unto *A*
Gen 3:17 unto *A* he said, Because thou hast
Gen 3:20 *A* called his wife's name Eve
Gen 3:21 Unto *A* also and to his wife did
Gen 4:1 And *A* knew Eve his wife
Gen 4:25 And *A* knew his wife again
Gen 5:1 the book of the generations of *A*
Gen 5:3 *A* lived an hundred and thirty
Deut 32:8 when he separated the sons of *A*
1Chr 1:1 *A*, Sheth, Enosh,
Job 31:33 I covered my transgressions as *A*
Lk 3:38 of Seth, which was the son of *A*
Rom 5:14 death reigned from *A* to Moses
1Cor 15:22 For as in *A* all die, even so in
1Cor 15:45 The first man *A* was made a living
1Ti 2:13 For *A* was first formed, then Eve
1Ti 2:14 *A* was not deceived, but the woman
Jude 14 And Enoch also, the seventh from *A*
*2. A town in Manasseh.*
Josh 3:16 an heap very far from the city *A*

**ADAMAH** *(ad'-am-ah) A walled city in Naphtali.*
Josh 19:36 And *A*, and Ramah, and Hazor,

**ADAMANT**
Eze 3:9 As an *a* harder than flint have I
Zec 7:12 made their hearts as an *a* stone

**ADAMI** *(ad'-am-i) A variant of Adamah.*
Josh 19:33 from Allon to Zaanannim, and *A*

**ADAM'S** *(ad'-ums)*
Rom 5:14 the similitude of *A* transgression

**ADAR** *(a'-dar)* See ADDAR, ATABOTH-ADAR.
*1. A city in southern Judah.*
Josh 15:3 along to Hezron, and went up to *A*
*2. Twelfth month of the Hebrew year.*
Ezr 6:15 on the third day of the month *A*
Est 3:7 month, that is, the month *A*
Est 3:13 month, which is the month *A*
Est 8:12 month, which is the month *A*
Est 9:1 month, that is, the month *A*
Est 9:15 day also of the month *A*, and slew
Est 9:17 the thirteenth day of the month *A*
Est 9:19 of the month *A* a day of gladness
Est 9:21 the fourteenth day of the month *A*

**ADBEEL** *(ad'-be-el) Son of Ishmael.*
Gen 25:13 and Kedar, and *A*, and Mibsam,
1Chr 1:29 then Kedar, and *A*, and Mibsam,

**ADD**
Gen 30:24 The LORD shall *a* to me another
Lev 5:16 shall *a* the fifth part thereto,
Lev 6:5 shall *a* the fifth part more
Lev 27:13 then he shall *a* a fifth part
Lev 27:31 he shall *a* thereto the fifth part
Num 5:7 *a* unto it the fifth part thereof,
Num 35:6 and to them ye shall *a* forty
Deut 4:2 Ye shall not *a* unto the word
Deut 12:32 thou shalt not *a* thereto, nor
Deut 19:9 then shalt thou *a* three cities
Deut 29:19 to *a* drunkenness to thirst
2Sa 24:3 LORD thy God *a* unto the people
1Kin 12:11 heavy yoke, I will *a* to your yoke
1Kin 12:14 heavy, and I will *a* to your yoke
2Kin 20:6 I will *a* unto thy days fifteen
1Chr 22:14 and thou mayest *a* thereto
2Chr 10:14 yoke heavy, but I will *a* thereto
2Chr 28:13 ye intend to *a* more to our sins
Ps 69:27 *A* iniquity unto their iniquity
Prov 3:2 and peace, shall they *a* to thee
Prov 30:6 *A* thou not unto his words, lest
Is 29:1 *a* ye year to year
Is 30:1 that they may *a* sin to sin
Is 38:5 I will *a* unto thy days fifteen
Mt 6:27 can *a* one cubit unto his stature
Lk 12:25 can *a* to his stature one cubit
Phil 1:16 supposing to *a* affliction to my
2Pet 1:5 diligence, *a* to your faith virtue
Rev 22:18 If any man shall *a* unto these
Rev 22:18 God shall *a* unto him the plagues

**ADDAN** *(ad'-dan) Home of some Exiles in Babylon.*
Ezr 2:59 Tel-melah, Tel-harsa, Cherub, *A*

**ADDAR** *(ad'-dar)* See ADAR, ATAROTH-ADDAR. *Son of Bela.*
1Chr 8:3 And the sons of Bela were, *A*

**ADDED**
Deut 5:22 and he *a* no more
1Sa 12:19 for we have *a* unto all our sins
Jer 36:32 there were *a* besides unto them
Jer 45:3 for the LORD hath *a* grief to my
Dan 4:36 excellent majesty was *a* unto me
Mt 6:33 these things shall be *a* unto you
Lk 3:20 *A* yet this above all, that he
Lk 12:31 these things shall be *a* unto you
Lk 19:11 as they heard these things, he *a*
Acts 2:41 the same day there were *a* unto
Acts 2:47 the Lord *a* to the church daily
Acts 5:14 were the more *a* to the Lord
Acts 11:24 much people was *a* unto the Lord
Gal 2:6 in conference *a* nothing to me
Gal 3:19 It was *a* because of

**ADDER**
Gen 49:17 an *a* in the path, that biteth the
Ps 58:4 the deaf *a* that stoppeth her ear
Ps 91:13 shalt tread upon the lion and *a*
Prov 23:32 a serpent, and stingeth like an *a*

**ADDERS'**
Ps 140:3 *a* poison is under their lips

**ADDETH**
Job 34:37 For he *a* rebellion unto his sin,
Prov 10:22 rich, and he *a* no sorrow with it
Prov 16:23 mouth, and *a* learning to his lips
Gal 3:15 no man disannulleth, or *a* thereto

**ADDI** *(ad'-di) Son of Cozam; ancestor of Jesus.*
Lk 3:28 of Melchi, which was the son of *A*

**ADDICTED**
1Cor 16:15 that they have *a* themselves to

**ADDITIONS**
1Kin 7:29 were certain *a* made of thin work
1Kin 7:36 of every one, and *a* round about

**ADDON** *(ad'-don) A form of Addan.*
Neh 7:61 Tel-melah, Tel-haresha, Cherub, *A*

**ADER** *(a'-dur) A son of Beriah.*
1Chr 8:15 And Zebadiah, and Arad, and *A*

**ADIEL** *(a'-de-el)*
*1. A descendant of Simeon.*
1Chr 4:36 and Jeshohaiah, and Asaiah, and *A*
*2. Father of Massiai.*
1Chr 9:12 and Maasiai the son of *A*, the son
*3. Father of Azmaveth.*
1Chr 27:25 was Azmaveth the son of *A*

**ADIN** *(a'-din)*
*1. Family who returned from exile.*
Ezr 2:15 The children of *A*, four hundred
Neh 7:20 The children of *A*, six hundred
*2. Family who sealed the covenant with Nehemiah.*
Neh 10:16 Adonijah, Bigvai, *A*,
*3. An exilic family with Ezra.*
Ezr 8:6 Of the sons also of *A*

**ADINA** *(ad'-in-ah) A "mighty man" of David.*
1Chr 11:42 *A* the son of Shiza the Reubenite,

**ADINO** *(ad'-in-o) A "mighty man" of David.*
2Sa 23:8 the same was *A* the Eznite

**ADITHAIM** *(ad-ith-a'-im) A city in the plain of Judah.*
Josh 15:36 Sharaim, and *A*, and Gederah, and

**ADJURE**
1Kin 22:16 How many times shall I *a* thee
2Chr 18:15 How many times shall I *a* thee
Mt 26:63 I *a* thee by the living God, that
Mk 5:7 I *a* thee by God, that thou
Acts 19:13 We *a* you by Jesus whom Paul

**ADJURED**
Josh 6:26 Joshua *a* them at that time,
1Sa 14:24 for Saul had *a* the people

**ADLAI** *(ad'-la-i) Father of Shapat.*
1Chr 27:29 valleys was Shaphat the son of *A*

**ADMAH** *(ad'-mah) A city destroyed with Sodom and Gomorrah.*
Gen 10:19 unto Sodom, and Gomorrah, and *A*
Gen 14:2 of Gomorrah, Shinab king of *A*
Gen 14:8 of Gomorrah, and the king of *A*
Deut 29:23 of Sodom, and Gomorrah, *A*, and
Hos 11:8 how shall I make thee as *A*

**ADMATHA** *(ad'-math-ah) A prince of Persia.*
Est 1:14 unto him was Carshena, Shethar, *A*

**ADMINISTERED**
2Cor 8:19 which is *a* by us to the glory of
2Cor 8:20 this abundance which is *a* by us

**ADMINISTRATION**
2Cor 9:12 For the *a* of this service not

**ADMINISTRATIONS**
1Cor 12:5 And there are differences of *a*

**ADMIRATION**
Jude 16 persons in *a* because of advantage
Rev 17:6 saw her, I wondered with great *a*

**ADMONISH**
Rom 15:14 able also to *a* one another
1Th 5:12 over you in the Lord, and *a* you
2Th 3:15 an enemy, but *a* him as a brother

**ADMONISHED**
Eccl 4:13 king, who will no more be *a*
Eccl 12:12 further, by these, my son, be *a*
Jer 42:19 that I have *a* you this day
Acts 27:9 was now already past, Paul *a* them
Heb 8:5 as Moses was *a* of God when he was

**ADMONITION**
1Cor 10:11 and they are written for our *a*
Eph 6:4 in the nurture and *a* of the Lord
Titus 3:10 the first and second *a* reject

**ADNA** *(ad'-nah)* See ADNAH.
*1. Married a foreigner while in exile.*
Ezr 10:30 *A*, and Chelal, Benaiah, Maaseiah,
*2. A priest during Joiakim's reign.*
Neh 12:15 Of Harim, *A*

**ADNAH** *(ad'-nah)* See ADNA.
*1. A captain in David's army.*
1Chr 12:20 there fell to him of Manasseh, *A*
*2. A commander in Jehoshaphat's army.*
2Chr 17:14 *A* the chief, and with him mighty

**ADO**
Mk 5:39 unto them, Why make ye this *a*

**ADONI-BEZEK** *(ad'-on-i-be'-zek) A lord of a Canaanite city.*
Judg 1:5 And they found *A* in Bezek
Judg 1:7 *A* said, Threescore and ten kings,

**ADONIJAH** *(ad-on-i'-jah)* See TOB-ADONIJAH.
*1. A son of David.*
2Sa 3:4 the fourth, A the son of Haggith
1Kin 1:5 Then A the son of Haggith exalted
1Kin 1:11 Hast thou not heard that A the
1Kin 1:13 why then doth A reign
1Kin 1:18 And now, behold, A reigneth
1Kin 1:24 A shall reign after me, and he
1Kin 1:43 And Jonathan answered and said to A
1Kin 1:49 that were with A were afraid
1Kin 1:50 A feared because of Solomon, and
1Kin 2:13 A the son of Haggith came to
1Kin 2:21 be given to A thy brother to wife
1Kin 2:22 ask Abishag the Shunammite for A
1Kin 2:24 A shall be put to death this day
1Kin 2:28 for Joab had turned after A
1Chr 3:2 the fourth, A the son of Haggith
*2. A Levite under King Jehoshaphat.*
2Chr 17:8 Shemiramoth, and Jehonathan, and A
*3. A clan leader who sealed the covenant with Nehemiah.*
Neh 10:16 A, Bigvai, Adin,

**ADONIKAM** *(ad-on-i'-kam) A family in exile.*
Ezr 2:13 The children of A, six hundred
Ezr 8:13 And of the last sons of A, whose
Neh 7:18 The children of A, six hundred

**ADONIRAM** *(ad-on-i'-ram)* See ADORAM. *A tribute officer under Solomon.*
1Kin 4:6 A the son of Abda was over the
1Kin 5:14 and A was over the levy

**ADONI-ZEDEK** *(ad'-on-i-ze'-dek) Canaanite king slain by Joshua.*
Josh 10:1 when A king of Jerusalem had
Josh 10:3 Wherefore A king of Jerusalem

**ADOPTION**
Rom 8:15 ye have received the Spirit of *a*
Rom 8:23 ourselves, waiting for the *a*
Rom 9:4 to whom pertaineth the *a*, and the
Gal 4:5 we might receive the *a* of sons
Eph 1:5 predestinated us unto the *a* of

**ADORAIM** *(ad-o-ra'-im) A city built by Rehoboam.*
2Chr 11:9 And A, and Lachish, and Azekah,

**ADORAM** *(ad-o'-ram)* See ADONIRAM.
*1. A tribute officer under David.*
2Sa 20:24 And A was over the tribute
*2. A tribute officer under Solomon.*
1Kin 12:18 Then king Rehoboam sent A

**ADORN**
1Ti 2:9 that women *a* themselves in modest
Titus 2:10 that they may *a* the doctrine of

**ADORNED**
Jer 31:4 shalt again be *a* with thy tabrets
Lk 21:5 how it was *a* with goodly stones
1Pet 3:5 *a* themselves, being in subjection
Rev 21:2 as a bride *a* for her husband

**ADORNETH**
Is 61:10 as a bride *a* herself with her

**ADORNING**
1Pet 3:3 Whose *a* let it not be that
1Pet 3:3 outward *a* of plaiting the hair

**ADRAMMELECH** *(a-dram'-mel-ek)*
*1. A god of the Avites.*
2Kin 17:31 burnt their children in fire to A
*2. A son of Sennacherib.*
2Kin 19:37 house of Nisroch his god, that A
Is 37:38 house of Nisroch his god, that A

**ADRAMYTTIAN** See ADRAMYTTIUM.

**ADRAMYTTIUM** *(a-dram-mit'-te-um) A seaport of Mysia in Asia Minor.*
Acts 27:2 And entering into a ship of A

**ADRIA** *(a'-dre-ah) The Adriatic Sea.*
Acts 27:27 as we were driven up and down in A

**ADRIEL** *(a'-dre-el) Husband of Merab, Saul's daughter.*
1Sa 18:19 unto A the Meholathite to wife
2Sa 21:8 whom she brought up for A the son

**ADULLAM** *(a-dul'-lam)* See ADULLAMITE.
*1. A city south of Jerusalem.*
Josh 12:15 the king of A, one
Josh 15:35 Jarmuth, and A, Socoh, and Azekah,
2Chr 11:7 And Beth-zur, and Shoco, and A
Neh 11:30 Zanoah, A, and in their villages,
Mic 1:15 he shall come unto A the glory of
*2. A large cave near the city of Adullam.*
1Sa 22:1 thence, and escaped to the cave A
2Sa 23:13 harvest time unto the cave of A
1Chr 11:15 rock to David, into the cave of A

**ADULLAMITE** *(a-dul'-lam-ite) A native of Adullam.*
Gen 38:1 and turned in to a certain A
Gen 38:12 he and his friend Hirah the A
Gen 38:20 by the hand of his friend the A

**ADULTERER**
Lev 20:10 with his neighbour's wife, the *a*
Job 24:15 The eye also of the *a* waiteth for
Is 57:3 the sorceress, the seed of the *a*

**ADULTERERS**
Ps 50:18 him, and hast been partaker with *a*
Jer 9:2 for they be all *a*, an assembly of
Jer 23:10 For the land is full of *a*
Hos 7:4 They are all *a*, as an oven heated
Mal 3:5 the sorcerers, and against the *a*
Lk 18:11 men are, extortioners, unjust, *a*
1Cor 6:9 fornicators, nor idolaters, nor *a*
Heb 13:4 whoremongers and *a* God will judge
Jas 4:4 Ye *a* and adulteresses, know ye not

**ADULTERESS**
Lev 20:10 the *a* shall surely be put to
Prov 6:26 the *a* will hunt for the precious
Hos 3:1 beloved of her friend, yet an *a*
Rom 7:3 man, she shall be called an *a*
Rom 7:3 so that she is no *a*, though she

**ADULTERESSES**
Eze 23:45 judge them after the manner of *a*
Eze 23:45 because they are *a*, and blood is
Jas 4:4 Ye adulterers and *a*, know ye not

**ADULTERIES**
Jer 13:27 I have seen thine *a*, and thy
Eze 23:43 said I unto her that was old in *a*
Hos 2:2 her *a* from between her breasts
Mt 15:19 proceed evil thoughts, murders, *a*
Mk 7:21 of men, proceed evil thoughts, *a*

**ADULTEROUS**
Prov 30:20 Such is the way of an *a* woman
Mt 12:39 *a* generation seeketh after a sign
Mt 16:4 *a* generation seeketh after a sign
Mk 8:38 of me and of my words in this *a*

**ADULTERY**
Ex 20:14 Thou shalt not commit *a*
Lev 20:10 *a* with another man's wife
Deut 5:18 Neither shalt thou commit *a*
Prov 6:32 committeth *a* with a woman lacketh
Jer 3:8 committed *a* I had put her away
Jer 3:9 committed *a* with stones and with
Jer 5:7 the full, they then committed *a*
Jer 7:9 ye steal, murder, and commit *a*
Jer 23:14 they commit *a*, and walk in lies
Jer 29:23 have committed *a* with their
Eze 16:32 But as a wife that committeth *a*
Eze 23:37 That they have committed *a*
Hos 4:2 and stealing, and committing *a*
Hos 4:13 and your spouses shall commit *a*
Hos 4:14 your spouses when they commit *a*
Mt 5:27 old time, Thou shalt not commit *a*
Mt 5:28 *a* with her already in his heart
Mt 5:32 causeth her to commit *a*
Mt 19:9 shall marry another, committeth *a*
Mt 19:18 murder, Thou shalt not commit *a*
Mk 10:11 another, committeth *a* against her
Mk 10:12 to another, she committeth *a*
Mk 10:19 the commandments, Do not commit *a*
Lk 16:18 and marrieth another, committeth *a*
Lk 18:20 the commandments, Do not commit *a*
Jn 8:3 unto him a woman taken in *a*
Jn 8:4 Master, this woman was taken in *a*
Rom 2:22 sayest a man should not commit *a*
Rom 13:9 For this, Thou shalt not commit *a*
Gal 5:19 A, fornication, uncleanness,
Jas 2:11 For he that said, Do not commit *a*
2Pet 2:14 Having eyes full of *a*, and that
Rev 2:22 them that commit *a* with her into

**ADUMMIM** *(a-dum'-mim)*
Josh 15:7 that is before the going up to A
Josh 18:17 is over against the going up of A

**ADVANCED**
1Sa 12:6 It is the LORD that *a* Moses
Est 3:1 *a* him, and set his seat above all
Est 5:11 how he had *a* him above the
Est 10:2 whereunto the king *a* him

**ADVANTAGE**
Job 35:3 What *a* will it be unto thee
Rom 3:1 What *a* then hath the Jew
2Cor 2:11 Lest Satan should get an *a* of us
Jude 16 in admiration because of *a*

**ADVERSARIES**
Ex 23:22 and an adversary unto thine *a*
Deut 32:27 lest their *a* should behave
Deut 32:43 and will render vengeance to his *a*
Josh 5:13 Art thou for us, or for our *a*
1Sa 2:10 The *a* of the LORD shall be broken
2Sa 19:22 ye should this day be *a* unto me
Ezr 4:1 Now when the *a* of Judah and
Neh 4:11 our *a* said, They shall not know,
Ps 38:20 render evil for good are mine *a*
Ps 69:19 mine *a* are all before thee
Ps 71:13 and consumed that are *a* to my soul
Ps 81:14 and turned my hand against their *a*
Ps 89:42 set up the right hand of his *a*
Ps 109:4 For my love they are my *a*
Ps 109:20 reward of mine *a* from the LORD
Ps 109:29 Let mine *a* be clothed with shame,
Is 1:24 Ah, I will ease me of mine *a*
Is 9:11 set up the *a* of Rezin against him
Is 11:13 the *a* of Judah shall be cut off
Is 59:18 he will repay, fury to his *a*
Is 63:18 our *a* have trodden down thy
Is 64:2 to make thy name known to thine *a*
Jer 30:16 and all thine *a*, every one of them
Jer 46:10 that he may avenge him of his *a*
Jer 50:7 and their *a* said, We offend not,
Lam 1:5 Her *a* are the chief, her enemies
Lam 1:7 the *a* saw her, and did mock at her
Lam 1:17 that his *a* should be round about
Lam 2:17 hath set up the horn of thine *a*
Mic 5:9 shall be lifted up upon thine *a*
Nah 1:2 LORD will take vengeance on his *a*
Lk 13:17 things, all his *a* were ashamed
Lk 21:15 which all your *a* shall not be
1Cor 16:9 unto me, and there are many *a*
Phil 1:28 And in nothing terrified by your *a*
Heb 10:27 which shall devour the *a*

**ADVERSARY**
Ex 23:22 an *a* unto thine adversaries
Num 22:22 in the way for an *a* against him
1Sa 1:6 her *a* also provoked her sore, for
1Sa 29:4 in the battle he be an *a* to us
1Kin 5:4 is neither *a* nor evil occurrent
1Kin 11:14 LORD stirred up an *a* unto Solomon
1Kin 11:23 And God stirred him up another *a*
1Kin 11:25 he was an *a* to Israel all the
Est 7:6 And Esther said, The *a* and enemy is
Job 31:35 that mine *a* had written a book
Ps 74:10 how long shall the *a* reproach
Is 50:8 who is mine *a*?
Lam 1:10 The *a* hath spread out his hand
Lam 2:4 stood with his right hand as an *a*
Lam 4:12 not have believed that the *a*
Amos 3:11 An *a* there shall be even round
Mt 5:25 Agree with thine *a* quickly
Mt 5:25 lest at any time the *a* deliver
Lk 12:58 with thine *a* to the magistrate
Lk 18:3 him, saying, Avenge me of mine *a*
1Ti 5:14 to the *a* to speak reproachfully
1Pet 5:8 because your *a* the devil, as a

**ADVERSITY**
2Sa 4:9 redeemed my soul out of all *a*
2Chr 15:6 for God did vex them with all *a*
Ps 10:6 for I shall never be in *a*
Ps 35:15 But in mine *a* they rejoiced, and
Ps 94:13 give him rest from the days of *a*
Prov 17:17 times, and a brother is born for *a*
Prov 24:10 If thou faint in the day of *a*
Eccl 7:14 but in the day of *a* consider
Is 30:20 the Lord give you the bread of *a*
Heb 13:3 and them which suffer *a*, as being

**ADVERTISE**
Num 24:14 I will *a* thee what this people
Ruth 4:4 And I thought to *a* thee, saying,

**ADVICE**
Judg 19:30 consider of it, take *a*, and speak
Judg 20:7 give here your *a* and counsel
1Sa 25:33 And blessed be thy *a*, and blessed
2Sa 19:43 that our *a* should not be first
2Chr 10:9 What *a* give ye that we may return
2Chr 10:14 them after the *a* of the young men

2Chr 25:17 Then Amaziah king of Judah took *a*
Prov 20:18 and with good *a* make war
2Cor 8:10 And herein I give my *a*

**ADVISE**
2Sa 24:13 now *a*, and see what answer I shall
1Kin 12:6 How do ye *a* that I may answer
1Chr 21:12 Now therefore *a* thyself what word

**ADVISED**
Prov 13:10 but with the well *a* is wisdom
Acts 27:12 the more part *a* to depart thence

**ADVOCATE**
1Jn 2:1 we have an *a* with the Father,

**AENEAS** *(e'-ne-as) A paralytic healed by Peter.*
Acts 9:33 he found a certain man named *A*
Acts 9:34 And Peter said unto him, *A*

**AENON** *(e'-non) A place in the valley of Shechem.*
Jn 3:23 was baptizing in *A* near to Salim

**AFFAIRS**
1Chr 26:32 to God, and *a* of the king
Ps 112:5 will guide his *a* with discretion
Dan 2:49 over the *a* of the province of
Dan 3:12 the *a* of the province of Babylon
Eph 6:21 But that ye also may know my *a*
Eph 6:22 purpose, that ye might know our *a*
Phil 1:27 be absent, I may hear of your *a*
2Ti 2:4 himself with the *a* of this life

**AFFECT**
Gal 4:17 They zealously *a* you, but not

**AFFECTED**
Acts 14:2 minds evil *a* against the brethren
Gal 4:18 *a* always in a good thing, and not

**AFFECTION**
1Chr 29:3 because I have set my *a* to the
Rom 1:31 without natural *a*, implacable,
2Cor 7:15 his inward *a* is more abundant
Col 3:2 Set your *a* on things above, not
Col 3:5 uncleanness, inordinate *a*
2Ti 3:3 Without natural *a*, trucebreakers,

**AFFECTIONS**
Rom 1:26 God gave them up unto vile *a*
Gal 5:24 crucified the flesh with the *a*

**AFFINITY**
1Kin 3:1 Solomon made *a* with Pharaoh king
2Chr 18:1 abundance, and joined *a* with Ahab
Ezr 9:14 join in *a* with the people of

**AFFIRM**
Rom 3:8 as some *a* that we say,) Let us do
1Ti 1:7 what they say, nor whereof they *a*
Titus 3:8 I will that thou *a* constantly

**AFFIRMED**
Lk 22:59 hour after another confidently *a*
Acts 12:15 But she constantly *a* that it was
Acts 25:19 was dead, whom Paul *a* to be alive

**AFFLICT**
Gen 15:13 they shall *a* them four hundred
Gen 31:50 If thou shalt *a* my daughters
Ex 1:11 to *a* them with their burdens
Ex 22:22 Ye shall not *a* any widow, or
Ex 22:23 If thou *a* them in any wise, and
Lev 16:29 ye shall *a* your souls, and do no
Lev 16:31 ye shall *a* your souls, by a
Lev 23:27 ye shall *a* your souls, and offer
Lev 23:32 of rest, and ye shall *a* your souls
Num 24:24 *a* Asshur, and shall *a* Eber
Num 29:7 and ye shall *a* your souls
Num 30:13 every binding oath to *a* the soul
Judg 16:5 that we may bind him to *a* him
Judg 16:6 thou mightest be bound to *a* thee
Judg 16:19 and she began to *a* him, and his
2Sa 7:10 of wickedness *a* them any more
1Kin 11:39 I will for this *a* the seed of
2Chr 6:26 their sin, when thou dost *a* them
Ezr 8:21 that we might *a* ourselves before
Job 37:23 he will not *a*
Ps 44:2 how thou didst *a* the people
Ps 55:19 *a* them, even he that abideth of
Ps 89:22 nor the son of wickedness *a* him
Ps 94:5 O LORD, and *a* thine heritage
Ps 143:12 destroy all them that *a* my soul
Is 9:1 *a* her by the way of the sea
Is 51:23 into the hand of them that *a* thee
Is 58:5 a day for a man to *a* his soul
Is 64:12 hold thy peace, and *a* us very sore
Jer 31:28 down, and to destroy, and to *a*
Lam 3:33 For he doth not *a* willingly nor
Amos 5:12 they *a* the just, they take a
Amos 6:14 they shall *a* you from the
Nah 1:12 thee, I will *a* thee no more
Zeph 3:19 time I will undo all that *a* thee

**AFFLICTED**
Ex 1:12 But the more they *a* them, the
Lev 23:29 shall not be *a* in that same day
Num 11:11 Wherefore hast thou *a* thy servant
Deut 26:6 *a* us, and laid upon us hard
Ruth 1:21 me, and the Almighty hath *a* me
2Sa 22:28 the *a* people thou wilt save
1Kin 2:26 because thou hast been *a* in all
1Kin 2:26 in all wherein my father was *a*
2Kin 17:20 *a* them, and delivered them into
Job 6:14 To him that is *a* pity should be
Job 30:11 *a* me, they have also let loose
Job 34:28 and he heareth the cry of the *a*
Ps 18:27 For thou wilt save the *a* people
Ps 22:24 abhorred the affliction of the *a*
Ps 25:16 for I am desolate and *a*
Ps 82:3 do justice to the *a* and needy
Ps 88:7 thou hast *a* me with all thy waves
Ps 88:15 I am *a* and ready to die from my
Ps 90:15 the days wherein thou hast *a* us
Ps 102:t A Prayer of the *a*, when he is
Ps 107:17 of their iniquities, are *a*
Ps 116:10 I was greatly *a*
Ps 119:67 Before I was *a* I went astray
Ps 119:71 is good for me that I have been *a*
Ps 119:75 thou in faithfulness hast *a* me
Ps 119:107 I am *a* very much
Ps 129:1 time have they *a* me from my youth
Ps 129:2 time have they *a* me from my youth
Ps 140:12 will maintain the cause of the *a*
Prov 15:15 All the days of the *a* are evil
Prov 22:22 neither oppress the *a* in the gate
Prov 26:28 hateth those that are *a* by it
Prov 31:5 the judgment of any of the *a*
Is 9:1 he lightly *a* the land of Zebulun
Is 49:13 and will have mercy upon his *a*
Is 51:21 Therefore hear now this, thou *a*
Is 53:4 stricken, smitten of God, and *a*
Is 53:7 He was oppressed, and he was *a*
Is 54:11 O thou *a*, tossed with tempest, and
Is 58:3 wherefore have we *a* our soul
Is 58:10 the hungry, and satisfy the *a* soul
Is 60:14 The sons also of them that *a* thee
Is 63:9 In all their affliction he was *a*
Lam 1:4 priests sigh, her virgins are *a*
Lam 1:5 for the LORD hath *a* her for the
Lam 1:12 wherewith the LORD hath *a* me in
Mic 4:6 driven out, and her that I have *a*
Nah 1:12 Though I have *a* thee, I will
Zeph 3:12 leave in the midst of thee an *a*
Mt 24:9 shall they deliver you up to be *a*
2Cor 1:6 And whether we be *a*, it is for
1Ti 5:10 feet, if she have relieved the *a*
Heb 11:37 being destitute, *a*, tormented
Jas 4:9 Be *a*, and mourn, and weep
Jas 5:13 Is any among you *a*

**AFFLICTION**
Gen 16:11 because the LORD hath heard thy *a*
Gen 29:32 the LORD hath looked upon my *a*
Gen 31:42 God hath seen mine *a* and the
Gen 41:52 be fruitful in the land of my *a*
Ex 3:7 I have surely seen the *a* of my
Ex 3:17 *a* of Egypt unto the land of the
Ex 4:31 that he had looked upon their *a*
Deut 16:3 therewith, even the bread of *a*
Deut 26:7 our voice, and looked on our *a*
1Sa 1:11 look on the *a* of thine handmaid
2Sa 16:12 that the LORD will look on mine *a*
1Kin 22:27 bread of *a* and with water of *a*
2Kin 14:26 For the LORD saw the *a* of Israel
2Chr 18:26 bread of *a* and with water of *a*
2Chr 20:9 house,) and cry unto thee in our *a*
2Chr 33:12 And when he was in *a*, he besought
Neh 1:3 in the province are in great *a*
Neh 9:9 didst see the *a* of our fathers in
Job 5:6 Although *a* cometh not forth of
Job 10:15 therefore see thou mine *a*
Job 30:16 the days of *a* have taken hold
Job 30:27 the days of *a* prevented me
Job 36:8 and be holden in cords of *a*
Job 36:15 He delivereth the poor in his *a*
Job 36:21 hast thou chosen rather than *a*
Ps 22:24 abhorred the *a* of the afflicted
Ps 25:18 Look upon mine *a* and my pain
Ps 44:24 thy face, and forgettest our *a*
Ps 66:11 thou laidst *a* upon our loins
Ps 88:9 Mine eye mourneth by reason of *a*
Ps 106:44 Nevertheless he regarded their *a*
Ps 107:10 shadow of death, being bound in *a*
Ps 107:39 brought low through oppression, *a*
Ps 107:41 he the poor on high from *a*
Ps 119:50 This is my comfort in my *a*
Ps 119:92 then have perished in mine *a*
Ps 119:153 Consider mine *a*, and deliver me
Is 30:20 of adversity, and the water of *a*
Is 48:10 chosen thee in the furnace of *a*
Is 63:9 In all their *a* he was afflicted,
Jer 4:15 publisheth *a* from mount Ephraim
Jer 15:11 time of evil and in the time of *a*
Jer 16:19 and my refuge in the day of *a*
Jer 30:15 Why criest thou for thine *a*
Jer 48:16 to come, and his *a* hasteth fast
Lam 1:3 gone into captivity because of *a*
Lam 1:7 remembered in the days of her *a*
Lam 1:9 O LORD, behold my *a*
Lam 3:1 seen *a* by the rod of his wrath
Lam 3:19 Remembering mine *a* and my misery,
Hos 5:15 in their *a* they will seek me
Amos 6:6 not grieved for the *a* of Joseph
Obad 13 not have looked on their *a* in the
Jonah 2:2 by reason of mine *a* unto the LORD
Nah 1:9 *a* shall not rise up the second
Hab 3:7 I saw the tents of Cushan in *a*
Zec 1:15 and they helped forward the *a*
Zec 8:10 out or came in because of the *a*
Zec 10:11 shall pass through the sea with *a*
Mk 4:17 when *a* or persecution ariseth for
Mk 13:19 For in those days shall be *a*
Acts 7:11 of Egypt and Chanaan, and great *a*
Acts 7:34 I have seen the *a* of my people
2Cor 2:4 For out of much *a* and anguish of
2Cor 4:17 For our light *a*, which is but for
2Cor 8:2 of *a* the abundance of their joy
Phil 1:16 supposing to add *a* to my bonds
Phil 4:14 that ye did communicate with my *a*
1Th 1:6 received the word in much *a*
1Th 3:7 comforted over you in all our *a*
Heb 11:25 suffer *a* with the people of God
Jas 1:27 fatherless and widows in their *a*
Jas 5:10 for an example of suffering *a*

**AFFLICTIONS**
Ps 34:19 Many are the *a* of the righteous
Ps 132:1 remember David, and all his *a*
Acts 7:10 And delivered him out of all his *a*
Acts 20:23 saying that bonds and *a* abide me
2Cor 6:4 of God, in much patience, in *a*
Col 1:24 *a* of Christ in my flesh for his
1Th 3:3 no man should be moved by these *a*
2Ti 1:8 but be thou partaker of the *a* of
2Ti 3:11 Persecutions, *a*, which came unto
2Ti 4:5 thou in all things, endure *a*
Heb 10:32 ye endured a great fight of *a*
Heb 10:33 both by reproaches and *a*
1Pet 5:9 knowing that the same *a* are

**AFFRIGHTED**
Deut 7:21 Thou shalt not be *a* at them
Job 18:20 as they that went before were *a*
Job 39:22 He mocketh at fear, and is not *a*
Is 21:4 My heart panted, fearfulness *a* me
Jer 51:32 fire, and the men of war are *a*
Mk 16:5 and they were *a*
Mk 16:6 And he saith unto them, Be not *a*
Lk 24:37 But they were terrified and *a*
Rev 11:13 and the remnant were *a*, and gave

**AFRAID**
Gen 3:10 voice in the garden, and I was *a*
Gen 18:15 for she was *a*
Gen 20:8 and the men were sore *a*
Gen 28:17 And he was *a*, and said, How
Gen 31:31 and said to Laban, Because I was *a*
Gen 32:7 Then Jacob was greatly *a* and
Gen 42:28 heart failed them, and they were *a*
Gen 42:35 the bundles of money, they were *a*
Gen 43:18 And the men were *a*, because they
Ex 3:6 for he was *a* to look upon God
Ex 14:10 and they were sore *a*
Ex 15:14 The people shall hear, and be *a*
Ex 34:30 they were *a* to come nigh him
Lev 26:6 down, and none shall make you *a*
Num 12:8 wherefore then were ye not *a* to
Num 22:3 And Moab was sore *a* of the people
Deut 1:17 ye shall not be *a* of the face of

Deut 1:29 Dread not, neither be *a* of them
Deut 2:4 and they shall be *a* of you
Deut 5:5 for ye were *a* by reason of the
Deut 7:18 Thou shalt not be *a* of them
Deut 7:19 all the people of whom thou art *a*
Deut 9:19 For I was *a* of the anger and hot
Deut 18:22 thou shalt not be *a* of him
Deut 20:1 more than thou, be not *a* of them
Deut 28:10 and they shall be *a* of thee
Deut 28:60 of Egypt, which thou wast *a* of
Deut 31:6 fear not, nor be *a* of them
Josh 1:9 be not *a*, neither be thou
Josh 9:24 therefore we were sore *a* of our
Josh 11:6 Joshua, Be not *a* because of them
Judg 7:3 saying, Whosoever is fearful and *a*
Ruth 3:8 at midnight, that the man was *a*
1Sa 4:7 And the Philistines were *a*
1Sa 7:7 they were *a* of the Philistines
1Sa 17:11 they were dismayed, and greatly *a*
1Sa 17:24 fled from him, and were sore *a*
1Sa 18:12 And Saul was *a* of David, because
1Sa 18:15 very wisely, he was *a* of him
1Sa 18:29 Saul was yet the more *a* of David
1Sa 21:1 Ahimelech was *a* at the meeting of
1Sa 21:12 was sore *a* of Achish the king of
1Sa 23:3 Behold, we be *a* here in Judah
1Sa 28:5 host of the Philistines, he was *a*
1Sa 28:13 the king said unto her, Be not *a*
1Sa 28:20 along on the earth, and was sore *a*
1Sa 31:4 for he was sore *a*
2Sa 1:14 How wast thou not *a* to stretch
2Sa 6:9 David was *a* of the LORD that day,
2Sa 14:15 because the people have made me *a*
2Sa 17:2 weak handed, and will make him *a*
2Sa 22:5 floods of ungodly men made me *a*
2Sa 22:46 they shall be *a* out of their
1Kin 1:49 that were with Adonijah were *a*
2Kin 1:15 be not *a* of him
2Kin 10:4 But they were exceedingly *a*
2Kin 19:6 Be not *a* of the words which thou
2Kin 25:26 for they were *a* of the Chaldees
1Chr 10:4 for he was sore *a*
1Chr 13:12 David was *a* of God that day,
1Chr 21:30 for he was *a* because of the sword
2Chr 20:15 Be not *a* nor dismayed by reason
2Chr 32:7 be not *a* nor dismayed for the
Neh 2:2 Then I was very sore *a*,
Neh 4:14 the people, Be not ye *a* of them
Neh 6:9 For they all made us *a*, saying,
Neh 6:13 was he hired, that I should be *a*
Est 7:6 Then Haman was *a* before the king
Job 3:25 that which I was *a* of is come
Job 5:21 neither shalt thou be *a* of
Job 5:22 neither shalt thou be *a* of the
Job 6:21 ye see my casting down, and are *a*
Job 9:28 I am *a* of all my sorrows, I know
Job 11:19 down, and none shall make thee *a*
Job 13:11 not his excellency make you *a*
Job 13:21 and let not thy dread make me *a*
Job 15:24 and anguish shall make him *a*
Job 18:11 shall make him *a* on every side
Job 19:29 Be ye *a* of the sword
Job 21:6 Even when I remember I am *a*
Job 23:15 when I consider, I am *a* of him
Job 32:6 wherefore I was *a*, and durst not
Job 33:7 my terror shall not make thee *a*
Job 39:20 thou make him *a* as a grasshopper
Job 41:25 up himself, the mighty are *a*
Ps 3:6 I will not be *a* of ten thousands
Ps 18:4 floods of ungodly men made me *a*
Ps 18:45 be *a* out of their close places
Ps 27:1 of whom shall I be *a*
Ps 49:16 Be not thou *a* when one is made
Ps 56:3 What time I am *a*, I will trust in
Ps 56:11 I will not be *a* what man can do
Ps 65:8 parts are *a* at thy tokens
Ps 77:16 they were *a*
Ps 83:15 make them *a* with thy storm
Ps 91:5 Thou shalt not be *a* for the
Ps 112:7 He shall not be *a* of evil tidings
Ps 112:8 is established, he shall not be *a*
Ps 119:120 and I am *a* of thy judgments
Prov 3:24 liest down, thou shalt not be *a*
Prov 3:25 Be not *a* of sudden fear, neither
Prov 31:21 She is not *a* of the snow for her
Eccl 12:5 shall be *a* of that which is high
Is 8:12 fear ye their fear, nor be *a*
Is 10:24 in Zion, be not *a* of the Assyrian
Is 10:29 Ramah is *a*
Is 12:2 I will trust, and not be *a*
Is 13:8 And they shall be *a*
Is 17:2 down, and none shall make them *a*
Is 19:16 and it shall be *a* and fear because
Is 19:17 thereof shall be *a* in himself
Is 20:5 And they shall be *a* and ashamed of
Is 31:4 he will not be *a* of their voice
Is 31:9 princes shall be *a* of the ensign
Is 33:14 The sinners in Zion are *a*
Is 37:6 Be not *a* of the words that thou
Is 40:9 lift it up, be not *a*
Is 41:5 the ends of the earth were *a*
Is 44:8 Fear ye not, neither be *a*
Is 51:7 of men, neither be ye *a* of their
Is 51:12 that thou shouldest be *a* of a man
Is 57:11 whom hast thou been *a* or feared
Jer 1:8 Be not *a* of their faces
Jer 2:12 at this, and be horribly *a*
Jer 10:5 Be not *a* of them
Jer 26:21 when Urijah heard it, he was *a*
Jer 30:10 quiet, and none shall make him *a*
Jer 36:16 the words, they were *a* both one
Jer 36:24 Yet they were not *a*, nor rent
Jer 38:19 I am *a* of the Jews that are
Jer 39:17 of the men of whom thou art *a*
Jer 41:18 for they were *a* of them, because
Jer 42:11 Be not *a* of the king of Babylon,
Jer 42:11 of whom ye are *a*
Jer 42:11 be not *a* of him, saith the LORD
Jer 42:16 and the famine, whereof ye were *a*
Jer 46:27 at ease, and none shall make him *a*
Eze 2:6 be not *a* of them
Eze 2:6 neither be *a* of their words,
Eze 2:6 be not *a* of their words, nor be
Eze 27:35 and their kings shall be sore *a*
Eze 30:9 to make the careless Ethiopians *a*
Eze 32:10 shall be horribly *a* for thee
Eze 34:28 safely, and none shall make them *a*
Eze 39:26 their land, and none made them *a*
Dan 4:5 I saw a dream which made me *a*
Dan 8:17 and when he came, I was *a*, and fell
Joel 2:22 Be not *a*, ye beasts of the field
Amos 3:6 the city, and the people not be *a*
Jonah 1:5 Then the mariners were *a*, and
Jonah 1:10 Then were the men exceedingly *a*
Mic 4:4 and none shall make them *a*
Mic 7:17 they shall be *a* of the LORD our
Nah 2:11 lion's whelp, and none made them *a*
Hab 2:17 of beasts, which made them *a*
Hab 3:2 I have heard thy speech, and was *a*
Zeph 3:13 down, and none shall make them *a*
Mal 2:5 me, and was *a* before my name
Mt 2:22 Herod, he was *a* to go thither
Mt 14:27 be not *a*
Mt 14:30 saw the wind boisterous, he was *a*
Mt 17:6 on their face, and were sore *a*
Mt 17:7 them, and said, Arise, and be not *a*
Mt 25:25 And I was *a*, and went and hid thy
Mt 28:10 said Jesus unto them, Be not *a*
Mk 5:15 and they were *a*
Mk 5:36 ruler of the synagogue, Be not *a*
Mk 6:50 be not *a*
Mk 9:6 for they were sore *a*
Mk 9:32 that saying, and were *a* to ask him
Mk 10:32 and as they followed, they were *a*
Mk 16:8 thing to any man for they were *a*
Lk 2:9 and they were sore *a*
Lk 8:25 And they being *a* wondered, saying
Lk 8:35 and they were *a*
Lk 12:4 Be not *a* of them that kill the
Lk 24:5 And as they were *a*, and bowed down
Jn 6:19 and they were *a*
Jn 6:20 be not *a*
Jn 14:27 be troubled, neither let it be *a*
Jn 19:8 that saying, he was the more *a*
Acts 9:26 but they were all *a* of him
Acts 10:4 when he looked on him, he was *a*
Acts 18:9 the night by a vision, Be not *a*
Acts 22:9 saw indeed the light, and were *a*
Acts 22:29 and the chief captain also was *a*
Rom 13:3 thou then not be *a* of the power
Rom 13:4 thou do that which is evil, be *a*
Gal 4:11 I am *a* of you, lest I have
Heb 11:23 they were not *a* of the king's
1Pet 3:6 are not *a* with any amazement
1Pet 3:14 be not *a* of their terror, neither
2Pet 2:10 they are not *a* to speak evil of

**AFTERNOON**
Judg 19:8 And they tarried until *a*, and they

**AGABUS** *(ag'-ab-us) A Christian prophet.*
Acts 11:28 stood up one of them named *A*
Acts 21:10 Judaea a certain prophet, named *A*

**AGAG** *(a'-gag)* See AGAGITE. *A king of Amalek during Exodus.*
Num 24:7 his king shall be higher than *A*
1Sa 15:9 But Saul and the people spared *A*
1Sa 15:20 have brought *A* the king of Amalek
1Sa 15:32 Bring ye hither to me *A* the king
1Sa 15:33 Samuel hewed *A* in pieces before

**AGAGITE** *(ag'-ag-ite) A member of an Amalekite tribe.*
Est 3:1 Haman the son of Hammedatha the *A*
Est 8:3 away the mischief of Haman the *A*
Est 9:24 the son of Hammedatha, the *A*

**AGAR** *(a'-gar)* See HAGAR. *Greek form of Hagar.*
Gal 4:24 gendereth to bondage, which is *A*
Gal 4:25 For this *A* is mount Sinai in

**AGATE**
Ex 28:19 And the third row a ligure, an *a*
Ex 39:12 And the third row, a ligure, an *a*
Eze 27:16 and fine linen, and coral, and *a*

**AGATES**
Is 54:12 And I will make thy windows of *a*

**AGE**
Gen 15:15 shalt be buried in a good old *a*
Gen 18:11 were old and well stricken in *a*
Gen 21:2 bare Abraham a son in his old *a*
Gen 21:7 have born him a son in his old *a*
Gen 24:1 was old, and well stricken in *a*
Gen 25:8 ghost, and died in a good old *a*
Gen 37:3 he was the son of his old *a*
Gen 44:20 old man, and a child of his old *a*
Gen 47:28 so the whole *a* of Jacob was an
Gen 48:10 the eyes of Israel were dim for *a*
Num 8:25 from the *a* of fifty years they
Josh 23:1 Joshua waxed old and stricken in *a*
Josh 23:2 them, I am old and stricken in *a*
Judg 8:32 son of Joash died in a good old *a*
Ruth 4:15 and a nourisher of thine old *a*
1Sa 2:33 die in the flower of their *a*
1Kin 14:4 eyes were set by reason of his *a*
1Kin 15:23 in the time of his old *a* he was
1Chr 23:3 from the *a* of thirty years
1Chr 23:24 from the *a* of twenty years and
1Chr 29:28 And he died in a good old *a*
2Chr 36:17 man, or him that stooped for *a*
Job 5:26 come to thy grave in a full *a*
Job 8:8 I pray thee, of the former *a*
Job 11:17 thine *a* shall be clearer than the
Job 30:2 in whom old *a* was perished
Ps 39:5 mine *a* is as nothing before thee
Ps 71:9 me not off in the time of old *a*
Ps 92:14 still bring forth fruit in old *a*
Is 38:12 Mine *a* is departed, and is removed
Is 46:4 And even to your old *a* I am he
Zec 8:4 his staff in his hand for very *a*
Mk 5:42 she was of the *a* of twelve years
Lk 1:36 also conceived a son in her old *a*
Lk 2:36 she was of a great *a*, and had
Lk 3:23 to be about thirty years of *a*
Lk 8:42 daughter, about twelve years of *a*
Jn 9:21 he is of *a*
Jn 9:23 said his parents, He is of *a*
1Cor 7:36 if she pass the flower of her *a*
Heb 5:14 to them that are of full *a*
Heb 11:11 of a child when she was past *a*

**AGED**
2Sa 19:32 Now Barzillai was a very *a* man
Job 12:20 away the understanding of the *a*
Job 15:10 both the grayheaded and very *a* men
Job 29:8 and the *a* arose, and stood up
Job 32:9 neither do the *a* understand
Jer 6:11 the *a* with him that is full of
Titus 2:2 That the *a* men be sober, grave,
Titus 2:3 The *a* women likewise, that they
Philem 9 being such an one as Paul the *a*

**AGEE** *(ag'-ee) Father of a "mighty man" of David.*
2Sa 23:11 Shammah the son of *A* the Hararite

**AGES**
Eph 2:7 That in the *a* to come he might
Eph 3:5 Which in other *a* was not made
Eph 3:21 by Christ Jesus throughout all *a*
Col 1:26 which hath been hid from *a*

**AGONY**
Lk 22:44 being in an *a* he prayed more

**AGREE**
Mt 5:25 *A* with thine adversary quickly,
Mt 18:19 That if two of you shall *a* on
Mt 20:13 didst not thou *a* with me for a
Mk 14:59 so did their witness *a* together
Acts 15:15 to this *a* the words of the
1Jn 5:8 and these three *a* in one
Rev 17:17 to fulfil his will, and to *a*

**AGREED**
Amos 3:3 walk together, except they be *a*
Mt 20:2 when he had *a* with the labourers
Mk 14:56 but their witness *a* not together
Jn 9:22 for the Jews had *a* already
Acts 5:9 How is it that ye have *a* together
Acts 5:40 And to him they *a*
Acts 23:20 The Jews have *a* to desire thee
Acts 28:25 when they *a* not among themselves,

**AGREEMENT**
2Kin 18:31 Make an *a* with me by a present,
Is 28:15 death, and with hell are we at *a*
Is 28:18 your *a* with hell shall not stand
Is 36:16 Make an *a* with me by a present,
Dan 11:6 king of the north to make an *a*
2Cor 6:16 what *a* hath the temple of God

**AGREETH**
Mk 14:70 and thy speech *a* thereto
Lk 5:36 out of the new *a* not with the old

**AGRIPPA** *(ag-rip'-pah) Great-grandson of Herod the Great.*
Acts 25:13 And after certain days king *A*
Acts 25:23 when *A* was come, and Bernice, with
Acts 25:24 And Festus said, King *A*, and all
Acts 26:1 Then *A* said unto Paul, Thou art
Acts 26:7 For which hope's sake, king *A*
Acts 26:19 Whereupon, O king *A*, I was not
Acts 26:27 King *A*, believest thou the

**AGROUND**
Acts 27:41 two seas met, they ran the ship *a*

**AGUE**
Lev 26:16 consumption, and the burning *a*

**AGUR** *(a'-gur) Son of Jakeh.*
Prov 30:1 The words of *A* the son of Jakeh,

**AHAB** *(a'-hab)* See AHAB'S.
*1. A king of Israel.*
1Kin 16:28 *A* his son reigned in his stead
1Kin 16:30 *A* the son of Omri did evil in the
1Kin 18:1 saying, Go, shew thyself unto *A*
1Kin 18:3 *A* called Obadiah, which was the
1Kin 18:5 *A* said unto Obadiah, Go into the
1Kin 18:16 and *A* went to meet Elijah
1Kin 18:17 when *A* saw Elijah, that *A* said
1Kin 18:20 So *A* sent unto all the children
1Kin 18:41 And Elijah said unto *A*, Get thee
1Kin 18:46 ran before *A* to the entrance of
1Kin 19:1 *A* told Jezebel all that Elijah
1Kin 20:2 he sent messengers to *A* king of
1Kin 20:13 a prophet unto *A* king of Israel
1Kin 20:34 Then said *A*, I will send thee
1Kin 21:2 *A* spake unto Naboth, saying, Give
1Kin 21:15 was dead, that Jezebel said to *A*
1Kin 21:16 when *A* heard that Naboth was dead
1Kin 21:20 *A* said to Elijah, Hast thou found
1Kin 21:21 will cut off from *A* him that
1Kin 21:29 Seest thou how *A* humbleth himself
1Kin 22:20 LORD said, Who shall persuade *A*
1Kin 22:39 Now the rest of the acts of *A*
1Kin 22:41 fourth year of *A* king of Israel
1Kin 22:49 the son of *A* unto Jehoshaphat
1Kin 22:51 Ahaziah the son of *A* began to
2Kin 1:1 Israel after the death of *A*
2Kin 8:16 Joram the son of *A* king of Israel
2Kin 8:18 the daughter of *A* was his wife
2Kin 8:25 year of Joram the son of *A* king
2Kin 9:7 smite the house of *A* thy master
2Kin 9:8 the whole house of *A* shall perish
2Kin 9:8 I will cut off from *A* him that
2Kin 9:25 rode together after *A* his father
2Kin 10:1 *A* had seventy sons in Samaria
2Kin 10:10 spake concerning the house of *A*
2Kin 10:17 that remained unto *A* in Samaria
2Kin 10:30 hast done unto the house of *A*
2Kin 21:3 a grove, as did *A* king of Israel
2Kin 21:13 and the plummet of the house of *A*
2Chr 18:1 and joined affinity with *A*
2Chr 18:19 Who shall entice *A* king of Israel
2Chr 21:6 like as did the house of *A*
2Chr 21:13 the whoredoms of the house of *A*
2Chr 22:5 went with Jehoram the son of *A*
2Chr 22:8 judgment upon the house of *A*
Mic 6:16 all the works of the house of *A*
*2. A false prophet during the Exile.*
Jer 29:21 of *A* the son of Kolaiah, and of
Jer 29:22 make thee like Zedekiah and like *A*

**AHAB'S** *(a'-habs)*
1Kin 21:8 So she wrote letters in *A* name
2Kin 10:1 them that brought up *A* children

**AHARAH** *(a-har'-ah)* See AHER, AHIRAM, EHI. *Third son of Benjamin.*
1Chr 8:1 the second, and *A* the third,

**AHARHEL** *(a-har'-hel) A descendant of Judah.*
1Chr 4:8 the families of *A* the son of

**AHASAI** *(a-ha'-sa-i) Family of returned exiles.*
Neh 11:13 the son of Azareel, the son of *A*

**AHASBAI** *(a-has'-ba-i) Father of a "mighty man" of David.*
2Sa 23:34 Eliphelet the son of *A*, the son

**AHASUERUS** *(a-has-u-e'-rus)* See AHASUERUS'.
*1. A Persian king, Cambyses.*
Ezr 4:6 And in the reign of *A*, in the
*2. Father of Darius the Mede.*
Dan 9:1 first year of Darius the son of *A*
*3. A king of Persia, Xerxes.*
Est 1:1 it came to pass in the days of *A*
Est 1:9 house which belonged to king *A*
Est 1:10 in the presence of *A* the king
Est 1:15 of the king *A* by the chamberlains
Est 1:19 Vashti come no more before king *A*
Est 2:1 the wrath of king *A* was appeased
Est 2:12 turn was come to go in to king *A*
Est 2:16 *A* into his house royal in the
Est 2:21 sought to lay hand on the king *A*
Est 3:1 king *A* promote Haman the son of
Est 3:12 the name of king *A* was it written
Est 6:2 sought to lay hand on the king *A*
Est 7:5 Then the king *A* answered and said
Est 8:1 On that day did the king *A* give
Est 10:1 the king *A* laid a tribute upon
Est 10:3 the Jew was next unto king *A*

**AHAVA** *(a-ha'-vah)* See IVA. *A river of Babylon.*
Ezr 8:15 to the river than runneth to *A*
Ezr 8:21 a fast there, at the river of *A*
Ezr 8:31 we departed from the river of *A*

**AHAZ** *(a'-haz)* See ACHAZ.
*1. A king of Judah.*
2Kin 15:38 *A* his son reigned in his stead
2Kin 16:1 of Pekah the son of Remaliah *A*
2Kin 16:2 Twenty years old was *A* when he
2Kin 16:5 and they besieged *A*, but could not
2Kin 16:8 *A* took the silver and gold that
2Kin 16:16 to all that king *A* commanded
2Kin 16:17 king *A* cut off the borders of the
2Kin 16:20 *A* slept with his fathers, and was
2Kin 17:1 In the twelfth year of *A* king of
2Kin 18:1 that Hezekiah the son of *A* king
2Kin 20:11 it had gone down in the dial of *A*
2Kin 23:12 the top of the upper chamber of *A*
1Chr 3:13 *A* his son, Hezekiah his son,
2Chr 27:9 *A* his son reigned in his stead
2Chr 28:1 *A* was twenty years old when he
2Chr 28:16 At that time did king *A* send unto
2Chr 28:24 *A* gathered together the vessels
2Chr 28:27 *A* slept with his fathers, and they
2Chr 29:19 which king *A* in his reign did
Is 1:1 in the days of Uzziah, Jotham, *A*
Is 7:3 Isaiah, Go forth now to meet *A*
Is 7:12 But *A* said, I will not ask,
Is 14:28 that king *A* died was this burden
Is 38:8 is gone down in the sun dial of *A*
Hos 1:1 in the days of Uzziah, Jotham, *A*
Mic 1:1 in the days of Jotham, *A*, and
*2. A Benjaminite and relative of Saul.*
1Chr 8:35 Pithon, and Melech, and Tarea, and *A*
1Chr 9:41 and Melech, and Tahrea, and *A*

**AHAZIAH** *(a-haz-i'-ah)* See AZARIAH, JEHOAHAZ.
*1. A king of Israel.*
1Kin 22:40 *A* his son reigned in his stead
1Kin 22:49 Then said *A* the son of Ahab unto
1Kin 22:51 *A* the son of Ahab began to reign
2Kin 1:2 *A* fell down through a lattice in
2Kin 1:18 of the acts of *A* which he did
1Chr 3:11 *A* his son, Joash his son,
2Chr 20:35 himself with *A* king of Israel
2Chr 20:37 thou hast joined thyself with *A*
*2. Son and successor of King Jehoram of Judah.*
2Kin 8:24 *A* his son reigned in his stead
2Kin 9:16 *A* king of Judah was come down to
2Kin 9:21 *A* king of Judah went out, each in
2Kin 9:27 But when *A* the king of Judah saw
2Kin 9:29 Ahab began *A* to reign over Judah
2Kin 10:13 the brethren of *A* king of Judah
2Kin 11:1 of *A* saw that her son was dead
2Kin 12:18 Jehoshaphat, and Jehoram, and *A*
2Kin 13:1 year of Joash the son of *A* king
2Kin 14:13 the son of Jehoash the son of *A*
2Chr 22:1 *A* his youngest son king in his
2Chr 22:7 the destruction of *A* was of God
2Chr 22:9 So the house of *A* had no power to
2Chr 22:10 of *A* saw that her son was dead

**AHBAN** *(ah'-ban) A descendant of Pharez.*
1Chr 2:29 was Abihail, and she bare him *A*

**AHER** *(a'-hur)* See AHARAH. *A descendant of Benjamin.*
1Chr 7:12 of Ir, and Hushim, the sons of *A*

**AHI** *(a'-hi)*
*1. A son of Abdiel.*
1Chr 5:15 *A* the son of Abdiel, the son of
*2. A chief of the Asherites.*
1Chr 7:34 *A*, and Rohgah, Jehubbah, and Aram

**AHIAH** *(a-hi'-ah)* See AHIJAH.
*1. Grandson of Phinehas.*
1Sa 14:3 And *A*, the son of Ahitub,
1Sa 14:18 And Saul said unto *A*, Bring hither
*2. A scribe of Solomon.*
1Kin 4:3 Elihoreph and *A*, the sons of
*3. A descendant of Benjamin.*
1Chr 8:7 And Naaman, and *A*, and Gera, he

**AHIAM** *(a-hi'-am) Son of Shahar.*
2Sa 23:33 *A* the son of Sharar the Hararite,
1Chr 11:35 *A* the son of Sacar the Hararite,

**AHIAN** *(a-hi'-an)*
1Chr 7:19 And the sons of Shemidah were, *A*

**AHIEZER** *(a-hi-e'-zer)*
*1. One who numbered the people.*
Num 1:12 *A* the son of Ammishaddai
Num 2:25 shall be *A* the son of Ammishaddai
Num 10:25 over his host was *A* the son of
*2. A chief of the Benjamites.*
1Chr 12:3 The chief was *A*, then Joash, the

**AHIHUD** *(a-hi'-hud)*
*1. A prince of Asher.*
Num 34:27 of Asher, *A* the son of Shelomi
*2. A Benjamite of the Ehud family.*
1Chr 8:7 removed them, and begat Uzza, and *A*

**AHIJAH** *(a-hi'-jah)* See AHIAH, AHIMELECH.
*1. A prophet during the reigns of Solomon and Rehoboam.*
1Kin 11:29 that the prophet *A* the Shilonite
1Kin 12:15 which the LORD spake by *A* the
1Kin 14:2 there is *A* the prophet, which
1Kin 14:4 Shiloh, and came to the house of *A*
1Kin 14:6 when *A* heard the sound of her
1Kin 14:18 hand of his servant *A* the prophet
1Kin 15:29 by his servant *A* the Shilonite
2Chr 9:29 the prophecy of *A* the Shilonite
2Chr 10:15 *A* the Shilonite to Jeroboam the
*2. Father of Baasha.*
1Kin 15:27 And Baasha the son of *A*, of the
1Kin 21:22 the house of Baasha the son of *A*
2Kin 9:9 the house of Baasha the son of *A*
*3. Son of Jerahmeel.*
1Chr 2:25 Bunah, and Oren, and Ozem, and *A*
*4. A "mighty man" of David.*
1Chr 11:36 the Mecherathite, *A* the Pelonite,
*5. A treasury official under David.*
1Chr 26:20 *A* was over the treasures of the
*6. A Levite who renewed the covenant.*
Neh 10:26 And *A*, Hanan, Anan,

**AHIKAM** *(a-hi'-kam) An officer in Josiah's court.*
2Kin 22:12 *A* the son of Shaphan, and Achbor
2Kin 22:14 So Hilkiah the priest, and *A*
2Kin 25:22 he made Gedaliah the son of *A*

2Chr 34:20 A the son of Shaphan, and Abdon
Jer 26:24 Nevertheless the hand of A the
Jer 39:14 the son of A the son of Shaphan
Jer 40:9 Gedaliah the son of A the son of
Jer 41:1 Gedaliah the son of A to Mizpah
Jer 41:2 smote Gedaliah the son of A the
Jer 43:6 the son of A the son of Shaphan

**AHILUD** *(a-hi'-lud) Father of a recorder under David and Solomon.*
2Sa 8:16 the son of A was recorder
2Sa 20:24 the son of A was recorder
1Kin 4:3 Jehoshaphat the son of A, the
1Kin 4:12 Baana the son of A
1Chr 18:15 and Jehoshaphat the son of A

**AHIMAAZ** *(a-him'-a-az)*
*1. Father of Ahinoam.*
1Sa 14:50 was Ahinoam, the daughter of A
*2. Son of Zadok.*
2Sa 15:27 A thy son, and Jonathan the son of
2Sa 15:36 A Zadok's son, and Jonathan
2Sa 17:17 Jonathan and A stayed by En-rogel
2Sa 18:27 the running of A the son of Zadok
2Sa 18:28 A called, and said unto the king,
1Chr 6:8 begat Zadok, and Zadok begat A
*3. An officer of Solomon.*
1Kin 4:15 A was in Naphtali

**AHIMAN** *(a-hi'-man)*
*1. A giant of Anak.*
Num 13:22 where A, Sheshai, and Talmai, the
Josh 15:14 three sons of Anak, Sheshai, and A
Judg 1:10 and they slew Sheshai, and A
*2. A Levite Temple servant.*
1Chr 9:17 and Akkub, and Talmon, and A

**AHIMELECH** *(a-him'-el-ek)*
*1. A priest.*
1Sa 21:1 came David to Nob to A the priest
1Sa 22:9 to Nob, to A the son of Ahitub
1Sa 22:11 king sent to call A the priest
1Sa 22:14 Then A answered the king, and said
1Sa 22:16 said, Thou shalt surely die, A
1Sa 23:6 son of A fled to David to Keilah
2Sa 8:17 A the son of Abiathar, were the
1Chr 24:3 A of the sons of Ithamar,
1Chr 24:31 of David the king, and Zadok, and A
Ps 52:t David is come to the house of A
*2. A Hittite officer.*
1Sa 26:6 said to A the Hittite, and to

**AHIMELECH'S** *(a-him'-el-eks) Refers to Ahimelech 1.*
1Sa 30:7 A son, I pray thee, bring me

**AHIMOTH**
1Chr 6:25 Amasai, and A

**AHINADAB** *(a-hin'-ad-ab) A son of Iddo.*
1Kin 4:14 A the son of Iddo had Mahanaim

**AHINOAM** *(a-hin'-o-am)*
*1. A wife of King Saul.*
1Sa 14:50 And the name of Saul's wife was A
*2. A wife of David.*
1Sa 25:43 David also took A of Jezreel
1Sa 27:3 A the Jezreelitess, and Abigail
2Sa 2:2 A the Jezreelitess, and Abigail
2Sa 3:2 was Amnon, of A the Jezreelitess
1Chr 3:1 Amnon, of A the Jezreelitess

**AHIO** *(a-hi'-o)*
*1. A son of Abinadab.*
2Sa 6:3 and Uzzah and A, the sons of
1Chr 13:7 and Uzza and A drave the cart
*2. A son of Beriah the Benjamite.*
1Chr 8:14 And A, Shashak, and Jeremoth,
*3. A son of Jehiel.*
1Chr 8:31 And Gedor, and A, and Zacher

**AHIRA** *(a-hi'-rah) A chief of Naphtali.*
Num 1:15 A the son of Enan
Num 2:29 shall be A the son of Enan
Num 7:78 the twelfth day A the son of Enan
Num 10:27 of Naphtali was A the son of Enan

**AHIRAM** *(a-hi'-rum)* See AHARAH, AHIRAMITES. *A descendant of Benjamin.*
Num 26:38 of A, the family of the

**AHIRAMITES** *(a-hi'-rum-ites) Descendants of Ahiram.*
Num 26:38 of Ahiram, the family of the A

**AHISAMACH** *(a-his'-am-ak) Father of Aholiab.*
Ex 31:6 with him Aholiab, the son of A
Ex 35:34 both he, and Aholiab, the son of A
Ex 38:23 And with him was Aholiab, son of A

**AHISHAHAR** *(a-hish'-a-har) A son of Bilhan.*
1Chr 7:10 and Zethan, and Tharshish, and A

**AHISHAR** *(a-hi'-shar) Governor of the palace under Solomon.*
1Kin 4:6 And A was over the household

**AHITHOPHEL** *(a-hith'-o-fel) A counsellor of David.*
2Sa 15:12 Absalom sent for A the Gilonite
2Sa 15:31 A is among the conspirators with
2Sa 16:15 came to Jerusalem, and A with him
2Sa 16:20 Then said Absalom to A, Give
2Sa 17:1 Moreover A said unto Absalom, Let
2Sa 17:14 is better than the counsel of A
2Sa 17:23 when A saw that his counsel was
2Sa 23:34 Eliam the son of A the Gilonite
1Chr 27:33 A was the king's counsellor

**AHITUB** *(a-hi'-tub)*
*1. The son of Phinehas.*
1Sa 14:3 And Ahiah, the son of A,
1Sa 22:9 to Nob, to Ahimelech the son of A
1Sa 22:20 sons of Ahimelech the son of A
*2. Father of the high priest during David's reign.*
2Sa 8:17 And Zadok the son of A, and
1Chr 6:52 son, Amariah his son, A his son,
1Chr 18:16 And Zadok the son of A, and
Ezr 7:2 the son of Zadok, the son of A
*3. A priest seven generations later than Ahitub 2.*
1Chr 6:11 begat Amariah, and Amariah begat A
*4. A priest in Nehemiah's time.*
1Chr 9:11 the son of Meraioth, the son of A
Neh 11:11 the son of Meraioth, the son of A

**AHLAB** *(ah'-lab) A city of Asher.*
Judg 1:31 inhabitants of Zidon, nor of A

**AHLAI** *(ah'-lahee)*
*1. A daughter of Sheshan.*
1Chr 2:31 And the children of Sheshan; A
*2. Father of a "mighty man" of David.*
1Chr 11:41 the Hittite, Zabad the son of A

**AHOAH** *(a-ho'-ah)* See AHOHITE. *The son of Bela.*
1Chr 8:4 And Abishua, and Naaman, and A

**AHOHITE** *(a-ho'-hite)*
*1. A descendant of Ahoah.*
2Sa 23:28 Zalmon the A, Maharai the
1Chr 11:12 Eleazar the son of Dodo, the A
1Chr 11:29 the Hushathite, Ilai the A
1Chr 27:4 the second month was Dodai an A
*2. A rendering of "son of Ahohi."*
2Sa 23:9 Eleazar the son of Dodo the A

**AHOLAH** *(a-ho'-lah) A name for Samaria and the Ten Tribes.*
Eze 23:4 names of them were A the elder
Eze 23:36 Son of man, wilt thou judge A
Eze 23:44 so went they in unto A and unto

**AHOLIAB** *(a-ho'-lee-ab) A Danite craftsman.*
Ex 31:6 behold, I have given with him A
Ex 35:34 that he may teach, both he, and A
Ex 36:1 Then wrought Bezaleel and A
Ex 36:2 And Moses called Bezaleel and A
Ex 38:23 And with him was A, son of

**AHOLIBAH** *(a-hol'-ib-ah) A name for Jerusalem and Judah.*
Eze 23:4 Aholah the elder, and A her sister
Eze 23:11 And when her sister A saw this
Eze 23:36 man, wilt thou judge Aholah and A

**AHOLIBAMAH** *(a-hol'-ib-a'-mah)*
*1. A wife of Esau.*
Gen 36:2 A the daughter of Anah the
Gen 36:5 A bare Jeush, and Jaalam, and Korah
Gen 36:14 And these were the sons of A
Gen 36:18 came of A the daughter of Anah
Gen 36:25 Dishon, and A the daughter of Anah
*2. A chief from Esau.*
Gen 36:41 Duke A, duke Elah, duke Pinon,
1Chr 1:52 Duke A, duke Elah, duke Pinon,

**AHUMAI** *(a-hoo'-mahee) Grandson of Shobal.*
1Chr 4:2 and Jahath begat A, and Lahad

**AHUZAM** *(a-hoo'-zam) A son of Ashur.*
1Chr 4:6 And Naarah bare him A, and Hepher,

**AHUZZATH** *(a-huz'-zath) A friend of Ahimilech the Philistine king.*
Gen 26:26 A one of his friends, and Phichol

**AI** *(a'-i)* See AIATH, AIJA, HAI. *A city near Bethel in Benjamin.*
Josh 7:2 Joshua sent men from Jericho to A
Josh 7:5 the men of A smote of them about
Josh 8:1 with thee, and arise, go up to A
Josh 8:9 and A, on the west side of A
Josh 8:16 all the people that were in A
Josh 8:17 not a man left in A or Beth-el
Josh 8:23 the king of A they took alive, and
Josh 8:28 And Joshua burnt A, and made it an
Josh 8:29 the king of A he hanged on a tree
Josh 9:3 had done unto Jericho and to A
Josh 10:1 had heard how Joshua had taken A
Josh 12:9 the king of A, which is beside
Ezr 2:28 The men of Beth-el and A, two
Neh 7:32 The men of Beth-el and A, an
Jer 49:3 Howl, O Heshbon, for A is spoiled

**AIAH** *(a-i'-ah)* See AJAH.
*1. A son of Zibeon the Horite.*
1Chr 1:40 A, and Anah
*2. The father of Saul's concubine.*
2Sa 3:7 was Rizpah, the daughter of A
2Sa 21:8 sons of Rizpah the daughter of A

**AIATH** *(a-i'-ath)* See AI. *A form of Ai.*
Is 10:28 He is come to A, he is passed to

**AIDED**
Judg 9:24 which *a* him in the killing of his

**AIJA** *(a-i'-jah)* See AI. *A form of Ai.*
Neh 11:31 from Geba dwelt at Michmash, and A

**AIJALON** *(a-ij'-el-on)* See AJALON.
*1. A Levitical city in Dan.*
Josh 21:24 A with her suburbs, Gath-rimmon
Judg 1:35 would dwell in mount Heres in A
*2. A place in Zebulun.*
Judg 12:12 was buried in A in the country of
*3. A town between Benjamin and Judah.*
1Sa 14:31 that day from Michmash to A
1Chr 8:13 fathers of the inhabitants of A
2Chr 11:10 And Zorah, and A, and Hebron, which
*4. A Levitical city in Ephraim.*
1Chr 6:69 And A with her suburbs, and

**AIJELETH** *(a-ij'-el-eth) A musical notation.*
Ps 22:t the chief Musician upon A Shahar

**AILETH**
Gen 21:17 and said unto her, What *a* thee
Judg 18:23 and said unto Micah, What *a* thee
Judg 18:24 that ye say unto me, What *a* thee
1Sa 11:5 What *a* the people that they weep
2Sa 14:5 king said unto her, What *a* thee
2Kin 6:28 king said unto her, What *a* thee
Is 22:1 What *a* thee now, that thou art

**AIN** *(ah'-yin)* See EN.
*1. A place between Riblah and the Sea of Chinnereth.*
Num 34:11 to Riblah, on the east side of A
*2. A Levitical city in Simeon.*
Josh 15:32 And Lebaoth, and Shilhim, and A
Josh 19:7 A, Remmon, and Ether, and Ashan
Josh 21:16 A with her suburbs, and Juttah
1Chr 4:32 their villages were, Etam, and A

**AIR**
Gen 1:26 sea, and over the fowl of the *a*
Gen 1:28 sea, and over the fowl of the *a*
Gen 1:30 earth, and to every fowl of the *a*
Gen 2:19 the field, and every fowl of the *a*
Gen 2:20 cattle, and to the fowl of the *a*
Gen 6:7 thing, and the fowls of the *a*
Gen 7:3 Of fowls also of the *a* by sevens
Gen 9:2 and upon every fowl of the *a*
Deut 4:17 winged fowl that flieth in the *a*
Deut 28:26 be meat unto all fowls of the *a*
1Sa 17:44 thy flesh unto the fowls of the *a*
1Sa 17:46 this day unto the fowls of the *a*
2Sa 21:10 of the *a* to rest on them by day
1Kin 14:11 shall the fowls of the *a* eat
1Kin 16:4 shall the fowls of the *a* eat
1Kin 21:24 shall the fowls of the *a* eat
Job 12:7 and the fowls of the *a*, and they
Job 28:21 close from the fowls of the *a*
Job 41:16 that no *a* can come between them
Ps 8:8 The fowl of the *a*, and the fish of

Prov 30:19 The way of an eagle in the *a*
Eccl 10:20 for a bird of the *a* shall carry
Mt 6:26 Behold the fowls of the *a*
Mt 8:20 and the birds of the *a* have nests
Mt 13:32 so that the birds of the *a* come
Mk 4:4 side, and the fowls of the *a* came
Mk 4:32 so that the fowls of the *a* may
Lk 8:5 and the fowls of the *a* devoured it
Lk 9:58 and birds of the *a* have nests
Lk 13:19 the fowls of the *a* lodged in the
Acts 10:12 things, and fowls of the *a*
Acts 11:6 things, and fowls of the *a*
Acts 22:23 clothes, and threw dust into the *a*
1Cor 9:26 I, not as one that beateth the *a*
1Cor 14:9 for ye shall speak into the *a*
Eph 2:2 the prince of the power of the *a*
1Th 4:17 clouds, to meet the Lord in the *a*
Rev 9:2 the *a* were darkened by reason of
Rev 16:17 poured out his vial into the *a*

**AJAH** *(a'-jah)* See AIAH. *A son of Zibeon the Horite.*
Gen 36:24 both *A*, and Anah

**AJALON** *(aj'-a-lon)* See AIJALON.
*1. A valley of Dan.*
Josh 10:12 and thou, Moon, in the valley of *A*
*2. A Levitical city in Dan.*
Josh 19:42 And Shaalabbin, and *A*, and Jethlah,
*3. A town between Benjamin and Judah.*
2Chr 28:18 and had taken Beth-shemesh, and *A*

**AKAN** *(a'-kan)* See JAAKAN, JAKAN. *A son of Ezer.*
Gen 36:27 Bilhan, and Zaavan, and *A*

**AKKUB** *(ak'-kub)*
*1. A descendant of David.*
1Chr 3:24 and Eliashib, and Pelaiah, and *A*
*2. A Levitical gatekeeper.*
1Chr 9:17 the porters were, Shallum, and *A*
Neh 11:19 Moreover the porters, *A*, Talmon,
Neh 12:25 Obadiah, Meshullam, Talmon, *A*
*3. A family of Levitical porters.*
Ezr 2:42 of Talmon, the children of *A*
Neh 7:45 of Talmon, the children of *A*
*4. A family of returned exiles.*
Ezr 2:45 of Hagabah, the children of *A*
*5. A priest in Ezra's time.*
Neh 8:7 and Bani, and Sherebiah, Jamin, *A*

**AKRABBIM** *(ac-rab'-bim)* See MAALE-ACRABBIM. *An ascent south of the Dead Sea.*
Num 34:4 from the south to the ascent of *A*
Judg 1:36 was from the going up to *A*

**ALABASTER**
Mt 26:7 *a* box of very precious ointment
Mk 14:3 an *a* box of ointment of spikenard
Lk 7:37 brought an *a* box of ointment,

**ALAMETH** *(al'-am-eth) A son of Becher.*
1Chr 7:8 and Abiah, and Anathoth, and *A*

**ALAMMELECH** *(a-lam'-mel-ek) A town in Asher.*
Josh 19:26 And *A*, and Amad, and Misheal

**ALAMOTH** *(al'-am-oth) A musical notation.*
1Chr 15:20 and Benaiah, with psalteries on *A*
Ps 46:*t* the sons of Korah, A Song upon *A*

**ALARM**
Num 10:5 When ye blow an *a*, then the camps
Num 10:6 When ye blow an *a* the second time
Num 10:7 blow, but ye shall not sound an *a*
Num 10:9 shall blow an *a* with the trumpets
2Chr 13:12 trumpets to cry *a* against you
Jer 4:19 of the trumpet, the *a* of war
Jer 49:2 that I will cause an *a* of war to
Joel 2:1 sound an *a* in my holy mountain
Zeph 1:16 *a* against the fenced cities, and

**ALBEIT**
Eze 13:7 *a* I have not spoken
Philem 19 *a* I do not say to thee how thou

**ALEMETH** *(al-e'-meth)*
*1. A Levitical city in Benjamin.*
1Chr 6:60 *A* with her suburbs, and Anathoth
*2. A descendant of Jonathan.*
1Chr 8:36 and Jehoadah begat *A*, and Azmaveth,
1Chr 9:42 Jarah begat *A*, and Azmaveth, and

**ALEXANDER** *(al-ex-an'-dur)*
*1. Son of Simeon who bore Jesus' cross.*
Mk 15:21 of the country, the father of *A*
*2. A Christian leader in Jerusalem.*
Acts 4:6 and Caiaphas, and John, and *A*
*3. A participant in the Ephesian riot.*
Acts 19:33 they drew *A* out of the multitude,
*4. An opponent of Paul.*
1Ti 1:20 Of whom is Hymenaeus and *A*
2Ti 4:14 *A* the coppersmith did me much

**ALEXANDRIA** *(al-ex-an'-dree-ah)* See ALEXANDRIANS. *A city in Egypt.*
Acts 18:24 Jew named Apollos, born at *A*
Acts 27:6 a ship of *A* sailing into Italy
Acts 28:11 months we departed in a ship of *A*

**ALEXANDRIANS** *(al-ex-an'-dree-uns) Residents of Alexandria.*
Acts 6:9 Libertines, and Cyrenians, and *A*

**ALGUM**
2Chr 2:8 trees, and *a* trees, out of Lebanon
2Chr 9:10 gold from Ophir, brought *a* trees

**ALIAH** *(a-li'-ah)* See ALVAH. *A chief of Edom.*
1Chr 1:51 duke Timnah, duke *A*, duke Jetheth

**ALIAN** *(a-li'-un)* See ALVAN. *A son of Shobal.*
1Chr 1:40 *A*, and Manahath, and Ebal, Shephi,

**ALIEN**
Ex 18:3 I have been an *a* in a strange
Deut 14:21 or thou mayest sell it unto an *a*
Job 19:15 I am an *a* in their sight
Ps 69:8 an *a* unto my mother's children
Is 61:5 the sons of the *a* shall be your

**ALIENATED**
Eze 23:17 them, and her mind was *a* from them
Eze 23:18 then my mind was *a* from her
Eze 23:22 thee, from whom thy mind is *a*
Eze 23:28 of them from whom thy mind is *a*
Eph 4:18 being *a* from the life of God
Col 1:21 And you, that were sometime *a*

**ALIENS**
Lam 5:2 to strangers, our houses to *a*
Eph 2:12 being *a* from the commonwealth of
Heb 11:34 to flight the armies of the *a*

**ALIVE**
Gen 6:19 the ark, to keep them *a* with thee
Gen 6:20 come unto thee, to keep them *a*
Gen 7:3 to keep seed *a* upon the face of
Gen 7:23 and Noah only remained *a*, and they
Gen 12:12 me, but they will save thee *a*
Gen 43:7 saying, Is your father yet *a*
Gen 43:27 Is he yet *a*
Gen 43:28 is in good health, he is yet *a*
Gen 45:26 told him, saying, Joseph is yet *a*
Gen 45:28 Joseph my son is yet *a*
Gen 46:30 thy face, because thou art yet *a*
Gen 50:20 this day, to save much people *a*
Ex 1:17 but saved the men children *a*
Ex 1:18 and have saved the men children *a*
Ex 1:22 and every daughter ye shall save *a*
Ex 4:18 and see whether they be yet *a*
Ex 22:4 be certainly found in his hand *a*
Lev 10:16 sons of Aaron which were left *a*
Lev 14:4 is to be cleansed two birds *a*
Lev 16:10 be presented *a* before the LORD
Lev 26:36 upon them that are left *a* of you
Num 16:33 went down *a* into the pit, and the
Num 21:35 until there was none left him *a*
Num 22:33 I had slain thee, and saved her *a*
Num 31:15 Have ye saved all the women *a*
Num 31:18 with him, keep *a* for yourselves
Deut 4:4 are *a* every one of you this day
Deut 5:3 who are all of us here *a* this day
Deut 6:24 that he might preserve us *a*
Deut 20:16 thou shalt save *a* nothing that
Deut 31:27 while I am yet *a* with you this
Deut 32:39 I kill, and I make *a*
Josh 2:13 And that ye will save *a* my father
Josh 6:25 Joshua saved Rahab the harlot *a*
Josh 8:23 And the king of Ai they took *a*
Josh 14:10 behold, the LORD hath kept me *a*
Judg 8:19 liveth, if ye had saved them *a*
Judg 21:14 *a* of the women of Jabesh-gilead
1Sa 2:6 The LORD killeth, and maketh *a*
1Sa 15:8 Agag the king of the Amalekites *a*
1Sa 27:9 and left neither man nor woman *a*
1Sa 27:11 saved neither man nor woman *a*
2Sa 8:2 and with one full line to keep *a*
2Sa 12:18 Behold, while the child was yet *a*
2Sa 12:21 for the child, while it was *a*
2Sa 12:22 said, While the child was yet *a*
2Sa 18:14 while he was yet *a* in the midst
1Kin 18:5 to save the horses and mules *a*
1Kin 20:18 come out for peace, take them *a*
1Kin 20:32 And he said, Is he yet *a*
1Kin 21:15 for Naboth is not *a*, but dead
2Kin 5:7 Am I God, to kill and to make *a*
2Kin 7:4 if they save us *a*, we shall live
2Kin 7:12 the city, we shall catch them *a*
2Kin 10:14 And he said, Take them *a*
2Chr 25:12 other ten thousand left *a* did the
Ps 22:29 and none can keep *a* his own soul
Ps 30:3 thou hast kept me *a*, that I
Ps 33:19 and to keep them *a* in famine
Ps 41:2 will preserve him, and keep him *a*
Prov 1:12 us swallow them up *a* as the grave
Eccl 4:2 than the living which are yet *a*
Jer 49:11 children, I will preserve them *a*
Eze 7:13 is sold, although they were yet *a*
Eze 13:18 the souls *a* that come unto you
Eze 13:19 to save the souls *a* that should
Eze 18:27 right, he shall save his soul *a*
Dan 5:19 and whom he would he kept *a*
Mt 27:63 deceiver said, while he was yet *a*
Mk 16:11 when they had heard that he was *a*
Lk 15:24 my son was dead, and is *a* again
Lk 15:32 brother was dead, and is *a* again
Lk 24:23 angels, which said that he was *a*
Acts 1:3 *a* after his passion by many
Acts 9:41 saints and widows, presented her *a*
Acts 20:12 And they brought the young man *a*
Acts 25:19 dead, whom Paul affirmed to be *a*
Rom 6:11 but *a* unto God through Jesus
Rom 6:13 as those that are *a* from the dead
Rom 7:9 For I was *a* without the law once
1Cor 15:22 so in Christ shall all be made *a*
1Th 4:15 of the Lord, that we which are *a*
1Th 4:17 Then we which are *a* and remain
Rev 1:18 I am *a* for evermore, Amen
Rev 2:8 the last, which was dead, and is *a*
Rev 19:20 These both were cast *a* into a

**ALLELUIA** *(al-le-loo'-yah) Greek form of Hallelujah.*
Rev 19:1 much people in heaven, saying, *A*
Rev 19:3 And again they said, *A*
Rev 19:4 saying, Amen; *A*.
Rev 19:6 of mighty thunderings, saying, *A*

**ALLON** *(al'-lon)* See ALLON-BACHUTH, ELON.
*1. A city in Naphtali.*
Josh 19:33 from *A* to Zaanannim, and Adami,
*2. A chief of a Simeonite family.*
1Chr 4:37 the son of Shiphi, the son of *A*

**ALLON-BACHUTH** *(al'-lon-bak'-ooth) A place near Bethel.*
Gen 35:8 and the name of it was called *A*

**ALLOW**
Lk 11:48 ye *a* the deeds of your fathers
Acts 24:15 God, which they themselves also *a*
Rom 7:15 For that which I do I *a* not

**ALMIGHTY** *A term for God meaning sufficient or all-powerful.*
Gen 17:1 and said unto him, I am the *A* God
Gen 28:3 God *A* bless thee, and make thee
Gen 35:11 And God said unto him, I am God *A*
Gen 43:14 God *A* give you mercy before the
Gen 48:3 God *A* appeared unto me at Luz in
Gen 49:25 and by the *A*, who shall bless thee
Ex 6:3 unto Jacob, by the name of God *A*
Num 24:4 which saw the vision of the *A*
Num 24:16 which saw the vision of the *A*
Ruth 1:20 for the *A* hath dealt very
Ruth 1:21 me, and the *A* hath afflicted me
Job 5:17 not thou the chastening of the *A*
Job 6:4 the arrows of the *A* are within me
Job 6:14 he forsaketh the fear of the *A*
Job 8:3 or doth the *A* pervert justice
Job 8:5 and make thy supplication to the *A*
Job 11:7 find out the *A* unto perfection
Job 13:3 Surely I would speak to the *A*
Job 15:25 himself against the *A*
Job 21:15 What is the *A*, that we should
Job 21:20 shall drink of the wrath of the *A*
Job 22:3 Is it any pleasure to the *A*
Job 22:17 and what can the *A* do for them
Job 22:23 If thou return to the *A*, thou
Job 22:25 the *A* shall be thy defence, and
Job 22:26 thou have thy delight in the *A*

Job 23:16 heart soft, and the *A* troubleth me
Job 24:1 times are not hidden from the *A*
Job 27:2 and the *A*, who hath vexed my soul
Job 27:10 Will he delight himself in the *A*
Job 27:11 is with the *A* will I not conceal
Job 27:13 which they shall receive of the *A*
Job 29:5 When the *A* was yet with me, when
Job 31:2 inheritance of the *A* from on high
Job 31:35 that the *A* would answer me, and
Job 32:8 the inspiration of the *A* giveth
Job 33:4 the breath of the *A* hath given me
Job 34:10 and from the *A*, that he should
Job 34:12 will the *A* pervert judgment
Job 35:13 neither will the *A* regard it
Job 37:23 Touching the *A*, we cannot find
Job 40:2 with the *A* instruct him
Ps 68:14 When the *A* scattered kings in it,
Ps 91:1 abide under the shadow of the *A*
Is 13:6 come as a destruction from the *A*
Eze 1:24 waters, as the voice of the *A*
Eze 10:5 as the voice of the *A* God when he
Joel 1:15 from the *A* shall it come
2Cor 6:18 and daughters, saith the Lord *A*
Rev 1:8 was, and which is to come, the *A*
Rev 4:8 Holy, holy, holy, Lord God *A*
Rev 11:17 We give thee thanks, O Lord God *A*
Rev 15:3 are thy works, Lord God *A*
Rev 16:7 altar say, Even so, Lord God *A*
Rev 16:14 battle of that great day of God *A*
Rev 19:15 the fierceness and wrath of *A* God
Rev 21:22 for the Lord God *A* and the Lamb

**ALMODAD** *(al-mo'-dad) A descendant of Shem.*
Gen 10:26 And Joktan begat *A*, and Sheleph, and
1Chr 1:20 And Joktan begat *A*, and Sheleph, and

**ALMON** *(al'-mon) A Levitical town in Benjamin.*
Josh 21:18 suburbs, and *A* with her suburbs

**ALMOND**
Eccl 12:5 the *a* tree shall flourish, and the
Jer 1:11 I said, I see a rod of an *a* tree

**ALMON-DIBLATHAIM** *(al'-mon-dib-lath-a'-im) An encampment of Israel in the Wilderness.*
Num 33:46 from Dibon-gad, and encamped in *A*
Num 33:47 And they removed from *A*, and

**ALMONDS**
Gen 43:11 spices, and myrrh, nuts, and *a*
Ex 25:33 Three bowls made like unto *a*
Ex 25:34 be four bowls made like unto *a*
Ex 37:19 the fashion of *a* in one branch
Ex 37:20 were four bowls made like *a*
Num 17:8 and bloomed blossoms, and yielded *a*

**ALMS**
Mt 6:1 that ye do not your *a* before men
Mt 6:2 Therefore when thou doest thine *a*
Mt 6:3 But when thou doest *a*, let not
Mt 6:4 That thine *a* may be in secret
Lk 11:41 But rather give *a* of such things
Lk 12:33 Sell that ye have, and give *a*
Acts 3:2 to ask *a* of them that entered
Acts 3:3 to go into the temple asked an *a*
Acts 3:10 *a* at the Beautiful gate of the
Acts 10:2 which gave much *a* to the people
Acts 10:4 thine *a* are come up for a
Acts 10:31 thine *a* are had in remembrance in
Acts 24:17 I came to bring *a* to my nation

**ALMSDEEDS**
Acts 9:36 of good works and *a* which she did

**ALMUG**
1Kin 10:11 Ophir great plenty of *a* trees
1Kin 10:12 the king made of the *a* trees

**ALOES**
Num 24:6 as the trees of lign *a* which the
Ps 45:8 thy garments smell of myrrh, and *a*
Prov 7:17 perfumed my bed with myrrh, *a*
Song 4:14 myrrh and *a*, with all the chief
Jn 19:39 brought a mixture of myrrh and *a*

**ALOTH** *(a'-loth)* See BEALOTH. *A region near Asher.*
1Kin 4:16 of Hushai was in Asher and in *A*

**ALOUD**
Gen 45:2 And he wept *a*
1Kin 18:27 mocked them, and said, Cry *a*
1Kin 18:28 And they cried *a*, and cut
Ezr 3:12 and many shouted *a* for joy
Job 19:7 I cry *a*, but there is no judgment
Ps 51:14 shall sing *a* of thy righteousness
Ps 55:17 and at noon, will I pray, and cry *a*
Ps 59:16 I will sing *a* of thy mercy in the
Ps 81:1 Sing *a* unto God our strength
Ps 132:16 her saints shall shout *a* for joy
Ps 149:5 let them sing *a* upon their beds
Is 24:14 they shall cry *a* from the sea
Is 54:1 forth into singing, and cry *a*
Is 58:1 Cry *a*, spare not, lift up thy
Dan 3:4 Then an herald cried *a*, To you it
Dan 4:14 He cried *a*, and said thus, Hew
Dan 5:7 The king cried *a* to bring in the
Hos 5:8 cry *a* at Beth-aven, after thee, O
Mic 4:9 Now why dost thou cry out *a*
Mk 15:8 the multitude crying *a* began to

**ALPHA** *(al'-fah) First letter of Greek alphabet.*
Rev 1:8 I am *A* and Omega, the beginning
Rev 1:11 Saying, I am *A* and Omega, the
Rev 21:6 I am *A* and Omega, the beginning
Rev 22:13 I am *A* and Omega, the beginning

**ALPHAEUS** *(al-fe'-us)* See CLEOPAS.
*1. Father of the apostle James.*
Mt 10:3 James the son of *A*, and Lebbaeus,
Mk 3:18 and Thomas, and James the son of *A*
Lk 6:15 and Thomas, James the son of *A*
Acts 1:13 and Matthew, James the son of *A*
*2. Father of the apostle Levi.*
Mk 2:14 he saw Levi the son of *A* sitting

**ALTAR**
Gen 8:20 Noah builded an *a* unto the LORD
Gen 12:7 builded he an *a* unto the LORD
Gen 12:8 he builded an *a* unto the LORD
Gen 13:4 Unto the place of the *a*, which he
Gen 13:18 and built there an *a* unto the LORD
Gen 22:9 and Abraham built an *a* there
Gen 26:25 And he builded an *a* there, and
Gen 33:20 And he erected there an *a*, and
Gen 35:1 and make there an *a* unto God
Gen 35:3 I will make there an *a* unto God
Gen 35:7 And he built there an *a*, and called
Ex 17:15 And Moses built an *a*, and called
Ex 20:24 An *a* of earth thou shalt make
Ex 20:26 thou go up by steps unto mine *a*
Ex 21:14 thou shalt take him from mine *a*
Ex 24:4 builded an *a* under the hill, and
Ex 24:6 the blood he sprinkled on the *a*
Ex 27:1 shalt make an *a* of shittim wood
Ex 27:5 the compass of the *a* beneath
Ex 27:6 thou shalt make staves for the *a*
Ex 27:7 be upon the two sides of the *a*
Ex 28:43 *a* to minister in the holy place
Ex 29:12 horns of the *a* with thy finger
Ex 29:13 them, and burn them upon the *a*
Ex 29:16 it round about upon the *a*
Ex 29:18 burn the whole ram upon the *a*
Ex 29:20 the blood upon the *a* round about
Ex 29:21 of the blood that is upon the *a*
Ex 29:25 burn them upon the *a* for a burnt
Ex 29:36 and thou shalt cleanse the *a*
Ex 29:37 shalt make an atonement for the *a*
Ex 29:38 which thou shalt offer upon the *a*
Ex 29:44 of the congregation, and the *a*
Ex 30:1 thou shalt make an *a* to burn
Ex 30:18 of the congregation and the *a*
Ex 30:20 come near to the *a* to minister
Ex 30:27 his vessels, and the *a* of incense,
Ex 30:28 the *a* of burnt offering with all
Ex 31:8 furniture, and the *a* of incense,
Ex 31:9 the *a* of burnt offering with all
Ex 32:5 saw it, he built an *a* before it
Ex 35:15 And the incense *a*, and his staves,
Ex 35:16 The *a* of burnt offering, with his
Ex 37:25 the incense *a* of shittim wood
Ex 38:1 he made the *a* of burnt offering
Ex 38:3 he made all the vessels of the *a*
Ex 38:4 he made for the *a* a brasen grate
Ex 38:7 the rings on the sides of the *a*
Ex 38:30 the congregation, and the brasen *a*
Ex 38:30 it, and all the vessels of the *a*
Ex 39:38 And the golden *a*, and the anointing
Ex 39:39 The brasen *a*, and his grate of
Ex 40:5 thou shalt set the *a* of gold for
Ex 40:7 tent of the congregation and the *a*
Ex 40:10 the *a* of the burnt offering
Ex 40:26 he put the golden *a* in the tent
Ex 40:29 he put the *a* of burnt offering by
Ex 40:30 tent of the congregation and the *a*
Ex 40:33 about the tabernacle and the *a*
Lev 1:5 the *a* that is by the door of the
Lev 1:7 priest shall put fire upon the *a*
Lev 1:9 priest shall burn all on the *a*
Lev 1:11 the *a* northward before the LORD
Lev 1:13 it all, and burn it upon the *a*
Lev 1:15 priest shall bring it unto the *a*
Lev 1:17 priest shall burn it upon the *a*
Lev 2:2 the memorial of it upon the *a*
Lev 2:8 he shall bring it unto the *a*
Lev 2:9 and shall burn it upon the *a*
Lev 2:12 burnt on the *a* for a sweet savour
Lev 3:2 the blood upon the *a* round about
Lev 3:5 on the *a* upon the burnt sacrifice
Lev 3:8 thereof round about upon the *a*
Lev 3:11 priest shall burn it upon the *a*
Lev 3:13 thereof upon the *a* round about
Lev 3:16 priest shall burn them upon the *a*
Lev 4:7 the *a* of sweet incense before the
Lev 4:10 upon the *a* of the burnt offering
Lev 4:18 of the *a* which is before the LORD
Lev 4:19 from him, and burn it upon the *a*
Lev 4:25 horns of the *a* of burnt offering
Lev 4:26 shall burn all his fat upon the *a*
Lev 4:30 horns of the *a* of burnt offering
Lev 4:31 the *a* for a sweet savour unto the
Lev 4:34 horns of the *a* of burnt offering
Lev 4:35 priest shall burn them upon the *a*
Lev 5:9 offering upon the side of the *a*
Lev 5:12 thereof, and burn it on the *a*
Lev 6:9 the *a* all night unto the morning
Lev 6:12 the fire upon the *a* shall be
Lev 6:13 shall ever be burning upon the *a*
Lev 6:15 it upon the *a* for a sweet savour
Lev 7:2 sprinkle round about upon the *a*
Lev 7:5 *a* for an offering made by fire
Lev 7:31 shall burn the fat upon the *a*
Lev 8:11 thereof upon the *a* seven times
Lev 8:15 the *a* round about with his finger
Lev 8:16 and Moses burned it upon the *a*
Lev 8:19 the blood upon the *a* round about
Lev 8:21 burnt the whole ram upon the *a*
Lev 8:24 the blood upon the *a* round about
Lev 8:28 burnt them on the *a* upon the
Lev 8:30 of the blood which was upon the *a*
Lev 9:7 said unto Aaron, Go unto the *a*
Lev 9:9 the blood at the bottom of the *a*
Lev 9:10 sin offering, he burnt upon the *a*
Lev 9:12 sprinkled round about upon the *a*
Lev 9:14 upon the burnt offering on the *a*
Lev 9:17 thereof, and burnt it upon the *a*
Lev 9:18 sprinkled upon the *a* round about
Lev 9:20 and he burnt the fat upon the *a*
Lev 9:24 consumed upon the *a* the burnt
Lev 10:12 it without leaven beside the *a*
Lev 14:20 and the meat offering upon the *a*
Lev 16:12 from off the *a* before the LORD
Lev 16:18 the *a* that is before the LORD
Lev 16:20 of the congregation, and the *a*
Lev 16:25 offering shall he burn upon the *a*
Lev 16:33 of the congregation, and for the *a*
Lev 17:6 sprinkle the blood upon the *a* of
Lev 17:11 *a* to make an atonement for your
Lev 21:23 vail, nor come nigh unto the *a*
Lev 22:22 of them upon the *a* unto the LORD
Num 3:26 by the *a* round about, and the
Num 4:11 upon the golden *a* they shall
Num 4:13 take away the ashes from the *a*
Num 4:14 basons, all the vessels of the *a*
Num 4:26 by the *a* round about, and their
Num 5:25 the LORD, and offer it upon the *a*
Num 5:26 thereof, and burn it upon the *a*
Num 7:1 instruments thereof, both the *a*
Num 7:10 offered for dedicating of the *a*
Num 7:11 day, for the dedicating of the *a*
Num 7:84 This was the dedication of the *a*
Num 7:88 This was the dedication of the *a*
Num 16:38 plates for a covering of the *a*
Num 16:39 plates for a covering of the *a*
Num 16:46 put fire therein from off the *a*
Num 18:3 vessels of the sanctuary and the *a*
Num 18:5 sanctuary, and the charge of the *a*
Num 18:7 office for every thing of the *a*
Num 18:17 sprinkle their blood upon the *a*
Deut 12:27 upon the *a* of the LORD thy God
Deut 16:21 unto the *a* of the LORD thy God
Deut 26:4 before the *a* of the LORD thy God
Deut 27:6 Thou shalt build the *a* of the
Deut 33:10 burnt sacrifice upon thine *a*
Josh 8:30 Then Joshua built an *a* unto the

Josh 8:31 an *a* of whole stones, over which
Josh 9:27 for the *a* of the LORD, even unto
Josh 22:10 *a* by Jordan, a great *a*
Josh 22:11 *a* over against the land of Canaan
Josh 22:16 in that ye have builded you an *a*
Josh 22:19 an *a* beside the *a* of the LORD
Josh 22:23 That we have built us an *a* to
Josh 22:26 us now prepare to build us an *a*
Josh 22:28 the pattern of the *a* of the LORD
Josh 22:29 to build an *a* for burnt offerings
Josh 22:34 children of Gad called the *a* Ed
Judg 6:24 built an *a* there unto the LORD
Judg 6:26 build an *a* unto the LORD thy God
Judg 6:28 the *a* of Baal was cast down, and
Judg 6:30 he hath cast down the *a* of Baal
Judg 6:31 because one hath cast down his *a*
Judg 6:32 because he hath thrown down his *a*
Judg 13:20 up toward heaven from off the *a*
Judg 21:4 rose early, and built there an *a*
1Sa 2:28 my priest, to offer upon mine *a*
1Sa 2:33 I shall not cut off from mine *a*
1Sa 7:17 there he built an *a* unto the LORD
1Sa 14:35 And Saul built an *a* unto the LORD
2Sa 24:18 rear an *a* unto the LORD in the
2Sa 24:21 to build an *a* unto the LORD, that
2Sa 24:25 built there an *a* unto the LORD
1Kin 1:50 caught hold on the horns of the *a*
1Kin 1:51 caught hold on the horns of the *a*
1Kin 1:53 they brought him down from the *a*
1Kin 2:28 caught hold on the horns of the *a*
1Kin 2:29 and, behold, he is by the *a*
1Kin 3:4 did Solomon offer upon that *a*
1Kin 6:20 so covered the *a* which was of
1Kin 6:22 also the whole *a* that was by the
1Kin 7:48 the *a* of gold, and the table of
1Kin 8:22 Solomon stood before the *a* of the
1Kin 8:31 come before thine *a* in this house
1Kin 8:54 from before the *a* of the LORD
1Kin 8:64 because the brasen *a* that was
1Kin 9:25 peace offerings upon the *a* which
1Kin 12:32 Judah, and he offered upon the *a*
1Kin 12:33 So he offered upon the *a* which he
1Kin 13:1 stood by the *a* to burn incense
1Kin 13:2 he cried against the *a* in the
1Kin 13:3 the *a* shall be rent, and the ashes
1Kin 13:4 cried against the *a* in Beth-el
1Kin 13:5 the ashes poured out from the *a*
1Kin 13:32 the LORD against the *a* in Beth-el
1Kin 18:26 leaped upon the *a* which was made
1Kin 18:30 he repaired the *a* of the LORD
1Kin 18:32 an *a* in the name of the LORD
1Kin 18:35 the water ran round about the *a*
2Kin 11:11 of the temple, along by the *a*
2Kin 12:9 lid of it, and set it beside the *a*
2Kin 16:10 saw an *a* that was at Damascus
2Kin 16:12 from Damascus, the king saw the *a*
2Kin 16:14 And he brought also the brasen *a*
2Kin 16:15 the brasen *a* shall be for me to
2Kin 23:9 to the *a* of the LORD in Jerusalem
2Kin 23:15 Moreover the *a* that was at
2Kin 23:17 done against the *a* of Beth-el
1Chr 6:49 upon the *a* of the burnt offering
1Chr 16:40 upon the *a* of the burnt offering
1Chr 21:18 set up an *a* unto the LORD in the
1Chr 21:22 that I may build an *a* therein
1Chr 21:26 built there an *a* unto the LORD
1Chr 21:29 the *a* of the burnt offering, were
1Chr 22:1 this is the *a* of the burnt
1Chr 28:18 for the *a* of incense refined gold
2Chr 1:5 Moreover the brasen *a*, that
2Chr 1:6 to the brasen *a* before the LORD
2Chr 4:1 Moreover he made an *a* of brass
2Chr 4:19 house of God, the golden *a* also
2Chr 5:12 stood at the east end of the *a*
2Chr 6:12 he stood before the *a* of the LORD
2Chr 6:22 come before thine *a* in this house
2Chr 7:7 because the brasen *a* which
2Chr 7:9 dedication of the *a* seven days
2Chr 8:12 the LORD on the *a* of the LORD
2Chr 15:8 and renewed the *a* of the LORD
2Chr 23:10 of the temple, along by the *a*
2Chr 26:16 incense upon the *a* of incense
2Chr 26:19 LORD, from beside the incense *a*
2Chr 29:18 the *a* of burnt offering, with all
2Chr 29:21 offer them on the *a* of the LORD
2Chr 29:22 blood, and sprinkled it on the *a*
2Chr 29:27 the burnt offering upon the *a*
2Chr 33:16 And he repaired the *a* of the LORD
Ezr 3:2 builded the *a* of the God of
Ezr 3:3 they set the *a* upon his bases
Ezr 7:17 offer them upon the *a* of the
Neh 10:34 to burn upon the *a* of the LORD
Ps 26:6 so will I compass thine *a*
Ps 43:4 Then will I go unto the *a* of God
Ps 51:19 they offer bullocks upon thine *a*
Ps 118:27 even unto the horns of the *a*
Is 6:6 with the tongs from off the *a*
Is 19:19 In that day shall there be an *a*
Is 27:9 *a* as chalkstones that are beaten
Is 56:7 shall be accepted upon mine *a*
Is 60:7 come up with acceptance on mine *a*
Lam 2:7 The Lord hath cast off his *a*
Eze 8:5 northward at the gate of the *a*
Eze 8:16 LORD, between the porch and the *a*
Eze 9:2 in, and stood beside the brasen *a*
Eze 40:46 keepers of the charge of the *a*
Eze 41:22 The *a* of wood was three cubits
Eze 43:13 of the *a* after the cubits
Eze 43:16 the *a* shall be twelve cubits long
Eze 43:22 and they shall cleanse the *a*
Eze 43:26 Seven days shall they purge the *a*
Eze 43:27 your burnt offerings upon the *a*
Eze 45:19 corners of the settle of the *a*
Eze 47:1 house, at the south side of the *a*
Joel 1:13 howl, ye ministers of the *a*
Joel 2:17 weep between the porch and the *a*
Amos 2:8 clothes laid to pledge by every *a*
Amos 3:14 horns of the *a* shall be cut off
Amos 9:1 saw the Lord standing upon the *a*
Zec 9:15 bowls, and as the corners of the *a*
Zec 14:20 be like the bowls before the *a*
Mal 1:7 offer polluted bread upon mine *a*
Mal 1:10 kindle fire on mine *a* for nought
Mal 2:13 covering the *a* of the LORD with
Mt 5:23 if thou bring thy gift to the *a*
Mt 5:24 Leave there thy gift before the *a*
Mt 23:18 Whosoever shall swear by the *a*
Mt 23:20 therefore shall swear by the *a*
Mt 23:35 slew between the temple and the *a*
Lk 1:11 right side of the *a* of incense
Lk 11:51 which perished between the *a*
Acts 17:23 devotions, I found an *a* with this
1Cor 9:13 *a* are partakers with the *a*
1Cor 10:18 the sacrifices partakers of the *a*
Heb 7:13 no man gave attendance at the *a*
Heb 13:10 We have an *a*, whereof they have
Jas 2:21 offered Isaac his son upon the *a*
Rev 6:9 I saw under the *a* the souls of
Rev 8:3 angel came and stood at the *a*
Rev 8:5 and filled it with fire of the *a*
Rev 9:13 the golden *a* which is before God
Rev 11:1 the temple of God, and the *a*
Rev 14:18 another angel came out from the *a*
Rev 16:7 I heard another out of the *a* say

### ALTARS

Ex 34:13 But ye shall destroy their *a*
Num 3:31 and the candlestick, and the *a*
Num 23:1 unto Balak, Build me here seven *a*
Num 23:14 top of Pisgah, and built seven *a*
Num 23:29 unto Balak, Build me here seven *a*
Deut 7:5 ye shall destroy their *a*, and
Deut 12:3 And ye shall overthrow their *a*
Judg 2:2 ye shall throw down their *a*
1Kin 19:10 thy covenant, thrown down thine *a*
1Kin 19:14 thy covenant, thrown down thine *a*
2Kin 11:18 his *a* and his images brake they in
2Kin 18:22 whose *a* Hezekiah hath taken away,
2Kin 21:3 and he reared up *a* for Baal
2Kin 21:4 he built *a* in the house of the
2Kin 21:5 he built *a* for all the host of
2Kin 23:12 the *a* that were on the top of the
2Kin 23:20 places that were there upon the *a*
2Chr 14:3 away the *a* of the strange gods
2Chr 23:17 and brake it down, and brake his *a*
2Chr 28:24 he made him *a* in every corner of
2Chr 30:14 took away the *a* that were in
2Chr 31:1 the *a* out of all Judah and
2Chr 32:12 away his high places and his *a*
2Chr 33:3 and he reared up *a* for Baalim
2Chr 33:4 Also he built *a* in the house of
2Chr 33:5 he built *a* for all the host of
2Chr 33:15 all the *a* that he had built in
2Chr 34:4 they brake down the *a* of Baalim
2Chr 34:5 bones of the priests upon their *a*
2Chr 34:7 And when he had broken down the *a*
Ps 84:3 may lay her young, even thine *a*
Is 17:8 And he shall not look to the *a*
Is 36:7 whose *a* Hezekiah hath taken away,
Is 65:3 burneth incense upon *a* of brick
Jer 11:13 set up *a* to that shameful thing
Jer 17:1 and upon the horns of your *a*
Jer 17:2 their children remember their *a*
Eze 6:4 your *a* shall be desolate, and your
Eze 6:6 that your *a* may be laid waste and
Eze 6:13 their idols round about their *a*
Hos 8:11 Ephraim hath made many *a* to sin
Hos 10:1 his fruit he hath increased the *a*
Hos 10:8 thistle shall come up on their *a*
Hos 12:11 their *a* are as heaps in the
Amos 3:14 will also visit the *a* of Beth-el
Rom 11:3 prophets, and digged down thine *a*

### ALTASCHITH

Ps 57:*t* To the chief Musician, *A*, Michtam
Ps 58:*t* To the chief Musician, *A*, Michtam
Ps 59:*t* To the chief Musician, *A*, Michtam
Ps 75:*t* To the chief Musician, *A*, A Psalm

### ALTER

Lev 27:10 He shall not *a* it, nor change it,
Ezr 6:11 that whosoever shall *a* this word
Ezr 6:12 that shall put to their hand to *a*
Ps 89:34 nor *a* the thing that is gone out

### ALTERED

Est 1:19 and the Medes, that it be not *a*
Lk 9:29 fashion of his countenance was *a*

### ALTERETH

Dan 6:8 Medes and Persians, which *a* not
Dan 6:12 Medes and Persians, which *a* not

**ALUSH** *(a'-lush) An Israelite encampment during the Exodus.*

Num 33:13 from Dophkah, and encamped in *A*
Num 33:14 And they removed from *A*, and

**ALVAH** *(al'-vah)* See ALIAH. *An Edomite chief.*

Gen 36:40 duke Timnah, duke *A*, duke Jetheth

**ALVAN** *(al'-van)* See ALIAN. *A son of Shobal the Horite.*

Gen 36:23 *A*, and Manahath, and Ebal, Shepho,

### ALWAY

Ex 25:30 the table shewbread before me *a*
Num 9:16 So it was *a*
Deut 11:1 and his commandments, *a*
Deut 28:33 be only oppressed and crushed *a*
2Sa 9:10 son shall eat bread *a* at my table
1Kin 11:36 a light *a* before me in Jerusalem
2Kin 8:19 him to give him *a* a light
Job 7:16 I would not live *a*
Ps 9:18 needy shall not *a* be forgotten
Ps 119:112 heart to perform thy statutes *a*
Prov 28:14 Happy is the man that feareth *a*
Mt 28:20 and, lo, I am with you *a*, even
Jn 7:6 but your time is *a* ready
Acts 10:2 to the people, and prayed to God *a*
Rom 11:10 not see, and bow down their back *a*
2Cor 4:11 For we which live are *a* delivered
2Cor 6:10 As sorrowful, yet *a* rejoicing
Phil 4:4 Rejoice in the Lord *a*
Col 4:6 Let your speech be *a* with grace
1Th 2:16 be saved, to fill up their sins *a*
2Th 2:13 to give thanks *a* to God for you
Titus 1:12 said, The Cretians are *a* liars
Heb 3:10 They do *a* err in their heart

### ALWAYS

Gen 6:3 shall not *a* strive with man
Ex 27:20 to cause the lamp to burn *a*
Ex 28:38 it shall be *a* upon his forehead,
Deut 5:29 keep all my commandments *a*
Deut 6:24 the LORD our God, for our good *a*
Deut 11:12 of the LORD thy God are *a* upon it
Deut 14:23 learn to fear the LORD thy God *a*

1Chr 16:15 Be ye mindful *a* of his covenant
2Chr 18:7 good unto me, but *a* evil
Job 27:10 will he *a* call upon God
Job 32:9 Great men are not *a* wise
Ps 10:5 His ways are *a* grievous
Ps 16:8 I have set the LORD *a* before me
Ps 103:9 He will not *a* chide
Prov 5:19 be thou ravished *a* with her love
Prov 8:30 delight, rejoicing *a* before him
Eccl 9:8 Let thy garments be *a* white
Is 57:16 ever, neither will I be *a* wroth
Jer 20:17 and her womb to be *a* great with me
Eze 38:8 Israel, which have been *a* waste
Mt 18:10 *a* behold the face of my Father
Mt 26:11 For ye have the poor *a* with you
Mk 5:5 And *a*, night and day, he was in the
Mk 14:7 For ye have the poor with you *a*
Lk 18:1 end, that men ought *a* to pray
Lk 21:36 ye therefore, and pray *a*
Jn 8:29 for I do *a* those things that
Jn 11:42 And I knew that thou hearest me *a*
Jn 12:8 For the poor *a* ye have with you
Jn 18:20 temple, whither the Jews *a* resort
Acts 2:25 the Lord *a* before my face
Acts 7:51 ye do *a* resist the Holy Ghost
Acts 24:3 We accept it *a*, and in all places,
Acts 24:16 to have *a* a conscience void of
Rom 1:9 mention of you *a* in my prayers
1Cor 1:4 I thank my God *a* on your behalf
1Cor 15:58 *a* abounding in the work of the
2Cor 2:14 which *a* causeth us to triumph in
2Cor 4:10 *A* bearing about in the body the
2Cor 5:6 Therefore we are *a* confident
2Cor 9:8 *a* having all sufficiency in all
Gal 4:18 affected *a* in a good thing
Eph 5:20 Giving thanks *a* for all things
Eph 6:18 Praying *a* with all prayer and
Phil 1:4 *A* in every prayer of mine for you
Phil 1:20 but that with all boldness, as *a*
Phil 2:12 my beloved, as ye have *a* obeyed
Col 1:3 Jesus Christ, praying *a* for you
Col 4:12 *a* labouring fervently for you in
1Th 1:2 give thanks to God *a* for you all
1Th 3:6 ye have good remembrance of us *a*
2Th 1:3 are bound to thank God *a* for you
2Th 1:11 Wherefore also we pray *a* for you
2Th 3:16 give you peace *a* by all means
Philem 4 mention of thee *a* in my prayers
Heb 9:6 the priests went *a* into the first
1Pet 3:15 be ready *a* to give an answer to
2Pet 1:12 not be negligent to put you *a* in
2Pet 1:15 these things *a* in remembrance

**AMAD** *(a'-mad) A town on the border of Asher.*
Josh 19:26 And Alammelech, and *A*, and Misheal

**AMAL** *(a'-mal) A descendant of Asher.*
1Chr 7:35 and Imna, and Shelesh, and *A*

**AMALEK** *(am'-al-ek)* See AMALEKITE.
*1. The son of Eliphaz.*
Gen 36:12 and she bare to Eliphaz *A*
Gen 36:16 Duke Korah, duke Gatam, and duke *A*
1Chr 1:36 and Gatam, Kenaz, and Timna, and *A*
*2. Descendants of Amalek.*
Ex 17:8 Then came *A*, and fought with
Ex 17:11 he let down his hand, *A* prevailed
Ex 17:13 And Joshua discomfited *A* and his
Ex 17:14 of *A* from under heaven
Ex 17:16 the LORD will have war with *A*
Num 24:20 And when he looked on *A*, he took
Deut 25:17 Remember what *A* did unto thee by
Judg 3:13 him the children of Ammon and *A*
Judg 5:14 there a root of them against *A*
1Sa 15:2 that which *A* did to Israel
1Sa 15:5 And Saul came to a city of *A*
1Sa 15:20 have brought Agag the king of *A*
1Sa 28:18 his fierce wrath upon *A*,
2Sa 8:12 and of the Philistines, and of *A*
1Chr 18:11 from the Philistinesand, from *A*
Ps 83:7 Gebal, and Ammon, and *A*

**AMALEKITE** *(am'-al-ek-ite)* See AMALEKITES. *A descendant of Amalek.*
1Sa 30:13 man of Egypt, servant to an *A*
2Sa 1:8 And I answered him, I am an *A*
2Sa 1:13 I am the son of a stranger, an *A*

**AMALEKITES** *(am'-al-ek-ites)*
Gen 14:7 and smote all the country of the *A*
Num 13:29 The *A* dwell in the land of the
Num 14:25 (Now the *A* and the Canaanites
Num 14:43 For the *A* and the Canaanites are
Judg 6:3 the Midianites came up, and the *A*
Judg 7:12 And the Midianites and the *A*
Judg 10:12 The Zidonians also, and the *A*
Judg 12:15 of Ephraim, in the mount of the *A*
1Sa 14:48 gathered an host, and smote the *A*
1Sa 15:6 get you down from among the *A*
1Sa 15:15 They have brought them from the *A*
1Sa 15:18 utterly destroy the sinners the *A*
1Sa 15:32 to me Agag the king of the *A*
1Sa 27:8 and the Gezrites, and the *A*
1Sa 30:1 that the *A* had invaded the south,
1Sa 30:18 all that the *A* had carried away
2Sa 1:1 from the slaughter of the *A*
1Chr 4:43 rest of the *A* that were escaped

**AMAM** *(a'-mam) A city near Shema and Moladah.*
Josh 15:26 *A*, and Shema, and Moladah,

**AMANA** *(am-a'-nah) A city in southern Judah.*
Song 4:8 look from the top of *A*, from the

**AMARIAH** *(am-a-ri'-ah)*
*1. A descendant of Aaron.*
1Chr 6:7 begat *A*, and *A* begat Ahitub,
1Chr 6:52 *A* his son, Ahitub his son,
Ezr 7:3 The son of *A*, the son of Azariah,
*2. A High Priest during Solomon's reign.*
1Chr 6:11 begat Amariah, and *A* begat Ahitub,
*3. A descendant of Kohath.*
1Chr 23:19 *A* the second, Jahaziel the third,
1Chr 24:23 *A* the second, Jahaziel the third,
*4. Chief priest during Jehoshaphat's reign.*
2Chr 19:11 *A* the chief priest is over you in
*5. A Levite in Hezekiah's time.*
2Chr 31:15 and Jeshua, and Shemaiah, *A*
*6. Married a foreign wife in exile.*
Ezr 10:42 Shallum, *A*, and Joseph
*7. A priest who sealed the covenant with Nehemiah.*
Neh 10:3 Pashur, *A*, Malchijah,
Neh 12:2 *A*, Malluch, Hattush,
Neh 12:13 of *A*, Jehohanan
*8. A descendant of Judah.*
Neh 11:4 son of Zechariah, the son of *A*
*9. An ancestor of Zephaniah the prophet.*
Zeph 1:1 the son of Gedaliah, the son of *A*

**AMASA** *(am'-a-sah)*
*1. David's nephew.*
2Sa 17:25 Absalom made *A* captain of the
2Sa 19:13 And say ye to *A*, Art thou not of
2Sa 20:4 Then said the king to *A*, Assemble
2Sa 20:8 is in Gibeon, *A* went before them
2Sa 20:9 And Joab said to *A*, Art thou in
2Sa 20:12 he removed *A* out of the highway
1Kin 2:5 unto *A* the son of Jether, whom he
1Kin 2:32 *A* the son of Jether, captain of
1Chr 2:17 And Abigail bare *A*
*2. An Ephraimite who opposed the slavery of the Jews.*
2Chr 28:12 *A* the son of Hadlai, stood up

**AMASAI** *(am'-as-ahee)*
*1. A descendant of Kohath.*
1Chr 6:25 *A*, and Ahimoth
2Chr 29:12 arose, Mahath the son of *A*
*2. A captain in David's army.*
1Chr 12:18 Then the spirit came upon *A*
*3. A Levite who helped relocate the Ark.*
1Chr 15:24 Jehoshaphat, and Nethaneel, and *A*

**AMASHAI** *(am'-ash-ahee) A priest of the Emmer family.*
Neh 11:13 *A* the son of Azareel, the son of

**AMASIAH** *(am-a-si'-ah) Chief captain of Jehoshaphat's army.*
2Chr 17:16 next him was *A* the son of Zichri,

**AMAZED**
Ex 15:15 Then the dukes of Edom shall be *a*
Judg 20:41 again, the men of Benjamin were *a*
Job 32:15 They were *a*, they answered no
Is 13:8 they shall be *a* one at another
Eze 32:10 I will make many people *a* at thee
Mt 12:23 And all the people were *a*, and said
Mt 19:25 heard it, they were exceedingly *a*
Mk 1:27 And they were all *a*, insomuch that
Mk 2:12 insomuch that they were all *a*
Mk 6:51 they were sore *a* in themselves
Mk 9:15 they beheld him, were greatly *a*
Mk 10:32 and they were *a*
Mk 14:33 and John, and began to be sore *a*
Mk 16:8 for they trembled and were *a*
Lk 2:48 And when they saw him, they were *a*
Lk 4:36 And they were all *a*, and spake
Lk 5:26 And they were all *a*, and they
Lk 9:43 they were all *a* at the mighty
Acts 2:7 And they were all *a* and marvelled,
Acts 2:12 And they were all *a*, and were in
Acts 9:21 But all that heard him were *a*

**AMAZEMENT**
Acts 3:10 *a* at that which had happened unto
1Pet 3:6 and are not afraid with any *a*

**AMAZIAH** *(am-a-zi'-ah)*
*1. Son and successor of King Joash of Judah.*
2Kin 12:21 *A* his son reigned in his stead
2Kin 13:12 he fought against *A* king of Judah
2Kin 14:1 *A* the son of Joash king of Judah
2Kin 14:8 Then *A* sent messengers to Jehoash
2Kin 14:9 of Israel sent to *A* king of Judah
2Kin 14:15 he fought with *A* king of Judah
2Kin 14:21 him king instead of his father *A*
2Kin 14:23 In the fifteenth year of *A* the
2Kin 15:1 son of *A* king of Judah to reign
1Chr 3:12 *A* his son, Azariah his son,
2Chr 24:27 *A* his son reigned in his stead
2Chr 25:1 *A* was twenty and five years old
2Chr 25:5 Moreover *A* gathered Judah
2Chr 25:11 *A* strengthened himself, and led
2Chr 25:13 of the army which *A* sent back
2Chr 25:18 of Israel sent to *A* king of Judah
2Chr 25:21 *A* king of Judah, at Beth-shemesh,
2Chr 25:27 Now after the time that *A* did
2Chr 26:1 king in the room of his father *A*
2Chr 26:4 to all that his father *A* did
*2. A Simeonite.*
1Chr 4:34 Jamlech, and Joshah the son of *A*
*3. A Levite from the Merari family.*
1Chr 6:45 son of Hashabiah, the son of *A*
*4. Priest of the idols at Bethel.*
Amos 7:10 Then *A* the priest of Beth-el sent
Amos 7:12 Also *A* said unto Amos, O thou

**AMBASSADOR**
Prov 13:17 but a faithful *a* is health
Jer 49:14 an *a* is sent unto the heathen,
Obad 1 an *a* is sent among the heathen,
Eph 6:20 For which I am an *a* in bonds

**AMBASSADORS**
Josh 9:4 and made as if they had been *a*
2Chr 32:31 the *a* of the princes of Babylon
2Chr 35:21 But he sent *a* to him, saying,
Is 18:2 That sendeth *a* by the sea
Is 30:4 at Zoan, and his *a* came to Hanes
Is 33:7 the *a* of peace shall weep
Eze 17:15 him in sending his *a* into Egypt
2Cor 5:20 Now then we are *a* for Christ

**AMBER**
Eze 1:4 midst thereof as the colour of *a*
Eze 1:27 And I saw as the colour of *a*
Eze 8:2 of brightness, as the colour of *a*

**AMBUSH**
Josh 8:2 lay thee an *a* for the city behind
Josh 8:7 Then ye shall rise up from the *a*
Josh 8:14 in *a* against him behind the city

**AMBUSHMENT**
2Chr 13:13 But Jeroboam caused an *a* to come
2Chr 13:13 Judah, and the *a* was behind them

**AMERCE**
Deut 22:19 they shall *a* him in an hundred

**AMETHYST**
Ex 28:19 row a ligure, an agate, and an *a*
Ex 39:12 row, a ligure, an agate, and an *a*
Rev 21:20 the twelfth, an *a*

**AMI** *(a'-mi) A family of returned exiles.*
Ezr 2:57 of Zebaim, the children of *A*

**AMIABLE**
Ps 84:1 How *a* are thy tabernacles, O LORD

**AMINADAB** *(a-min'-a-dab)* See AMMINADAB. *Son of Aram; ancestor of Jesus.*
Mt 1:4 And Aram begat *A*
Mt 1:4 and *A* begat Naasson
Lk 3:33 Which was the son of *A*, which was

**AMISS**
2Chr 6:37 We have sinned, we have done *a*
Dan 3:29 which speak any thing *a* against
Lk 23:41 but this man hath done nothing *a*
Jas 4:3 and receive not, because ye ask *a*

**AMITTAI** *(a-mit'-tahee) Father of Jonah.*
2Kin 14:25 his servant Jonah, the son of *A*
Jonah 1:1 LORD came unto Jonah the son of *A*

**AMMAH** *(am'-mah)* See METHEG-AMMAH. *A hill near Gibeon.*
2Sa 2:24 they were come to the hill of *A*

**AMMI** *(am'-mi)* See AMMI-NADIB, BEN-AMMI, LO-AMMI. *A name given to Israel by Hosea meaning "my people."*
Hos 2:1 Say ye unto your brethren, *A*

**AMMIEL** *(am'-me-el)* See ELIAM.
*1. A spy for Moses.*
Num 13:12 of Dan, *A* the son of Gemalli
*2. A Manassehite of Lodebar.*
2Sa 9:4 the house of Machir, the son of *A*
2Sa 9:5 the house of Machir, the son of *A*
2Sa 17:27 Machir the son of *A* of Lo-debar
*3. Father of a wife of David.*
1Chr 3:5 of Bath-shua the daughter of *A*
*4. A Levite Tabernacle servant.*
1Chr 26:5 *A* the sixth, Issachar the seventh

**AMMIHUD** *(am-mi'-hud)*
*1. Father of Elishama.*
Num 1:10 Elishama the son of *A*
Num 2:18 shall be Elishama the son of *A*
Num 7:48 seventh day Elishama the son of *A*
Num 10:22 host was Elishama the son of *A*
1Chr 7:26 *A* his son, Elishama his son,
*2. A Simeonite.*
Num 34:20 of Simeon, Shemuel the son of *A*
*3. A Naphtalite.*
Num 34:28 of Naphtali, Pedahel the son of *A*
*4. Father of the king of Geshur.*
2Sa 13:37 and went to Talmai, the son of *A*
*5. A son of Omri.*
1Chr 9:4 Uthai the son of *A*, the son of

**AMMINADAB** *(am-min'-a-dab)* See AMINADAB, AMMI-NADIB.
*1. Aaron's father-in-law.*
Ex 6:23 took him Elisheba, daughter of *A*
*2. A prince of Judah.*
Num 1:7 Nahshon the son of *A*
Num 7:12 day was Nahshon the son of *A*
Num 7:17 offering of Nahshon the son of *A*
Num 10:14 his host was Nahshon the son of *A*
Ruth 4:19 Hezron begat Ram, and Ram begat *A*
1Chr 2:10 And Ram begat *A*
*3. A son of Kohath.*
1Chr 6:22 *A* his son, Korah his son, Assir
*4. A Levite who relocated the Ark.*
1Chr 15:10 *A* the chief, and his brethren an
1Chr 15:11 and Joel, Shemaiah, and Eliel, and *A*

**AMMI-NADIB**
Song 6:12 made me like the chariots of *A*

**AMMISHADDAI** *(am-mi-shad'-dahee) Father of the chief of the tribe of Dan.*
Num 1:12 Ahiezer the son of *A*
Num 2:25 Dan shall be Ahiezer the son of *A*
Num 7:66 tenth day Ahiezer the son of *A*
Num 10:25 his host was Ahiezer the son of *A*

**AMMIZABAD** *(am-miz'-a-bad) Son of a captain of David.*
1Chr 27:6 and in his course was *A* his son

**AMMON** *(am'-mon) Territory in Jordan.*
Gen 19:38 the children of *A* unto this day
Num 21:24 even unto the children of *A*
Num 21:24 of the children of *A* was strong
Deut 2:37 the children of *A* thou camest not
Deut 3:11 in Rabbath of the children of *A*
Josh 12:2 the border of the children of *A*
Josh 13:10 the border of the children of *A*
Judg 3:13 unto him the children of *A*
Judg 10:6 and the gods of the children of *A*
Judg 10:9 Moreover the children of *A* passed
Judg 10:11 Amorites, from the children of *A*
Judg 10:17 Then the children of *A* were
Judg 10:18 fight against the children of *A*
Judg 11:4 that the children of *A* made war
Judg 11:27 of Israel and the children of *A*
Judg 12:1 fight against the children of *A*
1Sa 12:12 children of *A* came against you
1Sa 14:47 and against the children of *A*
2Sa 8:12 of Moab, and of the children of *A*
2Sa 10:1 king of the children of *A* died
2Sa 10:19 help the children of *A* any more
2Sa 11:1 they destroyed the children of *A*
2Sa 12:9 the sword of the children of *A*
2Sa 12:26 Rabbah of the children of *A*
2Sa 17:27 of Rabbah of the children of *A*
1Kin 11:7 abomination of the children of *A*
2Kin 23:13 abomination of the children of *A*
2Kin 24:2 and bands of the children of *A*
1Chr 18:11 Moab, and from the children of *A*
1Chr 19:1 king of the children of *A* died
1Chr 19:19 help the children of *A* any more
1Chr 20:1 the country of the children of *A*
2Chr 20:1 of Moab, and the children of *A*
2Chr 20:10 And now, behold, the children of *A*
2Chr 20:22 against the children of *A*
2Chr 27:5 the children of *A* gave him the
Neh 13:23 had married wives of Ashdod, of *A*
Ps 83:7 Gebal, and *A*, and Amalek
Is 11:14 the children of *A* shall obey them
Jer 9:26 and Edom, and the children of *A*
Jer 25:21 and Moab, and the children of *A*
Jer 49:6 captivity of the children of *A*
Dan 11:41 and the chief of the children of *A*
Amos 1:13 of the children of *A*, and for four
Zeph 2:8 revilings of the children of *A*
Zeph 2:9 and the children of *A* as Gomorrah

**AMMONITE** *(am'-mon-ite)* See AMMONITES, AMMONITESS. *A descendant of Ammon.*
Deut 23:3 An *A* or Moabite shall not enter
1Sa 11:1 Then Nahash the *A* came up
2Sa 23:37 Zelek the *A*, Nahari the
1Chr 11:39 Zelek the *A*, Naharai the
Neh 2:10 and Tobiah the servant, the *A*
Neh 2:19 and Tobiah the servant, the *A*
Neh 4:3 Now Tobiah the *A* was by him
Neh 13:1 was found written, that the *A*

**AMMONITES** *(am'-mon-ites)*
Deut 2:20 the *A* call them Zamzummims
1Sa 11:11 slew the *A* until the heat of the
1Kin 11:1 Pharaoh, women of the Moabites, *A*
1Kin 11:5 Milcom the abomination of the *A*
2Chr 20:1 and with them other beside the *A*
2Chr 26:8 the *A* gave gifts to Uzziah
2Chr 27:5 also with the king of the *A*
Ezr 9:1 Perizzites, the Jebusites, the *A*
Neh 4:7 Tobiah, and the Arabians, and the *A*
Jer 27:3 of Moab, and to the king of the *A*
Jer 40:11 that were in Moab, and among the *A*
Jer 41:10 and departed to go over to the *A*
Jer 41:15 with eight men, and went to the *A*
Jer 49:1 Concerning The *A*, thus saith the
Eze 21:20 may come to Rabbath of the *A*
Eze 21:28 the Lord GOD concerning the *A*
Eze 25:2 man, set thy face against the *A*
Eze 25:5 the *A* a couchingplace for flocks
Eze 25:10 the men of the east with the *A*

**AMMONITESS** *(am'-mon-i-tess)*
1Kin 14:21 his mother's name was Naamah an *A*
2Chr 12:13 his mother's name was Naamah an *A*
2Chr 24:26 Zabad the son of Shimeath an *A*

**AMNON** *(am'-non)* See AMNON'S.
*1. A son of David.*
2Sa 3:2 and his firstborn was *A*, of
2Sa 13:1 *A* the son of David loved her
2Sa 13:2 *A* was so vexed, that he fell sick
2Sa 13:10 into the chamber to *A* her brother
2Sa 13:15 Then *A* hated her exceedingly
2Sa 13:20 Hath *A* thy brother been with thee
2Sa 13:22 brother *A* neither good nor bad
2Sa 13:26 thee, let my brother *A* go with us
2Sa 13:32 for *A* only is dead
2Sa 13:39 for he was comforted concerning *A*
1Chr 3:1 the firstborn *A*, of Ahinoam the
*2. A son of Shimon.*
1Chr 4:20 And the sons of Shimon were, *A*

**AMNON'S** *(am'-nons) Refers to Amnon 1.*
2Sa 13:7 Go now to thy brother *A* house
2Sa 13:8 Tamar went to her brother *A* house
2Sa 13:28 Mark ye now when *A* heart is merry

**AMOK** *(a'-mok) A priest who returned from exile under Zerubbabel.*
Neh 12:7 Sallu, *A*, Hilkiah, Jedaiah
Neh 12:20 of *A*, Eber

**AMON** *(a'-mon)*
*1. A governor of Samaria.*
1Kin 22:26 carry him back unto *A* the
2Chr 18:25 carry him back to *A* the governor
*2. Son and successor of King Manasseh of Judah.*
2Kin 21:18 *A* his son reigned in his stead
2Kin 21:19 *A* was twenty and two years old
2Kin 21:23 the servants of *A* conspired
2Kin 21:25 of the acts of *A* which he did
1Chr 3:14 *A* his son, Josiah his son
2Chr 33:20 *A* his son reigned in his stead
2Chr 33:21 *A* was two and twenty years old
2Chr 33:25 that had conspired against king *A*
Jer 1:2 Josiah the son of *A* king of Judah
Jer 25:3 Josiah the son of *A* king of Judah
Zeph 1:1 the days of Josiah the son of *A*
Mt 1:10 and *A* begat Josias
*3. A descendant of Solomon who returned from the Exile under Zerubbabel.*
Neh 7:59 of Zebaim, the children of *A*

**AMORITE** *(am'-o-rite) A descendant of Canaan, Ham's son.*
Gen 10:16 And the Jebusite, and the *A*
Gen 14:13 dwelt in the plain of Mamre the *A*
Gen 48:22 the hand of the *A* with my sword
Ex 33:2 drive out the Canaanite, the *A*
Ex 34:11 I drive out before thee the *A*
Num 32:39 the *A* which was in it
Deut 2:24 given into thine hand Sihon the *A*
Josh 9:1 Lebanon, the Hittite, and the *A*
Josh 11:3 east and on the west, and to the *A*
1Chr 1:14 The Jebusite also, and the *A*
Eze 16:3 thy father was an *A*, and thy
Eze 16:45 an Hittite, and your father an *A*
Amos 2:9 Yet destroyed I the *A* before them
Amos 2:10 to possess the land of the *A*

**AMORITES** *(am'-o-rites)*
Gen 14:7 of the Amalekites, and also the *A*
Gen 15:16 iniquity of the *A* is not yet full
Gen 15:21 And the *A*, and the Canaanites, and
Ex 3:8 and the Hittites, and the *A*
Ex 23:23 thee, and bring thee in unto the *A*
Num 13:29 and the Jebusites, and the *A*
Num 21:13 of Moab, between Moab and the *A*
Num 21:21 unto Sihon king of the *A*, saying,
Num 21:25 dwelt in all the cities of the *A*
Num 21:29 unto Sihon king of the *A*
Num 21:31 Israel dwelt in the land of the *A*
Num 21:34 didst unto Sihon king of the *A*
Num 22:2 all that Israel had done to the *A*
Num 32:33 kingdom of Sihon king of the *A*
Deut 1:4 had slain Sihon the king of the *A*
Deut 1:44 And the *A*, which dwelt in that
Deut 3:2 didst unto Sihon king of the *A*
Deut 4:47 of Bashan, two kings of the *A*
Deut 7:1 and the Girgashites, and the *A*
Deut 20:17 namely, the Hittites, and the *A*
Deut 31:4 to Sihon and to Og, kings of the *A*
Josh 2:10 did unto the two kings of the *A*
Josh 3:10 and the Girgashites, and the *A*
Josh 5:1 pass, when all the kings of the *A*
Josh 9:10 he did to the two kings of the *A*
Josh 10:5 Therefore the five kings of the *A*
Josh 10:12 *A* before the children of Israel
Josh 12:2 Sihon king of the *A*, who dwelt in
Josh 13:4 Aphek, to the borders of the *A*
Josh 13:10 the cities of Sihon king of the *A*
Josh 24:8 you into the land of the *A*
Josh 24:12 you, even the two kings of the *A*
Josh 24:18 even the *A* which dwelt in the
Judg 1:34 the *A* forced the children of Dan
Judg 1:36 the coast of the *A* was from the
Judg 3:5 the Canaanites, Hittites, and *A*
Judg 6:10 fear not the gods of the *A*
Judg 10:8 side Jordan in the land of the *A*
Judg 10:11 from the Egyptians, and from the *A*
Judg 11:19 unto Sihon king of the *A*, the
Judg 11:21 possessed all the land of the *A*
1Sa 7:14 was peace between Israel and the *A*
2Sa 21:2 but of the remnant of the *A*
1Kin 4:19 country of Sihon king of the *A*
1Kin 9:20 people that were left of the *A*
1Kin 21:26 to all things as did the *A*
2Kin 21:11 wickedly above all that the *A* did
2Chr 8:7 left of the Hittites, and the *A*
Ezr 9:1 Moabites, the Egyptians, and the *A*
Neh 9:8 Canaanites, the Hittites, the *A*
Ps 135:11 Sihon king of the *A*, and Og king
Ps 136:19 Sihon king of the *A*

**AMOS** *(a'-mos)*
*1. A prophet during the reign of Uzziah.*
Amos 1:1 The words of A, who was among the
Amos 7:8 And the LORD said unto me, A
Amos 7:10 A hath conspired against thee in
Amos 7:12 Also Amaziah said unto A, O thou
Amos 8:2 And he said, A, what seest thou
*2. Son of Naum; an ancestor of Jesus.*
Lk 3:25 which was the son of A, which

**AMOZ** *(a'-moz) Father of Isaiah.*
2Kin 19:2 Isaiah the prophet the son of A
2Kin 20:1 Isaiah the son of A came to him
2Chr 26:22 Isaiah the prophet, the son of A
2Chr 32:20 the prophet Isaiah the son of A
2Chr 32:32 Isaiah the prophet, the son of A
Is 1:1 The vision of Isaiah the son of A
Is 13:1 which Isaiah the son of A did see
Is 20:2 the LORD by Isaiah the son of A
Is 37:2 Isaiah the prophet the son of A
Is 37:21 the son of A sent unto Hezekiah
Is 38:1 the son of A came unto him

**AMPHIPOLIS** *(am-fip'-o-lis) A city in Macedonia.*
Acts 17:1 when they had passed through A

**AMPLIAS** *(am'-ple-as) A Christian acquaintance of Paul's.*
Rom 16:8 Greet A my beloved in the Lord

**AMRAM** *(am'-ram)* See AMRAMITES, AMRAM'S, HEMDAN.
*1. Father of Moses and Aaron.*
Ex 6:18 A, and Izhar, and Hebron, and Uzziel
Num 3:19 A, and Izehar, Hebron, and Uzziel
Num 26:58 And Kohath begat A
1Chr 6:2 A, Izhar, and Hebron, and Uzziel
1Chr 6:18 And the sons of Kohath were, A
1Chr 23:12 A, Izhar, Hebron, and Uzziel, four
1Chr 24:20 Of the sons of A
*2. Married a foreign wife in Exile.*
Ezr 10:34 Maadai, A, and Uel,
*3. A son of Dishon.*
1Chr 1:41 A, and Eshban, and Ithran, and

**AMRAMITES** *(am'-ram-ites) Descendants of Amram 1.*
Num 3:27 of Kohath was the family of the A
1Chr 26:23 Of the A, and the Izharites, the

**AMRAM'S** *(am'-rams)*
Num 26:59 the name of A wife was Jochebed,

**AMRAPHEL** *(am'-raf-el) King of Shinar in Abraham's time.*
Gen 14:1 in the days of A king of Shinar
Gen 14:9 A king of Shinar, and Arioch king

**AMZI** *(am'-zi)*
*1. A son of Merari.*
1Chr 6:46 The son of A, the son of Bani,
*2. Ancestor of Adaiah.*
Neh 11:12 the son of Pelaliah, the son of A

**ANAB** *(a'-nab) A Canaanite city.*
Josh 11:21 from Hebron, from Debir, from A
Josh 15:50 And A, and Eshtemoh, and Anim,

**ANAH** *(a'-nah)*
*1. A daughter of Zibeon.*
Gen 36:2 of A the daughter of Zibeon the
Gen 36:18 of Aholibamah the daughter of A
Gen 36:25 And the children of A were these
*2. A son of Seir.*
Gen 36:20 Lotan, and Shobal, and Zibeon, and A
Gen 36:29 duke Shobal, duke Zibeon, duke A
1Chr 1:38 Lotan, and Shobal, and Zibeon, and A
*3. A son of Zibeon.*
Gen 36:24 both Ajah, and A
1Chr 1:40 Aiah, and A

**ANAHARATH** *(an-a-ha'-rath) A town in Issachar.*
Josh 19:19 And Haphraim, and Shihon, and A

**ANAIAH** *(an-a-i'-ah)*
*1. A priest who assisted Ezra.*
Neh 8:4 stood Mattithiah, and Shema, and A
*2. A Jew who sealed the covenant.*
Neh 10:22 Pelatiah, Hanan, A,

**ANAK** *(a'-nak)* See ANAKIMS. *The son of Arba.*
Num 13:22 and Talmai, the children of A
Num 13:33 we saw the giants, the sons of A
Deut 9:2 stand before the children of A
Josh 15:13 the city of Arba the father of A
Josh 15:14 drove thence the three sons of A
Josh 21:11 the city of Arba the father of A
Judg 1:20 thence the three sons of A

**ANAKIMS** *(an'-ak-ims) Descendants of Anak.*
Deut 1:28 have seen the sons of the A there
Deut 2:10 great, and many, and tall, as the A
Deut 2:21 great, and many, and tall, as the A
Deut 9:2 and tall, the children of the A
Josh 11:21 cut off the A from the mountains,
Josh 14:12 in that day how the A were there
Josh 14:15 Arba was a great man among the A

**ANAMIM** *(an'-am-im) A people of northern Egypt.*
Gen 10:13 And Mizraim begat Ludim, and A
1Chr 1:11 And Mizraim begat Ludim, and A

**ANAMMELECH** *(a-nam'-mel-ek) A god of the Babylonians.*
2Kin 17:31 in fire to Adrammelech and A

**ANAN** *(a'-nan) An Israelite who sealed the covenant under Nehemiah.*
Neh 10:26 And Ahijah, Hanan, A,

**ANANI** *(an-a'-ni) A son of Elioneai.*
1Chr 3:24 and Johanan, and Dalaiah, and A

**ANANIAH** *(an-an-i'-ah)* See ANANIAS.
*1. Grandfather of Azariah.*
Neh 3:23 the son of A by his house
*2. A town in Benjamin.*
Neh 11:32 And at Anathoth, Nob, A,

**ANANIAS** *(an-an-i'-as)* See ANANIAH.
*1. A Christian who tried to deceive the apostles.*
Acts 5:1 But a certain man named A
Acts 5:3 But Peter said, A, why hath Satan
Acts 5:5 A hearing these words fell down,
*2. A Christian who aided Paul.*
Acts 9:10 disciple at Damascus, named A
Acts 9:12 a vision a man named A coming in
Acts 9:17 A went his way, and entered into
Acts 22:12 And one A, a devout man according
*3. The High Priest who interrogated Paul.*
Acts 23:2 the high priest A commanded them
Acts 24:1 after five days A the high priest

**ANATH** *(a'-nath)* See BETH-ANATH. *Father of Shamgar the judge.*
Judg 3:31 him was Shamgar the son of A
Judg 5:6 the days of Shamgar the son of A

**ANATHEMA** *(a-nath'-em-ah) Greek word for "accursed."*
1Cor 16:22 Christ, let him be A Maranatha

**ANATHOTH** *(an'-a-thoth)* See ANETOTHITE.
*1. A Levitical city in Benjamin.*
Josh 21:18 A with her suburbs, and Almon with
1Kin 2:26 said the king, Get thee to A
1Chr 6:60 suburbs, and A with her suburbs
Ezr 2:23 The men of A, an hundred twenty
Neh 7:27 The men of A, an hundred twenty
Neh 11:32 And at A, Nob, Ananiah,
Is 10:30 to be heard unto Laish, O poor A
Jer 1:1 were in A in the land of Benjamin
Jer 11:21 saith the LORD of the men of A
Jer 29:27 thou not reproved Jeremiah of A
Jer 32:7 Buy thee my field that is in A
*2. A son of Becher.*
1Chr 7:8 Omri, and Jerimoth, and Abiah, and A
*3. An Israelite who sealed the covenant under Nehemiah.*
Neh 10:19 Hariph, A, Nebai,

**ANCESTORS**
Lev 26:45 remember the covenant of their *a*

**ANCHOR**
Heb 6:19 hope we have as an *a* of the soul

**ANCHORS**
Acts 27:29 they cast four *a* out of the stern
Acts 27:40 And when they had taken up the *a*

**ANCIENT**
Deut 33:15 chief things of the *a* mountains
Judg 5:21 that *a* river, the river Kishon
2Kin 19:25 of *a* times that I have formed it
1Chr 4:22 And these are *a* things
Ezr 3:12 of the fathers, who were *a* men
Job 12:12 With the *a* is wisdom
Ps 77:5 days of old, the years of *a* times
Prov 22:28 Remove not the *a* landmark
Is 3:2 prophet, and the prudent, and the *a*
Is 3:5 himself proudly against the *a*
Is 9:15 The *a* and honourable, he is the
Is 19:11 of the wise, the son of *a* kings
Is 23:7 whose antiquity is of *a* days
Is 37:26 of *a* times, that I have formed it
Is 44:7 since I appointed the *a* people
Is 45:21 hath declared this from *a* time
Is 46:10 from *a* times the things that are
Is 47:6 upon the *a* hast thou very heavily
Is 51:9 awake, as in the *a* days, in the
Jer 5:15 mighty nation, it is an *a* nation
Jer 18:15 in their ways from the *a* paths
Eze 9:6 Then they began at the *a* men
Eze 36:2 even the *a* high places are ours
Dan 7:9 the A of days did sit, whose
Dan 7:13 heaven, and came to the A of days
Dan 7:22 Until the A of days came, and

**ANCIENTS**
1Sa 24:13 As saith the proverb of the *a*
Ps 119:100 I understand more than the *a*
Is 3:14 judgment with the *a* of his people
Is 24:23 and before his *a* gloriously
Jer 19:1 take of the *a* of the people
Eze 7:26 the priest, and counsel from the *a*
Eze 8:11 of the *a* of the house of Israel
Eze 8:12 hast thou seen what the *a* of the
Eze 27:9 The *a* of Gebal and the wise men

**ANDREW** *(an'-drew) One of the twelve disciples.*
Mt 4:18 A his brother, casting a net into
Mt 10:2 is called Peter, and A his brother
Mk 1:16 A his brother casting a net into
Mk 1:29 into the house of Simon and A
Mk 3:18 And A, and Philip, and Bartholomew,
Mk 13:3 and John and A asked him privately,
Lk 6:14 A his brother, James and John,
Jn 1:40 speak, and followed him, was A
Jn 1:44 was of Bethsaida, the city of A
Jn 6:8 One of his disciples, A, Simon
Jn 12:22 Philip cometh and telleth A
Acts 1:13 Peter, and James, and John, and A

**ANDRONICUS** *(an-dro-ni'-cus) A relative of Paul.*
Rom 16:7 Salute A and Junia, my kinsmen, and

**ANEM** *(a'-nem)* See EN-GANNIM. *A Levitical city in Issachar.*
1Chr 6:73 suburbs, and A with her suburbs

**ANER** *(a'-nur)*
*1. An ally of Abraham.*
Gen 14:13 of Eshcol, and brother of A
Gen 14:24 of the men which went with me, A
*2. A Levitical city in Manasseh.*
1Chr 6:70 A with her suburbs, and Bileam

**ANETHOTHITE** *(an'-e-thoth-ite)* See ANETOTHITE. *A native of Anathoth.*
2Sa 23:27 Abiezer the A, Mebunnai the

**ANETOTHITE** *(an'-e-toth-ite)* See ANETHOTHITE, ANTOTHITE. *Same as Anethothite.*
1Chr 27:12 the ninth month was Abiezer the A

**ANGEL**
Gen 16:7 the *a* of the LORD found her by a
Gen 21:17 the *a* of God called to Hagar out
Gen 22:11 the *a* of the LORD called unto him
Gen 22:15 the *a* of the LORD called unto
Gen 24:7 he shall send his *a* before thee
Gen 24:40 I walk, will send his *a* with thee
Gen 31:11 the *a* of God spake unto me in a
Gen 48:16 The *a* which redeemed me from all
Ex 3:2 the *a* of the LORD appeared unto
Ex 14:19 the *a* of God, which went before
Ex 23:20 I send an A before thee, to keep
Ex 23:23 For mine A shall go before thee,
Ex 32:34 mine A shall go before thee
Ex 33:2 And I will send an *a* before thee
Num 20:16 he heard our voice, and sent an *a*
Num 22:22 the *a* of the LORD stood in the
Num 22:24 But the *a* of the LORD stood in a
Num 22:27 the ass saw the *a* of the LORD
Num 22:31 he saw the *a* of the LORD standing
Num 22:34 said unto the *a* of the LORD
Judg 2:1 an *a* of the LORD came up from
Judg 2:4 when the *a* of the LORD spake
Judg 5:23 said the *a* of the LORD, curse ye
Judg 6:11 And there came an *a* of the LORD
Judg 6:12 the *a* of the LORD appeared unto
Judg 6:20 the *a* of God said unto him, Take
Judg 6:21 Then the *a* of the LORD put forth

Judg 6:22 an *a* of the LORD face to face
Judg 13:3 the *a* of the LORD appeared unto
Judg 13:6 the countenance of an *a* of God
Judg 13:9 the *a* of God came again unto the
Judg 13:13 the *a* of the LORD said unto
Judg 13:15 said unto the *a* of the LORD
Judg 13:16 the *a* of the LORD said unto
Judg 13:20 that the *a* of the LORD ascended
Judg 13:21 But the *a* of the LORD did no more
1Sa 29:9 good in my sight, as an *a* of God
2Sa 14:17 for as an *a* of God, so is my lord
2Sa 14:20 to the wisdom of an *a* of God
2Sa 19:27 lord the king is as an *a* of God
2Sa 24:16 the *a* of the LORD was by the
2Sa 24:17 saw the *a* that smote the people
1Kin 13:18 an *a* spake unto me by the word of
1Kin 19:5 then an *a* touched him, and said
1Kin 19:7 the *a* of the LORD came again the
2Kin 1:3 But the *a* of the LORD said to
2Kin 1:15 the *a* of the LORD said unto
2Kin 19:35 that the *a* of the LORD went out,
1Chr 21:12 the *a* of the LORD destroying
1Chr 21:15 God sent an *a* unto Jerusalem to
1Chr 21:16 saw the *a* of the LORD stand
1Chr 21:20 Ornan turned back, and saw the *a*
1Chr 21:27 And the LORD commanded the *a*
1Chr 21:30 of the sword of the *a* of the LORD
2Chr 32:21 And the LORD sent an *a*, which cut
Ps 34:7 The *a* of the LORD encampeth round
Ps 35:5 let the *a* of the LORD chase them
Eccl 5:6 neither say thou before the *a*
Is 37:36 Then the *a* of the LORD went forth
Is 63:9 the *a* of his presence saved them
Dan 3:28 and Abed-nego, who hath sent his *a*
Dan 6:22 My God hath sent his *a*, and hath
Hos 12:4 Yea, he had power over the *a*
Zec 1:9 the *a* that talked with me said
Zec 1:11 they answered the *a* of the LORD
Zec 1:14 So the *a* that communed with me
Zec 1:19 I said unto the *a* that talked
Zec 2:3 the *a* that talked with me went
Zec 3:1 standing before the *a* of the LORD
Zec 3:3 garments, and stood before the *a*
Zec 4:1 the *a* that talked with me came
Zec 4:4 spake to the *a* that talked with
Zec 4:5 Then the *a* that talked with me
Zec 5:10 Then said I to the *a* that talked
Zec 6:4 said unto the *a* that talked with
Zec 12:8 as the *a* of the LORD before them
Mt 1:20 the *a* of the Lord appeared unto
Mt 1:24 the *a* of the Lord had bidden him
Mt 2:13 the *a* of the Lord appeareth to
Mt 2:19 an *a* of the Lord appeareth in a
Mt 28:2 for the *a* of the Lord descended
Mt 28:5 the *a* answered and said unto the
Lk 1:11 there appeared unto him an *a* of
Lk 1:13 But the *a* said unto him, Fear not
Lk 1:18 And Zacharias said unto the *a*
Lk 1:26 in the sixth month the *a* Gabriel
Lk 1:28 the *a* came in unto her, and said,
Lk 1:30 the *a* said unto her, Fear not,
Lk 1:34 Then said Mary unto the *a*
Lk 1:38 And the *a* departed from her
Lk 2:9 the *a* of the Lord came upon them,
Lk 2:10 the *a* said unto them, Fear not
Lk 2:13 the *a* a multitude of the heavenly
Lk 2:21 which was so named of the *a*
Lk 22:43 there appeared an *a* unto him from
Jn 5:4 For an *a* went down at a certain
Jn 12:29 others said, An *a* spake to him
Acts 5:19 But the *a* of the Lord by night
Acts 6:15 as it had been the face of an *a*
Acts 7:30 *a* of the Lord in a flame of fire
Acts 7:38 in the wilderness with the *a*
Acts 8:26 the *a* of the Lord spake unto
Acts 10:3 day an *a* of God coming in to him
Acts 10:7 when the *a* which spake unto
Acts 10:22 was warned from God by an holy *a*
Acts 11:13 how he had seen an *a* in his house
Acts 12:7 the *a* of the Lord came upon him,
Acts 12:9 was true which was done by the *a*
Acts 12:15 Then said they, It is his *a*
Acts 12:23 immediately the *a* of the Lord
Acts 23:8 is no resurrection, neither *a*
Acts 27:23 by me this night the *a* of God
2Cor 11:14 is transformed into an *a* of light
Gal 1:8 or an *a* from heaven, preach any
Gal 4:14 but received me as an *a* of God
Rev 1:1 signified it by his *a* unto his
Rev 2:1 Unto the *a* of the church of
Rev 2:8 unto the *a* of the church in
Rev 2:12 to the *a* of the church in
Rev 2:18 unto the *a* of the church in
Rev 3:1 unto the *a* of the church in
Rev 3:7 to the *a* of the church in
Rev 3:14 unto the *a* of the church of the
Rev 5:2 I saw a strong *a* proclaiming with
Rev 7:2 I saw another *a* ascending from
Rev 8:3 And another *a* came and stood at the
Rev 8:5 the *a* took the censer, and filled
Rev 8:7 The first *a* sounded, and there
Rev 8:10 And the third *a* sounded, and there
Rev 8:13 heard an *a* flying through the
Rev 9:1 And the fifth *a* sounded, and I saw
Rev 9:11 which is the *a* of the bottomless
Rev 9:13 And the sixth *a* sounded, and I
Rev 10:1 I saw another mighty *a* come down
Rev 10:5 the *a* which I saw stand upon the
Rev 10:7 of the voice of the seventh *a*
Rev 10:9 And I went unto the *a*, and said
Rev 11:1 the *a* stood, saying, Rise, and
Rev 11:15 And the seventh *a* sounded
Rev 14:6 I saw another *a* fly in the midst
Rev 14:9 the third *a* followed them, saying
Rev 14:19 the *a* thrust in his sickle into
Rev 16:3 the second *a* poured out his vial
Rev 16:8 the fourth *a* poured out his vial
Rev 17:7 the *a* said unto me, Wherefore
Rev 18:1 another *a* come down from heaven
Rev 18:21 a mighty *a* took up a stone like a
Rev 19:17 I saw an *a* standing in the sun
Rev 20:1 I saw an *a* come down from heaven,
Rev 21:17 of a man, that is, of the *a*
Rev 22:6 *a* to shew unto his servants the
Rev 22:8 *a* which shewed me these things
Rev 22:16 I Jesus have sent mine *a* to

## ANGELS

Gen 19:1 there came two *a* to Sodom at even
Gen 19:15 then the *a* hastened Lot, saying,
Gen 28:12 behold the *a* of God ascending and
Gen 32:1 his way, and the *a* of God met him
Job 4:18 his *a* he charged with folly
Ps 8:5 him a little lower than the *a*
Ps 68:17 thousand, even thousands of *a*
Ps 78:49 by sending evil *a* among them
Ps 91:11 shall give his *a* charge over thee
Ps 103:20 Bless the LORD, ye his *a*, that
Ps 104:4 Who maketh his *a* spirits
Ps 148:2 Praise ye him, all his *a*
Mt 4:6 He shall give his *a* charge
Mt 4:11 *a* came and ministered unto him
Mt 13:39 and the reapers are the *a*
Mt 13:41 Son of man shall send forth his *a*
Mt 13:49 the *a* shall come forth, and sever
Mt 16:27 glory of his Father with his *a*
Mt 18:10 That in heaven their *a* do always
Mt 22:30 but are as the *a* of God in heaven
Mt 24:36 not the *a* of heaven, but my
Mt 25:31 glory, and all the holy *a* with him
Mt 25:41 prepared for the devil and his *a*
Mt 26:53 me more than twelve legions of *a*
Mk 1:13 the *a* ministered unto him
Mk 8:38 of his Father with the holy *a*
Mk 12:25 but are as the *a* which are in
Mk 13:27 And then shall he send his *a*
Mk 13:32 not the *a* which are in heaven,
Lk 2:15 as the *a* were gone away from them
Lk 4:10 shall give his *a* charge over thee
Lk 9:26 in his Father's, and of the holy *a*
Lk 12:8 also confess before the *a* of God
Lk 12:9 be denied before the *a* of God
Lk 15:10 the *a* of God over one sinner that
Lk 16:22 was carried by the *a* into
Lk 20:36 for they are equal unto the *a*
Lk 24:23 they had also seen a vision of *a*
Jn 1:51 the *a* of God ascending and
Jn 20:12 seeth two *a* in white sitting, the
Acts 7:53 the law by the disposition of *a*
Rom 8:38 neither death, nor life, nor *a*
1Cor 4:9 spectacle unto the world, and to *a*
1Cor 6:3 Know ye not that we shall judge *a*
1Cor 11:10 on her head because of the *a*
1Cor 13:1 with the tongues of men and of *a*
Gal 3:19 it was ordained by *a* in the hand
Col 2:18 humility and worshipping of *a*
2Th 1:7 from heaven with his mighty *a*
1Ti 3:16 in the Spirit, seen of *a*,
1Ti 5:21 Lord Jesus Christ, and the elect *a*
Heb 1:4 made so much better than the *a*
Heb 1:6 let all the *a* of God worship him
Heb 1:7 of the *a* he saith
Heb 1:13 But to which of the *a* said he at
Heb 2:2 the word spoken by *a* was stedfast
Heb 2:5 For unto the *a* hath he not put in
Heb 2:7 him a little lower than the *a*
Heb 2:9 the *a* for the suffering of death
Heb 2:16 took not on him the nature of *a*
Heb 12:22 and to an innumerable company of *a*
Heb 13:2 some have entertained *a* unawares
1Pet 1:12 which things the *a* desire to look
1Pet 3:22 *a* and authorities and powers being
2Pet 2:4 God spared not the *a* that sinned
2Pet 2:11 Whereas *a*, which are greater in
Jude 6 the *a* which kept not their first
Rev 1:20 are the *a* of the seven churches
Rev 3:5 before my Father, and before his *a*
Rev 5:11 of many *a* round about the throne
Rev 7:1 after these things I saw four *a*
Rev 7:2 with a loud voice to the four *a*
Rev 7:11 all the *a* stood round about the
Rev 8:2 I saw the seven *a* which stood
Rev 8:6 the seven *a* which had the seven
Rev 8:13 of the trumpet of the three *a*
Rev 9:14 Loose the four *a* which are bound
Rev 9:15 the four *a* were loosed, which
Rev 12:7 his *a* fought against the dragon
Rev 12:9 his *a* were cast out with him
Rev 14:10 in the presence of the holy *a*
Rev 15:1 seven *a* having the seven last
Rev 15:6 the seven *a* came out of the
Rev 15:7 *a* seven golden vials full of the
Rev 15:8 of the seven *a* were fulfilled
Rev 16:1 the temple saying to the seven *a*
Rev 17:1 seven *a* which had the seven vials
Rev 21:9 came unto me one of the seven *a*
Rev 21:12 gates, and at the gates twelve *a*

## ANGER

Gen 27:45 brother's *a* turn away from thee
Gen 30:2 Jacob's *a* was kindled against
Gen 44:18 let not thine *a* burn against thy
Gen 49:6 for in their *a* they slew a man,
Ex 4:14 the *a* of the LORD was kindled
Ex 11:8 out from Pharaoh in a great *a*
Ex 32:19 Moses' *a* waxed hot, and he cast
Ex 32:22 Let not the *a* of my lord wax hot
Num 11:1 and his *a* was kindled
Num 11:10 the *a* of the LORD was kindled
Num 12:9 the *a* of the LORD was kindled
Num 22:22 God's *a* was kindled because he
Num 22:27 Balaam's *a* was kindled, and he
Num 24:10 Balak's *a* was kindled against
Num 25:3 the *a* of the LORD was kindled
Num 32:10 the LORD's *a* was kindled the same
Num 32:13 the LORD's *a* was kindled against
Num 32:14 *a* of the LORD toward Israel
Deut 4:25 LORD thy God, to provoke him to *a*
Deut 6:15 *a* of the LORD thy God be kindled
Deut 7:4 so will the *a* of the LORD be
Deut 9:18 of the LORD, to provoke him to *a*
Deut 13:17 turn from the fierceness of his *a*
Deut 29:20 him, but then the *a* of the LORD
Deut 29:23 which the LORD overthrew in his *a*
Deut 29:27 the *a* of the LORD was kindled
Deut 31:17 Then my *a* shall be kindled
Deut 31:29 to provoke him to *a* through the
Deut 32:16 provoked they him to *a*
Deut 32:21 me to *a* with their vanities
Josh 7:1 the *a* of the LORD was kindled
Josh 7:26 from the fierceness of his *a*
Josh 23:16 then shall the *a* of the LORD be
Judg 2:12 them, and provoked the LORD to *a*
Judg 2:14 the *a* of the LORD was hot against
Judg 2:20 the *a* of the LORD was hot against
Judg 3:8 Therefore the *a* of the LORD was
Judg 6:39 Let not thine *a* be hot against me
Judg 8:3 Then their *a* was abated toward
Judg 9:30 son of Ebed, his *a* was kindled
Judg 10:7 the *a* of the LORD was hot against
Judg 14:19 his *a* was kindled, and he went up
1Sa 11:6 his *a* was kindled greatly
1Sa 17:28 Eliab's *a* was kindled against
1Sa 20:30 Then Saul's *a* was kindled against
1Sa 20:34 arose from the table in fierce *a*
2Sa 6:7 the *a* of the LORD was kindled
2Sa 12:5 David's *a* was greatly kindled
2Sa 24:1 again the *a* of the LORD was
1Kin 14:9 molten images, to provoke me to *a*
1Kin 14:15 groves, provoking the LORD to *a*

1Kin 15:30 the LORD God of Israel to *a*
1Kin 16:2 provoke me to *a* with their sins
1Kin 16:7 in provoking him to *a* with the
1Kin 16:13 Israel to *a* with their vanities
1Kin 16:26 Israel to *a* with their vanities
1Kin 16:33 the LORD God of Israel to *a* than
1Kin 21:22 thou hast provoked me to *a*
1Kin 22:53 provoked to *a* the LORD God of
2Kin 13:3 the *a* of the LORD was kindled
2Kin 17:11 things to provoke the LORD to *a*
2Kin 17:17 of the LORD, to provoke him to *a*
2Kin 21:6 of the LORD, to provoke him to *a*
2Kin 21:15 sight, and have provoked me to *a*
2Kin 23:19 had made to provoke the LORD to *a*
2Kin 23:26 wherewith his *a* was kindled
2Kin 24:20 For through the *a* of the LORD it
1Chr 13:10 the *a* of the LORD was kindled
2Chr 25:10 wherefore their *a* was greatly
2Chr 25:15 Wherefore the *a* of the LORD was
2Chr 28:25 provoked to *a* the LORD God of his
2Chr 33:6 of the LORD, to provoke him to *a*
2Chr 34:25 to *a* with all the works of their
Neh 4:5 thee to *a* before the builders
Neh 9:17 gracious and merciful, slow to *a*
Est 1:12 wroth, and his *a* burned in him
Job 9:5 which overturneth them in his *a*
Job 9:13 If God will not withdraw his *a*
Job 18:4 He teareth himself in his *a*
Job 21:17 God distributeth sorrows in his *a*
Job 35:15 not so, he hath visited in his *a*
Ps 6:1 O lord, rebuke me not in thine *a*
Ps 7:6 Arise, O LORD, in thine *a*
Ps 21:9 fiery oven in the time of thine *a*
Ps 27:9 put not thy servant away in *a*
Ps 30:5 For his *a* endureth but a moment
Ps 37:8 Cease from *a*, and forsake wrath
Ps 38:3 in my flesh because of thine *a*
Ps 56:7 in thine *a* cast down the people,
Ps 69:24 let thy wrathful *a* take hold of
Ps 74:1 why doth thine *a* smoke against
Ps 77:9 hath he in *a* shut up his tender
Ps 78:21 *a* also came up against Israel
Ps 78:38 many a time turned he his *a* away
Ps 78:49 upon them the fierceness of his *a*
Ps 78:58 him to *a* with their high places
Ps 85:3 from the fierceness of thine *a*
Ps 90:7 For we are consumed by thine *a*
Ps 90:11 Who knoweth the power of thine *a*
Ps 103:8 merciful and gracious, slow to *a*
Ps 106:29 him to *a* with their inventions
Ps 145:8 slow to *a*, and of great mercy
Prov 15:1 but grievous words stir up *a*
Prov 15:18 is slow to *a* appeaseth strife
Prov 16:32 He that is slow to *a* is better
Prov 19:11 of a man deferreth his *a*
Prov 20:2 whoso provoketh him to *a* sinneth
Prov 21:14 A gift in secret pacifieth *a*
Prov 22:8 and the rod of his *a* shall fail
Prov 27:4 is cruel, and *a* is outrageous
Eccl 7:9 for *a* resteth in the bosom of
Is 1:4 the Holy One of Israel unto *a*
Is 5:25 Therefore is the *a* of the LORD
Is 7:4 for the fierce *a* of Rezin with
Is 9:12 For all this his *a* is not turned
Is 9:17 For all this his *a* is not turned
Is 9:21 For all this his *a* is not turned
Is 10:4 For all this his *a* is not turned
Is 10:25 mine *a* in their destruction
Is 12:1 thine *a* is turned away, and thou
Is 13:3 called my mighty ones for mine *a*
Is 13:9 cruel both with wrath and fierce *a*
Is 13:13 and in the day of his fierce *a*
Is 14:6 he that ruled the nations in *a*
Is 30:27 from far, burning with his *a*
Is 30:30 with the indignation of his *a*
Is 42:25 poured upon him the fury of his *a*
Is 48:9 name's sake will I defer mine *a*
Is 63:3 for I will tread them in mine *a*
Is 63:6 tread down the people in mine *a*
Is 65:3 me to *a* continually to my face
Is 66:15 to render his *a* with fury
Jer 2:35 surely his *a* shall turn from me
Jer 3:5 Will he reserve his *a* for ever
Jer 3:12 not cause mine *a* to fall upon you
Jer 4:8 for the fierce *a* of the LORD is
Jer 4:26 of the LORD, and by his fierce *a*
Jer 7:18 that they may provoke me to *a*
Jer 7:20 Behold, mine *a* and my fury shall
Jer 8:19 me to *a* with their graven images
Jer 10:24 not in thine *a*, lest thou bring
Jer 11:17 themselves to provoke me to *a* in
Jer 12:13 of the fierce *a* of the LORD
Jer 15:14 for a fire is kindled in mine *a*
Jer 17:4 ye have kindled a fire in mine *a*
Jer 18:23 with them in the time of thine *a*
Jer 21:5 and with a strong arm, even in *a*
Jer 23:20 The *a* of the LORD shall not
Jer 25:6 provoke me not to *a* with the
Jer 25:37 of the fierce *a* of the LORD
Jer 25:38 and because of his fierce *a*
Jer 30:24 The fierce *a* of the LORD shall
Jer 32:29 other gods, to provoke me to *a*
Jer 32:31 to me as a provocation of mine *a*
Jer 32:37 I have driven them in mine *a*
Jer 33:5 men, whom I have slain in mine *a*
Jer 36:7 for great is the *a* and the fury
Jer 42:18 As mine *a* and my fury hath been
Jer 44:3 have committed to provoke me to *a*
Jer 44:6 mine *a* was poured forth, and was
Jer 49:37 evil upon them, even my fierce *a*
Jer 51:45 from the fierce *a* of the LORD
Jer 52:3 For through the *a* of the LORD it
Lam 1:12 me in the day of his fierce *a*
Lam 2:1 of Zion with a cloud in his *a*
Lam 2:6 the indignation of his *a* the king
Lam 2:21 slain them in the day of thine *a*
Lam 3:43 Thou hast covered with *a*, and
Lam 3:66 destroy them in *a* from under the
Lam 4:11 he hath poured out his fierce *a*
Lam 4:16 The *a* of the LORD hath divided
Eze 5:13 Thus shall mine *a* be accomplished
Eze 5:15 execute judgments in thee in *a*
Eze 7:3 and I will send mine *a* upon thee
Eze 7:8 and accomplish mine *a* upon thee
Eze 8:17 have returned to provoke me to *a*
Eze 13:13 an overflowing shower in mine *a*
Eze 16:26 thy whoredoms, to provoke me to *a*
Eze 20:8 to accomplish my *a* against them
Eze 20:21 to accomplish my *a* against them
Eze 22:20 so will I gather you in mine *a*
Eze 25:14 do in Edom according to mine *a*
Eze 35:11 will even do according to thine *a*
Eze 43:8 I have consumed them in mine *a*
Dan 9:16 I beseech thee, let thine *a*
Dan 11:20 shall be destroyed, neither in *a*
Hos 8:5 mine *a* is kindled against them
Hos 11:9 execute the fierceness of mine *a*
Hos 12:14 provoked him to *a* most bitterly
Hos 13:11 I gave thee a king in mine *a*
Hos 14:4 for mine *a* is turned away from
Joel 2:13 gracious and merciful, slow to *a*
Amos 1:11 his *a* did tear perpetually, and he
Jonah 3:9 and turn away from his fierce *a*
Jonah 4:2 God, and merciful, slow to *a*
Mic 5:15 And I will execute vengeance in *a*
Mic 7:18 he retaineth not his *a* for ever
Nah 1:3 The LORD is slow to *a*, and great
Nah 1:6 abide in the fierceness of his *a*
Hab 3:8 was thine *a* against the rivers
Hab 3:12 didst thresh the heathen in *a*
Zeph 2:2 before the fierce *a* of the LORD
Zeph 2:2 day of the LORD's *a* come upon you
Zeph 2:3 be hid in the day of the LORD's *a*
Zeph 3:8 indignation, even all my fierce *a*
Zec 10:3 Mine *a* was kindled against the
Mk 3:5 looked round about on them with *a*
Rom 10:19 by a foolish nation I will *a* you
Eph 4:31 all bitterness, and wrath, and *a*
Col 3:8 *a*, wrath, malice, blasphemy,
Col 3:21 provoke not your children to *a*

**ANGLE**
Is 19:8 all they that cast *a* into the
Hab 1:15 take up all of them with the *a*

**ANGRY**
Gen 18:30 him, Oh let not the LORD be *a*
Gen 18:32 he said, Oh let not the Lord be *a*
Gen 45:5 nor *a* with yourselves, that ye
Lev 10:16 he was *a* with Eleazar and Ithamar,
Deut 1:37 Also the LORD was *a* with me for
Deut 4:21 LORD was *a* with me for your sakes
Deut 9:8 so that the LORD was *a* with you
Deut 9:20 the LORD was very *a* with Aaron to
Judg 18:25 lest *a* fellows run upon thee,
2Sa 19:42 then be ye *a* for this matter
1Kin 8:46 thou be *a* with them, and deliver
1Kin 11:9 And the LORD was *a* with Solomon
2Kin 17:18 the LORD was very *a* with Israel
2Chr 6:36 thou be *a* with them, and deliver
Ezr 9:14 wouldest not thou be *a* with us
Neh 5:6 I was very *a* when I heard their
Ps 2:12 Kiss the Son, lest he be *a*
Ps 7:11 God is *a* with the wicked every
Ps 76:7 in thy sight when once thou art *a*
Ps 79:5 wilt thou be *a* for ever
Ps 80:4 how long wilt thou be *a* against
Ps 85:5 Wilt thou be *a* with us for ever
Prov 14:17 He that is soon *a* dealeth
Prov 21:19 with a contentious and an *a* woman
Prov 22:24 Make no friendship with an *a* man
Prov 25:23 so doth an *a* countenance a
Prov 29:22 An *a* man stirreth up strife, and a
Eccl 5:6 should God be *a* at thy voice
Eccl 7:9 not hasty in thy spirit to be *a*
Song 1:6 mother's children were *a* with me
Is 12:1 though thou wast *a* with me
Eze 16:42 be quiet, and will be no more *a*
Dan 2:12 For this cause the king was *a*
Jonah 4:1 exceedingly, and he was very *a*
Jonah 4:4 the LORD, Doest thou well to be *a*
Jonah 4:9 thou well to be *a* for the gourd
Mt 5:22 That whosoever is *a* with his
Lk 14:21 house being *a* said to his servant
Lk 15:28 And he was *a*, and would not go in
Jn 7:23 are ye *a* at me, because I have
Eph 4:26 Be ye *a*, and sin not
Titus 1:7 not selfwilled, not soon *a*
Rev 11:18 And the nations were *a*, and thy

**ANGUISH**
Gen 42:21 in that we saw the *a* of his soul
Ex 6:9 not unto Moses for *a* of spirit
Deut 2:25 and be in *a* because of thee
2Sa 1:9 for *a* is come upon me, because my
Job 7:11 will speak in the *a* of my spirit
Job 15:24 and *a* shall make him afraid
Ps 119:143 and *a* have taken hold on me
Prov 1:27 distress and *a* cometh upon you
Is 8:22 trouble and darkness, dimness of *a*
Is 30:6 into the land of trouble and *a*
Jer 4:31 the *a* as of her that bringeth
Jer 6:24 *a* hath taken hold of us, and pain,
Jer 49:24 *a* and sorrows have taken her, as a
Jer 50:43 *a* took hold of him, and pangs as
Jn 16:21 she remembereth no more the *a*
Rom 2:9 Tribulation and *a*, upon every soul
2Cor 2:4 *a* of heart I wrote unto you with

**ANIAM** *(a'-ne-am) A son of Shemida.*
1Chr 7:19 Ahian, and Shechem, and Likhi, and *A*

**ANIM** *(a'-nim) A city in Judah.*
Josh 15:50 And Anab, and Eshtemoh, and *A*

**ANISE**
Mt 23:23 for ye pay tithe of mint and *a*

**ANNA** *(an'-nah) A prophetess.*
Lk 2:36 And there was one *A*, a prophetess,

**ANNAS** *(an'-nas) A High Priest during Jesus' ministry.*
Lk 3:2 *A* and Caiaphas being the high
Jn 18:13 And led him away to *A* first
Jn 18:24 Now *A* had sent him bound unto
Acts 4:6 *A* the high priest, and Caiaphas,

**ANOINT**
Ex 28:41 and shalt *a* them, and consecrate
Ex 29:7 pour it upon his head, and *a* him
Ex 29:36 for it, and thou shalt *a* it
Ex 30:26 thou shalt *a* the tabernacle of
Ex 30:30 And thou shalt *a* Aaron and his sons
Ex 40:9 *a* the tabernacle, and all that is
Ex 40:10 thou shalt *a* the altar of the
Ex 40:15 as thou didst *a* their father
Lev 16:32 And the priest, whom he shall *a*
Deut 28:40 but thou shalt not *a* thyself with
Judg 9:8 on a time to *a* a king over them
Judg 9:15 If in truth ye *a* me king over you
Ruth 3:3 *a* thee, and put thy raiment upon
1Sa 9:16 thou shalt *a* him to be captain
1Sa 15:1 The LORD sent me to *a* thee to be
1Sa 16:3 thou shalt *a* unto me him whom I
1Sa 16:12 And the LORD said, Arise, *a* him
2Sa 14:2 *a* not thyself with oil, but be as
1Kin 1:34 Nathan the prophet *a* him there
1Kin 19:15 *a* Hazael to be king over Syria
Is 21:5 ye princes, and *a* the shield
Dan 9:24 prophecy, and to *a* the most Holy
Dan 10:3 neither did I *a* myself at all
Amos 6:6 *a* themselves with the chief
Mic 6:15 thou shalt not *a* thee with oil
Mt 6:17 *a* thine head, and wash thy face

Mk 14:8 to *a* my body to the burying
Mk 16:1 that they might come and *a* him
Lk 7:46 My head with oil thou didst not *a*
Rev 3:18 *a* thine eyes with eyesalve, that

**ANOINTED**
Ex 29:2 and wafers unleavened *a* with oil
Ex 29:29 to be *a* therein, and to be
Lev 2:4 or unleavened wafers *a* with oil
Lev 4:3 If the priest that is *a* do sin
Lev 4:5 the priest that is *a* shall take
Lev 4:16 the priest that is *a* shall bring
Lev 6:20 the LORD in the day when he is *a*
Lev 6:22 is *a* in his stead shall offer it
Lev 7:12 and unleavened wafers *a* with oil
Lev 7:36 Israel, in the day that he *a* them
Lev 8:10 *a* the tabernacle and all that was
Lev 8:11 *a* the altar and all his vessels,
Num 3:3 Aaron, the priests which were *a*
Num 6:15 of unleavened bread *a* with oil
Num 7:1 up the tabernacle, and had *a* it
Num 7:10 altar in the day that it was *a*
Num 7:84 altar, in the day when it was *a*
Num 35:25 which was *a* with the holy oil
1Sa 2:10 king, and exalt the horn of his *a*
1Sa 2:35 shall walk before mine *a* for ever
1Sa 10:1 *a* thee to be captain over his
1Sa 12:5 his *a* is witness this day, that
1Sa 15:17 the LORD *a* thee king over Israel
1Sa 16:6 Surely the LORD's *a* is before him
1Sa 16:13 *a* him in the midst of his
1Sa 24:6 unto my master, the LORD's *a*
1Sa 24:10 for he is the LORD's *a*
1Sa 26:9 his hand against the LORD's *a*
1Sa 26:11 mine hand against the LORD's *a*
1Sa 26:16 kept your master, the LORD's *a*
1Sa 26:23 mine hand against the LORD's *a*
2Sa 1:14 hand to destroy the LORD's *a*
2Sa 1:16 saying, I have slain the LORD's *a*
2Sa 1:21 though he had not been *a* with oil
2Sa 2:4 there they *a* David king over the
2Sa 2:7 of Judah have *a* me king over them
2Sa 3:39 I am this day weak, though *a* king
2Sa 5:3 they *a* David king over Israel
2Sa 5:17 they had *a* David king over Israel
2Sa 12:7 I *a* thee king over Israel, and I
2Sa 12:20 *a* himself, and changed his apparel
2Sa 19:10 And Absalom, whom we *a* over us
2Sa 19:21 because he cursed the LORD's *a*
2Sa 22:51 and sheweth mercy to his *a*
2Sa 23:1 the *a* of the God of Jacob, and the
1Kin 1:39 of the tabernacle, and *a* Solomon
1Kin 1:45 prophet have *a* him king in Gihon
1Kin 5:1 had *a* him king in the room of his
2Kin 9:3 I have *a* thee king over Israel
2Kin 9:6 I have *a* thee king over the
2Kin 9:12 I have *a* thee king over Israel
2Kin 11:12 and they made him king, and *a* him
2Kin 23:30 *a* him, and made him king in his
1Chr 11:3 they *a* David king over Israel,
1Chr 14:8 David was *a* king over all Israel
1Chr 16:22 Saying, Touch not mine *a*, and do
1Chr 29:22 *a* him unto the LORD to be the
2Chr 6:42 turn not away the face of thine *a*
2Chr 22:7 whom the LORD had *a* to cut off
2Chr 23:11 And Jehoiada and his sons *a* him
2Chr 28:15 *a* them, and carried all the feeble
Ps 2:2 the LORD, and against his *a*
Ps 18:50 and sheweth mercy to his *a*
Ps 20:6 know I that the LORD saveth his *a*
Ps 28:8 is the saving strength of his *a*
Ps 45:7 hath *a* thee with the oil of
Ps 84:9 and look upon the face of thine *a*
Ps 89:20 with my holy oil have I *a* him
Ps 89:38 thou hast been wroth with thine *a*
Ps 89:51 the footsteps of thine *a*
Ps 92:10 I shall be *a* with fresh oil
Ps 105:15 Saying, Touch not mine *a*, and do
Ps 132:10 turn not away the face of thine *a*
Ps 132:17 I have ordained a lamp for mine *a*
Is 45:1 Thus saith the LORD to his *a*
Is 61:1 because the LORD hath *a* me to
Lam 4:20 the *a* of the LORD, was taken in
Eze 16:9 from thee, and I *a* thee with oil
Eze 28:14 Thou art the *a* cherub that
Hab 3:13 even for salvation with thine *a*
Zec 4:14 These are the two *a* ones
Mk 6:13 *a* with oil many that were sick,
Lk 4:18 because he hath *a* me to preach
Lk 7:38 feet, and *a* them with the ointment
Lk 7:46 but this woman hath *a* my feet
Jn 9:6 he *a* the eyes of the blind man
Jn 9:11 *a* mine eyes, and said unto me, Go
Jn 11:2 which *a* the Lord with ointment
Jn 12:3 *a* the feet of Jesus, and wiped his
Acts 4:27 child Jesus, whom thou hast *a*
Acts 10:38 How God *a* Jesus of Nazareth with
2Cor 1:21 with you in Christ, and hath *a* us
Heb 1:9 hath *a* thee with the oil of

**ANOINTING**
Ex 25:6 for the light, spices for *a* oil
Ex 29:21 upon the altar, and of the *a* oil
Ex 30:25 it shall be an holy *a* oil
Ex 30:31 This shall be an holy *a* oil unto
Ex 31:11 And the *a* oil, and sweet incense
Ex 35:8 the light, and spices for *a* oil
Ex 35:15 and his staves, and the *a* oil
Ex 35:28 for the light, and for the *a* oil
Ex 37:29 And he made the holy *a* oil
Ex 39:38 And the golden altar, and the *a* oil
Ex 40:9 And thou shalt take the *a* oil
Ex 40:15 for their *a* shall surely be an
Lev 7:35 is the portion of the *a* of Aaron
Lev 8:2 and the garments, and the *a* oil
Lev 8:10 And Moses took the *a* oil, and
Lev 8:12 he poured of the *a* oil upon
Lev 8:30 And Moses took of the *a* oil
Lev 10:7 for the *a* oil of the LORD is upon
Lev 21:10 whose head the *a* oil was poured
Lev 21:12 for the crown of the *a* oil of his
Num 4:16 daily meat offering, and the *a* oil
Num 18:8 I given them by reason of the *a*
Is 10:27 be destroyed because of the *a*
Jas 5:14 *a* him with oil in the name of the
1Jn 2:27 But the *a* which ye have received

**ANON**
Mt 13:20 word, and *a* with joy receiveth it
Mk 1:30 fever, and *a* they tell him of her

**ANT**
Prov 6:6 Go to the *a*, thou sluggard

**ANTICHRIST**
1Jn 2:18 ye have heard that *a* shall come
1Jn 2:22 He is *a*, that denieth the Father
1Jn 4:3 and this is that spirit of *a*
2Jn 7 This is a deceiver and an *a*

**ANTICHRISTS**
1Jn 2:18 come, even now are there many *a*

**ANTIOCH** *(an'-te-ok)*
*1. A city in Syria.*
Acts 6:5 and Nicolas a proselyte of *A*
Acts 11:19 far as Phenice, and Cyprus, and *A*
Acts 11:26 found him, he brought him unto *A*
Acts 11:27 prophets from Jerusalem unto *A*
Acts 13:1 that was at *A* certain prophets
Acts 14:26 And thence sailed to *A*, from
Acts 15:22 their own company to *A* with Paul
Acts 15:30 were dismissed, they came to *A*
Acts 15:35 also and Barnabas continued in *A*
Acts 18:22 the church, he went down to *A*
Gal 2:11 But when Peter was come to *A*
*2. A city in Pisidia.*
Acts 13:14 Perga, they came to *A* in Pisidia
Acts 14:19 came thither certain Jews from *A*
Acts 14:21 to Lystra, and to Iconium, and *A*
2Ti 3:11 which came unto me at *A*, at

**ANTIPAS** *(an'-tip-as) A Christian martyr.*
Rev 2:13 wherein *A* was my faithful martyr

**ANTIPATRIS** *(an-tip'-at-ris) A city in northern Palestine.*
Acts 23:31 and brought him by night to *A*

**ANTIQUITY**
Is 23:7 whose *a* is of ancient days

**ANTOTHIJAH** *(an-to-thi'-jah) Son of Shashak.*
1Chr 8:24 And Hananiah, and Elam, and *A*

**ANTOTHITE** *(an'-to-thite)* See ANETOTHITE. *A native of Anathoth.*
1Chr 11:28 Ikkesh the Tekoite, Abiezer the *A*
1Chr 12:3 and Berachah, and Jehu the *A*

**ANTS**
Prov 30:25 The *a* are a people not strong,

**ANUB** *(a'-nub) A descendant of Judah.*
1Chr 4:8 And Coz begat *A*, and Zobebah, and

**ANVIL**
Is 41:7 the hammer him that smote the *a*

**APACE**
2Sa 18:25 And he came *a*, and drew near
Ps 68:12 Kings of armies did flee *a*
Jer 46:5 are beaten down, and are fled *a*

**APELLES** *(a-pel'-leze) A Christian acquaintance of Paul.*
Rom 16:10 Salute *A* approved in Christ

**APES**
1Kin 10:22 gold, and silver, ivory, and *a*
2Chr 9:21 gold, and silver, ivory, and *a*

**APHARSACHITES** *(a-far'-sak-ites)* See APHARSATHCHITES. *An Assyrian tribe.*
Ezr 5:6 and his companions the *A*, which
Ezr 6:6 and your companions the *A*

**APHARSATHCHITES** *(a-far'-sath-kites)* See APHARSACHITES, APHARSITES. *Same as Apharsachites.*
Ezr 4:9 the Dinaites, the *A*, the

**APHARSITES** *(a-far'-sites)* See APHARSATHCHITES. *Same as Apharsachites*
Ezr 4:9 the Tarpelites, the *A*, the

**APHEK** *(a'-fek)* See APHIK.
*1. A Canaanite city.*
Josh 12:18 The king of *A*, one
1Sa 4:1 and the Philistines pitched in *A*
1Sa 29:1 together all their armies to *A*
*2. A city in Asher.*
Josh 13:4 is beside the Sidonians, unto *A*
Josh 19:30 Ummah also, and *A*, and Rehob
*3. Place where Ahab defeated Benhadad.*
1Kin 20:26 the Syrians, and went up to *A*
1Kin 20:30 But the rest fled to *A*, into the
2Kin 13:17 thou shalt smite the Syrians in *A*

**APHEKAH** *(af-e'-kah) A city in Judah.*
Josh 15:53 And Janum, and Beth-tappuah, and *A*

**APHIAH** *(af-i'-ah) An ancestor of Saul.*
1Sa 9:1 son of Bechorath, the son of *A*

**APHIK** *(a'-fik)* See APHEK. *Same as Aphek 2.*
Judg 1:31 Achzib, nor of Helbah, nor of *A*

**APHRAH** *(af'-rah)* See BETH-LEAPHRAH, OPHRAH. *A city in Benjamin.*
Mic 1:10 in the house of *A* roll thyself in

**APHSES** *(af'-seze) A Levite chief.*
1Chr 24:15 to Hezir, the eighteenth to *A*

**APIECE**
Num 3:47 take five shekels *a* by the poll
Num 7:86 incense, weighing ten shekels *a*
Num 17:6 of their princes gave him a rod *a*
1Kin 7:15 brass, of eighteen cubits high *a*
Eze 10:21 Every one had four faces *a*
Eze 41:24 And the doors had two leaves *a*
Lk 9:3 neither have two coats *a*
Jn 2:6 containing two or three firkins *a*

**APOLLONIA** *(ap-ol-lo'-ne-ah) A city in Macedonia.*
Acts 17:1 passed through Amphipolis and *A*

**APOLLOS** *(ap-ol'-los) A Christian Jew from Alexandria.*
Acts 18:24 And a certain Jew named *A*, born at
Acts 19:1 while *A* was at Corinth, Paul
1Cor 1:12 and I of *A*
1Cor 3:4 and another, I am of *A*
1Cor 3:6 I have planted, *A* watered
1Cor 3:22 Whether Paul, or *A*, or Cephas, or
1Cor 4:6 to myself and to *A* for your sakes
1Cor 16:12 As touching our brother *A*
Titus 3:13 *A* on their journey diligently,

**APOLLYON** *(ap-ol'-le-on) The angel of the Abyss.*
Rev 9:11 the Greek tongue hath his name *A*

**APOSTLE**
Rom 1:1 Jesus Christ, called to be an *a*
Rom 11:13 as I am the *a* of the Gentiles
1Cor 1:1 called to be an *a* of Jesus Christ
1Cor 9:1 Am I not an *a*
1Cor 15:9 am not meet to be called an *a*
2Cor 1:1 an *a* of Jesus Christ by the will
2Cor 12:12 Truly the signs of an *a* were
Gal 1:1 Paul, an *a*, (not of men, neither
Eph 1:1 an *a* of Jesus Christ by the will
Col 1:1 an *a* of Jesus Christ by the will
1Ti 1:1 an *a* of Jesus Christ by the
1Ti 2:7 I am ordained a preacher, and an *a*
2Ti 1:1 an *a* of Jesus Christ by the will

2Ti 1:11 am appointed a preacher, and an *a*
Titus 1:1 an *a* of Jesus Christ, according
Heb 3:1 heavenly calling, consider the *A*
1Pet 1:1 an *a* of Jesus Christ, to the
2Pet 1:1 an *a* of Jesus Christ, to them

## APOSTLES
Mt 10:2 names of the twelve *a* are these
Mk 6:30 the *a* gathered themselves
Lk 6:13 twelve, whom also he named *a*
Lk 9:10 And the *a*, when they were returned
Lk 11:49 I will send them prophets and *a*
Lk 17:5 the *a* said unto the Lord,
Lk 22:14 down, and the twelve *a* with him
Lk 24:10 told these things unto the *a*
Acts 1:2 unto the *a* whom he had chosen
Acts 1:26 he was numbered with the eleven *a*
Acts 2:37 Peter and to the rest of the *a*
Acts 2:43 and signs were done by the *a*
Acts 4:33 with great power gave the *a*
Acts 4:36 who by the *a* was surnamed
Acts 5:12 hands of the *a* were many signs
Acts 5:18 And laid their hands on the *a*
Acts 5:29 Peter and the other *a* answered
Acts 5:34 to put the *a* forth a little space
Acts 5:40 and when they had called the *a*
Acts 6:6 Whom they set before the *a*
Acts 8:1 Judaea and Samaria, except the *a*
Acts 8:14 Now when the *a* which were at
Acts 9:27 took him, and brought him to the *a*
Acts 11:1 And the *a* and brethren that were in
Acts 14:4 with the Jews, and part with the *a*
Acts 14:14 Which when the *a*, Barnabas and
Acts 15:2 go up to Jerusalem unto the *a*
Acts 15:4 of the church, and of the *a*
Acts 15:6 And the *a* and elders came together
Acts 15:22 Then pleased it the *a* and elders,
Acts 15:23 The *a* and elders and brethren send
Acts 15:33 from the brethren unto the *a*
Acts 16:4 keep, that were ordained of the *a*
Rom 16:7 who are of note among the *a*
1Cor 4:9 God hath set forth us the *a* last
1Cor 9:5 a wife, as well as other *a*
1Cor 12:28 set some in the church, first *a*
1Cor 12:29 Are all *a*?
1Cor 15:7 then of all the *a*
1Cor 15:9 For I am the least of the *a*
2Cor 11:5 a whit behind the very chiefest *a*
2Cor 11:13 For such are false *a*, deceitful
2Cor 12:11 am I behind the very chiefest *a*
Gal 1:17 to them which were *a* before me
Gal 1:19 But other of the *a* saw I none
Eph 2:20 upon the foundation of the *a*
Eph 3:5 is now revealed unto his holy *a*
Eph 4:11 And he gave some, *a*
1Th 2:6 burdensome, as the *a* of Christ
2Pet 3:2 of us the *a* of the Lord and
Jude 17 of the *a* of our Lord Jesus Christ
Rev 2:2 tried them which say they are *a*
Rev 18:20 her, thou heaven, and ye holy *a*
Rev 21:14 names of the twelve *a* of the Lamb

## APOSTLES'
Acts 2:42 stedfastly in the *a* doctrine
Acts 4:35 And laid them down at the *a* feet
Acts 4:37 money, and laid it at the *a* feet
Acts 5:2 part, and laid it at the *a* feet
Acts 8:18 that through laying on of the *a*

## APOSTLESHIP
Acts 1:25 take part of this ministry and *a*
Rom 1:5 whom we have received grace and *a*
1Cor 9:2 seal of mine *a* are ye in the Lord
Gal 2:8 to the *a* of the circumcision

## APOTHECARY
Ex 30:25 compound after the art of the *a*
Ex 30:35 confection after the art of the *a*
Ex 37:29 according to the work of the *a*
Eccl 10:1 *a* to send forth a stinking savour

## APPAIM *(ap'-pa-im) A son of Nadab.*
1Chr 2:30 Seled, and *A*
1Chr 2:31 And the sons of *A*

## APPAREL
Judg 17:10 by the year, and a suit of *a*
1Sa 27:9 asses, and the camels, and the *a*
2Sa 1:24 on ornaments of gold upon your *a*
2Sa 12:20 himself, and changed his *a*
2Sa 14:2 mourner, and put on now mourning *a*
1Kin 10:5 of his ministers, and their *a*
2Chr 9:4 of his ministers, and their *a*
Ezr 3:10 priests in their *a* with trumpets
Est 5:1 that Esther put on her royal *a*
Est 6:8 Let the royal *a* be brought which
Est 6:10 Haman, Make haste, and take the *a*
Est 8:15 of the king in royal *a* of blue
Is 3:22 The changeable suits of *a*
Is 4:1 our own bread, and wear our own *a*
Is 63:1 this that is glorious in his *a*
Is 63:2 Wherefore art thou red in thine *a*
Eze 27:24 work, and in chests of rich *a*
Zeph 1:8 as are clothed with strange *a*
Zec 14:14 together, gold, and silver, and *a*
Acts 1:10 two men stood by them in white *a*
Acts 12:21 set day Herod, arrayed in royal *a*
Acts 20:33 no man's silver, or gold, or *a*
1Ti 2:9 adorn themselves in modest *a*
Jas 2:2 man with a gold ring, in goodly *a*
1Pet 3:3 of gold, or of putting on of *a*

## APPARELLED
2Sa 13:18 daughters that were virgins *a*
Lk 7:25 they which are gorgeously *a*

## APPARENTLY
Num 12:8 I speak mouth to mouth, even *a*

## APPEAL
Acts 25:11 I *a* unto Caesar
Acts 28:19 was constrained to *a* unto Caesar

## APPEALED
Acts 25:12 answered, Hast thou *a* unto Caesar
Acts 25:21 But when Paul had *a* to be
Acts 25:25 he himself hath *a* to Augustus
Acts 26:32 if he had not *a* unto Caesar

## APPEAR
Gen 1:9 one place, and let the dry land *a*
Gen 30:37 made the white *a* which was in the
Ex 23:15 none shall *a* before me empty
Ex 23:17 males shall *a* before the Lord GOD
Ex 34:20 none shall *a* before me empty
Ex 34:23 children *a* before the Lord GOD
Lev 9:4 to day the LORD will *a* unto you
Lev 9:6 of the LORD shall *a* unto you
Lev 13:57 if it *a* still in the garment,
Lev 16:2 for I will *a* in the cloud upon
Deut 16:16 in a year shall all thy males *a*
Deut 31:11 When all Israel is come to *a*
Judg 13:21 the LORD did no more *a* to Manoah
1Sa 1:22 that he may *a* before the LORD, and
1Sa 2:27 Did I plainly *a* unto the house of
2Chr 1:7 that night did God *a* unto Solomon
Ps 42:2 when shall I come and *a* before God
Ps 90:16 Let thy work *a* unto thy servants,
Ps 102:16 up Zion, he shall *a* in his glory
Song 2:12 The flowers *a* on the earth
Song 4:1 goats, that *a* from mount Gilead
Song 6:5 flock of goats that *a* from Gilead
Song 7:12 whether the tender grape *a*
Is 1:12 When ye come to *a* before me
Is 66:5 but he shall *a* to your joy
Jer 13:26 thy face, that thy shame may *a*
Eze 21:24 in all your doings your sins do *a*
Mt 6:16 that they may *a* unto men to fast
Mt 6:18 That thou *a* not unto men to fast,
Mt 23:27 which indeed *a* beautiful outward,
Mt 24:30 then shall *a* the sign of the Son
Lk 11:44 for ye are as graves which *a* not
Lk 19:11 of God should immediately *a*
Acts 22:30 priests and all their council to *a*
Acts 26:16 in the which I will *a* unto thee
Rom 7:13 But sin, that it might *a* sin
2Cor 5:10 For we must all *a* before the
2Cor 7:12 the sight of God might *a* unto you
2Cor 13:7 not that we should *a* approved
Col 3:4 Christ, who is our life, shall *a*
1Ti 4:15 that thy profiting may *a* to all
Heb 9:24 now to *a* in the presence of God
Heb 9:28 he *a* the second time without sin
Heb 11:3 not made of things which do *a*
1Pet 4:18 shall the ungodly and the sinner *a*
1Pet 5:4 when the chief Shepherd shall *a*
1Jn 2:28 that, when he shall *a*, we may
1Jn 3:2 it doth not yet *a* what we shall
Rev 3:18 shame of thy nakedness do not *a*

## APPEARANCE
Num 9:15 as it were the *a* of fire, until
1Sa 16:7 for man looketh on the outward *a*
Eze 1:5 And this was their *a*
Eze 1:13 their *a* was like burning coals of
Eze 1:16 and their *a* and their work was as
Eze 1:26 as the *a* of a sapphire stone
Eze 1:28 This was the *a* of the likeness of
Eze 8:2 and lo a likeness as the *a* of fire
Eze 10:1 as the *a* of the likeness of a
Eze 10:9 the *a* of the wheels was as the
Eze 40:3 whose *a* was like the *a*
Eze 41:21 the *a* of the one as the *a*
Eze 42:11 the *a* of the chambers which were
Eze 43:3 it was according to the *a* of the
Dan 8:15 stood before me as the *a* of a man
Dan 10:6 and his face as the *a* of lightning
Dan 10:18 me one like the *a* of a man
Joel 2:4 *a* of them is as the *a* of horses
Jn 7:24 Judge not according to the *a*
2Cor 5:12 to answer them which glory in *a*
2Cor 10:7 on things after the outward *a*
1Th 5:22 Abstain from all *a* of evil

## APPEARED
Gen 12:7 the LORD *a* unto Abram, and said,
Gen 17:1 old and nine, the LORD *a* to Abram
Gen 18:1 the LORD *a* unto him in the plains
Gen 26:2 And the LORD *a* unto him, and said,
Gen 26:24 the LORD *a* unto him the same
Gen 35:1 that *a* unto thee when thou
Gen 35:7 because there God *a* unto him
Gen 35:9 God *a* unto Jacob again, when he
Gen 48:3 God Almighty *a* unto me at Luz in
Ex 3:2 the angel of the LORD *a* unto him
Ex 3:16 *a* unto me, saying, I have surely
Ex 4:1 The LORD hath not *a* unto thee
Ex 4:5 God of Jacob, hath *a* unto thee
Ex 6:3 I *a* unto Abraham, unto Isaac, and
Ex 14:27 his strength when the morning *a*
Ex 16:10 glory of the LORD *a* in the cloud
Lev 9:23 of the LORD *a* unto all the people
Num 14:10 the glory of the LORD *a* in the
Num 16:19 the glory of the LORD *a* unto all
Num 16:42 it, and the glory of the LORD *a*
Num 20:6 the glory of the LORD *a* unto them
Deut 31:15 the LORD *a* in the tabernacle in a
Judg 6:12 the angel of the LORD *a* unto him
Judg 13:3 of the LORD *a* unto the woman
Judg 13:10 Behold, the man hath *a* unto me
1Sa 3:21 the LORD *a* again in Shiloh
2Sa 22:16 And the channels of the sea *a*
1Kin 3:5 In Gibeon the LORD *a* to Solomon
1Kin 9:2 That the LORD *a* to Solomon the
1Kin 11:9 which had *a* unto him twice
2Kin 2:11 there *a* a chariot of fire, and
2Chr 3:1 where the LORD *a* unto David his
2Chr 7:12 the LORD *a* to Solomon by night,
Neh 4:21 of the morning till the stars *a*
Jer 31:3 The LORD hath *a* of old unto me,
Eze 10:1 *a* over them as it were a sapphire
Eze 10:8 there *a* in the cherubims the form
Eze 19:11 she *a* in her height with the
Dan 1:15 days their countenances *a* fairer
Dan 8:1 Belshazzar a vision *a* unto me
Mt 1:20 of the Lord *a* unto him in a dream
Mt 2:7 diligently what time the star *a*
Mt 13:26 fruit, then *a* the tares also
Mt 17:3 there *a* unto them Moses and Elias
Mt 27:53 the holy city, and *a* unto many
Mk 9:4 there *a* unto them Elias with
Mk 16:9 he *a* first to Mary Magdalene, out
Mk 16:12 After that he *a* in another form
Mk 16:14 Afterward he *a* unto the eleven as
Lk 1:11 there *a* unto him an angel of the
Lk 9:8 And of some, that Elias had *a*
Lk 9:31 Who *a* in glory, and spake of his
Lk 22:43 there *a* an angel unto him from
Lk 24:34 risen indeed, and hath *a* to Simon
Acts 2:3 there *a* unto them cloven tongues
Acts 7:2 The God of glory *a* unto our
Acts 7:30 there *a* to him in the wilderness
Acts 7:35 angel which *a* to him in the bush
Acts 9:17 that *a* unto thee in the way as
Acts 16:9 a vision *a* to Paul in the night
Acts 26:16 for I have *a* unto thee for this
Acts 27:20 sun nor stars in many days *a*
Titus 2:11 salvation hath *a* to all men
Titus 3:4 of God our Saviour toward man *a*
Heb 9:26 hath he *a* to put away sin by the
Rev 12:1 there *a* a great wonder in heaven
Rev 12:3 there *a* another wonder in heaven

## APPEARETH
Lev 13:14 But when raw flesh *a* in him
Lev 13:43 as the leprosy *a* in the skin of
Deut 2:30 him into thy hand, as *a* this day
Ps 84:7 one of them in Zion *a* before God
Prov 27:25 The hay *a*, and the tender grass

Jer 6:1 for evil *a* out of the north, and
Mal 3:2 and who shall stand when he *a*
Mt 2:13 the Lord *a* to Joseph in a dream
Mt 2:19 an angel of the Lord *a* in a dream
Jas 4:14 that *a* for a little time, and then

### APPEARING
1Ti 6:14 until the *a* of our Lord Jesus
2Ti 1:10 the *a* of our Saviour Jesus Christ
2Ti 4:1 the quick and the dead at his *a*
2Ti 4:8 all them also that love his *a*
Titus 2:13 the glorious *a* of the great God
1Pet 1:7 glory at the *a* of Jesus Christ

### APPERTAIN
Num 16:30 up, with all that *a* unto them
Jer 10:7 for to thee doth it *a*

### APPERTAINED
Num 16:32 and all the men that *a* unto Korah
Num 16:33 They, and all that *a* to them
Neh 2:8 the palace which *a* to the house

### APPERTAINETH
Lev 6:5 and give it unto him to whom it *a*
2Chr 26:18 It *a* not unto thee, Uzziah, to

### APPETITE
Job 38:39 or fill the *a* of the young lions,
Prov 23:2 if thou be a man given to *a*
Eccl 6:7 mouth, and yet the *a* is not filled
Is 29:8 he is faint, and his soul hath *a*

**APPHIA** *(af'-fee-ah) A Christian acquaintance of Paul.*
Philem 2 And to our beloved *A*, and Archippus

**APPII** *(ap'-pe-i) A place south of Rome.*
Acts 28:15 came to meet us as far as *A* forum

### APPLE
Deut 32:10 he kept him as the *a* of his eye
Ps 17:8 Keep me as the *a* of the eye
Prov 7:2 and my law as the *a* of thine eye
Song 2:3 As the *a* tree among the trees of
Song 8:5 I raised thee up under the *a* tree
Lam 2:18 let not the *a* of thine eye cease
Joel 1:12 the *a* tree, even all the trees of
Zec 2:8 you toucheth the *a* of his eye

### APPLES
Prov 25:11 A word fitly spoken is like *a* of
Song 2:5 with flagons, comfort me with *a*
Song 7:8 and the smell of thy nose like *a*

### APPLIED
Eccl 7:25 I *a* mine heart to know, and to
Eccl 8:9 *a* my heart unto every work that
Eccl 8:16 When I *a* mine heart to know

### APPLY
Ps 90:12 that we may *a* our hearts unto
Prov 2:2 *a* thine heart to understanding
Prov 22:17 *a* thine heart unto my knowledge
Prov 23:12 *A* thine heart unto instruction,

### APPOINT
Gen 30:28 *A* me thy wages, and I will give it
Gen 41:34 let him *a* officers over the land,
Ex 21:13 then I will *a* thee a place
Ex 30:16 shalt *a* it for the service of the
Lev 26:16 I will even *a* over you terror,
Num 1:50 But thou shalt *a* the Levites over
Num 3:10 And thou shalt *a* Aaron and his sons
Num 4:19 *a* them every one to his service
Num 4:27 ye shall *a* unto them in charge
Num 35:6 refuge, which ye shall *a* for the
Num 35:11 Then ye shall *a* you cities to be
Josh 20:2 *A* out for you cities of refuge,
1Sa 8:11 *a* them for himself, for his
2Sa 6:21 to *a* me ruler over the people of
2Sa 7:10 Moreover I will *a* a place for my
2Sa 15:15 my lord the king shall *a*
1Kin 5:6 to all that thou shalt *a*
1Kin 5:9 the place that thou shalt *a* me
1Chr 15:16 to *a* their brethren to be the
Neh 7:3 *a* watches of the inhabitants of
Est 2:3 let the king *a* officers in all
Job 14:13 thou wouldest *a* me a set time
Is 26:1 salvation will God *a* for walls
Is 61:3 To *a* unto them that mourn in Zion
Jer 15:3 I will *a* over them four kinds,
Jer 49:19 chosen man, that I may *a* over her
Jer 50:44 chosen man, that I may *a* over her
Jer 51:27 *a* a captain against her
Eze 21:19 *a* thee two ways, that the sword
Eze 21:20 *A* a way, that the sword may come
Eze 21:22 to *a* captains, to open the mouth
Eze 45:6 ye shall *a* the possession of the
Hos 1:11 *a* themselves one head, and they
Mt 24:51 *a* him his portion with the
Lk 12:46 will *a* him his portion with the
Lk 22:29 I *a* unto you a kingdom, as my
Acts 6:3 whom we may *a* over this business

### APPOINTED
Gen 4:25 hath *a* me another seed instead of
Gen 18:14 At the time *a* I will return unto
Gen 24:44 hath *a* out for my master's son
Ex 9:5 the LORD *a* a set time, saying, To
Ex 23:15 in the time *a* of the month Abib
Num 9:2 keep the passover at his *a* season
Num 9:7 *a* season among the children of
Num 9:13 of the LORD in his *a* season
Josh 8:14 he and all his people, at a time *a*
Josh 20:7 they *a* Kedesh in Galilee in mount
Josh 20:9 These were the cities *a* for all
Judg 18:11 six hundred men *a* with weapons of
Judg 18:16 the six hundred men *a* with their
Judg 20:38 Now there was an *a* sign between
1Sa 13:8 to the set time that Samuel had *a*
1Sa 13:11 thou camest not within the days *a*
1Sa 19:20 and Samuel standing as *a* over them
1Sa 20:35 field at the time *a* with David
1Sa 21:2 I have *a* my servants to such and
1Sa 25:30 shall have *a* thee ruler over
1Sa 29:4 his place which thou hast *a* him
2Sa 17:14 For the LORD had *a* to defeat the
2Sa 20:5 the set time which he had *a* him
2Sa 24:15 the morning even to the time *a*
1Kin 1:35 I have *a* him to be ruler over
1Kin 11:18 *a* him victuals, and gave him land
1Kin 12:12 the third day, as the king had *a*
1Kin 20:42 man whom I *a* to utter destruction
2Kin 7:17 the king *a* the lord on whose hand
2Kin 8:6 So the king *a* unto her a certain
2Kin 10:24 Jehu *a* fourscore men without, and
2Kin 11:18 the priest *a* officers over the
2Kin 18:14 the king of Assyria *a* unto
1Chr 6:48 *a* unto all manner of service of
1Chr 6:49 were *a* for all the work of the
1Chr 9:29 were *a* to oversee the vessels
1Chr 15:17 So the Levites *a* Heman the son of
1Chr 15:19 were *a* to sound with cymbals of
1Chr 16:4 he *a* certain of the Levites to
2Chr 8:14 And he *a*, according to the order
2Chr 20:21 he *a* singers unto the LORD, and
2Chr 23:18 Also Jehoiada *a* the offices of
2Chr 31:2 Hezekiah *a* the courses of the
2Chr 33:8 which I have *a* for your fathers
2Chr 34:22 and they that the king had *a*
Ezr 3:8 *a* the Levites, from twenty years
Ezr 8:20 the princes had *a* for the service
Ezr 10:14 in our cities come at *a* times
Neh 5:14 from the time that I was *a* to be
Neh 6:7 thou hast also *a* prophets to
Neh 7:1 the singers and the Levites were *a*
Neh 9:17 in their rebellion *a* a captain to
Neh 10:34 at times *a* year by year, to burn
Neh 12:31 *a* two great companies of them
Neh 12:44 at that time were some *a* over the
Neh 13:30 *a* the wards of the priests and the
Est 1:8 for so the king had *a* to all the
Est 2:15 the keeper of the women, *a*
Est 4:5 whom he had *a* to attend upon her,
Est 9:27 to their *a* time every year
Est 9:31 days of Purim in their times *a*
Job 7:1 Is there not an *a* time to man
Job 7:3 and wearisome nights are *a* to me
Job 14:5 thou hast *a* his bounds that he
Job 14:14 the days of my *a* time will I wait
Job 20:29 the heritage *a* unto him by God
Job 23:14 the thing that is *a* for me
Job 30:23 to the house *a* for all living
Ps 44:11 given us like sheep *a* for meat
Ps 78:5 *a* a law in Israel, which he
Ps 79:11 thou those that are *a* to die
Ps 81:3 in the new moon, in the time *a*
Ps 102:20 loose those that are *a* to death
Ps 104:19 He *a* the moon for seasons
Prov 7:20 and will come home at the day *a*
Prov 8:29 when he *a* the foundations of the
Prov 31:8 all such as are *a* to destruction
Is 1:14 your *a* feasts my soul hateth
Is 14:31 shall be alone in his *a* times
Is 28:25 the *a* barley and the rie in their
Is 44:7 since I *a* the ancient people
Jer 5:24 us the *a* weeks of the harvest
Jer 8:7 in the heaven knoweth her *a* times
Jer 33:25 if I have not *a* the ordinances of
Jer 46:17 he hath passed the time *a*
Jer 47:7 there hath he *a* it
Eze 4:6 I have *a* thee each day for a year
Eze 36:5 which have *a* my land into their
Eze 43:21 it in the *a* place of the house
Dan 1:5 the king *a* them a daily provision
Dan 1:10 who hath *a* your meat and your
Dan 8:19 for at the time *a* the end shall
Dan 10:1 was true, but the time *a* was long
Dan 11:27 the end shall be at the time *a*
Dan 11:29 At the time *a* he shall return, and
Dan 11:35 because it is yet for a time *a*
Mic 6:9 hear ye the rod, and who hath *a* it
Hab 2:3 the vision is yet for an *a* time
Mt 26:19 disciples did as Jesus had *a* them
Mt 27:10 potter's field, as the Lord *a* me
Mt 28:16 a mountain where Jesus had *a* them
Lk 3:13 no more than that which is *a* you
Lk 10:1 the Lord *a* other seventy also
Lk 22:29 as my Father hath *a* unto me
Acts 1:23 And they *a* two, Joseph called
Acts 7:44 in the wilderness, as he had *a*
Acts 17:26 determined the times before *a*
Acts 17:31 Because he hath *a* a day, in the
Acts 20:13 for so had he *a*, minding himself
Acts 22:10 things which are *a* for thee to do
Acts 28:23 And when they had *a* him a day
1Cor 4:9 last, as it were *a* to death
Gal 4:2 until the time *a* of the father
1Th 3:3 know that we are *a* thereunto
1Th 5:9 For God hath not *a* us to wrath
2Ti 1:11 Whereunto I am *a* a preacher
Titus 1:5 in every city, as I had *a* thee
Heb 1:2 whom he hath *a* heir of all things
Heb 3:2 was faithful to him that *a* him
Heb 9:27 as it is *a* unto men once to die,
1Pet 2:8 whereunto also they were *a*

### APPOINTETH
Dan 5:21 that he *a* over it whomsoever he

### APPOINTMENT
Num 4:27 At the *a* of Aaron and his sons
2Sa 13:32 for by the *a* of Absalom this hath
Ezr 6:9 according to the *a* of the priests
Job 2:11 for they had made an *a* together

### APPREHEND
2Cor 11:32 with a garrison, desirous to *a* me
Phil 3:12 if that I may *a* that for which

### APPREHENDED
Acts 12:4 And when he had *a* him, he put him
Phil 3:12 which also I am *a* of Christ Jesus
Phil 3:13 I count not myself to have *a*

### APPROACH
Lev 18:6 None of you shall *a* to any that
Lev 18:14 thou shalt not *a* to his wife
Lev 18:19 Also thou shalt not *a* unto a
Lev 20:16 if a woman *a* unto any beast, and
Lev 21:17 let him not *a* to offer the bread
Num 4:19 when they *a* unto the most holy
Deut 20:2 battle, that the priest shall *a*
Deut 31:14 thy days *a* that thou must die
Josh 8:5 are with me, will *a* unto the city
Job 40:19 can make his sword to *a* unto him
Ps 65:4 and causest to *a* unto thee
Jer 30:21 draw near, and he shall *a* unto me
Eze 42:13 where the priests that *a* unto the
Eze 43:19 which *a* unto me, to minister unto
1Ti 6:16 the light which no man can *a* unto

### APPROACHED
2Sa 11:20 Wherefore *a* ye so nigh unto the
2Kin 16:12 the king *a* to the altar, and

### APPROACHETH
Lk 12:33 faileth not, where no thief *a*

### APPROACHING
Is 58:2 they take delight in *a* to God
Heb 10:25 the more, as ye see the day *a*

### APPROVE
Ps 49:13 their posterity *a* their sayings
1Cor 16:3 ye shall *a* by your letters
Phil 1:10 That ye may *a* things that are

### APPROVED
Acts 2:22 a man *a* of God among you by
Rom 14:18 is acceptable to God, and *a* of men
Rom 16:10 Salute Apelles *a* in Christ
1Cor 11:19 that they which are *a* may be made

2Cor 7:11 In all things ye have *a*
2Cor 10:18 he that commendeth himself is *a*
2Cor 13:7 not that we should appear *a*
2Ti 2:15 Study to shew thyself *a* unto God

**APRONS**
Gen 3:7 together, and made themselves *a*
Acts 19:12 unto the sick handkerchiefs or *a*

**APT**
2Kin 24:16 *a* for war, even them the king of
1Chr 7:40 of them that were *a* to the war
1Ti 3:2 given to hospitality, *a* to teach
2Ti 2:24 all men, *a* to teach, patient,

**AQUILA** *(ac'-quil-ah) A Christian acquaintance of Paul.*
Acts 18:2 And found a certain Jew named *A*
Acts 18:18 Syria, and with him Priscilla and *A*
Acts 18:26 whom when *A* and Priscilla had
Rom 16:3 *A* my helpers in Christ Jesus
1Cor 16:19 *A* and Priscilla salute you much in
2Ti 4:19 Salute Prisca and *A*, and the

**AR** *(ar) The capital of Moab.*
Num 21:15 goeth down to the dwelling of *A*
Num 21:28 it hath consumed *A* of Moab
Deut 2:9 because I have given *A* unto the
Deut 2:18 Thou art to pass over through *A*
Deut 2:29 and the Moabites which dwell in *A*
Is 15:1 Because in the night *A* of Moab is

**ARA** *(a'-rah) A son of Jether.*
1Chr 7:38 Jephunneh, and Pispah, and *A*

**ARAB** *(a'-rab)* See ARBITE. *A city in Judah.*
Josh 15:52 *A*, and Dumah, and Eshean,

**ARABAH** *(ar'-ab-ah)* See BETH-ARABAH. *The Jordan Valley.*
Josh 18:18 the side over against *A* northward

**ARABIA** *(a-ra'-be-ah) The northern part of the Arabian peninsula.*
1Kin 10:15 and of all the kings of *A*
2Chr 9:14 And all the kings of *A* and
Is 21:13 The burden upon *A*
Jer 25:24 And all the kings of *A*, and all the
Eze 27:21 *A*, and all the princes of Kedar,
Gal 1:17 but I went into *A*, and returned
Gal 4:25 For this Agar is mount Sinai in *A*

**ARABIAN** *(a-ra'-be-un)* See ARABIANS. *An inhabitant of Arabia.*
Neh 2:19 the Ammonite, and Geshem the *A*
Neh 6:1 and Tobiah, and Geshem the *A*
Is 13:20 shall the *A* pitch tent there
Jer 3:2 as the *A* in the wilderness

**ARABIANS** *(a-ra'-be-uns)*
2Chr 17:11 the *A* brought him flocks, seven
2Chr 21:16 of the Philistines, and of the *A*
2Chr 22:1 *A* to the camp had slain all the
2Chr 26:7 against the *A* that dwelt in
Neh 4:7 Sanballat, and Tobiah, and the *A*
Acts 2:11 Cretes and *A*, we do hear them

**ARAD** *(a'-rad)*
*1. A Canaanite king.*
Num 21:1 when king *A* the Canaanite, which
Num 33:40 king *A* the Canaanite, which dwelt
*2. A district in Judah.*
Josh 12:14 the king of *A*, one
Judg 1:16 which lieth in the south of *A*
*3. A son of Beriah.*
1Chr 8:15 And Zebadiah, and *A*, and Ader,

**ARAH** *(a'-rah)*
*1. A son of Ulla.*
1Chr 7:39 *A*, and Haniel, and Rezia
*2. A family of exiles who returned under Zerubbabel.*
Ezr 2:5 The children of *A*, seven hundred
Neh 7:10 The children of *A*, six hundred
*3. Grandfather of Tobiah's wife.*
Neh 6:18 in law of Shechaniah the son of *A*

**ARAM** *(a'-ram)* See ARAMITESS, ARAM-NAHARAIM, ARAM-ZOBAH, BETH-ARAM, PADAN-ARAM, SYRIA.
*1. The son of Shem.*
Gen 10:22 and Arphaxad, and Lud, and *A*
1Chr 1:17 and Arphaxad, and Lud, and *A*
*2. The son of Kemuel.*
Gen 22:21 and Kemuel the father of *A*
*3. Another name for Syria.*
Num 23:7 of Moab hath brought me from *A*
*4. A district of Canaan.*
1Chr 2:23 And he took Geshur, and *A*, with the
*5. The son of Shamer.*
1Chr 7:34 Ahi, and Rohgah, Jehubbah, and *A*
Mt 1:3 and Esrom begat *A*
Lk 3:33 Aminadab, which was the son of *A*

**ARAMITESS** *(a'-ram-i-tes)* See SYRIAN. *Manasseh's concubine.*
1Chr 7:14 (but his concubine the *A* bare

**ARAM-NAHARAIM** *(a'-ram-na-ha-ra'-im)* See MESOPOTAMIA. *The area between the Tigris and Euphrates rivers.*
Ps 60:t when he strove with *A* and with

**ARAM-ZOBAH** *(a'-ram-zo'-bah) The area between the Orontes and Euphrates rivers.*
Ps 60:t with Aram-naharaim and with *A*

**ARAN** *(a'-ran)* See BETH-ARAN. *The son of Seir the Horite.*
Gen 36:28 of Dishan are these; Uz, and *A*
1Chr 1:42 sons of Dishan; Uz, and *A*

**ARARAT** *(ar'-ar-at)* See ARMENIA. *A district in Armenia.*
Gen 8:4 month, upon the mountains of *A*
Jer 51:27 against her the kingdoms of *A*

**ARAUNAH** *(a-raw'-nah)* See ORNAN. *A Jebusite.*
2Sa 24:16 threshingplace of *A* the Jebusite
2Sa 24:18 threshingfloor of *A* the Jebusite
2Sa 24:20 *A* looked, and saw the king and his
2Sa 24:21 *A* said, Wherefore is my lord the
2Sa 24:24 And the king said unto *A*, Nay

**ARBA** *(ar'-bah)* See ARBAH, ARBATHITE, ARBITE, KIRJATH-ABBA. *Father of Anakim.*
Josh 15:13 even the city of *A* the father of
Josh 21:11 the city of *A* the father of Anak

**ARBAH** *(ar'-bah)* See ARBA. *Another name for Hebron.*
Gen 35:27 unto Mamre, unto the city of *A*

**ARBATHITE** *(ar'-bath-ite) A native of Arbah.*
2Sa 23:31 Abi-albon the *A*, Azmaveth the
1Chr 11:32 the brooks of Gaash, Abiel the *A*

**ARBITE** *(ar'-bite) A native of Arab.*
2Sa 23:35 the Carmelite, Paarai the *A*

**ARCHANGEL**
1Th 4:16 a shout, with the voice of the *a*
Jude 9 Yet Michael the *a*, when

**ARCHELAUS** *(ar-ke-la'-us) A son of Herod the Great.*
Mt 2:22 But when he heard that *A* did

**ARCHER**
Gen 21:20 in the wilderness, and became an *a*
Jer 51:3 bendeth let the *a* bend his bow

**ARCHERS**
Gen 49:23 The *a* have sorely grieved him
Judg 5:11 *a* in the places of drawing water
1Sa 31:3 Saul, and the *a* hit him
1Chr 8:40 were mighty men of valour, *a*
1Chr 10:3 the *a* hit him
2Chr 35:23 the *a* shot at king Josiah
Job 16:13 His *a* compass me round about, he
Is 21:17 And the residue of the number of *a*
Is 22:3 together, they are bound by the *a*
Jer 50:29 together the *a* against Babylon

**ARCHES**
Eze 40:16 round about, and likewise to the *a*
Eze 40:21 the *a* thereof were after the
Eze 40:22 And their windows, and their *a*
Eze 40:25 in the *a* thereof round about,
Eze 40:26 the *a* thereof were before them
Eze 40:29 the *a* thereof, according to these
Eze 40:31 the *a* thereof were toward the
Eze 40:36 the *a* thereof, and the windows to

**ARCHEVITES** *(ar'-ke-vites) Chaldean settlers in Samaria.*
Ezr 4:9 Tarpelites, the Apharsites, the *A*

**ARCHI** *(ar'-kee)* See ARCHITE. *A border city of Ephraim.*
Josh 16:2 unto the borders of *A* to Ataroth

**ARCHIPPUS** *(ar-kip'-pus) A Christian acquaintance of Paul.*
Col 4:17 And say to *A*, Take heed to the
Philem 2 *A* our fellowsoldier, and to the

**ARCHITE** *(ar'-kite)* See ARCHI. *A friend of David.*
2Sa 15:32 Hushai the *A* came to meet him
2Sa 16:16 came to pass, when Hushai the *A*
2Sa 17:5 Call now Hushai the *A* also
2Sa 17:14 The counsel of Hushai the *A* is
1Chr 27:33 Hushai the *A* was the king's

**ARCTURUS** *(ark-tu'-rus) Another name for "the Great Bear."*
Job 9:9 Which maketh *A*, Orion, and
Job 38:32 canst thou guide *A* with his sons

**ARD** *(ard)* See ARDITES.
*1. A son of Benjamin.*
Gen 46:21 Rosh, Muppim, and Huppim, and *A*
*2. A son of Bela.*
Num 26:40 And the sons of Bela were *A*

**ARDITES** *(ar'-dites) Descendants of Bela.*
Num 26:40 of Ard, the family of the *A*

**ARDON** *(ar'-don) A son of Caleb.*
1Chr 2:18 Jesher, and Shobab, and *A*

**ARELI** *(a-re'-li)* See ARELITES. *A son of Gad.*
Gen 46:16 and Ezbon, Eri, and Arodi, and *A*
Num 26:17 of *A*, the family of the Arelites

**ARELITES** *(a-re'-lites)* See ARELI. *Descendants of Areli.*
Num 26:17 of Areli, the family of the *A*

**AREOPAGITE** *(a-re-op'-a-jite) A title of Dionysius.*
Acts 17:34 the which was Dionysius the *A*

**AREOPAGUS** *(a-re-op'-a-gus)* See AREOPAGITE, MARS'. *A plaza in Athens.*
Acts 17:19 took him, and brought him unto *A*

**ARETAS** *(ar'-e-tas) A north Arabian ruler.*
2Cor 11:32 *A* the king kept the city of the

**ARGOB** *(ar'-gob)*
*1. A district of Og in Bashan.*
Deut 3:4 cities, all the region of *A*
Deut 3:13 all the region of *A*, with all
1Kin 4:13 also pertained the region of *A*
*2. An official of King Pekah of Israel.*
2Kin 15:25 of the king's house, with *A*

**ARIDAI** *(a-rid'-a-i) A son of Haman.*
Est 9:9 And Parmashta, and Arisai, and *A*

**ARIDATHA** *(a-rid'-a-thah) A son of Haman.*
Est 9:8 And Poratha, and Adalia, and *A*

**ARIEH** *(a-ri'-eh) A companion of Argob.*
2Kin 15:25 the king's house, with Argob and *A*

**ARIEL** *(a'-re-el)* See JERUSALEM.
*1. An emissary of Ezra.*
Ezr 8:16 Then sent I for Eliezer, for *A*
*2. A name for Jerusalem.*
Is 29:1 Woe to Ariel, to *A*, the city
Is 29:7 the nations that fight against *A*

**ARIGHT**
Ps 50:23 *a* will I shew the salvation of
Ps 78:8 that set not their heart *a*
Prov 15:2 of the wise useth knowledge *a*
Prov 23:31 the cup, when it moveth itself *a*
Jer 8:6 and heard, but they spake not *a*

**ARIMATHAEA** *(ar-im-ath-e'-ah) Another name for Ramah.*
Mt 27:57 come, there came a rich man of *A*
Mk 15:43 Joseph of *A*, an honourable
Lk 23:51 he was of *A*, a city of the Jews
Jn 19:38 And after this Joseph of *A*

**ARIOCH** *(a'-re-ok)*
*1. King of Ellasar in Assyria.*
Gen 14:1 *A* king of Ellasar, Chedorlaomer
Gen 14:9 of Shinar, and *A* king of Ellasar
*2. Captain of Nebuchadnezzar's guard.*
Dan 2:14 wisdom to *A* the captain of the
Dan 2:25 Then *A* brought in Daniel before

**ARISAI** *(a-ris'-a-i) A son of Haman.*
Est 9:9 Parmashta, and *A*, and Aridai, and

**ARISE**
Gen 13:17 *A*, walk through the land in the
Gen 19:15 angels hastened Lot, saying, *A*

Gen 21:18 *A*, lift up the lad, and hold him
Gen 27:19 *a*, I pray thee, sit and eat of my
Gen 27:31 unto his father, Let my father *a*
Gen 27:43 and *a*, flee thou to Laban my
Gen 28:2 *A*, go to Padan-aram, to the house
Gen 31:13 now *a*, get thee out from this
Gen 35:1 And God said unto Jacob, *A*
Gen 35:3 And let us *a*, and go up to Beth-el
Gen 41:30 there shall *a* after them seven
Gen 43:8 the lad with me, and we will *a*
Gen 43:13 Take also your brother, and *a*
Deut 9:12 And the LORD said unto me, *A*
Deut 10:11 And the LORD said unto me, *A*
Deut 13:1 If there *a* among you a prophet,
Deut 17:8 If there *a* a matter too hard for
Josh 1:2 now therefore *a*, go over this
Josh 8:1 the people of war with thee, and *a*
Judg 5:12 *a*, Barak, and lead thy captivity
Judg 7:9 that the LORD said unto him, *A*
Judg 7:15 the host of Israel, and said, *A*
Judg 18:9 And they said, *A*, that we may go
Judg 20:40 to *a* up out of the city with a
1Sa 9:3 of the servants with thee, and *a*
1Sa 16:12 And the LORD said, *A*, anoint him
1Sa 23:4 the LORD answered him and said, *A*
2Sa 2:14 to Joab, Let the young men now *a*
2Sa 3:21 Abner said unto David, I will *a*
2Sa 11:20 if so be that the king's wrath *a*
2Sa 13:15 And Amnon said unto her, *A*
2Sa 15:14 were with him at Jerusalem, *A*
2Sa 17:1 twelve thousand men, and I will *a*
2Sa 17:21 king David, and said unto David, *A*
2Sa 19:7 Now therefore *a*, go forth, and
2Sa 22:39 them, that they could not *a*
1Kin 3:12 thee shall any *a* like unto thee
1Kin 14:2 And Jeroboam said to his wife, *A*
1Kin 14:12 *A* thou therefore, get thee to
1Kin 17:9 *A*, get thee to Zarephath, which
1Kin 19:5 touched him, and said unto him, *A*
1Kin 19:7 time, and touched him, and said, *A*
1Kin 21:7 *a*, and eat bread, and let thine
1Kin 21:15 that Jezebel said to Ahab, *A*
1Kin 21:18 *A*, go down to meet Ahab king of
2Kin 1:3 said to Elijah the Tishbite, *A*
2Kin 8:1 had restored to life, saying, *A*
2Kin 9:2 make him *a* up from among his
1Chr 22:16 *A* therefore, and be doing, and the
1Chr 22:19 *a* therefore, and build ye the
2Chr 6:41 Now therefore *a*, O LORD God, into
Ezr 10:4 *A*; for this matter belongeth
Neh 2:20 therefore we his servants will *a*
Est 1:18 Thus shall there *a* too much
Est 4:14 deliverance *a* to the Jews from
Job 7:4 I lie down, I say, When shall I *a*
Job 25:3 and upon whom doth not his light *a*
Ps 3:7 *A*, O LORD
Ps 7:6 *A*, O LORD, in thine anger, lift
Ps 9:19 *A*, O LORD
Ps 10:12 *A*, O LORD
Ps 12:5 of the needy, now will I *a*
Ps 17:13 *A*, O LORD, disappoint him, cast
Ps 44:23 *a*, cast us not off for ever
Ps 44:26 *A* for our help, and redeem us for
Ps 68:1 Let God *a*, let his enemies be
Ps 74:22 *A*, O God, plead thine own cause
Ps 78:6 who should *a* and declare them to
Ps 82:8 *A*, O God, judge the earth
Ps 88:10 shall the dead *a* and praise thee
Ps 89:9 when the waves thereof *a*, thou
Ps 102:13 Thou shalt *a*, and have mercy upon
Ps 109:28 when they *a*, let them be ashamed
Ps 132:8 *A*, O LORD, into thy rest
Prov 6:9 when wilt thou *a* out of thy sleep
Prov 31:28 Her children *a* up, and call her
Song 2:13 *A*, my love, my fair one, and come
Is 21:5 *a*, ye princes, and anoint the
Is 23:12 *a*, pass over to Chittim
Is 26:19 with my dead body shall they *a*
Is 31:2 but will *a* against the house of
Is 49:7 of rulers, Kings shall see and *a*
Is 52:2 *a*, and sit down, O Jerusalem
Is 60:2 but the LORD shall *a* upon thee
Jer 1:17 therefore gird up thy loins, and *a*
Jer 2:27 of their trouble they will say, *A*
Jer 6:4 *a*, and let us go up at noon
Jer 8:4 Shall they fall, and not *a*
Jer 13:4 which is upon thy loins, and *a*
Jer 13:6 that the LORD said unto me, *A*
Jer 18:2 *A*, and go down to the potter's
Jer 31:6 *A* ye, and let us go up to Zion
Jer 46:16 and they said, *A*, and let us go
Jer 49:28 *A* ye, go up to Kedar, and spoil
Jer 49:31 *A*, get you up unto the wealthy
Lam 2:19 *A*, cry out in the night
Eze 3:22 and he said unto me, *A*, go forth
Dan 2:39 after thee shall *a* another
Dan 7:5 and they said thus unto it, *A*
Dan 7:17 which shall *a* out of the earth
Dan 7:24 are ten kings that shall *a*
Hos 10:14 shall a tumult *a* among thy people
Amos 7:2 by whom shall Jacob *a*
Amos 7:5 by whom shall Jacob *a*
Obad 1 *A* ye, and let us rise up against
Jonah 1:2 *A*, go to Nineveh, that great city
Jonah 1:6 *a*, call upon thy God, if so be
Jonah 3:2 *A*, go unto Nineveh, that great
Jonah 4:8 came to pass, when the sun did *a*
Mic 2:10 *A* ye, and depart
Mic 4:13 *A* and thresh, O daughter of Zion
Mic 6:1 *A*, contend thou before the
Mic 7:8 when I fall, I shall *a*
Hab 2:19 to the dumb stone, *A*, it shall
Mal 4:2 *a* with healing in his wings
Mt 2:13 to Joseph in a dream, saying, *A*
Mt 2:20 Saying, *A*, and take the young
Mt 9:5 or to say, *A*, and walk
Mt 17:7 came and touched them, and said, *A*
Mt 24:24 For there shall *a* false Christs
Mk 2:9 or to say, *A*, and take up thy bed,
Mk 2:11 I say unto thee, *A*, and take up
Mk 5:41 Damsel, I say unto thee, *a*
Lk 5:24 of the palsy,) I say unto thee, *A*
Lk 7:14 Young man, I say unto thee, *A*
Lk 8:54 hand, and called, saying, Maid, *a*
Lk 15:18 I will *a* and go to my father, and
Lk 17:19 And he said unto him, *A*, go thy
Lk 24:38 why do thoughts *a* in your hearts
Jn 14:31 *A*, let us go hence
Acts 8:26 Lord spake unto Philip, saying, *A*
Acts 9:6 And the Lord said unto him, *A*
Acts 9:11 And the Lord said unto him, *A*
Acts 9:34 *a*, and make thy bed
Acts 9:40 him to the body said, Tabitha, *a*
Acts 10:20 *A* therefore, and get thee down, and
Acts 11:7 I heard a voice saying unto me, *A*
Acts 12:7 him up, saying, *A* up quickly
Acts 20:30 of your own selves shall men *a*
Acts 22:10 And the Lord said unto me, *A*
Acts 22:16 *a*, and be baptized, and wash away
Eph 5:14 *a* from the dead, and Christ shall
2Pet 1:19 the day star *a* in your hearts

**ARISETH**

1Kin 18:44 there *a* a little cloud out of the
Ps 104:22 The sun *a*, they gather themselves
Ps 112:4 there *a* light in the darkness
Eccl 1:5 The sun also *a*, and the sun goeth
Is 2:19 when he *a* to shake terribly the
Is 2:21 when he *a* to shake terribly the
Nah 3:17 but when the sun *a* they flee away
Mt 13:21 persecution *a* because of the word
Mk 4:17 persecution *a* for the word's sake
Jn 7:52 for out of Galilee *a* no prophet
Heb 7:15 there *a* another priest,

**ARISTARCHUS** *(ar-is-tar'-cus) A companion of Paul.*

Acts 19:29 and having caught Gaius and *A*
Acts 20:4 and of the Thessalonians, *A*
Acts 27:2 one *A*, a Macedonian of
Col 4:10 *A* my fellowprisoner saluteth you,
Philem 24 Marcus, *A*, Demas, Lucas, my

**ARISTOBULUS'** *(a-rus-to-bu'-luz) A Christian acquaintance of Paul.*

Rom 16:10 them which are of *A* household

**ARK**

Gen 6:14 Make thee an *a* of gopher wood
Gen 6:16 the door of the *a* shalt thou set
Gen 6:19 sort shalt thou bring into the *a*
Gen 7:1 thou and all thy house into the *a*
Gen 7:7 sons' wives with him, into the *a*
Gen 7:9 two and two unto Noah into the *a*
Gen 7:13 of his sons with them, into the *a*
Gen 7:17 increased, and bare up the *a*
Gen 7:23 they that were with him in the *a*
Gen 8:1 cattle that was with him in the *a*
Gen 8:4 the *a* rested in the seventh month
Gen 8:6 window of the *a* which he had made
Gen 8:9 she returned unto him into the *a*
Gen 8:13 removed the covering of the *a*
Gen 9:10 from all that go out of the *a*
Gen 9:18 of Noah, that went forth of the *a*
Ex 2:3 took for him an *a* of bulrushes
Ex 2:5 she saw the *a* among the flags
Ex 25:10 shall make an *a* of shittim wood
Ex 25:14 the rings by the sides of the *a*
Ex 25:16 thou shalt put into the *a* the
Ex 25:21 the mercy seat above upon the *a*
Ex 26:33 the vail the *a* of the testimony
Ex 26:34 put the mercy seat upon the *a* of
Ex 30:6 that is by the *a* of the testimony
Ex 30:26 and the *a* of the testimony,
Ex 31:7 the *a* of the testimony, and the
Ex 35:12 The *a*, and the staves thereof,
Ex 37:1 made the *a* of shittim wood
Ex 37:5 sides of the *a*, to bear the *a*
Ex 39:35 The *a* of the testimony, and the
Ex 40:3 therein the *a* of the testimony
Ex 40:5 before the *a* of the testimony
Ex 40:20 and put the testimony into the *a*
Ex 40:21 covered the *a* of the testimony
Lev 16:2 mercy seat, which is upon the *a*
Num 3:31 And their charge shall be the *a*
Num 4:5 cover the *a* of testimony with it
Num 7:89 that was upon the *a* of testimony
Num 10:33 the *a* of the covenant of the LORD
Num 10:35 when the *a* set forward, that
Num 14:44 nevertheless the *a* of the
Deut 10:1 mount, and make thee an *a* of wood
Deut 10:5 tables in the *a* which I had made
Deut 10:8 to bear the *a* of the covenant of
Deut 31:9 which bare the *a* of the covenant
Deut 31:25 which bare the *a* of the covenant
Josh 3:3 When ye see the *a* of the covenant
Josh 3:6 Take up the *a* of the covenant, and
Josh 3:8 that bear the *a* of the covenant
Josh 3:11 the *a* of the covenant of the Lord
Josh 3:13 that bear the *a* of the LORD
Josh 3:15 of the priests that bare the *a*
Josh 3:17 the priests that bare the *a* of
Josh 4:5 Pass over before the *a* of the
Josh 4:9 bare the *a* of the covenant stood
Josh 4:10 *a* stood in the midst of Jordan
Josh 4:18 the *a* of the covenant of the LORD
Josh 6:4 *a* seven trumpets of rams' horns
Josh 6:6 Take up the *a* of the covenant, and
Josh 6:9 and the rereward came after the *a*
Josh 6:11 So the *a* of the LORD compassed
Josh 6:13 came after the *a* of the LORD
Josh 7:6 *a* of the LORD until the eventide
Josh 8:33 judges, stood on this side the *a*
Judg 20:27 (for the *a* of the covenant of God
1Sa 3:3 where the *a* of God was, and Samuel
1Sa 4:3 Let us fetch the *a* of the
1Sa 4:6 they understood that the *a* of the
1Sa 4:11 And the *a* of God was taken
1Sa 4:13 heart trembled for the *a* of God
1Sa 4:17 dead, and the *a* of God is taken
1Sa 4:19 that the *a* of God was taken
1Sa 4:21 because the *a* of God was taken,
1Sa 5:1 the Philistines took the *a* of God
1Sa 5:3 earth before the *a* of the LORD
1Sa 5:4 ground before the *a* of the LORD
1Sa 5:7 The *a* of the God of Israel shall
1Sa 5:11 Send away the *a* of the God of
1Sa 6:1 the *a* of the LORD was in the
1Sa 6:8 take the *a* of the LORD, and lay it
1Sa 6:11 they laid the *a* of the LORD upon
1Sa 6:19 had looked into the *a* of the LORD
1Sa 6:21 brought again the *a* of the LORD
1Sa 7:1 and brought up the *a* of the LORD
1Sa 14:18 For the *a* of God was at that time
2Sa 6:2 bring up from thence the *a* of God
2Sa 6:7 and there he died by the *a* of God
2Sa 6:10 *a* of the LORD unto him into the
2Sa 6:13 that when they that bare the *a* of
2Sa 6:15 the *a* of the LORD with shouting
2Sa 6:17 they brought in the *a* of the LORD
2Sa 7:2 but the *a* of God dwelleth within
2Sa 11:11 And Uriah said unto David, The *a*
2Sa 15:24 bearing the *a* of the covenant of
2Sa 15:29 Abiathar carried the *a* of God
1Kin 2:26 because thou barest the *a* of the
1Kin 3:15 stood before the *a* of the
1Kin 6:19 to set there the *a* of the
1Kin 8:1 that they might bring up the *a* of
1Kin 8:3 and the priests took up the *a*
1Kin 8:7 two wings over the place of the *a*
1Kin 8:9 There was nothing in the *a* save
1Kin 8:21 have set there a place for the *a*

1Chr 6:31 LORD, after that the *a* had rest
1Chr 13:3 again the *a* of our God to us
1Chr 13:5 to bring the *a* of God from
1Chr 13:10 because he put his hand to the *a*
1Chr 13:13 So David brought not the *a* home
1Chr 13:14 the *a* of God remained with the
1Chr 15:1 prepared a place for the *a* of God
1Chr 15:2 the *a* of God but the Levites
1Chr 15:12 that ye may bring up the *a* of the
1Chr 15:14 the *a* of the LORD God of Israel
1Chr 15:23 were doorkeepers for the *a*
1Chr 15:24 the trumpets before the *a* of God
1Chr 15:27 all the Levites that bare the *a*
1Chr 15:29 as the *a* of the covenant of the
1Chr 16:1 So they brought the *a* of God
1Chr 16:4 minister before the *a* of the LORD
1Chr 16:6 the *a* of the covenant of God
1Chr 16:37 the *a* of the covenant of the LORD
1Chr 17:1 but the *a* of the covenant of the
1Chr 22:19 to bring the *a* of the covenant of
1Chr 28:2 the *a* of the covenant of the LORD
1Chr 28:18 covered the *a* of the covenant of
2Chr 1:4 But the *a* of God had David
2Chr 5:2 to bring up the *a* of the covenant
2Chr 5:4 and the Levites took up the *a*
2Chr 5:7 the priests brought in the *a* of
2Chr 5:9 seen from the *a* before the oracle
2Chr 6:11 And in it have I put the *a*
2Chr 6:41 thou, and the *a* of thy strength
2Chr 8:11 whereunto the *a* of the LORD hath
2Chr 35:3 Put the holy *a* in the house which
Ps 132:8 thou, and the *a* of thy strength
Jer 3:16 The *a* of the covenant of the LORD
Mt 24:38 day that Noe entered into the *a*
Lk 17:27 day that Noe entered into the *a*
Heb 9:4 the *a* of the covenant overlaid
Heb 11:7 prepared an *a* to the saving of
1Pet 3:20 while the *a* was a preparing,
Rev 11:19 his temple the *a* of his testament

**ARKITE** *(ar'-kite) A tribe descended from Canaan.*
Gen 10:17 And the Hivite, and the *A*, and the
1Chr 1:15 And the Hivite, and the *A*, and the

**ARM**
Ex 6:6 redeem you with a stretched out *a*
Ex 15:16 by the greatness of thine *a* they
Num 31:3 *A* some of yourselves unto the war
Deut 4:34 hand, and by a stretched out *a*
Deut 5:15 hand and by a stretched out *a*
Deut 7:19 hand, and the stretched out *a*
Deut 9:29 power and by thy stretched out *a*
Deut 11:2 hand, and his stretched out *a*
Deut 26:8 hand, and with an outstretched *a*
Deut 33:20 teareth the *a* with the crown of
1Sa 2:31 come, that I will cut off thine *a*
2Sa 1:10 and the bracelet that was on his *a*
1Kin 8:42 hand, and of thy stretched out *a*
2Kin 17:36 great power and a stretched out *a*
2Chr 6:32 hand, and thy stretched out *a*
2Chr 32:8 With his is an *a* of flesh
Job 26:2 how savest thou the *a* that hath
Job 31:22 Then let mine *a* fall from my
Job 35:9 by reason of the *a* of the mighty
Job 38:15 the high *a* shall be broken
Job 40:9 Hast thou an *a* like God
Ps 10:15 Break thou the *a* of the wicked
Ps 44:3 neither did their own *a* save them
Ps 77:15 with thine *a* redeemed thy people
Ps 89:10 thine enemies with thy strong *a*
Ps 89:13 Thou hast a mighty *a*
Ps 89:21 mine *a* also shall strengthen him
Ps 98:1 his right hand, and his holy *a*
Ps 136:12 hand, and with a stretched out *a*
Song 8:6 heart, as a seal upon thine *a*
Is 9:20 every man the flesh of his own *a*
Is 17:5 and reapeth the ears with his *a*
Is 30:30 shew the lighting down of his *a*
Is 33:2 be thou their *a* every morning
Is 40:10 hand, and his *a* shall rule for him
Is 48:14 his *a* shall be on the Chaldeans
Is 51:5 on mine *a* shall they trust
Is 51:9 put on strength, O *a* of the LORD
Is 52:10 LORD hath made bare his holy *a* in
Is 53:1 to whom is the *a* of the LORD
Is 59:16 therefore his *a* brought salvation
Is 62:8 by the *a* of his strength, Surely
Is 63:5 therefore mine own *a* brought
Is 63:12 hand of Moses with his glorious *a*
Jer 17:5 in man, and maketh flesh his *a*
Jer 21:5 hand and with a strong *a*, even in
Jer 27:5 power and by my outstretched *a*
Jer 32:17 great power and stretched out *a*
Jer 32:21 hand, and with a stretched out *a*
Jer 48:25 his *a* is broken, saith the LORD
Eze 4:7 thine *a* shall be uncovered, and
Eze 20:33 hand, and with a stretched out *a*
Eze 30:21 I have broken the *a* of Pharaoh
Eze 31:17 and they that were his *a*, that
Dan 11:6 not retain the power of the *a*
Zec 11:17 the sword shall be upon his *a*
Lk 1:51 hath shewed strength with his *a*
Jn 12:38 to whom hath the *a* of the Lord
Acts 13:17 with an high *a* brought he them
1Pet 4:1 *a* yourselves likewise with the

**ARMAGEDDON** *(ar-mag-ed'-don) Scene of the last great battle of time.*
Rev 16:16 called in the Hebrew tongue *A*

**ARMED**
Gen 14:14 he *a* his trained servants, born
Num 31:5 tribe, twelve thousand *a* for war
Num 32:17 *a* before the children of Israel
Num 32:20 if ye will go *a* before the LORD
Num 32:27 pass over, every man *a* for war
Num 32:29 Jordan, every man *a* to battle
Num 32:32 We will pass over *a* before the
Deut 3:18 ye shall pass over *a* before your
Josh 1:14 shall pass before your brethren *a*
Josh 4:12 passed over *a* before the children
Josh 6:7 let him that is *a* pass on before
Josh 6:9 the *a* men went before the priests
Josh 6:13 the *a* men went before them
Judg 7:11 the *a* men that were in the host
1Sa 17:5 he was *a* with a coat of mail
1Sa 17:38 Saul *a* David with his armour, and
1Chr 12:2 They were *a* with bows, and could
1Chr 12:23 that were ready *a* to the war
2Chr 17:17 with him *a* men with bow and shield
2Chr 28:14 So the *a* men left the captives and
Job 39:21 he goeth on to meet the *a* men
Ps 78:9 The children of Ephraim, being *a*
Prov 6:11 and thy want as an *a* man
Prov 24:34 and thy want as an *a* man
Is 15:4 therefore the *a* soldiers of Moab
Lk 11:21 When a strong man *a* keepeth his

**ARMENIA** *(ar-me'-ne-ah) A region between the lower ends of the Black and Caspian seas.*
2Kin 19:37 they escaped into the land of *A*
Is 37:38 they escaped into the land of *A*

**ARMHOLES**
Jer 38:12 under thine *a* under the cords
Eze 13:18 women that sew pillows to all *a*

**ARMIES**
Ex 6:26 of Egypt according to their *a*
Ex 7:4 upon Egypt, and bring forth mine *a*
Ex 12:17 day have I brought your *a* out of
Ex 12:51 of the land of Egypt by their *a*
Num 1:3 shall number them by their *a*
Num 2:3 of Judah pitch throughout their *a*
Num 2:9 four hundred, throughout their *a*
Num 2:16 and fifty, throughout their *a*
Num 2:18 of Ephraim according to their *a*
Num 2:24 and an hundred, throughout their *a*
Num 10:14 of Judah according to their *a*
Num 10:18 set forward according to their *a*
Num 10:22 set forward according to their *a*
Num 10:28 of Israel according to their *a*
Num 33:1 their *a* under the hand of Moses
Deut 20:9 of the *a* to lead the people
1Sa 17:1 together their *a* to battle
1Sa 17:8 and cried unto the *a* of Israel
1Sa 17:10 I defy the *a* of Israel this day
1Sa 17:23 out of the *a* of the Philistines,
1Sa 17:26 defy the *a* of the living God
1Sa 17:36 defied the *a* of the living God
1Sa 17:45 hosts, the God of the *a* of Israel
1Sa 23:3 against the *a* of the Philistines
1Sa 28:1 their *a* together for warfare
1Sa 29:1 together all their *a* to Aphek
2Kin 25:23 And when all the captains of the *a*
2Kin 25:26 great, and the captains of the *a*
1Chr 11:26 the valiant men of the *a* were
2Chr 16:4 sent the captains of his *a*
Job 25:3 Is there any number of his *a*
Ps 44:9 and goest not forth with our *a*
Ps 60:10 which didst not go out with our *a*
Ps 68:12 Kings of *a* did flee apace
Song 6:13 As it were the company of two *a*
Is 34:2 and his fury upon all their *a*
Mt 22:7 and he sent forth his *a*, and
Lk 21:20 see Jerusalem compassed with *a*
Heb 11:34 to flight the *a* of the aliens
Rev 19:14 the *a* which were in heaven
Rev 19:19 kings of the earth, and their *a*

**ARMONI** *(ar-mo'-ni) A son of King Saul.*
2Sa 21:8 Aiah, whom she bare unto Saul, *A*

**ARMOUR**
1Sa 14:1 the young man that bare his *a*
1Sa 14:6 to the young man that bare his *a*
1Sa 17:38 And Saul armed David with his *a*
1Sa 17:39 David girded his sword upon his *a*
1Sa 17:54 but he put his *a* in his tent
1Sa 31:9 his head, and stripped off his *a*
2Sa 2:21 the young men, and take thee his *a*
2Sa 18:15 bare Joab's *a* compassed about
1Kin 10:25 of gold, and garments, and *a*
1Kin 22:38 and they washed his *a*
2Kin 3:21 all that were able to put on *a*
2Kin 10:2 horses, a fenced city also, and *a*
2Kin 20:13 and all the house of his *a*
1Chr 10:9 him, they took his head, and his *a*
Is 22:8 the *a* of the house of the forest
Is 39:2 and all the house of his *a*
Eze 38:4 them clothed with all sorts of *a*
Lk 11:22 him all his *a* wherein he trusted
Rom 13:12 and let us put on the *a* of light
2Cor 6:7 by the *a* of righteousness on the
Eph 6:11 Put on the whole *a* of God
Eph 6:13 take unto you the whole *a* of God

**ARMOURBEARER**
Judg 9:54 unto the young man his *a*
1Sa 14:7 his *a* said unto him, Do all that
1Sa 14:12 answered Jonathan and his *a*
1Sa 14:13 and his *a* slew after him
1Sa 14:14 *a* made, was about twenty men,
1Sa 14:17 Jonathan and his *a* were not there
1Sa 16:21 and he became his *a*
1Sa 31:4 Then said Saul unto his *a*
1Sa 31:6 and his three sons, and his *a*
2Sa 23:37 *a* to Joab the son of Zeruiah,
1Chr 10:4 said Saul to his *a*, Draw thy
1Chr 11:39 the *a* of Joab the son of Zeruiah,

**ARMOURY**
Neh 3:19 the *a* at the turning of the wall
Song 4:4 tower of David builded for an *a*
Jer 50:25 The LORD hath opened his *a*

**ARMS**
Gen 49:24 the *a* of his hands were made
Deut 33:27 underneath are the everlasting *a*
Judg 15:14 the cords that were upon his *a*
Judg 16:12 them from off his *a* like a thread
2Sa 22:35 bow of steel is broken by mine *a*
2Kin 9:24 and smote Jehoram between his *a*
Job 22:9 the *a* of the fatherless have been
Ps 18:34 bow of steel is broken by mine *a*
Ps 37:17 For the *a* of the wicked shall be
Prov 31:17 strength, and strengtheneth her *a*
Is 44:12 it with the strength of his *a*
Is 49:22 shall bring thy sons in their *a*
Is 51:5 mine *a* shall judge the people
Eze 13:20 and I will tear them from your *a*
Eze 30:22 of Egypt, and will break his *a*
Eze 30:24 I will strengthen the *a* of the
Eze 30:25 the *a* of Pharaoh shall fall down
Dan 2:32 his *a* of silver, his belly and his
Dan 10:6 eyes as lamps of fire, and his *a*
Dan 11:15 the *a* of the south shall not
Dan 11:22 with the *a* of a flood shall they
Dan 11:31 *a* shall stand on his part, and
Hos 7:15 bound and strengthened their *a*
Hos 11:3 to go, taking them by their *a*
Mk 9:36 and when he had taken him in his *a*
Mk 10:16 And he took them up in his *a*
Lk 2:28 Then took he him up in his *a*

**ARMY**
Gen 26:26 the chief captain of his *a*
Ex 14:9 and his horsemen, and his *a*
Deut 11:4 what he did unto the *a* of Egypt
Judg 4:7 Sisera, the captain of Jabin's *a*
Judg 8:6 we should give bread unto thine *a*
Judg 9:29 to Abimelech, Increase thine *a*
1Sa 4:2 they slew of the *a* in the field
1Sa 4:12 a man of Benjamin out of the *a*
1Sa 4:16 I am he that came out of the *a*
1Sa 17:21 battle in array, *a* against *a*

1Sa 17:48 ran toward the *a* to meet the
1Kin 20:19 the *a* which followed them
1Kin 20:25 And number thee an *a*
1Kin 20:25 like the *a* that thou hast lost,
2Kin 25:5 all his *a* were scattered from him
2Kin 25:10 all the *a* of the Chaldees, that
1Chr 20:1 Joab led forth the power of the *a*
1Chr 27:34 general of the king's *a* was Joab
2Chr 13:3 with an *a* of valiant men of war
2Chr 14:8 Asa had an *a* of men that bare
2Chr 20:21 as they went out before the *a*
2Chr 24:24 For the *a* of the Syrians came
2Chr 25:7 let not the *a* of Israel go with
2Chr 25:9 I have given to the *a* of Israel
2Chr 25:10 the *a* that was come to him out of
2Chr 25:13 of the *a* which Amaziah sent back
2Chr 26:13 And under their hand was an *a*
Neh 2:9 king had sent captains of the *a*
Neh 4:2 the *a* of Samaria, and said, What
Job 29:25 and dwelt as a king in the *a*
Song 6:4 terrible as an *a* with banners
Song 6:10 and terrible as an *a* with banners
Is 36:2 unto king Hezekiah with a great *a*
Is 43:17 forth the chariot and horse, the *a*
Jer 32:2 of Babylon's *a* besieged Jerusalem
Jer 34:1 king of Babylon, and all his *a*
Jer 34:7 *a* fought against Jerusalem
Jer 34:21 hand of the king of Babylon's *a*
Jer 35:11 fear of the *a* of the Chaldeans
Jer 37:5 Then Pharaoh's *a* was come forth
Jer 37:7 Behold, Pharaoh's *a*, which is
Jer 37:10 *a* of the Chaldeans that fight
Jer 38:3 hand of the king of Babylon's *a*
Jer 39:1 all his *a* against Jerusalem, and
Jer 39:5 Chaldeans' *a* pursued after them
Jer 46:2 against the *a* of Pharaoh-necho
Jer 46:22 for they shall march with an *a*
Jer 52:4 of Babylon came, he and all his *a*
Jer 52:8 But the *a* of the Chaldeans
Jer 52:14 all the *a* of the Chaldeans, that
Eze 17:17 shall Pharaoh with his mighty *a*
Eze 27:10 of Lud and of Phut were in thine *a*
Eze 29:18 his *a* to serve a great service
Eze 32:31 all his *a* slain by the sword,
Eze 37:10 their feet, an exceeding great *a*
Eze 38:4 bring thee forth, and all thine *a*
Eze 38:15 a great company, and a mighty *a*
Dan 3:20 were in his *a* to bind Shadrach
Dan 4:35 to his will in the *a* of heaven
Dan 11:7 which shall come with an *a*
Dan 11:13 certain years with a great *a*
Dan 11:25 king of the south with a great *a*
Joel 2:11 utter his voice before his *a*
Joel 2:20 far off from you the northern *a*
Joel 2:25 my great *a* which I sent among you
Zec 9:8 about mine house because of the *a*
Acts 23:27 then came I with an *a*, and rescued
Rev 9:16 the number of the *a* of the
Rev 19:19 on the horse, and against his *a*

**ARNAN** *(ar'-nan) Descendants of David.*
1Chr 3:21 sons of Rephaiah, the sons of *A*

**ARNON** *(ar'-non) A river in southern Canaan.*
Num 21:13 and pitched on the other side of *A*
Num 21:24 his land from *A* unto Jabbok
Num 22:36 Moab, which is in the border of *A*
Deut 2:24 journey, and pass over the river *A*
Deut 2:36 is by the brink of the river of *A*
Deut 3:8 the river of *A* unto mount Hermon
Deut 4:48 is by the bank of the river *A*
Josh 12:1 from the river *A* unto mount
Josh 13:9 is upon the bank of the river *A*
Josh 13:16 is on the bank of the river *A*
Judg 11:13 from *A* even unto Jabbok, and unto
Judg 11:18 and pitched on the other side of *A*
2Kin 10:33 Aroer, which is by the river *A*
Is 16:2 Moab shall be at the fords of *A*
Jer 48:20 tell ye it in *A*, that Moab is

**AROD** *(a'-rod)* See ARODITES. *A son of Gad.*
Num 26:17 Of *A*, the family of the Arodites

**ARODI** *(ar'-o-di)* See ARODITES. *Descendants of Arod.*
Gen 46:16 Haggi, Shuni, and Ezbon, Eri, and *A*

**ARODITES** *(a'-ro-dites) Same as Arodi.*
Num 26:17 Of Arod, the family of the *A*

**AROER** *(ar'-o-ur)*
*1. A city in the valley of Jabbok.*
Num 32:34 Gad built Dibon, and Ataroth, and *A*
Josh 13:25 unto *A* that is before Rabbah
2Sa 24:5 over Jordan, and pitched in *A*
Is 17:2 The cities of *A* are forsaken
*2. An Amorite city.*
Deut 2:36 From *A*, which is by the brink of
Deut 3:12 we possessed at that time, from *A*
Deut 4:48 From *A*, which is by the bank of
Josh 12:2 dwelt in Heshbon, and ruled from *A*
Josh 13:9 From *A*, that is upon the bank of
Josh 13:16 And their coast was from *A*
Judg 11:26 in Heshbon and her towns, and in *A*
Judg 11:33 And he smote them from *A*, even
2Kin 10:33 and the Manassites, from *A*
1Chr 5:8 the son of Joel, who dwelt in *A*
Jer 48:19 O inhabitant of *A*, stand by the
*3. A city in southern Judah.*
1Sa 30:28 And to them which were in *A*

**AROERITE** *(ar'-o-ur-ite) A native of Aroer.*
1Chr 11:44 Jehiel the sons of Hothan the *A*

**AROSE**
Gen 19:15 And when the morning *a*, then the
Gen 19:33 when she lay down, nor when she *a*
Gen 19:35 and the younger *a*, and lay with him
Gen 19:35 when she lay down, nor when she *a*
Gen 24:10 and he *a*, and went to Mesopotamia,
Gen 24:61 And Rebekah *a*, and her damsels, and
Gen 37:7 in the field, and, lo, my sheaf *a*
Gen 38:19 And she *a*, and went away, and laid
Ex 1:8 Now there *a* up a new king over
Deut 34:10 there *a* not a prophet since in
Josh 8:3 So Joshua *a*, and all the people of
Josh 8:19 the ambush *a* quickly out of their
Josh 18:8 And the men *a*, and went away
Josh 24:9 son of Zippor, king of Moab, *a*
Judg 2:10 there *a* another generation after
Judg 3:20 And he *a* out of his seat
Judg 4:9 And Deborah *a*, and went with Barak
Judg 5:7 in Israel, until that I Deborah *a*
Judg 6:28 the city *a* early in the morning
Judg 8:21 And Gideon *a*, and slew Zebah and
Judg 10:1 after Abimelech there *a* to defend
Judg 10:3 And after him *a* Jair, a Gileadite,
Judg 13:11 And Manoah *a*, and went after his
Judg 16:3 *a* at midnight, and took the doors
Judg 19:3 And her husband *a*, and went after
Judg 19:5 when they *a* early in the morning,
Judg 19:8 he *a* early in the morning on the
Judg 20:8 And all the people *a* as one man
Judg 20:18 And the children of Israel *a*
Ruth 1:6 Then she *a* with her daughters in
1Sa 3:6 And Samuel *a* and went to Eli, and
1Sa 3:8 And he *a* and went to Eli, and said,
1Sa 5:3 of Ashdod *a* early on the morrow
1Sa 9:26 And Saul *a*, and they went out both
1Sa 13:15 And Samuel *a*, and gat him up from
1Sa 17:35 when he *a* against me, I caught
1Sa 17:48 to pass, when the Philistine *a*
1Sa 17:52 the men of Israel and of Judah *a*
1Sa 18:27 Wherefore David *a* and went, he and
1Sa 20:25 and Jonathan *a*, and Abner sat by
1Sa 20:34 So Jonathan *a* from the table in
1Sa 20:41 David *a* out of a place toward the
1Sa 21:10 And David *a*, and fled that day for
1Sa 23:13 which were about six hundred, *a*
1Sa 23:16 And Jonathan Saul's son *a*, and went
1Sa 23:24 And they *a*, and went to Ziph before
1Sa 24:4 Then David *a*, and cut off the
1Sa 24:8 David also *a* afterward, and went
1Sa 25:1 And David *a*, and went down to the
1Sa 25:41 And she *a*, and bowed herself on her
1Sa 26:2 Then Saul *a*, and went down to the
1Sa 26:5 And David *a*, and came to the place
1Sa 27:2 And David *a*, and he passed over
1Sa 28:23 So he *a* from the earth, and sat
1Sa 31:12 All the valiant men *a*, and went
2Sa 2:15 Then there *a* and went over by
2Sa 6:2 And David *a*, and went with all the
2Sa 11:2 that David *a* from off his bed, and
2Sa 12:17 And the elders of his house *a*
2Sa 12:20 Then David *a* from the earth, and
2Sa 13:29 Then all the king's sons *a*
2Sa 13:31 Then the king *a*, and tare his
2Sa 14:23 So Joab *a* and went to Geshur, and
2Sa 14:31 Then Joab *a*, and came to Absalom
2Sa 15:9 So he *a*, and went to Hebron
2Sa 17:22 Then David *a*, and all the people
2Sa 17:23 he saddled his ass, and *a*
2Sa 19:8 Then the king *a*, and sat in the
2Sa 23:10 He *a*, and smote the Philistines
1Kin 1:50 feared because of Solomon, and *a*
1Kin 2:40 And Shimei *a*, and saddled his ass,
1Kin 3:20 she *a* at midnight, and took my son
1Kin 8:54 he *a* from before the altar of the
1Kin 11:18 they *a* out of Midian, and came to
1Kin 11:40 And Jeroboam *a*, and fled into Egypt
1Kin 14:4 And Jeroboam's wife did so, and *a*
1Kin 14:17 And Jeroboam's wife *a*, and departed
1Kin 17:10 So he *a* and went to Zarephath
1Kin 19:3 And when he saw that, he *a*
1Kin 19:8 And he *a*, and did eat and drink, and
1Kin 19:21 Then he *a*, and went after Elijah,
2Kin 1:15 And he *a*, and went down with him
2Kin 4:30 And he *a*, and followed her
2Kin 7:7 Wherefore they *a* and fled in the
2Kin 7:12 the king *a* in the night, and said
2Kin 8:2 And the woman *a*, and did after the
2Kin 9:6 And he *a*, and went into the house
2Kin 10:12 And he *a* and departed, and came to
2Kin 11:1 saw that her son was dead, she *a*
2Kin 12:20 And his servants *a*, and made a
2Kin 19:35 when they *a* early in the morning,
2Kin 23:25 neither after him *a* there any
2Kin 25:26 and the captains of the armies, *a*
1Chr 10:12 They *a*, all the valiant men, and
1Chr 20:4 that there *a* war at Gezer with
2Chr 22:10 saw that her son was dead, she *a*
2Chr 29:12 Then the Levites *a*, Mahath the
2Chr 30:14 And they *a* and took away the altars
2Chr 30:27 Then the priests the Levites *a*
2Chr 36:16 of the LORD *a* against his people
Ezr 9:5 I *a* up from my heaviness
Ezr 10:5 Then *a* Ezra, and made the chief
Neh 2:12 I *a* in the night, I and some few
Est 8:4 So Esther *a*, and stood before the
Job 1:20 Then Job *a*, and rent his mantle,
Job 19:18 I *a*, and they spake against me
Job 29:8 and the aged *a*, and stood up
Ps 76:9 When God *a* to judgment, to save
Eccl 1:5 hasteth to his place where he *a*
Is 37:36 when they *a* early in the morning,
Jer 41:2 Then *a* Ishmael the son of
Eze 3:23 Then I *a*, and went forth into the
Dan 6:19 Then the king *a* very early in the
Jonah 3:3 So Jonah *a*, and went unto Nineveh,
Jonah 3:6 he *a* from his throne, and he laid
Mt 2:14 When he *a*, he took the young
Mt 2:21 And he *a*, and took the young child
Mt 8:15 and she *a*, and ministered unto them
Mt 8:24 there *a* a great tempest in the
Mt 8:26 Then he *a*, and rebuked the winds
Mt 9:7 And he *a*, and departed to his house
Mt 9:9 And he *a*, and followed him
Mt 9:19 And Jesus *a*, and followed him, and
Mt 9:25 her by the hand, and the maid *a*
Mt 25:7 Then all those virgins *a*, and
Mt 26:62 And the high priest *a*, and said
Mt 27:52 of the saints which slept *a*
Mk 2:12 And immediately he *a*, took up the
Mk 2:14 And he *a* and followed him
Mk 4:37 there *a* a great storm of wind, and
Mk 4:39 And he *a*, and rebuked the wind, and
Mk 5:42 And straightway the damsel *a*
Mk 7:24 And from thence he *a*, and went into
Mk 9:27 and he *a*
Mk 10:1 he *a* from thence, and cometh into
Mk 14:57 there *a* certain, and bare false
Lk 1:39 Mary *a* in those days, and went
Lk 4:38 he *a* out of the synagogue, and
Lk 6:8 And he *a* and stood forth
Lk 6:48 and when the flood *a*, the stream
Lk 8:24 Then he *a*, and rebuked the wind and
Lk 8:55 came again, and she *a* straightway
Lk 9:46 Then there *a* a reasoning among
Lk 15:14 there *a* a mighty famine in that
Lk 15:20 And he *a*, and came to his father
Lk 23:1 And the whole multitude of them *a*
Lk 24:12 Then *a* Peter, and ran unto the
Jn 3:25 Then there *a* a question between
Jn 6:18 the sea *a* by reason of a great
Jn 11:29 she *a* quickly, and came unto him
Acts 5:6 And the young men *a*, wound him up,
Acts 6:1 there *a* a murmuring of the
Acts 6:9 Then there *a* a certain of the
Acts 7:18 Till another king *a*, which knew
Acts 8:27 And he *a* and went

Acts 9:8 And Saul *a* from the earth
Acts 9:18 he received sight forthwith, and *a*
Acts 9:34 And he *a* immediately
Acts 9:39 Then Peter *a* and went with them
Acts 11:19 upon the persecution that *a* about
Acts 19:23 the same time there *a* no small
Acts 23:7 there *a* a dissension between the
Acts 23:9 And there *a* a great cry
Acts 23:10 when there *a* a great dissension,
Acts 27:14 But not long after there *a*
Rev 9:2 there *a* a smoke out of the pit,

**ARPAD** *(ar'-pad) A city near Hamath.*
2Kin 18:34 are the gods of Hamath, and of *A*
2Kin 19:13 king of Hamath, and the king of *A*
Is 10:9 is not Hamath as *A*
Jer 49:23 Hamath is confounded, and *A*

**ARPHAD** *(ar'-fad)* See ARPAD. *Same as Arpad.*
Is 36:19 Where are the gods of Hamath and *A*
Is 37:13 king of Hamath, and the king of *A*

**ARPHAXAD**
Gen 10:22 Elam, and Asshur, and *A*, and Lud,
Gen 10:24 And *A* begat Salah
Gen 11:10 begat *A* two years after the flood
Gen 11:13 *A* lived after he begat Salah four
1Chr 1:17 Elam, and Asshur, and *A*, and Lud,
1Chr 1:24 Shem, *A*, Shelah,
Lk 3:36 of Cainan, which was the son of *A*

**ARRAY**
Judg 20:20 *a* to fight against them at Gibeah
Judg 20:22 put themselves in *a* the first day
Judg 20:30 themselves in *a* against Gibeah
Judg 20:33 put themselves in *a* at Baal-tamar
1Sa 4:2 themselves in *a* against Israel
1Sa 17:2 set the battle in *a* against the
1Sa 17:8 come out to set your battle in *a*
1Sa 17:21 had put the battle in *a*, army
2Sa 10:8 put the battle in *a* at the
2Sa 10:10 that he might put them in *a*
2Sa 10:17 set themselves in *a* against David
1Kin 20:12 his servants, Set yourselves in *a*
1Chr 19:9 put the battle in *a* before the
1Chr 19:10 put them in *a* against the Syrians
1Chr 19:11 they set themselves in *a* against
1Chr 19:17 set the battle in *a* against them
2Chr 13:3 *a* against him with eight hundred
2Chr 14:10 they set the battle in *a* in the
Est 6:9 that they may *a* the man withal
Job 6:4 do set themselves in *a* against me
Job 40:10 *a* thyself with glory and beauty
Is 22:7 set themselves in *a* at the gate
Jer 6:23 set in *a* as men for war against
Jer 43:12 he shall *a* himself with the land
Jer 50:9 set themselves in *a* against her
Jer 50:14 Put yourselves in *a* against
Jer 50:42 upon horses, every one put in *a*
Joel 2:5 a strong people set in battle *a*
1Ti 2:9 or gold, or pearls, or costly *a*

**ARRAYED**
Gen 41:42 *a* him in vestures of fine linen,
2Chr 5:12 being *a* in white linen, having
2Chr 28:15 *a* them, and shod them, and gave
Est 6:11 *a* Mordecai, and brought him on
Mt 6:29 glory was not *a* like one of these
Lk 12:27 glory was not *a* like one of these
Lk 23:11 *a* him in a gorgeous robe, and sent
Acts 12:21 *a* in royal apparel, sat upon his
Rev 7:13 these which are *a* in white robes
Rev 17:4 And the woman was *a* in purple
Rev 19:8 she should be *a* in fine linen

**ARRIVED**
Lk 8:26 they *a* at the country of the
Acts 20:15 and the next day we *a* at Samos

**ARROGANCY**
1Sa 2:3 let not *a* come out of your mouth
Prov 8:13 pride, and *a*, and the evil way, and
Is 13:11 I will cause the *a* of the proud
Jer 48:29 proud) his loftiness, and his *a*

**ARROW**
1Sa 20:36 lad ran, he shot an *a* beyond him
2Kin 9:24 the *a* went out at his heart, and
2Kin 13:17 The *a* of the LORD's deliverance,
2Kin 19:32 this city, nor shoot an *a* there
Job 41:28 The *a* cannot make him flee
Ps 11:2 ready their *a* upon the string
Ps 64:7 God shall shoot at them with an *a*
Ps 91:5 nor for the *a* that flieth by day
Prov 25:18 a maul, and a sword, and a sharp *a*
Is 37:33 this city, nor shoot an *a* there
Jer 9:8 Their tongue is as an *a* shot out
Lam 3:12 and set me as a mark for the *a*
Zec 9:14 his *a* shall go forth as the

**ARROWS**
Num 24:8 and pierce them through with his *a*
Deut 32:23 I will spend mine *a* upon them
Deut 32:42 will make mine *a* drunk with blood
1Sa 20:20 I will shoot three *a* on the side
1Sa 20:22 Behold, the *a* are beyond thee
1Sa 20:36 find out now the *a* which I shoot
1Sa 20:38 Jonathan's lad gathered up the *a*
2Sa 22:15 And he sent out *a*, and scattered
2Kin 13:15 said unto him, Take bow and *a*
2Kin 13:18 And he said, Take the *a*
1Chr 12:2 shooting *a* out of a bow, even of
2Chr 26:15 and upon the bulwarks, to shoot *a*
Job 6:4 For the *a* of the Almighty are
Ps 7:13 he ordaineth his *a* against the
Ps 18:14 Yea, he sent out his *a*, and
Ps 21:12 thou shalt make ready thine *a*
Ps 38:2 For thine *a* stick fast in me, and
Ps 45:5 Thine *a* are sharp in the heart of
Ps 57:4 men, whose teeth are spears and *a*
Ps 58:7 he bendeth his bow to shoot his *a*
Ps 64:3 bend their bows to shoot their *a*
Ps 76:3 There brake he the *a* of the bow
Ps 77:17 thine *a* also went abroad
Ps 120:4 Sharp *a* of the mighty, with coals
Ps 127:4 As *a* are in the hand of a mighty
Ps 144:6 shoot out thine *a*, and destroy
Prov 26:18 mad man who casteth firebrands, *a*
Is 5:28 Whose *a* are sharp, and all their
Is 7:24 With *a* and with bows shall men
Jer 50:9 their *a* shall be as of a mighty
Jer 50:14 the bow, shoot at her, spare no *a*
Jer 51:11 Make bright the *a*
Lam 3:13 He hath caused the *a* of his
Eze 5:16 upon them the evil *a* of famine
Eze 21:21 he made his *a* bright, he
Eze 39:3 will cause thine *a* to fall out of
Eze 39:9 the bucklers, the bows and the *a*
Hab 3:11 at the light of thine *a* they went

**ARTAXERXES** *(ar-tax-erx'-ees)* See ARTAXERXES'.
*1. A Persian king known as Longimanus.*
Ezr 4:7 And in the days of *A* wrote Bishlam
Ezr 4:11 unto him, even unto *A* the king
*2. A Persian king known as Cambyses.*
Ezr 6:14 and Darius, and *A* king of Persia
*3. A Persian king known as Darius.*
Ezr 7:1 in the reign of *A* king of Persia
Ezr 7:7 in the seventh year of *A* the king
Ezr 7:11 king *A* gave unto Ezra the priest
Ezr 7:21 even I *A* the king, do make a
Ezr 8:1 in the reign of *A* the king
Neh 2:1 the twentieth year of *A* the king
Neh 5:14 and thirtieth year of *A* the king
Neh 13:6 thirtieth year of *A* king of

**ARTAXERXES'** *(ar-tax-erx'-eez) Refers to Artaxerxes 1.*
Ezr 4:23 Now when the copy of king *A*

**ARTEMAS** *(ar'-te-mas) A companion of Paul.*
Titus 3:12 When I shall send *A* unto thee

**ARTIFICER**
Gen 4:22 an instructer of every *a* in brass
Is 3:3 the counsellor, and the cunning *a*

**ARTIFICERS**
1Chr 29:5 work to be made by the hands of *a*
2Chr 34:11 Even to the *a* and builders gave

**ARTILLERY**
1Sa 20:40 Jonathan gave his *a* unto his lad

**ARTS**
Acts 19:19 *a* brought their books together

**ARUBOTH** *(ar'-u-both) A district of Solomon's rule.*
1Kin 4:10 The son of Hesed, in *A*

**ARUMAH** *(a-ru'-mah) A place in Ephraim.*
Judg 9:41 And Abimelech dwelt at *A*

**ARVAD** *(ar'-vad)* See ARVADITE. *An island near Zidon.*
Eze 27:8 of Zidon and *A* were thy mariners
Eze 27:11 The men of *A* with thine army were

**ARVADITE** *(ar'-vad-ite) Descendants of Canaan.*
Gen 10:18 And the *A*, and the Zemarite, and the
1Chr 1:16 And the *A*, and the Zemarite, and the

**ARZA** *(ar'-zah) A steward of King Elah of Israel.*
1Kin 16:9 himself drunk in the house of *A*

**ASA** *(a'-sah)* See ASA'S.
*1. A king of Judah.*
1Kin 15:8 *A* his son reigned in his stead
1Kin 15:11 *A* did that which was right in the
1Kin 15:18 king *A* sent them to Ben-hadad,
1Kin 15:24 *A* slept with his fathers, and was
1Kin 15:32 And there was war between *A*
1Kin 22:41 Jehoshaphat the son of *A* began to
1Kin 22:43 in all the ways of *A* his father
1Chr 3:10 *A* his son, Jehoshaphat his son,
2Chr 14:1 *A* his son reigned in his stead
2Chr 14:8 *A* had an army of men that bare
2Chr 14:10 Then *A* went out against him, and
2Chr 14:12 smote the Ethiopians before *A*
2Chr 14:13 And *A* and the people that were with
2Chr 15:2 And he went out to meet *A*, and said
2Chr 15:16 Maachah the mother of *A* the king
2Chr 15:19 thirtieth year of the reign of *A*
2Chr 16:1 *A* Baasha king of Israel came up
2Chr 16:4 Ben-hadad hearkened unto king *A*
2Chr 16:13 *A* slept with his fathers, and died
2Chr 17:2 which *A* his father had taken
2Chr 20:32 walked in the way of *A* his father
2Chr 21:12 in the ways of *A* king of Judah
Jer 41:9 was it which *A* the king had made
Mt 1:7 and Abia begat *A*
*2. Chief of a Levite family.*
1Chr 9:16 and Berechiah the son of *A*

**ASAHEL** *(as'-a-hel)*
*1. The son of Zeruiah, David's sister.*
2Sa 2:18 there, Joab, and Abishai, and *A*
2Sa 2:20 behind him, and said, Art thou *A*
2Sa 2:23 to the place where *A* fell down
2Sa 2:30 servants nineteen men and *A*
2Sa 2:32 And they took up *A*, and buried him
2Sa 3:27 for the blood of *A* his brother
2Sa 3:30 brother *A* at Gibeon in the battle
2Sa 23:24 *A* the brother of Joab was one of
1Chr 2:16 Abishai, and Joab, and *A*, three
1Chr 11:26 *A* the brother of Joab, Elhanan
1Chr 27:7 month was *A* the brother of Joab
*2. A Levite teacher.*
2Chr 17:8 and Nethaniah, and Zebadiah, and *A*
*3. A Levite officer.*
2Chr 31:13 and Azaziah, and Nahath, and *A*
*4. Father of Jonathan.*
Ezr 10:15 Only Jonathan the son of *A*

**ASAHIAH** *(as-a-hi'-ah)* See ASAIAH. *An officer of King Josiah.*
2Kin 22:12 *A* a servant of the king's, saying
2Kin 22:14 and Achbor, and Shaphan, and *A*

**ASAIAH** *(as-a'-yah)*
*1. A descendant of Simeon.*
1Chr 4:36 and Jaakobah, and Jeshohaiah, and *A*
*2. A descendant of Libni.*
1Chr 6:30 son, Haggiah his son, *A* his son
*3. A Shilonite of Jerusalem.*
1Chr 9:5 *A* the firstborn, and his sons
*4. A descendant of Merari.*
1Chr 15:6 *A* the chief, and his brethren two
1Chr 15:11 and for the Levites, for Uriel, *A*
*5. Same as Asahiah.*
2Chr 34:20 *A* a servant of the king's, saying

**ASAPH** *(a'-saf)* See ASAPH'S.
*1. Father of Joah.*
2Kin 18:18 and Joah the son of *A* the recorder
2Kin 18:37 and Joah the son of *A* the recorder
Is 36:22 the scribe, and Joah, the son of *A*
*2. A musician of David and Solomon.*
1Chr 6:39 And his brother *A*, who stood on
1Chr 15:17 brethren, *A* the son of Berechiah
1Chr 15:19 So the singers, Heman, *A*, and
1Chr 16:5 *A* the chief, and next to him
1Chr 16:7 thank the LORD into the hand of *A*
1Chr 16:37 ark of the covenant of the LORD *A*
1Chr 25:1 to the service of the sons of *A*
1Chr 25:6 to the king's order to *A*,
1Chr 25:9 lot came forth for *A* to Joseph
2Chr 29:30 words of David, and of *A* the seer
2Chr 35:15 the sons of *A* were in their place
Ezr 2:41 the children of *A*, an hundred

Neh 7:44 the children of *A*, an hundred
Neh 11:17 the son of Zabdi, the son of *A*
Neh 12:35 the son of Zaccur, the son of *A*
Neh 12:46 *A* of old there were chief of the
Ps 50:*t* A Psalm of *A*
Ps 73:*t* A Psalm of *A*
Ps 74:*t* Maschil of *A*
Ps 75:*t* Altaschith, A Psalm or Song of *A*
Ps 76:*t* on Neginoth, A Psalm or Song of *A*
Ps 77:*t* to Jeduthun, A Psalm of *A*
Ps 78:*t* Maschil of *A*
Ps 79:*t* A Psalm of *A*
Ps 80:*t* Shoshannim-Eduth, A Psalm of *A*
Ps 81:*t* upon Gittith, A Psalm of *A*
Ps 82:*t* A Psalm of *A*
Ps 83:*t* A Song or Psalm of *A*
*3. A Levite family in post-exilic Jerusalem.*
1Chr 9:15 the son of Zichri, the son of *A*
*4. Descendants of Merari.*
1Chr 26:1 the son of Kore, of the sons of *A*
*5. A Persian official.*
Neh 2:8 a letter unto *A* the keeper of the

**ASAPH'S** *(a'-safs) Refers to Asaph 1.*
Is 36:3 and Joah, *A* son, the recorder

**ASAREEL** *(a-sar'-e-el) A son of Jehaleleel.*
1Chr 4:16 Ziph, and Ziphah, Tiria, and *A*

**ASARELAH** *(as-a-re'-lah)* See JESHABELAH. *A son of a musician of David.*
1Chr 25:2 and Joseph, and Nethaniah, and *A*

**ASA'S** *(a'-sahz) Refers to Asa 1.*
1Kin 15:14 nevertheless *A* heart was perfect

**ASCEND**
Josh 6:5 the people shall *a* up every man
Ps 24:3 Who shall *a* into the hill of the
Ps 135:7 He causeth the vapours to *a* from
Ps 139:8 If I *a* up into heaven, thou art
Is 14:13 I will *a* into heaven, I will
Jer 10:13 he causeth the vapors to *a* from
Jer 51:16 he causeth the vapors to *a* from
Eze 38:9 Thou shalt *a* and come like a storm
Jn 6:62 of man *a* up where he was before
Jn 20:17 I *a* unto my Father, and your
Rom 10:6 heart, Who shall *a* into heaven
Rev 17:8 shall *a* out of the bottomless pit

**ASCENDED**
Ex 19:18 the smoke thereof *a* as the smoke
Num 13:22 they *a* by the south, and came unto
Josh 8:20 smoke of the city *a* up to heaven
Josh 10:7 So Joshua *a* from Gilgal, he, and
Josh 15:3 *a* up on the south side unto
Judg 13:20 LORD *a* in the flame of the altar
Judg 20:40 flame of the city *a* up to heaven
Ps 68:18 Thou hast *a* on high, thou hast
Prov 30:4 Who hath *a* up into heaven, or
Jn 3:13 no man hath *a* up to heaven, but
Jn 20:17 for I am not yet *a* to my Father
Acts 2:34 David is not *a* into the heavens
Acts 25:1 after three days he *a* from
Eph 4:8 When he *a* up on high, he led
Eph 4:10 that *a* up far above all heavens
Rev 8:4 *a* up before God out of the
Rev 11:12 they *a* up to heaven in a cloud

**ASCENDING**
Gen 28:12 and behold the angels of God *a*
Lk 19:28 he went before, *a* up to Jerusalem
Jn 1:51 open, and the angels of God *a*
Rev 7:2 saw another angel *a* from the east

**ASCENT**
Num 34:4 the south to the *a* of Akrabbim
2Sa 15:30 went up by the *a* of mount Olivet
1Kin 10:5 his *a* by which he went up unto
2Chr 9:4 his *a* by which he went up into

**ASCRIBE**
Deut 32:3 *a* ye greatness unto our God
Job 36:3 will *a* righteousness to my Maker
Ps 68:34 *A* ye strength unto God

**ASENATH** *(as'-e-nath) A great-grandson of Solomon.*
Gen 41:45 he gave him to wife *A* the
Gen 41:50 came, which *A* the daughter of
Gen 46:20 Ephraim, which *A* the daughter of

**ASER** *(a'-sur)* See ASHER. *Greek form of Asher.*
Lk 2:36 of Phanuel, of the tribe of *A*
Rev 7:6 Of the tribe of *A* were sealed

**ASHAMED**
Gen 2:25 man and his wife, and were not *a*
Num 12:14 should she not be *a* seven days
Judg 3:25 And they tarried till they were *a*
2Sa 10:5 because the men were greatly *a*
2Sa 19:3 as people being *a* steal away when
2Kin 2:17 when they urged him till he was *a*
2Kin 8:11 stedfastly, until he was *a*
1Chr 19:5 for the men were greatly *a*
2Chr 30:15 the priests and the Levites were *a*
Ezr 8:22 For I was *a* to require of the
Ezr 9:6 And said, O my God, I am *a*
Job 6:20 they came thither, and were *a*
Job 11:3 mockest, shall no man make thee *a*
Job 19:3 ye are not *a* that ye make
Ps 6:10 Let all mine enemies be *a*
Ps 25:2 let me not be *a*, let not mine
Ps 25:20 let me not be *a*
Ps 31:1 let me never be *a*
Ps 31:17 Let me not be *a*, O LORD
Ps 34:5 and their faces were not *a*
Ps 35:26 Let them be *a* and brought to
Ps 37:19 shall not be *a* in the evil time
Ps 40:14 Let them be *a* and confounded
Ps 69:6 GOD of hosts, be *a* for my sake
Ps 70:2 Let them be *a* and confounded that
Ps 74:21 O let not the oppressed return *a*
Ps 86:17 which hate me may see it, and be *a*
Ps 109:28 when they arise, let them be *a*
Ps 119:6 Then shall I not be *a*, when I
Ps 119:46 before kings, and will not be *a*
Ps 119:78 Let the proud be *a*
Ps 119:80 that I be not *a*
Ps 119:116 and let me not be *a* of my hope
Ps 127:5 they shall not be *a*, but they
Prov 12:4 but she that maketh *a* is as
Is 1:29 For they shall be *a* of the oaks
Is 20:5 *a* of Ethiopia their expectation,
Is 24:23 shall be confounded, and the sun *a*
Is 26:11 be *a* for their envy at the people
Is 29:22 Jacob, Jacob shall not now be *a*
Is 30:5 They were all *a* of a people that
Is 33:9 Lebanon is *a* and hewn down
Is 41:11 incensed against thee shall be *a*
Is 42:17 back, they shall be greatly *a*
Is 44:9 that they may be *a*
Is 44:11 all his fellows shall be *a*
Is 45:16 They shall be *a*, and also
Is 45:24 incensed against him shall be *a*
Is 49:23 shall not be *a* that wait for me
Is 50:7 and I know that I shall not be *a*
Is 54:4 for thou shalt not be *a*
Is 65:13 shall rejoice, but ye shall be *a*
Is 66:5 to your joy, and they shall be *a*
Jer 2:26 As the thief is *a* when he is
Jer 2:36 thou also shalt be *a* of Egypt
Jer 2:36 as thou wast *a* of Assyria
Jer 3:3 forehead, thou refusedst to be *a*
Jer 6:15 Were they *a* when they had
Jer 8:9 The wise men are *a*, they are
Jer 8:12 Were they *a* when they had
Jer 12:13 they shall be *a* of your revenues
Jer 14:3 they were *a* and confounded, and
Jer 15:9 she hath been *a* and confounded
Jer 17:13 all that forsake thee shall be *a*
Jer 20:11 they shall be greatly *a*
Jer 22:22 surely then shalt thou be *a*
Jer 31:19 I was *a*, yea, even confounded,
Jer 48:13 And Moab shall be *a* of Chemosh
Jer 48:13 as the house of Israel was *a* of
Jer 50:12 she that bare you shall be *a*
Eze 16:27 which are *a* of thy lewd way
Eze 16:61 shalt remember thy ways, and be *a*
Eze 32:30 terror they are *a* of their might
Eze 36:32 be *a* and confounded for your own
Eze 43:10 that they may be *a* of their
Eze 43:11 if they be *a* of all that they
Hos 4:19 they shall be *a* because of their
Hos 10:6 Israel shall be *a* of his own
Joel 1:11 Be ye *a*, O ye husbandmen
Joel 2:26 and my people shall never be *a*
Joel 2:27 and my people shall never be *a*
Mic 3:7 Then shall the seers be *a*
Zeph 3:11 thou not be *a* for all thy doings
Zec 9:5 for her expectation shall be *a*
Zec 13:4 be *a* every one of his vision
Mk 8:38 therefore shall be *a* of me
Lk 9:26 For whosoever shall be *a* of me
Lk 13:17 all his adversaries were *a*
Lk 16:3 to beg I am *a*
Rom 1:16 For I am not *a* of the gospel of
Rom 5:5 And hope maketh not *a*
Rom 6:21 those things whereof ye are now *a*
Rom 9:33 believeth on him shall not be *a*
Rom 10:11 believeth on him shall not be *a*
2Cor 7:14 thing to him of you, I am not *a*
2Cor 9:4 ye) should be *a* in this same
2Cor 10:8 destruction, I should not be *a*
Phil 1:20 that in nothing I shall be *a*
2Th 3:14 with him, that he may be *a*
2Ti 1:8 Be not thou therefore *a* of the
2Ti 1:12 nevertheless I am not *a*
2Ti 1:16 me, and was not *a* of my chain
2Ti 2:15 workman that needeth not to be *a*
Titus 2:8 is of the contrary part may be *a*
Heb 2:11 he is not *a* to call them brethren
Heb 11:16 wherefore God is not *a* to be
1Pet 3:16 they may be *a* that falsely accuse
1Pet 4:16 as a Christian, let him not be *a*
1Jn 2:28 not be *a* before him at his coming

**ASHAN** *(a'-shan)* See CHOR-ASHAN. *A Levitical city in Judah.*
Josh 15:42 Libnah, and Ether, and *A*,
Josh 19:7 Ain, Remmon, and Ether, and *A*
1Chr 4:32 and Ain, Rimmon, and Tochen, and *A*
1Chr 6:59 And *A* with her suburbs, and

**ASHBEA** *(ash'-be-ah) Descendants of Shelah.*
1Chr 4:21 fine linen, of the house of *A*

**ASHBEL** *(ash'-bel)* See ASHBELITES. *A son of Benjamin.*
Gen 46:21 were Belah, and Becher, and *A*
Num 26:38 of *A*, the family of the
1Chr 8:1 *A* the second, and Aharah the third

**ASHBELITES** *(ash'-bel-ites) Descendants of Ashbel.*
Num 26:38 of Ashbel, the family of the *A*

**ASHCHENAZ** *(ash'-ke-naz)* See ASHKENAZ.
*1. A son of Gomer.*
1Chr 1:6 *A*, and Riphath, and Togarmah
*2. A tribe near Armenia.*
Jer 51:27 kingdoms of Ararat, Minni, and *A*

**ASHDOD** *(ash'-dod)* See ASHDODITES, AZOTUS. *A Philistine city.*
Josh 11:22 only in Gaza, in Gath, and in *A*
Josh 15:46 unto the sea, all that lay near *A*
Josh 15:47 *A* with her towns and her villages,
1Sa 5:1 brought it from Eben-ezer unto *A*
1Sa 5:3 when they of *A* arose early on the
1Sa 5:5 of Dagon in *A* unto this day
1Sa 5:7 when the men of *A* saw that it was
1Sa 6:17 for *A* one, for Gaza one, for
2Chr 26:6 wall of Jabneh, and the wall of *A*
Neh 13:23 Jews that had married wives of *A*
Is 20:1 sent him,) and fought against *A*
Jer 25:20 and Ekron, and the remnant of *A*
Amos 1:8 cut off the inhabitant from *A*
Amos 3:9 Publish in the palaces at *A*
Zeph 2:4 shall drive out *A* at the noonday
Zec 9:6 And a bastard shall dwell in *A*

**ASHDODITES** *(ash'-dod-ites)* See ASHDOTHITES. *Inhabitants of Ashdod.*
Neh 4:7 and the Ammonites, and the *A*

**ASHDOTHITES** *(ash'-doth-ites)* See ASHDODITES. *Same as Ashdodites.*
Josh 13:3 the Gazathites, and the *A*, the

**ASHDOTH-PISGAH** *(ash'-doth-piz'-gah) The eastern slope of Mt. Pisgah.*
Deut 3:17 the salt sea, under *A* eastward
Josh 12:3 and from the south, under *A*
Josh 13:20 And Beth-peor, and *A*, and

**ASHER** *(ash'-ur)* See ASER, ASHERITES.
*1. A son of Jacob by Zilpah.*
Gen 30:13 and she called his name *A*
Gen 35:26 Gad, and *A*: these are the sons
Gen 46:17 And the sons of *A*
Gen 49:20 Out of *A* his bread shall be fat,
Ex 1:4 Dan, and Naphtali, Gad, and *A*
Num 26:46 of the daughter of *A* was Sarah
1Chr 2:2 and Benjamin, Naphtali, Gad, and *A*
1Chr 7:30 The sons of *A*; Imnah, and Isuah
1Chr 7:40 All these were the children of *A*
*2. A tribe descended from Asher 1.*
Num 1:13 Of *A*
Num 1:40 Of the children of *A*, by their

Num 2:27 of *A* shall be Pagiel the son of
Num 7:72 prince of the children of *A*
Num 10:26 of *A* was Pagiel the son of Ocran
Num 13:13 Of the tribe of *A*, Sethur the son
Num 26:44 Of the children of *A* after their
Num 26:47 of *A* according to those that were
Num 34:27 of the tribe of the children of *A*
Deut 27:13 Reuben, Gad, and *A*, and Zebulun,
Deut 33:24 of *A* he said, Let Asher be
Josh 19:34 reacheth to *A* on the west side,
Josh 21:6 and out of the tribe of *A*
Josh 21:30 And out of the tribe of *A*, Mishal
Judg 1:31 Neither did *A* drive out the
Judg 5:17 *A* continued on the sea shore, and
Judg 6:35 and he sent messengers unto *A*
Judg 7:23 out of Naphtali, and out of *A*
1Chr 6:62 and out of the tribe of *A*
1Chr 6:74 And out of the tribe of *A*
1Chr 12:36 And of *A*, such as went forth to
2Chr 30:11 Nevertheless divers of *A* and
Eze 48:2 the west side, a portion for *A*
Eze 48:34 one gate of Gad, one gate of *A*

*3. A town in Manasseh.*

Josh 17:7 Manasseh was from *A* to Michmethah
Josh 17:10 met together in *A* on the north
Josh 17:11 in *A* Beth-shean and her towns
1Kin 4:16 Baanah the son of Hushai was in *A*

**ASHERITES** *(ash'-ur-ites) Same as Asher 2.*

Judg 1:32 But the *A* dwelt among the

**ASHES**

Gen 18:27 the Lord, which am but dust and *a*
Ex 9:8 you handfuls of *a* of the furnace
Ex 9:10 they took *a* of the furnace, and
Ex 27:3 make his pans to receive his *a*
Lev 1:16 east part, by the place of the *a*
Lev 4:12 where the *a* are poured out, and
Lev 6:10 take up the *a* which the fire hath
Lev 6:11 carry forth the *a* without the
Num 4:13 take away the *a* from the altar
Num 19:9 gather up the *a* of the heifer
Num 19:17 of the *a* of the burnt heifer of
2Sa 13:19 Tamar put *a* on her head, and rent
1Kin 13:3 the *a* that are upon it shall be
1Kin 13:5 the *a* poured out from the altar,
1Kin 20:38 himself with *a* upon his face
1Kin 20:41 took the *a* away from his face
2Kin 23:4 carried the *a* of them unto
Est 4:1 and put on sackcloth with *a*
Est 4:3 and many lay in sackcloth and *a*
Job 2:8 and he sat down among the *a*
Job 13:12 Your remembrances are like unto *a*
Job 30:19 and I am become like dust and *a*
Job 42:6 myself, and repent in dust and *a*
Ps 102:9 For I have eaten *a* like bread
Ps 147:16 scattereth the hoar frost like *a*
Is 44:20 He feedeth on *a*
Is 58:5 spread sackcloth and *a* under him
Is 61:3 to give unto them beauty for *a*
Jer 6:26 sackcloth, and wallow thyself in *a*
Jer 25:34 and wallow yourselves in the *a*
Jer 31:40 of the dead bodies, and of the *a*
Lam 3:16 stones, he hath covered me with *a*
Eze 27:30 shall wallow themselves in the *a*
Eze 28:18 I will bring thee to *a* upon the
Dan 9:3 with fasting, and sackcloth, and *a*
Jonah 3:6 him with sackcloth, and sat in *a*
Mal 4:3 for they shall be *a* under the
Mt 11:21 long ago in sackcloth and *a*
Lk 10:13 sitting in sackcloth and *a*
Heb 9:13 the *a* of an heifer sprinkling the
2Pet 2:6 Gomorrah into *a* condemned them

**ASHIMA** *(ash'-im-ah) An idol of Hamath.*

2Kin 17:30 and the men of Hamath made *A*

**ASHKELON** *(ash'-ke-lon)* See ASKELON, ESHKALONITES. *A Philistine city.*

Judg 14:19 upon him, and he went down to *A*
Jer 25:20 the land of the Philistines, and *A*
Jer 47:5 *A* is cut off with the remnant of
Amos 1:8 that holdeth the sceptre from *A*
Zeph 2:4 be forsaken, and *A* a desolation
Zeph 2:7 in the houses of *A* shall they lie
Zec 9:5 *A* shall see it, and fear

**ASHKENAZ** *(ash'-ke-naz)* See ASHCHENAZ. *A son of Gomer.*

Gen 10:3 *A*, and Riphath, and Togarmah

**ASHNAH** *(ash'-nah)*

*1. A town in Judah near Dan.*

Josh 15:33 valley, Eshtaol, and Zoreah, and *A*

*2. A town in Judah on the plains.*

Josh 15:43 And Jiphtah, and *A*, and Nezib,

**ASHPENAZ** *(ash'-pe-naz) A prince of the eunuchs under Nebuchadnezzar.*

Dan 1:3 the king spake unto *A* the master

**ASHRIEL** *(ash'-re-el)* See ASRIEL. *A grandson of Manasseh.*

1Chr 7:14 *A*, whom she bare

**ASHTAROTH** *(ash'-ta-roth)* See ASHTERATHITE, ASHTEROTH, ASTORETH, ASTAROTH, BEESHTERAH.

*1. A god of the Philistines, Phoenicians, and Zidonians.*

Judg 2:13 the LORD, and served Baal and *A*
Judg 10:6 the LORD, and served Baalim, and *A*
1Sa 7:3 *A* from among you, and prepare your
1Sa 7:4 Israel did put away Baalim and *A*
1Sa 12:10 LORD, and have served Baalim and *A*
1Sa 31:10 put his armour in the house of *A*

*2. A city in Bashan.*

Josh 9:10 Og king of Bashan, which was at *A*
Josh 12:4 of the giants, that dwelt at *A*
Josh 13:12 Og in Bashan, which reigned in *A*
Josh 13:31 And half Gilead, and *A*, and Edrei,

*3. A Levitical city in Manasseh.*

1Chr 6:71 suburbs, and *A* with her suburbs

**ASHTERATHITE** *(ash'-ter-a-thite) Family name of Uzziah.*

1Chr 11:44 Uzzia the *A*, Shama and Jehiel the

**ASHTEROTH** *(ash'-te-roth) A city in Og.*

Gen 14:5 smote the Rephaims in *A* Karnaim

**ASHTORETH** *(ash'-to-reth)* See ASHTAROTH. *Same as Ashtaroth 1.*

1Kin 11:5 For Solomon went after *A* the
1Kin 11:33 have worshipped *A* the goddess of
2Kin 23:13 for *A* the abomination of the

**ASHUR** *(ash'-ur)* See ASHURITES, ASSHUR, ASSUR, ASSYRIA. *A son of Hezvon.*

1Chr 2:24 bare him *A* the father of Tekoa
1Chr 4:5 *A* the father of Tekoa had two

**ASHURITES** *(ash'-ur-ites)* See ASSHURIM. *A tribe in the plain of Esdraelon.*

2Sa 2:9 king over Gilead, and over the *A*
Eze 27:6 the company of the *A* have made

**ASHVATH** *(ash'-vath) A descendant of Asher.*

1Chr 7:33 Pasach, and Bimhal, and *A*

**ASIA** *(a'-she-ah)*

*1. A Roman province.*

Acts 2:9 and Cappadocia, in Pontus, and *A*
Acts 6:9 and of them of Cilicia and of *A*
Acts 16:6 Ghost to preach the word in *A*
Acts 19:10 in *A* heard the word of the Lord
Acts 19:22 himself stayed in *A* for a season
Acts 19:31 And certain of the chief of *A*
Acts 20:4 him into *A* Sopater of Berea
Acts 20:4 and of *A*, Tychicus and Trophimus
Acts 20:16 he would not spend the time in *A*
Acts 20:18 the first day that I came into *A*
1Cor 16:19 The churches of *A* salute you
2Cor 1:8 our trouble which came to us in *A*
2Ti 1:15 are in *A* be turned away from me
1Pet 1:1 Pontus, Galatia, Cappadocia, *A*
Rev 1:4 the seven churches which are in *A*
Rev 1:11 the seven churches which are in *A*

*2. Another name for Asia Minor.*

Acts 19:26 but almost throughout all *A*
Acts 19:27 should be destroyed, whom all *A*
Acts 21:27 ended, the Jews which were of *A*
Acts 24:18 Whereupon certain Jews from *A*
Acts 27:2 to sail by the coasts of *A*

**ASIEL** *(a'-se'-el) Grandfather of Jeha.*

1Chr 4:35 the son of Seraiah, the son of *A*

**ASKELON** *(as'-ke-lon)* See ASHKELON. *A Philistine city.*

Judg 1:18 *A* with the coast thereof, and
1Sa 6:17 one, for Gaza one, for *A* one
2Sa 1:20 it not in the streets of *A*

**ASLEEP**

Judg 4:21 for he was fast *a* and weary
1Sa 26:12 for they were all *a*
Song 7:9 lips of those that are *a* to speak
Jonah 1:5 and he lay, and was fast *a*
Mt 8:24 but he was *a*
Mt 26:40 the disciples, and findeth them *a*
Mt 26:43 And he came and found them *a* again
Mk 4:38 part of the ship, *a* on a pillow
Mk 14:40 returned, he found them *a* again
Lk 8:23 But as they sailed he fell *a*
Acts 7:60 when he had said this, he fell *a*
1Cor 15:6 present, but some are fallen *a*
1Cor 15:18 fallen *a* in Christ are perished
1Th 4:13 concerning them which are *a*
1Th 4:15 not prevent them which are *a*
2Pet 3:4 for since the fathers fell *a*

**ASNAH** *(as'-nah) A family of exiles.*

Ezr 2:50 The children of *A*, the children

**ASNAPPER** *(as-nap'-pur) An Assyrian king.*

Ezr 4:10 noble *A* brought over, and set in

**ASP**

Is 11:8 shall play on the hole of the *a*

**ASPATHA** *(as'-pa-thah) A son of Haman.*

Est 9:7 and Dalphon, and *A*

**ASPS**

Deut 32:33 dragons, and the cruel venom of *a*
Job 20:14 it is the gall of *a* within him
Job 20:16 He shall suck the poison of *a*
Rom 3:13 the poison of *a* is under their

**ASRIEL** *(as'-re-el)* See ASHRIEL, ASRIELITES. *A grandson of Manasseh.*

Num 26:31 And of *A*, the family of the
Josh 17:2 Helek, and for the children of *A*

**ASRIELITES** *(as'-re-el-ites) Descendants of Asriel.*

Num 26:31 And of Asriel, the family of the *A*

**ASS**

Gen 22:3 in the morning, and saddled his *a*
Gen 22:5 men, Abide ye here with the *a*
Gen 42:27 give his *a* provender in the inn
Gen 44:13 clothes, and laded every man his *a*
Gen 49:14 Issachar is a strong *a* couching
Ex 4:20 his sons, and set them upon an *a*
Ex 13:13 every firstling of an *a* thou
Ex 20:17 nor his ox, nor his *a*, nor any
Ex 21:33 an ox or an *a* fall therein
Ex 22:4 alive, whether it be ox, or *a*
Ex 22:9 whether it be for ox, for *a*
Ex 23:4 enemy's ox or his *a* going astray
Ex 23:12 thine *a* may rest, and the son of
Ex 34:20 But the firstling of an *a* thou
Num 16:15 I have not taken one *a* from them
Num 22:21 in the morning, and saddled his *a*
Num 22:25 when the *a* saw the angel of the
Num 22:27 when the *a* saw the angel of the
Num 22:30 Am not I thine *a*,
Num 22:32 smitten thine *a* these three times
Deut 5:14 nor thine ox, nor thine *a*
Deut 5:21 his maidservant, his ox, or his *a*
Deut 22:3 manner shalt thou do with his *a*
Deut 22:10 plow with an ox and an *a* together
Deut 28:31 thine *a* shall be violently taken
Josh 6:21 and old, and ox, and sheep, and *a*
Josh 15:18 and she lighted off her *a*
Judg 1:14 and she lighted from off her *a*
Judg 6:4 neither sheep, nor ox, nor *a*
Judg 10:4 sons that rode on thirty *a* colts
Judg 12:14 rode on threescore and ten *a* colts
Judg 15:15 And he found a new jawbone of an *a*
Judg 19:28 the man took her up upon an *a*
1Sa 12:3 or whose *a* have I taken
1Sa 15:3 suckling, ox and sheep, camel and *a*
1Sa 16:20 Jesse took an *a* laden with bread,
1Sa 25:20 it was so, as she rode on the *a*
1Sa 25:23 she hasted, and lighted off the *a*
1Sa 25:42 and arose, and rode upon an *a*
2Sa 17:23 not followed, he saddled his *a*
2Sa 19:26 said, I will saddle me an *a*
1Kin 2:40 And Shimei arose, and saddled his *a*
1Kin 13:13 unto his sons, Saddle me the *a*
1Kin 13:23 that he saddled for him the *a*
1Kin 13:24 the *a* stood by it, the lion also
1Kin 13:27 his sons, saying, Saddle me the *a*
1Kin 13:28 carcase cast in the way, and the *a*
2Kin 4:24 Then she saddled an *a*, and said to
Job 6:5 Doth the wild *a* bray when he hath
Job 24:3 away the *a* of the fatherless
Job 39:5 Who hath sent out the wild *a* free
Prov 26:3 for the horse, a bridle for the *a*
Is 1:3 owner, and the *a* his master's crib

Is 32:20 the feet of the ox and the *a*
Jer 2:24 A wild *a* used to the wilderness,
Jer 22:19 be buried with the burial of an *a*
Hos 8:9 a wild *a* alone by himself
Zec 9:9 lowly, and riding upon an *a*
Zec 9:9 and upon a colt the foal of an *a*
Zec 14:15 mule, of the camel, and of the *a*
Mt 21:2 ye shall find an *a* tied, and a
Mt 21:5 thee, meek, and sitting upon an *a*
Mt 21:5 and a colt the foal of an *a*
Mt 21:7 And brought the *a*, and the colt, and
Lk 13:15 his ox or his *a* from the stall
Lk 14:5 an *a* or an ox fallen into a pit
Jn 12:14 when he had found a young *a*
2Pet 2:16 the dumb *a* speaking with man's

**ASSAULT**
Est 8:11 and province that would *a* them
Acts 14:5 when there was an *a* made both of

**ASSAULTED**
Acts 17:5 *a* the house of Jason, and sought

**ASSAY**
Job 4:2 If we *a* to commune with thee,

**ASSAYED**
Deut 4:34 Or hath God *a* to go and take him a
1Sa 17:39 upon his armour, and he *a* to go
Acts 9:26 he *a* to join himself to the
Acts 16:7 they *a* to go into Bithynia

**ASSEMBLE**
Num 10:3 them, all the assembly shall *a*
2Sa 20:4 *A* me the men of Judah within
2Sa 20:5 Amasa went to *a* the men of Judah
Is 11:12 shall *a* the outcasts of Israel,
Is 45:20 *A* yourselves and come
Is 48:14 All ye, *a* yourselves, and hear
Jer 4:5 *A* yourselves, and let us go into
Jer 8:14 *a* yourselves, and let us enter
Jer 12:9 *a* all the beasts of the field,
Jer 21:4 I will *a* them into the midst of
Eze 11:17 *a* you out of the countries where
Eze 39:17 the field, *A* yourselves, and come
Dan 11:10 shall *a* a multitude of great
Hos 7:14 they *a* themselves for corn and
Joel 2:16 *a* the elders, gather the children
Joel 3:11 *A* yourselves, and come, all ye
Amos 3:9 *A* yourselves upon the mountains
Mic 2:12 I will surely *a*, O Jacob, all of
Mic 4:6 will I *a* her that halteth, and I
Zeph 3:8 that I may *a* the kingdoms, to

**ASSEMBLED**
Ex 38:8 which *a* at the door of the
Num 1:18 they *a* all the congregation
Josh 18:1 of Israel *a* together at Shiloh
Judg 10:17 of Israel *a* themselves together
1Sa 2:22 they lay with the women that *a* at
1Sa 14:20 that were with him *a* themselves
1Kin 8:1 Then Solomon *a* the elders of
1Kin 8:5 of Israel, that were *a* unto him
1Kin 12:21 he *a* all the house of Judah, with
1Chr 15:4 David *a* the children of Aaron, and
1Chr 28:1 David *a* all the princes of Israel
2Chr 5:2 Then Solomon *a* the elders of
2Chr 5:6 of Israel that were *a* unto him
2Chr 20:26 And on the fourth day they *a*
2Chr 30:13 there *a* at Jerusalem much people
Ezr 9:4 Then were *a* unto me every one
Ezr 10:1 there *a* unto him out of Israel a
Neh 9:1 of Israel were *a* with fasting
Est 9:18 the Jews that were at Shushan *a*
Ps 48:4 For, lo, the kings were *a*
Is 43:9 together, and let the people be *a*
Jer 5:7 *a* themselves by troops in the
Eze 38:7 thy company that are *a* unto thee
Dan 6:6 princes *a* together to the king,
Dan 6:11 Then these men *a*, and found Daniel
Dan 6:15 Then these men *a* unto the king
Mt 26:3 Then *a* together the chief priests
Mt 26:57 the scribes and the elders were *a*
Mt 28:12 when they were *a* with the elders,
Mk 14:53 with him were *a* all the chief
Jn 20:19 were *a* for fear of the Jews
Acts 1:4 being *a* together with them,
Acts 4:31 shaken where they were *a* together
Acts 11:26 to pass, that a whole year they *a*
Acts 15:25 being *a* with one accord, to send

**ASSEMBLIES**
Ps 86:14 the *a* of violent men have sought
Eccl 12:11 fastened by the masters of *a*
Is 1:13 and sabbaths, the calling of *a*
Is 4:5 of mount Zion, and upon her *a*
Eze 44:24 laws and my statutes in all mine *a*
Amos 5:21 I will not smell in your solemn *a*

**ASSEMBLY**
Gen 49:6 unto their *a*, mine honour, be not
Ex 12:6 the whole *a* of the congregation
Ex 16:3 to kill this whole *a* with hunger
Lev 4:13 be hid from the eyes of the *a*
Lev 8:4 the *a* was gathered together unto
Lev 23:36 it is a solemn *a*
Num 8:9 whole *a* of the children of Israel
Num 10:2 use them for the calling of the *a*
Num 14:5 the *a* of the congregation of the
Num 16:2 hundred and fifty princes of the *a*
Num 20:6 went from the presence of the *a*
Num 20:8 and gather thou the *a* together
Num 29:35 day ye shall have a solemn *a*
Deut 5:22 the LORD spake unto all your *a* in
Deut 9:10 of the fire in the day of the *a*
Deut 10:4 of the fire in the day of the *a*
Deut 16:8 be a solemn *a* to the LORD thy God
Deut 18:16 God in Horeb in the day of the *a*
Judg 20:2 in the *a* of the people of God
Judg 21:8 camp from Jabesh-gilead to the *a*
1Sa 17:47 all this *a* shall know that the
2Kin 10:20 Proclaim a solemn *a* for Baal
2Chr 7:9 eighth day they made a solemn *a*
2Chr 30:23 the whole *a* took counsel to keep
Neh 5:7 And I set a great *a* against them
Neh 8:18 on the eighth day was a solemn *a*
Ps 22:16 the *a* of the wicked have inclosed
Ps 89:7 be feared in the *a* of the saints
Ps 107:32 praise him in the *a* of the elders
Ps 111:1 in the *a* of the upright, and in
Prov 5:14 midst of the congregation and *a*
Jer 6:11 upon the *a* of young men together
Jer 9:2 an *a* of treacherous men
Jer 15:17 I sat not in the *a* of the mockers
Jer 26:17 spake to all the *a* of the people
Jer 50:9 to come up against Babylon an *a*
Lam 1:15 he hath called an *a* against me to
Lam 2:6 destroyed his places of the *a*
Eze 13:9 not be in the *a* of my people
Eze 23:24 with an *a* of people, which shall
Joel 1:14 ye a fast, call a solemn *a*
Joel 2:15 sanctify a fast, call a solemn *a*
Zeph 3:18 are sorrowful for the solemn *a*
Acts 19:32 for the *a* was confused
Acts 19:39 shall be determined in a lawful *a*
Acts 19:41 thus spoken, he dismissed the *a*
Heb 12:23 To the general *a* and church of the
Jas 2:2 your *a* a man with a gold ring

**ASSES**
Gen 12:16 and he had sheep, and oxen, and he *a*
Gen 24:35 and maidservants, and camels, and *a*
Gen 30:43 and menservants, and camels, and *a*
Gen 32:5 And I have oxen, and *a*, flocks, and
Gen 32:15 kine, and ten bulls, twenty she *a*
Gen 34:28 sheep, and their oxen, and their *a*
Gen 36:24 as he fed the *a* of Zibeon his
Gen 42:26 they laded their *a* with the corn
Gen 43:18 and take us for bondmen, and our *a*
Gen 43:24 and he gave their *a* provender
Gen 44:3 were sent away, they and their *a*
Gen 45:23 ten *a* laden with the good things
Gen 47:17 cattle of the herds, and for the *a*
Ex 9:3 upon the horses, upon the *a*
Num 31:28 and of the beeves, and of the *a*
Num 31:30 persons, of the beeves, of the *a*
Num 31:34 And threescore and one thousand *a*
Num 31:39 the *a* were thirty thousand and
Num 31:45 And thirty thousand *a* and five
Josh 7:24 daughters, and his oxen, and his *a*
Josh 9:4 and took old sacks upon their *a*
Judg 5:10 Speak, ye that ride on white *a*
Judg 19:3 with him, and a couple of *a*
Judg 19:10 there were with him two *a* saddled
Judg 19:19 both straw and provender for our *a*
Judg 19:21 and gave provender unto the *a*
1Sa 8:16 goodliest young men, and your *a*
1Sa 9:3 the *a* of Kish Saul's father were
1Sa 9:20 as for thine *a* that were lost
1Sa 10:2 The *a* which thou wentest to seek
1Sa 10:14 And he said, To seek the *a*
1Sa 10:16 us plainly that the *a* were found
1Sa 22:19 and sucklings, and oxen, and *a*
1Sa 25:18 cakes of figs, and laid them on *a*
1Sa 27:9 the sheep, and the oxen, and the *a*
2Sa 16:1 him, with a couple of *a* saddled
2Kin 4:22 of the young men, and one of the *a*
2Kin 7:7 and their horses, and their *a*
2Kin 7:10 *a* tied, and the tents as they were
1Chr 5:21 of *a* two thousand, and of men an
1Chr 12:40 and Naphtali, brought bread on *a*
1Chr 27:30 over the *a* was Jehdeiah the
2Chr 28:15 all the feeble of them upon *a*
Ezr 2:67 their *a*, six thousand seven
Neh 7:69 seven hundred and twenty *a*
Neh 13:15 bringing in sheaves, and lading *a*
Job 1:3 of oxen, and five hundred she *a*
Job 1:14 the *a* feeding beside them
Job 24:5 as wild *a* in the desert, go they
Job 42:12 yoke of oxen, and a thousand she *a*
Ps 104:11 the wild *a* quench their thirst
Is 21:7 of horsemen, a chariot of *a*
Is 30:6 upon the shoulders of young *a*
Is 30:24 the young *a* that ear the ground
Is 32:14 dens for ever, a joy of wild *a*
Jer 14:6 the wild *a* did stand in the high
Eze 23:20 whose flesh is as the flesh of *a*
Dan 5:21 his dwelling was with the wild *a*

**ASSHUR** *(ash'-ur)* See ASHUR, ASSUR, ASSYRIA.
*1. The builder of Nineveh.*
Gen 10:11 Out of that land went forth *A*
*2. A son of Shem.*
Gen 10:22 Elam, and *A*, and Arphaxad, and Lud,
1Chr 1:17 Elam, and *A*, and Arphaxad, and Lud,
*3. Another name for Assyria.*
Num 24:22 until *A* shall carry thee away
Eze 27:23 Eden, the merchants of Sheba, *A*
Eze 32:22 *A* is there and all her company
Hos 14:3 *A* shall not save us

**ASSHURIM** *(ash'-u-rim)* See ASHURITES. *Descendants of Dedan.*
Gen 25:3 And the sons of Dedan were *A*

**ASSIGNED**
Gen 47:22 had a portion *a* them of Pharaoh
Josh 20:8 they *a* Bezer in the wilderness
2Sa 11:16 that he *a* Uriah unto a place

**ASSIR** *(as'-sur)*
*1. A son of Korah.*
Ex 6:24 *A*, and Elkanah, and Abiasaph
1Chr 6:22 son, Korah his son, *A* his son,
*2. A son of Ebiasaph.*
1Chr 6:23 Ebiasaph his son, and *A* his son,
1Chr 6:37 The son of Tahath, the son of *A*
*3. A son of Jeconiah.*
1Chr 3:17 *A*, Salathiel his son,

**ASSOS** *(as'-sos) A seaport of Mysia in Asia Minor.*
Acts 20:13 before to ship, and sailed unto *A*
Acts 20:14 And when he met with us at *A*

**ASSUR** *(As'-sur)* See ASSHUR. *Same as Asshur 3.*
Ezr 4:2 the days of Esar-haddon king of *A*
Ps 83:8 *A* also is joined with them

**ASSURANCE**
Deut 28:66 and shalt have none *a* of thy life
Is 32:17 quietness and *a* for ever
Acts 17:31 he hath given *a* unto all men
Col 2:2 of the full *a* of understanding
1Th 1:5 in the Holy Ghost, and in much *a*
Heb 6:11 the full *a* of hope unto the end
Heb 10:22 a true heart in full *a* of faith

**ASSURED**
Lev 27:19 unto it, and it shall be *a* to him
Jer 14:13 give you *a* peace in this place
2Ti 3:14 hast learned and hast been *a* of

**ASSUREDLY**
1Sa 28:1 said unto David, Know thou *a*
1Kin 1:13 *A* Solomon thy son shall reign
1Kin 1:17 *A* Solomon thy son shall reign
1Kin 1:30 *A* Solomon thy son shall reign
Jer 32:41 this land *a* with my whole heart
Jer 38:17 If thou wilt *a* go forth unto the
Jer 49:12 drink of the cup have *a* drunken
Acts 2:36 all the house of Israel know *a*
Acts 16:10 *a* gathering that the Lord had

**ASSWAGED**
Gen 8:1 over the earth, and the waters *a*
Job 16:6 Though I speak, my grief is not *a*

**ASSYRIA** *(as-sir'-e-ah)* See ASSHUR, ASSYRIAN. *A Mesopotamian empire.*
Gen 2:14 which goeth toward the east of *A*
Gen 25:18 Egypt, as thou goest toward *A*
2Kin 15:19 Pul the king of *A* came against
2Kin 15:29 came Tiglath-pileser king of *A*
2Kin 16:7 to Tiglath-pileser king of *A*
2Kin 16:10 to meet Tiglath-pileser king of *A*
2Kin 16:18 of the LORD for the king of *A*
2Kin 17:3 him came up Shalmaneser king of *A*
2Kin 17:6 Hoshea the king of *A* took Samaria
2Kin 17:23 their own land to *A* unto this day
2Kin 17:26 they spake to the king of *A*
2Kin 18:7 he rebelled against the king of *A*
2Kin 18:9 king of *A* came up against Samaria
2Kin 18:11 the king of *A* did carry away
2Kin 18:13 did Sennacherib king of *A* come up
2Kin 18:17 And the king of *A* sent Tartan
2Kin 18:19 the great king, the king of *A*
2Kin 18:23 pledges to my lord the king of *A*
2Kin 18:28 of the great king, the king of *A*
2Kin 18:30 into the hand of the king of *A*
2Kin 18:33 out of the hand of the king of *A*
2Kin 19:4 whom the king of *A* his master
2Kin 19:6 the king of *A* have blasphemed me
2Kin 19:8 found the king of *A* warring
2Kin 19:10 into the hand of the king of *A*
2Kin 19:17 the kings of *A* have destroyed the
2Kin 19:20 king of *A* I have heard
2Kin 19:32 the LORD concerning the king of *A*
2Kin 19:36 So Sennacherib king of *A* departed
2Kin 20:6 out of the hand of the king of *A*
2Kin 23:29 king of *A* to the river Euphrates
1Chr 5:6 king of *A* carried away captive
1Chr 5:26 up the spirit of Pul king of *A*
2Chr 28:16 unto the kings of *A* to help him
2Chr 28:20 king of *A* came unto him, and
2Chr 30:6 out of the hand of the kings of *A*
2Chr 32:1 Sennacherib king of *A* came
2Chr 32:4 Why should the kings of *A* come
2Chr 32:7 nor dismayed for the king of *A*
2Chr 32:9 this did Sennacherib king of *A*
2Chr 32:21 in the camp of the king of *A*
2Chr 33:11 of the host of the king of *A*
Ezr 6:22 heart of the king of *A* unto them
Neh 9:32 of the kings of *A* unto this day
Is 7:17 even the king of *A*
Is 7:20 the river, by the king of *A*
Is 8:4 taken away before the king of *A*
Is 8:7 and many, even the king of *A*
Is 10:12 the stout heart of the king of *A*
Is 11:11 which shall be left, from *A*
Is 11:16 which shall be left, from *A*
Is 19:23 be a highway out of Egypt to *A*
Is 20:1 Sargon the king of *A* sent him
Is 20:4 So shall the king of *A* lead away
Is 20:6 be delivered from the king of *A*
Is 27:13 ready to perish in the land of *A*
Is 36:1 king of *A* came up against all the
Is 36:4 the great king, the king of *A*
Is 36:8 thee, to my master the king of *A*
Is 36:13 of the great king, the king of *A*
Is 36:15 into the hand of the king of *A*
Is 36:18 out of the hand of the king of *A*
Is 37:4 whom the king of *A* his master
Is 37:6 the king of *A* have blasphemed me
Is 37:8 found the king of *A* warring
Is 37:10 into the hand of the king of *A*
Is 37:18 the kings of *A* have laid waste
Is 37:21 me against Sennacherib king of *A*
Is 37:33 the LORD concerning the king of *A*
Is 37:37 So Sennacherib king of *A* departed
Is 38:6 out of the hand of the king of *A*
Jer 2:18 hast thou to do in the way of *A*
Jer 2:36 Egypt, as thou wast ashamed of *A*
Jer 50:17 the king of *A* hath devoured him
Eze 23:7 that were the chosen men of *A*
Hos 7:11 they call to Egypt, they go to *A*
Hos 8:9 For they are gone up to *A*
Hos 9:3 shall eat unclean things in *A*
Hos 10:6 *A* for a present to king Jareb
Hos 11:11 and as a dove out of the land of *A*
Mic 5:6 the land of *A* with the sword
Mic 7:12 he shall come even to thee from *A*
Nah 3:18 shepherds slumber, O king of *A*
Zeph 2:13 against the north, and destroy *A*
Zec 10:10 of Egypt, and gather them out of *A*

**ASSYRIAN** *(as-sir'-e'-un)* See ASSYRIANS. *An inhabitant of Assyria.*
Is 10:5 O *A*, the rod of mine anger, and
Is 10:24 in Zion, be not afraid of the *A*
Is 14:25 I will break the *A* in my land
Is 19:23 the *A* shall come into Egypt, and
Is 23:13 til the *A* founded it for them
Is 30:31 LORD shall the *A* be beaten down
Is 31:8 Then shall the *A* fall with the
Is 52:4 the *A* oppressed them without
Eze 31:3 the *A* was a cedar in Lebanon with
Hos 5:13 wound, then went Ephraim to the *A*
Hos 11:5 but the *A* shall be his king,
Mic 5:5 when the *A* shall come into our

**ASSYRIANS** *(as-sir'-e-uns)*
2Kin 19:35 of the *A* an hundred fourscore
Is 19:23 Egyptians shall serve with the *A*
Is 37:36 in the camp of the *A* an hundred
Lam 5:6 to the Egyptians, and to the *A*
Eze 16:28 played the whore also with the *A*
Eze 23:5 lovers, on the *A* her neighbours,
Eze 23:9 lovers, into the hand of the *A*
Eze 23:12 doted upon the *A* her neighbours
Eze 23:23 and Koa, and all the *A* with them
Hos 12:1 do make a covenant with the *A*

**ASTAROTH** *(as'-ta-roth)* See ASHTAROTH. *A city in Bashan.*
Deut 1:4 Bashan, which dwelt at *A* in Edrei

**ASTONIED**
Ezr 9:3 and of my beard, and sat down *a*
Ezr 9:4 I sat *a* until the evening
Job 17:8 Upright men shall be *a* at this
Job 18:20 after him shall be *a* at his day
Is 52:14 As many were *a* at thee
Jer 14:9 Why shouldest thou be as a man *a*
Eze 4:17 be *a* one with another, and consume
Dan 3:24 Nebuchadnezzar the king was *a*
Dan 4:19 was *a* for one hour, and his
Dan 5:9 in him, and his lords were *a*

**ASTONISHED**
Lev 26:32 dwell therein shall be *a* at it
1Kin 9:8 one that passeth by it shall be *a*
Job 21:5 Mark me, and be *a*, and lay your
Job 26:11 tremble, and are *a* at his reproof
Jer 2:12 Be *a*, O ye heavens, at this, and
Jer 4:9 and the priests shall be *a*
Jer 18:16 that passeth thereby shall be *a*
Jer 19:8 that passeth thereby shall be *a*
Jer 49:17 one that goeth by it shall be *a*
Jer 50:13 that goeth by Babylon shall be *a*
Eze 3:15 remained there *a* among them seven
Eze 26:16 at every moment, and be *a* at thee
Eze 27:35 of the isles shall be *a* at thee
Eze 28:19 the people shall be *a* at thee
Dan 8:27 I was *a* at the vision, but none
Mt 7:28 the people were *a* at his doctrine
Mt 13:54 insomuch that they were *a*
Mt 22:33 they were *a* at his doctrine
Mk 1:22 they were *a* at his doctrine
Mk 5:42 And they were *a* with a great
Mk 6:2 and many hearing him were *a*
Mk 7:37 And were beyond measure *a*, saying,
Mk 10:24 the disciples were *a* at his words
Mk 10:26 they were *a* out of measure,
Mk 11:18 the people was *a* at his doctrine
Lk 2:47 him were *a* at his understanding
Lk 4:32 they were *a* at his doctrine
Lk 5:9 For he was *a*, and all that were
Lk 8:56 And her parents were *a*
Lk 24:22 also of our company made us *a*
Acts 9:6 *a* said, Lord, what wilt thou have
Acts 10:45 which believed were *a*, as many as
Acts 12:16 the door, and saw him, they were *a*
Acts 13:12 being *a* at the doctrine of the

**ASTONISHMENT**
Deut 28:28 and blindness, and *a* of heart
Deut 28:37 And thou shalt become an *a*
2Chr 7:21 shall be an *a* to every one that
2Chr 29:8 delivered them to trouble, to *a*
Ps 60:3 made us to drink the wine of *a*
Jer 8:21 *a* hath taken hold on me
Jer 25:9 destroy them, and make them an *a*
Jer 25:11 shall be a desolation, and an *a*
Jer 25:18 to make them a desolation, an *a*
Jer 29:18 the earth, to be a curse, and an *a*
Jer 42:18 shall be an execration, and an *a*
Jer 44:12 shall be an execration, and an *a*
Jer 44:22 your land a desolation, and an *a*
Jer 51:37 dwelling place for dragons, an *a*
Jer 51:41 become an *a* among the nations
Eze 4:16 drink water by measure, and with *a*
Eze 5:15 an *a* unto the nations that are
Eze 12:19 and drink their water with *a*
Eze 23:33 and sorrow, with the cup of *a*
Zec 12:4 I will smite every horse with *a*
Mk 5:42 were astonished with a great *a*

**ASTRAY**
Ex 23:4 enemy's ox or his ass going *a*
Deut 22:1 brother's ox or his sheep go *a*
Ps 58:3 they go *a* as soon as they be born
Ps 119:67 Before I was afflicted I went *a*
Ps 119:176 I have gone *a* like a lost sheep
Prov 5:23 of his folly he shall go *a*
Prov 7:25 her ways, go not *a* in her paths
Prov 28:10 righteous to go *a* in an evil way
Is 53:6 All we like sheep have gone *a*
Jer 50:6 have caused them to go *a*, they
Eze 14:11 Israel may go no more *a* from me
Eze 44:10 far from me, when Israel went *a*
Eze 44:15 children of Israel went *a* from me
Eze 48:11 which went not *a* when the
Mt 18:12 sheep, and one of them be gone *a*
Mt 18:13 ninety and nine which went not *a*
1Pet 2:25 For ye were as sheep going *a*
2Pet 2:15 the right way, and are gone *a*

**ASTROLOGER**
Dan 2:10 such things at any magician, or *a*

**ASTROLOGERS**
Is 47:13 Let now the *a*, the stargazers,
Dan 1:20 *a* that were in all his realm
Dan 2:2 to call the magicians, and the *a*
Dan 2:27 cannot the wise men, the *a*
Dan 4:7 Then came in the magicians, the *a*
Dan 5:7 cried aloud to bring in the *a*
Dan 5:11 made master of the magicians, *a*
Dan 5:15 And now the wise men, the *a*

**ASUNDER**
Lev 1:17 but shall not divide it *a*
Lev 5:8 neck, but shall not divide it *a*
Num 16:31 clave *a* that was under them
2Kin 2:11 of fire, and parted them both *a*
Job 16:12 at ease, but he hath broken me *a*
Ps 2:3 Let us break their bands *a*
Ps 129:4 he hath cut *a* the cords of the
Jer 50:23 of the whole earth cut in *a*
Eze 30:16 great pain, and No shall be rent *a*
Hab 3:6 he beheld, and drove *a* the nations
Zec 11:10 staff, even Beauty, and cut it *a*
Zec 11:14 Then I cut *a* mine other staff,
Mt 19:6 together, let not man put *a*
Mt 24:51 And shall cut him *a*, and appoint
Mk 5:4 chains had been plucked *a* by him
Mk 10:9 together, let not man put *a*
Acts 1:18 he burst *a* in the midst, and all
Acts 15:39 departed in *a* one from the other
Heb 4:12 even to the dividing *a* of soul
Heb 11:37 were stoned, they were sawn *a*

**ASUPPIM** *Storage for temple gods.*
1Chr 26:15 and to his sons the house of *A*
1Chr 26:17 four a day, and toward *A* two

**ASYNCRITUS** *(a-sin'-cri-tus) A Christian acquaintance of Paul.*
Rom 16:14 Salute *A*, Phlegon, Hermas,

**ATAD** *(a'-tad)* See ABEL-MIZRAIM. *A place east of the Jordan.*
Gen 50:10 came to the threshingfloor of *A*
Gen 50:11 the mourning in the floor of *A*

**ATARAH** *(at'-a-rah) A wife of Jerahmeel.*
1Chr 2:26 another wife, whose name was *A*

**ATAROTH** *(at'-a-roth)* See ATAROTH-ADAR, ATROTH.
*1. A city east of the Jordan.*
Num 32:3 *A*, and Dibon, and Jazer, and Nimrah,
Num 32:34 children of Gad built Dibon, and *A*
*2. A city in Ephraim.*
Josh 16:2 unto the borders of Archi to *A*
Josh 16:7 And it went down from Janohah to *A*
*3. A city in Judah.*
1Chr 2:54 and the Netophathites, *A*, the

**ATAROTH-ADAR** *(at'-a-roth-a'-dar)* See ATAROTH-ADDAR. *A city on the border of Benjamin.*
Josh 18:13 and the border descended to *A*

**ATAROTH-ADDAR** *(at'-a-roth-ad'-dar)* See ATAROTH-ADAR. *Same as Ataroth-adar.*
Josh 16:5 on the east side was *A*, unto

**ATE**
Ps 106:28 *a* the sacrifices of the dead
Dan 10:3 I *a* no pleasant bread, neither
Rev 10:10 of the angel's hand, and *a* it up

**ATER** *(a'-tur)*
*1. An ancestor of an exiled family.*
Ezr 2:16 The children of *A* of Hezekiah
Neh 7:21 The children of *A* of Hezekiah
*2. An exiled family who returned under Zerubbabel.*
Ezr 2:42 of Shallum, the children of *A*
Neh 7:45 of Shallum, the children of *A*
*3. An Israelite who sealed the covenant with Nehemiah.*
Neh 10:17 *A*, Hizkijah, Azzur,

**ATHACH** *(a'-thak) A city in Judah.*
1Sa 30:30 and to them which were in *A*

**ATHAIAH** *(ath-a-i'-ah) A son of Uzziah*
Neh 11:4 *A* the son of Uzziah, the son of

**ATHALIAH** *(ath-a-li'-ah)*
*1. Daughter of Jezebel.*
2Kin 8:26 And his mother's name was *A*
2Kin 11:1 when *A* the mother of Ahaziah saw
2Kin 11:13 when *A* heard the noise of the
2Kin 11:20 they slew *A* with the sword beside
2Chr 22:2 also was *A* the daughter of Omri
2Chr 22:10 But when *A* the mother of Ahaziah
2Chr 23:13 Then *A* rent her clothes, and said,
2Chr 23:21 they had slain *A* with the sword
2Chr 24:7 For the sons of *A*, that wicked
*2. A son of Jeroham.*
1Chr 8:26 and Sheahariah, and *A*
*3. Father of Jeshiah.*
Ezr 8:7 Jeshaiah the son of *A*, and with

**ATHENIANS** *(a-the'-ne-uns) Citizens of Athens*
Acts 17:21 (For all the *A* and strangers which

**ATHENS** *(ath'-ens)* See ATHENIANS. *A city in Greece.*
Acts 17:15 conducted Paul brought him unto *A*
Acts 17:22 Mars' hill, and said, Ye men of *A*
Acts 18:1 these things Paul departed from *A*
1Th 3:1 it good to be left at *A* alone
1Th *s* Thessalonians was written from *A*
2Th *s* Thessalonians was written from *A*

**ATHIRST**
Judg 15:18 And he was sore *a*, and called on
Ruth 2:9 and when thou art *a*, go unto the
Mt 25:44 when saw we thee an hungred, or *a*
Rev 21:6 I will give unto him that is *a* of
Rev 22:17 And let him that is *a* come

**ATHLAI** *(ath'-lahee) Married a foreign wife in exile.*
Ezr 10:28 Jehohanan, Hananiah, Zabbai, and *A*

**ATONEMENT**
Ex 29:33 things wherewith the *a* was made
Ex 29:36 bullock for a sin offering for *a*
Ex 29:37 shalt make an *a* for the altar
Ex 30:10 Aaron shall make an *a* upon the
Ex 30:15 to make an *a* for your souls
Ex 32:30 I shall make an *a* for your sin
Lev 1:4 for him to make *a* for him
Lev 4:20 priest shall make an *a* for them
Lev 4:26 the priest shall make an *a* for
Lev 4:31 priest shall make an *a* for him
Lev 4:35 an *a* for his sin that he hath
Lev 5:6 the priest shall make an *a* for
Lev 5:10 the priest shall make an *a* for
Lev 5:13 the priest shall make an *a* for
Lev 5:16 the priest shall make an *a* for
Lev 5:18 make an *a* for him concerning his
Lev 6:7 make an *a* for him before the LORD
Lev 7:7 the priest that maketh *a*
Lev 8:34 to do, to make an *a* for you
Lev 9:7 make an *a* for thyself, and for the
Lev 10:17 to make *a* for them before the
Lev 12:7 the LORD, and make an *a* for her
Lev 14:18 make an *a* for him before the LORD
Lev 14:29 to make an *a* for him before the
Lev 14:31 the priest shall make an *a* for
Lev 14:53 and make an *a* for the house
Lev 15:15 the priest shall make an *a* for
Lev 15:30 the priest shall make an *a* for
Lev 16:6 make an *a* for himself, and for his
Lev 16:10 the LORD, to make an *a* with him
Lev 16:16 he shall make an *a* for the holy
Lev 16:24 make an *a* for himself, and for the
Lev 16:27 in to make *a* in the holy place
Lev 16:30 the priest make an *a* for you
Lev 16:32 father's stead, shall make the *a*
Lev 17:11 altar to make an *a* for your souls
Lev 17:11 that maketh an *a* for the soul
Lev 19:22 the priest shall make an *a* for
Lev 23:27 month there shall be a day of *a*
Lev 25:9 in the day of *a* shall ye make the
Num 5:8 beside the ram of the *a*
Num 6:11 offering, and make an *a* for him
Num 8:12 to make an *a* for the Levites
Num 8:19 to make an *a* for the children of
Num 8:21 Aaron made an *a* for them to
Num 15:25 the priest shall make an *a* for
Num 15:28 the priest shall make an *a* for
Num 16:46 and make an *a* for them
Num 16:47 and made an *a* for the people
Num 25:13 made an *a* for the children of
Num 28:22 offering, to make an *a* for you
Num 28:30 the goats, to make an *a* for you
Num 29:5 offering, to make an *a* for you
Num 29:11 beside the sin offering of *a*
Num 31:50 to make an *a* for our souls before
2Sa 21:3 and wherewith shall I make the *a*
1Chr 6:49 holy, and to make an *a* for Israel
2Chr 29:24 to make an *a* for all Israel
Neh 10:33 offerings to make an *a* for Israel
Rom 5:11 whom we have now received the *a*

**ATROTH** *(a'-troth)* See ATAROTH. *A city in Gad.*
Num 32:35 And *A*, Shophan, and Jaazer, and

**ATTAI** *(at'-tahee)*
*1. A grandson of Sheshan.*
1Chr 2:35 and she bare him *A*
1Chr 2:36 *A* begat Nathan, and Nathan begat
*2. A Gadite in David's army.*
1Chr 12:11 *A* the sixth, Eliel the seventh,
*3. A son of Rehoboam.*
2Chr 11:20 which bare him Abijah, and *A*

**ATTAIN**
Ps 139:6 it is high, I cannot *a* unto it
Prov 1:5 shall *a* unto wise counsels
Eze 46:7 as his hand shall *a* unto, and an
Hos 8:5 it be ere they *a* to innocency
Acts 27:12 any means they might *a* to Phenice
Phil 3:11 If by any means I might *a* unto

**ATTAINED**
Gen 47:9 have not *a* unto the days of the
2Sa 23:19 howbeit he *a* not unto the first
2Sa 23:23 but he *a* not to the first three
1Chr 11:21 howbeit he *a* not to the first
1Chr 11:25 but *a* not to the first three
Rom 9:30 have *a* to righteousness, even the
Rom 9:31 hath not *a* to the law of
Phil 3:12 Not as though I had already *a*
Phil 3:16 whereto we have already *a*
1Ti 4:6 doctrine, whereunto thou hast *a*

**ATTALIA** *(at-ta-li'-ah) A seaport near Perga.*
Acts 14:25 in Perga, they went down into *A*

**ATTEND**
Est 4:5 he had appointed to *a* upon her
Ps 17:1 *a* unto my cry, give ear unto my
Ps 55:2 *A* unto me, and hear me
Ps 61:1 *a* unto my prayer
Ps 86:6 and *a* to the voice of my
Ps 142:6 *A* unto my cry
Prov 4:1 and *a* to know understanding
Prov 4:20 My son, *a* to my words
Prov 5:1 *a* unto my wisdom, and bow thine
Prov 7:24 *a* to the words of my mouth
1Cor 7:35 that ye may *a* upon the Lord

**ATTENDANCE**
1Kin 10:5 the *a* of his ministers, and their
2Chr 9:4 the *a* of his ministers, and their
1Ti 4:13 give *a* to reading, to exhortation
Heb 7:13 which no man gave *a* at the altar

**ATTENDED**
Job 32:12 I *a* unto you, and, behold, there
Ps 66:19 he hath *a* to the voice of my
Acts 16:14 that she *a* unto the things which

**ATTENT**
2Chr 6:40 let thine ears be *a* unto the
2Chr 7:15 mine ears *a* unto the prayer that

**ATTENTIVE**
Neh 1:6 Let thine ear now be *a*, and thine
Neh 1:11 let now thine ear be *a* to the
Neh 8:3 were *a* unto the book of the law
Ps 130:2 let thine ears be *a* to the voice
Lk 19:48 people were very *a* to hear him

**ATTIRE**
Prov 7:10 a woman with the *a* of an harlot
Jer 2:32 her ornaments, or a bride her *a*
Eze 23:15 in dyed *a* upon their heads

**AUDIENCE**
Gen 23:10 in the *a* of the children of Heth
Gen 23:13 the *a* of the people of the land
Gen 23:16 in the *a* of the sons of Heth
Ex 24:7 read in the *a* of the people
1Sa 25:24 I pray thee, speak in thine *a*
1Chr 28:8 in the *a* of our God, keep and seek
Neh 13:1 of Moses in the *a* of the people
Lk 7:1 sayings in the *a* of the people
Lk 20:45 Then in the *a* of all the people
Acts 13:16 and ye that fear God, give *a*
Acts 15:12 gave *a* to Barnabas and Paul,
Acts 22:22 they gave him *a* unto this word,

**AUGUSTUS** *(aw-gus'-tus)* See AUGUSTUS', CAESAR. *An emperor of Rome.*
Lk 2:1 went out a decree from Caesar *A*
Acts 25:21 be reserved unto the hearing of *A*
Acts 25:25 he himself hath appealed to *A*

**AUGUSTUS'** *(aw-gus'-tus)*
Acts 27:1 Julius, a centurion of *A* band

**AUL**
Ex 21:6 bore his ear through with an *a*
Deut 15:17 Then thou shalt take an *a*

**AUNT**
Lev 18:14 she is thine *a*

**AUSTERE**
Lk 19:21 thee, because thou art an *a* man
Lk 19:22 Thou knewest that I was an *a* man

**AUTHOR**
1Cor 14:33 For God is not the *a* of confusion
Heb 5:9 he became the *a* of eternal
Heb 12:2 Looking unto Jesus the *a* and

**AUTHORITIES**
1Pet 3:22 angels and *a* and powers being made

**AUTHORITY**
Est 9:29 the Jew, wrote with all *a*
Prov 29:2 When the righteous are in *a*
Mt 7:29 he taught them as one having *a*
Mt 8:9 For I am a man under *a*, having
Mt 20:25 are great exercise *a* upon them
Mt 21:23 By what *a* doest thou these things
Mt 21:27 I you by what *a* I do these things
Mk 1:22 he taught them as one that had *a*
Mk 1:27 for with *a* commandeth he even the
Mk 10:42 great ones exercise *a* upon them
Mk 11:28 By what *a* doest thou these things
Mk 11:33 you by what *a* I do these things
Mk 13:34 gave *a* to his servants, and to
Lk 4:36 for with *a* and power he commandeth
Lk 7:8 For I also am a man set under *a*
Lk 9:1 *a* over all devils, and to cure
Lk 19:17 have thou *a* over ten cities
Lk 20:2 by what *a* doest thou these things
Lk 20:8 I you by what *a* I do these things
Lk 20:20 the power and *a* of the governor
Lk 22:25 they that exercise *a* upon them
Jn 5:27 hath given him *a* to execute
Acts 8:27 an eunuch of great *a* under
Acts 9:14 here he hath *a* from the chief
Acts 26:10 having received *a* from the chief
Acts 26:12 as I went to Damascus with *a*
1Cor 15:24 have put down all rule and all *a*
2Cor 10:8 boast somewhat more of our *a*
1Ti 2:2 kings, and for all that are in *a*
1Ti 2:12 nor to usurp *a* over the man
Titus 2:15 and exhort, and rebuke with all *a*
Rev 13:2 power, and his seat, and great *a*

**AVA** *(a'-vah)* See IVAH. *An area near Babylon.*
2Kin 17:24 and from Cuthah, and from *A*

**AVAILETH**
Est 5:13 Yet all this *a* me nothing
Gal 5:6 neither circumcision *a* any thing
Gal 6:15 neither circumcision *a* any thing
Jas 5:16 prayer of a righteous man *a* much

**AVEN** See BETH-AVEN. *Another name for Heliopolis, in Egypt.*
Eze 30:17 The young men of *A* and of
Hos 10:8 The high places also of *A*
Amos 1:5 inhabitant from the plain of *A*

**AVENGE**
Lev 19:18 Thou shalt not *a*, nor bear any
Lev 26:25 that shall *a* the quarrel of my
Num 31:2 *A* the children of Israel of the
Deut 32:43 for he will *a* the blood of his
1Sa 24:12 and thee, and the LORD *a* me of thee
2Kin 9:7 that I may *a* the blood of my
Est 8:13 to *a* themselves on their enemies
Is 1:24 and *a* me of mine enemies
Jer 46:10 that he may *a* him of his
Hos 1:4 I will *a* the blood of Jezreel
Lk 18:3 saying, *A* me of mine adversary
Lk 18:5 widow troubleth me, I will *a* her
Lk 18:7 shall not God *a* his own elect
Rom 12:19 *a* not yourselves, but rather give
Rev 6:10 *a* our blood on them that dwell on

**AVENGED**
Gen 4:24 If Cain shall be *a* sevenfold
Josh 10:13 until the people had *a* themselves
Judg 15:7 done this, yet will I be *a* of you
Judg 16:28 that I may be at once *a* of the
1Sa 14:24 that I may be *a* on mine enemies
1Sa 18:25 to be *a* of the king's enemies
1Sa 25:31 or that my lord hath *a* himself
2Sa 4:8 LORD hath *a* my lord the king
2Sa 18:19 LORD hath *a* him of his enemies
2Sa 18:31 for the LORD hath *a* thee this day
Jer 5:9 shall not my soul be *a* on such a
Jer 5:29 shall not my soul be *a* on such a
Jer 9:9 shall not my soul be *a* on such a
Acts 7:24 *a* him that was oppressed, and
Rev 18:20 for God hath *a* you on her
Rev 19:2 hath *a* the blood of his servants

**AVENGER**
Num 35:12 you cities for refuge from the *a*
Deut 19:6 Lest the *a* of the blood pursue
Deut 19:12 into the hand of the *a* of blood
Josh 20:3 your refuge from the *a* of blood
Josh 20:5 if the *a* of blood pursue after
Josh 20:9 die by the hand of the *a* of blood
Ps 8:2 mightest still the enemy and the *a*
Ps 44:16 by reason of the enemy and *a*
1Th 4:6 the Lord is the *a* of all such

**AVENGETH**
2Sa 22:48 It is God that *a* me, and that
Ps 18:47 It is God that *a* me, and subdueth

**AVENGING**
Judg 5:2 ye the LORD for the *a* of Israel
1Sa 25:26 from *a* thyself with thine own
1Sa 25:33 from *a* myself with mine own hand

**AVIM** *(a'-vim)* See AVIMS, AVITES. *A city near Bethel.*
Josh 18:23 And *A*, and Parah, and Ophrah,

**AVIMS** *(a'-vims)* See AVIM. *A Canaanite tribe.*
Deut 2:23 the *A* which dwelt in Hazerim,

**AVITES** *(a'-vites)* See AVIM.
*1. Same as Avims.*
Josh 13:3 and the Ekronites; also the *A*
*2. A tribe moved to Samaria.*
2Kin 17:31 the *A* made Nibhaz and Tartak, and

**AVITH** *(a'-vith) Capital of Edom.*
Gen 36:35 and the name of his city was *A*
1Chr 1:46 and the name of his city was *A*

**AVOID**
Prov 4:15 *A* it, pass not by it, turn from
Rom 16:17 and *a* them
1Cor 7:2 to *a* fornication, let every man
2Ti 2:23 foolish and unlearned questions *a*
Titus 3:9 But *a* foolish questions, and

**AWAKE**
Judg 5:12 *A*, *a*, Deborah
Job 8:6 surely now he would *a* for thee
Job 14:12 be no more, they shall not *a*
Ps 7:6 *a* for me to the judgment that
Ps 17:15 I shall be satisfied, when I *a*
Ps 35:23 *a* to my judgment, even unto my
Ps 44:23 *A*, why sleepest thou, O Lord
Ps 57:8 *A* up, my glory
Ps 59:4 *a* to help me, and behold
Ps 108:2 *A*, psaltery and harp
Ps 139:18 when I *a*, I am still with thee
Prov 23:35 when shall I *a*
Song 2:7 nor *a* my love, till he please
Song 3:5 nor *a* my love, till he please
Song 4:16 *A*, O north wind
Song 8:4 nor *a* my love, until he please
Is 26:19 *A* and sing, ye that dwell in dust
Is 51:9 *A*, *a*, put on strength, O arm
Is 51:17 *A*, *a*, stand up, O Jerusalem,
Is 52:1 *A*, *a*; put on thy strength
Dan 12:2 in the dust of the earth shall *a*
Joel 1:5 *A*, ye drunkards, and weep
Hab 2:7 *a* that shall vex thee, and thou
Hab 2:19 him that saith to the wood, *A*
Zec 13:7 *A*, O sword, against my shepherd,
Mk 4:38 and they *a* him, and say unto him,
Lk 9:32 and when they were *a*, they saw his
Jn 11:11 that I may *a* him out of sleep
Rom 13:11 it is high time to *a* out of sleep
1Cor 15:34 *A* to righteousness, and sin not
Eph 5:14 *A* thou that sleepest, and arise

**AWAKED**
Gen 28:16 Jacob *a* out of his sleep, and he
Judg 16:14 he *a* out of his sleep, and went
1Sa 26:12 saw it, nor knew it, neither *a*
1Kin 18:27 he sleepeth, and must be *a*
2Kin 4:31 him, saying, The child is not *a*
Ps 3:5 I *a*; for the LORD sustained me
Ps 78:65 Then the Lord *a* as one out of
Jer 31:26 Upon this I *a*, and beheld

**AWAKEST**
Ps 73:20 so, O Lord, when thou *a*, thou
Prov 6:22 and when thou *a*, it shall talk

**AWAKETH**
Ps 73:20 As a dream when one *a*
Is 29:8 but he *a*, and his soul is empty
Is 29:8 but he *a*, and, behold, he is faint

**AWARE**
Song 6:12 Or ever I was *a*, my soul made me
Jer 50:24 O Babylon, and thou wast not *a*
Mt 24:50 and in an hour that he is not *a* of
Lk 11:44 walk over them are not *a* of them
Lk 12:46 and at an hour when he is not *a*

**AWE**
Ps 4:4 Stand in *a*, and sin not
Ps 33:8 of the world stand in *a* of him
Ps 119:161 heart standeth in *a* of thy word

**AWOKE**
Gen 9:24 Noah *a* from his wine, and knew
Gen 41:4 So Pharaoh *a*
Gen 41:7 And Pharaoh *a*, and, behold, it was
Gen 41:21 So I *a*
Judg 16:20 he *a* out of his sleep, and said, I
1Kin 3:15 And Solomon *a*
Mt 8:25 *a* him, saying, Lord, save us
Lk 8:24 *a* him, saying, Master, master, we

**AX**
Deut 20:19 by forcing an *a* against them
1Sa 13:20 share, and his coulter, and his *a*
2Kin 6:5 the *a* head fell into the water
Is 10:15 Shall the *a* boast itself against
Jer 10:3 hands of the workman, with the *a*
Jer 51:20 Thou art my battle *a* and weapons
Mt 3:10 now also the *a* is laid unto the

**AXE**
Deut 19:5 with the *a* to cut down the tree
Judg 9:48 Abimelech took an *a* in his hand
1Kin 6:7 there was neither hammer nor *a*
Lk 3:9 now also the *a* is laid unto the

**AXES**
1Sa 13:21 and for the forks, and for the *a*
2Sa 12:31 under *a* of iron, and made them
1Chr 20:3 with harrows of iron, and with *a*
Ps 74:5 lifted up *a* upon the thick trees
Jer 46:22 army, and come against her with *a*
Eze 26:9 with his *a* he shall break down

**AXLETREES**
1Kin 7:32 the *a* of the wheels were joined
1Kin 7:33 their *a*, and their naves, and their

**AZAL** *(a'-zal) A place near Jerusalem.*
Zec 14:5 the mountains shall reach unto *A*

**AZALIAH** *(az-a-li'-ah) Father of Shaphan.*
2Kin 22:3 king sent Shaphan the son of *A*
2Chr 34:8 he sent Shaphan the son of *A*

**AZANIAH** *(az-a-ni'-ah) Father of Jeshua.*
Neh 10:9 both Jeshua the son of *A*, Binnui

**AZARAEL** *(a-zar'-a-el)* See AZAREEL. *A priest from the Immer family.*
Neh 12:36 And his brethren, Shemaiah, and *A*

**AZAREEL** *(a-zar'-e-el)* See AZARAEL.
*1. A Korahite in David's army.*
1Chr 12:6 Elkanah, and Jesiah, and *A*, and
*2. A priest during David's time.*
1Chr 25:18 The eleventh to *A*, he, his sons,
*3. A Danite prince during David's time.*
1Chr 27:22 Of Dan, *A* the son of Jeroham
*4. Married a foreign wife in exile.*
Ezr 10:41 *A*, and Shelemiah, Shemariah,
*5. Same as Azarael.*
Neh 11:13 and Amashai the son of *A*, the son

**AZARIAH** *(az-a-ri'-ah)* See AHAZIAH.
*1. A descendant of Zadok.*
1Kin 4:2 *A* the son of Zadok the priest,
*2. Captain of Solomon's guard.*
1Kin 4:5 *A* the son of Nathan was over the
*3. A king of Judah.*
2Kin 14:21 And all the people of Judah took *A*
2Kin 15:1 Jeroboam king of Israel began *A*
2Kin 15:6 And the rest of the acts of *A*
2Kin 15:17 thirtieth year of *A* king of Judah
2Kin 15:23 In the fiftieth year of *A* king of
2Kin 15:27 fiftieth year of *A* king of Judah
1Chr 3:12 *A* his son, Jotham his son,
*4. A descendant of Judah.*
1Chr 2:8 the sons of Ethan; *A*
*5. A descendant of Jerahmeel.*
1Chr 2:38 Obed begat Jehu, and Jehu begat *A*
1Chr 2:39 *A* begat Helez, and Helez begat
*6. A son of Ahimaaz.*
1Chr 6:9 And Ahimaaz begat *A*, and Azariah
*7. Grandson of Ahimaah.*
1Chr 6:10 And Johanan begat *A*, (he it is
1Chr 6:11 *A* begat Amariah, and Amariah begat
*8. A son of Hilkiah.*
1Chr 6:13 begat Hilkiah, and Hilkiah begat *A*
1Chr 6:14 *A* begat Seraiah, and Seraiah begat
1Chr 9:11 *A* the son of Hilkiah, the son of
Ezr 7:1 the son of Seraiah, the son of *A*
*9. A descendant of Kohath.*
1Chr 6:36 the son of Joel, the son of *A*
*10. A prophet sent to King Asa.*
2Chr 15:1 God came upon *A* the son of Oded
*11. A son of King Jehoshaphat.*
2Chr 21:2 the sons of Jehoshaphat, *A*
*12. A brother of King Jehoram.*
2Chr 21:2 and Jehiel, and Zechariah, and *A*
*13. A son of King Jehoram.*
2Chr 22:6 *A* the son of Jehoram king of
*14. A conspirator with Joash.*
2Chr 23:1 *A* the son of Jeroham, and Ishmael
*15. Another conspirator with Joash.*
2Chr 23:1 *A* the son of Obed, and Maaseiah
*16. A High Priest.*
2Chr 26:17 *A* the priest went in after him,
2Chr 26:20 *A* the chief priest, and all the
*17. A chief of Ephraim.*
2Chr 28:12 *A* the son of Johanan, Berechiah
*18. Father of Joel.*
2Chr 29:12 of Amasai, and Joel the son of *A*
*19. Helped cleanse the Temple.*
2Chr 29:12 Abdi, and *A* the son of Jehalelel
*20. A chief priest.*
2Chr 31:10 *A* the chief priest of the house
2Chr 31:13 *A* the ruler of the house of God
*21. Great-grandfather of Zadok.*
Ezr 7:3 The son of Amariah, the son of *A*
*22. A repairer of the Jerusalem walls.*
Neh 3:23 After him repaired *A* the son of
Neh 3:24 from the house of *A* unto the
*23. An exile with Zerubbabel.*
Neh 7:7 Zerubbabel, Jeshua, Nehemiah, *A*
*24. A priest with Ezra.*
Neh 8:7 Hodijah, Maaseiah, Kelita, *A*
*25. A priest who renewed the covenant.*
Neh 10:2 Seraiah, *A*, Jeremiah,
*26. A prince of Judah.*
Neh 12:33 And *A*, Ezra, and Meshullam,
*27. The son of Hoshaiah.*
Jer 43:2 Then spake *A* the son of Hoshaiah,

*28. A companion of Daniel.*
Dan 1:6 Daniel, Hananiah, Mishael, and *A*
Dan 1:7 and to *A*, of Abed-nego
Dan 1:11 Daniel, Hananiah, Mishael, and *A*
Dan 1:19 Daniel, Hananiah, Mishael, and *A*
Dan 2:17 known to Hananiah, Mishael, and *A*

**AZAZ** *(a'-zaz) Father of Bela.*
1Chr 5:8 And Bela the son of *A*, the son of

**AZAZIAH** *(az-a-zi'-ah)*
*1. A Levite who relocated the Ark.*
1Chr 15:21 and Obed-edom, and Jeiel, and *A*
*2. Father of Hoshea.*
1Chr 27:20 of Ephraim, Hoshea the son of *A*
*3. A Levite during Hezekiah's reign.*
2Chr 31:13 And Jehiel, and *A*, and Nahath, and

**AZBUK** *(az'-buk) Father of Nehemiah.*
Neh 3:16 repaired Nehemiah the son of *A*

**AZEKAH** *(a-ze'-kah) A town in Judah.*
Josh 10:10 to Beth-horon, and smote them to *A*
Josh 15:35 Jarmuth, and Adullam, Socoh, and *A*
1Sa 17:1 and pitched between Shochoh and *A*
2Chr 11:9 And Adoraim, and Lachish, and *A*
Neh 11:30 and the fields thereof, at *A*
Jer 34:7 against Lachish, and against *A*

**AZEL** *(a'-zel)* See JAAZIEL. *A descendant of King Saul.*
1Chr 8:37 son, Eleasah his son, *A* his son
1Chr 9:43 son, Eleasah his son, *A* his son

**AZEM** *(a'-zem)* See EZEM. *A city in Judah.*
Josh 15:29 Baalah, and Iim, and *A*,
Josh 19:3 And Hazar-shual, and Balah, and *A*

**AZGAD** *(az'-gad)*
*1. A family of exiles.*
Ezr 2:12 The children of *A*, a thousand two
Neh 7:17 The children of *A*, two thousand
*2. An exile with Ezra.*
Ezr 8:12 And of the sons of *A*
*3. A family who sealed the covenant.*
Neh 10:15 Bunni, *A*, Bebai,

**AZIEL** *(a'-ze-el) A Levite who relocated the Ark.*
1Chr 15:20 And Zechariah, and *A*, and

**AZIZA** *(a-zi'-zah) Married a foreigner in exile.*
Ezr 10:27 and Jeremoth, and Zabad, and *A*

**AZMAVETH** *(az-ma'-veth)* See BETH-AZMAVETH.
*1. A "mighty man" of David.*
2Sa 23:31 the Arbathite, *A* the Barhumite,
1Chr 11:33 *A* the Baharumite, Eliahba the
*2. A descendant of Jonathan.*
1Chr 8:36 and Jehoadah begat Alemeth, and *A*
1Chr 9:42 and Jarah begat Alemeth, and *A*
*3. Father of Jeziel and Pelet.*
1Chr 12:3 Jeziel, and Pelet, the sons of *A*
*4. A village on the border of Judah.*
Ezr 2:24 The children of *A*, forty and two
Neh 12:29 and out of the fields of Geba and *A*
*5. A treasurer of David.*
1Chr 27:25 treasures was *A* the son of Adiel

**AZMON** *(az'-mon)* See HESHMON. *A place in southern Canaan.*
Num 34:4 to Hazar-addar, and pass on to *A*
Num 34:5 from *A* unto the river of Egypt
Josh 15:4 From thence it passed toward *A*

**AZNOTH-TABOR** *(az'-noth-ta'-bor) Hills on the border of Naphtali.*
Josh 19:34 the coast turneth westward to *A*

**AZOR** *(a'-zor) Great-grandson of Zorobabel.*
Mt 1:13 and Eliakim begat *A*
Mt 1:14 And *A* begat Sadoc

**AZOTUS** *(a-zo'-tus)* See ASHDOD. *Greek form of Ashdod.*
Acts 8:40 But Philip was found at *A*

**AZRIEL** *(az'-re-el)*
*1. Chief of a family of Manasseh.*
1Chr 5:24 Epher, and Ishi, and Eliel, and *A*
*2. Father of Jerimoth*
1Chr 27:19 Naphtali, Jerimoth the son of *A*
*3. Father of Seraiah.*
Jer 36:26 and Seraiah the son of *A*, and

**AZRIKAM** *(az'-ri-kam)*
*1. A son of Neariah.*
1Chr 3:23 Elioenai, and Hezekiah, and *A*
*2. A son of Azel.*
1Chr 8:38 sons, whose names are these, *A*
1Chr 9:44 sons, whose names are these, *A*
*3. A descendant of Merari.*
1Chr 9:14 the son of Hasshub, the son of *A*
Neh 11:15 the son of Hashub, the son of *A*
*4. Governor of the house of King Ahaz.*
2Chr 28:7 *A* the governor of the house, and

**AZUBAH** *(a-zu'-bah)*
*1. Mother of King Jehoshaphat.*
1Kin 22:42 his mother's name was *A* the
2Chr 20:31 his mother's name was *A* the
*2. Wife of Caleb.*
1Chr 2:18 begat children of *A* his wife
1Chr 2:19 when *A* was dead, Caleb took unto

**AZUR** *(a'-zur)* See AZZUR.
*1. Father of Hananiah.*
Jer 28:1 Hananiah the son of *A* the prophet
*2. Father of Jaazaniah.*
Eze 11:1 whom I saw Jaazaniah the son of *A*

**AZZAH** *(az'-zah)* See GAZA. *A Philistine city.*
Deut 2:23 dwelt in Hazerim, even unto *A*
1Kin 4:24 the river, from Tiphsah even to *A*
Jer 25:20 Philistines, and Ashkelon, and *A*

**AZZAN** *(az'-zan) A prince of Issachar.*
Num 34:26 of Issachar, Paltiel the son of *A*

**AZZUR** *(az'-zur) An Israelite who sealed the covenant under Nehemiah.*
Neh 10:17 Ater, Hizkijah, *A*,

# B

**BAAL** *(ba'-al)* See BAAL-BERITH, BAALE, BAAL-GAD, BAAL-HAMON, BAAL-HANAN, BAAL-HAZOR, BAAL-HERMON, BAALIM, BAAL-MEON, BAAL-PEOR, BAAL-PERAZIM, BAAL-SHALISHA, BAAL-TAMAR.
*1. Chief god of the Canaanites.*
Num 22:41 him up into the high places of *B*
Judg 2:13 forsook the LORD, and served *B*
Judg 6:25 altar of *B* that thy father hath
Judg 6:28 the altar of *B* was cast down, and
Judg 6:30 he hath cast down the altar of *B*
Judg 6:32 Let *B* plead against him, because
1Kin 16:31 Zidonians, and went and served *B*
1Kin 18:19 and the prophets of *B* four hundred
1Kin 18:21 but if *B*, then follow him
1Kin 18:25 said unto the prophets of *B*
1Kin 18:40 unto them, Take the prophets of *B*
1Kin 19:18 knees which have not bowed unto *B*
1Kin 22:53 For he served *B*, and worshipped
2Kin 3:2 of *B* that his father had made
2Kin 10:18 unto them, Ahab served *B* a little
2Kin 10:21 and all the worshippers of *B* came
2Kin 10:25 to the city of the house of *B*
2Kin 11:18 the land went into the house of *B*
2Kin 17:16 the host of heaven, and served *B*
2Kin 21:3 and he reared up altars for *B*
2Kin 23:4 the vessels that were made for *B*
2Chr 23:17 the people went to the house of *B*
Jer 2:8 and the prophets prophesied by *B*
Jer 7:9 falsely, and burn incense unto *B*
Jer 11:13 altars to burn incense unto *B*
Jer 11:17 anger in offering incense unto *B*
Jer 12:16 taught my people to swear by *B*
Jer 19:5 built also the high places of *B*
Jer 23:13 they prophesied in *B*, and caused
Jer 23:27 have forgotten my name for *B*
Jer 32:29 they have offered incense unto *B*
Jer 32:35 they built the high places of *B*
Hos 2:8 gold, which they prepared for *B*
Hos 13:1 but when he offended in *B*
Zeph 1:4 the remnant of *B* from this place
Rom 11:4 bowed the knee to the image of *B*
*2. A city in Simeon.*
1Chr 4:33 about the same cities, unto *B*
*3. A descendant of Reuben.*
1Chr 5:5 son, Reaia his son, *B* his son,
*4. A descendant of Benjamin.*
1Chr 8:30 son Abdon, and Zur, and Kish, and *B*
1Chr 9:36 Abdon, then Zur, and Kish, and *B*

**BAALAH** *(ba'-al-ah)* See BAALE, BALEH, BILHAH, KIRJATH-BAAL.
*1. A city in Judah.*
Josh 15:9 and the border was drawn to *B*
Josh 15:10 from *B* westward unto mount Seir
Josh 15:29 *B*, and Iim, and Azem
1Chr 13:6 went up, and all Israel, to *B*
*2. A hill in Judah.*
Josh 15:11 and passed along to mount *B*

**BAALATH** *(ba'-al-ath)* See BAALATH-BEER. *A town in Dan.*
Josh 19:44 And Eltekeh, and Gibbethon, and *B*
1Kin 9:18 And *B*, and Tadmor in the wilderness
2Chr 8:6 And *B*, and all the store cities

**BAALATH-BEER** *(ba'-al-ath-be'-ur) A city in Simeon.*
Josh 19:8 round about these cities to *B*

**BAAL-BERITH** *(ba'-al-be'-rith) An idol.*
Judg 8:33 after Baalim, and made *B* their god
Judg 9:4 of silver out of the house of *B*

**BAALE** *(ba'-al-eh) A form of Baalah.*
2Sa 6:2 were with him from *B* of Judah

**BAAL-GAD** *(ba'-al-gad') A Canaanite city.*
Josh 11:17 even unto *B* in the valley of
Josh 12:7 from *B* in the valley of Lebanon
Josh 13:5 from *B* under mount Hermon unto

**BAAL-HAMON** *(ba'-al-ha'-mon) A place near Samaria.*
Song 8:11 Solomon had a vineyard at *B*

**BAAL-HANAN** *(ba'-al-ha'-nan)*
*1. A king of Edom.*
Gen 36:38 *B* the son of Achbor reigned in
Gen 36:39 *B* the son of Achbor died, and
1Chr 1:49 *B* the son of Achbor reigned in
1Chr 1:50 when *B* was dead, Hadad reigned in
*2. A superintendent for David.*
1Chr 27:28 the low plains was *B* the Gederite

**BAAL-HAZOR** *(ba'-al-ha'-zor)* See HAZOR. *A place near Ephraim.*
2Sa 13:23 Absalom had sheepshearers in *B*

**BAAL-HERMON** *(ba'-al-her'-mon) A city near Mt. Hermon.*
Judg 3:3 from mount *B* unto the entering in
1Chr 5:23 they increased from Bashan unto *B*

**BAALI** *(ba'-al-i) A rejected title of God.*
Hos 2:16 and shalt call me no more *B*

**BAALIM** *(ba'-al-im)* See BAAL. *Plural of Baal.*
Judg 2:11 sight of the LORD, and served *B*
Judg 3:7 the LORD their God, and served *B*
Judg 8:33 again, and went a whoring after *B*
Judg 10:6 sight of the LORD, and served *B*
Judg 10:10 our God, and also served *B*
1Sa 7:4 children of Israel did put away *B*
1Sa 12:10 the LORD, and have served *B*
1Kin 18:18 the LORD, and thou hast followed *B*
2Chr 17:3 David, and sought not unto *B*
2Chr 24:7 the LORD did they bestow upon *B*
2Chr 28:2 and made also molten images for *B*
2Chr 33:3 and he reared up altars for *B*
2Chr 34:4 the altars of *B* in his presence
Jer 2:23 polluted, I have not gone after *B*
Jer 9:14 of their own heart, and after *B*
Hos 2:13 will visit upon her the days of *B*

Hos 2:17 the names of *B* out of her mouth
Hos 11:2 they sacrificed unto *B*, and burned

**BAALIS** *(ba'-al-is) A king of the Ammonites.*
Jer 40:14 Dost thou certainly know that *B*

**BAAL-MEON** *(ba'-al-me'-on)* See BETH-BAAL-MEON. *A Reubenite town.*
Num 32:38 And Nebo, and *B*, (their names being
1Chr 5:8 in Aroer, even unto Nebo and *B*
Eze 25:9 of the country, Beth-jeshimoth, *B*

**BAAL-PEOR** *(ba'-al-pe'-or)* See PEOR. *A Moabite idol.*
Num 25:3 And Israel joined himself unto *B*
Num 25:5 his men that were joined unto *B*
Deut 4:3 what the LORD did because of *B*
Deut 4:3 for all the men that followed *B*
Ps 106:28 joined themselves also unto *B*
Hos 9:10 but they went to *B*, and separated

**BAAL-PERAZIM** *(ba'-al-per'-a-zim) A place near the valley of Rephaim.*
2Sa 5:20 And David came to *B*, and David
2Sa 5:20 called the name of that place *B*
1Chr 14:11 So they came up to *B*
1Chr 14:11 called the name of that place *B*

**BAAL'S** *(ba'-als)*
1Kin 18:22 but *B* prophets are four hundred

**BAAL-SHALISHA** *(ba'-al-shal'-i-shah) A place in Ephraim.*
2Kin 4:42 And there came a man from *B*

**BAAL-TAMAR** *(ba'-al-ta'-mar) A place in Benjamin.*
Judg 20:33 and put themselves in array at *B*

**BAAL-ZEBUB** *(ba'-al-ze'-bub)* See BEEL-ZEBUB. *A Philistine idol.*
2Kin 1:2 enquire of *B* the god of Ekron
2Kin 1:6 to enquire of *B* the god of Ekron
2Kin 1:16 to enquire of *B* the god of Ekron

**BAAL-ZEPHON** *(ba'-al-ze'-fon) A place near the Red Sea crossing.*
Ex 14:2 Migdol and the sea, over against *B*
Ex 14:9 sea, beside Pi-hahiroth, before *B*
Num 33:7 Pi-hahiroth, which is before *B*

**BAANA** *(ba'-an-ah)* See BAANAH.
*1. An officer in Solomon's army.*
1Kin 4:12 *B* the son of Ahilud
*2. Father of Zadok.*
Neh 3:4 them repaired Zadok the son of *B*

**BAANAH** *(ba'-an-ah)* See BAANA.
*1. A captain in Ishbosheth's army.*
2Sa 4:2 the name of the one was *B*
2Sa 4:5 the Beerothite, Rechab and *B*
2Sa 4:9 *B* his brother, the sons of Rimmon
*2. Father of Heleb.*
2Sa 23:29 Heleb the son of *B*, a
1Chr 11:30 the son of *B* the Netophathite
*3. An officer in Solomon's army.*
1Kin 4:16 *B* the son of Hushai was in Asher
*4. An exile who returned with Zerubbabel.*
Ezr 2:2 Bilshan, Mizpar, Bigvai, Rehum, *B*
Neh 7:7 Mispereth, Bigvai, Nehum, *B*
Neh 10:27 Malluch, Harim, *B*

**BAARA** *(ba'-ar-ah) A wife of Shaharaim.*
1Chr 8:8 Hushim and *B* were his wives

**BAASEIAH** *(ba-as-i'-ah) A Gersonite Levite.*
1Chr 6:40 The son of Michael, the son of *B*

**BAASHA** *(ba'-ash-ah) A king of Israel.*
1Kin 15:16 *B* king of Israel all their days
1Kin 15:17 *B* king of Israel went up against
1Kin 15:19 thy league with *B* king of Israel
1Kin 15:21 when *B* heard thereof, that he
1Kin 15:27 *B* the son of Ahijah, of the house
1Kin 15:27 *B* smote him at Gibbethon, which
1Kin 15:32 *B* king of Israel all their days
1Kin 16:1 Jehu the son of Hanani against *B*
1Kin 16:3 will take away the posterity of *B*
1Kin 16:8 *B* to reign over Israel in Tirzah
1Kin 16:11 that he slew all the house of *B*
1Kin 21:22 the house of *B* the son of Ahijah
2Kin 9:9 the house of *B* the son of Ahijah
2Chr 16:1 year of the reign of Asa *B* king
2Chr 16:3 thy league with *B* king of Israel
2Chr 16:6 thereof, wherewith *B* was building
Jer 41:9 made for fear of *B* king of Israel

**BABBLER**
Eccl 10:11 and a *b* is no better
Acts 17:18 some said, What will this *b* say

**BABE**
Ex 2:6 and, behold, the *b* wept
Lk 1:41 of Mary, the *b* leaped in her womb
Lk 1:44 the *b* leaped in my womb for joy
Lk 2:12 Ye shall find the *b* wrapped in
Lk 2:16 and the *b* lying in a manger
Heb 5:13 for he is a *b*

**BABEL** *(ba'-bel)* See BABYLON. *A city in the plain of Shinar.*
Gen 10:10 beginning of his kingdom was *B*
Gen 11:9 is the name of it called *B*

**BABES**
Ps 8:2 Out of the mouth of *b* and
Ps 17:14 of their substance to their *b*
Is 3:4 and *b* shall rule over them
Mt 11:25 and hast revealed them unto *b*
Mt 21:16 never read, Out of the mouth of *b*
Lk 10:21 and hast revealed them unto *b*
Rom 2:20 of the foolish, a teacher of *b*
1Cor 3:1 carnal, even as unto *b* in Christ
1Pet 2:2 As newborn *b*, desire the sincere

**BABYLON** *(bab'-il-un)* See BABEL, BABYLONIANS, BABYLONISH, BABYLON'S, CHALDEA, SHESHACH. *Capital of the Babylonian Empire; located on the Euphrates River.*
2Kin 17:24 of Assyria brought men from *B*
2Kin 17:30 the men of *B* made Succoth-benoth,
2Kin 20:12 the son of Baladan, king of *B*
2Kin 20:14 from a far country, even from *B*
2Kin 20:17 this day, shall be carried into *B*
2Kin 24:1 Nebuchadnezzar king of *B* came up
2Kin 24:7 for the king of *B* had taken from
2Kin 24:10 of *B* came up against Jerusalem
2Kin 24:15 he carried away Jehoiachin to *B*
2Kin 24:20 rebelled against the king of *B*
2Kin 25:1 Nebuchadnezzar king of *B* came
2Kin 25:6 him up to the king of *B* to Riblah
2Kin 25:11 that fell away to the king of *B*
2Kin 25:13 and carried the brass of them to *B*
2Kin 25:20 them to the king of *B* to Riblah
2Kin 25:27 that Evil-merodach king of *B* in
1Chr 9:1 away to *B* for their transgression
2Chr 32:31 ambassadors of the princes of *B*
2Chr 33:11 with fetters, and carried him to *B*
2Chr 36:6 came up Nebuchadnezzar king of *B*
2Chr 36:10 sent, and brought him to *B*
2Chr 36:18 all these he brought to *B*
2Chr 36:20 the sword carried he away to *B*
Ezr 1:11 brought up from *B* unto Jerusalem
Ezr 2:1 *B* had carried away unto *B*
Ezr 5:12 of Nebuchadnezzar the king of *B*
Ezr 5:17 house, which is there at *B*
Ezr 6:1 the treasures were laid up in *B*
Ezr 6:5 at Jerusalem, and brought unto *B*
Ezr 7:6 This Ezra went up from *B*
Ezr 7:9 month began he to go up from *B*
Ezr 7:16 find in all the province of *B*
Ezr 8:1 them that went up with me from *B*
Neh 7:6 the king of *B* had carried away
Neh 13:6 king of *B* came I unto the king
Est 2:6 the king of *B* had carried away
Ps 87:4 Rahab and *B* to them that know me
Ps 137:1 By the rivers of *B*, there we sat
Ps 137:8 O daughter of *B*, who art to be
Is 13:1 The burden of *B*, which Isaiah the
Is 13:19 And *B*, the glory of kingdoms, the
Is 14:4 proverb against the king of *B*
Is 14:22 hosts, and cut off from *B* the name
Is 21:9 and said, *B* is fallen, is fallen
Is 39:1 the son of Baladan, king of *B*
Is 39:3 far country unto me, even from *B*
Is 39:6 this day, shall be carried to *B*
Is 39:7 in the palace of the king of *B*
Is 43:14 For your sake I have sent to *B*
Is 47:1 the dust, O virgin daughter of *B*
Is 48:14 he will do his pleasure on *B*
Is 48:20 Go ye forth of *B*, flee ye from
Jer 20:4 into the hand of the king of *B*
Jer 21:2 king of *B* maketh war against us
Jer 21:4 ye fight against the king of *B*
Jer 21:7 hand of Nebuchadrezzar king of *B*
Jer 21:10 into the hand of the king of *B*
Jer 22:25 hand of Nebuchadrezzar king of *B*
Jer 24:1 of *B* had carried away captive
Jer 25:1 year of Nebuchadrezzar king of *B*
Jer 25:9 and Nebuchadrezzar the king of *B*
Jer 25:11 serve the king of *B* seventy years
Jer 27:6 of Nebuchadnezzar the king of *B*
Jer 27:8 same Nebuchadnezzar the king of *B*
Jer 27:11 under the yoke of the king of *B*
Jer 27:16 shortly be brought again from *B*
Jer 27:20 king of Judah from Jerusalem to *B*
Jer 27:22 They shall be carried to *B*
Jer 28:2 broken the yoke of the king of *B*
Jer 28:6 captive, from *B* into this place
Jer 28:11 of *B* from the neck of all nations
Jer 28:14 serve Nebuchadnezzar king of *B*
Jer 29:1 away captive from Jerusalem to *B*
Jer 29:3 king of Judah sent unto *B* to
Jer 29:10 at *B* I will visit you, and perform
Jer 29:15 hath raised us up prophets in *B*
Jer 29:20 I have sent from Jerusalem to *B*
Jer 29:28 therefore he sent unto us in *B*
Jer 32:3 into the hand of the king of *B*
Jer 32:28 hand of Nebuchadrezzar king of *B*
Jer 32:36 of the king of *B* by the sword
Jer 34:1 when Nebuchadnezzar king of *B*
Jer 35:11 king of *B* came up into the land
Jer 36:29 The king of *B* shall certainly
Jer 37:1 whom Nebuchadrezzar king of *B*
Jer 37:17 into the hand of the king of *B*
Jer 37:19 The king of *B* shall not come
Jer 38:23 by the hand of the king of *B*
Jer 39:1 came Nebuchadrezzar king of *B*
Jer 39:3 princes of the king of *B* came in
Jer 39:5 up to Nebuchadnezzar king of *B* to
Jer 39:9 *B* the remnant of the people that
Jer 39:11 Now Nebuchadrezzar king of *B* gave
Jer 40:1 were carried away captive unto *B*
Jer 40:4 unto thee to come with me into *B*
Jer 40:7 heard that the king of *B* had made
Jer 40:9 the land, and serve the king of *B*
Jer 40:11 heard that the king of *B* had left
Jer 41:2 whom the king of *B* had made
Jer 41:18 whom the king of *B* made governor
Jer 42:11 Be not afraid of the king of *B*
Jer 43:3 and carry us away captives into *B*
Jer 43:10 take Nebuchadrezzar the king of *B*
Jer 44:30 hand of Nebuchadrezzar king of *B*
Jer 46:2 of *B* smote in the fourth year of
Jer 46:13 king of *B* should come and smite
Jer 46:26 hand of Nebuchadrezzar king of *B*
Jer 49:28 king of *B* shall smite, thus saith
Jer 49:30 for Nebuchadrezzar king of *B* hath
Jer 50:1 that the LORD spake against *B*
Jer 50:8 Remove out of the midst of *B*
Jer 50:9 cause to come up against *B* an
Jer 50:13 goeth by *B* shall be astonished
Jer 50:16 Cut off the sower from *B*, and him
Jer 50:17 king of *B* hath broken his bones
Jer 50:23 how is *B* become a desolation
Jer 50:24 thee, and thou art also taken, O *B*
Jer 50:28 and escape out of the land of *B*
Jer 50:29 together the archers against *B*
Jer 50:34 and disquiet the inhabitants of *B*
Jer 50:42 against thee, O daughter of *B*
Jer 50:43 The king of *B* hath heard the
Jer 50:45 that he hath taken against *B*
Jer 51:1 Behold, I will raise up against *B*
Jer 51:2 And will send unto *B* fanners
Jer 51:6 Flee out of the midst of *B*
Jer 51:11 for his device is against *B*
Jer 51:24 And I will render unto *B* and to all
Jer 51:29 LORD shall be performed against *B*
Jer 51:33 The daughter of *B* is like a
Jer 51:37 *B* shall become heaps, a dwelling
Jer 51:41 how is *B* become an astonishment
Jer 51:44 And I will punish Bel in *B*
Jer 51:47 upon the graven images of *B*
Jer 51:48 that is therein, shall sing for *B*
Jer 51:53 Though *B* should mount up to
Jer 51:58 The broad walls of *B* shall be
Jer 51:64 thou shalt say, Thus shall *B* sink
Jer 52:3 rebelled against the king of *B*
Jer 52:4 Nebuchadrezzar king of *B* came
Jer 52:9 *B* to Riblah in the land of Hamath
Jer 52:15 away, that fell to the king of *B*
Jer 52:17 all the brass of them to *B*
Jer 52:26 them to the king of *B* to Riblah
Jer 52:31 that Evil-merodach king of *B* in
Jer 52:32 the kings that were with him in *B*
Jer 52:34 diet given him of the king of *B*
Eze 12:13 I will bring him to *B* to the land
Eze 17:12 Behold, the king of *B* is come to

Eze 17:16 in the midst of *B* he shall die
Eze 17:20 snare, and I will bring him to *B*
Eze 19:9 and brought him to the king of *B*
Eze 21:19 sword of the king of *B* may come
Eze 21:21 For the king of *B* stood at the
Eze 24:2 the king of *B* set himself against
Eze 26:7 Tyrus Nebuchadrezzar king of *B*
Eze 29:18 Nebuchadrezzar king of *B* caused
Eze 30:10 hand of Nebuchadrezzar king of *B*
Eze 30:24 the arms of the king of *B*
Eze 30:25 into the hand of the king of *B*
Eze 32:11 king of *B* shall come upon thee
Dan 1:1 king of *B* unto Jerusalem, and
Dan 2:12 to destroy all the wise men of *B*
Dan 2:14 forth to slay the wise men of *B*
Dan 2:18 the rest of the wise men of *B*
Dan 2:24 to destroy the wise men of *B*
Dan 2:48 over the whole province of *B*
Dan 2:48 over all the wise men of *B*
Dan 3:1 of Dura, in the province of *B*
Dan 3:12 the affairs of the province of *B*
Dan 3:30 Abed-nego, in the province of *B*
Dan 4:6 all the wise men of *B* before me
Dan 4:29 in the palace of the kingdom of *B*
Dan 5:7 and said to the wise men of *B*
Dan 7:1 king of *B* Daniel had a dream
Mic 4:10 field, and thou shalt go even to *B*
Zec 2:7 dwellest with the daughter of *B*
Zec 6:10 of Jedaiah, which are come from *B*
Mt 1:11 time they were carried away to *B*
Mt 1:12 And after they were brought to *B*
Mt 1:17 into *B* are fourteen generations
Acts 7:43 and I will carry you away beyond *B*
1Pet 5:13 The church that is at *B*, elected
Rev 14:8 *B* is fallen, is fallen, that
Rev 16:19 great *B* came in remembrance
Rev 17:5 *B* THE GREAT, THE MOTHER OF
Rev 18:2 *B* the great is fallen, is fallen,
Rev 18:10 Alas, alas that great city *B*
Rev 18:21 that great city *B* be thrown down

**BABYLONIANS** *(bab-il-o'-ne-ans)* See CHALDEANS. *Inhabitants of Babylonia.*
Ezr 4:9 Apharsites, the Archevites, the *B*
Eze 23:15 the manner of the *B* of Chaldea
Eze 23:17 the *B* came to her into the bed of
Eze 23:23 The *B*, and all the Chaldeans,

**BABYLONISH** *(bab-il-o'-nish)* See BABYLONIANS.
Josh 7:21 the spoils a goodly *B* garment

**BABYLON'S** *(bab'-il-ons)*
Jer 32:2 For then the king of *B* army
Jer 34:7 When the king of *B* army fought
Jer 34:21 the hand of the king of *B* army
Jer 38:3 the hand of the king of *B* army
Jer 38:17 forth unto the king of *B* princes
Jer 38:18 go forth to the king of *B* princes
Jer 38:22 forth to the king of *B* princes
Jer 39:13 and all the king of *B* princes

**BACA** *(ba'-cah) A valley near Jerusalem.*
Ps 84:6 the valley of *B* make it a well

**BACHRITES** *(bak'-rites) Descendants of Becher.*
Num 26:35 of Becher, the family of the *B*

**BACKS**
Ex 23:27 enemies turn their *b* unto thee
Josh 7:8 their *b* before their enemies
Josh 7:12 but turned their *b* before their
Judg 20:42 Therefore they turned their *b*
2Chr 29:6 of the LORD, and turned their *b*
Neh 9:26 and cast thy law behind their *b*
Eze 8:16 with their *b* toward the temple of
Eze 10:12 And their whole body, and their *b*

**BACKSIDE**
Ex 3:1 the flock to the *b* of the desert
Ex 26:12 hang over the *b* of the tabernacle
Rev 5:1 a book written within and on the *b*

**BACKSLIDING**
Jer 3:6 that which *b* Israel hath done
Jer 3:8 *b* Israel committed adultery I had
Jer 3:11 The *b* Israel hath justified
Jer 3:14 O *b* children, saith the LORD
Jer 3:22 ye *b* children, and I will heal
Jer 8:5 slidden back by a perpetual *b*
Jer 31:22 thou go about, O thou *b* daughter
Jer 49:4 thy flowing valley, O *b* daughter
Hos 4:16 Israel slideth back as a *b* heifer
Hos 11:7 my people are bent to *b* from me
Hos 14:4 I will heal their *b*, I will love

**BACKSLIDINGS**
Jer 2:19 thee, and thy *b* shall reprove thee
Jer 3:22 children, and I will heal your *b*
Jer 5:6 many, and their *b* are increased
Jer 14:7 for our *b* are many

**BACKWARD**
Gen 9:23 both their shoulders, and went *b*
Gen 49:17 so that his rider shall fall *b*
1Sa 4:18 seat *b* by the side of the gate
2Kin 20:10 the shadow return *b* ten degrees
Job 23:8 and *b*, but I cannot perceive him
Ps 40:14 let them be driven *b* and put to
Ps 70:2 let them be turned *b*, and put to
Is 1:4 unto anger, they are gone away *b*
Is 28:13 that they might go, and fall *b*
Is 38:8 sun dial of Ahaz, ten degrees *b*
Is 44:25 that turneth wise men *b*, and
Is 59:14 And judgment is turned away *b*
Jer 7:24 of their evil heart, and went *b*
Jer 15:6 saith the LORD, thou art gone *b*
Lam 1:8 yea, she sigheth, and turneth *b*
Jn 18:6 I am he, they went *b*

**BAD**
Gen 24:50 cannot speak unto thee *b* or good
Gen 31:24 not to Jacob either good or *b*
Gen 31:29 not to Jacob either good or *b*
Lev 27:10 good for a *b*, or a *b* for a good
Lev 27:12 value it, whether it be good or *b*
Lev 27:14 it, whether it be good or *b*
Lev 27:33 search whether it be good or *b*
Num 13:19 dwell in, whether it be good or *b*
Num 24:13 either good or *b* of mine own mind
2Sa 13:22 brother Amnon neither good nor *b*
2Sa 14:17 the king to discern good and *b*
1Kin 3:9 I may discern between good and *b*
Ezr 4:12 the *b* city, and have set up the
Jer 24:2 not be eaten, they were so *b*
Mt 13:48 into vessels, but cast the *b* away
Mt 22:10 all as many as they found, both *b*
2Cor 5:10 done, whether it be good or *b*

**BADE**
Gen 43:17 And the man did as Joseph *b*
Ex 16:24 up till the morning, as Moses *b*
Num 14:10 *b* stone them with stones
Josh 11:9 did unto them as the LORD *b* him
Ruth 3:6 all that her mother in law *b* her
1Sa 24:10 and some *b* me kill thee
2Sa 1:18 (Also he *b* them teach the
2Sa 14:19 for thy servant Joab, he *b* me
2Chr 10:12 on the third day, as the king *b*
Est 4:15 Then Esther *b* them return
Mt 16:12 understood they how that he *b*
Lk 14:9 And he that *b* thee and him come and
Lk 14:10 that when he that *b* thee cometh
Lk 14:12 said he also to him that *b* him
Lk 14:16 made a great supper, and *b* many
Acts 11:12 the Spirit *b* me go with them,
Acts 18:21 But *b* them farewell, saying, I
Acts 22:24 *b* that he should be examined by

**BADGERS'**
Ex 25:5 *b* skins, and shittim wood,
Ex 26:14 and a covering above of *b* skins
Ex 35:7 *b* skins, and shittim wood,
Ex 35:23 of rams, and *b* skins, brought them
Ex 36:19 a covering of *b* skins above that
Ex 39:34 red, and the covering of *b* skins
Num 4:6 thereon the covering of *b* skins
Num 4:8 same with a covering of *b* skins
Num 4:10 within a covering of *b* skins
Num 4:14 upon it a covering of *b* skins
Num 4:25 the covering of the *b* skins that
Eze 16:10 work, and shod thee with *b* skin

**BAG**
Deut 25:13 not have in thy *b* divers weights
1Sa 17:40 in a shepherd's *b* which he had
1Sa 17:49 And David put his hand in his *b*
Job 14:17 transgression is sealed up in a *b*
Prov 7:20 He hath taken a *b* of money with
Prov 16:11 the weights of the *b* are his work
Is 46:6 They lavish gold out of the *b*
Mic 6:11 with the *b* of deceitful weights
Hag 1:6 to put it into a *b* with holes
Jn 12:6 he was a thief, and had the *b*
Jn 13:29 thought, because Judas had the *b*

**BAGS**
2Kin 5:23 two talents of silver in two *b*
2Kin 12:10 came up, and they put up in *b*
Lk 12:33 yourselves *b* which wax not old

**BAHARUMITE** *(ba-ha'-rum-ite)* See BARHUMITE. *Inhabitants of Bahurim.*
1Chr 11:33 Azmaveth the *B*, Eliahba the

**BAHURIM** *(ba-hu'-rim)* See BAHARUMITE. *A village near Jerusalem.*
2Sa 3:16 her along weeping behind her to *B*
2Sa 16:5 And when king David came to *B*
2Sa 17:18 and came to a man's house in *B*
2Sa 19:16 Gera, a Benjamite, which was of *B*
1Kin 2:8 the son of Gera, a Benjamite of *B*

**BAJITH** *(ba'-jith) A temple in Moab.*
Is 15:2 He is gone up to *B*, and to Dibon,

**BAKBAKKAR** *(bak-bak'-kar) A Levite who returned from exile.*
1Chr 9:15 And *B*, Heresh, and Galal, and

**BAKBUK** *(bak'-buk) A family who returned from exile.*
Ezr 2:51 The children of *B*, the children
Neh 7:53 The children of *B*, the children

**BAKBUKIAH** *(bak-buk-i'-ah) A Levite exile who resettled in Jerusalem.*
Neh 11:17 *B* the second among his brethren,
Neh 12:9 Also *B* and Unni, their brethren,
Neh 12:25 Mattaniah, and *B*, Obadiah,

**BAKE**
Gen 19:3 did *b* unleavened bread, and they
Ex 16:23 *b* that which ye will *b* to day,
Lev 24:5 flour, and *b* twelve cakes thereof
Lev 26:26 ten women shall *b* your bread in
1Sa 28:24 did *b* unleavened bread thereof
2Sa 13:8 in his sight, and did *b* the cakes
Eze 4:12 thou shalt *b* it with dung that
Eze 46:20 where they shall *b* the meat

**BAKED**
Ex 12:39 they *b* unleavened cakes of the
Num 11:8 *b* it in pans, and made cakes of it
1Chr 23:29 and for that which is *b* in the pan
Is 44:19 also I have *b* bread upon the

**BAKEN**
Lev 2:4 of a meat offering *b* in the oven
Lev 2:7 meat offering *b* in the frying pan
Lev 6:17 It shall not be *b* with leaven
Lev 6:21 and when it is *b*, thou shalt bring
Lev 7:9 offering that is *b* in the oven
Lev 23:17 they shall be *b* with leaven
1Kin 19:6 there was a cake *b* on the coals

**BAKER**
Gen 40:1 his *b* had offended their lord the
Gen 40:5 the *b* of the king of Egypt, which
Gen 40:16 When the chief *b* saw that the
Gen 40:20 of the chief *b* among his servants
Gen 40:22 But he hanged the chief *b*
Gen 41:10 house, both me and the chief *b*
Hos 7:4 as an oven heated by the *b*
Hos 7:6 their *b* sleepeth all the night

**BALAAM** *(ba'-la-am)* See BALAAM'S. *Son of Beor.*
Num 22:5 unto *B* the son of Beor to Pethor
Num 22:7 and they came unto *B*, and spake
Num 22:12 And God said unto *B*, Thou shalt
Num 22:16 And they came to *B*, and said to him
Num 22:18 *B* answered and said unto the
Num 22:20 And God came unto *B* at night
Num 22:23 *B* smote the ass, to turn her into
Num 22:27 the LORD, she fell down under *B*
Num 22:34 *B* said unto the angel of the LORD
Num 22:41 on the morrow, that Balak took *B*
Num 23:1 *B* said unto Balak, Build me here
Num 23:11 And Balak said unto *B*, What hast
Num 23:16 And the LORD met *B*, and put a word
Num 23:25 And Balak said unto *B*, Neither
Num 24:1 when *B* saw that it pleased the
Num 24:10 anger was kindled against *B*
Num 24:12 *B* said unto Balak, Spake I not
Num 24:15 *B* the son of Beor hath said, and
Num 24:25 *B* rose up, and went and returned to
Num 31:8 *B* also the son of Beor they slew
Num 31:16 Israel, through the counsel of *B*
Deut 23:4 *B* the son of Beor of Pethor of
Deut 23:5 thy God would not hearken unto *B*
Josh 13:22 *B* also the son of Beor, the
Josh 24:9 called *B* the son of Beor to curse

Josh 24:10 But I would not hearken unto *B*
Neh 13:2 but hired *B* against them, that he
Mic 6:5 what *B* the son of Beor answered
2Pet 2:15 the way of *B* the son of Bosor
Jude 11 after the error of *B* for reward
Rev 2:14 them that hold the doctrine of *B*

**BALAAM'S**
Num 22:25 crushed *B* foot against the wall
Num 22:27 *B* anger was kindled, and he smote
Num 23:5 And the LORD put a word in *B* mouth

**BALAC** *(ba'-lak)* See BALAK. *Greek form of Balak.*
Rev 2:14 of Balaam, who taught *B* to cast a

**BALADAN** *(bal'-adan)* See BERODACH-BALADAN, MERODACH-BALADAN. *Father of a Babylonian king.*
2Kin 20:12 Berodach-baladan, the son of *B*
Is 39:1 Merodach-baladan, the son of *B*

**BALAH** *(ba'-lah)* See BAALAH. *A city in Simeon.*
Josh 19:3 And Hazar-shual, and *B*, and Azem,

**BALAK** *(ba'-lak)* See BALAC, BALAK'S. *A king of Moab.*
Num 22:2 *B* the son of Zippor saw all that
Num 22:4 *B* the son of Zippor was king of
Num 22:7 and spake unto him the words of *B*
Num 22:10 *B* the son of Zippor, king of Moab
Num 22:13 and said unto the princes of *B*
Num 22:18 and said unto the servants of *B*
Num 22:35 Balaam went with the princes of *B*
Num 23:1 And Balaam said unto *B*, Build me
Num 23:3 And Balaam said unto *B*, Stand by
Num 23:5 mouth, and said, Return unto *B*
Num 23:7 *B* the king of Moab hath brought
Num 23:11 *B* said unto Balaam, What hast
Num 23:13 *B* said unto him, Come, I pray
Num 23:15 And he said unto *B*, Stand here by
Num 23:25 *B* said unto Balaam, Neither curse
Num 24:10 *B* said unto Balaam, I called thee
Num 24:12 And Balaam said unto *B*, Spake I
Num 24:25 and *B* also went his way
Josh 24:9 Then *B* the son of Zippor, king of
Judg 11:25 better than *B* the son of Zippor
Mic 6:5 remember now what *B* king of Moab

**BALAK'S** *(ba'-laks)*
Num 24:10 *B* anger was kindled against

**BALANCE**
Job 31:6 Let me be weighed in an even *b*
Ps 62:9 to be laid in the *b*, they are
Prov 11:1 A false *b* is abomination to the
Prov 16:11 A just weight and *b* are the LORD's
Prov 20:23 and a false *b* is not good
Is 40:12 in scales, and the hills in a *b*
Is 40:15 as the small dust of the *b*
Is 46:6 the bag, and weigh silver in the *b*

**BALANCES**
Lev 19:36 Just *b*, just weights, a just
Job 6:2 calamity laid in the *b* together
Jer 32:10 and weighed him the money in the *b*
Eze 5:1 then take thee *b* to weigh
Eze 45:10 Ye shall have just *b*, and a just
Dan 5:27 Thou art weighed in the *b*
Hos 12:7 the *b* of deceit are in his hand
Amos 8:5 and falsifying the *b* by deceit
Mic 6:11 count them pure with the wicked *b*
Rev 6:5 him had a pair of *b* in his hand

**BALD**
Lev 11:22 the *b* locust after his kind, and
Lev 13:40 is fallen off his head, he is *b*
Lev 13:41 toward his face, he is forehead *b*
2Kin 2:23 said unto him, Go up, thou *b* head
Jer 16:6 nor make themselves *b* for them
Jer 48:37 For every head shall be *b*
Eze 27:31 themselves utterly *b* for thee
Eze 29:18 every head was made *b*, and every
Mic 1:16 Make thee *b*, and poll thee for thy

**BALDNESS**
Lev 21:5 shall not make *b* upon their head
Deut 14:1 nor make any *b* between your eyes
Is 3:24 and instead of well set hair *b*
Is 15:2 on all their heads shall be *b*
Is 22:12 weeping, and to mourning, and to *b*
Jer 47:5 *B* is come upon Gaza
Eze 7:18 faces, and *b* upon all their heads
Amos 8:10 all loins, and *b* upon every head
Mic 1:16 enlarge thy *b* as the eagle

**BALM**
Gen 37:25 their camels bearing spicery and *b*
Gen 43:11 the man a present, a little *b*
Jer 8:22 Is there no *b* in Gilead
Jer 46:11 Go up into Gilead, and take *b*
Jer 51:8 take *b* for her pain, if so be she
Eze 27:17 and Pannag, and honey, and oil, and *b*

**BAMAH** *(ba'-mah)* See BAMOTH. *Places where Israel sacrificed to idols.*
Eze 20:29 thereof is called *B* unto this day

**BAMOTH** *(ba'-moth)* See BAMOTH-BAAL. *A city on the Arnon River.*
Num 21:19 and from Nahaliel to *B*
Num 21:20 from *B* in the valley, that is in

**BAMOTH-BAAL** *(ba'-moth-ba'-al) A Moabite town.*
Josh 13:17 Dibon, and *B*, and Beth-baal-meon,

**BAND**
Ex 39:23 with a *b* round about the hole,
1Sa 10:26 and there went with him a *b* of men
1Kin 11:24 him, and became captain over a *b*
2Kin 13:21 behold, they spied a *b* of men
1Chr 12:18 and made them captains of the *b*
1Chr 12:21 David against the *b* of the rovers
2Chr 22:1 for the *b* of men that came with
Ezr 8:22 of the king a *b* of soldiers
Job 39:10 unicorn with his *b* in the furrow
Dan 4:15 the earth, even with a *b* of iron
Dan 4:23 the earth, even with a *b* of iron
Mt 27:27 unto him the whole *b* of soldiers
Mk 15:16 and they call together the whole *b*
Jn 18:3 then, having received a *b* of men
Jn 18:12 Then the *b* and the captain and
Acts 10:1 of the *b* called the Italian *b*
Acts 21:31 unto the chief captain of the *b*
Acts 27:1 a centurion of Augustus' *b*

**BANDED**
Acts 23:12 certain of the Jews *b* together

**BANDS**
Gen 32:7 herds, and the camels, into two *b*
Gen 32:10 and now I am become two *b*
Lev 26:13 I have broken the *b* of your yoke
Judg 15:14 his *b* loosed from off his hands
2Sa 4:2 two men that were captains of *b*
2Kin 6:23 So the *b* of Syria came no more
2Kin 13:20 the *b* of the Moabites invaded the
2Kin 23:33 Pharaoh-nechoh put him in *b* at
2Kin 24:2 against him *b* of the Chaldees
1Chr 7:4 were *b* of soldiers for war, six
1Chr 12:23 *b* that were ready armed to the
2Chr 26:11 men, that went out to war by *b*
Job 1:17 The Chaldeans made out three *b*
Job 38:31 Pleiades, or loose the *b* of Orion
Job 39:5 hath loosed the *b* of the wild ass
Ps 2:3 Let us break their *b* asunder
Ps 73:4 For there are no *b* in their death
Ps 107:14 death, and brake their *b* in sunder
Ps 119:61 The *b* of the wicked have robbed
Prov 30:27 go they forth all of them by *b*
Eccl 7:26 snares and nets, and her hands as *b*
Is 28:22 lest your *b* be made strong
Is 52:2 thyself from the *b* of thy neck
Is 58:6 to loose the *b* of wickedness, to
Jer 2:20 broken thy yoke, and burst thy *b*
Eze 3:25 they shall put *b* upon thee
Eze 4:8 behold, I will lay *b* upon thee
Eze 12:14 him to help him, and all his *b*
Eze 17:21 all his *b* shall fall by the sword
Eze 34:27 I have broken the *b* of their yoke
Eze 38:6 Gomer, and all his *b*
Eze 38:9 the land, thou, and all thy *b*
Eze 38:22 will rain upon him, and upon his *b*
Eze 39:4 of Israel, thou, and all thy *b*
Hos 11:4 cords of a man, with *b* of love
Zec 11:7 Beauty, and the other I called *B*
Zec 11:14 asunder mine other staff, even *B*
Lk 8:29 and he brake the *b*, and was driven
Acts 16:26 and every one's *b* were loosed
Acts 22:30 Jews, he loosed him from his *b*
Acts 27:40 the sea, and loosed the rudder *b*
Col 2:19 *b* having nourishment ministered,

**BANI** *(ba'-ni)*
*1. A "mighty man" of David.*
2Sa 23:36 of Nathan of Zobah, *B* the Gadite,
*2. A Levite descendant of Merari.*
1Chr 6:46 The son of Amzi, the son of *B*
*3. A descendant of Pharez.*
1Chr 9:4 the son of Imri, the son of *B*
*4. A family of exiles.*
Ezr 2:10 The children of *B*, six hundred
Ezr 10:29 And of the sons of *B*
*5. Father whose sons married foreign wives.*
Ezr 10:34 Of the sons of *B*
*6. A Jewish descendant of a foreign woman.*
Ezr 10:38 And *B*, and Binnui, Shimei,
*7. Father of Rehum.*
Neh 3:17 the Levites, Rehum the son of *B*
Neh 8:7 Also Jeshua, and *B*, and Sherebiah,
Neh 9:4 of the Levites, Jeshua, and *B*
*8. A priest who assisted Ezra.*
Neh 9:4 Shebaniah, Bunni, Sherebiah, *B*
Neh 10:13 Hodijah, *B*, Beninu
*9. An Israelite who renewed the covenant under Nehemiah.*
Neh 10:14 Pahath-moab, Elam, Zatthu, *B*
*10. A family of exiles.*
Neh 11:22 Jerusalem was Uzzi the son of *B*

**BANISHED**
2Sa 14:13 doth not fetch home again his *b*
2Sa 14:14 that his *b* be not expelled from

**BANISHMENT**
Ezr 7:26 whether it be unto death, or to *b*
Lam 2:14 thee false burdens and causes of *b*

**BANK**
Gen 41:17 I stood upon the *b* of the river
Deut 4:48 which is by the *b* of the river
Josh 12:2 which is upon the *b* of the river
Josh 13:9 that is upon the *b* of the river
Josh 13:16 that is on the *b* of the river
2Sa 20:15 they cast up a *b* against the city
2Kin 2:13 back, and stood by the *b* of Jordan
2Kin 19:32 shield, nor cast a *b* against it
Is 37:33 shields, nor cast a *b* against it
Eze 47:7 at the *b* of the river were very
Eze 47:12 by the river upon the *b* thereof
Dan 12:5 this side of the *b* of the river
Lk 19:23 not thou my money into the *b*

**BANKS**
Josh 3:15 all his *b* all the time of harvest
Josh 4:18 place, and flowed over all his *b*
1Chr 12:15 when it had overflown all his *b*
Is 8:7 channels, and go over all his *b*
Dan 8:16 man's voice between the *b* of Ulai

**BANNER**
Ps 60:4 Thou hast given a *b* to them that
Song 2:4 house, and his *b* over me was love
Is 13:2 Lift ye up a *b* upon the high

**BANNERS**
Ps 20:5 of our God we will set up our *b*
Song 6:4 terrible as an army with *b*
Song 6:10 and terrible as an army with *b*

**BANQUET**
Est 5:4 *b* that I have prepared for him
Est 5:5 Haman came to the *b* that Esther
Est 5:6 said unto Esther at the *b* of wine
Est 5:8 Haman come to the *b* that I shall
Est 5:12 the *b* that she had prepared but
Est 5:14 merrily with the king unto the *b*
Est 6:14 the *b* that Esther had prepared
Est 7:1 Haman came to *b* with Esther the
Est 7:2 the second day at the *b* of wine
Est 7:7 the king arising from the *b* of
Est 7:8 into the place of the *b* of wine
Job 41:6 the companions make a *b* of him
Dan 5:10 his lords, came into the *b* house
Amos 6:7 the *b* of them that stretched

**BAPTISM**
Mt 3:7 and Sadducees come to his *b*
Mt 20:22 the *b* that I am baptized with
Mt 21:25 The *b* of John, whence was it
Mk 1:4 preach the *b* of repentance for
Mk 10:38 be baptized with the *b* that I am
Mk 11:30 The *b* of John, was it from heaven
Lk 3:3 preaching the *b* of repentance for
Lk 7:29 being baptized with the *b* of John
Lk 12:50 But I have a *b* to be baptized
Lk 20:4 The *b* of John, was it from heaven
Acts 1:22 Beginning from the *b* of John
Acts 10:37 after the *b* which John preached
Acts 13:24 preached before his coming the *b*
Acts 18:25 Lord, knowing only the *b* of John
Acts 19:3 And they said, Unto John's *b*
Rom 6:4 buried with him by *b* into death

Eph 4:5 One Lord, one faith, one *b*
Col 2:12 Buried with him in *b*, wherein
1Pet 3:21 *b* doth also now save us (not the

**BAPTIST** *(bap'-tist)* See BAPTIST'S. *John, the forerunner of Jesus.*
Mt 3:1 In those days came John the *B*
Mt 11:11 risen a greater than John the *B*
Mt 14:2 his servants, This is John the *B*
Mt 16:14 Some say that thou art John the *B*
Mt 17:13 he spake unto them of John the *B*
Mk 6:14 That John the *B* was risen from
Mk 6:24 she said, The head of John the *B*
Mk 6:25 a charger the head of John the *B*
Mk 8:28 And they answered, John the *B*
Lk 7:20 John *B* hath sent us unto thee,
Lk 7:28 a greater prophet than John the *B*
Lk 7:33 For John the *B* came neither
Lk 9:19 They answering said, John the *B*

**BAPTIST'S** *(bap'-tists)*
Mt 14:8 me here John *B* head in a charger

**BAPTIZE**
Mt 3:11 I indeed *b* you with water unto
Mk 1:4 John did *b* in the wilderness, and
Mk 1:8 but he shall *b* you with the Holy
Lk 3:16 I indeed *b* you with water
Lk 3:16 he shall *b* you with the Holy
Jn 1:26 them, saying, I *b* with water
Jn 1:33 he that sent me to *b* with water
1Cor 1:17 For Christ sent me not to *b*

**BAPTIZED**
Mt 3:6 And were *b* of him in Jordan,
Mt 3:13 Jordan unto John, to be *b* of him
Mt 3:16 And Jesus, when he was *b*, went up
Mt 20:22 *b* with the baptism that I am *b*
Mt 20:23 *b* with the baptism that I am *b*
Mk 1:5 were all *b* of him in the river of
Mk 10:38 *b* with the baptism that I am *b*
Mk 16:16 believeth and is *b* shall be saved
Lk 3:7 that came forth to be *b* of him
Lk 3:12 Then came also publicans to be *b*
Lk 3:21 Now when all the people were *b*
Lk 7:29 being *b* with the baptism of John
Lk 7:30 themselves, being not *b* of him
Lk 12:50 But I have a baptism to be *b* with
Jn 3:22 there he tarried with them, and *b*
Jn 4:1 *b* more disciples than John,
Jn 10:40 the place where John at first *b*
Acts 1:5 For John truly *b* with water
Acts 2:38 be *b* every one of you in the name
Acts 2:41 gladly received his word were *b*
Acts 8:12 name of Jesus Christ, they were *b*
Acts 8:16 only they were *b* in the name of
Acts 8:36 what doth hinder me to be *b*
Acts 8:38 and he *b* him
Acts 9:18 forthwith, and arose, and was *b*
Acts 10:47 water, that these should not be *b*
Acts 11:16 he said, John indeed *b* with water
Acts 16:15 And when she was *b*, and her
Acts 16:33 and was *b*, he and all his,
Acts 18:8 hearing believed, and were *b*
Acts 19:3 them, Unto what then were ye *b*
Acts 22:16 arise, and be *b*, and wash away thy
Rom 6:3 that so many of us as were *b* into
1Cor 1:13 or were ye *b* in the name of Paul
1Cor 10:2 were all *b* unto Moses in the
1Cor 12:13 Spirit are we all *b* into one body
1Cor 15:29 they do which are *b* for the dead
1Cor 15:29 why are they then *b* for the dead
Gal 3:27 *b* into Christ have put on Christ

**BAPTIZING**
Mt 28:19 *b* them in the name of the Father,
Jn 1:28 beyond Jordan, where John was *b*
Jn 1:31 therefore am I come *b* with water
Jn 3:23 John also was *b* in Aenon near to

**BAR**
Ex 26:28 the middle *b* in the midst of the
Ex 36:33 he made the middle *b* to shoot
Num 4:10 skins, and shall put it upon a *b*
Num 4:12 skins, and shall put them on a *b*
Judg 16:3 posts, and went away with them, *b*
Neh 7:3 them shut the doors, and *b* them
Amos 1:5 will break also the *b* of Damascus

**BARABBAS** *(ba-rab'-bas) A criminal released instead of Jesus.*
Mt 27:16 then a notable prisoner, called *B*
Mt 27:20 multitude that they should ask *B*
Mt 27:26 Then released he *B* unto them
Mk 15:7 And there was one named *B*, which
Mk 15:11 should rather release *B* unto them
Mk 15:15 people, released *B* unto them, and
Lk 23:18 this man, and release unto us *B*
Jn 18:40 saying, Not this man, but *B*

**BARACHEL** *(bar'-ak-el) Father of Elihu.*
Job 32:2 of Elihu the son of *B* the Buzite
Job 32:6 Elihu the son of *B* the Buzite

**BARACHIAS** *(bar'-ak-i'-as) Father of Zachariah.*
Mt 23:35 the blood of Zacharias son of *B*

**BARAK** *(ba'-rak) A captain in Deborah's army.*
Judg 4:6 called *B* the son of Abinoam out
Judg 4:8 *B* said unto her, If thou wilt go
Judg 4:12 they shewed Sisera that *B* the son
Judg 4:14 And Deborah said unto *B*, Up
Judg 4:22 as *B* pursued Sisera, Jael came
Judg 5:1 *B* the son of Abinoam on that day,
Judg 5:12 arise, *B*, and lead thy captivity
Judg 5:15 even Issachar, and also *B*
Heb 11:32 me to tell of Gedeon, and of *B*

**BARBARIAN**
1Cor 14:11 be unto him that speaketh a *b*
1Cor 14:11 speaketh shall be a *b* unto me
Col 3:11 nor uncircumcision, *B*, Scythian,

**BARBARIANS**
Acts 28:4 when the *b* saw the venomous beast
Rom 1:14 both to the Greeks, and to the *B*

**BARE**
Gen 4:1 *b* Cain, and said, I have gotten a
Gen 4:2 she again *b* his brother Abel
Gen 4:17 and she conceived, and *b* Enoch
Gen 4:20 And Adah *b* Jabal
Gen 4:22 she also *b* Tubal-cain, an
Gen 4:25 she *b* a son, and called his name
Gen 6:4 they *b* children to them, the same
Gen 7:17 *b* up the ark, and it was lift up
Gen 16:1 Abram's wife *b* him no children
Gen 16:15 And Hagar *b* Abram a son
Gen 19:37 And the firstborn *b* a son, and
Gen 20:17 and they *b* children
Gen 21:2 *b* Abraham a son in his old age,
Gen 22:24 she *b* also Tebah, and Gaham, and
Gen 24:36 Sarah my master's wife *b* a son to
Gen 24:47 son, whom Milcah *b* unto him
Gen 25:2 she *b* him Zimran, and Jokshan, and
Gen 25:12 Sarah's handmaid, *b* unto Abraham
Gen 25:26 years old when she *b* them
Gen 29:32 *b* a son, and she called his name
Gen 30:1 saw that she *b* Jacob no children
Gen 30:5 conceived, and *b* Jacob a son
Gen 30:7 again, and *b* Jacob a second son
Gen 30:10 Zilpah Leah's maid *b* Jacob a son
Gen 30:12 Leah's maid *b* Jacob a second son
Gen 30:17 and *b* Jacob the fifth son
Gen 30:19 again, and *b* Jacob the sixth son
Gen 30:21 And afterwards she *b* a daughter
Gen 30:23 And she conceived, and *b* a son
Gen 31:8 then all the cattle *b* speckled
Gen 31:39 I *b* the loss of it
Gen 34:1 which she *b* unto Jacob, went out
Gen 36:4 And Adah *b* to Esau Eliphaz
Gen 36:12 and she *b* to Eliphaz Amalek
Gen 36:14 she *b* to Esau Jeush, and Jaalam,
Gen 38:3 And she conceived, and *b* a son
Gen 41:50 priest of On *b* unto him
Gen 44:27 know that my wife *b* me two sons
Gen 46:15 which she *b* unto Jacob in
Gen 46:18 these she *b* unto Jacob, even
Gen 46:20 priest of On *b* unto him
Gen 46:25 and she *b* these unto Jacob
Ex 2:2 the woman conceived, and *b* a son
Ex 2:22 she *b* him a son, and he called his
Ex 6:20 and she *b* him Aaron and Moses
Ex 6:23 she *b* him Nadab, and Abihu,
Ex 6:25 and she *b* him Phinehas
Ex 19:4 how I *b* you on eagles' wings, and
Lev 13:45 shall be rent, and his head *b*
Lev 13:55 whether it be *b* within or without
Num 13:23 they *b* it between two upon a
Num 26:59 whom her mother *b* to Levi in
Num 26:59 she *b* unto Amram Aaron and Moses,
Deut 1:31 how that the LORD thy God *b* thee
Deut 31:9 which *b* the ark of the covenant
Deut 31:25 which *b* the ark of the covenant
Josh 3:15 as they that *b* the ark were come
Josh 3:17 the priests that *b* the ark of the
Josh 4:9 *b* the ark of the covenant stood
Josh 4:18 when the priests that *b* the ark
Josh 8:33 which *b* the ark of the covenant
Judg 3:18 the people that *b* the present
Judg 8:31 she also *b* him a son, whose name
Judg 11:2 And Gilead's wife *b* him sons
Judg 13:2 and his wife was barren, and *b* not
Judg 13:24 And the woman *b* a son, and called
Ruth 4:12 Pharez, whom Tamar *b* unto Judah
Ruth 4:13 her conception, and she *b* a son
1Sa 1:20 had conceived, that she *b* a son
1Sa 2:21 *b* three sons and two daughters
1Sa 14:1 the young man that *b* his armour
1Sa 14:6 the young man that *b* his armour
1Sa 17:41 the man that *b* the shield went
2Sa 6:13 that when they that *b* the ark of
2Sa 11:27 became his wife, and *b* him a son
2Sa 12:15 that Uriah's wife *b* unto David
2Sa 12:24 she *b* a son, and he called his
2Sa 18:15 ten young men that *b* Joab's
2Sa 21:8 whom she *b* unto Saul, Armoni and
1Kin 1:6 his mother *b* him after Absalom
1Kin 5:15 and ten thousand that *b* burdens
1Kin 9:23 which *b* rule over the people that
1Kin 10:2 train, with camels that *b* spices
1Kin 11:20 Tahpenes *b* him Genubath his son
1Kin 14:28 the LORD, that the guard *b* them
2Kin 4:17 *b* a son at that season that
2Kin 5:23 and they *b* them before him
1Chr 1:32 she *b* Zimran, and Jokshan, and
1Chr 2:4 his daughter in law *b* him Pharez
1Chr 2:17 And Abigail *b* Amasa
1Chr 2:19 unto him Ephrath, which *b* him Hur
1Chr 2:21 and she *b* him Segub
1Chr 2:24 then Abiah Hezron's wife *b* him
1Chr 2:29 she *b* him Ahban, and Molid
1Chr 2:35 and she *b* him Attai
1Chr 2:46 *b* Haran, and Moza, and Gazez
1Chr 2:48 concubine, *b* Sheber, and Tirhanah
1Chr 4:6 Naarah *b* him Ahuzam, and Hepher,
1Chr 4:9 Because I *b* him with sorrow
1Chr 4:17 she *b* Miriam, and Shammai, and
1Chr 7:14 Ashriel, whom she *b*
1Chr 7:16 the wife of Machir *b* a son
1Chr 7:18 And his sister Hammoleketh *b* Ishod
1Chr 7:23 *b* a son, and he called his name
1Chr 12:24 children of Judah that *b* shield
1Chr 15:15 *b* the ark of God upon their
1Chr 15:26 God helped the Levites that *b* the
2Chr 8:10 that *b* rule over the people
2Chr 9:1 company, and camels that *b* spices
2Chr 11:19 Which *b* him children
2Chr 14:8 had an army of men that *b* targets
Neh 4:17 the wall, and they that *b* burdens
Neh 5:15 even their servants *b* rule over
Prov 17:25 and bitterness to her that *b* him
Prov 23:25 she that *b* thee shall rejoice
Song 6:9 the choice one of her that *b* her
Song 8:5 brought thee forth that *b* thee
Is 8:3 and she conceived, and *b* a son
Is 22:6 Elam *b* the quiver with chariots
Is 32:11 strip you, and make you *b*, and gird
Is 47:2 make *b* the leg, uncover the thigh
Is 51:2 father, and unto Sarah that *b* you
Is 52:10 The LORD hath made *b* his holy arm
Is 53:12 he *b* the sin of many, and made
Is 63:9 he *b* them, and carried them all
Jer 13:22 discovered, and thy heels made *b*
Jer 16:3 their mothers that *b* them
Jer 20:14 wherein my mother *b* me be blessed
Jer 22:26 out, and thy mother that *b* thee
Jer 49:10 But I have made Esau *b*, I have
Jer 50:12 she that *b* you shall be ashamed
Eze 12:7 I *b* it upon my shoulder in their
Eze 16:7 whereas thou wast naked and *b*
Eze 16:22 youth, when thou wast naked and *b*
Eze 16:39 jewels, and leave thee naked and *b*
Eze 19:11 the sceptres of them that *b* rule
Eze 23:4 and they were mine, and they *b* sons
Eze 23:29 and shall leave thee naked and *b*
Eze 23:37 their sons, whom they *b* unto me
Hos 1:3 which conceived, and *b* him a son
Hos 1:6 conceived again, and *b* a daughter
Hos 1:8 she conceived, and *b* a son
Joel 1:7 he hath made it clean *b*, and cast
Mt 8:17 infirmities, and *b* our sicknesses
Mk 14:56 For many *b* false witness against
Lk 4:22 all *b* him witness, and wondered at
Lk 7:14 they that *b* him stood still
Lk 8:8 up, and *b* fruit an hundredfold

Lk 11:27 Blessed is the womb that *b* thee
Lk 23:29 barren, and the wombs that never *b*
Jn 1:15 John *b* witness of him, and cried,
Jn 1:32 John *b* record, saying, I saw the
Jn 1:34 *b* record that this is the Son of
Jn 2:8 And they *b* it
Jn 5:33 he *b* witness unto the truth
Jn 12:6 bag, and *b* what was put therein
Jn 12:17 him from the dead, *b* record
Jn 19:35 And he that saw it *b* record
Acts 15:8 *b* them witness, giving them the
1Cor 15:37 but *b* grain, it may chance of
1Pet 2:24 Who his own self *b* our sins in
Rev 1:2 Who *b* record of the word of God,
Rev 22:2 which *b* twelve manner of fruits,

**BAREFOOT**
2Sa 15:30 his head covered, and he went *b*
Is 20:2 And he did so, walking naked and *b*

**BAREST**
1Kin 2:26 because thou *b* the ark of the
Is 63:19 thou never *b* rule over them
Jn 3:26 Jordan, to whom thou *b* witness

**BARHUMITE** *(bar'-hu-mite)* See BAHARUMITE. *A form of Baharumite.*
2Sa 23:31 the Arbathite, Azmaveth the *B*

**BARIAH** *(ba-ri'-ah) Grandson of Shechaniah.*
1Chr 3:22 Hattush, and Igeal, and *B*, and

**BAR-JESUS** *(bar-je'-sus)* See ELYMAS. *Another name of Elymas.*
Acts 13:6 prophet, a Jew, whose name was *B*

**BAR-JONA** *(bar-jo'-nah)* See SIMON. *Another name of Simon Peter.*
Mt 16:17 him, Blessed art thou, Simon *B*

**BARKOS** *(bar'-cos) A family who returned from the exile.*
Ezr 2:53 The children of *B*, the children
Neh 7:55 The children of *B*, the children

**BARLEY**
Ex 9:31 And the flax and the *b* was smitten
Lev 27:16 a homer of *b* seed shall be valued
Num 5:15 tenth part of an ephah of *b* meal
Deut 8:8 A land of wheat, and *b*, and vines,
Judg 7:13 a cake of *b* bread tumbled into
Ruth 1:22 in the beginning of *b* harvest
Ruth 2:17 and it was about an ephah of *b*
Ruth 2:23 glean unto the end of *b* harvest
Ruth 3:2 he winnoweth *b* to night in the
Ruth 3:15 it, he measured six measures of *b*
Ruth 3:17 six measures of *b* gave he me
2Sa 14:30 is near mine, and he hath *b* there
2Sa 17:28 earthen vessels, and wheat, and *b*
2Sa 21:9 in the beginning of *b* harvest
1Kin 4:28 *B* also and straw for the horses and
2Kin 4:42 firstfruits, twenty loaves of *b*
2Kin 7:1 and two measures of *b* for a shekel
2Kin 7:16 and two measures of *b* for a shekel
2Kin 7:18 Two measures of *b* for a shekel
1Chr 11:13 was a parcel of ground full of *b*
2Chr 2:10 and twenty thousand measures of *b*
2Chr 2:15 Now therefore the wheat, and the *b*
2Chr 27:5 of wheat, and ten thousand of *b*
Job 31:40 of wheat, and cockle instead of *b*
Is 28:25 wheat and the appointed *b* and the
Jer 41:8 in the field, of wheat, and of *b*
Eze 4:9 thou also unto thee wheat, and *b*
Eze 4:12 And thou shalt eat it as *b* cakes
Eze 13:19 among my people for handfuls of *b*
Eze 45:13 part of an ephah of an homer of *b*
Hos 3:2 of *b*, and an half homer of *b*
Joel 1:11 for the wheat and for the *b*
Jn 6:9 here, which hath five *b* loaves
Jn 6:13 fragments of the five *b* loaves
Rev 6:6 three measures of *b* for a penny

**BARN**
Job 39:12 thy seed, and gather it into thy *b*
Hag 2:19 Is the seed yet in the *b*
Mt 13:30 but gather the wheat into my *b*
Lk 12:24 neither have storehouse nor *b*

**BARNABAS** *(bar'-na-bas)* See JOSES. *A companion of Paul.*
Acts 4:36 by the apostles was surnamed *B*
Acts 9:27 But *B* took him, and brought him to
Acts 11:22 and they sent forth *B*, that he
Acts 11:25 Then departed *B* to Tarsus
Acts 11:30 to the elders by the hands of *B*
Acts 12:25 And *B* and Saul returned from
Acts 13:1 as *B*, and Simeon that was called
Acts 13:7 who called for *B* and Saul, and
Acts 13:43 proselytes followed Paul and *B*
Acts 13:46 *B* waxed bold, and said, It was
Acts 13:50 persecution against Paul and *B*
Acts 14:12 And they called *B*, Jupiter
Acts 14:14 Which when the apostles, *B*
Acts 14:20 day he departed with *B* to Derbe
Acts 15:2 *B* had no small dissension and
Acts 15:12 silence, and gave audience to *B*
Acts 15:22 company to Antioch with Paul and *B*
Acts 15:25 men unto you with our beloved *B*
Acts 15:35 *B* continued in Antioch, teaching
Acts 15:39 so *B* took Mark, and sailed unto
1Cor 9:6 Or I only and *B*, have not we power
Gal 2:1 went up again to Jerusalem with *B*
Gal 2:9 *B* the right hands of fellowship
Gal 2:13 insomuch that *B* also was carried
Col 4:10 you, and Marcus, sister's son to *B*

**BARNS**
Prov 3:10 So shall thy *b* be filled with
Joel 1:17 desolate, the *b* are broken down
Mt 6:26 do they reap, nor gather into *b*
Lk 12:18 I will pull down my *b*, and build

**BARREL**
1Kin 17:12 but an handful of meal in a *b*
1Kin 17:14 The *b* of meal shall not waste,
1Kin 17:16 the *b* of meal wasted not, neither

**BARREN**
Gen 11:30 But Sarai was *b*
Gen 25:21 for his wife, because she was *b*
Gen 29:31 but Rachel was *b*
Ex 23:26 cast their young, nor be *b*
Deut 7:14 not be male or female *b* among you
Judg 13:2 and his wife was *b*, and bare not
Judg 13:3 unto her, Behold now, thou art *b*
1Sa 2:5 so that the *b* hath born seven
2Kin 2:19 water is naught, and the ground *b*
2Kin 2:21 thence any more death or *b* land
Job 24:21 entreateth the *b* that beareth not
Job 39:6 and the *b* land his dwellings
Ps 113:9 He maketh the *b* woman to keep
Prov 30:16 and the *b* womb
Song 4:2 twins, and none is *b* among them
Song 6:6 and there is not one *b* among them
Is 54:1 Sing, O *b*, thou that didst not
Joel 2:20 and will drive him into a land *b*
Lk 1:7 because that Elisabeth was *b*
Lk 1:36 month with her, who was called *b*
Lk 23:29 they shall say, Blessed are the *b*
Gal 4:27 Rejoice, thou *b* that bearest not
2Pet 1:8 you that ye shall neither be *b*

**BARS**
Ex 26:26 thou shalt make *b* of shittim wood
Ex 26:27 five *b* for the boards of the
Ex 26:29 of gold for places for the *b*
Ex 35:11 his taches, and his boards, his *b*
Ex 36:31 he made *b* of shittim wood
Ex 36:32 five *b* for the boards of the
Ex 36:34 *b*, and overlaid the *b* with gold
Ex 39:33 his taches, his boards, his *b*
Ex 40:18 thereof, and put in the *b* thereof
Num 3:36 the *b* thereof, and the pillars
Num 4:31 the *b* thereof, and the pillars
Deut 3:5 with high walls, gates, and *b*
1Sa 23:7 into a town that hath gates and *b*
1Kin 4:13 cities with walls and brasen *b*
2Chr 8:5 cities, with walls, gates, and *b*
2Chr 14:7 walls, and towers, gates, and *b*
Neh 3:3 locks thereof, and the *b* thereof
Neh 3:6 locks thereof, and the *b* thereof
Neh 3:13 the *b* thereof, and a thousand
Job 17:16 shall go down to the *b* of the pit
Job 38:10 for it my decreed place, and set *b*
Job 40:18 his bones are like *b* of iron
Ps 107:16 cut the *b* of iron in sunder
Ps 147:13 strengthened the *b* of thy gates
Prov 18:19 are like the *b* of a castle
Is 45:2 and cut in sunder the *b* of iron
Jer 49:31 which have neither gates nor *b*
Jer 51:30 her *b* are broken
Lam 2:9 he hath destroyed and broken her *b*
Eze 38:11 and having neither *b* nor gates
Jonah 2:6 the earth with her *b* was about me
Nah 3:13 the fire shall devour thy *b*

**BARSABAS** *(bar'-sab-as)* See JOSEPH, JUDAS, JUSTUS.
*1. The successor of Judas as apostle.*
Acts 1:23 appointed two, Joseph called *B*
*2. A disciple sent to Antioch with Silas.*
Acts 15:22 namely, Judas surnamed *B*, and

**BARTHOLOMEW** *(bar-thol'-o-mew)* See NATHANAEL. *One of Jesus' twelve disciples.*
Mt 10:3 Philip, and *B*; Thomas, and
Mk 3:18 And Andrew, and Philip, and *B*
Lk 6:14 James and John, Philip and *B*
Acts 1:13 and Andrew, Philip, and Thomas, *B*

**BARTIMAEUS** *(bar-ti-me'-us) A blind beggar.*
Mk 10:46 a great number of people, blind *B*

**BARUCH** *(ba'-rook)*
*1. A son of Zabbai.*
Neh 3:20 After him *B* the son of Zabbai
Neh 10:6 Daniel, Ginnethon, *B*,
*2. A descendant of Perez.*
Neh 11:5 And Maaseiah the son of *B*, the son
*3. The scribe of Jeremiah.*
Jer 32:12 purchase unto *B* the son of Neriah
Jer 32:16 purchase unto *B* the son of Neriah
Jer 36:4 called *B* the son of Neriah
Jer 36:8 *B* the son of Neriah did according
Jer 36:10 Then read *B* in the book the words
Jer 36:13 when *B* read the book in the ears
Jer 36:26 to take *B* the scribe and Jeremiah
Jer 36:32 roll, and gave it to *B* the scribe
Jer 43:3 But *B* the son of Neriah setteth
Jer 43:6 prophet, and *B* the son of Neriah
Jer 45:1 spake unto *B* the son of Neriah

**BARZILLAI** *(bar-zil'-la-i)*
*1. A friend of David.*
2Sa 17:27 *B* the Gileadite of Rogelim,
2Sa 19:31 *B* the Gileadite came down from
2Sa 19:39 was come over, the king kissed *B*
1Kin 2:7 unto the sons of *B* the Gileadite
Ezr 2:61 of Koz, the children of *B*
Neh 7:63 of Koz, the children of *B*
*2. Husband of Merab.*
2Sa 21:8 the son of *B* the Meholathite

**BASE**
2Sa 6:22 will be *b* in mine own sight
1Kin 7:27 cubits was the length of one *b*
1Kin 7:29 the ledges there was a *b* above
1Kin 7:34 to the four corners of one *b*
Job 30:8 of fools, yea, children of *b* men
Is 3:5 the *b* against the honourable
Eze 17:14 That the kingdom might be *b*
Eze 29:14 they shall be there a *b* kingdom
Zec 5:11 and set there upon her own *b*
Mal 2:9 and *b* before all the people,
1Cor 1:28 *b* things of the world, and things
2Cor 10:1 who in presence am *b* among you

**BASES**
1Kin 7:27 And he made ten *b* of brass
1Kin 7:37 this manner he made the ten *b*
1Kin 7:43 ten *b*, and ten lavers on the *b*
2Kin 16:17 Ahaz cut off the borders of the *b*
2Kin 25:13 the house of the LORD, and the *b*
2Kin 25:16 the *b* which Solomon had made for
2Chr 4:14 *b*, and lavers made he upon the *b*
Ezr 3:3 And they set the altar upon his *b*
Jer 27:19 the sea, and concerning the *b*
Jer 52:17 the house of the LORD, and the *b*
Jer 52:20 bulls that were under the *b*

**BASEST**
Eze 29:15 It shall be the *b* of the kingdoms
Dan 4:17 setteth up over it the *b* of men

**BASHAN** *(ba'-shan)* See BASHAN-HAVOTH-JAIR. *Kingdom of King Og.*
Num 21:33 turned and went up by the way of *B*
Num 32:33 and the kingdom of Og king of *B*
Deut 1:4 in Heshbon, and Og the king of *B*
Deut 3:1 turned, and went up the way to *B*
Deut 3:3 our hands Og also, the king of *B*
Deut 3:10 plain, and all Gilead, and all *B*
Deut 3:13 And the rest of Gilead, and all *B*
Deut 4:43 and Golan in *B*, of the Manassites
Deut 4:47 land, and the land of Og king of *B*
Deut 29:7 of Heshbon, and Og the king of *B*
Deut 32:14 lambs, and rams of the breed of *B*
Deut 33:22 he shall leap from *B*
Josh 9:10 of Heshbon, and to Og king of *B*

Josh 12:4 And the coast of Og king of *B*
Josh 13:11 Hermon, and all *B* unto Salcah
Josh 13:30 coast was from Mahanaim, all *B*
Josh 17:1 war, therefore he had Gilead and *B*
Josh 17:5 beside the land of Gilead and *B*
Josh 20:8 Golan in *B* out of the tribe of
Josh 21:6 the half tribe of Manasseh in *B*
Josh 21:27 gave Golan in *B* with her suburbs
Josh 22:7 Moses had given possession in *B*
1Kin 4:13 region of Argob, which is in *B*
1Kin 4:19 the Amorites, and of Og king of *B*
2Kin 10:33 the river Arnon, even Gilead and *B*
1Chr 5:11 in the land of *B* unto Salchah
1Chr 5:16 And they dwelt in Gilead in *B*
1Chr 5:23 increased from *B* unto Baal-hermon
1Chr 6:62 out of the tribe of Manasseh in *B*
1Chr 6:71 Golan in *B* with her suburbs, and
Neh 9:22 and the land of Og king of *B*
Ps 22:12 strong bulls of *B* have beset me
Ps 68:15 hill of God is as the hill of *B*
Ps 68:22 said, I will bring again from *B*
Ps 135:11 of the Amorites, and Og king of *B*
Ps 136:20 And Og the king of *B*
Is 2:13 up, and upon all the oaks of *B*
Is 33:9 and *B* and Carmel shake off their
Jer 22:20 and lift up thy voice in *B*
Jer 50:19 and he shall feed on Carmel and *B*
Eze 27:6 Of the oaks of *B* have they made
Eze 39:18 all of them fatlings of *B*
Amos 4:1 Hear this word, ye kine of *B*
Mic 7:14 let them feed in *B* and Gilead, as
Nah 1:4 *B* languisheth, and Carmel, and the
Zec 11:2 howl, O ye oaks of *B*

**BASHAN-HAVOTH-JAIR** *(ba'-shan-ha'-voth-ja'-ur) Same as Argob.*
Deut 3:14 them after his own name, *B*

**BASHEMATH** *(bash'-e-math)* See BASMATH.
*1. Daughter of Elon the Hittite.*
Gen 26:34 *B* the daughter of Elon the
*2. Daughter of Ishmael.*
Gen 36:3 *B* Ishmael's daughter, sister of
Gen 36:10 the son of *B* the wife of Esau
Gen 36:13 were the sons of *B* Esau's wife
Gen 36:17 are the sons of *B* Esau's wife

**BASKET**
Gen 40:17 in the uppermost *b* there was of
Ex 29:3 *b*, and bring them in the *b*
Ex 29:23 one wafer out of the *b* of the
Ex 29:32 and the bread that is in the *b*
Lev 8:2 rams, and a *b* of unleavened bread
Lev 8:26 out of the *b* of unleavened bread,
Lev 8:31 that is in the *b* of consecrations
Num 6:15 a *b* of unleavened bread, cakes of
Num 6:17 with the *b* of unleavened bread
Num 6:19 one unleavened cake out of the *b*
Deut 26:2 thee, and shalt put it in a *b*
Deut 26:4 take the *b* out of thine hand
Deut 28:17 Cursed shall be thy *b* and thy
Judg 6:19 the flesh he put in a *b*, and he
Jer 24:2 One *b* had very good figs, even
Amos 8:1 behold a *b* of summer fruit
Acts 9:25 let him down by the wall in a *b*
2Cor 11:33 through a window in a *b* was I let

**BASKETS**
Gen 40:16 I had three white *b* on my head
Gen 40:18 The three *b* are three days
2Kin 10:7 persons, and put their heads in *b*
Jer 6:9 as a grapegatherer into the *b*
Jer 24:1 two *b* of figs were set before the
Mt 14:20 that remained twelve *b* full
Mt 15:37 meat that was left seven *b* full
Mt 16:9 and how many *b* ye took up
Mk 6:43 they took up twelve *b* full of the
Mk 8:8 broken meat that was left seven *b*
Mk 8:19 how many *b* full of fragments took
Lk 9:17 that remained to them twelve *b*
Jn 6:13 and filled twelve *b* with the

**BASMATH** *(bas'-math)* See BASHEMATH. *A daughter of Solomon.*
1Kin 4:15 he also took *B* the daughter of

**BASON**
Ex 12:22 it in the blood that is in the *b*
1Chr 28:17 gave gold by weight for every *b*
Jn 13:5 that he poureth water into a *b*

**BASONS**
Ex 24:6 half of the blood, and put it in *b*
Ex 27:3 ashes, and his shovels, and his *b*
Ex 38:3 pots, and the shovels, and the *b*
Num 4:14 and the shovels, and the *b*
2Sa 17:28 Brought beds, and *b*, and earthen
1Kin 7:40 lavers, and the shovels, and the *b*
1Kin 7:45 pots, and the shovels, and the *b*
1Kin 7:50 bowls, and the snuffers, and the *b*
2Kin 12:13 LORD bowls of silver, snuffers, *b*
1Chr 28:17 for the golden *b* he gave gold by
2Chr 4:8 And he made an hundred *b* of gold
2Chr 4:11 pots, and the shovels, and the *b*
2Chr 4:22 And the snuffers, and the *b*
Ezr 1:10 Thirty *b* of gold, silver *b*
Ezr 8:27 Also twenty *b* of gold, of a
Neh 7:70 a thousand drams of gold, fifty *b*
Jer 52:19 And the *b*, and the firepans, and the

**BASTARD**
Deut 23:2 A *b* shall not enter into the
Zec 9:6 a *b* shall dwell in Ashdod, and I

**BAT**
Lev 11:19 kind, and the lapwing, and the *b*
Deut 14:18 kind, and the lapwing, and the *b*

**BATH**
Is 5:10 of vineyard shall yield one *b*
Eze 45:10 and a just ephah, and a just *b*
Eze 45:11 that the *b* may contain the tenth
Eze 45:14 the *b* of oil, ye shall offer the

**BATHE**
Lev 15:5 *b* himself in water, and be unclean
Lev 15:10 *b* himself in water, and be unclean
Lev 15:13 *b* his flesh in running water, and
Lev 15:18 they shall both *b* themselves in
Lev 15:21 *b* himself in water, and be unclean
Lev 15:27 *b* himself in water, and be unclean
Lev 16:26 and *b* his flesh in water, and
Lev 16:28 and *b* his flesh in water, and
Lev 17:15 *b* himself in water, and be unclean
Num 19:7 he shall *b* his flesh in water, and
Num 19:19 *b* himself in water, and shall be

**BATH-RABBIM** *(bath-rab'-bim) A gate at Heshbon.*
Song 7:4 in Heshbon, by the gate of *B*

**BATHS**
1Kin 7:26 it contained two thousand *b*
1Kin 7:38 one laver contained forty *b*
2Chr 2:10 and twenty thousand *b* of wine
2Chr 4:5 received and held three thousand *b*
Ezr 7:22 wheat, and to an hundred *b* of wine
Eze 45:14 cor, which is an homer of ten *b*

**BATH-SHEBA** *(bath-she'-bah)* See BATH-SHUA. *A wife of David.*
2Sa 11:3 And one said, Is not this *B*
2Sa 12:24 And David comforted *B* his wife
1Kin 1:11 unto *B* the mother of Solomon
1Kin 1:15 *B* went in unto the king into the
1Kin 1:28 David answered and said, Call me *B*
1Kin 1:31 Then *B* bowed with her face to the
1Kin 2:13 came to *B* the mother of Solomon
1Kin 2:18 And *B* said, Well
Ps 51:*t* him, after he had gone in to *B*

**BATH-SHUA** *(bath'-shu-ah)* See BATH-SHEBA. *A form of Bath-sheba.*
1Chr 3:5 of *B* the daughter of Ammiel

**BATTLE**
Gen 14:8 they joined *b* with them in the
Num 21:33 all his people, to the *b* at Edrei
Num 31:14 which came from the *b*
Num 31:21 men of war which went to the *b*
Num 31:27 war upon them, who went out to *b*
Num 32:27 for war, before the LORD to *b*
Num 32:29 over Jordan, every man armed to *b*
Deut 2:9 neither contend with them in *b*
Deut 2:24 it, and contend with him in *b*
Deut 3:1 and all his people, to *b* at Edrei
Deut 20:1 out to *b* against thine enemies
Deut 20:5 his house, lest he die in the *b*
Deut 20:7 his house, lest he die in the *b*
Deut 29:7 came out against us unto *b*
Josh 4:13 over before the LORD unto *b*
Josh 8:14 city went out against Israel to *b*
Josh 11:19 all other they took in *b*
Josh 22:33 intend to go up against them in *b*
Judg 8:13 from *b* before the sun was up
Judg 20:14 to go out to *b* against the
Judg 20:18 to the *b* against the children of
Judg 20:20 went out to *b* against Benjamin
Judg 20:22 set their *b* again in array in the
Judg 20:28 out to *b* against the children of
Judg 20:34 of all Israel, and the *b* was sore
Judg 20:39 men of Israel retired in the *b*
Judg 20:42 but the *b* overtook them
1Sa 4:1 out against the Philistines to *b*
1Sa 7:10 drew near to *b* against Israel
1Sa 13:22 it came to pass in the day of *b*
1Sa 14:20 themselves, and they came to the *b*
1Sa 14:22 followed hard after them in the *b*
1Sa 17:1 together their armies to *b*
1Sa 17:8 come out to set your *b* in array
1Sa 17:13 went and followed Saul to the *b*
1Sa 17:20 the fight, and shouted for the *b*
1Sa 17:28 down that thou mightest see the *b*
1Sa 17:47 for the *b* is the LORD's, and he
1Sa 26:10 or he shall descend into *b*
1Sa 28:1 thou shalt go out with me to *b*
1Sa 29:4 let him not go down with us to *b*
1Sa 29:9 shall not go up with us to the *b*
1Sa 30:24 part is that goeth down to the *b*
1Sa 31:3 the *b* went sore against Saul, and
2Sa 1:4 the people are fled from the *b*
2Sa 1:25 fallen in the midst of the *b*
2Sa 2:17 there was a very sore *b* that day
2Sa 3:30 brother Asahel at Gibeon in the *b*
2Sa 10:8 put the *b* in array at the
2Sa 10:13 unto the *b* against the Syrians
2Sa 11:1 the time when kings go forth to *b*
2Sa 11:15 in the forefront of the hottest *b*
2Sa 11:25 make thy *b* more strong against
2Sa 17:11 that thou go to *b* in thine own
2Sa 18:6 the *b* was in the wood of Ephraim
2Sa 18:8 For the *b* was there scattered
2Sa 19:3 steal away when they flee in *b*
2Sa 19:10 we anointed over us, is dead in *b*
2Sa 21:17 shalt go no more out with us to *b*
2Sa 21:18 that there was again a *b* with the
2Sa 22:40 hast girded me with strength to *b*
2Sa 23:9 were there gathered together to *b*
1Kin 8:44 go out to *b* against their enemy
1Kin 20:14 he said, Who shall order the *b*
1Kin 20:29 the seventh day the *b* was joined
1Kin 20:39 went out into the midst of the *b*
1Kin 22:4 go with me to *b* to Ramoth-gilead
1Kin 22:6 I go against Ramoth-gilead to *b*
1Kin 22:15 we go against Ramoth-gilead to *b*
1Kin 22:30 myself, and enter into the *b*
1Kin 22:35 And the *b* increased that day
2Kin 3:7 thou go with me against Moab to *b*
2Kin 3:26 that the *b* was too sore for him
1Chr 5:20 for they cried to God in the *b*
1Chr 7:11 fit to go out for war and *b*
1Chr 7:40 to *b* was twenty and six thousand
1Chr 10:3 the *b* went sore against Saul, and
1Chr 11:13 were gathered together to *b*
1Chr 12:8 and men of war fit for the *b*
1Chr 12:19 the Philistines against Saul to *b*
1Chr 12:33 Zebulun, such as went forth to *b*
1Chr 12:36 of Asher, such as went forth to *b*
1Chr 14:15 that then thou shalt go out to *b*
1Chr 19:7 from their cities, and came to *b*
1Chr 19:9 put the *b* in array before the
1Chr 19:10 the *b* was set against him before
1Chr 19:14 before the Syrians unto the *b*
1Chr 19:17 set the *b* in array against them
1Chr 20:1 the time that kings go out to *b*
2Chr 13:3 Abijah set the *b* in array with an
2Chr 13:14 the *b* was before and behind
2Chr 14:10 they set the *b* in array in the
2Chr 18:5 Shall we go to Ramoth-gilead to *b*
2Chr 18:14 shall we go to Ramoth-gilead to *b*
2Chr 18:29 myself, and will go to the *b*
2Chr 18:34 And the *b* increased that day
2Chr 20:1 came against Jehoshaphat to *b*
2Chr 20:15 for the *b* is not yours, but God's
2Chr 20:17 shall not need to fight in this *b*
2Chr 25:8 go, do it, be strong for the *b*
2Chr 25:13 they should not go with him to *b*
Job 15:24 him, as a king ready to the *b*
Job 38:23 of trouble, against the day of *b*
Job 39:25 and he smelleth the *b* afar off
Job 41:8 hand upon him, remember the *b*
Ps 18:39 me with strength unto the *b*
Ps 24:8 and mighty, the LORD mighty in *b*
Ps 55:18 from the *b* that was against me
Ps 76:3 shield, and the sword, and the *b*
Ps 78:9 bows, turned back in the day of *b*
Ps 89:43 not made him to stand in the *b*

Ps 140:7 covered my head in the day of *b*
Prov 21:31 is prepared against the day of *b*
Eccl 9:11 nor the *b* to the strong, neither
Is 9:5 For every *b* of the warrior is
Is 13:4 hosts mustereth the host of the *b*
Is 22:2 with the sword, nor dead in *b*
Is 27:4 briers and thorns against me in *b*
Is 28:6 them that turn the *b* to the gate
Is 42:25 his anger, and the strength of *b*
Jer 8:6 as the horse rusheth into the *b*
Jer 18:21 men be slain by the sword in *b*
Jer 46:3 and shield, and draw near to *b*
Jer 49:14 against her, and rise up to the *b*
Jer 50:22 A sound of *b* is in the land, and
Jer 50:42 put in array, like a man to the *b*
Jer 51:20 Thou art my *b* ax and weapons of
Eze 7:14 but none goeth to the *b*
Eze 13:5 in the *b* in the day of the LORD
Dan 11:20 neither in anger, nor in *b*
Dan 11:25 stirred up to *b* with a very great
Hos 1:7 by bow, nor by sword, nor by *b*
Hos 2:18 the *b* out of the earth, and will
Hos 10:9 the *b* in Gibeah against the
Hos 10:14 Beth-arbel in the day of *b*
Joel 2:5 as a strong people set in *b* array
Amos 1:14 with shouting in the day of *b*
Obad 1 let us rise up against her in *b*
Zec 9:10 the *b* bow shall be cut off
Zec 10:3 them as his goodly horse in the *b*
Zec 14:2 nations against Jerusalem to *b*
1Cor 14:8 shall prepare himself to the *b*
Rev 9:7 like unto horses prepared unto *b*
Rev 9:9 of many horses running to *b*
Rev 16:14 to gather them to the *b* of that
Rev 20:8 to gather them together to *b*

**BATTLES**
1Sa 8:20 go out before us, and fight our *b*
1Sa 18:17 for me, and fight the LORD's *b*
1Sa 25:28 lord fighteth the *b* of the LORD
1Chr 26:27 Out of the spoils won in *b* did
2Chr 32:8 God to help us, and to fight our *b*
Is 30:32 in *b* of shaking will he fight

**BAVAI** *(bav'-a-i) A descendant of Henadad.*
Neh 3:18 *B* the son of Henadad, the ruler

**BAY**
Josh 15:2 from the *b* that looketh southward
Josh 15:5 the *b* of the sea at the uttermost
Josh 18:19 *b* of the salt sea at the south
Ps 37:35 himself like a green *b* tree
Zec 6:3 chariot grisled and *b* horses
Zec 6:7 the *b* went forth, and sought to go

**BAZLITH** *(baz'-lith)* See BAZLUTH. *A family who returned from exile.*
Neh 7:54 The children of *B*, the children

**BAZLUTH** *(baz'-luth)* See BAZLITH. *A form of Bazlith.*
Ezr 2:52 The children of *B*, the children

**BDELLIUM**
Gen 2:12 there is *b* and the onyx stone
Num 11:7 colour thereof as the colour of *b*

**BEALIAH** *(be-a-li'-ah) A warrior in David's army.*
1Chr 12:5 Eluzai, and Jerimoth, and *B*

**BEALOTH** *(be'-a-loth)* See ALOTH. *A city in Judah.*
Josh 15:24 Ziph, and Telem, and *B*,

**BEAM**
Judg 16:14 went away with the pin of the *b*
1Sa 17:7 his spear was like a weaver's *b*
2Sa 21:19 whose spear was like a weaver's *b*
1Kin 7:6 the thick *b* were before them
2Kin 6:2 and take thence every man a *b*
2Kin 6:5 But as one was felling a *b*
1Chr 11:23 was a spear like a weaver's *b*
1Chr 20:5 spear staff was like a weaver's *b*
Hab 2:11 the *b* out of the timber shall
Mt 7:3 but considerest not the *b* that is
Mt 7:4 behold, a *b* is in thine own eye
Lk 6:41 but perceivest not the *b* that is

**BEAMS**
1Kin 6:6 that the *b* should not be fastened
1Kin 6:9 and covered the house with *b*
1Kin 6:36 hewed stone, and a row of cedar *b*
1Kin 7:2 with cedar *b* upon the pillars
1Kin 7:12 hewed stones, and a row of cedar *b*
2Chr 3:7 He overlaid also the house, the *b*
Neh 2:8 *b* for the gates of the palace
Neh 3:3 who also laid the *b* thereof
Neh 3:6 they laid the *b* thereof, and set
Ps 104:3 Who layeth the *b* of his chambers
Song 1:17 The *b* of our house are cedar, and

**BEANS**
2Sa 17:28 and flour, and parched corn, and *b*
Eze 4:9 unto thee wheat, and barley, and *b*

**BEAR**
Gen 4:13 is greater than I can *b*
Gen 13:6 the land was not able to *b* them
Gen 16:11 art with child, and shalt *b* a son
Gen 17:17 that is ninety years old, *b*
Gen 17:19 wife shall *b* thee a son indeed
Gen 17:21 which Sarah shall *b* unto thee at
Gen 18:13 Shall I of a surety *b* a child
Gen 22:23 these eight Milcah did *b* to Nahor
Gen 30:3 she shall *b* upon my knees, that I
Gen 36:7 *b* them because of their cattle
Gen 43:9 then let me *b* the blame for ever
Gen 44:32 then I shall *b* the blame to my
Gen 49:15 and bowed his shoulder to *b*
Ex 18:22 they shall *b* the burden with thee
Ex 20:16 Thou shalt not *b* false witness
Ex 25:27 of the staves to *b* the table
Ex 27:7 two sides of the altar, to *b* it
Ex 28:12 Aaron shall *b* their names before
Ex 28:29 Aaron shall *b* the names of the
Ex 28:30 Aaron shall *b* the judgment of the
Ex 28:38 that Aaron may *b* the iniquity of
Ex 28:43 that they *b* not iniquity, and die
Ex 30:4 for the staves to *b* it withal
Ex 37:14 for the staves to *b* the table
Ex 37:27 for the staves to *b* it withal
Ex 38:7 of the altar, to *b* it withal
Lev 5:1 it, then he shall *b* his iniquity
Lev 5:17 guilty, and shall *b* his iniquity
Lev 10:17 it you to *b* the iniquity of the
Lev 12:5 But if she *b* a maid child, then
Lev 16:22 the goat shall *b* upon him all
Lev 17:16 then he shall *b* his iniquity
Lev 19:8 eateth it shall *b* his iniquity
Lev 19:18 nor *b* any grudge against the
Lev 20:17 he shall *b* his iniquity
Lev 20:19 they shall *b* their iniquity
Lev 22:9 lest they *b* sin for it, and die
Lev 22:16 Or suffer them to *b* the iniquity
Lev 24:15 curseth his God shall *b* his sin
Num 1:50 they shall *b* the tabernacle, and
Num 4:15 sons of Kohath shall come to *b* it
Num 4:25 they shall *b* the curtains of the
Num 5:31 this woman shall *b* her iniquity
Num 7:9 should *b* upon their shoulders
Num 9:13 season, that man shall *b* his sin
Num 11:14 I am not able to *b* all this
Num 11:17 they shall *b* the burden of the
Num 14:27 How long shall I *b* with this evil
Num 14:33 *b* your whoredoms, until your
Num 18:1 *b* the iniquity of the sanctuary
Num 18:22 the congregation, lest they *b* sin
Num 18:32 ye shall *b* no sin by reason of it
Num 30:15 then he shall *b* her iniquity
Deut 1:9 am not able to *b* you myself alone
Deut 1:12 I myself alone *b* your cumbrance
Deut 1:31 thee, as a man doth *b* his son
Deut 5:20 Neither shalt thou *b* false
Deut 10:8 to *b* the ark of the covenant of
Deut 28:57 her children which she shall *b*
Josh 3:8 that *b* the ark of the covenant
Josh 3:13 that *b* the ark of the LORD
Josh 4:16 that *b* the ark of the testimony
Josh 6:4 seven priests shall *b* before the
Josh 6:6 let seven priests *b* seven
Judg 13:3 thou shalt conceive, and *b* a son
Judg 13:5 thou shalt conceive, and *b* a son
Judg 13:7 thou shalt conceive, and *b* a son
Ruth 1:12 to night, and should also *b* sons
1Sa 17:34 and there came a lion, and a *b*
1Sa 17:36 slew both the lion and the *b*
2Sa 17:8 as a *b* robbed of her whelps in
2Sa 18:19 *b* the king tidings, how that the
1Kin 3:21 it was not my son, which I did *b*
1Kin 21:10 to *b* witness against him, saying,
2Kin 18:14 which thou puttest on me will I *b*
2Kin 19:30 root downward, and *b* fruit upward
1Chr 5:18 men, men able to *b* buckler
2Chr 2:2 and ten thousand men to *b* burdens
Est 1:22 should *b* rule in his own house
Ps 75:3 I *b* up the pillars of it
Ps 89:50 how I do *b* in my bosom the
Ps 91:12 They shall *b* thee up in their
Prov 9:12 scornest, thou alone shalt *b* it
Prov 12:24 hand of the diligent shall *b* rule
Prov 17:12 Let a *b* robbed of her whelps meet
Prov 18:14 but a wounded spirit who can *b*
Prov 28:15 As a roaring lion, and a ranging *b*
Prov 30:21 and for four which it cannot *b*
Song 4:2 whereof every one *b* twins
Is 1:14 I am weary to *b* them
Is 7:14 *b* a son, and shall call his name
Is 11:7 And the cow and the *b* shall feed
Is 37:31 root downward, and *b* fruit upward
Is 46:4 I have made, and I will *b*
Is 46:7 They *b* him upon the shoulder,
Is 52:11 that *b* the vessels of the LORD
Is 53:11 for he shall *b* their iniquities
Is 54:1 O barren, thou that didst not *b*
Jer 5:31 the priests *b* rule by their means
Jer 10:19 this is a grief, and I must *b* it
Jer 17:21 *b* no burden on the sabbath day,
Jer 17:27 not to *b* a burden, even entering
Jer 29:6 to husbands, that they may *b* sons
Jer 31:19 because I did *b* the reproach of
Jer 44:22 that the LORD could no longer *b*
Lam 3:10 was unto me as a *b* lying in wait
Lam 3:27 that he *b* the yoke in his youth
Eze 4:4 it thou shalt *b* their iniquity
Eze 12:6 thou *b* it upon thy shoulders
Eze 12:12 shall *b* upon his shoulder in the
Eze 14:10 they shall *b* the punishment of
Eze 16:52 *b* thine own shame for thy sins
Eze 16:54 thou mayest *b* thine own shame
Eze 17:8 and that it might *b* fruit
Eze 17:23 *b* fruit, and be a goodly cedar
Eze 18:19 doth not the son *b* the iniquity
Eze 23:35 therefore *b* thou also thy
Eze 23:49 ye shall *b* the sins of your idols
Eze 32:30 *b* their shame with them that go
Eze 34:29 neither *b* the shame of the
Eze 36:7 you, they shall *b* their shame
Eze 36:15 neither shalt thou *b* the reproach
Eze 44:10 they shall even *b* their iniquity
Eze 44:12 they shall *b* their iniquity
Eze 46:20 that they *b* them not out into the
Dan 2:39 which shall *b* rule over all the
Dan 7:5 beast, a second, like to a *b*
Hos 9:16 dried up, they shall *b* no fruit
Hos 13:8 I will meet them as a *b* that is
Amos 5:19 flee from a lion, and a *b* met him
Amos 7:10 is not able to *b* all his words
Mic 6:16 therefore ye shall *b* the reproach
Mic 7:9 I will *b* the indignation of the
Zeph 1:11 all they that *b* silver are cut
Hag 2:12 If one *b* holy flesh in the skirt
Zec 5:10 me, Whither do these *b* the ephah
Zec 6:13 he shall *b* the glory, and shall
Mt 3:11 whose shoes I am not worthy to *b*
Mt 4:6 their hands they shall *b* thee up
Mt 19:18 Thou shalt not *b* false witness
Mt 27:32 him they compelled to *b* his cross
Mk 10:19 Do not *b* false witness, Defraud
Mk 15:21 and Rufus, to *b* his cross
Lk 1:13 wife Elisabeth shall *b* thee a son
Lk 4:11 their hands they shall *b* thee up
Lk 11:48 Truly ye *b* witness that ye allow
Lk 13:9 And if it *b* fruit, well
Lk 14:27 And whosoever doth not *b* his cross
Lk 18:7 though he *b* long with them
Lk 18:20 Do not *b* false witness, Honour
Lk 23:26 that he might *b* it after Jesus
Jn 1:7 to *b* witness of the Light, that
Jn 1:8 but was sent to *b* witness of that
Jn 2:8 *b* unto the governor of the feast
Jn 3:28 Ye yourselves *b* me witness
Jn 5:31 If I *b* witness of myself, my
Jn 5:36 *b* witness of me, that the Father
Jn 8:14 Though I *b* record of myself, yet
Jn 8:18 I am one that *b* witness of myself
Jn 10:25 name, they *b* witness of me
Jn 15:4 branch cannot *b* fruit of itself
Jn 15:8 glorified, that ye *b* much fruit
Jn 15:27 And ye also shall *b* witness
Jn 16:12 you, but ye cannot *b* them now
Jn 18:23 evil, *b* witness of the evil
Jn 18:37 that I should *b* witness unto the
Acts 9:15 to *b* my name before the Gentiles,
Acts 15:10 our fathers nor we were able to *b*
Acts 18:14 would that I should *b* with you

Acts 22:5 the high priest doth *b* me witness
Acts 23:11 so must thou *b* witness also at
Acts 27:15 could not *b* up into the wind, we
Rom 10:2 For I *b* them record that they
Rom 13:9 Thou shalt not *b* false witness
Rom 15:1 to *b* the infirmities of the weak
1Cor 3:2 hitherto ye were not able to *b* it
1Cor 10:13 that ye may be able to *b* it
1Cor 15:49 we shall also *b* the image of the
2Cor 8:3 I *b* record, yea, and beyond their
2Cor 11:1 Would to God ye could *b* with me a
2Cor 11:4 ye might well *b* with him
Gal 4:15 for I *b* you record, that, if it
Gal 5:10 you shall *b* his judgment,
Gal 6:2 *B* ye one another's burdens, and so
Gal 6:5 every man shall *b* his own burden
Gal 6:17 for I *b* in my body the marks of
Col 4:13 For I *b* him record, that he hath
1Ti 5:14 *b* children, guide the house, give
Heb 9:28 offered to *b* the sins of many
Jas 3:12 my brethren, *b* olive berries
1Jn 1:2 *b* witness, and shew unto you that
1Jn 5:7 are three that *b* record in heaven
3Jn 12 yea, and we also *b* record
Rev 2:2 how thou canst not *b* them which
Rev 13:2 his feet were as the feet of a *b*

### BEARD
Lev 13:29 a plague upon the head or the *b*
Lev 14:9 his hair off his head and his *b*
Lev 19:27 thou mar the corners of thy *b*
Lev 21:5 shave off the corner of their *b*
1Sa 17:35 against me, I caught him by his *b*
1Sa 21:13 his spittle fall down upon his *b*
2Sa 19:24 his feet, nor trimmed his *b*
2Sa 20:9 by the *b* with the right hand to
Ezr 9:3 the hair of my head and of my *b*
Ps 133:2 upon the *b*, even Aaron's *b*
Is 7:20 and it shall also consume the *b*
Is 15:2 be baldness, and every *b* cut off
Jer 48:37 shall be bald, and every *b* clipped
Eze 5:1 upon thine head and upon thy *b*

### BEARDS
2Sa 10:4 off the one half of their *b*
1Chr 19:5 at Jericho until your *b* be grown
Jer 41:5 men, having their *b* shaven

### BEARERS
2Chr 2:18 of them to be *b* of burdens
2Chr 34:13 they were over the *b* of burdens
Neh 4:10 The strength of the *b* of burdens

### BEAREST
Judg 13:3 now, thou art barren, and *b* not
Ps 106:4 that thou *b* unto thy people
Jn 8:13 him, Thou *b* record of thyself
Rom 11:18 thou *b* not the root, but the root
Gal 4:27 Rejoice, thou barren that *b* not

### BEARETH
Lev 11:25 whosoever *b* ought of the carcase
Lev 11:28 he that *b* the carcase of them
Lev 11:40 he also that *b* the carcase of it
Lev 15:10 he that *b* any of those things
Num 11:12 father *b* the sucking child
Deut 25:6 *b* shall succeed in the name of
Deut 29:18 be among you a root that *b* gall
Deut 29:23 that it is not sown, nor *b*
Deut 32:11 taketh them, *b* them on her wings
Job 16:8 up in me *b* witness to my face
Job 24:21 entreateth the barren that *b* not
Prov 25:18 A man that *b* false witness
Prov 29:2 but when the wicked *b* rule
Song 6:6 whereof every one *b* twins
Joel 2:22 spring, for the tree *b* her fruit
Mt 13:23 which also *b* fruit, and bringeth
Jn 5:32 is another that *b* witness of me
Jn 8:18 that sent me *b* witness of me
Jn 15:2 Every branch in me that *b* not
Rom 8:16 The Spirit itself *b* witness with
Rom 13:4 for he *b* not the sword in vain
1Cor 13:7 *B* all things, believeth all
Heb 6:8 But that which *b* thorns and briers
1Jn 5:6 it is the Spirit that *b* witness

### BEARING
Gen 1:29 have given you every herb *b* seed
Gen 16:2 LORD hath restrained me from *b*
Gen 29:35 his name Judah; and left *b*
Gen 30:9 When Leah saw that she had left *b*
Gen 37:25 with their camels *b* spicery
Num 10:17 set forward, *b* the tabernacle
Num 10:21 set forward, *b* the sanctuary

Josh 3:3 and the priests the Levites *b* it
Josh 3:14 the priests *b* the ark of the
Josh 6:8 that the seven priests *b* the
Josh 6:13 seven priests *b* seven trumpets of
1Sa 17:7 one *b* a shield went before him
2Sa 15:24 *b* the ark of the covenant of God
Ps 126:6 *b* precious seed, shall doubtless
Mk 14:13 you a man *b* a pitcher of water
Lk 22:10 meet you, *b* a pitcher of water
Jn 19:17 he *b* his cross went forth into a
Rom 2:15 their conscience also *b* witness
Rom 9:1 my conscience also *b* me witness
2Cor 4:10 Always *b* about in the body the
Heb 2:4 God also *b* them witness, both
Heb 13:13 without the camp, *b* his reproach

### BEARS
2Kin 2:24 forth two she *b* out of the wood
Is 59:11 We roar all like *b*, and mourn sore

### BEAST
Gen 1:24 *b* of the earth after his kind
Gen 1:30 to every *b* of the earth, and to
Gen 2:19 God formed every *b* of the field
Gen 3:1 was more subtil than any *b* of the
Gen 3:14 above every *b* of the field
Gen 6:7 both man, and *b*, and the creeping
Gen 7:2 Of every clean *b* thou shalt take
Gen 7:14 every *b* after his kind, and all
Gen 7:21 of fowl, and of cattle, and of *b*
Gen 8:19 Every *b*, every creeping thing, and
Gen 9:2 be upon every *b* of the earth
Gen 9:5 hand of every *b* will I require it
Gen 9:10 of every *b* of the earth with you
Gen 34:23 every *b* of theirs be ours
Gen 37:20 Some evil *b* hath devoured him
Gen 37:33 an evil *b* hath devoured him
Ex 8:17 and it became lice in man, and in *b*
Ex 9:9 with blains upon man, and upon *b*
Ex 9:10 with blains upon man, and upon *b*
Ex 9:19 *b* which shall be found in the
Ex 9:22 of Egypt, upon man, and upon *b*
Ex 9:25 was in the field, both man and *b*
Ex 11:7 move his tongue, against man or *b*
Ex 12:12 the land of Egypt, both man and *b*
Ex 13:2 of Israel, both of man and of *b*
Ex 13:12 cometh of a *b* which thou hast
Ex 13:15 of man, and the firstborn of *b*
Ex 19:13 whether it be *b* or man, it shall
Ex 21:34 and the dead *b* shall be his
Ex 22:5 be eaten, and shall put in his *b*
Ex 22:10 or an ox, or a sheep, or any *b*
Ex 22:19 Whosoever lieth with a *b* shall
Ex 23:29 the *b* of the field multiply
Lev 5:2 it be a carcase of an unclean *b*
Lev 7:21 of man, or any unclean *b*, or any
Lev 7:24 the fat of the *b* that dieth of
Lev 11:26 The carcases of every *b* which
Lev 11:39 And if any *b*, of which ye may eat,
Lev 11:47 between the *b* that may be eaten
Lev 17:13 catcheth any *b* or fowl that may
Lev 18:23 any *b* to defile thyself therewith
Lev 20:15 And if a man lie with a *b*, he
Lev 20:25 make your souls abominable by *b*
Lev 24:18 he that killeth a *b* shall make it
Lev 24:21 And he that killeth a *b*, he shall
Lev 25:7 for the *b* that are in thy land,
Lev 27:9 And if it be a *b*, whereof men
Lev 27:27 And if it be of an unclean *b*
Num 3:13 in Israel, both man and *b*
Num 8:17 of Israel are mine, both man and *b*
Num 31:26 was taken, both of man and of *b*
Num 31:47 of fifty, both of man and of *b*
Deut 4:17 The likeness of any *b* that is on
Deut 14:6 every *b* that parteth the hoof, and
Deut 27:21 that lieth with any manner of *b*
Judg 20:48 the men of every city, as the *b*
2Kin 14:9 by a wild *b* that was in Lebanon
2Chr 25:18 by a wild *b* that was in Lebanon
Neh 2:12 neither was there any *b* with me
Neh 2:14 the *b* that was under me to pass
Job 39:15 or that the wild *b* may break them
Ps 36:6 O LORD, thou preservest man and *b*
Ps 50:10 For every *b* of the forest is mine
Ps 73:22 I was as a *b* before thee
Ps 80:13 the wild *b* of the field doth
Ps 104:11 drink to every *b* of the field
Ps 135:8 of Egypt, both of man and *b*
Ps 147:9 He giveth to the *b* his food
Prov 12:10 man regardeth the life of his *b*
Eccl 3:19 man hath no preeminence above a *b*

Eccl 3:21 the spirit of the *b* that goeth
Is 35:9 nor any ravenous *b* shall go up
Is 43:20 The *b* of the field shall honour
Is 46:1 they are a burden to the weary *b*
Is 63:14 As a *b* goeth down into the valley
Jer 7:20 this place, upon man, and upon *b*
Jer 9:10 of the heavens and the *b* are fled
Jer 21:6 of this city, both man and *b*
Jer 27:5 the *b* that are upon the ground,
Jer 31:27 of man, and with the seed of *b*
Jer 32:43 It is desolate without man or *b*
Jer 33:10 desolate without man and without *b*
Jer 33:12 desolate without man and without *b*
Jer 36:29 to cease from thence man and *b*
Jer 50:3 they shall depart, both man and *b*
Jer 51:62 remain in it, neither man nor *b*
Eze 14:13 and will cut off man and *b* from it
Eze 14:17 that I cut off man and *b* from it
Eze 14:19 to cut off from it man and *b*
Eze 14:21 and the famine, and the noisome *b*
Eze 25:13 and will cut off man and *b* from it
Eze 29:8 and cut off man and *b* out of thee
Eze 29:11 nor foot of *b* shall pass through
Eze 34:8 meat to every *b* of the field
Eze 34:28 neither shall the *b* of the land
Eze 36:11 I will multiply upon you man and *b*
Eze 39:17 to every *b* of the field, Assemble
Eze 44:31 or torn, whether it be fowl or *b*
Dan 7:5 And behold another *b*, a second,
Dan 7:7 visions, and behold a fourth *b*
Dan 7:11 beheld even till the *b* was slain
Dan 7:19 know the truth of the fourth *b*
Dan 7:23 The fourth *b* shall be the fourth
Hos 13:8 the wild *b* shall tear them
Jonah 3:7 saying, Let neither man nor *b*
Mic 1:13 bind the chariot to the swift *b*
Zeph 1:3 I will consume man and *b*
Zec 8:10 hire for man, nor any hire for *b*
Lk 10:34 and wine, and set him on his own *b*
Acts 28:4 the venomous *b* hang on his hand
Heb 12:20 if so much as a *b* touch the
Rev 4:7 the first *b* was like a lion, and
Rev 6:3 seal, I heard the second *b* say
Rev 6:5 seal, I heard the third *b* say
Rev 6:7 the voice of the fourth *b* say
Rev 11:7 the *b* that ascendeth out of the
Rev 13:1 saw a *b* rise up out of the sea,
Rev 13:11 I beheld another *b* coming up out
Rev 13:14 power to do in the sight of the *b*
Rev 13:17 the mark, or the name of the *b*
Rev 14:9 voice, If any man worship the *b*
Rev 14:11 day nor night, who worship the *b*
Rev 15:2 had gotten the victory over the *b*
Rev 16:2 men which had the mark of the *b*
Rev 16:10 his vial upon the seat of the *b*
Rev 16:13 and out of the mouth of the *b*
Rev 17:3 sit upon a scarlet coloured *b*
Rev 17:7 of the *b* that carrieth her, which
Rev 17:8 The *b* that thou sawest was, and is
Rev 17:11 the *b* that was, and is not, even
Rev 17:16 which thou sawest upon the *b*
Rev 17:17 and give their kingdom unto the *b*
Rev 19:19 And I saw the *b*, and the kings of
Rev 19:20 the *b* was taken, and with him the
Rev 19:20 had received the mark of the *b*
Rev 20:4 and which had not worshipped the *b*
Rev 20:10 of fire and brimstone, where the *b*

### BEAST'S
Dan 4:16 let a *b* heart be given unto him

### BEASTS
Gen 7:2 of *b* that are not clean by two,
Gen 7:8 Of clean *b*, and of *b* that are
Gen 31:39 That which was torn of *b* I
Gen 36:6 and his cattle, and all his *b*
Gen 45:17 lade your *b*, and go, get you unto
Ex 11:5 and all the firstborn of *b*
Ex 22:31 that is torn of *b* in the field
Ex 23:11 what they leave the *b* of the
Lev 7:24 fat of that which is torn with *b*
Lev 11:2 These are the *b* which ye shall
Lev 11:27 manner of *b* that go on all four
Lev 11:46 This is the law of the *b*, and of
Lev 17:15 or that which was torn with *b*
Lev 20:25 put difference between clean *b*
Lev 22:8 of itself, or is torn with *b*
Lev 26:6 I will rid evil *b* out of the land
Lev 26:22 I will also send wild *b* among you
Lev 27:26 Only the firstling of the *b*
Num 18:15 LORD, whether it be of men or *b*

Num 20:8 the congregation and their *b* drink
Num 20:11 drank, and their *b* also
Num 31:11 all the prey, both of men and of *b*
Num 31:30 of the flocks, of all manner of *b*
Num 35:3 their goods, and for all their *b*
Deut 7:22 lest the *b* of the field increase
Deut 14:4 These are the *b* which ye shall
Deut 14:6 and cheweth the cud among the *b*
Deut 28:26 unto the *b* of the earth, and no
Deut 32:24 send the teeth of *b* upon them
1Sa 17:44 the air, and to the *b* of the field
1Sa 17:46 to the wild *b* of the earth
2Sa 21:10 nor the *b* of the field by night
1Kin 4:33 he spake also of *b*, and of fowl,
1Kin 18:5 alive, that we lose not all the *b*
2Kin 3:17 ye, and your cattle, and your *b*
2Chr 32:28 and stalls for all manner of *b*
Ezr 1:4 gold, and with goods, and with *b*
Ezr 1:6 with gold, with goods, and with *b*
Job 5:22 be afraid of the *b* of the earth
Job 12:7 But ask now the *b*, and they shall
Job 18:3 Wherefore are we counted as *b*
Job 35:11 us more than the *b* of the earth
Job 37:8 Then the *b* go into dens, and
Job 40:20 where all the *b* of the field play
Ps 8:7 oxen, yea, and the *b* of the field
Ps 49:12 he is like the *b* that perish
Ps 49:20 not, is like the *b* that perish
Ps 50:11 the wild *b* of the field are mine
Ps 79:2 saints unto the *b* of the earth
Ps 104:20 wherein all the *b* of the forest
Ps 104:25 both small and great *b*
Ps 148:10 *B*, and all cattle
Prov 9:2 She hath killed her *b*
Prov 30:30 A lion which is strongest among *b*
Eccl 3:18 see that they themselves are *b*
Eccl 3:19 the sons of men befalleth *b*
Is 1:11 of rams, and the fat of fed *b*
Is 13:21 But wild *b* of the desert shall
Is 18:6 and to the *b* of the earth
Is 30:6 The burden of the *b* of the south
Is 34:14 The wild *b* of the desert shall
Is 40:16 nor the *b* thereof sufficient for
Is 46:1 their idols were upon the *b*
Is 56:9 All ye *b* of the field, come to
Is 66:20 and upon mules, and upon swift *b*
Jer 7:33 heaven, and for the *b* of the earth
Jer 12:4 the *b* are consumed, and the birds
Jer 12:9 assemble all the *b* of the field
Jer 15:3 the *b* of the earth, to devour and
Jer 19:7 heaven, and for the *b* of the earth
Jer 27:6 the *b* of the field have I given
Jer 28:14 given him the *b* of the field also
Jer 34:20 heaven, and to the *b* of the earth
Jer 50:39 Therefore the wild *b* of the
Eze 5:17 I send upon you famine and evil *b*
Eze 8:10 creeping things, and abominable *b*
Eze 14:15 If I cause noisome *b* to pass
Eze 29:5 for meat to the *b* of the field
Eze 31:6 *b* of the field bring forth their
Eze 31:13 all the *b* of the field shall be
Eze 32:4 I will fill the *b* of the whole
Eze 32:13 I will destroy also all the *b*
Eze 33:27 I give to the *b* to be devoured
Eze 34:5 meat to all the *b* of the field
Eze 34:25 will cause the evil *b* to cease
Eze 38:20 the *b* of the field, and all
Eze 39:4 to the *b* of the field to be
Dan 2:38 the *b* of the field and the fowls
Dan 4:12 the *b* of the field had shadow
Dan 4:14 let the *b* get away from under it,
Dan 4:15 the *b* in the grass of the earth
Dan 4:21 under which the *b* of the field
Dan 4:23 be with the *b* of the field
Dan 4:25 shall be with the *b* of the field
Dan 4:32 shall be with the *b* of the field
Dan 5:21 and his heart was made like the *b*
Dan 7:3 four great *b* came up from the sea
Dan 7:7 all the *b* that were before it
Dan 7:12 As concerning the rest of the *b*
Dan 7:17 These great *b*, which are four,
Dan 8:4 so that no *b* might stand before
Hos 2:12 the *b* of the field shall eat them
Hos 2:18 for them with the *b* of the field
Hos 4:3 with the *b* of the field, and with
Joel 1:18 How do the *b* groan
Joel 1:20 The *b* of the field cry also unto
Joel 2:22 Be not afraid, ye *b* of the field
Amos 5:22 the peace offerings of your fat *b*
Mic 5:8 a lion among the *b* of the forest
Hab 2:17 cover thee, and the spoil of *b*
Zeph 2:14 of her, all the *b* of the nations
Zec 14:15 of all the *b* that shall be in
Mk 1:13 and was with the wild *b*
Acts 7:42 have ye offered to me slain *b*
Acts 10:12 of fourfooted *b* of the earth
Acts 11:6 *b* of the earth, and wild *b*
Acts 23:24 And provide them *b*, that they may
Rom 1:23 man, and to birds, and fourfooted *b*
1Cor 15:32 I have fought with *b* at Ephesus
1Cor 15:39 flesh of men, another flesh of *b*
Titus 1:12 Cretians are alway liars, evil *b*
Heb 13:11 For the bodies of those *b*
Jas 3:7 For every kind of *b*, and of birds,
2Pet 2:12 But these, as natural brute *b*
Jude 10 they know naturally, as brute *b*
Rev 4:6 were four *b* full of eyes before
Rev 4:8 the four *b* had each of them six
Rev 5:6 of the throne and of the four *b*
Rev 5:8 he had taken the book, the four *b*
Rev 5:11 round about the throne and the *b*
Rev 5:14 And the four *b* said, Amen
Rev 6:1 thunder, one of the four *b* saying
Rev 6:6 in the midst of the four *b* say
Rev 6:8 death, and with the *b* of the earth
Rev 7:11 and about the elders and the four *b*
Rev 14:3 the throne, and before the four *b*
Rev 15:7 one of the four *b* gave unto the
Rev 18:13 and fine flour, and wheat, and *b*
Rev 19:4 elders and the four *b* fell down and

## BEAT
Ex 30:36 thou shalt *b* some of it very
Ex 39:3 they did *b* the gold into thin
Num 11:8 or *b* it in a mortar, and baked it
Deut 25:3 *b* him above these with many
Judg 8:17 he *b* down the tower of Penuel, and
Judg 9:45 *b* down the city, and sowed it with
Judg 19:22 *b* at the door, and spake to the
Ruth 2:17 *b* out that she had gleaned
2Sa 22:43 Then did I *b* them as small as the
2Kin 3:25 they *b* down the cities, and on
2Kin 13:25 Three times did Joash *b* him
2Kin 23:12 of the LORD, did the king *b* down
Ps 18:42 Then did I *b* them small as the
Ps 89:23 I will *b* down his foes before his
Prov 23:14 Thou shalt *b* him with the rod, and
Is 2:4 they shall *b* their swords into
Is 3:15 ye that ye *b* my people to pieces
Is 27:12 that the LORD shall *b* off from
Is 41:15 *b* them small, and shalt make the
Joel 3:10 *B* your plowshares into swords, and
Jonah 4:8 the sun *b* upon the head of Jonah,
Mic 4:3 they shall *b* their swords into
Mic 4:13 thou shalt *b* in pieces many
Mt 7:25 winds blew, and *b* upon that house
Mt 7:27 winds blew, and *b* upon that house
Mt 21:35 *b* one, and killed another, and
Mk 4:37 the waves *b* into the ship, so
Mk 12:3 *b* him, and sent him away empty
Lk 6:48 the stream *b* vehemently upon that
Lk 6:49 which the stream did *b* vehemently
Lk 12:45 shall begin to *b* the menservants
Lk 20:10 but the husbandmen *b* him, and sent
Acts 16:22 clothes, and commanded to *b* them
Acts 18:17 *b* him before the judgment seat
Acts 22:19 *b* in every synagogue them that

## BEATEN
Ex 5:14 had set over them, were *b*
Ex 5:16 and, behold, thy servants are *b*
Ex 25:18 of *b* work shalt thou make them,
Ex 25:31 of *b* work shall the candlestick
Ex 25:36 shall be one *b* work of pure gold
Ex 27:20 pure oil olive *b* for the light
Ex 29:40 fourth part of an hin of *b* oil
Ex 37:7 *b* out of one piece made he them,
Ex 37:17 of *b* work made he the candlestick
Ex 37:22 of it was one *b* work of pure gold
Lev 2:14 even corn *b* out of full ears
Lev 2:16 part of the *b* corn thereof, and
Lev 16:12 full of sweet incense *b* small
Lev 24:2 pure oil olive *b* for the light
Num 8:4 of the candlestick was of *b* gold
Num 28:5 fourth part of an hin of *b* oil
Deut 25:2 the wicked man be worthy to be *b*
Deut 25:2 down, and to be *b* before his face,
Josh 8:15 as if they were *b* before them
2Sa 2:17 and Abner was *b*, and the men of
1Kin 10:16 two hundred targets of *b* gold
2Chr 2:10 thousand measures of *b* wheat
2Chr 9:15 two hundred targets of *b* gold
2Chr 34:7 had *b* the graven images into
Prov 23:35 they have *b* me, and I felt it not
Is 27:9 chalkstones that are *b* in sunder
Is 28:27 fitches are *b* out with a staff
Is 30:31 LORD shall the Assyrian be *b* down
Jer 46:5 and their mighty ones are *b* down
Mic 1:7 thereof shall be *b* to pieces
Mk 13:9 in the synagogues ye shall be *b*
Lk 12:47 shall be *b* with many stripes
Acts 5:40 *b* them, they commanded that they
Acts 16:37 They have *b* us openly uncondemned
2Cor 11:25 Thrice was I *b* with rods, once

## BEATEST
Deut 24:20 When thou *b* thine olive tree,
Prov 23:13 for if thou *b* him with the rod,

## BEATETH
1Cor 9:26 I, not as one that *b* the air

## BEATING
1Sa 14:16 they went on *b* down one another
Mk 12:5 *b* some, and killing some
Acts 21:32 the soldiers, they left *b* of Paul

## BEAUTIES
Ps 110:3 in the *b* of holiness from the

## BEAUTIFUL
Gen 29:17 Rachel was *b* and well favoured
Deut 21:11 among the captives a *b* woman
1Sa 16:12 and withal of a *b* countenance
1Sa 25:3 and of a *b* countenance
2Sa 11:2 the woman was very *b* to look upon
Est 2:7 and the maid was fair and *b*
Ps 48:2 *B* for situation, the joy of the
Eccl 3:11 made every thing *b* in his time
Song 6:4 Thou art *b*, O my love, as Tirzah,
Song 7:1 How *b* are thy feet with shoes, O
Is 4:2 shall the branch of the LORD be *b*
Is 52:1 put on thy *b* garments, O
Is 52:7 How *b* upon the mountains are the
Is 64:11 our *b* house, where our fathers
Jer 13:20 that was given thee, thy *b* flock
Jer 48:17 strong staff broken, and the *b* rod
Eze 16:12 a *b* crown upon thine head
Eze 23:42 *b* crowns upon their heads
Mt 23:27 which indeed appear *b* outward
Acts 3:2 of the temple which is called *B*
Acts 3:10 alms at the *B* gate of the temple
Rom 10:15 How *b* are the feet of them that

## BEAUTIFY
Ezr 7:27 to *b* the house of the LORD which
Ps 149:4 he will *b* the meek with salvation
Is 60:13 to *b* the place of my sanctuary

## BEAUTY
Ex 28:2 thy brother for glory and for *b*
Ex 28:40 make for them, for glory and for *b*
2Sa 1:19 The *b* of Israel is slain upon thy
2Sa 14:25 much praised as Absalom for his *b*
1Chr 16:29 the LORD in the *b* of holiness
2Chr 3:6 house with precious stones for *b*
2Chr 20:21 should praise the *b* of holiness
Est 1:11 the people and the princes her *b*
Job 40:10 and array thyself with glory and *b*
Ps 27:4 life, to behold the *b* of the LORD
Ps 29:2 the LORD in the *b* of holiness
Ps 39:11 thou makest his *b* to consume away
Ps 45:11 the king greatly desire thy *b*
Ps 49:14 their *b* shall consume in the
Ps 50:2 Out of Zion, the perfection of *b*
Ps 90:17 let the *b* of the LORD our God be
Ps 96:6 and *b* are in his sanctuary
Ps 96:9 the LORD in the *b* of holiness
Prov 6:25 not after her *b* in thine heart
Prov 20:29 the *b* of old men is the grey head
Prov 31:30 Favour is deceitful, and *b* is vain
Is 3:24 and burning instead of *b*
Is 13:19 the *b* of the Chaldees' excellency
Is 28:1 whose glorious *b* is a fading
Is 28:4 And the glorious *b*, which is on
Is 33:17 eyes shall see the king in his *b*
Is 44:13 man, according to the *b* of a man
Is 53:2 there is no *b* that we should
Is 61:3 to give unto them *b* for ashes
Lam 1:6 of Zion all her *b* is departed
Lam 2:1 unto the earth the *b* of Israel
Lam 2:15 that men call The perfection of *b*
Eze 7:20 As for the *b* of his ornament, he
Eze 16:14 forth among the heathen for thy *b*
Eze 16:25 hast made thy *b* to be abhorred,

Eze 27:3 thou hast said, I am of perfect *b*
Eze 27:11 they have made thy *b* perfect
Eze 28:7 against the *b* of thy wisdom
Eze 28:12 full of wisdom, and perfect in *b*
Eze 28:17 was lifted up because of thy *b*
Eze 31:8 of God was like unto him in his *b*
Eze 32:19 Whom dost thou pass in *b*
Hos 14:6 his *b* shall be as the olive tree,
Zec 9:17 goodness, and how great is his *b*
Zec 11:7 the one I called *B*, and the other
Zec 11:10 And I took my staff, even *B*

**BEBAI** *(beb'-a-i)*
*1. Father of returned exiles.*
Ezr 2:11 The children of *B*, six hundred
Neh 7:16 The children of *B*, six hundred
*2. Father of returned exiles with Ezra.*
Ezr 8:11 And of the sons of *B*
Ezr 10:28 Of the sons also of *B*
*3. One who sealed the covenant.*
Neh 10:15 Bunni, Azgad, *B*,

**BECHER** *(be'-ker)* See BACHRITES.
*1. A son of Benjamin.*
Gen 46:21 sons of Benjamin were Belah, and *B*
1Chr 7:6 Bela, and *B*, and Jediael, three
1Chr 7:8 And the sons of *B*
*2. A son of Ephraim.*
Num 26:35 of *B*, the family of the Bachrites

**BECHORATH** *(be-ko'-rath) An ancestor of King Saul.*
1Sa 9:1 the son of Zeror, the son of *B*

**BECKONED**
Lk 1:22 for he *b* unto them, and remained
Lk 5:7 they *b* unto their partners, which
Jn 13:24 Simon Peter therefore *b* to him
Acts 19:33 Alexander *b* with the hand, and
Acts 21:40 *b* with the hand unto the people
Acts 24:10 governor had *b* unto him to speak

**BECKONING**
Acts 12:17 *b* unto them with the hand to hold
Acts 13:16 *b* with his hand said, Men of

**BED**
Gen 48:2 himself, and sat upon the *b*
Gen 49:4 thou wentest up to thy father's *b*
Gen 49:33 gathered up his feet into the *b*
Ex 8:3 thy bedchamber, and upon thy *b*
Ex 21:18 and he die not, but keepeth his *b*
Lev 15:4 Every *b*, whereon he lieth that
Lev 15:21 her *b* shall wash his clothes
Lev 15:23 And if it be on her *b*, or on any
Lev 15:26 Every *b* whereon she lieth all the
Lev 15:26 her as the *b* of her separation
1Sa 19:13 an image, and laid it in the *b*
1Sa 19:15 Bring him up to me in the *b*
1Sa 28:23 from the earth, and sat upon the *b*
2Sa 4:5 who lay on a *b* at noon
2Sa 4:7 he lay on his *b* in his bedchamber
2Sa 4:11 in his own house upon his *b*
2Sa 11:2 that David arose from off his *b*
2Sa 11:13 *b* with the servants of his lord
2Sa 13:5 unto him, Lay thee down on thy *b*
1Kin 1:47 the king bowed himself upon the *b*
1Kin 17:19 abode, and laid him upon his own *b*
1Kin 21:4 And he laid him down upon his *b*
2Kin 1:4 that *b* on which thou art gone up
2Kin 1:6 that *b* on which thou art gone up
2Kin 1:16 that *b* on which thou art gone up
2Kin 4:10 and let us set for him there a *b*
2Kin 4:21 laid him on the *b* of the man of
2Kin 4:32 was dead, and laid upon his *b*
1Chr 5:1 as he defiled his father's *b*
2Chr 16:14 laid him in the *b* which was
2Chr 24:25 the priest, and slew him on his *b*
Est 7:8 upon the *b* whereon Esther was
Job 7:13 My *b* shall comfort me, my couch
Job 17:13 I have made my *b* in the darkness
Job 33:15 men, in slumberings upon the *b*
Job 33:19 also with pain upon his *b*
Ps 4:4 with your own heart upon your *b*
Ps 6:6 all the night make I my *b* to swim
Ps 36:4 He deviseth mischief upon his *b*
Ps 41:3 him upon the *b* of languishing
Ps 63:6 When I remember thee upon my *b*
Ps 132:3 of my house, nor go up into my *b*
Ps 139:8 if I make my *b* in hell, behold,
Prov 7:16 I have decked my *b* with coverings
Prov 22:27 take away thy *b* from under thee
Prov 26:14 so doth the slothful upon his *b*
Song 1:16 also our *b* is green
Song 3:1 By night on my *b* I sought him
Song 3:7 Behold his *b*, which is Solomon's
Song 5:13 His cheeks are as a *b* of spices
Is 28:20 For the *b* is shorter than that a
Is 57:7 high mountain hast thou set thy *b*
Eze 23:17 came to her into the *b* of love
Eze 23:41 And satest upon a stately *b*
Eze 32:25 They have set her a *b* in the
Dan 2:28 visions of thy head upon thy *b*
Dan 2:29 came into thy mind upon thy *b*
Dan 4:5 afraid, and the thoughts upon my *b*
Dan 4:10 the visions of mine head in my *b*
Dan 4:13 the visions of my head upon my *b*
Dan 7:1 and visions of his head upon his *b*
Amos 3:12 in Samaria in the corner of a *b*
Mt 9:2 sick of the palsy, lying on a *b*
Mt 9:6 the palsy,) Arise, take up thy *b*
Mk 2:4 they let down the *b* wherein the
Mk 2:9 to say, Arise, and take up thy *b*
Mk 2:11 thee, Arise, and take up thy *b*
Mk 4:21 put under a bushel, or under a *b*
Mk 7:30 and her daughter laid upon the *b*
Lk 5:18 men brought in a *b* a man which
Lk 8:16 a vessel, or putteth it under a *b*
Lk 11:7 and my children are with me in *b*
Lk 17:34 there shall be two men in one *b*
Jn 5:8 unto him, Rise, take up thy *b*
Acts 9:33 which had kept his *b* eight years
Heb 13:4 in all, and the *b* undefiled
Rev 2:22 Behold, I will cast her into a *b*

**BEDAD** *(be'-dad) Father of Hadad.*
Gen 36:35 died, and Hadad the son of *B*
1Chr 1:46 was dead, Hadad the son of *B*

**BEDAN** *(be'-dan)*
*1. A judge of Israel.*
1Sa 12:11 And the LORD sent Jerubbaal, and *B*
*2. A descendant of Manasseh.*
1Chr 7:17 And the sons of Ulam; *B*

**BEDCHAMBER**
Ex 8:3 into thine house, and into thy *b*
2Sa 4:7 house, he lay on his bed in his *b*
2Kin 6:12 words that thou speakest in thy *b*
2Kin 11:2 in the *b* from Athaliah, so that
2Chr 22:11 and put him and his nurse in a *b*
Eccl 10:20 and curse not the rich in thy *b*

**BEDEIAH** *(be-de'-yah) Married a foreign wife in exile.*
Ezr 10:35 Benaiah, *B*, Chelluh,

**BEDS**
2Sa 17:28 Brought *b*, and basons, and earthen
Est 1:6 the *b* were of gold and silver,
Ps 149:5 let them sing aloud upon their *b*
Song 6:2 to the *b* of spices, to feed in
Is 57:2 they shall rest in their *b*
Hos 7:14 when they howled upon their *b*
Amos 6:4 That lie upon *b* of ivory, and
Mic 2:1 and work evil upon their *b*
Mk 6:55 about in *b* those that were sick
Acts 5:15 the streets, and laid them on *b*

**BEELIADA** *(be-e-li'-ad-ah) A son of David.*
1Chr 14:7 And Elishama, and *B*, and Eliphalet

**BEELZEBUB** *(be-el'-ze-bub)* See BAAL-ZEBUB. *Chief of evil spirits.*
Mt 10:25 called the master of the house *B*
Mt 12:24 but by *B* the prince of the devils
Mt 12:27 if I by *B* cast out devils, by
Mk 3:22 from Jerusalem said, He hath *B*
Lk 11:15 through *B* the chief of the devils
Lk 11:18 that I cast out devils through *B*

**BEER** *(be'-ur)* See BAALITH-BEER, BEER-ELIM, BEER-LAHAI-ROI, BEER-SHEBA.
*1. An Israelite post beyond the Arnon River.*
Num 21:16 And from thence they went to *B*
*2. A town in Judah.*
Judg 9:21 ran away, and fled, and went to *B*

**BEERA** *(be-e'-rah) Son of Zophah.*
1Chr 7:37 and Shilshah, and Ithran, and *B*

**BEERAH** *(be-e'-rah) A Reubenite prince.*
1Chr 5:6 *B* his son, whom Tilgath-pilneser

**BEER-ELIM** *(be'-ur-e'-lim) A well in Moab.*
Is 15:8 and the howling thereof unto *B*

**BEERI** *(be-e'-ri)*
*1. Father of Judith.*
Gen 26:34 the daughter of *B* the Hittite
*2. Father of Hosea.*
Hos 1:1 came unto Hosea, the son of *B*

**BEER-LAHAI-ROI** *(be'-ur-la'-hahe-ro'-e) A well.*
Gen 16:14 Wherefore the well was called *B*

**BEEROTH** *(be-e'-roth)* See BEROTHITE.
*1. An Israelite encampment during the Exodus.*
Deut 10:6 *B* of the children of Jaakan to
*2. A Hivite city in Canaan.*
Josh 9:17 were Gibeon, and Chephirah, and *B*
Josh 18:25 Gibeon, and Ramah, and *B*,
2Sa 4:2 (for *B* also was reckoned to
Ezr 2:25 of Kirjath-arim, Chephirah, and *B*
Neh 7:29 Kirjath-jearim, Chephirah, and *B*

**BEEROTHITE** *(be-er'-o-thite)* See BEEROTHITES, BEROTHITE. *An inhabitant of Beeroth.*
2Sa 4:2 Rechab, the sons of Rimmon a *B*
2Sa 4:5 And the sons of Rimmon the *B*
2Sa 4:9 brother, the sons of Rimmon the *B*
2Sa 23:37 Zelek the Ammonite, Nahari the *B*

**BEEROTHITES** *(be-er'-o-thites)*
2Sa 4:3 the *B* fled to Gittaim, and were

**BEER-SHEBA** *(be-ur'-she-bah) A Canaanite city.*
Gen 21:14 wandered in the wilderness of *B*
Gen 21:31 Wherefore he called that place *B*
Gen 22:19 rose up and went together to *B*
Gen 22:19 and Abraham dwelt at *B*
Gen 26:23 And he went up from thence to *B*
Gen 26:33 of the city is *B* unto this day
Gen 28:10 And Jacob went out from *B*, and went
Gen 46:1 all that he had, and came to *B*
Gen 46:5 And Jacob rose up from *B*
Josh 15:28 And Hazar-shual, and *B*, and
Josh 19:2 they had in their inheritance *B*
Judg 20:1 as one man, from Dan even to *B*
1Sa 3:20 even to *B* knew that Samuel was
1Sa 8:2 they were judges in *B*
2Sa 3:10 and over Judah, from Dan even to *B*
2Sa 17:11 unto thee, from Dan even to *B*
2Sa 24:2 of Israel, from Dan even to *B*
2Sa 24:7 to the south of Judah, even to *B*
2Sa 24:15 even to *B* seventy thousand men
1Kin 4:25 his fig tree, from Dan even to *B*
1Kin 19:3 went for his life, and came to *B*
2Kin 12:1 his mother's name was Zibiah of *B*
2Kin 23:8 burned incense, from Geba to *B*
1Chr 4:28 And they dwelt at *B*, and Moladah,
1Chr 21:2 number Israel from *B* even to Dan
2Chr 19:4 people from *B* to mount Ephraim
2Chr 24:1 name also was Zibiah of *B*
2Chr 30:5 from *B* even to Dan, that they
Neh 11:27 And at Hazar-shual, and at *B*
Neh 11:30 they dwelt from *B* unto the valley
Amos 5:5 into Gilgal, and pass not to *B*
Amos 8:14 and, The manner of *B* liveth

**BEES**
Deut 1:44 you, and chased you, as *b* do
Judg 14:8 behold, there was a swarm of *b*
Ps 118:12 They compassed me about like *b*

**BEESH-TERAH** *(be-esh'-te-rah)* See ASHTAROTH. *A Levitical city in Manasseh.*
Josh 21:27 and *B* with her suburbs

**BEEVES**
Lev 22:19 a male without blemish, of the *b*
Lev 22:21 a freewill offering in *b* or sheep
Num 31:28 both of the persons, and of the *b*
Num 31:30 fifty, of the persons, of the *b*
Num 31:33 threescore and twelve thousand *b*
Num 31:38 the *b* were thirty and six thousand
Num 31:44 And thirty and six thousand *b*

**BEFALL**
Gen 42:4 Lest peradventure mischief *b* him
Gen 42:38 if mischief *b* him by the way in
Gen 44:29 also from me, and mischief *b* him
Gen 49:1 shall *b* you in the last days
Deut 31:17 evils and troubles shall *b* them
Deut 31:29 evil will *b* you in the latter
Ps 91:10 There shall no evil *b* thee
Dan 10:14 *b* thy people in the latter days
Acts 20:22 the things that shall *b* me there

**BEFALLEN**
Lev 10:19 and such things have *b* me
Num 20:14 all the travel that hath *b* us
Deut 31:21 many evils and troubles are *b* them

Judg 6:13 us, why then is all this *b* us
1Sa 20:26 he thought, Something hath *b* him
Est 6:13 every thing that had *b* him
Mt 8:33 what was *b* to the possessed of

**BEFALLETH**
Eccl 3:19 *b* the sons of men *b* beasts
Eccl 3:19 even one thing *b* them

**BEFELL**
Gen 42:29 and told him all that *b* unto them
Josh 2:23 told him all things that *b* them
2Sa 19:7 thee than all the evil that *b*
Mk 5:16 that saw it told them how it *b* to
Acts 20:19 which *b* me by the lying in wait

**BEG**
Ps 109:10 be continually vagabonds, and *b*
Prov 20:4 therefore shall he *b* in harvest
Lk 16:3 to *b* I am ashamed

**BEGGAR**
1Sa 2:8 lifteth up the *b* from the
Lk 16:20 was a certain *b* named Lazarus
Lk 16:22 it came to pass, that the *b* died

**BEGGED**
Mt 27:58 to Pilate, and *b* the body of Jesus
Lk 23:52 Pilate, and *b* the body of Jesus
Jn 9:8 Is not this he that sat and *b*

**BEGGING**
Ps 37:25 forsaken, nor his seed *b* bread
Mk 10:46 sat by the highway side *b*
Lk 18:35 blind man sat by the way side *b*

**BEGINNINGS**
Num 10:10 in the *b* of your months, ye shall
Num 28:11 in the *b* of your months ye shall
Eze 36:11 do better unto you than at your *b*
Mk 13:8 these are the *b* of sorrows

**BEGOTTEN**
Gen 5:4 *b* Seth were eight hundred years
Lev 18:11 *b* of thy father, she is thy
Num 11:12 have I *b* them, that thou
Deut 23:8 The children that are *b* of them
Judg 8:30 and ten sons of his body *b*
Job 38:28 or who hath *b* the drops of dew
Ps 2:7 this day have I *b* thee
Is 49:21 thine heart, Who hath *b* me these
Hos 5:7 for they have *b* strange children
Jn 1:14 as of the only *b* of the Father
Jn 1:18 the only *b* Son, which is in the
Jn 3:16 that he gave his only *b* Son
Jn 3:18 the name of the only *b* Son of God
Acts 13:33 my Son, this day have I *b* thee
1Cor 4:15 I have *b* you through the gospel
Philem 10 whom I have *b* in my bonds
Heb 1:5 my Son, this day have I *b* thee
Heb 5:5 art my Son, to day have I *b* thee
Heb 11:17 offered up his only *b* son
1Pet 1:3 to his abundant mercy hath *b* us
1Jn 4:9 his only *b* Son into the world
1Jn 5:1 loveth him also that is *b* of him
1Jn 5:18 but he that is *b* of God keepeth
Rev 1:5 the first *b* of the dead, and the

**BEGUILE**
Col 2:4 lest any man should *b* you with
Col 2:18 Let no man *b* you of your reward

**BEGUILED**
Gen 3:13 the woman said, The serpent *b* me
Gen 29:25 wherefore then hast thou *b* me
Num 25:18 wherewith they have *b* you in the
Josh 9:22 saying, Wherefore have ye *b* us
2Cor 11:3 as the serpent *b* Eve through his

**BEHALF**
Ex 27:21 the *b* of the children of Israel
2Sa 3:12 sent messengers to David on his *b*
2Chr 16:9 to shew himself strong in the *b*
Job 36:2 I have yet to speak on God's *b*
Dan 11:18 own *b* shall cause the reproach
Rom 16:19 I am glad therefore on your *b*
1Cor 1:4 I thank my God always on your *b*
2Cor 1:11 may be given by many on our *b*
2Cor 5:12 you occasion to glory on our *b*
2Cor 8:24 and of our boasting on your *b*
2Cor 9:3 you should be in vain in this *b*
Phil 1:29 it is given in the *b* of Christ
1Pet 4:16 but let him glorify God on this *b*

**BEHAVE**
Deut 32:27 should *b* themselves strangely
1Chr 19:13 let us *b* ourselves valiantly for
Ps 101:2 I will *b* myself wisely in a
Is 3:5 the child shall *b* himself proudly
1Cor 13:5 Doth not *b* itself unseemly,
1Ti 3:15 know how thou oughtest to *b*

**BEHAVED**
1Sa 18:5 sent him, and *b* himself wisely
1Sa 18:14 David *b* himself wisely in all his
1Sa 18:30 that David *b* himself more wisely
Ps 35:14 I *b* myself as though he had been
Ps 131:2 Surely I have *b* and quieted myself
Mic 3:4 as they have *b* themselves ill in
1Th 2:10 unblameably we *b* ourselves among
2Th 3:7 for we *b* not ourselves disorderly

**BEHAVIOUR**
1Sa 21:13 And he changed his *b* before them
Ps 34:*t* he changed his *b* before Abimelech
1Ti 3:2 wife, vigilant, sober, of good *b*
Titus 2:3 that they be in *b* as becometh

**BEHEADED**
Deut 21:6 heifer that is *b* in the valley
2Sa 4:7 *b* him, and took his head, and
Mt 14:10 he sent, and *b* John in the prison
Mk 6:16 he said, It is John, whom I *b*
Mk 6:27 he went and *b* him in the prison,
Lk 9:9 And Herod said, John have I *b*
Rev 20:4 were *b* for the witness of Jesus

**BEHELD**
Gen 12:14 the Egyptians *b* the woman that
Gen 13:10 *b* all the plain of Jordan, that
Gen 19:28 all the land of the plain, and *b*
Gen 31:2 Jacob *b* the countenance of Laban,
Gen 48:8 Israel *b* Joseph's sons, and said,
Num 21:9 when he *b* the serpent of brass,
Num 23:21 He hath not *b* iniquity in Jacob,
Judg 16:27 that *b* while Samson made sport
1Sa 26:5 David *b* the place where Saul lay,
1Chr 21:15 as he was destroying, the LORD *b*
Job 31:26 If I *b* the sun when it shined, or
Ps 119:158 I *b* the transgressors, and was
Ps 142:4 I looked on my right hand, and *b*
Prov 7:7 *b* among the simple ones, I
Eccl 8:17 Then I *b* all the work of God,
Is 41:28 For I *b*, and there was no man
Jer 4:23 I *b* the earth, and, lo, it was
Jer 31:26 Upon this I awaked, and *b*
Eze 1:15 Now as I *b* the living creatures,
Eze 8:2 Then I *b*, and lo a likeness as the
Eze 37:8 And when I *b*, lo, the sinews and
Dan 7:4 I *b* till the wings thereof were
Dan 7:6 After this I *b*, and lo another,
Dan 7:9 I *b* till the thrones were cast
Dan 7:11 I *b* then because of the voice of
Dan 7:21 I *b*, and the same horn made war
Hab 3:6 he *b*, and drove asunder the
Mt 19:26 But Jesus *b* them, and said unto
Mk 9:15 all the people, when they *b* him
Mk 12:41 *b* how the people cast money into
Mk 15:47 of Joses *b* where he was laid
Lk 10:18 I *b* Satan as lightning fall from
Lk 19:41 he *b* the city, and wept over it,
Lk 20:17 he *b* them, and said, What is this
Lk 22:56 But a certain maid *b* him as he
Lk 23:55 *b* the sepulchre, and how his body
Lk 24:12 he *b* the linen clothes laid by
Jn 1:14 we *b* his glory, the glory as of
Jn 1:42 And when Jesus *b* him, he said,
Acts 1:9 spoken these things, while they *b*
Acts 17:23 *b* your devotions, I found an
Rev 5:6 And I *b*, and, lo, in the midst of
Rev 5:11 And I *b*, and I heard the voice of
Rev 6:5 And I *b*, and lo a black horse
Rev 6:12 I *b* when he had opened the sixth
Rev 7:9 After this I *b*, and, lo, a great
Rev 8:13 And I *b*, and heard an angel flying
Rev 11:12 and their enemies *b* them
Rev 13:11 I *b* another beast coming up out

**BEHEMOTH**
Job 40:15 Behold now *b*, which I made with

**BEKAH**
Ex 38:26 A *b* for every man, that is, half

**BEL** *(bel)* See BAAL. *A Babylonian god.*
Is 46:1 *B* boweth down, Nebo stoopeth,
Jer 50:2 *B* is confounded, Merodach is
Jer 51:44 And I will punish *B* in Babylon

**BELA** *(be'-lah)* See BELAH, BELAITES.
*1. Another name for Zoar.*
Gen 14:2 king of Zeboiim, and the king of *B*
Gen 14:8 the king of *B* (the same is Zoar
*2. An Edomite king.*
Gen 36:32 *B* the son of Beor reigned in Edom
1Chr 1:43 *B* the son of Beor
*3. A son of Benjamin.*
Num 26:38 of *B*, the family of the Belaites
Num 26:40 And the sons of *B* were Ard
1Chr 7:6 *B*, and Becher, and Jediael, three
1Chr 8:1 Benjamin begat *B* his firstborn
1Chr 8:3 And the sons of *B* were, Addar, and
*4. A son of Azaz the Reubenite.*
1Chr 5:8 *B* the son of Azaz, the son of

**BELAH** *(be'-lah)* See BELA. *A form of Bela.*
Gen 46:21 And the sons of Benjamin were *B*

**BELAITES** *(be'-lah-ites) Descendants of Bela.*
Num 26:38 of Bela, the family of the *B*

**BELCH**
Ps 59:7 they *b* out with their mouth

**BELIAL** *(be'-le-al) A title for a "worthless person."*
Deut 13:13 Certain men, the children of *B*
Judg 19:22 of the city, certain sons of *B*
Judg 20:13 us the men, the children of *B*
1Sa 1:16 handmaid for a daughter of *B*
1Sa 2:12 the sons of Eli were sons of *B*
1Sa 10:27 But the children of *B* said
1Sa 25:17 for he is such a son of *B*
1Sa 25:25 I pray thee, regard this man of *B*
1Sa 30:22 all the wicked men and men of *B*
2Sa 16:7 thou bloody man, and thou man of *B*
2Sa 20:1 happened to be there a man of *B*
2Sa 23:6 But the sons of *B* shall be all of
1Kin 21:10 And set two men, sons of *B*
1Kin 21:13 came in two men, children of *B*
2Chr 13:7 him vain men, the children of *B*
2Cor 6:15 what concord hath Christ with *B*

**BELIEVE**
Ex 4:1 But, behold, they will not *b* me
Ex 4:5 That they may *b* that the LORD God
Ex 4:8 to pass, if they will not *b* thee
Ex 19:9 with thee, and *b* thee for ever
Num 14:11 how long will it be ere they *b* me
Deut 1:32 ye did not *b* the LORD your God
2Kin 17:14 that did not *b* in the LORD their
2Chr 20:20 *B* in the LORD your God, so shall
2Chr 32:15 on this manner, neither yet *b* him
Job 9:16 yet would I not *b* that he had
Job 39:12 Wilt thou *b* him, that he will
Prov 26:25 When he speaketh fair, *b* him not
Is 7:9 If ye will not *b*, surely ye shall
Is 43:10 *b* me, and understand that I am he
Jer 12:6 *b* them not, though they speak
Hab 1:5 in your days, which ye will not *b*
Mt 9:28 *B* ye that I am able to do this
Mt 18:6 these little ones which *b* in me
Mt 21:25 us, Why did ye not then *b* him
Mt 21:32 afterward, that ye might *b* him
Mt 24:23 *b* it not
Mt 24:26 *b* it not
Mt 27:42 from the cross, and we will *b* him
Mk 1:15 repent ye, and *b* the gospel
Mk 5:36 synagogue, Be not afraid, only *b*
Mk 9:23 said unto him, If thou canst *b*
Mk 9:42 of these little ones that *b* in me
Mk 11:23 but shall *b* that those things
Mk 11:31 say, Why then did ye not *b* him
Mk 13:21 *b* him not
Mk 15:32 the cross, that we may see and *b*
Mk 16:17 signs shall follow them that *b*
Lk 8:12 their hearts, lest they should *b*
Lk 8:50 *b* only, and she shall be made
Lk 22:67 If I tell you, ye will not *b*
Lk 24:25 slow of heart to *b* all that the
Jn 1:7 that all men through him might *b*
Jn 1:12 even to them that *b* on his name
Jn 3:12 and ye *b* not, how shall ye *b*
Jn 4:21 *b* me, the hour cometh, when ye
Jn 4:42 And said unto the woman, Now we *b*
Jn 4:48 signs and wonders, ye will not *b*
Jn 5:38 whom he hath sent, him ye *b* not
Jn 5:44 How can ye *b*, which receive
Jn 5:47 But if ye *b* not his writings
Jn 6:29 that ye *b* on him whom he hath
Jn 6:30 then, that we may see, and *b* thee
Jn 6:36 ye also have seen me, and *b* not
Jn 6:64 there are some of you that *b* not
Jn 6:69 And we *b* and are sure that thou art

Jn 7:5 neither did his brethren *b* in him
Jn 7:39 which they that *b* on him should
Jn 8:24 for if ye *b* not that I am he, ye
Jn 8:45 I tell you the truth, ye *b* me not
Jn 9:18 the Jews did not *b* concerning him
Jn 9:35 Dost thou *b* on the Son of God
Jn 9:38 And he said, Lord, I *b*
Jn 10:26 But ye *b* not, because ye are not
Jn 11:15 not there, to the intent ye may *b*
Jn 11:27 I *b* that thou art the Christ, the
Jn 11:40 thee, that, if thou wouldest *b*
Jn 11:42 that they may *b* that thou hast
Jn 11:48 thus alone, all men will *b* on him
Jn 12:36 *b* in the light, that ye may be
Jn 12:39 Therefore they could not *b*
Jn 12:47 words, and *b* not, I judge him not
Jn 13:19 to pass, ye may *b* that I am he
Jn 14:1 ye *b* in God, *b* also in me
Jn 14:11 *B* me that I am in the Father, and
Jn 14:29 it is come to pass, ye might *b*
Jn 16:9 Of sin, because they *b* not on me
Jn 16:30 by this we *b* that thou camest
Jn 17:20 shall *b* on me through their word
Jn 17:21 that the world may *b* that thou
Jn 19:35 he saith true, that ye might *b*
Jn 20:25 hand into his side, I will not *b*
Jn 20:31 that ye might *b* that Jesus is the
Acts 8:37 I *b* that Jesus Christ is the Son
Acts 13:39 by him all that *b* are justified
Acts 13:41 work which ye shall in no wise *b*
Acts 15:7 hear the word of the gospel, and *b*
Acts 15:11 But we *b* that through the grace
Acts 16:31 *B* on the Lord Jesus Christ, and
Acts 19:4 that they should *b* on him which
Acts 21:20 of Jews there are which *b*
Acts 21:25 As touching the Gentiles which *b*
Acts 27:25 for I *b* God, that it shall be
Rom 3:3 For what if some did not *b*
Rom 3:22 unto all and upon all them that *b*
Rom 4:11 be the father of all them that *b*
Rom 4:24 if we *b* on him that raised up
Rom 6:8 we *b* that we shall also live with
Rom 10:9 shalt *b* in thine heart that God
Rom 10:14 how shall they *b* in him of whom
Rom 15:31 from them that do not *b* in Judaea
1Cor 1:21 of preaching to save them that *b*
1Cor 10:27 If any of them that *b* not bid you
1Cor 11:18 and I partly *b* it
1Cor 14:22 for a sign, not to them that *b*
2Cor 4:4 the minds of them which *b* not
2Cor 4:13 we also *b*, and therefore speak
Gal 3:22 might be given to them that *b*
Eph 1:19 of his power to us-ward who *b*
Phil 1:29 of Christ, not only to *b* on him
1Th 1:7 to all that *b* in Macedonia
1Th 2:10 ourselves among you that *b*
1Th 2:13 worketh also in you that *b*
1Th 4:14 For if we *b* that Jesus died and
2Th 1:10 *b* (because our testimony among
2Th 2:11 that they should *b* a lie
1Ti 1:16 *b* on him to life everlasting
1Ti 4:3 with thanksgiving of them which *b*
1Ti 4:10 men, specially of those that *b*
2Ti 2:13 If we *b* not, yet he abideth
Heb 10:39 but of them that *b* to the saving
Heb 11:6 cometh to God must *b* that he is
Jas 2:19 the devils also *b*, and tremble
1Pet 1:21 Who by him do *b* in God, that
1Pet 2:7 therefore which *b* he is precious
1Jn 3:23 That we should *b* on the name of
1Jn 4:1 *b* not every spirit, but try the
1Jn 5:13 have I written unto you that *b* on
1Jn 5:13 that ye may *b* on the name of the

**BELIEVED**

Gen 15:6 And he *b* in the LORD
Gen 45:26 heart fainted, for he *b* them not
Ex 4:31 And the people *b*
Ex 14:31 *b* the LORD, and his servant Moses
Num 20:12 and Aaron, Because ye *b* me not
Deut 9:23 ye *b* him not, nor hearkened to
1Sa 27:12 And Achish *b* David, saying, He
1Kin 10:7 Howbeit I *b* not the words, until
2Chr 9:6 Howbeit I *b* not their words,
Job 29:24 I laughed on them, they *b* it not
Ps 27:13 unless I had *b* to see the
Ps 78:22 Because they *b* not in God
Ps 78:32 *b* not for his wondrous works
Ps 106:12 Then *b* they his words
Ps 106:24 land, they *b* not his word
Ps 116:10 I *b*, therefore have I spoken
Ps 119:66 for I have *b* thy commandments
Is 53:1 Who hath *b* our report
Jer 40:14 the son of Ahikam *b* them not
Lam 4:12 would not have *b* that the
Dan 6:23 upon him, because he *b* in his God
Jonah 3:5 So the people of Nineveh *b* God
Mt 8:13 and as thou hast *b*, so be it done
Mt 21:32 of righteousness, and ye *b* him not
Mk 16:11 and had been seen of her, *b* not
Mk 16:13 neither *b* they them
Lk 1:1 which are most surely *b* among us
Lk 1:45 And blessed is she that *b*
Lk 20:5 will say, Why then *b* ye him not
Lk 24:11 as idle tales, and they *b* them not
Lk 24:41 And while they yet *b* not for joy
Jn 2:11 and his disciples *b* on him
Jn 2:22 they *b* the scripture, and the word
Jn 3:18 because he hath not *b* in the name
Jn 4:39 *b* on him for the saying of the
Jn 4:41 many more *b* because of his own
Jn 4:50 the man *b* the word that Jesus had
Jn 4:53 and himself *b*, and his whole house
Jn 5:46 *b* Moses, ye would have *b* me
Jn 6:64 who they were that *b* not, and who
Jn 7:31 And many of the people *b* on him
Jn 7:48 or of the Pharisees *b* on him
Jn 8:30 spake these words, many *b* on him
Jn 10:25 them, I told you, and ye *b* not
Jn 10:42 And many *b* on him there
Jn 11:45 things which Jesus did, *b* on him
Jn 12:11 the Jews went away, and *b* on Jesus
Jn 12:37 them, yet they *b* not on him
Jn 12:38 Lord, who hath *b* our report
Jn 12:42 chief rulers also many *b* on him
Jn 16:27 have *b* that I came out from God
Jn 17:8 they have *b* that thou didst send
Jn 20:8 to the sepulchre, and he saw, and *b*
Jn 20:29 thou hast seen me, thou hast *b*
Jn 20:29 that have not seen, and yet have *b*
Acts 2:44 all that *b* were together, and had
Acts 4:4 of them which heard the word *b*
Acts 4:32 of them that *b* were of one heart
Acts 8:12 But when they *b* Philip preaching
Acts 9:26 *b* not that he was a disciple
Acts 9:42 and many *b* in the Lord
Acts 10:45 which *b* were astonished, as many
Acts 11:17 who *b* on the Lord Jesus Christ
Acts 11:21 and a great number *b*, and turned
Acts 13:12 when he saw what was done, *b*
Acts 13:48 were ordained to eternal life *b*
Acts 14:1 the Jews and also of the Greeks *b*
Acts 14:23 them to the Lord, on whom they *b*
Acts 15:5 the sect of the Pharisees which *b*
Acts 16:1 woman, which was a Jewess, and *b*
Acts 17:4 And some of them *b*, and consorted
Acts 17:12 Therefore many of them *b*
Acts 17:34 certain men clave unto him, and *b*
Acts 18:8 *b* on the Lord with all his house
Acts 18:8 many of the Corinthians hearing *b*
Acts 18:27 much which had *b* through grace
Acts 19:2 the Holy Ghost since ye *b*
Acts 19:9 *b* not, but spake evil of that way
Acts 19:18 And many that *b* came, and confessed
Acts 22:19 synagogue them that *b* on thee
Acts 27:11 the centurion *b* the master
Acts 28:24 some *b* the things which were
Rom 4:3 *b* God, and it was counted
Rom 4:17 nations,) before him whom he *b*
Rom 4:18 Who against hope *b* in hope
Rom 10:14 on him in whom they have not *b*
Rom 10:16 Lord, who hath *b* our report
Rom 11:30 ye in times past have not *b* God
Rom 11:31 Even so have these also now not *b*
Rom 13:11 salvation nearer than when we *b*
1Cor 3:5 but ministers by whom ye *b*
1Cor 15:2 you, unless ye have *b* in vain
1Cor 15:11 or they, so we preach, and so ye *b*
2Cor 4:13 according as it is written, I *b*
Gal 2:16 even we have *b* in Jesus Christ,
Gal 3:6 Even as Abraham *b* God, and it was
Eph 1:13 in whom also after that ye *b*
2Th 1:10 among you was *b*) in that day
2Th 2:12 be damned who *b* not the truth
1Ti 3:16 *b* on in the world, received up
2Ti 1:12 for I know whom I have *b*, and am
Titus 3:8 that they which have *b* in God
Heb 3:18 his rest, but to them that *b* not
Heb 4:3 For we which have *b* do enter into
Heb 11:31 perished not with them that *b* not
Jas 2:23 which saith, Abraham *b* God
1Jn 4:16 *b* the love that God hath to us
Jude 5 destroyed them that *b* not

**BELIEVEST**

Lk 1:20 because thou *b* not my words
Jn 1:50 thee under the fig tree, *b* thou
Jn 11:26 *B* thou this
Jn 14:10 *B* thou not that I am in the
Acts 8:37 If thou *b* with all thine heart,
Acts 26:27 King Agrippa, *b* thou the prophets
Jas 2:19 Thou *b* that there is one God

**BELIEVETH**

Job 15:22 He *b* not that he shall return out
Job 39:24 neither *b* he that it is the sound
Prov 14:15 The simple *b* every word
Is 28:16 he that *b* shall not make haste
Mk 9:23 things are possible to him that *b*
Mk 16:16 He that *b* and is baptized shall be
Jn 3:15 That whosoever *b* in him should
Jn 3:16 that whosoever *b* in him should
Jn 3:18 He that *b* on him is not condemned
Jn 3:36 He that *b* on the Son hath
Jn 3:36 he that *b* not the Son shall not
Jn 6:35 he that *b* on me shall never
Jn 6:40 *b* on him, may have everlasting
Jn 6:47 He that *b* on me hath everlasting
Jn 7:38 He that *b* on me, as the scripture
Jn 11:25 he that *b* in me, though he were
Jn 12:44 cried and said, He that *b* on me
Jn 12:44 *b* not on me, but on him that sent
Jn 12:46 that whosoever *b* on me should not
Jn 14:12 I say unto you, He that *b* on me
Acts 10:43 *b* in him shall receive remission
Rom 1:16 salvation to every one that *b*
Rom 3:26 justifier of him which *b* in Jesus
Rom 4:5 but *b* on him that justifieth the
Rom 9:33 whosoever *b* on him shall not be
Rom 10:4 righteousness to every one that *b*
Rom 10:10 heart man *b* unto righteousness
Rom 10:11 Whosoever *b* on him shall not be
Rom 14:2 For one *b* that he may eat all
1Cor 7:12 brother hath a wife that *b* not
1Cor 7:13 which hath an husband that *b* not
1Cor 13:7 *b* all things, hopeth all things,
1Cor 14:24 and there come in one that *b* not
2Cor 6:15 hath he that *b* with an infidel
1Ti 5:16 man or woman that *b* have widows
1Pet 2:6 he that *b* on him shall not be
1Jn 5:1 Whosoever *b* that Jesus is the
1Jn 5:5 but he that *b* that Jesus is the
1Jn 5:10 He that *b* on the Son of God hath
1Jn 5:10 he that *b* not God hath made him a

**BELIEVING**

Mt 21:22 ye shall ask in prayer, *b*
Jn 20:27 and be not faithless, but *b*
Jn 20:31 that *b* ye might have life through
Acts 16:34 *b* in God with all his house
Acts 24:14 *b* all things which are written in
Rom 15:13 you with all joy and peace in *b*
1Ti 6:2 And they that have *b* masters
1Pet 1:8 though now ye see him not, yet *b*

**BELL**

Ex 28:34 A golden *b* and a pomegranate
Ex 39:26 A *b* and a pomegranate, a *b* and a

**BELLS**

Ex 28:33 *b* of gold between them round
Ex 39:25 they made *b* of pure gold
Zec 14:20 there be upon the *b* of the horses

**BELLY**

Gen 3:14 upon thy *b* shalt thou go, and dust
Lev 11:42 Whatsoever goeth upon the *b*
Num 5:21 thigh to rot, and thy *b* to swell
Num 5:22 bowels, to make thy *b* to swell
Num 5:27 her *b* shall swell, and her thigh
Num 25:8 and the woman through her *b*
Judg 3:21 thigh, and thrust it into his *b*
1Kin 7:20 over against the *b* which was by
Job 3:11 ghost when I came out of the *b*
Job 15:2 fill his *b* with the east wind
Job 15:35 and their *b* prepareth deceit
Job 20:15 God shall cast them out of his *b*
Job 20:20 shall not feel quietness in his *b*
Job 20:23 When he is about to fill his *b*
Job 32:19 my *b* is as wine which hath no
Job 40:16 force is in the navel of his *b*
Ps 17:14 whose *b* thou fillest with thy hid
Ps 22:10 art my God from my mother's *b*
Ps 31:9 with grief, yea, my soul and my *b*

Ps 44:25 our *b* cleaveth unto the earth
Prov 13:25 but the *b* of the wicked shall
Prov 18:8 into the innermost parts of the *b*
Prov 18:20 A man's *b* shall be satisfied with
Prov 20:27 all the inward parts of the *b*
Prov 20:30 stripes the inward parts of the *b*
Prov 26:22 into the innermost parts of the *b*
Song 5:14 his *b* is as bright ivory overlaid
Song 7:2 thy *b* is like an heap of wheat
Is 46:3 which are borne by me from the *b*
Jer 1:5 formed thee in the *b* I knew thee
Jer 51:34 filled his *b* with my delicates
Eze 3:3 Son of man, cause thy *b* to eat
Dan 2:32 and his arms of silver, his *b*
Jonah 1:17 Jonah was in the *b* of the fish
Jonah 2:1 LORD his God out of the fish's *b*
Jonah 2:2 out of the *b* of hell cried I, and
Hab 3:16 When I heard, my *b* trembled
Mt 12:40 and three nights in the whale's *b*
Mt 15:17 in at the mouth goeth into the *b*
Mk 7:19 into his heart, but into the *b*
Lk 15:16 *b* with the husks that the swine
Jn 7:38 out of his *b* shall flow rivers of
Rom 16:18 Jesus Christ, but their own *b*
1Cor 6:13 Meats for the *b*, and the *b* for
Phil 3:19 destruction, whose God is their *b*
Rev 10:9 and it shall make thy *b* bitter
Rev 10:10 I had eaten it, my *b* was bitter

### BELONG

Gen 40:8 Do not interpretations *b* to God
Lev 27:24 the possession of the land did *b*
Num 1:50 and over all things that *b* to it
Deut 29:29 The secret things *b* unto the LORD
Deut 29:29 which are revealed *b* unto us
Ps 47:9 shields of the earth *b* unto God
Ps 68:20 unto GOD the Lord *b* the issues
Prov 24:23 These things also *b* to the wise
Dan 9:9 To the Lord our God *b* mercies
Mk 9:41 my name, because ye *b* to Christ
Lk 19:42 the things which *b* unto thy peace
1Cor 7:32 for the things that *b* to the Lord

### BELONGED

Josh 17:8 on the border of Manasseh *b* to
1Sa 21:7 of the herdmen that *b* to Saul
1Kin 1:8 the mighty men which *b* to David
1Kin 15:27 which *b* to the Philistines
1Kin 16:15 which *b* to the Philistines
2Kin 14:28 which *b* to Judah, for Israel, are
1Chr 2:23 All these *b* to the sons of Machir
1Chr 13:6 which *b* to Judah, to bring up
2Chr 26:23 the burial which *b* to the kings
Est 1:9 house which *b* to king Ahasuerus
Est 2:9 with such things as *b* to her
Lk 23:7 he *b* unto Herod's jurisdiction

### BELONGETH

Num 8:24 This is it that *b* unto the
Deut 32:35 To me *b* vengeance, and recompence
Judg 19:14 by Gibeah, which *b* to Benjamin
Judg 20:4 into Gibeah that *b* to Benjamin
1Sa 17:1 which *b* to Judah, and pitched
1Sa 30:14 upon the coast which *b* to Judah
1Kin 17:9 which *b* to Zidon, and dwell there
1Kin 19:3 which *b* to Judah, and left his
2Kin 14:11 at Beth-shemesh, which *b* to Judah
2Chr 25:21 at Beth-shemesh, which *b* to Judah
Ezr 10:4 for this matter *b* unto thee
Ps 3:8 Salvation *b* unto the LORD
Ps 62:11 that power *b* unto God
Ps 94:1 O LORD God, to whom vengeance *b*
Dan 9:7 O Lord, righteousness *b* unto thee
Dan 9:8 to us *b* confusion of face, to our
Heb 5:14 But strong meat *b* to them that
Heb 10:30 hath said, Vengeance *b* unto me

### BELONGING

Num 7:9 the service of the sanctuary *b*
Ruth 2:3 a part of the field *b* unto Boaz
1Sa 6:18 Philistines *b* to the five lords
Prov 26:17 meddleth with strife *b* not to him
Lk 9:10 *b* to the city called Bethsaida

### BELOVED

Deut 21:15 If a man have two wives, one *b*
Deut 21:15 born him children, both the *b*
Deut 33:12 The *b* of the LORD shall dwell in
Neh 13:26 who was *b* of his God, and God made
Ps 60:5 That thy *b* may be delivered
Ps 108:6 That thy *b* may be delivered
Ps 127:2 for so he giveth his *b* sleep
Prov 4:3 only *b* in the sight of my mother
Song 1:14 My *b* is unto me as a cluster of
Song 1:16 Behold, thou art fair, my *b*
Song 2:3 so is my *b* among the sons
Song 2:8 The voice of my *b*
Song 2:16 My *b* is mine, and I am his
Song 2:17 the shadows flee away, turn, my *b*
Song 4:16 Let my *b* come into his garden, and
Song 5:1 drink, yea, drink abundantly, O *b*
Song 5:2 the voice of my *b* that knocketh
Song 5:4 My *b* put in his hand by the hole
Song 5:8 of Jerusalem, if ye find my *b*
Song 5:9 thy *b* more than another *b*
Song 5:16 This is my *b*, and this is my
Song 6:1 Whither is thy *b* gone, O thou
Song 6:1 whither is thy *b* turned aside
Song 6:2 My *b* is gone down into his garden
Song 6:3 am my beloved's, and my *b* is mine
Song 7:9 mouth like the best wine for my *b*
Song 7:11 Come, my *b*, let us go forth into
Song 7:13 I have laid up for thee, O my *b*
Song 8:5 wilderness, leaning upon her *b*
Song 8:14 Make haste, my *b*, and be thou like
Is 5:1 of my *b* touching his vineyard
Jer 11:15 What hath my *b* to do in mine
Jer 12:7 I have given the dearly *b* of my
Dan 9:23 for thou art greatly *b*
Dan 10:11 me, O Daniel, a man greatly *b*
Dan 10:19 And said, O man greatly *b*, fear
Hos 3:1 love a woman *b* of her friend, yet
Hos 9:16 even the *b* fruit of their womb
Mt 3:17 heaven, saying, This is my *b* Son
Mt 12:18 my *b*, in whom my soul is well
Mt 17:5 which said, This is my *b* Son
Mk 1:11 heaven, saying, Thou art my *b* Son
Mk 9:7 cloud, saying, This is my *b* Son
Lk 3:22 which said, Thou art my *b* Son
Lk 9:35 cloud, saying, This is my *b* Son
Lk 20:13 I will send my *b* son
Acts 15:25 men unto you with our *b* Barnabas
Rom 1:7 *b* of God, called to be saints
Rom 9:25 and her *b*, which was not *b*
Rom 11:28 they are *b* for the fathers' sakes
Rom 12:19 Dearly *b*, avenge not yourselves,
Rom 16:8 Greet Amplias my *b* in the Lord
Rom 16:12 Salute the *b* Persis, which
1Cor 4:14 but as my *b* sons I warn you
1Cor 4:17 you Timotheus, who is my *b* son
1Cor 10:14 Wherefore, my dearly *b*, flee from
1Cor 15:58 my *b* brethren, be ye stedfast,
2Cor 7:1 therefore these promises dearly *b*
2Cor 12:19 but we do all things, dearly *b*
Eph 1:6 he hath made us accepted in the *b*
Eph 6:21 a *b* brother and faithful minister
Phil 2:12 Wherefore, my *b*, as ye have
Phil 4:1 Therefore, my brethren dearly *b*
Col 3:12 as the elect of God, holy and *b*
Col 4:7 unto you, who is a *b* brother
Col 4:9 *b* brother, who is one of you
Col 4:14 the *b* physician, and Demas, greet
1Th 1:4 Knowing, brethren *b*, your
2Th 2:13 brethren *b* of the Lord, because
1Ti 6:2 because they are faithful and *b*
2Ti 1:2 To Timothy, my dearly *b* son
Philem 1 unto Philemon our dearly *b*
Philem 16 but above a servant, a brother *b*
Heb 6:9 But, *b*, we are persuaded better
Jas 1:16 Do not err, my *b* brethren
Jas 1:19 my *b* brethren, let every man be
Jas 2:5 my *b* brethren, Hath not God
1Pet 2:11 Dearly *b*, I beseech you as
2Pet 1:17 excellent glory, This is my *b* Son
2Pet 3:1 This second epistle, *b*, I now
2Pet 3:8 But, *b*, be not ignorant of this
2Pet 3:14 Wherefore, *b*, seeing that ye look
2Pet 3:17 Ye therefore, *b*, seeing ye know
1Jn 3:2 *B*, now are we the sons of God, and
1Jn 3:21 *B*, if our heart condemn us not,
1Jn 4:1 *B*, believe not every spirit, but
1Jn 4:7 *B*, let us love one another
1Jn 4:11 *B*, if God so loved us, we ought
3Jn 2 *B*, I wish above all things that
3Jn 5 *B*, thou doest faithfully
3Jn 11 *B*, follow not that which is evil,
Jude 3 *B*, when I gave all diligence to
Jude 17 But, *b*, remember ye the words
Jude 20 But ye, *b*, building up yourselves
Rev 20:9 the saints about, and the *b* city

### BELOVED'S

Song 6:3 I am my *b*, and my beloved is mine
Song 7:10 I am my *b*, and his desire is

### BELSHAZZAR *(bel-shaz'-ar) A Babylonian king.*

Dan 5:1 *B* the king made a great feast to
Dan 5:2 *B*, whiles he tasted the wine,
Dan 5:9 Then was king *B* greatly troubled,
Dan 5:22 And thou his son, O *B*, hast not
Dan 5:29 Then commanded *B*, and they clothed
Dan 7:1 In the first year of *B* king of
Dan 8:1 king *B* a vision appeared unto me

### BELTESHAZZAR *(bel-te-shaz'-ar)* See DANIEL. *The Babylonian name given to Daniel.*

Dan 1:7 he gave unto Daniel the name of *B*
Dan 2:26 said to Daniel, whose name was *B*
Dan 4:8 in before me, whose name was *B*
Dan 4:18 Now thou, O *B*, declare the
Dan 5:12 Daniel, whom the king named *B*
Dan 10:1 Daniel, whose name was called *B*

### BEMOAN

Jer 15:5 or who shall *b* thee
Jer 16:5 neither go to lament nor *b* them
Jer 22:10 not for the dead, neither *b* him
Jer 48:17 All ye that are about him, *b* him
Nah 3:7 who will *b* her

### BEN *(ben) A Levite.*

1Chr 15:18 the second degree, Zechariah, *B*

### BENAIAH *(ben-ay'-ah)*

*1. An officer of David.*
2Sa 8:18 *B* the son of Jehoiada was over
2Sa 20:23 *B* the son of Jehoiada was over
2Sa 23:20 *B* the son of Jehoiada, the son of
2Sa 23:22 These things did *B* the son of
1Kin 1:8 *B* the son of Jehoiada, and Nathan
1Kin 1:10 But Nathan the prophet, and *B*
1Kin 1:26 *B* the son of Jehoiada, and thy
1Kin 1:32 prophet, and *B* the son of Jehoiada
1Kin 1:36 *B* the son of Jehoiada answered
1Kin 1:38 *B* the son of Jehoiada, and the
1Kin 1:44 *B* the son of Jehoiada, and the
1Kin 2:25 the hand of *B* the son of Jehoiada
1Kin 2:29 Then Solomon sent *B* the son of
1Kin 2:30 *B* brought the king word again,
1Kin 2:34 So *B* the son of Jehoiada went up,
1Kin 2:46 commanded *B* the son of Jehoiada
1Kin 4:4 *B* the son of Jehoiada was over
1Chr 11:22 *B* the son of Jehoiada, the son of
1Chr 11:24 These things did *B* the son of
1Chr 18:17 *B* the son of Jehoiada was over
1Chr 27:5 month was *B* the son of Jehoiada
*2. A "mighty man" of David.*
2Sa 23:30 *B* the Pirathonite, Hiddai of the
1Chr 11:31 of Benjamin, *B* the Pirathonite,
1Chr 27:14 month was *B* the Pirathonite
*3. A Simeonite family chief.*
1Chr 4:36 and Adiel, and Jesimiel, and *B*
*4. A priest of David.*
1Chr 15:18 and Jehiel, and Unni, Eliab, and *B*
1Chr 15:20 Unni, and Eliab, and Maaseiah, and *B*
1Chr 15:24 and Amasai, and Zechariah, and *B*
1Chr 16:5 and Mattithiah, and Eliab, and *B*
1Chr 16:6 *B* also and Jahaziel the priests
*5. Father of Jehoida.*
1Chr 27:34 was Jehoiada the son of *B*
*6. Grandfather of Jehaziel.*
2Chr 20:14 son of Zechariah, the son of *B*
*7. A Levite during Hezekiah's reign.*
2Chr 31:13 and Ismachiah, and Mahath, and *B*
*8. A descendant of Parosh.*
Ezr 10:25 and Eleazar, and Malchijah, and *B*
*9. A son of Pahath-moab.*
Ezr 10:30 Adna, and Chelal, *B*, Maaseiah,
*10. A son of Bani.*
Ezr 10:35 *B*, Bedeiah, Chelluh,
*11. A son of Nebo.*
Ezr 10:43 Zabad, Zebina, Jadau, and Joel, *B*
*12. Father of Pelatiah.*
Eze 11:1 of Azur, and Pelatiah the son of *B*
Eze 11:13 that Pelatiah the son of *B* died

### BEN-AMMI *(ben-am'-mi) A son of Lot.*

Gen 19:38 bare a son, and called his name *B*

### BEND

Ps 11:2 For, lo, the wicked *b* their bow
Ps 64:3 *b* their bows to shoot their
Jer 9:3 they *b* their tongues like their

Jer 46:9 Lydians, that handle and *b* the bow
Jer 50:14 all ye that *b* the bow, shoot at
Jer 50:29 all ye that *b* the bow, camp
Jer 51:3 bendeth let the archer *b* his bow
Eze 17:7 this vine did *b* her roots toward

**BENDETH**
Ps 58:7 when he *b* his bow to shoot his
Jer 51:3 Against him that *b* let the archer

**BENDING**
Is 60:14 thee shall come *b* unto thee

**BENE-BERAK** *(be'-ne-be'-rak) A city in Dan.*
Josh 19:45 And Jehud, and *B*, and Gath-rimmon,

**BENEFACTORS**
Lk 22:25 authority upon them are called *b*

**BENEFIT**
2Chr 32:25 according to the *b* done unto him
Jer 18:10 wherewith I said I would *b* them
2Cor 1:15 that ye might have a second *b*
1Ti 6:2 and beloved, partakers of the *b*
Philem 14 that thy *b* should not be as it

**BENEFITS**
Ps 68:19 Lord, who daily loadeth us with *b*
Ps 103:2 my soul, and forget not all his *b*
Ps 116:12 the LORD for all his *b* toward me

**BENE-JAAKAN** *(be'-ne-ja'-a-kan) Namesake of several wells.*
Num 33:31 from Moseroth, and pitched in *B*
Num 33:32 And they removed from *B*, and

**BEN-HADAD** *(ben'-ha-dad)*
*1. A Syrian king, son of Tabrimon.*
1Kin 15:18 and king Asa sent them to *B*
1Kin 15:20 So *B* hearkened unto king Asa, and
2Chr 16:2 sent to *B* king of Syria, that
2Chr 16:4 *B* hearkened unto king Asa, and
*2. A Syrian king during Ahab's reign.*
1Kin 20:1 *B* the king of Syria gathered all
1Kin 20:5 again, and said, Thus speaketh *B*
1Kin 20:9 he said unto the messengers of *B*
1Kin 20:12 when *B* heard this message, as he
1Kin 20:16 But *B* was drinking himself drunk
1Kin 20:20 *B* the king of Syria escaped on an
1Kin 20:26 that *B* numbered the Syrians, and
1Kin 20:30 *B* fled, and came into the city,
1Kin 20:32 and said, Thy servant *B* saith
2Kin 6:24 that *B* king of Syria gathered all
2Kin 8:7 *B* the king of Syria was sick
2Kin 8:9 Thy son *B* king of Syria hath sent
*3. A Syrian king, son of Hazael.*
2Kin 13:3 into the hand of *B* the son of
2Kin 13:24 *B* his son reigned in his stead
Amos 1:4 shall devour the palaces of *B*
*4. A title for all the Syrian kings.*
Jer 49:27 it shall consume the palaces of *B*

**BEN-HAIL** *(ben-ha'-il) A prince of Judah.*
2Chr 17:7 he sent to his princes, even to *B*

**BEN-HANAN** *(ben-ha'-nan) A son of Shimon.*
1Chr 4:20 Shimon were, Amnon, and Rinnah, *B*

**BENINU** *(ben'-i-nu) A Levite who renewed the covenant.*
Neh 10:13 Hodijah, Bani, *B*

**BENJAMIN** *(ben'-ja-min)* See BENJAMIN'S, BENJAMITE.
*1. Youngest son of Jacob.*
Gen 35:18 but his father called him *B*
Gen 35:24 Joseph, and *B*
Gen 42:4 But *B*, Joseph's brother, Jacob
Gen 42:36 is not, and ye will take *B* away
Gen 43:14 away your other brother, and *B*
Gen 43:29 up his eyes, and saw his brother *B*
Gen 45:12 see, and the eyes of my brother *B*
Gen 45:14 and *B* wept upon his neck
Gen 45:22 but to *B* he gave three hundred
Gen 46:19 Joseph, and *B*
Gen 46:21 And the sons of *B* were Belah
Ex 1:3 Issachar, Zebulun, and *B*,
1Chr 2:2 Dan, Joseph, and *B*, Naphtali, Gad,
1Chr 7:6 The sons of *B*
1Chr 8:1 Now *B* begat Bela his firstborn,
*2. One of the twelve tribes comprising Israel.*
Gen 49:27 *B* shall ravin as a wolf:
Num 1:11 Of *B*
Num 1:36 Of the children of *B*, by their
Num 2:22 Then the tribe of *B*
Num 7:60 prince of the children of *B*
Num 10:24 *B* was Abidan the son of Gideoni
Num 13:9 Of the tribe of *B*, Palti the son
Num 34:21 Of the tribe of *B*, Elidad the son
Deut 27:12 and Issachar, and Joseph, and *B*
Deut 33:12 of *B* he said, The beloved of the
Josh 18:11 of *B* came up according to their
Josh 18:20 inheritance of the children of *B*
Josh 21:4 Simeon, and out of the tribe of *B*
Josh 21:17 And out of the tribe of *B*, Gibeon
Judg 1:21 the children of *B* did not drive
Judg 5:14 after thee, *B*, among thy people
Judg 10:9 also against Judah, and against *B*
Judg 19:14 by Gibeah, which belongeth to *B*
Judg 20:3 (Now the children of *B* heard that
Judg 20:10 do, when they come to Gibeah of *B*
Judg 20:12 men through all the tribe of *B*
Judg 20:17 And the men of Israel, beside *B*
Judg 20:20 went out to battle against *B*
Judg 20:23 the children of *B* my brother
Judg 20:28 the children of *B* my brother
Judg 20:30 children of *B* on the third day
Judg 20:35 And the LORD smote *B* before Israel
Judg 20:39 *B* began to smite and kill of the
Judg 20:41 again, the men of *B* were amazed
Judg 20:44 there fell of *B* eighteen thousand
Judg 20:46 fell that day of *B* were twenty
Judg 20:48 again upon the children of *B*
Judg 21:1 give his daughter unto *B* to wife
Judg 21:6 repented them for *B* their brother
Judg 21:13 to speak to the children of *B*
Judg 21:20 they commanded the children of *B*
1Sa 4:12 ran a man of *B* out of the army
1Sa 9:1 Now there was a man of *B*, whose
1Sa 9:16 thee a man out of the land of *B*
1Sa 10:2 in the border of *B* at Zelzah
1Sa 13:2 were with Jonathan in Gibeah of *B*
1Sa 13:15 up from Gilgal unto Gibeah of *B*
1Sa 14:16 of Saul in Gibeah of *B* looked
2Sa 2:9 and over Ephraim, and over *B*
2Sa 2:15 went over by number twelve of *B*
2Sa 2:31 of David had smitten of *B*
2Sa 3:19 Abner also spake in the ears of *B*
2Sa 4:2 Beerothite, of the children of *B*
2Sa 19:17 were a thousand men of *B* with him
2Sa 21:14 they in the country of *B* in Zelah
2Sa 23:29 of Gibeah of the children of *B*
1Kin 4:18 Shimei the son of Elah, in *B*
1Kin 12:21 of Judah, with the tribe of *B*
1Kin 15:22 Asa built with them Geba of *B*
1Chr 6:60 And out of the tribe of *B*
1Chr 8:40 All these are of the sons of *B*
1Chr 9:3 of Judah, and of the children of *B*
1Chr 11:31 pertained to the children of *B*
1Chr 12:2 bow, even of Saul's brethren of *B*
1Chr 21:6 *B* counted he not among them
1Chr 27:21 of *B*, Jaasiel the son of Abner
2Chr 14:8 and out of *B*, that bare shields and
2Chr 15:2 ye me, Asa, and all Judah and *B*
2Chr 17:17 And of *B*
2Chr 25:5 throughout all Judah and *B*
2Chr 31:1 the altars out of all Judah and *B*
2Chr 34:9 of Israel, and of all Judah and *B*
2Chr 34:32 in Jerusalem and *B* to stand to it
Ezr 1:5 of the fathers of Judah and *B*
Ezr 4:1 *B* heard that the children of the
Ezr 10:9 *B* gathered themselves together
Neh 11:4 of Judah, and of the children of *B*
Neh 11:31 The children also of *B* from Geba
Ps 68:27 There is little *B* with their
Ps 80:2 Before Ephraim and *B* and Manasseh
Jer 1:1 were in Anathoth in the land of *B*
Jer 6:1 O ye children of *B*, gather
Jer 17:26 Jerusalem, and from the land of *B*
Jer 32:8 which is in the country of *B*
Jer 32:44 take witnesses in the land of *B*
Jer 33:13 of the south, and in the land of *B*
Jer 37:12 to go into the land of *B*, to
Eze 48:22 of Judah and the border of *B*
Eze 48:32 one gate of Joseph, one gate of *B*
Hos 5:8 at Beth-aven, after thee, O *B*
Obad 19 and *B* shall possess Gilead
Acts 13:21 of Cis, a man of the tribe of *B*
Rom 11:1 of Abraham, of the tribe of *B*
Phil 3:5 of Israel, of the tribe of *B*
Rev 7:8 Of the tribe of *B* were sealed
*3. Great-grandson of Benjamin 1.*
1Chr 7:10 Jeush, and *B*, and Ehud, and
*4. A descendant of Harim.*
Ezr 10:32 *B*, Malluch, and Shemariah
*5. A repairer of the Jerusalem wall.*
Neh 3:23 After him repaired *B* and Hashub
*6. Purified the Jerusalem wall.*
Neh 12:34 Judah, and *B*, and Shemaiah, and
*7. A gate of Jerusalem.*
Jer 20:2 that were in the high gate of *B*
Jer 37:13 And when he was in the gate of *B*
Jer 38:7 then sitting in the gate of *B*

**BENJAMIN'S** *(ben'-ja-mins)*
*1. Refers to Benjamin 1.*
Gen 43:34 but *B* mess was five times so much
Gen 44:12 and the cup was found in *B* sack
Gen 45:14 he fell upon his brother *B* neck
*2. Refers to Benjamin 7.*
Zec 14:10 from *B* gate unto the place of the

**BENJAMITE** *(ben'-ja-mite)* See BENJAMITES. *A descendant of Benjamin.*
Judg 3:15 Ehud the son of Gera, a *B*
1Sa 9:1 Bechorath, the son of Aphiah, a *B*
1Sa 9:21 answered and said, Am not I a *B*
2Sa 16:11 much more now may this *B* do it
2Sa 19:16 And Shimei the son of Gera, a *B*
2Sa 20:1 was Sheba, the son of Bichri, a *B*
1Kin 2:8 a *B* of Bahurim, which cursed me
Est 2:5 of Shimei, the son of Kish, a *B*
Ps 7:*t* the words of Cush the *B*

**BENJAMITES** *(ben'-ja-mites)*
Judg 19:16 but the men of the place were *B*
Judg 20:35 of the *B* that day twenty and five
Judg 20:40 the *B* looked behind them, and,
1Sa 9:4 passed through the land of the *B*
1Sa 22:7 stood about him, Hear now, ye *B*
1Chr 27:12 Abiezer the Anetothite, of the *B*

**BENO** *(be'-no) A descendant of Merari.*
1Chr 24:26 sons of Jaaziah; *B*
1Chr 24:27 *B*, and Shoham, and Zaccur, and Ibri

**BEN-ONI** *(ben-o'-ni) Rachel's second son.*
Gen 35:18 died) that she called his name *B*

**BENT**
Ps 7:12 he hath *b* his bow, and made it
Ps 37:14 have *b* their bow, to cast down
Is 5:28 are sharp, and all their bows *b*
Is 21:15 drawn sword, and from the *b* bow
Lam 2:4 He hath *b* his bow like an enemy
Lam 3:12 He hath *b* his bow, and set me as a
Hos 11:7 my people are *b* to backsliding
Zec 9:13 When I have *b* Judah for me,

**BEN-ZOHETH** *(ben-zo'-heth) A descendant of Caleb.*
1Chr 4:20 sons of Ishi were, Zoheth, and *B*

**BEON** *(be'-on) A place east of the Jordan River.*
Num 32:3 and Shebam, and Nebo, and *B*

**BEOR** *(be'-or)*
*1. Father of Bela.*
Gen 36:32 Bela the son of *B* reigned in Edom
1Chr 1:43 Bela the son of *B*
*2. Father of Balaam.*
Num 22:5 Balaam the son of *B* to Pethor
Num 24:3 Balaam the son of *B* hath said
Num 24:15 Balaam the son of *B* hath said
Num 31:8 Balaam also the son of *B* they
Deut 23:4 son of *B* of Pethor of Mesopotamia
Josh 13:22 Balaam also the son of *B*, the
Josh 24:9 Balaam the son of *B* to curse you
Mic 6:5 what Balaam the son of *B* answered

**BERA** *(be'-rah) King of Sodom.*
Gen 14:2 made war with *B* king of Sodom

**BERACHAH** *(ber'-a-kah)*
*1. A Benjamite warrior in David's army.*
1Chr 12:3 and *B*, and Jehu the Antothite,
*2. A valley in Judah.*
2Chr 20:26 themselves in the valley of *B*
2Chr 20:26 place was called, The valley of *B*

**BERACHIAH** *(ber-a-ki'-ah)* See BERECHIAH. *Father of Asaph.*
1Chr 6:39 hand, even Asaph the son of *B*

**BERAIAH** *(ber-a-i'-ah) A son of Shimhi.*
1Chr 8:21 And Adaiah, and *B*, and Shimrath, the

**BEREA** *(be-re'-a) A city in Macedonia.*
Acts 17:10 Paul and Silas by night unto *B*
Acts 17:13 of God was preached of Paul at *B*
Acts 20:4 him into Asia Sopater of *B*

**BEREAVE**
Eccl 4:8 do I labour, and *b* my soul of good
Jer 15:7 I will *b* them of children, I will
Eze 5:17 evil beasts, and they shall *b* thee
Eze 36:12 no more henceforth *b* them of men
Eze 36:14 neither *b* thy nations any more,
Hos 9:12 their children, yet will I *b* them

**BEREAVED**
Gen 42:36 Me have ye *b* of my children
Gen 43:14 *b* of my children, I am *b*
Jer 18:21 wives be *b* of their children
Eze 36:13 up men, and hast *b* thy nations
Hos 13:8 as a bear that is *b* of her whelps

**BEREAVETH**
Lam 1:20 abroad the sword *b*, at home there

**BERECHIAH** *(ber-e-ki'-ah)* See BERACHIAH.
*1. A descendant of King Jehoiakim.*
1Chr 3:20 And Hashubah, and Ohel, and *B*
*2. Same as Berachiah.*
1Chr 15:17 his brethren, Asaph the son of *B*
*3. A Levite near Jerusalem.*
1Chr 9:16 *B* the son of Asa, the son of
*4. A Levite doorkeeper.*
1Chr 15:23 And *B* and Elkanah were doorkeepers
*5. An Ephraimite.*
2Chr 28:12 *B* the son of Meshillemoth, and
*6. Father of Meshullam.*
Neh 3:4 repaired Meshullam the son of *B*
Neh 3:30 son of *B* over against his chamber
Neh 6:18 of Meshullam the son of *B*
*7. Father of Zechariah.*
Zec 1:1 LORD unto Zechariah, the son of *B*
Zec 1:7 LORD unto Zechariah, the son of *B*

**BERED** *(be'-red)*
*1. A place in southern Canaan.*
Gen 16:14 behold, it is between Kadesh and *B*
*2. An Ephraimite.*
1Chr 7:20 *B* his son, and Tahath his son, and

**BERI** *(be'-ri)* See BERITES. *Son of Zophah.*
1Chr 7:36 and Harnepher, and Shual, and *B*

**BERIAH** *(be-ri'-ah)* See BERIITES.
*1. A son of Asher.*
Gen 46:17 Jimnah, and Ishuah, and Isui, and *B*
Num 26:44 of *B*, the family of the Beriites
1Chr 7:30 Imnah, and Isuah, and Ishuai, and *B*
*2. A son of Ephraim.*
1Chr 7:23 a son, and he called his name *B*
*3. A son of Elpaal.*
1Chr 8:13 *B* also, and Shema, who were heads
1Chr 8:16 and Ispah, and Joha, the sons of *B*
*4. A Levite.*
1Chr 23:10 Jahath, Zina, and Jeush, and *B*

**BERIITES** *(be-ri'-ites) Descendants of Beriah 1.*
Num 26:44 of Beriah, the family of the *B*

**BERITES** *(be'-rites) Descendants of Beri.*
2Sa 20:14 and to Beth-maachah, and all the *B*

**BERITH** *(be'-rith)* See BAAL-BERITH. *Idol at Shechem.*
Judg 9:46 an hold of the house of the god *B*

**BERNICE** *(bur-ni'-see) Daughter of Herod Agrippa.*
Acts 25:13 *B* came unto Caesarea to salute
Acts 25:23 when Agrippa was come, and *B*
Acts 26:30 rose up, and the governor, and *B*

**BERODACH-BALADAN** *(ber-o'-dak-bal'-a-dan)* See MERODACH-BALADAN. *A king of Babylon.*
2Kin 20:12 At that time *B*, the son of

**BEROTHAH** *(ber-o'-thah)* See BEROTHAI, BEROTHITE. *A city near Hamath.*
Eze 47:16 Hamath, *B*, Sibraim, which is

**BEROTHAI** *(ber'-o-thahee)* See BEROTHAH. *A city of Hadadezer.*
2Sa 8:8 And from Betah, and from *B*, cities

**BEROTHITE** *(be'-ro-thite)* See BEEROTHITE. *A native of Beeroth.*
1Chr 11:39 Zelek the Ammonite, Naharai the *B*

**BERRIES**
Is 17:6 two or three *b* in the top of the
Jas 3:12 tree, my brethren, bear olive *b*

**BERYL**
Ex 28:20 And the fourth row a *b*, and an onyx
Ex 39:13 And the fourth row, a *b*, an onyx,
Song 5:14 are as gold rings set with the *b*
Eze 1:16 was like unto the colour of a *b*
Eze 10:9 was as the colour of a *b* stone
Eze 28:13 topaz, and the diamond, the *b*
Dan 10:6 His body also was like the *b*
Rev 21:20 the eighth, *b*

**BESAI** *(be'-sahee) A family of exiles.*
Ezr 2:49 of Paseah, the children of *B*
Neh 7:52 The children of *B*, the children

**BESEECH**
Ex 3:18 we *b* thee, three days' journey
Ex 33:18 I *b* thee, shew me thy glory
Num 12:11 I *b* thee, lay not the sin upon us
Num 12:13 Heal her now, O God, I *b* thee
Num 14:17 I *b* thee, let the power of my
Num 14:19 I *b* thee, the iniquity of this
1Sa 23:11 I *b* thee, tell thy servant
2Sa 13:24 I *b* thee, and his servants go with
2Sa 16:4 I humbly *b* thee that I may find
2Sa 24:10 I *b* thee, O LORD, take away the
2Kin 19:19 I *b* thee, save thou us out of his
2Kin 20:3 I *b* thee, O LORD, remember now
1Chr 21:8 I *b* thee, do away the iniquity of
2Chr 6:40 I *b* thee, thine eyes be open, and
Neh 1:5 I *b* thee, O LORD God of heaven,
Neh 1:8 I *b* thee, the word that thou
Neh 1:11 I *b* thee, let now thine ear be
Job 10:9 I *b* thee, that thou hast made me
Job 42:4 I *b* thee, and I will speak
Ps 80:14 we *b* thee, O God of hosts
Ps 116:4 I *b* thee, deliver my soul
Ps 118:25 Save now, I *b* thee, O LORD
Ps 119:108 I *b* thee, the freewill offerings
Is 38:3 I *b* thee, how I have walked
Is 64:9 we *b* thee, we are all thy people
Jer 38:4 We *b* thee, let this man be put to
Jer 38:20 I *b* thee, the voice of the LORD,
Jer 42:2 we *b* thee, our supplication be
Dan 1:12 thy servants, I *b* thee, ten days
Dan 9:16 I *b* thee, let thine anger and thy
Amos 7:2 O Lord GOD, forgive, I *b* thee
Amos 7:5 I, O Lord GOD, cease, I *b* thee
Jonah 1:14 We *b* thee, O LORD, we *b*
Jonah 4:3 I *b* thee, my life from me
Mal 1:9 *b* God that he will be gracious
Mk 7:32 they *b* him to put his hand upon
Lk 8:28 I *b* thee, torment me not
Lk 9:38 I *b* thee, look upon my son
Acts 21:39 I *b* thee, suffer me to speak unto
Acts 26:3 wherefore I *b* thee to hear me
Rom 12:1 I *b* you therefore, brethren, by
Rom 15:30 Now I *b* you, brethren, for the
Rom 16:17 Now I *b* you, brethren, mark them
1Cor 1:10 Now I *b* you, brethren, by the
1Cor 4:16 Wherefore I *b* you, be ye
1Cor 16:15 I *b* you, brethren, (ye know the
2Cor 2:8 Wherefore I *b* you that ye would
2Cor 5:20 as though God did *b* you by us
2Cor 6:1 *b* you also that ye receive not
2Cor 10:1 Now I Paul myself *b* you by the
Gal 4:12 Brethren, I *b* you, be as I am
Eph 4:1 *b* you that ye walk worthy of the
Phil 4:2 I *b* Euodias, and *b* Syntyche,
1Th 4:1 Furthermore then we *b* you
1Th 4:10 but we *b* you, brethren, that ye
1Th 5:12 we *b* you, brethren, to know them
2Th 2:1 Now we *b* you, brethren, by the
Philem 9 for love's sake I rather *b* thee
Heb 13:19 But I *b* you the rather to do this
Heb 13:22 I *b* you, brethren, suffer the
1Pet 2:11 I *b* you as strangers and pilgrims,
2Jn 5 And now I *b* thee, lady, not as

**BESEECHING**
Mt 8:5 came unto him a centurion, *b* him,
Mk 1:40 *b* him, and kneeling down to him,
Lk 7:3 *b* him that he would come and heal

**BESET**
Judg 19:22 *b* the house round about, and beat
Judg 20:5 *b* the house round about upon me
Ps 22:12 bulls of Bashan have *b* me round
Ps 139:5 Thou hast *b* me behind and before,
Hos 7:2 own doings have *b* them about
Heb 12:1 the sin which doth so easily *b* us

**BESIEGE**
Deut 20:12 thee, then thou shalt *b* it
Deut 20:19 When thou shalt *b* a city a long
Deut 28:52 he shall *b* thee in all thy gates,
1Sa 23:8 to Keilah, to *b* David and his men
1Kin 8:37 if their enemy *b* them in the land
2Kin 24:11 city, and his servants did *b* it
2Chr 6:28 if their enemies *b* them in the
Is 21:2 *b*, O Media
Jer 21:4 which *b* you without the walls, and
Jer 21:9 to the Chaldeans that *b* you

**BESIEGED**
2Sa 11:1 children of Ammon, and *b* Rabbah
2Sa 20:15 *b* him in Abel of Beth-maachah, and
1Kin 16:17 Israel with him, and they *b* Tirzah
1Kin 20:1 *b* Samaria, and warred against it
2Kin 6:24 host, and went up, and *b* Samaria
2Kin 16:5 and they *b* Ahaz, but could not
2Kin 17:5 to Samaria, and *b* it three years
2Kin 18:9 came up against Samaria, and *b* it
2Kin 19:24 up all the rivers of *b* places
2Kin 24:10 Jerusalem, and the city was *b*
2Kin 25:2 the city was *b* unto the eleventh
1Chr 20:1 of Ammon, and came and *b* Rabbah
Eccl 9:14 *b* it, and built great bulwarks
Is 1:8 garden of cucumbers, as a *b* city
Is 37:25 up all the rivers of the *b* places
Jer 32:2 of Babylon's army *b* Jerusalem
Jer 37:5 when the Chaldeans that *b*
Jer 39:1 against Jerusalem, and they *b* it
Jer 52:5 So the city was *b* unto the
Eze 4:3 face against it, and it shall be *b*
Eze 6:12 is *b* shall die by the famine
Dan 1:1 Babylon unto Jerusalem, and *b* it

**BESODEIAH** *(bes-o-di'-ah) A repairer of Jerusalem's walls.*
Neh 3:6 Paseah, and Meshullam the son of *B*

**BESOM**
Is 14:23 it with the *b* of destruction

**BESOR** *(be'-sor) A brook in southern Judah.*
1Sa 30:9 with him, and came to the brook *B*
1Sa 30:21 made also to abide at the brook *B*

**BESOUGHT**
Gen 42:21 anguish of his soul, when he *b* us
Ex 32:11 Moses *b* the LORD his God, and said
Deut 3:23 I *b* the LORD at that time, saying
2Sa 12:16 David therefore *b* God for the
1Kin 13:6 And the man of God *b* the LORD
2Kin 1:13 *b* him, and said unto him, O man of
2Kin 13:4 And Jehoahaz *b* the LORD, and the
2Chr 33:12 he *b* the LORD his God, and humbled
Ezr 8:23 we fasted and *b* our God for this
Est 8:3 *b* him with tears to put away the
Jer 26:19 *b* the LORD, and the LORD repented
Mt 8:31 So the devils *b* him, saying, If
Mt 8:34 they *b* him that he would depart
Mt 14:36 *b* him that they might only touch
Mt 15:23 *b* him, saying, Send her away
Mt 18:29 *b* him, saying, Have patience with
Mk 5:10 he *b* him much that he would not
Mk 5:12 And all the devils *b* him, saying,
Mk 5:23 *b* him greatly, saying, My little
Mk 6:56 *b* him that they might touch if it
Mk 7:26 she *b* him that he would cast
Mk 8:22 unto him, and *b* him to touch him
Lk 4:38 and they *b* him for her
Lk 5:12 *b* him, saying, Lord, if thou wilt
Lk 7:4 they *b* him instantly, saying,
Lk 8:31 they *b* him that he would not
Lk 8:37 about *b* him to depart from them
Lk 8:41 *b* him that he would come into his
Lk 9:40 I *b* thy disciples to cast him out
Lk 11:37 a certain Pharisee *b* him to dine
Jn 4:40 they *b* him that he would tarry
Jn 4:47 *b* him that he would come down, and
Jn 19:31 *b* Pilate that their legs might
Jn 19:38 *b* Pilate that he might take away
Acts 13:42 the Gentiles *b* that these words
Acts 16:15 and her household, she *b* us
Acts 16:39 *b* them, and brought them out, and
Acts 21:12 *b* him not to go up to Jerusalem
Acts 25:2 him against Paul, and *b* him,
Acts 27:33 Paul *b* them all to take meat,
2Cor 12:8 this thing I *b* the Lord thrice
1Ti 1:3 As I *b* thee to abide still at

**BEST**
Gen 43:11 take of the *b* fruits in the land
Gen 47:6 in the *b* of the land make thy
Gen 47:11 in the *b* of the land, in the land
Ex 22:5 of the *b* of his own field
Num 18:12 All the *b* of the oil
Num 18:29 of the LORD, of all the *b* thereof

Num 18:30 have heaved the *b* thereof from it
Num 18:32 have heaved from it the *b* of it
Num 36:6 them marry to whom they think *b*
Deut 23:16 thy gates, where it liketh him *b*
1Sa 8:14 oliveyards, even the *b* of them
1Sa 15:9 the *b* of the sheep, and of the
1Sa 15:15 people spared the *b* of the sheep
2Sa 18:4 What seemeth you *b* I will do
1Kin 10:18 and overlaid it with the *b* gold
2Kin 10:3 Look even out the *b* and meetest of
Est 2:9 her maids unto the *b* place of the
Ps 39:5 verily every man at his *b* state
Song 7:9 like the *b* wine for my beloved
Eze 31:16 *b* of Lebanon, all that drink
Mic 7:4 The *b* of them is as a brier
Lk 15:22 servants, Bring forth the *b* robe
1Cor 12:31 But covet earnestly the *b* gifts

**BESTOW**
Ex 32:29 that he may *b* upon you a blessing
Deut 14:26 thou shalt *b* that money for
2Chr 24:7 the LORD did they *b* upon Baalim
Ezr 7:20 thou shalt have occasion to *b*
Lk 12:17 have no room where to *b* my fruits
1Cor 12:23 upon these we *b* more abundant
1Cor 13:3 though I *b* all my goods to feed

**BESTOWED**
1Kin 10:26 whom he *b* in the cities for
2Kin 5:24 hand, and *b* them in the house
2Kin 12:15 the money to be *b* on workmen
1Chr 29:25 *b* upon him such royal majesty as
2Chr 9:25 whom he *b* in the chariot cities,
Is 63:7 to all that the LORD hath *b* on us
Jn 4:38 reap that whereon ye *b* no labour
Rom 16:6 Mary, who *b* much labour on us
1Cor 15:10 his grace which was *b* upon me was
2Cor 1:11 that for the gift *b* upon us by
2Cor 8:1 *b* on the churches of Macedonia
Gal 4:11 lest I have *b* upon you labour in
1Jn 3:1 of love the Father hath *b* upon us

**BETAH** *(be'-tah) A city of Hadadezer.*
2Sa 8:8 And from *B*, and from Berothai,

**BETEN** *(be'-ten) A city in Asher.*
Josh 19:25 border was Helkath, and Hali, and *B*

**BETHABARA** *(beth-ab'-ar-ah)* See BETHBARAH. *A place east of the Jordan River.*
Jn 1:28 were done in *B* beyond Jordan

**BETH-ANATH** *(beth'-a-nath) A city in Naphtali.*
Josh 19:38 Iron, and Migdal-el, Horem, and *B*
Judg 1:33 nor the inhabitants of *B*

**BETH-ANOTH** *(beth'-a-noth) A city in Judah.*
Josh 15:59 And Maarath, and *B*, and Eltekon

**BETHANY** *(beth'-a-ny) A village near Jerusalem.*
Mt 21:17 and went out of the city into *B*
Mt 26:6 Now when Jesus was in *B*, in the
Mk 11:1 to Jerusalem, unto Bethphage and *B*
Mk 11:11 went out unto *B* with the twelve
Mk 14:3 being in *B* in the house of Simon
Lk 19:29 was come nigh to Bethphage and *B*
Lk 24:50 And he led them out as far as to *B*
Jn 11:1 man was sick, named Lazarus, of *B*
Jn 11:18 Now *B* was nigh unto Jerusalem,
Jn 12:1 before the passover came to *B*

**BETH-ARABAH** *(beth-ar'-ab-ah) A city of the Arabah.*
Josh 15:6 and passed along by the north of *B*
Josh 15:61 In the wilderness, *B*, Middin, and
Josh 18:22 And *B*, and Zemaraim, and Beth-el,

**BETH-ARAM** *(beth'-a-ram) A city in Gad.*
Josh 13:27 And in the valley, *B*, and

**BETH-ARBEL** *(beth-ar'-bel) A city destroyed by the Assyrians.*
Hos 10:14 as Shalman spoiled *B* in the day

**BETH-AVEN** *(beth-a'-ven) A town in Benjamin.*
Josh 7:2 Jericho to Ai, which is beside *B*
Josh 18:12 were at the wilderness of *B*
1Sa 13:5 in Michmash, eastward from *B*
1Sa 14:23 and the battle passed over unto *B*
Hos 4:15 Gilgal, neither go ye up to *B*
Hos 5:8 cry aloud at *B*, after thee, O
Hos 10:5 fear because of the calves of *B*

**BETH-AZMAVETH** *(beth-az'-maveth)* See AZMAVETH. *A village in Judah.*
Neh 7:28 The men of *B*, forty and two

**BETH-BAAL-MEON** *(beth-ba'-al-me'-on) A Moabite town.*
Josh 13:17 Dibon, and Bamoth-baal, and *B*

**BETH-BARAH** *(beth-ba'-rah)* See BETH-ABARA. *A place in Gad.*
Judg 7:24 before them the waters unto *B*
Judg 7:24 and took the waters unto *B*

**BETH-BIREI** *(beth-bir'-e-i)* See BETH-LEBAOTH. *A town in Simeon.*
1Chr 4:31 and Hazar-susim, and at *B*, and at

**BETH-CAR** *(beth'-car) A Philistine stronghold in Judah.*
1Sa 7:11 them, until they came under *B*

**BETH-DAGON** *(beth-da'-gon)*
*1. A town in Judah.*
Josh 15:41 And Gederoth, *B*, and Naamah, and
*2. A town in Asher.*
Josh 19:27 turneth toward the sunrising to *B*

**BETH-DIBLATHAIM** *(beth-dib-lath-a'-im) A Moabite town.*
Jer 48:22 Dibon, and upon Nebo, and upon *B*

**BETH-EL**
Gen 12:8 unto a mountain on the east of *B*
Gen 12:8 having *B* on the west, and Hai on
Gen 13:3 journeys from the south even to *B*
Gen 28:19 called the name of that place *B*
Gen 31:13 I am the God of *B*, where thou
Gen 35:1 unto Jacob, Arise, go up to *B*
Gen 35:3 And let us arise, and go up to *B*
Gen 35:6 in the land of Canaan, that is, *B*
Gen 35:8 was buried beneath *B* under an oak
Gen 35:15 place where God spake with him, *B*
Josh 7:2 Beth-aven, on the east side of *B*
Josh 8:9 lie in ambush, and abode between *B*
Josh 8:12 them to lie in ambush between *B*
Josh 8:17 was not a man left in Ai or *B*
Josh 12:9 the king of Ai, which is beside *B*
Josh 12:16 the king of *B*, one
Josh 16:1 from Jericho throughout mount *B*
Josh 18:13 to the side of Luz, which is *B*
Josh 18:22 Beth-arabah, and Zemaraim, and *B*
Judg 1:22 they also went up against *B*
Judg 4:5 Ramah and *B* in mount Ephraim
Judg 21:19 which is on the north side of *B*
1Sa 7:16 from year to year in circuit to *B*
1Sa 10:3 three men going up to God to *B*
1Sa 13:2 Saul in Michmash and in mount *B*
1Sa 30:27 To them which were in *B*, and to
1Kin 12:29 And he set the one in *B*, and the
1Kin 12:32 So did he in *B*, sacrificing unto
1Kin 13:1 by the word of the LORD unto *B*
1Kin 13:4 had cried against the altar in *B*
1Kin 13:10 not by the way that he came to *B*
1Kin 13:32 the LORD against the altar in *B*
2Kin 2:2 for the LORD hath sent me to *B*
2Kin 2:23 And he went up from thence unto *B*
2Kin 10:29 the golden calves that were in *B*
2Kin 17:28 from Samaria came and dwelt in *B*
2Kin 23:4 carried the ashes of them unto *B*
2Kin 23:15 Moreover the altar that was at *B*
2Kin 23:17 hast done against the altar of *B*
2Kin 23:19 the acts that he had done in *B*
1Chr 7:28 and habitations were, *B* and the
2Chr 13:19 *B* with the towns thereof, and
Ezr 2:28 The men of *B* and Ai, two hundred
Neh 7:32 The men of *B* and Ai, an hundred
Neh 11:31 dwelt at Michmash, and Aija, and *B*
Jer 48:13 was ashamed of *B* their confidence
Hos 10:15 So shall *B* do unto you because of
Hos 12:4 he found him in *B*, and there he
Amos 3:14 I will also visit the altars of *B*
Amos 4:4 Come to *B*, and transgress
Amos 7:10 Then Amaziah the priest of *B* sent
Amos 7:13 prophesy not again any more at *B*

**BETH-ELITE** *(beth'-el-ite) A native of Beth-el.*
1Kin 16:34 days did Hiel the *B* build Jericho

**BETH-EMEK** *(beth-e'-mek) A town in Asher.*
Josh 19:27 toward the north side of *B*

**BETHER** *(be'-thur) A district in the Jordan valley.*
Song 2:17 hart upon the mountains of *B*

**BETHESDA** *(beth-ez'-dah) A pool in Jerusalem.*
Jn 5:2 is called in the Hebrew tongue *B*

**BETH-EZEL** *(beth-e'-zel) A city in Judah.*
Mic 1:11 not forth in the mourning of *B*

**BETH-GADER** *(beth-ga'-der)* See GEDER. *A descendant of Caleb.*
1Chr 2:51 Hareph the father of *B*

**BETH-GAMUL** *(beth-ga'-mul) A Moabite town.*
Jer 48:23 And upon Kiriathaim, and upon *B*

**BETH-HACCEREM** *(beth-hak'-se-rem) A town in Judah.*
Neh 3:14 of Rechab, the ruler of part of *B*
Jer 6:1 and set up a sign of fire in *B*

**BETH-HARAN** *(beth-ha'-ran)* See ELON-BETH-HARAN. *A city in Gad.*
Num 32:36 And Beth-nimrah, and *B*, fenced

**BETH-HOGLA** *(beth-hog'-lah)* See BETH-HOGLAH. *A city in Benjamin.*
Josh 15:6 And the border went up to *B*

**BETH-HOGLAH** *(beth-hog'-lah)* See BETH-HOGLAH. *Same as Beth-hogla.*
Josh 18:19 along to the side of *B* northward
Josh 18:21 their families were Jericho, and *B*

**BETH-HORON** *(beth-ho'-ron) Two cities in Ephraim, near Benjamin.*
Josh 10:10 along the way that goeth up to *B*
Josh 16:3 unto the coast of *B* the nether
Josh 16:5 Ataroth-addar, unto *B* the upper
Josh 18:13 on the south side of the nether *B*
Josh 21:22 suburbs, and *B* with her suburbs
1Sa 13:18 company turned the way to *B*
1Kin 9:17 built Gezer, and *B* the nether,
1Chr 6:68 suburbs, and *B* with her suburbs,
1Chr 7:24 who built *B* the nether, and the
2Chr 8:5 Also he built *B* the upper
2Chr 25:13 Judah, from Samaria even unto *B*

**BETH-JESHIMOTH** *(beth-jesh'-im-oth)* See BETH-JESIMOTH. *Same as Beth-jesimoth.*
Josh 12:3 sea on the east, the way to *B*
Josh 13:20 and Ashdoth-pisgah, and *B*,
Eze 25:9 the glory of the country, *B*

**BETH-JESIMOTH** *(beth-jes'-im-oth)* See BETH-JESHIMOTH. *A Moabite city.*
Num 33:49 from *B* even unto Abel-shittim in

**BETH-LEBAOTH** *(beth-leb'-a-oth)* See BETH-BISEI. *A town in Simeon.*
Josh 19:6 And *B*, and Sharuhen

**BETH-LEHEM** *(beth'-le-hem)* See BETH-LEHEMITE, BETH-LEHEM-JUDAH.
*1. A city in Judah.*
Gen 35:19 in the way to Ephrath, which is *B*
Gen 48:7 the same is *B*
Ruth 1:19 two went until they came to *B*
Ruth 1:22 they came to *B* in the beginning
Ruth 2:4 And, behold, Boaz came from *B*
Ruth 4:11 in Ephratah, and be famous in *B*
1Sa 16:4 the LORD spake, and came to *B*
1Sa 17:15 to feed his father's sheep at *B*
1Sa 20:6 that he might run to *B* his city
1Sa 20:28 asked leave of me to go to *B*
2Sa 2:32 of his father, which was in *B*
2Sa 23:14 of the Philistines was then in *B*
2Sa 23:24 Elhanan the son of Dodo of *B*
1Chr 11:16 garrison was then at *B*
1Chr 11:26 Elhanan the son of Dodo of *B*
2Chr 11:6 He built even *B*, and Etam, and
Ezr 2:21 The children of *B*, an hundred
Neh 7:26 The men of *B* and Netophah, an
Mic 5:2 *B* Ephratah, though thou be little
*2. A town in Zebulun.*
Josh 19:15 and Shimron, and Idalah, and *B*
*3. A town in Ephraim.*
Judg 12:8 him Ibzan of *B* judged Israel
Judg 12:10 died Ibzan, and was buried at *B*
*4. A descendant of Caleb.*
1Chr 2:51 Salma the father of *B*, Hareph the
1Chr 4:4 of Ephratah, the father of *B*

**BETHLEHEM** *A town in Judea.*
Jer 41:17 of Chimham, which is by *B*
Mt 2:1 Now when Jesus was born in *B* of
Mt 2:5 said unto him, In *B* of Judaea
Mt 2:8 And he sent them to *B*, and said, Go
Mt 2:16 all the children that were in *B*

Lk 2:4 city of David, which is called *B*
Lk 2:15 Let us now go even unto *B*
Jn 7:42 of David, and out of the town of *B*

**BETH-LEHEMITE** *(beth'-le-hem-ite) A native of Bethlehem.*
1Sa 16:1 I will send thee to Jesse the *B*
1Sa 16:18 I have seen a son of Jesse the *B*
1Sa 17:58 son of thy servant Jesse the *B*
2Sa 21:19 the son of Jaare-oregim, a *B*

**BETH-LEHEM-JUDAH** *(beth'-le-hem-ju'-dah) Same as Beth-lehem 1.*
Judg 17:7 out of *B* of the family of Judah
Judg 19:1 took to him a concubine out of *B*
Judg 19:18 We are passing from *B* toward the
Ruth 1:1 a certain man of *B* went to
1Sa 17:12 the son of that Ephrathite of *B*

**BETH-MAACHAH** *(beth-ma'-a-kah)* See ABEL-BETH-MAACHAH. *A city in Manasseh.*
2Sa 20:14 of Israel unto Abel, and to *B*
2Sa 20:15 came and besieged him in Abel of *B*

**BETH-MARCABOTH** *(beth-mar'-cab-oth) A city in Judah.*
Josh 19:5 And Ziklag, and *B*, and Hazar-susah,
1Chr 4:31 And at *B*, and Hazar-susim, and at

**BETH-MEON** *(beth-me'-on)* See BETH-BAAL-MEON. *A Moabite city.*
Jer 48:23 and upon Beth-gamul, and upon *B*

**BETH-NIMRAH** *(beth-nim'-rah)* See NIMRAH. *A city in Gad.*
Num 32:36 And *B*, and Beth-haran, fenced
Josh 13:27 And in the valley, Beth-aram, and *B*

**BETH-PALET** *(beth-pa'-let)* See BETH-PELET. *A town in Judah.*
Josh 15:27 Hazar-gaddah, and Heshmon, and *B*

**BETH-PAZZEZ** *(beth-paz'-zez) A town in Issachar.*
Josh 19:21 and En-haddah, and *B*

**BETH-PEOR** *(beth-pe'-or) A Moabite city.*
Deut 3:29 in the valley over against *B*
Deut 4:46 in the valley over against *B*
Deut 34:6 the land of Moab, over against *B*
Josh 13:20 And *B*, and Ashdoth-pisgah, and

**BETHPHAGE** *(beth'-fa-je) A village near Jerusalem.*
Mt 21:1 unto Jerusalem, and were come to *B*
Mk 11:1 came nigh to Jerusalem, unto *B*
Lk 19:29 pass, when he was come nigh to *B*

**BETH-PHELET** *(beth'-fe-let)* See BETH-PALET. *A town in Judah.*
Neh 11:26 at Jeshua, and at Moladah, and at *B*

**BETH-RAPHA** *(beth'-ra-fah) Son of Eshton.*
1Chr 4:12 And Eshton begat *B*, and Paseah, and

**BETH-REHOB** *(beth'-re-hob) A place in northern Canaan.*
Judg 18:28 was in the valley that lieth by *B*
2Sa 10:6 sent and hired the Syrians of *B*

**BETHSAIDA** *(beth-sa'-dah)*
*1. A city in Galilee.*
Mt 11:21 woe unto thee, *B*
Mk 6:45 to the other side before unto *B*
Lk 10:13 woe unto thee, *B*
Jn 1:44 Now Philip was of *B*, the city of
Jn 12:21 Philip, which was of *B* of Galilee
*2. A place east of Lake Gennesareth.*
Mk 8:22 And he cometh to *B*
Lk 9:10 belonging to the city called *B*

**BETH-SHAN** *(beth'-shan)* See BETH-SHEAN. *A city in Manasseh.*
1Sa 31:10 his body to the wall of *B*
1Sa 31:12 of his sons from the wall of *B*
2Sa 21:12 stolen them from the street of *B*

**BETH-SHEAN** *(beth-she'-an)* See BETH-SHAN. *Same as Beth-shan.*
Josh 17:11 had in Issachar and in Asher *B*
Josh 17:16 of iron, both they who are of *B*
Judg 1:27 drive out the inhabitants of *B*
1Kin 4:12 Taanach and Megiddo, and all *B*
1Chr 7:29 of the children of Manasseh, *B*

**BETH-SHEMESH** *(beth'-she-mesh)* See BETH-SHEMITE.
*1. A town in Judah.*
Josh 15:10 the north side, and went down to *B*
Josh 21:16 suburbs, and *B* with her suburbs
1Sa 6:9 by the way of his own coast to *B*
1Sa 6:12 the straight way to the way of *B*
1Sa 6:15 the men of *B* offered burnt
1Sa 6:19 And he smote the men of *B*, because
1Kin 4:9 in Makaz, and in Shaalbim, and *B*
2Kin 14:11 one another in the face at *B*
2Kin 14:13 Jehoash the son of Ahaziah, at *B*
1Chr 6:59 suburbs, and *B* with her suburbs
2Chr 25:21 he and Amaziah king of Judah, at *B*
2Chr 25:23 Joash, the son of Jehoahaz, at *B*
2Chr 28:18 south of Judah, and had taken *B*
*2. A city in Issachar.*
Josh 19:22 to Tabor, and Shahazimah, and *B*
*3. A city in Naphtali.*
Josh 19:38 Horem, and Beth-anath, and *B*
Judg 1:33 drive out the inhabitants of *B*
*4. A temple in Egypt.*
Jer 43:13 shall break also the images of *B*

**BETH-SHEMITE** *(beth'-shem-ite) An inhabitant of Beth-shemesh.*
1Sa 6:14 into the field of Joshua, a *B*
1Sa 6:18 day in the field of Joshua, the *B*

**BETH-SHITTAH** *(beth-shit'-tah) A place in the Jordan valley.*
Judg 7:22 and the host fled to *B* in Zererath

**BETH-TAPPUAH** *(beth-tap'-pu-ah) A city in Judah.*
Josh 15:53 And Janum, and *B*, and Aphekah,

**BETHUEL** *(beth-u'-el)* See BETHUL.
*1. Son of Nahor.*
Gen 22:22 and Pildash, and Jidlaph, and *B*
Gen 24:15 came out, who was born to *B*
Gen 24:24 daughter of *B* the son of Milcah
Gen 24:47 And she said, The daughter of *B*
Gen 24:50 *B* answered and said, The thing
Gen 25:20 the daughter of *B* the Syrian of
Gen 28:2 to the house of *B* thy mother's
Gen 28:5 son of *B* the Syrian, the brother
*2. A town in Simeon.*
1Chr 4:30 And at *B*, and at Hormah, and at

**BETHUL** *(beth'-ul)* See BETHUEL. *A city in Simeon.*
Josh 19:4 And Eltolad, and *B*, and Hormah,

**BETH-ZUR** *(beth'-zur)*
*1. A town in Judah.*
Josh 15:58 Halhul, *B*, and Gedor,
2Chr 11:7 And *B*, and Shoco, and Adullam,
Neh 3:16 the ruler of the half part of *B*
*2. A descendant of Caleb.*
1Chr 2:45 and Maon was the father of *B*

**BETIMES**
Gen 26:31 they rose up *b* in the morning, and
2Chr 36:15 by his messengers, rising up *b*
Job 8:5 If thou wouldest seek unto God *b*
Job 24:5 rising *b* for a prey
Prov 13:24 that loveth him chasteneth him *b*

**BETONIM** *(bet'-o-nim) A town in Gad.*
Josh 13:26 Heshbon unto Ramath-mizpeh, and *B*

**BETRAY**
1Chr 12:17 be come to *b* me to mine enemies
Mt 24:10 shall *b* one another, and shall
Mt 26:16 he sought opportunity to *b* him
Mt 26:21 you, that one of you shall *b* me
Mt 26:23 in the dish, the same shall *b* me
Mt 26:46 he is at hand that doth *b* me
Mk 13:12 shall *b* the brother to death
Mk 14:10 chief priests, to *b* him unto them
Mk 14:11 how he might conveniently *b* him
Mk 14:18 which eateth with me shall *b* me
Lk 22:4 how he might *b* him unto them
Lk 22:6 sought opportunity to *b* him unto
Jn 6:64 believed not, and who should *b* him
Jn 6:71 for he it was that should *b* him
Jn 12:4 Simon's son, which should *b* him
Jn 13:2 Iscariot, Simon's son, to *b* him
Jn 13:11 For he knew who should *b* him
Jn 13:21 you, that one of you shall *b* me

**BETRAYED**
Mt 10:4 and Judas Iscariot, who also *b* him
Mt 17:22 shall be *b* into the hands of men
Mt 20:18 shall be *b* unto the chief priests
Mt 26:2 Son of man is *b* to be crucified
Mt 26:24 man by whom the Son of man is *b*
Mt 26:45 the Son of man is *b* into the
Mt 26:48 Now he that *b* him gave them a
Mt 27:4 that I have *b* the innocent blood
Mk 3:19 Judas Iscariot, which also *b* him
Mk 14:21 man by whom the Son of man is *b*
Mk 14:41 the Son of man is *b* into the
Mk 14:44 he that *b* him had given them a
Lk 21:16 ye shall be *b* both by parents, and
Lk 22:22 woe unto that man by whom he is *b*
Jn 18:2 And Judas also, which *b* him
Jn 18:5 And Judas also, which *b* him
1Cor 11:23 in which he was *b* took bread

**BETRAYETH**
Mt 27:3 Then Judas, which had *b* him
Mk 14:42 lo, he that *b* me is at hand
Lk 22:21 the hand of him that *b* me is with
Jn 21:20 Lord, which is he that *b* thee

**BETROTH**
Deut 28:30 Thou shalt *b* a wife, and another
Hos 2:19 I will *b* thee unto me for ever

**BETROTHED**
Ex 21:8 who hath *b* her to himself, then
Ex 22:16 a man entice a maid that is not *b*
Lev 19:20 *b* to an husband, and not at all
Deut 20:7 man is there that hath *b* a wife
Deut 22:23 is a virgin be *b* unto an husband
Deut 22:25 man find a *b* damsel in the field
Deut 22:27 the *b* damsel cried, and there was

**BEULAH** *(be-u'-lah) A name of restored Israel.*
Is 62:4 called Hephzi-bah, and thy land *B*

**BEWAIL**
Lev 10:6 *b* the burning which the LORD hath
Deut 21:13 *b* her father and her mother a full
Judg 11:37 *b* my virginity, I and my fellows
Is 16:9 Therefore I will *b* with the
2Cor 12:21 that I shall *b* many which have
Rev 18:9 deliciously with her, shall *b* her

**BEWARE**
Gen 24:6 *B* thou that thou bring not my son
Ex 23:21 *B* of him, and obey his voice,
Deut 6:12 Then *b* lest thou forget the LORD,
Deut 8:11 *B* that thou forget not the LORD
Deut 15:9 *B* that there be not a thought in
Judg 13:4 Now therefore *b*, I pray thee, and
Judg 13:13 I said unto the woman let her *b*
2Sa 18:12 *B* that none touch the young man
2Kin 6:9 *B* that thou pass not such a place
Job 36:18 *b* lest he take thee away with his
Prov 19:25 a scorner, and the simple will *b*
Is 36:18 *B* lest Hezekiah persuade you,
Mt 7:15 *B* of false prophets, which come
Mt 10:17 But *b* of men
Mt 16:6 *b* of the leaven of the Pharisees
Mt 16:11 that ye should *b* of the leaven of
Mk 8:15 *b* of the leaven of the Pharisees,
Mk 12:38 *B* of the scribes, which love to
Lk 12:1 *B* ye of the leaven of the
Lk 12:15 Take heed, and *b* of covetousness
Lk 20:46 *B* of the scribes, which desire to
Acts 13:40 *B* therefore, lest that come upon
Phil 3:2 *B* of dogs, *b* of evil workers
Col 2:8 *B* lest any man spoil you through
2Pet 3:17 *b* lest ye also, being led away

**BEWITCHED**
Acts 8:9 *b* the people of Samaria, giving
Acts 8:11 time he had *b* them with sorceries
Gal 3:1 foolish Galatians, who hath *b* you

**BEZAI** *(be'-zahee)*
*1. A family of exiles.*
Ezr 2:17 The children of *B*, three hundred
Neh 7:23 The children of *B*, three hundred
*2. A family who renewed the covenant.*
Neh 10:18 Hodijah, Hashum, *B*,

**BEZALEEL** *(be-zal'-e-el)*
*1. A craftsman.*
Ex 31:2 called by name *B* the son of Uri
Ex 35:30 called by name *B* the son of Uri
Ex 36:1 Then wrought *B* and Aholiab, and
Ex 37:1 *B* made the ark of shittim wood
Ex 38:22 *B* the son of Uri, the son of Hur,
1Chr 2:20 And Hur begat Uri, and Uri begat *B*
2Chr 1:5 that *B* the son of Uri, the son of
*2. Married a foreign wife in exile.*
Ezr 10:30 Benaiah, Maaseiah, Mattaniah, *B*

**BEZEK** *(be'-zek)* See ADONI-BEZEK. *A place in the Jordan valley.*
Judg 1:4 of them in *B* ten thousand men
Judg 1:5 And they found Adoni-bezek in *B*
1Sa 11:8 And when he numbered them in *B*

**BEZER** *(be'-zer)*
*1. A city of refuge.*
Deut 4:43 *B* in the wilderness, in the plain
Josh 20:8 they assigned *B* in the wilderness
Josh 21:36 *B* with her suburbs, and Jahazah
1Chr 6:78 *B* in the wilderness with her
*2. A son of Liph.*
1Chr 7:37 *B*, and Hod, and Shamma,

**BICHRI** *(bik'-ri) Father of Sheba.*
2Sa 20:1 name was Sheba, the son of *B*
2Sa 20:6 son of *B* do us more harm than did
2Sa 20:10 pursued after Sheba the son of *B*
2Sa 20:13 pursue after Sheba the son of *B*
2Sa 20:21 Sheba the son of *B* by name

**BID**
Num 15:38 *b* them that they make them
Josh 6:10 until the day I *b* you shout
1Sa 9:27 *B* the servant pass on before us,
2Sa 2:26 ere thou *b* the people return from
2Kin 4:24 riding for me, except I *b* thee
2Kin 5:13 if the prophet had *b* thee do some
2Kin 10:5 will do all that thou shalt *b* us
Jonah 3:2 it the preaching that I *b* thee
Zeph 1:7 a sacrifice, he hath *b* his guests
Mt 14:28 *b* me come unto thee on the water
Mt 22:9 ye shall find, *b* to the marriage
Mt 23:3 whatsoever they *b* you observe
Lk 9:61 let me first go *b* them farewell
Lk 10:40 *b* her therefore that she help me
Lk 14:12 lest they also *b* thee again
1Cor 10:27 that believe not *b* you to a feast
2Jn 10 house, neither *b* him God speed

**BIDDEN**
1Sa 9:13 and afterwards they eat that be *b*
1Sa 9:22 place among them that were *b*
2Sa 16:11 for the LORD hath *b* him
Mt 1:24 the angel of the Lord had *b* him
Mt 22:3 them that were *b* to the wedding
Mt 22:8 they which were *b* were not worthy
Lk 7:39 Pharisee which had *b* him saw it
Lk 14:7 a parable to those which were *b*
Lk 14:10 But when thou art *b*, go and sit
Lk 14:17 time to say to them that were *b*
Lk 14:24 were *b* shall taste of my supper

**BIDKAR** *(bid'-kar) A captain of Jehu.*
2Kin 9:25 Then said Jehu to *B* his captain

**BIER**
2Sa 3:31 king David himself followed the *b*
Lk 7:14 And he came and touched the *b*

**BIGTHA** *(big'-thah) A servant of Ahasuerus.*
Est 1:10 Mehuman, Biztha, Harbona, *B*

**BIGTHAN** *(big'-than)* See BIGTHANA. *A conspirator against Ahasuerus.*
Est 2:21 two of the king's chamberlains, *B*

**BIGTHANA** *(big'-than-ah)* See BIGTHAN. *Same as Bigthan.*
Est 6:2 that Mordecai had told of *B*

**BIGVAI** *(big'-vahee)*
*1. A family chief with Zerubbabel.*
Ezr 2:2 Mordecai, Bilshan, Mizpar, *B*
Neh 7:7 Mordecai, Bilshan, Mispereth, *B*
*2. A family of exiles with Zerubbabel.*
Ezr 2:14 The children of *B*, two thousand
Neh 7:19 The children of *B*, two thousand
*3. A family of exiles with Ezra.*
Ezr 8:14 Of the sons also of *B*
*4. A family who renewed the covenant.*
Neh 10:16 Adonijah, *B*, Adin,

**BILDAD** *(bil'-dad) A friend of Job.*
Job 2:11 *B* the Shuhite, and Zophar the
Job 8:1 Then answered *B* the Shuhite
Job 18:1 Then answered *B* the Shuhite
Job 25:1 Then answered *B* the Shuhite
Job 42:9 *B* the Shuhite and Zophar the

**BILEAM** *(bil'-e-am)* See IBLEAM. *A Levitical city in Manasseh.*
1Chr 6:70 *B* with her suburbs, for the

**BILGAH** *(bil'-gah)*
*1. A priest during David's time.*
1Chr 24:14 The fifteenth to *B*, the sixteenth
*2. A priest with Zerubbabel.*
Neh 12:5 Miamin, Maadiah, *B*,
Neh 12:18 Of *B*, Shammua

**BILGAI** *(bil'-gahee) A priest with Zerubbabel.*
Neh 10:8 Maaziah, *B*, Shemaiah

**BILHAH** *(bil'-hah)* See BALAH.
*1. Mother of Dan and Naphtali.*
Gen 29:29 *B* his handmaid to be her maid
Gen 30:3 And she said, Behold my maid *B*
Gen 30:7 *B* Rachel's maid conceived again,
Gen 35:22 lay with *B* his father's concubine
Gen 35:25 And the sons of *B*, Rachel's
Gen 37:2 and the lad was with the sons of *B*
Gen 46:25 These are the sons of *B*, which
1Chr 7:13 Jezer, and Shallum, the sons of *B*
*2. A town in Simeon.*
1Chr 4:29 And at *B*, and at Ezem, and at Tolad,

**BILHAN** *(bil'-han)*
*1. Son of Ezer.*
Gen 36:27 *B*, and Zaavan, and Akan
1Chr 1:42 *B*, and Zavan, and Jakan
*2. Son of Jediael.*
1Chr 7:10 also of Jediael; *B*

**BILL**
Deut 24:1 him write her a *b* of divorcement
Deut 24:3 write her a *b* of divorcement, and
Is 50:1 Where is the *b* of your mother's
Jer 3:8 away, and given her a *b* of divorce
Mk 10:4 to write a *b* of divorcement
Lk 16:6 And he said unto him, Take thy *b*

**BILLOWS**
Ps 42:7 waves and thy *b* are gone over me
Jonah 2:3 all thy *b* and thy waves passed

**BILSHAN** *(bil'-shan) A Jewish prince with Zerubbabel.*
Ezr 2:2 Seraiah, Reelaiah, Mordecai, *B*
Neh 7:7 Raamiah, Nahamani, Mordecai, *B*

**BIMHAL** *(bim'-hal) A son of Japlet.*
1Chr 7:33 Pasach, and *B*, and Ashvath

**BIND**
Ex 28:28 they shall *b* the breastplate by
Ex 39:21 they did *b* the breastplate by his
Num 30:2 or swear an oath to *b* his soul
Deut 6:8 thou shalt *b* them for a sign upon
Deut 11:18 *b* them for a sign upon your hand,
Deut 14:25 *b* up the money in thine hand, and
Josh 2:18 thou shalt *b* this line of scarlet
Judg 15:10 To *b* Samson are we come up, to do
Judg 15:12 him, We are come down to *b* thee
Judg 16:5 that we may *b* him to afflict him
Judg 16:11 If they *b* me fast with new ropes
Job 31:36 and *b* it as a crown to me
Job 38:31 Canst thou *b* the sweet influences
Job 39:10 Canst thou *b* the unicorn with his
Job 40:13 and *b* their faces in secret
Job 41:5 or wilt thou *b* him for thy
Ps 105:22 To *b* his princes at his pleasure
Ps 118:27 *b* the sacrifice with cords, even
Ps 149:8 To *b* their kings with chains, and
Prov 3:3 *b* them about thy neck
Prov 6:21 *B* them continually upon thine
Prov 7:3 *B* them upon thy fingers, write
Is 8:16 *B* up the testimony, seal the law
Is 49:18 *b* them on thee, as a bride doeth
Is 61:1 he hath sent me to *b* up the
Jer 51:63 that thou shalt *b* a stone to it
Eze 3:25 shall *b* thee with them, and thou
Eze 5:3 number, and *b* them in thy skirts
Eze 24:17 *b* the tire of thine head upon
Eze 30:21 healed, to put a roller to *b* it
Eze 34:16 will *b* up that which was broken,
Dan 3:20 were in his army to *b* Shadrach
Hos 6:1 hath smitten, and he will *b* us up
Hos 10:10 when they shall *b* themselves in
Mic 1:13 *b* the chariot to the swift beast
Mt 12:29 except he first *b* the strong man
Mt 13:30 *b* them in bundles to burn them
Mt 16:19 whatsoever thou shalt *b* on earth
Mt 18:18 Whatsoever ye shall *b* on earth
Mt 22:13 *B* him hand and foot, and take him
Mt 23:4 For they *b* heavy burdens and
Mk 3:27 he will first *b* the strong man
Mk 5:3 and no man could *b* him, no, not
Acts 9:14 to *b* all that call on thy name
Acts 12:8 Gird thyself, and *b* on thy sandals
Acts 21:11 So shall the Jews at Jerusalem *b*

**BINDETH**
Job 5:18 For he maketh sore, and *b* up
Job 26:8 He *b* up the waters in his thick
Job 28:11 He *b* the floods from overflowing
Job 30:18 it *b* me about as the collar of my
Job 36:13 they cry not when he *b* them
Ps 129:7 nor he that *b* sheaves his bosom
Ps 147:3 in heart, and *b* up their wounds
Prov 26:8 As he that *b* a stone in a sling,
Is 30:26 in the day that the LORD *b* up the

**BINDING**
Gen 37:7 we were *b* sheaves in the field,
Gen 49:11 *B* his foal unto the vine, and his
Ex 28:32 it shall have a *b* of woven work
Num 30:13 every *b* oath to afflict the soul,
Acts 22:4 this way unto the death, *b*

**BINEA** *(bin'-e-ah) A son of Moza.*
1Chr 8:37 And Moza begat *B*
1Chr 9:43 And Moza begat *B*

**BINNUI** *(bin'-nu-ee)*
*1. A Levite who returned from exile.*
Ezr 8:33 Jeshua, and Noadiah the son of *B*
*2. A descendant of Pahath-moab.*
Ezr 10:30 Mattaniah, Bezaleel, and *B*
*3. A descendant of Bani.*
Ezr 10:38 And Bani, and *B*, Shimei,
*4. A descendant of Henadad.*
Neh 3:24 After him repaired *B* the son of
Neh 10:9 *B* of the sons of Henadad, Kadmiel
*5. A family who returned from exile.*
Neh 7:15 The children of *B*, six hundred
*6. A Levite with Zerubbabel.*
Neh 12:8 Jeshua, *B*, Kadmiel, Sherebiah,

**BIRD**
Gen 7:14 his kind, every *b* of every sort
Lev 14:6 As for the living *b*, he shall
Lev 14:51 and the scarlet, and the living *b*
Job 41:5 thou play with him as with a *b*
Ps 11:1 Flee as a *b* to your mountain
Ps 124:7 Our soul is escaped as a *b* out of
Prov 1:17 is spread in the sight of any *b*
Prov 6:5 as a *b* from the hand of the
Prov 7:23 as a *b* hasteth to the snare, and
Prov 26:2 As the *b* by wandering, as the
Prov 27:8 As a *b* that wandereth from her
Eccl 10:20 for a *b* of the air shall carry
Eccl 12:4 rise up at the voice of the *b*
Is 16:2 as a wandering *b* cast out of the
Is 46:11 a ravenous *b* from the east
Jer 12:9 is unto me as a speckled *b*
Lam 3:52 enemies chased me sore, like a *b*
Hos 9:11 glory shall fly away like a *b*
Hos 11:11 shall tremble as a *b* out of Egypt
Amos 3:5 Can a *b* fall in a snare upon the
Rev 18:2 of every unclean and hateful *b*

**BIRDS**
Gen 15:10 but the *b* divided he not
Gen 40:17 the *b* did eat them out of the
Gen 40:19 the *b* shall eat thy flesh from
Lev 14:4 is to be cleansed two *b* alive
Lev 14:49 take to cleanse the house two *b*
Lev 14:50 the *b* in an earthen vessel over
Deut 14:11 Of all clean *b* ye shall eat
2Sa 21:10 suffered neither the *b* of the air
Ps 104:17 Where the *b* make their nests
Eccl 9:12 as the *b* that are caught in the
Song 2:12 time of the singing of *b* is come
Is 31:5 As *b* flying, so will the LORD of
Jer 4:25 all the *b* of the heavens were
Jer 5:27 As a cage is full of *b*, so are
Jer 12:4 the beasts are consumed, and the *b*
Jer 12:9 the *b* round about are against her
Eze 39:4 unto the ravenous *b* of every sort
Mt 8:20 the *b* of the air have nests
Mt 13:32 so that the *b* of the air come and
Lk 9:58 holes, and *b* of the air have nests
Rom 1:23 like to corruptible man, and to *b*
1Cor 15:39 of fishes, and another of *b*
Jas 3:7 For every kind of beasts, and of *b*

**BIRSHA** *(bur'-shah) A king of Gomorrah.*
Gen 14:2 with *B* king of Gomorrah, Shinab

**BIRTH**
Ex 28:10 other stone, according to their *b*
2Kin 19:3 the children are come to the *b*
Job 3:16 hidden untimely *b* I had not been
Ps 58:8 like the untimely *b* of a woman
Eccl 6:3 that an untimely *b* is better than

Eccl 7:1 of death than the day of one's *b*
Is 37:3 the children are come to the *b*
Is 66:9 Shall I bring to the *b*, and not
Eze 16:3 Thy *b* and thy nativity is of the
Hos 9:11 fly away like a bird, from the *b*
Mt 1:18 Now the *b* of Jesus Christ was on
Lk 1:14 and many shall rejoice at his *b*
Jn 9:1 a man which was blind from his *b*
Gal 4:19 of whom I travail in *b* again
Rev 12:2 with child cried, travailing in *b*

**BIRTHDAY**
Gen 40:20 third day, which was Pharaoh's *b*
Mt 14:6 But when Herod's *b* was kept
Mk 6:21 that Herod on his *b* made a supper

**BIRTHRIGHT**
Gen 25:31 said, Sell me this day thy *b*
Gen 27:36 he took away my *b*
Gen 43:33 the firstborn according to his *b*
1Chr 5:1 his *b* was given unto the sons of
Heb 12:16 for one morsel of meat sold his *b*

**BIRZAVITH** *(bur'-za-vith) A descendant of Asher.*
1Chr 7:31 Malchiel, who is the father of *B*

**BISHLAM** *(bish'-lam) A commissioner of Artaxerxes.*
Ezr 4:7 in the days of Artaxerxes wrote *B*

**BISHOP**
1Ti 3:1 If a man desire the office of a *b*
1Ti 3:2 A *b* then must be blameless, the
2Ti *s* ordained the first *b* of the
Titus 1:7 For a *b* must be blameless, as the
Titus *s* ordained the first *b* of the
1Pet 2:25 the Shepherd and *B* of your souls

**BISHOPRICK**
Acts 1:20 and his *b* let another take

**BISHOPS**
Phil 1:1 which are at Philippi, with the *b*

**BIT**
Num 21:6 the people, and they *b* the people
Ps 32:9 mouth must be held in with *b*
Amos 5:19 on the wall, and a serpent *b* him

**BITE**
Eccl 10:8 an hedge, a serpent shall *b* him
Eccl 10:11 will *b* without enchantment
Jer 8:17 be charmed, and they shall *b* you
Amos 9:3 the serpent, and he shall *b* them
Mic 3:5 that *b* with their teeth, and cry,
Hab 2:7 up suddenly that shall *b* thee
Gal 5:15 But if ye *b* and devour one another

**BITETH**
Gen 49:17 that *b* the horse heels, so that
Prov 23:32 At the last it *b* like a serpent

**BITHIAH** *(bith-i'-ah) Daughter of Pharaoh.*
1Chr 4:18 these are the sons of *B* the

**BITHRON** *(bith'-ron) A district in Arabah.*
2Sa 2:29 Jordan, and went through all *B*

**BITHYNIA** *(bith-in'-e-ah) A Roman province in Asia Minor.*
Acts 16:7 Mysia, they assayed to go into *B*
1Pet 1:1 Galatia, Cappadocia, Asia, and *B*

**BITTEN**
Num 21:8 to pass, that every one that is *b*
Num 21:9 that if a serpent had *b* any man

**BITTER**
Gen 27:34 with a great and exceeding *b* cry
Ex 1:14 their lives *b* with hard bondage
Ex 12:8 with *b* herbs they shall eat it
Ex 15:23 waters of Marah, for they were *b*
Num 5:18 shall have in his hand the *b*
Num 5:23 blot them out with the *b* water
Num 5:27 shall enter into her, and become *b*
Num 9:11 with unleavened bread and *b* herbs
Deut 32:24 heat, and with *b* destruction
Deut 32:32 of gall, their clusters are *b*
2Kin 14:26 of Israel, that it was very *b*
Est 4:1 and cried with a loud and a *b* cry
Job 3:20 and life unto the *b* in soul
Job 13:26 For thou writest *b* things against
Job 23:2 Even to day is my complaint *b*
Ps 64:3 shoot their arrows, even *b* words
Prov 5:4 But her end is *b* as wormwood
Prov 27:7 soul every *b* thing is sweet
Eccl 7:26 I find more *b* than death the
Is 5:20 *b* for sweet, and sweet for *b*
Is 24:9 shall be *b* to them that drink it
Jer 2:19 see that it is an evil thing and *b*
Jer 4:18 thy wickedness, because it is *b*
Jer 6:26 an only son, most *b* lamentation
Jer 31:15 Ramah, lamentation, and *b* weeping
Eze 27:31 bitterness of heart and *b* wailing
Amos 8:10 and the end thereof as a *b* day
Hab 1:6 I raise up the Chaldeans, that *b*
Col 3:19 wives, and be not *b* against them
Jas 3:11 the same place sweet water and *b*
Jas 3:14 But if ye have *b* envying and
Rev 8:11 waters, because they were made *b*
Rev 10:9 and it shall make thy belly *b*

**BITTERLY**
Judg 5:23 curse ye *b* the inhabitants
Ruth 1:20 hath dealt very *b* with me
Is 22:4 I will weep *b*, labour not to
Is 33:7 ambassadors of peace shall weep *b*
Eze 27:30 against thee, and shall cry *b*
Hos 12:14 provoked him to anger most *b*
Zeph 1:14 the mighty man shall cry there *b*
Mt 26:75 And he went out, and wept *b*
Lk 22:62 And Peter went out, and wept *b*

**BITTERN**
Is 14:23 make it a possession for the *b*
Is 34:11 and the *b* shall possess it
Zeph 2:14 the *b* shall lodge in the upper

**BITTERNESS**
1Sa 1:10 And she was in *b* of soul, and
1Sa 15:32 Surely the *b* of death is past
2Sa 2:26 it will be *b* in the latter end
Job 7:11 will complain in the *b* of my soul
Job 9:18 my breath, but filleth me with *b*
Job 10:1 I will speak in the *b* of my soul
Job 21:25 dieth in the *b* of his soul
Prov 14:10 The heart knoweth his own *b*
Prov 17:25 father, and *b* to her that bare him
Is 38:15 all my years in the *b* of my soul
Is 38:17 Behold, for peace I had great *b*
Lam 1:4 are afflicted, and she is in *b*
Lam 3:15 He hath filled me with *b*, he hath
Eze 3:14 and took me away, and I went in *b*
Eze 21:6 with *b* sigh before their eyes
Eze 27:31 weep for thee with *b* of heart
Zec 12:10 son, and shall be in *b* for him
Acts 8:23 that thou art in the gall of *b*
Rom 3:14 mouth is full of cursing and *b*
Eph 4:31 Let all *b*, and wrath, and anger, and
Heb 12:15 lest any root of *b* springing up

**BIZJOTHJAH** *(biz-joth'-jah) A town in Judah.*
Josh 15:28 Hazar-shual, and Beer-sheba, and *B*

**BIZTHA** *(biz'-thah) An eunuch of Ahasuerus.*
Est 1:10 wine, he commanded Mehuman, *B*

**BLACK**
Lev 13:31 and that there is no *b* hair in it
Lev 13:37 that there is *b* hair grown up
1Kin 18:45 that the heaven was *b* with clouds
Est 1:6 of red, and blue, and white, and *b*
Job 30:30 My skin is *b* upon me, and my bones
Prov 7:9 in the evening, in the *b*
Song 1:5 I am *b*, but comely, O ye
Song 5:11 locks are bushy, and *b* as a raven
Jer 4:28 mourn, and the heavens above be *b*
Jer 8:21 I am *b*
Jer 14:2 they are *b* unto the ground
Lam 5:10 Our skin was *b* like an oven
Zec 6:2 and in the second chariot *b* horses
Zec 6:6 The *b* horses which are therein go
Mt 5:36 not make one hair white or *b*
Rev 6:5 And I beheld, and lo a *b* horse
Rev 6:12 the sun became *b* as sackcloth of

**BLACKNESS**
Job 3:5 let the *b* of the day terrify it
Is 50:3 I clothe the heavens with *b*
Joel 2:6 all faces shall gather *b*
Nah 2:10 and the faces of them all gather *b*
Heb 12:18 that burned with fire, nor unto *b*
Jude 13 the *b* of darkness for ever

**BLADE**
Judg 3:22 the haft also went in after the *b*
Job 31:22 mine arm fall from my shoulder *b*
Mt 13:26 But when the *b* was sprung up, and
Mk 4:28 first the *b*, then the ear, after

**BLAINS**
Ex 9:9 breaking forth with *b* upon man
Ex 9:10 breaking forth with *b* upon man

**BLAME**
Gen 43:9 then let me bear the *b* for ever
Gen 44:32 bear the *b* to my father for ever
2Cor 8:20 that no man should *b* us in this
Eph 1:4 without *b* before him in love

**BLAMED**
2Cor 6:3 thing, that the ministry be not *b*
Gal 2:11 the face, because he was to be *b*

**BLAMELESS**
Gen 44:10 and ye shall be *b*
Josh 2:17 We will be *b* of this thine oath
Judg 15:3 Now shall I be more *b* than the
Mt 12:5 profane the sabbath, and are *b*
Lk 1:6 and ordinances of the Lord *b*
1Cor 1:8 that ye may be *b* in the day of
Phil 2:15 That ye may be *b* and harmless, the
Phil 3:6 which is in the law, *b*
1Th 5:23 body be preserved *b* unto the
1Ti 3:2 A bishop then must be *b*, the
1Ti 3:10 office of a deacon, being found *b*
1Ti 5:7 in charge, that they may be *b*
Titus 1:6 If any be *b*, the husband of one
2Pet 3:14 him in peace, without spot, and *b*

**BLASPHEME**
2Sa 12:14 to the enemies of the LORD to *b*
1Kin 21:10 him, saying, Thou didst *b* God
1Kin 21:13 people, saying, Naboth did *b* God
Ps 74:10 shall the enemy *b* thy name for
Mk 3:28 wherewith soever they shall *b*
Acts 26:11 synagogue, and compelled them to *b*
1Ti 1:20 that they may learn not to *b*
Jas 2:7 Do not they *b* that worthy name by
Rev 13:6 to *b* his name, and his tabernacle,

**BLASPHEMED**
Lev 24:11 son *b* the name of the LORD
2Kin 19:6 of the king of Assyria have *b* me
2Kin 19:22 Whom hast thou reproached and *b*
Ps 74:18 foolish people have *b* thy name
Is 37:6 of the king of Assyria have *b* me
Is 37:23 Whom hast thou reproached and *b*
Is 52:5 name continually every day is *b*
Is 65:7 mountains, and *b* me upon the hills
Eze 20:27 in this your fathers have *b* me
Acts 18:6 they opposed themselves, and *b*
Rom 2:24 For the name of God is *b* among
1Ti 6:1 of God and his doctrine be not *b*
Titus 2:5 that the word of God be not *b*
Rev 16:9 *b* the name of God, which hath
Rev 16:11 *b* the God of heaven because of
Rev 16:21 men *b* God because of the plague

**BLASPHEMER**
1Ti 1:13 Who was before a *b*, and a

**BLASPHEMERS**
Acts 19:37 nor yet *b* of your goddess
2Ti 3:2 covetous, boasters, proud, *b*

**BLASPHEMETH**
Lev 24:16 he that *b* the name of the LORD,
Ps 44:16 of him that reproacheth and *b*
Mt 9:3 within themselves, This man *b*
Lk 12:10 but unto him that *b* against the

**BLASPHEMIES**
Eze 35:12 that I have heard all thy *b* which
Mt 15:19 thefts, false witness, *b*
Mk 2:7 Why doth this man thus speak *b*
Mk 3:28 *b* wherewith soever they shall
Lk 5:21 Who is this which speaketh *b*
Rev 13:5 mouth speaking great things and *b*

**BLASPHEMOUS**
Acts 6:11 him speak *b* words against Moses
Acts 6:13 *b* words against this holy place

**BLASPHEMY**
2Kin 19:3 of trouble, and of rebuke, and *b*
Is 37:3 of trouble, and of rebuke, and of *b*
Mt 12:31 *b* shall be forgiven unto men
Mt 26:65 clothes, saying, He hath spoken *b*
Mt 26:65 behold, now ye have heard his *b*
Mk 7:22 lasciviousness, an evil eye, *b*
Mk 14:64 Ye have heard the *b*
Jn 10:33 stone thee not; but for *b*
Col 3:8 anger, wrath, malice, *b*, filthy
Rev 2:9 I know the *b* of them which say
Rev 13:1 and upon his heads the name of *b*

Rev 13:6 opened his mouth in *b* against God
Rev 17:3 beast, full of names of *b*

**BLAST**

Ex 15:8 with the *b* of thy nostrils the
Josh 6:5 make a long *b* with the ram's horn
2Sa 22:16 at the *b* of the breath of his
2Kin 19:7 Behold, I will send a *b* upon him
Job 4:9 By the *b* of God they perish, and
Ps 18:15 at the *b* of the breath of thy
Is 25:4 when the *b* of the terrible ones
Is 37:7 Behold, I will send a *b* upon him

**BLASTED**

Gen 41:6 *b* with the east wind sprung up
Gen 41:23 *b* with the east wind, sprung up
Gen 41:27 the seven empty ears *b* with the
2Kin 19:26 as corn *b* before it be grown up
Is 37:27 as corn *b* before it be grown up

**BLASTING**

Deut 28:22 and with the sword, and with *b*
1Kin 8:37 famine, if there be pestilence, *b*
2Chr 6:28 be pestilence, if there be *b*
Amos 4:9 I have smitten you with *b*
Hag 2:17 I smote you with *b* and with mildew

**BLASTUS** *(blas'-tus) A servant of Herod Agrippa I.*

Acts 12:20 him, and, having made *B* the king's

**BLEMISH**

Ex 12:5 Your lamb shall be without *b*
Ex 29:1 bullock, and two rams without *b*
Lev 1:3 let him offer a male without *b*
Lev 1:10 shall bring it a male without *b*
Lev 3:1 it without *b* before the LORD
Lev 3:6 he shall offer it without *b*
Lev 4:3 without *b* unto the LORD for a sin
Lev 4:23 of the goats, a male without *b*
Lev 4:28 of the goats, a female without *b*
Lev 4:32 shall bring it a female without *b*
Lev 5:15 a ram without *b* out of the flocks
Lev 5:18 a ram without *b* out of the flock
Lev 6:6 a ram without *b* out of the flock,
Lev 9:2 for a burnt offering, without *b*
Lev 9:3 both of the first year, without *b*
Lev 14:10 shall take two he lambs without *b*
Lev 21:17 their generations that hath any *b*
Lev 21:18 man he be that hath a *b*, he shall
Lev 21:20 or that hath a *b* in his eye
Lev 21:23 the altar, because he hath a *b*
Lev 22:19 at your own will a male without *b*
Lev 22:20 But whatsoever hath a *b*, that
Lev 23:12 the sheaf an he lamb without *b* of
Lev 23:18 lambs without *b* of the first year
Lev 24:19 a man cause a *b* in his neighbour
Lev 24:20 as he hath caused a *b* in a man
Num 6:14 without *b* for a burnt offering
Num 19:2 without spot, wherein is no *b*
Num 28:19 they shall be unto you without *b*
Num 28:31 they shall be unto you without *b*)
Num 29:2 lambs of the first year without *b*
Num 29:8 they shall be unto you without *b*
Num 29:13 they shall be without *b*
Num 29:20 lambs of the first year without *b*
Num 29:23 lambs of the first year without *b*
Num 29:29 lambs of the first year without *b*
Num 29:32 lambs of the first year without *b*
Num 29:36 lambs of the first year without *b*
Deut 15:21 And if there be any *b* therein
Deut 17:1 bullock, or sheep, wherein is *b*
2Sa 14:25 of his head there was no *b* in him
Eze 43:22 without *b* for a sin offering
Eze 43:25 a ram out of the flock, without *b*
Eze 45:18 take a young bullock without *b*
Eze 45:23 seven rams without *b* daily the
Eze 46:4 day shall be six lambs without *b*
Eze 46:6 be a young bullock without *b*
Eze 46:6 they shall be without *b*
Eze 46:13 lamb of the first year without *b*
Dan 1:4 Children in whom was no *b*
Eph 5:27 it should be holy and without *b*
1Pet 1:19 of Christ, as of a lamb without *b*

**BLEMISHES**

Lev 22:25 is in them, and *b* be in them
2Pet 2:13 Spots they are and *b*, sporting

**BLESS**

Gen 12:2 a great nation, and I will *b* thee
Gen 12:3 And I will *b* them that *b* thee
Gen 17:16 And I will *b* her, and give thee a
Gen 22:17 That in blessing I will *b* thee
Gen 26:3 will be with thee, and will *b* thee
Gen 26:24 I am with thee, and will *b* thee
Gen 27:4 that my soul may *b* thee before I
Gen 27:7 *b* thee before the LORD before my
Gen 27:10 that he may *b* thee before his
Gen 27:19 venison, that thy soul may *b* me
Gen 27:25 venison, that my soul may *b* thee
Gen 27:31 venison, that thy soul may *b* me
Gen 27:34 *B* me, even me also, O my father
Gen 27:38 *b* me, even me also, O my father
Gen 28:3 And God Almighty *b* thee, and make
Gen 32:26 not let thee go, except thou *b* me
Gen 48:9 thee, unto me, and I will *b* them
Gen 48:16 me from all evil, *b* the lads
Gen 48:20 saying, In thee shall Israel *b*
Gen 49:25 who shall *b* thee with blessings
Ex 12:32 and *b* me also
Ex 20:24 come unto thee, and I will *b* thee
Ex 23:25 he shall *b* thy bread, and thy
Num 6:23 On this wise ye shall *b* the
Num 6:27 and I will *b* them
Num 23:20 I have received commandment to *b*
Num 23:25 them at all, nor *b* them at all
Num 24:1 it pleased the LORD to *b* Israel
Deut 1:11 *b* you, as he hath promised you
Deut 7:13 thee, and *b* thee, and multiply thee
Deut 8:10 then thou shalt *b* the LORD thy
Deut 10:8 to *b* in his name, unto this day
Deut 14:29 that the LORD thy God may *b* thee
Deut 15:4 for the LORD shall greatly *b* thee
Deut 15:10 God shall *b* thee in all thy works
Deut 15:18 the LORD thy God shall *b* thee in
Deut 16:15 *b* thee in all thine increase
Deut 21:5 to *b* in the name of the LORD
Deut 23:20 that the LORD thy God may *b* thee
Deut 24:13 in his own raiment, and *b* thee
Deut 24:19 that the LORD thy God may *b* thee
Deut 26:15 *b* thy people Israel, and the land
Deut 27:12 mount Gerizim to *b* the people
Deut 28:8 he shall *b* thee in the land which
Deut 28:12 to *b* all the work of thine hand
Deut 29:19 that he *b* himself in his heart,
Deut 30:16 the LORD thy God shall *b* thee in
Deut 33:11 *B*, LORD, his substance, and accept
Josh 8:33 that they should *b* the people of
Judg 5:9 *B* ye the LORD
Ruth 2:4 answered him, The LORD *b* thee
1Sa 9:13 because he doth *b* the sacrifice
2Sa 6:20 David returned to *b* his household
2Sa 7:29 to *b* the house of thy servant
2Sa 8:10 to *b* him, because he had fought
2Sa 21:3 that ye may *b* the inheritance of
1Kin 1:47 came to *b* our lord king David
1Chr 4:10 Oh that thou wouldest *b* me indeed
1Chr 16:43 and David returned to *b* his house
1Chr 17:27 to *b* the house of thy servant
1Chr 23:13 to *b* in his name for ever
1Chr 29:20 Now *b* the LORD your God
Neh 9:5 *b* the LORD your God for ever and
Ps 5:12 thou, LORD, wilt *b* the righteous
Ps 16:7 I will *b* the LORD, who hath given
Ps 26:12 congregations will I *b* the LORD
Ps 28:9 people, and *b* thine inheritance
Ps 29:11 the LORD will *b* his people with
Ps 34:1 I will *b* the LORD at all times
Ps 62:4 they *b* with their mouth, but they
Ps 63:4 Thus will I *b* thee while I live
Ps 66:8 O *b* our God, ye people, and make
Ps 67:1 God be merciful unto us, and *b* us
Ps 67:6 God, even our own God, shall *b* us
Ps 67:7 God shall *b* us
Ps 68:26 *B* ye God in the congregations,
Ps 96:2 Sing unto the LORD, *b* his name
Ps 100:4 thankful unto him, and *b* his name
Ps 103:1 *B* the LORD, O my soul
Ps 103:2 *B* the LORD, O my soul, and forget
Ps 103:20 *B* the LORD, ye his angels, that
Ps 104:1 *B* the LORD, O my soul
Ps 104:35 *B* thou the LORD, O my soul
Ps 109:28 Let them curse, but *b* thou
Ps 115:12 he will *b* us
Ps 115:18 But we will *b* the LORD from this
Ps 128:5 The LORD shall *b* thee out of Zion
Ps 129:8 we *b* you in the name of the LORD
Ps 132:15 I will abundantly *b* her provision
Ps 134:1 *b* ye the LORD, all ye servants of
Ps 135:19 *B* the LORD, O house of Israel
Ps 145:1 I will *b* thy name for ever and
Ps 145:2 Every day will I *b* thee
Ps 145:10 and thy saints shall *b* thee
Ps 145:21 let all flesh *b* his holy name for
Prov 30:11 and doth not *b* their mother
Is 19:25 Whom the LORD of hosts shall *b*
Is 65:16 himself in the earth shall *b*
Jer 4:2 nations shall *b* themselves in him
Jer 31:23 The LORD *b* thee, O habitation of
Hag 2:19 from this day will I *b* you
Mt 5:44 *b* them that curse you, do good to
Lk 6:28 *B* them that curse you, and pray
Acts 3:26 his Son Jesus, sent him to *b* you
Rom 12:14 *B* them which persecute you
1Cor 4:12 being reviled, we *b*
1Cor 10:16 The cup of blessing which we *b*
Heb 6:14 Surely blessing I will *b* thee
Jas 3:9 Therewith *b* we God, even the

**BLESSED**

Gen 1:22 God *b* them, saying, Be fruitful,
Gen 1:28 God *b* them, and God said unto them
Gen 2:3 God *b* the seventh day, and
Gen 5:2 *b* them, and called their name Adam
Gen 9:1 God *b* Noah and his sons, and said
Gen 9:26 *B* be the LORD God of Shem
Gen 12:3 all families of the earth be *b*
Gen 14:19 he *b* him, and said
Gen 14:20 *b* be the most high God, which
Gen 17:20 Behold, I have *b* him, and will
Gen 18:18 of the earth shall be *b* in him
Gen 22:18 all the nations of the earth be *b*
Gen 24:1 the LORD had *b* Abraham in all
Gen 24:27 *B* be the LORD God of my master
Gen 24:31 said, Come in, thou *b* of the LORD
Gen 24:35 the LORD hath *b* my master greatly
Gen 24:48 *b* the LORD God of my master
Gen 24:60 they *b* Rebekah, and said unto her,
Gen 25:11 Abraham, that God *b* his son Isaac
Gen 26:4 all the nations of the earth be *b*
Gen 26:12 and the LORD *b* him
Gen 26:29 thou art now the *b* of the LORD
Gen 27:23 so he *b* him
Gen 27:27 *b* him, and said, See, the smell of
Gen 27:29 *b* be he that blesseth thee
Gen 27:33 before thou camest, and have *b* him
Gen 27:41 wherewith his father *b* him
Gen 28:1 *b* him, and charged him, and said
Gen 28:6 Esau saw that Isaac had *b* Jacob
Gen 28:6 that as he *b* him he gave him a
Gen 28:14 the families of the earth be *b*
Gen 30:13 for the daughters will call me *b*
Gen 30:27 the LORD hath *b* me for thy sake
Gen 30:30 the LORD hath *b* thee since my
Gen 31:55 sons and his daughters, and *b* them
Gen 32:29 And he *b* him there
Gen 35:9 came out of Padan-aram, and *b* him
Gen 39:5 that the LORD *b* the Egyptian's
Gen 47:7 and Jacob *b* Pharaoh
Gen 47:10 Jacob *b* Pharaoh, and went out from
Gen 48:3 in the land of Canaan, and *b* me,
Gen 48:15 he *b* Joseph, and said, God, before
Gen 48:20 he *b* them that day, saying, In
Gen 49:28 father spake unto them, and *b* them
Ex 18:10 *B* be the LORD, who hath delivered
Ex 20:11 the LORD *b* the sabbath day
Ex 39:43 and Moses *b* them
Lev 9:22 *b* them, and came down from
Lev 9:23 and came out, and *b* the people
Num 22:6 that he whom thou blessest is *b*
Num 22:12 for they are *b*
Num 23:11 thou hast *b* them altogether
Num 23:20 and he hath *b*
Num 24:9 *B* is he that blesseth thee, and
Deut 2:7 For the LORD thy God hath *b* thee
Deut 7:14 Thou shalt be *b* above all people
Deut 12:7 the LORD thy God hath *b* thee
Deut 14:24 when the LORD thy God hath *b* thee
Deut 15:14 *b* thee thou shalt give unto him
Deut 16:10 as the LORD thy God hath *b* thee
Deut 28:3 *B* shalt thou be in the city, and
Deut 33:1 *b* the children of Israel before
Deut 33:13 *B* of the LORD be his land, for
Deut 33:20 *B* be he that enlargeth Gad
Deut 33:24 Let Asher be *b* with children
Josh 14:13 And Joshua *b* him, and gave unto
Josh 17:14 as the LORD hath *b* me hitherto
Josh 22:6 So Joshua *b* them, and sent them
Josh 22:33 and the children of Israel *b* God
Josh 24:10 therefore he *b* you still
Judg 5:24 *B* above women shall Jael the wife
Judg 13:24 the child grew, and the LORD *b* him
Judg 17:2 *B* be thou of the LORD, my son

Ruth 2:19 *b* be he that did take knowledge
Ruth 3:10 *B* be thou of the LORD, my
Ruth 4:14 *B* be the LORD, which hath not
1Sa 2:20 Eli *b* Elkanah and his wife, and
1Sa 15:13 unto him, *B* be thou of the LORD
1Sa 23:21 And Saul said, *B* be ye of the LORD
1Sa 25:32 *B* be the LORD God of Israel,
1Sa 25:39 *B* be the LORD, that hath pleaded
1Sa 26:25 to David, *B* be thou, my son David
2Sa 2:5 *B* be ye of the LORD, that ye have
2Sa 6:11 the LORD *b* Obed-edom, and all his
2Sa 6:18 he *b* the people in the name of
2Sa 7:29 of thy servant be *b* for ever
2Sa 13:25 he would not go, but *b* him
2Sa 18:28 *B* be the LORD thy God, which hath
2Sa 19:39 king kissed Barzillai, and *b* him
2Sa 22:47 and *b* be my rock
1Kin 1:48 *B* be the LORD God of Israel,
1Kin 2:45 And king Solomon shall be *b*
1Kin 5:7 *B* be the LORD this day, which
1Kin 8:14 *b* all the congregation of Israel
1Kin 8:55 *b* all the congregation of Israel
1Kin 8:66 they *b* the king, and went unto
1Kin 10:9 *B* be the LORD thy God, which
1Chr 13:14 the LORD *b* the house of Obed-edom
1Chr 16:2 he *b* the people in the name of
1Chr 16:36 *B* be the LORD God of Israel for
1Chr 17:27 O LORD, and it shall be *b* for ever
1Chr 26:5 for God *b* him
1Chr 29:10 Wherefore David *b* the LORD before
1Chr 29:20 all the congregation *b* the LORD
2Chr 2:12 *B* be the LORD God of Israel, that
2Chr 6:3 *b* the whole congregation of
2Chr 6:4 *B* be the LORD God of Israel, who
2Chr 9:8 *B* be the LORD thy God, which
2Chr 20:26 for there they *b* the LORD
2Chr 31:8 they *b* the LORD, and his people
2Chr 31:10 for the LORD hath *b* his people
Ezr 7:27 *B* be the LORD God of our fathers,
Neh 8:6 Ezra *b* the LORD, the great God
Neh 9:5 *b* be thy glorious name, which is
Neh 11:2 the people *b* all the men, that
Job 1:10 thou hast *b* the work of his hands
Job 1:21 *b* be the name of the LORD
Job 29:11 the ear heard me, then it *b* me
Job 31:20 If his loins have not *b* me
Job 42:12 So the LORD *b* the latter end of
Ps 1:1 *B* is the man that walketh not in
Ps 2:12 *B* are all they that put their
Ps 18:46 and *b* be my rock
Ps 21:6 hast made him most *b* for ever
Ps 28:6 *B* be the LORD, because he hath
Ps 31:21 *B* be the LORD
Ps 32:1 *B* is he whose transgression is
Ps 33:12 *B* is the nation whose God is the
Ps 34:8 *b* is the man that trusteth in him
Ps 37:22 For such as be *b* of him shall
Ps 37:26 and his seed is *b*
Ps 40:4 *B* is that man that maketh the
Ps 41:1 *B* is he that considereth the poor
Ps 41:13 *B* be the LORD God of Israel from
Ps 45:2 God hath *b* thee for ever
Ps 49:18 while he lived he *b* his soul
Ps 65:4 *B* is the man whom thou choosest,
Ps 66:20 *B* be God, which hath not turned
Ps 68:19 *B* be the Lord, who daily loadeth
Ps 68:35 *B* be God
Ps 72:17 and men shall be *b* in him
Ps 84:4 *B* are they that dwell in thy
Ps 84:5 *B* is the man whose strength is in
Ps 84:12 *b* is the man that trusteth in
Ps 89:15 *B* is the people that know the
Ps 89:52 *B* be the LORD for evermore
Ps 94:12 *B* is the man whom thou chastenest
Ps 106:3 *B* are they that keep judgment, and
Ps 106:48 *B* be the LORD God of Israel from
Ps 112:1 *B* is the man that feareth the
Ps 113:2 *B* be the name of the LORD from
Ps 115:15 Ye are *b* of the LORD which made
Ps 118:26 *B* be he that cometh in the name
Ps 119:1 *B* are the undefiled in the way,
Ps 119:12 *B* art thou, O LORD
Ps 124:6 *B* be the LORD, who hath not given
Ps 128:1 *B* is every one that feareth the
Ps 128:4 man be *b* that feareth the LORD
Ps 135:21 *B* be the LORD out of Zion, which
Ps 144:1 *B* be the LORD my strength, which
Ps 147:13 he hath *b* thy children within
Prov 5:18 Let thy fountain be *b*
Prov 8:32 for *b* are they that keep my ways
Prov 8:34 *B* is the man that heareth me,
Prov 10:7 The memory of the just is *b*
Prov 20:7 his children are *b* after him
Prov 20:21 the end thereof shall not be *b*
Prov 22:9 hath a bountiful eye shall be *b*
Prov 31:28 children arise up, and call her *b*
Eccl 10:17 *B* art thou, O land, when thy king
Song 6:9 The daughters saw her, and *b* her
Is 19:25 *B* be Egypt my people, and Assyria
Is 30:18 *b* are all they that wait for him
Is 32:20 *B* are ye that sow beside all
Is 51:2 alone, and *b* him, and increased him
Is 56:2 *B* is the man that doeth this, and
Is 61:9 the seed which the LORD hath *b*
Is 65:23 are the seed of the *b* of the LORD
Is 66:3 incense, as if he *b* an idol
Jer 17:7 *B* is the man that trusteth in the
Jer 20:14 wherein my mother bare me be *b*
Eze 3:12 *B* be the glory of the LORD from
Dan 2:19 Then Daniel *b* the God of heaven
Dan 3:28 *B* be the God of Shadrach, Meshach
Dan 4:34 I *b* the most High, and I praised
Dan 12:12 *B* is he that waiteth, and cometh
Zec 11:5 that sell them say, *B* be the LORD
Mal 3:12 And all nations shall call you *b*
Mt 5:3 *B* are the poor in spirit
Mt 5:4 *B* are they that mourn
Mt 5:5 *B* are the meek
Mt 5:6 *B* are they which do hunger and
Mt 5:7 *B* are the merciful
Mt 5:8 *B* are the pure in heart
Mt 5:9 *B* are the peacemakers
Mt 5:10 *B* are they which are persecuted
Mt 5:11 *B* are ye, when men shall revile
Mt 11:6 *b* is he, whosoever shall not be
Mt 13:16 But *b* are your eyes, for they see
Mt 14:19 and looking up to heaven, he *b*
Mt 16:17 *B* art thou, Simon Bar-jona
Mt 21:9 *B* is he that cometh in the name
Mt 23:39 *B* is he that cometh in the name
Mt 24:46 *B* is that servant, whom his lord
Mt 25:34 ye *b* of my Father, inherit the
Mt 26:26 *b* it, and brake it, and gave it to
Mk 6:41 he looked up to heaven, and *b*
Mk 8:7 and he *b*, and commanded to set them
Mk 10:16 his hands upon them, and *b* them
Mk 11:9 *B* is he that cometh in the name
Mk 14:22 did eat, Jesus took bread, and *b*
Mk 14:61 thou the Christ, the Son of the *B*
Lk 1:28 *b* art thou among women
Lk 1:42 *B* art thou among women, and
Lk 1:42 *b* is the fruit of thy womb
Lk 1:45 And *b* is she that believed
Lk 1:48 all generations shall call me *b*
Lk 1:68 *B* be the Lord God of Israel
Lk 2:28 in his arms, and *b* God, and said,
Lk 2:34 And Simeon *b* them, and said unto
Lk 6:20 disciples, and said, *B* be ye poor
Lk 6:21 *B* are ye that hunger now
Lk 6:21 *B* are ye that weep now
Lk 6:22 *B* are ye, when men shall hate you
Lk 7:23 *b* is he, whosoever shall not be
Lk 9:16 he *b* them, and brake, and gave to
Lk 10:23 *B* are the eyes which see the
Lk 11:27 *B* is the womb that bare thee, and
Lk 11:28 *b* are they that hear the word of
Lk 12:37 *B* are those servants, whom the
Lk 12:38 them so, *b* are those servants
Lk 12:43 *B* is that servant, whom his lord
Lk 13:35 *B* is he that cometh in the name
Lk 14:14 And thou shalt be *b*
Lk 14:15 *B* is he that shall eat bread in
Lk 19:38 *B* be the King that cometh in the
Lk 23:29 *B* are the barren, and the wombs
Lk 24:30 *b* it, and brake, and gave to them
Lk 24:50 he lifted up his hands, and *b* them
Jn 12:13 *B* is the King of Israel that
Jn 20:29 *b* are they that have not seen, and
Acts 3:25 the kindreds of the earth be *b*
Acts 20:35 It is more *b* to give than to
Rom 1:25 the Creator, who is *b* for ever
Rom 4:7 *B* are they whose iniquities are
Rom 4:8 *B* is the man to whom the Lord
Rom 9:5 who is over all, God *b* for ever
2Cor 1:3 *B* be God, even the Father of our
2Cor 11:31 which is *b* for evermore, knoweth
Gal 3:8 In thee shall all nations be *b*
Eph 1:3 *B* be the God and Father of our
Eph 1:3 who hath *b* us with all spiritual
1Ti 1:11 the glorious gospel of the *b* God
1Ti 6:15 times he shall shew, who is the *b*
Titus 2:13 Looking for that *b* hope, and the
Heb 7:1 slaughter of the kings, and *b* him
Heb 7:6 *b* him that had the promises
Heb 11:20 By faith Isaac *b* Jacob and Esau
Heb 11:21 *b* both the sons of Joseph
Jas 1:12 *B* is the man that endureth
Jas 1:25 this man shall be *b* in his deed
1Pet 1:3 *B* be the God and Father of our
Rev 1:3 *B* is he that readeth, and they
Rev 14:13 *B* are the dead which die in the
Rev 16:15 *B* is he that watcheth, and keepeth
Rev 19:9 *B* are they which are called unto
Rev 20:6 *B* and holy is he that hath part in
Rev 22:7 *b* is he that keepeth the sayings
Rev 22:14 *B* are they that do his

## BLESSEDNESS

Rom 4:6 also describeth the *b* of the man
Rom 4:9 Cometh this *b* then upon the
Gal 4:15 Where is then the *b* ye spake of

## BLESSEST

Num 22:6 that he whom thou *b* is blessed
1Chr 17:27 for thou *b*, O LORD, and it shall
Ps 65:10 thou *b* the springing thereof

## BLESSETH

Gen 27:29 and blessed be he that *b* thee
Num 24:9 Blessed is he that *b* thee
Deut 15:6 For the LORD thy God *b* thee
Ps 10:3 *b* the covetous, whom the LORD
Ps 107:38 He *b* them also, so that they are
Prov 3:33 but he *b* the habitation of the
Prov 27:14 He that *b* his friend with a loud
Is 65:16 That he who *b* himself in the

## BLESSING

Gen 12:2 and thou shalt be a *b*
Gen 22:17 That in *b* I will bless thee, and
Gen 27:12 bring a curse upon me, and not a *b*
Gen 27:30 Isaac had made an end of *b* Jacob
Gen 27:35 and hath taken away thy *b*
Gen 27:36 Hast thou not reserved a *b* for me
Gen 27:38 his father, Hast thou but one *b*
Gen 27:41 *b* wherewith his father blessed
Gen 28:4 And give thee the *b* of Abraham
Gen 33:11 my *b* that is brought to thee
Gen 39:5 the *b* of the LORD was upon all
Gen 49:28 to his *b* he blessed them
Ex 32:29 may bestow upon you a *b* this day
Lev 25:21 Then I will command my *b* upon you
Deut 11:26 I set before you this day a *b*
Deut 11:29 put the *b* upon mount Gerizim
Deut 12:15 according to the *b* of the LORD
Deut 16:17 according to the *b* of the LORD
Deut 23:5 the curse into a *b* unto thee
Deut 28:8 The LORD shall command the *b* upon
Deut 30:1 things are come upon thee, the *b*
Deut 30:19 set before you life and death, *b*
Deut 33:1 And this is the *b*, wherewith Moses
Deut 33:7 And this is the *b* of Judah
Deut 33:16 let the *b* come upon the head of
Deut 33:23 and full with the *b* of the LORD
Josh 15:19 Who answered, Give me a *b*
Judg 1:15 And she said unto him, Give me a *b*
1Sa 25:27 now this *b* which thine handmaid
2Sa 7:29 with thy *b* let the house of thy
2Kin 5:15 thee, take a *b* of thy servant
Neh 9:5 which is exalted above all *b*
Neh 13:2 our God turned the curse into a *b*
Job 29:13 The *b* of him that was ready to
Ps 3:8 thy *b* is upon thy people
Ps 24:5 shall receive the *b* from the LORD
Ps 109:17 as he delighted not in *b*, so let
Ps 129:8 The *b* of the LORD be upon you
Ps 133:3 there the LORD commanded the *b*
Prov 10:22 The *b* of the LORD, it maketh rich
Prov 11:11 By the *b* of the upright the city
Prov 11:26 but *b* shall be upon the head of
Prov 24:25 a good *b* shall come upon them
Is 19:24 even a *b* in the midst of the land
Is 44:3 my *b* upon thine offspring
Is 65:8 for a *b* is in it
Eze 34:26 places round about my hill a *b*
Eze 44:30 that he may cause the *b* to rest
Joel 2:14 repent, and leave a *b* behind him
Zec 8:13 I save you, and ye shall be a *b*
Mal 3:10 of heaven, and pour you out a *b*
Lk 24:53 in the temple, praising and *b* God
Rom 15:29 of the *b* of the gospel of Christ
1Cor 10:16 The cup of *b* which we bless, is

Gal 3:14 That the *b* of Abraham might come
Heb 6:7 is dressed, receiveth *b* from God
Heb 6:14 Surely *b* I will bless thee, and
Heb 12:17 he would have inherited the *b*
Jas 3:10 of the same mouth proceedeth *b*
1Pet 3:9 but contrariwise *b*
Rev 5:12 and honour, and glory, and *b*
Rev 7:12 *B*, and glory, and wisdom, and

**BLESSINGS**
Gen 49:25 bless thee with *b* of heaven above
Deut 28:2 all these *b* shall come on thee,
Josh 8:34 all the words of the law, the *b*
Ps 21:3 him with the *b* of goodness
Prov 10:6 *B* are upon the head of the just
Prov 28:20 faithful man shall abound with *b*
Mal 2:2 upon you, and I will curse your *b*
Eph 1:3 *b* in heavenly places in Christ

**BLEW**
Josh 6:8 the LORD, and *b* with the trumpets
Josh 6:9 priests that *b* with the trumpets
Josh 6:13 and *b* with the trumpets
Josh 6:16 when the priests *b* with the
Josh 6:20 the priests *b* with the trumpets
Judg 3:27 that he *b* a trumpet in the
Judg 6:34 upon Gideon, and he *b* a trumpet
Judg 7:19 they *b* the trumpets, and brake the
Judg 7:22 the three hundred *b* the trumpets
1Sa 13:3 Saul *b* the trumpet throughout all
2Sa 2:28 So Joab *b* a trumpet, and all the
2Sa 18:16 Joab *b* the trumpet, and the people
2Sa 20:1 he *b* a trumpet, and said, We have
2Sa 20:22 he *b* a trumpet, and they retired
1Kin 1:39 And they *b* the trumpet
2Kin 9:13 *b* with trumpets, saying, Jehu is
2Kin 11:14 land rejoiced, and *b* with trumpets
Mt 7:25 the floods came, and the winds *b*
Mt 7:27 the floods came, and the winds *b*
Jn 6:18 by reason of a great wind that *b*
Acts 27:13 And when the south wind *b* softly
Acts 28:13 and after one day the south wind *b*

**BLIND**
Ex 4:11 or deaf, or the seeing, or the *b*
Lev 19:14 put a stumblingblock before the *b*
Lev 21:18 a *b* man, or a lame, or he that
Lev 22:22 *B*, or broken, or maimed, or
Deut 15:21 therein, as if it be lame, or *b*
Deut 16:19 for a gift doth *b* the eyes of the
Deut 27:18 the *b* to wander out of the way
Deut 28:29 as the *b* gropeth in darkness, and
1Sa 12:3 bribe to *b* mine eyes therewith
2Sa 5:6 Except thou take away the *b*
2Sa 5:8 Jebusites, and the lame and the *b*
Job 29:15 I was eyes to the *b*, and feet was
Ps 146:8 LORD openeth the eyes of the *b*
Is 29:18 the eyes of the *b* shall see out
Is 35:5 the eyes of the *b* shall be opened
Is 42:7 To open the *b* eyes, to bring out
Is 42:16 I will bring the *b* by a way that
Is 42:18 and look, ye *b*, that ye may see
Is 43:8 Bring forth the *b* people that
Is 56:10 His watchmen are *b*
Is 59:10 We grope for the wall like the *b*
Jer 31:8 of the earth, and with them the *b*
Lam 4:14 wandered as *b* men in the streets
Zeph 1:17 that they shall walk like *b* men
Mal 1:8 if ye offer the *b* for sacrifice
Mt 9:27 two *b* men followed him, crying,
Mt 11:5 The *b* receive their sight, and the
Mt 12:22 him one possessed with a devil, *b*
Mt 15:14 they be *b* leaders of the *b*
Mt 15:30 with them those that were lame, *b*
Mt 15:31 the lame to walk, and the *b* to see
Mt 20:30 two *b* men sitting by the way side
Mt 21:14 And the *b* and the lame came to him
Mt 23:16 ye *b* guides, which say, Whosoever
Mt 23:17 Ye fools and *b*:
Mt 23:19 Ye fools and *b*:
Mt 23:24 Ye *b* guides, which strain at a
Mt 23:26 Thou *b* Pharisee, cleanse first
Mk 8:22 and they bring a *b* man unto him
Mk 10:46 *b* Bartimaeus, the son of Timaeus,
Mk 10:49 And they call the *b* man, saying
Mk 10:51 The *b* man said unto him, Lord,
Lk 4:18 and recovering of sight to the *b*
Lk 6:39 them, Can the *b* lead the *b*
Lk 7:21 many that were *b* he gave sight
Lk 14:13 poor, the maimed, the lame, the *b*
Lk 14:21 the maimed, and the halt, and the *b*
Lk 18:35 a certain *b* man sat by the way
Jn 5:3 multitude of impotent folk, of *b*
Jn 9:1 a man which was *b* from his birth
Jn 9:2 his parents, that he was born *b*
Jn 9:6 eyes of the *b* man with the clay
Jn 9:8 before had seen him that he was *b*
Jn 9:13 him that aforetime was *b*
Jn 9:17 They say unto the *b* man again
Jn 9:24 called they the man that was *b*
Jn 9:25 I know, that, whereas I was *b*
Jn 9:32 the eyes of one that was born *b*
Jn 9:39 they which see might be made *b*
Jn 9:40 and said unto him, Are we *b* also
Jn 10:21 a devil open the eyes of the *b*
Jn 11:37 which opened the eyes of the *b*
Acts 13:11 is upon thee, and thou shalt be *b*
Rom 2:19 thou thyself art a guide of the *b*
2Pet 1:9 he that lacketh these things is *b*
Rev 3:17 and miserable, and poor, and *b*

**BLINDED**
Jn 12:40 He hath *b* their eyes, and hardened
Rom 11:7 obtained it, and the rest were *b*
2Cor 3:14 But their minds were *b*
2Cor 4:4 *b* the minds of them which believe
1Jn 2:11 that darkness hath *b* his eyes

**BLINDNESS**
Gen 19:11 at the door of the house with *b*
Deut 28:28 smite thee with madness, and *b*
2Kin 6:18 this people, I pray thee, with *b*
Zec 12:4 every horse of the people with *b*
Rom 11:25 that *b* in part is happened to
Eph 4:18 because of the *b* of their heart

**BLOOD**
Gen 4:10 the voice of thy brother's *b*
Gen 9:4 thereof, which is the *b* thereof
Gen 37:22 Reuben said unto them, Shed no *b*
Gen 37:26 our brother, and conceal his *b*
Gen 37:31 and dipped the coat in the *b*
Gen 42:22 behold, also his *b* is required
Gen 49:11 and his clothes in the *b* of grapes
Ex 4:9 shall become *b* upon the dry land
Ex 7:17 and they shall be turned to *b*
Ex 7:19 of water, that they may become *b*
Ex 12:7 And they shall take of the *b*
Ex 12:13 the *b* shall be to you for a token
Ex 12:22 dip it in the *b* that is in the
Ex 22:2 there shall no *b* be shed for him
Ex 23:18 Thou shalt not offer the *b* of my
Ex 24:6 And Moses took half of the *b*
Ex 29:12 take of the *b* of the bullock
Ex 29:20 kill the ram, and take of his *b*
Ex 30:10 with the *b* of the sin offering of
Ex 34:25 Thou shalt not offer the *b* of my
Lev 1:5 Aaron's sons, shall bring the *b*
Lev 1:11 shall sprinkle his *b* round about
Lev 1:15 the *b* thereof shall be wrung out
Lev 3:2 the *b* upon the altar round about
Lev 3:8 *b* thereof round about upon the
Lev 3:13 of Aaron shall sprinkle the *b*
Lev 3:17 that ye eat neither fat nor *b*
Lev 4:5 shall take of the bullock's *b*
Lev 4:16 *b* to the tabernacle of the
Lev 4:25 *b* of the sin offering with his
Lev 4:25 shall pour out his *b* at the
Lev 4:30 of the *b* thereof with his finger
Lev 4:34 *b* of the sin offering with his
Lev 5:9 he shall sprinkle of the *b* of the
Lev 5:9 the rest of the *b* shall be wrung
Lev 6:27 of the *b* thereof upon any garment
Lev 6:30 whereof any of the *b* is brought
Lev 7:2 the *b* thereof shall he sprinkle
Lev 7:14 the *b* of the peace offerings
Lev 7:26 ye shall eat no manner of *b*
Lev 7:33 that offereth the *b* of the peace
Lev 8:15 and Moses took the *b*, and put it
Lev 8:19 Moses sprinkled the *b* upon the
Lev 8:30 of the *b* which was upon the altar
Lev 9:9 of Aaron brought the *b* unto him
Lev 9:12 sons presented unto him the *b*
Lev 9:18 sons presented unto him the *b*
Lev 10:18 the *b* of it was not brought in
Lev 12:4 in the *b* of her purifying three
Lev 14:6 the living bird in the *b* of the
Lev 14:14 of the *b* of the trespass offering
Lev 14:25 of the *b* of the trespass offering
Lev 14:51 dip them in the *b* of the slain
Lev 14:52 the house with the *b* of the bird
Lev 15:19 and her issue in her flesh be *b*
Lev 16:14 take of the *b* of the bullock
Lev 16:18 take of the *b* of the bullock
Lev 16:27 whose *b* was brought in to make
Lev 17:4 *b* shall be imputed unto that man
Lev 19:16 against the *b* of thy neighbour
Lev 19:26 not eat any thing with the *b*
Lev 20:9 his *b* shall be upon him
Lev 20:27 their *b* shall be upon them
Num 18:17 sprinkle their *b* upon the altar
Num 19:4 take of her *b* with his finger
Num 23:24 prey, and drink the *b* of the slain
Num 35:19 The revenger of *b* himself shall
Num 35:25 of the hand of the revenger of *b*
Num 35:33 but by the *b* of him that shed it
Deut 12:16 Only ye shall not eat the *b*
Deut 12:23 be sure that thou eat not the *b*
Deut 12:27 offerings, the flesh and the *b*
Deut 15:23 thou shalt not eat the *b* thereof
Deut 17:8 in judgment, between *b* and *b*
Deut 19:6 of the *b* pursue the slayer
Deut 19:10 That innocent *b* be not shed in
Deut 21:7 Our hands have not shed this *b*
Deut 22:8 thou bring not *b* upon thine house
Deut 32:14 drink the pure *b* of the grape
Deut 32:42 make mine arrows drunk with *b*
Josh 2:19 his *b* shall be upon his head, and
Josh 20:3 your refuge from the avenger of *b*
Josh 20:5 the avenger of *b* pursue after him
Josh 20:9 by the hand of the avenger of *b*
Judg 9:24 their *b* be laid upon Abimelech
1Sa 14:32 people did eat them with the *b*
1Sa 19:5 wilt thou sin against innocent *b*
1Sa 25:26 thee from coming to shed *b*
1Sa 25:31 that thou hast shed *b* causeless
1Sa 26:20 let not my *b* fall to the earth
2Sa 1:16 unto him, Thy *b* be upon thy head
2Sa 1:22 From the *b* of the slain, from the
2Sa 3:27 for the *b* of Asahel his brother
2Sa 4:11 now require his *b* of your hand
2Sa 14:11 of *b* to destroy any more, lest
2Sa 16:8 all the *b* of the house of Saul
2Sa 20:12 Amasa wallowed in *b* in the midst
2Sa 23:17 is not this the *b* of the men that
1Kin 2:5 shed the *b* of war in peace, and
1Kin 2:9 thou down to the grave with *b*
1Kin 2:31 mayest take away the innocent *b*
1Kin 2:33 Their *b* shall therefore return
1Kin 2:37 thy *b* shall be upon thine own
1Kin 18:28 till the *b* gushed out upon them
1Kin 21:19 *b* of Naboth shall dogs lick thy
1Kin 22:35 the *b* ran out of the wound into
1Kin 22:38 and the dogs licked up his *b*
2Kin 3:22 on the other side as red as *b*
2Kin 9:7 that I may avenge the *b* of my
2Kin 9:26 the *b* of his sons, saith the LORD
2Kin 9:33 some of her *b* was sprinkled on
2Kin 16:13 sprinkled the *b* of his peace
2Kin 24:4 for the innocent *b* that he shed
1Chr 11:19 shall I drink the *b* of these men
1Chr 22:8 Thou hast shed *b* abundantly
1Chr 28:3 been a man of war, and hast shed *b*
2Chr 19:10 their cities, between *b* and *b*
2Chr 24:25 the *b* of the sons of Jehoiada the
2Chr 29:22 and the priests received the *b*
2Chr 30:16 the priests sprinkled the *b*
2Chr 35:11 sprinkled the *b* from their hands
Job 16:18 O earth, cover not thou my *b*
Job 39:30 Her young ones also suck up *b*
Ps 9:12 When he maketh inquisition for *b*
Ps 16:4 offerings of *b* will I not offer
Ps 30:9 What profit is there in my *b*
Ps 50:13 of bulls, or drink the *b* of goats
Ps 58:10 his feet in the *b* of the wicked
Ps 68:23 dipped in the *b* of thine enemies
Ps 72:14 shall their *b* be in his sight
Ps 78:44 And had turned their rivers into *b*
Ps 79:3 Their *b* have they shed like water
Ps 79:10 *b* of thy servants which is shed
Ps 94:21 and condemn the innocent *b*
Ps 105:29 He turned their waters into *b*
Ps 106:38 And shed innocent *b*
Prov 1:11 with us, let us lay wait for *b*
Prov 1:16 to evil, and make haste to shed *b*
Prov 6:17 and hands that shed innocent *b*
Prov 12:6 wicked are to lie in wait for *b*
Prov 28:17 man that doeth violence to the *b*
Prov 30:33 of the nose bringeth forth *b*
Is 1:11 delight not in the *b* of bullocks
Is 1:15 your hands are full of *b*
Is 4:4 shall have purged the *b* of
Is 9:5 noise, and garments rolled in *b*
Is 15:9 of Dimon shall be full of *b*

Is 26:21 earth also shall disclose her *b*
Is 33:15 his ears from hearing of *b*
Is 34:3 shall be melted with their *b*
Is 49:26 shall be drunken with their own *b*
Is 59:3 For your hands are defiled with *b*
Is 59:7 make haste to shed innocent *b*
Is 63:3 their *b* shall be sprinkled upon
Is 66:3 as if he offered swine's *b*
Jer 2:34 the *b* of the souls of the poor
Jer 7:6 shed not innocent *b* in this place
Jer 18:21 pour out their *b* by the force of
Jer 19:4 place with the *b* of innocents
Jer 22:3 shed innocent *b* in this place
Jer 22:17 and for to shed innocent *b*
Jer 26:15 bring innocent *b* upon yourselves
Jer 46:10 and made drunk with their *b*
Jer 48:10 keepeth back his sword from *b*
Jer 51:35 my *b* upon the inhabitants of
Lam 4:13 that have shed the *b* of the just
Eze 3:18 but his *b* will I require at thine
Eze 5:17 *b* shall pass through thee
Eze 9:9 great, and the land is full of *b*
Eze 14:19 and pour out my fury upon it in *b*
Eze 16:6 saw thee polluted in thine own *b*
Eze 16:22 bare, and wast polluted in thy *b*
Eze 16:36 by the *b* of thy children, which
Eze 18:10 that is a robber, a shedder of *b*
Eze 21:32 thy *b* shall be in the midst of
Eze 22:3 The city sheddeth *b* in the midst
Eze 22:9 men that carry tales to shed *b*
Eze 22:27 ravening the prey, to shed *b*
Eze 23:37 *b* is in their hands, and with
Eze 23:45 the manner of women that shed *b*
Eze 24:7 For her *b* is in the midst of her
Eze 28:23 pestilence, and *b* into her street
Eze 32:6 I will also water with thy *b* the
Eze 33:4 his *b* shall be upon his own head
Eze 33:25 Ye eat with the *b*, and lift up
Eze 35:5 hast shed the *b* of the children
Eze 36:18 my fury upon them for the *b* that
Eze 38:22 him with pestilence and with *b*
Eze 39:17 that ye may eat flesh, and drink *b*
Eze 43:18 thereon, and to sprinkle *b* thereon
Eze 44:7 offer my bread, the fat and the *b*
Eze 44:15 to offer unto me the fat and the *b*
Eze 45:19 take of the *b* of the sin offering
Hos 1:4 I will avenge the *b* of Jezreel
Hos 4:2 break out, and *b* toucheth *b*
Hos 6:8 iniquity, and is polluted with *b*
Hos 12:14 shall he leave his *b* upon him
Joel 2:30 in the heavens and in the earth, *b*
Joel 2:31 into darkness, and the moon into *b*
Joel 3:19 shed innocent *b* in their land
Jonah 1:14 and lay not upon us innocent *b*
Mic 3:10 They build up Zion with *b*
Mic 7:2 they all lie in wait for *b*
Hab 2:8 because of men's *b*, and for the
Zeph 1:17 their *b* shall be poured out as
Zec 9:7 take away his *b* out of his mouth
Mt 9:20 with an issue of *b* twelve years
Mt 16:17 *b* hath not revealed it unto thee,
Mt 23:30 them in the *b* of the prophets
Mt 26:28 For this is my *b* of the new
Mt 27:4 I have betrayed the innocent *b*
Mt 27:24 of the *b* of this just person
Mk 5:25 had an issue of *b* twelve years
Mk 5:29 fountain of her *b* was dried up
Mk 14:24 This is my *b* of the new testament
Lk 8:43 having an issue of *b* twelve years
Lk 11:50 That the *b* of all the prophets,
Lk 13:1 whose *b* Pilate had mingled with
Lk 22:20 cup is the new testament in my *b*
Lk 22:44 of *b* falling down to the ground
Jn 1:13 Which were born, not of *b*
Jn 6:53 of the Son of man, and drink his *b*
Jn 19:34 and forthwith came there out *b*
Acts 1:19 that is to say, The field of *b*
Acts 2:19 *b*, and fire, and vapour of smoke
Acts 2:20 into darkness, and the moon into *b*
Acts 5:28 to bring this man's *b* upon us
Acts 15:20 from things strangled, and from *b*
Acts 17:26 hath made of one *b* all nations of
Acts 18:6 Your *b* be upon your own heads
Acts 20:26 I am pure from the *b* of all men
Acts 21:25 offered to idols, and from *b*
Acts 22:20 when the *b* of thy martyr Stephen
Rom 3:15 Their feet are swift to shed *b*
Rom 5:9 being now justified by his *b*
1Cor 10:16 the communion of the *b* of Christ
1Cor 11:25 cup is the new testament in my *b*
1Cor 15:50 *b* cannot inherit the kingdom of
Gal 1:16 I conferred not with flesh and *b*
Eph 1:7 we have redemption through his *b*
Eph 2:13 are made nigh by the *b* of Christ
Eph 6:12 we wrestle not against flesh and *b*
Col 1:14 we have redemption through his *b*
Col 1:20 peace through the *b* of his cross
Heb 2:14 are partakers of flesh and *b*
Heb 9:7 once every year, not without *b*
Heb 9:12 Neither by the *b* of goats
Heb 9:25 place every year with *b* of others
Heb 10:4 not possible that the *b* of bulls
Heb 10:19 the holiest by the *b* of Jesus
Heb 12:4 Ye have not yet resisted unto *b*
Heb 12:24 to the *b* of sprinkling, that
Heb 13:11 whose *b* is brought into the
Heb 13:20 through the *b* of the everlasting
1Pet 1:2 of the *b* of Jesus Christ
1Pet 1:19 But with the precious *b* of Christ
1Jn 1:7 the *b* of Jesus Christ his Son
1Jn 5:6 is he that came by water and *b*
1Jn 5:6 by water only, but by water and *b*
1Jn 5:8 spirit, and the water, and the *b*
Rev 1:5 us from our sins in his own *b*
Rev 5:9 God by thy *b* out of every kindred
Rev 6:10 avenge our *b* on them that dwell
Rev 6:12 of hair, and the moon became as *b*
Rev 7:14 them white in the *b* of the Lamb
Rev 8:7 hail and fire mingled with *b*
Rev 8:8 third part of the sea became *b*
Rev 11:6 over waters to turn them to *b*
Rev 12:11 overcame him by the *b* of the Lamb
Rev 14:20 *b* came out of the winepress, even
Rev 16:3 it became as the *b* of a dead man
Rev 16:4 and they became *b*
Rev 16:6 they have shed the *b* of saints
Rev 16:6 thou hast given them *b* to drink
Rev 17:6 drunken with the *b* of the saints
Rev 17:6 with the *b* of the martyrs of
Rev 18:24 her was found the *b* of prophets
Rev 19:2 hath avenged the *b* of his
Rev 19:13 with a vesture dipped in *b*

## BLOODY
Ex 4:25 Surely a *b* husband art thou to me
2Sa 16:7 Come out, come out, thou *b* man
2Sa 21:1 is for Saul, and for his *b* house
Ps 5:6 the LORD will abhor the *b*
Ps 26:9 sinners, nor my life with *b* men
Ps 55:23 *b* and deceitful men shall not live
Ps 59:2 iniquity, and save me from *b* men
Ps 139:19 from me therefore, ye *b* men
Eze 7:23 for the land is full of *b* crimes
Eze 22:2 judge, wilt thou judge the *b* city
Eze 24:6 Woe to the *b* city, to the pot
Eze 24:9 Woe to the *b* city
Nah 3:1 Woe to the *b* city
Acts 28:8 sick of a fever and of a *b* flux

## BLOSSOM
Num 17:5 rod, whom I shall choose, shall *b*
Is 5:24 their *b* shall go up as dust
Is 27:6 Israel shall *b* and bud, and fill
Is 35:1 shall rejoice, and *b* as the rose
Hab 3:17 Although the fig tree shall not *b*

## BLOT
Ex 32:32 *b* me, I pray thee, out of thy
Num 5:23 he shall *b* them out with the
Deut 9:14 *b* out their name from under
Deut 25:19 that thou shalt *b* out the
Deut 29:20 the LORD shall *b* out his name
2Kin 14:27 *b* out the name of Israel from
Job 31:7 if any *b* hath cleaved to mine
Ps 51:1 mercies *b* out my transgressions
Ps 51:9 *b* out all mine iniquities
Prov 9:7 a wicked man getteth himself a *b*
Jer 18:23 neither *b* out their sin from thy
Rev 3:5 I will not *b* out his name out of

## BLOTTED
Neh 4:5 sin be *b* out from before thee
Ps 69:28 Let them be *b* out of the book of
Ps 109:13 following let their name be *b* out
Is 44:22 I have *b* out, as a thick cloud,
Acts 3:19 that your sins may be *b* out

## BLOW
Ex 15:10 Thou didst *b* with thy wind, the
Num 10:3 And when they shall *b* with them
Num 10:10 ye shall *b* with the trumpets over
Num 31:6 and the trumpets to *b* in his hand
Josh 6:4 priests shall *b* with the trumpets
Judg 7:18 When I *b* with a trumpet, I and all
1Kin 1:34 *b* ye with the trumpet, and say,
1Chr 15:24 did *b* with the trumpets before
Ps 39:10 consumed by the *b* of thine hand
Ps 78:26 an east wind to *b* in the heaven
Ps 81:3 *B* up the trumpet in the new moon,
Ps 147:18 he causeth his wind to *b*, and the
Song 4:16 *b* upon my garden, that the spices
Is 40:24 and he shall also *b* upon them
Jer 4:5 *B* ye the trumpet in the land
Jer 6:1 *b* the trumpet in Tekoa, and set up
Jer 14:17 breach, with a very grievous *b*
Jer 51:27 *b* the trumpet among the nations,
Eze 21:31 I will *b* against thee in the fire
Eze 22:20 to *b* the fire upon it, to melt it
Eze 33:3 he *b* the trumpet, and warn the
Hos 5:8 *B* ye the cornet in Gibeah, and the
Joel 2:1 *B* ye the trumpet in Zion, and
Joel 2:15 *B* the trumpet in Zion, sanctify a
Hag 1:9 brought it home, I did *b* upon it
Zec 9:14 the Lord GOD shall *b* the trumpet
Lk 12:55 And when ye see the south wind *b*
Rev 7:1 wind should not *b* on the earth

## BLOWETH
Is 18:3 when he *b* a trumpet, hear ye
Is 40:7 the spirit of the LORD *b* upon it
Is 54:16 that *b* the coals in the fire
Jn 3:8 The wind *b* where it listeth, and

## BLOWING
Lev 23:24 a memorial of *b* of trumpets
Num 29:1 it is a day of *b* the trumpets
Josh 6:9 going on, and *b* with the trumpets
Josh 6:13 going on, and *b* with the trumpets

## BLOWN
Job 20:26 a fire not *b* shall consume him
Is 27:13 that the great trumpet shall be *b*
Amos 3:6 Shall a trumpet be *b* in the city

## BLUE
Ex 25:4 And *b*, and purple, and scarlet, and
Ex 26:1 of fine twined linen, and *b*
Ex 26:4 of *b* upon the edge of the one
Ex 26:31 And thou shalt make a vail of *b*
Ex 26:36 for the door of the tent, of *b*
Ex 27:16 an hanging of twenty cubits, of *b*
Ex 28:5 And they shall take gold, and *b*
Ex 28:15 of gold, of *b*, and of purple, and
Ex 28:28 of the ephod with a lace of *b*
Ex 28:37 And thou shalt put it on a *b* lace
Ex 35:6 And *b*, and purple, and scarlet, and
Ex 35:23 every man, with whom was found *b*
Ex 36:8 of fine twined linen, and *b*
Ex 36:11 he made loops of *b* on the edge of
Ex 38:18 of the court was needlework, of *b*
Ex 38:23 workman, and an embroiderer in *b*
Ex 39:1 And of the *b*, and purple, and
Ex 39:8 of gold, *b*, and purple, and scarlet
Ex 39:21 of the ephod with a lace of *b*
Ex 39:29 girdle of fine twined linen, and *b*
Ex 39:31 And they tied unto it a lace of *b*
Num 4:9 And they shall take a cloth of *b*
Num 4:11 they shall spread a cloth of *b*
Num 15:38 of the borders a ribband of *b*
2Chr 2:7 and in purple, and crimson, and *b*
2Chr 2:14 and in timber, in purple, in *b*
Est 1:6 Where were white, green, and *b*
Est 8:15 of the king in royal apparel of *b*
Jer 10:9 *b* and purple is their clothing
Eze 23:6 Which were clothed with *b*
Eze 27:7 *b* and purple from the isles of
Eze 27:24 in *b* clothes, and broidered work,

## BLUSH
Ezr 9:6 *b* to lift up my face to thee, my
Jer 6:15 all ashamed, neither could they *b*
Jer 8:12 all ashamed, neither could they *b*

## BOANERGES *(bo-an-er'-jees) Surname of James and John, the sons of Zebedee.*
Mk 3:17 and he surnamed them *B*, which is,

## BOARD
Ex 26:16 cubits shall be the length of a *b*
Ex 26:19 another *b* for his two tenons
Ex 26:21 two sockets under one *b*
Ex 26:25 and two sockets under another *b*
Ex 36:21 The length of a *b* was ten cubits
Ex 36:24 under one *b* for his two tenons
Ex 36:26 and two sockets under another *b*
Ex 36:30 silver, under every *b* two sockets

**BOARDS**
Ex 26:15 thou shalt make *b* for the
Ex 26:22 westward thou shalt make six *b*
Ex 26:25 And they shall be eight *b*, and
Ex 27:8 Hollow with *b* shalt thou make it
Ex 35:11 covering, his taches, and his *b*
Ex 36:20 he made *b* for the tabernacle of
Ex 36:34 And he overlaid the *b* with gold
Ex 38:7 he made the altar hollow with *b*
Ex 39:33 his furniture, his taches, his *b*
Ex 40:18 sockets, and set up the *b* thereof
Num 3:36 shall be the *b* of the tabernacle
Num 4:31 the *b* of the tabernacle, and the
1Kin 6:9 house with beams and *b* of cedar
1Kin 6:15 the house within with *b* of cedar
Song 8:9 will inclose her with *b* of cedar
Eze 27:5 thy ship *b* of fir trees of Senir
Acts 27:44 And the rest, some on *b*, and some

**BOAST**
1Kin 20:11 *b* himself as he that putteth it
2Chr 25:19 thine heart lifteth thee up to *b*
Ps 34:2 soul shall make her *b* in the LORD
Ps 44:8 In God we *b* all the day long, and
Ps 49:6 *b* themselves in the multitude of
Ps 94:4 workers of iniquity *b* themselves
Ps 97:7 that *b* themselves of idols
Prov 27:1 *B* not thyself of to morrow
Is 10:15 Shall the ax *b* itself against him
Is 61:6 their glory shall ye *b* yourselves
Rom 2:17 the law, and makest thy *b* of God
Rom 2:23 Thou that makest thy *b* of the law
Rom 11:18 *B* not against the branches
2Cor 9:2 for which I *b* of you to them of
2Cor 10:8 For though I should *b* somewhat
2Cor 10:13 But we will not *b* of things
2Cor 10:16 not to *b* in another man's line of
Eph 2:9 of works, lest any man should *b*

**BOASTETH**
Ps 10:3 For the wicked *b* of his heart's
Prov 20:14 he is gone his way, then he *b*
Prov 25:14 Whoso *b* himself of a false gift
Jas 3:5 little member, and *b* great things

**BOASTING**
Acts 5:36 Theudas, *b* himself to be somebody
Rom 3:27 Where is *b* then
2Cor 7:14 to you in truth, even so our *b*
2Cor 8:24 love, and of our *b* on your behalf
2Cor 9:3 lest our *b* of you should be in
2Cor 10:15 Not *b* of things without our
2Cor 11:10 this *b* in the regions of Achaia
2Cor 11:17 in this confidence of *b*

**BOAT**
2Sa 19:18 there went over a ferry *b* to
Jn 6:22 that there was none other *b* there
Acts 27:16 we had much work to come by the *b*
Acts 27:30 had let down the *b* into the sea

**BOAZ** *(bo'-az)* See BOOZ.
*1. Husband of Ruth.*
Ruth 2:1 and his name was *B*
Ruth 2:11 *B* answered and said unto her, It
Ruth 2:14 *B* said unto her, At mealtime come
Ruth 2:19 with whom I wrought to day is *B*
Ruth 2:23 *B* to glean unto the end of barley
Ruth 3:2 now is not *B* of our kindred, with
Ruth 3:7 when *B* had eaten and drunk, and his
Ruth 4:1 Then went *B* up to the gate, and
Ruth 4:5 Then said *B*, What day thou buyest
Ruth 4:8 Therefore the kinsman said unto *B*
Ruth 4:13 So *B* took Ruth, and she was his
Ruth 4:21 And Salmon begat *B*
1Chr 2:11 begat Salma, and Salma begat *B*
*2. A pillar in Solomon's Temple.*
1Kin 7:21 and called the name thereof *B*
2Chr 3:17 and the name of that on the left *B*

**BOCHERU** *(bok'-er-u) A relative of Saul.*
1Chr 8:38 whose names are these, Azrikam, *B*
1Chr 9:44 whose names are these, Azrikam, *B*

**BOCHIM** *(bo'-kim) A place near Gilgal.*
Judg 2:1 the LORD came up from Gilgal to *B*
Judg 2:5 called the name of that place *B*

**BODIES**
Gen 47:18 the sight of my lord, but our *b*
1Sa 31:12 the *b* of his sons from the wall
1Chr 10:12 the *b* of his sons, and brought
2Chr 20:24 they were dead *b* fallen to the
Neh 9:37 they have dominion over our *b*
Job 13:12 ashes, your *b* to *b* of clay
Ps 79:2 The dead *b* of thy servants have
Ps 110:6 fill the places with the dead *b*
Jer 31:40 And the whole valley of the dead *b*
Jer 33:5 fill them with the dead *b* of men
Jer 34:20 their dead *b* shall be for meat
Jer 41:9 cast all the dead *b* of the men
Eze 1:11 another, and two covered their *b*
Eze 1:23 covered on that side, their *b*
Dan 3:27 upon whose *b* the fire had no
Amos 8:3 be many dead *b* in every place
Mt 27:52 many *b* of the saints which slept
Jn 19:31 that the *b* should not remain upon
Rom 1:24 their own *b* between themselves
Rom 8:11 *b* by his Spirit that dwelleth in
Rom 12:1 present your *b* a living sacrifice
1Cor 6:15 Know ye not that your *b* are the
1Cor 15:40 There are also celestial *b*
1Cor 15:40 and *b* terrestrial
Eph 5:28 love their wives as their own *b*
Heb 10:22 our *b* washed with pure water
Heb 13:11 For the *b* of those beasts, whose
Rev 11:8 their dead *b* shall lie in the

**BODILY**
Lk 3:22 in a *b* shape like a dove upon him
2Cor 10:10 but his *b* presence is weak, and
Col 2:9 all the fulness of the Godhead *b*
1Ti 4:8 For *b* exercise profiteth little

**BODY**
Ex 24:10 as it were the *b* of heaven in his
Lev 21:11 shall he go in to any dead *b*
Num 6:6 LORD he shall come at no dead *b*
Num 9:6 defiled by the dead *b* of a man
Num 9:10 be unclean by reason of a dead *b*
Num 19:11 He that toucheth the dead *b* of
Num 19:13 dead *b* of any man that is dead
Num 19:16 in the open fields, or a dead *b*
Deut 21:23 His *b* shall not remain all night
Deut 28:4 shall be the fruit of thy *b*
Deut 28:11 in goods, in the fruit of thy *b*
Deut 28:18 shall be the fruit of thy *b*
Deut 28:53 eat the fruit of thine own *b*
Deut 30:9 thine hand, in the fruit of thy *b*
Judg 8:30 and ten sons of his *b* begotten
1Sa 31:10 they fastened his *b* to the wall
1Sa 31:12 all night, and took the *b* of Saul
2Kin 8:5 he had restored a dead *b* to life
1Chr 10:12 men, and took away the *b* of Saul
Job 19:17 the children's sake of mine own *b*
Job 19:26 my skin worms destroy this *b*
Job 20:25 is drawn, and cometh out of the *b*
Ps 132:11 Of the fruit of thy *b* will I set
Prov 5:11 thy flesh and thy *b* are consumed,
Is 10:18 fruitful field, both soul and *b*
Is 26:19 with my dead *b* shall they arise
Is 51:23 hast laid thy *b* as the ground
Jer 26:23 cast his dead *b* into the graves
Jer 36:30 his dead *b* shall be cast out in
Lam 4:7 were more ruddy in *b* than rubies
Eze 10:12 And their whole *b*, and their backs,
Dan 4:33 his *b* was wet with the dew of
Dan 5:21 his *b* was wet with the dew of
Dan 7:11 his *b* destroyed, and given to the
Dan 7:15 in my spirit in the midst of my *b*
Dan 10:6 His *b* also was like the beryl, and
Mic 6:7 the fruit of my *b* for the sin of
Hag 2:13 by a dead *b* touch any of these
Mt 5:29 not that thy whole *b* should be
Mt 5:30 not that thy whole *b* should be
Mt 6:22 The light of the *b* is the eye
Mt 6:25 nor yet for your *b*, what ye shall
Mt 10:28 And fear not them which kill the *b*
Mt 14:12 disciples came, and took up the *b*
Mt 26:12 hath poured this ointment on my *b*
Mt 26:26 this is my *b*
Mt 27:58 Pilate, and begged the *b* of Jesus
Mt 27:58 commanded the *b* to be delivered
Mt 27:59 And when Joseph had taken the *b*
Mk 5:29 she felt in her *b* that she was
Mk 14:8 to anoint my *b* to the burying
Mk 14:22 this is my *b*
Mk 14:51 cloth cast about his naked *b*
Mk 15:43 Pilate, and craved the *b* of Jesus
Mk 15:45 he gave the *b* to Joseph
Lk 11:34 The light of the *b* is the eye
Lk 11:36 If thy whole *b* therefore be full
Lk 12:4 afraid of them that kill the *b*
Lk 12:22 neither for the *b*, what ye shall
Lk 17:37 unto them, Wheresoever the *b* is
Lk 22:19 This is my *b* which is given for
Lk 23:52 Pilate, and begged the *b* of Jesus
Lk 23:55 sepulchre, and how his *b* was laid
Lk 24:3 found not the *b* of the Lord Jesus
Lk 24:23 And when they found not his *b*
Jn 2:21 he spake of the temple of his *b*
Jn 19:38 he might take away the *b* of Jesus
Jn 19:40 Then took they the *b* of Jesus
Jn 20:12 where the *b* of Jesus had lain
Acts 9:40 and turning him to the *b* said
Acts 19:12 So that from his *b* were brought
Rom 4:19 considered not his own *b* now dead
Rom 6:6 that the *b* of sin might be
Rom 6:12 therefore reign in your mortal *b*
Rom 7:4 to the law by the *b* of Christ
Rom 7:24 me from the *b* of this death
Rom 8:10 the *b* is dead because of sin
Rom 8:13 do mortify the deeds of the *b*
Rom 8:23 to wit, the redemption of our *b*
Rom 12:4 as we have many members in one *b*
Rom 12:5 are one *b* in Christ, and every one
1Cor 5:3 For I verily, as absent in *b*
1Cor 6:13 Now the *b* is not for fornication,
1Cor 6:16 is joined to an harlot is one *b*
1Cor 6:18 that a man doeth is without the *b*
1Cor 7:4 wife hath not power of her own *b*
1Cor 7:34 that she may be holy both in *b*
1Cor 9:27 But I keep under my *b*, and bring
1Cor 10:16 the communion of the *b* of Christ
1Cor 11:24 this is my *b*, which is broken for
1Cor 11:27 shall be guilty of the *b*
1Cor 11:29 not discerning the Lord's *b*
1Cor 12:12 For as the *b* is one, and hath many
1Cor 12:20 they many members, yet but one *b*
1Cor 12:22 much more those members of the *b*
1Cor 13:3 though I give my *b* to be burned
1Cor 15:35 and with what *b* do they come
1Cor 15:37 sowest not that *b* that shall be
1Cor 15:38 But God giveth it a *b* as it hath
1Cor 15:44 It is sown a natural *b*
2Cor 4:10 the *b* the dying of the Lord Jesus
2Cor 5:6 whilst we are at home in the *b*
2Cor 5:8 rather to be absent from the *b*
2Cor 5:10 receive the things done in his *b*
2Cor 12:2 years ago, (whether in the *b*
2Cor 12:2 or whether out of the *b*, I cannot
Gal 6:17 for I bear in my *b* the marks of
Eph 1:23 Which is his *b*, the fulness of
Eph 2:16 unto God in one *b* by the cross
Eph 3:6 be fellowheirs, and of the same *b*
Eph 4:4 There is one *b*, and one Spirit,
Eph 4:12 the edifying of the *b* of Christ
Eph 4:16 From whom the whole *b* fitly
Eph 5:23 and he is the saviour of the *b*
Eph 5:30 For we are members of his *b*
Phil 1:20 Christ shall be magnified in my *b*
Phil 3:21 Who shall change our vile *b*
Col 1:18 And he is the head of the *b*
Col 1:22 In the *b* of his flesh through
Col 2:11 in putting off the *b* of the sins
Col 2:17 but the *b* is of Christ
Col 2:19 from which all the *b* by joints
Col 2:23 humility, and neglecting of the *b*
Col 3:15 which also ye are called in one *b*
1Th 5:23 *b* be preserved blameless unto the
Heb 10:5 but a *b* hast thou prepared me
Heb 10:10 through the offering of the *b* of
Heb 13:3 as being yourselves also in the *b*
Jas 2:16 things which are needful to the *b*
Jas 2:26 For as the *b* without the spirit
Jas 3:2 able also to bridle the whole *b*
Jas 3:6 that it defileth the whole *b*
1Pet 2:24 our sins in his own *b* on the tree
Jude 9 he disputed about the *b* of Moses

**BOHAN** *(bo'-han) A namesake of a border stone.*
Josh 15:6 the stone of *B* the son of Reuben
Josh 18:17 the stone of *B* the son of Reuben

**BOIL**
Ex 9:9 shall be a *b* breaking forth with
Lev 8:31 *B* the flesh at the door of the
Lev 13:18 even in the skin thereof, was a *b*
Lev 13:23 and spread not, it is a burning *b*
2Kin 20:7 And they took and laid it on the *b*
Job 41:31 maketh the deep to *b* like a pot
Is 38:21 lay it for a plaister upon the *b*
Is 64:2 the fire causeth the waters to *b*
Eze 24:5 bones under it, and make it *b* well
Eze 46:20 shall *b* the trespass offering
Eze 46:24 are the places of them that *b*

## BOILED
1Kin 19:21 them, and *b* their flesh with the
2Kin 6:29 So we *b* my son, and did eat him
Job 30:27 My bowels *b*, and rested not

## BOILS
Ex 9:11 before Moses because of the *b*
Job 2:7 smote Job with sore *b* from the

## BOLD
Prov 28:1 but the righteous are *b* as a lion
Acts 13:46 Then Paul and Barnabas waxed *b*
Rom 10:20 But Esaias is very *b*, and saith, I
2Cor 10:1 but being absent am *b* toward you
2Cor 11:21 Howbeit whereinsoever any is *b*
Phil 1:14 are much more *b* to speak the word
1Th 2:2 we were *b* in our God to speak
Philem 8 though I might be much *b* in

## BOLDLY
Gen 34:25 sword, and came upon the city *b*
Mk 15:43 went in *b* unto Pilate, and craved
Jn 7:26 But, lo, he speaketh *b*, and they
Acts 9:27 how he had preached *b* at Damascus
Acts 9:29 he spake *b* in the name of the
Acts 14:3 abode they speaking *b* in the Lord
Acts 18:26 began to speak *b* in the synagogue
Acts 19:8 spake *b* for the space of three
Rom 15:15 the more *b* unto you in some sort
Eph 6:19 me, that I may open my mouth *b*
Heb 4:16 Let us therefore come *b* unto the
Heb 13:6 So that we may *b* say, The Lord is

## BOLDNESS
Eccl 8:1 the *b* of his face shall be
Acts 4:13 Now when they saw the *b* of Peter
Acts 4:29 that with all *b* they may speak
Acts 4:31 they spake the word of God with *b*
2Cor 7:4 Great is my *b* of speech toward
Eph 3:12 In whom we have *b* and access with
Phil 1:20 be ashamed, but that with all *b*
1Ti 3:13 great *b* in the faith which is in
Heb 10:19 *b* to enter into the holiest by
1Jn 4:17 that we may have *b* in the day of

## BOLSTER
1Sa 19:13 a pillow of goats' hair for his *b*
1Sa 19:16 a pillow of goats' hair for his *b*
1Sa 26:7 stuck in the ground at his *b*
1Sa 26:11 now the spear that is at his *b*
1Sa 26:16 cruse of water that was at his *b*

## BOND
Num 30:2 an oath to bind his soul with a *b*
Num 30:10 her soul by a *b* with an oath
Num 30:11 every *b* wherewith she bound her
Job 12:18 He looseth the *b* of kings
Eze 20:37 you into the *b* of the covenant
Lk 13:16 from this *b* on the sabbath day
Acts 8:23 and in the *b* of iniquity
1Cor 12:13 Gentiles, whether we be *b* or free
Gal 3:28 there is neither *b* nor free
Eph 4:3 of the Spirit in the *b* of peace
Eph 6:8 the Lord, whether he be *b* or free
Col 3:11 Barbarian, Scythian, *b* nor free
Col 3:14 which is the *b* of perfectness
Rev 13:16 and great, rich and poor, free and *b*
Rev 19:18 flesh of all men, both free and *b*

## BONDAGE
Ex 1:14 their lives bitter with hard *b*
Ex 2:23 Israel sighed by reason of the *b*
Ex 6:5 whom the Egyptians keep in *b*
Ex 6:6 and I will rid you out of their *b*
Ex 6:9 anguish of spirit, and for cruel *b*
Ex 13:3 from Egypt, out of the house of *b*
Ex 13:14 from Egypt, from the house of *b*
Ex 20:2 of Egypt, out of the house of *b*
Deut 5:6 of Egypt, from the house of *b*
Deut 6:12 of Egypt, from the house of *b*
Deut 8:14 of Egypt, from the house of *b*
Deut 13:5 you out of the house of *b*
Deut 13:10 of Egypt, from the house of *b*
Deut 26:6 us, and laid upon us hard *b*
Josh 24:17 of Egypt, from the house of *b*
Judg 6:8 you forth out of the house of *b*
Ezr 9:8 us a little reviving in our *b*
Neh 5:5 and, lo, we bring into *b* our sons
Neh 5:18 because the *b* was heavy upon this
Neh 9:17 a captain to return to their *b*
Is 14:3 from the hard *b* wherein thou wast
Jn 8:33 and were never in *b* to any man
Acts 7:6 they should bring them into *b*
Rom 8:15 the spirit of *b* again to fear
Rom 8:21 shall be delivered from the *b* of
1Cor 7:15 is not under *b* in such cases
2Cor 11:20 suffer, if a man bring you into *b*
Gal 2:4 that they might bring us into *b*
Gal 4:3 were in *b* under the elements of
Gal 4:9 ye desire again to be in *b*
Gal 4:24 mount Sinai, which gendereth to *b*
Gal 4:25 is in *b* with her children
Gal 5:1 again with the yoke of *b*
Heb 2:15 all their lifetime subject to *b*
2Pet 2:19 of the same is he brought in *b*

## BONDMAID
Lev 19:20 with a woman, that is a *b*
Gal 4:22 had two sons, the one by a *b*

## BONDMAIDS
Lev 25:44 Both thy bondmen, and thy *b*
Lev 25:44 of them shall ye buy bondmen and *b*

## BONDMAN
Gen 44:33 instead of the lad a *b* to my lord
Deut 15:15 wast a *b* in the land of Egypt
Deut 16:12 that thou wast a *b* in Egypt
Deut 24:18 that thou wast a *b* in Egypt
Deut 24:22 wast a *b* in the land of Egypt
Rev 6:15 and the mighty men, and every *b*

## BONDMEN
Gen 43:18 and fall upon us, and take us for *b*
Gen 44:9 and we also will be my lord's *b*
Lev 25:42 they shall not be sold as *b*
Lev 25:46 they shall be your *b* for ever
Lev 26:13 that ye should not be their *b*
Deut 6:21 son, We were Pharaoh's *b* in Egypt
Deut 7:8 you out of the house of *b*
Deut 28:68 be sold unto your enemies for *b*
Josh 9:23 none of you be freed from being *b*
1Kin 9:22 of Israel did Solomon make no *b*
2Kin 4:1 take unto him my two sons to be *b*
2Chr 28:10 of Judah and Jerusalem for *b*
Ezr 9:9 For we were *b*
Est 7:4 But if we had been sold for *b*
Jer 34:13 of Egypt, out of the house of *b*

## BONDS
Num 30:5 or of her *b* wherewith she hath
Num 30:7 her *b* wherewith she bound her
Num 30:14 all her vows, or all her *b*
Ps 116:16 thou hast loosed my *b*
Jer 5:5 broken the yoke, and burst the *b*
Jer 27:2 Make thee *b* and yokes, and put them
Jer 30:8 off thy neck, and will burst thy *b*
Nah 1:13 and will burst thy *b* in sunder
Acts 20:23 in every city, saying that *b*
Acts 23:29 charge worthy of death or of *b*
Acts 25:14 a certain man left in *b* by Felix
Acts 26:29 such as I am, except these *b*
Acts 26:31 nothing worthy of death or of *b*
Eph 6:20 For which I am an ambassador in *b*
Phil 1:7 inasmuch as both in my *b*, and in
Phil 1:13 So that my *b* in Christ are
Phil 1:16 to add affliction to my *b*
Col 4:3 Christ, for which I am also in *b*
Col 4:18 Remember my *b*
2Ti 2:9 as an evil doer, even unto *b*
Philem 10 whom I have begotten in my *b*
Philem 13 unto me in the *b* of the gospel
Heb 10:34 ye had compassion of me in my *b*
Heb 11:36 and scourgings, yea, moreover of *b*
Heb 13:3 Remember them that are in *b*

## BONDWOMAN
Gen 21:10 unto Abraham, Cast out this *b*
Gen 21:13 son of the *b* will I make a nation
Gal 4:23 But he who was of the *b* was born
Gal 4:31 we are not children of the *b*

## BONDWOMEN
Deut 28:68 your enemies for bondmen and *b*
2Chr 28:10 for bondmen and *b* unto you
Est 7:4 we had been sold for bondmen and *b*

## BONE
Gen 2:23 said, This is now *b* of my bones
Gen 29:14 said to him, Surely thou art my *b*
Ex 12:46 shall ye break a *b* thereof
Num 9:12 morning, nor break any *b* of it
Num 19:16 or a *b* of a man, or a grave,
Num 19:18 and upon him that touched a *b*
Judg 9:2 remember also that I am your *b*
2Sa 5:1 saying, Behold, we are thy *b*
2Sa 19:13 ye to Amasa, Art thou not of my *b*
1Chr 11:1 saying, Behold, we are thy *b*
Job 2:5 thine hand now, and touch his *b*
Job 19:20 My *b* cleaveth to my skin and to my
Job 31:22 and mine arm be broken from the *b*
Ps 3:7 all mine enemies upon the cheek *b*
Prov 25:15 and a soft tongue breaketh the *b*
Eze 37:7 came together, *b* to his *b*
Eze 39:15 land, when any seeth a man's *b*
Jn 19:36 A *b* of him shall not be broken

## BONES
Gen 2:23 said, This is now bone of my *b*
Gen 50:25 ye shall carry up my *b* from hence
Ex 13:19 Moses took the *b* of Joseph with
Num 24:8 enemies, and shall break their *b*
Josh 24:32 the *b* of Joseph, which the
Judg 19:29 divided her, together with her *b*
1Sa 31:13 And they took their *b*, and buried
2Sa 19:12 Ye are my brethren, ye are my *b*
2Sa 21:12 David went and took the *b* of Saul
1Kin 13:2 men's *b* shall be burnt upon thee
1Kin 13:31 lay my *b* beside his *b*
2Kin 13:21 down, and touched the *b* of Elisha
2Kin 23:14 their places with the *b* of men
2Kin 23:16 took the *b* out of the sepulchres,
2Kin 23:20 and burned men's *b* upon them
1Chr 10:12 buried their *b* under the oak in
2Chr 34:5 he burnt the *b* of the priests
Job 4:14 which made all my *b* to shake
Job 10:11 flesh, and hast fenced me with *b*
Job 20:11 His *b* are full of the sin of his
Job 21:24 his *b* are moistened with marrow
Job 30:17 My *b* are pierced in me in the
Job 30:30 my *b* are burned with heat
Job 33:19 of his *b* with strong pain
Job 33:21 his *b* that were not seen stick
Job 40:18 His *b* are as strong pieces of
Ps 6:2 for my *b* are vexed
Ps 22:14 all my *b* are out of joint
Ps 22:17 I may tell all my *b*
Ps 31:10 iniquity, and my *b* are consumed
Ps 32:3 my *b* waxed old through my roaring
Ps 34:20 He keepeth all his *b*
Ps 35:10 All my *b* shall say, LORD, who is
Ps 38:3 rest in my *b* because of my sin
Ps 42:10 As with a sword in my *b*, mine
Ps 51:8 that the *b* which thou hast broken
Ps 53:5 for God hath scattered the *b* of
Ps 102:3 my *b* are burned as an hearth
Ps 102:5 groaning my *b* cleave to my skin
Ps 109:18 water, and like oil into his *b*
Ps 141:7 Our *b* are scattered at the
Prov 3:8 to thy navel, and marrow to thy *b*
Prov 12:4 ashamed is as rottenness in his *b*
Prov 14:30 but envy the rottenness of the *b*
Prov 15:30 and a good report maketh the *b* fat
Prov 16:24 to the soul, and health to the *b*
Prov 17:22 but a broken spirit drieth the *b*
Eccl 11:5 nor how the *b* do grow in the womb
Is 38:13 a lion, so will he break all my *b*
Is 58:11 in drought, and make fat thy *b*
Is 66:14 your *b* shall flourish like an
Jer 8:1 out the *b* of the kings of Judah
Jer 20:9 as a burning fire shut up in my *b*
Jer 23:9 all my *b* shake
Jer 50:17 king of Babylon hath broken his *b*
Lam 1:13 above hath he sent fire into my *b*
Lam 3:4 he hath broken my *b*
Lam 4:8 their skin cleaveth to their *b*
Eze 6:5 I will scatter your *b* round about
Eze 24:4 fill it with the choice *b*
Eze 24:10 it well, and let the *b* be burned
Eze 32:27 iniquities shall be upon their *b*
Eze 37:1 of the valley which was full of *b*
Eze 37:3 me, Son of man, can these *b* live
Eze 37:7 the *b* came together, bone to his
Eze 37:11 these *b* are the whole house of
Dan 6:24 brake all their *b* in pieces or
Amos 2:1 because he burned the *b* of the
Amos 6:10 bring out the *b* out of the house
Mic 3:2 and their flesh from off their *b*
Hab 3:16 rottenness entered into my *b*
Zeph 3:3 gnaw not the *b* till the morrow
Mt 23:27 are within full of dead men's *b*
Lk 24:39 for a spirit hath not flesh and *b*
Acts 3:7 ancle *b* received strength
Eph 5:30 body, of his flesh, and of his *b*
Heb 11:22 gave commandment concerning his *b*

## BONNETS
Ex 28:40 *b* shalt thou make for them, for
Ex 29:9 and his sons, and put the *b* on them
Ex 39:28 goodly *b* of fine linen, and linen

Lev 8:13 with girdles, and put *b* upon them
Is 3:20 The *b*, and the ornaments of the
Eze 44:18 have linen *b* upon their heads

**BOOK**
Gen 5:1 This is the *b* of the generations
Ex 17:14 Write this for a memorial in a *b*
Ex 24:7 he took the *b* of the covenant, and
Ex 32:32 out of thy *b* which thou hast
Num 5:23 shall write these curses in a *b*
Num 21:14 in the *b* of the wars of the LORD
Deut 17:18 him a copy of this law in a *b* out
Deut 28:58 law that are written in this *b*
Deut 28:61 not written in the *b* of this law
Deut 29:20 in this *b* shall lie upon him
Deut 29:27 curses that are written in this *b*
Deut 30:10 are written in this *b* of the law
Deut 31:24 the words of this law in a *b*
Deut 31:26 Take this *b* of the law, and put it
Josh 1:8 This *b* of the law shall not
Josh 8:31 in the *b* of the law of Moses
Josh 8:34 is written in the *b* of the law
Josh 10:13 this written in the *b* of Jasher
Josh 18:9 by cities into seven parts in a *b*
Josh 23:6 in the *b* of the law of Moses
Josh 24:26 words in the *b* of the law of God
1Sa 10:25 the kingdom, and wrote it in a *b*
2Sa 1:18 it is written in the *b* of Jasher
1Kin 11:41 in the *b* of the acts of Solomon
1Kin 14:19 they are written in the *b* of the
2Kin 14:6 in the *b* of the law of Moses
2Kin 15:11 they are written in the *b* of the
2Kin 15:15 they are written in the *b* of the
2Kin 15:21 are they not written in the *b* of
2Kin 15:26 they are written in the *b* of the
2Kin 15:31 they are written in the *b* of the
2Kin 21:25 *b* of the chronicles of the kings
2Kin 22:8 I have found the *b* of the law in
2Kin 22:8 And Hilkiah gave the *b* to Shaphan
2Kin 22:10 the priest hath delivered me a *b*
2Kin 22:11 the words of the *b* of the law
2Kin 23:2 *b* of the covenant which was found
2Kin 23:3 that were written in this *b*
2Kin 23:21 written in the *b* of this covenant
2Kin 23:24 *b* that Hilkiah the priest found
2Kin 23:28 are they not written in the *b* of
2Kin 24:5 are they not written in the *b* of
1Chr 9:1 in the *b* of the kings of Israel
1Chr 29:29 in the *b* of Samuel the seer
2Chr 9:29 in the *b* of Nathan the prophet
2Chr 12:15 in the *b* of Shemaiah the prophet
2Chr 16:11 in the *b* of the kings of Judah
2Chr 17:9 had the *b* of the law of the LORD
2Chr 20:34 they are written in the *b* of Jehu
2Chr 24:27 the story of the *b* of the kings
2Chr 25:4 in the law in the *b* of Moses
2Chr 34:14 Hilkiah the priest found a *b* of
2Chr 34:15 I have found the *b* of the law in
2Chr 34:16 Shaphan carried the *b* to the king
2Chr 34:18 the priest hath given me a *b*
2Chr 34:21 the words of the *b* that is found
2Chr 34:21 all that is written in this *b*
2Chr 34:24 curses that are written in the *b*
2Chr 34:30 *b* of the covenant that was found
2Chr 34:31 which are written in this *b*
2Chr 35:12 it is written in the *b* of Moses
2Chr 35:27 in the *b* of the kings of Israel
2Chr 36:8 in the *b* of the kings of Israel
Ezr 4:15 *b* of the records of thy fathers
Ezr 6:18 it is written in the *b* of Moses
Neh 8:1 bring the *b* of the law of Moses
Neh 8:3 attentive unto the *b* of the law
Neh 8:5 Ezra opened the *b* in the sight of
Neh 8:8 So they read in the *b* in the law
Neh 8:18 he read in the *b* of the law of
Neh 9:3 read in the *b* of the law of the
Neh 12:23 in the *b* of the chronicles
Neh 13:1 On that day they read in the *b* of
Est 2:23 it was written in the *b* of the
Est 6:1 he commanded to bring the *b* of
Est 9:32 and it was written in the *b*
Est 10:2 are they not written in the *b* of
Job 19:23 oh that they were printed in a *b*
Job 31:35 mine adversary had written a *b*
Ps 40:7 of the *b* it is written of me
Ps 56:8 are they not in thy *b*
Ps 69:28 out of the *b* of the living
Ps 139:16 in thy *b* all my members were
Is 29:11 the words of a *b* that is sealed
Is 29:18 the deaf hear the words of the *b*
Is 30:8 in a table, and note it in a *b*
Is 34:16 Seek ye out of the *b* of the LORD
Jer 25:13 all that is written in this *b*
Jer 30:2 I have spoken unto thee in a *b*
Jer 32:12 subscribed the *b* of the purchase
Jer 36:2 Take thee a roll of a *b*, and write
Jer 36:4 unto him, upon a roll of a *b*
Jer 36:8 reading in the *b* the words of the
Jer 36:10 Then read Baruch in the *b* the
Jer 36:13 when Baruch read the *b* in the
Jer 36:18 and I wrote them with ink in the *b*
Jer 36:32 *b* which Jehoiakim king of Judah
Jer 45:1 in a *b* at the mouth of Jeremiah
Jer 51:60 So Jeremiah wrote in a *b* all the
Jer 51:63 made an end of reading this *b*
Eze 2:9 and, lo, a roll of a *b* was therein
Dan 12:1 shall be found written in the *b*
Dan 12:4 shut up the words, and seal the *b*
Nah 1:1 The *b* of the vision of Nahum the
Mal 3:16 a *b* of remembrance was written
Mt 1:1 The *b* of the generation of Jesus
Mk 12:26 ye not read in the *b* of Moses
Lk 3:4 As it is written in the *b* of the
Lk 4:17 him the *b* of the prophet Esaias
Lk 4:20 And he closed the *b*, and he gave it
Lk 20:42 himself saith in the *b* of Psalms
Jn 20:30 which are not written in this *b*
Acts 1:20 it is written in the *b* of Psalms
Acts 7:42 written in the *b* of the prophets
Gal 3:10 in the *b* of the law to do them
Phil 4:3 whose names are in the *b* of life
Heb 9:19 hyssop, and sprinkled both the *b*
Heb 10:7 of the *b* it is written of me
Rev 1:11 and, What thou seest, write in a *b*
Rev 3:5 out his name out of the *b* of life
Rev 5:1 on the throne a *b* written within
Rev 5:2 Who is worthy to open the *b*
Rev 5:4 worthy to open and to read the *b*
Rev 5:7 took the *b* out of the right hand
Rev 5:9 Thou art worthy to take the *b*
Rev 10:2 had in his hand a little *b* open
Rev 10:8 take the little *b* which is open
Rev 10:9 unto him, Give me the little *b*
Rev 10:10 I took the little *b* out of the
Rev 13:8 names are not written in the *b* of
Rev 17:8 names were not written in the *b*
Rev 20:12 another *b* was opened
Rev 20:12 which is the *b* of life
Rev 20:15 was not found written in the *b* of
Rev 21:27 written in the Lamb's *b* of life
Rev 22:7 sayings of the prophecy of this *b*
Rev 22:9 which keep the sayings of this *b*
Rev 22:18 that are written in this *b*
Rev 22:19 words of the *b* of this prophecy
Rev 22:19 his part out of the *b* of life
Rev 22:19 which are written in this *b*

**BOOKS**
Eccl 12:12 of making many *b* there is no end
Dan 7:10 was set, and the *b* were opened
Dan 9:2 by *b* the number of the years
Jn 21:25 the *b* that should be written
Acts 19:19 arts brought their *b* together
2Ti 4:13 comest, bring with thee, and the *b*
Rev 20:12 and the *b* were opened
Rev 20:12 which were written in the *b*

**BOOTH**
Job 27:18 as a *b* that the keeper maketh
Jonah 4:5 the city, and there made him a *b*

**BOOTHS**
Gen 33:17 house, and made *b* for his cattle
Lev 23:42 Ye shall dwell in *b* seven days
Lev 23:43 children of Israel to dwell in *b*
Neh 8:14 of Israel should dwell in *b* in
Neh 8:15 of thick trees, to make *b*

**BOOTY**
Num 31:32 And the *b*, being the rest of the
Jer 49:32 And their camels shall be a *b*
Zeph 1:13 their goods shall become a *b*

**BOOZ** *(bo'-oz)* See BOAZ. *Greek form of Boaz.*
Mt 1:5 And Salmon begat *B* of Rachab
Lk 3:32 of Obed, which was the son of *B*

**BORDER**
Gen 10:19 the *b* of the Canaanites was from
Gen 49:13 his *b* shall be unto Zidon
Ex 19:12 the mount, or touch the *b* of it
Ex 25:25 thou shalt make unto it a *b* of an
Ex 25:27 Over against the *b* shall the
Ex 28:26 the breastplate in the *b* thereof
Ex 37:12 Also he made thereunto a *b* of an
Ex 37:14 Over against the *b* were the rings
Ex 39:19 the breastplate, upon the *b* of it
Num 20:16 a city in the uttermost of thy *b*
Num 20:21 give Israel passage through his *b*
Num 21:13 for Arnon is the *b* of Moab
Num 21:23 Israel to pass through his *b*
Num 22:36 Moab, which is in the *b* of Arnon
Num 33:44 in Ije-abarim, in the *b* of Moab
Num 34:3 your south *b* shall be the outmost
Num 35:26 the *b* of the city of his refuge
Deut 3:16 the *b* even unto the river Jabbok,
Deut 12:20 LORD thy God shall enlarge thy *b*
Josh 4:19 Gilgal, in the east *b* of Jericho
Josh 12:2 which is the *b* of the children of
Josh 12:5 unto the *b* of the Geshurites and
Josh 13:10 unto the *b* of the children of
Josh 13:11 the *b* of the Geshurites and
Josh 13:23 the *b* of the children of Reuben
Josh 13:26 from Mahanaim unto the *b* of Debir
Josh 15:1 even to the *b* of Edom the
Josh 15:12 the west *b* was to the great sea,
Josh 15:47 the great sea, and the *b* thereof
Josh 16:5 the *b* of the children of Ephraim
Josh 18:12 their *b* on the north side was
Josh 18:19 the outgoings of the *b* were at
Josh 19:10 the *b* of their inheritance was
Josh 19:11 their *b* went up toward the sea,
Josh 19:14 the *b* compasseth it on the north
Josh 19:18 their *b* was toward Jezreel, and
Josh 19:22 of their *b* were at Jordan
Josh 19:25 their *b* was Helkath, and Hali, and
Josh 19:46 Rakkon, with the *b* before Japho
Josh 22:25 hath made Jordan a *b* between us
Josh 24:30 in the *b* of his inheritance in
Judg 2:9 in the *b* of his inheritance in
Judg 7:22 to the *b* of Abel-meholah, unto
Judg 11:18 but came not within the *b* of Moab
1Sa 6:12 them unto the *b* of Beth-shemesh
1Sa 10:2 in the *b* of Benjamin at Zelzah
1Sa 13:18 turned to the way of the *b* that
2Sa 8:3 his *b* at the river Euphrates
1Kin 4:21 and unto the *b* of Egypt
2Kin 3:21 and upward, and stood in the *b*
2Chr 9:26 Philistines, and to the *b* of Egypt
Ps 78:54 them to the *b* of his sanctuary
Prov 15:25 will establish the *b* of the widow
Is 19:19 a pillar at the *b* thereof to the
Is 37:24 enter into the height of his *b*
Jer 31:17 shall come again to their own *b*
Jer 50:26 against her from the utmost *b*
Eze 11:10 will judge you in the *b* of Israel
Eze 29:10 Syene even unto the *b* of Ethiopia
Eze 43:13 the *b* thereof by the edge thereof
Eze 43:17 the *b* about it shall be half a
Eze 43:20 settle, and upon the *b* round about
Eze 45:7 the west *b* unto the east *b*
Eze 47:13 This shall be the *b*, whereby ye
Eze 47:15 this shall be the *b* of the land
Eze 48:1 the *b* of Damascus northward, to
Eze 48:3 by the *b* of Asher, from the east
Eze 48:12 most holy by the *b* of the Levites
Eze 48:21 of the oblation toward the east *b*
Eze 48:21 twenty thousand toward the west *b*
Eze 48:22 the *b* of Benjamin, shall be for
Eze 48:24 by the *b* of Benjamin, from the
Eze 48:27 by the *b* of Zebulun, from the
Joel 3:6 remove them far from their *b*
Amos 1:13 that they might enlarge their *b*
Amos 6:2 their *b* greater than your *b*
Obad 7 have brought thee even to the *b*
Zeph 2:8 themselves against their *b*
Zec 9:2 And Hamath also shall *b* thereby
Mal 1:4 The *b* of wickedness, and, The
Mk 6:56 it were but the *b* of his garment
Lk 8:44 touched the *b* of his garment

**BORDERS**
Gen 23:17 were in all the *b* round about
Gen 47:21 to cities from one end of the *b*
Ex 8:2 I will smite all thy *b* with frogs
Ex 16:35 unto the *b* of the land of Canaan
Ex 34:24 before thee, and enlarge thy *b*
Num 15:38 *b* of their garments throughout
Num 20:17 left, until we have passed thy *b*
Num 21:22 high way, until we be past thy *b*
Num 35:27 the *b* of the city of his refuge
Josh 11:2 in the *b* of Dor on the west,
Josh 13:2 all the *b* of the Philistines, and

Josh 16:2 unto the *b* of Archi to Ataroth
Josh 22:10 they came unto the *b* of Jordan
Josh 22:11 in the *b* of Jordan, at the
1Kin 7:28 they had *b*, and the *b* were
2Kin 16:17 Ahaz cut off the *b* of the bases
2Kin 18:8 the *b* thereof, from the tower of
2Kin 19:23 enter into the lodgings of his *b*
1Chr 5:16 suburbs of Sharon, upon their *b*
1Chr 7:29 by the *b* of the children of
Ps 74:17 hast set all the *b* of the earth
Ps 147:14 He maketh peace in thy *b*, and
Song 1:11 We will make thee *b* of gold with
Is 15:8 is gone round about the *b* of Moab
Is 54:12 all thy *b* of pleasant stones
Is 60:18 nor destruction within thy *b*
Jer 15:13 all thy sins, even in all thy *b*
Jer 17:3 for sin, throughout all thy *b*
Eze 27:4 Thy *b* are in the midst of the
Eze 45:1 in all the *b* thereof round about
Mic 5:6 and when he treadeth within our *b*
Mt 4:13 in the *b* of Zabulon and Nephthalim
Mt 23:5 enlarge the *b* of their garments,
Mk 7:24 arose, and went into the *b* of Tyre

**BORN**
Gen 4:18 And unto Enoch was *b* Irad
Gen 4:26 to him also there was *b* a son
Gen 6:1 and daughters were *b* unto them
Gen 10:1 them were sons *b* after the flood
Gen 10:21 even to him were children *b*
Gen 10:25 And unto Eber were *b* two sons
Gen 14:14 *b* in his own house, three hundred
Gen 15:3 one *b* in my house is mine heir
Gen 17:12 he that is *b* in the house, or
Gen 17:17 Shall a child be *b* unto him that
Gen 17:23 and all that were *b* in his house
Gen 17:27 *b* in the house, and bought with
Gen 21:3 of his son that was *b* unto him
Gen 21:5 when his son Isaac was *b* unto him
Gen 21:7 for I have *b* him a son in his old
Gen 21:9 which she had *b* unto Abraham
Gen 22:20 she hath also *b* children unto thy
Gen 24:15 who was *b* to Bethuel, son of
Gen 29:34 because I have *b* him three sons
Gen 30:20 me, because I have *b* him six sons
Gen 30:25 to pass, when Rachel had *b* Joseph
Gen 31:43 their children which they have *b*
Gen 35:26 which were *b* to him in Padan-aram
Gen 36:5 which were *b* unto him in the land
Gen 41:50 unto Joseph were *b* two sons
Gen 46:20 the land of Egypt were *b* Manasseh
Gen 46:22 of Rachel, which were *b* to Jacob
Gen 46:27 which were *b* him in Egypt, were
Gen 48:5 which were *b* unto thee in the
Ex 1:22 Every son that is *b* ye shall cast
Ex 12:19 be a stranger, or *b* in the land
Ex 12:48 be as one that is *b* in the land
Ex 21:4 she have *b* him sons or daughters
Lev 12:2 conceived seed, and *b* a man child
Lev 12:7 that hath *b* a male or a female
Lev 18:9 mother, whether she be *b* at home
Lev 19:34 be unto you as one *b* among you
Lev 22:11 he that is *b* in his house
Lev 23:42 *b* shall dwell in booths
Lev 24:16 as he that is *b* in the land
Num 9:14 and for him that was *b* in the land
Num 15:13 All that are *b* of the country
Num 15:29 both for him that is *b* among the
Num 26:60 And unto Aaron was *b* Nadab
Deut 21:15 they have *b* him children, both
Josh 5:5 but all the people that were *b* in
Josh 8:33 as he that was *b* among them
Judg 13:8 do unto the child that shall be *b*
Judg 18:29 father, who was *b* unto Israel
Ruth 4:15 thee than seven sons, hath *b* him
Ruth 4:17 saying, There is a son *b* to Naomi
1Sa 2:5 so that the barren hath *b* seven
1Sa 4:20 for thou hast *b* a son
1Sa 17:13 the battle were Eliab the first *b*
2Sa 3:2 unto David were sons *b* in Hebron
2Sa 3:5 These were *b* to David in Hebron
2Sa 5:13 yet sons and daughters *b* to David
2Sa 12:14 the child also that is *b* unto
2Sa 14:27 Absalom there were *b* three sons
2Sa 21:20 he also was *b* to the giant
2Sa 21:22 These four were *b* to the giant in
1Kin 13:2 a child shall be *b* unto the house
1Chr 1:19 And unto Eber were *b* two sons
1Chr 2:3 which three were *b* unto him of
1Chr 2:9 of Hezron, that were *b* unto him
1Chr 3:1 which were *b* unto him in Hebron
1Chr 3:4 These six were *b* unto him in
1Chr 7:21 that were *b* in that land slew
1Chr 20:8 These were *b* unto the giant in
1Chr 26:6 unto Shemaiah his son were sons *b*
Ezr 10:3 wives, and such as are *b* of them
Job 1:2 there were *b* unto him seven sons
Job 3:3 the day perish wherein I was *b*
Job 5:7 Yet man is *b* unto trouble, as the
Job 11:12 though man be *b* like a wild ass's
Job 14:1 Man that is *b* of a woman is of
Job 15:7 Art thou the first man that was *b*
Job 15:14 and he which is *b* of a woman
Job 25:4 he be clean that is *b* of a woman
Job 38:21 thou it, because thou wast then *b*
Ps 22:31 unto a people that shall be *b*
Ps 58:3 go astray as soon as they be *b*
Ps 78:6 the children which should be *b*
Ps 87:4 this man was *b* there
Ps 87:6 people, that this man was *b* there
Prov 17:17 a brother is *b* for adversity
Eccl 2:7 and had servants *b* in my house
Eccl 3:2 A time to be *b*, and a time to die
Eccl 4:14 whereas also he that is *b* in his
Is 9:6 For unto us a child is *b*, unto us
Is 66:8 or shall a nation be *b* at once
Jer 16:3 that are *b* in this place, and
Jer 20:14 Cursed be the day wherein I was *b*
Jer 22:26 country, where ye were not *b*
Eze 16:4 in the day thou wast *b* thy navel
Eze 47:22 you as *b* in the country among the
Hos 2:3 her as in the day that she was *b*
Mt 1:16 of Mary, of whom was *b* Jesus
Mt 2:1 Now when Jesus was *b* in Bethlehem
Mt 2:2 is he that is *b* King of the Jews
Mt 2:4 of them where Christ should be *b*
Mt 11:11 Among them that are *b* of women
Mt 19:12 which were so *b* from their
Mt 26:24 for that man if he had not been *b*
Mk 14:21 that man if he had never been *b*
Lk 1:35 that holy thing which shall be *b*
Lk 2:11 For unto you is *b* this day in the
Lk 7:28 Among those that are *b* of women
Jn 1:13 Which were *b*, not of blood, nor
Jn 3:3 thee, Except a man be *b* again
Jn 3:4 How can a man be *b* when he is old
Jn 3:4 into his mother's womb, and be *b*
Jn 3:5 thee, Except a man be *b* of water
Jn 3:6 That which is *b* of the flesh is
Jn 3:6 that which is *b* of the Spirit is
Jn 3:7 unto thee, Ye must be *b* again
Jn 3:8 every one that is *b* of the Spirit
Jn 8:41 We be not *b* of fornication
Jn 9:2 his parents, that he was *b* blind
Jn 9:19 your son, who ye say was *b* blind
Jn 9:20 our son, and that he was *b* blind
Jn 9:32 the eyes of one that was *b* blind
Jn 9:34 Thou wast altogether *b* in sins
Jn 16:21 that a man is *b* into the world
Jn 18:37 To this end was I *b*, and for this
Acts 2:8 our own tongue, wherein we were *b*
Acts 7:20 In which time Moses was *b*
Acts 18:2 *b* in Pontus, lately come from
Acts 18:24 *b* at Alexandria, an eloquent man,
Acts 22:3 *b* in Tarsus, a city in Cilicia,
Acts 22:28 And Paul said, But I was free *b*
Rom 9:11 (For the children being not yet *b*
1Cor 15:8 as of one *b* out of due time
Gal 4:23 bondwoman was *b* after the flesh
Gal 4:29 But as then he that was *b* after
Gal 4:29 him that was *b* after the Spirit
Heb 11:23 By faith Moses, when he was *b*
1Pet 1:23 Being *b* again, not of corruptible
1Jn 2:29 doeth righteousness is *b* of him
1Jn 3:9 Whosoever is *b* of God doth not
1Jn 3:9 sin, because he is *b* of God
1Jn 4:7 every one that loveth is *b* of God
1Jn 5:1 Jesus is the Christ is *b* of God
1Jn 5:4 For whatsoever is *b* of God
1Jn 5:18 whosoever is *b* of God sinneth not
Rev 12:4 her child as soon as it was *b*

**BORNE**
Ex 25:14 that the ark may be *b* with them
Ex 25:28 that the table may be *b* with them
Judg 16:29 stood, and on which it was *b* up
Job 34:31 I have *b* chastisement, I will not
Ps 55:12 then I could have *b* it
Ps 69:7 for thy sake I have *b* reproach
Is 46:3 which are *b* by me from the belly,
Is 53:4 Surely he hath *b* our griefs
Is 66:12 ye shall be *b* upon her sides, and
Jer 10:5 they must needs be *b*, because
Jer 15:9 She that hath *b* seven languisheth
Jer 15:10 that thou hast *b* me a man of
Lam 3:28 because he hath *b* it upon him
Lam 5:7 we have *b* their iniquities
Eze 16:20 whom thou hast *b* unto me
Eze 16:58 Thou hast *b* thy lewdness and thine
Eze 32:24 yet have they *b* their shame with
Eze 36:6 because ye have *b* the shame of
Eze 39:26 that they have *b* their shame
Amos 5:26 But ye have *b* the tabernacle of
Mt 20:12 unto us, which have *b* the burden
Mt 23:4 heavy burdens and grievous to be *b*
Mk 2:3 of the palsy, which was *b* of four
Lk 11:46 men with burdens grievous to be *b*
Jn 5:37 sent me, hath *b* witness of me
Jn 20:15 Sir, if thou have *b* him hence
Acts 21:35 that he was *b* of the soldiers for
1Cor 15:49 as we have *b* the image of the
3Jn 6 Which have *b* witness of thy
Rev 2:3 And hast *b*, and hast patience, and

**BORROW**
Ex 3:22 woman shall *b* of her neighbour
Ex 11:2 let every man *b* of his neighbour,
Ex 22:14 if a man *b* ought of his neighbour
Deut 15:6 nations, but thou shalt not *b*
Deut 28:12 many nations, and thou shalt not *b*
2Kin 4:3 *b* thee vessels abroad of all thy
Mt 5:42 from him that would *b* of thee

**BORROWED**
Ex 12:35 they *b* of the Egyptians jewels of
2Kin 6:5 for it was *b*
Neh 5:4 We have *b* money for the king's

**BORROWER**
Prov 22:7 the *b* is servant to the lender
Is 24:2 as with the lender, so with the *b*

**BORROWETH**
Ps 37:21 The wicked *b*, and payeth not again

**BOSCATH** *(bos'-cath)* See BOSKETH. *A city in Judah.*
2Kin 22:1 the daughter of Adaiah of *B*

**BOSOM**
Gen 16:5 I have given my maid into thy *b*
Ex 4:6 Put now thine hand into thy *b*
Num 11:12 say unto me, Carry them in thy *b*
Deut 13:6 daughter, or the wife of thy *b*
Deut 28:54 and toward the wife of his *b*
Deut 28:56 evil toward the husband of her *b*
Ruth 4:16 the child, and laid it in her *b*
2Sa 12:3 of his own cup, and lay in his *b*
2Sa 12:8 and thy master's wives into thy *b*
1Kin 1:2 him, and let her lie in thy *b*
1Kin 3:20 and laid her dead child in my *b*
1Kin 17:19 And he took him out of her *b*
Job 31:33 by hiding mine iniquity in my *b*
Ps 35:13 prayer returned into mine own *b*
Ps 74:11 pluck it out of thy *b*
Ps 79:12 into their *b* their reproach
Ps 89:50 how I do bear in my *b* the
Ps 129:7 nor he that bindeth sheaves his *b*
Prov 5:20 embrace the *b* of a stranger
Prov 6:27 Can a man take fire in his *b*
Prov 17:23 man taketh a gift out of the *b* to
Prov 19:24 man hideth his hand in his *b*
Prov 21:14 and a reward in the *b* strong wrath
Prov 26:15 slothful hideth his hand in his *b*
Eccl 7:9 anger resteth in the *b* of fools
Is 40:11 his arm, and carry them in his *b*
Is 65:6 even recompense into their *b*
Is 65:7 their former work into their *b*
Jer 32:18 of the fathers into the *b* of
Lam 2:12 poured out into their mothers' *b*
Mic 7:5 from her that lieth in thy *b*
Lk 6:38 over, shall men give into your *b*
Lk 16:22 by the angels into Abraham's *b*
Lk 16:23 afar off, and Lazarus in his *b*
Jn 1:18 which is in the *b* of the Father
Jn 13:23 on Jesus' *b* one of his disciples

**BOSOR** *(bo'-sor) Greek form of Besor.*
2Pet 2:15 the way of Balaam the son of *B*

**BOTTLE**
Gen 21:14 a *b* of water, and gave it unto
Gen 21:19 went, and filled the *b* with water
Judg 4:19 And she opened a *b* of milk
1Sa 1:24 a *b* of wine, and brought him unto

1Sa 10:3 and another carrying a *b* of wine
1Sa 16:20 a *b* of wine, and a kid, and sent
2Sa 16:1 of summer fruits, and a *b* of wine
Ps 56:8 put thou my tears into thy *b*
Ps 119:83 I am become like a *b* in the smoke
Jer 13:12 Every *b* shall be filled with wine
Jer 13:12 every *b* shall be filled with wine
Jer 19:1 Go and get a potter's earthen *b*
Jer 19:10 Then shalt thou break the *b* in
Hab 2:15 drink, that puttest thy *b* to him

**BOTTLES**
Josh 9:4 sacks upon their asses, and wine *b*
Josh 9:13 these *b* of wine, which we filled,
1Sa 25:18 two *b* of wine, and five sheep
Job 32:19 it is ready to burst like new *b*
Job 38:37 or who can stay the *b* of heaven
Jer 48:12 his vessels, and break their *b*
Hos 7:5 have made him sick with *b* of wine
Mt 9:17 do men put new wine into old *b*
Mk 2:22 man putteth new wine into old *b*
Lk 5:37 man putteth new wine into old *b*

**BOTTOM**
Ex 15:5 they sank into the *b* as a stone
Ex 29:12 blood beside the *b* of the altar
Lev 4:7 the *b* of the altar of the burnt
Lev 4:18 the *b* of the altar of the burnt
Lev 4:25 *b* of the altar of burnt offering
Lev 4:30 thereof at the *b* of the altar
Lev 4:34 thereof at the *b* of the altar
Lev 5:9 wrung out at the *b* of the altar
Lev 8:15 the blood at the *b* of the altar
Lev 9:9 the blood at the *b* of the altar
Job 36:30 it, and covereth the *b* of the sea
Song 3:10 the *b* thereof of gold, the
Eze 43:13 even the *b* shall be a cubit, and
Eze 43:14 from the *b* upon the ground even
Eze 43:17 the *b* thereof shall be a cubit
Dan 6:24 they came at the *b* of the den
Amos 9:3 from my sight in the *b* of the sea
Zec 1:8 myrtle trees that were in the *b*
Mt 27:51 in twain from the top to the *b*
Mk 15:38 in twain from the top to the *b*

**BOTTOMLESS**
Rev 9:1 was given the key of the *b* pit
Rev 9:11 which is the angel of the *b* pit
Rev 11:7 *b* pit shall make war against them
Rev 17:8 and shall ascend out of the *b* pit
Rev 20:1 having the key of the *b* pit
Rev 20:3 And cast him into the *b* pit

**BOUGH**
Gen 49:22 Joseph is a fruitful *b*
Judg 9:48 cut down a *b* from the trees, and
Is 10:33 shall lop the *b* with terror
Is 17:6 in the top of the uppermost *b*
Is 17:9 strong cities be as a forsaken *b*

**BOUGHS**
Lev 23:40 first day the *b* of goodly trees
Deut 24:20 shalt not go over the *b* again
2Sa 18:9 under the thick *b* of a great oak
Job 14:9 bring forth *b* like a plant
Ps 80:10 the *b* thereof were like the
Ps 80:11 She sent out her *b* unto the sea
Song 7:8 I will take hold of the *b* thereof
Is 27:11 When the *b* thereof are withered,
Eze 17:23 and it shall bring forth *b*
Eze 31:3 and his top was among the thick *b*
Eze 31:10 shot up his top among the thick *b*
Eze 31:12 his *b* are broken by all the
Eze 31:14 up their top among the thick *b*
Dan 4:12 the heaven dwelt in the *b* thereof

**BOUGHT**
Gen 17:12 or *b* with money of any stranger,
Gen 17:23 all that were *b* with his money,
Gen 17:27 *b* with money of the stranger,
Gen 33:19 he *b* a parcel of a field, where
Gen 39:1 *b* him of the hands of the
Gen 47:14 Canaan, for the corn which they *b*
Gen 47:20 Joseph *b* all the land of Egypt
Gen 47:22 the land of the priests *b* he not
Gen 49:30 which Abraham *b* with the field of
Gen 50:13 which Abraham *b* with the field
Ex 12:44 man's servant that is *b* for money
Lev 25:28 *b* it until the year of jubile
Lev 25:30 for ever to him that *b* it
Lev 25:50 *b* him from the year that he was
Lev 25:51 of the money that he was *b* for
Lev 27:22 the LORD a field which he hath *b*
Lev 27:24 return unto him of whom it was *b*
Deut 32:6 he thy father that hath *b* thee
Josh 24:32 a parcel of ground which Jacob *b*
Ruth 4:9 that I have *b* all that was
2Sa 12:3 little ewe lamb, which he had *b*
2Sa 24:24 So David *b* the threshingfloor and
1Kin 16:24 he *b* the hill Samaria of Shemer
Neh 5:16 this wall, neither *b* we any land
Is 43:24 Thou hast *b* me no sweet cane with
Jer 32:9 I *b* the field of Hanameel my
Jer 32:43 And fields shall be *b* in this land
Hos 3:2 So I *b* her to me for fifteen
Mt 13:46 and sold all that he had, and *b* it
Mt 21:12 *b* in the temple, and overthrew the
Mt 27:7 *b* with them the potter's field,
Mk 11:15 *b* in the temple, and overthrew the
Mk 15:46 he *b* fine linen, and took him down
Mk 16:1 had *b* sweet spices, that they
Lk 14:18 I have *b* a piece of ground, and I
Lk 17:28 they did eat, they drank, they *b*
Lk 19:45 that sold therein, and them that *b*
Acts 7:16 in the sepulchre that Abraham *b*
1Cor 6:20 For ye are *b* with a price
1Cor 7:23 Ye are *b* with a price
2Pet 2:1 even denying the Lord that *b* them

**BOUND**
Gen 22:9 *b* Isaac his son, and laid him on
Gen 38:28 *b* upon his hand a scarlet thread,
Gen 39:20 where the king's prisoners were *b*
Gen 40:3 the place where Joseph was *b*
Gen 40:5 which were *b* in the prison
Gen 42:19 be *b* in the house of your prison
Gen 42:24 and *b* him before their eyes
Gen 44:30 life is *b* up in the lad's life
Gen 49:26 utmost *b* of the everlasting hills
Ex 12:34 their kneadingtroughs being *b* up
Lev 8:7 ephod, and *b* it unto him therewith
Num 19:15 which hath no covering *b* upon it
Num 30:4 wherewith she hath *b* her soul
Num 30:4 she hath *b* her soul shall stand
Num 30:11 she *b* her soul shall stand
Josh 2:21 she *b* the scarlet line in the
Josh 9:4 bottles, old, and rent, and *b* up
Judg 15:13 they *b* him with two new cords, and
Judg 16:6 mightest be *b* to afflict thee
Judg 16:8 dried, and she *b* him with them
Judg 16:10 wherewith thou mightest be *b*
Judg 16:13 me wherewith thou mightest be *b*
Judg 16:21 *b* him with fetters of brass
1Sa 25:29 the soul of my lord shall be *b* in
2Sa 3:34 Thy hands were not *b*, nor thy
2Kin 5:23 *b* two talents of silver in two
2Kin 17:4 shut him up, and *b* him in prison
2Kin 25:7 *b* him with fetters of brass, and
2Chr 33:11 *b* him with fetters, and carried
2Chr 36:6 *b* him in fetters, to carry him to
Job 36:8 And if they be *b* in fetters
Job 38:20 take it to the *b* thereof, and that
Ps 68:6 out those which are *b* with chains
Ps 104:9 Thou hast set a *b* that they may
Ps 107:10 being *b* in affliction and iron
Prov 22:15 Foolishness is *b* in the heart of
Prov 30:4 who hath *b* the waters in a
Is 1:6 not been closed, neither *b* up
Is 22:3 they are *b* by the archers
Is 61:1 of the prison to them that are *b*
Jer 5:22 the *b* of the sea by a perpetual
Jer 30:13 cause, that thou mayest be *b* up
Jer 39:7 *b* him with chains, to carry him
Jer 40:1 when he had taken him being *b* in
Jer 52:11 king of Babylon *b* him in chains
Lam 1:14 transgressions is *b* by his hand
Eze 27:24 *b* with cords, and made of cedar,
Eze 30:21 it shall not be *b* up to be healed
Eze 34:4 neither have ye *b* up that which
Dan 3:21 these men were *b* in their coats
Dan 3:23 fell down *b* into the midst of the
Dan 3:24 Did not we cast three men *b* into
Hos 4:19 The wind hath *b* her up in her
Hos 5:10 were like them that remove the *b*
Hos 7:15 Though I have *b* and strengthened
Hos 13:12 The iniquity of Ephraim is *b* up
Nah 3:10 her great men were *b* in chains
Mt 14:3 *b* him, and put him in prison for
Mt 16:19 on earth shall be *b* in heaven
Mt 18:18 on earth shall be *b* in heaven
Mt 27:2 And when they had *b* him, they led
Mk 5:4 he had been often *b* with fetters
Mk 6:17 *b* him in prison for Herodias'
Mk 15:1 *b* Jesus, and carried him away, and
Mk 15:7 which lay *b* with them that had
Lk 8:29 and he was kept *b* with chains
Lk 10:34 *b* up his wounds, pouring in oil
Lk 13:16 of Abraham, whom Satan hath *b*
Jn 11:44 *b* hand and foot with graveclothes
Jn 18:12 of the Jews took Jesus, and *b* him,
Jn 18:24 Now Annas had sent him *b* unto
Acts 9:2 might bring them *b* unto Jerusalem
Acts 9:21 them *b* unto the chief priests
Acts 12:6 two soldiers, *b* with two chains
Acts 20:22 I go *b* in the spirit unto
Acts 21:11 *b* his own hands and feet, and said,
Acts 21:13 for I am ready not to be *b* only
Acts 21:33 him to be *b* with two chains
Acts 22:5 which were there *b* unto Jerusalem
Acts 22:25 as they *b* him with thongs, Paul
Acts 22:29 a Roman, and because he had *b* him
Acts 23:12 *b* themselves under a curse,
Acts 23:14 We have *b* ourselves under a great
Acts 23:21 which have *b* themselves with an
Acts 24:27 the Jews a pleasure, left Paul *b*
Acts 28:20 of Israel I am *b* with this chain
Rom 7:2 is *b* by the law to her husband so
1Cor 7:27 Art thou *b* unto a wife
1Cor 7:39 The wife is *b* by the law as long
2Th 1:3 We are *b* to thank God always for
2Th 2:13 But we are *b* to give thanks alway
2Ti 2:9 but the word of God is not *b*
Heb 13:3 that are in bonds, as *b* with them
Rev 9:14 *b* in the great river Euphrates
Rev 20:2 Satan, and *b* him a thousand years,

**BOUNDS**
Ex 19:12 thou shalt set *b* unto the people
Ex 19:23 Set *b* about the mount, and
Ex 23:31 I will set thy *b* from the Red sea
Deut 32:8 he set the *b* of the people
Job 14:5 his *b* that he cannot pass
Job 26:10 hath compassed the waters with *b*
Is 10:13 have removed the *b* of the people
Acts 17:26 the *b* of their habitation

**BOUNTIFUL**
Prov 22:9 He that hath a *b* eye shall be
Is 32:5 nor the churl said to be *b*

**BOUNTIFULLY**
Ps 13:6 because he hath dealt *b* with me
Ps 116:7 the LORD hath dealt *b* with thee
Ps 119:17 Deal *b* with thy servant, that I
Ps 142:7 for thou shalt deal *b* with me
2Cor 9:6 soweth *b* shall reap also *b*

**BOUNTY**
1Kin 10:13 Solomon gave her of his royal *b*
2Cor 9:5 you, and make up beforehand your *b*

**BOW** See also WORSHIP.
Gen 9:13 I do set my *b* in the cloud, and it
Gen 9:16 the *b* shall be in the cloud
Gen 27:3 thy weapons, thy quiver and thy *b*
Gen 27:29 thee, and nations *b* down to thee
Gen 37:10 thy brethren indeed come to *b*
Gen 41:43 they cried before him, *B* the knee
Gen 48:22 with my sword and with my *b*
Gen 49:8 children shall *b* down before thee
Gen 49:24 But his *b* abode in strength, and
Ex 11:8 *b* down themselves unto me, saying
Ex 20:5 Thou shalt not *b* down thyself to
Ex 23:24 Thou shalt not *b* down to their
Lev 26:1 in your land, to *b* down unto it
Deut 5:9 Thou shalt not *b* down thyself
Josh 23:7 nor *b* yourselves unto them
Josh 24:12 with thy sword, nor with thy *b*
Judg 2:19 them, and to *b* down unto them
1Sa 18:4 even to his sword, and to his *b*
2Sa 1:18 of Judah the use of the *b*
2Sa 1:22 the *b* of Jonathan turned not back
2Sa 22:35 so that a *b* of steel is broken by
1Kin 22:34 certain man drew a *b* at a venture
2Kin 5:18 I *b* myself in the house of Rimmon
2Kin 6:22 with thy sword and with thy *b*
2Kin 9:24 Jehu drew a *b* with his full
2Kin 13:15 And Elisha said unto him, Take *b*
2Kin 13:16 Israel, Put thine hand upon the *b*
2Kin 17:35 nor *b* yourselves to them, nor
2Kin 19:16 *b* down thine ear, and hear
1Chr 5:18 and sword, and to shoot with *b*
1Chr 12:2 and shooting arrows out of a *b*
2Chr 17:17 and with him armed men with *b*
2Chr 18:33 certain man drew a *b* at a venture
Job 20:24 the *b* of steel shall strike him
Job 29:20 my *b* was renewed in my hand

Job 31:10 let others *b* down upon her
Job 39:3 They *b* themselves, they bring
Ps 7:12 he hath bent his *b*, and made it
Ps 11:2 For, lo, the wicked bend their *b*
Ps 18:34 so that a *b* of steel is broken by
Ps 22:29 to the dust shall *b* before him
Ps 31:2 *B* down thine ear to me
Ps 37:14 the sword, and have bent their *b*
Ps 44:6 For I will not trust in my *b*
Ps 46:9 he breaketh the *b*, and cutteth the
Ps 58:7 bendeth his *b* to shoot his arrows
Ps 72:9 the wilderness shall *b* before him
Ps 76:3 brake he the arrows of the *b*
Ps 78:57 turned aside like a deceitful *b*
Ps 86:1 *B* down thine ear, O LORD, hear me
Ps 95:6 O come, let us worship and *b* down
Ps 144:5 *B* thy heavens, O LORD, and come
Prov 5:1 *b* thine ear to my understanding
Prov 14:19 The evil *b* before the good
Prov 22:17 *B* down thine ear, and hear the
Eccl 12:3 the strong men shall *b* themselves
Is 10:4 Without me they shall *b* down
Is 21:15 drawn sword, and from the bent *b*
Is 41:2 and as driven stubble to his *b*
Is 45:23 That unto me every knee shall *b*
Is 46:2 They stoop, they *b* down together
Is 49:23 they shall *b* down to thee with
Is 51:23 *B* down, that we may go over
Is 58:5 is it to *b* down his head as a
Is 60:14 they that despised thee shall *b*
Is 65:12 ye shall all *b* down to the
Is 66:19 Pul, and Lud, that draw the *b*
Jer 6:23 They shall lay hold on *b* and spear
Jer 9:3 tongues like their *b* for lies
Jer 46:9 that handle and bend the *b*
Jer 49:35 I will break the *b* of Elam
Jer 50:14 all ye that bend the *b*, shoot at
Jer 50:29 all ye that bend the *b*, camp
Jer 50:42 They shall hold the *b* and the
Jer 51:3 bendeth let the archer bend his *b*
Lam 2:4 He hath bent his *b* like an enemy
Lam 3:12 He hath bent his *b*, and set me as
Eze 1:28 As the appearance of the *b* that
Eze 39:3 I will smite thy *b* out of thy
Hos 1:5 that I will break the *b* of Israel
Hos 1:7 God, and will not save them by *b*
Hos 2:18 and I will break the *b* and the
Hos 7:16 they are like a deceitful *b*
Amos 2:15 he stand that handleth the *b*
Mic 6:6 *b* myself before the high God
Hab 3:6 the perpetual hills did *b*
Hab 3:9 Thy *b* was made quite naked,
Zec 9:10 the battle *b* shall be cut off
Zec 9:13 filled the *b* with Ephraim, and
Zec 10:4 the nail, out of him the battle *b*
Rom 11:10 see, and *b* down their back alway
Rom 14:11 Lord, every knee shall *b* to me
Eph 3:14 For this cause I *b* my knees unto
Phil 2:10 name of Jesus every knee should *b*
Rev 6:2 and he that sat on him had a *b*

## BOWED

Gen 18:2 *b* himself toward the ground,
Gen 19:1 he *b* himself with his face toward
Gen 23:7 *b* himself to the people of the
Gen 23:12 Abraham *b* down himself before the
Gen 24:26 the man *b* down his head, and
Gen 24:48 I *b* down my head, and worshipped
Gen 33:3 *b* himself to the ground seven
Gen 42:6 *b* down themselves before him with
Gen 43:26 *b* themselves to him to the earth
Gen 43:28 they *b* down their heads, and made
Gen 47:31 Israel *b* himself upon the bed's
Gen 48:12 he *b* himself with his face to the
Gen 49:15 *b* his shoulder to bear, and became
Ex 4:31 then they *b* their heads and
Ex 12:27 And the people *b* the head and
Ex 34:8 *b* his head toward the earth, and
Num 22:31 he *b* down his head, and fell flat
Num 25:2 did eat, and *b* down to their gods
Josh 23:16 gods, and *b* yourselves to them
Judg 2:12 *b* themselves unto them, and
Judg 2:17 gods, and *b* themselves unto them
Judg 5:27 At her feet he *b*, he fell, he lay
Judg 7:6 *b* down upon their knees to drink
Judg 16:30 he *b* himself with all his might
Ruth 2:10 *b* herself to the ground, and said
1Sa 4:19 she *b* herself and travailed
1Sa 20:41 ground, and *b* himself three times
1Sa 24:8 face to the earth, and *b* himself
1Sa 25:23 face, and *b* herself to the ground,
1Sa 25:41 *b* herself on her face to the
1Sa 28:14 face to the ground, and *b* himself
2Sa 9:8 he *b* himself, and said, What is
2Sa 14:22 *b* himself, and thanked the king
2Sa 14:33 *b* himself on his face to the
2Sa 18:21 Cushi *b* himself unto Joab, and ran
2Sa 19:14 he *b* the heart of all the men of
2Sa 22:10 He *b* the heavens also, and came
2Sa 24:20 *b* himself before the king on his
1Kin 1:16 And Bath-sheba *b*, and did obeisance
1Kin 1:23 he *b* himself before the king with
1Kin 1:31 Then Bath-sheba *b* with her face
1Kin 1:47 the king *b* himself upon the bed
1Kin 1:53 *b* himself to king Solomon
1Kin 2:19 *b* himself unto her, and sat down
1Kin 19:18 knees which have not *b* unto Baal
2Kin 2:15 *b* themselves to the ground before
2Kin 4:37 *b* herself to the ground, and took
1Chr 21:21 *b* himself to David with his face
1Chr 29:20 *b* down their heads, and worshipped
2Chr 7:3 they *b* themselves with their
2Chr 20:18 Jehoshaphat *b* his head with his
2Chr 25:14 *b* down himself before them, and
2Chr 29:29 present with him *b* themselves
2Chr 29:30 they *b* their heads and worshipped
Neh 8:6 they *b* their heads, and worshipped
Est 3:2 that were in the king's gate, *b*
Est 3:5 Haman saw that Mordecai *b* not
Ps 18:9 He *b* the heavens also, and came
Ps 35:14 I *b* down heavily, as one that
Ps 38:6 I am *b* down greatly
Ps 44:25 For our soul is *b* down to the
Ps 57:6 my soul is *b* down
Ps 145:14 up all those that be *b* down
Ps 146:8 LORD raiseth them that are *b* down
Is 2:11 of men shall be *b* down, and the
Is 2:17 loftiness of man shall be *b* down
Is 21:3 I was *b* down at the hearing of it
Mt 27:29 they *b* the knee before him, and
Lk 13:11 was *b* together, and could in no
Lk 24:5 *b* down their faces to the earth,
Jn 19:30 he *b* his head, and gave up the
Rom 11:4 who have not *b* the knee to the

## BOWELS

Gen 15:4 thine own *b* shall be thine heir
Gen 25:23 shall be separated from thy *b*
Gen 43:30 for his *b* did yearn upon his
Num 5:22 the curse shall go into thy *b*
2Sa 7:12 which shall proceed out of thy *b*
2Sa 16:11 my son, which came forth of my *b*
2Sa 20:10 shed out his *b* to the ground, and
1Kin 3:26 for her *b* yearned upon her son,
2Chr 21:15 sickness by disease of thy *b*
2Chr 21:18 his *b* with an incurable disease
2Chr 21:19 his *b* fell out by reason of his
2Chr 32:21 *b* slew him there with the sword
Job 20:14 Yet his meat in his *b* is turned
Job 30:27 My *b* boiled, and rested not
Ps 22:14 it is melted in the midst of my *b*
Ps 71:6 that took me out of my mother's *b*
Ps 109:18 let it come into his *b* like water
Song 5:4 door, and my *b* were moved for him
Is 16:11 Wherefore my *b* shall sound like
Is 48:19 the offspring of thy *b* like the
Is 49:1 from the *b* of my mother hath he
Is 63:15 strength, the sounding of thy *b*
Jer 4:19 My *b*, my *b*
Jer 31:20 therefore my *b* are troubled for
Lam 1:20 my *b* are troubled
Lam 2:11 my *b* are troubled, my liver is
Eze 3:3 fill thy *b* with this roll that I
Eze 7:19 their souls, neither fill their *b*
Acts 1:18 midst, and all his *b* gushed out
2Cor 6:12 ye are straitened in your own *b*
Phil 1:8 you all in the *b* of Jesus Christ
Phil 2:1 of the Spirit, if any *b* and
Col 3:12 beloved, *b* of mercies, kindness,
Philem 7 because the *b* of the saints are
Philem 12 receive him, that is, mine own *b*
Philem 20 refresh my *b* in the Lord
1Jn 3:17 shutteth up his *b* of compassion

## BOWETH

Judg 7:5 likewise every one that *b* down
Is 2:9 And the mean man *b* down, and the
Is 46:1 Bel *b* down, Nebo stoopeth, their

## BOWING

Gen 24:52 the LORD, *b* himself to the earth
Ps 17:11 their eyes *b* down to the earth
Ps 62:3 as a *b* wall shall ye be, and as a
Mk 15:19 *b* their knees worshipped him

## BOWL

Num 7:13 one silver *b* of seventy shekels,
Num 7:43 a silver *b* of seventy shekels,
Num 7:49 one silver *b* of seventy shekels,
Num 7:85 and thirty shekels, each *b* seventy
Judg 6:38 of the fleece, a *b* full of water
Eccl 12:6 loosed, or the golden *b* be broken
Zec 4:2 with a *b* upon the top of it, and

## BOWLS

Ex 25:29 *b* thereof, to cover withal
Ex 25:31 his shaft, and his branches, his *b*
Ex 37:16 dishes, and his spoons, and his *b*
Ex 37:19 Three *b* made after the fashion of
Ex 37:20 were four *b* made like almonds
Num 4:7 dishes, and the spoons, and the *b*
Num 7:84 of silver, twelve silver *b*
1Kin 7:41 the two *b* of the chapiters that
1Kin 7:42 to cover the two *b* of the
1Kin 7:50 And the *b*, and the snuffers, and the
2Kin 12:13 the house of the LORD *b* of silver
2Kin 25:15 And the firepans, and the *b*
1Chr 28:17 gold for the fleshhooks, and the *b*
Jer 52:18 and the snuffers, and the *b*
Amos 6:6 That drink wine in *b*, and anoint
Zec 9:15 and they shall be filled like *b*
Zec 14:20 be like the *b* before the altar

## BOWS

1Sa 2:4 The *b* of the mighty men are
1Chr 12:2 They were armed with *b*, and could
2Chr 14:8 that bare shields and drew *b*
2Chr 26:14 and helmets, and habergeons, and *b*
Neh 4:13 swords, their spears, and their *b*
Neh 4:16 the spears, the shields, and the *b*
Ps 37:15 heart, and their *b* shall be broken
Ps 64:3 bend their *b* to shoot their
Ps 78:9 being armed, and carrying *b*
Is 5:28 are sharp, and all their *b* bent
Is 7:24 with *b* shall men come thither
Is 13:18 Their *b* also shall dash the young
Jer 51:56 every one of their *b* is broken
Eze 39:9 shields and the bucklers, the *b*

## BOX

2Kin 9:1 take this *b* of oil in thine hand,
2Kin 9:3 Then take the *b* of oil, and pour
Is 41:19 the pine, and the *b* tree together
Is 60:13 the *b* together, to beautify the
Mt 26:7 *b* of very precious ointment
Mk 14:3 a woman having an alabaster *b* of
Lk 7:37 an alabaster *b* of ointment

## BOYS

Gen 25:27 And the *b* grew
Zec 8:5 of the city shall be full of *b*

## BOZEZ *(bo'-zez) A rock near Michmash.*

1Sa 14:4 and the name of the one was *B*

## BOZKATH *(boz'-kath) A city in Judah.*

Josh 15:39 Lachish, and *B*, and Eglon,

## BOZRAH *(boz'-rah)*

*1. The capital city of Edom.*
Gen 36:33 Zerah of *B* reigned in his stead
1Chr 1:44 Zerah of *B* reigned in his stead
Is 34:6 the LORD hath a sacrifice in *B*
Is 63:1 Edom, with dyed garments from *B*
Jer 49:13 that *B* shall become a desolation,
Jer 49:22 eagle, and spread his wings over *B*
Amos 1:12 shall devour the palaces of *B*
Mic 2:12 them together as the sheep of *B*
*2. A place in Moab.*
Jer 48:24 And upon Kerioth, and upon *B*

## BRACELETS

Gen 24:22 two *b* for her hands of ten
Gen 24:30 *b* upon his sister's hands, and
Gen 24:47 her face, and the *b* upon her hands
Gen 38:18 And she said, Thy signet, and thy *b*
Gen 38:25 whose are these, the signet, and *b*
Ex 35:22 willing hearted, and brought *b*
Num 31:50 of jewels of gold, chains, and *b*
Is 3:19 The chains, and the *b*, and the
Eze 16:11 I put *b* upon thy hands, and a
Eze 23:42 which put *b* upon their hands, and

## BRAKE

Ex 9:25 *b* every tree of the field
Ex 32:3 all the people *b* off the golden
Ex 32:19 and *b* them beneath the mount
Deut 9:17 hands, and *b* them before your eyes

Judg 7:19 *b* the pitchers that were in their
Judg 9:53 head, and all to *b* his skull
Judg 16:9 he *b* the withs, as a thread of
Judg 16:12 he *b* them from off his arms like
1Sa 4:18 side of the gate, and his neck *b*
2Sa 23:16 the three mighty men *b* through
1Kin 19:11 *b* in pieces the rocks before the
2Kin 10:27 *b* down the house of Baal, and made
2Kin 11:18 the house of Baal, and *b* it down
2Kin 14:13 *b* down the wall of Jerusalem from
2Kin 18:4 *b* the images, and cut down the
2Kin 23:7 he *b* down the houses of the
2Kin 23:8 *b* down the high places of the
2Kin 23:12 *b* them down from thence, and cast
2Kin 23:14 he *b* in pieces the images, and cut
2Kin 23:15 altar and the high place he *b* down
2Kin 25:10 *b* down the walls of Jerusalem
1Chr 11:18 the three *b* through the host of
2Chr 14:3 *b* down the images, and cut down
2Chr 21:17 *b* into it, and carried away all
2Chr 25:23 *b* down the wall of Jerusalem from
2Chr 26:6 *b* down the wall of Gath, and the
2Chr 31:1 *b* the images in pieces, and cut
2Chr 34:4 they *b* down the altars of Baalim
2Chr 36:19 *b* down the wall of Jerusalem, and
Job 29:17 I *b* the jaws of the wicked, and
Job 38:8 sea with doors, when it *b* forth
Job 38:10 *b* up for it my decreed place, and
Ps 76:3 There *b* he the arrows of the bow,
Ps 105:16 he *b* the whole staff of bread
Ps 105:33 *b* the trees of their coasts
Ps 106:29 the plague *b* in upon them
Ps 107:14 death, and *b* their bands in sunder
Jer 28:10 prophet Jeremiah's neck, and *b* it
Jer 31:32 which my covenant they *b*,
Jer 39:8 *b* down the walls of Jerusalem
Jer 52:14 *b* down all the walls of Jerusalem
Jer 52:17 of the LORD, the Chaldeans *b*
Eze 17:16 despised, and whose covenant he *b*
Dan 2:1 troubled, and his sleep *b* from him
Dan 2:34 iron and clay, and *b* them to pieces
Dan 2:45 that it *b* in pieces the iron, the
Dan 6:24 *b* all their bones in pieces or
Dan 7:7 *b* in pieces, and stamped the
Dan 7:19 *b* in pieces, and stamped the
Dan 8:7 smote the ram, and *b* his two horns
Mt 14:19 up to heaven, he blessed, and *b*
Mt 15:36 *b* them, and gave to his disciples,
Mt 26:26 *b* it, and gave it to the disciples
Mk 6:41 *b* the loaves, and gave them to his
Mk 8:6 loaves, and gave thanks, and *b*
Mk 8:19 When I *b* the five loaves among
Mk 14:3 she *b* the box, and poured it on
Mk 14:22 *b* it and gave to them, and said,
Lk 5:6 and their net *b*
Lk 8:29 he *b* the bands, and was driven of
Lk 9:16 to heaven, he blessed them, and *b*
Lk 22:19 *b* it, and gave unto them, saying,
Lk 24:30 took bread, and blessed it, and *b*
Jn 19:32 *b* the legs of the first, and of
Jn 19:33 dead already, they *b* not his legs
1Cor 11:24 when he had given thanks, he *b* it

### BRAKEST
Ex 34:1 in the first tables, which thou *b*
Deut 10:2 in the first tables which thou *b*
Ps 74:13 thou *b* the heads of the dragons
Ps 74:14 Thou *b* the heads of leviathan in
Eze 29:7 they leaned upon thee, thou *b*

### BRAMBLE
Judg 9:14 said all the trees unto the *b*
Judg 9:15 the *b* said unto the trees, If in
Lk 6:44 nor of a *b* bush gather they

### BRANCH
Ex 25:33 with a knop and a flower in one *b*
Ex 37:17 his shaft, and his *b*, his bowls,
Ex 37:19 the fashion of almonds in one *b*
Num 13:23 cut down from thence a *b* with one
Job 8:16 his *b* shooteth forth in his
Job 14:7 that the tender *b* thereof will
Job 15:32 time, and his *b* shall not be green
Job 18:16 and above shall his *b* be cut off
Job 29:19 the dew lay all night upon my *b*
Ps 80:15 the *b* that thou madest strong for
Prov 11:28 righteous shall flourish as a *b*
Is 4:2 In that day shall the *b* of the
Is 9:14 off from Israel head and tail, *b*
Is 11:1 a *B* shall grow out of his roots
Is 14:19 of thy grave like an abominable *b*
Is 17:9 forsaken bough, and an uppermost *b*
Is 19:15 head or tail, *b* or rush, may do
Is 25:5 the *b* of the terrible ones shall
Is 60:21 the *b* of my planting, the work of
Jer 23:5 raise unto David a righteous *B*
Jer 33:15 that time, will I cause the *B* of
Eze 8:17 they put the *b* to their nose
Eze 15:2 or than a *b* which is among the
Eze 17:3 took the highest *b* of the cedar
Eze 17:22 the highest *b* of the high cedar
Dan 11:7 But out of a *b* of her roots shall
Zec 3:8 will bring forth my servant the *B*
Zec 6:12 the man whose name is The *B*
Mal 4:1 leave them neither root nor *b*
Mt 24:32 When his *b* is yet tender, and
Mk 13:28 When her *b* is yet tender, and
Jn 15:2 Every *b* in me that beareth not
Jn 15:2 every *b* that beareth fruit, he
Jn 15:4 As the *b* cannot bear fruit of
Jn 15:6 in me, he is cast forth as a *b*

### BRANCHES
Gen 40:10 And in the vine were three *b*
Gen 40:12 The three *b* are three days
Gen 49:22 whose *b* run over the wall
Ex 25:31 his shaft, and his *b*, his bowls,
Ex 25:32 six *b* shall come out of the sides
Ex 25:35 be a knop under two *b* of the same
Ex 25:35 according to the six *b* that
Ex 25:36 their *b* shall be of the same
Ex 37:18 six *b* going out of the sides
Ex 37:21 And a knop under two *b* of the same
Lev 23:40 *b* of palm trees, and the boughs of
Neh 8:15 fetch olive *b*, and pine *b*
Job 15:30 the flame shall dry up his *b*
Ps 80:11 the sea, and her *b* unto the river
Ps 104:12 which sing among the *b*
Is 16:8 her *b* are stretched out, they are
Is 17:6 in the outmost fruitful *b* thereof
Is 18:5 and take away and cut down the *b*
Is 27:10 down, and consume the *b* thereof
Jer 11:16 it, and the *b* of it are broken
Eze 17:6 whose *b* turned toward him, and the
Eze 17:23 in the shadow of the *b* thereof
Eze 19:10 full of *b* by reason of many
Eze 19:11 with the multitude of her *b*
Eze 19:14 is gone out of a rod of her *b*
Eze 31:3 a cedar in Lebanon with fair *b*
Eze 31:5 his *b* became long because of the
Eze 31:12 all the valleys his *b* are fallen
Eze 31:13 of the field shall be upon his *b*
Eze 36:8 ye shall shoot forth your *b*
Dan 4:14 down the tree, and cut off his *b*
Dan 4:21 upon whose *b* the fowls of the
Hos 11:6 cities, and shall consume his *b*
Hos 14:6 His *b* shall spread, and his beauty
Joel 1:7 the *b* thereof are made white
Nah 2:2 them out, and marred their vine *b*
Zec 4:12 What be these two olive *b* which
Mt 13:32 come and lodge in the *b* thereof
Mt 21:8 others cut down *b* from the trees
Mk 4:32 herbs, and shooteth out great *b*
Mk 11:8 others cut down *b* off the trees
Lk 13:19 of the air lodged in the *b* of it
Jn 12:13 Took *b* of palm trees, and went
Jn 15:5 I am the vine, ye are the *b*
Rom 11:16 if the root be holy, so are the *b*
Rom 11:21 if God spared not the natural *b*
Rom 11:24 these, which be the natural *b*

### BRASEN
Ex 27:4 four *b* rings in the four corners
Ex 35:16 burnt offering, with his *b* grate
Ex 38:4 he made for the altar a *b* grate
Ex 38:10 twenty, and their *b* sockets twenty
Ex 38:30 the *b* altar, and the *b* grate
Ex 39:39 The *b* altar, and his grate of
Lev 6:28 and if it be sodden in a *b* pot
Num 16:39 the priest took the *b* censers
1Kin 4:13 great cities with walls and *b* bars
1Kin 7:30 And every base had four *b* wheels
1Kin 8:64 because the *b* altar that was
1Kin 14:27 made in their stead *b* shields
2Kin 16:14 And he brought also the *b* altar
2Kin 16:17 off the *b* oxen that were under it
2Kin 18:4 brake in pieces the *b* serpent
2Kin 25:13 the *b* sea that was in the house
1Chr 18:8 wherewith Solomon made the *b* sea
2Chr 1:5 Moreover the *b* altar, that
2Chr 1:6 to the *b* altar before the LORD
2Chr 6:13 For Solomon had made a *b* scaffold
2Chr 7:7 because the *b* altar which Solomon
Jer 1:18 *b* walls against the whole land,
Jer 15:20 unto this people a fenced *b* wall
Jer 52:17 the *b* sea that was in the house
Jer 52:20 twelve *b* bulls that were under
Eze 9:2 in, and stood beside the *b* altar
Mk 7:4 and pots, *b* vessels, and of tables

### BRASS
Gen 4:22 of every artificer in *b* and iron
Ex 25:3 gold, and silver, and *b*,
Ex 26:11 thou shalt make fifty taches of *b*
Ex 26:37 cast five sockets of *b* for them
Ex 27:2 and thou shalt overlay it with *b*
Ex 27:10 twenty sockets shall be of *b*
Ex 27:17 of silver, and their sockets of *b*
Ex 30:18 Thou shalt also make a laver of *b*
Ex 31:4 in gold, and in silver, and in *b*
Ex 35:24 *b* brought the LORD's offering
Ex 35:32 in gold, and in silver, and in *b*
Ex 36:18 he made fifty taches of *b* to
Ex 36:38 but their five sockets were of *b*
Ex 38:2 and he overlaid it with *b*
Ex 38:8 and the foot of it of *b*
Ex 38:11 and their sockets of *b* twenty
Ex 38:17 sockets for the pillars were of *b*
Ex 38:19 four, and their sockets of *b* four
Ex 38:29 the *b* of the offering was seventy
Ex 39:39 brasen altar, and his grate of *b*
Lev 26:19 as iron, and your earth as *b*
Num 21:9 And Moses made a serpent of *b*
Num 31:22 the gold, and the silver, the *b*
Deut 8:9 of whose hills thou mayest dig *b*
Deut 28:23 that is over thy head shall be *b*
Deut 33:25 Thy shoes shall be iron and *b*
Josh 6:19 silver, and gold, and vessels of *b*
Josh 6:24 and the gold, and the vessels of *b*
Josh 22:8 silver, and with gold, and with *b*
Judg 16:21 and bound him with fetters of *b*
1Sa 17:5 had an helmet of *b* upon his head
1Sa 17:38 put an helmet of *b* upon his head
2Sa 8:8 king David took exceeding much *b*
2Sa 21:16 hundred shekels of *b* in weight
1Kin 7:14 was a man of Tyre, a worker in *b*
1Kin 7:27 And he made ten bases of *b*
1Kin 7:30 brasen wheels, and plates of *b*
1Kin 7:38 Then made he ten lavers of *b*
1Kin 7:45 of the LORD, were of bright *b*
2Kin 25:7 and bound him with fetters of *b*
2Kin 25:13 the pillars of *b* that were in the
1Chr 18:8 brought David very much *b*
1Chr 22:3 *b* in abundance without weight
1Chr 22:14 and of *b* and iron without weight
1Chr 29:2 and the *b* for things of *b*
1Chr 29:7 of *b* eighteen thousand talents,
2Chr 2:7 in gold, and in silver, and in *b*
2Chr 2:14 work in gold, and in silver, in *b*
2Chr 4:1 Moreover he made an altar of *b*
2Chr 4:9 overlaid the doors of them with *b*
2Chr 4:16 the house of the LORD of bright *b*
2Chr 12:10 king Rehoboam made shields of *b*
2Chr 24:12 *b* to mend the house of the LORD
Job 6:12 or is my flesh of *b*
Job 28:2 *b* is molten out of the stone
Job 40:18 bones are as strong pieces of *b*
Job 41:27 as straw, and *b* as rotten wood
Ps 107:16 For he hath broken the gates of *b*
Is 45:2 break in pieces the gates of *b*
Is 48:4 is an iron sinew, and thy brow *b*
Is 60:17 For *b* I will bring gold, and for
Jer 6:28 they are *b* and iron
Jer 52:17 Also the pillars of *b* that were
Eze 1:7 like the colour of burnished *b*
Eze 22:18 all they are *b*, and tin, and iron,
Eze 24:11 that the *b* of it may be hot, and
Eze 27:13 vessels of *b* in thy market
Eze 40:3 was like the appearance of *b*
Dan 2:32 his belly and his thighs of *b*
Dan 2:35 was the iron, the clay, the *b*
Dan 2:39 and another third kingdom of *b*
Dan 2:45 brake in pieces the iron, the *b*
Dan 4:15 even with a band of iron and *b*
Dan 4:23 even with a band of iron and *b*
Dan 5:4 gods of gold, and of silver, of *b*
Dan 5:23 the gods of silver, and gold, of *b*
Dan 7:19 were of iron, and his nails of *b*
Dan 10:6 feet like in colour to polished *b*
Mic 4:13 iron, and I will make thy hoofs *b*
Zec 6:1 the mountains were mountains of *b*
Mt 10:9 nor silver, nor *b* in your purses,
1Cor 13:1 I am become as sounding *b*

Rev 1:15 And his feet like unto fine *b*
Rev 2:18 fire, and his feet are like fine *b*
Rev 9:20 and idols of gold, and silver, and *b*
Rev 18:12 of most precious wood, and of *b*

## BRAY

Job 6:5 Doth the wild ass *b* when he hath
Prov 27:22 Though thou shouldest *b* a fool in

## BREACH

Gen 38:29 this *b* be upon thee
Lev 24:20 *B* for *b*, eye for eye, tooth
Num 14:34 and ye shall know my *b* of promise
Judg 21:15 made a *b* in the tribes of Israel
2Sa 5:20 before me, as the *b* of waters
2Sa 6:8 the LORD had made a *b* upon Uzzah
2Kin 12:5 wheresoever any *b* shall be found
1Chr 13:11 the LORD had made a *b* upon Uzza
1Chr 15:13 the LORD our God made a *b* upon us
Neh 6:1 that there was no *b* left therein
Job 16:14 He breaketh me with *b* upon *b*
Ps 106:23 chosen stood before him in the *b*
Prov 15:4 therein is a *b* in the spirit
Is 7:6 let us make a *b* therein for us,
Is 30:13 be to you as a *b* ready to fall
Is 30:26 bindeth up the *b* of his people
Is 58:12 be called, The repairer of the *b*
Jer 14:17 people is broken with a great *b*
Lam 2:13 for thy *b* is great like the sea
Eze 26:10 into a city wherein is made a *b*

## BREACHES

Judg 5:17 the sea shore, and abode in his *b*
1Kin 11:27 repaired the *b* of the city of
2Kin 12:5 them repair the *b* of the house
2Kin 12:7 repair ye not the *b* of the house
2Kin 12:8 to repair the *b* of the house
2Kin 12:12 the *b* of the house of the LORD
2Kin 22:5 to repair the *b* of the house
Neh 4:7 that the *b* began to be stopped,
Ps 60:2 heal the *b* thereof
Is 22:9 also the *b* of the city of David
Amos 4:3 And ye shall go out at the *b*
Amos 6:11 will smite the great house with *b*
Amos 9:11 fallen, and close up the *b* thereof

## BREAD

Gen 3:19 of thy face shalt thou eat *b*
Gen 14:18 king of Salem brought forth *b*
Gen 18:5 And I will fetch a morsel of *b*
Gen 19:3 a feast, and did bake unleavened *b*
Gen 21:14 early in the morning, and took *b*
Gen 25:34 Then Jacob gave Esau *b* and pottage
Gen 27:17 gave the savoury meat and the *b*
Gen 28:20 I go, and will give me *b* to eat
Gen 31:54 and called his brethren to eat *b*
Gen 37:25 And they sat down to eat *b*
Gen 39:6 save the *b* which he did eat
Gen 41:54 all the land of Egypt there was *b*
Gen 43:25 that they should eat *b* there
Gen 43:31 himself, and said, Set on *b*
Gen 45:23 she asses laden with corn and *b*
Gen 47:12 his father's household, with *b*
Gen 47:13 there was no *b* in all the land
Gen 47:15 unto Joseph, and said, Give us *b*
Gen 47:17 Joseph gave them *b* in exchange
Gen 47:19 buy us and our land for *b*, and we
Ex 2:20 call him, that he may eat *b*
Ex 12:8 roast with fire, and unleavened *b*
Ex 12:15 days shall ye eat unleavened *b*
Ex 12:17 observe the feast of unleavened *b*
Ex 12:20 shall ye eat unleavened *b*
Ex 13:3 shall no leavened *b* be eaten
Ex 13:6 days thou shalt eat unleavened *b*
Ex 16:3 and when we did eat *b* to the full
Ex 16:8 and in the morning *b* to the full
Ex 16:12 morning ye shall be filled with *b*
Ex 16:15 This is the *b* which the LORD hath
Ex 16:22 day they gathered twice as much *b*
Ex 16:29 the sixth day the *b* of two days
Ex 16:32 that they may see the *b* wherewith
Ex 18:12 to eat *b* with Moses' father in
Ex 23:15 keep the feast of unleavened *b*
Ex 23:18 of my sacrifice with leavened *b*
Ex 23:25 your God, and he shall bless thy *b*
Ex 29:2 And unleavened *b*, and cakes
Ex 29:23 one loaf of *b*, and one cake of oiled
Ex 29:32 the *b* that is in the basket, by
Ex 29:34 of the consecrations, or of the *b*
Ex 34:18 of unleavened *b* shalt thou keep
Ex 34:28 he did neither eat *b*, nor drink
Ex 40:23 he set the *b* in order upon it
Lev 6:16 with unleavened *b* shall it be
Lev 7:13 leavened *b* with the sacrifice of
Lev 8:2 rams, and a basket of unleavened *b*
Lev 8:26 out of the basket of unleavened *b*
Lev 8:31 there eat it with the *b* that is
Lev 8:32 of the *b* shall ye burn with fire
Lev 21:6 the *b* of their God, they do offer
Lev 21:8 for he offereth the *b* of thy God
Lev 21:17 to offer the *b* of his God
Lev 21:21 nigh to offer the *b* of his God
Lev 22:25 hand shall ye offer the *b* of your
Lev 23:6 of unleavened *b* unto the LORD
Lev 23:14 And ye shall eat neither *b*
Lev 23:18 ye shall offer with the *b* seven
Lev 23:20 *b* of the first fruits for a wave
Lev 24:7 it may be on the *b* for a memorial
Lev 26:5 ye shall eat your *b* to the full
Lev 26:26 I have broken the staff of your *b*
Num 4:7 the continual *b* shall be thereon
Num 6:15 And a basket of unleavened *b*
Num 6:17 with the basket of unleavened *b*
Num 9:11 it, and eat it with unleavened *b*
Num 14:9 for they are *b* for us
Num 15:19 when ye eat of the *b* of the land
Num 21:5 for there is no *b*, neither is
Num 28:2 my *b* for my sacrifices made by
Num 28:17 days shall unleavened *b* be eaten
Deut 8:3 that man doth not live by *b* only
Deut 8:9 shalt eat *b* without scarceness
Deut 9:9 neither did eat *b* nor drink water
Deut 9:18 I did neither eat *b*, nor drink
Deut 16:3 shalt eat no leavened *b* with it
Deut 16:8 days thou shalt eat unleavened *b*
Deut 16:16 in the feast of unleavened *b*
Deut 23:4 Because they met you not with *b*
Deut 29:6 Ye have not eaten *b*, neither have
Josh 9:5 all the *b* of their provision was
Josh 9:12 This our *b* we took hot for our
Judg 7:13 a cake of barley *b* tumbled into
Judg 8:5 loaves of *b* unto the people that
Judg 8:15 that we should give *b* unto thy
Judg 13:16 me, I will not eat of thy *b*
Judg 19:5 thine heart with a morsel of *b*
Judg 19:19 and there is *b* and wine also for me
Ruth 1:6 his people in giving them *b*
Ruth 2:14 come thou hither, and eat of the *b*
1Sa 2:5 have hired out themselves for *b*
1Sa 2:36 piece of silver and a morsel of *b*
1Sa 9:7 for the *b* is spent in our vessels
1Sa 10:3 carrying three loaves of *b*
1Sa 16:20 And Jesse took an ass laden with *b*
1Sa 21:3 me five loaves of *b* in mine hand
1Sa 21:5 the *b* is in a manner common, yea,
1Sa 22:13 in that thou hast given him *b*
1Sa 25:11 Shall I then take my *b*, and my
1Sa 28:20 for he had eaten no *b* all the day
1Sa 28:22 me set a morsel of *b* before thee
1Sa 28:24 and did bake unleavened *b* thereof
1Sa 30:11 him to David, and gave him *b*
2Sa 3:29 on the sword, or that lacketh *b*
2Sa 3:35 to me, and more also, if I taste *b*
2Sa 6:19 as men, to every one a cake of *b*
2Sa 9:7 thou shalt eat *b* at my table
2Sa 9:10 son shall eat *b* alway at my table
2Sa 12:17 neither did he eat *b* with them
2Sa 12:20 they set *b* before him, and he did
2Sa 16:1 upon them two hundred loaves of *b*
1Kin 13:8 neither will I eat *b* nor drink
1Kin 13:15 him, Come home with me, and eat *b*
1Kin 13:22 But camest back, and hast eaten *b*
1Kin 17:6 And the ravens brought him *b*
1Kin 17:11 a morsel of *b* in thine hand
1Kin 18:4 in a cave, and fed them with *b*
1Kin 18:13 in a cave, and fed them with *b*
1Kin 21:4 away his face, and would eat no *b*
1Kin 21:7 arise, and eat *b*, and let thine
1Kin 22:27 and feed him with *b* of affliction
2Kin 4:8 and she constrained him to eat *b*
2Kin 4:42 man of God *b* of the firstfruits
2Kin 6:22 set *b* and water before them, that
2Kin 18:32 land of corn and wine, a land of *b*
2Kin 23:9 unleavened *b* among their brethren
2Kin 25:3 there was no *b* for the people of
2Kin 25:29 he did eat *b* continually before
1Chr 12:40 brought *b* on asses, and on camels,
1Chr 16:3 woman, to every one a loaf of *b*
2Chr 8:13 even in the feast of unleavened *b*
2Chr 18:26 and feed him with *b* of affliction
2Chr 30:13 unleavened *b* in the second month
2Chr 30:21 kept the feast of unleavened *b*
2Chr 35:17 feast of unleavened *b* seven days
Ezr 6:22 unleavened *b* seven days with joy
Ezr 10:6 he came thither, he did eat no *b*
Neh 5:14 not eaten the *b* of the governor
Neh 5:18 not I the *b* of the governor
Neh 9:15 gavest them *b* from heaven for
Neh 13:2 not the children of Israel with *b*
Job 15:23 He wandereth abroad for *b*
Job 22:7 hast withholden *b* from the hungry
Job 27:14 shall not be satisfied with *b*
Job 28:5 for the earth, out of it cometh *b*
Job 33:20 So that his life abhorreth *b*
Job 42:11 did eat *b* with him in his house
Ps 14:4 eat up my people as they eat *b*
Ps 37:25 forsaken, nor his seed begging *b*
Ps 41:9 I trusted, which did eat of my *b*
Ps 53:4 eat up my people as they eat *b*
Ps 78:20 can he give *b* also
Ps 80:5 feedest them with the *b* of tears
Ps 102:4 so that I forget to eat my *b*
Ps 102:9 For I have eaten ashes like *b*
Ps 104:15 *b* which strengtheneth man's heart
Ps 105:40 them with the *b* of heaven
Ps 109:10 let them seek their *b* also out of
Ps 127:2 up late, to eat the *b* of sorrows
Ps 132:15 I will satisfy her poor with *b*
Prov 4:17 For they eat the *b* of wickedness
Prov 6:26 a man is brought to a piece of *b*
Prov 9:5 Come, eat of my *b*, and drink of
Prov 9:17 *b* eaten in secret is pleasant
Prov 12:9 honoureth himself, and lacketh *b*
Prov 12:11 land shall be satisfied with *b*
Prov 20:13 and thou shalt be satisfied with *b*
Prov 20:17 *B* of deceit is sweet to a man
Prov 22:9 he giveth of his *b* to the poor
Prov 23:6 Eat thou not the *b* of him that
Prov 25:21 be hungry, give him *b* to eat
Prov 28:19 his land shall have plenty of *b*
Prov 28:21 for for a piece of *b* that man
Prov 31:27 and eateth not the *b* of idleness
Eccl 9:7 eat thy *b* with joy, and drink thy
Eccl 9:11 strong, neither yet *b* to the wise
Eccl 11:1 Cast thy *b* upon the waters
Is 3:1 and the staff, the whole stay of *b*
Is 3:7 house is neither *b* nor clothing
Is 4:1 saying, We will eat our own *b*
Is 21:14 with their *b* him that fled
Is 28:28 *B* corn is bruised
Is 30:20 Lord give you the *b* of adversity
Is 30:23 *b* of the increase of the earth,
Is 33:16 *b* shall be given him
Is 36:17 land of corn and wine, a land of *b*
Is 44:15 yea, he kindleth it, and baketh *b*
Is 44:19 also I have baked *b* upon the
Is 51:14 pit, nor that his *b* should fail
Is 55:2 money for that which is not *b*
Is 55:10 to the sower, and *b* to the eater
Is 58:7 not to deal thy *b* to the hungry
Jer 5:17 eat up thine harvest, and thy *b*
Jer 37:21 of *b* out of the bakers' street
Jer 38:9 there is no more *b* in the city
Jer 41:1 they did eat *b* together in Mizpah
Jer 42:14 the trumpet, nor have hunger of *b*
Jer 52:6 so that there was no *b* for the
Jer 52:33 he did continually eat *b* before
Lam 1:11 All her people sigh, they seek *b*
Lam 4:4 the young children ask *b*, and no
Lam 5:6 Assyrians, to be satisfied with *b*
Lam 5:9 We gat our *b* with the peril of
Eze 4:9 vessel, and make thee *b* thereof
Eze 4:13 defiled *b* among the Gentiles
Eze 4:15 shalt prepare thy *b* therewith
Eze 5:16 and will break your staff of *b*
Eze 12:18 eat thy *b* with quaking, and drink
Eze 14:13 break the staff of the *b* thereof
Eze 16:49 sister Sodom, pride, fulness of *b*
Eze 18:7 hath given his *b* to the hungry
Eze 24:17 thy lips, and eat not the *b* of men
Eze 24:22 your lips, nor eat the *b* of men
Eze 44:3 in it to eat *b* before the LORD
Eze 44:7 even my house, when ye offer my *b*
Eze 45:21 unleavened *b* shall be eaten
Dan 10:3 I ate no pleasant *b*, neither came
Hos 2:5 my lovers, that give me my *b*
Hos 9:4 be unto them as the *b* of mourners
Amos 4:6 want of *b* in all your places
Amos 7:12 the land of Judah, and there eat *b*
Amos 8:11 in the land, not a famine of *b*
Obad 7 they that eat thy *b* have laid a
Hag 2:12 and with his skirt do touch *b*

Mal 1:7 offer polluted *b* upon mine altar
Mt 4:3 that these stones be made *b*
Mt 4:4 Man shall not live by *b* alone
Mt 6:11 Give us this day our daily *b*
Mt 7:9 of you, whom if his son ask *b*
Mt 15:2 not their hands when they eat *b*
Mt 15:26 not meet to take the children's *b*
Mt 15:33 have so much *b* in the wilderness
Mt 16:5 they had forgotten to take *b*
Mt 16:7 It is because we have taken no *b*
Mt 16:8 because ye have brought no *b*
Mt 16:11 spake it not to you concerning *b*
Mt 26:17 *b* the disciples came to Jesus
Mt 26:26 as they were eating, Jesus took *b*
Mk 3:20 they could not so much as eat *b*
Mk 6:8 no scrip, no *b*, no money in their
Mk 6:36 the villages, and buy themselves *b*
Mk 6:37 buy two hundred pennyworth of *b*
Mk 7:2 his disciples eat *b* with defiled
Mk 7:5 but eat *b* with unwashen hands
Mk 7:27 not meet to take the children's *b*
Mk 8:4 men with *b* here in the wilderness
Mk 8:14 disciples had forgotten to take *b*
Mk 8:16 It is because we have no *b*
Mk 14:1 the passover, and of unleavened *b*
Mk 14:12 And the first day of unleavened *b*
Mk 14:22 And as they did eat, Jesus took *b*
Lk 4:3 this stone that it be made *b*
Lk 4:4 man shall not live by *b* alone
Lk 7:33 eating *b* nor drinking wine
Lk 9:3 staves, nor scrip, neither *b*
Lk 11:3 Give us day by day our daily *b*
Lk 11:11 If a son shall ask *b* of any of
Lk 14:1 to eat *b* on the sabbath day
Lk 14:15 shall eat *b* in the kingdom of God
Lk 15:17 of my father's have *b* enough
Lk 22:1 feast of unleavened *b* drew nigh
Lk 22:7 Then came the day of unleavened *b*
Lk 22:19 And he took *b*, and gave thanks, and
Lk 24:30 sat at meat with them, he took *b*
Lk 24:35 known of them in breaking of *b*
Jn 6:5 Philip, Whence shall we buy *b*
Jn 6:7 Two hundred pennyworth of *b* is
Jn 6:23 the place where they did eat *b*
Jn 6:31 He gave them *b* from heaven to eat
Jn 6:32 gave you not that *b* from heaven
Jn 6:32 giveth you the true *b* from heaven
Jn 6:33 For the *b* of God is he which
Jn 6:34 Lord, evermore give us this *b*
Jn 6:35 unto them, I am the *b* of life
Jn 6:41 I am the *b* which came down from
Jn 6:48 I am that *b* of life
Jn 6:50 This is the *b* which cometh down
Jn 6:51 I am the living *b* which came down
Jn 6:58 This is that *b* which came down
Jn 13:18 He that eateth *b* with me hath
Jn 21:9 there, and fish laid thereon, and *b*
Jn 21:13 Jesus then cometh, and taketh *b*
Acts 2:42 fellowship, and in breaking of *b*
Acts 2:46 breaking *b* from house to house,
Acts 12:3 were the days of unleavened *b*
Acts 20:6 after the days of unleavened *b*
Acts 20:7 came together to break *b*, Paul
Acts 20:11 come up again, and had broken *b*
Acts 27:35 he had thus spoken, he took *b*
1Cor 5:8 the unleavened *b* of sincerity
1Cor 10:16 The *b* which we break, is it not
1Cor 10:17 For we being many are one *b*
1Cor 11:23 in which he was betrayed took *b*
1Cor 11:26 For as often as ye eat this *b*
1Cor 11:27 whosoever shall eat this *b*
1Cor 11:28 and so let him eat of that *b*
2Cor 9:10 both minister *b* for your food
2Th 3:8 did we eat any man's *b* for nought
2Th 3:12 they work, and eat their own *b*

## BREADTH

Gen 6:15 the *b* of it fifty cubits, and the
Gen 13:17 length of it and in the *b* of it
Ex 25:10 a cubit and a half the *b* thereof
Ex 25:23 thereof, and a cubit the *b* thereof
Ex 26:2 the *b* of one curtain four cubits
Ex 26:16 half shall be the *b* of one board
Ex 27:12 for the *b* of the court on the
Ex 27:18 the *b* fifty every where, and the
Ex 28:16 and a span shall be the *b* thereof
Ex 30:2 thereof, and a cubit the *b* thereof
Ex 36:9 the *b* of one curtain four cubits
Ex 37:1 and a cubit and a half the *b* of it
Ex 37:25 a cubit, and the *b* of it a cubit
Ex 38:1 and five cubits the *b* thereof
Ex 38:18 height in the *b* was five cubits
Ex 39:9 thereof, and a span the *b* thereof
Deut 3:11 and four cubits the *b* of it
Judg 20:16 could sling stones at an hair *b*
1Kin 6:2 the *b* thereof twenty cubits, and
1Kin 6:20 in length, and twenty cubits in *b*
1Kin 7:2 the *b* thereof fifty cubits, and
1Kin 7:26 And it was an hand *b* thick
2Chr 3:3 cubits, and the *b* twenty cubits
2Chr 3:8 according to the *b* of the house
2Chr 4:1 and twenty cubits the *b* thereof
Ezr 6:3 the *b* thereof threescore cubits
Job 37:10 the *b* of the waters is straitened
Job 38:18 thou perceived the *b* of the earth
Is 8:8 shall fill the *b* of thy land
Eze 40:5 long by the cubit and an hand *b*
Eze 40:11 he measured the *b* of the entry of
Eze 40:19 Then he measured the *b* from the
Eze 41:1 which was the *b* of the tabernacle
Eze 41:11 the *b* of the place that was left
Eze 41:14 Also the *b* of the face of the
Eze 42:2 door, and the *b* was fifty cubits
Eze 42:4 was a walk of ten cubits *b* inward
Eze 43:13 The cubit is a cubit and an hand *b*
Eze 45:1 the *b* shall be ten thousand
Dan 3:1 and the *b* thereof six cubits
Hab 1:6 march through the *b* of the land
Zec 2:2 to see what is the *b* thereof
Zec 5:2 and the *b* thereof ten cubits
Eph 3:18 with all saints what is the *b*
Rev 20:9 went up on the *b* of the earth
Rev 21:16 the length is as large as the *b*
Rev 21:16 The length and the *b* and the height

## BREAK

Gen 19:9 Lot, and came near to *b* the door
Gen 27:40 that thou shalt *b* his yoke from
Ex 12:46 neither shall ye *b* a bone thereof
Ex 13:13 it, then thou shalt *b* his neck
Ex 19:21 lest they *b* through unto the LORD
Ex 19:24 the people *b* through to come up
Ex 22:6 If fire *b* out, and catch in thorns
Ex 23:24 quite *b* down their images
Ex 32:2 *B* off the golden earrings, which
Ex 32:24 hath any gold, let them *b* it off
Ex 34:13 *b* their images, and cut down their
Ex 34:20 not, then shalt thou *b* his neck
Lev 11:33 and ye shall *b* it
Lev 13:12 if a leprosy *b* out abroad in the
Lev 14:43 *b* out in the house, after that he
Lev 14:45 he shall *b* down the house, the
Lev 26:15 but that ye *b* my covenant
Lev 26:19 I will *b* the pride of your power
Lev 26:44 to *b* my covenant with them
Num 9:12 the morning, nor *b* any bone of it
Num 24:8 shall *b* their bones, and pierce
Num 30:2 he shall not *b* his word, he shall
Deut 7:5 *b* down their images, and cut down
Deut 12:3 *b* their pillars, and burn their
Deut 31:16 *b* my covenant which I have made
Deut 31:20 and provoke me, and *b* my covenant
Judg 2:1 I will never *b* my covenant with
Judg 8:9 peace, I will *b* down this tower
1Sa 25:10 many servants now a days that *b*
2Sa 2:32 they came to Hebron at *b* of day
1Kin 15:19 *b* thy league with Baasha king of
2Kin 3:26 to *b* through even unto the king
2Kin 25:13 did the Chaldees *b* in pieces
2Chr 16:3 *b* thy league with Baasha king of
Ezr 9:14 Should we again *b* thy
Neh 4:3 he shall even *b* down their stone
Job 13:25 Wilt thou *b* a leaf driven to and
Job 19:2 *b* me in pieces with words
Job 34:24 He shall *b* in pieces mighty men
Job 39:15 or that the wild beast may *b* them
Ps 2:3 Let us *b* their bands asunder, and
Ps 2:9 Thou shalt *b* them with a rod of
Ps 10:15 *B* thou the arm of the wicked and
Ps 58:6 *B* their teeth, O God, in their
Ps 72:4 shall *b* in pieces the oppressor
Ps 74:6 But now they *b* down the carved
Ps 89:31 If they *b* my statutes, and keep
Ps 89:34 My covenant will I not *b*, nor
Ps 94:5 They *b* in pieces thy people, O
Ps 141:5 oil, which shall not *b* my head
Eccl 3:3 a time to *b* down, and a time to
Song 2:17 Until the day *b*, and the shadows
Song 4:6 Until the day *b*, and the shadows
Is 5:5 *b* down the wall thereof, and it
Is 14:7 they *b* forth into singing
Is 14:25 That I will *b* the Assyrian in my
Is 28:24 *b* the clods of his ground
Is 28:28 nor *b* it with the wheel of his
Is 30:14 he shall *b* it as the breaking of
Is 35:6 the wilderness shall waters *b* out
Is 38:13 so will he *b* all my bones
Is 42:3 A bruised reed shall he not *b*
Is 44:23 *b* forth into singing, ye
Is 45:2 I will *b* in pieces the gates of
Is 49:13 *b* forth into singing, O mountains
Is 52:9 *B* forth into joy, sing together,
Is 54:1 *b* forth into singing, and cry
Is 54:3 For thou shalt *b* forth on the
Is 55:12 the hills shall *b* forth before
Is 58:6 go free, and that ye *b* every yoke
Is 58:8 thy light *b* forth as the morning
Jer 1:14 *b* forth upon all the inhabitants
Jer 4:3 *B* up your fallow ground, and sow
Jer 14:21 *b* not thy covenant with us
Jer 15:12 Shall iron *b* the northern iron and
Jer 19:10 Then shalt thou *b* the bottle in
Jer 28:4 for I will *b* the yoke of the king
Jer 28:11 Even so will I *b* the yoke of
Jer 30:8 that I will *b* his yoke from off
Jer 31:28 to *b* down, and to throw down, and
Jer 33:20 If ye can *b* my covenant of the
Jer 43:13 He shall *b* also the images of
Jer 45:4 which I have built will I *b* down
Jer 48:12 his vessels, and *b* their bottles
Jer 49:35 I will *b* the bow of Elam, the
Jer 51:20 for with thee will I *b* in pieces
Eze 4:16 I will *b* the staff of bread in
Eze 5:16 will *b* your staff of bread
Eze 13:14 So will I *b* down the wall that ye
Eze 14:13 will *b* the staff of the bread
Eze 16:38 thee, as women that *b* wedlock
Eze 17:15 or shall he *b* the covenant, and be
Eze 23:34 thou shalt *b* the sherds thereof,
Eze 26:4 of Tyrus, and *b* down her towers
Eze 26:9 axes he shall *b* down thy towers
Eze 26:12 they shall *b* down thy walls, and
Eze 29:7 of thee by thy hand, thou didst *b*
Eze 30:18 when I shall *b* there the yokes of
Eze 30:22 will *b* his arms, the strong, and
Eze 30:24 but I will *b* Pharaoh's arms, and
Dan 2:40 shall it *b* in pieces and bruise
Dan 2:44 people, but it shall *b* in pieces
Dan 4:27 *b* off thy sins by righteousness,
Dan 7:23 tread it down, and *b* it in pieces
Hos 1:5 that I will *b* the bow of Israel
Hos 2:18 I will *b* the bow and the sword and
Hos 4:2 committing adultery, they *b* out
Hos 10:2 he shall *b* down their altars, he
Hos 10:11 plow, and Jacob shall *b* his clods
Joel 2:7 and they shall not *b* their ranks
Amos 1:5 I will *b* also the bar of Damascus
Amos 5:6 lest he *b* out like fire in the
Mic 3:3 they *b* their bones, and chop them
Nah 1:13 For now will I *b* his yoke from
Zec 11:10 that I might *b* my covenant which
Zec 11:14 that I might *b* the brotherhood
Mt 5:19 Whosoever therefore shall *b* one
Mt 6:19 and where thieves *b* through
Mt 9:17 else the bottles *b*, and the wine
Mt 12:20 A bruised reed shall he not *b*
Acts 20:7 came together to *b* bread, Paul
Acts 20:11 a long while, even till *b* of day
Acts 21:13 ye to weep and to *b* mine heart
1Cor 10:16 The bread which we *b*, is it not
Gal 4:27 *b* forth and cry, thou that

## BREAKETH

Gen 32:26 he said, Let me go, for the day *b*
Job 9:17 For he *b* me with a tempest, and
Job 12:14 he *b* down, and it cannot be built
Job 16:14 He *b* me with breach upon breach,
Job 28:4 The flood *b* out from the
Ps 29:5 voice of the LORD *b* the cedars
Ps 46:9 he *b* the bow, and cutteth the
Ps 119:20 My soul *b* for the longing that it
Prov 25:15 and a soft tongue *b* the bone
Eccl 10:8 whoso *b* an hedge, a serpent shall
Is 59:5 is crushed *b* out into a viper
Jer 19:11 as one *b* a potter's vessel, that
Jer 23:29 hammer that *b* the rock in pieces
Lam 4:4 bread, and no man *b* it unto them
Dan 2:40 forasmuch as iron *b* in pieces

### BREAKING
Gen 32:24 with him until the *b* of the day
Ex 9:9 shall be a boil *b* forth with
Ex 22:2 If a thief be found *b* up, and be
1Chr 14:11 hand like the *b* forth of waters
Job 30:14 upon me as a wide *b* in of waters
Ps 144:14 that there be no *b* in, nor going
Is 22:5 *b* down the walls, and of crying to
Is 30:13 whose *b* cometh suddenly at an
Eze 16:59 the oath in *b* the covenant
Eze 17:18 the oath by *b* the covenant
Eze 21:6 of man, with the *b* of thy loins
Hos 13:13 place of the *b* forth of children
Lk 24:35 was known of them in *b* of bread
Acts 2:42 in *b* of bread, and in prayers
Acts 2:46 *b* bread from house to house, did
Rom 2:23 through *b* the law dishonourest

### BREAST
Ex 29:26 thou shalt take the *b* of the ram
Lev 7:30 made by fire, the fat with the *b*
Lev 7:34 For the wave *b* and the heave
Lev 8:29 And Moses took the *b*, and waved it
Lev 10:14 And the wave *b* and heave shoulder
Num 6:20 for the priest, with the wave *b*
Num 18:18 shall be thine, as the wave *b*
Job 24:9 pluck the fatherless from the *b*
Is 60:16 and shalt suck the *b* of kings
Lam 4:3 the sea monsters draw out the *b*
Dan 2:32 head was of fine gold, his *b*
Lk 18:13 unto heaven, but smote upon his *b*
Jn 13:25 lying on Jesus' *b* saith unto him
Jn 21:20 also leaned on his *b* at supper

### BREASTPLATE
Ex 25:7 be set in the ephod, and in the *b*
Ex 28:4 a *b*, and an ephod, and a robe, and a
Ex 28:15 thou shalt make the *b* of judgment
Ex 28:26 of the *b* in the border thereof
Ex 28:28 they shall bind the *b* by the
Ex 29:5 the ephod, and the ephod, and the *b*
Ex 35:9 set for the ephod, and for the *b*
Ex 35:27 set, for the ephod, and for the *b*
Ex 39:8 he made the *b* of cunning work,
Ex 39:15 upon the *b* chains at the ends
Ex 39:19 put them on the two ends of the *b*
Ex 39:21 they did bind the *b* by his rings
Lev 8:8 And he put the *b* upon him
Is 59:17 he put on righteousness as a *b*
Eph 6:14 having on the *b* of righteousness
1Th 5:8 sober, putting on the *b* of faith

### BREASTPLATES
Rev 9:9 And they had *b*
Rev 9:17 having *b* of fire, and of jacinth,

### BREASTS
Gen 49:25 lieth under, blessings of the *b*
Lev 9:20 And they put the fat upon the *b*
Job 3:12 or why the *b* that I should suck
Job 21:24 His *b* are full of milk, and his
Ps 22:9 when I was upon my mother's *b*
Prov 5:19 let her *b* satisfy thee at all
Song 1:13 shall lie all night betwixt my *b*
Song 4:5 Thy two *b* are like two young roes
Song 7:3 Thy two *b* are like two young roes
Song 7:7 thy *b* to clusters of grapes
Song 8:1 that sucked the *b* of my mother
Song 8:8 a little sister, and she hath no *b*
Song 8:10 I am a wall, and my *b* like towers
Is 28:9 the milk, and drawn from the *b*
Is 66:11 with the *b* of her consolations
Eze 16:7 thy *b* are fashioned, and thine
Eze 23:3 there were their *b* pressed
Eze 23:8 bruised the *b* of her virginity
Eze 23:34 thereof, and pluck off thine own *b*
Hos 2:2 her adulteries from between her *b*
Hos 9:14 them a miscarrying womb and dry *b*
Joel 2:16 and those that suck the *b*
Nah 2:7 of doves, tabering upon their *b*
Lk 23:48 which were done, smote their *b*
Rev 15:6 having their *b* girded with golden

### BREATH
Gen 2:7 into his nostrils the *b* of life
Gen 6:17 flesh, wherein is the *b* of life
Gen 7:15 flesh, wherein is the *b* of life
Gen 7:22 whose nostrils was the *b* of life
2Sa 22:16 blast of the *b* of his nostrils
1Kin 17:17 that there was no *b* left in him
Job 4:9 by the *b* of his nostrils are they
Job 9:18 will not suffer me to take my *b*
Job 12:10 thing, and the *b* of all mankind
Job 15:30 by the *b* of his mouth shall he go
Job 17:1 My *b* is corrupt, my days are
Job 19:17 My *b* is strange to my wife,
Job 27:3 All the while my *b* is in me
Job 33:4 the *b* of the Almighty hath given
Job 34:14 unto himself his spirit and his *b*
Job 37:10 By the *b* of God frost is given
Job 41:21 His *b* kindleth coals, and a flame
Ps 18:15 blast of the *b* of thy nostrils
Ps 33:6 of them by the *b* of his mouth
Ps 104:29 thou takest away their *b*, they
Ps 135:17 is there any *b* in their mouths
Ps 146:4 His *b* goeth forth, he returneth
Ps 150:6 thing that hath *b* praise the LORD
Eccl 3:19 yea, they have all one *b*
Is 2:22 whose *b* is in his nostrils
Is 11:4 with the *b* of his lips shall he
Is 30:28 And his *b*, as an overflowing
Is 30:33 the *b* of the LORD, like a stream
Is 33:11 your *b*, as fire, shall devour you
Is 42:5 he that giveth *b* unto the people
Jer 10:14 and there is no *b* in them
Jer 51:17 and there is no *b* in them
Lam 4:20 The *b* of our nostrils, the
Eze 37:5 I will cause *b* to enter into you,
Eze 37:9 Come from the four winds, O *b*
Dan 5:23 and the God in whose hand thy *b* is
Dan 10:17 me, neither is there *b* left in me
Hab 2:19 there is no *b* at all in the midst
Acts 17:25 he giveth to all life, and *b*

### BREATHE
Josh 11:11 there was not any left to *b*
Josh 11:14 them, neither left they any to *b*
Ps 27:12 me, and such as *b* out cruelty
Eze 37:9 *b* upon these slain, that they may

### BREATHED
Gen 2:7 *b* into his nostrils the breath of
Josh 10:40 but utterly destroyed all that *b*
1Kin 15:29 left not to Jeroboam any that *b*
Jn 20:22 he *b* on them, and saith unto them,

### BREECHES
Ex 28:42 linen *b* to cover their nakedness
Ex 39:28 linen *b* of fine twined linen,
Lev 6:10 his linen *b* shall he put upon his
Lev 16:4 have the linen *b* upon his flesh
Eze 44:18 have linen *b* upon their loins

### BREED
Gen 8:17 that they may *b* abundantly in the
Deut 32:14 lambs, and rams of the *b* of Bashan

### BRETHREN
Gen 9:22 father, and told his two *b* without
Gen 9:25 servants shall he be unto his *b*
Gen 13:8 for we be *b*
Gen 16:12 in the presence of all his *b*
Gen 19:7 And said, I pray you, *b*, do not so
Gen 24:27 me to the house of my master's *b*
Gen 25:18 died in the presence of all his *b*
Gen 27:29 be lord over thy *b*, and let thy
Gen 27:37 all his *b* have I given to him for
Gen 29:4 And Jacob said unto them, My *b*
Gen 31:23 And he took his *b* with him
Gen 31:25 Laban with his *b* pitched in the
Gen 31:46 And Jacob said unto his *b*, Gather
Gen 34:11 unto her father and unto her *b*
Gen 34:25 Jacob, Simeon and Levi, Dinah's *b*
Gen 37:2 was feeding the flock with his *b*
Gen 37:8 his *b* said to him, Shalt thou
Gen 37:10 thy *b* indeed come to bow down
Gen 37:13 Do not thy *b* feed the flock in
Gen 37:17 And Joseph went after his *b*
Gen 37:23 when Joseph was come unto his *b*
Gen 37:26 And Judah said unto his *b*, What
Gen 37:30 And he returned unto his *b*
Gen 38:1 that Judah went down from his *b*
Gen 42:3 Joseph's ten *b* went down to buy
Gen 42:6 and Joseph's *b* came, and bowed down
Gen 42:7 And Joseph saw his *b*, and he knew
Gen 42:13 said, Thy servants are twelve *b*
Gen 42:32 We be twelve *b*, sons of our
Gen 42:33 leave one of your *b* here with me
Gen 44:14 his *b* came to Joseph's house
Gen 44:33 and let the lad go up with his *b*
Gen 45:1 made himself known unto his *b*
Gen 45:15 Moreover he kissed all his *b*
Gen 45:24 So he sent his *b* away, and they
Gen 47:1 and said, My father and my *b*
Gen 47:5 and thy *b* are come unto thee
Gen 47:11 Joseph placed his father and his *b*
Gen 48:6 of their *b* in their inheritance
Gen 48:22 to thee one portion above thy *b*
Gen 49:5 Simeon and Levi are *b*
Gen 49:8 art he whom thy *b* shall praise
Gen 49:26 him that was separate from his *b*
Gen 50:8 all the house of Joseph, and his *b*
Gen 50:17 thee now, the trespass of thy *b*
Ex 1:6 And Joseph died, and all his *b*
Ex 2:11 that he went out unto his *b*
Ex 4:18 return unto my *b* which are in
Lev 10:4 carry your *b* from before the
Lev 21:10 is the high priest among his *b*
Lev 25:46 but over your *b* the children of
Lev 25:48 one of his *b* may redeem him
Num 8:26 their *b* in the tabernacle of the
Num 16:10 all thy *b* the sons of Levi with
Num 18:2 thy *b* also of the tribe of Levi,
Num 20:3 when our *b* died before the LORD
Num 25:6 brought unto his *b* a Midianitish
Num 27:4 among the *b* of our father
Num 32:6 of Reuben, Shall your *b* go to war
Deut 1:16 Hear the causes between your *b*
Deut 1:28 our *b* have discouraged our heart,
Deut 2:4 of your *b* the children of Esau
Deut 3:18 your *b* the children of Israel
Deut 10:9 part nor inheritance with his *b*
Deut 15:7 you a poor man of one of thy *b*
Deut 18:2 have no inheritance among their *b*
Deut 18:7 as all his *b* the Levites do,
Deut 18:18 up a Prophet from among their *b*
Deut 24:7 his *b* of the children of Israel
Deut 24:14 and needy, whether he be of thy *b*
Deut 25:5 If *b* dwell together, and one of
Deut 33:9 neither did he acknowledge his *b*
Deut 33:16 him that was separated from his *b*
Josh 1:14 ye shall pass before your *b* armed
Josh 2:13 my father, and my mother, and my *b*
Josh 6:23 father, and her mother, and her *b*
Josh 14:8 Nevertheless my *b* that went up
Josh 17:4 us an inheritance among our *b*
Josh 22:3 Ye have not left your *b* these
Judg 8:19 And he said, They were my *b*
Judg 9:1 to Shechem unto his mother's *b*
Judg 9:5 slew his *b* the sons of Jerubbaal,
Judg 9:24 aided him in the killing of his *b*
Judg 9:26 the son of Ebed came with his *b*
Judg 9:31 Ebed and his *b* be come to Shechem
Judg 9:41 and Zebul thrust out Gaal and his *b*
Judg 9:56 father, in slaying his seventy *b*
Judg 11:3 Then Jephthah fled from his *b*
Judg 14:3 among the daughters of thy *b*
Judg 16:31 Then his *b* and all the house of
Judg 18:8 they came unto their *b* to Zorah
Judg 18:14 of Laish, and said unto their *b*
Judg 19:23 and said unto them, Nay, my *b*
Judg 20:13 of their *b* the children of Israel
Judg 21:22 their *b* come unto us to complain
Ruth 4:10 be not cut off from among his *b*
1Sa 16:13 him in the midst of his *b*
1Sa 17:17 Take now for thy *b* an ephah of
1Sa 17:22 army, and came and saluted his *b*
1Sa 20:29 away, I pray thee, and see my *b*
1Sa 22:1 and when his *b* and all his father's
1Sa 30:23 David, Ye shall not do so, my *b*
2Sa 2:26 return from following their *b*
2Sa 3:8 of Saul thy father, to his *b*
2Sa 15:20 return thou, and take back thy *b*
2Sa 19:12 Ye are my *b*, ye are my bones and
2Sa 19:41 Why have our *b* the men of Judah
1Kin 1:9 called all his *b* the king's sons,
1Kin 12:24 your *b* the children of Israel
2Kin 9:2 him arise up from among his *b*
2Kin 10:13 Jehu met with the *b* of Ahaziah
2Kin 23:9 unleavened bread among their *b*
1Chr 4:9 was more honourable than his *b*
1Chr 4:27 but his *b* had not many children,
1Chr 5:2 For Judah prevailed above his *b*
1Chr 5:7 his *b* by their families, when the
1Chr 6:44 their *b* the sons of Merari stood
1Chr 7:5 their *b* among all the families of
1Chr 7:22 his *b* came to comfort him
1Chr 8:32 dwelt with their *b* in Jerusalem
1Chr 9:6 Jeuel, and their *b*, six hundred and
1Chr 9:17 and Talmon, and Ahiman, and their *b*
1Chr 12:2 bow, even of Saul's *b* of Benjamin
1Chr 13:2 abroad unto our *b* every where
1Chr 15:7 his *b* an hundred and thirty
1Chr 15:12 yourselves, both ye and your *b*
1Chr 16:7 into the hand of Asaph and his *b*
1Chr 16:37 of the LORD Asaph and his *b*

1Chr 16:38 And Obed-edom with their *b*
1Chr 23:22 their *b* the sons of Kish took
1Chr 25:7 with their *b* that were instructed
1Chr 25:9 to Gedaliah, who with his *b*
1Chr 25:10 to Zaccur, he, his sons, and his *b*
1Chr 26:7 whose *b* were strong men, Elihu,
1Chr 26:11 sons and *b* of Hosah were thirteen
1Chr 26:25 And his *b* by Eliezer
1Chr 26:32 And his *b*, men of valour, were two
1Chr 27:18 Elihu, one of the *b* of David
1Chr 28:2 his feet, and said, Hear me, my *b*
2Chr 5:12 with their sons and their *b*
2Chr 11:4 go up, nor fight against your *b*
2Chr 19:10 shall come to you of your *b* that
2Chr 21:2 he had *b* the sons of Jehoshaphat,
2Chr 22:8 and the sons of the *b* of Ahaziah
2Chr 28:11 ye have taken captive of your *b*
2Chr 29:34 wherefore their *b* the Levites did
2Chr 30:7 like your fathers, and like your *b*
2Chr 31:15 to give to their *b* by courses
2Chr 35:5 the fathers of your *b* the people
Ezr 3:2 his *b* the priests, and Zerubbabel
Ezr 6:20 for their *b* the priests, and for
Ezr 7:18 seem good to thee, and to thy *b*
Ezr 8:17 to his *b* the Nethinims, at the
Ezr 10:18 the son of Jozadak, and his *b*
Neh 1:2 That Hanani, one of my *b*, came,
Neh 3:1 rose up with his *b* the priests
Neh 3:18 After him repaired their *b*
Neh 4:2 And he spake before his *b* and the
Neh 4:14 and terrible, and fight for your *b*
Neh 4:23 So neither I, nor my *b*, nor my
Neh 5:1 wives against their *b* the Jews
Neh 5:5 flesh is as the flesh of our *b*
Neh 5:8 have redeemed our *b* the Jews
Neh 5:8 and will ye even sell your *b*
Neh 5:14 my *b* have not eaten the bread of
Neh 10:10 And their *b*, Shebaniah, Hodijah,
Neh 10:29 They clave to their *b*, their
Neh 11:12 their *b* that did the work of the
Neh 12:7 of their *b* in the days of Jeshua
Neh 12:24 with their *b* over against them,
Neh 12:36 And his *b*, Shemaiah, and Azarael,
Neh 13:13 was to distribute unto their *b*
Est 10:3 of the multitude of his *b*
Job 6:15 My *b* have dealt deceitfully as a
Job 19:13 He hath put my *b* far from me
Job 42:11 came there unto him all his *b*
Job 42:15 them inheritance among their *b*
Ps 22:22 I will declare thy name unto my *b*
Ps 69:8 I am become a stranger unto my *b*
Ps 122:8 For my *b* and companions' sakes, I
Ps 133:1 how pleasant it is for *b* to dwell
Prov 6:19 and he that soweth discord among *b*
Prov 17:2 of the inheritance among the *b*
Prov 19:7 All the *b* of the poor do hate him
Is 66:5 Your *b* that hated you, that cast
Is 66:20 they shall bring all your *b* for
Jer 7:15 as I have cast out all your *b*
Jer 12:6 For even thy *b*, and the house of
Jer 29:16 of your *b* that are not gone forth
Jer 35:3 the son of Habaziniah, and his *b*
Jer 41:8 and slew them not among their *b*
Jer 49:10 his seed is spoiled, and his *b*
Eze 11:15 of man, thy *b*, even thy *b*
Hos 2:1 Say ye unto your *b*, Ammi
Hos 13:15 Though he be fruitful among his *b*
Mic 5:3 then the remnant of his *b* shall
Mt 1:2 and Jacob begat Judas and his *b*
Mt 1:11 Josias begat Jechonias and his *b*
Mt 4:18 by the sea of Galilee, saw two *b*
Mt 4:21 from thence, he saw other two *b*
Mt 5:47 And if ye salute your *b* only
Mt 12:46 his *b* stood without, desiring to
Mt 12:48 and who are my *b*
Mt 12:49 and said, Behold my mother and my *b*
Mt 13:55 and his *b*, James, and Joses, and
Mt 19:29 that hath forsaken houses, or *b*
Mt 20:24 indignation against the two *b*
Mt 22:25 Now there were with us seven *b*
Mt 23:8 and all ye are *b*
Mt 25:40 one of the least of these my *b*
Mt 28:10 go tell my *b* that they go into
Mk 3:31 There came then his *b* and his
Mk 3:33 saying, Who is my mother, or my *b*
Mk 3:34 and said, Behold my mother and my *b*
Mk 10:29 no man that hath left house, or *b*
Mk 10:30 now in this time, houses, and *b*
Mk 12:20 Now there were seven *b*
Lk 8:19 came to him his mother and his *b*
Lk 8:20 thy *b* stand without, desiring to
Lk 8:21 my *b* are these which hear the
Lk 14:12 call not thy friends, nor thy *b*
Lk 14:26 and wife, and children, and *b*
Lk 16:28 For I have five *b*
Lk 18:29 hath left house, or parents, or *b*
Lk 20:29 There were therefore seven *b*
Lk 21:16 be betrayed both by parents, and *b*
Lk 22:32 art converted, strengthen thy *b*
Jn 2:12 he, and his mother, and his *b*
Jn 7:3 His *b* therefore said unto him,
Jn 7:5 neither did his *b* believe in him
Jn 7:10 But when his *b* were gone up
Jn 20:17 but go to my *b*, and say unto them,
Jn 21:23 this saying abroad among the *b*
Acts 1:14 mother of Jesus, and with his *b*
Acts 1:16 Men and *b*, this scripture must
Acts 2:29 Men and *b*, let me freely speak
Acts 2:37 rest of the apostles, Men and *b*
Acts 3:17 And now, *b*, I wot that through
Acts 3:22 God raise up unto you of your *b*
Acts 6:3 Wherefore, *b*, look ye out among
Acts 7:2 And he said, Men, *b*, and fathers,
Acts 7:13 Joseph was made known to his *b*
Acts 7:23 his *b* the children of Israel
Acts 9:30 Which when the *b* knew, they
Acts 10:23 certain *b* from Joppa accompanied
Acts 11:1 *b* that were in Judaea heard that
Acts 11:12 these six *b* accompanied me
Acts 11:29 unto the *b* which dwelt in Judaea
Acts 12:17 things unto James, and to the *b*
Acts 13:15 unto them, saying, Ye men and *b*
Acts 13:26 Men and *b*, children of the stock
Acts 13:38 unto you therefore, men and *b*
Acts 14:2 minds evil affected against the *b*
Acts 15:1 down from Judaea taught the *b*
Acts 15:3 caused great joy unto all the *b*
Acts 15:7 up, and said unto them, Men and *b*
Acts 15:13 James answered, saying, Men and *b*
Acts 15:22 and Silas, chief men among the *b*
Acts 15:36 visit our *b* in every city where
Acts 15:40 by the *b* unto the grace of God
Acts 16:2 of by the *b* that were at Lystra
Acts 16:40 and when they had seen the *b*
Acts 17:6 certain *b* unto the rulers of the
Acts 17:10 the *b* immediately sent away Paul
Acts 17:14 then immediately the *b* sent away
Acts 18:18 and then took his leave of the *b*
Acts 18:27 the *b* wrote, exhorting the
Acts 20:32 And now, *b*, I commend you to God,
Acts 21:7 to Ptolemais, and saluted the *b*
Acts 21:17 the *b* received us gladly
Acts 22:1 Men, *b*, and fathers, hear ye my
Acts 22:5 I received letters unto the *b*
Acts 23:1 the council, said, Men and *b*
Acts 23:5 Then said Paul, I wist not, *b*
Acts 28:14 Where we found *b*, and were desired
Acts 28:21 neither any of the *b* that came
Rom 1:13 I would not have you ignorant, *b*
Rom 7:1 Know ye not, *b*, (for I speak to
Rom 8:12 Therefore, *b*, we are debtors, not
Rom 8:29 be the firstborn among many *b*
Rom 9:3 accursed from Christ for my *b*
Rom 10:1 *B*, my heart's desire and prayer to
Rom 11:25 For I would not, *b*, that ye
Rom 12:1 I beseech you therefore, *b*
Rom 15:14 also am persuaded of you, my *b*
Rom 15:30 Now I beseech you, *b*, for the
Rom 16:14 the *b* which are with them
1Cor 1:10 Now I beseech you, *b*, by the name
1Cor 1:11 declared unto me of you, my *b*
1Cor 1:26 For ye see your calling, *b*
1Cor 2:1 And I, *b*, when I came to you, came
1Cor 3:1 And I, *b*, could not speak unto you
1Cor 4:6 And these things, *b*, I have in a
1Cor 6:5 be able to judge between his *b*
1Cor 6:8 wrong, and defraud, and that your *b*
1Cor 7:24 *B*, let every man, wherein he is
1Cor 7:29 But this I say, *b*, the time is
1Cor 8:12 But when ye sin so against the *b*
1Cor 9:5 as the *b* of the Lord, and Cephas
1Cor 10:1 Moreover, *b*, I would not that ye
1Cor 11:2 Now I praise you, *b*, that ye
1Cor 11:33 Wherefore, my *b*, when ye come
1Cor 12:1 Now concerning spiritual gifts, *b*
1Cor 14:6 Now, *b*, if I come unto you
1Cor 14:20 *B*, be not children in
1Cor 14:26 How is it then, *b*
1Cor 14:39 Wherefore, *b*, covet to prophesy,
1Cor 15:1 Moreover, *b*, I declare unto you
1Cor 15:6 of above five hundred *b* at once
1Cor 15:50 Now this I say, *b*, that flesh and
1Cor 15:58 Therefore, my beloved *b*, be ye
1Cor 16:11 for I look for him with the *b*
1Cor 16:20 All the *b* greet you
2Cor 1:8 For we would not, *b*, have you
2Cor 8:1 Moreover, *b*, we do you to wit of
2Cor 8:23 or our *b* be enquired of, they are
2Cor 9:3 Yet have I sent the *b*, lest our
2Cor 9:5 it necessary to exhort the *b*
2Cor 11:9 the *b* which came from Macedonia
2Cor 11:26 the sea, in perils among false *b*
2Cor 13:11 Finally, *b*, farewell
Gal 1:2 all the *b* which are with me, unto
Gal 1:11 But I certify you, *b*, that the
Gal 2:4 of false *b* unawares brought in
Gal 3:15 *B*, I speak after the manner of
Gal 4:12 *B*, I beseech you, be as I am
Gal 4:28 Now we, *b*, as Isaac was, are the
Gal 4:31 So then, *b*, we are not children
Gal 5:11 And I, *b*, if I yet preach
Gal 5:13 For, *b*, ye have been called unto
Gal 6:1 *B*, if a man be overtaken in a
Gal 6:18 *B*, the grace of our Lord Jesus
Eph 6:10 Finally, my *b*, be strong in the
Eph 6:23 Peace be to the *b*, and love with
Phil 1:12 I would ye should understand, *b*
Phil 1:14 And many of the *b* in the Lord
Phil 3:1 Finally, my *b*, rejoice in the
Phil 3:13 *B*, I count not myself to have
Phil 3:17 *B*, be followers together of me,
Phil 4:1 my *b* dearly beloved and longed for
Phil 4:8 Finally, *b*, whatsoever things are
Phil 4:21 The *b* which are with me greet you
Col 1:2 faithful *b* in Christ which are at
Col 4:15 Salute the *b* which are in
1Th 1:4 *b* beloved, your election of God
1Th 2:1 For yourselves, *b*, know our
1Th 2:9 For ye remember, *b*, our labour and
1Th 2:14 For ye, *b*, became followers of
1Th 2:17 But we, *b*, being taken from you
1Th 3:7 Therefore, *b*, we were comforted
1Th 4:1 then we beseech you, *b*, and exhort
1Th 4:10 the *b* which are in all Macedonia
1Th 4:13 not have you to be ignorant, *b*
1Th 5:1 of the times and the seasons, *b*
1Th 5:4 But ye, *b*, are not in darkness,
1Th 5:12 And we beseech you, *b*, to know
1Th 5:14 Now we exhort you, *b*, warn them
1Th 5:26 Greet all the *b* with an holy kiss
1Th 5:27 be read unto all the holy *b*
2Th 1:3 to thank God always for you, *b*
2Th 2:1 Now we beseech you, *b*, by the
2Th 2:15 Therefore, *b*, stand fast, and hold
2Th 3:1 Finally, *b*, pray for us, that the
2Th 3:6 Now we command you, *b*, in the
2Th 3:13 But ye, *b*, be not weary in well
1Ti 4:6 If thou put the *b* in remembrance
1Ti 5:1 and the younger men as *b*
1Ti 6:2 despise them, because they are *b*
2Ti 4:21 Linus, and Claudia, and all the *b*
Heb 2:11 he is not ashamed to call them *b*
Heb 2:12 I will declare thy name unto my *b*
Heb 2:17 him to be made like unto his *b*
Heb 3:1 Wherefore, holy *b*, partakers of
Heb 3:12 Take heed, *b*, lest there be in
Heb 7:5 to the law, that is, of their *b*
Heb 10:19 Having therefore, *b*, boldness to
Heb 13:22 And I beseech you, *b*, suffer the
Jas 1:2 My *b*, count it all joy when ye
Jas 1:16 Do not err, my beloved *b*
Jas 1:19 Wherefore, my beloved *b*, let
Jas 2:1 My *b*, have not the faith of our
Jas 2:5 Hearken, my beloved *b*, Hath not
Jas 2:14 What doth it profit, my *b*
Jas 3:1 My *b*, be not many masters,
Jas 3:10 My *b*, these things ought not so
Jas 3:12 Can the fig tree, my *b*, bear
Jas 4:11 Speak not evil one of another, *b*
Jas 5:7 Be patient therefore, *b*, unto the
Jas 5:9 Grudge not one against another, *b*
Jas 5:10 Take, my *b*, the prophets, who
Jas 5:19 *B*, if any of you do err from the
1Pet 1:22 unto unfeigned love of the *b*
1Pet 3:8 one of another, love as *b*
1Pet 5:9 in your *b* that are in the world
2Pet 1:10 Wherefore the rather, *b*, give
1Jn 2:7 *B*, I write no new commandment
1Jn 3:13 Marvel not, my *b*, if the world
1Jn 3:14 unto life, because we love the *b*

1Jn 3:16 to lay down our lives for the *b*
3Jn 3 rejoiced greatly, when the *b* came
3Jn 5 whatsoever thou doest to the *b*
3Jn 10 doth he himself receive the *b*
Rev 6:11 fellowservants also and their *b*
Rev 12:10 the accuser of our *b* is cast down
Rev 19:10 of thy *b* that have the testimony
Rev 22:9 of thy *b* the prophets, and of them

## BRIBES
1Sa 8:3 aside after lucre, and took *b*
Ps 26:10 and their right hand is full of *b*
Is 33:15 his hands from holding of *b*

## BRICK
Gen 11:3 to another, Go to, let us make *b*
Ex 1:14 hard bondage, in morter, and in *b*
Ex 5:7 give the people straw to make *b*
Ex 5:14 task in making *b* both yesterday
Ex 5:16 and they say to us, Make *b*
Is 65:3 burneth incense upon altars of *b*

## BRICKKILN
2Sa 12:31 and made them pass through the *b*
Jer 43:9 and hide them in the clay in the *b*
Nah 3:14 the morter, make strong the *b*

## BRICKS
Ex 5:8 And the tale of the *b*, which they
Ex 5:18 shall ye deliver the tale of *b*
Is 9:10 The *b* are fallen down, but we

## BRIDE
Is 49:18 bind them on thee, as a *b* doeth
Is 61:10 as a *b* adorneth herself with her
Is 62:5 bridegroom rejoiceth over the *b*
Jer 2:32 her ornaments, or a *b* her attire
Jer 7:34 bridegroom, and the voice of the *b*
Jer 16:9 bridegroom, and the voice of the *b*
Jer 25:10 bridegroom, and the voice of the *b*
Jer 33:11 bridegroom, and the voice of the *b*
Joel 2:16 and the *b* out of her closet
Jn 3:29 He that hath the *b* is the
Rev 18:23 of the *b* shall be heard no more
Rev 21:2 prepared as a *b* adorned for her
Rev 21:9 hither, I will shew thee the *b*
Rev 22:17 And the Spirit and the *b* say

## BRIDECHAMBER
Mt 9:15 Can the children of the *b* mourn
Mk 2:19 Can the children of the *b* fast
Lk 5:34 make the children of the *b* fast

## BRIDEGROOM
Ps 19:5 Which is as a *b* coming out of his
Is 61:10 as a *b* decketh himself with
Is 62:5 as the *b* rejoiceth over the bride
Jer 7:34 of gladness, the voice of the *b*
Jer 16:9 of gladness, the voice of the *b*
Jer 25:10 of gladness, the voice of the *b*
Jer 33:11 of gladness, the voice of the *b*
Joel 2:16 let the *b* go forth of his chamber
Mt 9:15 as long as the *b* is with them
Mt 9:15 when the *b* shall be taken from
Mt 25:1 and went forth to meet the *b*
Mt 25:5 While the *b* tarried, they all
Mt 25:6 a cry made, Behold, the *b* cometh
Mt 25:10 they went to buy, the *b* came
Mk 2:19 fast, while the *b* is with them
Mk 2:19 long as they have the *b* with them
Mk 2:20 when the *b* shall be taken away
Lk 5:34 fast, while the *b* is with them
Lk 5:35 when the *b* shall be taken away
Jn 2:9 of the feast called the *b*
Jn 3:29 He that hath the bride is the *b*
Jn 3:29 but the friend of the *b*, which
Rev 18:23 and the voice of the *b* and of the

## BRIDLE
2Kin 19:28 my *b* in thy lips, and I will turn
Job 30:11 also let loose the *b* before me
Job 41:13 can come to him with his double *b*
Ps 32:9 must be held in with bit and *b*
Ps 39:1 I will keep my mouth with a *b*
Prov 26:3 a *b* for the ass, and a rod for the
Is 30:28 there shall be a *b* in the jaws of
Is 37:29 my *b* in thy lips, and I will turn
Jas 3:2 able also to *b* the whole body

## BRIER
Is 55:13 instead of the *b* shall come up
Eze 28:24 *b* unto the house of Israel
Mic 7:4 The best of them is as a *b*

## BRIERS
Judg 8:7 of the wilderness and with *b*
Judg 8:16 and thorns of the wilderness and *b*
Is 5:6 but there shall come up *b*
Is 7:23 it shall even be for *b* and thorns
Is 9:18 it shall devour the *b* and thorns,
Is 10:17 his thorns and his *b* in one day
Is 27:4 who would set the *b* and thorns
Is 32:13 people shall come up thorns and *b*
Eze 2:6 afraid of their words, though *b*
Heb 6:8 *b* is rejected, and is nigh unto

## BRIGHT
Lev 13:2 or *b* spot, and it be in the skin
Lev 13:4 If the *b* spot be white in the
Lev 13:19 be a white rising, or a *b* spot
Lev 13:23 But if the *b* spot stay in his
Lev 14:56 and for a scab, and for a *b* spot
1Kin 7:45 of the LORD, were of *b* brass
2Chr 4:16 the house of the LORD of *b* brass
Job 37:11 he scattereth his *b* cloud
Job 37:21 now men see not the *b* light which
Song 5:14 his belly is as *b* ivory overlaid
Jer 51:11 Make *b* the arrows
Eze 1:13 and the fire was *b*, and out of the
Eze 21:15 it is made *b*, it is wrapped up
Eze 21:21 he made his arrows *b*, he
Eze 27:19 *b* iron, cassia, and calamus, were
Eze 32:8 All the *b* lights of heaven will I
Nah 3:3 lifteth up both the *b* sword
Zec 10:1 so the LORD shall make *b* clouds
Mt 17:5 a *b* cloud overshadowed them
Lk 11:36 as when the *b* shining of a candle
Acts 10:30 man stood before me in *b* clothing
Rev 22:16 the offspring of David, and the *b*

## BRIGHTNESS
2Sa 22:13 Through the *b* before him were
Job 31:26 shined, or the moon walking in *b*
Ps 18:12 At the *b* that was before him his
Is 59:9 for *b*, but we walk in darkness
Is 60:3 kings to the *b* of thy rising
Is 60:19 neither for *b* shall the moon give
Is 62:1 thereof go forth as *b*, and the
Eze 1:4 a *b* was about it, and out of the
Eze 1:27 of fire, and it had *b* round about
Eze 8:2 upward, as the appearance of *b*
Eze 10:4 full of the *b* of the LORD's glory
Eze 28:7 and they shall defile thy *b*
Eze 28:17 thy wisdom by reason of thy *b*
Dan 2:31 whose *b* was excellent, stood
Dan 4:36 mine honour and *b* returned unto me
Dan 12:3 shine as the *b* of the firmament
Amos 5:20 even very dark, and no *b* in it
Hab 3:4 And his *b* was as the light
Acts 26:13 above the *b* of the sun, shining
2Th 2:8 destroy with the *b* of his coming
Heb 1:3 Who being the *b* of his glory

## BRIM
Josh 3:15 were dipped in the *b* of the water
1Kin 7:23 from the one *b* to the other
1Kin 7:26 was wrought like the *b* of a cup
2Chr 4:2 sea of ten cubits from *b* to *b*
2Chr 4:5 the *b* of it like the work of the
Jn 2:7 And they filled them up to the *b*

## BRIMSTONE
Gen 19:24 upon Sodom and upon Gomorrah *b*
Deut 29:23 that the whole land thereof is *b*
Job 18:15 *b* shall be scattered upon his
Ps 11:6 he shall rain snares, fire and *b*
Is 30:33 of the LORD, like a stream of *b*
Is 34:9 pitch, and the dust thereof into *b*
Eze 38:22 and great hailstones, fire, and *b*
Lk 17:29 *b* from heaven, and destroyed them
Rev 9:17 of fire, and of jacinth, and *b*
Rev 14:10 *b* in the presence of the holy
Rev 19:20 a lake of fire burning with *b*
Rev 20:10 cast into the lake of fire and *b*
Rev 21:8 lake which burneth with fire and *b*

## BRINK
Gen 41:3 kine upon the *b* of the river
Ex 2:3 it in the flags by the river's *b*
Ex 7:15 by the river's *b* against he come
Deut 2:36 which is by the *b* of the river of
Josh 3:8 to the *b* of the water of Jordan
Eze 47:6 to return to the *b* of the river

## BROAD
Ex 27:1 cubits long, and five cubits *b*
Num 16:38 let them make them *b* plates for a
1Kin 6:6 chamber was five cubits *b*
2Chr 6:13 cubits long, and five cubits *b*
Neh 3:8 Jerusalem unto the *b* wall
Neh 12:38 the furnaces even unto the *b* wall
Job 36:16 out of the strait into a *b* place
Ps 119:96 thy commandment is exceeding *b*
Song 3:2 in the *b* ways I will seek him
Is 33:21 be unto us a place of *b* rivers
Jer 5:1 seek in the *b* places thereof, if
Jer 51:58 The *b* walls of Babylon shall be
Eze 40:6 of the gate, which was one reed *b*
Eze 40:29 long, and five and twenty cubits *b*
Eze 40:30 cubits long, and five cubits *b*
Eze 41:1 six cubits *b* on the one side, and
Eze 43:16 be twelve cubits long, twelve *b*
Eze 43:17 fourteen *b* in the four squares
Eze 45:6 of the city five thousand *b*
Eze 46:22 of forty cubits long and thirty *b*
Nah 2:4 one against another in the *b* ways
Mt 7:13 *b* is the way, that leadeth to
Mt 23:5 they make *b* their phylacteries,

## BROIDERED
Ex 28:4 a *b* coat, a mitre, and a girdle
Eze 16:10 I clothed thee also with *b* work
Eze 16:13 of fine linen, and silk, and *b* work
Eze 16:18 And tookest thy *b* garments
Eze 26:16 and put off their *b* garments
Eze 27:7 Fine linen with *b* work from Egypt
Eze 27:16 *b* work, and fine linen, and coral,
Eze 27:24 *b* work, and in chests of rich

## BROKEN
Gen 7:11 fountains of the great deep *b* up
Gen 17:14 he hath *b* my covenant
Gen 38:29 she said, How hast thou *b* forth
Lev 6:28 wherein it is sodden shall be *b*
Lev 11:35 for pots, they shall be *b* down
Lev 13:20 of leprosy *b* out of the boil
Lev 13:25 it is a leprosy *b* out of the
Lev 15:12 which hath the issue, shall be *b*
Lev 21:20 or scabbed, or hath his stones *b*
Lev 22:22 Blind, or *b*, or maimed, or having
Lev 22:24 is bruised, or crushed, or *b*
Lev 26:13 I have *b* the bands of your yoke,
Lev 26:26 when I have *b* the staff of your
Num 15:31 hath *b* his commandment, that soul
Judg 5:22 Then were the horsehoofs *b* by the
Judg 16:9 as a thread of tow is *b* when it
1Sa 2:4 The bows of the mighty men are *b*
1Sa 2:10 of the LORD shall be *b* to pieces
2Sa 5:20 The LORD hath *b* forth upon mine
2Sa 22:35 a bow of steel is *b* by mine arms
1Kin 18:30 altar of the LORD that was *b* down
1Kin 22:48 the ships were *b* at Ezion-geber
2Kin 11:6 the house, that it be not *b* down
2Kin 25:4 And the city was *b* up, and all the
1Chr 14:11 God hath *b* in upon mine enemies
2Chr 20:37 the LORD hath *b* thy works
2Chr 20:37 And the ships were *b*, that they
2Chr 24:7 had *b* up the house of God
2Chr 25:12 that they all were *b* in pieces
2Chr 32:5 built up all the wall that was *b*
2Chr 33:3 Hezekiah his father had *b* down
2Chr 34:7 when he had *b* down the altars and
Neh 1:3 wall of Jerusalem also is *b* down
Neh 2:13 of Jerusalem, which were *b* down
Job 4:10 teeth of the young lions, are *b*
Job 7:5 my skin is *b*, and become loathsome
Job 16:12 at ease, but he hath *b* me asunder
Job 17:11 are past, my purposes are *b* off
Job 22:9 of the fatherless have been *b*
Job 24:20 wickedness shall be *b* as a tree
Job 31:22 mine arm be *b* from the bone
Job 38:15 and the high arm shall be *b*
Ps 3:7 thou hast *b* the teeth of the
Ps 18:34 a bow of steel is *b* by mine arms
Ps 31:12 I am like a *b* vessel
Ps 34:18 unto them that are of a *b* heart
Ps 34:20 not one of them is *b*
Ps 37:15 heart, and their bows shall be *b*
Ps 37:17 the arms of the wicked shall be *b*
Ps 38:8 I am feeble and sore *b*
Ps 44:19 Though thou hast sore *b* us in the
Ps 51:8 which thou hast *b* may rejoice
Ps 51:17 sacrifices of God are a *b* spirit
Ps 51:17 a *b* and a contrite heart, O God,
Ps 55:20 he hath *b* his covenant
Ps 60:2 thou hast *b* it
Ps 69:20 Reproach hath *b* my heart
Ps 80:12 hast thou then *b* down her hedges
Ps 89:10 Thou hast *b* Rahab in pieces, as

Ps 89:40 Thou hast *b* down all his hedges
Ps 107:16 For he hath *b* the gates of brass,
Ps 109:16 he might even slay the *b* in heart
Ps 124:7 the snare is *b*, and we are escaped
Ps 147:3 He healeth the *b* in heart
Prov 3:20 his knowledge the depths are *b* up
Prov 6:15 shall he be *b* without remedy
Prov 15:13 of the heart the spirit is *b*
Prov 17:22 but a *b* spirit drieth the bones
Prov 24:31 the stone wall thereof was *b* down
Prov 25:19 time of trouble is like a *b* tooth
Prov 25:28 is like a city that is *b* down
Eccl 4:12 a threefold cord is not quickly *b*
Eccl 12:6 loosed, or the golden bowl be *b*
Is 5:27 the latchet of their shoes be *b*
Is 7:8 and five years shall Ephraim be *b*
Is 8:9 and ye shall be *b* in pieces
Is 8:15 shall stumble, and fall, and be *b*
Is 9:4 For thou hast *b* the yoke of his
Is 14:5 The LORD hath *b* the staff of the
Is 14:29 rod of him that smote thee is *b*
Is 16:8 have *b* down the principal plants
Is 19:10 they shall be *b* in the purposes
Is 21:9 gods he hath *b* unto the ground
Is 22:10 the houses have ye *b* down to
Is 24:5 *b* the everlasting covenant
Is 24:10 The city of confusion is *b* down
Is 24:19 The earth is utterly *b* down
Is 27:11 are withered, they shall be *b* off
Is 28:13 go, and fall backward, and be *b*
Is 30:14 vessel that is *b* in pieces
Is 33:8 he hath *b* the covenant, he hath
Is 33:20 any of the cords thereof be *b*
Is 36:6 in the staff of this *b* reed
Jer 2:13 *b* cisterns, that can hold no
Jer 2:16 Tahapanes have *b* the crown of thy
Jer 2:20 For of old time I have *b* thy yoke
Jer 4:26 *b* down at the presence of the
Jer 5:5 these have altogether *b* the yoke
Jer 10:20 is spoiled, and all my cords are *b*
Jer 11:10 the house of Judah have *b* my
Jer 11:16 it, and the branches of it are *b*
Jer 14:17 people is *b* with a great breach
Jer 22:28 this man Coniah a despised *b* idol
Jer 23:9 me is *b* because of the prophets
Jer 28:2 I have *b* the yoke of the king of
Jer 28:12 *b* the yoke from off the neck of
Jer 33:21 be *b* with David my servant
Jer 37:11 *b* up from Jerusalem for fear of
Jer 39:2 of the month, the city was *b* up
Jer 48:17 say, How is the strong staff *b*
Jer 48:25 Moab is cut off, and his arm is *b*
Jer 48:38 for I have *b* Moab like a vessel
Jer 50:2 Merodach is *b* in pieces
Jer 50:17 king of Babylon hath *b* his bones
Jer 50:23 whole earth cut in asunder and *b*
Jer 51:30 her bars are *b*
Jer 51:56 every one of their bows is *b*
Jer 51:58 of Babylon shall be utterly *b*
Jer 52:7 Then the city was *b* up, and all
Lam 2:9 he hath destroyed and *b* her bars
Lam 3:4 he hath *b* my bones
Lam 3:16 He hath also *b* my teeth with
Eze 6:4 and your images shall be *b*
Eze 6:9 because I am *b* with their whorish
Eze 17:19 and my covenant that he hath *b*
Eze 19:12 her strong rods were *b* and
Eze 26:2 she is *b* that was the gates of
Eze 27:26 the east wind hath *b* thee in the
Eze 27:34 be *b* by the seas in the depths of
Eze 30:4 her foundations shall be *b* down
Eze 30:21 I have *b* the arm of Pharaoh king
Eze 31:12 his boughs are *b* by all the
Eze 32:28 thou shalt be *b* in the midst of
Eze 34:4 have ye bound up that which was *b*
Eze 34:16 and will bind up that which was *b*
Eze 34:27 when I have *b* the bands of their
Eze 44:7 they have *b* my covenant because
Dan 2:35 *b* to pieces together, and became
Dan 2:42 be partly strong, and partly *b*
Dan 8:8 was strong, the great horn was *b*
Dan 8:22 Now that being *b*, whereas four
Dan 8:25 but he shall be *b* without hand
Dan 11:4 stand up, his kingdom shall be *b*
Dan 11:22 from before him, and shall be *b*
Hos 5:11 *b* in judgment, because he
Hos 8:6 of Samaria shall be *b* in pieces
Joel 1:17 desolate, the barns are *b* down
Jonah 1:4 so that the ship was like to be *b*
Mic 2:13 they have *b* up, and have passed
Zec 11:11 And it was *b* in that day
Zec 11:16 one, nor heal that that is *b*
Mt 15:37 they took up of the *b* meat that
Mt 21:44 fall on this stone shall be *b*
Mt 24:43 suffered his house to be *b* up
Mk 2:4 and when they had *b* it up, they
Mk 5:4 him, and the fetters *b* in pieces
Mk 8:8 they took up of the *b* meat that
Lk 12:39 his house to be *b* through
Lk 20:18 fall upon that stone shall be *b*
Jn 5:18 he not only had *b* the sabbath
Jn 7:23 the law of Moses should not be *b*
Jn 10:35 and the scripture cannot be *b*
Jn 19:31 Pilate that their legs might be *b*
Jn 19:36 A bone of him shall not be *b*
Jn 21:11 so many, yet was not the net *b*
Acts 13:43 when the congregation was *b* up
Acts 20:11 had *b* bread, and eaten, and talked
Acts 27:35 and when he had *b* it, he began to
Rom 11:17 if some of the branches be *b* off
1Cor 11:24 is my body, which is *b* for you
Eph 2:14 hath *b* down the middle wall of
Rev 2:27 potter shall they be *b* to shivers

## BROOK

Gen 32:23 them, and sent them over the *b*
Lev 23:40 thick trees, and willows of the *b*
Num 13:23 And they came unto the *b* of Eshcol
Deut 2:13 I, and get you over the *b* Zered
Deut 9:21 cast the dust thereof into the *b*
1Sa 17:40 five smooth stones out of the *b*
1Sa 30:9 with him, and came to the *b* Besor
1Sa 30:10 could not go over the *b* Besor
1Sa 30:21 made also to abide at the *b* Besor
2Sa 15:23 himself passed over the *b* Kidron
2Sa 17:20 They be gone over the *b* of water
1Kin 2:37 out, and passest over the *b* Kidron
1Kin 15:13 idol, and burnt it by the *b* Kidron
1Kin 17:3 and hide thyself by the *b* Cherith
1Kin 17:7 a while, that the *b* dried up
1Kin 18:40 brought them down to the *b* Kishon
2Kin 23:6 Jerusalem, unto the *b* Kidron
2Kin 23:12 dust of them into the *b* Kidron
2Chr 15:16 it, and burnt it at the *b* Kidron
2Chr 20:16 find them at the end of the *b*
2Chr 29:16 it out abroad into the *b* Kidron
2Chr 30:14 and cast them into the *b* Kidron
2Chr 32:4 the *b* that ran through the midst
Neh 2:15 went I up in the night by the *b*
Job 6:15 have dealt deceitfully as a *b*
Job 40:22 of the *b* compass him about
Ps 83:9 as to Jabin, at the *b* of Kison
Ps 110:7 shall drink of the *b* in the way
Prov 18:4 of wisdom as a flowing *b*
Is 15:7 away to the *b* of the willows
Jer 31:40 the fields unto the *b* of Kidron
Jn 18:1 his disciples over the *b* Cedron

## BROOKS

Num 21:14 Red sea, and in the *b* of Arnon,
Deut 8:7 a good land, a land of *b* of water
2Sa 23:30 Hiddai of the *b* of Gaash
1Kin 18:5 fountains of water, and unto all *b*
1Chr 11:32 Hurai of the *b* of Gaash, Abiel
Job 6:15 as the stream of *b* they pass away
Job 20:17 floods, the *b* of honey and butter
Job 22:24 of Ophir as the stones of the *b*
Ps 42:1 hart panteth after the water *b*
Is 19:6 the *b* of defence shall be emptied

## BROTH

Judg 6:19 basket, and he put the *b* in a pot
Judg 6:20 upon this rock, and pour out the *b*
Is 65:4 *b* of abominable things is in

## BROTHER

Gen 4:2 And she again bare his *b* Abel
Gen 4:8 And Cain talked with Abel his *b*
Gen 9:5 at the hand of every man's *b* will
Gen 10:21 the *b* of Japheth the elder, even
Gen 14:13 *b* of Eshcol, and *b* of Aner
Gen 20:5 even she herself said, He is my *b*
Gen 20:13 shall come, say of me, He is my *b*
Gen 20:16 I have given thy *b* a thousand
Gen 22:20 born children unto thy *b* Nahor
Gen 22:23 did bear to Nahor, Abraham's *b*
Gen 24:15 the wife of Nahor, Abraham's *b*
Gen 24:29 And Rebekah had a *b*, and his name
Gen 24:53 he gave also to her *b* and to her
Gen 25:26 And after that came his *b* out
Gen 27:6 thy father speak unto Esau thy *b*
Gen 27:11 Esau my *b* is a hairy man, and I am
Gen 27:23 were hairy, as his *b* Esau's hands
Gen 27:30 that Esau his *b* came in from his
Gen 27:41 then will I slay my *b* Jacob
Gen 27:42 thy *b* Esau, as touching thee,
Gen 27:43 flee thou to Laban my *b* to Haran
Gen 28:2 daughters of Laban thy mother's *b*
Gen 28:5 the *b* of Rebekah, Jacob's and
Gen 29:10 the flock of Laban his mother's *b*
Gen 29:12 Rachel that he was her father's *b*
Gen 29:15 unto Jacob, Because thou art my *b*
Gen 32:3 Esau his *b* unto the land of Seir
Gen 32:6 saying, We came to thy *b* Esau
Gen 32:11 pray thee, from the hand of my *b*
Gen 32:13 his hand a present for Esau his *b*
Gen 32:17 When Esau my *b* meeteth thee
Gen 33:3 until he came near to his *b*
Gen 33:9 And Esau said, I have enough, my *b*
Gen 35:1 from the face of Esau thy *b*
Gen 35:7 he fled from the face of his *b*
Gen 36:6 from the face of his *b* Jacob
Gen 37:26 profit is it if we slay our *b*
Gen 37:27 for he is our *b* and our flesh
Gen 38:8 her, and raise up seed to thy *b*
Gen 38:29 that, behold, his *b* came out
Gen 42:4 But Benjamin, Joseph's *b*, Jacob
Gen 42:15 your youngest *b* come hither
Gen 42:20 But bring your youngest *b* unto me
Gen 42:21 verily guilty concerning our *b*
Gen 42:34 And bring your youngest *b* unto me
Gen 42:38 for his *b* is dead, and he is left
Gen 43:3 face, except your *b* be with you
Gen 43:13 Take also your *b*, and arise, go
Gen 43:29 saw his *b* Benjamin, his mother's
Gen 44:19 saying, Have ye a father, or a *b*
Gen 45:4 And he said, I am Joseph your *b*
Gen 45:12 see, and the eyes of my *b* Benjamin
Gen 48:19 but truly his younger *b* shall be
Ex 4:14 Is not Aaron the Levite thy *b*
Ex 7:1 Aaron thy *b* shall be thy prophet
Ex 28:1 take thou unto thee Aaron thy *b*
Ex 28:4 holy garments for Aaron thy *b*
Ex 28:41 shalt put them upon Aaron thy *b*
Ex 32:27 the camp, and slay every man his *b*
Ex 32:29 man upon his son, and upon his *b*
Lev 16:2 Moses, Speak unto Aaron thy *b*
Lev 18:14 the nakedness of thy father's *b*
Lev 19:17 not hate thy *b* in thine heart
Lev 21:2 and for his daughter, and for his *b*
Lev 25:25 If thy *b* be waxen poor, and hath
Lev 25:35 if thy *b* be waxen poor, and fallen
Lev 25:39 if thy *b* that dwelleth by thee be
Lev 25:47 thy *b* that dwelleth by him wax
Num 6:7 or for his mother, for his *b*
Num 20:8 together, thou, and Aaron thy *b*
Num 20:14 of Edom, Thus saith thy *b* Israel
Num 27:13 as Aaron thy *b* was gathered
Num 36:2 our *b* unto his daughters
Deut 1:16 between every man and his *b*
Deut 13:6 If thy *b*, the son of thy mother,
Deut 15:2 it of his neighbour, or of his *b*
Deut 15:7 shut thine hand from thy poor *b*
Deut 15:9 eye be evil against thy poor *b*
Deut 17:15 over thee, which is not thy *b*
Deut 19:18 testified falsely against his *b*
Deut 22:1 case bring them again unto thy *b*
Deut 23:7 for he is thy *b*
Deut 23:19 not lend upon usury to thy *b*
Deut 24:10 thou dost lend thy *b* any thing
Deut 25:3 then thy *b* should seem vile unto
Deut 25:5 her husband's *b* shall go in unto
Deut 25:5 duty of an husband's *b* unto her
Deut 25:6 the name of his *b* which is dead
Deut 25:7 My husband's *b* refuseth to raise
Deut 25:7 up unto his *b* a name in Israel
Deut 25:7 the duty of my husband's *b*
Deut 28:54 eye shall be evil toward his *b*
Deut 32:50 as Aaron thy *b* died in mount Hor,
Josh 15:17 of Kenaz, the *b* of Caleb, took it
Judg 1:3 And Judah said unto Simeon his *b*
Judg 1:13 son of Kenaz, Caleb's younger *b*
Judg 1:17 And Judah went with Simeon his *b*
Judg 3:9 son of Kenaz, Caleb's younger *b*
Judg 9:3 for they said, He is our *b*
Judg 9:18 of Shechem, because he is your *b*
Judg 9:21 for fear of Abimelech his *b*
Judg 9:24 be laid upon Abimelech their *b*
Judg 20:23 the children of Benjamin my *b*
Judg 20:28 the children of Benjamin my *b*
Judg 21:6 them for Benjamin their *b*
Ruth 4:3 land, which was our *b* Elimelech's

1Sa 14:3 the son of Ahitub, I-chabod's *b*
1Sa 17:28 Eliab his eldest *b* heard when he
1Sa 20:29 and my *b*, he hath commanded me to
1Sa 26:6 *b* to Joab, saying, Who will go
2Sa 1:26 for thee, my *b* Jonathan
2Sa 2:22 I hold up my face to Joab thy *b*
2Sa 2:27 up every one from following his *b*
2Sa 3:30 Joab and Abishai his *b* slew Abner
2Sa 4:6 Rechab and Baanah his *b* escaped
2Sa 4:9 answered Rechab and Baanah his *b*
2Sa 10:10 into the hand of Abishai his *b*
2Sa 13:3 the son of Shimeah David's *b*
2Sa 13:4 love Tamar, my *b* Absalom's sister
2Sa 13:7 Go now to thy *b* Amnon's house
2Sa 13:8 Tamar went to her *b* Amnon's house
2Sa 13:10 into the chamber to Amnon her *b*
2Sa 13:12 And she answered him, Nay, my *b*
2Sa 14:7 Deliver him that smote his *b*
2Sa 18:2 the son of Zeruiah, Joab's *b*
2Sa 20:9 Amasa, Art thou in health, my *b*
2Sa 20:10 Abishai his *b* pursued after Sheba
2Sa 21:19 slew the *b* of Goliath the Gittite
2Sa 21:21 Shimeah the *b* of David slew him
2Sa 23:18 the *b* of Joab, the son of Zeruiah
2Sa 23:24 Asahel the *b* of Joab was one of
1Kin 1:10 the mighty men, and Solomon his *b*
1Kin 2:7 I fled because of Absalom thy *b*
1Kin 2:21 given to Adonijah thy *b* to wife
1Kin 9:13 which thou hast given me, my *b*
1Kin 13:30 over him, saying, Alas, my *b*
1Kin 20:32 he is my *b*
1Kin 20:33 and they said, Thy *b* Ben-hadad
2Kin 24:17 his father's *b* king in his stead
1Chr 2:32 the sons of Jada the *b* of Shammai
1Chr 2:42 of Caleb the *b* of Jerahmeel were
1Chr 4:11 Chelub the *b* of Shuah begat Mehir
1Chr 6:39 his *b* Asaph, who stood on his
1Chr 7:16 and the name of his *b* was Sheresh
1Chr 7:35 And the sons of his *b* Helem
1Chr 8:39 And the sons of Eshek his *b* were
1Chr 11:20 And Abishai the *b* of Joab, he was
1Chr 11:26 armies were, Asahel the *b* of Joab
1Chr 11:38 Joel the *b* of Nathan, Mibhar the
1Chr 11:45 the son of Shimri, and Joha his *b*
1Chr 19:11 unto the hand of Abishai his *b*
1Chr 19:15 fled before Abishai his *b*
1Chr 20:5 the *b* of Goliath the Gittite
1Chr 20:7 son of Shimea David's *b* slew him
1Chr 24:25 The *b* of Michah was Isshiah
1Chr 26:22 Zetham, and Joel his *b*, which were
1Chr 27:7 month was Asahel the *b* of Joab
2Chr 31:12 Shimei his *b* was the next
2Chr 31:13 hand of Cononiah and Shimei his *b*
2Chr 36:4 Eliakim his *b* king over Judah
2Chr 36:4 And Necho took Jehoahaz his *b*
2Chr 36:10 Zedekiah his *b* king over Judah
Neh 5:7 exact usury, every one of his *b*
Neh 7:2 That I gave my *b* Hanani, and
Job 22:6 a pledge from thy *b* for nought
Job 30:29 I am a *b* to dragons, and a
Ps 35:14 though he had been my friend or *b*
Ps 49:7 can by any means redeem his *b*
Ps 50:20 sittest and speakest against thy *b*
Prov 17:17 a *b* is born for adversity
Prov 18:9 *b* to him that is a great waster
Prov 18:19 A *b* offended is harder to be won
Prov 18:24 that sticketh closer than a *b*
Prov 27:10 that is near than a *b* far off
Eccl 4:8 yea, he hath neither child nor *b*
Song 8:1 O that thou wert as my *b*, that
Is 3:6 his *b* of the house of his father
Is 9:19 no man shall spare his *b*
Is 19:2 fight every one against his *b*
Is 41:6 and every one said to his *b*
Jer 9:4 and trust ye not in any *b*
Jer 22:18 lament for him, saying, Ah my *b*
Jer 23:35 neighbour, and every one to his *b*
Jer 31:34 his neighbour, and every man his *b*
Jer 34:9 of them, to wit, of a Jew his *b*
Jer 34:14 ye go every man his *b* an Hebrew
Jer 34:17 liberty, every one to his *b*
Eze 18:18 spoiled his *b* by violence
Eze 33:30 to another, every one to his *b*
Eze 38:21 sword shall be against his *b*
Eze 44:25 for son, or for daughter, for *b*
Hos 12:3 He took his *b* by the heel in the
Amos 1:11 did pursue his *b* with the sword
Obad 10 *b* Jacob shame shall cover thee
Obad 12 thy *b* in the day that he became a
Mic 7:2 hunt every man his *b* with a net
Hag 2:22 every one by the sword of his *b*
Zec 7:9 and compassions every man to his *b*
Zec 7:10 evil against his *b* in your heart
Mal 1:2 Was not Esau Jacob's *b*
Mal 2:10 every man against his *b*, by
Mt 4:18 called Peter, and Andrew his *b*
Mt 4:21 the son of Zebedee, and John his *b*
Mt 5:22 his *b* without a cause shall be in
Mt 5:23 thy *b* hath ought against thee
Mt 5:24 first be reconciled to thy *b*
Mt 7:4 Or how wilt thou say to thy *b*
Mt 10:2 is called Peter, and Andrew his *b*
Mt 10:21 *b* shall deliver up the *b* to death
Mt 12:50 is in heaven, the same is my *b*
Mt 14:3 sake, his *b* Philip's wife
Mt 17:1 Peter, James, and John his *b*
Mt 18:15 Moreover if thy *b* shall trespass
Mt 18:21 how oft shall my *b* sin against me
Mt 18:35 every one his *b* their trespasses
Mt 22:24 his *b* shall marry his wife
Mt 22:25 issue, left his wife unto his *b*
Mk 1:16 Andrew his *b* casting a net into
Mk 1:19 the son of Zebedee, and John his *b*
Mk 3:17 Zebedee, and John the *b* of James
Mk 3:35 the will of God, the same is my *b*
Mk 5:37 and James, and John the *b* of James
Mk 6:3 the *b* of James, and Joses, and of
Mk 6:17 sake, his *b* Philip's wife
Mk 12:19 wrote unto us, If a man's *b* die
Mk 13:12 *b* shall betray the *b* to death
Lk 3:1 his *b* Philip tetrarch of Ituraea
Lk 3:19 for Herodias his *b* Philip's wife
Lk 6:14 named Peter,) and Andrew his *b*
Lk 6:16 And Judas the *b* of James, and Judas
Lk 6:42 canst thou say to thy *b*, *B*
Lk 12:13 unto him, Master, speak to my *b*
Lk 15:27 he said unto him, Thy *b* is come
Lk 15:32 for this thy *b* was dead, and is
Lk 17:3 If thy *b* trespass against thee,
Lk 20:28 wrote unto us, If any man's *b* die
Jn 1:40 him, was Andrew, Simon Peter's *b*
Jn 1:41 He first findeth his own *b* Simon
Jn 6:8 Andrew, Simon Peter's *b*, saith
Jn 11:2 hair, whose *b* Lazarus was sick
Jn 11:19 comfort them concerning their *b*
Jn 11:21 been here, my *b* had not died
Jn 11:23 unto her, Thy *b* shall rise again
Jn 11:32 been here, my *b* had not died
Acts 1:13 Zelotes, and Judas the *b* of James
Acts 9:17 *B* Saul, the Lord, even Jesus,
Acts 12:2 he killed James the *b* of John
Acts 21:20 and said unto him, Thou seest, *b*
Acts 22:13 *B* Saul, receive thy sight
Rom 14:10 But why dost thou judge thy *b*
Rom 14:15 But if thy *b* be grieved with thy
Rom 14:21 any thing whereby thy *b* stumbleth
Rom 16:23 city saluteth you, and Quartus a *b*
1Cor 1:1 will of God, and Sosthenes our *b*
1Cor 5:11 is called a *b* be a fornicator
1Cor 6:6 But *b* goeth to law with *b*,
1Cor 7:12 If any *b* hath a wife that
1Cor 7:15 A *b* or a sister is not under
1Cor 8:11 knowledge shall the weak *b* perish
1Cor 8:13 if meat make my *b* to offend
1Cor 8:13 lest I make my *b* to offend
1Cor 16:12 As touching our *b* Apollos
2Cor 1:1 the will of God, and Timothy our *b*
2Cor 2:13 because I found not Titus my *b*
2Cor 8:18 And we have sent with him the *b*
2Cor 8:22 And we have sent with them our *b*
2Cor 12:18 Titus, and with him I sent a *b*
Gal 1:19 I none, save James the Lord's *b*
Eph 6:21 how I do, Tychicus, a beloved *b*
Phil 2:25 to send to you Epaphroditus, my *b*
Col 1:1 will of God, and Timotheus our *b*
Col 4:7 unto you, who is a beloved *b*
Col 4:9 Onesimus, a faithful and beloved *b*
1Th 3:2 And sent Timotheus, our *b*, and
1Th 4:6 defraud his *b* in any matter
2Th 3:6 every *b* that walketh disorderly
2Th 3:15 an enemy, but admonish him as a *b*
Philem 1 of Jesus Christ, and Timothy our *b*
Philem 7 saints are refreshed by thee, *b*
Philem 16 a *b* beloved, specially to me, but
Philem 20 Yea, *b*, let me have joy of thee
Heb 8:11 his neighbour, and every man his *b*
Heb 13:23 Know ye that our *b* Timothy is set
Jas 1:9 Let the *b* of low degree rejoice
Jas 2:15 If a *b* or sister be naked, and
Jas 4:11 He that speaketh evil of his *b*
Jas 4:11 of his *b*, and judgeth his *b*
1Pet 5:12 Silvanus, a faithful *b* unto you
2Pet 3:15 even as our beloved *b* Paul also
1Jn 2:9 is in the light, and hateth his *b*
1Jn 2:10 He that loveth his *b* abideth in
1Jn 2:11 that hateth his *b* is in darkness
1Jn 3:10 neither he that loveth not his *b*
1Jn 3:12 of that wicked one, and slew his *b*
1Jn 3:14 loveth not his *b* abideth in death
1Jn 3:15 hateth his *b* is a murderer
1Jn 3:17 good, and seeth his *b* have need
1Jn 4:20 say, I love God, and hateth his *b*
1Jn 4:21 he who loveth God love his *b* also
1Jn 5:16 If any man see his *b* sin a sin
Jude 1 *b* of James, to them that are
Rev 1:9 I John, who also am your *b*

## BROTHERLY

Amos 1:9 and remembered not the *b* covenant
Rom 12:10 one to another with *b* love
1Th 4:9 But as touching *b* love ye need
Heb 13:1 Let *b* love continue
2Pet 1:7 And to godliness *b* kindness
2Pet 1:7 and to *b* kindness charity

## BROTHER'S

Gen 4:9 Am I my *b* keeper
Gen 4:10 the voice of thy *b* blood crieth
Gen 4:21 And his *b* name was Jubal
Gen 10:25 and his *b* name was Joktan
Gen 12:5 Sarai his wife, and Lot his *b* son
Gen 14:12 And they took Lot, Abram's *b* son
Gen 24:48 master's *b* daughter unto his son
Gen 27:44 until thy *b* fury turn away
Gen 38:8 unto Onan, Go in unto thy *b* wife
Lev 18:16 the nakedness of thy *b* wife
Lev 20:21 And if a man shall take his *b* wife
Deut 22:1 Thou shalt not see thy *b* ox or
Deut 22:3 and with all lost things of thy *b*
Deut 22:4 Thou shalt not see thy *b* ass or
Deut 25:7 man like not to take his *b* wife
Deut 25:9 Then shall his *b* wife come unto
Deut 25:9 will not build up his *b* house
1Kin 2:15 turned about, and is become my *b*
1Chr 1:19 and his *b* name was Joktan
Job 1:13 wine in their eldest *b* house
Job 1:18 wine in their eldest *b* house
Prov 27:10 neither go into thy *b* house in
Mt 7:3 the mote that is in thy *b* eye
Mt 7:5 out the mote out of thy *b* eye
Mk 6:18 for thee to have thy *b* wife
Lk 6:41 the mote that is in thy *b* eye
Lk 6:42 out the mote that is in thy *b* eye
Rom 14:13 an occasion to fall in his *b* way
1Jn 3:12 were evil, and his *b* righteous

## BROWN

Gen 30:32 all the *b* cattle among the sheep,
Gen 30:33 *b* among the sheep, that shall be
Gen 30:35 all the *b* among the sheep, and
Gen 30:40 all the *b* in the flock of Laban

## BRUISE

Gen 3:15 it shall *b* thy head, and thou
Is 28:28 nor *b* it with his horsemen
Is 53:10 Yet it pleased the LORD to *b* him
Jer 30:12 Thy *b* is incurable, and thy wound
Dan 2:40 shall it break in pieces and *b*
Nah 3:19 There is no healing of thy *b*
Rom 16:20 the God of peace shall *b* Satan

## BRUISED

Lev 22:24 unto the LORD that which is *b*
2Kin 18:21 upon the staff of this *b* reed
Is 28:28 Bread corn is *b*
Is 42:3 A *b* reed shall he not break, and
Is 53:5 he was *b* for our iniquities
Eze 23:3 there they *b* the teats of their
Eze 23:8 they *b* the breasts of her
Mt 12:20 A *b* reed shall he not break, and
Lk 4:18 to set at liberty them that are *b*

## BRUTISH

Ps 49:10 the *b* person perish, and leave
Ps 92:6 A *b* man knoweth not
Ps 94:8 Understand, ye *b* among the people
Prov 12:1 but he that hateth reproof is *b*
Prov 30:2 Surely I am more *b* than any man
Is 19:11 of Pharaoh is become *b*
Jer 10:8 But they are altogether *b*
Jer 10:14 Every man is *b* in his knowledge
Jer 10:21 For the pastors are become *b*
Jer 51:17 Every man is *b* by his knowledge
Eze 21:31 thee into the hand of *b* men

## BUCKLER
2Sa 22:31 he is a *b* to all them that trust
1Chr 5:18 valiant men, men able to bear *b*
1Chr 12:8 that could handle shield and *b*
Ps 18:2 my *b*, and the horn of my salvation
Ps 18:30 he is a *b* to all those that trust
Ps 35:2 Take hold of shield and *b*, and
Ps 91:4 truth shall be thy shield and *b*
Prov 2:7 he is a *b* to them that walk
Jer 46:3 Order ye the *b* and shield, and draw
Eze 23:24 which shall set against thee *b*
Eze 26:8 lift up the *b* against thee

## BUCKLERS
2Chr 23:9 captains of hundreds spears, and *b*
Job 15:26 upon the thick bosses of his *b*
Song 4:4 whereon there hang a thousand *b*
Eze 38:4 even a great company with *b*
Eze 39:9 both the shields and the *b*

## BUD
Job 14:9 the scent of water it will *b*
Job 38:27 to cause the *b* of the tender herb
Ps 132:17 I make the horn of David to *b*
Song 7:12 and the pomegranates *b* forth
Is 18:5 when the *b* is perfect, and the
Is 27:6 Israel shall blossom and *b*
Is 55:10 and maketh it bring forth and *b*
Is 61:11 as the earth bringeth forth her *b*
Eze 16:7 to multiply as the *b* of the field
Eze 29:21 of the house of Israel to *b* forth
Hos 8:7 the *b* shall yield no meal

## BUDDED
Gen 40:10 and it was as though it *b*, and her
Num 17:8 Aaron for the house of Levi was *b*
Song 6:11 flourished, and the pomegranates *b*
Eze 7:10 rod hath blossomed, pride hath *b*
Heb 9:4 had manna, and Aaron's rod that *b*

## BUFFETED
Mt 26:67 they spit in his face, and *b* him
1Cor 4:11 and thirst, and are naked, and are *b*
1Pet 2:20 when ye be *b* for your faults, ye

## BUILD
Gen 11:4 let us *b* us a city and a tower,
Gen 11:8 and they left off to *b* the city
Ex 20:25 thou shalt not *b* it of hewn stone
Num 23:1 *B* me here seven altars, and
Num 23:29 *B* me here seven altars, and
Num 32:16 We will *b* sheepfolds here for our
Num 32:24 *B* you cities for your little ones
Deut 20:20 thou shalt *b* bulwarks against the
Deut 25:9 will not *b* up his brother's house
Deut 27:5 there shalt thou *b* an altar unto
Deut 27:6 Thou shalt *b* the altar of the
Deut 28:30 thou shalt *b* an house, and thou
Josh 22:26 us now prepare to *b* us an altar
Josh 22:29 to *b* an altar for burnt offerings
Judg 6:26 *b* an altar unto the LORD thy God
Ruth 4:11 which two did *b* the house of
1Sa 2:35 I will *b* him a sure house
2Sa 7:5 Shalt thou *b* me an house for me
2Sa 7:7 Why *b* ye not me an house of cedar
2Sa 7:13 He shall *b* an house for my name,
2Sa 7:27 saying, I will *b* thee an house
2Sa 24:21 to *b* an altar unto the LORD, that
1Kin 2:36 *B* thee an house in Jerusalem, and
1Kin 5:3 *b* an house unto the name of the
1Kin 5:18 timber and stones to *b* the house
1Kin 6:1 that he began to *b* the house of
1Kin 8:16 tribes of Israel to *b* an house
1Kin 9:15 for to *b* the house of the LORD,
1Kin 9:19 Solomon desired to *b* in Jerusalem
1Kin 9:24 then did he *b* Millo
1Kin 11:7 Then did Solomon *b* an high place
1Kin 11:38 *b* thee a sure house, as I built
1Kin 16:34 did Hiel the Beth-elite *b* Jericho
1Chr 14:1 and carpenters, to *b* him an house
1Chr 17:4 Thou shalt not *b* me an house to
1Chr 17:10 the LORD will *b* thee an house
1Chr 17:12 He shall *b* me an house, and I will
1Chr 17:25 that thou wilt *b* him an house
1Chr 21:22 that I may *b* an altar therein
1Chr 22:2 stones to *b* the house of God
1Chr 22:6 charged him to *b* an house for the
1Chr 28:2 I had in mine heart to *b* an house
1Chr 29:16 to *b* thee an house for thine holy
2Chr 2:1 Solomon determined to *b* an house
2Chr 2:3 didst send him cedars to *b* him an
2Chr 2:9 to *b* shall be wonderful great
2Chr 2:12 that might *b* an house for the
2Chr 3:1 Then Solomon began to *b* the house
2Chr 6:5 tribes of Israel to *b* an house in
2Chr 8:6 Solomon desired to *b* in Jerusalem
2Chr 14:7 Let us *b* these cities, and make
2Chr 35:3 son of David king of Israel did *b*
2Chr 36:23 he hath charged me to *b* him an
Ezr 1:2 he hath charged me to *b* him an
Ezr 4:2 said unto them, Let us *b* with you
Ezr 5:2 began to *b* the house of God which
Ezr 6:7 the elders of the Jews *b* this
Neh 2:5 sepulchres, that I may *b* it
Neh 2:17 let us *b* up the wall of Jerusalem
Neh 3:3 gate did the sons of Hassenaah *b*
Neh 4:3 he said, Even that which they *b*
Neh 4:10 we are not able to *b* the wall
Ps 28:5 destroy them, and not *b* them up
Ps 51:18 *b* thou the walls of Jerusalem
Ps 69:35 will *b* the cities of Judah
Ps 89:4 ever, and *b* up thy throne to all
Ps 102:16 When the LORD shall *b* up Zion
Ps 127:1 Except the LORD *b* the house
Ps 127:1 they labour in vain that *b* it
Ps 147:2 The LORD doth *b* up Jerusalem
Prov 24:27 and afterwards *b* thine house
Eccl 3:3 to break down, and a time to *b* up
Song 8:9 we will *b* upon her a palace of
Is 9:10 but we will *b* with hewn stones
Is 45:13 he shall *b* my city, and he shall
Is 58:12 thee shall *b* the old waste places
Is 60:10 of strangers shall *b* up thy walls
Is 61:4 they shall *b* the old wastes, they
Is 65:21 And they shall *b* houses, and
Is 66:1 is the house that ye *b* unto me
Jer 1:10 destroy, and to throw down, to *b*
Jer 18:9 and concerning a kingdom, to *b*
Jer 22:14 I will *b* me a wide house and large
Jer 24:6 and I will *b* them, and not pull
Jer 29:5 *B* ye houses, and dwell in them
Jer 29:28 *b* ye houses, and dwell in them
Jer 31:4 Again I will *b* thee, and thou
Jer 31:28 so will I watch over them, to *b*
Jer 33:7 Israel to return, and will *b* them
Jer 35:7 Neither shall ye *b* house, nor sow
Jer 35:9 Nor to *b* houses for us to dwell
Jer 42:10 in this land, then will I *b* you
Eze 4:2 *b* a fort against it, and cast a
Eze 11:3 let us *b* houses
Eze 21:22 to cast a mount, and to *b* a fort
Eze 28:26 and shall *b* houses, and plant
Eze 36:36 I the LORD *b* the ruined places
Dan 9:25 to *b* Jerusalem unto the Messiah
Amos 9:11 I will *b* it as in the days of old
Amos 9:14 they shall *b* the waste cities, and
Mic 3:10 They *b* up Zion with blood, and
Zeph 1:13 they shall also *b* houses, but not
Hag 1:8 and bring wood, and *b* the house
Zec 5:11 To *b* it an house in the land of
Zec 6:12 he shall *b* the temple of the LORD
Zec 9:3 Tyrus did *b* herself a strong hold
Mal 1:4 return and *b* the desolate places
Mt 16:18 upon this rock I will *b* my church
Mt 23:29 because ye *b* the tombs of the
Mt 26:61 of God, and to *b* it in three days
Mk 14:58 within three days I will *b*
Lk 11:47 Woe unto you! for ye *b* the
Lk 12:18 pull down my barns, and *b* greater
Lk 14:28 of you, intending to *b* a tower
Lk 14:30 Saying, This man began to *b*
Acts 7:49 what house will ye *b* me
Acts 15:16 will *b* again the tabernacle of
Acts 20:32 grace, which is able to *b* you up
Rom 15:20 lest I should *b* upon another
1Cor 3:12 Now if any man *b* upon this
Gal 2:18 For if I *b* again the things which

## BUILDED
Gen 4:17 he *b* a city, and called the name
Gen 8:20 Noah *b* an altar unto the LORD
Gen 10:11 *b* Nineveh, and the city Rehoboth,
Gen 11:5 which the children of men *b*
Gen 12:7 there *b* he an altar unto the LORD
Gen 26:25 he *b* an altar there, and called
Ex 24:4 *b* an altar under the hill, and
Num 32:38 unto the cities which they *b*
Josh 22:16 in that ye have *b* you an altar
1Kin 8:27 less this house that I have *b*
1Kin 8:43 that this house, which I have *b*
1Kin 15:22 thereof, wherewith Baasha had *b*
2Kin 23:13 *b* for Ashtoreth the abomination
1Chr 22:5 the house that is to be *b* for the
Ezr 3:2 *b* the altar of the God of Israel,
Ezr 4:1 the children of the captivity *b*
Ezr 4:13 the king, that, if this city be *b*
Ezr 4:16 that, if this city be *b* again
Ezr 4:21 cease, and that this city be not *b*
Ezr 5:8 which is *b* with great stones, and
Ezr 5:11 that was *b* these many years ago
Ezr 5:15 house of God be *b* in his place
Ezr 6:3 at Jerusalem, Let the house be *b*
Ezr 6:14 And the elders of the Jews *b*
Neh 3:1 priests, and they *b* the sheep gate
Neh 4:1 heard that we *b* the wall, he was
Neh 4:17 They which *b* on the wall, and they
Neh 6:1 heard that I had *b* the wall
Neh 7:4 therein, and the houses were not *b*
Neh 12:29 for the singers had *b* them
Job 20:19 away an house which he *b* not
Ps 122:3 Jerusalem is *b* as a city that is
Prov 9:1 Wisdom hath *b* her house, she hath
Prov 24:3 Through wisdom is an house *b*
Eccl 2:4 I *b* me houses
Song 4:4 tower of David *b* for an armoury
Jer 30:18 city shall be *b* upon her own heap
Lam 3:5 He hath *b* against me, and
Eze 36:10 and the wastes shall be *b*
Eze 36:33 cities, and the wastes shall be *b*
Lk 17:28 they sold, they planted, they *b*
Eph 2:22 In whom ye also are *b* together
Heb 3:3 inasmuch as he who hath *b* the

## BUILDERS
1Kin 5:18 Solomon's *b* and Hiram's *b*
2Kin 12:11 it out to the carpenters and *b*
2Kin 22:6 Unto carpenters, and *b*, and masons,
2Chr 34:11 *b* gave they it, to buy hewn stone
Ezr 3:10 when the *b* laid the foundation of
Neh 4:5 thee to anger before the *b*
Neh 4:18 For the *b*, every one had his
Ps 118:22 The stone which the *b* refused is
Eze 27:4 thy *b* have perfected thy beauty
Mt 21:42 The stone which the *b* rejected
Mk 12:10 The stone which the *b* rejected is
Lk 20:17 The stone which the *b* rejected
Acts 4:11 which was set at nought of you *b*
1Pet 2:7 the stone which the *b* disallowed

## BUILDEST
Deut 22:8 When thou *b* a new house, then
Neh 6:6 for which cause thou *b* the wall
Eze 16:31 In that thou *b* thine eminent
Mt 27:40 *b* it in three days, save thyself
Mk 15:29 temple, and *b* it in three days,

## BUILDETH
Josh 6:26 riseth up and *b* this city Jericho
Job 27:18 He *b* his house as a moth, and as a
Prov 14:1 Every wise woman *b* her house
Jer 22:13 Woe unto him that *b* his house by
Hos 8:14 forgotten his Maker, and *b* temples
Amos 9:6 It is he that *b* his stories in
Hab 2:12 Woe to him that *b* a town with
1Cor 3:10 foundation, and another *b* thereon
1Cor 3:10 man take heed how he *b* thereupon

## BUILDING
Josh 22:19 in *b* you an altar beside the
1Kin 3:1 made an end of *b* his own house
1Kin 6:7 And the house, when it was in *b*
1Kin 6:12 this house which thou art in *b*
1Kin 6:38 So was he seven years in *b* it
1Kin 7:1 But Solomon was *b* his own house
1Kin 9:1 the *b* of the house of the LORD
1Kin 15:21 that he left off *b* of Ramah
1Chr 28:2 God, and had made ready for the *b*
2Chr 3:3 for the *b* of the house of God
2Chr 16:5 it, that he left off *b* of Ramah
2Chr 16:6 thereof, wherewith Baasha was *b*
Ezr 4:4 of Judah, and troubled them in *b*
Ezr 4:12 *b* the rebellious and the bad city,
Ezr 5:4 names of the men that make this *b*
Ezr 5:16 even until now hath it been in *b*
Ezr 6:8 for the *b* of this house of God
Eccl 10:18 much slothfulness the *b* decayeth
Eze 17:17 *b* forts, to cut off many persons
Eze 40:5 he measured the breadth of the *b*
Eze 41:12 Now the *b* that was before the
Eze 42:1 was before the *b* toward the north
Eze 42:10 place, and over against the *b*
Eze 46:23 there was a row of *b* round about
Jn 2:20 and six years was this temple in *b*
1Cor 3:9 God's husbandry, ye are God's *b*
2Cor 5:1 dissolved, we have a *b* of God

Eph 2:21 In whom all the *b* fitly framed
Heb 9:11 that is to say, not of this *b*
Jude 20 *b* up yourselves on your most holy
Rev 21:18 the *b* of the wall of it was of

**BUILDINGS**
Mt 24:1 to shew him the *b* of the temple
Mk 13:1 of stones and what *b* are here
Mk 13:2 him, Seest thou these great *b*

**BUILT**
Gen 13:18 *b* there an altar unto the LORD
Gen 22:9 Abraham *b* an altar there, and laid
Gen 33:17 *b* him an house, and made booths
Gen 35:7 he *b* there an altar, and called
Ex 1:11 they *b* for Pharaoh treasure
Ex 17:15 Moses *b* an altar, and called the
Ex 32:5 saw it, he *b* an altar before it
Num 13:22 (Now Hebron was *b* seven years
Num 21:27 let the city of Sihon be *b*
Num 23:14 *b* seven altars, and offered a
Num 32:34 And the children of Gad *b* Dibon
Num 32:37 the children of Reuben *b* Heshbon
Deut 8:12 hast *b* goodly houses, and dwelt
Deut 13:16 it shall not be *b* again
Deut 20:5 is there that hath *b* a new house
Josh 8:30 Then Joshua *b* an altar unto the
Josh 19:50 he *b* the city, and dwelt therein
Josh 22:10 *b* there an altar by Jordan
Josh 22:11 *b* an altar over against the land
Josh 22:23 That we have *b* us an altar to
Josh 24:13 labour, and cities which ye *b* not
Judg 1:26 *b* a city, and called the name
Judg 6:24 Then Gideon *b* an altar there unto
Judg 6:28 offered upon the altar that was *b*
Judg 18:28 they *b* a city, and dwelt therein
Judg 21:4 *b* there an altar, and offered
1Sa 7:17 there he *b* an altar unto the LORD
1Sa 14:35 Saul *b* an altar unto the LORD
2Sa 5:9 David *b* round about from Millo and
2Sa 5:11 and they *b* David an house
2Sa 24:25 David *b* there an altar unto the
1Kin 3:2 house *b* unto the name of the LORD
1Kin 6:2 which king Solomon *b* for the LORD
1Kin 7:2 He *b* also the house of the forest
1Kin 8:13 I have surely *b* thee an house to
1Kin 9:3 this house, which thou hast *b*
1Kin 9:10 when Solomon had *b* the two houses
1Kin 9:17 And Solomon *b* Gezer, and Beth-horon
1Kin 9:24 house which Solomon had *b* for her
1Kin 10:4 and the house that he had *b*
1Kin 11:27 Solomon *b* Millo, and repaired the
1Kin 11:38 as I *b* for David, and will give
1Kin 12:25 Then Jeroboam *b* Shechem in mount
1Kin 14:23 For they also *b* them high places,
1Kin 15:17 *b* Ramah, that he might not suffer
1Kin 15:22 king Asa *b* with them Geba of
1Kin 16:32 Baal, which he had *b* in Samaria
1Kin 18:32 with the stones he *b* an altar in
1Kin 22:39 made, and all the cities that he *b*
2Kin 14:22 He *b* Elath, and restored it to
2Kin 15:35 He *b* the higher gate of the house
2Kin 16:11 Urijah the priest *b* an altar
2Kin 16:18 that they had *b* in the house
2Kin 17:9 they *b* them high places in all
2Kin 21:3 For he *b* up again the high places
2Kin 25:1 they *b* forts against it round
1Chr 6:10 that Solomon *b* in Jerusalem
1Chr 6:32 until Solomon had *b* the house of
1Chr 7:24 who *b* Beth-horon the nether, and
1Chr 8:12 and Misham, and Shamed, who *b* Ono
1Chr 11:8 he *b* the city round about, even
1Chr 17:6 Why have ye not *b* me an house of
1Chr 21:26 David *b* there an altar unto the
1Chr 22:19 to be *b* to the name of the LORD
2Chr 6:2 But I have *b* an house of
2Chr 8:1 wherein Solomon had *b* the house
2Chr 8:2 to Solomon, Solomon *b* them
2Chr 8:4 he *b* Tadmor in the wilderness, and
2Chr 8:5 Also he *b* Beth-horon the upper,
2Chr 8:11 the house that he had *b* for her
2Chr 9:3 and the house that he had *b*
2Chr 11:5 *b* cities for defence in Judah
2Chr 14:6 he *b* fenced cities in Judah
2Chr 14:7 So they *b* and prospered
2Chr 16:1 *b* Ramah, to the intent that he
2Chr 16:6 he *b* therewith Geba and Mizpah
2Chr 17:12 he *b* in Judah castles, and cities
2Chr 20:8 have *b* thee a sanctuary therein
2Chr 26:2 He *b* Eloth, and restored it to
2Chr 26:6 *b* cities about Ashdod, and among
2Chr 26:9 Moreover Uzziah *b* towers in
2Chr 26:10 Also he *b* towers in the desert,
2Chr 27:3 He *b* the high gate of the house
2Chr 32:5 *b* up all the wall that was broken
2Chr 33:3 For he *b* again the high places
2Chr 33:14 Now after this he *b* a wall
2Chr 33:19 places wherein he *b* high places
Neh 3:13 they *b* it, and set up the doors
Neh 4:6 So *b* we the wall
Neh 7:1 came to pass, when the wall was *b*
Job 3:14 which *b* desolate places for
Job 12:14 down, and it cannot be *b* again
Job 22:23 the Almighty, thou shalt be *b* up
Ps 78:69 he *b* his sanctuary like high
Ps 89:2 Mercy shall be *b* up for ever
Eccl 9:14 *b* great bulwarks against it
Is 5:2 *b* a tower in the midst of it, and
Is 25:2 it shall never be *b*
Is 44:26 cities of Judah, Ye shall be *b*
Is 44:28 to Jerusalem, Thou shalt be *b*
Jer 7:31 they have *b* the high places of
Jer 12:16 then shall they be *b* in the midst
Jer 19:5 They have *b* also the high places
Jer 31:4 build thee, and thou shalt be *b*
Jer 31:38 that the city shall be *b* to the
Jer 32:31 that they *b* it even unto this day
Jer 32:35 they *b* the high places of Baal,
Jer 45:4 which I have *b* will I break down
Jer 52:4 *b* forts against it round about
Eze 13:10 one *b* up a wall, and, lo, others
Eze 16:24 That thou hast also *b* unto thee
Eze 26:14 thou shalt be *b* no more
Dan 4:30 that I have *b* for the house of
Dan 9:25 the street shall be *b* again
Amos 5:11 ye have *b* houses of hewn stone,
Mic 7:11 day that thy walls are to be *b*
Hag 1:2 that the LORD's house should be *b*
Zec 1:16 my house shall be *b* in it
Zec 8:9 laid, that the temple might be *b*
Mt 7:24 which *b* his house upon a rock
Mt 7:26 which *b* his house upon the sand
Mt 21:33 *b* a tower, and let it out to
Mk 12:1 *b* a tower, and let it out to
Lk 4:29 the hill whereon their city was *b*
Lk 6:48 He is like a man which *b* an house
Lk 7:5 and he hath *b* us a synagogue
Acts 7:47 But Solomon *b* him an house
1Cor 3:14 abide which he hath *b* thereupon
Eph 2:20 are *b* upon the foundation of the
Col 2:7 *b* up in him, and stablished in the
Heb 3:4 but he that *b* all things is God
1Pet 2:5 are *b* up a spiritual house, an

**BUKKI** *(buk'-ki)*
*1. A high priest.*
1Chr 6:5 And Abishua begat *B*
1Chr 6:51 *B* his son, Uzzi his son, Zerahiah
Ezr 7:4 the son of Uzzi, the son of *B*
*2. A Danite prince.*
Num 34:22 of Dan, *B* the son of Jogli

**BUKKIAH** *(buk-ki'-ah) A Levite musician.*
1Chr 25:4 *B*, Mattaniah, Uzziel, Shebuel, and
1Chr 25:13 The sixth to *B*, he, his sons, and

**BUL** *(bul) Eighth month of the Hebrew year.*
1Kin 6:38 the eleventh year, in the month *B*

**BULL**
Job 21:10 Their *b* gendereth, and faileth not
Is 51:20 the streets, as a wild *b* in a net

**BULLOCK**
Ex 29:1 Take one young *b*, and two rams
Ex 29:3 them in the basket, with the *b*
Ex 29:10 thou shalt cause a *b* to be
Ex 29:36 day a *b* for a sin offering for
Lev 1:5 shall kill the *b* before the LORD
Lev 4:3 a young *b* without blemish unto
Lev 4:4 he shall bring the *b* unto the
Lev 8:2 a *b* for the sin offering, and two
Lev 8:14 he brought the *b* for the sin
Lev 9:4 Also a *b* and a ram for peace
Lev 9:18 He slew also the *b* and the ram for
Lev 16:3 with a young *b* for a sin offering
Lev 16:6 offer his *b* of the sin offering
Lev 16:27 the *b* for the sin offering, and
Lev 22:23 Either a *b* or a lamb that hath
Lev 22:27 When a *b*, or a sheep, or a goat,
Lev 23:18 of the first year, and one young *b*
Num 7:15 One young *b*, one ram, one lamb of
Num 8:8 a young *b* with his meat offering
Num 15:8 a *b* for a burnt offering, or for
Num 15:24 one young *b* for a burnt offering
Num 23:2 Balaam offered on every altar a *b*
Num 23:30 Balaam had said, and offered a *b*
Num 28:12 mingled with oil, for one *b*
Num 29:2 one young *b*, one ram, and seven
Deut 15:19 work with the firstling of thy *b*
Deut 17:1 unto the LORD thy God any *b*
Deut 33:17 is like the firstling of his *b*
Judg 6:25 him, Take thy father's young *b*
1Sa 1:25 And they slew a *b*, and brought the
1Kin 18:23 them choose one *b* for themselves
2Chr 13:9 consecrate himself with a young *b*
Ps 50:9 I will take no *b* out of thy house
Ps 69:31 than an ox or *b* that hath horns
Is 65:25 lion shall eat straw like the *b*
Jer 31:18 as a *b* unaccustomed to the yoke
Eze 43:19 a young *b* for a sin offering
Eze 43:21 Thou shalt take the *b* also of the
Eze 45:18 take a young *b* without blemish
Eze 46:6 be a young *b* without blemish

**BULLOCK'S**
Lev 4:4 lay his hand upon the *b* head
Lev 4:5 shall take of the *b* blood
Lev 4:16 *b* blood to the tabernacle of the

**BULLOCKS**
Num 7:87 the burnt offering were twelve *b*
Num 8:12 hands upon the heads of the *b*
Num 23:29 and prepare me here seven *b*
Num 28:11 two young *b*, and one ram, seven
Num 29:13 thirteen young *b*, two rams, and
1Sa 1:24 him up with her, with three *b*
1Kin 18:23 Let them therefore give us two *b*
1Chr 15:26 LORD, that they offered seven *b*
1Chr 29:21 after that day, even a thousand *b*
2Chr 30:24 to the congregation a thousand *b*
2Chr 35:7 thousand, and three thousand *b*
Ezr 6:9 they have need of, both young *b*
Ezr 6:17 of this house of God an hundred *b*
Ezr 8:35 twelve *b* for all Israel, ninety
Job 42:8 take unto you now seven *b*
Ps 51:19 they offer *b* upon thine altar
Ps 66:15 I will offer *b* with goats
Is 1:11 I delight not in the blood of *b*
Is 34:7 them, and the *b* with the bulls
Jer 46:21 in the midst of her like fatted *b*
Jer 50:27 Slay all her *b*
Eze 39:18 rams, of lambs, and of goats, of *b*
Eze 45:23 offering to the LORD, seven *b*
Hos 12:11 they sacrifice *b* in Gilgal

**BULLS**
Gen 32:15 their colts, forty kine, and ten *b*
Ps 22:12 Many *b* have compassed me
Ps 50:13 Will I eat the flesh of *b*
Ps 68:30 spearmen, the multitude of the *b*
Is 34:7 them, and the bullocks with the *b*
Jer 50:11 heifer at grass, and bellow as *b*
Jer 52:20 twelve brasen *b* that were under
Heb 9:13 For if the blood of *b* and of goats
Heb 10:4 not possible that the blood of *b*

**BULWARKS**
Deut 20:20 thou shalt build *b* against the
2Chr 26:15 to be on the towers and upon the *b*
Ps 48:13 Mark ye well her *b*, consider her
Eccl 9:14 it, and built great *b* against it
Is 26:1 will God appoint for walls and *b*

**BUNAH** *(boo'-nah) Son of Jerahmeel.*
1Chr 2:25 were, Ram the firstborn, and *B*

**BUNCHES**
2Sa 16:1 bread, and an hundred *b* of raisins
1Chr 12:40 *b* of raisins, and wine, and oil, and
Is 30:6 treasures upon the *b* of camels

**BUNDLE**
Gen 42:35 every man's *b* of money was in his
1Sa 25:29 *b* of life with the LORD thy God
Song 1:13 A *b* of myrrh is my wellbeloved
Acts 28:3 Paul had gathered a *b* of sticks

**BUNDLES**
Gen 42:35 their father saw the *b* of money
Mt 13:30 and bind them in *b* to burn them

**BUNNI** *(bun'-ni)*
*1. A Levite with Ezra.*
Neh 9:4 and Bani, Kadmiel, Shebaniah, *B*
*2. Father of Hashabiah.*
Neh 11:15 son of Hashabiah, the son of *B*
*3. A family who renewed the covenant.*
Neh 10:15 *B*, Azgad, Bebai,

**BURDEN**
Ex 18:22 they shall bear the *b* with thee
Ex 23:5 hateth thee lying under his *b*
Num 4:15 These things are the *b* of the
Num 11:11 that thou layest the *b* of all
Deut 1:12 bear your cumbrance, and your *b*
2Sa 15:33 then thou shalt be a *b* unto me
2Sa 19:35 be yet a *b* unto my lord the king
2Kin 5:17 thy servant two mules' *b* of earth
2Kin 8:9 of Damascus, forty camels' *b*
2Kin 9:25 the LORD laid this *b* upon him
2Chr 35:3 it shall not be a *b* upon your
Neh 13:19 that there should no *b* be brought
Job 7:20 thee, so that I am a *b* to myself
Ps 38:4 as an heavy *b* they are too heavy
Ps 55:22 Cast thy *b* upon the LORD, and he
Ps 81:6 I removed his shoulder from the *b*
Eccl 12:5 and the grasshopper shall be a *b*
Is 9:4 hast broken the yoke of his *b*
Is 10:27 that his *b* shall be taken away
Is 13:1 The *b* of Babylon, which Isaiah
Is 14:25 his *b* depart from off their
Is 14:28 that king Ahaz died was this *b*
Is 15:1 The *b* of Moab
Is 17:1 The *b* of Damascus
Is 19:1 The *b* of Egypt
Is 21:1 The *b* of the desert of the sea
Is 21:11 The *b* of Dumah
Is 21:13 The *b* upon Arabia
Is 22:1 The *b* of the valley of vision
Is 22:25 the *b* that was upon it shall be
Is 23:1 The *b* of Tyre
Is 30:6 The *b* of the beasts of the south
Is 30:27 anger, and the *b* thereof is heavy
Is 46:1 they are a *b* to the weary beast
Is 46:2 they could not deliver the *b*
Jer 17:21 bear no *b* on the sabbath day, nor
Jer 23:33 saying, What is the *b* of the LORD
Jer 23:38 shall not say, The *b* of the LORD
Eze 12:10 This *b* concerneth the prince in
Hos 8:10 for the *b* of the king of princes
Nah 1:1 The *b* of Nineveh
Hab 1:1 The *b* which Habakkuk the prophet
Zeph 3:18 whom the reproach of it was a *b*
Zec 9:1 The *b* of the word of the LORD in
Zec 12:1 The *b* of the word of the LORD for
Zec 12:3 all that *b* themselves with it
Mal 1:1 The *b* of the word of the LORD to
Mt 11:30 my yoke is easy, and my *b* is light
Mt 20:12 unto us, which have borne the *b*
Acts 15:28 to lay upon you no greater *b* than
Acts 21:3 the ship was to unlade her *b*
2Cor 12:16 But be it so, I did not *b* you
Gal 6:5 every man shall bear his own *b*
Rev 2:24 I will put upon you none other *b*

**BURDENS**
Gen 49:14 ass couching down between two *b*
Ex 1:11 to afflict them with their *b*
Ex 2:11 brethren, and looked on their *b*
Ex 5:4 get you unto your *b*
Ex 6:6 from under the *b* of the Egyptians
Num 4:24 Gershonites, to serve, and for *b*
1Kin 5:15 and ten thousand that bare *b*
2Chr 2:2 and ten thousand men to bear *b*
2Chr 2:18 of them to be bearers of *b*
2Chr 24:27 greatness of the *b* laid upon him
2Chr 34:13 they were over the bearers of *b*
Neh 4:10 of the bearers of *b* is decayed
Neh 4:17 on the wall, and they that bare *b*
Neh 13:15 and figs, and all manner of *b*
Is 58:6 wickedness, to undo the heavy *b*
Lam 2:14 but have seen for thee false *b*
Amos 5:11 and ye take from him *b* of wheat
Mt 23:4 For they bind heavy *b* and grievous
Lk 11:46 men with *b* grievous to be borne
Gal 6:2 Bear ye one another's *b*, and so

**BURDENSOME**
Zec 12:3 a *b* stone for all people
2Cor 11:9 kept myself from being *b* unto you
2Cor 12:13 be that I myself was not *b* to you
1Th 2:6 when we might have been *b*

**BURIAL**
2Chr 26:23 the *b* which belonged to the kings
Eccl 6:3 good, and also that he have no *b*
Is 14:20 not be joined with them in *b*
Jer 22:19 be buried with the *b* of an ass
Mt 26:12 on my body, she did it for my *b*
Acts 8:2 men carried Stephen to his *b*

**BURIED**
Gen 15:15 thou shalt be *b* in a good old age
Gen 23:19 Abraham *b* Sarah his wife in the
Gen 25:9 Ishmael *b* him in the cave of
Gen 25:10 there was Abraham *b*, and Sarah his
Gen 35:8 she was *b* beneath Beth-el under
Gen 35:19 was *b* in the way to Ephrath,
Gen 35:29 and his sons Esau and Jacob *b* him
Gen 48:7 I *b* her there in the way of
Gen 49:31 There they *b* Abraham and Sarah his
Gen 49:31 there they *b* Isaac and Rebekah his
Gen 49:31 and there I *b* Leah
Gen 50:13 *b* him in the cave of the field of
Gen 50:14 father, after he had *b* his father
Num 11:34 because there they *b* the people
Num 20:1 Miriam died there, and was *b* there
Num 33:4 For the Egyptians *b* all their
Deut 10:6 Aaron died, and there he was *b*
Deut 34:6 he *b* him in a valley in the land
Josh 24:30 they *b* him in the border of his
Josh 24:32 *b* they in Shechem, in a parcel of
Josh 24:33 they *b* him in a hill that
Judg 2:9 they *b* him in the border of his
Judg 8:32 was *b* in the sepulchre of Joash
Judg 10:2 and died, and was *b* in Shamir
Judg 12:7 was *b* in one of the cities of
Judg 12:10 Ibzan, and was *b* at Beth-lehem
Judg 16:31 *b* him between Zorah and Eshtaol in
Ruth 1:17 will I die, and there will I be *b*
1Sa 25:1 *b* him in his house at Ramah
1Sa 28:3 *b* him in Ramah, even in his own
1Sa 31:13 *b* them under a tree at Jabesh, and
2Sa 2:4 were they that *b* Saul
2Sa 2:5 even unto Saul, and have *b* him
2Sa 2:32 *b* him in the sepulchre of his
2Sa 4:12 *b* it in the sepulchre of Abner in
2Sa 17:23 was *b* in the sepulchre of his
2Sa 19:37 be *b* by the grave of my father and
2Sa 21:14 Jonathan his son *b* they in the
1Kin 2:10 was *b* in the city of David
1Kin 2:34 he was *b* in his own house in the
1Kin 11:43 was *b* in the city of David his
1Kin 13:31 came to pass, after he had *b* him
1Kin 14:18 And they *b* him
1Kin 14:31 was *b* with his fathers in the
1Kin 15:8 they *b* him in the city of David
1Kin 15:24 was *b* with his fathers in the
1Kin 16:6 his fathers, and was *b* in Tirzah
1Kin 16:28 his fathers, and was *b* in Samaria
1Kin 22:37 they *b* the king in Samaria
1Kin 22:50 was *b* with his fathers in the
2Kin 8:24 was *b* with his fathers in the
2Kin 9:28 *b* him in his sepulchre with his
2Kin 10:35 and they *b* him in Samaria
2Kin 12:21 they *b* him with his fathers in
2Kin 13:9 and they *b* him in Samaria
2Kin 13:13 Joash was *b* in Samaria with the
2Kin 13:20 And Elisha died, and they *b* him
2Kin 14:16 was *b* in Samaria with the kings
2Kin 14:20 he was *b* at Jerusalem with his
2Kin 15:7 they *b* him with his fathers in
2Kin 15:38 was *b* with his fathers in the
2Kin 16:20 was *b* with his fathers in the
2Kin 21:18 was *b* in the garden of his own
2Kin 21:26 he was *b* in his sepulchre in the
2Kin 23:30 *b* him in his own sepulchre
1Chr 10:12 *b* their bones under the oak in
2Chr 9:31 he was *b* in the city of David his
2Chr 12:16 was *b* in the city of David
2Chr 14:1 they *b* him in the city of David
2Chr 16:14 they *b* him in his own sepulchres,
2Chr 21:1 was *b* with his fathers in the
2Chr 21:20 Howbeit they *b* him in the city of
2Chr 22:9 they had slain him, they *b* him
2Chr 24:16 they *b* him in the city of David
2Chr 24:25 they *b* him in the city of David,
2Chr 24:25 but they *b* him not in the
2Chr 25:28 *b* him with his fathers in the
2Chr 26:23 they *b* him with his fathers in
Job 27:15 remain of him shall be *b* in death
Eccl 8:10 And so I saw the wicked *b*, who had
Jer 8:2 shall not be gathered, nor be *b*
Jer 16:4 neither shall they be *b*
Jer 16:6 they shall not be *b*, neither
Jer 20:6 shalt die, and shalt be *b* there
Jer 22:19 He shall be *b* with the burial of
Jer 25:33 lamented, neither gathered, nor *b*
Eze 39:15 till the buriers have *b* it in the
Mt 14:12 *b* it, and went and told Jesus
Lk 16:22 the rich man also died, and was *b*
Acts 2:29 David, that he is both dead and *b*
Acts 5:6 up, and carried him out, and *b* him
Acts 5:9 *b* thy husband are at the door
Acts 5:10 her forth, *b* her by her husband
Rom 6:4 Therefore we are *b* with him by
1Cor 15:4 And that he was *b*, and that he rose
Col 2:12 *B* with him in baptism, wherein

**BURN**
Gen 11:3 make brick, and *b* them throughly
Gen 44:18 thine anger *b* against thy servant
Ex 12:10 the morning ye shall *b* with fire
Ex 27:20 to cause the lamp to *b* always
Ex 29:13 them, and *b* them upon the altar
Ex 29:18 thou shalt *b* the whole ram upon
Ex 29:25 *b* them upon the altar for a burnt
Ex 29:34 then thou shalt *b* the remainder
Ex 30:1 make an altar to *b* incense upon
Ex 30:7 Aaron shall *b* thereon sweet
Ex 30:20 to *b* offering made by fire unto
Lev 1:9 priest shall *b* all on the altar
Lev 1:13 it all, and *b* it upon the altar
Lev 2:2 the priest shall *b* the memorial
Lev 2:9 shall *b* it upon the altar
Lev 2:11 for ye shall *b* no leaven, nor any
Lev 2:16 the priest shall *b* the memorial
Lev 3:5 Aaron's sons shall *b* it on the
Lev 4:12 *b* him on the wood with fire
Lev 4:19 from him, and *b* it upon the altar
Lev 4:21 *b* him as he burned the first
Lev 5:12 *b* it on the altar, according to
Lev 6:12 the priest shall *b* wood on it
Lev 7:5 the priest shall *b* them upon the
Lev 7:31 the priest shall *b* the fat upon
Lev 8:32 of the bread shall ye *b* with fire
Lev 13:52 He shall therefore *b* that garment
Lev 16:25 shall he *b* upon the altar
Lev 17:6 *b* the fat for a sweet savour unto
Lev 24:2 cause the lamps to *b* continually
Num 5:26 *b* it upon the altar, and afterward
Num 18:17 shalt *b* their fat for an offering
Num 19:5 one shall *b* the heifer in his
Deut 5:23 (for the mountain did *b* with fire
Deut 7:5 *b* their graven images with fire
Deut 7:25 their gods shall ye *b* with fire
Deut 12:3 and *b* their groves with fire
Deut 13:16 shalt *b* with fire the city, and
Deut 32:22 shall *b* unto the lowest hell, and
Josh 11:6 *b* their chariots with fire
Josh 11:13 that did Joshua *b*
Judg 9:52 of the tower to *b* it with fire
Judg 12:1 we will *b* thine house upon thee
Judg 14:15 us the riddle, lest we *b* thee
1Sa 2:16 not fail to *b* the fat presently
1Sa 2:28 to *b* incense, to wear an ephod
1Kin 13:1 stood by the altar to *b* incense
2Kin 16:15 Upon the great altar *b* the
2Kin 18:4 of Israel did *b* incense to it
1Chr 23:13 to *b* incense before the LORD, to
2Chr 2:4 to *b* before him sweet incense, and
2Chr 2:6 save only to *b* sacrifice before
2Chr 4:20 that they should *b* after the
2Chr 13:11 they *b* unto the LORD every
2Chr 28:25 to *b* incense unto other gods
2Chr 29:11 minister unto him, and *b* incense
2Chr 32:12 one altar, and *b* incense upon it
Neh 10:34 to *b* upon the altar of the LORD
Ps 79:5 shall thy jealousy *b* like fire
Ps 89:46 shall thy wrath *b* like fire
Is 1:31 and they shall both *b* together
Is 10:17 and it shall *b* and devour his
Is 27:4 them, I would *b* them together
Is 40:16 And Lebanon is not sufficient to *b*
Is 44:15 Then shall it be for a man to *b*
Is 47:14 the fire shall *b* them
Jer 4:4 *b* that none can quench it because
Jer 7:9 *b* incense unto Baal, and walk
Jer 7:20 and it shall *b*, and shall not be
Jer 7:31 Hinnom, to *b* their sons and their
Jer 11:13 even altars to *b* incense unto
Jer 15:14 anger, which shall *b* upon you
Jer 17:4 anger, which shall *b* for ever
Jer 19:5 to *b* their sons with fire for
Jer 21:10 and he shall *b* it with fire
Jer 21:12 *b* that none can quench it,
Jer 32:29 *b* it with the houses, upon whose
Jer 34:2 and he shall *b* it with fire
Jer 34:5 so shall they *b* odours for thee
Jer 34:22 and take it, and *b* it with fire
Jer 36:25 king that he would not *b* the roll

| | |
|---|---|
| Jer 37:8 | and take it, and *b* it with fire |
| Jer 37:10 | tent, and *b* this city with fire |
| Jer 38:18 | they shall *b* it with fire, and |
| Jer 43:12 | and he shall *b* them, and carry them |
| Jer 44:3 | in that they went to *b* incense |
| Jer 44:5 | to *b* no incense unto other gods |
| Jer 44:17 | to *b* incense unto the queen of |
| Jer 44:25 | to *b* incense to the queen of |
| Eze 5:2 | Thou shalt *b* with fire a third |
| Eze 5:4 | the fire, and *b* them in the fire |
| Eze 16:41 | they shall *b* thine houses with |
| Eze 23:47 | *b* up their houses with fire |
| Eze 24:5 | *b* also the bones under it, and |
| Eze 24:11 | brass of it may be hot, and may *b* |
| Eze 39:9 | *b* the weapons, both the shields |
| Eze 43:21 | he shall *b* it in the appointed |
| Hos 4:13 | *b* incense upon the hills, under |
| Nah 2:13 | I will *b* her chariots in the |
| Hab 1:16 | *b* incense unto their drag |
| Mal 4:1 | cometh, that shall *b* as an oven |
| Mt 3:12 | but he will *b* up the chaff with |
| Mt 13:30 | and bind them in bundles to *b* them |
| Lk 1:9 | his lot was to *b* incense when he |
| Lk 3:17 | but the chaff he will *b* with fire |
| Lk 24:32 | Did not our heart *b* within us |
| 1Cor 7:9 | it is better to marry than to *b* |
| 2Cor 11:29 | who is offended, and I *b* not |
| Rev 17:16 | eat her flesh, and *b* her with fire |

**BURNED**

| | |
|---|---|
| Ex 3:2 | the bush *b* with fire, and the bush |
| Lev 4:21 | burn him as he *b* the first |
| Lev 8:16 | Moses *b* it upon the altar |
| Deut 4:11 | the mountain *b* with fire unto the |
| Deut 9:15 | mount, and the mount *b* with fire |
| Josh 7:25 | *b* them with fire, after they had |
| Josh 11:13 | Israel *b* none of them, save Hazor |
| 1Sa 30:1 | smitten Ziklag, and *b* it with fire |
| 1Sa 30:3 | and, behold, it was *b* with fire |
| 1Sa 30:14 | and we *b* Ziklag with fire |
| 2Sa 5:21 | and David and his men *b* them |
| 2Sa 23:7 | they shall be utterly *b* with fire |
| 2Kin 10:26 | of the house of Baal, and *b* them |
| 2Kin 15:35 | *b* incense still in the high |
| 2Kin 22:17 | have *b* incense unto other gods, |
| 2Kin 23:4 | he *b* them without Jerusalem in |
| 2Kin 23:11 | *b* the chariots of the sun with |
| 2Kin 23:20 | *b* men's bones upon them, and |
| 1Chr 14:12 | and they were *b* with fire |
| 2Chr 25:14 | them, and *b* incense unto them |
| 2Chr 29:7 | have not *b* incense nor offered |
| 2Chr 34:25 | have *b* incense unto other gods, |
| Neh 1:3 | the gates thereof are *b* with fire |
| Neh 2:17 | he gates thereof are *b* with fire |
| Neh 4:2 | heaps of the rubbish which are *b* |
| Est 1:12 | very wroth, and his anger *b* in him |
| Job 1:16 | hath *b* up the sheep, and the |
| Job 30:30 | me, and my bones are *b* with heat |
| Ps 39:3 | while I was musing the fire *b* |
| Ps 74:8 | they have *b* up all the synagogues |
| Ps 80:16 | It is *b* with fire, it is cut down |
| Ps 102:3 | and my bones are *b* as an hearth |
| Ps 106:18 | the flame *b* up the wicked |
| Prov 6:27 | bosom, and his clothes not be *b* |
| Prov 6:28 | hot coals, and his feet not be *b* |
| Is 1:7 | your cities are *b* with fire |
| Is 24:6 | inhabitants of the earth are *b* |
| Is 33:12 | up shall they be *b* in the fire |
| Is 42:25 | it *b* him, yet he laid it not to |
| Is 43:2 | the fire, thou shalt not be *b* |
| Is 44:19 | I have *b* part of it in the fire |
| Is 64:11 | praised thee, is *b* up with fire |
| Is 65:7 | which have *b* incense upon the |
| Jer 1:16 | have *b* incense unto other gods, |
| Jer 2:15 | his cities are *b* without |
| Jer 6:29 | The bellows are *b*, the lead is |
| Jer 9:10 | because they are *b* up, so that |
| Jer 18:15 | they have *b* incense to vanity, and |
| Jer 19:4 | have *b* incense in it unto other |
| Jer 19:13 | upon whose roofs they have *b* |
| Jer 36:27 | that the king had *b* the roll |
| Jer 36:28 | the king of Judah hath *b* |
| Jer 36:32 | king of Judah had *b* in the fire |
| Jer 38:17 | city shall not be *b* with fire |
| Jer 38:23 | cause this city to be *b* with fire |
| Jer 39:8 | the Chaldeans *b* the king's house, |
| Jer 44:15 | had *b* incense unto other gods |
| Jer 44:19 | when we *b* incense to the queen of |
| Jer 44:21 | The incense that ye *b* in the |
| Jer 44:23 | Because ye have *b* incense |
| Jer 49:2 | daughters shall be *b* with fire |
| Jer 51:30 | they have *b* her dwellingplaces |
| Jer 51:32 | the reeds they have *b* with fire |
| Jer 51:58 | high gates shall be *b* with fire |
| Jer 52:13 | *b* the house of the LORD, and the |
| Lam 2:3 | he *b* against Jacob like a flaming |
| Eze 15:4 | of it, and the midst of it is *b* |
| Eze 20:47 | to the north shall be *b* therein |
| Eze 24:10 | it well, and let the bones be *b* |
| Hos 2:13 | wherein she *b* incense to them, and |
| Hos 11:2 | *b* incense to graven images |
| Joel 1:19 | the flame hath *b* all the trees of |
| Amos 2:1 | because he *b* the bones of the |
| Mic 1:7 | thereof shall be *b* with the fire |
| Nah 1:5 | the earth is *b* at his presence, |
| Mt 13:40 | are gathered and *b* in the fire |
| Mt 22:7 | murderers, and *b* up their city |
| Jn 15:6 | them into the fire, and they are *b* |
| Acts 19:19 | and *b* them before all men |
| Rom 1:27 | *b* in their lust one toward |
| 1Cor 3:15 | If any man's work shall be *b* |
| 1Cor 13:3 | and though I give my body to be *b* |
| Heb 6:8 | whose end is to be *b* |
| Heb 12:18 | that *b* with fire, nor unto |
| Heb 13:11 | for sin, are *b* without the camp |
| 2Pet 3:10 | that are therein shall be *b* up |
| Rev 1:15 | as if they *b* in a furnace |
| Rev 18:8 | she shall be utterly *b* with fire |

**BURNETH**

| | |
|---|---|
| Lev 13:24 | the quick flesh that *b* have a |
| Lev 16:28 | he that *b* them shall wash his |
| Num 19:8 | he that *b* her shall wash his |
| Ps 46:9 | he *b* the chariot in the fire |
| Ps 83:14 | As the fire *b* a wood, and as the |
| Ps 97:3 | *b* up his enemies round about |
| Is 9:18 | For wickedness *b* as the fire |
| Is 44:16 | He *b* part thereof in the fire |
| Is 62:1 | thereof as a lamp that *b* |
| Is 64:2 | As when the melting fire *b* |
| Is 65:3 | *b* incense upon altars of brick |
| Is 65:5 | nose, a fire that *b* all the day |
| Is 66:3 | he that *b* incense, as if he |
| Jer 48:35 | him that *b* incense to his gods |
| Hos 7:6 | morning it *b* as a flaming fire |
| Joel 2:3 | and behind them a flame *b* |
| Amos 6:10 | take him up, and he that *b* him |
| Rev 21:8 | in the lake which *b* with fire |

**BURNING**

| | |
|---|---|
| Gen 15:17 | a *b* lamp that passed between |
| Ex 21:25 | *B* for *b*, wound for wound, |
| Lev 6:9 | because of the *b* upon the altar |
| Lev 10:6 | bewail the *b* which the LORD hath |
| Lev 13:23 | and spread not, it is a *b* boil |
| Lev 16:12 | of *b* coals of fire from off the |
| Lev 26:16 | the *b* ague, that shall consume |
| Num 16:37 | take up the censers out of the *b* |
| Num 19:6 | the midst of the *b* of the heifer |
| Deut 28:22 | and with an extreme *b*, and with |
| Deut 29:23 | is brimstone, and salt, and *b* |
| Deut 32:24 | hunger, and devoured with *b* heat |
| 2Chr 16:14 | they made a very great *b* for him |
| 2Chr 21:19 | And his people made no *b* for him |
| 2Chr 21:19 | like the *b* of his fathers |
| Job 41:19 | Out of his mouth go *b* lamps |
| Ps 140:10 | Let *b* coals fall upon them |
| Prov 16:27 | in his lips there is as a *b* fire |
| Prov 26:21 | As coals are to *b* coals, and wood |
| Prov 26:23 | *B* lips and a wicked heart are like |
| Is 3:24 | and *b* instead of beauty |
| Is 4:4 | judgment, and by the spirit of *b* |
| Is 9:5 | but this shall be with *b* and fuel |
| Is 10:16 | a *b* like |
| Is 30:27 | *b* with his anger, and the burden |
| Is 34:9 | land thereof shall become *b* pitch |
| Jer 20:9 | as a *b* fire shut up in my bones |
| Jer 36:22 | a fire on the hearth *b* before him |
| Jer 44:8 | *b* incense unto other gods in the |
| Eze 1:13 | was like *b* coals of fire, and like |
| Dan 3:6 | the midst of a *b* fiery furnace |
| Dan 3:11 | the midst of a *b* fiery furnace |
| Dan 3:17 | us from *b* fiery furnace |
| Dan 3:20 | them into the *b* fiery furnace |
| Dan 3:21 | the midst of the *b* fiery furnace |
| Dan 3:26 | the mouth of the *b* fiery furnace |
| Dan 7:9 | flame, and his wheels as *b* fire |
| Dan 7:11 | and given to the *b* flame |
| Amos 4:11 | a firebrand plucked out of the *b* |
| Hab 3:5 | *b* coals went forth at his feet |
| Lk 12:35 | be girded about, and your lights *b* |
| Jn 5:35 | He was a *b* and a shining light |
| Jas 1:11 | is no sooner risen with a *b* heat |
| Rev 4:5 | lamps of fire *b* before the throne |
| Rev 8:8 | as it were a great mountain *b* |
| Rev 8:10 | *b* as it were a lamp, and it fell |
| Rev 18:9 | they shall see the smoke of her *b* |
| Rev 18:18 | when they saw the smoke of her *b* |
| Rev 19:20 | a lake of fire *b* with brimstone |

**BURNT**

| | |
|---|---|
| Gen 8:20 | offered *b* offerings on the altar |
| Gen 22:2 | offer him there for a *b* offering |
| Gen 22:13 | offered him up for a *b* offering |
| Gen 38:24 | Bring her forth, and let her be *b* |
| Ex 3:3 | sight, why the bush is not *b* |
| Ex 10:25 | and *b* offerings, that we may |
| Ex 18:12 | took a *b* offering and sacrifices |
| Ex 20:24 | sacrifice thereon thy *b* offerings |
| Ex 24:5 | Israel, which offered *b* offerings |
| Ex 29:18 | it is a *b* offering unto the LORD |
| Ex 29:25 | upon the altar for a *b* offering |
| Ex 29:42 | *b* offering throughout your |
| Ex 30:9 | nor *b* sacrifice, nor meat |
| Ex 30:28 | the altar of *b* offering with all |
| Ex 31:9 | the altar of *b* offering with all |
| Ex 32:6 | offered *b* offerings, and brought |
| Ex 32:20 | *b* it in the fire, and ground it to |
| Ex 35:16 | The altar of *b* offering, with his |
| Ex 38:1 | he made the altar of *b* offering |
| Ex 40:6 | *b* offering before the door of the |
| Ex 40:10 | the altar of the *b* offering |
| Ex 40:27 | he *b* sweet incense thereon |
| Ex 40:29 | he put the altar of *b* offering by |
| Lev 1:3 | If his offering be a *b* sacrifice |
| Lev 2:12 | but they shall not be *b* on the |
| Lev 3:5 | on the altar upon the *b* sacrifice |
| Lev 4:7 | of the altar of the *b* offering |
| Lev 5:7 | and the other for a *b* offering |
| Lev 5:10 | offer the second for a *b* offering |
| Lev 6:9 | This is the law of the *b* offering |
| Lev 7:2 | *b* offering shall they kill the |
| Lev 8:17 | he *b* with fire without the camp |
| Lev 9:2 | and a ram for a *b* offering |
| Lev 10:16 | offering, and, behold, it was *b* |
| Lev 10:19 | their *b* offering before the LORD |
| Lev 12:6 | the first year for a *b* offering |
| Lev 12:8 | the one for the *b* offering |
| Lev 13:52 | it shall be *b* in the fire |
| Lev 14:13 | the *b* offering, in the holy place |
| Lev 14:19 | he shall kill the *b* offering |
| Lev 14:20 | priest shall offer the *b* offering |
| Lev 16:3 | and a ram for a *b* offering |
| Lev 16:5 | and one ram for a *b* offering |
| Lev 17:8 | that offereth a *b* offering or |
| Lev 19:6 | day, it shall be *b* in the fire |
| Lev 20:14 | they shall be *b* with fire |
| Lev 21:9 | she shall be *b* with fire |
| Lev 22:18 | unto the LORD for a *b* offering |
| Lev 23:12 | for a *b* offering unto the LORD |
| Lev 23:18 | they shall be for a *b* offering |
| Lev 23:37 | a *b* offering, and a meat offering, |
| Num 6:11 | and the other for a *b* offering |
| Num 6:14 | without blemish for a *b* offering |
| Num 6:16 | sin offering, and his *b* offering |
| Num 10:10 | trumpets over your *b* offerings |
| Num 11:1 | the fire of the LORD *b* among them |
| Num 15:8 | a bullock for a *b* offering |
| Num 15:24 | young bullock for a *b* offering |
| Num 16:39 | they that were *b* had offered |
| Num 19:17 | *b* heifer of purification for sin |
| Num 23:3 | Balak, Stand by thy *b* offering |
| Num 23:6 | lo, he stood by his *b* sacrifice |
| Num 28:3 | day, for a continual *b* offering |
| Num 28:6 | It is a continual *b* offering |
| Num 29:2 | ye shall offer a *b* offering for a |
| Num 31:10 | they *b* all their cities wherein |
| Deut 9:21 | *b* it with fire, and stamped it, and |
| Deut 12:6 | ye shall bring your *b* offerings |
| Deut 12:11 | your *b* offerings, and your |
| Deut 12:27 | thou shalt offer thy *b* offerings |
| Deut 12:31 | have *b* in the fire to their gods |
| Deut 27:6 | thou shalt offer *b* offerings |
| Deut 32:24 | They shall be *b* with hunger |
| Deut 33:10 | whole *b* sacrifice upon thine |
| Josh 6:24 | they *b* the city with fire, and all |
| Josh 7:15 | thing shall be *b* with fire |
| Josh 8:28 | And Joshua *b* Ai, and made it an |
| Josh 8:31 | they offered thereon *b* offerings |
| Josh 11:9 | *b* their chariots with fire |
| Josh 11:11 | and he *b* Hazor with fire |

Josh 22:23 or if to offer thereon *b* offering
Judg 6:26 offer a *b* sacrifice with the wood
Judg 11:31 will offer it up for a *b* offering
Judg 13:16 if thou wilt offer a *b* offering
Judg 13:23 not have received a *b* offering
Judg 15:5 *b* up both the shocks, and also the
Judg 18:27 sword, and *b* the city with fire
Judg 20:26 offered *b* offerings and peace
Judg 21:4 offered *b* offerings and peace
1Sa 2:15 Also before they *b* the fat
1Sa 6:14 offered the kine a *b* offering
1Sa 7:9 offered it for a *b* offering
1Sa 10:8 to offer *b* offerings, and to
1Sa 13:9 Bring hither a *b* offering to me
1Sa 15:22 as great delight in *b* offerings
1Sa 31:12 came to Jabesh, and *b* them there
2Sa 6:17 and David offered *b* offerings
2Sa 24:22 here be oxen for *b* sacrifice
1Kin 3:3 and *b* incense in high places
1Kin 3:15 LORD, and offered up *b* offerings
1Kin 8:64 for there he offered *b* offerings
1Kin 9:16 *b* it with fire, and slain the
1Kin 11:8 which *b* incense and sacrificed
1Kin 12:33 upon the altar, and *b* incense
1Kin 13:2 men's bones shall be *b* upon thee
1Kin 15:13 idol, and *b* it by the brook Kidron
1Kin 16:18 *b* the king's house over him with
1Kin 18:33 and pour it on the *b* sacrifice
1Kin 18:38 fell, and consumed the *b* sacrifice
1Kin 22:43 *b* incense yet in the high places
2Kin 1:14 *b* up the two captains of the
2Kin 3:27 offered him for a *b* offering upon
2Kin 5:17 *b* offering nor sacrifice unto
2Kin 10:24 *b* offerings, Jehu appointed
2Kin 16:13 And he *b* his *b* offering
2Kin 17:11 there they *b* incense in all the
2Kin 17:31 the Sepharvites *b* their children
2Kin 25:9 great man's house *b* he with fire
1Chr 6:49 upon the altar of the *b* offering
1Chr 16:1 and they offered *b* sacrifices
1Chr 16:40 To offer *b* offerings unto the
1Chr 21:23 the oxen also for *b* offerings
1Chr 22:1 of the *b* offering for Israel
1Chr 23:31 to offer all *b* sacrifices unto
1Chr 29:21 offered *b* offerings unto the LORD
2Chr 1:6 a thousand *b* offerings upon it
2Chr 2:4 for the *b* offerings morning and
2Chr 4:6 *b* offering they washed in them
2Chr 7:1 and consumed the *b* offering
2Chr 8:12 Then Solomon offered *b* offerings
2Chr 13:11 and every evening *b* sacrifices
2Chr 15:16 it, and *b* it at the brook Kidron
2Chr 23:18 to offer the *b* offerings of the
2Chr 24:14 they offered *b* offerings in the
2Chr 28:3 Moreover he *b* incense in the
2Chr 29:18 LORD, and the altar of *b* offering
2Chr 30:15 brought in the *b* offerings into
2Chr 31:2 and Levites for *b* offerings
2Chr 31:3 his substance for the *b* offerings
2Chr 35:12 And they removed the *b* offerings
Ezr 3:2 to offer *b* offerings thereon, as
Ezr 8:35 offered *b* offerings unto the God
Neh 10:33 and for the continual *b* offering
Job 1:5 offered *b* offerings according to
Job 42:8 up for yourselves a *b* offering
Ps 20:3 and accept thy *b* sacrifice
Ps 40:6 *b* offering and sin offering hast
Ps 50:8 thy sacrifices or thy *b* offerings
Ps 51:16 thou delightest not in *b* offering
Ps 51:19 *b* offering and whole *b* offering
Ps 66:13 into thy house with *b* offerings
Ps 66:15 thee *b* sacrifices of fatlings
Is 1:11 I am full of the *b* offerings of
Is 40:16 sufficient for a *b* offering
Is 43:23 small cattle of thy *b* offerings
Is 56:7 their *b* offerings and their
Is 61:8 I hate robbery for *b* offering
Jer 6:20 your *b* offerings are not
Jer 7:21 Put your *b* offerings unto your
Jer 14:12 and when they offer *b* offering
Jer 17:26 south, bringing *b* offerings, and
Jer 19:5 fire for *b* offerings unto Baal
Jer 33:18 before me to offer *b* offerings
Jer 51:25 and will make thee a *b* mountain
Eze 40:38 where they washed the *b* offering
Eze 43:18 to offer *b* offerings thereon, and
Eze 44:11 they shall slay the *b* offering
Eze 45:15 for a *b* offering, and for peace
Eze 46:2 shall prepare his *b* offering
Eze 46:15 for a continual *b* offering
Hos 6:6 of God more than *b* offerings
Amos 5:22 Though ye offer me *b* offerings
Mic 6:6 come before him with *b* offerings
Mk 12:33 more than all whole *b* offerings
Heb 10:6 In *b* offerings and sacrifices for
Heb 10:8 *b* offerings and offering for sin
Rev 8:7 the third part of trees was *b* up
Rev 8:7 and all green grass was *b* up

### BURST

Job 32:19 it is ready to *b* like new bottles
Prov 3:10 presses shall *b* out with new wine
Jer 2:20 broken thy yoke, and *b* thy bands
Jer 5:5 broken the yoke, and *b* the bonds
Jer 30:8 will *b* thy bonds, and strangers
Nah 1:13 will *b* thy bonds in sunder
Mk 2:22 the new wine doth *b* the bottles
Lk 5:37 the new wine will *b* the bottles
Acts 1:18 he *b* asunder in the midst, and all

### BURY

Gen 23:4 that I may *b* my dead out of my
Gen 23:6 of our sepulchres *b* thy dead
Gen 23:8 should *b* my dead out of my sight
Gen 23:11 *b* thy dead
Gen 23:13 of me, and I will *b* my dead there
Gen 23:15 *b* therefore thy dead
Gen 47:29 *b* me not, I pray thee, in Egypt
Gen 47:30 *b* me in their buryingplace
Gen 49:29 *b* me with my fathers in the cave
Gen 50:5 of Canaan, there shalt thou *b* me
Gen 50:7 And Joseph went up to *b* his father
Gen 50:14 went up with him to *b* his father
Deut 21:23 shalt in any wise *b* him that day
1Kin 2:31 said, and fall upon him, and *b* him
1Kin 11:15 host was gone up to *b* the slain
1Kin 13:29 to the city, to mourn and to *b* him
1Kin 13:31 then *b* me in the sepulchre
1Kin 14:13 shall mourn for him, and *b* him
2Kin 9:10 and there shall be none to *b* her
2Kin 9:34 now this cursed woman, and *b* her
Ps 79:3 and there was none to *b* them
Jer 7:32 for they shall *b* in Tophet
Jer 14:16 and they shall have none to *b* them
Jer 19:11 they shall *b* them in Tophet
Jer 19:11 till there be no place to *b*
Eze 39:11 and there shall they *b* Gog
Hos 9:6 them up, Memphis shall *b* them
Mt 8:21 me first to go and *b* my father
Mt 8:22 and let the dead *b* their dead
Mt 27:7 potter's field, to *b* strangers in
Lk 9:59 me first to go and *b* my father
Lk 9:60 him, Let the dead *b* their dead
Jn 19:40 as the manner of the Jews is to *b*

### BURYING

2Kin 13:21 to pass, as they were *b* a man
Eze 39:12 the house of Israel be *b* of them
Mk 14:8 to anoint my body to the *b*
Jn 12:7 day of my *b* hath she kept this

### BURYINGPLACE

Gen 23:4 me a possession of a *b* with you
Gen 23:9 a possession of a *b* amongst you
Gen 23:20 of a *b* by the sons of Heth
Gen 47:30 of Egypt, and bury me in their *b*
Gen 49:30 Hittite for a possession of a *b*
Gen 50:13 of a *b* of Ephron the Hittite
Judg 16:31 Eshtaol in the *b* of Manoah his

### BUSH

Ex 3:2 of fire out of the midst of a *b*
Ex 3:2 the *b* burned with fire
Ex 3:2 and the *b* was not consumed
Ex 3:3 sight, why the *b* is not burnt
Ex 3:4 him out of the midst of the *b*
Deut 33:16 will of him that dwelt in the *b*
Mk 12:26 how in the *b* God spake unto him,
Lk 6:44 nor of a bramble *b* gather they
Lk 20:37 even Moses shewed at the *b*
Acts 7:30 Lord in a flame of fire in a *b*
Acts 7:35 which appeared to him in the *b*

### BUSINESS

Gen 39:11 went into the house to do his *b*
Deut 24:5 shall he be charged with any *b*
Josh 2:14 yours, if ye utter not this our *b*
Josh 2:20 And if thou utter this our *b*
Judg 18:7 and had no *b* with any man
Judg 18:28 they had no *b* with any man
1Sa 20:19 thyself when the *b* was in hand
1Sa 21:2 The king hath commanded me a *b*
1Sa 21:2 of the *b* whereabout I send thee
1Sa 21:8 the king's *b* required haste
1Chr 26:29 for the outward *b* over Israel
1Chr 26:30 westward in all the *b* of the LORD
2Chr 13:10 and the Levites wait upon their *b*
2Chr 17:13 he had much *b* in the cities of
2Chr 32:31 Howbeit in the *b* of the
Neh 11:16 the outward *b* of the house of God
Neh 11:22 over the *b* of the house of God
Neh 13:30 the Levites, every one in his *b*
Est 3:9 that have the charge of the *b*
Ps 107:23 that do *b* in great waters
Prov 22:29 thou a man diligent in his *b*
Eccl 5:3 cometh through the multitude of *b*
Eccl 8:16 to see the *b* that is done upon
Dan 8:27 I rose up, and did the king's *b*
Lk 2:49 I must be about my Father's *b*
Acts 6:3 whom we may appoint over this *b*
Rom 12:11 Not slothful in *b*
Rom 16:2 whatsoever *b* she hath need of you
1Th 4:11 to be quiet, and to do your own *b*

### BUTLER

Gen 40:1 that the *b* of the king of Egypt
Gen 40:5 of his dream, the *b* and the baker
Gen 40:9 the chief *b* told his dream to
Gen 40:13 manner when thou wast his *b*
Gen 40:20 lifted up the head of the chief *b*
Gen 40:21 he restored the chief *b* unto his
Gen 40:23 not the chief *b* remember Joseph
Gen 41:9 spake the chief *b* unto Pharaoh

### BUTTER

Gen 18:8 And he took *b*, and milk, and the
Deut 32:14 *B* of kine, and milk of sheep, with
Judg 5:25 brought forth *b* in a lordly dish
2Sa 17:29 And honey, and *b*, and sheep, and
Job 20:17 floods, the brooks of honey and *b*
Job 29:6 When I washed my steps with *b*
Ps 55:21 of his mouth were smoother than *b*
Prov 30:33 churning of milk bringeth forth *b*
Is 7:15 *B* and honey shall he eat, that he
Is 7:22 they shall give, he shall eat *b*

### BUTTOCKS

2Sa 10:4 in the middle, even to their *b*
1Chr 19:4 in the midst hard by their *b*
Is 20:4 even with their *b* uncovered

### BUY

Gen 41:57 Egypt to Joseph for to *b* corn
Gen 42:2 thither, and *b* for us from thence
Gen 42:5 to *b* corn among those that came
Gen 42:7 From the land of Canaan to *b* food
Gen 42:10 but to *b* food are thy servants
Gen 43:2 Go again, *b* us a little food
Gen 43:20 down at the first time to *b* food
Gen 43:22 down in our hands to *b* food
Gen 44:25 Go again, and *b* us a little food
Gen 47:19 *b* us and our land for bread, and we
Ex 21:2 If thou *b* an Hebrew servant, six
Lev 22:11 But if the priest *b* any soul with
Lev 25:15 thou shalt *b* of thy neighbour
Lev 25:44 of them shall ye *b* bondmen
Lev 25:45 among you, of them shall ye *b*
Deut 2:6 ye shall also *b* water of them for
Deut 28:68 bondwomen, and no man shall *b* you
Ruth 4:4 *B* it before the inhabitants, and
Ruth 4:8 said unto Boaz, *B* it for thee
2Sa 24:21 To *b* the threshingfloor of thee,
2Sa 24:24 but I will surely *b* it of thee at
2Kin 12:12 to *b* timber and hewed stone to
2Kin 22:6 to *b* timber and hewn stone to
1Chr 21:24 but I will verily *b* it for the
2Chr 34:11 to *b* hewn stone, and timber for
Ezr 7:17 That thou mayest *b* speedily with
Neh 5:3 and houses, that we might *b* corn
Neh 10:31 that we would not *b* it of them on
Prov 23:23 *B* the truth, and sell it not
Is 55:1 come ye, *b*, and eat
Is 55:1 *b* wine and milk without money and
Jer 32:7 *B* thee my field that is in
Jer 32:7 of redemption is thine to *b* it
Jer 32:8 *B* my field, I pray thee, that is
Jer 32:8 *b* it for thyself
Jer 32:25 *B* thee the field for money, and
Jer 32:44 Men shall *b* fields for money, and
Amos 8:6 That we may *b* the poor for silver
Mt 14:15 and *b* themselves victuals
Mt 25:9 that sell, and *b* for yourselves
Mt 25:10 And while they went to *b*, the
Mk 6:36 villages, and *b* themselves bread

Mk 6:37 *b* two hundred pennyworth of bread
Lk 9:13 *b* meat for all this people
Lk 22:36 him sell his garment, and *b* one
Jn 4:8 gone away unto the city to *b* meat
Jn 6:5 Philip, Whence shall we *b* bread
Jn 13:29 *B* those things that we have need
1Cor 7:30 and they that *b*, as though they
Jas 4:13 and continue there a year, and *b*
Rev 3:18 I counsel thee to *b* of me gold
Rev 13:17 And that no man might *b* or sell

**BUZ** *(buz)*
*1. Son of Nahor.*
Gen 22:21 *B* his brother, and Kemuel the
*2. A Gadite.*
1Chr 5:14 the son of Jahdo, the son of *B*
*3. A tribe in northern Arabia.*
Jer 25:23 Dedan, and Tema, and *B*, and all that

**BUZI** *(boo'-zi)* See BUZITE. *Father of Ezekiel.*
Eze 1:3 Ezekiel the priest, the son of *B*

**BUZITE** *(boo'-zite) A member of Buz 3.*
Job 32:2 Elihu the son of Barachel the *B*
Job 32:6 son of Barachel the *B* answered

**BYWORD**
Deut 28:37 astonishment, a proverb, and a *b*
1Kin 9:7 a proverb and a *b* among all people
2Chr 7:20 proverb and a *b* among all nations
Job 17:6 made me also a *b* of the people
Job 30:9 I their song, yea, I am their *b*
Ps 44:14 Thou makest us a *b* among the

# C

**CABBON** *(cab'-bon) A town in Judah.*
Josh 15:40 And C, and Lahmam, and Kithlish,

**CABUL** *(ca'-bul) A town in Asher.*
Josh 19:27 goeth out to C on the left hand,
1Kin 9:13 them the land of C unto this day

**CAESAR** *(se'-zur)* See CAESAR'S. *Title for the Roman Emperor.*
Mt 22:17 it lawful to give tribute unto C
Mt 22:21 Render therefore unto C the
Mk 12:14 Is it lawful to give tribute to C
Mk 12:17 Render to C the things that are
Lk 2:1 went out a decree from C Augustus
Lk 3:1 year of the reign of Tiberius C
Lk 20:22 for us to give tribute unto C
Lk 20:25 Render therefore unto C the
Lk 23:2 forbidding to give tribute to C
Jn 19:12 himself a king speaketh against C
Jn 19:15 answered, We have no king but C
Acts 11:28 to pass in the days of Claudius C
Acts 17:7 do contrary to the decrees of C
Acts 25:8 the temple, nor yet against C
Acts 25:11 I appeal unto C
Acts 25:21 kept till I might send him to C
Acts 26:32 if he had not appealed unto C
Acts 27:24 thou must be brought before C
Acts 28:19 was constrained to appeal unto C

**CAESAREA** *(ses-a-re'-ah)*
*1. A town north of Galilee.*
Mt 16:13 into the coasts of C Philippi
Mk 8:27 into the towns of C Philippi
*2. A Judean Mediterranean port.*
Acts 8:40 all the cities, till he came to C
Acts 9:30 knew, they brought him down to C
Acts 10:1 certain man in C called Cornelius
Acts 10:24 morrow after they entered into C
Acts 11:11 where I was, sent from C unto me
Acts 12:19 And he went down from Judaea to C
Acts 18:22 And when he had landed at C
Acts 21:8 company departed, and came unto C
Acts 21:16 certain of the disciples of C
Acts 23:23 two hundred soldiers to go to C
Acts 23:33 Who, when they came to C, and
Acts 25:1 he ascended from C to Jerusalem
Acts 25:4 that Paul should be kept at C
Acts 25:6 ten days, he went down unto C
Acts 25:13 came unto C to salute Festus

**CAESAR'S** *(se'-zurs)*
Mt 22:21 They say unto him, C
Mt 22:21 Caesar the things which are C
Mk 12:16 And they said unto him, C
Mk 12:17 to Caesar the things that are C
Lk 20:24 They answered and said, C
Lk 20:25 unto Caesar the things which be C
Jn 19:12 man go, thou art not C friend
Acts 25:10 I stand at C judgment seat, where
Phil 4:22 they that are of C household

**CAIAPHAS** *(cah'-ya-fus) A High Priest during Jesus' time.*
Mt 26:3 the high priest, who was called C
Mt 26:57 led him away to C the high priest
Lk 3:2 C being the high priests, the
Jn 11:49 And one of them, named C, being
Jn 18:13 for he was father in law to C
Jn 18:14 Now C was he, which gave counsel
Jn 18:24 him bound unto C the high priest
Jn 18:28 Then led they Jesus from C unto
Acts 4:6 And Annas the high priest, and C

**CAIN** See TUBAL-CAIN.
*1. Eldest son of Adam and Eve.*
Gen 4:1 and she conceived, and bare C
Gen 4:2 but C was a tiller of the ground
Gen 4:5 But unto C and to his offering he
Gen 4:6 And the LORD said unto C, Why art
Gen 4:8 C talked with Abel his brother
Gen 4:9 And the LORD said unto C, Where is
Gen 4:13 And C said unto the LORD, My
Gen 4:15 Therefore whosoever slayeth C
Gen 4:15 And the LORD set a mark upon C
Gen 4:16 C went out from the presence of
Gen 4:17 And C knew his wife
Gen 4:24 If C shall be avenged sevenfold,
Gen 4:25 seed instead of Abel, whom C slew
Heb 11:4 a more excellent sacrifice than C
1Jn 3:12 Not as C, who was of that wicked
Jude 11 they have gone in the way of C
*2. A town in Judah.*
Josh 15:57 C, Gibeah, and Timnah

**CAINAN** *(ca'-nun)* See KENAN. *Son of Enos.*
Gen 5:9 lived ninety years, and begat C
Gen 5:10 after he begat C eight hundred
Gen 5:12 C lived seventy years, and begat
Gen 5:14 all the days of C were nine
Lk 3:36 Which was the son of C, which was
Lk 3:37 Maleleel, which was the son of C

**CAKE**
Ex 29:23 one *c* of oiled bread, and one
Lev 8:26 LORD, he took one unleavened *c*
Lev 24:5 two tenth deals shall be in one *c*
Num 6:19 one unleavened *c* out of the
Num 15:20 Ye shall offer up a *c* of the
Judg 7:13 a *c* of barley bread tumbled into
1Sa 30:12 gave him a piece of a *c* of figs
2Sa 6:19 as men, to every one a *c* of bread
1Kin 17:12 thy God liveth, I have not a *c*
1Kin 19:6 there was a *c* baken on the coals,
Hos 7:8 Ephraim is a *c* not turned

**CAKES**
Gen 18:6 it, and make *c* upon the hearth
Ex 12:39 they baked unleavened *c* of the
Ex 29:2 *c* unleavened tempered with oil,
Lev 2:4 it shall be unleavened *c* of fine
Lev 7:12 unleavened *c* mingled with oil
Lev 24:5 flour, and bake twelve *c* thereof
Num 6:15 *c* of fine flour mingled with oil,
Num 11:8 baked it in pans, and made *c* of it
Josh 5:11 after the passover, unleavened *c*
Judg 6:19 unleavened *c* of an ephah of flour
1Sa 25:18 raisins, and two hundred *c* of figs
2Sa 13:6 make me a couple of *c* in my sight
2Sa 13:10 Tamar took the *c* which she had
1Chr 12:40 *c* of figs, and bunches of raisins,
1Chr 23:29 offering, and for the unleavened *c*
Jer 7:18 to make *c* to the queen of heaven,
Jer 44:19 did we make her *c* to worship her
Eze 4:12 And thou shalt eat it as barley *c*

**CALAH** *(ca'-lah) An Assyrian city.*
Gen 10:11 and the city Rehoboth, and C
Gen 10:12 And Resen between Nineveh and C

**CALAMITIES**
Ps 57:1 refuge, until these *c* be overpast
Ps 141:5 prayer also shall be in their *c*
Prov 17:5 he that is glad at *c* shall not be

**CALAMITY**
Deut 32:35 for the day of their *c* is at hand
2Sa 22:19 prevented me in the day of my *c*
Job 6:2 my *c* laid in the balances
Job 30:13 my path, they set forward my *c*
Ps 18:18 prevented me in the day of my *c*
Prov 1:26 I also will laugh at your *c*
Prov 6:15 shall his *c* come suddenly
Prov 19:13 son is the *c* of his father
Prov 24:22 For their *c* shall rise suddenly
Prov 27:10 house in the day of thy *c*
Jer 18:17 the face, in the day of their *c*
Jer 46:21 day of their *c* was come upon them
Jer 48:16 The *c* of Moab is near to come, and
Jer 49:8 will bring the *c* of Esau upon him
Jer 49:32 I will bring their *c* from all
Eze 35:5 the sword in the time of their *c*
Obad 13 my people in the day of their *c*

**CALAMUS**
Ex 30:23 of sweet *c* two hundred and fifty
Song 4:14 *c* and cinnamon, with all trees of
Eze 27:19 bright iron, cassia, and *c*

**CALCOL** *(cal'-col)* See CHALCOL. *A son of Zerah.*
1Chr 2:6 Zimri, and Ethan, and Heman, and C

**CALDRON**
1Sa 2:14 it into the pan, or kettle, or *c*
Job 41:20 as out of a seething pot or *c*
Eze 11:3 this city is the *c*, and we be the
Eze 11:7 the flesh, and this city is the *c*
Eze 11:11 This city shall not be your *c*
Mic 3:3 the pot, and as flesh within the *c*

**CALDRONS**
2Chr 35:13 sod they in pots, and in *c*
Jer 52:18 The *c* also, and the shovels, and
Jer 52:19 firepans, and the bowls, and the *c*

**CALEB** *(ca'-leb)* See CALEB'S, CALEB-EPHRATAH, CHELUBAI.
*1. A son of Jephunneh.*
Num 13:6 of Judah, C the son of Jephunneh
Num 13:30 C stilled the people before Moses
Num 14:6 C the son of Jephunneh, which
Num 14:24 But my servant C, because he had
Num 14:30 save C the son of Jephunneh, and
Num 14:38 C the son of Jephunneh, which
Num 26:65 save C the son of Jephunneh, and
Num 32:12 Save C the son of Jephunneh the
Num 34:19 of Judah, C the son of Jephunneh
Deut 1:36 Save C the son of Jephunneh
Josh 14:6 C the son of Jephunneh the
Josh 14:13 gave unto C the son of Jephunneh
Josh 15:13 unto C the son of Jephunneh he
Josh 15:17 son of Kenaz, the brother of C
Josh 21:12 gave they to C the son of
Judg 1:12 And C said, He that smiteth
Judg 1:14 C said unto her, What wilt thou
Judg 1:20 And they gave Hebron unto C
1Sa 25:3 and he was of the house of C
1Sa 30:14 to Judah, and upon the south of C
1Chr 2:49 and the daughter of C was Achsa
1Chr 4:15 And the sons of C the son of
1Chr 6:56 they gave to C the son of
*2. A son of Hezron.*
1Chr 2:18 C the son of Hezron begat
1Chr 2:19 C took unto him Ephrath, which
1Chr 2:42 Now the sons of C the brother of
*3. A son of Hur.*
1Chr 2:50 were the sons of C the son of Hur

**CALEB-EPHRATAH** *(ca'-leb-ef'-ra-tah) The place where Hezron died.*
1Chr 2:24 after that Hezron was dead in C

**CALEB'S** *(ca'-lebs) Refers to Caleb 1.*
Judg 1:13 C younger brother, took it
Judg 3:9 son of Kenaz, C younger brother
1Chr 2:46 C concubine, bare Haran, and Moza,
1Chr 2:48 C concubine, bare Sheber, and

**CALF**
Gen 18:7 the herd, and fetcht a c tender
Ex 32:4 after he had made it a molten c
Ex 32:8 they have made them a molten c
Ex 32:19 unto the camp, that he saw the c
Lev 9:2 Take thee a young c for a sin
Lev 9:8 slew the c of the sin offering,
Deut 9:16 God, and had made you a molten c
Deut 9:21 the c which ye had made, and burnt
1Sa 28:24 woman had a fat c in the house
Neh 9:18 they had made them a molten c
Job 21:10 cow calveth, and casteth not her c
Ps 29:6 maketh them also to skip like a c
Ps 106:19 They made a c in Horeb, and
Is 11:6 and the c and the young lion and the
Is 27:10 there shall the c feed, and there
Jer 34:18 me, when they cut the c in twain
Hos 8:5 Thy c, O Samaria, hath cast thee
Lk 15:23 And bring hither the fatted c
Lk 15:27 father hath killed the fatted c
Lk 15:30 hast killed for him the fatted c
Acts 7:41 they made a c in those days, and
Rev 4:7 and the second beast like a c

**CALL**
Gen 2:19 Adam to see what he would c them
Gen 4:26 then began men to c upon the name
Gen 16:11 son, and shalt c his name Ishmael
Gen 17:15 thou shalt not c her name Sarai
Gen 17:19 thou shalt c his name Isaac
Gen 24:57 We will c the damsel, and enquire
Gen 30:13 the daughters will c me blessed
Gen 46:33 to pass, when Pharaoh shall c you
Ex 2:7 c to thee a nurse of the Hebrew
Ex 2:20 c him, that he may eat bread
Ex 34:15 one c thee, and thou eat of his
Num 16:12 And Moses sent to c Dathan
Num 22:5 to c him, saying, Behold, there
Num 22:20 him, If the men come to c thee
Num 22:37 send unto thee to c thee
Deut 2:11 but the Moabites c them Emims
Deut 2:20 the Ammonites c them Zamzummims
Deut 3:9 Hermon the Sidonians c Sirion
Deut 3:9 and the Amorites c it Shenir
Deut 4:7 all things that we c upon him for
Deut 4:26 I c heaven and earth to witness
Deut 25:8 elders of his city shall c him
Deut 30:1 thou shalt c them to mind among
Deut 30:19 I c heaven and earth to record
Deut 31:14 c Joshua, and present yourselves
Deut 31:28 c heaven and earth to record
Deut 33:19 They shall c the people unto the
Judg 12:1 didst not c us to go with thee
Judg 16:25 C for Samson, that he may make us
Judg 21:13 and to c peaceably unto them
Ruth 1:20 C me not Naomi, c me Mara
Ruth 1:21 why then c ye me Naomi, seeing
1Sa 3:6 for thou didst c me
1Sa 12:17 I will c unto the LORD, and he
1Sa 16:3 c Jesse to the sacrifice, and I
1Sa 22:11 sent to c Ahimelech the priest
2Sa 17:5 C now Hushai the Archite also, and
2Sa 22:4 I will c on the LORD, who is
1Kin 1:28 answered and said, C me Bath-sheba
1Kin 1:32 C me Zadok the priest, and Nathan
1Kin 8:52 in all that they c for unto thee
1Kin 17:18 me to c my sin to remembrance
1Kin 18:24 c ye on the name of your gods, and
1Kin 18:24 I will c on the name of the LORD
1Kin 18:25 c on the name of your gods, but
1Kin 22:13 gone to c Micaiah spake unto him
2Kin 4:12 his servant, C this Shunammite
2Kin 5:11 c on the name of the LORD his God
2Kin 10:19 Now therefore c unto me all the
1Chr 16:8 c upon his name, make known his
2Chr 18:12 went to c Micaiah spake to him
Job 5:1 C now, if there be any that will
Job 13:22 Then c thou, and I will answer
Job 14:15 Thou shalt c, and I will answer
Job 27:10 will he always c upon God
Ps 4:1 Hear me when I c, O God of my
Ps 14:4 eat bread, and c not upon the LORD
Ps 18:3 I will c upon the LORD, who is
Ps 20:9 let the king hear us when we c
Ps 49:11 they c their lands after their
Ps 50:4 He shall c to the heavens from
Ps 50:15 c upon me in the day of trouble
Ps 55:16 As for me, I will c upon God
Ps 72:17 all nations shall c him blessed
Ps 77:6 I c to remembrance my song in the
Ps 80:18 us, and we will c upon thy name
Ps 86:5 unto all them that c upon thee
Ps 86:7 of my trouble I will c upon thee
Ps 91:15 He shall c upon me, and I will
Ps 99:6 among them that c upon his name
Ps 102:2 in the day when I c answer me
Ps 105:1 c upon his name
Ps 116:2 therefore will I c upon him as
Ps 116:13 c upon the name of the LORD
Ps 116:17 will c upon the name of the LORD
Ps 145:18 unto all them that c upon him
Prov 1:28 Then shall they c upon me
Prov 7:4 c understanding thy kinswoman
Prov 8:4 Unto you, O men, I c
Prov 9:15 To c passengers who go right on
Prov 31:28 arise up, and c her blessed
Is 5:20 Woe unto them that c evil good
Is 7:14 shall c his name Immanuel
Is 8:3 C his name Maher-shalal-hash-baz
Is 12:4 c upon his name, declare his
Is 22:12 Lord GOD of hosts c to weeping
Is 22:20 that I will c my servant Eliakim
Is 31:2 will not c back his words
Is 34:12 They shall c the nobles thereof
Is 41:25 the sun shall he c upon my name
Is 44:5 another shall c himself by the
Is 44:7 And who, as I, shall c, and shall
Is 45:3 which c thee by thy name, am the
Is 48:2 For they c themselves of the holy
Is 48:13 when I c unto them, they stand up
Is 55:5 thou shalt c a nation that thou
Is 58:5 wilt thou c this a fast, and an
Is 58:9 Then shalt thou c, and the LORD
Is 58:13 c the sabbath a delight, the holy
Is 60:14 and they shall c thee, The city of
Is 60:18 but thou shalt c thy walls
Is 61:6 shall c you the Ministers of our
Is 62:12 And they shall c them, The holy
Is 65:15 c his servants by another name
Is 65:24 come to pass, that before they c
Jer 1:15 I will c all the families of the
Jer 3:17 At that time they shall c
Jer 3:19 and I said, Thou shalt c me
Jer 6:30 Reprobate silver shall men c them
Jer 7:27 thou shalt also c unto them
Jer 9:17 c for the mourning women, that
Jer 10:25 families that c not on thy name
Jer 25:29 for I will c for a sword upon all
Jer 29:12 Then shall ye c upon me, and ye
Jer 33:3 C unto me, and I will answer thee,
Jer 50:29 C together the archers against
Jer 51:27 c together against her the
Lam 2:15 men c The perfection of beauty
Eze 21:23 but he will c to remembrance the
Eze 36:29 I will c for the corn, and will
Eze 38:21 I will c for a sword against him
Eze 39:11 they shall c it The valley of
Dan 2:2 king commanded to c the magicians
Hos 1:4 said unto him, C his name Jezreel
Hos 1:6 unto him, C her name Lo-ruhamah
Hos 1:9 Then said God, C his name Lo-ammi
Hos 2:16 LORD, that thou shalt c me Ishi
Hos 7:11 they c to Egypt, they go to
Joel 1:14 c a solemn assembly, gather the
Joel 2:15 a fast, c a solemn assembly
Joel 2:32 that whosoever shall c on the
Amos 5:16 they shall c the husbandman to
Jonah 1:6 c upon thy God, if so be that God
Zeph 3:9 that they may all c upon the name
Zec 3:10 hosts, shall ye c every man his
Zec 13:9 they shall c on my name, and I
Mal 1:4 and they shall c them, The border
Mal 3:12 all nations shall c you blessed
Mal 3:15 And now we c the proud happy
Mt 1:21 thou shalt c his name JESUS
Mt 1:23 they shall c his name Emmanuel,
Mt 9:13 I am not come to c the righteous
Mt 10:25 they c them of his household
Mt 20:8 C the labourers, and give them
Mt 22:3 sent forth his servants to c them
Mt 22:43 doth David in spirit c him Lord
Mt 22:45 If David then c him Lord
Mt 23:9 c no man your father upon the
Mk 2:17 I came not to c the righteous
Mk 10:49 they c the blind man, saying unto
Mk 15:12 whom ye c the King of the Jews
Mk 15:16 they c together the whole band
Lk 1:13 thou shalt c his name John
Lk 1:31 a son, and shalt c his name JESUS
Lk 1:48 generations shall c me blessed
Lk 5:32 I came not to c the righteous
Lk 6:46 why c ye me, Lord, Lord, and do
Lk 14:12 c not thy friends, nor thy
Jn 4:16 c thy husband, and come hither
Jn 13:13 Ye c me Master and Lord
Jn 15:15 Henceforth I c you not servants
Acts 2:21 that whosoever shall c on the
Acts 2:39 many as the Lord our God shall c
Acts 9:14 to bind all that c on thy name
Acts 10:5 c for one Simon, whose surname is
Acts 10:15 cleansed, that c not thou common
Acts 10:28 not c any man common or unclean
Acts 10:32 c hither Simon, whose surname is
Acts 11:9 cleansed, that c not thou common
Acts 11:13 c for Simon, whose surname is
Acts 19:13 took upon them to c over them
Acts 24:14 after the way which they c heresy
Acts 24:25 season, I will c for thee
Rom 9:25 I will c them my people, which
Rom 10:12 is rich unto all that c upon him
Rom 10:13 For whosoever shall c upon the
Rom 10:14 How then shall they c on him in
1Cor 1:2 with all that in every place c
2Cor 1:23 Moreover I c God for a record
2Ti 1:5 When I c to remembrance the
2Ti 2:22 with them that c on the Lord out
Heb 2:11 is not ashamed to c them brethren
Heb 10:32 But c to remembrance the former
Jas 5:14 let him c for the elders of the
1Pet 1:17 if ye c on the Father, who

**CALLETH**
1Kin 8:43 that the stranger c to thee for
2Chr 6:33 that the stranger c to thee for
Job 12:4 who c upon God, and he answereth
Ps 42:7 Deep c unto deep at the noise of
Ps 147:4 he c them all by their names
Prov 18:6 and his mouth c for strokes
Is 21:11 He c to me out of Seir, Watchman,
Is 40:26 he c them all by names by the
Is 59:4 None c for justice, nor any
Is 64:7 is none that c upon thy name
Hos 7:7 is none among them that c unto me
Amos 5:8 that c for the waters of the sea,
Amos 9:6 he that c for the waters of the
Mt 27:47 that, said, This man c for Elias
Mk 3:13 and c unto him whom he would
Mk 10:49 he c thee
Mk 12:37 therefore himself c him Lord
Mk 15:35 heard it said, Behold, he c Elias
Lk 15:6 he c together his friends and
Lk 15:9 it, she c her friends and her
Lk 20:37 when he c the Lord the God of
Lk 20:44 David therefore c him Lord
Jn 10:3 he c his own sheep by name, and
Jn 11:28 The Master is come, and c for thee
Rom 4:17 c those things which be not as
Rom 9:11 not of works, but of him that c
1Cor 12:3 Spirit of God c Jesus accursed
Gal 5:8 cometh not of him that c you
1Th 5:24 Faithful is he that c you
Rev 2:20 which c herself a prophetess, to

**CALLING**
Num 10:2 them for the c of the assembly
Is 1:13 the c of assemblies, I cannot
Is 41:4 c the generations from the
Is 46:11 C a ravenous bird from the east,
Eze 23:19 in c to remembrance the days of
Mt 11:16 markets, and c unto their fellows,
Mk 3:31 without, sent unto him, c him
Mk 11:21 Peter c to remembrance saith unto
Mk 15:44 c unto him the centurion, he
Lk 7:19 John c unto him two of his
Lk 7:32 c one to another, and saying, We
Acts 7:59 c upon God, and saying, Lord Jesus
Acts 22:16 c on the name of the Lord
Rom 11:29 c of God are without repentance
1Cor 1:26 For ye see your c, brethren, how
1Cor 7:20 the same c wherein he was called
Eph 1:18 know what is the hope of his c
Eph 4:4 are called in one hope of your c
Phil 3:14 the high c of God in Christ Jesus
2Th 1:11 would count you worthy of this c
2Ti 1:9 us, and called us with an holy c
Heb 3:1 partakers of the heavenly c

1Pet 3:6 Sarah obeyed Abraham, c him lord
2Pet 1:10 give diligence to make your c

**CALM**

Ps 107:29 He maketh the storm a c, so that
Jonah 1:11 that the sea may be c unto us
Jonah 1:12 so shall the sea be c unto you
Mt 8:26 and there was a great c
Mk 4:39 ceased, and there was a great c
Lk 8:24 and they ceased, and there was a c

**CALNEH** *(cal'-neh)* See CALNO, CANNEH. *A center of Babylonian worship.*

Gen 10:10 Babel, and Erech, and Accad, and C
Amos 6:2 Pass ye unto C, and see

**CALNO** *(cal'-no)* See CALNEH. *Same as Calneh.*

Is 10:9 Is not C as Carchemish

**CALVARY**

Lk 23:33 to the place, which is called C

**CALVES**

1Sa 6:7 bring their c home from them
1Sa 6:10 cart, and shut up their c at home
1Sa 14:32 and took sheep, and oxen, and c
1Kin 12:28 counsel, and made two c of gold
1Kin 12:32 unto the c that he had made
2Kin 10:29 the golden c that were in Beth-el
2Kin 17:16 them molten images, even two c
2Chr 11:15 for the c which he had made
2Chr 13:8 and there are with you golden c
Ps 68:30 with the c of the people, till
Hos 10:5 because of the c of Beth-aven
Hos 13:2 the men that sacrifice kiss the c
Hos 14:2 will we render the c of our lips
Amos 6:4 the c out of the midst of the
Mic 6:6 offerings, with c of a year old
Mal 4:2 grow up as c of the stall
Heb 9:12 by the blood of goats and c
Heb 9:19 the law, he took the blood of c

**CAMEL**

Gen 24:64 saw Isaac, she lighted off the c
Lev 11:4 as the c, because he cheweth the
Deut 14:7 as the c, and the hare, and the
1Sa 15:3 and suckling, ox and sheep, c
Zec 14:15 the horse, of the mule, of the c
Mt 19:24 It is easier for a c to go
Mt 23:24 strain at a gnat, and swallow a c
Mk 10:25 It is easier for a c to go
Lk 18:25 For it is easier for a c to go

**CAMELS**

Gen 12:16 maidservants, and she asses, and c
Gen 24:10 ten c of the c of his master
Gen 24:14 and I will give thy c drink also
Gen 24:20 draw water, and drew for all his c
Gen 24:22 as the c had done drinking, that
Gen 24:30 he stood by the c at the well
Gen 24:32 gave straw and provender for the c
Gen 24:35 and maidservants, and c, and asses
Gen 24:46 and she made the c drink also
Gen 24:61 damsels, and they rode upon the c
Gen 24:63 and, behold, the c were coming
Gen 30:43 and menservants, and c, and asses
Gen 31:17 set his sons and his wives upon c
Gen 32:7 and the flocks, and herds, and the c
Gen 32:15 Thirty milch c with their colts,
Gen 37:25 with their c bearing spicery
Ex 9:3 upon the asses, upon the c
Judg 6:5 their c were without number
Judg 7:12 their c were without number, as
1Sa 27:9 the oxen, and the asses, and the c
1Sa 30:17 young men, which rode upon c
1Kin 10:2 with c that bare spices, and very
1Chr 5:21 of their c fifty thousand, and of
1Chr 12:40 brought bread on asses, and on c
1Chr 27:30 Over the c also was Obil the
2Chr 9:1 c that bare spices, and gold in
2Chr 14:15 c in abundance, and returned to
Ezr 2:67 Their c, four hundred thirty and
Neh 7:69 Their c, four hundred thirty and
Est 8:10 horseback, and riders on mules, c
Est 8:14 c went out, being hastened and
Job 1:3 sheep, and three thousand c
Job 1:17 three bands, and fell upon the c
Job 42:12 thousand sheep, and six thousand c
Is 21:7 of asses, and a chariot of c
Is 30:6 treasures upon the bunches of c
Is 60:6 multitude of c shall cover thee
Jer 49:29 and all their vessels, and their c
Jer 49:32 their c shall be a booty, and the
Eze 25:5 I will make Rabbah a stable for c

**CAMON** *(ca'-mon) A town in Gilead.*

Judg 10:5 And Jair died, and was buried in C

**CAMP**

Ex 14:19 which went before the c of Israel
Ex 16:13 quails came up, and covered the c
Ex 19:16 people that was in the c trembled
Ex 19:17 out of the c to meet with God
Ex 29:14 thou burn with fire without the c
Ex 32:17 There is a noise of war in the c
Ex 32:19 soon as he came nigh unto the c
Ex 32:26 Moses stood in the gate of the c
Ex 33:7 the c, afar off from the c
Ex 33:11 And he turned again into the c
Ex 36:6 to be proclaimed throughout the c
Lev 4:12 without the c unto a clean place
Lev 4:21 forth the bullock without the c
Lev 6:11 without the c unto a clean place
Lev 8:17 he burnt with fire without the c
Lev 9:11 he burnt with fire without the c
Lev 10:4 before the sanctuary out of the c
Lev 13:46 without the c shall his
Lev 14:3 shall go forth out of the c
Lev 14:8 that he shall come into the c
Lev 16:26 and afterward come into the c
Lev 16:28 he shall come into the c
Lev 17:3 an ox, or lamb, or goat, in the c
Lev 24:10 Israel strove together in the c
Lev 24:14 that hath cursed without the c
Lev 24:23 him that had cursed out of the c
Num 1:52 tents, every man by his own c
Num 2:3 they of the standard of the c of
Num 2:9 in the c of Judah were an hundred
Num 2:10 c of Reuben according to their
Num 2:16 the c of Reuben were an hundred
Num 2:17 shall set forward with the c of
Num 2:24 the c of Ephraim were an hundred
Num 2:31 they that were numbered in the c
Num 4:5 when the c setteth forward, Aaron
Num 4:15 as the c is to set forward
Num 5:2 they put out of the c every leper
Num 10:14 of the c of the children of Judah
Num 10:34 day, when they went out of the c
Num 11:1 in the uttermost parts of the c
Num 11:9 dew fell upon the c in the night
Num 11:26 remained two of the men in the c
Num 11:26 and they prophesied in the c
Num 11:30 And Moses gat him into the c
Num 11:31 sea, and let them fall by the c
Num 12:14 be shut out from the c seven days
Num 12:15 shut out from the c seven days
Num 14:44 Moses, departed not out of the c
Num 15:35 him with stones without the c
Num 19:3 may bring her forth without the c
Num 19:7 he shall come into the c, and the
Num 19:9 up without the c in a clean place
Num 31:12 unto the c at the plains of Moab,
Num 31:19 ye abide without the c seven days
Num 31:24 ye shall come into the c
Deut 23:10 shall he go abroad out of the c
Deut 23:11 he shall come into the c again
Deut 23:12 have a place also without the c
Deut 23:14 God walketh in the midst of thy c
Deut 29:11 and thy stranger that is in thy c
Josh 5:8 abode in their places in the c
Josh 6:11 into the c, and lodged in the c
Josh 6:14 city once, and returned into the c
Josh 6:18 make the c of Israel a curse, and
Josh 6:23 left them without the c of Israel
Josh 9:6 to Joshua unto the c at Gilgal
Josh 10:6 unto Joshua to the c to Gilgal
Josh 10:15 with him, unto the c to Gilgal
Josh 10:21 c to Joshua at Makkedah in peace
Josh 10:43 with him, unto the c to Gilgal
Judg 7:17 I come to the outside of the c
Judg 13:25 in the c of Dan between Zorah
Judg 21:8 there came none to the c from
Judg 21:12 brought them unto the c to Shiloh
1Sa 4:3 the people were come into the c
1Sa 13:17 the c of the Philistines in three
1Sa 14:21 went up with them into the c from
1Sa 17:4 out of the c of the Philistines
1Sa 17:17 run to the c to thy brethren
1Sa 26:6 go down with me to Saul to the c
2Sa 1:2 a man came out of the c from Saul
1Kin 16:16 over Israel that day in the c
2Kin 3:24 when they came to the c of Israel
2Kin 6:8 and such a place shall be my c
2Kin 7:5 uttermost part of the c of Syria
2Kin 7:7 even the c as it was, and fled for
2Kin 7:10 We came to the c of the Syrians
2Kin 7:12 are they gone out of the c to
2Kin 19:35 smote in the c of the Assyrians
2Chr 22:1 to the c had slain all the eldest
2Chr 32:21 captains in the c of the king of
Ps 78:28 it fall in the midst of their c
Ps 106:16 They envied Moses also in the c
Is 29:3 I will c against thee round about
Is 37:36 smote in the c of the Assyrians
Jer 50:29 the bow, c against it round about
Eze 4:2 set the c also against it, and set
Joel 2:11 for his c is very great
Nah 3:17 which c in the hedges in the cold
Heb 13:11 for sin, are burned without the c
Heb 13:13 therefore unto him without the c
Rev 20:9 compassed the c of the saints

**CAMPS**

Num 2:32 c throughout their hosts were six
Num 5:3 that they defile not their c
Num 10:2 and for the journeying of the c
Num 10:25 all the c throughout their hosts
Amos 4:10 c to come up unto your nostrils

**CANA** *(ca'-nah) A village in Galilee.*

Jn 2:1 was a marriage in C of Galilee
Jn 2:11 did Jesus in C of Galilee
Jn 4:46 came again into C of Galilee
Jn 21:2 and Nathanael of C in Galilee

**CANAAN** *(ca'-na-an)* See CANAANITE.

*1. Son of Ham.*

Gen 9:18 and Ham is the father of C
Gen 9:22 And Ham, the father of C, saw the
Gen 9:25 And he said, Cursed be C
Gen 10:6 Cush, and Mizraim, and Phut, and C
Gen 10:15 C begat Sidon his firstborn, and
1Chr 1:8 Cush, and Mizraim, Put, and C
1Chr 1:13 C begat Zidon his firstborn, and

*2. Place where Canaanites dwell.*

Gen 11:31 to go into the land of C
Gen 12:5 forth to go into the land of C
Gen 13:12 Abram dwelled in the land of C
Gen 16:3 dwelt ten years in the land of C
Gen 17:8 art a stranger, all the land of C
Gen 23:2 same is Hebron in the land of C
Gen 23:19 same is Hebron in the land of C
Gen 28:1 take a wife of the daughters of C
Gen 28:6 take a wife of the daughters of C
Gen 28:8 of C pleased not Isaac his father
Gen 31:18 Isaac his father in the land of C
Gen 33:18 which is in the land of C
Gen 35:6 to Luz, which is in the land of C
Gen 36:2 his wives of the daughters of C
Gen 36:5 born unto him in the land of C
Gen 36:6 which he had got in the land of C
Gen 37:1 was a stranger, in the land of C
Gen 42:5 the famine was in the land of C
Gen 42:7 From the land of C to buy food
Gen 42:13 sons of one man in the land of C
Gen 42:29 their father unto the land of C
Gen 42:32 with our father in the land of C
Gen 44:8 unto thee out of the land of C
Gen 45:17 and go, get you unto the land of C
Gen 45:25 came into the land of C unto
Gen 46:6 they had gotten in the land of C
Gen 46:12 Er and Onan died in the land of C
Gen 46:31 which were in the land of C
Gen 47:1 are come out of the land of C
Gen 47:4 famine is sore in the land of C
Gen 47:13 all the land of C fainted by
Gen 47:14 of Egypt, and in the land of C
Gen 47:15 of Egypt, and in the land of C
Gen 48:3 unto me at Luz in the land of C
Gen 48:7 by me in the land of C in the way
Gen 49:30 is before Mamre, in the land of C
Gen 50:5 digged for me in the land of C
Gen 50:13 carried him into the land of C
Ex 6:4 them, to give them the land of C
Ex 15:15 inhabitants of C shall melt away
Ex 16:35 unto the borders of the land of C
Lev 14:34 ye be come into the land of C
Lev 18:3 after the doings of the land of C
Lev 25:38 Egypt, to give you the land of C
Num 13:2 they may search the land of C
Num 13:17 them to spy out the land of C
Num 26:19 Er and Onan died in the land of C
Num 32:30 among you in the land of C
Num 32:32 the LORD into the land of C
Num 33:40 in the south in the land of C

Num 33:51 over Jordan into the land of C
Num 34:2 When ye come into the land of C
Num 34:2 even the land of C with the
Num 34:29 of Israel in the land of C
Num 35:10 over Jordan into the land of C
Num 35:14 shall ye give in the land of C
Deut 32:49 and behold the land of C, which I
Josh 5:12 fruit of the land of C that year
Josh 14:1 Israel inherited in the land of C
Josh 21:2 them at Shiloh in the land of C
Josh 22:9 Shiloh, which is in the land of C
Josh 22:10 Jordan, that are in the land of C
Josh 22:32 of Gilead, unto the land of C
Josh 24:3 him throughout all the land of C
Judg 3:1 had not known all the wars of C
Judg 4:2 into the hand of Jabin king of C
Judg 4:23 C before the children of Israel
Judg 4:24 had destroyed Jabin king of C
Judg 5:19 then fought the kings of C in
Judg 21:12 Shiloh, which is in the land of C
1Chr 16:18 thee will I give the land of C
Ps 105:11 thee will I give the land of C
Ps 106:38 sacrificed unto the idols of C
Ps 135:11 Bashan, and all the kingdoms of C
Is 19:18 of Egypt speak the language of C
Eze 16:3 thy nativity is of the land of C
Eze 16:29 in the land of C unto Chaldea
Zeph 2:5 O C, the land of the Philistines,
Mt 15:22 a woman of C came out of the same

**CANAANITE** *(ca'-na-an-ite)* See CANAANITES, CANAANITESS, CANAANITISH, ZELOTES. *Descendants of Canaan.*
Gen 12:6 the C was then in the land
Gen 13:7 and the C and the Perizzite dwelled
Gen 38:2 there a daughter of a certain C
Ex 23:28 shall drive out the Hivite, the C
Ex 33:2 and I will drive out the C
Ex 34:11 before thee the Amorite, and the C
Num 21:1 And when king Arad the C, which
Num 33:40 And king Arad the C, which dwelt
Josh 9:1 Hittite, and the Amorite, the C
Josh 11:3 to the C on the east and on the
Josh 13:3 which is counted to the C
Zec 14:21 the C in the house of the LORD of
Mt 10:4 Simon the C, and Judas Iscariot,
Mk 3:18 and Thaddaeus, and Simon the C

**CANAANITES** *(ca'-na-an-ites)*
Gen 10:18 families of the C spread abroad
Gen 15:21 And the Amorites, and the C
Gen 24:3 my son of the daughters of the C
Gen 24:37 my son of the daughters of the C
Gen 34:30 of the land, among the C and the
Gen 50:11 inhabitants of the land, the C
Ex 3:8 unto the place of the C, and the
Ex 3:17 of Egypt unto the land of the C
Ex 13:5 bring thee into the land of the C
Ex 13:11 bring thee into the land of the C
Ex 23:23 and the Perizzites, and the C
Num 13:29 the C dwell by the sea, and by the
Num 14:25 the C dwelt in the valley
Num 21:3 of Israel, and delivered up the C
Deut 1:7 sea side, to the land of the C
Deut 7:1 and the Amorites, and the C
Deut 11:30 goeth down, in the land of the C
Deut 20:17 Hittites, and the Amorites, the C
Josh 3:10 drive out from before you the C
Josh 5:1 and all the kings of the C
Josh 7:9 For the C and all the inhabitants
Josh 12:8 Hittites, the Amorites, and the C
Josh 13:4 the south, all the land of the C
Josh 16:10 not out the C that dwelt in Gezer
Josh 17:12 but the C would dwell in that
Josh 24:11 and the Perizzites, and the C
Judg 1:1 go up for us against the C first
Judg 3:3 of the Philistines, and all the C
Judg 3:5 of Israel dwelt among the C
2Sa 24:7 of the Hivites, and of the C
1Kin 9:16 slain the C that dwelt in the
Ezr 9:1 their abominations, even of the C
Neh 9:8 him to give the land of the C
Neh 9:24 inhabitants of the land, the C
Obad 20 shall possess that of the C

**CANAANITESS** *(ca'-na-an-ite-ess)*
1Chr 2:3 him of the daughter of Shua the C

**CANAANITISH** *(ca'-na-an-i-tish)*
Gen 46:10 and Shaul the son of a C woman
Ex 6:15 and Shaul the son of a C woman

**CANDACE** *(can'-da-see) Name for a dynasty of Ethiopian queens.*
Acts 8:27 under C queen of the Ethiopians

**CANDLE**
Job 18:6 his c shall be put out with him
Job 21:17 How oft is the c of the wicked
Job 29:3 When his c shined upon my head,
Ps 18:28 For thou wilt light my c
Prov 20:27 of man is the c of the LORD
Prov 24:20 the c of the wicked shall be put
Prov 31:18 her c goeth not out by night
Jer 25:10 millstones, and the light of the c
Mt 5:15 Neither do men light a c, and put
Mk 4:21 Is a c brought to be put under a
Lk 8:16 No man, when he hath lighted a c
Lk 11:33 No man, when he hath lighted a c
Lk 11:36 of a c doth give thee light
Lk 15:8 one piece, doth not light a c
Rev 18:23 the light of a c shall shine no
Rev 22:5 and they need no c, neither light

**CANDLESTICK**
Ex 25:31 thou shalt make a c of pure gold
Ex 26:35 the c over against the table on
Ex 30:27 and all his vessels, and the c
Ex 31:8 the pure c with all his furniture
Ex 35:14 The c also for the light, and his
Ex 39:37 The pure c, with the lamps
Ex 40:4 and thou shalt bring in the c
Ex 40:24 he put the c in the tent of the
Lev 24:4 c before the LORD continually
Num 3:31 the ark, and the table, and the c
Num 4:9 cover the c of the light, and his
Num 8:2 give light over against the c
2Kin 4:10 and a table, and a stool, and a c
1Chr 28:15 of gold, by weight for every c
2Chr 13:11 the c of gold with the lamps
Dan 5:5 wrote over against the c upon the
Zec 4:2 behold a c all of gold, with a
Zec 4:11 upon the right side of the c
Mt 5:15 put it under a bushel, but on a c
Mk 4:21 and not to be set on a c
Lk 8:16 but setteth it on a c, that they
Lk 11:33 under a bushel, but on a c
Heb 9:2 the first, wherein was the c
Rev 2:5 will remove thy c out of his

**CANDLESTICKS**
1Kin 7:49 the c of pure gold, five on the
1Chr 28:15 Even the weight for the c of gold
1Chr 28:15 for the c of silver by weight,
2Chr 4:7 he made ten c of gold according
2Chr 4:20 Moreover the c with their lamps,
Jer 52:19 bowls, and the caldrons, and the c
Rev 1:12 turned, I saw seven golden c
Rev 1:13 in the midst of the seven c one
Rev 1:20 right hand, and the seven golden c
Rev 1:20 the seven c which thou sawest are
Rev 2:1 the midst of the seven golden c
Rev 11:4 the two c standing before the God

**CANKERWORM**
Joel 1:4 locust hath left hath the c eaten
Joel 2:25 that the locust hath eaten, the c
Nah 3:15 it shall eat thee up like the c
Nah 3:16 the c spoileth, and fleeth away

**CANNEH** *(can'-neh)* See CALNEH. *A place in southern Arabia.*
Eze 27:23 Haran, and C, and Eden, the

**CAPERNAUM** *(ca-pur'-na-um) A city in Galilee.*
Mt 4:13 Nazareth, he came and dwelt in C
Mt 8:5 And when Jesus was entered into C
Mt 11:23 And thou, C, which art exalted
Mt 17:24 And when they were come to C
Mk 1:21 And they went into C
Mk 2:1 he entered into C after some days
Mk 9:33 And he came to C
Lk 4:23 we have heard done in C, do also
Lk 4:31 And came down to C, a city of
Lk 7:1 of the people, he entered into C
Lk 10:15 And thou, C, which art exalted to
Jn 2:12 After this he went down to C
Jn 4:46 nobleman, whose son was sick at C
Jn 6:17 and went over the sea toward C
Jn 6:24 also took shipping, and came to C
Jn 6:59 the synagogue, as he taught in C

**CAPHTHORIM** *(caf'-tho-rim)* See CAPHTORIM. *People of Caphtor.*
1Chr 1:12 whom came the Philistines,) and C

**CAPHTOR** *(caf'-tor)* See CAPHTORIM. *Original land of the Philistines.*
Deut 2:23 which came forth out of C
Jer 47:4 the remnant of the country of C
Amos 9:7 and the Philistines from C

**CAPHTORIM** *(caf'-to-rim)* See CAPHTHORIM, CAPHTORIMS. *Same as Caphthorim.*
Gen 10:14 out of whom came Philistim,) and C

**CAPHTORIMS** *(caf'-to-rims)* See CAPHTORIM.
Deut 2:23 Hazerim, even unto Azzah, the C

**CAPPADOCIA** *(cap-pa-do'-she-ah) A Roman province in Asia Minor.*
Acts 2:9 Mesopotamia, and in Judaea, and C
1Pet 1:1 throughout Pontus, Galatia, C

**CAPTAIN**
Gen 21:22 Phichol the chief c of his host
Gen 21:32 Phichol the chief c of his host
Gen 26:26 Phichol the chief c of his army
Gen 37:36 of Pharaoh's, and c of the guard
Gen 39:1 c of the guard, an Egyptian,
Gen 40:3 the house of the c of the guard
Gen 40:4 the c of the guard charged Joseph
Gen 41:10 in the c of the guard's house
Gen 41:12 servant to the c of the guard
Num 2:3 be c of the children of Judah
Num 2:5 the son of Zuar shall be c of the
Num 2:7 be c of the children of Zebulun
Num 14:4 one to another, Let us make a c
Josh 5:14 but as c of the host of the LORD
Judg 4:2 the c of whose host was Sisera,
Judg 4:7 the c of Jabin's army, with his
Judg 11:6 unto Jephthah, Come, and be our c
Judg 11:11 made him head and c over them
1Sa 9:16 him to be c over my people Israel
1Sa 10:1 thee to be c over his inheritance
1Sa 12:9 c of the host of Hazor, and into
1Sa 13:14 him to be c over his people
1Sa 14:50 the name of the c of his host was
1Sa 17:18 unto the c of their thousand
1Sa 17:55 the c of the host, Abner, whose
1Sa 18:13 made him his c over a thousand
1Sa 22:2 and he became a c over them
1Sa 26:5 the son of Ner, the c of his host
2Sa 2:8 of Ner, c of Saul's host, took
2Sa 5:2 and thou shalt be a c over Israel
2Sa 5:8 soul, he shall be chief and c
2Sa 10:16 Shobach the c of the host of
2Sa 10:18 smote Shobach the c of their host
2Sa 17:25 Absalom made Amasa c of the host
2Sa 19:13 if thou be not c of the host
2Sa 23:19 therefore he was their c
2Sa 24:2 said to Joab the c of the host
1Kin 1:19 priest, and Joab the c of the host
1Kin 2:32 c of the host of Israel, and Amasa
1Kin 11:15 Joab the c of the host was gone
1Kin 11:21 that Joab the c of the host was
1Kin 11:24 became c over a band, when David
1Kin 16:9 c of half his chariots, conspired
1Kin 16:16 the c of the host, king over
2Kin 1:9 him a c of fifty with his fifty
2Kin 1:10 and said to the c of fifty
2Kin 1:11 another c of fifty with his fifty
2Kin 1:13 he sent again a c of the third
2Kin 4:13 the king, or to the c of the host
2Kin 5:1 c of the host of the king of
2Kin 9:5 I have an errand to thee, O c
2Kin 9:25 Then said Jehu to Bidkar his c
2Kin 15:25 a c of his, conspired against him
2Kin 18:24 one c of the least of my master's
2Kin 20:5 tell Hezekiah the c of my people
2Kin 25:8 c of the guard, a servant of the
2Kin 25:10 that were with the c of the guard
1Chr 11:6 first shall be chief and c
1Chr 11:21 for he was their c
1Chr 11:42 a c of the Reubenites, and thirty
1Chr 19:16 Shophach the c of the host of
1Chr 19:18 killed Shophach the c of the host
1Chr 27:5 The third c of the host for the
2Chr 13:12 God himself is with us for our c
2Chr 17:15 next to him was Jehohanan the c
Neh 9:17 a c to return to their bondage
Is 3:3 The c of fifty, and the honourable
Is 36:9 one c of the least of my master's
Jer 37:13 a c of the ward was there, whose
Jer 39:9 Then Nebuzar-adan the c of the
Jer 40:1 the c of the guard had let him go
Jer 40:5 So the c of the guard gave him

Jer 41:10 whom Nebuzar-adan the c of the
Jer 43:6 the c of the guard had left with
Jer 51:27 appoint a c against her
Jer 52:12 c of the guard, which served the
Jer 52:14 that were with the c of the guard
Jer 52:24 the c of the guard took Seraiah
Jer 52:26 So Nebuzar-adan the c of the
Jer 52:30 the c of the guard carried away
Dan 2:14 Arioch the c of the king's guard
Dan 2:15 and said to Arioch the king's c
Jn 18:12 Then the band and the c and
Acts 4:1 the c of the temple, and the
Acts 5:24 the c of the temple and the chief
Acts 5:26 Then went the c with the officers
Acts 21:31 came unto the chief c of the band
Acts 21:37 castle, he said unto the chief c
Acts 22:24 The chief c commanded him to be
Acts 22:26 that, he went and told the chief c
Acts 22:27 Then the chief c came, and said
Acts 22:29 the chief c also was afraid,
Acts 23:10 a great dissension, the chief c
Acts 23:15 council signify to the chief c
Acts 23:17 this young man unto the chief c
Acts 23:22 So the chief c then let the young
Acts 24:7 But the chief c Lysias came upon
Acts 24:22 the chief c shall come down
Acts 28:16 prisoners to the c of the guard
Heb 2:10 to make the c of their salvation

## CAPTAINS

Ex 14:7 and c over every one of them
Ex 15:4 his chosen c also are drowned in
Num 31:14 with the c over thousands, and
Deut 1:15 c over thousands, and c
Deut 20:9 that they shall make c of the
Deut 29:10 your c of your tribes, your
Josh 10:24 said unto the c of the men of war
1Sa 8:12 will appoint him c over thousands
1Sa 22:7 and make you all c of thousands
2Sa 4:2 had two men that were c of bands
2Sa 18:1 set c of thousands and c of
2Sa 18:5 the c charge concerning Absalom
2Sa 23:8 in the seat, chief among the c
2Sa 24:4 and against the c of the host
1Kin 1:25 the c of the host, and Abiathar
1Kin 2:5 the two c of the hosts of Israel
1Kin 9:22 and his princes, and his c
1Kin 15:20 sent the c of the hosts which he
1Kin 20:24 place, and put c in their rooms
1Kin 22:31 two c that had rule over his
1Kin 22:32 when the c of the chariots saw
2Kin 1:14 burnt up the two c of the former
2Kin 8:21 about, and the c of the chariots
2Kin 9:5 the c of the host were sitting
2Kin 10:25 said to the guard and to the c
2Kin 11:4 rulers over hundreds, with the c
2Kin 11:19 rulers over hundreds, and the c
2Kin 25:23 when all the c of the armies,
2Kin 25:26 the c of the armies, arose, and
1Chr 4:42 Seir, having for their c Pelatiah
1Chr 11:11 a Hachmonite, the chief of the c
1Chr 11:15 Now three of the thirty c went
1Chr 12:14 of the sons of Gad, c of the host
1Chr 12:20 c of the thousands that were of
1Chr 12:21 of valour, and were c in the host
1Chr 12:28 father's house twenty and two c
1Chr 12:34 And of Naphtali a thousand c
1Chr 13:1 consulted with the c of thousands
1Chr 15:25 the c over thousands, went to
1Chr 25:1 the c of the host separated to
1Chr 26:26 the c over thousands and hundreds,
1Chr 27:1 c of thousands and hundreds, and
1Chr 27:3 Perez was the chief of all the c
1Chr 28:1 the c of the companies that
1Chr 29:6 the c of thousands and of hundreds
2Chr 1:2 to the c of thousands and of
2Chr 8:9 men of war, and chief of his c
2Chr 11:11 put c in them, and store of
2Chr 16:4 sent the c of his armies against
2Chr 17:14 Of Judah, the c of thousands
2Chr 18:30 c of the chariots that were with
2Chr 21:9 him in, and the c of the chariots
2Chr 23:1 took the c of hundreds, Azariah
2Chr 23:9 to the c of hundreds spears
2Chr 23:14 the priest brought out the c of
2Chr 23:20 And he took the c of hundreds
2Chr 25:5 made them c over thousands, and
2Chr 25:5 c over hundreds, according to the
2Chr 26:11 of Hananiah, one of the king's c
2Chr 32:6 he set c of war over the people,
2Chr 32:21 c in the camp of the king of
2Chr 33:11 the c of the host of the king of
2Chr 33:14 put c of war in all the fenced
Neh 2:9 the king had sent c of the army
Job 39:25 afar off, the thunder of the c
Jer 13:21 for thou hast taught them to be c
Jer 40:7 Now when all the c of the forces
Jer 42:1 Then all the c of the forces, and
Jer 51:23 thee will I break in pieces c
Jer 51:28 the c thereof, and all the rulers
Jer 51:57 princes, and her wise men, her c
Eze 21:22 for Jerusalem, to appoint c
Eze 23:6 Which were clothed with blue, c
Eze 23:12 the Assyrians her neighbours, c
Eze 23:23 of them desirable young men, c
Dan 3:2 princes, the governors, and the c
Dan 3:3 the princes, the governors, and c
Dan 3:27 And the princes, governors, and c
Dan 6:7 the counsellors, and the c
Nah 3:17 thy c as the great grasshoppers,
Mk 6:21 a supper to his lords, high c
Lk 22:4 with the chief priests and c
Lk 22:52 c of the temple, and the elders,
Acts 25:23 of hearing, with the chief c
Rev 6:15 and the rich men, and the chief c
Rev 19:18 flesh of kings, and the flesh of c

## CAPTIVE

Gen 14:14 that his brother was taken c
Gen 34:29 ones, and their wives took they c
Ex 12:29 of the c that was in the dungeon
Num 24:22 Asshur shall carry thee away c
Deut 21:10 hands, and thou hast taken them c
Judg 5:12 Barak, and lead thy captivity c
1Kin 8:48 enemies, which led them away c
1Kin 8:50 before them who carried them c
2Kin 5:2 had brought away c out of the
2Kin 6:22 thou hast taken c with thy sword
2Kin 15:29 and carried them c to Assyria
2Kin 16:9 carried the people of it c to Kir
2Kin 24:16 of Babylon brought c to Babylon
1Chr 5:6 king of Assyria carried away c
2Chr 6:37 land whither they are carried c
2Chr 25:12 children of Judah carry away c
2Chr 28:8 c of their brethren two hundred
2Chr 28:11 ye have taken c of your brethren
2Chr 30:9 before them that lead them c
Ps 68:18 high, thou hast led captivity c
Ps 137:3 us away c required of us a song
Is 49:21 my children, and am desolate, a c
Is 49:24 mighty, or the lawful c delivered
Is 51:14 The c exile hasteneth that he may
Is 52:2 of thy neck, O c daughter of Zion
Jer 1:3 of Jerusalem c in the fifth month
Jer 13:17 LORD's flock is carried away c
Jer 13:19 shall be carried away c all of it
Jer 20:4 shall carry them c into Babylon
Jer 22:12 place whither they have led him c
Jer 24:1 of Babylon had carried away c
Jer 24:5 that are carried away c of Judah
Jer 27:20 when he carried away c Jeconiah
Jer 28:6 and all that is carried away c
Jer 29:1 away c from Jerusalem to Babylon
Jer 29:14 I caused you to be carried away c
Jer 39:9 of the guard carried away c into
Jer 40:1 were carried away c of Jerusalem
Jer 41:10 Then Ishmael carried away c all
Jer 41:14 away c from Mizpah cast about
Jer 52:15 of the guard carried away c
Jer 52:27 away c out of his own land
Amos 1:6 away c the whole captivity
Amos 6:7 Therefore now shall they go c
Amos 7:11 led away c out of their own land
Obad 11 carried away c his forces
Nah 2:7 And Huzzab shall be led away c
Lk 21:24 be led away c into all nations
Eph 4:8 up on high, he led captivity c
2Ti 2:26 who are taken c by him at his
2Ti 3:6 lead c silly women laden with

## CAPTIVES

Gen 31:26 as c taken with the sword
Num 31:9 took all the women of Midian c
Num 31:12 And they brought the c, and the
Num 31:19 your c on the third day, and on
Deut 21:11 seest among the c a beautiful
Deut 32:42 blood of the slain and of the c
1Sa 30:2 And had taken the women c, that
1Kin 8:46 away c unto the land of the enemy
2Kin 24:14 of valour, even ten thousand c
2Chr 6:36 they carry them away c unto a
2Chr 6:38 whither they have carried them c
2Chr 28:5 away a great multitude of them c
2Chr 28:11 therefore, and deliver the c again
2Chr 28:13 shall not bring in the c hither
Ps 106:46 of all those that carried them c
Is 14:2 and they shall take them c
Is 14:2 them c, whose c they were
Is 20:4 prisoners, and the Ethiopians c
Is 45:13 my city, and he shall let go my c
Is 49:25 Even the c of the mighty shall be
Is 61:1 to proclaim liberty to the c
Jer 28:4 of Judah, with all the c of Judah
Jer 29:1 elders which were carried away c
Jer 43:3 and carry us away c into Babylon
Jer 43:12 burn them, and carry them away c
Jer 48:46 for thy sons are taken c, and thy
Jer 50:33 that took them c held them fast
Eze 1:1 as I was among the c by the river
Eze 6:9 whither they shall be carried c
Eze 16:53 of thy c in the midst of them
Dan 2:25 found a man of the c of Judah
Dan 11:8 shall also carry c into Egypt
Lk 4:18 to preach deliverance to the c

## CAPTIVITY

Num 21:29 into c unto Sihon king of the
Deut 21:13 the raiment of her c from off her
Deut 28:41 for they shall go into c
Deut 30:3 the LORD thy God will turn thy c
Judg 5:12 Barak, and lead thy c captive
Judg 18:30 the day of the c of the land
2Kin 24:15 those carried he into c from
2Kin 25:27 thirtieth year of the c of
1Chr 5:22 dwelt in their steads until the c
1Chr 6:15 And Jehozadak went into c, when
2Chr 6:37 unto thee in the land of their c
2Chr 6:38 their soul in the land of their c
2Chr 29:9 and our wives are in c for this
Ezr 1:11 the c that were brought up from
Ezr 2:1 that went up out of the c
Ezr 3:8 come out of the c unto Jerusalem
Ezr 4:1 the c builded the temple unto the
Ezr 6:16 the rest of the children of the c
Ezr 6:19 the children of the c kept the
Ezr 8:35 which were come out of the c
Ezr 9:7 of the lands, to the sword, to c
Ezr 10:7 unto all the children of the c
Ezr 10:16 And the children of the c did so
Neh 1:2 escaped, which were left of the c
Neh 1:3 c there in the province are in
Neh 4:4 them for a prey in the land of c
Neh 7:6 that went up out of the c
Neh 8:17 again out of the c made booths
Est 2:6 the c which had been carried away
Job 42:10 And the LORD turned the c of Job
Ps 14:7 bringeth back the c of his people
Ps 53:6 bringeth back the c of his people
Ps 68:18 on high, thou hast led c captive
Ps 78:61 And delivered his strength into c
Ps 85:1 hast brought back the c of Jacob
Ps 126:1 LORD turned again the c of Zion
Ps 126:4 Turn again our c, O LORD, as the
Is 5:13 my people are gone into c
Is 22:17 carry thee away with a mighty c
Is 46:2 but themselves are gone into c
Jer 15:2 are for the c, to the c
Jer 20:6 in thine house shall go into c
Jer 22:22 and thy lovers shall go into c
Jer 30:3 again the c of my people Israel
Jer 30:10 thy seed from the land of their c
Jer 32:44 I will cause their c to return
Jer 33:7 And I will cause the c of Judah
Jer 33:11 cause to return the c of the land
Jer 33:26 I will cause their c to return
Jer 43:11 and such as are for c to c
Jer 46:19 furnish thyself to go into c
Jer 46:27 thy seed from the land of their c
Jer 48:7 go forth into c with his priests
Jer 48:11 neither hath he gone into c
Jer 48:47 the c of Moab in the latter days
Jer 49:3 for their king shall go into c
Jer 49:6 I will bring again the c of the
Jer 49:39 I will bring again the c of Elam
Jer 52:31 thirtieth year of the c of
Lam 1:3 Judah is gone into c because of
Lam 1:5 are gone into c before the enemy
Lam 1:18 and my young men are gone into c
Lam 2:14 iniquity, to turn away thy c
Lam 4:22 no more carry thee away into c
Eze 1:2 fifth year of king Jehoiachin's c

Eze 3:11 And go, get thee to them of the c
Eze 3:15 came to them of the c at Tel-abib
Eze 11:24 into Chaldea, to them of the c
Eze 12:4 as they that go forth into c
Eze 12:7 my stuff by day, as stuff for c
Eze 12:11 they shall remove and go into c
Eze 16:53 the c of Samaria and her daughters
Eze 16:53 then will I bring again the c of
Eze 25:3 of Judah, when they went into c
Eze 29:14 I will bring again the c of Egypt
Eze 30:17 and these cities shall go into c
Eze 30:18 and her daughters shall go into c
Eze 33:21 pass in the twelfth year of our c
Eze 39:23 went into c for their iniquity
Eze 39:25 will I bring again the c of Jacob
Eze 39:28 be led into c among the heathen
Eze 40:1 five and twentieth year of our c
Dan 5:13 of the children of the c of Judah
Dan 6:13 of the children of the c of Judah
Dan 11:33 by the sword, and by flame, by c
Hos 6:11 I returned the c of my people
Joel 3:1 shall bring again the c of Judah
Amos 1:5 of Syria shall go into c unto Kir
Amos 1:9 delivered up the whole c to Edom
Amos 1:15 And their king shall go into c
Amos 5:5 for Gilgal shall surely go into c
Amos 5:27 you to go into c beyond Damascus
Amos 7:17 go into c forth of his land
Amos 9:4 though they go into c before
Amos 9:14 the c of my people of Israel
Obad 20 the c of this host of the
Obad 20 the c of Jerusalem, which is in
Mic 1:16 they are gone into c from thee
Nah 3:10 she carried away, she went into c
Hab 1:9 shall gather the c as the sand
Zeph 2:7 visit them, and turn away their c
Zeph 3:20 turn back your c before your eyes
Zec 6:10 Take of them of the c, even of
Zec 14:2 of the city shall go forth into c
Rom 7:23 bringing me into c to the law of
2Cor 10:5 bringing into c every thought to
Eph 4:8 he led c captive, and gave gifts
Rev 13:10 into c shall go into c

**CARCAS** *(car'-cas) A servant of King Ahasuerus.*
Est 1:10 Bigtha, and Abagtha, Zethar, and C

**CARCASE**
Lev 5:2 whether it be a c of an unclean
Lev 11:8 their c shall ye not touch
Lev 11:24 whosoever toucheth the c of them
Deut 14:8 flesh, nor touch their dead c
Deut 28:26 thy c shall be meat unto all
Josh 8:29 take his c down from the tree
Judg 14:8 aside to see the c of the lion
Judg 14:8 and honey in the c of the lion
1Kin 13:22 thy c shall not come unto the
1Kin 13:24 his c was cast in the way, and the
2Kin 9:37 the c of Jezebel shall be as dung
Is 14:19 as a c trodden under feet
Mt 24:28 For wheresoever the c is, there

**CARCASES**
Gen 15:11 the fowls came down upon the c
Lev 11:11 shall have their c in abomination
Lev 11:26 The c of every beast which
Lev 26:30 cast your c upon the c of
Num 14:29 Your c shall fall in this
Num 14:32 But as for you, your c, they
Num 14:33 until your c be wasted in the
1Sa 17:46 I will give the c of the host of
Is 5:25 their c were torn in the midst of
Is 34:3 shall come up out of their c
Is 66:24 look upon the c of the men that
Jer 7:33 the c of this people shall be
Jer 9:22 Even the c of men shall fall as
Jer 16:4 their c shall be meat for the
Jer 16:18 with the c of their detestable
Jer 19:7 their c will I give to be meat
Eze 6:5 I will lay the dead c of the
Eze 43:7 nor by the c of their kings in
Eze 43:9 the c of their kings, far from me
Nah 3:3 of slain, and a great number of c
Heb 3:17 whose c fell in the wilderness

**CARCHEMISH** *(car'-ke-mish)* See CHARCHEMISH. *A city on the Euphrates River.*
Is 10:9 Is not Calno as C
Jer 46:2 was by the river Euphrates in C

**CARE**
1Sa 10:2 hath left the c of the asses
2Sa 18:3 flee away, they will not c for us
2Kin 4:13 careful for us with all this c
Jer 49:31 nation, that dwelleth without c
Eze 4:16 eat bread by weight, and with c
Mt 13:22 the c of this world, and the
Lk 10:34 him to an inn, and took c of him
Lk 10:40 dost thou not c that my sister
1Cor 7:21 c not for it
1Cor 9:9 Doth God take c for oxen
1Cor 12:25 have the same c one for another
2Cor 7:12 but that our c for you in the
2Cor 8:16 which put the same earnest c into
2Cor 11:28 the c of all the churches
Phil 2:20 will naturally c for your state
Phil 4:10 that now at the last your c of me
1Ti 3:5 how shall he take c of the church
1Pet 5:7 Casting all your c upon him

**CAREAH** *(ca-re'-ah)* See KAREAH. *Father of Johanan.*
2Kin 25:23 and Johanan the son of C, and

**CARED**
Ps 142:4 no man c for my soul
Jn 12:6 not that he c for the poor
Acts 18:17 Gallio c for none of those things

**CAREFUL**
2Kin 4:13 thou hast been c for us with all
Jer 17:8 shall not be c in the year of
Dan 3:16 we are not c to answer thee in
Lk 10:41 her, Martha, Martha, thou art c
Phil 4:6 Be c for nothing
Phil 4:10 wherein ye were also c, but ye
Titus 3:8 might be c to maintain good works

**CAREFULLY**
Deut 15:5 Only if thou c hearken unto the
Mic 1:12 of Maroth waited c for good
Phil 2:28 I sent him therefore the more c
Heb 12:17 though he sought it c with tears

**CAREFULNESS**
Eze 12:18 water with trembling and with c
Eze 12:19 They shall eat their bread with c
1Cor 7:32 But I would have you without c
2Cor 7:11 what c it wrought in you, yea,

**CARELESS**
Judg 18:7 were therein, how they dwelt c
Is 32:9 hear my voice, ye c daughters
Is 32:10 shall ye be troubled, ye c women
Is 32:11 be troubled, ye c ones
Eze 30:9 to make the c Ethiopians afraid

**CARELESSLY**
Is 47:8 to pleasures, that dwellest c
Eze 39:6 them that dwell c in the isles
Zeph 2:15 the rejoicing city that dwelt c

**CARES**
Mk 4:19 the c of this world, and the
Lk 8:14 go forth, and are choked with c
Lk 21:34 c of this life, and so that day

**CAREST**
Mt 22:16 neither c thou for any man
Mk 4:38 c thou not that we perish
Mk 12:14 thou art true, and c for no man

**CARETH**
Deut 11:12 land which the LORD thy God c for
Jn 10:13 hireling, and c not for the sheep
1Cor 7:32 He that is unmarried c for the
1Cor 7:33 But he that is married c for the
1Cor 7:34 The unmarried woman c for the
1Cor 7:34 but she that is married c for the
1Pet 5:7 for he c for you

**CARMEL** *(car'-mel)* See CARMELITE.
*1. A mountain range in Canaan.*
Josh 12:22 the king of Jokneam of C, one
Josh 19:26 and reacheth to C westward
1Sa 15:12 Samuel, saying, Saul came to C
1Kin 18:19 to me all Israel unto mount C
1Kin 18:42 And Elijah went up to the top of C
2Kin 2:25 And he went from thence to mount C
2Kin 4:25 unto the man of God to mount C
2Kin 19:23 and into the forest of his C
2Chr 26:10 in the mountains, and in C
Song 7:5 Thine head upon thee is like C
Is 33:9 and C shake off their fruits
Is 35:2 unto it, the excellency of C
Is 37:24 border, and the forest of his C
Jer 46:18 as C by the sea, so shall he come
Jer 50:19 habitation, and he shall feed on C
Amos 1:2 the top of C shall wither
Amos 9:3 hide themselves in the top of C
Mic 7:14 in the wood, in the midst of C
Nah 1:4 Bashan languisheth, and C, and the
*2. A town in Judah.*
Josh 15:55 Maon, C, and Ziph, and Juttah,
1Sa 25:2 Maon, whose possessions were in C
1Sa 25:5 the young men, Get you up to C
1Sa 25:7 all the while they were in C
1Sa 25:40 David were come to Abigail to C

**CARMELITE** *(car'-mel-ite)* See CARMELITESS. *An inhabitant of Carmel 2.*
1Sa 30:5 Abigail the wife of Nabal the C
2Sa 2:2 and Abigail Nabal's wife the C
2Sa 23:35 Hezrai the C, Paarai the Arbite,
1Chr 11:37 Hezro the C, Naarai the son of

**CARMELITESS** *(car'-mel-i-tess)*
1Sa 27:3 Jezreelitess, and Abigail the C
1Chr 3:1 second Daniel, of Abigail the C

**CARMI** *(car'-mi)* See CARMITES.
*1. Father of Achan.*
Josh 7:1 for Achan, the son of C, the son
Josh 7:18 and Achan, the son of C, the son
1Chr 2:7 And the sons of C
1Chr 4:1 Pharez, Hezron, and C, and Hur, and
*2. A son of Reuben.*
Gen 46:9 and Phallu, and Hezron, and C
Ex 6:14 Hanoch, and Pallu, Hezron, and C
Num 26:6 of C, the family of the Carmites
1Chr 5:3 Hanoch, and Pallu, Hezron, and C

**CARMITES** *(car'-mites) Descendants of Carmi 2.*
Num 26:6 of Carmi, the family of the C

**CARNAL**
Rom 7:14 but I am c, sold under sin
Rom 8:7 Because the c mind is enmity
Rom 15:27 to minister unto them in c things
1Cor 3:1 as unto spiritual, but as unto c
1Cor 3:3 For ye are yet c
1Cor 3:3 and divisions, are ye not c
1Cor 3:4 are ye not c?
1Cor 9:11 if we shall reap your c things
2Cor 10:4 weapons of our warfare are not c
Heb 7:16 after the law of a c commandment
Heb 9:10 c ordinances, imposed on them

**CARNALLY**
Lev 18:20 lie c with thy neighbour's wife
Lev 19:20 whosoever lieth c with a woman
Num 5:13 a man lie with her c, and it be
Rom 8:6 For to be c minded is death

**CARPENTER**
Is 41:7 So the c encouraged the goldsmith
Is 44:13 The c stretcheth out his rule
Mk 6:3 Is not this the c, the son of

**CARPENTER'S**
Mt 13:55 Is not this the c son

**CARPENTERS**
2Sa 5:11 to David, and cedar trees, and c
2Kin 12:11 and they laid it out to the c
2Kin 22:6 Unto c, and builders, and masons,
1Chr 14:1 of cedars, with masons and c
2Chr 24:12 c to repair the house of the LORD
Ezr 3:7 also unto the masons, and to the c
Jer 24:1 the princes of Judah, with the c
Jer 29:2 of Judah and Jerusalem, and the c
Zec 1:20 And the LORD shewed me four c

**CARPUS** *(car'-pus) A friend of Paul.*
2Ti 4:13 cloke that I left at Troas with C

**CARRIED**
Gen 31:18 he c away all his cattle, and all
Gen 31:26 c away my daughters, as captives
Gen 46:5 of Israel c Jacob their father
Gen 50:13 For his sons c him into the land
Lev 10:5 c them in their coats out of the
Josh 4:8 c them over with them unto the
Judg 16:3 c them up to the top of an hill
1Sa 5:8 of Israel be c about unto Gath
1Sa 30:2 but c them away, and went on their
1Sa 30:18 that the Amalekites had c away
2Sa 6:10 but David c it aside into the
2Sa 15:29 Abiathar c the ark of God again
1Kin 8:47 land whither they were c captives
1Kin 17:19 c him up into a loft, where he
1Kin 21:13 Then they c him forth out of the
2Kin 7:8 c thence silver, and gold, and

2Kin 9:28 his servants c him in a chariot
2Kin 15:29 c them captive to Assyria
2Kin 16:9 c the people of it captive to Kir
2Kin 17:6 c Israel away into Assyria, and
2Kin 17:11 whom the LORD c away before them
2Kin 17:23 So was Israel c away out of their
2Kin 17:28 they had c away from Samaria came
2Kin 17:33 whom they c away from thence
2Kin 20:17 this day, shall be c into Babylon
2Kin 23:4 c the ashes of them unto Beth-el
2Kin 23:30 his servants c him in a chariot
2Kin 24:13 he c out thence all the treasures
2Kin 25:7 of brass, and c him to Babylon
2Kin 25:13 c the brass of them to Babylon
2Kin 25:21 So Judah was c away out of their
1Chr 5:6 king of Assyria c away captive
1Chr 5:26 and he c them away, even the
1Chr 6:15 when the LORD c away Judah
1Chr 9:1 who were c away to Babylon for
1Chr 13:7 they c the ark of God in a new
1Chr 13:13 but c it aside into the house of
2Chr 6:37 land whither they are c captive
2Chr 12:9 he c away also the shields of
2Chr 14:13 they c away very much spoil
2Chr 16:6 they c away the stones of Ramah,
2Chr 21:17 c away all the substance that was
2Chr 24:11 it, and c it to his place again
2Chr 28:5 c away a great multitude of them
2Chr 28:8 the children of Israel c away
2Chr 28:15 c all the feeble of them upon
2Chr 28:17 smitten Judah, and c away captives
2Chr 33:11 with fetters, and c him to Babylon
2Chr 34:16 Shaphan c the book to the king,
2Chr 36:4 his brother, and c him to Egypt
2Chr 36:7 Nebuchadnezzar also c of the
2Chr 36:20 the sword c he away to Babylon
Ezr 2:1 of those which had been c away
Ezr 2:1 Babylon had c away unto Babylon
Ezr 5:12 c the people away into Babylon
Neh 7:6 the king of Babylon had c away
Est 2:6 Who had been c away from
Est 2:6 been c away with Jeconiah king of
Est 2:6 the king of Babylon had c away
Job 1:17 have c them away, yea, and slain
Job 5:13 of the froward is c headlong
Job 10:19 I should have been c from the
Ps 46:2 though the mountains be c into
Ps 106:46 of all those that c them captives
Ps 137:3 For there they that c us away
Is 39:6 this day, shall be c to Babylon
Is 46:3 which are c from the womb
Is 49:22 shall be c upon their shoulders
Is 53:4 our griefs, and c our sorrows
Is 63:9 c them all the days of old
Jer 13:17 LORD's flock is c away captive
Jer 13:19 Judah shall be c away captive all
Jer 24:1 king of Babylon had c away
Jer 24:5 that are c away captive of Judah
Jer 27:20 when he c away captive Jeconiah
Jer 27:22 They shall be c to Babylon
Jer 28:3 this place, and c them to Babylon
Jer 28:6 all that is c away captive, from
Jer 29:1 elders which were c away captives
Jer 29:7 caused you to be c away captives
Jer 29:14 I caused you to be c away captive
Jer 39:9 the captain of the guard c away
Jer 40:1 were c away captive of Jerusalem
Jer 40:7 of them that were not c away
Jer 41:10 Then Ishmael c away captive all
Jer 41:14 c away captive from Mizpah cast
Jer 52:9 c him up unto the king of Babylon
Jer 52:11 c him to Babylon, and put him in
Jer 52:15 the captain of the guard c away
Jer 52:17 c all the brass of them to
Jer 52:27 Thus Judah was c away captive out
Jer 52:28 Nebuchadrezzar c away captive
Jer 52:30 the captain of the guard c away
Eze 6:9 whither they shall be c captives
Eze 17:4 c it into a land of traffick
Eze 37:1 c me out in the spirit of the
Dan 1:2 which he c into the land of
Dan 2:35 the wind c them away, that no
Hos 10:6 It shall be also c unto Assyria
Hos 12:1 Assyrians, and oil is c into Egypt
Joel 3:5 have c into your temples my
Amos 1:6 because they c away captive the
Obad 11 c away captive his forces
Nah 3:10 Yet was she c away, she went into
Mt 1:11 time they were c away to Babylon
Mk 15:1 c him away, and delivered him to
Lk 7:12 there was a dead man c out
Lk 16:22 died, and was c by the angels into
Lk 24:51 from them, and c up into heaven
Acts 3:2 lame from his mother's womb was c
Acts 5:6 up, and c him out, and buried him
Acts 7:16 were c over into Sychem, and laid
Acts 8:2 devout men c Stephen to his
Acts 21:34 him to be c into the castle
1Cor 12:2 c away unto these dumb idols,
Gal 2:13 c away with their dissimulation
Eph 4:14 c about with every wind of
Heb 13:9 Be not c about with divers and
2Pet 2:17 clouds that are c with a tempest
Jude 12 without water, c about of winds
Rev 12:15 her to be c away of the flood
Rev 17:3 So he c me away in the spirit
Rev 21:10 he c me away in the spirit to a

**CARRY**
Gen 37:25 going to c it down to Egypt
Gen 42:19 c corn for the famine of your
Gen 43:11 c down the man a present, a
Gen 44:1 with food, as much as they can c
Gen 45:27 which Joseph had sent to c him
Gen 46:5 which Pharaoh had sent to c him
Gen 47:30 thou shalt c me out of Egypt, and
Gen 50:25 ye shall c up my bones from hence
Ex 12:46 thou shalt not c forth ought of
Ex 13:19 ye shall c up my bones away hence
Ex 14:11 to c us forth out of Egypt
Ex 33:15 go not with me, c us not up hence
Lev 4:12 c forth without the camp unto a
Lev 4:21 he shall c forth the bullock
Lev 6:11 c forth the ashes without the
Lev 10:4 c your brethren from before the
Lev 14:45 he shall c them forth out of the
Lev 16:27 shall one c forth without the
Num 11:12 C them in thy bosom, as a nursing
Num 24:22 Asshur shall c thee away captive
Deut 14:24 so that thou art not able to c it
Deut 28:38 Thou shalt c much seed out into
Josh 4:3 ye shall c them over with you, and
1Sa 17:18 c these ten cheeses unto the
1Sa 20:40 unto him, Go, c them to the city
2Sa 15:25 C back the ark of God into the
2Sa 19:18 to c over the king's household
1Kin 8:46 so that they c them away captives
1Kin 18:12 shall c thee whither I know not
1Kin 21:10 then c him out, and stone him,
1Kin 22:26 c him back unto Amon the governor
1Kin 22:34 hand, and c me out of the host
2Kin 4:19 to a lad, C him to his mother
2Kin 9:2 c him to an inner chamber
2Kin 17:27 C thither one of the priests whom
2Kin 18:11 the king of Assyria did c away
2Kin 25:11 the captain of the guard c away
1Chr 10:9 to c tidings unto their idols, and
1Chr 15:2 None ought to c the ark of God
1Chr 23:26 shall no more c the tabernacle
2Chr 2:16 thou shalt c it up to Jerusalem
2Chr 6:36 they c them away captives unto a
2Chr 18:25 c him back to Amon the governor
2Chr 18:33 that thou mayest c me out of the
2Chr 20:25 more than they could c away
2Chr 25:12 children of Judah c away captive
2Chr 29:5 c forth the filthiness out of the
2Chr 29:16 to c it out abroad into the brook
2Chr 36:6 in fetters, to c him to Babylon
Ezr 5:15 c them into the temple that is in
Ezr 7:15 to c the silver and gold, which
Job 15:12 Why doth thine heart c thee away
Ps 49:17 he dieth he shall c nothing away
Eccl 5:15 which he may c away in his hand
Eccl 10:20 bird of the air shall c the voice
Is 5:29 shall c it away safe, and none
Is 15:7 shall they c away to the brook of
Is 22:17 the LORD will c thee away with a
Is 23:7 her own feet shall c her afar off
Is 30:6 they will c their riches upon the
Is 40:11 c them in his bosom, and shall
Is 41:16 and the wind shall c them away
Is 46:4 even to hoar hairs will I c you
Is 46:7 him upon the shoulder, they c him
Is 57:13 the wind shall c them all away
Jer 17:22 Neither c forth a burden out of
Jer 20:4 he shall c them captive into
Jer 39:7 with chains, to c him to Babylon
Jer 39:14 that he should c him home
Jer 43:3 c us away captives into Babylon
Jer 43:12 them, and c them away captives
Lam 4:22 he will no more c thee away into
Eze 12:5 in their sight, and c out thereby
Eze 12:12 through the wall to c out thereby
Eze 22:9 men that c tales to shed blood
Eze 38:13 to c away silver and gold, to take
Dan 11:8 shall also c captives into Egypt
Mk 6:55 began to c about in beds those
Mk 11:16 c any vessel through the temple
Lk 10:4 C neither purse, nor scrip, nor
Jn 5:10 not lawful for thee to c thy bed
Jn 21:18 c thee whither thou wouldest not
Acts 5:9 at the door, and shall c thee out
Acts 7:43 I will c you away beyond Babylon
1Ti 6:7 is certain we can c nothing out

**CARRYING**
1Sa 10:3 one c three kids, and another
Ps 78:9 c bows, turned back in the day of
Jer 1:3 unto the c away of Jerusalem
Mt 1:17 from David until the c away into
Acts 5:10 c her forth, buried her by her

**CARSHENA** *(car-she'-nah) A Persian prince.*
Est 1:14 And the next unto him was C

**CART**
1Sa 6:7 Now therefore make a new c
1Sa 6:10 milch kine, and tied them to the c
1Sa 6:14 the c came into the field of
2Sa 6:3 set the ark of God upon a new c
1Chr 13:7 c out of the house of Abinadab
Is 5:18 and sin as it were with a c rope
Is 28:27 neither is a c wheel turned about
Amos 2:13 as a c is pressed that is full of

**CARVED**
Judg 18:18 house, and fetched the c image
1Kin 6:18 the house within was c with knops
1Kin 6:29 he c all the walls of the house
1Kin 6:32 he c upon them carvings of
1Kin 6:35 he c thereon cherubims and palm
2Chr 33:7 And he set a c image, the idol
2Chr 33:22 the c images which Manasseh his
2Chr 34:3 the c images, and the molten
Ps 74:6 But now they break down the c
Prov 7:16 with c works, with fine linen of

**CASE**
Ex 5:19 did see that they were in evil c
Deut 19:4 this is the c of the slayer,
Deut 22:1 thou shalt in any c bring them
Deut 24:13 In any c thou shalt deliver him
Ps 144:15 that people, that is in such a c
Mt 5:20 ye shall in no c enter into the
Mt 19:10 If the c of the man be so with
Jn 5:6 been now a long time in that c

**CASIPHIA** *(cas-if'-e-ah) A place in Syria.*
Ezr 8:17 Iddo the chief at the place C

**CASLUHIM** *(cas'-loo-him) Descendants of Mizraim.*
Gen 10:14 And Pathrusim, and C, (out of whom
1Chr 1:12 And Pathrusim, and C, (of whom came

**CASSIA**
Ex 30:24 of c five hundred shekels, after
Ps 45:8 smell of myrrh, and aloes, and c
Eze 27:19 bright iron, c, and calamus, were

**CAST**
Gen 21:10 C out this bondwoman and her son
Gen 21:15 she c the child under one of the
Gen 31:38 she goats have not c their young
Gen 31:51 pillar, which I have c betwixt me
Gen 37:20 c him into some pit, and we will
Gen 37:22 but c him into this pit that is
Gen 37:24 took him, and c him into a pit
Gen 39:7 wife c her eyes upon Joseph
Ex 1:22 is born ye shall c into the river
Ex 4:3 And he said, C it on the ground
Ex 4:25 c it at his feet, and said, Surely
Ex 7:9 c it before Pharaoh, and it shall
Ex 7:10 Aaron c down his rod before
Ex 7:12 For they c down every man his rod
Ex 10:19 and c them into the Red sea
Ex 15:4 his host hath he c into the sea
Ex 15:25 when he had c into the waters
Ex 22:31 ye shall c it to the dogs
Ex 23:26 There shall nothing c their young
Ex 25:12 thou shalt c four rings of gold
Ex 26:37 thou shalt c five sockets of
Ex 32:19 he c the tables out of his hands,
Ex 32:24 then I c it into the fire, and
Ex 38:27 c the sockets of the sanctuary

Lev 1:16 c it beside the altar on the east
Lev 14:40 they shall c them into an unclean
Lev 16:8 Aaron shall c lots upon the two
Lev 18:24 defiled which I c out before you
Lev 20:23 nation, which I c out before you
Lev 26:30 c your carcases upon the carcases
Lev 26:44 enemies, I will not c them away
Num 19:6 c it into the midst of the
Num 35:22 or have c upon him any thing
Deut 6:19 To c out all thine enemies from
Deut 7:1 hath c out many nations before
Deut 9:4 hath c them out from before thee
Deut 28:40 for thine olive shall c his fruit
Deut 29:28 c them into another land, as it
Josh 8:29 c it at the entering of the gate
Josh 10:11 that the LORD c down great stones
Josh 10:27 c them into the cave wherein they
Josh 13:12 did Moses smite, and c them out
Josh 18:6 that I may c lots for you here
Judg 6:28 the altar of Baal was c down
Judg 8:25 did c therein every man the
Judg 9:53 a certain woman c a piece of a
Judg 15:17 that he c away the jawbone out of
1Sa 14:42 C lots between me and Jonathan my
1Sa 18:11 And Saul c the javelin
1Sa 20:33 Saul c a javelin at him to smite
2Sa 1:21 of the mighty is vilely c away
2Sa 11:21 did not a woman c a piece of a
2Sa 16:6 he c stones at David, and at all
2Sa 20:12 c a cloth upon him, when he saw
1Kin 7:15 For he c two pillars of brass, of
1Kin 9:7 my name, will I c out of my sight
1Kin 13:24 and his carcase was c in the way
1Kin 14:9 hast c me behind thy back
1Kin 14:24 LORD c out before the children of
1Kin 18:42 he c himself down upon the earth,
1Kin 19:19 by him, and c his mantle upon him
1Kin 21:26 whom the LORD c out before the
2Kin 2:16 c him upon some mountain, or into
2Kin 4:41 And he c it into the pot
2Kin 6:6 down a stick, and c it in thither
2Kin 7:15 Syrians had c away in their haste
2Kin 9:25 c him in the portion of the field
2Kin 10:25 guard and the captains c them out
2Kin 13:21 they c the man into the sepulchre
2Kin 16:3 whom the LORD c out from before
2Kin 17:8 whom the LORD c out from before
2Kin 17:20 until he had c them out of his
2Kin 19:18 have c their gods into the fire
2Kin 21:2 whom the LORD c out before the
2Kin 23:6 c the powder thereof upon the
2Kin 24:20 until he had c them out from his
1Chr 24:31 These likewise c lots over
1Chr 25:8 And they c lots, ward against ward
1Chr 26:13 And they c lots, as well the small
1Chr 28:9 he will c thee off for ever
2Chr 4:3 Two rows of oxen were c
2Chr 4:17 of Jordan did the king c them
2Chr 7:20 will I c out of my sight, and will
2Chr 11:14 his sons had c them off from
2Chr 13:9 Have ye not c out the priests of
2Chr 20:11 to come to c us out of thy
2Chr 24:10 c into the chest, until they had
2Chr 25:8 hath power to help, and to c down
2Chr 28:3 had c out before the children of
2Chr 29:19 did c away in his transgression
2Chr 30:14 c them into the brook Kidron
2Chr 33:2 whom the LORD had c out before
2Chr 33:15 and c them out of the city
Neh 1:9 though there were of you c out
Neh 6:16 they were much c down in their
Neh 9:26 c thy law behind their backs, and
Neh 10:34 we c the lots among the priests,
Neh 11:1 rest of the people also c lots
Neh 13:8 therefore I c forth all the
Est 3:7 of king Ahasuerus, they c Pur
Est 9:24 to destroy them, and had c Pur
Job 8:4 he have c them away for their
Job 8:20 God will not c away a perfect man
Job 15:33 shall c off his flower as the
Job 18:7 his own counsel shall c him down
Job 20:15 God shall c them out of his belly
Job 27:22 For God shall c upon him, and not
Job 29:24 of my countenance they c not down
Job 30:19 He hath c me into the mire, and I
Job 39:3 ones, they c out their sorrows
Job 40:11 C abroad the rage of thy wrath
Job 41:9 shall not one be c down even at
Ps 2:3 c away their cords from us
Ps 5:10 c them out in the multitude of
Ps 17:13 LORD, disappoint him, c him down
Ps 18:42 I did c them out as the dirt in
Ps 22:10 I was c upon thee from the womb
Ps 36:12 they are c down, and shall not be
Ps 37:14 to c down the poor and needy, and
Ps 42:5 Why art thou c down, O my soul
Ps 42:6 my soul is c down within me
Ps 42:11 Why art thou c down, O my soul
Ps 43:2 why dost thou c me off
Ps 44:2 afflict the people, and c them out
Ps 51:11 C me not away from thy presence
Ps 55:3 for they c iniquity upon me, and
Ps 55:22 C thy burden upon the LORD, and he
Ps 56:7 in thine anger c down the people,
Ps 60:1 O God, thou hast c us off
Ps 60:8 over Edom will I c out my shoe
Ps 62:4 They only consult to c him down
Ps 71:9 C me not off in the time of old
Ps 74:1 why hast thou c us off for ever
Ps 76:6 horse are c into a dead sleep
Ps 77:7 Will the Lord c off for ever
Ps 78:49 He c upon them the fierceness of
Ps 78:55 He c out the heathen also before
Ps 80:8 thou hast c out the heathen, and
Ps 89:38 But thou hast c off and abhorred,
Ps 94:14 LORD will not c off his people
Ps 102:10 hast lifted me up, and c me down
Ps 108:9 over Edom will I c out my shoe
Ps 140:10 let them be c into the fire
Ps 144:6 C forth lightning, and scatter
Prov 1:14 C in thy lot among us
Prov 7:26 For she hath c down many wounded
Prov 16:33 The lot is c into the lap
Prov 22:10 C out the scorner, and contention
Eccl 3:5 A time to c away stones, and a
Eccl 11:1 C thy bread upon the waters
Is 2:20 a man shall c his idols of silver
Is 5:24 because they have c away the law
Is 6:13 in them, when they c their leaves
Is 14:19 But thou art c out of thy grave
Is 16:2 wandering bird c out of the nest
Is 19:8 all they that c angle into the
Is 25:7 of the covering c over all people
Is 26:19 and the earth shall c out the dead
Is 28:2 shall c down to the earth with
Is 28:25 doth he not c abroad the fitches,
Is 30:22 thou shalt c them away as a
Is 31:7 shall c away his idols of silver
Is 34:3 Their slain also shall be c out
Is 37:33 shields, nor c a bank against it
Is 38:17 for thou hast c all my sins
Is 41:9 chosen thee, and not c thee away
Is 57:14 C ye up, c ye up, prepare the
Is 58:7 poor that are c out to thy house
Is 62:10 c up, c up the highways
Is 66:5 that c you out for my name's sake
Jer 6:6 c a mount against Jerusalem
Jer 6:15 I visit them they shall be c down
Jer 7:15 I will c you out of my sight, as
Jer 7:29 and c it away, and take up a
Jer 8:12 visitation they shall be c down
Jer 9:19 our dwellings have c us out
Jer 14:16 to whom they prophesy shall be c
Jer 15:1 c them out of my sight, and let
Jer 16:13 Therefore will I c you out of
Jer 18:15 walk in paths, in a way not c up
Jer 22:7 cedars, and c them into the fire
Jer 22:19 c forth beyond the gates of
Jer 23:39 and c you out of my presence
Jer 26:23 c his dead body into the graves
Jer 28:16 I will c thee from off the face
Jer 31:37 I will also c off all the seed of
Jer 33:24 chosen, he hath even c them off
Jer 36:23 c it into the fire that was on
Jer 36:30 his dead body shall be c out in
Jer 38:6 c him into the dungeon of
Jer 38:9 whom they have c into the dungeon
Jer 41:7 c them into the midst of the pit,
Jer 41:14 away captive from Mizpah c about
Jer 50:26 c her up as heaps, and destroy her
Jer 51:34 my delicates, he hath c me out
Jer 52:3 till he had c them out from his
Lam 2:1 c down from heaven unto the earth
Lam 2:7 The Lord hath c off his altar
Lam 3:31 the Lord will not c off for ever
Lam 3:53 the dungeon, and c a stone upon me
Eze 4:2 it, and c a mount against it
Eze 5:4 c them into the midst of the fire
Eze 6:4 I will c down your slain men
Eze 7:19 They shall c their silver in the
Eze 11:16 Although I have c them far off
Eze 15:4 it is c into the fire for fuel
Eze 16:5 but thou wast c out in the open
Eze 18:31 C away from you all your
Eze 19:12 she was c down to the ground, and
Eze 20:7 them, C ye away every man the
Eze 21:22 to c a mount, and to build a fort
Eze 23:35 c me behind thy back, therefore
Eze 26:8 c a mount against thee, and lift
Eze 27:30 shall c up dust upon their heads,
Eze 28:16 therefore I will c thee as
Eze 31:16 when I c him down to hell with
Eze 32:4 I will c thee forth upon the open
Eze 32:18 c them down, even her, and the
Eze 36:5 minds, to c it out for a prey
Eze 43:24 priests shall c salt upon them
Dan 3:6 shall the same hour be c into the
Dan 3:11 that he should be c into the
Dan 3:20 to c them into the burning fiery
Dan 3:24 Did not we c three men bound into
Dan 6:7 he shall be c into the den of
Dan 6:12 shall be c into the den of lions
Dan 6:16 c him into the den of lions
Dan 6:24 they c them into the den of lions
Dan 7:9 till the thrones were c down
Dan 8:7 but he c him down to the ground,
Dan 11:12 and he shall c down many ten
Hos 8:3 Israel hath c off the thing that
Hos 9:17 My God will c them away, because
Hos 14:5 c forth his roots as Lebanon
Joel 1:7 made it clean bare, and c it away
Joel 3:3 they have c lots for my people
Amos 1:11 did c off all pity, and his anger
Amos 4:3 ye shall c them into the palace,
Amos 8:3 they shall c them forth with
Obad 11 c lots upon Jerusalem, even thou
Jonah 1:5 c forth the wares that were in
Jonah 1:12 me up, and c me forth into the sea
Jonah 2:3 For thou hadst c me into the deep
Mic 2:5 that shall c a cord by lot in the
Mic 4:7 her that was c far off a strong
Mic 7:19 thou wilt c all their sins into
Nah 3:6 I will c abominable filth upon
Zeph 3:15 he hath c out thine enemy
Zec 1:21 to c out the horns of the
Zec 5:8 he c it into the midst of the
Zec 9:4 Behold, the Lord will c her out
Zec 10:6 be as though I had not c them off
Zec 11:13 c them to the potter in the house
Mal 3:11 neither shall your vine c her
Mt 3:10 is hewn down, and c into the fire
Mt 4:6 be the Son of God, c thyself down
Mt 4:12 heard that John was c into prison
Mt 5:13 good for nothing, but to be c out
Mt 5:25 officer, and thou be c into prison
Mt 6:30 to morrow is c into the oven,
Mt 7:5 first c out the beam out of thine
Mt 7:19 is hewn down, and c into the fire
Mt 7:22 and in thy name have c out devils
Mt 8:12 be c out into outer darkness
Mt 8:16 he c out the spirits with his
Mt 8:31 him, saying, If thou c us out
Mt 9:33 And when the devil was c out
Mt 10:1 to c them out, and to heal all
Mt 10:8 raise the dead, c out devils
Mt 12:24 This fellow doth not c out devils
Mt 12:26 if Satan c out Satan, he is
Mt 12:27 And if I by Beelzebub c out devils
Mt 13:42 shall c them into a furnace of
Mt 13:47 that was c into the sea, and
Mt 13:50 shall c them into the furnace of
Mt 15:17 is c out into the draught
Mt 15:26 bread, and to c it to dogs
Mt 15:30 c them down at Jesus' feet
Mt 17:19 said, Why could not we c him out
Mt 17:27 c an hook, and take up the fish
Mt 18:8 cut them off, and c them from thee
Mt 18:30 c him into prison, till he should
Mt 21:12 c out all them that sold and
Mt 21:21 and be thou c into the sea
Mt 21:39 c him out of the vineyard, and
Mt 22:13 c him into outer darkness
Mt 25:30 c ye the unprofitable servant
Mt 27:5 he c down the pieces of silver in
Mt 27:35 upon my vesture did they c lots
Mt 27:44 with him, c the same in his teeth
Mk 1:34 diseases, and c out many devils
Mk 1:39 all Galilee, and c out devils
Mk 3:15 sicknesses, and to c out devils
Mk 3:23 How can Satan c out Satan

Mk 4:26 as if a man should c seed into
Mk 6:13 they c out many devils, and
Mk 7:26 c forth the devil out of her
Mk 9:18 that they should c him out
Mk 9:22 ofttimes it hath c him into the
Mk 9:28 Why could not we c him out
Mk 9:42 neck, and he were c into the sea
Mk 9:45 having two feet to be c into hell
Mk 9:47 two eyes to be c into hell fire
Mk 11:7 Jesus, and c their garments on him
Mk 11:15 began to c out them that sold and
Mk 11:23 and be thou c into the sea
Mk 12:4 and at him they c stones, and
Mk 12:8 c him out of the vineyard
Mk 12:41 beheld how the people c money
Mk 12:43 this poor widow hath c more in
Mk 14:51 cloth c about his naked body
Mk 16:9 out of whom he had c seven devils
Mk 16:17 my name shall they c out devils
Lk 1:29 c in her mind what manner of
Lk 3:9 is hewn down, and c into the fire
Lk 4:9 c thyself down from hence
Lk 4:29 that they might c him down
Lk 6:22 c out your name as evil, for the
Lk 6:42 c out first the beam out of thine
Lk 9:25 and lose himself, or be c away
Lk 9:40 thy disciples to c him out
Lk 11:18 because ye say that I c out
Lk 12:5 killed hath power to c into hell
Lk 12:28 to morrow is c into the oven
Lk 12:58 the officer c thee into prison
Lk 13:19 a man took, and c into his garden
Lk 13:32 I c out devils, and I do cures to
Lk 14:35 but men c it out
Lk 17:2 he c into the sea, than that he
Lk 19:35 they c their garments upon the
Lk 19:43 shall c a trench about thee
Lk 19:45 began to c out them that sold
Lk 20:12 wounded him also, and c him out
Lk 20:15 So they c him out of the vineyard
Lk 21:3 hath c in more than they all
Lk 22:41 from them about a stone's c
Lk 23:19 and for murder, was c into prison
Lk 23:25 murder was c into prison, whom
Lk 23:34 parted his raiment, and c lots
Jn 3:24 John was not yet c into prison
Jn 6:37 to me I will in no wise c out
Jn 8:7 let him first c a stone at her
Jn 8:59 took they up stones to c at him
Jn 9:34 And they c him out
Jn 12:31 the prince of this world be c out
Jn 15:6 he is c forth as a branch, and is
Jn 19:24 and for my vesture they did c lots
Jn 21:6 C the net on the right side of
Acts 7:19 so that they c out their young
Acts 7:21 And when he was c out, Pharaoh's
Acts 7:58 c him out of the city, and stoned
Acts 12:8 C thy garment about thee, and
Acts 16:23 they c them into prison, charging
Acts 16:37 Romans, and have c us into prison
Acts 22:23 c off their clothes, and threw
Acts 27:19 the third day we c out with our
Acts 27:26 Howbeit we must be c upon a
Acts 27:29 they c four anchors out of the
Acts 27:38 c out the wheat into the sea
Acts 27:43 they which could swim should c
Rom 11:1 Hath God c away his people
Rom 13:12 let us therefore c off the works
1Cor 7:35 not that I may c a snare upon you
2Cor 4:9 c down, but not destroyed
2Cor 7:6 comforteth those that are c down
Gal 4:30 C out the bondwoman and her son
1Ti 5:12 because they have c off their
Heb 10:35 C not away therefore your
2Pet 2:4 but c them down to hell, and
Rev 2:10 the devil shall c some of you
Rev 2:14 Balaam, who taught Balac to c a
Rev 2:22 I will c her into a bed, and them
Rev 4:10 c their crowns before the throne,
Rev 8:5 the altar, and c it into the earth
Rev 8:7 they were c upon the earth
Rev 12:4 and did c them to the earth
Rev 12:9 And the great dragon was c out
Rev 12:13 saw that he was c unto the earth
Rev 12:15 the serpent c out of his mouth
Rev 14:19 c it into the great winepress of
Rev 18:19 they c dust on their heads, and
Rev 18:21 c it into the sea, saying, Thus
Rev 19:20 These both were c alive into a
Rev 20:3 c him into the bottomless pit, and
Rev 20:10 them was c into the lake of fire
Rev 20:14 hell were c into the lake of fire
Rev 20:15 life was c into the lake of fire

### CASTETH

Job 21:10 cow calveth, and c not her calf
Ps 147:6 he c the wicked down to the
Ps 147:17 He c forth his ice like morsels
Prov 10:3 but he c away the substance of
Prov 19:15 Slothfulness c into a deep sleep
Prov 21:22 c down the strength of the
Prov 26:18 As a mad man who c firebrands
Is 40:19 with gold, and c silver chains
Jer 6:7 As a fountain c out her waters,
Mt 9:34 He c out devils through the
Mk 3:22 of the devils c he out devils
Lk 11:15 He c out devils through Beelzebub
1Jn 4:18 but perfect love c out fear
3Jn 10 and c them out of the church
Rev 6:13 as a fig tree c her untimely figs

### CASTING

2Sa 8:2 c them down to the ground
1Kin 7:37 all of them had one c, one
Ezr 10:1 c himself down before the house
Job 6:21 ye see my c down, and are afraid
Ps 74:7 they have defiled by c down the
Ps 89:39 his crown by c it to the ground
Eze 17:17 by c up mounts, and building forts
Mic 6:14 thy c down shall be in the midst
Mt 4:18 his brother, c a net into the sea
Mt 27:35 and parted his garments, c lots
Mk 1:16 his brother c a net into the sea
Mk 9:38 we saw one c out devils in thy
Mk 10:50 c away his garment, rose, and came
Mk 15:24 c lots upon them, what every man
Lk 9:49 we saw one c out devils in thy
Lk 11:14 he was c out a devil, and it was
Lk 21:1 saw the rich men c their gifts
Lk 21:2 poor widow c in thither two mites
Rom 11:15 For if the c away of them be the
2Cor 10:5 C down imaginations, and every
1Pet 5:7 C all your care upon him

### CASTLE

1Chr 11:5 David took the c of Zion, which
1Chr 11:7 And David dwelt in the c
Prov 18:19 are like the bars of a c
Acts 21:34 him to be carried into the c
Acts 21:37 as Paul was to be led into the c
Acts 22:24 him to be brought into the c
Acts 23:10 them, and to bring him into the c
Acts 23:16 he went and entered into the c
Acts 23:32 go with him, and returned to the c

### CASTLES

Gen 25:16 by their towns, and by their c
Num 31:10 they dwelt, and all their goodly c
1Chr 6:54 their c in their coasts, of the
1Chr 27:25 and in the villages, and in the c
2Chr 17:12 and he built in Judah c, and cities
2Chr 27:4 and in the forests he built c

### CASTOR *(cas'-tor) Patron god of sailors.*

Acts 28:11 in the isle, whose sign was C

### CATCH

Ex 22:6 c in thorns, so that the stacks
Judg 21:21 c you every man his wife of the
1Kin 20:33 from him, and did hastily c it
2Kin 7:12 we shall c them alive, and get
Ps 10:9 he lieth in wait to c the poor
Ps 35:8 net that he hath hid c himself
Ps 109:11 extortioner c all that he hath
Jer 5:26 they set a trap, they c men
Eze 19:3 lion, and it learned to c the prey
Eze 19:6 lion, and learned to c the prey
Hab 1:15 they c them in their net, and
Mk 12:13 Herodians, to c him in his words
Lk 5:10 from henceforth thou shalt c men
Lk 11:54 seeking to c something out of his

### CATERPILLAR

1Kin 8:37 mildew, locust, or if there be c
Ps 78:46 also their increase unto the c
Is 33:4 like the gathering of the c
Joel 1:4 hath left hath the c eaten
Joel 2:25 eaten, the cankerworm, and the c

### CATERPILLARS

2Chr 6:28 or mildew, locusts, or c
Ps 105:34 spake, and the locusts came, and c
Jer 51:14 fill thee with men, as with c
Jer 51:27 horses to come up as the rough c

### CATTLE

Gen 1:24 living creature after his kind, c
Gen 2:20 And Adam gave names to all c
Gen 3:14 this, thou art cursed above all c
Gen 4:20 in tents, and of such as have c
Gen 6:20 of c after their kind, of every
Gen 7:14 all the c after their kind, and
Gen 7:21 the earth, both of fowl, and of c
Gen 8:1 all the c that was with him in
Gen 8:17 all flesh, both of fowl, and of c
Gen 9:10 with you, of the fowl, of the c
Gen 13:2 And Abram was very rich in c
Gen 13:7 c and the herdmen of Lot's c
Gen 30:29 thee, and how thy c was with me
Gen 30:32 all the speckled and spotted c
Gen 30:39 and brought forth c ringstraked
Gen 30:41 the stronger c did conceive
Gen 30:43 exceedingly, and had much c
Gen 31:8 then all the c bare speckled
Gen 31:10 upon the c were ringstraked
Gen 31:12 leap upon the c are ringstraked
Gen 31:18 And he carried away all his c
Gen 31:41 daughters, and six years for thy c
Gen 33:14 according as the c that goeth
Gen 34:5 sons were with his c in the field
Gen 34:23 Shall not their c and their
Gen 36:6 persons of his house, and his c
Gen 46:6 And they took their c, and their
Gen 46:32 their trade hath been to feed c
Gen 47:6 then make them rulers over my c
Gen 47:16 And Joseph said, Give your c
Gen 47:17 for the c of the herds, and for
Gen 47:18 my lord also hath our herds of c
Ex 9:3 upon thy c which is in the field
Ex 9:4 sever between the c of Israel
Ex 9:4 of Israel and the c of Egypt
Ex 9:19 therefore now, and gather thy c
Ex 10:26 Our c also shall go with us
Ex 12:29 and all the firstborn of c
Ex 17:3 our children and our c with thirst
Ex 20:10 nor thy maidservant, nor thy c
Ex 34:19 and every firstling among thy c
Lev 1:2 bring your offering of the c
Lev 5:2 beast, or a carcase of unclean c
Lev 19:19 Thou shalt not let thy c gender
Lev 25:7 And for thy c, and for the beast
Lev 26:22 your children, and destroy your c
Num 3:41 the c of the Levites instead of
Num 20:4 that we and our c should die there
Num 20:19 my c drink of thy water, then I
Num 31:9 and took the spoil of all their c
Num 32:1 had a very great multitude of c
Num 32:16 build sheepfolds here for our c
Num 35:3 of them shall be for their c
Deut 2:35 Only the c we took for a prey
Deut 3:7 But all the c, and the spoil of
Deut 3:19 and your little ones, and your c
Deut 5:14 nor thine ass, nor any of thy c
Deut 7:14 barren among you, or among your c
Deut 11:15 grass in thy fields for thy c
Deut 13:15 the c thereof, with the edge of
Deut 20:14 and the little ones, and the c
Deut 28:4 thy ground, and the fruit of thy c
Deut 28:51 he shall eat the fruit of thy c
Deut 30:9 body, and in the fruit of thy c
Josh 1:14 your little ones, and your c
Josh 8:2 the c thereof, shall ye take for
Josh 8:27 Only the c and the spoil of that
Josh 11:14 spoil of these cities, and the c
Josh 14:4 with their suburbs for their c
Josh 21:2 the suburbs thereof for our c
Judg 6:5 For they came up with their c
Judg 18:21 and put the little ones and the c
1Sa 23:5 and brought away their c, and
1Sa 30:20 they drave before those other c
1Kin 1:9 fat c by the stone of Zoheleth,
1Kin 1:19 And he hath slain oxen and fat c
2Kin 3:9 for the c that followed them
2Kin 3:17 ye may drink, both ye, and your c
1Chr 5:9 because their c were multiplied
1Chr 5:21 And they took away their c
1Chr 7:21 came down to take away their c
2Chr 14:15 They smote also the tents of c
2Chr 26:10 for he had much c, both in the
2Chr 35:8 thousand and six hundred small c
Neh 9:37 over our bodies, and over our c
Neh 10:36 of our sons, and of our c, as it
Job 36:33 the c also concerning the vapour
Ps 50:10 the c upon a thousand hills
Ps 78:48 gave up their c also to the hail

Ps 104:14 the grass to grow for the c
Ps 107:38 suffereth not their c to decrease
Ps 148:10 Beasts, and all c
Eccl 2:7 small c above all that were in
Is 7:25 and for the treading of lesser c
Is 30:23 in that day shall thy c feed in
Is 43:23 small c of thy burnt offerings
Is 46:1 upon the beasts, and upon the c
Jer 9:10 can men hear the voice of the c
Jer 49:32 the multitude of their c a spoil
Eze 34:17 I judge between c and c
Eze 38:12 the nations, which have gotten c
Joel 1:18 the herds of c are perplexed,
Jonah 4:11 and also much c
Hag 1:11 forth, and upon men, and upon c
Zec 2:4 the multitude of men and c therein
Zec 13:5 taught me to keep c from my youth
Lk 17:7 a servant plowing or feeding c
Jn 4:12 and his children, and his c

**CAUGHT**

Gen 22:13 behold behind him a ram c in a
Gen 39:12 she c him by his garment, saying,
Ex 4:4 c it, and it became a rod in his
Num 31:32 prey which the men of war had c
Judg 1:6 c him, and cut off his thumbs and
Judg 8:14 c a young man of the men of
Judg 15:4 c three hundred foxes, and took
Judg 21:23 of them that danced, whom they c
1Sa 17:35 I c him by his beard, and smote
2Sa 2:16 they c every one his fellow by
2Sa 18:9 his head c hold of the oak, and he
1Kin 1:50 c hold on the horns of the altar
1Kin 2:28 c hold on the horns of the altar
1Kin 11:30 Ahijah c the new garment that was
2Kin 4:27 the hill, she c him by the feet
2Chr 22:9 and they c him, (for he was hid in
Prov 7:13 So she c him, and kissed him, and
Eccl 9:12 the birds that are c in the snare
Jer 50:24 thou art found, and also c
Mt 14:31 c him, and said unto him, O thou
Mt 21:39 And they c him, and cast him out of
Mk 12:3 And they c him, and beat him, and
Lk 8:29 For oftentimes it had c him
Jn 21:3 and that night they c nothing
Jn 21:10 of the fish which ye have now c
Acts 6:12 c him, and brought him to the
Acts 8:39 Spirit of the Lord c away Philip
Acts 16:19 their gains was gone, they c Paul
Acts 19:29 and having c Gaius and Aristarchus,
Acts 26:21 the Jews c me in the temple
Acts 27:15 And when the ship was c, and could
2Cor 12:2 such an one c up to the third
2Cor 12:4 How that he was c up into
2Cor 12:16 being crafty, I c you with guile
1Th 4:17 remain shall be c up together
Rev 12:5 and her child was c up unto God

**CAUL**

Ex 29:13 the c that is above the liver, and
Lev 3:4 the c above the liver, with the
Lev 7:4 the c that is above the liver,
Lev 8:16 the c above the liver, and the two
Lev 9:10 the c above the liver of the sin
Hos 13:8 will rend the c of their heart,

**CAUSE**

Gen 7:4 I will c it to rain upon the
Gen 45:1 C every man to go out from me
Ex 8:5 c frogs to come up upon the land
Ex 9:16 for this c have I raised thee up
Ex 21:19 shall c him to be thoroughly
Ex 22:5 If a man shall c a field or
Ex 22:9 the c of both parties shall come
Ex 23:2 neither shalt thou speak in a c
Ex 23:6 the judgment of thy poor in his c
Ex 27:20 to c the lamp to burn always
Ex 29:10 thou shalt c a bullock to be
Lev 14:41 he shall c the house to be
Lev 19:29 daughter, to c her to be a whore
Lev 24:2 the light, to c the lamps to burn
Lev 24:19 if a man c a blemish in his
Lev 25:9 Then shalt thou c the trumpet of
Lev 26:16 the eyes, and c sorrow of heart
Num 5:24 he shall c the woman to drink the
Num 16:5 will c him to come near unto him
Num 16:11 For which c both thou and all thy
Num 27:5 brought their c before the LORD
Num 28:7 c the strong wine to be poured
Num 35:30 any person to c him to die
Deut 1:17 the c that is too hard for you,
Deut 3:28 he shall c them to inherit the
Deut 12:11 to c his name to dwell there
Deut 17:16 nor c the people to return to
Deut 24:4 thou shalt not c the land to sin,
Deut 25:2 the judge shall c him to lie down
Deut 28:7 The LORD shall c thine enemies
Deut 28:25 The LORD shall c thee to be
Deut 31:7 thou shalt c them to inherit it
Josh 5:4 this is the c why Joshua did
Josh 20:4 shall declare his c in the ears
Josh 23:7 nor c to swear by them, neither
1Sa 17:29 Is there not a c?
1Sa 19:5 blood, to slay David without a c
1Sa 24:15 me and thee, and see, and plead my c
1Sa 25:39 that hath pleaded the c of my
1Sa 28:9 snare for my life, to c me to die
2Sa 3:35 when all the people came to c
2Sa 13:13 whither shall I c my shame to go
2Sa 15:4 any suit or c might come unto me
1Kin 1:33 c Solomon my son to ride upon
1Kin 5:9 will c them to be discharged
1Kin 8:31 laid upon him to c him to swear
1Kin 8:45 supplication, and maintain their c
1Kin 11:27 this was the c that he lifted up
1Kin 12:15 for the c was from the LORD, that
2Kin 19:7 I will c him to fall by the sword
1Chr 21:3 why will he be a c of trespass to
2Chr 6:35 supplication, and maintain their c
2Chr 10:15 for the c was of God, that the
2Chr 19:10 what c soever shall come to you
2Chr 32:20 for this c Hezekiah the king, and
Ezr 4:15 for which c was this city
Ezr 5:5 they could not c them to cease
Neh 4:11 slay them, and c the work to cease
Neh 6:6 for which c thou buildest the
Neh 13:26 him did outlandish women c to sin
Est 3:13 to c to perish, all Jews, both
Est 5:5 C Haman to make haste, that he
Est 8:11 to c to perish, all the power of
Job 2:3 him, to destroy him without c
Job 5:8 and unto God would I commit my c
Job 6:24 c me to understand wherein I have
Job 9:17 multiplieth my wounds without c
Job 13:18 Behold now, I have ordered my c
Job 20:2 do my thoughts c me to answer
Job 23:4 I would order my c before him
Job 24:7 They c the naked to lodge without
Job 29:16 the c which I knew not I searched
Job 31:13 If I did despise the c of my
Job 34:11 c every man to find according to
Job 38:26 To c it to rain on the earth,
Ps 7:4 him that without c is mine enemy
Ps 9:4 hast maintained my right and my c
Ps 10:17 thou wilt c thine ear to hear
Ps 25:3 which transgress without c
Ps 35:1 Plead my c, O LORD, with them
Ps 35:7 For without c have they hid for
Ps 35:19 the eye that hate me without a c
Ps 43:1 plead my c against an ungodly
Ps 67:1 c his face to shine upon us
Ps 69:4 They that hate me without a c are
Ps 71:2 righteousness, and c me to escape
Ps 74:22 Arise, O God, plead thine own c
Ps 76:8 Thou didst c judgment to be heard
Ps 80:3 O God, and c thy face to shine
Ps 80:19 God of hosts, c thy face to shine
Ps 85:4 c thine anger toward us to cease
Ps 109:3 and fought against me without a c
Ps 119:78 perversely with me without a c
Ps 119:154 Plead my c, and deliver me
Ps 119:161 have persecuted me without a c
Ps 140:12 maintain the c of the afflicted
Ps 143:8 C me to hear thy lovingkindness
Prov 1:11 for the innocent without c
Prov 3:30 Strive not with a man without c
Prov 4:16 unless they c some to fall
Prov 8:21 That I may c those that love me
Prov 18:17 first in his own c seemeth just
Prov 22:23 For the LORD will plead their c
Prov 23:11 he shall plead their c with thee
Prov 23:29 who hath wounds without c
Prov 24:28 against thy neighbour without c
Prov 25:9 Debate thy c with thy neighbour
Prov 29:7 considereth the c of the poor
Prov 31:8 thy mouth for the dumb in the c
Eccl 2:20 Therefore I went about to c my
Eccl 5:6 thy mouth to c thy flesh to sin
Eccl 7:10 What is the c that the former
Eccl 10:1 Dead flies c the ointment of the
Song 8:2 I would c thee to drink of spiced
Is 1:23 neither doth the c of the widow
Is 3:12 which lead thee c thee to err
Is 9:16 of this people c them to err
Is 10:30 c it to be heard unto Laish, O
Is 13:10 shall not c her light to shine
Is 27:6 He shall c them that come of
Is 28:12 ye may c the weary to rest
Is 30:11 c the Holy One of Israel to cease
Is 32:6 he will c the drink of the
Is 37:7 I will c him to fall by the sword
Is 41:21 Produce your c, saith the LORD
Is 42:2 nor c his voice to be heard in
Is 49:8 to c to inherit the desolate
Is 51:22 that pleadeth the c of his people
Is 52:4 Assyrian oppressed them without c
Is 58:14 I will c thee to ride upon the
Is 61:11 the Lord GOD will c righteousness
Is 66:9 birth, and not c to bring forth
Jer 3:12 I will not c mine anger to fall
Jer 5:28 they judge not the c
Jer 7:3 I will c you to dwell in this
Jer 11:20 unto thee have I revealed my c
Jer 13:16 your God, before he c darkness
Jer 14:22 of the Gentiles that can c rain
Jer 15:4 I will c them to be removed into
Jer 16:9 I will c to cease out of this
Jer 16:21 I will this once c them to know
Jer 17:4 I will c thee to serve thine
Jer 18:2 there I will c thee to hear my
Jer 19:7 I will c them to fall by the
Jer 20:12 for unto thee have I opened my c
Jer 22:16 He judged the c of the poor
Jer 23:27 Which think to c my people to
Jer 25:15 c all the nations, to whom I send
Jer 29:8 dreams which ye c to be dreamed
Jer 30:3 I will c them to return to the
Jer 31:2 when I went to c him to rest
Jer 32:35 Hinnom, to c their sons and their
Jer 33:7 I will c the captivity of Judah
Jer 34:22 c them to return to this city
Jer 36:29 shall c to cease from thence man
Jer 37:20 that thou c me not to return to
Jer 38:23 thou shalt c this city to be
Jer 42:12 c you to return to your own land
Jer 48:12 that shall c him to wander, and
Jer 49:2 that I will c an alarm of war to
Jer 50:9 c to come up against Babylon an
Jer 51:27 c the horses to come up as the
Lam 3:32 But though he c grief, yet will
Eze 3:3 c thy belly to eat, and fill thy
Eze 5:1 c it to pass upon thine head and
Eze 9:1 C them that have charge over the
Eze 14:15 If I c noisome beasts to pass
Eze 16:2 of man, c Jerusalem to know her
Eze 20:4 c them to know the abominations
Eze 21:17 and I will c my fury to rest
Eze 23:48 Thus will I c lewdness to cease
Eze 24:8 That it might c fury to come up
Eze 25:7 I will c thee to perish out of
Eze 26:3 will c many nations to come up
Eze 27:30 shall c their voice to be heard
Eze 29:4 I will c the fish of thy rivers
Eze 30:13 I will c their images to cease
Eze 32:4 will c all the fowls of the
Eze 34:10 c them to cease from feeding the
Eze 36:12 I will c men to walk upon you,
Eze 36:27 c you to walk in my statutes, and
Eze 37:5 I will c breath to enter into you
Eze 39:2 will c thee to come up from the
Eze 44:30 that he may c the blessing to
Dan 2:12 For this c the king was angry and
Dan 8:25 his policy also he shall c craft
Dan 9:17 c thy face to shine upon thy
Dan 9:27 the week he shall c the sacrifice
Dan 11:18 c the reproach offered by him to
Dan 11:39 he shall c them to rule over many
Hos 1:4 will c to cease the kingdom of
Hos 2:11 I will also c all her mirth to
Joel 3:11 thither c thy mighty ones to come
Amos 5:27 Therefore will I c you to go into
Amos 6:3 c the seat of violence to come
Amos 8:9 that I will c the sun to go down
Jonah 1:7 for whose c this evil is upon us
Mic 7:9 against him, until he plead my c
Hab 1:3 and c me to behold grievance
Zec 8:12 I will c the remnant of this
Zec 13:2 also I will c the prophets and the
Mt 5:22 a c shall be in danger of the
Mt 5:32 saving for the c of fornication
Mt 10:21 c them to be put to death
Mt 19:3 to put away his wife for every c

Mt 19:5 For this c shall a man leave
Mk 10:7 For this c shall a man leave his
Mk 13:12 shall c them to be put to death
Lk 8:47 for what c she had touched him
Lk 21:16 shall they c to be put to death
Lk 23:22 I have found no c of death in him
Jn 12:18 For this c the people also met
Jn 12:27 but for this c came I unto this
Jn 15:25 law, They hated me without a c
Jn 18:37 for this c came I into the world,
Acts 10:21 what is the c wherefore ye are
Acts 13:28 they found no c of death in him
Acts 19:40 there being no c whereby we may
Acts 23:28 the c wherefore they accused him
Acts 25:14 declared Paul's c unto the king
Acts 28:18 there was no c of death in me
Rom 1:26 For this c God gave them up unto
Rom 13:6 For for this c pay ye tribute
Rom 15:9 For this c I will confess to thee
Rom 16:17 mark them which c divisions
1Cor 4:17 For this c have I sent unto you
1Cor 11:10 For this c ought the woman to
2Cor 4:16 For which c we faint not
2Cor 5:13 we be sober, it is for your c
2Cor 7:12 I did it not for his c that had
Eph 3:1 For this c I Paul, the prisoner
Eph 3:14 For this c I bow my knees unto
Eph 5:31 For this c shall a man leave his
Phil 2:18 For the same c also do ye joy, and
Col 1:9 For this c we also, since the day
Col 4:16 c that it be read also in the
1Th 2:13 For this c also thank we God
1Th 3:5 For this c, when I could no
2Th 2:11 for this c God shall send them
1Ti 1:16 for this c I obtained mercy
2Ti 1:12 For the which c I also suffer
Titus 1:5 For this c left I thee in Crete,
Heb 2:11 for which c he is not ashamed to
Heb 9:15 for this c he is the mediator of
1Pet 4:6 For for this c was the gospel
Rev 12:15 that he might c her to be carried
Rev 13:15 c that as many as would not

**CAUSED**

Gen 2:5 for the LORD God had not c it to
Gen 2:21 the LORD God c a deep sleep to
Gen 20:13 when God c me to wander from my
Gen 41:52 For God hath c me to be fruitful
Ex 14:21 the LORD c the sea to go back by
Ex 36:6 they c it to be proclaimed
Lev 24:20 as he hath c a blemish in a man,
Num 31:16 these c the children of Israel,
Deut 34:4 I have c thee to see it with
Judg 16:19 she c him to shave off the seven
1Sa 10:20 when Samuel had c all the tribes
1Sa 20:17 Jonathan c David to swear again,
2Sa 7:11 have c thee to rest from all
1Kin 1:38 c Solomon to ride upon king
1Kin 2:19 c a seat to be set for the king's
1Kin 20:33 he c him to come up into the
2Kin 17:17 they c their sons and their
2Chr 8:2 c the children of Israel to dwell
2Chr 13:13 But Jeroboam c an ambushment to
2Chr 21:11 c the inhabitants of Jerusalem to
2Chr 33:6 he c his children to pass through
2Chr 34:32 he c all that were present in
Ezr 6:12 the God that hath c his name to
Neh 8:7 c the people to understand the
Est 5:14 he c the gallows to be made
Job 29:13 I c the widow's heart to sing for
Job 31:16 or have c the eyes of the widow
Job 31:39 or have c the owners thereof to
Job 37:15 c the light of his cloud to shine
Job 38:12 c the dayspring to know his place
Ps 66:12 Thou hast c men to ride over our
Ps 78:13 sea, and c them to pass through
Ps 119:49 upon which thou hast c me to hope
Prov 7:21 fair speech she c him to yield
Is 19:14 they have c Egypt to err in every
Is 43:23 I have not c thee to serve with
Is 48:21 he c the waters to flow out of
Is 63:14 Spirit of the LORD c him to rest
Jer 12:14 c my people Israel to inherit
Jer 13:11 so have I c to cleave unto me the
Jer 15:8 I have c him to fall upon it
Jer 18:15 they have c them to stumble in
Jer 23:13 c my people Israel to err
Jer 29:4 whom I have c to be carried away
Jer 32:23 therefore thou hast c all this
Jer 34:11 c the servants and the handmaids,
Jer 48:4 ones have c a cry to be heard
Jer 48:33 I have c wine to fail from the
Jer 50:6 have c them to go astray, they
Jer 51:49 As Babylon hath c the slain of
Lam 2:6 the LORD hath c the solemn feasts
Lam 2:17 he hath c thine enemy to rejoice
Lam 3:13 He hath c the arrows of his
Eze 3:2 and he c me to eat that roll
Eze 16:7 I have c thee to multiply as the
Eze 20:10 Wherefore I c them to go forth
Eze 22:4 thou hast c thy days to draw near
Eze 23:37 have also c their sons, whom they
Eze 24:13 till I have c my fury to rest
Eze 29:18 c his army to serve a great
Eze 31:15 down to the grave I c a mourning
Eze 32:23 which c terror in the land of the
Eze 32:26 though they c their terror in the
Eze 32:32 For I have c my terror in the
Eze 37:2 c me to pass by them round about
Eze 39:28 which c them to be led into
Eze 44:12 c the house of Israel to fall
Eze 46:21 c me to pass by the four corners
Eze 47:6 c me to return to the brink of
Dan 9:21 being c to fly swiftly, touched
Hos 4:12 of whoredoms hath c them to err
Amos 2:4 their lies c them to err, after
Amos 4:7 I c it to rain upon one city, and
Jonah 3:7 he c it to be proclaimed and
Zec 3:4 I have c thine iniquity to pass
Mal 2:8 ye have c many to stumble at the
Jn 11:37 have c that even this man should
Acts 15:3 they c great joy unto all the
2Cor 2:5 But if any have c grief, he hath

**CAUSES**

Ex 18:19 thou mayest bring the c unto God
Deut 1:16 Hear the c between your brethren,
Jer 3:8 when for all the c whereby
Lam 2:14 false burdens and c of banishment
Lam 3:58 hast pleaded the c of my soul
Acts 26:21 For these c the Jews caught me in

**CAUSETH**

Num 5:18 the bitter water that c the curse
Job 12:24 c them to wander in a wilderness
Job 20:3 my understanding c me to answer
Job 37:13 He c it to come, whether for
Ps 104:14 He c the grass to grow for the
Ps 107:40 and c them to wander in the
Ps 135:7 He c the vapours to ascend from
Ps 147:18 he c his wind to blow, and the
Prov 10:5 in harvest is a son that c shame
Prov 10:10 winketh with the eye c sorrow
Prov 14:35 wrath is against him that c shame
Prov 17:2 have rule over a son that c shame
Prov 18:18 The lot c contentions to cease,
Prov 19:26 his mother, is a son that c shame
Prov 28:10 Whoso c the righteous to go
Is 61:11 as the garden c the things that
Is 64:2 the fire c the waters to boil, to
Jer 10:13 he c the vapors to ascend from
Jer 51:16 he c the vapors to ascend from
Eze 26:3 as the sea c his waves to come up
Eze 44:18 with any thing that c sweat
Mt 5:32 c her to commit adultery
2Cor 2:14 which always c us to triumph in
2Cor 9:11 which c through us thanksgiving
Rev 13:12 c the earth and them which dwell
Rev 13:16 he c all, both small and great,

**CAVE**

Gen 19:30 and he dwelt in a c, he and his two
Gen 23:9 he may give me the c of Machpelah
Gen 23:19 the c of the field of Machpelah
Gen 25:9 buried him in the c of Machpelah
Gen 49:29 c that is in the field of Ephron
Gen 50:13 buried him in the c of the field
Josh 10:16 hid themselves in a c at Makkedah
Josh 10:22 Joshua, Open the mouth of the c
1Sa 22:1 and escaped to the c Adullam
1Sa 24:3 by the way, where was a c
1Sa 24:7 But Saul rose up out of the c
2Sa 23:13 time unto the c of Adullam
1Kin 18:4 and hid them by fifty in a c
1Kin 18:13 LORD's prophets by fifty in a c
1Kin 19:9 And he came thither unto a c
1Kin 19:13 stood in the entering in of the c
1Chr 11:15 to David, into the c of Adullam
Ps 57:*t* when he fled from Saul in the c
Ps 142:*t* A Prayer when he was in the c
Jn 11:38 It was a c, and a stone lay upon

**CAVES**

Judg 6:2 which are in the mountains, and c
1Sa 13:6 people did hide themselves in c
Job 30:6 in c of the earth, and in the
Is 2:19 into the c of the earth, for fear
Eze 33:27 in the c shall die of the
Heb 11:38 and in dens and c of the earth

**CEASE**

Gen 8:22 and day and night shall not c
Ex 9:29 and the thunder shall c, neither
Num 8:25 shall c waiting upon the service
Num 11:25 they prophesied, and did not c
Num 17:5 I will make to c from me the
Deut 15:11 shall never c out of the land
Deut 32:26 of them to c from among men
Josh 22:25 children c from fearing the LORD
Judg 15:7 of you, and after that I will c
Judg 20:28 Benjamin my brother, or shall I c
1Sa 7:8 C not to cry unto the LORD our
2Chr 16:5 of Ramah, and let his work c
Ezr 4:21 to cause these men to c, and that
Ezr 5:5 they could not cause them to c
Neh 4:11 slay them, and cause the work to c
Neh 6:3 why should the work c, whilst I
Job 3:17 There the wicked c from troubling
Job 10:20 c then, and let me alone, that I
Job 14:7 tender branch thereof will not c
Ps 37:8 C from anger, and forsake wrath
Ps 46:9 He maketh wars to c unto the end
Ps 85:4 cause thine anger toward us to c
Ps 89:44 Thou hast made his glory to c
Prov 18:18 The lot causeth contentions to c
Prov 19:27 C, my son, to hear the
Prov 20:3 honour for a man to c from strife
Prov 22:10 yea, strife and reproach shall c
Prov 23:4 c from thine own wisdom
Eccl 12:3 the grinders c because they are
Is 1:16 c to do evil
Is 2:22 C ye from man, whose breath is in
Is 10:25 while, and the indignation shall c
Is 13:11 the arrogancy of the proud to c
Is 16:10 made their vintage shouting to c
Is 17:3 also shall c from Ephraim
Is 21:2 sighing thereof have I made to c
Is 30:11 One of Israel to c from before us
Is 33:1 when thou shalt c to spoil
Jer 7:34 Then will I cause to c from the
Jer 14:17 night and day, and let them not c
Jer 16:9 I will cause to c out of this
Jer 17:8 neither shall c from yielding
Jer 31:36 c from being a nation before me
Jer 36:29 shall cause to c from thence man
Jer 48:35 I will cause to c in Moab
Lam 2:18 let not the apple of thine eye c
Eze 6:6 and your idols may be broken and c
Eze 7:24 make the pomp of the strong to c
Eze 12:23 I will make this proverb to c
Eze 16:41 I will cause thee to c from
Eze 23:27 make thy lewdness to c from thee
Eze 26:13 cause the noise of thy songs to c
Eze 30:10 c by the hand of Nebuchadrezzar
Eze 33:28 the pomp of her strength shall c
Eze 34:10 cause them to c from feeding the
Eze 34:25 evil beasts to c out of the land
Dan 9:27 sacrifice and the oblation to c
Dan 11:18 the reproach offered by him to c
Hos 1:4 will cause to c the kingdom of
Hos 2:11 also cause all her mirth to c
Amos 7:5 Then said I, O Lord GOD, c
Acts 13:10 wilt thou not c to pervert the
1Cor 13:8 there be tongues, they shall c
Eph 1:16 C not to give thanks for you,
Col 1:9 do not c to pray for you, and to
2Pet 2:14 and that cannot c from sin

**CEASED**

Gen 18:11 it c to be with Sarah after the
Ex 9:33 and the thunders and hail c
Josh 5:12 the manna c on the morrow after
Judg 2:19 they c not from their own doings,
Judg 5:7 The inhabitants of the villages c
1Sa 2:5 and they that were hungry c
1Sa 25:9 words in the name of David, and c
Ezr 4:24 Then c the work of the house of
Job 32:1 these three men c to answer Job
Ps 35:15 they did tear me, and c not
Ps 77:2 sore ran in the night, and c not
Is 14:4 and say, How hath the oppressor c
Lam 5:14 The elders have c from the gate
Jonah 1:15 the sea c from her raging

Mt 14:32 come into the ship, the wind c
Mk 4:39 And the wind c, and there was a
Mk 6:51 and the wind c
Lk 7:45 in hath not c to kiss my feet
Lk 8:24 and they c, and there was a calm
Lk 11:1 in a certain place, when he c
Acts 5:42 they c not to teach and preach
Acts 20:1 And after the uproar was c
Acts 20:31 I c not to warn every one night
Acts 21:14 he would not be persuaded, we c
Gal 5:11 is the offence of the cross c
Heb 4:10 he also hath c from his own works
Heb 10:2 they not have c to be offered
1Pet 4:1 in the flesh hath c from sin

**CEASING**
1Sa 12:23 the LORD in c to pray for you
Acts 12:5 but prayer was made without c of
Rom 1:9 that without c I make mention of
1Th 1:3 without c your work of faith
1Th 2:13 cause also thank we God without c
1Th 5:17 Pray without c
2Ti 1:3 that without c I have remembrance

**CEDAR**
Lev 14:4 c wood, and scarlet, and hyssop
Lev 14:49 c wood, and scarlet, and hyssop
Num 19:6 And the priest shall take c wood
Num 24:6 as c trees beside the waters
2Sa 5:11 c trees, and carpenters, and masons
2Sa 7:2 See now, I dwell in an house of c
1Kin 4:33 from the c tree that is in
1Kin 5:6 hew me c trees out of Lebanon
1Kin 6:9 house with beams and boards of c
1Kin 6:20 covered the altar which was of c
1Kin 6:36 hewed stone, and a row of c beams
1Kin 7:2 upon four rows of c pillars
1Kin 7:12 hewed stones, and a row of c beams
1Kin 9:11 furnished Solomon with c trees
2Kin 14:9 sent to the c that was in Lebanon
2Kin 19:23 cut down the tall c trees thereof
1Chr 22:4 Also c trees in abundance
2Chr 1:15 c trees made he as the sycomore
2Chr 2:8 Send me also c trees, fir trees,
2Chr 9:27 c trees made he as the sycomore
2Chr 25:18 sent to the c that was in Lebanon
Ezr 3:7 to bring c trees from Lebanon to
Job 40:17 He moveth his tail like a c
Ps 92:12 he shall grow like a c in Lebanon
Song 1:17 The beams of our house are c
Song 8:9 will inclose her with boards of c
Is 41:19 plant in the wilderness the c
Jer 22:14 and it is cieled with c, and
Eze 17:3 took the highest branch of the c
Eze 17:22 the highest branch of the high c
Eze 27:24 bound with cords, and made of c
Eze 31:3 the Assyrian was a c in Lebanon
Zeph 2:14 for he shall uncover the c work
Zec 11:2 for the c is fallen

**CEDARS**
Judg 9:15 and devour the c of Lebanon
1Kin 7:11 measures of hewed stones, and c
1Kin 10:27 c made he to be as the sycomore
1Chr 14:1 to David, and timber of c, with
1Chr 17:1 Lo, I dwell in an house of c
2Chr 2:3 didst send him c to build him an
Ps 29:5 voice of the LORD breaketh the c
Ps 80:10 thereof were like the goodly c
Ps 104:16 the c of Lebanon, which he hath
Ps 148:9 fruitful trees, and all c
Song 5:15 is as Lebanon, excellent as the c
Is 2:13 And upon all the c of Lebanon
Is 9:10 but we will change them into c
Is 14:8 the c of Lebanon, saying, Since
Is 37:24 will cut down the tall c thereof
Is 44:14 He heweth him down c, and taketh
Jer 22:7 they shall cut down thy choice c
Jer 22:23 that makest thy nest in the c
Eze 27:5 they have taken c from Lebanon to
Eze 31:8 The c in the garden of God could
Amos 2:9 was like the height of the c
Zec 11:1 that the fire may devour thy c

**CEDRON** *(se'-drun)* See KIDRON. *Same as Kidron.*
Jn 18:1 his disciples over the brook C

**CENCHREA** *(sen'-kre-ah) Harbor city for Corinth.*
Acts 18:18 having shorn his head in C
Rom 16:1 of the church which is at C
Rom *s* Phebe servant of the church at C

**CENSER**
Lev 10:1 Aaron, took either of them his c
Lev 16:12 he shall take a c full of burning
Num 16:17 And take every man his c, and put
Num 16:46 Moses said unto Aaron, Take a c
2Chr 26:19 had a c in his hand to burn
Eze 8:11 with every man his c in his hand
Heb 9:4 Which had the golden c, and the
Rev 8:3 at the altar, having a golden c
Rev 8:5 And the angel took the c, and

**CENSERS**
Num 4:14 minister about it, even the c
Num 16:6 Take you c, Korah, and all his
Num 16:17 censer, two hundred and fifty c
Num 16:37 take up the c out of the burning
1Kin 7:50 the spoons, and the c of pure gold
2Chr 4:22 basons, and the spoons, and the c

**CENTURION**
Mt 8:5 there came unto him a c,
Mt 8:8 The c answered and said, Lord, I
Mt 8:13 And Jesus said unto the c, Go thy
Mt 27:54 Now when the c, and they that were
Mk 15:39 And when the c, which stood over
Mk 15:44 and calling unto him the c
Lk 7:6 the c sent friends to him, saying
Lk 23:47 Now when the c saw what was done,
Acts 10:1 a c of the band called the
Acts 10:22 And they said, Cornelius the c
Acts 22:25 said unto the c that stood by
Acts 24:23 And he commanded a c to keep Paul
Acts 27:1 Julius, a c of Augustus' band
Acts 27:11 Nevertheless the c believed the
Acts 27:31 Paul said to the c and to the
Acts 27:43 But the c, willing to save Paul,
Acts 28:16 the c delivered the prisoners to

**CEPHAS** *(se'-fas)* See PETER. *Name given to Simon Peter.*
Jn 1:42 thou shalt be called C, which is
1Cor 1:12 and I of C
1Cor 3:22 Whether Paul, or Apollos, or C
1Cor 9:5 as the brethren of the Lord, and C
1Cor 15:5 And that he was seen of C, then of
Gal 2:9 And when James, C, and John, who

**CERTAIN**
Gen 28:11 And he lighted upon a c place
Gen 37:15 a c man found him, and, behold, he
Gen 38:1 and turned in to a c Adullamite
Ex 16:4 gather a c rate every day, that I
Num 9:6 And there were c men, who were
Num 16:2 with c of the children of Israel,
Deut 13:13 C men, the children of Belial,
Deut 17:4 it be true, and the thing c
Deut 25:2 to his fault, by a c number
Judg 9:53 a c woman cast a piece of a
Judg 13:2 there was a c man of Zorah, of
Judg 19:1 that there was a c Levite
Judg 19:22 c sons of Belial, beset the house
Ruth 1:1 a c man of Beth-lehem-judah went
1Sa 1:1 Now there was a c man of
1Sa 21:7 Now a c man of the servants of
2Sa 18:10 a c man saw it, and told Joab, and
1Kin 2:37 thou shalt know for c that thou
1Kin 7:29 oxen were c additions made of
1Kin 11:17 c Edomites of his father's
1Kin 20:35 a c man of the sons of the
1Kin 22:34 a c man drew a bow at a venture,
2Kin 4:1 Now there cried a c woman of the
2Kin 8:6 appointed unto her a c officer
1Chr 9:28 c of them had the charge of the
1Chr 16:4 he appointed c of the Levites to
1Chr 19:5 Then there went c, and told David
2Chr 8:13 Even after a c rate every day,
2Chr 18:2 after c years he went down to
2Chr 18:33 a c man drew a bow at a venture,
2Chr 28:12 Then c of the heads of the
Ezr 10:16 with c chief of the fathers,
Neh 1:2 came, he and c men of Judah
Neh 11:4 at Jerusalem dwelt c of the
Neh 11:23 that a c portion should be for
Neh 12:35 c of the priests' sons with
Neh 13:6 after c days obtained I leave of
Neh 13:25 smote c of them, and plucked off
Est 2:5 the palace there was a c Jew
Est 3:8 There is a c people scattered
Jer 26:15 But know ye for c, that if ye put
Jer 26:17 Then rose up c of the elders of
Jer 41:5 That there came c from Shechem
Jer 52:15 c of the poor of the people
Eze 14:1 Then came c of the elders of
Eze 20:1 that c of the elders of Israel
Dan 1:3 that he should bring c of the
Dan 2:45 and the dream is c, and the
Dan 3:8 that time c Chaldeans came near
Dan 3:12 There are c Jews whom thou hast
Dan 8:13 unto that c saint which spake
Dan 10:5 behold a c man clothed in linen,
Dan 11:13 after c years with a great army
Mt 8:19 a c scribe came, and said unto him
Mt 9:3 c of the scribes said within
Mt 9:18 behold, there came a c ruler
Mt 12:38 Then c of the scribes and of the
Mt 17:14 there came to him a c man
Mt 18:23 of heaven likened unto a c king
Mt 20:20 desiring a c thing of him
Mt 21:28 A c man had two sons
Mt 21:33 There was a c householder
Mt 22:2 of heaven is like unto a c king
Mk 2:6 But there were c of the scribes
Mk 5:25 a c woman, which had an issue of
Mk 5:35 synagogue's house c which said
Mk 7:1 c of the scribes, which came from
Mk 7:25 For a c woman, whose young
Mk 11:5 c of them that stood there said
Mk 12:1 A c man planted a vineyard, and
Mk 12:13 send unto him c of the Pharisees
Mk 12:42 And there came a c poor widow
Mk 14:51 there followed him a c young man
Mk 14:57 And there arose c, and bare false
Lk 1:5 a c priest named Zacharias, of
Lk 5:12 to pass, when he was in a c city
Lk 5:17 And it came to pass on a c day
Lk 6:2 c of the Pharisees said unto them
Lk 7:2 a c centurion's servant, who was
Lk 7:41 There was a c creditor which had
Lk 8:2 c women, which had been healed of
Lk 8:20 it was told him by c which said
Lk 8:27 met him out of the city a c man
Lk 9:57 a c man said unto him, Lord, I
Lk 10:25 a c lawyer stood up, and tempted
Lk 10:30 A c man went down from Jerusalem
Lk 10:33 But a c Samaritan, as he
Lk 10:38 that he entered into a c village
Lk 11:1 as he was praying in a c place
Lk 11:27 a c woman of the company lifted
Lk 11:37 a c Pharisee besought him to dine
Lk 12:16 The ground of a c rich man
Lk 13:6 A c man had a fig tree planted in
Lk 13:31 day there came c of the Pharisees
Lk 14:2 there was a c man before him
Lk 14:16 A c man made a great supper, and
Lk 15:11 And he said, A c man had two sons
Lk 16:1 disciples, There was a c rich man
Lk 16:19 There was a c rich man, which was
Lk 17:12 And as he entered into a c village
Lk 18:9 he spake this parable unto c
Lk 18:18 a c ruler asked him, saying, Good
Lk 18:35 a c blind man sat by the way side
Lk 19:12 A c nobleman went into a far
Lk 20:9 A c man planted a vineyard, and
Lk 20:27 came to him c of the Sadducees
Lk 20:39 Then c of the scribes answering
Lk 21:2 he saw also a c poor widow
Lk 22:56 But a c maid beheld him as he sat
Lk 23:19 (Who for a c sedition made in the
Lk 24:1 prepared, and c others with them
Lk 24:22 c women also of our company made
Jn 4:46 And there was a c nobleman
Jn 5:4 down at a c season into the pool
Jn 11:1 Now a c man was sick, named
Jn 12:20 there were c Greeks among them
Acts 3:2 a c man lame from his mother's
Acts 5:1 But a c man named Ananias, with
Acts 6:9 there arose c of the synagogue
Acts 8:9 But there was a c man, called
Acts 8:36 way, they came unto a c water
Acts 9:10 there was a c disciple at
Acts 9:19 Then was Saul c days with the
Acts 9:33 he found a c man named Aeneas
Acts 10:1 There was a c man in Caesarea
Acts 10:11 a c vessel descending unto him,
Acts 10:23 c brethren from Joppa accompanied
Acts 10:48 prayed they him to tarry c days
Acts 11:5 A c vessel descend, as it had
Acts 12:1 his hands to vex c of the church
Acts 13:1 that was at Antioch c prophets
Acts 13:6 Paphos, they found a c sorcerer
Acts 14:8 there sat a c man at Lystra,
Acts 14:19 came thither c Jews from Antioch

Acts 15:1 c men which came down from Judaea
Acts 15:5 But there rose up c of the sect
Acts 15:24 that c which went out from us
Acts 16:1 a c disciple was there, named
Acts 16:12 were in that city abiding c days
Acts 16:14 a c woman named Lydia, a seller
Acts 17:5 took unto them c lewd fellows of
Acts 17:18 Then c philosophers of the
Acts 17:20 For thou bringest c strange
Acts 17:28 as c also of your own poets have
Acts 18:2 found a c Jew named Aquila, born
Acts 18:24 a c Jew named Apollos, born at
Acts 19:24 For a c man named Demetrius, a
Acts 20:9 there sat in a window a c young
Acts 21:10 came down from Judaea a c prophet
Acts 23:12 c of the Jews banded together, and
Acts 24:1 with a c orator named Tertullus,
Acts 25:13 after c days king Agrippa and
Acts 27:1 c other prisoners unto one named
Acts 27:16 running under a c island which is
Acts 27:26 we must be cast upon a c island
Acts 27:39 discovered a c creek with a shore
Rom 15:26 Achaia to make a c contribution
1Cor 4:11 have no c dwellingplace
Gal 2:12 For before that c came from James
1Ti 6:7 it is c we can carry nothing out
Heb 2:6 But one in a c place testified,
Heb 4:4 For he spake in a c place of the
Heb 10:27 But a c fearful looking for of
Jude 4 For there are c men crept in

**CERTAINLY**

Gen 18:10 I will c return unto thee
Gen 26:28 We saw c that the LORD was with
Gen 43:7 could we c know that he would say
Gen 44:15 that such a man as I can c divine
Gen 50:15 will c requite us all the evil
Ex 3:12 And he said, C I will be with thee
Ex 22:4 If the theft be c found in his
Lev 5:19 he hath c trespassed against the
Lev 24:16 congregation shall c stone him
Josh 9:24 Because it was c told thy
Judg 14:12 if ye can c declare it me within
1Sa 20:3 Thy father c knoweth that I have
1Sa 23:10 thy servant hath c heard that
1Sa 25:28 for the LORD will c make my lord
1Kin 1:30 even so will I c do this day
2Kin 8:10 unto him, Thou mayest c recover
2Chr 18:27 If thou c return in peace, then
Prov 23:5 for riches c make themselves
Jer 8:8 Lo, c in vain made he it
Jer 13:12 Do we not c know that every
Jer 25:28 Ye shall c drink
Jer 36:29 The king of Babylon shall c come
Jer 40:14 Dost thou c know that Baalis the
Jer 42:19 know c that I have admonished you
Jer 44:17 But we will c do whatsoever thing
Lam 2:16 c this is the day that we looked
Dan 11:10 and one shall c come, and overflow,
Lk 23:47 C this was a righteous man

**CERTAINTY**

Josh 23:13 Know for a c that the LORD your
1Sa 23:23 and come ye again to me with the c
Prov 22:21 know the c of the words of truth
Dan 2:8 I know of c that ye would gain
Lk 1:4 know the c of those things
Acts 21:34 not know the c for the tumult
Acts 22:30 c wherefore he was accused of the

**CERTIFY**

2Sa 15:28 there come word from you to c me
Ezr 4:16 We c the king that, if this city
Ezr 5:10 to c thee, that we might write
Ezr 7:24 Also we c you, that touching any
Gal 1:11 But I c you, brethren, that the

**CHAFF**

Job 21:18 as c that the storm carrieth away
Ps 1:4 but are like the c which the wind
Ps 35:5 Let them be as c before the wind
Is 5:24 and the flame consumeth the c
Is 17:13 shall be chased as the c of the
Is 29:5 shall be as c that passeth away
Is 33:11 Ye shall conceive c, ye shall
Is 41:15 and shalt make the hills as c
Jer 23:28 What is the c to the wheat
Dan 2:35 became like the c of the summer
Hos 13:3 as the c that is driven with the
Zeph 2:2 before the day pass as the c
Mt 3:12 up the c with unquenchable fire
Lk 3:17 but the c he will burn with fire

**CHAIN**

Gen 41:42 put a gold c about his neck
1Kin 7:17 work, and wreaths of c work
Ps 73:6 compasseth them about as a c
Song 4:9 eyes, with one c of thy neck
Lam 3:7 he hath made my c heavy
Eze 7:23 Make a c
Eze 16:11 thy hands, and a c on thy neck
Dan 5:29 put a c of gold about his neck,
Acts 28:20 of Israel I am bound with this c
2Ti 1:16 me, and was not ashamed of my c
Rev 20:1 pit and a great c in his hand

**CHAINS**

Ex 28:14 two c of pure gold at the ends
Ex 39:15 the breastplate c at the ends
Num 31:50 hath gotten, of jewels of gold, c
Judg 8:26 beside the c that were about
1Kin 6:21 the c of gold before the oracle
2Chr 3:5 and set thereon palm trees and c
2Chr 3:16 And he made c, as in the oracle,
Ps 68:6 out those which are bound with c
Ps 149:8 To bind their kings with c
Prov 1:9 thy head, and c about thy neck
Song 1:10 jewels, thy neck with c of gold
Is 3:19 The c, and the bracelets, and the
Is 40:19 with gold, and casteth silver c
Is 45:14 in c they shall come over, and
Jer 39:7 eyes, and bound him with c
Jer 40:1 in c among all that were carried
Jer 52:11 king of Babylon bound him in c
Eze 19:4 they brought him with c unto the
Nah 3:10 all her great men were bound in c
Mk 5:3 could bind him, no, not with c
Mk 5:4 often bound with fetters and c
Lk 8:29 and he was kept bound with c
Acts 12:6 two soldiers, bound with two c
Acts 21:33 him to be bound with two c
2Pet 2:4 delivered them into c of darkness
Jude 6 c under darkness unto the

**CHALCOL** *(kal'-kol)* See CALCOL. *Son of Mahol.*

1Kin 4:31 the Ezrahite, and Heman, and C

**CHALDAEANS** *(kal-de'-uns)* See CHALDEANS. *Inhabitants of southern Babylonia.*

Acts 7:4 came he out of the land of the C

**CHALDEA** *(kal-de'-ah)* See BABYLON, CHALDEAN. *Southern portion of Babylonia.*

Jer 50:10 And C shall be a spoil
Jer 51:24 to all the inhabitants of C all
Jer 51:35 blood upon the inhabitants of C
Eze 11:24 by the Spirit of God into C
Eze 16:29 in the land of Canaan unto C
Eze 23:15 manner of the Babylonians of C

**CHALDEAN** *(kal-de'-un)* See BABYLONIAN, CHALDEANS, CHALDEANS'.

Ezr 5:12 the king of Babylon, the C
Dan 2:10 any magician, or astrologer, or C

**CHALDEANS** *(kal-de'-uns)* See BABYLONIANS, CHALDAEANS, CHALDEANS', CHALDEES. *Same as Chaldaeans.*

Job 1:17 The C made out three bands, and
Is 23:13 Behold the land of the C
Is 43:14 down all their nobles, and the C
Is 47:1 is no throne, O daughter of the C
Is 47:5 darkness, O daughter of the C
Is 48:14 and his arm shall be on the C
Is 48:20 of Babylon, flee ye from the C
Jer 21:4 king of Babylon, and against the C
Jer 21:9 falleth to the C that besiege you
Jer 22:25 and into the hand of the C
Jer 24:5 the land of the C for their good
Jer 25:12 iniquity, and the land of the C
Jer 32:4 escape out of the hand of the C
Jer 32:24 is given into the hand of the C
Jer 32:29 And the C, that fight against this
Jer 32:43 is given into the hand of the C
Jer 33:5 They come to fight with the C
Jer 35:11 for fear of the army of the C
Jer 37:5 and when the C that besieged
Jer 37:8 the C shall come again, and fight
Jer 37:13 Thou fallest away to the C
Jer 38:2 goeth forth to the C shall live
Jer 38:18 be given into the hand of the C
Jer 39:8 the C burned the king's house, and
Jer 40:9 saying, Fear not to serve the C
Jer 41:3 the C that were found there, and
Jer 43:3 deliver us into the hand of the C
Jer 50:1 of the C by Jeremiah the prophet
Jer 51:4 shall fall in the land of the C
Jer 51:54 from the land of the C
Jer 52:7 (now the C were by the city round
Jer 52:8 But the army of the C pursued
Eze 1:3 in the land of the C by the river
Eze 12:13 to Babylon to the land of the C
Eze 23:14 the images of the C pourtrayed
Dan 1:4 learning and the tongue of the C
Dan 2:2 and the sorcerers, and the C
Dan 2:4 Then spake the C to the king in
Dan 2:10 The C answered before the king,
Dan 3:8 at that time certain C came near
Dan 4:7 magicians, the astrologers, the C
Dan 5:7 bring in the astrologers, the C
Dan 5:11 of the magicians, astrologers, C
Dan 5:30 the king of the C slain
Dan 9:1 made king over the realm of the C
Hab 1:6 For, lo, I raise up the C

**CHALDEANS'** *(kal-de'-uns)*

Jer 39:5 But the C army pursued after them

**CHALDEES** *(kal'-dees)* See CHALDEES'. *Same as Chaldeans.*

Gen 11:28 of his nativity, in Ur of the C
Gen 11:31 forth with them from Ur of the C
Gen 15:7 brought thee out of Ur of the C
2Kin 24:2 sent against him bands of the C
2Kin 25:4 (now the C were against the city
2Kin 25:10 And all the army of the C, that
2Kin 25:24 not to be the servants of the C
2Chr 36:17 upon them the king of the C
Neh 9:7 him forth out of Ur of the C

**CHALDEES'** *(kal'-dees)* See CHALDEANS.

Is 13:19 the beauty of the C excellency

**CHAMBER**

Gen 43:30 and he entered into his c, and wept
Judg 3:24 covereth his feet in his summer c
Judg 15:1 will go in to my wife into the c
Judg 16:9 wait, abiding with her in the c
Judg 16:12 liers in wait abiding in the c
2Sa 13:10 into the c to Amnon her brother
2Sa 18:33 and went up to the c over the gate
1Kin 1:15 went in unto the king into the c
1Kin 6:6 The nethermost c was five cubits
1Kin 14:28 them back into the guard c
1Kin 17:23 down out of the c into the house
1Kin 20:30 into the city, into an inner c
1Kin 22:25 into an inner c to hide thyself
2Kin 1:2 his upper c that was in Samaria
2Kin 4:10 Let us make a little c, I pray
2Kin 9:2 and carry him to an inner c
2Kin 23:11 by the c of Nathan-melech the
2Chr 12:11 them again into the guard c
2Chr 18:24 into an inner c to hide thyself
Ezr 10:6 went into the c of Johanan the
Neh 3:30 of Berechiah over against his c
Neh 13:4 of the c of the house of our God
Ps 19:5 a bridegroom coming out of his c
Song 3:4 into the c of her that conceived
Jer 35:4 into the c of the sons of Hanan,
Jer 36:10 in the c of Gemariah the son of
Jer 36:12 king's house, into the scribe's c
Jer 36:20 in the c of Elishama the scribe
Eze 40:7 every little c was one reed long,
Eze 40:13 little c to the roof of another
Eze 40:45 And he said unto me, This c
Eze 41:5 and the breadth of every side c
Eze 41:7 c to the highest by the midst
Eze 41:9 which was for the side c without
Eze 42:1 he brought me into the c that was
Dan 6:10 open in his c toward Jerusalem
Joel 2:16 the bridegroom go forth of his c
Acts 9:37 they laid her in an upper c
Acts 9:39 they brought him into the upper c
Acts 20:8 were many lights in the upper c

**CHAMBERLAIN**

2Kin 23:11 chamber of Nathan-melech the c
Est 2:3 the custody of Hege the king's c
Est 2:14 of Shaashgaz, the king's c
Est 2:15 but what Hegai the king's c
Acts 12:20 the king's c their friend
Rom 16:23 Erastus the c of the city

**CHAMBERLAINS**

Est 1:10 the seven c that served in the
Est 1:12 the king's commandment by his c
Est 1:15 of the king Ahasuerus by the c

Est 2:21 king's gate, two of the king's c
Est 4:4 her c came and told it her
Est 4:5 for Hatach, one of the king's c
Est 6:2 and Teresh, two of the king's c
Est 6:14 with him, came the king's c
Est 7:9 And Harbonah, one of the c

**CHAMBERS**
1Kin 6:5 the house he built c round about
1Kin 6:10 then he built c against all the
1Chr 9:26 set office, and were over the c
1Chr 9:33 who remaining in the c were free
1Chr 23:28 LORD, in the courts, and in the c
1Chr 28:11 and of the upper c thereof
1Chr 28:12 of all the c round about, of the
2Chr 3:9 he overlaid the upper c with gold
2Chr 31:11 c in the house of the LORD
Ezr 8:29 in the c of the house of the LORD
Neh 10:37 to the c of the house of our God
Neh 12:44 over the c for the treasures
Neh 13:9 commanded, and they cleansed the c
Job 9:9 Pleiades, and the c of the south
Ps 104:3 the beams of his c in the waters
Ps 104:13 He watereth the hills from his c
Ps 105:30 in the c of their kings
Prov 7:27 going down to the c of death
Prov 24:4 by knowledge shall the c be
Song 1:4 king hath brought me into his c
Is 26:20 my people, enter thou into thy c
Jer 22:13 and his c by wrong
Jer 35:2 of the LORD, into one of the c
Eze 8:12 every man in the c of his imagery
Eze 21:14 which entereth into their privy c
Eze 40:7 the little c were five cubits
Eze 40:16 narrow windows to the little c
Eze 40:44 the c of the singers in the inner
Eze 41:26 and upon the side c of the house
Eze 42:4 before the c was a walk of ten
Eze 44:19 and lay them in the holy c
Eze 45:5 for a possession for twenty c
Eze 46:19 into the holy c of the priests,
Mt 24:26 behold, he is in the secret c

**CHANAAN** *(ka'-na-un)* See CANAAN. *Greek form of Canaan.*
Acts 7:11 over all the land of Egypt and C
Acts 13:19 seven nations in the land of C

**CHANCE**
Deut 22:6 If a bird's nest c to be before
1Sa 6:9 it was a c that happened to us
2Sa 1:6 As I happened by c upon mount
Eccl 9:11 time and c happeneth to them all
Lk 10:31 by c there came down a certain
1Cor 15:37 it may c of wheat, or of some

**CHANGE**
Gen 35:2 and be clean, and c your garments
Lev 27:10 He shall not alter it, nor c it
Lev 27:33 or bad, neither shall he c it
Judg 14:12 sheets and thirty c of garments
Judg 14:19 gave c of garments unto them
Job 14:14 time will I wait, till my c come
Job 17:12 They c the night into day
Ps 102:26 as a vesture shalt thou c them
Prov 24:21 not with them that are given to c
Is 9:10 but we will c them into cedars
Jer 2:36 thou about so much to c thy way
Jer 13:23 Can the Ethiopian c his skin
Dan 7:25 most High, and think to c times
Hos 4:7 therefore will I c their glory
Hab 1:11 Then shall his mind c, and he
Zec 3:4 clothe thee with c of raiment
Mal 3:6 For I am the LORD, I c not
Acts 6:14 shall c the customs which Moses
Rom 1:26 for even their women did c the
Gal 4:20 with you now, and to c my voice
Phil 3:21 Who shall c our vile body, that
Heb 7:12 of necessity a c also of the law

**CHANGED**
Gen 31:7 me, and c my wages ten times
Gen 31:41 thou hast c my wages ten times
Gen 41:14 c his raiment, and came in unto
Lev 13:16 be c unto white, he shall come
Lev 13:55 the plague have not c his colour
Num 32:38 Baal-meon, (their names being c
1Sa 21:13 he c his behaviour before them,
2Sa 12:20 c his apparel, and came into the
2Kin 24:17 stead, and c his name to Zedekiah
2Kin 25:29 And c his prison garments
Job 30:18 of my disease is my garment c
Ps 34:*t* when he c his behaviour before
Ps 102:26 change them, and they shall be c
Ps 106:20 Thus they c their glory into the
Eccl 8:1 boldness of his face shall be c
Is 24:5 c the ordinance, broken the
Jer 2:11 Hath a nation c their gods
Jer 48:11 in him, and his scent is not c
Jer 52:33 And c his prison garments
Lam 4:1 how is the most fine gold c
Eze 5:6 she hath c my judgments into
Dan 2:9 before me, till the time be c
Dan 3:19 his visage was c against Shadrach
Dan 3:27 neither were their coats c
Dan 3:28 have c the king's word, and
Dan 4:16 Let his heart be c from man's
Dan 5:6 Then the king's countenance was c
Dan 5:9 and his countenance was c in him
Dan 5:10 nor let thy countenance be c
Dan 6:8 the writing, that it be not c
Dan 6:15 the king establisheth may be c
Dan 6:17 might not be c concerning Daniel
Dan 7:28 me, and my countenance c in me
Mic 2:4 he hath c the portion of my
Acts 28:6 they c their minds, and said that
Rom 1:23 c the glory of the uncorruptible
Rom 1:25 Who c the truth of God into a lie
1Cor 15:51 all sleep, but we shall all be c
1Cor 15:52 incorruptible, and we shall be c
2Cor 3:18 are c into the same image from
Heb 1:12 fold them up, and they shall be c

**CHANGES**
Gen 45:22 he gave each man c of raiment
2Kin 5:5 of gold, and ten c of raiment
2Kin 5:22 of silver, and two c of garments
Job 10:17 c and war are against me
Ps 55:19

**CHAPITER**
1Kin 7:16 of the one c was five cubits
1Kin 7:31 And the mouth of it within the c
2Kin 25:17 and the c upon it was brass
2Chr 3:15 the c that was on the top of each
Jer 52:22 And a c of brass was upon it

**CHAPITERS**
Ex 36:38 and he overlaid their c and their
Ex 38:17 overlaying of their c of silver
Ex 38:28 the pillars, and overlaid their c
1Kin 7:16 he made two c of molten brass, to
1Kin 7:41 the two bowls of the c that were
2Chr 4:12 the c which were on the top of
Jer 52:22 upon the c round about, all of

**CHARASHIM** *(car'-a-shim) Place founded by Joab.*
1Chr 4:14 the father of the valley of C

**CHARCHEMISH** *(car'-ke-mish)* See CARCHEMISH. *Same as Carchemish.*
2Chr 35:20 to fight against C by Euphrates

**CHARGE**
Gen 26:5 obeyed my voice, and kept my c
Gen 28:6 as he blessed him he gave him a c
Ex 6:13 gave them a c unto the children
Ex 19:21 c the people, lest they break
Lev 8:35 keep the c of the LORD, that ye
Num 1:53 the Levites shall keep the c of
Num 3:7 And they shall keep his c, and the
Num 3:25 the c of the sons of Gershon in
Num 3:28 keeping the c of the sanctuary
Num 3:31 their c shall be the ark, and the
Num 4:27 unto them in c all their burdens
Num 5:19 the priest shall c her by an oath
Num 5:21 Then the priest shall c the woman
Num 8:26 the congregation, to keep the c
Num 9:19 of Israel kept the c of the LORD
Num 9:23 they kept the c of the LORD
Num 18:3 And they shall keep thy c, and the
Num 27:19 give him a c in their sight
Num 27:23 hands upon him, and gave him a c
Num 31:30 Levites, which keep the c of the
Num 31:47 Levites, which kept the c of the
Num 31:49 men of war which are under our c
Deut 3:28 But c Joshua, and encourage him,
Deut 11:1 the LORD thy God, and keep his c
Deut 21:8 unto thy people of Israel's c
Deut 31:14 that I may give him a c
Deut 31:23 he gave Joshua the son of Nun a c
Josh 22:3 but have kept the c of the
2Sa 14:8 I will give c concerning thee
2Sa 18:5 the captains c concerning Absalom
1Kin 2:3 keep the c of the LORD thy God,
1Kin 4:28 every man according to his c
1Kin 11:28 all the c of the house of Joseph
2Kin 7:17 leaned to have the c of the gate
1Chr 9:27 because the c was upon them, and
1Chr 22:12 give thee c concerning Israel,
1Chr 23:32 the c of the tabernacle of the
2Chr 13:11 for we keep the c of the LORD our
2Chr 30:17 therefore the Levites had the c
Neh 7:2 of the palace, c over Jerusalem
Neh 10:32 to c ourselves yearly with the
Est 3:9 that have the c of the business
Est 4:8 to c her that she should go in
Job 34:13 hath given him a c over the earth
Ps 35:11 they laid to my c things that I
Ps 91:11 shall give his angels c over thee
Song 2:7 I c you, O ye daughters of
Song 3:5 I c you, O ye daughters of
Song 5:8 I c you, O daughters of Jerusalem
Song 8:4 I c you, O daughters of Jerusalem
Is 10:6 of my wrath will I give him a c
Jer 39:11 king of Babylon gave c concerning
Jer 47:7 given it a c against Ashkelon
Jer 52:25 which had the c of the men of war
Eze 9:1 Cause them that have c over the
Eze 40:45 the keepers of the c of the house
Eze 44:8 kept the c of mine holy things
Eze 44:11 having c at the gates of the
Eze 48:11 which have kept my c, which went
Zec 3:7 ways, and if thou wilt keep my c
Mt 4:6 give his angels c concerning thee
Mk 9:25 I c thee, come out of him, and
Lk 4:10 shall give his angels c over thee
Acts 7:60 Lord, lay not this sin to their c
Acts 8:27 who had the c of all her treasure
Acts 16:24 Who, having received such a c
Acts 23:29 his c worthy of death or of bonds
Rom 8:33 any thing to the c of God's elect
1Cor 9:18 the gospel of Christ without c
1Th 5:27 I c you by the Lord that this
1Ti 1:3 that thou mightest c some that
1Ti 1:18 This c I commit unto thee, son
1Ti 5:7 And these things give in c
1Ti 5:21 I c thee before God, and the Lord
1Ti 6:13 I give thee c in the sight of God
1Ti 6:17 C them that are rich in this
2Ti 4:1 I c thee therefore before God, and
2Ti 4:16 it may not be laid to their c

**CHARGEABLE**
2Sa 13:25 now go, lest we be c unto thee
Neh 5:15 before me were c unto the people
2Cor 11:9 you, and wanted, I was c to no man
1Th 2:9 we would not be c unto any of you
2Th 3:8 we might not be c to any of you

**CHARGED**
Gen 26:11 Abimelech c all his people,
Gen 28:1 c him, and said unto him, Thou
Gen 40:4 of the guard c Joseph with them
Gen 49:29 he c them, and said unto them, I
Ex 1:22 Pharaoh c all his people, saying,
Deut 1:16 I c your judges at that time,
Deut 24:5 shall he be c with any business
Deut 27:11 Moses c the people the same day,
Josh 18:8 Joshua c them that went to
Josh 22:5 the servant of the LORD c you
Ruth 2:9 have I not c the young men that
1Sa 14:27 father c the people with the oath
2Sa 11:19 c the messenger, saying, When
2Sa 18:12 in our hearing the king c thee
1Kin 2:1 he c Solomon his son, saying,
1Kin 2:43 that I have c thee with
1Kin 13:9 For so was it c me by the word of
2Kin 17:15 whom the LORD had c them, that
2Kin 17:35 c them, saying, Ye shall not fear
1Chr 22:6 c him to build an house for the
1Chr 22:13 judgments which the LORD c Moses
2Chr 19:9 he c them, saying, Thus shall ye
2Chr 36:23 he hath c me to build him an
Ezr 1:2 he hath c me to build him an
Neh 13:19 c that they should not be opened
Est 2:10 for Mordecai had c her that she
Est 2:20 as Mordecai had c her
Job 1:22 sinned not, nor c God foolishly
Job 4:18 and his angels he c with folly
Jer 32:13 I c Baruch before them, saying,
Jer 35:8 father in all that he hath c us
Mt 9:30 and Jesus straitly c them, saying,
Mt 12:16 c them that they should not make
Mt 16:20 Then c he his disciples that they
Mt 17:9 from the mountain, Jesus c them
Mk 1:43 And he straitly c him, and

Mk 3:12 he straitly c them that they
Mk 5:43 he c them straitly that no man
Mk 7:36 he c them that they should tell
Mk 7:36 but the more he c them, so much
Mk 8:15 he c them, saying, Take heed,
Mk 8:30 he c them that they should tell
Mk 9:9 he c them that they should tell
Mk 10:48 many c him that he should hold
Lk 5:14 And he c him to tell no man
Lk 8:56 but he c them that they should
Lk 9:21 And he straitly c them, and
Acts 23:22 c him, See thou tell no man that
1Th 2:11 c every one of you, as a father
1Ti 5:16 them, and let not the church be c

## CHARGER

Num 7:13 And his offering was one silver c
Num 7:19 for his offering one silver c
Num 7:25 His offering was one silver c
Num 7:31 c of the weight of an hundred
Num 7:37 His offering was one silver c
Num 7:43 c of the weight of an hundred
Num 7:49 His offering was one silver c
Num 7:55 c of the weight of an hundred
Num 7:85 Each c of silver weighing an
Mt 14:8 here John Baptist's head in a c
Mt 14:11 And his head was brought in a c
Mk 6:25 by in a c the head of John the
Mk 6:28 And brought his head in a c

## CHARGES

2Chr 8:14 and the Levites to their c
2Chr 31:16 c according to their courses
2Chr 31:17 in their c by their courses
2Chr 35:2 And he set the priests in their c
Acts 21:24 be at c with them, that they may
1Cor 9:7 a warfare any time at his own c

## CHARIOT

Gen 41:43 ride in the second c which he had
Gen 46:29 And Joseph made ready his c
Ex 14:6 And he made ready his c, and took
Ex 14:25 And took off their c wheels
Judg 4:15 Sisera lighted down off his c
Judg 5:28 Why is his c so long in coming
2Sa 8:4 and David houghed all the c horses
1Kin 7:33 was like the work of a c wheel
1Kin 10:29 a c came up and went out of Egypt
1Kin 12:18 made speed to get him up to his c
1Kin 18:44 up, say unto Ahab, Prepare thy c
1Kin 20:25 horse for horse, and c for c
1Kin 20:33 caused him to come up into the c
1Kin 22:34 he said unto the driver of his c
2Kin 2:11 there appeared a c of fire
2Kin 2:12 the c of Israel, and the horsemen
2Kin 5:9 with his horses and with his c
2Kin 5:21 down from the c to meet him
2Kin 5:26 again from his c to meet thee
2Kin 7:14 They took therefore two c horses
2Kin 9:16 So Jehu rode in a c, and went to
2Kin 9:21 And his c was made ready
2Kin 10:15 he took him up to him into the c
2Kin 13:14 the c of Israel, and the horsemen
2Kin 23:30 him in a c dead from Megiddo
1Chr 18:4 also houghed all the c horses
1Chr 28:18 pattern of the c of the cherubims
2Chr 1:14 which he placed in the c cities
2Chr 1:17 a c for six hundred shekels of
2Chr 8:6 Solomon had, and all the c cities
2Chr 9:25 whom he bestowed in the c cities
2Chr 10:18 made speed to get him up to his c
2Chr 18:33 therefore he said to his c man
2Chr 18:34 c against the Syrians until the
2Chr 35:24 therefore took him out of that c
Ps 46:9 he burneth the c in the fire
Ps 76:6 O God of Jacob, both the c
Ps 104:3 who maketh the clouds his c
Song 3:9 a c of the wood of Lebanon
Is 21:7 he saw a c with a couple of
Is 43:17 Which bringeth forth the c
Jer 51:21 thee will I break in pieces the c
Mic 1:13 bind the c to the swift beast
Zec 6:2 In the first c were red horses
Zec 9:10 I will cut off the c from Ephraim
Acts 8:28 sitting in his c read Esaias the
Acts 8:38 he commanded the c to stand still

## CHARIOTS

Gen 50:9 And there went up with him both c
Ex 14:7 And he took six hundred chosen c
Ex 14:17 and upon all his host, upon his c
Ex 15:4 Pharaoh's c and his host hath he
Ex 15:19 of Pharaoh went in with his c
Deut 11:4 unto their horses, and to their c
Deut 20:1 enemies, and seest horses, and c
Josh 11:4 with horses and c very many
Josh 17:16 land of the valley have c of iron
Josh 17:18 though they have iron c, and
Josh 24:6 pursued after your fathers with c
Judg 1:19 because they had c of iron
Judg 4:3 for he had nine hundred c of iron
Judg 4:7 of Jabin's army, with his c
Judg 4:13 gathered together all his c
Judg 5:28 Why tarry the wheels of his c
1Sa 8:11 them for himself, for his c
1Sa 13:5 with Israel, thirty thousand c
2Sa 1:6 and, lo, the c and horsemen
2Sa 8:4 David took from him a thousand c
2Sa 10:18 of seven hundred c of the Syrians
2Sa 15:1 this, that Absalom prepared him c
1Kin 1:5 and he prepared him c and horsemen,
1Kin 4:26 stalls of horses for his c
1Kin 9:19 Solomon had, and cities for his c
1Kin 9:22 his captains, and rulers of his c
1Kin 10:26 And Solomon gathered together c
1Kin 16:9 Zimri, captain of half his c
1Kin 20:1 kings with him, and horses, and c
1Kin 20:21 out, and smote the horses and c
1Kin 22:31 captains that had rule over his c
2Kin 6:14 sent he thither horses, and c
2Kin 7:6 the Syrians to hear a noise of c
2Kin 8:21 to Zair, and all the c with him
2Kin 10:2 with you, and there are with you c
2Kin 13:7 but fifty horsemen, and ten c
2Kin 18:24 and put thy trust on Egypt for c
2Kin 19:23 With the multitude of my c I am
2Kin 23:11 burned the c of the sun with fire
1Chr 18:4 David took from him a thousand c
1Chr 19:6 talents of silver to hire them c
1Chr 19:18 thousand men which fought in c
2Chr 1:14 Solomon gathered c and horsemen
2Chr 8:9 captains, and captains of his c
2Chr 9:25 thousand stalls for horses and c
2Chr 12:3 With twelve hundred c, and
2Chr 14:9 thousand, and three hundred c
2Chr 16:8 a huge host, with very many c
2Chr 18:30 of the c that were with him
2Chr 21:9 princes, and all his c with him
Ps 20:7 Some trust in c, and some in
Ps 68:17 The c of God are twenty thousand,
Song 1:9 company of horses in Pharaoh's c
Song 6:12 made me like the c of Ammi-nadib
Is 2:7 is there any end of their c
Is 22:6 bare the quiver with c of men
Is 22:7 valleys shall be full of c
Is 22:18 there the c of thy glory shall be
Is 31:1 and stay on horses, and trust in c
Is 36:9 and put thy trust on Egypt for c
Is 37:24 By the multitude of my c am I
Is 66:15 with his c like a whirlwind, to
Is 66:20 all nations upon horses, and in c
Jer 4:13 his c shall be as a whirlwind
Jer 17:25 the throne of David, riding in c
Jer 22:4 the throne of David, riding in c
Jer 46:9 and rage, ye c
Jer 47:3 horses, at the rushing of his c
Jer 50:37 their horses, and upon their c
Eze 23:24 shall come against thee with c
Eze 26:7 the north, with horses, and with c
Eze 26:10 and of the wheels, and of the c
Eze 27:20 in precious clothes for c
Eze 39:20 at my table with horses and c
Dan 11:40 him like a whirlwind, with c
Joel 2:5 Like the noise of c on the tops
Mic 5:10 of thee, and I will destroy thy c
Nah 2:3 the c shall be with flaming
Nah 2:13 and I will burn her c in the smoke
Nah 3:2 horses, and of the jumping c
Hab 3:8 horses and thy c of salvation
Hag 2:22 and I will overthrow the c
Zec 6:1 there came four c out from
Rev 9:9 of c of many horses running to
Rev 18:13 beasts, and sheep, and horses, and c

## CHARITY

1Cor 8:1 puffeth up, but c edifieth
1Cor 13:1 men and of angels, and have not c
1Cor 13:4 c vaunteth not itself, is not
1Cor 13:8 C never faileth
1Cor 13:13 And now abideth faith, hope, c
1Cor 13:13 but the greatest of these is c
1Cor 14:1 Follow after c, and desire
1Cor 16:14 all your things be done with c
Col 3:14 above all these things put on c
1Th 3:6 good tidings of your faith and c
2Th 1:3 the c of every one of you all
1Ti 1:5 is c out of a pure heart, and of a
1Ti 2:15 if they continue in faith and c
1Ti 4:12 in word, in conversation, in c
2Ti 2:22 follow righteousness, faith, c
2Ti 3:10 purpose, faith, longsuffering, c
Titus 2:2 temperate, sound in faith, in c
1Pet 4:8 have fervent c among yourselves
1Pet 5:14 ye one another with a kiss of c
2Pet 1:7 and to brotherly kindness c
3Jn 6 of thy c before the church
Jude 12 are spots in your feasts of c
Rev 2:19 I know thy works, and c, and

## CHARRAN *(car'-ran)* See HARAN. *Greek form of Haran.*

Acts 7:2 Mesopotamia, before he dwelt in C
Acts 7:4 of the Chaldaeans, and dwelt in C

## CHASE

Lev 26:7 ye shall c your enemies, and they
Lev 26:8 And five of you shall c an hundred
Lev 26:36 of a shaken leaf shall c them
Deut 32:30 How should one c a thousand
Josh 23:10 One man of you shall c a thousand
Ps 35:5 let the angel of the LORD c them

## CHASED

Deut 1:44 c you, as bees do, and destroyed
Josh 7:5 for they c them from before the
Josh 8:24 wilderness wherein they c them
Josh 10:10 c them along the way that goeth
Josh 11:8 c them unto great Zidon, and unto
Judg 9:40 And Abimelech c him, and he fled
Judg 20:43 c them, and trode them down with
Neh 13:28 therefore I c him from me
Job 18:18 darkness, and c out of the world
Job 20:8 he shall be c away as a vision of
Is 13:14 And it shall be as the c roe
Is 17:13 shall be c as the chaff of the
Lam 3:52 Mine enemies c me sore, like a

## CHASTEN

2Sa 7:14 I will c him with the rod of men,
Ps 6:1 anger, neither c me in thy hot
Ps 38:1 neither c me in thy hot
Prov 19:18 C thy son while there is hope, and
Dan 10:12 to c thyself before thy God, thy
Rev 3:19 As many as I love, I rebuke and c

## CHASTENED

Deut 21:18 and that, when they have c him
Job 33:19 He is c also with pain upon his
Ps 69:10 c my soul with fasting, that was
Ps 73:14 been plagued, and c every morning
Ps 118:18 The LORD hath c me sore
1Cor 11:32 we are c of the Lord, that we
2Cor 6:9 as c, and not killed
Heb 12:10 c us after their own pleasure

## CHASTENETH

Deut 8:5 heart, that, as a man c his son
Prov 13:24 he that loveth him c him betimes
Heb 12:6 For whom the Lord loveth he c
Heb 12:7 son is he whom the father c not

## CHASTENING

Job 5:17 not thou the c of the Almighty
Prov 3:11 despise not the c of the LORD
Is 26:16 a prayer when thy c was upon them
Heb 12:5 not thou the c of the Lord
Heb 12:7 If ye endure c, God dealeth with
Heb 12:11 Now no c for the present seemeth

## CHASTISE

Lev 26:28 will c you seven times for your
Deut 22:18 city shall take that man and c him
1Kin 12:11 but I will c you with scorpions
2Chr 10:11 but I will c you with scorpions
Hos 7:12 I will c them, as their
Hos 10:10 in my desire that I should c them
Lk 23:16 I will therefore c him, and
Lk 23:22 I will therefore c him, and let

## CHASTISED

1Kin 12:11 my father hath c you with whips
2Chr 10:11 my father c you with whips, but I
Jer 31:18 hast c me, and I was c

## CHASTISEMENT

Deut 11:2 seen the c of the LORD your God
Job 34:31 be said unto God, I have borne c
Is 53:5 the c of our peace was upon him

Jer 30:14 with the c of a cruel one, for
Heb 12:8 But if ye be without c, whereof

**CHEBAR** *(ke'-bar) A river in Mesopotamia.*
Eze 1:1 the captives by the river of C
Eze 1:3 of the Chaldeans by the river C
Eze 3:15 that dwelt by the river of C
Eze 3:23 which I saw by the river of C
Eze 10:15 that I saw by the river of C
Eze 10:20 God of Israel by the river of C
Eze 10:22 which I saw by the river of C
Eze 43:3 vision that I saw by the river C

**CHEDORLAOMER** *(ke'-dor-la'-o-mer) An Elamite king.*
Gen 14:1 C king of Elam, and Tidal king of
Gen 14:4 Twelve years they served C
Gen 14:5 And in the fourteenth year came C
Gen 14:9 With C the king of Elam, and with
Gen 14:17 return from the slaughter of C

**CHEEK**
1Kin 22:24 near, and smote Micaiah on the c
2Chr 18:23 near, and smote Micaiah upon the c
Job 16:10 me upon the c reproachfully
Ps 3:7 all mine enemies upon the c bone
Lam 3:30 He giveth his c to him that
Joel 1:6 he hath the c teeth of a great
Mic 5:1 of Israel with a rod upon the c
Mt 5:39 shall smite thee on thy right c
Lk 6:29 on the one c offer also the other

**CHEEKS**
Deut 18:3 priest the shoulder, and the two c
Song 1:10 Thy c are comely with rows of
Song 5:13 His c are as a bed of spices, as
Is 50:6 my c to them that plucked off the
Lam 1:2 night, and her tears are on her c

**CHEER**
Deut 24:5 shall c up his wife which he hath
Eccl 11:9 let thy heart c thee in the days
Mt 9:2 Son, be of good c
Mt 14:27 unto them, saying, Be of good c
Mk 6:50 and saith unto them, Be of good c
Jn 16:33 but be of good c
Acts 23:11 by him, and said, Be of good c
Acts 27:22 now I exhort you to be of good c
Acts 27:25 Wherefore, sirs, be of good c
Acts 27:36 Then were they all of good c

**CHEERFUL**
Prov 15:13 heart maketh a c countenance
Zec 8:19 joy and gladness, and c feasts
Zec 9:17 corn shall make the young men c
2Cor 9:7 for God loveth a c giver

**CHELAL** *(ke'-lal) Married a foreign wife in exile.*
Ezr 10:30 Adna, and C, Benaiah, Maaseiah,

**CHELLUH** *(kel'-loo) Married a foreign wife in exile.*
Ezr 10:35 Benaiah, Bedeiah, C,

**CHELUB** *(ke'-lub)*
*1. A descendant of Caleb.*
1Chr 4:11 C the brother of Shuah begat
*2. Father of Ezri.*
1Chr 27:26 the ground was Ezri the son of C

**CHELUBAI** *(ke-loo'-bahee) Son of Hezron.*
1Chr 2:9 Jerahmeel, and Ram, and C

**CHEMARIMS** *(kem'-a-rims) Idolatrous priests of Judah.*
Zeph 1:4 the name of the C with the

**CHEMOSH** *(ke'-mosh) A Moabite god.*
Num 21:29 thou art undone, O people of C
Judg 11:24 not thou possess that which C thy
1Kin 11:7 Solomon build an high place for C
1Kin 11:33 C the god of the Moabites, and
2Kin 23:13 for C the abomination of the
Jer 48:7 C shall go forth into captivity
Jer 48:13 And Moab shall be ashamed of C
Jer 48:46 the people of C perisheth

**CHENAANAH** *(ke-na'-a-nah)*
*1. Father of Zedekiah.*
1Kin 22:11 Zedekiah the son of C made him
1Kin 22:24 Zedekiah the son of C went near
2Chr 18:10 Zedekiah the son of C had made
2Chr 18:23 Zedekiah the son of C came near
*2. Brother of Ehud.*
1Chr 7:10 Jeush, and Benjamin, and Ehud, and C

**CHENANI** *(ken'-a-ni) A Levite helper of Ezra.*
Neh 9:4 Bunni, Sherebiah, Bani, and C

**CHENANIAH** *(ken-a-ni'-ah)* See CONONIAH.
*1. A chief Levite during David's reign.*
1Chr 15:22 And C, chief of the Levites, was
1Chr 15:27 C the master of the song with the
*2. An officer in David's army.*
1Chr 26:29 Of the Izharites, C and his sons

**CHEPHAR-HAAMMONAI** *(ke'-far-ha-am'-mo-nahee) A town in Benjamin.*
Josh 18:24 And C, and Ophni, and Gaba

**CHEPHIRAH** *(ke-fi'-rah) A Hittite village in Benjamin.*
Josh 9:17 their cities were Gibeon, and C
Josh 18:26 And Mizpeh, and C, and Mozah,
Ezr 2:25 The children of Kirjath-arim, C
Neh 7:29 The men of Kirjath-jearim, C

**CHERAN** *(ke'-ran) Son of Dishon.*
Gen 36:26 and Eshban, and Ithran, and C
1Chr 1:41 and Eshban, and Ithran, and C

**CHERETHIMS** *(ker'-e-thims)* See CHERETHITES. *A Philistine tribe.*
Eze 25:16 and I will cut off the C, and

**CHERETHITES** *(ker'-e-thites)* See CHERETHIMS.
*1. Same as Cherethims.*
1Sa 30:14 invasion upon the south of the C
Zeph 2:5 sea coast, the nation of the C
*2. Executioners and runners in David's army.*
2Sa 8:18 of Jehoiada was over both the C
2Sa 15:18 and all the C, and all the
2Sa 20:7 after him Joab's men, and the C
2Sa 20:23 son of Jehoiada was over the C
1Kin 1:38 the son of Jehoiada, and the C
1Kin 1:44 the son of Jehoiada, and the C
1Chr 18:17 son of Jehoiada was over the C

**CHERITH** *(ke'-rith) A brook in Gilead.*
1Kin 17:3 and hide thyself by the brook C
1Kin 17:5 he went and dwelt by the brook C

**CHERUB** *(ke'-rub)*
*1. A winged celestial being.*
Ex 25:19 make one c on the one end, and the
Ex 25:19 the other c on the other end
Ex 37:8 One c on the end on this side, and
2Sa 22:11 And he rode upon a c, and did fly
1Kin 6:24 cubits was the one wing of the c
2Chr 3:11 wing of the one c was five cubits
Ps 18:10 And he rode upon a c, and did fly
Eze 9:3 of Israel was gone up from the c
Eze 10:2 the wheels, even under the c
Eze 10:4 of the LORD went up from the c
Eze 10:7 one c stretched forth his hand
Eze 10:9 the cherubims, one wheel by one c
Eze 10:14 first face was the face of a c
Eze 28:14 art the anointed c that covereth
Eze 28:16 I will destroy thee, O covering c
Eze 41:18 tree was between a c and a c
*2. An exile who returned with Zerubbabel.*
Ezr 2:59 up from Tel-melah, Tel-harsa, C
Neh 7:61 from Tel-melah, Tel-haresha, C

**CHERUBIMS**
Ex 25:18 And thou shalt make two c of gold
Ex 25:20 seat shall the faces of the c be
Ex 25:22 from between the two c which are
Ex 26:1 with c of cunning work shalt thou
Ex 26:31 with c shall it be made
Ex 36:8 with c of cunning work made he
Ex 36:35 with c made he it of cunning work
Ex 37:7 And he made two c of gold, beaten
Num 7:89 testimony, from between the two c
1Sa 4:4 which dwelleth between the c
2Sa 6:2 hosts that dwelleth between the c
1Kin 6:23 he made two c of olive tree
1Kin 6:25 both the c were of one measure and
1Kin 6:35 And he carved thereon c and palm
1Kin 7:29 the ledges were lions, oxen, and c
1Kin 7:36 the borders thereof, he graved c
1Kin 8:6 even under the wings of the c
2Kin 19:15 which dwellest between the c
1Chr 13:6 LORD, that dwelleth between the c
1Chr 28:18 pattern of the chariot of the c
2Chr 3:7 and graved c on the walls
2Chr 3:10 house he made two c of image work
2Chr 3:14 fine linen, and wrought c thereon
2Chr 5:7 even under the wings of the c
Ps 80:1 thou that dwellest between the c
Ps 99:1 he sitteth between the c
Is 37:16 that dwellest between the c
Eze 10:1 c there appeared over them as it
Eze 10:6 the wheels, from between the c
Eze 10:9 behold the four wheels by the c
Eze 10:15 And the c were lifted up
Eze 10:18 of the house, and stood over the c
Eze 11:22 Then did the c lift up their
Eze 41:18 And it was made with c and palm
Eze 41:20 ground unto above the door were c
Eze 41:25 on the doors of the temple, c
Heb 9:5 over it the c of glory shadowing

**CHESALON** *(kes'-a-lon) A landmark in Judah.*
Josh 15:10 side of mount Jearim, which is C

**CHESED** *(ke'-sed) A son of Nahor.*
Gen 22:22 And C, and Hazo, and Pildash, and

**CHESIL** *(ke'-sil) A Canaanite town.*
Josh 15:30 And Eltolad, and C, and Hormah,

**CHEST**
2Kin 12:9 But Jehoiada the priest took a c
2Kin 12:10 there was much money in the c
2Chr 24:8 king's commandment they made a c
2Chr 24:10 and brought in, and cast into the c

**CHESULLOTH** *(ke-sul'-loth)* See CHISLOTH-TABOR. *A town in Issachar.*
Josh 19:18 border was toward Jezreel, and C

**CHEWETH**
Lev 11:3 c the cud, among the beasts, that
Lev 11:7 yet he c not the cud
Lev 11:26 nor c the cud, are unclean unto
Deut 14:6 c the cud among the beasts, that

**CHEZIB** *(ke'-zib)* See ACHZIB, CHOZEBA. *A Canaanite village.*
Gen 38:5 and he was at C, when she bare him

**CHIDON** *(ki'-don)* See NACHON. *Place where Uzzah died.*
1Chr 13:9 came unto the threshingfloor of C

**CHIEF**
Gen 21:22 Phichol the c captain of his host
Gen 26:26 Phichol the c captain of his army
Gen 40:2 against the c of the butlers, and
Gen 40:9 the c butler told his dream to
Gen 40:16 When the c baker saw that the
Gen 40:20 up the head of the c butler
Gen 41:9 Then spake the c butler unto
Lev 21:4 being a c man among his people,
Num 3:24 the c of the house of the father
Num 3:30 the c of the house of the father
Num 4:46 the c of Israel numbered, after
Num 25:14 a prince of a c house among the
Num 31:26 the c fathers of the congregation
Deut 1:15 So I took the c of your tribes,
Deut 33:15 for the c things of the ancient
Josh 22:14 princes, of each c house a prince
Judg 20:2 the c of all the people, even of
1Sa 14:38 hither, all the c of the people
1Sa 15:21 the c of the things which should
2Sa 5:8 of David's soul, he shall be c
2Sa 8:18 and David's sons were c rulers
2Sa 20:26 Jairite was a c ruler about David
2Sa 23:8 in the seat, c among the captains
2Sa 23:13 three of the thirty c went down
2Sa 23:18 son of Zeruiah, was c among three
1Kin 5:16 Beside the c of Solomon's
1Kin 8:1 the c of the fathers of the
1Kin 9:23 These were the c of the officers
1Kin 14:27 the hands of the c of the guard
2Kin 25:18 guard took Seraiah the c priest
1Chr 5:2 and of him came the c ruler
1Chr 5:7 was reckoned, were the c, Jeiel,
1Chr 5:12 Joel the c, and Shapham the next,
1Chr 5:15 c of the house of their fathers
1Chr 7:3 all of them c men
1Chr 7:40 men of valour, c of the princes
1Chr 8:28 by their generations, c men
1Chr 9:9 All these men were c of the
1Chr 9:17 Shallum was the c
1Chr 9:26 these Levites, the four c porters
1Chr 11:6 the Jebusites first shall be c
1Chr 11:6 Zeruiah went first up, and was c
1Chr 11:20 of Joab, he was c of the three
1Chr 12:3 The c was Ahiezer, then Joash,
1Chr 12:18 who was c of the captains, and he
1Chr 15:5 Uriel the c, and his brethren an
1Chr 16:5 Asaph the c, and next to him

| | |
|---|---|
| 1Chr 18:17 | of David were c about the king |
| 1Chr 23:8 | the c was Jehiel, and Zetham, and |
| 1Chr 24:4 | there were more c men found of |
| 1Chr 24:31 | the c of the fathers of the |
| 1Chr 26:10 | Simri the c, (for though he was |
| 1Chr 27:1 | the c fathers and captains of |
| 1Chr 29:6 | Then the c of the fathers and |
| 1Chr 29:22 | the LORD to be the c governor |
| 2Chr 1:2 | all Israel, the c of the fathers |
| 2Chr 5:2 | the c of the fathers of the |
| 2Chr 8:9 | c of his captains, and captains of |
| 2Chr 11:22 | Abijah the son of Maachah the c |
| 2Chr 12:10 | the hands of the c of the guard |
| 2Chr 17:14 | Adnah the c, and with him mighty |
| 2Chr 19:8 | of the c of the fathers of Israel |
| 2Chr 19:11 | Amariah the c priest is over you |
| 2Chr 23:2 | the c of the fathers of Israel, |
| 2Chr 24:6 | king called for Jehoiada the c |
| 2Chr 26:12 | The whole number of the c of the |
| 2Chr 26:20 | And Azariah the c priest, and all |
| 2Chr 31:10 | Azariah the c priest of the house |
| 2Chr 35:9 | c of the Levites, gave unto the |
| 2Chr 36:14 | Moreover all the c of the priests |
| Ezr 1:5 | Then rose up the c of the fathers |
| Ezr 2:68 | some of the c of the fathers, |
| Ezr 3:12 | c of the fathers, who were |
| Ezr 4:2 | to the c of the fathers, and said |
| Ezr 5:10 | the men that were the c of them |
| Ezr 7:5 | the son of Aaron the c priest |
| Ezr 7:28 | of Israel c men to go up with me |
| Ezr 8:1 | are now the c of their fathers |
| Ezr 9:2 | hath been c in this trespass |
| Ezr 10:5 | arose Ezra, and made the c priests |
| Ezr 10:16 | with certain c of the fathers, |
| Neh 7:70 | some of the c of the fathers gave |
| Neh 8:13 | the c of the fathers of all the |
| Neh 10:14 | The c of the people |
| Neh 11:3 | Now these are the c of the |
| Neh 12:7 | These were the c of the priests |
| Job 12:24 | the c of the people of the earth |
| Job 29:25 | I chose out their way, and sat c |
| Job 40:19 | He is the c of the ways of God |
| Ps 4:*t* | To the c Musician on Neginoth, A |
| Ps 88:*t* | for the sons of Korah to the c |
| Ps 105:36 | the c of all their strength |
| Ps 109:*t* | To the c Musician, A Psalm of |
| Ps 137:6 | not Jerusalem above my c joy |
| Ps 139:*t* | To the c Musician, A Psalm of |
| Ps 140:*t* | To the c Musician, A Psalm of |
| Prov 1:21 | She crieth in the c place of |
| Prov 16:28 | a whisperer separateth c friends |
| Song 4:14 | and aloes, with all the c spices |
| Is 14:9 | even all the c ones of the earth |
| Is 41:9 | thee from the c men thereof |
| Jer 13:21 | to be captains, and as c over thee |
| Jer 20:1 | who was also c governor in the |
| Jer 31:7 | shout among the c of the nations |
| Jer 49:35 | bow of Elam, the c of their might |
| Jer 52:24 | guard took Seraiah the c priest |
| Lam 1:5 | Her adversaries are the c |
| Eze 27:22 | in thy fairs with c of all spices |
| Eze 38:2 | the c prince of Meshech and Tubal, |
| Eze 39:1 | the c prince of Meshech and Tubal |
| Dan 2:48 | c of the governors over all the |
| Dan 10:13 | lo, Michael, one of the c princes |
| Dan 11:41 | the c of the children of Ammon |
| Amos 6:1 | which are named c of the nations |
| Amos 6:6 | themselves with the c ointments |
| Hab 3:19 | To the c singer on my stringed |
| Mt 2:4 | he had gathered all the c priests |
| Mt 16:21 | c priests and scribes, and be |
| Mt 20:18 | be betrayed unto the c priests |
| Mt 20:27 | And whosoever will be c among you |
| Mt 21:15 | And when the c priests and scribes |
| Mt 21:23 | the c priests and the elders of |
| Mt 21:45 | And when the c priests and |
| Mt 23:6 | the c seats in the synagogues, |
| Mt 26:3 | assembled together the c priests |
| Mt 26:14 | Iscariot, went unto the c priests |
| Mt 26:47 | and staves, from the c priests |
| Mt 26:59 | Now the c priests, and elders, and |
| Mt 27:1 | was come, all the c priests |
| Mt 27:3 | pieces of silver to the c priests |
| Mt 27:6 | the c priests took the silver |
| Mt 27:12 | he was accused of the c priests |
| Mt 27:20 | But the c priests and elders |
| Mt 27:41 | Likewise also the c priests |
| Mt 27:62 | the c priests and Pharisees came |
| Mt 28:11 | shewed unto the c priests all the |
| Mk 6:21 | captains, and c estates of Galilee |
| Mk 8:31 | of the c priests, and scribes, and |
| Mk 10:33 | be delivered unto the c priests |
| Mk 11:18 | c priests heard it, and sought how |
| Mk 11:27 | there come to him the c priests |
| Mk 12:39 | the c seats in the synagogues, and |
| Mk 14:1 | the c priests and the scribes |
| Mk 14:10 | twelve, went unto the c priests |
| Mk 14:43 | and staves, from the c priest |
| Mk 14:53 | were assembled all the c priests |
| Mk 14:55 | the c priests and all the council |
| Mk 15:1 | the c priests held a consultation |
| Mk 15:3 | the c priests accused him of many |
| Mk 15:10 | For he knew that the c priests |
| Mk 15:11 | But the c priests moved the |
| Mk 15:31 | Likewise also the c priests |
| Lk 9:22 | c priests and scribes, and be slain |
| Lk 11:15 | Beelzebub the c of the devils |
| Lk 14:1 | into the house of one of the c |
| Lk 14:7 | how they chose out the c rooms |
| Lk 19:2 | which was the c among the |
| Lk 19:47 | But the c priests and the scribes |
| Lk 20:1 | the c priests and the scribes came |
| Lk 20:19 | the c priests and the scribes the |
| Lk 20:46 | and the c rooms at feasts |
| Lk 22:2 | the c priests and scribes sought |
| Lk 22:4 | and communed with the c priests |
| Lk 22:26 | and he that is c, as he that doth |
| Lk 22:52 | Jesus said unto the c priests |
| Lk 22:66 | the c priests and the scribes came |
| Lk 23:4 | Then said Pilate to the c priests |
| Lk 23:10 | the c priests and scribes stood and |
| Lk 23:13 | had called together the c priests |
| Lk 23:23 | of the c priests prevailed |
| Lk 24:20 | And how the c priests and our |
| Jn 7:32 | the c priests sent officers to |
| Jn 7:45 | the officers to the c priests |
| Jn 11:47 | Then gathered the c priests |
| Jn 11:57 | Now both the c priests and the |
| Jn 12:10 | But the c priests consulted that |
| Jn 12:42 | Nevertheless among the c rulers |
| Jn 18:3 | and officers from the c priests |
| Jn 18:35 | the c priests have delivered thee |
| Jn 19:6 | When the c priests therefore and |
| Jn 19:15 | The c priests answered, We have |
| Jn 19:21 | Then said the c priests of the |
| Acts 4:23 | reported all that the c priests |
| Acts 5:24 | the c priests heard these things, |
| Acts 9:14 | c priests to bind all that call |
| Acts 9:21 | them bound unto the c priests |
| Acts 13:50 | the c men of the city, and raised |
| Acts 14:12 | because he was the c speaker |
| Acts 15:22 | Silas, c men among the brethren |
| Acts 16:12 | which is the c city of that part |
| Acts 17:4 | and of the c women not a few |
| Acts 18:8 | the c ruler of the synagogue, |
| Acts 18:17 | the c ruler of the synagogue, and |
| Acts 19:14 | c of the priests, which did so |
| Acts 19:31 | And certain of the c of Asia |
| Acts 21:31 | unto the c captain of the band |
| Acts 21:37 | he said unto the c captain |
| Acts 22:24 | The c captain commanded him to be |
| Acts 23:10 | the c captain, fearing lest Paul |
| Acts 23:14 | And they came to the c priests |
| Acts 24:7 | But the c captain Lysias came |
| Acts 24:22 | When Lysias the c captain shall |
| Acts 25:2 | the c of the Jews informed him |
| Acts 25:15 | the c priests and the elders of |
| Acts 25:23 | of hearing, with the c captains |
| Acts 26:10 | authority from the c priests |
| Acts 26:12 | and commission from the c priests |
| Acts 28:7 | of the c man of the island |
| Acts 28:17 | called the c of the Jews together |
| Eph 2:20 | himself being the c corner stone |
| 1Ti 1:15 | of whom I am c |
| 1Pet 2:6 | I lay in Sion a c corner stone |
| 1Pet 5:4 | when the c Shepherd shall appear, |
| Rev 6:15 | the c captains, and the mighty men |

## CHIEFEST

| | |
|---|---|
| 1Sa 2:29 | c of all the offerings of Israel |
| 1Sa 9:22 | made them sit in the c place |
| 1Sa 21:7 | the c of the herdmen that |
| 2Chr 32:33 | they buried him in the c of the |
| Song 5:10 | ruddy, the c among ten thousand |
| Mk 10:44 | And whosoever of you will be the c |
| 2Cor 11:5 | a whit behind the very c apostles |
| 2Cor 12:11 | am I behind the very c apostles |
| 1Ti s | the c city of Phrygia Pacatiana |

## CHILD

| | |
|---|---|
| Gen 11:30 | she had no c |
| Gen 16:11 | unto her, Behold, thou art with c |
| Gen 17:10 | Every man c among you shall be |
| Gen 17:12 | every man c in your generations, |
| Gen 17:14 | the uncircumcised man c whose |
| Gen 17:17 | Shall a c be born unto him that |
| Gen 18:13 | Shall I of a surety bear a c |
| Gen 19:36 | of Lot with c by their father |
| Gen 21:8 | the c grew, and was weaned |
| Gen 21:14 | it on her shoulder, and the c |
| Gen 37:30 | brethren, and said, The c is not |
| Gen 38:24 | behold, she is with c by whoredom |
| Gen 42:22 | saying, Do not sin against the c |
| Gen 44:20 | a c of his old age, a little one |
| Ex 2:2 | saw him that he was a goodly c |
| Ex 21:22 | strive, and hurt a woman with c |
| Ex 22:22 | any widow, or fatherless c |
| Lev 12:2 | conceived seed, and born a man c |
| Lev 12:5 | But if she bear a maid c, then |
| Lev 22:13 | widow, or divorced, and have no c |
| Num 11:12 | father beareth the sucking c |
| Deut 25:5 | and one of them die, and have no c |
| Judg 11:34 | and she was his only c |
| Judg 13:5 | for the c shall be a Nazarite |
| Judg 13:7 | for the c shall be a Nazarite to |
| Judg 13:12 | How shall we order the c, and how |
| Judg 13:24 | the c grew, and the LORD blessed |
| Ruth 4:16 | And Naomi took the c, and laid it |
| 1Sa 1:11 | give unto thine handmaid a man c |
| 1Sa 1:22 | not go up until the c be weaned |
| 1Sa 2:11 | the c did minister unto the LORD |
| 1Sa 2:18 | before the LORD, being a c |
| 1Sa 2:21 | the c Samuel grew before the LORD |
| 1Sa 2:26 | the c Samuel grew on, and was in |
| 1Sa 3:1 | the c Samuel ministered unto the |
| 1Sa 3:8 | that the LORD had called the c |
| 1Sa 4:19 | law, Phinehas' wife, was with c |
| 1Sa 4:21 | And she named the c I-chabod |
| 2Sa 6:23 | no c unto the day of her death |
| 2Sa 11:5 | told David, and said, I am with c |
| 2Sa 12:14 | the c also that is born unto thee |
| 2Sa 12:21 | thou didst fast and weep for the c |
| 1Kin 3:7 | and I am but a little c |
| 1Kin 3:17 | I was delivered of a c with her |
| 1Kin 3:19 | this woman's c died in the night |
| 1Kin 3:25 | said, Divide the living c in two |
| 1Kin 3:26 | O my lord, give her the living c |
| 1Kin 11:17 | Hadad being yet a little c |
| 1Kin 13:2 | a c shall be born unto the house |
| 1Kin 14:12 | into the city, the c shall die |
| 1Kin 14:17 | threshold of the door, the c died |
| 1Kin 17:21 | himself upon the c three times |
| 1Kin 17:23 | And Elijah took the c, and brought |
| 2Kin 4:14 | answered, Verily she hath no c |
| 2Kin 4:18 | when the c was grown, it fell on |
| 2Kin 4:26 | is it well with the c |
| 2Kin 4:29 | my staff upon the face of the c |
| 2Kin 4:32 | the c was dead, and laid upon his |
| 2Kin 4:34 | And he went up, and lay upon the c |
| 2Kin 4:34 | he stretched himself upon the c |
| 2Kin 4:35 | the c sneezed seven times |
| 2Kin 5:14 | like unto the flesh of a little c |
| 2Kin 8:12 | and rip up their women with c |
| 2Kin 15:16 | that were with c he ripped up |
| Job 3:3 | said, There is a man c conceived |
| Ps 131:2 | as a c that is weaned of his |
| Prov 20:11 | Even a c is known by his doings, |
| Prov 22:6 | Train up a c in the way he should |
| Prov 22:15 | is bound in the heart of a c |
| Prov 23:13 | not correction from the c |
| Prov 23:24 | a wise c shall have joy of him |
| Prov 29:15 | but a c left to himself bringeth |
| Prov 29:21 | a c shall have him become his son |
| Eccl 4:8 | he hath neither c nor brother |
| Eccl 4:13 | a wise c than an old and foolish |
| Eccl 4:15 | with the second c that shall |
| Eccl 10:16 | O land, when thy king is a c |
| Eccl 11:5 | in the womb of her that is with c |
| Is 3:5 | the c shall behave himself |
| Is 7:16 | For before the c shall know to |
| Is 8:4 | For before the c shall have |
| Is 9:6 | For unto us a c is born, unto us |
| Is 10:19 | be few, that a c may write them |
| Is 11:6 | a little c shall lead them |
| Is 26:17 | Like as a woman with c, that |
| Is 49:15 | Can a woman forget her sucking c |
| Is 54:1 | that didst not travail with c |
| Is 65:20 | for the c shall die an hundred |
| Is 66:7 | she was delivered of a man c |

Jer 1:6 for I am a c
Jer 1:7 said unto me, Say not, I am a c
Jer 4:31 that bringeth forth her first c
Jer 20:15 A man c is born unto thee
Jer 30:6 whether a man doth travail with c
Jer 31:8 and the lame, the woman with c
Jer 31:20 is he a pleasant c
Jer 44:7 cut off from you man and woman, c
Lam 4:4 The tongue of the sucking c
Hos 11:1 When Israel was a c, then I loved
Hos 13:16 their women with c shall be
Amos 1:13 up the women with c of Gilead
Mt 1:18 found with c of the Holy Ghost
Mt 1:23 a virgin shall be with c
Mt 2:8 search diligently for the young c
Mt 2:9 stood over where the young c was
Mt 2:11 they saw the young c with Mary
Mt 2:13 Arise, and take the young c
Mt 2:14 he arose, he took the young c
Mt 2:20 Arise, and take the young c
Mt 2:21 And he arose, and took the young c
Mt 10:21 to death, and the father the c
Mt 17:18 the c was cured from that very
Mt 18:2 Jesus called a little c unto him
Mt 18:4 humble himself as this little c
Mt 18:5 little c in my name receiveth me
Mt 23:15 the c of hell than yourselves
Mt 24:19 woe unto them that are with c
Mk 9:21 And he said, Of a c
Mk 9:24 the father of the c cried out
Mk 9:36 And he took a c, and set him in the
Mk 10:15 the kingdom of God as a little c
Mk 13:17 woe to them that are with c
Lk 1:7 And they had no c, because that
Lk 1:59 day they came to circumcise the c
Lk 1:66 What manner of c shall this be
Lk 1:76 And thou, c, shalt be called the
Lk 1:80 the c grew, and waxed strong in
Lk 2:5 espoused wife, being great with c
Lk 2:17 was told them concerning this c
Lk 2:21 for the circumcising of the c
Lk 2:27 parents brought in the c Jesus
Lk 2:34 this c is set for the fall and
Lk 2:40 the c grew, and waxed strong in
Lk 2:43 the c Jesus tarried behind in
Lk 9:38 for he is mine only c
Lk 9:42 unclean spirit, and healed the c
Lk 9:47 thought of their heart, took a c
Lk 9:48 this c in my name receiveth me
Lk 18:17 c shall in no wise enter therein
Lk 21:23 woe unto them that are with c
Jn 4:49 him, Sir, come down ere my c die
Jn 16:21 soon as she is delivered of the c
Acts 4:27 a truth against thy holy c Jesus
Acts 4:30 by the name of thy holy c Jesus
Acts 7:5 him, when as yet he had no c
Acts 13:10 thou c of the devil, thou enemy
1Cor 13:11 I was a c, I spake as a c
1Cor 13:11 I understood as a c
1Cor 13:11 I thought as a c
Gal 4:1 the heir, as long as he is a c
1Th 5:3 travail upon a woman with c
2Ti 3:15 that from a c thou hast known the
Heb 11:11 was delivered of a c when she was
Heb 11:23 they saw he was a proper c
Rev 12:2 And she being with c cried
Rev 12:5 her c was caught up unto God, and
Rev 12:13 which brought forth the man c

## CHILDLESS

Gen 15:2 wilt thou give me, seeing I go c
Lev 20:20 they shall die c
1Sa 15:33 As thy sword hath made women c
Jer 22:30 the LORD, Write ye this man c
Lk 20:30 took her to wife, and he died c

## CHILDREN

Gen 3:16 sorrow thou shalt bring forth c
Gen 6:4 of men, and they bare c to them
Gen 10:21 the father of all the c of Eber
Gen 11:5 which the c of men builded
Gen 16:1 Sarai Abram's wife bare him no c
Gen 18:19 him, that he will command his c
Gen 19:38 of the c of Ammon unto this day
Gen 20:17 and they bare c
Gen 21:7 Sarah should have given c suck
Gen 22:20 she hath also born c unto thy
Gen 23:5 the c of Heth answered Abraham,
Gen 23:7 the land, even to the c of Heth
Gen 23:10 Ephron dwelt among the c of Heth
Gen 23:18 in the presence of the c of Heth
Gen 25:4 All these were the c of Keturah
Gen 25:22 the c struggled together within
Gen 30:1 saw that she bare Jacob no c
Gen 30:26 Give me my wives and my c, for
Gen 31:43 and these c are my c
Gen 32:11 me, and the mother with the c
Gen 32:32 Therefore the c of Israel eat not
Gen 33:1 And he divided the c unto Leah
Gen 33:13 knoweth that the c are tender
Gen 33:19 at the hand of the c of Hamor
Gen 36:21 the c of Seir in the land of Edom
Gen 36:31 any king over the c of Israel
Gen 37:3 loved Joseph more than all his c
Gen 42:36 them, Me have ye bereaved of my c
Gen 43:14 If I be bereaved of my c, I am
Gen 45:10 thy c, and thy children's c
Gen 45:21 And the c of Israel did so
Gen 46:8 are the names of the c of Israel
Gen 49:8 thy father's c shall bow down
Gen 49:32 is therein was from the c of Heth
Gen 50:23 Joseph saw Ephraim's c of the
Ex 1:1 are the names of the c of Israel
Ex 2:6 This is one of the Hebrews' c
Ex 2:23 the c of Israel sighed by reason
Ex 2:25 God looked upon the c of Israel
Ex 3:9 the cry of the c of Israel is
Ex 4:29 all the elders of the c of Israel
Ex 4:31 LORD had visited the c of Israel
Ex 5:14 the officers of the c of Israel
Ex 5:19 the officers of the c of Israel
Ex 6:5 the groaning of the c of Israel
Ex 7:2 that he send the c of Israel out
Ex 9:6 of the c of Israel died not one
Ex 9:26 where the c of Israel were, was
Ex 9:35 would he let the c of Israel go
Ex 10:20 would not let the c of Israel go
Ex 10:23 but all the c of Israel had light
Ex 11:7 But against any of the c of
Ex 11:10 c of Israel go out of his land
Ex 12:26 when your c shall say unto you,
Ex 12:27 of the c of Israel in Egypt
Ex 13:2 the womb among the c of Israel
Ex 14:2 Speak unto the c of Israel
Ex 14:15 speak unto the c of Israel
Ex 14:16 the c of Israel shall go on dry
Ex 14:22 the c of Israel went into the
Ex 14:29 But the c of Israel walked upon
Ex 15:1 the c of Israel this song unto
Ex 15:19 but the c of Israel went on dry
Ex 16:1 of the c of Israel came unto the
Ex 17:1 all the congregation of the c of
Ex 17:3 out of Egypt, to kill us and our c
Ex 17:7 of the chiding of the c of Israel
Ex 19:1 when the c of Israel were gone
Ex 19:3 of Jacob, and tell the c of Israel
Ex 19:6 shalt speak unto the c of Israel
Ex 20:5 fathers upon the c unto the third
Ex 20:22 shalt say unto the c of Israel
Ex 21:4 her c shall be her master's, and
Ex 22:24 be widows, and your c fatherless
Ex 24:5 sent young men of the c of Israel
Ex 24:11 upon the nobles of the c of
Ex 24:17 in the eyes of the c of Israel
Ex 25:2 Speak unto the c of Israel
Ex 25:22 commandment unto the c of Israel
Ex 27:20 shalt command the c of Israel
Ex 28:38 which the c of Israel shall
Ex 29:28 c of Israel of the sacrifice of
Ex 29:43 I will meet with the c of Israel
Ex 29:45 will dwell among the c of Israel
Ex 30:12 c of Israel after their number
Ex 31:13 thou also unto the c of Israel
Ex 32:20 made the c of Israel drink of it
Ex 32:28 the c of Levi did according to
Ex 33:5 Moses, Say unto the c of Israel
Ex 34:23 men c appear before the Lord GOD
Ex 34:30 all the c of Israel saw Moses,
Ex 35:1 of the c of Israel together
Ex 35:4 congregation of the c of Israel
Ex 35:20 the c of Israel departed from the
Ex 35:29 The c of Israel brought a willing
Ex 35:30 Moses said unto the c of Israel
Ex 36:3 which the c of Israel had brought
Ex 40:36 the c of Israel went onward in
Lev 1:2 Speak unto the c of Israel
Lev 4:2 Speak unto the c of Israel
Lev 6:18 All the males among the c of
Lev 7:23 Speak unto the c of Israel
Lev 9:3 unto the c of Israel thou shalt
Lev 10:11 that ye may teach the c of Israel
Lev 10:14 offerings of the c of Israel
Lev 15:31 the c of Israel from their
Lev 16:5 c of Israel two kids of the goats
Lev 16:16 uncleanness of the c of Israel
Lev 16:21 the iniquities of the c of Israel
Lev 16:34 c of Israel for all their sins
Lev 17:2 sons, and unto all the c of Israel
Lev 17:5 To the end that the c of Israel
Lev 17:12 I said unto the c of Israel
Lev 18:2 Speak unto the c of Israel
Lev 19:2 congregation of the c of Israel
Lev 19:18 against the c of thy people
Lev 20:2 thou shalt say to the c of Israel
Lev 21:24 sons, and unto all the c of Israel
Lev 22:2 holy things of the c of Israel
Lev 22:15 holy things of the c of Israel
Lev 22:18 sons, and unto all the c of Israel
Lev 22:32 be hallowed among the c of Israel
Lev 23:43 may know that I made the c of
Lev 24:2 Command the c of Israel, that
Lev 24:8 being taken from the c of Israel
Lev 24:10 went out among the c of Israel
Lev 24:15 shalt speak unto the c of Israel
Lev 24:23 And Moses spake to the c of Israel
Lev 25:2 Speak unto the c of Israel
Lev 25:33 possession among the c of Israel
Lev 26:22 which shall rob you of your c
Lev 26:46 the c of Israel in mount Sinai by
Lev 27:2 Speak unto the c of Israel
Lev 27:34 the c of Israel in mount Sinai
Num 1:2 congregation of the c of Israel
Num 1:45 were numbered of the c of Israel
Num 1:49 sum of them among the c of Israel
Num 1:52 the c of Israel shall pitch their
Num 2:33 numbered among the c of Israel
Num 3:4 of Sinai, and they had no c
Num 3:8 and the charge of the c of Israel
Num 5:2 Command the c of Israel, that
Num 6:23 ye shall bless the c of Israel
Num 6:27 put my name upon the c of Israel
Num 7:24 Helon, prince of the c of Zebulun
Num 8:6 from among the c of Israel
Num 8:9 of the c of Israel together
Num 8:19 an atonement for the c of Israel
Num 8:19 no plague among the c of Israel
Num 8:20 congregation of the c of Israel
Num 9:2 Let the c of Israel also keep the
Num 10:12 the c of Israel took their
Num 10:28 were the journeyings of the c of
Num 11:4 the c of Israel also wept again,
Num 13:2 which I give unto the c of Israel
Num 14:2 all the c of Israel murmured
Num 15:32 while the c of Israel were in the
Num 15:38 Speak unto the c of Israel
Num 16:2 with certain of the c of Israel
Num 16:27 and their sons, and their little c
Num 17:12 the c of Israel spake unto Moses,
Num 18:5 any more upon the c of Israel
Num 18:11 wave offerings of the c of Israel
Num 18:19 which the c of Israel offer unto
Num 19:2 Speak unto the c of Israel
Num 20:1 Then came the c of Israel
Num 20:22 the c of Israel, even the whole
Num 25:6 one of the c of Israel came and
Num 26:2 congregation of the c of Israel
Num 27:20 the c of Israel may be obedient
Num 31:18 But all the women c, that have
Num 31:54 for a memorial for the c of
Num 33:1 the journeys of the c of Israel
Num 35:2 Command the c of Israel, that
Num 36:13 by the hand of Moses unto the c
Deut 1:3 Moses spake unto the c of Israel
Deut 1:36 he hath trodden upon, and to his c
Deut 1:39 said should be a prey, and your c
Deut 3:16 is the border of the c of Ammon
Deut 3:18 your brethren the c of Israel
Deut 4:10 and that they may teach their c
Deut 4:25 beget c, and children's c
Deut 4:40 with thy c after thee, and that
Deut 5:9 fathers upon the c unto the third
Deut 5:29 them, and with their c for ever
Deut 6:7 teach them diligently unto thy c
Deut 9:2 the c of the Anakims, whom thou
Deut 10:6 the c of Israel took their
Deut 11:2 with your c which have not known
Deut 11:19 And ye shall teach them your c
Deut 14:1 Ye are the c of the LORD your God
Deut 17:20 days in his kingdom, he, and his c
Deut 21:15 hated, and they have born him c
Deut 23:8 The c that are begotten of them

Deut 24:7 his brethren of the c of Israel
Deut 24:16 not be put to death for the c
Deut 28:54 of his c which he shall leave
Deut 31:19 you, and teach it the c of Israel
Deut 31:22 day, and taught it the c of Israel
Deut 32:20 generation, c in whom is no faith
Deut 32:46 command your c to observe to do
Deut 32:49 which I give unto the c of Israel
Deut 32:51 the c of Israel at the waters of
Deut 33:1 the c of Israel before his death
Josh 2:2 the c of Israel to search out the
Josh 4:12 over armed before the c of Israel
Josh 5:2 circumcise again the c of Israel
Josh 5:10 the c of Israel encamped in
Josh 5:12 neither had the c of Israel manna
Josh 6:1 up because of the c of Israel
Josh 7:1 But the c of Israel committed a
Josh 7:12 Therefore the c of Israel could
Josh 7:23 and unto all the c of Israel
Josh 8:31 LORD commanded the c of Israel
Josh 9:17 the c of Israel journeyed, and
Josh 10:4 Joshua and with the c of Israel
Josh 10:11 c of Israel slew with the sword
Josh 11:14 the c of Israel took for a prey
Josh 12:1 which the c of Israel smote, and
Josh 13:10 unto the border of the c of Ammon
Josh 13:13 Nevertheless the c of Israel
Josh 15:63 the Jebusites dwell with the c of
Josh 21:41 of the c of Israel were forty
Josh 22:11 at the passage of the c of Israel
Josh 22:12 when the c of Israel heard of it,
Judg 3:2 of the c of Israel might know
Judg 4:3 oppressed the c of Israel
Judg 6:2 c of Israel made them the dens
Judg 8:18 one resembled the c of a king
Judg 8:28 subdued before the c of Israel
Judg 10:10 the c of Israel cried unto the
Judg 10:11 LORD said unto the c of Israel
Judg 13:1 the c of Israel did evil again in
Judg 14:16 a riddle unto the c of my people
Judg 20:15 the c of Benjamin were numbered
Judg 21:24 the c of Israel departed thence
1Sa 1:2 had c, but Hannah had no c
1Sa 2:5 that hath many c is waxed feeble
1Sa 2:28 made by fire of the c of Israel
1Sa 7:4 Then the c of Israel did put away
1Sa 7:6 Samuel judged the c of Israel in
1Sa 9:2 there was not among the c of
1Sa 10:18 And said unto the c of Israel
1Sa 10:27 But the c of Belial said, How
1Sa 11:8 the c of Israel were three
1Sa 12:12 the c of Ammon came against you
1Sa 14:18 at that time with the c of Israel
1Sa 14:47 Moab, and against the c of Ammon
1Sa 15:6 kindness to all the c of Israel
1Sa 16:11 unto Jesse, Are here all thy c
1Sa 17:53 the c of Israel returned from
1Sa 22:19 the sword, both men and women, c
1Sa 26:19 but if they be the c of men
1Sa 30:22 to every man his wife and his c
2Sa 1:18 the c of Judah the use of the bow
2Sa 2:25 the c of Benjamin gathered
2Sa 4:2 Beerothite, of the c of Benjamin
1Kin 2:4 If thy c take heed to their way,
1Kin 9:21 Their c that were left after them
1Kin 11:2 LORD said unto the c of Israel
1Kin 11:7 the abomination of the c of Ammon
1Kin 11:33 Milcom the god of the c of Ammon
1Kin 12:17 But as for the c of Israel which
1Kin 12:24 your brethren the c of Israel
1Kin 19:10 for the c of Israel have forsaken
1Kin 19:14 because the c of Israel have
1Kin 20:3 thy wives also and thy c, even the
1Kin 21:26 cast out before the c of Israel
2Kin 2:24 and tare forty and two c of them
2Kin 4:7 and live thou and thy c of the rest
2Kin 8:12 thou wilt do unto the c of Israel
2Kin 9:1 one of the c of the prophets
2Kin 10:1 to them that brought up Ahab's c
2Kin 10:5 also, and the bringers up of the c
2Kin 10:13 down to salute the c of the king
2Kin 10:13 of the king and the c of the queen
2Kin 10:30 thy c of the fourth generation
2Kin 13:5 the c of Israel dwelt in their
2Kin 14:6 But the c of the murderers he
2Kin 16:3 out from before the c of Israel
2Kin 17:7 that the c of Israel had sinned
2Kin 17:41 c, and their children's c
2Kin 18:4 for unto those days the c of
2Kin 19:3 for the c are come to the birth,
2Kin 19:12 the c of Eden which were in
2Kin 21:2 cast out before the c of Israel
2Kin 24:2 and bands of the c of Ammon
1Chr 1:43 king reigned over the c of Israel
1Chr 2:18 Hezron begat c of Azubah his wife
1Chr 2:30 but Seled died without c
1Chr 2:32 and Jether died without c
1Chr 4:27 but his brethren had not many c
1Chr 5:11 the c of Gad dwelt over against
1Chr 5:14 These are the c of Abihail the
1Chr 5:23 the c of the half tribe of
1Chr 6:3 And the c of Amram
1Chr 6:33 are they that waited with their c
1Chr 14:4 his c which he had in Jerusalem
1Chr 15:4 And David assembled the c of Aaron
1Chr 15:15 the c of the Levites bare the ark
1Chr 16:13 ye c of Jacob, his chosen ones
1Chr 17:9 neither shall the c of wickedness
1Chr 18:11 from Moab, and from the c of Ammon
1Chr 19:1 the king of the c of Ammon died
1Chr 20:4 that was of the c of the giant
1Chr 24:2 before their father, and had no c
1Chr 26:10 of the c of Merari, had sons
1Chr 27:1 Now the c of Israel after their
1Chr 27:3 Of the c of Perez was the chief
1Chr 27:20 Of the c of Ephraim, Hoshea the
1Chr 28:8 for your c after you for ever
2Chr 5:2 of the fathers of the c of Israel
2Chr 5:10 a covenant with the c of Israel
2Chr 6:11 that he made with the c of Israel
2Chr 6:16 yet so that thy c take heed to
2Chr 6:30 the hearts of the c of men
2Chr 7:3 when all the c of Israel saw how
2Chr 8:2 caused the c of Israel to dwell
2Chr 11:19 Which bare him c
2Chr 11:23 dispersed of all his c throughout
2Chr 13:7 men, the c of Belial, and have
Ezr 6:16 and the rest of the c of the
Ezr 6:19 the c of the captivity kept the
Ezr 6:20 for all the c of the captivity
Ezr 6:21 the c of Israel, which were come
Ezr 7:7 went up some of the c of Israel
Ezr 8:35 Also the c of those that had been
Ezr 9:12 an inheritance to your c for ever
Ezr 10:1 congregation of men and women and c
Ezr 10:7 unto all the c of the captivity
Ezr 10:16 the c of the captivity did so
Ezr 10:44 them had wives by whom they had c
Neh 1:6 for the c of Israel thy servants,
Neh 1:6 the sins of the c of Israel
Neh 2:10 the welfare of the c of Israel
Neh 5:5 brethren, our c as their c
Neh 8:17 had not the c of Israel done so
Neh 9:1 fourth day of this month the c of
Neh 9:23 Their c also multipliedst thou as
Neh 9:24 So the c went in and possessed the
Neh 10:39 the c of Levi shall bring the
Neh 11:3 the c of Solomon's servants
Neh 12:43 the wives also and the c rejoiced
Neh 12:47 them unto the c of Aaron
Neh 13:2 not the c of Israel with bread
Neh 13:16 the sabbath unto the c of Judah
Neh 13:24 their c spake half in the speech
Est 3:13 Jews, both young and old, little c
Est 5:11 riches, and the multitude of his c
Job 5:4 His c are far from safety, and
Job 8:4 If thy c have sinned against him,
Job 17:5 even the eyes of his c shall fail
Job 19:18 Yea, young c despised me
Job 20:10 His c shall seek to please the
Job 21:11 like a flock, and their c dance
Job 21:19 layeth up his iniquity for his c
Job 24:5 food for them and for their c
Job 27:14 If his c be multiplied, it is for
Job 29:5 with me, when my c were about me
Job 30:8 They were c of fools
Job 41:34 is a king over all the c of pride
Ps 11:4 his eyelids try, the c of men
Ps 12:1 fail from among the c of men
Ps 14:2 from heaven upon the c of men
Ps 17:14 they are full of c, and leave the
Ps 21:10 seed from among the c of men
Ps 34:11 Come, ye c, hearken unto me
Ps 36:7 therefore the c of men put their
Ps 45:2 Thou art fairer than the c of men
Ps 45:16 of thy fathers shall be thy c
Ps 53:2 from heaven upon the c of men
Ps 66:5 in his doing toward the c of men
Ps 69:8 and an alien unto my mother's c
Ps 72:4 he shall save the c of the needy
Ps 73:15 against the generation of thy c
Ps 78:4 will not hide them from their c
Ps 78:5 should make them known to their c
Ps 78:6 even the c which should be born
Ps 78:6 arise and declare them to their c
Ps 78:9 The c of Ephraim, being armed, and
Ps 82:6 all of you are c of the most High
Ps 83:8 they have holpen the c of Lot
Ps 89:30 If his c forsake my law, and walk
Ps 90:3 and sayest, Return, ye c of men
Ps 90:16 and thy glory unto their c
Ps 102:28 The c of thy servants shall
Ps 103:7 his acts unto the c of Israel
Ps 103:13 Like as a father pitieth his c
Ps 103:17 righteousness unto children's c
Ps 105:6 servant, ye c of Jacob his chosen
Ps 107:8 wonderful works to the c of men
Ps 109:9 Let his c be fatherless, and his
Ps 109:10 Let his c be continually
Ps 109:12 be any to favour his fatherless c
Ps 113:9 and to be a joyful mother of c
Ps 115:14 you more and more, you and your c
Ps 115:16 hath he given to the c of men
Ps 127:3 c are an heritage of the LORD
Ps 127:4 so are c of the youth
Ps 128:3 thy c like olive plants round
Ps 128:6 thou shalt see thy children's c
Ps 132:12 If thy c will keep my covenant and
Ps 132:12 their c shall also sit upon thy
Ps 137:7 the c of Edom in the day of
Ps 144:7 from the hand of strange c
Ps 144:11 me from the hand of strange c
Ps 147:13 he hath blessed thy c within thee
Ps 148:12 old men, and c
Ps 148:14 even of the c of Israel, a people
Ps 149:2 let the c of Zion be joyful in
Prov 4:1 Hear, ye c, the instruction of a
Prov 5:7 Hear me now therefore, O ye c
Prov 7:24 unto me now therefore, O ye c
Prov 8:32 therefore hearken unto me, O ye c
Prov 13:22 inheritance to his children's c
Prov 14:26 his c shall have a place of
Prov 15:11 then the hearts of the c of men
Prov 17:6 Children's c are the crown of old
Prov 17:6 the glory of c are their fathers
Prov 20:7 his c are blessed after him
Prov 31:28 Her c arise up, and call her
Eccl 6:3 If a man beget an hundred c
Song 1:6 my mother's c were angry with me
Is 1:2 I have nourished and brought up c
Is 1:4 evildoers, c that are corrupters
Is 2:6 themselves in the c of strangers
Is 3:4 I will give c to be their princes
Is 3:12 c are their oppressors, and women
Is 8:18 the c whom the LORD hath given me
Is 11:14 the c of Ammon shall obey them
Is 13:16 Their c also shall be dashed to
Is 13:18 their eye shall not spare c
Is 14:21 his c for the iniquity of their
Is 17:3 as the glory of the c of Israel
Is 17:9 left because of the c of Israel
Is 21:17 the mighty men of the c of Kedar
Is 23:4 I travail not, nor bring forth c
Is 27:12 one by one, O ye c of Israel
Is 29:23 But when he seeth his c, the work
Is 30:1 Woe to the rebellious c, saith
Is 30:9 is a rebellious people, lying c
Is 31:6 c of Israel have deeply revolted
Is 37:3 for the c are come to the birth,
Is 37:12 the c of Eden which were in
Is 38:19 the father to the c shall make
Is 47:8 shall I know the loss of c
Is 49:17 Thy c shall make haste
Is 49:20 The c which thou shalt have,
Is 49:21 me these, seeing I have lost my c
Is 49:25 with thee, and I will save thy c
Is 54:1 for more are the c of the
Is 54:13 all thy c shall be taught of the
Is 57:4 are ye not c of transgression, a
Is 63:8 my people, c that will not lie
Is 66:8 she brought forth her c
Is 66:20 as the c of Israel bring an
Jer 2:9 your children's c will I plead
Jer 2:16 Also the c of Noph and Tahapanes
Jer 2:30 In vain have I smitten your c
Jer 3:14 Turn, O backsliding c, saith the
Jer 3:19 How shall I put thee among the c
Jer 3:21 supplications of the c of Israel
Jer 4:22 they are sottish c, and they have
Jer 5:7 thy c have forsaken me, and sworn

Jer 6:1 O ye c of Benjamin, gather
Jer 6:11 pour it out upon the c abroad
Jer 7:18 The c gather wood, and the fathers
Jer 7:30 For the c of Judah have done evil
Jer 9:21 to cut off the c from without
Jer 9:26 the c of Ammon, and Moab, and all
Jer 10:20 my c are gone forth of me, and
Jer 15:7 I will bereave them of c, I will
Jer 17:2 Whilst their c remember their
Jer 17:19 the gate of the c of the people
Jer 18:21 deliver up their c to the famine
Jer 31:15 Rahel weeping for her c refused
Jer 32:18 the bosom of their c after them
Jer 32:30 For the c of Israel and the
Jer 32:39 of them, and of their c after them
Jer 38:23 wives and thy c to the Chaldeans
Jer 40:7 unto him men, and women, and c
Jer 41:16 of war, and the women, and the c
Jer 43:6 Even men, and women, and c, and the
Jer 47:3 their c for feebleness of hands
Jer 49:6 the captivity of the c of Ammon
Jer 49:11 Leave thy fatherless c, I will
Jer 50:4 the c of Israel shall come, they
Jer 50:33 c of Israel and the c of Judah
Lam 1:5 her c are gone into captivity
Lam 1:16 my c are desolate, because the
Lam 2:11 because the c and the sucklings
Lam 2:19 him for the life of thy young c
Lam 3:33 willingly nor grieve the c of men
Lam 4:4 the young c ask bread, and no man
Lam 4:10 women have sodden their own c
Lam 5:13 the c fell under the wood
Eze 2:3 I send thee to the c of Israel
Eze 3:11 unto the c of thy people, and
Eze 4:13 Even thus shall the c of Israel
Eze 6:5 c of Israel before their idols
Eze 9:6 and young, both maids, and little c
Eze 16:21 That thou hast slain my c
Eze 16:36 and by the blood of thy c
Eze 16:45 that lotheth her husband and her c
Eze 20:18 unto their c in the wilderness
Eze 20:21 the c rebelled against me
Eze 23:39 had slain their c to their idols
Eze 31:14 in the midst of the c of men
Eze 33:2 speak to the c of thy people, and
Eze 33:12 say unto the c of thy people, The
Eze 33:17 Yet the c of thy people say, The
Eze 33:30 the c of thy people still are
Eze 35:5 hast shed the blood of the c of
Eze 37:16 Judah, and for the c of Israel his
Eze 37:18 when the c of thy people shall
Eze 37:21 I will take the c of Israel from
Eze 37:25 therein, even they, and their c
Eze 43:7 midst of the c of Israel for ever
Eze 44:9 that is among the c of Israel
Eze 44:15 c of Israel went astray from me
Eze 47:22 which shall beget c among you
Eze 48:11 when the c of Israel went astray
Dan 1:3 bring certain of the c of Israel
Dan 1:6 these were of the c of Judah
Dan 1:10 than the c which are of your sort
Dan 1:13 the countenance of the c that eat
Dan 1:15 c which did eat the portion of
Dan 1:17 As for these four c, God gave
Dan 2:38 And wheresoever the c of men dwell
Dan 5:13 which art of the c of the
Dan 6:13 Daniel, which is of the c of the
Dan 6:24 the den of lions, them, their c
Dan 11:41 and the chief of the c of Ammon
Dan 12:1 standeth for the c of thy people
Hos 1:2 of whoredoms and c of whoredoms
Hos 1:10 Yet the number of the c of Israel
Hos 2:4 I will not have mercy upon her c
Hos 3:1 the LORD toward the c of Israel
Hos 4:1 word of the LORD, ye c of Israel
Hos 4:6 thy God, I will also forget thy c
Hos 5:7 for they have begotten strange c
Hos 9:12 Though they bring up their c
Hos 9:13 bring forth his c to the murderer
Hos 10:9 c of iniquity did not overtake
Hos 10:14 was dashed in pieces upon her c
Hos 11:10 then the c shall tremble from the
Hos 13:13 place of the breaking forth of c
Joel 1:3 Tell ye your c of it
Joel 2:16 assemble the elders, gather the c
Joel 2:23 ye c of Zion, and rejoice in the
Joel 3:6 The c also of Judah and the
Joel 3:8 into the hand of the c of Judah
Joel 3:16 the strength of the c of Israel
Joel 3:19 violence against the c of Judah
Amos 1:13 transgressions of the c of Ammon
Amos 2:11 not even thus, O ye c of Israel
Amos 3:1 O c of Israel, against the whole
Amos 3:12 so shall the c of Israel be taken
Amos 4:5 O ye c of Israel, saith the Lord
Amos 9:7 Are ye not as c of the Ethiopians
Obad 12 thou have rejoiced over the c of
Obad 20 captivity of this host of the c
Mic 1:16 and poll thee for thy delicate c
Mic 2:9 from their c have ye taken away
Mic 5:3 shall return unto the c of Israel
Nah 3:10 her young c also were dashed in
Zeph 1:8 the princes, and the king's c
Zeph 2:8 the revilings of the c of Ammon
Zec 10:7 their c shall see it, and be glad
Mal 4:6 the heart of the fathers to the c
Mal 4:6 heart of the c to their fathers
Mt 2:16 slew all the c that were in
Mt 2:18 Rachel weeping for her c
Mt 3:9 stones to raise up c unto Abraham
Mt 5:9 they shall be called the c of God
Mt 5:45 That ye may be the c of your
Mt 7:11 to give good gifts unto your c
Mt 8:12 But the c of the kingdom shall be
Mt 9:15 Can the c of the bridechamber
Mt 10:21 the c shall rise up against their
Mt 11:16 It is like unto c sitting in the
Mt 11:19 But wisdom is justified of her c
Mt 12:27 by whom do your c cast them out
Mt 13:38 seed are the c of the kingdom
Mt 14:21 thousand men, beside women and c
Mt 15:38 thousand men, beside women and c
Mt 17:25 of their own c, or of strangers
Mt 17:26 unto him, Then are the c free
Mt 18:3 converted, and become as little c
Mt 18:25 him to be sold, and his wife, and c
Mt 19:13 there brought unto him little c
Mt 19:14 But Jesus said, Suffer little c
Mt 19:29 father, or mother, or wife, or c
Mt 20:20 of Zebedee's c with her sons
Mt 21:15 the c crying in the temple, and
Mt 22:24 said, If a man die, having no c
Mt 23:31 that ye are the c of them which
Mt 23:37 I have gathered thy c together
Mt 27:9 whom they of the c of Israel did
Mt 27:25 His blood be on us, and on our c
Mt 27:56 and the mother of Zebedee's c
Mk 2:19 Can the c of the bridechamber
Mk 7:27 Let the c first be filled
Mk 9:37 receive one of such c in my name
Mk 10:13 And they brought young c to him
Mk 10:14 the little c to come unto me
Mk 10:24 again, and saith unto them, C
Mk 10:29 father, or mother, or wife, or c
Mk 10:30 and sisters, and mothers, and c
Mk 12:19 wife behind him, and leave no c
Mk 13:12 c shall rise up against their
Lk 1:16 many of the c of Israel shall he
Lk 1:17 hearts of the fathers to the c
Lk 3:8 stones to raise up c unto Abraham
Lk 5:34 them, Can ye make the c of the
Lk 6:35 ye shall be the c of the Highest
Lk 7:32 They are like unto c sitting in
Lk 7:35 wisdom is justified of all her c
Lk 11:7 shut, and my c are with me in bed
Lk 11:13 to give good gifts unto your c
Lk 13:34 I have gathered thy c together
Lk 14:26 father, and mother, and wife, and c
Lk 16:8 for the c of this world are in
Lk 18:16 Suffer little c to come unto me,
Lk 18:29 or brethren, or wife, or c
Lk 19:44 the ground, and thy c within thee
Lk 20:28 a wife, and he die without c
Lk 20:29 took a wife, and died without c
Lk 20:31 and they left no c, and died
Lk 20:34 The c of this world marry, and are
Lk 20:36 and are the c of God, being the
Lk 20:36 being the c of the resurrection
Lk 23:28 for yourselves, and for your c
Jn 4:12 drank thereof himself, and his c
Jn 8:39 unto them, If ye were Abraham's c
Jn 11:52 the c of God that were scattered
Jn 12:36 that ye may be the c of light
Jn 13:33 Little c, yet a little while I am
Jn 21:5 Then Jesus saith unto them, C
Acts 2:39 promise is unto you, and to your c
Acts 3:25 Ye are the c of the prophets, and
Acts 5:21 all the senate of the c of Israel
Acts 7:19 that they cast out their young c
Acts 7:23 his brethren the c of Israel
Acts 7:37 which said unto the c of Israel
Acts 9:15 and kings, and the c of Israel
Acts 10:36 God sent unto the c of Israel
Acts 13:26 c of the stock of Abraham, and
Acts 13:33 the same unto us their c, in that
Acts 21:5 us on our way, with wives and c
Acts 21:21 ought not to circumcise their c
Rom 8:16 spirit, that we are the c of God
Rom 8:17 And if c, then heirs
Rom 8:21 glorious liberty of the c of God
Rom 9:7 seed of Abraham, are they all c
Rom 9:8 They which are the c of the flesh
Rom 9:8 these are not the c of God
Rom 9:8 but the c of the promise are
Rom 9:11 (For the c being not yet born,
Rom 9:26 be called the c of the living God
Rom 9:27 Though the number of the c of
1Cor 7:14 else were your c unclean
1Cor 14:20 be not c in understanding
2Cor 3:7 so that the c of Israel could not
2Cor 3:13 that the c of Israel could not
2Cor 6:13 the same, (I speak as unto my c
2Cor 12:14 for the c ought not to lay up for
2Cor 12:14 but the parents for the c
Gal 3:7 the same are the c of Abraham
Gal 3:26 For ye are all the c of God by
Gal 4:3 Even so we, when we were c
Gal 4:19 My little c, of whom I travail in
Gal 4:25 is, and is in bondage with her c
Gal 4:27 c than she which hath a husband
Gal 4:28 Isaac was, are the c of promise
Gal 4:31 we are not c of the bondwoman,
Eph 1:5 us unto the adoption of c by
Eph 2:2 worketh in the c of disobedience
Eph 2:3 and were by nature the c of wrath
Eph 4:14 That we henceforth be no more c
Eph 5:1 followers of God, as dear c
Eph 5:6 of God upon the c of disobedience
Eph 5:8 walk as c of light
Eph 6:1 C, obey your parents in the Lord
Eph 6:4 provoke not your c to wrath
Col 3:6 cometh on the c of disobedience
Col 3:20 C, obey your parents in all
Col 3:21 provoke not your c to anger
1Th 2:7 even as a nurse cherisheth her c
1Th 2:11 of you, as a father doth his c
1Th 5:5 c of light, and the c of the day
1Ti 3:4 having his c in subjection with
1Ti 3:12 of one wife, ruling their c
1Ti 5:4 if any widow have c or nephews
1Ti 5:10 if she have brought up c, if she
1Ti 5:14 the younger women marry, bear c
Titus 1:6 having faithful c not accused of
Titus 2:4 their husbands, to love their c
Heb 2:13 the c which God hath given me
Heb 2:14 Forasmuch then as the c are
Heb 11:22 the departing of the c of Israel
Heb 12:5 which speaketh unto you as unto c
1Pet 1:14 As obedient c, not fashioning
2Pet 2:14 with covetous practices; cursed c
1Jn 2:1 My little c, these things write I
1Jn 2:12 I write unto you, little c
1Jn 2:18 Little c, it is the last time
1Jn 2:28 And now, little c, abide in him
1Jn 3:7 Little c, let no man deceive you
1Jn 3:10 In this the c of God are manifest
1Jn 3:10 and the c of the devil
1Jn 3:18 My little c, let us not love in
1Jn 4:4 Ye are of God, little c, and have
1Jn 5:2 we know that we love the c of God
1Jn 5:21 Little c, keep yourselves from
2Jn 1 unto the elect lady and her c
2Jn 4 I found of thy c walking in truth
2Jn 13 The c of thy elect sister greet
3Jn 4 to hear that my c walk in truth
Rev 2:14 before the c of Israel, to eat
Rev 2:23 And I will kill her c with death
Rev 7:4 all the tribes of the c of Israel
Rev 21:12 twelve tribes of the c of Israel

**CHILEAB** *(kil'-e-ab)* See DANIEL. *A son of David.*
2Sa 3:3 And his second, C, of Abigail the

**CHILION** *(kil'-e-on)* See CHILION'S. *A son of Elimelech.*
Ruth 1:2 name of his two sons Mahlon and C
Ruth 1:5 and C died also both of them

**CHILION'S** *(kil'-e-ons)*
Ruth 4:9 Elimelech's, and all that was C

**CHILMAD** *(kil'-mad) An area between Assyria and Arabia.*
Eze 27:23 merchants of Sheba, Asshur, and C

**CHIMHAM** *(kim'-ham) A servant of David.*
2Sa 19:37 But behold thy servant C
2Sa 19:38 C shall go over with me, and I
2Sa 19:40 to Gilgal, and C went on with him
Jer 41:17 and dwelt in the habitation of C

**CHINNERETH** *(kin'-ne-reth)* See CHINNEROTH, CINNEROTH, GENNESARET. *A district around the Sea of Galilee.*
Num 34:11 the side of the sea of C eastward
Deut 3:17 from C even unto the sea of the
Josh 13:27 sea of C on the other side Jordan
Josh 19:35 Zer, and Hammath, Rakkath, and C

**CHINNEROTH** *(kin'-ne-roth)* See CHINNERETH. *Same as Chinnereth.*
Josh 11:2 and of the plains south of C
Josh 12:3 plain to the sea of C on the east

**CHIOS** *(ki'-os) An island near Greece.*
Acts 20:15 came the next day over against C

**CHISLEU** *(kis'-lew) Ninth month of the Hebrew year.*
Neh 1:1 And it came to pass in the month C
Zec 7:1 day of the ninth month, even in C

**CHISLON** *(kis'-lon) Father of Elidad.*
Num 34:21 of Benjamin, Elidad the son of C

**CHISLOTH-TABOR** *(kis'-loth-ta'-bor)* See CHESULLOTH. *A city in Zebulon.*
Josh 19:12 sunrising unto the border of C

**CHITTIM** *(kit'-tim)* See KITTIM. *Descendants of Javan.*
Num 24:24 come from the coast of C
Is 23:1 from the land of C it is revealed
Is 23:12 arise, pass over to C
Jer 2:10 For pass over the isles of C
Eze 27:6 brought out of the isles of C
Dan 11:30 For the ships of C shall come

**CHIUN** *(ki'-un)* See REMPHAN. *Another name for the god Saturn.*
Amos 5:26 C your images, the star of your

**CHLOE** *(clo'-e) A Christian acquaintance of Paul.*
1Cor 1:11 them which are of the house of C

**CHOICE**
Gen 23:6 in the c of our sepulchres bury
Gen 49:11 and his ass's colt unto the c vine
Deut 12:11 all your c vows which ye vow unto
1Sa 9:2 a c young man, and a goodly
2Sa 10:9 chose of all the c men of Israel
2Kin 3:19 fenced city, and every c city
2Kin 19:23 and the c fir trees thereof
1Chr 7:40 heads of their father's house, c
1Chr 19:10 chose out of all the c of Israel
2Chr 25:5 them three hundred thousand c men
Neh 5:18 daily was one ox and six c sheep
Prov 8:10 and knowledge rather than c gold
Prov 8:19 and my revenue than c silver
Prov 10:20 tongue of the just is as c silver
Song 6:9 she is the c one of her that bare
Is 37:24 and the c fir trees thereof
Jer 22:7 they shall cut down thy c cedars
Eze 24:4 fill it with the c bones
Eze 24:5 Take the c of the flock, and burn
Eze 31:16 and all the trees of Eden, the c
Acts 15:7 while ago God made c among us

**CHOKED**
Mt 13:7 the thorns sprung up, and c them
Mk 4:7 c it, and it yielded no fruit
Mk 5:13 and were c in the sea
Lk 8:7 thorns sprang up with it, and c it
Lk 8:14 are c with cares and riches and
Lk 8:33 place into the lake, and were c

**CHOOSE**
Ex 17:9 C us out men, and go out, fight
Num 16:7 that the man whom the LORD doth c
Num 17:5 the man's rod, whom I shall c
Deut 7:7 set his love upon you, nor c you
Deut 12:5 c out of all your tribes to put
Deut 12:11 c to cause his name to dwell
Deut 12:14 LORD shall c in one of thy tribes
Deut 12:18 which the LORD thy God shall c
Deut 12:26 the place which the LORD shall c
Deut 14:23 shall c to place his name there
Deut 14:24 God shall c to set his name there
Deut 14:25 which the LORD thy God shall c
Deut 15:20 the place which the LORD shall c
Deut 16:2 shall c to place his name there
Deut 16:6 God shall c to place his name in
Deut 16:7 which the LORD thy God shall c
Deut 16:15 the place which the LORD shall c
Deut 16:16 God in the place which he shall c
Deut 17:8 which the LORD thy God shall c
Deut 17:10 the LORD shall c shall shew thee
Deut 17:15 whom the LORD thy God shall c
Deut 18:6 the place which the LORD shall c
Deut 23:16 he shall c in one of thy gates
Deut 26:2 shall c to place his name there
Deut 30:19 therefore c life, that both thou
Deut 31:11 God in the place which he shall c
Josh 9:27 in the place which he should c
Josh 24:15 c you this day whom ye will serve
1Sa 2:28 did I c him out of all the tribes
1Sa 17:8 c you a man for you, and let him
2Sa 16:18 and all the men of Israel, c
2Sa 17:1 Let me now c out twelve thousand
2Sa 21:6 of Saul, whom the LORD did c
2Sa 24:12 c thee one of them, that I may do
1Kin 14:21 the city which the LORD did c out
1Kin 18:23 let them c one bullock for
1Kin 18:25 C you one bullock for yourselves,
1Chr 21:10 c thee one of them, that I may do
1Chr 21:11 him, Thus saith the LORD, C thee
Neh 9:7 LORD the God, who didst c Abram
Job 9:14 c out my words to reason with him
Job 34:4 Let us c to us judgment
Job 34:33 thou refuse, or whether thou c
Ps 25:12 teach in the way that he shall c
Ps 47:4 He shall c our inheritance for us
Prov 1:29 did not c the fear of the LORD
Prov 3:31 oppressor, and c none of his ways
Is 7:15 to refuse the evil, and c the good
Is 7:16 c the good, the land that thou
Is 14:1 on Jacob, and will yet c Israel
Is 49:7 One of Israel, and he shall c thee
Is 56:4 c the things that please me, and
Is 65:12 did c that wherein I delighted
Is 66:4 I also will c their delusions, and
Eze 21:19 c thou a place, c it at the
Eze 21:19 c it at the head of the way to
Zec 1:17 Zion, and shall yet c Jerusalem
Zec 2:12 land, and shall c Jerusalem again
Phil 1:22 yet what I shall c I wot not

**CHOR-ASHAN** *(cor-a'-shan) A town in Judah.*
1Sa 30:30 and to them which were in C

**CHORAZIN** *(co-ra'-zin) A city near Capernaum.*
Mt 11:21 Woe unto thee, C
Lk 10:13 Woe unto thee, C

**CHOSE**
Gen 6:2 them wives of all which they c
Gen 13:11 Then Lot c him all the plain of
Ex 18:25 Moses c able men out of all
Deut 4:37 therefore he c their seed after
Deut 10:15 he c their seed after them, even
Josh 8:3 Joshua c out thirty thousand
Judg 5:8 They c new gods
1Sa 13:2 Saul c him three thousand men of
1Sa 17:40 c him five smooth stones out of
2Sa 6:21 which c me before thy father, and
2Sa 10:9 he c of all the choice men of
1Kin 8:16 I c no city out of all the tribes
1Kin 8:16 but I c David to be over my
1Kin 11:34 David my servant's sake, whom I c
1Chr 19:10 he c out of all the choice of
1Chr 28:4 c me before all the house of my
2Chr 6:5 out of the land of Egypt I c no
2Chr 6:5 neither c I any man to be a ruler
Job 29:25 I c out their way, and sat chief,
Ps 78:67 c not the tribe of Ephraim
Ps 78:68 But c the tribe of Judah, the
Ps 78:70 He c David also his servant, and
Is 66:4 c that in which I delighted not
Eze 20:5 In the day when I c Israel
Lk 6:13 and of them he c twelve, whom also
Lk 14:7 how they c out the chief rooms
Acts 6:5 they c Stephen, a man full of
Acts 13:17 people of Israel c our fathers
Acts 15:40 Paul c Silas, and departed, being

**CHOSEN**
Ex 14:7 And he took six hundred c chariots
Ex 15:4 his c captains also are drowned
Num 16:5 even him whom he hath c will he
Deut 7:6 the LORD thy God hath c thee to
Deut 12:21 which the LORD thy God hath c to
Deut 14:2 the LORD hath c thee to be a
Deut 16:11 hath c to place his name there
Deut 18:5 hath c him out of all thy tribes
Deut 21:5 God hath c to minister unto him
Josh 24:22 that ye have c you the LORD
Judg 10:14 cry unto the gods which ye have c
Judg 20:15 were numbered seven hundred c men
Judg 20:16 seven hundred c men lefthanded
Judg 20:34 thousand c men out of all Israel
1Sa 8:18 king which ye shall have c you
1Sa 10:24 See ye him whom the LORD hath c
1Sa 12:13 behold the king whom ye have c
1Sa 16:8 Neither hath the LORD c this
1Sa 16:9 Neither hath the LORD c this
1Sa 16:10 Jesse, The LORD hath not c these
1Sa 20:30 do not I know that thou hast c
1Sa 24:2 thousand c men out of all Israel
1Sa 26:2 having three thousand c men of
2Sa 6:1 together all the c men of Israel
1Kin 3:8 of thy people which thou hast c
1Kin 8:44 toward the city which thou hast c
1Kin 8:48 the city which thou hast c
1Kin 11:13 Jerusalem's sake which I have c
1Kin 11:32 the city which I have c out of
1Kin 11:36 the city which I have c me to put
1Kin 12:21 and fourscore thousand c men
2Kin 21:7 which I have c out of all tribes
2Kin 23:27 city Jerusalem which I have c
1Chr 9:22 All these which were c to be
1Chr 15:2 for them hath the LORD c to carry
1Chr 16:13 ye children of Jacob, his c ones
1Chr 16:41 Jeduthun, and the rest that were c
1Chr 28:4 for he hath c Judah to be the
1Chr 28:5 he hath c Solomon my son to sit
1Chr 28:6 for I have c him to be my son, and
1Chr 28:10 for the LORD hath c thee to build
1Chr 29:1 my son, whom alone God hath c
2Chr 6:6 But I have c Jerusalem, that my
2Chr 6:6 have c David to be over my people
2Chr 6:34 this city which thou hast c
2Chr 6:38 toward the city which thou hast c
2Chr 7:12 have c this place to myself for
2Chr 7:16 For now have I c and sanctified
2Chr 11:1 and fourscore thousand c men
2Chr 12:13 the city which the LORD had c out
2Chr 13:3 even four hundred thousand c men
2Chr 13:3 with eight hundred thousand c men
2Chr 13:17 five hundred thousand c men
2Chr 29:11 for the LORD hath c you to stand
2Chr 33:7 which I have c before all the
Neh 1:9 I have c to set my name there
Job 36:21 for this hast thou c rather than
Ps 33:12 he hath c for his own inheritance
Ps 78:31 and smote down the c men of Israel
Ps 89:3 I have made a covenant with my c
Ps 89:19 exalted one c out of the people
Ps 105:6 ye children of Jacob his c
Ps 105:26 and Aaron whom he had c
Ps 105:43 with joy, and his c with gladness
Ps 106:5 That I may see the good of thy c
Ps 106:23 had not Moses his c stood before
Ps 119:30 I have c the way of truth
Ps 119:173 for I have c thy precepts
Ps 132:13 For the LORD hath c Zion
Ps 135:4 For the LORD hath c Jacob unto
Prov 16:16 rather to be c than silver
Prov 22:1 rather to be c than great riches
Is 1:29 for the gardens that ye have c
Is 41:8 my servant, Jacob whom I have c
Is 41:9 I have c thee, and not cast thee
Is 43:10 LORD, and my servant whom I have c
Is 43:20 to give drink to my people, my c
Is 44:1 and Israel, whom I have c
Is 44:2 and thou, Jesurun, whom I have c
Is 48:10 I have c thee in the furnace of
Is 58:5 Is it such a fast that I have c
Is 58:6 not this the fast that I have c
Is 65:15 your name for a curse unto my c
Is 66:3 they have c their own ways, and
Jer 8:3 death shall be c rather than life
Jer 33:24 families which the LORD hath c
Jer 48:15 his c young men are gone down to
Jer 49:19 and who is a c man, that I may
Jer 50:44 and who is a c man, that I may
Eze 23:7 that were the c men of Assyria
Dan 11:15 withstand, neither his c people
Hag 2:23 for I have c thee, saith the LORD

Zec 3:2 that hath c Jerusalem rebuke thee
Mt 12:18 Behold my servant, whom I have c
Mt 20:16 for many be called, but few c
Mt 22:14 many are called, but few are c
Mk 13:20 the elect's sake, whom he hath c
Lk 10:42 Mary hath c that good part, which
Lk 23:35 if he be Christ, the c of God
Jn 6:70 them, Have not I c you twelve
Jn 13:18 I know whom I have c
Jn 15:16 not c me, but I have c you
Jn 15:19 but I have c you out of the world
Acts 1:2 unto the apostles whom he had c
Acts 1:24 whether of these two thou hast c
Acts 9:15 for he is a c vessel unto me, to
Acts 10:41 unto witnesses c before of God
Acts 15:22 to send c men of their own
Acts 15:25 to send c men unto you with our
Acts 22:14 God of our fathers hath c thee
Rom 16:13 Salute Rufus c in the Lord
1Cor 1:27 But God hath c the foolish things
1Cor 1:27 God hath c the weak things of the
1Cor 1:28 which are despised, hath God c
2Cor 8:19 but who was also c of the
Eph 1:4 According as he hath c us in him
2Th 2:13 c you to salvation through
2Ti 2:4 who hath c him to be a soldier
Jas 2:5 Hath not God c the poor of this
1Pet 2:4 but c of God, and precious,
1Pet 2:9 But ye are a c generation
Rev 17:14 are with him are called, and c

**CHOZEBA** *(ko-ze'-bah)* See CHEZIB. *A city in Judah.*
1Chr 4:22 And Jokim, and the men of C

**CHRIST** *(krist)* See ANTICHRIST, CHRISTIAN, CHRIST'S, CHRISTS, JESUS, MESSIAH. *A title of Jesus of Nazareth; Greek for Messiah.*
Mt 1:1 book of the generation of Jesus C
Mt 1:16 was born Jesus, who is called C
Mt 1:17 unto C are fourteen generations
Mt 1:18 birth of Jesus C was on this wise
Mt 2:4 of them where C should be born
Mt 11:2 in the prison the works of C
Mt 16:16 answered and said, Thou art the C
Mt 16:20 no man that he was Jesus the C
Mt 22:42 Saying, What think ye of C
Mt 23:8 for one is your Master, even C
Mt 23:10 for one is your Master, even C
Mt 24:5 come in my name, saying, I am C
Mt 24:23 shall say unto you, Lo, here is C
Mt 26:63 tell us whether thou be the C
Mt 26:68 Saying, Prophesy unto us, thou C
Mt 27:17 or Jesus which is called C
Mt 27:22 then with Jesus which is called C
Mk 1:1 of the gospel of Jesus C, the Son
Mk 8:29 and saith unto him, Thou art the C
Mk 9:41 my name, because ye belong to C
Mk 12:35 that C is the son of David
Mk 13:6 come in my name, saying, I am C
Mk 13:21 shall say to you, Lo, here is C
Mk 14:61 and said unto him, Art thou the C
Mk 15:32 Let C the King of Israel descend
Lk 2:11 a Saviour, which is C the Lord
Lk 2:26 before he had seen the Lord's C
Lk 3:15 of John, whether he were the C
Lk 4:41 Thou art C the Son of God
Lk 4:41 for they knew that he was C
Lk 9:20 answering said, The C of God
Lk 20:41 say they that C is David's son
Lk 21:8 come in my name, saying, I am C
Lk 22:67 Art thou the C
Lk 23:2 that he himself is C a King
Lk 23:35 let him save himself, if he be C
Lk 23:39 on him, saying, If thou be C
Lk 24:26 Ought not C to have suffered
Lk 24:46 and thus it behoved C to suffer
Jn 1:17 grace and truth came by Jesus C
Jn 1:20 but confessed, I am not the C
Jn 1:25 thou then, if thou be not that C
Jn 1:41 is, being interpreted, the C
Jn 3:28 that I said, I am not the C
Jn 4:25 Messias cometh, which is called C
Jn 4:29 is not this the C
Jn 4:42 and know that this is indeed the C
Jn 6:69 and are sure that thou art that C
Jn 7:26 indeed that this is the very C
Jn 7:27 but when C cometh, no man knoweth
Jn 7:31 When C cometh, will he do more
Jn 7:41 Others said, This is the C
Jn 7:41 Shall C come out of Galilee
Jn 7:42 That C cometh of the seed of
Jn 9:22 any man did confess that he was C
Jn 10:24 If thou be the C, tell us plainly
Jn 11:27 I believe that thou art the C
Jn 12:34 the law that C abideth for ever
Jn 17:3 the only true God, and Jesus C
Jn 20:31 might believe that Jesus is the C
Acts 2:30 he would raise up C to sit on his
Acts 2:31 spake of the resurrection of C
Acts 2:36 ye have crucified, both Lord and C
Acts 2:38 Jesus C for the remission of sins
Acts 3:6 of Jesus C of Nazareth rise up
Acts 3:18 that C should suffer, he hath so
Acts 3:20 And he shall send Jesus C, which
Acts 4:10 the name of Jesus C of Nazareth
Acts 4:26 the Lord, and against his C
Acts 5:42 not to teach and preach Jesus C
Acts 8:5 Samaria, and preached C unto them
Acts 8:12 of God, and the name of Jesus C
Acts 8:37 that Jesus C is the Son of God
Acts 9:20 he preached C in the synagogues
Acts 9:22 proving that this is very C
Acts 9:34 Jesus C maketh thee whole
Acts 10:36 preaching peace by Jesus C
Acts 11:17 who believed on the Lord Jesus C
Acts 15:11 Lord Jesus C we shall be saved
Acts 15:26 for the name of our Lord Jesus C
Acts 16:18 of Jesus C to come out of her
Acts 16:31 said, Believe on the Lord Jesus C
Acts 17:3 that C must needs have suffered,
Acts 17:3 whom I preach unto you, is C
Acts 18:5 to the Jews that Jesus was C
Acts 18:28 the scriptures that Jesus was C
Acts 19:4 after him, that is, on C Jesus
Acts 20:21 and faith toward our Lord Jesus C
Acts 24:24 him concerning the faith in C
Acts 26:23 That C should suffer, and that he
Acts 28:31 which concern the Lord Jesus C
Rom 1:1 Paul, a servant of Jesus C
Rom 1:3 his Son Jesus C our Lord, which
Rom 1:6 are ye also the called of Jesus C
Rom 1:7 our Father, and the Lord Jesus C
Rom 1:8 God through Jesus C for you all
Rom 1:16 am not ashamed of the gospel of C
Rom 2:16 by Jesus C according to my gospel
Rom 3:22 is by faith of Jesus C unto all
Rom 3:24 the redemption that is in C Jesus
Rom 5:1 with God through our Lord Jesus C
Rom 5:6 in due time C died for the
Rom 5:8 were yet sinners, C died for us
Rom 5:11 in God through our Lord Jesus C
Rom 5:15 which is by one man, Jesus C
Rom 5:17 reign in life by one, Jesus C
Rom 5:21 eternal life by Jesus C our Lord
Rom 6:3 C were baptized into his death
Rom 6:4 that like as C was raised up from
Rom 6:8 Now if we be dead with C, we
Rom 6:9 Knowing that C being raised from
Rom 6:11 unto God through Jesus C our Lord
Rom 6:23 life through Jesus C our Lord
Rom 7:4 dead to the law by the body of C
Rom 7:25 God through Jesus C our Lord
Rom 8:1 to them which are in C Jesus
Rom 8:2 in C Jesus hath made me free from
Rom 8:9 any man have not the Spirit of C
Rom 8:10 if C be in you, the body is dead
Rom 8:11 he that raised up C from the dead
Rom 8:17 of God, and joint-heirs with C
Rom 8:34 It is C that died, yea rather,
Rom 8:35 separate us from the love of C
Rom 8:39 which is in C Jesus our Lord
Rom 9:1 I say the truth in C, I lie not,
Rom 9:3 accursed from C for my brethren
Rom 9:5 as concerning the flesh C came
Rom 10:4 For C is the end of the law for
Rom 10:6 to bring C down from above
Rom 10:7 to bring up C again from the dead
Rom 12:5 we, being many, are one body in C
Rom 13:14 But put ye on the Lord Jesus C
Rom 14:9 For to this end C both died
Rom 14:10 before the judgment seat of C
Rom 14:15 with thy meat, for whom C died
Rom 14:18 serveth C is acceptable to God
Rom 15:3 For even C pleased not himself
Rom 15:5 another according to C Jesus
Rom 15:6 the Father of our Lord Jesus C
Rom 15:7 as C also received us to the
Rom 15:8 Now I say that Jesus C was a
Rom 15:16 of Jesus C to the Gentiles
Rom 15:17 I may glory through Jesus C in
Rom 15:18 which C hath not wrought by me
Rom 15:19 fully preached the gospel of C
Rom 15:20 the gospel, not where C was named
Rom 15:29 the blessing of the gospel of C
Rom 16:3 and Aquila my helpers in C Jesus
Rom 16:5 the firstfruits of Achaia unto C
Rom 16:7 who also were in C before me
Rom 16:9 Salute Urbane, our helper in C
Rom 16:10 Salute Apelles approved in C
Rom 16:16 The churches of C salute you
Rom 16:18 such serve not our Lord Jesus C
Rom 16:20 of our Lord Jesus C be with you
Rom 16:24 our Lord Jesus C be with you all
Rom 16:25 and the preaching of Jesus C
Rom 16:27 be glory through Jesus C for ever
1Cor 1:1 Jesus C through the will of God
1Cor 1:2 that are sanctified in C Jesus
1Cor 1:2 upon the name of Jesus C our Lord
1Cor 1:3 Father, and from the Lord Jesus C
1Cor 1:4 God which is given you by Jesus C
1Cor 1:6 of C was confirmed in you
1Cor 1:7 the coming of our Lord Jesus C
1Cor 1:8 in the day of our Lord Jesus C
1Cor 1:9 of his Son Jesus C our Lord
1Cor 1:10 by the name of our Lord Jesus C
1Cor 1:12 and I of C
1Cor 1:13 Is C divided?
1Cor 1:17 For C sent me not to baptize, but
1Cor 1:17 lest the cross of C should be
1Cor 1:23 But we preach C crucified
1Cor 1:24 C the power of God, and the wisdom
1Cor 1:30 But of him are ye in C Jesus
1Cor 2:2 any thing among you, save Jesus C
1Cor 2:16 But we have the mind of C
1Cor 3:1 carnal, even as unto babes in C
1Cor 3:11 that is laid, which is Jesus C
1Cor 3:23 and C is God's
1Cor 4:1 of us, as of the ministers of C
1Cor 4:10 sake, but ye are wise in C
1Cor 4:15 ten thousand instructers in C
1Cor 4:15 for in C Jesus I have begotten
1Cor 4:17 of my ways which be in C, as I
1Cor 5:4 In the name of our Lord Jesus C
1Cor 5:4 the power of our Lord Jesus C
1Cor 5:7 For even C our passover is
1Cor 6:15 your bodies are the members of C
1Cor 6:15 I then take the members of C
1Cor 8:6 and one Lord Jesus C, by whom are
1Cor 8:11 brother perish, for whom C died
1Cor 8:12 weak conscience, ye sin against C
1Cor 9:1 have I not seen Jesus C our Lord
1Cor 9:12 we should hinder the gospel of C
1Cor 9:18 the gospel of C without charge
1Cor 9:21 to God, but under the law to C
1Cor 10:4 and that Rock was C
1Cor 10:9 Neither let us tempt C, as some
1Cor 10:16 the communion of the blood of C
1Cor 10:16 the communion of the body of C
1Cor 11:1 of me, even as I also am of C
1Cor 11:3 that the head of every man is C
1Cor 11:3 and the head of C is God
1Cor 12:12 so also is C
1Cor 12:27 Now ye are the body of C, and
1Cor 15:3 how that C died for our sins
1Cor 15:12 Now if C be preached that he rose
1Cor 15:13 of the dead, then is C not risen
1Cor 15:14 if C be not risen, then is our
1Cor 15:15 of God that he raised up C
1Cor 15:16 rise not, then is not C raised
1Cor 15:17 if C be not raised, your faith is
1Cor 15:18 fallen asleep in C are perished
1Cor 15:19 this life only we have hope in C
1Cor 15:20 But now is C risen from the dead,
1Cor 15:22 even so in C shall all be made
1Cor 15:23 C the firstfruits
1Cor 15:31 which I have in C Jesus our Lord
1Cor 15:57 victory through our Lord Jesus C
1Cor 16:22 any man love not the Lord Jesus C
1Cor 16:23 of our Lord Jesus C be with you
1Cor 16:24 love be with you all in C Jesus
2Cor 1:1 of Jesus C by the will of God
2Cor 1:2 Father, and from the Lord Jesus C
2Cor 1:3 the Father of our Lord Jesus C
2Cor 1:5 the sufferings of C abound in us
2Cor 1:5 consolation also aboundeth by C
2Cor 1:19 For the Son of God, Jesus C
2Cor 1:21 stablisheth us with you in C
2Cor 2:10 forgave I it in the person of C
2Cor 2:14 always causeth us to triumph in C

| | |
|---|---|
| 2Cor 2:15 | are unto God a sweet savour of C |
| 2Cor 2:17 | in the sight of God speak we in C |
| 2Cor 3:3 | the epistle of C ministered by us |
| 2Cor 3:4 | have we through C to God-ward |
| 2Cor 3:14 | which vail is done away in C |
| 2Cor 4:4 | light of the glorious gospel of C |
| 2Cor 4:5 | ourselves, but C Jesus the Lord |
| 2Cor 4:6 | of God in the face of Jesus C |
| 2Cor 5:10 | before the judgment seat of C |
| 2Cor 5:14 | For the love of C constraineth us |
| 2Cor 5:16 | we have known C after the flesh |
| 2Cor 5:17 | Therefore if any man be in C |
| 2Cor 5:18 | us to himself by Jesus C, and hath |
| 2Cor 5:19 | To wit, that God was in C |
| 2Cor 5:20 | Now then we are ambassadors for C |
| 2Cor 6:15 | what concord hath C with Belial |
| 2Cor 8:9 | the grace of our Lord Jesus C |
| 2Cor 8:23 | the churches, and the glory of C |
| 2Cor 9:13 | subjection into the gospel of C |
| 2Cor 10:1 | the meekness and gentleness of C |
| 2Cor 10:5 | thought to the obedience of C |
| 2Cor 10:14 | also in preaching the gospel of C |
| 2Cor 11:2 | you as a chaste virgin to C |
| 2Cor 11:3 | from the simplicity that is in C |
| 2Cor 11:10 | As the truth of C is in me |
| 2Cor 11:13 | themselves into the apostles of C |
| 2Cor 11:23 | Are they ministers of C |
| 2Cor 11:31 | God and Father of our Lord Jesus C |
| 2Cor 12:2 | I knew a man in C above fourteen |
| 2Cor 12:9 | the power of C may rest upon me |
| 2Cor 12:19 | we speak before God in C |
| 2Cor 13:3 | seek a proof of C speaking in me |
| 2Cor 13:5 | how that Jesus C is in you |
| 2Cor 13:14 | The grace of the Lord Jesus C |
| Gal 1:1 | neither by man, but by Jesus C |
| Gal 1:3 | Father, and from our Lord Jesus C |
| Gal 1:6 | grace of C unto another gospel |
| Gal 1:7 | and would pervert the gospel of C |
| Gal 1:10 | I should not be the servant of C |
| Gal 1:12 | but by the revelation of Jesus C |
| Gal 1:22 | of Judaea which were in C |
| Gal 2:4 | liberty which we have in C Jesus |
| Gal 2:16 | law, but by the faith of Jesus C |
| Gal 2:16 | even we have believed in Jesus C |
| Gal 2:16 | be justified by the faith of C |
| Gal 2:17 | we seek to be justified by C |
| Gal 2:17 | is therefore C the minister of |
| Gal 2:20 | I am crucified with C |
| Gal 2:20 | yet not I, but C liveth in me |
| Gal 2:21 | the law, then C is dead in vain |
| Gal 3:1 | before whose eyes Jesus C hath |
| Gal 3:13 | C hath redeemed us from the curse |
| Gal 3:14 | on the Gentiles through Jesus C |
| Gal 3:16 | one, And to thy seed, which is C |
| Gal 3:17 | was confirmed before of God in C |
| Gal 3:22 | C might be given to them that |
| Gal 3:24 | schoolmaster to bring us unto C |
| Gal 3:26 | of God by faith in C Jesus |
| Gal 3:27 | baptized into C have put on C |
| Gal 3:28 | for ye are all one in C Jesus |
| Gal 4:7 | then an heir of God through C |
| Gal 4:14 | an angel of God, even as C Jesus |
| Gal 4:19 | again until C be formed in you |
| Gal 5:1 | wherewith C hath made us free |
| Gal 5:2 | C shall profit you nothing |
| Gal 5:4 | C is become of no effect unto you |
| Gal 5:6 | For in Jesus C neither |
| Gal 6:2 | and so fulfil the law of C |
| Gal 6:12 | persecution for the cross of C |
| Gal 6:14 | in the cross of our Lord Jesus C |
| Gal 6:15 | For in C Jesus neither |
| Gal 6:18 | Lord Jesus C be with your spirit |
| Eph 1:1 | of Jesus C by the will of God |
| Eph 1:1 | and to the faithful in C Jesus |
| Eph 1:2 | Father, and from the Lord Jesus C |
| Eph 1:3 | God and Father of our Lord Jesus C |
| Eph 1:3 | blessings in heavenly places in C |
| Eph 1:5 | of children by Jesus C to himself |
| Eph 1:10 | together in one all things in C |
| Eph 1:12 | his glory, who first trusted in C |
| Eph 1:17 | That the God of our Lord Jesus C |
| Eph 1:20 | Which he wrought in C, when he |
| Eph 2:5 | hath quickened us together with C |
| Eph 2:6 | in heavenly places in C Jesus |
| Eph 2:7 | toward us through C Jesus |
| Eph 2:10 | created in C Jesus unto good |
| Eph 2:12 | at that time ye were without C |
| Eph 2:13 | But now in C Jesus ye who |
| Eph 2:13 | are made nigh by the blood of C |
| Eph 2:20 | Jesus C himself being the chief |
| Eph 3:1 | of Jesus C for you Gentiles |
| Eph 3:4 | my knowledge in the mystery of C) |
| Eph 3:6 | of his promise in C by the gospel |
| Eph 3:8 | the unsearchable riches of C |
| Eph 3:9 | who created all things by Jesus C |
| Eph 3:11 | he purposed in C Jesus our Lord |
| Eph 3:14 | the Father of our Lord Jesus C |
| Eph 3:17 | That C may dwell in your hearts |
| Eph 3:19 | And to know the love of C, which |
| Eph 3:21 | by C Jesus throughout all ages |
| Eph 4:7 | to the measure of the gift of C |
| Eph 4:12 | for the edifying of the body of C |
| Eph 4:13 | the stature of the fulness of C |
| Eph 4:15 | things, which is the head, even C |
| Eph 4:20 | But ye have not so learned C |
| Eph 5:2 | as C also hath loved us, and hath |
| Eph 5:5 | inheritance in the kingdom of C |
| Eph 5:14 | dead, and C shall give thee light |
| Eph 5:20 | in the name of our Lord Jesus C |
| Eph 5:23 | even as C is the head of the |
| Eph 5:24 | as the church is subject unto C |
| Eph 5:25 | even as C also loved the church, |
| Eph 5:32 | but I speak concerning C and the |
| Eph 6:5 | of your heart, as unto C |
| Eph 6:6 | but as the servants of C, doing |
| Eph 6:23 | the Father and the Lord Jesus C |
| Eph 6:24 | our Lord Jesus C in sincerity |
| Phil 1:1 | the servants of Jesus C, to all |
| Phil 1:1 | to all the saints in C Jesus |
| Phil 1:2 | Father, and from the Lord Jesus C |
| Phil 1:6 | it until the day of Jesus C |
| Phil 1:8 | you all in the bowels of Jesus C |
| Phil 1:10 | without offence till the day of C |
| Phil 1:11 | which are by Jesus C, unto the |
| Phil 1:13 | So that my bonds in C are |
| Phil 1:15 | Some indeed preach C even of envy |
| Phil 1:16 | The one preach C of contention |
| Phil 1:18 | or in truth, C is preached |
| Phil 1:19 | supply of the Spirit of Jesus C |
| Phil 1:20 | so now also C shall be magnified |
| Phil 1:21 | For to me to live is C, and to die |
| Phil 1:23 | desire to depart, and to be with C |
| Phil 1:26 | C for me by my coming to you |
| Phil 1:27 | be as it becometh the gospel of C |
| Phil 1:29 | it is given in the behalf of C |
| Phil 2:1 | be therefore any consolation in C |
| Phil 2:5 | in you, which was also in C Jesus |
| Phil 2:11 | confess that Jesus C is Lord |
| Phil 2:16 | I may rejoice in the day of C |
| Phil 2:30 | work of C he was nigh unto death |
| Phil 3:3 | the spirit, and rejoice in C Jesus |
| Phil 3:7 | to me, those I counted loss for C |
| Phil 3:8 | the knowledge of C Jesus my Lord |
| Phil 3:8 | them but dung, that I may win C |
| Phil 3:9 | which is through the faith of C |
| Phil 3:12 | also I am apprehended of C Jesus |
| Phil 3:14 | high calling of God in C Jesus |
| Phil 3:18 | are the enemies of the cross of C |
| Phil 3:20 | for the Saviour, the Lord Jesus C |
| Phil 4:7 | hearts and minds through C Jesus |
| Phil 4:13 | through C which strengtheneth me |
| Phil 4:19 | to his riches in glory by C Jesus |
| Phil 4:21 | Salute every saint in C Jesus |
| Phil 4:23 | our Lord Jesus C be with you all |
| Col 1:1 | of Jesus C by the will of God |
| Col 1:2 | in C which are at Colosse |
| Col 1:2 | our Father and the Lord Jesus C |
| Col 1:3 | and the Father of our Lord Jesus C |
| Col 1:4 | we heard of your faith in C Jesus |
| Col 1:7 | for you a faithful minister of C |
| Col 1:24 | C in my flesh for his body's sake |
| Col 1:27 | which is C in you, the hope of |
| Col 1:28 | every man perfect in C Jesus |
| Col 2:2 | of God, and of the Father, and of C |
| Col 2:5 | stedfastness of your faith in C |
| Col 2:6 | received C Jesus the Lord |
| Col 2:8 | of the world, and not after C |
| Col 2:11 | flesh by the circumcision of C |
| Col 2:17 | but the body is of C |
| Col 2:20 | Wherefore if ye be dead with C |
| Col 3:1 | If ye then be risen with C |
| Col 3:1 | where C sitteth on the right hand |
| Col 3:3 | and your life is hid with C in God |
| Col 3:4 | When C, who is our life, shall |
| Col 3:11 | but C is all, and in all |
| Col 3:13 | even as C forgave you, so also do |
| Col 3:16 | Let the word of C dwell in you |
| Col 3:24 | for ye serve the Lord C |
| Col 4:3 | to speak the mystery of C |
| Col 4:12 | who is one of you, a servant of C |
| 1Th 1:1 | the Father and in the Lord Jesus C |
| 1Th 1:1 | our Father, and the Lord Jesus C |
| 1Th 1:3 | of hope in our Lord Jesus C |
| 1Th 2:6 | burdensome, as the apostles of C |
| 1Th 2:14 | which in Judaea are in C Jesus |
| 1Th 2:19 | of our Lord Jesus C at his coming |
| 1Th 3:2 | fellowlabourer in the gospel of C |
| 1Th 3:11 | our Father, and our Lord Jesus C |
| 1Th 3:13 | Lord Jesus C with all his saints |
| 1Th 4:16 | the dead in C shall rise first |
| 1Th 5:9 | salvation by our Lord Jesus C |
| 1Th 5:18 | of God in C Jesus concerning you |
| 1Th 5:23 | the coming of our Lord Jesus C |
| 1Th 5:28 | of our Lord Jesus C be with you |
| 2Th 1:1 | our Father and the Lord Jesus C |
| 2Th 1:2 | our Father and the Lord Jesus C |
| 2Th 1:8 | the gospel of our Lord Jesus C |
| 2Th 1:12 | Jesus C may be glorified in you |
| 2Th 1:12 | of our God and the Lord Jesus C |
| 2Th 2:1 | by the coming of our Lord Jesus C |
| 2Th 2:2 | as that the day of C is at hand |
| 2Th 2:14 | of the glory of our Lord Jesus C |
| 2Th 2:16 | Now our Lord Jesus C himself |
| 2Th 3:5 | and into the patient waiting for C |
| 2Th 3:6 | in the name of our Lord Jesus C |
| 2Th 3:12 | and exhort by our Lord Jesus C |
| 2Th 3:18 | our Lord Jesus C be with you all |
| 1Ti 1:1 | an apostle of Jesus C by the |
| 1Ti 1:1 | God our Saviour, and Lord Jesus C |
| 1Ti 1:2 | our Father and Jesus C our Lord |
| 1Ti 1:12 | I thank C Jesus our Lord, who |
| 1Ti 1:14 | faith and love which is in C Jesus |
| 1Ti 1:15 | that C Jesus came into the world |
| 1Ti 1:16 | Jesus C might shew forth all |
| 1Ti 2:5 | God and men, the man C Jesus |
| 1Ti 2:7 | apostle, (I speak the truth in C |
| 1Ti 3:13 | in the faith which is in C Jesus |
| 1Ti 4:6 | be a good minister of Jesus C |
| 1Ti 5:11 | begun to wax wanton against C |
| 1Ti 5:21 | before God, and the Lord Jesus C |
| 1Ti 6:3 | the words of our Lord Jesus C |
| 1Ti 6:13 | all things, and before C Jesus |
| 1Ti 6:14 | the appearing of our Lord Jesus C |
| 2Ti 1:1 | of Jesus C by the will of God |
| 2Ti 1:1 | of life which is in C Jesus |
| 2Ti 1:2 | the Father and C Jesus our Lord |
| 2Ti 1:9 | which was given us in C Jesus |
| 2Ti 1:10 | appearing of our Saviour Jesus C |
| 2Ti 1:13 | faith and love which is in C Jesus |
| 2Ti 2:1 | in the grace that is in C Jesus |
| 2Ti 2:3 | as a good soldier of Jesus C |
| 2Ti 2:8 | Remember that Jesus C of the seed |
| 2Ti 2:10 | is in C Jesus with eternal glory |
| 2Ti 2:19 | name of C depart from iniquity |
| 2Ti 3:12 | all that will live godly in C |
| 2Ti 3:15 | through faith which is in C Jesus |
| 2Ti 4:1 | before God, and the Lord Jesus C |
| 2Ti 4:22 | The Lord Jesus C be with thy |
| Titus 1:1 | of God, and an apostle of Jesus C |
| Titus 1:4 | and the Lord Jesus C our Saviour |
| Titus 2:13 | great God and our Saviour Jesus C |
| Titus 3:6 | through Jesus C our Saviour |
| Philem 1 | Paul, a prisoner of Jesus C |
| Philem 3 | our Father and the Lord Jesus C |
| Philem 6 | thing which is in you in C Jesus |
| Philem 8 | in C to enjoin thee that which is |
| Philem 9 | and now also a prisoner of Jesus C |
| Philem 23 | my fellowprisoner in C Jesus |
| Philem 25 | Lord Jesus C be with your spirit |
| Heb 3:1 | Priest of our profession, C Jesus |
| Heb 3:6 | But C as a son over his own house |
| Heb 3:14 | For we are made partakers of C |
| Heb 5:5 | So also C glorified not himself |
| Heb 6:1 | principles of the doctrine of C |
| Heb 9:11 | But C being come an high priest |
| Heb 9:14 | much more shall the blood of C |
| Heb 9:24 | For C is not entered into the |
| Heb 9:28 | So C was once offered to bear the |
| Heb 10:10 | the body of Jesus C once for all |
| Heb 11:26 | of C greater riches than the |
| Heb 13:8 | Jesus C the same yesterday, and to |
| Heb 13:21 | in his sight, through Jesus C |
| Jas 1:1 | of God and of the Lord Jesus C |
| Jas 2:1 | not the faith of our Lord Jesus C |
| 1Pet 1:1 | Peter, an apostle of Jesus C |
| 1Pet 1:2 | of the blood of Jesus C |
| 1Pet 1:3 | God and Father of our Lord Jesus C |
| 1Pet 1:3 | of Jesus C from the dead, |
| 1Pet 1:7 | glory at the appearing of Jesus C |
| 1Pet 1:11 | manner of time the Spirit of C |

1Pet 1:11 beforehand the sufferings of C
1Pet 1:13 you at the revelation of Jesus C
1Pet 1:19 But with the precious blood of C
1Pet 2:5 acceptable to God by Jesus C
1Pet 2:21 because C also suffered for us,
1Pet 3:16 your good conversation in C
1Pet 3:18 For C also hath once suffered for
1Pet 3:21 by the resurrection of Jesus C
1Pet 4:1 Forasmuch then as C hath suffered
1Pet 4:11 may be glorified through Jesus C
1Pet 4:14 be reproached for the name of C
1Pet 5:1 a witness of the sufferings of C
1Pet 5:10 unto his eternal glory by C Jesus
1Pet 5:14 with you all that are in C Jesus
2Pet 1:1 servant and an apostle of Jesus C
2Pet 1:1 of God and our Saviour Jesus C
2Pet 1:8 the knowledge of our Lord Jesus C
2Pet 1:11 of our Lord and Saviour Jesus C
2Pet 1:14 our Lord Jesus C hath shewed me
2Pet 1:16 and coming of our Lord Jesus C
2Pet 2:20 of the Lord and Saviour Jesus C
2Pet 3:18 of our Lord and Saviour Jesus C
1Jn 1:3 Father, and with his Son Jesus C
1Jn 1:7 the blood of Jesus C his Son
1Jn 2:1 the Father, Jesus C the righteous
1Jn 2:22 that denieth that Jesus is the C
1Jn 3:23 on the name of his Son Jesus C
1Jn 4:2 that confesseth that Jesus C is
1Jn 4:3 C is come in the flesh is not of
1Jn 5:1 Jesus is the C is born of God
1Jn 5:6 by water and blood, even Jesus C
1Jn 5:20 is true, even in his Son Jesus C
2Jn 3 Father, and from the Lord Jesus C
2Jn 7 that Jesus C is come in the flesh
2Jn 9 abideth not in the doctrine of C
2Jn 9 that abideth in the doctrine of C
Jude 1 Jude, the servant of Jesus C
Jude 1 Father, and preserved in Jesus C
Jude 4 Lord God, and our Lord Jesus C
Jude 17 the apostles of our Lord Jesus C
Jude 21 Lord Jesus C unto eternal life
Rev 1:1 The Revelation of Jesus C
Rev 1:2 and of the testimony of Jesus C
Rev 1:5 And from Jesus C, who is the
Rev 1:9 kingdom and patience of Jesus C
Rev 1:9 and for the testimony of Jesus C
Rev 11:15 kingdoms of our Lord, and of his C
Rev 12:10 of our God, and the power of his C
Rev 12:17 and have the testimony of Jesus C
Rev 20:4 reigned with C a thousand years
Rev 20:6 shall be priests of God and of C
Rev 22:21 our Lord Jesus C be with you all

**CHRISTIAN** *(kris'-tyan)* See CHRISTIANS. *A follower of Jesus Christ.*
Acts 26:28 thou persuadest me to be a C
1Pet 4:16 Yet if any man suffer as a C

**CHRISTIANS** *(kris'-tyans)*
Acts 11:26 were called C first in Antioch

**CHRIST'S** *(krists)*
Rom 15:30 for the Lord Jesus C sake
1Cor 3:23 And ye are C
1Cor 4:10 We are fools for C sake, but ye
1Cor 7:22 called, being free, is C servant
1Cor 15:23 they that are C at his coming
2Cor 2:12 came to Troas to preach C gospel
2Cor 5:20 we pray you in C stead, be ye
2Cor 10:7 man trust to himself that he is C
2Cor 10:7 he is C, even so are we C
2Cor 12:10 in distresses for C sake
Gal 3:29 And if ye be C, then are ye
Gal 5:24 they that are C have crucified
Eph 4:32 even as God for C sake hath
Phil 2:21 not the things which are Jesus C
1Pet 4:13 ye are partakers of C sufferings

**CHRISTS** *(krists)*
Mt 24:24 For there shall arise false C
Mk 13:22 For false C and false prophets

**CHRONICLES**
1Kin 14:19 of the c of the kings of Israel
1Chr 27:24 account of the c of king David
Neh 12:23 were written in the book of the c
Est 2:23 the book of the c before the king
Est 6:1 the book of records of the c
Est 10:2 of the c of the kings of Media

**CHRYSOLITE**
Rev 21:20 the seventh, c

**CHRYSOPRASUS**
Rev 21:20 the tenth, a c

**CHUB** *(cub) Allies of Egypt.*
Eze 30:5 and all the mingled people, and C

**CHUN** *(kun) A city in Aran-zobah.*
1Chr 18:8 Likewise from Tibhath, and from C

**CHURCH**
Mt 16:18 upon this rock I will build my c
Mt 18:17 to hear them, tell it unto the c
Mt 18:17 but if he neglect to hear the c
Acts 2:47 the Lord added to the c daily
Acts 5:11 And great fear came upon all the c
Acts 7:38 is he, that was in the c in the
Acts 8:1 the c which was at Jerusalem
Acts 8:3 for Saul, he made havock of the c
Acts 11:22 of the c which was in Jerusalem
Acts 11:26 assembled themselves with the c
Acts 12:1 his hands to vex certain of the c
Acts 12:5 ceasing of the c unto God for him
Acts 13:1 Now there were in the c that was
Acts 14:23 ordained them elders in every c
Acts 14:27 and had gathered the c together
Acts 15:3 brought on their way by the c
Acts 15:4 they were received of the c
Acts 15:22 and elders, with the whole c
Acts 18:22 and gone up, and saluted the c
Acts 20:17 and called the elders of the c
Acts 20:28 overseers, to feed the c of God
Rom 16:1 of the c which is at Cenchrea
Rom 16:5 Likewise greet the c that is in
Rom 16:23 mine host, and of the whole c
Rom s servant of the c at Cenchrea
1Cor 1:2 Unto the c of God which is at
1Cor 4:17 as I teach every where in every c
1Cor 6:4 who are least esteemed in the c
1Cor 10:32 the Gentiles, nor to the c of God
1Cor 11:18 when ye come together in the c
1Cor 11:22 or despise ye the c of God
1Cor 12:28 And God hath set some in the c
1Cor 14:4 that prophesieth edifieth the c
1Cor 14:5 that the c may receive edifying
1Cor 14:12 excel to the edifying of the c
1Cor 14:19 Yet in the c I had rather speak
1Cor 14:23 If therefore the whole c be come
1Cor 14:28 let him keep silence in the c
1Cor 14:35 shame for women to speak in the c
1Cor 15:9 because I persecuted the c of God
1Cor 16:19 with the c that is in their house
2Cor 1:1 unto the c of God which is at
Gal 1:13 measure I persecuted the c of God
Eph 1:22 the head over all things to the c
Eph 3:10 the c the manifold wisdom of God
Eph 3:21 Unto him be glory in the c by
Eph 5:23 as Christ is the head of the c
Eph 5:24 Therefore as the c is subject
Eph 5:25 even as Christ also loved the c
Eph 5:27 it to himself a glorious c
Eph 5:29 it, even as the Lord the c
Eph 5:32 speak concerning Christ and the c
Phil 3:6 zeal, persecuting the c
Phil 4:15 no c communicated with me as
Col 1:18 he is the head of the body, the c
Col 1:24 his body's sake, which is the c
Col 4:15 the c which is in his house
Col 4:16 also in the c of the Laodiceans
1Th 1:1 unto the c of the Thessalonians
2Th 1:1 unto the c of the Thessalonians
1Ti 3:5 he take care of the c of God
1Ti 3:15 which is the c of the living God,
1Ti 5:16 them, and let not the c be charged
2Ti s bishop of the c of the Ephesians
Titus s bishop of the c of the Cretians
Philem 2 and to the c in thy house
Heb 2:12 in the midst of the c will I sing
Heb 12:23 c of the firstborn, which are
Jas 5:14 him call for the elders of the c
1Pet 5:13 The c that is at Babylon, elected
3Jn 6 of thy charity before the c
3Jn 9 I wrote unto the c
3Jn 10 and casteth them out of the c
Rev 2:1 angel of the c of Ephesus write
Rev 2:8 angel of the c in Smyrna write
Rev 2:12 angel of the c in Pergamos write
Rev 2:18 angel of the c in Thyatira write
Rev 3:1 angel of the c in Sardis write
Rev 3:7 And to the angel of the c in
Rev 3:14 unto the angel of the c of the

**CHURCHES**
Acts 9:31 Then had the c rest throughout
Acts 15:41 and Cilicia, confirming the c
Acts 16:5 so were the c established in the
Acts 19:37 which are neither robbers of c
Rom 16:4 also all the c of the Gentiles
Rom 16:16 The c of Christ salute you
1Cor 7:17 And so ordain I in all c
1Cor 11:16 such custom, neither the c of God
1Cor 14:33 as in all c of the saints
1Cor 14:34 your women keep silence in the c
1Cor 16:1 given order to the c of Galatia
1Cor 16:19 The c of Asia salute you
2Cor 8:1 bestowed on the c of Macedonia
2Cor 8:18 the gospel throughout all the c
2Cor 8:19 the c to travel with us with this
2Cor 8:23 they are the messengers of the c
2Cor 8:24 shew ye to them, and before the c
2Cor 11:8 I robbed other c, taking wages of
2Cor 11:28 me daily, the care of all the c
2Cor 12:13 ye were inferior to other c
Gal 1:2 with me, unto the c of Galatia
Gal 1:22 was unknown by face unto the c of
1Th 2:14 became followers of the c of God
2Th 1:4 in the c of God for your patience
Rev 1:4 to the seven c which are in Asia
Rev 1:11 the seven c which are in Asia
Rev 1:20 are the angels of the seven c
Rev 1:20 which thou sawest are the seven c
Rev 2:7 what the Spirit saith unto the c
Rev 2:11 what the Spirit saith unto the c
Rev 2:17 what the Spirit saith unto the c
Rev 2:23 all the c shall know that I am he
Rev 2:29 what the Spirit saith unto the c
Rev 3:6 what the Spirit saith unto the c
Rev 3:13 what the Spirit saith unto the c
Rev 3:22 what the Spirit saith unto the c
Rev 22:16 unto you these things in the c

**CHUSHAN-RISHATHAIM** *(cu'-shan-rish-a-tha'-im) A king of Mesopotamia.*
Judg 3:8 the hand of C king of Mesopotamia
Judg 3:8 of Israel served C eight years
Judg 3:10 the LORD delivered C king of
Judg 3:10 and his hand prevailed against C

**CHUZA** *(cu'-zah) A steward of Herod Antipas.*
Lk 8:3 the wife of C Herod's steward

**CILICIA** *(sil-ish'-yah) A Roman province in Asia Minor.*
Acts 6:9 and Alexandrians, and of them of C
Acts 15:23 Gentiles in Antioch and Syria and C
Acts 15:41 And he went through Syria and C
Acts 21:39 am a Jew of Tarsus, a city in C
Acts 22:3 Jew, born in Tarsus, a city in C
Acts 23:34 he understood that he was of C
Acts 27:5 we had sailed over the sea of C
Gal 1:21 into the regions of Syria and C

**CINNAMON**
Ex 30:23 of sweet c half so much, even two
Prov 7:17 my bed with myrrh, aloes, and c
Song 4:14 calamus and c, with all trees of
Rev 18:13 And c, and odours, and ointments, and

**CINNEROTH** *(sin'-ne-roth)* See CHINNEROTH. *Same as Chinneroth.*
1Kin 15:20 and Abel-beth-maachah, and all C

**CIRCUMCISE**
Gen 17:11 ye shall c the flesh of your
Deut 10:16 C therefore the foreskin of your
Deut 30:6 LORD thy God will c thine heart
Josh 5:2 c again the children of Israel
Josh 5:4 is the cause why Joshua did c
Jer 4:4 C yourselves to the LORD, and take
Lk 1:59 day they came to c the child
Jn 7:22 and ye on the sabbath day c a man
Acts 15:5 That it was needful to c them
Acts 21:21 ought not to c their children

**CIRCUMCISED**
Gen 17:10 man child among you shall be c
Gen 17:12 days old shall be c among you
Gen 17:13 with thy money, must needs be c
Gen 17:14 flesh of his foreskin is not c
Gen 17:23 c the flesh of their foreskin in
Gen 17:24 when he was c in the flesh of his
Gen 17:25 when he was c in the flesh of his
Gen 17:26 In the selfsame day was Abraham c
Gen 17:27 of the stranger, were c with him
Gen 21:4 Abraham c his son Isaac being

Gen 34:15 be, that every male of you be c
Gen 34:17 will not hearken unto us, to be c
Gen 34:22 us be c, as they are c
Gen 34:24 and every male was c, all that
Ex 12:44 for money, when thou hast c him
Ex 12:48 the LORD, let all his males be c
Lev 12:3 flesh of his foreskin shall be c
Josh 5:3 c the children of Israel at the
Josh 5:5 the people that came out were c
Josh 5:5 out of Egypt, them they had not c
Josh 5:7 up in their stead, them Joshua c
Josh 5:7 they had not c them by the way
Jer 9:25 are c with the uncircumcised
Acts 7:8 Isaac, and c him the eighth day
Acts 15:1 Except ye be c after the manner
Acts 15:24 your souls, saying, Ye must be c
Acts 16:3 c him because of the Jews which
Rom 4:11 believe, though they be not c
1Cor 7:18 Is any man called being c
1Cor 7:18 let him not be c
Gal 2:3 a Greek, was compelled to be c
Gal 5:2 say unto you, that if ye be c
Gal 5:3 again to every man that is c
Gal 6:12 flesh, they constrain you to be c
Gal 6:13 themselves who are c keep the law
Gal 6:13 but desire to have you c, that
Phil 3:5 C the eighth day, of the stock of
Col 2:11 In whom also ye are c with the

## CIRCUMCISION

Ex 4:26 thou art, because of the c
Jn 7:22 Moses therefore gave unto you c
Jn 7:23 man on the sabbath day receive c
Acts 7:8 And he gave him the covenant of c
Acts 10:45 they of the c which believed were
Acts 11:2 were of the c contended with him
Rom 2:25 For c verily profiteth, if thou
Rom 2:25 thy c is made uncircumcision
Rom 2:26 uncircumcision be counted for c
Rom 2:27 c dost transgress the law
Rom 2:28 neither is that c, which is
Rom 2:29 c is that of the heart, in the
Rom 3:1 or what profit is there of c
Rom 3:30 shall justify the c by faith
Rom 4:9 blessedness then upon the c only
Rom 4:10 when he was in c, or in
Rom 4:10 Not in c, but in uncircumcision
Rom 4:11 And he received the sign of c
Rom 4:12 the father of c to them who are
Rom 4:12 to them who are not of the c only
Rom 15:8 of the c for the truth of God
1Cor 7:19 C is nothing, and uncircumcision
Gal 2:7 gospel of the c was unto Peter
Gal 2:8 Peter to the apostleship of the c
Gal 2:9 the heathen, and they unto the c
Gal 2:12 fearing them which were of the c
Gal 5:6 neither c availeth any thing
Gal 5:11 And I, brethren, if I yet preach c
Gal 6:15 neither c availeth any thing
Eph 2:11 the C in the flesh made by hands
Phil 3:3 For we are the c, which worship
Col 2:11 with the c made without hands
Col 2:11 of the flesh by the c of Christ
Col 3:11 c nor uncircumcision, Barbarian,
Col 4:11 called Justus, who are of the c
Titus 1:10 specially they of the c

## CIS *(sis)* See KISH. *Father of King Saul.*

Acts 13:21 gave unto them Saul the son of C

## CISTERN

2Kin 18:31 ye every one the waters of his c
Prov 5:15 Drink waters out of thine own c
Eccl 12:6 or the wheel broken at the c
Is 36:16 every one the waters of his own c

## CLAP

Job 27:23 Men shall c their hands at him,
Ps 47:1 O c your hands, all ye people
Ps 98:8 Let the floods c their hands
Is 55:12 of the field shall c their hands
Lam 2:15 All that pass by c their hands at
Nah 3:19 thee shall c the hands over thee

## CLAUDA *(claw'-dah) An island near Crete.*

Acts 27:16 certain island which is called C

## CLAUDIA *(claw'-de-ah) A Roman Christian.*

2Ti 4:21 thee, and Pudens, and Linus, and C

## CLAUDIUS *(claw'-de-us)*

*1. A Roman emperor.*
Acts 11:28 to pass in the days of C Caesar
Acts 18:2 (because that C had commanded all
*2. A Roman officer in Jerusalem.*
Acts 23:26 C Lysias unto the most excellent

## CLAVE

Gen 22:3 c the wood for the burnt offering
Gen 34:3 his soul c unto Dinah the
Num 16:31 that the ground c asunder that
Judg 15:19 But God c an hollow place that
Ruth 1:14 but Ruth c unto her
1Sa 6:14 they c the wood of the cart, and
2Sa 20:2 men of Judah c unto their king
2Sa 23:10 his hand c unto the sword
1Kin 11:2 Solomon c unto these in love
2Kin 18:6 For he c to the LORD, and departed
Neh 10:29 They c to their brethren, their
Ps 78:15 He c the rocks in the wilderness,
Is 48:21 he c the rock also, and the waters
Acts 17:34 Howbeit certain men c unto him

## CLAY

1Kin 7:46 in the c ground between Succoth
2Chr 4:17 in the c ground between Succoth
Job 4:19 in them that dwell in houses of c
Job 10:9 that thou hast made me as the c
Job 13:12 ashes, your bodies to bodies of c
Job 27:16 dust, and prepare raiment as the c
Job 33:6 I also am formed out of the c
Job 38:14 It is turned as c to the seal
Ps 40:2 horrible pit, out of the miry c
Is 29:16 be esteemed as the potter's c
Is 41:25 and as the potter treadeth c
Is 45:9 Shall the c say to him that
Is 64:8 we are the c, and thou our potter
Jer 18:4 the vessel that he made of c was
Jer 18:6 as the c is in the potter's hand,
Jer 43:9 them in the c in the brickkiln
Dan 2:33 feet part of iron and part of c
Dan 2:34 his feet that were of iron and c
Dan 2:35 Then was the iron, the c, the
Dan 2:41 feet and toes, part of potters' c
Dan 2:41 sawest the iron mixed with miry c
Dan 2:42 were part of iron, and part of c
Dan 2:43 sawest iron mixed with miry c
Dan 2:43 even as iron is not mixed with c
Dan 2:45 pieces the iron, the brass, the c
Nah 3:14 go into c, and tread the morter,
Hab 2:6 that ladeth himself with thick c
Jn 9:6 made c of the spittle, and he
Jn 9:6 eyes of the blind man with the c
Jn 9:11 A man that is called Jesus made c
Jn 9:14 sabbath day when Jesus made the c
Jn 9:15 He put c upon mine eyes, and I
Rom 9:21 not the potter power over the c

## CLEAN

Gen 7:2 Of every c beast thou shalt take
Gen 7:2 of beasts that are not c by two
Gen 7:8 Of c beasts, and of beasts that
Gen 7:8 and of beasts that are not c
Gen 8:20 c beast, and of every c fowl
Gen 35:2 gods that are among you, and be c
Lev 4:12 without the camp unto a c place
Lev 6:11 without the camp unto a c place
Lev 7:19 all that be c shall eat thereof
Lev 10:10 unholy, and between unclean and c
Lev 10:14 shall ye eat in a c place
Lev 11:36 is plenty of water, shall be c
Lev 11:37 is to be sown, it shall be c
Lev 11:47 between the unclean and the c
Lev 12:8 for her, and she shall be c
Lev 13:6 the priest shall pronounce him c
Lev 13:6 shall wash his clothes, and be c
Lev 13:13 him c that hath the plague
Lev 13:13 he is c
Lev 13:17 him c that hath the plague
Lev 13:17 he is c
Lev 13:23 the priest shall pronounce him c
Lev 13:28 the priest shall pronounce him c
Lev 13:34 the priest shall pronounce him c
Lev 13:34 shall wash his clothes, and be c
Lev 13:37 the scall is healed, he is c
Lev 13:37 the priest shall pronounce him c
Lev 13:39 he is c
Lev 13:40 yet is he c
Lev 13:41 yet is he c
Lev 13:58 the second time, and shall be c
Lev 13:59 thing of skins, to pronounce it c
Lev 14:4 be cleansed two birds alive and c
Lev 14:7 times, and shall pronounce him c
Lev 14:8 in water, that he may be c
Lev 14:9 flesh in water, and he shall be c
Lev 14:11 the priest that maketh him c
Lev 14:11 the man that is to be made c
Lev 14:20 for him, and he shall be c
Lev 14:48 shall pronounce the house c
Lev 14:53 and it shall be c
Lev 14:57 it is unclean, and when it is c
Lev 15:8 the issue spit upon him that is c
Lev 15:13 in running water, and shall be c
Lev 15:28 and after that she shall be c
Lev 16:30 that ye may be c from all your
Lev 17:15 then shall he be c
Lev 20:25 put difference between c beasts
Lev 20:25 and between unclean fowls and c
Lev 22:4 of the holy things, until he be c
Lev 22:7 the sun is down, he shall be c
Lev 23:22 thou shalt not make c riddance of
Num 5:28 woman be not defiled, but be c
Num 8:7 clothes, and so make themselves c
Num 9:13 But the man that is c, and is not
Num 18:11 every one that is c in thy house
Num 18:13 every one that is c in thine
Num 19:9 a man that is c shall gather up
Num 19:9 up without the camp in a c place
Num 19:12 on the seventh day he shall be c
Num 19:12 the seventh day he shall not be c
Num 19:18 a c person shall take hyssop, and
Num 19:19 the c person shall sprinkle upon
Num 19:19 in water, and shall be c at even
Num 31:23 the fire, and it shall be c
Num 31:24 the seventh day, and ye shall be c
Deut 12:15 the c may eat thereof, as of the
Deut 12:22 the c shall eat of them alike
Deut 14:11 Of all c birds ye shall eat
Deut 14:20 But of all c fowls ye may eat
Deut 15:22 the c person shall eat it alike,
Deut 23:10 that is not c by reason of
Josh 3:17 people were passed c over Jordan
Josh 4:1 people were c passed over Jordan
Josh 4:11 all the people were c passed over
1Sa 20:26 hath befallen him, he is not c
1Sa 20:26 surely he is not c
2Kin 5:10 again to thee, and thou shalt be c
2Kin 5:12 may I not wash in them, and be c
2Kin 5:13 he saith to thee, Wash, and be c
2Kin 5:14 of a little child, and he was c
2Chr 30:17 for every one that was not c
Job 9:30 and make my hands never so c
Job 11:4 is pure, and I am c in thine eyes
Job 14:4 Who can bring a c thing out of an
Job 15:14 What is man, that he should be c
Job 15:15 heavens are not c in his sight
Job 17:9 he that hath c hands shall be
Job 25:4 or how can he be c that is born
Job 33:9 I am c without transgression, I
Ps 19:9 The fear of the LORD is c
Ps 24:4 He that hath c hands, and a pure
Ps 51:7 me with hyssop, and I shall be c
Ps 51:10 Create in me a c heart, O God
Ps 73:1 even to such as are of a c heart
Ps 77:8 Is his mercy c gone for ever
Prov 14:4 Where no oxen are, the crib is c
Prov 16:2 of a man are c in his own eyes
Prov 20:9 can say, I have made my heart c
Eccl 9:2 to the good and to the c, and to
Is 1:16 Wash you, make you c
Is 24:19 down, the earth is c dissolved
Is 28:8 so that there is no place c
Is 30:24 the ground shall eat c provender
Is 52:11 be ye c, that bear the vessels of
Is 66:20 a c vessel into the house of the
Jer 13:27 wilt thou not be made c
Eze 22:26 between the unclean and the c
Eze 36:25 will I sprinkle c water upon you
Eze 36:25 and ye shall be c
Eze 44:23 between the unclean and the c
Joel 1:7 he hath made it c bare, and cast
Zec 11:17 his arm shall be c dried up
Mt 8:2 thou wilt, thou canst make me c
Mt 8:3 be thou c
Mt 23:25 for ye make c the outside of the
Mt 23:26 the outside of them may be c also
Mt 27:59 he wrapped it in a c linen cloth
Mk 1:40 thou wilt, thou canst make me c
Mk 1:41 be thou c
Lk 5:12 thou wilt, thou canst make me c
Lk 5:13 be thou c
Lk 11:39 make c the outside of the cup

Lk 11:41 behold, all things are c unto you
Jn 13:10 his feet, but is c every whit
Jn 13:10 and ye are c, but not all
Jn 13:11 said he, Ye are not all c
Jn 15:3 Now ye are c through the word
Acts 18:6 I am c
2Pet 2:18 those that were c escaped from
Rev 19:8 be arrayed in fine linen, c
Rev 19:14 clothed in fine linen, white and c

**CLEANSE**
Ex 29:36 and thou shalt c the altar
Lev 14:49 he shall take to c the house two
Lev 14:52 he shall c the house with the
Lev 16:19 c it, and hallow it from the
Lev 16:30 to c you, that ye may be clean
Num 8:6 the children of Israel, and c them
Num 8:7 thou do unto them, to c them
Num 8:15 and thou shalt c them, and offer
Num 8:21 an atonement for them to c them
2Chr 29:15 to c the house of the LORD
2Chr 29:16 of the house of the LORD, to c it
Neh 13:22 that they should c themselves
Ps 19:12 c thou me from secret faults
Ps 51:2 iniquity, and c me from my sin
Ps 119:9 shall a young man c his way
Jer 4:11 my people, not to fan, nor to c
Jer 33:8 I will c them from all their
Eze 36:25 from all your idols, will I c you
Eze 37:23 they have sinned, and will c them
Eze 39:12 of them, that they may c the land
Eze 39:14 the face of the earth, to c it
Eze 39:16 Thus shall they c the land
Eze 43:20 thus shalt thou c and purge it
Eze 43:22 and they shall c the altar
Eze 43:22 as they did c it with the bullock
Eze 45:18 blemish, and c the sanctuary
Joel 3:21 For I will c their blood that I
Mt 10:8 c the lepers, raise the dead,
Mt 23:26 c first that which is within the
2Cor 7:1 let us c ourselves from all
Eph 5:26 c it with the washing of water by
Jas 4:8 C your hands, ye sinners
1Jn 1:9 to c us from all unrighteousness

**CLEANSED**
Lev 11:32 so it shall be c
Lev 12:7 she shall be c from the issue of
Lev 14:4 that is to be c two birds alive
Lev 14:7 be c from the leprosy seven times
Lev 14:8 he that is to be c shall wash his
Lev 14:14 right ear of him that is to be c
Lev 14:17 right ear of him that is to be c
Lev 14:18 the head of him that is to be c
Lev 14:19 is to be c from his uncleanness
Lev 14:25 right ear of him that is to be c
Lev 14:28 right ear of him that is to be c
Lev 14:29 the head of him that is to be c
Lev 14:31 that is to be c before the LORD
Lev 15:13 hath an issue is c of his issue
Lev 15:28 But if she be c of her issue
Num 35:33 the land cannot be c of the blood
Josh 22:17 which we are not c until this day
2Chr 29:18 We have c all the house of the
2Chr 30:18 had not c themselves, yet did
2Chr 30:19 though he be not c according to
2Chr 34:5 altars, and c Judah and Jerusalem
Neh 13:9 commanded, and they c the chambers
Neh 13:30 Thus c I them from all strangers,
Job 35:3 I have, if I be c from my sin
Ps 73:13 Verily I have c my heart in vain,
Eze 22:24 Thou art the land that is not c
Eze 36:33 In the day that I shall have c
Eze 44:26 And after he is c, they shall
Dan 8:14 then shall the sanctuary be c
Joel 3:21 their blood that I have not c
Mt 8:3 And immediately his leprosy was c
Mt 11:5 the lame walk, the lepers are c
Mk 1:42 departed from him, and he was c
Lk 4:27 and none of them was c, saving
Lk 7:22 the lame walk, the lepers are c
Lk 17:14 that, as they went, they were c
Lk 17:17 said, Were there not ten c
Acts 10:15 the second time, What God hath c
Acts 11:9 from heaven, What God hath c

**CLEANSING**
Lev 13:7 been seen of the priest for his c
Lev 13:35 much in the skin after his c
Lev 14:2 of the leper in the day of his c
Lev 14:23 day for his c unto the priest
Lev 14:32 that which pertaineth to his c
Lev 15:13 to himself seven days for his c
Num 6:9 his head in the day of his c
Eze 43:23 thou hast made an end of c it
Mk 1:44 offer for thy c those things
Lk 5:14 to the priest, and offer for thy c

**CLEAR**
Gen 24:8 thou shalt be c from this my oath
Gen 24:41 shalt thou be c from this my oath
Gen 24:41 one, thou shalt be c from my oath
Gen 44:16 or how shall we c ourselves
Ex 34:7 will by no means c the guilty
2Sa 23:4 the earth by c shining after rain
Ps 51:4 and be c when thou judgest
Song 6:10 c as the sun, and terrible as an
Is 18:4 place like a c heat upon herbs
Amos 8:9 darken the earth in the c day
Zec 14:6 that the light shall not be c
2Cor 7:11 yourselves to be c in this matter
Rev 21:11 like a jasper stone, c as crystal
Rev 21:18 was pure gold, like unto c glass
Rev 22:1 c as crystal, proceeding out of

**CLEARLY**
Job 33:3 my lips shall utter knowledge c
Mt 7:5 then shalt thou see c to cast out
Mk 8:25 was restored, and saw every man c
Lk 6:42 then shalt thou see c to pull out
Rom 1:20 creation of the world are c seen

**CLEAVE**
Gen 2:24 mother, and shall c unto his wife
Lev 1:17 he shall c it with the wings
Deut 4:4 But ye that did c unto the LORD
Deut 10:20 serve, and to him shalt thou c
Deut 11:22 in all his ways, and to c unto him
Deut 13:4 ye shall serve him, and c unto him
Deut 13:17 there shall c nought of the
Deut 28:21 make the pestilence c unto thee
Deut 28:60 and they shall c unto thee
Deut 30:20 and that thou mayest c unto him
Josh 22:5 to c unto him, and to serve him
Josh 23:8 But c unto the LORD your God, as
Josh 23:12 c unto the remnant of these
2Kin 5:27 of Naaman shall c unto thee
Job 38:38 the clods c fast together
Ps 74:15 Thou didst c the fountain and the
Ps 101:3 it shall not c to me
Ps 102:5 my groaning my bones c to my skin
Ps 137:6 let my tongue c to the roof of my
Is 14:1 they shall c to the house of
Jer 13:11 so have I caused to c unto me the
Eze 3:26 I will make thy tongue c to the
Dan 2:43 they shall not c one to another
Dan 11:34 but many shall c to them with
Hab 3:9 Thou didst c the earth with
Zec 14:4 the mount of Olives shall c in
Mt 19:5 and mother, and shall c to his wife
Mk 10:7 and mother, and c to his wife
Acts 11:23 heart they would c unto the Lord
Rom 12:9 c to that which is good

**CLEAVETH**
Deut 14:6 c the cleft into two claws, and
Job 16:13 he c my reins asunder, and doth
Job 19:20 My bone c to my skin and to my
Ps 22:15 and my tongue c to my jaws
Ps 41:8 say they, c fast unto him
Ps 44:25 our belly c unto the earth
Ps 119:25 My soul c unto the dust
Ps 141:7 cutteth and c wood upon the earth
Eccl 10:9 and he that c wood shall be
Jer 13:11 For as the girdle c to the loins
Lam 4:4 c to the roof of his mouth for
Lam 4:8 their skin c to their bones
Lk 10:11 dust of your city, which c on us

**CLEFTS**
Song 2:14 that art in the c of the rock
Is 2:21 To go into the c of the rocks
Jer 49:16 dwellest in the c of the rock
Amos 6:11 and the little house with c
Obad 3 dwellest in the c of the rock

**CLEMENT** *(clem'-ent) A companion of Paul.*
Phil 4:3 me in the gospel, with C also

**CLEOPAS** *(cle'-o-pas)* See ALPHAEUS, CLEOPHAS. *A disciple on Emmaus Road.*
Lk 24:18 the one of them, whose name was C

**CLEOPHAS** *(cle'-o-fas)* See CLEOPAS. *Husband of Mary.*
Jn 19:25 sister, Mary the wife of C

**CLODS**
Job 7:5 clothed with worms and c of dust
Job 21:33 The c of the valley shall be
Job 38:38 the c cleave fast together
Is 28:24 break the c of his ground
Hos 10:11 plow, and Jacob shall break his c
Joel 1:17 The seed is rotten under their c

**CLOKE**
Is 59:17 and was clad with zeal as a c
Mt 5:40 thy coat, let him have thy c also
Lk 6:29 him that taketh away thy c forbid
Jn 15:22 now they have no c for their sin
1Th 2:5 ye know, nor a c of covetousness
2Ti 4:13 The c that I left at Troas with
1Pet 2:16 liberty for a c of maliciousness

**CLOSE**
Num 5:13 eyes of her husband, and be kept c
2Sa 22:46 be afraid out of their c places
1Chr 12:1 while he yet kept himself c
Job 28:21 kept c from the fowls of the air
Job 41:15 shut up together as with a c seal
Ps 18:45 be afraid out of their c places
Jer 42:16 shall follow c after you there in
Dan 8:7 And I saw him come c unto the ram
Amos 9:11 c up the breaches thereof
Lk 9:36 And they kept it c, and told no man
Acts 27:13 thence, they sailed c by Crete

**CLOSED**
Gen 2:21 c up the flesh instead thereof
Gen 20:18 For the LORD had fast c up all
Num 16:33 the pit, and the earth c upon them
Judg 3:22 the fat c upon the blade, so that
Is 1:6 they have not been c, neither
Is 29:10 deep sleep, and hath c your eyes
Dan 12:9 for the words are c up and sealed
Jonah 2:5 the depth c me round about, the
Mt 13:15 and their eyes they have c
Lk 4:20 he c the book, and he gave it
Acts 28:27 and their eyes have they c

**CLOTH**
Num 4:6 spread over it a c wholly of blue
Num 4:7 they shall spread a c of blue
Num 4:8 spread upon them a c of scarlet
Num 4:9 And they shall take a c of blue
Num 4:11 they shall spread a c of blue
Num 4:12 and put them in a c of blue
Num 4:13 and spread a purple c thereon
Deut 22:17 they shall spread the c before
1Sa 19:13 bolster, and covered it with a c
1Sa 21:9 wrapped in a c behind the ephod
2Sa 20:12 cast a c upon him, when he saw
2Kin 8:15 morrow, that he took a thick c
Is 30:22 cast them away as a menstruous c
Mt 9:16 of new c unto an old garment
Mt 27:59 he wrapped it in a clean linen c
Mk 2:21 piece of new c on an old garment
Mk 14:51 having a linen c cast about his
Mk 14:52 And he left the linen c, and fled

**CLOTHE**
Ex 40:14 his sons, and c them with coats
Est 4:4 and she sent raiment to c Mordecai
Ps 132:16 I will also c her priests with
Ps 132:18 His enemies will I c with shame
Prov 23:21 shall c a man with rags
Is 22:21 I will c him with thy robe, and
Is 49:18 thou shalt surely c thee with
Is 50:3 I c the heavens with blackness,
Eze 26:16 they shall c themselves with
Eze 34:3 ye c you with the wool, ye kill
Hag 1:6 ye c you, but there is none warm
Zec 3:4 I will c thee with change of
Mt 6:30 if God so c the grass of the
Mt 6:30 shall he not much more c you
Lk 12:28 If then God so c the grass
Lk 12:28 how much more will he c you

**CLOTHED**
Gen 3:21 make coats of skins, and c them
Lev 8:7 c him with the robe, and put the
2Sa 1:24 who c you in scarlet, with other
1Chr 15:27 David was c with a robe of fine
1Chr 21:16 who were c in sackcloth, fell
2Chr 6:41 be c with salvation, and let thy
2Chr 18:9 c in their robes, and they sat in
2Chr 28:15 with the spoil c all that were

Est 4:2 the king's gate c with sackcloth
Job 7:5 My flesh is c with worms and clods
Job 8:22 hate thee shall be c with shame
Job 10:11 Thou hast c me with skin and flesh
Job 29:14 put on righteousness, and it c me
Job 39:19 hast thou c his neck with thunder
Ps 35:26 let them be c with shame and
Ps 65:13 The pastures are c with flocks
Ps 93:1 reigneth, he is c with majesty
Ps 93:1 the LORD is c with strength,
Ps 104:1 thou art c with honour and majesty
Ps 109:18 As he c himself with cursing like
Ps 109:29 mine adversaries be c with shame
Ps 132:9 priests be c with righteousness
Prov 31:21 her household are c with scarlet
Is 61:10 for he hath c me with the
Eze 7:27 prince shall be c with desolation
Eze 9:2 man among them was c with linen
Eze 9:3 he called to the man c with linen
Eze 9:11 the man c with linen, which had
Eze 10:2 spake unto the man c with linen
Eze 10:6 commanded the man c with linen
Eze 10:7 of him that was c with linen
Eze 16:10 I c thee also with broidered work
Eze 23:6 Which were c with blue, captains
Eze 23:12 rulers c most gorgeously,
Eze 38:4 all of them c with all sorts of
Eze 44:17 they shall be c with linen
Dan 5:7 shall be c with scarlet, and have
Dan 5:16 thou shalt be c with scarlet
Dan 5:29 they c Daniel with scarlet, and
Dan 10:5 behold a certain man c in linen
Dan 12:6 And one said to the man c in linen
Dan 12:7 And I heard the man c in linen
Zeph 1:8 all such as are c with strange
Zec 3:3 Now Joshua was c with filthy
Zec 3:5 his head, and c him with garments
Mt 6:31 or, Wherewithal shall we be c
Mt 11:8 A man c in soft raiment
Mt 25:36 Naked, and ye c me
Mt 25:38 or naked, and c thee
Mt 25:43 naked, and ye c me not
Mk 1:6 John was c with camel's hair, and
Mk 5:15 and had the legion, sitting, and c
Mk 15:17 they c him with purple, and
Mk 16:5 c in a long white garment
Lk 7:25 A man c in soft raiment
Lk 8:35 sitting at the feet of Jesus, c
Lk 16:19 rich man, which was c in purple
2Cor 5:2 earnestly desiring to be c upon
2Cor 5:3 If so be that being c we shall
2Cor 5:4 but c upon, that mortality might
1Pet 5:5 to another, and be c with humility
Rev 1:13 c with a garment down to the foot
Rev 3:5 same shall be c in white raiment
Rev 3:18 raiment, that thou mayest be c
Rev 4:4 sitting, c in white raiment
Rev 7:9 c with white robes, and palms in
Rev 10:1 down from heaven, c with a cloud
Rev 11:3 threescore days, c in sackcloth
Rev 12:1 a woman c with the sun, and the
Rev 15:6 c in pure and white linen, and
Rev 18:16 that was c in fine linen, and
Rev 19:13 he was c with a vesture dipped in
Rev 19:14 c in fine linen, white and clean

## CLOTHES

Gen 37:29 and he rent his c
Gen 37:34 And Jacob rent his c, and put
Gen 44:13 Then they rent their c, and laded
Gen 49:11 his c in the blood of grapes
Ex 12:34 in their c upon their shoulders
Ex 19:10 morrow, and let them wash their c
Ex 19:14 and they washed their c
Lev 10:6 your heads, neither rend your c
Lev 11:25 carcase of them shall wash his c
Lev 11:28 carcase of them shall wash his c
Lev 11:40 carcase of it shall wash his c
Lev 11:40 carcase of it shall wash his c
Lev 13:6 and he shall wash his c, and be
Lev 13:34 and he shall wash his c, and be
Lev 13:45 his c shall be rent, and his head
Lev 14:8 to be cleansed shall wash his c
Lev 14:9 and he shall wash his c, also he
Lev 14:47 in the house shall wash his c
Lev 14:47 in the house shall wash his c
Lev 15:5 toucheth his bed shall wash his c
Lev 15:6 hath the issue shall wash his c
Lev 15:7 hath the issue shall wash his c
Lev 15:8 then he shall wash his c, and
Lev 15:10 of those things shall wash his c
Lev 15:11 in water, he shall wash his c
Lev 15:13 for his cleansing, and wash his c
Lev 15:21 toucheth her bed shall wash his c
Lev 15:22 she sat upon shall wash his c
Lev 15:27 be unclean, and shall wash his c
Lev 16:26 the scapegoat shall wash his c
Lev 16:28 burneth them shall wash his c
Lev 16:32 and shall put on the linen c
Lev 17:15 he shall both wash his c
Lev 21:10 uncover his head, nor rend his c
Num 8:7 flesh, and let them wash their c
Num 8:21 purified, and they washed their c
Num 14:6 searched the land, rent their c
Num 19:7 Then the priest shall wash his c
Num 19:8 her shall wash his c in water
Num 19:10 of the heifer shall wash his c
Num 19:19 purify himself, and wash his c
Num 19:21 of separation shall wash his c
Num 31:24 wash your c on the seventh day
Deut 29:5 your c are not waxen old upon you
Josh 7:6 And Joshua rent his c, and fell to
Judg 11:35 he saw her, that he rent his c
1Sa 4:12 the same day with his c rent
1Sa 19:24 And he stript off his c also
2Sa 1:2 camp from Saul with his c rent
2Sa 1:11 Then David took hold on his c
2Sa 3:31 that were with him, Rend your c
2Sa 13:31 stood by with their c rent
2Sa 19:24 his beard, nor washed his c
1Kin 1:1 and they covered him with c
1Kin 21:27 those words, that he rent his c
2Kin 2:12 and he took hold of his own c
2Kin 5:7 the letter, that he rent his c
2Kin 5:8 the king of Israel had rent his c
2Kin 5:8 Wherefore hast thou rent thy c
2Kin 6:30 of the woman, that he rent his c
2Kin 11:14 and Athaliah rent her c, and cried,
2Kin 18:37 to Hezekiah with their c rent
2Kin 19:1 heard it, that he rent his c
2Kin 22:11 of the law, that he rent his c
2Kin 22:19 and a curse, and hast rent thy c
2Chr 23:13 Then Athaliah rent her c, and said
2Chr 34:19 of the law, that he rent his c
2Chr 34:27 before me, and didst rend thy c
Neh 4:23 me, none of us put off our c
Neh 9:21 their c waxed not old, and their
Est 4:1 was done, Mordecai rent his c
Job 9:31 mine own c shall abhor me
Prov 6:27 his bosom, and his c not be burned
Is 36:22 to Hezekiah with their c rent
Is 37:1 heard it, that he rent his c
Jer 41:5 beards shaven, and their c rent
Eze 16:39 shall strip thee also of thy c
Eze 23:26 also strip thee out of thy c
Eze 27:20 in precious c for chariots
Eze 27:24 in all sorts of things, in blue c
Amos 2:8 c laid to pledge by every altar
Mt 21:7 the colt, and put on them their c
Mt 24:18 field return back to take his c
Mt 26:65 Then the high priest rent his c
Mk 5:28 said, If I may touch but his c
Mk 5:30 press, and said, Who touched my c
Mk 14:63 Then the high priest rent his c
Mk 15:20 from him, and put his own c on him
Lk 2:7 and wrapped him in swaddling c
Lk 2:12 the babe wrapped in swaddling c
Lk 8:27 devils long time, and ware no c
Lk 19:36 they spread their c in the way
Lk 24:12 the linen c laid by themselves
Jn 19:40 it in linen c with the spices
Jn 20:5 looking in, saw the linen c lying
Jn 20:6 and seeth the linen c lie
Jn 20:7 head, not lying with the linen c
Acts 7:58 their c at a young man's feet
Acts 14:14 Paul, heard of, they rent their c
Acts 16:22 the magistrates rent off their c
Acts 22:23 cried out, and cast off their c

## CLOTHING

Job 22:6 and stripped the naked of their c
Job 24:7 the naked to lodge without c
Job 24:10 cause him to go naked without c
Job 31:19 seen any perish for want of c
Ps 35:13 were sick, my c was sackcloth
Ps 45:13 her c is of wrought gold
Prov 27:26 The lambs are for thy c, and the
Prov 31:22 her c is silk and purple
Prov 31:25 Strength and honour are her c
Is 3:6 his father, saying, Thou hast c
Is 3:7 my house is neither bread nor c
Is 23:18 sufficiently, and for durable c
Is 59:17 the garments of vengeance for c
Jer 10:9 blue and purple is their c
Mt 7:15 which come to you in sheep's c
Mt 11:8 they that wear soft c are in
Mk 12:38 which love to go in long c
Acts 10:30 a man stood before me in bright c
Jas 2:3 to him that weareth the gay c

## CLOUD

Gen 9:13 I do set my bow in the c, and it
Gen 9:14 when I bring a c over the earth
Gen 9:14 the bow shall be seen in the c
Gen 9:16 And the bow shall be in the c
Ex 13:21 them by day in a pillar of a c
Ex 13:22 away the pillar of the c by day
Ex 14:19 the pillar of the c went from
Ex 14:20 and it was a c and darkness to them
Ex 14:24 the pillar of fire and of the c
Ex 16:10 of the LORD appeared in the c
Ex 19:9 Lo, I come unto thee in a thick c
Ex 19:16 a thick c upon the mount, and the
Ex 24:15 mount, and a c covered the mount
Ex 24:16 the c covered it six days
Ex 24:16 Moses out of the midst of the c
Ex 24:18 went into the midst of the c
Ex 34:5 And the LORD descended in the c
Ex 40:34 Then a c covered the tent of the
Ex 40:35 because the c abode thereon, and
Ex 40:36 when the c was taken up from over
Ex 40:37 But if the c were not taken up,
Ex 40:38 For the c of the LORD was upon
Lev 16:2 in the c upon the mercy seat
Lev 16:13 that the c of the incense may
Num 9:15 up the c covered the tabernacle
Num 9:16 the c covered it by day, and the
Num 9:17 when the c was taken up from the
Num 9:17 and in the place where the c abode
Num 9:18 as long as the c abode upon the
Num 9:19 when the c tarried long upon the
Num 9:20 when the c was a few days upon
Num 9:21 when the c abode from even unto
Num 9:21 that the c was taken up in the
Num 9:21 by night that the c was taken up
Num 9:22 that the c tarried upon the
Num 10:11 that the c was taken up from off
Num 10:12 the c rested in the wilderness of
Num 10:34 the c of the LORD was upon them
Num 11:25 And the LORD came down in a c
Num 12:5 came down in the pillar of the c
Num 12:10 the c departed from off the
Num 14:14 that thy c standeth over them, and
Num 14:14 by daytime in a pillar of a c
Num 16:42 the c covered it, and the glory of
Deut 1:33 ye should go, and in a c by day
Deut 5:22 the midst of the fire, of the c
Deut 31:15 the tabernacle in a pillar of a c
Deut 31:15 the pillar of the c stood over
1Kin 8:10 that the c filled the house of
1Kin 8:11 to minister because of the c
1Kin 18:44 ariseth a little c out of the sea
2Chr 5:13 the house was filled with a c
2Chr 5:14 to minister by reason of the c
Neh 9:19 the pillar of the c departed not
Job 3:5 let a c dwell upon it
Job 7:9 As the c is consumed and vanisheth
Job 22:13 can he judge through the dark c
Job 26:8 the c is not rent under them
Job 26:9 and spreadeth his c upon it
Job 30:15 and my welfare passeth away as a c
Job 36:32 by the c that cometh betwixt
Job 37:11 watering he wearieth the thick c
Job 37:11 he scattereth his bright c
Job 37:15 the light of his c to shine
Job 38:9 When I made the c the garment
Ps 78:14 daytime also he led them with a c
Ps 105:39 He spread a c for a covering
Prov 16:15 is as a c of the latter rain
Is 4:5 Zion, and upon her assemblies, a c
Is 18:4 like a c of dew in the heat of
Is 19:1 the LORD rideth upon a swift c
Is 25:5 the heat with the shadow of a c
Is 44:22 I have blotted out, as a thick c
Is 44:22 thy transgressions, and, as a c
Is 60:8 Who are these that fly as a c
Lam 2:1 of Zion with a c in his anger
Lam 3:44 hast covered thyself with a c
Eze 1:4 came out of the north, a great c
Eze 1:28 is in the c in the day of rain

Eze 8:11 a thick c of incense went up
Eze 10:3 the c filled the inner court
Eze 10:4 the house was filled with the c
Eze 30:18 a c shall cover her, and her
Eze 32:7 I will cover the sun with a c
Eze 38:9 be like a c to cover the land
Eze 38:16 Israel, as a c to cover the land
Hos 6:4 your goodness is as a morning c
Hos 13:3 they shall be as the morning c
Mt 17:5 a bright c overshadowed them
Mt 17:5 and behold a voice out of the c
Mk 9:7 there was a c that overshadowed
Mk 9:7 and a voice came out of the c
Lk 9:34 he thus spake, there came a c
Lk 9:34 feared as they entered into the c
Lk 9:35 there came a voice out of the c
Lk 12:54 When ye see a c rise out of the
Lk 21:27 of man coming in a c with power
Acts 1:9 a c received him out of their
1Cor 10:1 all our fathers were under the c
1Cor 10:2 all baptized unto Moses in the c
Heb 12:1 with so great a c of witnesses
Rev 10:1 from heaven, clothed with a c
Rev 11:12 they ascended up to heaven in a c
Rev 14:14 And I looked, and behold a white c
Rev 14:14 upon the c one sat like unto the
Rev 14:15 voice to him that sat on the c
Rev 14:16 he that sat on the c thrust in

## CLOUDS

Deut 4:11 midst of heaven, with darkness, c
Judg 5:4 dropped, the c also dropped water
2Sa 22:12 waters, and thick c of the skies
2Sa 23:4 riseth, even a morning without c
1Kin 18:45 that the heaven was black with c
Job 20:6 and his head reach unto the c
Job 22:14 Thick c are a covering to him,
Job 26:8 up the waters in his thick c
Job 35:5 behold the c which are higher
Job 36:28 Which the c do drop and distil
Job 36:29 the spreadings of the c, or the
Job 36:32 With c he covereth the light
Job 37:16 thou know the balancings of the c
Job 37:21 bright light which is in the c
Job 38:34 thou lift up thy voice to the c
Job 38:37 Who can number the c in wisdom
Ps 18:11 waters and thick c of the skies
Ps 18:12 was before him his thick c passed
Ps 36:5 faithfulness reacheth unto the c
Ps 57:10 heavens, and thy truth unto the c
Ps 68:34 and his strength is in the c
Ps 77:17 The c poured out water
Ps 78:23 he had commanded the c from above
Ps 97:2 C and darkness are round about him
Ps 104:3 who maketh the c his chariot
Ps 108:4 and thy truth reacheth unto the c
Ps 147:8 Who covereth the heaven with c
Prov 3:20 up, and the c drop down the dew
Prov 8:28 When he established the c above
Prov 25:14 himself of a false gift is like c
Eccl 11:3 If the c be full of rain, they
Eccl 11:4 regardeth the c shall not reap
Eccl 12:2 nor the c return after the rain
Is 5:6 I will also command the c that
Is 14:14 ascend above the heights of the c
Jer 4:13 Behold, he shall come up as c
Dan 7:13 of man came with the c of heaven
Joel 2:2 and of gloominess, a day of c
Nah 1:3 the c are the dust of his feet
Zeph 1:15 and gloominess, a day of c
Zec 10:1 so the LORD shall make bright c
Mt 24:30 in the c of heaven with power
Mt 26:64 and coming in the c of heaven
Mk 13:26 coming in the c with great power
Mk 14:62 and coming in the c of heaven
1Th 4:17 up together with them in the c
2Pet 2:17 c that are carried with a tempest
Jude 12 c they are without water, carried
Rev 1:7 Behold, he cometh with c

## CNIDUS *(ni'-dus) A port town in south-western Asia Minor.*

Acts 27:7 scarce were come over against C

## COALS

Lev 16:12 c of fire from off the altar
2Sa 22:9 c were kindled by it
2Sa 22:13 before him were c of fire kindled
1Kin 19:6 there was a cake baken on the c
Job 41:21 His breath kindleth c, and a flame
Ps 18:8 c were kindled by it
Ps 18:12 passed, hail stones and c of fire
Ps 18:13 hail stones and c of fire
Ps 120:4 of the mighty, with c of juniper
Ps 140:10 Let burning c fall upon them
Prov 6:28 Can one go upon hot c, and his
Prov 25:22 For thou shalt heap c of fire
Prov 26:21 As c are to burning c, and
Prov 26:21 As c are to burning c
Song 8:6 the c thereof are c of fire
Is 44:12 the tongs both worketh in the c
Is 44:19 baked bread upon the c thereof
Is 54:16 that bloweth the c in the fire
Eze 1:13 was like burning c of fire
Eze 10:2 fill thine hand with c of fire
Eze 24:11 set it empty upon the c thereof
Hab 3:5 burning c went forth at his feet
Jn 18:18 there, who had made a fire of c
Jn 21:9 land, they saw a fire of c there
Rom 12:20 shalt heap c of fire on his head

## COAST

Ex 10:4 I bring the locusts into thy c
Num 13:29 by the sea, and by the c of Jordan
Num 20:23 by the c of the land of Edom,
Num 22:36 Arnon, which is in the utmost c
Num 24:24 come come from the c of Chittim
Num 34:3 of Zin along by the c of Edom
Num 34:3 c of the salt sea eastward
Num 34:11 the c shall go down from Shepham
Deut 2:4 Ye are to pass through the c of
Deut 2:18 Ar, the c of Moab, this day
Deut 3:17 the c thereof, from Chinnereth
Deut 11:24 the uttermost sea shall your c be
Deut 16:4 with thee in all thy c seven days
Deut 19:8 if the LORD thy God enlarge thy c
Josh 1:4 down of the sun, shall be your c
Josh 12:4 the c of Og king of Bashan, which
Josh 12:23 The king of Dor in the c of Dor
Josh 13:16 their c was from Aroer, that is
Josh 13:25 their c was Jazer, and all the
Josh 13:30 their c was from Mahanaim, all
Josh 15:1 the uttermost part of the south c
Josh 15:4 out of that c were at the sea
Josh 15:4 this shall be your south c
Josh 15:12 the great sea, and the c thereof
Josh 15:12 This is the c of the children of
Josh 15:21 children of Judah toward the c of
Josh 16:3 westward to the c of Japhleti
Josh 16:3 unto the c of Beth-horon the
Josh 17:7 the c of Manasseh was from Asher
Josh 17:9 the c descended unto the river
Josh 17:9 the c of Manasseh also was on the
Josh 18:5 abide in their c on the south
Josh 18:11 the c of their lot came forth
Josh 18:19 this was the south c
Josh 19:22 the c reacheth to Tabor, and
Josh 19:29 then the c turneth to Ramah, and
Josh 19:29 and the c turneth to Hosah
Josh 19:29 at the sea from the c to Achzib
Josh 19:33 their c was from Heleph, from
Josh 19:34 then the c turneth westward to
Josh 19:41 the c of their inheritance was
Josh 19:47 the c of the children of Dan went
Judg 1:18 took Gaza with the c thereof
Judg 1:18 and Askelon with the c thereof
Judg 1:18 and Ekron with the c thereof
Judg 1:36 the c of the Amorites was from
Judg 11:20 not Israel to pass through his c
1Sa 6:9 way of his own c to Beth-shemesh
1Sa 7:13 came no more into the c of Israel
1Sa 27:1 me any more in any c of Israel
1Sa 30:14 upon the c which belongeth to
2Kin 14:25 He restored the c of Israel from
1Chr 4:10 bless me indeed, and enlarge my c
Eze 25:16 destroy the remnant of the sea c
Eze 47:16 which is by the c of Hauran
Eze 48:1 to the c of the way of Hethlon
Eze 48:1 northward, to the c of Hamath
Zeph 2:5 unto the inhabitants of the sea c
Zeph 2:6 the sea c shall be dwellings and
Zeph 2:7 the c shall be for the remnant of
Mt 4:13 which is upon the sea c, in the
Lk 6:17 and from the sea c of Tyre

## COASTS

Ex 10:14 and rested in all the c of Egypt
Ex 10:19 one locust in all the c of Egypt
Num 21:13 out of the c of the Amorites
Num 32:33 with the cities thereof in the c
Num 34:2 land of Canaan with the c thereof
Num 34:12 with the c thereof round about
Deut 3:14 of Argob unto the c of Geshuri
Deut 19:3 divide the c of thy land, which
Deut 28:40 olive trees throughout all thy c
Josh 9:1 in all the c of the great sea
Josh 18:5 abide in their c on the north
Josh 18:20 by the c thereof round about,
Josh 19:49 land for inheritance by their c
Judg 11:22 all the c of the Amorites
Judg 11:26 that be along by the c of Arnon
Judg 18:2 family five men from their c
Judg 19:29 sent her into all the c of Israel
1Sa 5:6 even Ashdod and the c thereof
1Sa 7:14 the c thereof did Israel deliver
1Sa 11:3 unto all the c of Israel
1Sa 11:7 the c of Israel by the hands of
2Sa 21:5 in any of the c of Israel
1Kin 1:3 throughout all the c of Israel
2Kin 10:32 smote them in all the c of Israel
2Kin 15:16 the c thereof from Tirzah
1Chr 6:54 their castles in their c, of the
1Chr 6:66 c out of the tribe of Ephraim
1Chr 21:12 throughout all the c of Israel
2Chr 11:13 to him out of all their c
Ps 105:31 of flies, and lice in all their c
Ps 105:33 and brake the trees of their c
Jer 25:32 raised up from the c of the earth
Jer 31:8 them from the c of the earth
Jer 50:41 raised up from the c of the earth
Eze 33:2 of the land take a man of their c
Joel 3:4 Zidon, and all the c of Palestine
Mt 2:16 and in all the c thereof, from
Mt 8:34 he would depart out of their c
Mt 15:21 and departed into the c of Tyre
Mt 15:22 of Canaan came out of the same c
Mt 15:39 and came into the c of Magdala
Mt 16:13 into the c of Caesarea Philippi
Mt 19:1 came into the c of Judaea beyond
Mk 5:17 pray him to depart out of their c
Mk 7:31 departing from the c of Tyre
Mk 7:31 the midst of the c of Decapolis
Mk 10:1 cometh into the c of Judaea by
Acts 13:50 and expelled them out of their c
Acts 19:1 the upper c came to Ephesus
Acts 26:20 and throughout all the c of Judaea
Acts 27:2 meaning to sail by the c of Asia

## COAT

Gen 37:3 he made him a c of many colours
Gen 37:23 they stript Joseph out of his c
Gen 37:23 his c of many colours that was on
Gen 37:31 And they took Joseph's c, and
Gen 37:31 dipped the c in the blood
Gen 37:32 they sent the c of many colours,
Gen 37:32 whether it be thy son's c or no
Gen 37:33 it, and said, It is my son's c
Ex 28:4 and a robe, and a broidered c
Ex 28:39 embroider the c of fine linen
Ex 29:5 garments, and put upon Aaron the c
Lev 8:7 And he put upon him the c, and
Lev 16:4 He shall put on the holy linen c
1Sa 2:19 his mother made him a little c
1Sa 17:5 and he was armed with a c of mail
1Sa 17:5 the weight of the c was five
1Sa 17:38 he armed him with a c of mail
2Sa 15:32 came to meet him with his c rent
Job 30:18 me about as the collar of my c
Song 5:3 I have put off my c
Mt 5:40 at the law, and take away thy c
Lk 6:29 forbid not to take thy c also
Jn 19:23 and also his c
Jn 19:23 now the c was without seam, woven
Jn 21:7 he girt his fisher's c unto him

## COATS

Gen 3:21 did the LORD God make c of skins
Ex 28:40 Aaron's sons thou shalt make c
Ex 29:8 his sons, and put c upon them
Ex 39:27 they made c of fine linen of
Ex 40:14 his sons, and clothe them with c
Lev 8:13 put c upon them, and girded them
Lev 10:5 them in their c out of the camp
Dan 3:21 these men were bound in their c
Dan 3:27 neither were their c changed
Mt 10:10 for your journey, neither two c
Mk 6:9 and not put on two c
Lk 3:11 unto them, He that hath two c
Lk 9:3 neither have two c apiece
Acts 9:39 by him weeping, and shewing the c

## COCK

Mt 26:34 this night, before the c crow
Mt 26:74 And immediately the c crew
Mt 26:75 said unto him, Before the c crow

Mk 14:30 night, before the c crow twice
Mk 14:68 and the c crew
Mk 14:72 And the second time the c crew
Mk 14:72 unto him, Before the c crow twice
Lk 22:34 the c shall not crow this day,
Lk 22:60 while he yet spake, the c crew
Lk 22:61 said unto him, Before the c crow
Jn 13:38 The c shall not crow, till thou
Jn 18:27 and immediately the c crew

**COLD**
Gen 8:22 seedtime and harvest, and c
Job 24:7 they have no covering in the c
Job 37:9 and c out of the north
Ps 147:17 who can stand before his c
Prov 20:4 will not plow by reason of the c
Prov 25:13 As the c of snow in the time of
Prov 25:20 away a garment in c weather
Prov 25:25 As c waters to a thirsty soul, so
Jer 18:14 or shall the c flowing waters
Nah 3:17 camp in the hedges in the c day
Mt 10:42 of c water only in the name of a
Mt 24:12 the love of many shall wax c
Jn 18:18 for it was c
Acts 28:2 present rain, and because of the c
2Cor 11:27 thirst, in fastings often, in c
Rev 3:15 that thou art neither c nor hot
Rev 3:15 I would thou wert c or hot
Rev 3:16 lukewarm, and neither c nor hot

**COLHOZEH** *(col-ho'-zeh)*
Neh 3:15 repaired Shallun the son of C
Neh 11:5 the son of Baruch, the son of C

**COLLAR**
Job 30:18 me about as the c of my coat

**COLLARS**
Judg 8:26 beside ornaments, and c, and purple

**COLLECTION**
2Chr 24:6 Judah and out of Jerusalem the c
2Chr 24:9 to bring in to the LORD the c
1Cor 16:1 concerning the c for the saints

**COLLEGE**
2Kin 22:14 she dwelt in Jerusalem in the c
2Chr 34:22 she dwelt in Jerusalem in the c

**COLLOPS**
Job 15:27 maketh c of fat on his flanks

**COLONY**
Acts 16:12 of that part of Macedonia, and a c

**COLORS**
Is 54:11 I will lay thy stones with fair c

**COLOSSE** *(co-los'-see)* See COLOSSIANS. *A city in Phrygia.*
Col 1:2 brethren in Christ which are at C

**COLOSSIANS** *(co-los'-yans) Residents of Colosse.*
Col s from Rome to the C by Tychicus

**COLOUR**
Lev 13:55 the plague have not changed his c
Num 11:7 the c thereof as the c of
Prov 23:31 when it giveth his c in the cup
Eze 1:4 midst thereof as the c of amber
Eze 1:7 like the c of burnished brass
Eze 1:16 was like unto the c of a beryl
Eze 1:22 as the c of the terrible crystal
Eze 1:27 And I saw as the c of amber
Eze 8:2 of brightness, as the c of amber
Eze 10:9 was as the c of a beryl stone
Dan 10:6 his feet like in c to polished
Acts 27:30 under c as though they would have
Rev 17:4 arrayed in purple and scarlet c

**COLOURS**
Gen 37:3 and he made him a coat of many c
Gen 37:23 coat of many c that was on him
Gen 37:32 And they sent the coat of many c
Judg 5:30 to Sisera a prey of divers c
Judg 5:30 a prey of divers c of needlework
Judg 5:30 of divers c of needlework on both
2Sa 13:18 a garment of divers c upon her
2Sa 13:19 of divers c that was on her
1Chr 29:2 glistering stones, and of divers c
Eze 16:16 thy high places with divers c
Eze 17:3 of feathers, which had divers c

**COLT**
Gen 49:11 his ass's c unto the choice vine
Job 11:12 man be born like a wild ass's c
Zec 9:9 upon a c the foal of an ass
Mt 21:2 find an ass tied, and a c with her
Mt 21:5 an ass, and a c the foal of an ass
Mt 21:7 And brought the ass, and the c
Mk 11:2 into it, ye shall find a c tied
Mk 11:4 found the c tied by the door
Mk 11:5 them, What do ye, loosing the c
Mk 11:7 And they brought the c to Jesus
Lk 19:30 entering ye shall find a c tied
Lk 19:33 And as they were loosing the c
Lk 19:33 unto them, Why loose ye the c
Lk 19:35 cast their garments upon the c
Jn 12:15 cometh, sitting on an ass's c

**COMELINESS**
Is 53:2 he hath no form nor c
Eze 16:14 for it was perfect through my c
Eze 27:10 they set forth thy c
Dan 10:8 for my c was turned in me into
1Cor 12:23 parts have more abundant c

**COMELY**
1Sa 16:18 a c person, and the LORD is with
Job 41:12 his power, nor his c proportion
Ps 33:1 for praise is c for the upright
Ps 147:1 and praise is c
Prov 30:29 go well, yea, four are c in going
Eccl 5:18 c for one to eat and to drink, and
Song 1:5 I am black, but c, O ye daughters
Song 1:10 Thy cheeks are c with rows of
Song 2:14 voice, and thy countenance is c
Song 4:3 of scarlet, and thy speech is c
Song 6:4 c as Jerusalem, terrible as an
Is 4:2 c for them that are escaped of
Jer 6:2 the daughter of Zion to a c
1Cor 7:35 upon you, but for that which is c
1Cor 11:13 is it c that a woman pray unto
1Cor 12:24 For our c parts have no need

**COMFORT**
Gen 5:29 This same shall c us concerning
Gen 18:5 of bread, and c ye your hearts
Gen 27:42 doth c himself, purposing to kill
Gen 37:35 his daughters rose up to c him
Judg 19:5 C thine heart with a morsel of
Judg 19:8 C thine heart, I pray thee
2Sa 10:2 David sent to c him by the hand
1Chr 7:22 and his brethren came to c him
1Chr 19:2 David sent messengers to c him
1Chr 19:2 of Ammon to Hanun, to c him
Job 2:11 to mourn with him and to c him
Job 6:10 Then should I yet have c
Job 7:13 When I say, My bed shall c me
Job 9:27 off my heaviness, and c myself
Job 10:20 alone, that I may take c a little
Job 21:34 How then c ye me in vain, seeing
Ps 23:4 thy rod and thy staff they c me
Ps 71:21 greatness, and c me on every side
Ps 119:50 This is my c in my affliction
Ps 119:76 thy merciful kindness be for my c
Ps 119:82 word, saying, When wilt thou c me
Song 2:5 me with flagons, c me with apples
Is 22:4 weep bitterly, labour not to c me
Is 40:1 C ye, c ye my people, saith
Is 51:3 For the LORD shall c Zion
Is 51:3 he will c all her waste places
Is 51:19 by whom shall I c thee
Is 57:6 Should I receive c in these
Is 61:2 to c all that mourn
Is 66:13 comforteth, so will I c you
Jer 8:18 When I would c myself against
Jer 16:7 mourning, to c them for the dead
Jer 31:13 mourning into joy, and will c them
Lam 1:2 her lovers she hath none to c her
Lam 1:17 hands, and there is none to c her
Lam 1:21 there is none to c me
Lam 2:13 equal to thee, that I may c thee
Eze 14:23 And they shall c you, when ye see
Eze 16:54 in that thou art a c unto them
Zec 1:17 and the LORD shall yet c Zion
Zec 10:2 they c in vain
Mt 9:22 he said, Daughter, be of good c
Mk 10:49 saying unto him, Be of good c
Lk 8:48 unto her, Daughter, be of good c
Jn 11:19 to c them concerning their
Acts 9:31 in the c of the Holy Ghost, were
Rom 15:4 c of the scriptures might have
1Cor 14:3 edification, and exhortation, and c
2Cor 1:3 of mercies, and the God of all c
2Cor 1:4 that we may be able to c them
2Cor 1:4 by the c wherewith we ourselves
2Cor 2:7 c him, lest perhaps such a one
2Cor 7:4 I am filled with c, I am
2Cor 7:13 we were comforted in your c
2Cor 13:11 Be perfect, be of good c, be of
Eph 6:22 and that he might c your hearts
Phil 2:1 Christ, if any c of love, if any
Phil 2:19 you, that I also may be of good c
Col 4:8 your estate, and c your hearts
Col 4:11 God, which have been a c unto me
1Th 3:2 to c you concerning your faith
1Th 4:18 Wherefore c one another with
1Th 5:11 Wherefore c yourselves together,
1Th 5:14 c the feebleminded, support the
2Th 2:17 C your hearts, and stablish you in

**COMFORTED**
Gen 24:67 Isaac was c after his mother's
Gen 37:35 but he refused to be c
Gen 38:12 and Judah was c, and went up unto
Gen 50:21 he c them, and spake kindly unto
Ruth 2:13 for that thou hast c me, and for
2Sa 12:24 David c Bath-sheba his wife, and
2Sa 13:39 for he was c concerning Amnon,
Job 42:11 c him over all the evil that the
Ps 77:2 my soul refused to be c
Ps 86:17 LORD, hast holpen me, and c me
Ps 119:52 and have c myself
Is 49:13 for the LORD hath c his people
Is 52:9 for the LORD hath c his people
Is 54:11 tossed with tempest, and not c
Is 66:13 ye shall be c in Jerusalem
Jer 31:15 refused to be c for her children
Eze 5:13 to rest upon them, and I will be c
Eze 14:22 ye shall be c concerning the evil
Eze 31:16 shall be c in the nether parts of
Eze 32:31 shall be c over all his multitude
Mt 2:18 her children, and would not be c
Mt 5:4 for they shall be c
Lk 16:25 but now he is c, and thou art
Jn 11:31 c her, when they saw Mary, that
Acts 16:40 seen the brethren, they c them
Acts 20:12 man alive, and were not a little c
Rom 1:12 that I may be c together with you
1Cor 14:31 all may learn, and all may be c
2Cor 1:4 we ourselves are c of God
2Cor 1:6 or whether we be c, it is for
2Cor 7:6 c us by the coming of Titus
2Cor 7:7 wherewith he was c in you
2Cor 7:13 we were c in your comfort
Col 2:2 That their hearts might be c
1Th 2:11 As ye know how we exhorted and c
1Th 3:7 we were c over you in all our

**COMFORTER**
Eccl 4:1 were oppressed, and they had no c
Eccl 4:1 but they had no c
Lam 1:9 she had no c
Lam 1:16 because the c that should relieve
Jn 14:16 and he shall give you another C
Jn 14:26 But the C, which is the Holy
Jn 15:26 But when the C is come, whom I
Jn 16:7 the C will not come unto you

**COMFORTERS**
2Sa 10:3 that he hath sent c unto thee
1Chr 19:3 that he hath sent c unto thee
Job 16:2 miserable c are ye all
Ps 69:20 and for c, but I found none
Nah 3:7 whence shall I seek c for thee

**COMMAND**
Gen 18:19 him, that he will c his children
Gen 27:8 according to that which I c thee
Gen 50:16 Thy father did c before he died
Ex 7:2 shalt speak all that I c thee
Ex 8:27 LORD our God, as he shall c us
Ex 18:23 God c thee so, then thou shalt be
Ex 27:20 thou shalt c the children of
Ex 34:11 thou that which I c thee this day
Lev 6:9 C Aaron and his sons, saying, This
Lev 13:54 Then the priest shall c that they
Lev 14:4 Then shall the priest c to take
Lev 14:5 the priest shall c that one of
Lev 14:36 Then the priest shall c that they
Lev 14:40 Then the priest shall c that they
Lev 24:2 C the children of Israel, that
Lev 25:21 Then I will c my blessing upon
Num 5:2 C the children of Israel, that
Num 9:8 the LORD will c concerning you
Num 28:2 C the children of Israel, and say
Num 34:2 C the children of Israel, and say
Num 35:2 C the children of Israel, that
Num 36:6 c concerning the daughters of
Deut 2:4 c thou the people, saying, Ye are
Deut 4:2 add unto the word which I c you

Deut 4:2 the LORD your God which I c you
Deut 4:40 which I c thee this day, that it
Deut 6:2 his commandments, which I c thee
Deut 6:6 which I c thee this day, shall be
Deut 7:11 which I c thee this day, to do
Deut 8:1 All the commandments which I c
Deut 8:11 statutes, which I c thee this day
Deut 10:13 which I c thee this day for thy
Deut 11:8 which I c you this day, that ye
Deut 11:13 which I c you this day, to love
Deut 11:22 these commandments which I c you
Deut 11:27 your God, which I c you this day
Deut 11:28 of the way which I c you this day
Deut 12:11 shall ye bring all that I c you
Deut 12:14 thou shalt do all that I c thee
Deut 12:28 all these words which I c thee
Deut 12:32 What thing soever I c you
Deut 13:18 which I c thee this day, to do
Deut 15:5 which I c thee this day
Deut 15:11 therefore I c thee, saying, Thou
Deut 15:15 therefore I c thee this thing to
Deut 18:18 unto them all that I shall c him
Deut 19:7 Wherefore I c thee, saying, Thou
Deut 19:9 which I c thee this day, to love
Deut 24:18 therefore I c thee to do this
Deut 24:22 therefore I c thee to do this
Deut 27:1 which I c you this day
Deut 27:4 which I c you this day, in mount
Deut 27:10 statutes, which I c thee this day
Deut 28:1 which I c thee this day, that the
Deut 28:8 The LORD shall c the blessing
Deut 28:13 which I c thee this day, to
Deut 28:14 the words which I c thee this day
Deut 28:15 statutes which I c thee this day
Deut 30:2 to all that I c thee this day
Deut 30:8 which I c thee this day
Deut 30:11 which I c thee this day, it is
Deut 30:16 In that I c thee this day to love
Deut 32:46 which ye shall c your children to
Josh 1:11 c the people, saying, Prepare you
Josh 3:8 thou shalt c the priests that
Josh 4:3 c ye them, saying, Take you hence
Josh 4:16 C the priests that bear the ark
Josh 11:15 servant, so did Moses c Joshua
1Sa 16:16 Let our lord now c thy servants
1Kin 5:6 Now therefore c thou that they
1Kin 11:38 hearken unto all that I c thee
2Chr 7:13 or if I c the locusts to devour
Job 39:27 Doth the eagle mount up at thy c
Ps 42:8 Yet the LORD will c his
Ps 44:4 c deliverances for Jacob
Is 5:6 I will also c the clouds that
Is 45:11 the work of my hands c ye me
Jer 1:7 whatsoever I c thee thou shalt
Jer 1:17 speak unto them all that I c thee
Jer 11:4 according to all which I c you
Jer 26:2 all the words that I c thee to
Jer 27:4 c them to say unto their masters,
Jer 34:22 Behold, I will c, saith the LORD,
Lam 1:10 whom thou didst c that they
Amos 9:3 sea, thence will I c the serpent
Amos 9:4 thence will I c the sword
Amos 9:9 For, lo, I will c, and I will sift
Mt 4:3 c that these stones be made bread
Mt 19:7 Why did Moses then c to give a
Mt 27:64 C therefore that the sepulchre be
Mk 10:3 unto them, What did Moses c you
Lk 4:3 c this stone that it be made
Lk 8:31 c them to go out into the deep
Lk 9:54 wilt thou that we c fire to come
Jn 15:14 if ye do whatsoever I c you
Jn 15:17 These things I c you, that ye
Acts 5:28 Did not we straitly c you that ye
Acts 15:5 to c them to keep the law of
Acts 16:18 I c thee in the name of Jesus
1Cor 7:10 And unto the married I c, yet not
2Th 3:4 will do the things which we c you
2Th 3:6 Now we c you, brethren, in the
2Th 3:12 Now them that are such we c
1Ti 4:11 These things c and teach

## COMMANDMENT

Gen 45:21 according to the c of Pharaoh
Ex 17:1 according to the c of the LORD
Ex 25:22 which I will give thee in c unto
Ex 34:32 he gave them in c all that the
Ex 36:6 And Moses gave c, and they caused
Ex 38:21 according to the c of Moses
Num 3:39 numbered at the c of the LORD
Num 4:37 the c of the LORD by the hand of
Num 4:41 according to the c of the LORD
Num 4:49 According to the c of the LORD
Num 9:18 At the c of the LORD the children
Num 9:18 at the c of the LORD they pitched
Num 9:20 according to the c of the LORD
Num 9:20 according to the c of the LORD
Num 9:23 At the c of the LORD they rested
Num 9:23 at the c of the LORD they
Num 9:23 at the c of the LORD by the hand
Num 10:13 the c of the LORD by the hand of
Num 13:3 Moses by the c of the LORD sent
Num 14:41 ye transgress the c of the LORD
Num 15:31 of the LORD, and hath broken his c
Num 23:20 I have received c to bless
Num 24:13 go beyond the c of the LORD
Num 27:14 against my c in the desert of Zin
Num 33:2 journeys by the c of the LORD
Num 33:38 mount Hor at the c of the LORD
Deut 1:3 LORD had given him in c unto them
Deut 1:26 the c of the LORD your God
Deut 1:43 against the c of the LORD
Deut 9:23 the c of the LORD your God
Deut 17:20 that he turn not aside from the c
Deut 30:11 For this c which I command thee
Josh 1:18 be that doth rebel against thy c
Josh 8:8 according to the c of the LORD
Josh 15:13 according to the c of the LORD to
Josh 17:4 Therefore according to the c of
Josh 21:3 at the c of the LORD, these
Josh 22:3 of the c of the LORD your God
Josh 22:5 take diligent heed to do the c
1Sa 12:14 not rebel against the c of the
1Sa 12:15 rebel against the c of the LORD
1Sa 13:13 kept the c of the LORD thy God
1Sa 15:13 have performed the c of the LORD
1Sa 15:24 transgressed the c of the LORD
2Sa 12:9 thou despised the c of the LORD
1Kin 2:43 the c that I have charged thee
1Kin 13:21 hast not kept the c which the
2Kin 17:34 c which the LORD commanded the
2Kin 17:37 ordinances, and the law, and the c
2Kin 18:36 for the king's c was, saying,
2Kin 23:35 according to the c of Pharaoh
2Kin 24:3 Surely at the c of the LORD came
1Chr 12:32 their brethren were at their c
1Chr 14:12 their gods there, David gave a c
1Chr 28:21 people will be wholly at thy c
2Chr 8:13 according to the c of Moses
2Chr 8:15 they departed not from the c of
2Chr 14:4 and to do the law and the c
2Chr 19:10 blood and blood, between law and c
2Chr 24:6 according to the c of Moses the
2Chr 24:8 at the king's c they made a chest
2Chr 24:21 stoned him with stones at the c
2Chr 29:15 according to the c of the king
2Chr 29:25 according to the c of David
2Chr 29:25 for so was the c of the LORD by
2Chr 30:6 and according to the c of the king
2Chr 30:12 one heart to do the c of the king
2Chr 31:5 And as soon as the c came abroad
2Chr 31:13 at the c of Hezekiah the king, and
2Chr 35:10 according to the king's c
2Chr 35:15 according to the c of David
2Chr 35:16 according to the c of king Josiah
Ezr 4:21 Give ye now c to cause these men
Ezr 4:21 until another c shall be given
Ezr 6:14 according to the c of the God of
Ezr 6:14 and according to the c of Cyrus
Ezr 8:17 I sent them with c unto Iddo the
Ezr 10:3 that tremble at the c of our God
Neh 11:23 was the king's c concerning them
Neh 12:24 according to the c of David the
Neh 12:45 according to the c of David
Est 1:12 the king's c by his chamberlains
Est 1:15 she hath not performed the c of
Est 1:19 let there go a royal c from him
Est 2:8 came to pass, when the king's c
Est 2:20 for Esther did the c of Mordecai
Est 3:3 transgressest thou the king's c
Est 3:14 a c to be given in every province
Est 3:15 being hastened by the king's c
Est 4:3 whithersoever the king's c
Est 4:5 gave him a c to Mordecai, to know
Est 4:10 and gave him c unto Mordecai
Est 8:13 a c to be given in every province
Est 8:14 and pressed on by the king's c
Est 8:17 city, whithersoever the king's c
Est 9:1 of the same, when the king's c
Job 23:12 gone back from the c of his lips
Ps 19:8 the c of the LORD is pure,
Ps 71:3 thou hast given c to save me
Ps 119:96 but thy c is exceeding broad
Ps 147:15 He sendeth forth his c upon earth
Prov 6:20 My son, keep thy father's c
Prov 6:23 For the c is a lamp
Prov 8:29 the waters should not pass his c
Prov 13:13 feareth the c shall be rewarded
Prov 19:16 He that keepeth the c keepeth his
Eccl 8:2 counsel thee to keep the king's c
Eccl 8:5 Whoso keepeth the c shall feel no
Is 23:11 the LORD hath given a c against
Is 36:21 for the king's c was, saying,
Jer 35:14 none, but obey their father's c
Jer 35:16 performed the c of their father
Jer 35:18 the c of Jonadab your father
Lam 1:18 for I have rebelled against his c
Dan 3:22 because the king's c was urgent
Dan 9:23 supplications the c came forth
Dan 9:25 going forth of the c to restore
Hos 5:11 he willingly walked after the c
Nah 1:14 hath given a c concerning thee
Mal 2:1 O ye priests, this c is for you
Mal 2:4 that I have sent this c unto you
Mt 8:18 he gave c to depart unto the
Mt 15:3 the c of God by your tradition
Mt 15:6 Thus have ye made the c of God of
Mt 22:36 which is the great c in the law
Mt 22:38 This is the first and great c
Mk 7:8 For laying aside the c of God
Mk 7:9 Full well ye reject the c of God
Mk 12:28 him, Which is the first c of all
Mk 12:30 this is the first c
Mk 12:31 none other c greater than these
Lk 15:29 transgressed I at any time thy c
Lk 23:56 sabbath day according to the c
Jn 10:18 This c have I received of my
Jn 11:57 and the Pharisees had given a c
Jn 12:49 which sent me, he gave me a c
Jn 12:50 I know that his c is life
Jn 13:34 A new c I give unto you, That ye
Jn 14:31 and as the Father gave me c
Jn 15:12 This is my c, That ye love one
Acts 15:24 to whom we gave no such c
Acts 17:15 and receiving a c unto Silas
Acts 23:30 gave c to his accusers also to
Acts 25:23 at Festus' c Paul was brought
Rom 7:8 But sin, taking occasion by the c
Rom 7:9 but when the c came, sin revived,
Rom 7:10 And the c, which was ordained to
Rom 7:11 For sin, taking occasion by the c
Rom 7:12 the c holy, and just, and good
Rom 7:13 that sin by the c might become
Rom 13:9 and if there be any other c
Rom 16:26 according to the c of the
1Cor 7:6 this by permission, and not of c
1Cor 7:25 virgins I have no c of the Lord
2Cor 8:8 I speak not by c, but by occasion
Eph 6:2 which is the first c with promise
1Ti 1:1 by the c of God our Saviour
1Ti 1:5 Now the end of the c is charity
1Ti 6:14 thou keep this c without spot
Titus 1:3 to the c of God our Saviour
Heb 7:5 have a c to take tithes of the
Heb 7:16 not after the law of a carnal c
Heb 7:18 c going before for the weakness
Heb 11:22 gave c concerning his bones
Heb 11:23 were not afraid of the king's c
2Pet 2:21 the holy c delivered unto them
2Pet 3:2 of the c of us the apostles of
1Jn 2:7 I write no new c unto you
1Jn 2:7 but an old c which ye had from
1Jn 2:7 The old c is the word which ye
1Jn 2:8 a new c I write unto you, which
1Jn 3:23 And this is his c, That we should
1Jn 3:23 love one another, as he gave us c
1Jn 4:21 this c have we from him, That he
2Jn 4 have received a c from the Father
2Jn 5 though I wrote a new c unto thee
2Jn 6 This is the c, That, as ye have

## COMMANDMENTS

Gen 26:5 my voice, and kept my charge, my c
Ex 15:26 sight, and wilt give ear to his c
Ex 16:28 How long refuse ye to keep my c
Ex 20:6 them that love me, and keep my c
Ex 24:12 a law, and c which I have written
Ex 34:28 words of the covenant, the ten c
Lev 4:2 ignorance against any of the c of
Lev 4:13 somewhat against any of the c of
Lev 4:22 ignorance against any of the c of

Lev 4:27 somewhat against any of the c of
Lev 5:17 to be done by the c of the LORD
Lev 22:31 Therefore shall ye keep my c
Lev 26:3 walk in my statutes, and keep my c
Lev 26:14 me, and will not do all these c
Lev 26:15 so that ye will not do all my c
Lev 27:34 These are the c, which the LORD
Num 15:22 and not observed all these c
Num 15:39 and remember all the c of the LORD
Num 15:40 ye may remember, and do all my c
Num 36:13 These are the c and the judgments,
Deut 4:2 that ye may keep the c of the
Deut 4:13 you to perform, even ten c
Deut 4:40 therefore his statutes, and his c
Deut 5:10 of them that love me and keep my c
Deut 5:29 fear me, and keep all my c always
Deut 5:31 I will speak unto thee all the c
Deut 6:1 Now these are the c, the statutes
Deut 6:2 to keep all his statutes and his c
Deut 6:17 keep the c of the LORD your God
Deut 6:25 these c before the LORD our God
Deut 7:9 him and keep his c to a thousand
Deut 7:11 Thou shalt therefore keep the c
Deut 8:1 All the c which I command thee
Deut 8:2 whether thou wouldest keep his c
Deut 8:6 keep the c of the LORD thy God
Deut 8:11 thy God, in not keeping his c
Deut 10:4 to the first writing, the ten c
Deut 10:13 To keep the c of the LORD
Deut 11:1 and his judgments, and his c
Deut 11:8 c which I command you this day
Deut 11:13 hearken diligently unto my c
Deut 11:22 all these c which I command you
Deut 11:27 if ye obey the c of the LORD your
Deut 11:28 obey the c of the LORD your God
Deut 13:4 God, and fear him, and keep his c
Deut 13:18 to keep all his c which I command
Deut 15:5 to observe to do all these c
Deut 19:9 shalt keep all these c to do them
Deut 26:13 according to all thy c which thou
Deut 26:13 I have not transgressed thy c
Deut 26:17 and to keep his statutes, and his c
Deut 26:18 thou shouldest keep all his c
Deut 27:1 Keep all the c which I command
Deut 27:10 of the LORD thy God, and do his c
Deut 28:1 to do all his c which I command
Deut 28:9 keep the c of the LORD thy God
Deut 28:13 unto the c of the LORD thy God
Deut 28:15 God, to observe to do all his c
Deut 28:45 the LORD thy God, to keep his c
Deut 30:8 do all his c which I command thee
Deut 30:10 the LORD thy God, to keep his c
Deut 30:16 in his ways, and to keep his c
Deut 31:5 the c which I have commanded you
Josh 22:5 in all his ways, and to keep his c
Judg 2:17 in, obeying the c of the LORD
Judg 3:4 hearken unto the c of the LORD
1Sa 15:11 me, and hath not performed my c
1Kin 2:3 to keep his statutes, and his c
1Kin 3:14 ways, to keep my statutes and my c
1Kin 6:12 keep all my c to walk in them
1Kin 8:58 in all his ways, and to keep his c
1Kin 8:61 in his statutes, and to keep his c
1Kin 9:6 children, and will not keep my c
1Kin 11:34 I chose, because he kept my c
1Kin 11:38 to keep my statutes and my c
1Kin 14:8 my servant David, who kept my c
1Kin 18:18 have forsaken the c of the LORD
2Kin 17:13 from your evil ways, and keep my c
2Kin 17:16 they left all the c of the LORD
2Kin 17:19 not the c of the LORD their God
2Kin 18:6 following him, but kept his c
2Kin 23:3 after the LORD, and to keep his c
1Chr 28:7 if he be constant to do my c
1Chr 28:8 seek for all the c of the LORD
1Chr 29:19 a perfect heart, to keep thy c
2Chr 7:19 and forsake my statutes and my c
2Chr 17:4 of his father, and walked in his c
2Chr 24:20 transgress ye the c of the LORD
2Chr 31:21 God, and in the law, and in the c
2Chr 34:31 after the LORD, and to keep his c
Ezr 7:11 of the words of the c of the LORD
Ezr 9:10 for we have forsaken thy c
Ezr 9:14 Should we again break thy c
Neh 1:5 that love him and observe his c
Neh 1:7 thee, and have not kept the c
Neh 1:9 if ye turn unto me, and keep my c
Neh 9:13 and true laws, good statutes and c
Neh 9:16 necks, and hearkened not to thy c
Neh 9:29 and hearkened not unto thy c
Neh 9:34 thy law, nor hearkened unto thy c
Neh 10:29 do all the c of the LORD our Lord
Ps 78:7 the works of God, but keep his c
Ps 89:31 my statutes, and keep not my c
Ps 103:18 that remember his c to do them
Ps 103:20 excel in strength, that do his c
Ps 111:7 all his c are sure
Ps 111:10 have all they that do his c
Ps 112:1 that delighteth greatly in his c
Ps 119:6 I have respect unto all thy c
Ps 119:10 O let me not wander from thy c
Ps 119:19 hide not thy c from me
Ps 119:21 cursed, which do err from thy c
Ps 119:32 I will run the way of thy c
Ps 119:35 me to go in the path of thy c
Ps 119:47 And I will delight myself in thy c
Ps 119:48 also will I lift up unto thy c
Ps 119:60 and delayed not to keep thy c
Ps 119:66 for I have believed thy c
Ps 119:73 that I may learn thy c
Ps 119:86 All thy c are faithful
Ps 119:98 Thou through thy c hast made me
Ps 119:115 for I will keep the c of my God
Ps 119:127 Therefore I love thy c above gold
Ps 119:131 for I longed for thy c
Ps 119:143 yet thy c are my delights
Ps 119:151 and all thy c are truth
Ps 119:166 for thy salvation, and done thy c
Ps 119:172 for all thy c are righteousness
Ps 119:176 for I do not forget thy c
Prov 2:1 my words, and hide my c with thee
Prov 3:1 but let thine heart keep my c
Prov 4:4 keep my c, and live
Prov 7:1 words, and lay up my c with thee
Prov 7:2 Keep my c, and live
Prov 10:8 The wise in heart will receive c
Eccl 12:13 Fear God, and keep his c
Is 48:18 that thou hadst hearkened to my c
Dan 9:4 him, and to them that keep his c
Amos 2:4 the LORD, and have not kept his c
Mt 5:19 shall break one of these least c
Mt 15:9 for doctrines the c of men
Mt 19:17 wilt enter into life, keep the c
Mt 22:40 On these two c hang all the law
Mk 7:7 for doctrines the c of men
Mk 10:19 Thou knowest the c, Do not commit
Mk 12:29 him, The first of all the c is
Lk 1:6 before God, walking in all the c
Lk 18:20 Thou knowest the c, Do not commit
Jn 14:15 If ye love me, keep my c
Jn 14:21 He that hath my c, and keepeth
Jn 15:10 If ye keep my c, ye shall abide
Jn 15:10 even as I have kept my Father's c
Acts 1:2 the Holy Ghost had given c unto
1Cor 7:19 but the keeping of the c of God
1Cor 14:37 unto you are the c of the Lord
Eph 2:15 even the law of c contained in
Col 2:22 after the c and doctrines of men
Col 4:10 (touching whom ye received c
1Th 4:2 For ye know what c we gave you by
Titus 1:14 c of men, that turn from the
1Jn 2:3 we know him, if we keep his c
1Jn 2:4 I know him, and keepeth not his c
1Jn 3:22 of him, because we keep his c
1Jn 3:24 keepeth his c dwelleth in him
1Jn 5:2 when we love God, and keep his c
1Jn 5:3 love of God, that we keep his c
1Jn 5:3 and his c are not grievous
2Jn 6 is love, that we walk after his c
Rev 12:17 her seed, which keep the c of God
Rev 14:12 are they that keep the c of God
Rev 22:14 Blessed are they that do his c

## COMMEND

Lk 23:46 into thy hands I c my spirit
Acts 20:32 I c you to God, and to the word of
Rom 3:5 c the righteousness of God
Rom 16:1 I c unto you Phebe our sister,
2Cor 3:1 Do we begin again to c ourselves
2Cor 5:12 For we c not ourselves again unto
2Cor 10:12 with some that c themselves

## COMMENDED

Gen 12:15 saw her, and c her before Pharaoh
Prov 12:8 A man shall be c according to his
Eccl 8:15 Then I c mirth, because a man
Lk 16:8 the lord c the unjust steward,
Acts 14:23 they c them to the Lord, on whom
2Cor 12:11 for I ought to have been c of you

## COMMIT

Ex 20:14 Thou shalt not c adultery
Lev 5:15 If a soul c a trespass, and sin
Lev 5:17 c any of these things which are
Lev 6:2 c a trespass against the LORD, and
Lev 18:26 and shall not c any of these
Lev 18:29 For whosoever shall c any of
Lev 18:29 even the souls that c them shall
Lev 18:30 that ye c not any one of these
Lev 20:5 to c whoredom with Molech, from
Num 5:6 When a man or woman shall c
Num 5:6 any sin that men c, to do
Num 5:12 c a trespass against him,
Num 25:1 the people began to c whoredom
Num 31:16 to c trespass against the LORD in
Deut 5:18 Neither shalt thou c adultery
Deut 19:20 shall henceforth c no more any
Josh 22:20 c a trespass in the accursed
2Sa 7:14 If he c iniquity, I will chasten
2Chr 21:11 of Jerusalem to c fornication
Job 5:8 and unto God would I c my cause
Job 34:10 that he should c iniquity
Ps 31:5 Into thine hand I c my spirit
Ps 37:5 C thy way unto the LORD
Prov 16:3 C thy works unto the LORD, and thy
Prov 16:12 to kings to c wickedness
Is 22:21 I will c thy government into his
Is 23:17 shall c fornication with all the
Jer 7:9 c adultery, and swear falsely, and
Jer 9:5 and weary themselves to c iniquity
Jer 23:14 they c adultery, and walk in lies
Jer 37:21 c Jeremiah into the court of the
Jer 44:7 Wherefore c ye this great evil
Eze 3:20 and c iniquity, and I lay a
Eze 8:17 c the abominations which they c
Eze 16:17 didst c whoredom with them,
Eze 16:34 followeth thee to c whoredoms
Eze 16:43 thou shalt not c this lewdness
Eze 20:30 c ye whoredom after their
Eze 22:9 the midst of thee they c lewdness
Eze 23:43 Will they now c whoredoms with
Eze 33:13 and c iniquity, all his
Hos 4:10 they shall c whoredom, and shall
Hos 4:13 your daughters shall c whoredom
Hos 4:13 and your spouses shall c adultery
Hos 4:14 daughters when they c whoredom
Hos 4:14 your spouses when they c adultery
Hos 6:9 for they c lewdness
Hos 7:1 for they c falsehood
Mt 5:27 time, Thou shalt not c adultery
Mt 5:32 causeth her to c adultery
Mt 19:9 which is put away doth c adultery
Mt 19:18 murder, Thou shalt not c adultery
Mk 10:19 Do not c adultery, Do not kill,
Lk 12:48 did c things worthy of stripes,
Lk 16:11 who will c to your trust the true
Lk 18:20 Do not c adultery, Do not kill,
Jn 2:24 Jesus did not c himself unto them
Rom 1:32 that they which c such things are
Rom 2:2 against them which c such things
Rom 2:22 a man should not c adultery
Rom 2:22 dost thou c adultery
Rom 2:22 idols, dost thou c sacrilege
Rom 13:9 this, Thou shalt not c adultery
1Cor 10:8 Neither let us c fornication
1Ti 1:18 This charge I c unto thee
2Ti 2:2 the same c thou to faithful men,
Jas 2:9 ye c sin, and are convinced of the
Jas 2:11 Do not c adultery, said also, Do
Jas 2:11 Now if thou c no adultery
1Pet 4:19 according to the will of God c
1Jn 3:9 is born of God doth not c sin
Rev 2:14 unto idols, and to c fornication
Rev 2:20 my servants to c fornication
Rev 2:22 them that c adultery with her

## COMMITTED

Gen 39:8 he hath c all that he hath to my
Gen 39:22 prison c to Joseph's hand all the
Lev 4:35 for his sin that he hath c
Lev 5:7 for his trespass, which he hath c
Lev 18:30 customs, which were c before you
Lev 20:13 of them have c an abomination
Lev 20:23 for they c all these things, and
Num 15:24 if ought be c by ignorance
Deut 17:5 which have c that wicked thing,
Deut 21:22 if a man have c a sin worthy of
Josh 7:1 c a trespass in the accursed
Josh 22:16 have c against the God of Israel
Josh 22:31 because ye have not c this

Judg 20:6 for they have c lewdness and folly
1Kin 8:47 perversely, we have c wickedness
1Kin 14:22 with their sins which they had c
1Kin 14:27 c them unto the hands of the
1Chr 10:13 which he c against the LORD
2Chr 12:10 c them to the hands of the chief
2Chr 34:16 All that was c to thy servants,
Ps 106:6 we have c iniquity, we have done
Jer 2:13 For my people have c two evils
Jer 3:8 whereby backsliding Israel c
Jer 3:9 c adultery with stones and with
Jer 5:7 to the full, they then c adultery
Jer 5:30 horrible thing is c in the land
Jer 6:15 when they had c abomination
Jer 8:12 when they had c abomination
Jer 16:10 have c against the LORD our God
Jer 29:23 they have c villany in Israel
Jer 29:23 have c adultery with their
Jer 39:14 c him unto Gedaliah the son of
Jer 40:7 had c unto him men, and women, and
Jer 41:10 the captain of the guard had c to
Jer 44:3 have c to provoke me to anger
Jer 44:9 which they have c in the land of
Jer 44:22 the abominations which ye have c
Eze 6:9 have c in all their abominations
Eze 15:8 because they have c a trespass
Eze 16:26 Thou hast also c fornication with
Eze 16:50 and c abomination before me
Eze 16:51 hath Samaria c half of thy sins
Eze 16:52 hast c more abominable than they
Eze 18:12 to the idols, hath c abomination,
Eze 18:21 from all his sins that he hath c
Eze 18:22 his transgressions that he hath c
Eze 18:27 his wickedness that he hath c
Eze 18:28 his transgressions that he hath c
Eze 20:27 in that they have c a trespass
Eze 20:43 for all your evils that ye have c
Eze 22:11 one hath c abomination with his
Eze 23:3 they c whoredoms in Egypt
Eze 23:3 they c whoredoms in their youth
Eze 23:7 Thus she c her whoredoms with
Eze 23:37 That they have c adultery
Eze 23:37 their idols have they c adultery
Eze 33:13 for his iniquity that he hath c
Eze 33:16 c shall be mentioned unto him
Eze 33:29 abominations which they have c
Eze 43:8 abominations that they have c
Eze 44:13 abominations which they have c
Dan 9:5 have c iniquity, and have done
Hos 1:2 the land hath c great whoredom
Hos 4:18 they have c whoredom continually
Mal 2:11 and an abomination is c in Israel
Mt 5:28 c adultery with her already in
Mk 15:7 with him, who had c murder in the
Lk 12:48 and to whom men have c much
Jn 5:22 but hath c all judgment unto the
Acts 8:3 men and women c them to prison
Acts 25:11 or have c any thing worthy of
Acts 25:25 he had c nothing worthy of death
Acts 27:40 they c themselves unto the sea,
Acts 28:17 though I have c nothing against
Rom 3:2 them were c the oracles of God
1Cor 9:17 of the gospel is c unto me
1Cor 10:8 fornication, as some of them c
2Cor 5:19 hath c unto us the word of
2Cor 11:7 Have I c an offence in abasing
2Cor 12:21 lasciviousness which they have c
Gal 2:7 the uncircumcision was c unto me
1Ti 1:11 God, which was c to my trust
1Ti 6:20 keep that which is c to thy trust
2Ti 1:12 have c unto him against that day
2Ti 1:14 That good thing which was c unto
Titus 1:3 which is c unto me according to
Jas 5:15 and if he have c sins, they shall
1Pet 2:23 but c himself to him that judgeth
Jude 15 deeds which they have ungodly c
Rev 17:2 of the earth have c fornication
Rev 18:3 earth have c fornication with her
Rev 18:9 who have c fornication and lived

## COMMITTETH

Lev 20:10 the man that c adultery with
Lev 20:10 even he that c adultery with his
Ps 10:14 the poor c himself unto thee
Prov 6:32 But whoso c adultery with a woman
Eze 8:6 that the house of Israel c here
Eze 16:32 But as a wife that c adultery
Eze 18:24 c iniquity, and doeth according to
Eze 18:26 c iniquity, and dieth in them
Eze 33:18 c iniquity, he shall even die
Mt 5:32 her that is divorced c adultery
Mt 19:9 shall marry another, c adultery
Mk 10:11 another, c adultery against her
Mk 10:12 to another, she c adultery
Lk 16:18 and marrieth another, c adultery
Lk 16:18 away from her husband c adultery
Jn 8:34 Whosoever c sin is the servant of
1Cor 6:18 but he that c fornication sinneth
1Jn 3:4 Whosoever c sin transgresseth
1Jn 3:8 He that c sin is of the devil

## COMMON

Lev 4:27 if any one of the c people sin
Num 16:29 men die the c death of all men
1Sa 21:4 There is no c bread under mine
1Sa 21:5 and the bread is in a manner c
Eccl 6:1 the sun, and it is c among men
Jer 26:23 into the graves of the c people
Jer 31:5 and shall eat them as c things
Eze 23:42 with the men of the c sort were
Mt 27:27 took Jesus into the c hall
Mk 12:37 the c people heard him gladly
Acts 2:44 together, and had all things c
Acts 4:32 but they had all things c
Acts 5:18 and put them in the c prison
Acts 10:14 any thing that is c or unclean
Acts 10:15 cleansed, that call not thou c
Acts 10:28 not call any man c or unclean
Acts 11:8 for nothing c or unclean hath at
Acts 11:9 cleansed, that call not thou c
1Cor 10:13 taken you but such as is c to man
Titus 1:4 mine own son after the c faith
Jude 3 write unto you of the c salvation

## COMMUNE

Gen 34:6 went out unto Jacob to c with him
Ex 25:22 I will c with thee from above the
1Sa 18:22 C with David secretly, and say,
1Sa 19:3 I will c with my father of thee
Job 4:2 If we assay to c with thee
Ps 4:4 c with your own heart upon your
Ps 64:5 they c of laying snares privily
Ps 77:6 I c with mine own heart

## COMMUNED

Gen 23:8 he c with them, saying, If it be
Gen 34:8 Hamor c with them, saying, The
Gen 34:20 c with the men of their city,
Gen 42:24 c with them, and took from them
Gen 43:19 they c with him at the door of
Judg 9:1 c with them, and with all the
1Sa 9:25 Samuel c with Saul upon the top
1Sa 25:39 c with Abigail, to take her to
1Kin 10:2 she c with him of all that was in
2Kin 22:14 and they c with her
2Chr 9:1 she c with him of all that was in
Eccl 1:16 I c with mine own heart, saying,
Dan 1:19 And the king c with them
Zec 1:14 So the angel that c with me said
Lk 6:11 c one with another what they
Lk 22:4 c with the chief priests and
Lk 24:15 pass, that, while they c together
Acts 24:26 him the oftener, and c with him

## COMMUNICATION

2Sa 3:17 Abner had c with the elders of
2Kin 9:11 them, Ye know the man, and his c
Mt 5:37 But let your c be, Yea, yea
Eph 4:29 Let no corrupt c proceed out of
Col 3:8 filthy c out of your mouth
Philem 6 That the c of thy faith may

## COMMUNION

1Cor 10:16 is it not the c of the blood of
1Cor 10:16 is it not the c of the body of
2Cor 6:14 what c hath light with darkness
2Cor 13:14 the c of the Holy Ghost, be with

## COMPANIES

Judg 7:16 three hundred men into three c
Judg 7:20 the three c blew the trumpets, and
Judg 9:34 wait against Shechem in four c
Judg 9:43 and divided them into three c
Judg 9:44 the two other c ran upon all the
1Sa 11:11 Saul put the people in three c
1Sa 13:17 of the Philistines in three c
2Kin 5:2 And the Syrians had gone out by c
1Chr 9:18 in the c of the children of Levi
1Chr 28:1 the captains of the c that
Neh 12:31 appointed two great c of them
Neh 12:40 So stood the two c of them that
Job 6:19 the c of Sheba waited for them
Is 21:13 O ye travelling c of Dedanim
Is 57:13 criest, let thy c deliver thee
Eze 26:7 chariots, and with horsemen, and c
Mk 6:39 down by c upon the green grass

## COMPANION

Ex 32:27 his brother, and every man his c
Judg 14:20 Samson's wife was given to his c
Judg 15:2 therefore I gave her to thy c
Judg 15:6 his wife, and given her to his c
1Chr 27:33 the Archite was the king's c
Job 30:29 to dragons, and a c to owls
Ps 119:63 I am a c of all them that fear
Prov 13:20 but a c of fools shall be
Prov 28:7 but he that is a c of riotous men
Prov 28:24 the same is the c of a destroyer
Mal 2:14 yet is she thy c, and the wife of
Phil 2:25 c in labour, and fellow soldier,
Rev 1:9 c in tribulation, and in the

## COMPANIONS

Judg 11:38 and she went with her c, and
Judg 14:11 brought thirty c to be with him
Ezr 4:7 Tabeel, and the rest of their c
Ezr 4:9 scribe, and the rest of their c
Ezr 4:17 to the rest of their c that dwell
Ezr 4:23 Shimshai the scribe, and their c
Ezr 5:3 and Shethar-boznai, and their c
Ezr 5:6 his c the Apharsachites, which
Ezr 6:6 your c the Apharsachites, which
Ezr 6:13 river, Shethar-boznai, and their c
Job 35:4 answer thee, and thy c with thee
Job 41:6 Shall the c make a banquet of him
Ps 45:14 the virgins her c that follow her
Song 1:7 aside by the flocks of thy c
Song 8:13 the c hearken to thy voice
Is 1:23 are rebellious, and c of thieves
Eze 37:16 for the children of Israel his c
Eze 37:16 for all the house of Israel his c
Dan 2:17 Mishael, and Azariah, his c
Acts 19:29 Paul's c in travel, they rushed
Heb 10:33 whilst ye became c of them that

## COMPANY

Gen 32:8 said, If Esau come to the one c
Gen 32:8 then the other c which is left
Gen 32:21 lodged that night in the c
Gen 35:11 a c of nations shall be of thee,
Gen 37:25 a c of Ishmeelites came from
Gen 50:9 and it was a very great c
Num 14:7 they spake unto all the c of the
Num 16:5 unto Korah and unto all his c
Num 16:6 you censers, Korah, and all his c
Num 16:11 all thy c are gathered together
Num 16:16 all thy c before the LORD, thou,
Num 16:40 he be not as Korah, and as his c
Num 22:4 Now shall this c lick up all that
Num 26:9 against Aaron in the c of Korah
Num 26:10 with Korah, when that c died
Num 27:3 he was not in the c of them that
Num 27:3 the LORD in the c of Korah
Judg 9:37 another c come along by the plain
Judg 9:44 the c that was with him, rushed
Judg 18:23 that thou comest with such a c
1Sa 10:5 that thou shalt meet a c of
1Sa 10:10 behold, a c of prophets met him
1Sa 13:17 one c turned unto the way that
1Sa 13:18 another c turned the way to
1Sa 13:18 another c turned to the way of
1Sa 19:20 when they saw the c of the
1Sa 30:15 thou bring me down to this c
1Sa 30:15 I will bring thee down to this c
1Sa 30:23 delivered the c that came against
2Kin 5:15 the man of God, he and all his c
2Kin 9:17 he spied the c of Jehu as he came
2Kin 9:17 and said, I see a c
2Chr 9:1 at Jerusalem, with a very great c
2Chr 20:12 great c that cometh against us
2Chr 24:24 came with a small c of men
Neh 12:38 the other c of them that gave
Job 16:7 thou hast made desolate all my c
Job 34:8 Which goeth in c with the workers
Ps 55:14 walked unto the house of God in c
Ps 68:11 great was the c of those that
Ps 68:30 Rebuke the c of spearmen, the
Ps 106:17 and covered the c of Abiram
Ps 106:18 And a fire was kindled in their c
Prov 29:3 but he that keepeth c with
Song 1:9 to a c of horses in Pharaoh's
Song 6:13 As it were the c of two armies
Jer 31:8 a great c shall return thither
Eze 16:40 also bring up a c against thee
Eze 17:17 great c make for him in the war,
Eze 23:46 I will bring up a c upon them

Eze 23:47 the c shall stone them with
Eze 27:6 the c of the Ashurites have made
Eze 27:27 in all thy c which is in the
Eze 27:34 all thy c in the midst of thee
Eze 32:3 over thee with a c of many people
Eze 32:22 Asshur is there and all her c
Eze 32:23 her c is round about her grave
Eze 38:4 even a great c with bucklers and
Eze 38:7 all thy c that are assembled unto
Eze 38:13 gathered thy c to take a prey
Eze 38:15 riding upon horses, a great c
Hos 6:9 so the c of priests murder in the
Lk 2:44 him to have been in the c
Lk 5:29 there was a great c of publicans
Lk 6:17 the c of his disciples, and a
Lk 6:22 shall separate you from their c
Lk 9:14 them sit down by fifties in a c
Lk 9:38 behold, a man of the c cried out
Lk 11:27 of the c lifted up her voice
Lk 12:13 one of the c said unto him,
Lk 23:27 followed him a great c of people
Lk 24:22 also of our c made us astonished
Jn 6:5 saw a great c come unto him, he
Acts 4:23 let go, they went to their own c
Acts 6:7 a great c of the priests were
Acts 10:28 for a man that is a Jew to keep c
Acts 13:13 his c loosed from Paphos, they
Acts 15:22 their own c to Antioch with Paul
Acts 17:5 the baser sort, and gathered a c
Acts 21:8 we that were of Paul's c departed
Rom 15:24 I be somewhat filled with your c
1Cor 5:9 epistle not to c with fornicators
1Cor 5:11 written unto you not to keep c
2Th 3:14 have no c with him, that he may
Heb 12:22 and to an innumerable c of angels
Rev 18:17 all the c in ships, and sailors,

**COMPASS**

Ex 27:5 under the c of the altar beneath
Ex 38:4 grate of network under the c
Num 21:4 Red sea, to c the land of Edom
Num 34:5 the border shall fetch a c from
Josh 6:3 And ye shall c the city, all ye
Josh 6:4 ye shall c the city seven times
Josh 6:7 c the city, and let him that is
Josh 15:3 to Adar, and fetched a c to Karkaa
2Sa 5:23 but fetch a c behind them
1Kin 7:15 cubits did c either of them about
1Kin 7:23 cubits did c it round about
1Kin 7:35 a round c of half a cubit high
2Kin 3:9 they fetched a c of seven days'
2Kin 11:8 ye shall c the king round about,
2Chr 4:2 from brim to brim, round in c
2Chr 4:2 cubits did c it round about
2Chr 4:3 which did c it round about
2Chr 23:7 the Levites shall c the king
Job 16:13 His archers c me round about, he
Job 40:22 willows of the brook c him about
Ps 5:12 wilt thou c him as with a shield
Ps 7:7 of the people c thee about
Ps 17:9 my deadly enemies, who c me about
Ps 26:6 so will I c thine altar, O LORD
Ps 32:7 thou shalt c me about with songs
Ps 32:10 the LORD, mercy shall c him about
Ps 49:5 of my heels shall c me about
Ps 140:9 the head of those that c me about
Ps 142:7 the righteous shall c me about
Prov 8:27 when he set a c upon the face of
Is 44:13 and he marketh it out with the c
Is 50:11 that c yourselves about with
Jer 31:22 the earth, A woman shall c a man
Jer 31:39 Gareb, and shall c about to Goath
Jer 52:21 fillet of twelve cubits did c it
Hab 1:4 wicked doth c about the righteous
Mt 23:15 for ye c sea and land to make one
Lk 19:43 c thee round, and keep thee in on
Acts 28:13 And from thence we fetched a c

**COMPASSED**

Gen 19:4 c the house round, both old and
Deut 2:1 we c mount Seir many days
Deut 2:3 Ye have c this mountain long
Josh 6:11 So the ark of the LORD c the city
Josh 6:14 second day they c the city once
Josh 6:15 c the city after the same manner
Josh 6:15 day they c the city seven times
Josh 15:10 the border c from Baalah westward
Josh 18:14 c the corner of the sea southward
Judg 11:18 c the land of Edom, and the land
Judg 16:2 they c him in, and laid wait for
1Sa 23:26 for Saul and his men c David
2Sa 18:15 that bare Joab's armour c about
2Sa 22:5 When the waves of death c me
2Sa 22:6 The sorrows of hell c me about
2Kin 6:14 by night, and c the city about
2Kin 6:15 an host c the city both with
2Kin 8:21 the Edomites which c him about
2Chr 18:31 Therefore they c about him to
2Chr 21:9 smote the Edomites which c him in
2Chr 33:14 c about Ophel, and raised it up a
Job 19:6 me, and hath c me with his net
Job 26:10 He hath c the waters with bounds,
Ps 17:11 They have now c us in our steps
Ps 18:4 The sorrows of death c me
Ps 18:5 The sorrows of hell c me about
Ps 22:12 Many bulls have c me
Ps 22:16 For dogs have c me
Ps 40:12 innumerable evils have c me about
Ps 88:17 they c me about together
Ps 109:3 They c me about also with words
Ps 116:3 The sorrows of death c me
Ps 118:10 All nations c me about
Ps 118:11 They c me about
Ps 118:11 yea, they c me about
Ps 118:12 They c me about like bees
Lam 3:5 me, and c me with gall and travel
Jonah 2:3 and the floods c me about
Jonah 2:5 The waters c me about, even to
Lk 21:20 shall see Jerusalem c with armies
Heb 5:2 himself also is c with infirmity
Heb 11:30 after they were c about seven
Heb 12:1 Wherefore seeing we also are c
Rev 20:9 c the camp of the saints about,

**COMPASSION**

Ex 2:6 And she had c on him, and said,
Deut 13:17 have c upon thee, and multiply
Deut 30:3 have c upon thee, and will return
1Sa 23:21 for ye have c on me
1Kin 8:50 give them c before them who
1Kin 8:50 that they may have c on them
2Kin 13:23 had c on them, and had respect
2Chr 30:9 your children shall find c before
2Chr 36:15 because he had c on his people
2Chr 36:17 had no c upon young man or maiden
Ps 78:38 But he, being full of c, forgave
Ps 86:15 thou, O Lord, art a God full of c
Ps 111:4 the LORD is gracious and full of c
Ps 112:4 he is gracious, and full of c
Ps 145:8 LORD is gracious, and full of c
Is 49:15 not have c on the son of her womb
Jer 12:15 have c on them, and will bring
Lam 3:32 yet will he have c according to
Eze 16:5 unto thee, to have c upon thee
Mic 7:19 again, he will have c upon us
Mt 9:36 he was moved with c on them
Mt 14:14 and was moved with c toward them
Mt 15:32 I have c on the multitude,
Mt 18:27 of that servant was moved with c
Mt 18:33 have had c on thy fellowservant
Mt 20:34 So Jesus had c on them, and
Mk 1:41 And Jesus, moved with c, put forth
Mk 5:19 for thee, and hath had c on thee
Mk 6:34 and was moved with c toward them
Mk 8:2 I have c on the multitude,
Mk 9:22 thing, have c on us, and help us
Lk 7:13 the Lord saw her, he had c on her
Lk 10:33 when he saw him, he had c on him
Lk 15:20 off, his father saw him, and had c
Rom 9:15 have c on whom I will have c
Heb 5:2 Who can have c on the ignorant,
Heb 10:34 For ye had c of me in my bonds,
1Pet 3:8 having c one of another, love as
1Jn 3:17 up his bowels of c from him
Jude 22 And of some have c, making a

**COMPEL**

Lev 25:39 thou shalt not c him to serve as
Est 1:8 none did c
Mt 5:41 whosoever shall c thee to go a
Mk 15:21 they c one Simon a Cyrenian, who
Lk 14:23 c them to come in, that my house

**COMPELLED**

1Sa 28:23 together with the woman, c him
2Chr 21:11 fornication, and c Judah thereto
Mt 27:32 him they c to bear his cross
Acts 26:11 synagogue, and c them to blaspheme
2Cor 12:11 ye have c me
Gal 2:3 a Greek, was c to be circumcised

**COMPLAIN**

Judg 21:22 their brethren come unto us to c
Job 7:11 I will c in the bitterness of my
Job 31:38 the furrows likewise thereof c
Lam 3:39 Wherefore doth a living man c

**COMPLAINT**

1Sa 1:16 for out of the abundance of my c
Job 7:13 me, my couch shall ease my c
Job 9:27 If I say, I will forget my c
Job 10:1 I will leave my c upon myself
Job 21:4 As for me, is my c to man
Job 23:2 Even to day is my c bitter
Ps 55:2 I mourn in my c, and make a noise
Ps 102:*t* poureth out his c before the LORD
Ps 142:2 I poured out my c before him

**CONANIAH** *(co-na-ni'-ah)* See CONONIAH. *A chief Levite during Josiah's time.*

2Chr 35:9 C also, and Shemaiah and Nethaneel,

**CONCEIT**

Prov 18:11 and as an high wall in his own c
Prov 26:5 lest he be wise in his own c
Prov 26:12 thou a man wise in his own c
Prov 26:16 sluggard is wiser in his own c
Prov 28:11 The rich man is wise in his own c

**CONCEIVE**

Gen 30:38 that they should c when they came
Gen 30:41 the stronger cattle did c
Gen 30:41 that they might c among the rods
Num 5:28 shall be free, and shall c seed
Judg 13:3 but thou shalt c, and bear a son
Judg 13:5 For, lo, thou shalt c, and bear a
Judg 13:7 unto me, Behold, thou shalt c
Job 15:35 They c mischief, and bring forth
Ps 51:5 and in sin did my mother c me
Is 7:14 Behold, a virgin shall c, and bear
Is 33:11 Ye shall c chaff, ye shall bring
Is 59:4 they c mischief, and bring forth
Lk 1:31 thou shalt c in thy womb, and
Heb 11:11 received strength to c seed

**CONCEIVED**

Gen 4:1 and she c, and bare Cain, and said,
Gen 4:17 and she c, and bare Enoch
Gen 16:4 he went in unto Hagar, and she c
Gen 16:4 and when she saw that she had c
Gen 16:5 and when she saw that she had c
Gen 21:2 For Sarah c, and bare Abraham a
Gen 25:21 of him, and Rebekah his wife c
Gen 29:32 And Leah c, and bare a son, and she
Gen 29:33 she c again, and bare a son
Gen 29:34 she c again, and bare a son
Gen 29:35 she c again, and bare a son
Gen 30:5 And Bilhah c, and bare Jacob a son
Gen 30:7 And Bilhah Rachel's maid c again
Gen 30:17 God hearkened unto Leah, and she c
Gen 30:19 Leah c again, and bare Jacob the
Gen 30:23 And she c, and bare a son
Gen 30:39 the flocks c before the rods, and
Gen 31:10 at the time that the cattle c
Gen 38:3 And she c, and bare a son
Gen 38:4 she c again, and bare a son
Gen 38:5 And she yet again c, and bare a son
Gen 38:18 came in unto her, and she c by him
Ex 2:2 And the woman c, and bare a son
Lev 12:2 saying, If a woman have c seed
Num 11:12 Have I c all this people
1Sa 1:20 was come about after Hannah had c
1Sa 2:21 visited Hannah, so that she c
2Sa 11:5 And the woman c, and sent and told
2Kin 4:17 And the woman c, and bare a son at
1Chr 7:23 he went in to his wife, she c
Job 3:3 was said, There is a man child c
Ps 7:14 hath c mischief, and brought forth
Song 3:4 into the chamber of her that c me
Is 8:3 and she c, and bare a son
Jer 49:30 hath c a purpose against you
Hos 1:3 which c, and bare him a son
Hos 1:6 she c again, and bare a daughter
Hos 1:8 she had weaned Lo-ruhamah, she c
Hos 2:5 she that c them hath done
Mt 1:20 for that which is c in her is of
Lk 1:24 those days his wife Elisabeth c
Lk 1:36 she hath also c a son in her old
Lk 2:21 angel before he was c in the womb
Acts 5:4 why hast thou c this thing in
Rom 9:10 when Rebecca also had c by one
Jas 1:15 Then when lust hath c, it

## CONCUBINE

Gen 22:24 And his c, whose name was Reumah,
Gen 35:22 and lay with Bilhah his father's c
Gen 36:12 Timna was c to Eliphaz Esau's son
Judg 8:31 his c that was in Shechem, she
Judg 19:1 who took to him a c out of
Judg 19:2 his c played the whore against
Judg 19:9 rose up to depart, he, and his c
Judg 19:10 saddled, his c also was with him
Judg 19:24 is my daughter a maiden, and his c
Judg 19:25 so the man took his c, and brought
Judg 19:27 the woman his c was fallen down
Judg 19:29 a knife, and laid hold on his c
Judg 20:4 belongeth to Benjamin, I and my c
Judg 20:5 my c have they forced, that she
Judg 20:6 And I took my c, and cut her in
2Sa 3:7 And Saul had a c, whose name was
2Sa 3:7 thou gone in unto my father's c
2Sa 21:11 of Aiah, the c of Saul, had done
1Chr 1:32 the sons of Keturah, Abraham's c
1Chr 2:46 And Ephah, Caleb's c, bare Haran,
1Chr 2:48 Maachah, Caleb's c, bare Sheber,
1Chr 7:14 (but his c the Aramitess bare

## CONCUBINES

Gen 25:6 But unto the sons of the c
2Sa 5:13 And David took him more c and wives
2Sa 15:16 king left ten women, which were c
2Sa 16:21 Go in unto thy father's c
2Sa 16:22 went in unto his father's c in
2Sa 19:5 thy wives, and the lives of thy c
2Sa 20:3 the king took the ten women his c
1Kin 11:3 princesses, and three hundred c
1Chr 3:9 David, beside the sons of the c
2Chr 11:21 above all his wives and his c
2Chr 11:21 eighteen wives, and threescore c
Est 2:14 chamberlain, which kept the c
Song 6:8 threescore queens, and fourscore c
Song 6:9 yea, the queens and the c, and they
Dan 5:2 his princes, his wives, and his c
Dan 5:3 his princes, his wives, and his c
Dan 5:23 and thy lords, thy wives, and thy c

## CONDEMN

Ex 22:9 and whom the judges shall c
Deut 25:1 the righteous, and c the wicked
Job 9:20 myself, mine own mouth shall c me
Job 10:2 I will say unto God, Do not c me
Job 34:17 wilt thou c him that is most just
Job 40:8 wilt thou c me, that thou mayest
Ps 37:33 nor c him when he is judged
Ps 94:21 and c the innocent blood
Ps 109:31 him from those that c his soul
Prov 12:2 a man of wicked devices will he c
Is 50:9 who is he that shall c me
Is 54:17 thee in judgment thou shalt c
Mt 12:41 this generation, and shall c it
Mt 12:42 this generation, and shall c it
Mt 20:18 they shall c him to death,
Mk 10:33 they shall c him to death, and
Lk 6:37 c not, and ye shall not be
Lk 11:31 men of this generation, and c them
Lk 11:32 this generation, and shall c it
Jn 3:17 Son into the world to c the world
Jn 8:11 unto her, Neither do I c thee
2Cor 7:3 I speak not this to c you
1Jn 3:20 For if our heart c us, God is
1Jn 3:21 Beloved, if our heart c us not

## CONDEMNATION

Lk 23:40 seeing thou art in the same c
Jn 3:19 And this is the c, that light is
Jn 5:24 life, and shall not come into c
Rom 5:16 for the judgment was by one to c
Rom 5:18 judgment came upon all men to c
Rom 8:1 There is therefore now no c to
1Cor 11:34 that ye come not together unto c
2Cor 3:9 if the ministration of c be glory
1Ti 3:6 he fall into the c of the devil
Jas 3:1 we shall receive the greater c
Jas 5:12 lest ye fall into c
Jude 4 before of old ordained to this c

## CONDEMNED

2Chr 36:3 c the land in an hundred talents
Job 32:3 found no answer, and yet had c Job
Ps 109:7 he shall be judged, let him be c
Amos 2:8 the c in the house of their god
Mt 12:7 ye would not have c the guiltless
Mt 12:37 and by thy words thou shalt be c
Mt 27:3 him, when he saw that he was c
Mk 14:64 they all c him to be guilty of
Lk 6:37 condemn not, and ye shall not be c
Lk 24:20 delivered him to be c to death
Jn 3:18 He that believeth on him is not c
Jn 3:18 that believeth not is c already
Jn 8:10 hath no man c thee
Rom 8:3 and for sin, c sin in the flesh
1Cor 11:32 we should not be c with the world
Titus 2:8 Sound speech, that cannot be c
Titus 3:11 and sinneth, being c of himself
Heb 11:7 by the which he c the world
Jas 5:6 Ye have c and killed the just
Jas 5:9 another, brethren, lest ye be c
2Pet 2:6 Gomorrah into ashes c them with

## CONFERRED

1Kin 1:7 he c with Joab the son of Zeruiah
Acts 4:15 council, they c among themselves,
Acts 25:12 when he had c with the council,
Gal 1:16 immediately I c not with flesh and

## CONFESS

Lev 5:5 that he shall c that he hath
Lev 16:21 c over him all the iniquities of
Lev 26:40 If they shall c their iniquity,
Num 5:7 Then they shall c their sin which
1Kin 8:33 c thy name, and pray, and make
1Kin 8:35 c thy name, and turn from their
2Chr 6:24 c thy name, and pray and make
2Chr 6:26 c thy name, and turn from their
Neh 1:6 c the sins of the children of
Job 40:14 Then will I also c unto thee that
Ps 32:5 I will c my transgressions unto
Mt 10:32 therefore shall c me before men
Mt 10:32 him will I c also before my
Lk 12:8 Whosoever shall c me before men
Lk 12:8 also c before the angels of God
Jn 9:22 any man did c that he was Christ
Jn 12:42 the Pharisees they did not c him
Acts 23:8 but the Pharisees c both
Acts 24:14 But this I c unto thee, that
Rom 10:9 That if thou shalt c with thy
Rom 14:11 and every tongue shall c to God
Rom 15:9 For this cause I will c to thee
Phil 2:11 that every tongue should c that
Jas 5:16 C your faults one to another, and
1Jn 1:9 If we c our sins, he is faithful
1Jn 4:15 Whosoever shall c that Jesus is
2Jn 7 who c not that Jesus Christ is
Rev 3:5 but I will c his name before my

## CONFESSED

Ezr 10:1 Ezra had prayed, and when he had c
Neh 9:2 c their sins, and the iniquities
Neh 9:3 and another fourth part they c
Jn 1:20 And he c, and denied not
Jn 1:20 but c, I am not the Christ
Acts 19:18 And many that believed came, and c
Heb 11:13 c that they were strangers and

## CONFESSION

Josh 7:19 God of Israel, and make c unto him
2Chr 30:22 making c to the LORD God of their
Ezr 10:11 Now therefore make c unto the
Dan 9:4 the LORD my God, and made my c
Rom 10:10 with the mouth c is made unto
1Ti 6:13 Pontius Pilate witnessed a good c

## CONFIDENCE

Judg 9:26 men of Shechem put their c in him
2Kin 18:19 What c is this wherein thou
Job 4:6 Is not this thy fear, thy c
Job 18:14 His c shall be rooted out of his
Job 31:24 to the fine gold, Thou art my c
Ps 65:5 who art the c of all the ends of
Ps 118:8 in the LORD than to put c in man
Ps 118:9 the LORD than to put c in princes
Prov 3:26 For the LORD shall be thy c
Prov 14:26 the fear of the LORD is strong c
Prov 21:22 the strength of the c thereof
Prov 25:19 C in an unfaithful man in time of
Is 30:15 in c shall be your strength
Is 36:4 What c is this wherein thou
Jer 48:13 was ashamed of Beth-el their c
Eze 28:26 yea, they shall dwell with c
Eze 29:16 more the c of the house of Israel
Mic 7:5 a friend, put ye not c in a guide
Acts 28:31 the Lord Jesus Christ, with all c
2Cor 1:15 in this c I was minded to come
2Cor 2:3 having c in you all, that my joy
2Cor 7:16 I have c in you in all things
2Cor 8:22 upon the great c which I have in
2Cor 10:2 when I am present with that c
2Cor 11:17 foolishly, in this c of boasting
Gal 5:10 I have c in you through the Lord,
Eph 3:12 access with c by the faith of him
Phil 1:25 And having this c, I know that I
Phil 3:3 Jesus, and have no c in the flesh
Phil 3:4 I might also have c in the flesh
2Th 3:4 we have c in the Lord touching
Philem 21 Having c in thy obedience I wrote
Heb 3:6 are we, if we hold fast the c
Heb 3:14 of our c stedfast unto the end
Heb 10:35 Cast not away therefore your c
1Jn 2:28 he shall appear, we may have c
1Jn 3:21 us not, then have we c toward God
1Jn 5:14 this is the c that we have in him

## CONFIDENT

Ps 27:3 against me, in this will I be c
Prov 14:16 but the fool rageth, and is c
Rom 2:19 art c that thou thyself art a
2Cor 5:6 Therefore we are always c
2Cor 5:8 We are c, I say, and willing
2Cor 9:4 ashamed in this same c boasting
Phil 1:6 Being c of this very thing, that
Phil 1:14 waxing c by my bonds, are much

## CONFIDENTLY

Lk 22:59 one hour after another c affirmed

## CONFIRM

Ruth 4:7 changing, for to c all things
1Kin 1:14 in after thee, and c thy words
2Kin 15:19 him to c the kingdom in his hand
Est 9:29 to c this second letter of Purim
Est 9:31 To c these days of Purim in their
Ps 68:9 thou didst c thine inheritance
Is 35:3 weak hands, and c the feeble knees
Eze 13:6 hope that they would c the word
Dan 9:27 he shall c the covenant with many
Dan 11:1 the Mede, even I, stood to c
Rom 15:8 to c the promises made unto the
1Cor 1:8 Who shall also c you unto the end
2Cor 2:8 ye would c your love toward him

## CONFIRMED

2Sa 7:24 For thou hast c to thyself thy
2Kin 14:5 as the kingdom was c in his hand
1Chr 14:2 LORD had c him king over Israel
1Chr 16:17 hath c the same to Jacob for a
Est 9:32 the decree of Esther c these
Ps 105:10 c the same unto Jacob for a law,
Dan 9:12 he hath c his words, which he
Acts 15:32 with many words, and c them
1Cor 1:6 testimony of Christ was c in you
Gal 3:15 a man's covenant, yet if it be c
Gal 3:17 that was c before of God in
Heb 2:3 was c unto us by them that heard
Heb 6:17 of his counsel, c it by an oath

## CONFOUND

Gen 11:7 there c their language, that they
Gen 11:9 because the LORD did there c the
Jer 1:17 lest I c thee before them
1Cor 1:27 things of the world to c the wise
1Cor 1:27 to c the things which are mighty

## CONFOUNDED

2Kin 19:26 power, they were dismayed and c
Job 6:20 They were c because they had
Ps 22:5 trusted in thee, and were not c
Ps 35:4 Let them be c and put to shame
Ps 40:14 c together that seek after my
Ps 69:6 that seek thee be c for my sake
Ps 70:2 c that seek after my soul
Ps 71:13 Let them be c and consumed that
Ps 71:24 for they are c, for they are
Ps 83:17 Let them be c and troubled for
Ps 97:7 C be all they that serve graven
Ps 129:5 Let them all be c and turned back
Is 1:29 ye shall be c for the gardens
Is 19:9 that weave networks, shall be c
Is 24:23 Then the moon shall be c, and the
Is 37:27 power, they were dismayed and c
Is 41:11 thee shall be ashamed and c
Is 45:16 They shall be ashamed, and also c
Is 45:17 ashamed nor c world without end
Is 50:7 therefore shall I not be c
Is 54:4 neither be thou c
Jer 9:19 we are greatly c, because we have
Jer 10:14 every founder is c by the graven
Jer 14:3 they were ashamed and c, and
Jer 15:9 she hath been ashamed and c
Jer 17:18 Let them be c that persecute me,
Jer 17:18 but let not me be c
Jer 22:22 and c for all thy wickedness
Jer 31:19 I was ashamed, yea, even c

Jer 46:24 The daughter of Egypt shall be c
Jer 48:1 Kiriathaim is c and taken
Jer 48:1 Misgab is c and dismayed
Jer 48:20 Moab is c
Jer 49:23 Hamath is c, and Arpad
Jer 50:2 say, Babylon is taken, Bel is c
Jer 50:2 her idols are c, her images are
Jer 50:12 Your mother shall be sore c
Jer 51:17 every founder is c by the graven
Jer 51:47 and her whole land shall be c
Jer 51:51 We are c, because we have heard
Eze 16:52 yea, be thou c also, and bear thy
Eze 16:54 mayest be c in all that thou hast
Eze 16:63 thou mayest remember, and be c
Eze 36:32 c for your own ways, O house of
Mic 3:7 be ashamed, and the diviners c
Mic 7:16 see and be c at all their might
Zec 10:5 the riders on horses shall be c
Acts 2:6 came together, and were c, because
Acts 9:22 c the Jews which dwelt at
1Pet 2:6 believeth on him shall not be c

### CONFUSION
Lev 18:23 it is c
Lev 20:12 they have wrought c
1Sa 20:30 the son of Jesse to thine own c
1Sa 20:30 unto the c of thy mother's
Ezr 9:7 to c of face, as it is this day
Job 10:15 I am full of c
Ps 35:4 brought to c that devise my hurt
Ps 35:26 brought to c together that
Ps 44:15 My c is continually before me, and
Ps 70:2 be turned backward, and put to c
Ps 71:1 let me never be put to c
Ps 109:29 cover themselves with their own c
Is 24:10 The city of c is broken down
Is 30:3 in the shadow of Egypt your c
Is 34:11 stretch out upon it the line of c
Is 41:29 their molten images are wind and c
Is 45:16 they shall go to c together that
Is 61:7 for c they shall rejoice in their
Jer 3:25 our shame, and our c covereth us
Jer 7:19 to the c of their own faces
Jer 20:11 their everlasting c shall never
Dan 9:7 unto thee, but unto us c of faces
Dan 9:8 O Lord, to us belongeth c of face
Acts 19:29 the whole city was filled with c
1Cor 14:33 For God is not the author of c
Jas 3:16 envying and strife is, there is c

### CONIAH *(co-ni'-ah)* See JEHOIACHIN. *Another name for Jehoiachin.*
Jer 22:24 though C the son of Jehoiakim
Jer 22:28 Is this man C a despised broken
Jer 37:1 instead of C the son of Jehoiakim

### CONIES
Ps 104:18 and the rocks for the c
Prov 30:26 The c are but a feeble folk, yet

### CONONIAH *(co-no-ni'-ah)* See CONANIAH. *A Levite during Hezekiah's time.*
2Chr 31:12 over which C the Levite was ruler
2Chr 31:13 overseers under the hand of C

### CONQUER
Rev 6:2 he went forth conquering, and to c

### CONQUERING
Rev 6:2 and he went forth c, and to conquer

### CONQUERORS
Rom 8:37 than c through him that loved us

### CONSCIENCE
Jn 8:9 being convicted by their own c
Acts 23:1 I have lived in all good c before
Acts 24:16 to have always a c void of
Rom 2:15 their c also bearing witness, and
Rom 9:1 my c also bearing me witness in
Rom 13:5 for wrath, but also for c sake
1Cor 8:7 for some with c of the idol unto
1Cor 8:7 their c being weak is defiled
1Cor 8:10 shall not the c of him which is
1Cor 8:12 brethren, and wound their weak c
1Cor 10:25 asking no question for c sake
1Cor 10:27 asking no question for c sake
1Cor 10:28 that shewed it, and for c sake
1Cor 10:29 C, I say, not thine own, but of
1Cor 10:29 liberty judged of another man's c
2Cor 1:12 is this, the testimony of our c
2Cor 4:2 every man's c in the sight of God
1Ti 1:5 of a pure heart, and of a good c
1Ti 1:19 Holding faith, and a good c
1Ti 3:9 mystery of the faith in a pure c
1Ti 4:2 having their c seared with a hot
2Ti 1:3 from my forefathers with pure c
Titus 1:15 even their mind and c is defiled
Heb 9:9 perfect, as pertaining to the c
Heb 9:14 purge your c from dead works to
Heb 10:2 should have had no more c of sins
Heb 10:22 hearts sprinkled from an evil c
Heb 13:18 for we trust we have a good c
1Pet 2:19 if a man for c toward God endure
1Pet 3:16 Having a good c
1Pet 3:21 the answer of a good c toward God

### CONSECRATE
Ex 28:3 make Aaron's garments to c him
Ex 28:41 c them, and sanctify them, that
Ex 29:9 shalt c Aaron and his sons
Ex 29:33 the atonement was made, to c
Ex 29:35 seven days shalt thou c them
Ex 30:30 c them, that they may minister
Ex 32:29 C yourselves to day to the LORD,
Lev 8:33 for seven days shall he c you
Lev 16:32 whom he shall c to minister in
Num 6:12 he shall c unto the LORD the days
1Chr 29:5 who then is willing to c his
2Chr 13:9 so that whosoever cometh to c
Eze 43:26 and they shall c themselves
Mic 4:13 I will c their gain unto the LORD

### CONSECRATED
Ex 29:29 therein, and to be c in them
Lev 21:10 that is c to put on the garments,
Num 3:3 whom he c to minister in the
Josh 6:19 and iron, are c unto the LORD
Judg 17:5 c one of his sons, who became
Judg 17:12 And Micah c the Levite
1Kin 13:33 c him, and he became one of the
2Chr 26:18 that are c to burn incense
2Chr 29:31 ye have c yourselves unto the
2Chr 29:33 the c things were six hundred
2Chr 31:6 were c unto the LORD their God
Ezr 3:5 feasts of the LORD that were c
Heb 7:28 the Son, who is c for evermore
Heb 10:20 way, which he hath c for us

### CONSECRATION
Ex 29:22 for it is a ram of c
Ex 29:26 breast of the ram of Aaron's c
Ex 29:27 is heaved up, of the ram of the c
Ex 29:31 thou shalt take the ram of the c
Lev 8:22 the other ram, the ram of c
Lev 8:29 for of the ram of c it was Moses'
Lev 8:33 the days of your c be at an end
Num 6:7 because the c of his God is upon
Num 6:9 he hath defiled the head of his c

### CONSENT
Gen 34:15 But in this will we c unto you
Gen 34:22 Only herein will the men c unto
Gen 34:23 only let us c unto them, and they
Deut 13:8 Thou shalt not c unto him
Judg 11:17 but he would not c
1Sa 11:7 and they came out with one c
1Kin 20:8 him, Hearken not unto him, nor c
Ps 83:5 consulted together with one c
Prov 1:10 sinners entice thee, c thou not
Hos 6:9 of priests murder in the way by c
Zeph 3:9 the LORD, to serve him with one c
Lk 14:18 they all with one c began to make
Rom 7:16 I c unto the law that it is good
1Cor 7:5 except it be with c for a time
1Ti 6:3 c not to wholesome words, even

### CONSIDER
Ex 33:13 c that this nation is thy people
Lev 13:13 Then the priest shall c
Deut 4:39 c it in thine heart, that the
Deut 8:5 Thou shalt also c in thine heart
Deut 32:7 c the years of many generations
Deut 32:29 that they would c their latter
Judg 18:14 now therefore c what ye have to
Judg 19:30 c of it, take advice, and speak
1Sa 12:24 for c how great things he hath
1Sa 25:17 know and c what thou wilt do
2Kin 5:7 wherefore c, I pray you, and see
Job 11:11 will he not then c it
Job 23:15 when I c, I am afraid of him
Job 34:27 would not c any of his ways
Job 37:14 c the wondrous works of God
Ps 5:1 c my meditation
Ps 8:3 When I c thy heavens, the work of
Ps 9:13 c my trouble which I suffer of
Ps 13:3 C and hear me, O LORD my God
Ps 25:19 C mine enemies
Ps 37:10 thou shalt diligently c his place
Ps 45:10 Hearken, O daughter, and c
Ps 48:13 well her bulwarks, c her palaces
Ps 50:22 Now c this, ye that forget God,
Ps 64:9 they shall wisely c of his doing
Ps 119:95 but I will c thy testimonies
Ps 119:153 C mine affliction, and deliver me
Ps 119:159 C how I love thy precepts
Prov 6:6 c her ways, and be wise
Prov 23:1 c diligently what is before thee
Prov 24:12 he that pondereth the heart c it
Eccl 5:1 for they c not that they do evil
Eccl 7:13 C the work of God
Eccl 7:14 but in the day of adversity c
Is 1:3 not know, my people doth not c
Is 5:12 neither c the operation of his
Is 14:16 c thee, saying, Is this the man
Is 18:4 I will c in my dwelling place
Is 41:20 That they may see, and know, and c
Is 41:22 what they be, that we may c them
Is 43:18 neither c the things of old
Is 52:15 they had not heard shall they c
Jer 2:10 c diligently, and see if there be
Jer 9:17 C ye, and call for the mourning
Jer 23:20 days ye shall c it perfectly
Jer 30:24 in the latter days ye shall c it
Lam 1:11 see, O LORD, and c
Lam 2:20 c to whom thou hast done this
Lam 5:1 c, and behold our reproach
Eze 12:3 it may be they will c, though
Dan 9:23 the matter, and c the vision
Hos 7:2 they c not in their hearts that I
Hag 1:5 C your ways
Hag 1:7 C your ways
Hag 2:15 c from this day and upward, from
Hag 2:18 C now from this day and upward,
Hag 2:18 the LORD's temple was laid, c it
Mt 6:28 C the lilies of the field, how
Lk 12:24 C the ravens
Lk 12:27 C the lilies how they grow
Jn 11:50 Nor c that it is expedient for us
Acts 15:6 together for to c of this matter
2Ti 2:7 C what I say
Heb 3:1 c the Apostle and High Priest of
Heb 7:4 Now c how great this man was,
Heb 10:24 let us c one another to provoke
Heb 12:3 For c him that endured such

### CONSIDERED
1Kin 3:21 but when I had c it in the
1Kin 5:8 I have c the things which thou
Job 1:8 Hast thou c my servant Job, that
Job 2:3 Hast thou c my servant Job, that
Ps 31:7 for thou hast c my trouble
Ps 77:5 I have c the days of old, the
Prov 24:32 Then I saw, and c it well
Eccl 4:1 c all the oppressions that are
Eccl 4:4 I c all travail, and every right
Eccl 4:15 I c all the living which walk
Eccl 9:1 For all this I c in my heart even
Dan 7:8 I c the horns, and, behold, there
Mk 6:52 For they c not the miracle of the
Acts 11:6 I had fastened mine eyes, I c
Acts 12:12 And when he had c the thing
Rom 4:19 he c not his own body now dead,

### CONSIDERETH
Ps 33:15 he c all their works
Ps 41:1 Blessed is he that c the poor
Prov 21:12 wisely c the house of the wicked
Prov 28:22 c not that poverty shall come
Prov 29:7 The righteous c the cause of the
Prov 31:16 She c a field, and buyeth it
Is 44:19 none c in his heart, neither is
Eze 18:14 sins which he hath done, and c
Eze 18:28 Because he c, and turneth away

### CONSOLATION
Jer 16:7 of c to drink for their father or
Lk 2:25 waiting for the c of Israel
Lk 6:24 for ye have received your c
Acts 4:36 being interpreted, The son of c
Acts 15:31 had read, they rejoiced for the c
Rom 15:5 c grant you to be likeminded one
2Cor 1:5 so our c also aboundeth by Christ
2Cor 1:6 we be afflicted, it is for your c
2Cor 1:6 we be comforted, it is for your c
2Cor 1:7 so shall ye be also of the c
2Cor 7:7 but by the c wherewith he was
Phil 2:1 be therefore any c in Christ
2Th 2:16 and hath given us everlasting c

Philem 7 c in thy love, because the bowels
Heb 6:18 to lie, we might have a strong c

### CONSPIRACY

2Sa 15:12 And the c was strong
2Kin 12:20 his servants arose, and made a c
2Kin 14:19 Now they made a c against him in
2Kin 15:15 his c which he made, behold, they
2Kin 15:30 made a c against Pekah the son of
2Kin 17:4 king of Assyria found c in Hoshea
2Chr 25:27 made a c against him in Jerusalem
Jer 11:9 A c is found among the men of
Eze 22:25 There is a c of her prophets in
Acts 23:13 than forty which had made this c

### CONSPIRED

Gen 37:18 they c against him to slay him
1Sa 22:8 That all of you have c against me
1Sa 22:13 him, Why have ye c against me
1Kin 15:27 house of Issachar, c against him
1Kin 16:9 c against him, as he was in
1Kin 16:16 encamped heard say, Zimri hath c
2Kin 9:14 the son of Nimshi c against Joram
2Kin 10:9 I c against my master, and slew
2Kin 15:10 the son of Jabesh c against him
2Kin 15:25 c against him, and smote him in
2Kin 21:23 servants of Amon c against him
2Kin 21:24 them that had c against king Amon
2Chr 24:21 they c against him, and stoned him
2Chr 24:25 his own servants c against him
2Chr 24:26 these are they that c against him
2Chr 33:24 And his servants c against him
2Chr 33:25 them that had c against king Amon
Neh 4:8 c all of them together to come and
Amos 7:10 Amos hath c against thee in the

### CONSTRAINED

2Kin 4:8 and she c him to eat bread
Mt 14:22 straightway Jesus c his disciples
Mk 6:45 straightway he c his disciples to
Lk 24:29 But they c him, saying, Abide
Acts 16:15 And she c us
Acts 28:19 I was c to appeal unto Caesar

### CONSULTED

1Kin 12:6 king Rehoboam c with the old men,
1Kin 12:8 c with the young men that were
1Chr 13:1 David c with the captains of
2Chr 20:21 when he had c with the people, he
Neh 5:7 Then I c with myself, and I
Ps 83:3 c against thy hidden ones
Ps 83:5 For they have c together with one
Eze 21:21 he c with images, he looked in
Dan 6:7 have c together to establish a
Mic 6:5 now what Balak king of Moab c
Hab 2:10 Thou hast c shame to thy house by
Mt 26:4 c that they might take Jesus by
Jn 12:10 But the chief priests c that they

### CONSUME

Gen 41:30 and the famine shall c the land
Ex 32:10 them, and that I may c them
Ex 32:12 to c them from the face of the
Ex 33:3 lest I c thee in the way
Ex 33:5 of thee in a moment, and c thee
Lev 26:16 ague, that shall c the eyes
Num 16:21 that I may c them in a moment
Num 16:45 that I may c them as in a moment
Deut 5:25 for this great fire will c us
Deut 7:16 thou shalt c all the people which
Deut 7:22 thou mayest not c them at once
Deut 28:38 for the locust shall c it
Deut 28:42 of thy land shall the locust c
Deut 32:22 shall c the earth with her
Josh 24:20 c you, after that he hath done
1Sa 2:33 altar, shall be to c thine eyes
2Kin 1:10 heaven, and c thee and thy fifty
2Kin 1:12 heaven, and c thee and thy fifty
Neh 9:31 thou didst not utterly c them
Est 9:24 to c them, and to destroy them
Job 15:34 fire shall c the tabernacles of
Job 20:26 a fire not blown shall c him
Job 24:19 Drought and heat c the snow waters
Ps 37:20 they shall c
Ps 37:20 into smoke shall they c away
Ps 39:11 his beauty to c away like a moth
Ps 49:14 their beauty shall c in the grave
Ps 59:13 C them in wrath, c them,
Ps 78:33 their days did he c in vanity
Is 7:20 and it shall also c the beard
Is 10:18 shall c the glory of his forest,
Is 27:10 down, and c the branches thereof
Jer 8:13 I will surely c them, saith the
Jer 14:12 but I will c them by the sword,
Jer 49:27 it shall c the palaces of
Eze 4:17 c away for their iniquity
Eze 13:13 hailstones in my fury to c it
Eze 20:13 them in the wilderness, to c them
Eze 21:28 to c because of the glittering
Eze 22:15 will c thy filthiness out of thee
Eze 24:10 c the flesh, and spice it well, and
Eze 35:12 desolate, they are given us to c
Dan 2:44 c all these kingdoms, and it shall
Dan 7:26 take away his dominion, to c
Hos 11:6 shall c his branches, and devour
Zeph 1:2 I will utterly c all things from
Zeph 1:3 I will c man and beast
Zeph 1:3 I will c the fowls of the heaven,
Zec 5:4 shall c it with the timber
Zec 14:12 Their flesh shall c away while
Zec 14:12 their eyes shall c away in their
Zec 14:12 their tongue shall c away in
Lk 9:54 c them, even as Elias did
2Th 2:8 whom the Lord shall c with the
Jas 4:3 that ye may c it upon your lusts

### CONSUMED

Gen 19:15 lest thou be c in the iniquity of
Gen 19:17 to the mountain, lest thou be c
Gen 31:40 in the day the drought c me
Ex 3:2 with fire, and the bush was not c
Ex 15:7 wrath, which c them as stubble
Ex 22:6 or the field, be c therewith
Lev 6:10 the ashes which the fire hath c
Lev 9:24 c upon the altar the burnt
Num 11:1 c them that were in the uttermost
Num 12:12 half c when he cometh out of his
Num 14:35 this wilderness they shall be c
Num 16:26 lest ye be c in all their sins
Num 16:35 c the two hundred and fifty men
Num 17:13 shall we be c with dying
Num 21:28 it hath c Ar of Moab, and the
Num 25:11 that I c not the children of
Num 32:13 in the sight of the LORD, was c
Deut 2:15 among the host, until they were c
Deut 2:16 when all the men of war were c
Deut 28:21 until he have c thee from off the
Josh 5:6 which came out of Egypt, were c
Josh 8:24 of the sword, until they were c
Josh 10:20 great slaughter, till they were c
Judg 6:21 c the flesh and the unleavened
1Sa 12:25 still do wickedly, ye shall be c
1Sa 15:18 against them until they be c
2Sa 21:5 the king, The man that c us
2Sa 22:38 not again until I had c them
2Sa 22:39 And I have c them, and wounded them
1Kin 18:38 c the burnt sacrifice, and the
1Kin 22:11 Syrians, until thou have c them
2Kin 1:10 heaven, and c him and his fifty
2Kin 1:12 heaven, and c him and his fifty
2Kin 7:13 of the Israelites that are c
2Kin 13:17 in Aphek, till thou have c them
2Kin 13:19 Syria till thou hadst c it
2Chr 7:1 c the burnt offering and the
2Chr 8:8 whom the children of Israel c not
2Chr 18:10 shalt push Syria until they be c
Ezr 9:14 with us till thou hadst c us
Neh 2:3 the gates thereof are c with fire
Neh 2:13 gates thereof were c with fire
Job 1:16 sheep, and the servants, and c them
Job 4:9 breath of his nostrils are they c
Job 6:17 they are c out of their place
Job 7:9 As the cloud is c and vanisheth
Job 19:27 though my reins be c within me
Job 33:21 His flesh is c away, that it
Ps 6:7 Mine eye is c because of grief
Ps 18:37 did I turn again till they were c
Ps 31:9 mine eye is c with grief, yea, my
Ps 31:10 mine iniquity, and my bones are c
Ps 39:10 I am c by the blow of thine hand
Ps 71:13 c that are adversaries to my soul
Ps 73:19 they are utterly c with terrors
Ps 78:63 The fire c their young men
Ps 90:7 For we are c by thine anger, and
Ps 102:3 For my days are c like smoke
Ps 104:35 the sinners be c out of the earth
Ps 119:87 They had almost c me upon earth
Ps 119:139 My zeal hath c me, because mine
Prov 5:11 when thy flesh and thy body are c
Is 1:28 that forsake the LORD shall be c
Is 16:4 oppressors are c out of the land
Is 29:20 to nought, and the scorner is c
Is 64:7 thy face from us, and hast c us
Is 66:17 and the mouse, shall be c together
Jer 5:3 thou hast c them, but they have
Jer 6:29 burned, the lead is c of the fire
Jer 9:16 after them, till I have c them
Jer 10:25 him, and c him, and have made his
Jer 12:4 the beasts are c, and the birds
Jer 14:15 famine shall those prophets be c
Jer 16:4 and they shall be c by the sword
Jer 20:18 my days should be c with shame
Jer 24:10 till they be c from off the land
Jer 27:8 until I have c them by his hand
Jer 36:23 until all the roll was c in the
Jer 44:12 there, and they shall all be c
Jer 44:12 they shall even be c by the sword
Jer 44:18 have been c by the sword and by
Jer 44:27 of Egypt shall be c by the sword
Jer 49:37 after them, till I have c them
Lam 2:22 and brought up hath mine enemy c
Lam 3:22 LORD's mercies that we are not c
Eze 5:12 they be c in the midst of thee
Eze 13:14 ye shall be c in the midst
Eze 19:12 the fire c them
Eze 22:31 I have c them with the fire of my
Eze 24:11 it, that the scum of it may be c
Eze 34:29 they shall be no more c with
Eze 43:8 wherefore I have c them in mine
Eze 47:12 shall the fruit thereof be c
Dan 11:16 which by his hand shall be c
Mal 3:6 ye sons of Jacob are not c
Gal 5:15 that ye be not c one of another

### CONSUMPTION

Lev 26:16 even appoint over you terror, c
Deut 28:22 LORD shall smite thee with a c
Is 10:22 the c decreed shall overflow with
Is 10:23 Lord GOD of hosts shall make a c
Is 28:22 from the Lord GOD of hosts a c

### CONTAIN

1Kin 8:27 heaven of heavens cannot c thee
1Kin 18:32 as great as would c two measures
2Chr 2:6 and heaven of heavens cannot c him
2Chr 6:18 heaven of heavens cannot c thee
Eze 45:11 that the bath may c the tenth
Jn 21:25 not c the books that should be
1Cor 7:9 But if they cannot c, let them

### CONTAINED

1Kin 7:26 it c two thousand baths
1Kin 7:38 one laver c forty baths
Rom 2:14 by nature the things c in the law
Eph 2:15 of commandments c in ordinances
1Pet 2:6 also it is c in the scripture

### CONTEMPT

Est 1:18 Thus shall there arise too much c
Job 12:21 He poureth c upon princes, and
Job 31:34 or did the c of families terrify
Ps 107:40 He poureth c upon princes, and
Ps 119:22 Remove from me reproach and c
Ps 123:3 we are exceedingly filled with c
Ps 123:4 ease, and with the c of the proud
Prov 18:3 wicked cometh, then cometh also c
Is 23:9 glory, and to bring into c all the
Dan 12:2 and some to shame and everlasting c

### CONTEMPTIBLE

Mal 1:7 say, The table of the LORD is c
Mal 1:12 thereof, even his meat, is c
Mal 2:9 Therefore have I also made you c
2Cor 10:10 presence is weak, and his speech c

### CONTEND

Deut 2:9 neither c with them in battle
Deut 2:24 it, and c with him in battle
Job 9:3 If he will c with him, he cannot
Job 13:8 will ye c for God
Prov 28:4 such as keep the law c with them
Eccl 6:10 neither may he c with him that is
Is 49:25 for I will c with him that
Is 50:8 who will c with me
Is 57:16 For I will not c for ever
Jer 12:5 then how canst thou c with horses
Jer 18:19 the voice of them that c with me
Amos 7:4 the Lord GOD called to c by fire
Mic 6:1 c thou before the mountains, and
Jude 3 c for the faith which was once

### CONTENDED

Neh 13:11 Then c I with the rulers, and said
Neh 13:17 Then I c with the nobles of Judah
Neh 13:25 I c with them, and cursed them, and
Job 31:13 maidservant, when they c with me

Is 41:12 them, even them that c with thee
Acts 11:2 of the circumcision c with him

**CONTENT**
Gen 37:27 And his brethren were c
Ex 2:21 Moses was c to dwell with the man
Lev 10:20 Moses heard that, he was c
Josh 7:7 would to God we had been c
Judg 17:11 the Levite was c to dwell with
Judg 19:6 had said unto the man, Be c
2Kin 5:23 And Naaman said, Be c, take two
2Kin 6:3 And one said, Be c, I pray thee,
Job 6:28 Now therefore be c, look upon me
Prov 6:35 neither will he rest c, though
Mk 15:15 Pilate, willing to c the people
Lk 3:14 and be c with your wages
Phil 4:11 state I am, therewith to be c
1Ti 6:8 and raiment let us be therewith c
Heb 13:5 be c with such things as ye have
3Jn 10 not c therewith, neither doth he

**CONTENTION**
Prov 13:10 Only by pride cometh c
Prov 17:14 therefore leave off c, before it
Prov 18:6 A fool's lips enter into c
Prov 22:10 the scorner, and c shall go out
Jer 15:10 a man of c to the whole earth
Hab 1:3 are that raise up strife and c
Acts 15:39 the c was so sharp between them,
Phil 1:16 The one preach Christ of c
1Th 2:2 you the gospel of God with much c

**CONTENTIONS**
Prov 18:18 The lot causeth c to cease
Prov 18:19 their c are like the bars of a
Prov 19:13 the c of a wife are a continual
Prov 23:29 who hath c
1Cor 1:11 Chloe, that there are c among you
Titus 3:9 questions, and genealogies, and c

**CONTENTIOUS**
Prov 21:19 in the wilderness, than with a c
Prov 26:21 so is a c man to kindle strife
Prov 27:15 rainy day and a c woman are alike
Rom 2:8 But unto them that are c, and do
1Cor 11:16 But if any man seem to be c

**CONTINUAL**
Ex 29:42 This shall be a c burnt offering
Num 4:7 the c bread shall be thereon
Num 28:3 by day, for a c burnt offering
Num 28:6 It is a c burnt offering, which
Num 28:10 beside the c burnt offering, and
Num 28:15 beside the c burnt offering, and
Num 28:23 which is for a c burnt offering
Num 28:24 beside the c burnt offering
Num 28:31 them beside the c burnt offering
Num 29:11 the c burnt offering, and the meat
Num 29:16 beside the c burnt offering, his
Num 29:19 beside the c burnt offering, and
Num 29:22 beside the c burnt offering, and
Num 29:25 beside the c burnt offering, his
Num 29:28 beside the c burnt offering, and
Num 29:31 beside the c burnt offering, his
Num 29:34 beside the c burnt offering, his
Num 29:38 beside the c burnt offering, and
2Kin 25:30 his allowance was a c allowance
2Chr 2:4 for the c shewbread, and for the
Ezr 3:5 offered the c burnt offering
Neh 10:33 for the c meat offering, and for
Neh 10:33 for the c burnt offering, of the
Prov 15:15 of a merry heart hath a c feast
Prov 19:13 of a wife are a c dropping
Prov 27:15 A c dropping in a very rainy day
Is 14:6 people in wrath with a c stroke
Jer 48:5 of Luhith c weeping shall go up
Jer 52:34 there was a c diet given him of
Eze 39:14 sever out men of c employment
Eze 46:15 morning for a c burnt offering
Lk 18:5 by her c coming she weary me
Rom 9:2 heaviness and c sorrow in my heart

**CONTINUALLY**
Gen 6:5 of his heart was only evil c
Gen 8:3 returned from off the earth c
Gen 8:5 the waters decreased c until the
Ex 28:29 for a memorial before the LORD c
Ex 28:30 upon his heart before the LORD c
Ex 29:38 of the first year day by day c
Lev 24:2 to cause the lamps to burn c
Lev 24:3 the morning before the LORD c
Lev 24:4 candlestick before the LORD c
Lev 24:8 set it in order before the LORD c
Josh 6:13 the ark of the LORD went on c
1Sa 18:29 and Saul became David's enemy c
2Sa 9:7 shalt eat bread at my table c
2Sa 9:13 for he did eat c at the king's
2Sa 15:12 people increased c with Absalom
2Sa 19:13 before me c in the room of Joab
1Kin 10:8 which stand c before thee
2Kin 4:9 man of God, which passeth by us c
2Kin 25:29 he did eat bread c before him all
1Chr 16:6 the priests with trumpets c
1Chr 16:11 and his strength, seek his face c
1Chr 16:37 to minister before the ark c
1Chr 16:40 of the burnt offering c morning
1Chr 23:31 unto them, c before the LORD
2Chr 9:7 which stand c before thee
2Chr 12:15 Rehoboam and Jeroboam c
2Chr 24:14 LORD c all the days of Jehoiada
Job 1:5 Thus did Job c
Ps 34:1 his praise shall c be in my mouth
Ps 35:27 yea, let them say c, Let the LORD
Ps 38:17 halt, and my sorrow is c before me
Ps 40:11 and thy truth c preserve me
Ps 40:16 such as love thy salvation say c
Ps 42:3 while they c say unto me, Where
Ps 44:15 My confusion is c before me
Ps 50:8 to have been c before me
Ps 52:1 the goodness of God endureth c
Ps 58:7 melt away as waters which run c
Ps 69:23 and make their loins c to shake
Ps 70:4 such as love thy salvation say c
Ps 71:3 whereunto I may c resort
Ps 71:6 my praise shall be c of thee
Ps 71:14 But I will hope c, and will yet
Ps 72:15 also shall be made for him c
Ps 73:23 Nevertheless I am c with thee
Ps 74:23 rise up against thee increaseth c
Ps 109:10 Let his children be c vagabonds
Ps 109:15 Let them be before the LORD c
Ps 109:19 a girdle wherewith he is girded c
Ps 119:44 shall I keep thy law c for ever
Ps 119:109 My soul is c in my hand
Ps 119:117 have respect unto thy statutes c
Ps 140:2 c are they gathered together for
Prov 6:14 his heart, he deviseth mischief c
Prov 6:21 Bind them c upon thine heart, and
Eccl 1:6 it whirleth about c, and the wind
Is 21:8 I stand c upon the watchtower in
Is 49:16 thy walls are c before me
Is 51:13 hast feared c every day because
Is 52:5 my name c every day is blasphemed
Is 58:11 And the LORD shall guide thee c
Is 60:11 thy gates shall be open c
Is 65:3 me to anger c to my face
Jer 6:7 before me c is grief and wounds
Jer 33:18 offerings, and to do sacrifice c
Jer 52:33 he did c eat bread before him all
Eze 46:14 a meat offering c by a perpetual
Dan 6:16 Thy God whom thou servest c
Dan 6:20 is thy God, whom thou servest c
Hos 4:18 they have committed whoredom c
Hos 12:6 and judgment, and wait on thy God c
Obad 16 so shall all the heathen drink c
Nah 3:19 hath not thy wickedness passed c
Hab 1:17 not spare c to slay the nations
Lk 24:53 were c in the temple, praising and
Acts 6:4 will give ourselves c to prayer
Acts 10:7 of them that waited on him c
Rom 13:6 attending c upon this very thing
Heb 7:3 abideth a priest c
Heb 10:1 year c make the comers thereunto
Heb 13:15 the sacrifice of praise to God c

**CONTINUANCE**
Deut 28:59 even great plagues, and of long c
Deut 28:59 and sore sicknesses, and of long c
Ps 139:16 which in c were fashioned, when
Is 64:5 in those is c, and we shall be
Rom 2:7 To them who by patient c in well

**CONTINUE**
Ex 21:21 if he c a day or two, he shall
Lev 12:4 she shall then c in the blood of
Lev 12:5 she shall c in the blood of her
1Sa 12:14 you c following the LORD your God
1Sa 13:14 But now thy kingdom shall not c
2Sa 7:29 that it may c for ever before
1Kin 2:4 That the LORD may c his word
Job 15:29 neither shall his substance c
Job 17:2 doth not mine eye c in their
Ps 36:10 O c thy lovingkindness unto them
Ps 49:11 their houses shall c for ever
Ps 102:28 children of thy servants shall c
Ps 119:91 They c this day according to
Is 5:11 that c until night, till wine
Jer 32:14 vessel, that they may c many days
Dan 11:8 he shall c more years than the
Mt 15:32 because they c with me now three
Jn 8:31 If ye c in my word, then are ye
Jn 15:9 c ye in my love
Acts 13:43 persuaded them to c in the grace
Acts 14:22 exhorting them to c in the faith
Acts 26:22 I c unto this day, witnessing
Rom 6:1 Shall we c in sin, that grace may
Rom 11:22 if thou c in his goodness
Gal 2:5 of the gospel might c with you
Phil 1:25 abide and c with you all for your
Col 1:23 If ye c in the faith grounded and
Col 4:2 C in prayer, and watch in the same
1Ti 2:15 if they c in faith and charity and
1Ti 4:16 c in them
2Ti 3:14 But c thou in the things which
Heb 7:23 suffered to c by reason of death
Heb 13:1 Let brotherly love c
Jas 4:13 c there a year, and buy and sell,
2Pet 3:4 all things c as they were from
1Jn 2:24 you, ye also shall c in the Son
Rev 13:5 was given unto him to c forty
Rev 17:10 cometh, he must c a short space

**CONTINUED**
Gen 40:4 and they c a season in ward
Judg 5:17 Asher c on the sea shore, and
Ruth 1:2 the country of Moab, and c there
Ruth 2:7 hath c even from the morning
1Sa 1:12 as she c praying before the LORD,
2Sa 6:11 the ark of the LORD c in the
1Kin 22:1 they c three years without war
2Chr 29:28 all this c until the burnt
Neh 5:16 also I c in the work of this wall
Job 27:1 Moreover Job c his parable
Job 29:1 Moreover Job c his parable
Ps 72:17 his name shall be c as long as
Dan 1:21 Daniel c even unto the first year
Lk 6:12 c all night in prayer to God
Lk 22:28 Ye are they which have c with me
Jn 2:12 they c there not many days
Jn 8:7 So when they c asking him
Jn 11:54 there c with his disciples
Acts 1:14 These all c with one accord in
Acts 2:42 And they c stedfastly in the
Acts 8:13 he c with Philip, and wondered,
Acts 12:16 But Peter c knocking
Acts 15:35 Barnabas c in Antioch, teaching
Acts 18:11 he c there a year and six months,
Acts 19:10 this c by the space of two years
Acts 20:7 c his speech until midnight
Acts 27:33 c fasting, having taken nothing
Heb 8:9 because they c not in my covenant
1Jn 2:19 would no doubt have c with us

**CONTRARY**
Lev 26:21 And if ye walk c unto me, and will
Lev 26:23 things, but will walk c unto me
Lev 26:24 Then will I also walk c unto you
Lev 26:27 unto me, but walk c unto me
Lev 26:28 Then I will walk c unto you also
Lev 26:40 also they have walked c unto me
Lev 26:41 I also have walked c unto them
Est 9:1 (though it was turned to the c
Eze 16:34 the c is in thee from other women
Eze 16:34 unto thee, therefore thou art c
Mt 14:24 for the wind was c
Mk 6:48 for the wind was c unto them
Acts 17:7 these all do c to the decrees of
Acts 18:13 men to worship God c to the law
Acts 23:3 me to be smitten c to the law
Acts 26:9 things c to the name of Jesus of
Acts 27:4 Cyprus, because the winds were c
Rom 11:24 wert graffed c to nature into a
Rom 16:17 offences c to the doctrine which
Gal 5:17 these are c the one to the other
Col 2:14 was against us, which was c to us
1Th 2:15 not God, and are c to all men
1Ti 1:10 thing that is c to sound doctrine
Titus 2:8 is of the c part may be ashamed

**CONTRITE**
Ps 34:18 saveth such as be of a c spirit
Ps 51:17 a c heart, O God, thou wilt not
Is 57:15 with him also that is of a c
Is 57:15 to revive the heart of the c ones
Is 66:2 of a c spirit, and trembleth at my

**CONTROVERSY**
Deut 17:8 matters of c within thy gates
Deut 19:17 the men, between whom the c is
Deut 21:5 and by their word shall every c
Deut 25:1 If there be a c between men
2Sa 15:2 that when any man that had a c
Is 34:8 of recompences for the c of Zion
Jer 25:31 LORD hath a c with the nations
Eze 44:24 in c they shall stand in judgment
Hos 4:1 for the LORD hath a c with the
Hos 12:2 The LORD hath also a c with Judah
Mic 6:2 ye, O mountains, the LORD's c
Mic 6:2 the LORD hath a c with his people
1Ti 3:16 without c great is the mystery of

**CONVENIENT**
Prov 30:8 feed me with food c for me
Jer 40:4 c for thee to go, thither go
Jer 40:5 it seemeth c unto thee to go
Mk 6:21 when a c day was come, that Herod
Acts 24:25 when I have a c season, I will
Rom 1:28 do those things which are not c
1Cor 16:12 come when he shall have c time
Eph 5:4 nor jesting, which are not c
Philem 8 to enjoin thee that which is c

**CONVERSATION**
Ps 37:14 to slay such as be of upright c
Ps 50:23 his c aright will I shew the
2Cor 1:12 we have had our c in the world
Gal 1:13 For ye have heard of my c in time
Eph 2:3 c in times past in the lusts of
Eph 4:22 the former c the old man, which
Phil 1:27 Only let your c be as it becometh
Phil 3:20 For our c is in heaven
1Ti 4:12 of the believers, in word, in c
Heb 13:5 Let your c be without
Heb 13:7 considering the end of their c
Jas 3:13 good c his works with meekness of
1Pet 1:15 so be ye holy in all manner of c
1Pet 1:18 from your vain c received by
1Pet 2:12 Having your c honest among the
1Pet 3:1 word be won by the c of the wives
1Pet 3:2 your chaste c coupled with fear
1Pet 3:16 accuse your good c in Christ
2Pet 2:7 with the filthy c of the wicked
2Pet 3:11 ought ye to be in all holy c

**CONVERTED**
Ps 51:13 and sinners shall be c unto thee
Is 60:5 of the sea shall be c unto thee
Mt 13:15 with their heart, and should be c
Mt 18:3 I say unto you, Except ye be c
Mk 4:12 lest at any time they should be c
Lk 22:32 and when thou art c, strengthen
Jn 12:40 with their heart, and be c
Acts 3:19 Repent ye therefore, and be c
Acts 28:27 with their heart, and should be c

**CONVINCED**
Job 32:12 there was none of you that c Job
Acts 18:28 For he mightily c the Jews
1Cor 14:24 he is c of all, he is judged of
Jas 2:9 are c of the law as transgressors

**CONVOCATION**
Ex 12:16 day there shall be an holy c
Ex 12:16 there shall be an holy c to you
Lev 23:3 is the sabbath of rest, an holy c
Lev 23:7 first day ye shall have an holy c
Lev 23:8 in the seventh day is an holy c
Lev 23:21 that it may be an holy c unto you
Lev 23:24 of blowing of trumpets, an holy c
Lev 23:27 it shall be an holy c unto you
Lev 23:35 the first day shall be an holy c
Lev 23:36 day shall be an holy c unto you
Num 28:18 the first day shall be an holy c
Num 28:25 day ye shall have an holy c
Num 28:26 be out, ye shall have an holy c
Num 29:1 month, ye shall have an holy c
Num 29:7 of this seventh month an holy c

**CONVOCATIONS**
Lev 23:2 ye shall proclaim to be holy c
Lev 23:4 feasts of the LORD, even holy c
Lev 23:37 ye shall proclaim to be holy c

**COPY**
Deut 17:18 that he shall write him a c of
Josh 8:32 stones a c of the law of Moses
Ezr 4:11 This is the c of the letter that
Ezr 4:23 Now when the c of king
Ezr 5:6 The c of the letter that Tatnai,
Ezr 7:11 Now this is the c of the letter
Est 3:14 The c of the writing for a
Est 4:8 Also he gave him the c of the
Est 8:13 The c of the writing for a

**CORD**
Josh 2:15 down by a c through the window
Job 30:11 Because he hath loosed my c
Job 41:1 or his tongue with a c which thou
Eccl 4:12 a threefold c is not quickly
Eccl 12:6 Or ever the silver c be loosed
Mic 2:5 have none that shall cast a c by

**CORDS**
Ex 35:18 the pins of the court, and their c
Ex 39:40 hanging for the court gate, his c
Num 3:26 the c of it for all the service
Num 3:37 and their pins, and their c
Num 4:26 the altar round about, and their c
Num 4:32 and their pins, and their c
Judg 15:13 And they bound him with two new c
Judg 15:14 the c that were upon his arms
Est 1:6 fastened with c of fine linen
Job 36:8 be holden in c of affliction
Ps 2:3 and cast away their c from us
Ps 118:27 bind the sacrifice with c
Ps 129:4 cut asunder the c of the wicked
Ps 140:5 have hid a snare for me, and c
Prov 5:22 be holden with the c of his sins
Is 5:18 draw iniquity with c of vanity
Is 33:20 any of the c thereof be broken
Is 54:2 spare not, lengthen thy c
Jer 10:20 spoiled, and all my c are broken
Jer 38:6 and they let down Jeremiah with c
Jer 38:11 let them down by c into the
Jer 38:12 under thine armholes under the c
Jer 38:13 So they drew up Jeremiah with c
Eze 27:24 of rich apparel, bound with c
Hos 11:4 I drew them with c of a man
Jn 2:15 he had made a scourge of small c

**CORINTH** *(cor'-inth)* See CORINTHIANS, CORINTHUS. *Capital of Achaia.*
Acts 18:1 from Athens, and came to C
Acts 19:1 that, while Apollos was at C
1Cor 1:2 the church of God which is at C
2Cor 1:1 the church of God which is at C
2Cor 1:23 you I came not as yet unto C
2Ti 4:20 Erastus abode at C

**CORINTHIANS** *(co-rin'-the-uns) Residents of Corinth.*
Acts 18:8 many of the C hearing believed,
1Cor s The first epistle to the C was
2Cor 6:11 O ye C, our mouth is open unto
2Cor s the C was written from Philippi

**CORINTHUS** *(co-rin'-thus)* See CORINTH. *Same as Corinth.*
Rom s Written to the Romans from C

**CORMORANT**
Lev 11:17 And the little owl, and the c
Deut 14:17 and the gier eagle, and the c
Is 34:11 But the c and the bittern shall
Zeph 2:14 both the c and the bittern shall

**CORN**
Gen 27:28 of the earth, and plenty of c
Gen 27:37 and with c and wine have I
Gen 41:5 seven ears of c came up upon one
Gen 41:35 lay up c under the hand of
Gen 41:49 Joseph gathered c as the sand of
Gen 41:57 into Egypt to Joseph for to buy c
Gen 42:1 saw that there was c in Egypt
Gen 42:2 heard that there is c in Egypt
Gen 42:3 went down to buy c in Egypt
Gen 42:5 to buy c among those that came
Gen 42:19 carry c for the famine of your
Gen 42:25 to fill their sacks with c
Gen 42:26 they laded their asses with the c
Gen 43:2 when they had eaten up the c
Gen 44:2 of the youngest, and his c money
Gen 45:23 and ten she asses laden with c
Gen 47:14 for the c which they bought
Ex 22:6 thorns, so that the stacks of c
Ex 22:6 or the standing c, or the field
Lev 2:14 green ears of c dried by the fire
Lev 2:14 even c beaten out of full ears
Lev 2:16 it, part of the beaten c thereof
Lev 23:14 eat neither bread, nor parched c
Num 18:27 were the c of the threshingfloor
Deut 7:13 and the fruit of thy land, thy c
Deut 11:14 that thou mayest gather in thy c
Deut 12:17 thy gates the tithe of thy c
Deut 14:23 name there, the tithe of thy c
Deut 16:9 to put the sickle to the c
Deut 16:13 that thou hast gathered in thy c
Deut 18:4 The firstfruit also of thy c
Deut 23:25 the standing c of thy neighbour
Deut 23:25 unto thy neighbour's standing c
Deut 25:4 the ox when he treadeth out the c
Deut 28:51 shall not leave thee either c
Deut 33:28 Jacob shall be upon a land of c
Josh 5:11 they did eat of the old c of the
Josh 5:11 parched c in the selfsame day
Josh 5:12 eaten of the old c of the land
Judg 15:5 the standing c of the Philistines
Judg 15:5 shocks, and also the standing c
Ruth 2:2 glean ears of c after him in
Ruth 2:14 and he reached her parched c
Ruth 3:7 down at the end of the heap of c
1Sa 17:17 an ephah of this parched c
1Sa 25:18 and five measures of parched c
2Sa 17:19 mouth, and spread ground c thereon
2Sa 17:28 and barley, and flour, and parched c
2Kin 4:42 full ears of c in the husk
2Kin 18:32 like your own land, a land of c
2Kin 19:26 as c blasted before it be grown
2Chr 31:5 in abundance the firstfruits of c
2Chr 32:28 also for the increase of c
Neh 5:2 therefore we take up c for them
Neh 5:3 and houses, that we might buy c
Neh 5:10 might exact of them money and c
Neh 5:11 part of the money, and of the c
Neh 10:39 shall bring the offering of the c
Neh 13:5 vessels, and the tithes of the c
Neh 13:12 all Judah the tithe of the c
Job 5:26 like as a shock of c cometh in in
Job 24:6 reap every one his c in the field
Job 24:24 off as the tops of the ears of c
Job 39:4 good liking, they grow up with c
Ps 4:7 than in the time that their c
Ps 65:9 thou preparest them c, when thou
Ps 65:13 also are covered over with c
Ps 72:16 of c in the earth upon the top of
Ps 78:24 had given them of the c of heaven
Prov 11:26 He that withholdeth c, the people
Is 17:5 the harvestman gathereth the c
Is 21:10 threshing, and the c of my floor
Is 28:28 Bread c is bruised
Is 36:17 like your own land, a land of c
Is 37:27 as c blasted before it be grown
Is 62:8 c to be meat for thine enemies
Lam 2:12 say to their mothers, Where is c
Eze 36:29 and I will call for the c, and will
Hos 2:8 did not know that I gave her c
Hos 2:9 take away my c in the time
Hos 2:22 And the earth shall hear the c
Hos 7:14 they assemble themselves for c
Hos 10:11 and loveth to tread out the c
Hos 14:7 they shall revive as the c
Joel 1:10 for the c is wasted
Joel 1:17 for the c is withered
Joel 2:19 people, Behold, I will send you c
Amos 8:5 moon be gone, that we may sell c
Amos 9:9 like as c is sifted in a sieve,
Hag 1:11 upon the mountains, and upon the c
Zec 9:17 c shall make the young men
Mt 12:1 on the sabbath day through the c
Mt 12:1 and began to pluck the ears of c
Mk 2:23 that he went through the c fields
Mk 2:23 they went, to pluck the ears of c
Mk 4:28 after that the full c in the ear
Lk 6:1 that he went through the c fields
Lk 6:1 disciples plucked the ears of c
Jn 12:24 Except a c of wheat fall into the
Acts 7:12 heard that there was c in Egypt
1Cor 9:9 of the ox that treadeth out the c
1Ti 5:18 the ox that treadeth out the c

**CORNELIUS** *(cor-ne'-le-us) A Roman centurion converted by Peter.*
Acts 10:1 certain man in Caesarea called C
Acts 10:3 in to him, and saying unto him, C
Acts 10:7 which spake unto C was departed
Acts 10:17 C had made enquiry for Simon's
Acts 10:21 which were sent unto him from C
Acts 10:22 C the centurion, a just man, and
Acts 10:24 C waited for them, and had called
Acts 10:25 C met him, and fell down at his
Acts 10:30 C said, Four days ago I was
Acts 10:31 And said, C, thy prayer is heard,

**CORNER**
Ex 36:25 which is toward the north c
Lev 21:5 shave off the c of their beard
Josh 18:14 compassed the c of the sea
2Kin 11:11 from the right c of the temple to
2Kin 11:11 to the left c of the temple
2Kin 14:13 gate of Ephraim unto the c gate
2Chr 25:23 the gate of Ephraim to the c gate
2Chr 26:9 towers in Jerusalem at the c gate
2Chr 28:24 altars in every c of Jerusalem
Neh 3:24 of the wall, even unto the c
Neh 3:31 and to the going up of the c
Neh 3:32 between the going up of the c
Job 38:6 or who laid the c stone thereof
Ps 118:22 is become the head stone of the c
Ps 144:12 our daughters may be as c stones
Prov 7:8 through the street near her c
Prov 7:12 and lieth in wait at every c
Prov 21:9 to dwell in a c of the housetop
Prov 25:24 to dwell in the c of the housetop
Is 28:16 a tried stone, a precious c stone
Is 30:20 be removed into a c any more
Jer 31:38 Hananeel unto the gate of the c
Jer 31:40 unto the c of the horse gate
Jer 48:45 and shall devour the c of Moab
Jer 51:26 not take of thee a stone for a c
Eze 46:21 in every c of the court there was
Amos 3:12 in Samaria in the c of a bed
Zec 10:4 Out of him came forth the c
Zec 14:10 the first gate, unto the c gate
Mt 21:42 same is become the head of the c
Mk 12:10 is become the head of the c
Lk 20:17 same is become the head of the c
Acts 4:11 which is become the head of the c
Acts 26:26 this thing was not done in a c
Eph 2:20 himself being the chief c stone
1Pet 2:6 I lay in Sion a chief c stone
1Pet 2:7 same is made the head of the c

**CORNERS**
Ex 25:12 and put them in the four c thereof
Ex 25:26 four c that are on the four feet
Ex 26:23 c of the tabernacle in the two
Ex 26:24 they shall be for the two c
Ex 27:2 of it upon the four c thereof
Ex 27:4 rings in the four c thereof
Ex 30:4 crown of it, by the two c thereof
Ex 36:28 two boards made he for the c of
Ex 36:29 did to both of them in both the c
Ex 37:3 to be set by the four c of it
Ex 37:13 four c that were in the four feet
Ex 37:27 crown thereof, by the two c of it
Ex 38:2 horns thereof on the four c of it
Lev 19:9 wholly reap the c of thy field
Lev 19:27 not round the c of your heads
Lev 19:27 shalt thou mar the c of thy beard
Lev 23:22 c of thy field when thou reapest
Num 24:17 and shall smite the c of Moab
Deut 32:26 said, I would scatter them into c
1Kin 7:30 and the four c thereof had
1Kin 7:34 to the four c of one base
Neh 9:22 and didst divide them into c
Job 1:19 and smote the four c of the house
Is 11:12 from the four c of the earth
Jer 9:26 and all that are in the utmost c
Jer 25:23 and all that are in the utmost c
Jer 49:32 them that are in the utmost c
Eze 7:2 come upon the four c of the land
Eze 41:22 the c thereof, and the length
Eze 43:20 on the four c of the settle, and
Eze 45:19 upon the four c of the settle of
Eze 46:21 pass by the four c of the court
Eze 46:22 In the four c of the court there
Eze 46:22 these four c were of one measure
Zec 9:15 bowls, and as the c of the altar
Mt 6:5 in the c of the streets, that
Acts 10:11 a great sheet knit at the four c
Acts 11:5 let down from heaven by four c
Rev 7:1 on the four c of the earth

**CORRECT**
Ps 39:11 rebukes dost c man for iniquity
Ps 94:10 the heathen, shall not he c
Prov 29:17 C thy son, and he shall give thee
Jer 2:19 Thine own wickedness shall c thee
Jer 10:24 O LORD, c me, but with judgment
Jer 30:11 but I will c thee in measure, and
Jer 46:28 of thee, but c thee in measure

**CORRECTION**
Job 37:13 causeth it to come, whether for c
Prov 3:11 neither be weary of his c
Prov 7:22 as a fool to the c of the stocks
Prov 15:10 C is grievous unto him that
Prov 22:15 but the rod of c shall drive it
Prov 23:13 Withhold not c from the child
Jer 2:30 they received no c
Jer 5:3 they have refused to receive c
Jer 7:28 LORD their God, nor receiveth c
Hab 1:12 thou hast established them for c
Zeph 3:2 she received not c
2Ti 3:16 for doctrine, for reproof, for c

**CORRUPT**
Gen 6:11 The earth also was c before God
Gen 6:12 the earth, and, behold, it was c
Deut 4:16 Lest ye c yourselves, and make you
Deut 4:25 shall c yourselves, and make a
Deut 31:29 ye will utterly c yourselves
Job 17:1 My breath is c, my days are
Ps 14:1 They are c, they have done
Ps 38:5 are c because of my foolishness
Ps 53:1 C are they, and have done
Ps 73:8 They are c, and speak wickedly
Prov 25:26 troubled fountain, and a c spring
Eze 20:44 nor according to your c doings
Eze 23:11 she was more c in her inordinate
Dan 2:9 c words to speak before me, till
Dan 11:32 covenant shall he c by flatteries
Mal 1:14 unto the Lord a c thing
Mal 2:3 I will c your seed, and spread
Mt 6:19 earth, where moth and rust doth c
Mt 6:20 neither moth nor rust doth c
Mt 7:17 but a c tree bringeth forth evil
Mt 7:18 neither can a c tree bring forth
Mt 12:33 the tree c, and his fruit c
Lk 6:43 tree bringeth not forth c fruit
Lk 6:43 neither doth a c tree bring forth
1Cor 15:33 communications c good manners
2Cor 2:17 as many, which c the word of God
Eph 4:22 which is c according to the
Eph 4:29 Let no c communication proceed
1Ti 6:5 disputings of men of c minds
2Ti 3:8 men of c minds, reprobate
Jude 10 in those things they c themselves
Rev 19:2 which did c the earth with her

**CORRUPTED**
Gen 6:12 for all flesh had c his way upon
Ex 8:24 the land was c by reason of the
Ex 32:7 land of Egypt, have c themselves
Deut 9:12 out of Egypt have c themselves
Deut 32:5 They have c themselves, their
Judg 2:19 c themselves more than their
Eze 16:47 thou wast c more than they in all
Eze 28:17 thou hast c thy wisdom by reason
Hos 9:9 They have deeply c themselves
Zeph 3:7 rose early, and c all their doings
Mal 2:8 ye have c the covenant of Levi,
2Cor 7:2 wronged no man, we have c no man
2Cor 11:3 so your minds should be c from
Jas 5:2 Your riches are c, and your

**CORRUPTIBLE**
Rom 1:23 into an image made like to c man
1Cor 9:25 they do it to obtain a c crown
1Cor 15:53 For this c must put on
1Cor 15:54 So when this c shall have put on
1Pet 1:18 were not redeemed with c things
1Pet 1:23 Being born again, not of c seed
1Pet 3:4 the heart, in that which is not c

**CORRUPTION**
Lev 22:25 because their c is in them
2Kin 23:13 the right hand of the mount of c
Job 17:14 I have said to c, Thou art my
Ps 16:10 suffer thine Holy One to see c
Ps 49:9 still live for ever, and not see c
Is 38:17 delivered it from the pit of c
Dan 10:8 was turned in me into c, and I
Jonah 2:6 thou brought up my life from c
Acts 2:27 suffer thine Holy One to see c
Acts 2:31 hell, neither his flesh did see c
Acts 13:34 dead, now no more to return to c
Acts 13:35 suffer thine Holy One to see c
Acts 13:36 laid unto his fathers, and saw c
Acts 13:37 whom God raised again, saw no c
Rom 8:21 of c into the glorious liberty of
1Cor 15:42 It is sown in c
1Cor 15:50 neither doth c inherit
Gal 6:8 flesh shall of the flesh reap c
2Pet 1:4 having escaped the c that is in
2Pet 2:12 utterly perish in their own c
2Pet 2:19 themselves are the servants of c

**COSAM** *(co'-sam) Son of Elmodam; ancestor of Jesus*
Lk 3:28 of Addi, which was the son of C

**COST**
2Sa 19:42 we eaten at all of the king's c
2Sa 24:24 of that which doth c me nothing
1Chr 21:24 offer burnt offerings without c
Lk 14:28 not down first, and counteth the c

**COUCH**
Gen 49:4 he went up to my c
Job 7:13 my c shall ease my complaint
Job 38:40 When they c in their dens, and
Ps 6:6 I water my c with my tears
Amos 3:12 of a bed, and in Damascus in a c
Lk 5:19 his c into the midst before Jesus
Lk 5:24 thee, Arise, and take up thy c

**COUNCIL**
Ps 68:27 the princes of Judah and their c
Mt 5:22 Raca, shall be in danger of the c
Mt 12:14 held a c against him, how they
Mt 26:59 priests, and elders, and all the c
Mk 14:55 all the c sought for witness
Mk 15:1 elders and scribes and the whole c
Lk 22:66 together, and led him into their c
Jn 11:47 priests and the Pharisees a c
Acts 4:15 them to go aside out of the c
Acts 5:21 him, and called the c together
Acts 5:27 them, they set them before the c
Acts 5:34 Then stood there up one in the c
Acts 5:41 from the presence of the c
Acts 6:12 him, and brought him to the c
Acts 6:15 And all that sat in the c, looking
Acts 22:30 priests and all their c to appear
Acts 23:1 Paul, earnestly beholding the c
Acts 23:6 Pharisees, he cried out in the c
Acts 23:15 Now therefore ye with the c
Acts 23:20 down Paul to morrow into the c
Acts 23:28 I brought him forth into their c
Acts 24:20 in me, while I stood before the c
Acts 25:12 when he had conferred with the c

**COUNSEL**
Ex 18:19 unto my voice, I will give thee c
Num 27:21 who shall ask c for him after the
Num 31:16 Israel, through the c of Balaam
Deut 32:28 For they are a nation void of c
Josh 9:14 asked not c at the mouth of the
Judg 18:5 And they said unto him, Ask c
Judg 20:7 give here your advice and c
Judg 20:18 asked c of God, and said, Which of
Judg 20:23 asked c of the LORD, saying,
1Sa 14:37 And Saul asked c of God, Shall I
2Sa 15:31 turn the c of Ahithophel into
2Sa 15:34 for me defeat the c of Ahithophel
2Sa 16:20 Give c among you what we shall do
2Sa 16:23 the c of Ahithophel, which he
2Sa 16:23 so was all the c of Ahithophel
2Sa 17:7 The c that Ahithophel hath given
2Sa 17:11 Therefore I c that all Israel be
2Sa 17:14 The c of Hushai the Archite is
2Sa 17:14 better than the c of Ahithophel
2Sa 17:14 defeat the good c of Ahithophel
2Sa 17:15 and thus did Ahithophel c Absalom
2Sa 17:23 saw that his c was not followed
2Sa 20:18 They shall surely ask c at Abel
1Kin 1:12 let me, I pray thee, give thee c
1Kin 12:8 he forsook the c of the old men
1Kin 12:9 What c give ye that we may answer
1Kin 12:13 old men's c that they gave him
1Kin 12:14 them after the c of the young men
1Kin 12:28 Whereupon the king took c
2Kin 6:8 took c with his servants, saying,
2Kin 18:20 are but vain words,) I have c
1Chr 10:13 also for asking c of one that had
2Chr 10:6 king Rehoboam took c with the old
2Chr 10:6 What c give ye me to return
2Chr 10:8 But he forsook the c which the
2Chr 10:8 took c with the young men that
2Chr 10:13 forsook the c of the old men
2Chr 22:5 He walked also after their c
2Chr 25:16 Art thou made of the king's c
2Chr 25:16 and hast not hearkened unto my c
2Chr 30:2 For the king had taken c, and his
2Chr 30:23 the whole assembly took c to keep
2Chr 32:3 He took c with his princes and his
Ezr 10:3 according to the c of my lord
Ezr 10:8 according to the c of the princes
Neh 4:15 God had brought their c to nought
Neh 6:7 and let us take c together

Job 5:13 the c of the froward is carried
Job 10:3 and shine upon the c of the wicked
Job 12:13 is wisdom and strength, he hath c
Job 18:7 his own c shall cast him down
Job 21:16 the c of the wicked is far from
Job 22:18 but the c of the wicked is far
Job 29:21 waited, and kept silence at my c
Job 38:2 c by words without knowledge
Job 42:3 that hideth c without knowledge
Ps 1:1 not in the c of the ungodly
Ps 2:2 and the rulers take c together
Ps 13:2 long shall I take c in my soul
Ps 14:6 Ye have shamed the c of the poor
Ps 16:7 the LORD, who hath given me c
Ps 20:4 own heart, and fulfil all thy c
Ps 31:13 while they took c together
Ps 33:10 The LORD bringeth the c of the
Ps 33:11 The c of the LORD standeth for
Ps 55:14 We took sweet c together, and
Ps 64:2 from the secret c of the wicked
Ps 71:10 wait for my soul take c together
Ps 73:24 Thou shalt guide me with thy c
Ps 83:3 taken crafty c against thy people
Ps 106:13 they waited not for his c
Ps 106:43 they provoked him with their c
Ps 107:11 contemned the c of the most High
Prov 1:25 ye have set at nought all my c
Prov 1:30 They would none of my c
Prov 8:14 C is mine, and sound wisdom
Prov 11:14 Where no c is, the people fall
Prov 12:15 he that hearkeneth unto c is wise
Prov 15:22 Without c purposes are
Prov 19:20 Hear c, and receive instruction,
Prov 19:21 nevertheless the c of the LORD
Prov 20:5 C in the heart of man is like
Prov 20:18 Every purpose is established by c
Prov 21:30 nor c against the LORD
Prov 24:6 For by wise c thou shalt make thy
Prov 27:9 of a man's friend by hearty c
Eccl 8:2 I c thee to keep the king's
Is 5:19 let the c of the Holy One of
Is 7:5 have taken evil c against thee
Is 8:10 Take c together, and it shall come
Is 11:2 and understanding, the spirit of c
Is 16:3 Take c, execute judgment
Is 19:3 and I will destroy the c thereof
Is 19:11 the c of the wise counsellors of
Is 19:17 because of the c of the LORD of
Is 23:8 hath taken this c against Tyre
Is 28:29 of hosts, which is wonderful in c
Is 29:15 to hide their c from the LORD
Is 30:1 saith the LORD, that take c
Is 36:5 they are but vain words) I have c
Is 40:14 With whom took he c, and who
Is 44:26 and performeth the c of his
Is 45:21 yea, let them take c together
Is 46:10 My c shall stand, and I will do
Is 46:11 executeth my c from a far country
Jer 18:18 nor c from the wise, nor the word
Jer 18:23 all their c against me to slay me
Jer 19:7 I will make void the c of Judah
Jer 23:18 hath stood in the c of the LORD
Jer 23:22 But if they had stood in my c
Jer 32:19 Great in c, and mighty in work
Jer 38:15 and if I give thee c, wilt thou
Jer 49:7 is c perished from the prudent
Jer 49:20 Therefore hear the c of the LORD
Jer 49:30 Babylon hath taken c against you
Jer 50:45 hear ye the c of the LORD
Eze 7:26 priest, and c from the ancients
Eze 11:2 give wicked c in this city
Dan 2:14 Then Daniel answered with c
Dan 4:27 let my c be acceptable unto thee,
Hos 4:12 My people ask c at their stocks,
Hos 10:6 shall be ashamed of his own c
Mic 4:12 neither understand they his c
Zec 6:13 the c of peace shall be between
Mt 22:15 took c how they might entangle
Mt 27:1 elders of the people took c
Mt 27:7 And they took c, and bought with
Mt 28:12 with the elders, and had taken c
Mk 3:6 straightway took c with the
Lk 7:30 lawyers rejected the c of God
Lk 23:51 same had not consented to the c
Jn 11:53 took c together for to put him to
Jn 18:14 which gave c to the Jews, that it
Acts 2:23 delivered by the determinate c
Acts 4:28 thy c determined before to be
Acts 5:33 the heart, and took c to slay them
Acts 5:38 for if this c or this work be of
Acts 9:23 the Jews took c to kill him
Acts 20:27 declare unto you all the c of God
Acts 27:42 the soldiers' c was to kill the
Eph 1:11 after the c of his own will
Heb 6:17 promise the immutability of his c
Rev 3:18 I c thee to buy of me gold tried

## COUNSELLOR

2Sa 15:12 the Gilonite, David's c, from his
1Chr 26:14 for Zechariah his son, a wise c
1Chr 27:32 Jonathan David's uncle was a c
1Chr 27:33 And Ahithophel was the king's c
2Chr 22:3 mother was his c to do wickedly
Is 3:3 and the honourable man, and the c
Is 9:6 name shall be called Wonderful, C
Is 40:13 or being his c hath taught him
Is 41:28 among them, and there was no c
Mic 4:9 is thy c perished?
Nah 1:11 evil against the LORD, a wicked c
Mk 15:43 of Arimathaea, an honourable c
Lk 23:50 there was a man named Joseph, a c
Rom 11:34 or who hath been his c

## COUNSELLORS

2Chr 22:4 for they were his c after the
Ezr 4:5 And hired c against them, to
Ezr 7:14 of the king, and of his seven c
Ezr 7:15 his c have freely offered unto
Ezr 7:28 unto me before the king, and his c
Ezr 8:25 our God, which the king, and his c
Job 3:14 c of the earth, which built
Job 12:17 He leadeth c away spoiled, and
Ps 119:24 also are my delight, and my c
Prov 11:14 multitude of c there is safety
Prov 12:20 but to the c of peace is joy
Prov 15:22 of c they are established
Prov 24:6 in multitude of c there is safety
Is 1:26 thy c as at the beginning
Is 19:11 the counsel of the wise c of
Dan 3:2 the judges, the treasurers, the c
Dan 3:3 the judges, the treasurers, the c
Dan 3:24 and spake, and said unto his c
Dan 3:27 and captains, and the king's c
Dan 4:36 and my c and my lords sought unto
Dan 6:7 governors, and the princes, the c

## COUNSELS

Job 37:12 it is turned round about by his c
Ps 5:10 let them fall by their own c
Ps 81:12 and they walked in their own c
Prov 1:5 shall attain unto wise c
Prov 12:5 but the c of the wicked are
Prov 22:20 to thee excellent things in c
Is 25:1 thy c of old are faithfulness and
Is 47:13 wearied in the multitude of thy c
Jer 7:24 their ear, but walked in the c
Hos 11:6 them, because of their own c
Mic 6:16 of Ahab, and ye walk in their c
1Cor 4:5 make manifest the c of the hearts

## COUNT

Ex 12:4 shall make your c for the lamb
Lev 19:23 then ye shall c the fruit thereof
Lev 23:15 ye shall c unto you from the
Lev 25:27 Then let him c the years of the
Lev 25:52 jubile, then he shall c with him
Num 23:10 Who can c the dust of Jacob, and
1Sa 1:16 C not thine handmaid for a
Job 19:15 and my maids, c me for a stranger
Job 31:4 he see my ways, and c all my steps
Ps 87:6 The LORD shall c, when he writeth
Ps 139:18 If I should c them, they are more
Ps 139:22 I c them mine enemies
Mic 6:11 Shall I c them pure with the
Acts 20:24 neither c I my life dear unto
Phil 3:8 I c all things but loss for the
Phil 3:8 do c them but dung, that I may
Phil 3:13 Brethren, I c not myself to have
2Th 1:11 that our God would c you worthy
2Th 3:15 Yet c him not as an enemy, but
1Ti 6:1 servants as are under the yoke c
Philem 17 If thou c me therefore a partner,
Jas 1:2 c it all joy when ye fall into
Jas 5:11 we c them happy which endure
2Pet 2:13 as they that c it pleasure to
2Pet 3:9 promise, as some men c slackness
Rev 13:18 c the number of the beast

## COUNTED

Gen 15:6 he c it to him for righteousness
Gen 30:33 that shall be c stolen with me
Gen 31:15 Are we not c of him strangers
Ex 38:21 of testimony, as it was c
Lev 25:31 be c as the fields of the country
Num 18:30 then it shall be c unto the
Josh 13:3 which is c to the Canaanite
1Kin 1:21 son Solomon shall be c offenders
1Kin 3:8 be numbered nor c for multitude
1Chr 21:6 Benjamin c he not among them
1Chr 23:24 as they were c by number of names
Neh 13:13 for they were c faithful, and
Job 18:3 Wherefore are we c as beasts
Job 41:29 Darts are c as stubble
Ps 44:22 we are c as sheep for the
Ps 88:4 I am c with them that go down
Ps 106:31 And that was c unto him for
Prov 17:28 he holdeth his peace, is c wise
Prov 27:14 it shall be c a curse to him
Is 5:28 hoofs shall be c like flint
Is 32:15 fruitful field be c for a forest
Is 33:18 where is he that c the towers
Is 40:15 are c as the small dust of the
Is 40:17 they are c to him less than
Hos 8:12 but they were c as a strange
Mt 14:5 because they c him as a prophet
Mk 11:32 for all men c John, that he was a
Acts 5:41 rejoicing that they were c worthy
Acts 19:19 they c the price of them, and
Rom 2:26 be c for circumcision
Rom 4:3 God, and it was c unto him for
Rom 4:5 his faith is c for righteousness
Rom 9:8 of the promise are c for the seed
Phil 3:7 those I c loss for Christ
2Th 1:5 that ye may be c worthy of the
1Ti 1:12 me, for that he c me faithful
1Ti 5:17 well be c worthy of double honour
Heb 3:3 For this man was c worthy of more
Heb 7:6 But he whose descent is not c
Heb 10:29 hath c the blood of the covenant,

## COUNTENANCE

Gen 4:5 was very wroth, and his c fell
Gen 4:6 and why is thy c fallen
Gen 31:2 And Jacob beheld the c of Laban
Gen 31:5 unto them, I see your father's c
Ex 23:3 Neither shalt thou c a poor man
Num 6:26 The LORD lift up his c upon thee
Deut 28:50 A nation of fierce c, which shall
Judg 13:6 his c was like the c of
1Sa 1:18 did eat, and her c was no more sad
1Sa 16:7 unto Samuel, Look not on his c
1Sa 16:12 ruddy, and withal of a beautiful c
1Sa 17:42 a youth, and ruddy, and of a fair c
1Sa 25:3 and of a beautiful c
2Sa 14:27 she was a woman of a fair c
2Kin 8:11 And he settled his c stedfastly
Neh 2:2 said unto me, Why is thy c sad
Neh 2:3 why should not my c be sad
Job 14:20 thou changest his c, and sendest
Job 29:24 the light of my c they cast not
Ps 4:6 up the light of thy c upon us
Ps 10:4 through the pride of his c
Ps 11:7 his c doth behold the upright
Ps 21:6 him exceeding glad with thy c
Ps 42:5 praise him for the help of his c
Ps 42:11 him, who is the health of my c
Ps 43:5 him, who is the health of my c
Ps 44:3 thine arm, and the light of thy c
Ps 80:16 perish at the rebuke of thy c
Ps 89:15 O LORD, in the light of thy c
Ps 90:8 secret sins in the light of thy c
Prov 15:13 A merry heart maketh a cheerful c
Prov 16:15 the light of the king's c is life
Prov 25:23 so doth an angry c a backbiting
Prov 27:17 sharpeneth the c of his friend
Eccl 7:3 of the c the heart is made better
Song 2:14 of the stairs, let me see thy c
Song 2:14 is thy voice, and thy c is comely
Song 5:15 his c is as Lebanon, excellent as
Is 3:9 The shew of their c doth witness
Eze 27:35 they shall be troubled in their c
Dan 1:13 the c of the children that eat of
Dan 5:6 Then the king's c was changed
Dan 5:9 his c was changed in him, and his
Dan 5:10 thee, nor let thy c be changed
Dan 7:28 me, and my c changed in me
Dan 8:23 to the full, a king of fierce c
Mt 6:16 as the hypocrites, of a sad c
Mt 28:3 His c was like lightning, and his
Lk 9:29 the fashion of his c was altered
Acts 2:28 make me full of joy with thy c
2Cor 3:7 of Moses for the glory of his c
Rev 1:16 his c was as the sun shineth in

### COUPLE
Ex 26:6 c the curtains together with the
Ex 26:9 thou shalt c five curtains by
Ex 26:11 c the tent together, that it may
Ex 36:18 of brass to c the tent together
Ex 39:4 for it, to c it together
Judg 19:3 servant with him, and a c of asses
2Sa 13:6 make me a c of cakes in my sight,
2Sa 16:1 with a c of asses saddled, and
Is 21:7 a chariot with a c of horsemen
Is 21:9 of men, with a c of horsemen

### COUPLED
Ex 26:3 be c together one to another
Ex 26:3 shall be c one to another
Ex 26:24 they shall be c together beneath,
Ex 26:24 they shall be c together above
Ex 36:10 he c the five curtains one unto
Ex 36:10 curtains he c one unto another
Ex 36:13 c the curtains one unto another
Ex 36:16 he c five curtains by themselves,
Ex 36:29 And they were c beneath, and
Ex 36:29 c together at the head thereof,
Ex 39:4 the two edges was it c together
1Pet 3:2 chaste conversation c with fear

### COUPLING
Ex 26:4 from the selvedge in the c
Ex 26:4 curtain, in the c of the second
Ex 26:5 that is in the c of the second
Ex 26:10 curtain that is outmost in the c
Ex 28:27 over against the other c thereof
Ex 36:11 from the selvedge in the c
Ex 36:11 curtain, in the c of the second
Ex 36:12 which was in the c of the second
Ex 36:17 edge of the curtain in the c
Ex 39:20 over against the other c thereof

### COURAGE
Num 13:20 And be ye of good c, and bring of
Deut 31:6 Be strong and of a good c, fear
Deut 31:7 Israel, Be strong and of a good c
Deut 31:23 and said, Be strong and of a good c
Josh 1:6 Be strong and of a good c
Josh 1:9 Be strong and of a good c
Josh 1:18 only be strong and of a good c
Josh 2:11 remain any more c in any man
Josh 10:25 dismayed, be strong and of good c
2Sa 10:12 Be of good c, and let us play the
1Chr 19:13 Be of good c, and let us behave
1Chr 22:13 be strong, and of good c
1Chr 28:20 his son, Be strong and of good c
2Chr 15:8 of Oded the prophet, he took c
Ezr 10:4 be of good c, and do it
Ps 27:14 be of good c, and he shall
Ps 31:24 Be of good c, and he shall
Is 41:6 said to his brother, Be of good c
Dan 11:25 his c against the king of the
Acts 28:15 saw, he thanked God, and took c

### COURAGEOUS
Josh 1:7 Only be thou strong and very c
Josh 23:6 Be ye therefore very c to keep
2Sa 13:28 be c, and be valiant
2Chr 32:7 Be strong and c, be not afraid nor
Amos 2:16 he that is c among the mighty

### COURSE
1Chr 27:1 of every c were twenty and four
1Chr 27:4 over the c of the second month
1Chr 28:1 that ministered to the king by c
2Chr 5:11 and did not then wait by c
Ezr 3:11 sang together by c in praising
Ps 82:5 of the earth are out of c
Jer 8:6 every one turned to his c
Jer 23:10 their c is evil, and their force
Lk 1:5 named Zacharias, of the c of Abia
Lk 1:8 before God in the order of his c
Acts 13:25 And as John fulfilled his c
Acts 16:11 with a straight c to Samothracia
Acts 20:24 that I might finish my c with joy
Acts 21:1 came with a straight c unto Coos
Acts 21:7 we had finished our c from Tyre
1Cor 14:27 the most by three, and that by c
Eph 2:2 according to the c of this world
2Th 3:1 word of the Lord may have free c
2Ti 4:7 good fight, I have finished my c
Jas 3:6 setteth on fire the c of nature

### COURSES
Judg 5:20 the stars in their c fought
1Kin 5:14 ten thousand a month by c
1Chr 23:6 into c among the sons of Levi
1Chr 27:1 the king in any matter of the c
1Chr 28:13 Also for the c of the priests and
1Chr 28:21 the c of the priests and the
2Chr 8:14 the c of the priests to their
2Chr 8:14 also by their c at every gate
2Chr 23:8 the priest dismissed not the c
2Chr 31:2 appointed the c of the priests
2Chr 31:2 and the Levites after their c
2Chr 31:15 to give to their brethren by c
2Chr 31:16 charges according to their c
2Chr 31:17 in their charges by their c
2Chr 35:4 of your fathers, after your c
2Chr 35:10 place, and the Levites in their c
Ezr 6:18 and the Levites in their c
Is 44:4 grass, as willows by the water c

### COURT
Ex 40:33 he reared up the c round about

### COVENANT
Gen 6:18 with thee will I establish my c
Gen 9:9 behold, I establish my c with you
Gen 9:11 And I will establish my c with you
Gen 9:12 of the c which I make between me
Gen 9:13 be for a token of a c between me
Gen 9:15 And I will remember my c, which is
Gen 9:16 the everlasting c between God
Gen 9:17 Noah, This is the token of the c
Gen 15:18 day the LORD made a c with Abram
Gen 17:2 And I will make my c between me
Gen 17:4 my c is with thee, and thou shalt
Gen 17:7 I will establish my c between me
Gen 17:7 generations for an everlasting c
Gen 17:9 Thou shalt keep my c therefore
Gen 17:10 This is my c, which ye shall keep
Gen 17:11 be a token of the c betwixt me
Gen 17:13 my c shall be in your flesh for
Gen 17:13 your flesh for an everlasting c
Gen 17:14 he hath broken my c
Gen 17:19 I will establish my c with him
Gen 17:19 with him for an everlasting c
Gen 17:21 But my c will I establish with
Gen 21:27 and both of them made a c
Gen 21:32 Thus they made a c at Beer-sheba
Gen 26:28 and let us make a c with thee
Gen 31:44 come thou, let us make a c
Ex 2:24 God remembered his c with Abraham
Ex 6:4 also established my c with them
Ex 6:5 and I have remembered my c
Ex 19:5 my voice indeed, and keep my c
Ex 23:32 Thou shalt make no c with them
Ex 24:7 And he took the book of the c
Ex 24:8 said, Behold the blood of the c
Ex 31:16 generations, for a perpetual c
Ex 34:10 And he said, Behold, I make a c
Ex 34:12 lest thou make a c with the
Ex 34:15 Lest thou make a c with the
Ex 34:27 words I have made a c with thee
Ex 34:28 the tables the words of the c
Lev 2:13 thou suffer the salt of the c of
Lev 24:8 of Israel by an everlasting c
Lev 26:9 you, and establish my c with you
Lev 26:15 but that ye break my c
Lev 26:25 shall avenge the quarrel of my c
Lev 26:42 will I remember my c with Jacob
Lev 26:42 also my c with Isaac
Lev 26:42 also my c with Abraham will I
Lev 26:44 and to break my c with them
Lev 26:45 remember the c of their ancestors
Num 10:33 the ark of the c of the LORD went
Num 14:44 the ark of the c of the LORD
Num 18:19 it is a c of salt for ever before
Num 25:12 I give unto him my c of peace
Num 25:13 even the c of an everlasting
Deut 4:13 And he declared unto you his c
Deut 4:23 lest ye forget the c of the LORD
Deut 4:31 nor forget the c of thy fathers
Deut 5:2 our God made a c with us in Horeb
Deut 5:3 made not this c with our fathers
Deut 7:2 thou shalt make no c with them
Deut 7:9 the faithful God, which keepeth c
Deut 7:12 God shall keep unto thee the c
Deut 8:18 that he may establish his c which
Deut 9:9 even the tables of the c which
Deut 9:11 stone, even the tables of the c
Deut 9:15 of the c were in my two hands
Deut 10:8 bear the ark of the c of the LORD
Deut 17:2 thy God, in transgressing his c
Deut 29:1 These are the words of the c
Deut 29:1 beside the c which he made with
Deut 29:9 therefore the words of this c
Deut 29:12 into c with the LORD thy God
Deut 29:14 with you only do I make this c
Deut 29:21 to all the curses of the c that
Deut 29:25 the c of the LORD God of their
Deut 31:9 bare the ark of the c of the LORD
Deut 31:16 break my c which I have made with
Deut 31:20 and provoke me, and break my c
Deut 31:25 bare the ark of the c of the LORD
Deut 31:26 ark of the c of the LORD your God
Deut 33:9 observed thy word, and kept thy c
Josh 3:3 ark of the c of the LORD your God
Josh 3:6 saying, Take up the ark of the c
Josh 3:6 And they took up the ark of the c
Josh 3:8 that bear the ark of the c
Josh 3:11 the ark of the c of the Lord of
Josh 3:14 ark of the c before the people
Josh 3:17 that bare the ark of the c of the
Josh 4:7 the ark of the c of the LORD
Josh 4:9 which bare the ark of the c stood
Josh 4:18 that bare the ark of the c of the
Josh 6:6 them, Take up the ark of the c
Josh 6:8 the ark of the c of the LORD
Josh 7:11 my c which I commanded them
Josh 7:15 transgressed the c of the LORD
Josh 8:33 bare the ark of the c of the LORD
Josh 23:16 the c of the LORD your God
Josh 24:25 So Joshua made a c with the
Judg 2:1 I will never break my c with you
Judg 2:20 people hath transgressed my c
Judg 20:27 (for the ark of the c of God was
1Sa 4:3 Let us fetch the ark of the c of
1Sa 4:4 ark of the c of the LORD of hosts
1Sa 4:4 with the ark of the c of God
1Sa 4:5 when the ark of the c of the LORD
1Sa 11:1 Make a c with us, and we will
1Sa 11:2 will I make a c with you, that I
1Sa 18:3 Then Jonathan and David made a c
1Sa 20:8 into a c of the LORD with thee
1Sa 20:16 So Jonathan made a c with the
1Sa 23:18 they two made a c before the LORD
2Sa 15:24 bearing the ark of the c of God
2Sa 23:5 made with me an everlasting c
1Kin 3:15 the ark of the c of the LORD
1Kin 6:19 the ark of the c of the LORD
1Kin 8:1 might bring up the ark of the c
1Kin 8:6 brought in the ark of the c of
1Kin 8:9 when the LORD made a c with the
1Kin 8:21 ark, wherein is the c of the LORD
1Kin 8:23 on earth beneath, who keepest c
1Kin 11:11 thee, and thou hast not kept my c
1Kin 19:10 of Israel have forsaken thy c
1Kin 19:14 of Israel have forsaken thy c
1Kin 20:34 I will send thee away with this c
1Kin 20:34 So he made a c with him, and sent
2Kin 11:4 made a c with them, and took an
2Kin 11:17 Jehoiada made a c between the
2Kin 13:23 because of his c with Abraham
2Kin 17:15 his c that he made with their
2Kin 17:35 With whom the LORD had made a c
2Kin 17:38 the c that I have made with you
2Kin 18:12 their God, but transgressed his c
2Kin 23:2 the words of the book of the c
2Kin 23:3 made a c before the LORD, to walk
2Kin 23:3 to perform the words of this c
2Kin 23:3 And all the people stood to the c
2Kin 23:21 is written in the book of this c
1Chr 11:3 David made a c with them in
1Chr 15:25 c of the LORD out of the house of
1Chr 15:26 bare the ark of the c of the LORD
1Chr 15:28 the c of the LORD with shouting
1Chr 15:29 as the ark of the c of the LORD
1Chr 16:6 before the ark of the c of God
1Chr 16:15 Be ye mindful always of his c
1Chr 16:16 Even of the c which he made with
1Chr 16:17 and to Israel for an everlasting c
1Chr 16:37 ark of the c of the LORD Asaph
1Chr 17:1 but the ark of the c of the LORD
1Chr 22:19 the ark of the c of the LORD
1Chr 28:2 for the ark of the c of the LORD
1Chr 28:18 the ark of the c of the LORD
2Chr 5:2 to bring up the ark of the c of
2Chr 5:7 brought in the ark of the c of
2Chr 5:10 when the LORD made a c with the
2Chr 6:11 ark, wherein is the c of the LORD
2Chr 6:14 which keepest c, and shewest mercy
2Chr 13:5 him and to his sons by a c of salt
2Chr 15:12 they entered into a c to seek the
2Chr 21:7 because of the c that he had made
2Chr 23:1 son of Zichri, into c with him
2Chr 23:3 all the congregation made a c
2Chr 23:16 And Jehoiada made a c between him

2Chr 29:10 a c with the LORD God of Israel
2Chr 34:30 the words of the book of the c
2Chr 34:31 made a c before the LORD, to walk
2Chr 34:31 to perform the words of the c
2Chr 34:32 did according to the c of God
Ezr 10:3 Now therefore let us make a c
Neh 1:5 and terrible God, that keepeth c
Neh 9:8 madest a c with him to give the
Neh 9:32 the terrible God, who keepest c
Neh 9:38 of all this we make a sure c
Neh 13:29 the c of the priesthood, and of
Job 31:1 I made a c with mine eyes
Job 41:4 Will he make a c with thee
Ps 25:10 and truth unto such as keep his c
Ps 25:14 and he will shew them his c
Ps 44:17 have we dealt falsely in thy c
Ps 50:5 made a c with me by sacrifice
Ps 50:16 shouldest take my c in thy mouth
Ps 55:20 he hath broken his c
Ps 74:20 Have respect unto the c
Ps 78:10 They kept not the c of God
Ps 78:37 were they stedfast in his c
Ps 89:3 I have made a c with my chosen, I
Ps 89:28 my c shall stand fast with him
Ps 89:34 My c will I not break, nor alter
Ps 89:39 made void the c of thy servant
Ps 103:18 To such as keep his c, and to
Ps 105:8 He hath remembered his c for ever
Ps 105:9 Which c he made with Abraham, and
Ps 105:10 and to Israel for an everlasting c
Ps 106:45 And he remembered for them his c
Ps 111:5 he will ever be mindful of his c
Ps 111:9 he hath commanded his c for ever
Ps 132:12 If thy children will keep my c
Prov 2:17 and forgetteth the c of her God
Is 24:5 broken the everlasting c
Is 28:15 said, We have made a c with death
Is 28:18 your c with death shall be
Is 33:8 he hath broken the c, he hath
Is 42:6 give thee for a c of the people
Is 49:8 give thee for a c of the people
Is 54:10 neither shall the c of my peace
Is 55:3 make an everlasting c with you
Is 56:4 please me, and take hold of my c
Is 56:6 it, and taketh hold of my c
Is 57:8 bed, and made thee a c with them
Is 59:21 As for me, this is my c with them
Is 61:8 make an everlasting c with them
Jer 3:16 The ark of the c of the LORD
Jer 11:2 Hear ye the words of this c
Jer 11:3 obeyeth not the words of this c
Jer 11:6 Hear ye the words of this c
Jer 11:8 upon them all the words of this c
Jer 11:10 house of Judah have broken my c
Jer 14:21 remember, break not thy c with us
Jer 22:9 the c of the LORD their God
Jer 31:31 that I will make a new c with the
Jer 31:32 Not according to the c that I
Jer 31:32 which my c they brake, although I
Jer 31:33 But this shall be the c that I
Jer 32:40 make an everlasting c with them
Jer 33:20 If ye can break my c of the day
Jer 33:20 my c of the night, and that there
Jer 33:21 Then may also my c be broken with
Jer 33:25 If my c be not with day and night,
Jer 34:8 the king Zedekiah had made a c
Jer 34:10 which had entered into the c
Jer 34:13 I made a c with your fathers in
Jer 34:15 ye had made a c before me in the
Jer 34:18 men that have transgressed my c
Jer 34:18 c which they had made before me
Jer 50:5 to the LORD in a perpetual c that
Eze 16:8 and entered into a c with thee
Eze 16:59 the oath in breaking the c
Eze 16:60 my c with thee in the days of thy
Eze 16:60 unto thee an everlasting c
Eze 16:61 for daughters, but not by thy c
Eze 16:62 I will establish my c with thee
Eze 17:13 made a c with him, and hath taken
Eze 17:14 keeping of his c it might stand
Eze 17:15 or shall he break the c, and be
Eze 17:16 whose c he brake, even with him
Eze 17:18 the oath by breaking the c
Eze 17:19 my c that he hath broken, even it
Eze 20:37 bring you into the bond of the c
Eze 34:25 will make with them a c of peace
Eze 37:26 will make a c of peace with them
Eze 37:26 be an everlasting c with them
Eze 44:7 broken my c because of all your
Dan 9:4 and dreadful God, keeping the c
Dan 9:27 he shall confirm the c with many
Dan 11:22 yea, also the prince of the c
Dan 11:28 heart shall be against the holy c
Dan 11:30 indignation against the holy c
Dan 11:30 with them that forsake the holy c
Dan 11:32 c shall he corrupt by flatteries
Hos 2:18 in that day will I make a c for
Hos 6:7 like men have transgressed the c
Hos 8:1 they have transgressed my c
Hos 10:4 swearing falsely in making a c
Hos 12:1 they do make a c with the
Amos 1:9 and remembered not the brotherly c
Zec 9:11 by the blood of thy c I have sent
Zec 11:10 that I might break my c which I
Mal 2:4 that my c might be with Levi,
Mal 2:5 My c was with him of life and
Mal 2:8 ye have corrupted the c of Levi
Mal 2:10 by profaning the c of our fathers
Mal 2:14 companion, and the wife of thy c
Mal 3:1 even the messenger of the c
Lk 1:72 and to remember his holy c
Acts 3:25 of the c which God made with our
Acts 7:8 he gave him the c of circumcision
Rom 11:27 For this is my c unto them
Gal 3:15 Though it be but a man's c
Gal 3:17 And this I say, that the c
Heb 8:6 he is the mediator of a better c
Heb 8:7 For if that first c had been
Heb 8:8 when I will make a new c with the
Heb 8:9 Not according to the c that I
Heb 8:9 they continued not in my c
Heb 8:10 For this is the c that I will
Heb 8:13 In that he saith, A new c
Heb 9:1 Then verily the first c had also
Heb 9:4 the ark of the c overlaid round
Heb 9:4 budded, and the tables of the c
Heb 10:16 This is the c that I will make
Heb 10:29 hath counted the blood of the c
Heb 12:24 Jesus the mediator of the new c
Heb 13:20 the blood of the everlasting c

## COVER

Ex 10:5 they shall c the face of the
Ex 21:33 man shall dig a pit, and not c it
Ex 25:29 and bowls thereof, to c withal
Ex 26:13 side and on that side, to c it
Ex 28:42 breeches to c their nakedness
Ex 33:22 will c thee with my hand while I
Ex 37:16 bowls, and his covers to c withal
Ex 40:3 and c the ark with the vail
Lev 13:12 the leprosy c all the skin of him
Lev 16:13 the cloud of the incense may c
Lev 17:13 blood thereof, and c it with dust
Num 4:5 c the ark of testimony with it
Num 4:7 the bowls, and covers to c withal
Num 4:8 c the same with a covering of
Num 4:9 c the candlestick of the light,
Num 4:11 c it with a covering of badgers'
Num 4:12 c them with a covering of
Num 22:5 they c the face of the earth, and
Deut 23:13 c that which cometh from thee
Deut 33:12 the LORD shall c him all the day
1Sa 24:3 and Saul went in to c his feet
1Kin 7:18 to c the chapiters that were upon
1Kin 7:41 to c the two bowls of the
1Kin 7:42 to c the two bowls of the
2Chr 4:12 the two wreaths to c the two
2Chr 4:13 to c the two pommels of the
Neh 4:5 c not their iniquity, and let not
Job 16:18 c not thou my blood, and let my
Job 21:26 dust, and the worms shall c them
Job 22:11 and abundance of waters c thee
Job 38:34 abundance of waters may c thee
Job 40:22 The shady trees c him with their
Ps 91:4 He shall c thee with his feathers
Ps 104:9 turn not again to c the earth
Ps 109:29 let them c themselves with their
Ps 139:11 Surely the darkness shall c me
Ps 140:9 mischief of their own lips c them
Is 11:9 the LORD, as the waters c the sea
Is 14:11 under thee, and the worms c thee
Is 22:17 captivity, and will surely c thee
Is 26:21 and shall no more c her slain
Is 30:1 that c with a covering, but not
Is 58:7 seest the naked, that thou c him
Is 59:6 neither shall they c themselves
Is 60:2 the darkness shall c the earth
Is 60:6 multitude of camels shall c thee
Jer 46:8 I will go up, and will c the earth
Eze 7:18 sackcloth, and horror shall c them
Eze 12:6 thou shalt c thy face, that thou
Eze 12:12 he shall c his face, that he see
Eze 24:7 the ground, to c it with dust
Eze 24:17 c not thy lips, and eat not the
Eze 24:22 ye shall not c your lips, nor eat
Eze 26:10 horses their dust shall c thee
Eze 26:19 and great waters shall c thee
Eze 30:18 as for her, a cloud shall c her
Eze 32:7 I will c the heaven, and make the
Eze 32:7 I will c the sun with a cloud, and
Eze 37:6 c you with skin, and put breath in
Eze 38:9 be like a cloud to c the land
Eze 38:16 Israel, as a cloud to c the land
Hos 2:9 my flax given to c her nakedness
Hos 10:8 shall say to the mountains, C us
Obad 10 brother Jacob shame shall c thee
Mic 3:7 yea, they shall all c their lips
Mic 7:10 shame shall c her which said unto
Hab 2:14 the LORD, as the waters c the sea
Hab 2:17 violence of Lebanon shall c thee
Mk 14:65 to c his face, and to buffet him,
Lk 23:30 and to the hills, C us
1Cor 11:7 indeed ought not to c his head
1Pet 4:8 for charity shall c the multitude

## COVERED

Gen 7:19 under the whole heaven, were c
Gen 7:20 and the mountains were c
Gen 9:23 c the nakedness of their father
Gen 24:65 she took a vail, and c herself
Gen 38:14 c her with a vail, and wrapped
Gen 38:15 because she had c her face
Ex 8:6 came up, and c the land of Egypt
Ex 10:15 For they c the face of the whole
Ex 14:28 c the chariots, and the horsemen,
Ex 15:5 The depths have c them
Ex 15:10 with thy wind, the sea c them
Ex 16:13 the quails came up, and c the camp
Ex 24:15 the mount, and a cloud c the mount
Ex 24:16 Sinai, and the cloud c it six days
Ex 37:9 c with their wings over the mercy
Ex 40:21 c the ark of the testimony
Ex 40:34 Then a cloud c the tent of the
Lev 13:13 the leprosy have c all his flesh
Num 4:20 to see when the holy things are c
Num 7:3 six c wagons, and twelve oxen
Num 9:15 up the cloud c the tabernacle
Num 9:16 the cloud c it by day, and the
Num 16:42 and, behold, the cloud c it
Deut 32:15 thick, thou art c with fatness
Josh 24:7 the sea upon them, and c them
Judg 4:18 the tent, she c him with a mantle
Judg 4:19 milk, and gave him drink, and c him
1Sa 19:13 his bolster, and c it with a cloth
1Sa 28:14 and he is c with a mantle
2Sa 15:30 as he went up, and had his head c
2Sa 15:30 was with him c every man his head
2Sa 19:4 But the king c his face, and the
1Kin 1:1 they c him with clothes, but he
1Kin 6:9 c the house with beams and boards
1Kin 6:15 he c them on the inside with wood
1Kin 6:15 c the floor of the house with
1Kin 6:20 so c the altar which was of cedar
1Kin 6:35 c them with gold fitted upon the
1Kin 7:3 it was c with cedar above upon
1Kin 7:7 it was c with cedar from one side
1Kin 8:7 ark, and the cherubims c the ark
2Kin 19:1 c himself with sackcloth, and went
2Kin 19:2 c with sackcloth, to Isaiah the
1Chr 28:18 c the ark of the covenant of the
2Chr 5:8 ark, and the cherubims c the ark
Neh 3:15 c it, and set up the doors thereof
Est 6:12 mourning, and having his head c
Est 7:8 king's mouth, they c Haman's face
Job 23:17 neither hath he c the darkness
Job 31:33 If I c my transgressions as Adam,
Ps 32:1 is forgiven, whose sin is c
Ps 44:15 and the shame of my face hath c me
Ps 44:19 c us with the shadow of death
Ps 65:13 valleys also are c over with corn
Ps 68:13 the wings of a dove c with silver
Ps 69:7 shame hath c my face
Ps 71:13 let them be c with reproach and
Ps 80:10 The hills were c with the shadow
Ps 85:2 thou hast c all their sin
Ps 89:45 thou hast c him with shame
Ps 106:11 the waters c their enemies
Ps 106:17 and c the company of Abiram
Ps 139:13 thou hast c me in my mother's
Ps 140:7 thou hast c my head in the day of

Prov 24:31 nettles had c the face thereof,
Prov 26:23 a potsherd c with silver dross
Prov 26:26 Whose hatred is c by deceit
Eccl 6:4 his name shall be c with darkness
Is 6:2 with twain he c his face
Is 6:2 and with twain he c his feet
Is 29:10 your rulers, the seers hath he c
Is 37:1 c himself with sackcloth, and went
Is 37:2 of the priests c with sackcloth
Is 51:16 I have c thee in the shadow of
Is 61:10 he hath c me with the robe of
Jer 14:3 and confounded, and c their heads
Jer 14:4 were ashamed, they c their heads
Jer 51:42 she is c with the multitude of
Jer 51:51 shame hath c our faces
Lam 2:1 How hath the Lord c the daughter
Lam 3:16 stones, he hath c me with ashes
Lam 3:43 Thou hast c with anger, and
Lam 3:44 Thou hast c thyself with a cloud,
Eze 1:11 to another, and two c their bodies
Eze 1:23 which c on this side, and every
Eze 1:23 which c on that side, their
Eze 16:8 over thee, and c thy nakedness
Eze 16:10 fine linen, and I c thee with silk
Eze 18:7 hath c the naked with a garment
Eze 18:16 hath c the naked with a garment,
Eze 24:8 a rock, that it should not be c
Eze 27:7 of Elishah was that which c thee
Eze 31:15 I c the deep for him, and I
Eze 37:8 them, and the skin c them above
Eze 41:16 windows, and the windows were c
Jonah 3:6 c him with sackcloth, and sat in
Jonah 3:8 beast be c with sackcloth, and cry
Hab 3:3 His glory c the heavens, and the
Mt 8:24 the ship was c with the waves
Mt 10:26 for there is nothing c, that
Lk 12:2 For there is nothing c, that
Rom 4:7 are forgiven, and whose sins are c
1Cor 11:4 or prophesying, having his head c
1Cor 11:6 For if the woman be not c
1Cor 11:6 be shorn or shaven, let her be c

### COVERETH
Ex 29:13 all the fat that c the inwards
Ex 29:22 and the fat that c the inwards
Lev 3:3 the fat that c the inwards
Lev 3:9 and the fat that c the inwards
Lev 3:14 the fat that c the inwards
Lev 4:8 the fat that c the inwards
Lev 7:3 and the fat that c the inwards
Lev 9:19 that which c the inwards, and the
Num 22:11 which c the face of the earth
Judg 3:24 Surely he c his feet in his
Job 9:24 he c the faces of the judges
Job 15:27 Because he c his face with his
Job 36:30 it, and c the bottom of the sea
Job 36:32 With clouds he c the light
Ps 73:6 violence c them as a garment
Ps 109:19 him as the garment which c him
Ps 147:8 Who c the heaven with clouds, who
Prov 10:6 but violence c the mouth of the
Prov 10:11 but violence c the mouth of the
Prov 10:12 but love c all sins
Prov 12:16 but a prudent man c shame
Prov 17:9 He that c a transgression seeketh
Prov 28:13 He that c his sins shall not
Jer 3:25 our shame, and our confusion c us
Eze 28:14 art the anointed cherub that c
Mal 2:16 for one c violence with his
Lk 8:16 c it with a vessel, or putteth it

### COVERING
Gen 8:13 and Noah removed the c of the ark
Gen 20:16 he is to thee a c of the eyes
Ex 22:27 For that is his c only, it is his
Ex 25:20 c the mercy seat with their wings
Ex 26:7 to be a c upon the tabernacle
Ex 26:14 thou shalt make a c for the tent
Ex 26:14 a c above of badgers' skins
Ex 35:11 tabernacle, his tent, and his c
Ex 35:12 mercy seat, and the vail of the c
Ex 36:19 he made a c for the tent of rams'
Ex 36:19 a c of badgers' skins above that
Ex 39:34 the c of rams' skins dyed red, and
Ex 39:34 the c of badgers' skins
Ex 39:34 and the vail of the c
Ex 40:19 put the c of the tent above upon
Ex 40:21 and set up the vail of the c
Lev 13:45 he shall put a c upon his upper
Num 3:25 the c thereof, and the hanging for
Num 4:5 they shall take down the c vail
Num 4:6 thereon the c of badgers' skins
Num 4:8 same with a c of badgers' skins
Num 4:10 within a c of badgers' skins
Num 4:11 cover it with a c of badgers'
Num 4:12 them with a c of badgers' skins
Num 4:14 upon it a c of badgers' skins
Num 4:15 made an end of c the sanctuary
Num 4:25 of the congregation, his c
Num 4:25 the c of the badgers' skins that
Num 16:38 broad plates for a c of the altar
Num 16:39 broad plates for a c of the altar
Num 19:15 which hath no c bound upon it
2Sa 17:19 spread a c over the well's mouth,
Job 22:14 Thick clouds are a c to him
Job 24:7 that they have no c in the cold
Job 26:6 him, and destruction hath no c
Job 31:19 clothing, or any poor without c
Ps 105:39 He spread a cloud for a c
Song 3:10 the c of it of purple, the midst
Is 22:8 And he discovered the c of Judah
Is 25:7 of the c cast over all people
Is 28:20 the c narrower than that he can
Is 30:1 and that cover with a c, but not
Is 30:22 Ye shall defile also the c of thy
Is 50:3 and I make sackcloth their c
Eze 28:13 every precious stone was thy c
Eze 28:16 O c cherub, from the midst of the
Mal 2:13 c the altar of the LORD with
1Cor 11:15 for her hair is given her for a c

### COVERT
1Sa 25:20 came down by the c of the hill
2Kin 16:18 the c for the sabbath that they
Job 38:40 abide in the c to lie in wait
Job 40:21 in the c of the reed, and fens
Ps 61:4 will trust in the c of thy wings
Is 4:6 for a c from storm and from rain
Is 16:4 be thou a c to them from the face
Is 32:2 the wind, and a c from the tempest
Jer 25:38 He hath forsaken his c, as the

### COVET
Ex 20:17 Thou shalt not c thy neighbour's
Ex 20:17 thou shalt not c thy neighbour's
Deut 5:21 wife, neither shalt thou c thy
Mic 2:2 they c fields, and take them by
Rom 7:7 law had said, Thou shalt not c
Rom 13:9 false witness, Thou shalt not c
1Cor 12:31 But c earnestly the best gifts
1Cor 14:39 c to prophesy, and forbid not to

### COVETOUS
Ps 10:3 heart's desire, and blesseth the c
Lk 16:14 And the Pharisees also, who were c
1Cor 5:10 of this world, or with the c
1Cor 5:11 a brother be a fornicator, or c
1Cor 6:10 Nor thieves, nor c, nor drunkards
Eph 5:5 nor unclean person, nor c man
1Ti 3:3 but patient, not a brawler, not c
2Ti 3:2 be lovers of their own selves, c
2Pet 2:14 have exercised with c practices

### COVETOUSNESS
Ex 18:21 fear God, men of truth, hating c
Ps 119:36 unto thy testimonies, and not to c
Prov 28:16 but he that hateth c shall
Is 57:17 the iniquity of his c was I wroth
Jer 6:13 of them every one is given to c
Jer 8:10 unto the greatest is given to c
Jer 22:17 thine heart are not but for thy c
Jer 51:13 is come, and the measure of thy c
Eze 33:31 their heart goeth after their c
Hab 2:9 coveteth an evil c to his house
Mk 7:22 Thefts, c, wickedness, deceit,
Lk 12:15 them, Take heed, and beware of c
Rom 1:29 fornication, wickedness, c
2Cor 9:5 matter of bounty, and not as of c
Eph 5:3 and all uncleanness, or c
Col 3:5 evil concupiscence, and c
1Th 2:5 as ye know, nor a cloke of c
Heb 13:5 your conversation be without c
2Pet 2:3 through c shall they with feigned

### COW
Lev 22:28 And whether it be c or ewe
Num 18:17 But the firstling of a c, or the
Job 21:10 their c calveth, and casteth not
Is 7:21 a man shall nourish a young c
Is 11:7 And the c and the bear shall feed
Amos 4:3 every c at that which is before

### COZ *(coz) A descendant of Caleb.*
1Chr 4:8 C begat Anub, and Zobebah, and the

### COZBI *(coz'-bi) A Midianite woman.*
Num 25:15 woman that was slain was C
Num 25:18 of Peor, and in the matter of C

### CRAFT
Dan 8:25 cause c to prosper in his hand
Mk 14:1 how they might take him by c
Acts 18:3 And because he was of the same c
Acts 19:25 that by this c we have our wealth
Acts 19:27 our c is in danger to be set at
Rev 18:22 craftsman, of whatsoever c he be

### CRAFTINESS
Job 5:13 He taketh the wise in their own c
Lk 20:23 But he perceived their c, and said
1Cor 3:19 He taketh the wise in their own c
2Cor 4:2 of dishonesty, not walking in c
Eph 4:14 the sleight of men, and cunning c

### CRAFTSMEN
2Kin 24:14 thousand captives, and all the c
2Kin 24:16 might, even seven thousand, and c
1Chr 4:14 for they were c
Neh 11:35 Lod, and Ono, the valley of c
Hos 13:2 all of it the work of the c
Acts 19:24 brought no small gain unto the c
Acts 19:38 the c which are with him, have a

### CREATE
Ps 51:10 C in me a clean heart, O God
Is 4:5 the LORD will c upon every
Is 45:7 I form the light, and c darkness
Is 45:7 I make peace, and c evil
Is 57:19 I c the fruit of the lips
Is 65:17 I c new heavens and a new earth
Is 65:18 for ever in that which I c
Is 65:18 I c Jerusalem a rejoicing, and her

### CREATED
Gen 1:1 In the beginning God c the heaven
Gen 1:21 God c great whales, and every
Gen 1:27 So God c man in his own image
Gen 1:27 in the image of God c he him
Gen 1:27 male and female c he them
Gen 2:3 from all his work which God c
Gen 2:4 and of the earth when they were c
Gen 5:1 In the day that God c man
Gen 5:2 Male and female c he them
Gen 5:2 Adam, in the day when they were c
Gen 6:7 have c from the face of the earth
Deut 4:32 day that God c man upon the earth
Ps 89:12 and the south thou hast c them
Ps 102:18 shall be c shall praise the LORD
Ps 104:30 forth thy spirit, they are c
Ps 148:5 for he commanded, and they were c
Is 40:26 and behold who hath c these things
Is 41:20 the Holy One of Israel hath c it
Is 42:5 he that c the heavens, and
Is 43:1 thus saith the LORD that c thee
Is 43:7 for I have c him for my glory, I
Is 45:8 I the LORD have c it
Is 45:12 made the earth, and c man upon it
Is 45:18 saith the LORD that c the heavens
Is 45:18 he c it not in vain, he formed it
Is 48:7 They are c now, and not from the
Is 54:16 I have c the smith that bloweth
Is 54:16 I have c the waster to destroy
Jer 31:22 for the LORD hath c a new thing
Eze 21:30 in the place where thou wast c
Eze 28:13 thee in the day that thou wast c
Eze 28:15 from the day that thou wast c
Mal 2:10 hath not one God c us
Mk 13:19 which God c unto this time
1Cor 11:9 was the man c for the woman
Eph 2:10 c in Christ Jesus unto good works
Eph 3:9 who c all things by Jesus Christ
Eph 4:24 after God is c in righteousness
Col 1:16 For by him were all things c
Col 1:16 all things were c by him, and for
Col 3:10 after the image of him that c him
1Ti 4:3 which God hath c to be received
Rev 4:11 for thou hast c all things
Rev 4:11 thy pleasure they are and were c
Rev 10:6 who c heaven, and the things that

### CREATION
Mk 10:6 of the c God made them male
Mk 13:19 the c which God created unto this
Rom 1:20 things of him from the c of the
Rom 8:22 we know that the whole c groaneth
2Pet 3:4 were from the beginning of the c
Rev 3:14 the beginning of the c of God

### CREATOR
Eccl 12:1 Remember now thy C in the days of
Is 40:28 the C of the ends of the earth,
Is 43:15 the c of Israel, your King
Rom 1:25 the creature more than the C
1Pet 4:19 well doing, as unto a faithful C

### CREATURE
Gen 1:20 the moving c that hath life
Gen 1:21 and every living c that moveth
Gen 1:24 forth the living c after his kind
Gen 2:19 Adam called every living c
Gen 9:10 every living c that is with you
Gen 9:12 every living c that is with you,
Gen 9:15 and every living c of all flesh
Gen 9:16 every living c of all flesh that
Lev 11:46 of every living c that moveth in
Lev 11:46 of every c that creepeth upon the
Eze 1:20 of the living c was in the wheels
Eze 1:21 of the living c was in the wheels
Eze 1:22 living c was as the colour of the
Eze 10:15 This is the living c that I saw
Eze 10:17 of the living c was in them
Eze 10:20 This is the living c that I saw
Mk 16:15 and preach the gospel to every c
Rom 1:25 served the c more than the
Rom 8:19 c waiteth for the manifestation
Rom 8:20 For the c was made subject to
Rom 8:21 Because the c itself also shall
Rom 8:39 nor depth, nor any other c
2Cor 5:17 man be in Christ, he is a new c
Gal 6:15 nor uncircumcision, but a new c
Col 1:15 God, the firstborn of every c
Col 1:23 to every c which is under heaven
1Ti 4:4 For every c of God is good, and
Heb 4:13 Neither is there any c that is
Rev 5:13 every c which is in heaven, and on

### CREATURES
Is 13:21 houses shall be full of doleful c
Eze 1:5 the likeness of four living c
Eze 1:13 for the likeness of the living c
Eze 1:13 up and down among the living c
Eze 1:14 And the living c ran and returned
Eze 1:15 Now as I beheld the living c
Eze 1:15 upon the earth by the living c
Eze 1:19 And when the living c went
Eze 1:19 when the living c were lifted up
Eze 3:13 living c that touched one another
Jas 1:18 be a kind of firstfruits of his c
Rev 8:9 of the c which were in the sea

### CREEP
Lev 11:20 All fowls that c, going upon all
Lev 11:29 things that c upon the earth
Lev 11:31 unclean to you among all that c
Lev 11:42 things that c upon the earth
Ps 104:20 beasts of the forest do c forth
Eze 38:20 things that c upon the earth
2Ti 3:6 sort are they which c into houses

### CREEPETH
Gen 1:25 every thing that c upon the earth
Gen 1:26 thing that c upon the earth
Gen 1:30 every thing that c upon the earth
Gen 7:8 every thing that c upon the earth
Gen 7:14 every creeping thing that c upon
Gen 7:21 thing that c upon the earth
Gen 8:17 thing that c upon the earth
Gen 8:19 whatsoever c upon the earth,
Lev 11:41 every creeping thing that c upon
Lev 11:43 with any creeping thing that c
Lev 11:44 thing that c upon the earth
Lev 11:46 creature that c upon the earth
Lev 20:25 living thing that c on the ground
Deut 4:18 of any thing that c on the ground

### CREEPING
Gen 1:24 c thing, and beast of the earth
Gen 1:26 over every c thing that creepeth
Gen 6:7 the c thing, and the fowls of the
Gen 6:20 of every c thing of the earth
Gen 7:14 every c thing that creepeth upon
Gen 7:21 of every c thing that creepeth
Gen 7:23 the c things, and the fowl of the
Gen 8:17 of every c thing that creepeth
Gen 8:19 Every beast, every c thing
Lev 5:2 the carcase of unclean c things
Lev 11:21 may ye eat of every flying c
Lev 11:23 But all other flying c things
Lev 11:29 the c things that creep upon the
Lev 11:41 every c thing that creepeth upon
Lev 11:42 hath more feet among all c things
Lev 11:43 with any c thing that creepeth
Lev 11:44 of c thing that creepeth upon the
Lev 22:5 Or whosoever toucheth any c thing
Deut 14:19 every c thing that flieth is
1Kin 4:33 of c things, and of fishes
Ps 104:25 wherein are things c innumerable
Ps 148:10 c things, and flying fowl
Eze 8:10 and behold every form of c things
Eze 38:20 all c things that creep upon the
Hos 2:18 with the c things of the ground
Hab 1:14 of the sea, as the c things
Acts 10:12 c things, and fowls of the air
Acts 11:6 c things, and fowls of the air
Rom 1:23 and fourfooted beasts, and c things

### CRESCENS *(cres'-sens) A companion of Paul.*
2Ti 4:10 C to Galatia, Titus unto Dalmatia

### CRETE *(creet)* See CRETES. *An island south of Greece.*
Acts 27:7 suffering us, we sailed under C
Acts 27:12 which is an haven of C, and lieth
Acts 27:13 thence, they sailed close by C
Acts 27:21 me, and not have loosed from C
Titus 1:5 For this cause left I thee in C

### CRETES *(creets)* See CRETIANS. *Inhabitants of Crete.*
Acts 2:11 C and Arabians, we do hear them

### CRETIANS *(cre'-shuns)* See CRETES. *Same as Cretes.*
Titus 1:12 The C are alway liars, evil
Titus s bishop of the church of the C

### CREW
Mt 26:74 And immediately the cock c
Mk 14:68 and the cock c
Mk 14:72 And the second time the cock c
Lk 22:60 while he yet spake, the cock c
Jn 18:27 and immediately the cock c

### CRIED
Gen 27:34 he c with a great and exceeding
Gen 39:14 with me, and I c with a loud voice
Gen 39:15 that I lifted up my voice and c
Gen 39:18 as I lifted up my voice and c
Gen 41:43 they c before him, Bow the knee
Gen 41:55 the people c to Pharaoh for bread
Gen 45:1 and he c, Cause every man to go
Ex 2:23 reason of the bondage, and they c
Ex 5:15 c unto Pharaoh, saying, Wherefore
Ex 8:12 Moses c unto the LORD because of
Ex 14:10 of Israel c out unto the LORD
Ex 15:25 And he c unto the LORD
Ex 17:4 Moses c unto the LORD, saying,
Num 11:2 And the people c unto Moses
Num 12:13 Moses c unto the LORD, saying,
Num 14:1 lifted up their voice, and c
Num 20:16 when we c unto the LORD, he heard
Deut 22:24 the damsel, because she c not
Deut 22:27 field, and the betrothed damsel c
Deut 26:7 when we c unto the LORD God of
Josh 24:7 when they c unto the LORD, he put
Judg 3:9 of Israel c unto the LORD
Judg 3:15 of Israel c unto the LORD
Judg 4:3 of Israel c unto the LORD
Judg 5:28 c through the lattice, Why is his
Judg 6:6 of Israel c unto the LORD
Judg 6:7 when the children of Israel c
Judg 7:20 and they c, The sword of the LORD,
Judg 7:21 and all the host ran, and c
Judg 9:7 and lifted up his voice, and c
Judg 10:10 of Israel c unto the LORD
Judg 10:12 ye c to me, and I delivered you
Judg 18:23 they c unto the children of Dan
1Sa 4:13 and told it, all the city c out
1Sa 5:10 Ekron, that the Ekronites c out
1Sa 7:9 Samuel c unto the LORD for Israel
1Sa 12:8 your fathers c unto the LORD,
1Sa 12:10 they c unto the LORD, and said, We
1Sa 15:11 he c unto the LORD all night
1Sa 17:8 c unto the armies of Israel, and
1Sa 20:37 Jonathan c after the lad, and said
1Sa 20:38 Jonathan c after the lad, Make
1Sa 24:8 c after Saul, saying, My lord the
1Sa 26:14 David c to the people, and to
1Sa 28:12 Samuel, she c with a loud voice
2Sa 18:25 And the watchman c, and told the
2Sa 19:4 the king c with a loud voice, O
2Sa 20:16 Then c a wise woman out of the
2Sa 22:7 upon the LORD, and c to my God
1Kin 13:2 he c against the altar in the
1Kin 13:4 which had c against the altar in
1Kin 13:21 he c unto the man of God that
1Kin 13:32 For the saying which he c by the
1Kin 17:20 he c unto the LORD, and said, O
1Kin 17:21 c unto the LORD, and said, O LORD
1Kin 18:28 they c aloud, and cut themselves
1Kin 20:39 passed by, he c unto the king
1Kin 22:32 and Jehoshaphat c out
2Kin 2:12 And Elisha saw it, and he c
2Kin 4:1 Now there c a certain woman of
2Kin 4:40 of the pottage, that they c out
2Kin 6:5 and he c, and said, Alas, master
2Kin 6:26 there c a woman unto him, saying,
2Kin 8:5 c to the king for her house and
2Kin 11:14 Athaliah rent her clothes, and c
2Kin 18:28 c with a loud voice in the Jews'
2Kin 20:11 the prophet c unto the LORD
1Chr 5:20 for they c to God in the battle,
2Chr 13:14 they c unto the LORD, and the
2Chr 14:11 Asa c unto the LORD his God, and
2Chr 18:31 but Jehoshaphat c out, and the
2Chr 32:18 Then they c with a loud voice in
2Chr 32:20 of Amoz, prayed and c to heaven
Neh 9:4 c with a loud voice unto the LORD
Neh 9:27 trouble, when they c unto thee
Neh 9:28 c unto thee, thou heardest them
Est 4:1 c with a loud and a bitter cry
Job 29:12 I delivered the poor that c
Job 30:5 (they c after them as after a
Job 30:28 up, and I c in the congregation
Ps 3:4 I c unto the LORD with my voice,
Ps 18:6 upon the LORD, and c unto my God
Ps 18:41 They c, but there was none to
Ps 22:5 They c unto thee, and were
Ps 22:24 but when he c unto him, he heard
Ps 30:2 I c unto thee, and thou hast
Ps 30:8 I c to thee, O LORD
Ps 31:22 supplications when I c unto thee
Ps 34:6 This poor man c, and the LORD
Ps 66:17 I c unto him with my mouth, and he
Ps 77:1 I c unto God with my voice, even
Ps 88:1 God of my salvation, I have c day
Ps 88:13 But unto thee have I c, O LORD
Ps 107:6 Then they c unto the LORD in
Ps 107:13 Then they c unto the LORD in
Ps 119:145 I c with my whole heart
Ps 119:146 I c unto thee
Ps 119:147 the dawning of the morning, and c
Ps 120:1 In my distress I c unto the LORD
Ps 130:1 of the depths have I c unto thee
Ps 138:3 In the day when I c thou
Ps 142:1 I c unto the LORD with my voice
Ps 142:5 I c unto thee, O LORD
Is 6:3 one c unto another, and said, Holy
Is 6:4 moved at the voice of him that c
Is 21:8 And he c, A lion
Is 30:7 have I c concerning this, Their
Is 36:13 c with a loud voice in the Jews'
Jer 4:20 Destruction upon destruction is c
Jer 20:8 I c out, I c violence and
Jer 20:8 c out, I c violence and spoil
Lam 2:18 Their heart c unto the Lord, O
Lam 4:15 They c unto them, Depart ye
Eze 9:1 He c also in mine ears with a
Eze 9:8 that I fell upon my face, and c
Eze 10:13 it was c unto them in my hearing,
Eze 11:13 c with a loud voice, and said, Ah
Dan 3:4 Then an herald c aloud, To you it
Dan 4:14 He c aloud, and said thus, Hew
Dan 5:7 The king c aloud to bring in the
Dan 6:20 he c with a lamentable voice unto
Hos 7:14 they have not c unto me with
Jonah 1:5 c every man unto his god, and cast
Jonah 1:14 Wherefore they c unto the LORD
Jonah 2:2 I c by reason of mine affliction
Jonah 2:2 out of the belly of hell c I
Jonah 3:4 the city a day's journey, and he c
Zec 1:4 whom the former prophets have c
Zec 6:8 Then c he upon me, and spake unto
Zec 7:7 hath c by the former prophets
Zec 7:13 it is come to pass, that as he c
Zec 7:13 so they c, and I would not hear,
Mt 8:29 And, behold, they c out, saying,
Mt 14:26 and they c out for fear
Mt 14:30 and beginning to sink, he c
Mt 15:22 c unto him, saying, Have mercy on
Mt 20:30 c out, saying, Have mercy on us,
Mt 20:31 but they c the more, saying, Have
Mt 21:9 went before, and that followed, c
Mt 27:23 But they c out the more, saying,

Mt 27:46 hour Jesus c with a loud voice
Mt 27:50 when he had c again with a loud
Mk 1:23 an unclean spirit; and he c out
Mk 1:26 c with a loud voice, he came out
Mk 3:11 him, fell down before him, and c
Mk 5:7 c with a loud voice, and said,
Mk 6:49 it had been a spirit, and c out
Mk 9:24 the father of the child c out
Mk 9:26 And the spirit c, and rent him sore
Mk 10:48 but he c the more a great deal,
Mk 11:9 before, and they that followed, c
Mk 15:13 they c out again, Crucify him
Mk 15:14 they c out the more exceedingly,
Mk 15:34 hour Jesus c with a loud voice
Mk 15:37 Jesus c with a loud voice, and
Mk 15:39 against him, saw that he so c out
Lk 4:33 and c out with a loud voice,
Lk 8:8 he had said these things, he c
Lk 8:28 he c out, and fell down before him
Lk 9:38 a man of the company c out
Lk 16:24 And he c and said, Father Abraham,
Lk 18:38 And he c, saying, Jesus, thou son
Lk 18:39 but he c so much the more, Thou
Lk 23:18 they c out all at once, saying,
Lk 23:21 But they c, saying, Crucify him,
Lk 23:46 when Jesus had c with a loud
Jn 1:15 John bare witness of him, and c
Jn 7:28 Then c Jesus in the temple as he
Jn 7:37 of the feast, Jesus stood and c
Jn 11:43 he c with a loud voice, Lazarus,
Jn 12:13 and went forth to meet him, and c
Jn 12:44 Jesus c and said, He that
Jn 18:40 Then c they all again, saying,
Jn 19:6 and officers saw him, they c out
Jn 19:12 but the Jews c out, saying, If
Jn 19:15 But they c out, Away with him,
Acts 7:57 Then they c out with a loud voice
Acts 7:60 c with a loud voice, Lord, lay
Acts 16:17 same followed Paul and us, and c
Acts 16:28 But Paul c with a loud voice,
Acts 19:28 c out, saying, Great is Diana of
Acts 19:32 Some therefore c one thing
Acts 19:34 the space of two hours c out
Acts 21:34 some c one thing, some another,
Acts 22:23 And as they c out, and cast off
Acts 22:24 wherefore they c so against him
Acts 23:6 he c out in the council, Men and
Acts 24:21 that I c standing among them,
Rev 6:10 they c with a loud voice, saying,
Rev 7:2 he c with a loud voice to the
Rev 7:10 c with a loud voice, saying,
Rev 10:3 c with a loud voice, as when a
Rev 10:3 and when he had c, seven thunders
Rev 12:2 And she being with child c
Rev 14:18 c with a loud cry to him that had
Rev 18:2 he c mightily with a strong voice
Rev 18:18 c when they saw the smoke of her
Rev 18:19 cast dust on their heads, and c
Rev 19:17 he c with a loud voice, saying to

## CRIES

Jas 5:4 the c of them which have reaped

## CRIEST

Ex 14:15 Moses, Wherefore c thou unto me
1Sa 26:14 Who art thou that c to the king
Prov 2:3 if thou c after knowledge, and
Is 57:13 When thou c, let thy companies
Jer 30:15 Why c thou for thine affliction

## CRIETH

Gen 4:10 blood c unto me from the ground
Ex 22:27 come to pass, when he c unto me
Job 24:12 and the soul of the wounded c out
Ps 72:12 shall deliver the needy when he c
Ps 84:2 my flesh c out for the living God
Prov 1:20 Wisdom c without
Prov 1:21 She c in the chief place of
Prov 8:3 She c at the gates, at the entry
Prov 9:3 she c upon the highest places of
Is 26:17 is in pain, and c out in her pangs
Is 40:3 of him that c in the wilderness
Jer 12:8 it c out against me
Mic 6:9 The LORD's voice c unto the city
Mt 15:23 for she c after us
Lk 9:39 taketh him, and he suddenly c out
Rom 9:27 Esaias also c concerning Israel,
Jas 5:4 is of you kept back by fraud, c

## CRIMSON

2Chr 2:7 and in iron, and in purple, and c
2Chr 2:14 blue, and in fine linen, and in c
2Chr 3:14 the vail of blue, and purple, and c
Is 1:18 though they be red like c
Jer 4:30 thou clothest thyself with c

## CROOKED

Deut 32:5 are a perverse and c generation
Job 26:13 hand hath formed the c serpent
Ps 125:5 as turn aside unto their c ways
Prov 2:15 Whose ways are c, and they froward
Eccl 1:15 That which is c cannot be made
Eccl 7:13 straight, which he hath made c
Is 27:1 even leviathan that c serpent
Is 40:4 the c shall be made straight, and
Is 42:16 before them, and c things straight
Is 45:2 make the c places straight
Is 59:8 they have made them c paths
Lam 3:9 stone, he hath made my paths c
Lk 3:5 the c shall be made straight, and
Phil 2:15 rebuke, in the midst of a c

## CROSS

Mt 10:38 And he that taketh not his c
Mt 16:24 deny himself, and take up his c
Mt 27:32 him they compelled to bear his c
Mt 27:40 Son of God, come down from the c
Mt 27:42 let him now come down from the c
Mk 8:34 deny himself, and take up his c
Mk 10:21 and come, take up the c, and follow
Mk 15:21 Alexander and Rufus, to bear his c
Mk 15:30 thyself, and come down from the c
Mk 15:32 of Israel descend now from the c
Lk 9:23 himself, and take up his c daily
Lk 14:27 And whosoever doth not bear his c
Lk 23:26 and on him they laid the c
Jn 19:17 he bearing his c went forth into
Jn 19:19 wrote a title, and put it on the c
Jn 19:25 by the c of Jesus his mother
Jn 19:31 upon the c on the sabbath day
1Cor 1:17 lest the c of Christ should be
1Cor 1:18 of the c is to them that perish
Gal 5:11 is the offence of the c ceased
Gal 6:12 persecution for the c of Christ
Gal 6:14 save in the c of our Lord Jesus
Eph 2:16 unto God in one body by the c
Phil 2:8 death, even the death of the c
Phil 3:18 the enemies of the c of Christ
Col 1:20 peace through the blood of his c
Col 2:14 of the way, nailing it to his c
Heb 12:2 was set before him endured the c

## CROW

Mt 26:34 this night, before the cock c
Mt 26:75 said unto him, Before the cock c
Mk 14:30 night, before the cock c twice
Mk 14:72 unto him, Before the cock c twice
Lk 22:34 the cock shall not c this day
Lk 22:61 said unto him, Before the cock c
Jn 13:38 unto thee, The cock shall not c

## CROWN

Gen 49:26 on the c of the head of him that
Ex 25:11 upon it a c of gold round about
Ex 25:24 make thereto a c of gold round
Ex 25:25 thou shalt make a golden c to the
Ex 29:6 put the holy c upon the mitre
Ex 30:3 unto it a c of gold round about
Ex 30:4 thou make to it under the c of it
Ex 37:2 made a c of gold to it round
Ex 37:11 made thereunto a c of gold round
Ex 37:12 made a c of gold for the border
Ex 37:26 unto it a c of gold round about
Ex 37:27 gold for it under the c thereof
Ex 39:30 plate of the holy c of pure gold
Lev 8:9 put the golden plate, the holy c
Lev 21:12 for the c of the anointing oil of
Deut 33:20 the arm with the c of the head
2Sa 1:10 I took the c that was upon his
2Sa 12:30 their king's c from off his head
2Sa 14:25 to the c of his head there was no
2Kin 11:12 put the c upon him, and gave him
1Chr 20:2 David took the c of their king
2Chr 23:11 king's son, and put upon him the c
Est 1:11 before the king with the c royal
Est 2:17 he set the royal c upon her head
Est 6:8 the c royal which is set upon his
Est 8:15 white, and with a great c of gold
Job 2:7 the sole of his foot unto his c
Job 19:9 and taken the c from my head
Job 31:36 shoulder, and bind it as a c to me
Ps 21:3 thou settest a c of pure gold on
Ps 89:39 thou hast profaned his c by
Ps 132:18 upon himself shall his c flourish
Prov 4:9 a c of glory shall she deliver to
Prov 12:4 woman is a c to her husband
Prov 14:24 The c of the wise is their riches
Prov 16:31 The hoary head is a c of glory
Prov 17:6 children are the c of old men
Prov 27:24 doth the c endure to every
Song 3:11 c wherewith his mother crowned
Is 3:17 c of the head of the daughters of
Is 28:1 Woe to the c of pride, to the
Is 28:3 The c of pride, the drunkards of
Is 28:5 LORD of hosts be for a c of glory
Is 62:3 Thou shalt also be a c of glory
Jer 2:16 have broken the c of thy head
Jer 13:18 down, even the c of your glory
Jer 48:45 Moab, and the c of the head of the
Lam 5:16 The c is fallen from our head
Eze 16:12 a beautiful c upon thine head
Eze 21:26 the diadem, and take off the c
Zec 9:16 shall be as the stones of a c
Mt 27:29 they had platted a c of thorns
Mk 15:17 purple, and platted a c of thorns
Jn 19:2 soldiers platted a c of thorns
Jn 19:5 forth, wearing the c of thorns
1Cor 9:25 do it to obtain a corruptible c
Phil 4:1 and longed for, my joy and c
1Th 2:19 hope, or joy, or c of rejoicing
2Ti 4:8 up for me a c of righteousness
Jas 1:12 he shall receive the c of life
1Pet 5:4 ye shall receive a c of glory
Rev 2:10 and I will give thee a c of life
Rev 3:11 thou hast, that no man take thy c
Rev 6:2 and a c was given unto him
Rev 12:1 upon her head a c of twelve stars
Rev 14:14 having on his head a golden c

## CROWNED

Ps 8:5 hast c him with glory and honour
Prov 14:18 the prudent are c with knowledge
Song 3:11 the crown wherewith his mother c
Nah 3:17 Thy c are as the locusts, and thy
2Ti 2:5 for masteries, yet is he not c
Heb 2:9 of death, c with glory and honour

## CROWNS

Eze 23:42 beautiful c upon their heads
Zec 6:11 take silver and gold, and make c
Zec 6:14 the c shall be to Helem, and to
Rev 4:4 they had on their heads c of gold
Rev 4:10 cast their c before the throne,
Rev 9:7 heads were as it were c like gold
Rev 12:3 horns, and seven c upon his heads
Rev 13:1 horns, and upon his horns ten c
Rev 19:12 fire, and on his head were many c

## CRUCIFIED

Mt 26:2 Son of man is betrayed to be c
Mt 27:22 all say unto him, Let him be c
Mt 27:23 the more, saying, Let him be c
Mt 27:26 Jesus, he delivered him to be c
Mt 27:35 And they c him, and parted his
Mt 27:38 were there two thieves c with him
Mt 27:44 also, which were c with him
Mt 28:5 that ye seek Jesus, which was c
Mk 15:15 when he had scourged him, to be c
Mk 15:24 And when they had c him, they
Mk 15:25 was the third hour, and they c him
Mk 15:32 they that were c with him reviled
Mk 16:6 Jesus of Nazareth, which was c
Lk 23:23 requiring that he might be c
Lk 23:33 called Calvary, there they c him
Lk 24:7 the hands of sinful men, and be c
Lk 24:20 condemned to death, and have c him
Jn 19:16 him therefore unto them to be c
Jn 19:18 Where they c him, and two others
Jn 19:20 Jesus was c was nigh to the city
Jn 19:23 soldiers, when they had c Jesus
Jn 19:32 of the other which was c with him
Jn 19:41 where he was c there was a garden
Acts 2:23 taken, and by wicked hands have c
Acts 2:36 that same Jesus, whom ye have c
Acts 4:10 Christ of Nazareth, whom ye c
Rom 6:6 that our old man is c with him
1Cor 1:13 was Paul c for you?
1Cor 1:23 But we preach Christ c, unto the
1Cor 2:2 you, save Jesus Christ, and him c
1Cor 2:8 not have c the Lord of glory
2Cor 13:4 though he was c through weakness
Gal 2:20 I am c with Christ
Gal 3:1 evidently set forth, c among you
Gal 5:24 they that are Christ's have c the
Gal 6:14 by whom the world is c unto me
Rev 11:8 Egypt, where also our Lord was c

## CRUCIFY
Mt 20:19 mock, and to scourge, and to c him
Mt 23:34 some of them ye shall kill and c
Mt 27:31 on him, and led him away to c him
Mk 15:13 And they cried out again, C him
Mk 15:14 out the more exceedingly, C him
Mk 15:20 on him, and led him out to c him
Mk 15:27 And with him they c two thieves
Lk 23:21 cried, saying, C him, c him
Jn 19:6 out, saying, C him, c him
Jn 19:6 unto them, Take ye him, and c him
Jn 19:10 not that I have power to c thee
Jn 19:15 with him, away with him, c him
Jn 19:15 unto them, Shall I c your King
Heb 6:6 seeing they c to themselves the

## CRUEL
Gen 49:7 and their wrath, for it was c
Ex 6:9 of spirit, and for c bondage
Deut 32:33 dragons, and the c venom of asps
Job 30:21 Thou art become c to me
Ps 25:19 and they hate me with c hatred
Ps 71:4 hand of the unrighteous and c man
Prov 5:9 others, and thy years unto the c
Prov 11:17 but he that is c troubleth his
Prov 12:10 mercies of the wicked are c
Prov 17:11 therefore a c messenger shall be
Prov 27:4 Wrath is c, and anger is
Song 8:6 jealousy is c as the grave
Is 13:9 c both with wrath and fierce anger
Is 19:4 over into the hand of a c lord
Jer 6:23 they are c, and have no mercy
Jer 30:14 with the chastisement of a c one
Jer 50:42 they are c, and will not shew
Lam 4:3 daughter of my people is become c
Heb 11:36 And others had trial of c mockings

## CRUELTY
Gen 49:5 instruments of c are in their
Judg 9:24 That the c done to the threescore
Ps 27:12 me, and such as breathe out c
Ps 74:20 are full of the habitations of c
Eze 34:4 with c have ye ruled them

## CRUSE
1Sa 26:11 the c of water, and let us go
1Sa 26:12 the c of water from Saul's
1Sa 26:16 the c of water that was at his
1Kin 14:3 a c of honey, and go to him
1Kin 17:12 a barrel, and a little oil in a c
1Kin 17:14 neither shall the c of oil fail
1Kin 17:16 neither did the c of oil fail
1Kin 19:6 and a c of water at his head
2Kin 2:20 And he said, Bring me a new c

## CRUSH
Job 39:15 that the foot may c them, or that
Lam 1:15 against me to c my young men
Lam 3:34 To c under his feet all the
Amos 4:1 which c the needy, which say to

## CRUSHED
Lev 22:24 LORD that which is bruised, or c
Num 22:25 c Balaam's foot against the wall
Deut 28:33 be only oppressed and c alway
Job 4:19 which are c before the moth
Job 5:4 they are c in the gate, neither
Is 59:5 that which is c breaketh out into
Jer 51:34 hath devoured me, he hath c me

## CRY
Gen 18:20 LORD said, Because the c of Sodom
Gen 18:21 according to the c of it, which
Gen 19:13 because the c of them is waxen
Gen 27:34 a great and exceeding bitter c
Ex 2:23 their c came up unto God by
Ex 3:7 have heard their c by reason of
Ex 3:9 the c of the children of Israel
Ex 5:8 therefore they c, saying, Let us
Ex 11:6 And there shall be a great c
Ex 12:30 and there was a great c in Egypt
Ex 22:23 they c at all unto me
Ex 22:23 I will surely hear their c
Ex 32:18 of them that c for being overcome
Lev 13:45 upon his upper lip, and shall c
Num 16:34 about them fled at the c of them
Deut 15:9 he c unto the LORD against thee,
Deut 24:15 lest he c against thee unto the
Judg 10:14 c unto the gods which ye have
1Sa 5:12 the c of the city went up to
1Sa 7:8 Cease not to c unto the LORD our
1Sa 8:18 ye shall c out in that day
1Sa 9:16 because their c is come unto me
2Sa 19:28 I yet to c any more unto the king
2Sa 22:7 my c did enter into his ears
1Kin 8:28 my God, to hearken unto the c
1Kin 18:27 mocked them, and said, C aloud
2Kin 8:3 she went forth to c unto the king
2Chr 6:19 my God, to hearken unto the c
2Chr 13:12 trumpets to c alarm against you
2Chr 20:9 c unto thee in our affliction,
Neh 5:1 there was a great c of the people
Neh 5:6 very angry when I heard their c
Neh 9:9 heardest their c by the Red sea
Est 4:1 cried with a loud and a bitter c
Est 9:31 of the fastings and their c
Job 16:18 blood, and let my c have no place
Job 19:7 I c out of wrong, but I am not
Job 19:7 I c aloud, but there is no
Job 27:9 Will God hear his c when trouble
Job 30:20 I c unto thee, and thou dost not
Job 30:24 though they c in his destruction
Job 31:38 If my land c against me, or that
Job 34:28 So that they cause the c of the
Job 34:28 he heareth the c of the afflicted
Job 35:9 they make the oppressed to c
Job 35:9 they c out by reason of the arm
Job 35:12 There they c, but none giveth
Job 36:13 they c not when he bindeth them
Job 38:41 when his young ones c unto God
Ps 5:2 Hearken unto the voice of my c
Ps 9:12 not the c of the humble
Ps 17:1 right, O LORD, attend unto my c
Ps 18:6 my c came before him, even into
Ps 22:2 I c in the daytime, but thou
Ps 27:7 O LORD, when I c with my voice
Ps 28:1 Unto thee will I c, O LORD my
Ps 28:2 when I c unto thee, when I lift
Ps 34:15 and his ears are open unto their c
Ps 34:17 The righteous c, and the LORD
Ps 39:12 O LORD, and give ear unto my c
Ps 40:1 inclined unto me, and heard my c
Ps 55:17 at noon, will I pray, and c aloud
Ps 56:9 When I c unto thee, then shall
Ps 57:2 I will c unto God most high
Ps 61:1 Hear my c, O God
Ps 61:2 of the earth will I c unto thee
Ps 86:3 for I c unto thee daily
Ps 88:2 incline thine ear unto my c
Ps 89:26 He shall c unto me, Thou art my
Ps 102:1 LORD, and let my c come unto thee
Ps 106:44 affliction, when he heard their c
Ps 107:19 Then they c unto the LORD in
Ps 107:28 Then they c unto the LORD in
Ps 119:169 Let my c come near before thee, O
Ps 141:1 Lord, I c unto thee
Ps 141:1 unto my voice, when I c unto thee
Ps 142:6 Attend unto my c
Ps 145:19 he also will hear their c
Ps 147:9 and to the young ravens which c
Prov 8:1 Doth not wisdom c
Prov 21:13 his ears at the c of the poor
Prov 21:13 he also shall c himself
Eccl 9:17 heard in quiet more than the c of
Is 5:7 for righteousness, but behold a c
Is 8:4 child shall have knowledge to c
Is 12:6 C out and shout, thou inhabitant
Is 13:22 shall c in their desolate houses
Is 14:31 c, O city
Is 15:4 And Heshbon shall c, and Elealeh
Is 15:4 soldiers of Moab shall c out
Is 15:5 My heart shall c out for Moab
Is 15:5 shall raise up a c of destruction
Is 15:8 For the c is gone round about the
Is 19:20 for they shall c unto the LORD
Is 24:14 they shall c aloud from the sea
Is 29:9 c ye out, and c
Is 30:19 unto thee at the voice of thy c
Is 33:7 valiant ones shall c without
Is 34:14 the satyr shall c to his fellow
Is 40:2 c unto her, that her warfare is
Is 40:6 The voice said, C
Is 40:6 And he said, What shall I c
Is 42:2 He shall not c, nor lift up, nor
Is 42:13 he shall c, yea, roar
Is 42:14 now will I c like a travailing
Is 43:14 whose c is in the ships
Is 46:7 yea, one shall c unto him
Is 54:1 c aloud, thou that didst not
Is 58:1 C aloud, spare not, lift up thy
Is 58:9 thou shalt c, and he shall say,
Is 65:14 but ye shall c for sorrow of
Jer 2:2 c in the ears of Jerusalem,
Jer 3:4 thou not from this time c unto me
Jer 4:5 c, gather together, and say,
Jer 7:16 neither lift up c nor prayer for
Jer 8:19 Behold the voice of the c of the
Jer 11:11 and though they shall c unto me
Jer 11:12 c unto the gods unto whom they
Jer 11:14 neither lift up a c or prayer for
Jer 11:14 they c unto me for their trouble
Jer 14:2 the c of Jerusalem is gone up
Jer 14:12 fast, I will not hear their c
Jer 18:22 Let a c be heard from their
Jer 20:16 let him hear the c in the morning
Jer 22:20 Go up to Lebanon, and c
Jer 22:20 in Bashan, and c from the passages
Jer 25:34 Howl, ye shepherds, and c
Jer 25:36 A voice of the c of the shepherds
Jer 31:6 upon the mount Ephraim shall c
Jer 46:12 thy c hath filled the land
Jer 46:17 They did c there, Pharaoh king of
Jer 47:2 then the men shall c, and all the
Jer 48:4 ones have caused a c to be heard
Jer 48:5 have heard a c of destruction
Jer 48:20 howl and c; tell ye it in Arnon
Jer 48:31 I will c out for all Moab
Jer 48:34 From the c of Heshbon even unto
Jer 49:3 c, ye daughters of Rabbah, gird
Jer 49:21 at the c the noise thereof was
Jer 49:29 and they shall c unto them
Jer 50:46 the c is heard among the nations
Jer 51:54 A sound of a c cometh from
Lam 2:19 Arise, c out in the night
Lam 3:8 Also when I c and shout, he
Lam 3:56 ear at my breathing, at my c
Eze 8:18 though they c in mine ears with a
Eze 9:4 that c for all the abominations
Eze 21:12 C and howl, son of man
Eze 24:17 Forbear to c, make no mourning
Eze 26:15 of thy fall, when the wounded c
Eze 27:28 the sound of the c of thy pilots
Eze 27:30 shall c bitterly, and shall cast
Hos 5:8 c aloud at Beth-aven, after thee,
Hos 8:2 Israel shall c unto me, My God,
Joel 1:14 your God, and c unto the LORD,
Joel 1:19 O LORD, to thee will I c
Joel 1:20 of the field c also unto thee
Amos 3:4 a young lion c out of his den
Jonah 1:2 that great city, and c against it
Jonah 3:8 sackcloth, and c mightily unto God
Mic 3:4 Then shall they c unto the LORD
Mic 3:5 that bite with their teeth, and c
Mic 4:9 Now why dost thou c out aloud
Nah 2:8 Stand, stand, shall they c
Hab 1:2 O LORD, how long shall I c
Hab 1:2 even c out unto thee of violence,
Hab 2:11 the stone shall c out of the wall
Zeph 1:10 noise of a c from the fish gate
Zeph 1:14 mighty man shall c there bitterly
Zec 1:14 C thou, saying, Thus saith the
Zec 1:17 C yet, saying, Thus saith the
Mt 12:19 He shall not strive, nor c
Mt 25:6 And at midnight there was a c made
Mk 10:47 of Nazareth, he began to c out
Lk 18:7 avenge his own elect, which c day
Lk 19:40 stones would immediately c out
Acts 23:9 And there arose a great c
Rom 8:15 Spirit of adoption, whereby we c
Gal 4:27 break forth and c, thou that
Rev 14:18 cried with a loud c to him that

## CRYING
1Sa 4:14 when Eli heard the noise of the c
2Sa 13:19 hand on her head, and went on c
Job 39:7 regardeth he the c of the driver
Ps 69:3 I am weary of my c
Prov 19:18 let not thy soul spare for his c
Prov 30:15 horseleach hath two daughters, c
Is 22:5 walls, and of c to the mountains
Is 24:11 There is a c for wine in the
Is 65:19 heard in her, nor the voice of c
Jer 48:3 A voice of c shall be from
Zec 4:7 thereof with shoutings, c
Mal 2:13 with weeping, and with c out
Mt 3:3 The voice of one c in the
Mt 9:27 two blind men followed him, c
Mt 21:15 the children c in the temple, and
Mk 1:3 The voice of one c in the
Mk 5:5 the mountains, and in the tombs, c
Mk 15:8 the multitude c aloud began to
Lk 3:4 The voice of one c in the
Lk 4:41 c out, and saying, Thou art Christ
Jn 1:23 voice of one c in the wilderness

Acts 8:7 c with loud voice, came out of
Acts 14:14 ran in among the people, c out,
Acts 17:6 unto the rulers of the city, c
Acts 21:28 C out, Men of Israel, help
Acts 21:36 of the people followed after, c
Acts 25:24 c that he ought not to live any
Gal 4:6 of his Son into your hearts, c
Heb 5:7 and supplications with strong c
Rev 14:15 c with a loud voice to him that
Rev 21:4 more death, neither sorrow, nor c

## CRYSTAL
Job 28:17 The gold and the c cannot equal it
Eze 1:22 as the colour of the terrible c
Rev 4:6 was a sea of glass like unto c
Rev 21:11 like a jasper stone, clear as c
Rev 22:1 of water of life, clear as c

## CUD
Lev 11:3 is clovenfooted, and cheweth the c
Lev 11:4 not eat of them that chew the c
Lev 11:4 camel, because he cheweth the c
Lev 11:5 coney, because he cheweth the c
Lev 11:6 hare, because he cheweth the c
Lev 11:7 yet he cheweth not the c
Lev 11:26 clovenfooted, nor cheweth the c
Deut 14:6 cheweth the c among the beasts,
Deut 14:7 not eat of them that chew the c
Deut 14:7 for they chew the c, but divide
Deut 14:8 the hoof, yet cheweth not the c

## CUMMIN
Is 28:25 the fitches, and scatter the c
Is 28:27 wheel turned about upon the c
Is 28:27 with a staff, and the c with a rod
Mt 23:23 pay tithe of mint and anise and c

## CUNNING
Gen 25:27 and Esau was a c hunter, a man of
Ex 26:1 with cherubims of c work shalt
Ex 26:31 and fine twined linen of c work
Ex 28:6 and fine twined linen, with c work
Ex 28:15 of judgment with c work
Ex 31:4 To devise c works, to work in
Ex 35:33 to make any manner of c work
Ex 35:35 of the c workman, and of the
Ex 35:35 and of those that devise c work
Ex 36:8 cherubims of c work made he them
Ex 36:35 cherubims made he it of c work
Ex 38:23 a c workman, and an embroiderer in
Ex 39:3 and in the fine linen, with c work
Ex 39:8 he made the breastplate of c work
1Sa 16:16 who is a c player on an harp
1Sa 16:18 that is c in playing, and a mighty
1Kin 7:14 c to work all works in brass
1Chr 22:15 all manner of c men for every
1Chr 25:7 of the LORD, even all that were c
2Chr 2:7 therefore a man c to work in gold
2Chr 2:7 can skill to grave with the c men
2Chr 2:13 And now I have sent a c man
2Chr 2:14 be put to him, with thy c men
2Chr 2:14 with the c men of my lord David
2Chr 26:15 engines, invented by c men
Ps 137:5 let my right hand forget her c
Song 7:1 work of the hands of a c workman
Is 3:3 the c artificer, and the eloquent
Is 40:20 he seeketh unto him a c workman
Jer 9:17 and send for c women, that they
Jer 10:9 they are all the work of c men
Dan 1:4 c in knowledge, and understanding
Eph 4:14 c craftiness, whereby they lie in

## CUP
Gen 40:11 Pharaoh's c was in my hand
Gen 40:11 and pressed them into Pharaoh's c
Gen 40:11 I gave the c into Pharaoh's hand
Gen 40:13 deliver Pharaoh's c into his hand
Gen 40:21 he gave the c into Pharaoh's hand
Gen 44:2 And put my c, the silver c
Gen 44:12 the c was found in Benjamin's
Gen 44:16 he also with whom the c is found
Gen 44:17 man in whose hand the c is found
2Sa 12:3 own meat, and drank of his own c
1Kin 7:26 was wrought like the brim of a c
2Chr 4:5 like the work of the brim of a c
Ps 11:6 shall be the portion of their c
Ps 16:5 of mine inheritance and of my c
Ps 23:5 my c runneth over
Ps 73:10 waters of a full c are wrung out
Ps 75:8 the hand of the LORD there is a c
Ps 116:13 I will take the c of salvation
Prov 23:31 it giveth his colour in the c
Is 51:17 of the LORD the c of his fury
Is 51:17 the dregs of the c of trembling
Is 51:22 of thine hand the c of trembling
Is 51:22 the dregs of the c of my fury
Jer 16:7 the c of consolation to drink for
Jer 25:15 Take the wine c of this fury at
Jer 25:17 Then took I the c at the LORD's
Jer 25:28 take the c at thine hand to drink
Jer 49:12 of the c have assuredly drunken
Jer 51:7 a golden c in the LORD's hand
Lam 4:21 the c also shall pass through
Eze 23:31 will I give her c into thine hand
Eze 23:32 drink of thy sister's c deep
Eze 23:33 with the c of astonishment and
Eze 23:33 with the c of thy sister Samaria
Hab 2:16 the c of the LORD's right hand
Zec 12:2 I will make Jerusalem a c of
Mt 10:42 c of cold water only in the name
Mt 20:22 of the c that I shall drink of
Mt 20:23 Ye shall drink indeed of my c
Mt 23:25 make clean the outside of the c
Mt 23:26 first that which is within the c
Mt 26:27 And he took the c, and gave thanks,
Mt 26:39 possible, let this c pass from me
Mt 26:42 if this c may not pass away from
Mk 9:41 a c of water to drink in my name
Mk 10:38 ye drink of the c that I drink of
Mk 10:39 drink of the c that I drink of
Mk 14:23 And he took the c, and when he had
Mk 14:36 take away this c from me
Lk 11:39 make clean the outside of the c
Lk 22:17 And he took the c, and gave thanks,
Lk 22:20 Likewise also the c after supper
Lk 22:20 This c is the new testament in my
Lk 22:42 be willing, remove this c from me
Jn 18:11 the c which my Father hath given
1Cor 10:16 The c of blessing which we bless,
1Cor 10:21 Ye cannot drink the c of the Lord
1Cor 10:21 and the c of devils
1Cor 11:25 same manner also he took the c
1Cor 11:25 This c is the new testament in my
1Cor 11:26 eat this bread, and drink this c
1Cor 11:27 drink this c of the Lord,
1Cor 11:28 of that bread, and drink of that c
Rev 14:10 into the c of his indignation
Rev 16:19 to give unto her the c of the
Rev 17:4 having a golden c in her hand
Rev 18:6 in the c which she hath filled

## CUPS
1Chr 28:17 and the bowls, and the c
Is 22:24 quantity, from the vessels of c
Jer 35:5 pots full of wine, and c, and I
Jer 52:19 and the spoons, and the c
Mk 7:4 to hold, as the washing of c
Mk 7:8 men, as the washing of pots and c

## CURE
Jer 33:6 health and c, and I will c them
Hos 5:13 heal you, nor c you of your wound
Mt 17:16 and they could not c him
Lk 9:1 over all devils, and to c diseases

## CURED
Jer 46:11 for thou shalt not be c
Mt 17:18 the child was c from that very
Lk 7:21 in that same hour he c many of
Jn 5:10 said unto him that was c, It is

## CURIOUS
Ex 28:8 the c girdle of the ephod, which
Ex 28:27 above the c girdle of the ephod
Ex 28:28 above the c girdle of the ephod
Ex 29:5 gird him with the c girdle of the
Ex 35:32 And to devise c works, to work in
Ex 39:5 the c girdle of his ephod, that
Ex 39:20 above the c girdle of the ephod
Ex 39:21 above the c girdle of the ephod
Lev 8:7 with the c girdle of the ephod
Acts 19:19 used c arts brought their books

## CURSE
Gen 8:21 I will not again c the ground any
Gen 12:3 thee, and c him that curseth thee
Gen 27:12 and I shall bring a c upon me
Gen 27:13 said unto him, Upon me be thy c
Ex 22:28 nor c the ruler of thy people
Lev 19:14 Thou shalt not c the deaf
Num 5:18 bitter water that causeth the c
Num 5:19 bitter water that causeth the c
Num 5:21 the woman, The LORD make thee a c
Num 5:22 the c shall go into thy bowels
Num 5:24 bitter water that causeth the c
Num 5:24 the c shall enter into her
Num 5:27 the c shall enter into her
Num 5:27 shall be a c among her people
Num 22:6 I pray thee, c me this people
Num 22:11 come now, c me them
Num 22:12 thou shalt not c the people
Num 22:17 I pray thee, c me this people
Num 23:7 c me Jacob, and come, defy Israel
Num 23:8 How shall I c, whom God hath not
Num 23:11 I took thee to c mine enemies
Num 23:13 and c me them from thence
Num 23:25 Neither c them at all, nor bless
Num 23:27 thou mayest c me them from thence
Num 24:10 I called thee to c mine enemies
Deut 11:26 you this day a blessing and a c
Deut 11:28 And a c, if ye will not obey the
Deut 11:29 Gerizim, and the c upon mount Ebal
Deut 23:4 Pethor of Mesopotamia, to c thee
Deut 23:5 the c into a blessing unto thee
Deut 27:13 shall stand upon mount Ebal to c
Deut 29:19 he heareth the words of this c
Deut 30:1 upon thee, the blessing and the c
Josh 6:18 and make the camp of Israel a c
Josh 24:9 Balaam the son of Beor to c you
Judg 5:23 C ye Meroz, said the angel of the
Judg 5:23 c ye bitterly the inhabitants
Judg 9:57 upon them came the c of Jotham
2Sa 16:9 this dead dog c my lord the king
2Sa 16:10 so let him c, because the LORD
2Sa 16:10 LORD hath said unto him, C David
2Sa 16:11 let him alone, and let him c
1Kin 2:8 c in the day when I went to
2Kin 22:19 should become a desolation and a c
Neh 10:29 their nobles, and entered into a c
Neh 13:2 them, that he should c them
Neh 13:2 God turned the c into a blessing
Job 1:11 he will c thee to thy face
Job 2:5 he will c thee to thy face
Job 2:9 c God, and die
Job 3:8 Let them c it
Job 3:8 that c the day, who are ready
Job 31:30 to sin by wishing a c to his soul
Ps 62:4 their mouth, but they c inwardly
Ps 109:28 Let them c, but bless thou
Prov 3:33 The c of the LORD is in the house
Prov 11:26 corn, the people shall c him
Prov 24:24 him shall the people c, nations
Prov 26:2 so the c causeless shall not come
Prov 27:14 it shall be counted a c to him
Prov 28:27 his eyes shall have many a c
Prov 30:10 unto his master, lest he c thee
Eccl 7:21 lest thou hear thy servant c thee
Eccl 10:20 C not the king, no not in thy
Eccl 10:20 c not the rich in thy bedchamber
Is 8:21 c their king and their God, and
Is 24:6 hath the c devoured the earth
Is 34:5 and upon the people of my c
Is 43:28 and have given Jacob to the c
Is 65:15 your name for a c unto my chosen
Jer 15:10 yet every one of them doth c me
Jer 24:9 and a proverb, a taunt and a c
Jer 25:18 astonishment, an hissing, and a c
Jer 26:6 will make this city a c to all
Jer 29:18 kingdoms of the earth, to be a c
Jer 29:22 of them shall be taken up a c by
Jer 42:18 and an astonishment, and a c
Jer 44:8 off, and that ye might be a c
Jer 44:12 and an astonishment, and a c
Jer 44:22 and an astonishment, and a c
Jer 49:13 a reproach, a waste, and a c
Lam 3:65 sorrow of heart, thy c unto them
Dan 9:11 therefore the c is poured upon us
Zec 5:3 This is the c that goeth forth
Zec 8:13 as ye were a c among the heathen
Mal 2:2 I will even send a c upon you
Mal 2:2 and I will c your blessings
Mal 3:9 Ye are cursed with a c
Mal 4:6 come and smite the earth with a c
Mt 5:44 enemies, bless them that c you
Mt 26:74 Then began he to c and to swear,
Mk 14:71 But he began to c and to swear,
Lk 6:28 Bless them that c you, and pray
Acts 23:12 and bound themselves under a c
Acts 23:14 bound ourselves under a great c
Rom 12:14 bless, and c not
Gal 3:10 works of the law are under the c
Gal 3:13 redeemed us from the c of the law
Gal 3:13 being made a c for us
Jas 3:9 and therewith c we men, which are
Rev 22:3 And there shall be no more c

## CURSED

Gen 3:14 thou art c above all cattle, and
Gen 3:17 c is the ground for thy sake
Gen 4:11 now art thou c from the earth,
Gen 5:29 the ground which the LORD hath c
Gen 9:25 And he said, C be Canaan
Gen 27:29 c be every one that curseth thee,
Gen 49:7 C be their anger, for it was
Lev 20:9 he hath c his father or his
Lev 24:11 the name of the LORD, and c
Lev 24:14 him that hath c without the camp
Lev 24:23 him that had c out of the camp
Num 22:6 and he whom thou cursest is c
Num 23:8 I curse, whom God hath not c
Num 24:9 c is he that curseth thee
Deut 7:26 lest thou be a c thing like it
Deut 7:26 for it is a c thing
Deut 13:17 of the c thing to thine hand
Deut 27:15 C be the man that maketh any
Deut 27:16 C be he that setteth light by his
Deut 27:17 C be he that removeth his
Deut 27:18 C be he that maketh the blind to
Deut 27:19 C be he that perverteth the
Deut 27:20 C be he that lieth with his
Deut 27:21 C be he that lieth with any
Deut 27:22 C be he that lieth with his
Deut 27:23 C be he that lieth with his
Deut 27:24 C be he that smiteth his
Deut 27:25 C be he that taketh reward to
Deut 27:26 C be he that confirmeth not all
Deut 28:16 C shalt thou be in the city, and
Deut 28:16 c shalt thou be in the field
Deut 28:17 C shall be thy basket and thy
Deut 28:18 C shall be the fruit of thy body,
Deut 28:19 C shalt thou be when thou comest
Deut 28:19 c shalt thou be when thou goest
Josh 6:26 C be the man before the LORD,
Josh 9:23 Now therefore ye are c, and there
Judg 9:27 did eat and drink, and c Abimelech
Judg 21:18 C be he that giveth a wife to
1Sa 14:24 C be the man that eateth any food
1Sa 14:28 C be the man that eateth any food
1Sa 17:43 the Philistine c David by his
1Sa 26:19 c be they before the LORD
2Sa 16:5 came forth, and c still as he came
2Sa 16:7 And thus said Shimei when he c
2Sa 16:13 c as he went, and threw stones at
2Sa 19:21 because he c the LORD's anointed
1Kin 2:8 which c me with a grievous curse
2Kin 2:24 c them in the name of the LORD
2Kin 9:34 and said, Go, see now this c woman
Neh 13:25 c them, and smote certain of them,
Job 1:5 sinned, and c God in their hearts
Job 3:1 Job his mouth, and c his day
Job 5:3 but suddenly I c his habitation
Job 24:18 their portion is c in the earth
Ps 37:22 they that be c of him shall be
Ps 119:21 hast rebuked the proud that are c
Eccl 7:22 thyself likewise hast c others
Jer 11:3 C be the man that obeyeth not the
Jer 17:5 C be the man that trusteth in man
Jer 20:14 C be the day wherein I was born
Jer 20:15 C be the man who brought tidings
Jer 48:10 C be he that doeth the work of
Jer 48:10 c be he that keepeth back his
Mal 1:14 But c be the deceiver, which hath
Mal 2:2 I have c them already, because ye
Mal 3:9 Ye are c with a curse
Mt 25:41 left hand, Depart from me, ye c
Jn 7:49 who knoweth not the law are c
Gal 3:10 C is every one that continueth
Gal 3:13 C is every one that hangeth on a
2Pet 2:14 with covetous practices; c children

## CURSES

Num 5:23 shall write these c in a book
Deut 28:15 that all these c shall come upon
Deut 28:45 Moreover all these c shall come
Deut 29:20 all the c that are written in
Deut 29:21 according to all the c of the
Deut 29:27 to bring upon it all the c that
Deut 30:7 all these c upon thine enemies
2Chr 34:24 even all the c that are written

## CURSETH

Gen 12:3 thee, and curse him that c thee
Gen 27:29 cursed be every one that c thee
Ex 21:17 he that c his father, or his
Lev 20:9 For every one that c his father
Lev 24:15 Whosoever c his God shall bear
Num 24:9 thee, and cursed is he that c thee
Prov 20:20 Whoso c his father or his mother,
Prov 30:11 a generation that c their father
Mt 15:4 He that c father or mother, let
Mk 7:10 Whoso c father or mother, let him

## CURSING

Num 5:21 the woman with an oath of c
Deut 28:20 The LORD shall send upon thee c
Deut 30:19 you life and death, blessing and c
2Sa 16:12 me good for his c this day
Ps 10:7 His mouth is full of c and deceit
Ps 59:12 and for c and lying which they
Ps 109:17 As he loved c, so let it come
Ps 109:18 with c like as with his garment
Prov 29:24 he heareth c, and bewrayeth it not
Rom 3:14 Whose mouth is full of c and
Heb 6:8 is rejected, and is nigh unto c
Jas 3:10 mouth proceedeth blessing and c

## CURTAIN

Ex 26:2 length of one c shall be eight
Ex 26:2 the breadth of one c four cubits
Ex 26:4 one c from the selvedge in the
Ex 26:4 the uttermost edge of another c
Ex 26:5 shalt thou make in the one c
Ex 26:5 thou make in the edge of the c
Ex 26:8 The length of one c shall be
Ex 26:8 the breadth of one c four cubits
Ex 26:9 shalt double the sixth c in the
Ex 26:10 loops on the edge of the one c
Ex 26:10 the c which coupleth the second
Ex 26:12 the half c that remaineth, shall
Ex 36:9 The length of one c was twenty
Ex 36:9 the breadth of one c four cubits
Ex 36:11 of one c from the selvedge in the
Ex 36:11 the uttermost side of another c
Ex 36:12 Fifty loops made he in one c
Ex 36:12 made he in the edge of the c
Ex 36:12 the loops held one c to another
Ex 36:15 length of one c was thirty cubits
Ex 36:15 cubits was the breadth of one c
Ex 36:17 edge of the c in the coupling
Ex 36:17 the c which coupleth the second
Num 3:26 the c for the door of the court,
Ps 104:2 out the heavens like a c
Is 40:22 stretcheth out the heavens as a c

## CURTAINS

Ex 26:1 with ten c of fine twined linen
Ex 26:2 every one of the c shall have one
Ex 26:3 The five c shall be coupled
Ex 26:3 other five c shall be coupled one
Ex 26:6 couple the c together with the
Ex 26:7 thou shalt make c of goats' hair
Ex 26:7 eleven c shalt thou make
Ex 26:8 the eleven c shall be all of one
Ex 26:9 shalt couple five c by themselves
Ex 26:9 six c by themselves, and shalt
Ex 26:12 remaineth of the c of the tent
Ex 26:13 the length of the c of the tent
Ex 36:8 made ten c of fine twined linen
Ex 36:9 the c were all of one size
Ex 36:10 the five c one unto another
Ex 36:10 the other five c he coupled one
Ex 36:13 coupled the c one unto another
Ex 36:14 he made c of goats' hair for the
Ex 36:14 eleven c he made them
Ex 36:15 the eleven c were of one size
Ex 36:16 he coupled five c by themselves
Ex 36:16 and six c by themselves
Num 4:25 bear the c of the tabernacle
2Sa 7:2 the ark of God dwelleth within c
1Chr 17:1 of the LORD remaineth under c
Song 1:5 of Kedar, as the c of Solomon
Is 54:2 forth the c of thine habitations
Jer 4:20 spoiled, and my c in a moment
Jer 10:20 tent any more, and to set up my c
Jer 49:29 shall take to themselves their c
Hab 3:7 the c of the land of Midian did

## CUSH *(cush)* See ETHIOPIA.

*1. A son of Ham.*
Gen 10:6 C, and Mizraim, and Phut, and
Gen 10:7 the sons of C; Seba, and Havilah
Gen 10:8 And C begat Nimrod
1Chr 1:8 C, and Mizraim, Put, and Canaan
1Chr 1:9 the sons of C; Seba, and Havilah
1Chr 1:10 And C begat Nimrod

*2. A Benjaminite.*
Ps 7:t the words of C the Benjamite

*3. Land of descendants of Cush.*
Is 11:11 Egypt, and from Pathros, and from C

## CUSHAN *(cu'-shan)* See CHUSHAN-RISHATHAIM. *Same as Chushan-rishathaim.*

Hab 3:7 saw the tents of C in affliction

## CUSHI *(cu'-shi)*

*1. Messenger of David.*
2Sa 18:21 Then said Joab to C, Go tell the
2Sa 18:21 C bowed himself unto Joab, and ran
2Sa 18:22 me, I pray thee, also run after C
2Sa 18:23 way of the plain, and overran C
2Sa 18:31 And, behold, C came
2Sa 18:31 C said, Tidings, my lord the king
2Sa 18:32 And the king said unto C, Is the
2Sa 18:32 C answered, The enemies of my

*2. Ancestor of Jehudi.*
Jer 36:14 son of Shelemiah, the son of C

*3. Father of Zephaniah.*
Zeph 1:1 came unto Zephaniah the son of C

## CUSTODY

Num 3:36 And under the c and charge of the
Est 2:3 unto the c of Hege the king's
Est 2:8 to the c of Hegai, that Esther
Est 2:8 to the c of Hegai, keeper of the
Est 2:14 to the c of Shaashgaz, the king's

## CUSTOM

Gen 31:35 for the c of women is upon me
Judg 11:39 And it was a c in Israel,
1Sa 2:13 the priest's c with the people
Ezr 3:4 by number, according to the c
Ezr 4:13 they not pay toll, tribute, and c
Ezr 4:20 and toll, tribute, and c, was paid
Ezr 7:24 to impose toll, tribute, or c
Jer 32:11 sealed according to the law and c
Mt 9:9 sitting at the receipt of c
Mt 17:25 of the earth take c or tribute
Mk 2:14 sitting at the receipt of c
Lk 1:9 According to the c of the
Lk 2:27 do for him after the c of the law
Lk 2:42 after the c of the feast
Lk 4:16 and, as his c was, he went into
Lk 5:27 Levi, sitting at the receipt of c
Jn 18:39 But ye have a c, that I should
Rom 13:7 c to whom c; fear to whom fear
1Cor 11:16 be contentious, we have no such c

## CUSTOMS

Lev 18:30 not any one of these abominable c
Jer 10:3 For the c of the people are vain
Acts 6:14 shall change the c which Moses
Acts 16:21 And teach c, which are not lawful
Acts 21:21 neither to walk after the c
Acts 26:3 I know thee to be expert in all c
Acts 28:17 or c of our fathers, yet was I

## CUT

Gen 9:11 neither shall all flesh be c off
Gen 17:14 that soul shall be c off from his
Ex 4:25 c off the foreskin of her son, and
Ex 9:15 thou shalt be c off from the
Ex 12:15 soul shall be c off from Israel
Ex 12:19 even that soul shall be c off
Ex 23:23 and I will c them off
Ex 29:17 thou shalt c the ram in pieces,
Ex 30:33 shall even be c off from his
Ex 30:38 shall even be c off from his
Ex 31:14 that soul shall be c off from
Ex 34:13 images, and c down their groves
Ex 39:3 c it into wires, to work it in
Lev 1:6 offering, and c it into his pieces
Lev 1:12 he shall c it into his pieces,
Lev 7:20 shall be c off from his people
Lev 7:21 shall be c off from his people
Lev 7:25 it shall be c off from his people
Lev 7:27 shall be c off from his people
Lev 8:20 And he c the ram into pieces
Lev 17:4 that man shall be c off from
Lev 17:9 even that man shall be c off from
Lev 17:10 will c him off from among his
Lev 17:14 eateth it shall be c off
Lev 18:29 be c off from among their people
Lev 19:8 that soul shall be c off from
Lev 20:3 will c him off from among his
Lev 20:5 will c him off, and all that go a
Lev 20:6 will c him off from among his
Lev 20:17 they shall be c off in the sight
Lev 20:18 both of them shall be c off from
Lev 22:3 that soul shall be c off from my
Lev 22:24 or crushed, or broken, or c
Lev 23:29 he shall be c off from among his
Lev 26:30 c down your images, and cast your

Num 4:18 C ye not off the tribe of the
Num 9:13 be c off from among his people
Num 13:23 c down from thence a branch with
Num 13:24 of Israel c down from thence
Num 15:30 that soul shall be c off from
Num 15:31 that soul shall utterly be c off
Num 19:13 soul shall be c off from Israel
Num 19:20 that soul shall be c off from
Deut 7:5 c down their groves, and burn
Deut 12:29 c off the nations from before
Deut 14:1 ye shall not c yourselves
Deut 19:1 thy God hath c off the nations
Deut 19:5 with the axe to c down the tree
Deut 20:19 thou shalt not c them down (for
Deut 20:20 thou shalt destroy and c them down
Deut 23:1 or hath his privy member c off
Deut 25:12 Then thou shalt c off her hand
Josh 3:13 c off from the waters that come
Josh 3:16 salt sea, failed, and were c off
Josh 4:7 were c off before the ark of the
Josh 4:7 the waters of Jordan were c off
Josh 7:9 c off our name from the earth
Josh 11:21 c off the Anakims from the
Josh 17:15 c down for thyself there in the
Josh 17:18 a wood, and thou shalt c it down
Josh 23:4 all the nations that I have c off
Judg 1:6 c off his thumbs and his great
Judg 1:7 thumbs and their great toes c off
Judg 6:25 c down the grove that is by it
Judg 6:26 the grove which thou shalt c down
Judg 6:28 the grove was c down that was by
Judg 6:30 because he hath c down the grove
Judg 9:48 c down a bough from the trees, and
Judg 9:49 all the people likewise c down
Judg 20:6 c her in pieces, and sent her
Judg 21:6 There is one tribe c off from
Ruth 4:10 not c off from among his brethren
1Sa 2:31 that I will c off thine arm, and
1Sa 2:33 whom I shall not c off from mine
1Sa 5:4 were c off upon the threshold
1Sa 17:51 him, and c off his head therewith
1Sa 20:15 But also thou shalt not c off thy
1Sa 20:15 not when the LORD hath c off the
1Sa 24:4 c off the skirt of Saul's robe
1Sa 24:5 because he had c off Saul's skirt
1Sa 24:11 for in that I c off the skirt of
1Sa 24:21 that thou wilt not c off my seed
1Sa 28:9 how he hath c off those that have
1Sa 31:9 they c off his head, and stripped
2Sa 4:12 c off their hands and their feet,
2Sa 7:9 have c off all thine enemies out
2Sa 10:4 c off their garments in the
2Sa 20:22 they c off the head of Sheba the
1Kin 9:7 Then will I c off Israel out of
1Kin 11:16 until he had c off every male in
1Kin 13:34 of Jeroboam, even to c it off
1Kin 14:10 will c off from Jeroboam him that
1Kin 14:14 who shall c off the house of
1Kin 18:4 when Jezebel c off the prophets
1Kin 18:23 c it in pieces, and lay it on wood
1Kin 18:28 c themselves after their manner
1Kin 18:33 c the bullock in pieces, and laid
1Kin 21:21 will c off from Ahab him that
2Kin 6:4 came to Jordan, they c down wood
2Kin 6:6 he c down a stick, and cast it in
2Kin 9:8 I will c off from Ahab him that
2Kin 10:32 the LORD began to c Israel short
2Kin 16:17 king Ahaz c off the borders of
2Kin 18:4 c down the groves, and brake in
2Kin 18:16 At that time did Hezekiah c off
2Kin 19:23 will c down the tall cedar trees
2Kin 23:14 c down the groves, and filled
2Kin 24:13 c in pieces all the vessels of
1Chr 17:8 have c off all thine enemies from
1Chr 19:4 c off their garments in the midst
1Chr 20:3 c them with saws, and with harrows
2Chr 2:8 can skill to c timber in Lebanon
2Chr 2:10 the hewers that c timber
2Chr 2:16 we will c wood out of Lebanon, as
2Chr 14:3 the images, and c down the groves
2Chr 15:16 Asa c down her idol, and stamped
2Chr 22:7 to c off the house of Ahab
2Chr 26:21 for he was c off from the house
2Chr 28:24 c in pieces the vessels of the
2Chr 31:1 c down the groves, and threw down
2Chr 32:21 which c off all the mighty men of
2Chr 34:4 on high above them, he c down
2Chr 34:7 c down all the idols throughout
Job 4:7 or where were the righteous c off
Job 6:9 let loose his hand, and c me off
Job 8:12 not c down, it withereth before
Job 8:14 Whose hope shall be c off
Job 11:10 If he c off, and shut up, or
Job 14:2 forth like a flower, and is c down
Job 14:7 hope of a tree, if it be c down
Job 18:16 above shall his branch be c off
Job 21:21 his months is c off in the midst
Job 22:16 Which were c down out of time,
Job 22:20 our substance is not c down
Job 23:17 Because I was not c off before
Job 24:24 c off as the tops of the ears of
Job 30:4 Who c up mallows by the bushes,
Job 36:20 when people are c off in their
Ps 12:3 The LORD shall c off all
Ps 31:22 I am c off from before thine eyes
Ps 34:16 to c off the remembrance of them
Ps 37:2 soon be c down like the grass
Ps 37:9 For evildoers shall be c off
Ps 37:22 be cursed of him shall be c off
Ps 37:28 seed of the wicked shall be c off
Ps 37:34 when the wicked are c off
Ps 37:38 end of the wicked shall be c off
Ps 54:5 c them off in thy truth
Ps 58:7 let them be as c in pieces
Ps 75:10 of the wicked also will I c off
Ps 76:12 He shall c off the spirit of
Ps 80:16 is burned with fire, it is c down
Ps 83:4 let us c them off from being a
Ps 88:5 they are c off from thy hand
Ps 88:16 thy terrors have c me off
Ps 90:6 in the evening it is c down
Ps 90:10 for it is soon c off, and we fly
Ps 94:23 shall c them off in their own
Ps 94:23 the LORD our God shall c them off
Ps 101:5 his neighbour, him will I c off
Ps 101:8 that I may c off all wicked doers
Ps 107:16 c the bars of iron in sunder
Ps 109:13 Let his posterity be c off
Ps 109:15 that he may c off the memory of
Ps 129:4 he hath c asunder the cords of
Ps 143:12 of thy mercy c off mine enemies,
Prov 2:22 shall be c off from the earth
Prov 10:31 the froward tongue shall be c out
Prov 23:18 expectation shall not be c off
Prov 24:14 expectation shall not be c off
Is 9:10 the sycomores are c down, but we
Is 9:14 LORD will c off from Israel head
Is 10:7 and c off nations not a few
Is 10:34 he shall c down the thickets of
Is 11:13 of Judah shall be c off
Is 14:12 how art thou c down to the ground
Is 14:22 c off from Babylon the name, and
Is 15:2 be baldness, and every beard c off
Is 18:5 he shall both c off the sprigs
Is 18:5 take away and c down the branches
Is 22:25 be removed, and be c down, and fall
Is 22:25 that was upon it shall be c off
Is 29:20 that watch for iniquity are c off
Is 33:12 as thorns c up shall they be
Is 37:24 I will c down the tall cedars
Is 38:12 I have c off like a weaver my
Is 38:12 he will c me off with pining
Is 45:2 c in sunder the bars of iron
Is 48:9 for thee, that I c thee not off
Is 48:19 c off nor destroyed from before
Is 51:9 Art thou not it that hath c Rahab
Is 53:8 for he was c off out of the land
Is 55:13 sign that shall not be c off
Is 56:5 name, that shall not be c off
Is 66:3 as if he c off a dog's neck
Jer 7:28 is c off from their mouth
Jer 7:29 C off thine hair, O Jerusalem, and
Jer 9:21 to c off the children from
Jer 11:19 let us c him off from the land of
Jer 16:6 nor c themselves, nor make
Jer 22:7 they shall c down thy choice
Jer 25:37 are c down because of the fierce
Jer 34:18 when they c the calf in twain, and
Jer 36:23 he c it with the penknife, and
Jer 41:5 having c themselves, with
Jer 44:7 to c off from you man and woman,
Jer 44:8 that ye might c yourselves off,
Jer 44:11 for evil, and to c off all Judah
Jer 46:23 They shall c down her forest,
Jer 47:4 to c off from Tyrus and Zidon
Jer 47:5 Ashkelon is c off with the
Jer 47:5 how long wilt thou c thyself
Jer 48:2 let us c it off from being a
Jer 48:2 Also thou shalt be c down
Jer 48:25 The horn of Moab is c off
Jer 49:26 of war shall be c off in that day
Jer 50:16 C off the sower from Babylon, and
Jer 50:23 of the whole earth c in asunder
Jer 50:30 of war shall be c off in that day
Jer 51:6 be not c off in her iniquity
Jer 51:62 to c it off, that none shall
Lam 2:3 He hath c off in his fierce anger
Lam 3:53 They have c off my life in the
Lam 3:54 then I said, I am c off
Eze 6:6 and your images may be c down
Eze 14:8 I will c him off from the midst
Eze 14:13 will c off man and beast from it
Eze 14:17 so that I c off man and beast from
Eze 14:19 to c off from it man and beast
Eze 14:21 to c off from it man and beast
Eze 16:4 wast born thy navel was not c
Eze 17:9 c off the fruit thereof, that it
Eze 17:17 forts, to c off many persons
Eze 21:3 and will c off from thee the
Eze 21:4 Seeing then that I will c off
Eze 25:7 I will c thee off from the people
Eze 25:13 will c off man and beast from it
Eze 25:16 I will c off the Cherethims, and
Eze 29:8 c off man and beast out of thee
Eze 30:15 I will c off the multitude of No
Eze 31:12 have c him off, and have left him
Eze 35:7 c off from it him that passeth
Eze 37:11 we are c off for our parts
Eze 39:10 neither c down any out of the
Dan 2:5 thereof, ye shall be c in pieces
Dan 2:34 a stone was c out without hands
Dan 2:45 was c out of the mountain without
Dan 3:29 shall be c in pieces, and their
Dan 4:14 c off his branches, shake off his
Dan 9:26 two weeks shall Messiah be c off
Hos 8:4 idols, that they may be c off
Hos 10:7 her king is c off as the foam
Hos 10:15 king of Israel utterly be c off
Joel 1:5 for it is c off from your mouth
Joel 1:9 the drink offering is c off from
Joel 1:16 Is not the meat c off before our
Amos 1:5 c off the inhabitant from the
Amos 1:8 I will c off the inhabitant from
Amos 2:3 I will c off the judge from the
Amos 3:14 horns of the altar shall be c off
Amos 9:1 c them in the head, all of them
Obad 5 by night, (how art thou c off
Obad 9 of Esau may be c off by slaughter
Obad 10 and thou shalt be c off for ever
Obad 14 to c off those of his that did
Mic 5:9 all thine enemies shall be c off
Mic 5:10 that I will c off thy horses out
Mic 5:11 I will c off the cities of thy
Mic 5:12 I will c off witchcrafts out of
Mic 5:13 graven images also will I c off
Nah 1:12 yet thus shall they be c down
Nah 1:14 will I c off the graven image
Nah 1:15 he is utterly c off
Nah 2:13 I will c off thy prey from the
Nah 3:15 the sword shall c thee off
Hab 3:17 shall be c off from the fold
Zeph 1:3 I will c off man from off the
Zeph 1:4 I will c off the remnant of Baal
Zeph 1:11 the merchant people are c down
Zeph 1:11 they that bear silver are c off
Zeph 3:6 I have c off the nations
Zeph 3:7 dwelling should not be c off
Zec 5:3 one that stealeth shall be c off
Zec 5:3 one that sweareth shall be c off
Zec 9:6 I will c off the pride of the
Zec 9:10 I will c off the chariot from
Zec 9:10 and the battle bow shall be c off
Zec 11:8 also I c off in one month
Zec 11:9 is to be c off, let it be c off
Zec 11:10 c it asunder, that I might break
Zec 11:14 Then I c asunder mine other staff
Zec 11:16 not visit those that be c off
Zec 12:3 with it shall be c in pieces
Zec 13:2 that I will c off the names of
Zec 13:8 two parts therein shall be c off
Zec 14:2 shall not be c off from the city
Mal 2:12 The LORD will c off the man that
Mt 5:30 c it off, and cast it from thee
Mt 18:8 c them off, and cast them from
Mt 21:8 others c down branches from the
Mt 24:51 shall c him asunder, and appoint
Mk 9:43 if thy hand offend thee, c it off

Mk 9:45 if thy foot offend thee, *c* it off
Mk 11:8 others *c* down branches off the
Mk 14:47 the high priest, and *c* off his ear
Lk 12:46 will *c* him in sunder, and will
Lk 13:7 *c* it down
Lk 13:9 after that thou shalt *c* it down
Lk 22:50 priest, and *c* off his right ear
Jn 18:10 servant, and *c* off his right ear
Jn 18:26 his kinsman whose ear Peter *c* off
Acts 5:33 they were *c* to the heart, and took
Acts 7:54 they were *c* to the heart, and they
Acts 27:32 Then the soldiers *c* off the ropes
Rom 9:28 *c* it short in righteousness
Rom 11:22 thou also shalt be *c* off
Rom 11:24 For if thou wert *c* out of the
2Cor 11:12 that I may *c* off occasion from
Gal 5:12 were even *c* off which trouble you

**CUTH** *(cuth)* See CUTHAH. *A Babylonian city.*
2Kin 17:30 the men of C made Nergal, and the

**CUTHAH** *(cu'-thah)* See CUTH. *Same as Cuth.*
2Kin 17:24 men from Babylon, and from C

**CUTTETH**
Job 28:10 He *c* out rivers among the rocks
Ps 46:9 the bow, and *c* the spear in sunder
Ps 141:7 the grave's mouth, as when one *c*
Prov 26:6 the hand of a fool *c* off the feet
Jer 10:3 for one *c* a tree out of the
Jer 22:14 chambers, and *c* him out windows

**CUTTING**
Ex 31:5 in *c* of stones, to set them, and
Ex 35:33 in the *c* of stones, to set them,
Is 38:10 I said in the *c* off of my days, I
Hab 2:10 to thy house by *c* off many people
Mk 5:5 crying, and *c* himself with stones

**CYMBALS**
2Sa 6:5 timbrels, and on cornets, and on *c*
1Chr 13:8 and with timbrels, and with *c*
1Chr 15:16 musick, psalteries and harps and *c*
1Chr 15:19 to sound with *c* of brass
1Chr 15:28 and with trumpets, and with *c*
1Chr 16:5 but Asaph made a sound with *c*
1Chr 16:42 *c* for those that should make a
1Chr 25:1 harps, with psalteries, and with *c*
1Chr 25:6 in the house of the LORD, with *c*
2Chr 5:12 arrayed in white linen, having *c*
2Chr 5:13 voice with the trumpets and *c*
2Chr 29:25 in the house of the LORD with *c*
Ezr 3:10 Levites the sons of Asaph with *c*
Neh 12:27 and with singing, with *c*,
Ps 150:5 Praise him upon the loud *c*
Ps 150:5 him upon the high sounding *c*

**CYPRESS**
Is 44:14 him down cedars, and taketh the *c*

**CYPRUS** *(si'-prus) An island off the Syrian coast.*
Acts 4:36 a Levite, and of the country of C
Acts 11:19 travelled as far as Phenice, and C
Acts 11:20 And some of them were men of C
Acts 13:4 and from thence they sailed to C
Acts 15:39 took Mark, and sailed unto C
Acts 21:3 Now when we had discovered C
Acts 21:16 brought with them one Mnason of C
Acts 27:4 from thence, we sailed under C

**CYRENE** *(si-re'-ne)* See CYRENIAN. *A Libyan city.*
Mt 27:32 came out, they found a man of C
Acts 2:10 and in the parts of Libya about C
Acts 11:20 of them were men of Cyprus and C
Acts 13:1 was called Niger, and Lucius of C

**CYRENIAN** *(si-re'-ne-an)* See CYRENIANS. *A native of Cyrene.*
Mk 15:21 And they compel one Simon a C
Lk 23:26 laid hold upon one Simon, a C

**CYRENIANS** *(si-re'-ne-ans)*
Acts 6:9 synagogue of the Libertines, and C

**CYRENIUS** *(si-re'-ne-us) A Roman governor of Syria.*
Lk 2:2 made when C was governor of Syria

**CYRUS** *(si'-rus) Founder of the Persian Empire.*
2Chr 36:22 first year of C king of Persia
2Chr 36:22 up the spirit of C king of Persia
2Chr 36:23 Thus saith C king of Persia, All
Ezr 1:1 first year of C king of Persia
Ezr 1:1 up the spirit of C king of Persia
Ezr 1:2 Thus saith C king of Persia, The
Ezr 1:7 Also C the king brought forth the
Ezr 1:8 Even those did C king of Persia
Ezr 3:7 that they had of C king of Persia
Ezr 4:3 as king C the king of Persia hath
Ezr 4:5 all the days of C king of Persia
Ezr 5:13 But in the first year of C the
Ezr 5:13 C made a decree to build this
Ezr 5:14 those did C the king take out of
Ezr 5:17 that a decree was made of C the
Ezr 6:3 In the first year of C the king
Ezr 6:3 the same C the king made a decree
Ezr 6:14 according to the commandment of C
Is 44:28 That saith of C, He is my
Is 45:1 the LORD to his anointed, to C
Dan 1:21 unto the first year of king C
Dan 6:28 and in the reign of C the Persian
Dan 10:1 In the third year of C king of

# D

**DABAREH** *(dab'-a-reh)* See DABERATH. *A Levitical city in Issachar.*
Josh 21:28 her suburbs, D with her suburbs,

**DABBASHETH** *(dab'-ba-sheth) A border city of Issachar.*
Josh 19:11 sea, and Maralah, and reached to D

**DABERATH** *(dab'-e-rath)* See DABAREH. *Same as Dabareh.*
Josh 19:12 and then goeth out to D, and goeth
1Chr 6:72 her suburbs, D with her suburbs,

**DAGON** See BETH-DAGON, DAGON'S. *A Philistine god.*
Judg 16:23 great sacrifice unto D their god
1Sa 5:2 house of D, and set it by D
1Sa 5:3 D was fallen upon his face to the
1Sa 5:3 And they took D, and set him in his
1Sa 5:4 D was fallen upon his face to the
1Sa 5:4 and the head of D and both the
1Sa 5:4 the stump of D was left to him
1Sa 5:5 neither the priests of D, nor any
1Sa 5:5 of D in Ashdod unto this day
1Sa 5:7 sore upon us, and upon D our god
1Chr 10:10 his head in the temple of D

**DAILY**
Ex 5:13 your *d* tasks, as when there was
Ex 5:19 from your bricks of your *d* task
Ex 16:5 be twice as much as they gather *d*
Num 4:16 the *d* meat offering, and the
Num 28:24 this manner ye shall offer *d*
Num 29:6 the *d* burnt offering, and his meat
Judg 16:16 she pressed him *d* with her words
2Kin 25:30 a *d* rate for every day, all the
2Chr 31:16 his *d* portion for their service
Ezr 3:4 offered the *d* burnt offerings by
Neh 5:18 prepared for me *d* was one ox
Est 3:4 pass, when they spake *d* unto him
Ps 13:2 soul, having sorrow in my heart *d*
Ps 42:10 they say *d* unto me, Where
Ps 56:1 he fighting *d* oppresseth me
Ps 56:2 enemies would *d* swallow me up
Ps 61:8 that I may *d* perform my vows
Ps 68:19 who *d* loadeth us with benefits,
Ps 72:15 and *d* shall he be praised
Ps 74:22 foolish man reproacheth thee *d*
Ps 86:3 for I cry unto thee *d*
Ps 88:9 LORD, I have called *d* upon thee
Ps 88:17 round about me *d* like water
Prov 8:30 I was *d* his delight, rejoicing
Prov 8:34 watching *d* at my gates, waiting
Is 58:2 Yet they seek me *d*, and delight to
Jer 7:25 *d* rising up early and sending them
Jer 20:7 I am in derision *d*, every one
Jer 20:8 unto me, and a derision, *d*
Jer 37:21 that they should give him *d* a
Eze 30:16 and Noph shall have distresses *d*
Eze 45:23 without blemish *d* the seven days
Eze 45:23 of the goats *d* for a sin offering
Eze 46:13 Thou shalt *d* prepare a burnt
Dan 1:5 the king appointed them a *d*
Dan 8:11 by him the *d* sacrifice was taken
Dan 8:12 the *d* sacrifice by reason of
Dan 8:13 vision concerning the *d* sacrifice
Dan 11:31 shall take away the *d* sacrifice
Dan 12:11 And from the time that the *d*
Hos 12:1 he *d* increaseth lies and
Mt 6:11 Give us this day our *d* bread
Mt 26:55 I sat *d* with you teaching in the
Mk 14:49 I was *d* with you in the temple
Lk 9:23 himself, and take up his cross *d*
Lk 11:3 Give us day by day our *d* bread
Lk 19:47 he taught *d* in the temple
Lk 22:53 When I was *d* with you in the
Acts 2:46 continuing *d* with one accord in
Acts 2:47 church *d* such as should be saved
Acts 3:2 whom they laid *d* at the gate of
Acts 5:42 *d* in the temple, and in every
Acts 6:1 neglected in the *d* ministration
Acts 16:5 faith, and increased in number *d*
Acts 17:11 and searched the scriptures *d*
Acts 17:17 in the market *d* with them
Acts 19:9 disputing *d* in the school of one
1Cor 15:31 in Christ Jesus our Lord, I die *d*
2Cor 11:28 that which cometh upon me *d*
Heb 3:13 But exhort one another *d*,
Heb 7:27 Who needeth not *d*, as those high
Heb 10:11 priest standeth *d* ministering
Jas 2:15 be naked, and destitute of *d* food

**DALAIAH** *(dal-a-i'-ah)* See DELAIAH. *A descendant of Judah.*
1Chr 3:24 and Akkub, and Johanan, and D

**DALMANUTHA** *(dal-ma-nu'-thah) A village in Galilee.*
Mk 8:10 and came into the parts of D

**DALMATIA** *(dal-ma'-she-ah) A Roman province west of Macedonia.*
2Ti 4:10 Crescens to Galatia, Titus unto D

**DALPHON** *(dal'-fon) A son of Haman.*
Est 9:7 And Parshandatha, and D,

**DAM**
Ex 22:30 seven days it shall be with his *d*
Lev 22:27 shall be seven days under the *d*
Deut 22:6 the *d* sitting upon the young, or
Deut 22:6 not take the *d* with the young
Deut 22:7 shalt in any wise let the *d* go

**DAMAGE**
Ezr 4:22 why should *d* grow to the hurt of
Est 7:4 not countervail the king's *d*
Prov 26:6 off the feet, and drinketh *d*
Dan 6:2 and the king should have no *d*
Acts 27:10 will be with hurt and much *d*
2Cor 7:9 might receive *d* by us in nothing

**DAMARIS** *(dam'-a-ris) An Athenian convert of Paul.*
Acts 17:34 Areopagite, and a woman named D

**DAMASCENES** *(dam-as-senes') Inhabitants of Damascus.*
2Cor 11:32 the city of the D with a garrison

**DAMASCUS** *(da-mas'-cus)* See DAMASCENES, SYRIA-DAMASCUS. *A city in Syria.*
Gen 14:15 which is on the left hand of D
Gen 15:2 of my house is this Eliezer of D
2Sa 8:5 when the Syrians of D came to
2Sa 8:6 David put garrisons in Syria of D
1Kin 11:24 and they went to D, and dwelt
1Kin 11:24 and dwelt therein, and reigned in D
1Kin 15:18 king of Syria, that dwelt at D
1Kin 19:15 on thy way to the wilderness of D
1Kin 20:34 shalt make streets for thee in D
2Kin 5:12 not Abana and Pharpar, rivers of D

2Kin 8:7 And Elisha came to *D*
2Kin 8:9 even of every good thing of *D*
2Kin 14:28 he warred, and how he recovered *D*
2Kin 16:9 king of Assyria went up against *D*
2Kin 16:10 king Ahaz went to *D* to meet
2Kin 16:10 and saw an altar that was at *D*
2Kin 16:11 that king Ahaz had sent from *D*
2Kin 16:11 it against king Ahaz came from *D*
2Kin 16:12 And when the king was come from *D*
1Chr 18:5 when the Syrians of *D* came to
2Chr 16:2 king of Syria, that dwelt at *D*
2Chr 24:23 spoil of them unto the king of *D*
2Chr 28:5 captives, and brought them to *D*
2Chr 28:23 he sacrificed unto the gods of *D*
Song 7:4 of Lebanon which looketh toward *D*
Is 7:8 For the head of Syria is *D*
Is 7:8 and the head of *D* is Rezin
Is 8:4 and my mother, the riches of *D*
Is 10:9 is not Samaria as *D*
Is 17:1 The burden of *D*
Is 17:1 *D* is taken away from being a city
Is 17:3 Ephraim, and the kingdom from *D*
Jer 49:23 Concerning *D*. Hamath is confounded
Jer 49:24 *D* is waxed feeble, and turneth
Jer 49:27 kindle a fire in the wall of *D*
Eze 27:18 *D* was thy merchant in the
Eze 47:16 which is between the border of *D*
Eze 47:17 be Hazar-enan, the border of *D*
Eze 47:18 measure from Hauran, and from *D*
Eze 48:1 the border of *D* northward
Amos 1:3 For three transgressions of *D*
Amos 1:5 I will break also the bar of *D*
Amos 3:12 of a bed, and in *D* in a couch
Amos 5:27 you to go into captivity beyond *D*
Zec 9:1 *D* shall be the rest thereof
Acts 9:2 letters to *D* to the synagogues
Acts 9:3 as he journeyed, he came near *D*
Acts 9:8 the hand, and brought him into *D*
Acts 9:10 there was a certain disciple at *D*
Acts 9:19 the disciples which were at *D*
Acts 9:22 the Jews which dwelt at *D*
Acts 9:27 boldly at *D* in the name of Jesus
Acts 22:5 unto the brethren, and went to *D*
Acts 22:6 was come nigh unto *D* about noon
Acts 22:10 said unto me, Arise, and go into *D*
Acts 22:11 that were with me, I came into *D*
Acts 26:12 as I went to *D* with authority
Acts 26:20 But shewed first unto them of *D*
2Cor 11:32 In *D* the governor under Aretas
Gal 1:17 Arabia, and returned again unto *D*

**DAMNATION**
Mt 23:14 ye shall receive the greater *d*
Mt 23:33 how can ye escape the *d* of hell
Mk 3:29 but is in danger of eternal *d*
Mk 12:40 these shall receive greater *d*
Lk 20:47 the same shall receive greater *d*
Jn 5:29 evil, unto the resurrection of *d*
Rom 3:8 whose *d* is just
Rom 13:2 shall receive to themselves *d*
1Cor 11:29 drinketh *d* to himself, not
1Ti 5:12 Having *d*, because they have cast
2Pet 2:3 not, and their *d* slumbereth not

**DAMNED**
Mk 16:16 he that believeth not shall be *d*
Rom 14:23 he that doubteth is *d* if he eat
2Th 2:12 That they all might be *d* who

**DAMSEL**
Gen 24:14 that the *d* to whom I shall say,
Gen 24:16 the *d* was very fair to look upon,
Gen 24:28 And the *d* ran, and told them of her
Gen 24:55 Let the *d* abide with us a few
Gen 24:57 And they said, We will call the *d*
Gen 34:3 of Jacob, and he loved the *d*
Gen 34:3 and spake kindly unto the *d*
Gen 34:4 saying, Get me this *d* to wife
Gen 34:12 but give me the *d* to wife
Deut 22:15 Then shall the father of the *d*
Deut 22:19 them unto the father of the *d*
Deut 22:20 virginity be not found for the *d*
Deut 22:21 the *d* to the door of her father's
Deut 22:23 If a *d* that is a virgin be
Deut 22:24 the *d*, because she cried not,
Deut 22:25 find a betrothed *d* in the field
Deut 22:26 But unto the *d* thou shalt do
Deut 22:26 there is in the *d* no sin worthy
Deut 22:27 field, and the betrothed *d* cried
Deut 22:28 If a man find a *d* that is a
Judg 5:30 to every man a *d* or two
Judg 19:3 when the father of the *d* saw him
Ruth 2:5 over the reapers, Whose *d* is this
Ruth 2:6 It is the Moabitish *d* that came
1Kin 1:3 So they sought for a fair *d*
1Kin 1:4 the *d* was very fair, and cherished
Mt 14:11 in a charger, and given to the *d*
Mt 26:69 a *d* came unto him, saying, Thou
Mk 5:39 the *d* is not dead, but sleepeth
Mk 5:40 the father and the mother of the *d*
Mk 5:40 entereth in where the *d* was lying
Mk 5:41 And he took the *d* by the hand
Mk 5:41 which is, being interpreted, *D*
Mk 5:42 And straightway the *d* arose
Mk 6:22 him, the king said unto the *d*
Mk 6:28 in a charger, and gave it to the *d*
Mk 6:28 the *d* gave it to her mother
Jn 18:17 Then saith the *d* that kept the
Acts 12:13 a *d* came to hearken, named Rhoda
Acts 16:16 a certain *d* possessed with a

**DAN** *(dan)* See DANITES, DAN-JAAN, LAISH, MAHANEH-DAN.
*1. A son of Jacob.*
Gen 30:6 therefore called she his name *D*
Gen 35:25 *D*, and Naphtali
Gen 46:23 And the sons of *D*
Gen 49:16 *D* shall judge his people, as one
Gen 49:17 *D* shall be a serpent by the way,
Ex 1:4 *D*, and Naphtali, Gad, and Asher
Josh 19:47 therein, and called Leshem, *D*
Josh 19:47 after the name of *D* their father
Judg 18:29 after the name of *D* their father
1Chr 2:2 *D*, Joseph, and Benjamin, Naphtali,
Eze 27:19 *D* also and Javan going to and fro
*2. A city and tribal territory in northern Canaan.*
Gen 14:14 eighteen, and pursued them unto *D*
Deut 34:1 all the land of Gilead, unto *D*
Judg 18:29 called the name of the city *D*
Judg 20:1 from *D* even to Beer-sheba, with
1Sa 3:20 all Israel from *D* even to
2Sa 3:10 from *D* even to Beer-sheba
2Sa 17:11 from *D* even to Beer-sheba, as the
2Sa 24:2 from *D* even to Beer-sheba, and
2Sa 24:15 from *D* even to Beer-sheba seventy
1Kin 4:25 from *D* even to Beer-sheba, all
1Kin 12:29 Beth-el, and the other put he in *D*
1Kin 12:30 before the one, even unto *D*
1Kin 15:20 of Israel, and smote Ijon, and *D*
2Kin 10:29 in Beth-el, and that were in *D*
1Chr 21:2 Israel from Beer-sheba even to *D*
2Chr 16:4 and they smote Ijon, and *D*, and
2Chr 30:5 Israel, from Beer-sheba even to *D*
Jer 4:15 For a voice declareth from *D*
Jer 8:16 of his horses was heard from *D*
Eze 48:1 a portion for *D*
Eze 48:2 And by the border of *D*, from the
Eze 48:32 gate of Benjamin, one gate of *D*
Amos 8:14 of Samaria, and say, Thy god, O *D*
*3. Tribe descended from Dan 1.*
Ex 31:6 of Ahisamach, of the tribe of *D*
Ex 35:34 of Ahisamach, of the tribe of *D*
Ex 38:23 of Ahisamach, of the tribe of *D*
Lev 24:11 of Dibri, of the tribe of *D*
Num 1:12 Of *D*; Ahiezer the son
Num 1:38 Of the children of *D*, by their
Num 1:39 of them, even of the tribe of *D*
Num 2:25 The standard of the camp of *D*
Num 2:25 of *D* shall be Ahiezer the son of
Num 2:31 of *D* were an hundred thousand
Num 7:66 prince of the children of *D*
Num 10:25 of the children of *D* set forward
Num 13:12 Of the tribe of *D*, Ammiel the son
Num 26:42 sons of *D* after their families
Num 26:42 of *D* after their families
Num 34:22 of the tribe of the children of *D*
Deut 27:13 Gad, and Asher, and Zebulun, *D*
Deut 33:22 Dan he said, *D* is a lion's whelp
Josh 19:40 of *D* according to their families
Josh 19:47 of *D* went out too little for them
Josh 19:47 therefore the children of *D* went
Josh 19:48 of *D* according to their families
Josh 21:5 Ephraim, and out of the tribe of *D*
Josh 21:23 And out of the tribe of *D*, Eltekeh
Judg 1:34 children of *D* into the mountain
Judg 5:17 why did *D* remain in ships
Judg 13:25 in the camp of *D* between Zorah
Judg 18:2 the children of *D* sent of their
Judg 18:16 which were of the children of *D*
Judg 18:22 and overtook the children of *D*
Judg 18:23 they cried unto the children of *D*
Judg 18:25 the children of *D* said unto him
Judg 18:26 the children of *D* went their way
Judg 18:30 the children of *D* set up the
Judg 18:30 were priests to the tribe of *D*
1Chr 27:22 Of *D*, Azareel the son of Jeroham
2Chr 2:14 of a woman of the daughters of *D*

**DANCE**
Judg 21:21 of Shiloh come out to *d* in dances
Job 21:11 like a flock, and their children *d*
Ps 149:3 Let them praise his name in the *d*
Ps 150:4 Praise him with the timbrel and *d*
Eccl 3:4 a time to mourn, and a time to *d*
Is 13:21 there, and satyrs shall *d* there
Jer 31:13 shall the virgin rejoice in the *d*
Lam 5:15 our *d* is turned into mourning

**DANCED**
Judg 21:23 to their number, of them that *d*
2Sa 6:14 David *d* before the LORD with all
Mt 11:17 piped unto you, and ye have not *d*
Mt 14:6 of Herodias *d* before them
Mk 6:22 the said Herodias came in, and *d*
Lk 7:32 piped unto you, and ye have not *d*

**DANCES**
Ex 15:20 after her with timbrels and with *d*
Judg 11:34 meet him with timbrels and with *d*
Judg 21:21 of Shiloh come out to dance in *d*
1Sa 21:11 sing one to another of him in *d*
1Sa 29:5 they sang one to another in *d*
Jer 31:4 shalt go forth in the *d* of them

**DANCING**
Ex 32:19 that he saw the calf, and the *d*
1Sa 18:6 cities of Israel, singing and *d*
1Sa 30:16 earth, eating and drinking, and *d*
2Sa 6:16 leaping and *d* before the LORD
1Chr 15:29 out at a window saw king David *d*
Ps 30:11 turned for me my mourning into *d*
Lk 15:25 the house, he heard musick and *d*

**DANGER**
Mt 5:21 shall be in *d* of the judgment
Mt 5:22 shall be in *d* of the judgment
Mt 5:22 shall be in *d* of the council
Mt 5:22 shall be in *d* of hell fire
Mk 3:29 but is in *d* of eternal damnation
Acts 19:27 craft is in *d* to be set at nought
Acts 19:40 For we are in *d* to be called in

**DANIEL** See BELTESHAZZAR.
*1. A son of David.*
1Chr 3:1 the second *D*, of Abigail the
*2. An Israelite who renewed the covenant.*
Ezr 8:2 of the sons of Ithamar; *D*
Neh 10:6 *D*, Ginnethon, Baruch,
*3. A major prophet.*
Eze 14:14 Though these three men, Noah, *D*
Eze 14:20 Though Noah, *D*, and Job, were in
Eze 28:3 Behold, thou art wiser than *D*
Dan 1:6 were of the children of Judah, *D*
Dan 1:7 for he gave unto *D* the name of
Dan 1:8 But *D* purposed in his heart that
Dan 1:9 Now God had brought *D* into favour
Dan 1:10 prince of the eunuchs said unto *D*
Dan 1:11 Then said *D* to Melzar, whom the
Dan 1:11 of the eunuchs had set over *D*
Dan 1:17 *D* had understanding in all
Dan 1:19 them all was found none like *D*
Dan 1:21 *D* continued even unto the first
Dan 2:13 and they sought *D* and his fellows
Dan 2:14 Then *D* answered with counsel and
Dan 2:15 Arioch made the thing known to *D*
Dan 2:16 Then *D* went in, and desired of the
Dan 2:17 Then *D* went to his house, and made
Dan 2:18 that *D* and his fellows should not
Dan 2:19 revealed unto *D* in a night vision
Dan 2:19 Then *D* blessed the God of heaven
Dan 2:20 *D* answered and said, Blessed be
Dan 2:24 Therefore *D* went in unto Arioch,
Dan 2:25 Then Arioch brought in *D* before
Dan 2:26 The king answered and said to *D*
Dan 2:27 *D* answered in the presence of the
Dan 2:46 upon his face, and worshipped *D*
Dan 2:47 The king answered unto *D*, and said
Dan 2:48 Then the king made *D* a great man
Dan 2:49 Then *D* requested of the king, and
Dan 2:49 but *D* sat in the gate of the king
Dan 4:8 But at the last *D* came in before
Dan 4:19 Then *D*, whose name was
Dan 5:12 doubts, were found in the same *D*
Dan 5:12 now let *D* be called, and he will
Dan 5:13 Then was *D* brought in before the

Dan 5:13 said unto Daniel, Art thou that *D*
Dan 5:17 Then *D* answered and said before
Dan 5:29 and they clothed *D* with scarlet
Dan 6:2 of whom *D* was first
Dan 6:3 Then this *D* was preferred above
Dan 6:4 against *D* concerning the kingdom
Dan 6:5 find any occasion against this *D*
Dan 6:10 Now when *D* knew that the writing
Dan 6:11 found *D* praying and making
Dan 6:13 and said before the king, That *D*
Dan 6:14 set his heart on *D* to deliver him
Dan 6:16 king commanded, and they brought *D*
Dan 6:16 Now the king spake and said unto *D*
Dan 6:17 might not be changed concerning *D*
Dan 6:20 with a lamentable voice unto *D*
Dan 6:20 king spake and said to Daniel, O *D*
Dan 6:21 Then said *D* unto the king, O king
Dan 6:23 should take *D* up out of the den
Dan 6:23 So *D* was taken up out of the den,
Dan 6:24 those men which had accused *D*
Dan 6:26 and fear before the God of *D*
Dan 6:27 who hath delivered *D* from the
Dan 6:28 So this *D* prospered in the reign
Dan 7:1 king of Babylon *D* had a dream
Dan 7:2 *D* spake and said, I saw in my
Dan 7:15 I *D* was grieved in my spirit in
Dan 7:28 As for me *D*, my cogitations much
Dan 8:1 appeared unto me, even unto me *D*
Dan 8:15 it came to pass, when I, even I *D*
Dan 8:27 I *D* fainted, and was sick certain
Dan 9:2 the first year of his reign I *D*
Dan 9:22 and talked with me, and said, O *D*
Dan 10:1 a thing was revealed unto *D*
Dan 10:2 In those days I *D* was mourning
Dan 10:7 And I *D* alone saw the vision
Dan 10:11 And he said unto me, O *D*, a man
Dan 10:12 Then said he unto me, Fear not, *D*
Dan 12:4 But thou, O *D*, shut up the words,
Dan 12:5 Then I *D* looked, and, behold,
Dan 12:9 And he said, Go thy way, *D*
Mt 24:15 spoken of by *D* the prophet
Mk 13:14 spoken of by *D* the prophet

**DANITES** *(dan'-ites) Descendants of Dan 1.*

Judg 13:2 of Zorah, of the family of the *D*
Judg 18:1 *D* sought them an inheritance to
Judg 18:11 thence of the family of the *D*
1Chr 12:35 of the *D* expert in war twenty and

**DAN-JAAN** *(dan-ja'-an) A place between Gilead and Zidon.*

2Sa 24:6 and they came to *D*, and about to

**DANNAH** *(dan'-nah) A city in Judah.*

Josh 15:49 And *D*, and Kirjath-sannah, which is

**DARA** *(da'-rah)* See DARDA. *A son of Zerah.*

1Chr 2:6 Ethan, and Heman, and Calcol, and *D*

**DARDA** *(dar'-dah)* See DARA. *A wise man.*

1Kin 4:31 and Heman, and Chalcol, and *D*

**DARIUS** *(da-ri'-us)*

*1. Darius Hystaspes, king of Persia.*

Ezr 4:5 the reign of *D* king of Persia
Ezr 4:24 of the reign of *D* king of Persia
Ezr 5:5 cease, till the matter came to *D*
Ezr 5:6 the river, sent unto *D* the king
Ezr 5:7 Unto *D* the king, all peace
Ezr 6:1 Then *D* the king made a decree, and
Ezr 6:12 I *D* have made a decree
Ezr 6:13 to that which *D* the king had sent
Ezr 6:14 to the commandment of Cyrus, and *D*
Ezr 6:15 year of the reign of *D* the king
Hag 1:1 In the second year of *D* the king
Hag 1:15 in the second year of *D* the king
Hag 2:10 month, in the second year of *D*
Zec 1:1 month, in the second year of *D*
Zec 1:7 Sebat, in the second year of *D*
Zec 7:1 pass in the fourth year of king *D*

*2. Darius Nothus, king of Persia.*

Neh 12:22 to the reign of *D* the Persian

*3. Cyaxares, king of Media.*

Dan 5:31 *D* the Median took the kingdom,
Dan 6:1 It pleased *D* to set over the
Dan 6:6 and said thus unto him, King *D*
Dan 6:9 Wherefore king *D* signed the
Dan 6:25 Then king *D* wrote unto all people
Dan 6:28 prospered in the reign of *D*
Dan 9:1 year of *D* the son of Ahasuerus
Dan 11:1 I in the first year of *D* the Mede

**DARK**

Gen 15:17 the sun went down, and it was *d*
Lev 13:6 if the plague be somewhat *d*
Lev 13:21 than the skin, but be somewhat *d*
Lev 13:26 the other skin, but be somewhat *d*
Lev 13:28 in the skin, but it be somewhat *d*
Lev 13:56 the plague be somewhat *d* after
Num 12:8 apparently, and not in *d* speeches
Josh 2:5 of the gate, when it was *d*
2Sa 22:12 *d* waters, and thick clouds of the
Neh 13:19 began to be *d* before the sabbath
Job 3:9 of the twilight thereof be *d*
Job 12:25 They grope in the *d* without light
Job 18:6 shall be *d* in his tabernacle
Job 22:13 can he judge through the *d* cloud
Job 24:16 In the *d* they dig through houses,
Ps 18:11 round about him were *d* waters
Ps 35:6 Let their way be *d* and slippery
Ps 49:4 I will open my *d* saying upon the
Ps 74:20 for the *d* places of the earth are
Ps 78:2 I will utter *d* sayings of old
Ps 88:12 thy wonders be known in the *d*
Ps 105:28 He sent darkness, and made it *d*
Prov 1:6 of the wise, and their *d* sayings
Prov 7:9 evening, in the black and *d* night
Is 29:15 LORD, and their works are in the *d*
Is 45:19 in a *d* place of the earth
Jer 13:16 feet stumble upon the *d* mountains
Lam 3:6 He hath set me in *d* places
Eze 8:12 the house of Israel do in the *d*
Eze 32:7 and make the stars thereof *d*
Eze 32:8 of heaven will I make *d* over thee
Eze 34:12 scattered in the cloudy and *d* day
Dan 8:23 and understanding *d* sentences
Joel 2:10 the sun and the moon shall be *d*
Amos 5:8 and maketh the day *d* with night
Amos 5:20 even very *d*, and no brightness in
Mic 3:6 and it shall be *d* unto you
Mic 3:6 and the day shall be *d* over them
Zec 14:6 light shall not be clear, nor *d*
Lk 11:36 full of light, having no part *d*
Jn 6:17 And it was now *d*, and Jesus was not
Jn 20:1 early, when it was yet *d*, unto
2Pet 1:19 a light that shineth in a *d* place

**DARKENED**

Ex 10:15 earth, so that the land was *d*
Ps 69:23 Let their eyes be *d*, that they
Eccl 12:2 the moon, or the stars, be not *d*
Eccl 12:3 that look out of the windows be *d*
Is 5:30 the light is *d* in the heavens
Is 9:19 the LORD of hosts is the land *d*
Is 13:10 the sun shall be *d* in his going
Is 24:11 all joy is *d*, the mirth of the
Eze 30:18 also the day shall be *d*, when I
Joel 3:15 The sun and the moon shall be *d*
Zec 11:17 his right eye shall be utterly *d*
Mt 24:29 of those days shall the sun be *d*
Mk 13:24 tribulation, the sun shall be *d*
Lk 23:45 And the sun was *d*, and the veil of
Rom 1:21 and their foolish heart was *d*
Rom 11:10 Let their eyes be *d*, that they
Eph 4:18 Having the understanding *d*
Rev 8:12 as the third part of them was *d*
Rev 9:2 the air were *d* by reason of the

**DARKNESS**

Gen 1:2 *d* was upon the face of the deep
Gen 1:4 God divided the light from the *d*
Gen 1:5 Day, and the *d* he called Night
Gen 1:18 and to divide the light from the *d*
Gen 15:12 horror of great *d* fell upon him
Ex 10:21 that there may be *d* over the land
Ex 10:21 Egypt, even *d* which may be felt
Ex 10:22 there was a thick *d* in all the
Ex 14:20 *d* to them, but it gave light by
Ex 20:21 unto the thick *d* where God was
Deut 4:11 with *d*, clouds, and thick *d*
Deut 5:22 of the cloud, and of the thick *d*
Deut 5:23 voice out of the midst of the *d*
Deut 28:29 as the blind gropeth in *d*
Josh 24:7 he put *d* between you and the
1Sa 2:9 the wicked shall be silent in *d*
2Sa 22:10 and *d* was under his feet
2Sa 22:12 he made *d* pavilions round about
2Sa 22:29 and the LORD will lighten my *d*
1Kin 8:12 he would dwell in the thick *d*
2Chr 6:1 he would dwell in the thick *d*
Job 3:4 Let that day be *d*
Job 3:5 Let *d* and the shadow of death
Job 3:6 that night, let *d* seize upon it
Job 5:14 They meet with *d* in the daytime
Job 10:21 not return, even to the land of *d*
Job 10:22 A land of *d*, as *d* itself
Job 10:22 order, and where the light is as *d*
Job 12:22 discovereth deep things out of *d*
Job 15:22 not that he shall return out of *d*
Job 15:23 the day of *d* is ready at his hand
Job 15:30 He shall not depart out of *d*
Job 17:12 the light is short because of *d*
Job 17:13 I have made my bed in the *d*
Job 18:18 shall be driven from light into *d*
Job 19:8 and he hath set *d* in my paths
Job 20:26 All *d* shall be hid in his secret
Job 22:11 Or *d*, that thou canst not see
Job 23:17 I was not cut off before the *d*
Job 23:17 he covered the *d* from my face
Job 28:3 He setteth an end to *d*, and
Job 28:3 the stones of *d*, and the shadow of
Job 29:3 by his light I walked through *d*
Job 30:26 I waited for light, there came *d*
Job 34:22 There is no *d*, nor shadow of
Job 37:19 order our speech by reason of *d*
Job 38:9 thick *d* a swaddlingband for it,
Job 38:19 and as for *d*, where is the place
Ps 18:9 and *d* was under his feet
Ps 18:11 He made *d* his secret place
Ps 18:28 LORD my God will enlighten my *d*
Ps 82:5 they walk on in *d*
Ps 88:6 laid me in the lowest pit, in *d*
Ps 88:18 me, and mine acquaintance into *d*
Ps 91:6 the pestilence that walketh in *d*
Ps 97:2 Clouds and *d* are round about him
Ps 104:20 Thou makest *d*, and it is night
Ps 105:28 He sent *d*, and made it dark
Ps 107:10 Such as sit in *d* and in the shadow
Ps 107:14 He brought them out of *d* and the
Ps 112:4 there ariseth light in the *d*
Ps 139:11 Surely the *d* shall cover me
Ps 139:12 the *d* hideth not from thee
Ps 139:12 the *d* and the light are both alike
Ps 143:3 he hath made me to dwell in *d*
Prov 2:13 to walk in the ways of *d*
Prov 4:19 The way of the wicked is as *d*
Prov 20:20 shall be put out in obscure *d*
Eccl 2:13 as far as light excelleth *d*
Eccl 2:14 but the fool walketh in *d*
Eccl 5:17 All his days also he eateth in *d*
Eccl 6:4 in with vanity, and departeth in *d*
Eccl 6:4 his name shall be covered with *d*
Eccl 11:8 let him remember the days of *d*
Is 5:20 that put *d* for light, and light
Is 5:20 for light, and light for *d*
Is 5:30 one look unto the land, behold *d*
Is 8:22 and behold trouble and *d*, dimness
Is 8:22 and they shall be driven to *d*
Is 9:2 in *d* have seen a great light
Is 29:18 see out of obscurity, and out of *d*
Is 42:7 them that sit in *d* out of the
Is 42:16 I will make *d* light before them,
Is 45:3 will give thee the treasures of *d*
Is 45:7 I form the light, and create *d*
Is 47:5 thou silent, and get thee into *d*
Is 49:9 to them that are in *d*, Shew
Is 50:10 of his servant, that walketh in *d*
Is 58:10 and thy *d* be as the noonday
Is 59:9 for brightness, but we walk in *d*
Is 60:2 the *d* shall cover the earth, and
Is 60:2 the earth, and gross *d* the people
Jer 2:31 a land of *d*
Jer 13:16 LORD your God, before he cause *d*
Jer 13:16 of death, and make it gross *d*
Jer 23:12 them as slippery ways in the *d*
Lam 3:2 hath led me, and brought me into *d*
Eze 32:8 set *d* upon thy land, saith the
Dan 2:22 he knoweth what is in the *d*
Joel 2:2 A day of *d* and of gloominess, a
Joel 2:2 a day of clouds and of thick *d*
Joel 2:31 The sun shall be turned into *d*
Amos 4:13 that maketh the morning *d*
Amos 5:18 the day of the LORD is *d*, and not
Amos 5:20 not the day of the LORD be *d*
Mic 7:8 when I sit in *d*, the LORD shall
Nah 1:8 *d* shall pursue his enemies
Zeph 1:15 and desolation, a day of *d*
Zeph 1:15 a day of clouds and thick *d*
Mt 4:16 which sat in *d* saw great light
Mt 6:23 thy whole body shall be full of *d*
Mt 6:23 be *d*, how great is that *d*
Mt 8:12 shall be cast out into outer *d*
Mt 10:27 What I tell you in *d*, that speak

Mt 22:13 away, and cast him into outer *d*
Mt 25:30 unprofitable servant into outer *d*
Mt 27:45 was *d* over all the land unto the
Mk 15:33 there was *d* over the whole land
Lk 1:79 give light to them that sit in *d*
Lk 11:34 evil, thy body also is full of *d*
Lk 11:35 light which is in thee be not *d*
Lk 12:3 in *d* shall be heard in the light
Lk 22:53 is your hour, and the power of *d*
Lk 23:44 there was a *d* over all the earth
Jn 1:5 And the light shineth in *d*
Jn 1:5 the *d* comprehended it not
Jn 3:19 men loved *d* rather than light,
Jn 8:12 followeth me shall not walk in *d*
Jn 12:35 the light, lest *d* come upon you
Jn 12:35 for he that walketh in *d* knoweth
Jn 12:46 on me should not abide in *d*
Acts 2:20 The sun shall be turned into *d*
Acts 13:11 there fell on him a mist and a *d*
Acts 26:18 and to turn them from *d* to light
Rom 2:19 a light of them which are in *d*
Rom 13:12 therefore cast off the works of *d*
1Cor 4:5 to light the hidden things of *d*
2Cor 4:6 the light to shine out of *d*
2Cor 6:14 what communion hath light with *d*
Eph 5:8 For ye were sometimes *d*, but now
Eph 5:11 with the unfruitful works of *d*
Eph 6:12 the rulers of the *d* of this world
Col 1:13 delivered us from the power of *d*
1Th 5:4 But ye, brethren, are not in *d*
1Th 5:5 we are not of the night, nor of *d*
Heb 12:18 fire, nor unto blackness, and *d*
1Pet 2:9 of *d* into his marvellous light
2Pet 2:4 delivered them into chains of *d*
2Pet 2:17 to whom the mist of *d* is reserved
1Jn 1:5 light, and in him is no *d* at all
1Jn 1:6 fellowship with him, and walk in *d*
1Jn 2:8 because the *d* is past, and the
1Jn 2:9 brother, is in *d* even until now
1Jn 2:11 is in *d*, and walketh in *d*
1Jn 2:11 because that *d* hath blinded his
Jude 6 in everlasting chains under *d*
Jude 13 the blackness of *d* for ever
Rev 16:10 and his kingdom was full of *d*

**DARKON** *(dar'-kon) A family of exiles.*
Ezr 2:56 of Jaalah, the children of *D*
Neh 7:58 of Jaala, the children of *D*

**DASH**
2Kin 8:12 wilt *d* their children, and rip up
Ps 2:9 thou shalt *d* them in pieces like
Ps 91:12 lest thou *d* thy foot against a
Is 13:18 Their bows also shall *d* the young
Jer 13:14 I will *d* them one against another
Mt 4:6 lest at any time thou *d* thy foot
Lk 4:11 lest at any time thou *d* thy foot

**DASHED**
Ex 15:6 hath *d* in pieces the enemy
Is 13:16 be *d* to pieces before their eyes
Hos 10:14 the mother was *d* in pieces upon
Hos 13:16 infants shall be *d* in pieces
Nah 3:10 her young children also were *d* in

**DATHAN** *(da'-than) A conspirator against Moses.*
Num 16:1 of Kohath, the son of Levi, and *D*
Num 16:12 And Moses sent to call *D* and Abiram
Num 16:24 about the tabernacle of Korah, *D*
Num 16:25 And Moses rose up and went unto *D*
Num 16:27 from the tabernacle of Korah, *D*
Num 16:27 *D* and Abiram came out, and stood
Num 26:9 Nemuel, and *D*, and Abiram
Num 26:9 This is that *D* and Abiram, which
Deut 11:6 And what he did unto *D* and Abiram,
Ps 106:17 earth opened and swallowed up *D*

**DAUBED**
Ex 2:3 *d* it with slime and with pitch, and
Eze 13:10 others *d* it with untempered
Eze 13:12 daubing wherewith ye have *d* it
Eze 13:14 ye have *d* with untempered morter
Eze 13:15 upon them that have *d* it with
Eze 13:15 no more, neither they that *d* it
Eze 22:28 her prophets have *d* them with

**DAUGHTER**
Gen 11:29 the *d* of Haran, the father of
Gen 11:31 son's son, and Sarai his *d* in law
Gen 20:12 she is the *d* of my father, but
Gen 20:12 but not the *d* of my mother
Gen 24:23 And said, Whose *d* art thou
Gen 24:24 I am the *d* of Bethuel the son of
Gen 24:47 her, and said, Whose *d* art thou
Gen 24:47 The *d* of Bethuel, Nahor's son,
Gen 24:48 master's brother's *d* unto his son
Gen 25:20 the *d* of Bethuel the Syrian of
Gen 26:34 Judith the *d* of Beeri the Hittite
Gen 26:34 Bashemath the *d* of Elon the
Gen 28:9 the *d* of Ishmael Abraham's son
Gen 29:6 Rachel his *d* cometh with the
Gen 29:10 when Jacob saw Rachel the *d* of
Gen 29:18 years for Rachel thy younger *d*
Gen 29:23 evening, that he took Leah his *d*
Gen 29:24 Laban gave unto his *d* Leah Zilpah
Gen 29:28 him Rachel his *d* to wife also
Gen 29:29 Laban gave to Rachel his *d* Bilhah
Gen 30:21 And afterwards she bare a *d*
Gen 34:1 And Dinah the *d* of Leah, which she
Gen 34:3 clave unto Dinah the *d* of Jacob
Gen 34:5 that he had defiled Dinah his *d*
Gen 34:7 in Israel in lying with Jacob's *d*
Gen 34:8 my son Shechem longeth for your *d*
Gen 34:17 then will we take our *d*, and we
Gen 34:19 he had delight in Jacob's *d*
Gen 36:2 Adah the *d* of Elon the Hittite,
Gen 36:2 Aholibamah the *d* of Anah the
Gen 36:2 Anah the *d* of Zibeon the Hivite
Gen 36:3 And Bashemath Ishmael's *d*, sister
Gen 36:14 *d* of Anah the *d* of Zibeon
Gen 36:18 came of Aholibamah the *d* of Anah
Gen 36:25 and Aholibamah the *d* of Anah
Gen 36:39 the *d* of Matred, the *d* of
Gen 38:2 Judah saw there a *d* of a certain
Gen 38:11 said Judah to Tamar his *d* in law
Gen 38:12 in process of time the *d* of Shuah
Gen 38:16 not that she was his *d* in law
Gen 38:24 Tamar thy *d* in law hath played
Gen 41:45 the *d* of Poti-pherah priest of On
Gen 41:50 came, which Asenath the *d* of
Gen 46:15 in Padan-aram, with his *d* Dinah
Gen 46:18 whom Laban gave to Leah his *d*
Gen 46:20 Ephraim, which Asenath the *d* of
Gen 46:25 Laban gave unto Rachel his *d*
Ex 1:16 but if it be a *d*, then she shall
Ex 1:22 every *d* ye shall save alive
Ex 2:1 Levi, and took to wife a *d* of Levi
Ex 2:5 the *d* of Pharaoh came down to
Ex 2:7 said his sister to Pharaoh's *d*
Ex 2:8 Pharaoh's *d* said to her, Go
Ex 2:9 Pharaoh's *d* said unto her, Take
Ex 2:10 she brought him unto Pharaoh's *d*
Ex 2:21 and he gave Moses Zipporah his *d*
Ex 6:23 *d* of Amminadab, sister of Naashon
Ex 20:10 thou, nor thy son, nor thy *d*
Ex 21:7 if a man sell his *d* to be a
Ex 21:31 gored a son, or have gored a *d*
Lev 12:6 fulfilled, for a son, or for a *d*
Lev 18:9 the *d* of thy father, or *d*
Lev 18:10 *d*, or of thy daughter's *d*
Lev 18:11 of thy father's wife's *d*,
Lev 18:15 the nakedness of thy *d* in law
Lev 18:17 the nakedness of a woman and her *d*
Lev 18:17 son's *d*, or her daughter's *d*
Lev 19:29 Do not prostitute thy *d*, to cause
Lev 20:12 And if a man lie with his *d* in law
Lev 20:17 father's *d*, or his mother's *d*
Lev 21:2 and for his son, and for his *d*
Lev 21:9 the *d* of any priest, if she
Lev 22:12 If the priest's *d* also be married
Lev 22:13 But if the priest's *d* be a widow
Lev 24:11 the *d* of Dibri, of the tribe of
Num 25:15 was slain was Cozbi, the *d* of Zur
Num 25:18 the *d* of a prince of Midian,
Num 26:46 the name of the *d* of Asher was
Num 26:59 the *d* of Levi, whom her mother
Num 27:8 inheritance to pass unto his *d*
Num 27:9 And if he have no *d*, then ye shall
Num 30:16 wife, between the father and his *d*
Num 36:8 And every *d*, that possesseth an
Deut 5:14 thou, nor thy son, nor thy *d*
Deut 7:3 thy *d* thou shalt not give unto
Deut 7:3 nor his *d* shalt thou take unto
Deut 12:18 thou, and thy son, and thy *d*
Deut 13:6 thy mother, or thy son, or thy *d*
Deut 16:11 God, thou, and thy son, and thy *d*
Deut 16:14 feast, thou, and thy son, and thy *d*
Deut 18:10 or his *d* to pass through the fire
Deut 22:16 I gave my *d* unto this man to wife
Deut 22:17 saying, I found not thy *d* a maid
Deut 27:22 the *d* of his father, or the
Deut 27:22 father, or the *d* of his mother
Deut 28:56 toward her son, and toward her *d*
Josh 15:16 will I give Achsah my *d* to wife
Josh 15:17 he gave him Achsah his *d* to wife
Judg 1:12 will I give Achsah my *d* to wife
Judg 1:13 he gave him Achsah his *d* to wife
Judg 11:34 his *d* came out to meet him with
Judg 11:34 her he had neither son nor *d*
Judg 11:35 his clothes, and said, Alas, my *d*
Judg 11:40 went yearly to lament the *d* of
Judg 19:24 Behold, here is my *d* a maiden
Judg 21:1 give his *d* unto Benjamin to wife
Ruth 1:22 her *d* in law, with her, which
Ruth 2:2 And she said unto her, Go, my *d*
Ruth 2:8 unto Ruth, Hearest thou not, my *d*
Ruth 2:20 And Naomi said unto her *d* in law
Ruth 2:22 *d* in law, It is good, my *d*
Ruth 3:1 mother in law said unto her, My *d*
Ruth 3:10 Blessed be thou of the LORD, my *d*
Ruth 3:11 And now, my *d*, fear not
Ruth 3:16 law, she said, Who art thou, my *d*
Ruth 3:18 Then said she, Sit still, my *d*
Ruth 4:15 for thy *d* in law, which loveth
1Sa 1:16 thine handmaid for a *d* of Belial
1Sa 4:19 his *d* in law, Phinehas' wife, was
1Sa 14:50 was Ahinoam, the *d* of Ahimaaz
1Sa 17:25 riches, and will give him his *d*
1Sa 18:17 to David, Behold my elder *d* Merab
1Sa 18:19 at the time when Merab Saul's *d*
1Sa 18:20 And Michal Saul's *d* loved David
1Sa 18:27 gave him Michal his *d* to wife
1Sa 18:28 and that Michal Saul's *d* loved him
1Sa 25:44 But Saul had given Michal his *d*
2Sa 3:3 the *d* of Talmai king of Geshur
2Sa 3:7 name was Rizpah, the *d* of Aiah
2Sa 3:13 thou first bring Michal Saul's *d*
2Sa 6:16 Michal Saul's *d* looked through a
2Sa 6:20 Michal the *d* of Saul came out to
2Sa 6:23 Therefore Michal the *d* of Saul
2Sa 11:3 the *d* of Eliam, the wife of Uriah
2Sa 12:3 his bosom, and was unto him as a *d*
2Sa 14:27 were born three sons, and one *d*
2Sa 17:25 in to Abigail the *d* of Nahash
2Sa 21:8 two sons of Rizpah the *d* of Aiah
2Sa 21:8 five sons of Michal the *d* of Saul
2Sa 21:10 Rizpah the *d* of Aiah took
2Sa 21:11 David what Rizpah the *d* of Aiah
1Kin 3:1 of Egypt, and took Pharaoh's *d*
1Kin 4:11 Taphath the *d* of Solomon to wife
1Kin 4:15 Basmath the *d* of Solomon to wife
1Kin 7:8 also an house for Pharaoh's *d*
1Kin 9:16 given it for a present unto his *d*
1Kin 9:24 But Pharaoh's *d* came up out of
1Kin 11:1 together with the *d* of Pharaoh
1Kin 15:2 was Maachah, the *d* of Abishalom
1Kin 15:10 was Maachah, the *d* of Abishalom
1Kin 16:31 the *d* of Ethbaal king of the
1Kin 22:42 name was Azubah the *d* of Shilhi
2Kin 8:18 for the *d* of Ahab was his wife
2Kin 8:26 the *d* of Omri king of Israel
2Kin 9:34 for she is a king's *d*
2Kin 11:2 the *d* of king Joram, sister of
2Kin 14:9 Give thy *d* to my son to wife
2Kin 15:33 name was Jerusha, the *d* of Zadok
2Kin 18:2 also was Abi, the *d* of Zachariah
2Kin 19:21 The virgin the *d* of Zion hath
2Kin 19:21 the *d* of Jerusalem hath shaken
2Kin 21:19 the *d* of Haruz of Jotbah
2Kin 22:1 the *d* of Adaiah of Boscath
2Kin 23:10 his *d* to pass through the fire to
2Kin 23:31 the *d* of Jeremiah of Libnah
2Kin 23:36 the *d* of Pedaiah of Rumah
2Kin 24:8 the *d* of Elnathan of Jerusalem
2Kin 24:18 the *d* of Jeremiah of Libnah
1Chr 1:50 the *d* of Matred, the *d* of
1Chr 2:3 of the *d* of Shua the Canaanitess
1Chr 2:4 Tamar his *d* in law bare him
1Chr 2:21 *d* of Machir the father of Gilead
1Chr 2:35 Sheshan gave his *d* to Jarha his
1Chr 2:49 and the *d* of Caleb was Achsa
1Chr 3:2 the *d* of Talmai king of Geshur
1Chr 3:5 of Bath-shua the *d* of Ammiel
1Chr 4:18 sons of Bithiah the *d* of Pharaoh
1Chr 7:24 his *d* was Sherah, who built
1Chr 15:29 that Michal the *d* of Saul looking
2Chr 8:11 Solomon brought up the *d* of
2Chr 11:18 Rehoboam took him Mahalath the *d*
2Chr 11:18 Abihail the *d* of Eliab the son of
2Chr 11:20 he took Maachah the *d* of Absalom
2Chr 11:21 Rehoboam loved Maachah the *d* of
2Chr 13:2 Michaiah the *d* of Uriel of Gibeah
2Chr 20:31 name was Azubah the *d* of Shilhi

2Chr 21:6 for he had the *d* of Ahab to wife
2Chr 22:2 also was Athaliah the *d* of Omri
2Chr 22:11 the *d* of the king, took Joash the
2Chr 22:11 the *d* of king Jehoram, the wife
2Chr 25:18 Give thy *d* to my son to wife
2Chr 27:1 also was Jerushah, the *d* of Zadok
2Chr 29:1 was Abijah, the *d* of Zechariah
Neh 6:18 the *d* of Meshullam the son of
Est 2:7 that is, Esther, his uncle's *d*
Est 2:7 were dead, took for his own *d*
Est 2:15 the *d* of Abihail the uncle of
Est 2:15 who had taken her for his *d*
Est 9:29 the *d* of Abihail, and Mordecai the
Ps 9:14 in the gates of the *d* of Zion
Ps 45:10 Hearken, O *d*, and consider, and
Ps 45:12 the *d* of Tyre shall be there with
Ps 45:13 The king's *d* is all glorious
Ps 137:8 O *d* of Babylon, who art to be
Song 7:1 thy feet with shoes, O prince's *d*
Is 1:8 the *d* of Zion is left as a
Is 10:30 Lift up thy voice, O *d* of Gallim
Is 10:32 the mount of the *d* of Zion
Is 16:1 unto the mount of the *d* of Zion
Is 22:4 spoiling of the *d* of my people
Is 23:10 land as a river, O *d* of Tarshish
Is 23:12 thou oppressed virgin, *d* of Zidon
Is 37:22 the *d* of Zion, hath despised thee
Is 37:22 the *d* of Jerusalem hath shaken
Is 47:1 O virgin *d* of Babylon, sit on the
Is 47:1 no throne, O *d* of the Chaldeans
Is 47:5 darkness, O *d* of the Chaldeans
Is 52:2 of thy neck, O captive *d* of Zion
Is 62:11 world, Say ye to the *d* of Zion
Jer 4:11 toward the *d* of my people
Jer 4:31 child, the voice of the *d* of Zion
Jer 6:2 I have likened the *d* of Zion to a
Jer 6:14 of the *d* of my people slightly
Jer 6:23 for war against thee, O *d* of Zion
Jer 6:26 O *d* of my people, gird thee with
Jer 8:11 of the *d* of my people slightly
Jer 8:19 the voice of the cry of the *d* of
Jer 8:21 For the hurt of the *d* of my
Jer 8:22 of the *d* of my people recovered
Jer 9:1 the slain of the *d* of my people
Jer 9:7 shall I do for the *d* of my people
Jer 14:17 for the virgin *d* of my people is
Jer 31:22 go about, O thou backsliding *d*
Jer 46:11 balm, O virgin, the *d* of Egypt
Jer 46:19 O thou *d* dwelling in Egypt,
Jer 46:24 The *d* of Egypt shall be
Jer 48:18 Thou *d* that dost inhabit Dibon,
Jer 49:4 flowing valley, O backsliding *d*
Jer 50:42 against thee, O *d* of Babylon
Jer 51:33 The *d* of Babylon is like a
Jer 52:1 the *d* of Jeremiah of Libnah
Lam 1:6 from the *d* of Zion all her beauty
Lam 1:15 the *d* of Judah, as in a winepress
Lam 2:1 the *d* of Zion with a cloud in his
Lam 2:2 strong holds of the *d* of Judah
Lam 2:4 the tabernacle of the *d* of Zion
Lam 2:5 in the *d* of Judah mourning
Lam 2:8 destroy the wall of the *d* of Zion
Lam 2:10 The elders of the *d* of Zion sit
Lam 2:11 destruction of the *d* of my people
Lam 2:13 I liken to thee, O *d* of Jerusalem
Lam 2:13 comfort thee, O virgin *d* of Zion
Lam 2:15 their head at the *d* of Jerusalem
Lam 2:18 the Lord, O wall of the *d* of Zion
Lam 3:48 destruction of the *d* of my people
Lam 4:3 the *d* of my people is become
Lam 4:6 of the iniquity of the *d* of my
Lam 4:10 destruction of the *d* of my people
Lam 4:21 O *d* of Edom, that dwellest in the
Lam 4:22 is accomplished, O *d* of Zion
Lam 4:22 visit thine iniquity, O *d* of Edom
Eze 14:20 shall deliver neither son nor *d*
Eze 16:44 As is the mother, so is her *d*
Eze 16:45 Thou art thy mother's *d*, that
Eze 22:11 hath lewdly defiled his *d* in law
Eze 22:11 his sister, his father's *d*
Eze 44:25 for mother, or for son, or for *d*
Dan 11:6 for the king's *d* of the south
Dan 11:17 he shall give him the *d* of women
Hos 1:3 and took Gomer the *d* of Diblaim
Hos 1:6 she conceived again, and bare a *d*
Mic 1:13 of the sin to the *d* of Zion
Mic 4:8 the strong hold of the *d* of Zion
Mic 4:8 shall come to the *d* of Jerusalem
Mic 4:10 O *d* of Zion, like a woman in
Mic 4:13 Arise and thresh, O *d* of Zion
Mic 5:1 thyself in troops, O *d* of troops
Mic 7:6 the *d* riseth up against her
Mic 7:6 the *d* in law against her mother
Zeph 3:10 even the *d* of my dispersed, shall
Zeph 3:14 Sing, O *d* of Zion
Zeph 3:14 all the heart, O *d* of Jerusalem
Zec 2:7 dwellest with the *d* of Babylon
Zec 2:10 Sing and rejoice, O *d* of Zion
Zec 9:9 Rejoice greatly, O *d* of Zion
Zec 9:9 shout, O *d* of Jerusalem
Mal 2:11 married the *d* of a strange god
Mt 9:18 saying, My *d* is even now dead
Mt 9:22 and when he saw her, he said, *D*
Mt 10:35 the *d* against her mother, and the
Mt 10:35 the *d* in law against her mother
Mt 10:37 he that loveth son or *d* more than
Mt 14:6 the *d* of Herodias danced before
Mt 15:22 my *d* is grievously vexed with a
Mt 15:28 her *d* was made whole from that
Mt 21:5 Tell ye the *d* of Sion, Behold,
Mk 5:23 My little *d* lieth at the point of
Mk 5:34 And he said unto her, *D*, thy faith
Mk 5:35 certain which said, Thy *d* is dead
Mk 6:22 when the *d* of the said Herodias
Mk 7:25 whose young *d* had an unclean
Mk 7:26 cast forth the devil out of her *d*
Mk 7:29 the devil is gone out of thy *d*
Mk 7:30 out, and her *d* laid upon the bed
Lk 2:36 the *d* of Phanuel, of the tribe of
Lk 8:42 For he had one only *d*, about
Lk 8:48 And he said unto her, *D*, be of
Lk 8:49 saying to him, Thy *d* is dead
Lk 12:53 the mother against the *d*
Lk 12:53 and the *d* against the mother
Lk 12:53 in law against her *d* in law
Lk 12:53 the *d* in law against her mother
Lk 13:16 being a *d* of Abraham, whom Satan
Jn 12:15 Fear not, *d* of Sion
Acts 7:21 Pharaoh's *d* took him up, and
Heb 11:24 be called the son of Pharaoh's *d*

**DAUGHTERS**

Gen 5:4 and he begat sons and *d*
Gen 5:7 seven years, and begat sons and *d*
Gen 5:10 fifteen years, and begat sons and *d*
Gen 5:13 forty years, and begat sons and *d*
Gen 5:16 thirty years, and begat sons and *d*
Gen 5:19 hundred years, and begat sons and *d*
Gen 5:22 hundred years, and begat sons and *d*
Gen 5:26 and two years, and begat sons and *d*
Gen 5:30 and five years, and begat sons and *d*
Gen 6:1 earth, and *d* were born unto them,
Gen 6:2 the *d* of men that they were fair
Gen 6:4 of God came in unto the *d* of men
Gen 11:11 hundred years, and begat sons and *d*
Gen 11:13 three years, and begat sons and *d*
Gen 11:15 three years, and begat sons and *d*
Gen 11:17 thirty years, and begat sons and *d*
Gen 11:19 and nine years, and begat sons and *d*
Gen 11:21 seven years, and begat sons and *d*
Gen 11:23 hundred years, and begat sons and *d*
Gen 11:25 years, and begat sons and *d*
Gen 19:8 I have two *d* which have not known
Gen 19:12 son in law, and thy sons, and thy *d*
Gen 19:14 sons in law, which married his *d*
Gen 19:15 take thy wife, and thy two *d*
Gen 19:16 and upon the hand of his two *d*
Gen 19:30 mountain, and his two *d* with him
Gen 19:30 dwelt in a cave, he and his two *d*
Gen 19:36 Thus were both the *d* of Lot with
Gen 24:3 my son of the *d* of the Canaanites
Gen 24:13 the *d* of the men of the city come
Gen 24:37 my son of the *d* of the Canaanites
Gen 27:46 my life because of the *d* of Heth
Gen 27:46 take a wife of the *d* of Heth
Gen 27:46 which are of the *d* of the land
Gen 28:1 take a wife of the *d* of Canaan
Gen 28:2 *d* of Laban thy mother's brother
Gen 28:6 take a wife of the *d* of Canaan
Gen 28:8 Esau seeing that the *d* of Canaan
Gen 29:16 And Laban had two *d*
Gen 30:13 for the *d* will call me blessed
Gen 31:26 to me, and carried away my *d*
Gen 31:28 me to kiss my sons and my *d*
Gen 31:31 take by force thy *d* from me
Gen 31:41 thee fourteen years for thy two *d*
Gen 31:43 These *d* are my *d*, and
Gen 31:43 Jacob, These *d* are my *d*
Gen 31:43 can I do this day unto these my *d*
Gen 31:50 If thou shalt afflict my *d*
Gen 31:50 take other wives beside my *d*
Gen 31:55 up, and kissed his sons and his *d*
Gen 34:1 went out to see the *d* of the land
Gen 34:9 with us, and give your *d* unto us
Gen 34:9 unto us, and take our *d* unto you
Gen 34:16 Then will we give our *d* unto you
Gen 34:16 and we will take your *d* to us
Gen 34:21 us take their *d* to us for wives
Gen 34:21 and let us give them our *d*
Gen 36:2 took his wives of the *d* of Canaan
Gen 36:6 his wives, and his sons, and his *d*
Gen 37:35 all his *d* rose up to comfort him
Gen 46:7 his *d*, and his sons' *d*
Gen 46:15 his *d* were thirty and three
Ex 2:16 the priest of Midian had seven *d*
Ex 2:20 And he said unto his *d*, And where
Ex 3:22 upon your sons, and upon your *d*
Ex 6:25 one of the *d* of Putiel to wife
Ex 10:9 old, with our sons and with our *d*
Ex 21:4 and she have born him sons or *d*
Ex 21:9 with her after the manner of *d*
Ex 32:2 wives, of your sons, and of your *d*
Ex 34:16 take of their *d* unto thy sons
Ex 34:16 their *d* go a whoring after their
Lev 10:14 and thy sons, and thy *d* with thee
Lev 26:29 the flesh of your *d* shall ye eat
Num 18:11 to thy *d* with thee, by a statute
Num 18:19 thy *d* with thee, by a statute for
Num 21:29 his sons that escaped, and his *d*
Num 25:1 whoredom with the *d* of Moab
Num 26:33 son of Hepher had no sons, but *d*
Num 26:33 the names of the *d* of Zelophehad
Num 27:1 Then came the *d* of Zelophehad
Num 27:1 and these are the names of his *d*
Num 27:7 The *d* of Zelophehad speak right
Num 36:2 Zelophehad our brother unto his *d*
Num 36:6 concerning the *d* of Zelophehad
Num 36:10 so did the *d* of Zelophehad
Num 36:11 the *d* of Zelophehad, were married
Deut 12:12 God, ye, and your sons, and your *d*
Deut 12:31 their *d* they have burnt in the
Deut 23:17 be no whore of the *d* of Israel
Deut 28:32 thy *d* shall be given unto another
Deut 28:41 Thou shalt beget sons and *d*
Deut 28:53 the flesh of thy sons and of thy *d*
Deut 32:19 of his sons, and of his *d*
Josh 7:24 of gold, and his sons, and his *d*
Josh 17:3 of Manasseh, had no sons, but *d*
Josh 17:3 and these are the names of his *d*
Josh 17:6 Because the *d* of Manasseh had an
Judg 3:6 they took their *d* to be their
Judg 3:6 gave their *d* to their sons, and
Judg 11:40 That the *d* of Israel went yearly
Judg 12:9 he had thirty sons, and thirty *d*
Judg 12:9 took in thirty *d* from abroad for
Judg 14:1 of the *d* of the Philistines
Judg 14:2 of the *d* of the Philistines
Judg 14:3 woman among the *d* of thy brethren
Judg 21:7 not give them of our *d* to wives
Judg 21:18 may not give them wives of our *d*
Judg 21:21 if the *d* of Shiloh come out to
Judg 21:21 man his wife of the *d* of Shiloh
Ruth 1:6 Then she arose with her *d* in law
Ruth 1:7 her two *d* in law with her
Ruth 1:8 Naomi said unto her two *d* in law
Ruth 1:11 And Naomi said, Turn again, my *d*
Ruth 1:12 Turn again, my *d*, go your way
Ruth 1:13 nay, my *d*
1Sa 1:4 wife, and to all her sons and her *d*
1Sa 2:21 and bare three sons and two *d*
1Sa 8:13 he will take your *d* to be
1Sa 14:49 the names of his two *d* were these
1Sa 30:3 wives, and their sons, and their *d*
1Sa 30:6 man for his sons and for his *d*
1Sa 30:19 nor great, neither sons nor *d*
2Sa 1:20 lest the *d* of the Philistines
2Sa 1:20 lest the *d* of the uncircumcised
2Sa 1:24 Ye *d* of Israel, weep over Saul,
2Sa 5:13 were yet sons and *d* born to David
2Sa 13:18 *d* that were virgins apparelled
2Sa 19:5 the lives of thy sons and of thy *d*
2Kin 17:17 their *d* to pass through the fire,
1Chr 2:34 Now Sheshan had no sons, but *d*
1Chr 4:27 Shimei had sixteen sons and six *d*
1Chr 7:15 and Zelophehad had *d*
1Chr 14:3 and David begat more sons and *d*
1Chr 23:22 died, and had no sons, but *d*
1Chr 25:5 to Heman fourteen sons and three *d*
2Chr 2:14 son of a woman of the *d* of Dan
2Chr 11:21 and eight sons, and threescore *d*

2Chr 13:21 twenty and two sons, and sixteen *d*
2Chr 24:3 and he begat sons and *d*
2Chr 28:8 thousand, women, sons, and *d*
2Chr 29:9 the sword, and our sons and our *d*
2Chr 31:18 wives, and their sons, and their *d*
Ezr 2:61 which took a wife of the *d* of
Ezr 9:2 taken of their *d* for themselves
Ezr 9:12 give not your *d* unto their sons
Ezr 9:12 take their *d* unto your sons
Neh 3:12 part of Jerusalem, he and his *d*
Neh 4:14 brethren, your sons, and your *d*
Neh 5:2 that said, We, our sons, and our *d*
Neh 5:5 our *d* to be servants
Neh 5:5 some of our *d* are brought unto
Neh 7:63 which took one of the *d* of
Neh 10:28 wives, their sons, and their *d*
Neh 10:30 that we would not give our *d* unto
Neh 10:30 nor take their *d* for our sons
Neh 13:25 not give your *d* unto their sons
Neh 13:25 nor take their *d* unto your sons
Job 1:2 unto him seven sons and three *d*
Job 1:13 his *d* were eating and drinking
Job 1:18 thy *d* were eating and drinking
Job 42:13 He had also seven sons and three *d*
Job 42:15 found so fair as the *d* of Job
Ps 45:9 Kings' *d* were among thy
Ps 48:11 let the *d* of Judah be glad,
Ps 97:8 the *d* of Judah rejoiced because
Ps 106:37 sons and their *d* unto devils,
Ps 106:38 blood of their sons and of their *d*
Ps 144:12 that our *d* may be as corner
Prov 30:15 The horseleach hath two *d*
Prov 31:29 Many *d* have done virtuously, but
Eccl 12:4 all the *d* of musick shall be
Song 1:5 O ye *d* of Jerusalem, as the tents
Song 2:2 thorns, so is my love among the *d*
Song 2:7 O ye *d* of Jerusalem, by the roes,
Song 3:5 O ye *d* of Jerusalem, by the roes,
Song 3:10 with love, for the *d* of Jerusalem
Song 3:11 O ye *d* of Zion, and behold king
Song 5:8 O *d* of Jerusalem, if ye find my
Song 5:16 is my friend, O *d* of Jerusalem
Song 6:9 The *d* saw her, and blessed her
Song 8:4 O *d* of Jerusalem, that ye stir
Is 3:16 Because the *d* of Zion are haughty
Is 3:17 of the head of the *d* of Zion
Is 4:4 away the filth of the *d* of Zion
Is 16:2 so the *d* of Moab shall be at the
Is 32:9 hear my voice, ye careless *d*
Is 43:6 my *d* from the ends of the earth
Is 49:22 thy *d* shall be carried upon their
Is 56:5 name better than of sons and of *d*
Is 60:4 thy *d* shall be nursed at thy side
Jer 3:24 herds, their sons and their *d*
Jer 5:17 thy sons and thy *d* should eat
Jer 7:31 their sons and their *d* in the fire
Jer 9:20 mouth, and teach your *d* wailing
Jer 11:22 their *d* shall die by famine
Jer 14:16 nor their sons, nor their *d*
Jer 16:2 thou have sons or *d* in this place
Jer 16:3 concerning the *d* that are born in
Jer 19:9 sons and the flesh of their *d*
Jer 29:6 Take ye wives, and beget sons and *d*
Jer 29:6 give your *d* to husbands
Jer 29:6 that they may bear sons and *d*
Jer 32:35 their *d* to pass through the fire
Jer 35:8 our wives, our sons, nor our *d*
Jer 41:10 were in Mizpah, even the king's *d*
Jer 43:6 and children, and the king's *d*
Jer 48:46 taken captives, and thy *d* captives
Jer 49:2 her *d* shall be burned with fire
Jer 49:3 ye *d* of Rabbah, gird you with
Lam 3:51 because of all the *d* of my city
Eze 13:17 face against the *d* of thy people
Eze 14:16 shall deliver neither sons nor *d*
Eze 14:18 shall deliver neither sons nor *d*
Eze 14:22 be brought forth, both sons and *d*
Eze 16:20 thou hast taken thy sons and thy *d*
Eze 16:27 the *d* of the Philistines, which
Eze 16:46 her *d* that dwell at thy left hand
Eze 16:46 thy right hand, is Sodom and her *d*
Eze 16:48 hath not done, she nor her *d*
Eze 16:48 as thou hast done, thou and thy *d*
Eze 16:49 idleness was in her and in her *d*
Eze 16:53 the captivity of Sodom and her *d*
Eze 16:53 the captivity of Samaria and her *d*
Eze 16:55 When thy sisters, Sodom and her *d*
Eze 16:55 her *d* shall return to their
Eze 16:55 thy *d* shall return to your former
Eze 16:57 of thy reproach of the *d* of Syria
Eze 16:57 the *d* of the Philistines, which
Eze 16:61 I will give them unto thee for *d*
Eze 23:2 two women, the *d* of one mother
Eze 23:4 were mine, and they bare sons and *d*
Eze 23:10 they took her sons and her *d*
Eze 23:25 they shall take thy sons and thy *d*
Eze 23:47 shall slay their sons and their *d*
Eze 24:21 your *d* whom ye have left shall
Eze 24:25 minds, their sons and their *d*
Eze 26:6 her *d* which are in the field
Eze 26:8 with the sword thy *d* in the field
Eze 30:18 her *d* shall go into captivity
Eze 32:16 the *d* of the nations shall lament
Eze 32:18 the *d* of the famous nations, unto
Hos 4:13 therefore your *d* shall commit
Hos 4:14 I will not punish your *d* when
Joel 2:28 your *d* shall prophesy, your old
Joel 3:8 your *d* into the hand of the
Amos 7:17 thy *d* shall fall by the sword, and
Lk 1:5 and his wife was of the *d* of Aaron
Lk 23:28 *D* of Jerusalem, weep not for me,
Acts 2:17 your *d* shall prophesy, and your
Acts 21:9 And the same man had four *d*
2Cor 6:18 you, and ye shall be my sons and *d*
1Pet 3:6 whose *d* ye are, as long as ye do

**DAVID** See DAVID'S. *Second king of Israel.*

Ruth 4:17 father of Jesse, the father of *D*
Ruth 4:22 begat Jesse, and Jesse begat *D*
1Sa 16:13 came upon *D* from that day forward
1Sa 16:19 Jesse, and said, Send me *D* thy son
1Sa 16:20 sent them by *D* his son unto Saul
1Sa 16:21 *D* came to Saul, and stood before
1Sa 16:22 Saul sent to Jesse, saying, Let *D*
1Sa 16:23 that *D* took an harp, and played
1Sa 17:12 Now *D* was the son of that
1Sa 17:14 And *D* was the youngest
1Sa 17:15 But *D* went and returned from Saul
1Sa 17:17 And Jesse said unto *D* his son
1Sa 17:20 *D* rose up early in the morning,
1Sa 17:22 *D* left his carriage in the hand
1Sa 17:23 and *D* heard them
1Sa 17:26 *D* spake to the men that stood by
1Sa 17:28 anger was kindled against *D*
1Sa 17:29 *D* said, What have I now done
1Sa 17:31 words were heard which *D* spake
1Sa 17:32 *D* said to Saul, Let no man's
1Sa 17:33 And Saul said to *D*, Thou art not
1Sa 17:34 *D* said unto Saul, Thy servant
1Sa 17:37 *D* said moreover, The LORD that
1Sa 17:37 And Saul said unto *D*, Go, and the
1Sa 17:38 Saul armed *D* with his armour, and
1Sa 17:39 *D* girded his sword upon his
1Sa 17:39 *D* said unto Saul, I cannot go
1Sa 17:39 And *D* put them off him
1Sa 17:41 came on and drew near unto *D*
1Sa 17:42 Philistine looked about, and saw *D*
1Sa 17:43 And the Philistine said unto *D*
1Sa 17:43 Philistine cursed *D* by his gods
1Sa 17:44 And the Philistine said to *D*
1Sa 17:45 Then said *D* to the Philistine,
1Sa 17:48 and came and drew nigh to meet *D*
1Sa 17:48 that *D* hasted, and ran toward the
1Sa 17:49 *D* put his hand in his bag, and
1Sa 17:50 So *D* prevailed over the
1Sa 17:50 was no sword in the hand of *D*
1Sa 17:51 Therefore *D* ran, and stood upon
1Sa 17:54 *D* took the head of the Philistine
1Sa 17:55 when Saul saw *D* go forth against
1Sa 17:57 as *D* returned from the slaughter
1Sa 17:58 *D* answered, I am the son of thy
1Sa 18:1 was knit with the soul of *D*
1Sa 18:3 *D* made a covenant, because he
1Sa 18:4 was upon him, and gave it to *D*
1Sa 18:5 *D* went out whithersoever Saul
1Sa 18:6 when *D* was returned from the
1Sa 18:7 thousands, and *D* his ten thousands
1Sa 18:8 ascribed unto *D* ten thousands
1Sa 18:9 Saul eyed *D* from that day and
1Sa 18:10 *D* played with his hand, as at
1Sa 18:11 I will smite *D* even to the wall
1Sa 18:11 *D* avoided out of his presence
1Sa 18:12 And Saul was afraid of *D*, because
1Sa 18:14 *D* behaved himself wisely in all
1Sa 18:16 But all Israel and Judah loved *D*
1Sa 18:17 And Saul said to *D*, Behold my
1Sa 18:18 *D* said unto Saul, Who am I
1Sa 18:19 should have been given to *D*
1Sa 18:20 And Michal Saul's daughter loved *D*
1Sa 18:21 Wherefore Saul said to *D*, Thou
1Sa 18:22 saying, Commune with *D* secretly
1Sa 18:23 those words in the ears of *D*
1Sa 18:23 *D* said, Seemeth it to you a light
1Sa 18:24 saying, On this manner spake *D*
1Sa 18:25 Saul said, Thus shall ye say to *D*
1Sa 18:25 to make *D* fall by the hand of the
1Sa 18:26 his servants told *D* these words
1Sa 18:26 it pleased *D* well to be the
1Sa 18:27 Wherefore *D* arose and went, he and
1Sa 18:27 *D* brought their foreskins, and
1Sa 18:28 and knew that the LORD was with *D*
1Sa 18:29 Saul was yet the more afraid of *D*
1Sa 18:30 that *D* behaved himself more
1Sa 19:1 servants, that they should kill *D*
1Sa 19:2 Saul's son delighted much in *D*
1Sa 19:2 and Jonathan told *D*, saying, Saul
1Sa 19:4 good of *D* unto Saul his father
1Sa 19:4 against his servant, against *D*
1Sa 19:5 to slay *D* without a cause
1Sa 19:7 And Jonathan called *D*
1Sa 19:7 And Jonathan brought *D* to Saul
1Sa 19:8 *D* went out, and fought with the
1Sa 19:9 and *D* played with his hand
1Sa 19:10 Saul sought to smite *D* even to
1Sa 19:10 *D* fled, and escaped that night
1Sa 19:12 So Michal let *D* down through a
1Sa 19:14 Saul sent messengers to take *D*
1Sa 19:15 the messengers again to see *D*
1Sa 19:18 So *D* fled, and escaped, and came to
1Sa 19:19 Behold, *D* is at Naioth in Ramah
1Sa 19:20 And Saul sent messengers to take *D*
1Sa 19:22 and said, Where are Samuel and *D*
1Sa 20:1 *D* fled from Naioth in Ramah, and
1Sa 20:3 *D* sware moreover, and said, Thy
1Sa 20:4 Then said Jonathan unto *D*
1Sa 20:5 *D* said unto Jonathan, Behold, to
1Sa 20:6 *D* earnestly asked leave of me
1Sa 20:10 Then said *D* to Jonathan, Who
1Sa 20:11 And Jonathan said unto *D*, Come, and
1Sa 20:12 And Jonathan said unto *D*, O LORD
1Sa 20:12 behold, if there be good toward *D*
1Sa 20:15 hath cut off the enemies of *D*
1Sa 20:16 a covenant with the house of *D*
1Sa 20:17 Jonathan caused *D* to swear again
1Sa 20:18 Then Jonathan said to *D*, To
1Sa 20:24 So *D* hid himself in the field
1Sa 20:28 *D* earnestly asked leave of me to
1Sa 20:33 of his father to slay *D*
1Sa 20:34 for he was grieved for *D*, because
1Sa 20:35 at the time appointed with *D*
1Sa 20:39 Jonathan and *D* knew the matter
1Sa 20:41 *D* arose out of a place toward the
1Sa 20:41 with another, until *D* exceeded
1Sa 20:42 And Jonathan said to *D*, Go in
1Sa 21:1 Then came *D* to Nob to Ahimelech
1Sa 21:1 was afraid at the meeting of *D*
1Sa 21:2 *D* said unto Ahimelech the priest,
1Sa 21:4 And the priest answered *D*, and said
1Sa 21:5 *D* answered the priest, and said
1Sa 21:8 *D* said unto Ahimelech, And is
1Sa 21:9 *D* said, There is none like that
1Sa 21:10 *D* arose, and fled that day for
1Sa 21:11 Is not this *D* the king of the
1Sa 21:11 thousands, and *D* his ten thousands
1Sa 21:12 *D* laid up these words in his
1Sa 22:1 *D* therefore departed thence, and
1Sa 22:3 *D* went thence to Mizpeh of Moab
1Sa 22:4 the while that *D* was in the hold
1Sa 22:5 And the prophet Gad said unto *D*
1Sa 22:5 Then *D* departed, and came into the
1Sa 22:6 Saul heard that *D* was discovered
1Sa 22:14 among all thy servants as *D*
1Sa 22:17 because their hand also is with *D*
1Sa 22:20 escaped, and fled after *D*
1Sa 22:21 Abiathar shewed *D* that Saul had
1Sa 22:22 *D* said unto Abiathar, I knew it
1Sa 23:1 Then they told *D*, saying, Behold,
1Sa 23:2 Therefore *D* enquired of the LORD,
1Sa 23:2 And the LORD said unto *D*, Go, and
1Sa 23:4 Then *D* enquired of the LORD yet
1Sa 23:5 So *D* and his men went to Keilah,
1Sa 23:5 So *D* saved the inhabitants of
1Sa 23:6 of Ahimelech fled to *D* to Keilah
1Sa 23:7 Saul that *D* was come to Keilah
1Sa 23:8 go down to Keilah, to besiege *D*
1Sa 23:9 *D* knew that Saul secretly
1Sa 23:10 Then said *D*, O LORD God of Israel
1Sa 23:12 Then said *D*, Will the men of
1Sa 23:13 Then *D* and his men, which were

1Sa 23:13 it was told Saul that *D* was
1Sa 23:14 *D* abode in the wilderness in
1Sa 23:15 *D* saw that Saul was come out to
1Sa 23:15 *D* was in the wilderness of Ziph
1Sa 23:16 went to *D* into the wood, and
1Sa 23:18 *D* abode in the wood, and Jonathan
1Sa 23:19 Doth not *D* hide himself with us
1Sa 23:24 but *D* and his men were in the
1Sa 23:25 And they told *D*
1Sa 23:25 he pursued after *D* in the
1Sa 23:26 this side of the mountain, and *D*
1Sa 23:26 *D* made haste to get away for fear
1Sa 23:26 for Saul and his men compassed *D*
1Sa 23:28 returned from pursuing after *D*
1Sa 23:29 *D* went up from thence, and dwelt
1Sa 24:1 *D* is in the wilderness of En-gedi
1Sa 24:2 of all Israel, and went to seek *D*
1Sa 24:3 and *D* and his men remained in the
1Sa 24:4 the men of *D* said unto him,
1Sa 24:4 Then *D* arose, and cut off the
1Sa 24:7 So *D* stayed his servants with
1Sa 24:8 *D* also arose afterward, and went
1Sa 24:8 *D* stooped with his face to the
1Sa 24:9 *D* said to Saul, Wherefore hearest
1Sa 24:9 Behold, *D* seeketh thy hurt
1Sa 24:16 when *D* had made an end of
1Sa 24:16 said, Is this thy voice, my son *D*
1Sa 24:17 And he said to *D*, Thou art more
1Sa 24:22 And *D* sware unto Saul
1Sa 24:22 but *D* and his men gat them up unto
1Sa 25:1 *D* arose, and went down to the
1Sa 25:4 *D* heard in the wilderness that
1Sa 25:5 *D* sent out ten young men, and
1Sa 25:5 *D* said unto the young men, Get
1Sa 25:8 thy servants, and to thy son *D*
1Sa 25:9 all those words in the name of *D*
1Sa 25:10 servants, and said, Who is *D*
1Sa 25:13 *D* said unto his men, Gird ye on
1Sa 25:13 *D* also girded on his sword
1Sa 25:13 there went up after *D* about four
1Sa 25:14 *D* sent messengers out of the
1Sa 25:20 covert of the hill, and, behold, *D*
1Sa 25:21 Now *D* had said, Surely in vain
1Sa 25:22 also do God unto the enemies of *D*
1Sa 25:23 And when Abigail saw *D*, she hasted
1Sa 25:23 ass, and fell before *D* on her face
1Sa 25:32 *D* said to Abigail, Blessed be the
1Sa 25:35 So *D* received of her hand that
1Sa 25:39 when *D* heard that Nabal was dead,
1Sa 25:39 *D* sent and communed with Abigail,
1Sa 25:40 when the servants of *D* were come
1Sa 25:40 *D* sent us unto thee, to take thee
1Sa 25:42 went after the messengers of *D*
1Sa 25:43 *D* also took Ahinoam of Jezreel
1Sa 26:1 Doth not *D* hide himself in the
1Sa 26:2 to seek *D* in the wilderness of
1Sa 26:3 But *D* abode in the wilderness, and
1Sa 26:4 *D* therefore sent out spies, and
1Sa 26:5 *D* arose, and came to the place
1Sa 26:5 *D* beheld the place where Saul lay
1Sa 26:6 Then answered *D* and said to
1Sa 26:7 So *D* and Abishai came to the
1Sa 26:8 Then said Abishai to *D*, God hath
1Sa 26:9 *D* said to Abishai, Destroy him
1Sa 26:10 *D* said furthermore, As the LORD
1Sa 26:12 So *D* took the spear and the cruse
1Sa 26:13 Then *D* went over to the other
1Sa 26:14 *D* cried to the people, and to
1Sa 26:15 *D* said to Abner, Art not thou a
1Sa 26:17 said, Is this thy voice, my son *D*
1Sa 26:17 *D* said, It is my voice, my lord,
1Sa 26:21 return, my son *D*
1Sa 26:22 *D* answered and said, Behold the
1Sa 26:25 *D*, Blessed be thou, my son *D*
1Sa 26:25 So *D* went on his way, and Saul
1Sa 27:1 *D* said in his heart, I shall now
1Sa 27:2 *D* arose, and he passed over with
1Sa 27:3 *D* dwelt with Achish at Gath, he
1Sa 27:3 even *D* with his two wives,
1Sa 27:4 told Saul that *D* was fled to Gath
1Sa 27:5 *D* said unto Achish, If I have now
1Sa 27:7 the time that *D* dwelt in the
1Sa 27:8 And *D* and his men went up, and
1Sa 27:9 *D* smote the land, and left neither
1Sa 27:10 *D* said, Against the south of
1Sa 27:11 *D* saved neither man nor woman
1Sa 27:11 tell on us, saying, So did *D*
1Sa 27:12 And Achish believed *D*, saying, He
1Sa 28:1 And Achish said unto *D*, Know thou
1Sa 28:2 *D* said to Achish, Surely thou
1Sa 28:2 And Achish said to *D*, Therefore
1Sa 28:17 it to thy neighbour, even to *D*
1Sa 29:2 but *D* and his men passed on in the
1Sa 29:3 of the Philistines, Is not this *D*
1Sa 29:5 Is not this *D*, of whom they sang
1Sa 29:5 thousands, and *D* his ten thousands
1Sa 29:6 Then Achish called *D*, and said
1Sa 29:8 *D* said unto Achish, But what have
1Sa 29:9 And Achish answered and said to *D*
1Sa 29:11 So *D* and his men rose up early to
1Sa 30:1 And it came to pass, when *D*
1Sa 30:3 So *D* and his men came to the city,
1Sa 30:4 Then *D* and the people that were
1Sa 30:6 And *D* was greatly distressed
1Sa 30:6 but *D* encouraged himself in the
1Sa 30:7 *D* said to Abiathar the priest,
1Sa 30:7 brought thither the ephod to *D*
1Sa 30:8 *D* enquired at the LORD, saying,
1Sa 30:9 So *D* went, he and the six hundred
1Sa 30:10 But *D* pursued, he and four hundred
1Sa 30:11 in the field, and brought him to *D*
1Sa 30:13 And *D* said unto him, To whom
1Sa 30:15 *D* said to him, Canst thou bring
1Sa 30:17 *D* smote them from the twilight
1Sa 30:18 And *D* recovered all that the
1Sa 30:18 and *D* rescued his two wives
1Sa 30:19 *D* recovered all
1Sa 30:20 *D* took all the flocks and the
1Sa 30:21 *D* came to the two hundred men,
1Sa 30:21 that they could not follow *D*
1Sa 30:21 and they went forth to meet *D*
1Sa 30:21 when *D* came near to the people,
1Sa 30:22 Belial, of those that went with *D*
1Sa 30:23 Then said *D*, Ye shall not do so,
1Sa 30:26 when *D* came to Ziklag, he sent of
1Sa 30:31 to all the places where *D* himself
2Sa 1:1 when *D* was returned from the
2Sa 1:1 *D* had abode two days in Ziklag
2Sa 1:2 and so it was, when he came to *D*
2Sa 1:3 *D* said unto him, From whence
2Sa 1:4 *D* said unto him, How went the
2Sa 1:5 *D* said unto the young man that
2Sa 1:11 Then *D* took hold on his clothes,
2Sa 1:13 *D* said unto the young man that
2Sa 1:14 *D* said unto him, How wast thou
2Sa 1:15 *D* called one of the young men, and
2Sa 1:16 *D* said unto him, Thy blood be
2Sa 1:17 *D* lamented with this lamentation
2Sa 2:1 that *D* enquired of the LORD,
2Sa 2:1 *D* said, Whither shall I go up
2Sa 2:2 So *D* went up thither, and his two
2Sa 2:3 that were with him did *D* bring up
2Sa 2:4 there they anointed *D* king over
2Sa 2:4 And they told *D*, saying, That the
2Sa 2:5 *D* sent messengers unto the men of
2Sa 2:10 But the house of Judah followed *D*
2Sa 2:11 the time that *D* was king in
2Sa 2:13 of Zeruiah, and the servants of *D*
2Sa 2:15 and twelve of the servants of *D*
2Sa 2:17 Israel, before the servants of *D*
2Sa 2:31 But the servants of *D* had smitten
2Sa 3:1 house of Saul and the house of *D*
2Sa 3:1 but *D* waxed stronger and stronger,
2Sa 3:2 unto *D* were sons born in Hebron
2Sa 3:5 These were born to *D* in Hebron
2Sa 3:6 house of Saul and the house of *D*
2Sa 3:8 delivered thee into the hand of *D*
2Sa 3:9 as the LORD hath sworn to *D*
2Sa 3:10 up the throne of *D* over Israel
2Sa 3:12 messengers to *D* on his behalf
2Sa 3:14 *D* sent messengers to Ish-bosheth
2Sa 3:17 Ye sought for *D* in times past to
2Sa 3:18 for the LORD hath spoken of *D*
2Sa 3:18 By the hand of my servant *D* I
2Sa 3:19 also to speak in the ears of *D* in
2Sa 3:20 So Abner came to *D* to Hebron
2Sa 3:20 *D* made Abner and the men that were
2Sa 3:21 And Abner said unto *D*, I will
2Sa 3:21 And *D* sent Abner away
2Sa 3:22 And, behold, the servants of *D*
2Sa 3:22 Abner was not with *D* in Hebron
2Sa 3:26 And when Joab was come out from *D*
2Sa 3:26 but *D* knew it not
2Sa 3:28 And afterward when *D* heard it
2Sa 3:31 *D* said to Joab, and to all the
2Sa 3:31 king *D* himself followed the bier
2Sa 3:35 *D* to eat meat while it was yet
2Sa 3:35 *D* sware, saying, So do God to me,
2Sa 4:8 of Ish-bosheth unto *D* to Hebron
2Sa 4:9 *D* answered Rechab and Baanah his
2Sa 4:12 *D* commanded his young men, and
2Sa 5:1 tribes of Israel to *D* unto Hebron
2Sa 5:3 king *D* made a league with them in
2Sa 5:3 they anointed *D* king over Israel
2Sa 5:4 *D* was thirty years old when he
2Sa 5:6 which spake unto *D*, saying,
2Sa 5:6 thinking, *D* cannot come in
2Sa 5:7 Nevertheless *D* took the strong
2Sa 5:7 the same is the city of *D*
2Sa 5:8 *D* said on that day, Whosoever
2Sa 5:9 So *D* dwelt in the fort
2Sa 5:9 and called it the city of *D*
2Sa 5:9 *D* built round about from Millo and
2Sa 5:10 *D* went on, and grew great, and the
2Sa 5:11 king of Tyre sent messengers to *D*
2Sa 5:11 and they built *D* an house
2Sa 5:12 *D* perceived that the LORD had
2Sa 5:13 *D* took him more concubines and
2Sa 5:13 yet sons and daughters born to *D*
2Sa 5:17 had anointed *D* king over Israel
2Sa 5:17 the Philistines came up to seek *D*
2Sa 5:17 *D* heard of it, and went down to
2Sa 5:19 *D* enquired of the LORD, saying,
2Sa 5:19 And the LORD said unto *D*, Go up
2Sa 5:20 *D* came to Baal-perazim
2Sa 5:20 *D* smote them there, and said, The
2Sa 5:21 they left their images, and *D*
2Sa 5:23 when *D* enquired of the LORD, he
2Sa 5:25 *D* did so, as the LORD had
2Sa 6:1 *D* gathered together all the
2Sa 6:2 *D* arose, and went with all the
2Sa 6:5 And *D* and all the house of Israel
2Sa 6:8 *D* was displeased, because the
2Sa 6:9 *D* was afraid of the LORD that day
2Sa 6:10 So *D* would not remove the ark of
2Sa 6:10 LORD unto him into the city of *D*
2Sa 6:10 but *D* carried it aside into the
2Sa 6:12 And it was told king *D*, saying,
2Sa 6:12 So *D* went and brought up the ark
2Sa 6:12 into the city of *D* with gladness
2Sa 6:14 *D* danced before the LORD with all
2Sa 6:14 *D* was girded with a linen ephod
2Sa 6:15 So *D* and all the house of Israel
2Sa 6:16 the LORD came into the city of *D*
2Sa 6:16 a window, and saw king *D* leaping
2Sa 6:17 that *D* had pitched for it
2Sa 6:17 *D* offered burnt offerings and
2Sa 6:18 as soon as *D* had made an end of
2Sa 6:20 Then *D* returned to bless his
2Sa 6:20 of Saul came out to meet *D*
2Sa 6:21 *D* said unto Michal, It was before
2Sa 7:5 Go and tell my servant *D*, Thus
2Sa 7:8 shalt thou say unto my servant *D*
2Sa 7:17 so did Nathan speak unto *D*
2Sa 7:18 Then went king *D* in, and sat
2Sa 7:20 what can *D* say more unto thee
2Sa 7:26 *D* be established before thee
2Sa 8:1 that *D* smote the Philistines, and
2Sa 8:1 *D* took Metheg-ammah out of the
2Sa 8:3 *D* smote also Hadadezer, the son
2Sa 8:4 *D* took from him a thousand
2Sa 8:4 *D* houghed all the chariot horses,
2Sa 8:5 *D* slew of the Syrians two and
2Sa 8:6 Then *D* put garrisons in Syria of
2Sa 8:6 the Syrians became servants to *D*
2Sa 8:6 And the LORD preserved *D*
2Sa 8:7 *D* took the shields of gold that
2Sa 8:8 king *D* took exceeding much brass
2Sa 8:9 *D* had smitten all the host of
2Sa 8:10 sent Joram his son unto king *D*
2Sa 8:11 Which also king *D* did dedicate
2Sa 8:13 *D* gat him a name when he returned
2Sa 8:14 And the LORD preserved *D*
2Sa 8:15 *D* reigned over all Israel
2Sa 8:15 *D* executed judgment and justice
2Sa 9:1 *D* said, Is there yet any that is
2Sa 9:2 when they had called him unto *D*
2Sa 9:5 Then king *D* sent, and fetched him
2Sa 9:6 the son of Saul, was come unto *D*
2Sa 9:6 And *D* said, Mephibosheth
2Sa 9:7 *D* said unto him, Fear not
2Sa 10:2 Then said *D*, I will shew kindness
2Sa 10:2 *D* sent to comfort him by the hand
2Sa 10:3 Thinkest thou that *D* doth honour
2Sa 10:3 hath not *D* rather sent his
2Sa 10:5 When they told it unto *D*, he sent
2Sa 10:6 saw that they stank before *D*
2Sa 10:7 when *D* heard of it, he sent Joab,
2Sa 10:17 And when it was told *D*, he
2Sa 10:17 set themselves in array against *D*

2Sa 10:18 *D* slew the men of seven hundred
2Sa 11:1 that *D* sent Joab, and his servants
2Sa 11:1 But *D* tarried still at Jerusalem
2Sa 11:2 that *D* arose from off his bed, and
2Sa 11:3 *D* sent and enquired after the
2Sa 11:4 *D* sent messengers, and took her
2Sa 11:5 conceived, and sent and told *D*
2Sa 11:6 *D* sent to Joab, saying, Send me
2Sa 11:6 And Joab sent Uriah to *D*
2Sa 11:7 *D* demanded of him how Joab did,
2Sa 11:8 *D* said to Uriah, Go down to thy
2Sa 11:10 And when they had told *D*, saying,
2Sa 11:10 *D* said unto Uriah, Camest thou
2Sa 11:11 And Uriah said unto *D*, The ark, and
2Sa 11:12 *D* said to Uriah, Tarry here to
2Sa 11:13 when *D* had called him, he did eat
2Sa 11:14 that *D* wrote a letter to Joab, and
2Sa 11:17 the people of the servants of *D*
2Sa 11:18 told *D* all the things concerning
2Sa 11:22 shewed *D* all that Joab had sent
2Sa 11:23 And the messenger said unto *D*
2Sa 11:25 Then *D* said unto the messenger,
2Sa 11:27 *D* sent and fetched her to his
2Sa 11:27 But the thing that *D* had done
2Sa 12:1 And the LORD sent Nathan unto *D*
2Sa 12:7 And Nathan said to *D*, Thou art the
2Sa 12:13 *D* said unto Nathan, I have sinned
2Sa 12:13 And Nathan said unto *D*, The LORD
2Sa 12:15 that Uriah's wife bare unto *D*
2Sa 12:16 *D* therefore besought God for the
2Sa 12:16 *D* fasted, and went in, and lay all
2Sa 12:18 the servants of *D* feared to tell
2Sa 12:19 But when *D* saw that his servants
2Sa 12:19 *D* perceived that the child was
2Sa 12:19 therefore *D* said unto his
2Sa 12:20 Then *D* arose from the earth, and
2Sa 12:24 *D* comforted Bath-sheba his wife,
2Sa 12:27 And Joab sent messengers to *D*
2Sa 12:29 *D* gathered all the people
2Sa 12:31 So *D* and all the people returned
2Sa 13:1 the son of *D* had a fair sister
2Sa 13:1 and Amnon the son of *D* loved her
2Sa 13:7 Then *D* sent home to Tamar, saying
2Sa 13:21 But when king *D* heard of all
2Sa 13:30 the way, that tidings came to *D*
2Sa 13:37 *D* mourned for his son every day
2Sa 13:39 the soul of king *D* longed to go
2Sa 15:13 And there came a messenger to *D*
2Sa 15:14 *D* said unto all his servants that
2Sa 15:22 *D* said to Ittai, Go and pass over
2Sa 15:30 *D* went up by the ascent of mount
2Sa 15:31 And one told *D*, saying, Ahithophel
2Sa 15:31 *D* said, O LORD, I pray thee, turn
2Sa 15:32 that when *D* was come to the top
2Sa 15:33 Unto whom *D* said, If thou passest
2Sa 16:1 when *D* was a little past the top
2Sa 16:5 when king *D* came to Bahurim,
2Sa 16:6 And he cast stones at *D*, and at all
2Sa 16:6 and at all the servants of king *D*
2Sa 16:10 LORD hath said unto him, Curse *D*
2Sa 16:11 *D* said to Abishai, and to all his
2Sa 16:13 And as *D* and his men went by the
2Sa 16:23 counsel of Ahithophel both with *D*
2Sa 17:1 and pursue after *D* this night
2Sa 17:16 therefore send quickly, and tell *D*
2Sa 17:17 and they went and told king *D*
2Sa 17:21 told king *D*, and said unto *D*
2Sa 17:22 Then *D* arose, and all the people
2Sa 17:24 Then *D* came to Mahanaim
2Sa 17:27 when *D* was come to Mahanaim, that
2Sa 17:29 sheep, and cheese of kine, for *D*
2Sa 18:1 *D* numbered the people that were
2Sa 18:2 *D* sent forth a third part of the
2Sa 18:7 slain before the servants of *D*
2Sa 18:9 And Absalom met the servants of *D*
2Sa 18:24 *D* sat between the two gates
2Sa 19:11 king *D* sent to Zadok and to
2Sa 19:16 the men of Judah to meet king *D*
2Sa 19:22 *D* said, What have I to do with
2Sa 19:43 have also more right in *D* than ye
2Sa 20:1 and said, We have no part in *D*
2Sa 20:2 of Israel went up from after *D*
2Sa 20:3 *D* came to his house at Jerusalem
2Sa 20:6 *D* said to Abishai, Now shall
2Sa 20:11 Joab, and he that is for *D*
2Sa 20:21 against the king, even against *D*
2Sa 20:26 Jairite was a chief ruler about *D*
2Sa 21:1 in the days of *D* three years
2Sa 21:1 and *D* enquired of the LORD
2Sa 21:3 Wherefore *D* said unto the
2Sa 21:7 that was between them, between *D*
2Sa 21:11 it was told *D* what Rizpah the
2Sa 21:12 *D* went and took the bones of Saul
2Sa 21:15 *D* went down, and his servants with
2Sa 21:15 and *D* waxed faint
2Sa 21:16 sword, thought to have slain *D*
2Sa 21:17 Then the men of *D* sware unto him
2Sa 21:21 Shimeah the brother of *D* slew him
2Sa 21:22 in Gath, and fell by the hand of *D*
2Sa 22:1 *D* spake unto the LORD the words
2Sa 22:51 mercy to his anointed, unto *D*
2Sa 23:1 Now these be the last words of *D*
2Sa 23:1 *D* the son of Jesse said, and the
2Sa 23:8 of the mighty men whom *D* had
2Sa 23:9 of the three mighty men with *D*
2Sa 23:13 came to *D* in the harvest time
2Sa 23:14 *D* was then in an hold, and the
2Sa 23:15 *D* longed, and said, Oh that one
2Sa 23:16 and took it, and brought it to *D*
2Sa 23:23 And *D* set him over his guard
2Sa 24:1 he moved *D* against them to say,
2Sa 24:10 *D* said unto the LORD, I have
2Sa 24:11 For when *D* was up in the morning,
2Sa 24:12 Go and say unto *D*, Thus saith the
2Sa 24:13 So Gad came to *D*, and told him, and
2Sa 24:14 *D* said unto Gad, I am in a great
2Sa 24:17 *D* spake unto the LORD when he saw
2Sa 24:18 And Gad came that day to *D*
2Sa 24:19 And *D*, according to the saying of
2Sa 24:21 *D* said, To buy the threshingfloor
2Sa 24:22 And Araunah said unto *D*, Let my
2Sa 24:24 So *D* bought the threshingfloor and
2Sa 24:25 *D* built there an altar unto the
1Kin 1:1 Now king *D* was old and stricken in
1Kin 1:8 mighty men which belonged to *D*
1Kin 1:11 *D* our lord knoweth it not
1Kin 1:13 Go and get thee in unto king *D*
1Kin 1:28 Then king *D* answered and said,
1Kin 1:31 Let my lord king *D* live for ever
1Kin 1:32 And king *D* said, Call me Zadok the
1Kin 1:37 than the throne of my lord king *D*
1Kin 1:43 Verily our lord king *D* hath made
1Kin 1:47 came to bless our lord king *D*
1Kin 2:1 Now the days of *D* drew nigh that
1Kin 2:10 So *D* slept with his fathers
1Kin 2:10 and was buried in the city of *D*
1Kin 2:11 the days that *D* reigned over
1Kin 2:12 upon the throne of *D* his father
1Kin 2:24 me on the throne of *D* my father
1Kin 2:26 the Lord GOD before *D* my father
1Kin 2:32 my father *D* not knowing thereof,
1Kin 2:33 but upon *D*, and upon his seed, and
1Kin 2:44 that thou didst to *D* my father
1Kin 2:45 and the throne of *D* shall be
1Kin 3:1 and brought her into the city of *D*
1Kin 3:3 in the statutes of *D* his father
1Kin 3:6 servant *D* my father great mercy
1Kin 3:7 king instead of *D* my father
1Kin 3:14 as thy father *D* did walk
1Kin 5:1 for Hiram was ever a lover of *D*
1Kin 5:3 Thou knowest how that *D* my father
1Kin 5:5 the LORD spake unto *D* my father
1Kin 5:7 which hath given unto *D* a wise
1Kin 6:12 which I spake unto *D* thy father
1Kin 7:51 which *D* his father had dedicated
1Kin 8:1 of the LORD out of the city of *D*
1Kin 8:15 with his mouth unto *D* my father
1Kin 8:16 but I chose *D* to be over my
1Kin 8:17 it was in the heart of *D* my
1Kin 8:18 And the LORD said unto *D* my father
1Kin 8:20 up in the room of *D* my father
1Kin 8:24 *D* my father that thou promisedst
1Kin 8:25 keep with thy servant *D* my father
1Kin 8:26 unto thy servant *D* my father
1Kin 8:66 LORD had done for *D* his servant
1Kin 9:4 as *D* thy father walked, in
1Kin 9:5 as I promised to *D* thy father
1Kin 9:24 came up out of the city of *D* unto
1Kin 11:4 as was the heart of *D* his father
1Kin 11:6 the LORD, as did *D* his father
1Kin 11:12 not do it for *D* thy father's sake
1Kin 11:13 thy son for *D* my servant's sake
1Kin 11:15 when *D* was in Edom, and Joab the
1Kin 11:21 that *D* slept with his fathers
1Kin 11:24 when *D* slew them of Zobah
1Kin 11:27 of the city of *D* his father
1Kin 11:33 my judgments, as did *D* his father
1Kin 11:34 his life for *D* my servant's sake
1Kin 11:36 that *D* my servant may have a
1Kin 11:38 commandments, as *D* my servant did
1Kin 11:38 a sure house, as I built for *D*
1Kin 11:39 for this afflict the seed of *D*
1Kin 11:43 in the city of *D* his father
1Kin 12:16 saying, What portion have we in *D*
1Kin 12:16 now see to thine own house, *D*
1Kin 12:19 the house of *D* unto this day
1Kin 12:20 none that followed the house of *D*
1Kin 12:26 kingdom return to the house of *D*
1Kin 13:2 shall be born unto the house of *D*
1Kin 14:8 kingdom away from the house of *D*
1Kin 14:8 hast not been as my servant *D*
1Kin 14:31 with his fathers in the city of *D*
1Kin 15:3 God, as the heart of *D* his father
1Kin 15:5 Because *D* did that which was
1Kin 15:8 they buried him in the city of *D*
1Kin 15:11 of the LORD, as did *D* his father
1Kin 15:24 in the city of *D* his father
1Kin 22:50 in the city of *D* his father
2Kin 8:19 Judah for *D* his servant's sake
2Kin 8:24 with his fathers in the city of *D*
2Kin 9:28 with his fathers in the city of *D*
2Kin 12:21 with his fathers in the city of *D*
2Kin 14:3 LORD, yet not like *D* his father
2Kin 14:20 with his fathers in the city of *D*
2Kin 15:7 with his fathers in the city of *D*
2Kin 15:38 in the city of *D* his father
2Kin 16:2 LORD his God, like *D* his father
2Kin 16:20 with his fathers in the city of *D*
2Kin 17:21 rent Israel from the house of *D*
2Kin 18:3 to all that *D* his father did
2Kin 20:5 the LORD, the God of *D* thy father
2Kin 21:7 of which the LORD said to *D*
2Kin 22:2 in all the way of *D* his father
1Chr 2:15 Ozem the sixth, *D* the seventh
1Chr 3:1 Now these were the sons of *D*
1Chr 3:9 These were all the sons of *D*
1Chr 4:31 their cities unto the reign of *D*
1Chr 6:31 these are they whom *D* set over
1Chr 7:2 number was in the days of *D* two
1Chr 9:22 in their villages, whom *D*
1Chr 10:14 kingdom unto *D* the son of Jesse
1Chr 11:1 themselves to *D* unto Hebron
1Chr 11:3 *D* made a covenant with them in
1Chr 11:3 they anointed *D* king over Israel,
1Chr 11:4 And *D* and all Israel went to
1Chr 11:5 inhabitants of Jebus said to *D*
1Chr 11:5 Nevertheless *D* took the castle of
1Chr 11:5 of Zion, which is the city of *D*
1Chr 11:6 *D* said, Whosoever smiteth the
1Chr 11:7 And *D* dwelt in the castle
1Chr 11:7 they called it the city of *D*
1Chr 11:9 So *D* waxed greater and greater
1Chr 11:10 of the mighty men whom *D* had
1Chr 11:11 of the mighty men whom *D* had
1Chr 11:13 He was with *D* at Pas-dammim, and
1Chr 11:15 went down to the rock to *D*
1Chr 11:16 *D* was then in the hold, and the
1Chr 11:17 *D* longed, and said, Oh that one
1Chr 11:18 and took it, and brought it to *D*
1Chr 11:18 but *D* would not drink of it, but
1Chr 11:25 and *D* set him over his guard
1Chr 12:1 are they that came to *D* to Ziklag
1Chr 12:8 *D* into the hold to the wilderness
1Chr 12:16 and Judah to the hold unto *D*
1Chr 12:17 *D* went out to meet them, and
1Chr 12:18 and he said, Thine are we, *D*
1Chr 12:18 Then *D* received them, and made
1Chr 12:19 there fell some of Manasseh to *D*
1Chr 12:21 they helped *D* against the band of
1Chr 12:22 day there came to *D* to help him
1Chr 12:23 came to *D* to Hebron, to turn the
1Chr 12:31 by name, to come and make *D* king
1Chr 12:38 to make *D* king over all Israel
1Chr 12:38 were of one heart to make *D* king
1Chr 12:39 there they were with *D* three days
1Chr 13:1 *D* consulted with the captains of
1Chr 13:2 *D* said unto all the congregation
1Chr 13:5 So *D* gathered all Israel together
1Chr 13:6 *D* went up, and all Israel, to
1Chr 13:8 And *D* and all Israel played before
1Chr 13:11 *D* was displeased, because the
1Chr 13:12 *D* was afraid of God that day,
1Chr 13:13 So *D* brought not the ark home to
1Chr 13:13 home to himself to the city of *D*
1Chr 14:1 king of Tyre sent messengers to *D*
1Chr 14:2 *D* perceived that the LORD had
1Chr 14:3 *D* took more wives at Jerusalem
1Chr 14:3 *D* begat more sons and daughters
1Chr 14:8 that *D* was anointed king over all
1Chr 14:8 the Philistines went up to seek *D*

1Chr 14:8 *D* heard of it, and went out
1Chr 14:10 *D* enquired of God, saying, Shall
1Chr 14:11 and *D* smote them there
1Chr 14:11 Then *D* said, God hath broken in
1Chr 14:12 *D* gave a commandment, and they
1Chr 14:14 Therefore *D* enquired again of God
1Chr 14:16 *D* therefore did as God commanded
1Chr 14:17 the fame of *D* went out into all
1Chr 15:1 *D* made him houses in the city of
1Chr 15:1 made him houses in the city of *D*
1Chr 15:2 Then *D* said, None ought to carry
1Chr 15:3 *D* gathered all Israel together to
1Chr 15:4 *D* assembled the children of Aaron
1Chr 15:11 *D* called for Zadok and Abiathar
1Chr 15:16 *D* spake to the chief of the
1Chr 15:25 So *D*, and the elders of Israel, and
1Chr 15:27 *D* was clothed with a robe of fine
1Chr 15:27 *D* also had upon him an ephod of
1Chr 15:29 of the Lord came to the city of *D*
1Chr 15:29 at a window saw king *D* dancing
1Chr 16:1 tent that *D* had pitched for it
1Chr 16:2 when *D* had made an end of
1Chr 16:7 Then on that day *D* delivered
1Chr 16:43 *D* returned to bless his house
1Chr 17:1 as *D* sat in his house
1Chr 17:1 that *D* said to Nathan the prophet
1Chr 17:2 Then Nathan said unto *D*, Do all
1Chr 17:4 tell *D* my servant, Thus saith the
1Chr 17:7 shalt thou say unto my servant *D*
1Chr 17:15 so did Nathan speak unto *D*
1Chr 17:16 *D* the king came and sat before the
1Chr 17:18 What can *D* speak more to thee for
1Chr 17:24 let the house of *D* thy servant be
1Chr 18:1 that *D* smote the Philistines, and
1Chr 18:3 *D* smote Hadarezer king of Zobah
1Chr 18:4 *D* took from him a thousand
1Chr 18:4 *D* also houghed all the chariot
1Chr 18:5 *D* slew of the Syrians two and
1Chr 18:6 Then *D* put garrisons in
1Chr 18:6 preserved *D* whithersoever he went
1Chr 18:7 *D* took the shields of gold that
1Chr 18:8 brought *D* very much brass,
1Chr 18:9 how *D* had smitten all the host of
1Chr 18:10 He sent Hadoram his son to king *D*
1Chr 18:11 Them also king *D* dedicated unto
1Chr 18:13 preserved *D* whithersoever he went
1Chr 18:14 So *D* reigned over all Israel, and
1Chr 18:17 the sons of *D* were chief about
1Chr 19:2 *D* said, I will shew kindness unto
1Chr 19:2 *D* sent messengers to comfort him
1Chr 19:2 So the servants of *D* came into
1Chr 19:3 Thinkest thou that *D* doth honour
1Chr 19:5 told *D* how the men were served
1Chr 19:6 had made themselves odious to *D*
1Chr 19:8 when *D* heard of it, he sent Joab,
1Chr 19:17 And it was told *D*
1Chr 19:17 So when *D* had put the battle in
1Chr 19:18 *D* slew of the Syrians seven
1Chr 19:19 Israel, they made peace with *D*
1Chr 20:1 But *D* tarried at Jerusalem
1Chr 20:2 *D* took the crown of their king
1Chr 20:3 Even so dealt *D* with all the
1Chr 20:3 And *D* and all the people returned
1Chr 20:8 and they fell by the hand of *D*
1Chr 21:1 provoked *D* to number Israel
1Chr 21:2 *D* said to Joab and to the rulers
1Chr 21:5 the number of the people unto *D*
1Chr 21:8 *D* said unto God, I have sinned
1Chr 21:10 Go and tell *D*, saying, Thus saith
1Chr 21:11 So Gad came to *D*, and said unto
1Chr 21:13 *D* said unto Gad, I am in a great
1Chr 21:16 *D* lifted up his eyes, and saw the
1Chr 21:16 Then *D* and the elders of Israel,
1Chr 21:17 *D* said unto God, Is it not I that
1Chr 21:18 Lord commanded Gad to say to *D*
1Chr 21:18 that *D* should go up, and set up an
1Chr 21:19 *D* went up at the saying of Gad,
1Chr 21:21 as *D* came to Ornan
1Chr 21:21 Ornan looked and saw *D*
1Chr 21:21 bowed himself to *D* with his face
1Chr 21:22 Then *D* said to Ornan, Grant me
1Chr 21:23 And Ornan said unto *D*, Take it to
1Chr 21:24 king *D* said to Ornan, Nay
1Chr 21:25 So *D* gave to Ornan for the place
1Chr 21:26 *D* built there an altar unto the
1Chr 21:28 At that time when *D* saw that the
1Chr 21:30 But *D* could not go before it to
1Chr 22:1 Then *D* said, This is the house of
1Chr 22:2 *D* commanded to gather together
1Chr 22:3 *D* prepared iron in abundance for
1Chr 22:4 Tyre brought much cedar wood to *D*
1Chr 22:5 *D* said, Solomon my son is young
1Chr 22:5 So *D* prepared abundantly before
1Chr 22:7 *D* said to Solomon, My son, as for
1Chr 22:17 *D* also commanded all the princes
1Chr 23:1 So when *D* was old and full of days
1Chr 23:5 instruments which I made, said *D*
1Chr 23:6 *D* divided them into courses among
1Chr 23:25 For *D* said, The Lord God of
1Chr 23:27 For by the last words of *D* the
1Chr 24:3 *D* distributed them, both Zadok of
1Chr 24:31 in the presence of *D* the king
1Chr 25:1 Moreover *D* and the captains of the
1Chr 26:26 which *D* the king, and the chief
1Chr 26:31 reign of *D* they were sought for
1Chr 26:32 whom king *D* made rulers over the
1Chr 27:18 Elihu, one of the brethren of *D*
1Chr 27:23 But *D* took not the number of them
1Chr 27:24 of the Chronicles of king *D*
1Chr 28:1 *D* assembled all the princes of
1Chr 28:2 Then *D* the king stood up upon his
1Chr 28:11 Then *D* gave to Solomon his son
1Chr 28:19 All this, said *D*, the Lord made
1Chr 28:20 *D* said to Solomon his son, Be
1Chr 29:1 Furthermore *D* the king said unto
1Chr 29:9 *D* the king also rejoiced with
1Chr 29:10 Wherefore *D* blessed the Lord
1Chr 29:10 *D* said, Blessed be thou, Lord God
1Chr 29:20 *D* said to all the congregation,
1Chr 29:22 the son of *D* king the second time
1Chr 29:23 as king instead of *D* his father
1Chr 29:24 all the sons likewise of king *D*
1Chr 29:26 Thus *D* the son of Jesse reigned
1Chr 29:29 Now the acts of *D* the king
2Chr 1:1 And Solomon the son of *D* was
2Chr 1:4 But the ark of God had *D* brought
2Chr 1:4 to the place which *D* had prepared
2Chr 1:8 great mercy unto *D* my father
2Chr 1:9 let thy promise unto *D* my father
2Chr 2:3 thou didst deal with *D* my father
2Chr 2:7 whom *D* my father did provide
2Chr 2:12 who hath given to *D* the king a
2Chr 2:14 men of my lord *D* thy father
2Chr 2:17 *D* his father had numbered them
2Chr 3:1 Lord appeared unto *D* his father
2Chr 3:1 in the place that *D* had prepared
2Chr 5:1 that *D* his father had dedicated
2Chr 5:2 of the Lord out of the city of *D*
2Chr 6:4 with his mouth to my father *D*
2Chr 6:6 have chosen *D* to be over my
2Chr 6:7 Now it was in the heart of *D* my
2Chr 6:8 But the Lord said to *D* my father
2Chr 6:10 up in the room of *D* my father
2Chr 6:15 hast kept with thy servant *D* my
2Chr 6:16 keep with thy servant *D* my father
2Chr 6:17 hast spoken unto thy servant *D*
2Chr 6:42 the mercies of *D* thy servant
2Chr 7:6 which *D* the king had made to
2Chr 7:6 when *D* praised by their ministry
2Chr 7:10 that the Lord had shewed unto *D*
2Chr 7:17 as *D* thy father walked, and do
2Chr 7:18 have covenanted with *D* thy father
2Chr 8:11 of *D* unto the house that he had
2Chr 8:11 in the house of *D* king of Israel
2Chr 8:14 to the order of *D* his father
2Chr 8:14 for so had *D* the man of God
2Chr 9:31 in the city of *D* his father
2Chr 10:16 saying, What portion have we in *D*
2Chr 10:16 your tents, O Israel, and now, *D*
2Chr 10:19 the house of *D* unto this day
2Chr 11:17 years they walked in the way of *D*
2Chr 11:18 of Jerimoth the son of *D* to wife
2Chr 12:16 and was buried in the city of *D*
2Chr 13:5 kingdom over Israel to *D* for ever
2Chr 13:6 servant of Solomon the son of *D*
2Chr 13:8 Lord in the hand of the sons of *D*
2Chr 14:1 they buried him in the city of *D*
2Chr 16:14 made for himself in the city of *D*
2Chr 17:3 in the first ways of his father *D*
2Chr 21:1 with his fathers in the city of *D*
2Chr 21:7 would not destroy the house of *D*
2Chr 21:7 covenant that he had made with *D*
2Chr 21:12 the Lord God of *D* thy father
2Chr 21:20 they buried him in the city of *D*
2Chr 23:3 Lord hath said of the sons of *D*
2Chr 23:18 whom *D* had distributed in the
2Chr 23:18 singing, as it was ordained by *D*
2Chr 24:16 in the city of *D* among the kings
2Chr 24:25 they buried him in the city of *D*
2Chr 27:9 they buried him in the city of *D*
2Chr 28:1 of the Lord, like *D* his father
2Chr 29:2 to all that *D* his father had done
2Chr 29:25 according to the commandment of *D*
2Chr 29:26 stood with the instruments of *D*
2Chr 29:27 ordained by *D* king of Israel
2Chr 29:30 unto the Lord with the words of *D*
2Chr 30:26 of *D* king of Israel there was not
2Chr 32:5 repaired Millo in the city of *D*
2Chr 32:30 to the west side of the city of *D*
2Chr 32:33 the sepulchres of the sons of *D*
2Chr 33:7 God, of which God had said to *D*
2Chr 33:14 a wall without the city of *D*
2Chr 34:2 in the ways of *D* his father
2Chr 34:3 after the God of *D* his father
2Chr 35:3 son of *D* king of Israel did build
2Chr 35:4 the writing of *D* king of Israel
2Chr 35:15 according to the commandment of *D*
Ezr 3:10 the ordinance of *D* king of Israel
Ezr 8:2 of the sons of *D*
Ezr 8:20 Also of the Nethinims, whom *D*
Neh 3:15 that go down from the city of *D*
Neh 3:16 over against the sepulchres of *D*
Neh 12:24 commandment of *D* the man of God
Neh 12:36 instruments of *D* the man of God
Neh 12:37 up by the stairs of the city of *D*
Neh 12:37 of the wall, above the house of *D*
Neh 12:45 according to the commandment of *D*
Neh 12:46 For in the days of *D* and Asaph of
Ps 3:*t* A Psalm of *D*, when he fled from
Ps 4:*t* on Neginoth, A Psalm of *D*
Ps 5:*t* upon Nehiloth, A Psalm of *D*
Ps 6:*t* upon Sheminith, A Psalm of *D*
Ps 7:*t* Shiggaion of *D*, which he sang
Ps 8:*t* upon Gittith, A Psalm of *D*
Ps 9:*t* upon Muth-labben, A Psalm of *D*
Ps 11:*t* the chief Musician, A Psalm of *D*
Ps 12:*t* upon Sheminith, A Psalm of *D*
Ps 13:*t* the chief Musician, A Psalm of *D*
Ps 14:*t* the chief Musician, A Psalm of *D*
Ps 15:*t* A Psalm of *D*
Ps 16:*t* Michtam of *D*
Ps 17:*t* A Prayer of *D*
Ps 18:*t* the chief Musician, A Psalm of *D*
Ps 18:50 mercy to his anointed, to *D*
Ps 19:*t* the chief Musician, A Psalm of *D*
Ps 20:*t* the chief Musician, A Psalm of *D*
Ps 21:*t* the chief Musician, A Psalm of *D*
Ps 22:*t* Aijeleth Shahar, A Psalm of *D*
Ps 23:*t* A Psalm of *D*
Ps 24:*t* A Psalm of *D*
Ps 25:*t* A Psalm of *D*
Ps 26:*t* A Psalm of *D*
Ps 27:*t* A Psalm of *D*
Ps 28:*t* A Psalm of *D*
Ps 29:*t* A Psalm of *D*
Ps 30:*t* the dedication of the house of *D*
Ps 31:*t* the chief Musician, A Psalm of *D*
Ps 32:*t* A Psalm of *D*, A Maschil
Ps 34:*t* A Psalm of *D*, when he changed his
Ps 35:*t* A Psalm of *D*
Ps 36:*t* the chief Musician, A Psalm of *D*
Ps 37:*t* A Psalm of *D*
Ps 38:*t* A Psalm of *D*, to bring to
Ps 39:*t* even to Jeduthun, A Psalm of *D*
Ps 40:*t* the chief Musician, A Psalm of *D*
Ps 41:*t* the chief Musician, A Psalm of *D*
Ps 51:*t* the chief Musician, A Psalm of *D*
Ps 52:*t* Musician, Maschil, A Psalm of *D*
Ps 52:*t* *D* is come to the house of
Ps 53:*t* Mahalath, Maschil, A Psalm of *D*
Ps 54:*t* Neginoth, Maschil, A Psalm of *D*
Ps 54:*t* Doth not *D* hide himself with us
Ps 55:*t* Neginoth, Maschil, A Psalm of *D*
Ps 56:*t* a Michtam of *D*, when the
Ps 57:*t* Altaschith, Michtam of *D*
Ps 58:*t* Altaschith, Michtam of *D*
Ps 59:*t* Altaschith, Michtam of *D*
Ps 60:*t* upon Shushan-eduth, Michtam of *D*
Ps 61:*t* upon Neginah, A Psalm of *D*
Ps 62:*t* to Jeduthun, A Psalm of *D*
Ps 63:*t* A Psalm of *D*, when he was in the
Ps 64:*t* the chief Musician, A Psalm of *D*
Ps 65:*t* Musician, A Psalm and Song of *D*
Ps 68:*t* Musician, A Psalm or Song of *D*
Ps 69:*t* upon Shoshannim, A Psalm of *D*
Ps 70:*t* the chief Musician, A Psalm of *D*
Ps 72:20 The prayers of *D* the son of Jesse
Ps 78:70 He chose *D* also his servant, and
Ps 86:*t* A Prayer of *D*
Ps 89:3 I have sworn unto *D* my servant

Ps 89:20 I have found *D* my servant
Ps 89:35 that I will not lie unto *D*
Ps 89:49 thou swarest unto *D* in thy truth
Ps 101:*t* A Psalm of *D*
Ps 103:*t* A Psalm of *D*
Ps 108:*t* A Song or Psalm of *D*
Ps 109:*t* the chief Musician, A Psalm of *D*
Ps 110:*t* A Psalm of *D*
Ps 122:*t* A Song of degrees of *D*
Ps 122:5 the thrones of the house of *D*
Ps 124:*t* A Song of degrees of *D*
Ps 131:*t* A Song of degrees of *D*
Ps 132:1 Lord, remember *D*, and all his
Ps 132:11 LORD hath sworn in truth unto *D*
Ps 132:17 will I make the horn of *D* to bud
Ps 133:*t* A Song of degrees of *D*
Ps 138:*t* A Psalm of *D*
Ps 139:*t* the chief Musician, A Psalm of *D*
Ps 140:*t* the chief Musician, A Psalm of *D*
Ps 141:*t* A Psalm of *D*
Ps 142:*t* Maschil of *D*
Ps 143:*t* A Psalm of *D*
Ps 144:*t* A Psalm of *D*
Ps 144:10 who delivereth *D* his servant from
Prov 1:1 Proverbs of Solomon the son of *D*
Eccl 1:1 of the Preacher, the son of *D*
Song 4:4 tower of *D* builded for an armoury
Is 7:2 And it was told the house of *D*
Is 7:13 said, Hear ye now, O house of *D*
Is 9:7 be no end, upon the throne of *D*
Is 16:5 in truth in the tabernacle of *D*
Is 22:9 the breaches of the city of *D*
Is 22:22 the key of the house of *D* will I
Is 29:1 to Ariel, the city where *D* dwelt
Is 38:5 the LORD, the God of *D* thy father
Is 55:3 you, even the sure mercies of *D*
Jer 17:25 sitting upon the throne of *D*
Jer 21:12 O house of *D*, thus saith the LORD
Jer 22:2 that sittest upon the throne of *D*
Jer 22:4 sitting upon the throne of *D*
Jer 22:30 sitting upon the throne of *D*
Jer 23:5 raise unto *D* a righteous Branch
Jer 29:16 that sitteth upon the throne of *D*
Jer 30:9 *D* their king, whom I will raise
Jer 33:15 righteousness to grow up unto *D*
Jer 33:17 *D* shall never want a man to sit
Jer 33:21 be broken with *D* my servant
Jer 33:22 multiply the seed of *D* my servant
Jer 33:26 *D* my servant, so that I will not
Jer 36:30 none to sit upon the throne of *D*
Eze 34:23 feed them, even my servant *D*
Eze 34:24 my servant *D* a prince among them
Eze 37:24 *D* my servant shall be king over
Eze 37:25 my servant *D* shall be their
Hos 3:5 LORD their God, and *D* their king
Amos 6:5 instruments of musick, like *D*
Amos 9:11 tabernacle of *D* that is fallen
Zec 12:7 that the glory of the house of *D*
Zec 12:8 them at that day shall be as *D*
Zec 12:8 the house of *D* shall be as God,
Zec 12:10 I will pour upon the house of *D*
Zec 12:12 family of the house of *D* apart
Zec 13:1 fountain opened to the house of *D*
Mt 1:1 of Jesus Christ, the son of *D*
Mt 1:6 And Jesse begat *D* the king
Mt 1:6 *D* the king begat Solomon of her
Mt 1:17 to *D* are fourteen generations
Mt 1:17 from *D* until the carrying away
Mt 1:20 saying, Joseph, thou son of *D*
Mt 9:27 crying, and saying, Thou son of *D*
Mt 12:3 them, Have ye not read what *D* did
Mt 12:23 and said, Is not this the son of *D*
Mt 15:22 on me, O Lord, thou son of *D*
Mt 20:30 on us, O Lord, thou son of *D*
Mt 20:31 on us, O Lord, thou son of *D*
Mt 21:9 saying, Hosanna to the son of *D*
Mt 21:15 saying, Hosanna to the son of *D*
Mt 22:42 They say unto him, The son of *D*
Mt 22:43 How then doth *D* in spirit call
Mt 22:45 If *D* then call him Lord
Mk 2:25 Have ye never read what *D* did
Mk 10:47 out, and say, Jesus, thou son of *D*
Mk 10:48 more a great deal, Thou son of *D*
Mk 11:10 be the kingdom of our father *D*
Mk 12:35 that Christ is the son of *D*
Mk 12:36 For *D* himself said by the Holy
Mk 12:37 *D* therefore himself calleth him
Lk 1:27 was Joseph, of the house of *D*
Lk 1:32 him the throne of his father *D*
Lk 1:69 us in the house of his servant *D*
Lk 2:4 into Judaea, unto the city of *D*
Lk 2:4 was of the house and lineage of *D*
Lk 2:11 day in the city of *D* a Saviour
Lk 3:31 of Nathan, which was the son of *D*
Lk 6:3 read so much as this, what *D* did
Lk 18:38 saying, Jesus, thou son of *D*
Lk 18:39 so much the more, Thou son of *D*
Lk 20:42 *D* himself saith in the book of
Lk 20:44 *D* therefore calleth him Lord, how
Jn 7:42 Christ cometh of the seed of *D*
Jn 7:42 town of Bethlehem, where *D* was
Acts 1:16 *D* spake before concerning Judas
Acts 2:25 For *D* speaketh concerning him, I
Acts 2:29 speak unto you of the patriarch *D*
Acts 2:34 For *D* is not ascended into the
Acts 4:25 mouth of thy servant *D* hast said
Acts 7:45 our fathers, unto the days of *D*
Acts 13:22 up unto them *D* to be their king
Acts 13:22 I have found *D* the son of Jesse,
Acts 13:34 give you the sure mercies of *D*
Acts 13:36 For *D*, after he had served his
Acts 15:16 build again the tabernacle of *D*
Rom 1:3 seed of *D* according to the flesh
Rom 4:6 Even as *D* also describeth the
Rom 11:9 *D* saith, Let their table be made
2Ti 2:8 of *D* was raised from the dead
Heb 4:7 a certain day, saying in *D*
Heb 11:32 of *D* also, and Samuel, and of the
Rev 3:7 true, he that hath the key of *D*
Rev 5:5 the tribe of Juda, the Root of *D*
Rev 22:16 am the root and the offspring of *D*

## DAWNING

Josh 6:15 rose early about the *d* of the day
Judg 19:26 the woman in the *d* of the day
Job 3:9 let it see the *d* of the day
Job 7:4 to and fro unto the *d* of the day
Ps 119:147 I prevented the *d* of the morning

## DAYTIME

Num 14:14 by *d* in a pillar of a cloud, and
Job 5:14 They meet with darkness in the *d*
Job 24:16 marked for themselves in the *d*
Ps 22:2 O my God, I cry in the *d*, but
Ps 42:8 his lovingkindness in the *d*
Ps 78:14 In the *d* also he led them with a
Is 4:6 a shadow in the *d* from the heat
Is 21:8 upon the watchtower in the *d*
2Pet 2:13 it pleasure to riot in the *d*

## DEACON

1Ti 3:10 let them use the office of a *d*
1Ti 3:13 a *d* well purchase to themselves a

## DEACONS

Phil 1:1 Philippi, with the bishops and *d*
1Ti 3:8 Likewise must the *d* be grave
1Ti 3:12 Let the *d* be the husbands of one

## DEAD

Gen 20:3 him, Behold, thou art but a *d* man
Gen 23:3 stood up from before his *d*
Gen 23:4 I may bury my *d* out of my sight
Gen 23:6 of our sepulchres bury thy *d*
Gen 23:6 but that thou mayest bury thy *d*
Gen 23:8 should bury my *d* out of my sight
Gen 23:11 bury thy *d*
Gen 23:13 of me, and I will bury my *d* there
Gen 23:15 bury therefore thy *d*
Gen 42:38 for his brother is *d*, and he is
Gen 44:20 and his brother is *d*, and he alone
Gen 50:15 saw that their father was *d*
Ex 4:19 for all the men are *d* which
Ex 9:7 of the cattle of the Israelites *d*
Ex 12:30 a house where there was not one *d*
Ex 12:33 for they said, We be all *d* men
Ex 14:30 Egyptians *d* upon the sea shore
Ex 21:34 and the *d* beast shall be his
Ex 21:35 the *d* ox also they shall divide
Ex 21:36 and the *d* shall be his own
Lev 11:31 doth touch them, when they be *d*
Lev 11:32 any of them, when they are *d*
Lev 19:28 cuttings in your flesh for the *d*
Lev 21:1 for the *d* among his people
Lev 21:11 shall he go in to any *d* body
Lev 22:4 thing that is unclean by the *d*
Num 5:2 and whosoever is defiled by the *d*
Num 6:6 LORD he shall come at no *d* body
Num 6:11 him, for that he sinned by the *d*
Num 9:6 defiled by the *d* body of a man
Num 9:7 defiled by the *d* body of a man
Num 9:10 be unclean by reason of a *d* body
Num 12:12 Let her not be as one *d*, of whom
Num 16:48 And he stood between the *d*
Num 19:11 He that toucheth the *d* body of
Num 19:13 Whosoever toucheth the *d* body of
Num 19:13 *d* body of any man that is *d*
Num 19:16 in the open fields, or a *d* body
Num 19:18 a bone, or one slain, or one *d*
Num 20:29 congregation saw that Aaron was *d*
Deut 2:16 and *d* from among the people,
Deut 14:1 between your eyes for the *d*
Deut 14:8 flesh, nor touch their *d* carcase
Deut 25:5 the wife of the *d* shall not marry
Deut 25:6 name of his brother which is *d*
Deut 26:14 nor given ought thereof for the *d*
Josh 1:2 Moses my servant is *d*
Judg 2:19 to pass, when the judge was *d*
Judg 3:25 was fallen down *d* on the earth
Judg 4:1 of the LORD, when Ehud was *d*
Judg 4:22 her tent, behold, Sisera lay *d*
Judg 5:27 he bowed, there he fell down *d*
Judg 8:33 to pass, as soon as Gideon was *d*
Judg 9:55 Israel saw that Abimelech was *d*
Judg 16:30 So the *d* which he slew at his
Judg 20:5 have they forced, that she is *d*
Ruth 1:8 you, as ye have dealt with the *d*
Ruth 2:20 to the living and to the *d*
Ruth 4:5 the Moabitess, the wife of the *d*
Ruth 4:5 of the *d* upon his inheritance
Ruth 4:10 of the *d* upon his inheritance
Ruth 4:10 that the name of the *d* be not cut
1Sa 4:17 also, Hophni and Phinehas, are *d*
1Sa 4:19 in law and her husband were *d*
1Sa 17:51 saw their champion was *d*, they
1Sa 24:14 after a *d* dog, after a flea
1Sa 25:39 when David heard that Nabal was *d*
1Sa 28:3 Now Samuel was *d*, and all Israel
1Sa 31:5 armourbearer saw that Saul was *d*
1Sa 31:7 and that Saul and his sons were *d*
2Sa 1:4 the people also are fallen and *d*
2Sa 1:4 and Jonathan his son are *d* also
2Sa 1:5 Saul and Jonathan his son be *d*
2Sa 2:7 for your master Saul is *d*
2Sa 4:1 heard that Abner was *d* in Hebron
2Sa 4:10 me, saying, Behold, Saul is *d*
2Sa 9:8 look upon such a *d* dog as I am
2Sa 11:21 Uriah the Hittite is *d* also
2Sa 11:24 some of the king's servants be *d*
2Sa 11:24 Uriah the Hittite is *d* also
2Sa 11:26 that Uriah her husband was *d*
2Sa 12:18 to tell him that the child was *d*
2Sa 12:18 we tell him that the child is *d*
2Sa 12:19 perceived that the child was *d*
2Sa 12:19 unto his servants, Is the child *d*
2Sa 12:19 And they said, He is *d*
2Sa 12:21 but when the child was *d*, thou
2Sa 12:23 But now he is *d*, wherefore should
2Sa 13:32 for Amnon only is *d*
2Sa 13:33 that all the king's sons are *d*
2Sa 13:33 for Amnon only is *d*
2Sa 13:39 concerning Amnon, seeing he was *d*
2Sa 14:2 had a long time mourned for the *d*
2Sa 14:5 widow woman, and mine husband is *d*
2Sa 16:9 Why should this *d* dog curse my
2Sa 18:20 because the king's son is *d*
2Sa 19:10 anointed over us, is *d* in battle
2Sa 19:28 but *d* men before my lord the king
1Kin 3:20 laid her *d* child in my bosom
1Kin 3:21 my child suck, behold, it was *d*
1Kin 3:22 is my son, and the *d* is thy son
1Kin 3:22 but the *d* is thy son, and the
1Kin 3:23 that liveth, and thy son is the *d*
1Kin 3:23 but thy son is the *d*, and my son
1Kin 11:21 the captain of the host was *d*
1Kin 13:31 to his sons, saying, When I am *d*
1Kin 21:14 saying, Naboth is stoned, and is *d*
1Kin 21:15 that Naboth was stoned, and was *d*
1Kin 21:15 for Naboth is not alive, but *d*
1Kin 21:16 when Ahab heard that Naboth was *d*
2Kin 3:5 it came to pass, when Ahab was *d*
2Kin 4:1 Thy servant my husband is *d*
2Kin 4:32 house, behold, the child was *d*
2Kin 8:5 he had restored a *d* body to life
2Kin 11:1 of Ahaziah saw that her son was *d*
2Kin 19:35 behold, they were all *d* corpses
2Kin 23:30 him in a chariot *d* from Megiddo
1Chr 1:44 And when Bela was *d*, Jobab the son
1Chr 1:45 And when Jobab was *d*, Husham of
1Chr 1:46 And when Husham was *d*, Hadad the
1Chr 1:47 And when Hadad was *d*, Samlah of
1Chr 1:48 And when Samlah was *d*, Shaul of
1Chr 1:49 And when Shaul was *d*, Baal-hanan

1Chr 1:50 And when Baal-hanan was *d*, Hadad
1Chr 2:19 And when Azubah was *d*, Caleb took
1Chr 2:24 Hezron was *d* in Caleb-ephratah
1Chr 10:5 armourbearer saw that Saul was *d*
1Chr 10:7 and that Saul and his sons were *d*
2Chr 20:24 they were *d* bodies fallen to the
2Chr 20:25 both riches with the *d* bodies
2Chr 22:10 of Ahaziah saw that her son was *d*
Est 2:7 when her father and mother were *d*
Job 1:19 upon the young men, and they are *d*
Job 26:5 *D* things are formed from under
Ps 31:12 forgotten as a *d* man out of mind
Ps 76:6 and horse are cast into a *d* sleep
Ps 79:2 The *d* bodies of thy servants have
Ps 88:5 Free among the *d*, like the slain
Ps 88:10 Wilt thou shew wonders to the *d*
Ps 88:10 shall the *d* arise and praise thee
Ps 106:28 and ate the sacrifices of the *d*
Ps 110:6 fill the places with the *d* bodies
Ps 115:17 The *d* praise not the LORD,
Ps 143:3 as those that have been long *d*
Prov 2:18 death, and her paths unto the *d*
Prov 9:18 knoweth not that the *d* are there
Prov 21:16 in the congregation of the *d*
Eccl 4:2 Wherefore I praised the *d* which
Eccl 4:2 the *d* which are already *d* more
Eccl 9:3 and after that they go to the *d*
Eccl 9:4 dog is better than a *d* lion
Eccl 9:5 but the *d* know not any thing,
Eccl 10:1 *D* flies cause the ointment of the
Is 8:19 for the living to the *d*
Is 14:9 it stirreth up the *d* for thee
Is 22:2 with the sword, nor *d* in battle
Is 26:14 They are *d*, they shall not live
Is 26:19 Thy *d* men shall live, together
Is 26:19 together with my *d* body shall
Is 26:19 and the earth shall cast out the *d*
Is 37:36 behold, they were all *d* corpses
Is 59:10 are in desolate places as *d* men
Jer 16:7 to comfort them for the *d*
Jer 22:10 Weep ye not for the *d*, neither
Jer 26:23 cast his *d* body into the graves
Jer 31:40 the whole valley of the *d* bodies
Jer 33:5 them with the *d* bodies of men
Jer 34:20 their *d* bodies shall be for meat
Jer 36:30 his *d* body shall be cast out in
Jer 41:9 cast all the *d* bodies of the men
Lam 3:6 places, as they that be *d* of old
Eze 6:5 I will lay the *d* carcases of the
Eze 24:17 cry, make no mourning for the *d*
Eze 44:25 they shall come at no *d* person to
Eze 44:31 of any thing that is *d* of itself
Amos 8:3 there shall be many *d* bodies in
Hag 2:13 by a *d* body touch any of these
Mt 2:19 But when Herod was *d*, behold, an
Mt 2:20 for they are *d* which sought the
Mt 8:22 and let the *d* bury their *d*
Mt 9:18 saying, My daughter is even now *d*
Mt 9:24 for the maid is not *d*, but
Mt 10:8 cleanse the lepers, raise the *d*
Mt 11:5 the *d* are raised up, and the poor
Mt 14:2 he is risen from the *d*
Mt 17:9 of man be risen again from the *d*
Mt 22:31 the resurrection of the *d*
Mt 22:32 God is not the God of the *d*
Mt 23:27 are within full of *d* men's bones
Mt 27:64 people, He is risen from the *d*
Mt 28:4 did shake, and became as *d* men
Mt 28:7 that he is risen from the *d*
Mk 5:35 which said, Thy daughter is *d*
Mk 5:39 the damsel is not *d*, but sleepeth
Mk 6:14 the Baptist was risen from the *d*
Mk 6:16 he is risen from the *d*
Mk 9:9 Son of man were risen from the *d*
Mk 9:10 the rising from the *d* should mean
Mk 9:26 and he was as one *d*
Mk 9:26 insomuch that many said, He is *d*
Mk 12:25 when they shall rise from the *d*
Mk 12:26 And as touching the *d*, that they
Mk 12:27 He is not the God of the *d*
Mk 15:44 marvelled if he were already *d*
Mk 15:44 whether he had been any while *d*
Lk 7:12 there was a *d* man carried out,
Lk 7:15 And he that was *d* sat up, and began
Lk 7:22 the *d* are raised, to the poor the
Lk 8:49 saying to him, Thy daughter is *d*
Lk 8:52 she is not *d*, but sleepeth
Lk 8:53 to scorn, knowing that she was *d*
Lk 9:7 that John was risen from the *d*
Lk 9:60 Let the *d* bury their *d*
Lk 10:30 and departed, leaving him half *d*
Lk 15:24 For this my son was *d*, and is
Lk 15:32 for this thy brother was *d*
Lk 16:30 if one went unto them from the *d*
Lk 16:31 though one rose from the *d*
Lk 20:35 and the resurrection from the *d*
Lk 20:37 Now that the *d* are raised
Lk 20:38 For he is not a God of the *d*
Lk 24:5 seek ye the living among the *d*
Lk 24:46 to rise from the *d* the third day
Jn 2:22 therefore he was risen from the *d*
Jn 5:21 as the Father raiseth up the *d*
Jn 5:25 when the *d* shall hear the voice
Jn 6:49 manna in the wilderness, and are *d*
Jn 6:58 fathers did eat manna, and are *d*
Jn 8:52 Abraham is *d*, and the prophets
Jn 8:53 our father Abraham, which is *d*
Jn 8:53 and the prophets are *d*
Jn 11:14 unto them plainly, Lazarus is *d*
Jn 11:25 believeth in me, though he were *d*
Jn 11:39 the sister of him that was *d*
Jn 11:39 for he hath been *d* four days
Jn 11:41 the place where the *d* was laid
Jn 11:44 And he that was *d* came forth
Jn 12:1 Lazarus was which had been *d*
Jn 12:1 *d*, whom he raised from the *d*
Jn 12:9 whom he had raised from the *d*
Jn 12:17 grave, and raised him from the *d*
Jn 19:33 and saw that he was *d* already
Jn 20:9 he must rise again from the *d*
Jn 21:14 that he was risen from the *d*
Acts 2:29 David, that he is both *d* and
Acts 3:15 whom God hath raised from the *d*
Acts 4:2 Jesus the resurrection from the *d*
Acts 4:10 whom God raised from the *d*
Acts 5:10 young men came in, and found her *d*
Acts 7:4 thence, when his father was *d*
Acts 10:41 with him after he rose from the *d*
Acts 10:42 God to be the Judge of quick and *d*
Acts 13:30 But God raised him from the *d*
Acts 13:34 that he raised him up from the *d*
Acts 14:19 the city, supposing he had been *d*
Acts 17:3 and risen again from the *d*
Acts 17:31 he hath raised him from the *d*
Acts 17:32 of the resurrection of the *d*
Acts 20:9 the third loft, and was taken up *d*
Acts 23:6 resurrection of the *d* I am called
Acts 24:15 shall be a resurrection of the *d*
Acts 24:21 the resurrection of the *d* I am
Acts 25:19 and of one Jesus, which was *d*
Acts 26:8 you, that God should raise the *d*
Acts 26:23 first that should rise from the *d*
Acts 28:6 or fallen down *d* suddenly
Rom 1:4 by the resurrection from the *d*
Rom 4:17 even God, who quickeneth the *d*
Rom 4:19 considered not his own body now *d*
Rom 4:24 up Jesus our Lord from the *d*
Rom 5:15 the offence of one many be *d*
Rom 6:2 How shall we, that are *d* to sin
Rom 6:4 the *d* by the glory of the Father
Rom 6:7 For he that is *d* is freed from
Rom 6:8 Now if we be *d* with Christ
Rom 6:9 raised from the *d* dieth no more
Rom 6:11 to be *d* indeed unto sin, but
Rom 6:13 those that are alive from the *d*
Rom 7:2 but if the husband be *d*, she is
Rom 7:3 but if her husband be *d*, she is
Rom 7:4 ye also are become *d* to the law
Rom 7:4 to him who is raised from the *d*
Rom 7:6 that being *d* wherein we were held
Rom 7:8 For without the law sin was *d*
Rom 8:10 the body is *d* because of sin
Rom 8:11 up Jesus from the *d* dwell in you
Rom 8:11 *d* shall also quicken your mortal
Rom 10:7 bring up Christ again from the *d*
Rom 10:9 God hath raised him from the *d*
Rom 11:15 of them be, but life from the *d*
Rom 14:9 he might be Lord both of the *d*
1Cor 7:39 but if her husband be *d*, she is
1Cor 15:12 preached that he rose from the *d*
1Cor 15:12 there is no resurrection of the *d*
1Cor 15:13 there be no resurrection of the *d*
1Cor 15:15 up, if so be that the *d* rise not
1Cor 15:16 For if the *d* rise not, then is
1Cor 15:20 now is Christ risen from the *d*
1Cor 15:21 also the resurrection of the *d*
1Cor 15:29 do which are baptized for the *d*
1Cor 15:29 if the *d* rise not at all
1Cor 15:29 are they then baptized for the *d*
1Cor 15:32 it me, if the *d* rise not
1Cor 15:35 will say, How are the *d* raised up
1Cor 15:42 also is the resurrection of the *d*
1Cor 15:52 sound, and the *d* shall be raised
2Cor 1:9 but in God which raiseth the *d*
2Cor 5:14 one died for all, then were all *d*
Gal 1:1 Father, who raised him from the *d*
Gal 2:19 I through the law am *d* to the law
Gal 2:21 the law, then Christ is *d* in vain
Eph 1:20 when he raised him from the *d*
Eph 2:1 who were *d* in trespasses and sins
Eph 2:5 Even when we were *d* in sins
Eph 5:14 sleepest, and arise from the *d*
Phil 3:11 unto the resurrection of the *d*
Col 1:18 the firstborn from the *d*
Col 2:12 who hath raised him from the *d*
Col 2:13 being *d* in your sins and the
Col 2:20 Wherefore if ye be *d* with Christ
Col 3:3 For ye are *d*, and your life is hid
1Th 1:10 heaven, whom he raised from the *d*
1Th 4:16 the *d* in Christ shall rise first
1Ti 5:6 in pleasure is *d* while she liveth
2Ti 2:8 from the *d* according to my gospel
2Ti 2:11 For if we be *d* with him, we shall
2Ti 4:1 the *d* at his appearing and his
Heb 6:1 of repentance from *d* works
Heb 6:2 and of resurrection of the *d*
Heb 9:14 purge your conscience from *d*
Heb 9:17 is of force after men are *d*
Heb 11:4 and by it he being *d* yet speaketh
Heb 11:12 even of one, and him as good as *d*
Heb 11:19 to raise him up, even from the *d*
Heb 11:35 their *d* raised to life again
Heb 13:20 again from the *d* our Lord Jesus
Jas 2:17 faith, if it hath not works, is *d*
Jas 2:20 that faith without works is *d*
Jas 2:26 the body without the spirit is *d*
Jas 2:26 so faith without works is *d* also
1Pet 1:3 of Jesus Christ from the *d*
1Pet 1:21 that raised him up from the *d*
1Pet 2:24 being *d* to sins, should live unto
1Pet 4:5 ready to judge the quick and the *d*
1Pet 4:6 preached also to them that are *d*
Jude 12 withereth, without fruit, twice *d*
Rev 1:5 and the first begotten of the *d*
Rev 1:17 saw him, I fell at his feet as *d*
Rev 1:18 I am he that liveth, and was *d*
Rev 2:8 first and the last, which was *d*
Rev 3:1 a name that thou livest, and art *d*
Rev 11:8 their *d* bodies shall lie in the
Rev 11:9 see their *d* bodies three days
Rev 11:9 shall not suffer their *d* bodies
Rev 11:18 is come, and the time of the *d*
Rev 14:13 Blessed are the *d* which die in
Rev 16:3 it became as the blood of a *d* man
Rev 20:5 But the rest of the *d* lived not
Rev 20:12 And I saw the *d*, small and great,
Rev 20:12 the *d* were judged out of those
Rev 20:13 gave up the *d* which were in it
Rev 20:13 up the *d* which were in them

## DEADLY

1Sa 5:11 for there was a *d* destruction
Ps 17:9 oppress me, from my *d* enemies
Eze 30:24 the groanings of a *d* wounded man
Mk 16:18 and if they drink any *d* thing
Jas 3:8 an unruly evil, full of *d* poison
Rev 13:3 and his *d* wound was healed
Rev 13:12 beast, whose *d* wound was healed

## DEAF

Ex 4:11 or who maketh the dumb, or *d*
Lev 19:14 Thou shalt not curse the *d*
Ps 38:13 But I, as a *d* man, heard not
Ps 58:4 they are like the *d* adder that
Is 29:18 in that day shall the *d* hear the
Is 35:5 the ears of the *d* shall be
Is 42:18 Hear, ye *d*
Is 42:19 or *d*, as my messenger that I sent
Is 43:8 eyes, and the *d* that have ears
Mic 7:16 mouth, their ears shall be *d*
Mt 11:5 the *d* hear, the dead are raised
Mk 7:32 bring unto him one that was *d*
Mk 7:37 he maketh both the *d* to hear
Mk 9:25 *d* spirit, I charge thee, come out
Lk 7:22 the *d* hear, the dead are raised,

## DEAL

Gen 19:9 now will we *d* worse with thee,
Gen 21:23 thou wilt not *d* falsely with me
Gen 24:49 And now if ye will *d* kindly
Gen 32:9 and I will *d* well with thee
Gen 34:31 Should he *d* with our sister as

Gen 47:29 *d* kindly and truly with me
Ex 1:10 let us *d* wisely with them
Ex 8:29 but let not Pharaoh *d* deceitfully
Ex 21:9 he shall *d* with her after the
Ex 23:11 thou shalt *d* with thy vineyard
Ex 29:40 tenth *d* of flour mingled with the
Lev 14:21 one tenth *d* of fine flour mingled
Lev 19:11 not steal, neither *d* falsely
Num 11:15 if thou *d* thus with me, kill me,
Num 15:4 tenth *d* of flour mingled with the
Num 28:13 a several tenth *d* of flour
Num 28:21 A several tenth *d* shalt thou
Num 28:29 A several tenth *d* unto one lamb
Num 29:4 one tenth *d* for one lamb,
Num 29:10 A several tenth *d* for one lamb
Num 29:15 a several tenth *d* to each lamb of
Deut 7:5 But thus shall ye *d* with them
Josh 2:14 the land, that we will *d* kindly
Ruth 1:8 the LORD *d* kindly with you, as ye
1Sa 20:8 Therefore thou shalt *d* kindly
2Sa 18:5 *D* gently for my sake with the
2Chr 2:3 As thou didst *d* with David my
2Chr 2:3 dwell therein, even so *d* with me
2Chr 19:11 *D* courageously, and the LORD shall
Job 42:8 lest I *d* with you after your
Ps 75:4 unto the fools, *D* not foolishly
Ps 105:25 to *d* subtilly with his servants
Ps 119:17 *D* bountifully with thy servant,
Ps 119:124 *D* with thy servant according unto
Ps 142:7 for thou shalt *d* bountifully with
Prov 12:22 but they that *d* truly are his
Is 26:10 of uprightness will he *d* unjustly
Is 33:1 make an end to *d* treacherously
Is 33:1 they shall *d* treacherously with
Is 48:8 wouldest *d* very treacherously
Is 52:13 my servant shall *d* prudently
Is 58:7 Is it not to *d* thy bread to the
Jer 12:1 happy that *d* very treacherously
Jer 18:23 *d* thus with them in the time of
Jer 21:2 if so be that the LORD will *d*
Eze 8:18 Therefore will I also *d* in fury
Eze 16:59 I will even *d* with thee as thou
Eze 18:9 kept my judgments, to *d* truly
Eze 22:14 the days that I shall *d* with thee
Eze 23:25 they shall *d* furiously with thee
Eze 23:29 they shall *d* with thee hatefully,
Eze 31:11 he shall surely *d* with him
Dan 1:13 thou seest, *d* with thy servants
Dan 11:7 shall *d* against them, and shall
Hab 1:13 upon them that *d* treacherously
Mal 2:10 why do we *d* treacherously every
Mal 2:15 let none *d* treacherously against
Mal 2:16 that ye *d* not treacherously
Mk 7:36 more a great *d* they published it
Mk 10:48 but he cried the more a great *d*

### DEALEST

Ex 5:15 Wherefore *d* thou thus with thy
Is 33:1 *d* treacherously, and they dealt

### DEALETH

Judg 18:4 thus *d* Micah with me, and hath
1Sa 23:22 told me that he *d* very subtilly
Prov 10:4 poor that *d* with a slack hand
Prov 13:16 prudent man *d* with knowledge
Prov 14:17 He that is soon angry *d* foolishly
Prov 21:24 is his name, who *d* in proud wrath
Is 21:2 dealer *d* treacherously, and the
Jer 6:13 the priest every one *d* falsely
Jer 8:10 the priest every one *d* falsely
Heb 12:7 God *d* with you as with sons

### DEALS

Lev 14:10 three tenth *d* of fine flour for a
Lev 23:13 thereof shall be two tenth *d* of
Lev 23:17 two wave loaves of two tenth *d*
Lev 24:5 two tenth *d* shall be in one cake
Num 15:6 for a meat offering two tenth *d*
Num 15:9 *d* of flour mingled with half an
Num 28:9 two tenth *d* of flour for a meat
Num 28:12 three tenth *d* of flour for a meat
Num 28:12 two tenth *d* of flour for a meat
Num 28:20 three tenth *d* shall ye offer for
Num 28:20 bullock, and two tenth *d* for a ram
Num 28:28 three tenth *d* unto one bullock,
Num 28:28 two tenth *d* unto one ram,
Num 29:3 three tenth *d* for a bullock
Num 29:3 and two tenth *d* for a ram
Num 29:9 three tenth *d* to a bullock
Num 29:9 and two tenth *d* to one ram,
Num 29:14 three tenth *d* unto every bullock
Num 29:14 two tenth *d* to each ram of the

### DEALT

Gen 16:6 when Sarai *d* hardly with her, she
Gen 33:11 because God hath *d* graciously
Gen 43:6 Wherefore *d* ye so ill with me, as
Ex 1:20 Therefore God *d* well with the
Ex 14:11 hast thou *d* thus with us, to
Ex 18:11 they *d* proudly he was above them
Ex 21:8 seeing he hath *d* deceitfully with
Judg 9:16 if ye have *d* well with Jerubbaal
Judg 9:19 If ye then have *d* truly and
Judg 9:23 and the men of Shechem *d*
Ruth 1:8 as ye have *d* with the dead, and
Ruth 1:20 hath *d* very bitterly with me
1Sa 24:18 how that thou hast *d* well with me
1Sa 25:31 shall have *d* well with my lord
2Sa 6:19 he *d* among all the people, even
2Kin 12:15 for they *d* faithfully
2Kin 21:6 *d* with familiar spirits and
2Kin 22:7 hand, because they *d* faithfully
1Chr 16:3 he *d* to every one of Israel, both
1Chr 20:3 Even so *d* David with all the
2Chr 6:37 done amiss, and have *d* wickedly
2Chr 11:23 he *d* wisely, and dispersed of all
2Chr 33:6 *d* with a familiar spirit, and with
Neh 1:7 We have *d* very corruptly against
Neh 9:10 that they *d* proudly against them
Neh 9:16 But they and our fathers *d* proudly
Neh 9:29 yet they *d* proudly, and hearkened
Job 6:15 My brethren have *d* deceitfully as
Ps 13:6 because he hath *d* bountifully
Ps 44:17 neither have we *d* falsely in thy
Ps 78:57 *d* unfaithfully like their fathers
Ps 103:10 He hath not *d* with us after our
Ps 116:7 for the LORD hath *d* bountifully
Ps 119:65 Thou hast *d* well with thy servant
Ps 119:78 for they *d* perversely with me
Ps 147:20 He hath not *d* so with any nation
Is 24:16 dealers have *d* treacherously
Is 24:16 dealers have *d* very treacherously
Is 33:1 they *d* not treacherously with
Jer 3:20 so have ye *d* treacherously with
Jer 5:11 the house of Judah have *d* very
Jer 12:6 even they have *d* treacherously
Lam 1:2 all her friends have *d*
Eze 22:7 in the midst of thee have they *d*
Eze 25:12 Because that Edom hath *d* against
Eze 25:15 the Philistines have *d* by revenge
Hos 5:7 They have *d* treacherously against
Hos 6:7 there have they *d* treacherously
Joel 2:26 that hath *d* wondrously with you
Zec 1:6 our doings, so hath he *d* with us
Mal 2:11 Judah hath *d* treacherously, and an
Mal 2:14 whom thou hast *d* treacherously
Lk 1:25 Thus hath the Lord *d* with me in
Lk 2:48 Son, why hast thou thus *d* with us
Acts 7:19 The same *d* subtilly with our
Acts 25:24 of the Jews have *d* with me
Rom 12:3 according as God hath *d* to every

### DEAR

Jer 31:20 Is Ephraim my *d* son
Lk 7:2 who was *d* unto him, was sick, and
Acts 20:24 count I my life *d* unto myself
Eph 5:1 followers of God, as *d* children
Col 1:7 of Epaphras our *d* fellowservant
Col 1:13 us into the kingdom of his *d* Son
1Th 2:8 souls, because ye were *d* unto us

### DEARLY

Jer 12:7 I have given the *d* beloved of my
Rom 12:19 *D* beloved, avenge not yourselves,
1Cor 10:14 my *d* beloved, flee from idolatry
2Cor 7:1 these promises *d* beloved, let us
2Cor 12:19 *d* beloved, for your edifying
Phil 4:1 Therefore, my brethren *d* beloved
Phil 4:1 fast in the Lord, my *d* beloved
2Ti 1:2 To Timothy, my *d* beloved son
Philem 1 unto Philemon our *d* beloved
1Pet 2:11 *D* beloved, I beseech you as

### DEARTH

Gen 41:54 seven years of *d* began to come
Gen 41:54 and the *d* was in all lands
2Kin 4:38 and there was a *d* in the land
2Chr 6:28 If there be *d* in the land
Neh 5:3 might buy corn, because of the *d*
Jer 14:1 came to Jeremiah concerning the *d*
Acts 7:11 Now there came a *d* over all the
Acts 11:28 great *d* throughout all the world

### DEATH

Gen 21:16 Let me not see the *d* of the child
Gen 24:67 comforted after his mother's *d*
Gen 25:11 to pass after the *d* of Abraham
Gen 26:11 his wife shall surely be put to *d*
Gen 26:18 them after the *d* of Abraham
Gen 27:2 old, I know not the day of my *d*
Gen 27:7 thee before the LORD before my *d*
Gen 27:10 he may bless thee before his *d*
Ex 10:17 may take away from me this *d* only
Ex 19:12 mount shall be surely put to *d*
Ex 21:12 he die, shall be surely put to *d*
Ex 21:15 mother, shall be surely put to *d*
Ex 21:16 hand, he shall surely be put to *d*
Ex 21:17 mother, shall surely be put to *d*
Ex 21:29 his owner also shall be put to *d*
Ex 22:19 a beast shall surely be put to *d*
Ex 31:14 it shall surely be put to *d*
Ex 31:15 day, he shall surely be put to *d*
Ex 35:2 work therein shall be put to *d*
Lev 16:1 the *d* of the two sons of Aaron
Lev 19:20 they shall not be put to *d*
Lev 20:2 he shall surely be put to *d*
Lev 20:9 mother shall be surely put to *d*
Lev 20:10 shall surely be put to *d*
Lev 20:11 of them shall surely be put to *d*
Lev 20:12 of them shall surely be put to *d*
Lev 20:13 they shall surely be put to *d*
Lev 20:15 he shall surely be put to *d*
Lev 20:16 they shall surely be put to *d*
Lev 20:27 wizard, shall surely be put to *d*
Lev 24:16 LORD, he shall surely be put to *d*
Lev 24:16 of the LORD, shall be put to *d*
Lev 24:17 any man shall surely be put to *d*
Lev 24:21 a man, he shall be put to *d*
Lev 27:29 but shall surely be put to *d*
Num 1:51 cometh nigh shall be put to *d*
Num 3:10 cometh nigh shall be put to *d*
Num 3:38 cometh nigh shall be put to *d*
Num 15:35 The man shall be surely put to *d*
Num 16:29 men die the common *d* of all men
Num 18:7 cometh nigh shall be put to *d*
Num 23:10 Let me die the *d* of the righteous
Num 35:16 murderer shall surely be put to *d*
Num 35:17 murderer shall surely be put to *d*
Num 35:18 murderer shall surely be put to *d*
Num 35:21 him shall surely be put to *d*
Num 35:25 it unto the *d* of the high priest
Num 35:28 until the *d* of the high priest
Num 35:28 but after the *d* of the high
Num 35:30 to *d* by the mouth of witnesses
Num 35:31 a murderer, which is guilty of *d*
Num 35:31 but he shall be surely put to *d*
Num 35:32 until the *d* of the priest
Deut 13:5 of dreams, shall be put to *d*
Deut 13:9 be first upon him to put him to *d*
Deut 17:6 is worthy of *d* be put to *d*
Deut 17:6 witness he shall not be put to *d*
Deut 17:7 be first upon him to put him to *d*
Deut 19:6 whereas he was not worthy of *d*
Deut 21:22 have committed a sin worthy of *d*
Deut 21:22 and he be to be put to *d*
Deut 22:26 in the damsel no sin worthy of *d*
Deut 24:16 not be put to *d* for the children
Deut 24:16 be put to *d* for the fathers
Deut 24:16 shall be put to *d* for his own sin
Deut 30:15 thee this day life and good, and *d*
Deut 30:19 I have set before you life and *d*
Deut 31:27 and how much more after my *d*
Deut 31:29 my *d* ye will utterly corrupt
Deut 33:1 children of Israel before his *d*
Josh 1:1 Now after the *d* of Moses the
Josh 1:18 him, he shall be put to *d*
Josh 2:13 have, and deliver our lives from *d*
Josh 20:6 until the *d* of the high priest
Judg 1:1 Now after the *d* of Joshua it came
Judg 5:18 jeoparded their lives unto the *d*
Judg 6:31 let him be put to *d* whilst it is
Judg 13:7 from the womb to the day of his *d*
Judg 16:16 so that his soul was vexed unto *d*
Judg 16:30 *d* were more than they which he
Judg 20:13 Gibeah, that we may put them to *d*
Judg 21:5 He shall surely be put to *d*
Ruth 1:17 also, if ought but *d* part thee
Ruth 2:11 law since the *d* of thine husband
1Sa 4:20 about the time of her *d* the women
1Sa 11:12 men, that we may put them to *d*
1Sa 11:13 not a man be put to *d* this day
1Sa 15:32 the bitterness of *d* is past
1Sa 15:35 see Saul until the day of his *d*

1Sa 20:3 is but a step between me and *d*
1Sa 22:22 I have occasioned the *d* of all
2Sa 1:1 came to pass after the *d* of Saul
2Sa 1:23 in their *d* they were not divided
2Sa 6:23 no child unto the day of her *d*
2Sa 8:2 two lines measured he to put to *d*
2Sa 15:21 shall be, whether in *d* or life
2Sa 19:21 not Shimei be put to *d* for this
2Sa 19:22 be put to *d* this day in Israel
2Sa 20:3 shut up unto the day of their *d*
2Sa 21:9 were put to *d* in the days of
2Sa 22:5 When the waves of *d* compassed me
2Sa 22:6 the snares of *d* prevented me
1Kin 2:8 not put thee to *d* with the sword
1Kin 2:24 shall be put to *d* this day
1Kin 2:26 for thou art worthy of *d*
1Kin 2:26 not at this time put thee to *d*
1Kin 11:40 in Egypt until the *d* of Solomon
2Kin 1:1 Israel after the *d* of Ahab
2Kin 2:21 thence any more *d* or barren land
2Kin 4:40 man of God, there is *d* in the pot
2Kin 14:6 not be put to *d* for the children
2Kin 14:6 be put to *d* for the fathers
2Kin 14:6 shall be put to *d* for his own sin
2Kin 14:17 king of Judah lived after the *d*
2Kin 15:5 was a leper unto the day of his *d*
2Kin 20:1 days was Hezekiah sick unto *d*
1Chr 22:5 prepared abundantly before his *d*
2Chr 15:13 God of Israel should be put to *d*
2Chr 22:4 after the *d* of his father to his
2Chr 23:7 the house, he shall be put to *d*
2Chr 24:17 Now after the *d* of Jehoiada came
2Chr 25:25 *d* of Joash son of Jehoahaz king
2Chr 26:21 was a leper unto the day of his *d*
2Chr 32:24 days Hezekiah was sick to the *d*
2Chr 32:33 Jerusalem did him honour at his *d*
Ezr 7:26 upon him, whether it be unto *d*
Est 4:11 is one law of his to put him to *d*
Job 3:5 and the shadow of *d* stain it
Job 3:21 Which long for *d*, but it cometh
Job 5:20 he shall redeem thee from *d*
Job 7:15 and *d* rather than my life
Job 10:21 of darkness and the shadow of *d*
Job 10:22 and of the shadow of *d*, without
Job 12:22 out to light the shadow of *d*
Job 16:16 on my eyelids is the shadow of *d*
Job 18:13 even the firstborn of *d* shall
Job 24:17 to them even as the shadow of *d*
Job 24:17 in the terrors of the shadow of *d*
Job 27:15 of him shall be buried in *d*
Job 28:3 of darkness, and the shadow of *d*
Job 28:22 *d* say, We have heard the fame
Job 30:23 know that thou wilt bring me to *d*
Job 34:22 is no darkness, nor shadow of *d*
Job 38:17 Have the gates of *d* been opened
Job 38:17 seen the doors of the shadow of *d*
Ps 6:5 For in *d* there is no remembrance
Ps 7:13 for him the instruments of *d*
Ps 9:13 liftest me up from the gates of *d*
Ps 13:3 eyes, lest I sleep the sleep of *d*
Ps 18:4 The sorrows of *d* compassed me
Ps 18:5 the snares of *d* prevented me
Ps 22:15 brought me into the dust of *d*
Ps 23:4 the valley of the shadow of *d*
Ps 33:19 To deliver their soul from *d*
Ps 44:19 covered us with the shadow of *d*
Ps 48:14 he will be our guide even unto *d*
Ps 49:14 *d* shall feed on them
Ps 55:4 the terrors of *d* are fallen upon
Ps 55:15 Let *d* seize upon them, and let
Ps 56:13 hast delivered my soul from *d*
Ps 68:20 the Lord belong the issues from *d*
Ps 73:4 For there are no bands in their *d*
Ps 78:50 he spared not their soul from *d*
Ps 89:48 that liveth, and shall not see *d*
Ps 102:20 those that are appointed to *d*
Ps 107:10 in darkness and in the shadow of *d*
Ps 107:14 of darkness and the shadow of *d*
Ps 107:18 draw near unto the gates of *d*
Ps 116:3 The sorrows of *d* compassed me
Ps 116:8 hast delivered my soul from *d*
Ps 116:15 the LORD is the *d* of his saints
Ps 118:18 he hath not given me over unto *d*
Prov 2:18 For her house inclineth unto *d*
Prov 5:5 Her feet go down to *d*
Prov 7:27 going down to the chambers of *d*
Prov 8:36 all they that hate me love *d*
Prov 10:2 righteousness delivereth from *d*
Prov 11:4 righteousness delivereth from *d*
Prov 11:19 evil pursueth it to his own *d*
Prov 12:28 the pathway thereof there is no *d*
Prov 13:14 to depart from the snares of *d*
Prov 14:12 the end thereof are the ways of *d*
Prov 14:27 to depart from the snares of *d*
Prov 14:32 the righteous hath hope in his *d*
Prov 16:14 of a king is as messengers of *d*
Prov 16:25 the end thereof are the ways of *d*
Prov 18:21 *D* and life are in the power of the
Prov 21:6 to and fro of them that seek *d*
Prov 24:11 them that are drawn unto *d*
Prov 26:18 casteth firebrands, arrows, and *d*
Eccl 7:1 the day of *d* than the day of
Eccl 7:26 find more bitter than *d* the woman
Eccl 8:8 hath he power in the day of *d*
Song 8:6 for love is strong as *d*
Is 9:2 in the land of the shadow of *d*
Is 25:8 He will swallow up *d* in victory
Is 28:15 We have made a covenant with *d*
Is 28:18 your covenant with *d* shall be
Is 38:1 days was Hezekiah sick unto *d*
Is 38:18 thee, *d* can not celebrate thee
Is 53:9 wicked, and with the rich in his *d*
Is 53:12 hath poured out his soul unto *d*
Jer 2:6 of drought, and of the shadow of *d*
Jer 8:3 *d* shall be chosen rather than
Jer 9:21 For *d* is come up into our windows
Jer 13:16 he turn it into the shadow of *d*
Jer 15:2 Such as are for *d*, to *d*
Jer 15:2 Such as are for *d*, to *d*
Jer 18:21 and let their men be put to *d*
Jer 21:8 the way of life, and the way of *d*
Jer 26:15 certain, that if ye put me to *d*
Jer 26:19 and all Judah put him at all to *d*
Jer 26:21 the king sought to put him to *d*
Jer 26:24 of the people to put him to *d*
Jer 38:4 thee, let this man be put to *d*
Jer 38:15 wilt thou not surely put me to *d*
Jer 38:16 soul, I will not put thee to *d*
Jer 38:25 us, and we will not put thee to *d*
Jer 43:3 that they might put us to *d*
Jer 43:11 such as are for *d* to *d*
Jer 52:11 in prison till the day of his *d*
Jer 52:27 put them to *d* in Riblah in the
Jer 52:34 a portion until the day of his *d*
Lam 1:20 bereaveth, at home there is as *d*
Eze 18:32 in the *d* of him that dieth
Eze 31:14 for they are all delivered unto *d*
Eze 33:11 pleasure in the *d* of the wicked
Hos 13:14 I will redeem them from *d*
Hos 13:14 O *d*, I will be thy plagues
Amos 5:8 the shadow of *d* into the morning
Jonah 4:9 do well to be angry, even unto *d*
Hab 2:5 his desire as hell, and is as *d*
Mt 2:15 And was there until the *d* of Herod
Mt 4:16 shadow of *d* light is sprung up
Mt 10:21 shall deliver up the brother to *d*
Mt 10:21 and cause them to be put to *d*
Mt 14:5 when he would have put him to *d*
Mt 15:4 or mother, let him die the *d*
Mt 16:28 here, which shall not taste of *d*
Mt 20:18 and they shall condemn him to *d*
Mt 26:38 exceeding sorrowful, even unto *d*
Mt 26:59 against Jesus, to put him to *d*
Mt 26:66 and said, He is guilty of *d*
Mt 27:1 against Jesus to put him to *d*
Mk 5:23 daughter lieth at the point of *d*
Mk 7:10 or mother, let him die the *d*
Mk 9:1 here, which shall not taste of *d*
Mk 10:33 and they shall condemn him to *d*
Mk 13:12 shall betray the brother to *d*
Mk 13:12 shall cause them to be put to *d*
Mk 14:1 him by craft, and put him to *d*
Mk 14:34 is exceeding sorrowful unto *d*
Mk 14:55 against Jesus to put him to *d*
Mk 14:64 condemned him to be guilty of *d*
Lk 1:79 in darkness and in the shadow of *d*
Lk 2:26 Ghost, that he should not see *d*
Lk 9:27 here, which shall not taste of *d*
Lk 18:33 scourge him, and put him to *d*
Lk 21:16 shall they cause to be put to *d*
Lk 22:33 thee, both into prison, and to *d*
Lk 23:15 worthy of *d* is done unto him
Lk 23:22 I have found no cause of *d* in him
Lk 23:32 led with him to be put to *d*
Lk 24:20 him to be condemned to *d*, and have
Jn 4:47 for he was at the point of *d*
Jn 5:24 but is passed from *d* unto life
Jn 8:51 my saying, he shall never see *d*
Jn 8:52 saying, he shall never taste of *d*
Jn 11:4 said, This sickness is not unto *d*
Jn 11:13 Howbeit Jesus spake of his *d*
Jn 11:53 together for to put him to *d*
Jn 12:10 they might put Lazarus also to *d*
Jn 12:33 signifying what *d* he should die
Jn 18:31 lawful for us to put any man to *d*
Jn 18:32 signifying what *d* he should die
Jn 21:19 signifying by what *d* he should
Acts 2:24 up, having loosed the pains of *d*
Acts 8:1 And Saul was consenting unto his *d*
Acts 12:19 that they should be put to *d*
Acts 13:28 they found no cause of *d* in him
Acts 22:4 I persecuted this way unto the *d*
Acts 22:20 by, and consenting unto his *d*
Acts 23:29 charge worthy of *d* or of bonds
Acts 25:11 committed any thing worthy of *d*
Acts 25:25 had committed nothing worthy of *d*
Acts 26:10 and when they were put to *d*
Acts 26:31 nothing worthy of *d* or of bonds
Acts 28:18 there was no cause of *d* in me
Rom 1:32 such things are worthy of *d*
Rom 5:10 to God by the *d* of his Son
Rom 5:12 into the world, and *d* by sin
Rom 5:12 so *d* passed upon all men, for
Rom 5:14 Nevertheless *d* reigned from Adam
Rom 5:17 man's offence *d* reigned by one
Rom 5:21 That as sin hath reigned unto *d*
Rom 6:3 Christ were baptized into his *d*
Rom 6:4 buried with him by baptism into *d*
Rom 6:5 together in the likeness of his *d*
Rom 6:9 *d* hath no more dominion over him
Rom 6:16 whether of sin unto *d*, or of
Rom 6:21 for the end of those things is *d*
Rom 6:23 For the wages of sin is *d*
Rom 7:5 to bring forth fruit unto *d*
Rom 7:10 to life, I found to be unto *d*
Rom 7:13 that which is good made *d* unto me
Rom 7:13 working *d* in me by that which is
Rom 7:24 me from the body of this *d*
Rom 8:2 me free from the law of sin and *d*
Rom 8:6 For to be carnally minded is *d*
Rom 8:38 I am persuaded, that neither *d*
1Cor 3:22 or the world, or life, or *d*
1Cor 4:9 last, as it were appointed to *d*
1Cor 11:26 do shew the Lord's *d* till he come
1Cor 15:21 For since by man came *d*, by man
1Cor 15:26 that shall be destroyed is *d*
1Cor 15:54 *D* is swallowed up in victory
1Cor 15:55 O *d*, where is thy sting
1Cor 15:56 The sting of *d* is sin
2Cor 1:9 the sentence of *d* in ourselves
2Cor 1:10 delivered us from so great a *d*
2Cor 2:16 we are the savour of *d* unto *d*
2Cor 2:16 we are the savour of *d* unto *d*
2Cor 3:7 But if the ministration of *d*
2Cor 4:11 delivered unto *d* for Jesus' sake
2Cor 4:12 So then *d* worketh in us, but life
2Cor 7:10 the sorrow of the world worketh *d*
Phil 1:20 whether it be by life, or by *d*
Phil 2:8 and became obedient unto *d*
Phil 2:8 even the *d* of the cross
Phil 2:27 indeed he was sick nigh unto *d*
Phil 2:30 work of Christ he was nigh unto *d*
Phil 3:10 being made conformable unto his *d*
Col 1:22 the body of his flesh through *d*
2Ti 1:10 Christ, who hath abolished *d*
Heb 2:9 the angels for the suffering of *d*
Heb 2:9 God should taste *d* for every man
Heb 2:14 that through *d* he might destroy
Heb 2:14 him that had the power of *d*
Heb 2:15 them who through fear of *d* were
Heb 5:7 that was able to save him from *d*
Heb 7:23 to continue by reason of *d*
Heb 9:15 new testament, that by means of *d*
Heb 9:16 be the *d* of the testator
Heb 11:5 that he should not see *d*
Jas 1:15 it is finished, bringeth forth *d*
Jas 5:20 his way shall save a soul from *d*
1Pet 3:18 God, being put to *d* in the flesh
1Jn 3:14 we have passed from *d* unto life
1Jn 3:14 not his brother abideth in *d*
1Jn 5:16 sin a sin which is not unto *d*
1Jn 5:16 life for them that sin not unto *d*
1Jn 5:16 There is a sin unto *d*
1Jn 5:17 and there is a sin not unto *d*
Rev 1:18 and have the keys of hell and of *d*
Rev 2:10 be thou faithful unto *d*, and I
Rev 2:11 shall not be hurt of the second *d*
Rev 2:23 I will kill her children with *d*
Rev 6:8 and his name that sat on him was *D*
Rev 6:8 sword, and with hunger, and with *d*

Rev 9:6 And in those days shall men seek *d*
Rev 9:6 to die, and *d* shall flee from them
Rev 12:11 loved not their lives unto the *d*
Rev 13:3 his heads as it were wounded to *d*
Rev 18:8 her plagues come in one day, *d*
Rev 20:6 such the second *d* hath no power
Rev 20:13 and *d* and hell delivered up the
Rev 20:14 And *d* and hell were cast into the
Rev 20:14 This is the second *d*
Rev 21:4 and there shall be no more *d*
Rev 21:8 which is the second *d*

**DEBATE**
Prov 25:9 *D* thy cause with thy neighbour
Is 27:8 forth, thou wilt *d* with it
Is 58:4 Behold, ye fast for strife and *d*
Rom 1:29 full of envy, murder, *d*, deceit,

**DEBIR** *(de'-bur)* See KIRJATH-SANNAH, KIRJATH-SEPHER.
*1. An Amorite king.*
Josh 10:3 unto *D* king of Eglon, saying,
*2. A city in Judah.*
Josh 10:38 and all Israel with him, to *D*
Josh 10:39 done to Hebron, so he did to *D*
Josh 11:21 mountains, from Hebron, from *D*
Josh 12:13 The king of *D*, one
Josh 15:7 toward *D* from the valley of Achor
Josh 15:15 up thence to the inhabitants of *D*
Josh 15:15 and the name of *D* before was
Josh 15:49 and Kirjath-sannah, which is *D*
Josh 21:15 suburbs, and *D* with her suburbs,
Judg 1:11 went against the inhabitants of *D*
Judg 1:11 and the name of *D* before was
1Chr 6:58 her suburbs, *D* with her suburbs,
*3. The boundary of Gad.*
Josh 13:26 Mahanaim unto the border of *D*

**DEBORAH** *(deb'-o-rah)*
*1. Rebekah's nurse.*
Gen 35:8 But *D* Rebekah's nurse died, and
*2. A judge of Israel.*
Judg 4:4 And *D*, a prophetess, the wife of
Judg 4:5 the palm tree of *D* between Ramah
Judg 4:9 *D* arose, and went with Barak to
Judg 4:10 and *D* went up with him
Judg 4:14 And *D* said unto Barak, Up
Judg 5:1 Then sang *D* and Barak the son of
Judg 5:7 in Israel, until that I *D* arose
Judg 5:12 Awake, awake, *D*
Judg 5:15 princes of Issachar were with *D*

**DEBT**
1Sa 22:2 and every one that was in *d*
2Kin 4:7 Go, sell the oil, and pay thy *d*
Neh 10:31 year, and the exaction of every *d*
Mt 18:27 loosed him, and forgave him the *d*
Mt 18:30 prison, till he should pay the *d*
Mt 18:32 I forgave thee all that *d*
Rom 4:4 not reckoned of grace, but of *d*

**DEBTOR**
Eze 18:7 hath restored to the *d* his pledge
Mt 23:16 the gold of the temple, he is a *d*
Rom 1:14 I am *d* both to the Greeks, and to
Gal 5:3 that he is a *d* to do the whole

**DEBTORS**
Mt 6:12 us our debts, as we forgive our *d*
Lk 7:41 certain creditor which had two *d*
Lk 16:5 one of his lord's *d* unto him
Rom 8:12 Therefore, brethren, we are *d*
Rom 15:27 and their *d* they are

**DECAPOLIS** *(de-cap'-o-lis) A district east of the Jordan River.*
Mt 4:25 of people from Galilee, and from *D*
Mk 5:20 began to publish in *D* how great
Mk 7:31 the midst of the coasts of *D*

**DECEIT**
Job 15:35 and their belly prepareth *d*
Job 27:4 wickedness, nor my tongue utter *d*
Job 31:5 or if my foot hath hasted to *d*
Ps 10:7 His mouth is full of cursing and *d*
Ps 36:3 of his mouth are iniquity and *d*
Ps 50:19 to evil, and thy tongue frameth *d*
Ps 55:11 *d* and guile depart not from her
Ps 72:14 He shall redeem their soul from *d*
Ps 101:7 He that worketh *d* shall not dwell
Ps 119:118 for their *d* is falsehood
Prov 12:5 the counsels of the wicked are *d*
Prov 12:17 but a false witness *d*
Prov 12:20 *D* is in the heart of them that
Prov 14:8 but the folly of fools is *d*
Prov 20:17 Bread of *d* is sweet to a man
Prov 26:24 lips, and layeth up *d* within him
Prov 26:26 Whose hatred is covered by *d*
Is 53:9 neither was any *d* in his mouth
Jer 5:27 so are their houses full of *d*
Jer 8:5 they hold fast *d*, they refuse to
Jer 9:6 habitation is in the midst of *d*
Jer 9:6 through *d* they refuse to know me,
Jer 9:8 it speaketh *d*
Jer 14:14 nought, and the *d* of their heart
Jer 23:26 of the *d* of their own heart
Hos 11:12 and the house of Israel with *d*
Hos 12:7 the balances of *d* are in his hand
Amos 8:5 and falsifying the balances by *d*
Zeph 1:9 houses with violence and *d*
Mk 7:22 covetousness, wickedness, *d*
Rom 1:29 full of envy, murder, debate, *d*
Rom 3:13 their tongues they have used *d*
Col 2:8 you through philosophy and vain *d*
1Th 2:3 For our exhortation was not of *d*

**DECEITFUL**
Ps 5:6 will abhor the bloody and *d* man
Ps 35:20 but they devise *d* matters against
Ps 43:1 O deliver me from the *d* and unjust
Ps 52:4 devouring words, O thou *d* tongue
Ps 55:23 *d* men shall not live out half
Ps 78:57 were turned aside like a *d* bow
Ps 109:2 the mouth of the *d* are opened
Ps 120:2 lying lips, and from a *d* tongue
Prov 11:18 The wicked worketh a *d* work
Prov 14:25 but a *d* witness speaketh lies
Prov 23:3 for they are *d* meat
Prov 27:6 but the kisses of an enemy are *d*
Prov 29:13 poor and the *d* man meet together
Prov 31:30 Favour is *d*, and beauty is vain
Jer 17:9 The heart is *d* above all things,
Hos 7:16 they are like a *d* bow
Mic 6:11 and with the bag of *d* weights
Mic 6:12 their tongue is *d* in their mouth
Zeph 3:13 neither shall a *d* tongue be found
2Cor 11:13 apostles, *d* workers, transforming
Eph 4:22 corrupt according to the *d* lusts

**DECEITFULLY**
Gen 34:13 Shechem and Hamor his father *d*
Ex 8:29 but let not Pharaoh deal *d* any
Ex 21:8 seeing he hath dealt *d* with her
Lev 6:4 the thing which he hath *d* gotten
Job 6:15 brethren have dealt *d* as a brook
Job 13:7 and talk *d* for him
Ps 24:4 his soul unto vanity, nor sworn *d*
Ps 52:2 like a sharp rasor, working *d*
Jer 48:10 that doeth the work of the LORD *d*
Dan 11:23 made with him he shall work *d*
2Cor 4:2 nor handling the word of God *d*

**DECEIVE**
2Sa 3:25 of Ner, that he came to *d* thee
2Kin 4:28 did I not say, Do not *d* me
2Kin 18:29 the king, Let not Hezekiah *d* you
2Kin 19:10 God in whom thou trustest *d* thee
2Chr 32:15 therefore let not Hezekiah *d* you
Prov 24:28 and *d* not with thy lips
Is 36:14 the king, Let not Hezekiah *d* you
Is 37:10 *d* thee, saying, Jerusalem shall
Jer 9:5 they will *d* every one his
Jer 29:8 *d* you, neither hearken to your
Jer 37:9 *D* not yourselves, saying, The
Zec 13:4 they wear a rough garment to *d*
Mt 24:4 them, Take heed that no man *d* you
Mt 24:5 and shall *d* many
Mt 24:11 shall rise, and shall *d* many
Mt 24:24 they shall *d* the very elect
Mk 13:5 say, Take heed lest any man *d* you
Mk 13:6 and shall *d* many
Rom 16:18 fair speeches *d* the hearts of the
1Cor 3:18 Let no man *d* himself
Eph 4:14 whereby they lie in wait to *d*
Eph 5:6 Let no man *d* you with vain words
2Th 2:3 Let no man *d* you by any means
1Jn 1:8 we *d* ourselves, and the truth is
1Jn 3:7 Little children, let no man *d* you
Rev 20:3 that he should *d* the nations no
Rev 20:8 shall go out to *d* the nations

**DECEIVED**
Gen 31:7 And your father hath *d* me, and
Lev 6:2 violence, or hath *d* his neighbour
Deut 11:16 that your heart be not *d*
1Sa 19:17 Michal, Why hast thou *d* me so
1Sa 28:12 Saul, saying, Why hast thou *d* me
2Sa 19:26 My lord, O king, my servant *d* me
Job 12:16 the *d* and the deceiver are his
Job 15:31 not him that is *d* trust in vanity
Job 31:9 mine heart have been *d* by a woman
Prov 20:1 whosoever is *d* thereby is not
Is 19:13 fools, the princes of Noph are *d*
Is 44:20 a *d* heart hath turned him aside,
Jer 4:10 thou hast greatly *d* this people
Jer 20:7 O LORD, thou hast *d* me, and I was
Jer 20:7 thou hast *d* me, and I was *d*
Jer 49:16 Thy terribleness hath *d* thee
Lam 1:19 for my lovers, but they *d* me
Eze 14:9 if the prophet be *d* when he hath
Eze 14:9 I the LORD have *d* that prophet
Obad 3 pride of thine heart hath *d* thee
Obad 7 at peace with thee have *d* thee
Lk 21:8 said, Take heed that ye be not *d*
Jn 7:47 them the Pharisees, Are ye also *d*
Rom 7:11 *d* me, and by it slew me
1Cor 6:9 Be not *d*: neither fornicators
1Cor 15:33 Be not *d*: evil communications
Gal 6:7 Be not *d*; God is not
1Ti 2:14 And Adam was not *d*, but the woman
1Ti 2:14 but the woman being *d* was in the
2Ti 3:13 and worse, deceiving, and being *d*
Titus 3:3 sometimes foolish, disobedient, *d*
Rev 18:23 thy sorceries were all nations *d*
Rev 19:20 with which he *d* them that had
Rev 20:10 the devil that *d* them was cast

**DECEIVER**
Gen 27:12 me, and I shall seem to him as a *d*
Job 12:16 the deceived and the *d* are his
Mal 1:14 But cursed be the *d*, which hath
Mt 27:63 Sir, we remember that that *d* said
2Jn 7 This is a *d* and an antichrist

**DECEIVETH**
Prov 26:19 is the man that *d* his neighbour
Jn 7:12 but he *d* the people
Gal 6:3 when he is nothing, he *d* himself
Jas 1:26 but *d* his own heart, this man's
Rev 12:9 and Satan, which *d* the whole world
Rev 13:14 *d* them that dwell on the earth by

**DECKED**
Prov 7:16 I have *d* my bed with coverings of
Eze 16:11 I *d* thee also with ornaments, and
Eze 16:13 Thus wast thou *d* with gold
Hos 2:13 she *d* herself with her earrings
Rev 17:4 *d* with gold and precious stones and
Rev 18:16 *d* with gold, and precious stones,

**DECLARATION**
Est 10:2 the *d* of the greatness of
Job 13:17 my speech, and my *d* with your ears
Lk 1:1 *d* of those things which are most
2Cor 8:19 Lord, and *d* of your ready mind

**DECLARE**
Gen 41:24 was none that could *d* it to me
Deut 1:5 Moab, began Moses to *d* this law
Josh 20:4 shall *d* his cause in the ears of
Judg 14:12 if ye can certainly *d* it me
Judg 14:13 But if ye cannot *d* it me, then
Judg 14:15 that he may *d* unto us the riddle,
1Kin 22:13 the words of the prophets *d* good
1Chr 16:24 *D* his glory among the heathen
2Chr 18:12 *d* good to the king with one
Est 4:8 to *d* it unto her, and to charge
Job 12:8 of the sea shall *d* unto thee
Job 15:17 that which I have seen I will *d*
Job 21:31 Who shall *d* his way to his face
Job 28:27 Then did he see it, and *d* it
Job 31:37 I would *d* unto him the number of
Job 38:4 *d*, if thou hast understanding
Job 38:18 *d* if thou knowest it all
Job 40:7 demand of thee, and *d* thou unto me
Job 42:4 demand of thee, and *d* thou unto me
Ps 2:7 I will *d* the decree
Ps 9:11 *d* among the people his doings
Ps 19:1 The heavens *d* the glory of God
Ps 22:22 I will *d* thy name unto my
Ps 22:31 shall *d* his righteousness unto a
Ps 30:9 shall it *d* thy truth
Ps 38:18 For I will *d* mine iniquity
Ps 40:5 if I would *d* and speak of them,
Ps 50:6 heavens shall *d* his righteousness
Ps 50:16 hast thou to do to *d* my statutes
Ps 64:9 fear, and shall *d* the work of God
Ps 66:16 I will *d* what he hath done for my
Ps 73:28 that I may *d* all thy works
Ps 75:1 name is near thy wondrous works *d*

Ps 75:9 But I will *d* for ever
Ps 78:6 arise and *d* them to their children
Ps 96:3 *D* his glory among the heathen,
Ps 97:6 The heavens *d* his righteousness,
Ps 102:21 To *d* the name of the LORD in Zion
Ps 107:22 *d* his works with rejoicing
Ps 118:17 live, and *d* the works of the LORD
Ps 145:4 and shall *d* thy mighty acts
Ps 145:6 and I will *d* thy greatness
Eccl 9:1 in my heart even to *d* all this
Is 3:9 they *d* their sin as Sodom, they
Is 12:4 *d* his doings among the people,
Is 21:6 watchman, let him *d* what he seeth
Is 41:22 or *d* us things for to come
Is 42:9 to pass, and new things do I *d*
Is 42:12 *d* his praise in the islands
Is 43:9 who among them can *d* this
Is 43:26 *d* thou, that thou mayest be
Is 44:7 as I, shall call, and shall *d* it
Is 45:19 I *d* things that are right
Is 48:6 and will not ye *d* it
Is 48:20 with a voice of singing *d* ye
Is 53:8 who shall *d* his generation
Is 57:12 I will *d* thy righteousness, and
Is 66:19 they shall *d* my glory among the
Jer 4:5 *D* ye in Judah, and publish in
Jer 5:20 *D* this in the house of Jacob, and
Jer 9:12 hath spoken, that he may *d* it
Jer 31:10 *d* it in the isles afar off, and
Jer 38:15 If I *d* it unto thee, wilt thou
Jer 38:25 *D* unto us now what thou hast said
Jer 42:4 answer you, I will *d* it unto you
Jer 42:20 so *d* unto us, and we will do it
Jer 46:14 *D* ye in Egypt, and publish in
Jer 50:2 *D* ye among the nations, and
Jer 50:28 to *d* in Zion the vengeance of the
Jer 51:10 let us *d* in Zion the work of the
Eze 12:16 that they may *d* all their
Eze 23:36 *d* unto them their abominations
Eze 40:4 *d* all that thou seest to the
Dan 4:18 *d* the interpretation thereof,
Mic 1:10 *D* ye it not at Gath, weep ye not
Mic 3:8 to *d* unto Jacob his transgression
Zec 9:12 even to day do I *d* that I will
Mt 13:36 *D* unto us the parable of the
Mt 15:15 unto him, *D* unto us this parable
Jn 17:26 unto them thy name, and will *d* it
Acts 8:33 who shall *d* his generation
Acts 13:32 we *d* unto you glad tidings, how
Acts 13:41 though a man *d* it unto you
Acts 17:23 worship, him *d* I unto you
Acts 20:27 For I have not shunned to *d* unto
Rom 3:25 to *d* his righteousness for the
Rom 3:26 To *d*, I say, at this time his
1Cor 3:13 for the day shall *d* it, because
1Cor 11:17 Now in this that I *d* unto you I
1Cor 15:1 I *d* unto you the gospel which I
Col 4:7 state shall Tychicus *d* unto you
Heb 2:12 I will *d* thy name unto my
Heb 11:14 things *d* plainly that they seek a
1Jn 1:3 heard *d* we unto you, that ye also
1Jn 1:5 *d* unto you, that God is light, and

**DECLARED**
Ex 9:16 that my name may be *d* throughout
Lev 23:44 Moses *d* unto the children of
Num 1:18 they *d* their pedigrees after
Num 15:34 because it was not *d* what should
Deut 4:13 he *d* unto you his covenant, which
2Sa 19:6 For thou hast *d* this day, that
Neh 8:12 the words that were *d* unto them
Job 26:3 plentifully *d* the thing as it is
Ps 40:10 I have *d* thy faithfulness and thy
Ps 71:17 hitherto have I *d* thy wondrous
Ps 77:14 thou hast *d* thy strength among
Ps 88:11 lovingkindness be *d* in the grave
Ps 119:13 With my lips have I *d* all the
Ps 119:26 I have *d* my ways, and thou
Is 21:2 A grievous vision is *d* unto me
Is 21:10 God of Israel, have I *d* unto you
Is 41:26 Who hath *d* from the beginning,
Is 43:12 I have *d*, and have saved, and I
Is 44:8 thee from that time, and have *d* it
Is 45:21 who hath *d* this from ancient time
Is 48:3 I have *d* the former things from
Is 48:5 from the beginning *d* it to thee
Is 48:14 among them hath *d* these things
Jer 36:13 Then Michaiah *d* unto them all the
Jer 42:21 now I have this day *d* it to you
Lk 8:47 she *d* unto him before all the
Jn 1:18 of the Father, he hath *d* him
Jn 17:26 I have *d* unto them thy name, and
Acts 9:27 *d* unto them how he had seen the
Acts 10:8 when he had *d* all these things
Acts 12:17 *d* unto them how the Lord had
Acts 15:4 they *d* all things that God had
Acts 15:14 Simeon hath *d* how God at the
Acts 21:19 he *d* particularly what things God
Acts 25:14 Festus *d* Paul's cause unto the
Rom 1:4 *d* to be the Son of God with power
Rom 9:17 thee, and that my name might be *d*
1Cor 1:11 For it hath been *d* unto me of you
2Cor 3:3 *d* to be the epistle of Christ
Col 1:8 Who also *d* unto us your love in
Rev 10:7 as he hath *d* to his servants the

**DECLINE**
Ex 23:2 to *d* after many to wrest judgment
Deut 17:11 thou shalt not *d* from the
Ps 119:157 yet do I not *d* from thy
Prov 4:5 neither *d* from the words of my
Prov 7:25 Let not thine heart *d* to her ways

**DECLINED**
2Chr 34:2 *d* neither to the right hand, nor
Job 23:11 his way have I kept, and not *d*
Ps 44:18 have our steps *d* from thy way
Ps 119:51 yet have I not *d* from thy law

**DECREE**
2Chr 30:5 So they established a *d* to make
Ezr 5:13 a *d* to build this house of God
Ezr 5:17 that a *d* was made of Cyrus the
Ezr 6:1 Then Darius the king made a *d*
Ezr 6:3 *d* concerning the house of God at
Ezr 6:8 Moreover I make a *d* what ye shall
Ezr 6:11 Also I have made a *d*, that
Ezr 6:12 I Darius have made a *d*
Ezr 7:13 I make a *d*, that all they of the
Ezr 7:21 do make a *d* to all the treasurers
Est 1:20 when the king's *d* which he shall
Est 2:8 his *d* was heard, and when many
Est 3:15 the *d* was given in Shushan the
Est 4:3 his *d* came, there was great
Est 4:8 *d* that was given at Shushan to
Est 8:14 the *d* was given at Shushan the
Est 8:17 his *d* came, the Jews had joy and
Est 9:1 his *d* drew near to be put in
Est 9:13 also according unto this day's *d*
Est 9:14 the *d* was given at Shushan
Est 9:32 the *d* of Esther confirmed these
Job 22:28 Thou shalt also *d* a thing
Job 28:26 When he made a *d* for the rain
Ps 2:7 I will declare the *d*
Ps 148:6 he hath made a *d* which shall not
Prov 8:15 kings reign, and princes *d* justice
Prov 8:29 When he gave to the sea his *d*
Is 10:1 Woe unto them that *d* unrighteous
Jer 5:22 bound of the sea by a perpetual *d*
Dan 2:9 dream, there is but one *d* for you
Dan 2:13 the *d* went forth that the wise
Dan 2:15 Why is the *d* so hasty from the
Dan 3:10 Thou, O king, hast made a *d*
Dan 3:29 Therefore I make a *d*, That every
Dan 4:6 Therefore made I a *d* to bring in
Dan 4:17 is by the *d* of the watchers
Dan 4:24 this is the *d* of the most High,
Dan 6:7 statute, and to make a firm *d*
Dan 6:8 Now, O king, establish the *d*
Dan 6:9 signed the writing and the *d*
Dan 6:12 the king concerning the king's *d*
Dan 6:12 Hast thou not signed a *d*, that
Dan 6:13 nor the *d* that thou hast signed,
Dan 6:15 That no *d* nor statute which the
Dan 6:26 I make a *d*, That in every
Jonah 3:7 Nineveh by the *d* of the king
Mic 7:11 day shall the *d* be far removed
Zeph 2:2 Before the *d* bring forth, before
Lk 2:1 went out a *d* from Caesar Augustus

**DECREED**
Est 2:1 done, and what was *d* against her
Est 9:31 as they had *d* for themselves and
Job 38:10 And brake up for it my *d* place
Is 10:22 the consumption *d* shall overflow
1Cor 7:37 hath so *d* in his heart that he

**DEDAN** *(de'-dan)* See DEDANIM.
*1. A grandson of Cush.*
Gen 10:7 sons of Raamah; Sheba, and *D*
1Chr 1:9 sons of Raamah; Sheba, and *D*
*2. A son of Jokshan.*
Gen 25:3 And Jokshan begat Sheba, and *D*
Gen 25:3 the sons of *D* were Asshurim, and
1Chr 1:32 sons of Jokshan; Sheba, and *D*
*3. A district between Sela and the Salt Sea.*
Jer 25:23 *D*, and Tema, and Buz, and all that
Jer 49:8 dwell deep, O inhabitants of *D*
Eze 25:13 they of *D* shall fall by the sword
Eze 27:15 The men of *D* were thy merchants
Eze 27:20 *D* was thy merchant in precious
Eze 38:13 Sheba, and *D*, and the merchants of

**DEDANIM** *(ded'-a-nim)* See DODANIM.
*Descendants of Raamah.*
Is 21:13 O ye travelling companies of *D*

**DEDICATE**
Deut 20:5 the battle, and another man *d* it
2Sa 8:11 king David did *d* unto the LORD
1Chr 26:27 *d* to maintain the house of the
2Chr 2:4 to *d* it to him, and to burn before

**DEDICATED**
Deut 20:5 a new house, and hath not *d* it
Judg 17:3 I had wholly *d* the silver unto
2Sa 8:11 gold that he had *d* of all nations
1Kin 7:51 which David his father had *d*
1Kin 8:63 of Israel *d* the house of the LORD
1Kin 15:15 the things which his father had *d*
1Kin 15:15 and the things which himself had *d*
2Kin 12:4 All the money of the *d* things
2Kin 12:18 fathers, kings of Judah, had *d*
1Chr 18:11 also king David *d* unto the LORD
1Chr 26:20 the treasures of the *d* things
1Chr 26:26 all the treasures of the *d* things
1Chr 26:26 the captains of the host, had *d*
1Chr 26:28 and Joab the son of Zeruiah, had *d*
1Chr 26:28 and whosoever had *d* any thing
1Chr 28:12 of the treasuries of the *d* things
2Chr 5:1 that David his father had *d*
2Chr 7:5 all the people *d* the house of God
2Chr 15:18 the things that his father had *d*
2Chr 15:18 and that he himself had *d*
2Chr 24:7 also all the *d* things of the
2Chr 31:12 tithes and the *d* things faithfully
Eze 44:29 every *d* thing in Israel shall be
Heb 9:18 testament was *d* without blood

**DEDICATION**
Num 7:84 This was the *d* of the altar
Num 7:88 This was the *d* of the altar
2Chr 7:9 for they kept the *d* of the altar
Ezr 6:16 kept the *d* of this house of God
Ezr 6:17 offered at the *d* of this house of
Neh 12:27 at the *d* of the wall of Jerusalem
Neh 12:27 to keep the *d* with gladness, both
Ps 30:*t* Song at the *d* of the house of
Dan 3:2 to come to the *d* of the image
Dan 3:3 unto the *d* of the image that
Jn 10:22 at Jerusalem the feast of the *d*

**DEED**
Gen 44:15 What *d* is this that ye have done
Ex 9:16 in very *d* for this cause have I
Judg 19:30 There was no such *d* done nor seen
1Sa 25:34 For in very *d*, as the LORD God of
1Sa 26:4 that Saul was come in very *d*
2Sa 12:14 because by this *d* thou hast given
2Chr 6:18 But will God in very *d* dwell with
Est 1:17 For this *d* of the queen shall
Est 1:18 have heard of the *d* of the queen
Lk 23:51 to the counsel and *d* of them
Lk 24:19 which was a prophet mighty in *d*
Acts 4:9 good *d* done to the impotent man
Rom 15:18 Gentiles obedient, by word and *d*
1Cor 5:2 that he that hath done this *d*
1Cor 5:3 him that hath so done this *d*
2Cor 10:11 be also in *d* when we are present
Col 3:17 And whatsoever ye do in word or *d*
Jas 1:25 man shall be blessed in his *d*
1Jn 3:18 but in *d* and in truth

**DEEDS**
Gen 20:9 thou hast done *d* unto me that
1Chr 16:8 make known his *d* among the people
2Chr 35:27 And his *d*, first and last, behold,
Ezr 9:13 is come upon us for our evil *d*
Neh 6:19 reported his good *d* before me
Neh 13:14 wipe not out my good *d* that I
Ps 28:4 Give them according to their *d*
Ps 105:1 make known his *d* among the people
Is 59:18 According to their *d*, accordingly
Jer 5:28 they overpass the *d* of the wicked
Jer 25:14 them according to their *d*

Lk 11:48 ye allow the *d* of your fathers
Lk 23:41 receive the due reward of our *d*
Jn 3:19 light, because their *d* were evil
Jn 3:20 lest his *d* should be reproved
Jn 3:21 that his *d* may be made manifest,
Jn 8:41 Ye do the *d* of your father
Acts 7:22 and was mighty in words and in *d*
Acts 19:18 and confessed, and shewed their *d*
Acts 24:2 that very worthy *d* are done unto
Rom 2:6 to every man according to his *d*
Rom 3:20 Therefore by the *d* of the law
Rom 3:28 by faith without the *d* of the law
Rom 8:13 do mortify the *d* of the body
2Cor 12:12 in signs, and wonders, and mighty *d*
Col 3:9 put off the old man with his *d*
2Pet 2:8 day to day with their unlawful *d*
2Jn 11 speed is partaker of his evil *d*
3Jn 10 remember his *d* which he doeth
Jude 15 ungodly *d* which they have ungodly
Rev 2:6 hatest the *d* of the Nicolaitanes
Rev 2:22 except they repent of their *d*
Rev 16:11 sores, and repented not of their *d*

## DEEP

Gen 1:2 was upon the face of the *d*
Gen 2:21 the LORD God caused a *d* sleep to
Gen 7:11 of the great *d* broken up, and the
Gen 8:2 The fountains also of the *d*
Gen 15:12 a *d* sleep fell upon Abram
Gen 49:25 of the *d* that lieth under
Deut 33:13 for the *d* that coucheth beneath,
1Sa 26:12 because a *d* sleep from the LORD
Job 4:13 when *d* sleep falleth on men,
Job 12:22 He discovereth *d* things out of
Job 33:15 when *d* sleep falleth upon men, in
Job 38:30 and the face of the *d* is frozen
Job 41:31 He maketh the *d* to boil like a
Job 41:32 one would think the *d* to be hoary
Ps 36:6 thy judgments are a great *d*
Ps 42:7 *D* calleth unto *d* at the noise
Ps 42:7 *D* calleth unto *d* at the noise
Ps 64:6 one of them, and the heart, is *d*
Ps 69:2 I sink in *d* mire, where there is
Ps 69:2 I am come into *d* waters, where
Ps 69:14 hate me, and out of the *d* waters
Ps 69:15 neither let the *d* swallow me up
Ps 80:9 and didst cause it to take *d* root
Ps 92:5 and thy thoughts are very *d*
Ps 95:4 are the *d* places of the earth
Ps 104:6 it with the *d* as with a garment
Ps 107:24 the LORD, and his wonders in the *d*
Ps 135:6 in the seas, and all *d* places
Ps 140:10 into *d* pits, that they rise not
Prov 8:28 the fountains of the *d*
Prov 18:4 of a man's mouth are as *d* waters
Prov 19:15 casteth into a *d* sleep
Prov 20:5 the heart of man is like *d* water
Prov 22:14 mouth of strange women is a *d* pit
Prov 23:27 For a whore is a *d* ditch
Eccl 7:24 which is far off, and exceeding *d*
Is 29:10 upon you the spirit of *d* sleep
Is 29:15 Woe unto them that seek *d* to hide
Is 30:33 he hath made it *d* and large
Is 44:27 That saith to the *d*, Be dry, and I
Is 51:10 sea, the waters of the great *d*
Is 63:13 That led them through the *d*
Jer 49:8 Flee ye, turn back, dwell *d*
Jer 49:30 Flee, get you far off, dwell *d*
Eze 23:32 shalt drink of thy sister's cup *d*
Eze 26:19 I shall bring up the *d* upon thee
Eze 31:4 the *d* set him up on high with her
Eze 31:15 I covered the *d* for him, and I
Eze 32:14 Then will I make their waters *d*
Eze 34:18 and to have drunk of the *d* waters
Dan 2:22 He revealeth the *d* and secret
Dan 8:18 I was in a *d* sleep on my face
Dan 10:9 then was I in a *d* sleep on my
Amos 7:4 fire, and it devoured the great *d*
Jonah 2:3 For thou hadst cast me into the *d*
Hab 3:10 the *d* uttered his voice, and
Lk 5:4 unto Simon, Launch out into the *d*
Lk 6:48 built an house, and digged *d*
Lk 8:31 command them to go out into the *d*
Jn 4:11 to draw with, and the well is *d*
Acts 20:9 being fallen into a *d* sleep
Rom 10:7 Or, Who shall descend into the *d*
1Cor 2:10 things, yea, the *d* things of God
2Cor 8:2 their *d* poverty abounded unto the
2Cor 11:25 and a day I have been in the *d*

## DEFENCE

Num 14:9 their *d* is departed from them, and
2Chr 11:5 and built cities for *d* in Judah
Job 22:25 Yea, the Almighty shall be thy *d*
Ps 7:10 My *d* is of God, which saveth the
Ps 31:2 for an house of *d* to save me
Ps 59:9 for God is my *d*
Ps 59:16 for thou hast been my *d* and refuge
Ps 59:17 for God is my *d*, and the God of my
Ps 62:2 he is my *d*
Ps 62:6 he is my *d*
Ps 89:18 For the LORD is our *d*
Ps 94:22 But the LORD is my *d*
Eccl 7:12 For wisdom is a *d*
Eccl 7:12 and money is a *d*
Is 4:5 upon all the glory shall be a *d*
Is 19:6 the brooks of *d* shall be emptied
Is 33:16 his place of *d* shall be the
Nah 2:5 and the *d* shall be prepared
Acts 19:33 have made his *d* unto the people
Acts 22:1 hear ye my *d* which I make now
Phil 1:7 as both in my bonds, and in the *d*
Phil 1:17 I am set for the *d* of the gospel

## DEFENCED

Is 25:2 of a *d* city a ruin
Is 27:10 Yet the *d* city shall be desolate,
Is 36:1 against all the *d* cities of Judah
Is 37:26 waste *d* cities into ruinous heaps
Jer 1:18 have made thee this day a *d* city
Jer 4:5 and let us go into the *d* cities
Jer 8:14 and let us enter into the *d* cities
Jer 34:7 for these *d* cities remained of
Eze 21:20 and to Judah in Jerusalem the *d*

## DEFEND

Judg 10:1 to *d* Israel Tola the son of Puah
2Kin 19:34 For I will *d* this city, to save
2Kin 20:6 I will *d* this city for mine own
Ps 20:1 name of the God of Jacob *d* thee
Ps 59:1 *d* me from them that rise up
Ps 82:3 *D* the poor and fatherless
Is 31:5 the LORD of hosts *d* Jerusalem
Is 37:35 For I will *d* this city to save it
Is 38:6 and I will *d* this city
Zec 9:15 The LORD of hosts shall *d* them
Zec 12:8 In that day shall the LORD *d* the

## DEFIED

Num 23:8 I defy, whom the LORD hath not *d*
1Sa 17:36 seeing he hath *d* the armies of
1Sa 17:45 of Israel, whom thou hast *d*
2Sa 21:21 And when he *d* Israel, Jonathan the
2Sa 23:9 when they *d* the Philistines that
1Chr 20:7 But when he *d* Israel, Jonathan

## DEFILE

Lev 11:44 neither shall ye *d* yourselves
Lev 15:31 when they *d* my tabernacle that is
Lev 18:20 wife, to *d* thyself with her
Lev 18:23 any beast to *d* thyself therewith
Lev 18:24 *D* not ye yourselves in any of
Lev 18:28 not you out also, when ye *d* it
Lev 18:30 that ye *d* not yourselves therein
Lev 20:3 to *d* my sanctuary, and to profane
Lev 21:4 But he shall not *d* himself
Lev 21:11 nor *d* himself for his father, or
Lev 22:8 not eat to *d* himself therewith
Num 5:3 that they *d* not their camps, in
Num 35:34 *D* not therefore the land which ye
2Kin 23:13 children of Ammon, did the king *d*
Song 5:3 how shall I *d* them?
Is 30:22 Ye shall *d* also the covering of
Jer 32:34 is called by my name, to *d* it
Eze 7:22 shall enter into it, and *d* it
Eze 9:7 *D* the house, and fill the courts
Eze 20:7 *d* not yourselves with the idols
Eze 20:18 nor *d* yourselves with their idols
Eze 22:3 against herself to *d* herself
Eze 28:7 they shall *d* thy brightness
Eze 33:26 ye *d* every one his neighbour's
Eze 37:23 Neither shall they *d* themselves
Eze 43:7 the house of Israel no more *d*
Eze 44:25 at no dead person to *d* themselves
Eze 44:25 no husband, they may *d* themselves
Dan 1:8 in his heart that he would not *d*
Dan 1:8 that he might not *d* himself
Mt 15:18 and they *d* the man
Mt 15:20 are the things which *d* a man
Mk 7:15 that entering into him can *d* him
Mk 7:15 those are they that *d* the man
Mk 7:18 into the man, it cannot *d* him
Mk 7:23 come from within, and *d* the man
1Cor 3:17 If any man *d* the temple of God,
1Ti 1:10 for them that *d* themselves with
Jude 8 these filthy dreamers *d* the flesh

## DEFILED

Gen 34:2 her, and lay with her, and *d* her
Gen 34:5 that he had *d* Dinah his daughter
Gen 34:13 because he had *d* Dinah their
Gen 34:27 because they had *d* their sister
Lev 5:3 be that a man shall be *d* withal
Lev 11:43 them, that ye should be *d* thereby
Lev 13:46 shall be in him he shall be *d*
Lev 15:32 goeth from him, and is *d* therewith
Lev 18:24 are *d* which I cast out before you
Lev 18:25 And the land is *d*
Lev 18:27 were before you, and the land is *d*
Lev 19:31 after wizards, to be *d* by them
Lev 21:1 There shall none be *d* for the
Lev 21:3 for her may he be *d*
Num 5:2 and whosoever is *d* by the dead
Num 5:13 and be kept close, and she be *d*
Num 5:14 jealous of his wife, and she be *d*
Num 5:14 of his wife, and she be not *d*
Num 5:20 of thy husband, and if thou be *d*
Num 5:27 come to pass, that, if she be *d*
Num 5:28 And if the woman be not *d*, but be
Num 5:29 instead of her husband, and is *d*
Num 6:9 he hath *d* the head of his
Num 6:12 because his separation was *d*
Num 9:6 who were *d* by the dead body of a
Num 9:7 We are *d* by the dead body of a
Num 19:20 because he hath *d* the sanctuary
Deut 21:23 that thy land be not *d*, which
Deut 22:9 the fruit of thy vineyard, be *d*
Deut 24:4 be his wife, after that she is *d*
2Kin 23:8 *d* the high places where the
2Kin 23:10 he *d* Topheth, which is in the
1Chr 5:1 forasmuch as he *d* his father's
Neh 13:29 they have *d* the priesthood
Job 16:15 my skin, and *d* my horn in the dust
Ps 74:7 they have *d* by casting down the
Ps 79:1 thy holy temple have they *d*
Ps 106:39 Thus were they *d* with their own
Is 24:5 The earth also is *d* under the
Is 59:3 For your hands are *d* with blood
Jer 2:7 ye *d* my land, and made mine
Jer 3:9 her whoredom, that she *d* the land
Jer 16:18 because they have *d* my land
Jer 19:13 shall be *d* as the place of Tophet
Eze 4:13 their *d* bread among the Gentiles
Eze 5:11 because thou hast *d* my sanctuary
Eze 7:24 and their holy places shall be *d*
Eze 18:6 neither hath *d* his neighbour's
Eze 18:11 and *d* his neighbour's wife,
Eze 18:15 hath not *d* his neighbour's wife,
Eze 20:43 doings, wherein ye have been *d*
Eze 22:4 hast *d* thyself in thine idols
Eze 22:11 hath lewdly *d* his daughter in law
Eze 23:7 all their idols she *d* herself
Eze 23:13 Then I saw that she was *d*
Eze 23:17 they *d* her with their whoredom,
Eze 23:38 they have *d* my sanctuary in the
Eze 28:18 Thou hast *d* thy sanctuaries by
Eze 36:17 they *d* it by their own way and by
Eze 43:8 they have even *d* my holy name by
Hos 5:3 whoredom, and Israel is *d*
Hos 6:10 whoredom of Ephraim, Israel is *d*
Mic 4:11 thee, that say, Let her be *d*
Mk 7:2 of his disciples eat bread with *d*
Jn 18:28 hall, lest they should be *d*
1Cor 8:7 their conscience being weak is *d*
Titus 1:15 but unto them that are *d* and
Titus 1:15 their mind and conscience is *d*
Heb 12:15 trouble you, and thereby many be *d*
Rev 3:4 which have not *d* their garments
Rev 14:4 they which were not *d* with women

## DEFILETH

Ex 31:14 every one that *d* it shall surely
Num 19:13 *d* the tabernacle of the LORD
Num 35:33 for blood it *d* the land
Mt 15:11 goeth into the mouth *d* a man
Mt 15:11 out of the mouth, this *d* a man
Mt 15:20 with unwashen hands *d* not a man
Mk 7:20 out of the man, that *d* the man
Jas 3:6 that it *d* the whole body, and
Rev 21:27 enter into it any thing that *d*

## DEFRAUD

Lev 19:13 Thou shalt not *d* thy neighbour
Mk 10:19 *D* not, Honour thy father and

1Cor 6:8 Nay, ye do wrong, and *d*, and that
1Cor 7:5 *D* ye not one the other, except it
1Th 4:6 *d* his brother in any matter

**DEFRAUDED**
1Sa 12:3 or whom have I *d*?
1Sa 12:4 And they said, Thou hast not *d* us
1Cor 6:7 rather suffer yourselves to be *d*
2Cor 7:2 no man, we have *d* no man

**DEFY**
Num 23:7 curse me Jacob, and come, *d* Israel
Num 23:8 or how shall I *d*, whom the LORD
1Sa 17:10 I *d* the armies of Israel this day
1Sa 17:25 surely to *d* Israel is he come up
1Sa 17:26 that he should *d* the armies of

**DEGREE**
1Chr 15:18 their brethren of the second *d*
1Chr 17:17 to the estate of a man of high *d*
Ps 62:9 Surely men of low *d* are vanity
Ps 62:9 and men of high *d* are a lie
Lk 1:52 seats, and exalted them of low *d*
1Ti 3:13 purchase to themselves a good *d*
Jas 1:9 Let the brother of low *d* rejoice

**DEGREES**
2Kin 20:9 shall the shadow go forward ten *d*
2Kin 20:9 or go back ten *d*
2Kin 20:10 for the shadow to go down ten *d*
2Kin 20:10 the shadow return backward ten *d*
2Kin 20:11 brought the shadow ten *d* backward
Ps 120:*t* A Song of *d*
Ps 121:*t* A Song of *d*
Ps 122:*t* A Song of *d* of David
Ps 123:*t* A Song of *d*
Ps 124:*t* A Song of *d* of David
Ps 125:*t* A Song of *d*
Ps 126:*t* A Song of *d*
Ps 127:*t* A Song of *d* for Solomon
Ps 128:*t* A Song of *d*
Ps 129:*t* A Song of *d*
Ps 130:*t* A Song of *d*
Ps 131:*t* A Song of *d* of David
Ps 132:*t* A Song of *d*
Ps 133:*t* A Song of *d* of David
Ps 134:*t* A Song of *d*
Is 38:8 bring again the shadow of the *d*
Is 38:8 sun dial of Ahaz, ten *d* backward
Is 38:8 So the sun returned ten *d*
Is 38:8 by which *d* it was gone down

**DEHAVITES** *(de-ha'-vites) Foreign settlers in Samaria.*
Ezr 4:9 the Susanchites, the *D*, and the

**DEKAR** *(de'-kar) Father of an officer of Solomon.*
1Kin 4:9 The son of *D*, in Makaz, and in

**DELAIAH** *(del-a-i'-ah)* See DALAIAH.
*1. A priest of David.*
1Chr 24:18 The three and twentieth to *D*
*2. A family with a lost genealogy.*
Ezr 2:60 The children of *D*, the children
Neh 7:62 The children of *D*, the children
*3. An opponent of Nehemiah.*
Neh 6:10 son of *D* the son of Mehetabeel
*4. A prince of Judah.*
Jer 36:12 *D* the son of Shemaiah, and
Jer 36:25 Nevertheless Elnathan and *D*

**DELICATE**
Deut 28:54 is tender among you, and very *d*
Deut 28:56 *d* woman among you, which would
Is 47:1 no more be called tender and *d*
Jer 6:2 of Zion to a comely and *d* woman
Mic 1:16 and poll thee for thy *d* children

**DELICATELY**
1Sa 15:32 And Agag came unto him *d*
Prov 29:21 He that *d* bringeth up his servant
Lam 4:5 They that did feed *d* are desolate
Lk 7:25 gorgeously apparelled, and live *d*

**DELIGHT**
Gen 34:19 because he had *d* in Jacob's
Num 14:8 If the LORD *d* in us, then he will
Deut 10:15 Only the LORD had a *d* in thy
Deut 21:14 be, if thou have no *d* in her
1Sa 15:22 as great *d* in burnt offerings
1Sa 18:22 Behold, the king hath *d* in thee
2Sa 15:26 he thus say, I have no *d* in thee
2Sa 24:3 my lord the king *d* in this thing
Est 6:6 To whom would the king *d* to do
Job 22:26 thou have thy *d* in the Almighty
Job 27:10 Will he *d* himself in the Almighty
Job 34:9 that he should *d* himself with God
Ps 1:2 But his *d* is in the law of the
Ps 16:3 excellent, in whom is all my *d*
Ps 37:4 *D* thyself also in the LORD
Ps 37:11 shall *d* themselves in the
Ps 40:8 I *d* to do thy will, O my God
Ps 62:4 they *d* in lies
Ps 68:30 thou the people that *d* in war
Ps 94:19 within me thy comforts *d* my soul
Ps 119:16 I will *d* myself in thy statutes
Ps 119:24 Thy testimonies also are my *d*
Ps 119:35 for therein do I *d*
Ps 119:47 And I will *d* myself in thy
Ps 119:70 but I *d* in thy law
Ps 119:77 for thy law is my *d*
Ps 119:174 and thy law is my *d*
Prov 1:22 the scorners *d* in their scorning,
Prov 2:14 *d* in the frowardness of the
Prov 8:30 and I was daily his *d*, rejoicing
Prov 11:1 but a just weight is his *d*
Prov 11:20 upright in their way are his *d*
Prov 12:22 they that deal truly are his *d*
Prov 15:8 prayer of the upright is his *d*
Prov 16:13 Righteous lips are the *d* of kings
Prov 18:2 A fool hath no *d* in understanding
Prov 19:10 *D* is not seemly for a fool
Prov 24:25 them that rebuke him shall be *d*
Prov 29:17 he shall give *d* unto thy soul
Song 2:3 under his shadow with great *d*
Is 1:11 I *d* not in the blood of bullocks,
Is 13:17 for gold, they shall not *d* in it
Is 55:2 let your soul *d* itself in fatness
Is 58:2 *d* to know my ways, as a nation
Is 58:2 they take *d* in approaching to God
Is 58:13 and call the sabbath a *d*, the holy
Is 58:14 Then shalt thou *d* thyself in the
Jer 6:10 they have no *d* in it
Jer 9:24 for in these things I *d*, saith
Mal 3:1 of the covenant, whom ye *d* in
Rom 7:22 For I *d* in the law of God after

**DELIGHTED**
1Sa 19:2 Saul's son *d* much in David
2Sa 22:20 delivered me, because he *d* in me
1Kin 10:9 which *d* in thee, to set thee on
2Chr 9:8 which *d* in thee to set thee on
Neh 9:25 *d* themselves in thy great
Est 2:14 no more, except the king *d* in her
Ps 18:19 delivered me, because he *d* in me
Ps 22:8 deliver him, seeing he *d* in him
Ps 109:17 as he *d* not in blessing, so let
Is 65:12 did choose that wherein I *d* not
Is 66:4 and chose that in which I *d* not
Is 66:11 be *d* with the abundance of her

**DELIGHTETH**
Est 6:6 the man whom the king *d* to honour
Est 6:7 the man whom the king *d* to honour
Est 6:9 withal whom the king *d* to honour
Est 6:9 the man whom the king *d* to honour
Est 6:11 the man whom the king *d* to honour
Ps 37:23 and he *d* in his way
Ps 112:1 the LORD, that *d* greatly in his
Ps 147:10 He *d* not in the strength of the
Prov 3:12 as a father the son in whom he *d*
Is 42:1 mine elect, in whom my soul *d*
Is 62:4 for the LORD *d* in thee, and thy
Is 66:3 ways, and their soul *d* in their
Mic 7:18 for ever, because he *d* in mercy
Mal 2:17 of the LORD, and he *d* in them

**DELIGHTS**
2Sa 1:24 you in scarlet, with other *d*
Ps 119:92 Unless thy law had been my *d*
Ps 119:143 yet thy commandments are my *d*
Prov 8:31 my *d* were with the sons of men
Eccl 2:8 the *d* of the sons of men, as
Song 7:6 pleasant art thou, O love, for *d*

**DELILAH** *(de-li'-lah) Woman who betrayed Samson.*
Judg 16:4 valley of Sorek, whose name was *D*
Judg 16:6 *D* said to Samson, Tell me, I pray
Judg 16:10 *D* said unto Samson, Behold, thou
Judg 16:12 *D* therefore took new ropes, and
Judg 16:13 *D* said unto Samson, Hitherto thou
Judg 16:18 when *D* saw that he had told her

**DELIVER**
Gen 32:11 *D* me, I pray thee, from the hand
Gen 37:22 to *d* him to his father again
Gen 40:13 thou shalt *d* Pharaoh's cup into
Gen 42:34 so will I *d* you your brother, and
Gen 42:37 *d* him into my hand, and I will
Ex 3:8 I am come down to *d* them out of
Ex 5:18 yet shall ye *d* the tale of bricks
Ex 21:13 but God *d* him into his hand
Ex 22:7 If a man shall *d* unto his
Ex 22:10 If a man *d* unto his neighbour an
Ex 22:26 thou shalt *d* it unto him by that
Ex 23:31 for I will *d* the inhabitants of
Lev 26:26 they shall *d* you your bread again
Num 21:2 If thou wilt indeed *d* this people
Num 35:25 the congregation shall *d* the
Deut 1:27 to *d* us into the hand of the
Deut 2:30 that he might *d* him into thy hand
Deut 3:2 for I will *d* him, and all his
Deut 7:2 thy God shall *d* them before thee
Deut 7:16 the LORD thy God shall *d* thee
Deut 7:23 thy God shall *d* them unto thee
Deut 7:24 he shall *d* their kings into thine
Deut 19:12 *d* him into the hand of the
Deut 23:14 to *d* thee, and to give up thine
Deut 23:15 Thou shalt not *d* unto his master
Deut 24:13 In any case thou shalt *d* him the
Deut 25:11 *d* her husband out of the hand of
Deut 32:39 any that can *d* out of my hand
Josh 2:13 have, and *d* our lives from death
Josh 7:7 to *d* us into the hand of the
Josh 8:7 your God will *d* it into your hand
Josh 11:6 morrow about this time will I *d*
Josh 20:5 then they shall not *d* the slayer
Judg 4:7 I will *d* him into thine hand
Judg 7:7 *d* the Midianites into thine hand
Judg 10:11 Israel, Did not I *d* you from the
Judg 10:13 wherefore I will *d* you no more
Judg 10:14 let them *d* you in the time of
Judg 10:15 *d* us only, we pray thee, this day
Judg 11:9 the LORD *d* them before me, shall
Judg 11:30 If thou shalt without fail *d* the
Judg 13:5 he shall begin to *d* Israel out of
Judg 15:12 that we may *d* thee into the hand
Judg 15:13 fast, and *d* thee into their hand
Judg 20:13 Now therefore *d* us the men
Judg 20:28 I will *d* them into thine hand
1Sa 4:8 who shall *d* us out of the hand of
1Sa 7:3 he will *d* you out of the hand of
1Sa 7:14 Israel *d* out of the hands of the
1Sa 12:10 but now *d* us out of the hand of
1Sa 12:21 things, which cannot profit nor *d*
1Sa 14:37 wilt thou *d* them into the hand of
1Sa 17:37 he will *d* me out of the hand of
1Sa 17:46 the LORD *d* thee into mine hand
1Sa 23:4 for I will *d* the Philistines into
1Sa 23:11 of Keilah *d* me up into his hand
1Sa 23:12 Will the men of Keilah *d* me
1Sa 23:12 LORD said, They will *d* thee up
1Sa 23:20 our part shall be to *d* him into
1Sa 24:4 I will *d* thine enemy into thine
1Sa 24:15 cause, and *d* me out of thine hand
1Sa 26:24 LORD, and let him *d* me out of all
1Sa 28:19 Moreover the LORD will also *d*
1Sa 28:19 the LORD also shall *d* the host of
1Sa 30:15 nor *d* me into the hands of my
2Sa 3:14 *D* me my wife Michal, which I
2Sa 5:19 wilt thou *d* them into mine hand
2Sa 5:19 for I will doubtless *d* the
2Sa 14:7 *D* him that smote his brother,
2Sa 14:16 to *d* his handmaid out of the hand
2Sa 20:21 *d* him only, and I will depart from
1Kin 8:46 *d* them to the enemy, so that they
1Kin 18:9 that thou wouldest *d* thy servant
1Kin 20:5 Thou shalt *d* me thy silver, and
1Kin 20:13 I will *d* it into thine hand this
1Kin 20:28 therefore will I *d* all this great
1Kin 22:6 for the Lord shall *d* it into the
1Kin 22:12 for the LORD shall *d* it into the
1Kin 22:15 for the LORD shall *d* it into the
2Kin 3:10 to *d* them into the hand of Moab
2Kin 3:13 to *d* them into the hand of Moab
2Kin 3:18 he will *d* the Moabites also into
2Kin 12:7 but *d* it for the breaches of the
2Kin 17:39 he shall *d* you out of the hand of
2Kin 18:23 I will *d* thee two thousand horses
2Kin 18:29 be able to *d* you out of his hand
2Kin 18:30 saying, The LORD will surely *d* us
2Kin 18:32 you, saying, The LORD will *d* us
2Kin 18:35 that the LORD should *d* Jerusalem
2Kin 20:6 and I will *d* thee and this city out
2Kin 21:14 *d* them into the hand of their
2Kin 22:5 let them *d* it into the hand of
1Chr 14:10 wilt thou *d* them into mine hand

1Chr 14:10 for I will *d* them into thine hand
1Chr 16:35 *d* us from the heathen, that we
2Chr 6:36 *d* them over before their enemies,
2Chr 18:5 for God will *d* it into the king's
2Chr 18:11 for the LORD shall *d* it into the
2Chr 25:15 which could not *d* their own
2Chr 25:20 that he might *d* them into the
2Chr 28:11 *d* the captives again, which ye
2Chr 32:11 The LORD our God shall *d* us out
2Chr 32:13 to *d* their lands out of mine hand
2Chr 32:14 that could *d* his people out of
2Chr 32:14 be able to *d* you out of mine hand
2Chr 32:15 to *d* his people out of mine hand
2Chr 32:15 your God *d* you out of mine hand
2Chr 32:17 *d* his people out of mine hand
Ezr 7:19 those *d* thou before the God of
Neh 9:28 many times didst thou *d* them
Job 5:4 neither is there any to *d* them
Job 5:19 He shall *d* thee in six troubles
Job 6:23 *D* me from the enemy's hand
Job 10:7 none that can *d* out of thine hand
Job 22:30 He shall *d* the island of the
Job 33:24 *D* him from going down to the pit
Job 33:28 He will *d* his soul from going
Job 36:18 then a great ransom cannot *d* thee
Ps 6:4 Return, O LORD, *d* my soul
Ps 7:1 them that persecute me, and *d* me
Ps 7:2 pieces, while there is none to *d*
Ps 17:13 *d* my soul from the wicked, which
Ps 22:4 trusted, and thou didst *d* them
Ps 22:8 on the LORD that he would *d* him
Ps 22:8 let him *d* him, seeing he
Ps 22:20 *D* my soul from the sword
Ps 25:20 O keep my soul, and *d* me
Ps 27:12 *D* me not over unto the will of
Ps 31:1 *d* me in thy righteousness
Ps 31:2 *d* me speedily
Ps 31:15 *d* me from the hand of mine
Ps 33:17 neither shall he *d* any by his
Ps 33:19 To *d* their soul from death, and to
Ps 37:40 LORD shall help them, and *d* them
Ps 37:40 he shall *d* them from the wicked,
Ps 39:8 *D* me from all my transgressions
Ps 40:13 Be pleased, O LORD, to *d* me
Ps 41:1 the LORD will *d* him in time of
Ps 41:2 thou wilt not *d* him unto the will
Ps 43:1 O *d* me from the deceitful and
Ps 50:15 I will *d* thee, and thou shalt
Ps 50:22 in pieces, and there be none to *d*
Ps 51:14 *D* me from bloodguiltiness, O God,
Ps 56:13 wilt not thou *d* my feet from
Ps 59:1 *D* me from mine enemies, O my God
Ps 59:2 *D* me from the workers of iniquity
Ps 69:14 *D* me out of the mire, and let me
Ps 69:18 *d* me because of mine enemies
Ps 70:1 Make haste, O God, to *d* me
Ps 71:2 *D* me in thy righteousness, and
Ps 71:4 *D* me, O my God, out of the hand
Ps 71:11 for there is none to *d* him
Ps 72:12 For he shall *d* the needy when he
Ps 74:19 O *d* not the soul of thy
Ps 79:9 *d* us, and purge away our sins, for
Ps 82:4 *D* the poor and needy
Ps 89:48 shall he *d* his soul from the hand
Ps 91:3 Surely he shall *d* thee from the
Ps 91:14 upon me, therefore will I *d* him
Ps 91:15 I will *d* him, and honour him
Ps 106:43 Many times did he *d* them
Ps 109:21 thy mercy is good, *d* thou me
Ps 116:4 O LORD, I beseech thee, *d* my soul
Ps 119:134 *D* me from the oppression of man
Ps 119:153 Consider mine affliction, and *d* me
Ps 119:154 Plead my cause, and *d* me
Ps 119:170 *d* me according to thy word
Ps 120:2 *D* my soul, O LORD, from lying
Ps 140:1 *D* me, O LORD, from the evil man
Ps 142:6 *d* me from my persecutors
Ps 143:9 *D* me, O LORD, from mine enemies
Ps 144:7 *d* me out of great waters, from
Ps 144:11 *d* me from the hand of strange
Prov 2:12 To *d* thee from the way of the
Prov 2:16 To *d* thee from the strange woman,
Prov 4:9 of glory shall she *d* to thee
Prov 6:3 *d* thyself, when thou art come
Prov 6:5 *D* thyself as a roe from the hand
Prov 11:6 of the upright shall *d* them
Prov 12:6 mouth of the upright shall *d* them
Prov 19:19 for if thou *d* him, yet thou must
Prov 23:14 shalt *d* his soul from hell
Prov 24:11 If thou forbear to *d* them that
Eccl 8:8 neither shall wickedness *d* those
Is 5:29 it away safe, and none shall *d* it
Is 19:20 a great one, and he shall *d* them
Is 29:11 which men *d* to one that is
Is 31:5 defending also he will *d* it
Is 36:14 for he shall not be able to *d* you
Is 36:15 saying, The LORD will surely *d* us
Is 36:18 you, saying, The LORD will *d* us
Is 36:20 that the LORD should *d* Jerusalem
Is 38:6 And I will *d* thee and this city out
Is 43:13 is none that can *d* out of my hand
Is 44:17 prayeth unto it, and saith, *D* me
Is 44:20 aside, that he cannot *d* his soul
Is 46:2 they could not *d* the burden
Is 46:4 even I will carry, and will *d* you
Is 47:14 they shall not *d* themselves from
Is 50:2 or have I no power to *d*
Is 57:13 criest, let thy companies *d* thee
Jer 1:8 for I am with thee to *d* thee
Jer 1:19 thee, saith the LORD, to *d* thee
Jer 15:9 I *d* to the sword before their
Jer 15:20 to *d* thee, saith the LORD
Jer 15:21 I will *d* thee out of the hand of
Jer 18:21 Therefore *d* up their children to
Jer 20:5 Moreover I will *d* all the
Jer 21:7 I will *d* Zedekiah king of Judah,
Jer 21:12 *d* him that is spoiled out of the
Jer 22:3 *d* the spoiled out of the hand of
Jer 24:9 I will *d* them to be removed into
Jer 29:18 will *d* them to be removed to all
Jer 29:21 I will *d* them into the hand of
Jer 38:19 lest they *d* me into their hand,
Jer 38:20 said, They shall not *d* thee
Jer 39:17 But I will *d* thee in that day,
Jer 39:18 For I will surely *d* thee, and thou
Jer 42:11 you, and to *d* you from his hand
Jer 43:3 for to *d* us into the hand of the
Jer 43:11 *d* such as are for death to death
Jer 46:26 I will *d* them into the hand of
Jer 51:6 Babylon, and *d* every man his soul
Jer 51:45 *d* ye every man his soul from the
Lam 5:8 that doth *d* us out of their hand
Eze 7:19 *d* them in the day of the wrath of
Eze 11:9 *d* you into the hands of strangers
Eze 13:21 *d* my people out of your hand, and
Eze 13:23 for I will *d* my people out of
Eze 14:14 they should *d* but their own souls
Eze 14:16 they shall *d* neither sons nor
Eze 14:18 they shall *d* neither sons nor
Eze 14:20 they shall *d* neither son nor
Eze 14:20 they shall but *d* their own souls
Eze 21:31 *d* thee into the hand of brutish
Eze 23:28 I will *d* thee into the hand of
Eze 25:4 therefore I will *d* thee to the
Eze 25:7 will *d* thee for a spoil to the
Eze 33:5 taketh warning shall *d* his soul
Eze 33:12 shall not *d* him in the day of his
Eze 34:10 for I will *d* my flock from their
Eze 34:12 will *d* them out of all places
Dan 3:15 that shall *d* you out of my hands
Dan 3:17 to *d* us from the burning fiery
Dan 3:17 he will *d* us out of thine hand, O
Dan 3:29 God that can *d* after this sort
Dan 6:14 set his heart on Daniel to *d* him
Dan 6:14 going down of the sun to *d* him
Dan 6:16 continually, he will *d* thee
Dan 6:20 able to *d* thee from the lions
Dan 8:4 any that could *d* out of his hand
Dan 8:7 could *d* the ram out of his hand
Hos 2:10 none shall *d* her out of mine hand
Hos 11:8 how shall I *d* thee, Israel
Amos 1:6 captivity, to *d* them up to Edom
Amos 2:14 shall the mighty *d* himself
Amos 2:15 swift of foot shall not *d* himself
Amos 2:15 that rideth the horse *d* himself
Amos 6:8 therefore will I *d* up the city
Jonah 4:6 his head, to *d* him from his grief
Mic 5:6 thus shall he *d* us from the
Mic 5:8 teareth in pieces, and none can *d*
Mic 6:14 shalt take hold, but shalt not *d*
Zeph 1:18 *d* them in the day of the LORD's
Zec 2:7 *D* thyself, O Zion, that dwellest
Zec 11:6 I will *d* the men every one into
Zec 11:6 of their hand I will not *d* them
Mt 5:25 the adversary *d* thee to the judge
Mt 5:25 the judge *d* thee to the officer,
Mt 6:13 temptation, but *d* us from evil
Mt 10:17 for they will *d* you up to the
Mt 10:19 But when they *d* you up, take no
Mt 10:21 the brother shall *d* up the
Mt 20:19 shall *d* him to the Gentiles to
Mt 24:9 Then shall they *d* you up to be
Mt 26:15 give me, and I will *d* him unto you
Mt 27:43 let him *d* him now, if he will
Mk 10:33 shall *d* him to the Gentiles
Mk 13:9 for they shall *d* you up to
Mk 13:11 *d* you up, take no thought
Lk 11:4 but *d* us from evil
Lk 12:58 the judge *d* thee to the officer,
Lk 20:20 they might *d* him unto the power
Acts 7:25 that God by his hand would *d* them
Acts 7:34 and am come down to *d* them
Acts 21:11 shall *d* him into the hands of the
Acts 25:11 no man may *d* me unto them
Acts 25:16 of the Romans to *d* any man to die
Rom 7:24 who shall *d* me from the body of
1Cor 5:5 To *d* such a one unto Satan for
2Cor 1:10 from so great a death, and doth *d*
2Cor 1:10 we trust that he will yet *d* us
Gal 1:4 that he might *d* us from this
2Ti 4:18 the Lord shall *d* me from every
Heb 2:15 *d* them who through fear of death
2Pet 2:9 The Lord knoweth how to *d* the

## DELIVERANCE

Gen 45:7 to save your lives by a great *d*
Judg 15:18 Thou hast given this great *d* into
2Kin 5:1 the LORD had given *d* unto Syria
2Kin 13:17 said, The arrow of the LORD's *d*
2Kin 13:17 and the arrow of *d* from Syria
1Chr 11:14 the LORD saved them by a great *d*
2Chr 12:7 but I will grant them some *d*
Ezr 9:13 and hast given us such *d* as this
Est 4:14 *d* arise to the Jews from another
Ps 18:50 Great *d* giveth he to his king
Ps 32:7 compass me about with songs of *d*
Is 26:18 not wrought any *d* in the earth
Joel 2:32 Zion and in Jerusalem shall be *d*
Obad 17 But upon mount Zion shall be *d*
Lk 4:18 to preach *d* to the captives, and
Heb 11:35 were tortured, not accepting *d*

## DELIVERED

Gen 9:2 into your hand are they *d*
Gen 14:20 which hath *d* thine enemies into
Gen 25:24 her days to be *d* were fulfilled
Gen 32:16 he *d* them into the hand of his
Gen 37:21 he *d* him out of their hands
Ex 1:19 are *d* ere the midwives come in
Ex 2:19 An Egyptian *d* us out of the hand
Ex 5:23 hast thou *d* thy people at all
Ex 12:27 the Egyptians, and *d* our houses
Ex 18:4 *d* me from the sword of Pharaoh
Ex 18:8 the way, and how the LORD *d* them
Ex 18:9 whom he had *d* out of the hand of
Ex 18:10 who hath *d* you out of the hand of
Ex 18:10 who hath *d* the people from under
Lev 6:2 in that which was *d* him to keep
Lev 6:4 or that which was *d* him to keep
Lev 26:25 ye shall be *d* into the hand of
Num 21:3 of Israel, and *d* up the Canaanites
Num 21:34 for I have *d* him into thy hand,
Num 31:5 So there were *d* out of the
Deut 2:33 the LORD our God *d* him before us
Deut 2:36 the LORD our God *d* all unto us
Deut 3:3 So the LORD our God *d* into our
Deut 5:22 of stone, and *d* them unto me
Deut 9:10 the LORD *d* unto me two tables of
Deut 20:13 God hath *d* it into thine hands
Deut 21:10 God hath *d* them into thine hands
Deut 31:9 *d* it unto the priests the sons of
Josh 2:24 Truly the LORD hath *d* into our
Josh 9:26 *d* them out of the hand of the
Josh 10:8 for I have *d* them into thine hand
Josh 10:12 LORD *d* up the Amorites before the
Josh 10:19 God hath *d* them into your hand
Josh 10:30 And the LORD *d* it also, and the
Josh 10:32 the LORD *d* Lachish into the hand
Josh 11:8 the LORD *d* them into the hand of
Josh 21:44 the LORD *d* all their enemies into
Josh 22:31 now ye have *d* the children of
Josh 24:10 so I *d* you out of his hand
Josh 24:11 and I *d* them into your hand
Judg 1:2 I have *d* the land into his hand
Judg 1:4 the LORD *d* the Canaanites and the
Judg 2:14 he *d* them into the hands of
Judg 2:16 which *d* them out of the hand of
Judg 2:18 *d* them out of the hand of their
Judg 2:23 neither *d* he them into the hand
Judg 3:9 who *d* them, even Othniel the son
Judg 3:10 the LORD *d* Chushan-rishathaim

Judg 3:28 for the LORD hath *d* your enemies
Judg 3:31 and he also *d* Israel
Judg 4:14 hath *d* Sisera into thine hand
Judg 5:11 They that are *d* from the noise of
Judg 6:1 the LORD *d* them into the hand of
Judg 6:9 I *d* you out of the hand of the
Judg 6:13 *d* us into the hands of the
Judg 7:9 for I have *d* it into thine hand
Judg 7:14 into his hand hath God *d* Midian
Judg 7:15 for the LORD hath *d* into your
Judg 8:3 God hath *d* into your hands the
Judg 8:7 when the LORD hath *d* Zebah
Judg 8:22 for thou hast *d* us from the hand
Judg 8:34 who had *d* them out of the hands
Judg 9:17 *d* you out of the hand of Midian
Judg 10:12 I *d* you out of their hand
Judg 11:21 And the LORD God of Israel *d* Sihon
Judg 11:32 the LORD *d* them into his hands
Judg 12:2 ye *d* me not out of their hands
Judg 12:3 And when I saw that ye *d* me not
Judg 12:3 the LORD *d* them into my hand
Judg 13:1 the LORD *d* them into the hand of
Judg 16:23 Our god hath *d* Samson our enemy
Judg 16:24 Our god hath *d* into our hands our
1Sa 4:19 was with child, near to be *d*
1Sa 10:18 *d* you out of the hand of the
1Sa 12:11 *d* you out of the hand of your
1Sa 14:10 for the LORD hath *d* them into our
1Sa 14:12 for the LORD hath *d* them into the
1Sa 14:48 *d* Israel out of the hands of them
1Sa 17:35 him, and *d* it out of his mouth
1Sa 17:37 The LORD that *d* me out of the paw
1Sa 23:7 God hath *d* him into mine hand
1Sa 23:14 but God *d* him not into his hand
1Sa 24:10 *d* thee to day into mine hand in
1Sa 24:18 the LORD had *d* me into thine hand
1Sa 26:8 God hath *d* thine enemy into thine
1Sa 26:23 for the LORD *d* thee into my hand
1Sa 30:23 *d* the company that came against
2Sa 3:8 have not *d* thee into the hand of
2Sa 10:10 the rest of the people he *d* into
2Sa 12:7 I *d* thee out of the hand of Saul
2Sa 16:8 the LORD hath *d* the kingdom into
2Sa 18:28 which hath *d* up the men that
2Sa 19:9 he *d* us out of the hand of the
2Sa 21:6 men of his sons be *d* unto us
2Sa 21:9 he *d* them into the hands of the
2Sa 22:1 in the day that the LORD had *d*
2Sa 22:18 He *d* me from my strong enemy, and
2Sa 22:20 he *d* me, because he delighted in
2Sa 22:44 Thou also hast *d* me from the
2Sa 22:49 thou hast *d* me from the violent
1Kin 3:17 I was *d* of a child with her in
1Kin 3:18 the third day after that I was *d*
1Kin 3:18 that this woman was *d* also
1Kin 13:26 the LORD hath *d* him unto the lion
1Kin 15:18 *d* them into the hand of his
1Kin 17:23 house, and *d* him unto his mother
2Kin 12:15 into whose hand they *d* the money
2Kin 13:3 he *d* them into the hand of Hazael
2Kin 17:20 *d* them into the hand of spoilers,
2Kin 18:30 this city shall not be *d* into the
2Kin 18:33 any of the gods of the nations *d*
2Kin 18:34 have they *d* Samaria out of mine
2Kin 18:35 that have *d* their country out of
2Kin 19:10 Jerusalem shall not be *d* into the
2Kin 19:11 and shalt thou be *d*
2Kin 19:12 *d* them which my fathers have
2Kin 22:7 money that was *d* into their hand
2Kin 22:9 have *d* it into the hand of them
2Kin 22:10 the priest hath *d* me a book
1Chr 5:20 Hagarites were *d* into their hand
1Chr 11:14 *d* it, and slew the Philistines
1Chr 16:7 Then on that day David *d* first
1Chr 19:11 the rest of the people he *d* unto
2Chr 13:16 God *d* them into their hand
2Chr 16:8 he *d* them into thine hand
2Chr 18:14 they shall be *d* into your hand
2Chr 23:9 *d* to the captains of hundreds
2Chr 24:24 the LORD *d* a very great host into
2Chr 28:5 Wherefore the LORD his God *d* him
2Chr 28:5 he was also *d* into the hand of
2Chr 28:9 he hath *d* them into your hand, and
2Chr 29:8 he hath *d* them to trouble, to
2Chr 32:17 *d* their people out of mine hand
2Chr 34:9 they *d* the money that was brought
2Chr 34:15 Hilkiah *d* the book to Shaphan
2Chr 34:17 have *d* it into the hand of the
Ezr 5:14 Babylon, and they were *d* unto one
Ezr 8:31 he *d* us from the hand of the
Ezr 8:36 they *d* the king's commissions
Ezr 9:7 been *d* into the hand of the kings
Est 6:9 horse be *d* to the hand of one of
Job 16:11 God hath *d* me to the ungodly, and
Job 22:30 it is *d* by the pureness of thine
Job 23:7 so should I be *d* for ever from my
Job 29:12 Because I *d* the poor that cried,
Ps 7:4 I have *d* him that without cause
Ps 18:*t* *d* him from the hand of all his
Ps 18:17 He *d* me from my strong enemy, and
Ps 18:19 he *d* me, because he delighted in
Ps 18:43 Thou hast *d* me from the strivings
Ps 18:48 thou hast *d* me from the violent
Ps 22:5 They cried unto thee, and were *d*
Ps 33:16 man is not *d* by much strength
Ps 34:4 me, and *d* me from all my fears
Ps 54:7 For he hath *d* me out of all
Ps 55:18 He hath *d* my soul in peace from
Ps 56:13 For thou hast *d* my soul from
Ps 60:5 That thy beloved may be *d*
Ps 69:14 let me be *d* from them that hate
Ps 78:42 day when he *d* them from the enemy
Ps 78:61 *d* his strength into captivity, and
Ps 81:6 his hands were *d* from the pots
Ps 81:7 calledst in trouble, and I *d* thee
Ps 86:13 thou hast *d* my soul from the
Ps 107:6 he *d* them out of their distresses
Ps 107:20 *d* them from their destructions
Ps 108:6 That thy beloved may be *d*
Ps 116:8 For thou hast *d* my soul from
Prov 11:8 The righteous is *d* out of trouble
Prov 11:9 knowledge shall the just be *d*
Prov 11:21 seed of the righteous shall be *d*
Prov 28:26 walketh wisely, he shall be *d*
Eccl 9:15 and he by his wisdom *d* the city
Is 20:6 to be *d* from the king of Assyria
Is 29:12 the book is *d* to him that is not
Is 34:2 he hath *d* them to the slaughter
Is 36:15 this city shall not be *d* into the
Is 36:18 any of the gods of the nations *d*
Is 36:19 have they *d* Samaria out of my
Is 36:20 that have *d* their land out of my
Is 37:11 and shalt thou be *d*
Is 37:12 *d* them which my fathers have
Is 38:17 thou hast in love to my soul *d* it
Is 49:24 mighty, or the lawful captive *d*
Is 49:25 prey of the terrible shall be *d*
Is 66:7 came, she was *d* of a man child
Jer 7:10 and say, We are *d* to do all these
Jer 20:13 for he hath *d* the soul of the
Jer 32:4 but shall surely be *d* into the
Jer 32:16 Now when I had *d* the evidence of
Jer 32:36 It shall be *d* into the hand of
Jer 34:3 be taken, and *d* into his hand
Jer 37:17 thou shalt be *d* into the hand of
Jer 46:24 she shall be *d* into the hand of
Lam 1:14 the Lord hath *d* me into their
Eze 3:19 but thou hast *d* thy soul
Eze 3:21 also thou hast *d* thy soul
Eze 14:16 they only shall be *d*, but the
Eze 14:18 they only shall be *d* themselves
Eze 16:21 *d* them to cause them to pass
Eze 16:27 *d* thee unto the will of them that
Eze 17:15 he break the covenant, and be *d*
Eze 23:9 Wherefore I have *d* her into the
Eze 31:11 I have therefore *d* him into the
Eze 31:14 for they are all *d* unto death
Eze 32:20 she is *d* to the sword
Eze 33:9 but thou hast *d* thy soul
Eze 34:27 *d* them out of the hand of those
Dan 3:28 *d* his servants that trusted in
Dan 6:27 who hath *d* Daniel from the power
Dan 12:1 that time thy people shall be *d*
Joel 2:32 the name of the LORD shall be *d*
Amos 1:9 because they *d* up the whole
Amos 9:1 escapeth of them shall not be *d*
Obad 14 neither shouldest thou have *d* up
Mic 4:10 there shalt thou be *d*
Hab 2:9 that he may be *d* from the power
Mal 3:15 they that tempt God are even *d*
Mt 11:27 All things are *d* unto me of my
Mt 18:34 *d* him to the tormentors, till he
Mt 25:14 and *d* unto them his goods
Mt 27:2 *d* him to Pontius Pilate the
Mt 27:18 knew that for envy they had *d* him
Mt 27:26 Jesus, he *d* him to be crucified
Mt 27:58 Pilate commanded the body to be *d*
Mk 7:13 your tradition, which ye have *d*
Mk 9:31 The Son of man is *d* into the
Mk 10:33 shall be *d* unto the chief priests
Mk 15:1 him away, and *d* him to Pilate
Mk 15:10 chief priests had *d* him for envy
Mk 15:15 *d* Jesus, when he had scourged him
Lk 1:2 Even as they *d* them unto us
Lk 1:57 time came that she should be *d*
Lk 1:74 being *d* out of the hand of our
Lk 2:6 accomplished that she should be *d*
Lk 4:6 for that is *d* unto me
Lk 4:17 there was *d* unto him the book of
Lk 7:15 And he *d* him to his mother
Lk 9:42 *d* him again to his father
Lk 9:44 shall be *d* into the hands of men
Lk 10:22 All things are *d* to me of my
Lk 12:58 that thou mayest be *d* from him
Lk 18:32 For he shall be *d* unto the
Lk 19:13 *d* them ten pounds, and said unto
Lk 23:25 but he *d* Jesus to their will
Lk 24:7 The Son of man must be *d* into the
Lk 24:20 our rulers *d* him to be condemned
Jn 16:21 as soon as she is *d* of the child
Jn 18:30 would not have *d* him up unto thee
Jn 18:35 chief priests have *d* thee unto me
Jn 18:36 I should not be *d* to the Jews
Jn 19:11 therefore he that *d* me unto thee
Jn 19:16 Then *d* he him therefore unto them
Acts 2:23 being *d* by the determinate
Acts 3:13 whom ye *d* up, and denied him in
Acts 6:14 the customs which Moses *d* us
Acts 7:10 *d* him out of all his afflictions,
Acts 12:4 *d* him to four quaternions of
Acts 12:11 hath *d* me out of the hand of
Acts 15:30 together, they *d* the epistle
Acts 16:4 they *d* them the decrees for to
Acts 23:33 *d* the epistle to the governor,
Acts 27:1 sail into Italy, they *d* Paul
Acts 28:16 the centurion *d* the prisoners to
Acts 28:17 yet was I *d* prisoner from
Rom 4:25 Who was *d* for our offences, and
Rom 6:17 form of doctrine which was *d* you
Rom 7:6 But now we are *d* from the law
Rom 8:21 creature itself also shall be *d*
Rom 8:32 but *d* him up for us all, how
Rom 15:31 That I may be *d* from them that do
1Cor 11:2 ordinances, as I *d* them to you
1Cor 11:23 Lord that which also I *d* unto you
1Cor 15:3 For I *d* unto you first of all
1Cor 15:24 when he shall have *d* up the
2Cor 1:10 Who *d* us from so great a death,
2Cor 4:11 *d* unto death for Jesus' sake
Col 1:13 Who hath *d* us from the power of
1Th 1:10 which *d* us from the wrath to come
2Th 3:2 And that we may be *d* from
1Ti 1:20 whom I have *d* unto Satan, that
2Ti 3:11 but out of them all the Lord *d* me
2Ti 4:17 I was *d* out of the mouth of the
Heb 11:11 was *d* of a child when she was
2Pet 2:4 *d* them into chains of darkness,
2Pet 2:7 *d* just Lot, vexed with the filthy
2Pet 2:21 the holy commandment *d* unto them
Jude 3 which was once *d* unto the saints
Rev 12:2 in birth, and pained to be *d*
Rev 12:4 the woman which was ready to be *d*
Rev 20:13 hell *d* up the dead which were in

## DELIVERER

Judg 3:9 the LORD raised up a *d* to the
Judg 3:15 LORD, the LORD raised them up a *d*
Judg 18:28 And there was no *d*, because it was
2Sa 22:2 my rock, and my fortress, and my *d*
Ps 18:2 my rock, and my fortress, and my *d*
Ps 40:17 thou art my help and my *d*
Ps 70:5 thou art my help and my *d*
Ps 144:2 my high tower, and my *d*
Acts 7:35 a *d* by the hand of the angel
Rom 11:26 shall come out of Sion the *D*

## DELIVERETH

Job 36:15 He *d* the poor in his affliction,
Ps 18:48 He *d* me from mine enemies
Ps 34:7 them that fear him, and *d* them
Ps 34:17 *d* them out of all their troubles
Ps 34:19 but the LORD *d* him out of them
Ps 97:10 he *d* them out of the hand of the
Ps 144:10 who *d* David his servant from the
Prov 10:2 but righteousness *d* from death
Prov 11:4 but righteousness *d* from death
Prov 14:25 A true witness *d* souls
Prov 31:24 *d* girdles unto the merchant
Is 42:22 they are for a prey, and none *d*
Dan 6:27 He *d* and rescueth, and he worketh

### DEMAND
Job 38:3 for I will *d* of thee, and answer
Job 40:7 I will *d* of thee, and declare thou
Job 42:4 I will *d* of thee, and declare thou
Dan 4:17 the *d* by the word of the holy

### DEMANDED
Ex 5:14 set over them, were beaten, and *d*
2Sa 11:7 David *d* of him how Joab did, and
Dan 2:27 king hath *d* cannot the wise men
Mt 2:4 he *d* of them where Christ should
Lk 3:14 And the soldiers likewise *d* of him
Lk 17:20 when he was *d* of the Pharisees,
Acts 21:33 *d* who he was, and what he had done

### DEMAS *(de'-mas) A companion of Paul.*
Col 4:14 Luke, the beloved physician, and *D*
2Ti 4:10 For *D* hath forsaken me, having
Philem 24 Marcus, Aristarchus, *D*, Lucas, my

### DEMETRIUS *(de-me'-tre-us)*
*1. An opponent of Paul.*
Acts 19:24 For a certain man named *D*
Acts 19:38 Wherefore if *D*, and the craftsmen
*2. Disciple commended by John.*
3Jn 12 *D* hath good report of all men, and

### DEN
Ps 10:9 wait secretly as a lion in his *d*
Is 11:8 put his hand on the cockatrice' *d*
Jer 7:11 become a *d* of robbers in your
Jer 9:11 heaps, and a *d* of dragons
Jer 10:22 Judah desolate, and a *d* of dragons
Dan 6:7 shall be cast into the *d* of lions
Dan 6:12 shall be cast into the *d* of lions
Dan 6:16 and cast him into the *d* of lions
Dan 6:17 and laid upon the mouth of the *d*
Dan 6:19 went in haste unto the *d* of lions
Dan 6:20 And when he came to the *d*, he
Dan 6:23 take Daniel up out of the *d*
Dan 6:23 Daniel was taken up out of the *d*
Dan 6:24 cast them into the *d* of lions
Dan 6:24 they came at the bottom of the *d*
Amos 3:4 a young lion cry out of his *d*
Mt 21:13 ye have made it a *d* of thieves
Mk 11:17 ye have made it a *d* of thieves
Lk 19:46 ye have made it a *d* of thieves

### DENIED
Gen 18:15 Then Sarah *d*, saying, I laughed
1Kin 20:7 and I *d* him not
Job 31:28 for I should have *d* the God that
Mt 26:70 But he *d* before them all, saying,
Mt 26:72 again he *d* with an oath, I do not
Mk 14:68 But he *d*, saying, I know not,
Mk 14:70 And he *d* it again
Lk 8:45 When all *d*, Peter and they that
Lk 12:9 be *d* before the angels of God
Lk 22:57 he *d* him, saying, Woman, I know
Jn 1:20 And he confessed, and *d* not
Jn 13:38 crow, till thou hast *d* me thrice
Jn 18:25 He *d* it, and said, I am not
Jn 18:27 Peter then *d* again
Acts 3:13 *d* him in the presence of Pilate,
Acts 3:14 But ye *d* the Holy One and the Just
1Ti 5:8 he hath *d* the faith, and is worse
Rev 2:13 my name, and hast not *d* my faith
Rev 3:8 my word, and hast not *d* my name

### DENS
Judg 6:2 of Israel made them the *d* which
Job 37:8 Then the beasts go into *d*
Job 38:40 When they couch in their *d*
Ps 104:22 and lay them down in their *d*
Song 4:8 and Hermon, from the lions' *d*
Is 32:14 and towers shall be for *d* for ever
Nah 2:12 with prey, and his *d* with ravin
Heb 11:38 deserts, and in mountains, and in *d*
Rev 6:15 free man, hid themselves in the *d*

### DENY
Josh 24:27 unto you, lest ye *d* your God
1Kin 2:16 one petition of thee, *d* me not
Job 8:18 his place, then it shall *d* him
Prov 30:7 *d* me them not before I die
Prov 30:9 *d* thee, and say, Who is the LORD
Mt 10:33 whosoever shall *d* me before men
Mt 10:33 him will I also *d* before my
Mt 16:24 come after me, let him *d* himself
Mt 26:34 cock crow, thou shalt *d* me thrice
Mt 26:35 with thee, yet will I not *d* thee
Mt 26:75 cock crow, thou shalt *d* me thrice
Mk 8:34 come after me, let him *d* himself
Mk 14:30 twice, thou shalt *d* me thrice
Mk 14:31 I will not *d* thee in any wise
Mk 14:72 twice, thou shalt *d* me thrice
Lk 9:23 come after me, let him *d* himself
Lk 20:27 which *d* that there is any
Lk 22:34 thrice *d* that thou knowest me
Lk 22:61 cock crow, thou shalt *d* me thrice
Acts 4:16 and we cannot *d* it
2Ti 2:12 if we *d* him, he also will *d* us
2Ti 2:13 he cannot *d* himself
Titus 1:16 but in works they *d* him, being

### DENYING
2Ti 3:5 but *d* the power thereof
Titus 2:12 *d* ungodliness and worldly lusts,
2Pet 2:1 even *d* the Lord that bought them,
Jude 4 *d* the only Lord God, and our Lord

### DEPART
Gen 13:9 or if thou *d* to the right hand,
Gen 49:10 sceptre shall not *d* from Judah
Ex 8:11 And the frogs shall *d* from thee
Ex 8:29 of flies may *d* from Pharaoh
Ex 18:27 And Moses let his father in law *d*
Ex 21:22 so that her fruit *d* from her
Ex 33:1 And the LORD said unto Moses, *D*
Lev 25:41 And then shall he *d* from thee
Num 10:30 but I will *d* to mine own land, and
Num 16:26 unto the congregation, saying, *D*
Deut 4:9 lest they *d* from thy heart all
Deut 9:7 didst *d* out of the land of Egypt
Josh 1:8 law shall not *d* out of thy mouth
Josh 24:28 So Joshua let the people *d*
Judg 6:18 *D* not hence, I pray thee, until I
Judg 7:3 *d* early from mount Gilead
Judg 19:5 the morning, that he rose up to *d*
Judg 19:7 And when the man rose up to *d*
Judg 19:8 the morning on the fifth day to *d*
Judg 19:9 And when the man rose up to *d*
1Sa 15:6 Saul said unto the Kenites, Go, *d*
1Sa 22:5 *d*, and get thee into the land of
1Sa 29:10 in the morning, and have light, *d*
1Sa 29:11 rose up early to *d* in the morning
1Sa 30:22 they may lead them away, and *d*
2Sa 7:15 mercy shall not *d* away from him
2Sa 11:12 and to morrow I will let thee *d*
2Sa 12:10 shall never *d* from thine house
2Sa 15:14 make speed to *d*, lest he overtake
2Sa 20:21 only, and I will *d* from the city
2Sa 22:23 statutes, I did not *d* from them
1Kin 11:21 Hadad said to Pharaoh, Let me *d*
1Kin 12:5 *D* yet for three days, then come
1Kin 12:24 of the LORD, and returned to *d*
1Kin 15:19 of Israel, that he may *d* from me
2Chr 16:3 of Israel, that he may *d* from me
2Chr 18:31 and God moved them to *d* from him
2Chr 35:15 they might not *d* from their
Job 7:19 How long wilt thou not *d* from me
Job 15:30 He shall not *d* out of darkness
Job 20:28 The increase of his house shall *d*
Job 21:14 they say unto God, *D* from us
Job 22:17 Which said unto God, *D* from us
Job 28:28 to *d* from evil is understanding
Ps 6:8 *D* from me, all ye workers of
Ps 34:14 *D* from evil, and do good
Ps 37:27 *D* from evil, and do good
Ps 55:11 guile *d* not from her streets
Ps 101:4 A froward heart shall *d* from me
Ps 119:115 *D* from me, ye evildoers
Ps 139:19 *d* from me therefore, ye bloody
Prov 3:7 fear the LORD, and *d* from evil
Prov 3:21 let not them *d* from thine eyes
Prov 4:21 Let them not *d* from thine eyes
Prov 5:7 *d* not from the words of my mouth
Prov 13:14 to *d* from the snares of death
Prov 13:19 to fools to *d* from evil
Prov 14:27 to *d* from the snares of death
Prov 15:24 that he may *d* from hell beneath
Prov 16:6 fear of the LORD men *d* from evil
Prov 16:17 of the upright is to *d* from evil
Prov 17:13 evil shall not *d* from his house
Prov 22:6 he is old, he will not *d* from it
Prov 27:22 not his foolishness *d* from him
Is 11:13 The envy also of Ephraim shall *d*
Is 14:25 shall his yoke *d* from off them
Is 14:25 his burden *d* from off their
Is 52:11 *D* ye, *d* ye, go ye out from
Is 52:11 *d* ye, go ye out from thence,
Is 54:10 For the mountains shall *d*
Is 54:10 my kindness shall not *d* from thee
Is 59:21 shall not *d* out of thy mouth, nor
Jer 6:8 lest my soul *d* from thee
Jer 17:13 they that *d* from me shall be
Jer 31:36 those ordinances *d* from before me
Jer 32:40 that they shall not *d* from me
Jer 37:9 Chaldeans shall surely *d* from us
Jer 37:9 for they shall not *d*
Jer 50:3 they shall remove, they shall *d*
Lam 4:15 They cried unto them, *D* ye
Lam 4:15 *d*, *d*, touch not
Lam 4:15 *d*, *d*, touch not
Eze 16:42 and my jealousy shall *d* from thee
Hos 9:12 also to them when I *d* from them
Mic 2:10 Arise ye, and *d*
Zec 10:11 the sceptre of Egypt shall *d* away
Mt 7:23 *d* from me, ye that work iniquity
Mt 8:18 to *d* unto the other side
Mt 8:34 he would *d* out of their coasts
Mt 10:14 when ye *d* out of that house or
Mt 14:16 said unto them, They need not *d*
Mt 25:41 *D* from me, ye cursed, into
Mk 5:17 pray him to *d* out of their coasts
Mk 6:10 abide till ye *d* from that place
Mk 6:11 nor hear you, when ye *d* thence
Lk 2:29 thou thy servant *d* in peace
Lk 4:42 that he should not *d* from them
Lk 5:8 Jesus' knees, saying, *D* from me
Lk 8:37 about besought him to *d* from them
Lk 9:4 into, there abide, and thence *d*
Lk 12:59 thee, thou shalt not *d* thence
Lk 13:27 *d* from me, all ye workers of
Lk 13:31 him, Get thee out, and *d* hence
Lk 21:21 are in the midst of it *d* out
Jn 7:3 *D* hence, and go into Judaea, that
Jn 13:1 *d* out of this world unto the
Jn 16:7 but if I *d*, I will send him unto
Acts 1:4 they should not *d* from Jerusalem
Acts 16:36 now therefore *d*, and go in peace
Acts 16:39 desired them to *d* out of the city
Acts 18:2 commanded all Jews to *d* from Rome
Acts 20:7 them, ready to *d* on the morrow
Acts 22:21 And he said unto me, *D*
Acts 23:22 captain then let the young man *d*
Acts 25:4 himself would *d* shortly thither
Acts 27:12 part advised to *d* thence also
1Cor 7:10 not the wife *d* from her husband
1Cor 7:11 But and if she *d*, let her remain
1Cor 7:15 But if the unbelieving *d*, let him
1Cor 7:15 the unbelieving *d*, let him *d*
2Cor 12:8 thrice, that it might *d* from me
Phil 1:23 betwixt two, having a desire to *d*
1Ti 4:1 times some shall *d* from the faith
2Ti 2:19 name of Christ *d* from iniquity
Jas 2:16 *D* in peace, be ye warmed and

### DEPARTED
Gen 12:4 So Abram *d*, as the LORD had
Gen 12:4 years old when he *d* out of Haran
Gen 14:12 in Sodom, and his goods, and *d*
Gen 21:14 and she *d*, and wandered in the
Gen 24:10 of the camels of his master, and *d*
Gen 26:17 Isaac *d* thence, and pitched his
Gen 26:31 away, and they *d* from him in peace
Gen 31:40 my sleep *d* from mine eyes
Gen 31:55 and Laban *d*, and returned unto his
Gen 37:17 And the man said, They are *d* hence
Gen 42:26 asses with the corn, and *d* thence
Gen 45:24 sent his brethren away, and they *d*
Ex 19:2 For they were *d* from Rephidim
Ex 33:11 *d* not out of the tabernacle
Ex 35:20 of the children of Israel *d* from
Lev 13:58 if the plague be *d* from them
Num 10:33 they *d* from the mount of the LORD
Num 12:9 kindled against them; and he *d*
Num 12:10 And the cloud *d* from off the
Num 14:9 their defence is *d* from them
Num 14:44 and Moses, *d* not out of the camp
Num 22:7 the elders of Midian *d* with the
Num 33:3 they *d* from Rameses in the first
Num 33:6 they *d* from Succoth, and pitched
Num 33:8 they *d* from before Pi-hahiroth,
Num 33:13 they *d* from Dophkah, and encamped
Num 33:15 they *d* from Rephidim, and pitched
Num 33:17 they *d* from Kibroth-hattaavah, and
Num 33:18 they *d* from Hazeroth, and pitched
Num 33:19 they *d* from Rithmah, and pitched
Num 33:20 they *d* from Rimmon-parez, and
Num 33:27 they *d* from Tahath, and pitched at
Num 33:30 they *d* from Hashmonah, and
Num 33:31 they *d* from Moseroth, and pitched
Num 33:35 they *d* from Ebronah, and encamped
Num 33:41 they *d* from mount Hor, and pitched

| | |
|---|---|
| Num 33:42 | they *d* from Zalmonah, and pitched |
| Num 33:43 | they *d* from Punon, and pitched in |
| Num 33:44 | they *d* from Oboth, and pitched in |
| Num 33:45 | they *d* from Iim, and pitched in |
| Num 33:48 | they *d* from the mountains of |
| Deut 1:19 | when we *d* from Horeb, we went |
| Deut 24:2 | when she is *d* out of his house, |
| Josh 2:21 | And she sent them away, and they *d* |
| Josh 22:9 | *d* from the children of Israel out |
| Judg 6:21 | of the LORD *d* out of his sight |
| Judg 9:55 | they *d* every man unto his place |
| Judg 16:20 | not that the LORD was *d* from him |
| Judg 17:8 | the man *d* out of the city from |
| Judg 18:7 | Then the five men *d*, and came to |
| Judg 18:21 | So they turned and *d*, and put the |
| Judg 19:10 | that night, but he rose up and *d* |
| Judg 21:24 | of Israel *d* thence at that time |
| 1Sa 4:21 | The glory is *d* from Israel |
| 1Sa 4:22 | said, The glory is *d* from Israel |
| 1Sa 6:6 | not let the people go, and they *d* |
| 1Sa 10:2 | When thou art *d* from me to day, |
| 1Sa 15:6 | So the Kenites *d* from among the |
| 1Sa 16:14 | Spirit of the LORD *d* from Saul |
| 1Sa 16:23 | and the evil spirit *d* from him |
| 1Sa 18:12 | was with him, and was *d* from Saul |
| 1Sa 20:42 | And he arose and *d* |
| 1Sa 22:1 | David therefore *d* thence, and |
| 1Sa 22:5 | Then David *d*, and came into the |
| 1Sa 23:13 | arose and *d* out of Keilah, and went |
| 1Sa 28:15 | God is *d* from me, and answereth me |
| 1Sa 28:16 | seeing the LORD is *d* from thee |
| 2Sa 6:19 | So all the people *d* every one to |
| 2Sa 11:8 | Uriah *d* out of the king's house, |
| 2Sa 12:15 | And Nathan *d* unto his house |
| 2Sa 17:21 | came to pass, after they were *d* |
| 2Sa 19:24 | from the day the king *d* until the |
| 2Sa 22:22 | have not wickedly *d* from my God |
| 1Kin 12:5 | And the people *d* |
| 1Kin 12:16 | So Israel *d* unto their tents |
| 1Kin 14:17 | And Jeroboam's wife arose, and *d* |
| 1Kin 19:19 | So he *d* thence, and found Elisha |
| 1Kin 20:9 | And the messengers *d*, and brought |
| 1Kin 20:36 | as soon as thou art *d* from me |
| 1Kin 20:36 | And as soon as he was *d* from him |
| 1Kin 20:38 | So the prophet *d*, and waited for |
| 2Kin 1:4 | And Elijah *d* |
| 2Kin 3:3 | he *d* not therefrom |
| 2Kin 3:27 | they *d* from him, and returned to |
| 2Kin 5:5 | And he *d*, and took with him ten |
| 2Kin 5:19 | So he *d* from him a little way |
| 2Kin 5:24 | and he let the men go, and they *d* |
| 2Kin 8:14 | So he *d* from Elisha, and came to |
| 2Kin 10:12 | And he arose and *d*, and came to |
| 2Kin 10:15 | And when he was *d* thence, he |
| 2Kin 10:29 | Jehu *d* not from after them, to |
| 2Kin 10:31 | for he *d* not from the sins of |
| 2Kin 13:2 | he *d* not therefrom |
| 2Kin 13:6 | Nevertheless they *d* not from the |
| 2Kin 13:11 | he *d* not from all the sins of |
| 2Kin 14:24 | he *d* not from all the sins of |
| 2Kin 15:9 | he *d* not from the sins of |
| 2Kin 15:18 | he *d* not all his days from the |
| 2Kin 15:24 | he *d* not from the sins of |
| 2Kin 15:28 | he *d* not from the sins of |
| 2Kin 17:22 | they *d* not from them |
| 2Kin 18:6 | *d* not from following him, but |
| 2Kin 19:8 | heard that he was *d* from Lachish |
| 2Kin 19:36 | So Sennacherib king of Assyria *d* |
| 1Chr 16:43 | all the people *d* every man to his |
| 1Chr 21:4 | Wherefore Joab *d*, and went |
| 2Chr 8:15 | they *d* not from the commandment |
| 2Chr 10:5 | And the people *d* |
| 2Chr 20:32 | *d* not from it, doing that which |
| 2Chr 21:20 | years, and *d* without being desired |
| 2Chr 24:25 | And when they were *d* from him |
| 2Chr 34:33 | all his days they *d* not from |
| Ezr 8:31 | Then we *d* from the river of Ahava |
| Neh 9:19 | the cloud *d* not from them by day |
| Ps 18:21 | have not wickedly *d* from my God |
| Ps 34:*t* | who drove him away, and he *d* |
| Ps 105:38 | Egypt was glad when they *d* |
| Ps 119:102 | I have not *d* from thy judgments |
| Is 7:17 | the day that Ephraim *d* from Judah |
| Is 37:8 | heard that he was *d* from Lachish |
| Is 37:37 | So Sennacherib king of Assyria *d* |
| Is 38:12 | Mine age is *d*, and is removed from |
| Jer 29:2 | the smiths, were *d* from Jerusalem |
| Jer 37:5 | of them, they *d* from Jerusalem |
| Jer 41:10 | *d* to go over to the Ammonites |
| Jer 41:17 | And they *d*, and dwelt in the |
| Lam 1:6 | of Zion all her beauty is *d* |
| Eze 6:9 | heart, which hath *d* from me |
| Eze 10:18 | Then the glory of the LORD *d* from |
| Dan 4:31 | The kingdom is *d* from thee |
| Hos 10:5 | thereof, because it is *d* from it |
| Mal 2:8 | But ye are *d* out of the way |
| Mt 2:9 | they had heard the king, they *d* |
| Mt 2:12 | they *d* into their own country |
| Mt 2:13 | And when they were *d*, behold, the |
| Mt 2:14 | mother by night, and *d* into Egypt |
| Mt 4:12 | into prison, he *d* into Galilee |
| Mt 9:7 | And he arose, and *d* to his house |
| Mt 9:27 | And when Jesus *d* thence, two blind |
| Mt 9:31 | But they, when they were *d* |
| Mt 11:1 | he *d* thence to teach and to preach |
| Mt 11:7 | And as they *d*, Jesus began to say |
| Mt 12:9 | And when he was *d* thence, he went |
| Mt 13:53 | these parables, he *d* thence |
| Mt 14:13 | he *d* thence by ship into a desert |
| Mt 15:21 | *d* into the coasts of Tyre and |
| Mt 15:29 | Jesus *d* from thence, and came nigh |
| Mt 16:4 | And he left them, and *d* |
| Mt 17:18 | and he *d* out of him |
| Mt 19:1 | he *d* from Galilee, and came into |
| Mt 19:15 | his hands on them, and *d* thence |
| Mt 20:29 | as they *d* from Jericho, a great |
| Mt 24:1 | went out, and *d* from the temple |
| Mt 27:5 | of silver in the temple, and *d* |
| Mt 27:60 | the door of the sepulchre, and *d* |
| Mt 28:8 | they *d* quickly from the sepulchre |
| Mk 1:35 | *d* into a solitary place, and there |
| Mk 1:42 | the leprosy *d* from him, and he was |
| Mk 5:20 | And he *d*, and began to publish in |
| Mk 6:32 | they *d* into a desert place by |
| Mk 6:46 | he *d* into a mountain to pray |
| Mk 8:13 | ship again *d* to the other side |
| Mk 9:30 | they *d* thence, and passed through |
| Lk 1:23 | he *d* to his own house |
| Lk 1:38 | And the angel *d* from her |
| Lk 2:37 | which *d* not from the temple, but |
| Lk 4:13 | he *d* from him for a season |
| Lk 4:42 | And when it was day, he *d* and went |
| Lk 5:13 | the leprosy *d* from him |
| Lk 5:25 | *d* to his own house, glorifying |
| Lk 7:24 | the messengers of John were *d* |
| Lk 8:35 | out of whom the devils were *d* |
| Lk 8:38 | *d* besought him that he might be |
| Lk 9:6 | And they *d*, and went through the |
| Lk 9:33 | as they *d* from him, Peter said |
| Lk 10:30 | his raiment, and wounded him, and *d* |
| Lk 10:35 | And on the morrow when he *d* |
| Lk 24:12 | clothes laid by themselves, and *d* |
| Jn 4:3 | Judaea, and *d* again into Galilee |
| Jn 4:43 | Now after two days he *d* thence |
| Jn 5:15 | The man *d*, and told the Jews that |
| Jn 6:15 | he *d* again into a mountain |
| Jn 12:36 | These things spake Jesus, and *d* |
| Acts 5:41 | they *d* from the presence of the |
| Acts 10:7 | which spake unto Cornelius was *d* |
| Acts 11:25 | Then *d* Barnabas to Tarsus, for to |
| Acts 12:10 | and forthwith the angel *d* from him |
| Acts 12:17 | And he *d*, and went into another |
| Acts 13:4 | the Holy Ghost, *d* unto Seleucia |
| Acts 13:14 | But when they *d* from Perga |
| Acts 14:20 | the next day he *d* with Barnabas |
| Acts 15:38 | who *d* from them from Pamphylia, |
| Acts 15:39 | that they *d* in asunder one from |
| Acts 15:40 | And Paul chose Silas, and *d* |
| Acts 16:40 | they comforted them, and *d* |
| Acts 17:15 | to him with all speed, they *d* |
| Acts 17:33 | So Paul *d* from among them |
| Acts 18:1 | these things Paul *d* from Athens |
| Acts 18:7 | he *d* thence, and entered into a |
| Acts 18:23 | had spent some time there, he *d* |
| Acts 19:9 | he *d* from them, and separated the |
| Acts 19:12 | and the diseases *d* from them |
| Acts 20:1 | *d* for to go into Macedonia |
| Acts 20:11 | even till break of day, so he *d* |
| Acts 21:5 | had accomplished those days, we *d* |
| Acts 21:8 | we that were of Paul's company *d* |
| Acts 22:29 | Then straightway they *d* from him |
| Acts 28:10 | and when we *d*, they laded us with |
| Acts 28:11 | after three months we *d* in a ship |
| Acts 28:25 | not among themselves, they *d* |
| Acts 28:29 | had said these words, the Jews *d* |
| Phil 4:15 | when I *d* from Macedonia, no |
| 2Ti 4:10 | world, and is *d* unto Thessalonica |
| Philem 15 | he therefore *d* for a season |
| Rev 6:14 | the heaven *d* as a scroll when it |
| Rev 18:14 | soul lusted after are *d* from thee |
| Rev 18:14 | dainty and goodly are *d* from thee |

## DEPARTETH

| | |
|---|---|
| Job 27:21 | wind carrieth him away, and he *d* |
| Prov 14:16 | wise man feareth, and *d* from evil |
| Eccl 6:4 | *d* in darkness, and his name shall |
| Is 59:15 | he that *d* from evil maketh |
| Jer 3:20 | treacherously *d* from her husband |
| Jer 17:5 | whose heart *d* from the LORD |
| Nah 3:1 | the prey *d* not |
| Lk 9:39 | and bruising him hardly *d* from him |

## DEPARTING

| | |
|---|---|
| Gen 35:18 | to pass, as her soul was in *d* |
| Ex 16:1 | their *d* out of the land of Egypt |
| Is 59:13 | *d* away from our God, speaking |
| Dan 9:5 | even by *d* from thy precepts and |
| Dan 9:11 | transgressed thy law, even by *d* |
| Hos 1:2 | great whoredom, *d* from the LORD |
| Mk 6:33 | And the people saw them *d*, and many |
| Mk 7:31 | *d* from the coasts of Tyre and |
| Acts 13:13 | John *d* from them returned to |
| Acts 20:29 | that after my *d* shall grievous |
| Heb 3:12 | in *d* from the living God |
| Heb 11:22 | made mention of the *d* of the |

## DEPTH

| | |
|---|---|
| Job 28:14 | The *d* saith, It is not in me |
| Job 38:16 | walked in the search of the *d* |
| Ps 33:7 | he layeth up the *d* in storehouses |
| Prov 8:27 | a compass upon the face of the *d* |
| Prov 25:3 | for height, and the earth for *d* |
| Is 7:11 | ask it either in the *d*, or in the |
| Jonah 2:5 | the *d* closed me round about, the |
| Mt 18:6 | were drowned in the *d* of the sea |
| Mk 4:5 | up, because it had no *d* of earth |
| Rom 8:39 | Nor height, nor *d*, nor any other |
| Rom 11:33 | O the *d* of the riches both of the |
| Eph 3:18 | is the breadth, and length, and *d* |

## DEPTHS

| | |
|---|---|
| Ex 15:5 | The *d* have covered them |
| Ex 15:8 | the *d* were congealed in the heart |
| Deut 8:7 | *d* that spring out of valleys and |
| Ps 68:22 | again from the *d* of the sea |
| Ps 71:20 | up again from the *d* of the earth |
| Ps 77:16 | the *d* also were troubled |
| Ps 78:15 | them drink as out of the great *d* |
| Ps 106:9 | so he led them through the *d* |
| Ps 107:26 | they go down again to the *d* |
| Ps 130:1 | Out of the *d* have I cried unto |
| Prov 3:20 | his knowledge the *d* are broken up |
| Prov 8:24 | When there were no *d*, I was |
| Prov 9:18 | her guests are in the *d* of hell |
| Is 51:10 | that hath made the *d* of the sea a |
| Eze 27:34 | be broken by the seas in the *d* of |
| Mic 7:19 | their sins into the *d* of the sea |
| Rev 2:24 | have not known the *d* of Satan |

## DEPUTY

| | |
|---|---|
| 1Kin 22:47 | a *d* was king |
| Acts 13:7 | was with the *d* of the country |
| Acts 13:8 | to turn away the *d* from the faith |
| Acts 13:12 | Then the *d*, when he saw what was |
| Acts 18:12 | when Gallio was the *d* of Achaia |

## DERBE *(der'-by) A south Galatian town.*

| | |
|---|---|
| Acts 14:6 | of it, and fled unto Lystra and *D* |
| Acts 14:20 | he departed with Barnabas to *D* |
| Acts 16:1 | Then came he to *D* and Lystra |
| Acts 20:4 | and Gaius of *D*, and Timotheus |

## DERISION

| | |
|---|---|
| Job 30:1 | are younger than I have me in *d* |
| Ps 2:4 | the Lord shall have them in *d* |
| Ps 44:13 | a *d* to them that are round about |
| Ps 59:8 | shalt have all the heathen in *d* |
| Ps 79:4 | *d* to them that are round about us |
| Ps 119:51 | proud have had me greatly in *d* |
| Jer 20:7 | I am in *d* daily, every one |
| Jer 20:8 | made a reproach unto me, and a *d* |
| Jer 48:26 | vomit, and he also shall be in *d* |
| Jer 48:27 | For was not Israel a *d* unto thee |
| Jer 48:39 | so shall Moab be a *d* and a |
| Lam 3:14 | I was a *d* to all my people |
| Eze 23:32 | be laughed to scorn and had in *d* |
| Eze 36:4 | *d* to the residue of the heathen |
| Hos 7:16 | this shall be their *d* in the land |

## DESCEND

| | |
|---|---|
| Num 34:11 | and the border shall *d*, and shall |
| 1Sa 26:10 | or he shall *d* into battle |
| Ps 49:17 | his glory shall not *d* after him |
| Is 5:14 | that rejoiceth, shall *d* into it |

Eze 26:20 with them that *d* into the pit
Eze 31:16 with them that *d* into the pit
Mk 15:32 of Israel *d* now from the cross
Acts 11:5 saw a vision, A certain vessel *d*
Rom 10:7 Who shall *d* into the deep
1Th 4:16 shall *d* from heaven with a shout

### DESCENDED
Ex 19:18 the LORD *d* upon it in fire
Ex 33:9 tabernacle, the cloudy pillar *d*
Ex 34:5 the LORD *d* in the cloud, and stood
Deut 9:21 the brook that *d* out of the mount
Josh 2:23 *d* from the mountain, and passed
Josh 17:9 the coast *d* unto the river Kanah,
Josh 18:13 the border *d* to Ataroth-adar,
Josh 18:16 *d* to the valley of Hinnom, to the
Josh 18:16 on the south, and *d* to En-rogel,
Josh 18:17 *d* to the stone of Bohan the son
Ps 133:3 as the dew that *d* upon the
Prov 30:4 ascended up into heaven, or *d*
Mt 7:25 And the rain *d*, and the floods came
Mt 7:27 And the rain *d*, and the floods came
Mt 28:2 angel of the Lord *d* from heaven
Lk 3:22 the Holy Ghost *d* in a bodily
Acts 24:1 the high priest *d* with the elders
Eph 4:9 what is it but that he also *d*
Eph 4:10 He that *d* is the same also that

### DESCENDING
Gen 28:12 of God ascending and *d* on it
Mt 3:16 the Spirit of God *d* like a dove
Mk 1:10 the Spirit like a dove *d* upon him
Jn 1:32 I saw the Spirit *d* from heaven
Jn 1:33 whom thou shalt see the Spirit *d*
Jn 1:51 and *d* upon the Son of man
Acts 10:11 and a certain vessel *d* unto him
Rev 21:10 *d* out of heaven from God,

### DESERT
Ex 3:1 flock to the backside of the *d*
Ex 5:3 three days' journey into the *d*
Ex 19:2 and were come to the *d* of Sinai
Ex 23:31 from the *d* unto the river
Num 20:1 into the *d* of Zin in the first
Num 27:14 my commandment in the *d* of Zin
Num 33:16 they removed from the *d* of Sinai
Deut 32:10 He found him in a *d* land, and in
2Chr 26:10 Also he built towers in the *d*
Job 24:5 Behold, as wild asses in the *d*
Ps 28:4 render to them their *d*
Ps 78:40 and grieve him in the *d*
Ps 102:6 I am like an owl of the *d*
Ps 106:14 and tempted God in the *d*
Is 13:21 beasts of the *d* shall lie there
Is 21:1 The burden of the *d* of the sea
Is 21:1 so it cometh from the *d*, from a
Is 34:14 The wild beasts of the *d* shall
Is 35:1 the *d* shall rejoice, and blossom
Is 35:6 break out, and streams in the *d*
Is 40:3 make straight in the *d* a highway
Is 41:19 I will set in the *d* the fir tree
Is 43:19 wilderness, and rivers in the *d*
Is 43:20 wilderness, and rivers in the *d*
Is 51:3 her *d* like the garden of the LORD
Jer 17:6 shall be like the heath in the *d*
Jer 25:24 people that dwell in the *d*
Jer 50:12 a wilderness, a dry land, and a *d*
Jer 50:39 the wild beasts of the *d* with the
Eze 47:8 country, and go down into the *d*
Mt 14:13 by ship into a *d* place apart
Mt 14:15 to him, saying, This is a *d* place
Mt 24:26 unto you, Behold, he is in the *d*
Mk 1:45 city, but was without in *d* places
Mk 6:31 yourselves apart into a *d* place
Mk 6:32 they departed into a *d* place by
Mk 6:35 him, and said, This is a *d* place
Lk 4:42 departed and went into a *d* place
Lk 9:10 a *d* place belonging to the city
Lk 9:12 for we are here in a *d* place
Jn 6:31 fathers did eat manna in the *d*
Acts 8:26 Jerusalem unto Gaza, which is *d*

### DESERTS
Is 48:21 when he led them through the *d*
Jer 2:6 wilderness, through a land of *d*
Eze 7:27 to their *d* will I judge them
Eze 13:4 are like the foxes in the *d*
Lk 1:80 was in the *d* till the day of his
Heb 11:38 they wandered in *d*, and in

### DESERVETH
Job 11:6 thee less than thine iniquity *d*

### DESIRE
Gen 3:16 thy *d* shall be to thy husband, and
Gen 4:7 And unto thee shall be his *d*
Ex 10:11 for that ye did *d*
Ex 34:24 neither shall any man *d* thy land
Deut 5:21 Neither shalt thou *d* thy
Deut 7:25 thou shalt not *d* the silver or
Deut 18:6 come with all the *d* of his mind
Deut 21:11 hast a *d* unto her, that thou
Judg 8:24 I would *d* a request of you, that
1Sa 9:20 And on whom is all the *d* of Israel
1Sa 23:20 the *d* of thy soul to come down
2Sa 23:5 is all my salvation, and all my *d*
1Kin 2:20 I *d* one small petition of thee
1Kin 5:8 I will do all thy *d* concerning
1Kin 5:9 and thou shalt accomplish my *d*
1Kin 5:10 fir trees according to all his *d*
1Kin 9:1 all Solomon's *d* which he was
1Kin 9:11 with gold, according to all his *d*
1Kin 10:13 unto the queen of Sheba all her *d*
2Kin 4:28 said, Did I *d* a son of my lord
2Chr 9:12 to the queen of Sheba all her *d*
2Chr 15:15 and sought him with their whole *d*
Neh 1:11 servants, who *d* to fear thy name
Job 13:3 and I *d* to reason with God
Job 14:15 thou wilt have a *d* to the work of
Job 21:14 for we *d* not the knowledge of thy
Job 31:16 withheld the poor from their *d*
Job 31:35 behold, my *d* is, that the
Job 33:32 speak, for I *d* to justify thee
Job 34:36 My *d* is that Job may be tried
Job 36:20 *D* not the night, when people are
Ps 10:3 wicked boasteth of his heart's *d*
Ps 10:17 hast heard the *d* of the humble
Ps 21:2 Thou hast given him his heart's *d*
Ps 38:9 Lord, all my *d* is before thee
Ps 40:6 and offering thou didst not *d*
Ps 45:11 the king greatly *d* thy beauty
Ps 54:7 hath seen his *d* upon mine enemies
Ps 59:10 let me see my *d* upon mine enemies
Ps 70:2 put to confusion, that *d* my hurt
Ps 73:25 upon earth that I *d* beside thee
Ps 78:29 for he gave them their own *d*
Ps 92:11 shall see my *d* on mine enemies
Ps 92:11 mine ears shall hear my *d* of the
Ps 112:8 he see his *d* upon his enemies
Ps 112:10 the *d* of the wicked shall perish
Ps 118:7 I see my *d* upon them that hate me
Ps 145:16 satisfiest the *d* of every living
Ps 145:19 He will fulfil the *d* of them that
Prov 3:15 all the things thou canst *d* are
Prov 10:24 but the *d* of the righteous shall
Prov 11:23 The *d* of the righteous is only
Prov 13:12 heart sick, but when the *d* cometh
Prov 13:19 The *d* accomplished is sweet to
Prov 18:1 Through *d* a man, having separated
Prov 19:22 The *d* of a man is his kindness
Prov 21:25 The *d* of the slothful killeth him
Prov 23:6 neither *d* thou his dainty meats
Prov 24:1 neither *d* to be with them
Eccl 6:9 eyes than the wandering of the *d*
Eccl 12:5 be a burden, and *d* shall fail
Song 7:10 beloved's, and his *d* is toward me
Is 26:8 the *d* of our soul is to thy name,
Is 53:2 is no beauty that we should *d* him
Jer 22:27 land whereunto they *d* to return
Jer 42:22 in the place whither ye *d* to go
Jer 44:14 have a *d* to return to dwell there
Eze 24:16 I take away from thee the *d* of
Eze 24:21 the *d* of your eyes, and that which
Eze 24:25 the *d* of their eyes, and that
Dan 2:18 That they would *d* mercies of the
Dan 11:37 nor the *d* of women, nor regard
Hos 10:10 It is in my *d* that I should
Amos 5:18 Woe unto you that *d* the day of
Mic 7:3 he uttereth his mischievous *d*
Hab 2:5 home, who enlargeth his *d* as hell
Hag 2:7 the *d* of all nations shall come
Mk 9:35 If any man *d* to be first, the
Mk 10:35 do for us whatsoever we shall *d*
Mk 11:24 unto you, What things soever ye *d*
Mk 15:8 *d* him to do as he had ever done
Lk 17:22 when ye shall *d* to see one of the
Lk 20:46 which *d* to walk in long robes, and
Lk 22:15 With *d* I have desired to eat this
Acts 23:20 The Jews have agreed to *d* thee
Acts 28:22 But we *d* to hear of thee what
Rom 10:1 Brethren, my heart's *d* and prayer
Rom 15:23 having a great *d* these many years
1Cor 14:1 *d* spiritual gifts, but rather
2Cor 7:7 when he told us your earnest *d*
2Cor 7:11 what fear, yea, what vehement *d*
2Cor 11:12 from them which *d* occasion
2Cor 12:6 For though I would *d* to glory
Gal 4:9 whereunto ye *d* again to be in
Gal 4:20 I *d* to be present with you now,
Gal 4:21 ye that *d* to be under the law, do
Gal 6:12 As many as *d* to make a fair shew
Gal 6:13 but *d* to have you circumcised,
Eph 3:13 Wherefore I *d* that ye faint not
Phil 1:23 having a *d* to depart, and to be
Phil 4:17 Not because I *d* a gift
Phil 4:17 but I *d* fruit that may abound to
Col 1:9 to *d* that ye might be filled with
1Th 2:17 to see your face with great *d*
1Ti 3:1 If a man *d* the office of a bishop
Heb 6:11 we *d* that every one of you do
Heb 11:16 But now they *d* a better country,
Jas 4:2 *d* to have, and cannot obtain
1Pet 1:12 things the angels *d* to look into
1Pet 2:2 *d* the sincere milk of the word,
Rev 9:6 shall *d* to die, and death shall

### DESIRED
Gen 3:6 a tree to be *d* to make one wise,
1Sa 12:13 ye have chosen, and whom ye have *d*
1Kin 9:19 that which Solomon *d* to build in
2Chr 8:6 all that Solomon *d* to build in
2Chr 11:23 And he *d* many wives
2Chr 21:20 and departed without being *d*
Est 2:13 whatsoever she *d* was given her to
Job 20:20 shall not save of that which he *d*
Ps 19:10 More to be *d* are they than gold,
Ps 27:4 One thing have I *d* of the LORD
Ps 107:30 bringeth them unto their *d* haven
Ps 132:13 he hath *d* it for his habitation
Ps 132:14 for I have *d* it
Prov 8:11 all the things that may be *d* are
Prov 21:20 There is treasure to be *d*
Eccl 2:10 mine eyes *d* I kept not from them
Is 1:29 of the oaks which ye have *d*
Is 26:9 soul have I *d* thee in the night
Jer 17:16 neither have I *d* the woeful day
Dan 2:16 *d* of the king that he would give
Dan 2:23 unto me now what we *d* of thee
Hos 6:6 For I *d* mercy, and not sacrifice
Mic 7:1 my soul *d* the firstripe fruit
Zeph 2:1 gather together, O nation not *d*
Mt 13:17 righteous men have *d* to see those
Mt 16:1 tempting *d* him that he would shew
Mk 15:6 one prisoner, whomsoever they *d*
Lk 7:36 one of the Pharisees *d* him that
Lk 9:9 And he *d* to see him
Lk 10:24 kings have *d* to see those things
Lk 22:15 With desire I have *d* to eat this
Lk 22:31 Satan hath *d* to have you, that he
Lk 23:25 cast into prison, whom they had *d*
Jn 12:21 *d* him, saying, Sir, we would see
Acts 3:14 *d* a murderer to be granted unto
Acts 7:46 *d* to find a tabernacle for the
Acts 8:31 he *d* Philip that he would come up
Acts 9:2 *d* of him letters to Damascus to
Acts 12:20 chamberlain their friend, *d* peace
Acts 13:7 *d* to hear the word of God
Acts 13:21 And afterward they *d* a king
Acts 13:28 yet *d* they Pilate that he should
Acts 16:39 *d* them to depart out of the city
Acts 18:20 When they *d* him to tarry longer
Acts 25:3 *d* favour against him, that he
Acts 28:14 were *d* to tarry with them seven
1Cor 16:12 I greatly *d* him to come unto you
2Cor 8:6 Insomuch that we *d* Titus, that as
2Cor 12:18 I *d* Titus, and with him I sent a
1Jn 5:15 the petitions that we *d* of him
Ps 140:8 not, O LORD, the *d* of the wicked
Eph 2:3 fulfilling the *d* of the flesh

### DESIRETH
Deut 14:26 or for whatsoever thy soul *d*
1Sa 2:16 then take as much as thy soul *d*
1Sa 18:25 The king *d* not any dowry, but an
1Sa 20:4 unto David, Whatsoever thy soul *d*
2Sa 3:21 reign over all that thine heart *d*
1Kin 11:37 according to all that thy soul *d*
Job 7:2 a servant earnestly *d* the shadow
Job 23:13 And what his soul *d*, even that he
Ps 34:12 What man is he that *d* life
Ps 68:16 the hill which God *d* to dwell in
Prov 12:12 The wicked *d* the net of evil men
Prov 13:4 The soul of the sluggard *d*
Prov 21:10 The soul of the wicked *d* evil

Eccl 6:2 for his soul of all that he *d*
Lk 5:39 drunk old wine straightway *d* new
Lk 14:32 and *d* conditions of peace
1Ti 3:1 of a bishop, he *d* a good work

## DESIRING

Mt 12:46 without, *d* to speak with him
Mt 12:47 without, *d* to speak with thee
Mt 20:20 him, and *d* a certain thing of him
Lk 8:20 stand without, *d* to see thee
Lk 16:21 *d* to be fed with the crumbs which
Acts 9:38 *d* him that he would not delay to
Acts 19:31 *d* him that he would not adventure
Acts 25:15 *d* to have judgment against him
2Cor 5:2 earnestly *d* to be clothed upon
1Th 3:6 *d* greatly to see us, as we also
1Ti 1:7 *D* to be teachers of the law
2Ti 1:4 Greatly *d* to see thee, being

## DESIROUS

Prov 23:3 Be not *d* of his dainties
Lk 23:8 for he was *d* to see him of a long
Jn 16:19 knew that they were *d* to ask him
2Cor 11:32 a garrison, *d* to apprehend me
Gal 5:26 Let us not be *d* of vain glory
1Th 2:8 So being affectionately *d* of you

## DESOLATE

Gen 47:19 not die, that the land be not *d*
Ex 23:29 lest the land become *d*, and the
Lev 26:22 and your high ways shall be *d*
Lev 26:33 and your land shall be *d*, and your
Lev 26:34 sabbaths, as long as it lieth *d*
Lev 26:35 long as it lieth *d* it shall rest
Lev 26:43 while she lieth *d* without them
2Sa 13:20 So Tamar remained *d* in her
2Chr 36:21 as she lay *d* she kept sabbath
Job 3:14 earth, which built *d* places for
Job 15:28 And he dwelleth in *d* cities
Job 15:34 of hypocrites shall be *d*, and fire
Job 16:7 thou hast made *d* all my company
Job 30:3 the wilderness in former time *d*
Job 38:27 To satisfy the *d* and waste ground
Ps 25:16 for I am *d* and afflicted
Ps 34:21 hate the righteous shall be *d*
Ps 34:22 them that trust in him shall be *d*
Ps 40:15 Let them be *d* for a reward of
Ps 69:25 Let their habitation be *d*
Ps 109:10 bread also out of their *d* places
Ps 143:4 my heart within me is *d*
Is 1:7 Your country is *d*, your cities
Is 1:7 it in your presence, and it is *d*
Is 3:26 she being *d* shall sit upon the
Is 5:9 Of a truth many houses shall be *d*
Is 6:11 man, and the land be utterly *d*
Is 7:19 rest all of them in the *d* valleys
Is 13:9 fierce anger, to lay the land *d*
Is 13:22 shall cry in their *d* houses
Is 15:6 the waters of Nimrim shall be *d*
Is 24:6 and they that dwell therein are *d*
Is 27:10 Yet the defenced city shall be *d*
Is 49:8 cause to inherit the *d* heritages
Is 49:19 thy *d* places, and the land of thy
Is 49:21 I have lost my children, and am *d*
Is 54:1 of the *d* than the children of the
Is 54:3 make the *d* cities to be inhabited
Is 59:10 we are in *d* places as dead men
Is 62:4 thy land any more be termed *D*
Jer 2:12 be horribly afraid, be ye very *d*
Jer 4:7 from his place to make thy land *d*
Jer 4:27 said, The whole land shall be *d*
Jer 6:8 lest I make thee *d*, a land not
Jer 7:34 for the land shall be *d*
Jer 9:11 I will make the cities of Judah *d*
Jer 10:22 to make the cities of Judah *d*
Jer 10:25 and have made his habitation *d*
Jer 12:10 pleasant portion a *d* wilderness
Jer 12:11 They have made it *d*
Jer 12:11 being *d* it mourneth unto me
Jer 12:11 the whole land is made *d*, because
Jer 18:16 To make their land *d*, and a
Jer 19:8 And I will make this city *d*
Jer 25:38 for their land is *d* because of
Jer 26:9 this city shall be *d* without an
Jer 32:43 It is *d* without man or beast
Jer 33:10 ye say shall be *d* without man
Jer 33:10 streets of Jerusalem, that are *d*
Jer 33:12 which is *d* without man and without
Jer 44:6 and they are wasted and *d*, as at
Jer 46:19 waste and *d* without an inhabitant
Jer 48:9 for the cities thereof shall be *d*
Jer 48:34 waters also of Nimrim shall be *d*
Jer 49:2 and it shall be a *d* heap, and her
Jer 49:20 their habitations *d* with them
Jer 50:3 her, which shall make her land *d*
Jer 50:13 but it shall be wholly *d*
Jer 50:45 make their habitation *d* with them
Jer 51:26 but thou shalt be *d* for ever
Jer 51:62 but that it shall be *d* for ever
Lam 1:4 all her gates are *d*
Lam 1:13 he hath made me *d* and faint all
Lam 1:16 my children are *d*, because the
Lam 3:11 he hath made me *d*
Lam 4:5 delicately are *d* in the streets
Lam 5:18 the mountain of Zion, which is *d*
Eze 6:4 And your altars shall be *d*
Eze 6:6 and the high places shall be *d*
Eze 6:6 may be laid waste and made *d*
Eze 6:14 upon them, and make the land *d*
Eze 6:14 more *d* than the wilderness toward
Eze 12:19 that her land may be *d* from all
Eze 12:20 waste, and the land shall be *d*
Eze 14:15 and they spoil it, so that it be *d*
Eze 14:16 but the land shall be *d*
Eze 15:8 And I will make the land *d*
Eze 19:7 And he knew their *d* palaces
Eze 19:7 and the land was *d*, and the fulness
Eze 20:26 womb, that I might make them *d*
Eze 25:3 the land of Israel, when it was *d*
Eze 25:13 and I will make it *d* from Teman
Eze 26:19 When I shall make thee a *d* city
Eze 26:20 of the earth, in places *d* of old
Eze 29:9 And the land of Egypt shall be *d*
Eze 29:10 land of Egypt utterly waste and *d*
Eze 29:12 *d* in the midst of the countries
Eze 29:12 midst of the countries that are *d*
Eze 29:12 laid waste shall be *d* forty years
Eze 30:7 they shall be *d* in the midst of
Eze 30:7 midst of the countries that are *d*
Eze 30:14 And I will make Pathros *d*, and will
Eze 32:15 I shall make the land of Egypt *d*
Eze 33:28 For I will lay the land most *d*
Eze 33:28 mountains of Israel shall be *d*
Eze 33:29 land most *d* because of all their
Eze 35:3 thee, and I will make thee most *d*
Eze 35:4 cities waste, and thou shalt be *d*
Eze 35:7 will I make mount Seir most *d*
Eze 35:12 Israel, saying, They are laid *d*
Eze 35:14 rejoiceth, I will make thee *d*
Eze 35:15 house of Israel, because it was *d*
Eze 35:15 thou shalt be *d*, O mount Seir, and
Eze 36:3 Because they have made you *d*
Eze 36:4 to the valleys, to the *d* wastes
Eze 36:34 the *d* land shall be tilled,
Eze 36:34 whereas it lay *d* in the sight of
Eze 36:35 This land that was *d* is become
Eze 36:35 and the waste and *d* and ruined
Eze 36:36 places, and plant that that was *d*
Eze 38:12 to turn thine hand upon the *d*
Dan 9:17 upon thy sanctuary that is *d*
Dan 9:27 abominations he shall make it *d*
Dan 9:27 shall be poured upon the *d*
Dan 11:31 the abomination that maketh *d*
Dan 12:11 abomination that maketh *d* set up
Hos 5:9 Ephraim shall be *d* in the day of
Hos 13:16 Samaria shall become *d*
Joel 1:17 clods, the garners are laid *d*
Joel 1:18 the flocks of sheep are made *d*
Joel 2:3 and behind them a *d* wilderness
Joel 2:20 drive him into a land barren and *d*
Joel 3:19 and Edom shall be a *d* wilderness
Amos 7:9 high places of Isaac shall be *d*
Mic 1:7 the idols thereof will I lay *d*
Mic 6:13 in making thee *d* because of thy
Mic 7:13 the land shall be *d* because of
Zeph 3:6 their towers are *d*
Zec 7:14 Thus the land was *d* after them
Zec 7:14 for they laid the pleasant land *d*
Mal 1:4 will return and build the *d* places
Mt 23:38 your house is left unto you *d*
Lk 13:35 your house is left unto you *d*
Acts 1:20 Psalms, Let his habitation be *d*
Gal 4:27 for the *d* hath many more children
1Ti 5:5 she that is a widow indeed, and *d*
Rev 17:16 the whore, and shall make her *d*
Rev 18:19 for in one hour is she made *d*

## DESOLATION

Lev 26:31 and bring your sanctuaries unto *d*
Lev 26:32 And I will bring the land into *d*
Josh 8:28 for ever, even a *d* unto this day
2Kin 22:19 that they should become a *d*
2Chr 30:7 who therefore gave them up to *d*
Job 30:14 in the *d* they rolled themselves
Ps 73:19 How are they brought into *d*
Prov 1:27 When your fear cometh as *d*
Prov 3:25 neither of the *d* of the wicked
Is 10:3 in the *d* which shall come from
Is 17:9 and there shall be *d*
Is 24:12 In the city is left *d*, and the
Is 47:11 *d* shall come upon thee suddenly,
Is 51:19 *d*, and destruction, and the famine,
Is 64:10 is a wilderness, Jerusalem a *d*
Jer 22:5 that this house shall become a *d*
Jer 25:11 And this whole land shall be a *d*
Jer 25:18 princes thereof, to make them a *d*
Jer 34:22 Judah a *d* without an inhabitant
Jer 44:2 and, behold, this day they are a *d*
Jer 44:22 therefore is your land a *d*
Jer 49:13 that Bozrah shall become a *d*
Jer 49:17 Also Edom shall be a *d*
Jer 49:33 for dragons, and a *d* for ever
Jer 50:23 become a *d* among the nations
Jer 51:29 Babylon a *d* without an inhabitant
Jer 51:43 Her cities are a *d*, a dry land,
Lam 3:47 and a snare is come upon us, *d*
Eze 7:27 prince shall be clothed with *d*
Eze 23:33 with the cup of astonishment and *d*
Dan 8:13 and the transgression of *d*
Hos 12:1 he daily increaseth lies and *d*
Joel 3:19 Egypt shall be a *d*, and Edom shall
Mic 6:16 that I should make thee a *d*
Zeph 1:13 a booty, and their houses a *d*
Zeph 1:15 distress, a day of wasteness and *d*
Zeph 2:4 be forsaken, and Ashkelon a *d*
Zeph 2:9 and saltpits, and a perpetual *d*
Zeph 2:13 and will make Nineveh a *d*, and dry
Zeph 2:14 *d* shall be in the thresholds
Zeph 2:15 how is she become a *d*, a place
Mt 12:25 against itself is brought to *d*
Mt 24:15 shall see the abomination of *d*
Mk 13:14 ye shall see the abomination of *d*
Lk 11:17 against itself is brought to *d*
Lk 21:20 know that the *d* thereof is nigh

## DESOLATIONS

Ezr 9:9 God, and to repair the *d* thereof
Ps 46:8 what *d* he hath made in the earth
Ps 74:3 up thy feet unto the perpetual *d*
Is 61:4 they shall raise up the former *d*
Is 61:4 the *d* of many generations
Jer 25:9 and an hissing, and perpetual *d*
Jer 25:12 and will make it perpetual *d*
Eze 35:9 I will make thee perpetual *d*
Dan 9:2 years in the *d* of Jerusalem
Dan 9:18 open thine eyes, and behold our *d*
Dan 9:26 end of the war *d* are determined

## DESPAIR

1Sa 27:1 and Saul shall *d* of me, to seek me
Eccl 2:20 *d* of all the labour which I took
2Cor 4:8 we are perplexed, but not in *d*

## DESPISE

Lev 26:15 And if ye shall *d* my statutes
1Sa 2:30 they that *d* me shall be lightly
2Sa 19:43 why then did ye *d* us, that our
Est 1:17 so that they shall *d* their
Job 5:17 therefore *d* not thou the
Job 9:21 I would *d* my life
Job 10:3 that thou shouldest *d* the work of
Job 31:13 If I did *d* the cause of my
Ps 51:17 heart, O God, thou wilt not *d*
Ps 73:20 awakest, thou shalt *d* their image
Ps 102:17 destitute, and not *d* their prayer
Prov 1:7 but fools *d* wisdom and instruction
Prov 3:11 *d* not the chastening of the LORD
Prov 6:30 Men do not *d* a thief, if he steal
Prov 23:9 for he will *d* the wisdom of thy
Prov 23:22 *d* not thy mother when she is old
Is 30:12 of Israel, Because ye *d* this word
Jer 4:30 thy lovers will *d* thee, they will
Jer 23:17 say still unto them that *d* me
Lam 1:8 all that honoured her *d* her
Eze 16:57 which *d* thee round about
Eze 28:26 that *d* them round about them
Amos 5:21 I *d* your feast days, and I will
Mal 1:6 you, O priests, that *d* my name
Mt 6:24 hold to the one, and *d* the other
Mt 18:10 Take heed that ye *d* not one of
Lk 16:13 hold to the one, and *d* the other
Rom 14:3 that eateth *d* him that eateth not
1Cor 11:22 or *d* ye the church of God, and
1Cor 16:11 Let no man therefore *d* him

1Th 5:20 *D* not prophesyings
1Ti 4:12 Let no man *d* thy youth
1Ti 6:2 masters, let them not *d* them
Titus 2:15 Let no man *d* thee
Heb 12:5 *d* not thou the chastening of the
2Pet 2:10 of uncleanness, and *d* government
Jude 8 *d* dominion, and speak evil of

### DESPISED

Gen 16:4 her mistress was *d* in her eyes
Gen 16:5 conceived, I was *d* in her eyes
Gen 25:34 thus Esau *d* his birthright
Lev 26:43 even because they *d* my judgments
Num 11:20 because that ye have *d* the LORD
Num 14:31 know the land which ye have *d*
Num 15:31 Because he hath *d* the word of the
Judg 9:38 this the people that thou hast *d*
1Sa 10:27 And they *d* him, and brought him no
2Sa 6:16 and she *d* him in her heart
2Sa 12:9 Wherefore hast thou *d* the
2Sa 12:10 because thou hast *d* me, and hast
2Kin 19:21 the daughter of Zion hath *d* thee
1Chr 15:29 and she *d* him in her heart
2Chr 36:16 *d* his words, and misused his
Neh 2:19 *d* us, and said, What is this thing
Neh 4:4 for we are *d*
Job 12:5 *d* in the thought of him that is
Job 19:18 Yea, young children *d* me
Ps 22:6 of men, and *d* of the people
Ps 22:24 For he hath not *d* nor abhorred
Ps 53:5 to shame, because God hath *d* them
Ps 106:24 they *d* the pleasant land, they
Ps 119:141 I am small and *d*
Prov 1:30 they *d* all my reproof
Prov 5:12 and my heart *d* reproof
Prov 12:8 is of a perverse heart shall be *d*
Prov 12:9 He that is *d*, and hath a servant,
Eccl 9:16 the poor man's wisdom is *d*
Song 8:1 yea, I should not be *d*
Is 5:24 *d* the word of the Holy One of
Is 33:8 he hath *d* the cities, he
Is 37:22 the daughter of Zion, hath *d* thee
Is 53:3 He is *d* and rejected of men
Is 53:3 he was *d*, and we esteemed him not
Is 60:14 all they that *d* thee shall bow
Jer 22:28 this man Coniah a *d* broken idol
Jer 33:24 thus they have *d* my people
Jer 49:15 among the heathen, and *d* among men
Lam 2:6 hath *d* in the indignation of his
Eze 16:59 which hast *d* the oath in breaking
Eze 17:16 made him king, whose oath he *d*
Eze 17:18 Seeing he *d* the oath by breaking
Eze 17:19 surely mine oath that he hath *d*
Eze 20:13 they *d* my judgments, which if a
Eze 20:16 Because they *d* my judgments
Eze 20:24 but had *d* my statutes, and had
Eze 22:8 Thou hast *d* mine holy things, and
Eze 28:24 are round about them, that *d* them
Amos 2:4 because they have *d* the law of
Obad 2 thou art greatly *d*
Zec 4:10 For who hath *d* the day of small
Mal 1:6 say, Wherein have we *d* thy name
Lk 18:9 they were righteous, and *d* others
Acts 19:27 goddess Diana should be *d*
1Cor 1:28 the world, and things which are *d*
1Cor 4:10 ye are honourable, but we are *d*
Gal 4:14 which was in my flesh ye *d* not
Heb 10:28 He that *d* Moses' law died without
Jas 2:6 But ye have *d* the poor

### DESPISETH

Job 36:5 God is mighty, and *d* not any
Ps 69:33 the poor, and *d* not his prisoners
Prov 11:12 is void of wisdom *d* his neighbour
Prov 13:13 Whoso *d* the word shall be
Prov 14:2 is perverse in his ways *d* him
Prov 14:21 He that *d* his neighbour sinneth
Prov 15:5 A fool *d* his father's instruction
Prov 15:20 but a foolish man *d* his mother
Prov 15:32 instruction *d* his own soul
Prov 19:16 but he that *d* his ways shall die
Prov 30:17 *d* to obey his mother, the ravens
Is 33:15 he that *d* the gain of oppressions
Is 49:7 his Holy One, to him whom man *d*
Lk 10:16 he that *d* you *d* me
Lk 10:16 *d* me *d* him that sent me
1Th 4:8 He therefore that *d*, *d* not man

### DESTITUTE

Gen 24:27 who hath not left *d* my master of
Ps 102:17 will regard the prayer of the *d*
Ps 141:8 leave not my soul *d*
Prov 15:21 is joy to him that is *d* of wisdom
Eze 32:15 the country shall be *d* of that
1Ti 6:5 *d* of the truth, supposing that
Heb 11:37 being *d*, afflicted, tormented
Jas 2:15 be naked, and *d* of daily food,

### DESTROY

Gen 6:7 I will *d* man whom I have created
Gen 6:13 I will *d* them with the earth
Gen 6:17 to *d* all flesh, wherein is the
Gen 7:4 that I have made will I *d* from
Gen 9:11 more be a flood to *d* the earth
Gen 9:15 become a flood to *d* all flesh
Gen 18:23 Wilt thou also *d* the righteous
Gen 18:24 wilt thou also *d* and not spare the
Gen 18:28 wilt thou *d* all the city for lack
Gen 18:28 forty and five, I will not *d* it
Gen 18:31 I will not *d* it for twenty's sake
Gen 18:32 I will not *d* it for ten's sake
Gen 19:13 For we will *d* this place, because
Gen 19:13 and the LORD hath sent us to *d* it
Gen 19:14 for the LORD will *d* this city
Ex 8:9 to *d* the frogs from thee and thy
Ex 12:13 shall not be upon you to *d* you
Ex 15:9 my sword, my hand shall *d* them
Ex 23:27 will *d* all the people to whom
Ex 34:13 But ye shall *d* their altars
Lev 23:30 the same soul will I *d* from among
Lev 26:22 *d* your cattle, and make you few in
Lev 26:30 I will *d* your high places, and cut
Lev 26:44 to *d* them utterly, and to break my
Num 21:2 I will utterly *d* their cities
Num 24:17 *d* all the children of Sheth
Num 24:19 shall *d* him that remaineth of the
Num 32:15 ye shall *d* all this people
Num 33:52 *d* all their pictures, and *d*
Deut 1:27 the hand of the Amorites, to *d* us
Deut 2:15 to *d* them from among the host,
Deut 4:31 not forsake thee, neither *d* thee
Deut 6:15 *d* thee from off the face of the
Deut 7:2 smite them, and utterly *d* them
Deut 7:4 against you, and *d* thee suddenly
Deut 7:5 ye shall *d* their altars, and break
Deut 7:10 hate him to their face, to *d* them
Deut 7:23 shall *d* them with a mighty
Deut 7:24 thou shalt *d* their name from
Deut 9:3 a consuming fire he shall *d* them
Deut 9:3 *d* them quickly, as the LORD hath
Deut 9:14 Let me alone, that I may *d* them
Deut 9:19 was wroth against you to *d* you
Deut 9:25 the LORD had said he would *d* you
Deut 9:26 *d* not thy people and thine
Deut 10:10 and the LORD would not *d* thee
Deut 12:2 Ye shall utterly *d* all the places
Deut 12:3 *d* the names of them out of that
Deut 20:17 But thou shalt utterly *d* them
Deut 20:19 thou shalt not *d* the trees
Deut 20:20 not trees for meat, thou shalt *d*
Deut 28:63 will rejoice over you to *d* you
Deut 31:3 he will *d* these nations from
Deut 32:25 shall *d* both the young man and the
Deut 33:27 and shall say, *D* them
Josh 7:7 the hand of the Amorites, to *d* us
Josh 7:12 except ye *d* the accursed from
Josh 9:24 to *d* all the inhabitants of the
Josh 11:20 that he might *d* them utterly
Josh 11:20 favour, but that he might *d* them
Josh 22:33 to *d* the land wherein the
Judg 6:5 entered into the land to *d* it
Judg 21:11 do, Ye shall utterly *d* every male
1Sa 15:3 utterly *d* all that they have, and
1Sa 15:6 lest I *d* you with them
1Sa 15:9 good, and would not utterly *d* them
1Sa 15:18 utterly *d* the sinners the
1Sa 23:10 to *d* the city for my sake
1Sa 24:21 that thou wilt not *d* my name out
1Sa 26:9 David said to Abishai, *D* him not
1Sa 26:15 people in to *d* the king thy lord
2Sa 1:14 hand to *d* the LORD's anointed
2Sa 14:7 and we will *d* the heir also
2Sa 14:11 revengers of blood to *d* any more
2Sa 14:11 lest they *d* my son
2Sa 14:16 hand of the man that would *d* me
2Sa 20:19 thou seekest to *d* a city and a
2Sa 20:20 me, that I should swallow up or *d*
2Sa 22:41 that I might *d* them that hate me
2Sa 24:16 his hand upon Jerusalem to *d* it
1Kin 9:21 also were not able utterly to *d*
1Kin 13:34 to *d* it from off the face of the
1Kin 16:12 Thus did Zimri *d* all the house of
2Kin 8:19 Yet the LORD would not *d* Judah
2Kin 10:19 might *d* the worshippers of Baal
2Kin 13:23 and Jacob, and would not *d* them
2Kin 18:25 LORD against this place to *d* it
2Kin 18:25 Go up against this land, and *d* it
2Kin 24:2 sent them against Judah to *d* it
1Chr 21:15 an angel unto Jerusalem to *d* it
2Chr 12:7 therefore I will not *d* them
2Chr 12:12 he would not *d* him altogether
2Chr 20:23 Seir, utterly to slay and *d* them
2Chr 20:23 every one helped to *d* another
2Chr 21:7 would not *d* the house of David
2Chr 25:16 God hath determined to *d* thee
2Chr 35:21 is with me, that he *d* thee not
Ezr 6:12 name to dwell there *d* all kings
Ezr 6:12 to *d* this house of God which is
Est 3:6 to *d* all the Jews that were
Est 3:13 all the king's provinces, to *d*
Est 4:7 for the Jews, to *d* them
Est 4:8 was given at Shushan to *d* them
Est 8:5 which he wrote to *d* the Jews
Est 8:11 and to stand for their life, to *d*
Est 9:24 against the Jews to *d* them
Est 9:24 to consume them, and to *d* them
Job 2:3 him, to *d* him without cause
Job 6:9 that it would please God to *d* me
Job 8:18 If he *d* him from his place, then
Job 10:8 yet thou dost *d* me
Job 19:26 after my skin worms *d* this body
Ps 5:6 Thou shalt *d* them that speak
Ps 5:10 *D* thou them, O God
Ps 18:40 that I might *d* them that hate me
Ps 21:10 fruit shalt thou *d* from the earth
Ps 28:5 of his hands, he shall *d* them
Ps 40:14 that seek after my soul to *d* it
Ps 52:5 shall likewise *d* thee for ever
Ps 55:9 *D*, O Lord, and divide their
Ps 63:9 those that seek my soul, to *d* it
Ps 69:4 they that would *d* me, being mine
Ps 74:8 hearts, Let us *d* them together
Ps 101:8 I will early *d* all the wicked of
Ps 106:23 he said that he would *d* them
Ps 106:23 his wrath, lest he should *d* them
Ps 106:34 They did not *d* the nations
Ps 118:10 name of the LORD will I *d* them
Ps 118:11 name of the LORD I will *d* them
Ps 118:12 name of the LORD I will *d* them
Ps 119:95 wicked have waited for me to *d* me
Ps 143:12 *d* all them that afflict my soul
Ps 144:6 shoot out thine arrows, and *d* them
Ps 145:20 but all the wicked will he *d*
Prov 1:32 prosperity of fools shall *d* them
Prov 11:3 of transgressors shall *d* them
Prov 15:25 The LORD will *d* the house of the
Prov 21:7 of the wicked shall *d* them
Eccl 5:6 *d* the work of thine hands
Eccl 7:16 why shouldest thou *d* thyself
Is 3:12 to err, and *d* the way of thy paths
Is 10:7 but it is in his heart to *d*
Is 11:9 nor *d* in all my holy mountain
Is 11:15 the LORD shall utterly *d* the
Is 13:5 indignation, to *d* the whole land
Is 13:9 he shall *d* the sinners thereof
Is 19:3 I will *d* the counsel thereof
Is 23:11 to *d* the strong holds thereof
Is 25:7 he will *d* in this mountain the
Is 32:7 to *d* the poor with lying words
Is 36:10 LORD against this land to *d* it
Is 36:10 Go up against this land, and *d* it
Is 42:14 I will *d* and devour at once
Is 51:13 as if he were ready to *d*
Is 54:16 and I have created the waster to *d*
Is 65:8 cluster, and one saith, *D* it not
Is 65:8 sakes, that I may not *d* them all
Is 65:25 nor *d* in all my holy mountain
Jer 1:10 out, and to pull down, and to *d*
Jer 5:10 Go ye up upon her walls, and *d*
Jer 6:5 by night, and let us *d* her palaces
Jer 11:19 Let us *d* the tree with the fruit
Jer 12:17 *d* that nation, saith the LORD
Jer 13:14 spare, nor have mercy, but *d* them
Jer 15:3 of the earth, to devour and *d*
Jer 15:6 my hand against thee, and *d* thee
Jer 15:7 I will *d* my people, since they
Jer 17:18 *d* them with double destruction
Jer 18:7 up, and to pull down, and to *d* it
Jer 23:1 Woe be unto the pastors that *d*
Jer 25:9 about, and will utterly *d* them
Jer 31:28 down, and to throw down, and to *d*
Jer 36:29 *d* this land, and shall cause to

Jer 46:8 I will *d* the city and the
Jer 48:18 he shall *d* thy strong holds
Jer 49:9 they will *d* till they have enough
Jer 49:38 will *d* from thence the king and
Jer 50:21 utterly *d* after them, saith the
Jer 50:26 her up as heaps, and *d* her utterly
Jer 51:3 *d* ye utterly all her host
Jer 51:11 is against Babylon, to *d* it
Jer 51:20 and with thee will I *d* kingdoms
Lam 2:8 The LORD hath purposed to *d* the
Lam 3:66 *d* them in anger from under the
Eze 5:16 and which I will send to *d* you
Eze 6:3 I will *d* your high places
Eze 9:8 wilt thou *d* all the residue of
Eze 14:9 will *d* him from the midst of my
Eze 21:31 of brutish men, and skilful to *d*
Eze 22:27 to *d* souls, to get dishonest gain
Eze 22:30 the land, that I should not *d* it
Eze 25:7 I will *d* thee
Eze 25:15 to *d* it for the old hatred
Eze 25:16 *d* the remnant of the sea coast
Eze 26:4 they shall *d* the walls of Tyrus,
Eze 26:12 walls, and *d* thy pleasant houses
Eze 28:16 and I will *d* thee, O covering
Eze 30:11 shall be brought to *d* the land
Eze 30:13 I will also *d* the idols, and I
Eze 32:13 I will *d* also all the beasts
Eze 34:16 but I will *d* the fat and the
Eze 43:3 I saw when I came to *d* the city
Dan 2:12 commanded to *d* all the wise men
Dan 2:24 to *d* the wise men of Babylon
Dan 2:24 *D* not the wise men of Babylon
Dan 4:23 Hew the tree down, and *d* it
Dan 7:26 consume and to *d* it unto the end
Dan 8:24 he shall *d* wonderfully, and shall
Dan 8:24 shall *d* the mighty and the holy
Dan 8:25 heart, and by peace shall *d* many
Dan 9:26 that shall come shall *d* the city
Dan 11:26 portion of his meat shall *d* him
Dan 11:44 go forth with great fury to *d*
Hos 2:12 I will *d* her vines and her fig
Hos 4:5 the night, and I will *d* thy mother
Hos 11:9 I will not return to *d* Ephraim
Amos 9:8 I will *d* it from off the face of
Amos 9:8 not utterly *d* the house of Jacob
Obad 8 even *d* the wise men out of Edom,
Mic 2:10 it is polluted, it shall *d* you
Mic 5:10 of thee, and I will *d* thy chariots
Mic 5:14 so will I *d* thy cities
Zeph 2:5 Philistines, I will even *d* thee
Zeph 2:13 against the north, and *d* Assyria
Hag 2:22 I will *d* the strength of the
Zec 12:9 that I will seek to *d* all the
Mal 3:11 he shall not *d* the fruits of your
Mt 2:13 seek the young child to *d* him
Mt 5:17 not that I am come to *d* the law
Mt 5:17 I am not come to *d*, but to fulfil
Mt 10:28 him which is able to *d* both soul
Mt 12:14 against him, how they might *d* him
Mt 21:41 will miserably *d* those wicked men
Mt 26:61 I am able to *d* the temple of God,
Mt 27:20 should ask Barabbas, and *d* Jesus
Mk 1:24 art thou come to *d* us
Mk 3:6 against him, how they might *d* him
Mk 9:22 and into the waters, to *d* him
Mk 11:18 and sought how they might *d* him
Mk 12:9 *d* the husbandmen, and will give
Mk 14:58 I will *d* this temple that is made
Lk 4:34 art thou come to *d* us
Lk 6:9 to save life, or to *d* it
Lk 9:56 man is not come to *d* men's lives
Lk 19:47 of the people sought to *d* him
Lk 20:16 *d* these husbandmen, and shall give
Jn 2:19 *D* this temple, and in three days I
Jn 10:10 for to steal, and to kill, and to *d*
Acts 6:14 of Nazareth shall *d* this place
Rom 14:15 *D* not him with thy meat, for whom
Rom 14:20 For meat *d* not the work of God
1Cor 1:19 I will *d* the wisdom of the wise,
1Cor 3:17 temple of God, him shall God *d*
1Cor 6:13 but God shall *d* both it and them
2Th 2:8 shall *d* with the brightness of
Heb 2:14 that through death he might *d* him
Jas 4:12 who is able to save and to *d*
1Jn 3:8 that he might *d* the works of the
Rev 11:18 *d* them which *d* the earth

### DESTROYED

Gen 7:23 every living substance was *d*
Gen 7:23 they were *d* from the earth
Gen 13:10 where, before the LORD *d* Sodom
Gen 19:29 when God *d* the cities of the
Gen 34:30 and I shall be *d*, I and my house
Ex 10:7 thou not yet that Egypt is *d*
Ex 22:20 LORD only, he shall be utterly *d*
Num 21:3 and they utterly *d* them and their
Deut 1:44 *d* you in Seir, even unto Hormah
Deut 2:12 when they had *d* them from before
Deut 2:21 but the LORD *d* them before them
Deut 2:22 when he *d* the Horims from before
Deut 2:23 *d* them, and dwelt in their stead
Deut 2:34 that time, and utterly *d* the men
Deut 3:6 And we utterly *d* them, as we did
Deut 4:3 God hath *d* them from among you
Deut 4:26 upon it, but shall utterly be *d*
Deut 7:20 hide themselves from thee, be *d*
Deut 7:23 destruction, until they be *d*
Deut 7:24 thee, until thou have *d* them
Deut 9:8 was angry with you to have *d* you
Deut 9:20 angry with Aaron to have *d* him
Deut 11:4 how the LORD hath *d* them unto
Deut 12:30 that they be *d* from before thee
Deut 28:20 unto for to do, until thou be *d*
Deut 28:24 down upon thee, until thou be *d*
Deut 28:45 and overtake thee, till thou be *d*
Deut 28:48 thy neck, until he have *d* thee
Deut 28:51 of thy land, until thou be *d*
Deut 28:51 thy sheep, until he have *d* thee
Deut 28:61 bring upon thee, until thou be *d*
Deut 31:4 unto the land of them, whom he *d*
Josh 2:10 Sihon and Og, whom ye utterly *d*
Josh 6:21 they utterly *d* all that was in
Josh 8:26 until he had utterly *d* all the
Josh 10:1 had taken Ai, and had utterly *d* it
Josh 10:28 and the king thereof he utterly *d*
Josh 10:35 therein he utterly *d* that day
Josh 10:37 but *d* it utterly, and all the
Josh 10:39 utterly *d* all the souls that were
Josh 10:40 but utterly *d* all that breathed,
Josh 11:12 the sword, and he utterly *d* them
Josh 11:14 the sword, until they had *d* them
Josh 11:21 Joshua *d* them utterly with their
Josh 23:15 until he have *d* you from off this
Josh 24:8 and I *d* them from before you
Judg 1:17 Zephath, and utterly *d* it
Judg 4:24 until they had *d* Jabin king of
Judg 6:4 *d* the increase of the earth, till
Judg 20:21 *d* down to the ground of the
Judg 20:25 *d* down to the ground of the
Judg 20:35 the children of Israel *d* of the
Judg 20:42 they *d* in the midst of them
Judg 21:16 the women are *d* out of Benjamin
Judg 21:17 a tribe be not *d* out of Israel
1Sa 5:6 he *d* them, and smote them with
1Sa 15:8 utterly *d* all the people with the
1Sa 15:9 and refuse, that they *d* utterly
1Sa 15:15 and the rest we have utterly *d*
1Sa 15:20 have utterly *d* the Amalekites
1Sa 15:21 which should have been utterly *d*
2Sa 11:1 they *d* the children of Ammon, and
2Sa 21:5 be *d* from remaining in any of the
2Sa 22:38 pursued mine enemies, and *d* them
2Sa 24:16 to the angel that *d* the people
1Kin 15:13 Asa *d* her idol, and burnt it by
1Kin 15:29 that breathed, until he had *d* him
2Kin 10:17 in Samaria, till he had *d* him
2Kin 10:28 Thus Jehu *d* Baal out of Israel
2Kin 11:1 she arose and *d* all the seed royal
2Kin 13:7 for the king of Syria had *d* them
2Kin 19:12 them which my fathers have *d*
2Kin 19:17 of Assyria have *d* the nations
2Kin 19:18 therefore they have *d* them
2Kin 21:3 which Hezekiah his father had *d*
2Kin 21:9 *d* before the children of Israel
1Chr 4:41 *d* them utterly unto this day, and
1Chr 5:25 the land, whom God *d* before them
1Chr 20:1 And Joab smote Rabbah, and *d* it
1Chr 21:12 months to be *d* before thy foes
1Chr 21:15 evil, and said to the angel that *d*
2Chr 14:13 for they were *d* before the LORD,
2Chr 15:6 And nation was *d* of nation
2Chr 20:10 turned from them, and *d* them not
2Chr 22:10 *d* all the seed royal of the house
2Chr 24:23 *d* all the princes of the people
2Chr 31:1 until they had utterly *d* them all
2Chr 32:14 nations that my fathers utterly *d*
2Chr 33:9 whom the LORD had *d* before the
2Chr 34:11 which the kings of Judah had *d*
2Chr 36:19 *d* all the goodly vessels thereof
Ezr 4:15 for which cause was this city *d*
Ezr 5:12 who *d* this house, and carried the
Est 3:9 it be written that they may be *d*
Est 4:14 and thy father's house shall be *d*
Est 7:4 are sold, I and my people, to be *d*
Est 9:6 Jews slew and *d* five hundred men
Est 9:12 *d* five hundred men in Shushan the
Job 4:20 They are *d* from morning to
Job 19:10 He hath *d* me on every side, and I
Job 34:25 in the night, so that they are *d*
Ps 9:5 thou hast *d* the wicked, thou hast
Ps 9:6 and thou hast *d* cities
Ps 11:3 If the foundations be *d*, what can
Ps 37:38 transgressors shall be *d* together
Ps 73:27 thou hast *d* all them that go a
Ps 78:38 their iniquity, and *d* them not
Ps 78:45 and frogs, which *d* them
Ps 78:47 He *d* their vines with hail, and
Ps 92:7 is that they shall be *d* for ever
Ps 137:8 of Babylon, who art to be *d*
Prov 13:13 despiseth the word shall be *d*
Prov 13:20 a companion of fools shall be *d*
Prov 13:23 is that is *d* for want of judgment
Prov 29:1 his neck, shall suddenly be *d*
Is 9:16 they that are led of them are *d*
Is 10:27 the yoke shall be *d* because of
Is 14:17 and *d* the cities thereof
Is 14:20 because thou hast *d* thy land
Is 26:14 *d* them, and made all their memory
Is 34:2 he hath utterly *d* them, he hath
Is 37:12 them which my fathers have *d*
Is 37:19 therefore they have *d* them
Is 48:19 been cut off nor *d* from before me
Jer 12:10 Many pastors have *d* my vineyard
Jer 22:20 for all thy lovers are *d*
Jer 48:4 Moab is *d*
Jer 48:8 perish, and the plain shall be *d*
Jer 48:42 Moab shall be *d* from being a
Jer 51:8 Babylon is suddenly fallen and *d*
Jer 51:55 *d* out of her the great voice
Lam 2:5 he hath *d* his strong holds, and
Lam 2:6 he hath *d* his places of the
Lam 2:9 he hath *d* and broken her bars
Eze 26:17 and say to thee, How art thou *d*
Eze 27:32 like the *d* in the midst of the
Eze 30:8 when all her helpers shall be *d*
Eze 32:12 the multitude thereof shall be *d*
Dan 2:44 a kingdom, which shall never be *d*
Dan 6:26 kingdom that which shall not be *d*
Dan 7:11 beast was slain, and his body *d*
Dan 7:14 kingdom that which shall not be *d*
Dan 11:20 but within few days he shall be *d*
Hos 4:6 My people are *d* for lack of
Hos 10:8 the sin of Israel, shall be *d*
Hos 13:9 O Israel, thou hast *d* thyself
Amos 2:9 Yet *d* I the Amorite before them,
Amos 2:9 yet I *d* his fruit from above, and
Zeph 3:6 their cities are *d*, so that there
Mt 22:7 *d* those murderers, and burned up
Lk 17:27 and the flood came, and *d* them all
Lk 17:29 from heaven, and *d* them all
Acts 3:23 shall be *d* from among the people
Acts 9:21 Is not this he that *d* them which
Acts 13:19 when he had *d* seven nations in
Acts 19:27 and her magnificence should be *d*
Rom 6:6 that the body of sin might be *d*
1Cor 10:9 tempted, and were *d* of serpents
1Cor 10:10 and were *d* of the destroyer
1Cor 15:26 enemy that shall be *d* is death
2Cor 4:9 cast down, but not *d*
Gal 1:23 the faith which once he *d*
Gal 2:18 build again the things which I *d*
Heb 11:28 lest he that *d* the firstborn
2Pet 2:12 beasts, made to be taken and *d*
Jude 5 afterward *d* them that believed
Rev 8:9 third part of the ships were *d*

### DESTROYER

Ex 12:23 will not suffer the *d* to come in
Judg 16:24 the *d* of our country, which slew
Job 15:21 in prosperity the *d* shall come
Ps 17:4 kept me from the paths of the *d*
Prov 28:24 the same is the companion of a *d*
Jer 4:7 the *d* of the Gentiles is on his
1Cor 10:10 and were destroyed of the *d*

### DESTROYETH

Deut 8:20 which the LORD *d* before your face
Job 9:22 He *d* the perfect and the wicked
Job 12:23 increaseth the nations, and *d* them
Prov 6:32 he that doeth it *d* his own soul
Prov 11:9 with his mouth *d* his neighbour

Prov 31:3 thy ways to that which *d* kings
Eccl 7:7 and a gift *d* the heart
Eccl 9:18 but one sinner *d* much good

## DESTROYING

Deut 3:6 of Heshbon, utterly *d* the men
Deut 13:15 *d* it utterly, and all that is
Josh 11:11 edge of the sword, utterly *d* them
2Kin 19:11 to all lands, by *d* them utterly
1Chr 21:12 land, and the angel of the LORD *d*
1Chr 21:15 and as he was *d*, the LORD beheld,
Is 28:2 a *d* storm, as a flood of mighty
Is 37:11 to all lands by *d* them utterly
Jer 2:30 your prophets, like a *d* lion
Jer 51:1 that rise up against me, a *d* wind
Jer 51:25 O *d* mountain, saith the LORD,
Lam 2:8 not withdrawn his hand from *d*
Eze 9:1 man with his *d* weapon in his hand
Eze 20:17 mine eye spared them from *d* them

## DESTRUCTION

Deut 7:23 destroy them with a mighty *d*
Deut 32:24 burning heat, and with bitter *d*
1Sa 5:9 the city with a very great *d*
1Sa 5:11 for there was a deadly *d*
1Kin 20:42 a man whom I appointed to utter *d*
2Chr 22:4 the death of his father to his *d*
2Chr 22:7 the *d* of Ahaziah was of God by
2Chr 26:16 his heart was lifted up to his *d*
Est 8:6 endure to see the *d* of my kindred
Est 9:5 of the sword, and slaughter, and *d*
Job 5:21 be afraid of *d* when it cometh
Job 5:22 At *d* and famine thou shalt laugh
Job 18:12 *d* shall be ready at his side
Job 21:17 how oft cometh their *d* upon them
Job 21:20 His eyes shall see his *d*, and he
Job 21:30 is reserved to the day of *d*
Job 26:6 before him, and *d* hath no covering
Job 28:22 *D* and death say, We have heard the
Job 30:12 up against me the ways of their *d*
Job 30:24 grave, though they cry in his *d*
Job 31:3 Is not *d* to the wicked
Job 31:12 it is a fire that consumeth to *d*
Job 31:23 For *d* from God was a terror to me
Job 31:29 at the *d* of him that hated me
Ps 35:8 Let *d* come upon him at unawares
Ps 35:8 into that very *d* let him fall
Ps 55:23 bring them down into the pit of *d*
Ps 73:18 thou castedst them down into *d*
Ps 88:11 or thy faithfulness in *d*
Ps 90:3 Thou turnest man to *d*
Ps 91:6 nor for the *d* that wasteth at
Ps 103:4 Who redeemeth thy life from *d*
Prov 1:27 your *d* cometh as a whirlwind
Prov 10:14 mouth of the foolish is near *d*
Prov 10:15 the *d* of the poor is their
Prov 10:29 but *d* shall be to the workers of
Prov 13:3 wide his lips shall have *d*
Prov 14:28 of people is the *d* of the prince
Prov 15:11 Hell and *d* are before the LORD
Prov 16:18 Pride goeth before *d*, and an
Prov 17:19 that exalteth his gate seeketh *d*
Prov 18:7 A fool's mouth is his *d*, and his
Prov 18:12 Before *d* the heart of man is
Prov 21:15 but *d* shall be to the workers of
Prov 24:2 For their heart studieth *d*
Prov 27:20 Hell and *d* are never full
Prov 31:8 of all such as are appointed to *d*
Is 1:28 the *d* of the transgressors and of
Is 10:25 cease, and mine anger in their *d*
Is 13:6 come as a *d* from the Almighty
Is 14:23 will sweep it with the besom of *d*
Is 15:5 they shall raise up a cry of *d*
Is 19:18 shall be called, The city of *d*
Is 24:12 and the gate is smitten with *d*
Is 49:19 places, and the land of thy *d*
Is 51:19 desolation, and *d*, and the famine,
Is 59:7 wasting and *d* are in their paths
Is 60:18 wasting nor *d* within thy borders
Jer 4:6 evil from the north, and a great *d*
Jer 4:20 *D* upon *d* is cried
Jer 6:1 out of the north, and great *d*
Jer 17:18 and destroy them with double *d*
Jer 46:20 a very fair heifer, but *d* cometh
Jer 48:3 Horonaim, spoiling and great *d*
Jer 48:5 the enemies have heard a cry of *d*
Jer 50:22 is in the land, and of great *d*
Jer 51:54 great *d* from the land of the
Lam 2:11 for the *d* of the daughter of my
Lam 3:47 is come upon us, desolation and *d*
Lam 3:48 *d* of the daughter of my people
Lam 4:10 they were their meat in the *d* of
Eze 5:16 which shall be for their *d*
Eze 7:25 *D* cometh; and they shall seek
Eze 32:9 bring thy *d* among the nations
Hos 7:13 fled from me: *d* unto them
Hos 9:6 lo, they are gone because of *d*
Hos 13:14 O grave, I will be thy *d*
Joel 1:15 as a *d* from the Almighty shall it
Obad 12 of Judah in the day of their *d*
Mic 2:10 destroy you, even with a sore *d*
Zec 14:11 and there shall be no more utter *d*
Mt 7:13 is the way, that leadeth to *d*
Rom 3:16 *D* and misery are in their ways
Rom 9:22 the vessels of wrath fitted to *d*
1Cor 5:5 unto Satan for the *d* of the flesh
2Cor 10:8 edification, and not for your *d*
2Cor 13:10 me to edification, and not to *d*
Phil 3:19 Whose end is *d*, whose God is
1Th 5:3 then sudden *d* cometh upon them,
2Th 1:9 be punished with everlasting *d*
1Ti 6:9 lusts, which drown men in *d*
2Pet 2:1 and bring upon themselves swift *d*
2Pet 3:16 scriptures, unto their own *d*

## DETERMINED

1Sa 20:7 be sure that evil is *d* by him
1Sa 20:9 *d* by my father to come upon thee
1Sa 20:33 Jonathan knew that it was *d* of
1Sa 25:17 for evil is *d* against our master,
2Sa 13:32 of Absalom this hath been *d* from
2Chr 2:1 Solomon *d* to build an house for
2Chr 25:16 that God hath *d* to destroy thee
Est 7:7 evil *d* against him by the king
Job 14:5 Seeing his days are *d*, the number
Is 10:23 shall make a consumption, even *d*
Is 19:17 hosts, which he hath *d* against it
Is 28:22 even *d* upon the whole earth
Dan 9:24 weeks are *d* upon thy people
Dan 9:26 end of the war desolations are *d*
Dan 9:27 that *d* shall be poured upon the
Dan 11:36 for that that is *d* shall be done
Lk 22:22 the Son of man goeth, as it was *d*
Acts 3:13 when he was *d* to let him go
Acts 4:28 thy counsel *d* before to be done
Acts 11:29 *d* to send relief unto the
Acts 15:2 they *d* that Paul and Barnabas, and
Acts 15:37 Barnabas *d* to take with them John
Acts 17:26 hath *d* the times before appointed
Acts 19:39 it shall be *d* in a lawful
Acts 20:16 For Paul had *d* to sail by Ephesus
Acts 25:25 to Augustus, I have *d* to send him
Acts 27:1 when it was *d* that we should sail
1Cor 2:2 For I *d* not to know any thing
2Cor 2:1 But I *d* this with myself, that I
Titus 3:12 for I have *d* there to winter

## DETESTABLE

Jer 16:18 with the carcases of their *d*
Eze 5:11 sanctuary with all thy *d* things
Eze 7:20 of their *d* things therein
Eze 11:18 away all the *d* things thereof
Eze 11:21 after the heart of their *d* things
Eze 37:23 idols, nor with their *d* things

**DEUEL** *(de-oo'-el)* See REUEL. *Father of Eliasaph.*

Num 1:14 Eliasaph the son of *D*
Num 7:42 sixth day Eliasaph the son of *D*
Num 7:47 offering of Eliasaph the son of *D*
Num 10:20 of Gad was Eliasaph the son of *D*

## DEVICE

2Chr 2:14 to find out every *d* which shall
Est 8:3 his *d* that he had devised against
Est 9:25 by letters that his wicked *d*
Ps 21:11 they imagined a mischievous *d*
Ps 140:8 further not his wicked *d*
Eccl 9:10 for there is no work, nor *d*
Jer 18:11 you, and devise a *d* against you
Jer 51:11 for his *d* is against Babylon, to
Lam 3:62 their *d* against me all the day
Acts 17:29 stone, graven by art and man's *d*

## DEVICES

Job 5:12 disappointeth the *d* of the crafty
Job 21:27 the *d* which ye wrongfully imagine
Ps 10:2 in the *d* that they have imagined
Ps 33:10 he maketh the *d* of the people of
Ps 37:7 man who bringeth wicked *d* to pass
Prov 1:31 and be filled with their own *d*
Prov 12:2 a man of wicked *d* will he condemn
Prov 14:17 and a man of wicked *d* is hated
Prov 19:21 There are many *d* in a man's heart
Is 32:7 he deviseth wicked *d* to destroy
Jer 11:19 they had devised *d* against me
Jer 18:12 but we will walk after our own *d*
Jer 18:18 let us devise *d* against Jeremiah
Dan 11:24 he shall forecast his *d* against
Dan 11:25 they shall forecast *d* against him
2Cor 2:11 for we are not ignorant of his *d*

## DEVIL

Mt 4:1 wilderness to be tempted of the *d*
Mt 4:5 Then the *d* taketh him up into the
Mt 4:8 the *d* taketh him up into an
Mt 4:11 Then the *d* leaveth him, and,
Mt 9:32 him a dumb man possessed with a *d*
Mt 9:33 when the *d* was cast out, the dumb
Mt 11:18 and they say, He hath a *d*
Mt 12:22 unto him one possessed with a *d*
Mt 13:39 enemy that sowed them is the *d*
Mt 15:22 is grievously vexed with a *d*
Mt 17:18 And Jesus rebuked the *d*
Mt 25:41 fire, prepared for the *d* and his
Mk 5:15 him that was possessed with the *d*
Mk 5:16 him that was possessed with the *d*
Mk 5:18 the *d* prayed him that he might be
Mk 7:26 forth the *d* out of her daughter
Mk 7:29 the *d* is gone out of thy daughter
Mk 7:30 house, she found the *d* gone out
Lk 4:2 Being forty days tempted of the *d*
Lk 4:3 the *d* said unto him, If thou be
Lk 4:5 And the *d*, taking him up into an
Lk 4:6 the *d* said unto him, All this
Lk 4:13 when the *d* had ended all the
Lk 4:33 had a spirit of an unclean *d*
Lk 4:35 when the *d* had thrown him in the
Lk 7:33 and ye say, He hath a *d*
Lk 8:12 then cometh the *d*, and taketh away
Lk 8:29 was driven of the *d* into the
Lk 9:42 the *d* threw him down, and tare him
Lk 11:14 And he was casting out a *d*
Lk 11:14 when the *d* was gone out, the dumb
Jn 6:70 you twelve, and one of you is a *d*
Jn 7:20 answered and said, Thou hast a *d*
Jn 8:44 Ye are of your father the *d*
Jn 8:48 thou art a Samaritan, and hast a *d*
Jn 8:49 Jesus answered, I have not a *d*
Jn 8:52 Now we know that thou hast a *d*
Jn 10:20 And many of them said, He hath a *d*
Jn 10:21 the words of him that hath a *d*
Jn 10:21 Can a *d* open the eyes of the
Jn 13:2 the *d* having now put into the
Acts 10:38 all that were oppressed of the *d*
Acts 13:10 all mischief, thou child of the *d*
Eph 4:27 Neither give place to the *d*
Eph 6:11 stand against the wiles of the *d*
1Ti 3:6 into the condemnation of the *d*
1Ti 3:7 reproach and the snare of the *d*
2Ti 2:26 out of the snare of the *d*
Heb 2:14 power of death, that is, the *d*
Jas 4:7 Resist the *d*, and he will flee
1Pet 5:8 because your adversary the *d*
1Jn 3:8 that committeth sin is of the *d*
1Jn 3:8 for the *d* sinneth from the
1Jn 3:8 might destroy the works of the *d*
1Jn 3:10 and the children of the *d*
Jude 9 when contending with the *d* he
Rev 2:10 the *d* shall cast some of you into
Rev 12:9 that old serpent, called the *D*
Rev 12:12 for the *d* is come down unto you,
Rev 20:2 that old serpent, which is the *D*
Rev 20:10 the *d* that deceived them was cast

## DEVILS

Lev 17:7 offer their sacrifices unto *d*
Deut 32:17 They sacrificed unto *d*, not to
2Chr 11:15 for the high places, and for the *d*
Ps 106:37 sons and their daughters unto *d*
Mt 4:24 those which were possessed with *d*
Mt 7:22 and in thy name have cast out *d*
Mt 8:16 many that were possessed with *d*
Mt 8:28 met him two possessed with *d*
Mt 8:31 So the *d* besought him, saying, If
Mt 8:33 to the possessed of the *d*
Mt 9:34 He casteth out *d* through the
Mt 9:34 through the prince of the *d*
Mt 10:8 raise the dead, cast out *d*
Mt 12:24 This fellow doth not cast out *d*
Mt 12:24 by Beelzebub the prince of the *d*
Mt 12:27 And if I by Beelzebub cast out *d*
Mt 12:28 But if I cast out *d* by the Spirit
Mk 1:32 them that were possessed with *d*
Mk 1:34 diseases, and cast out many *d*

Mk 1:34 and suffered not the *d* to speak
Mk 1:39 all Galilee, and cast out *d*
Mk 3:15 heal sicknesses, and to cast out *d*
Mk 3:22 of the *d* casteth he out *d*
Mk 5:12 all the *d* besought him, saying,
Mk 6:13 And they cast out many *d*, and
Mk 9:38 saw one casting out *d* in thy name
Mk 16:9 out of whom he had cast seven *d*
Mk 16:17 In my name shall they cast out *d*
Lk 4:41 *d* also came out of many, crying
Lk 8:2 out of whom went seven *d*
Lk 8:27 man, which had *d* long time
Lk 8:30 because many *d* were entered into
Lk 8:33 Then went the *d* out of the man,
Lk 8:35 out of whom the *d* were departed
Lk 8:36 was possessed of the *d* was healed
Lk 8:38 Now the man out of whom the *d*
Lk 9:1 power and authority over all *d*
Lk 9:49 saw one casting out *d* in thy name
Lk 10:17 even the *d* are subject unto us
Lk 11:15 said, He casteth out *d* through
Lk 11:15 Beelzebub the chief of the *d*
Lk 11:18 I cast out *d* through Beelzebub
Lk 11:19 And if I by Beelzebub cast out *d*
Lk 11:20 with the finger of God cast out *d*
Lk 13:32 that fox, Behold, I cast out *d*
1Cor 10:20 sacrifice, they sacrifice to *d*
1Cor 10:20 ye should have fellowship with *d*
1Cor 10:21 cup of the Lord, and the cup of *d*
1Cor 10:21 table, and of the table of *d*
1Ti 4:1 spirits, and doctrines of *d*
Jas 2:19 the *d* also believe, and tremble
Rev 9:20 that they should not worship *d*
Rev 16:14 For they are the spirits of *d*
Rev 18:2 and is become the habitation of *d*

**DEVISE**
Ex 31:4 To *d* cunning works, to work in
Ex 35:32 to *d* curious works, to work in
Ex 35:35 and of those that *d* cunning work
2Sa 14:14 yet doth he *d* means, that his
Ps 35:4 to confusion that *d* my hurt
Ps 35:20 but they *d* deceitful matters
Ps 41:7 against me do they *d* my hurt
Prov 3:29 *D* not evil against thy neighbour,
Prov 14:22 Do they not err that *d* evil
Prov 14:22 shall be to them that *d* good
Prov 16:30 his eyes to *d* froward things
Jer 18:11 you, and *d* a device against you
Jer 18:18 let us *d* devices against Jeremiah
Eze 11:2 these are the men that *d* mischief
Mic 2:1 Woe to them that *d* iniquity
Mic 2:3 this family do I *d* an evil

**DEVISED**
2Sa 21:5 that *d* against us that we should
1Kin 12:33 which he had *d* of his own heart
Est 8:3 that he had *d* against the Jews
Est 8:5 *d* by Haman the son of Hammedatha
Est 9:24 had *d* against the Jews to destroy
Est 9:25 which he *d* against the Jews,
Ps 31:13 they *d* to take away my life
Jer 11:19 they had *d* devices against me
Jer 48:2 they have *d* evil against it
Jer 51:12 for the LORD hath both *d* and done
Lam 2:17 hath done that which he had *d*
2Pet 1:16 not followed cunningly *d* fables

**DEVISETH**
Ps 36:4 He *d* mischief upon his bed
Ps 52:2 Thy tongue *d* mischiefs
Prov 6:14 he *d* mischief continually
Prov 6:18 An heart that *d* wicked
Prov 16:9 A man's heart *d* his way
Prov 24:8 He that *d* to do evil shall be
Is 32:7 he *d* wicked devices to destroy
Is 32:8 But the liberal *d* liberal things

**DEVOTED**
Lev 27:21 holy unto the LORD, as a field *d*
Lev 27:28 Notwithstanding no *d* thing
Lev 27:28 every *d* thing is most holy unto
Lev 27:29 None *d*, which shall be
Lev 27:29 which shall be *d* of men
Num 18:14 Every thing *d* in Israel shall be
Ps 119:38 thy servant, who is *d* to thy fear

**DEVOUR**
Gen 49:27 the morning he shall *d* the prey
Deut 32:42 blood, and my sword shall *d* flesh
Judg 9:15 and *d* the cedars of Lebanon
Judg 9:20 *d* the men of Shechem, and the
Judg 9:20 house of Millo, and *d* Abimelech
2Sa 2:26 said, Shall the sword *d* for ever
2Chr 7:13 command the locusts to *d* the land
Job 18:13 It shall *d* the strength of his
Job 18:13 of death shall *d* his strength
Ps 21:9 wrath, and the fire shall *d* them
Ps 50:3 a fire shall *d* before him
Ps 80:13 wild beast of the field doth *d* it
Prov 30:14 to *d* the poor from off the earth,
Is 1:7 strangers *d* it in your presence,
Is 9:12 they shall *d* Israel with open
Is 9:18 it shall *d* the briers and thorns,
Is 10:17 *d* his thorns and his briers in one
Is 26:11 of thine enemies shall *d* them
Is 31:8 not of a mean man, shall *d* him
Is 33:11 your breath, as fire, shall *d* you
Is 42:14 I will destroy and *d* at once
Is 56:9 ye beasts of the field, come to *d*
Jer 2:3 all that *d* him shall offend
Jer 5:14 people wood, and it shall *d* them
Jer 12:9 beasts of the field, come to *d*
Jer 12:12 *d* from the one end of the land
Jer 15:3 and the beasts of the earth, to *d*
Jer 17:27 it shall *d* the palaces of
Jer 21:14 it shall *d* all things round about
Jer 30:16 that *d* thee shall be devoured
Jer 46:10 and the sword shall *d*, and it shall
Jer 46:14 sword shall *d* round about thee
Jer 48:45 shall *d* the corner of Moab, and
Jer 50:32 it shall *d* all round about him
Eze 7:15 famine and pestilence shall *d* him
Eze 15:7 and another fire shall *d* them
Eze 20:47 it shall *d* every green tree in
Eze 23:37 them through the fire, to *d* them
Eze 28:18 midst of thee, it shall *d* thee
Eze 34:28 the beast of the land *d* them
Eze 36:14 thou shalt *d* men no more, neither
Dan 7:5 thus unto it, Arise, *d* much flesh
Dan 7:23 shall *d* the whole earth, and shall
Hos 5:7 now shall a month *d* them with
Hos 8:14 it shall *d* the palaces thereof
Hos 11:6 *d* them, because of their own
Hos 13:8 there will I *d* them like a lion
Amos 1:4 which shall *d* the palaces of
Amos 1:7 which shall *d* the palaces thereof
Amos 1:10 which shall *d* the palaces thereof
Amos 1:12 which shall *d* the palaces of
Amos 1:14 it shall *d* the palaces thereof,
Amos 2:2 it shall *d* the palaces of Kirioth
Amos 2:5 it shall *d* the palaces of
Amos 5:6 *d* it, and there be none to quench
Obad 18 shall kindle in them, and *d* them
Nah 2:13 the sword shall *d* thy young lions
Nah 3:13 the fire shall *d* thy bars
Nah 3:15 There shall the fire *d* thee
Hab 3:14 was as to *d* the poor secretly
Zec 9:15 and they shall *d*, and subdue with
Zec 11:1 that the fire may *d* thy cedars
Zec 12:6 they shall *d* all the people round
Mt 23:14 for ye *d* widows' houses, and for a
Mk 12:40 Which *d* widows' houses, and for a
Lk 20:47 Which *d* widows' houses, and for a
2Cor 11:20 you into bondage, if a man *d* you
Gal 5:15 *d* one another, take heed that ye
Heb 10:27 which shall *d* the adversaries
1Pet 5:8 about, seeking whom he may *d*
Rev 12:4 for to *d* her child as soon as it

**DEVOURED**
Gen 31:15 hath quite *d* also our money
Gen 37:20 say, Some evil beast hath *d* him
Gen 37:33 an evil beast hath *d* him
Gen 41:7 seven thin ears *d* the seven rank
Gen 41:24 the thin ears *d* the seven good
Lev 10:2 *d* them, and they died before the
Num 26:10 what time the fire *d* two hundred
Deut 31:17 from them, and they shall be *d*
Deut 32:24 *d* with burning heat, and with
2Sa 18:8 the wood *d* more people that day
2Sa 18:8 people that day than the sword *d*
2Sa 22:9 and fire out of his mouth *d*
Ps 18:8 and fire out of his mouth *d*
Ps 78:45 of flies among them, which *d* them
Ps 79:7 For they have *d* Jacob, and laid
Ps 105:35 *d* the fruit of their ground
Is 1:20 ye shall be *d* with the sword
Is 24:6 hath the curse *d* the earth
Jer 2:30 own sword hath *d* your prophets
Jer 3:24 For shame hath *d* the labour of
Jer 8:16 have *d* the land, and all that is
Jer 10:25 *d* him, and consumed him, and have
Jer 30:16 they that devour thee shall be *d*
Jer 50:7 All that found them have *d* them
Jer 50:17 the king of Assyria hath *d* him
Jer 51:34 the king of Babylon hath *d* me
Lam 4:11 it hath *d* the foundations thereof
Eze 15:5 any work, when the fire hath *d* it
Eze 16:20 thou sacrificed unto them to be *d*
Eze 19:3 to catch the prey; it *d* men
Eze 19:6 to catch the prey, and *d* men
Eze 19:14 branches, which hath *d* her fruit
Eze 22:25 they have *d* souls
Eze 23:25 residue shall be *d* by the fire
Eze 33:27 will I give to the beasts to be *d*
Eze 39:4 the beasts of the field to be *d*
Dan 7:7 it *d* and brake in pieces, and
Dan 7:19 which *d*, brake in pieces, and
Hos 7:7 an oven, and have *d* their judges
Hos 7:9 Strangers have *d* his strength
Joel 1:19 for the fire hath *d* the pastures
Joel 1:20 the fire hath *d* the pastures of
Amos 4:9 increased, the palmerworm *d* them
Amos 7:4 it *d* the great deep, and did eat
Nah 1:10 they shall be *d* as stubble fully
Zeph 1:18 be *d* by the fire of his jealousy
Zeph 3:8 for all the earth shall be *d* with
Zec 9:4 and she shall be *d* with fire
Mt 13:4 and the fowls came and *d* them up
Mk 4:4 fowls of the air came and *d* it up
Lk 8:5 and the fowls of the air *d* it
Lk 15:30 which hath *d* thy living with
Rev 20:9 from God out of heaven, and *d* them

**DEVOUT**
Lk 2:25 and the same man was just and *d*
Acts 2:5 *d* men, out of every nation under
Acts 8:2 *d* men carried Stephen to his
Acts 10:2 A *d* man, and one that feared God
Acts 10:7 a *d* soldier of them that waited
Acts 13:50 But the Jews stirred up the *d*
Acts 17:4 of the *d* Greeks a great multitude
Acts 17:17 the Jews, and with the *d* persons
Acts 22:12 a *d* man according to the law,

**DEW**
Gen 27:28 God give thee of the *d* of heaven
Gen 27:39 of the *d* of heaven from above
Ex 16:13 in the morning the *d* lay round
Ex 16:14 when the *d* that lay was gone up,
Num 11:9 when the *d* fell upon the camp in
Deut 32:2 my speech shall distil as the *d*
Deut 33:13 things of heaven, for the *d*
Deut 33:28 his heavens shall drop down *d*
Judg 6:37 if the *d* be on the fleece only,
Judg 6:38 wringed the *d* out of the fleece,
Judg 6:39 all the ground let there be *d*
Judg 6:40 there was *d* on all the ground
2Sa 1:21 of Gilboa, let there be no *d*
2Sa 17:12 as the *d* falleth on the ground
1Kin 17:1 there shall not be *d* nor rain
Job 29:19 the *d* lay all night upon my
Job 38:28 who hath begotten the drops of *d*
Ps 110:3 thou hast the *d* of thy youth
Ps 133:3 As the *d* of Hermon, and as the *d*
Prov 3:20 up, and the clouds drop down the *d*
Prov 19:12 his favour is as *d* upon the grass
Song 5:2 for my head is filled with *d*
Is 18:4 like a cloud of *d* in the heat of
Is 26:19 for thy *d* is as the *d* of herbs,
Dan 4:15 it be wet with the *d* of heaven
Dan 4:23 it be wet with the *d* of heaven
Dan 4:25 wet thee with the *d* of heaven
Dan 4:33 body was wet with the *d* of heaven
Dan 5:21 body was wet with the *d* of heaven
Hos 6:4 as the early *d* it goeth away
Hos 13:3 as the early *d* that passeth away,
Hos 14:5 I will be as the *d* unto Israel
Mic 5:7 many people as a *d* from the LORD
Hag 1:10 heaven over you is stayed from *d*
Zec 8:12 and the heavens shall give their *d*

**DIADEM**
Job 29:14 my judgment was as a robe and a *d*
Is 28:5 for a *d* of beauty, unto the
Is 62:3 a royal *d* in the hand of thy God
Eze 21:26 Remove the *d*, and take off the

**DIAMOND**
Ex 28:18 be an emerald, a sapphire, and a *d*
Ex 39:11 an emerald, a sapphire, and a *d*
Jer 17:1 of iron, and with the point of a *d*
Eze 28:13 the sardius, topaz, and the *d*

**DIANA** *(di-an'-ah) A Greek goddess.*
Acts 19:24 which made silver shrines for *D*
Acts 19:27 goddess *D* should be despised
Acts 19:28 Great is *D* of the Ephesians
Acts 19:34 Great is *D* of the Ephesians
Acts 19:35 worshipper of the great goddess *D*

**DIBLAIM** *(dib'-la-im) Father of Gomer.*
Hos 1:3 and took Gomer the daughter of *D*

**DIBLATH** *(dib'-lath) A place in northern Canaan.*
Eze 6:14 than the wilderness toward *D*

**DIBON** *(di'-bon)* See DIBON-GAD, DIMON.
*1. A Moabite city.*
Num 21:30 Heshbon is perished even unto *D*
Num 32:3 Ataroth, and *D*, and Jazer, and
Num 32:34 And the children of Gad built *D*
Josh 13:9 and all the plain of Medeba unto *D*
Josh 13:17 *D*, and Bamoth-baal, and
Jer 48:18 Thou daughter that dost inhabit *D*
Jer 48:22 upon *D*, and upon Nebo, and upon
Is 15:2 He is gone up to Bajith, and to *D*
*2. A town in Judah.*
Neh 11:25 in the villages thereof, and at *D*

**DIBON-GAD** *(di'-bon-gad') An encampment during the Exodus.*
Num 33:45 from Iim, and pitched in *D*
Num 33:46 And they removed from *D*, and

**DIBRI** *(dib'-ri) Father of Shelomith.*
Lev 24:11 was Shelomith, the daughter of *D*

**DIDYMUS** *(did'-i-mus)* See THOMAS. *Another name for Thomas the apostle.*
Jn 11:16 said Thomas, which is called *D*
Jn 20:24 one of the twelve, called *D*
Jn 21:2 Simon Peter, and Thomas called *D*

**DIE**
Gen 2:17 thereof thou shalt surely *d*
Gen 3:3 shall ye touch it, lest ye *d*
Gen 3:4 the woman, Ye shall not surely *d*
Gen 6:17 that is in the earth shall *d*
Gen 19:19 lest some evil take me, and I *d*
Gen 20:7 thou that thou shalt surely *d*
Gen 25:32 Behold, I am at the point to *d*
Gen 26:9 Because I said, Lest I *d* for her
Gen 27:4 my soul may bless thee before I *d*
Gen 30:1 Give me children, or else I *d*
Gen 33:13 one day, all the flock will *d*
Gen 38:11 said, Lest peradventure he *d* also
Gen 42:2 that we may live, and not *d*
Gen 42:20 be verified, and ye shall not *d*
Gen 43:8 that we may live, and not *d*
Gen 44:9 it be found, both let him *d*
Gen 44:22 his father, his father would *d*
Gen 44:31 is not with us, that he will *d*
Gen 45:28 I will go and see him before I *d*
Gen 46:30 said unto Joseph, Now let me *d*
Gen 47:15 why should we *d* in thy presence
Gen 47:19 shall we *d* before thine eyes
Gen 47:19 seed, that we may live, and not *d*
Gen 47:29 time drew nigh that Israel must *d*
Gen 48:21 said unto Joseph, Behold, I *d*
Gen 50:5 made me swear, saying, Lo, I *d*
Gen 50:24 said unto his brethren, I *d*
Ex 7:18 fish that is in the river shall *d*
Ex 9:4 there shall nothing *d* of all that
Ex 9:19 down upon them, and they shall *d*
Ex 10:28 thou seest my face thou shalt *d*
Ex 11:5 in the land of Egypt shall *d*
Ex 14:11 us away to *d* in the wilderness
Ex 14:12 we should *d* in the wilderness
Ex 20:19 not God speak with us, lest we *d*
Ex 21:12 that smiteth a man, so that he *d*
Ex 21:14 from mine altar, that he may *d*
Ex 21:18 he *d* not, but keepeth his bed
Ex 21:20 a rod, and he *d* under his hand
Ex 21:28 a man or a woman, that they *d*
Ex 21:35 ox hurt another's, that he *d*
Ex 22:2 up, and be smitten that he *d*
Ex 22:10 and it *d*, or be hurt, or driven
Ex 22:14 neighbour, and it be hurt, or *d*
Ex 28:35 when he cometh out, that he *d* not
Ex 28:43 that they bear not iniquity, and *d*
Ex 30:20 wash with water, that they *d* not
Ex 30:21 and their feet, that they *d* not
Lev 8:35 charge of the LORD, that ye *d* not
Lev 10:6 lest ye *d*, and lest wrath come
Lev 10:7 of the congregation, lest ye *d*
Lev 10:9 of the congregation, lest ye *d*
Lev 11:39 any beast, of which ye may eat, *d*
Lev 15:31 that they *d* not in their
Lev 16:2 that he *d* not
Lev 16:13 upon the testimony, that he *d* not
Lev 20:20 they shall *d* childless
Lev 22:9 *d* therefore, if they profane it
Num 4:15 touch any holy thing, lest they *d*
Num 4:19 that they may live, and not *d*
Num 4:20 things are covered, lest they *d*
Num 6:7 or for his sister, when they *d*
Num 6:9 if any man *d* very suddenly by him
Num 14:35 consumed, and there they shall *d*
Num 16:29 If these men *d* the common death
Num 17:10 from me, that they *d* not
Num 17:12 unto Moses, saying, Behold, we *d*
Num 17:13 tabernacle of the LORD shall *d*
Num 18:3 that neither they, nor ye also, *d*
Num 18:22 lest they bear sin, and *d*
Num 18:32 the children of Israel, lest ye *d*
Num 20:4 we and our cattle should *d* there
Num 20:26 unto his people, and shall *d* there
Num 21:5 of Egypt to *d* in the wilderness
Num 23:10 Let me *d* the death of the
Num 26:65 shall surely *d* in the wilderness
Num 27:8 of Israel, saying, If a man *d*
Num 35:12 that the manslayer *d* not, until
Num 35:16 instrument of iron, so that he *d*
Num 35:17 wherewith he may *d*, and he *d*
Num 35:18 wherewith he may *d*, and he *d*
Num 35:20 him by laying of wait, that he *d*
Num 35:21 him with his hand, that he *d*
Num 35:23 any stone, wherewith a man may *d*
Num 35:23 and cast it upon him, that he *d*
Num 35:30 any person to cause him to *d*
Deut 4:22 But I must *d* in this land, I must
Deut 5:25 Now therefore why should we *d*
Deut 5:25 our God any more, then we shall *d*
Deut 13:10 stone him with stones, that he *d*
Deut 17:5 them with stones, till they *d*
Deut 17:12 the judge, even that man shall *d*
Deut 18:16 great fire any more, that I *d* not
Deut 18:20 gods, even that prophet shall *d*
Deut 19:5 upon his neighbour, that he *d*
Deut 19:11 and smite him mortally that he *d*
Deut 19:12 avenger of blood, that he may *d*
Deut 20:5 lest he *d* in the battle, and
Deut 20:6 lest he *d* in the battle, and
Deut 20:7 lest he *d* in the battle, and
Deut 21:21 stone him with stones, that he *d*
Deut 22:21 stone her with stones that she *d*
Deut 22:22 then they shall both of them *d*
Deut 22:24 them with stones that they *d*
Deut 22:25 only that lay with her shall *d*
Deut 24:3 or if the latter husband *d*
Deut 24:7 then that thief shall *d*
Deut 25:5 dwell together, and one of them *d*
Deut 31:14 days approach that thou must *d*
Deut 32:50 *d* in the mount whither thou goest
Deut 33:6 Let Reuben live, and not *d*
Josh 20:9 not *d* by the hand of the avenger
Judg 6:23 thou shalt not *d*
Judg 6:30 Bring out thy son, that he may *d*
Judg 13:22 unto his wife, We shall surely *d*
Judg 15:18 and now shall I *d* for thirst
Judg 16:30 Let me *d* with the Philistines
Ruth 1:17 Where thou diest, will I *d*
1Sa 2:33 *d* in the flower of their age
1Sa 2:34 one day they shall *d* both of them
1Sa 12:19 the LORD thy God, that we *d* not
1Sa 14:39 my son, he shall surely *d*
1Sa 14:43 in mine hand, and, lo, I must *d*
1Sa 14:44 for thou shalt surely *d*, Jonathan
1Sa 14:45 said unto Saul, Shall Jonathan *d*
1Sa 20:2 thou shalt not *d*
1Sa 20:14 of the LORD, that I *d* not
1Sa 20:31 unto me, for he shall surely *d*
1Sa 22:16 king said, Thou shalt surely *d*
1Sa 26:10 or his day shall come to *d*
1Sa 26:16 LORD liveth, ye are worthy to *d*
1Sa 28:9 for my life, to cause me to *d*
2Sa 11:15 him, that he may be smitten, and *d*
2Sa 12:5 done this thing shall surely *d*
2Sa 12:13 thou shalt not *d*
2Sa 12:14 is born unto thee shall surely *d*
2Sa 14:14 For we must needs *d*, and are as
2Sa 18:3 neither if half of us *d*, will
2Sa 19:23 unto Shimei, Thou shalt not *d*
2Sa 19:37 that I may *d* in mine own city, and
1Kin 1:52 shall be found in him, he shall *d*
1Kin 2:1 David drew nigh that he should *d*
1Kin 2:30 but I will *d* here
1Kin 2:37 certain that thou shalt surely *d*
1Kin 2:42 whither, that thou shalt surely *d*
1Kin 14:12 into the city, the child shall *d*
1Kin 17:12 my son, that we may eat it, and *d*
1Kin 19:4 for himself that he might *d*
1Kin 21:10 out, and stone him, that he may *d*
2Kin 1:4 art gone up, but shalt surely *d*
2Kin 1:6 art gone up, but shalt surely *d*
2Kin 1:16 art gone up, but shalt surely *d*
2Kin 7:3 Why sit we here until we *d*
2Kin 7:4 in the city, and we shall *d* there
2Kin 7:4 if we sit still here, we *d* also
2Kin 7:4 if they kill us, we shall but *d*
2Kin 8:10 shewed me that he shall surely *d*
2Kin 18:32 honey, that ye may live, and not *d*
2Kin 20:1 for thou shalt *d*, and not live
2Chr 25:4 shall not *d* for the children
2Chr 25:4 the children *d* for the fathers
2Chr 25:4 every man shall *d* for his own sin
2Chr 32:11 over yourselves to *d* by famine
Job 2:9 curse God, and *d*
Job 4:21 they *d*, even without wisdom
Job 12:2 and wisdom shall *d* with you
Job 14:8 the stock thereof *d* in the ground
Job 14:14 If a man *d*, shall he live again
Job 27:5 till I *d* I will not remove mine
Job 29:18 I shall *d* in my nest, and I shall
Job 34:20 In a moment shall they *d*, and the
Job 36:12 they shall *d* without knowledge
Job 36:14 They *d* in youth, and their life is
Ps 41:5 speak evil of me, When shall he *d*
Ps 49:10 For he seeth that wise men *d*
Ps 79:11 those that are appointed to *d*
Ps 82:7 But ye shall *d* like men, and fall
Ps 88:15 ready to *d* from my youth up
Ps 104:29 takest away their breath, they *d*
Ps 118:17 I shall not *d*, but live, and
Prov 5:23 He shall *d* without instruction
Prov 10:21 but fools *d* for want of wisdom
Prov 15:10 and he that hateth reproof shall *d*
Prov 19:16 that despiseth his ways shall *d*
Prov 23:13 him with the rod, he shall not *d*
Prov 30:7 deny me them not before I *d*
Eccl 3:2 A time to be born, and a time to *d*
Eccl 7:17 shouldest thou *d* before thy time
Eccl 9:5 the living know that they shall *d*
Is 22:13 for to morrow we shall *d*
Is 22:14 not be purged from you till ye *d*
Is 22:18 there shalt thou *d*, and there the
Is 38:1 for thou shalt *d*, and not live
Is 51:6 therein shall *d* in like manner
Is 51:12 be afraid of a man that shall *d*
Is 51:14 that he should not *d* in the pit
Is 65:20 for the child shall *d* an hundred
Is 66:24 for their worm shall not *d*
Jer 11:21 that thou *d* not by our hand
Jer 11:22 young men shall *d* by the sword
Jer 11:22 their daughters shall *d* by famine
Jer 16:4 They shall *d* of grievous deaths
Jer 16:6 and the small shall *d* in this land
Jer 20:6 to Babylon, and there thou shalt *d*
Jer 21:6 they shall *d* of a great
Jer 21:9 in this city shall *d* by the sword
Jer 22:12 But he shall *d* in the place
Jer 22:26 and there shall ye *d*
Jer 26:8 him, saying, Thou shalt surely *d*
Jer 26:11 saying, This man is worthy to *d*
Jer 26:16 This man is not worthy to *d*
Jer 27:13 Why will ye *d*, thou and thy people
Jer 28:16 this year thou shalt *d*, because
Jer 31:30 But every one shall *d* for his own
Jer 34:4 Thou shalt not *d* by the sword
Jer 34:5 But thou shalt *d* in peace
Jer 37:20 the scribe, lest I *d* there
Jer 38:2 in this city shall *d* by the sword
Jer 38:9 he is like to *d* for hunger in the
Jer 38:10 out of the dungeon, before he *d*
Jer 38:24 these words, and thou shalt not *d*
Jer 38:26 to Jonathan's house, to *d* there
Jer 42:16 and there ye shall *d*
Jer 42:17 they shall *d* by the sword, by the
Jer 42:22 that ye shall *d* by the sword
Jer 44:12 they shall *d*, from the least even
Eze 3:18 the wicked, Thou shalt surely *d*
Eze 3:18 man shall *d* in his iniquity
Eze 3:19 he shall *d* in his iniquity
Eze 3:20 before him, he shall *d*
Eze 3:20 he shall *d* in his sin, and his
Eze 5:12 thee shall *d* with the pestilence

Eze 6:12 far off shall *d* of the pestilence
Eze 6:12 is besieged shall *d* by the famine
Eze 7:15 the field shall *d* with the sword
Eze 12:13 see it, though he shall *d* there
Eze 13:19 slay the souls that should not *d*
Eze 17:16 the midst of Babylon he shall *d*
Eze 18:4 the soul that sinneth, it shall *d*
Eze 18:13 he shall surely *d*
Eze 18:17 he shall not *d* for the iniquity
Eze 18:18 even he shall *d* in his iniquity
Eze 18:20 The soul that sinneth, it shall *d*
Eze 18:21 shall surely live, he shall not *d*
Eze 18:23 at all that the wicked should *d*
Eze 18:24 hath sinned, in them shall he *d*
Eze 18:26 that he hath done shall he *d*
Eze 18:28 shall surely live, he shall not *d*
Eze 18:31 for why will ye *d*, O house of
Eze 28:8 thou shalt *d* the deaths of them
Eze 28:10 Thou shalt *d* the deaths of the
Eze 33:8 O wicked man, thou shalt surely *d*
Eze 33:8 man shall *d* in his iniquity
Eze 33:9 he shall *d* in his iniquity
Eze 33:11 for why will ye *d*, O house of
Eze 33:13 hath committed, he shall *d* for it
Eze 33:14 the wicked, Thou shalt surely *d*
Eze 33:15 shall surely live, he shall not *d*
Eze 33:18 iniquity, he shall even *d* thereby
Eze 33:27 caves shall *d* of the pestilence
Amos 2:2 Moab shall *d* with tumult, with
Amos 6:9 in one house, that they shall *d*
Amos 7:11 Jeroboam shall *d* by the sword
Amos 7:17 thou shalt *d* in a polluted land
Amos 9:10 of my people shall *d* by the sword
Jonah 4:3 better for me to *d* than to live
Jonah 4:8 and wished in himself to *d*
Jonah 4:8 better for me to *d* than to live
Hab 1:12 we shall not *d*
Zec 11:9 that that dieth, let it *d*
Zec 13:8 therein shall be cut off and *d*
Mt 15:4 or mother, let him *d* the death
Mt 22:24 Master, Moses said, If a man *d*
Mt 26:35 him, Though I should *d* with thee
Mk 7:10 or mother, let him *d* the death
Mk 12:19 unto us, If a man's brother *d*
Mk 14:31 If I should *d* with thee, I will
Lk 7:2 unto him, was sick, and ready to *d*
Lk 20:28 unto us, If any man's brother *d*
Lk 20:28 he *d* without children, that his
Lk 20:36 Neither can they *d* any more
Jn 4:49 Sir, come down ere my child *d*
Jn 6:50 a man may eat thereof, and not *d*
Jn 8:21 seek me, and shall *d* in your sins
Jn 8:24 you, that ye shall *d* in your sins
Jn 8:24 I am he, ye shall *d* in your sins
Jn 11:16 also go, that we may *d* with him
Jn 11:26 and believeth in me shall never *d*
Jn 11:50 one man should *d* for the people
Jn 11:51 Jesus should *d* for that nation
Jn 12:24 wheat fall into the ground and *d*
Jn 12:24 but if it *d*, it bringeth forth
Jn 12:33 signifying what death he should *d*
Jn 18:14 one man should *d* for the people
Jn 18:32 signifying what death he should *d*
Jn 19:7 law, and by our law he ought to *d*
Jn 21:23 that that disciple should not *d*
Jn 21:23 said not unto him, He shall not *d*
Acts 21:13 but also to *d* at Jerusalem for
Acts 25:11 of death, I refuse not to *d*
Acts 25:16 Romans to deliver any man to *d*
Rom 5:7 for a righteous man will one *d*
Rom 5:7 man some would even dare to *d*
Rom 8:13 live after the flesh, ye shall *d*
Rom 14:8 we *d*, we *d* unto the Lord
Rom 14:8 whether we live therefore, or *d*
1Cor 9:15 for it were better for me to *d*
1Cor 15:22 For as in Adam all *d*, even so in
1Cor 15:31 Christ Jesus our Lord, I *d* daily
1Cor 15:32 for to morrow we *d*
1Cor 15:36 is not quickened, except it *d*
2Cor 7:3 that ye are in our hearts to *d*
Phil 1:21 live is Christ, and to *d* is gain
Heb 7:8 here men that *d* receive tithes
Heb 9:27 is appointed unto men once to *d*
Rev 3:2 which remain, that are ready to *d*
Rev 9:6 and shall desire to *d*, and death
Rev 14:13 Blessed are the dead which *d* in

## DIED

Gen 5:5 and thirty years: and he *d*
Gen 5:8 and twelve years: and he *d*
Gen 5:11 and five years: and he *d*
Gen 5:14 and ten years: and he *d*
Gen 5:17 and five years: and he *d*
Gen 5:20 and two years: and he *d*.
Gen 5:27 and nine years: and he *d*
Gen 5:31 and seven years: and he *d*
Gen 7:21 all flesh *d* that moved upon the
Gen 7:22 all that was in the dry land, *d*
Gen 9:29 and fifty years: and he *d*
Gen 11:28 Haran *d* before his father Terah
Gen 11:32 and Terah *d* in Haran
Gen 23:2 And Sarah *d* in Kirjath-arba
Gen 25:8 *d* in a good old age, an old man,
Gen 25:17 and he gave up the ghost and *d*
Gen 25:18 he *d* in the presence of all his
Gen 35:8 But Deborah Rebekah's nurse *d*
Gen 35:18 (for she *d*) that she called his
Gen 35:19 And Rachel *d*, and was buried in the
Gen 35:29 And Isaac gave up the ghost, and *d*
Gen 36:33 And Bela *d*, and Jobab the son of
Gen 36:34 And Jobab *d*, and Husham of the land
Gen 36:35 And Husham *d*, and Hadad the son of
Gen 36:36 Hadad *d*, and Samlah of Masrekah
Gen 36:37 And Samlah *d*, and Saul of Rehoboth
Gen 36:38 And Saul *d*, and Baal-hanan the son
Gen 36:39 And Baal-hanan the son of Achbor *d*
Gen 38:12 daughter of Shuah Judah's wife *d*
Gen 46:12 Onan *d* in the land of Canaan
Gen 48:7 Rachel *d* by me in the land of
Gen 50:16 father did command before he *d*
Gen 50:26 So Joseph *d*, being an hundred and
Ex 1:6 And Joseph *d*, and all his brethren,
Ex 2:23 of time, that the king of Egypt *d*
Ex 7:21 the fish that was in the river *d*
Ex 8:13 the frogs *d* out of the houses,
Ex 9:6 and all the cattle of Egypt *d*
Ex 9:6 the children of Israel *d* not one
Ex 16:3 Would to God we had *d* by the hand
Lev 10:2 them, and they *d* before the LORD
Lev 16:1 offered before the LORD, and *d*
Lev 17:15 eateth that which *d* of itself
Num 3:4 Abihu *d* before the LORD, when
Num 14:2 we had *d* in the land of Egypt
Num 14:2 God we had *d* in this wilderness
Num 14:37 *d* by the plague before the LORD
Num 15:36 stoned him with stones, and he *d*
Num 16:49 Now they that *d* in the plague
Num 16:49 beside them that *d* about the
Num 20:1 and Miriam *d* there, and was buried
Num 20:3 Would God that we had *d* when our
Num 20:3 our brethren *d* before the LORD
Num 20:28 Aaron *d* there in the top of the
Num 21:6 and much people of Israel *d*
Num 25:9 those that *d* in the plague were
Num 26:10 with Korah, when that company *d*
Num 26:11 the children of Korah *d* not
Num 26:19 Onan *d* in the land of Canaan
Num 26:61 And Nadab and Abihu *d*, when they
Num 27:3 Our father *d* in the wilderness,
Num 27:3 but *d* in his own sin, and had no
Num 33:38 *d* there, in the fortieth year
Num 33:39 years old when he *d* in mount Hor
Deut 10:6 there Aaron *d*, and there he was
Deut 32:50 Aaron thy brother *d* in mount Hor
Deut 34:5 LORD *d* there in the land of Moab
Deut 34:7 and twenty years old when he *d*
Josh 5:4 *d* in the wilderness by the way,
Josh 10:11 upon them unto Azekah, and they *d*
Josh 10:11 they were more which *d* with
Josh 24:29 Nun, the servant of the LORD, *d*
Josh 24:33 And Eleazar the son of Aaron *d*
Judg 1:7 him to Jerusalem, and there he *d*
Judg 2:8 Nun, the servant of the LORD, *d*
Judg 2:21 which Joshua left when he *d*
Judg 3:11 And Othniel the son of Kenaz *d*
Judg 4:21 asleep and weary. So he *d*
Judg 8:32 son of Joash *d* in a good old age
Judg 9:49 of the tower of Shechem *d* also
Judg 9:54 man thrust him through, and he *d*
Judg 10:2 twenty and three years, and *d*
Judg 10:5 And Jair *d*, and was buried in Camon
Judg 12:7 Then *d* Jephthah the Gileadite, and
Judg 12:10 Then *d* Ibzan, and was buried at
Judg 12:12 And Elon the Zebulonite *d*, and was
Judg 12:15 son of Hillel the Pirathonite *d*
Ruth 1:3 And Elimelech Naomi's husband *d*
Ruth 1:5 Chilion *d* also both of them
1Sa 4:18 gate, and his neck brake, and he *d*
1Sa 5:12 the men that *d* not were smitten
1Sa 14:45 rescued Jonathan, that he *d* not
1Sa 25:1 And Samuel *d*; and all the Israelites
1Sa 25:37 that his heart *d* within him
1Sa 25:38 the LORD smote Nabal, that he *d*
1Sa 31:5 upon his sword, and *d* with him
1Sa 31:6 So Saul *d*, and his three sons, and
2Sa 1:15 And he smote him that he *d*
2Sa 2:23 there, and *d* in the same place
2Sa 2:23 Asahel fell down and *d* stood still
2Sa 2:31 three hundred and threescore men *d*
2Sa 3:27 under the fifth rib, that he *d*
2Sa 3:33 and said, *D* Abner as a fool dieth
2Sa 6:7 there he *d* by the ark of God
2Sa 10:1 king of the children of Ammon *d*
2Sa 10:18 of their host, who *d* there
2Sa 11:17 and Uriah the Hittite *d* also
2Sa 11:21 the wall, that he *d* in Thebez
2Sa 12:18 the seventh day, that the child *d*
2Sa 17:23 in order, and hanged himself, and *d*
2Sa 18:33 would God I had *d* for thee
2Sa 19:6 lived, and all we had *d* this day
2Sa 20:10 him not again; and he *d*
2Sa 24:15 there *d* of the people from Dan
1Kin 2:25 and he fell upon him that he *d*
1Kin 2:46 out, and fell upon him, that he *d*
1Kin 3:19 this woman's child *d* in the night
1Kin 12:18 stoned him with stones, that he *d*
1Kin 14:17 of the door, the child *d*
1Kin 16:18 house over him with fire, and *d*
1Kin 16:22 so Tibni *d*, and Omri reigned
1Kin 21:13 stoned him with stones, that he *d*
1Kin 22:35 against the Syrians, and *d* at even
1Kin 22:37 So the king *d*, and was brought to
2Kin 1:17 So he *d* according to the word of
2Kin 4:20 on her knees till noon, and then *d*
2Kin 7:17 upon him in the gate, and he *d*
2Kin 7:20 upon him in the gate, and he *d*
2Kin 8:15 it on his face, so that he *d*
2Kin 9:27 And he fled to Megiddo, and *d* there
2Kin 12:21 his servants, smote him, and he *d*
2Kin 13:14 sick of his sickness whereof he *d*
2Kin 13:20 And Elisha *d*, and they buried him
2Kin 13:24 So Hazael king of Syria *d*
2Kin 23:34 and he came to Egypt, and *d* there
2Kin 25:25 him, and smote Gedaliah, that he *d*
1Chr 1:51 Hadad *d* also. And the dukes
1Chr 2:30 but Seled *d* without children
1Chr 2:32 Jether *d* without children
1Chr 10:5 fell likewise on the sword, and *d*
1Chr 10:6 So Saul *d*, and his three sons
1Chr 10:6 and all his house *d* together
1Chr 10:13 So Saul *d* for his transgression
1Chr 13:10 and there he *d* before God
1Chr 19:1 king of the children of Ammon *d*
1Chr 23:22 And Eleazar *d*, and had no sons, but
1Chr 24:2 Abihu *d* before their father, and
1Chr 29:28 he *d* in a good old age, full of
2Chr 10:18 stoned him with stones, that he *d*
2Chr 13:20 and the LORD struck him, and he *d*
2Chr 16:13 *d* in the one and fortieth year of
2Chr 18:34 time of the sun going down he *d*
2Chr 21:19 so he *d* of sore diseases
2Chr 24:15 and was full of days when he *d*
2Chr 24:15 thirty years old was he when he *d*
2Chr 24:22 And when he *d*, he said, The LORD
2Chr 24:25 and slew him on his bed, and he *d*
2Chr 35:24 brought him to Jerusalem, and he *d*
Job 3:11 Why *d* I not from the womb
Job 42:17 So Job *d*, being old and full of
Is 6:1 *d* I saw also the Lord sitting
Is 14:28 that king Ahaz *d* was this burden
Jer 28:17 So Hananiah the prophet *d* the
Eze 11:13 Pelatiah the son of Benaiah *d*
Eze 24:18 and at even my wife *d*
Hos 13:1 when he offended in Baal, he *d*
Mt 22:27 And last of all the woman *d* also
Mk 12:21 And the second took her, and *d*
Mk 12:22 last of all the woman *d* also
Lk 16:22 came to pass, that the beggar *d*
Lk 16:22 the rich man also *d*, and was
Lk 20:29 a wife, and *d* without children
Lk 20:30 her to wife, and he *d* childless
Lk 20:31 and they left no children, and *d*
Lk 20:32 Last of all the woman *d* also
Jn 11:21 been here, my brother had not *d*
Jn 11:32 been here, my brother had not *d*
Jn 11:37 even this man should not have *d*
Acts 7:15 Jacob went down into Egypt, and *d*
Acts 9:37 days, that she was sick, and *d*
Rom 5:6 due time Christ *d* for the ungodly
Rom 5:8 were yet sinners, Christ *d* for us

Rom 6:10 that he *d*, he *d* unto sin once
Rom 7:9 came, sin revived, and I *d*
Rom 8:34 It is Christ that *d*, yea rather,
Rom 14:9 For to this end Christ both *d*
Rom 14:15 with thy meat, for whom Christ *d*
1Cor 8:11 brother perish, for whom Christ *d*
1Cor 15:3 how that Christ *d* for our sins
2Cor 5:14 thus judge, that if one *d* for all
2Cor 5:15 And that he *d* for all, that they
2Cor 5:15 but unto him which *d* for them
1Th 4:14 For if we believe that Jesus *d*
1Th 5:10 Who *d* for us, that, whether we
Heb 10:28 law *d* without mercy under two or
Heb 11:13 These all *d* in faith, not having
Heb 11:22 By faith Joseph, when he *d*
Rev 8:9 were in the sea, and had life, *d*
Rev 8:11 many men *d* of the waters, because
Rev 16:3 and every living soul *d* in the sea

**DIFFERENCE**
Ex 11:7 put a *d* between the Egyptians
Lev 10:10 And that ye may put *d* between holy
Lev 11:47 To make a *d* between the unclean
Lev 20:25 put *d* between clean beasts
Eze 22:26 have put no *d* between the holy
Eze 22:26 they shewed *d* between the unclean
Eze 44:23 my people the *d* between the holy
Acts 15:9 put no *d* between us and them,
Rom 3:22 for there is no *d*
Rom 10:12 For there is no *d* between the Jew
1Cor 7:34 There is *d* also between a wife and
Jude 22 some have compassion, making a *d*

**DIG**
Ex 21:33 a pit, or if a man shall *d* a pit
Deut 8:9 whose hills thou mayest *d* brass
Deut 23:13 abroad, thou shalt *d* therewith
Job 3:21 *d* for it more than for hid
Job 6:27 ye *d* a pit for your friend
Job 11:18 yea, thou shalt *d* about thee
Job 24:16 In the dark they *d* through houses
Eze 8:8 me, Son of man, *d* now in the wall
Eze 12:5 *D* thou through the wall in their
Eze 12:12 they shall *d* through the wall to
Amos 9:2 Though they *d* into hell, thence
Lk 13:8 also, till I shall *d* about it
Lk 16:3 I cannot *d*

**DIGGED**
Gen 21:30 unto me, that I have *d* this well
Gen 26:15 had *d* in the days of Abraham his
Gen 26:18 Isaac *d* again the wells of water,
Gen 26:18 which they had *d* in the days of
Gen 26:19 Isaac's servants *d* in the valley
Gen 26:21 they *d* another well, and strove
Gen 26:22 from thence, and *d* another well
Gen 26:25 there Isaac's servants *d* a well
Gen 26:32 the well which they had *d*
Gen 49:6 their selfwill they *d* down a wall
Gen 50:5 in my grave which I have *d* for me
Ex 7:24 all the Egyptians *d* round about
Num 21:18 The princes *d* the well
Num 21:18 the nobles of the people *d* it
Deut 6:11 thou filledst not, and wells *d*
2Kin 19:24 I have *d* and drunk strange waters,
2Chr 26:10 in the desert, and *d* many wells
Neh 9:25 houses full of all goods, wells *d*
Ps 7:15 *d* it, and is fallen into the ditch
Ps 35:7 cause they have *d* for my soul
Ps 57:6 they have *d* a pit before me, into
Ps 94:13 until the pit be *d* for the wicked
Ps 119:85 The proud have *d* pits for me
Is 5:6 it shall not be pruned, nor *d*
Is 7:25 that shall be *d* with the mattock
Is 37:25 I have *d*, and drunk water
Is 51:1 hole of the pit whence ye are *d*
Jer 13:7 Then I went to Euphrates, and *d*
Jer 18:20 for they have *d* a pit for my soul
Jer 18:22 for they have *d* a pit to take me,
Eze 8:8 when I had *d* in the wall, behold
Eze 12:7 in the even I *d* through the wall
Mt 21:33 *d* a winepress in it, and built a
Mt 25:18 *d* in the earth, and hid his lord's
Mk 12:1 *d* a place for the winefat, and
Lk 6:48 *d* deep, and laid the foundation on
Rom 11:3 prophets, and *d* down thine altars

**DIGNITY**
Gen 49:3 my strength, the excellency of *d*
Est 6:3 *d* hath been done to Mordecai for
Eccl 10:6 Folly is set in great *d*, and the
Hab 1:7 and their *d* shall proceed of

**DIKLAH** *(dik'-lah) A son of Joktan.*
Gen 10:27 And Hadoram, and Uzal, and *D*
1Chr 1:21 Hadoram also, and Uzal, and *D*

**DILEAN** *(dil'-e-an) A city in Judah.*
Josh 15:38 And *D*, and Mizpeh, and Joktheel,

**DILIGENCE**
Prov 4:23 Keep thy heart with all *d*
Lk 12:58 give *d* that thou mayest be
Rom 12:8 he that ruleth, with *d*
2Cor 8:7 and knowledge, and in all *d*
2Ti 4:9 Do thy *d* to come shortly unto me
2Ti 4:21 Do thy *d* to come before winter
Heb 6:11 one of you do shew the same *d* to
2Pet 1:5 And beside this, giving all *d*
2Pet 1:10 give *d* to make your calling and
Jude 3 when I gave all *d* to write unto

**DILIGENT**
Deut 19:18 judges shall make *d* inquisition
Josh 22:5 But take *d* heed to do the
Ps 64:6 they accomplish a *d* search
Ps 77:6 and my spirit made *d* search
Prov 10:4 but the hand of the *d* maketh rich
Prov 12:24 The hand of the *d* shall bear rule
Prov 12:27 substance of a *d* man is precious
Prov 13:4 soul of the *d* shall be made fat
Prov 21:5 The thoughts of the *d* tend only
Prov 22:29 thou a man *d* in his business
Prov 27:23 Be thou *d* to know the state of
2Cor 8:22 proved *d* in many things
2Cor 8:22 but now much more *d*
Titus 3:12 be *d* to come unto me to Nicopolis
2Pet 3:14 be *d* that ye may be found of him

**DILIGENTLY**
Ex 15:26 If thou wilt *d* hearken to the
Lev 10:16 Moses *d* sought the goat of the
Deut 4:9 to thyself, and keep thy soul *d*
Deut 6:7 teach them *d* unto thy children
Deut 6:17 Ye shall *d* keep the commandments
Deut 11:13 if ye shall hearken *d* unto my
Deut 11:22 For if ye shall *d* keep all these
Deut 13:14 enquire, and make search, and ask *d*
Deut 17:4 hast heard of it, and enquired *d*
Deut 24:8 of leprosy, that thou observe *d*
Deut 28:1 if thou shalt hearken *d* unto the
1Kin 20:33 Now the men did *d* observe whether
Ezr 7:23 let it be *d* done for the house of
Job 13:17 Hear *d* my speech, and my
Job 21:2 Hear *d* my speech, and let this be
Ps 37:10 thou shalt *d* consider his place,
Ps 119:4 us to keep thy precepts *d*
Prov 7:15 *d* to seek thy face, and I have
Prov 11:27 He that *d* seeketh good procureth
Prov 23:1 consider *d* what is before thee
Is 21:7 he hearkened *d* with much heed
Is 55:2 hearken *d* unto me, and eat ye that
Jer 2:10 and send unto Kedar, and consider *d*
Jer 12:16 if they will *d* learn the ways of
Jer 17:24 if ye *d* hearken unto me, saith
Zec 6:15 if ye will *d* obey the voice of
Mt 2:7 enquired of them *d* what time the
Mt 2:8 search *d* for the young child
Mt 2:16 he had *d* enquired of the wise men
Lk 15:8 house, and seek *d* till she find it
Acts 18:25 taught *d* the things of the Lord,
1Ti 5:10 if she have *d* followed every good
2Ti 1:17 in Rome, he sought me out very *d*
Titus 3:13 and Apollos on their journey *d*
Heb 11:6 rewarder of them that *d* seek him
Heb 12:15 Looking *d* lest any man fail of
1Pet 1:10 have enquired and searched *d*

**DIM**
Gen 27:1 Isaac was old, and his eyes were *d*
Gen 48:10 the eyes of Israel were *d* for age
Deut 34:7 his eye was not *d*, nor his
1Sa 3:2 place, and his eyes began to wax *d*
1Sa 4:15 and his eyes were *d*, that he could
Job 17:7 Mine eye also is *d* by reason of
Is 32:3 of them that see shall not be *d*
Lam 4:1 How is the gold become *d*
Lam 5:17 for these things our eyes are *d*

**DIMINISH**
Ex 5:8 ye shall not *d* ought thereof
Ex 21:10 duty of marriage, shall he not *d*
Lev 25:16 thou shalt *d* the price of it
Deut 4:2 neither shall ye *d* ought from it
Deut 12:32 not add thereto, nor *d* from it
Jer 26:2 *d* not a word
Eze 5:11 therefore will I also *d* thee
Eze 29:15 for I will *d* them, that they

**DIMINISHED**
Ex 5:11 not ought of your work shall be *d*
Prov 13:11 gotten by vanity shall be *d*
Is 21:17 the children of Kedar, shall be *d*
Jer 29:6 may be increased there, and not *d*
Eze 16:27 have *d* thine ordinary food, and

**DIMNAH** *(dim'-nah) A Levitical city in Zebulun.*
Josh 21:35 *D* with her suburbs, Nahalal with

**DIMON** *(di'-mon)* See DIBON, DIMONAH. *A Moabite city.*
Is 15:9 For the waters of *D* shall be full
Is 15:9 for I will bring more upon *D*

**DIMONAH** *(di-mo'-nah)* See DIMON. *A city in Judah.*
Josh 15:22 And Kinah, and *D*, and Adadah,

**DINAH** See DINAH'S. *A daughter of Jacob.*
Gen 30:21 a daughter, and called her name *D*
Gen 34:1 *D* the daughter of Leah, which she
Gen 34:3 his soul clave unto *D* the
Gen 34:5 he had defiled *D* his daughter
Gen 34:13 he had defiled *D* their sister
Gen 34:26 took *D* out of Shechem's house, and
Gen 46:15 Padan-aram, with his daughter *D*

**DINAH'S**
Gen 34:25 *D* brethren, took each man his

**DINAITES** *(di'-na-ites) Foreign settlers in Samaria.*
Ezr 4:9 the *D*, the Apharsathchites, the

**DINHABAH** *(din'-ha-bah) Capital of Edom.*
Gen 36:32 and the name of his city was *D*
1Chr 1:43 and the name of his city was *D*

**DIONYSIUS** *(di-on-ish'-yus) An Athenian convert of Paul.*
Acts 17:34 the which was *D* the Areopagite

**DIOTREPHES** *(di-ot'-re-feez) A believer condemned by John.*
3Jn 9 but *D*, who loveth to have the

**DIP**
Ex 12:22 *d* it in the blood that is in the
Lev 4:6 the priest shall *d* his finger in
Lev 4:17 the priest shall *d* his finger in
Lev 14:6 and the hyssop, and shall *d* them
Lev 14:16 the priest shall *d* his right
Lev 14:51 *d* them in the blood of the slain
Num 19:18 *d* it in the water, and sprinkle it
Deut 33:24 let him *d* his foot in oil
Ruth 2:14 *d* thy morsel in the vinegar
Lk 16:24 that he may *d* the tip of his

**DIPPED**
Gen 37:31 goats, and *d* the coat in the blood
Lev 9:9 he *d* his finger in the blood, and
Josh 3:15 were *d* in the brim of the water
1Sa 14:27 *d* it in an honeycomb, and put his
2Kin 5:14 *d* himself seven times in Jordan,
2Kin 8:15 *d* it in water, and spread it on
Ps 68:23 That thy foot may be *d* in the
Jn 13:26 give a sop, when I have *d* it
Jn 13:26 And when he had *d* the sop, he gave
Rev 19:13 clothed with a vesture *d* in blood

**DIRECT**
Gen 46:28 to *d* his face unto Goshen
Ps 5:3 will I *d* my prayer unto thee
Prov 3:6 him, and he shall *d* thy paths
Prov 11:5 of the perfect shall *d* his way
Eccl 10:10 but wisdom is profitable to *d*
Is 45:13 and I will *d* all his ways
Is 61:8 I will *d* their work in truth, and
Jer 10:23 man that walketh to *d* his steps
1Th 3:11 Jesus Christ, *d* our way unto you
2Th 3:5 the Lord *d* your hearts into the

**DISALLOWED**
Num 30:5 her, because her father *d* her
Num 30:8 But if her husband *d* her on the
Num 30:11 his peace at her, and *d* her not
1Pet 2:4 *d* indeed of men, but chosen of
1Pet 2:7 the stone which the builders *d*

**DISCERN**
Gen 31:32 before our brethren *d* thou what
Gen 38:25 and she said, *D*, I pray thee,
2Sa 14:17 so is my lord the king to *d* good

| | |
|---|---|
| 2Sa 19:35 | can I *d* between good and evil |
| 1Kin 3:9 | that I may *d* between good and bad |
| 1Kin 3:11 | understanding to *d* judgment |
| Ezr 3:13 | So that the people could not *d* |
| Job 4:16 | but I could not *d* the form |
| Job 6:30 | cannot my taste *d* perverse things |
| Eze 44:23 | cause them to *d* between the |
| Jonah 4:11 | cannot *d* between their right hand |
| Mal 3:18 | *d* between the righteous and the |
| Mt 16:3 | ye can *d* the face of the sky |
| Mt 16:3 | but can ye not *d* the signs of the |
| Lk 12:56 | ye can *d* the face of the sky and |
| Lk 12:56 | is it that ye do not *d* this time |
| Heb 5:14 | senses exercised to *d* both good |

## DISCERNED

| | |
|---|---|
| Gen 27:23 | he *d* him not, because his hands |
| 1Kin 20:41 | the king of Israel *d* him that he |
| Prov 7:7 | I *d* among the youths, a young man |
| 1Cor 2:14 | because they are spiritually *d* |

## DISCIPLE

| | |
|---|---|
| Mt 10:24 | The *d* is not above his master, |
| Mt 10:25 | It is enough for the *d* that he be |
| Mt 10:42 | water only in the name of a *d* |
| Mt 27:57 | who also himself was Jesus' *d* |
| Lk 6:40 | The *d* is not above his master |
| Lk 14:26 | own life also, he cannot be my *d* |
| Lk 14:27 | and come after me, cannot be my *d* |
| Lk 14:33 | that he hath, he cannot be my *d* |
| Jn 9:28 | him, and said, Thou art his *d* |
| Jn 18:15 | Jesus, and so did another *d* |
| Jn 18:15 | that *d* was known unto the high |
| Jn 18:16 | Then went out that other *d* |
| Jn 19:26 | the *d* standing by, whom he loved, |
| Jn 19:27 | Then saith he to the *d*, Behold |
| Jn 19:27 | from that hour that *d* took her |
| Jn 19:38 | being a *d* of Jesus, but secretly |
| Jn 20:2 | to Simon Peter, and to the other *d* |
| Jn 20:3 | went forth, and that other *d* |
| Jn 20:4 | the other *d* did outrun Peter, and |
| Jn 20:8 | Then went in also that other *d* |
| Jn 21:7 | Therefore that *d* whom Jesus loved |
| Jn 21:20 | seeth the *d* whom Jesus loved |
| Jn 21:23 | that that *d* should not die |
| Jn 21:24 | This is the *d* which testifieth of |
| Acts 9:10 | there was a certain *d* at Damascus |
| Acts 9:26 | and believed not that he was a *d* |
| Acts 9:36 | Joppa a certain *d* named Tabitha |
| Acts 16:1 | and, behold, a certain *d* was there |
| Acts 21:16 | one Mnason of Cyprus, an old *d* |

## DISCIPLES

| | |
|---|---|
| Is 8:16 | seal the law among my *d* |
| Mt 5:1 | he was set, his *d* came unto him |
| Mt 8:21 | And another of his *d* said unto him |
| Mt 8:23 | into a ship, his *d* followed him |
| Mt 8:25 | his *d* came to him, and awoke him, |
| Mt 9:10 | and sat down with him and his *d* |
| Mt 9:11 | saw it, they said unto his *d* |
| Mt 9:14 | Then came to him the *d* of John |
| Mt 9:14 | fast oft, but thy *d* fast not |
| Mt 9:19 | and followed him, and so did his *d* |
| Mt 9:37 | Then saith he unto his *d*, The |
| Mt 10:1 | had called unto him his twelve *d* |
| Mt 11:1 | an end of commanding his twelve *d* |
| Mt 11:2 | of Christ, he sent two of his *d* |
| Mt 12:1 | his *d* were an hungred, and began |
| Mt 12:2 | thy *d* do that which is not lawful |
| Mt 12:49 | forth his hand toward his *d* |
| Mt 13:10 | the *d* came, and said unto him, Why |
| Mt 13:36 | his *d* came unto him, saying, |
| Mt 14:12 | his *d* came, and took up the body, |
| Mt 14:15 | his *d* came to him, saying, This |
| Mt 14:19 | and gave the loaves to his *d* |
| Mt 14:19 | and the *d* to the multitude |
| Mt 14:22 | his *d* to get into a ship, and to |
| Mt 14:26 | when the *d* saw him walking on the |
| Mt 15:2 | Why do thy *d* transgress the |
| Mt 15:12 | Then came his *d*, and said unto him |
| Mt 15:23 | his *d* came and besought him, |
| Mt 15:32 | Then Jesus called his *d* unto him |
| Mt 15:33 | his *d* say unto him, Whence should |
| Mt 15:36 | and brake them, and gave to his *d* |
| Mt 15:36 | and the *d* to the multitude |
| Mt 16:5 | when his *d* were come to the other |
| Mt 16:13 | Caesarea Philippi, he asked his *d* |
| Mt 16:20 | Then charged he his *d* that they |
| Mt 16:21 | began Jesus to shew unto his *d* |
| Mt 16:24 | Then said Jesus unto his *d* |
| Mt 17:6 | And when the *d* heard it, they fell |
| Mt 17:10 | his *d* asked him, saying, Why then |
| Mt 17:13 | Then the *d* understood that he |
| Mt 17:16 | And I brought him to thy *d* |
| Mt 17:19 | Then came the *d* to Jesus apart, |
| Mt 18:1 | same time came the *d* unto Jesus |
| Mt 19:10 | His *d* say unto him, If the case |
| Mt 19:13 | and the *d* rebuked them |
| Mt 19:23 | Then said Jesus unto his *d* |
| Mt 19:25 | When his *d* heard it, they were |
| Mt 20:17 | the twelve *d* apart in the way |
| Mt 21:1 | of Olives, then sent Jesus two *d* |
| Mt 21:6 | the *d* went, and did as Jesus |
| Mt 21:20 | And when the *d* saw it, they |
| Mt 22:16 | him their *d* with the Herodians |
| Mt 23:1 | to the multitude, and to his *d* |
| Mt 24:1 | his *d* came to him for to shew him |
| Mt 24:3 | the *d* came unto him privately, |
| Mt 26:1 | these sayings, he said unto his *d* |
| Mt 26:8 | But when his *d* saw it, they had |
| Mt 26:17 | bread the *d* came to Jesus |
| Mt 26:18 | passover at thy house with my *d* |
| Mt 26:19 | the *d* did as Jesus had appointed |
| Mt 26:26 | and brake it, and gave it to the *d* |
| Mt 26:35 | Likewise also said all the *d* |
| Mt 26:36 | Gethsemane, and saith unto the *d* |
| Mt 26:40 | And he cometh unto the *d*, and |
| Mt 26:45 | Then cometh he to his *d*, and saith |
| Mt 26:56 | Then all the *d* forsook him |
| Mt 27:64 | lest his *d* come by night, and |
| Mt 28:7 | tell his *d* that he is risen from |
| Mt 28:8 | and did run to bring his *d* word |
| Mt 28:9 | And as they went to tell his *d* |
| Mt 28:13 | His *d* came by night, and stole him |
| Mt 28:16 | Then the eleven *d* went away into |
| Mk 2:15 | also together with Jesus and his *d* |
| Mk 2:16 | and sinners, they said unto his *d* |
| Mk 2:18 | the *d* of John and of the Pharisees |
| Mk 2:18 | unto him, Why do the *d* of John |
| Mk 2:18 | fast, but thy *d* fast not |
| Mk 2:23 | his *d* began, as they went, to |
| Mk 3:7 | himself with his *d* to the sea |
| Mk 3:9 | And he spake to his *d*, that a |
| Mk 4:34 | he expounded all things to his *d* |
| Mk 5:31 | his *d* said unto him, Thou seest |
| Mk 6:1 | and his *d* follow him |
| Mk 6:29 | when his *d* heard of it, they came |
| Mk 6:35 | his *d* came unto him, and said, |
| Mk 6:41 | gave them to his *d* to set before |
| Mk 6:45 | his *d* to get into the ship |
| Mk 7:2 | of his *d* eat bread with defiled |
| Mk 7:5 | Why walk not thy *d* according to |
| Mk 7:17 | his *d* asked him concerning the |
| Mk 8:1 | eat, Jesus called his *d* unto him |
| Mk 8:4 | his *d* answered him, From whence |
| Mk 8:6 | gave to his *d* to set before them |
| Mk 8:10 | he entered into a ship with his *d* |
| Mk 8:14 | Now the *d* had forgotten to take |
| Mk 8:27 | And Jesus went out, and his *d* |
| Mk 8:27 | and by the way he asked his *d* |
| Mk 8:33 | turned about and looked on his *d* |
| Mk 8:34 | people unto him with his *d* also |
| Mk 9:14 | And when he came to his *d*, he saw |
| Mk 9:18 | I spake to thy *d* that they should |
| Mk 9:28 | his *d* asked him privately, Why |
| Mk 9:31 | For he taught his *d*, and said unto |
| Mk 10:10 | in the house his *d* asked him |
| Mk 10:13 | his *d* rebuked those that brought |
| Mk 10:23 | round about, and saith unto his *d* |
| Mk 10:24 | the *d* were astonished at his |
| Mk 10:46 | he went out of Jericho with his *d* |
| Mk 11:1 | he sendeth forth two of his *d* |
| Mk 11:14 | And his *d* heard it |
| Mk 12:43 | And he called unto him his *d* |
| Mk 13:1 | one of his *d* saith unto him, |
| Mk 14:12 | his *d* said unto him, Where wilt |
| Mk 14:13 | And he sendeth forth two of his *d* |
| Mk 14:14 | shall eat the passover with my *d* |
| Mk 14:16 | his *d* went forth, and came into |
| Mk 14:32 | and he saith to his *d*, Sit ye here |
| Mk 16:7 | But go your way, tell his *d* |
| Lk 5:30 | Pharisees murmured against his *d* |
| Lk 5:33 | Why do the *d* of John fast often, |
| Lk 5:33 | likewise the *d* of the Pharisees |
| Lk 6:1 | his *d* plucked the ears of corn, |
| Lk 6:13 | was day, he called unto him his *d* |
| Lk 6:17 | plain, and the company of his *d* |
| Lk 6:20 | And he lifted up his eyes on his *d* |
| Lk 7:11 | many of his *d* went with him, and |
| Lk 7:18 | the *d* of John shewed him of all |
| Lk 7:19 | two of his *d* sent them to Jesus |
| Lk 8:9 | his *d* asked him, saying, What |
| Lk 8:22 | he went into a ship with his *d* |
| Lk 9:1 | he called his twelve *d* together |
| Lk 9:14 | And he said to his *d*, Make them |
| Lk 9:16 | gave to the *d* to set before the |
| Lk 9:18 | praying, his *d* were with him |
| Lk 9:40 | I besought thy *d* to cast him out |
| Lk 9:43 | Jesus did, he said unto his *d* |
| Lk 9:54 | And when his *d* James and John saw |
| Lk 10:23 | And he turned him unto his *d* |
| Lk 11:1 | one of his *d* said unto him, Lord, |
| Lk 11:1 | pray, as John also taught his *d* |
| Lk 12:1 | to say unto his *d* first of all |
| Lk 12:22 | And he said unto his *d*, Therefore |
| Lk 16:1 | And he said also unto his *d* |
| Lk 17:1 | Then said he unto the *d*, It is |
| Lk 17:22 | And he said unto the *d*, The days |
| Lk 18:15 | but when his *d* saw it, they |
| Lk 19:29 | of Olives, he sent two of his *d* |
| Lk 19:37 | of the *d* began to rejoice |
| Lk 19:39 | unto him, Master, rebuke thy *d* |
| Lk 20:45 | all the people he said unto his *d* |
| Lk 22:11 | shall eat the passover with my *d* |
| Lk 22:39 | and his *d* also followed him |
| Lk 22:45 | from prayer, and was come to his *d* |
| Jn 1:35 | after John stood, and two of his *d* |
| Jn 1:37 | the two *d* heard him speak, and |
| Jn 2:2 | both Jesus was called, and his *d* |
| Jn 2:11 | and his *d* believed on him |
| Jn 2:12 | mother, and his brethren, and his *d* |
| Jn 2:17 | his *d* remembered that it was |
| Jn 2:22 | his *d* remembered that he had said |
| Jn 3:22 | his *d* into the land of Judaea |
| Jn 3:25 | question between some of John's *d* |
| Jn 4:1 | made and baptized more *d* than John |
| Jn 4:2 | himself baptized not, but his *d* |
| Jn 4:8 | (For his *d* were gone away unto |
| Jn 4:27 | And upon this came his *d*, and |
| Jn 4:31 | the mean while his *d* prayed him |
| Jn 4:33 | said the *d* one to another |
| Jn 6:3 | and there he sat with his *d* |
| Jn 6:8 | One of his *d*, Andrew, Simon |
| Jn 6:11 | thanks, he distributed to the *d* |
| Jn 6:11 | the *d* to them that were set down |
| Jn 6:12 | were filled, he said unto his *d* |
| Jn 6:16 | his *d* went down unto the sea, |
| Jn 6:22 | one whereinto his *d* were entered |
| Jn 6:22 | went not with his *d* into the boat |
| Jn 6:22 | but that his *d* were gone away |
| Jn 6:24 | was not there, neither his *d* |
| Jn 6:60 | Many therefore of his *d*, when |
| Jn 6:61 | himself that his *d* murmured at it |
| Jn 6:66 | that time many of his *d* went back |
| Jn 7:3 | that thy *d* also may see the works |
| Jn 8:31 | my word, then are ye my *d* indeed |
| Jn 9:2 | his *d* asked him, saying, Master, |
| Jn 9:27 | will ye also be his *d* |
| Jn 9:28 | but we are Moses' *d* |
| Jn 11:7 | Then after that saith he to his *d* |
| Jn 11:8 | His *d* say unto him, Master, the |
| Jn 11:12 | Then said his *d*, Lord, if he |
| Jn 11:54 | and there continued with his *d* |
| Jn 12:4 | Then saith one of his *d*, Judas |
| Jn 12:16 | understood not his *d* at the first |
| Jn 13:22 | Then the *d* looked one on another, |
| Jn 13:23 | on Jesus' bosom one of his *d* |
| Jn 13:35 | all men know that ye are my *d* |
| Jn 15:8 | so shall ye be my *d* |
| Jn 16:17 | some of his *d* among themselves |
| Jn 16:29 | His *d* said unto him, Lo, now |
| Jn 18:1 | with his *d* over the brook Cedron |
| Jn 18:1 | the which he entered, and his *d* |
| Jn 18:2 | resorted thither with his *d* |
| Jn 18:17 | not thou also one of this man's *d* |
| Jn 18:19 | priest then asked Jesus of his *d* |
| Jn 18:25 | Art not thou also one of his *d* |
| Jn 20:10 | Then the *d* went away again unto |
| Jn 20:18 | told the *d* that she had seen the |
| Jn 20:19 | the doors were shut where the *d* |
| Jn 20:20 | Then were the *d* glad, when they |
| Jn 20:25 | The other *d* therefore said unto |
| Jn 20:26 | days again his *d* were within |
| Jn 20:30 | Jesus in the presence of his *d* |
| Jn 21:1 | to the *d* at the sea of Tiberias |
| Jn 21:2 | of Zebedee, and two other of his *d* |
| Jn 21:4 | but the *d* knew not that it was |
| Jn 21:8 | the other *d* came in a little ship |
| Jn 21:12 | none of the *d* durst ask him, Who |
| Jn 21:14 | Jesus shewed himself to his *d* |
| Acts 1:15 | stood up in the midst of the *d* |
| Acts 6:1 | number of the *d* was multiplied |

Acts 6:2 the multitude of the *d* unto them
Acts 6:7 the number of the *d* multiplied in
Acts 9:1 against the *d* of the Lord
Acts 9:19 with the *d* which were at Damascus
Acts 9:25 Then the *d* took him by night, and
Acts 9:26 assayed to join himself to the *d*
Acts 9:38 the *d* had heard that Peter was
Acts 11:26 the *d* were called Christians
Acts 11:29 Then the *d*, every man according
Acts 13:52 the *d* were filled with joy, and
Acts 14:20 as the *d* stood round about him,
Acts 14:22 Confirming the souls of the *d*
Acts 14:28 they abode long time with the *d*
Acts 15:10 put a yoke upon the neck of the *d*
Acts 18:23 in order, strengthening all the *d*
Acts 18:27 exhorting the *d* to receive him
Acts 19:1 and finding certain *d*,
Acts 19:9 from them, and separated the *d*
Acts 19:30 people, the *d* suffered him not
Acts 20:1 Paul called unto him the *d*
Acts 20:7 when the *d* came together to break
Acts 20:30 things, to draw away *d* after them
Acts 21:4 And finding *d*, we tarried there
Acts 21:16 also certain of the *d* of Caesarea

## DISCOMFITED
Ex 17:13 And Joshua *d* Amalek and his people
Num 14:45 them, and *d* them, even unto Hormah
Josh 10:10 the LORD *d* them before Israel, and
Judg 4:15 And the LORD *d* Sisera, and all his
Judg 8:12 and Zalmunna, and *d* all the host
1Sa 7:10 upon the Philistines, and *d* them
2Sa 22:15 lightning, and *d* them
Ps 18:14 he shot out lightnings, and *d* them
Is 31:8 and his young men shall be *d*

## DISCOURAGED
Num 21:4 was much *d* because of the way
Num 32:9 they *d* the heart of the children
Deut 1:21 fear not, neither be *d*
Deut 1:28 our brethren have *d* our heart
Is 42:4 He shall not fail nor be *d*
Col 3:21 children to anger, lest they be *d*

## DISCOVER
Deut 22:30 wife, nor *d* his father's skirt
1Sa 14:8 we will *d* ourselves unto them
Job 41:13 Who can *d* the face of his garment
Prov 18:2 but that his heart may *d* itself
Prov 25:9 *d* not a secret to another
Is 3:17 the LORD will *d* their secret
Jer 13:26 Therefore will I *d* thy skirts
Lam 4:22 he will *d* thy sins
Eze 16:37 will *d* thy nakedness unto them,
Hos 2:10 now will I *d* her lewdness in the
Mic 1:6 I will *d* the foundations thereof
Nah 3:5 I will *d* thy skirts upon thy face

## DISCOVERED
Ex 20:26 thy nakedness be not *d* thereon
Lev 20:18 he hath *d* her fountain, and she
1Sa 14:11 both of them *d* themselves unto
1Sa 22:6 When Saul heard that David was *d*
2Sa 22:16 foundations of the world were *d*
Ps 18:15 of the world were *d* at thy rebuke
Is 22:8 he *d* the covering of Judah, and
Is 57:8 for thou hast *d* thyself to
Jer 13:22 thine iniquity are thy skirts *d*
Lam 2:14 they have not *d* thine iniquity,
Eze 13:14 the foundation thereof shall be *d*
Eze 16:36 thy nakedness *d* through thy
Eze 16:57 Before thy wickedness was *d*
Eze 21:24 in that your transgressions are *d*
Eze 22:10 In thee have they *d* their
Eze 23:10 These *d* her nakedness
Eze 23:18 So she *d* her whoredoms, and
Eze 23:18 her whoredoms, and *d* her nakedness
Eze 23:29 of thy whoredoms shall be *d*
Hos 7:1 the iniquity of Ephraim was *d*
Acts 21:3 Now when we had *d* Cyprus, we left
Acts 27:39 but they *d* a certain creek with a

## DISCRETION
Ps 112:5 he will guide his affairs with *d*
Prov 1:4 to the young man knowledge and *d*
Prov 2:11 *D* shall preserve thee,
Prov 3:21 keep sound wisdom and *d*
Prov 5:2 That thou mayest regard *d*
Prov 11:22 a fair woman which is without *d*
Prov 19:11 The *d* of a man deferreth his
Is 28:26 his God doth instruct him to *d*
Jer 10:12 out the heavens by his *d*

## DISEASE
2Kin 1:2 whether I shall recover of this *d*
2Kin 8:8 saying, Shall I recover of this *d*
2Kin 8:9 saying, Shall I recover of this *d*
2Chr 16:12 until his *d* was exceeding great
2Chr 16:12 yet in his *d* he sought not to the
2Chr 21:15 great sickness by *d* of thy bowels
2Chr 21:18 in his bowels with an incurable *d*
Job 30:18 of my *d* is my garment changed
Ps 38:7 are filled with a loathsome *d*
Ps 41:8 An evil *d*, say they, cleaveth
Eccl 6:2 is vanity, and it is an evil *d*
Mt 4:23 all manner of *d* among the people
Mt 9:35 and every *d* among the people
Mt 10:1 of sickness and all manner of *d*
Jn 5:4 made whole of whatsoever *d* he had

## DISEASED
1Kin 15:23 his old age he was *d* in his feet
2Chr 16:12 of his reign was *d* in his feet
Eze 34:4 The *d* have ye not strengthened,
Eze 34:21 pushed all the *d* with your horns,
Mt 9:20 which was *d* with an issue of
Mt 14:35 brought unto him all that were *d*
Mk 1:32 brought unto him all that were *d*
Jn 6:2 which he did on them that were *d*

## DISEASES
Ex 15:26 put none of these *d* upon thee
Deut 7:15 put none of the evil *d* of Egypt
Deut 28:60 upon thee all the *d* of Egypt
2Chr 21:19 so he died of sore *d*
2Chr 24:25 (for they left him in great *d*
Ps 103:3 who healeth all thy *d*
Mt 4:24 that were taken with divers *d*
Mk 1:34 many that were sick of divers *d*
Lk 4:40 divers *d* brought them unto him
Lk 6:17 him, and to be healed of their *d*
Lk 9:1 over all devils, and to cure *d*
Acts 19:12 the *d* departed from them, and the
Acts 28:9 which had *d* in the island, came,

## DISGUISED
1Sa 28:8 Saul *d* himself, and put on other
1Kin 20:38 *d* himself with ashes upon his
1Kin 22:30 And the king of Israel *d* himself
2Chr 18:29 So the king of Israel *d* himself
2Chr 35:22 but *d* himself, that he might

## DISHAN *(di'-shan)* See DISHON. *A son of Seir.*
Gen 36:21 And Dishon, and Ezer, and *D*
Gen 36:28 The children of *D* are these
Gen 36:30 Duke Dishon, duke Ezer, duke *D*
1Chr 1:38 Anah, and Dishon, and Ezar, and *D*
1Chr 1:42 The sons of *D*

## DISHON *(di'-shon)* See DISHAN.
*1. A son of Seir.*
Gen 36:21 And *D*, and Ezer, and Dishan
Gen 36:26 And these are the children of *D*
Gen 36:30 Duke *D*, duke Ezer, duke Dishan
1Chr 1:38 Shobal, and Zibeon, and Anah, and *D*
*2. A son of Anah.*
Gen 36:25 *D*, and Aholibamah the daughter of
1Chr 1:41 The sons of Anah; *D*
1Chr 1:41 And the sons of *D*

## DISHONOUR
Ezr 4:14 meet for us to see the king's *d*
Ps 35:26 *d* that magnify themselves against
Ps 69:19 and my shame, and my *d*
Ps 71:13 reproach and *d* that seek my hurt
Prov 6:33 A wound and *d* shall he get
Jn 8:49 I honour my Father, and ye do *d* me
Rom 1:24 to *d* their own bodies between
Rom 9:21 unto honour, and another unto *d*
1Cor 15:43 It is sown in *d*
2Cor 6:8 By honour and *d*, by evil report and
2Ti 2:20 and some to honour, and some to *d*

## DISMAYED
Deut 31:8 fear not, neither be *d*
Josh 1:9 be not afraid, neither be thou *d*
Josh 8:1 Fear not, neither be thou *d*
Josh 10:25 unto them, Fear not, nor be *d*
1Sa 17:11 of the Philistine, they were *d*
2Kin 19:26 were of small power, they were *d*
1Chr 22:13 dread not, nor be *d*
1Chr 28:20 fear not, nor be *d*
2Chr 20:15 Be not afraid nor *d* by reason of
2Chr 20:17 fear not, nor be *d*
2Chr 32:7 be not afraid nor *d* for the king
Is 21:3 I was *d* at the seeing of it
Is 37:27 were of small power, they were *d*
Is 41:10 be not *d*
Is 41:23 or do evil, that we may be *d*
Jer 1:17 be not *d* at their faces, lest I
Jer 8:9 wise men are ashamed, they are *d*
Jer 10:2 be not *d* at the signs of heaven
Jer 10:2 for the heathen are *d* at them
Jer 17:18 be *d*, but let not me be *d*
Jer 23:4 they shall fear no more, nor be *d*
Jer 30:10 neither be *d*, O Israel
Jer 46:5 Wherefore have I seen them *d*
Jer 46:27 O my servant Jacob, and be not *d*
Jer 48:1 Misgab is confounded and *d*
Jer 49:37 Elam to be *d* before their enemies
Jer 50:36 and they shall be *d*
Eze 2:6 nor be *d* at their looks, though
Eze 3:9 neither be *d* at their looks,
Obad 9 mighty men, O Teman, shall be *d*

## DISOBEDIENCE
Rom 5:19 For as by one man's *d* many were
2Cor 10:6 in a readiness to revenge all *d*
Eph 2:2 now worketh in the children of *d*
Eph 5:6 of God upon the children of *d*
Col 3:6 God cometh on the children of *d*
Heb 2:2 *d* received a just recompence of

## DISOBEDIENT
1Kin 13:26 who was *d* unto the word of the
Neh 9:26 Nevertheless they were *d*, and
Lk 1:17 the *d* to the wisdom of the just
Acts 26:19 I was not *d* unto the heavenly
Rom 1:30 of evil things, *d* to parents,
Rom 10:21 stretched forth my hands unto a *d*
1Ti 1:9 man, but for the lawless and *d*
2Ti 3:2 *d* to parents, unthankful, unholy,
Titus 1:16 deny him, being abominable, and *d*
Titus 3:3 also were sometimes foolish, *d*
1Pet 2:7 but unto them which be *d*, the
1Pet 2:8 stumble at the word, being *d*
1Pet 3:20 Which sometime were *d*, when once

## DISPENSATION
1Cor 9:17 a *d* of the gospel is committed
Eph 1:10 That in the *d* of the fulness of
Eph 3:2 If ye have heard of the *d* of the
Col 1:25 according to the *d* of God which

## DISPERSE
1Sa 14:34 *D* yourselves among the people, and
Prov 15:7 The lips of the wise *d* knowledge
Eze 12:15 and *d* them in the countries
Eze 20:23 *d* them through the countries
Eze 22:15 *d* thee in the countries, and will
Eze 29:12 will *d* them through the countries
Eze 30:23 will *d* them through the countries
Eze 30:26 *d* them among the countries

## DISPERSED
2Chr 11:23 *d* of all his children throughout
Est 3:8 *d* among the people in all the
Ps 112:9 He hath *d*, he hath given to the
Prov 5:16 Let thy fountains be *d* abroad
Is 11:12 gather together the *d* of Judah
Eze 36:19 they were *d* through the countries
Zeph 3:10 even the daughter of my *d*
Jn 7:35 go unto the *d* among the Gentiles
Acts 5:37 as many as obeyed him, were *d*
2Cor 9:9 it is written, He hath *d* abroad

## DISPLEASE
Gen 31:35 Let it not *d* my lord that I
Num 22:34 now therefore, if it *d* thee
1Sa 29:7 that thou *d* not the lords of the
2Sa 11:25 Joab, Let not this thing *d* thee
Prov 24:18 it *d* him, and he turn away his

## DISPLEASED
Gen 38:10 thing which he did *d* the LORD
Gen 48:17 the head of Ephraim, it *d* him
Num 11:1 people complained, it *d* the LORD
Num 11:10 Moses also was *d*
1Sa 8:6 the thing *d* Samuel, when they
1Sa 18:8 very wroth, and the saying *d* him
2Sa 6:8 And David was *d*, because the LORD
2Sa 11:27 that David had done *d* the LORD
1Kin 1:6 his father had not *d* him at any
1Kin 20:43 went to his house heavy and *d*
1Kin 21:4 *d* because of the word which
1Chr 13:11 And David was *d*, because the LORD
1Chr 21:7 God was *d* with this thing
Ps 60:1 scattered us, thou hast been *d*
Is 59:15 it *d* him that there was no
Dan 6:14 was sore *d* with himself, and set

Jonah 4:1 it *d* Jonah exceedingly, and he
Hab 3:8 Was the LORD *d* against the rivers
Zec 1:2 been sore *d* with your fathers
Zec 1:15 I am very sore *d* with the heathen
Zec 1:15 for I was but a little *d*, and they
Mt 21:15 they were sore *d*,
Mk 10:14 when Jesus saw it, he was much *d*
Mk 10:41 began to be much *d* with James
Acts 12:20 Herod was highly *d* with them of

## DISPLEASURE

Deut 9:19 was afraid of the anger and hot *d*
Judg 15:3 Philistines, though I do them a *d*
Ps 2:5 wrath, and vex them in his sore *d*
Ps 6:1 neither chasten me in thy hot *d*
Ps 38:1 neither chasten me in thy hot *d*

## DISPOSED

Job 34:13 Or who hath *d* the whole world
Job 37:15 Dost thou know when God *d* them
Acts 18:27 when he was *d* to pass into Achaia
1Cor 10:27 you to a feast, and ye be *d* to go

## DISPUTED

Mk 9:33 What was it that ye *d* among
Mk 9:34 way they had *d* among themselves
Acts 9:29 Jesus, and *d* against the Grecians
Acts 17:17 Therefore *d* he in the synagogue
Jude 9 he *d* about the body of Moses

## DISPUTING

Acts 6:9 and of Asia, *d* with Stephen
Acts 15:7 And when there had been much *d*
Acts 19:8 for the space of three months, *d*
Acts 19:9 *d* daily in the school of one
Acts 24:12 me in the temple *d* with any man

## DISQUIETED

1Sa 28:15 said to Saul, Why hast thou *d* me
Ps 39:6 surely they are *d* in vain
Ps 42:5 and why art thou *d* in me
Ps 42:11 and why art thou *d* within me
Ps 43:5 and why art thou *d* within me
Prov 30:21 For three things the earth is *d*

## DISSOLVED

Ps 75:3 all the inhabitants thereof are *d*
Is 14:31 thou, whole Palestina, art *d*
Is 24:19 broken down, the earth is clean *d*
Is 34:4 all the host of heaven shall be *d*
Nah 2:6 opened, and the palace shall be *d*
2Cor 5:1 house of this tabernacle were *d*
2Pet 3:11 that all these things shall be *d*
2Pet 3:12 heavens being on fire shall be *d*

## DISTRESS

Gen 35:3 answered me in the day of my *d*
Gen 42:21 therefore is this *d* come upon us
Deut 2:9 *D* not the Moabites, neither
Deut 2:19 *d* them not, nor meddle with them
Deut 28:53 thine enemies shall *d* thee
Deut 28:55 shall *d* thee in all thy gates
Deut 28:57 enemy shall *d* thee in thy gates
Judg 11:7 come unto me now when ye are in *d*
1Sa 22:2 And every one that was in *d*
2Sa 22:7 In my *d* I called upon the LORD,
1Kin 1:29 redeemed my soul out of all *d*
2Chr 28:22 in the time of his *d* did he
Neh 2:17 Ye see the *d* that we are in, how
Neh 9:37 pleasure, and we are in great *d*
Ps 4:1 hast enlarged me when I was in *d*
Ps 18:6 In my *d* I called upon the LORD,
Ps 118:5 I called upon the LORD in *d*
Ps 120:1 In my *d* I cried unto the LORD, and
Prov 1:27 when *d* and anguish cometh upon you
Is 25:4 a strength to the needy in his *d*
Is 29:2 Yet I will *d* Ariel, and there
Is 29:7 and her munition, and that *d* her
Jer 10:18 land at this once, and will *d* them
Lam 1:20 for I am in *d*
Obad 12 spoken proudly in the day of *d*
Obad 14 that did remain in the day of *d*
Zeph 1:15 of wrath, a day of trouble and *d*
Zeph 1:17 And I will bring *d* upon men
Lk 21:23 shall be great *d* in the land
Lk 21:25 and upon the earth *d* of nations
Rom 8:35 shall tribulation, or *d*, or
1Cor 7:26 this is good for the present *d*
1Th 3:7 our affliction and *d* by your faith

## DISTRESSED

Gen 32:7 Jacob was greatly afraid and *d*
Num 22:3 Moab was *d* because of the
Judg 2:15 and they were greatly *d*
Judg 10:9 so that Israel was sore *d*
1Sa 13:6 a strait, (for the people were *d*
1Sa 14:24 the men of Israel were *d* that day
1Sa 28:15 And Saul answered, I am sore *d*
1Sa 30:6 And David was greatly *d*
2Sa 1:26 I am *d* for thee, my brother
2Chr 28:20 *d* him, but strengthened him not
2Cor 4:8 troubled on every side, yet not *d*

## DISTRESSES

Ps 25:17 O bring thou me out of my *d*
Ps 107:6 he delivered them out of their *d*
Ps 107:13 and he saved them out of their *d*
Ps 107:19 and he saveth them out of their *d*
Ps 107:28 he bringeth them out of their *d*
Eze 30:16 and Noph shall have *d* daily
2Cor 6:4 afflictions, in necessities, in *d*
2Cor 12:10 in *d* for Christ's sake

## DISTRIBUTE

Josh 13:32 *d* for inheritance in the plains
2Chr 31:14 to *d* the oblations of the LORD,
Neh 13:13 was to *d* unto their brethren
Lk 18:22 *d* unto the poor, and thou shalt
1Ti 6:18 be rich in good works, ready to *d*

## DISTRIBUTED

Josh 14:1 *d* for inheritance to them
1Chr 24:3 And David *d* them, both Zadok of
2Chr 23:18 whom David had *d* in the house of
Jn 6:11 he *d* to the disciples, and the
1Cor 7:17 But as God hath *d* to every man
2Cor 10:13 the rule which God hath *d* to us

## DITCH

Job 9:31 Yet shalt thou plunge me in the *d*
Ps 7:15 fallen into the *d* which he made
Prov 23:27 For a whore is a deep *d*
Is 22:11 Ye made also a *d* between the two
Mt 15:14 blind, both shall fall into the *d*
Lk 6:39 they not both fall into the *d*

## DIVERS

Deut 22:9 not sow thy vineyard with *d* seeds
Deut 22:11 not wear a garment of *d* sorts
Deut 25:13 not have in thy bag *d* weights
Deut 25:14 have in thine house *d* measures
Judg 5:30 to Sisera a prey of *d* colours
Judg 5:30 a prey of *d* colours of needlework
Judg 5:30 of *d* colours of needlework on
2Sa 13:18 a garment of *d* colours upon her
2Sa 13:19 rent her garment of *d* colours
1Chr 29:2 of *d* colours, and all manner of
2Chr 16:14 *d* kinds of spices prepared by the
2Chr 21:4 *d* also of the princes of Israel
2Chr 30:11 Nevertheless *d* of Asher and
Ps 78:45 He sent *d* sorts of flies among
Ps 105:31 there came *d* sorts of flies, and
Prov 20:10 *D* weights, and *d* measures,
Prov 20:23 *D* weights are an abomination unto
Eccl 5:7 words there are also *d* vanities
Eze 16:16 thy high places with *d* colours
Eze 17:3 of feathers, which had *d* colours
Mt 4:24 that were taken with *d* diseases
Mt 24:7 and earthquakes, in *d* places
Mk 1:34 many that were sick of *d* diseases
Mk 8:3 for *d* of them came from far
Mk 13:8 shall be earthquakes in *d* places
Lk 4:40 *d* diseases brought them unto him
Lk 21:11 earthquakes shall be in *d* places
Acts 19:9 But when *d* were hardened, and
1Cor 12:10 to another *d* kinds of tongues
2Ti 3:6 with sins, led away with *d* lusts
Titus 3:3 deceived, serving *d* lusts
Heb 1:1 in *d* manners spake in time past
Heb 2:4 with *d* miracles, and gifts of the
Heb 9:10 *d* washings, and carnal ordinances,
Heb 13:9 Be not carried about with *d*
Jas 1:2 when ye fall into *d* temptations

## DIVERSE

Lev 19:19 thy cattle gender with a *d* kind
Est 1:7 vessels being *d* one from another
Est 3:8 their laws are *d* from all people
Dan 7:3 from the sea, *d* one from another
Dan 7:7 it was *d* from all the beasts that
Dan 7:19 which was *d* from all the others,
Dan 7:23 which shall be *d* from all
Dan 7:24 he shall be *d* from the first, and

## DIVIDE

Gen 1:6 let it *d* the waters from the
Gen 1:14 to *d* the day from the night
Gen 1:18 to *d* the light from the darkness
Gen 49:7 I will *d* them in Jacob, and
Gen 49:27 and at night he shall *d* the spoil
Ex 14:16 thine hand over the sea, and *d* it
Ex 15:9 will overtake, I will *d* the spoil
Ex 21:35 the live ox, and *d* the money of it
Ex 21:35 and the dead ox also they shall *d*
Ex 26:33 the vail shall *d* unto you between
Lev 1:17 but shall not *d* it asunder
Lev 5:8 neck, but shall not *d* it asunder
Lev 11:4 cud, or of them that *d* the hoof
Lev 11:7 the swine, though he *d* the hoof
Num 31:27 *d* the prey into two parts
Num 33:54 ye shall *d* the land by lot for an
Num 34:17 which shall *d* the land unto you
Num 34:18 to *d* the land by inheritance
Num 34:29 to *d* the inheritance unto the
Deut 14:7 or of them that *d* the cloven hoof
Deut 14:7 chew the cud, but *d* not the hoof
Deut 19:3 *d* the coasts of thy land, which
Josh 1:6 *d* for an inheritance the land
Josh 13:6 only *d* thou it by lot unto the
Josh 13:7 Now therefore *d* this land for an
Josh 18:5 they shall *d* it into seven parts
Josh 22:8 *d* the spoil of your enemies with
2Sa 19:29 said, Thou and Ziba *d* the land
1Kin 3:25 *D* the living child in two, and
1Kin 3:26 neither mine nor thine, but *d* it
Neh 9:11 thou didst *d* the sea before them,
Neh 9:22 didst *d* them into corners
Job 27:17 the innocent shall *d* the silver
Ps 55:9 O Lord, and *d* their tongues
Ps 60:6 I will *d* Shechem, and mete out the
Ps 74:13 Thou didst *d* the sea by thy
Ps 108:7 I will *d* Shechem, and mete out the
Prov 16:19 than to *d* the spoil with the
Is 9:3 men rejoice when they *d* the spoil
Is 53:12 Therefore will I *d* him a portion
Is 53:12 he shall *d* the spoil with the
Eze 5:1 balances to weigh, and *d* the hair
Eze 45:1 when ye shall *d* by lot the land
Eze 47:21 So shall ye *d* this land unto you
Eze 47:22 that ye shall *d* it by lot for an
Eze 48:29 shall *d* by lot unto the tribes of
Dan 11:39 shall *d* the land for gain
Lk 12:13 that he *d* the inheritance with me
Lk 22:17 this, and *d* it among yourselves

## DIVIDED

Gen 1:4 God *d* the light from the darkness
Gen 1:7 *d* the waters which were under the
Gen 10:5 of the Gentiles *d* in their lands
Gen 10:25 for in his days was the earth *d*
Gen 10:32 by these were the nations *d* in
Gen 14:15 he *d* himself against them, he and
Gen 15:10 *d* them in the midst, and laid each
Gen 15:10 but the birds *d* he not
Gen 32:7 he *d* the people that was with him
Gen 33:1 he *d* the children unto Leah, and
Ex 14:21 dry land, and the waters were *d*
Num 26:53 Unto these the land shall be *d*
Num 26:55 the land shall be *d* by lot
Num 26:56 thereof be *d* between many
Num 31:42 which Moses *d* from the men that
Deut 4:19 hath *d* unto all nations under the
Deut 32:8 When the Most High *d* to the
Josh 14:5 of Israel did, and they *d* the land
Josh 18:10 there Joshua *d* the land unto the
Josh 19:51 *d* for an inheritance by lot in
Josh 23:4 I have *d* unto you by lot these
Judg 5:30 have they not *d* the prey
Judg 7:16 he *d* the three hundred men into
Judg 9:43 *d* them into three companies, and
Judg 19:29 *d* her, together with her bones,
2Sa 1:23 and in their death they were not *d*
1Kin 16:21 people of Israel *d* into two parts
1Kin 18:6 So they *d* the land between them
2Kin 2:8 the waters, and they were *d* hither
1Chr 1:19 in his days the earth was *d*
1Chr 23:6 David *d* them into courses among
1Chr 24:4 and thus were they *d*
1Chr 24:5 Thus were they *d* by lot, one sort
2Chr 35:13 *d* them speedily among all the
Job 38:25 Who hath *d* a watercourse for the
Ps 68:12 that tarried at home *d* the spoil
Ps 78:13 He *d* the sea, and caused them to
Ps 78:55 *d* them an inheritance by line, and
Ps 136:13 To him which *d* the Red sea into
Is 33:23 is the prey of a great spoil *d*
Is 34:17 his hand hath *d* it unto them by
Is 51:15 that *d* the sea, whose waves
Lam 4:16 The anger of the LORD hath *d* them

Eze 37:22 neither shall they be *d* into two
Dan 2:41 of iron, the kingdom shall be *d*
Dan 5:28 Thy kingdom is *d*, and given to the
Dan 11:4 shall be *d* toward the four winds
Hos 10:2 Their heart is *d*
Amos 7:17 and thy land shall be *d* by line
Mic 2:4 turning away he hath *d* our fields
Zec 14:1 thy spoil shall be *d* in the midst
Mt 12:25 Every kingdom *d* against itself is
Mt 12:25 every city or house *d* against
Mt 12:26 Satan, he is *d* against himself
Mk 3:24 if a kingdom be *d* against itself
Mk 3:25 if a house be *d* against itself,
Mk 3:26 rise up against himself, and be *d*
Mk 6:41 the two fishes *d* he among them
Lk 11:17 Every kingdom *d* against itself is
Lk 11:17 a house *d* against a house falleth
Lk 11:18 Satan also be *d* against himself
Lk 12:52 shall be five in one house *d*
Lk 12:53 father shall be *d* against the son
Lk 15:12 he *d* unto them his living
Acts 13:19 he *d* their land to them by lot
Acts 14:4 the multitude of the city was *d*
Acts 23:7 and the multitude was *d*
1Cor 1:13 Is Christ *d*?
Rev 16:19 great city was *d* into three parts

**DIVIDETH**
Lev 11:4 the cud, but *d* not the hoof
Lev 11:5 the cud, but *d* not the hoof
Lev 11:6 the cud, but *d* not the hoof
Lev 11:26 of every beast which *d* the hoof
Deut 14:8 the swine, because it *d* the hoof
Job 26:12 He *d* the sea with his power, and
Ps 29:7 of the LORD *d* the flames of fire
Jer 31:35 which *d* the sea when the waves
Mt 25:32 as a shepherd *d* his sheep from
Lk 11:22 he trusted, and *d* his spoils

**DIVIDING**
Josh 19:49 of *d* the land for inheritance by
Josh 19:51 they made an end of *d* the country
Is 63:12 *d* the water before them, to make
Dan 7:25 a time and times and the *d* of time
1Cor 12:11 *d* to every man severally as he
2Ti 2:15 rightly *d* the word of truth
Heb 4:12 even to the *d* asunder of soul

**DIVINATION**
Num 22:7 the rewards of *d* in their hand
Num 23:23 is there any *d* against Israel
Deut 18:10 through the fire, or that useth *d*
2Kin 17:17 pass through the fire, and used *d*
Jer 14:14 unto you a false vision and *d*
Eze 12:24 *d* within the house of Israel
Eze 13:6 They have seen vanity and lying *d*
Eze 13:7 and have ye not spoken a lying *d*
Eze 21:21 head of the two ways, to use *d*
Eze 21:22 hand was the *d* for Jerusalem
Eze 21:23 them as a false *d* in their sight
Acts 16:16 with a spirit of *d* met us

**DIVINE**
Gen 44:15 such a man as I can certainly *d*
1Sa 28:8 *d* unto me by the familiar spirit,
Prov 16:10 A *d* sentence is in the lips of
Eze 13:9 that see vanity, and that *d* lies
Eze 13:23 no more vanity, nor *d* divinations
Eze 21:29 whiles they *d* a lie unto thee, to
Mic 3:6 unto you, that ye shall not *d*
Mic 3:11 the prophets thereof *d* for money
Heb 9:1 had also ordinances of *d* service
2Pet 1:3 According as his *d* power hath
2Pet 1:4 be partakers of the *d* nature

**DIVINERS**
Deut 18:14 observers of times, and unto *d*
1Sa 6:2 called for the priests and the *d*
Is 44:25 of the liars, and maketh *d* mad
Jer 27:9 to your prophets, nor to your *d*
Jer 29:8 Let not your prophets and your *d*
Mic 3:7 be ashamed, and the *d* confounded
Zec 10:2 the *d* have seen a lie, and have

**DIVISION**
Ex 8:23 I will put a *d* between my people
2Chr 35:5 after the *d* of the families of
Lk 12:51 you, Nay; but rather *d*
Jn 7:43 So there was a *d* among the people
Jn 9:16 And there was a *d* among them
Jn 10:19 There was a *d* therefore again

**DIVISIONS**
Josh 11:23 to their *d* by their tribes
Josh 12:7 a possession according to their *d*
Josh 18:10 of Israel according to their *d*
Judg 5:15 For the *d* of Reuben there were
Judg 5:16 For the *d* of Reuben there were
1Chr 24:1 Now these are the *d* of the sons
1Chr 26:1 Concerning the *d* of the porters
1Chr 26:12 these were the *d* of the porters
1Chr 26:19 These are the *d* of the porters
2Chr 35:5 *d* of the families of the fathers
2Chr 35:12 might give according to the *d* of
Ezr 6:18 they set the priests in their *d*
Neh 11:36 And of the Levites were *d* in Judah
Rom 16:17 brethren, mark them which cause *d*
1Cor 1:10 and that there be no *d* among you
1Cor 3:3 you envying, and strife, and *d*
1Cor 11:18 I hear that there be *d* among you

**DIVORCE**
Jer 3:8 away, and given her a bill of *d*

**DIVORCED**
Lev 21:14 or a *d* woman, or profane, or an
Lev 22:13 daughter be a widow, or *d*
Num 30:9 of a widow, and of her that is *d*
Mt 5:32 her that is *d* committeth adultery

**DIVORCEMENT**
Deut 24:1 let him write her a bill of *d*
Deut 24:3 her, and write her a bill of *d*
Is 50:1 is the bill of your mother's *d*
Mt 5:31 let him give her a writing of *d*
Mt 19:7 command to give a writing of *d*
Mk 10:4 suffered to write a bill of *d*

**DIZAHAB** *(diz'-a-hab) A place in the Sinai wilderness.*
Deut 1:1 and Laban, and Hazeroth, and *D*

**DOCTOR**
Acts 5:34 a *d* of the law, had in reputation

**DOCTORS**
Lk 2:46 sitting in the midst of the *d*
Lk 5:17 *d* of the law sitting by, which

**DOCTRINE**
Deut 32:2 My *d* shall drop as the rain, my
Job 11:4 My *d* is pure, and I am clean in
Prov 4:2 For I give you good *d*, forsake ye
Is 28:9 shall he make to understand *d*
Is 29:24 they that murmured shall learn *d*
Jer 10:8 the stock is a *d* of vanities
Mt 7:28 people were astonished at his *d*
Mt 16:12 but of the *d* of the Pharisees and
Mt 22:33 they were astonished at his *d*
Mk 1:22 And they were astonished at his *d*
Mk 1:27 what new *d* is this
Mk 4:2 and said unto them in his *d*
Mk 11:18 people was astonished at his *d*
Mk 12:38 And he said unto them in his *d*
Lk 4:32 And they were astonished at his *d*
Jn 7:16 My *d* is not mine, but his that
Jn 7:17 his will, he shall know of the *d*
Jn 18:19 of his disciples, and of his *d*
Acts 2:42 stedfastly in the apostles' *d*
Acts 5:28 have filled Jerusalem with your *d*
Acts 13:12 astonished at the *d* of the Lord
Acts 17:19 May we know what this new *d*
Rom 6:17 form of *d* which was delivered you
Rom 16:17 to the *d* which ye have learned
1Cor 14:6 or by prophesying, or by *d*
1Cor 14:26 one of you hath a psalm, hath a *d*
Eph 4:14 about with every wind of *d*
1Ti 1:3 some that they teach no other *d*
1Ti 1:10 thing that is contrary to sound *d*
1Ti 4:6 the words of faith and of good *d*
1Ti 4:13 to reading, to exhortation, to *d*
1Ti 4:16 heed unto thyself, and unto the *d*
1Ti 5:17 they who labour in the word and *d*
1Ti 6:1 of God and his *d* be not blasphemed
1Ti 6:3 to the *d* which is according to
2Ti 3:10 But thou hast fully known my *d*
2Ti 3:16 of God, and is profitable for *d*
2Ti 4:2 with all longsuffering and *d*
2Ti 4:3 when they will not endure sound *d*
Titus 1:9 be able by sound *d* both to exhort
Titus 2:1 the things which become sound *d*
Titus 2:7 in *d* shewing uncorruptness,
Titus 2:10 that they may adorn the *d* of God
Heb 6:1 the principles of the *d* of Christ
Heb 6:2 Of the *d* of baptisms, and of
2Jn 9 and abideth not in the *d* of Christ
2Jn 9 that abideth in the *d* of Christ
2Jn 10 any unto you, and bring not this *d*
Rev 2:14 them that hold the *d* of Balaam
Rev 2:15 hold the *d* of the Nicolaitanes
Rev 2:24 as many as have not this *d*

**DOCTRINES**
Mt 15:9 teaching for *d* the commandments
Mk 7:7 teaching for *d* the commandments
Col 2:22 the commandments and *d* of men
1Ti 4:1 seducing spirits, and *d* of devils
Heb 13:9 about with divers and strange *d*

**DODAI** *(do'-dahee)* See DODO. *A captain in David's army.*
1Chr 27:4 the second month was *D* an Ahohite

**DODANIM** *(do'-da-nim)* See RODANIM. *Descendants of Javan.*
Gen 10:4 and Tarshish, Kittim, and *D*
1Chr 1:7 and Tarshish, Kittim, and *D*

**DODAVAH** *(do'-da-vah) Father of Eliezer.*
2Chr 20:37 Then Eliezer the son of *D* of

**DODO** *(do'-do)* See DODAI.
*1. Grandfather of Tola.*
Judg 10:1 the son of Puah, the son of *D*
*2. Father of Eleazar.*
2Sa 23:9 Eleazar the son of *D* the Ahohite
1Chr 11:12 him was Eleazar the son of *D*
*3. Father of Elhanan.*
2Sa 23:24 the son of *D* of Beth-lehem
1Chr 11:26 the son of *D* of Beth-lehem

**DOEG** *(do'-eg) Chief herdsman of King Saul.*
1Sa 21:7 and his name was *D*, an Edomite,
1Sa 22:9 Then answered *D* the Edomite
1Sa 22:18 And the king said to *D*, Turn thou,
1Sa 22:18 *D* the Edomite turned, and he fell
1Sa 22:22 when *D* the Edomite was there,
Ps 52:*t* when *D* the Edomite came and told

**DOER**
Gen 39:22 did there, he was the *d* of it
2Sa 3:39 the *d* of evil according to his
Ps 31:23 plentifully rewardeth the proud *d*
Prov 17:4 A wicked *d* giveth heed to false
2Ti 2:9 I suffer trouble, as an evil *d*
Jas 1:23 a hearer of the word, and not a *d*
Jas 1:25 but a *d* of the work, this man
Jas 4:11 law, thou art not a *d* of the law

**DOERS**
2Kin 22:5 the hand of the *d* of the work
2Kin 22:5 let them give it to the *d* of the
Job 8:20 neither will he help the evil *d*
Ps 101:8 *d* from the city of the LORD
Rom 2:13 but the *d* of the law shall be
Jas 1:22 But be ye *d* of the word, and not

**DOG**
Ex 11:7 shall not a *d* move his tongue
Deut 23:18 of a whore, or the price of a *d*
Judg 7:5 as a *d* lappeth, him shalt thou
1Sa 17:43 said unto David, Am I a *d*
1Sa 24:14 after a dead *d*, after a flea
2Sa 9:8 look upon such a dead *d* as I am
2Sa 16:9 Why should this dead *d* curse my
2Kin 8:13 But what, is thy servant a *d*
Ps 22:20 darling from the power of the *d*
Ps 59:6 they make a noise like a *d*
Ps 59:14 and let them make a noise like a *d*
Prov 26:11 As a *d* returneth to his vomit, so
Prov 26:17 one that taketh a *d* by the ears
Eccl 9:4 for a living *d* is better than a
2Pet 2:22 The *d* is turned to his own vomit

**DOGS**
Ex 22:31 ye shall cast it to the *d*
1Kin 14:11 in the city shall the *d* eat
1Kin 16:4 in the city shall the *d* eat
1Kin 21:19 In the place where *d* licked the
1Kin 21:19 of Naboth shall *d* lick thy blood
1Kin 21:23 The *d* shall eat Jezebel by the
1Kin 21:24 Ahab in the city the *d* shall eat
1Kin 22:38 the *d* licked up his blood
2Kin 9:10 the *d* shall eat Jezebel in the
2Kin 9:36 shall *d* eat the flesh of Jezebel
Job 30:1 have set with the *d* of my flock
Ps 22:16 For *d* have compassed me
Ps 68:23 the tongue of thy *d* in the same
Is 56:10 all ignorant, they are all dumb *d*
Is 56:11 they are greedy *d* which can never
Jer 15:3 the *d* to tear, and the fowls of

Mt 7:6 not that which is holy unto the *d*
Mt 15:26 bread, and to cast it to *d*
Mt 15:27 yet the *d* eat of the crumbs which
Mk 7:27 bread, and to cast it unto the *d*
Mk 7:28 yet the *d* under the table eat of
Lk 16:21 moreover the *d* came and licked his
Phil 3:2 Beware of *d*, beware of evil
Rev 22:15 For without are *d*, and sorcerers,

## DOING

Gen 31:28 hast now done foolishly in so *d*
Gen 44:5 ye have done evil in so *d*
Ex 15:11 fearful in praises, *d* wonders
Num 20:19 without *d* any thing else, go
Deut 9:18 in *d* wickedly in the sight of the
1Kin 7:40 So Hiram made an end of *d* all the
1Kin 16:19 *d* evil in the sight of the LORD
1Kin 22:43 *d* that which was right in the
2Kin 21:16 in *d* that which was evil in the
1Chr 22:16 Arise therefore, and be *d*, and the
2Chr 20:32 *d* that which was right in the
Ezr 9:1 *d* according to their abominations
Neh 6:3 I am *d* a great work, so that I
Job 32:22 in so *d* my maker would soon take
Ps 64:9 shall wisely consider of his *d*
Ps 66:5 he is terrible in his *d* toward
Ps 118:23 This is the LORD's *d*
Is 56:2 keepeth his hand from *d* any evil
Is 58:13 from *d* thy pleasure on my holy
Is 58:13 not *d* thine own ways, nor finding
Mt 21:42 this is the Lord's *d*, and it is
Mt 24:46 when he cometh shall find so *d*
Mk 12:11 This was the Lord's *d*, and it is
Lk 12:43 when he cometh shall find so *d*
Acts 10:38 who went about *d* good, and healing
Acts 24:20 they have found any evil *d* in me
Rom 2:7 in well *d* seek for glory and
Rom 12:20 for in so *d* thou shalt heap coals
2Cor 8:11 Now therefore perform the *d* of it
Gal 6:9 And let us not be weary in well *d*
Eph 6:6 *d* the will of God from the heart
Eph 6:7 With good will *d* service, as to
2Th 3:13 brethren, be not weary in well *d*
1Ti 4:16 for in *d* this thou shalt both
1Ti 5:21 another, *d* nothing by partiality
1Pet 2:15 that with well *d* ye may put to
1Pet 3:17 be so, that ye suffer for well *d*
1Pet 3:17 for well *d*, than for evil *d*
1Pet 4:19 of their souls to him in well *d*

## DOMINION

Gen 1:26 let them have *d* over the fish of
Gen 1:28 have *d* over the fish of the sea,
Gen 27:40 pass when thou shalt have the *d*
Gen 37:8 shalt thou indeed have *d* over us
Num 24:19 shall come he that shall have *d*
Judg 5:13 have *d* over the nobles among the
Judg 5:13 made me have *d* over the mighty
Judg 14:4 the Philistines had *d* over Israel
1Kin 4:24 For he had *d* over all the region
1Kin 9:19 and in all the land of his *d*
2Kin 20:13 in his house, nor in all his *d*
1Chr 4:22 and Saraph, who had the *d* in Moab
1Chr 18:3 his *d* by the river Euphrates
2Chr 8:6 throughout all the land of his *d*
2Chr 21:8 from under the *d* of Judah
Neh 9:28 so that they had the *d* over them
Neh 9:37 also they have *d* over our bodies,
Job 25:2 *D* and fear are with him
Job 38:33 canst thou set the *d* thereof in
Ps 8:6 Thou madest him to have *d* over
Ps 19:13 let them not have *d* over me
Ps 49:14 the upright shall have *d* over
Ps 72:8 He shall have *d* also from sea to
Ps 103:22 his works in all places of his *d*
Ps 114:2 his sanctuary, and Israel his *d*
Ps 119:133 not any iniquity have *d* over me
Ps 145:13 thy *d* endureth throughout all
Is 26:13 besides thee have had *d* over us
Is 39:2 in his house, nor in all his *d*
Jer 34:1 kingdoms of the earth of his *d*
Jer 51:28 thereof, and all the land of his *d*
Dan 4:3 his *d* is from generation to
Dan 4:22 thy *d* to the end of the earth
Dan 4:34 whose *d* is an everlasting *d*
Dan 6:26 That in every *d* of my kingdom men
Dan 6:26 his *d* shall be even unto the end
Dan 7:6 and *d* was given to it
Dan 7:12 they had their *d* taken away
Dan 7:14 And there was given him *d*, and
Dan 7:14 his *d* is an everlasting *d*,
Dan 7:26 and they shall take away his *d*
Dan 7:27 And the kingdom and *d*, and the
Dan 11:3 up, that shall rule with great *d*
Dan 11:4 according to his *d* which he ruled
Dan 11:5 be strong above him, and have *d*
Dan 11:5 his *d* shall be a great *d*
Mic 4:8 shall it come, even the first *d*
Zec 9:10 his *d* shall be from sea even to
Mt 20:25 the Gentiles exercise *d* over them
Rom 6:9 death hath no more *d* over him
Rom 6:14 For sin shall not have *d* over you
Rom 7:1 how that the law hath *d* over a
2Cor 1:24 that we have *d* over your faith
Eph 1:21 and power, and might, and *d*
1Pet 4:11 be praise and *d* for ever and ever
1Pet 5:11 be glory and *d* for ever and ever
Jude 8 defile the flesh, despise *d*
Jude 25 Saviour, be glory and majesty, *d*
Rev 1:6 be glory and *d* for ever and ever

## DOOR

Gen 4:7 not well, sin lieth at the *d*
Gen 6:16 the *d* of the ark shalt thou set
Gen 18:1 he sat in the tent *d* in the heat
Gen 18:2 ran to meet them from the tent *d*
Gen 18:10 And Sarah heard it in the tent *d*
Gen 19:6 Lot went out at the *d* unto them
Gen 19:6 and shut the *d* after him
Gen 19:9 Lot, and came near to break the *d*
Gen 19:10 house to them, and shut to the *d*
Gen 19:11 the *d* of the house with blindness
Gen 19:11 wearied themselves to find the *d*
Gen 43:19 with him at the *d* of the house
Ex 12:7 on the upper *d* post of the houses
Ex 12:22 *d* of his house until the morning
Ex 12:23 the LORD will pass over the *d*
Ex 21:6 he shall also bring him to the *d*
Ex 21:6 or unto the *d* post
Ex 26:36 an hanging for the *d* of the tent
Ex 29:4 the *d* of the tabernacle of the
Ex 29:11 by the *d* of the tabernacle of the
Ex 29:32 by the *d* of the tabernacle of the
Ex 29:42 your generations at the *d* of the
Ex 33:8 and stood every man at his tent *d*
Ex 33:9 stood at the *d* of the tabernacle,
Ex 33:10 pillar stand at the tabernacle *d*
Ex 33:10 every man in his tent *d*
Ex 35:15 the hanging for the *d* at the
Ex 35:17 hanging for the *d* of the court
Ex 36:37 for the tabernacle *d* of blue
Ex 38:8 which assembled at the *d* of the
Ex 38:30 to the *d* of the tabernacle of the
Ex 39:38 the hanging for the tabernacle *d*
Ex 40:5 of the *d* to the tabernacle
Ex 40:6 *d* of the tabernacle of the tent
Ex 40:12 his sons unto the *d* of the
Ex 40:28 at the *d* of the tabernacle
Ex 40:29 *d* of the tabernacle of the tent
Lev 1:3 at the *d* of the tabernacle of the
Lev 1:5 by the *d* of the tabernacle of the
Lev 3:2 and kill it at the *d* of the
Lev 4:4 the *d* of the tabernacle of the
Lev 4:7 which is at the *d* of the
Lev 4:18 which is at the *d* of the
Lev 8:3 the *d* of the tabernacle of the
Lev 8:4 the *d* of the tabernacle of the
Lev 8:31 Boil the flesh at the *d* of the
Lev 8:33 of the *d* of the tabernacle of the
Lev 8:35 at the *d* of the tabernacle of the
Lev 10:7 the *d* of the tabernacle of the
Lev 12:6 unto the *d* of the tabernacle of
Lev 14:11 at the *d* of the tabernacle of the
Lev 14:23 unto the *d* of the tabernacle of
Lev 14:38 the house to the *d* of the house
Lev 15:14 the *d* of the tabernacle of the
Lev 15:29 to the *d* of the tabernacle of the
Lev 16:7 at the *d* of the tabernacle of the
Lev 17:4 the *d* of the tabernacle of the
Lev 17:5 unto the *d* of the tabernacle of
Lev 17:6 at the *d* of the tabernacle of the
Lev 17:9 the *d* of the tabernacle of the
Lev 19:21 unto the *d* of the tabernacle of
Num 3:25 the hanging for the *d* of the
Num 3:26 curtain for the *d* of the court
Num 4:25 the hanging for the *d* of the
Num 4:26 the hanging for the *d* of the gate
Num 6:10 to the *d* of the tabernacle of the
Num 6:13 the *d* of the tabernacle of the
Num 6:18 at the *d* of the tabernacle of the
Num 10:3 at the *d* of the tabernacle of the
Num 11:10 every man in the *d* of his tent
Num 12:5 stood in the *d* of the tabernacle,
Num 16:18 stood in the *d* of the tabernacle
Num 16:19 against them unto the *d* of the
Num 16:27 stood in the *d* of their tents, and
Num 16:50 the *d* of the tabernacle of the
Num 20:6 the *d* of the tabernacle of the
Num 25:6 the *d* of the tabernacle of the
Num 27:2 by the *d* of the tabernacle of the
Deut 11:20 upon the *d* posts of thine house
Deut 15:17 it through his ear unto the *d*
Deut 22:21 to the *d* of her father's house
Deut 31:15 over the *d* of the tabernacle
Josh 19:51 at the *d* of the tabernacle of the
Judg 4:20 her, Stand in the *d* of the tent
Judg 9:52 went hard unto the *d* of the tower
Judg 19:22 round about, and beat at the *d*
Judg 19:26 fell down at the *d* of the man's
Judg 19:27 fallen down at the *d* of the house
1Sa 2:22 at the *d* of the tabernacle of the
2Sa 11:9 But Uriah slept at the *d* of the
2Sa 13:17 from me, and bolt the *d* after her
2Sa 13:18 out, and bolted the *d* after her
1Kin 6:8 The *d* for the middle chamber was
1Kin 6:33 So also made he for the *d* of the
1Kin 6:34 leaves of the one *d* were folding
1Kin 6:34 of the other *d* were folding
1Kin 14:6 her feet, as she came in at the *d*
1Kin 14:17 came to the threshold of the *d*
1Kin 14:27 which kept the *d* of the king's
2Kin 4:4 thou shalt shut the *d* upon thee
2Kin 4:5 from him, and shut the *d* upon her
2Kin 4:15 called her, she stood in the *d*
2Kin 4:21 of God, and shut the *d* upon him
2Kin 4:33 shut the *d* upon them twain, and
2Kin 5:9 stood at the *d* of the house of
2Kin 6:32 *d*, and hold him fast at the *d*
2Kin 9:3 Then open the *d*, and flee, and
2Kin 9:10 And he opened the *d*, and fled
2Kin 12:9 the priests that kept the *d* put
2Kin 22:4 which the keepers of the *d* have
2Kin 23:4 order, and the keepers of the *d*
2Kin 25:18 and the three keepers of the *d*
1Chr 9:21 of the *d* of the tabernacle of the
Neh 3:20 *d* of the house of Eliashib the
Neh 3:21 from the *d* of the house of
Est 2:21 Teresh, of those which kept the *d*
Est 6:2 the keepers of the *d*, who sought
Job 31:9 laid wait at my neighbour's *d*
Job 31:34 silence, and went not out of the *d*
Ps 141:3 Keep the *d* of my lips
Prov 5:8 come not nigh the *d* of her house
Prov 9:14 she sitteth at the *d* of her house
Prov 26:14 As the *d* turneth upon his hinges,
Song 5:4 in his hand by the hole of the *d*
Song 8:9 and if she be a *d*, we will inclose
Is 6:4 the posts of the *d* moved at the
Jer 35:4 of Shallum, the keeper of the *d*
Jer 52:24 and the three keepers of the *d*
Eze 8:3 to the *d* of the inner gate, that
Eze 8:7 brought me to the *d* of the court
Eze 8:8 digged in the wall, behold a *d*
Eze 8:14 Then he brought me to the *d* of
Eze 8:16 at the *d* of the temple of the
Eze 10:19 every one stood at the *d* of the
Eze 11:1 behold at the *d* of the gate five
Eze 40:13 and twenty cubits, *d* against *d*
Eze 41:2 breadth of the *d* was ten cubits
Eze 41:2 the sides of the *d* were five
Eze 41:3 and measured the post of the *d*
Eze 41:3 and the *d*, six cubits
Eze 41:3 and the breadth of the *d*, seven
Eze 41:11 one *d* toward the north, and
Eze 41:11 another *d* toward the south
Eze 41:16 The *d* posts, and the narrow
Eze 41:16 three stories, over against the *d*
Eze 41:17 To that above the *d*, even unto
Eze 41:20 unto above the *d* were cherubims
Eze 41:24 two leaves for the one *d*
Eze 41:24 and two leaves for the other *d*
Eze 42:2 an hundred cubits was the north *d*
Eze 42:12 was a *d* in the head of the way
Eze 46:3 the land shall worship at the *d*
Eze 47:1 me again unto the *d* of the house
Hos 2:15 valley of Achor for a *d* of hope
Amos 9:1 said, Smite the lintel of the *d*
Mt 6:6 and when thou hast shut thy *d*
Mt 25:10 and the *d* was shut
Mt 27:60 stone to the *d* of the sepulchre
Mt 28:2 rolled back the stone from the *d*

Mk 1:33 was gathered together at the *d*
Mk 2:2 no, not so much as about the *d*
Mk 11:4 found the colt tied by the *d*
Mk 15:46 stone unto the *d* of the sepulchre
Mk 16:3 stone from the *d* of the sepulchre
Lk 11:7 the *d* is now shut, and my children
Lk 13:25 risen up, and hath shut to the *d*
Lk 13:25 without, and to knock at the *d*
Jn 10:1 not by the *d* into the sheepfold
Jn 10:2 *d* is the shepherd of the sheep
Jn 10:7 unto you, I am the *d* of the sheep
Jn 10:9 I am the *d*
Jn 18:16 But Peter stood at the *d* without
Jn 18:16 and spake unto her that kept the *d*
Jn 18:17 damsel that kept the *d* unto Peter
Acts 5:9 buried thy husband are at the *d*
Acts 12:6 before the *d* kept the prison
Acts 12:13 knocked at the *d* of the gate
Acts 12:16 and when they had opened the *d*
Acts 14:27 how he had opened the *d* of faith
1Cor 16:9 For a great *d* and effectual is
2Cor 2:12 a *d* was opened unto me of the
Col 4:3 open unto us a *d* of utterance
Jas 5:9 the judge standeth before the *d*
Rev 3:8 I have set before thee an open *d*
Rev 3:20 Behold, I stand at the *d*, and
Rev 3:20 man hear my voice, and open the *d*
Rev 4:1 behold, a *d* was opened in heaven

**DOORKEEPER**
Ps 84:10 I had rather be a *d* in the house

**DOORS**
Josh 2:19 *d* of thy house into the street
Judg 3:23 shut the *d* of the parlour upon
Judg 3:24 the *d* of the parlour were locked,
Judg 3:25 opened not the *d* of the parlour
Judg 11:31 of the *d* of my house to meet me
Judg 16:3 took the *d* of the gate of the
Judg 19:27 opened the *d* of the house, and
1Sa 3:15 opened the *d* of the house of the
1Sa 21:13 and scrabbled on the *d* of the gate
1Kin 6:31 oracle he made *d* of olive tree
1Kin 6:32 The two *d* also were of olive tree
1Kin 6:34 the two *d* were of fir tree
1Kin 7:5 And all the *d* and posts were square
1Kin 7:50 both for the *d* of the inner house
1Kin 7:50 for the *d* of the house, to wit,
2Kin 18:16 the *d* of the temple of the LORD
1Chr 22:3 the nails for the *d* of the gates
2Chr 3:7 and the *d* thereof, with gold
2Chr 4:9 great court, and *d* for the court
2Chr 4:9 overlaid the *d* of them with brass
2Chr 4:22 the inner *d* thereof for the most
2Chr 4:22 the *d* of the house of the temple,
2Chr 23:4 shall be porters of the *d*
2Chr 28:24 shut up the *d* of the house of the
2Chr 29:3 opened the *d* of the house of the
2Chr 29:7 have shut up the *d* of the porch
2Chr 34:9 the *d* had gathered of the hand of
Neh 3:1 it, and set up the *d* of it
Neh 3:3 thereof, and set up the *d* thereof
Neh 3:6 thereof, and set up the *d* thereof
Neh 3:13 built it, and set up the *d* thereof
Neh 3:14 build it, and set up the *d* thereof
Neh 3:15 it, and set up the *d* thereof
Neh 6:1 not set up the *d* upon the gates
Neh 6:10 let us shut the *d* of the temple
Neh 7:1 was built, and I had set up the *d*
Neh 7:3 stand by, let them shut the *d*
Job 3:10 not up the *d* of my mother's womb
Job 31:32 but I opened my *d* to the
Job 38:8 Or who shut up the sea with *d*
Job 38:10 decreed place, and set bars and *d*
Job 38:17 or hast thou seen the *d* of the
Job 41:14 Who can open the *d* of his face
Ps 24:7 be ye lifted up, ye everlasting *d*
Ps 24:9 lift them up, ye everlasting *d*
Ps 78:23 above, and opened the *d* of heaven
Prov 8:3 city, at the coming in at the *d*
Prov 8:34 waiting at the posts of my *d*
Eccl 12:4 the *d* shall be shut in the
Is 26:20 and shut thy *d* about thee
Is 57:8 Behind the *d* also and the posts
Eze 33:30 in the *d* of the houses, and speak
Eze 41:11 the *d* of the side chambers were
Eze 41:23 temple and the sanctuary had two *d*
Eze 41:24 the *d* had two leaves apiece, two
Eze 41:25 on the *d* of the temple, cherubims
Eze 42:4 and their *d* toward the north
Eze 42:11 fashions, and according to their *d*
Eze 42:12 according to the *d* of the
Mic 7:5 keep the *d* of thy mouth from her
Zec 11:1 Open thy *d*, O Lebanon, that the
Mal 1:10 that would shut the *d* for nought
Mt 24:33 that it is near, even at the *d*
Mk 13:29 that it is nigh, even at the *d*
Jn 20:19 when the *d* were shut where the
Jn 20:26 the *d* being shut, and stood in the
Acts 5:19 Lord by night opened the prison *d*
Acts 5:23 standing without before the *d*
Acts 16:26 immediately all the *d* were opened
Acts 16:27 and seeing the prison *d* open
Acts 21:30 and forthwith the *d* were shut

**DOPHKAH** *(dof'-kah) An encampment during the Exodus.*
Num 33:12 of Sin, and encamped in *D*
Num 33:13 And they departed from *D*, and

**DOR** *(dor)* See EN-DOR. *A Canaanite city.*
Josh 11:2 in the borders of *D* on the west
Josh 12:23 The king of *D* in the coast of *D*
Josh 17:11 towns, and the inhabitants of *D*
Judg 1:27 towns, nor the inhabitants of *D*
1Kin 4:11 Abinadab, in all the region of *D*
1Chr 7:29 towns, Megiddo and her towns, *D*

**DORCAS** *(dor'-cas)* See TABITHA. *Disciple raised from the dead by Peter.*
Acts 9:36 by interpretation is called *D*
Acts 9:39 coats and garments which *D* made

**DOST**
Gen 32:29 it that thou *d* ask after my name
Gen 44:4 when thou *d* overtake them, say
Deut 9:5 *d* thou go to possess their land
Deut 24:10 When thou *d* lend thy brother any
Deut 24:11 the man to whom thou *d* lend shall
Judg 14:16 Thou *d* but hate me, and lovest me
1Sa 24:14 after whom *d* thou pursue
1Sa 28:16 Wherefore then *d* thou ask of me
1Kin 2:22 why *d* thou ask Abishag the
1Kin 21:7 *D* thou now govern the kingdom of
2Kin 18:20 Now on whom *d* thou trust, that
2Chr 6:26 sin, when thou *d* afflict them
Neh 2:4 For what *d* thou make request
Job 2:9 *D* thou still retain thine
Job 7:21 And why *d* thou not pardon my
Job 10:8 yet thou *d* destroy me
Job 14:3 *d* thou open thine eyes upon such
Job 14:16 *d* thou not watch over my sin
Job 15:8 *d* thou restrain wisdom to thyself
Job 30:20 unto thee, and thou *d* not hear me
Job 33:13 Why *d* thou strive against him
Job 37:15 *D* thou know when God disposed
Job 37:16 *D* thou know the balancings of the
Ps 39:11 When thou with rebukes *d* correct
Ps 43:2 why *d* thou cast me off
Ps 44:12 *d* not increase thy wealth by
Ps 99:4 thou *d* establish equity, thou
Prov 4:8 honour, when thou *d* embrace her
Eccl 7:10 for thou *d* not enquire wisely
Song 5:9 beloved, that thou *d* so charge us
Is 26:7 *d* weigh the path of the just
Is 36:5 now on whom *d* thou trust, that
Jer 32:3 Wherefore *d* thou prophesy, and say
Jer 40:14 *D* thou certainly know that Baalis
Jer 48:18 daughter that *d* inhabit Dibon
Lam 5:20 Wherefore *d* thou forget us for
Eze 2:6 thou *d* dwell among scorpions
Eze 32:19 Whom *d* thou pass in beauty
Eze 33:8 if thou *d* not speak to warn the
Mic 4:9 Now why *d* thou cry out aloud
Hab 1:3 Why *d* thou shew me iniquity, and
Lk 10:40 *d* thou not care that my sister
Lk 23:40 *D* not thou fear God, seeing thou
Jn 6:30 what *d* thou work?
Jn 9:34 born in sins, and *d* thou teach us
Jn 9:35 *D* thou believe on the Son of God
Jn 10:24 How long *d* thou make us to doubt
Jn 13:6 him, Lord, *d* thou wash my feet
Rom 2:21 should not steal, *d* thou steal
Rom 2:22 adultery, *d* thou commit adultery
Rom 2:22 idols, *d* thou commit sacrilege
Rom 2:27 circumcision *d* transgress the law
Rom 14:10 But why *d* thou judge thy brother
Rom 14:10 or why *d* thou set at nought thy
1Cor 4:7 why *d* thou glory, as if thou
Rev 6:10 *d* thou not judge and avenge our

**DOTHAN** *(do'-than) A city in Manasseh.*
Gen 37:17 I heard them say, Let us go to *D*
Gen 37:17 his brethren, and found them in *D*
2Kin 6:13 him, saying, Behold, he is in *D*

**DOUBLE**
Gen 43:12 take *d* money in your hand
Gen 43:15 they took *d* money in their hand,
Ex 22:4 he shall restore *d*
Ex 22:7 the thief be found, let him pay *d*
Ex 22:9 he shall pay *d* unto his neighbour
Ex 26:9 shalt *d* the sixth curtain in the
Ex 39:9 they made the breastplate *d*
Deut 15:18 worth a *d* hired servant to thee
Deut 21:17 by giving him a *d* portion of all
2Kin 2:9 let a *d* portion of thy spirit be
1Chr 12:33 they were not of *d* heart
Job 11:6 that they are *d* to that which is
Job 41:13 can come to him with his *d* bridle
Ps 12:2 with a *d* heart do they speak
Is 40:2 LORD's hand *d* for all her sins
Is 61:7 For your shame ye shall have *d*
Is 61:7 land they shall possess the *d*
Jer 16:18 their iniquity and their sin *d*
Jer 17:18 destroy them with *d* destruction
Zec 9:12 that I will render *d* unto thee
1Ti 5:17 be counted worthy of *d* honour
Jas 1:8 A *d* minded man is unstable in all
Jas 4:8 purify your hearts, ye *d* minded
Rev 18:6 *d* unto her *d* according to
Rev 18:6 she hath filled fill to her *d*

**DOUBLED**
Gen 41:32 dream was *d* unto Pharaoh twice
Ex 28:16 Foursquare it shall be being *d*
Ex 39:9 span the breadth thereof, being *d*
Eze 21:14 let the sword be *d* the third time

**DOUBT**
Gen 37:33 is without *d* rent in pieces
Deut 28:66 life shall hang in *d* before thee
Job 12:2 No *d* but ye are the people, and
Mt 14:31 faith, wherefore didst thou *d*
Mt 21:21 *d* not, ye shall not only do this
Mk 11:23 shall not *d* in his heart, but
Lk 11:20 no *d* the kingdom of God is come
Jn 10:24 How long dost thou make us to *d*
Acts 2:12 were all amazed, and were in *d*
Acts 28:4 No *d* this man is a murderer, whom
1Cor 9:10 For our sakes, no *d*, this is
Gal 4:20 for I stand in *d* of you
1Jn 2:19 they would no *d* have continued

**DOUBTED**
Mt 28:17 but some *d*
Acts 5:24 they *d* of them whereunto this
Acts 10:17 Now while Peter *d* in himself what
Acts 25:20 because I *d* of such manner of

**DOUBTING**
Jn 13:22 on another, *d* of whom he spake
Acts 10:20 down, and go with them, *d* nothing
Acts 11:12 bade me go with them, nothing *d*
1Ti 2:8 up holy hands, without wrath and *d*

**DOUBTLESS**
Num 14:30 *D* ye shall not come into the land
2Sa 5:19 for I will *d* deliver the
Ps 126:6 shall *d* come again with rejoicing
Is 63:16 *D* thou art our father, though
1Cor 9:2 unto others, yet *d* I am to you
2Cor 12:1 not expedient for me *d* to glory
Phil 3:8 Yea *d*, and I count all things but

**DOUGH**
Ex 12:34 the people took their *d* before it
Ex 12:39 baked unleavened cakes of the *d*
Num 15:20 of your *d* for an heave offering
Num 15:21 Of the first of your *d* ye shall
Neh 10:37 bring the firstfruits of our *d*
Jer 7:18 fire, and the women knead their *d*
Eze 44:30 the priest the first of your *d*
Hos 7:4 after he hath kneaded the *d*

**DOVE**
Gen 8:8 Also he sent forth a *d* from him
Gen 8:9 But the *d* found no rest for the
Gen 8:10 sent forth the *d* out of the ark
Gen 8:11 the *d* came in to him in the
Gen 8:12 and sent forth the *d*
Ps 55:6 Oh that I had wings like a *d*
Ps 68:13 wings of a *d* covered with silver
Song 2:14 O my *d*, that art in the clefts of
Song 5:2 to me, my sister, my love, my *d*
Song 6:9 My *d*, my undefiled is but one

Is 38:14 I did mourn as a *d*
Jer 48:28 be like the *d* that maketh her
Hos 7:11 is like a silly *d* without heart
Hos 11:11 as a *d* out of the land of Assyria
Mt 3:16 Spirit of God descending like a *d*
Mk 1:10 the Spirit like a *d* descending
Lk 3:22 a bodily shape like a *d* upon him
Jn 1:32 descending from heaven like a *d*

## DOVES
Song 5:12 eyes of *d* by the rivers of waters
Is 59:11 like bears, and mourn sore like *d*
Is 60:8 as the *d* to their windows
Eze 7:16 mountains like *d* of the valleys
Nah 2:7 lead her as with the voice of *d*
Mt 10:16 as serpents, and harmless as *d*
Mt 21:12 and the seats of them that sold *d*
Mk 11:15 and the seats of them that sold *d*
Jn 2:14 that sold oxen and sheep and *d*
Jn 2:16 And said unto them that sold *d*

## DOWRY
Gen 30:20 God hath endued me with a good *d*
Gen 34:12 Ask me never so much *d* and gift,
Ex 22:17 according to the *d* of virgins
1Sa 18:25 The king desireth not any *d*

## DRAGON
Neh 2:13 valley, even before the *d* well
Ps 91:13 the *d* shalt thou trample under
Is 27:1 he shall slay the *d* that is in
Is 51:9 hath cut Rahab, and wounded the *d*
Jer 51:34 he hath swallowed me up like a *d*
Eze 29:3 the great *d* that lieth in the
Rev 12:3 and behold a great red *d*, having
Rev 12:4 the *d* stood before the woman
Rev 12:7 his angels fought against the *d*
Rev 12:7 the *d* fought and his angels,
Rev 12:9 the great *d* was cast out, that
Rev 12:13 when the *d* saw that he was cast
Rev 12:16 which the *d* cast out of his mouth
Rev 12:17 the *d* was wroth with the woman,
Rev 13:2 the *d* gave him his power, and his
Rev 13:4 they worshipped the *d* which gave
Rev 13:11 like a lamb, and he spake as a *d*
Rev 16:13 come out of the mouth of the *d*
Rev 20:2 And he laid hold on the *d*, that

## DRAGONS
Deut 32:33 Their wine is the poison of *d*
Job 30:29 I am a brother to *d*, and a
Ps 44:19 sore broken us in the place of *d*
Ps 74:13 the heads of the *d* in the waters
Ps 148:7 the LORD from the earth, ye *d*
Is 13:22 *d* in their pleasant palaces
Is 34:13 and it shall be an habitation of *d*
Is 35:7 in the habitation of *d*, where
Is 43:20 the field shall honour me, the *d*
Jer 9:11 Jerusalem heaps, and a den of *d*
Jer 10:22 of Judah desolate, and a den of *d*
Jer 14:6 they snuffed up the wind like *d*
Jer 49:33 Hazor shall be a dwelling for *d*
Jer 51:37 heaps, a dwelling place for *d*
Mic 1:8 I will make a wailing like the *d*
Mal 1:3 waste for the *d* of the wilderness

## DRAMS
1Chr 29:7 talents and ten thousand *d*
Ezr 2:69 and one thousand *d* of gold
Ezr 8:27 basons of gold, of a thousand *d*
Neh 7:70 the treasure a thousand *d* of gold
Neh 7:71 work twenty thousand *d* of gold
Neh 7:72 was twenty thousand *d* of gold

## DRANK
Gen 9:21 he *d* of the wine, and was drunken
Gen 24:46 so I *d*, and she made the camels
Gen 27:25 and he brought him wine, and he *d*
Gen 43:34 And they *d*, and were merry with him
Num 20:11 abundantly, and the congregation *d*
Deut 32:38 *d* the wine of their drink
2Sa 12:3 *d* of his own cup, and lay in his
1Kin 13:19 bread in his house, and *d* water
1Kin 17:6 and he *d* of the brook
Dan 1:5 meat, and of the wine which he *d*
Dan 1:8 nor with the wine which he *d*
Dan 5:1 *d* wine before the thousand
Dan 5:3 and his concubines, *d* in them
Dan 5:4 They *d* wine, and praised the gods
Mk 14:23 and they all *d* of it
Lk 17:27 They did eat, they *d*, they
Lk 17:28 they did eat, they *d*, they bought
Jn 4:12 *d* thereof himself, and his
1Cor 10:4 for they *d* of that spiritual Rock

## DRAUGHT
2Kin 10:27 made it a *d* house unto this day
Mt 15:17 belly, and is cast out into the *d*
Mk 7:19 belly, and goeth out into the *d*
Lk 5:4 and let down your nets for a *d*
Lk 5:9 at the *d* of the fishes which they

## DRAVE
Ex 14:25 wheels, that they *d* them heavily
Josh 16:10 they *d* not out the Canaanites
Josh 24:12 which *d* them out from before you,
Josh 24:18 the LORD *d* out from before us all
Judg 1:19 he *d* out the inhabitants of the
Judg 6:9 *d* them out from before you, and
1Sa 30:20 which they *d* before those other
2Sa 6:3 sons of Abinadab, *d* the new cart
2Kin 16:6 Syria, and *d* the Jews from Elath
2Kin 17:21 Jeroboam *d* Israel from following
1Chr 13:7 and Uzza and Ahio *d* the cart
Acts 7:45 whom God *d* out before the face of
Acts 18:16 he *d* them from the judgment seat

## DRAW
Gen 24:11 time that women go out to *d* water
Gen 24:13 of the city come out to *d* water
Gen 24:19 I will *d* water for thy camels
Gen 24:20 again unto the well to *d* water
Gen 24:43 virgin cometh forth to *d* water
Gen 24:44 I will also *d* for thy camels
Ex 3:5 And he said, *D* not nigh hither
Ex 12:21 them, *D* out and take you a lamb
Ex 15:9 I will *d* my sword, my hand shall
Lev 26:33 will *d* out a sword after you
Judg 3:22 so that he could not *d* the dagger
Judg 4:6 *d* toward mount Tabor, and take
Judg 4:7 I will *d* unto thee to the river
Judg 9:54 *D* thy sword, and slay me, that men
Judg 19:13 let us *d* near to one of these
Judg 20:32 *d* them from the city unto the
1Sa 9:11 maidens going out to *d* water
1Sa 14:36 Let us *d* near hither unto God
1Sa 14:38 *D* ye near hither, all the chief
1Sa 31:4 *D* thy sword, and thrust me through
2Sa 17:13 we will *d* it into the river,
1Chr 10:4 *D* thy sword, and thrust me through
Job 21:33 and every man shall *d* after him
Job 40:23 he trusteth that he can *d* up
Job 41:1 Canst thou *d* out leviathan with
Ps 28:3 *D* me not away with the wicked, and
Ps 35:3 *D* out also the spear, and stop the
Ps 69:18 *D* nigh unto my soul, and redeem it
Ps 73:28 is good for me to *d* near to God
Ps 85:5 wilt thou *d* out thine anger to
Ps 107:18 they *d* near unto the gates of
Ps 119:150 They *d* nigh that follow after
Prov 20:5 of understanding will *d* it out
Eccl 12:1 come not, nor the years *d* nigh
Song 1:4 *D* me, we will run after thee
Is 5:18 Woe unto them that *d* iniquity
Is 5:19 of the Holy One of Israel *d* nigh
Is 12:3 ye *d* water out of the wells of
Is 29:13 people *d* near me with their mouth
Is 45:20 *d* near together, ye that are
Is 57:3 But *d* near hither, ye sons of the
Is 57:4 a wide mouth, and *d* out the tongue
Is 58:10 if thou *d* out thy soul to the
Is 66:19 that *d* the bow, to Tubal, and
Jer 30:21 and I will cause him to *d* near
Jer 46:3 and shield, and *d* near to battle
Jer 49:20 of the flock shall *d* them out
Jer 50:45 of the flock shall *d* them out
Lam 4:3 the sea monsters *d* out the breast
Eze 5:2 I will *d* out a sword after them
Eze 5:12 I will *d* out a sword after them
Eze 9:1 charge over the city to *d* near
Eze 12:14 I will *d* out the sword after them
Eze 21:3 will *d* forth my sword out of his
Eze 22:4 hast caused thy days to *d* near
Eze 28:7 they shall *d* their swords against
Eze 30:11 they shall *d* their swords against
Eze 32:20 *d* her and all her multitudes
Joel 3:9 let all the men of war *d* near
Nah 3:14 *D* thee waters for the siege,
Hag 2:16 to *d* out fifty vessels out of the
Jn 2:8 *D* out now, and bear unto the
Jn 4:7 a woman of Samaria to *d* water
Jn 4:11 Sir, thou hast nothing to *d* with
Jn 4:15 not, neither come hither to *d*
Jn 6:44 Father which hath sent me *d* him
Jn 12:32 the earth, will *d* all men unto me
Jn 21:6 now they were not able to *d* it
Acts 20:30 to *d* away disciples after them
Heb 7:19 by the which we *d* nigh unto God
Heb 10:22 Let us *d* near with a true heart
Heb 10:38 but if any man *d* back, my soul
Heb 10:39 of them who *d* back unto perdition
Jas 2:6 *d* you before the judgment seats
Jas 4:8 *D* nigh to God, and he will *d*

## DRAWETH
Deut 25:11 the wife of the one *d* near for to
Judg 19:9 now the day *d* toward evening, I
Job 24:22 He *d* also the mighty with his
Job 33:22 his soul *d* near unto the grave,
Ps 10:9 when he *d* him into his net
Ps 88:3 my life *d* nigh unto the grave
Is 26:17 that *d* near the time of her
Eze 7:12 The time is come, the day *d* near
Mt 15:8 This people *d* nigh unto me with
Lk 21:8 and the time *d* near
Lk 21:28 for your redemption *d* nigh
Jas 5:8 for the coming of the Lord *d* nigh

## DRAWN
Num 22:23 way, and his sword *d* in his hand
Num 22:31 way, and his sword *d* in his hand
Deut 21:3 and which hath not *d* in the yoke
Deut 30:17 not hear, but shalt be *d* away
Josh 5:13 him with his sword *d* in his hand
Josh 8:6 till we have *d* them from the city
Josh 8:16 were *d* away from the city
Josh 15:9 the border was *d* from the top of
Josh 15:9 and the border was *d* to Baalah
Josh 15:11 and the border was *d* to Shicron
Josh 18:14 And the border was *d* thence
Josh 18:17 was *d* from the north, and went
Judg 20:31 were *d* away from the city
Ruth 2:9 that which the young men have *d*
1Chr 21:16 having a *d* sword in his hand
Job 20:25 It is *d*, and cometh out of the
Ps 37:14 The wicked have *d* out the sword
Ps 55:21 than oil, yet were they *d* swords
Prov 24:11 them that are *d* unto death
Is 21:15 from the swords, from the *d* sword
Is 28:9 the milk, and *d* from the breasts
Jer 22:19 with the burial of an ass, *d*
Jer 31:3 with lovingkindness have I *d* thee
Lam 2:3 he hath *d* back his right hand
Eze 21:5 have *d* forth my sword out of his
Eze 21:28 thou, The sword, the sword is *d*
Acts 11:10 all were *d* up again into heaven
Jas 1:14 when he is *d* away of his own lust

## DREAD
Gen 9:2 the *d* of you shall be upon every
Ex 15:16 Fear and *d* shall fall upon them
Deut 1:29 *D* not, neither be afraid of them
Deut 2:25 will I begin to put the *d* of thee
Deut 11:25 the *d* of you upon all the land
1Chr 22:13 *d* not, nor be dismayed
Job 13:11 and his *d* fall upon you
Job 13:21 let not thy *d* make me afraid
Is 8:13 your fear, and let him be your *d*

## DREADFUL
Gen 28:17 and said, How *d* is this place
Job 15:21 A *d* sound is in his ears
Eze 1:18 were so high that they were *d*
Dan 7:7 and behold a fourth beast, *d*
Dan 7:19 from all the others, exceeding *d*
Dan 9:4 *d* God, keeping the covenant and
Hab 1:7 They are terrible and *d*
Mal 1:14 my name is *d* among the heathen
Mal 4:5 of the great and *d* day of the LORD

## DREAM
Gen 20:3 came to Abimelech in a *d* by night
Gen 20:6 And God said unto him in a *d*
Gen 31:10 up mine eyes, and saw in a *d*
Gen 31:11 angel of God spake unto me in a *d*
Gen 31:24 Laban the Syrian in a *d* by night
Gen 37:5 And Joseph dreamed a *d*, and he told
Gen 37:6 this *d* which I have dreamed
Gen 37:9 And he dreamed yet another *d*
Gen 37:9 Behold, I have dreamed a *d* more
Gen 37:10 What is this *d* that thou hast
Gen 40:5 And they dreamed a *d* both of them
Gen 40:5 each man his *d* in one night
Gen 40:5 to the interpretation of his *d*
Gen 40:8 unto him, We have dreamed a *d*
Gen 40:9 chief butler told his *d* to Joseph
Gen 40:9 and said to him, In my *d*
Gen 40:16 unto Joseph, I also was in my *d*
Gen 41:7 awoke, and, behold, it was a *d*

Gen 41:8 and Pharaoh told them his *d*
Gen 41:11 And we dreamed a *d* in one night
Gen 41:11 to the interpretation of his *d*
Gen 41:12 to his *d* he did interpret
Gen 41:15 unto Joseph, I have dreamed a *d*
Gen 41:15 understand a *d* to interpret it
Gen 41:17 Pharaoh said unto Joseph, In my *d*
Gen 41:22 And I saw in my *d*, and, behold,
Gen 41:25 Pharaoh, The *d* of Pharaoh is one
Gen 41:26 are seven years: the *d* is one
Gen 41:32 for that the *d* was doubled unto
Num 12:6 and will speak unto him in a *d*
Judg 7:13 man that told a *d* unto his fellow
Judg 7:13 and said, Behold, I dreamed a *d*
Judg 7:15 Gideon heard the telling of the *d*
1Kin 3:5 to Solomon in a *d* by night
1Kin 3:15 and, behold, it was a *d*
Job 20:8 He shall fly away as a *d*, and
Job 33:15 In a *d*, in a vision of the night,
Ps 73:20 As a *d* when one awaketh
Ps 126:1 of Zion, we were like them that *d*
Eccl 5:3 For a *d* cometh through the
Is 29:7 shall be as a *d* of a night vision
Jer 23:28 hath a *d*, let him tell a *d*
Dan 2:3 unto them, I have dreamed a *d*
Dan 2:3 spirit was troubled to know the *d*
Dan 2:4 tell thy servants the *d*, and we
Dan 2:5 will not make known unto me the *d*
Dan 2:6 But if ye shew the *d*, and the
Dan 2:6 therefore shew me the *d*, and the
Dan 2:7 the king tell his servants the *d*
Dan 2:9 will not make known unto me the *d*
Dan 2:9 therefore tell me the *d*, and I
Dan 2:26 unto me the *d* which I have seen
Dan 2:28 Thy *d*, and the visions of thy head
Dan 2:36 This is the *d*; and we will
Dan 2:45 and the *d* is certain, and the
Dan 4:5 I saw a *d* which made me afraid,
Dan 4:6 me the interpretation of the *d*
Dan 4:7 and I told the *d* before them
Dan 4:8 and before him I told the *d*
Dan 4:9 visions of my *d* that I have seen
Dan 4:18 This *d* I king Nebuchadnezzar have
Dan 4:19 said, Belteshazzar, let not the *d*
Dan 4:19 the *d* be to them that hate thee,
Dan 7:1 king of Babylon Daniel had a *d*
Dan 7:1 then he wrote the *d*, and told the
Joel 2:28 your old men shall *d* dreams
Mt 1:20 the Lord appeared unto him in a *d*
Mt 2:12 being warned of God in a *d* that
Mt 2:13 Lord appeareth to Joseph in a *d*
Mt 2:19 in a *d* to Joseph in Egypt
Mt 2:22 being warned of God in a *d*
Mt 27:19 this day in a *d* because of him
Acts 2:17 and your old men shall *d* dreams

## DREAMED

Gen 28:12 And he *d*, and behold a ladder set
Gen 37:5 Joseph *d* a dream, and he told it
Gen 37:6 you, this dream which I have *d*
Gen 37:9 he *d* yet another dream, and told
Gen 37:9 Behold, I have *d* a dream more
Gen 37:10 is this dream that thou hast *d*
Gen 40:5 they *d* a dream both of them, each
Gen 40:8 said unto him, We have *d* a dream
Gen 41:1 of two full years, that Pharaoh *d*
Gen 41:5 And he slept and *d* the second time
Gen 41:11 we *d* a dream in one night, I and
Gen 41:11 we *d* each man according to the
Gen 41:15 I have *d* a dream, and there is
Gen 42:9 the dreams which he *d* of them
Judg 7:13 I *d* a dream, and, lo, a cake of
Jer 23:25 saying, I have *d*, I have *d*
Jer 29:8 dreams which ye cause to be *d*
Dan 2:1 Nebuchadnezzar *d* dreams,
Dan 2:3 I have *d* a dream, and my spirit

## DREAMER

Gen 37:19 to another, Behold, this *d* cometh
Deut 13:1 or a *d* of dreams, and giveth thee
Deut 13:3 that prophet, or that *d* of dreams
Deut 13:5 or that *d* of dreams, shall be put

## DREAMS

Gen 37:8 hated him yet the more for his *d*
Gen 37:20 see what will become of his *d*
Gen 41:12 and he interpreted to us our *d*
Gen 42:9 Joseph remembered the *d* which he
Deut 13:1 you a prophet, or a dreamer of *d*
Deut 13:3 prophet, or that dreamer of *d*
Deut 13:5 prophet, or that dreamer of *d*
1Sa 28:6 answered him not, neither by *d*
1Sa 28:15 neither by prophets, nor by *d*
Job 7:14 Then thou scarest me with *d*
Eccl 5:7 For in the multitude of *d*
Jer 23:27 to forget my name by their *d*
Jer 23:32 them that prophesy false *d*
Jer 29:8 neither hearken to your *d* which
Dan 1:17 understanding in all visions and *d*
Dan 2:1 Nebuchadnezzar dreamed *d*
Dan 2:2 for to shew the king his *d*
Dan 5:12 understanding, interpreting of *d*
Joel 2:28 your old men shall dream *d*
Zec 10:2 seen a lie, and have told false *d*
Acts 2:17 and your old men shall dream *d*

## DRESS

Gen 2:15 into the garden of Eden to *d* it
Gen 18:7 and he hasted to *d* it
Deut 28:39 *d* them, but shalt neither drink
2Sa 12:4 to *d* for the wayfaring man that
2Sa 13:5 *d* the meat in my sight, that I
2Sa 13:7 Amnon's house, and *d* him meat
1Kin 17:12 *d* it for me and my son, that we
1Kin 18:23 I will *d* the other bullock, and
1Kin 18:25 for yourselves, and *d* it first

## DRESSED

Gen 18:8 milk, and the calf which he had *d*
Lev 7:9 all that is *d* in the fryingpan,
1Sa 25:18 of wine, and five sheep ready *d*
2Sa 12:4 *d* it for the man that was come to
2Sa 19:24 king, and had neither *d* his feet
1Kin 18:26 was given them, and they *d* it
Heb 6:7 meet for them by whom it is *d*

## DREW

Gen 18:23 And Abraham *d* near, and said, Wilt
Gen 24:20 water, and *d* for all his camels
Gen 24:45 down unto the well, and *d* water
Gen 37:28 and they *d* and lifted up Joseph out
Gen 38:29 as he *d* back his hand, that,
Gen 47:29 the time *d* nigh that Israel must
Ex 2:10 Because I *d* him out of the water
Ex 2:16 *d* water, and filled the troughs to
Ex 2:19 also *d* water enough for us, and
Ex 14:10 And when Pharaoh *d* nigh, the
Ex 20:21 Moses *d* near unto the thick
Lev 9:5 and all the congregation *d* near
Josh 8:11 *d* nigh, and came before the city,
Josh 8:26 For Joshua *d* not his hand back,
Judg 8:10 twenty thousand men that *d* sword
Judg 8:20 But the youth *d* not his sword
Judg 20:2 thousand footmen that *d* sword
Judg 20:15 and six thousand men that *d* sword
Judg 20:17 hundred thousand men that *d* sword
Judg 20:25 all these *d* the sword
Judg 20:35 all these *d* the sword
Judg 20:37 liers in wait *d* themselves along
Judg 20:46 thousand men that *d* the sword
Ruth 4:8 So he *d* off his shoe
1Sa 7:6 *d* water, and poured it out before
1Sa 7:10 the Philistines *d* near to battle
1Sa 9:18 Then Saul *d* near to Samuel in the
1Sa 17:16 And the Philistine *d* near morning
1Sa 17:40 he *d* near to the Philistine
1Sa 17:41 came on and *d* near unto David
1Sa 17:48 *d* nigh to meet David, that David
1Sa 17:51 *d* it out of the sheath thereof,
2Sa 10:13 And Joab *d* nigh, and the people
2Sa 18:25 And he came apace, and *d* near
2Sa 22:17 he *d* me out of many waters
2Sa 23:16 *d* water out of the well of
2Sa 24:9 valiant men that *d* the sword
1Kin 2:1 Now the days of David *d* nigh that
1Kin 8:8 they *d* out the staves, that the
1Kin 22:34 a certain man *d* a bow at a
2Kin 3:26 seven hundred men that *d* swords
2Kin 9:24 Jehu *d* a bow with his full
1Chr 11:18 *d* water out of the well of
1Chr 19:14 *d* nigh before the Syrians unto
1Chr 19:16 *d* forth the Syrians that were
1Chr 21:5 hundred thousand men that *d* sword
1Chr 21:5 and ten thousand men that *d* sword
2Chr 5:9 they *d* out the staves of the ark,
2Chr 14:8 *d* bows, two hundred and fourscore
2Chr 18:33 a certain man *d* a bow at a
Est 5:2 So Esther *d* near, and touched the
Est 9:1 his decree *d* near to be put in
Ps 18:16 he *d* me out of many waters
Is 41:5 were afraid, *d* near, and came
Jer 38:13 So they *d* up Jeremiah with cords,
Hos 11:4 I *d* them with cords of a man,
Zeph 3:2 she *d* not near to her God
Mt 13:48 they *d* to shore, and sat down, and
Mt 21:1 when they *d* nigh unto Jerusalem,
Mt 21:34 when the time of the fruit *d* near
Mt 26:51 *d* his sword, and struck a servant
Mk 6:53 of Gennesaret, and *d* to the shore
Mk 14:47 of them that stood by *d* a sword
Lk 15:1 Then *d* near unto him all the
Lk 15:25 *d* nigh to the house, he heard
Lk 22:1 feast of unleavened bread *d* nigh
Lk 22:47 *d* near unto Jesus to kiss him
Lk 23:54 preparation, and the sabbath *d* on
Lk 24:15 and reasoned, Jesus himself *d* near
Lk 24:28 they *d* nigh unto the village,
Jn 2:9 servants which *d* the water knew
Jn 18:10 Simon Peter having a sword *d* it
Jn 21:11 *d* the net to land full of great
Acts 5:37 *d* away much people after him
Acts 7:17 the time of the promise *d* nigh
Acts 7:31 as he *d* near to behold it, the
Acts 10:9 *d* nigh unto the city, Peter went
Acts 14:19 *d* him out of the city, supposing
Acts 16:19 *d* them into the marketplace unto
Acts 16:27 he *d* out his sword, and would have
Acts 17:6 they *d* Jason and certain brethren
Acts 19:33 they *d* Alexander out of the
Acts 21:30 Paul, and *d* him out of the temple
Acts 27:27 that they *d* near to some country
Rev 12:4 his tail *d* the third part of the

## DRIED

Gen 8:7 were *d* up from off the earth
Gen 8:13 the waters were *d* up from off the
Gen 8:14 day of the month, was the earth *d*
Lev 2:14 green ears of corn *d* by the fire
Num 6:3 nor eat moist grapes, or *d*
Num 11:6 But now our soul is *d* away
Josh 2:10 For we have heard how the LORD *d*
Josh 4:23 For the LORD your God *d* up the
Josh 4:23 which he *d* up from before us,
Josh 5:1 heard that the LORD had *d* up the
Judg 16:7 green withs that were never *d*
Judg 16:8 green withs which had not been *d*
1Kin 13:4 *d* up, so that he could not pull
1Kin 17:7 a while, that the brook *d* up
2Kin 19:24 I *d* up all the rivers of besieged
Job 18:16 His roots shall be *d* up beneath
Job 28:4 they are *d* up, they are gone away
Ps 22:15 My strength is *d* up like a
Ps 69:3 my throat is *d*
Ps 106:9 the Red sea also, and it was *d* up
Is 5:13 their multitude *d* up with thirst
Is 19:5 the river shall be wasted and *d* up
Is 19:6 defence shall be emptied and *d* up
Is 37:25 have I *d* up all the rivers of the
Is 51:10 thou not it which hath *d* the sea
Jer 23:10 places of the wilderness are *d* up
Jer 50:38 and they shall be *d* up
Eze 17:24 have *d* up the green tree, and have
Eze 19:12 and the east wind *d* up her fruit
Eze 37:11 behold, they say, Our bones are *d*
Hos 9:16 is smitten, their root is *d* up
Hos 13:15 and his fountain shall be *d* up
Joel 1:10 the new wine is *d* up, the oil
Joel 1:12 The vine is *d* up, and the fig tree
Joel 1:20 for the rivers of waters are *d* up
Zec 11:17 his arm shall be clean *d* up
Mk 5:29 fountain of her blood was *d* up
Mk 11:20 the fig tree *d* up from the roots
Rev 16:12 and the water thereof was *d* up

## DRINK

Gen 19:32 let us make our father *d* wine
Gen 19:33 their father *d* wine that night
Gen 19:34 let us make him *d* wine this night
Gen 19:35 father *d* wine that night also
Gen 21:19 with water, and gave the lad *d*
Gen 24:14 I pray thee, that I may *d*
Gen 24:14 and she shall say, *D*
Gen 24:14 and I will give thy camels *d* also
Gen 24:17 *d* a little water of thy pitcher
Gen 24:18 And she said, *D*, my lord
Gen 24:18 upon her hand, and gave him *d*
Gen 24:19 And when she had done giving him *d*
Gen 24:43 little water of thy pitcher to *d*
Gen 24:44 And she say to me, Both *d* thou
Gen 24:45 and I said unto her, Let me *d*
Gen 24:46 from her shoulder, and said, *D*
Gen 24:46 and I will give thy camels *d* also
Gen 24:46 and she made the camels *d* also
Gen 24:54 And they did eat and *d*, he and the
Gen 25:34 and he did eat and *d*, and rose up,

Gen 26:30 a feast, and they did eat and *d*
Gen 30:38 troughs when the flocks came to *d*
Gen 30:38 conceive when they came to *d*
Gen 35:14 he poured a *d* offering thereon,
Ex 7:18 to *d* of the water of the river
Ex 7:21 the Egyptians could not *d* of the
Ex 7:24 about the river for water to *d*
Ex 7:24 for they could not *d* of the water
Ex 15:23 they could not *d* of the waters of
Ex 15:24 Moses, saying, What shall we *d*
Ex 17:1 was no water for the people to *d*
Ex 17:2 said, Give us water that we may *d*
Ex 17:6 out of it, that the people may *d*
Ex 24:11 they saw God, and did eat and *d*
Ex 29:40 an hin of wine for a *d* offering
Ex 29:41 to the *d* offering thereof
Ex 30:9 shall ye pour *d* offering thereon
Ex 32:6 people sat down to eat and to *d*
Ex 32:20 the children of Israel *d* of it
Ex 34:28 neither eat bread, nor *d* water
Lev 10:9 Do not *d* wine nor strong *d*,
Lev 10:9 Do not *d* wine nor strong *d*
Lev 11:34 all *d* that may be drunk in every
Lev 23:13 the *d* offering thereof shall be
Lev 23:18 their *d* offerings, even an
Lev 23:37 *d* offerings, every thing upon his
Num 5:24 he shall cause the woman to *d* the
Num 5:26 cause the woman to *d* the water
Num 5:27 he hath made her to *d* the water
Num 6:3 himself from wine and strong *d*
Num 6:3 shall *d* no vinegar of wine, or
Num 6:3 of wine, or vinegar of strong *d*
Num 6:3 neither shall he *d* any liquor of
Num 6:15 offering, and their *d* offerings
Num 6:17 meat offering, and his *d* offering
Num 6:20 that the Nazarite may *d* wine
Num 15:5 a *d* offering shalt thou prepare
Num 15:7 for a *d* offering thou shalt offer
Num 15:10 thou shalt bring for a *d* offering
Num 15:24 his *d* offering, according to the
Num 20:5 neither is there any water to *d*
Num 20:8 congregation and their beasts *d*
Num 20:17 neither will we *d* of the water of
Num 20:19 my cattle *d* of thy water, then I
Num 21:22 we will not *d* of the waters of
Num 23:24 prey, and *d* the blood of the slain
Num 28:7 the *d* offering thereof shall be
Num 28:7 unto the LORD for a *d* offering
Num 28:8 as the *d* offering thereof, thou
Num 28:9 oil, and the *d* offering thereof
Num 28:10 burnt offering, and his *d* offering
Num 28:14 their *d* offerings shall be half
Num 28:15 burnt offering, and his *d* offering
Num 28:24 burnt offering, and his *d* offering
Num 28:31 blemish) and their *d* offerings
Num 29:6 their *d* offerings, according unto
Num 29:11 of it, and their *d* offerings
Num 29:16 meat offering, and his *d* offering
Num 29:18 their *d* offerings for the
Num 29:19 thereof, and their *d* offerings
Num 29:21 their *d* offerings for the
Num 29:22 meat offering, and his *d* offering
Num 29:24 their *d* offerings for the
Num 29:25 meat offering, and his *d* offering
Num 29:27 their *d* offerings for the
Num 29:28 meat offering, and his *d* offering
Num 29:30 their *d* offerings for the
Num 29:31 meat offering, and his *d* offering
Num 29:33 their *d* offerings for the
Num 29:34 meat offering, and his *d* offering
Num 29:37 their *d* offerings for the bullock
Num 29:38 meat offering, and his *d* offering
Num 29:39 for your *d* offerings, and for your
Num 33:14 was no water for the people to *d*
Deut 2:6 of them for money, that ye may *d*
Deut 2:28 me water for money, that I may *d*
Deut 9:9 neither did eat bread nor *d* water
Deut 9:18 nor *d* water, because of all your
Deut 14:26 or for wine, or for strong *d*
Deut 28:39 but shalt neither *d* of the wine
Deut 29:6 have ye drunk wine or strong *d*
Deut 32:14 thou didst *d* the pure blood of
Deut 32:38 the wine of their *d* offerings
Judg 4:19 I pray thee, a little water to *d*
Judg 4:19 a bottle of milk, and gave him *d*
Judg 7:5 boweth down upon his knees to *d*
Judg 7:6 down upon their knees to *d* water
Judg 9:27 of their god, and did eat and *d*
Judg 13:4 *d* not wine nor strong *d*
Judg 13:4 and *d* not wine nor strong *d*
Judg 13:7 now *d* no wine nor strong
Judg 13:7 no wine nor strong *d*
Judg 13:14 neither let her *d* wine or strong
Judg 13:14 let her *d* wine or strong *d*
Judg 19:4 so they did eat and *d*, and lodged
Judg 19:6 eat and *d* both of them together
Judg 19:21 their feet, and did eat and *d*
Ruth 2:9 *d* of that which the young men
1Sa 1:15 drunken neither wine nor strong *d*
1Sa 30:11 and they made him *d* water
2Sa 11:11 into mine house, to eat and to *d*
2Sa 11:13 him, he did eat and *d* before him
2Sa 16:2 be faint in the wilderness may *d*
2Sa 19:35 taste what I eat or what I *d*
2Sa 23:15 Oh that one would give me *d* of
2Sa 23:16 he would not *d* thereof, but
2Sa 23:17 therefore he would not *d* it
1Kin 1:25 *d* before him, and say, God save
1Kin 13:8 bread nor *d* water in this place
1Kin 13:9 nor *d* water, nor turn again by
1Kin 13:16 neither will I eat bread nor *d*
1Kin 13:17 eat no bread nor *d* water there
1Kin 13:18 that he may eat bread and *d* water
1Kin 13:22 thee, Eat no bread, and *d* no water
1Kin 17:4 that thou shalt *d* of the brook
1Kin 17:10 water in a vessel, that I may *d*
1Kin 18:41 unto Ahab, Get thee up, eat and *d*
1Kin 18:42 So Ahab went up to eat and to *d*
1Kin 19:6 And he did eat and *d*, and laid him
1Kin 19:8 And he arose, and did eat and *d*
2Kin 3:17 filled with water, that ye may *d*
2Kin 6:22 them, that they may eat and *d*
2Kin 7:8 into one tent, and did eat and *d*
2Kin 9:34 he was come in, he did eat and *d*
2Kin 16:13 and poured his *d* offering
2Kin 16:15 offering, and their *d* offerings
2Kin 18:27 *d* their own piss with you
2Kin 18:31 *d* ye every one the waters of his
1Chr 11:17 Oh that one would give me *d* of
1Chr 11:18 but David would not *d* of it
1Chr 11:19 shall I *d* the blood of these men
1Chr 11:19 Therefore he would not *d* it
1Chr 29:21 lambs, with their *d* offerings
1Chr 29:22 *d* before the LORD on that day
2Chr 28:15 them, and gave them to eat and to *d*
2Chr 29:35 the *d* offerings for every burnt
Ezr 3:7 and meat, and *d*, and oil, unto them
Ezr 7:17 their *d* offerings, and offer them
Ezr 10:6 he did eat no bread, nor *d* water
Neh 8:10 *d* the sweet, and send portions
Neh 8:12 went their way to eat, and to *d*
Est 1:7 they gave them *d* in vessels of
Est 3:15 the king and Haman sat down to *d*
Est 4:16 and neither eat nor *d* three days
Job 1:4 sisters to eat and to *d* with them
Job 21:20 he shall *d* of the wrath of the
Job 22:7 not given water to the weary to *d*
Ps 16:4 their *d* offerings of blood will I
Ps 36:8 thou shalt make them *d* of the
Ps 50:13 of bulls, or *d* the blood of goats
Ps 60:3 thou hast made us to *d* the wine
Ps 69:21 thirst they gave me vinegar to *d*
Ps 75:8 shall wring them out, and *d* them
Ps 78:15 gave them *d* as out of the great
Ps 78:44 floods, that they could not *d*
Ps 80:5 them tears to *d* in great measure
Ps 102:9 mingled my *d* with weeping,
Ps 104:11 They give *d* to every beast of the
Ps 110:7 He shall *d* of the brook in the
Prov 4:17 and *d* the wine of violence
Prov 5:15 *D* waters out of thine own cistern
Prov 9:5 *d* of the wine which I have
Prov 20:1 is a mocker, strong *d* is raging
Prov 23:7 Eat and *d*, saith he to thee
Prov 25:21 be thirsty, give him water to *d*
Prov 31:4 it is not for kings to *d* wine
Prov 31:4 nor for princes strong *d*
Prov 31:5 Lest they *d*, and forget the law,
Prov 31:6 Give strong *d* unto him that is
Prov 31:7 Let him *d*, and forget his poverty,
Eccl 2:24 man, than that he should eat and *d*
Eccl 3:13 that every man should eat and *d*
Eccl 5:18 and comely for one to eat and to *d*
Eccl 8:15 the sun, than to eat, and to *d*
Eccl 9:7 *d* thy wine with a merry heart
Song 5:1 *d*, yea, *d* abundantly, O
Song 5:1 yea, *d* abundantly, O beloved
Song 8:2 I would cause thee to *d* of spiced
Is 5:11 that they may follow strong *d*
Is 5:22 them that are mighty to *d* wine
Is 5:22 of strength to mingle strong *d*
Is 21:5 watch in the watchtower, eat, *d*
Is 22:13 let us eat and *d*
Is 24:9 They shall not *d* wine with a song
Is 24:9 strong *d* shall be bitter to them
Is 24:9 shall be bitter to them that *d* it
Is 28:7 through strong *d* are out of the
Is 28:7 have erred through strong *d*
Is 28:7 out of the way through strong *d*
Is 29:9 stagger, but not with strong *d*
Is 32:6 he will cause the *d* of the
Is 36:12 *d* their own piss with you
Is 36:16 *d* ye every one the waters of his
Is 43:20 to give *d* to my people, my chosen
Is 51:22 thou shalt no more *d* it again
Is 56:12 will fill ourselves with strong *d*
Is 57:6 hast thou poured a *d* offering
Is 62:8 the stranger shall not *d* thy wine
Is 62:9 have brought it together shall *d*
Is 65:11 that furnish the *d* offering unto
Is 65:13 behold, my servants shall *d*
Jer 2:18 Egypt, to *d* the waters of Sihor
Jer 2:18 to *d* the waters of the river
Jer 7:18 to pour out *d* offerings unto
Jer 8:14 and given us water of gall to *d*
Jer 9:15 and give them water of gall to *d*
Jer 16:7 *d* for their father or for their
Jer 16:8 to sit with them to eat and to *d*
Jer 19:13 have poured out *d* offerings unto
Jer 22:15 did not thy father eat and *d*
Jer 23:15 make them *d* the water of gall
Jer 25:15 to whom I send thee, to *d* it
Jer 25:16 And they shall *d*, and be moved, and
Jer 25:17 and made all the nations to *d*
Jer 25:26 of Sheshach shall *d* after them
Jer 25:27 *D* ye, and be drunken, and spue, and
Jer 25:28 take the cup at thine hand to *d*
Jer 25:28 Ye shall certainly *d*
Jer 32:29 poured out *d* offerings unto other
Jer 35:2 chambers, and give them wine to *d*
Jer 35:5 and I said unto them, *D* ye wine
Jer 35:6 But they said, We will *d* no wine
Jer 35:6 us, saying, Ye shall *d* no wine
Jer 35:8 to *d* no wine all our days, we,
Jer 35:14 commanded his sons not to *d* wine
Jer 35:14 for unto this day they *d* none
Jer 44:17 to pour out *d* offerings unto her,
Jer 44:18 to pour out *d* offerings unto her,
Jer 44:19 poured out *d* offerings unto her,
Jer 44:19 pour out *d* offerings unto her,
Jer 44:25 to pour out *d* offerings unto her
Jer 49:12 to *d* of the cup have assuredly
Jer 49:12 but thou shalt surely *d* of it
Eze 4:11 Thou shalt *d* also water by
Eze 4:11 from time to time shalt thou *d*
Eze 4:16 they shall *d* water by measure, and
Eze 12:18 *d* thy water with trembling and
Eze 12:19 *d* their water with astonishment,
Eze 20:28 out there their *d* offerings
Eze 23:32 Thou shalt *d* of thy sister's cup
Eze 23:34 Thou shalt even *d* it and suck it
Eze 25:4 fruit, and they shall *d* thy milk
Eze 31:14 in their height, all that *d* water
Eze 31:16 best of Lebanon, all that *d* water
Eze 34:19 they *d* that which ye have fouled
Eze 39:17 that ye may eat flesh, and *d* blood
Eze 39:18 *d* the blood of the princes of the
Eze 39:19 *d* blood till ye be drunken, of my
Eze 44:21 Neither shall any priest *d* wine
Eze 45:17 *d* offerings, in the feasts, and in
Dan 1:10 appointed your meat and your *d*
Dan 1:12 us pulse to eat, and water to *d*
Dan 1:16 and the wine that they should *d*
Dan 5:2 his concubines, might *d* therein
Hos 2:5 wool and my flax, mine oil and my *d*
Hos 4:18 Their *d* is sour
Joel 1:9 the *d* offering is cut off from
Joel 1:13 the *d* offering is withholden from
Joel 2:14 a *d* offering unto the LORD your
Joel 3:3 girl for wine, that they might *d*
Amos 2:8 they *d* the wine of the condemned
Amos 2:12 ye gave the Nazarites wine to *d*
Amos 4:1 their masters, Bring, and let us *d*
Amos 4:8 unto one city, to *d* water
Amos 5:11 but ye shall not *d* wine of them
Amos 6:6 That *d* wine in bowls, and anoint
Amos 9:14 vineyards, and *d* the wine thereof
Obad 16 *d* continually, yea, they shall *d*
Jonah 3:7 let them not feed, nor *d* water
Mic 2:11 unto thee of wine and of strong *d*

Mic 6:15 sweet wine, but shalt not *d* wine
Hab 2:15 him that giveth his neighbour *d*
Hab 2:16 *d* thou also, and let thy foreskin
Zeph 1:13 but not *d* the wine thereof
Hag 1:6 ye *d*, but ye are not filled with
Hag 1:6 but ye are not filled with *d*
Zec 7:6 when ye did eat, and when ye did *d*
Zec 7:6 yourselves, and *d* for yourselves
Zec 9:15 and they shall *d*, and make a noise
Mt 6:25 ye shall eat, or what ye shall *d*
Mt 6:31 or, What shall we *d*
Mt 10:42 whosoever shall give to *d* unto
Mt 20:22 *d* of the cup that I shall *d*
Mt 20:23 Ye shall *d* indeed of my cup, and
Mt 24:49 and to eat and *d* with the drunken
Mt 25:35 I was thirsty, and ye gave me *d*
Mt 25:37 or thirsty, and gave thee *d*
Mt 25:42 I was thirsty, and ye gave me no *d*
Mt 26:27 to them, saying, *D* ye all of it
Mt 26:29 I will not *d* henceforth of this
Mt 26:29 until that day when I *d* it new
Mt 26:42 pass away from me, except I *d* it
Mt 27:34 vinegar to *d* mingled with gall
Mt 27:34 tasted thereof, he would not *d*
Mt 27:48 it on a reed, and gave him to *d*
Mk 9:41 a cup of water to *d* in my name
Mk 10:38 can ye *d* of the cup that I *d*
Mk 10:39 *d* of the cup that I *d* of
Mk 14:25 I will *d* no more of the fruit of
Mk 14:25 until that day that I *d* it new in
Mk 15:23 they gave him to *d* wine mingled
Mk 15:36 it on a reed, and gave him to *d*
Mk 16:18 if they *d* any deadly thing, it
Lk 1:15 shall *d* neither wine nor strong
Lk 1:15 neither wine nor strong *d*
Lk 5:30 *d* with publicans and sinners
Lk 5:33 but thine eat and *d*
Lk 12:19 take thine ease, eat, *d*, and be
Lk 12:29 ye shall eat, or what ye shall *d*
Lk 12:45 and maidens, and to eat and *d*
Lk 17:8 and afterward thou shalt eat and *d*
Lk 22:18 I will not *d* of the fruit of the
Lk 22:30 *d* at my table in my kingdom, and
Jn 4:7 saith unto her, Give me to *d*
Jn 4:9 thou, being a Jew, askest *d* of me
Jn 4:10 that saith to thee, Give me to *d*
Jn 6:53 *d* his blood, ye have no life in
Jn 6:55 indeed, and my blood is *d* indeed
Jn 7:37 let him come unto me, and *d*
Jn 18:11 hath given me, shall I not *d* it
Acts 9:9 sight, and neither did eat nor *d*
Acts 10:41 *d* with him after he rose from the
Acts 23:12 nor *d* till they had killed Paul
Acts 23:21 nor *d* till they have killed him
Rom 12:20 if he thirst, give him *d*
Rom 14:17 kingdom of God is not meat and *d*
Rom 14:21 to eat flesh, nor to *d* wine
1Cor 9:4 Have we not power to eat and to *d*
1Cor 10:4 all *d* the same spiritual *d*
1Cor 10:4 all *d* the same spiritual *d*
1Cor 10:7 The people sat down to eat and *d*
1Cor 10:21 Ye cannot *d* the cup of the Lord,
1Cor 10:31 Whether therefore ye eat, or *d*
1Cor 11:22 ye not houses to eat and to *d* in
1Cor 11:25 this do ye, as oft as ye *d* it
1Cor 11:26 *d* this cup, ye do shew the Lord's
1Cor 11:27 bread, and *d* this cup of the Lord,
1Cor 11:28 of that bread, and *d* of that cup
1Cor 12:13 all made to *d* into one Spirit
1Cor 15:32 let us eat and *d*
Col 2:16 judge you in meat, or in *d*
1Ti 5:23 *D* no longer water, but use a
Rev 14:8 because she made all nations *d* of
Rev 14:10 The same shall *d* of the wine of
Rev 16:6 thou hast given them blood to *d*

### DRINKETH

Gen 44:5 Is not this it in which my lord *d*
Deut 11:11 *d* water of the rain of heaven
Job 6:4 the poison whereof *d* up my spirit
Job 15:16 which *d* iniquity like water
Job 34:7 who *d* up scorning like water
Job 40:23 he *d* up a river, and hasteth not
Prov 26:6 cutteth off the feet, and *d* damage
Is 29:8 man dreameth, and, behold, he *d*
Is 44:12 he *d* no water, and is faint
Mk 2:16 *d* with publicans and sinners
Jn 4:13 Whosoever *d* of this water shall
Jn 4:14 But whosoever *d* of the water that
Jn 6:54 *d* my blood, hath eternal life
Jn 6:56 *d* my blood, dwelleth in me, and I
1Cor 11:29 *d* unworthily, eateth and *d*
Heb 6:7 For the earth which *d* in the rain

### DRINKING

Gen 24:19 also, until they have done *d*
Gen 24:22 to pass, as the camels had done *d*
Ruth 3:3 he shall have done eating and *d*
1Sa 30:16 upon all the earth, eating and *d*
1Kin 4:20 the sea in multitude, eating and *d*
1Kin 10:21 all king Solomon's *d* vessels were
1Kin 16:9 *d* himself drunk in the house of
1Kin 20:12 heard this message, as he was *d*
1Kin 20:16 But Ben-hadad was *d* himself drunk
1Chr 12:39 David three days, eating and *d*
2Chr 9:20 all the *d* vessels of king Solomon
Est 1:8 the *d* was according to the law
Job 1:13 *d* wine in their eldest brother's
Job 1:18 *d* wine in their eldest brother's
Is 22:13 sheep, eating flesh, and *d* wine
Mt 11:18 John came neither eating nor *d*
Mt 11:19 The Son of man came eating and *d*
Mt 24:38 the flood they were eating and *d*
Lk 7:33 neither eating bread nor *d* wine
Lk 7:34 Son of man is come eating and *d*
Lk 10:7 *d* such things as they give

### DRIVE

Ex 6:1 shall he *d* them out of his land
Ex 23:28 which shall *d* out the Hivite, the
Ex 23:29 I will not *d* them out from before
Ex 23:30 little I will *d* them out from
Ex 23:31 thou shalt *d* them out before thee
Ex 33:2 I will *d* out the Canaanite, the
Ex 34:11 I *d* out before thee the Amorite,
Num 22:6 that I may *d* them out of the land
Num 22:11 to overcome them, and *d* them out
Num 33:52 Then ye shall *d* out all the
Num 33:55 But if ye will not *d* out the
Deut 4:38 To *d* out nations from before thee
Deut 9:3 so shalt thou *d* them out, and
Deut 9:4 doth *d* them out from before thee
Deut 9:5 doth *d* them out from before thee
Deut 11:23 Then will the LORD *d* out all
Deut 18:12 the LORD thy God doth *d* them out
Josh 3:10 fail *d* out from before you the
Josh 13:6 them will I *d* out from before the
Josh 14:12 I shall be able to *d* them out
Josh 15:63 of Judah could not *d* them out
Josh 17:12 *d* out the inhabitants of those
Josh 17:13 but did not utterly *d* them out
Josh 17:18 for thou shalt *d* out the
Josh 23:5 *d* them from out of your sight
Josh 23:13 *d* out any of these nations from
Judg 1:19 but could not *d* out the
Judg 1:21 did not *d* out the Jebusites that
Judg 1:27 Neither did Manasseh *d* out the
Judg 1:28 and did not utterly *d* them out
Judg 1:29 Neither did Ephraim *d* out the
Judg 1:30 Neither did Zebulun *d* out the
Judg 1:31 Neither did Asher *d* out the
Judg 1:32 for they did not *d* them out
Judg 1:33 Neither did Naphtali *d* out the
Judg 2:3 I will not *d* them out from before
Judg 2:21 I also will not henceforth *d* out
Judg 11:24 God shall *d* out from before us
2Kin 4:24 an ass, and said to her servant, *D*
2Chr 20:7 who didst *d* out the inhabitants
Job 18:11 side, and shall *d* him to his feet
Job 24:3 They *d* away the ass of the
Ps 44:2 How thou didst *d* out the heathen
Ps 68:2 is driven away, so *d* them away
Prov 22:15 shall *d* it far from him
Is 22:19 I will *d* thee from thy station,
Jer 24:9 all places whither I shall *d* them
Jer 27:10 and that I should *d* you out
Jer 27:15 that I might *d* you out, and that
Jer 46:15 not, because the LORD did *d* them
Eze 4:13 Gentiles, whither I will *d* them
Dan 4:25 That they shall *d* thee from men
Dan 4:32 they shall *d* thee from men, and
Hos 9:15 I will *d* them out of mine house
Joel 2:20 will *d* him into a land barren and
Zeph 2:4 they shall *d* out Ashdod at the
Acts 27:15 up into the wind, we let her *d*

### DRIVEN

Gen 4:14 thou hast *d* me out this day from
Ex 10:11 they were *d* out from Pharaoh's
Ex 22:10 or *d* away, no man seeing it
Num 32:21 until he hath *d* out his enemies
Deut 4:19 shouldest be *d* to worship them,
Deut 30:1 the LORD thy God hath *d* thee
Deut 30:4 If any of thine be *d* out unto the
Josh 23:9 For the LORD hath *d* out from
1Sa 26:19 for they have *d* me out this day
Job 6:13 is wisdom *d* quite from me
Job 13:25 Wilt thou break a leaf *d* to
Job 18:18 He shall be *d* from light into
Job 30:5 They were *d* forth from among men,
Ps 40:14 let them be *d* backward and put to
Ps 68:2 As smoke is *d* away, so drive them
Ps 114:3 Jordan was *d* back
Ps 114:5 Jordan, that thou wast *d* back
Prov 14:32 The wicked is *d* away in his
Is 8:22 and they shall be *d* to darkness
Is 19:7 wither, be *d* away, and be no more
Is 41:2 sword, and as *d* stubble to his bow
Jer 8:3 the places whither I have *d* them
Jer 16:15 the lands whither he had *d* them
Jer 23:2 *d* them away, and have not visited
Jer 23:3 countries whither I have *d* them
Jer 23:8 countries whither I had *d* them
Jer 23:12 they shall be *d* on, and fall
Jer 29:14 the places whither I have *d* you
Jer 29:18 the nations whither I have *d* them
Jer 32:37 whither I have *d* them in mine
Jer 40:12 of all places whither they were *d*
Jer 43:5 nations, whither they had been *d*
Jer 46:28 the nations whither I have *d* thee
Jer 49:5 ye shall be *d* out every man right
Jer 50:17 the lions have *d* him away
Eze 31:11 I have *d* him out for his
Eze 34:4 again that which was *d* away
Eze 34:16 bring again that which was *d* away
Dan 4:33 he was *d* from men, and did eat
Dan 5:21 he was *d* from the sons of men
Dan 9:7 whither thou hast *d* them, because
Hos 13:3 as the chaff that is *d* with the
Mic 4:6 I will gather her that is *d* out
Zeph 3:19 and gather her that was *d* out
Lk 8:29 was *d* of the devil into the
Acts 27:17 strake sail, and so were *d*
Acts 27:27 night was come, as we were *d* up
Jas 1:6 a wave of the sea *d* with the wind
Jas 3:4 are *d* of fierce winds, yet are

### DROP

Deut 32:2 My doctrine shall *d* as the rain
Deut 33:28 also his heavens shall *d* down dew
Job 36:28 Which the clouds do *d* and distil
Ps 65:11 and thy paths *d* fatness
Ps 65:12 They *d* upon the pastures of the
Prov 3:20 the clouds *d* down the dew
Prov 5:3 a strange woman *d* as an honeycomb
Song 4:11 O my spouse, *d* as the honeycomb
Is 40:15 nations are as a *d* of a bucket
Is 45:8 *D* down, ye heavens, from above,
Eze 20:46 *d* thy word toward the south, and
Eze 21:2 *d* thy word toward the holy places
Joel 3:18 mountains shall *d* down new wine
Amos 7:16 *d* not thy word against the house
Amos 9:13 the mountains shall *d* sweet wine

### DROPPED

Judg 5:4 earth trembled, and the heavens *d*
Judg 5:4 the clouds also *d* water
1Sa 14:26 the wood, behold, the honey *d*
2Sa 21:10 of harvest until water *d* upon
Job 29:22 and my speech *d* upon them
Ps 68:8 the heavens also *d* at the
Song 5:5 my hands *d* with myrrh, and my

### DROPPING

Prov 19:13 of a wife are a continual *d*
Prov 27:15 A continual *d* in a very rainy day
Song 5:13 lilies, *d* sweet smelling myrrh

### DROSS

Ps 119:119 the wicked of the earth like *d*
Prov 25:4 Take away the *d* from the silver,
Prov 26:23 a potsherd covered with silver *d*
Is 1:22 Thy silver is become *d*, thy wine
Is 1:25 thee, and purely purge away thy *d*
Eze 22:18 house of Israel is to me become *d*
Eze 22:18 they are even the *d* of silver
Eze 22:19 Because ye are all become *d*

### DROUGHT

Gen 31:40 in the day the *d* consumed me
Deut 8:15 serpents, and scorpions, and *d*
Job 24:19 *D* and heat consume the snow waters
Ps 32:4 is turned into the *d* of summer
Is 58:11 and satisfy thy soul in *d*
Jer 2:6 and of pits, through a land of *d*

Jer 17:8 not be careful in the year of *d*
Jer 50:38 A *d* is upon her waters
Hos 13:5 in the land of great *d*
Hag 1:11 And I called for a *d* upon the land

## DROVE
Gen 3:24 So he *d* out the man
Gen 15:11 the carcases, Abram *d* them away
Gen 32:16 servants, every *d* by themselves
Gen 32:16 me, and put a space betwixt *d*
Gen 32:16 and put a space betwixt *d* and *d*
Gen 33:8 thou by all this *d* which I met
Ex 2:17 the shepherds came and *d* them away
Num 21:32 *d* out the Amorites that were
Josh 15:14 Caleb *d* thence the three sons of
1Chr 8:13 who *d* away the inhabitants of
Ps 34:*t* who *d* him away, and he departed
Hab 3:6 beheld, and *d* asunder the nations
Jn 2:15 he *d* them all out of the temple,

## DROWNED
Ex 15:4 also are *d* in the Red sea
Amos 8:8 and it shall be cast out and *d*
Amos 9:5 and shall be *d*, as by the flood of
Mt 18:6 that he were *d* in the depth of
Heb 11:29 Egyptians assaying to do were *d*

## DRUNK
Lev 11:34 all drink that may be *d* in every
Deut 29:6 neither have ye *d* wine or strong
Deut 32:42 make mine arrows *d* with blood
Judg 15:19 and when he had *d*, his spirit came
Ruth 3:7 And when Boaz had eaten and *d*
1Sa 1:9 in Shiloh, and after they had *d*
1Sa 30:12 nor *d* any water, three days and
2Sa 11:13 and he made him *d*
1Kin 13:22 *d* water in the place, of the
1Kin 13:23 eaten bread, and after he had *d*
1Kin 16:9 drinking himself *d* in the house
1Kin 20:16 himself *d* in the pavilions
2Kin 6:23 and when they had eaten and *d*
2Kin 19:24 *d* strange waters, and with the
Song 5:1 I have *d* my wine with my milk
Is 37:25 I have digged, and *d* water
Is 51:17 which hast *d* at the hand of the
Is 63:6 make them *d* in my fury, and I will
Jer 46:10 and made *d* with their blood
Jer 51:57 And I will make *d* her princes
Eze 34:18 to have *d* of the deep waters, but
Dan 5:23 concubines, have *d* wine in them
Obad 16 For as ye have *d* upon my holy
Lk 5:39 No man also having *d* old wine
Lk 13:26 *d* in thy presence, and thou hast
Jn 2:10 and when men have well *d*, then
Eph 5:18 be not *d* with wine, wherein is
Rev 17:2 been made *d* with the wine of her
Rev 18:3 For all nations have *d* of the

## DRUNKARD
Deut 21:20 he is a glutton, and a *d*
Prov 23:21 For the *d* and the glutton shall
Prov 26:9 goeth up into the hand of a *d*
Is 24:20 shall reel to and fro like a *d*
1Cor 5:11 an idolater, or a railer, or a *d*

## DRUNKARDS
Ps 69:12 and I was the song of the *d*
Is 28:1 to the *d* of Ephraim, whose
Is 28:3 the *d* of Ephraim, shall be
Joel 1:5 Awake, ye *d*, and weep
Nah 1:10 and while they are drunken as *d*
1Cor 6:10 Nor thieves, nor covetous, nor *d*

## DRUNKEN
Gen 9:21 And he drank of the wine, and was *d*
1Sa 1:13 Eli thought she had been *d*
1Sa 1:14 unto her, How long wilt thou be *d*
1Sa 1:15 I have *d* neither wine nor strong
1Sa 25:36 within him for he was very *d*
Job 12:25 them to stagger like a *d* man
Ps 107:27 and fro, and stagger like a *d* man
Is 19:14 as a *d* man staggereth in his
Is 29:9 they are *d*, but not with wine
Is 49:26 they shall be *d* with their own
Is 51:17 thou hast *d* the dregs of the cup
Is 51:21 now this, thou afflicted, and *d*
Jer 23:9 I am like a *d* man, and like a man
Jer 25:27 Drink ye, and be *d*, and spue, and
Jer 48:26 Make ye him *d*: for he magnified
Jer 49:12 drink of the cup have assuredly *d*
Jer 51:7 hand, that made all the earth *d*
Jer 51:7 the nations have *d* of her wine
Jer 51:39 feasts, and I will make them *d*
Lam 3:15 he hath made me *d* with wormwood
Lam 4:21 thou shalt be *d*, and shalt make
Lam 5:4 We have *d* our water for money
Eze 39:19 full, and drink blood till ye be *d*
Nah 1:10 and while they are *d* as drunkards
Nah 3:11 Thou also shalt be *d*
Hab 2:15 to him, and makest him *d* also
Mt 24:49 and to eat and drink with the *d*
Lk 12:45 and to eat and drink, and to be *d*
Lk 17:8 serve me, till I have eaten and *d*
Acts 2:15 For these are not *d*, as ye
1Cor 11:21 and one is hungry, and another is *d*
1Th 5:7 be *d* are *d* in the night
Rev 17:6 I saw the woman *d* with the blood

## DRUNKENNESS
Deut 29:19 of mine heart, to add *d* to thirst
Eccl 10:17 for strength, and not for *d*
Jer 13:13 inhabitants of Jerusalem, with *d*
Eze 23:33 Thou shalt be filled with *d*
Lk 21:34 overcharged with surfeiting, and *d*
Rom 13:13 not in rioting and *d*, not in
Gal 5:21 Envyings, murders, *d*, revellings,

## DRUSILLA *(dru-sil'-lah) Wife of Felix.*
Acts 24:24 when Felix came with his wife *D*

## DRY
Gen 1:9 place, and let the *d* land appear
Gen 1:10 And God called the *d* land Earth
Gen 7:22 of all that was in the *d* land
Gen 8:13 the face of the ground was *d*
Ex 4:9 river, and pour it upon the *d* land
Ex 4:9 become blood upon the *d* land
Ex 14:16 children of Israel shall go on *d*
Ex 14:21 night, and made the sea *d* land
Ex 14:22 of the sea upon the *d* ground
Ex 14:29 *d* land in the midst of the sea
Ex 15:19 on *d* land in the midst of the sea
Lev 7:10 offering, mingled with oil, and *d*
Lev 13:30 it is a *d* scall, even a leprosy
Josh 3:17 of the LORD stood firm on *d*
Josh 3:17 passed over on *d* ground, until
Josh 4:18 were lifted up unto the *d* land
Josh 4:22 came over this Jordan on *d* land
Josh 9:5 bread of their provision was *d*
Josh 9:12 but now, behold, it is *d*, and it
Judg 6:37 it be *d* upon all the earth beside
Judg 6:39 let it now be *d* only upon the
Judg 6:40 for it was *d* upon the fleece only
2Kin 2:8 they two went over on *d* ground
Neh 9:11 midst of the sea on the *d* land
Job 12:15 the waters, and they *d* up
Job 13:25 and wilt thou pursue the *d* stubble
Job 15:30 the flame shall *d* up his branches
Ps 63:1 my flesh longeth for thee in a *d*
Ps 66:6 He turned the sea into *d* land
Ps 68:6 the rebellious dwell in a *d* land
Ps 95:5 and his hands formed the *d* land
Ps 105:41 they ran in the *d* places like a
Ps 107:33 and the watersprings into *d* ground
Ps 107:35 *d* ground into watersprings
Prov 17:1 Better is a *d* morsel, and
Is 25:5 as the heat in a *d* place
Is 32:2 as rivers of water in a *d* place
Is 41:18 the *d* land springs of water
Is 42:15 and hills, and *d* up all their herbs
Is 42:15 islands, and I will *d* up the pools
Is 44:3 and floods upon the *d* ground
Is 44:27 That saith to the deep, Be *d*
Is 44:27 and I will *d* up thy rivers
Is 50:2 at my rebuke I *d* up the sea
Is 53:2 and as a root out of a *d* ground
Is 56:3 eunuch say, Behold, I am a *d* tree
Jer 4:11 A *d* wind of the high places in
Jer 50:12 wilderness, a *d* land, and a desert
Jer 51:36 I will *d* up her sea
Jer 51:36 and make her springs *d*
Jer 51:43 a *d* land, and a wilderness, a land
Eze 17:24 have made the *d* tree to flourish
Eze 19:13 planted in the wilderness, in a *d*
Eze 20:47 tree in thee, and every *d* tree
Eze 30:12 And I will make the rivers *d*
Eze 37:2 and, lo, they were very *d*
Eze 37:4 O ye *d* bones, hear the word of
Hos 2:3 and set her like a *d* land
Hos 9:14 a miscarrying womb and *d* breasts
Hos 13:15 and his spring shall become *d*
Jonah 1:9 hath made the sea and the *d* land
Jonah 2:10 vomited out Jonah upon the *d* land
Nah 1:4 rebuketh the sea, and maketh it *d*
Nah 1:10 be devoured as stubble fully *d*
Zeph 2:13 and *d* like a wilderness
Hag 2:6 earth, and the sea, and the *d* land
Zec 10:11 the deeps of the river shall *d* up
Mt 12:43 man, he walketh through *d* places
Lk 11:24 man, he walketh through *d* places
Lk 23:31 tree, what shall be done in the *d*
Heb 11:29 through the Red sea as by *d* land

## DUE
Lev 10:13 it is thy *d*, and thy sons' *d*
Lev 10:14 they be thy *d*, and thy sons' *d*
Lev 26:4 I will give you rain in *d* season
Num 28:2 offer unto me in their *d* season
Deut 11:14 rain of your land in his *d* season
Deut 18:3 be the priest's *d* from the people
Deut 32:35 their foot shall slide in *d* time
1Chr 15:13 sought him not after the *d* order
1Chr 16:29 LORD the glory *d* unto his name
Neh 11:23 for the singers, *d* for every day
Ps 29:2 LORD the glory *d* unto his name
Ps 96:8 LORD the glory *d* unto his name
Ps 104:27 give them their meat in *d* season
Ps 145:15 them their meat in *d* season
Prov 3:27 good from them to whom it is *d*
Prov 15:23 and a word spoken in *d* season
Eccl 10:17 and thy princes eat in *d* season
Mt 18:34 pay all that was *d* unto him
Mt 24:45 to give them meat in *d* season
Lk 12:42 their portion of meat in *d* season
Lk 23:41 for we receive the *d* reward of
Rom 5:6 in *d* time Christ died for the
Rom 13:7 tribute to whom tribute is *d*
1Cor 7:3 unto the wife *d* benevolence
1Cor 15:8 as of one born out of *d* time
Gal 6:9 for in *d* season we shall reap, if
1Ti 2:6 all, to be testified in *d* time
Titus 1:3 But hath in *d* times manifested
1Pet 5:6 that he may exalt you in *d* time

## DUMAH *(doo'-mah)*
*1. Son of Ishmael.*
Gen 25:14 And Mishma, and *D*, and Massa,
1Chr 1:30 Mishma, and *D*, Massa, Hadad, and
*2. A city in Judah.*
Josh 15:52 Arab, and *D*, and Eshean,
*3. An undetermined city.*
Is 21:11 The burden of *D*. He calleth to

## DUMB
Ex 4:11 or who maketh the *d*, or deaf, or
Ps 38:13 I was as a *d* man that openeth not
Ps 39:2 I was *d* with silence, I held my
Ps 39:9 I was *d*, I opened not my mouth
Prov 31:8 Open thy mouth for the *d* in the
Is 35:6 hart, and the tongue of the *d* sing
Is 53:7 a sheep before her shearers is *d*
Is 56:10 all ignorant, they are all *d* dogs
Eze 3:26 thy mouth, that thou shalt be *d*
Eze 24:27 thou shalt speak, and be no more *d*
Eze 33:22 was opened, and I was no more *d*
Dan 10:15 toward the ground, and I became *d*
Hab 2:18 trusteth therein, to make *d* idols
Hab 2:19 to the *d* stone, Arise, it shall
Mt 9:32 they brought to him a *d* man
Mt 9:33 devil was cast out, the *d* spake
Mt 12:22 with a devil, blind, and *d*
Mt 12:22 the blind and *d* both spake and saw
Mt 15:30 those that were lame, blind, *d*
Mt 15:31 when they saw the *d* to speak
Mk 7:37 deaf to hear, and the *d* to speak
Mk 9:17 my son, which hath a *d* spirit
Mk 9:25 spirit, saying unto him, Thou *d*
Lk 1:20 And, behold, thou shalt be *d*
Lk 11:14 casting out a devil, and it was *d*
Lk 11:14 devil was gone out, the *d* spake
Acts 8:32 like a lamb *d* before his shearer,
1Cor 12:2 carried away unto these *d* idols
2Pet 2:16 the *d* ass speaking with man's

## DUNG
Ex 29:14 bullock, and his skin, and his *d*
Lev 4:11 legs, and his inwards, and his *d*
Lev 8:17 and his hide, his flesh, and his *d*
Lev 16:27 skins, and their flesh, and their *d*
Num 19:5 flesh, and her blood, with her *d*
1Kin 14:10 Jeroboam, as a man taketh away *d*
2Kin 6:25 *d* for five pieces of silver
2Kin 9:37 *d* upon the face of the field in
2Kin 18:27 that they may eat their own *d*
Neh 2:13 the dragon well, and to the *d* port
Neh 3:13 on the wall unto the *d* gate
Neh 3:14 But the *d* gate repaired Malchiah
Neh 12:31 upon the wall toward the *d* gate

Job 20:7 perish for ever like his own *d*
Ps 83:10 they became as *d* for the earth
Is 36:12 that they may eat their own *d*
Jer 8:2 they shall be for *d* upon the face
Jer 9:22 fall as *d* upon the open field
Jer 16:4 but they shall be as *d* upon the
Jer 25:33 they shall be *d* upon the ground
Eze 4:12 it with *d* that cometh out of man
Eze 4:15 given thee cow's *d* for man's *d*
Eze 4:15 given thee cow's *d* for man's *d*
Zeph 1:17 as dust, and their flesh as the *d*
Mal 2:3 spread *d* upon your faces
Mal 2:3 even the *d* of your solemn feasts
Lk 13:8 I shall dig about it, and *d* it
Phil 3:8 things, and do count them but *d*

**DUNGEON**
Gen 40:15 they should put me into the *d*
Gen 41:14 brought him hastily out of the *d*
Ex 12:29 of the captive that was in the *d*
Jer 37:16 Jeremiah was entered into the *d*
Jer 38:6 cast him into the *d* of Malchiah
Jer 38:6 in the *d* there was no water, but
Jer 38:7 they had put Jeremiah in the *d*
Jer 38:9 whom they have cast into the *d*
Jer 38:10 Jeremiah the prophet out of the *d*
Jer 38:11 by cords into the *d* to Jeremiah
Jer 38:13 and took him up out of the *d*
Lam 3:53 have cut off my life in the *d*
Lam 3:55 name, O LORD, out of the low *d*

**DUNGHILL**
1Sa 2:8 lifteth up the beggar from the *d*
Ezr 6:11 his house be made a *d* for this
Ps 113:7 and lifteth the needy out of the *d*
Is 25:10 straw is trodden down for the *d*
Dan 2:5 and your houses shall be made a *d*
Dan 3:29 and their houses shall be made a *d*
Lk 14:35 for the land, nor yet for the *d*

**DURA** *(doo'-rah) A plain in Babylonia.*
Dan 3:1 he set it up in the plain of *D*

**DURST**
Est 7:5 that *d* presume in his heart to do
Job 32:6 *d* not shew you mine opinion
Mt 22:46 neither *d* any man from that day
Mk 12:34 no man after that *d* ask him any
Lk 20:40 after that they *d* not ask him any
Jn 21:12 none of the disciples *d* ask him
Acts 5:13 of the rest *d* no man join himself
Acts 7:32 Moses trembled, and *d* not behold
Jude 9 *d* not bring against him a railing

**DUST**
Gen 2:7 formed man of the *d* of the ground
Gen 3:14 *d* shalt thou eat all the days of
Gen 3:19 for *d* thou art, and unto *d*
Gen 13:16 thy seed as the *d* of the earth
Gen 13:16 man can number the *d* of the earth
Gen 18:27 unto the Lord, which am but *d*
Gen 28:14 shall be as the *d* of the earth
Ex 8:16 smite the *d* of the land, that it
Ex 8:17 smote the *d* of the earth, and it
Ex 8:17 all the *d* of the land became lice
Ex 9:9 it shall become small *d* in all
Lev 14:41 they shall pour out the *d* that
Lev 17:13 blood thereof, and cover it with *d*
Num 5:17 of the *d* that is in the floor of
Num 23:10 Who can count the *d* of Jacob
Deut 9:21 even until it was as small as *d*
Deut 9:21 I cast the *d* thereof into the
Deut 28:24 the rain of thy land powder and *d*
Deut 32:24 the poison of serpents of the *d*
Josh 7:6 Israel, and put *d* upon their heads
1Sa 2:8 raiseth up the poor out of the *d*
2Sa 16:13 and threw stones at him, and cast *d*
2Sa 22:43 as small as the *d* of the earth
1Kin 16:2 as I exalted thee out of the *d*
1Kin 18:38 the wood, and the stones, and the *d*
1Kin 20:10 if the *d* of Samaria shall suffice
2Kin 13:7 made them like the *d* by threshing
2Kin 23:12 cast the *d* of them into the brook
2Chr 1:9 the *d* of the earth in multitude
2Chr 34:4 made *d* of them, and strowed it
Job 2:12 sprinkled *d* upon their heads
Job 4:19 whose foundation is in the *d*
Job 5:6 cometh not forth of the *d*
Job 7:5 clothed with worms and clods of *d*
Job 7:21 for now shall I sleep in the *d*
Job 10:9 wilt thou bring me into *d* again
Job 14:19 grow out of the *d* of the earth
Job 16:15 skin, and defiled my horn in the *d*
Job 17:16 our rest together is in the *d*
Job 20:11 shall lie down with him in the *d*
Job 21:26 shall lie down alike in the *d*
Job 22:24 Then shalt thou lay up gold as *d*
Job 27:16 Though he heap up silver as the *d*
Job 28:6 and it hath *d* of gold
Job 30:19 the mire, and I am become like *d*
Job 34:15 and man shall turn again unto *d*
Job 38:38 When the *d* groweth into hardness,
Job 39:14 earth, and warmeth them in the *d*
Job 40:13 Hide them in the *d* together
Job 42:6 I abhor myself, and repent in *d*
Ps 7:5 and lay mine honour in the *d*
Ps 18:42 small as the *d* before the wind
Ps 22:15 brought me into the *d* of death
Ps 22:29 to the *d* shall bow before him
Ps 30:9 shall the *d* praise thee
Ps 44:25 our soul is bowed down to the *d*
Ps 72:9 and his enemies shall lick the *d*
Ps 78:27 rained flesh also upon them as *d*
Ps 102:14 stones, and favour the *d* thereof
Ps 103:14 he remembereth that we are *d*
Ps 104:29 they die, and return to their *d*
Ps 113:7 raiseth up the poor out of the *d*
Ps 119:25 My soul cleaveth unto the *d*
Prov 8:26 part of the *d* of the world
Eccl 3:20 the *d*, and all turn to *d* again
Eccl 12:7 Then shall the *d* return to the
Is 2:10 the rock, and hide thee in the *d*
Is 5:24 and their blossom shall go up as *d*
Is 25:12 to the ground, even to the *d*
Is 26:5 he bringeth it even to the *d*
Is 26:19 Awake and sing, ye that dwell in *d*
Is 29:4 speech shall be low out of the *d*
Is 29:4 speech shall whisper out of the *d*
Is 29:5 strangers shall be like small *d*
Is 34:7 their *d* made fat with fatness
Is 34:9 the *d* thereof into brimstone, and
Is 40:12 comprehended the *d* of the earth
Is 40:15 as the small *d* of the balance
Is 41:2 gave them as the *d* to his sword
Is 47:1 Come down, and sit in the *d*
Is 49:23 and lick up the *d* of thy feet
Is 52:2 Shake thyself from the *d*
Is 65:25 *d* shall be the serpent's meat
Lam 2:10 have cast up *d* upon their heads
Lam 3:29 He putteth his mouth in the *d*
Eze 24:7 the ground, to cover it with *d*
Eze 26:4 I will also scrape her *d* from her
Eze 26:10 horses their *d* shall cover thee
Eze 26:12 thy *d* in the midst of the water
Eze 27:30 shall cast up *d* upon their heads,
Dan 12:2 in the *d* of the earth shall awake
Amos 2:7 That pant after the *d* of the
Mic 1:10 of Aphrah roll thyself in the *d*
Mic 7:17 shall lick the *d* like a serpent
Nah 1:3 the clouds are the *d* of his feet
Nah 3:18 thy nobles shall dwell in the *d*
Hab 1:10 for they shall heap *d*, and take it
Zeph 1:17 blood shall be poured out as *d*
Zec 9:3 and heaped up silver as the *d*
Mt 10:14 shake off the *d* of your feet
Mk 6:11 shake off the *d* under your feet
Lk 9:5 shake off the very *d* from your
Lk 10:11 Even the very *d* of your city
Acts 13:51 But they shook off the *d* of their
Acts 22:23 clothes, and threw *d* into the air,
Rev 18:19 they cast *d* on their heads, and

**DUTY**
Ex 21:10 her *d* of marriage, shall he not
Deut 25:5 perform the *d* of an husband's
Deut 25:7 the *d* of my husband's brother
2Chr 8:14 as the *d* of every day required
Ezr 3:4 as the *d* of every day required
Eccl 12:13 for this is the whole *d* of man
Lk 17:10 done that which was our *d* to do
Rom 15:27 their *d* is also to minister unto

**DWARF**
Lev 21:20 Or crookbackt, or a *d*, or that

**DWELL**
Gen 4:20 the father of such as *d* in tents
Gen 9:27 he shall *d* in the tents of Shem
Gen 13:6 them, that they might *d* together
Gen 13:6 so that they could not *d* together
Gen 16:12 he shall *d* in the presence of all
Gen 19:30 for he feared to *d* in Zoar
Gen 20:15 *d* where it pleaseth thee
Gen 24:3 of the Canaanites, among whom I *d*
Gen 24:37 the Canaanites, in whose land I *d*
Gen 26:2 *d* in the land which I shall tell
Gen 30:20 now will my husband *d* with me
Gen 34:10 And ye shall *d* with us
Gen 34:10 *d* and trade ye therein, and get you
Gen 34:16 we will *d* with you, and we will
Gen 34:21 therefore let them *d* in the land
Gen 34:22 consent unto us for to *d* with us
Gen 34:23 unto them, and they will *d* with us
Gen 35:1 go up to Beth-el, and *d* there
Gen 36:7 than that they might *d* together
Gen 45:10 thou shalt *d* in the land of
Gen 46:34 that ye may *d* in the land of
Gen 47:4 let thy servants *d* in the land of
Gen 47:6 make thy father and brethren to *d*
Gen 47:6 in the land of Goshen let them *d*
Gen 49:13 Zebulun shall *d* at the haven of
Ex 2:21 was content to *d* with the man
Ex 8:22 of Goshen, in which my people *d*
Ex 15:17 thou hast made for thee to *d* in
Ex 23:33 They shall not *d* in thy land
Ex 25:8 that I may *d* among them
Ex 29:45 I will *d* among the children of
Ex 29:46 of Egypt, that I may *d* among them
Lev 13:46 he shall *d* alone
Lev 20:22 whither I bring you to *d* therein
Lev 23:42 Ye shall *d* in booths seven days
Lev 23:42 Israelites born shall *d* in booths
Lev 23:43 children of Israel to *d* in booths
Lev 25:18 ye shall *d* in the land in safety
Lev 25:19 your fill, and *d* therein in safety
Lev 26:5 full, and *d* in your land safely
Lev 26:32 your enemies which *d* therein
Num 5:3 camps, in the midst whereof I *d*
Num 13:19 what the land is that they *d* in
Num 13:19 cities they be that they *d* in
Num 13:28 be strong that *d* in the land
Num 13:29 The Amalekites *d* in the land of
Num 13:29 the Amorites, *d* in the mountains
Num 13:29 and the Canaanites *d* by the sea
Num 14:30 I sware to make you *d* therein
Num 23:9 lo, the people shall *d* alone
Num 32:17 our little ones shall *d* in the
Num 33:53 of the land, and *d* therein
Num 33:55 vex you in the land wherein ye *d*
Num 35:2 their possession cities to *d* in
Num 35:3 cities shall they have to *d* in
Num 35:32 come again to *d* in the land
Num 35:34 ye shall inhabit, wherein I *d*
Num 35:34 for I the LORD *d* among the
Deut 2:4 children of Esau, which *d* in Seir
Deut 2:29 children of Esau which *d* in Seir
Deut 2:29 and the Moabites which *d* in Ar
Deut 11:30 which *d* in the champaign over
Deut 11:31 ye shall possess it, and *d* therein
Deut 12:10 *d* in the land which the LORD your
Deut 12:10 about, so that ye *d* in safety
Deut 12:11 to cause his name to *d* there
Deut 13:12 God hath given thee to *d* there
Deut 17:14 shalt *d* therein, and shalt say, I
Deut 23:16 He shall *d* with thee, even among
Deut 25:5 If brethren *d* together, and one of
Deut 28:30 and thou shalt not *d* therein
Deut 30:20 that thou mayest *d* in the land
Deut 33:12 the LORD shall *d* in safety by him
Deut 33:12 he shall *d* between his shoulders
Deut 33:28 then shall *d* in safety alone
Josh 9:7 Peradventure ye *d* among us
Josh 9:22 when ye *d* among us
Josh 10:6 *d* in the mountains are gathered
Josh 13:13 the Maachathites *d* among the
Josh 14:4 in the land, save cities to *d* in
Josh 15:63 but the Jebusites *d* with the
Josh 16:10 but the Canaanites *d* among the
Josh 17:12 Canaanites would *d* in that land
Josh 17:16 all the Canaanites that *d* in the
Josh 20:4 a place, that he may *d* among them
Josh 20:6 he shall *d* in that city, until he
Josh 21:2 Moses to give us cities to *d* in
Josh 24:13 ye built not, and ye *d* in them
Josh 24:15 the Amorites, in whose land ye *d*
Judg 1:21 but the Jebusites *d* with the
Judg 1:27 Canaanites would *d* in that land
Judg 1:35 But the Amorites would *d* in mount
Judg 6:10 the Amorites, in whose land ye *d*
Judg 9:41 that they should not *d* in Shechem
Judg 17:10 *D* with me, and be unto me a father
Judg 17:11 was content to *d* with the man
Judg 18:1 them an inheritance to *d* in
1Sa 12:8 made them *d* in this place
1Sa 27:5 the country, that I may *d* there

1Sa 27:5 for why should thy servant *d* in
2Sa 7:2 I *d* in an house of cedar, but the
2Sa 7:5 build me an house for me to *d* in
2Sa 7:10 that they may *d* in a place of
1Kin 2:36 *d* there, and go not forth thence
1Kin 3:17 this woman *d* in one house
1Kin 6:13 I will *d* among the children of
1Kin 8:12 he would *d* in the thick darkness
1Kin 8:13 built thee an house to *d* in
1Kin 8:27 will God indeed *d* on the earth
1Kin 17:9 belongeth to Zidon, and *d* there
2Kin 4:13 I *d* among mine own people
2Kin 6:1 the place where we *d* with thee is
2Kin 6:2 us a place there, where we may *d*
2Kin 17:27 *d* there, and let him teach them
2Kin 25:24 *d* in the land, and serve the king
1Chr 17:1 I *d* in an house of cedars, but
1Chr 17:4 not build me an house to *d* in
1Chr 17:9 they shall *d* in their place, and
1Chr 23:25 that they may *d* in Jerusalem for
2Chr 2:3 build him an house to *d* therein
2Chr 6:1 he would *d* in the thick darkness
2Chr 6:18 very deed *d* with men on the earth
2Chr 8:2 the children of Israel to *d* there
2Chr 8:11 My wife shall not *d* in the house
2Chr 19:10 brethren that *d* in their cities
Ezr 4:17 companions that *d* in Samaria
Ezr 6:12 name to *d* there destroy all kings
Neh 8:14 *d* in booths in the feast of the
Neh 11:1 to bring one of ten to *d* in
Neh 11:1 nine parts to *d* in other cities
Neh 11:2 themselves to *d* at Jerusalem
Job 3:5 let a cloud *d* upon it
Job 4:19 in them that *d* in houses of clay
Job 11:14 wickedness *d* in thy tabernacles
Job 18:15 It shall *d* in his tabernacle,
Job 19:15 They that *d* in mine house, and my
Job 30:6 To *d* in the cliffs of the valleys
Ps 4:8 LORD, only makest me *d* in safety
Ps 5:4 neither shall evil *d* with thee
Ps 15:1 who shall *d* in thy holy hill
Ps 23:6 I will *d* in the house of the LORD
Ps 24:1 the world, and they that *d* therein
Ps 25:13 His soul shall *d* at ease
Ps 27:4 that I may *d* in the house of the
Ps 37:3 so shalt thou *d* in the land
Ps 37:27 and *d* for evermore
Ps 37:29 the land, and *d* therein for ever
Ps 65:4 that he may *d* in thy courts
Ps 65:8 They also that *d* in the uttermost
Ps 68:6 the rebellious *d* in a dry land
Ps 68:16 hill which God desireth to *d* in
Ps 68:16 the LORD will *d* in it for ever
Ps 68:18 the LORD God might *d* among them
Ps 69:25 let none *d* in their tents
Ps 69:35 that they may *d* there, and have it
Ps 69:36 love his name shall *d* therein
Ps 72:9 They that *d* in the wilderness
Ps 78:55 of Israel to *d* in their tents
Ps 84:4 are they that *d* in thy house
Ps 84:10 than to *d* in the tents of
Ps 85:9 that glory may *d* in our land
Ps 98:7 the world, and they that *d* therein
Ps 101:6 the land, that they may *d* with me
Ps 101:7 shall not *d* within my house
Ps 107:4 they found no city to *d* in
Ps 107:34 wickedness of them that *d* therein
Ps 107:36 there he maketh the hungry to *d*
Ps 120:5 that I *d* in the tents of Kedar
Ps 132:14 here will I *d*; for I have
Ps 133:1 brethren to *d* together in unity
Ps 139:9 *d* in the uttermost parts of the
Ps 140:13 upright shall *d* in thy presence
Ps 143:3 he hath made me to *d* in darkness
Prov 1:33 hearkeneth unto me shall *d* safely
Prov 2:21 the upright shall *d* in the land
Prov 8:12 I wisdom *d* with prudence, and find
Prov 21:9 It is better to *d* in a corner of
Prov 21:19 It is better to *d* in the
Prov 25:24 It is better to *d* in the corner
Is 6:5 I *d* in the midst of a people of
Is 9:2 they that *d* in the land of the
Is 11:6 wolf also shall *d* with the lamb
Is 13:21 and owls shall *d* there, and satyrs
Is 16:4 Let mine outcasts *d* with thee
Is 23:13 for them that *d* in the wilderness
Is 23:18 for them that *d* before the LORD
Is 24:6 they that *d* therein are desolate
Is 26:5 bringeth down them that *d* on high
Is 26:19 Awake and sing, ye that *d* in dust
Is 30:19 shall *d* in Zion at Jerusalem
Is 32:16 shall *d* in the wilderness
Is 32:18 my people shall *d* in a peaceable
Is 33:14 Who among us shall *d* with the
Is 33:14 who among us shall *d* with
Is 33:16 He shall *d* on high
Is 33:24 the people that *d* therein shall
Is 34:11 also and the raven shall *d* in it
Is 34:17 generation shall they *d* therein
Is 40:22 them out as a tent to *d* in
Is 49:20 give place to me that I may *d*
Is 51:6 they that *d* therein shall die in
Is 57:15 I *d* in the high and holy place,
Is 58:12 The restorer of paths to *d* in
Is 65:9 it, and my servants shall *d* there
Jer 4:29 forsaken, and not a man *d* therein
Jer 7:3 will cause you to *d* in this place
Jer 7:7 I cause you to *d* in this place
Jer 8:16 the city, and those that *d* therein
Jer 8:19 of them that *d* in a far country
Jer 9:26 corners, that *d* in the wilderness
Jer 12:4 wickedness of them that *d* therein
Jer 20:6 all that *d* in thine house shall
Jer 23:6 saved, and Israel shall *d* safely
Jer 23:8 they shall *d* in their own land
Jer 24:8 them that *d* in the land of Egypt
Jer 25:5 *d* in the land that the LORD hath
Jer 25:24 people that *d* in the desert
Jer 27:11 they shall till it, and *d* therein
Jer 29:5 Build ye houses, and *d* in them
Jer 29:28 build ye houses, and *d* in them
Jer 29:32 have a man to *d* among this people
Jer 31:24 there shall *d* in Judah itself, and
Jer 32:37 and I will cause them to *d* safely
Jer 33:16 and Jerusalem shall *d* safely
Jer 35:7 all your days ye shall *d* in tents
Jer 35:9 to build houses for us to *d* in
Jer 35:11 so we *d* at Jerusalem
Jer 35:15 ye shall *d* in the land which I
Jer 40:5 *d* with him among the people
Jer 40:9 *d* in the land, and serve the king
Jer 40:10 I will *d* at Mizpah to serve the
Jer 40:10 *d* in your cities that ye have
Jer 42:13 We will not *d* in this land,
Jer 42:14 and there will we *d*
Jer 43:4 to *d* in the land of Judah
Jer 43:5 to *d* in the land of Judah
Jer 44:1 Jews which *d* in the land of Egypt
Jer 44:1 which *d* at Migdol, and at
Jer 44:8 of Egypt, whither ye be gone to *d*
Jer 44:13 them that *d* in the land of Egypt
Jer 44:14 a desire to return to *d* there
Jer 44:26 all Judah that *d* in the land of
Jer 47:2 the city, and them that *d* therein
Jer 48:9 without any to *d* therein
Jer 48:28 O ye that *d* in Moab, leave the
Jer 48:28 *d* in the rock, and be like the
Jer 49:1 his people *d* in his cities
Jer 49:8 *d* deep, O inhabitants of Dedan
Jer 49:18 shall a son of man *d* in it
Jer 49:30 *d* deep, O ye inhabitants of Hazor
Jer 49:31 gates nor bars, which *d* alone
Jer 49:33 there, nor any son of man *d* in it
Jer 50:3 desolate, and none shall *d* therein
Jer 50:39 of the islands shall *d* there
Jer 50:39 and the owls shall *d* therein
Jer 50:40 shall any son of man *d* therein
Jer 51:1 against them that *d* in the midst
Eze 2:6 thou dost *d* among scorpions
Eze 12:19 of all them that *d* therein
Eze 16:46 daughters that *d* at thy left hand
Eze 17:23 under it shall *d* all fowl of
Eze 17:23 the branches thereof shall they *d*
Eze 28:25 then shall they *d* in their land
Eze 28:26 they shall *d* safely therein, and
Eze 28:26 they shall *d* with confidence,
Eze 32:15 smite all them that *d* therein
Eze 34:25 they shall *d* safely in the
Eze 34:28 but they shall *d* safely, and none
Eze 36:28 ye shall *d* in the land that I
Eze 36:33 also cause you to *d* in the cities
Eze 37:25 they shall *d* in the land that I
Eze 37:25 and they shall *d* therein, even
Eze 38:8 they shall *d* safely all of them
Eze 38:11 that *d* safely, all of them
Eze 38:12 that *d* in the midst of the land
Eze 39:6 among them that *d* carelessly in
Eze 39:9 they that *d* in the cities of
Eze 43:7 where I will *d* in the midst of
Eze 43:9 I will *d* in the midst of them for
Dan 2:38 wheresoever the children of men *d*
Dan 4:1 that *d* in all the earth
Dan 6:25 that *d* in all the earth
Hos 9:3 They shall not *d* in the LORD's
Hos 12:9 yet make thee to *d* in tabernacles
Hos 14:7 They that *d* under his shadow
Joel 3:20 But Judah shall *d* for ever
Amos 3:12 of Israel be taken out that *d* in
Amos 5:11 stone, but ye shall not *d* in them
Amos 9:5 all that *d* therein shall mourn
Mic 4:10 thou shalt *d* in the field, and
Mic 7:13 because of them that *d* therein
Mic 7:14 which *d* solitarily in the wood,
Nah 1:5 the world, and all that *d* therein
Nah 3:18 thy nobles shall *d* in the dust
Hab 2:8 city, and of all that *d* therein
Hab 2:17 city, and of all that *d* therein
Zeph 1:18 of all them that *d* in the land
Hag 1:4 to *d* in your cieled houses, and
Zec 2:10 I will *d* in the midst of thee,
Zec 2:11 I will *d* in the midst of thee, and
Zec 8:3 will *d* in the midst of Jerusalem
Zec 8:4 old women *d* in the streets of
Zec 8:8 they shall *d* in the midst of
Zec 9:6 And a bastard shall *d* in Ashdod
Zec 14:11 And men shall *d* in it, and there
Mt 12:45 and they enter in and *d* there
Lk 11:26 and they enter in, and *d* there
Lk 21:35 *d* on the face of the whole earth
Acts 1:20 desolate, and let no man *d* therein
Acts 2:14 all ye that *d* at Jerusalem, be
Acts 4:16 to all them that *d* in Jerusalem
Acts 7:4 into this land, wherein ye now *d*
Acts 13:27 For they that *d* at Jerusalem
Acts 17:26 to *d* on all the face of the earth
Acts 28:16 but Paul was suffered to *d* by
Rom 8:9 that the Spirit of God *d* in you
Rom 8:11 up Jesus from the dead *d* in you
1Cor 7:12 and she be pleased to *d* with him
1Cor 7:13 and if he be pleased to *d* with her
2Cor 6:16 I will *d* in them, and walk in them
Eph 3:17 That Christ may *d* in your hearts
Col 1:19 that in him should all fulness *d*
Col 3:16 Let the word of Christ *d* in you
1Pet 3:7 *d* with them according to
1Jn 4:13 Hereby know we that we *d* in him
Rev 3:10 to try them that *d* upon the earth
Rev 6:10 blood on them that *d* on the earth
Rev 7:15 on the throne shall *d* among them
Rev 11:10 they that *d* upon the earth shall
Rev 12:12 ye heavens, and ye that *d* in them
Rev 13:6 and them that *d* in heaven
Rev 13:8 all that *d* upon the earth shall
Rev 13:12 them which *d* therein to worship
Rev 13:14 deceiveth them that *d* on the
Rev 13:14 to them that *d* on the earth
Rev 14:6 unto them that *d* on the earth
Rev 17:8 they that *d* on the earth shall
Rev 21:3 he will *d* with them, and they

## DWELLED

Gen 13:7 the Perizzite *d* then in the land
Gen 13:12 Abram *d* in the land of Canaan, and
Gen 13:12 Lot *d* in the cities of the plain,
Gen 20:1 *d* between Kadesh and Shur, and
Ruth 1:4 they *d* there about ten years
1Sa 12:11 on every side, and ye *d* safe

## DWELLEST

Deut 12:29 them, and *d* in their land
Deut 19:1 *d* in their cities, and in their
Deut 26:1 and possessest it, and *d* therein
2Kin 19:15 which *d* between the cherubims,
Ps 80:1 thou that *d* between the cherubims
Ps 123:1 O thou that *d* in the heavens
Song 8:13 Thou that *d* in the gardens, the
Is 10:24 hosts, O my people that *d* in Zion
Is 37:16 that *d* between the cherubims,
Is 47:8 that *d* carelessly, that sayest in
Jer 49:16 O thou that *d* in the clefts of
Jer 51:13 O thou that *d* upon many waters,
Lam 4:21 of Edom, that *d* in the land of Uz
Eze 7:7 thee, O thou that *d* in the land
Eze 12:2 of man, thou *d* in the midst of a
Obad 3 thou that *d* in the clefts of the
Zec 2:7 that *d* with the daughter of
Jn 1:38 Master,) where *d* thou
Rev 2:13 I know thy works, and where thou *d*

## DWELLETH

Lev 19:34 But the stranger that *d* with you
Lev 25:39 if thy brother that *d* by thee be

Lev 25:47 brother that *d* by him wax poor
Num 13:18 and the people that *d* therein
Deut 33:20 he *d* as a lion, and teareth the
Josh 6:25 she *d* in Israel even unto this
Josh 22:19 wherein the LORD's tabernacle *d*
1Sa 4:4 which *d* between the cherubims
1Sa 27:11 while he *d* in the country of the
2Sa 6:2 that *d* between the cherubims
2Sa 7:2 the ark of God *d* within curtains
1Chr 13:6 that *d* between the cherubims,
Job 15:28 he *d* in desolate cities, and in
Job 38:19 Where is the way where light *d*
Job 39:28 She *d* and abideth on the rock,
Ps 9:11 to the LORD, which *d* in Zion
Ps 26:8 and the place where thine honour *d*
Ps 91:1 He that *d* in the secret place of
Ps 113:5 the LORD our God, who *d* on high,
Ps 135:21 out of Zion, which *d* at Jerusalem
Prov 3:29 seeing he *d* securely by thee
Is 8:18 of hosts, which *d* in mount Zion
Is 33:5 for he *d* on high
Jer 29:16 the people that *d* in this city
Jer 44:2 desolation, and no man *d* therein,
Jer 49:31 that *d* without care, saith the
Jer 51:43 a land wherein no man *d*, neither
Lam 1:3 she *d* among the heathen, she
Eze 16:46 that *d* at thy right hand, is
Eze 17:16 the king *d* that made him king
Eze 38:14 when my people of Israel *d* safely
Dan 2:22 darkness, and the light *d* with him
Hos 4:3 every one that *d* therein shall
Joel 3:21 for the LORD *d* in Zion
Amos 8:8 and every one mourn that *d* therein
Mt 23:21 by it, and by him that *d* therein
Jn 6:56 my blood, *d* in me, and I in him
Jn 14:10 but the Father that *d* in me
Jn 14:17 for he *d* with you, and shall be in
Acts 7:48 Howbeit the most High *d* not in
Acts 17:24 *d* not in temples made with hands
Rom 7:17 that do it, but sin that *d* in me
Rom 7:18 is, in my flesh,) *d* no good thing
Rom 7:20 that do it, but sin that *d* in me
Rom 8:11 by his Spirit that *d* in you
1Cor 3:16 that the Spirit of God *d* in you
Col 2:9 For in him *d* all the fulness of
2Ti 1:14 by the Holy Ghost which *d* in us
Jas 4:5 The spirit that *d* in us lusteth
2Pet 3:13 earth, wherein *d* righteousness
1Jn 3:17 how *d* the love of God in him
1Jn 3:24 keepeth his commandments *d* in him
1Jn 4:12 God *d* in us, and his love is
1Jn 4:15 God *d* in him, and he in God
1Jn 4:16 he that *d* in love *d* in God
2Jn 2 the truth's sake, which *d* in us
Rev 2:13 slain among you, where Satan *d*

### DWELLING

Gen 10:30 their *d* was from Mesha, as thou
Gen 25:27 Jacob was a plain man, *d* in tents
Gen 27:39 thy *d* shall be the fatness of the
Lev 25:29 if a man sell a *d* house in a
Num 21:15 that goeth down to the *d* of Ar
Josh 13:21 dukes of Sihon, *d* in the country
1Kin 8:30 hear thou in heaven thy *d* place
1Kin 8:39 hear thou in heaven thy *d* place
1Kin 8:43 Hear thou in heaven thy *d* place
1Kin 8:49 in heaven thy *d* place, and
1Kin 21:8 were in his city, *d* with Naboth
2Kin 17:25 at the beginning of their *d* there
1Chr 6:32 they ministered before the *d*
1Chr 6:54 Now these are their *d* places
2Chr 6:2 and a place for thy *d* for ever
2Chr 6:21 hear thou from thy *d* place
2Chr 6:30 hear thou from heaven thy *d* place
2Chr 6:33 heavens, even from thy *d* place
2Chr 6:39 heavens, even from thy *d* place
2Chr 30:27 came up to his holy *d* place
2Chr 36:15 on his people, and on his *d* place
Job 8:22 the *d* place of the wicked shall
Job 21:28 where are the *d* places of the
Ps 49:11 their *d* places to all generations
Ps 49:14 consume in the grave from their *d*
Ps 52:5 and pluck thee out of thy *d* place
Ps 74:7 defiled by casting down the *d*
Ps 76:2 and his *d* place in Zion
Ps 79:7 Jacob, and laid waste his *d* place
Ps 90:1 thou hast been our *d* place in all
Ps 91:10 shall any plague come nigh thy *d*
Prov 21:20 and oil in the *d* of the wise
Prov 24:15 against the *d* of the righteous
Is 4:5 upon every *d* place of mount Zion
Is 18:4 I will consider in my *d* place
Jer 46:19 O thou daughter *d* in Egypt
Jer 49:33 And Hazor shall be a *d* for dragons
Jer 51:37 a *d* place for dragons, an
Eze 38:11 all of them *d* without walls, and
Eze 48:15 profane place for the city, for *d*
Dan 2:11 whose *d* is not with flesh
Dan 4:25 thy *d* shall be with the beasts of
Dan 4:32 thy *d* shall be with the beasts of
Dan 5:21 his *d* was with the wild asses
Joel 3:17 I am the LORD your God *d* in Zion
Nah 2:11 Where is the *d* of the lions
Zeph 3:7 so their *d* should not be cut off,
Mk 5:3 Who had his *d* among the tombs
Acts 2:5 there were *d* at Jerusalem Jews,
Acts 19:17 Jews and Greeks also *d* at Ephesus
1Ti 6:16 *d* in the light which no man can
Heb 11:9 *d* in tabernacles with Isaac and
2Pet 2:8 that righteous man *d* among them

### DWELLINGPLACES

Jer 30:18 tents, and have mercy on his *d*
Jer 51:30 they have burned her *d*
Eze 6:6 In all your *d* the cities shall be
Eze 37:23 will save them out of all their *d*
Hab 1:6 to possess the *d* that are not

### DWELLINGS

Ex 10:23 of Israel had light in their *d*
Lev 3:17 generations throughout all your *d*
Lev 7:26 or of beast, in any of your *d*
Lev 23:3 sabbath of the LORD in all your *d*
Lev 23:14 your generations in all your *d*
Lev 23:21 *d* throughout your generations
Lev 23:31 your generations in all your *d*
Num 35:29 your generations in all your *d*
Job 18:19 nor any remaining in his *d*
Job 18:21 such are the *d* of the wicked
Job 39:6 and the barren land his *d*
Ps 55:15 for wickedness is in their *d*
Ps 87:2 Zion more than all the *d* of Jacob
Is 32:18 habitation, and in sure *d*, and in
Jer 9:19 because our *d* have cast us out
Eze 25:4 in thee, and make their *d* in thee
Zeph 2:6 And the sea coast shall be *d*

### DWELT

Gen 4:16 *d* in the land of Nod, on the east
Gen 11:2 and they *d* there
Gen 11:31 they came unto Haran, and *d* there
Gen 13:18 *d* in the plain of Mamre, which is
Gen 14:7 Amorites, that *d* in Hazezon-tamar
Gen 14:12 who *d* in Sodom, and his goods, and
Gen 14:13 for he *d* in the plain of Mamre
Gen 16:3 after Abram had *d* ten years in
Gen 19:29 the cities in the which Lot *d*
Gen 19:30 *d* in the mountain, and his two
Gen 19:30 he *d* in a cave, he and his two
Gen 21:20 *d* in the wilderness, and became an
Gen 21:21 he *d* in the wilderness of Paran
Gen 22:19 and Abraham *d* at Beer-sheba
Gen 23:10 Ephron *d* among the children of
Gen 24:62 for he *d* in the south country
Gen 25:11 Isaac *d* by the well Lahai-roi
Gen 25:18 they *d* from Havilah unto Shur,
Gen 26:6 And Isaac *d* in Gerar
Gen 26:17 the valley of Gerar, and *d* there
Gen 35:22 when Israel *d* in that land, that
Gen 36:8 Thus *d* Esau in mount Seir
Gen 37:1 Jacob *d* in the land wherein his
Gen 38:11 went and *d* in her father's house
Gen 47:27 Israel *d* in the land of Egypt, in
Gen 50:22 Joseph *d* in Egypt, he, and his
Ex 2:15 and *d* in the land of Midian
Ex 12:40 who *d* in Egypt, was four hundred
Lev 18:3 the land of Egypt, wherein ye *d*
Lev 26:35 your sabbaths, when ye *d* upon it
Num 14:25 and the Canaanites *d* in the valley
Num 14:45 Canaanites which *d* in that hill
Num 20:15 we have *d* in Egypt a long time
Num 21:1 which *d* in the south, heard tell
Num 21:25 Israel *d* in all the cities of the
Num 21:31 Thus Israel *d* in the land of the
Num 21:34 the Amorites, which *d* at Heshbon
Num 31:10 all their cities wherein they *d*
Num 32:40 and he *d* therein
Num 33:40 which *d* in the south in the land
Deut 1:4 which *d* in Heshbon, and Og the
Deut 1:4 which *d* at Astaroth in Edrei
Deut 1:6 Ye have *d* long enough in this
Deut 1:44 which *d* in that mountain, came
Deut 2:8 which *d* in Seir, through the way
Deut 2:10 The Emims *d* therein in times past
Deut 2:12 The Horims also *d* in Seir
Deut 2:12 before them, and *d* in their stead
Deut 2:20 giants *d* therein in old time
Deut 2:21 them, and *d* in their stead
Deut 2:22 of Esau, which *d* in Seir, when he
Deut 2:22 *d* in their stead even unto this
Deut 2:23 And the Avims which *d* in Hazerim
Deut 2:23 them, and *d* in their stead
Deut 3:2 the Amorites, which *d* at Heshbon
Deut 4:46 who *d* at Heshbon, whom Moses and
Deut 8:12 built goodly houses, and *d* therein
Deut 29:16 we have *d* in the land of Egypt
Deut 33:16 will of him that *d* in the bush
Josh 2:15 town wall, and she *d* upon the wall
Josh 7:7 *d* on the other side Jordan
Josh 9:16 and that they *d* among them
Josh 12:2 who *d* in Heshbon, and ruled from
Josh 12:4 that *d* at Ashtaroth and at Edrei,
Josh 16:10 the Canaanites that *d* in Gezer
Josh 19:47 *d* therein, and called Leshem, Dan,
Josh 19:50 he built the city, and *d* therein
Josh 21:43 they possessed it, and *d* therein
Josh 22:33 the children of Reuben and Gad *d*
Josh 24:2 Your fathers *d* on the other side
Josh 24:7 ye *d* in the wilderness a long
Josh 24:8 which *d* on the other side Jordan
Josh 24:18 the Amorites which *d* in the land
Judg 1:9 that *d* in the mountain, and in the
Judg 1:10 the Canaanites that *d* in Hebron
Judg 1:16 they went and *d* among the people
Judg 1:29 the Canaanites that *d* in Gezer
Judg 1:29 but the Canaanites *d* in Gezer
Judg 1:30 but the Canaanites *d* among them
Judg 1:32 But the Asherites *d* among the
Judg 1:33 but he *d* among the Canaanites,
Judg 3:3 Hivites that *d* in mount Lebanon
Judg 3:5 of Israel *d* among the Canaanites
Judg 4:2 which *d* in Harosheth of the
Judg 4:5 she *d* under the palm tree of
Judg 8:11 *d* in tents on the east of Nobah
Judg 8:29 Joash went and *d* in his own house
Judg 9:21 *d* there, for fear of Abimelech
Judg 9:41 And Abimelech *d* at Arumah
Judg 10:1 he *d* in Shamir in mount Ephraim
Judg 11:3 brethren, and *d* in the land of Tob
Judg 11:26 While Israel *d* in Heshbon
Judg 15:8 *d* in the top of the rock Etam
Judg 18:7 were therein, how they *d* careless
Judg 18:28 they built a city, and *d* therein
Judg 21:23 repaired the cities, and *d* in them
Ruth 2:23 and *d* with her mother in law
1Sa 19:18 he and Samuel went and *d* in Naioth
1Sa 22:4 they *d* with him all the while
1Sa 23:29 *d* in strong holds at En-gedi
1Sa 27:3 David *d* with Achish at Gath, he
1Sa 27:7 the time that David *d* in the
1Sa 31:7 the Philistines came and *d* in them
2Sa 2:3 they *d* in the cities of Hebron
2Sa 5:9 So David *d* in the fort, and called
2Sa 7:6 Whereas I have not *d* in any house
2Sa 9:12 all that *d* in the house of Ziba
2Sa 9:13 So Mephibosheth *d* in Jerusalem
2Sa 14:28 So Absalom *d* two full years in
1Kin 2:38 Shimei *d* in Jerusalem many days
1Kin 4:25 And Judah and Israel *d* safely
1Kin 7:8 his house where he *d* had another
1Kin 9:16 the Canaanites that *d* in the city
1Kin 11:24 *d* therein, and reigned in Damascus
1Kin 12:2 Solomon, and Jeroboam *d* in Egypt
1Kin 12:17 which *d* in the cities of Judah
1Kin 12:25 in mount Ephraim, and *d* therein
1Kin 13:11 Now there *d* an old prophet in
1Kin 13:25 the city where the old prophet *d*
1Kin 15:18 that *d* at Damascus, saying,
1Kin 15:21 building of Ramah, and *d* in Tirzah
1Kin 17:5 *d* by the brook Cherith, that is
2Kin 13:5 of Israel *d* in their tents
2Kin 15:5 death, and *d* in a several house
2Kin 16:6 Elath, and *d* there unto this day
2Kin 17:24 and *d* in the cities thereof
2Kin 17:28 *d* in Beth-el, and taught them how
2Kin 17:29 in their cities wherein they *d*
2Kin 19:36 went and returned, and *d* at Nineveh
2Kin 22:14 (now she *d* in Jerusalem in the
1Chr 2:55 of the scribes which *d* at Jabez
1Chr 4:23 those that *d* among plants and
1Chr 4:23 there they *d* with the king for
1Chr 4:28 they *d* at Beer-sheba, and Moladah,

1Chr 4:40 they of Ham had *d* there of old
1Chr 4:41 this day, and *d* in their rooms
1Chr 4:43 escaped, and *d* there unto this day
1Chr 5:8 who *d* in Aroer, even unto Nebo and
1Chr 5:10 they *d* in their tents throughout
1Chr 5:11 of Gad *d* over against them
1Chr 5:16 they *d* in Gilead in Bashan, and in
1Chr 5:22 they *d* in their steads until the
1Chr 5:23 tribe of Manasseh *d* in the land
1Chr 7:29 In these *d* the children of Joseph
1Chr 8:28 These *d* in Jerusalem
1Chr 8:29 at Gibeon *d* the father of Gibeon
1Chr 8:32 these also *d* with their brethren
1Chr 9:2 *d* in their possessions in their
1Chr 9:3 in Jerusalem *d* of the children of
1Chr 9:16 that *d* in the villages of the
1Chr 9:34 these *d* at Jerusalem
1Chr 9:35 in Gibeon *d* the father of Gibeon,
1Chr 9:38 they also *d* with their brethren
1Chr 10:7 the Philistines came and *d* in them
1Chr 11:7 And David *d* in the castle
1Chr 17:5 For I have not *d* in an house
2Chr 10:17 that *d* in the cities of Judah
2Chr 11:5 Rehoboam *d* in Jerusalem, and built
2Chr 16:2 that *d* at Damascus, saying,
2Chr 19:4 Jehoshaphat *d* at Jerusalem
2Chr 20:8 they *d* therein, and have built
2Chr 26:7 the Arabians that *d* in Gur-baal
2Chr 26:21 *d* in a several house, being a
2Chr 28:18 and they *d* there
2Chr 30:25 that *d* in Judah, rejoiced
2Chr 31:4 that *d* in Jerusalem to give the
2Chr 31:6 that *d* in the cities of Judah,
2Chr 34:22 (now she *d* in Jerusalem in the
Ezr 2:70 *d* in their cities, and all Israel
Neh 3:26 Moreover the Nethinims *d* in Ophel
Neh 4:12 the Jews which *d* by them came
Neh 7:73 and all Israel, *d* in their cities
Neh 11:1 of the people *d* at Jerusalem
Neh 11:3 the province that *d* in Jerusalem
Neh 11:3 but in the cities of Judah *d*
Neh 11:4 at Jerusalem *d* certain of the
Neh 11:6 All the sons of Perez that *d* at
Neh 11:21 But the Nethinims *d* in Ophel
Neh 11:25 of Judah *d* at Kirjath-arba
Neh 11:30 they *d* from Beer-sheba unto the
Neh 11:31 Benjamin from Geba *d* at Michmash
Neh 13:16 There *d* men of Tyre also therein,
Est 9:19 that *d* in the unwalled towns,
Job 22:8 and the honourable man *d* in it
Job 29:25 *d* as a king in the army, as one
Ps 68:10 Thy congregation hath *d* therein
Ps 74:2 mount Zion, wherein thou hast *d*
Ps 94:17 my soul had almost *d* in silence
Ps 120:6 My soul hath long *d* with him that
Is 13:20 neither shall it be *d* in from
Is 29:1 to Ariel, the city where David *d*
Is 37:37 went and returned, and *d* at Nineveh
Jer 2:6 passed through, and where no man *d*
Jer 35:10 But we have *d* in tents, and have
Jer 39:14 so he *d* among the people
Jer 40:6 *d* with him among the people that
Jer 41:17 *d* in the habitation of Chimham,
Jer 44:15 that *d* in the land of Egypt
Jer 50:39 neither shall it be *d* in from
Eze 3:15 that *d* by the river of Chebar, and
Eze 31:6 under his shadow *d* all great
Eze 31:17 that *d* under his shadow in the
Eze 36:17 of Israel *d* in their own land
Eze 37:25 wherein your fathers have *d*
Eze 39:26 when they *d* safely in their land,
Dan 4:12 heaven *d* in the boughs thereof
Dan 4:21 which the beasts of the field *d*
Zeph 2:15 rejoicing city that *d* carelessly
Mt 2:23 *d* in a city called Nazareth
Mt 4:13 *d* in Capernaum, which is upon the
Lk 1:65 on all that *d* round about them
Lk 13:4 above all men that *d* in Jerusalem
Jn 1:14 *d* among us, (and we beheld his
Jn 1:39 They came and saw where he *d*
Acts 7:2 before he *d* in Charran,
Acts 7:4 the Chaldaeans, and *d* in Charran
Acts 9:22 the Jews which *d* at Damascus
Acts 9:32 to the saints which *d* at Lydda
Acts 9:35 And all that *d* at Lydda and Saron
Acts 11:29 the brethren which *d* in Judaea
Acts 13:17 *d* as strangers in the land of
Acts 19:10 so that all they which *d* in Asia
Acts 22:12 of all the Jews which *d* there
Acts 28:30 Paul *d* two whole years in his own
2Ti 1:5 which *d* first in thy grandmother
Rev 11:10 them that *d* on the earth

**DYED**
Ex 25:5 And rams' skins *d* red, and badgers'
Ex 26:14 for the tent of rams' skins *d* red
Ex 35:7 And rams' skins *d* red, and badgers'
Ex 36:19 for the tent of rams' skins *d* red
Ex 39:34 the covering of rams' skins *d* red
Is 63:1 with *d* garments from Bozrah
Eze 23:15 exceeding in *d* attire upon their

**DYING**
Num 17:13 shall we be consumed with *d*
Mk 12:20 took a wife, and *d* left no seed
Lk 8:42 years of age, and she lay a *d*
2Cor 4:10 the body the *d* of the Lord Jesus
2Cor 6:9 as *d*, and, behold, we live
Heb 11:21 By faith Jacob, when he was a *d*

# E

**EAGLE**
Lev 11:13 the *e*, and the ossifrage, and the
Lev 11:18 and the pelican, and the gier *e*
Deut 14:12 the *e*, and the ossifrage, and the
Deut 14:17 And the pelican, and the gier *e*
Deut 28:49 earth, as swift as the *e* flieth
Deut 32:11 As an *e* stirreth up her nest,
Job 9:26 as the *e* that hasteth to the prey
Job 39:27 Doth the *e* mount up at thy
Prov 23:5 fly away as an *e* toward heaven
Prov 30:19 The way of an *e* in the air
Jer 48:40 Behold, he shall fly as an *e*
Jer 49:16 make thy nest as high as the *e*
Jer 49:22 he shall come up and fly as the *e*
Eze 1:10 four also had the face of an *e*
Eze 10:14 and the fourth the face of an *e*
Eze 17:3 A great *e* with great wings,
Eze 17:7 another great *e* with great wings
Hos 8:1 He shall come as an *e* against the
Obad 4 thou exalt thyself as the *e*
Mic 1:16 enlarge thy baldness as the *e*
Hab 1:8 fly as the *e* that hasteth to eat
Rev 4:7 fourth beast was like a flying *e*
Rev 12:14 were given two wings of a great *e*

**EAGLES**
2Sa 1:23 they were swifter than *e*, they
Prov 30:17 out, and the young *e* shall eat it
Is 40:31 shall mount up with wings as *e*
Jer 4:13 his horses are swifter than *e*
Lam 4:19 swifter than the *e* of the heaven
Mt 24:28 there will the *e* be gathered
Lk 17:37 thither will the *e* be gathered

**EAR**
Ex 9:31 for the barley was in the *e*
Ex 15:26 wilt give *e* to his commandments,
Ex 21:6 bore his *e* through with an aul
Ex 29:20 the tip of the right *e* of Aaron
Ex 29:20 tip of the right *e* of his sons
Lev 8:23 upon the tip of Aaron's right *e*
Lev 8:24 upon the tip of their right *e*
Lev 14:14 it upon the tip of the right *e* of
Lev 14:17 *e* of him that is to be cleansed
Lev 14:25 it upon the tip of the right *e* of
Lev 14:28 *e* of him that is to be cleansed
Deut 1:45 your voice, nor give *e* unto you
Deut 15:17 it through his *e* unto the door
Deut 32:1 Give *e*, O ye heavens, and I will
Judg 5:3 give *e*, O ye princes
1Sa 8:12 and will set them to *e* his ground
1Sa 9:15 in his *e* a day before Saul came
2Kin 19:16 LORD, bow down thine *e*, and hear
2Chr 24:19 but they would not give *e*
Neh 1:6 Let thine *e* now be attentive, and
Neh 1:11 let now thine *e* be attentive to
Neh 9:30 yet would they not give *e*
Job 4:12 mine *e* received a little thereof
Job 12:11 Doth not the *e* try words
Job 13:1 mine *e* hath heard and understood
Job 29:11 When the *e* heard me, then it
Job 29:21 Unto me men gave *e*, and waited, and
Job 32:11 I gave *e* to your reasons, whilst
Job 34:2 give *e* unto me, ye that have
Job 34:3 For the *e* trieth words, as the
Job 36:10 also their *e* to discipline
Job 42:5 of thee by the hearing of the *e*
Ps 5:1 Give *e* to my words, O LORD
Ps 10:17 thou wilt cause thine *e* to hear
Ps 17:1 give *e* unto my prayer, that goeth
Ps 17:6 incline thine *e* unto me, and hear
Ps 31:2 Bow down thine *e* to me
Ps 39:12 O LORD, and give *e* unto my cry
Ps 45:10 and consider, and incline thine *e*
Ps 49:1 give *e*, all ye inhabitants of the
Ps 49:4 will incline mine *e* to a parable
Ps 54:2 give *e* to the words of my mouth
Ps 55:1 Give *e* to my prayer, O God
Ps 58:4 deaf adder that stoppeth her *e*
Ps 71:2 incline thine *e* unto me, and save
Ps 77:1 and he gave *e* unto me
Ps 78:1 Give *e*, O my people, to my law
Ps 80:1 Give *e*, O Shepherd of Israel,
Ps 84:8 give *e*, O God of Jacob
Ps 86:1 Bow down thine *e*, O LORD, hear me
Ps 86:6 Give *e*, O LORD, unto my prayer
Ps 88:2 incline thine *e* unto my cry
Ps 94:9 He that planted the *e*, shall he
Ps 102:2 incline thine *e* unto me
Ps 116:2 he hath inclined his *e* unto me
Ps 141:1 give *e* unto my voice, when I cry
Ps 143:1 give *e* to my supplications
Prov 2:2 thou incline thine *e* unto wisdom
Prov 4:20 incline thine *e* unto my sayings
Prov 5:1 bow thine *e* to my understanding
Prov 5:13 nor inclined mine *e* to them that
Prov 15:31 The *e* that heareth the reproof of
Prov 17:4 a liar giveth *e* to a naughty
Prov 18:15 the *e* of the wise seeketh
Prov 20:12 The hearing *e*, and the seeing eye,
Prov 22:17 Bow down thine *e*, and hear the
Prov 25:12 wise reprover upon an obedient *e*
Prov 28:9 away his *e* from hearing the law
Eccl 1:8 nor the *e* filled with hearing
Is 1:2 Hear, O heavens, and give *e*
Is 1:10 give *e* unto the law of our God,
Is 8:9 and give *e*, all ye of far
Is 28:23 Give ye *e*, and hear my voice
Is 30:24 the young asses that *e* the ground
Is 32:9 give *e* unto my speech
Is 37:17 Incline thine *e*, O LORD, and hear
Is 42:23 Who among you will give *e* to this
Is 48:8 time that thine *e* was not opened
Is 50:4 he wakeneth mine *e* to hear as the
Is 50:5 The Lord GOD hath opened mine *e*
Is 51:4 give *e* unto me, O my nation
Is 55:3 Incline your *e*, and come unto me
Is 59:1 neither his *e* heavy, that it
Is 64:4 not heard, nor perceived by the *e*
Jer 6:10 their *e* is uncircumcised, and they
Jer 7:24 not, nor inclined their *e*
Jer 7:26 not unto me, nor inclined their *e*
Jer 9:20 let your *e* receive the word of
Jer 11:8 obeyed not, nor inclined their *e*
Jer 13:15 Hear ye, and give *e*
Jer 17:23 not, neither inclined their *e*
Jer 25:4 nor inclined your *e* to hear
Jer 34:14 unto me, neither inclined their *e*
Jer 35:15 but ye have not inclined your *e*
Jer 44:5 nor inclined their *e* to turn from
Lam 3:56 hide not thine *e* at my breathing,
Dan 9:18 O my God, incline thine *e*
Hos 5:1 and give ye *e*, O house of the king
Joel 1:2 Hear this, ye old men, and give *e*
Amos 3:12 lion two legs, or a piece of an *e*
Mt 10:27 and what ye hear in the *e*, that
Mt 26:51 high priest's, and smote off his *e*

Mk 4:28 first the blade, then the e
Mk 4:28 after that the full corn in the e
Mk 14:47 the high priest, and cut off his e
Lk 12:3 which ye have spoken in the e in
Lk 22:50 priest, and cut off his right e
Lk 22:51 And he touched his e, and healed
Jn 18:10 servant, and cut off his right e
Jn 18:26 his kinsman whose e Peter cut off
1Cor 2:9 nor e heard, neither have entered
1Cor 12:16 if the e shall say, Because I am
Rev 2:7 He that hath an e, let him hear
Rev 2:11 He that hath an e, let him hear
Rev 2:17 He that hath an e, let him hear
Rev 2:29 He that hath an e, let him hear
Rev 3:6 He that hath an e, let him hear
Rev 3:13 He that hath an e, let him hear
Rev 3:22 He that hath an e, let him hear
Rev 13:9 If any man have an e, let him

## EARLY

Gen 19:2 your feet, and ye shall rise up e
Gen 19:27 Abraham gat up e in the morning
Gen 20:8 Abimelech rose e in the morning
Gen 21:14 Abraham rose up e in the morning
Gen 22:3 Abraham rose up e in the morning
Gen 28:18 Jacob rose up e in the morning,
Gen 31:55 e in the morning Laban rose up,
Ex 8:20 Rise up e in the morning, and
Ex 9:13 Rise up e in the morning, and
Ex 24:4 rose up e in the morning, and
Ex 32:6 they rose up e on the morrow, and
Ex 34:4 Moses rose up e in the morning,
Num 14:40 they rose up e in the morning, and
Josh 3:1 Joshua rose e in the morning
Josh 6:12 Joshua rose e in the morning, and
Josh 6:15 that they rose e about the
Josh 7:16 Joshua rose up e in the morning
Josh 8:10 Joshua rose up e in the morning
Josh 8:14 it, that they hasted and rose up e
Judg 6:28 the city arose e in the morning
Judg 6:38 for he rose up e on the morrow
Judg 7:1 that were with him, rose up e
Judg 7:3 depart e from mount Gilead
Judg 9:33 the sun is up, thou shalt rise e
Judg 19:5 when they arose e in the morning
Judg 19:8 he arose e in the morning on the
Judg 19:9 to morrow get you e on your way
Judg 21:4 morrow, that the people rose e
1Sa 1:19 And they rose up in the morning e
1Sa 5:3 of Ashdod arose e on the morrow
1Sa 5:4 when they arose e on the morrow
1Sa 9:26 And they arose e
1Sa 15:12 when Samuel rose e to meet Saul
1Sa 17:20 David rose up e in the morning,
1Sa 29:10 Wherefore now rise up e in the
1Sa 29:10 soon as ye be up e in the morning
1Sa 29:11 his men rose up e to depart in
2Sa 15:2 And Absalom rose up e, and stood
2Kin 3:22 they rose up e in the morning, and
2Kin 6:15 of the man of God was risen e
2Kin 19:35 when they arose e in the morning
2Chr 20:20 they rose e in the morning, and
2Chr 29:20 Then Hezekiah the king rose e
Job 1:5 rose up e in the morning, and
Ps 46:5 shall help her, and that right e
Ps 57:8 I myself will awake e
Ps 63:1 e will I seek thee
Ps 78:34 returned and enquired e after God
Ps 90:14 O satisfy us e with thy mercy
Ps 101:8 I will e destroy all the wicked
Ps 108:2 I myself will awake e
Ps 127:2 It is vain for you to rise up e
Prov 1:28 they shall seek me e, but they
Prov 8:17 that seek me e shall find me
Prov 27:14 rising e in the morning, it shall
Song 7:12 Let us get up e to the vineyards
Is 5:11 that rise up e in the morning
Is 26:9 within me will I seek thee e
Is 37:36 when they arose e in the morning
Jer 7:13 and I spake unto you, rising up e
Jer 7:25 the prophets, daily rising up e
Jer 11:7 even unto this day, rising e
Jer 25:3 I have spoken unto you, rising e
Jer 25:4 servants the prophets, rising e
Jer 26:5 I sent unto you, both rising up e
Jer 29:19 the prophets, rising up e
Jer 32:33 though I taught them, rising up e
Jer 35:14 I have spoken unto you, rising e
Jer 35:15 the prophets, rising up e
Jer 44:4 servants the prophets, rising e
Dan 6:19 king arose very e in the morning
Hos 5:15 affliction they will seek me e
Hos 6:4 as the e dew it goeth away
Hos 13:3 as the e dew that passeth away,
Zeph 3:7 but they rose e, and corrupted all
Mt 20:1 which went out e in the morning
Mk 16:2 very e in the morning the first
Mk 16:9 Now when Jesus was risen e the
Lk 21:38 all the people came e in the
Lk 24:1 very e in the morning, they came
Lk 24:22 which were e at the sepulchre
Jn 8:2 e in the morning he came again
Jn 18:28 of judgment: and it was e
Jn 20:1 the week cometh Mary Magdalene e
Acts 5:21 into the temple e in the morning
Jas 5:7 for it, until he receive the e

## EARNEST

Rom 8:19 For the e expectation of the
2Cor 1:22 given the e of the Spirit in our
2Cor 5:5 given unto us the e of the Spirit
2Cor 7:7 when he told us your e desire
2Cor 8:16 which put the same e care into
Eph 1:14 Which is the e of our inheritance
Phil 1:20 According to my e expectation
Heb 2:1 we ought to give the more e heed

## EARNESTLY

Num 22:37 Did I not e send unto thee to
1Sa 20:6 David e asked leave of me that he
1Sa 20:28 David e asked leave of me to go
Neh 3:20 Zabbai e repaired the other piece
Job 7:2 As a servant e desireth the
Jer 11:7 For I e protested unto your
Jer 31:20 I do e remember him still
Mic 7:3 may do evil with both hands e
Lk 22:44 in an agony he prayed more e
Lk 22:56 e looked upon him, and said, This
Acts 3:12 or why look ye so e on us
Acts 23:1 e beholding the council, said,
1Cor 12:31 But covet e the best gifts
2Cor 5:2 e desiring to be clothed upon
Jas 5:17 he prayed e that it might not
Jude 3 exhort you that ye should e

## EARRING

Gen 24:22 golden e of half a shekel weight
Gen 24:30 came to pass, when he saw the e
Gen 24:47 I put the e upon her face, and the
Job 42:11 money, and every one an e of gold
Prov 25:12 As an e of gold, and an ornament

## EARRINGS

Gen 35:4 all their e which were in their
Ex 32:2 unto them, Break off the golden e
Ex 32:3 golden e which were in their ears
Ex 35:22 and brought bracelets, and e
Num 31:50 chains, and bracelets, rings, e
Judg 8:24 me every man the e of his prey
Judg 8:24 (For they had golden e, because
Judg 8:25 every man the e of his prey
Judg 8:26 golden e that he requested was a
Is 3:20 and the tablets, and the e
Eze 16:12 e in thine ears, and a beautiful
Hos 2:13 and she decked herself with her e

## EARS

Gen 20:8 told all these things in their e
Gen 35:4 earrings which were in their e
Gen 41:5 seven e of corn came up upon one
Gen 41:6 And, behold, seven thin e and
Gen 41:7 the seven thin e devoured the
Gen 41:7 devoured the seven rank and full e
Gen 41:22 seven e came up in one stalk,
Gen 41:23 And, behold, seven e, withered,
Gen 41:24 e devoured the seven good e
Gen 41:26 the seven good e are seven years
Gen 41:27 the seven empty e blasted with
Gen 44:18 thee, speak a word in my lord's e
Gen 50:4 in the e of Pharaoh, saying,
Ex 10:2 mayest tell in the e of thy son
Ex 11:2 Speak now in the e of the people
Ex 17:14 and rehearse it in the e of Joshua
Ex 32:2 which are in the e of your wives
Ex 32:3 earrings which were in their e
Lev 2:14 of thy firstfruits green e of
Lev 2:14 even corn beaten out of full e
Lev 23:14 nor parched corn, nor green e
Num 11:18 ye have wept in the e of the LORD
Num 14:28 LORD, as ye have spoken in mine e
Deut 5:1 which I speak in your e this day
Deut 23:25 pluck the e with thine hand
Deut 29:4 see, and e to hear, unto this day
Deut 31:28 may speak these words in their e
Deut 31:30 Moses spake in the e of all the
Deut 32:44 this song in the e of the people
Josh 20:4 the e of the elders of that city
Judg 7:3 proclaim in the e of the people
Judg 9:2 in the e of all the men of
Judg 9:3 brethren spake of him in the e of
Judg 17:2 and spakest of also in mine e
Ruth 2:2 glean e of corn after him in
1Sa 3:11 at which both the e of every one
1Sa 8:21 them in the e of the LORD
1Sa 11:4 tidings in the e of the people
1Sa 15:14 bleating of the sheep in mine e
1Sa 18:23 those words in the e of David
2Sa 3:19 also spake in the e of Benjamin
2Sa 3:19 the e of David in Hebron all that
2Sa 7:22 all that we have heard with our e
2Sa 22:7 and my cry did enter into his e
2Kin 4:42 full e of corn in the husk
2Kin 18:26 e of the people that are on the
2Kin 19:28 thy tumult is come up into mine e
2Kin 21:12 of it, both his e shall tingle
2Kin 23:2 he read in their e all the words
1Chr 17:20 all that we have heard with our e
2Chr 6:40 let thine e be attent unto the
2Chr 7:15 mine e attent unto the prayer
2Chr 34:30 he read in their e all the words
Neh 8:3 the e of all the people were
Job 13:17 and my declaration with your e
Job 15:21 A dreadful sound is in his e
Job 24:24 off as the tops of the e of corn
Job 28:22 heard the fame thereof with our e
Job 33:16 Then he openeth the e of men
Job 36:15 and openeth their e in oppression
Ps 18:6 came before him, even into his e
Ps 34:15 his e are open unto their cry
Ps 40:6 mine e hast thou opened
Ps 44:1 We have heard with our e, O God,
Ps 78:1 incline your e to the words of my
Ps 92:11 mine e shall hear my desire of
Ps 115:6 They have e, but they hear not
Ps 130:2 let thine e be attentive to the
Ps 135:17 They have e, but they hear not
Prov 21:13 Whoso stoppeth his e at the cry
Prov 23:9 Speak not in the e of a fool
Prov 23:12 thine e to the words of knowledge
Prov 26:17 one that taketh a dog by the e
Is 5:9 In mine e said the LORD of hosts,
Is 6:10 people fat, and make their e heavy
Is 6:10 their eyes, and hear with their e
Is 11:3 after the hearing of his e
Is 17:5 reapeth the e with his arm
Is 17:5 e in the valley of Rephaim
Is 22:14 in mine e by the LORD of hosts
Is 30:21 thine e shall hear a word behind
Is 32:3 the e of them that hear shall
Is 33:15 that stoppeth his e from hearing
Is 35:5 the e of the deaf shall be
Is 36:11 in the e of the people that are
Is 37:29 tumult, is come up into mine e
Is 42:20 opening the e, but he heareth not
Is 43:8 eyes, and the deaf that have e
Is 49:20 other, shall say again in thine e
Jer 2:2 cry in the e of Jerusalem, saying
Jer 5:21 which have e, and hear not
Jer 19:3 heareth, his e shall tingle
Jer 26:11 as ye have heard with your e
Jer 26:15 speak all these words in your e
Jer 28:7 this word that I speak in thine e
Jer 28:7 in the e of all the people
Jer 29:29 in the e of Jeremiah the prophet
Jer 36:6 the e of the people in the LORD's
Jer 36:6 thou shalt read them in the e of
Jer 36:10 in the e of all the people
Jer 36:13 the book in the e of the people
Jer 36:14 hast read in the e of the people
Jer 36:15 Sit down now, and read it in our e
Jer 36:15 So Baruch read it in their e
Jer 36:20 the words in the e of the king
Jer 36:21 read it in the e of the king
Jer 36:21 in the e of all the princes which
Eze 3:10 thine heart, and hear with thine e
Eze 8:18 cry in mine e with a loud voice
Eze 9:1 also in mine e with a loud voice
Eze 12:2 they have e to hear, and hear not
Eze 16:12 forehead, and earrings in thine e
Eze 23:25 take away thy nose and thine e
Eze 24:26 thee to hear it with thine e
Eze 40:4 thine eyes, and hear with thine e
Eze 44:5 hear with thine e all that I say

Mic 7:16 mouth, their *e* shall be deaf
Zec 7:11 the shoulder, and stopped their *e*
Mt 11:15 He that hath *e* to hear, let him
Mt 12:1 and began to pluck the *e* of corn
Mt 13:9 Who hath *e* to hear, let him hear
Mt 13:15 their *e* are dull of hearing, and
Mt 13:15 their eyes, and hear with their *e*
Mt 13:16 and your *e*, for they hear
Mt 13:43 Who hath *e* to hear, let him hear
Mt 28:14 if this come to the governor's *e*
Mk 2:23 they went, to pluck the *e* of corn
Mk 4:9 unto them, He that hath *e* to hear
Mk 4:23 If any man have *e* to hear
Mk 7:16 If any man have *e* to hear
Mk 7:33 and put his fingers into his *e*
Mk 7:35 And straightway his *e* were opened
Mk 8:18 and having *e*, hear ye not
Lk 1:44 thy salutation sounded in mine *e*
Lk 4:21 scripture fulfilled in your *e*
Lk 6:1 disciples plucked the *e* of corn
Lk 8:8 he cried, He that hath *e* to hear
Lk 9:44 sayings sink down into your *e*
Lk 14:35 He that hath *e* to hear, let him
Acts 7:51 and uncircumcised in heart and *e*
Acts 7:57 a loud voice, and stopped their *e*
Acts 11:22 the *e* of the church which was in
Acts 17:20 certain strange things to our *e*
Acts 28:27 their *e* are dull of hearing, and
Acts 28:27 their eyes, and hear with their *e*
Rom 11:8 *e* that they should not hear
2Ti 4:3 teachers, having itching *e*
2Ti 4:4 turn away their *e* from the truth
Jas 5:4 into the *e* of the Lord of Sabaoth
1Pet 3:12 his *e* are open unto their prayers

## EARTHEN

Lev 6:28 But the *e* vessel wherein it is
Lev 11:33 every *e* vessel, whereinto any of
Lev 14:5 in an *e* vessel over running water
Lev 14:50 in an *e* vessel over running water
Num 5:17 take holy water in an *e* vessel
2Sa 17:28 *e* vessels, and wheat, and barley,
Jer 19:1 Go and get a potter's *e* bottle
Jer 32:14 and put them in an *e* vessel
Lam 4:2 are they esteemed as *e* pitchers
2Cor 4:7 have this treasure in *e* vessels

## EARTHLY

Jn 3:12 If I have told you *e* things
Jn 3:31 he that is of the earth is *e*
2Cor 5:1 For we know that if our *e* house
Phil 3:19 in their shame, who mind *e* things
Jas 3:15 not from above, but is *e*, sensual

## EARTHQUAKE

1Kin 19:11 and after the wind an *e*
1Kin 19:11 but the LORD was not in the *e*
1Kin 19:12 And after the *e* a fire
Is 29:6 of hosts with thunder, and with *e*
Amos 1:1 of Israel, two years before the *e*
Zec 14:5 *e* in the days of Uzziah king of
Mt 27:54 him, watching Jesus, saw the *e*
Mt 28:2 And, behold, there was a great *e*
Acts 16:26 And suddenly there was a great *e*
Rev 6:12 seal, and, lo, there was a great *e*
Rev 8:5 and lightnings, and an *e*
Rev 11:13 the same hour was there a great *e*
Rev 11:13 in the *e* were slain of men seven
Rev 11:19 voices, and thunderings, and an *e*
Rev 16:18 and there was a great *e*, such as
Rev 16:18 upon the earth, so mighty an *e*

## EARTHQUAKES

Mt 24:7 be famines, and pestilences, and *e*
Mk 13:8 there shall be *e* in divers places
Lk 21:11 great *e* shall be in divers places

## EASE

Deut 23:13 when thou wilt *e* thyself abroad
Deut 28:65 nations shalt thou find no *e*
Judg 20:43 trode them down with *e* over
2Chr 10:4 now therefore *e* thou somewhat the
2Chr 10:9 *E* somewhat the yoke that thy
Job 7:13 me, my couch shall *e* my complaint
Job 12:5 the thought of him that is at *e*
Job 16:12 I was at *e*, but he hath broken me
Job 21:23 full strength, being wholly at *e*
Ps 25:13 His soul shall dwell at *e*
Ps 123:4 scorning of those that are at *e*
Is 1:24 I will *e* me of mine adversaries,
Is 32:9 Rise up, ye women that are at *e*
Is 32:11 Tremble, ye women that are at *e*
Jer 46:27 return, and be in rest and at *e*
Jer 48:11 hath been at *e* from his youth
Eze 23:42 multitude being at *e* was with her
Amos 6:1 Woe to them that are at *e* in Zion
Zec 1:15 with the heathen that are at *e*
Lk 12:19 take thine *e*, eat, drink, and be

## EASIER

Ex 18:22 so shall it be *e* for thyself
Mt 9:5 For whether is *e*, to say, Thy
Mt 19:24 It is *e* for a camel to go through
Mk 2:9 Whether is it *e* to say to the
Mk 10:25 It is *e* for a camel to go through
Lk 5:23 Whether is *e*, to say, Thy sins be
Lk 16:17 it is *e* for heaven and earth to
Lk 18:25 For it is *e* for a camel to go

## EASTER *Passover.*

Acts 12:4 intending after *E* to bring him

## EASTWARD

Gen 2:8 God planted a garden *e* in Eden
Gen 13:14 art northward, and southward, and *e*
Gen 25:6 his son, while he yet lived, *e*
Ex 27:13 east side *e* shall be fifty cubits
Ex 38:13 for the east side *e* fifty cubits
Lev 16:14 his finger upon the mercy seat *e*
Num 3:38 tabernacle of the congregation *e*
Num 32:19 to us on this side Jordan *e*
Num 34:3 outmost coast of the salt sea *e*
Num 34:11 side of the sea of Chinnereth *e*
Num 34:15 this side Jordan near Jericho *e*
Deut 3:17 salt sea, under Ashdoth-pisgah *e*
Deut 3:27 and northward, and southward, and *e*
Deut 4:49 the plain on this side Jordan *e*
Josh 11:8 and unto the valley of Mizpeh *e*
Josh 13:8 Moses gave them, beyond Jordan *e*
Josh 13:27 on the other side Jordan *e*
Josh 13:32 other side Jordan, by Jericho, *e*
Josh 16:6 went about *e* unto Taanath-shiloh
Josh 19:12 turned from Sarid *e* toward the
Josh 20:8 other side Jordan by Jericho *e*
1Sa 13:5 in Michmash, *e* from Beth-aven
1Kin 7:39 house *e* over against the south
1Kin 17:3 Get thee hence, and turn thee *e*
2Kin 10:33 From Jordan *e*, all the land of
2Kin 13:17 And he said, Open the window *e*
1Chr 5:9 *e* he inhabited unto the entering
1Chr 7:28 *e* Naaran, and westward Gezer, with
1Chr 9:18 waited in the king's gate *e*
1Chr 26:14 the lot *e* fell to Shelemiah
1Chr 26:17 *E* were six Levites, northward
Neh 12:37 David, even unto the water gate *e*
Eze 11:1 the LORD's house, which looketh *e*
Eze 40:10 gate *e* were three on this side
Eze 40:19 without, an hundred cubits *e*
Eze 45:7 westward, and from the east side *e*
Eze 47:1 the threshold of the house *e*
Eze 47:2 gate by the way that looketh *e*
Eze 47:3 the line in his hand went forth *e*
Eze 48:18 portion shall be ten thousand *e*

## EASY

Prov 14:6 but knowledge is *e* unto him that
Mt 11:30 For my yoke is *e*, and my burden is
1Cor 14:9 tongue words *e* to be understood
Jas 3:17 *e* to be intreated, full of mercy

## EAT

Gen 2:16 the garden thou mayest freely *e*
Gen 2:17 and evil, thou shalt not *e* of it
Gen 3:1 Ye shall not *e* of every tree of
Gen 3:2 We may *e* of the fruit of the
Gen 3:3 hath said, Ye shall not *e* of it
Gen 3:5 know that in the day ye *e* thereof
Gen 3:6 of the fruit thereof, and did *e*
Gen 3:6 and he did *e*
Gen 3:11 thee that thou shouldest not *e*
Gen 3:12 gave me of the tree, and I did *e*
Gen 3:13 serpent beguiled me, and I did *e*
Gen 3:14 dust shalt thou *e* all the days of
Gen 3:17 saying, Thou shalt not *e* of it
Gen 3:17 in sorrow shalt thou *e* of it all
Gen 3:18 thou shalt *e* the herb of the
Gen 3:19 of thy face shalt thou *e* bread
Gen 3:22 also of the tree of life, and *e*
Gen 9:4 the blood thereof, shall ye not *e*
Gen 18:8 under the tree, and they did *e*
Gen 19:3 unleavened bread, and they did *e*
Gen 24:33 was set meat before him to *e*
Gen 24:33 but he said, I will not *e*
Gen 24:54 And they did *e* and drink, he and the
Gen 25:28 because he did *e* of his venison
Gen 25:34 and he did *e* and drink, and rose up,
Gen 26:30 made them a feast, and they did *e*
Gen 27:4 and bring it to me, that I may *e*
Gen 27:7 me savoury meat, that I may *e*
Gen 27:10 it to thy father, that he may *e*
Gen 27:19 *e* of my venison, that thy soul
Gen 27:25 I will *e* of my son's venison,
Gen 27:25 it near to him, and he did *e*
Gen 27:31 *e* of his son's venison, that thy
Gen 28:20 I go, and will give me bread to *e*
Gen 31:46 they did *e* there upon the heap
Gen 31:54 and called his brethren to *e* bread
Gen 31:54 and they did *e* bread, and tarried
Gen 32:32 the children of Israel *e* not of
Gen 37:25 And they sat down to *e* bread
Gen 39:6 save the bread which he did *e*
Gen 40:17 the birds did *e* them out of the
Gen 40:19 the birds shall *e* thy flesh from
Gen 41:4 leanfleshed kine did *e* up the
Gen 41:20 the ill favoured kine did *e* up
Gen 43:25 that they should *e* bread there
Gen 43:32 Egyptians, which did *e* with him
Gen 43:32 not *e* bread with the Hebrews
Gen 45:18 ye shall *e* the fat of the land
Gen 47:22 did *e* their portion which Pharaoh
Ex 2:20 call him, that he may *e* bread
Ex 10:5 they shall *e* the residue of that
Ex 10:5 shall *e* every tree which groweth
Ex 10:12 *e* every herb of the land, even
Ex 10:15 they did *e* every herb of the land
Ex 12:7 houses, wherein they shall *e* it
Ex 12:8 they shall *e* the flesh in that
Ex 12:8 with bitter herbs they shall *e* it
Ex 12:9 *E* not of it raw, nor sodden at
Ex 12:11 And thus shall ye *e* it
Ex 12:11 and ye shall *e* it in haste
Ex 12:15 days shall ye *e* unleavened bread
Ex 12:16 save that which every man must *e*
Ex 12:18 ye shall *e* unleavened bread,
Ex 12:20 Ye shall *e* nothing leavened
Ex 12:20 shall ye *e* unleavened bread
Ex 12:43 There shall no stranger *e* thereof
Ex 12:44 him, then shall he *e* thereof
Ex 12:45 hired servant shall not *e* thereof
Ex 12:48 person shall *e* thereof
Ex 13:6 thou shalt *e* unleavened bread
Ex 16:3 when we did *e* bread to the full
Ex 16:8 you in the evening flesh to *e*
Ex 16:12 saying, At even ye shall *e* flesh
Ex 16:15 the LORD hath given you to *e*
Ex 16:25 And Moses said, *E* that to day
Ex 16:35 of Israel did *e* manna forty years
Ex 16:35 they did *e* manna, until they came
Ex 18:12 to *e* bread with Moses' father in
Ex 22:31 neither shall ye *e* any flesh that
Ex 23:11 that the poor of thy people may *e*
Ex 23:11 the beasts of the field shall *e*
Ex 23:15 (thou shalt *e* unleavened bread
Ex 24:11 also they saw God, and did *e*
Ex 29:32 his sons shall *e* the flesh of the
Ex 29:33 they shall *e* those things
Ex 29:33 a stranger shall not *e* thereof
Ex 32:6 and the people sat down to *e*
Ex 34:15 thee, and thou *e* of his sacrifice
Ex 34:18 thou shalt *e* unleavened bread
Ex 34:28 he did neither *e* bread, nor drink
Lev 3:17 that ye *e* neither fat nor blood
Lev 6:16 thereof shall Aaron and his sons *e*
Lev 6:16 the congregation they shall *e* it
Lev 6:18 children of Aaron shall *e* of it
Lev 6:26 offereth it for sin shall *e* it
Lev 6:29 among the priests shall *e* thereof
Lev 7:6 among the priests shall *e* thereof
Lev 7:19 all that be clean shall *e* thereof
Lev 7:21 *e* of the flesh of the sacrifice
Lev 7:23 Ye shall *e* no manner of fat, of
Lev 7:24 but ye shall in no wise *e* of it
Lev 7:26 Moreover ye shall *e* no manner of
Lev 8:31 there *e* it with the bread that is
Lev 8:31 Aaron and his sons shall *e* it
Lev 10:12 *e* it without leaven beside the
Lev 10:13 ye shall *e* it in the holy place,
Lev 10:14 shall ye *e* in a clean place
Lev 11:2 *e* among all the beasts that are
Lev 11:3 among the beasts, that shall ye *e*
Lev 11:4 not *e* of them that chew the cud
Lev 11:8 Of their flesh shall ye not *e*
Lev 11:9 These shall ye *e* of all that are
Lev 11:9 and in the rivers, them shall ye *e*
Lev 11:11 ye shall not *e* of their flesh,
Lev 11:21 Yet these may ye *e* of every

Lev 11:22 Even these of them ye may *e*
Lev 11:39 if any beast, of which ye may *e*
Lev 11:42 the earth, them ye shall not *e*
Lev 17:12 No soul of you shall *e* blood
Lev 17:12 that sojourneth among you *e* blood
Lev 17:14 Ye shall *e* the blood of no manner
Lev 19:25 shall ye *e* of the fruit thereof
Lev 19:26 Ye shall not *e* any thing with the
Lev 21:22 He shall *e* the bread of his God,
Lev 22:4 he shall not *e* of the holy things
Lev 22:6 shall not *e* of the holy things,
Lev 22:7 shall afterward *e* of the holy
Lev 22:8 he shall not *e* to defile himself
Lev 22:10 no stranger *e* of the holy thing
Lev 22:10 shall not *e* of the holy thing
Lev 22:11 with his money, he shall *e* of it
Lev 22:11 they shall *e* of his meat
Lev 22:12 she may not *e* of an offering of
Lev 22:13 she shall *e* of her father's meat
Lev 22:13 there shall no stranger *e* thereof
Lev 22:14 if a man *e* of the holy thing
Lev 22:16 when they *e* their holy things
Lev 23:6 days ye must *e* unleavened bread
Lev 23:14 ye shall *e* neither bread, nor
Lev 24:9 they shall *e* it in the holy place
Lev 25:12 ye shall *e* the increase thereof
Lev 25:19 ye shall *e* your fill, and dwell
Lev 25:20 What shall we *e* the seventh year
Lev 25:22 *e* yet of old fruit until the
Lev 25:22 in ye shall *e* of the old store
Lev 26:5 ye shall *e* your bread to the full
Lev 26:10 ye shall *e* old store, and bring
Lev 26:16 vain, for your enemies shall *e* it
Lev 26:26 and ye shall *e*, and not be
Lev 26:29 ye shall *e* the flesh of your sons
Lev 26:29 of your daughters shall ye *e*
Lev 26:38 of your enemies shall *e* you up
Num 6:3 nor *e* moist grapes, or dried
Num 6:4 he *e* nothing that is made of the
Num 9:11 *e* it with unleavened bread and
Num 11:4 Who shall give us flesh to *e*
Num 11:5 which we did *e* in Egypt freely
Num 11:13 Give us flesh, that we may *e*
Num 11:18 to morrow, and ye shall *e* flesh
Num 11:18 Who shall give us flesh to *e*
Num 11:18 give you flesh, and ye shall *e*
Num 11:19 Ye shall not *e* one day, nor two
Num 11:21 that they may *e* a whole month
Num 15:19 when ye *e* of the bread of the
Num 18:10 most holy place shalt thou *e* it
Num 18:10 every male shall *e* it
Num 18:11 clean in thy house shall *e* of it
Num 18:13 in thine house shall *e* of it
Num 18:31 ye shall *e* it in every place, ye
Num 23:24 lie down until he *e* of the prey
Num 24:8 he shall *e* up the nations his
Num 25:2 and the people did *e*, and bowed
Deut 2:6 of them for money, that ye may *e*
Deut 2:28 me meat for money, that I may *e*
Deut 4:28 neither see, nor hear, nor *e*
Deut 8:9 shalt *e* bread without scarceness
Deut 9:9 I neither did *e* bread nor drink
Deut 9:18 I did neither *e* bread, nor drink
Deut 11:15 thy cattle, that thou mayest *e*
Deut 12:7 there ye shall *e* before the LORD
Deut 12:15 *e* flesh in all thy gates,
Deut 12:15 and the clean may *e* thereof
Deut 12:16 Only ye shall not *e* the blood
Deut 12:17 Thou mayest not *e* within thy
Deut 12:18 But thou must *e* them before the
Deut 12:20 and thou shalt say, I will *e* flesh
Deut 12:20 thy soul longeth to *e* flesh
Deut 12:20 thou mayest *e* flesh, whatsoever
Deut 12:21 thou shalt *e* in thy gates
Deut 12:22 is eaten, so thou shalt *e* them
Deut 12:22 the clean shall *e* of them alike
Deut 12:23 be sure that thou *e* not the blood
Deut 12:23 thou mayest not *e* the life with
Deut 12:24 Thou shalt not *e* it
Deut 12:25 Thou shalt not *e* it
Deut 12:27 God, and thou shalt *e* the flesh
Deut 14:3 Thou shalt not *e* any abominable
Deut 14:4 are the beasts which ye shall *e*
Deut 14:6 among the beasts, that ye shall *e*
Deut 14:7 not *e* of them that chew the cud
Deut 14:8 ye shall not *e* of their flesh,
Deut 14:9 These ye shall *e* of all that are
Deut 14:9 have fins and scales shall ye *e*
Deut 14:10 not fins and scales ye may not *e*
Deut 14:11 Of all clean birds ye shall *e*
Deut 14:12 are they of which ye shall not *e*
Deut 14:20 But of all clean fowls ye may *e*
Deut 14:21 Ye shall not *e* of any thing that
Deut 14:21 is in thy gates, that he may *e* it
Deut 14:23 thou shalt *e* before the LORD thy
Deut 14:26 thou shalt *e* there before the
Deut 14:29 thy gates, shall come, and shall *e*
Deut 15:20 Thou shalt *e* it before the LORD
Deut 15:22 Thou shalt *e* it within thy gates
Deut 15:22 the clean person shall *e* it alike
Deut 15:23 shalt not *e* the blood thereof
Deut 16:3 Thou shalt *e* no leavened bread
Deut 16:3 seven days shalt thou *e*
Deut 16:7 *e* it in the place which the LORD
Deut 16:8 thou shalt *e* unleavened bread
Deut 18:1 they shall *e* the offerings of the
Deut 18:8 shall have like portions to *e*
Deut 20:6 battle, and another man *e* of it
Deut 20:14 thou shalt *e* the spoil of thine
Deut 20:19 for thou mayest *e* of them
Deut 23:24 then thou mayest *e* grapes thy
Deut 26:12 that they may *e* within thy gates,
Deut 27:7 peace offerings, and shalt *e* there
Deut 28:31 eyes, and thou shalt not *e* thereof
Deut 28:33 which thou knowest not *e* up
Deut 28:39 for the worms shall *e* them
Deut 28:51 he shall *e* the fruit of thy
Deut 28:53 thou shalt *e* the fruit of thine
Deut 28:55 of his children whom he shall *e*
Deut 28:57 for she shall *e* them for want of
Deut 32:13 that he might *e* the increase of
Deut 32:38 Which did *e* the fat of their
Josh 5:11 they did *e* of the old corn of the
Josh 5:12 but they did *e* of the fruit of
Josh 24:13 which ye planted not do ye *e*
Judg 9:27 the house of their god, and did *e*
Judg 13:4 drink, and *e* not any unclean thing
Judg 13:7 neither *e* any unclean thing
Judg 13:14 She may not *e* of any thing that
Judg 13:14 drink, nor *e* any unclean thing
Judg 13:16 I will not *e* of thy bread
Judg 14:9 and gave them, and they did *e*
Judg 19:4 so they did *e* and drink, and lodged
Judg 19:6 And they sat down, and did *e*
Judg 19:8 and they did *e* both of them
Judg 19:21 they washed their feet, and did *e*
Ruth 2:14 *e* of the bread, and dip thy morsel
Ruth 2:14 her parched corn, and she did *e*
1Sa 1:7 therefore she wept, and did not *e*
1Sa 1:18 the woman went her way, and did *e*
1Sa 2:36 that I may *e* a piece of bread
1Sa 9:13 he go up to the high place to *e*
1Sa 9:13 people will not *e* until he come
1Sa 9:13 afterwards they *e* that be bidden
1Sa 9:19 for ye shall *e* with me to day, and
1Sa 9:24 set it before thee, and *e*
1Sa 9:24 So Saul did *e* with Samuel that
1Sa 14:32 the people did *e* them with the
1Sa 14:33 in that they *e* with the blood
1Sa 14:34 sheep, and slay them here, and *e*
1Sa 20:24 the king sat him down to *e* meat
1Sa 20:34 did *e* no meat the second day of
1Sa 28:22 and *e*, that thou mayest have
1Sa 28:23 he refused, and said, I will not *e*
1Sa 28:25 and they did *e*
1Sa 30:11 and gave him bread, and he did *e*
2Sa 3:35 to *e* meat while it was yet day
2Sa 9:7 thou shalt *e* bread at my table
2Sa 9:10 master's son may have food to *e*
2Sa 9:10 thy master's son shall *e* bread
2Sa 9:11 he shall *e* at my table, as one of
2Sa 9:13 for he did *e* continually at the
2Sa 11:11 I then go into mine house, to *e*
2Sa 11:13 David had called him, he did *e*
2Sa 12:3 it did *e* of his own meat, and
2Sa 12:17 neither did he *e* bread with them
2Sa 12:20 set bread before him, and he did *e*
2Sa 12:21 dead, thou didst rise and *e* bread
2Sa 13:5 I may see it, and *e* it at her hand
2Sa 13:6 sight, that I may *e* at her hand
2Sa 13:9 but he refused to *e*
2Sa 13:10 that I may *e* of thine hand
2Sa 13:11 had brought them unto him to *e*
2Sa 16:2 fruit for the young men to *e*
2Sa 17:29 people that were with him, to *e*
2Sa 19:28 that did *e* at thine own table
2Sa 19:35 taste what I *e* or what I drink
1Kin 1:25 and, behold, they *e* and drink
1Kin 2:7 be of those that *e* at thy table
1Kin 13:8 neither will I *e* bread nor drink
1Kin 13:9 *E* no bread, nor drink water, nor
1Kin 13:15 Come home with me, and *e* bread
1Kin 13:16 neither will I *e* bread nor drink
1Kin 13:17 Thou shalt *e* no bread nor drink
1Kin 13:18 thine house, that he may *e* bread
1Kin 13:19 did *e* bread in his house, and
1Kin 13:22 *E* no bread, and drink no water
1Kin 14:11 in the city shall the dogs *e*
1Kin 14:11 shall the fowls of the air *e*
1Kin 16:4 in the city shall the dogs *e*
1Kin 16:4 shall the fowls of the air *e*
1Kin 17:12 me and my son, that we may *e* it
1Kin 17:15 he, and her house, did *e* many days
1Kin 18:19 which *e* at Jezebel's table
1Kin 18:41 said unto Ahab, Get thee up, *e*
1Kin 18:42 So Ahab went up to *e* and to drink
1Kin 19:5 him, and said unto him, Arise and *e*
1Kin 19:6 And he did *e* and drink, and laid him
1Kin 19:7 touched him, and said, Arise and *e*
1Kin 19:8 And he arose, and did *e* and drink,
1Kin 19:21 unto the people, and they did *e*
1Kin 21:4 his face, and would *e* no bread
1Kin 21:7 *e* bread, and let thine heart be
1Kin 21:23 The dogs shall *e* Jezebel by the
1Kin 21:24 Ahab in the city the dogs shall *e*
1Kin 21:24 shall the fowls of the air *e*
2Kin 4:8 and she constrained him to *e* bread
2Kin 4:8 he turned in thither to *e* bread
2Kin 4:40 they poured out for the men to *e*
2Kin 4:40 And they could not *e* thereof
2Kin 4:41 for the people, that they may *e*
2Kin 4:42 unto the people, that they may *e*
2Kin 4:43 Give the people, that they may *e*
2Kin 4:43 thus saith the LORD, They shall *e*
2Kin 4:44 set it before them, and they did *e*
2Kin 6:22 before them, that they may *e*
2Kin 6:28 thy son, that we may *e* him to day
2Kin 6:28 we will *e* my son to morrow
2Kin 6:29 So we boiled my son, and did *e* him
2Kin 6:29 Give thy son, that we may *e* him
2Kin 7:2 eyes, but shalt not *e* thereof
2Kin 7:8 they went into one tent, and did *e*
2Kin 7:19 eyes, but shalt not *e* thereof
2Kin 9:10 the dogs shall *e* Jezebel in the
2Kin 9:34 And when he was come in, he did *e*
2Kin 9:36 shall dogs *e* the flesh of Jezebel
2Kin 18:27 that they may *e* their own dung,
2Kin 18:31 then *e* ye every man of his own
2Kin 19:29 Ye shall *e* this year such things
2Kin 19:29 and *e* the fruits thereof
2Kin 23:9 but they did *e* of the unleavened
2Kin 25:29 he did *e* bread continually before
1Chr 29:22 And did *e* and drink before the LORD
2Chr 28:15 and shod them, and gave them to *e*
2Chr 30:18 yet did they *e* the passover
2Chr 30:22 they did *e* throughout the feast
2Chr 31:10 the LORD, we have had enough to *e*
Ezr 2:63 that they should not *e* of the
Ezr 6:21 the LORD God of Israel, did *e*
Ezr 9:12 *e* the good of the land, and leave
Ezr 10:6 he did *e* no bread, nor drink
Neh 5:2 up corn for them, that we may *e*
Neh 7:65 that they should not *e* of the
Neh 8:10 *e* the fat, and drink the sweet, and
Neh 8:12 the people went their way to *e*
Neh 9:25 so they did *e*, and were filled, and
Neh 9:36 fathers to *e* the fruit thereof
Est 4:16 neither *e* nor drink three days,
Job 1:4 for their three sisters to *e*
Job 3:24 For my sighing cometh before I *e*
Job 31:8 Then let me sow, and let another *e*
Job 42:11 did *e* bread with him in his house
Ps 14:4 *e* up my people as they *e* bread
Ps 22:26 The meek shall *e* and be satisfied
Ps 22:29 that be fat upon earth shall *e*
Ps 27:2 came upon me to *e* up my flesh
Ps 41:9 which did *e* of my bread, hath
Ps 50:13 Will I *e* the flesh of bulls, or
Ps 53:4 *e* up my people as they *e* bread
Ps 78:24 rained down manna upon them to *e*
Ps 78:25 Man did *e* angels' food
Ps 78:29 So they did *e*, and were well
Ps 102:4 so that I forget to *e* my bread
Ps 105:35 did *e* up all the herbs in their
Ps 127:2 to *e* the bread of sorrows
Ps 128:2 For thou shalt *e* the labour of
Ps 141:4 let me not *e* of their dainties
Prov 1:31 Therefore shall they *e* of the
Prov 4:17 For they *e* the bread of
Prov 9:5 *e* of my bread, and drink of the

Prov 13:2 A man shall *e* good by the fruit
Prov 13:2 transgressors shall *e* violence
Prov 18:21 love it shall *e* the fruit thereof
Prov 23:1 thou sittest to *e* with a ruler
Prov 23:6 *E* thou not the bread of him that
Prov 23:7 *E* and drink, saith he to thee
Prov 24:13 *e* thou honey, because it is good
Prov 25:16 *e* so much as is sufficient for
Prov 25:21 be hungry, give him bread to *e*
Prov 25:27 It is not good to *e* much honey
Prov 27:18 tree shall *e* the fruit thereof
Prov 30:17 and the young eagles shall *e* it
Eccl 2:24 for a man, than that he should *e*
Eccl 2:25 For who can *e*, or who else can
Eccl 3:13 And also that every man should *e*
Eccl 5:11 they are increased that *e* them
Eccl 5:12 whether he *e* little or much
Eccl 5:18 it is good and comely for one to *e*
Eccl 5:19 hath given him power to *e* thereof
Eccl 6:2 giveth him not power to *e* thereof
Eccl 8:15 thing under the sun, than to *e*
Eccl 9:7 *e* thy bread with joy, and drink
Eccl 10:16 thy princes *e* in the morning
Eccl 10:17 thy princes *e* in due season, for
Song 4:16 garden, and *e* his pleasant fruits
Song 5:1 *e*, O friends
Is 1:19 ye shall *e* the good of the land
Is 3:10 for they shall *e* the fruit of
Is 4:1 We will *e* our own bread, and wear
Is 5:17 of the fat ones shall strangers *e*
Is 7:15 Butter and honey shall he *e*
Is 7:22 shall give, he shall *e* butter
Is 7:22 honey shall every one *e* that is
Is 9:20 he shall *e* on the left hand, and
Is 9:20 they shall *e* every man the flesh
Is 11:7 the lion shall *e* straw like the
Is 21:5 table, watch in the watchtower, *e*
Is 22:13 let us *e* and drink
Is 23:18 to *e* sufficiently, and for durable
Is 30:24 ground shall *e* clean provender
Is 36:12 that they may *e* their own dung,
Is 36:16 *e* ye every one of his vine, and
Is 37:30 Ye shall *e* this year such as
Is 37:30 vineyards, and *e* the fruit thereof
Is 50:9 the moth shall *e* them up
Is 51:8 For the moth shall *e* them up like
Is 51:8 the worm shall *e* them like wool
Is 55:1 come ye, buy, and *e*
Is 55:2 *e* ye that which is good, and let
Is 61:6 ye shall *e* the riches of the
Is 62:9 that have gathered it shall *e* it
Is 65:4 which *e* swine's flesh, and broth
Is 65:13 GOD, Behold, my servants shall *e*
Is 65:21 vineyards, and *e* the fruit of them
Is 65:22 shall not plant, and another *e*
Is 65:25 the lion shall *e* straw like the
Jer 2:7 to *e* the fruit thereof and the
Jer 5:17 they shall *e* up thine harvest, and
Jer 5:17 sons and thy daughters should *e*
Jer 5:17 they shall *e* up thy flocks and
Jer 5:17 they shall *e* up thy vines and thy
Jer 7:21 unto your sacrifices, and *e* flesh
Jer 15:16 words were found, and I did *e* them
Jer 16:8 feasting, to sit with them to *e*
Jer 19:9 I will cause them to *e* the flesh
Jer 19:9 they shall *e* every one the flesh
Jer 22:15 did not thy father *e* and drink, and
Jer 22:22 The wind shall *e* up all thy
Jer 29:5 gardens, and *e* the fruit of them
Jer 29:28 gardens, and *e* the fruit of them
Jer 31:5 shall *e* them as common things
Jer 41:1 there they did *e* bread together
Jer 52:33 he did continually *e* bread before
Lam 2:20 Shall the women *e* their fruit
Eze 2:8 thy mouth, and *e* that I give thee
Eze 3:1 Son of man, *e* that thou findest
Eze 3:1 *e* this roll, and go speak unto the
Eze 3:2 and he caused me to *e* that roll
Eze 3:3 Son of man, cause thy belly to *e*
Eze 3:3 Then did I *e* it
Eze 4:9 ninety days shalt thou *e* thereof
Eze 4:10 thou shalt *e* shall be by weight
Eze 4:10 from time to time shalt thou *e* it
Eze 4:12 thou shalt *e* it as barley cakes,
Eze 4:13 shall the children of Israel *e*
Eze 4:16 they shall *e* bread by weight, and
Eze 5:10 Therefore the fathers shall *e* the
Eze 5:10 and the sons shall *e* their fathers
Eze 12:18 *e* thy bread with quaking, and
Eze 12:19 They shall *e* their bread with
Eze 16:13 thou didst *e* fine flour, and honey
Eze 22:9 in thee they *e* upon the mountains
Eze 24:17 lips, and *e* not the bread of men
Eze 24:22 your lips, nor *e* the bread of men
Eze 25:4 they shall *e* thy fruit, and they
Eze 33:25 Ye *e* with the blood, and lift up
Eze 34:3 Ye *e* the fat, and ye clothe you
Eze 34:19 they *e* that which ye have trodden
Eze 39:17 of Israel, that ye may *e* flesh
Eze 39:18 Ye shall *e* the flesh of the
Eze 39:19 ye shall *e* fat till ye be full,
Eze 42:13 LORD shall *e* the most holy things
Eze 44:3 in it to *e* bread before the LORD
Eze 44:29 They shall *e* the meat offering,
Eze 44:31 The priests shall not *e* of any
Dan 1:12 and let them give us pulse to *e*
Dan 1:13 of the children that *e* of the
Dan 1:15 *e* the portion of the king's meat
Dan 4:25 make thee to *e* grass as oxen
Dan 4:32 make thee to *e* grass as oxen
Dan 4:33 did *e* grass as oxen, and his body
Hos 2:12 beasts of the field shall *e* them
Hos 4:8 They *e* up the sin of my people,
Hos 4:10 For they shall *e*, and not have
Hos 8:13 of mine offerings, and *e* it
Hos 9:3 they shall *e* unclean things in
Hos 9:4 all that *e* thereof shall be
Joel 2:26 ye shall *e* in plenty, and be
Amos 6:4 *e* the lambs out of the flock, and
Amos 7:4 great deep, and did *e* up a part
Amos 7:12 land of Judah, and there *e* bread
Amos 9:14 gardens, and *e* the fruit of them
Obad 7 they that *e* thy bread have laid a
Mic 3:3 Who also *e* the flesh of my people
Mic 6:14 Thou shalt *e*, but not be
Mic 7:1 there is no cluster to *e*
Nah 3:15 it shall *e* thee up like the
Hab 1:8 as the eagle that hasteth to *e*
Hag 1:6 ye *e*, but ye have not enough
Zec 7:6 And when ye did *e*, and when ye did
Zec 7:6 did not ye *e* for yourselves, and
Zec 11:9 let the rest *e* every one the
Zec 11:16 but he shall *e* the flesh of the
Mt 6:25 for your life, what ye shall *e*
Mt 6:31 thought, saying, What shall we *e*
Mt 12:1 pluck the ears of corn, and to *e*
Mt 12:4 did *e* the shewbread, which was
Mt 12:4 which was not lawful for him to *e*
Mt 14:16 give ye them to *e*
Mt 14:20 And they did all *e*, and were filled
Mt 15:2 not their hands when they *e* bread
Mt 15:20 but to *e* with unwashen hands
Mt 15:27 yet the dogs *e* of the crumbs
Mt 15:32 three days, and have nothing to *e*
Mt 15:37 And they did all *e*, and were filled
Mt 15:38 they that did *e* were four
Mt 24:49 smite his fellowservants, and to *e*
Mt 26:17 for thee to *e* the passover
Mt 26:21 And as they did *e*, he said, Verily
Mt 26:26 the disciples, and said, Take, *e*
Mk 1:6 he did *e* locusts and wild honey
Mk 2:16 saw him *e* with publicans and
Mk 2:26 did *e* the shewbread, which is not
Mk 2:26 lawful to *e* but for the priests
Mk 3:20 they could not so much as *e* bread
Mk 5:43 should be given her to *e*
Mk 6:31 had no leisure so much as to *e*
Mk 6:36 for they have nothing to *e*
Mk 6:37 said unto them, Give ye them to *e*
Mk 6:37 of bread, and give them to *e*
Mk 6:42 And they did all *e*, and were filled
Mk 6:44 they that did *e* of the loaves
Mk 7:2 disciples *e* bread with defiled
Mk 7:3 *e* not, holding the tradition of
Mk 7:4 except they wash, they *e* not
Mk 7:5 but *e* bread with unwashen hands
Mk 7:28 table *e* of the children's crumbs
Mk 8:1 great, and having nothing to *e*
Mk 8:2 three days, and have nothing to *e*
Mk 8:8 So they did *e*, and were filled
Mk 11:14 No man *e* fruit of thee hereafter
Mk 14:12 that thou mayest *e* the passover
Mk 14:14 where I shall *e* the passover with
Mk 14:18 And as they sat and did *e*, Jesus
Mk 14:22 And as they did *e*, Jesus took
Mk 14:22 and gave to them, and said, Take, *e*
Lk 4:2 And in those days he did *e* nothing
Lk 5:30 disciples, saying, Why do ye *e*
Lk 5:33 but thine *e* and drink
Lk 6:1 the ears of corn, and did *e*
Lk 6:4 *e* the shewbread, and gave also to
Lk 6:4 to *e* but for the priests alone
Lk 7:36 him that he would *e* with him
Lk 9:13 said unto them, Give ye them to *e*
Lk 9:17 And they did *e*, and were all filled
Lk 10:8 *e* such things as are set before
Lk 12:19 take thine ease, *e*, drink, and be
Lk 12:22 for your life, what ye shall *e*
Lk 12:29 And seek not ye what ye shall *e*
Lk 12:45 menservants and maidens, and to *e*
Lk 14:1 to *e* bread on the sabbath day
Lk 14:15 Blessed is he that shall *e* bread
Lk 15:16 the husks that the swine did *e*
Lk 15:23 and let us *e*, and be merry
Lk 17:8 and afterward thou shalt *e*
Lk 17:27 They did *e*, they drank, they
Lk 17:28 they did *e*, they drank, they
Lk 22:8 us the passover, that we may *e*
Lk 22:11 where I shall *e* the passover with
Lk 22:15 With desire I have desired to *e*
Lk 22:16 I will not any more *e* thereof
Lk 22:30 That ye may *e* and drink at my
Lk 24:43 he took it, and did *e* before them
Jn 4:31 prayed him, saying, Master, *e*
Jn 4:32 I have meat to *e* that ye know not
Jn 4:33 any man brought him ought to *e*
Jn 6:5 we buy bread, that these may *e*
Jn 6:23 the place where they did *e* bread
Jn 6:26 because ye did *e* of the loaves
Jn 6:31 Our fathers did *e* manna in the
Jn 6:31 gave them bread from heaven to *e*
Jn 6:49 Your fathers did *e* manna in the
Jn 6:50 heaven, that a man may *e* thereof
Jn 6:51 if any man *e* of this bread, he
Jn 6:52 this man give us his flesh to *e*
Jn 6:53 Except ye *e* the flesh of the Son
Jn 6:58 not as your fathers did *e* manna
Jn 18:28 that they might *e* the passover
Acts 2:46 did *e* their meat with gladness and
Acts 9:9 sight, and neither did *e* nor drink
Acts 10:13 Rise, Peter; kill, and *e*
Acts 10:41 of God, even to us, who did *e*
Acts 11:3 and didst *e* with them
Acts 11:7 Arise, Peter; slay and *e*
Acts 23:12 *e* nor drink till they had killed
Acts 23:14 that we will *e* nothing until we
Acts 23:21 that they will neither *e* nor
Acts 27:35 he had broken it, he began to *e*
Rom 14:2 that he may *e* all things
Rom 14:21 It is good neither to *e* flesh
Rom 14:23 that doubteth is damned if he *e*
1Cor 5:11 with such an one, no not to *e*
1Cor 8:7 of the idol unto this hour *e* it
1Cor 8:8 for neither, if we *e*, are we the
1Cor 8:8 neither, if we *e* not, are we the
1Cor 8:10 *e* those things which are offered
1Cor 8:13 I will *e* no flesh while the world
1Cor 9:4 Have we not power to *e* and to
1Cor 10:3 did all *e* the same spiritual meat
1Cor 10:7 written, The people sat down to *e*
1Cor 10:18 are not they which *e* of the
1Cor 10:25 is sold in the shambles, that *e*
1Cor 10:27 whatsoever is set before you, *e*
1Cor 10:28 *e* not for his sake that shewed it
1Cor 10:31 Whether therefore ye *e*, or drink,
1Cor 11:20 this is not to *e* the Lord's
1Cor 11:22 have ye not houses to *e* and to
1Cor 11:24 he brake it, and said, Take, *e*
1Cor 11:26 For as often as ye *e* this bread
1Cor 11:27 whosoever shall *e* this bread
1Cor 11:28 so let him *e* of that bread, and
1Cor 11:33 when ye come together to *e*
1Cor 11:34 any man hunger, let him *e* at home
1Cor 15:32 let us *e* and drink
Gal 2:12 he did *e* with the Gentiles
2Th 3:8 Neither did we *e* any man's bread
2Th 3:10 not work, neither should he *e*
2Th 3:12 they work, and *e* their own bread
2Ti 2:17 their word will *e* as doth a
Heb 13:10 to *e* which serve the tabernacle
Jas 5:3 shall *e* your flesh as it were
Rev 2:7 I give to *e* of the tree of life
Rev 2:14 to *e* things sacrificed unto idols
Rev 2:17 I give to *e* of the hidden manna
Rev 2:20 to *e* things sacrificed unto idols
Rev 10:9 said unto me, Take it, and *e* it up
Rev 17:16 shall *e* her flesh, and burn her
Rev 19:18 That ye may *e* the flesh of kings,

**EATEN**
Gen 3:11 Hast thou *e* of the tree, whereof
Gen 3:17 hast *e* of the tree, of which I
Gen 6:21 unto thee of all food that is *e*
Gen 14:24 that which the young men have *e*
Gen 27:33 I have *e* of all before thou
Gen 31:38 rams of thy flock have I not *e*
Gen 41:21 And when they had *e* them up
Gen 41:21 known that they had *e* them
Gen 43:2 when they had *e* up the corn which
Ex 12:46 In one house shall it be *e*
Ex 13:3 shall no leavened bread be *e*
Ex 13:7 bread shall be *e* seven days
Ex 21:28 and his flesh shall not be *e*
Ex 22:5 cause a field or vineyard to be *e*
Ex 29:34 it shall not be *e*, because it is
Lev 6:16 shall it be *e* in the holy place
Lev 6:23 it shall not be *e*
Lev 6:26 in the holy place shall it be *e*
Lev 6:30 in the holy place, shall be *e*
Lev 7:6 it shall be *e* in the holy place
Lev 7:15 for thanksgiving shall be *e* the
Lev 7:16 it shall be *e* the same day that
Lev 7:16 the remainder of it shall be *e*
Lev 7:18 be *e* at all on the third day
Lev 7:19 any unclean thing shall not be *e*
Lev 10:17 Wherefore have ye not *e* the sin
Lev 10:18 have *e* it in the holy place
Lev 10:19 if I had *e* the sin offering to
Lev 11:13 they shall not be *e*, they are an
Lev 11:34 Of all meat which may be *e*
Lev 11:41 it shall not be *e*
Lev 11:47 between the beast that may be *e*
Lev 11:47 and the beast that may not be *e*
Lev 17:13 any beast or fowl that may be *e*
Lev 19:6 It shall be *e* the same day ye
Lev 19:7 if it be *e* at all on the third
Lev 19:23 it shall not be *e* of
Lev 22:30 On the same day it shall be *e* up
Num 28:17 days shall unleavened bread be *e*
Deut 6:11 when thou shalt have *e* and be full
Deut 8:10 When thou hast *e* and art full,
Deut 8:12 Lest when thou hast *e* and art full
Deut 12:22 as the roebuck and the hart is *e*
Deut 14:19 they shall not be *e*
Deut 20:6 vineyard, and hath not yet *e* of it
Deut 26:14 I have not *e* thereof in my
Deut 29:6 Ye have not *e* bread, neither have
Deut 31:20 and they shall have *e* and filled
Josh 5:12 had *e* of the old corn of the land
Ruth 3:7 And when Boaz had *e* and drunk, and
1Sa 1:9 up after they had *e* in Shiloh
1Sa 14:30 if haply the people had *e* freely
1Sa 28:20 for he had *e* no bread all the day
1Sa 30:12 and when he had *e*, his spirit came
1Sa 30:12 for he had *e* no bread, nor drunk
2Sa 19:42 have we *e* at all of the king's
1Kin 13:22 hast *e* bread and drunk water in
1Kin 13:23 to pass, after he had *e* bread
1Kin 13:28 the lion had not *e* the carcase
2Kin 6:23 and when they had *e* and drunk, he
Neh 5:14 my brethren have not *e* the bread
Job 6:6 is unsavoury be *e* without salt
Job 13:28 as a garment that is moth *e*
Job 31:17 Or have *e* my morsel myself alone,
Job 31:17 the fatherless hath not *e* thereof
Job 31:39 If I have *e* the fruits thereof
Ps 69:9 zeal of thine house hath *e* me up
Ps 102:9 For I have *e* ashes like bread, and
Prov 9:17 bread *e* in secret is pleasant
Prov 23:8 thou hast *e* shalt thou vomit up
Song 5:1 I have *e* my honeycomb with my
Is 3:14 for ye have *e* up the vineyard
Is 5:5 thereof, and it shall be *e* up
Is 6:13 and it shall return, and shall be *e*
Is 44:19 I have roasted flesh, and *e* it
Jer 10:25 for they have *e* up Jacob, and
Jer 24:2 figs, which could not be *e*
Jer 24:3 evil, very evil, that cannot be *e*
Jer 24:8 the evil figs, which cannot be *e*
Jer 29:17 like vile figs, that cannot be *e*
Jer 31:29 The fathers have *e* a sour grape
Eze 4:14 up even till now have I not *e* of
Eze 18:2 The fathers have *e* sour grapes
Eze 18:6 hath not *e* upon the mountains,
Eze 18:11 duties, but even hath *e* upon the
Eze 18:15 That hath not *e* upon the
Eze 34:18 you to have *e* up the good pasture
Eze 45:21 unleavened bread shall be *e*
Hos 10:13 ye have *e* the fruit of lies
Joel 1:4 hath left hath the locust *e*
Joel 1:4 hath left hath the cankerworm *e*
Joel 1:4 hath left hath the caterpiller *e*
Joel 2:25 the years that the locust hath *e*
Mt 14:21 they that had *e* were about five
Mk 8:9 they that had *e* were about four
Lk 13:26 shall ye begin to say, We have *e*
Lk 17:8 and serve me, till I have *e*
Jn 2:17 zeal of thine house hath *e* me up
Jn 6:13 and above unto them that had *e*
Acts 10:10 very hungry, and would have *e*
Acts 10:14 for I have never *e* any thing that
Acts 12:23 he was *e* of worms, and gave up the
Acts 20:11 again, and had broken bread, and *e*
Acts 27:38 And when they had *e* enough
Rev 10:10 and as soon as I had *e* it, my

**EATETH**
Ex 12:15 for whosoever *e* leavened bread
Ex 12:19 for whosoever *e* that which is
Lev 7:18 the soul that *e* of it shall bear
Lev 7:20 But the soul that *e* of the flesh
Lev 7:25 For whosoever *e* the fat of the
Lev 7:25 even the soul that *e* it shall be
Lev 7:27 it be that *e* any manner of blood
Lev 11:40 he that *e* of the carcase of it
Lev 14:47 he that *e* in the house shall wash
Lev 17:10 that *e* any manner of blood
Lev 17:10 against that soul that *e* blood
Lev 17:14 whosoever *e* it shall be cut off
Lev 17:15 every soul that *e* that which died
Lev 19:8 Therefore every one that *e* it
Num 13:32 it, is a land that *e* up the
1Sa 14:24 man that *e* any food until evening
1Sa 14:28 the man that *e* any food this day
Job 5:5 Whose harvest the hungry *e* up
Job 21:25 soul, and never *e* with pleasure
Job 40:15 he *e* grass as an ox
Ps 106:20 similitude of an ox that *e* grass
Prov 13:25 The righteous *e* to the satisfying
Prov 30:20 she *e*, and wipeth her mouth, and
Prov 31:27 *e* not the bread of idleness
Eccl 4:5 together, and *e* his own flesh
Eccl 5:17 his days also he *e* in darkness
Eccl 6:2 eat thereof, but a stranger *e* it
Is 28:4 it is yet in his hand he *e* it up
Is 29:8 man dreameth, and, behold, he *e*
Is 44:16 with part thereof he *e* flesh
Is 59:5 he that *e* of their eggs dieth, and
Jer 31:30 every man that *e* the sour grape
Mt 9:11 Why *e* your Master with publicans
Mk 2:16 disciples, How is it that he *e*
Mk 14:18 One of you which *e* with me shall
Lk 15:2 receiveth sinners, and *e* with them
Jn 6:54 Whoso *e* my flesh, and drinketh my
Jn 6:56 He that *e* my flesh, and drinketh
Jn 6:57 so he that *e* me, even he shall
Jn 6:58 he that *e* of this bread shall
Jn 13:18 He that *e* bread with me hath
Rom 14:2 another, who is weak, *e* herbs
Rom 14:3 *e* despise him that *e* not
Rom 14:3 which *e* not judge him that *e*
Rom 14:6 He that *e*, *e* to the Lord,
Rom 14:6 *e* not, to the Lord he *e* not
Rom 14:20 for that man who *e* with offence
Rom 14:23 because he *e* not of faith
1Cor 9:7 *e* not of the fruit thereof
1Cor 9:7 *e* not of the milk of the flock
1Cor 11:29 *e* and drinketh unworthily, *e*

**EATING**
Ex 12:4 every man according to his *e*
Ex 16:16 it every man according to his *e*
Ex 16:18 every man according to his *e*
Ex 16:21 every man according to his *e*
Judg 14:9 in his hands, and went on *e*
Ruth 3:3 man, until he shall have done *e*
1Sa 14:34 the LORD in *e* with the blood
1Sa 30:16 abroad upon all the earth, *e*
1Kin 1:41 it as they had made an end of *e*
1Kin 4:20 is by the sea in multitude, *e*
2Kin 4:40 as they were *e* of the pottage,
1Chr 12:39 were with David three days, *e*
Job 1:13 his sons and his daughters were *e*
Job 1:18 Thy sons and thy daughters were *e*
Job 20:23 rain it upon him while he is *e*
Is 22:13 *e* flesh, and drinking wine
Is 66:17 midst, *e* swine's flesh, and the
Amos 7:2 an end of *e* the grass of the land
Mt 11:18 John came neither *e* nor drinking
Mt 11:19 The Son of man came *e* and drinking
Mt 24:38 were before the flood they were *e*
Mt 26:26 And as they were *e*, Jesus took
Lk 7:33 neither *e* bread nor drinking wine
Lk 7:34 The Son of man is come *e* and
Lk 10:7 And in the same house remain, *e*
1Cor 8:4 the *e* of those things that are
1Cor 11:21 For in *e* every one taketh before

**EBAL** *(e'-bal) Son of Shobal.*
Gen 36:23 Alvan, and Manahath, and *E*, Shepho,
Deut 11:29 and the curse upon mount *E*
Deut 27:4 command you this day, in mount *E*
Deut 27:13 shall stand upon mount *E* to curse
Josh 8:30 the LORD God of Israel in mount *E*
Josh 8:33 half of them over against mount *E*
1Chr 1:22 And *E*, and Abimael, and Sheba,
1Chr 1:40 Alian, and Manahath, and *E*, Shephi,

**EBED** *(e'-bed)* See EBED-MELECH.
*1. Father of Gaal.*
Judg 9:26 Gaal the son of *E* came with his
Judg 9:28 And Gaal the son of *E* said
Judg 9:30 the words of Gaal the son of *E*
Judg 9:31 saying, Behold, Gaal the son of *E*
Judg 9:35 And Gaal the son of *E* went out
*2. A family of exiles.*
Ezr 8:6 *E* the son of Jonathan, and with

**EBED-MELECH** *(e'-bed-me'-lek) An Ethiopian eunuch.*
Jer 38:7 Now when *E* the Ethiopian, one of
Jer 38:8 *E* went forth out of the king's
Jer 38:10 king commanded *E* the Ethiopian
Jer 38:11 So *E* took the men with him, and
Jer 38:12 *E* the Ethiopian said unto
Jer 39:16 speak to *E* the Ethiopian, saying,

**EBEN-EZER** *A Philistine city.*
1Sa 4:1 to battle, and pitched beside *E*
1Sa 5:1 and brought it from *E* unto Ashdod
1Sa 7:12 Shen, and called the name of it *E*

**EBER** *(e'-bur)* See HEBER.
*1. A great-grandson of Shem.*
Gen 10:21 father of all the children of *E*
Gen 10:24 and Salah begat *E*
Gen 10:25 unto *E* were born two sons
Gen 11:14 lived thirty years, and begat *E*
Gen 11:15 after he begat *E* four hundred
Gen 11:16 *E* lived four and thirty years, and
Gen 11:17 *E* lived after he begat Peleg four
1Chr 1:18 begat Shelah, and Shelah begat *E*
1Chr 1:19 unto *E* were born two sons
1Chr 1:25 *E*, Peleg, Reu,
*2. Descendants of Eber 1.*
Num 24:24 Asshur, and shall afflict *E*
*3. Son of Elpaal.*
1Chr 8:12 *E*, and Misham, and Shamed, who
*4. A priest of the Amok family.*
Neh 12:20 Kallai; of Amok, *E*

**EBIASAPH** *(e-bi'-a-saf)* See ABIASAPH. *A great-grandson of Korah.*
1Chr 6:23 *E* his son, and Assir his son,
1Chr 6:37 the son of Assir, the son of *E*
1Chr 9:19 the son of Kore, the son of *E*

**EBRONAH** *(eb-ro'-nah) An encampment during the Exodus.*
Num 33:34 from Jotbathah, and encamped at *E*
Num 33:35 And they departed from *E*, and

**ED** *(ed) Name of an altar.*
Josh 22:34 of Gad called the altar *E*

**EDAR** *(e'-dar)* See EDER. *A name of a watchtower.*
Gen 35:21 his tent beyond the tower of *E*

**EDEN** *(e'-dun)*
*1. Original land of Adam and Eve.*
Gen 2:8 planted a garden eastward in *E*
Gen 2:10 went out of *E* to water the garden
Gen 2:15 into the garden of *E* to dress it
Gen 3:23 him forth from the garden of *E*
Gen 3:24 east of the garden of *E* Cherubim
Gen 4:16 the land of Nod, on the east of *E*
Is 51:3 will make her wilderness like *E*
Eze 28:13 hast been in *E* the garden of God
Eze 31:9 so that all the trees of *E*
Eze 31:16 and all the trees of *E*, the choice
Eze 31:18 in greatness among the trees of *E*
Eze 31:18 of *E* unto the nether parts of the
Eze 36:35 is become like the garden of *E*
Joel 2:3 is as the garden of *E* before them

*2. An undetermined place.*
2Kin 19:12 the children of *E* which were in
Is 37:12 the children of *E* which were in
Eze 27:23 Haran, and Canneh, and *E*, the
Amos 1:5 the sceptre from the house of *E*
*3. Son of Joah.*
2Chr 29:12 of Zimmah, and *E* the son of Joah
*4. A Levite during Hezekiah's time.*
2Chr 31:15 And next him were *E*, and Miniamin,

**EDER** *(e'-dur)* See EDAR. *A city in southern Judah.*
Josh 15:21 Edom southward were Kabzeel, and *E*
*2. A grandson of Merari.*
1Chr 23:23 Mahli, and *E*, and Jeremoth, three
1Chr 24:30 Mahli, and *E*, and Jerimoth

**EDGE**
Gen 34:26 his son with the *e* of the sword
Ex 13:20 in the *e* of the wilderness
Ex 17:13 people with the *e* of the sword
Ex 26:4 the *e* of the one curtain from the
Ex 26:4 uttermost *e* of another curtain
Ex 26:5 loops shalt thou make in the *e* of
Ex 26:10 the *e* of the one curtain that is
Ex 26:10 fifty loops in the *e* of the
Ex 36:11 on the *e* of one curtain from the
Ex 36:12 fifty loops made he in the *e* of
Ex 36:17 *e* of the curtain in the coupling
Ex 36:17 fifty loops made he upon the *e* of
Num 21:24 smote him with the *e* of the sword
Num 33:6 Etham, which is in the *e* of the
Num 33:37 in the *e* of the land of Edom
Deut 13:15 that city with the *e* of the sword
Deut 13:15 thereof, with the *e* of the sword
Deut 20:13 thereof with the *e* of the sword
Josh 6:21 and ass, with the *e* of the sword
Josh 8:24 all fallen on the *e* of the sword
Josh 8:24 smote it with the *e* of the sword
Josh 10:28 smote it with the *e* of the sword
Josh 10:30 smote it with the *e* of the sword
Josh 10:32 smote it with the *e* of the sword
Josh 10:35 smote it with the *e* of the sword
Josh 10:37 smote it with the *e* of the sword
Josh 10:39 them with the *e* of the sword
Josh 11:11 therein with the *e* of the sword
Josh 11:12 them with the *e* of the sword
Josh 11:14 smote with the *e* of the sword
Josh 13:27 even unto the *e* of the sea of
Josh 19:47 smote it with the *e* of the sword
Judg 1:8 it with the *e* of the sword
Judg 1:25 the city with the *e* of the sword
Judg 4:15 with the *e* of the sword before
Judg 4:16 fell upon the *e* of the sword
Judg 18:27 them with the *e* of the sword
Judg 20:37 the city with the *e* of the sword
Judg 20:48 them with the *e* of the sword
Judg 21:10 with the *e* of the sword, with the
1Sa 15:8 people with the *e* of the sword
1Sa 22:19 smote he with the *e* of the sword
1Sa 22:19 and sheep, with the *e* of the sword
2Sa 15:14 the city with the *e* of the sword
2Kin 10:25 them with the *e* of the sword
Job 1:15 servants with the *e* of the sword
Job 1:17 servants with the *e* of the sword
Ps 89:43 also turned the *e* of his sword
Eccl 10:10 be blunt, and he do not whet the *e*
Jer 21:7 them with the *e* of the sword
Jer 31:29 the children's teeth are set on *e*
Jer 31:30 his teeth shall be set on *e*
Eze 18:2 the children's teeth are set on *e*
Eze 43:13 the border thereof by the *e*
Lk 21:24 shall fall by the *e* of the sword
Heb 11:34 escaped the *e* of the sword, out

**EDIFICATION**
Rom 15:2 his neighbour for his good to *e*
1Cor 14:3 speaketh unto men to *e*, and
2Cor 10:8 the Lord hath given us for *e*
2Cor 13:10 which the Lord hath given me to *e*

**EDIFYING**
1Cor 14:5 that the church may receive *e*
1Cor 14:12 may excel to the *e* of the church
1Cor 14:26 Let all things be done unto *e*
2Cor 12:19 dearly beloved, for your *e*
Eph 4:12 for the *e* of the body of Christ
Eph 4:16 body unto the *e* of itself in love
Eph 4:29 which is good to the use of *e*
1Ti 1:4 than godly *e* which is in faith

**EDOM** *(e'-dum)* See EDOMITES, ESAU, IDUMEA, OBED-EDOM.
*1. Another name for Esau.*
Gen 36:21 children of Seir in the land of *E*
Gen 36:31 that reigned in the land of *E*
Gen 36:32 Bela the son of Beor reigned in *E*
Gen 36:43 these be the dukes of *E*,
Ex 15:15 the dukes of *E* shall be amazed
Num 20:14 from Kadesh unto the king of *E*
Num 20:18 *E* said unto him, Thou shalt not
Num 20:20 *E* came out against him with much
Num 20:21 Thus *E* refused to give Israel
Num 20:23 by the coast of the land of *E*
Num 21:4 Red sea, to compass the land of *E*
Num 24:18 *E* shall be a possession, Seir
Num 33:37 Hor, in the edge of the land of *E*
Num 34:3 of Zin along by the coast of *E*
Josh 15:1 even to the border of *E* the
Josh 15:21 coast of *E* southward were Kabzeel
Judg 5:4 marchedst out of the field of *E*
Judg 11:17 messengers unto the king of *E*
Judg 11:17 but the king of *E* would not
Judg 11:18 and compassed the land of *E*
1Sa 14:47 children of Ammon, and against *E*
2Sa 8:14 And he put garrisons in *E*
2Sa 8:14 throughout all *E* put he garrisons
2Sa 8:14 all they of *E* became David's
1Kin 9:26 of the Red sea, in the land of *E*
1Kin 11:14 he was of the king's seed in *E*
1Kin 11:15 came to pass, when David was in *E*
1Kin 11:15 he had smitten every male in *E*
1Kin 11:16 he had cut off every male in *E*
1Kin 22:47 There was then no king in *E*
2Kin 3:8 way through the wilderness of *E*
2Kin 3:9 king of Judah, and the king of *E*
2Kin 3:12 the king of *E* went down to him
2Kin 3:20 there came water by the way of *E*
2Kin 3:26 through even unto the king of *E*
2Kin 8:20 In his days *E* revolted from under
2Kin 8:22 Yet *E* revolted from under the
2Kin 14:7 He slew of *E* in the valley of
2Kin 14:10 Thou hast indeed smitten *E*
1Chr 1:43 that reigned in the land of *E*
1Chr 1:51 And the dukes of *E* were
1Chr 1:54 These are the dukes of *E*
1Chr 18:11 from *E*, and from Moab, and from the
1Chr 18:13 And he put garrisons in *E*
2Chr 8:17 at the sea side in the land of *E*
2Chr 25:20 they sought after the gods of *E*
Ps 60:*t* smote of *E* in the valley of salt
Ps 60:8 over *E* will I cast out my shoe
Ps 60:9 who will lead me into *E*
Ps 83:6 The tabernacles of *E*, and the
Ps 108:9 over *E* will I cast out my shoe
Ps 108:10 who will lead me into *E*
Ps 137:7 the children of *E* in the day of
Is 11:14 they shall lay their hand upon *E*
Is 63:1 Who is this that cometh from *E*
Jer 9:26 Egypt, and Judah, and *E*, and the
Jer 25:21 *E*, and Moab, and the children of
Jer 27:3 And send them to the king of *E*
Jer 40:11 and among the Ammonites, and in *E*
Jer 49:7 Concerning *E*, thus saith the LORD
Jer 49:17 Also *E* shall be a desolation
Jer 49:20 that he hath taken against *E*
Jer 49:22 *E* be as the heart of a woman in
Lam 4:21 and be glad, O daughter of *E*
Lam 4:22 thine iniquity, O daughter of *E*
Eze 25:12 Because that *E* hath dealt against
Eze 25:13 also stretch out mine hand upon *E*
Eze 25:14 I will lay my vengeance upon *E* by
Eze 25:14 they shall do in *E* according to
Eze 32:29 There is *E*, her kings, and all her
Dan 11:41 escape out of his hand, even *E*
Joel 3:19 *E* shall be a desolate wilderness,
Amos 1:6 to deliver them up to *E*
Amos 1:9 up the whole captivity to *E*
Amos 1:11 For three transgressions of *E*
Amos 2:1 bones of the king of *E* into lime
Amos 9:12 they may possess the remnant of *E*
Obad 1 saith the Lord GOD concerning *E*
Obad 8 destroy the wise men out of *E*
Mal 1:4 Whereas *E* saith, We are
*2. Descendants of Esau.*
Gen 25:30 therefore was his name called *E*
Gen 32:3 land of Seir, the country of *E*
Gen 36:1 the generations of Esau, who is *E*
Gen 36:8 Esau is *E*
Gen 36:16 came of Eliphaz in the land of *E*
Gen 36:17 came of Reuel in the land of *E*
Gen 36:19 are the sons of Esau, who is *E*

**EDOMITE** *(e'-dum-ite)* See EDOMITES. *A descendant of Esau.*
Deut 23:7 Thou shalt not abhor an *E*
1Sa 21:7 and his name was Doeg, an *E*
1Sa 22:9 Then answered Doeg the *E*, which
1Sa 22:18 And Doeg the *E* turned, and he fell
1Sa 22:22 day, when Doeg the *E* was there
1Kin 11:14 unto Solomon, Hadad the *E*
Ps 52:*t* of David, when Doeg the *E* came

**EDOMITES** *(e'-dum-ites)*
Gen 36:9 the father of the *E* in mount Seir
Gen 36:43 he is Esau the father of the *E*
1Kin 11:1 of the Moabites, Ammonites, *E*
1Kin 11:17 certain *E* of his father's
2Kin 8:21 smote the *E* which compassed him
1Chr 18:12 the son Zeruiah slew of the *E* in
1Chr 18:13 all the *E* became David's servants
2Chr 21:8 In his days the *E* revolted from
2Chr 21:9 smote the *E* which compassed him
2Chr 21:10 So the *E* revolted from under the
2Chr 25:14 come from the slaughter of the *E*
2Chr 25:19 Lo, thou hast smitten the *E*
2Chr 28:17 For again the *E* had come and

**EDREI** *(ed'-re-i)*
*1. A city in Bashan.*
Num 21:33 his people, to the battle at *E*
Deut 1:4 which dwelt at Astaroth in *E*
Deut 3:1 and all his people, to battle at *E*
Deut 3:10 and all Bashan, unto Salchah and *E*
Josh 12:4 that dwelt at Ashtaroth and at *E*
Josh 13:12 reigned in Ashtaroth and in *E*
Josh 13:31 half Gilead, and Ashtaroth, and *E*
*2. A city in Naphtali.*
Josh 19:37 And Kedesh, and *E*, and En-hazor,

**EFFECT**
Num 30:8 she bound her soul, of none *e*
2Chr 34:22 and they spake to her to that *e*
Ps 33:10 devices of the people of none *e*
Is 32:17 the *e* of righteousness quietness
Jer 48:30 his lies shall not so *e* it
Eze 12:23 at hand, and the *e* of every vision
Mt 15:6 God of none *e* by your tradition
Mk 7:13 of none *e* through your tradition
Rom 3:3 make the faith of God without *e*
Rom 4:14 and the promise made of none *e*
Rom 9:6 the word of God hath taken none *e*
1Cor 1:17 Christ should be made of none *e*
Gal 3:17 should make the promise of none *e*
Gal 5:4 Christ is become of no *e* unto you

**EFFECTUAL**
1Cor 16:9 *e* is opened unto me, and there are
2Cor 1:6 which is *e* in the enduring of the
Eph 3:7 me by the *e* working of his power
Eph 4:16 according to the *e* working in the
Philem 6 of thy faith may become *e* by the
Jas 5:16 The *e* fervent prayer of a

**EGGS**
Deut 22:6 whether they be young ones, or *e*
Deut 22:6 upon the young, or upon the *e*
Job 39:14 Which leaveth her *e* in the earth
Is 10:14 as one gathereth *e* that are left
Is 59:5 They hatch cockatrice' *e*, and
Is 59:5 he that eateth of their *e* dieth
Jer 17:11 As the partridge sitteth on *e*

**EGLAH** *(eg'-lah)* See MICHAL. *A wife of David.*
2Sa 3:5 sixth, Ithream, by *E* David's wife
1Chr 3:3 the sixth, Ithream by *E* his wife

**EGLAIM** *(eg'-la-im)* See EN-EGLAIM. *A Moabite city.*
Is 15:8 the howling thereof unto *E*

**EGLON** *(eg'-lon)*
*1. An Amorite city.*
Josh 10:3 Lachish, and unto Debir king of *E*
Josh 10:5 king of Lachish, the king of *E*
Josh 10:23 king of Lachish, and the king of *E*
Josh 10:34 from Lachish Joshua passed unto *E*
Josh 10:36 And Joshua went up from *E*, and all
Josh 10:37 to all that he had done to *E*
Josh 12:12 The king of *E*, one
Josh 15:39 Lachish, and Bozkath, and *E*
*2. A Moabite king.*
Judg 3:12 the LORD strengthened *E* the king
Judg 3:14 the children of Israel served *E*
Judg 3:15 a present unto *E* the king of Moab

Judg 3:17 the present unto *E* king of Moab
Judg 3:17 and *E* was a very fat man

**EGYPT** *(e'-jipt)* See EGYPTIAN, MIZRAIM.
*Kingdom in northeast Africa.*

Gen 12:10 went down into *E* to sojourn there
Gen 12:11 he was come near to enter into *E*
Gen 12:14 that, when Abram was come into *E*
Gen 13:1 And Abram went up out of *E*
Gen 13:10 of the LORD, like the land of *E*
Gen 15:18 from the river of *E* unto the
Gen 21:21 him a wife out of the land of *E*
Gen 25:18 unto Shur, that is before *E*
Gen 26:2 him, and said, Go not down into *E*
Gen 37:25 going to carry it down to *E*
Gen 37:28 and they brought Joseph into *E*
Gen 37:36 sold him into *E* unto Potiphar
Gen 39:1 And Joseph was brought down to *E*
Gen 40:1 that the butler of the king of *E*
Gen 40:1 offended their lord the king of *E*
Gen 40:5 and the baker of the king of *E*
Gen 41:8 called for all the magicians of *E*
Gen 41:19 in all the land of *E* for badness
Gen 41:29 throughout all the land of *E*
Gen 41:30 be forgotten in the land of *E*
Gen 41:33 and set him over the land of *E*
Gen 41:34 of *E* in the seven plenteous years
Gen 41:36 which shall be in the land of *E*
Gen 41:41 set thee over all the land of *E*
Gen 41:43 him ruler over all the land of *E*
Gen 41:44 hand or foot in all the land of *E*
Gen 41:45 went out over all the land of *E*
Gen 41:46 he stood before Pharaoh king of *E*
Gen 41:46 went throughout all the land of *E*
Gen 41:48 which were in the land of *E*
Gen 41:53 that was in the land of *E*
Gen 41:54 all the land of *E* there was bread
Gen 41:55 all the land of *E* was famished
Gen 41:56 waxed sore in the land of *E*
Gen 41:57 all countries came into *E* to
Gen 42:1 saw that there was corn in *E*
Gen 42:2 heard that there is corn in *E*
Gen 42:3 went down to buy corn in *E*
Gen 43:2 which they had brought out of *E*
Gen 43:15 and rose up, and went down to *E*
Gen 45:4 your brother, whom ye sold into *E*
Gen 45:8 throughout all the land of *E*
Gen 45:9 God hath made me lord of all *E*
Gen 45:13 my father of all my glory in *E*
Gen 45:18 you the good of the land of *E*
Gen 45:19 land of *E* for your little ones
Gen 45:20 of all the land of *E* is yours
Gen 45:23 laden with the good things of *E*
Gen 45:25 And they went up out of *E*, and came
Gen 45:26 governor over all the land of *E*
Gen 46:3 fear not to go down into *E*
Gen 46:4 I will go down with thee into *E*
Gen 46:6 land of Canaan, and came into *E*
Gen 46:7 seed brought he with him into *E*
Gen 46:8 of Israel, which came into *E*
Gen 46:20 the land of *E* were born Manasseh
Gen 46:26 souls that came with Jacob into *E*
Gen 46:27 Joseph, which were born him in *E*
Gen 46:27 house of Jacob, which came into *E*
Gen 47:6 The land of *E* is before thee
Gen 47:11 a possession in the land of *E*
Gen 47:13 very sore, so that the land of *E*
Gen 47:14 that was found in the land of *E*
Gen 47:15 money failed in the land of *E*
Gen 47:20 all the land of *E* for Pharaoh
Gen 47:21 *E* even to the other end thereof
Gen 47:26 over the land of *E* unto this day
Gen 47:27 And Israel dwelt in the land of *E*
Gen 47:28 in the land of *E* seventeen years
Gen 47:29 bury me not, I pray thee, in *E*
Gen 47:30 and thou shalt carry me out of *E*
Gen 48:5 of *E* before I came unto thee into
Gen 48:5 before I came unto thee into *E*
Gen 50:7 all the elders of the land of *E*
Gen 50:14 And Joseph returned into *E*
Gen 50:22 And Joseph dwelt in *E*, he, and his
Gen 50:26 and he was put in a coffin in *E*
Ex 1:1 of Israel, which came into *E*
Ex 1:5 for Joseph was in *E* already
Ex 1:8 there arose up a new king over *E*
Ex 1:15 the king of *E* spake to the Hebrew
Ex 1:17 as the king of *E* commanded them
Ex 1:18 the king of *E* called for the
Ex 2:23 of time, that the king of *E* died
Ex 3:7 of my people which are in *E*
Ex 3:10 the children of Israel out of *E*
Ex 3:11 the children of Israel out of *E*
Ex 3:12 brought forth the people out of *E*
Ex 3:16 that which is done to you in *E*
Ex 3:17 *E* unto the land of the Canaanites
Ex 3:18 of Israel, unto the king of *E*
Ex 3:19 the king of *E* will not let you go
Ex 3:20 smite *E* with all my wonders which
Ex 4:18 unto my brethren which are in *E*
Ex 4:19 in Midian, Go, return into *E*
Ex 4:20 and he returned to the land of *E*
Ex 4:21 When thou goest to return into *E*
Ex 5:4 the king of *E* said unto them,
Ex 5:12 throughout all the land of *E* to
Ex 6:11 in, speak unto Pharaoh king of *E*
Ex 6:13 Israel, and unto Pharaoh king of *E*
Ex 6:13 of Israel out of the land of *E*
Ex 6:26 of *E* according to their armies
Ex 6:27 which spake to Pharaoh king of *E*
Ex 6:27 out the children of Israel from *E*
Ex 6:28 spake unto Moses in the land of *E*
Ex 6:29 of *E* all that I say unto thee
Ex 7:3 and my wonders in the land of *E*
Ex 7:4 that I may lay my hand upon *E*
Ex 7:4 the land of *E* by great judgments
Ex 7:5 I stretch forth mine hand upon *E*
Ex 7:11 now the magicians of *E*, they also
Ex 7:19 thine hand upon the waters of *E*
Ex 7:19 throughout all the land of *E*
Ex 7:21 throughout all the land of *E*
Ex 7:22 the magicians of *E* did so with
Ex 8:5 to come up upon the land of *E*
Ex 8:6 out his hand over the waters of *E*
Ex 8:6 came up, and covered the land of *E*
Ex 8:7 up frogs upon the land of *E*
Ex 8:16 lice throughout all the land of *E*
Ex 8:17 lice throughout all the land of *E*
Ex 8:24 houses, and into all the land of *E*
Ex 9:4 of Israel and the cattle of *E*
Ex 9:6 and all the cattle of *E* died
Ex 9:9 small dust in all the land of *E*
Ex 9:9 throughout all the land of *E*
Ex 9:18 such as hath not been in *E* since
Ex 9:22 may be hail in all the land of *E*
Ex 9:22 field, throughout the land of *E*
Ex 9:23 rained hail upon the land of *E*
Ex 9:24 of *E* since it became a nation
Ex 9:25 of *E* all that was in the field
Ex 10:2 what things I have wrought in *E*
Ex 10:7 thou not yet that *E* is destroyed
Ex 10:12 the land of *E* for the locusts
Ex 10:12 may come up upon the land of *E*
Ex 10:13 forth his rod over the land of *E*
Ex 10:14 went up over all the land of *E*
Ex 10:14 and rested in all the coasts of *E*
Ex 10:15 field, through all the land of *E*
Ex 10:19 one locust in all the coasts of *E*
Ex 10:21 be darkness over the land of *E*
Ex 10:22 in all the land of *E* three days
Ex 11:1 more upon Pharaoh, and upon *E*
Ex 11:3 was very great in the land of *E*
Ex 11:4 will I go out into the midst of *E*
Ex 11:5 in the land of *E* shall die
Ex 11:6 cry throughout all the land of *E*
Ex 11:9 be multiplied in the land of *E*
Ex 12:1 Moses and Aaron in the land of *E*
Ex 12:12 through the land of *E* this night
Ex 12:12 the firstborn in the land of *E*
Ex 12:12 gods of *E* I will execute judgment
Ex 12:13 you, when I smite the land of *E*
Ex 12:17 your armies out of the land of *E*
Ex 12:27 of the children of Israel in *E*
Ex 12:29 the firstborn in the land of *E*
Ex 12:30 and there was a great cry in *E*
Ex 12:39 which they brought forth out of *E*
Ex 12:39 because they were thrust out of *E*
Ex 12:40 of Israel, who dwelt in *E*
Ex 12:41 LORD went out from the land of *E*
Ex 12:42 them out from the land of *E*
Ex 12:51 of the land of *E* by their armies
Ex 13:3 day, in which ye came out from *E*
Ex 13:8 me when I came forth out of *E*
Ex 13:9 the LORD brought thee out of *E*
Ex 13:14 the LORD brought us out from *E*
Ex 13:15 the firstborn in the land of *E*
Ex 13:16 LORD brought us forth out of *E*
Ex 13:17 they see war, and they return to *E*
Ex 13:18 up harnessed out of the land of *E*
Ex 14:5 king of *E* that the people fled
Ex 14:7 and all the chariots of *E*
Ex 14:8 the heart of Pharaoh king of *E*
Ex 14:11 Because there were no graves in *E*
Ex 14:11 us, to carry us forth out of *E*
Ex 14:12 word that we did tell thee in *E*
Ex 16:1 departing out of the land of *E*
Ex 16:3 hand of the LORD in the land of *E*
Ex 16:6 you out from the land of *E*
Ex 16:32 you forth from the land of *E*
Ex 17:3 thou hast brought us up out of *E*
Ex 18:1 LORD had brought Israel out of *E*
Ex 19:1 gone forth out of the land of *E*
Ex 20:2 brought thee out of the land of *E*
Ex 22:21 were strangers in the land of *E*
Ex 23:9 were strangers in the land of *E*
Ex 23:15 for in it thou camest out from *E*
Ex 29:46 them forth out of the land of *E*
Ex 32:1 us up out of the land of *E*
Ex 32:4 thee up out of the land of *E*
Ex 32:7 broughtest out of the land of *E*
Ex 32:8 thee up out of the land of *E*
Ex 32:11 of the land of *E* with great power
Ex 32:23 us up out of the land of *E*
Ex 33:1 brought up out of the land of *E*
Ex 34:18 month Abib thou camest out from *E*
Lev 11:45 you up out of the land of *E*
Lev 18:3 After the doings of the land of *E*
Lev 19:34 were strangers in the land of *E*
Lev 19:36 brought you out of the land of *E*
Lev 22:33 brought you out of the land of *E*
Lev 23:43 brought them out of the land of *E*
Lev 25:38 you forth out of the land of *E*
Lev 25:42 forth out of the land of *E*
Lev 25:55 forth out of the land of *E*
Lev 26:13 you forth out of the land of *E*
Lev 26:45 forth out of the land of *E* in the
Num 1:1 were come out of the land of *E*
Num 3:13 of *E* I hallowed unto me all the
Num 8:17 of *E* I sanctified them for myself
Num 9:1 were come out of the land of *E*
Num 11:5 which we did eat in *E* freely
Num 11:18 for it was well with us in *E*
Num 11:20 Why came we forth out of *E*
Num 13:22 seven years before Zoan in *E*
Num 14:2 that we had died in the land of *E*
Num 14:3 better for us to return into *E*
Num 14:4 captain, and let us return into *E*
Num 14:19 people, from *E* even until now
Num 14:22 and my miracles, which I did in *E*
Num 15:41 brought you out of the land of *E*
Num 20:5 ye made us to come up out of *E*
Num 20:15 How our fathers went down into *E*
Num 20:15 and we have dwelt in *E* a long time
Num 20:16 and hath brought us forth out of *E*
Num 21:5 out of *E* to die in the wilderness
Num 22:5 there is a people come out from *E*
Num 22:11 there is a people come out of *E*
Num 23:22 God brought them out of *E*
Num 24:8 God brought him forth out of *E*
Num 26:4 went forth out of the land of *E*
Num 26:59 whom her mother bare to Levi in *E*
Num 32:11 of the men that came up out of *E*
Num 33:1 of *E* with their armies under the
Num 33:38 were come out of the land of *E*
Num 34:5 from Azmon unto the river of *E*
Deut 1:27 us forth out of the land of *E*
Deut 1:30 did for you in *E* before your eyes
Deut 4:20 the iron furnace, even out of *E*
Deut 4:34 did for you in *E* before your eyes
Deut 4:37 with his mighty power out of *E*
Deut 4:45 after they came forth out of *E*
Deut 4:46 they were come forth out of *E*
Deut 5:6 brought thee out of the land of *E*
Deut 5:15 wast a servant in the land of *E*
Deut 6:12 thee forth out of the land of *E*
Deut 6:21 We were Pharaoh's bondmen in *E*
Deut 6:21 us out of *E* with a mighty hand
Deut 6:22 and wonders, great and sore, upon *E*
Deut 7:8 the hand of Pharaoh king of *E*
Deut 7:15 none of the evil diseases of *E*
Deut 7:18 did unto Pharaoh, and unto all *E*
Deut 8:14 thee forth out of the land of *E*
Deut 9:7 didst depart out of the land of *E*
Deut 9:12 of *E* have corrupted themselves
Deut 9:26 forth out of *E* with a mighty hand
Deut 10:19 were strangers in the land of *E*
Deut 10:22 went down into *E* with threescore
Deut 11:3 which he did in the midst of *E*
Deut 11:3 unto Pharaoh the king of *E*
Deut 11:4 And what he did unto the army of *E*
Deut 11:10 it, is not as the land of *E*

Deut 13:5 brought you out of the land of *E*
Deut 13:10 brought thee out of the land of *E*
Deut 15:15 wast a bondman in the land of *E*
Deut 16:1 thee forth out of *E* by night
Deut 16:3 out of the land of *E* in haste
Deut 16:3 of *E* all the days of thy life
Deut 16:6 that thou camest forth out of *E*
Deut 16:12 that thou wast a bondman in *E*
Deut 17:16 cause the people to return to *E*
Deut 20:1 thee up out of the land of *E*
Deut 23:4 way, when ye came forth out of *E*
Deut 24:9 that ye were come forth out of *E*
Deut 24:18 that thou wast a bondman in *E*
Deut 24:22 wast a bondman in the land of *E*
Deut 25:17 when ye were come forth out of *E*
Deut 26:5 my father, and he went down into *E*
Deut 26:8 forth out of *E* with a mighty hand
Deut 28:27 smite thee with the botch of *E*
Deut 28:60 upon thee all the diseases of *E*
Deut 28:68 thee into *E* again with ships
Deut 29:2 in the land of *E* unto Pharaoh
Deut 29:16 we have dwelt in the land of *E*
Deut 29:25 them forth out of the land of *E*
Deut 34:11 to do in the land of *E* to Pharaoh
Josh 2:10 for you, when ye came out of *E*
Josh 5:4 All the people that came out of *E*
Josh 5:4 the way, after they came out of *E*
Josh 5:5 way as they came forth out of *E*
Josh 5:6 men of war, which came out of *E*
Josh 5:9 the reproach of *E* from off you
Josh 9:9 of him, and all that he did in *E*
Josh 13:3 From Sihor, which is before *E*
Josh 15:4 and went out unto the river of *E*
Josh 15:47 her villages, unto the river of *E*
Josh 24:4 and his children went down into *E*
Josh 24:5 also and Aaron, and I plagued *E*
Josh 24:6 I brought your fathers out of *E*
Josh 24:7 have seen what I have done in *E*
Josh 24:14 other side of the flood, and in *E*
Josh 24:17 our fathers out of the land of *E*
Josh 24:32 of Israel brought up out of *E*
Judg 2:1 I made you to go up out of *E*
Judg 2:12 brought them out of the land of *E*
Judg 6:8 Israel, I brought you up from *E*
Judg 6:13 not the LORD bring us up from *E*
Judg 11:13 land, when they came up out of *E*
Judg 11:16 But when Israel came up from *E*
Judg 19:30 of the land of *E* unto this day
1Sa 2:27 when they were in *E* in Pharaoh's
1Sa 8:8 up out of *E* even unto this day
1Sa 10:18 I brought up Israel out of *E*
1Sa 12:6 fathers up out of the land of *E*
1Sa 12:8 When Jacob was come into *E*
1Sa 12:8 forth your fathers out of *E*
1Sa 15:2 the way, when he came up from *E*
1Sa 15:6 when they came up out of *E*
1Sa 15:7 to Shur, that is over against *E*
1Sa 27:8 to Shur, even unto the land of *E*
1Sa 30:13 And he said, I am a young man of *E*
2Sa 7:6 the children of Israel out of *E*
2Sa 7:23 thou redeemedst to thee from *E*
1Kin 3:1 affinity with Pharaoh king of *E*
1Kin 4:21 and unto the border of *E*
1Kin 4:30 country, and all the wisdom of *E*
1Kin 6:1 were come out of the land of *E*
1Kin 8:9 they came out of the land of *E*
1Kin 8:16 forth my people Israel out of *E*
1Kin 8:21 brought them out of the land of *E*
1Kin 8:51 thou broughtest forth out of *E*
1Kin 8:53 broughtest our fathers out of *E*
1Kin 8:65 in of Hamath unto the river of *E*
1Kin 9:9 fathers out of the land of *E*
1Kin 9:16 For Pharaoh king of *E* had gone up
1Kin 10:28 had horses brought out of *E*
1Kin 10:29 went out of *E* for six hundred
1Kin 11:17 servants with him, to go into *E*
1Kin 11:18 to *E*, unto Pharaoh king of *E*
1Kin 11:21 when Hadad heard in *E* that David
1Kin 11:40 And Jeroboam arose, and fled into *E*
1Kin 11:40 unto Shishak king of *E*
1Kin 11:40 was in *E* until the death of
1Kin 12:2 son of Nebat, who was yet in *E*
1Kin 12:2 Solomon, and Jeroboam dwelt in *E*
1Kin 12:28 thee up out of the land of *E*
1Kin 14:25 that Shishak king of *E* came up
2Kin 17:4 sent messengers to So king of *E*
2Kin 17:7 them up out of the land of *E*
2Kin 17:7 the hand of Pharaoh king of *E*
2Kin 17:36 of the land of *E* with great power
2Kin 18:21 of this bruised reed, even upon *E*
2Kin 18:21 so is Pharaoh king of *E* unto all
2Kin 18:24 put thy trust on *E* for chariots
2Kin 21:15 their fathers came forth out of *E*
2Kin 23:29 of *E* went up against the king of
2Kin 23:34 and he came to *E*, and died there
2Kin 24:7 the king of *E* came not again any
2Kin 24:7 had taken from the river of *E*
2Kin 24:7 that pertained to the king of *E*
2Kin 25:26 the armies, arose, and came to *E*
1Chr 13:5 from Shihor of *E* even unto the
1Chr 17:21 whom thou hast redeemed out of *E*
2Chr 1:16 had horses brought out of *E*
2Chr 1:17 brought forth out of *E* a chariot
2Chr 5:10 Israel, when they came out of *E*
2Chr 6:5 my people out of the land of *E* I
2Chr 7:8 in of Hamath unto the river of *E*
2Chr 7:22 them forth out of the land of *E*
2Chr 9:26 and to the border of *E*
2Chr 9:28 unto Solomon horses out of *E*
2Chr 10:2 the son of Nebat, who was in *E*
2Chr 10:2 that Jeroboam returned out of *E*
2Chr 12:2 of *E* came up against Jerusalem
2Chr 12:3 that came with him out of *E*
2Chr 12:9 So Shishak king of *E* came up
2Chr 20:10 they came out of the land of *E*
2Chr 26:8 even to the entering in of *E*
2Chr 35:20 Necho king of *E* came up to fight
2Chr 36:3 the king of *E* put him down at
2Chr 36:4 the king of *E* made Eliakim his
2Chr 36:4 his brother, and carried him to *E*
Neh 9:9 affliction of our fathers in *E*
Neh 9:18 God that brought thee up out of *E*
Ps 68:31 Princes shall come out of *E*
Ps 78:12 their fathers, in the land of *E*
Ps 78:43 How he had wrought his signs in *E*
Ps 78:51 And smote all the firstborn in *E*
Ps 80:8 Thou hast brought a vine out of *E*
Ps 81:5 he went out through the land of *E*
Ps 81:10 brought thee out of the land of *E*
Ps 105:23 Israel also came into *E*
Ps 105:38 *E* was glad when they departed
Ps 106:7 understood not thy wonders in *E*
Ps 106:21 which had done great things in *E*
Ps 114:1 When Israel went out of *E*
Ps 135:8 Who smote the firstborn of *E*
Ps 135:9 into the midst of thee, O *E*
Ps 136:10 To him that smote *E* in their
Prov 7:16 works, with fine linen of *E*
Is 7:18 uttermost part of the rivers of *E*
Is 10:24 thee, after the manner of *E*
Is 10:26 lift it up after the manner of *E*
Is 11:11 be left, from Assyria, and from *E*
Is 11:16 he came up out of the land of *E*
Is 19:1 The burden of *E*
Is 19:1 swift cloud, and shall come into *E*
Is 19:1 the idols of *E* shall be moved at
Is 19:1 the heart of *E* shall melt in the
Is 19:3 the spirit of *E* shall fail in the
Is 19:12 of hosts hath purposed upon *E*
Is 19:13 they have also seduced *E*, even
Is 19:14 they have caused *E* to err in
Is 19:15 shall there be any work for *E*
Is 19:16 In that day shall *E* be like unto
Is 19:17 of Judah shall be a terror unto *E*
Is 19:18 five cities in the land of *E*
Is 19:19 in the midst of the land of *E*
Is 19:20 LORD of hosts in the land of *E*
Is 19:21 And the LORD shall be known to *E*
Is 19:22 And the LORD shall smite *E*
Is 19:23 be a highway out of *E* to Assyria
Is 19:23 and the Assyrian shall come into *E*
Is 19:24 shall Israel be the third with *E*
Is 19:25 saying, Blessed be *E* my people
Is 20:3 years for a sign and wonder upon *E*
Is 20:4 uncovered, to the shame of *E*
Is 20:5 expectation, and of *E* their glory
Is 23:5 As at the report concerning *E*
Is 27:12 of the river unto the stream of *E*
Is 27:13 and the outcasts in the land of *E*
Is 30:2 That walk to go down into *E*
Is 30:2 and to trust in the shadow of *E*
Is 30:3 in the shadow of *E* your confusion
Is 31:1 them that go down to *E* for help
Is 36:6 staff of this broken reed, on *E*
Is 36:6 so is Pharaoh king of *E* to all
Is 36:9 put thy trust on *E* for chariots
Is 43:3 I gave *E* for thy ransom, Ethiopia
Is 45:14 saith the LORD, The labour of *E*
Is 52:4 aforetime into *E* to sojourn there
Jer 2:6 us up out of the land of *E*
Jer 2:18 hast thou to do in the way of *E*
Jer 2:36 thou also shalt be ashamed of *E*
Jer 7:22 brought them out of the land of *E*
Jer 7:25 came forth out of the land of *E*
Jer 9:26 *E*, and Judah, and Edom, and the
Jer 11:4 them forth out of the land of *E*
Jer 11:7 them up out of the land of *E*
Jer 16:14 of Israel out of the land of *E*
Jer 23:7 of Israel out of the land of *E*
Jer 24:8 them that dwell in the land of *E*
Jer 25:19 Pharaoh king of *E*, and his
Jer 26:21 afraid, and fled, and went into *E*
Jer 26:22 the king sent men into *E*, namely,
Jer 26:22 and certain men with him into *E*
Jer 26:23 fetched forth Urijah out of *E*
Jer 31:32 bring them out of the land of *E*
Jer 32:20 signs and wonders in the land of *E*
Jer 32:21 out of the land of *E* with signs
Jer 34:13 them forth out of the land of *E*
Jer 37:5 army was come forth out of *E*
Jer 37:7 shall return to *E* into their own
Jer 41:17 Bethlehem, to go to enter into *E*
Jer 42:14 but we will go into the land of *E*
Jer 42:15 set your faces to enter into *E*
Jer 42:16 you there in the land of *E*
Jer 42:16 follow close after you there in *E*
Jer 42:17 to go into *E* to sojourn there
Jer 42:18 you, when ye shall enter into *E*
Jer 42:19 Go ye not into *E*
Jer 43:2 Go not into *E* to sojourn there
Jer 43:7 So they came into the land of *E*
Jer 43:11 he shall smite the land of *E*
Jer 43:12 in the houses of the gods of *E*
Jer 43:12 array himself with the land of *E*
Jer 43:13 that is in the land of *E*
Jer 44:1 Jews which dwell in the land of *E*
Jer 44:8 unto other gods in the land of *E*
Jer 44:12 the land of *E* to sojourn there
Jer 44:12 and fall in the land of *E*
Jer 44:13 them that dwell in the land of *E*
Jer 44:14 the land of *E* to sojourn there
Jer 44:15 that dwelt in the land of *E*
Jer 44:24 Judah that are in the land of *E*
Jer 44:26 Judah that dwell in the land of *E*
Jer 44:26 man of Judah in all the land of *E*
Jer 44:27 Judah that are in the land of *E*
Jer 44:28 land of *E* into the land of Judah
Jer 44:28 the land of *E* to sojourn there
Jer 44:30 give Pharaoh-hophra king of *E*
Jer 46:2 Against *E*, against the army of
Jer 46:2 army of Pharaoh-necho king of *E*
Jer 46:8 *E* riseth up like a flood, and his
Jer 46:11 balm, O virgin, the daughter of *E*
Jer 46:13 come and smite the land of *E*
Jer 46:14 Declare ye in *E*, and publish in
Jer 46:17 Pharaoh king of *E* is but a noise
Jer 46:19 O thou daughter dwelling in *E*
Jer 46:20 *E* is like a very fair heifer, but
Jer 46:24 The daughter of *E* shall be
Jer 46:25 multitude of No, and Pharaoh, and *E*
Eze 17:15 in sending his ambassadors into *E*
Eze 19:4 with chains unto the land of *E*
Eze 20:5 known unto them in the land of *E*
Eze 20:6 *E* into a land that I had espied
Eze 20:7 yourselves with the idols of *E*
Eze 20:8 did they forsake the idols of *E*
Eze 20:8 in the midst of the land of *E*
Eze 20:9 them forth out of the land of *E*
Eze 20:10 to go forth out of the land of *E*
Eze 20:36 the wilderness of the land of *E*
Eze 23:3 And they committed whoredoms in *E*
Eze 23:8 she her whoredoms brought from *E*
Eze 23:19 the harlot in the land of *E*
Eze 23:27 brought from the land of *E*
Eze 23:27 them, nor remember *E* any more
Eze 27:7 *E* was that which thou spreadest
Eze 29:2 face against Pharaoh king of *E*
Eze 29:2 against him, and against all *E*
Eze 29:3 against thee, Pharaoh king of *E*
Eze 29:6 all the inhabitants of *E* shall
Eze 29:9 the land of *E* shall be desolate
Eze 29:10 make the land of *E* utterly waste
Eze 29:12 I will make the land of *E*
Eze 29:14 bring again the captivity of *E*
Eze 29:19 I will give the land of *E* unto
Eze 29:20 of *E* for his labour wherewith he
Eze 30:4 And the sword shall come upon *E*
Eze 30:4 when the slain shall fall in *E*
Eze 30:6 also that uphold *E* shall fall
Eze 30:8 LORD, when I have set a fire in *E*

Eze 30:9 upon them, as in the day of E
Eze 30:10 of E to cease by the hand of
Eze 30:11 shall draw their swords against E
Eze 30:13 no more a prince of the land of E
Eze 30:13 will put a fear in the land of E
Eze 30:15 fury upon Sin, the strength of E
Eze 30:16 And I will set fire in E
Eze 30:18 shall break there the yokes of E
Eze 30:19 will I execute judgments in E
Eze 30:21 the arm of Pharaoh king of E
Eze 30:22 I am against Pharaoh king of E
Eze 30:25 stretch it out upon the land of E
Eze 31:2 man, speak unto Pharaoh king of E
Eze 32:2 lamentation for Pharaoh king of E
Eze 32:12 and they shall spoil the pomp of E
Eze 32:15 shall make the land of E desolate
Eze 32:16 shall lament for her, even for E
Eze 32:18 man, wail for the multitude of E
Dan 9:15 the land of E with a mighty hand
Dan 11:8 carry captives into E their gods
Dan 11:42 the land of E shall not escape
Dan 11:43 over all the precious things of E
Hos 2:15 she came up out of the land of E
Hos 7:11 they call to E, they go to
Hos 7:16 their derision in the land of E
Hos 8:13 they shall return to E
Hos 9:3 but Ephraim shall return to E
Hos 9:6 E shall gather them up, Memphis
Hos 11:1 him, and called my son out of E
Hos 11:5 not return into the land of E
Hos 11:11 shall tremble as a bird out of E
Hos 12:1 and oil is carried into E
Hos 12:9 LORD thy God from the land of E
Hos 12:13 the LORD brought Israel out of E
Hos 13:4 LORD thy God from the land of E
Joel 3:19 E shall be a desolation, and Edom
Amos 2:10 brought you up from the land of E
Amos 3:1 I brought up from the land of E
Amos 3:9 in the palaces in the land of E
Amos 4:10 pestilence after the manner of E
Amos 8:8 and drowned, as by the flood of E
Amos 9:5 be drowned, as by the flood of E
Amos 9:7 up Israel out of the land of E
Mic 6:4 thee up out of the land of E
Mic 7:15 thy coming out of the land of E
Nah 3:9 E were her strength, and it was
Hag 2:5 with you when ye came out of E
Zec 10:10 again also out of the land of E
Zec 10:11 the sceptre of E shall depart
Zec 14:18 And if the family of E go not up
Zec 14:19 This shall be the punishment of E
Mt 2:13 and his mother, and flee into E
Mt 2:14 by night, and departed into E
Mt 2:15 Out of E have I called my son
Mt 2:19 in a dream to Joseph in E
Acts 2:10 Phrygia, and Pamphylia, in E
Acts 7:9 with envy, sold Joseph into E
Acts 7:10 in the sight of Pharaoh king of E
Acts 7:10 and he made him governor over E
Acts 7:11 a dearth over all the land of E
Acts 7:12 heard that there was corn in E
Acts 7:15 So Jacob went down into E
Acts 7:17 people grew and multiplied in E
Acts 7:34 of my people which is in E
Acts 7:34 now come, I will send thee into E
Acts 7:36 wonders and signs in the land of E
Acts 7:39 hearts turned back again into E
Acts 7:40 brought us out of the land of E
Acts 13:17 as strangers in the land of E
Heb 3:16 all that came out of E by Moses
Heb 8:9 to lead them out of the land of E
Heb 11:26 riches than the treasures in E
Heb 11:27 By faith he forsook E, not
Jude 5 the people out of the land of E
Rev 11:8 spiritually is called Sodom and E

**EGYPTIAN** *(e-jip'-shun)* See EGYPTIAN'S, EGYPTIANS.

*1. An inhabitant of Egypt.*
Gen 16:1 and she had an handmaid, an E
Gen 16:3 wife took Hagar her maid the E
Gen 21:9 Sarah saw the son of Hagar the E
Gen 25:12 Abraham's son, whom Hagar the E
Gen 39:1 captain of the guard, an E
Gen 39:2 in the house of his master the E
Ex 1:19 women are not as the E women
Ex 2:11 he spied an E smiting an Hebrew,
Ex 2:12 there was no man, he slew the E
Ex 2:14 kill me, as thou killedst the E
Ex 2:19 An E delivered us out of the hand
Lev 24:10 woman, whose father was an E
Deut 23:7 thou shalt not abhor an E
1Sa 30:11 And they found an E in the field
2Sa 23:21 And he slew an E, a goodly man
2Sa 23:21 the E had a spear in his hand
1Chr 2:34 And Sheshan had a servant, an E
1Chr 11:23 And he slew an E, a man of great
Is 19:23 the E into Assyria, and the
Acts 7:24 was oppressed, and smote the E
Acts 7:28 as thou diddest the E yesterday
Acts 21:38 Art not thou that E, which before

*2. The Red Sea.*
Is 11:15 destroy the tongue of the E sea

**EGYPTIANS** *(e-jip'-shuns)*
Gen 12:12 when the E shall see thee, that
Gen 12:14 the E beheld the woman that she
Gen 41:55 and Pharaoh said unto all the E
Gen 41:56 storehouses, and sold unto the E
Gen 43:32 them by themselves, and for the E
Gen 43:32 because the E might not eat bread
Gen 43:32 that is an abomination unto the E
Gen 45:2 and the E and the house of Pharaoh
Gen 46:34 is an abomination unto the E
Gen 47:15 all the E came unto Joseph, and
Gen 47:20 for the E sold every man his
Gen 50:3 the E mourned for him threescore
Gen 50:11 is a grievous mourning to the E
Ex 1:13 the E made the children of Israel
Ex 3:8 them out of the hand of the E
Ex 3:9 wherewith the E oppress them
Ex 3:21 favour in the sight of the E
Ex 3:22 and ye shall spoil the E
Ex 6:5 whom the E keep in bondage
Ex 6:6 from under the burdens of the E
Ex 6:7 from under the burdens of the E
Ex 7:5 the E shall know that I am the
Ex 7:18 the E shall lothe to drink of the
Ex 7:21 the E could not drink of the
Ex 7:24 all the E digged round about the
Ex 8:21 the houses of the E shall be full
Ex 8:26 of the E to the LORD our God
Ex 8:26 of the E before their eyes
Ex 9:11 the magicians, and upon all the E
Ex 10:6 and the houses of all the E
Ex 11:3 favour in the sight of the E
Ex 11:7 put a difference between the E
Ex 12:23 will pass through to smite the E
Ex 12:27 in Egypt, when he smote the E
Ex 12:30 and all his servants, and all the E
Ex 12:33 the E were urgent upon the people
Ex 12:35 of the E jewels of silver
Ex 12:36 favour in the sight of the E
Ex 12:36 And they spoiled the E
Ex 14:4 that the E may know that I am the
Ex 14:9 But the E pursued after them, all
Ex 14:10 behold, the E marched after them
Ex 14:12 us alone, that we may serve the E
Ex 14:12 been better for us to serve the E
Ex 14:13 for the E whom ye have seen to
Ex 14:17 I will harden the hearts of the E
Ex 14:18 the E shall know that I am the
Ex 14:20 it came between the camp of the E
Ex 14:23 the E pursued, and went in after
Ex 14:24 the E through the pillar of fire
Ex 14:24 and troubled the host of the E
Ex 14:25 so that the E said, Let us flee
Ex 14:25 fighteth for them against the E
Ex 14:26 waters may come again upon the E
Ex 14:27 and the E fled against it
Ex 14:27 the LORD overthrew the E in the
Ex 14:30 that day out of the hand of the E
Ex 14:30 Israel saw the E dead upon the
Ex 14:31 which the LORD did upon the E
Ex 15:26 which I have brought upon the E
Ex 18:8 to the E for Israel's sake, and
Ex 18:9 out of the hand of the E
Ex 18:10 you out of the hand of the E
Ex 18:10 from under the hand of the E
Ex 19:4 have seen what I did unto the E
Ex 32:12 Wherefore should the E speak
Num 14:13 Then the E shall hear it, (for
Num 20:15 the E vexed us, and our fathers
Num 33:3 hand in the sight of all the E
Num 33:4 For the E buried all their
Deut 26:6 the E evil entreated us, and
Josh 24:6 the E pursued after your fathers
Josh 24:7 put darkness between you and the E
Judg 6:9 you out of the hand of the E
Judg 10:11 Did not I deliver you from the E
1Sa 4:8 the E with all the plagues in the
1Sa 6:6 ye harden your hearts, as the E
1Sa 10:18 you out of the hand of the E
2Kin 7:6 Hittites, and the kings of the E
Ezr 9:1 Ammonites, the Moabites, the E
Is 19:2 set the E against the E
Is 19:4 the E will I give over into the
Is 19:21 the E shall know the LORD in that
Is 19:23 the E shall serve with the
Is 20:4 Assyria lead away the E prisoners
Is 30:7 For the E shall help in vain, and
Is 31:3 Now the E are men, and not God
Jer 43:13 of the E shall he burn with fire
Lam 5:6 We have given the hand to the E
Eze 16:26 with the E thy neighbours
Eze 23:21 the E for the paps of thy youth
Eze 29:12 scatter the E among the nations
Eze 29:13 E from the people whither they
Eze 30:23 scatter the E among the nations
Eze 30:26 scatter the E among the nations
Acts 7:22 in all the wisdom of the E
Heb 11:29 which the E assaying to do were

**EHI** *(e'-hi)* See AHARAH. *A son of Benjamin.*
Gen 46:21 and Ashbel, Gera, and Naaman, E

**EHUD** *(e'-hud)*

*1. A son of Gera.*
Judg 3:15 E the son of Gera, a Benjamite, a
Judg 3:16 But E made him a dagger which had
Judg 3:20 And E came unto him
Judg 3:20 E said, I have a message from God
Judg 3:21 E put forth his left hand, and
Judg 3:23 Then E went forth through the
Judg 3:26 E escaped while they tarried, and
Judg 4:1 of the LORD, when E was dead

*2. A great-grandson of Benjamin.*
1Chr 7:10 Jeush, and Benjamin, and E, and
1Chr 8:6 And these are the sons of E

**EIGHT**
Gen 5:4 Seth were e hundred years
Gen 5:7 after he begat Enos e hundred
Gen 5:10 after he begat Cainan e hundred
Gen 5:13 he begat Mahalaleel e hundred
Gen 5:16 after he begat Jared e hundred
Gen 5:17 Mahalaleel were e hundred ninety
Gen 5:19 he begat Enoch e hundred years
Gen 17:12 he that is e days old shall be
Gen 21:4 his son Isaac being e days old
Gen 22:23 these e Milcah did bear to Nahor,
Ex 26:2 length of one curtain shall be e
Ex 26:25 And they shall be e boards
Ex 36:9 e cubits, and the breadth of one
Ex 36:30 And there were e boards
Num 2:24 e thousand and an hundred,
Num 3:28 were e thousand and six hundred,
Num 4:48 were e thousand and five hundred
Num 7:8 e oxen he gave unto the sons of
Num 29:29 And on the sixth day e bullocks
Num 35:7 shall be forty and e cities
Deut 2:14 Zered, was thirty and e years
Josh 21:41 e cities with their suburbs
Judg 3:8 served Chushan-rishathaim e years
Judg 12:14 and he judged Israel e years
1Sa 4:15 Now Eli was ninety and e years old
1Sa 17:12 and he had e sons
2Sa 23:8 up his spear against e hundred
2Sa 24:9 there were in Israel e hundred
1Kin 7:10 ten cubits, and stones of e cubits
2Kin 8:17 he reigned e years in Jerusalem
2Kin 10:36 in Samaria was twenty and e years
2Kin 22:1 Josiah was e years old when he
1Chr 12:24 e hundred, ready armed to the war
1Chr 12:30 e hundred, mighty men of valour,
1Chr 12:35 e thousand and six hundred
1Chr 16:38 their brethren, threescore and e
1Chr 23:3 by man, was thirty and e thousand
1Chr 24:4 e among the sons of Ithamar
1Chr 25:7 was two hundred fourscore and e
2Chr 11:21 e sons, and threescore daughters
2Chr 13:3 in array against him with e
2Chr 21:5 he reigned e years in Jerusalem
2Chr 21:20 he reigned in Jerusalem e years
2Chr 29:17 the house of the LORD in e days
2Chr 34:1 Josiah was e years old when he
2Chr 36:9 Jehoiachin was e years old when
Ezr 2:6 and Joab, two thousand e hundred
Ezr 2:16 of Ater of Hezekiah, ninety and e
Ezr 2:23 Anathoth, an hundred twenty and e
Ezr 2:41 of Asaph, an hundred twenty and e

Ezr 8:11 and with him twenty and *e* males
Neh 7:11 thousand and *e* hundred and eighteen
Neh 7:13 of Zattu, *e* hundred forty and five
Neh 7:15 of Binnui, six hundred forty and *e*
Neh 7:16 of Bebai, six hundred twenty and *e*
Neh 7:21 of Ater of Hezekiah, ninety and *e*
Neh 7:22 Hashum, three hundred twenty and *e*
Neh 7:26 an hundred fourscore and *e*
Neh 7:27 Anathoth, an hundred twenty and *e*
Neh 7:44 of Asaph, an hundred forty and *e*
Neh 7:45 of Shobai, an hundred thirty and *e*
Neh 11:6 threescore and *e* valiant men
Neh 11:8 Sallai, nine hundred twenty and *e*
Neh 11:12 the house were *e* hundred twenty
Neh 11:14 of valour, an hundred twenty and *e*
Eccl 11:2 a portion to seven, and also to *e*
Jer 41:15 escaped from Johanan with *e* men
Jer 52:29 from Jerusalem *e* hundred thirty
Eze 40:9 the porch of the gate, *e* cubits
Eze 40:31 and the going up to it had *e* steps
Eze 40:34 and the going up to it had *e* steps
Eze 40:37 and the going up to it had *e* steps
Eze 40:41 *e* tables, whereupon they slew
Mic 5:5 shepherds, and *e* principal men
Lk 2:21 when *e* days were accomplished for
Lk 9:28 an *e* days after these sayings
Jn 5:5 an infirmity thirty and *e* years
Jn 20:26 after *e* days again his disciples
Acts 9:33 which had kept his bed *e* years
1Pet 3:20 *e* souls were saved by water

**EIGHTEEN**
Gen 14:14 house, three hundred and *e*
Judg 3:14 Eglon the king of Moab *e* years
Judg 10:8 *e* years, all the children of
Judg 20:25 of Israel again *e* thousand men
Judg 20:44 fell of Benjamin *e* thousand men
2Sa 8:13 of salt, being *e* thousand men
1Kin 7:15 of brass, of *e* cubits high apiece
2Kin 24:8 Jehoiachin was *e* years old when
2Kin 25:17 of the one pillar was *e* cubits
1Chr 12:31 tribe of Manasseh *e* thousand
1Chr 18:12 in the valley of salt *e* thousand
1Chr 26:9 sons and brethren, strong men, *e*
1Chr 29:7 of brass *e* thousand talents, and
2Chr 11:21 (for he took *e* wives, and
Ezr 8:9 with him two hundred and *e* males
Ezr 8:18 with his sons and his brethren, *e*
Neh 7:11 thousand and eight hundred and *e*
Jer 52:21 height of one pillar was *e* cubits
Eze 48:35 round about *e* thousand measures
Lk 13:4 those *e*, upon whom the tower
Lk 13:11 a spirit of infirmity *e* years
Lk 13:16 hath bound, lo, these *e* years

**EIGHTEENTH**
1Kin 15:1 Now in the *e* year of king
2Kin 3:1 over Israel in Samaria the *e* year
2Kin 22:3 pass in the *e* year of king Josiah
2Kin 23:23 But in the *e* year of king Josiah,
1Chr 24:15 to Hezir, the *e* to Aphses,
1Chr 25:25 The *e* to Hanani, he, his sons
2Chr 13:1 Now in the *e* year of king
2Chr 34:8 Now in the *e* year of his reign,
2Chr 35:19 In the *e* year of the reign of
Jer 32:1 of Judah, which was the *e* year of
Jer 52:29 In the *e* year of Nebuchadrezzar

**EIGHTH**
Ex 22:30 on the *e* day thou shalt give it
Lev 9:1 And it came to pass on the *e* day
Lev 12:3 in the *e* day the flesh of his
Lev 14:10 on the *e* day he shall take two he
Lev 14:23 he shall bring them on the *e* day
Lev 15:14 on the *e* day he shall take to him
Lev 15:29 on the *e* day she shall take unto
Lev 22:27 and from the *e* day and thenceforth
Lev 23:36 on the *e* day shall be an holy
Lev 23:39 on the *e* day shall be a sabbath
Lev 25:22 And ye shall sow the *e* year
Num 6:10 on the *e* day he shall bring two
Num 7:54 On the *e* day offered Gamaliel the
Num 29:35 On the *e* day ye shall have a
1Kin 6:38 month Bul, which is the *e* month
1Kin 8:66 On the *e* day he sent the people
1Kin 12:32 ordained a feast in the *e* month
1Kin 12:33 the fifteenth day of the *e* month
1Kin 16:29 *e* year of Asa king of Judah began
2Kin 15:8 *e* year of Azariah king of Judah
2Kin 24:12 him in the *e* year of his reign
1Chr 12:12 Johanan the *e*, Elzabad the ninth,
1Chr 24:10 to Hakkoz, the *e* to Abijah,
1Chr 25:15 The *e* to Jeshaiah, he, his sons,
1Chr 26:5 the seventh, Peulthai the *e*
1Chr 27:11 *e* captain for the *e* month
2Chr 7:9 in the *e* day they made a solemn
2Chr 29:17 on the *e* day of the month came
2Chr 34:3 For in the *e* year of his reign,
Neh 8:18 on the *e* day was a solemn
Eze 43:27 it shall be, that upon the *e* day
Zec 1:1 In the *e* month, in the second
Lk 1:59 that on the *e* day they came to
Acts 7:8 and circumcised him the *e* day
Phil 3:5 Circumcised the *e* day, of the
2Pet 2:5 but saved Noah the *e* person
Rev 17:11 was, and is not, even he is the *e*
Rev 21:20 the *e*, beryl

**EKER** *(e'-ker) Descendant of Judah.*
1Chr 2:27 were, Maaz, and Jamin, and *E*

**EKRON** *(ec'-ron)* See EKRONITES. *A Philistine city.*
Josh 13:3 unto the borders of *E* northward
Josh 15:11 out unto the side of *E* northward
Josh 15:45 *E*, with her towns and her villages
Josh 15:46 From *E* even unto the sea, all
Josh 19:43 And Elon, and Thimnathah, and *E*
Judg 1:18 and *E* with the coast thereof
1Sa 5:10 they sent the ark of God to *E*
1Sa 5:10 pass, as the ark of God came to *E*
1Sa 6:16 they returned to *E* the same day
1Sa 6:17 one, for Gath one, for *E* one
1Sa 7:14 to Israel, from *E* even unto Gath
1Sa 17:52 the valley, and to the gates of *E*
1Sa 17:52 even unto Gath, and unto *E*
2Kin 1:2 of Baal-zebub the god of *E*
2Kin 1:3 of Baal-zebub the god of *E*
2Kin 1:6 of Baal-zebub the god of *E*
2Kin 1:16 of Baal-zebub the god of *E*
Jer 25:20 and Ashkelon, and Azzah, and *E*
Amos 1:8 I will turn mine hand against *E*
Zeph 2:4 noonday, and *E* shall be rooted up
Zec 9:5 it, and be very sorrowful, and *E*
Zec 9:7 in Judah, and *E* as a Jebusite

**EKRONITES** *(ek'-ron-ites) Inhabitants of Ekron.*
Josh 13:3 the Gittites, and the *E*
1Sa 5:10 that the *E* cried out, saying,

**ELADAH** *(el'-a-dah) A descendant of Ephraim.*
1Chr 7:20 *E* his son, and Tahath his son,

**ELAH** *(e'-lah)*
*1. An Edomite prince.*
Gen 36:41 Duke Aholibamah, duke *E*, duke
1Chr 1:52 Duke Aholibamah, duke *E*, duke
*2. A valley in Judah.*
1Sa 17:2 and pitched by the valley of *E*
1Sa 17:19 Israel, were in the valley of *E*
1Sa 21:9 thou slewest in the valley of *E*
*3. Father of Shimei.*
1Kin 4:18 Shimei the son of *E*, in Benjamin
*4. Son of King Baasha of Israel.*
1Kin 16:6 *E* his son reigned in his stead
1Kin 16:8 *E* the son of Baasha to reign over
1Kin 16:13 Baasha, and the sins of *E* his son
1Kin 16:14 Now the rest of the acts of *E*
*5. Father of King Hoshea of Israel.*
2Kin 15:30 Hoshea the son of *E* made a
2Kin 17:1 Judah began Hoshea the son of *E*
2Kin 18:1 of Hoshea son of *E* king of Israel
2Kin 18:9 of Hoshea son of *E* king of Israel
*6. A son of Caleb.*
1Chr 4:15 of Jephunneh; Iru, *E*
1Chr 4:15 and the sons of *E*, even Kenaz
*7. A Benjamite.*
1Chr 9:8 *E* the son of Uzzi, the son of

**ELAM** *(e'-lam)* See ELAMITES, PERSIA.
*1. A son of Shem.*
Gen 10:22 *E*, and Asshur, and Arphaxad, and Lud
1Chr 1:17 *E*, and Asshur, and Arphaxad, and Lud
*2. Land of the Elamites.*
Gen 14:1 Ellasar, Chedorlaomer king of *E*
Gen 14:9 With Chedorlaomer the king of *E*
Is 11:11 Pathros, and from Cush, and from *E*
Is 21:2 Go up, O *E*:
Is 22:6 *E* bare the quiver with chariots
Jer 25:25 of Zimri, and all the kings of *E*
Jer 49:34 *E* in the beginning of the reign
Jer 49:35 Behold, I will break the bow of *E*
Jer 49:36 upon *E* will I bring the four
Jer 49:36 the outcasts of *E* shall not come
Jer 49:37 For I will cause *E* to be dismayed
Jer 49:38 And I will set my throne in *E*
Jer 49:39 bring again the captivity of *E*
Eze 32:24 There is *E* and all her multitude
Dan 8:2 which is in the province of *E*
*3. Son of Shashak.*
1Chr 8:24 And Hananiah, and *E*, and Antothijah,
*4. A son of Meshelemiah.*
1Chr 26:3 *E* the fifth, Jehohanan the sixth,
*5. A family of exiles with Zerubbabel.*
Ezr 2:7 The children of *E*, a thousand two
Neh 7:12 The children of *E*, a thousand two
*6. A family of exiles with Zerubbabel.*
Ezr 2:31 The children of the other *E*
Neh 7:34 The children of the other *E*
*7. A family of exiles with Ezra.*
Ezr 8:7 And of the sons of *E*
*8. An ancestor of Shechaniah.*
Ezr 10:2 of Jehiel, one of the sons of *E*
Ezr 10:26 And of the sons of *E*
*9. A chief who renewed the covenant.*
Neh 10:14 Parosh, Pahath-moab, *E*, Zatthu,
*10. A priest who purified the wall.*
Neh 12:42 and Jehohanan, and Malchijah, and *E*

**ELAMITES** *(e'-lam-ites)* See PERSIANS. *Foreign settlers in Samaria.*
Ezr 4:9 the Dehavites, and the *E*,
Acts 2:9 Parthians, and Medes, and *E*

**ELASAH** *(el'-a-sah)* See ELEASAH.
*1. Married a foreign wife.*
Ezr 10:22 Ishmael, Nethaneel, Jozabad, and *E*
*2. An ambassador of Hezekiah.*
Jer 29:3 By the hand of *E* the son of

**ELATH** *(e'-lath)* See ELOTH. *An Elamite port.*
Deut 2:8 the way of the plain from *E*
2Kin 14:22 He built *E*, and restored it to
2Kin 16:6 of Syria recovered *E* to Syria
2Kin 16:6 and drave the Jews from *E*
2Kin 16:6 and the Syrians came to *E*, and

**EL-BETH-EL** *Another name for Bethel.*
Gen 35:7 an altar, and called the place *E*

**ELDAAH** *(el'-da-ah) A son of Midian.*
Gen 25:4 Epher, and Hanoch, and Abidah, and *E*
1Chr 1:33 Epher, and Henoch, and Abida, and *E*

**ELDAD** *(el'-dad) An elder and prophet with Moses.*
Num 11:26 camp, the name of the one was *E*
Num 11:27 man, and told Moses, and said, *E*

**ELDER**
Gen 10:21 the brother of Japheth the *e*
Gen 25:23 the *e* shall serve the younger
Gen 27:42 these words of Esau her *e* son
Gen 29:16 the name of the *e* was Leah
1Sa 18:17 Behold my *e* daughter Merab, her
1Kin 2:22 for he is mine *e* brother
Job 15:10 aged men, much *e* than thy father
Job 32:4 because they were *e* than he
Eze 16:46 thine *e* sister is Samaria, she and
Eze 16:61 receive thy sisters, thine *e*
Eze 23:4 names of them were Aholah the *e*
Lk 15:25 Now his *e* son was in the field
Rom 9:12 The *e* shall serve the younger
1Ti 5:1 Rebuke not an *e*, but intreat him
1Ti 5:2 The *e* women as mothers
1Ti 5:19 Against an *e* receive not an
1Pet 5:1 you I exhort, who am also an *e*
1Pet 5:5 submit yourselves unto the *e*
2Jn 1 The *e* unto the elect lady and her
3Jn 1 The *e* unto the wellbeloved Gaius,

**ELDERS**
Gen 50:7 of Pharaoh, the *e* of his house
Gen 50:7 all the *e* of the land of Egypt,
Ex 3:16 gather the *e* of Israel together,
Ex 3:18 the *e* of Israel, unto the king of
Ex 4:29 the *e* of the children of Israel
Ex 12:21 called for all the *e* of Israel
Ex 17:5 take with thee of the *e* of Israel
Ex 17:6 in the sight of the *e* of Israel
Ex 18:12 all the *e* of Israel, to eat bread
Ex 19:7 and called for the *e* of the people
Ex 24:1 and seventy of the *e* of Israel
Ex 24:9 and seventy of the *e* of Israel
Ex 24:14 And he said unto the *e*, Tarry ye
Lev 4:15 the *e* of the congregation shall
Lev 9:1 and his sons, and the *e* of Israel
Num 11:16 me seventy men of the *e* of Israel

Num 11:16 knowest to be the *e* of the people
Num 11:24 men of the *e* of the people
Num 11:25 and gave it unto the seventy *e*
Num 11:30 the camp, he and the *e* of Israel
Num 16:25 the *e* of Israel followed him
Num 22:4 And Moab said unto the *e* of Midian
Num 22:7 *e* of Moab and the *e* of Midian
Deut 5:23 heads of your tribes, and your *e*
Deut 19:12 Then the *e* of his city shall send
Deut 21:2 Then thy *e* and thy judges shall
Deut 21:3 even the *e* of that city shall
Deut 21:4 the *e* of that city shall bring
Deut 21:6 all the *e* of that city, that are
Deut 21:19 him out unto the *e* of his city
Deut 21:20 shall say unto the *e* of his city
Deut 22:15 the *e* of the city in the gate
Deut 22:16 father shall say unto the *e*
Deut 22:17 cloth before the *e* of the city
Deut 22:18 the *e* of that city shall take
Deut 25:7 wife go up to the gate unto the *e*
Deut 25:8 Then the *e* of his city shall call
Deut 25:9 unto him in the presence of the *e*
Deut 27:1 Moses with the *e* of Israel
Deut 29:10 captains of your tribes, your *e*
Deut 31:9 LORD, and unto all the *e* of Israel
Deut 31:28 unto me all the *e* of your tribes
Deut 32:7 thy *e*, and they will tell thee
Josh 7:6 the *e* of Israel, and put dust upon
Josh 8:10 the *e* of Israel, before the
Josh 8:33 And all Israel, and their *e*
Josh 9:11 Wherefore our *e* and all the
Josh 20:4 in the ears of the *e* of that city
Josh 23:2 for all Israel, and for their *e*
Josh 24:1 and called for the *e* of Israel
Josh 24:31 all the days of the *e* that
Judg 2:7 all the days of the *e* that
Judg 8:14 the *e* thereof, even threescore and
Judg 8:16 And he took the *e* of the city
Judg 11:5 the *e* of Gilead went to fetch
Judg 11:7 said unto the *e* of Gilead
Judg 11:8 the *e* of Gilead said unto
Judg 11:9 said unto the *e* of Gilead
Judg 11:10 the *e* of Gilead said unto
Judg 11:11 went with the *e* of Gilead
Judg 21:16 Then the *e* of the congregation
Ruth 4:2 took ten men of the *e* of the city
Ruth 4:4 before the *e* of my people
Ruth 4:9 And Boaz said unto the *e*, and unto
Ruth 4:11 that were in the gate, and the *e*
1Sa 4:3 the *e* of Israel said, Wherefore
1Sa 8:4 Then all the *e* of Israel gathered
1Sa 11:3 the *e* of Jabesh said unto him,
1Sa 15:30 before the *e* of my people, and
1Sa 16:4 the *e* of the town trembled at his
1Sa 30:26 of the spoil unto the *e* of Judah
2Sa 3:17 with the *e* of Israel, saying, Ye
2Sa 5:3 So all the *e* of Israel came to
2Sa 12:17 the *e* of his house arose, and went
2Sa 17:4 well, and all the *e* of Israel
2Sa 17:15 Absalom and the *e* of Israel
2Sa 19:11 saying, Speak unto the *e* of Judah
1Kin 8:1 Solomon assembled the *e* of Israel
1Kin 8:3 all the *e* of Israel came, and the
1Kin 20:7 called all the *e* of the land
1Kin 20:8 And all the *e* and all the people
1Kin 21:8 and sent the letters unto the *e*
1Kin 21:11 the men of his city, even the *e*
2Kin 6:32 his house, and the *e* sat with him
2Kin 6:32 came to him, he said to the *e*
2Kin 10:1 the rulers of Jezreel, to the *e*
2Kin 10:5 the *e* also, and the bringers up of
2Kin 19:2 the *e* of the priests, covered
2Kin 23:1 unto him all the *e* of Judah
1Chr 11:3 Therefore came all the *e* of
1Chr 15:25 the *e* of Israel, and the captains
1Chr 21:16 the *e* of Israel, who were clothed
2Chr 5:2 Solomon assembled the *e* of Israel
2Chr 5:4 And all the *e* of Israel came
2Chr 34:29 together all the *e* of Judah
Ezr 5:5 God was upon the *e* of the Jews
Ezr 5:9 Then asked we those *e*, and said
Ezr 6:7 the *e* of the Jews build this
Ezr 6:8 *e* of these Jews for the building
Ezr 6:14 the *e* of the Jews builded, and
Ezr 10:8 counsel of the princes and the *e*
Ezr 10:14 and with them the *e* of every city
Ps 107:32 him in the assembly of the *e*
Prov 31:23 sitteth among the *e* of the land
Is 37:2 the *e* of the priests covered with
Jer 26:17 up certain of the *e* of the land
Jer 29:1 of the *e* which were carried away
Lam 1:19 mine *e* gave up the ghost in the
Lam 2:10 The *e* of the daughter of Zion sit
Lam 4:16 priests, they favoured not the *e*
Lam 5:12 the faces of *e* were not honoured
Lam 5:14 The *e* have ceased from the gate,
Eze 8:1 the *e* of Judah sat before me,
Eze 14:1 of the *e* of Israel unto me
Eze 20:1 that certain of the *e* of Israel
Eze 20:3 man, speak unto the *e* of Israel
Joel 1:14 a solemn assembly, gather the *e*
Joel 2:16 the congregation, assemble the *e*
Mt 15:2 transgress the tradition of the *e*
Mt 16:21 and suffer many things of the *e*
Mt 21:23 the *e* of the people came unto him
Mt 26:3 the *e* of the people, unto the
Mt 26:47 chief priests and *e* of the people
Mt 26:57 scribes and the *e* were assembled
Mt 26:59 Now the chief priests, and *e*
Mt 27:1 *e* of the people took counsel
Mt 27:3 silver to the chief priests and *e*
Mt 27:12 accused of the chief priests and *e*
Mt 27:20 *e* persuaded the multitude that
Mt 27:41 him, with the scribes and *e*
Mt 28:12 they were assembled with the *e*
Mk 7:3 holding the tradition of the *e*
Mk 7:5 to the tradition of the *e*
Mk 8:31 things, and be rejected of the *e*
Mk 11:27 priests, and the scribes, and the *e*
Mk 14:43 priest and the scribes and the *e*
Mk 14:53 all the chief priests and the *e*
Mk 15:1 held a consultation with the *e*
Lk 7:3 sent unto him the *e* of the Jews
Lk 9:22 things, and be rejected of the *e*
Lk 20:1 scribes came upon him with the *e*
Lk 22:52 captains of the temple, and the *e*
Lk 22:66 the *e* of the people and the chief
Acts 4:5 morrow, that their rulers, and *e*
Acts 4:8 of the people, and *e* of Israel,
Acts 4:23 priests and *e* had said unto them
Acts 6:12 stirred up the people, and the *e*
Acts 11:30 sent it to the *e* by the hands of
Acts 14:23 ordained them *e* in every church
Acts 15:2 apostles and *e* about this question
Acts 15:4 church, and of the apostles and *e*
Acts 15:6 *e* came together for to consider
Acts 15:22 Then pleased it the apostles and *e*
Acts 15:23 The apostles and *e* and brethren
Acts 16:4 *e* which were at Jerusalem
Acts 20:17 called the *e* of the church
Acts 21:18 and all the *e* were present
Acts 22:5 and all the estate of the *e*
Acts 23:14 came to the chief priests and *e*
Acts 24:1 high priest descended with the *e*
Acts 25:15 the *e* of the Jews informed me,
1Ti 5:17 Let the *e* that rule well be
Titus 1:5 ordain *e* in every city, as I had
Heb 11:2 For by it the *e* obtained a good
Jas 5:14 him call for the *e* of the church
1Pet 5:1 The *e* which are among you I
Rev 4:4 twenty *e* sitting, clothed in
Rev 4:10 twenty *e* fall down before him
Rev 5:5 one of the *e* saith unto me, Weep
Rev 5:6 beasts, and in the midst of the *e*
Rev 5:8 twenty *e* fell down before the
Rev 5:11 the throne and the beasts and the *e*
Rev 5:14 twenty *e* fell down and worshipped
Rev 7:11 about the throne, and about the *e*
Rev 7:13 And one of the *e* answered, saying
Rev 11:16 And the four and twenty *e*, which
Rev 14:3 before the four beasts, and the *e*
Rev 19:4 And the four and twenty *e* and the

**ELDEST**
Gen 24:2 unto his *e* servant of his house
Gen 27:1 not see, he called Esau his *e* son
Gen 27:15 goodly raiment of her *e* son Esau
Gen 44:12 And he searched, and began at the *e*
Num 1:20 of Reuben, Israel's *e* son
Num 26:5 Reuben, the *e* son of Israel
1Sa 17:13 the three *e* sons of Jesse went and
1Sa 17:14 the three *e* followed Saul
1Sa 17:28 Eliab his *e* brother heard when he
2Kin 3:27 Then he took his *e* son that
2Chr 22:1 to the camp had slain all the *e*
Job 1:13 wine in their *e* brother's house
Job 1:18 wine in their *e* brother's house
Jn 8:9 one by one, beginning at the *e*

**ELEAD** *(e'-le-ad) A descendant of Ephraim.*
1Chr 7:21 Shuthelah his son, and Ezer, and *E*

**ELEALEH** *(el-e-a'-leh) An Amorite village.*
Num 32:3 and Nimrah, and Heshbon, and *E*
Num 32:37 of Reuben built Heshbon, and *E*
Is 15:4 And Heshbon shall cry, and *E*
Is 16:9 with my tears, O Heshbon, and *E*
Jer 48:34 the cry of Heshbon even unto *E*

**ELEASAH** *(el-e'-a-sah)* See ELASAH.
*1. A son of Helez.*
1Chr 2:39 begat Helez, and Helez begat *E*
1Chr 2:40 *E* begat Sisamai, and Sisamai begat
*2. A descendant of King Saul.*
1Chr 8:37 his son, *E* his son, Azel his son
1Chr 9:43 his son, *E* his son, Azel his son

**ELEAZAR** *(el-e-a'-zar)*
*1. A son of Aaron.*
Ex 6:23 she bare him Nadab, and Abihu, *E*
Ex 6:25 *E* Aaron's son took him one of the
Ex 28:1 even Aaron, Nadab and Abihu, *E*
Lev 10:6 Moses said unto Aaron, and unto *E*
Lev 10:12 Moses spake unto Aaron, and unto *E*
Lev 10:16 and he was angry with *E* and Ithamar
Num 3:2 Nadab the firstborn, and Abihu, *E*
Num 3:4 and *E* and Ithamar ministered in the
Num 3:32 *E* the son of Aaron the priest
Num 4:16 to the office of *E* the son of
Num 16:37 Speak unto *E* the son of Aaron the
Num 16:39 *E* the priest took the brasen
Num 19:3 shall give her unto *E* the priest
Num 19:4 *E* the priest shall take of her
Num 20:25 *E* his son, and bring them up unto
Num 20:26 and put them upon *E* his son
Num 20:28 and put them upon *E* his son
Num 20:28 *E* came down from the mount
Num 25:7 And when Phinehas, the son of *E*
Num 25:11 Phinehas, the son of *E*, the son
Num 26:1 unto *E* the son of Aaron the
Num 26:3 *E* the priest spake with them in
Num 26:60 Aaron was born Nadab, and Abihu, *E*
Num 26:63 *E* the priest, who numbered the
Num 27:2 before *E* the priest, and before
Num 27:19 And set him before *E* the priest
Num 27:21 shall stand before *E* the priest
Num 27:22 and set him before *E* the priest
Num 31:6 Phinehas the son of *E* the priest
Num 31:12 *E* the priest, and unto the
Num 31:13 *E* the priest, and all the princes
Num 31:21 *E* the priest said unto the men of
Num 31:26 *E* the priest, and the chief
Num 31:29 and give it unto *E* the priest
Num 31:31 *E* the priest did as the LORD
Num 31:41 unto *E* the priest, as the LORD
Num 31:51 *E* the priest took the gold of
Num 31:54 *E* the priest took the gold of the
Num 32:2 to *E* the priest, and unto the
Num 32:28 them Moses commanded *E* the priest
Num 34:17 *E* the priest, and Joshua the son
Deut 10:6 *E* his son ministered in the
Josh 14:1 which *E* the priest, and Joshua the
Josh 17:4 came near before *E* the priest
Josh 19:51 which *E* the priest, and Joshua the
Josh 21:1 of the Levites unto *E* the priest
Josh 22:13 Phinehas the son of *E* the priest
Josh 22:31 Phinehas the son of *E* the priest
Josh 22:32 Phinehas the son of *E* the priest
Josh 24:33 And *E* the son of Aaron died
Judg 20:28 And Phinehas, the son of *E*
1Chr 6:3 Nadab, and Abihu, *E*, and Ithamar
1Chr 6:4 *E* begat Phinehas, Phinehas begat
1Chr 6:50 *E* his son, Phinehas his son,
1Chr 9:20 Phinehas the son of *E* was the
1Chr 24:1 Nadab, and Abihu, *E*, and Ithamar
1Chr 24:2 therefore *E* and Ithamar executed
1Chr 24:3 them, both Zadok of the sons of *E*
1Chr 24:4 of *E* than of the sons of Ithamar
1Chr 24:4 Among the sons of *E* there were
1Chr 24:5 of God, were of the sons of *E*
1Chr 24:6 household being taken for *E*
Ezr 7:5 the son of Phinehas, the son of *E*
*2. Son of Abinadab.*
1Sa 7:1 sanctified *E* his son to keep the
*3. A son of Dodo.*
2Sa 23:9 after him was *E* the son of Dodo
1Chr 11:12 after him was *E* the son of Dodo,

*4. Son of Mahli.*
1Chr 23:21 The sons of Mahli; *E*, and Kish
1Chr 23:22 *E* died, and had no sons, but
1Chr 24:28 Of Mahli came *E*, who had no sons
*5. Son of Phinehas.*
Ezr 8:33 with him was *E* the son of
*6. Married a foreign wife.*
Ezr 10:25 and Malchiah, and Miamin, and *E*
*7. A priest in Nehemiah's time.*
Neh 12:42 And Maaseiah, and Shemaiah, and *E*
*8. Son of Eliud; ancestor of Jesus.*
Mt 1:15 And Eliud begat *E*
Mt 1:15 and *E* begat Matthan

**ELECT**
Is 42:1 mine *e*, in whom my soul
Is 45:4 servant's sake, and Israel mine *e*
Is 65:9 mine *e* shall inherit it, and my
Is 65:22 mine *e* shall long enjoy the work
Mt 24:24 they shall deceive the very *e*
Mt 24:31 his *e* from the four winds
Mk 13:22 if it were possible, even the *e*
Mk 13:27 his *e* from the four winds
Lk 18:7 And shall not God avenge his own *e*
Rom 8:33 thing to the charge of God's *e*
Col 3:12 Put on therefore, as the *e* of God
1Ti 5:21 the *e* angels, that thou observe
Titus 1:1 according to the faith of God's *e*
1Pet 1:2 *E* according to the foreknowledge
1Pet 2:6 in Sion a chief corner stone, *e*
2Jn 1 The elder unto the *e* lady
2Jn 13 of thy *e* sister greet thee

**ELECTION**
Rom 9:11 of God according to *e* might stand
Rom 11:5 according to the *e* of grace
Rom 11:7 but the *e* hath obtained it, and
Rom 11:28 but as touching the *e*, they are
1Th 1:4 brethren beloved, your *e* of God
2Pet 1:10 to make your calling and *e* sure

**ELECT'S**
Mt 24:22 but for the *e* sake those days
Mk 13:20 but for the *e* sake, whom he hath
2Ti 2:10 endure all things for the *e* sakes

**EL-ELOHE-ISRAEL** *(el-el-o'-he-iz'-rah-el) An altar of Jacob near Shechem.*
Gen 33:20 there an altar, and called it *E*

**ELEMENTS**
Gal 4:3 bondage under the *e* of the world
Gal 4:9 again to the weak and beggarly *e*
2Pet 3:10 the *e* shall melt with fervent
2Pet 3:12 the *e* shall melt with fervent

**ELEPH** *(e'-lef) A town in Benjamin.*
Josh 18:28 And Zelah, *E*, and Jebusi, which is

**ELEVEN**
Gen 32:22 his *e* sons, and passed over the
Gen 37:9 the *e* stars made obeisance to me
Ex 26:7 *e* curtains shalt thou make
Ex 26:8 the *e* curtains shall be all of
Ex 36:14 *e* curtains he made them
Ex 36:15 the *e* curtains were of one size
Num 29:20 And on the third day *e* bullocks
Deut 1:2 (There are *e* days' journey from
Josh 15:51 *e* cities with their villages
Judg 16:5 of us *e* hundred pieces of silver
Judg 17:2 The *e* hundred shekels of silver
Judg 17:3 when he had restored the *e*
2Kin 23:36 he reigned *e* years in Jerusalem
2Kin 24:18 he reigned *e* years in Jerusalem
2Chr 36:5 he reigned *e* years in Jerusalem
2Chr 36:11 reigned *e* years in Jerusalem
Jer 52:1 he reigned *e* years in Jerusalem
Eze 40:49 cubits, and the breadth *e* cubits
Mt 28:16 Then the *e* disciples went away
Mk 16:14 unto the *e* as they sat at meat
Lk 24:9 told all these things unto the *e*
Lk 24:33 found the *e* gathered together, and
Acts 1:26 was numbered with the *e* apostles
Acts 2:14 But Peter, standing up with the *e*

**ELEVENTH**
Num 7:72 On the *e* day Pagiel the son of
Deut 1:3 the fortieth year, in the *e* month
1Kin 6:38 And in the *e* year, in the month
2Kin 9:29 in the *e* year of Joram the son of
2Kin 25:2 unto the *e* year of king Zedekiah
1Chr 12:13 the tenth, Machbanai the *e*
1Chr 24:12 The *e* to Eliashib, the twelfth to
1Chr 25:18 The *e* to Azareel, he, his sons,
1Chr 27:14 The *e* captain for the *e*
Jer 1:3 unto the end of the *e* year of
Jer 39:2 in the *e* year of Zedekiah, in the
Jer 52:5 unto the *e* year of king Zedekiah
Eze 26:1 And it came to pass in the *e* year
Eze 30:20 And it came to pass in the *e* year
Eze 31:1 And it came to pass in the *e* year
Zec 1:7 and twentieth day of the *e* month
Mt 20:6 about the *e* hour he went out, and
Mt 20:9 that were hired about the *e* hour
Rev 21:20 the *e*, a jacinth

**ELHANAN** *(el-ha'-nan)*
*1. Son of Jair.*
2Sa 21:19 where *E* the son of Jaare-oregim,
1Chr 20:5 *E* the son of Jair slew Lahmi the
*2. Son of Dodo.*
2Sa 23:24 *E* the son of Dodo of Beth-lehem,
1Chr 11:26 *E* the son of Dodo of Beth-lehem,

**ELI** *(e'-li)* See ELI'S, ELOI.
*1. A High Priest of Israel.*
1Sa 1:3 And the two sons of *E*, Hophni and
1Sa 1:9 Now *E* the priest sat upon a seat
1Sa 1:12 the LORD, that *E* marked her mouth
1Sa 1:13 therefore *E* thought she had been
1Sa 1:14 *E* said unto her, How long wilt
1Sa 1:17 Then *E* answered and said, Go in
1Sa 1:25 and brought the child to *E*
1Sa 2:11 unto the LORD before *E* the priest
1Sa 2:12 Now the sons of *E* were sons of
1Sa 2:20 *E* blessed Elkanah and his wife, and
1Sa 2:22 Now *E* was very old, and heard all
1Sa 2:27 And there came a man of God unto *E*
1Sa 3:1 ministered unto the LORD before *E*
1Sa 3:2 when *E* was laid down in his place
1Sa 3:5 And he ran unto *E*, and said, Here
1Sa 3:6 And Samuel arose and went to *E*
1Sa 3:8 And he arose and went to *E*, and said
1Sa 3:8 *E* perceived that the LORD had
1Sa 3:9 Therefore *E* said unto Samuel, Go,
1Sa 3:12 *E* all things which I have spoken
1Sa 3:14 I have sworn unto the house of *E*
1Sa 3:15 feared to shew *E* the vision
1Sa 3:16 Then *E* called Samuel, and said,
1Sa 4:4 and the two sons of *E*, Hophni and
1Sa 4:11 and the two sons of *E*, Hophni and
1Sa 4:13 *E* sat upon a seat by the wayside
1Sa 4:14 when *E* heard the noise of the
1Sa 4:14 man came in hastily, and told *E*
1Sa 4:15 Now *E* was ninety and eight years
1Sa 4:16 And the man said unto *E*, I am he
1Sa 14:3 the son of Phinehas, the son of *E*
1Kin 2:27 the house of *E* in Shiloh
*2. An Aramaic term for God.*
Mt 27:46 with a loud voice, saying, Eli, *E*

**ELIAB** *(e'-le-ab)* See ELIAB'S, ELIEL.
*1. Son of Helon.*
Num 1:9 *E* the son of Helon
Num 2:7 *E* the son of Helon shall be
Num 7:24 the third day *E* the son of Helon
Num 7:29 offering of *E* the son of Helon
Num 10:16 of Zebulun was *E* the son of Helon
*2. Father of Dathan.*
Num 16:1 Dathan and Abiram, the sons of *E*
Num 16:12 Dathan and Abiram, the sons of *E*
Num 26:8 the sons of Pallu; *E*
Num 26:9 And the sons of *E*
Deut 11:6 Dathan and Abiram, the sons of *E*
*3. A son of Jesse.*
1Sa 16:6 were come, that he looked on *E*
1Sa 17:13 the battle were *E* the first born
1Sa 17:28 *E* his eldest brother heard when
1Chr 2:13 And Jesse begat his firstborn *E*
2Chr 11:18 daughter of *E* the son of Jesse
*4. A Levite ancestor of Samuel.*
1Chr 6:27 *E* his son, Jeroham his son,
*5. A leader in David's army.*
1Chr 12:9 Obadiah the second, *E* the third,
*6. A Levite in David's time.*
1Chr 15:18 and Jehiel, and Unni, *E*, and
1Chr 15:20 and Jehiel, and Unni, and *E*
1Chr 16:5 and Jehiel, and Mattithiah, and *E*

**ELIAB'S** *(e'-le-abs)*
1Sa 17:28 *E* anger was kindled against David

**ELIADA** *(e'-li'-a-dah)* See ELIADAH.
*1. A son of David.*
2Sa 5:16 And Elishama, and *E*, and Eliphalet
1Chr 3:8 And Elishama, and *E*, and Eliphelet,
2Chr 17:17 *E* a mighty man of valour, and with

**ELIADAH** *(e-li'-a-dah)* See ELIADA. *An opponent of King Saul.*
1Kin 11:23 adversary, Rezon the son of *E*

**ELIAH** *(e-li'-ah)* See ELIJAH. *A son of Jeroham.*
1Chr 8:27 And Jaresiah, and *E*, and Zichri, the
Ezr 10:26 and Abdi, and Jeremoth, and *E*

**ELIAHBA** *(e-li'-ah-bah) A "mighty man" of David.*
2Sa 23:32 *E* the Shaalbonite, of the sons of
1Chr 11:33 Baharumite, *E* the Shaalbonite,

**ELIAKIM** *(e-li'-a-kim)* See JEHOIAKIM.
*1. A son of Hilkiah.*
2Kin 18:18 out to them *E* the son of Hilkiah
2Kin 18:26 Then said *E* the son of Hilkiah,
2Kin 18:37 Then came *E* the son of Hilkiah,
2Kin 19:2 And he sent *E*, which was over the
Is 22:20 my servant *E* the son of Hilkiah
Is 36:3 Then came forth unto him *E*
Is 36:11 Then said *E* and Shebna and Joah
Is 36:22 Then came *E*, the son of Hilkiah,
Is 37:2 And he sent *E*, who was over the
*2. Original name of Jehoiakim.*
2Kin 23:34 Pharaoh-nechoh made *E* the son of
2Chr 36:4 the king of Egypt made *E* his
*3. A priest who dedicated the wall.*
Neh 12:41 *E*, Maaseiah, Miniamin, Michaiah,
*4. Son of Abiud; ancestor of Jesus.*
Mt 1:13 and Abiud begat *E*
Mt 1:13 and *E* begat Azor
Lk 3:30 of Jonan, which was the son of *E*

**ELIAM** *(e'-le-am)*
*1. Father of Bathsheba.*
2Sa 11:3 Bath-sheba, the daughter of *E*
*2. A "mighty man" of David.*
2Sa 23:34 *E* the son of Ahithophel the

**ELIAS** *(e-li'-as)* See ELIJAH. *Greek form of Elijah.*
Mt 11:14 if ye will receive it, this is *E*
Mt 16:14 some, *E*; and others, Jeremias
Mt 17:3 them Moses and *E* talking with him
Mt 17:4 and one for Moses, and one for *E*
Mt 17:10 scribes that *E* must first come
Mt 17:11 *E* truly shall first come, and
Mt 17:12 That *E* is come already, and they
Mt 27:47 said, This man calleth for *E*
Mt 27:49 let us see whether *E* will come to
Mk 6:15 Others said, That it is *E*
Mk 8:28 but some say, *E*
Mk 9:4 appeared unto them *E* with Moses
Mk 9:5 and one for Moses, and one for *E*
Mk 9:11 scribes that *E* must first come
Mk 9:12 *E* verily cometh first, and
Mk 9:13 That *E* is indeed come, and they
Mk 15:35 it said, Behold, he calleth *E*
Mk 15:36 let us see whether *E* will come to
Lk 1:17 him in the spirit and power of *E*
Lk 4:25 were in Israel in the days of *E*
Lk 4:26 But unto none of them was *E* sent
Lk 9:8 And of some, that *E* had appeared
Lk 9:19 but some say *E*
Lk 9:30 two men, which were Moses and *E*
Lk 9:33 and one for Moses, and one for *E*
Lk 9:54 and consume them, even as *E* did
Jn 1:21 Art thou *E*?
Jn 1:25 if thou be not that Christ, nor *E*
Rom 11:2 not what the scripture saith of *E*
Jas 5:17 *E* was a man subject to like

**ELIASAPH** *(e-li'-a-saf)*
*1. A chief of Gad.*
Num 1:14 *E* the son of Deuel
Num 2:14 Gad shall be *E* the son of Reuel
Num 7:42 the sixth day *E* the son of Deuel
Num 7:47 offering of *E* the son of Deuel
Num 10:20 of Gad was *E* the son of Deuel
*2. A Gershonite leader.*
Num 3:24 shall be *E* the son of Lael

**ELIASHIB** *(e-li'-a-shib)*
*1. A descendant of Judah.*
1Chr 3:24 of Elioenai were, Hodaiah, and *E*
*2. A priest in David's time.*
1Chr 24:12 The eleventh to *E*, the twelfth to
*3. Son of Joiakim.*
Ezr 10:6 chamber of Johanan the son of *E*
Neh 12:10 Joiakim, Joiakim also begat *E*
Neh 12:10 and *E* begat Joiada

Neh 12:22 The Levites in the days of *E*
Neh 12:23 the days of Johanan the son of *E*
*4. Married a foreign wife.*
Ezr 10:24 Of the singers also; *E*
*5. Son of Zotta.*
Ezr 10:27 Elioenai, *E*, Mattaniah, and
*6. Son of Bani.*
Ezr 10:36 Vaniah, Meremoth, *E*,
*7. High Priest during Nehemiah's time.*
Neh 3:1 Then *E* the high priest rose up
Neh 3:20 of the house of *E* the high priest
Neh 3:21 from the door of the house of *E*
Neh 3:21 even to the end of the house of *E*
Neh 13:4 this, *E* the priest, having the
Neh 13:7 of the evil that *E* did for Tobiah
Neh 13:28 the son of *E* the high priest, was

**ELIATHAH** *(e-li'-a-thah) A son of Heman.*
1Chr 25:4 and Jerimoth, Hananiah, Hanani, *E*
1Chr 25:27 The twentieth to *E*, he, his sons,

**ELIDAD** *(e-li'-dad) Son of Chislon.*
Num 34:21 of Benjamin, *E* the son of Chislon

**ELIEL** *(e'-le-el)* See ELIAH.
*1. Head of the house of Manasseh.*
1Chr 5:24 even Epher, and Ishi, and *E*
*2. Son of Jeroham.*
1Chr 6:34 the son of Jeroham, the son of *E*
*3. A son of Shimhi.*
1Chr 8:20 And Elienai, and Zilthai, and *E*
*4. A son of Shashak.*
1Chr 8:22 And Ishpan, and Heber, and *E*
*5. A captain in David's army.*
1Chr 11:46 *E* the Mahavite, and Jeribai, and
*6. A "mighty man" of David.*
1Chr 11:47 *E*, and Obed, and Jasiel the
*7. A Gadite ally of David.*
1Chr 12:11 Attai the sixth, *E* the seventh,
*8. A chief of Judah.*
1Chr 15:9 *E* the chief, and his brethren
*9. A chief Levite.*
1Chr 15:11 Asaiah, and Joel, Shemaiah, and *E*
*10. A Levite in Hezekiah's time.*
2Chr 31:13 and Jerimoth, and Jozabad, and *E*

**ELIENAI** *(e-li-e'-nahee) A son of Shimhi.*
1Chr 8:20 And *E*, and Zilthai, and Eliel,

**ELIEZER**
Gen 15:2 of my house is this *E* of Damascus
Ex 18:4 And the name of the other was *E*
1Chr 7:8 Zemira, and Joash, and *E*, and
1Chr 15:24 and Zechariah, and Benaiah, and *E*
1Chr 23:15 sons of Moses were, Gershom, and *E*
1Chr 23:17 And the sons of *E* were, Rehabiah
1Chr 23:17 And *E* had none other sons
1Chr 26:25 And his brethren by *E*
1Chr 27:16 was *E* the son of Zichri
2Chr 20:37 Then *E* the son of Dodavah of
Ezr 8:16 Then sent I for *E*, for Ariel, for
Ezr 10:18 Maaseiah, and *E*, and Jarib, and
Ezr 10:23 Kelita,) Pethahiah, Judah, and *E*
Ezr 10:31 *E*, Ishijah, Malchiah, Shemaiah,
Lk 3:29 of Jose, which was the son of *E*

**ELIHOENAI** *(e-li-ho-e'-nahee)* See ELIOENAI. *A family of exiles.*
Ezr 8:4 *E* the son of Zerahiah, and with

**ELIHOREPH** *(e-li-ho'-ref) A scribe of Solomon.*
1Kin 4:3 *E* and Ahiah, the sons of Shisha,

**ELIHU** *(e-li'-hew)*
*1. Great-grandfather of Samuel.*
1Sa 1:1 the son of Jeroham, the son of *E*
*2. A soldier of David.*
1Chr 12:20 and Michael, and Jozabad, and *E*
*3. A Tabernacle servant.*
1Chr 26:7 whose brethren were strong men, *E*
*4. Brother of David.*
1Chr 27:18 Of Judah, *E*, one of the brethren
*5. A friend of Job.*
Job 32:2 Then was kindled the wrath of *E*
Job 32:4 Now *E* had waited till Job had
Job 32:5 When *E* saw that there was no
Job 32:6 *E* the son of Barachel the Buzite
Job 34:1 Furthermore *E* answered and said,
Job 35:1 *E* spake moreover, and said,
Job 36:1 *E* also proceeded, and said,

**ELIJAH** *(e-li'-jah)* See ELIAH, ELIAS.
*1. The prophet.*
1Kin 17:1 *E* the Tishbite, who was of the
1Kin 17:13 *E* said unto her, Fear not
1Kin 17:15 did according to the saying of *E*
1Kin 17:16 of the LORD, which he spake by *E*
1Kin 17:18 And she said unto *E*, What have I
1Kin 17:22 And the LORD heard the voice of *E*
1Kin 17:23 *E* took the child, and brought him
1Kin 17:23 *E* said, See, thy son liveth
1Kin 17:24 And the woman said to *E*, Now by
1Kin 18:1 LORD came to *E* in the third year
1Kin 18:2 *E* went to shew himself unto Ahab
1Kin 18:7 was in the way, behold, *E* met him
1Kin 18:7 and said, Art thou that my lord *E*
1Kin 18:8 tell thy lord, Behold, *E* is here
1Kin 18:11 tell thy lord, Behold, *E* is here
1Kin 18:14 tell thy lord, Behold, *E* is here
1Kin 18:15 *E* said, As the LORD of hosts
1Kin 18:16 and Ahab went to meet *E*
1Kin 18:17 it came to pass, when Ahab saw *E*
1Kin 18:21 *E* came unto all the people, and
1Kin 18:22 Then said *E* unto the people, I,
1Kin 18:25 *E* said unto the prophets of Baal,
1Kin 18:27 that *E* mocked them, and said, Cry
1Kin 18:30 *E* said unto all the people, Come
1Kin 18:31 *E* took twelve stones, according
1Kin 18:36 that *E* the prophet came near, and
1Kin 18:40 *E* said unto them, Take the
1Kin 18:40 *E* brought them down to the brook
1Kin 18:41 *E* said unto Ahab, Get thee up,
1Kin 18:42 *E* went up to the top of Carmel
1Kin 18:46 And the hand of the LORD was on *E*
1Kin 19:1 told Jezebel all that *E* had done
1Kin 19:2 Jezebel sent a messenger unto *E*
1Kin 19:9 unto him, What doest thou here, *E*
1Kin 19:13 when *E* heard it, that he wrapped
1Kin 19:13 and said, What doest thou here, *E*
1Kin 19:19 *E* passed by him, and cast his
1Kin 19:20 he left the oxen, and ran after *E*
1Kin 19:21 Then he arose, and went after *E*
1Kin 21:17 the LORD came to *E* the Tishbite
1Kin 21:20 And Ahab said to *E*, Hast thou
1Kin 21:28 the LORD came to *E* the Tishbite
2Kin 1:3 the LORD said to *E* the Tishbite
2Kin 1:4 And *E* departed.
2Kin 1:8 And he said, It is *E* the Tishbite
2Kin 1:10 *E* answered and said to the captain
2Kin 1:12 *E* answered and said unto them, If
2Kin 1:13 and fell on his knees before *E*
2Kin 1:15 the angel of the LORD said unto *E*
2Kin 1:17 of the LORD which *E* had spoken
2Kin 2:1 up *E* into heaven by a whirlwind
2Kin 2:1 that *E* went with Elisha from
2Kin 2:2 *E* said unto Elisha, Tarry here, I
2Kin 2:4 *E* said unto him, Elisha, tarry
2Kin 2:6 *E* said unto him, Tarry, I pray
2Kin 2:8 *E* took his mantle, and wrapped it
2Kin 2:9 that *E* said unto Elisha, Ask what
2Kin 2:11 *E* went up by a whirlwind into
2Kin 2:13 mantle of *E* that fell from him
2Kin 2:14 mantle of *E* that fell from him
2Kin 2:14 said, Where is the LORD God of *E*
2Kin 2:15 The spirit of *E* doth rest on
2Kin 3:11 poured water on the hands of *E*
2Kin 9:36 by his servant *E* the Tishbite
2Kin 10:10 which he spake by his servant *E*
2Kin 10:17 of the LORD, which he spake to *E*
2Chr 21:12 writing to him from *E* the prophet
Mal 4:5 I will send you *E* the prophet
*2. Married a foreign wife.*
Ezr 10:21 Maaseiah, and *E*, and Shemaiah, and

**ELIKA** *(e-li'-kah) A guard of David.*
2Sa 23:25 the Harodite, *E* the Harodite,

**ELIM** *(e'-lim)* See BEER-ELIM. *An encampment during the Exodus.*
Ex 15:27 And they came to *E*, where were
Ex 16:1 And they took their journey from *E*
Ex 16:1 of Sin, which is between *E*
Num 33:9 from Marah, and came unto *E*
Num 33:9 in *E* were twelve fountains of
Num 33:10 And they removed from *E*, and

**ELIMELECH** *(e-lim'-e-lek)* See ELIMELECH'S. *Husband of Naomi.*
Ruth 1:2 And the name of the man was *E*
Ruth 1:3 And *E* Naomi's husband died
Ruth 2:1 man of wealth, of the family of *E*
Ruth 2:3 Boaz, who was of the kindred of *E*

**ELIMELECH'S**
Ruth 4:3 of land, which was our brother *E*
Ruth 4:9 that I have bought all that was *E*

**ELIOENAI** *(e-li-o-e'-nahee)* See ELIHOENAI.
*1. A son of Neariah.*
1Chr 3:23 *E*, and Hezekiah, and Azrikam, three
1Chr 3:24 And the sons of *E* were, Hodaiah,
*2. A Simeonite prince.*
1Chr 4:36 And *E*, and Jaakobah, and
*3. A son of Becher.*
1Chr 7:8 and Joash, and Eliezer, and *E*
*4. A Temple servant.*
1Chr 26:3 the sixth, *E* the seventh
*5. Married a foreign wife.*
Ezr 10:22 *E*, Maaseiah, Ishmael, Nethaneel,
*6. A son of Zattu.*
Ezr 10:27 *E*, Eliashib, Mattaniah, and
*7. A priest during Nehemiah's time.*
Neh 12:41 Maaseiah, Miniamin, Michaiah, *E*

**ELIPHAL** *(el'-i-fal) A captain in David's army.*
1Chr 11:35 the Hararite, *E* the son of Ur,

**ELIPHALET** *(e-lif'-a-let)* See ELIPHELET, ELPALET. *A son of David.*
2Sa 5:16 And Elishama, and Eliada, and *E*
1Chr 14:7 And Elishama, and Beeliada, and *E*

**ELIPHAZ** *(el'-if-az)*
*1. A son of Esau.*
Gen 36:4 And Adah bare to Esau *E*
Gen 36:10 *E* the son of Adah the wife of
Gen 36:11 And the sons of *E* were Teman
Gen 36:12 was concubine to *E* Esau's son
Gen 36:12 and she bare to *E* Amalek
Gen 36:15 the sons of *E* the firstborn son
Gen 36:16 came of *E* in the land of Edom
1Chr 1:35 *E*, Reuel, and Jeush, and Jaalam, and
1Chr 1:36 The sons of *E*; Teman, and
*2. A friend of Job.*
Job 2:11 *E* the Temanite, and Bildad the
Job 4:1 Then *E* the Temanite answered and
Job 15:1 Then answered *E* the Temanite
Job 22:1 Then *E* the Temanite answered and
Job 42:7 the LORD said to *E* the Temanite
Job 42:9 So *E* the Temanite and Bildad the

**ELIPHELEH** *(e-lif'-e-leh) A Levite singer.*
1Chr 15:18 and Maaseiah, and Mattithiah, and *E*
1Chr 15:21 And Mattithiah, and *E*, and Mikneiah,

**ELIPHELET** *(e-lif-e-let)* See ELIPHALET.
*1. A "mighty man" of David.*
2Sa 23:34 *E* the son of Ahasbai, the son of
*2. A son of David.*
1Chr 3:6 Ibhar also, and Elishama, and *E*
*3. Same as Eliphat.*
1Chr 3:8 And Elishama, and Eliada, and *E*
*4. A descendant of King Saul.*
1Chr 8:39 Jehush the second, and *E* the third
*5. A family of exiles.*
Ezr 8:13 whose names are these, *E*
*6. A son of Hashum.*
Ezr 10:33 Mattenai, Mattathah, Zabad, *E*

**ELI'S** *(e'-lize) Refers to Eli 1.*
1Sa 3:14 that the iniquity of *E* house

**ELISABETH** *(e-liz'-a-beth)* See ELISABETH'S. *Mother of John the Baptist.*
Lk 1:5 of Aaron, and her name was *E*
Lk 1:7 child, because that *E* was barren
Lk 1:13 thy wife *E* shall bear thee a son,
Lk 1:24 those days his wife *E* conceived
Lk 1:36 And, behold, thy cousin *E*, she
Lk 1:40 house of Zacharias, and saluted *E*
Lk 1:41 when *E* heard the salutation of
Lk 1:41 *E* was filled with the Holy Ghost

**ELISABETH'S** *(e-liz'-a-beths)*
Lk 1:57 Now *E* full time came that she

**ELISEUS** *(el-i-se'-us)* See ELISHA. *Greek form of Elisha.*
Lk 4:27 in the time of *E* the prophet

**ELISHA** *(e-li'-shah)* See ELISEUS. *A prophet.*
1Kin 19:16 and *E* the son of Shaphat of
1Kin 19:17 the sword of Jehu shall *E* slay
1Kin 19:19 found *E* the son of Shaphat, who
2Kin 2:1 Elijah went with *E* from Gilgal
2Kin 2:2 And Elijah said unto *E*, Tarry here
2Kin 2:2 *E* said unto him, As the LORD
2Kin 2:3 were at Beth-el came forth to *E*
2Kin 2:4 And Elijah said unto him, *E*
2Kin 2:5 that were at Jericho came to *E*

2Kin 2:9 over, that Elijah said unto *E*
2Kin 2:9 *E* said, I pray thee, let a double
2Kin 2:12 *E* saw it, and he cried, My father,
2Kin 2:14 and thither: and *E* went over.
2Kin 2:15 spirit of Elijah doth rest on *E*
2Kin 2:19 the men of the city said unto *E*
2Kin 2:22 to the saying of *E* which he spake
2Kin 3:11 Here is *E* the son of Shaphat,
2Kin 3:13 *E* said unto the king of Israel,
2Kin 3:14 *E* said, As the LORD of hosts
2Kin 4:1 the sons of the prophets unto *E*
2Kin 4:2 *E* said unto her, What shall I do
2Kin 4:8 that *E* passed to Shunem, where
2Kin 4:17 season that *E* had said unto her
2Kin 4:32 when *E* was come into the house,
2Kin 4:38 And *E* came again to Gilgal
2Kin 5:8 when *E* the man of God had heard
2Kin 5:9 at the door of the house of *E*
2Kin 5:10 *E* sent a messenger unto him,
2Kin 5:20 the servant of *E* the man of God
2Kin 5:25 *E* said unto him, Whence comest
2Kin 6:1 sons of the prophets said unto *E*
2Kin 6:12 but *E*, the prophet that is in
2Kin 6:17 *E* prayed, and said, LORD, I pray
2Kin 6:17 and chariots of fire round about *E*
2Kin 6:18 *E* prayed unto the LORD, and said,
2Kin 6:18 according to the word of *E*
2Kin 6:19 *E* said unto them, This is not the
2Kin 6:20 come into Samaria, that *E* said
2Kin 6:21 And the king of Israel said unto *E*
2Kin 6:31 if the head of *E* the son of
2Kin 6:32 But *E* sat in his house, and the
2Kin 7:1 Then *E* said, Hear ye the word of
2Kin 8:1 Then spake *E* unto the woman,
2Kin 8:4 the great things that *E* hath done
2Kin 8:5 her son, whom *E* restored to life
2Kin 8:7 And *E* came to Damascus
2Kin 8:10 *E* said unto him, Go, say unto him
2Kin 8:13 *E* answered, The LORD hath shewed
2Kin 8:14 So he departed from *E*, and came to
2Kin 8:14 said to him, What said *E* to thee
2Kin 9:1 *E* the prophet called one of the
2Kin 13:14 Now *E* was fallen sick of his
2Kin 13:15 *E* said unto him, Take bow and
2Kin 13:16 *E* put his hands upon the king's
2Kin 13:17 Then *E* said, Shoot
2Kin 13:20 *E* died, and they buried him
2Kin 13:21 the man into the sepulchre of *E*
2Kin 13:21 down, and touched the bones of *E*

**ELISHAH** *(e-li'-shah) A son of Javan.*
Gen 10:4 *E*, and Tarshish, Kittim, and
1Chr 1:7 *E*, and Tarshish, Kittim, and
Eze 27:7 purple from the isles of *E* was

**ELISHAMA** *(e-lish'-a-mah)* See ELISHUA.
*1. Grandfather of Joshua.*
Num 1:10 *E* the son of Ammihud
Num 2:18 shall be *E* the son of Ammihud
Num 7:48 seventh day *E* the son of Ammihud
Num 7:53 offering of *E* the son of Ammihud
Num 10:22 over his host was *E* the son of
1Chr 7:26 son, Ammihud his son, *E* his son,
*2. A son of David.*
2Sa 5:16 And *E*, and Eliada, and Eliphalet
1Chr 3:6 Ibhar also, and *E*, and Eliphelet,
1Chr 3:8 And *E*, and Eliada, and Eliphelet,
1Chr 14:7 And *E*, and Beeliada, and Eliphalet
*3. A descendant of Judah.*
Jer 41:1 the son of Nethaniah the son of *E*
*4. Son of Jekamiah.*
1Chr 2:41 Jekamiah, and Jekamiah begat *E*
*5. Same as Elishua.*
2Kin 25:25 son of Nethaniah, the son of *E*
*6. A priest who taught the law.*
2Chr 17:8 and with them *E* and Jehoram,
*7. A scribe of Jehoiakim.*
Jer 36:12 even *E* the scribe, and Delaiah the
Jer 36:20 in the chamber of *E* the scribe
Jer 36:21 he took it out of *E* the scribe's

**ELISHAPHAT** *(e-lish'-a-fat) Assisted in making Joash king.*
2Chr 23:1 *E* the son of Zichri, into

**ELISHEBA** *(e-lish'-e-bah) Daughter of Amminadab.*
Ex 6:23 And Aaron took him *E*, daughter of

**ELISHUA** *(e-lish'-oo-ah)* See ELISHAMA. *A son of David.*
2Sa 5:15 Ibhar also, and *E*, and Nepheg, and
1Chr 14:5 And Ibhar, and *E*, and Elpalet,

**ELIUD** *(e-li'-ud) Son of Achim; ancestor of Jesus.*
Mt 1:14 and Achim begat *E*
Mt 1:15 And *E* begat Eleazar

**ELIZAPHAN** *(e-liz'-a-fan)* See ELZAPHAN.
*1. Son of Uzziel.*
Num 3:30 shall be *E* the son of Uzziel
1Chr 15:8 Of the sons of *E*
*2. Son of Parnach.*
Num 34:25 of Zebulun, *E* the son of Parnach
*3. A family of Levites.*
2Chr 29:13 And of the sons of *E*

**ELIZUR** *(e-li'-zur) Son of Shedeur.*
Num 1:5 *E* the son of Shedeur
Num 2:10 shall be *E* the son of Shedeur
Num 7:30 On the fourth day *E* the son of
Num 7:35 offering of *E* the son of Shedeur
Num 10:18 over his host was *E* the son of

**ELKANAH** *(el-ka'-nah)*
*1. A grandson of Korah.*
Ex 6:24 Assir, and *E*, and Abiasaph
1Chr 6:23 *E* his son, and Ebiasaph his son,
*2. Father of Samuel.*
1Sa 1:1 mount Ephraim, and his name was *E*
1Sa 1:4 when the time was that *E* offered
1Sa 1:8 Then said *E* her husband to her,
1Sa 1:19 and *E* knew Hannah his wife
1Sa 1:21 And the man *E*, and all his house,
1Sa 1:23 *E* her husband said unto her, Do
1Sa 2:11 *E* went to Ramah to his house
1Sa 2:20 And Eli blessed *E* and his wife, and
1Chr 6:27 son, Jeroham his son, *E* his son
1Chr 6:34 The son of *E*, the son of Jeroham,
*3. A Levite.*
1Chr 6:25 the sons of *E*; Amasai, and
1Chr 6:36 The son of *E*, the son of Joel,
*4. A descendant of Kohath.*
1Chr 6:26 the sons of *E*
1Chr 6:35 The son of Zuph, the son of *E*
*5. Father of Asa.*
1Chr 9:16 the son of Asa, the son of *E*
*6. A soldier in David's army.*
1Chr 12:6 *E*, and Jesiah, and Azareel, and
*7. A Levite doorkeeper.*
1Chr 15:23 *E* were doorkeepers for the ark
*8. An officer of King Ahaz.*
2Chr 28:7 *E* that was next to the king

**ELKOSHITE**
Nah 1:1 book of the vision of Nahum the *E*

**ELLASAR** *(el'-la-sar) A Babylonian city.*
Gen 14:1 king of Shinar, Arioch king of *E*
Gen 14:9 of Shinar, and Arioch king of *E*

**ELMODAM** *(el-mo'-dam) Son of Er.*
Lk 3:28 of Cosam, which was the son of *E*

**ELNAAM** *(el-na'-am) Father of two of David's "mighty men."*
1Chr 11:46 and Joshaviah, the sons of *E*

**ELNATHAN** *(el-na'-than)*
*1. Father of Nehushta.*
2Kin 24:8 the daughter of *E* of Jerusalem
Jer 26:22 *E* the son of Achbor, and certain
Jer 36:12 *E* the son of Achbor, and Gemariah
Jer 36:25 Nevertheless *E* and Delaiah and
*2. Name of three Levites during Ezra's time.*
Ezr 8:16 for Ariel, for Shemaiah, and for *E*
Ezr 8:16 and for Jarib, and for *E*
Ezr 8:16 also for Joiarib, and for *E*

**ELOI** *(e-lo'-ee)* See ELI. *Same as Eli 2.*
Mk 15:34 a loud voice, saying, *E*, *E*

**ELON** *(e'-lon)* See ELONITES.
*1. Esau's father-in-law.*
Gen 26:34 the daughter of *E* the Hittite
Gen 36:2 the daughter of *E* the Hittite
*2. A son of Zebulun.*
Gen 46:14 Sered, and *E*, and Jahleel
Num 26:26 of *E*, the family of the Elonites
*3. A Danite town.*
Josh 19:43 And *E*, and Thimnathah, and Ekron,
*4. A judge of Israel.*
Judg 12:11 And after him *E*, a Zebulonite,
Judg 12:12 *E* the Zebulonite died, and was

**ELON-BETH-HANAN** *(e'-lon-beth-ha'-nan) A Danite town.*
1Kin 4:9 Shaalbim, and Beth-shemesh, and *E*

**ELONITES** *(e'-lon-ites) Descendants of Elon 2.*
Num 26:26 of Elon, the family of the *E*

**ELOTH** *(e'-loth)* See ELATH. *Same as Elath.*
1Kin 9:26 in Ezion-geber, which is beside *E*
2Chr 8:17 Solomon to Ezion-geber, and to *E*
2Chr 26:2 He built *E*, and restored it to

**ELPAAL** *(el-pa'-al) A son of Shaharaim.*
1Chr 8:11 of Hushim he begat Abitub, and *E*
1Chr 8:12 The sons of *E*; Eber, and Misham
1Chr 8:18 Jezliah, and Jobab, the sons of *E*

**ELPALET** *(el-pa'-let)* See ELIPHALET. *A son of David.*
1Chr 14:5 And Ibhar, and Elishua, and *E*

**EL-PARAN** *(el-pa'-ran) A place in southern Canaan.*
Gen 14:6 in their mount Seir, unto *E*

**ELTEKEH** *(el'-te-keh) A Danite city.*
Josh 19:44 And *E*, and Gibbethon, and Baalath,
Josh 21:23 *E* with her suburbs, Gibbethon

**ELTEKON** *(el'-te-kon) A city in Judah.*
Josh 15:59 And Maarath, and Beth-anoth, and *E*

**ELTOLAD** *(el-to'-lad) A city in Judah.*
Josh 15:30 And *E*, and Chesil, and Hormah,
Josh 19:4 And *E*, and Bethul, and Hormah,

**ELUL** *(e'-lul) Sixth month of the Hebrew year.*
Neh 6:15 and fifth day of the month *E*

**ELUZAI** *(e-loo'-zahee) A soldier in David's army.*
1Chr 12:5 *E*, and Jerimoth, and Bealiah, and

**ELYMAS** *(el'-i-mas)* See BAR-JESUS. *A sorcerer.*
Acts 13:8 But *E* the sorcerer (for so is his

**ELZABAD** *(el'-za-bad)*
*1. A soldier in David's army.*
1Chr 12:12 Johanan the eighth, *E* the ninth,
*2. Son of Shemaiah.*
1Chr 26:7 Othni, and Rephael, and Obed, *E*

**ELZAPHAN** *(el'-za-fan)* See ELIZAPHAN. *A son of Uzziel.*
Ex 6:22 Mishael, and *E*, and Zithri
Lev 10:4 And Moses called Mishael and *E*

**EMBRACE**
2Kin 4:16 time of life, thou shalt *e* a son
Job 24:8 *e* the rock for want of a shelter
Prov 4:8 to honour, when thou dost *e* her
Prov 5:20 *e* the bosom of a stranger
Eccl 3:5 a time to *e*, and a time to refrain
Song 2:6 head, and his right hand doth *e* me
Song 8:3 and his right hand should *e* me
Lam 4:5 brought up in scarlet *e* dunghills

**EMBRACED**
Gen 29:13 *e* him, and kissed him, and brought
Gen 33:4 *e* him, and fell on his neck, and
Gen 48:10 and he kissed them, and *e* them
Acts 20:1 *e* them, and departed for to go
Heb 11:13 *e* them, and confessed that they

**EMERALD**
Ex 28:18 And the second row shall be an *e*
Ex 39:11 And the second row, an *e*, a
Eze 28:13 the jasper, the sapphire, the *e*
Rev 4:3 throne, in sight like unto an *e*
Rev 21:19 a chalcedony; the fourth, an *e*

**EMERODS**
Deut 28:27 the botch of Egypt, and with the *e*
1Sa 5:6 them, and smote them with *e*
1Sa 5:9 they had *e* in their secret parts
1Sa 5:12 died not were smitten with the *e*
1Sa 6:4 They answered, Five golden *e*
1Sa 6:5 ye shall make images of your *e*
1Sa 6:11 of gold and the images of their *e*
1Sa 6:17 these are the golden *e* which the

**EMIMS** *(e'-mims) A race of giants.*
Gen 14:5 the *E* in Shaveh Kiriathaim,
Deut 2:10 The *E* dwelt therein in times past
Deut 2:11 but the Moabites call them *E*

**EMINENT**
Eze 16:24 also built unto thee an *e* place
Eze 16:31 In that thou buildest thine *e*
Eze 16:39 shall throw down thine *e* place
Eze 17:22 it upon an high mountain and *e*

**EMMANUEL** *(em-man'-uel)* See IMMANUEL. *A Messianic name.*
Mt 1:23 and they shall call his name *E*

**EMMAUS** *(em'-ma-us) A village near Jerusalem.*
Lk 24:13 same day to a village called *E*

**EMMOR** *(em'-mor)* See HAMOR. *Father of Sychem.*
Acts 7:16 sons of *E* the father of Sychem

**EMPTIED**
Gen 24:20 *e* her pitcher into the trough, and
Gen 42:35 to pass as they *e* their sacks
2Chr 24:11 *e* the chest, and took it, and
Neh 5:13 even thus be he shaken out, and *e*
Is 19:6 the brooks of defence shall be *e*
Is 24:3 The land shall be utterly *e*
Jer 48:11 hath not been *e* from vessel to
Nah 2:2 for the emptiers have *e* them out

**EMPTY**
Gen 31:42 thou hadst sent me away now *e*
Gen 37:24 and the pit was *e*, there was no
Gen 41:27 the seven *e* ears blasted with the
Ex 3:21 when ye go, ye shall not go *e*
Ex 23:15 and none shall appear before me *e*
Ex 34:20 And none shall appear before me *e*
Lev 14:36 command that they *e* the house
Deut 15:13 thou shalt not let him go away *e*
Deut 16:16 not appear before the LORD *e*
Judg 7:16 with *e* pitchers, and lamps within
Ruth 1:21 LORD hath brought me home again *e*
Ruth 3:17 Go not *e* unto thy mother in law
1Sa 6:3 the God of Israel, send it not *e*
1Sa 20:18 because thy seat will be *e*
1Sa 20:25 side, and David's place was *e*
1Sa 20:27 month, that David's place was *e*
2Sa 1:22 the sword of Saul returned not *e*
2Kin 4:3 thy neighbours, even *e* vessels
Job 22:9 Thou hast sent widows away *e*
Job 26:7 out the north over the *e* place
Eccl 11:3 they *e* themselves upon the earth
Is 24:1 the LORD maketh the earth *e*
Is 29:8 but he awaketh, and his soul is *e*
Is 32:6 to make *e* the soul of the hungry,
Jer 14:3 returned with their vessels *e*
Jer 48:12 shall *e* his vessels, and break
Jer 51:2 fan her, and shall *e* her land
Jer 51:34 me, he hath made me an *e* vessel
Eze 24:11 Then set it *e* upon the coals
Hos 10:1 Israel is an *e* vine, he bringeth
Nah 2:10 She is *e*, and void, and waste
Hab 1:17 Shall they therefore *e* their net
Zec 4:12 pipes *e* the golden oil out of
Mt 12:44 when he is come, he findeth it *e*
Mk 12:3 and beat him, and sent him away *e*
Lk 1:53 and the rich he hath sent *e* away
Lk 20:10 beat him, and sent him away *e*
Lk 20:11 shamefully, and sent him away *e*

**ENAM** *(e'-nam) A city in Judah.*
Josh 15:34 and En-gannim, Tappuah, and *E*

**ENAN** *(e'-nan)* See HAZAR-ENAN. *Father of Ahira.*
Num 1:15 Ahira the son of *E*
Num 2:29 shall be Ahira the son of *E*
Num 7:78 twelfth day Ahira the son of *E*
Num 7:83 offering of Ahira the son of *E*
Num 10:27 Naphtali was Ahira the son of *E*

**ENCAMP**
Ex 14:2 *e* before Pi-hahiroth, between
Ex 14:2 before it shall ye *e* by the sea
Num 1:50 it, and shall *e* round about the
Num 2:17 as they *e*, so shall they set
Num 2:27 those that *e* by him shall be the
Num 3:38 But those that *e* before the
Num 10:31 how we are to *e* in the wilderness
2Sa 12:28 *e* against the city, and take it
Job 19:12 *e* round about my tabernacle
Ps 27:3 an host should *e* against me
Zec 9:8 I will *e* about mine house because

**ENCAMPED**
Ex 13:20 *e* in Etham, in the edge of the
Ex 15:27 they *e* there by the waters
Ex 18:5 where he *e* at the mount of God
Num 33:10 from Elim, and *e* by the Red sea
Num 33:11 *e* in the wilderness of Sin
Num 33:12 of Sin, and *e* in Dophkah
Num 33:13 from Dophkah, and *e* in Alush
Num 33:14 *e* at Rephidim, where was no water
Num 33:17 and *e* at Hazeroth.
Num 33:24 mount Shapher, and *e* in Haradah
Num 33:26 from Makheloth, and *e* at Tahath
Num 33:30 from Hashmonah, and *e* at Moseroth
Num 33:32 Bene-jaakan, and *e* at Hor-hagidgad
Num 33:34 from Jotbathah, and *e* at Ebronah
Num 33:35 from Ebronah, and *e* at Ezion-gaber
Num 33:46 and *e* in Almon-diblathaim
Josh 4:19 *e* in Gilgal, in the east border
Josh 5:10 children of Israel *e* in Gilgal
Josh 10:5 *e* before Gibeon, and made war
Josh 10:31 *e* against it, and fought against
Josh 10:34 they *e* against it, and fought
Judg 6:4 they *e* against them, and destroyed
Judg 9:50 *e* against Thebez, and took it
Judg 10:17 gathered together, and *e* in Gilead
Judg 10:17 together, and *e* in Mizpeh
Judg 20:19 the morning, and *e* against Gibeah
1Sa 11:1 up, and *e* against Jabesh-gilead
1Sa 13:16 but the Philistines *e* in Michmash
2Sa 11:11 my lord, are *e* in the open fields
1Kin 16:15 the people were *e* against
1Kin 16:16 the people that were *e* heard say
1Chr 11:15 *e* in the valley of Rephaim
2Chr 32:1 *e* against the fenced cities, and

**ENCHANTMENTS**
Ex 7:11 did in like manner with their *e*
Ex 7:22 of Egypt did so with their *e*
Ex 8:7 the magicians did so with their *e*
Ex 8:18 with their *e* to bring forth lice
Num 24:1 as at other times, to seek for *e*
2Kin 17:17 the fire, and used divination and *e*
2Kin 21:6 and observed times, and used *e*
2Chr 33:6 also he observed times, and used *e*
Is 47:9 the great abundance of thine *e*
Is 47:12 Stand now with thine *e*, and with

**ENCOURAGE**
Deut 1:38 *e* him: for he shall cause
Deut 3:28 and *e* him, and strengthen him
2Sa 11:25 overthrow it: and *e* thou him
Ps 64:5 They *e* themselves in an evil

**ENCOURAGED**
Judg 20:22 the men of Israel *e* themselves
1Sa 30:6 but David *e* himself in the LORD
2Chr 31:4 that they might be *e* in the law
2Chr 35:2 *e* them to the service of the
Is 41:7 So the carpenter *e* the goldsmith

**END**
Gen 6:13 The *e* of all flesh is come before
Gen 8:3 after the *e* of the hundred and
Gen 8:6 to pass at the *e* of forty days
Gen 23:9 which is in the *e* of his field
Gen 27:30 had made an *e* of blessing Jacob
Gen 41:1 pass at the *e* of two full years
Gen 47:21 *e* of the borders of Egypt even to
Gen 47:21 Egypt even to the other *e* thereof
Gen 49:33 made an *e* of commanding his sons
Ex 8:22 to the *e* thou mayest know that I
Ex 12:41 pass at the *e* of the four hundred
Ex 23:16 which is in the *e* of the year
Ex 25:19 And make one cherub on the one *e*
Ex 25:19 the other cherub on the other *e*
Ex 26:28 boards shall reach from *e* to *e*
Ex 31:18 Moses, when he had made an *e* of
Ex 34:22 of ingathering at the year's *e*
Ex 36:33 from the one *e* to the other
Ex 37:8 One cherub on the *e* on this side
Ex 37:8 on the other *e* on that side
Lev 8:33 of your consecration be at an *e*
Lev 16:20 when he hath made an *e* of
Lev 17:5 To the *e* that the children of
Num 4:15 his sons have made an *e* of
Num 16:31 as he had made an *e* of speaking
Num 23:10 and let my last *e* be like his
Num 24:20 but his latter *e* shall be that he
Deut 8:16 to do thee good at thy latter *e*
Deut 9:11 to pass at the *e* of forty days
Deut 11:12 year even unto the *e* of the year
Deut 13:7 from the one *e* of the earth even
Deut 13:7 unto the other *e* of the earth
Deut 14:28 At the *e* of three years thou
Deut 15:1 At the *e* of every seven years
Deut 17:16 to the *e* that he should multiply
Deut 17:20 to the *e* that he may prolong his
Deut 20:9 an *e* of speaking unto the people
Deut 26:12 When thou hast made an *e* of
Deut 28:49 from the *e* of the earth, as swift
Deut 28:64 from the one *e* of the earth even
Deut 31:10 At the *e* of every seven years, in
Deut 31:24 when Moses had made an *e* of
Deut 32:20 I will see what their *e* shall be
Deut 32:29 would consider their latter *e*
Deut 32:45 Moses made an *e* of speaking all
Josh 8:24 when Israel had made an *e* of
Josh 9:16 it came to pass at the *e* of three
Josh 10:20 an *e* of slaying them with a very
Josh 15:5 sea, even unto the *e* of Jordan
Josh 15:8 which is at the *e* of the valley
Josh 18:15 was from the *e* of Kirjath-jearim
Josh 18:16 the *e* of the mountain that lieth
Josh 18:19 salt sea at the south *e* of Jordan
Josh 19:49 When they had made an *e* of
Josh 19:51 So they made an *e* of dividing the
Judg 3:18 when he had made an *e* to offer
Judg 6:21 *e* of the staff that was in his
Judg 11:39 to pass at the *e* of two months
Judg 15:17 when he had made an *e* of speaking
Judg 19:9 behold, the day groweth to an *e*
Ruth 2:23 unto the *e* of barley harvest
Ruth 3:7 down at the *e* of the heap of corn
Ruth 3:10 latter *e* than at the beginning
1Sa 3:12 I begin, I will also make an *e*
1Sa 9:27 going down to the *e* of the city
1Sa 10:13 he had made an *e* of prophesying
1Sa 13:10 *e* of offering the burnt offering
1Sa 14:27 wherefore he put forth the *e* of
1Sa 14:43 the *e* of the rod that was in mine
1Sa 18:1 when he had made an *e* of speaking
1Sa 24:16 when David had made an *e* of
2Sa 2:23 *e* of the spear smote him under
2Sa 2:26 be bitterness in the latter *e*
2Sa 6:18 an *e* of offering burnt offerings
2Sa 11:19 When thou hast made an *e* of
2Sa 13:36 as he had made an *e* of speaking
2Sa 14:26 every year's *e* that he polled it
2Sa 24:8 Jerusalem at the *e* of nine months
1Kin 1:41 as they had made an *e* of eating
1Kin 2:39 to pass at the *e* of three years
1Kin 3:1 until he had made an *e* of
1Kin 7:40 So Hiram made an *e* of doing all
1Kin 8:54 an *e* of praying all this prayer
1Kin 9:10 to pass at the *e* of twenty years
2Kin 8:3 to pass at the seven years' *e*
2Kin 10:21 was full from one *e* to another
2Kin 10:25 as soon as he had made an *e* of
2Kin 18:10 at the *e* of three years they took
2Kin 21:16 Jerusalem from one *e* to another
1Chr 16:2 when David had made an *e* of
2Chr 4:10 on the right side of the east *e*
2Chr 5:12 stood at the east *e* of the altar
2Chr 7:1 Solomon had made an *e* of praying
2Chr 8:1 to pass at the *e* of twenty years
2Chr 20:16 find them at the *e* of the brook
2Chr 20:23 when they had made an *e* of the
2Chr 21:19 after the *e* of two years, his
2Chr 24:10 chest, until they had made an *e*
2Chr 24:23 came to pass at the *e* of the year
2Chr 29:17 of the first month they made an *e*
2Chr 29:29 they had made an *e* of offering
Ezr 9:11 from one *e* to another with their
Ezr 10:17 they made an *e* with all the men
Neh 3:21 to the *e* of the house of Eliashib
Neh 4:2 will they make an *e* in a day
Job 6:11 and what is mine *e*, that I should
Job 8:7 yet thy latter *e* should greatly
Job 16:3 Shall vain words have an *e*
Job 18:2 it be ere ye make an *e* of words
Job 26:10 the day and night come to an *e*
Job 28:3 He setteth an *e* to darkness
Job 34:36 that Job may be tried unto the *e*
Job 42:12 *e* of Job more than his beginning
Ps 7:9 of the wicked come to an *e*
Ps 9:6 are come to a perpetual *e*
Ps 19:4 their words to the *e* of the world
Ps 19:6 forth is from the *e* of the heaven
Ps 30:12 To the *e* that my glory may sing
Ps 37:37 for the *e* of that man is peace
Ps 37:38 the *e* of the wicked shall be cut
Ps 39:4 LORD, make me to know mine *e*
Ps 46:9 to cease unto the *e* of the earth
Ps 61:2 From the *e* of the earth will I
Ps 73:17 then understood I their *e*
Ps 102:27 and thy years shall have no *e*
Ps 107:27 man, and are at their wit's *e*
Ps 119:33 and I shall keep it unto the *e*
Ps 119:96 I have seen an *e* of all
Ps 119:112 statutes alway, even unto the *e*
Prov 5:4 But her *e* is bitter as wormwood,

Prov 14:12 but the *e* thereof are the ways of
Prov 14:13 the *e* of that mirth is heaviness
Prov 16:25 but the *e* thereof are the ways of
Prov 19:20 mayest be wise in thy latter *e*
Prov 20:21 but the *e* thereof shall not be
Prov 23:18 For surely there is an *e*
Prov 25:8 not what to do in the *e* thereof
Eccl 3:11 from the beginning to the *e*
Eccl 4:8 yet is there no *e* of all his
Eccl 4:16 There is no *e* of all the people,
Eccl 7:2 for that is the *e* of all men
Eccl 7:8 Better is the *e* of a thing than
Eccl 7:14 to the *e* that man should find
Eccl 10:13 the *e* of his talk is mischievous
Eccl 12:12 making many books there is no *e*
Is 2:7 is there any *e* of their treasures
Is 2:7 is there any *e* of their chariots
Is 5:26 unto them from the *e* of the earth
Is 7:3 at the *e* of the conduit of the
Is 9:7 and peace there shall be no *e*
Is 13:5 from the *e* of heaven, even the
Is 16:4 for the extortioner is at an *e*
Is 23:15 after the *e* of seventy years
Is 23:17 pass after the *e* of seventy years
Is 33:1 make an *e* to deal treacherously
Is 38:12 night wilt thou make an *e* of me
Is 38:13 night wilt thou make an *e* of me
Is 41:22 and know the latter *e* of them
Is 42:10 praise from the *e* of the earth
Is 45:17 confounded world without *e*
Is 46:10 Declaring the *e* from the
Is 47:7 didst remember the latter *e* of it
Is 48:20 it even to the *e* of the earth
Is 49:6 salvation unto the *e* of the earth
Is 62:11 unto the *e* of the world, Say ye
Jer 1:3 unto the *e* of the eleventh year
Jer 3:5 will he keep it to the *e*
Jer 4:27 yet will I not make a full *e*
Jer 5:10 but make not a full *e*
Jer 5:18 I will not make a full *e* with you
Jer 5:31 will ye do in the *e* thereof
Jer 12:4 said, He shall not see our last *e*
Jer 12:12 *e* of the land even to the other
Jer 12:12 even to the other *e* of the land
Jer 17:11 days, and at his *e* shall be a fool
Jer 25:33 one *e* of the earth even unto the
Jer 25:33 unto the other *e* of the earth
Jer 26:8 when Jeremiah had made an *e* of
Jer 29:11 evil, to give you an expected *e*
Jer 30:11 though I make a full *e* of all
Jer 30:11 will I not make a full *e* of thee
Jer 31:17 And there is hope in thine *e*
Jer 34:14 At the *e* of seven years let ye go
Jer 43:1 that when Jeremiah had made an *e*
Jer 44:27 until there be an *e* of them
Jer 46:28 for I will make a full *e* of all
Jer 46:28 I will not make a full *e* of thee
Jer 51:13 thine *e* is come, and the measure
Jer 51:31 that his city is taken at one *e*
Jer 51:63 made an *e* of reading this book
Lam 1:9 she remembereth not her last *e*
Lam 4:18 our *e* is near, our days are
Lam 4:18 for our *e* is come
Eze 3:16 to pass at the *e* of seven days
Eze 7:2 An *e*, the *e* is come upon the
Eze 7:3 Now is the *e* come upon thee, and I
Eze 7:6 An *e* is come, the *e* is come
Eze 11:13 wilt thou make a full *e* of the
Eze 20:17 neither did I make an *e* of them
Eze 20:26 to the *e* that they might know
Eze 21:25 when iniquity shall have an *e*
Eze 21:29 their iniquity shall have an *e*
Eze 29:13 At the *e* of forty years will I
Eze 31:14 To the *e* that none of all the
Eze 35:5 time that their iniquity had an *e*
Eze 39:14 after the *e* of seven months shall
Eze 41:12 the separate place at the *e*
Eze 42:15 Now when he had made an *e* of
Eze 43:23 hast made an *e* of cleansing it
Eze 48:1 From the north *e* to the coast of
Dan 1:5 that at the *e* thereof they might
Dan 1:15 at the *e* of ten days their
Dan 1:18 Now at the *e* of the days that the
Dan 4:11 thereof to the *e* of all the earth
Dan 4:22 dominion to the *e* of the earth
Dan 4:29 At the *e* of twelve months he
Dan 4:34 And at the *e* of the days I
Dan 6:26 dominion shall be even unto the *e*
Dan 7:26 and to destroy it unto the *e*
Dan 7:28 Hitherto is the *e* of the matter
Dan 8:17 time of the *e* shall be the vision
Dan 8:19 in the last *e* of the indignation
Dan 8:19 the time appointed the *e* shall be
Dan 9:24 and to make an *e* of sins, and to
Dan 9:26 the *e* thereof shall be with a
Dan 9:26 unto the *e* of the war desolations
Dan 11:6 in the *e* of years they shall join
Dan 11:27 for yet the *e* shall be at the
Dan 11:35 white, even to the time of the *e*
Dan 11:40 at the time of the *e* shall the
Dan 11:45 yet he shall come to his *e*
Dan 12:4 book, even to the time of the *e*
Dan 12:6 it be to the *e* of these wonders
Dan 12:8 shall be the *e* of these things
Dan 12:9 and sealed till the time of the *e*
Dan 12:13 But go thou thy way till the *e* be
Dan 12:13 in thy lot at the *e* of the days
Amos 3:15 the great houses shall have an *e*
Amos 5:18 to what *e* is it for you
Amos 7:2 that when they had made an *e* of
Amos 8:2 The *e* is come upon my people of
Amos 8:10 the *e* thereof as a bitter day
Obad 9 to the *e* that every one of the
Nah 1:8 an utter *e* of the place thereof
Nah 1:9 he will make an utter *e*
Nah 2:9 for there is none *e* of the store
Nah 3:3 there is none *e* of their corpses
Hab 2:3 but at the *e* it shall speak, and
Mt 10:22 endureth to the *e* shall be saved
Mt 11:1 when Jesus had made an *e* of
Mt 13:39 the harvest is the *e* of the world
Mt 13:40 it be in the *e* of this world
Mt 13:49 shall it be at the *e* of the world
Mt 24:3 coming, and of the *e* of the world
Mt 24:6 to pass, but the *e* is not yet
Mt 24:13 he that shall endure unto the *e*
Mt 24:14 and then shall the *e* come
Mt 24:31 from one *e* of heaven to the other
Mt 26:58 with the servants, to see the *e*
Mt 28:1 In the *e* of the sabbath, as it
Mt 28:20 even unto the *e* of the world
Mk 3:26 he cannot stand, but hath an *e*
Mk 13:7 but the *e* shall not be yet
Mk 13:13 he that shall endure unto the *e*
Lk 1:33 his kingdom there shall be no *e*
Lk 18:1 a parable unto them to this *e*
Lk 21:9 but the *e* is not by and by
Lk 22:37 things concerning me have an *e*
Jn 13:1 world, he loved them unto the *e*
Jn 18:37 To this *e* was I born, and for this
Acts 7:19 to the *e* they might not live
Rom 1:11 to the *e* ye may be established
Rom 4:16 to the *e* the promise might be
Rom 6:21 for the *e* of those things is
Rom 6:22 and the *e* everlasting life
Rom 10:4 For Christ is the *e* of the law
Rom 14:9 For to this *e* Christ both died,
1Cor 1:8 shall also confirm you unto the *e*
1Cor 15:24 Then cometh the *e*, when he shall
2Cor 1:13 shall acknowledge even to the *e*
2Cor 2:9 For to this *e* also did I write,
2Cor 3:13 the *e* of that which is abolished
2Cor 11:15 whose *e* shall be according to
Eph 3:21 all ages, world without *e*
Phil 3:19 Whose *e* is destruction, whose God
1Th 3:13 To the *e* he may stablish your
1Ti 1:5 Now the *e* of the commandment is
Heb 3:6 of the hope firm unto the *e*
Heb 3:14 confidence stedfast unto the *e*
Heb 6:8 whose *e* is to be burned
Heb 6:11 full assurance of hope unto the *e*
Heb 6:16 is to them an *e* of all strife
Heb 7:3 beginning of days, nor *e* of life
Heb 9:26 but now once in the *e* of the
Heb 13:7 considering the *e* of their
Jas 5:11 and have seen the *e* of the Lord
1Pet 1:9 Receiving the *e* of your faith
1Pet 1:13 hope to the *e* for the grace that
1Pet 4:7 But the *e* of all things is at
1Pet 4:17 what shall the *e* be of them that
2Pet 2:20 the latter *e* is worse with them
Rev 2:26 and keepeth my works unto the *e*
Rev 21:6 and Omega, the beginning and the *e*
Rev 22:13 and Omega, the beginning and the *e*

**ENDED**

Gen 2:2 on the seventh day God *e* his work
Gen 41:53 was in the land of Egypt, were *e*
Gen 47:18 When that year was *e*, they came
Deut 31:30 of this song, until they were *e*
Deut 34:8 and mourning for Moses were *e*
Ruth 2:21 until they have *e* all my harvest
2Sa 20:18 and so they *e* the matter
1Kin 7:51 So was *e* all the work that king
2Chr 29:34 help them, till the work was *e*
Job 31:40 The words of Job are *e*
Ps 72:20 of David the son of Jesse are *e*
Is 60:20 days of thy mourning shall be *e*
Jer 8:20 harvest is past, the summer is *e*
Eze 4:8 till thou hast *e* the days of thy
Mt 7:28 when Jesus had *e* these sayings
Lk 4:2 and when they were *e*, he afterward
Lk 4:13 devil had *e* all the temptation
Lk 7:1 Now when he had *e* all his sayings
Jn 13:2 And supper being *e*, the devil
Acts 19:21 After these things were *e*
Acts 21:27 when the seven days were almost *e*

**EN-DOR** *(en'-dor) A village near Mt. Tabor.*

Josh 17:11 towns, and the inhabitants of *E*
1Sa 28:7 that hath a familiar spirit at *E*
Ps 83:10 Which perished at *E*: they became

**ENDS**

Ex 25:18 in the two *e* of the mercy seat
Ex 25:19 cherubims on the two *e* thereof
Ex 28:14 two chains of pure gold at the *e*
Ex 28:22 *e* of wreathen work of pure gold
Ex 28:23 on the two *e* of the breastplate
Ex 28:24 are on the *e* of the breastplate
Ex 28:25 the other two *e* of the two
Ex 28:26 two *e* of the breastplate in the
Ex 37:7 on the two *e* of the mercy seat
Ex 37:8 cherubims on the two *e* thereof
Ex 38:5 the four *e* of the grate of brass
Ex 39:15 the breastplate chains at the *e*
Ex 39:16 in the two *e* of the breastplate
Ex 39:17 rings on the *e* of the breastplate
Ex 39:18 the two *e* of the two wreathen
Ex 39:19 on the two *e* of the breastplate
Deut 33:17 together to the *e* of the earth
1Sa 2:10 shall judge the *e* of the earth
1Kin 8:8 that the *e* of the staves were
2Chr 5:9 that the *e* of the staves were
Job 28:24 he looketh to the *e* of the earth
Job 37:3 lightning unto the *e* of the earth
Job 38:13 take hold of the *e* of the earth
Ps 19:6 and his circuit unto the *e* of it
Ps 22:27 All the *e* of the world shall
Ps 48:10 praise unto the *e* of the earth
Ps 59:13 in Jacob unto the *e* of the earth
Ps 65:5 of all the *e* of the earth
Ps 67:7 all the *e* of the earth shall fear
Ps 72:8 the river unto the *e* of the earth
Ps 98:3 all the *e* of the earth have seen
Ps 135:7 to ascend from the *e* of the earth
Prov 17:24 a fool are in the *e* of the earth
Prov 30:4 all the *e* of the earth
Is 26:15 far unto all the *e* of the earth
Is 40:28 the Creator of the *e* of the earth
Is 41:5 the *e* of the earth were afraid,
Is 41:9 taken from the *e* of the earth
Is 43:6 daughters from the *e* of the earth
Is 45:22 ye saved, all the *e* of the earth
Is 52:10 all the *e* of the earth shall see
Jer 10:13 to ascend from the *e* of the earth
Jer 16:19 unto thee from the *e* of the earth
Jer 25:31 come even to the *e* of the earth
Jer 51:16 to ascend from the *e* of the earth
Eze 15:4 fire devoureth both the *e* of it
Mic 5:4 be great unto the *e* of the earth
Zec 9:10 river even to the *e* of the earth
Acts 13:47 salvation unto the *e* of the earth
Rom 10:18 words unto the *e* of the world
1Cor 10:11 upon whom the *e* of the world are

**ENDUED**

Gen 30:20 God hath *e* me with a good dowry
2Chr 2:12 *e* with prudence and understanding,
2Chr 2:13 *e* with understanding, of Huram my
Lk 24:49 until ye be *e* with power from on
Jas 3:13 *e* with knowledge among you

**ENDURE**

Gen 33:14 me and the children be able to *e*
Ex 18:23 so, then thou shalt be able to *e*
Est 8:6 For how can I *e* to see the evil
Est 8:6 or how can I *e* to see the
Job 8:15 hold it fast, but it shall not *e*
Job 31:23 of his highness I could not *e*
Ps 9:7 But the LORD shall *e* for ever

Ps 30:5 weeping may *e* for a night
Ps 72:5 thee as long as the sun and moon *e*
Ps 72:17 His name shall *e* for ever
Ps 89:29 also will I make to *e* for ever
Ps 89:36 His seed shall *e* for ever
Ps 102:12 thou, O LORD, shalt *e* for ever
Ps 102:26 shall perish, but thou shalt *e*
Ps 104:31 of the LORD shall *e* for ever
Prov 27:24 doth the crown *e* to every
Eze 22:14 Can thine heart *e*, or can thine
Mt 24:13 But he that shall *e* unto the end
Mk 4:17 and so *e* but for a time
Mk 13:13 but he that shall *e* unto the end
2Th 1:4 and tribulations that ye *e*
2Ti 2:3 Thou therefore *e* hardness
2Ti 2:10 Therefore I *e* all things for the
2Ti 4:3 they will not *e* sound doctrine
2Ti 4:5 *e* afflictions, do the work of an
Heb 12:7 If ye *e* chastening, God dealeth
Heb 12:20 (For they could not *e* that which
Jas 5:11 we count them happy which *e*
1Pet 2:19 for conscience toward God *e* grief

## ENDURED

Ps 81:15 their time should have *e* for ever
Rom 9:22 *e* with much longsuffering the
2Ti 3:11 what persecutions I *e*
Heb 6:15 And so, after he had patiently *e*
Heb 10:32 ye *e* a great fight of afflictions
Heb 11:27 for he *e*, as seeing him who is
Heb 12:2 was set before him *e* the cross
Heb 12:3 For consider him that *e* such

## ENDURETH

1Chr 16:34 for his mercy *e* for ever
1Chr 16:41 because his mercy *e* for ever
2Chr 5:13 for his mercy *e* for ever
2Chr 7:3 for his mercy *e* for ever
2Chr 7:6 because his mercy *e* for ever
2Chr 20:21 for his mercy *e* for ever
Ezr 3:11 for his mercy *e* for ever toward
Ps 30:5 For his anger *e* but a moment
Ps 52:1 the goodness of God *e* continually
Ps 72:7 of peace so long as the moon *e*
Ps 100:5 his truth *e* to all generations
Ps 106:1 for his mercy *e* for ever
Ps 107:1 for his mercy *e* for ever
Ps 111:3 and his righteousness *e* for ever
Ps 111:10 his praise *e* for ever
Ps 112:3 and his righteousness *e* for ever
Ps 112:9 his righteousness *e* for ever
Ps 117:2 the truth of the LORD *e* for ever
Ps 118:1 because his mercy *e* for ever
Ps 118:2 say, that his mercy *e* for ever
Ps 118:3 say, that his mercy *e* for ever
Ps 118:4 say, that his mercy *e* for ever
Ps 118:29 for his mercy *e* for ever
Ps 119:160 righteous judgments *e* for ever
Ps 135:13 Thy name, O LORD, *e* for ever
Ps 136:1 for his mercy *e* for ever
Ps 136:2 for his mercy *e* for ever
Ps 136:3 for his mercy *e* for ever
Ps 136:4 for his mercy *e* for ever
Ps 136:5 for his mercy *e* for ever
Ps 136:6 for his mercy *e* for ever
Ps 136:7 for his mercy *e* for ever
Ps 136:8 for his mercy *e* for ever
Ps 136:9 for his mercy *e* for ever
Ps 136:10 for his mercy *e* for ever
Ps 136:11 for his mercy *e* for ever
Ps 136:12 for his mercy *e* for ever
Ps 136:13 for his mercy *e* for ever
Ps 136:14 for his mercy *e* for ever
Ps 136:15 for his mercy *e* for ever
Ps 136:16 for his mercy *e* for ever
Ps 136:17 for his mercy *e* for ever
Ps 136:18 for his mercy *e* for ever
Ps 136:19 for his mercy *e* for ever
Ps 136:20 for his mercy *e* for ever
Ps 136:21 for his mercy *e* for ever
Ps 136:22 for his mercy *e* for ever
Ps 136:23 for his mercy *e* for ever
Ps 136:24 for his mercy *e* for ever
Ps 136:25 for his mercy *e* for ever
Ps 136:26 for his mercy *e* for ever
Ps 138:8 thy mercy, O LORD, *e* for ever
Ps 145:13 thy dominion *e* throughout all
Jer 33:11 for his mercy *e* for ever
Mt 10:22 but he that *e* to the end shall be
Jn 6:27 which *e* unto everlasting life
1Cor 13:7 hopeth all things, *e* all things
Jas 1:12 is the man that *e* temptation
1Pet 1:25 the word of the Lord *e* for ever

## EN-EGLAIM *(en-eg'-la-im) A place near the Salt Sea.*

Eze 47:10 upon it from En-gedi even unto E

## ENEMIES

Gen 14:20 delivered thine *e* into thy hand
Gen 22:17 shall possess the gate of his *e*
Gen 49:8 shall be in the neck of thine *e*
Ex 1:10 war, they join also unto our *e*
Ex 23:22 I will be an enemy unto thine *e*
Ex 23:27 I will make all thine *e* turn
Ex 32:25 unto their shame among their *e*
Lev 26:7 And ye shall chase your *e*, and they
Lev 26:8 your *e* shall fall before you by
Lev 26:16 in vain, for your *e* shall eat it
Lev 26:17 ye shall be slain before your *e*
Lev 26:32 your *e* which dwell therein shall
Lev 26:36 hearts in the lands of their *e*
Lev 26:37 no power to stand before your *e*
Lev 26:38 land of your *e* shall eat you up
Lev 26:41 them into the land of their *e*
Lev 26:44 they be in the land of their *e*
Num 10:9 and ye shall be saved from your *e*
Num 10:35 LORD, and let thine *e* be scattered
Num 14:42 ye be not smitten before your *e*
Num 23:11 I took thee to curse mine *e*
Num 24:8 he shall eat up the nations his *e*
Num 24:10 I called thee to curse mine *e*
Num 24:18 shall be a possession for his *e*
Num 32:21 driven out his *e* from before him
Deut 1:42 lest ye be smitten before your *e*
Deut 6:19 out all thine *e* from before thee
Deut 12:10 rest from all your *e* round about
Deut 20:1 out to battle against thine *e*
Deut 20:3 day unto battle against your *e*
Deut 20:4 to fight for you against your *e*
Deut 20:14 shalt eat the spoil of thine *e*
Deut 21:10 forth to war against thine *e*
Deut 23:9 host goeth forth against thine *e*
Deut 23:14 and to give up thine *e* before thee
Deut 25:19 rest from all thine *e* round about
Deut 28:7 The LORD shall cause thine *e* that
Deut 28:25 thee to be smitten before thine *e*
Deut 28:31 sheep shall be given unto thine *e*
Deut 28:48 shalt thou serve thine *e* which
Deut 28:53 wherewith thine *e* shall distress
Deut 28:55 wherewith thine *e* shall distress
Deut 28:68 be sold unto your *e* for bondmen
Deut 30:7 put all these curses upon thine *e*
Deut 32:31 even our *e* themselves being
Deut 32:41 I will render vengeance to mine *e*
Deut 33:7 be thou an help to him from his *e*
Deut 33:29 thine *e* shall be found liars unto
Josh 7:8 their backs before their *e*
Josh 7:12 could not stand before their *e*
Josh 7:12 turned their backs before their *e*
Josh 7:13 canst not stand before thine *e*
Josh 10:13 avenged themselves upon their *e*
Josh 10:19 ye not, but pursue after your *e*
Josh 10:25 all your *e* against whom ye fight
Josh 21:44 a man of all their *e* before them
Josh 21:44 all their *e* into their hand
Josh 22:8 of your *e* with your brethren
Josh 23:1 from all their *e* round about
Judg 2:14 the hands of their *e* round about
Judg 2:14 any longer stand before their *e*
Judg 2:18 their *e* all the days of the judge
Judg 3:28 *e* the Moabites into your hand
Judg 5:31 So let all thine *e* perish
Judg 8:34 of all their *e* on every side
Judg 11:36 vengeance for thee of thine *e*
1Sa 2:1 my mouth is enlarged over mine *e*
1Sa 4:3 save us out of the hand of our *e*
1Sa 12:10 us out of the hand of our *e*
1Sa 12:11 the hand of your *e* on every side
1Sa 14:24 that I may be avenged on mine *e*
1Sa 14:30 spoil of their *e* which they found
1Sa 14:47 against all his *e* on every side
1Sa 18:25 to be avenged of the king's *e*
1Sa 20:15 the *e* of David every one from the
1Sa 20:16 it at the hand of David's *e*
1Sa 25:22 also do God unto the *e* of David
1Sa 25:26 thine own hand, now let thine *e*
1Sa 25:29 and the souls of thine *e*, them
1Sa 29:8 against the *e* of my lord the king
1Sa 30:26 of the spoil of the *e* of the LORD
2Sa 3:18 and out of the hand of all their *e*
2Sa 5:20 forth upon mine *e* before me
2Sa 7:1 rest round about from all his *e*
2Sa 7:9 off all thine *e* out of thy sight
2Sa 7:11 thee to rest from all thine *e*
2Sa 12:14 to the *e* of the LORD to blaspheme
2Sa 18:19 LORD hath avenged him of his *e*
2Sa 18:32 The *e* of my lord the king, and all
2Sa 19:6 In that thou lovest thine *e*
2Sa 19:9 saved us out of the hand of our *e*
2Sa 22:1 him out of the hand of all his *e*
2Sa 22:4 so shall I be saved from mine *e*
2Sa 22:38 I have pursued mine *e*, and
2Sa 22:41 also given me the necks of mine *e*
2Sa 22:49 bringeth me forth from mine *e*
2Sa 24:13 flee three months before thine *e*
1Kin 3:11 hast asked the life of thine *e*
1Kin 8:48 soul, in the land of their *e*
2Kin 17:39 you out of the hand of all your *e*
2Kin 21:14 them into the hand of their *e*
2Kin 21:14 a prey and a spoil to all their *e*
1Chr 12:17 ye be come to betray me to mine *e*
1Chr 14:11 God hath broken in upon mine *e* by
1Chr 17:8 off all thine *e* from before thee
1Chr 17:10 I will subdue all thine *e*
1Chr 21:12 sword of thine *e* overtaketh thee
1Chr 22:9 rest from all his *e* round about
2Chr 1:11 honour, nor the life of thine *e*
2Chr 6:28 if their *e* besiege them in the
2Chr 6:34 go out to war against their *e* by
2Chr 6:36 deliver them over before their *e*
2Chr 20:27 made them to rejoice over their *e*
2Chr 20:29 fought against the *e* of Israel
2Chr 25:20 them into the hand of their *e*
Neh 4:15 when our *e* heard that it was
Neh 5:9 the reproach of the heathen our *e*
Neh 6:1 the Arabian, and the rest of our *e*
Neh 6:16 that when all our *e* heard thereof
Neh 9:27 them into the hand of their *e*
Neh 9:27 them out of the hand of their *e*
Neh 9:28 thou them in the hand of their *e*
Est 8:13 to avenge themselves on their *e*
Est 9:1 in the day that the *e* of the Jews
Est 9:5 *e* with the stroke of the sword
Est 9:16 lives, and had rest from their *e*
Est 9:22 the Jews rested from their *e*
Job 19:11 me unto him as one of his *e*
Ps 3:7 all mine *e* upon the cheek bone
Ps 5:8 righteousness because of mine *e*
Ps 6:7 waxeth old because of all mine *e*
Ps 6:10 Let all mine *e* be ashamed
Ps 7:6 because of the rage of mine *e*
Ps 8:2 strength because of thine *e*
Ps 9:3 When mine *e* are turned back, they
Ps 10:5 as for all his *e*, he puffeth at
Ps 17:9 that oppress me, from my deadly *e*
Ps 18:*t* him from the hand of all his *e*
Ps 18:3 so shall I be saved from mine *e*
Ps 18:37 I have pursued mine *e*, and
Ps 18:40 also given me the necks of mine *e*
Ps 18:48 He delivereth me from mine *e*
Ps 21:8 hand shall find out all thine *e*
Ps 23:5 me in the presence of mine *e*
Ps 25:2 let not mine *e* triumph over me
Ps 25:19 Consider mine *e*; for they are
Ps 27:2 When the wicked, even mine *e*
Ps 27:6 up above mine *e* round about me
Ps 27:11 a plain path, because of mine *e*
Ps 27:12 not over unto the will of mine *e*
Ps 31:11 I was a reproach among all mine *e*
Ps 31:15 me from the hand of mine *e*
Ps 35:19 mine *e* wrongfully rejoice over me
Ps 37:20 the *e* of the LORD shall be as the
Ps 38:19 But mine *e* are lively, and they
Ps 41:2 him unto the will of his *e*
Ps 41:5 Mine *e* speak evil of me, When
Ps 42:10 in my bones, mine *e* reproach me
Ps 44:5 thee will we push down our *e*
Ps 44:7 But thou hast saved us from our *e*
Ps 45:5 in the heart of the king's *e*
Ps 54:5 He shall reward evil unto mine *e*
Ps 54:7 hath seen his desire upon mine *e*
Ps 56:2 Mine *e* would daily swallow me up
Ps 56:9 thee, then shall mine *e* turn back
Ps 59:1 Deliver me from mine *e*, O my God
Ps 59:10 let me see my desire upon mine *e*
Ps 60:12 it is that shall tread down our *e*
Ps 66:3 of thy power shall thine *e* submit
Ps 68:1 God arise, let his *e* be scattered
Ps 68:21 God shall wound the head of his *e*
Ps 68:23 be dipped in the blood of thine *e*
Ps 69:4 me, being mine *e* wrongfully

Ps 69:18 deliver me because of mine *e*
Ps 71:10 For mine *e* speak against me
Ps 72:9 his *e* shall lick the dust
Ps 74:4 Thine *e* roar in the midst of thy
Ps 74:23 Forget not the voice of thine *e*
Ps 78:53 but the sea overwhelmed their *e*
Ps 78:66 he smote his *e* in the hinder
Ps 80:6 our *e* laugh among themselves
Ps 81:14 should soon have subdued their *e*
Ps 83:2 For, lo, thine *e* make a tumult
Ps 89:10 thine *e* with thy strong arm
Ps 89:42 hast made all his *e* to rejoice
Ps 89:51 Wherewith thine *e* have reproached
Ps 92:9 For, lo, thine *e*, O LORD, for, lo
Ps 92:9 for, lo, thine *e* shall perish
Ps 92:11 shall see my desire on mine *e*
Ps 97:3 and burneth up his *e* round about
Ps 102:8 Mine *e* reproach me all the day
Ps 105:24 made them stronger than their *e*
Ps 106:11 And the waters covered their *e*
Ps 106:42 Their *e* also oppressed them, and
Ps 108:13 it is that shall tread down our *e*
Ps 110:1 I make thine *e* thy footstool
Ps 110:2 rule thou in the midst of thine *e*
Ps 112:8 he see his desire upon his *e*
Ps 119:98 hast made me wiser than mine *e*
Ps 119:139 because mine *e* have forgotten thy
Ps 119:157 Many are my persecutors and mine *e*
Ps 127:5 speak with the *e* in the gate
Ps 132:18 His *e* will I clothe with shame
Ps 136:24 And hath redeemed us from our *e*
Ps 138:7 hand against the wrath of mine *e*
Ps 139:20 thine *e* take thy name in vain
Ps 139:22 I count them mine *e*
Ps 143:9 Deliver me, O LORD, from mine *e*
Ps 143:12 And of thy mercy cut off mine *e*
Prov 16:7 he maketh even his *e* to be at
Is 1:24 and avenge me of mine *e*
Is 9:11 him, and join his *e* together
Is 26:11 fire of thine *e* shall devour them
Is 42:13 he shall prevail against his *e*
Is 59:18 adversaries, recompence to his *e*
Is 62:8 thy corn to be meat for thine *e*
Is 66:6 rendereth recompence to his *e*
Is 66:14 and his indignation toward his *e*
Jer 12:7 of my soul into the hand of her *e*
Jer 15:9 to the sword before their *e*
Jer 15:14 make thee to pass with thine *e*
Jer 17:4 *e* in the land which thou knowest
Jer 19:7 fall by the sword before their *e*
Jer 19:9 and straitness, wherewith their *e*
Jer 20:4 fall by the sword of their *e*
Jer 20:5 I give into the hand of their *e*
Jer 21:7 and into the hand of their *e*
Jer 34:20 them into the hand of their *e*
Jer 34:21 I give into the hand of their *e*
Jer 44:30 of Egypt into the hand of his *e*
Jer 48:5 the going down of Horonaim the *e*
Jer 49:37 to be dismayed before their *e*
Lam 1:2 with her, they are become her *e*
Lam 1:5 are the chief, her *e* prosper
Lam 1:21 all mine *e* have heard of my
Lam 2:16 All thine *e* have opened their
Lam 3:46 All our *e* have opened their
Lam 3:52 Mine *e* chased me sore, like a
Eze 39:23 them into the hand of their *e*
Dan 4:19 interpretation thereof to thine *e*
Amos 9:4 go into captivity before their *e*
Mic 4:10 thee from the hand of thine *e*
Mic 5:9 all thine *e* shall be cut off
Mic 7:6 a man's *e* are the men of his own
Nah 1:2 and he reserveth wrath for his *e*
Nah 1:8 and darkness shall pursue his *e*
Nah 3:13 be set wide open unto thine *e*
Zec 10:5 which tread down their *e* in the
Mt 5:44 But I say unto you, Love your *e*
Mt 22:44 till I make thine *e* thy footstool
Mk 12:36 till I make thine *e* thy footstool
Lk 1:71 we should be saved from our *e*
Lk 1:74 out of the hand of our *e* might
Lk 6:27 unto you which hear, Love your *e*
Lk 6:35 But love ye your *e*, and do good,
Lk 19:27 But those mine *e*, which would not
Lk 19:43 that thine *e* shall cast a trench
Lk 20:43 Till I make thine *e* thy footstool
Rom 5:10 For if, when we were *e*, we were
Rom 11:28 they are *e* for your sakes
1Cor 15:25 he hath put all *e* under his feet
Phil 3:18 that they are the *e* of the cross
Col 1:21 *e* in your mind by wicked works,
Heb 1:13 I make thine *e* thy footstool
Heb 10:13 till his *e* be made his footstool
Rev 11:5 their mouth, and devoureth their *e*
Rev 11:12 and their *e* beheld them

**ENEMY**
Ex 15:6 LORD, hath dashed in pieces the *e*
Ex 15:9 The *e* said, I will pursue, I will
Ex 23:22 then I will be an *e* unto thine
Lev 26:25 delivered into the hand of the *e*
Num 10:9 against the *e* that oppresseth you
Num 35:23 that he die, and was not his *e*
Deut 28:57 wherewith thine *e* shall distress
Deut 32:27 that I feared the wrath of the *e*
Deut 32:42 beginning of revenges upon the *e*
Deut 33:27 thrust out the *e* from before thee
Judg 16:23 Samson our *e* into our hand
Judg 16:24 delivered into our hands our *e*
1Sa 2:32 shalt see an *e* in my habitation
1Sa 18:29 Saul became David's *e* continually
1Sa 19:17 me so, and sent away mine *e*
1Sa 24:4 deliver thine *e* into thine hand
1Sa 24:19 For if a man find his *e*, will he
1Sa 26:8 thine *e* into thine hand this day
1Sa 28:16 from thee, and is become thine *e*
2Sa 4:8 the son of Saul thine *e*, which
2Sa 22:18 He delivered me from my strong *e*
1Kin 8:33 be smitten down before the *e*
1Kin 8:37 if their *e* besiege them in the
1Kin 8:44 go out to battle against their *e*
1Kin 8:46 them, and deliver them to the *e*
1Kin 8:46 captives unto the land of the *e*
1Kin 21:20 Hast thou found me, O mine *e*
2Chr 6:24 be put to the worse before the *e*
2Chr 25:8 shall make thee fall before the *e*
2Chr 26:13 to help the king against the *e*
Ezr 8:22 help us against the *e* in the way
Ezr 8:31 us from the hand of the *e*
Est 3:10 the Agagite, the Jews' *e*
Est 7:4 tongue, although the *e* could not
Est 7:6 and *e* is this wicked Haman
Est 8:1 the Jews' *e* unto Esther the queen
Est 9:10 the *e* of the Jews, slew they
Est 9:24 the *e* of all the Jews, had
Job 13:24 face, and holdest me for thine *e*
Job 16:9 mine *e* sharpeneth his eyes upon
Job 27:7 Let mine *e* be as the wicked, and
Job 33:10 me, he counteth me for his *e*
Ps 7:4 him that without cause is mine *e*
Ps 7:5 Let the *e* persecute my soul, and
Ps 8:2 that thou mightest still the *e*
Ps 9:6 O thou *e*, destructions are come
Ps 13:2 shall mine *e* be exalted over me
Ps 13:4 Lest mine *e* say, I have prevailed
Ps 18:17 He delivered me from my strong *e*
Ps 31:8 shut me up into the hand of the *e*
Ps 41:11 because mine *e* doth not triumph
Ps 42:9 of the oppression of the *e*
Ps 43:2 of the oppression of the *e*
Ps 44:10 makest us to turn back from the *e*
Ps 44:16 by reason of the *e* and avenger
Ps 55:3 Because of the voice of the *e*
Ps 55:12 For it was not an *e* that
Ps 61:3 me, and a strong tower from the *e*
Ps 64:1 my life from fear of the *e*
Ps 74:3 even all that the *e* hath done
Ps 74:10 shall the *e* blaspheme thy name
Ps 74:18 that the *e* hath reproached, O
Ps 78:42 when he delivered them from the *e*
Ps 89:22 The *e* shall not exact upon him
Ps 106:10 them from the hand of the *e*
Ps 107:2 redeemed from the hand of the *e*
Ps 143:3 For the *e* hath persecuted my soul
Prov 24:17 Rejoice not when thine *e* falleth
Prov 25:21 If thine *e* be hungry, give him
Prov 27:6 the kisses of an *e* are deceitful
Is 59:19 When the *e* shall come in like a
Is 63:10 he was turned to be their *e*
Jer 6:25 for the sword of the *e* and fear is
Jer 15:11 verily I will cause the *e* to
Jer 18:17 as with an east wind before the *e*
Jer 30:14 thee with the wound of an *e*
Jer 31:16 come again from the land of the *e*
Jer 44:30 king of Babylon, his *e*, and that
Lam 1:5 gone into captivity before the *e*
Lam 1:7 fell into the hand of the *e*
Lam 1:9 for the *e* hath magnified himself
Lam 1:16 desolate, because the *e* prevailed
Lam 2:3 his right hand from before the *e*
Lam 2:4 He hath bent his bow like an *e*
Lam 2:5 The Lord was as an *e*
Lam 2:7 of the *e* the walls of her palaces
Lam 2:17 thine *e* to rejoice over thee
Lam 2:22 brought up hath mine *e* consumed
Lam 4:12 the *e* should have entered into
Eze 36:2 Because the *e* hath said against
Hos 8:3 the *e* shall pursue him
Mic 2:8 my people is risen up as an *e*
Mic 7:8 Rejoice not against me, O mine *e*
Mic 7:10 she that is mine *e* shall see it
Nah 3:11 seek strength because of the *e*
Zeph 3:15 he hath cast out thine *e*
Mt 5:43 thy neighbour, and hate thine *e*
Mt 13:25 his *e* came and sowed tares among
Mt 13:28 unto them, An *e* hath done this
Mt 13:39 The *e* that sowed them is the
Lk 10:19 and over all the power of the *e*
Acts 13:10 thou *e* of all righteousness, wilt
Rom 12:20 Therefore if thine *e* hunger
1Cor 15:26 The last *e* that shall be
Gal 4:16 Am I therefore become your *e*
2Th 3:15 Yet count him not as an *e*
Jas 4:4 of the world is the *e* of God

**EN-GANNIM** *(en-gan'-nim)*
*1. A city in Judah.*
Josh 15:34 and *E*, Tappuah, and Enam
*2. A city in Issachar.*
Josh 19:21 And Remeth, and *E*, and En-haddah,
Josh 21:29 her suburbs, *E* with her suburbs

**EN-GEDI** *(en-ghe'-di)* See HAZAZON-TAMAR. *A town on the Salt Sea.*
Josh 15:62 and the city of Salt, and *E*
1Sa 23:29 and dwelt in strong holds at *E*
1Sa 24:1 David is in the wilderness of *E*
2Chr 20:2 be in Hazazon-tamar, which is *E*
Song 1:14 of camphire in the vineyards of *E*
Eze 47:10 it from *E* even unto En-eglaim

**ENGRAVINGS**
Ex 28:11 like the *e* of a signet, shalt
Ex 28:21 names, like the *e* of a signet
Ex 28:36 like the *e* of a signet, HOLINESS
Ex 39:14 like the *e* of a signet, every one
Ex 39:30 like to the *e* of a signet

**EN-HADDAH** *(en-had'-dah) A city in Issachar.*
Josh 19:21 And Remeth, and En-gannim, and *E*

**EN-HAKKORE** *(en-hak'-ko-re) A spring.*
Judg 15:19 he called the name thereof *E*

**EN-HAZOR** *(en-ha'-zor) A city in Naphtali.*
Josh 19:37 And Kedesh, and Edrei, and *E*

**ENJOY**
Lev 26:34 shall the land *e* her sabbaths
Lev 26:34 the land rest, and *e* her sabbaths
Lev 26:43 shall *e* her sabbaths, while she
Num 36:8 *e* every man the inheritance of
Deut 28:41 but thou shalt not *e* them
Josh 1:15 *e* it, which Moses the LORD's
Eccl 2:1 with mirth, therefore *e* pleasure
Eccl 2:24 his soul *e* good in his labour
Eccl 3:13 *e* the good of all his labour, it
Eccl 5:18 to *e* the good of all his labour
Is 65:22 mine elect shall long *e* the work
Acts 24:2 that by thee we *e* great quietness
1Ti 6:17 giveth us richly all things to *e*
Heb 11:25 than to *e* the pleasures of sin

**ENLIGHTENED**
1Sa 14:27 and his eyes were *e*
1Sa 14:29 you, how mine eyes have been *e*
Job 33:30 to be *e* with the light of the
Ps 97:4 His lightnings *e* the world
Eph 1:18 of your understanding being *e*
Heb 6:4 for those who were once *e*

**EN-MISHPAT** *Another name for Kadesh.*
Gen 14:7 And they returned, and came to *E*

**ENMITY**
Gen 3:15 I will put *e* between thee and the
Num 35:21 Or in *e* smite him with his hand,
Num 35:22 he thrust him suddenly without *e*
Lk 23:12 they were at *e* between themselves
Rom 8:7 the carnal mind is *e* against God
Eph 2:15 abolished in his flesh the *e*
Eph 2:16 cross, having slain the *e* thereby
Jas 4:4 of the world is *e* with God

**ENOCH** *(e'-nok)* See HENOCH.
*1. A son of Cain.*
Gen 4:17 and she conceived, and bare *E*
Gen 4:18 And unto *E* was born Irad
*2. A city built by Cain.*
Gen 4:17 after the name of his son, *E*
*3. A son of Jared.*
Gen 5:18 sixty and two years, and he begat *E*
Gen 5:19 he begat *E* eight hundred years
Gen 5:21 *E* lived sixty and five years, and
Gen 5:22 *E* walked with God after he begat
Gen 5:23 all the days of *E* were three
Gen 5:24 And *E* walked with God
Lk 3:37 Mathusala, which was the son of *E*
Heb 11:5 By faith *E* was translated that he
Jude 14 *E* also, the seventh from Adam,

**ENOS** *(e'-nos)* See ENOSH. *Son of Seth.*
Gen 4:26 and he called his name *E*
Gen 5:6 hundred and five years, and begat *E*
Gen 5:7 after he begat *E* eight hundred
Gen 5:9 *E* lived ninety years, and begat
Gen 5:10 *E* lived after he begat Cainan
Gen 5:11 all the days of *E* were nine
Lk 3:38 Which was the son of *E*, which was

**ENOSH** *(e'-nosh)* See ENOS. *Same as Enos.*
1Chr 1:1 Adam, Sheth, *E*,

**ENQUIRE**
Gen 24:57 the damsel, and *e* at her mouth
Gen 25:22 And she went to *e* of the LORD
Ex 18:15 people come unto me to *e* of God
Deut 12:30 that thou *e* not after their gods,
Deut 13:14 Then shalt thou *e*, and make search
Deut 17:9 that shall be in those days, and *e*
Judg 4:20 *e* of thee, and say, Is there any
1Sa 9:9 when a man went to *e* of God
1Sa 17:56 *E* thou whose son the stripling is
1Sa 22:15 I then begin to *e* of God for him
1Sa 28:7 that I may go to her, and *e* of her
1Kin 22:5 said unto the king of Israel, *E*
1Kin 22:7 besides, that we might *e* of him
1Kin 22:8 by whom we may *e* of the LORD
2Kin 1:2 *e* of Baal-zebub the god of Ekron
2Kin 1:3 that ye go to *e* of Baal-zebub the
2Kin 1:6 that thou sendest to *e* of
2Kin 1:16 *e* of Baal-zebub the god of Ekron
2Kin 1:16 no God in Israel to *e* of his word
2Kin 3:11 that we may *e* of the LORD by him
2Kin 8:8 *e* of the LORD by him, saying,
2Kin 16:15 altar shall be for me to *e* by
2Kin 22:13 *e* of the LORD for me, and for the
2Kin 22:18 which sent you to *e* of the LORD
1Chr 10:13 had a familiar spirit, to *e* of it
1Chr 18:10 to *e* of his welfare, and to
1Chr 21:30 not go before it to *e* of God
2Chr 18:4 said unto the king of Israel, *E*
2Chr 18:6 besides, that we might *e* of him
2Chr 18:7 man, by whom we may *e* of the LORD
2Chr 32:31 who sent unto him to *e* of the
2Chr 34:21 *e* of the LORD for me, and for them
2Chr 34:26 who sent you to *e* of the LORD
Ezr 7:14 to *e* concerning Judah and
Job 8:8 For *e*, I pray thee, of the former
Ps 27:4 the LORD, and to *e* in his temple
Eccl 7:10 for thou dost not *e* wisely
Is 21:12 also the night: if ye will *e*
Is 21:12 *e* ye: return, come
Jer 21:2 *E*, I pray thee, of the LORD for
Jer 37:7 that sent you unto me to *e* of me
Eze 14:7 prophet to *e* of him concerning me
Eze 20:1 of Israel came to *e* of the LORD
Eze 20:3 Are ye come to *e* of me
Mt 10:11 enter, *e* who in it is worthy
Lk 22:23 they began to *e* among themselves,
Jn 16:19 Do ye *e* among yourselves of that
Acts 9:11 *e* in the house of Judas for one
Acts 19:39 But if ye *e* any thing concerning
Acts 23:15 as though ye would *e* something
Acts 23:20 as though they would *e* somewhat
2Cor 8:23 Whether any do *e* of Titus

**ENQUIRED**
Deut 17:4 *e* diligently, and, behold, it be
Judg 6:29 And when they *e* and asked, they
Judg 8:14 the men of Succoth, and *e* of him
Judg 20:27 children of Israel *e* of the LORD
1Sa 10:22 Therefore they *e* of the LORD
1Sa 22:10 he *e* of the LORD for him, and gave
1Sa 22:13 hast *e* of God for him, that he
1Sa 23:2 Therefore David *e* of the LORD
1Sa 23:4 Then David *e* of the LORD yet
1Sa 28:6 when Saul *e* of the LORD, the LORD
1Sa 30:8 David *e* at the LORD, saying,
2Sa 2:1 that David *e* of the LORD, saying,
2Sa 5:19 David *e* of the LORD, saying,
2Sa 5:23 when David *e* of the LORD, he said
2Sa 11:3 David sent and *e* after the woman
2Sa 16:23 was as if a man had *e* at the
2Sa 21:1 and David *e* of the LORD
1Chr 10:14 And *e* not of the LORD
1Chr 13:3 for we *e* not at it in the days of
1Chr 14:10 David *e* of God, saying, Shall I
1Chr 14:14 Therefore David *e* again of God
Ps 78:34 returned and *e* early after God
Eze 14:3 should I be *e* of at all by them
Eze 20:3 GOD, I will not be *e* of by you
Eze 20:31 and shall I be *e* of by you
Eze 20:31 GOD, I will not be *e* of by you
Eze 36:37 I will yet for this be *e* of by
Dan 1:20 that the king *e* of them, he
Zeph 1:6 sought the LORD, nor *e* for him
Mt 2:7 *e* of them diligently what time
Mt 2:16 had diligently *e* of the wise men
Jn 4:52 Then *e* he of them the hour when
2Cor 8:23 or our brethren be *e* of, they are
1Pet 1:10 salvation the prophets have *e*

**EN-RIMMON** *(en-rim'-mon)* See AIN, RIMMON. *A city in Judah.*
Neh 11:29 And at *E*, and at Zareah, and at

**EN-ROGEL** *(en-ro'-ghel) A fountain near Jerusalem.*
Josh 15:7 the goings out thereof were at *E*
Josh 18:16 on the south, and descended to *E*
2Sa 17:17 Jonathan and Ahimaaz stayed by *E*
1Kin 1:9 stone of Zoheleth, which is by *E*

**EN-SHEMESH** *(en-she'-mesh) A spring.*
Josh 15:7 passed toward the waters of *E*
Josh 18:17 the north, and went forth to *E*

**ENSIGN**
Num 2:2 with the *e* of their father's
Is 5:26 he will lift up an *e* to the
Is 11:10 stand for an *e* of the people
Is 11:12 shall set up an *e* for the nations
Is 18:3 lifteth up an *e* on the mountains
Is 30:17 a mountain, and as an *e* on an hill
Is 31:9 princes shall be afraid of the *e*
Zec 9:16 lifted up as an *e* upon his land

**EN-TAPPUAH** *(en-tap'-poo-ah) A town in Manasseh.*
Josh 17:7 hand unto the inhabitants of *E*

**ENTER**
Gen 12:11 he was come near to *e* into Egypt
Ex 40:35 able to *e* into the tent of the
Num 4:3 all that *e* into the host, to do
Num 4:23 all that *e* in to perform the
Num 5:24 the curse shall *e* into her
Num 5:27 the curse shall *e* into her
Num 20:24 for he shall not *e* into the land
Deut 23:1 shall not *e* into the congregation
Deut 23:2 A bastard shall not *e* into the
Deut 23:2 *e* into the congregation of the
Deut 23:3 *e* into the congregation of the
Deut 23:3 *e* into the congregation of the
Deut 23:8 *e* into the congregation of the
Deut 29:12 That thou shouldest *e* into
Josh 10:19 them not to *e* into their cities
Judg 18:9 go, and to *e* to possess the land
2Sa 22:7 my cry did *e* into his ears
1Kin 14:12 and when thy feet *e* into the city
1Kin 22:30 myself, and *e* into the battle
2Kin 7:4 We will *e* into the city, then the
2Kin 11:5 A third part of you that *e* in on
2Kin 19:23 I will *e* into the lodgings of his
2Chr 7:2 the priests could not *e* into the
2Chr 23:19 unclean in any thing should *e* in
2Chr 30:8 *e* into his sanctuary, which he
Neh 2:8 for the house that I shall *e* into
Est 4:2 for none might *e* into the king's
Job 22:4 will he *e* with thee into judgment
Job 34:23 that he should *e* into judgment
Ps 37:15 Their sword shall *e* into their
Ps 45:15 they shall *e* into the king's
Ps 95:11 they should not *e* into my rest
Ps 100:4 *E* into his gates with
Ps 118:20 into which the righteous shall *e*
Ps 143:2 *e* not into judgment with thy
Prov 4:14 *E* not into the path of the wicked
Prov 18:6 A fool's lips *e* into contention,
Prov 23:10 *e* not into the fields of the
Is 2:10 *E* into the rock, and hide thee in
Is 3:14 The LORD will *e* into judgment
Is 26:2 which keepeth the truth may *e* in
Is 26:20 *e* thou into thy chambers, and shut
Is 37:24 I will *e* into the height of his
Is 57:2 He shall *e* into peace
Is 59:14 in the street, and equity cannot *e*
Jer 7:2 that *e* in at these gates to
Jer 8:14 let us *e* into the defenced cities
Jer 14:18 if I *e* into the city, then behold
Jer 16:5 *E* not into the house of mourning,
Jer 17:20 that *e* in by these gates
Jer 17:25 Then shall there *e* into the gates
Jer 21:13 or who shall *e* into our
Jer 22:2 thy people that *e* in by these
Jer 22:4 then shall there *e* in by the
Jer 41:17 Bethlehem, to go to *e* into Egypt,
Jer 42:15 set your faces to *e* into Egypt
Jer 42:18 you, when ye shall *e* into Egypt
Lam 1:10 not *e* into thy congregation
Lam 3:13 of his quiver to *e* into my reins
Eze 7:22 for the robbers shall *e* into it
Eze 13:9 neither shall they *e* into the
Eze 20:38 they shall not *e* into the land of
Eze 26:10 when he shall *e* into thy gates,
Eze 26:10 as men *e* into a city wherein is
Eze 37:5 I will cause breath to *e* into you
Eze 42:14 When the priests *e* therein
Eze 44:2 and no man shall *e* in by it
Eze 44:3 he shall *e* by the way of the
Eze 44:9 shall *e* into my sanctuary, of any
Eze 44:16 They shall *e* into my sanctuary,
Eze 44:17 that when they *e* in at the gates
Eze 44:21 when they *e* into the inner court
Eze 46:2 the prince shall *e* by the way of
Eze 46:8 And when the prince shall *e*
Dan 11:7 shall *e* into the fortress of the
Dan 11:17 He shall also set his face to *e*
Dan 11:24 He shall *e* peaceably even upon
Dan 11:40 he shall *e* into the countries, and
Dan 11:41 He shall *e* also into the glorious
Hos 11:9 I will not *e* into the city
Joel 2:9 they shall *e* in at the windows
Amos 5:5 nor *e* into Gilgal, and pass not to
Jonah 3:4 Jonah began to *e* into the city a
Zec 5:4 it shall *e* into the house of the
Mt 5:20 ye shall in no case *e* into the
Mt 6:6 *e* into thy closet, and when thou
Mt 7:13 *E* ye in at the strait gate
Mt 7:21 shall *e* into the kingdom of
Mt 10:5 city of the Samaritans *e* ye not
Mt 10:11 city or town ye shall *e*, enquire
Mt 12:29 Or else how can one *e* into a
Mt 12:45 wicked than himself, and they *e* in
Mt 18:3 ye shall not *e* into the kingdom
Mt 18:8 to *e* into life halt or maimed
Mt 18:9 thee to *e* into life with one eye
Mt 19:17 but if thou wilt *e* into life
Mt 19:23 *e* into the kingdom of heaven
Mt 19:24 than for a rich man to *e* into the
Mt 25:21 *e* thou into the joy of thy lord
Mt 25:23 *e* thou into the joy of thy lord
Mt 26:41 that ye *e* not into temptation
Mk 1:45 no more openly *e* into the city
Mk 3:27 No man can *e* into a strong man's
Mk 5:12 swine, that we may *e* into them
Mk 6:10 place soever ye *e* into a house
Mk 9:25 out of him, and *e* no more into him
Mk 9:43 for thee to *e* into life maimed
Mk 9:45 for thee to *e* halt into life
Mk 9:47 it is better for thee to *e* into
Mk 10:15 child, he shall not *e* therein
Mk 10:23 riches *e* into the kingdom of God
Mk 10:24 to *e* into the kingdom of God
Mk 10:25 than for a rich man to *e* into the
Mk 13:15 into the house, neither *e* therein
Mk 14:38 lest ye *e* into temptation
Lk 7:6 thou shouldest *e* under my roof
Lk 8:16 that they which *e* in may see the
Lk 8:32 would suffer them to *e* into them
Lk 9:4 And whatsoever house ye *e* into
Lk 10:5 And into whatsoever house ye *e*
Lk 10:8 And into whatsoever city ye *e*
Lk 10:10 But into whatsoever city ye *e*
Lk 11:26 and they *e* in, and dwell there
Lk 13:24 Strive to *e* in at the strait gate
Lk 13:24 I say unto you, will seek to *e* in
Lk 18:17 child shall in no wise *e* therein

Lk 18:24 riches *e* into the kingdom of God
Lk 18:25 than for a rich man to *e* into the
Lk 21:21 are in the countries *e* thereinto
Lk 22:40 them, Pray that ye *e* not into
Lk 22:46 lest ye *e* into temptation
Lk 24:26 things, and to *e* into his glory
Jn 3:4 can he *e* the second time into his
Jn 3:5 he cannot *e* into the kingdom of
Jn 10:9 by me if any man *e* in, he shall
Acts 14:22 *e* into the kingdom of God
Acts 20:29 grievous wolves *e* in among you
Heb 3:11 They shall not *e* into my rest
Heb 3:18 they should not *e* into his rest
Heb 3:19 not *e* in because of unbelief
Heb 4:3 have believed do *e* into rest
Heb 4:3 if they shall *e* into my rest
Heb 4:5 If they shall *e* into my rest
Heb 4:6 that some must *e* therein, and they
Heb 4:11 therefore to *e* into that rest
Heb 10:19 boldness to *e* into the holiest by
Rev 15:8 man was able to *e* into the temple
Rev 21:27 there shall in no wise *e* into it
Rev 22:14 may *e* in through the gates into

## ENTERED

Gen 7:13 In the selfsame day *e* Noah
Gen 19:3 in unto him, and *e* into his house
Gen 19:23 the earth when Lot *e* into Zoar
Gen 31:33 tent, and *e* into Rachel's tent
Gen 43:30 he *e* into his chamber, and wept
Ex 33:9 as Moses *e* into the tabernacle,
Josh 2:3 which are *e* into thine house
Josh 8:19 they *e* into the city, and took it,
Josh 10:20 of them *e* into fenced cities
Judg 6:5 they *e* into the land to destroy
Judg 9:46 they *e* into an hold of the house
2Sa 10:14 Abishai, and *e* into the city
2Kin 7:8 *e* into another tent, and carried
2Kin 9:31 as Jehu *e* in at the gate, she
1Chr 19:15 his brother, and *e* into the city
2Chr 12:11 when the king *e* into the house of
2Chr 15:12 they *e* into a covenant to seek
2Chr 27:2 howbeit he *e* not into the temple
2Chr 32:1 *e* into Judah, and encamped against
Neh 2:15 *e* by the gate of the valley, and
Neh 10:29 *e* into a curse, and into an oath,
Job 38:16 Hast thou *e* into the springs of
Job 38:22 Hast thou *e* into the treasures of
Jer 2:7 but when ye *e*, ye defiled my land
Jer 9:21 is *e* into our palaces, to cut off
Jer 34:10 which had *e* into the covenant,
Jer 37:16 Jeremiah was *e* into the dungeon
Lam 1:10 the heathen *e* into her sanctuary
Lam 4:12 the enemy should have *e* into the
Eze 2:2 the spirit *e* into me when he
Eze 3:24 Then the spirit *e* into me
Eze 16:8 *e* into a covenant with thee,
Eze 36:20 when they *e* unto the heathen,
Eze 41:6 they *e* into the wall which was of
Eze 44:2 hath *e* in by it, therefore it
Obad 11 foreigners *e* into his gates, and
Obad 13 Thou shouldest not have *e* into
Hab 3:16 rottenness *e* into my bones, and I
Mt 8:5 when Jesus was *e* into Capernaum
Mt 8:23 And when he was *e* into a ship
Mt 9:1 he *e* into a ship, and passed over,
Mt 12:4 How he *e* into the house of God,
Mt 24:38 the day that Noe *e* into the ark
Mk 1:21 day he *e* into the synagogue
Mk 1:29 they *e* into the house of Simon and
Mk 2:1 again he *e* into Capernaum after
Mk 3:1 he *e* again into the synagogue
Mk 4:1 so that he *e* into a ship, and sat
Mk 5:13 went out, and *e* into the swine
Mk 6:56 And whithersoever he *e*, into
Mk 7:17 when he was *e* into the house from
Mk 7:24 *e* into an house, and would have no
Mk 8:10 straightway he *e* into a ship with
Mk 11:2 and as soon as ye be *e* into it
Mk 11:11 Jesus *e* into Jerusalem, and into
Lk 1:40 *e* into the house of Zacharias, and
Lk 4:38 and *e* into Simon's house
Lk 5:3 he *e* into one of the ships, which
Lk 6:6 that he *e* into the synagogue and
Lk 7:1 the people, he *e* into Capernaum
Lk 7:44 I *e* into thine house, thou gavest
Lk 8:30 many devils were *e* into him
Lk 8:33 of the man, and *e* into the swine
Lk 9:34 feared as they *e* into the cloud
Lk 9:52 went, and *e* into a village of the
Lk 10:38 that he *e* into a certain village
Lk 11:52 ye *e* not in yourselves, and them
Lk 17:12 as he *e* into a certain village,
Lk 17:27 the day that Noe *e* into the ark
Lk 19:1 And Jesus *e* and passed through
Lk 22:3 Then *e* Satan into Judas surnamed
Lk 22:10 when ye are *e* into the city,
Lk 24:3 And they *e* in, and found not the
Jn 4:38 ye are *e* into their labours
Jn 6:17 *e* into a ship, and went over the
Jn 6:22 whereinto his disciples were *e*
Jn 13:27 And after the sop Satan *e* into him
Jn 18:1 was a garden, into the which he *e*
Jn 18:33 Then Pilate *e* into the judgment
Jn 21:3 *e* into a ship immediately
Acts 3:2 of them that *e* into the temple
Acts 3:8 *e* with them into the temple,
Acts 5:21 they *e* into the temple early in
Acts 9:17 went his way, and *e* into the house
Acts 10:24 morrow after they *e* into Caesarea
Acts 11:8 hath at any time *e* into my mouth
Acts 11:12 we *e* into the man's house
Acts 16:40 *e* into the house of Lydia
Acts 18:7 *e* into a certain man's house,
Acts 18:19 but he himself *e* into the
Acts 19:30 would have *e* in unto the people
Acts 21:8 we *e* into the house of Philip the
Acts 21:26 with them *e* into the temple
Acts 23:16 *e* into the castle, and told Paul
Acts 25:23 was *e* into the place of hearing,
Acts 28:8 to whom Paul *e* in, and prayed, and
Rom 5:12 by one man sin *e* into the world
Rom 5:20 Moreover the law *e*, that the
1Cor 2:9 neither have *e* into the heart of
Heb 4:6 *e* not in because of unbelief
Heb 4:10 For he that is *e* into his rest
Heb 6:20 the forerunner is for us *e*
Heb 9:12 but by his own blood he *e* in once
Heb 9:24 For Christ is not *e* into the holy
Jas 5:4 *e* into the ears of the Lord of
2Jn 7 deceivers are *e* into the world
Rev 11:11 of life from God *e* into them

## ENTERETH

Num 4:30 every one that *e* into the service
Num 4:35 every one that *e* into the service
Num 4:39 every one that *e* into the service
Num 4:43 every one that *e* into the service
2Chr 31:16 even unto every one that *e* into
Prov 2:10 When wisdom *e* into thine heart,
Prov 17:10 A reproof *e* more into a wise man
Eze 21:14 which *e* into their privy chambers
Eze 42:12 the east, as one *e* into them
Eze 46:9 he that *e* in by the way of the
Eze 46:9 he that *e* by the way of the south
Mt 15:17 that whatsoever *e* in at the mouth
Mk 5:40 *e* in where the damsel was lying
Mk 7:18 thing from without *e* into the man
Mk 7:19 Because it *e* not into his heart,
Lk 22:10 him into the house where he *e* in
Jn 10:1 He that *e* not by the door into
Jn 10:2 But he that *e* in by the door is
Heb 6:19 which *e* into that within the veil
Heb 9:25 as the high priest *e* into the

## ENTERING

Ex 35:15 at the *e* in of the tabernacle
Josh 8:29 cast it at the *e* of the gate of
Josh 13:5 Hermon unto the *e* into Hamath
Josh 20:4 at the *e* of the gate of the city
Judg 3:3 unto the *e* in of Hamath
Judg 9:35 stood in the *e* of the gate of the
Judg 9:40 even unto the *e* of the gate
Judg 9:44 stood in the *e* of the gate of the
Judg 18:16 Dan, stood by the *e* of the gate
Judg 18:17 the priest stood in the *e* of the
1Sa 23:7 by *e* into a town that hath gates
2Sa 10:8 in array at the *e* in of the gate
2Sa 11:23 them even unto the *e* of the gate
1Kin 6:31 for the *e* of the oracle he made
1Kin 8:65 from the *e* in of Hamath unto the
1Kin 19:13 stood in the *e* in of the cave
2Kin 7:3 men at the *e* in of the gate
2Kin 10:8 at the *e* in of the gate until the
2Kin 14:25 the coast of Israel from the *e* of
2Kin 23:8 *e* in of the gate of Joshua the
2Kin 23:11 at the *e* in of the house of the
1Chr 5:9 *e* in of the wilderness from the
1Chr 13:5 Egypt even unto the *e* of Hemath
2Chr 7:8 from the *e* in of Hamath unto the
2Chr 18:9 the *e* in of the gate of Samaria
2Chr 23:4 part of you *e* on the sabbath
2Chr 23:13 stood at his pillar at the *e* in
2Chr 23:15 when she was come to the *e* of the
2Chr 26:8 abroad even to the *e* in of Egypt
2Chr 33:14 even to the *e* in at the fish gate
Is 23:1 that there is no house, no *e* in
Jer 1:15 the *e* of the gates of Jerusalem
Jer 17:27 even *e* in at the gates of
Eze 44:5 mark well the *e* in of the house,
Amos 6:14 *e* in of Hemath unto the river of
Mt 23:13 ye them that are *e* to go in
Mk 4:19 and the lusts of other things *e* in
Mk 7:15 that *e* into him can defile him
Mk 8:13 *e* into the ship again departed to
Mk 16:5 *e* into the sepulchre, they saw a
Lk 11:52 them that were *e* in ye hindered
Lk 19:30 in the which at your *e* ye shall
Acts 8:3 *e* into every house, and haling men
Acts 27:2 *e* into a ship of Adramyttium, we
1Th 1:9 manner of *e* in we had unto you
Heb 4:1 being left us of *e* into his rest

## ENTICE

Ex 22:16 if a man *e* a maid that is not
Deut 13:6 *e* thee secretly, saying, Let us
Judg 14:15 *E* thy husband, that he may
Judg 16:5 *E* him, and see wherein his great
2Chr 18:19 Who shall *e* Ahab king of Israel,
2Chr 18:20 the LORD, and said, I will *e* him
2Chr 18:21 the LORD said, Thou shalt *e* him
Prov 1:10 My son, if sinners *e* thee

## ENTRANCE

Num 34:8 your border unto the *e* of Hamath
Judg 1:24 the *e* into the city, and we will
Judg 1:25 shewed them the *e* into the city
1Kin 18:46 before Ahab to the *e* of Jezreel
1Kin 22:10 in the *e* of the gate of Samaria
1Chr 4:39 And they went to the *e* of Gedor
2Chr 12:10 that kept the *e* of the king's
Ps 119:130 The *e* of thy words giveth light
Eze 40:15 the face of the gate of the *e*
1Th 2:1 know our *e* in unto you, that it
2Pet 1:11 For so an *e* shall be ministered

## ENTREATED

Gen 12:16 he *e* Abram well for her sake
Ex 5:22 hast thou so evil *e* this people
Deut 26:6 And the Egyptians evil *e* us
Mt 22:6 *e* them spitefully, and slew them
Lk 18:32 shall be mocked, and spitefully *e*
Lk 20:11 *e* him shamefully, and sent him
Acts 7:19 evil *e* our fathers, so that they
Acts 27:3 And Julius courteously *e* Paul
1Th 2:2 before, and were shamefully *e*

## ENTRY

2Kin 16:18 house, and the king's *e* without
1Chr 9:19 the LORD, were keepers of the *e*
2Chr 4:22 the *e* of the house, the inner
Prov 8:3 at the *e* of the city, at the
Jer 19:2 which is by the *e* of the east
Jer 26:10 sat down in the *e* of the new gate
Jer 36:10 at the *e* of the new gate of the
Jer 38:14 *e* that is in the house of the
Jer 43:9 which is at the *e* of Pharaoh's
Eze 8:5 this image of jealousy in the *e*
Eze 27:3 art situate at the *e* of the sea
Eze 40:11 the breadth of the *e* of the gate
Eze 40:40 up to the *e* of the north gate
Eze 42:9 was the *e* on the east side
Eze 46:19 After he brought me through the *e*

## ENVIED

Gen 26:14 and the Philistines *e* him
Gen 30:1 no children, Rachel *e* her sister
Gen 37:11 And his brethren *e* him
Ps 106:16 They *e* Moses also in the camp, and
Eccl 4:4 this a man is *e* of his neighbour
Eze 31:9 were in the garden of God, *e* him

## ENVIOUS

Ps 37:1 neither be thou *e* against the
Ps 73:3 For I was *e* at the foolish, when
Prov 24:1 Be not thou *e* against evil men,
Prov 24:19 neither be thou *e* at the wicked

## ENVY

Job 5:2 man, and *e* slayeth the silly one
Prov 3:31 *E* thou not the oppressor, and
Prov 14:30 but *e* the rottenness of the bones
Prov 23:17 Let not thine heart *e* sinners
Prov 27:4 but who is able to stand before *e*
Eccl 9:6 love, and their hatred, and their *e*

Is 11:13 The *e* also of Ephraim shall
Is 11:13 Ephraim shall not *e* Judah
Is 26:11 ashamed for their *e* at the people
Eze 35:11 according to thine *e* which thou
Mt 27:18 For he knew that for *e* they had
Mk 15:10 priests had delivered him for *e*
Acts 7:9 And the patriarchs, moved with *e*
Acts 13:45 they were filled with *e*, and
Acts 17:5 which believed not, moved with *e*
Rom 1:29 full of *e*, murder, debate, deceit
Phil 1:15 indeed preach Christ even of *e*
1Ti 6:4 of words, whereof cometh *e*
Titus 3:3 pleasures, living in malice and *e*
Jas 4:5 that dwelleth in us lusteth to *e*

**ENVYING**
Rom 13:13 and wantonness, not in strife and *e*
1Cor 3:3 for whereas there is among you *e*
Gal 5:26 one another, *e* one another
Jas 3:14 But if ye have bitter *e* and strife
Jas 3:16 For where *e* and strife is, there

**ENVYINGS**
2Cor 12:20 lest there be debates, *e*, wraths,
Gal 5:21 *E*, murders, drunkenness,

**EPAENETUS** *(ep-en'-e-tus) A Christian acquaintance of Paul.*
Rom 16:5 Salute my wellbeloved *E*, who is

**EPAPHRAS** *(ep'-a-fras) A Christian acquaintance of Paul.*
Col 1:7 As ye also learned of *E* our dear
Col 4:12 *E*, who is one of you, a servant
Philem 23 There salute thee *E*, my

**EPAPHRODITUS** *(e-paf-ro-di'-tus) A fellow-worker with Paul.*
Phil 2:25 it necessary to send to you *E*
Phil 4:18 having received of *E* the things
Phil *s* to the Philippians from Rome by *E*

**EPHAH** *(e'-fah)*
*1. A son of Midian; grandson of Abraham.*
Gen 25:4 *E*, and Epher, and Hanoch, and Abidah
1Chr 1:33 *E*, and Epher, and Henoch, and Abida,
Is 60:6 the dromedaries of Midian and *E*
*2. A concubine of Caleb.*
1Chr 2:46 And *E*, Caleb's concubine, bare
*3. A son of Jahdai.*
1Chr 2:47 Jotham, and Gesham, and Pelet, and *E*
*4. A grain measure.*
Ex 16:36 an omer is the tenth part of an *e*
Lev 5:11 of an *e* of fine flour for a sin
Lev 6:20 the tenth part of an *e* of fine
Lev 19:36 balances, just weights, a just *e*
Num 5:15 tenth part of an *e* of barley meal
Num 28:5 a tenth part of an *e* of flour for
Judg 6:19 unleavened cakes of an *e* of flour
Ruth 2:17 and it was about an *e* of barley
1Sa 1:24 one *e* of flour, and a bottle of
1Sa 17:17 an *e* of this parched corn
Is 5:10 seed of an homer shall yield an *e*
Eze 45:10 have just balances, and a just *e*
Eze 45:11 The *e* and the bath shall be of one
Eze 45:11 the *e* the tenth part of an homer
Eze 45:13 part of an *e* of an homer of wheat
Eze 45:13 of an *e* of an homer of barley
Eze 45:24 offering of an *e* for a bullock
Eze 45:24 an *e* for a ram, and an hin of oil
Eze 45:24 a ram, and an hin of oil for an *e*
Eze 46:5 offering shall be an *e* for a ram
Eze 46:5 to give, and an hin of oil to an *e*
Eze 46:7 an *e* for a bullock, and
Eze 46:7 an *e* for a ram, and for the lambs
Eze 46:7 unto, and an hin of oil to an *e*
Eze 46:11 shall be an *e* to a bullock
Eze 46:11 an *e* to a ram, and to the lambs as
Eze 46:11 to give, and an hin of oil to an *e*
Eze 46:14 morning, the sixth part of an *e*
Amos 8:5 forth wheat, making the *e* small
Zec 5:6 This is an *e* that goeth forth
Zec 5:7 sitteth in the midst of the *e*
Zec 5:8 cast it into the midst of the *e*
Zec 5:9 lifted up the *e* between the earth
Zec 5:10 me, Whither do these bear the *e*

**EPHAI** *(e'-fahee) Family who remained in Jerusalem during captivity.*
Jer 40:8 the sons of *E* the Netophathite,

**EPHER** *(e'-fur)*
*1. A son of Midian; grandson of Abraham.*
Gen 25:4 and *E*, and Hanoch, and Abidah
1Chr 1:33 Ephah, and *E*, and Henoch, and Abida,
*2. A descendant of Judah.*
1Chr 4:17 Ezra were, Jether, and Mered, and *E*
*3. A chief of Manasseh.*
1Chr 5:24 house of their fathers, even *E*

**EPHES-DAMMIM** *A city in Judah.*
1Sa 17:1 between Shochoh and Azekah, in *E*

**EPHESIAN** *(e-fe'-zheun)* See EPHESIANS. *A resident of Ephesus.*
Acts 21:29 him in the city Trophimus an *E*

**EPHESIANS** *(e-fe'-zheuns)*
Acts 19:28 saying, Great is Diana of the *E*
Acts 19:34 out, Great is Diana of the *E*
Acts 19:35 *E* is a worshipper of the great
Eph *s* from Rome unto the *E* by Tychicus
2Ti *s* bishop of the church of the *E*

**EPHESUS** *(ef'-e-sus)* See EPHESIAN. *Capital of Roman province of Asia.*
Acts 18:19 And he came to *E*, and left them
Acts 18:21 And he sailed from *E*
Acts 18:24 in the scriptures, came to *E*
Acts 19:1 the upper coasts came to *E*
Acts 19:17 Jews and Greeks also dwelling at *E*
Acts 19:26 see and hear, that not alone at *E*
Acts 19:35 the people, he said, Ye men of *E*
Acts 20:16 Paul had determined to sail by *E*
Acts 20:17 And from Miletus he sent to *E*
1Cor 15:32 I have fought with beasts at *E*
1Cor 16:8 I will tarry at *E* until Pentecost
Eph 1:1 God, to the saints which are at *E*
1Ti 1:3 besought thee to abide still at *E*
2Ti 1:18 things he ministered unto me at *E*
2Ti 4:12 And Tychicus have I sent to *E*
Rev 1:11 unto *E*, and unto Smyrna, and unto
Rev 2:1 angel of the church of *E* write

**EPHLAL** *(ef'-lal) A descendant of Pharez.*
1Chr 2:37 And Zabad begat *E*, and *E* begat
1Chr 2:37 begat *E*, and *E* begat Obed,

**EPHOD** *(e'-fod)*
*1. Father of Hanniel.*
Num 34:23 of Manasseh, Hanniel the son of *E*
*2. A priestly garment.*
Ex 25:7 and stones to be set in the *e*
Ex 28:4 a breastplate, and an *e*, and a robe
Ex 28:6 And they shall make the *e* of gold
Ex 28:8 And the curious girdle of the *e*
Ex 28:12 upon the shoulders of the *e* for
Ex 28:15 work of the *e* thou shalt make it
Ex 28:25 shoulderpieces of the *e* before it
Ex 28:26 is in the side of the *e* inward
Ex 28:27 the two sides of the *e* underneath
Ex 28:27 above the curious girdle of the *e*
Ex 28:28 of the *e* with a lace of blue
Ex 28:28 above the curious girdle of the *e*
Ex 28:28 be not loosed from the *e*
Ex 28:31 the robe of the *e* all of blue
Ex 29:5 the coat, and the robe of the *e*
Ex 29:5 and the *e*, and the breastplate
Ex 29:5 with the curious girdle of the *e*
Ex 35:9 and stones to be set for the *e*
Ex 35:27 and stones to be set, for the *e*
Ex 39:2 And he made the *e* of gold, blue,
Ex 39:5 And the curious girdle of his *e*
Ex 39:7 them on the shoulders of the *e*
Ex 39:8 work, like the work of the *e*
Ex 39:18 on the shoulderpieces of the *e*
Ex 39:19 was on the side of the *e* inward
Ex 39:20 the two sides of the *e* underneath
Ex 39:20 above the curious girdle of the *e*
Ex 39:21 of the *e* with a lace of blue
Ex 39:21 above the curious girdle of the *e*
Ex 39:21 might not be loosed from the *e*
Ex 39:22 the robe of the *e* of woven work
Lev 8:7 put the *e* upon him, and he girded
Lev 8:7 with the curious girdle of the *e*
Judg 8:27 And Gideon made an *e* thereof
Judg 17:5 an house of gods, and made an *e*
Judg 18:14 there is in these houses an *e*
Judg 18:17 took the graven image, and the *e*
Judg 18:18 fetched the carved image, the *e*
Judg 18:20 heart was glad, and he took the *e*
1Sa 2:18 a child, girded with a linen *e*
1Sa 2:28 incense, to wear an *e* before me
1Sa 14:3 priest in Shiloh, wearing an *e*
1Sa 21:9 wrapped in a cloth behind the *e*
1Sa 22:18 persons that did wear a linen *e*
1Sa 23:6 came down with an *e* in his hand
1Sa 23:9 the priest, Bring hither the *e*
1Sa 30:7 pray thee, bring me hither the *e*
1Sa 30:7 brought thither the *e* to David
2Sa 6:14 David was girded with a linen *e*
1Chr 15:27 also had upon him an *e* of linen
Hos 3:4 without an image, and without an *e*

**EPHPHATHA**
Mk 7:34 he sighed, and saith unto him, *E*

**EPHRAIM** *(e'-fra-im)* See EPHRAIMITE, EPHRAIM'S, EPHRAIN.
*1. A son of Joseph.*
Gen 41:52 name of the second called he *E*
Gen 46:20 of Egypt were born Manasseh and *E*
Gen 48:1 him his two sons, Manasseh and *E*
Gen 48:5 And now thy two sons, *E* and
Gen 48:13 *E* in his right hand toward
Gen 48:17 his right hand upon the head of *E*
Gen 48:20 bless, saying, God make thee as *E*
Gen 48:20 and he set *E* before Manasseh
Num 26:28 their families were Manasseh and *E*
1Chr 7:20 And the sons of *E*
1Chr 7:22 *E* their father mourned many days,
*2. One of the twelve tribes comprising Israel.*
Num 1:10 children of Joseph: of *E*
Num 1:32 namely, of the children of *E*
Num 1:33 of them, even of the tribe of *E*
Num 2:18 of *E* according to their armies
Num 2:18 the captain of the sons of *E*
Num 2:24 of *E* were an hundred thousand
Num 7:48 prince of the children of *E*
Num 10:22 *E* set forward according to their
Num 13:8 Of the tribe of *E*, Oshea the son
Num 26:35 sons of *E* after their families
Num 26:37 of *E* according to those that were
Num 34:24 of the tribe of the children of *E*
Deut 33:17 they are the ten thousands of *E*
Deut 34:2 And all Naphtali, and the land of *E*
Josh 14:4 were two tribes, Manasseh and *E*
Josh 16:4 children of Joseph, Manasseh and *E*
Josh 16:5 the border of the children of *E*
Josh 16:8 children of *E* by their families
Josh 16:9 cities for the children of *E* were
Josh 17:8 belonged to the children of *E*
Josh 17:9 these cities of *E* are among the
Josh 17:17 the house of Joseph, even to *E*
Josh 21:5 of the families of the tribe of *E*
Josh 21:20 their lot out of the tribe of *E*
Judg 1:29 Neither did *E* drive out the
Judg 5:14 Out of *E* was there a root of them
Judg 7:24 Then all the men of *E* gathered
Judg 8:1 the men of *E* said unto him, Why
Judg 8:2 of *E* better than the vintage of
Judg 10:9 and against the house of *E*
Judg 12:1 the men of *E* gathered themselves
Judg 12:4 men of Gilead, and fought with *E*
Judg 12:4 and the men of Gilead smote *E*
Judg 12:4 of *E* among the Ephraimites
Judg 12:15 in Pirathon in the land of *E*
2Sa 2:9 and over Jezreel, and over *E*
1Chr 6:66 coasts out of the tribe of *E*
1Chr 9:3 Benjamin, and of the children of *E*
1Chr 12:30 the children of *E* twenty thousand
1Chr 27:10 Pelonite, of the children of *E*
1Chr 27:14 Pirathonite, of the children of *E*
1Chr 27:20 Of the children of *E*, Hoshea the
2Chr 15:9 the strangers with them out of *E*
2Chr 17:2 of Judah, and in the cities of *E*
2Chr 25:7 wit, with all the children of *E*
2Chr 25:10 that was come to him out of *E*
2Chr 28:7 And Zichri, a mighty man of *E*
2Chr 28:12 of the heads of the children of *E*
2Chr 30:1 Judah, and wrote letters also to *E*
2Chr 30:10 to city through the country of *E*
2Chr 30:18 of the people, even many of *E*
2Chr 31:1 in *E* also and Manasseh, until they
2Chr 34:6 in the cities of Manasseh, and *E*
2Chr 34:9 of the hand of Manasseh and *E*
Ps 60:7 *E* also is the strength of mine
Ps 78:9 The children of *E*, being armed,
Ps 78:67 and chose not the tribe of *E*
Ps 80:2 Before *E* and Benjamin and Manasseh
Ps 108:8 *E* also is the strength of mine
Is 7:2 Syria is confederate with *E*
Is 7:5 Because Syria, *E*, and the son of
Is 7:8 and five years shall *E* be broken
Is 7:9 And the head of *E* is Samaria
Is 7:17 from the day that *E* departed from
Is 9:9 all the people shall know, even *E*
Is 9:21 Manasseh, *E*
Is 9:21 and *E*, Manasseh
Is 11:13 The envy also of *E* shall depart

Is 11:13 *E* shall not envy Judah
Is 11:13 and Judah shall not vex *E*
Is 17:3 fortress also shall cease from *E*
Is 28:1 of pride, to the drunkards of *E*
Is 28:3 of pride, the drunkards of *E*
Jer 7:15 even the whole seed of *E*
Jer 31:9 to Israel, and *E* is my firstborn
Jer 31:18 I have surely heard *E* bemoaning
Jer 31:20 Is *E* my dear son
Eze 37:16 it, For Joseph, the stick of *E*
Eze 37:19 Joseph, which is in the hand of *E*
Eze 48:5 the west side, a portion for *E*
Eze 48:6 And by the border of *E*, from the
Hos 4:17 *E* is joined to idols
Hos 5:3 I know *E*, and Israel is not hid
Hos 5:3 for now, O *E*, thou committest
Hos 5:5 and *E* fall in their iniquity
Hos 5:9 *E* shall be desolate in the day of
Hos 5:11 *E* is oppressed and broken in
Hos 5:12 will I be unto *E* as a moth
Hos 5:13 When *E* saw his sickness, and Judah
Hos 5:13 then went *E* to the Assyrian, and
Hos 5:14 For I will be unto *E* as a lion
Hos 6:4 O *E*, what shall I do unto thee
Hos 6:10 there is the whoredom of *E*
Hos 7:1 the iniquity of *E* was discovered
Hos 7:8 *E*, he hath mixed himself among
Hos 7:8 *E* is a cake not turned
Hos 7:11 *E* also is like a silly dove
Hos 8:9 *E* hath hired lovers
Hos 8:11 Because *E* hath made many altars
Hos 9:3 but *E* shall return to Egypt, and
Hos 9:8 The watchman of *E* was with my God
Hos 9:11 As for *E*, their glory shall fly
Hos 9:13 *E*, as I saw Tyrus, is planted in
Hos 9:13 but *E* shall bring forth his
Hos 9:16 *E* is smitten, their root is dried
Hos 10:6 *E* shall receive shame, and Israel
Hos 10:11 *E* is as an heifer that is taught,
Hos 10:11 I will make *E* to ride
Hos 11:3 I taught *E* also to go, taking
Hos 11:8 How shall I give thee up, *E*
Hos 11:9 I will not return to destroy *E*
Hos 11:12 *E* compasseth me about with lies,
Hos 12:1 *E* feedeth on wind, and followeth
Hos 12:8 *E* said, Yet I am become rich, I
Hos 12:14 *E* provoked him to anger most
Hos 13:1 When *E* spake trembling, he
Hos 13:12 The iniquity of *E* is bound up
Hos 14:8 *E* shall say, What have I to do
Obad 19 shall possess the fields of *E*
Zec 9:10 I will cut off the chariot from *E*
Zec 9:13 for me, filled the bow with *E*
Zec 10:7 they of *E* shall be like a mighty

*3. Mountains in Samaria.*

Josh 17:15 if mount *E* be too narrow for thee
Josh 19:50 even Timnath-serah in mount *E*
Josh 20:7 Naphtali, and Shechem in mount *E*
Josh 21:21 with her suburbs in mount *E*
Josh 24:30 which is in mount *E*, on the
Josh 24:33 which was given him in mount *E*
Judg 2:9 Timnath-heres, in the mount of *E*
Judg 3:27 a trumpet in the mountain of *E*
Judg 4:5 Ramah and Beth-el in mount *E*
Judg 7:24 messengers throughout all mount *E*
Judg 10:1 and he dwelt in Shamir in mount *E*
Judg 17:1 And there was a man of mount *E*
Judg 17:8 he came to mount *E* to the house
Judg 18:2 who when they came to mount *E*
Judg 18:13 they passed thence unto mount *E*
Judg 19:1 sojourning on the side of mount *E*
Judg 19:16 even, which was also of mount *E*
Judg 19:18 toward the side of mount *E*
1Sa 1:1 of Ramathaim-zophim, of mount *E*
1Sa 9:4 And he passed through mount *E*
1Sa 14:22 had hid themselves in mount *E*
2Sa 20:21 but a man of mount *E*, Sheba the
1Kin 4:8 The son of Hur, in mount *E*
1Kin 12:25 Jeroboam built Shechem in mount *E*
2Kin 5:22 *E* two young men of the sons of
1Chr 6:67 in mount *E* with her suburbs
2Chr 13:4 Zemaraim, which is in mount *E*
2Chr 15:8 which he had taken from mount *E*
2Chr 19:4 people from Beer-sheba to mount *E*
Jer 4:15 affliction from mount *E*
Jer 31:6 upon the mount *E* shall cry
Jer 50:19 shall be satisfied upon mount *E*

*4. A town near Absalom's farm.*

2Sa 13:23 in Baal-hazor, which is beside *E*

*5. Battle site between David's and Absalom's armies.*

2Sa 18:6 the battle was in the wood of *E*

*6. A northern gate at Jerusalem.*

2Kin 14:13 gate of *E* unto the corner gate
2Chr 25:23 the gate of *E* to the corner gate
Neh 8:16 and in the street of the gate of *E*
Neh 12:39 And from above the gate of *E*

*7. A city near Jerusalem.*

Jn 11:54 wilderness, into a city called *E*

**EPHRAIMITE** *(e'-fra-im-ite)* See EPHRAIMITES. *A descendant of Ephraim.*

Judg 12:5 said unto him, Art thou an *E*

**EPHRAIMITES** *(e'-fra-im-ites)*

Josh 16:10 dwell among the *E* unto this day
Judg 12:4 fugitives of Ephraim among the *E*
Judg 12:5 passages of Jordan before the *E*
Judg 12:5 that when those *E* which were
Judg 12:6 fell at that time of the *E* forty

**EPHRAIM'S** *(e'-fra-ims)*

*1. Refers to Ephraim 1.*

Gen 48:14 hand, and laid it upon *E* head
Gen 48:17 to remove it from *E* head unto
Gen 50:23 Joseph saw *E* children of the

*2. Refers to Ephraim 2.*

Josh 17:10 Southward it was *E*, and northward

**EPHRAIN** *(e'-fra-in)* See EPHRAIM, EPHRON. *A city in Benjamin.*

2Chr 13:19 and *E* with the towns thereof

**EPHRATAH** *(ef'-rat-ah)* See BETHLEHEM, CALEB-EPHRATAH, EPHRATH, EPHRATHITE.

*1. Another name for Bethlehem-judah.*

Ruth 4:11 and do thou worthily in *E*, and be
Ps 132:6 Lo, we heard of it at *E*
Mic 5:2 But thou, Beth-lehem *E*, though

*2. A wife of Caleb.*

1Chr 2:50 son of Hur, the firstborn of *E*
1Chr 4:4 sons of Hur, the firstborn of *E*

**EPHRATH** *(e'-frath)* See EPHRATAH.

*1. A city in Judah.*

Gen 35:16 was but a little way to come to *E*
Gen 35:19 and was buried in the way to *E*
Gen 48:7 but a little way to come unto *E*
Gen 48:7 buried her there in the way of *E*

*2. Same as Ephratah 2.*

1Chr 2:19 was dead, Caleb took unto him *E*

**EPHRATHITE** *(ef'-rath-ite)* See EPHRATHITES. *An inhabitant of Bethlehem-judah.*

1Sa 1:1 of Tohu, the son of Zuph, an *E*
1Sa 17:12 son of that *E* of Beth-lehem-judah
1Kin 11:26 an *E* of Zereda, Solomon's servant

**EPHRATHITES** *(ef'-rath-ites)*

Ruth 1:2 and Chilion, *E* of Beth-lehem-judah

**EPHRON** *(e'-fron)* See EPHRAIM, EPHRAIN.

*1. Son of Zohar.*

Gen 23:8 for me to *E* the son of Zohar
Gen 23:10 *E* dwelt among the children of
Gen 23:10 *E* the Hittite answered Abraham in
Gen 23:13 he spake unto *E* in the audience
Gen 23:14 *E* answered Abraham, saying unto
Gen 23:16 And Abraham hearkened unto *E*
Gen 23:16 Abraham weighed to *E* the silver
Gen 23:17 And the field of *E*, which was in
Gen 25:9 in the field of *E* the son of
Gen 49:29 is in the field of *E* the Hittite
Gen 49:30 bought with the field of *E* the
Gen 50:13 a buryingplace of *E* the Hittite

*2. A mountain between Judah and Benjamin.*

Josh 15:9 went out to the cities of mount *E*

**EPICUREANS** *(ep-i-cu-re'-ans) Followers of the philosopher Epicurus.*

Acts 17:18 certain philosophers of the *E*

**EPISTLE**

Acts 15:30 together, they delivered the *e*
Acts 23:33 delivered the *e* to the governor,
Rom 16:22 I Tertius, who wrote this *e*
1Cor 5:9 I wrote unto you in an *e* not to
1Cor s The first *e* to the Corinthians
2Cor 3:2 Ye are our *e* written in our
2Cor 3:3 the *e* of Christ ministered by us
2Cor 7:8 the same *e* hath made you sorry
2Cor s The second *e* to the Corinthians
Col 4:16 when this *e* is read among you,
Col 4:16 likewise read the *e* from Laodicea
1Th 5:27 this *e* be read unto all the holy
1Th s The first *e* unto the
2Th 2:15 taught, whether by word, or our *e*
2Th 3:14 man obey not our word by this *e*
2Th 3:17 which is the token in every *e*
2Th s The second *e* to the Thessalonians
2Ti s The second *e* unto Timotheus,
2Pet 3:1 This second *e*, beloved, I now

**EQUAL**

Job 28:17 gold and the crystal cannot *e* it
Job 28:19 topaz of Ethiopia shall not *e* it
Ps 17:2 eyes behold the things that are *e*
Ps 55:13 But it was thou, a man mine *e*
Prov 26:7 The legs of the lame are not *e*
Is 40:25 will ye liken me, or shall I be *e*
Is 46:5 will ye liken me, and make me *e*
Lam 2:13 what shall I *e* to thee, that I
Eze 18:25 say, The way of the Lord is not *e*
Eze 18:25 Is not my way *e*
Eze 18:29 The way of the Lord is not *e*
Eze 18:29 of Israel, are not my ways *e*
Eze 33:17 say, The way of the Lord is not *e*
Eze 33:17 as for them, their way is not *e*
Eze 33:20 say, The way of the Lord is not *e*
Mt 20:12 and thou hast made them *e* unto us
Lk 20:36 for they are *e* unto the angels
Jn 5:18 Father, making himself *e* with God
Phil 2:6 it not robbery to be *e* with God
Col 4:1 servants that which is just and *e*
Rev 21:16 breadth and the height of it are *e*

**EQUITY**

Ps 98:9 the world, and the people with *e*
Ps 99:4 thou dost establish *e*, thou
Prov 1:3 justice, and judgment, and *e*
Prov 2:9 righteousness, and judgment, and *e*
Prov 17:26 good, nor to strike princes for *e*
Eccl 2:21 wisdom, and in knowledge, and in *e*
Is 11:4 reprove with *e* for the meek of
Is 59:14 in the street, and *e* cannot enter
Mic 3:9 abhor judgment, and pervert all *e*
Mal 2:6 he walked with me in peace and *e*

**ER** *(ur)*

*1. A son of Judah.*

Gen 38:3 and he called his name *E*
Gen 38:6 took a wife for *E* his firstborn
Gen 38:7 And *E*, Judah's firstborn, was
Gen 46:12 *E*, and Onan, and Shelah, and Pharez,
Gen 46:12 but *E* and Onan died in the land of
Num 26:19 The sons of Judah were *E* and Onan
Num 26:19 and *E* and Onan died in the land of
1Chr 2:3 *E*, and Onan, and Shelah
1Chr 2:3 And *E*, the firstborn of Judah, was

*2. A son of Shelah.*

1Chr 4:21 *E* the father of Lecah, and Laadah

*3. Father of Elmodan; ancestor of Jesus.*

Lk 3:28 Elmodam, which was the son of *E*

**ERAN** *(e'-ran)* See ERANITES. *A son of Shath-elah.*

Num 26:36 of *E*, the family of the Eranites

**ERANITES** *(e'-ran-ites) Descendants of Eran.*

Num 26:36 of Eran, the family of the *E*

**ERASTUS** *(e-ras'-tus)*

*1. A fellow-worker with Paul.*

Acts 19:22 unto him, Timotheus and *E*
2Ti 4:20 *E* abode at Corinth

*2. A Corinthian city official.*

Rom 16:23 *E* the chamberlain of the city

**ERE**

Ex 1:19 are delivered *e* the midwives come
Num 11:33 *e* it was chewed, the wrath of the
Num 14:11 long will it be *e* they believe me
1Sa 3:3 *e* the lamp of God went out in the
2Sa 2:26 *e* thou bid the people return from
2Kin 6:32 but *e* the messenger came to him,
Job 18:2 How long will it be *e* ye make an
Jer 47:6 long will it be *e* thou be quiet
Hos 8:5 how long will it be *e* they attain
Jn 4:49 Sir, come down *e* my child die

**ERECH** *(e'-rek)* See ARCHEVITES. *A city in Shinar.*

Gen 10:10 of his kingdom was Babel, and *E*

**ERI** *(e'-ri)* See ERITES. *A son of Gad.*

Gen 46:16 and Haggi, Shuni, and Ezbon, *E*
Num 26:16 of *E*, the family of the Erites

**ERITES** *(e'-rites) Descendants of Eri.*
Num 26:16 of Eri, the family of the E

**ERR**
2Chr 33:9 the inhabitants of Jerusalem to e
Ps 95:10 a people that do e in their heart
Ps 119:21 which do e from thy commandments
Ps 119:118 all them that e from thy statutes
Prov 14:22 Do they not e that devise evil
Prov 19:27 to e from the words of knowledge
Is 3:12 which lead thee cause thee to e
Is 9:16 of this people cause them to e
Is 19:14 Egypt to e in every work thereof
Is 28:7 they e in vision, they stumble in
Is 30:28 of the people, causing them to e
Is 35:8 though fools, shall not e therein
Is 63:17 thou made us to e from thy ways
Jer 23:13 and caused my people Israel to e
Jer 23:32 my people to e by their lies
Hos 4:12 whoredoms hath caused them to e
Amos 2:4 and their lies caused them to e
Mic 3:5 prophets that make my people e
Mt 22:29 and said unto them, Ye do e
Mk 12:24 unto them, Do ye not therefore e
Mk 12:27 ye therefore do greatly e
Heb 3:10 They do alway e in their heart
Jas 1:16 Do not e, my beloved brethren
Jas 5:19 if any of you do e from the truth

**ERRED**
Lev 5:18 his ignorance wherein he e
Num 15:22 And if ye have e, and not observed
1Sa 26:21 the fool, and have e exceedingly
Job 6:24 me to understand wherein I have e
Job 19:4 And be it indeed that I have e
Ps 119:110 yet I e not from thy precepts
Is 28:7 But they also have e through wine
Is 28:7 the prophet have e through strong
Is 29:24 They also that e in spirit shall
1Ti 6:10 they have e from the faith, and
1Ti 6:21 have e concerning the faith
2Ti 2:18 Who concerning the truth have e

**ERROR**
2Sa 6:7 and God smote him there for his e
Job 19:4 mine e remaineth with myself
Eccl 5:6 the angel, that it was an e
Eccl 10:5 as an e which proceedeth from the
Is 32:6 to utter e against the LORD, to
Dan 6:4 there any e or fault found in him
Mt 27:64 so the last e shall be worse than
Rom 1:27 of their e which was meet
Jas 5:20 e of his way shall save a soul
2Pet 2:18 escaped from them who live in e
2Pet 3:17 led away with the e of the wicked
1Jn 4:6 of truth, and the spirit of e
Jude 11 after the e of Balaam for reward

**ESAIAS** *(e-sah'-yas)* See ISAIAH. *Greek form of Isaiah.*
Mt 3:3 was spoken of by the prophet E
Mt 4:14 which was spoken by E the prophet
Mt 8:17 which was spoken by E the prophet
Mt 12:17 which was spoken by E the prophet
Mt 13:14 is fulfilled the prophecy of E
Mt 15:7 well did E prophesy of you,
Mk 7:6 Well hath E prophesied of you
Lk 3:4 of the words of E the prophet
Lk 4:17 him the book of the prophet E
Jn 1:23 the Lord, as said the prophet E
Jn 12:38 That the saying of E the prophet
Jn 12:39 because that E said again
Jn 12:41 These things said E, when he saw
Acts 8:28 in his chariot read E the prophet
Acts 8:30 and heard him read the prophet E
Acts 28:25 by E the prophet unto our fathers
Rom 9:27 E also crieth concerning Israel,
Rom 9:29 as E said before, Except the Lord
Rom 10:16 For E saith, Lord, who hath
Rom 10:20 But E is very bold, and saith, I
Rom 15:12 E saith, There shall be a root of

**ESAR-HADDON** *(e'-zar-had'-dun) An Assyrian king.*
2Kin 19:37 E his son reigned in his stead
Ezr 4:2 since the days of E king of Assur
Is 37:38 E his son reigned in his stead

**ESAU** *(e'-saw)*
*1. A son of Isaac.*
Gen 25:25 and they called his name E
Gen 25:27 E was a cunning hunter, a man of
Gen 25:28 And Isaac loved E, because he did
Gen 25:29 E came from the field, and he was
Gen 25:30 E said to Jacob, Feed me, I pray
Gen 25:32 E said, Behold, I am at the point
Gen 25:34 Then Jacob gave E bread and
Gen 25:34 thus E despised his birthright
Gen 26:34 E was forty years old when he
Gen 27:1 he called E his eldest son, and
Gen 27:5 when Isaac spake to E his son
Gen 27:5 E went to the field to hunt for
Gen 27:6 father speak unto E thy brother
Gen 27:11 E my brother is a hairy man, and I
Gen 27:15 raiment of her eldest son E
Gen 27:19 his father, I am E thy firstborn
Gen 27:21 thou be my very son E or not
Gen 27:22 but the hands are the hands of E
Gen 27:24 he said, Art thou my very son E
Gen 27:30 that E his brother came in from
Gen 27:32 I am thy son, thy firstborn E
Gen 27:34 when E heard the words of his
Gen 27:37 And Isaac answered and said unto E
Gen 27:38 E said unto his father, Hast thou
Gen 27:38 E lifted up his voice, and wept
Gen 27:41 E hated Jacob because of the
Gen 27:41 E said in his heart, The days of
Gen 27:42 these words of E her elder son
Gen 27:42 unto him, Behold, thy brother E
Gen 28:6 When E saw that Isaac had blessed
Gen 28:8 E seeing that the daughters of
Gen 28:9 Then went E unto Ishmael, and took
Gen 32:3 to E his brother unto the land of
Gen 32:4 shall ye speak unto my lord E
Gen 32:6 saying, We came to thy brother E
Gen 32:8 If E come to the one company, and
Gen 32:11 of my brother, from the hand of E
Gen 32:13 hand a present for E his brother
Gen 32:17 When E my brother meeteth thee,
Gen 32:18 is a present sent unto my lord E
Gen 32:19 this manner shall ye speak unto E
Gen 33:1 E came, and with him four hundred
Gen 33:4 E ran to meet him, and embraced
Gen 33:9 E said, I have enough, my brother
Gen 33:15 E said, Let me now leave with
Gen 33:16 So E returned that day on his way
Gen 35:1 from the face of E thy brother
Gen 35:29 and his sons E and Jacob buried him
Gen 36:1 these are the generations of E
Gen 36:2 E took his wives of the daughters
Gen 36:4 And Adah bare to E Eliphaz
Gen 36:5 these are the sons of E, which
Gen 36:6 E took his wives, and his sons, and
Gen 36:8 E in mount Seir: E is Edom
Gen 36:9 these are the generations of E
Gen 36:10 the son of Adah the wife of E
Gen 36:10 son of Bashemath the wife of E
Gen 36:14 and she bare to E Jeush, and Jaalam
Gen 36:15 These were dukes of the sons of E
Gen 36:15 of Eliphaz the firstborn son of E
Gen 36:19 These are the sons of E, who is
Gen 36:40 names of the dukes that came of E
Gen 36:43 he is E the father of the
Josh 24:4 And I gave unto Isaac Jacob and E
Josh 24:4 and I gave unto E mount Seir
1Chr 1:34 sons of Isaac; E and Israel
Mal 1:2 Was not E Jacob's brother
Mal 1:3 And I hated E, and laid his
Heb 12:16 or profane person, as E, who for
*2. Descendants of Esau.*
Deut 2:4 your brethren the children of E
Deut 2:5 Seir unto E for a possession
Deut 2:8 our brethren the children of E
Deut 2:12 the children of E succeeded them
Deut 2:22 As he did to the children of E
Deut 2:29 children of E which dwell in Seir
1Chr 1:35 The sons of E
Jer 49:8 bring the calamity of E upon him
Jer 49:10 But I have made E bare, I have
Obad 6 are the things of E searched out
Obad 18 and the house of E for stubble
Obad 18 any remaining of the house of E
Rom 9:13 have I loved, but E have I hated
Heb 11:20 E concerning things to come
*3. A mountain.*
Obad 8 out of the mount of E
Obad 9 of E may be cut off by slaughter
Obad 19 shall possess the mount of E
Obad 21 Zion to judge the mount of E

**ESAU'S** *(e'-saws) Refers to Esau 1.*
Gen 25:26 and his hand took hold on E heel
Gen 27:23 hairy, as his brother E hands
Gen 28:5 of Rebekah, Jacob's and E mother
Gen 36:10 These are the names of E sons
Gen 36:12 was concubine to Eliphaz E son
Gen 36:12 were the sons of Adah E wife
Gen 36:13 were the sons of Bashemath E wife
Gen 36:14 the daughter of Zibeon, E wife
Gen 36:17 these are the sons of Reuel E son
Gen 36:17 are the sons of Bashemath E wife
Gen 36:18 are the sons of Aholibamah E wife
Gen 36:18 the daughter of Anah, E wife

**ESCAPE**
Gen 19:17 that he said, E for thy life
Gen 19:17 e to the mountain, lest thou be
Gen 19:19 I cannot e to the mountain, lest
Gen 19:20 let me e thither, (is it not a
Gen 19:22 Haste thee, e thither
Gen 32:8 company which is left shall e
Josh 8:22 they let none of them remain or e
1Sa 27:1 speedily e into the land of the
1Sa 27:1 so shall I e out of his hand
2Sa 15:14 we shall not else e from Absalom
2Sa 20:6 he get him fenced cities, and e us
1Kin 18:40 let not one of them e
2Kin 9:15 then let none go forth nor e out
2Kin 10:24 I have brought into your hands e
2Kin 19:31 they that e out of mount Zion
Ezr 9:8 God, to leave us a remnant to e
Est 4:13 thou shalt e in the king's house
Job 11:20 shall fail, and they shall not e
Ps 55:8 I would hasten my e from the
Ps 56:7 Shall they e by iniquity
Ps 71:2 righteousness, and cause me to e
Ps 141:10 own nets, whilst that I withal e
Prov 19:5 he that speaketh lies shall not e
Eccl 7:26 pleaseth God shall e from her
Is 20:6 and how shall we e
Is 37:32 they that e out of mount Zion
Is 66:19 I will send those that e of them
Jer 11:11 which they shall not be able to e
Jer 25:35 the principal of the flock to e
Jer 32:4 not e out of the hand of the
Jer 34:3 thou shalt not e out of his hand,
Jer 38:18 thou shalt not e out of their
Jer 38:23 thou shalt not e out of their
Jer 42:17 none of them shall remain or e
Jer 44:14 shall e or remain, that they
Jer 44:14 shall return but such as shall e
Jer 44:28 Yet a small number that e the
Jer 46:6 flee away, nor the mighty man e
Jer 48:8 every city, and no city shall e
Jer 50:28 e out of the land of Babylon, to
Jer 50:29 let none thereof e
Eze 6:8 e the sword among the nations
Eze 6:9 they that e of you shall remember
Eze 7:16 But they that e of them shall
Eze 7:16 shall e, and shall be on the
Eze 17:15 shall he e that doeth such things
Eze 17:18 all these things, he shall not e
Dan 11:41 but these shall e out of his hand
Dan 11:42 and the land of Egypt shall not e
Joel 2:3 yea, and nothing shall e them
Obad 14 cut off those of his that did e
Mt 23:33 how can ye e the damnation of
Lk 21:36 to e all these things that shall
Acts 27:42 any of them should swim out, and e
Rom 2:3 that thou shalt e the judgment of
1Cor 10:13 temptation also make a way to e
1Th 5:3 and they shall not e
Heb 2:3 How shall we e, if we neglect so
Heb 12:25 earth, much more shall not we e

**ESCAPED**
Gen 14:13 And there came one that had e
Ex 10:5 the residue of that which is e
Num 21:29 he hath given his sons that e
Deut 23:15 is e from his master unto thee
Judg 3:26 Ehud e while they tarried, and
Judg 3:26 the quarries, and e unto Seirath
Judg 3:29 and there e not a man
Judg 12:5 Ephraimites which were e said
Judg 21:17 for them that be e of Benjamin
1Sa 14:41 but the people e
1Sa 19:10 and David fled, and e that night
1Sa 19:12 and he went, and fled, and e
1Sa 19:17 away mine enemy, that he is e
1Sa 19:18 So David fled, and e, and came to
1Sa 22:1 thence, and e to the cave Adullam
1Sa 22:20 son of Ahitub, named Abiathar, e
1Sa 23:13 Saul that David was e from Keilah
1Sa 30:17 there e not a man of them, save
2Sa 1:3 Out of the camp of Israel am I e

2Sa 4:6 and Rechab and Baanah his brother *e*
1Kin 20:20 Ben-hadad the king of Syria *e* on
2Kin 19:30 the remnant that is *e* of the
2Kin 19:37 they *e* into the land of Armenia
1Chr 4:43 of the Amalekites that were *e*
2Chr 16:7 king of Syria *e* out of thine hand
2Chr 20:24 fallen to the earth, and none *e*
2Chr 30:6 that are *e* out of the hand of the
2Chr 36:20 them that had *e* from the sword
Ezr 9:15 for we remain yet *e*, as it is
Neh 1:2 concerning the Jews that had *e*
Job 1:15 I only am *e* alone to tell thee
Job 1:16 I only am *e* alone to tell thee
Job 1:17 I only am *e* alone to tell thee
Job 1:19 I only am *e* alone to tell thee
Job 19:20 I am *e* with the skin of my teeth
Ps 124:7 Our soul is *e* as a bird out of
Ps 124:7 the snare is broken, and we are *e*
Is 4:2 for them that are *e* of Israel
Is 10:20 such as are *e* of the house of
Is 37:31 the remnant that is *e* of the
Is 37:38 they *e* into the land of Armenia
Is 45:20 ye that are *e* of the nations
Jer 41:15 *e* from Johanan with eight men
Jer 51:50 Ye that have *e* the sword, go away
Lam 2:22 LORD's anger none *e* nor remained
Eze 24:27 mouth be opened to him which is *e*
Eze 33:21 that one that had *e* out of
Eze 33:22 evening, afore he that was *e* came
Jn 10:39 but he *e* out of their hand,
Acts 27:44 that they *e* all safe to land
Acts 28:1 And when they were *e*, then they
Acts 28:4 whom, though he hath *e* the sea
2Cor 11:33 down by the wall, and *e* his hands
Heb 11:34 *e* the edge of the sword, out of
Heb 12:25 For if they *e* not who refused him
2Pet 1:4 having *e* the corruption that is
2Pet 2:18 those that were clean *e* from them
2Pet 2:20 For if after they have *e* the

**ESCAPETH**
1Kin 19:17 that him that *e* the sword of
1Kin 19:17 him that *e* from the sword of Jehu
Is 15:9 lions upon him that *e* of Moab
Jer 48:19 him that fleeth, and her that *e*
Eze 24:26 That he that *e* in that day shall
Amos 9:1 he that *e* of them shall not be

**ESEK** *(e'-sek) A well in the valley of Geran.*
Gen 26:20 he called the name of the well *E*

**ESH-BAAL** *(esh'-ba-al)* See ISH-BOSHETH. *A son of King Saul.*
1Chr 8:33 Malchi-shua, and Abinadab, and *E*
1Chr 9:39 Malchi-shua, and Abinadab, and *E*

**ESHBAN** A son of Dishon.
Gen 36:26 Hemdan, and *E*, and Ithran, and
1Chr 1:41 and *E*, and Ithran, and Cheran

**ESHCOL** *(esh'-col)*
*1. Brother of Mamre and Aner.*
Gen 14:13 Mamre the Amorite, brother of *E*
Gen 14:24 men which went with me, Aner, *E*
*2. A valley or brook in Hebron.*
Num 13:23 And they came unto the brook of *E*
Num 13:24 The place was called the brook *E*
Num 32:9 they went up unto the valley of *E*
Deut 1:24 and came unto the valley of *E*

**ESHEAN** *(esh'-e-an) A city in Judea.*
Josh 15:52 Arab, and Dumah, and *E*,

**ESHEK** *(e'-shek) A descendant of King Saul.*
1Chr 8:39 the sons of *E* his brother were,

**ESHKALONITES** *(esh'-ka-lon-ites) Inhabitants of Ashkelon.*
Josh 13:3 and the Ashdothites, the *E*

**ESHTAOL** *(esh'-ta-ol)* See ESHTAULITES. *A town in Judah.*
Josh 15:33 And in the valley, *E*, and Zoreah,
Josh 19:41 their inheritance was Zorah, and *E*
Judg 13:25 camp of Dan between Zorah and *E*
Judg 16:31 *E* in the buryingplace of Manoah
Judg 18:2 of valour, from Zorah, and from *E*
Judg 18:8 unto their brethren to Zorah and *E*
Judg 18:11 Danites, out of Zorah and out of *E*

**ESHTAULITES** *(esh'-ta-u-lites) Inhabitants of Eshtaol.*
1Chr 2:53 came the Zareathites, and the *E*

**ESHTEMOA** *(esh-te-mo'-ah)* See ESHTEMOH.
*1. A Levitical town in Judah.*
Josh 21:14 suburbs, and *E* with her suburbs,
1Sa 30:28 and to them which were in *E*
1Chr 6:57 with her suburbs, and Jattir, and *E*
*2. A descendant of Ezra.*
1Chr 4:17 and Ishbah the father of *E*
1Chr 4:19 the Garmite, and *E* the Maachathite

**ESHTEMOH** *(esh'-te-moh)* See ESHTEMOA. *Same as Eshtemoa 1.*
Josh 15:50 And Anab, and *E*, and Anim,

**ESHTON** *(esh'-ton) Grandson of Chelub.*
1Chr 4:11 Mehir, which was the father of *E*
1Chr 4:12 *E* begat Beth-rapha, and Paseah, and

**ESLI** *(es'-li) Father of Naum; ancestor of Jesus.*
Lk 3:25 of Naum, which was the son of *E*

**ESPECIALLY**
Ps 31:11 but *e* among my neighbours, and a
Acts 26:3 *E* because I know thee to be
Gal 6:10 *e* unto them who are of the
1Ti 5:17 *e* they who labour in the word and
2Ti 4:13 the books, but *e* the parchments

**ESPOUSED**
2Sa 3:14 which I *e* to me for an hundred
Mt 1:18 his mother Mary was *e* to Joseph
Lk 1:27 To a virgin *e* to a man whose name
Lk 2:5 To be taxed with Mary his *e* wife
2Cor 11:2 for I have *e* you to one husband,

**ESROM** *(es'-rom)* See HEZRON. *Son of Phares; ancestor of Jesus.*
Mt 1:3 and Phares begat *E*
Mt 1:3 and *E* begat Aram
Lk 3:33 of Aram, which was the son of *E*

**ESTABLISH**
Gen 6:18 with thee will I *e* my covenant
Gen 9:9 I *e* my covenant with you, and with
Gen 9:11 I will *e* my covenant with you
Gen 17:7 I will *e* my covenant between me
Gen 17:19 I will *e* my covenant with him for
Gen 17:21 my covenant will I *e* with Isaac
Lev 26:9 you, and *e* my covenant with you
Num 30:13 the soul, her husband may *e* it
Deut 8:18 that he may *e* his covenant which
Deut 28:9 The LORD shall *e* thee an holy
Deut 29:13 That he may *e* thee to day for a
1Sa 1:23 only the LORD *e* his word
2Sa 7:12 bowels, and I will *e* his kingdom
2Sa 7:25 *e* it for ever, and do as thou hast
1Kin 9:5 Then I will *e* the throne of thy
1Kin 15:4 son after him, and to *e* Jerusalem
1Chr 17:11 and I will *e* his kingdom
1Chr 22:10 I will *e* the throne of his
1Chr 28:7 Moreover I will *e* his kingdom for
2Chr 9:8 to *e* them for ever, therefore
Job 36:7 he doth *e* them for ever, and they
Ps 7:9 but *e* the just: for the righteous
Ps 48:8 God will *e* it for ever
Ps 87:5 the highest himself shall *e* her
Ps 89:2 shalt thou *e* in the very heavens
Ps 89:4 Thy seed will I *e* for ever
Ps 90:17 *e* thou the work of our hands upon
Ps 90:17 the work of our hands *e* thou it
Ps 99:4 thou dost *e* equity, thou
Prov 15:25 but he will *e* the border of the
Is 9:7 to *e* it with judgment and with
Is 49:8 to *e* the earth, to cause to
Is 62:7 And give him no rest, till he *e*
Jer 33:2 the LORD that formed it, to *e* it
Eze 16:60 I will *e* unto thee an everlasting
Eze 16:62 I will *e* my covenant with thee
Dan 6:7 together to *e* a royal statute
Dan 6:8 *e* the decree, and sign the writing
Dan 11:14 exalt themselves to *e* the vision
Amos 5:15 good, and *e* judgment in the gate
Rom 3:31 yea, we *e* the law
Rom 10:3 going about to *e* their own
1Th 3:2 to *e* you, and to comfort you
Heb 10:9 first, that he may *e* the second

**ESTABLISHED**
Gen 9:17 which I have *e* between me
Gen 41:32 is because the thing is *e* by God
Ex 6:4 I have also *e* my covenant with
Ex 15:17 O Lord, which thy hands have *e*
Lev 25:30 *e* for ever to him that bought it
Deut 19:15 witnesses, shall the matter be *e*
Deut 32:6 Hath he not made thee, and *e* thee
1Sa 3:20 was *e* to be a prophet of the LORD
1Sa 13:13 *e* thy kingdom upon Israel for
1Sa 20:31 the ground, thou shalt not be *e*
1Sa 24:20 Israel shall be *e* in thine hand
2Sa 5:12 LORD had *e* him king over Israel
2Sa 7:16 shall be *e* for ever before thee
2Sa 7:16 thy throne shall be *e* for ever
2Sa 7:26 servant David be *e* before thee
1Kin 2:12 and his kingdom was *e* greatly
1Kin 2:24 the LORD liveth, which hath *e* me
1Kin 2:45 be *e* before the LORD for ever
1Kin 2:46 the kingdom was *e* in the hand of
1Chr 17:14 throne shall be *e* for evermore
1Chr 17:23 his house be *e* for ever, and do as
1Chr 17:24 Let it even be *e*, that thy name
1Chr 17:24 thy servant be *e* before thee
2Chr 1:9 promise unto David my father be *e*
2Chr 12:1 when Rehoboam had *e* the kingdom
2Chr 20:20 LORD your God, so shall ye be *e*
2Chr 25:3 when the kingdom was *e* to him
2Chr 30:5 So they *e* a decree to make
Job 21:8 Their seed is *e* in their sight
Job 22:28 thing, and it shall be *e* unto thee
Ps 24:2 the seas, and *e* it upon the floods
Ps 40:2 feet upon a rock, and *e* my goings
Ps 78:5 For he *e* a testimony in Jacob, and
Ps 78:69 earth which he hath *e* for ever
Ps 89:21 With whom my hand shall be *e*
Ps 89:37 It shall be *e* for ever as the
Ps 93:2 Thy throne is *e* of old
Ps 96:10 the world also shall be *e* that it
Ps 102:28 their seed shall be *e* before thee
Ps 112:8 His heart is *e*, he shall not be
Ps 119:90 thou hast *e* the earth, and it
Ps 140:11 an evil speaker be *e* in the earth
Prov 3:19 hath he *e* the heavens
Prov 4:26 feet, and let all thy ways be *e*
Prov 8:28 When he *e* the clouds above
Prov 12:3 man shall not be *e* by wickedness
Prov 12:19 lip of truth shall be *e* for ever
Prov 15:22 of counsellors they are *e*
Prov 16:3 LORD, and thy thoughts shall be *e*
Prov 16:12 the throne is *e* by righteousness
Prov 20:18 Every purpose is *e* by counsel
Prov 24:3 and by understanding it is *e*
Prov 25:5 shall be *e* in righteousness
Prov 29:14 his throne shall be *e* for ever
Prov 30:4 who hath *e* all the ends of the
Is 2:2 be *e* in the top of the mountains
Is 7:9 believe, surely ye shall not be *e*
Is 16:5 And in mercy shall the throne be *e*
Is 45:18 he hath *e* it, he created it not
Is 54:14 In righteousness shalt thou be *e*
Jer 10:12 he hath *e* the world by his wisdom
Jer 30:20 congregation shall be *e* before me
Jer 51:15 he hath *e* the world by his wisdom
Dan 4:36 I was *e* in my kingdom, and
Mic 4:1 be *e* in the top of the mountains
Hab 1:12 thou hast *e* them for correction
Zec 5:11 and it shall be *e*, and set there
Mt 18:16 witnesses every word may be *e*
Acts 16:5 were the churches *e* in the faith
Rom 1:11 gift, to the end ye may be *e*
2Cor 13:1 witnesses shall every word be *e*
Heb 8:6 which was *e* upon better promises
Heb 13:9 that the heart be *e* with grace
2Pet 1:12 be *e* in the present truth

**ESTATE**
1Chr 17:17 to the *e* of a man of high degree
Est 1:19 *e* unto another that is better
Ps 136:23 Who remembered us in our low *e*
Eccl 1:16 saying, Lo, I am come to great *e*
Eccl 3:18 the *e* of the sons of men, that
Eze 16:55 shall return to their former *e*
Eze 16:55 shall return to their former *e*
Eze 16:55 shall return to your former *e*
Dan 11:7 roots shall one stand up in his *e*
Dan 11:20 Then shall stand up in his *e* a
Dan 11:21 in his *e* shall stand up a vile
Dan 11:38 But in his *e* shall he honour the
Lk 1:48 the low *e* of his handmaiden
Acts 22:5 and all the *e* of the elders
Rom 12:16 but condescend to men of low *e*
Col 4:8 that he might know your *e*
Jude 6 which kept not their first *e*

**ESTEEM**
Job 36:19 Will he *e* thy riches
Ps 119:128 Therefore I *e* all thy precepts

Is 53:4 yet we did *e* him stricken,
Phil 2:3 *e* other better than themselves
1Th 5:13 to *e* them very highly in love for

**ESTEEMED**
Deut 32:15 lightly *e* the Rock of his
1Sa 2:30 despise me shall be lightly *e*
1Sa 18:23 I am a poor man, and lightly *e*
Job 23:12 I have *e* the words of his mouth
Prov 17:28 lips is *e* a man of understanding
Is 29:16 shall be *e* as the potter's clay
Is 29:17 field shall be *e* as a forest
Is 53:3 he was despised, and we *e* him not
Lam 4:2 how are they *e* as earthen
Lk 16:15 for that which is highly *e* among
1Cor 6:4 who are least *e* in the church

**ESTEEMETH**
Job 41:27 He *e* iron as straw, and brass as
Rom 14:5 One man *e* one day above another
Rom 14:5 another *e* every day alike
Rom 14:14 but to him that *e* any thing to be

**ESTHER** *(est'-thur)* See ESTHER'S, HADASSAH. *A Jewish queen.*
Est 2:7 brought up Hadassah, that is, *E*
Est 2:8 that *E* was brought also unto the
Est 2:10 *E* had not shewed her people nor
Est 2:11 women's house, to know how *E* did
Est 2:15 Now when the turn of *E*, the
Est 2:15 *E* obtained favour in the sight of
Est 2:16 So *E* was taken unto king
Est 2:17 the king loved *E* above all the
Est 2:20 *E* had not yet shewed her kindred
Est 2:20 for *E* did the commandment of
Est 2:22 who told it unto *E* the queen
Est 2:22 *E* certified the king thereof in
Est 4:5 Then called *E* for Hatach, one of
Est 4:8 destroy them, to shew it unto *E*
Est 4:9 told *E* the words of Mordecai
Est 4:10 Again *E* spake unto Hatach, and
Est 4:13 Mordecai commanded to answer *E*
Est 4:15 Then *E* bade them return Mordecai
Est 4:17 to all that *E* had commanded him
Est 5:1 that *E* put on her royal apparel,
Est 5:2 when the king saw *E* the queen
Est 5:2 the king held out to *E* the golden
Est 5:2 So *E* drew near, and touched the
Est 5:3 unto her, What wilt thou, queen *E*
Est 5:4 *E* answered, If it seem good unto
Est 5:5 that he may do as *E* hath said
Est 5:5 the banquet that *E* had prepared
Est 5:6 the king said unto *E* at the
Est 5:7 Then answered *E*, and said, My
Est 5:12 *E* the queen did let no man come
Est 6:14 the banquet that *E* had prepared
Est 7:1 came to banquet with *E* the queen
Est 7:2 unto *E* on the second day at the
Est 7:2 What is thy petition, queen *E*
Est 7:3 Then *E* the queen answered and said
Est 7:5 answered and said unto *E* the queen
Est 7:6 *E* said, The adversary and enemy is
Est 7:7 for his life to *E* the queen
Est 7:8 fallen upon the bed whereon *E* was
Est 8:1 the Jews' enemy unto *E* the queen
Est 8:1 for *E* had told what he was unto
Est 8:2 *E* set Mordecai over the house of
Est 8:3 *E* spake yet again before the king
Est 8:4 out the golden sceptre toward *E*
Est 8:4 So *E* arose, and stood before the
Est 8:7 Ahasuerus said unto *E* the queen
Est 8:7 I have given *E* the house of Haman
Est 9:12 And the king said unto *E* the queen
Est 9:13 Then said *E*, If it please the
Est 9:25 But when *E* came before the king,
Est 9:29 Then *E* the queen, the daughter of
Est 9:31 *E* the queen had enjoined them, and
Est 9:32 the decree of *E* confirmed these

**ESTHER'S** *(es'-thurs)*
Est 2:18 and his servants, even *E* feast
Est 4:4 So *E* maids and her chamberlains
Est 4:12 And they told to Mordecai *E* words

**ESTIMATION**
Lev 5:15 with thy *e* by shekels of silver,
Lev 5:18 out of the flock, with thy *e*
Lev 6:6 out of the flock, with thy *e*
Lev 27:2 shall be for the LORD by thy *e*
Lev 27:3 thy *e* shall be of the male from
Lev 27:3 even thy *e* shall be fifty shekels
Lev 27:4 then thy *e* shall be thirty
Lev 27:5 then thy *e* shall be of the male
Lev 27:6 then thy *e* shall be of the male
Lev 27:6 for the female thy *e* shall be
Lev 27:7 then thy *e* shall be fifteen
Lev 27:8 But if he be poorer than thy *e*
Lev 27:13 a fifth part thereof unto thy *e*
Lev 27:15 of the money of thy *e* unto it
Lev 27:16 then thy *e* shall be according to
Lev 27:17 according to thy *e* it shall stand
Lev 27:18 and it shall be abated from thy *e*
Lev 27:19 of the money of thy *e* unto it
Lev 27:23 unto him the worth of thy *e*
Lev 27:23 he shall give thine *e* in that day
Lev 27:27 redeem it according to thine *e*
Lev 27:27 shall be sold according to thy *e*
Num 18:16 thou redeem, according to thine *e*

**ESTRANGED**
Job 19:13 acquaintance are verily *e* from me
Ps 58:3 The wicked are *e* from the womb
Ps 78:30 They were not *e* from their lust
Jer 19:4 have *e* this place, and have burned
Eze 14:5 because they are all *e* from me

**ETAM** *(e'-tam)*
*1. An area in western Judah.*
Judg 15:8 and dwelt in the top of the rock *E*
Judg 15:11 went to the top of the rock *E*
*2. A descendant of Judah.*
1Chr 4:3 And these were of the father of *E*
*3. A village in Simeon.*
1Chr 4:32 And their villages were, *E*
*4. A town in Judah.*
2Chr 11:6 He built even Beth-lehem, and *E*

**ETERNAL**
Deut 33:27 The *e* God is thy refuge, and
Is 60:15 I will make thee an *e* excellency
Mt 19:16 I do, that I may have *e* life
Mt 25:46 but the righteous into life *e*
Mk 3:29 but is in danger of *e* damnation
Mk 10:17 I do that I may inherit *e* life
Mk 10:30 and in the world to come *e* life
Lk 10:25 what shall I do to inherit *e* life
Lk 18:18 what shall I do to inherit *e* life
Jn 3:15 not perish, but have *e* life
Jn 4:36 and gathereth fruit unto life *e*
Jn 5:39 in them ye think ye have *e* life
Jn 6:54 and drinketh my blood, hath *e* life
Jn 6:68 thou hast the words of *e* life
Jn 10:28 And I give unto them *e* life
Jn 12:25 world shall keep it unto life *e*
Jn 17:2 that he should give *e* life to as
Jn 17:3 And this is life *e*, that they
Acts 13:48 were ordained to *e* life believed
Rom 1:20 that are made, even his *e* power
Rom 2:7 and honour and immortality, *e* life
Rom 5:21 through righteousness unto *e* life
Rom 6:23 but the gift of God is *e* life
2Cor 4:17 exceeding and *e* weight of glory
2Cor 4:18 things which are not seen are *e*
2Cor 5:1 made with hands, *e* in the heavens
Eph 3:11 According to the *e* purpose which
1Ti 1:17 Now unto the King *e*, immortal,
1Ti 6:12 of faith, lay hold on *e* life
1Ti 6:19 that they may lay hold on *e* life
2Ti 2:10 is in Christ Jesus with *e* glory
Titus 1:2 In hope of *e* life, which God,
Titus 3:7 according to the hope of *e* life
Heb 5:9 he became the author of *e*
Heb 6:2 of the dead, and of *e* judgment
Heb 9:12 having obtained *e* redemption for
Heb 9:14 who through the *e* Spirit offered
Heb 9:15 the promise of *e* inheritance
1Pet 5:10 unto his *e* glory by Christ Jesus
1Jn 1:2 and shew unto you that *e* life
1Jn 2:25 he hath promised us, even *e* life
1Jn 3:15 hath *e* life abiding in him
1Jn 5:11 that God hath given to us *e* life
1Jn 5:13 ye may know that ye have *e* life
1Jn 5:20 This is the true God, and *e* life
Jude 7 suffering the vengeance of *e* fire
Jude 21 our Lord Jesus Christ unto *e* life

**ETHAM** *(e'-tham) An encampment during the Exodus.*
Ex 13:20 from Succoth, and encamped in *E*
Num 33:6 from Succoth, and pitched in *E*
Num 33:7 And they removed from *E*, and turned
Num 33:8 journey in the wilderness of *E*

**ETHAN** *(e'-than)*
*1. A wise man in Solomon's time.*
1Kin 4:31 than *E* the Ezrahite, and Heman, and
Ps 89:*t* Maschil of *E* the Ezrahite
*2. A son of Zerah.*
1Chr 2:6 Zimri, and *E*, and Heman, and Calcol,
1Chr 2:8 And the sons of *E*
*3. A descendant of Gershon.*
1Chr 6:42 The son of *E*, the son of Zimmah,
*4. A descendant of Merari.*
1Chr 6:44 *E* the son of Kishi, the son of
1Chr 15:17 brethren, *E* the son of Kushaiah
1Chr 15:19 the singers, Heman, Asaph, and *E*

**ETHANIM** *(eth'-a-nim) Seventh month of the Hebrew year.*
1Kin 8:2 at the feast in the month *E*

**ETHBAAL** *(eth'-ba-al) Father of Jezebel.*
1Kin 16:31 of *E* king of the Zidonians

**ETHER** *(e'-ther) A city in Judah.*
Josh 15:42 Libnah, and *E*, and Ashan,
Josh 19:7 Ain, Remmon, and *E*, and Ashan

**ETHIOPIA** *(e-the-o'-pe-ah)* See CUSH, ETHIOPIAN.
*1. The land south of Egypt.*
Gen 2:13 compasseth the whole land of *E*
Est 1:1 reigned from India even unto *E*
Est 8:9 which are from India unto *E*
Job 28:19 The topaz of *E* shall not equal it
Ps 87:4 behold Philistia, and Tyre, with *E*
Is 18:1 which is beyond the rivers of *E*
Eze 29:10 Syene even unto the border of *E*
Zeph 3:10 the rivers of *E* my suppliants
Acts 8:27 and, behold, a man of *E*, an eunuch
*2. Inhabitants of Ethiopia.*
2Kin 19:9 heard say of Tirhakah king of *E*
Ps 68:31 *E* shall soon stretch out her
Is 20:3 and wonder upon Egypt and upon *E*
Is 20:5 ashamed of *E* their expectation,
Is 37:9 say concerning Tirhakah king of *E*
Is 43:3 I gave Egypt for thy ransom, *E*
Is 45:14 of Egypt, and merchandise of *E*
Eze 30:4 and great pain shall be in *E*
Eze 30:5 *E*, and Libya, and Lydia, and all the
Eze 38:5 Persia, *E*, and Libya with them
Nah 3:9 *E* and Egypt were her strength, and

**ETHIOPIAN**
Num 12:1 the *E* woman whom he had married
Num 12:1 for he had married an *E* woman
2Chr 14:9 the *E* with an host of a thousand
Jer 13:23 Can the *E* change his skin, or the
Jer 38:7 Now when Ebed-melech the *E*
Jer 38:10 king commanded Ebed-melech the *E*
Jer 38:12 Ebed-melech the *E* said unto
Jer 39:16 Go and speak to Ebed-melech the *E*

**ETHIOPIANS** *Inhabitants of Ethiopia.*
2Chr 12:3 the Lubim, the Sukkiims, and the *E*
2Chr 14:12 the LORD smote the *E* before Asa
2Chr 14:12 before Judah; and the *E* fled
2Chr 14:13 the *E* were overthrown, that they
2Chr 16:8 Were not the *E* and the Lubims a
2Chr 21:16 Arabians, that were near the *E*
Is 20:4 the *E* captives, young and old,
Jer 46:9 the *E* and the Libyans, that handle
Eze 30:9 to make the careless *E* afraid
Dan 11:43 the *E* shall be at his steps
Amos 9:7 not as children of the *E* unto me
Zeph 2:12 Ye *E* also, ye shall be slain by
Acts 8:27 under Candace queen of the *E*

**ETHNAN** *(eth'-nan) Grandson of Ashur.*
1Chr 4:7 were, Zereth, and Jezoar, and *E*

**ETHNI** *(eth'-ni)* See JEATERAI. *Ancestor of Asaph.*
1Chr 6:41 The son of *E*, the son of Zerah,

**EUBULUS** *(yu-bu'-lus) A Christian acquaintance of Paul.*
2Ti 4:21 *E* greeteth thee, and Pudens, and

**EUNICE** *(yu-ni'-see) Mother of Timothy.*
2Ti 1:5 grandmother Lois, and thy mother *E*

**EUNUCH**
Is 56:3 neither let the *e* say, Behold, I
Jer 52:25 He took also out of the city an *e*
Acts 8:27 an *e* of great authority under
Acts 8:34 the *e* answered Philip, and said, I
Acts 8:36 the *e* said, See, here is water
Acts 8:38 the water, both Philip and the *e*
Acts 8:39 that the *e* saw him no more

**EUNUCHS**
2Kin 9:32 looked out to him two or three *e*
2Kin 20:18 they shall be *e* in the palace of
Is 39:7 they shalt be *e* in the palace of
Is 56:4 unto the *e* that keep my sabbaths
Jer 29:2 the king, and the queen, and the *e*
Jer 34:19 the princes of Jerusalem, the *e*
Jer 38:7 one of the *e* which was in the
Jer 41:16 women, and the children, and the *e*
Dan 1:3 unto Ashpenaz the master of his *e*
Dan 1:7 the prince of the *e* gave names
Dan 1:8 of the *e* that he might not defile
Dan 1:9 love with the prince of the *e*
Dan 1:10 prince of the *e* said unto Daniel
Dan 1:11 of the *e* had set over Daniel
Dan 1:18 of the *e* brought them in before
Mt 19:12 For there are some *e*, which were
Mt 19:12 and there are some *e*, which were
Mt 19:12 *e*, which were made *e* of men
Mt 19:12 and there be *e*, which have made
Mt 19:12 which have made themselves *e* for

**EUODIAS** *(yu-o'-de-as) A Christian at Philippi.*
Phil 4:2 I beseech *E*, and beseech Syntyche,

**EUPHRATES** *(yu-fra'-teze) A river in Mesopotamia.*
Gen 2:14 And the fourth river is *E*
Gen 15:18 unto the great river, the river *E*
Deut 1:7 unto the great river, the river *E*
Deut 11:24 from the river, the river *E*
Josh 1:4 unto the great river, the river *E*
2Sa 8:3 recover his border at the river *E*
2Kin 23:29 king of Assyria to the river *E*
2Kin 24:7 river of Egypt unto the river *E*
1Chr 5:9 the wilderness from the river *E*
1Chr 18:3 his dominion by the river *E*
2Chr 35:20 to fight against Charchemish by *E*
Jer 13:4 upon thy loins, and arise, go to *E*
Jer 13:5 So I went, and hid it by *E*
Jer 13:6 LORD said unto me, Arise, go to *E*
Jer 13:7 Then I went to *E*, and digged, and
Jer 46:2 was by the river *E* in Carchemish
Jer 46:6 toward the north by the river *E*
Jer 46:10 the north country by the river *E*
Jer 51:63 and cast it into the midst of *E*
Rev 9:14 are bound in the great river *E*
Rev 16:12 his vial upon the great river *E*

**EUROCLYDON** *(yu-roc'-lid-on) A Mediterranean wind.*
Acts 27:14 it a tempestuous wind, called *E*

**EUTYCHUS** *(yu'-tik-us) Youth restored to life.*
Acts 20:9 a certain young man named *E*

**EVE** *(eev) Wife of Adam.*
Gen 3:20 And Adam called his wife's name *E*
Gen 4:1 And Adam knew *E* his wife
2Cor 11:3 beguiled *E* through his subtilty
1Ti 2:13 For Adam was first formed, then *E*

**EVENING**
Gen 1:5 And the *e* and the morning were the
Gen 1:8 And the *e* and the morning were the
Gen 1:13 And the *e* and the morning were the
Gen 1:19 And the *e* and the morning were the
Gen 1:23 And the *e* and the morning were the
Gen 1:31 And the *e* and the morning were the
Gen 8:11 the dove came in to him in the *e*
Gen 24:11 of water at the time of the *e*
Gen 29:23 And it came to pass in the *e*
Gen 30:16 came out of the field in the *e*
Ex 12:6 of Israel shall kill it in the *e*
Ex 16:8 give you in the *e* flesh to eat
Ex 18:13 Moses from the morning unto the *e*
Ex 27:21 from *e* to morning before the LORD
Lev 24:3 the *e* unto the morning before the
Deut 23:11 when *e* cometh on, he shall wash
Josh 10:26 upon the trees until the *e*
Judg 19:9 now the day draweth toward *e*
1Sa 14:24 man that eateth any food until *e*
1Sa 17:16 Philistine drew near morning and *e*
1Sa 30:17 even unto the *e* of the next day
1Kin 17:6 and bread and flesh in the *e*
1Kin 18:29 the offering of the *e* sacrifice
1Kin 18:36 the offering of the *e* sacrifice
2Kin 16:15 the *e* meat offering, and the
1Chr 16:40 offering continually morning and *e*
2Chr 2:4 the burnt offerings morning and *e*
2Chr 13:11 every *e* burnt sacrifices and sweet
2Chr 13:11 lamps thereof, to burn every *e*
2Chr 31:3 *e* burnt offerings, and the burnt
Ezr 3:3 even burnt offerings morning and *e*
Ezr 9:4 astonied until the *e* sacrifice
Ezr 9:5 at the *e* sacrifice I arose up
Est 2:14 In the *e* she went, and on the
Job 4:20 are destroyed from morning to *e*
Ps 55:17 *E*, and morning, and at noon, will I
Ps 59:6 They return at *e*: they make a
Ps 59:14 And at *e* let them return
Ps 65:8 of the morning and *e* to rejoice
Ps 90:6 in the *e* it is cut down, and
Ps 104:23 work and to his labour until the *e*
Ps 141:2 up of my hands as the *e* sacrifice
Prov 7:9 In the twilight, in the *e*
Eccl 11:6 in the *e* withhold not thine hand
Jer 6:4 of the *e* are stretched out
Eze 33:22 of the LORD was upon me in the *e*
Eze 46:2 shall not be shut until the *e*
Dan 8:26 And the vision of the *e* and the
Dan 9:21 about the time of the *e* oblation
Hab 1:8 are more fierce than the *e* wolves
Zeph 2:7 shall they lie down in the *e*
Zeph 3:3 her judges are *e* wolves
Zec 14:7 that at *e* time it shall be light
Mt 14:15 And when it was *e*, his disciples
Mt 14:23 and when the *e* was come, he was
Mt 16:2 and said unto them, When it is *e*
Mk 14:17 in the *e* he cometh with the
Lk 24:29 for it is toward *e*, and the day is
Jn 20:19 Then the same day at *e*, being the
Acts 28:23 the prophets, from morning till *e*

**EVENTIDE**
Gen 24:63 to meditate in the field at the *e*
Josh 7:6 the ark of the LORD until the *e*
Josh 8:29 of Ai he hanged on a tree until *e*
Mk 11:11 now the *e* was come, he went out
Acts 4:3 for it was now *e*

**EVERLASTING**
Gen 9:16 the *e* covenant between God
Gen 17:7 generations for an *e* covenant
Gen 17:8 of Canaan, for an *e* possession
Gen 17:13 in your flesh for an *e* covenant
Gen 17:19 with him for an *e* covenant
Gen 21:33 the name of the LORD, the *e* God
Gen 48:4 after thee for an *e* possession
Gen 49:26 the utmost bound of the *e* hills
Ex 40:15 an *e* priesthood throughout their
Lev 16:34 shall be an *e* statute unto you
Lev 24:8 of Israel by an *e* covenant
Num 25:13 the covenant of an *e* priesthood
Deut 33:27 and underneath are the *e* arms
2Sa 23:5 hath made with me an *e* covenant
1Chr 16:17 and to Israel for an *e* covenant
Ps 24:7 and be ye lifted up, ye *e* doors
Ps 24:9 even lift them up, ye *e* doors
Ps 41:13 Israel from *e*, and to *e*
Ps 90:2 world, even from *e* to *e*
Ps 93:2 thou art from *e*
Ps 100:5 his mercy is *e*
Ps 103:17 *e* to *e* upon them that
Ps 105:10 and to Israel for an *e* covenant
Ps 106:48 of Israel from *e* to *e*
Ps 112:6 shall be in *e* remembrance
Ps 119:142 is an *e* righteousness, and thy law
Ps 119:144 of thy testimonies is *e*
Ps 139:24 in me, and lead me in the way *e*
Ps 145:13 Thy kingdom is an *e* kingdom
Prov 8:23 I was set up from *e*, from the
Prov 10:25 the righteous is an *e* foundation
Is 9:6 The *e* Father, The Prince of Peace
Is 24:5 ordinance, broken the *e* covenant
Is 26:4 in the LORD JEHOVAH is *e* strength
Is 33:14 us shall dwell with *e* burnings
Is 35:10 songs and *e* joy upon their heads
Is 40:28 thou not heard, that the *e* God
Is 45:17 in the LORD with an *e* salvation
Is 51:11 *e* joy shall be upon their head
Is 54:8 but with *e* kindness will I have
Is 55:3 I will make an *e* covenant with
Is 55:13 for an *e* sign that shall not be
Is 56:5 I will give them an *e* name
Is 60:19 shall be unto thee an *e* light
Is 60:20 the LORD shall be thine *e* light
Is 61:7 *e* joy shall be unto them
Is 61:8 I will make an *e* covenant with
Is 63:12 them, to make himself an *e* name
Is 63:16 thy name is from *e*
Jer 10:10 is the living God, and an *e* king
Jer 20:11 their *e* confusion shall never be
Jer 23:40 I will bring an *e* reproach upon
Jer 31:3 I have loved thee with an *e* love
Jer 32:40 I will make an *e* covenant with
Eze 16:60 establish unto thee an *e* covenant
Eze 37:26 it shall be an *e* covenant with
Dan 4:3 his kingdom is an *e* kingdom
Dan 4:34 whose dominion is an *e* dominion
Dan 7:14 his dominion is an *e* dominion
Dan 7:27 whose kingdom is an *e* kingdom
Dan 9:24 to bring in *e* righteousness, and
Dan 12:2 earth shall awake, some to *e* life
Dan 12:2 and some to shame and *e* contempt
Mic 5:2 have been from of old, from *e*
Hab 1:12 Art thou not from *e*, O LORD my
Hab 3:6 the *e* mountains were scattered,
Hab 3:6 his ways are *e*
Mt 18:8 two feet to be cast into *e* fire
Mt 19:29 and shall inherit *e* life
Mt 25:41 from me, ye cursed, into *e* fire
Mt 25:46 shall go away into *e* punishment
Lk 16:9 receive you into *e* habitations
Lk 18:30 and in the world to come life *e*
Jn 3:16 not perish, but have *e* life
Jn 3:36 believeth on the Son hath *e* life
Jn 4:14 of water springing up into *e* life
Jn 5:24 on him that sent me, hath *e* life
Jn 6:27 meat which endureth unto *e* life
Jn 6:40 believeth on him, may have *e* life
Jn 6:47 that believeth on me hath *e* life
Jn 12:50 that his commandment is life *e*
Acts 13:46 yourselves unworthy of *e* life
Rom 6:22 unto holiness, and the end *e* life
Rom 16:26 to the commandment of the *e* God
Gal 6:8 shall of the Spirit reap life *e*
2Th 1:9 Who shall be punished with *e*
2Th 2:16 and hath given us *e* consolation
1Ti 1:16 believe on him to life *e*
1Ti 6:16 to whom be honour and power *e*
Heb 13:20 the blood of the *e* covenant
2Pet 1:11 into the *e* kingdom of our Lord
Jude 6 he hath reserved in *e* chains
Rev 14:6 having the *e* gospel to preach

**EVERMORE**
Deut 28:29 be only oppressed and spoiled *e*
2Sa 22:51 unto David, and to his seed for *e*
2Kin 17:37 you, ye shall observe to do for *e*
1Chr 17:14 throne shall be established for *e*
Ps 16:11 hand there are pleasures for *e*
Ps 18:50 to David, and to his seed for *e*
Ps 37:27 and dwell for *e*
Ps 77:8 doth his promise fail for *e*
Ps 86:12 and I will glorify thy name for *e*
Ps 89:28 mercy will I keep for him for *e*
Ps 89:52 Blessed be the LORD for *e*
Ps 92:8 thou, LORD, art most high for *e*
Ps 105:4 seek his face *e*
Ps 106:31 unto all generations for *e*
Ps 113:2 from this time forth and for *e*
Ps 115:18 from this time forth and for *e*
Ps 121:8 this time forth, and even for *e*
Ps 132:12 also sit upon thy throne for *e*
Ps 133:3 the blessing, even life for *e*
Eze 37:26 in the midst of them for *e*
Eze 37:28 be in the midst of them for *e*
Jn 6:34 him, Lord, *e* give us this bread
2Cor 11:31 Christ, which is blessed for *e*
1Th 5:16 Rejoice *e*
Heb 7:28 the Son, who is consecrated for *e*
Rev 1:18 and, behold, I am alive for *e*

**EVI** *(e'-vi) A Midian prince.*
Num 31:8 namely, *E*, and Rekem, and Zur, and
Josh 13:21 with the princes of Midian, *E*

**EVIDENCE**
Jer 32:10 And I subscribed the *e*, and sealed
Jer 32:11 So I took the *e* of the purchase,
Jer 32:12 I gave the *e* of the purchase unto
Jer 32:14 this *e* of the purchase, both
Jer 32:14 sealed, and this *e* which is open
Jer 32:16 Now when I had delivered the *e* of
Heb 11:1 for, the *e* of things not seen

**EVIDENT**
Job 6:28 for it is *e* unto you if I lie
Gal 3:11 law in the sight of God, it is *e*
Phil 1:28 to them an *e* token of perdition
Heb 7:14 For it is *e* that our Lord sprang
Heb 7:15 And it is yet far more *e*

## EVIL

Gen 2:9 tree of knowledge of good and *e*
Gen 2:17 of the knowledge of good and *e*
Gen 3:5 be as gods, knowing good and *e*
Gen 3:22 as one of us, to know good and *e*
Gen 6:5 his heart was only *e* continually
Gen 8:21 man's heart is *e* from his youth
Gen 19:19 the mountain, lest some *e* take me
Gen 37:2 unto his father their *e* report
Gen 37:20 Some *e* beast hath devoured him
Gen 37:33 an *e* beast hath devoured him
Gen 44:4 have ye rewarded *e* for good
Gen 44:5 ye have done *e* in so doing
Gen 44:34 lest peradventure I see the *e*
Gen 47:9 *e* have the days of the years of
Gen 48:16 which redeemed me from all *e*
Gen 50:15 all the *e* which we did unto him
Gen 50:17 for they did unto thee *e*
Gen 50:20 for you, ye thought *e* against me
Ex 5:19 did see that they were in *e* case
Ex 5:22 thou so *e* entreated this people
Ex 5:23 he hath done *e* to this people
Ex 10:10 for *e* is before you
Ex 23:2 not follow a multitude to do *e*
Ex 32:12 repent of this *e* against thy
Ex 32:14 the LORD repented of the *e* which
Ex 33:4 the people heard these *e* tidings
Lev 5:4 pronouncing with his lips to do *e*
Lev 26:6 I will rid *e* beasts out of the
Num 13:32 they brought up an *e* report of
Num 14:27 I bear with this *e* congregation
Num 14:35 it unto all this *e* congregation
Num 14:37 up the *e* report upon the land
Num 20:5 to bring us in unto this *e* place
Num 32:13 that had done *e* in the sight of
Deut 1:35 not one of these men of this *e*
Deut 1:39 no knowledge between good and *e*
Deut 4:25 shall do *e* in the sight of the
Deut 7:15 none of the *e* diseases of Egypt
Deut 13:5 So shalt thou put the *e* away from
Deut 15:9 thine eye be *e* against thy poor
Deut 17:7 put the *e* away from among you
Deut 17:12 shalt put away the *e* from Israel
Deut 19:19 put the *e* away from among you
Deut 19:20 no more any such *e* among you
Deut 21:21 so shalt thou put *e* away from
Deut 22:14 bring up an *e* name upon her, and
Deut 22:19 an *e* name upon a virgin of Israel
Deut 22:21 so shalt thou put *e* away from
Deut 22:22 shalt thou put away *e* from Israel
Deut 22:24 shalt put away *e* from among you
Deut 24:7 thou shalt put *e* away from among
Deut 26:6 And the Egyptians *e* entreated us
Deut 28:54 his eye shall be *e* toward his
Deut 28:56 her eye shall be *e* toward the
Deut 29:21 LORD shall separate him unto *e*
Deut 30:15 day life and good, and death and *e*
Deut 31:29 *e* will befall you in the latter
Deut 31:29 because ye will do *e* in the sight
Josh 23:15 LORD bring upon you all *e* things
Josh 24:15 if it seem *e* unto you to serve
Judg 2:11 did *e* in the sight of the LORD
Judg 2:15 the LORD was against them for *e*
Judg 3:7 did *e* in the sight of the LORD
Judg 3:12 the children of Israel did *e*
Judg 3:12 because they had done *e* in the
Judg 4:1 did *e* in the sight of the LORD
Judg 6:1 did *e* in the sight of the LORD
Judg 9:23 Then God sent an *e* spirit between
Judg 9:57 all the *e* of the men of Shechem
Judg 10:6 the children of Israel did *e*
Judg 13:1 the children of Israel did *e*
Judg 20:13 death, and put away *e* from Israel
Judg 20:34 knew not that *e* was near them
Judg 20:41 for they saw that *e* was come upon
1Sa 2:23 for I hear of your *e* dealings by
1Sa 6:9 then he hath done us this great *e*
1Sa 12:19 added unto all our sins this *e*
1Sa 15:19 didst *e* in the sight of the LORD
1Sa 16:14 an *e* spirit from the LORD
1Sa 16:15 an *e* spirit from God troubleth
1Sa 16:16 when the *e* spirit from God is
1Sa 16:23 when the *e* spirit from God was
1Sa 16:23 the *e* spirit departed from him
1Sa 18:10 that the *e* spirit from God came
1Sa 19:9 the *e* spirit from the LORD was
1Sa 20:7 then be sure that *e* is determined
1Sa 20:9 for if I knew certainly that *e*
1Sa 20:13 it please my father to do thee *e*
1Sa 24:11 see that there is neither *e* nor
1Sa 24:17 whereas I have rewarded thee *e*
1Sa 25:3 was churlish and *e* in his doings
1Sa 25:17 for *e* is determined against our
1Sa 25:21 and he hath requited me *e* for good
1Sa 25:26 and they that seek *e* to my lord
1Sa 25:28 *e* hath not been found in thee all
1Sa 25:39 and hath kept his servant from *e*
1Sa 26:18 or what *e* is in mine hand
1Sa 29:6 for I have not found *e* in thee
2Sa 3:39 of *e* according to his wickedness
2Sa 12:9 of the LORD, to do *e* in his sight
2Sa 12:11 I will raise up *e* against thee
2Sa 13:16 this *e* in sending me away is
2Sa 15:14 bring *e* upon us, and smite the
2Sa 17:14 LORD might bring *e* upon Absalom
2Sa 19:7 *e* that befell thee from thy youth
2Sa 19:35 can I discern between good and *e*
2Sa 24:16 the LORD repented him of the *e*
1Kin 5:4 neither adversary nor *e* occurrent
1Kin 9:9 LORD brought upon them all this *e*
1Kin 11:6 Solomon did *e* in the sight of the
1Kin 13:33 returned not from his *e* way
1Kin 14:9 But hast done *e* above all that
1Kin 14:10 I will bring *e* upon the house of
1Kin 14:22 Judah did *e* in the sight of the
1Kin 15:26 he did *e* in the sight of the LORD
1Kin 15:34 he did *e* in the sight of the LORD
1Kin 16:7 even for all the *e* that he did in
1Kin 16:19 doing *e* in the sight of the LORD
1Kin 16:25 But Omri wrought *e* in the eyes of
1Kin 16:30 Ahab the son of Omri did *e* in the
1Kin 17:20 hast thou also brought *e* upon the
1Kin 21:20 work *e* in the sight of the LORD
1Kin 21:21 Behold, I will bring *e* upon thee
1Kin 21:29 will not bring the *e* in his days
1Kin 21:29 will I bring the *e* upon his house
1Kin 22:8 good concerning me, but *e*
1Kin 22:18 no good concerning me, but *e*
1Kin 22:23 hath spoken *e* concerning thee
1Kin 22:52 he did *e* in the sight of the LORD
2Kin 3:2 he wrought *e* in the sight of the
2Kin 6:33 Behold, this *e* is of the LORD
2Kin 8:12 Because I know the *e* that thou
2Kin 8:18 he did *e* in the sight of the LORD
2Kin 8:27 did *e* in the sight of the LORD,
2Kin 13:2 he did that which was *e* in the
2Kin 13:11 he did that which was *e* in the
2Kin 14:24 he did that which was *e* in the
2Kin 15:9 he did that which was *e* in the
2Kin 15:18 he did that which was *e* in the
2Kin 15:24 he did that which was *e* in the
2Kin 15:28 he did that which was *e* in the
2Kin 17:2 he did that which was *e* in the
2Kin 17:13 saying, Turn ye from your *e* ways
2Kin 17:17 sold themselves to do *e* in the
2Kin 21:2 he did that which was *e* in the
2Kin 21:9 seduced them to do more *e* than
2Kin 21:12 am bringing such *e* upon Jerusalem
2Kin 21:15 done that which was *e* in my sight
2Kin 21:16 in doing that which was *e* in the
2Kin 21:20 he did that which was *e* in the
2Kin 22:16 I will bring *e* upon this place,
2Kin 22:20 eyes shall not see all the *e*
2Kin 23:32 he did that which was *e* in the
2Kin 23:37 he did that which was *e* in the
2Kin 24:9 he did that which was *e* in the
2Kin 24:19 he did that which was *e* in the
1Chr 2:3 was *e* in the sight of the LORD
1Chr 4:10 that thou wouldest keep me from *e*
1Chr 7:23 because it went *e* with his house
1Chr 21:15 and he repented him of the *e*
1Chr 21:17 that have sinned and done *e* indeed
2Chr 7:22 he brought all this *e* upon them
2Chr 12:14 And he did *e*, because he prepared
2Chr 18:7 good unto me, but always *e*
2Chr 18:17 not prophesy good unto me, but *e*
2Chr 18:22 LORD hath spoken *e* against thee
2Chr 20:9 when *e* cometh upon us, as the
2Chr 21:6 was *e* in the eyes of the LORD
2Chr 22:4 Wherefore he did *e* in the sight
2Chr 29:6 done that which was *e* in the eyes
2Chr 33:2 But did that which was *e* in the
2Chr 33:6 he wrought much *e* in the sight of
2Chr 33:22 was *e* in the sight of the LORD
2Chr 34:24 I will bring *e* upon this place,
2Chr 34:28 the *e* that I will bring upon this
2Chr 36:5 he did that which was *e* in the
2Chr 36:9 he did that which was *e* in the
2Chr 36:12 he did that which was *e* in the
Ezr 9:13 is come upon us for our *e* deeds
Neh 6:13 might have matter for an *e* report
Neh 9:28 they did *e* again before thee
Neh 13:7 understood of the *e* that Eliashib
Neh 13:17 What *e* thing is this that ye do,
Neh 13:18 our God bring all this *e* upon us
Neh 13:27 unto you to do all this great *e*
Est 7:7 for he saw that there was *e*
Est 8:6 *e* that shall come unto my people
Job 1:1 that feared God, and eschewed *e*
Job 1:8 that feareth God, and escheweth *e*
Job 2:3 that feareth God, and escheweth *e*
Job 2:10 of God, and shall we not receive *e*
Job 2:11 all this *e* that was come upon him
Job 5:19 seven there shall no *e* touch thee
Job 8:20 neither will he help the *e* doers
Job 24:21 He *e* entreateth the barren that
Job 28:28 to depart from *e* is understanding
Job 30:26 for good, then *e* came unto me
Job 31:29 lifted up myself when *e* found him
Job 35:12 because of the pride of *e* men
Job 42:11 comforted him over all the *e* that
Ps 5:4 neither shall *e* dwell with thee
Ps 7:4 If I have rewarded *e* unto him
Ps 10:15 arm of the wicked and the *e* man
Ps 15:3 nor doeth *e* to his neighbour, nor
Ps 21:11 For they intended *e* against thee
Ps 23:4 shadow of death, I will fear no *e*
Ps 34:13 Keep thy tongue from *e*, and thy
Ps 34:14 Depart from *e*, and do good
Ps 34:16 LORD is against them that do *e*
Ps 34:21 *E* shall slay the wicked
Ps 35:12 They rewarded me *e* for good to
Ps 36:4 he abhorreth not *e*
Ps 37:8 not thyself in any wise to do *e*
Ps 37:19 not be ashamed in the *e* time
Ps 37:27 Depart from *e*, and do good
Ps 38:20 They also that render *e* for good
Ps 40:14 and put to shame that wish me *e*
Ps 41:5 Mine enemies speak *e* of me
Ps 41:8 An *e* disease, say they, cleaveth
Ps 49:5 should I fear in the days of *e*
Ps 50:19 Thou givest thy mouth to *e*
Ps 51:4 and done this *e* in thy sight
Ps 52:3 Thou lovest *e* more than good
Ps 54:5 He shall reward *e* unto mine
Ps 56:5 thoughts are against me for *e*
Ps 64:5 themselves in an *e* matter
Ps 78:49 by sending *e* angels among them
Ps 90:15 the years wherein we have seen *e*
Ps 91:10 There shall no *e* befall thee
Ps 97:10 Ye that love the LORD, hate *e*
Ps 109:5 they have rewarded me *e* for good
Ps 109:20 them that speak *e* against my soul
Ps 112:7 shall not be afraid of *e* tidings
Ps 119:101 my feet from every *e* way, that I
Ps 121:7 shall preserve thee from all *e*
Ps 140:1 me, O LORD, from the *e* man
Ps 140:11 Let not an *e* speaker be
Ps 140:11 *e* shall hunt the violent man to
Ps 141:4 not my heart to any *e* thing
Prov 1:16 For their feet run to *e*, and make
Prov 1:33 and shall be quiet from fear of *e*
Prov 2:12 thee from the way of the *e* man
Prov 2:14 Who rejoice to do *e*, and delight
Prov 3:7 fear the LORD, and depart from *e*
Prov 3:29 Devise not *e* against thy
Prov 4:14 and go not in the way of *e* men
Prov 4:27 remove thy foot from *e*
Prov 5:14 in all *e* in the midst of the
Prov 6:24 To keep thee from the *e* woman
Prov 8:13 The fear of the LORD is to hate *e*
Prov 8:13 pride, and arrogancy, and the *e* way
Prov 11:19 so he that pursueth *e* pursueth it
Prov 12:12 wicked desireth the net of *e* men
Prov 12:20 the heart of them that imagine *e*
Prov 12:21 There shall no *e* happen to the
Prov 13:19 to fools to depart from *e*
Prov 13:21 *E* pursueth sinners
Prov 14:16 man feareth, and departeth from *e*
Prov 14:19 The *e* bow before the good
Prov 14:22 Do they not err that devise *e*
Prov 15:3 in every place, beholding the *e*
Prov 15:15 the days of the afflicted are *e*
Prov 15:28 the wicked poureth out *e* things
Prov 16:4 even the wicked for the day of *e*
Prov 16:6 of the LORD men depart from *e*
Prov 16:17 the upright is to depart from *e*
Prov 16:27 An ungodly man diggeth up *e*
Prov 16:30 his lips he bringeth *e* to pass
Prov 17:11 An *e* man seeketh only rebellion

Prov 17:13 Whoso rewardeth *e* for good
Prov 17:13 *e* shall not depart from his house
Prov 19:23 he shall not be visited with *e*
Prov 20:8 away all *e* with his eyes
Prov 20:22 Say not thou, I will recompense *e*
Prov 20:30 of a wound cleanseth away *e*
Prov 21:10 The soul of the wicked desireth *e*
Prov 22:3 A prudent man foreseeth the *e*
Prov 23:6 bread of him that hath an *e* eye
Prov 24:1 Be not thou envious against *e* men
Prov 24:8 He that deviseth to do *e* shall be
Prov 24:19 Fret not thyself because of *e* men
Prov 24:20 shall be no reward to the *e* man
Prov 27:12 A prudent man foreseeth the *e*
Prov 28:5 *E* men understand not judgment
Prov 28:10 to go astray in an *e* way, he
Prov 28:22 hasteth to be rich hath an *e* eye
Prov 29:6 of an *e* man there is a snare
Prov 30:32 or if thou hast thought *e*
Prov 31:12 not *e* all the days of her life
Eccl 2:21 This also is vanity and a great *e*
Eccl 4:3 who hath not seen the *e* work that
Eccl 5:1 they consider not that they do *e*
Eccl 5:13 There is a sore *e* which I have
Eccl 5:14 those riches perish by *e* travail
Eccl 5:16 And this also is a sore *e*, that in
Eccl 6:1 There is an *e* which I have seen
Eccl 6:2 is vanity, and it is an *e* disease
Eccl 8:3 stand not in an *e* thing
Eccl 8:5 commandment shall feel no *e* thing
Eccl 8:11 Because sentence against an *e*
Eccl 8:11 men is fully set in them to do *e*
Eccl 8:12 a sinner do *e* an hundred times
Eccl 9:3 This is an *e* among all things
Eccl 9:3 of the sons of men is full of *e*
Eccl 9:12 fishes that are taken in an *e* net
Eccl 9:12 sons of men snared in an *e* time
Eccl 10:5 There is an *e* which I have seen
Eccl 11:2 what *e* shall be upon the earth
Eccl 11:10 put away *e* from thy flesh
Eccl 12:1 while the *e* days come not, nor
Eccl 12:14 it be good, or whether it be *e*
Is 1:16 put away the *e* of your doings
Is 1:16 cease to do *e*
Is 3:9 have rewarded *e* unto themselves
Is 5:20 that call *e* good, and good *e*
Is 7:5 have taken *e* counsel against thee
Is 7:15 that he may know to refuse the *e*
Is 7:16 child shall know to refuse the *e*
Is 13:11 will punish the world for their *e*
Is 31:2 he also is wise, and will bring *e*
Is 32:7 also of the churl are *e*
Is 33:15 shutteth his eyes from seeing *e*
Is 41:23 yea, do good, or do *e*, that we
Is 45:7 I make peace, and create *e*
Is 47:11 Therefore shall *e* come upon thee
Is 56:2 keepeth his hand from doing any *e*
Is 57:1 is taken away from the *e* to come
Is 59:7 Their feet run to *e*, and they make
Is 59:15 from *e* maketh himself a prey
Is 65:12 but did *e* before mine eyes, and
Is 66:4 but they did *e* before mine eyes,
Jer 1:14 Out of the north an *e* shall break
Jer 2:3 *e* shall come upon them, saith the
Jer 2:19 and see that it is an *e* thing
Jer 3:5 done *e* things as thou couldest
Jer 3:17 the imagination of their *e* heart
Jer 4:4 because of the *e* of your doings
Jer 4:6 for I will bring *e* from the north
Jer 4:22 they are wise to do *e*, but to do
Jer 5:12 neither shall *e* come upon us
Jer 6:1 for *e* appeareth out of the north,
Jer 6:19 I will bring *e* upon this people,
Jer 7:24 the imagination of their *e* heart
Jer 7:30 of Judah have done *e* in my sight
Jer 8:3 them that remain of this *e* family
Jer 9:3 for they proceed from *e* to *e*
Jer 10:5 for they cannot do *e*, neither
Jer 11:8 the imagination of their *e* heart
Jer 11:11 Behold, I will bring *e* upon them
Jer 11:15 when thou doest *e*, then thou
Jer 11:17 hath pronounced *e* against thee
Jer 11:17 for the *e* of the house of Israel
Jer 11:23 for I will bring *e* upon the men
Jer 12:14 against all mine *e* neighbours
Jer 13:10 This *e* people, which refuse to
Jer 13:23 good, that are accustomed to do *e*
Jer 15:11 thee well in the time of *e*
Jer 16:10 all this great *e* against us
Jer 16:12 the imagination of his *e* heart

Jer 17:17 thou art my hope in the day of *e*
Jer 17:18 bring upon them the day of *e*
Jer 18:8 pronounced, turn from their *e*
Jer 18:8 I will repent of the *e* that I
Jer 18:10 If it do *e* in my sight, that it
Jer 18:11 I frame *e* against you, and devise
Jer 18:11 ye now every one from his *e* way
Jer 18:12 do the imagination of his *e* heart
Jer 18:20 Shall *e* be recompensed for good
Jer 19:3 I will bring *e* upon this place,
Jer 19:15 upon all her towns all the *e* that
Jer 21:10 my face against this city for *e*
Jer 21:12 because of the *e* of your doings
Jer 23:2 upon you the *e* of your doings
Jer 23:10 dried up, and their course is *e*
Jer 23:12 for I will bring *e* upon them
Jer 23:17 heart, No *e* shall come upon you
Jer 23:22 have turned them from their *e* way
Jer 23:22 from the *e* of their doings
Jer 24:3 and the *e*, very *e*
Jer 24:3 cannot be eaten, they are so *e*
Jer 24:8 And as the *e* figs, which cannot be
Jer 24:8 cannot be eaten, they are so *e*
Jer 25:5 now every one from his *e* way
Jer 25:5 from the *e* of your doings, and
Jer 25:29 I begin to bring *e* on the city
Jer 25:32 *e* shall go forth from nation to
Jer 26:3 and turn every man from his *e* way
Jer 26:3 that I may repent me of the *e*
Jer 26:3 because of the *e* of their doings
Jer 26:13 *e* that he hath pronounced against
Jer 26:19 the LORD repented him of the *e*
Jer 26:19 procure great *e* against our souls
Jer 28:8 great kingdoms, of war, and of *e*
Jer 29:11 thoughts of peace, and not of *e*
Jer 29:17 cannot be eaten, they are so *e*
Jer 32:23 all this *e* to come upon them
Jer 32:30 of Judah have only done *e* before
Jer 32:32 Because of all the *e* of the
Jer 32:42 all this great *e* upon this people
Jer 35:15 ye now every man from his *e* way
Jer 35:17 of Jerusalem all the *e* that I
Jer 36:3 of Judah will hear all the *e*
Jer 36:3 return every man from his *e* way
Jer 36:7 return every one from his *e* way
Jer 36:31 all the *e* that I have pronounced
Jer 38:9 these men have done *e* in all that
Jer 39:16 my words upon this city for *e*
Jer 40:2 pronounced this *e* upon this place
Jer 41:11 heard of all the *e* that Ishmael
Jer 42:6 it be good, or whether it be *e*
Jer 42:10 for I repent me of the *e* that I
Jer 42:17 the *e* that I will bring upon them
Jer 44:2 Ye have seen all the *e* that I
Jer 44:7 this great *e* against your souls
Jer 44:11 set my face against you for *e*
Jer 44:17 and were well, and saw no *e*
Jer 44:22 because of the *e* of your doings
Jer 44:23 therefore this *e* is happened unto
Jer 44:27 I will watch over them for *e*
Jer 44:29 surely stand against you for *e*
Jer 45:5 I will bring *e* upon all flesh,
Jer 48:2 they have devised *e* against it
Jer 49:23 for they have heard *e* tidings
Jer 49:37 and I will bring *e* upon them
Jer 51:24 of Chaldea all their *e* that they
Jer 51:60 wrote in a book all the *e* that
Jer 51:64 shall not rise from the *e* that I
Jer 52:2 he did that which was *e* in the
Lam 3:38 of the most High proceedeth not *e*
Eze 5:16 upon them the *e* arrows of famine
Eze 5:17 *e* beasts, and they shall bereave
Eze 6:10 that I would do this *e* unto them
Eze 6:11 Alas for all the *e* abominations
Eze 7:5 An *e*, an only *e*, behold, is
Eze 14:22 the *e* that I have brought upon
Eze 33:11 turn ye, turn ye from your *e* ways
Eze 34:25 will cause the *e* beasts to cease
Eze 36:31 shall ye remember your own *e* ways
Eze 38:10 and thou shalt think an *e* thought
Dan 9:12 us, by bringing upon us a great *e*
Dan 9:13 all this *e* is come upon us
Dan 9:14 hath the LORD watched upon the *e*
Joel 2:13 and repenteth him of the *e*
Amos 3:6 shall there be *e* in a city
Amos 5:13 for it is an *e* time
Amos 5:14 Seek good, and not *e*, that ye may
Amos 5:15 Hate the *e*, and love the good, and
Amos 6:3 Ye that put far away the *e* day
Amos 9:4 set mine eyes upon them for *e*

Amos 9:10 The *e* shall not overtake nor
Jonah 1:7 for whose cause this *e* is upon us
Jonah 1:8 for whose cause this *e* is upon us
Jonah 3:8 turn every one from his *e* way
Jonah 3:10 that they turned from their *e* way
Jonah 3:10 and God repented of the *e*, that he
Jonah 4:2 and repentest thee of the *e*
Mic 1:12 but *e* came down from the LORD
Mic 2:1 and work *e* upon their beds
Mic 2:3 this family do I devise an *e*
Mic 2:3 for this time is *e*
Mic 3:2 Who hate the good, and love the *e*
Mic 3:11 none *e* can come upon us
Mic 7:3 That they may do *e* with both
Nah 1:11 that imagineth *e* against the LORD
Hab 1:13 of purer eyes than to behold *e*
Hab 2:9 an *e* covetousness to his house
Hab 2:9 be delivered from the power of *e*
Zeph 1:12 not do good, neither will he do *e*
Zeph 3:15 thou shalt not see *e* any more
Zec 1:4 *e* ways, and from your *e* doings
Zec 7:10 let none of you imagine *e* against
Zec 8:17 let none of you imagine *e* in your
Mal 1:8 blind for sacrifice, is it not *e*
Mal 1:8 the lame and sick, is it not *e*
Mal 2:17 Every one that doeth *e* is good in
Mt 5:11 manner of *e* against you falsely
Mt 5:37 is more than these cometh of *e*
Mt 5:39 unto you, That ye resist not *e*
Mt 5:45 maketh his sun to rise on the *e*
Mt 6:13 temptation, but deliver us from *e*
Mt 6:23 But if thine eye be *e*, thy whole
Mt 6:34 unto the day is the *e* thereof
Mt 7:11 If ye then, being *e*, know how to
Mt 7:17 tree bringeth forth *e* fruit
Mt 7:18 tree cannot bring forth *e* fruit
Mt 9:4 think ye *e* in your hearts
Mt 12:34 of vipers, how can ye, being *e*
Mt 12:35 an *e* man out of the *e* treasure
Mt 12:35 bringeth forth *e* things
Mt 12:39 answered and said unto them, An *e*
Mt 15:19 of the heart proceed *e* thoughts
Mt 20:15 Is thine eye *e*, because I am good
Mt 24:48 if that *e* servant shall say in
Mt 27:23 said, Why, what *e* hath he done
Mk 3:4 on the sabbath days, or to do *e*
Mk 7:21 proceed *e* thoughts, adulteries,
Mk 7:22 an *e* eye, blasphemy, pride,
Mk 7:23 All these *e* things come from
Mk 9:39 that can lightly speak *e* of me
Mk 15:14 them, Why, what *e* hath he done
Lk 6:9 days to do good, or to do *e*
Lk 6:22 you, and cast out your name as *e*
Lk 6:35 unto the unthankful and to the *e*
Lk 6:45 an *e* man out of the *e* treasure
Lk 6:45 bringeth forth that which is *e*
Lk 7:21 and plagues, and of *e* spirits
Lk 8:2 had been healed of *e* spirits
Lk 11:4 but deliver us from *e*
Lk 11:13 If ye then, being *e*, know how to
Lk 11:29 to say, This is an *e* generation
Lk 11:34 but when thine eye is *e*, thy body
Lk 16:25 and likewise Lazarus *e* things
Lk 23:22 time, Why, what *e* hath he done
Jn 3:19 light, because their deeds were *e*
Jn 3:20 one that doeth *e* hateth the light
Jn 5:29 and they that have done *e*, unto
Jn 7:7 it, that the works thereof are *e*
Jn 17:15 shouldest keep them from the *e*
Jn 18:23 answered him, If I have spoken *e*
Jn 18:23 bear witness of the *e*
Acts 7:6 entreat them *e* four hundred years
Acts 7:19 *e* entreated our fathers, so that
Acts 9:13 how much *e* he hath done to thy
Acts 14:2 made their minds *e* affected
Acts 19:9 but spake *e* of that way before
Acts 19:12 the *e* spirits went out of them
Acts 19:13 to call over them which had *e*
Acts 19:15 the *e* spirit answered and said,
Acts 19:16 the man in whom the *e* spirit was
Acts 23:5 Thou shalt not speak *e* of the
Acts 23:9 saying, We find no *e* in this man
Acts 24:20 they have found any *e* doing in me
Rom 1:30 boasters, inventors of *e* things
Rom 2:9 every soul of man that doeth *e*
Rom 3:8 affirm that we say,) Let us do *e*
Rom 7:19 but the *e* which I would not, that
Rom 7:21 do good, *e* is present with me
Rom 9:11 neither having done any good or *e*
Rom 12:9 Abhor that which is *e*

Rom 12:17 Recompense to no man *e* for *e*
Rom 12:17 Recompense to no man *e* for *e*
Rom 12:21 Be not overcome of *e*
Rom 12:21 but overcome *e* with good
Rom 13:3 to good works, but to the *e*
Rom 13:4 But if thou do that which is *e*
Rom 13:4 wrath upon him that doeth *e*
Rom 14:16 not then your good be *e* spoken of
Rom 14:20 but it is *e* for that man who
Rom 16:19 is good, and simple concerning *e*
1Cor 10:6 we should not lust after *e* things
1Cor 10:30 why am I *e* spoken of for that for
1Cor 13:5 easily provoked, thinketh no *e*
1Cor 15:33 *e* communications corrupt good
2Cor 6:8 by *e* report and good report
2Cor 13:7 Now I pray to God that ye do no *e*
Gal 1:4 us from this present *e* world
Eph 4:31 *e* speaking, be put away from you,
Eph 5:16 the time, because the days are *e*
Eph 6:13 be able to withstand in the *e* day
Phil 3:2 of dogs, beware of *e* workers
Col 3:5 *e* concupiscence, and covetousness,
1Th 5:15 See that none render *e* for *e*
1Th 5:22 Abstain from all appearance of *e*
2Th 3:3 stablish you, and keep you from *e*
1Ti 6:4 strife, railings, *e* surmisings,
1Ti 6:10 of money is the root of all *e*
2Ti 2:9 I suffer trouble, as an *e* doer
2Ti 3:13 But *e* men and seducers shall wax
2Ti 4:14 the coppersmith did me much *e*
2Ti 4:18 deliver me from every *e* work
Titus 1:12 liars, *e* beasts, slow bellies
Titus 2:8 having no *e* thing to say of you
Titus 3:2 To speak *e* of no man, to be no
Heb 3:12 any of you an *e* heart of unbelief
Heb 5:14 to discern both good and *e*
Heb 10:22 sprinkled from an *e* conscience
Jas 1:13 for God cannot be tempted with *e*
Jas 2:4 are become judges of *e* thoughts
Jas 3:8 it is an unruly *e*, full of deadly
Jas 3:16 is confusion and every *e* work
Jas 4:11 Speak not *e* one of another,
Jas 4:11 He that speaketh *e* of his brother
Jas 4:11 speaketh *e* of the law, and judgeth
Jas 4:16 all such rejoicing is *e*
1Pet 2:1 and envies, and all *e* speakings,
1Pet 3:9 Not rendering *e* for *e*, or
1Pet 3:9 Not rendering *e* for *e*, or
1Pet 3:10 let him refrain his tongue from *e*
1Pet 3:11 Let him eschew *e*, and do good
1Pet 3:12 Lord is against them that do *e*
1Pet 3:16 that, whereas they speak *e* of you
1Pet 3:17 for well doing, than for *e* doing
1Pet 4:4 excess of riot, speaking *e* of you
1Pet 4:14 on their part he is *e* spoken of
2Pet 2:2 way of truth shall be *e* spoken of
2Pet 2:10 afraid to speak *e* of dignities
2Pet 2:12 speak *e* of the things that they
1Jn 3:12 Because his own works were *e*
2Jn 11 speed is partaker of his *e* deeds
3Jn 11 follow not that which is *e*
3Jn 11 he that doeth *e* hath not seen God
Jude 8 dominion, and speak *e* of dignities
Jude 10 But these speak *e* of those things
Rev 2:2 canst not bear them which are *e*

**EVILDOERS**
Ps 26:5 have hated the congregation of *e*
Ps 37:1 Fret not thyself because of *e*
Ps 37:9 For *e* shall be cut off
Ps 94:16 will rise up for me against the *e*
Ps 119:115 Depart from me, ye *e*
Is 1:4 laden with iniquity, a seed of *e*
Is 14:20 the seed of *e* shall never be
Is 31:2 arise against the house of the *e*
Jer 20:13 of the poor from the hand of *e*
Jer 23:14 strengthen also the hands of *e*
1Pet 2:12 they speak against you as *e*
1Pet 2:14 by him for the punishment of *e*
1Pet 3:16 they speak evil of you, as of *e*

**EVIL-MERODACH** *(e'-vil-mer'-o-dak)*
*Son of Nebuchadnezzar.*
2Kin 25:27 that *E* king of Babylon in the
Jer 52:31 that *E* king of Babylon in the

**EVILS**
Deut 31:17 they shall be devoured, and many *e*
Deut 31:17 day, Are not these *e* come upon us
Deut 31:18 *e* which they shall have wrought
Deut 31:21 shall come to pass, when many *e*
Ps 40:12 For innumerable *e* have compassed
Jer 2:13 my people have committed two *e*
Eze 6:9 *e* which they have committed in
Eze 20:43 all your *e* that ye have committed
Lk 3:19 for all the *e* which Herod had

**EWE**
Gen 21:28 Abraham set seven *e* lambs of the
Gen 21:29 What mean these seven *e* lambs
Gen 21:30 For these seven *e* lambs shalt
Lev 14:10 one *e* lamb of the first year
Lev 22:28 And whether it be cow or *e*
Num 6:14 one *e* lamb of the first year
2Sa 12:3 nothing, save one little *e* lamb

**EXACT**
Deut 15:2 he shall not *e* it of his
Deut 15:3 foreigner thou mayest *e* it again
Neh 5:7 Ye *e* usury, every one of his
Neh 5:10 might *e* of them money and corn
Neh 5:11 and the oil, that ye *e* of them
Ps 89:22 The enemy shall not *e* upon him
Is 58:3 pleasure, and *e* all your labours
Lk 3:13 *E* no more than that which is

**EXALT**
Ex 15:2 my father's God, and I will *e* him
1Sa 2:10 *e* the horn of his anointed
Job 17:4 therefore shalt thou not *e* them
Ps 34:3 let us *e* his name together
Ps 37:34 he shall *e* thee to inherit the
Ps 66:7 not the rebellious *e* themselves
Ps 92:10 But my horn shalt thou *e* like the
Ps 99:5 *E* ye the LORD our God, and worship
Ps 99:9 *E* the LORD our God, and worship at
Ps 107:32 Let them *e* him also in the
Ps 118:28 thou art my God, I will *e* thee
Ps 140:8 lest they *e* themselves
Prov 4:8 *E* her, and she shall promote thee
Is 13:2 *e* the voice unto them, shake the
Is 14:13 I will *e* my throne above the
Is 25:1 I will *e* thee, I will praise thy
Eze 21:26 *e* him that is low, and abase him
Eze 29:15 neither shall it *e* itself any
Eze 31:14 *e* themselves for their height
Dan 11:14 *e* themselves to establish the
Dan 11:36 and he shall *e* himself, and magnify
Hos 11:7 High, none at all would *e* him
Obad 4 Though thou *e* thyself as the
Mt 23:12 whosoever shall *e* himself shall
2Cor 11:20 take of you, if a man *e* himself
1Pet 5:6 that he may *e* you in due time

**EXALTED**
Num 24:7 Agag, and his kingdom shall be *e*
1Sa 2:1 LORD, mine horn is *e* in the LORD
2Sa 5:12 that he had *e* his kingdom for his
2Sa 22:47 *e* be the God of the rock of my
1Kin 1:5 the son of Haggith *e* himself
1Kin 14:7 Forasmuch as I *e* thee from among
1Kin 16:2 Forasmuch as I *e* thee out of the
2Kin 19:22 whom hast thou *e* thy voice
1Chr 29:11 thou art *e* as head above all
Neh 9:5 which is *e* above all blessing and
Job 5:11 which mourn may be *e* to safety
Job 24:24 They are *e* for a little while,
Job 36:7 them for ever, and they are *e*
Ps 12:8 side, when the vilest men are *e*
Ps 13:2 shall mine enemy be *e* over me
Ps 18:46 let the God of my salvation be *e*
Ps 21:13 Be thou *e*, LORD, in thine own
Ps 46:10 I will be *e* among the heathen
Ps 46:10 I will be *e* in the earth
Ps 47:9 he is greatly *e*
Ps 57:5 Be thou *e*, O God, above the
Ps 57:11 Be thou *e*, O God, above the
Ps 75:10 horns of the righteous shall be *e*
Ps 89:16 thy righteousness shall they be *e*
Ps 89:17 in thy favour our horn shall be *e*
Ps 89:19 I have *e* one chosen out of the
Ps 89:24 and in my name shall his horn be *e*
Ps 97:9 thou art *e* far above all gods
Ps 108:5 Be thou *e*, O God, above the
Ps 112:9 his horn shall be *e* with honour
Ps 118:16 The right hand of the LORD is *e*
Prov 11:11 of the upright the city is *e*
Is 2:2 shall be *e* above the hills
Is 2:11 LORD alone shall be *e* in that day
Is 2:17 LORD alone shall be *e* in that day
Is 5:16 of hosts shall be *e* in judgment
Is 12:4 make mention that his name is *e*
Is 30:18 you, and therefore will he be *e*
Is 33:5 The LORD is *e*
Is 33:10 now will I be *e*
Is 37:23 whom hast thou *e* thy voice
Is 40:4 Every valley shall be *e*, and every
Is 49:11 a way, and my highways shall be *e*
Is 52:13 deal prudently, he shall be *e*
Eze 17:24 have *e* the low tree, have dried
Eze 19:11 her stature was *e* among the thick
Eze 31:5 Therefore his height was *e* above
Hos 13:1 trembling, he *e* himself in Israel
Hos 13:6 were filled, and their heart was *e*
Mic 4:1 it shall be *e* above the hills
Mt 11:23 which art *e* unto heaven, shalt be
Mt 23:12 shall humble himself shall be *e*
Lk 1:52 seats, and *e* them of low degree
Lk 10:15 Capernaum, which art *e* to heaven
Lk 14:11 that humbleth himself shall be *e*
Lk 18:14 that humbleth himself shall be *e*
Acts 2:33 being by the right hand of God *e*
Acts 5:31 Him hath God *e* with his right
Acts 13:17 *e* the people when they dwelt as
2Cor 11:7 abasing myself that ye might be *e*
2Cor 12:7 lest I should be *e* above measure
2Cor 12:7 lest I should be *e* above measure
Phil 2:9 God also hath highly *e* him
Jas 1:9 degree rejoice in that he is *e*

**EXALTETH**
Job 36:22 Behold, God *e* by his power
Ps 148:14 He also *e* the horn of his people,
Prov 14:29 that is hasty of spirit *e* folly
Prov 14:34 Righteousness *e* a nation
Prov 17:19 he that *e* his gate seeketh
Lk 14:11 For whosoever *e* himself shall be
Lk 18:14 for every one that *e* himself
2Cor 10:5 every high thing that *e* itself
2Th 2:4 *e* himself above all that is

**EXAMINE**
Ezr 10:16 the tenth month to *e* the matter
Ps 26:2 *E* me, O LORD, and prove me
1Cor 9:3 to them that do *e* me is this
1Cor 11:28 But let a man *e* himself, and so
2Cor 13:5 *E* yourselves, whether ye be in

**EXAMINED**
Lk 23:14 having *e* him before you, have
Acts 4:9 If we this day be *e* of the good
Acts 12:19 he *e* the keepers, and commanded
Acts 22:24 that he should be *e* by scourging
Acts 22:29 from him which should have *e* him
Acts 28:18 Who, when they had *e* me, would

**EXAMPLE**
Mt 1:19 willing to make her a publick *e*
Jn 13:15 For I have given you an *e*
1Ti 4:12 but be thou an *e* of the believers
Heb 4:11 fall after the same *e* of unbelief
Heb 8:5 Who serve unto the *e* and shadow of
Jas 5:10 for an *e* of suffering affliction,
1Pet 2:21 suffered for us, leaving us an *e*
Jude 7 flesh, are set forth for an *e*

**EXCEED**
Deut 25:3 stripes he may give him, and not *e*
Deut 25:3 lest, if he should *e*, and beat him
Mt 5:20 shall *e* the righteousness of the
2Cor 3:9 of righteousness *e* in glory

**EXCEEDING**
Gen 15:1 thy shield, and thy *e* great reward
Gen 17:6 And I will make thee *e* fruitful
Gen 27:34 *e* bitter cry, and said unto his
Ex 1:7 and multiplied, and waxed *e* mighty
Ex 19:16 the voice of the trumpet *e* loud
Num 14:7 to search it, is an *e* good land
1Sa 2:3 Talk no more so *e* proudly
2Sa 8:8 king David took *e* much brass
2Sa 12:2 The rich man had *e* many flocks
1Kin 4:29 wisdom and understanding *e* much
1Kin 7:47 because they were *e* many
1Chr 20:2 he brought also *e* much spoil out
1Chr 22:5 for the LORD must be *e* magnifical
2Chr 11:12 spears, and made them *e* strong
2Chr 14:14 for there was *e* much spoil in
2Chr 16:12 until his disease was *e* great
2Chr 32:27 And Hezekiah had *e* much riches
Ps 21:6 thou hast made him *e* glad with
Ps 43:4 altar of God, unto God my *e* joy
Ps 119:96 but thy commandment is *e* broad
Prov 30:24 the earth, but they are *e* wise
Eccl 7:24 *e* deep, who can find it out
Jer 48:29 (he is *e* proud) his loftiness, and
Eze 9:9 of Israel and Judah is *e* great
Eze 16:13 and thou wast *e* beautiful, and thou

Eze 23:15 *e* in dyed attire upon their heads
Eze 37:10 upon their feet, an *e* great army
Eze 47:10 the fish of the great sea, *e* many
Dan 3:22 was urgent, and the furnace *e* hot
Dan 6:23 Then was the king *e* glad for him
Dan 7:19 *e* dreadful, whose teeth were of
Dan 8:9 little horn, which waxed *e* great
Jonah 3:3 Now Nineveh was an *e* great city
Jonah 4:6 So Jonah was *e* glad of the gourd
Mt 2:10 they rejoiced with *e* great joy
Mt 2:16 was *e* wroth, and sent forth, and
Mt 4:8 him up into an *e* high mountain
Mt 5:12 Rejoice, and be *e* glad
Mt 8:28 *e* fierce, so that no man might
Mt 17:23 And they were *e* sorry
Mt 26:22 And they were *e* sorrowful, and
Mt 26:38 unto them, My soul is *e* sorrowful
Mk 6:26 And the king was *e* sorry
Mk 9:3 became shining, *e* white as snow
Mk 14:34 My soul is *e* sorrowful unto death
Lk 23:8 Herod saw Jesus, he was *e* glad
Acts 7:20 was *e* fair, and nourished up in
Rom 7:13 commandment might become *e*
2Cor 4:17 worketh for us a far more *e*
2Cor 7:4 comfort, I am *e* joyful in all our
2Cor 9:14 you for the *e* grace of God in you
Eph 1:19 what is the *e* greatness of his
Eph 2:7 the *e* riches of his grace in his
Eph 3:20 do *e* abundantly above all that we
1Ti 1:14 Lord was *e* abundant with faith
1Pet 4:13 ye may be glad also with *e* joy
2Pet 1:4 Whereby are given unto us *e* great
Jude 24 presence of his glory with *e* joy
Rev 16:21 the plague thereof was *e* great

**EXCEEDINGLY**

Gen 7:19 waters prevailed *e* upon the earth
Gen 13:13 and sinners before the LORD *e*
Gen 16:10 her, I will multiply thy seed *e*
Gen 17:2 and thee, and will multiply thee *e*
Gen 17:20 fruitful, and will multiply him *e*
Gen 27:33 And Isaac trembled very *e*, and said
Gen 30:43 And the man increased *e*, and had
Gen 47:27 therein, and grew, and multiplied *e*
1Sa 26:21 played the fool, and have erred *e*
2Sa 13:15 Then Amnon hated her *e*
2Kin 10:4 But they were *e* afraid, and said,
1Chr 29:25 *e* in the sight of all Israel
2Chr 1:1 was with him, and magnified him *e*
2Chr 17:12 And Jehoshaphat waxed great *e*
2Chr 26:8 for he strengthened himself *e*
Neh 2:10 it grieved them *e* that there was
Est 4:4 Then was the queen *e* grieved
Job 3:22 Which rejoice *e*, and are glad,
Ps 68:3 yea, let them *e* rejoice
Ps 106:14 But lusted *e* in the wilderness,
Ps 119:167 and I love them *e*
Ps 123:3 for we are *e* filled with contempt
Ps 123:4 Our soul is *e* filled with the
Is 24:19 dissolved, the earth is moved *e*
Dan 7:7 dreadful and terrible, and strong *e*
Jonah 1:10 Then were the men *e* afraid
Jonah 1:16 Then the men feared the LORD *e*
Jonah 4:1 But it displeased Jonah *e*
Mt 19:25 heard it, they were *e* amazed
Mk 4:41 And they feared *e*, and said one to
Mk 15:14 And they cried out the more *e*
Acts 16:20 Jews, do *e* trouble our city,
Acts 26:11 being *e* mad against them, I
Acts 27:18 we being *e* tossed with a tempest,
2Cor 7:13 *e* the more joyed we for the joy
Gal 1:14 being more *e* zealous of the
1Th 3:10 praying *e* that we might see
2Th 1:3 because that your faith groweth *e*
Heb 12:21 Moses said, I *e* fear and quake

**EXCEL**

Gen 49:4 as water, thou shalt not *e*
1Chr 15:21 with harps on the Sheminith to *e*
Ps 103:20 that *e* in strength, that do his
Is 10:10 images did *e* them of Jerusalem
1Cor 14:12 seek that ye may *e* to the

**EXCELLENCY**

Gen 49:3 *e* of dignity, and the *e* of power
Ex 15:7 in the greatness of thine *e* thou
Deut 33:26 thy help, and in his *e* on the sky
Deut 33:29 and who is the sword of thy *e*
Job 4:21 Doth not their *e* which is in them
Job 13:11 Shall not his *e* make you afraid
Job 20:6 Though his *e* mount up to the
Job 37:4 with the voice of his *e*
Job 40:10 thyself now with majesty and *e*
Ps 47:4 the *e* of Jacob whom he loved
Ps 62:4 to cast him down from his *e*
Ps 68:34 his *e* is over Israel, and his
Eccl 7:12 but the *e* of knowledge is, that
Is 13:19 the beauty of the Chaldees' *e*
Is 35:2 the *e* of Carmel and Sharon, they
Is 35:2 of the LORD, and the *e* of our God
Is 60:15 I will make thee an eternal *e*
Eze 24:21 the *e* of your strength, the
Amos 6:8 of hosts, I abhor the *e* of Jacob
Amos 8:7 LORD hath sworn by the *e* of Jacob
Nah 2:2 hath turned away the *e* of Jacob
Nah 2:2 of Jacob, as the *e* of Israel
1Cor 2:1 came not with *e* of speech or of
2Cor 4:7 that the *e* of the power may be of
Phil 3:8 the *e* of the knowledge of Christ

**EXCELLENT**

Est 1:4 honour of his *e* majesty many days
Job 37:23 he is *e* in power, and in judgment,
Ps 8:1 how *e* is thy name in all the
Ps 8:9 how *e* is thy name in all the
Ps 16:3 are in the earth, and to the *e*
Ps 36:7 How *e* is thy lovingkindness, O
Ps 76:4 *e* than the mountains of prey
Ps 141:5 it shall be an *e* oil, which shall
Ps 148:13 for his name alone is *e*
Ps 150:2 him according to his *e* greatness
Prov 8:6 for I will speak of *e* things
Prov 12:26 is more *e* than his neighbour
Prov 17:7 *E* speech becometh not a fool
Prov 17:27 understanding is of an *e* spirit
Prov 22:20 to thee *e* things in counsels
Song 5:15 is as Lebanon, *e* as the cedars
Is 4:2 the fruit of the earth shall be *e*
Is 12:5 for he hath done *e* things
Is 28:29 in counsel, and *e* in working
Eze 16:7 and thou art come to *e* ornaments
Dan 2:31 image, whose brightness was *e*
Dan 4:36 *e* majesty was added unto me
Dan 5:12 Forasmuch as an *e* spirit, and
Dan 5:14 *e* wisdom is found in thee
Dan 6:3 because an *e* spirit was in him
Lk 1:3 thee in order, most *e* Theophilus,
Acts 23:26 Claudius Lysias unto the most *e*
Rom 2:18 the things that are more *e*
1Cor 12:31 yet shew I unto you a more *e* way
Phil 1:10 ye may approve things that are *e*
Heb 1:4 obtained a more *e* name than they
Heb 8:6 he obtained a more *e* ministry
Heb 11:4 God a more *e* sacrifice than Cain
2Pet 1:17 a voice to him from the *e* glory

**EXCESS**

Mt 23:25 they are full of extortion and *e*
Eph 5:18 not drunk with wine, wherein is *e*
1Pet 4:3 lusts, *e* of wine, revellings,
1Pet 4:4 with them to the same *e* of riot

**EXCHANGE**

Gen 47:17 gave them bread in *e* for horses
Lev 27:10 the *e* thereof shall be holy
Job 28:17 the *e* of it shall not be for
Eze 48:14 shall not sell of it, neither *e*
Mt 16:26 a man give in *e* for his soul
Mk 8:37 a man give in *e* for his soul

**EXECUTE**

Ex 12:12 gods of Egypt I will *e* judgment
Num 5:30 the priest shall *e* upon her all
Num 8:11 that they may *e* the service of
Deut 10:18 He doth *e* the judgment of the
1Kin 6:12 *e* my judgments, and keep all my
Ps 119:84 when wilt thou *e* judgment on them
Ps 149:7 To *e* vengeance upon the heathen,
Ps 149:9 To *e* upon them the judgment
Is 16:3 Take counsel, *e* judgment
Jer 7:5 if ye throughly *e* judgment
Jer 21:12 *E* judgment in the morning, and
Jer 22:3 *E* ye judgment and righteousness,
Jer 23:5 shall *e* judgment and justice in
Jer 33:15 and he shall *e* judgment and
Eze 5:8 will *e* judgments in the midst of
Eze 5:10 I will *e* judgments in thee, and
Eze 5:15 when I shall *e* judgments in thee
Eze 11:9 will *e* judgments among you
Eze 16:41 *e* judgments upon thee in the
Eze 25:11 I will *e* judgments upon Moab
Eze 25:17 I will *e* great vengeance upon
Eze 30:14 Zoan, and will *e* judgments in No
Eze 30:19 Thus will I *e* judgments in Egypt
Eze 45:9 *e* judgment and justice, take away
Hos 11:9 I will not *e* the fierceness of
Mic 5:15 I will *e* vengeance in anger and
Mic 7:9 my cause, and *e* judgment for me
Zec 7:9 *E* true judgment, and shew mercy and
Zec 8:16 *e* the judgment of truth and peace
Jn 5:27 him authority to *e* judgment also
Rom 13:4 a revenger to *e* wrath upon him
Jude 15 To *e* judgment upon all, and to

**EXECUTED**

Num 33:4 gods also the LORD *e* judgments
Deut 33:21 he *e* the justice of the LORD, and
2Sa 8:15 David *e* judgment and justice unto
1Chr 6:10 (he it is that *e* the priest's
1Chr 18:14 *e* judgment and justice among all
1Chr 24:2 Ithamar *e* the priest's office
2Chr 24:24 So they *e* judgment against Joash
Ezr 7:26 let judgment be *e* speedily upon
Ps 106:30 stood up Phinehas, and *e* judgment
Eccl 8:11 an evil work is not *e* speedily
Jer 23:20 shall not return, until he have *e*
Eze 11:12 neither *e* my judgments, but have
Eze 18:8 hath *e* true judgment between man
Eze 18:17 hath *e* my judgments, hath walked
Eze 20:24 they had not *e* my judgments
Eze 23:10 for they had *e* judgment upon her
Eze 28:22 I shall have *e* judgments in her
Eze 28:26 when I have *e* judgments upon all
Eze 39:21 see my judgment that I have *e*
Lk 1:8 that while he *e* the priest's

**EXECUTETH**

Ps 9:16 known by the judgment which he *e*
Ps 103:6 The LORD *e* righteousness and
Ps 146:7 Which *e* judgment for the
Is 46:11 the man that *e* my counsel from a
Jer 5:1 if there be any that *e* judgment
Joel 2:11 for he is strong that *e* his word

**EXERCISE**

Ps 131:1 neither do I *e* myself in great
Jer 9:24 the LORD which *e* lovingkindness
Mt 20:25 the Gentiles *e* dominion over them
Mt 20:25 are great *e* authority upon them
Mk 10:42 the Gentiles *e* lordship over them
Mk 10:42 their great ones *e* authority upon
Lk 22:25 the Gentiles *e* lordship over them
Lk 22:25 they that *e* authority upon them
Acts 24:16 And herein do I *e* myself, to have
1Ti 4:7 *e* thyself rather unto godliness
1Ti 4:8 For bodily *e* profiteth little

**EXERCISED**

Eccl 1:13 the sons of man to be *e* therewith
Eccl 3:10 to the sons of men to be *e* in it
Eze 22:29 *e* robbery, and have vexed the poor
Heb 5:14 senses *e* to discern both good
Heb 12:11 unto them which are *e* thereby
2Pet 2:14 an heart they have *e* with

**EXHORT**

Acts 2:40 other words did he testify and *e*
Acts 27:22 now I *e* you to be of good cheer
2Cor 9:5 it necessary to *e* the brethren
1Th 4:1 *e* you by the Lord Jesus, that as
1Th 5:14 Now we *e* you, brethren, warn them
2Th 3:12 *e* by our Lord Jesus Christ, that
1Ti 2:1 I *e* therefore, that, first of all
1Ti 6:2 These things teach and *e*
2Ti 4:2 *e* with all longsuffering and
Titus 1:9 able by sound doctrine both to *e*
Titus 2:6 men likewise *e* to be sober minded
Titus 2:9 *E* servants to be obedient unto
Titus 2:15 These things speak, and *e*, and
Heb 3:13 But *e* one another daily, while it
1Pet 5:1 elders which are among you I *e*
Jude 3 *e* you that ye should earnestly

**EXHORTATION**

Lk 3:18 many other things in his *e*
Acts 13:15 have any word of *e* for the people
Acts 20:2 parts, and had given them much *e*
Rom 12:8 Or he that exhorteth, on *e*
1Cor 14:3 unto men to edification, and *e*
2Cor 8:17 For indeed he accepted the *e*
1Th 2:3 For our *e* was not of deceit, nor
1Ti 4:13 give attendance to reading, to *e*
Heb 12:5 ye have forgotten the *e* which
Heb 13:22 brethren, suffer the word of *e*

**EXHORTING**

Acts 14:22 *e* them to continue in the faith,
Acts 18:27 *e* the disciples to receive him

Heb 10:25 but e one another
1Pet 5:12 I have written briefly, e

## EXPECTATION
Ps 9:18 the e of the poor shall not
Ps 62:5 for my e is from him
Prov 10:28 but the e of the wicked shall
Prov 11:7 man dieth, his e shall perish
Prov 11:23 but the e of the wicked is wrath
Prov 23:18 thine e shall not be cut off
Prov 24:14 thy e shall not be cut off
Is 20:5 and ashamed of Ethiopia their e
Is 20:6 that day, Behold, such is our e
Zec 9:5 for her e shall be ashamed
Lk 3:15 And as the people were in e
Acts 12:11 from all the e of the people of
Rom 8:19 For the earnest e of the creature
Phil 1:20 According to my earnest e

## EXPEDIENT
Jn 11:50 Nor consider that it is e for us
Jn 16:7 It is e for you that I go away
Jn 18:14 that it was e that one man should
1Cor 6:12 unto me, but all things are not e
1Cor 10:23 for me, but all things are not e
2Cor 8:10 for this is e for you, who have
2Cor 12:1 It is not e for me doubtless to

## EXPELLED
Josh 13:13 of Israel e not the Geshurites
Judg 1:20 he e thence the three sons of
2Sa 14:14 his banished be not e from him
Acts 13:50 e them out of their coasts

## EXPERIENCE
Gen 30:27 for I have learned by e that the
Eccl 1:16 my heart had great e of wisdom
Rom 5:4 And patience, e
Rom 5:4 and e, hope

## EXPERT
1Chr 12:33 e in war, with all instruments of
1Chr 12:35 And of the Danites e in war twenty
1Chr 12:36 battle, e in war, forty thousand
Song 3:8 all hold swords, being e in war
Jer 50:9 shall be as of a mighty e man
Acts 26:3 know thee to be e in all customs

## EXPIRED
1Sa 18:26 and the days were not e
2Sa 11:1 to pass, after the year was e
1Chr 17:11 when thy days be e that thou must
1Chr 20:1 pass, that after the year was e
2Chr 36:10 And when the year was e, king
Est 1:5 And when these days were e
Eze 43:27 And when these days are e, it
Acts 7:30 And when forty years were e
Rev 20:7 And when the thousand years are e

## EXPOUNDED
Judg 14:19 unto them which e the riddle
Mk 4:34 he e all things to his disciples
Lk 24:27 he e unto them in all the
Acts 11:4 e it by order unto them, saying,
Acts 18:26 e unto him the way of God more
Acts 28:23 to whom he e and testified the

## EXPRESSED
Num 1:17 men which are e by their names
1Chr 12:31 thousand, which were e by name
1Chr 16:41 were chosen, who were e by name
2Chr 28:15 men which were e by name rose up
2Chr 31:19 city, the men that were e by name
Ezr 8:20 all of them were e by name

## EXTOL
Ps 30:1 I will e thee, O LORD
Ps 68:4 e him that rideth upon the
Ps 145:1 I will e thee, my God, O king
Dan 4:37 Now I Nebuchadnezzar praise and e

## EYE
Ex 21:24 E for e, tooth for tooth, hand
Ex 21:26 a man smite the e of his servant
Ex 21:26 or the e of his maid, that it
Lev 21:20 or that hath a blemish in his e
Lev 24:20 e for e, tooth for tooth
Deut 7:16 thine e shall have no pity upon
Deut 13:8 neither shall thine e pity him
Deut 15:9 thine e be evil against thy poor
Deut 19:13 Thine e shall not pity him, but
Deut 19:21 And thine e shall not pity
Deut 19:21 e for e, tooth for tooth, hand
Deut 25:12 thine e shall not pity her
Deut 28:54 his e shall be evil toward his
Deut 28:56 her e shall be evil toward the
Deut 32:10 he kept him as the apple of his e
Deut 34:7 his e was not dim, nor his
1Sa 24:10 but mine e spared thee
2Sa 22:25 to my cleanness in his e sight
Ezr 5:5 But the e of their God was upon
Job 7:7 mine e shall no more see good
Job 7:8 The e of him that hath seen me
Job 10:18 up the ghost, and no e had seen me
Job 13:1 mine e hath seen all this, mine
Job 16:20 but mine e poureth out tears unto
Job 17:2 doth not mine e continue in their
Job 17:7 Mine e also is dim by reason of
Job 20:9 The e also which saw him shall
Job 24:15 The e also of the adulterer
Job 24:15 saying, No e shall see me
Job 28:7 the vulture's e hath not seen
Job 28:10 his e seeth every precious thing
Job 29:11 and when the e saw me, it gave
Job 42:5 but now mine e seeth thee
Ps 6:7 Mine e is consumed because of
Ps 17:8 Keep me as the apple of the e
Ps 31:9 mine e is consumed with grief,
Ps 32:8 I will guide thee with mine e
Ps 33:18 the e of the LORD is upon them
Ps 35:19 e that hate me without a cause
Ps 35:21 Aha, aha, our e hath seen it
Ps 54:7 mine e hath seen his desire upon
Ps 88:9 Mine e mourneth by reason of
Ps 92:11 Mine e also shall see my desire
Ps 94:9 he that formed the e, shall he
Prov 7:2 and my law as the apple of thine e
Prov 10:10 winketh with the e causeth sorrow
Prov 20:12 The hearing ear, and the seeing e
Prov 22:9 a bountiful e shall be blessed
Prov 23:6 bread of him that hath an evil e
Prov 28:22 hasteth to be rich hath an evil e
Prov 30:17 The e that mocketh at his father,
Eccl 1:8 the e is not satisfied with
Eccl 4:8 neither is his e satisfied with
Is 13:18 their e shall not spare children
Is 52:8 for they shall see e to e
Is 64:4 the ear, neither hath the e seen
Jer 13:17 mine e shall weep sore, and run
Lam 1:16 mine e, mine e runneth down
Lam 2:4 to the e in the tabernacle of the
Lam 2:18 not the apple of thine e cease
Lam 3:48 Mine e runneth down with rivers
Lam 3:49 Mine e trickleth down, and ceaseth
Lam 3:51 Mine e affecteth mine heart
Eze 5:11 neither shall mine e spare
Eze 7:4 mine e shall not spare thee,
Eze 7:9 mine e shall not spare, neither
Eze 8:18 mine e shall not spare, neither
Eze 9:5 let not your e spare, neither
Eze 9:10 mine e shall not spare, neither
Eze 16:5 None e pitied thee, to do any of
Eze 20:17 Nevertheless mine e spared them
Mic 4:11 and let our e look upon Zion
Zec 2:8 you toucheth the apple of his e
Zec 11:17 upon his arm, and upon his right e
Zec 11:17 his right e shall be utterly
Mt 5:29 And if thy right e offend thee
Mt 5:38 hath been said, An e for an e
Mt 6:22 The light of the body is the e
Mt 6:22 if therefore thine e be single
Mt 6:23 But if thine e be evil, thy whole
Mt 7:3 mote that is in thy brother's e
Mt 7:3 the beam that is in thine own e
Mt 7:4 pull out the mote out of thine e
Mt 7:4 behold, a beam is in thine own e
Mt 7:5 out the beam out of thine own e
Mt 7:5 the mote out of thy brother's e
Mt 18:9 if thine e offend thee, pluck it
Mt 18:9 to enter into life with one e
Mt 19:24 to go through the e of a needle
Mt 20:15 Is thine e evil, because I am
Mk 7:22 deceit, lasciviousness, an evil e
Mk 9:47 if thine e offend thee, pluck it
Mk 9:47 the kingdom of God with one e
Mk 10:25 to go through the e of a needle
Lk 6:41 mote that is in thy brother's e
Lk 6:41 the beam that is in thine own e
Lk 6:42 out the mote that is in thine e
Lk 6:42 the beam that is in thine own e
Lk 6:42 first the beam out of thine own e
Lk 6:42 mote that is in thy brother's e
Lk 11:34 The light of the body is the e
Lk 11:34 therefore when thine e is single
Lk 11:34 but when thine e is evil, thy
Lk 18:25 camel to go through a needle's e
1Cor 2:9 E hath not seen, nor ear heard,
1Cor 12:16 shall say, Because I am not the e
1Cor 12:17 If the whole body were an e
1Cor 12:21 the e cannot say unto the hand, I
1Cor 15:52 moment, in the twinkling of an e
Rev 1:7 every e shall see him, and they

## EYELIDS
Job 16:16 on my e is the shadow of death
Job 41:18 are like the e of the morning
Ps 11:4 his eyes behold, his e try
Ps 132:4 mine eyes, or slumber to mine e
Prov 4:25 let thine e look straight before
Prov 6:4 eyes, nor slumber to thine e
Prov 6:25 let her take thee with her e
Prov 30:13 and their e are lifted up
Jer 9:18 our e gush out with waters

## EYES
Gen 3:5 then your e shall be opened, and
Gen 3:6 and that it was pleasant to the e
Gen 3:7 the e of them both were opened,
Gen 6:8 found grace in the e of the LORD
Gen 13:10 And Lot lifted up his e, and beheld
Gen 13:14 from him, Lift up now thine e
Gen 16:4 mistress was despised in her e
Gen 16:5 I was despised in her e
Gen 18:2 And he lift up his e and looked, and
Gen 19:8 ye to them as is good in your e
Gen 20:16 he is to thee a covering of the e
Gen 21:19 And God opened her e, and she saw a
Gen 22:4 third day Abraham lifted up his e
Gen 22:13 And Abraham lifted up his e
Gen 24:63 and he lifted up his e, and saw, and
Gen 24:64 And Rebekah lifted up her e
Gen 27:1 his e were dim, so that he could
Gen 30:27 if I have found favour in thine e
Gen 30:41 e of the cattle in the gutters
Gen 31:10 that I lifted up mine e, and saw
Gen 31:12 And he said, Lift up now thine e
Gen 31:40 and my sleep departed from mine e
Gen 33:1 And Jacob lifted up his e, and
Gen 33:5 And he lifted up his e, and saw the
Gen 34:11 Let me find grace in your e
Gen 37:25 and they lifted up their e
Gen 39:7 wife cast her e upon Joseph
Gen 41:37 was good in the e of Pharaoh
Gen 41:37 in the e of all his servants
Gen 42:24 and bound him before their e
Gen 43:29 And he lifted up his e, and saw his
Gen 44:21 that I may set mine e upon him
Gen 45:12 And, behold, your e see, and the
Gen 45:12 the e of my brother Benjamin,
Gen 46:4 shall put his hand upon thine e
Gen 47:19 shall we die before thine e
Gen 48:10 Now the e of Israel were dim for
Gen 49:12 His e shall be red with wine, and
Gen 50:4 now I have found grace in your e
Ex 5:21 be abhorred in the e of Pharaoh
Ex 5:21 in the e of his servants, to put
Ex 8:26 of the Egyptians before their e
Ex 13:9 and for a memorial between thine e
Ex 13:16 and for frontlets between thine e
Ex 14:10 of Israel lifted up their e
Ex 24:17 the e of the children of Israel
Lev 4:13 be hid from the e of the assembly
Lev 20:4 ways hide their e from the man
Lev 26:16 ague, that shall consume the e
Num 5:13 be hid from the e of her husband
Num 10:31 thou mayest be to us instead of e
Num 11:6 beside this manna, before our e
Num 15:39 your own heart and your own e
Num 16:14 thou put out the e of these men
Num 20:8 ye unto the rock before their e
Num 20:12 to sanctify me in the e of the
Num 22:31 the LORD opened the e of Balaam
Num 24:2 And Balaam lifted up his e
Num 24:3 the man whose e are open hath
Num 24:4 a trance, but having his e open
Num 24:15 the man whose e are open hath
Num 24:16 a trance, but having his e open
Num 27:14 me at the water before their e
Num 33:55 of them shall be pricks in your e
Deut 1:30 for you in Egypt before your e
Deut 3:21 Thine e have seen all that the
Deut 3:27 and lift up thine e westward
Deut 3:27 and behold it with thine e
Deut 4:3 Your e have seen what the LORD
Deut 4:9 things which thine e have seen
Deut 4:19 thou lift up thine e unto heaven
Deut 4:34 for you in Egypt before your e

| | |
|---|---|
| Deut 6:8 | be as frontlets between thine *e* |
| Deut 6:22 | all his household, before our *e* |
| Deut 7:19 | temptations which thine *e* saw |
| Deut 9:17 | and brake them before your *e* |
| Deut 10:21 | things, which thine *e* have seen |
| Deut 11:7 | But your *e* have seen all the |
| Deut 11:12 | the *e* of the LORD thy God are |
| Deut 11:18 | be as frontlets between your *e* |
| Deut 12:8 | whatsoever is right in his own *e* |
| Deut 13:18 | in the *e* of the LORD thy God |
| Deut 14:1 | between your *e* for the dead |
| Deut 16:19 | gift doth blind the *e* of the wise |
| Deut 21:7 | blood, neither have our *e* seen it |
| Deut 24:1 | that she find no favour in his *e* |
| Deut 28:31 | ox shall be slain before thine *e* |
| Deut 28:32 | thine *e* shall look, and fail with |
| Deut 28:34 | of thine *e* which thou shalt see |
| Deut 28:65 | trembling heart, and failing of *e* |
| Deut 28:67 | of thine *e* which thou shalt see |
| Deut 29:2 | your *e* in the land of Egypt unto |
| Deut 29:3 | which thine *e* have seen, the |
| Deut 29:4 | *e* to see, and ears to hear, unto |
| Deut 34:4 | thee to see it with thine *e* |
| Josh 5:13 | Jericho, that he lifted up his *e* |
| Josh 23:13 | your sides, and thorns in your *e* |
| Josh 24:7 | your *e* have seen what I have done |
| Judg 16:21 | took him, and put out his *e* |
| Judg 16:28 | of the Philistines for my two *e* |
| Judg 17:6 | that which was right in his own *e* |
| Judg 19:17 | And when he had lifted up his *e* |
| Judg 21:25 | that which was right in his own *e* |
| Ruth 2:9 | Let thine *e* be on the field that |
| Ruth 2:10 | Why have I found grace in thine *e* |
| 1Sa 2:33 | shall be to consume thine *e* |
| 1Sa 3:2 | his *e* began to wax dim, that he |
| 1Sa 4:15 | his *e* were dim, that he could not |
| 1Sa 6:13 | and they lifted up their *e* |
| 1Sa 11:2 | I may thrust out all your right *e* |
| 1Sa 12:3 | bribe to blind mine *e* therewith |
| 1Sa 12:16 | the LORD will do before your *e* |
| 1Sa 14:27 | and his *e* were enlightened |
| 1Sa 14:29 | how mine *e* have been enlightened, |
| 1Sa 20:3 | I have found grace in thine *e* |
| 1Sa 20:29 | if I have found favour in thine *e* |
| 1Sa 24:10 | this day thine *e* have seen how |
| 1Sa 25:8 | young men find favour in thine *e* |
| 1Sa 26:21 | was precious in thine *e* this day |
| 1Sa 26:24 | much set by this day in mine *e* |
| 1Sa 26:24 | much set by in the *e* of the LORD |
| 1Sa 27:5 | I have now found grace in thine *e* |
| 2Sa 6:20 | to day in the *e* of the handmaids |
| 2Sa 12:11 | take thy wives before thine *e* |
| 2Sa 13:34 | kept the watch lifted up his *e* |
| 2Sa 15:25 | find favour in the *e* of the LORD |
| 2Sa 18:24 | unto the wall, and lifted up his *e* |
| 2Sa 19:27 | therefore what is good in thine *e* |
| 2Sa 22:28 | but thine *e* are upon the haughty, |
| 2Sa 24:3 | that the *e* of my lord the king |
| 1Kin 1:20 | the *e* of all Israel are upon thee |
| 1Kin 1:48 | this day, mine *e* even seeing it |
| 1Kin 8:29 | That thine *e* may be open toward |
| 1Kin 8:52 | That thine *e* may be open unto the |
| 1Kin 9:3 | and mine *e* and mine heart shall be |
| 1Kin 10:7 | I came, and mine *e* had seen it |
| 1Kin 11:33 | do that which is right in mine *e* |
| 1Kin 14:4 | for his *e* were set by reason of |
| 1Kin 14:8 | only which was right in mine *e* |
| 1Kin 15:5 | was right in the *e* of the LORD |
| 1Kin 15:11 | was right in the *e* of the LORD |
| 1Kin 16:25 | wrought evil in the *e* of the LORD |
| 1Kin 20:6 | whatsoever is pleasant in thine *e* |
| 1Kin 22:43 | was right in the *e* of the LORD |
| 2Kin 4:34 | his *e* upon his *e*, and his hands |
| 2Kin 4:35 | times, and the child opened his *e* |
| 2Kin 6:17 | LORD, I pray thee, open his *e* |
| 2Kin 6:17 | opened the *e* of the young man |
| 2Kin 6:20 | open the *e* of these men, that |
| 2Kin 6:20 | And the LORD opened their *e* |
| 2Kin 7:2 | thou shalt see it with thine *e* |
| 2Kin 7:19 | thou shalt see it with thine *e* |
| 2Kin 10:5 | that which is good in thine *e* |
| 2Kin 10:30 | that which is right in mine *e* |
| 2Kin 19:16 | open, LORD, thine *e*, and see |
| 2Kin 19:22 | and lifted up thine *e* on high |
| 2Kin 22:20 | thine *e* shall not see all the |
| 2Kin 25:7 | the sons of Zedekiah before his *e* |
| 2Kin 25:7 | and put out the *e* of Zedekiah |
| 1Chr 13:4 | right in the *e* of all the people |
| 1Chr 17:17 | this was a small thing in thine *e* |
| 1Chr 21:16 | And David lifted up his *e*, and saw |
| 1Chr 21:23 | do that which is good in his *e* |
| 2Chr 6:20 | That thine *e* may be open upon |
| 2Chr 6:40 | thine *e* be open, and let thine |
| 2Chr 7:15 | Now mine *e* shall be open, and mine |
| 2Chr 7:16 | and mine *e* and mine heart shall be |
| 2Chr 9:6 | I came, and mine *e* had seen it |
| 2Chr 14:2 | right in the *e* of the LORD his |
| 2Chr 16:9 | For the *e* of the LORD run to and |
| 2Chr 20:12 | but our *e* are upon thee |
| 2Chr 21:6 | was evil in the *e* of the LORD |
| 2Chr 29:6 | evil in the *e* of the LORD our God |
| 2Chr 29:8 | to hissing, as ye see with your *e* |
| 2Chr 34:28 | neither shall thine *e* see all the |
| Ezr 3:12 | house was laid before their *e* |
| Ezr 9:8 | that our God may lighten our *e* |
| Neh 1:6 | now be attentive, and thine *e* open |
| Neh 6:16 | much cast down in their own *e* |
| Est 1:17 | despise their husbands in their *e* |
| Est 8:5 | king, and I be pleasing in his *e* |
| Job 2:12 | they lifted up their *e* afar off |
| Job 3:10 | womb, nor hid sorrow from mine *e* |
| Job 4:16 | an image was before mine *e* |
| Job 7:8 | thine *e* are upon me, and I am not |
| Job 10:4 | Hast thou *e* of flesh |
| Job 11:4 | is pure, and I am clean in thine *e* |
| Job 11:20 | But the *e* of the wicked shall |
| Job 14:3 | open thine *e* upon such an one |
| Job 15:12 | and what do thy *e* wink at, |
| Job 16:9 | enemy sharpeneth his *e* upon me |
| Job 17:5 | even the *e* of his children shall |
| Job 19:27 | mine *e* shall behold, and not |
| Job 21:8 | and their offspring before their *e* |
| Job 21:20 | His *e* shall see his destruction, |
| Job 24:23 | yet his *e* are upon their ways |
| Job 27:19 | he openeth his *e*, and he is not |
| Job 28:21 | is hid from the *e* of all living |
| Job 29:15 | I was *e* to the blind, and feet was |
| Job 31:1 | I made a covenant with mine *e* |
| Job 31:7 | and mine heart walked after mine *e* |
| Job 31:16 | or have caused the *e* of the widow |
| Job 32:1 | he was righteous in his own *e* |
| Job 34:21 | For his *e* are upon the ways of |
| Job 36:7 | not his *e* from the righteous |
| Job 39:29 | prey, and her *e* behold afar off |
| Job 40:24 | He taketh it with his *e* |
| Job 41:18 | his *e* are like the eyelids of the |
| Ps 10:8 | his *e* are privily set against the |
| Ps 11:4 | his *e* behold, his eyelids try, |
| Ps 13:3 | lighten mine *e*, lest I sleep the |
| Ps 15:4 | In whose *e* a vile person is |
| Ps 17:2 | let thine *e* behold the things |
| Ps 17:11 | they have set their *e* bowing down |
| Ps 19:8 | LORD is pure, enlightening the *e* |
| Ps 25:15 | Mine *e* are ever toward the LORD |
| Ps 26:3 | lovingkindness is before mine *e* |
| Ps 31:22 | I am cut off from before thine *e* |
| Ps 34:15 | The *e* of the LORD are upon the |
| Ps 36:1 | is no fear of God before his *e* |
| Ps 36:2 | flattereth himself in his own *e* |
| Ps 38:10 | as for the light of mine *e* |
| Ps 50:21 | set them in order before thine *e* |
| Ps 66:7 | his *e* behold the nations |
| Ps 69:3 | mine *e* fail while I wait for my |
| Ps 69:23 | Let their *e* be darkened, that |
| Ps 73:7 | Their *e* stand out with fatness |
| Ps 77:4 | Thou holdest mine *e* waking |
| Ps 91:8 | Only with thine *e* shalt thou |
| Ps 101:3 | set no wicked thing before mine *e* |
| Ps 101:6 | Mine *e* shall be upon the faithful |
| Ps 115:5 | *e* have they, but they see not |
| Ps 116:8 | mine *e* from tears, and my feet |
| Ps 118:23 | it is marvellous in our *e* |
| Ps 119:18 | Open thou mine *e*, that I may |
| Ps 119:37 | Turn away mine *e* from beholding |
| Ps 119:82 | Mine *e* fail for thy word, saying, |
| Ps 119:123 | Mine *e* fail for thy salvation, and |
| Ps 119:136 | Rivers of waters run down mine *e* |
| Ps 119:148 | Mine *e* prevent the night watches, |
| Ps 121:1 | lift up mine *e* unto the hills |
| Ps 123:1 | Unto thee lift I up mine *e* |
| Ps 123:2 | as the *e* of servants look unto |
| Ps 123:2 | as the *e* of a maiden unto the |
| Ps 123:2 | so our *e* wait upon the LORD our |
| Ps 131:1 | is not haughty, nor mine *e* lofty |
| Ps 132:4 | I will not give sleep to mine *e* |
| Ps 135:16 | *e* have they, but they see not |
| Ps 139:16 | Thine *e* did see my substance, yet |
| Ps 141:8 | But mine *e* are unto thee, O GOD |
| Ps 145:15 | The *e* of all wait upon thee |
| Ps 146:8 | LORD openeth the *e* of the blind |
| Prov 3:7 | Be not wise in thine own *e* |
| Prov 3:21 | let not them depart from thine *e* |
| Prov 4:21 | Let them not depart from thine *e* |
| Prov 4:25 | Let thine *e* look right on, and let |
| Prov 5:21 | man are before the *e* of the LORD |
| Prov 6:4 | Give not sleep to thine *e* |
| Prov 6:13 | He winketh with his *e*, he |
| Prov 10:26 | the teeth, and as smoke to the *e* |
| Prov 12:15 | of a fool is right in his own *e* |
| Prov 15:3 | The *e* of the LORD are in every |
| Prov 15:30 | The light of the *e* rejoiceth the |
| Prov 16:2 | of a man are clean in his own *e* |
| Prov 16:30 | He shutteth his *e* to devise |
| Prov 17:8 | in the *e* of him that hath it |
| Prov 17:24 | but the *e* of a fool are in the |
| Prov 20:8 | away all evil with his *e* |
| Prov 20:13 | open thine *e*, and thou shalt be |
| Prov 21:2 | of a man is right in his own *e* |
| Prov 21:10 | findeth no favour in his *e* |
| Prov 22:12 | The *e* of the LORD preserve |
| Prov 23:5 | Wilt thou set thine *e* upon that |
| Prov 23:26 | let thine *e* observe my ways |
| Prov 23:29 | who hath redness of *e* |
| Prov 23:33 | Thine *e* shall behold strange |
| Prov 25:7 | the prince whom thine *e* have seen |
| Prov 27:20 | so the *e* of man are never |
| Prov 28:27 | but he that hideth his *e* shall |
| Prov 29:13 | the LORD lighteneth both their *e* |
| Prov 30:12 | that are pure in their own *e* |
| Prov 30:13 | O how lofty are their *e* |
| Eccl 2:10 | whatsoever mine *e* desired I kept |
| Eccl 2:14 | The wise man's *e* are in his head |
| Eccl 5:11 | beholding of them with their *e* |
| Eccl 6:9 | the *e* than the wandering of the |
| Eccl 8:16 | nor night seeth sleep with his *e* |
| Eccl 11:7 | it is for the *e* to behold the sun |
| Eccl 11:9 | heart, and in the sight of thine *e* |
| Song 1:15 | thou hast doves' *e* |
| Song 4:1 | hast doves' *e* within thy locks |
| Song 4:9 | my heart with one of thine *e* |
| Song 5:12 | His *e* are as the *e* of doves by |
| Song 6:5 | Turn away thine *e* from me |
| Song 7:4 | thine *e* like the fishpools in |
| Song 8:10 | then was I in his *e* as one that |
| Is 1:15 | I will hide mine *e* from you |
| Is 1:16 | of your doings from before mine *e* |
| Is 3:8 | to provoke the *e* of his glory |
| Is 3:16 | stretched forth necks and wanton *e* |
| Is 5:15 | the *e* of the lofty shall be |
| Is 5:21 | them that are wise in their own *e* |
| Is 6:5 | for mine *e* have seen the King, |
| Is 6:10 | their ears heavy, and shut their *e* |
| Is 6:10 | lest they see with their *e* |
| Is 11:3 | judge after the sight of his *e* |
| Is 13:16 | dashed to pieces before their *e* |
| Is 17:7 | his *e* shall have respect to the |
| Is 29:10 | deep sleep, and hath closed your *e* |
| Is 29:18 | the *e* of the blind shall see out |
| Is 30:20 | but thine *e* shall see thy |
| Is 32:3 | the *e* of them that see shall not |
| Is 33:15 | shutteth his *e* from seeing evil |
| Is 33:17 | Thine *e* shall see the king in his |
| Is 33:20 | thine *e* shall see Jerusalem a |
| Is 35:5 | Then the *e* of the blind shall be |
| Is 37:17 | open thine *e*, O LORD, and see |
| Is 37:23 | and lifted up thine *e* on high |
| Is 38:14 | mine *e* fail with looking upward |
| Is 40:26 | Lift up your *e* on high, and behold |
| Is 42:7 | To open the blind *e*, to bring out |
| Is 43:8 | the blind people that have *e* |
| Is 44:18 | for he hath shut their *e*, that |
| Is 49:5 | be glorious in the *e* of the LORD |
| Is 49:18 | Lift up thine *e* round about |
| Is 51:6 | Lift up your *e* to the heavens, and |
| Is 52:10 | arm in the *e* of all the nations |
| Is 59:10 | and we grope as if we had no *e* |
| Is 60:4 | Lift up thine *e* round about |
| Is 65:12 | but did evil before mine *e* |
| Is 65:16 | because they are hid from mine *e* |
| Is 66:4 | but they did evil before mine *e* |
| Jer 3:2 | Lift up thine *e* unto the high |
| Jer 5:3 | are not thine *e* upon the truth |
| Jer 5:21 | which have *e*, and see not |
| Jer 7:11 | become a den of robbers in your *e* |
| Jer 9:1 | mine *e* a fountain of tears, that |
| Jer 9:18 | that our *e* may run down with |
| Jer 13:20 | Lift up your *e*, and behold them |
| Jer 14:6 | their *e* did fail, because there |
| Jer 14:17 | Let mine *e* run down with tears |
| Jer 16:9 | cease out of this place in your *e* |

Jer 16:17 For mine *e* are upon all their
Jer 16:17 is their iniquity hid from mine *e*
Jer 20:4 and thine *e* shall behold it
Jer 22:17 But thine *e* and thine heart are
Jer 24:6 set mine *e* upon them for good
Jer 29:21 he shall slay them before your *e*
Jer 31:16 weeping, and thine *e* from tears
Jer 32:4 his *e* shall behold his *e*
Jer 32:19 for thine *e* are open upon all the
Jer 34:3 thine *e* shall behold the *e* of
Jer 34:3 the *e* of the king of Babylon
Jer 39:6 Zedekiah in Riblah before his *e*
Jer 39:7 Moreover he put out Zedekiah's *e*
Jer 42:2 of many, as thine *e* do behold us
Jer 52:2 was evil in the *e* of the LORD
Jer 52:10 the sons of Zedekiah before his *e*
Jer 52:11 Then he put out the *e* of Zedekiah
Lam 2:11 Mine *e* do fail with tears, my
Lam 4:17 our *e* as yet failed for our vain
Lam 5:17 for these things our *e* are dim
Eze 1:18 full of *e* round about them four
Eze 6:9 departed from me, and with their *e*
Eze 8:5 lift up thine *e* now the way
Eze 8:5 So I lifted up mine *e* the way
Eze 10:12 were full of *e* round about
Eze 12:2 house, which have *e* to see
Eze 12:12 he see not the ground with his *e*
Eze 18:6 neither hath lifted up his *e* to
Eze 18:12 hath lifted up his *e* to the idols
Eze 18:15 neither hath lifted up his *e* to
Eze 20:7 man the abominations of his *e*
Eze 20:8 away the abominations of their *e*
Eze 20:24 their *e* were after their fathers'
Eze 21:6 bitterness sigh before their *e*
Eze 22:26 have hid their *e* from my sabbaths
Eze 23:16 soon as she saw them with her *e*
Eze 23:27 not lift up thine *e* unto them
Eze 23:40 wash thyself, paintedst thy *e*
Eze 24:16 desire of thine *e* with a stroke
Eze 24:21 strength, the desire of your *e*
Eze 24:25 glory, the desire of their *e*
Eze 33:25 lift up your *e* toward your idols,
Eze 36:23 sanctified in you before their *e*
Eze 37:20 be in thine hand before their *e*
Eze 38:16 in thee, O Gog, before their *e*
Eze 38:23 be known in the *e* of many nations
Eze 40:4 Son of man, behold with thine *e*
Eze 44:5 mark well, and behold with thine *e*
Dan 4:34 lifted up mine *e* unto heaven
Dan 7:8 in this horn were *e* like the *e*
Dan 7:8 horn were *e* like the *e* of man
Dan 7:20 even of that horn that had *e*
Dan 8:3 Then I lifted up mine *e*, and saw,
Dan 8:5 had a notable horn between his *e*
Dan 8:21 between his *e* is the first king
Dan 9:18 open thine *e*, and behold our
Dan 10:5 Then I lifted up mine *e*, and
Dan 10:6 his *e* as lamps of fire, and his
Hos 13:14 shall be hid from mine *e*
Joel 1:16 not the meat cut off before our *e*
Amos 9:4 I will set mine *e* upon them for
Amos 9:8 the *e* of the Lord GOD are upon
Mic 7:10 mine *e* shall behold her
Hab 1:13 Thou art of purer *e* than to
Zeph 3:20 back your captivity before your *e*
Hag 2:3 is it not in your *e* in comparison
Zec 1:18 Then lifted I up mine *e*, and saw,
Zec 2:1 I lifted up mine *e* again, and
Zec 3:9 upon one stone shall be seven *e*
Zec 4:10 they are the *e* of the LORD
Zec 5:1 I turned, and lifted up mine *e*
Zec 5:5 said unto me, Lift up now thine *e*
Zec 5:9 Then lifted I up mine *e*, and
Zec 6:1 And I turned, and lifted up mine *e*
Zec 8:6 If it be marvellous in the *e* of
Zec 8:6 it also be marvellous in mine *e*
Zec 9:1 when the *e* of man, as of all the
Zec 9:8 for now have I seen with mine *e*
Zec 12:4 I will open mine *e* upon the house
Zec 14:12 their *e* shall consume away in
Mal 1:5 your *e* shall see, and ye shall say
Mt 9:29 Then touched he their *e*, saying,
Mt 9:30 And their *e* were opened
Mt 13:15 and their *e* they have closed
Mt 13:15 time they should see with their *e*
Mt 13:16 But blessed are your *e*, for they
Mt 17:8 when they had lifted up their *e*
Mt 18:9 rather than having two *e* to be
Mt 20:33 Lord, that our *e* may be opened
Mt 20:34 on them, and touched their *e*
Mt 20:34 their *e* received sight, and they
Mt 21:42 and it is marvellous in our *e*
Mt 26:43 for their *e* were heavy
Mk 8:18 Having *e*, see ye not
Mk 8:23 and when he had spit on his *e*
Mk 8:25 he put his hands again upon his *e*
Mk 9:47 than having two *e* to be cast into
Mk 12:11 and it is marvellous in our *e*
Mk 14:40 again, (for their *e* were heavy
Lk 2:30 For mine *e* have seen thy
Lk 4:20 the *e* of all them that were in
Lk 6:20 lifted up his *e* on his disciples
Lk 10:23 Blessed are the *e* which see the
Lk 16:23 And in hell he lift up his *e*
Lk 18:13 up so much as his *e* unto heaven
Lk 19:42 but now they are hid from thine *e*
Lk 24:16 But their *e* were holden that they
Lk 24:31 their *e* were opened, and they knew
Jn 4:35 I say unto you, Lift up your *e*
Jn 6:5 When Jesus then lifted up his *e*
Jn 9:6 he anointed the *e* of the blind
Jn 9:10 unto him, How were thine *e* opened
Jn 9:11 made clay, and anointed mine *e*
Jn 9:14 made the clay, and opened his *e*
Jn 9:15 them, He put clay upon mine *e*
Jn 9:17 him, that he hath opened thine *e*
Jn 9:21 or who hath opened his *e*, we know
Jn 9:26 how opened he thine *e*
Jn 9:30 is, and yet he hath opened mine *e*
Jn 9:32 the *e* of one that was born blind
Jn 10:21 a devil open the *e* of the blind
Jn 11:37 which opened the *e* of the blind
Jn 11:41 And Jesus lifted up his *e*, and said
Jn 12:40 He hath blinded their *e*, and
Jn 12:40 they should not see with their *e*
Jn 17:1 and lifted up his *e* to heaven
Acts 3:4 fastening his *e* upon him with
Acts 9:8 when his *e* were opened, he saw no
Acts 9:18 from his *e* as it had been scales
Acts 9:40 And she opened her *e*
Acts 11:6 which when I had fastened mine *e*
Acts 13:9 the Holy Ghost, set his *e* on him
Acts 26:18 To open their *e*, and to turn them
Acts 28:27 and their *e* have they closed
Acts 28:27 lest they should see with their *e*
Rom 3:18 is no fear of God before their *e*
Rom 11:8 *e* that they should not see, and
Rom 11:10 Let their *e* be darkened, that
Gal 3:1 before whose *e* Jesus Christ hath
Gal 4:15 would have plucked out your own *e*
Eph 1:18 The *e* of your understanding being
Heb 4:13 opened unto the *e* of him with
1Pet 3:12 For the *e* of the Lord are over
2Pet 2:14 Having *e* full of adultery, and
1Jn 1:1 which we have seen with our *e*
1Jn 2:11 that darkness hath blinded his *e*
1Jn 2:16 the flesh, and the lust of the *e*
Rev 1:14 his *e* were as a flame of fire
Rev 2:18 who hath his *e* like unto a flame
Rev 3:18 anoint thine *e* with eyesalve,
Rev 4:6 were four beasts full of *e* before
Rev 4:8 and they were full of *e* within
Rev 5:6 having seven horns and seven *e*
Rev 7:17 wipe away all tears from their *e*
Rev 19:12 His *e* were as a flame of fire, and
Rev 21:4 wipe away all tears from their *e*

**EZAR** *(e'-zar)* See EZER. *A son of Seir.*
1Chr 1:38 Zibeon, and Anah, and Dishon, and *E*

**EZBAI** *(ez'-bahee) Father of Naarai.*
1Chr 11:37 Carmelite, Naarai the son of *E*

**EZBON** *(ez'-bon)*
*1. Son of Gad.*
Gen 46:16 Ziphion, and Haggi, Shuni, and *E*
*2. Son of Bela.*
1Chr 7:7 *E*, and Uzzi, and Uzziel, and

**EZEKIAS** *(ez-e-ki'-as)* See HEZEKIAH. *Greek form of Hezekiah.*
Mt 1:9 and Achaz begat *E*
Mt 1:10 And *E* begat Manasses

**EZEKIEL** *A priest and prophet.*
Eze 1:3 came expressly unto *E* the priest
Eze 24:24 Thus *E* is unto you a sign

**EZEL** *A boundary stone.*
1Sa 20:19 and shalt remain by the stone *E*

**EZEM** *A city in Judah.*
1Chr 4:29 And at Bilhah, and at *E*, and at

**EZER**
*1. Son of Seir the Horite.*
Gen 36:21 And Dishon, and *E*, and Dishan
Gen 36:27 The children of *E* are these
Gen 36:30 Duke Dishon, duke *E*, duke Dishan
1Chr 1:42 The sons of *E*; Bilhan
*2. A descendant of Judah.*
1Chr 4:4 Gedor, and *E* the father of Hushah
*3. A son of Ephraim.*
1Chr 7:21 son, and Shuthelah his son, and *E*
*4. A Gadite who fought for David.*
1Chr 12:9 *E* the first, Obadiah the second,
*5. A Levite who repaired the Jerusalem wall.*
Neh 3:19 him repaired *E* the son of Jeshua
*6. A priest in the time of Nehemiah.*
Neh 12:42 and Malchijah, and Elam, and *E*

**EZION-GABER** *Same as Ezion-geber.*
Num 33:35 from Ebronah, and encamped at *E*
Num 33:36 And they removed from *E*, and
Deut 2:8 the plain from Elath, and from *E*
2Chr 20:36 and they made the ships in *E*

**EZION-GEBER** *(e'-ze-on-ghe'-bur)* See EZION-GABER. *An Israelite seaport.*
1Kin 9:26 Solomon made a navy of ships in *E*
1Kin 22:48 for the ships were broken at *E*
2Chr 8:17 Then went Solomon to *E*, and to

**EZNITE** *(ez'-nite) Descendant of Adino.*
2Sa 23:8 the same was Adino the *E*

**EZRA** *(ez'-rah)* See AZARIAH, EZRAHITE.
*1. A descendant of Judah.*
1Chr 4:17 And the sons of *E* were, Jether, and
*2. Priest who led exiles back to Jerusalem.*
Ezr 7:1 *E* the son of Seraiah, the son of
Ezr 7:6 This *E* went up from Babylon
Ezr 7:10 For *E* had prepared his heart to
Ezr 7:11 Artaxerxes gave unto *E* the priest
Ezr 7:12 unto *E* the priest, a scribe of
Ezr 7:21 that whatsoever *E* the priest
Ezr 7:25 And thou, *E*, after the wisdom of
Ezr 10:1 Now when *E* had prayed, and when he
Ezr 10:2 of Elam, answered and said unto *E*
Ezr 10:5 Then arose *E*, and made the chief
Ezr 10:6 Then *E* rose up from before the
Ezr 10:10 *E* the priest stood up, and said
Ezr 10:16 *E* the priest, with certain chief
Neh 8:1 they spake unto *E* the scribe to
Neh 8:2 *E* the priest brought the law
Neh 8:4 *E* the scribe stood upon a pulpit
Neh 8:5 *E* opened the book in the sight of
Neh 8:6 *E* blessed the LORD, the great God
Neh 8:9 *E* the priest the scribe, and the
Neh 8:13 unto *E* the scribe, even to
Neh 12:13 Of *E*, Meshullam
Neh 12:26 of *E* the priest, the scribe
Neh 12:33 And Azariah, *E*, and Meshullam,
Neh 12:36 God, and *E* the scribe before them
*3. A priest who returned from exile.*
Neh 12:1 Seraiah, Jeremiah, *E*,

**EZRAHITE** *(ez'-rah-hite)*
1Kin 4:31 than Ethan the *E*, and Heman, and
Ps 88:t Leannoth, Maschil of Heman the *E*
Ps 89:t Maschil of Ethan the *E*

**EZRI** *(ez'-ri) A superindendent of David.*
1Chr 27:26 ground was *E* the son of Chelub

# F

**FABLES**
1Ti 1:4 Neither give heed to *f* and endless
1Ti 4:7 refuse profane and old wives' *f*
2Ti 4:4 truth, and shall be turned unto *f*
Titus 1:14 Not giving heed to Jewish *f*
2Pet 1:16 not followed cunningly devised *f*

**FACE**
Gen 1:2 was upon the *f* of the deep
Gen 1:2 moved upon the *f* of the waters
Gen 1:29 is upon the *f* of all the earth
Gen 2:6 watered the whole *f* of the ground
Gen 3:19 In the sweat of thy *f* shalt thou
Gen 4:14 this day from the *f* of the earth
Gen 4:14 from thy *f* shall I be hid
Gen 6:1 to multiply on the *f* of the earth
Gen 6:7 created from the *f* of the earth
Gen 7:3 alive upon the *f* of all the earth
Gen 7:4 from off the *f* of the earth
Gen 7:18 ark went upon the *f* of the waters
Gen 7:23 was upon the *f* of the ground
Gen 8:8 from off the *f* of the ground
Gen 8:9 were on the *f* of the whole earth
Gen 8:13 the *f* of the ground was dry
Gen 11:4 upon the *f* of the whole earth
Gen 11:8 upon the *f* of all the earth
Gen 11:9 upon the *f* of all the earth
Gen 16:6 with her, she fled from her *f*
Gen 16:8 I flee from the *f* of my mistress
Gen 17:3 And Abram fell on his *f*
Gen 17:17 Then Abraham fell upon his *f*
Gen 19:1 with his *f* toward the ground
Gen 19:13 great before the *f* of the LORD
Gen 24:47 and I put the earring upon her *f*
Gen 30:33 come for my hire before thy *f*
Gen 31:21 set his *f* toward the mount Gilead
Gen 32:20 me, and afterward I will see his *f*
Gen 32:30 for I have seen God *f* to *f*
Gen 33:10 for therefore I have seen thy *f*
Gen 33:10 as though I had seen the *f* of God
Gen 35:1 from the *f* of Esau thy brother
Gen 35:7 he fled from the *f* of his brother
Gen 36:6 from the *f* of his brother Jacob
Gen 38:15 because she had covered her *f*
Gen 41:56 was over all the *f* of the earth
Gen 43:3 us, saying, Ye shall not see my *f*
Gen 43:5 unto us, Ye shall not see my *f*
Gen 43:31 And he washed his *f*, and went out,
Gen 44:23 you, ye shall see my *f* no more
Gen 44:26 for we may not see the man's *f*
Gen 46:28 to direct his *f* unto Goshen
Gen 46:30 me die, since I have seen thy *f*
Gen 48:11 I had not thought to see thy *f*
Gen 48:12 himself with his *f* to the earth
Gen 50:1 Joseph fell upon his father's *f*
Gen 50:18 went and fell down before his *f*
Ex 2:15 Moses fled from the *f* of Pharaoh
Ex 3:6 And Moses hid his *f*
Ex 10:5 shall cover the *f* of the earth
Ex 10:15 covered the *f* of the whole earth
Ex 10:28 heed to thyself, see my *f* no more
Ex 10:28 thou seest my *f* thou shalt die
Ex 10:29 I will see thy *f* again no more
Ex 14:19 cloud went from before their *f*
Ex 14:25 Let us flee from the *f* of Israel
Ex 16:14 upon the *f* of the wilderness
Ex 32:12 them from the *f* of the earth
Ex 33:11 LORD spake unto Moses *f* to *f*
Ex 33:16 that are upon the *f* of the earth
Ex 33:20 he said, Thou canst not see my *f*
Ex 33:23 but my *f* shall not be seen
Ex 34:29 wist not that the skin of his *f*
Ex 34:30 behold, the skin of his *f* shone
Ex 34:33 with them, he put a vail on his *f*
Ex 34:35 of Israel saw the *f* of Moses
Ex 34:35 that the skin of Moses' *f* shone
Ex 34:35 put the vail upon his *f* again
Lev 13:41 the part of his head toward his *f*
Lev 17:10 I will even set my *f* against that
Lev 19:32 honour the *f* of the old man, and
Lev 20:3 I will set my *f* against that man,
Lev 20:5 I will set my *f* against that man
Lev 20:6 even set my *f* against that soul
Lev 26:17 And I will set my *f* against you
Num 6:25 LORD make his *f* shine upon thee
Num 11:31 high upon the *f* of the earth
Num 12:3 were upon the *f* of the earth
Num 12:14 her father had but spit in her *f*
Num 14:14 that thou LORD art seen *f* to *f*
Num 16:4 heard it, he fell upon his *f*
Num 19:3 one shall slay her before his *f*
Num 22:5 they cover the *f* of the earth
Num 22:11 which covereth the *f* of the earth
Num 22:31 his head, and fell flat on his *f*
Num 24:1 but he set his *f* toward the
Deut 1:17 not be afraid of the *f* of man
Deut 5:4 LORD talked with you *f* to *f* in
Deut 6:15 thee from off the *f* of the earth
Deut 7:6 that are upon the *f* of the earth
Deut 7:10 them that hate him to their *f*
Deut 7:10 him, he will repay him to his *f*
Deut 8:20 the LORD destroyeth before your *f*
Deut 9:3 bring them down before thy *f*
Deut 25:2 and to be beaten before his *f*
Deut 25:9 off his foot, and spit in his *f*
Deut 28:7 thee to be smitten before thy *f*
Deut 28:31 taken away from before thy *f*
Deut 31:5 shall give them up before your *f*
Deut 31:17 and I will hide my *f* from them
Deut 31:18 I will surely hide my *f* in that
Deut 32:20 said, I will hide my *f* from them
Deut 34:10 whom the LORD knew *f* to *f*
Josh 5:14 Joshua fell on his *f* to the earth
Josh 7:6 his *f* before the ark of the LORD
Josh 7:10 liest thou thus upon thy *f*
Judg 6:22 an angel of the LORD *f* to *f*
Ruth 2:10 Then she fell on her *f*, and bowed
1Sa 5:3 Dagon was fallen upon his *f* to
1Sa 5:4 Dagon was fallen upon his *f* to
1Sa 17:49 he fell upon his *f* to the earth
1Sa 20:15 every one from the *f* of the earth
1Sa 20:41 fell on his *f* to the ground, and
1Sa 24:8 stooped with his *f* to the earth
1Sa 25:23 and fell before David on her *f*
1Sa 25:41 herself on her *f* to the earth
1Sa 26:20 earth before the *f* of the LORD
1Sa 28:14 stooped with his *f* to the ground
2Sa 2:22 hold up my *f* to Joab thy brother
2Sa 3:13 that is, Thou shalt not see my *f*
2Sa 3:13 when thou comest to see my *f*
2Sa 9:6 come unto David, he fell on his *f*
2Sa 14:4 she fell on her *f* to the ground
2Sa 14:22 Joab fell to the ground on his *f*
2Sa 14:24 house, and let him not see my *f*
2Sa 14:24 house, and saw not the king's *f*
2Sa 14:28 and saw not the king's *f*
2Sa 14:32 therefore let me see the king's *f*
2Sa 14:33 bowed himself on his *f* to the
2Sa 18:8 over the *f* of all the country
2Sa 18:28 earth upon his *f* before the king
2Sa 19:4 But the king covered his *f*
2Sa 24:20 the king on his *f* upon the ground
1Kin 1:23 the king with his *f* to the ground
1Kin 1:31 bowed with her *f* to the earth
1Kin 8:14 And the king turned his *f* about
1Kin 13:6 Intreat now the *f* of the LORD thy
1Kin 13:34 it from off the *f* of the earth
1Kin 18:7 and he knew him, and fell on his *f*
1Kin 18:42 put his *f* between his knees,
1Kin 19:13 he wrapped his *f* in his mantle
1Kin 20:38 himself with ashes upon his *f*
1Kin 20:41 and took the ashes away from his *f*
1Kin 21:4 his bed, and turned away his *f*
2Kin 4:29 my staff upon the *f* of the child
2Kin 4:31 the staff upon the *f* of the child
2Kin 8:15 in water, and spread it on his *f*
2Kin 9:30 and she painted her *f*, and tired
2Kin 9:32 he lifted up his *f* to the window
2Kin 9:37 shall be as dung upon the *f* of
2Kin 12:17 Hazael set his *f* to go up to
2Kin 13:14 down unto him, and wept over his *f*
2Kin 14:8 let us look one another in the *f*
2Kin 14:11 another in the *f* at Beth-shemesh
2Kin 18:24 then wilt thou turn away the *f* of
2Kin 20:2 Then he turned his *f* to the wall
1Chr 16:11 strength, seek his *f* continually
1Chr 21:21 to David with his *f* to the ground
2Chr 6:3 And the king turned his *f*, and
2Chr 6:42 not away the *f* of thine anointed
2Chr 7:14 themselves, and pray, and seek my *f*
2Chr 20:18 his head with his *f* to the ground
2Chr 25:17 let us see one another in the *f*
2Chr 25:21 and they saw one another in the *f*
2Chr 30:9 will not turn away his *f* from you
2Chr 32:21 with shame of *f* to his own land
2Chr 35:22 would not turn his *f* from him
Ezr 9:6 and blush to lift up my *f* to thee
Ezr 9:7 to a spoil, and to confusion of *f*
Est 1:14 and Media, which saw the king's *f*
Est 7:8 mouth, they covered Haman's *f*
Job 1:11 and he will curse thee to thy *f*
Job 2:5 and he will curse thee to thy *f*
Job 4:15 Then a spirit passed before my *f*
Job 11:15 thou lift up thy *f* without spot
Job 13:24 Wherefore hidest thou thy *f*
Job 15:27 covereth his *f* with his fatness
Job 16:8 up in me beareth witness to my *f*
Job 16:16 My *f* is foul with weeping, and on
Job 21:31 shall declare his way to his *f*
Job 22:26 and shalt lift up thy *f* unto God
Job 23:17 he covered the darkness from my *f*
Job 24:15 and disguiseth his *f*
Job 26:9 holdeth back the *f* of his throne
Job 30:10 me, and spare not to spit in my *f*
Job 33:26 and he shall see his *f* with joy
Job 34:29 and when he hideth his *f*, who then
Job 37:12 the *f* of the world in the earth
Job 38:30 the *f* of the deep is frozen
Job 41:13 can discover the *f* of his garment
Job 41:14 Who can open the doors of his *f*
Ps 5:8 make thy way straight before my *f*
Ps 10:11 he hideth his *f*
Ps 13:1 long wilt thou hide thy *f* from me
Ps 17:15 behold thy *f* in righteousness
Ps 21:12 thy strings against the *f* of them
Ps 22:24 hath he hid his *f* from him
Ps 24:6 that seek him, that seek thy *f*
Ps 27:8 When thou saidst, Seek ye my *f*
Ps 27:8 my heart said unto thee, Thy *f*
Ps 27:9 Hide not thy *f* far from me
Ps 30:7 thou didst hide thy *f*, and I was
Ps 31:16 Make thy *f* to shine upon thy
Ps 34:16 The *f* of the LORD is against them
Ps 41:12 settest me before thy *f* for ever
Ps 44:15 the shame of my *f* hath covered me
Ps 44:24 Wherefore hidest thou thy *f*
Ps 51:9 Hide thy *f* from my sins, and blot
Ps 67:1 cause his *f* to shine upon us
Ps 69:7 shame hath covered my *f*
Ps 69:17 hide not thy *f* from thy servant
Ps 80:3 O God, and cause thy *f* to shine
Ps 80:7 of hosts, and cause thy *f* to shine
Ps 80:19 of hosts, cause thy *f* to shine
Ps 84:9 look upon the *f* of thine anointed
Ps 88:14 why hidest thou thy *f* from me
Ps 89:14 and truth shall go before thy *f*
Ps 89:23 beat down his foes before his *f*
Ps 102:2 Hide not thy *f* from me in the day
Ps 104:15 and oil to make his *f* to shine
Ps 104:29 Thou hidest thy *f*, they are
Ps 104:30 thou renewest the *f* of the earth
Ps 105:4 seek his *f* evermore
Ps 119:135 Make thy *f* to shine upon thy
Ps 132:10 not away the *f* of thine anointed
Ps 143:7 hide not thy *f* from me, lest I be
Prov 7:13 with an impudent *f* said unto him
Prov 7:15 thee, diligently to seek thy *f*
Prov 8:27 a compass upon the *f* of the depth
Prov 21:29 A wicked man hardeneth his *f*
Prov 24:31 nettles had covered the *f* thereof
Prov 27:19 As in water *f* answereth to *f*,
Eccl 8:1 wisdom maketh his *f* to shine
Eccl 8:1 of his *f* shall be changed
Is 6:2 with twain he covered his *f*
Is 8:17 that hideth his *f* from the house
Is 14:21 nor fill the *f* of the world with
Is 16:4 to them from the *f* of the spoiler
Is 23:17 the world upon the *f* of the earth
Is 25:7 destroy in this mountain the *f* of
Is 27:6 fill the *f* of the world with
Is 28:25 he hath made plain the *f* thereof
Is 29:22 neither shall his *f* now wax pale
Is 36:9 then wilt thou turn away the *f* of
Is 38:2 turned his *f* toward the wall
Is 49:23 with their *f* toward the earth
Is 50:6 I hid not my *f* from shame

Is 50:7 have I set my f like a flint
Is 54:8 I hid my f from thee for a moment
Is 59:2 your sins have hid his f from you
Is 64:7 for thou hast hid thy f from us
Is 65:3 me to anger continually to my f
Jer 1:13 the f thereof is toward the north
Jer 2:27 back unto me, and not their f
Jer 4:30 thou rentest thy f with painting
Jer 8:2 for dung upon the f of the earth
Jer 13:26 I discover thy skirts upon thy f
Jer 16:4 as dung upon the f of the earth
Jer 16:17 they are not hid from my f
Jer 18:17 shew them the back, and not the f
Jer 21:10 For I have set my f against this
Jer 22:25 hand of them whose f thou fearest
Jer 25:26 which are upon the f of the earth
Jer 28:16 thee from off the f of the earth
Jer 32:31 should remove it from before my f
Jer 32:33 unto me the back, and not the f
Jer 33:5 I have hid my f from this city
Jer 44:11 I will set my f against you for
Lam 2:19 water before the f of the Lord
Lam 3:35 man before the f of the most High
Eze 1:10 they four had the f of a man
Eze 1:10 the f of a lion, on the right
Eze 1:10 they four had the f of an ox on
Eze 1:10 four also had the f of an eagle
Eze 1:28 when I saw it, I fell upon my f
Eze 3:8 I have made thy f strong against
Eze 3:23 and I fell on my f
Eze 4:3 set thy f against it, and it shall
Eze 4:7 Therefore thou shalt set thy f
Eze 6:2 set thy f toward the mountains of
Eze 7:22 My f will I turn also from them,
Eze 9:8 I was left, that I fell upon my f
Eze 10:14 first f was the f of a cherub
Eze 10:14 second f was the f of a man
Eze 10:14 and the third the f of a lion
Eze 10:14 and the fourth the f of an eagle
Eze 11:13 Then fell I down upon my f
Eze 12:6 thou shalt cover thy f, that thou
Eze 12:12 he shall cover his f, that he see
Eze 13:17 set thy f against the daughters
Eze 14:3 of their iniquity before their f
Eze 14:4 of his iniquity before his f
Eze 14:7 of his iniquity before his f
Eze 14:8 I will set my f against that man,
Eze 15:7 And I will set my f against them
Eze 15:7 when I set my f against them
Eze 20:35 will I plead with you f to f
Eze 20:35 will I plead with you f to f
Eze 20:46 set thy f toward the south, and
Eze 21:2 set thy f toward Jerusalem, and
Eze 21:16 left, whithersoever thy f is set
Eze 25:2 set thy f against the Ammonites,
Eze 28:21 set thy f against Zidon, and
Eze 29:2 set thy f against Pharaoh king of
Eze 34:6 upon all the f of the earth
Eze 35:2 set thy f against mount Seir, and
Eze 38:2 set thy f against Gog, the land
Eze 38:18 my fury shall come up in my f
Eze 38:20 that are upon the f of the earth
Eze 39:14 remain upon the f of the earth
Eze 39:23 therefore hid I my f from them
Eze 39:24 unto them, and hid my f from them
Eze 39:29 I hide my f any more from them
Eze 40:15 from the f of the gate of the
Eze 40:15 gate of the entrance unto the f
Eze 41:14 the breadth of the f of the house
Eze 41:19 So that the f of a man was toward
Eze 41:19 the f of a young lion toward the
Eze 41:21 and the f of the sanctuary
Eze 41:25 upon the f of the porch without
Eze 43:3 and I fell upon my f
Eze 44:4 and I fell upon my f
Dan 2:46 Nebuchadnezzar fell upon his f
Dan 8:5 west on the f of the whole earth
Dan 8:17 I was afraid, and fell upon my f
Dan 8:18 sleep on my f toward the ground
Dan 9:3 I set my f unto the Lord God, to
Dan 9:8 to us belongeth confusion of f
Dan 9:17 cause thy f to shine upon thy
Dan 10:6 his f as the appearance of
Dan 10:9 was I in a deep sleep on my f
Dan 10:9 and my f toward the ground
Dan 10:15 I set my f toward the ground, and
Dan 11:17 He shall also set his f to enter
Dan 11:18 he turn his f unto the isles
Dan 11:19 Then he shall turn his f toward
Hos 5:5 of Israel doth testify to his f
Hos 5:15 their offence, and seek my f
Hos 7:2 they are before my f
Hos 7:10 of Israel testifieth to his f
Joel 2:6 Before their f the people shall
Joel 2:20 with his f toward the east sea,
Amos 5:8 them out upon the f of the earth
Amos 9:6 them out upon the f of the earth
Amos 9:8 it from off the f of the earth
Mic 3:4 he will even hide his f from them
Nah 2:1 in pieces is come up before thy f
Nah 3:5 discover thy skirts upon thy f
Zec 5:3 over the f of the whole earth
Mt 6:17 anoint thine head, and wash thy f
Mt 11:10 I send my messenger before thy f
Mt 16:3 ye can discern the f of the sky
Mt 17:2 his f did shine as the sun, and
Mt 17:6 heard it, they fell on their f
Mt 18:10 angels do always behold the f of
Mt 26:39 little farther, and fell on his f
Mt 26:67 Then did they spit in his f
Mk 1:2 I send my messenger before thy f
Mk 14:65 to spit on him, and to cover his f
Lk 1:76 for thou shalt go before the f of
Lk 2:31 before the f of all people
Lk 5:12 who seeing Jesus fell on his f
Lk 7:27 I send my messenger before thy f
Lk 9:51 set his f to go to Jerusalem
Lk 9:52 And sent messengers before his f
Lk 9:53 because his f was as though he
Lk 10:1 two before his f into every city
Lk 12:56 ye can discern the f of the sky
Lk 17:16 And fell down on his f at his feet
Lk 21:35 dwell on the f of the whole earth
Lk 22:64 him, they struck him on the f
Jn 11:44 his f was bound about with a
Acts 2:25 the Lord always before my f
Acts 6:15 saw his f as it had been the f
Acts 7:45 out before the f of our fathers
Acts 17:26 dwell on all the f of the earth
Acts 20:25 of God, shall see my f no more
Acts 20:38 they should see his f no more
Acts 25:16 have the accusers f to f
1Cor 13:12 but then f to f
1Cor 14:25 down on his f he will worship God
2Cor 3:7 f of Moses for the glory of his
2Cor 3:13 which put a vail over his f
2Cor 3:18 with open f beholding as in a
2Cor 4:6 of God in the f of Jesus Christ
2Cor 11:20 if a man smite you on the f
Gal 1:22 was unknown by f unto the
Gal 2:11 Antioch, I withstood him to the f
Col 2:1 have not seen my f in the flesh
1Th 2:17 to see your f with great desire
1Th 3:10 that we might see your f, and
Jas 1:23 his natural f in a glass
1Pet 3:12 but the f of the Lord is against
2Jn 12 speak f to f, that our joy may
2Jn 12 come unto you, and speak f to f
3Jn 14 thee, and we shall speak f to f
3Jn 14 thee, and we shall speak f to f
Rev 4:7 the third beast had a f as a man
Rev 6:16 hide us from the f of him that
Rev 10:1 his f was as it were the sun, and
Rev 12:14 from the f of the serpent
Rev 20:11 sat on it, from whose f the earth
Rev 22:4 And they shall see his f

## FACES

Gen 9:23 their f were backward, and they
Gen 18:22 men turned their f from thence
Gen 30:40 set the f of the flocks toward
Gen 42:6 him with their f to the earth
Ex 19:7 laid before their f all these
Ex 20:20 his fear may be before your f
Ex 25:20 their f shall look one to another
Ex 25:20 shall the f of the cherubims be
Ex 37:9 with their f one to another
Ex 37:9 were the f of the cherubims
Lev 9:24 they shouted, and fell on their f
Num 14:5 Aaron fell on their f before all
Num 16:22 And they fell upon their f
Num 16:45 And they fell upon their f
Num 20:6 and they fell upon their f
Judg 13:20 and fell on their f to the ground
Judg 18:23 And they turned their f, and said
2Sa 19:5 day the f of all thy servants
1Kin 2:15 that all Israel set their f on me
1Kin 18:39 saw it, they fell on their f
1Chr 12:8 f were like the f of lions
1Chr 21:16 in sackcloth, fell upon their f
2Chr 3:13 feet, and their f were inward
2Chr 7:3 bowed themselves with their f to
2Chr 29:6 have turned away their f from the
Neh 8:6 LORD with their f to the ground
Job 9:24 he covereth the f of the judges
Job 40:13 and bind their f in secret
Ps 34:5 and their f were not ashamed
Ps 83:16 Fill their f with shame
Is 3:15 and grind the f of the poor
Is 13:8 their f shall be as flames
Is 25:8 wipe away tears from off all f
Is 53:3 we hid as it were our f from him
Jer 1:8 Be not afraid of their f
Jer 1:17 be not dismayed at their f
Jer 5:3 made their f harder than a rock
Jer 7:19 to the confusion of their own f
Jer 30:6 all f are turned into paleness
Jer 42:15 set your f to enter into Egypt
Jer 42:17 f to go into Egypt to sojourn
Jer 44:12 that have set their f to go into
Jer 50:5 to Zion with their f thitherward
Jer 51:51 shame hath covered our f
Lam 5:12 the f of elders were not honoured
Eze 1:6 And every one had four f, and every
Eze 1:8 and they four had their f and their
Eze 1:10 As for the likeness of their f
Eze 1:11 Thus were their f
Eze 1:15 living creatures, with his four f
Eze 3:8 thy face strong against their f
Eze 7:18 and shame shall be upon all f
Eze 8:16 LORD, and their f toward the east
Eze 10:14 And every one had four f
Eze 10:21 Every one had four f apiece
Eze 10:22 the likeness of their f was the
Eze 10:22 f which I saw by the river of
Eze 14:6 turn away your f from all your
Eze 20:47 all f from the south to the north
Eze 41:18 and every cherub had two f
Dan 1:10 for why should he see your f
Dan 9:7 thee, but unto us confusion of f
Joel 2:6 all f shall gather blackness
Nah 2:10 and the f of them all gather
Hab 1:9 their f shall sup up as the east
Mal 2:3 seed, and spread dung upon your f
Mt 6:16 for they disfigure their f
Lk 24:5 bowed down their f to the earth
Rev 7:11 fell before the throne on their f
Rev 9:7 their f were as the f of men
Rev 11:16 on their seats, fell upon their f

## FADE

2Sa 22:46 Strangers shall f away, and they
Ps 18:45 The strangers shall f away
Is 64:6 and we all do f as a leaf
Jer 8:13 the fig tree, and the leaf shall f
Eze 47:12 for meat, whose leaf shall not f
Jas 1:11 the rich man f away in his ways

## FADETH

Is 1:30 shall be as an oak whose leaf f
Is 24:4 f away, the world languisheth and
Is 24:4 f away, the haughty people of the
Is 40:7 The grass withereth, the flower f
Is 40:8 The grass withereth, the flower f
1Pet 1:4 that f not away, reserved in
1Pet 5:4 a crown of glory that f not away

## FAIL

Gen 47:16 you for your cattle, if money f
Deut 28:32 f with longing for them all the
Deut 31:6 he will not f thee, nor forsake
Deut 31:8 be with thee, he will not f thee
Josh 1:5 I will not f thee, nor forsake
Josh 3:10 that he will without f drive out
Judg 11:30 If thou shalt without f deliver
1Sa 2:16 Let them not f to burn the fat
1Sa 17:32 no man's heart f because of him
1Sa 20:5 I should not f to sit with the
1Sa 30:8 them, and without f recover all
2Sa 3:29 let there not f from the house of
1Kin 2:4 there shall not f thee (said he)
1Kin 8:25 There shall not f thee a man in
1Kin 9:5 There shall not f thee a man upon
1Kin 17:14 neither shall the cruse of oil f
1Kin 17:16 neither did the cruse of oil f
1Chr 28:20 he will not f thee, nor forsake
2Chr 6:16 There shall not f thee a man in
2Chr 7:18 There shall not f thee a man to
Ezr 4:22 heed now that ye f not to do this
Ezr 6:9 given them day by day without f
Est 6:10 let nothing f of all that thou
Est 9:27 unto them, so as it should not f

Est 9:28 should not *f* from among the Jews
Job 11:20 the eyes of the wicked shall *f*
Job 14:11 As the waters *f* from the sea
Job 17:5 the eyes of his children shall *f*
Job 31:16 caused the eyes of the widow to *f*
Ps 12:1 for the faithful *f* from among the
Ps 69:3 mine eyes *f* while I wait for my
Ps 77:8 doth his promise *f* for evermore
Ps 89:33 nor suffer my faithfulness to *f*
Ps 119:82 Mine eyes *f* for thy word, saying,
Ps 119:123 Mine eyes *f* for thy salvation, and
Prov 22:8 and the rod of his anger shall *f*
Eccl 12:5 be a burden, and desire shall *f*
Is 19:3 shall *f* in the midst thereof
Is 19:5 the waters shall *f* from the sea
Is 21:16 and all the glory of Kedar shall *f*
Is 31:3 and they all shall *f* together
Is 32:6 the drink of the thirsty to *f*
Is 32:10 for the vintage shall *f*, the
Is 34:16 no one of these shall *f*, none
Is 38:14 mine eyes *f* with looking upward
Is 42:4 He shall not *f* nor be discouraged
Is 51:14 pit, nor that his bread should *f*
Is 57:16 for the spirit should *f* before me
Is 58:11 of water, whose waters *f* not
Jer 14:6 their eyes did *f*, because there
Jer 15:18 me as a liar, and as waters that *f*
Jer 48:33 wine to *f* from the winepresses
Lam 2:11 Mine eyes do *f* with tears
Lam 3:22 because his compassions *f* not
Hos 9:2 and the new wine shall *f* in her
Amos 8:4 to make the poor of the land to *f*
Hab 3:17 the labour of the olive shall *f*
Lk 16:9 that, when ye *f*, they may receive
Lk 16:17 than one tittle of the law to *f*
Lk 22:32 for thee, that thy faith *f* not
1Cor 13:8 there be prophecies, they shall *f*
Heb 1:12 same, and thy years shall not *f*
Heb 11:32 for the time would *f* me to tell
Heb 12:15 any man *f* of the grace of God

## FAILED

Gen 42:28 and their heart *f* them, and they
Gen 47:15 when money *f* in the land of Egypt
Josh 3:16 the plain, even the salt sea, *f*
Josh 21:45 There *f* not ought of any good
Josh 23:14 that not one thing hath *f* of all
Josh 23:14 and not one thing hath *f* thereof
1Kin 8:56 there hath not *f* one word of all
Job 19:14 My kinsfolk have *f*, and my
Ps 142:4 refuge *f* me; no man cared
Song 5:6 my soul *f* when he spake
Jer 51:30 their might hath *f*
Lam 4:17 our eyes as yet *f* for our vain

## FAILETH

Gen 47:15 for the money *f*
Job 21:10 Their bull gendereth, and *f* not
Ps 31:10 my strength *f* because of mine
Ps 38:10 heart panteth, my strength *f* me
Ps 40:12 therefore my heart *f* me
Ps 71:9 forsake me not when my strength *f*
Ps 73:26 My flesh and my heart *f*
Ps 109:24 and my flesh *f* of fatness
Ps 143:7 my spirit *f*
Eccl 10:3 by the way, his wisdom *f* him
Is 15:6 hay is withered away, the grass *f*
Is 40:26 strong in power; not one *f*
Is 41:17 and their tongue *f* for thirst
Is 44:12 he is hungry, and his strength *f*
Is 59:15 Yea, truth *f*
Eze 12:22 are prolonged, and every vision *f*
Zeph 3:5 his judgment to light, he *f* not
Lk 12:33 in the heavens that *f* not
1Cor 13:8 Charity never *f*

## FAINT

Gen 25:29 came from the field, and he was *f*
Gen 25:30 red pottage; for I am *f*
Deut 20:3 let not your hearts *f*, fear not,
Deut 20:8 heart *f* as well as his heart
Deut 25:18 behind thee, when thou wast *f*
Josh 2:9 of the land *f* because of you
Josh 2:24 of the country do *f* because of us
Judg 8:4 hundred men that were with him, *f*
Judg 8:5 for they be *f*, and I am pursuing
1Sa 14:28 And the people were *f*
1Sa 14:31 and the people were very *f*
1Sa 30:10 which were so *f* that they could
1Sa 30:21 which were so *f* that they could
2Sa 16:2 wine, that such as be *f* in the
2Sa 21:15 and David waxed *f*
Prov 24:10 If thou *f* in the day of adversity
Is 1:5 is sick, and the whole heart *f*
Is 13:7 Therefore shall all hands be *f*
Is 29:8 he awaketh, and, behold, he is *f*
Is 40:29 He giveth power to the *f*
Is 40:30 Even the youths shall *f* and be
Is 40:31 and they shall walk, and not *f*
Is 44:12 he drinketh no water, and is *f*
Jer 8:18 sorrow, my heart is *f* in me
Jer 51:46 And lest your heart *f*, and ye fear
Lam 1:13 made me desolate and *f* all the day
Lam 1:22 sighs are many, and my heart is *f*
Lam 2:19 that *f* for hunger in the top of
Lam 5:17 For this our heart is *f*
Eze 21:7 feeble, and every spirit shall *f*
Eze 21:15 gates, that their heart may *f*
Amos 8:13 virgins and young men *f* for thirst
Mt 15:32 fasting, lest they *f* in the way
Mk 8:3 houses, they will *f* by the way
Lk 18:1 ought always to pray, and not to *f*
2Cor 4:1 we have received mercy, we *f* not
2Cor 4:16 For which cause we *f* not
Gal 6:9 season we shall reap, if we *f* not
Eph 3:13 Wherefore I desire that ye *f* not
Heb 12:3 ye be wearied and *f* in your minds
Heb 12:5 nor *f* when thou art rebuked of

## FAINTED

Gen 45:26 And Jacob's heart *f*, for he
Gen 47:13 all the land of Canaan *f* by
Ps 27:13 I had *f*, unless I had believed to
Ps 107:5 and thirsty, their soul *f* in them
Is 51:20 Thy sons have *f*, they lie at the
Jer 45:3 I *f* in my sighing, and I find no
Eze 31:15 the trees of the field *f* for him
Dan 8:27 And I Daniel *f*, and was sick
Jonah 2:7 When my soul *f* within me I
Jonah 4:8 upon the head of Jonah, that he *f*
Mt 9:36 on them, because they *f*, and were
Rev 2:3 sake hast laboured, and hast not *f*

## FAINTETH

Ps 84:2 even *f* for the courts of the LORD
Ps 119:81 My soul *f* for thy salvation
Is 10:18 be as when a standard-bearer *f*
Is 40:28 earth, *f* not, neither is weary

## FAIR

Gen 6:2 daughters of men that they were *f*
Gen 12:11 thou art a *f* woman to look upon
Gen 12:14 the woman that she was very *f*
Gen 24:16 damsel was very *f* to look upon
Gen 26:7 because she was *f* to look upon
1Sa 17:42 and ruddy, and of a *f* countenance
2Sa 13:1 the son of David had a *f* sister
2Sa 14:27 was a woman of a *f* countenance
1Kin 1:3 So they sought for a *f* damsel
1Kin 1:4 And the damsel was very *f*, and
Est 1:11 for she was *f* to look on
Est 2:2 Let there be *f* young virgins
Est 2:3 may gather together all the *f*
Est 2:7 nor mother, and the maid was *f*
Job 37:22 *F* weather cometh out of the north
Job 42:15 so *f* as the daughters of Job
Prov 7:21 With her much *f* speech she caused
Prov 11:22 so is a *f* woman which is without
Prov 26:25 When he speaketh *f*, believe him
Song 1:15 Behold, thou art *f*, my love
Song 1:15 behold, thou art *f*
Song 1:16 Behold, thou art *f*, my beloved,
Song 2:10 my love, my *f* one, and come away
Song 2:13 my love, my *f* one, and come away
Song 4:1 Behold, thou art *f*, my love
Song 4:1 behold, thou art *f*
Song 4:7 Thou art all *f*, my love
Song 4:10 How *f* is thy love, my sister, my
Song 6:10 *f* as the moon, clear as the sun,
Song 7:6 How *f* and how pleasant art thou, O
Is 5:9 be desolate, even great and *f*
Is 54:11 will lay thy stones with *f* colors
Jer 4:30 in vain shalt thou make thyself *f*
Jer 11:16 thy name, A green olive tree, *f*
Jer 12:6 they speak *f* words unto thee
Jer 46:20 Egypt is like a very *f* heifer
Eze 16:17 taken thy *f* jewels of my gold
Eze 16:39 and shall take thy *f* jewels
Eze 23:26 and take away thy *f* jewels
Eze 31:3 cedar in Lebanon with *f* branches
Eze 31:7 Thus was he *f* in his greatness,
Eze 31:9 I have made him *f* by the
Dan 4:12 The leaves thereof were *f*
Dan 4:21 Whose leaves were *f*, and the fruit
Hos 10:11 but I passed over upon her *f* neck
Amos 8:13 In that day shall the *f* virgins
Zec 3:5 Let them set a *f* mitre upon his
Zec 3:5 So they set a *f* mitre upon his
Mt 16:2 ye say, It will be *f* weather
Acts 7:20 was born, and was exceeding *f*
Acts 27:8 which is called The *f* havens
Rom 16:18 *f* speeches deceive the hearts of
Gal 6:12 to make a *f* shew in the flesh

## FAIRS

Eze 27:12 and lead, they traded in thy *f*
Eze 27:14 traded in thy *f* with horses
Eze 27:16 occupied in thy *f* with emeralds
Eze 27:19 going to and fro occupied in thy *f*
Eze 27:22 they occupied in thy *f* with chief
Eze 27:27 Thy riches, and thy *f*, thy

## FAITH

Deut 32:20 children in whom is no *f*
Hab 2:4 but the just shall live by his *f*
Mt 6:30 more clothe you, O ye of little *f*
Mt 8:10 you, I have not found so great *f*
Mt 8:26 are ye fearful, O ye of little *f*
Mt 9:2 Jesus seeing their *f* said unto
Mt 9:22 thy *f* hath made thee whole
Mt 9:29 to your *f* be it unto you
Mt 14:31 said unto him, O thou of little *f*
Mt 15:28 unto her, O woman, great is thy *f*
Mt 16:8 said unto them, O ye of little *f*
Mt 17:20 If ye have *f* as a grain of
Mt 21:21 I say unto you, If ye have *f*
Mt 23:23 of the law, judgment, mercy, and *f*
Mk 2:5 When Jesus saw their *f*, he said
Mk 4:40 how is it that ye have no *f*
Mk 5:34 thy *f* hath made thee whole
Mk 10:52 thy *f* hath made thee whole
Mk 11:22 saith unto them, Have *f* in God
Lk 5:20 And when he saw their *f*, he said
Lk 7:9 you, I have not found so great *f*
Lk 7:50 the woman, Thy *f* hath saved thee
Lk 8:25 said unto them, Where is your *f*
Lk 8:48 thy *f* hath made thee whole
Lk 12:28 he clothe you, O ye of little *f*
Lk 17:5 unto the Lord, Increase our *f*
Lk 17:6 If ye had *f* as a grain of mustard
Lk 17:19 thy *f* hath made thee whole
Lk 18:8 shall he find *f* on the earth
Lk 18:42 thy *f* hath saved thee
Lk 22:32 for thee, that thy *f* fail not
Acts 3:16 his name through *f* in his name
Acts 3:16 the *f* which is by him hath given
Acts 6:5 chose Stephen, a man full of *f*
Acts 6:7 priests were obedient to the *f*
Acts 6:8 And Stephen, full of *f* and power,
Acts 11:24 and full of the Holy Ghost and of *f*
Acts 13:8 turn away the deputy from the *f*
Acts 14:9 that he had *f* to be healed
Acts 14:22 them to continue in the *f*
Acts 14:27 the door of *f* unto the Gentiles
Acts 15:9 them, purifying their hearts by *f*
Acts 16:5 the churches established in the *f*
Acts 20:21 *f* toward our Lord Jesus Christ
Acts 24:24 him concerning the *f* in Christ
Acts 26:18 are sanctified by *f* that is in me
Rom 1:5 to the *f* among all nations
Rom 1:8 you all, that your *f* is spoken of
Rom 1:12 you by the mutual *f* both of you
Rom 1:17 of God revealed from *f* to *f*
Rom 1:17 written, The just shall live by *f*
Rom 3:3 make the *f* of God without effect
Rom 3:22 of God which is by *f* of Jesus
Rom 3:25 through *f* in his blood, to
Rom 3:27 but by the law of *f*
Rom 3:28 that a man is justified by *f*
Rom 3:30 justify the circumcision by *f*
Rom 3:30 and uncircumcision through *f*
Rom 3:31 then make void the law through *f*
Rom 4:5 the ungodly, his *f* is counted for
Rom 4:9 for we say that *f* was reckoned to
Rom 4:11 of the *f* which he had yet being
Rom 4:12 of that *f* of our father Abraham
Rom 4:13 through the righteousness of *f*
Rom 4:14 *f* is made void, and the promise
Rom 4:16 Therefore it is of *f*, that it
Rom 4:16 also which is of the *f* of Abraham
Rom 4:19 And being not weak in *f*, he
Rom 4:20 but was strong in *f*, giving glory
Rom 5:1 Therefore being justified by *f*
Rom 5:2 by *f* into this grace wherein we
Rom 9:30 the righteousness which is of *f*

Rom 9:32 Because they sought it not by *f*
Rom 10:6 is of *f* speaketh on this wise
Rom 10:8 that is, the word of *f*, which we
Rom 10:17 So then *f* cometh by hearing, and
Rom 11:20 broken off, and thou standest by *f*
Rom 12:3 to every man the measure of *f*
Rom 12:6 according to the proportion of *f*
Rom 14:1 that is weak in the *f* receive ye
Rom 14:22 Hast thou *f*?
Rom 14:23 eat, because he eateth not of *f*
Rom 14:23 for whatsoever is not of *f* is sin
Rom 16:26 nations for the obedience of *f*
1Cor 2:5 That your *f* should not stand in
1Cor 12:9 To another *f* by the same Spirit
1Cor 13:2 and though I have all *f*, so that I
1Cor 13:13 And now abideth *f*, hope, charity,
1Cor 15:14 vain, and your *f* is also vain
1Cor 15:17 be not raised, your *f* is vain
1Cor 16:13 Watch ye, stand fast in the *f*
2Cor 1:24 that we have dominion over your *f*
2Cor 1:24 for by *f* ye stand
2Cor 4:13 We having the same spirit of *f*
2Cor 5:7 (For we walk by *f*, not by sight
2Cor 8:7 as ye abound in every thing, in *f*
2Cor 10:15 when your *f* is increased, that we
2Cor 13:5 whether ye be in the *f*
Gal 1:23 the *f* which once he destroyed
Gal 2:16 but by the *f* of Jesus Christ,
Gal 2:16 be justified by the *f* of Christ
Gal 2:20 I live by the *f* of the Son of God
Gal 3:2 the law, or by the hearing of *f*
Gal 3:5 the law, or by the hearing of *f*
Gal 3:7 that they which are of *f*, the
Gal 3:8 justify the heathen through *f*
Gal 3:9 So then they which be of *f* are
Gal 3:11 for, The just shall live by *f*
Gal 3:12 And the law is not of *f*
Gal 3:14 promise of the Spirit through *f*
Gal 3:22 that the promise by *f* of Jesus
Gal 3:23 But before *f* came, we were kept
Gal 3:23 shut up unto the *f* which should
Gal 3:24 that we might be justified by *f*
Gal 3:25 But after that *f* is come, we are
Gal 3:26 of God by *f* in Christ Jesus
Gal 5:5 the hope of righteousness by *f*
Gal 5:6 but *f* which worketh by love
Gal 5:22 gentleness, goodness, *f*,
Gal 6:10 who are of the household of *f*
Eph 1:15 heard of your *f* in the Lord Jesus
Eph 2:8 by grace are ye saved through *f*
Eph 3:12 with confidence by the *f* of him
Eph 3:17 may dwell in your hearts by *f*
Eph 4:5 One Lord, one *f*, one baptism,
Eph 4:13 we all come in the unity of the *f*
Eph 6:16 Above all, taking the shield of *f*
Eph 6:23 to the brethren, and love with *f*
Phil 1:25 for your furtherance and joy of *f*
Phil 1:27 together for the *f* of the gospel
Phil 2:17 sacrifice and service of your *f*
Phil 3:9 which is through the *f* of Christ
Phil 3:9 which is of God by *f*
Col 1:4 heard of your *f* in Christ Jesus
Col 1:23 If ye continue in the *f* grounded
Col 2:5 stedfastness of your *f* in Christ
Col 2:7 up in him, and stablished in the *f*
Col 2:12 the *f* of the operation of God
1Th 1:3 without ceasing your work of *f*
1Th 1:8 *f* to God-ward is spread abroad
1Th 3:2 to comfort you concerning your *f*
1Th 3:5 forbear, I sent to know your *f*
1Th 3:6 brought us good tidings of your *f*
1Th 3:7 affliction and distress by your *f*
1Th 3:10 that which is lacking in your *f*
1Th 5:8 putting on the breastplate of *f*
2Th 1:3 because that your *f* groweth
2Th 1:4 *f* in all your persecutions and
2Th 1:11 and the work of *f* with power
2Th 3:2 for all men have not *f*
1Ti 1:2 Unto Timothy, my own son in the *f*
1Ti 1:4 than godly edifying which is in *f*
1Ti 1:5 conscience, and of *f* unfeigned
1Ti 1:14 was exceeding abundant with *f*
1Ti 1:19 Holding *f*, and a good conscience
1Ti 1:19 concerning *f* have made shipwreck
1Ti 2:7 a teacher of the Gentiles in *f*
1Ti 2:15 if they continue in *f* and charity
1Ti 3:9 of the *f* in a pure conscience
1Ti 3:13 great boldness in the *f* which is
1Ti 4:1 some shall depart from the *f*
1Ti 4:6 nourished up in the words of *f*
1Ti 4:12 in charity, in spirit, in *f*
1Ti 5:8 own house, he hath denied the *f*
1Ti 5:12 they have cast off their first *f*
1Ti 6:10 after, they have erred from the *f*
1Ti 6:11 after righteousness, godliness, *f*
1Ti 6:12 Fight the good fight of *f*
1Ti 6:21 have erred concerning the *f*
2Ti 1:5 the unfeigned *f* that is in thee
2Ti 1:13 which thou hast heard of me, in *f*
2Ti 2:18 and overthrow the *f* of some
2Ti 2:22 but follow righteousness, *f*
2Ti 3:8 minds, reprobate concerning the *f*
2Ti 3:10 manner of life, purpose, *f*
2Ti 3:15 *f* which is in Christ Jesus
2Ti 4:7 my course, I have kept the *f*
Titus 1:1 according to the *f* of God's elect
Titus 1:4 mine own son after the common *f*
Titus 1:13 that they may be sound in the *f*
Titus 2:2 grave, temperate, sound in *f*
Titus 3:15 Greet them that love us in the *f*
Philem 5 Hearing of thy love and *f*, which
Philem 6 thy *f* may become effectual by the
Heb 4:2 not being mixed with *f* in them
Heb 6:1 dead works, and of *f* toward God,
Heb 6:12 followers of them who through *f*
Heb 10:22 true heart in full assurance of *f*
Heb 10:23 of our *f* without wavering
Heb 10:38 Now the just shall live by *f*
Heb 11:1 Now *f* is the substance of things
Heb 11:3 Through *f* we understand that the
Heb 11:4 By *f* Abel offered unto God a more
Heb 11:5 By *f* Enoch was translated that he
Heb 11:6 But without *f* it is impossible to
Heb 11:7 By *f* Noah, being warned of God of
Heb 11:7 the righteousness which is by *f*
Heb 11:8 By *f* Abraham, when he was called
Heb 11:9 By *f* he sojourned in the land of
Heb 11:11 Through *f* also Sara herself
Heb 11:13 These all died in *f*, not having
Heb 11:17 By *f* Abraham, when he was tried,
Heb 11:20 By *f* Isaac blessed Jacob and Esau
Heb 11:21 By *f* Jacob, when he was a dying,
Heb 11:22 By *f* Joseph, when he died, made
Heb 11:23 By *f* Moses, when he was born, was
Heb 11:24 By *f* Moses, when he was come to
Heb 11:27 By *f* he forsook Egypt, not
Heb 11:28 Through *f* he kept the passover,
Heb 11:29 By *f* they passed through the Red
Heb 11:30 By *f* the walls of Jericho fell
Heb 11:31 By *f* the harlot Rahab perished
Heb 11:33 Who through *f* subdued kingdoms,
Heb 11:39 obtained a good report through *f*
Heb 12:2 the author and finisher of our *f*
Heb 13:7 whose *f* follow, considering the
Jas 1:3 trying of your *f* worketh patience
Jas 1:6 But let him ask in *f*, nothing
Jas 2:1 have not the *f* of our Lord Jesus
Jas 2:5 the poor of this world rich in *f*
Jas 2:14 though a man say he hath *f*
Jas 2:14 can *f* save him?
Jas 2:17 Even so *f*, if it hath not works,
Jas 2:18 Yea, a man may say, Thou hast *f*
Jas 2:18 shew me thy *f* without thy works,
Jas 2:18 I will shew thee my *f* by my works
Jas 2:20 that *f* without works is dead
Jas 2:22 Seest thou how *f* wrought with his
Jas 2:22 and by works was *f* made perfect
Jas 2:24 is justified, and not by *f* only
Jas 2:26 so *f* without works is dead also
Jas 5:15 the prayer of *f* shall save the
1Pet 1:5 *f* unto salvation ready to be
1Pet 1:7 That the trial of your *f*, being
1Pet 1:9 Receiving the end of your *f*
1Pet 1:21 that your *f* and hope might be in
1Pet 5:9 Whom resist stedfast in the *f*
2Pet 1:1 precious *f* with us through the
2Pet 1:5 diligence, add to your *f* virtue
1Jn 5:4 overcometh the world, even our *f*
Jude 3 earnestly contend for the *f* which
Jude 20 up yourselves on your most holy *f*
Rev 2:13 my name, and hast not denied my *f*
Rev 2:19 and charity, and service, and *f*
Rev 13:10 patience and the *f* of the saints
Rev 14:12 of God, and the *f* of Jesus

**FAITHFUL**

Num 12:7 who is *f* in all mine house
Deut 7:9 thy God, he is God, the *f* God
1Sa 2:35 And I will raise me up a *f* priest
1Sa 22:14 who is so *f* among all thy
2Sa 20:19 that are peaceable and *f* in Israel
Neh 7:2 for he was a *f* man, and feared God
Neh 9:8 foundest his heart *f* before thee
Neh 13:13 for they were counted *f*, and their
Ps 12:1 for the *f* fail from among the
Ps 31:23 for the LORD preserveth the *f*
Ps 89:37 moon, and as a *f* witness in heaven
Ps 101:6 shall be upon the *f* of the land
Ps 119:86 All thy commandments are *f*
Ps 119:138 commanded are righteous and very *f*
Prov 11:13 but he that is of a *f* spirit
Prov 13:17 but a *f* ambassador is health
Prov 14:5 A *f* witness will not lie
Prov 20:6 but a *f* man who can find
Prov 25:13 so is a *f* messenger to them that
Prov 27:6 *F* are the wounds of a friend
Prov 28:20 A *f* man shall abound with
Is 1:21 How is the *f* city become an
Is 1:26 city of righteousness, the *f* city
Is 8:2 I took unto me *f* witnesses to
Is 49:7 because of the LORD that is *f*
Jer 42:5 *f* witness between us, if we do
Dan 6:4 forasmuch as he was *f*, neither
Hos 11:12 with God, and is *f* with the saints
Mt 24:45 Who then is a *f* and wise servant,
Mt 25:21 Well done, thou good and *f* servant
Mt 25:21 thou hast been *f* over a few
Mt 25:23 him, Well done, good and *f* servant
Mt 25:23 thou hast been *f* over a few
Lk 12:42 the Lord said, Who then is that *f*
Lk 16:10 He that is *f* in that which is
Lk 16:10 which is least is *f* also in much
Lk 16:11 been *f* in the unrighteous mammon
Lk 16:12 if ye have not been *f* in that
Lk 19:17 thou hast been *f* in a very little
Acts 16:15 judged me to be *f* to the Lord
1Cor 1:9 God is *f*, by whom ye were called
1Cor 4:2 stewards, that a man be found *f*
1Cor 4:17 *f* in the Lord, who shall bring
1Cor 7:25 mercy of the Lord to be *f*
1Cor 10:13 but God is *f*, who will not suffer
Gal 3:9 faith are blessed with *f* Abraham
Eph 1:1 and to the *f* in Christ Jesus
Eph 6:21 *f* minister in the Lord, shall
Col 1:2 *f* brethren in Christ which are at
Col 1:7 who is for you a *f* minister of
Col 4:7 a *f* minister and fellowservant in
Col 4:9 With Onesimus, a *f* and beloved
1Th 5:24 *F* is he that calleth you, who
2Th 3:3 But the Lord is *f*, who shall
1Ti 1:12 me, for that he counted me *f*
1Ti 1:15 This is a *f* saying, and worthy of
1Ti 3:11 sober, *f* in all things
1Ti 4:9 This is a *f* saying and worthy of
1Ti 6:2 them service, because they are *f*
2Ti 2:2 the same commit thou to *f* men
2Ti 2:11 It is a *f* saying
2Ti 2:13 we believe not, yet he abideth *f*
Titus 1:6 having *f* children not accused of
Titus 1:9 Holding fast the *f* word as he
Titus 3:8 This is a *f* saying, and these
Heb 2:17 and *f* high priest in things
Heb 3:2 Who was *f* to him that appointed
Heb 3:2 also Moses was *f* in all his house
Heb 3:5 verily was *f* in all his house
Heb 10:23 (for he is *f* that promised
Heb 11:11 she judged him *f* who had promised
1Pet 4:19 well doing, as unto a *f* Creator
1Pet 5:12 a *f* brother unto you, as I
1Jn 1:9 If we confess our sins, he is *f*
Rev 1:5 Christ, who is the *f* witness
Rev 2:10 be thou *f* unto death, and I will
Rev 2:13 wherein Antipas was my *f* martyr
Rev 3:14 things saith the Amen, the *f*
Rev 17:14 him are called, and chosen, and *f*
Rev 19:11 he that sat upon him was called *F*
Rev 21:5 for these words are true and *f*
Rev 22:6 said unto me, These sayings are *f*

**FAITHFULLY**

2Kin 12:15 for they dealt *f*
2Kin 22:7 their hand, because they dealt *f*
2Chr 19:9 ye do in the fear of the LORD, *f*
2Chr 31:12 tithes and the dedicated things *f*
2Chr 34:12 And the men did the work *f*
Prov 29:14 The king that *f* judgeth the poor,
Jer 23:28 my word, let him speak my word *f*
3Jn 5 thou doest *f* whatsoever thou

## FAITHFULNESS
1Sa 26:23 man his righteousness and his f
Ps 5:9 For there is no f in their mouth
Ps 36:5 thy f reacheth unto the clouds
Ps 40:10 I have declared thy f and thy
Ps 88:11 or thy f in destruction
Ps 89:1 known thy f to all generations
Ps 89:2 thy f shalt thou establish in the
Ps 89:5 thy f also in the congregation of
Ps 89:8 or to thy f round about thee
Ps 89:24 But my f and my mercy shall be
Ps 89:33 from him, nor suffer my f to fail
Ps 92:2 morning, and thy f every night,
Ps 119:75 that thou in f hast afflicted me
Ps 119:90 Thy f is unto all generations
Ps 143:1 in thy f answer me, and in thy
Is 11:5 f the girdle of his reins
Is 25:1 thy counsels of old are f
Lam 3:23 great is thy f
Hos 2:20 even betroth thee unto me in f

## FAITHLESS
Mt 17:17 Then Jesus answered and said, O f
Mk 9:19 O f generation, how long shall I
Lk 9:41 And Jesus answering said, O f
Jn 20:27 and be not f, but believing

## FALL
Gen 2:21 a deep sleep to f upon Adam
Gen 43:18 f upon us, and take us for bondmen
Gen 45:24 See that ye f not out by the way
Gen 49:17 that his rider shall f backward
Ex 5:3 lest he f upon us with pestilence
Ex 15:16 Fear and dread shall f upon them
Ex 21:33 it, and an ox or an ass f therein
Lev 11:32 them, when they are dead, doth f
Lev 11:37 if any part of their carcase f
Lev 11:38 part of their carcase f thereon
Lev 19:29 lest the land f to whoredom
Lev 26:7 they shall f before you by the
Lev 26:8 your enemies shall f before you
Lev 26:36 they shall f when none pursueth
Lev 26:37 they shall f one upon another, as
Num 11:31 let them f by the camp, as it
Num 14:3 to f by the sword, that our wives
Num 14:29 shall f in this wilderness
Num 14:32 they shall f in this wilderness
Num 14:43 you, and ye shall f by the sword
Num 34:2 f unto you for an inheritance
Deut 22:4 ass or his ox f down by the way
Deut 22:8 house, if any man f from thence
Josh 6:5 of the city shall f down flat
Judg 8:21 said, Rise thou, and f upon us
Judg 15:12 that ye will not f upon me
Judg 15:18 thirst, and f into the hand of the
Ruth 2:16 let f also some of the handfuls
Ruth 3:18 thou know how the matter will f
1Sa 3:19 none of his words f to the ground
1Sa 14:45 hair of his head f to the ground
1Sa 18:25 f by the hand of the Philistines
1Sa 21:13 let his spittle f down upon his
1Sa 22:17 not put forth their hand to f
1Sa 22:18 Turn thou, and f upon the priests
1Sa 26:20 let not my blood f to the earth
2Sa 1:15 and said, Go near, and f upon him
2Sa 14:11 hair of thy son f to the earth
2Sa 24:14 let us f now into the hand of the
2Sa 24:14 let me not f into the hand of man
1Kin 1:52 not an hair of him f to the earth
1Kin 2:29 Jehoiada, saying, Go, f upon him
1Kin 2:31 said, and f upon him, and bury him
1Kin 22:20 may go up and f at Ramoth-gilead
2Kin 7:4 let us f unto the host of the
2Kin 10:10 Know now that there shall f unto
2Kin 14:10 thy hurt, that thou shouldest f
2Kin 19:7 I will cause him to f by the
1Chr 12:19 He will f to his master Saul to
1Chr 21:13 let me f now into the hand of the
1Chr 21:13 but let me not f into the hand of
2Chr 18:19 may go up and f at Ramoth-gilead
2Chr 21:15 until thy bowels f out by reason
2Chr 25:8 make thee f before the enemy
2Chr 25:19 thine hurt, that thou shouldest f
Est 6:13 before whom thou hast begun to f
Est 6:13 but shalt surely f before him
Job 13:11 and his dread f upon you
Job 31:22 Then let mine arm f from my
Ps 5:10 let them f by their own counsels
Ps 9:3 are turned back, they shall f
Ps 10:10 that the poor may f by his strong
Ps 35:8 that very destruction let him f
Ps 37:24 Though he f, he shall not be
Ps 45:5 whereby the people f under thee
Ps 63:10 They shall f by the sword
Ps 64:8 own tongue to f upon themselves
Ps 72:11 all kings shall f down before him
Ps 78:28 he let it f in the midst of their
Ps 82:7 f like one of the princes
Ps 91:7 A thousand shall f at thy side
Ps 118:13 thrust sore at me that I might f
Ps 140:10 Let burning coals f upon them
Ps 141:10 Let the wicked f into their own
Ps 145:14 The LORD upholdeth all that f
Prov 4:16 away, unless they cause some to f
Prov 10:8 but a prating fool shall f
Prov 10:10 but a prating fool shall f
Prov 11:5 but the wicked shall f by his own
Prov 11:14 Where no counsel is, the people f
Prov 11:28 trusteth in his riches shall f
Prov 16:18 and an haughty spirit before a f
Prov 22:14 of the LORD shall f therein
Prov 24:16 the wicked shall f into mischief
Prov 26:27 diggeth a pit shall f therein
Prov 28:10 he shall f himself into his own
Prov 28:14 his heart shall f into mischief
Prov 28:18 in his ways shall f at once
Prov 29:16 the righteous shall see their f
Eccl 4:10 For if they f, the one will lift
Eccl 10:8 diggeth a pit shall f into it
Eccl 11:3 if the tree f toward the south,
Is 3:25 Thy men shall f by the sword
Is 8:15 among them shall stumble, and f
Is 10:4 they shall f under the slain
Is 10:34 Lebanon shall f by a mighty one
Is 13:15 unto them shall f by the sword
Is 22:25 be removed, and be cut down, and f
Is 24:18 of the fear shall f into the pit
Is 24:20 and it shall f, and not rise again
Is 28:13 f backward, and be broken, and
Is 30:13 be to you as a breach ready to f
Is 30:25 slaughter, when the towers f
Is 31:3 both he that helpeth shall f
Is 31:3 and he that is holpen shall f down
Is 31:8 the Assyrian f with the sword
Is 34:4 and all their host shall f down
Is 37:7 I will cause him to f by the
Is 40:30 and the young men shall utterly f
Is 44:19 shall I f down to the stock of a
Is 45:14 they shall f down unto thee, they
Is 46:6 they f down, yea, they worship
Is 47:11 and mischief shall f upon thee
Is 54:15 against thee shall f for thy sake
Jer 3:12 cause mine anger to f upon you
Jer 6:15 they shall f among them that f
Jer 6:21 sons together shall f upon them
Jer 8:4 Shall they f, and not arise
Jer 8:12 shall they f among them that f
Jer 9:22 f as dung upon the open field
Jer 15:8 caused him to f upon it suddenly
Jer 19:7 I will cause them to f by the
Jer 20:4 they shall f by the sword of
Jer 23:12 shall be driven on, and f therein
Jer 23:19 it shall f grievously upon the
Jer 25:27 ye, and be drunken, and spue, and f
Jer 25:34 ye shall f like a pleasant vessel
Jer 30:23 it shall f with pain upon the
Jer 37:14 I f not away to the Chaldeans
Jer 39:18 and thou shalt not f by the sword
Jer 44:12 and f in the land of Egypt
Jer 46:6 f toward the north by the river
Jer 46:16 He made many to f, yea, one fell
Jer 48:44 the fear shall f into the pit
Jer 49:21 is moved at the noise of their f
Jer 49:26 young men shall f in her streets
Jer 50:30 her young men f in the streets
Jer 50:32 the most proud shall stumble and f
Jer 51:4 Thus the slain shall f in the
Jer 51:44 yea, the wall of Babylon shall f
Jer 51:47 slain shall f in the midst of her
Jer 51:49 caused the slain of Israel to f
Jer 51:49 so at Babylon shall f the slain
Lam 1:14 he hath made my strength to f
Eze 5:12 a third part shall f by the sword
Eze 6:7 the slain shall f in the midst of
Eze 6:11 for they shall f by the sword
Eze 6:12 that is near shall f by the sword
Eze 11:10 Ye shall f by the sword
Eze 13:11 morter, that it shall f
Eze 13:11 ye, O great hailstones, shall f
Eze 13:14 be discovered, and it shall f
Eze 17:21 his bands shall f by the sword
Eze 23:25 thy remnant shall f by the sword
Eze 24:6 let no lot f upon it
Eze 24:21 ye have left shall f by the sword
Eze 25:13 of Dedan shall f by the sword
Eze 26:15 isles shake at the sound of thy f
Eze 26:18 isles tremble in the day of thy f
Eze 27:27 shall f into the midst of the
Eze 27:34 in the midst of thee shall f
Eze 29:5 thou shalt f upon the open fields
Eze 30:4 when the slain shall f in Egypt
Eze 30:5 shall f with them by the sword
Eze 30:6 also that uphold Egypt shall f
Eze 30:6 shall they f in it by the sword
Eze 30:17 of Pi-beseth shall f by the sword
Eze 30:22 the sword to f out of his hand
Eze 30:25 the arms of Pharaoh shall f down
Eze 31:16 to shake at the sound of his f
Eze 32:10 his own life, in the day of thy f
Eze 32:12 will I cause thy multitude to f
Eze 32:20 They shall f in the midst of them
Eze 33:12 he shall not f thereby in the day
Eze 33:27 the wastes shall f by the sword
Eze 35:8 shall they f that are slain with
Eze 36:15 cause thy nations to f any more
Eze 38:20 down, and the steep places shall f
Eze 38:20 every wall shall f to the ground
Eze 39:3 arrows to f out of thy right hand
Eze 39:4 Thou shalt f upon the mountains
Eze 39:5 Thou shalt f upon the open field
Eze 44:12 of Israel to f into iniquity
Eze 47:14 this land shall f unto you for
Dan 3:5 ye f down and worship the golden
Dan 3:10 all kinds of musick, shall f down
Dan 3:15 ye f down and worship the image
Dan 11:14 but they shall f
Dan 11:19 but he shall stumble and f
Dan 11:26 and many shall f down slain
Dan 11:33 yet they shall f by the sword
Dan 11:34 Now when they shall f, they shall
Dan 11:35 of them of understanding shall f
Hos 4:5 Therefore shalt thou f in the day
Hos 4:5 shall f with thee in the night
Hos 4:14 that doth not understand shall f
Hos 5:5 Ephraim f in their iniquity
Hos 5:5 Judah also shall f with them
Hos 7:16 their princes shall f by the
Hos 10:8 and to the hills, F on us
Hos 13:16 they shall f by the sword
Hos 14:9 the transgressors shall f therein
Joel 2:8 when they f upon the sword, they
Amos 3:5 Can a bird f in a snare upon the
Amos 3:14 be cut off, and f to the ground
Amos 7:17 daughters shall f by the sword
Amos 8:14 even they shall f, and never rise
Amos 9:9 the least grain f upon the earth
Mic 7:8 when I f, I shall arise
Nah 3:12 they shall even f into the mouth
Mt 4:9 I give thee, if thou wilt f down
Mt 7:27 and great was the f of it
Mt 10:29 one of them shall not f on the
Mt 12:11 if it f into a pit on the sabbath
Mt 15:14 both shall f into the ditch
Mt 15:27 which f from their masters' table
Mt 21:44 whosoever shall f on this stone
Mt 21:44 but on whomsoever it shall f
Mt 24:29 and the stars shall f from heaven
Mk 13:25 And the stars of heaven shall f
Lk 2:34 this child is set for the f
Lk 6:39 they not both f into the ditch
Lk 8:13 and in time of temptation f away
Lk 10:18 Satan as lightning f from heaven
Lk 20:18 Whosoever shall f upon that stone
Lk 20:18 but on whomsoever it shall f
Lk 21:24 they shall f by the edge of the
Lk 23:30 to say to the mountains, F on us
Jn 12:24 a corn of wheat f into the ground
Acts 27:17 they should f into the quicksands
Acts 27:32 of the boat, and let her f off
Acts 27:34 f from the head of any of you
Rom 11:11 they stumbled that they should f
Rom 11:11 but rather through their f
Rom 11:12 Now if the f of them be the
Rom 14:13 or an occasion to f in his
1Cor 10:12 he standeth take heed lest he f
1Ti 3:6 he f into the condemnation of the
1Ti 3:7 lest he f into reproach and the
1Ti 6:9 will be rich f into temptation
Heb 4:11 lest any man f after the same
Heb 6:6 If they shall f away, to renew
Heb 10:31 It is a fearful thing to f into

2Kin 21:6 and dealt with f spirits and
2Kin 23:24 the workers with f spirits
1Chr 10:13 of one that had a f spirit
2Chr 33:6 and dealt with a f spirit
Job 19:14 my f friends have forgotten me
Ps 41:9 Yea, mine own f friend, in whom I
Is 8:19 unto them that have f spirits
Is 19:3 and to them that have f spirits
Is 29:4 as of one that hath a f spirit

**FAMILIARS**

Jer 20:10 All my f watched for my halting,

**FAMINE**

Gen 12:10 And there was a f in the land
Gen 12:10 for the f was grievous in the
Gen 26:1 And there was a f in the land
Gen 26:1 beside the first f that was in
Gen 41:27 wind shall be seven years of f
Gen 41:30 arise after them seven years of f
Gen 41:30 the f shall consume the land
Gen 41:31 by reason of that f following
Gen 41:36 land against the seven years of f
Gen 41:36 the land perish not through the f
Gen 41:50 sons before the years of f came
Gen 41:56 the f was over all the face of
Gen 41:56 the f waxed sore in the land of
Gen 41:57 because that the f was so sore in
Gen 42:5 for the f was in the land of
Gen 42:19 corn for the f of your houses
Gen 42:33 take food for the f of your
Gen 43:1 the f was sore in the land
Gen 45:6 years hath the f been in the land
Gen 45:11 for yet there are five years of f
Gen 47:4 for the f is sore in the land of
Gen 47:13 for the f was very sore, so that
Gen 47:13 Canaan fainted by reason of the f
Gen 47:20 because the f prevailed over them
Ruth 1:1 that there was a f in the land
2Sa 21:1 Then there was a f in the days of
2Sa 24:13 Shall seven years of f come unto
1Kin 8:37 If there be in the land f
1Kin 18:2 And there was a sore f in Samaria
2Kin 6:25 And there was a great f in Samaria
2Kin 7:4 then the f is in the city, and we
2Kin 8:1 for the LORD hath called for a f
2Kin 25:3 month the f prevailed in the city
1Chr 21:12 Either three years' f
2Chr 20:9 judgment, or pestilence, or f
2Chr 32:11 give over yourselves to die by f
Job 5:20 In f he shall redeem thee from
Job 5:22 destruction and f thou shalt laugh
Job 30:3 For want and f they were solitary
Ps 33:19 death, and to keep them alive in f
Ps 37:19 in the days of f they shall be
Ps 105:16 he called for a f upon the land
Is 14:30 and I will kill thy root with f
Is 51:19 and destruction, and the f
Jer 5:12 neither shall we see sword nor f
Jer 11:22 and their daughters shall die by f
Jer 14:12 them by the sword, and by the f
Jer 14:13 sword, neither shall ye have f
Jer 14:15 f shall not be in this land
Jer 14:15 f shall those prophets be
Jer 14:16 of Jerusalem because of the f
Jer 14:18 behold them that are sick with f
Jer 15:2 as are for the f, to the f
Jer 16:4 be consumed by the sword, and by f
Jer 18:21 up their children to the f
Jer 21:7 from the sword, and from the f
Jer 21:9 die by the sword, and by the f
Jer 24:10 And I will send the sword, the f
Jer 27:8 with the sword, and with the f
Jer 27:13 people, by the sword, by the f
Jer 29:17 send upon them the sword, the f
Jer 29:18 them with the sword, with the f
Jer 32:24 because of the sword, and of the f
Jer 32:36 Babylon by the sword, and by the f
Jer 34:17 to the pestilence, and to the f
Jer 38:2 shall die by the sword, by the f
Jer 42:16 in the land of Egypt, and the f
Jer 42:17 shall die by the sword, by the f
Jer 42:22 shall die by the sword, by the f
Jer 44:12 consumed by the sword and by the f
Jer 44:12 by the sword and by the f
Jer 44:13 Jerusalem, by the sword, by the f
Jer 44:18 consumed by the sword and by the f
Jer 44:27 consumed by the sword and by the f
Jer 52:6 the f was sore in the city, so
Lam 5:10 an oven because of the terrible f
Eze 5:12 with f shall they be consumed in
Eze 5:16 upon them the evil arrows of f
Eze 5:16 and I will increase the f upon you
Eze 5:17 So will I send upon you f
Eze 6:11 shall fall by the sword, by the f
Eze 6:12 and is besieged shall die by the f
Eze 7:15 and the pestilence and the f within
Eze 7:15 and he that is in the city, f
Eze 12:16 them from the sword, from the f
Eze 14:13 thereof, and will send f upon it
Eze 14:21 Jerusalem, the sword, and the f
Eze 36:29 increase it, and lay no f upon you
Eze 36:30 reproach of f among the heathen
Amos 8:11 that I will send a f in the land
Amos 8:11 not a f of bread, nor a thirst
Lk 4:25 when great f was throughout all
Lk 15:14 arose a mighty f in that land
Rom 8:35 or distress, or persecution, or f
Rev 18:8 one day, death, and mourning, and f

**FAMINES**

Mt 24:7 and there shall be f, and
Mk 13:8 places, and there shall be f
Lk 21:11 shall be in divers places, and f

**FAMOUS**

Num 16:2 f in the congregation, men of
Num 26:9 which were f in the congregation,
Ruth 4:11 Ephratah, and be f in Beth-lehem
Ruth 4:14 that his name may be f in Israel
1Chr 5:24 f men, and heads of the house of
1Chr 12:30 f throughout the house of their
Ps 74:5 A man was f according as he had
Ps 136:18 And slew f kings
Eze 23:10 and she became f among women
Eze 32:18 and the daughters of the f nations

**FAN**

Is 30:24 with the shovel and with the f
Is 41:16 Thou shalt f them, and the wind
Jer 4:11 daughter of my people, not to f
Jer 15:7 I will f them with a f in the
Jer 51:2 Babylon fanners, that shall f her
Mt 3:12 Whose f is in his hand, and he
Lk 3:17 Whose f is in his hand, and he

**FAREWELL**

Lk 9:61 but let me first go bid them f
Acts 18:21 But bade them f, saying, I must
Acts 23:30 what they had against him. F.
2Cor 13:11 Finally, brethren, f

**FASHION**

Gen 6:15 this is the f which thou shalt
Ex 26:30 f thereof which was shewed thee
Ex 37:19 the f of almonds in one branch
1Kin 6:38 and according to all the f of it
2Kin 16:10 the priest the f of the altar
Job 31:15 did not one f us in the womb
Eze 43:11 the f thereof, and the goings out
Mk 2:12 saying, We never saw it on this f
Lk 9:29 the f of his countenance was
Acts 7:44 to the f that he had seen
1Cor 7:31 for the f of this world passeth
Phil 2:8 And being found in f as a man
Jas 1:11 grace of the f of it perisheth

**FASHIONED**

Ex 32:4 f it with a graving tool, after
Job 10:8 f me together round about
Ps 119:73 Thy hands have made me and f me
Ps 139:16 which in continuance were f
Is 22:11 unto him that f it long ago
Eze 16:7 thy breasts are f, and thine hair
Phil 3:21 that it may be f like unto his

**FAST**

Gen 20:18 For the LORD had f closed up all
Judg 4:21 for he was f asleep and weary
Judg 15:13 but we will bind thee f, and
Judg 16:11 If they bind me f with new ropes
Ruth 2:8 but abide here f by my maidens
Ruth 2:21 Thou shalt keep f by my young men
Ruth 2:23 So she kept f by the maidens of
2Sa 12:21 thou didst f and weep for the
2Sa 12:23 he is dead, wherefore should I f
1Kin 21:9 the letters, saying, Proclaim a f
1Kin 21:12 They proclaimed a f, and set
2Kin 6:32 door, and hold him f at the door
2Chr 20:3 proclaimed a f throughout all
Ezr 5:8 walls, and this work goeth f on
Ezr 8:21 Then I proclaimed a f there
Est 4:16 f ye for me, and neither eat nor
Est 4:16 and my maidens will f likewise
Job 2:3 still he holdeth f his integrity
Job 8:15 he shall hold it f, but it shall
Job 27:6 My righteousness I hold f
Job 38:38 and the clods cleave f together
Ps 33:9 he commanded, and it stood f
Ps 38:2 For thine arrows stick f in me
Ps 41:8 say they, cleaveth f unto him
Ps 65:6 strength setteth f the mountains
Ps 89:28 covenant shall stand f with him
Ps 111:8 They stand f for ever and ever, and
Prov 4:13 Take f hold of instruction
Is 58:3 day of your f ye find pleasure
Is 58:4 ye f for strife and debate, and to
Is 58:4 ye shall not f as ye do this day,
Is 58:5 Is it such a f that I have chosen
Is 58:5 wilt thou call this a f, and an
Is 58:6 Is not this the f that I have
Jer 8:5 they hold f deceit, they refuse
Jer 14:12 When they f, I will not hear
Jer 36:9 that they proclaimed a f before
Jer 46:14 say ye, Stand f, and prepare thee
Jer 48:16 come, and his affliction hasteth f
Jer 50:33 took them captives held them f
Joel 1:14 Sanctify ye a f, call a solemn
Joel 2:15 the trumpet in Zion, sanctify a f
Jonah 1:5 and he lay, and was f asleep
Jonah 3:5 believed God, and proclaimed a f
Zec 7:5 years, did ye at all f unto me
Zec 8:19 The f of the fourth month, and the
Zec 8:19 the f of the fifth
Zec 8:19 the f of the seventh
Zec 8:19 and the f of
Mt 6:16 Moreover when ye f, be not, as
Mt 6:16 they may appear unto men to f
Mt 6:18 thou appear not unto men to f
Mt 9:14 Why do we and the Pharisees f oft
Mt 9:14 f oft, but thy disciples f not
Mt 9:15 from them, and then shall they f
Mt 26:48 hold him f
Mk 2:18 and of the Pharisees used to f
Mk 2:18 of John and of the Pharisees f
Mk 2:18 but thy disciples f not
Mk 2:19 children of the bridechamber f
Mk 2:19 with them, they cannot f
Mk 2:20 then shall they f in those days
Lk 5:33 do the disciples of John f often
Lk 5:34 children of the bridechamber f
Lk 5:35 then shall they f in those days
Lk 18:12 I f twice in the week, I give
Acts 16:24 made their feet f in the stocks
Acts 27:9 because the f was now already
Acts 27:41 and the forepart stuck f, and
1Cor 16:13 stand f in the faith, quit you
Gal 5:1 Stand f therefore in the liberty
Phil 1:27 that ye stand f in one spirit
Phil 4:1 so stand f in the Lord, my dearly
1Th 3:8 live, if ye stand f in the Lord
1Th 5:21 hold f that which is good
2Th 2:15 Therefore, brethren, stand f
2Ti 1:13 Hold f the form of sound words,
Titus 1:9 Holding f the faithful word as he
Heb 3:6 if we hold f the confidence and
Heb 4:14 let us hold f our profession
Heb 10:23 Let us hold f the profession of
Rev 2:13 and thou holdest f my name
Rev 2:25 have already hold f till I come
Rev 3:3 hast received and heard, and hold f
Rev 3:11 hold that f which thou hast, that

**FASTED**

Judg 20:26 f that day until even, and offered
1Sa 7:6 f on that day, and said there, We
1Sa 31:13 a tree at Jabesh, and f seven days
2Sa 1:12 f until even, for Saul, and for
2Sa 12:16 and David f, and went in, and lay
2Sa 12:22 the child was yet alive, I f
1Kin 21:27 sackcloth upon his flesh, and f
1Chr 10:12 oak in Jabesh, and f seven days
Ezr 8:23 So we f and besought our God for
Neh 1:4 and mourned certain days, and f
Is 58:3 Wherefore have we f, say they, and
Zec 7:5 to the priests, saying, When ye f
Mt 4:2 And when he had f forty days
Acts 13:2 they ministered to the Lord, and f
Acts 13:3 And when they had f and prayed, and

**FASTEN**

Ex 28:14 f the wreathen chains to the
Ex 28:25 thou shalt f in the two ouches
Ex 39:31 to f it on high upon the mitre
Is 22:23 I will f him as a nail in a sure
Jer 10:4 they f it with nails and with

### FASTENED
Ex 39:18 chains they *f* in the two ouches
Ex 40:18 *f* his sockets, and set up the
Judg 4:21 temples, and *f* it into the ground
Judg 16:14 she *f* it with the pin, and said
1Sa 31:10 they *f* his body to the wall of
2Sa 20:8 *f* upon his loins in the sheath
1Kin 6:6 be *f* in the walls of the house
1Chr 10:10 *f* his head in the temple of Dagon
2Chr 9:18 which were *f* to the throne, and
Est 1:6 *f* with cords of fine linen and
Job 38:6 are the foundations thereof *f*
Eccl 12:11 as nails *f* by the masters of
Is 22:25 shall the nail that is *f* in the
Is 41:7 he *f* it with nails, that it
Eze 40:43 an hand broad, *f* round about
Lk 4:20 in the synagogue were *f* on him
Acts 11:6 the which when I had *f* mine eyes
Acts 28:3 out of the heat, and *f* on his hand

### FASTING
Neh 9:1 of Israel were assembled with *f*
Est 4:3 mourning among the Jews, and *f*
Ps 35:13 I humbled my soul with *f*
Ps 69:10 wept, and chastened my soul with *f*
Ps 109:24 My knees are weak through *f*
Jer 36:6 the LORD's house upon the *f* day
Dan 6:18 his palace, and passed the night *f*
Dan 9:3 prayer and supplications, with *f*
Joel 2:12 me with all your heart, and with *f*
Mt 15:32 and I will not send them away *f*
Mt 17:21 goeth not out but by prayer and *f*
Mk 8:3 them away *f* to their own houses
Mk 9:29 by nothing, but by prayer and *f*
Acts 10:30 days ago I was *f* until this hour
Acts 14:23 church, and had prayed with *f*
Acts 27:33 ye have tarried and continued *f*
1Cor 7:5 that ye may give yourselves to *f*

### FASTINGS
Est 9:31 their seed, the matters of the *f*
Lk 2:37 the temple, but served God with *f*
2Cor 6:5 in labours, in watchings, in *f*
2Cor 11:27 in *f* often, in cold and nakedness

### FAT
Gen 4:4 of his flock and of the *f* thereof
Gen 41:4 the seven well favoured and *f* kine
Gen 41:20 did eat up the first seven *f* kine
Gen 45:18 and ye shall eat the *f* of the land
Gen 49:20 Out of Asher his bread shall be *f*
Ex 23:18 neither shall the *f* of my
Ex 29:13 thou shalt take all the *f* that
Ex 29:13 the *f* that is upon them, and burn
Ex 29:22 thou shalt take of the ram the *f*
Ex 29:22 the *f* that covereth the inwards,
Ex 29:22 the *f* that is upon them, and the
Lev 1:8 lay the parts, the head, and the *f*
Lev 1:12 pieces, with his head and his *f*
Lev 3:3 the *f* that covereth the inwards,
Lev 3:3 all the *f* that is upon the
Lev 3:4 the *f* that is on them, which is
Lev 3:9 the *f* thereof, and the whole rump,
Lev 3:9 the *f* that covereth the inwards,
Lev 3:9 all the *f* that is upon the
Lev 3:10 the *f* that is upon them, which is
Lev 3:14 the *f* that covereth the inwards,
Lev 3:14 all the *f* that is upon the
Lev 3:15 the *f* that is upon them, which is
Lev 3:16 all the *f* is the LORD's
Lev 3:17 that ye eat neither *f* nor blood
Lev 4:8 the *f* of the bullock for the sin
Lev 4:8 the *f* that covereth the inwards,
Lev 4:8 all the *f* that is upon the
Lev 4:9 the *f* that is upon them, which is
Lev 4:19 he shall take all his *f* from him
Lev 4:26 burn all his *f* upon the altar
Lev 4:26 as the *f* of the sacrifice of
Lev 4:31 shall take away all the *f* thereof
Lev 4:31 as the *f* is taken away from off
Lev 4:35 shall take away all the *f* thereof
Lev 4:35 as the *f* of the lamb is taken
Lev 6:12 the *f* of the peace offerings
Lev 7:3 offer of it all the *f* thereof
Lev 7:3 the *f* that covereth the inwards,
Lev 7:4 the *f* that is on them, which is
Lev 7:23 Ye shall eat no manner of *f*
Lev 7:24 the *f* of the beast that dieth of
Lev 7:24 the *f* of that which is torn with
Lev 7:25 eateth the *f* of the beast
Lev 7:30 the *f* with the breast, it shall
Lev 7:31 shall burn the *f* upon the altar
Lev 7:33 of the peace offerings, and the *f*
Lev 8:16 he took all the *f* that was upon
Lev 8:16 and the two kidneys, and their *f*
Lev 8:20 the head, and the pieces, and the *f*
Lev 8:25 And he took the *f*, and the rump, and
Lev 8:25 all the *f* that was upon the
Lev 8:25 and the two kidneys, and their *f*
Lev 8:26 one wafer, and put them on the *f*
Lev 9:10 But the *f*, and the kidneys, and the
Lev 9:19 the *f* of the bullock and of the
Lev 9:20 they put the *f* upon the breasts,
Lev 9:20 he burnt the *f* upon the altar
Lev 9:24 altar the burnt offering and the *f*
Lev 10:15 offerings made by fire of the *f*
Lev 16:25 the *f* of the sin offering shall
Lev 17:6 burn the *f* for a sweet savour
Num 13:20 land is, whether it be *f* or lean
Num 18:17 shalt burn their *f* for an
Deut 31:20 and filled themselves, and waxen *f*
Deut 32:14 with *f* of lambs, and rams of the
Deut 32:14 with the *f* of kidneys of wheat
Deut 32:15 But Jeshurun waxed *f*, and kicked
Deut 32:15 thou art waxen *f*, thou art grown
Deut 32:38 Which did eat the *f* of their
Judg 3:17 and Eglon was a very *f* man
Judg 3:22 the *f* closed upon the blade, so
1Sa 2:15 Also before they burnt the *f*
1Sa 2:16 not fail to burn the *f* presently
1Sa 2:29 to make yourselves *f* with the
1Sa 15:22 and to hearken than the *f* of rams
1Sa 28:24 the woman had a *f* calf in the
2Sa 1:22 from the *f* of the mighty, the bow
1Kin 1:9 *f* cattle by the stone of Zoheleth
1Kin 1:19 *f* cattle and sheep in abundance,
1Kin 1:25 *f* cattle and sheep in abundance,
1Kin 4:23 Ten *f* oxen, and twenty oxen out of
1Kin 8:64 the *f* of the peace offerings
1Kin 8:64 the *f* of the peace offerings
1Chr 4:40 And they found *f* pasture and good,
2Chr 7:7 the *f* of the peace offerings,
2Chr 7:7 and the meat offerings, and the *f*
2Chr 29:35 with the *f* of the peace offerings
2Chr 35:14 offerings and the *f* until night
Neh 8:10 unto them, Go your way, eat the *f*
Neh 9:25 a *f* land, and possessed houses
Neh 9:25 eat, and were filled, and became *f*
Neh 9:35 *f* land which thou gavest before
Job 15:27 maketh collops of *f* on his flanks
Ps 17:10 They are inclosed in their own *f*
Ps 22:29 All they that be *f* upon earth
Ps 37:20 LORD shall be as the *f* of lambs
Ps 92:14 they shall be *f* and flourishing
Ps 119:70 Their heart is as *f* as grease
Prov 11:25 The liberal soul shall be made *f*
Prov 13:4 of the diligent shall be made *f*
Prov 15:30 a good report maketh the bones *f*
Prov 28:25 trust in the LORD shall be made *f*
Is 1:11 of rams, and the *f* of fed beasts
Is 5:17 the waste places of the *f* ones
Is 6:10 Make the heart of this people *f*
Is 10:16 send among his *f* ones leanness
Is 25:6 all people a feast of *f* things
Is 25:6 of *f* things full of marrow, of
Is 28:1 of the *f* valleys of them that are
Is 28:4 is on the head of the *f* valley
Is 30:23 of the earth, and it shall be *f*
Is 34:6 it is made *f* with fatness, and
Is 34:6 with the *f* of the kidneys of rams
Is 34:7 and their dust made *f* with fatness
Is 43:24 me with the *f* of thy sacrifices
Is 58:11 in drought, and make *f* thy bones
Jer 5:28 They are waxen *f*, they shine
Jer 50:11 because ye are grown *f* as the
Eze 34:3 Ye eat the *f*, and ye clothe you
Eze 34:14 in a *f* pasture shall they feed
Eze 34:16 but I will destroy the *f* and the
Eze 34:20 will judge between the *f* cattle
Eze 39:19 ye shall eat *f* till ye be full,
Eze 44:7 when ye offer my bread, the *f*
Eze 44:15 before me to offer unto me the *f*
Eze 45:15 out of the *f* pastures of Israel
Amos 5:22 peace offerings of your *f* beasts
Hab 1:16 by them their portion is *f*
Zec 11:16 he shall eat the flesh of the *f*

### FATHERLESS
Ex 22:22 not afflict any widow, or *f* child
Ex 22:24 be widows, and your children *f*
Deut 10:18 execute the judgment of the *f*
Deut 14:29 thee,) and the stranger, and the *f*
Deut 16:11 gates, and the stranger, and the *f*
Deut 16:14 Levite, the stranger, and the *f*
Deut 24:17 of the stranger, nor of the *f*
Deut 24:19 be for the stranger, for the *f*
Deut 24:20 be for the stranger, for the *f*
Deut 24:21 be for the stranger, for the *f*
Deut 26:12 the Levite, the stranger, the *f*
Deut 26:13 and unto the stranger, to the *f*
Deut 27:19 the judgment of the stranger, *f*
Job 6:27 Yea, ye overwhelm the *f*, and ye
Job 22:9 the arms of the *f* have been
Job 24:3 They drive away the ass of the *f*
Job 24:9 They pluck the *f* from the breast,
Job 29:12 the poor that cried, and the *f*
Job 31:17 the *f* hath not eaten thereof
Job 31:21 lifted up my hand against the *f*
Ps 10:14 thou art the helper of the *f*
Ps 10:18 To judge the *f* and the oppressed,
Ps 68:5 A father of the *f*, and a judge of
Ps 82:3 Defend the poor and *f*
Ps 94:6 and the stranger, and murder the *f*
Ps 109:9 Let his children be *f*, and his
Ps 109:12 be any to favour his *f* children
Ps 146:9 he relieveth the *f* and widow
Prov 23:10 not into the fields of the *f*
Is 1:17 the oppressed, judge the *f*
Is 1:23 they judge not the *f*, neither
Is 9:17 shall have mercy on their *f*
Is 10:2 prey, and that they may rob the *f*
Jer 5:28 not the cause, the cause of the *f*
Jer 7:6 oppress not the stranger, the *f*
Jer 22:3 violence to the stranger, the *f*
Jer 49:11 Leave thy *f* children, I will
Lam 5:3 We are orphans and *f*,
Eze 22:7 in thee have they vexed the *f*
Hos 14:3 for in thee the *f* findeth mercy
Zec 7:10 oppress not the widow, nor the *f*
Mal 3:5 in his wages, the widow, and the *f*
Jas 1:27 Father is this, To visit the *f*

### FATHER'S
Gen 9:23 and they saw not their *f* nakedness
Gen 12:1 thy kindred, and from thy *f* house
Gen 20:13 me to wander from my *f* house
Gen 24:7 which took me from my *f* house
Gen 24:23 is there room in thy *f* house for
Gen 24:38 But thou shalt go unto my *f* house
Gen 24:40 of my kindred, and of my *f* house
Gen 26:15 For all the wells which his *f*
Gen 28:21 come again to my *f* house in peace
Gen 29:9 Rachel came with her *f* sheep
Gen 29:12 Rachel that he was her *f* brother
Gen 31:1 taken away all that was our *f*
Gen 31:1 of that which was our *f* hath he
Gen 31:5 I see your *f* countenance, that it
Gen 31:14 inheritance for us in our *f* house
Gen 31:19 stolen the images that were her *f*
Gen 31:30 sore longedst after thy *f* house
Gen 35:22 lay with Bilhah his *f* concubine
Gen 37:2 the sons of Zilpah, his *f* wives
Gen 37:12 to feed their *f* flock in Shechem
Gen 38:11 Remain a widow at thy *f* house
Gen 38:11 went and dwelt in her *f* house
Gen 41:51 all my toil, and all my *f* house
Gen 46:31 his brethren, and unto his *f* house
Gen 46:31 my *f* house, which were in the
Gen 47:12 all his *f* household, with bread,
Gen 48:17 and he held up his *f* hand, to
Gen 49:4 thou wentest up to thy *f* bed
Gen 49:8 thy *f* children shall bow down
Gen 50:1 And Joseph fell upon his *f* face
Gen 50:8 and his brethren, and his *f* house
Gen 50:22 in Egypt, he, and his *f* house
Ex 2:16 troughs to water their *f* flock
Ex 6:20 him Jochebed his *f* sister to wife
Ex 15:2 my *f* God, and I will exalt him
Lev 16:32 priest's office in his *f* stead
Lev 18:8 The nakedness of thy *f* wife shalt
Lev 18:8 it is thy *f* nakedness
Lev 18:11 of thy *f* wife's daughter,
Lev 18:12 the nakedness of thy *f* sister
Lev 18:12 she is thy *f* near kinswoman
Lev 18:14 the nakedness of thy *f* brother
Lev 20:11 his *f* wife hath uncovered his
Lev 20:11 hath uncovered his *f* nakedness
Lev 20:17 his *f* daughter, or his mother's
Lev 20:19 sister, nor of thy *f* sister
Lev 22:13 and is returned unto her *f* house
Lev 22:13 she shall eat of her *f* meat
Num 2:2 with the ensign of their *f* house

Num 18:1 thy f house with thee shall bear
Num 27:7 among their f brethren
Num 27:10 inheritance unto his f brethren
Num 30:3 being in her f house in her youth
Num 30:16 yet in her youth in her f house
Num 36:11 unto their f brothers' sons
Deut 22:21 damsel to the door of her f house
Deut 22:21 to play the whore in her f house
Deut 22:30 A man shall not take his f wife
Deut 22:30 nor discover his f skirt
Deut 27:20 be he that lieth with his f wife
Deut 27:20 because he uncovereth his f skirt
Josh 2:12 shew kindness unto my f house
Josh 2:18 all thy f household, home unto
Josh 6:25 her f household, and all that she
Judg 6:15 and I am the least in my f house
Judg 6:25 Take thy f young bullock, even
Judg 6:27 because he feared his f household
Judg 9:5 went unto his f house at Ophrah
Judg 9:18 up against my f house this day
Judg 11:2 shalt not inherit in our f house
Judg 11:7 me, and expel me out of my f house
Judg 14:15 thee and thy f house with fire
Judg 14:19 and he went up to his f house
Judg 19:2 her f house to Beth-lehem-judah
Judg 19:3 she brought him into her f house
1Sa 2:31 arm, and the arm of thy f house
1Sa 9:20 on thee, and on all thy f house
1Sa 17:15 to feed his f sheep at Beth-lehem
1Sa 17:25 make his f house free in Israel
1Sa 17:34 Thy servant kept his f sheep
1Sa 18:2 go no more home to his f house
1Sa 18:18 or my f family in Israel, that I
1Sa 22:1 all his f house heard it, they
1Sa 22:11 son of Ahitub, and all his f house
1Sa 22:16 thou, and all thy f house
1Sa 22:22 of all the persons of thy f house
1Sa 24:21 destroy my name out of my f house
2Sa 3:7 thou gone in unto my f concubine
2Sa 3:29 of Joab, and on all his f house
2Sa 9:7 kindness for Jonathan thy f sake
2Sa 14:9 be on me, and on my f house
2Sa 15:34 have been thy f servant hitherto
2Sa 16:19 I have served in thy f presence
2Sa 16:21 Go in unto thy f concubines
2Sa 16:22 Absalom went in unto his f
2Sa 19:28 For all of my f house were but
2Sa 24:17 against me, and against my f house
1Kin 11:12 not do it for David thy f sake
1Kin 11:17 of his f servants with him
1Kin 12:10 shall be thicker than my f loins
1Kin 18:18 thy f house, in that ye have
2Kin 10:3 sons, and set him on his f throne
2Kin 23:30 and made him king in his f stead
2Kin 24:17 his f brother king in his stead
1Chr 5:1 forasmuch as he defiled his f bed
1Chr 7:2 Shemuel, heads of their f house
1Chr 7:40 of Asher, heads of their f house
1Chr 12:28 of his f house twenty and two
1Chr 21:17 God, be on me, and on my f house
1Chr 23:11 according to their f house
2Chr 2:13 with understanding, of Huram my f
2Chr 10:10 shall be thicker than my f loins
2Chr 21:13 slain thy brethren of thy f house
2Chr 36:1 king in his f stead in Jerusalem
Ezr 2:59 they could not shew their f house
Neh 1:6 both I and my f house have sinned
Neh 7:61 they could not shew their f house
Est 4:14 thy f house shall be destroyed
Ps 45:10 thine own people, and thy f house
Prov 4:3 For I was my f son, tender and
Prov 6:20 keep thy f commandment, and
Prov 13:1 son heareth his f instruction
Prov 15:5 fool despiseth his f instruction
Prov 27:10 thy f friend, forsake not
Is 7:17 thy people, and upon thy f house
Is 22:23 a glorious throne to his f house
Is 22:24 him all the glory of his f house
Jer 35:14 but obey their f commandment
Eze 18:14 that seeth all his f sins which
Eze 22:11 his sister, his f daughter
Mt 26:29 it new with you in my F kingdom
Lk 2:49 I must be about my F business
Lk 9:26 in his own glory, and in his F
Lk 12:32 for it is your F good pleasure to
Lk 15:17 of my f have bread enough
Lk 16:27 wouldest send him to my f house
Jn 2:16 make not my F house an house of
Jn 5:43 I am come in my F name, and ye
Jn 6:39 this is the F will which hath
Jn 10:25 the works that I do in my F name
Jn 10:29 to pluck them out of my F hand
Jn 14:2 In my F house are many mansions
Jn 14:24 not mine, but the F which sent me
Jn 15:10 as I have kept my F commandments
Acts 7:20 up in his f house three months
1Cor 5:1 that one should have his f wife
Rev 14:1 having his F name written in

## FATHERS'

Ex 6:14 be the heads of their f houses
Ex 10:6 nor thy f fathers have seen,
Num 17:6 one, according to their f houses
Num 26:2 upward, throughout their f house
Num 32:14 ye are risen up in your f stead
Neh 2:3 the place of my f sepulchres
Neh 2:5 unto the city of my f sepulchres
Eze 20:24 eyes were after their f idols
Eze 22:10 they discovered their f nakedness
Dan 11:24 have not done, nor his f fathers
Rom 11:28 they are beloved for the f sakes

## FATLINGS

1Sa 15:9 and of the oxen, and of the f
2Sa 6:13 paces, he sacrificed oxen and f
Ps 66:15 unto thee burnt sacrifices of f
Eze 39:18 bullocks, all of them f of Bashan
Mt 22:4 my f are killed, and all things

## FATNESS

Gen 27:28 the f of the earth, and plenty of
Gen 27:39 shall be the f of the earth
Deut 32:15 thick, thou art covered with f
Judg 9:9 unto them, Should I leave my f
Job 15:27 he covereth his face with his f
Job 36:16 on thy table should be full of f
Ps 36:8 satisfied with the f of thy house
Ps 63:5 be satisfied as with marrow and f
Ps 65:11 and thy paths drop f
Ps 73:7 Their eyes stand out with f
Ps 109:24 and my flesh faileth of f
Is 17:4 the f of his flesh shall wax lean
Is 34:6 with blood, it is made fat with f
Is 34:7 and their dust made fat with f
Is 55:2 let your soul delight itself in f
Jer 31:14 the soul of the priests with f
Rom 11:17 the root and f of the olive tree

## FATTED

1Kin 4:23 and fallowdeer, and f fowl
Jer 46:21 the midst of her like f bullocks
Lk 15:23 And bring hither the f calf
Lk 15:27 thy father hath killed the f calf
Lk 15:30 hast killed for him the f calf

## FAULT

Ex 5:16 but the f is in thine own people
Deut 25:2 his face, according to his f
1Sa 29:3 I have found no f in him since he
2Sa 3:8 with a f concerning this woman
Ps 59:4 prepare themselves without my f
Dan 6:4 could find none occasion nor f
Dan 6:4 there any error or f found in him
Mt 18:15 go and tell him his f between thee
Mk 7:2 unwashen, hands, they found f
Lk 23:4 people, I find no f in this man
Lk 23:14 have found no f in this man
Jn 18:38 them, I find in him no f at all
Jn 19:4 may know that I find no f in him
Jn 19:6 for I find no f in him
Rom 9:19 unto me, Why doth he yet find f
1Cor 6:7 there is utterly a f among you
Gal 6:1 if a man be overtaken in a f
Heb 8:8 For finding f with them, he saith
Rev 14:5 for they are without f before the

## FAULTS

Gen 41:9 I do remember my f this day
Ps 19:12 cleanse thou me from secret f
Jas 5:16 Confess your f one to another, and
1Pet 2:20 when ye be buffeted for your f

## FAVOUR

Gen 18:3 now I have found f in thy sight
Gen 30:27 if I have found f in thine eyes
Gen 39:21 gave him f in the sight of the
Ex 3:21 I will give this people f in the
Ex 11:3 the LORD gave the people f in the
Ex 12:36 the LORD gave the people f in the
Num 11:11 have I not found f in thy sight
Num 11:15 if I have found f in thy sight
Deut 24:1 that she find no f in his eyes
Deut 28:50 the old, nor shew f to the young
Deut 33:23 O Naphtali, satisfied with f
Josh 11:20 and that they might have no f
Ruth 2:13 Let me find f in thy sight, my
1Sa 2:26 was in f both with the LORD, and
1Sa 16:22 for he hath found f in my sight
1Sa 20:29 if I have found f in thine eyes
1Sa 25:8 young men find f in thine eyes
1Sa 29:6 nevertheless the lords f thee not
2Sa 15:25 if I shall find f in the eyes of
1Kin 11:19 Hadad found great f in the sight
Neh 2:5 servant have found f in thy sight
Est 2:15 Esther obtained f in the sight of
Est 2:17 f in his sight more than all the
Est 5:2 that she obtained f in his sight
Est 5:8 If I have found f in the sight of
Est 7:3 If I have found f in thy sight
Est 8:5 and if I have found f in his sight
Job 10:12 Thou hast granted me life and f
Ps 5:12 with f wilt thou compass him as
Ps 30:5 in his f is life
Ps 30:7 by thy f thou hast made my
Ps 35:27 that f my righteous cause
Ps 44:3 because thou hadst a f unto them
Ps 45:12 the people shall intreat thy f
Ps 89:17 in thy f our horn shall be
Ps 102:13 for the time to f her, yea, the
Ps 102:14 her stones, and f the dust thereof
Ps 106:4 with the f that thou bearest unto
Ps 109:12 any to f his fatherless children
Ps 112:5 A good man sheweth f, and lendeth
Ps 119:58 I intreated thy f with my whole
Prov 3:4 So shalt thou find f and good
Prov 8:35 and shall obtain f of the LORD
Prov 11:27 seeketh good procureth f
Prov 12:2 good man obtaineth f of the LORD
Prov 13:15 Good understanding giveth f
Prov 14:9 among the righteous there is f
Prov 14:35 The king's f is toward a wise
Prov 16:15 his f is as a cloud of the latter
Prov 18:22 thing, and obtaineth f of the LORD
Prov 19:6 will intreat the f of the prince
Prov 19:12 but his f is as dew upon the
Prov 21:10 findeth no f in his eyes
Prov 22:1 loving f rather than silver and
Prov 28:23 f than he that flattereth with
Prov 29:26 Many seek the ruler's f
Prov 31:30 F is deceitful, and beauty is vain
Eccl 9:11 nor yet f to men of skill
Song 8:10 I in his eyes as one that found f
Is 26:10 Let f be shewed to the wicked,
Is 27:11 formed them will shew them no f
Is 60:10 but in my f have I had mercy on
Jer 16:13 where I will not shew you f
Dan 1:9 Now God had brought Daniel into f
Lk 1:30 for thou hast found f with God
Lk 2:52 stature, and in f with God and man
Acts 2:47 having f with all the people
Acts 7:10 his afflictions, and gave him f
Acts 7:46 Who found f before God, and
Acts 25:3 desired f against him, that he

## FAVOURED

Gen 29:17 Rachel was beautiful and well f
Gen 39:6 was a goodly person, and well f
Gen 41:2 of the river seven well f kine
Gen 41:3 them out of the river, ill f
Gen 41:4 And the ill f and leanfleshed kine
Gen 41:4 kine did eat up the seven well f
Gen 41:18 seven kine, fatfleshed and well f
Gen 41:19 up after them, poor and very ill f
Gen 41:20 the ill f kine did eat up the
Gen 41:21 but they were still ill f
Gen 41:27 ill f kine that came up after
Lam 4:16 priests, they f not the elders
Dan 1:4 whom was no blemish, but well f
Lk 1:28 Hail, thou that art highly f

## FEAR

Gen 9:2 the f of you and the dread of you
Gen 15:1 in a vision, saying, F not, Abram
Gen 20:11 Surely the f of God is not in
Gen 21:17 f not; for God hath heard
Gen 26:24 f not, for I am with thee, and
Gen 31:42 the f of Isaac, had been with me,
Gen 31:53 Jacob sware by the f of his
Gen 32:11 for I f him, lest he will come and
Gen 35:17 the midwife said unto her, F not
Gen 42:18 for I f God
Gen 43:23 he said, Peace be to you, f not
Gen 46:3 f not to go down into Egypt
Gen 50:19 And Joseph said unto them, F not
Gen 50:21 Now therefore f ye not

| | |
|---|---|
| Ex 9:30 | ye will not yet *f* the LORD God |
| Ex 14:13 | *F* ye not, stand still, and see the |
| Ex 15:16 | *F* and dread shall fall upon them |
| Ex 18:21 | people able men, such as *f* God |
| Ex 20:20 | Moses said unto the people, *F* not |
| Ex 20:20 | that his *f* may be before your |
| Ex 23:27 | I will send my *f* before thee |
| Lev 19:3 | Ye shall *f* every man his mother, |
| Lev 19:14 | the blind, but shalt *f* thy God |
| Lev 19:32 | face of the old man, and *f* thy God |
| Lev 25:17 | but thou shalt *f* thy God |
| Lev 25:36 | but *f* thy God |
| Lev 25:43 | but shalt *f* thy God |
| Num 14:9 | neither *f* ye the people of the |
| Num 14:9 | LORD is with us: *f* them not |
| Num 21:34 | LORD said unto Moses, *F* him not |
| Deut 1:21 | *f* not, neither be discouraged |
| Deut 2:25 | the *f* of thee upon the nations |
| Deut 3:2 | the LORD said unto me, *F* him not |
| Deut 3:22 | Ye shall not *f* them |
| Deut 4:10 | that they may learn to *f* me all |
| Deut 5:29 | in them, that they would *f* me |
| Deut 6:2 | thou mightest *f* the LORD thy God |
| Deut 6:13 | Thou shalt *f* the LORD thy God, and |
| Deut 6:24 | to *f* the LORD our God, for our |
| Deut 8:6 | to walk in his ways, and to *f* him |
| Deut 10:12 | but to *f* the LORD thy God, to |
| Deut 10:20 | Thou shalt *f* the LORD thy God |
| Deut 11:25 | your God shall lay the *f* of you |
| Deut 13:4 | *f* him, and keep his commandments, |
| Deut 13:11 | And all Israel shall hear, and *f* |
| Deut 14:23 | to *f* the LORD thy God always |
| Deut 17:13 | all the people shall hear, and *f* |
| Deut 17:19 | may learn to *f* the LORD his God |
| Deut 19:20 | which remain shall hear, and *f* |
| Deut 20:3 | *f* not, and do not tremble, neither |
| Deut 21:21 | and all Israel shall hear, and *f* |
| Deut 28:58 | that thou mayest *f* this glorious |
| Deut 28:66 | and thou shalt *f* day and night, and |
| Deut 28:67 | for the *f* of thine heart |
| Deut 28:67 | heart wherewith thou shalt *f* |
| Deut 31:6 | *f* not, nor be afraid of them |
| Deut 31:8 | *f* not, neither be dismayed |
| Deut 31:12 | *f* the LORD your God, and observe |
| Deut 31:13 | learn to *f* the LORD your God, as |
| Josh 4:24 | that ye might *f* the LORD your God |
| Josh 8:1 | *F* not, neither be thou dismayed |
| Josh 10:8 | LORD said unto Joshua, *F* them not |
| Josh 10:25 | *F* not, nor be dismayed, be strong |
| Josh 22:24 | done it for *f* of this thing |
| Josh 24:14 | Now therefore *f* the LORD, and |
| Judg 4:18 | turn in to me; *f* not |
| Judg 6:10 | *f* not the gods of the Amorites, |
| Judg 6:23 | *f* not: thou shalt not die |
| Judg 7:10 | But if thou *f* to go down, go thou |
| Judg 9:21 | for *f* of Abimelech his brother |
| Ruth 3:11 | And now, my daughter, *f* not |
| 1Sa 4:20 | stood by her said unto her, *F* not |
| 1Sa 11:7 | the *f* of the LORD fell on the |
| 1Sa 12:14 | If ye will *f* the LORD, and serve |
| 1Sa 12:20 | said unto the people, *F* not |
| 1Sa 12:24 | Only *f* the LORD, and serve him in |
| 1Sa 21:10 | and fled that day for *f* of Saul |
| 1Sa 22:23 | Abide thou with me, *f* not |
| 1Sa 23:17 | And he said unto him, *F* not |
| 1Sa 23:26 | haste to get away for *f* of Saul |
| 2Sa 9:7 | And David said unto him, *F* not |
| 2Sa 13:28 | then kill him, *f* not |
| 2Sa 23:3 | be just, ruling in the *f* of God |
| 1Kin 8:40 | That they may *f* thee all the days |
| 1Kin 8:43 | to *f* thee, as do thy people |
| 1Kin 17:13 | And Elijah said unto her, *F* not |
| 1Kin 18:12 | but I thy servant *f* the LORD from |
| 2Kin 4:1 | that thy servant did *f* the LORD |
| 2Kin 6:16 | And he answered, *F* not |
| 2Kin 17:28 | them how they should *f* the LORD |
| 2Kin 17:34 | they *f* not the LORD, neither do |
| 2Kin 17:35 | saying, Ye shall not *f* other gods |
| 2Kin 17:36 | stretched out arm, him shall ye *f* |
| 2Kin 17:37 | and ye shall not *f* other gods |
| 2Kin 17:38 | neither shall ye *f* other gods |
| 2Kin 17:39 | But the LORD your God ye shall *f* |
| 2Kin 25:24 | *F* not to be the servants of the |
| 1Chr 14:17 | the LORD brought the *f* of him |
| 1Chr 16:30 | *F* before him, all the earth |
| 1Chr 28:20 | *f* not, nor be dismayed |
| 2Chr 6:31 | That they may *f* thee, to walk in |
| 2Chr 6:33 | *f* thee, as doth thy people Israel |
| 2Chr 14:14 | for the *f* of the LORD came upon |
| 2Chr 17:10 | the *f* of the LORD fell upon all |
| 2Chr 19:7 | Wherefore now let the *f* of the |
| 2Chr 19:9 | shall ye do in the *f* of the LORD |
| 2Chr 20:17 | *f* not, nor be dismayed |
| 2Chr 20:29 | the *f* of God was on all the |
| Ezr 3:3 | for *f* was upon them because of |
| Neh 1:11 | who desire to *f* thy name |
| Neh 5:9 | the *f* of our God because of the |
| Neh 5:15 | not I, because of the *f* of God |
| Neh 6:14 | that would have put me in *f* |
| Neh 6:19 | sent letters to put me in *f* |
| Est 8:17 | for the *f* of the Jews fell upon |
| Est 9:2 | for the *f* of them fell upon all |
| Est 9:3 | because the *f* of Mordecai fell |
| Job 1:9 | Doth Job *f* God for nought |
| Job 4:6 | Is not this thy *f*, thy confidence |
| Job 4:14 | *F* came upon me, and trembling, |
| Job 6:14 | forsaketh the *f* of the Almighty |
| Job 9:34 | me, and let not his *f* terrify me |
| Job 9:35 | Then would I speak, and not *f* him |
| Job 11:15 | shalt be stedfast, and shalt not *f* |
| Job 15:4 | Yea, thou castest off *f*, and |
| Job 21:9 | Their houses are safe from *f* |
| Job 22:4 | he reprove thee for *f* of thee |
| Job 22:10 | thee, and sudden *f* troubleth thee |
| Job 25:2 | Dominion and *f* are with him |
| Job 28:28 | the *f* of the LORD, that is wisdom |
| Job 31:34 | Did I *f* a great multitude, or did |
| Job 37:24 | Men do therefore *f* him |
| Job 39:16 | her labour is in vain without *f* |
| Job 39:22 | He mocketh at *f*, and is not |
| Job 41:33 | his like, who is made without *f* |
| Ps 2:11 | Serve the LORD with *f*, and rejoice |
| Ps 5:7 | in thy *f* will I worship toward |
| Ps 9:20 | Put them in *f*, O LORD |
| Ps 14:5 | There were they in great *f* |
| Ps 15:4 | he honoureth them that *f* the LORD |
| Ps 19:9 | The *f* of the LORD is clean, |
| Ps 22:23 | Ye that *f* the LORD, praise him |
| Ps 22:23 | *f* him, all ye the seed of Israel |
| Ps 22:25 | my vows before them that *f* him |
| Ps 23:4 | shadow of death, I will *f* no evil |
| Ps 25:14 | the LORD is with them that *f* him |
| Ps 27:1 | whom shall I *f*? |
| Ps 27:3 | against me, my heart shall not *f* |
| Ps 31:11 | and a *f* to mine acquaintance |
| Ps 31:13 | *f* was on every side |
| Ps 31:19 | hast laid up for them that *f* thee |
| Ps 33:8 | Let all the earth *f* the LORD |
| Ps 33:18 | the LORD is upon them that *f* him |
| Ps 34:7 | round about them that *f* him |
| Ps 34:9 | O *f* the LORD, ye his saints |
| Ps 34:9 | is no want to them that *f* him |
| Ps 34:11 | will teach you the *f* of the LORD |
| Ps 36:1 | that there is no *f* of God before |
| Ps 40:3 | many shall see it, and *f*, and shall |
| Ps 46:2 | Therefore will not we *f*, though |
| Ps 48:6 | *F* took hold upon them there, and |
| Ps 49:5 | Wherefore should I *f* in the days |
| Ps 52:6 | righteous also shall see, and *f* |
| Ps 53:5 | There were they in great *f* |
| Ps 53:5 | in great *f*, where no *f* was |
| Ps 55:19 | changes, therefore they *f* not God |
| Ps 56:4 | I will not *f* what flesh can do |
| Ps 60:4 | a banner to them that *f* thee |
| Ps 61:5 | heritage of those that *f* thy name |
| Ps 64:1 | my life from *f* of the enemy |
| Ps 64:4 | do they shoot at him, and *f* not |
| Ps 64:9 | And all men shall *f*, and shall |
| Ps 66:16 | Come and hear, all ye that *f* God |
| Ps 67:7 | the ends of the earth shall *f* him |
| Ps 72:5 | They shall *f* thee as long as the |
| Ps 85:9 | salvation is nigh them that *f* him |
| Ps 86:11 | unite my heart to *f* thy name |
| Ps 90:11 | even according to thy *f*, so is |
| Ps 96:9 | *f* before him, all the earth |
| Ps 102:15 | shall *f* the name of the LORD |
| Ps 103:11 | his mercy toward them that *f* him |
| Ps 103:13 | the LORD pitieth them that *f* him |
| Ps 103:17 | everlasting upon them that *f* him |
| Ps 105:38 | for the *f* of them fell upon them |
| Ps 111:5 | given meat unto them that *f* him |
| Ps 111:10 | The *f* of the LORD is the |
| Ps 115:11 | Ye that *f* the LORD, trust in the |
| Ps 115:13 | will bless them that *f* the LORD |
| Ps 118:4 | Let them now that *f* the LORD say |
| Ps 118:6 | I will not *f* |
| Ps 119:38 | servant, who is devoted to thy *f* |
| Ps 119:39 | Turn away my reproach which I *f* |
| Ps 119:63 | companion of all them that *f* thee |
| Ps 119:74 | They that *f* thee will be glad |
| Ps 119:79 | Let those that *f* thee turn unto |
| Ps 119:120 | My flesh trembleth for *f* of thee |
| Ps 135:20 | ye that *f* the LORD, bless the |
| Ps 145:19 | the desire of them that *f* him |
| Ps 147:11 | pleasure in them that *f* him |
| Prov 1:7 | The *f* of the LORD is the |
| Prov 1:26 | I will mock when your *f* cometh |
| Prov 1:27 | When your *f* cometh as desolation, |
| Prov 1:29 | did not choose the *f* of the LORD |
| Prov 1:33 | and shall be quiet from *f* of evil |
| Prov 2:5 | thou understand the *f* of the LORD |
| Prov 3:7 | *f* the LORD, and depart from evil |
| Prov 3:25 | Be not afraid of sudden *f* |
| Prov 8:13 | The *f* of the LORD is to hate evil |
| Prov 9:10 | The *f* of the LORD is the |
| Prov 10:24 | The *f* of the wicked, it shall |
| Prov 10:27 | The *f* of the LORD prolongeth days |
| Prov 14:26 | In the *f* of the LORD is strong |
| Prov 14:27 | The *f* of the LORD is a fountain |
| Prov 15:16 | Better is little with the *f* of |
| Prov 15:33 | The *f* of the LORD is the |
| Prov 16:6 | by the *f* of the LORD men depart |
| Prov 19:23 | The *f* of the LORD tendeth to life |
| Prov 20:2 | The *f* of a king is as the roaring |
| Prov 22:4 | the *f* of the LORD are riches, and |
| Prov 23:17 | but be thou in the *f* of the LORD |
| Prov 24:21 | *f* thou the LORD and the king |
| Prov 29:25 | The *f* of man bringeth a snare |
| Eccl 3:14 | it, that men should *f* before him |
| Eccl 5:7 | but *f* thou God |
| Eccl 8:12 | be well with them that *f* God |
| Eccl 8:12 | that *f* God, which *f* before him |
| Eccl 12:13 | *F* God, and keep his commandments |
| Song 3:8 | thigh because of *f* in the night |
| Is 2:10 | for *f* of the LORD, and for the |
| Is 2:19 | for *f* of the LORD, and for the |
| Is 2:21 | for *f* of the LORD, and for the |
| Is 7:4 | *f* not, neither be fainthearted |
| Is 7:25 | not come thither the *f* of briers |
| Is 8:12 | neither *f* ye their *f*, nor be |
| Is 8:12 | neither *f* ye their *f*, nor be |
| Is 8:13 | and let him be your *f*, and let him |
| Is 11:2 | knowledge and of the *f* of the LORD |
| Is 11:3 | in the *f* of the LORD |
| Is 14:3 | from thy sorrow, and from thy *f* |
| Is 19:16 | *f* because of the shaking of the |
| Is 21:4 | hath he turned into *f* unto me |
| Is 24:17 | *F*, and the pit, and the snare, are |
| Is 24:18 | of the *f* shall fall into the pit |
| Is 25:3 | the terrible nations shall *f* thee |
| Is 29:13 | their *f* toward me is taught by |
| Is 29:23 | shall *f* the God of Israel |
| Is 31:9 | over to his strong hold for *f* |
| Is 33:6 | the *f* of the LORD is his treasure |
| Is 35:4 | a fearful heart, Be strong, *f* not |
| Is 41:10 | *F* thou not; for I am |
| Is 41:13 | hand, saying unto thee, *F* not |
| Is 41:14 | *F* not, thou worm Jacob, and ye men |
| Is 43:1 | that formed thee, O Israel, *F* not |
| Is 43:5 | *F* not: for I am with thee |
| Is 44:2 | *F* not, O Jacob, my servant |
| Is 44:8 | *F* ye not, neither be afraid |
| Is 44:11 | yet they shall *f*, and they shall |
| Is 51:7 | *f* ye not the reproach of men, |
| Is 54:4 | *F* not; for thou shalt not be ashamed |
| Is 54:14 | for thou shalt not *f* |
| Is 59:19 | So shall they *f* the name of the |
| Is 60:5 | together, and thine heart shall *f* |
| Is 63:17 | and hardened our heart from thy *f* |
| Jer 2:19 | that my *f* is not in thee, saith |
| Jer 5:22 | *F* ye not me? saith the LORD |
| Jer 5:24 | Let us now *f* the LORD our God, |
| Jer 6:25 | the enemy and *f* is on every side |
| Jer 10:7 | Who would not *f* thee, O King of |
| Jer 20:10 | defaming of many, *f* on every side |
| Jer 23:4 | and they shall *f* no more, nor be |
| Jer 26:19 | did he not *f* the LORD, and |
| Jer 30:5 | heard a voice of trembling, of *f* |
| Jer 30:10 | Therefore *f* thou not, O my |
| Jer 32:39 | way, that they may *f* me for ever |
| Jer 32:40 | I will put my *f* in their hearts |
| Jer 33:9 | and they shall *f* and tremble for |
| Jer 35:11 | let us go to Jerusalem for *f* of |
| Jer 35:11 | for *f* of the army of the Syrians |
| Jer 37:11 | Jerusalem for *f* of Pharaoh's army |
| Jer 40:9 | *F* not to serve the Chaldeans |
| Jer 41:9 | for *f* of Baasha king of Israel |
| Jer 46:5 | for *f* was round about, saith the |
| Jer 46:27 | But *f* not thou, O my servant |
| Jer 46:28 | *F* thou not, O Jacob my servant, |

Jer 48:43 *F*, and the pit, and the snare,
Jer 48:44 the *f* shall fall into the pit
Jer 49:5 I will bring a *f* upon thee
Jer 49:24 to flee, and *f* hath seized on her
Jer 49:29 cry unto them, *F* is on every side
Jer 50:16 for *f* of the oppressing sword
Jer 51:46 ye *f* for the rumour that shall be
Lam 3:47 *F* and a snare is come upon us,
Lam 3:57 thou saidst, *F* not
Eze 3:9 *f* them not, neither be dismayed
Eze 30:13 I will put a *f* in the land of
Dan 1:10 I *f* my lord the king, who hath
Dan 6:26 *f* before the God of Daniel
Dan 10:12 said he unto me, *F* not, Daniel
Dan 10:19 O man greatly beloved, *f* not
Hos 3:5 shall *f* the LORD and his goodness
Hos 10:5 shall *f* because of the calves of
Joel 2:21 *F* not, O land
Amos 3:8 lion hath roared, who will not *f*
Jonah 1:9 I *f* the LORD, the God of heaven,
Mic 7:17 God, and shall *f* because of thee
Zeph 3:7 I said, Surely thou wilt *f* me
Zeph 3:16 be said to Jerusalem, *F* thou not
Hag 1:12 the people did *f* before the LORD
Hag 2:5 remaineth among you: *f* ye not
Zec 8:13 *f* not, but let your hands be
Zec 8:15 to the house of Judah: *f* ye not
Zec 9:5 Ashkelon shall see it, and *f*
Mal 1:6 if I be a master, where is my *f*
Mal 2:5 for the *f* wherewith he feared me
Mal 3:5 *f* not me, saith the LORD of hosts
Mal 4:2 But unto you that *f* my name shall
Mt 1:20 *f* not to take unto thee Mary thy
Mt 10:26 *F* them not therefore
Mt 10:28 *f* not them which kill the body,
Mt 10:28 but rather *f* him which is able to
Mt 10:31 *F* ye not therefore, ye are of
Mt 14:26 and they cried out for *f*
Mt 21:26 we *f* the people
Mt 28:4 for *f* of him the keepers did
Mt 28:5 and said unto the women, *F* not ye
Mt 28:8 quickly from the sepulchre with *f*
Lk 1:12 was troubled, and *f* fell upon him
Lk 1:13 said unto him, *F* not, Zacharias
Lk 1:30 angel said unto her, *F* not, Mary
Lk 1:50 that *f* him from generation to
Lk 1:65 *f* came on all that dwelt round
Lk 1:74 enemies might serve him without *f*
Lk 2:10 the angel said unto them, *F* not
Lk 5:10 And Jesus said unto Simon, *F* not
Lk 5:26 God, and were filled with *f*
Lk 7:16 And there came a *f* on all
Lk 8:37 for they were taken with great *f*
Lk 8:50 he answered him, saying, *F* not
Lk 12:5 will forewarn you whom ye shall *f*
Lk 12:5 *F* him, which after he hath killed
Lk 12:5 yea, I say unto you, *F* him
Lk 12:7 *F* not therefore
Lk 12:32 *F* not, little flock
Lk 18:4 himself, Though I *f* not God
Lk 21:26 Men's hearts failing them for *f*
Lk 23:40 him, saying, Dost not thou *f* God
Jn 7:13 openly of him for *f* of the Jews
Jn 12:15 *F* not, daughter of Sion
Jn 19:38 but secretly for *f* of the Jews
Jn 20:19 were assembled for *f* of the Jews
Acts 2:43 And *f* came upon every soul
Acts 5:5 great *f* came on all them that
Acts 5:11 great *f* came upon all the church,
Acts 9:31 and walking in the *f* of the Lord
Acts 13:16 Men of Israel, and ye that *f* God
Acts 19:17 *f* fell on them all, and the name
Acts 27:24 Saying, *F* not, Paul
Rom 3:18 There is no *f* of God before their
Rom 8:15 the spirit of bondage again to *f*
Rom 11:20 Be not highminded, but *f*
Rom 13:7 to whom custom; *f* to whom
Rom 13:7 to whom *f*; honour to whom
1Cor 2:3 was with you in weakness, and in *f*
1Cor 16:10 that he may be with you without *f*
2Cor 7:1 holiness in the *f* of God
2Cor 7:11 what indignation, yea, what *f*
2Cor 7:15 obedience of you all, how with *f*
2Cor 11:3 But I *f*, lest by any means, as
2Cor 12:20 For I *f*, lest, when I come, I
Eph 5:21 one to another in the *f* of God
Eph 6:5 according to the flesh, with *f*
Phil 1:14 bold to speak the word without *f*
Phil 2:12 out your own salvation with *f*
1Ti 5:20 all, that others also may *f*
2Ti 1:7 hath not given us the spirit of *f*
Heb 2:15 through *f* of death were all their
Heb 4:1 Let us therefore *f*, lest, a
Heb 11:7 not seen as yet, moved with *f*
Heb 12:21 that Moses said, I exceedingly *f*
Heb 12:28 with reverence and godly *f*
Heb 13:6 I will not *f* what man shall do
1Pet 1:17 time of your sojourning here in *f*
1Pet 2:17 *F* God. Honour the king
1Pet 2:18 to your masters with all *f*
1Pet 3:2 conversation coupled with *f*
1Pet 3:15 that is in you with meekness and *f*
1Jn 4:18 There is no *f* in love
1Jn 4:18 but perfect love casteth out *f*
1Jn 4:18 because *f* hath torment
Jude 12 you, feeding themselves without *f*
Jude 23 And others save with *f*, pulling
Rev 1:17 upon me, saying unto me, *F* not
Rev 2:10 *F* none of those things which thou
Rev 11:11 great *f* fell upon them which saw
Rev 11:18 saints, and them that *f* thy name
Rev 14:7 *F* God, and give glory to him
Rev 15:4 Who shall not *f* thee, O Lord, and
Rev 18:10 afar off for the *f* of her torment
Rev 18:15 afar off for the *f* of her torment
Rev 19:5 ye his servants, and ye that *f* him

## FEARED

Gen 19:30 for he *f* to dwell in Zoar
Gen 26:7 for he *f* to say, She is my wife
Ex 1:17 But the midwives *f* God, and did
Ex 1:21 pass, because the midwives *f* God
Ex 2:14 And Moses *f*, and said, Surely this
Ex 9:20 He that *f* the word of the LORD
Ex 14:31 and the people *f* the LORD, and
Deut 25:18 and he *f* not God
Deut 32:17 newly up, whom your fathers *f* not
Deut 32:27 Were it not that I *f* the wrath of
Josh 4:14 and they *f* him, as they *f*
Josh 10:2 That they *f* greatly, because
Judg 6:27 because he *f* his father's
Judg 8:20 for he *f*, because he was yet a
1Sa 3:15 Samuel *f* to shew Eli the vision
1Sa 12:18 all the people greatly *f* the LORD
1Sa 14:26 for the people *f* the oath
1Sa 15:24 because I *f* the people, and obeyed
2Sa 3:11 a word again, because he *f* him
2Sa 10:19 So the Syrians *f* to help the
2Sa 12:18 the servants of David *f* to tell
1Kin 1:50 Adonijah *f* because of Solomon, and
1Kin 3:28 and they *f* the king
1Kin 18:3 (Now Obadiah *f* the LORD greatly
2Kin 17:7 of Egypt, and had *f* other gods,
2Kin 17:25 there, that they *f* not the LORD
2Kin 17:32 So they *f* the LORD, and made unto
2Kin 17:33 They *f* the LORD, and served their
2Kin 17:41 So these nations *f* the LORD
1Chr 16:25 he also is to be *f* above all gods
2Chr 20:3 And Jehoshaphat *f*, and set himself
Neh 7:2 faithful man, and *f* God above many
Job 1:1 and upright, and one that *f* God
Job 3:25 which I greatly *f* is come upon me
Ps 76:7 Thou, even thou, art to be *f*
Ps 76:8 the earth *f*, and was still,
Ps 76:11 unto him that ought to be *f*
Ps 78:53 on safely, so that they *f* not
Ps 89:7 God is greatly to be *f* in the
Ps 96:4 he is to be *f* above all gods
Ps 130:4 with thee, that thou mayest be *f*
Is 41:5 The isles saw it, and *f*
Is 51:13 hast *f* continually every day
Is 57:11 whom hast thou been afraid or *f*
Jer 3:8 treacherous sister Judah *f* not
Jer 42:16 pass, that the sword, which ye *f*
Jer 44:10 this day, neither have they *f*
Eze 11:8 Ye have *f* the sword
Dan 5:19 trembled and *f* before him
Hos 10:3 because we *f* not the LORD
Jonah 1:16 Then the men *f* the LORD
Mal 2:5 for the fear wherewith he *f* me
Mal 3:16 Then they that *f* the LORD spake
Mal 3:16 him for them that *f* the LORD
Mt 14:5 he *f* the multitude, because they
Mt 21:46 they *f* the multitude, because
Mt 27:54 they *f* greatly, saying, Truly
Mk 4:41 they *f* exceedingly, and said one
Mk 6:20 For Herod *f* John, knowing that he
Mk 11:18 for they *f* him, because all the
Mk 11:32 they *f* the people
Mk 12:12 lay hold on him, but *f* the people
Lk 9:34 they *f* as they entered into the
Lk 9:45 they *f* to ask him of that saying
Lk 18:2 which *f* not God, neither regarded
Lk 19:21 For I *f* thee, because thou art an
Lk 20:19 and they *f* the people
Lk 22:2 for they *f* the people
Jn 9:22 parents, because they *f* the Jews
Acts 5:26 for they *f* the people, lest they
Acts 10:2 one that *f* God with all his house
Acts 16:38 and they *f*, when they heard that
Heb 5:7 death, and was heard in that he *f*

## FEAREST

Gen 22:12 for now I know that thou *f* God
Is 57:11 even of old, and thou *f* me not
Jer 22:25 hand of them whose face thou *f*

## FEARETH

1Kin 1:51 Behold, Adonijah *f* king Solomon
Job 1:8 and an upright man, one that *f* God
Job 2:3 and an upright man, one that *f* God
Ps 25:12 What man is he that *f* the LORD
Ps 112:1 is the man that *f* the LORD
Ps 128:1 is every one that *f* the Lord
Ps 128:4 man be blessed that *f* the LORD
Prov 13:13 but he that *f* the commandment
Prov 14:2 in his uprightness *f* the LORD
Prov 14:16 A wise man *f*, and departeth from
Prov 28:14 Happy is the man that *f* alway
Prov 31:30 but a woman that *f* the LORD
Eccl 7:18 for he that *f* God shall come
Eccl 8:13 because he *f* not before God
Eccl 9:2 sweareth, as he that *f* an oath
Is 50:10 Who is among you that *f* the LORD
Acts 10:22 a just man, and one that *f* God
Acts 10:35 But in every nation he that *f* him
Acts 13:26 and whosoever among you *f* God
1Jn 4:18 He that *f* is not made perfect in

## FEARFUL

Ex 15:11 *f* in praises, doing wonders
Deut 20:8 say, What man is there that is *f*
Deut 28:58 and *f* name, THE LORD THY GOD
Judg 7:3 people, saying, Whosoever is *f*
Is 35:4 Say to them that are of a *f* heart
Mt 8:26 he saith unto them, Why are ye *f*
Mk 4:40 said unto them, Why are ye so *f*
Lk 21:11 *f* sights and great signs shall
Heb 10:27 But a certain *f* looking for of
Heb 10:31 It is a *f* thing to fall into the
Rev 21:8 But the *f*, and unbelieving, and the

## FEARING

Josh 22:25 children cease from *f* the LORD
Mk 5:33 But the woman *f* and trembling,
Acts 23:10 *f* lest Paul should have been
Acts 27:17 *f* lest they should fall into the
Acts 27:29 Then *f* lest we should have fallen
Gal 2:12 himself, *f* them which were of the
Col 3:22 but in singleness of heart, *f* God
Heb 11:27 not *f* the wrath of the king

## FEAST

Gen 19:3 and he made them a *f*, and did bake
Gen 21:8 Abraham made a great *f* the same
Gen 26:30 And he made them a *f*, and they did
Gen 29:22 the men of the place, and made a *f*
Gen 40:20 that he made a *f* unto all his
Ex 5:1 that they may hold a *f* unto me in
Ex 10:9 we must hold a *f* unto the LORD
Ex 12:14 ye shall keep it a *f* to the LORD
Ex 12:14 ye shall keep it a *f* by an
Ex 12:17 observe the *f* of unleavened bread
Ex 13:6 day shall be a *f* to the LORD
Ex 23:14 keep a *f* unto me in the year
Ex 23:15 keep the *f* of unleavened bread
Ex 23:16 the *f* of harvest, the firstfruits
Ex 23:16 the *f* of ingathering, which is in
Ex 32:5 To morrow is a *f* to the LORD
Ex 34:18 The *f* of unleavened bread shalt
Ex 34:22 thou shalt observe the *f* of weeks
Ex 34:22 the *f* of ingathering at the
Ex 34:25 shall the sacrifice of the *f* of
Lev 23:6 *f* of unleavened bread unto the
Lev 23:34 *f* of tabernacles for seven days
Lev 23:39 ye shall keep a *f* unto the LORD
Lev 23:41 ye shall keep it a *f* unto the
Num 28:17 day of this month is the *f*
Num 29:12 ye shall keep a *f* unto the LORD
Deut 16:10 thou shalt keep the *f* of weeks
Deut 16:13 Thou shalt observe the *f* of
Deut 16:14 And thou shalt rejoice in thy *f*
Deut 16:15 *f* unto the LORD thy God in the

Deut 16:16 in the *f* of unleavened bread, and
Deut 16:16 bread, and in the *f* of weeks
Deut 16:16 and in the *f* of tabernacles
Deut 31:10 release, in the *f* of tabernacles,
Judg 14:10 and Samson made there a *f*
Judg 14:12 me within the seven days of the *f*
Judg 14:17 seven days, while their *f* lasted
Judg 21:19 there is a *f* of the LORD in
1Sa 25:36 he held a *f* in his house, like
1Sa 25:36 his house, like the *f* of a king
2Sa 3:20 and the men that were with him a *f*
1Kin 3:15 made a *f* to all his servants
1Kin 8:2 at the *f* in the month Ethanim
1Kin 8:65 And at that time Solomon held a *f*
1Kin 12:32 ordained a *f* in the eighth month
1Kin 12:32 like unto the *f* that is in Judah,
1Kin 12:33 ordained a *f* unto the children of
2Chr 5:3 *f* which was in the seventh month
2Chr 7:8 Solomon kept the *f* seven days
2Chr 7:9 seven days, and the *f* seven days
2Chr 8:13 even in the *f* of unleavened bread
2Chr 8:13 bread, and in the *f* of weeks
2Chr 8:13 and in the *f* of tabernacles
2Chr 30:13 much people to keep the *f* of
2Chr 30:21 present at Jerusalem kept the *f*
2Chr 30:22 eat throughout the *f* seven days
2Chr 35:17 the *f* of unleavened bread seven
Ezr 3:4 kept also the *f* of tabernacles
Ezr 6:22 kept the *f* of unleavened bread
Neh 8:14 in the *f* of the seventh month
Neh 8:18 And they kept the *f* seven days
Est 1:3 he made a *f* unto all his princes
Est 1:5 the king made a *f* unto all the
Est 1:9 a *f* for the women in the royal
Est 2:18 a great *f* unto all his princes
Est 2:18 and his servants, even Esther's *f*
Est 8:17 the Jews had joy and gladness, a *f*
Ps 81:3 appointed, on our solemn *f* day
Prov 15:15 a merry heart hath a continual *f*
Eccl 10:19 A *f* is made for laughter, and wine
Is 25:6 unto all people a *f* of fat things
Is 25:6 a *f* of wines on the lees, of fat
Lam 2:7 LORD, as in the day of a solemn *f*
Eze 45:21 the passover, a *f* of seven days
Eze 45:23 seven days of the *f* he shall
Eze 45:25 like in the *f* of the seven days
Dan 5:1 the king made a great *f* to a
Hos 2:11 her *f* days, her new moons, and her
Hos 9:5 in the day of the *f* of the LORD
Hos 12:9 as in the days of the solemn *f*
Amos 5:21 I hate, I despise your *f* days
Zec 14:16 to keep the *f* of tabernacles
Zec 14:18 up to keep the *f* of tabernacles
Zec 14:19 up to keep the *f* of tabernacles
Mt 26:2 two days is the *f* of the passover
Mt 26:5 But they said, Not on the *f* day
Mt 26:17 of the *f* of unleavened bread the
Mt 27:15 Now at that *f* the governor was
Mk 14:1 days was the *f* of the passover
Mk 14:2 But they said, Not on the *f* day
Mk 15:6 Now at that *f* he released unto
Lk 2:41 year at the *f* of the passover
Lk 2:42 after the custom of the *f*
Lk 5:29 him a great *f* in his own house
Lk 14:13 But when thou makest a *f*, call
Lk 22:1 Now the *f* of unleavened bread
Lk 23:17 release one unto them at the *f*
Jn 2:8 bear unto the governor of the *f*
Jn 2:9 When the ruler of the *f* had
Jn 2:9 the governor of the *f* called the
Jn 2:23 at the passover, in the *f* day
Jn 4:45 that he did at Jerusalem at the *f*
Jn 4:45 for they also went unto the *f*
Jn 5:1 this there was a *f* of the Jews
Jn 6:4 a *f* of the Jews, was nigh
Jn 7:2 Now the Jews' *f* of tabernacles
Jn 7:8 Go ye up unto this *f*
Jn 7:8 I go not up yet unto this *f*
Jn 7:10 then went he also up unto the *f*
Jn 7:11 Then the Jews sought him at the *f*
Jn 7:14 Now about the midst of the *f*
Jn 7:37 last day, that great day of the *f*
Jn 10:22 Jerusalem the *f* of the dedication
Jn 11:56 that he will not come to the *f*
Jn 12:12 people that were come to the *f*
Jn 12:20 that came up to worship at the *f*
Jn 13:1 Now before the *f* of the passover,
Jn 13:29 we have need of against the *f*
Acts 18:21 this *f* that cometh in Jerusalem
1Cor 5:8 Therefore let us keep the *f*
1Cor 10:27 that believe not bid you to a *f*
2Pet 2:13 deceivings while they *f* with you
Jude 12 of charity, when they *f* with you

## FEASTING

Est 9:17 they, and made it a day of *f*
Est 9:18 rested, and made it a day of *f*
Est 9:19 month Adar a day of gladness and *f*
Est 9:22 they should make them days of *f*
Job 1:5 days of their *f* were gone about
Eccl 7:2 than to go to the house of *f*
Jer 16:8 not also go into the house of *f*

## FEASTS

Lev 23:2 Concerning the *f* of the LORD
Lev 23:2 convocations, even these are my *f*
Lev 23:4 These are the *f* of the LORD
Lev 23:37 These are the *f* of the LORD
Lev 23:44 of Israel the *f* of the LORD
Num 15:3 offering, or in your solemn *f*
Num 29:39 do unto the LORD in your set *f*
1Chr 23:31 in the new moons, and on the set *f*
2Chr 2:4 on the solemn *f* of the LORD our
2Chr 8:13 the new moons, and on the solemn *f*
2Chr 31:3 the new moons, and for the set *f*
Ezr 3:5 of all the set *f* of the LORD that
Neh 10:33 of the new moons, for the set *f*
Ps 35:16 With hypocritical mockers in *f*
Is 1:14 your appointed *f* my soul hateth
Is 5:12 and pipe, and wine, are in their *f*
Jer 51:39 In their heat I will make their *f*
Lam 1:4 because none come to the solemn *f*
Lam 2:6 the LORD hath caused the solemn *f*
Eze 36:38 of Jerusalem in her solemn *f*
Eze 45:17 and drink offerings, in the *f*
Eze 46:9 before the LORD in the solemn *f*
Eze 46:11 And in the *f* and in the solemnities
Hos 2:11 her sabbaths, and all her solemn *f*
Amos 8:10 I will turn your *f* into mourning
Nah 1:15 O Judah, keep thy solemn *f*
Zec 8:19 joy and gladness, and cheerful *f*
Mal 2:3 even the dung of your solemn *f*
Mt 23:6 And love the uppermost rooms at *f*
Mk 12:39 and the uppermost rooms at *f*
Lk 20:46 and the chief rooms at *f*
Jude 12 are spots in your *f* of charity

## FEATHERS

Lev 1:16 pluck away his crop with his *f*
Job 39:13 or wings and *f* unto the ostrich
Ps 68:13 silver, and her *f* with yellow gold
Ps 91:4 He shall cover thee with his *f*
Eze 17:3 wings, longwinged, full of *f*
Eze 17:7 eagle with great wings and many *f*
Dan 4:33 hairs were grown like eagles' *f*

## FED

Gen 30:36 Jacob *f* the rest of Laban's
Gen 36:24 as he *f* the asses of Zibeon his
Gen 41:2 and they *f* in a meadow
Gen 41:18 and they *f* in a meadow
Gen 47:17 he *f* them with bread for all
Gen 48:15 the God which *f* me all my life
Ex 16:32 I have *f* you in the wilderness
Deut 8:3 *f* thee with manna, which thou
Deut 8:16 Who *f* thee in the wilderness with
2Sa 20:3 *f* them, but went not in unto them
1Kin 18:4 *f* them with bread and water
1Kin 18:13 *f* them with bread and water
1Chr 27:29 over the herds that *f* in Sharon
Ps 37:3 land, and verily thou shalt be *f*
Ps 78:72 So he *f* them according to the
Ps 81:16 He should have *f* them also with
Is 1:11 of rams, and the fat of *f* beasts
Jer 5:7 when I had *f* them to the full,
Jer 5:8 They were as *f* horses in the
Eze 16:19 oil, and honey, wherewith I *f* thee
Eze 34:3 the wool, ye kill them that are *f*
Eze 34:8 *f* themselves, and *f* not my flock
Dan 4:12 thereof, and all flesh was *f* of it
Dan 5:21 they *f* him with grass like oxen,
Zec 11:7 and I *f* the flock
Mt 25:37 saw we thee an hungred, and *f* thee
Mk 5:14 they that *f* the swine fled, and
Lk 8:34 When they that *f* them saw what
Lk 16:21 desiring to be *f* with the crumbs
1Cor 3:2 I have *f* you with milk, and not

## FEEBLE

Gen 30:42 But when the cattle were *f*
Deut 25:18 even all that were *f* behind thee
1Sa 2:5 hath many children is waxed *f*
2Sa 4:1 dead in Hebron, his hands were *f*
2Chr 28:15 carried all the *f* of them upon
Neh 4:2 and said, What do these *f* Jews
Job 4:4 hast strengthened the *f* knees
Ps 38:8 I am *f* and sore broken
Ps 105:37 there was not one *f* person among
Prov 30:26 The conies are but a *f* folk
Is 16:14 remnant shall be very small and *f*
Is 35:3 hands, and confirm the *f* knees
Jer 6:24 our hands wax *f*
Jer 49:24 Damascus is waxed *f*, and turneth
Jer 50:43 of them, and his hands waxed *f*
Eze 7:17 All hands shall be *f*, and all
Eze 21:7 melt, and all hands shall be *f*
Zec 12:8 he that is *f* among them at that
1Cor 12:22 the body, which seem to be more *f*
Heb 12:12 which hang down, and the *f* knees

## FEED

Gen 25:30 *F* me, I pray thee, with that same
Gen 29:7 ye the sheep, and go and *f* them
Gen 30:31 this thing for me, I will again *f*
Gen 37:12 his brethren went to *f* their
Gen 37:13 Do not thy brethren *f* the flock
Gen 37:16 where they *f* their flocks
Gen 46:32 their trade hath been to *f* cattle
Ex 22:5 shall *f* in another man's field
Ex 34:3 nor herds *f* before that mount
1Sa 17:15 Saul to *f* his father's sheep at
2Sa 5:2 Thou shalt *f* my people Israel, and
2Sa 7:7 I commanded to *f* my people Israel
2Sa 19:33 me, and I will *f* thee with me in
1Kin 17:4 the ravens to *f* thee there
1Kin 22:27 *f* him with bread of affliction and
1Chr 11:2 Thou shalt *f* my people Israel, and
1Chr 17:6 whom I commanded to *f* my people
2Chr 18:26 *f* him with bread of affliction and
Job 24:2 take away flocks, and *f* thereof
Job 24:20 the worm shall *f* sweetly on him
Ps 28:9 *f* them also, and lift them up for
Ps 49:14 death shall *f* on them
Ps 78:71 brought him to *f* Jacob his people
Prov 10:21 The lips of the righteous *f* many
Prov 30:8 *f* me with food convenient for me
Song 1:8 *f* thy kids beside the shepherds'
Song 4:5 twins, which *f* among the lilies
Song 6:2 to *f* in the gardens, and to gather
Is 5:17 the lambs *f* after their manner
Is 11:7 And the cow and the bear shall *f*
Is 14:30 the firstborn of the poor shall *f*
Is 27:10 there shall the calf *f*, and there
Is 30:23 thy cattle *f* in large pastures
Is 40:11 He shall *f* his flock like a
Is 49:9 They shall *f* in the ways, and
Is 49:26 I will *f* them that oppress thee
Is 58:14 *f* thee with the heritage of Jacob
Is 61:5 *f* your flocks, and the sons of the
Is 65:25 wolf and the lamb shall *f* together
Jer 3:15 which shall *f* you with knowledge
Jer 6:3 they shall *f* every one in his
Jer 9:15 Behold, I will *f* them, even this
Jer 23:2 the pastors that *f* my people
Jer 23:4 over them which shall *f* them
Jer 23:15 I will *f* them with wormwood, and
Jer 50:19 he shall *f* on Carmel and Bashan,
Lam 4:5 They that did *f* delicately are
Eze 34:2 of Israel that do *f* themselves
Eze 34:2 not the shepherds *f* the flocks
Eze 34:3 but ye *f* not the flock
Eze 34:10 shepherds *f* themselves any more
Eze 34:13 *f* them upon the mountains of
Eze 34:14 I will *f* them in a good pasture,
Eze 34:14 in a fat pasture shall they *f*
Eze 34:15 I will *f* my flock, and I will
Eze 34:16 I will *f* them with judgment
Eze 34:23 over them, and he shall *f* them
Eze 34:23 he shall *f* them, and he shall be
Dan 11:26 they that *f* of the portion of his
Hos 4:16 now the LORD will *f* them as a
Hos 9:2 and the winepress shall not *f* them
Jonah 3:7 let them not *f*, nor drink water
Mic 5:4 *f* in the strength of the LORD, in
Mic 7:14 *F* thy people with thy rod, the
Mic 7:14 let them *f* in Bashan and Gilead,
Zeph 2:7 they shall *f* thereupon
Zeph 3:13 for they shall *f* and lie down, and
Zec 11:4 *F* the flock of the slaughter
Zec 11:7 I will *f* the flock of slaughter,
Zec 11:9 Then said I, I will not *f* you
Zec 11:16 nor *f* that that standeth still
Lk 15:15 him into his fields to *f* swine

Jn 21:15 He saith unto him, *F* my lambs
Jn 21:16 He saith unto him, *F* my sheep
Jn 21:17 Jesus saith unto him, *F* my sheep
Acts 20:28 to *f* the church of God, which he
Rom 12:20 if thine enemy hunger, *f* him
1Cor 13:3 bestow all my goods to *f* the poor
1Pet 5:2 *F* the flock of God which is among
Rev 7:17 midst of the throne shall *f* them
Rev 12:6 that they should *f* her there a

## FEEDETH

Prov 15:14 mouth of fools *f* on foolishness
Song 2:16 he *f* among the lilies
Song 6:3 he *f* among the lilies
Is 44:20 He *f* on ashes
Hos 12:1 Ephraim *f* on wind, and followeth
Mt 6:26 yet your heavenly Father *f* them
Lk 12:24 and God *f* them
1Cor 9:7 or who *f* a flock, and eateth not

## FEEDING

Gen 37:2 was *f* the flock with his brethren
Job 1:14 and the asses *f* beside them
Eze 34:10 them to cease from *f* the flock
Nah 2:11 the *f* place of the young lions,
Mt 8:30 from them an herd of many swine *f*
Mk 5:11 mountains a great herd of swine *f*
Lk 8:32 of many swine *f* on the mountain
Lk 17:7 a servant plowing or *f* cattle
Jude 12 *f* themselves without fear

## FEEL

Gen 27:12 My father peradventure will *f* me
Gen 27:21 I pray thee, that I may *f* thee
Judg 16:26 Suffer me that I may *f* the
Job 20:20 Surely he shall not *f* quietness
Ps 58:9 Before your pots can *f* the thorns
Eccl 8:5 commandment shall *f* no evil thing
Acts 17:27 if haply they might *f* after him

## FEET

Gen 18:4 you, be fetched, and wash your *f*
Gen 19:2 tarry all night, and wash your *f*
Gen 24:32 camels, and water to wash his *f*
Gen 24:32 the men's *f* that were with him
Gen 43:24 water, and they washed their *f*
Gen 49:10 nor a lawgiver from between his *f*
Gen 49:33 he gathered up his *f* into the bed
Ex 3:5 put off thy shoes from off thy *f*
Ex 4:25 of her son, and cast it at his *f*
Ex 12:11 girded, your shoes on your *f*
Ex 24:10 there was under his *f* as it were
Ex 25:26 that are on the four *f* thereof
Ex 30:19 their hands and their *f* thereat
Ex 30:21 shall wash their hands and their *f*
Ex 37:13 that were in the four *f* thereof
Ex 40:31 their hands and their *f* thereat
Lev 8:24 the great toes of their right *f*
Lev 11:21 which have legs above their *f*
Lev 11:23 things, which have four *f*
Lev 11:42 or whatsoever hath more *f* among
Num 20:19 thing else, go through on my *f*
Deut 2:28 only I will pass through on my *f*
Deut 11:24 your *f* shall tread shall be yours
Deut 28:57 cometh out from between her *f*
Deut 33:3 and they sat down at thy *f*
Josh 3:13 as soon as the soles of the *f* of
Josh 3:15 the *f* of the priests that bare
Josh 4:3 where the priests' *f* stood firm
Josh 4:9 in the place where the *f* of the
Josh 4:18 the soles of the priests' *f* were
Josh 9:5 old shoes and clouted upon their *f*
Josh 10:24 put your *f* upon the necks of
Josh 10:24 put their *f* upon the necks of
Josh 14:9 thy *f* have trodden shall be thine
Judg 3:24 his *f* in his summer chamber
Judg 4:10 up with ten thousand men at his *f*
Judg 4:15 chariot, and fled away on his *f*
Judg 4:17 *f* to the tent of Jael the wife of
Judg 5:27 At her *f* he bowed, he fell, he
Judg 5:27 at her *f* he bowed, he fell
Judg 19:21 and they washed their *f*, and did
Ruth 3:4 shalt go in, and uncover his *f*
Ruth 3:7 came softly, and uncovered his *f*
Ruth 3:8 and, behold, a woman lay at his *f*
Ruth 3:14 she lay at his *f* until the
1Sa 2:9 He will keep the *f* of his saints
1Sa 14:13 up upon his hands and upon his *f*
1Sa 24:3 and Saul went in to cover his *f*
1Sa 25:24 And fell at his *f*, and said, Upon
1Sa 25:41 be a servant to wash the *f* of the
2Sa 3:34 nor thy *f* put into fetters
2Sa 4:4 had a son that was lame of his *f*
2Sa 4:12 and cut off their hands and their *f*
2Sa 9:3 yet a son, which is lame on his *f*
2Sa 9:13 and was lame on both his *f*
2Sa 11:8 down to thy house, and wash thy *f*
2Sa 19:24 and had neither dressed his *f*
2Sa 22:10 and darkness was under his *f*
2Sa 22:34 He maketh my *f* like hinds' *f*
2Sa 22:37 so that my *f* did not slip
2Sa 22:39 yea, they are fallen under my *f*
1Kin 2:5 in his shoes that were on his *f*
1Kin 5:3 put them under the soles of his *f*
1Kin 14:6 Ahijah heard the sound of her *f*
1Kin 14:12 when thy *f* enter into the city,
1Kin 15:23 old age he was diseased in his *f*
2Kin 4:27 the hill, she caught him by the *f*
2Kin 4:37 she went in, and fell at his *f*
2Kin 6:32 of his master's *f* behind him
2Kin 9:35 of her than the skull, and the *f*
2Kin 13:21 he revived, and stood up on his *f*
2Kin 19:24 with the sole of my *f* have I
2Kin 21:8 Neither will I make the *f* of
1Chr 28:2 the king stood up upon his *f*
2Chr 3:13 and they stood on their *f*, and
2Chr 16:12 his reign was diseased in his *f*
Neh 9:21 not old, and their *f* swelled not
Est 8:3 the king, and fell down at his *f*
Job 12:5 *f* is as a lamp despised in the
Job 13:27 Thou puttest my *f* also in the
Job 13:27 a print upon the heels of my *f*
Job 18:8 is cast into a net by his own *f*
Job 18:11 side, and shall drive him to his *f*
Job 29:15 the blind, and *f* was I to the lame
Job 30:12 they push away my *f*, and they
Job 33:11 He putteth my *f* in the stocks
Ps 8:6 hast put all things under his *f*
Ps 18:9 and darkness was under his *f*
Ps 18:33 He maketh my *f* like hinds' *f*,
Ps 18:36 under me, that my *f* did not slip
Ps 18:38 they are fallen under my *f*
Ps 22:16 they pierced my hands and my *f*
Ps 25:15 shall pluck my *f* out of the net
Ps 31:8 hast set my *f* in a large room
Ps 40:2 clay, and set my *f* upon a rock, and
Ps 47:3 us, and the nations under our *f*
Ps 56:13 thou deliver my *f* from falling
Ps 58:10 he shall wash his *f* in the blood
Ps 66:9 suffereth not our *f* to be moved
Ps 73:2 as for me, my *f* were almost gone
Ps 74:3 Lift up thy *f* unto the perpetual
Ps 91:13 dragon shalt thou trample under *f*
Ps 105:18 Whose *f* they hurt with fetters
Ps 115:7 *f* have they, but they walk not
Ps 116:8 from tears, and my *f* from falling
Ps 119:59 turned my *f* unto thy testimonies
Ps 119:101 my *f* from every evil way, that I
Ps 119:105 Thy word is a lamp unto my *f*
Ps 122:2 Our *f* shall stand within thy
Prov 1:16 For their *f* run to evil, and make
Prov 4:26 Ponder the path of thy *f*, and let
Prov 5:5 Her *f* go down to death
Prov 6:13 his eyes, he speaketh with his *f*
Prov 6:18 *f* that be swift in running to
Prov 6:28 hot coals, and his *f* not be burned
Prov 7:11 her *f* abide not in her house
Prov 19:2 that hasteth with his *f* sinneth
Prov 26:6 hand of a fool cutteth off the *f*
Prov 29:5 spreadeth a net for his *f*
Song 5:3 I have washed my *f*
Song 7:1 beautiful are thy *f* with shoes
Is 3:16 and making a tinkling with their *f*
Is 3:18 tinkling ornaments about their *f*
Is 6:2 and with twain he covered his *f*
Is 7:20 the head, and the hair of the *f*
Is 14:19 as a carcase trodden under *f*
Is 23:7 her own *f* shall carry her afar
Is 26:6 even the *f* of the poor, and the
Is 28:3 Ephraim, shall be trodden under *f*
Is 32:20 forth thither the *f* of the ox
Is 37:25 with the sole of my *f* have I
Is 41:3 that he had not gone with his *f*
Is 49:23 and lick up the dust of thy *f*
Is 52:7 the *f* of him that bringeth good
Is 59:7 Their *f* run to evil, and they make
Is 60:13 make the place of my *f* glorious
Is 60:14 down at the soles of thy *f*
Jer 13:16 before your *f* stumble upon the
Jer 14:10 they have not refrained their *f*
Jer 18:22 take me, and hid snares for my *f*
Jer 38:22 thy *f* are sunk in the mire, and
Lam 1:13 he hath spread a net for my *f*
Lam 3:34 To crush under his *f* all the
Eze 1:7 And their *f* were straight *f*
Eze 1:7 the sole of their *f* was like the
Eze 2:1 me, Son of man, stand upon thy *f*
Eze 2:2 unto me, and set me upon my *f*
Eze 3:24 into me, and set me upon my *f*
Eze 16:25 hast opened thy *f* to every one
Eze 24:17 and put on thy shoes upon thy *f*
Eze 24:23 heads, and your shoes upon your *f*
Eze 25:6 hands, and stamped with the *f*
Eze 32:2 troubledst the waters with thy *f*
Eze 34:18 *f* the residue of your pastures
Eze 34:18 must foul the residue with your *f*
Eze 34:19 which ye have trodden with your *f*
Eze 34:19 which ye have fouled with your *f*
Eze 37:10 lived, and stood up upon their *f*
Eze 43:7 and the place of the soles of my *f*
Dan 2:33 his *f* part of iron and part of
Dan 2:34 upon his *f* that were of iron
Dan 2:41 And whereas thou sawest the *f*
Dan 2:42 toes of the *f* were part of iron
Dan 7:4 and made stand upon the *f* as a man
Dan 7:7 the residue with the *f* of it
Dan 7:19 and stamped the residue with his *f*
Dan 10:6 his *f* like in colour to polished
Nah 1:3 the clouds are the dust of his *f*
Nah 1:15 the *f* of him that bringeth good
Hab 3:5 burning coals went forth at his *f*
Hab 3:19 will make my *f* like hinds' *f*
Zec 14:4 his *f* shall stand in that day
Zec 14:12 while they stand upon their *f*
Mal 4:3 ashes under the soles of your *f*
Mt 7:6 they trample them under their *f*
Mt 10:14 shake off the dust of your *f*
Mt 15:30 and cast them down at Jesus' *f*
Mt 18:8 two *f* to be cast into everlasting
Mt 18:29 fellowservant fell down at his *f*
Mt 28:9 And they came and held him by the *f*
Mk 5:22 when he saw him, he fell at his *f*
Mk 6:11 *f* for a testimony against them
Mk 7:25 of him, and came and fell at his *f*
Mk 9:45 than having two *f* to be cast into
Lk 1:79 to guide our *f* into the way of
Lk 7:38 stood at his *f* behind him weeping
Lk 7:38 and began to wash his *f* with tears
Lk 7:38 of her head, and kissed his *f*
Lk 7:44 thou gavest me no water for my *f*
Lk 7:44 she hath washed my *f* with tears
Lk 7:45 in hath not ceased to kiss my *f*
Lk 7:46 hath anointed my *f* with ointment
Lk 8:35 sitting at the *f* of Jesus
Lk 8:41 and he fell down at Jesus' *f*
Lk 9:5 off the very dust from your *f* for
Lk 10:39 Mary, which also sat at Jesus' *f*
Lk 15:22 on his hand, and shoes on his *f*
Lk 17:16 And fell down on his face at his *f*
Lk 24:39 Behold my hands and my *f*, that it
Lk 24:40 he shewed them his hands and his *f*
Jn 11:2 wiped his *f* with her hair, whose
Jn 11:32 saw him, she fell down at his *f*
Jn 12:3 and anointed the *f* of Jesus
Jn 12:3 wiped his *f* with her hair
Jn 13:5 and began to wash the disciples' *f*
Jn 13:6 him, Lord, dost thou wash my *f*
Jn 13:8 him, Thou shalt never wash my *f*
Jn 13:9 unto him, Lord, not my *f* only
Jn 13:10 needeth not save to wash his *f*
Jn 13:12 So after he had washed their *f*
Jn 13:14 and Master, have washed your *f*
Jn 13:14 ought to wash one another's *f*
Jn 20:12 the head, and the other at the *f*
Acts 3:7 and immediately his *f* and ancle
Acts 4:35 laid them down at the apostles' *f*
Acts 4:37 and laid it at the apostles' *f*
Acts 5:2 and laid it at the apostles' *f*
Acts 5:9 the *f* of them which have buried
Acts 5:10 she down straightway at his *f*
Acts 7:33 him, Put off thy shoes from thy *f*
Acts 7:58 their clothes at a young man's *f*
Acts 10:25 met him, and fell down at his *f*
Acts 13:25 whose shoes of his *f* I am not
Acts 13:51 the dust of their *f* against them
Acts 14:8 man at Lystra, impotent in his *f*
Acts 14:10 voice, Stand upright on thy *f*
Acts 16:24 made their *f* fast in the stocks
Acts 21:11 and bound his own hands and *f*
Acts 22:3 in this city at the *f* of Gamaliel
Acts 26:16 But rise, and stand upon thy *f*
Rom 3:15 Their *f* are swift to shed blood

Rom 10:15 How beautiful are the *f* of them
Rom 16:20 bruise Satan under your *f* shortly
1Cor 12:21 nor again the head to the *f*
1Cor 15:25 hath put all enemies under his *f*
1Cor 15:27 hath put all things under his *f*
Eph 1:22 hath put all things under his *f*
Eph 6:15 your *f* shod with the preparation
1Ti 5:10 if she have washed the saints' *f*
Heb 2:8 things in subjection under his *f*
Heb 12:13 And make straight paths for your *f*
Rev 1:15 his *f* like unto fine brass, as if
Rev 1:17 saw him, I fell at his *f* as dead
Rev 2:18 his *f* are like fine brass
Rev 3:9 to come and worship before thy *f*
Rev 10:1 sun, and his *f* as pillars of fire
Rev 11:11 them, and they stood upon their *f*
Rev 12:1 the sun, and the moon under her *f*
Rev 13:2 his *f* were as the *f* of a bear
Rev 19:10 I fell at his *f* to worship him
Rev 22:8 *f* of the angel which shewed me

**FELIX** *(fe'-lix)* See FELIX'. *A Roman procurator of Judea.*
Acts 23:24 him safe unto *F* the governor
Acts 23:26 governor *F* sendeth greeting
Acts 24:3 and in all places, most noble *F*
Acts 24:22 when *F* heard these things, having
Acts 24:24 when *F* came with his wife
Acts 24:25 *F* trembled, and answered, Go thy
Acts 24:27 and *F*, willing to shew the Jews a
Acts 25:14 a certain man left in bonds by *F*

**FELL**
Gen 4:5 very wroth, and his countenance *f*
Gen 14:10 and Gomorrah fled, and *f* there
Gen 15:12 down, a deep sleep *f* upon Abram
Gen 15:12 of great darkness *f* upon him
Gen 17:3 And Abram *f* on his face
Gen 17:17 Then Abraham *f* upon his face, and
Gen 33:4 *f* on his neck, and kissed him
Gen 44:14 they *f* before him on the ground
Gen 45:14 he *f* upon his brother Benjamin's
Gen 46:29 he *f* on his neck, and wept on his
Gen 50:1 Joseph *f* upon his father's face,
Gen 50:18 went and *f* down before his face
Ex 32:28 there *f* of the people that day
Lev 9:24 they shouted, and *f* on their faces
Lev 16:9 goat upon which the LORD's lot *f*
Lev 16:10 on which the lot *f* to be the
Num 11:4 that was among them *f* a lusting
Num 11:9 when the dew *f* upon the camp in
Num 11:9 in the night, the manna *f* upon it
Num 14:5 Aaron *f* on their faces before all
Num 16:4 heard it, he *f* upon his face
Num 16:22 they *f* upon their faces, and said,
Num 16:45 And they *f* upon their faces
Num 20:6 and they *f* upon their faces
Num 22:27 the LORD, she *f* down under Balaam
Num 22:31 his head, and *f* flat on his face
Deut 9:18 I *f* down before the LORD, as at
Deut 9:25 Thus I *f* down before the LORD
Deut 9:25 nights, as I *f* down at the first
Josh 5:14 Joshua *f* on his face to the earth
Josh 6:20 shout, that the wall *f* down flat
Josh 7:6 *f* to the earth upon his face
Josh 8:25 it was, that all that *f* that day
Josh 11:7 and they *f* upon them
Josh 16:1 Joseph *f* from Jordan by Jericho
Josh 17:5 there *f* ten portions to Manasseh,
Josh 22:20 wrath *f* on all the congregation
Judg 4:16 all the host of Sisera *f* upon the
Judg 5:27 At her feet he bowed, he *f*
Judg 5:27 at her feet he bowed, he *f*
Judg 5:27 he bowed, there he *f* down dead,
Judg 7:13 a tent, and smote it that it *f*
Judg 8:10 for there *f* an hundred and twenty
Judg 12:6 there *f* at that time of the
Judg 13:20 *f* on their faces to the ground
Judg 16:30 the house *f* upon the lords, and
Judg 19:26 *f* down at the door of the man's
Judg 20:44 there *f* of Benjamin eighteen
Judg 20:46 So that all which *f* that day of
Ruth 2:10 Then she *f* on her face, and bowed
1Sa 4:10 for there *f* of Israel thirty
1Sa 4:18 that he *f* from off the seat
1Sa 11:7 fear of the LORD *f* on the people
1Sa 14:13 and they *f* before Jonathan
1Sa 17:49 he *f* upon his face to the earth
1Sa 17:52 *f* down by the way to Shaaraim
1Sa 20:41 *f* on his face to the ground, and
1Sa 22:18 he *f* upon the priests, and slew on
1Sa 25:23 *f* before David on her face, and
1Sa 25:24 *f* at his feet, and said, Upon me,
1Sa 28:20 Then Saul *f* straightway all along
1Sa 29:3 since he *f* unto me unto this day
1Sa 30:13 because three days agone I *f* sick
1Sa 31:1 *f* down slain in mount Gilboa
1Sa 31:4 Saul took a sword, and *f* upon it
1Sa 31:5 he *f* likewise upon his sword, and
2Sa 1:2 that he *f* to the earth, and did
2Sa 2:16 so they *f* down together
2Sa 2:23 he *f* down there, and died in the
2Sa 2:23 to the place where Asahel *f* down
2Sa 4:4 she made haste to flee, that he *f*
2Sa 9:6 David, he *f* on his face, and did
2Sa 11:17 there *f* some of the people of the
2Sa 13:2 that he *f* sick for his sister
2Sa 14:4 she *f* on her face to the ground,
2Sa 14:22 Joab *f* to the ground on his face,
2Sa 18:28 he *f* down to the earth upon his
2Sa 19:18 of Gera *f* down before the king
2Sa 20:8 and as he went forth it *f* out
2Sa 21:9 they *f* all seven together, and
2Sa 21:22 *f* by the hand of David, and by the
1Kin 2:25 he *f* upon him that he died
1Kin 2:32 who *f* upon two men more righteous
1Kin 2:34 up, and *f* upon him, and slew him
1Kin 2:46 out, and *f* upon him, that he died
1Kin 14:1 Abijah the son of Jeroboam *f* sick
1Kin 17:17 the mistress of the house, *f* sick
1Kin 18:7 *f* on his face, and said, Art thou
1Kin 18:38 Then the fire of the LORD *f*
1Kin 18:39 saw it, they *f* on their faces
1Kin 20:30 and there a wall *f* upon twenty
2Kin 1:2 Ahaziah *f* down through a lattice
2Kin 1:13 *f* on his knees before Elijah, and
2Kin 2:13 mantle of Elijah that *f* from him
2Kin 2:14 mantle of Elijah that *f* from him
2Kin 3:19 shall *f* every good tree, and stop
2Kin 4:8 it *f* on a day, that Elisha passed
2Kin 4:11 it *f* on a day, that he came
2Kin 4:18 it *f* on a day, that he went out
2Kin 4:37 *f* at his feet, and bowed herself
2Kin 6:5 the ax head *f* into the water
2Kin 6:6 the man of God said, Where *f* it
2Kin 7:20 And so it *f* out unto him
2Kin 25:11 the fugitives that *f* away to the
1Chr 5:10 Hagarites, who *f* by their hand
1Chr 5:22 For there *f* down many slain,
1Chr 10:1 *f* down slain in mount Gilboa
1Chr 10:4 Saul took a sword, and *f* upon it
1Chr 10:5 he *f* likewise on the sword, and
1Chr 12:19 there *f* some of Manasseh to David
1Chr 12:20 there *f* to him of Manasseh, Adnah
1Chr 20:8 they *f* by the hand of David, and
1Chr 21:14 there *f* of Israel seventy
1Chr 21:16 in sackcloth, *f* upon their faces
1Chr 26:14 the lot eastward *f* to Shelemiah
1Chr 27:24 because there *f* wrath for it
2Chr 13:17 so there *f* down slain of Israel
2Chr 15:9 for they *f* to him out of Israel
2Chr 17:10 the fear of the LORD *f* upon all
2Chr 20:18 of Jerusalem *f* before the LORD
2Chr 21:19 his bowels *f* out by reason of his
2Chr 25:13 *f* upon the cities of Judah, from
Ezr 9:5 I *f* upon my knees, and spread out
Est 8:3 *f* down at his feet, and besought
Est 8:17 the fear of the Jews *f* upon them
Est 9:2 fear of them *f* upon all people
Est 9:3 the fear of Mordecai *f* upon them
Job 1:15 And the Sabeans *f* upon them
Job 1:17 *f* upon the camels, and have
Job 1:19 it *f* upon the young men, and they
Job 1:20 *f* down upon the ground, and
Ps 27:2 up my flesh, they stumbled and *f*
Ps 78:64 Their priests *f* by the sword
Ps 105:38 for the fear of them *f* upon them
Ps 107:12 they *f* down, and there was none to
Jer 39:9 in the city, and those that *f* away
Jer 39:9 that *f* to him, with the rest of
Jer 46:16 to fall, yea, one *f* upon another
Jer 52:15 in the city, and those that *f* away
Jer 52:15 that *f* to the king of Babylon, and
Lam 1:7 when her people *f* into the hand
Lam 5:13 the children *f* under the wood
Eze 1:28 I *f* upon my face, and I heard a
Eze 3:23 and I *f* on my face
Eze 8:1 of the Lord GOD *f* there upon me
Eze 9:8 that I *f* upon my face, and cried,
Eze 11:5 the Spirit of the LORD *f* upon me
Eze 11:13 Then *f* I down upon my face, and
Eze 39:23 so *f* they all by the sword
Eze 43:3 and I *f* upon my face
Eze 44:4 and I *f* upon my face
Dan 2:46 Nebuchadnezzar *f* upon his face
Dan 3:7 *f* down and worshipped the golden
Dan 3:23 *f* down bound into the midst of
Dan 4:31 there *f* a voice from heaven,
Dan 7:20 came up, and before whom three *f*
Dan 8:17 I was afraid, and *f* upon my face
Dan 10:7 but a great quaking *f* upon them
Jonah 1:7 lots, and the lot *f* upon Jonah
Mt 2:11 *f* down, and worshipped him
Mt 7:25 and it *f* not: for it was founded
Mt 7:27 and it *f*: and great was the fall
Mt 13:4 some seeds *f* by the way side, and
Mt 13:5 Some *f* upon stony places, where
Mt 13:7 And some *f* among thorns
Mt 13:8 But other *f* into good ground, and
Mt 17:6 they *f* on their face, and were
Mt 18:26 The servant therefore *f* down
Mt 18:29 fellowservant *f* down at his feet
Mt 26:39 *f* on his face, and prayed, saying,
Mk 3:11 *f* down before him, and cried,
Mk 4:4 some *f* by the way side, and the
Mk 4:5 some *f* on stony ground, where it
Mk 4:7 some *f* among thorns, and the
Mk 4:8 other *f* on good ground, and did
Mk 5:22 he saw him, he *f* at his feet,
Mk 5:33 *f* down before him, and told him
Mk 7:25 of him, and came and *f* at his feet
Mk 9:20 he *f* on the ground, and wallowed
Mk 14:35 *f* on the ground, and prayed that,
Lk 1:12 was troubled, and fear *f* upon him
Lk 5:8 he *f* down at Jesus' knees, saying
Lk 5:12 who seeing Jesus *f* on his face
Lk 6:49 vehemently, and immediately it *f*
Lk 8:5 he sowed, some *f* by the way side
Lk 8:6 And some *f* upon a rock
Lk 8:7 And some *f* among thorns
Lk 8:8 other *f* on good ground, and sprang
Lk 8:14 that which *f* among thorns are
Lk 8:23 But as they sailed he *f* asleep
Lk 8:28 *f* down before him, and with a loud
Lk 8:41 he *f* down at Jesus' feet, and
Lk 10:30 *f* among thieves, which stripped
Lk 10:36 unto him that *f* among the thieves
Lk 13:4 upon whom the tower in Siloam *f*
Lk 15:20 *f* on his neck, and kissed him
Lk 16:21 which *f* from the rich man's table
Lk 17:16 *f* down on his face at his feet,
Jn 11:32 she *f* down at his feet, saying
Jn 18:6 went backward, and *f* to the ground
Acts 1:25 which Judas by transgression *f*
Acts 1:26 and the lot *f* upon Matthias
Acts 5:5 hearing these words *f* down
Acts 5:10 Then *f* she down straightway at
Acts 7:60 he had said this, he *f* asleep
Acts 9:4 he *f* to the earth, and heard a
Acts 9:18 immediately there *f* from his eyes
Acts 10:10 made ready, he *f* into a trance,
Acts 10:25 *f* down at his feet, and worshipped
Acts 10:44 the Holy Ghost *f* on all them
Acts 11:15 speak, the Holy Ghost *f* on them
Acts 12:7 his chains *f* off from his hands
Acts 13:11 immediately there *f* on him a mist
Acts 13:36 *f* on sleep, and was laid unto his
Acts 16:29 *f* down before Paul and Silas,
Acts 19:17 fear *f* on them all, and the name
Acts 19:35 image which *f* down from Jupiter
Acts 20:9 *f* down from the third loft, and
Acts 20:10 *f* on him, and embracing him said,
Acts 20:37 *f* on Paul's neck, and kissed him,
Acts 22:7 I *f* unto the ground, and heard a
Rom 11:22 on them which *f*, severity
Rom 15:3 them that reproached thee *f* on me
1Cor 10:8 *f* in one day three and twenty
Heb 3:17 sinned, whose carcases *f* in the
Heb 11:30 faith the walls of Jericho *f* down
2Pet 3:4 for since the fathers *f* asleep
Rev 1:17 saw him, I *f* at his feet as dead
Rev 5:8 twenty elders *f* down before the
Rev 5:14 the four and twenty elders *f* down
Rev 6:13 stars of heaven *f* unto the earth
Rev 7:11 *f* before the throne on their
Rev 8:10 there *f* a great star from heaven,
Rev 8:10 it *f* upon the third part of the
Rev 11:11 great fear *f* upon them which saw
Rev 11:13 and the tenth part of the city *f*
Rev 11:16 *f* upon their faces, and worshipped
Rev 16:2 there *f* a noisome and grievous

Rev 16:19 and the cities of the nations *f*
Rev 16:21 there *f* upon men a great hail out
Rev 19:4 elders and the four beasts *f* down
Rev 19:10 I *f* at his feet to worship him
Rev 22:8 I *f* down to worship before the

### FELLOW
Gen 19:9 This one *f* came in to sojourn, and
Ex 2:13 Wherefore smitest thou thy *f*
Judg 7:13 man that told a dream unto his *f*
Judg 7:14 his *f* answered and said, This is
Judg 7:22 every man's sword against his *f*
1Sa 14:20 man's sword was against his *f*
1Sa 21:15 this *f* to play the mad man in my
1Sa 21:15 shall this *f* come into my house
1Sa 25:21 this *f* hath in the wilderness
1Sa 29:4 said unto him, Make this *f* return
2Sa 2:16 every one his *f* by the head
1Kin 22:27 Put this *f* in the prison, and feed
2Kin 9:11 wherefore came this mad *f* to thee
2Chr 18:26 Put this *f* in the prison, and feed
Eccl 4:10 fall, the one will lift up his *f*
Is 34:14 and the satyr shall cry to his *f*
Jonah 1:7 And they said every one to his *f*
Zec 13:7 and against the man that is my *f*
Mt 12:24 This *f* doth not cast out devils,
Mt 26:61 And said, This *f* said, I am able
Mt 26:71 This *f* was also with Jesus of
Lk 22:59 Of a truth this *f* also was with
Lk 23:2 We found this *f* perverting the
Jn 9:29 as for this *f*, we know not from
Acts 18:13 This *f* persuadeth men to worship
Acts 22:22 Away with such a *f* from the earth
Acts 24:5 have found this man a pestilent *f*
Phil 2:25 *f* soldier, but your messenger, and
Col 4:11 These only are my *f* workers unto

### FELLOWS
Judg 11:37 and bewail my virginity, I and my *f*
Judg 18:25 lest angry *f* run upon thee, and
2Sa 6:20 as one of the vain *f* shamelessly
Ps 45:7 the oil of gladness above thy *f*
Is 44:11 all his *f* shall be ashamed
Eze 37:19 and the tribes of Israel his *f*
Dan 2:13 Daniel and his *f* to be slain
Dan 2:18 his *f* should not perish with the
Dan 7:20 look was more stout than his *f*
Zec 3:8 thy *f* that sit before thee
Mt 11:16 markets, and calling unto their *f*
Acts 17:5 certain lewd *f* of the baser sort
Heb 1:9 the oil of gladness above thy *f*

### FELLOWSERVANT
Mt 18:29 his *f* fell down at his feet, and
Mt 18:33 also have had compassion on thy *f*
Col 1:7 learned of Epaphras our dear *f*
Col 4:7 minister and *f* in the Lord
Rev 19:10 I am thy *f*, and of thy brethren
Rev 22:9 for I am thy *f*, and of thy

### FELLOWSERVANTS
Mt 18:28 went out, and found one of his *f*
Mt 18:31 So when his *f* saw what was done,
Mt 24:49 And shall begin to smite his *f*
Rev 6:11 little season, until their *f* also

### FELLOWSHIP
Lev 6:2 delivered him to keep, or in *f*
Ps 94:20 of iniquity have *f* with thee
Acts 2:42 in the apostles' doctrine and *f*
1Cor 1:9 the *f* of his Son Jesus Christ our
1Cor 10:20 that ye should have *f* with devils
2Cor 6:14 for what *f* hath righteousness
2Cor 8:4 take upon us the *f* of the
Gal 2:9 and Barnabas the right hands of *f*
Eph 3:9 see what is the *f* of the mystery
Eph 5:11 have no *f* with the unfruitful
Phil 1:5 For your *f* in the gospel from the
Phil 2:1 if any *f* of the Spirit, if any
Phil 3:10 the *f* of his sufferings, being
1Jn 1:3 that ye also may have *f* with us
1Jn 1:3 truly our *f* is with the Father,
1Jn 1:6 If we say that we have *f* with him
1Jn 1:7 we have *f* one with another, and

### FELT
Gen 27:22 he *f* him, and said, The voice is
Ex 10:21 even darkness which may be *f*
Prov 23:35 have beaten me, and I *f* it not
Mk 5:29 she *f* in her body that she was
Acts 28:5 beast into the fire, and *f* no harm

### FEMALE
Gen 1:27 male and *f* created he them
Gen 5:2 Male and *f* created he them
Gen 6:19 they shall be male and *f*
Gen 7:2 thee by sevens, the male and his *f*
Gen 7:2 clean by two, the male and his *f*
Gen 7:3 air by sevens, the male and the *f*
Gen 7:9 into the ark, the male and the *f*
Gen 7:16 *f* of all flesh, as God had
Lev 3:1 whether it be a male or *f*
Lev 3:6 male or *f*, he shall offer it
Lev 4:28 a *f* without blemish, for his sin
Lev 4:32 bring it a *f* without blemish
Lev 5:6 a *f* from the flock, a lamb or a
Lev 12:7 her that hath born a male or a *f*
Lev 27:4 And if it be a *f*, then thy
Lev 27:5 shekels, and for the *f* ten shekels
Lev 27:6 for the *f* thy estimation shall be
Lev 27:7 shekels, and for the *f* ten shekels
Num 5:3 *f* shall ye put out, without the
Deut 4:16 figure, the likeness of male or *f*
Deut 7:14 not be male or *f* barren among you
Mt 19:4 the beginning made them male and *f*
Mk 10:6 creation God made them male and *f*
Gal 3:28 free, there is neither male nor *f*

### FENCED
Num 32:17 in the *f* cities because of the
Num 32:36 and Beth-haran, *f* cities
Deut 3:5 cities were *f* with high walls
Deut 9:1 cities great and *f* up to heaven,
Deut 28:52 *f* walls come down, wherein thou
Josh 10:20 of them entered into *f* cities
Josh 14:12 that the cities were great and *f*
Josh 19:35 the *f* cities are Ziddim, Zer, and
1Sa 6:18 the five lords, both of *f* cities
2Sa 20:6 him, lest he get him *f* cities
2Sa 23:7 touch them must be *f* with iron
2Kin 3:19 And ye shall smite every *f* city
2Kin 10:2 horses, a *f* city also, and armour
2Kin 17:9 of the watchmen to the *f* city
2Kin 18:8 of the watchmen to the *f* city
2Kin 18:13 against all the *f* cities of Judah
2Kin 19:25 waste *f* cities into ruinous heaps
2Chr 8:5 *f* cities, with walls, gates, and
2Chr 11:10 in Judah and in Benjamin *f* cities
2Chr 11:23 and Benjamin, unto every *f* city
2Chr 12:4 he took the *f* cities which
2Chr 14:6 he built *f* cities in Judah
2Chr 17:2 in all the *f* cities of Judah
2Chr 17:19 the *f* cities throughout all Judah
2Chr 19:5 all the *f* cities of Judah
2Chr 21:3 things, with *f* cities in Judah
2Chr 32:1 and encamped against the *f* cities
2Chr 33:14 war in all the *f* cities of Judah
Job 10:11 hast *f* me with bones and sinews
Job 19:8 He hath *f* up my way that I cannot
Is 2:15 high tower, and upon every *f* wall
Is 5:2 And he *f* it, and gathered out the
Jer 5:17 shall impoverish thy *f* cities
Jer 15:20 unto this people a *f* brasen wall
Eze 36:35 and ruined cities are become *f*
Dan 11:15 mount, and take the most *f* cities
Hos 8:14 and Judah hath multiplied *f* cities
Zeph 1:16 and alarm against the *f* cities

### FERVENT
Acts 18:25 being *f* in the spirit, he spake
Rom 12:11 *f* in spirit; serving the Lord
2Cor 7:7 mourning, your *f* mind toward me
Jas 5:16 The effectual *f* prayer of a
1Pet 4:8 above all things have *f* charity
2Pet 3:10 elements shall melt with *f* heat
2Pet 3:12 elements shall melt with *f* heat

### FESTUS *(fes'-tus)* See FESTUS'. *A Roman procurator of Judea.*
Acts 24:27 Porcius *F* came into Felix' room
Acts 25:1 Now when *F* was come into the
Acts 25:4 But *F* answered, that Paul should
Acts 25:9 But *F*, willing to do the Jews a
Acts 25:12 Then *F*, when he had conferred
Acts 25:13 came unto Caesarea to salute *F*
Acts 25:14 *F* declared Paul's cause unto the
Acts 25:22 Then Agrippa said unto *F*, I would
Acts 25:24 *F* said, King Agrippa, and all men
Acts 26:24 *F* said with a loud voice, Paul,
Acts 26:25 said, I am not mad, most noble *F*
Acts 26:32 Then said Agrippa unto *F*, This

### FETCH
Gen 18:5 I will *f* a morsel of bread, and
Gen 27:9 *f* me from thence two good kids of
Gen 27:13 obey my voice, and go *f* me them
Gen 27:45 will send, and *f* thee from thence
Gen 42:16 let him *f* your brother, and ye
Ex 2:5 flags, she sent her maid to *f* it
Num 20:10 must we *f* you water out of this
Num 34:5 the border shall *f* a compass from
Deut 19:12 *f* him thence, and deliver him into
Deut 24:10 go into his house to *f* his pledge
Deut 24:19 thou shalt not go again to *f* it
Deut 30:4 and from thence will he *f* thee
Judg 11:5 the elders of Gilead went to *f*
Judg 20:10 to *f* victual for the people, that
1Sa 4:3 Let us *f* the ark of the covenant
1Sa 6:21 come ye down, and *f* it up to you
1Sa 16:11 said unto Jesse, Send and *f* him
1Sa 20:31 *f* him unto me, for he shall
1Sa 26:22 the young men come over and *f* it
2Sa 5:23 but *f* a compass behind them, and
2Sa 14:13 not *f* home again his banished
2Sa 14:20 To *f* about this form of speech
1Kin 17:10 *F* me, I pray thee, a little water
1Kin 17:11 And as she was going to *f* it
2Kin 6:13 he is, that I may send and *f* him
2Chr 18:8 *F* quickly Micaiah the son of Imla
Neh 8:15 *f* olive branches, and pine
Job 36:3 I will *f* my knowledge from afar,
Is 56:12 Come ye, say they, I will *f* wine
Jer 36:21 king sent Jehudi to *f* the roll
Acts 16:37 them come themselves and *f* us out

### FETCHED
Gen 18:4 a little water, I pray you, be *f*
Gen 27:14 And he went, and *f*, and brought them
Josh 15:3 to Adar, and *f* a compass to Karkaa
Judg 18:18 *f* the carved image, the ephod, and
1Sa 10:23 And they ran and *f* him thence
2Sa 4:6 as though they would have *f* wheat
2Sa 9:5 *f* him out of the house of Machir,
2Sa 11:27 *f* her to his house, and she became
2Sa 14:2 *f* thence a wise woman, and said
1Kin 7:13 sent and *f* Hiram out of Tyre
1Kin 9:28 *f* from thence gold, four hundred
2Kin 3:9 they *f* a compass of seven days'
2Kin 11:4 *f* the rulers over hundreds, with
2Chr 1:17 And they *f* up, and brought forth
2Chr 12:11 *f* them, and brought them again
Jer 26:23 they *f* forth Urijah out of Egypt,
Acts 28:13 And from thence we *f* a compass

### FETTERS
Judg 16:21 and bound him with *f* of brass
2Sa 3:34 bound, nor thy feet put into *f*
2Kin 25:7 and bound him with *f* of brass
2Chr 33:11 the thorns, and bound him with *f*
2Chr 36:6 of Babylon, and bound him in *f*
Job 36:8 And if they be bound in *f*, and be
Ps 105:18 Whose feet they hurt with *f*
Ps 149:8 and their nobles with *f* of iron
Mk 5:4 he had been often bound with *f*
Mk 5:4 by him, and the *f* broken in pieces
Lk 8:29 kept bound with chains and in *f*

### FEVER
Deut 28:22 with a consumption, and with a *f*
Mt 8:14 mother laid, and sick of a *f*
Mt 8:15 her hand, and the *f* left her
Mk 1:30 wife's mother lay sick of a *f*
Mk 1:31 and immediately the *f* left her
Lk 4:38 mother was taken with a great *f*
Lk 4:39 stood over her, and rebuked the *f*
Jn 4:52 the seventh hour the *f* left him
Acts 28:8 father of Publius lay sick of a *f*

### FIELD
Gen 2:5 every plant of the *f* before it
Gen 2:5 herb of the *f* before it grew
Gen 2:19 God formed every beast of the *f*
Gen 2:20 air, and to every beast of the *f*
Gen 3:1 the *f* which the LORD God had made
Gen 3:14 and above every beast of the *f*
Gen 3:18 thou shalt eat the herb of the *f*
Gen 4:8 to pass, when they were in the *f*
Gen 23:9 which is in the end of his *f*
Gen 23:11 the *f* give I thee, and the cave
Gen 23:13 I will give thee money for the *f*
Gen 23:17 the *f* of Ephron, which was in
Gen 23:17 which was before Mamre, the *f*
Gen 23:17 all the trees that were in the *f*
Gen 23:19 the *f* of Machpelah before Mamre

Gen 23:20 And the *f*, and the cave that is
Gen 24:63 meditate in the *f* at the eventide
Gen 24:65 that walketh in the *f* to meet us
Gen 25:9 in the *f* of Ephron the son of
Gen 25:10 The *f* which Abraham purchased of
Gen 25:27 a cunning hunter, a man of the *f*
Gen 25:29 and Esau came from the *f*, and he
Gen 27:3 and thy bow, and go out to the *f*
Gen 27:5 Esau went to the *f* to hunt for
Gen 27:27 a *f* which the LORD hath blessed
Gen 29:2 looked, and behold a well in the *f*
Gen 30:14 and found mandrakes in the *f*
Gen 30:16 came out of the *f* in the evening
Gen 31:4 Leah to the *f* unto his flock,
Gen 33:19 And he bought a parcel of a *f*
Gen 34:5 were with his cattle in the *f*
Gen 34:7 out of the *f* when they heard it
Gen 34:28 city, and that which was in the *f*
Gen 36:35 who smote Midian in the *f* of Moab
Gen 37:7 we were binding sheaves in the *f*
Gen 37:15 behold, he was wandering in the *f*
Gen 39:5 he had in the house, and in the *f*
Gen 41:48 the food of the *f*, which was
Gen 47:20 Egyptians sold every man his *f*
Gen 47:24 be your own, for seed of the *f*
Gen 49:29 is in the *f* of Ephron the Hittite
Gen 49:30 that is in the *f* of Machpelah
Gen 49:30 the *f* of Ephron the Hittite for a
Gen 49:32 The purchase of the *f* and of the
Gen 50:13 in the cave of the *f* of Machpelah
Gen 50:13 with the *f* for a possession of a
Ex 1:14 in all manner of service in the *f*
Ex 9:3 upon thy cattle which is in the *f*
Ex 9:19 and all that thou hast in the *f*
Ex 9:19 which shall be found in the *f*
Ex 9:21 servants and his cattle in the *f*
Ex 9:22 and upon every herb of the *f*
Ex 9:25 of Egypt all that was in the *f*
Ex 9:25 hail smote every herb of the *f*
Ex 9:25 and brake every tree of the *f*
Ex 10:5 groweth for you out of the *f*
Ex 10:15 trees, or in the herbs of the *f*
Ex 16:25 day ye shall not find it in the *f*
Ex 22:5 If a man shall cause a *f* or
Ex 22:5 and shall feed in another man's *f*
Ex 22:5 of the best of his own *f*, and of
Ex 22:6 or the standing corn, or the *f*
Ex 22:31 that is torn of beasts in the *f*
Ex 23:11 the beasts of the *f* shall eat
Ex 23:16 which thou hast sown in the *f*
Ex 23:16 in thy labours out of the *f*
Ex 23:29 the beast of the *f* multiply
Lev 14:7 living bird loose into the open *f*
Lev 17:5 which they offer in the open *f*
Lev 19:9 wholly reap the corners of thy *f*
Lev 19:19 not sow thy *f* with mingled seed
Lev 23:22 of thy *f* when thou reapest
Lev 25:3 Six years thou shalt sow thy *f*
Lev 25:4 thou shalt neither sow thy *f*
Lev 25:12 the increase thereof out of the *f*
Lev 25:34 But the *f* of the suburbs of their
Lev 26:4 the trees of the *f* shall yield
Lev 27:16 part of a *f* of his possession
Lev 27:17 If he sanctify his *f* from the
Lev 27:18 sanctify his *f* after the jubile
Lev 27:19 if he that sanctified the *f* will
Lev 27:20 And if he will not redeem the *f*
Lev 27:20 he have sold the *f* to another man
Lev 27:21 But the *f*, when it goeth out in
Lev 27:21 unto the LORD, as a *f* devoted
Lev 27:22 the LORD a *f* which he hath bought
Lev 27:24 *f* shall return unto him of whom
Lev 27:28 of the *f* of his possession, shall
Num 22:4 ox licketh up the grass of the *f*
Num 22:23 of the way, and went into the *f*
Num 23:14 brought him into the *f* of Zophim
Deut 5:21 thy neighbour's house, his *f*
Deut 7:22 of the *f* increase upon thee
Deut 14:22 that the *f* bringeth forth year by
Deut 20:19 *f* is man's life) to employ them
Deut 21:1 to possess it, lying in the *f*
Deut 22:25 find a betrothed damsel in the *f*
Deut 22:27 For he found her in the *f*
Deut 24:19 down thine harvest in thy *f*
Deut 24:19 and hast forgot a sheaf in the *f*
Deut 28:3 and blessed shalt thou be in the *f*
Deut 28:16 and cursed shalt thou be in the *f*
Deut 28:38 carry much seed out into the *f*
Josh 8:24 the inhabitants of Ai in the *f*
Josh 15:18 him to ask of her father a *f*
Judg 1:14 him to ask of her father a *f*
Judg 5:4 marchedst out of the *f* of Edom
Judg 5:18 death in the high places of the *f*
Judg 9:32 thee, and lie in wait in the *f*
Judg 9:42 the people went out into the *f*
Judg 9:43 companies, and laid wait in the *f*
Judg 13:9 the woman as she sat in the *f*
Judg 19:16 his work out of the *f* at even
Judg 20:31 and the other to Gibeah in the *f*
Ruth 2:2 Naomi, Let me now go to the *f*
Ruth 2:3 gleaned in the *f* after the
Ruth 2:3 part of the *f* belonging unto Boaz
Ruth 2:8 Go not to glean in another *f*
Ruth 2:9 be on the *f* that they do reap
Ruth 2:17 she gleaned in the *f* until even
Ruth 2:22 they meet thee not in any other *f*
Ruth 4:5 buyest the *f* of the hand of Naomi
1Sa 4:2 in the *f* about four thousand men
1Sa 6:14 cart came into the *f* of Joshua
1Sa 6:18 unto this day in the *f* of Joshua
1Sa 11:5 came after the herd out of the *f*
1Sa 14:15 trembling in the host, in the *f*
1Sa 17:44 air, and to the beasts of the *f*
1Sa 19:3 my father in the *f* where thou art
1Sa 20:5 the *f* unto the third day at even
1Sa 20:11 Come, and let us go out into the *f*
1Sa 20:11 went out both of them into the *f*
1Sa 20:24 So David hid himself in the *f*
1Sa 20:35 the *f* at the time appointed with
1Sa 30:11 they found an Egyptian in the *f*
2Sa 10:8 were by themselves in the *f*
2Sa 11:23 and came out unto us into the *f*
2Sa 14:6 they two strove together in the *f*
2Sa 14:30 Joab's *f* is near mine, and he hath
2Sa 14:30 servants set the *f* on fire
2Sa 14:31 thy servants set my *f* on fire
2Sa 17:8 robbed of her whelps in the *f*
2Sa 18:6 out into the *f* against Israel
2Sa 20:12 out of the highway into the *f*
2Sa 21:10 nor the beasts of the *f* by night
1Kin 11:29 and they two were alone in the *f*
1Kin 14:11 him that dieth in the *f* shall the
1Kin 21:24 him that dieth in the *f* shall the
2Kin 4:39 out into the *f* to gather herbs
2Kin 7:12 camp to hide themselves in the *f*
2Kin 8:6 all the fruits of the *f* since the
2Kin 9:25 of the *f* of Naboth the Jezreelite
2Kin 9:37 the *f* in the portion of Jezreel
2Kin 18:17 in the highway of the fuller's *f*
2Kin 19:26 they were as the grass of the *f*
1Chr 1:46 smote Midian in the *f* of Moab
1Chr 19:9 come were by themselves in the *f*
1Chr 27:26 *f* for tillage of the ground was
2Chr 26:23 him with his fathers in the *f* of
2Chr 31:5 and of all the increase of the *f*
Neh 13:10 were fled every one to his *f*
Job 5:23 league with the stones of the *f*
Job 5:23 the beasts of the *f* shall be at
Job 24:6 reap every one his corn in the *f*
Job 40:20 all the beasts of the *f* play
Ps 8:7 oxen, yea, and the beasts of the *f*
Ps 50:11 the wild beasts of the *f* are mine
Ps 78:12 land of Egypt, in the *f* of Zoan
Ps 78:43 and his wonders in the *f* of Zoan
Ps 80:13 beast of the *f* doth devour it
Ps 96:12 Let the *f* be joyful, and all that
Ps 103:15 as a flower of the *f*, so he
Ps 104:11 drink to every beast of the *f*
Prov 24:27 make it fit for thyself in the *f*
Prov 24:30 I went by the *f* of the slothful,
Prov 27:26 the goats are the price of the *f*
Prov 31:16 She considereth a *f*, and buyeth it
Eccl 5:9 king himself is served by the *f*
Song 2:7 roes, and by the hinds of the *f*
Song 3:5 roes, and by the hinds of the *f*
Song 7:11 let us go forth into the *f*
Is 5:8 to house, that lay *f* to *f*
Is 5:8 to house, that lay *f* to *f*
Is 7:3 in the highway of the fuller's *f*
Is 10:18 his forest, and of his fruitful *f*
Is 16:10 and joy out of the plentiful *f*
Is 29:17 shall be turned into a fruitful *f*
Is 29:17 the fruitful *f* shall be esteemed
Is 32:15 and the wilderness be a fruitful *f*
Is 32:15 the fruitful *f* be counted for a
Is 32:16 remain in the fruitful *f*
Is 36:2 in the highway of the fuller's *f*
Is 37:27 they were as the grass of the *f*
Is 40:6 thereof is as the flower of the *f*
Is 43:20 beast of the *f* shall honour me
Is 55:12 all the trees of the *f* shall clap
Is 56:9 All ye beasts of the *f*, come to
Jer 4:17 As keepers of a *f*, are they
Jer 6:25 Go not forth into the *f*, nor walk
Jer 7:20 beast, and upon the trees of the *f*
Jer 9:22 fall as dung upon the open *f*
Jer 12:4 and the herbs of every *f* wither
Jer 12:9 assemble all the beasts of the *f*
Jer 14:5 the hind also calved in the *f*
Jer 14:18 If I go forth into the *f*, then
Jer 17:3 O my mountain in the *f*, I will
Jer 18:14 cometh from the rock of the *f*
Jer 26:18 Zion shall be plowed like a *f*
Jer 27:6 the beasts of the *f* have I given
Jer 28:14 him the beasts of the *f* also
Jer 32:7 Buy thee my *f* that is in Anathoth
Jer 32:8 LORD, and said unto me, Buy my *f*
Jer 32:9 I bought the *f* of Hanameel my
Jer 32:25 GOD, Buy thee the *f* for money
Jer 35:9 neither have we vineyard, nor *f*
Jer 41:8 for we have treasures in the *f*
Jer 48:33 is taken from the plentiful *f*
Lam 4:9 for want of the fruits of the *f*
Eze 7:15 he that is in the *f* shall die
Eze 16:5 thou wast cast out in the open *f*
Eze 16:7 to multiply as the bud of the *f*
Eze 17:5 and planted it in a fruitful *f*
Eze 17:24 all the trees of the *f* shall know
Eze 20:46 against the forest of the south *f*
Eze 26:6 the *f* shall be slain by the sword
Eze 26:8 the sword thy daughters in the *f*
Eze 29:5 for meat to the beasts of the *f*
Eze 31:4 unto all the trees of the *f*
Eze 31:5 above all the trees of the *f*
Eze 31:6 of the *f* bring forth their young
Eze 31:13 all the beasts of the *f* shall be
Eze 31:15 trees of the *f* fainted for him
Eze 32:4 cast thee forth upon the open *f*
Eze 33:27 him that is in the open *f* will I
Eze 34:5 meat to all the beasts of the *f*
Eze 34:8 meat to every beast of the *f*
Eze 34:27 the tree of the *f* shall yield her
Eze 36:30 tree, and the increase of the *f*
Eze 38:20 heaven, and the beasts of the *f*
Eze 39:4 beasts of the *f* to be devoured
Eze 39:5 Thou shalt fall upon the open *f*
Eze 39:10 shall take no wood out of the *f*
Eze 39:17 fowl, and to every beast of the *f*
Dan 2:38 of men dwell, the beasts of the *f*
Dan 4:12 the beasts of the *f* had shadow
Dan 4:15 in the tender grass of the *f*
Dan 4:21 which the beasts of the *f* dwelt
Dan 4:23 in the tender grass of the *f*
Dan 4:23 be with the beasts of the *f*
Dan 4:25 shall be with the beasts of the *f*
Dan 4:32 shall be with the beasts of the *f*
Hos 2:12 beasts of the *f* shall eat them
Hos 2:18 for them with the beasts of the *f*
Hos 4:3 with the beasts of the *f*
Hos 10:4 hemlock in the furrows of the *f*
Joel 1:10 The *f* is wasted, the land
Joel 1:11 the harvest of the *f* is perished
Joel 1:12 tree, even all the trees of the *f*
Joel 1:19 burned all the trees of the *f*
Joel 1:20 The beasts of the *f* cry also unto
Joel 2:22 Be not afraid, ye beasts of the *f*
Mic 1:6 make Samaria as an heap of the *f*
Mic 3:12 for your sake be plowed as a *f*
Mic 4:10 and thou shalt dwell in the *f*
Zec 10:1 rain, to every one grass in the *f*
Mal 3:11 fruit before the time in the *f*
Mt 6:28 Consider the lilies of the *f*
Mt 6:30 God so clothe the grass of the *f*
Mt 13:24 which sowed good seed in his *f*
Mt 13:27 not thou sow good seed in thy *f*
Mt 13:31 a man took, and sowed in his *f*
Mt 13:36 the parable of the tares of the *f*
Mt 13:38 The *f* is the world
Mt 13:44 is like unto treasure hid in a *f*
Mt 13:44 that he hath, and buyeth that *f*
Mt 24:18 *f* return back to take his clothes
Mt 24:40 Then shall two be in the *f*
Mt 27:7 bought with them the potter's *f*
Mt 27:8 Wherefore that *f* was called
Mt 27:8 The *f* of blood, unto this day
Mt 27:10 And gave them for the potter's *f*
Mk 13:16 let him that is in the *f* not turn
Lk 2:8 shepherds abiding in the *f*
Lk 12:28 grass, which is to day in the *f*
Lk 15:25 Now his elder son was in the *f*

Lk 17:7 and by, when he is come from the f
Lk 17:31 and he that is in the f, let him
Lk 17:36 Two men shall be in the f
Acts 1:18 Now this man purchased a f with
Acts 1:19 insomuch as that f is called in
Acts 1:19 that is to say, The f of blood

### FIELDS
Ex 8:13 of the villages, and out of the f
Lev 14:53 out of the city into the open f
Lev 25:31 counted as the f of the country
Lev 27:22 is not of the f of his possession
Num 16:14 or given us inheritance of f
Num 19:16 slain with a sword in the open f
Num 20:17 we will not pass through the f
Num 21:22 we will not turn into the f
Deut 11:15 grass in thy f for thy cattle
Deut 32:13 might eat the increase of the f
Deut 32:32 of Sodom, and of the f of Gomorrah
Josh 21:12 But the f of the city, and the
Judg 9:27 And they went out into the f
Judg 9:44 all the people that were in the f
1Sa 8:14 And he will take your f, and your
1Sa 22:7 of Jesse give every one of you f
1Sa 25:15 with them, when we were in the f
2Sa 1:21 upon you, nor f of offerings
2Sa 11:11 lord, are encamped in the open f
1Kin 2:26 to Anathoth, unto thine own f
1Kin 16:4 him that dieth of his in the f
2Kin 23:4 Jerusalem in the f of Kidron
1Chr 6:56 But the f of the city, and the
1Chr 16:32 let the f rejoice, and all that is
1Chr 27:25 and over the storehouses in the f
2Chr 31:19 which were in the f of the
Neh 11:25 And for the villages, with their f
Neh 11:30 the f thereof, at Azekah, and in
Neh 12:29 Gilgal, and out of the f of Geba
Neh 12:44 f of the cities the portions of
Job 5:10 and sendeth waters upon the f
Ps 107:37 And sow the f, and plant vineyards,
Ps 132:6 we found it in the f of the wood
Prov 8:26 had not made the earth, nor the f
Prov 23:10 not into the f of the fatherless
Is 16:8 For the f of Heshbon languish, and
Is 32:12 for the teats, for the pleasant f
Jer 6:12 turned unto others, with their f
Jer 8:10 their f to them that shall
Jer 13:27 on the hills in the f
Jer 31:40 all the f unto the brook of
Jer 32:15 Houses and f and vineyards shall be
Jer 32:43 f shall be bought in this land,
Jer 32:44 Men shall buy f for money
Jer 39:10 vineyards and f at the same time
Jer 40:7 of the forces which were in the f
Jer 40:13 of the forces that were in the f
Eze 29:5 thou shalt fall upon the open f
Hos 12:11 as heaps in the furrows of the f
Obad 19 shall possess the f of Ephraim
Obad 19 of Ephraim, and the f of Samaria
Mic 2:2 And they covet f, and take them by
Mic 2:4 away he hath divided our f
Hab 3:17 the f shall yield no meat
Mk 2:23 the corn f on the sabbath day
Lk 6:1 that he went through the corn f
Lk 15:15 sent him into his f to feed swine
Jn 4:35 up your eyes, and look on the f
Jas 5:4 who have reaped down your f

### FIERCE
Gen 49:7 be their anger, for it was f
Ex 32:12 Turn from thy f wrath, and repent
Num 25:4 that the f anger of the LORD may
Num 32:14 to augment yet the f anger of the
Deut 28:50 A nation of f countenance
1Sa 20:34 arose from the table in f anger
1Sa 28:18 his f wrath upon Amalek,
2Chr 28:11 for the f wrath of the LORD is
2Chr 28:13 there is f wrath against Israel
2Chr 29:10 that his f wrath may turn away
Ezr 10:14 until the f wrath of our God for
Job 4:10 lion, and the voice of the f lion
Job 10:16 Thou huntest me as a f lion
Job 28:8 nor the f lion passed by it
Job 41:10 None is so f that dare stir him
Ps 88:16 Thy f wrath goeth over me
Is 7:4 for the f anger of Rezin with
Is 13:9 f anger, to lay the land desolate
Is 13:13 and in the day of his f anger
Is 19:4 a f king shall rule over them,
Is 33:19 Thou shalt not see a f people
Jer 4:8 for the f anger of the LORD is
Jer 4:26 of the LORD, and by his f anger
Jer 12:13 of the f anger of the LORD
Jer 25:37 of the f anger of the LORD
Jer 25:38 and because of his f anger
Jer 30:24 The f anger of the LORD shall not
Jer 49:37 evil upon them, even my f anger
Jer 51:45 soul from the f anger of the LORD
Lam 1:12 me in the day of his f anger
Lam 2:3 He hath cut off in his f anger
Lam 4:11 he hath poured out his f anger
Dan 8:23 a king of f countenance, and
Jonah 3:9 and turn away from his f anger
Hab 1:8 are more f than the evening
Zeph 2:2 before the f anger of the LORD
Zeph 3:8 indignation, even all my f anger
Mt 8:28 out of the tombs, exceeding f
Lk 23:5 And they were the more f, saying,
2Ti 3:3 false accusers, incontinent, f
Jas 3:4 great, and are driven of f winds

### FIERCENESS
Deut 13:17 may turn from the f of his anger
Josh 7:26 turned from the f of his anger
2Kin 23:26 not from the f of his great wrath
2Chr 30:8 that the f of his wrath may turn
Job 39:24 He swalloweth the ground with f
Ps 78:49 cast upon them the f of his anger
Ps 85:3 thyself from the f of thine anger
Jer 25:38 because of the f of the oppressor
Hos 11:9 not execute the f of mine anger
Nah 1:6 can abide in the f of his anger
Rev 16:19 of the wine of the f of his wrath
Rev 19:15 treadeth the winepress of the f

### FIERY
Num 21:6 the LORD sent f serpents among
Num 21:8 unto Moses, Make thee a f serpent
Deut 8:15 wherein were f serpents, and
Deut 33:2 right hand went a f law for them
Ps 21:9 Thou shalt make them as a f oven
Is 14:29 fruit shall be a f flying serpent
Is 30:6 f flying serpent, they will carry
Dan 3:6 the midst of a burning f furnace
Dan 3:11 the midst of a burning f furnace
Dan 3:15 the midst of a burning f furnace
Dan 3:17 us from the burning f furnace
Dan 3:20 them into the burning f furnace
Dan 3:21 midst of the burning f furnace
Dan 3:23 midst of the burning f furnace
Dan 3:26 mouth of the burning f furnace
Dan 7:9 his throne was like the f flame
Dan 7:10 A f stream issued and came forth
Eph 6:16 all the f darts of the wicked
Heb 10:27 f indignation, which shall devour
1Pet 4:12 the f trial which is to try you

### FIFTEEN
Gen 5:10 f years, and begat sons and
Gen 7:20 F cubits upward did the waters
Gen 25:7 an hundred threescore and f years
Ex 27:14 of the gate shall be f cubits
Ex 27:15 side shall be hangings f cubits
Ex 38:14 side of the gate were f cubits
Ex 38:15 hand, were hangings of f cubits
Ex 38:25 f shekels, after the shekel of
Lev 27:7 thy estimation shall be f shekels
Num 31:37 six hundred and threescore and f
Judg 8:10 about f thousand men, all that
2Sa 9:10 Now Ziba had f sons and twenty
2Sa 19:17 his f sons and his twenty servants
1Kin 7:3 on forty five pillars, f in a row
2Kin 14:17 Jehoahaz king of Israel f years
2Kin 20:6 I will add unto thy days f years
2Chr 25:25 Jehoahaz king of Israel f years
Is 38:5 I will add unto thy days f years
Eze 45:12 f shekels, shall be your maneh
Hos 3:2 her to me for f pieces of silver
Jn 11:18 Jerusalem, about f furlongs off
Acts 7:14 kindred, threescore and f souls
Acts 27:28 again, and found it f fathoms
Gal 1:18 Peter, and abode with him f days

### FIFTEENTH
Ex 16:1 on the f day of the second month
Lev 23:6 on the f day of the same month is
Lev 23:34 The f day of this seventh month
Lev 23:39 Also in the f day of the seventh
Num 28:17 in the f day of this month is the
Num 29:12 on the f day of the seventh month
Num 33:3 on the f day of the first month
1Kin 12:32 on the f day of the month, like
1Kin 12:33 the f day of the eighth month
2Kin 14:23 In the f year of Amaziah the son
1Chr 24:14 The f to Bilgah, the sixteenth to
1Chr 25:22 The f to Jeremoth, he, his sons,
2Chr 15:10 in the f year of the reign of Asa
Est 9:18 on the f day of the same they
Est 9:21 the f day of the same, yearly,
Eze 32:17 in the f day of the month, that
Eze 45:25 in the f day of the month, shall
Lk 3:1 Now in the f year of the reign of

### FIFTH
Gen 1:23 and the morning were the f day
Gen 30:17 and bare Jacob the f son
Gen 41:34 take up the f part of the land of
Gen 47:24 give the f part unto Pharaoh
Gen 47:26 Pharaoh should have the f part
Lev 5:16 and shall add the f part thereto
Lev 6:5 shall add the f part more thereto
Lev 19:25 in the f year shall ye eat of the
Lev 22:14 put the f part thereof unto it
Lev 27:13 then he shall add a f part
Lev 27:15 then he shall add the f part of
Lev 27:19 then he shall add the f part of
Lev 27:27 shall add a f part of it thereto
Lev 27:31 add thereto the f part thereof
Num 5:7 and add unto it the f part thereof
Num 7:36 On the f day Shelumiel the son of
Num 29:26 on the f day nine bullocks, two
Num 33:38 in the first day of the f month
Josh 19:24 the f lot came out for the tribe
Judg 19:8 morning on the f day to depart
2Sa 2:23 spear smote him under the f rib
2Sa 3:4 and the f, Shephatiah the son of
2Sa 3:27 smote him there under the f rib
2Sa 4:6 and they smote him under the f rib
2Sa 20:10 smote him therewith in the f rib
1Kin 6:31 posts were a f part of the wall
1Kin 14:25 in the f year of king Rehoboam
2Kin 8:16 in the f year of Joram the son of
2Kin 25:8 And in the f month, on the seventh
1Chr 2:14 the fourth, Raddai the f,
1Chr 3:3 The f, Shephatiah of Abital
1Chr 8:2 Nohah the fourth, and Rapha the f
1Chr 12:10 the fourth, Jeremiah the f
1Chr 24:9 The f to Malchijah, the sixth to
1Chr 25:12 The f to Nethaniah, he, his sons,
1Chr 26:3 Elam the f, Jehohanan the sixth,
1Chr 26:4 the fourth, and Nethaneel the f
1Chr 27:8 The f captain for the f month
2Chr 12:2 that in the f year of king
Ezr 7:8 came to Jerusalem in the f month
Ezr 7:9 on the first day of the f month
Neh 6:5 unto me in like manner the f time
Neh 6:15 f day of the month Elul, in fifty
Jer 1:3 Jerusalem captive in the f month
Jer 28:1 fourth year, and in the f month
Jer 36:9 it came to pass in the f year of
Jer 52:12 Now in the f month, in the tenth
Eze 1:1 in thc f day of the month, as I
Eze 1:2 In the f day of the month
Eze 1:2 which was the f year of king
Eze 8:1 in the f day of the month, as I
Eze 20:1 the seventh year, in the f month
Eze 33:21 in the f day of the month, that
Zec 7:3 Should I weep in the f month
Zec 7:5 ye fasted and mourned in the f
Zec 8:19 month, and the fast of the f
Rev 6:9 And when he had opened the f seal
Rev 9:1 the f angel sounded, and I saw a
Rev 16:10 the f angel poured out his vial
Rev 21:20 The f, sardonyx; the sixth

### FIFTIES
Ex 18:21 rulers of hundreds, rulers of f
Ex 18:25 rulers of hundreds, rulers of f
Deut 1:15 over hundreds, and captains over f
1Sa 8:12 thousands, and captains over f
2Kin 1:14 the former f with their f
Mk 6:40 in ranks, by hundreds, and by f
Lk 9:14 them sit down by f in a company

### FIFTIETH
Lev 25:10 And ye shall hallow the f year
Lev 25:11 shall that f year be unto you
2Kin 15:23 In the f year of Azariah king of
2Kin 15:27 f year of Azariah king of Judah

### FIFTY
Gen 6:15 the breadth of it f cubits
Gen 7:24 the earth an hundred and f days
Gen 8:3 f days the waters were abated
Gen 9:28 flood three hundred and f years

Gen 9:29 Noah were nine hundred and *f* years
Gen 18:24 Peradventure there be *f* righteous
Gen 18:24 the *f* righteous that are therein
Gen 18:26 If I find in Sodom *f* righteous
Gen 18:28 lack five of the *f* righteous
Ex 26:5 *F* loops shalt thou make in the
Ex 26:5 *f* loops shalt thou make in the
Ex 26:6 thou shalt make *f* taches of gold
Ex 26:10 thou shalt make *f* loops on the
Ex 26:10 *f* loops in the edge of the
Ex 26:11 thou shalt make *f* taches of brass
Ex 27:12 shall be hangings of *f* cubits
Ex 27:13 side eastward shall be *f* cubits
Ex 27:18 and the breadth *f* every where
Ex 30:23 *f* shekels, and of sweet calamus
Ex 30:23 calamus two hundred and *f* shekels,
Ex 36:12 *F* loops made he in one curtain,
Ex 36:12 *f* loops made he in the edge of
Ex 36:13 he made *f* taches of gold, and
Ex 36:17 And he made *f* loops upon the
Ex 36:17 *f* loops made he upon the edge of
Ex 36:18 he made *f* taches of brass to
Ex 38:12 side were hangings of *f* cubits
Ex 38:13 the east side eastward *f* cubits
Ex 38:26 thousand and five hundred and *f* men
Lev 23:16 sabbath shall ye number *f* days
Lev 27:3 shall be *f* shekels of silver
Lev 27:16 be valued at *f* shekels of silver
Num 1:23 of the tribe of Simeon, were *f*
Num 1:25 and five thousand six hundred and *f*
Num 1:29 of the tribe of Issachar, were *f*
Num 1:31 of the tribe of Zebulun, were *f*
Num 1:43 of the tribe of Naphtali, were *f*
Num 1:46 thousand and five hundred and *f*
Num 2:6 were numbered thereof, were *f*
Num 2:8 were numbered thereof, were *f*
Num 2:13 were numbered of them, were *f*
Num 2:15 five thousand and six hundred and *f*
Num 2:16 were an hundred thousand and *f*
Num 2:16 one thousand and four hundred and *f*
Num 2:30 were numbered of them, were *f*
Num 2:31 Dan were an hundred thousand and *f*
Num 2:32 thousand and five hundred and *f*
Num 4:3 and upward even until *f* years old
Num 4:23 upward until *f* years old shalt
Num 4:30 upward even unto *f* years old
Num 4:35 and upward even unto *f* years old
Num 4:36 two thousand seven hundred and *f*
Num 4:39 and upward even unto *f* years old
Num 4:43 and upward even unto *f* years old
Num 4:47 and upward even unto *f* years old
Num 8:25 from the age of *f* years they
Num 16:2 *f* princes of the assembly, famous
Num 16:17 censer, two hundred and *f* censers
Num 16:35 *f* men that offered incense
Num 26:10 devoured two hundred and *f* men
Num 26:34 that were numbered of them, *f*
Num 26:47 who were *f* and three thousand and
Num 31:30 thou shalt take one portion of *f*
Num 31:47 half, Moses took one portion of *f*
Num 31:52 seven hundred and *f* shekels
Deut 22:29 father *f* shekels of silver
Josh 7:21 wedge of gold of *f* shekels weight
1Sa 6:19 he smote of the people *f* thousand
2Sa 15:1 and *f* men to run before him
2Sa 24:24 the oxen for *f* shekels of silver
1Kin 1:5 and *f* men to run before him
1Kin 7:2 and the breadth thereof *f* cubits
1Kin 7:6 the length thereof was *f* cubits
1Kin 9:23 Solomon's work, five hundred and *f*
1Kin 10:29 and an horse for an hundred and *f*
1Kin 18:4 and hid them by *f* in a cave
1Kin 18:13 LORD's prophets by *f* in a cave
1Kin 18:19 of Baal four hundred and *f*
1Kin 18:22 are four hundred and *f* men
2Kin 1:9 him a captain of *f* with his *f*
2Kin 1:10 and said to the captain of *f*
2Kin 1:10 heaven, and consume thee and thy *f*
2Kin 1:10 heaven, and consumed him and his *f*
2Kin 1:11 captain of *f* with his *f*
2Kin 1:12 heaven, and consume thee and thy *f*
2Kin 1:12 heaven, and consumed him and his *f*
2Kin 1:13 of the third *f* with his *f*
2Kin 1:13 And the third captain of *f* went up
2Kin 1:13 the life of these *f* thy servants
2Kin 2:7 *f* men of the sons of the prophets
2Kin 2:16 be with thy servants *f* strong men
2Kin 2:17 They sent therefore *f* men
2Kin 13:7 people to Jehoahaz but *f* horsemen
2Kin 15:2 two and *f* years in Jerusalem
2Kin 15:20 of each man *f* shekels of silver,
2Kin 15:25 with him *f* men of the Gileadites
2Kin 21:1 he began to reign, and reigned *f*
1Chr 5:21 of their camels *f* thousand
1Chr 5:21 *f* thousand, and of asses two
1Chr 8:40 and sons' sons, an hundred and *f*
1Chr 9:9 generations, nine hundred and *f*
1Chr 12:33 *f* thousand, which could keep rank
2Chr 1:17 and an horse for an hundred and *f*
2Chr 2:17 *f* thousand and three thousand and
2Chr 3:9 the nails was *f* shekels of gold
2Chr 8:10 officers, even two hundred and *f*
2Chr 8:18 *f* talents of gold, and brought
2Chr 26:3 began to reign, and he reigned *f*
2Chr 33:1 began to reign, and he reigned *f*
Ezr 2:7 of Elam, a thousand two hundred *f*
Ezr 2:14 of Bigvai, two thousand *f*
Ezr 2:15 children of Adin, four hundred *f*
Ezr 2:22 The men of Netophah, *f* and six
Ezr 2:29 The children of Nebo, *f* and two
Ezr 2:30 children of Magbish, an hundred *f*
Ezr 2:31 Elam, a thousand two hundred *f*
Ezr 2:37 children of Immer, a thousand *f*
Ezr 2:60 children of Nekoda, six hundred *f*
Ezr 8:3 of the males an hundred and *f*
Ezr 8:6 of Jonathan, and with him *f* males
Ezr 8:26 *f* talents of silver, and silver
Neh 5:17 *f* of the Jews and rulers, beside
Neh 6:15 fifth day of the month Elul, in *f*
Neh 7:10 children of Arah, six hundred *f*
Neh 7:12 of Elam, a thousand two hundred *f*
Neh 7:20 children of Adin, six hundred *f*
Neh 7:33 The men of the other Nebo, *f*
Neh 7:34 Elam, a thousand two hundred *f*
Neh 7:40 children of Immer, a thousand *f*
Neh 7:70 *f* basons, five hundred and thirty
Est 5:14 gallows be made of *f* cubits high
Est 7:9 also, the gallows *f* cubits high
Is 3:3 The captain of *f*, and the
Eze 40:15 of the inner gate were *f* cubits
Eze 40:21 the length thereof was *f* cubits
Eze 40:25 the length was *f* cubits, and the
Eze 40:29 it was *f* cubits long, and five and
Eze 40:33 it was *f* cubits long, and five and
Eze 40:36 the length was *f* cubits, and the
Eze 42:2 door, and the breadth was *f* cubits
Eze 42:7 the length thereof was *f* cubits
Eze 42:8 in the utter court was *f* cubits
Eze 45:2 *f* cubits round about for the
Eze 48:17 toward the north two hundred and *f*
Eze 48:17 toward the south two hundred and *f*
Eze 48:17 toward the east two hundred and *f*
Eze 48:17 toward the west two hundred and *f*
Hag 2:16 out *f* vessels out of the press
Lk 7:41 hundred pence, and the other *f*
Lk 16:6 and sit down quickly, and write *f*
Jn 8:57 him, Thou art not yet *f* years old
Jn 21:11 of great fishes, an hundred and *f*
Acts 13:20 *f* years, until Samuel the prophet
Acts 19:19 found it *f* thousand pieces of

**FIG**
Gen 3:7 they sewed *f* leaves together, and
Deut 8:8 and *f* trees, and pomegranates
Judg 9:10 And the trees said to the *f* tree
Judg 9:11 But the *f* tree said unto them,
1Kin 4:25 his vine and under his *f* tree
2Kin 18:31 vine, and every one of his *f* tree
Ps 105:33 their vines also and their *f* trees
Prov 27:18 Whoso keepeth the *f* tree shall
Song 2:13 The *f* tree putteth forth her
Is 34:4 as a falling *f* from the *f* tree
Is 36:16 vine, and every one of his *f* tree
Jer 5:17 eat up thy vines and thy *f* trees
Jer 8:13 the vine, nor figs on the *f* tree
Hos 2:12 her *f* trees, whereof she hath
Hos 9:10 in the *f* tree at her first time
Joel 1:7 vine waste, and barked my *f* tree
Joel 1:12 up, and the *f* tree languisheth
Joel 2:22 the *f* tree and the vine do yield
Amos 4:9 your *f* trees and your olive trees
Mic 4:4 his vine and under his *f* tree
Nah 3:12 *f* trees with the firstripe figs
Hab 3:17 Although the *f* tree shall not
Hag 2:19 the *f* tree, and the pomegranate,
Zec 3:10 the vine and under the *f* tree
Mt 21:19 when he saw a *f* tree in the way,
Mt 21:19 presently the *f* tree withered
Mt 21:20 How soon is the *f* tree withered
Mt 21:21 this which is done to the *f* tree
Mt 24:32 Now learn a parable of the *f* tree
Mk 11:13 seeing a *f* tree afar off having
Mk 11:20 they saw the *f* tree dried up from
Mk 11:21 the *f* tree which thou cursedst is
Mk 13:28 Now learn a parable of the *f* tree
Lk 13:6 A certain man had a *f* tree
Lk 13:7 come seeking fruit on this *f* tree
Lk 21:29 Behold the *f* tree, and all the
Jn 1:48 when thou wast under the *f* tree
Jn 1:50 thee, I saw thee under the *f* tree
Jas 3:12 Can the *f* tree, my brethren, bear
Rev 6:13 even as a *f* tree casteth her

**FIGHT**
Ex 1:10 *f* against us, and so get them up
Ex 14:14 The LORD shall *f* for you, and ye
Ex 17:9 out men, and go out, *f* with Amalek
Deut 1:30 before you, he shall *f* for you
Deut 1:41 the LORD, we will go up and *f*
Deut 1:42 unto them, Go not up, neither *f*
Deut 2:32 and all his people, to *f* at Jahaz
Deut 3:22 LORD your God he shall *f* for you
Deut 20:4 to *f* for you against your enemies
Deut 20:10 nigh unto a city to *f* against it
Josh 9:2 to *f* with Joshua and with Israel,
Josh 10:25 your enemies against whom ye *f*
Josh 11:5 of Merom, to *f* against Israel
Josh 19:47 Dan went up to *f* against Leshem
Judg 1:1 first, to *f* against them
Judg 1:3 that we may *f* against the
Judg 1:9 down to *f* against the Canaanites
Judg 8:1 wentest to *f* with the Midianites
Judg 9:38 out, I pray now, and *f* with them
Judg 10:9 Jordan to *f* also against Judah
Judg 10:18 man is he that will begin to *f*
Judg 11:6 that we may *f* with the children
Judg 11:8 *f* against the children of Ammon,
Judg 11:9 If ye bring me home again to *f*
Judg 11:12 come against me to *f* in my land
Judg 11:25 or did he ever *f* against them
Judg 11:32 of Ammon to *f* against them
Judg 12:1 *f* against the children of Ammon
Judg 12:3 unto me this day, to *f* against me
Judg 20:20 array to *f* against them at Gibeah
1Sa 4:9 quit yourselves like men, and *f*
1Sa 8:20 out before us, and *f* our battles
1Sa 13:5 together to *f* with Israel
1Sa 15:18 *f* against them until they be
1Sa 17:9 If he be able to *f* with me
1Sa 17:10 me a man, that we may *f* together
1Sa 17:20 the host was going forth to the *f*
1Sa 17:32 will go and *f* with this Philistine
1Sa 17:33 this Philistine to *f* with him
1Sa 18:17 for me, and *f* the LORD's battles
1Sa 23:1 the Philistines *f* against Keilah
1Sa 28:1 for warfare, to *f* with Israel
1Sa 29:8 that I may not go *f* against the
2Sa 11:20 nigh unto the city when ye did *f*
1Kin 12:21 to *f* against the house of Israel,
1Kin 12:24 nor *f* against your brethren the
1Kin 20:23 but let us *f* against them in the
1Kin 20:25 we will *f* against them in the
1Kin 20:26 up to Aphek, to *f* against Israel
1Kin 22:31 *F* neither with small nor great,
1Kin 22:32 turned aside to *f* against him
2Kin 3:21 were come up to *f* against them
2Kin 10:3 *f* for your master's house
2Kin 19:9 he is come out to *f* against thee
2Chr 11:1 to *f* against Israel, that he
2Chr 11:4 nor *f* against your brethren
2Chr 13:12 *f* ye not against the LORD God of
2Chr 18:30 *F* ye not with small or great,
2Chr 18:31 they compassed about him to *f*
2Chr 20:17 not need to *f* in this battle
2Chr 32:2 purposed to *f* against Jerusalem
2Chr 32:8 to help us, and to *f* our battles
2Chr 35:20 up to *f* against Charchemish by
2Chr 35:22 himself, that he might *f* with him
2Chr 35:22 came to *f* in the valley of
Neh 4:8 to *f* against Jerusalem, and to
Neh 4:14 *f* for your brethren, your sons,
Neh 4:20 our God shall *f* for us
Ps 35:1 *f* against them that *f* against
Ps 56:2 they be many that *f* against me
Ps 144:1 hands to war, and my fingers to *f*
Is 19:2 they shall *f* every one against
Is 29:7 the nations that *f* against Ariel
Is 29:7 even all that *f* against her
Is 29:8 that *f* against mount Zion
Is 30:32 of shaking will he *f* with it

Is 31:4 come down to *f* for mount Zion
Jer 1:19 they shall *f* against thee
Jer 15:20 they shall *f* against thee, but
Jer 21:4 wherewith ye *f* against the king
Jer 21:5 I myself will *f* against you with
Jer 32:5 though ye *f* with the Chaldeans,
Jer 32:24 that *f* against it, because of the
Jer 32:29 that *f* against this city, shall
Jer 33:5 They come to *f* with the Chaldeans
Jer 34:22 and they shall *f* against it
Jer 37:8 *f* against this city, and take it,
Jer 37:10 the Chaldeans that *f* against you
Jer 41:12 went to *f* with Ishmael the son of
Jer 51:30 men of Babylon have forborn to *f*
Dan 10:20 now will I return to *f* with the
Dan 11:11 *f* with him, even with the king of
Zec 10:5 and they shall *f*, because the LORD
Zec 14:3 *f* against those nations, as when
Zec 14:14 Judah also shall *f* at Jerusalem
Jn 18:36 world, then would my servants *f*
Acts 5:39 ye be found even to *f* against God
Acts 23:9 to him, let us not *f* against God
1Cor 9:26 so *f* I, not as one that beateth
1Ti 6:12 *F* the good *f* of faith
2Ti 4:7 I have fought a good *f*, I have
Heb 10:32 endured a great *f* of afflictions
Heb 11:34 made strong, waxed valiant in *f*
Jas 4:2 ye *f* and war, yet ye have not,
Rev 2:16 will *f* against them with the

## FIGS

Num 13:23 of the pomegranates, and of the *f*
Num 20:5 it is no place of seed, or of *f*
1Sa 25:18 and two hundred cakes of *f*
1Sa 30:12 gave him a piece of a cake of *f*
2Kin 20:7 And Isaiah said, Take a lump of *f*
1Chr 12:40 oxen, and meat, meal, cakes of *f*
Neh 13:15 as also wine, grapes, and *f*
Song 2:13 tree putteth forth her green *f*
Is 38:21 said, Let them take a lump of *f*
Jer 8:13 nor *f* on the fig tree, and the
Jer 24:1 two baskets of *f* were set before
Jer 24:2 One basket had very good *f*
Jer 24:2 even like the *f* that are first
Jer 24:2 other basket had very naughty *f*
Jer 24:3 And I said, *F*
Jer 24:3 the good *f*, very good
Jer 24:5 Like these good *f*, so will I
Jer 24:8 And as the evil *f*, which cannot be
Jer 29:17 and will make them like vile *f*
Nah 3:12 fig trees with the firstripe *f*
Mt 7:16 of thorns, or *f* of thistles
Mk 11:13 for the time of *f* was not yet
Lk 6:44 For of thorns men do not gather *f*
Jas 3:12 either a vine, *f*?
Rev 6:13 a fig tree casteth her untimely *f*

## FIGURE

Deut 4:16 image, the similitude of any *f*
Is 44:13 and maketh it after the *f* of a man
Rom 5:14 who is the *f* of him that was to
1Cor 4:6 I have in a *f* transferred to
Heb 9:9 Which was a *f* for the time then
Heb 11:19 also he received him in a *f*
1Pet 3:21 The like *f* whereunto even baptism

## FILL

Gen 1:22 *f* the waters in the seas, and let
Gen 42:25 to *f* their sacks with corn
Gen 44:1 *F* the men's sacks with food, as
Ex 10:6 And they shall *f* thy houses
Ex 16:32 *F* an omer of it to be kept for
Lev 25:19 her fruit, and ye shall eat your *f*
Deut 23:24 thy *f* at thine own pleasure
1Sa 16:1 *f* thine horn with oil, and go, I
1Kin 18:33 *F* four barrels with water, and
Job 8:21 Till he *f* thy mouth with laughing
Job 15:2 *f* his belly with the east wind
Job 20:23 When he is about to *f* his belly
Job 23:4 *f* my mouth with arguments
Job 38:39 or *f* the appetite of the young
Job 41:7 Canst thou *f* his skin with barbed
Ps 81:10 thy mouth wide, and I will *f* it
Ps 83:16 *F* their faces with shame
Ps 110:6 he shall *f* the places with the
Prov 1:13 we shall *f* our houses with spoil
Prov 7:18 let us take our *f* of love until
Prov 8:21 and I will *f* their treasures
Is 8:8 out of his wings shall *f* the
Is 14:21 nor *f* the face of the world with
Is 27:6 *f* the face of the world with
Is 56:12 we will *f* ourselves with strong
Jer 13:13 I will *f* all the inhabitants of
Jer 23:24 Do not I *f* heaven and earth
Jer 33:5 but it is to *f* them with the dead
Jer 51:14 Surely I will *f* thee with men
Eze 3:3 *f* thy bowels with this roll that
Eze 7:19 souls, neither *f* their bowels
Eze 9:7 *f* the courts with the slain
Eze 10:2 *f* thine hand with coals of fire
Eze 24:4 *f* it with the choice bones
Eze 30:11 *f* the land with the slain
Eze 32:4 I will *f* the beasts of the whole
Eze 32:5 *f* the valleys with thy height
Eze 35:8 I will *f* his mountains with his
Zeph 1:9 which *f* their masters' houses
Hag 2:7 I will *f* this house with glory,
Mt 9:16 for that which is put in to *f* it
Mt 15:33 as to *f* so great a multitude
Mt 23:32 *F* ye up then the measure of your
Jn 2:7 *F* the waterpots with water
Rom 15:13 God of hope *f* you with all joy
Eph 4:10 that he might *f* all things
Col 1:24 *f* up that which is behind of the
1Th 2:16 saved, to *f* up their sins alway
Rev 18:6 she hath filled *f* to her double

## FILLED

Gen 6:11 and the earth was *f* with violence
Gen 6:13 for the earth is *f* with violence
Gen 21:19 *f* the bottle with water, and gave
Gen 24:16 *f* her pitcher, and came up
Gen 26:15 them, and *f* them with earth
Ex 1:7 and the land was *f* with them
Ex 2:16 *f* the troughs to water their
Ex 16:12 morning ye shall be *f* with bread
Ex 28:3 whom I have *f* with the spirit of
Ex 31:3 I have *f* him with the spirit of
Ex 35:31 he hath *f* him with the spirit of
Ex 35:35 Them hath he *f* with wisdom of
Ex 40:34 of the LORD *f* the tabernacle
Ex 40:35 of the LORD *f* the tabernacle
Num 14:21 all the earth shall be *f* with the
Deut 26:12 may eat within thy gates, and be *f*
Deut 31:20 *f* themselves, and waxen fat
Josh 9:13 these bottles of wine, which we *f*
1Kin 7:14 and he was *f* with wisdom, and
1Kin 8:10 that the cloud *f* the house of the
1Kin 8:11 LORD had *f* the house of the LORD
1Kin 18:35 he *f* the trench also with water
1Kin 20:27 but the Syrians *f* the country
2Kin 3:17 that valley shall be *f* with water
2Kin 3:20 and the country was *f* with water
2Kin 3:25 cast every man his stone, and *f* it
2Kin 21:16 till he had *f* Jerusalem from one
2Kin 23:14 *f* their places with the bones of
2Kin 24:4 for he *f* Jerusalem with innocent
2Chr 5:13 then the house was *f* with a cloud
2Chr 5:14 the LORD had *f* the house of God
2Chr 7:1 the glory of the LORD *f* the house
2Chr 7:2 the LORD had *f* the LORD's house
2Chr 16:14 bed which was *f* with sweet odours
Ezr 9:11 which have *f* it from one end to
Neh 9:25 so they did eat, and were *f*
Job 3:15 who *f* their houses with silver
Job 16:8 thou hast *f* me with wrinkles,
Job 22:18 Yet he *f* their houses with good
Ps 38:7 For my loins are *f* with a
Ps 71:8 Let my mouth be *f* with thy praise
Ps 72:19 whole earth be *f* with his glory
Ps 78:29 So they did eat, and were well *f*
Ps 80:9 take deep root, and it *f* the land
Ps 104:28 thine hand, they are *f* with good
Ps 123:3 are exceedingly *f* with contempt
Ps 123:4 Our soul is exceedingly *f* with
Ps 126:2 was our mouth *f* with laughter
Prov 1:31 be *f* with their own devices
Prov 3:10 shall thy barns be *f* with plenty
Prov 5:10 strangers be *f* with thy wealth
Prov 12:21 wicked shall be *f* with mischief
Prov 14:14 shall be *f* with his own ways
Prov 18:20 of his lips shall he be *f*
Prov 20:17 his mouth shall be *f* with gravel
Prov 24:4 chambers be *f* with all precious
Prov 25:16 thee, lest thou be *f* therewith
Prov 30:16 earth that is not *f* with water
Prov 30:22 and a fool when he is *f* with meat
Eccl 1:8 nor the ear *f* with hearing
Eccl 6:3 and his soul be not *f* with good
Eccl 6:7 and yet the appetite is not *f*
Song 5:2 for my head is *f* with dew
Is 6:1 up, and his train *f* the temple
Is 6:4 and the house was *f* with smoke
Is 21:3 are my loins *f* with pain
Is 33:5 he hath *f* Zion with judgment and
Is 34:6 sword of the LORD is *f* with blood
Is 43:24 neither hast thou *f* me with the
Is 65:20 old man that hath not *f* his days
Jer 13:12 Every bottle shall be *f* with wine
Jer 13:12 every bottle shall be *f* with wine
Jer 15:17 for thou hast *f* me with
Jer 16:18 they have *f* mine inheritance with
Jer 19:4 have *f* this place with the blood
Jer 41:9 *f* it with them that were slain
Jer 46:12 shame, and thy cry hath *f* the land
Jer 51:5 though their land was *f* with sin
Jer 51:34 he hath *f* his belly with my
Lam 3:15 He hath *f* me with bitterness, he
Lam 3:30 he is *f* full with reproach
Eze 8:17 for they have *f* the land with
Eze 10:3 the cloud *f* the inner court
Eze 10:4 the house was *f* with the cloud,
Eze 11:6 ye have *f* the streets thereof
Eze 23:33 Thou shalt be *f* with drunkenness
Eze 28:16 of thy merchandise they have *f*
Eze 36:38 cities be *f* with flocks of men
Eze 39:20 Thus ye shall be *f* at my table
Eze 43:5 the glory of the LORD *f* the house
Eze 44:4 the LORD *f* the house of the LORD
Dan 2:35 mountain, and *f* the whole earth
Hos 13:6 to their pasture, so were they *f*
Hos 13:6 they were *f*, and their heart was
Nah 2:12 *f* his holes with prey, and his
Hab 2:14 For the earth shall be *f* with the
Hab 2:16 Thou art *f* with shame for glory
Hag 1:6 but ye are not *f* with drink
Zec 9:13 *f* the bow with Ephraim, and raised
Zec 9:15 and they shall be *f* like bowls
Mt 5:6 for they shall be *f*
Mt 14:20 And they did all eat, and were *f*
Mt 15:37 And they did all eat, and were *f*
Mt 27:48 *f* it with vinegar, and put it on a
Mk 2:21 else the new piece that *f* it up
Mk 6:42 And they did all eat, and were *f*
Mk 7:27 her, Let the children first be *f*
Mk 8:8 So they did eat, and were *f*
Mk 15:36 *f* a spunge full of vinegar, and
Lk 1:15 he shall be *f* with the Holy Ghost
Lk 1:41 Elisabeth was *f* with the Holy
Lk 1:53 He hath *f* the hungry with good
Lk 1:67 was *f* with the Holy Ghost
Lk 2:40 strong in spirit, *f* with wisdom
Lk 3:5 Every valley shall be *f*, and every
Lk 4:28 these things, were *f* with wrath,
Lk 5:7 *f* both the ships, so that they
Lk 5:26 were *f* with fear, saying, We have
Lk 6:11 And they were *f* with madness
Lk 6:21 for ye shall be *f*
Lk 8:23 they were *f* with water, and were
Lk 9:17 And they did eat, and were all *f*
Lk 14:23 come in, that my house may be *f*
Lk 15:16 he would fain have *f* his belly
Jn 2:7 they *f* them up to the brim
Jn 6:12 When they were *f*, he said unto
Jn 6:13 *f* twelve baskets with the
Jn 6:26 did eat of the loaves, and were *f*
Jn 12:3 the house was *f* with the odour of
Jn 16:6 you, sorrow hath *f* your heart
Jn 19:29 they *f* a spunge with vinegar, and
Acts 2:2 it *f* all the house where they
Acts 2:4 they were all *f* with the Holy
Acts 3:10 they were *f* with wonder and
Acts 4:8 *f* with the Holy Ghost, said unto
Acts 4:31 they were all *f* with the Holy
Acts 5:3 why hath Satan *f* thine heart to
Acts 5:17 and were *f* with indignation,
Acts 5:28 ye have *f* Jerusalem with your
Acts 9:17 and be *f* with the Holy Ghost
Acts 13:9 *f* with the Holy Ghost, set his
Acts 13:45 multitudes, they were *f* with envy
Acts 13:52 And the disciples were *f* with joy
Acts 19:29 whole city was *f* with confusion
Rom 1:29 Being *f* with all unrighteousness,
Rom 15:14 *f* with all knowledge, able also
Rom 15:24 I be somewhat *f* with your company
2Cor 7:4 I am *f* with comfort, I am
Eph 3:19 that ye might be *f* with all the
Eph 5:18 but be *f* with the Spirit
Phil 1:11 Being *f* with the fruits of
Col 1:9 to desire that ye might be *f* with
2Ti 1:4 tears, that I may be *f* with joy
Jas 2:16 in peace, be ye warmed and *f*

Rev 8:5 *f* it with fire of the altar, and
Rev 15:1 for in them is *f* up the wrath of
Rev 15:8 the temple was *f* with smoke from
Rev 18:6 she hath *f* fill to her double
Rev 19:21 the fowls were *f* with their flesh

**FILLETH**
Job 9:18 breath, but *f* me with bitterness
Ps 84:6 the rain also *f* the pools
Ps 107:9 *f* the hungry soul with goodness
Ps 129:7 the mower *f* not his hand
Ps 147:14 *f* thee with the finest of the
Eph 1:23 fulness of him that *f* all in all

**FILLETS**
Ex 27:10 their *f* shall be of silver
Ex 27:11 the pillars and their *f* of silver
Ex 36:38 chapiters and their *f* with gold
Ex 38:10 pillars and their *f* were of silver
Ex 38:11 the pillars and their *f* of silver
Ex 38:12 the pillars and their *f* of silver
Ex 38:17 the pillars and their *f* of silver
Ex 38:19 chapiters and their *f* of silver

**FILTH**
Is 4:4 the *f* of the daughters of Zion
Nah 3:6 will cast abominable *f* upon thee
1Cor 4:13 we are made as the *f* of the world
1Pet 3:21 away of the *f* of the flesh

**FILTHINESS**
2Chr 29:5 carry forth the *f* out of the holy
Ezr 6:21 the *f* of the heathen of the land
Ezr 9:11 the *f* of the people of the lands
Prov 30:12 and yet is not washed from their *f*
Is 28:8 all tables are full of vomit and *f*
Lam 1:9 Her *f* is in her skirts
Eze 16:36 Because thy *f* was poured out, and
Eze 22:15 and will consume thy *f* out of thee
Eze 24:11 that the *f* of it may be molten in
Eze 24:13 In thy *f* is lewdness
Eze 24:13 not be purged from thy *f* any more
Eze 36:25 from all your *f*, and from all your
2Cor 7:1 ourselves from all *f* of the flesh
Eph 5:4 Neither *f*, nor foolish talking,
Jas 1:21 Wherefore lay apart all *f*
Rev 17:4 and *f* of her fornication

**FILTHY**
Job 15:16 *f* is man, which drinketh iniquity
Ps 14:3 they are all together become *f*
Ps 53:3 they are altogether become *f*
Is 64:6 our righteousnesses are as *f* rags
Zeph 3:1 Woe to her that is *f* and polluted,
Zec 3:3 was clothed with *f* garments
Zec 3:4 Take away the *f* garments from him
Col 3:8 *f* communication out of your mouth
1Ti 3:3 no striker, not greedy of *f* lucre
1Ti 3:8 much wine, not greedy of *f* lucre
Titus 1:7 no striker, not given to *f* lucre
Titus 1:11 ought not, for *f* lucre's sake
1Pet 5:2 not for *f* lucre, but of a ready
2Pet 2:7 vexed with the *f* conversation of
Jude 8 Likewise also these *f* dreamers
Rev 22:11 and he which is *f*, let him be
Rev 22:11 let him be *f* still

**FINALLY**
2Cor 13:11 *F*, brethren, farewell
Eph 6:10 *F*, my brethren, be strong in the
Phil 3:1 *F*, my brethren, rejoice in the
Phil 4:8 *F*, brethren, whatsoever things
2Th 3:1 *F*, brethren, pray for us, that
1Pet 3:8 *F*, be ye all of one mind, having

**FIND**
Gen 18:26 If I *f* in Sodom fifty righteous
Gen 18:28 If I *f* there forty and five, I
Gen 18:30 not do it, if I *f* thirty there
Gen 19:11 wearied themselves to *f* the door
Gen 32:5 that I may *f* grace in thy sight
Gen 32:19 ye speak unto Esau, when ye *f* him
Gen 33:8 These are to *f* grace in the sight
Gen 33:15 let me *f* grace in the sight of my
Gen 34:11 Let me *f* grace in your eyes, and
Gen 38:22 to Judah, and said, I cannot *f* her
Gen 41:38 Can we *f* such a one as this is, a
Gen 47:25 let us *f* grace in the sight of my
Ex 5:11 get you straw where ye can *f* it
Ex 16:25 ye shall not *f* it in the field
Ex 33:13 that I may *f* grace in thy sight
Num 32:23 be sure your sin will *f* you out
Num 35:27 the revenger of blood *f* him
Deut 4:29 LORD thy God, thou shalt *f* him
Deut 22:23 a man *f* her in the city, and lie
Deut 22:25 But if a man *f* a betrothed damsel
Deut 22:28 If a man *f* a damsel that is a
Deut 24:1 that she *f* no favour in his eyes
Deut 28:65 nations shalt thou *f* no ease
Judg 9:33 to them as thou shalt *f* occasion
Judg 14:12 *f* it out, then I will give you
Judg 17:8 sojourn where he could *f* a place
Judg 17:9 to sojourn where I may *f* a place
Ruth 1:9 LORD grant you that ye may *f* rest
Ruth 2:2 in whose sight I shall *f* grace
Ruth 2:13 Let me *f* favour in thy sight, my
1Sa 1:18 handmaid *f* grace in thy sight
1Sa 9:13 city, ye shall straightway *f* him
1Sa 9:13 about this time ye shall *f* him
1Sa 10:2 then thou shalt *f* two men by
1Sa 20:21 lad, saying, Go, *f* out the arrows
1Sa 20:36 *f* out now the arrows which I
1Sa 23:17 Saul my father shall not *f* thee
1Sa 24:19 For if a man *f* his enemy, will he
1Sa 25:8 young men *f* favour in thine eyes
2Sa 15:25 if I shall *f* favour in the eyes
2Sa 16:4 that I may *f* grace in thy sight
2Sa 17:20 had sought and could not *f* them
1Kin 18:5 peradventure we may *f* grass to
1Kin 18:12 and tell Ahab, and he cannot *f* thee
2Chr 2:14 to *f* out every device which shall
2Chr 20:16 ye shall *f* them at the end of the
2Chr 30:9 your children shall *f* compassion
2Chr 32:4 of Assyria come, and *f* much water
Ezr 4:15 so shalt thou *f* in the book of
Ezr 7:16 gold that thou canst *f* in all the
Job 3:22 glad, when they can *f* the grave
Job 11:7 Canst thou by searching *f* out God
Job 11:7 canst thou *f* out the Almighty
Job 17:10 for I cannot *f* one wise man among
Job 23:3 that I knew where I might *f* him
Job 34:11 cause every man to *f* according to
Job 37:23 the Almighty, we cannot *f* him out
Ps 10:15 his wickedness till thou *f* none
Ps 17:3 hast tried me, and shalt *f* nothing
Ps 21:8 Thine hand shall *f* out all thine
Ps 21:8 thy right hand shall *f* out those
Ps 132:5 Until I *f* out a place for the
Prov 1:13 We shall *f* all precious substance
Prov 1:28 me early, but they shall not *f* me
Prov 2:5 LORD, and *f* the knowledge of God
Prov 3:4 So shalt thou *f* favour and good
Prov 4:22 are life unto those that *f* them
Prov 8:9 and right to them that *f* knowledge
Prov 8:12 and *f* out knowledge of witty
Prov 8:17 that seek me early shall *f* me
Prov 16:20 a matter wisely shall *f* good
Prov 19:8 understanding shall *f* good
Prov 20:6 but a faithful man who can *f*
Prov 28:23 shall *f* more favour than he that
Prov 31:10 Who can *f* a virtuous woman
Eccl 3:11 so that no man can *f* out the work
Eccl 7:14 man should *f* nothing after him
Eccl 7:24 exceeding deep, who can *f* it out
Eccl 7:26 I *f* more bitter than death the
Eccl 7:27 one by one, to *f* out the account
Eccl 7:28 yet my soul seeketh, but I *f* not
Eccl 8:17 that a man cannot *f* out the work
Eccl 8:17 it out, yet he shall not *f* it
Eccl 8:17 yet shall he not be able to *f* it
Eccl 11:1 for thou shalt *f* it after many
Eccl 12:10 sought to *f* out acceptable words
Song 5:6 sought him, but I could not *f* him
Song 5:8 if ye *f* my beloved, that ye tell
Song 8:1 when I should *f* thee without
Is 34:14 *f* for herself a place of rest
Is 41:12 seek them, and shalt not *f* them
Is 58:3 day of your fast ye *f* pleasure
Jer 2:24 in her month they shall *f* her
Jer 5:1 places thereof, if ye can *f* a man
Jer 6:16 ye shall *f* rest for your souls
Jer 10:18 them, that they may *f* it so
Jer 29:13 *f* me, when ye shall search for me
Jer 45:3 in my sighing, and I *f* no rest
Lam 1:6 like harts that *f* no pasture
Lam 2:9 her prophets also *f* no vision
Dan 6:4 princes sought to *f* occasion
Dan 6:4 but they could *f* none occasion
Dan 6:5 We shall not *f* any occasion
Dan 6:5 except we *f* it against him
Hos 2:6 that she shall not *f* her paths
Hos 2:7 seek them, but shall not *f* them
Hos 5:6 but they shall not *f* him
Hos 12:8 in all my labours they shall *f*
Amos 8:12 of the LORD, and shall not *f* it
Mt 7:7 seek, and ye shall *f*
Mt 7:14 life, and few there be that *f* it
Mt 10:39 his life for my sake shall *f* it
Mt 11:29 ye shall *f* rest unto your souls
Mt 16:25 his life for my sake shall *f* it
Mt 17:27 thou shalt *f* a piece of money
Mt 18:13 And if so be that he *f* it, verily
Mt 21:2 ye shall *f* an ass tied, and a colt
Mt 22:9 and as many as ye shall *f*
Mt 24:46 when he cometh shall *f* so doing
Mk 11:2 ye shall *f* a colt tied, whereon
Mk 11:13 he might *f* any thing thereon
Mk 13:36 coming suddenly he *f* you sleeping
Lk 2:12 Ye shall *f* the babe wrapped in
Lk 5:19 when they could not *f* by what way
Lk 6:7 that they might *f* an accusation
Lk 11:9 seek, and ye shall *f*
Lk 12:37 when he cometh shall *f* watching
Lk 12:38 *f* them so, blessed are those
Lk 12:43 when he cometh shall *f* so doing
Lk 13:7 fruit on this fig tree, and *f* none
Lk 15:4 that which is lost, until he *f* it
Lk 15:8 and seek diligently till she *f* it
Lk 18:8 shall he *f* faith on the earth
Lk 19:30 entering ye shall *f* a colt tied
Lk 19:48 could not *f* what they might do
Lk 23:4 people, I *f* no fault in this man
Jn 7:34 shall seek me, and shall not *f* me
Jn 7:35 he go, that we shall not *f* him
Jn 7:36 shall seek me, and shall not *f* me
Jn 10:9 shall go in and out, and *f* pasture
Jn 18:38 I *f* in him no fault at all
Jn 19:4 may know that I *f* no fault in him
Jn 19:6 for I *f* no fault in him
Jn 21:6 side of the ship, and ye shall *f*
Acts 7:46 desired to *f* a tabernacle for the
Acts 17:27 *f* him, though he be not far from
Acts 23:9 saying, We *f* no evil in this man
Rom 7:18 that which is good I *f* not
Rom 7:21 I *f* then a law, that, when I
Rom 9:19 unto me, Why doth he yet *f* fault
2Cor 9:4 *f* you unprepared, we (that we say
2Cor 12:20 I shall not *f* you such as I would
2Ti 1:18 *f* mercy of the Lord in that day
Heb 4:16 *f* grace to help in time of need
Rev 9:6 men seek death, and shall not *f* it
Rev 18:14 thou shalt *f* them no more at all

**FINDETH**
Gen 4:14 every one that *f* me shall slay me
Job 33:10 he *f* occasions against me, he
Ps 119:162 word, as one that *f* great spoil
Prov 3:13 Happy is the man that *f* wisdom
Prov 8:35 For whoso *f* me *f* life
Prov 14:6 seeketh wisdom, and *f* it not
Prov 17:20 hath a froward heart *f* no good
Prov 18:22 Whoso *f* a wife *f* a good
Prov 21:10 his neighbour *f* no favour in his
Prov 21:21 righteousness and mercy *f* life
Eccl 9:10 Whatsoever thy hand *f* to do
Lam 1:3 among the heathen, she *f* no rest
Hos 14:3 in thee the fatherless *f* mercy
Mt 7:8 and he that seeketh *f*
Mt 10:39 He that *f* his life shall lose it
Mt 12:43 places, seeking rest, and *f* none
Mt 12:44 is come, he *f* it empty, swept, and
Mt 26:40 *f* them asleep, and saith unto
Mk 14:37 *f* them sleeping, and saith unto
Lk 11:10 and he that seeketh *f*
Lk 11:25 he *f* it swept and garnished
Jn 1:41 He first *f* his own brother Simon,
Jn 1:43 *f* Philip, and saith unto him,
Jn 1:45 Philip *f* Nathanael, and saith unto
Jn 5:14 Afterward Jesus *f* him in the

**FINDING**
Gen 4:15 lest any *f* him should kill him
Job 9:10 doeth great things past *f* out
Is 58:13 nor *f* thine own pleasure, nor
Lk 11:24 *f* none, he saith, I will return
Acts 4:21 *f* nothing how they might punish
Acts 19:1 and *f* certain disciples,
Acts 21:2 *f* a ship sailing over unto
Acts 21:4 *f* disciples, we tarried there
Rom 11:33 judgments, and his ways past *f* out
Heb 8:8 For *f* fault with them, he saith,

**FINE**
Gen 18:6 quickly three measures of *f* meal
Gen 41:42 him in vestures of *f* linen
Ex 25:4 and *f* linen, and goats' hair,

Ex 26:1 ten curtains of *f* twined linen
Ex 26:31 *f* twined linen of cunning work
Ex 26:36 *f* twined linen, wrought with
Ex 27:9 of *f* twined linen of an hundred
Ex 27:16 *f* twined linen, wrought with
Ex 27:18 five cubits of *f* twined linen
Ex 28:5 and purple, and scarlet, and *f* linen
Ex 28:6 *f* twined linen, with cunning work
Ex 28:8 and scarlet, and *f* twined linen
Ex 28:15 of *f* twined linen, shalt thou
Ex 28:39 embroider the coat of *f* linen
Ex 28:39 shalt make the mitre of *f* linen
Ex 35:6 and *f* linen, and goats' hair,
Ex 35:23 *f* linen, and goats' hair, and red
Ex 35:25 and of scarlet, and of *f* linen
Ex 35:35 in *f* linen, and of the weaver,
Ex 36:8 ten curtains of *f* twined linen
Ex 36:35 and scarlet, and *f* twined linen
Ex 36:37 *f* twined linen, of needlework
Ex 38:9 the court were of *f* twined linen
Ex 38:16 about were of *f* twined linen
Ex 38:18 and scarlet, and *f* twined linen
Ex 38:23 purple, and in scarlet, and *f* linen
Ex 39:2 and scarlet, and *f* twined linen
Ex 39:3 in the scarlet, and in the *f* linen
Ex 39:5 and scarlet, and *f* twined linen
Ex 39:8 and scarlet, and *f* twined linen
Ex 39:27 they made coats of *f* linen of
Ex 39:28 And a mitre of *f* linen
Ex 39:28 and goodly bonnets of *f* linen
Ex 39:28 linen breeches of *f* twined linen
Ex 39:29 a girdle of *f* twined linen, and
Lev 2:1 his offering shall be of *f* flour
Lev 2:4 cakes of *f* flour mingled with oil
Lev 2:5 it shall be of *f* flour unleavened
Lev 2:7 shall be made of *f* flour with oil
Lev 5:11 of *f* flour for a sin offering
Lev 6:20 of *f* flour for a meat offering
Lev 7:12 with oil, of *f* flour, fried
Lev 14:10 three tenth deals of *f* flour for
Lev 14:21 one tenth deal of *f* flour mingled
Lev 23:13 deals of *f* flour mingled with oil
Lev 23:17 they shall be of *f* flour
Lev 24:5 And thou shalt take *f* flour
Num 6:15 cakes of *f* flour mingled with oil
Num 7:13 both of them were full of *f* flour
Num 7:19 both of them full of *f* flour
Num 7:25 both of them full of *f* flour
Num 7:31 both of them full of *f* flour
Num 7:37 both of them full of *f* flour
Num 7:43 both of them full of *f* flour
Num 7:49 both of them full of *f* flour
Num 7:55 both of them full of *f* flour
Num 7:61 both of them full of *f* flour
Num 7:67 both of them full of *f* flour
Num 7:73 both of them full of *f* flour
Num 7:79 both of them full of *f* flour
Num 8:8 even *f* flour mingled with oil, and
1Kin 4:22 was thirty measures of *f* flour
2Kin 7:1 of *f* flour be sold for a shekel
2Kin 7:16 So a measure of *f* flour was sold
2Kin 7:18 a measure of *f* flour for a shekel
1Chr 4:21 of them that wrought *f* linen
1Chr 9:29 the *f* flour, and the wine, and the
1Chr 15:27 clothed with a robe of *f* linen
1Chr 23:29 for the *f* flour for meat offering
2Chr 2:14 in *f* linen, and in crimson
2Chr 3:5 which he overlaid with *f* gold
2Chr 3:8 and he overlaid it with *f* gold
2Chr 3:14 *f* linen, and wrought cherubims
Ezr 8:27 and two vessels of *f* copper
Est 1:6 fastened with cords of *f* linen
Est 8:15 and with a garment of *f* linen
Job 28:1 a place for gold where they *f* it
Job 28:17 shall not be for jewels of *f* gold
Job 31:24 hope, or have said to the *f* gold
Ps 19:10 than gold, yea, than much *f* gold
Ps 119:127 yea, above *f* gold
Prov 3:14 and the gain thereof than *f* gold
Prov 7:16 works, with *f* linen of Egypt
Prov 8:19 than gold, yea, than *f* gold
Prov 25:12 of gold, and an ornament of *f* gold
Prov 31:24 She maketh *f* linen, and selleth it
Song 5:11 His head is as the most *f* gold
Song 5:15 set upon sockets of *f* gold
Is 3:23 the *f* linen, and the hoods, and the
Is 13:12 a man more precious than *f* gold
Is 19:9 Moreover they that work in *f* flax
Lam 4:1 how is the most *f* gold changed
Lam 4:2 of Zion, comparable to *f* gold
Eze 16:10 I girded thee about with *f* linen
Eze 16:13 and thy raiment was of *f* linen
Eze 16:13 thou didst eat *f* flour, and honey,
Eze 16:19 *f* flour, and oil, and honey,
Eze 27:7 *F* linen with broidered work from
Eze 27:16 *f* linen, and coral, and agate
Eze 46:14 oil, to temper with the *f* flour
Dan 2:32 This image's head was of *f* gold
Dan 10:5 were girded with *f* gold of Uphaz
Zec 9:3 *f* gold as the mire of the streets
Mk 15:46 And he bought *f* linen, and took him
Lk 16:19 *f* linen, and fared sumptuously
Rev 1:15 And his feet like unto *f* brass
Rev 2:18 and his feet are like *f* brass
Rev 18:12 *f* linen, and purple, and silk, and
Rev 18:13 *f* flour, and wheat, and beasts, and
Rev 18:16 city, that was clothed in *f* linen
Rev 19:8 she should be arrayed in *f* linen
Rev 19:8 for the *f* linen is the
Rev 19:14 white horses, clothed in *f* linen

**FINGER**

Ex 8:19 Pharaoh, This is the *f* of God
Ex 29:12 the horns of the altar with thy *f*
Ex 31:18 stone, written with the *f* of God
Lev 4:6 shall dip his *f* in the blood
Lev 4:17 dip his *f* in some of the blood
Lev 4:25 of the sin offering with his *f*
Lev 4:30 of the blood thereof with his *f*
Lev 4:34 of the sin offering with his *f*
Lev 8:15 the altar round about with his *f*
Lev 9:9 and he dipped his *f* in the blood
Lev 14:16 *f* in the oil that is in his left
Lev 14:16 his *f* seven times before the LORD
Lev 14:27 shall sprinkle with his right *f*
Lev 16:14 sprinkle it with his *f* upon the
Lev 16:14 the blood with his *f* seven times
Lev 16:19 upon it with his *f* seven times
Num 19:4 take of her blood with his *f*
Deut 9:10 stone written with the *f* of God
1Kin 12:10 My little *f* shall be thicker than
2Chr 10:10 My little *f* shall be thicker than
Is 58:9 yoke, the putting forth of the *f*
Lk 11:20 But if I with the *f* of God cast
Lk 16:24 may dip the tip of his *f* in water
Jn 8:6 with his *f* wrote on the ground,
Jn 20:25 put my *f* into the print of the
Jn 20:27 he to Thomas, Reach hither thy *f*

**FINGERS**

2Sa 21:20 that had on every hand six *f*
1Chr 20:6 a man of great stature, whose *f*
Ps 8:3 thy heavens, the work of thy *f*
Ps 144:1 my hands to war, and my *f* to fight
Prov 6:13 his feet, he teacheth with his *f*
Prov 7:3 Bind them upon thy *f*, write them
Song 5:5 my *f* with sweet smelling myrrh,
Is 2:8 that which their own *f* have made
Is 17:8 that which his *f* have made
Is 59:3 blood, and your *f* with iniquity
Jer 52:21 the thickness thereof was four *f*
Dan 5:5 hour came forth *f* of a man's hand
Mt 23:4 not move them with one of their *f*
Mk 7:33 put his *f* into his ears, and he
Lk 11:46 the burdens with one of your *f*

**FINISH**

Gen 6:16 in a cubit shalt thou *f* it above
Dan 9:24 to *f* the transgression, and to
Zec 4:9 his hands shall also *f* it
Lk 14:28 he have sufficient to *f* it
Lk 14:29 and is not able to *f* it, all that
Lk 14:30 to build, and was not able to *f*
Jn 4:34 that sent me, and to *f* his work
Jn 5:36 the Father hath given me to *f*
Acts 20:24 so that I might *f* my course with
Rom 9:28 For he will *f* the work, and cut it
2Cor 8:6 so he would also *f* in you the

**FINISHED**

Gen 2:1 the heavens and the earth were *f*
Ex 39:32 of the tent of the congregation *f*
Ex 40:33 So Moses *f* the work
Deut 31:24 law in a book, until they were *f*
Josh 4:10 until every thing was *f* that the
Ruth 3:18 until he have *f* the thing this
1Kin 6:9 So he built the house, and *f* it
1Kin 6:14 Solomon built the house, and *f* it
1Kin 6:22 until he had *f* all the house
1Kin 6:38 was the house *f* throughout all
1Kin 7:1 years, and he *f* all his house
1Kin 7:22 so was the work of the pillars *f*
1Kin 9:1 when Solomon had *f* the building
1Kin 9:25 So he *f* the house
1Chr 27:24 began to number, but he *f* not
1Chr 28:20 until thou hast *f* all the work
2Chr 4:11 Huram *f* the work that he was to
2Chr 5:1 for the house of the LORD was *f*
2Chr 7:11 Thus Solomon *f* the house of the
2Chr 8:16 of the LORD, and until it was *f*
2Chr 24:14 And when they had *f* it, they
2Chr 29:28 until the burnt offering was *f*
2Chr 31:1 Now when all this was *f*, all
2Chr 31:7 *f* them in the seventh month
Ezr 5:16 in building, and yet it is not *f*
Ezr 6:14 and *f* it, according to the
Ezr 6:15 this house was *f* on the third day
Neh 6:15 So the wall was *f* in the twenty
Dan 5:26 numbered thy kingdom, and *f* it
Dan 12:7 all these things shall be *f*
Mt 13:53 when Jesus had *f* these parables
Mt 19:1 when Jesus had *f* these sayings
Mt 26:1 when Jesus had *f* all these
Jn 17:4 I have *f* the work which thou
Jn 19:30 the vinegar, he said, It is *f*
Acts 21:7 when we had *f* our course from
2Ti 4:7 I have *f* my course, I have kept
Heb 4:3 although the works were *f* from
Jas 1:15 and sin, when it is *f*, bringeth
Rev 10:7 the mystery of God should be *f*
Rev 11:7 they shall have *f* their testimony
Rev 20:5 until the thousand years were *f*

**FINS**

Lev 11:9 whatsoever hath *f* and scales in
Lev 11:10 And all that have not *f* and scales
Lev 11:12 Whatsoever hath no *f* nor scales
Deut 14:9 all that have *f* and scales shall
Deut 14:10 And whatsoever hath not *f* and

**FIR**

2Sa 6:5 of instruments made of *f* wood
1Kin 5:8 cedar, and concerning timber of *f*
1Kin 5:10 *f* trees according to all his
1Kin 6:15 of the house with planks of *f*
1Kin 6:34 And the two doors were of *f* tree
1Kin 9:11 *f* trees, and with gold, according
2Kin 19:23 the choice *f* trees thereof
2Chr 2:8 *f* trees, and algum trees, out of
2Chr 3:5 house he cieled with *f* tree
Ps 104:17 the *f* trees are her house
Song 1:17 are cedar, and our rafters of *f*
Is 14:8 the *f* trees rejoice at thee, and
Is 37:24 the choice *f* trees thereof
Is 41:19 will set in the desert the *f* tree
Is 55:13 thorn shall come up the *f* tree
Is 60:13 the *f* tree, the pine tree, and the
Eze 27:5 ship boards of *f* trees of Senir
Eze 31:8 the *f* trees were not like his
Hos 14:8 I am like a green *f* tree
Nah 2:3 the *f* trees shall be terribly
Zec 11:2 Howl, *f* tree

**FIRE**

Gen 19:24 *f* from the LORD out of heaven
Gen 22:6 and he took the *f* in his hand
Gen 22:7 And he said, Behold the *f* and the
Ex 3:2 of *f* out of the midst of a bush
Ex 3:2 behold, the bush burned with *f*
Ex 9:23 the *f* ran along upon the ground
Ex 9:24 *f* mingled with the hail, very
Ex 12:8 flesh in that night, roast with *f*
Ex 12:9 all with water, but roast with *f*
Ex 12:10 the morning ye shall burn with *f*
Ex 13:21 and by night in a pillar of *f*
Ex 13:22 day, nor the pillar of *f* by night
Ex 14:24 Egyptians through the pillar of *f*
Ex 19:18 the LORD descended upon it in *f*
Ex 22:6 If *f* break out, and catch in
Ex 22:6 he that kindled the *f* shall
Ex 24:17 *f* on the top of the mount in the
Ex 29:14 thou burn with *f* without the camp
Ex 29:18 offering made by *f* unto the LORD
Ex 29:25 offering made by *f* unto the LORD
Ex 29:34 shalt burn the remainder with *f*
Ex 29:41 offering made by *f* unto the LORD
Ex 30:20 offering made by *f* unto the LORD
Ex 32:20 had made, and burnt it in the *f*
Ex 32:24 then I cast it into the *f*
Ex 35:3 Ye shall kindle no *f* throughout
Ex 40:38 *f* was on it by night, in the
Lev 1:7 priest shall put *f* upon the altar
Lev 1:7 lay the wood in order upon the *f*
Lev 1:8 on the *f* which is upon the altar

Lev 1:9 sacrifice, an offering made by *f*
Lev 1:12 on the *f* which is upon the altar
Lev 1:13 sacrifice, an offering made by *f*
Lev 1:17 upon the wood that is upon the *f*
Lev 1:17 sacrifice, an offering made by *f*
Lev 2:2 to be an offering made by *f*
Lev 2:3 offerings of the LORD made by *f*
Lev 2:9 it is an offering made by *f*
Lev 2:10 offerings of the LORD made by *f*
Lev 2:11 offering of the LORD made by *f*
Lev 2:14 green ears of corn dried by the *f*
Lev 2:16 offering made by *f* unto the LORD
Lev 3:3 offering made by *f* unto the LORD
Lev 3:5 is upon the wood that is on the *f*
Lev 3:5 it is an offering made by *f*
Lev 3:9 offering made by *f* unto the LORD
Lev 3:11 offering made by *f* unto the LORD
Lev 3:14 offering made by *f* unto the LORD
Lev 3:16 made by *f* for a sweet savour
Lev 4:12 and burn him on the wood with *f*
Lev 4:35 offerings made by *f* unto the LORD
Lev 5:12 offerings made by *f* unto the LORD
Lev 6:9 the *f* of the altar shall be
Lev 6:10 take up the ashes which the *f*
Lev 6:12 the *f* upon the altar shall be
Lev 6:13 The *f* shall ever be burning upon
Lev 6:17 portion of my offerings made by *f*
Lev 6:18 offerings of the LORD made by *f*
Lev 6:30 it shall be burnt in the *f*
Lev 7:5 offering made by *f* unto the LORD
Lev 7:17 third day shall be burnt with *f*
Lev 7:19 it shall be burnt with *f*
Lev 7:25 offering made by *f* unto the LORD
Lev 7:30 offerings of the LORD made by *f*
Lev 7:35 offerings of the LORD made by *f*
Lev 8:17 he burnt with *f* without the camp
Lev 8:21 offering made by *f* unto the LORD
Lev 8:28 offering made by *f* unto the LORD
Lev 8:32 of the bread shall ye burn with *f*
Lev 9:11 he burnt with *f* without the camp
Lev 9:24 there came a *f* out from before
Lev 10:1 put *f* therein, and put incense
Lev 10:1 offered strange *f* before the LORD
Lev 10:2 And there went out *f* from the LORD
Lev 10:12 offerings of the LORD made by *f*
Lev 10:13 sacrifices of the LORD made by *f*
Lev 10:15 offerings made by *f* of the fat
Lev 13:52 it shall be burnt in the *f*
Lev 13:55 thou shalt burn it in the *f*
Lev 13:57 that wherein the plague is with *f*
Lev 16:12 *f* from off the altar before the
Lev 16:13 upon the *f* before the LORD
Lev 16:27 shall burn in the *f* their skins
Lev 18:21 seed pass through the *f* to Molech
Lev 19:6 day, it shall be burnt in the *f*
Lev 20:14 they shall be burnt with *f*
Lev 21:6 offerings of the LORD made by *f*
Lev 21:9 she shall be burnt with *f*
Lev 21:21 offerings of the LORD made by *f*
Lev 22:22 nor make an offering by *f* of them
Lev 22:27 offering made by *f* unto the LORD
Lev 23:8 by *f* unto the LORD seven days
Lev 23:13 an offering made by *f* unto the
Lev 23:18 even an offering made by *f*
Lev 23:25 offering made by *f* unto the LORD
Lev 23:27 offering made by *f* unto the LORD
Lev 23:36 offering made by *f* unto the LORD
Lev 23:36 offering made by *f* unto the LORD
Lev 23:37 offering made by *f* unto the LORD
Lev 24:7 offering made by *f* unto the LORD
Lev 24:9 made by *f* by a perpetual statute
Num 3:4 offered strange *f* before the LORD
Num 6:18 put it in the *f* which is under
Num 9:15 as it were the appearance of *f*
Num 9:16 and the appearance of *f* by night
Num 11:1 the *f* of the LORD burnt among
Num 11:2 unto the LORD, the *f* was quenched
Num 11:3 because the *f* of the LORD burnt
Num 14:14 and in a pillar of *f* by night
Num 15:3 an offering by *f* unto the LORD
Num 15:10 wine, for an offering made by *f*
Num 15:13 in offering an offering made by *f*
Num 15:14 will offer an offering made by *f*
Num 15:25 sacrifice made by *f* unto the LORD
Num 16:7 put *f* therein, and put incense in
Num 16:18 put *f* in them, and laid incense
Num 16:35 there came out a *f* from the LORD
Num 16:37 and scatter thou the *f* yonder
Num 16:46 put *f* therein from off the altar,
Num 18:9 holy things, reserved from the *f*
Num 18:17 fat for an offering made by *f*
Num 21:28 For there is a *f* gone out of
Num 26:10 what time the *f* devoured two
Num 26:61 offered strange *f* before the LORD
Num 28:2 bread for my sacrifices made by *f*
Num 28:3 This is the offering made by *f*
Num 28:6 sacrifice made by *f* unto the LORD
Num 28:8 offer it, a sacrifice made by *f*
Num 28:13 sacrifice made by *f* unto the LORD
Num 28:19 *f* for a burnt offering unto the
Num 28:24 meat of the sacrifice made by *f*
Num 29:6 sacrifice made by *f* unto the LORD
Num 29:13 offering, a sacrifice made by *f*
Num 29:36 offering, a sacrifice made by *f*
Num 31:10 all their goodly castles, with *f*
Num 31:23 Every thing that may abide the *f*
Num 31:23 ye shall make it go through the *f*
Num 31:23 all that abideth not the *f* ye
Deut 1:33 in *f* by night, to shew you by
Deut 4:11 with *f* unto the midst of heaven
Deut 4:12 you out of the midst of the *f*
Deut 4:15 Horeb out of the midst of the *f*
Deut 4:24 the LORD thy God is a consuming *f*
Deut 4:33 out of the midst of the *f*
Deut 4:36 earth he shewed thee his great *f*
Deut 4:36 words out of the midst of the *f*
Deut 5:4 mount out of the midst of the *f*
Deut 5:5 ye were afraid by reason of the *f*
Deut 5:22 mount out of the midst of the *f*
Deut 5:23 (for the mountain did burn with *f*
Deut 5:24 voice out of the midst of the *f*
Deut 5:25 for this great *f* will consume us
Deut 5:26 out of the midst of the *f*
Deut 7:5 burn their graven images with *f*
Deut 7:25 their gods shall ye burn with *f*
Deut 9:3 as a consuming *f* he shall destroy
Deut 9:10 the *f* in the day of the assembly
Deut 9:15 mount, and the mount burned with *f*
Deut 9:21 ye had made, and burnt it with *f*
Deut 10:4 the *f* in the day of the assembly
Deut 12:3 and burn their groves with *f*
Deut 12:31 have burnt in the *f* to their gods
Deut 13:16 and shalt burn with *f* the city
Deut 18:1 offerings of the LORD made by *f*
Deut 18:10 daughter to pass through the *f*
Deut 18:16 let me see this great *f* any more
Deut 32:22 For a *f* is kindled in mine anger,
Deut 32:22 set on *f* the foundations of the
Josh 6:24 And they burnt the city with *f*
Josh 7:15 thing shall be burnt with *f*
Josh 7:25 stones, and burned them with *f*
Josh 8:8 that ye shall set the city on *f*
Josh 8:19 and hasted and set the city on *f*
Josh 11:6 and burn their chariots with *f*
Josh 11:9 and burnt their chariots with *f*
Josh 11:11 and he burnt Hazor with *f*
Josh 13:14 made by *f* are their inheritance
Judg 1:8 the sword, and set the city on *f*
Judg 6:21 there rose up *f* out of the rock,
Judg 9:15 let *f* come out of the bramble, and
Judg 9:20 let *f* come out from Abimelech, and
Judg 9:20 let *f* come out from the men of
Judg 9:49 and set the hold on *f* upon them
Judg 9:52 of the tower to burn it with *f*
Judg 12:1 burn thine house upon thee with *f*
Judg 14:15 thee and thy father's house with *f*
Judg 15:5 when he had set the brands on *f*
Judg 15:6 and burnt her and her father with *f*
Judg 15:14 as flax that was burnt with *f*
Judg 16:9 is broken when it toucheth the *f*
Judg 18:27 sword, and burnt the city with *f*
Judg 20:48 also they set on *f* all the cities
1Sa 2:28 by *f* of the children of Israel
1Sa 30:1 Ziklag, and burned it with *f*
1Sa 30:3 and, behold, it was burned with *f*
1Sa 30:14 and we burned Ziklag with *f*
2Sa 14:30 go and set it on *f*
2Sa 14:30 servants set the field on *f*
2Sa 14:31 thy servants set my field on *f*
2Sa 22:9 *f* out of his mouth devoured
2Sa 22:13 him were coals of *f* kindled
2Sa 23:7 burned with *f* in the same place
1Kin 9:16 taken Gezer, and burnt it with *f*
1Kin 16:18 the king's house over him with *f*
1Kin 18:23 lay it on wood, and put no *f* under
1Kin 18:23 lay it on wood, and put no *f* under
1Kin 18:24 and the God that answereth by *f*
1Kin 18:25 of your gods, but put no *f* under
1Kin 18:38 Then the *f* of the LORD fell, and
1Kin 19:12 And after the earthquake a *f*
1Kin 19:12 but the LORD was not in the *f*
1Kin 19:12 after the *f* a still small voice
2Kin 1:10 then let *f* come down from heaven,
2Kin 1:10 And there came down *f* from heaven
2Kin 1:12 let *f* come down from heaven, and
2Kin 1:12 the *f* of God came down from
2Kin 1:14 there came *f* down from heaven, and
2Kin 2:11 a chariot of *f*, and horses of *f*
2Kin 6:17 chariots of *f* round about Elisha
2Kin 8:12 strong holds wilt thou set on *f*
2Kin 16:3 his son to pass through the *f*
2Kin 17:17 daughters to pass through the *f*
2Kin 17:31 children in *f* to Adrammelech
2Kin 19:18 have cast their gods into the *f*
2Kin 21:6 made his son pass through the *f*
2Kin 23:10 to pass through the *f* to Molech
2Kin 23:11 the chariots of the sun with *f*
2Kin 25:9 great man's house burnt he with *f*
1Chr 14:12 and they were burned with *f*
1Chr 21:26 by *f* upon the altar of burnt
2Chr 7:1 the *f* came down from heaven, and
2Chr 7:3 of Israel saw how the *f* came down
2Chr 28:3 and burnt his children in the *f*
2Chr 33:6 the *f* in the valley of the son of
2Chr 35:13 with *f* according to the ordinance
2Chr 36:19 all the palaces thereof with *f*
Neh 1:3 gates thereof are burned with *f*
Neh 2:3 gates thereof are consumed with *f*
Neh 2:13 thereof were consumed with *f*
Neh 2:17 gates thereof are burned with *f*
Neh 9:12 and in the night by a pillar of *f*
Neh 9:19 neither the pillar of *f* by night
Job 1:16 The *f* of God is fallen from
Job 15:34 *f* shall consume the tabernacles
Job 18:5 spark of his *f* shall not shine
Job 20:26 a *f* not blown shall consume him
Job 22:20 remnant of them the *f* consumeth
Job 28:5 it is turned up as it were *f*
Job 31:12 For it is a *f* that consumeth to
Job 41:19 lamps, and sparks of *f* leap out
Ps 11:6 wicked he shall rain snares, *f*
Ps 18:8 *f* out of his mouth devoured
Ps 18:12 passed, hail stones and coals of *f*
Ps 18:13 hail stones and coals of *f*
Ps 21:9 wrath, and the *f* shall devour them
Ps 29:7 the LORD divideth the flames of *f*
Ps 39:3 while I was musing the *f* burned
Ps 46:9 he burneth the chariot in the *f*
Ps 50:3 a *f* shall devour before him, and
Ps 57:4 even among them that are set on *f*
Ps 66:12 we went through *f* and through
Ps 68:2 as wax melteth before the *f*
Ps 74:7 They have cast *f* into thy
Ps 78:14 all the night with a light of *f*
Ps 78:21 so a *f* was kindled against Jacob,
Ps 78:63 The *f* consumed their young men
Ps 79:5 shall thy jealousy burn like *f*
Ps 80:16 It is burned with *f*, it is cut
Ps 83:14 As the *f* burneth a wood, and as
Ps 83:14 flame setteth the mountains on *f*
Ps 89:46 shall thy wrath burn like *f*
Ps 97:3 A *f* goeth before him, and burneth
Ps 104:4 his ministers a flaming *f*
Ps 105:32 rain, and flaming *f* in their land
Ps 105:39 *f* to give light in the night
Ps 106:18 a *f* was kindled in their company
Ps 118:12 are quenched as the *f* of thorns
Ps 140:10 let them be cast into the *f*
Ps 148:8 *F*, and hail; snow, and
Prov 6:27 Can a man take *f* in his bosom
Prov 16:27 his lips there is as a burning *f*
Prov 25:22 heap coals of *f* upon his head
Prov 26:20 no wood is, there the *f* goeth out
Prov 26:21 to burning coals, and wood to *f*
Prov 30:16 the *f* that saith not, It is
Song 8:6 the coals thereof are coals of *f*
Is 1:7 your cities are burned with *f*
Is 4:5 shining of a flaming *f* by night
Is 5:24 Therefore as the *f* devoureth the
Is 9:5 be with burning and fuel of *f*
Is 9:18 For wickedness burneth as the *f*
Is 9:19 shall be as the fuel of the *f*
Is 10:16 a burning like the burning of a *f*
Is 10:17 light of Israel shall be for a *f*
Is 26:11 the *f* of thine enemies shall
Is 27:11 the women come, and set them on *f*
Is 29:6 and the flame of devouring *f*
Is 30:14 a sherd to take *f* from the hearth
Is 30:27 and his tongue as a devouring *f*
Is 30:30 with the flame of a devouring *f*

Is 30:33 the pile thereof is f and much
Is 31:9 whose f is in Zion, and his
Is 33:11 your breath, as f, shall devour
Is 33:12 up shall they be burned in the f
Is 33:14 shall dwell with the devouring f
Is 37:19 have cast their gods into the f
Is 42:25 it hath set him on f round about
Is 43:2 when thou walkest through the f
Is 44:16 He burneth part thereof in the f
Is 44:16 Aha, I am warm, I have seen the f
Is 44:19 I have burned part of it in the f
Is 47:14 the f shall burn them
Is 47:14 warm at, nor f to sit before it
Is 50:11 Behold, all ye that kindle a f
Is 50:11 walk in the light of your f
Is 54:16 that bloweth the coals in the f
Is 64:2 As when the melting f burneth
Is 64:2 the f causeth the waters to boil,
Is 64:11 praised thee, is burned up with f
Is 65:5 a f that burneth all the day
Is 66:15 behold, the LORD will come with f
Is 66:15 and his rebuke with flames of f
Is 66:16 For by f and by his sword will the
Is 66:24 neither shall their f be quenched
Jer 4:4 lest my fury come forth like f
Jer 5:14 will make my words in thy mouth f
Jer 6:1 up a sign of f in Beth-haccerem
Jer 6:29 the lead is consumed of the f
Jer 7:18 wood, and the fathers kindle the f
Jer 7:31 sons and their daughters in the f
Jer 11:16 tumult he hath kindled f upon it
Jer 15:14 for a f is kindled in mine anger,
Jer 17:4 ye have kindled a f in mine anger
Jer 17:27 I kindle a f in the gates thereof
Jer 19:5 to burn their sons with f for
Jer 20:9 a burning f shut up in my bones
Jer 21:10 and he shall burn it with f
Jer 21:12 lest my fury go out like f
Jer 21:14 I will kindle a f in the forest
Jer 22:7 cedars, and cast them into the f
Jer 23:29 Is not my word like as a f
Jer 29:22 king of Babylon roasted in the f
Jer 32:29 set f on this city, and burn it
Jer 32:35 to pass through the f unto Molech
Jer 34:2 and he shall burn it with f
Jer 34:22 and take it, and burn it with f
Jer 36:22 there was a f on the hearth
Jer 36:23 cast it into the f that was on
Jer 36:23 in the f that was on the hearth
Jer 36:32 king of Judah had burned in the f
Jer 37:8 and take it, and burn it with f
Jer 37:10 tent, and burn this city with f
Jer 38:17 city shall not be burned with f
Jer 38:18 and they shall burn it with f
Jer 38:23 this city to be burned with f
Jer 39:8 the houses of the people, with f
Jer 43:12 I will kindle a f in the houses
Jer 43:13 Egyptians shall he burn with f
Jer 48:45 but a f shall come forth out of
Jer 49:2 daughters shall be burned with f
Jer 49:27 I will kindle a f in the wall of
Jer 50:32 I will kindle a f in his cities
Jer 51:32 the reeds they have burned with f
Jer 51:58 high gates shall be burned with f
Jer 51:58 in vain, and the folk in the f
Jer 52:13 the great men, burned he with f
Lam 1:13 hath he sent f into my bones
Lam 2:3 against Jacob like a flaming f
Lam 2:4 he poured out his fury like f
Lam 4:11 and hath kindled a f in Zion
Eze 1:4 a f infolding itself, and a
Eze 1:4 amber, out of the midst of the f
Eze 1:13 was like burning coals of f
Eze 1:13 living creatures; and the f was bright
Eze 1:13 out of the f went forth lightning
Eze 1:27 as the appearance of f round
Eze 1:27 as it were the appearance of f
Eze 5:2 Thou shalt burn with f a third
Eze 5:4 cast them into the midst of the f
Eze 5:4 and burn them in the f
Eze 5:4 for thereof shall a f come forth
Eze 8:2 a likeness as the appearance of f
Eze 8:2 of his loins even downward, f
Eze 10:2 of f from between the cherubims
Eze 10:6 Take f from between the wheels,
Eze 10:7 f that was between the cherubims
Eze 15:4 it is cast into the f for fuel
Eze 15:4 the f devoureth both the ends of
Eze 15:5 when the f hath devoured it, and
Eze 15:6 I have given to the f for fuel
Eze 15:7 they shall go out from one f
Eze 15:7 another f shall devour them
Eze 16:21 to pass through the f for them
Eze 16:41 shall burn thine houses with f
Eze 19:12 the f consumed them
Eze 19:14 f is gone out of a rod of her
Eze 20:26 the f all that openeth the womb
Eze 20:31 your sons to pass through the f
Eze 20:47 Behold, I will kindle a f in thee
Eze 21:31 against thee in the f of my wrath
Eze 21:32 Thou shalt be for fuel to the f
Eze 22:20 furnace, to blow the f upon it
Eze 22:21 upon you in the f of my wrath
Eze 22:31 them with the f of my wrath
Eze 23:25 shall be devoured by the f
Eze 23:37 to pass for them through the f
Eze 23:47 and burn up their houses with f
Eze 24:9 even make the pile for f great
Eze 24:10 Heap on wood, kindle the f
Eze 24:12 her scum shall be in the f
Eze 28:14 in the midst of the stones of f
Eze 28:16 from the midst of the stones of f
Eze 28:18 forth a f from the midst of thee
Eze 30:8 when I have set a f in Egypt
Eze 30:14 desolate, and will set f in Zoan
Eze 30:16 And I will set f in Egypt
Eze 36:5 Surely in the f of my jealousy
Eze 38:19 in the f of my wrath have I
Eze 38:22 rain, and great hailstones, f
Eze 39:6 And I will send a f on Magog
Eze 39:9 shall go forth, and shall set on f
Eze 39:9 burn them with f seven years
Eze 39:10 shall burn the weapons with f
Dan 3:22 the flame of the f slew those men
Dan 3:24 men bound into the midst of the f
Dan 3:25 walking in the midst of the f
Dan 3:26 came forth of the midst of the f
Dan 3:27 whose bodies the f had no power
Dan 3:27 nor the smell of f had passed on
Dan 7:9 flame, and his wheels as burning f
Dan 10:6 and his eyes as lamps of f
Hos 7:6 morning it burneth as a flaming f
Hos 8:14 I will send a f upon his cities
Joel 1:19 for the f hath devoured the
Joel 1:20 the f hath devoured the pastures
Joel 2:3 A f devoureth before them
Joel 2:5 of f that devoureth the stubble
Joel 2:30 and in the earth, blood, and f
Amos 1:4 But I will send a f into the
Amos 1:7 But I will send a f on the wall
Amos 1:10 But I will send a f on the wall
Amos 1:12 But I will send a f upon Teman
Amos 1:14 But I will kindle a f in the wall
Amos 2:2 But I will send a f upon Moab
Amos 2:5 But I will send a f upon Judah
Amos 5:6 out like f in the house of Joseph
Amos 7:4 Lord GOD called to contend by f
Obad 18 the house of Jacob shall be a f
Mic 1:4 be cleft, as wax before the f
Mic 1:7 shall be burned with the f
Nah 1:6 his fury is poured out like f
Nah 3:13 the f shall devour thy bars
Nah 3:15 There shall the f devour thee
Hab 2:13 people shall labour in the very f
Zeph 1:18 devoured by the f of his jealousy
Zeph 3:8 with the f of my jealousy
Zec 2:5 unto her a wall of f round about
Zec 3:2 this a brand plucked out of the f
Zec 9:4 and she shall be devoured with f
Zec 11:1 that the f may devour thy cedars
Zec 12:6 an hearth of f among the wood
Zec 12:6 and like a torch of f in a sheaf
Zec 13:9 the third part through the f
Mal 1:10 neither do ye kindle f on mine
Mal 3:2 for he is like a refiner's f
Mt 3:10 is hewn down, and cast into the f
Mt 3:11 with the Holy Ghost, and with f
Mt 3:12 up the chaff with unquenchable f
Mt 5:22 shall be in danger of hell f
Mt 7:19 is hewn down, and cast into the f
Mt 13:40 are gathered and burned in the f
Mt 13:42 cast them into a furnace of f
Mt 13:50 cast them into the furnace of f
Mt 17:15 ofttimes he falleth into the f
Mt 18:8 to be cast into everlasting f
Mt 18:9 two eyes to be cast into hell f
Mt 25:41 me, ye cursed, into everlasting f
Mk 9:22 it hath cast him into the f
Mk 9:43 into the f that never shall be
Mk 9:44 not, and the f is not quenched
Mk 9:45 into the f that never shall be
Mk 9:46 not, and the f is not quenched
Mk 9:47 two eyes to be cast into hell f
Mk 9:48 not, and the f is not quenched
Mk 9:49 every one shall be salted with f
Mk 14:54 and warmed himself at the f
Lk 3:9 is hewn down, and cast into the f
Lk 3:16 you with the Holy Ghost and with f
Lk 3:17 he will burn with f unquenchable
Lk 9:54 f to come down from heaven
Lk 12:49 I am come to send f on the earth
Lk 17:29 Lot went out of Sodom it rained f
Lk 22:55 when they had kindled a f in the
Lk 22:56 beheld him as he sat by the f
Jn 15:6 them, and cast them into the f
Jn 18:18 there, who had made a f of coals
Jn 21:9 they saw a f of coals there, and
Acts 2:3 them cloven tongues like as of f
Acts 2:19 blood, and f, and vapour of smoke
Acts 7:30 Lord in a flame of f in a bush
Acts 28:2 for they kindled a f, and received
Acts 28:3 of sticks, and laid them on the f
Acts 28:5 he shook off the beast into the f
Rom 12:20 shalt heap coals of f on his head
1Cor 3:13 because it shall be revealed by f
1Cor 3:13 the f shall try every man's work
1Cor 3:15 yet so as by f
2Th 1:8 In flaming f taking vengeance on
Heb 1:7 and his ministers a flame of f
Heb 11:34 Quenched the violence of f
Heb 12:18 be touched, and that burned with f
Heb 12:29 For our God is a consuming f
Jas 3:5 a matter a little f kindleth
Jas 3:6 And the tongue is a f, a world of
Jas 3:6 setteth on f the course of nature
Jas 3:6 and it is set on f of hell
Jas 5:3 shall eat your flesh as it were f
1Pet 1:7 though it be tried with f
2Pet 3:7 reserved unto f against the day
2Pet 3:12 being on f shall be dissolved
Jude 7 the vengeance of eternal f
Jude 23 fear, pulling them out of the f
Rev 1:14 and his eyes were as a flame of f
Rev 2:18 his eyes like unto a flame of f
Rev 3:18 to buy of me gold tried in the f
Rev 4:5 of f burning before the throne
Rev 8:5 and filled it with f of the altar
Rev 8:7 f mingled with blood, and they
Rev 8:8 with f was cast into the sea
Rev 9:17 on them, having breastplates of f
Rev 9:17 and out of their mouths issued f
Rev 9:18 part of men killed, by the f
Rev 10:1 sun, and his feet as pillars of f
Rev 11:5 f proceedeth out of their mouth,
Rev 13:13 so that he maketh f come down
Rev 14:10 and he shall be tormented with f
Rev 14:18 the altar, which had power over f
Rev 15:2 a sea of glass mingled with f
Rev 16:8 unto him to scorch men with f
Rev 17:16 eat her flesh, and burn her with f
Rev 18:8 shall be utterly burned with f
Rev 19:12 His eyes were as a flame of f
Rev 19:20 lake of f burning with brimstone
Rev 20:9 f came down from God out of
Rev 20:10 them was cast into the lake of f
Rev 20:14 hell were cast into the lake of f
Rev 20:15 life was cast into the lake of f
Rev 21:8 in the lake which burneth with f

## FIRM

Josh 3:17 f on dry ground in the midst of
Josh 4:3 where the priests' feet stood f
Job 41:23 they are f in themselves
Job 41:24 His heart is as f as a stone
Ps 73:4 but their strength is f
Dan 6:7 statute, and to make a f decree
Heb 3:6 of the hope f unto the end

## FIRMAMENT

Gen 1:6 Let there be a f in the midst of
Gen 1:7 And God made the f, and divided the
Gen 1:7 the f from the waters which were
Gen 1:7 the waters which were above the f
Gen 1:8 And God called the f Heaven
Gen 1:14 Let there be lights in the f of
Gen 1:15 the f of the heaven to give light
Gen 1:17 God set them in the f of the
Gen 1:20 the earth in the open f of heaven
Ps 19:1 the f sheweth his handywork
Ps 150:1 praise him in the f of his power
Eze 1:22 the likeness of the f upon the

Eze 1:23 under the *f* were their wings
Eze 1:25 the *f* that was over their heads
Eze 1:26 above the *f* that was over their
Eze 10:1 in the *f* that was above the head
Dan 12:3 shine as the brightness of the *f*

**FIRST**

Gen 1:5 and the morning were the *f* day
Gen 2:11 The name of the *f* is Pison
Gen 8:5 on the *f* day of the month, were
Gen 8:13 and *f* year, in the *f* month
Gen 8:13 the *f* day of the month, the
Gen 13:4 which he had made there at the *f*
Gen 25:25 the *f* came out red, all over like
Gen 26:1 beside the *f* famine that was in
Gen 28:19 that city was called Luz at the *f*
Gen 38:28 thread, saying, This came out *f*
Gen 41:20 did eat up the *f* seven fat kine
Gen 43:18 at the *f* time are we brought in
Gen 43:20 down at the *f* time to buy food
Ex 4:8 to the voice of the *f* sign
Ex 12:2 it shall be the *f* month of the
Ex 12:5 blemish, a male of the *f* year
Ex 12:15 even the *f* day ye shall put away
Ex 12:15 the *f* day until the seventh day
Ex 12:16 in the *f* day there shall be an
Ex 12:18 In the *f* month, on the fourteenth
Ex 22:29 to offer the *f* of thy ripe fruits
Ex 23:19 The *f* of the firstfruits of thy
Ex 28:17 the *f* row shall be a sardius, a
Ex 28:17 this shall be the *f* row
Ex 29:38 two lambs of the *f* year day by
Ex 34:1 tables of stone like unto the *f*
Ex 34:1 words that were in the *f* tables
Ex 34:4 tables of stone like unto the *f*
Ex 34:26 The *f* of the firstfruits of thy
Ex 39:10 the *f* row was a sardius, a topaz,
Ex 39:10 this was the *f* row
Ex 40:2 On the *f* day of the *f* month
Ex 40:2 On the *f* day of the *f* month
Ex 40:17 it came to pass in the *f* month in
Ex 40:17 on the *f* day of the month, that
Lev 4:21 him as he burned the *f* bullock
Lev 5:8 which is for the sin offering *f*
Lev 9:3 and a lamb, both of the *f* year
Lev 9:15 and offered it for sin, as the *f*
Lev 12:6 the *f* year for a burnt offering
Lev 14:10 one ewe lamb of the *f* year
Lev 23:5 the *f* month at even is the LORD's
Lev 23:7 In the *f* day ye shall have an
Lev 23:12 *f* year for a burnt offering unto
Lev 23:18 without blemish of the *f* year
Lev 23:19 two lambs of the *f* year for a
Lev 23:20 the *f* fruits for a wave offering
Lev 23:24 in the *f* day of the month, shall
Lev 23:35 On the *f* day shall be an holy
Lev 23:39 on the *f* day shall be a sabbath,
Lev 23:40 ye shall take you on the *f* day
Num 1:1 on the *f* day of the second month,
Num 1:18 on the *f* day of the second month
Num 2:9 These shall *f* set forth
Num 6:12 shall bring a lamb of the *f* year
Num 6:14 one he lamb of the *f* year without
Num 6:14 one ewe lamb of the *f* year
Num 7:12 the *f* day was Nahshon the son of
Num 7:15 one ram, one lamb of the *f* year
Num 7:17 goats, five lambs of the *f* year
Num 7:21 one ram, one lamb of the *f* year
Num 7:23 goats, five lambs of the *f* year
Num 7:27 one ram, one lamb of the *f* year
Num 7:29 goats, five lambs of the *f* year
Num 7:33 one ram, one lamb of the *f* year
Num 7:35 goats, five lambs of the *f* year
Num 7:39 one ram, one lamb of the *f* year
Num 7:41 goats, five lambs of the *f* year
Num 7:45 one ram, one lamb of the *f* year
Num 7:47 goats, five lambs of the *f* year
Num 7:51 one ram, one lamb of the *f* year
Num 7:53 goats, five lambs of the *f* year
Num 7:57 one ram, one lamb of the *f* year
Num 7:59 goats, five lambs of the *f* year
Num 7:63 one ram, one lamb of the *f* year
Num 7:65 goats, five lambs of the *f* year
Num 7:69 one ram, one lamb of the *f* year
Num 7:71 goats, five lambs of the *f* year
Num 7:75 one ram, one lamb of the *f* year
Num 7:77 goats, five lambs of the *f* year
Num 7:81 one ram, one lamb of the *f* year
Num 7:83 goats, five lambs of the *f* year
Num 7:87 the lambs of the *f* year twelve
Num 7:88 the lambs of the *f* year sixty
Num 9:1 in the *f* month of the second year
Num 9:5 on the fourteenth day of the *f*
Num 10:13 they *f* took their journey
Num 10:14 In the *f* place went the standard
Num 15:20 the *f* of your dough for an heave
Num 15:21 Of the *f* of your dough ye shall
Num 15:27 of the *f* year for a sin offering
Num 18:13 whatsoever is *f* ripe in the land,
Num 20:1 the desert of Zin in the *f* month
Num 24:20 Amalek was the *f* of the nations
Num 28:3 two lambs of the *f* year without
Num 28:9 lambs of the *f* year without spot
Num 28:11 lambs of the *f* year without spot
Num 28:16 *f* month is the passover of the
Num 28:18 In the *f* day shall be an holy
Num 28:19 ram, and seven lambs of the *f* year
Num 28:27 ram, seven lambs of the *f* year
Num 29:1 on the *f* day of the month, ye
Num 29:2 seven lambs of the *f* year without
Num 29:8 ram, and seven lambs of the *f* year
Num 29:13 and fourteen lambs of the *f* year
Num 29:17 lambs of the *f* year without spot
Num 29:20 of the *f* year without blemish
Num 29:23 of the *f* year without blemish
Num 29:26 lambs of the *f* year without spot
Num 29:29 of the *f* year without blemish
Num 29:32 of the *f* year without blemish
Num 29:36 seven lambs of the *f* year without
Num 33:3 from Rameses in the *f* month
Num 33:3 the fifteenth day of the *f* month
Num 33:38 in the *f* day of the fifth month
Deut 1:3 on the *f* day of the month, that
Deut 9:18 down before the LORD, as at the *f*
Deut 9:25 nights, as I fell down at the *f*
Deut 10:1 tables of stone like unto the *f*
Deut 10:2 the *f* tables which thou brakest
Deut 10:3 tables of stone like unto the *f*
Deut 10:4 according to the *f* writing
Deut 10:10 mount, according to the *f* time
Deut 11:14 the *f* rain and the latter rain,
Deut 13:9 thine hand shall be *f* upon him to
Deut 16:4 sacrificedst the *f* day at even
Deut 17:7 be *f* upon him to put him to death
Deut 18:4 the *f* of the fleece of thy sheep,
Deut 26:2 That thou shalt take of the *f* of
Deut 33:21 he provided the *f* part for
Josh 4:19 on the tenth day of the *f* month
Josh 8:5 come out against us, as at the *f*
Josh 8:6 They flee before us, as at the *f*
Josh 21:10 for theirs was the *f* lot
Judg 1:1 for us against the Canaanites *f*
Judg 18:29 of the city was Laish at the *f*
Judg 20:18 Which of us shall go up *f* to the
Judg 20:18 LORD said, Judah shall go up *f*
Judg 20:22 put themselves in array the *f* day
Judg 20:32 down before us, as at the *f*
Judg 20:39 before us, as in the *f* battle
1Sa 14:14 that *f* slaughter, which Jonathan
1Sa 14:35 the same was the *f* altar that he
1Sa 17:13 the battle were Eliab the *f* born
2Sa 3:13 except thou *f* bring Michal Saul's
2Sa 17:9 of them be overthrown at the *f*
2Sa 19:20 I am come the *f* this day of all
2Sa 19:43 *f* had in bringing back our king
2Sa 21:9 days of harvest, in the *f* days
2Sa 23:19 he attained not unto the *f* three
2Sa 23:23 he attained not to the *f* three
1Kin 16:23 *f* year of Asa king of Judah began
1Kin 17:13 make me thereof a little cake *f*
1Kin 18:25 for yourselves, and dress it *f*
1Kin 20:9 to thy servant at the *f* I will do
1Kin 20:17 of the provinces went out *f*
1Chr 9:2 Now the *f* inhabitants that dwelt
1Chr 11:6 the Jebusites *f* shall be chief
1Chr 11:6 Joab the son of Zeruiah went *f* up
1Chr 11:21 he attained not to the *f* three
1Chr 11:25 but attained not to the *f* three
1Chr 12:9 Ezer the *f*, Obadiah the second,
1Chr 12:15 went over Jordan in the *f* month
1Chr 15:13 because ye did it not at the *f*
1Chr 16:7 on that day David delivered *f*
1Chr 23:19 Jeriah the *f*, Amariah the second,
1Chr 23:20 Micah the *f*, and Jesiah the second
1Chr 24:7 Now the *f* lot came forth to
1Chr 24:21 of Rehabiah, the *f* was Isshiah
1Chr 24:23 Jeriah the *f*, Amariah the second,
1Chr 25:9 Now the *f* lot came forth for
1Chr 27:2 Over the *f* course for the *f*
1Chr 27:3 of the host for the *f* month
1Chr 29:29 Now the acts of David the king, *f*
2Chr 3:3 *f* measure was threescore cubits
2Chr 9:29 rest of the acts of Solomon, *f*
2Chr 12:15 Now the acts of Rehoboam, *f*
2Chr 16:11 And, behold, the acts of Asa, *f*
2Chr 17:3 in the *f* ways of his father David
2Chr 20:34 of the acts of Jehoshaphat, *f*
2Chr 25:26 rest of the acts of Amaziah, *f*
2Chr 26:22 the rest of the acts of Uzziah, *f*
2Chr 28:26 of his acts and of all his ways, *f*
2Chr 29:3 He in the *f* year of his reign, in
2Chr 29:3 year of his reign, in the *f* month
2Chr 29:17 Now they began on the *f* day of
2Chr 29:17 day of the *f* month to sanctify
2Chr 29:17 of the *f* month they made an end
2Chr 35:1 the fourteenth day of the *f* month
2Chr 35:27 And his deeds, *f* and last, behold,
2Chr 36:22 Now in the *f* year of Cyrus king
Ezr 1:1 Now in the *f* year of Cyrus king
Ezr 3:6 From the *f* day of the seventh
Ezr 3:12 men, that had seen the *f* house
Ezr 5:13 But in the *f* year of Cyrus the
Ezr 6:3 In the *f* year of Cyrus the king
Ezr 6:19 the fourteenth day of the *f* month
Ezr 7:9 For upon the *f* day of the
Ezr 7:9 *f* month began he to go up from
Ezr 7:9 on the *f* day of the fifth month
Ezr 8:31 on the twelfth day of the *f* month
Ezr 10:16 sat down in the *f* day of the
Ezr 10:17 by the *f* day of the *f* month
Ezr 10:17 by the *f* day of the *f* month
Neh 7:5 of them which came up at the *f*
Neh 8:2 upon the *f* day of the seventh
Neh 8:18 from the *f* day unto the last day,
Est 1:14 which sat the *f* in the kingdom
Est 3:7 In the *f* month, that is, the
Est 3:12 the thirteenth day of the *f* month
Job 15:7 Art thou the *f* man that was born
Job 42:14 And he called the name of the *f*
Prov 18:17 He that is *f* in his own cause
Is 1:26 restore thy judges as at the *f*
Is 9:1 when at the *f* he lightly
Is 41:4 I the LORD, the *f*, and with the
Is 41:27 The *f* shall say to Zion, Behold,
Is 43:27 Thy *f* father hath sinned, and thy
Is 44:6 I am the *f*, and I am the last
Is 48:12 I am the *f*, I also am the last
Is 60:9 me, and the ships of Tarshish *f*
Jer 4:31 that bringeth forth her *f* child
Jer 7:12 where I set my name at the *f*
Jer 16:18 *f* I will recompense their
Jer 24:2 like the figs that are *f* ripe
Jer 25:1 of Judah, that was the *f* year of
Jer 33:7 and will build them, as at the *f*
Jer 33:11 of the land, as at the *f*, saith
Jer 36:28 words that were in the *f* roll
Jer 50:17 *f* the king of Assyria hath
Jer 52:31 king of Babylon in the *f* year of
Eze 10:14 the *f* face was the face of a
Eze 26:1 in the *f* day of the month, that
Eze 29:17 and twentieth year, in the *f* month
Eze 29:17 in the *f* day of the month, the
Eze 30:20 the eleventh year, in the *f* month
Eze 31:1 in the *f* day of the month, that
Eze 32:1 in the *f* day of the month, that
Eze 40:21 after the measure of the *f* gate
Eze 44:30 the *f* of all the firstfruits of
Eze 44:30 the priest the *f* of your dough
Eze 45:18 In the *f* month, in the
Eze 45:18 in the *f* day of the month, thou
Eze 45:21 In the *f* month, in the fourteenth
Eze 46:13 of the *f* year without blemish
Dan 1:21 unto the *f* year of king Cyrus
Dan 6:2 of whom Daniel was *f*
Dan 7:1 In the *f* year of Belshazzar king
Dan 7:4 The *f* was like a lion, and had
Dan 7:8 whom there were three of the *f*
Dan 7:24 and he shall be diverse from the *f*
Dan 8:1 which appeared unto me at the *f*
Dan 8:21 is between his eyes is the *f* king
Dan 9:1 In the *f* year of Darius the son
Dan 9:2 In the *f* year of his reign I
Dan 10:4 and twentieth day of the *f* month
Dan 10:12 for from the *f* day that thou
Dan 11:1 Also I in the *f* year of Darius
Hos 2:7 will go and return to my *f* husband
Hos 9:10 in the fig tree at her *f* time
Joel 2:23 and the latter rain in the *f* month
Amos 6:7 with the *f* that go captive
Mic 4:8 it come, even the *f* dominion

Hag 1:1 in the *f* day of the month, came
Hag 2:3 saw this house in her *f* glory
Zec 6:2 In the *f* chariot were red horses
Zec 12:7 shall save the tents of Judah *f*
Zec 14:10 gate unto the place of the *f* gate
Mt 5:24 *f* be reconciled to thy brother,
Mt 6:33 But seek ye *f* the kingdom of God,
Mt 7:5 *f* cast out the beam out of thine
Mt 8:21 unto him, Lord, suffer me *f* to go
Mt 10:2 The *f*, Simon, who is called Peter
Mt 12:29 except he *f* bind the strong man
Mt 12:45 of that man is worse than the *f*
Mt 13:30 Gather ye together *f* the tares
Mt 17:10 scribes that Elias must *f* come
Mt 17:11 them, Elias truly shall *f* come
Mt 17:27 take up the fish that *f* cometh up
Mt 19:30 But many that are *f* shall be last
Mt 19:30 and the last shall be *f*
Mt 20:8 from the last unto the *f*
Mt 20:10 But when the *f* came, they
Mt 20:16 shall be *f*, and the *f* last
Mt 21:28 and he came to the *f*, and said, Son
Mt 21:31 They say unto him, The *f*
Mt 21:36 other servants more than the *f*
Mt 22:25 and the *f*, when he had married a
Mt 22:38 This is the *f* and great
Mt 23:26 cleanse *f* that which is within
Mt 26:17 Now the *f* day of the feast of
Mt 27:64 error shall be worse than the *f*
Mt 28:1 dawn toward the *f* day of the week
Mk 3:27 except he will *f* bind the strong
Mk 4:28 *f* the blade, then the ear, after
Mk 7:27 her, Let the children *f* be filled
Mk 9:11 scribes that Elias must *f* come
Mk 9:12 told them, Elias verily cometh *f*
Mk 9:35 them, If any man desire to be *f*
Mk 10:31 But many that are *f* shall be last
Mk 10:31 and the last *f*
Mk 12:20 the *f* took a wife, and dying left
Mk 12:28 Which is the *f* commandment of all
Mk 12:29 The *f* of all the commandments is,
Mk 12:30 this is the *f* commandment
Mk 13:10 the gospel must *f* be published
Mk 14:12 the *f* day of unleavened bread,
Mk 16:2 the morning the *f* day of the week
Mk 16:9 risen early the *f* day of the week
Mk 16:9 he appeared *f* to Mary Magdalene,
Lk 1:3 of all things from the very *f*
Lk 2:2 this taxing was *f* made when
Lk 6:1 on the second sabbath after the *f*
Lk 6:42 cast out *f* the beam out of thine
Lk 9:59 he said, Lord, suffer me *f* to go
Lk 9:61 but let me *f* go bid them farewell
Lk 10:5 *f* say, Peace be to this house
Lk 11:26 of that man is worse than the *f*
Lk 11:38 he had not *f* washed before dinner
Lk 12:1 say unto his disciples *f* of all
Lk 13:30 there are last which shall be *f*
Lk 13:30 there are *f* which shall be last
Lk 14:18 The *f* said unto him, I have
Lk 14:28 build a tower, sitteth not down *f*
Lk 14:31 another king, sitteth not down *f*
Lk 16:5 unto him, and said unto the *f*
Lk 17:25 But *f* must he suffer many things,
Lk 19:16 Then came the *f*, saying, Lord,
Lk 20:29 the *f* took a wife, and died
Lk 21:9 these things must *f* come to pass
Lk 24:1 Now upon the *f* day of the week,
Jn 1:41 He *f* findeth his own brother
Jn 5:4 whosoever then *f* after the
Jn 8:7 let him *f* cast a stone at her
Jn 10:40 place where John at *f* baptized
Jn 12:16 not his disciples at the *f*
Jn 18:13 And led him away to Annas *f*
Jn 19:32 and brake the legs of the *f*
Jn 19:39 which at the *f* came to Jesus by
Jn 20:1 The *f* day of the week cometh Mary
Jn 20:4 Peter, and came *f* to the sepulchre
Jn 20:8 which came *f* to the sepulchre, and
Jn 20:19 being the *f* day of the week, when
Acts 3:26 Unto you *f* God, having raised up
Acts 7:12 Egypt, he sent out our fathers *f*
Acts 11:26 called Christians *f* in Antioch
Acts 12:10 When they were past the *f*
Acts 13:24 When John had *f* preached before
Acts 13:46 should *f* have been spoken to you
Acts 15:14 at the *f* did visit the Gentiles
Acts 20:7 upon the *f* day of the week, when
Acts 20:18 from the *f* day that I came into
Acts 26:4 which was at the *f* among mine own
Acts 26:20 But shewed *f* unto them of
Acts 26:23 that he should be the *f* that
Acts 27:43 cast themselves *f* into the sea
Rom 1:8 *F*, I thank my God through Jesus
Rom 1:16 to the Jew *f*, and also to the
Rom 2:9 man that doeth evil, of the Jew *f*
Rom 2:10 that worketh good, to the Jew *f*
Rom 10:19 *F* Moses saith, I will provoke you
Rom 11:35 Or who hath *f* given to him, and it
Rom 15:24 if *f* I be somewhat filled with
1Cor 11:18 For *f* of all, when ye come
1Cor 12:28 *f* apostles, secondarily prophets,
1Cor 14:30 by, let the *f* hold his peace
1Cor 15:3 you *f* of all that which I also
1Cor 15:45 The *f* man Adam was made a living
1Cor 15:46 that was not *f* which is spiritual
1Cor 15:47 The *f* man is of the earth, earthy
1Cor 16:2 Upon the *f* day of the week let
1Cor *s* The *f* epistle to the Corinthians
2Cor 8:5 but *f* gave their own selves to
2Cor 8:12 For if there be *f* a willing mind
Gal 4:13 the gospel unto you at the *f*
Eph 1:12 glory, who *f* trusted in Christ
Eph 4:9 *f* into the lower parts of the
Eph 6:2 which is the *f* commandment with
Phil 1:5 gospel from the *f* day until now
1Th 4:16 the dead in Christ shall rise *f*
1Th *s* The *f* epistle unto the
2Th 2:3 there come a falling away *f*
1Ti 1:16 that in me *f* Jesus Christ might
1Ti 2:1 *f* of all, supplications, prayers,
1Ti 2:13 For Adam was *f* formed, then Eve
1Ti 3:10 And let these also *f* be proved
1Ti 5:4 let them learn *f* to shew piety at
1Ti 5:12 they have cast off their *f* faith
1Ti *s* The *f* to Timothy was written from
2Ti 1:5 which dwelt *f* in thy grandmother
2Ti 2:6 must be *f* partaker of the fruits
2Ti 4:16 At my *f* answer no man stood with
2Ti *s* ordained the *f* bishop of the
Titus 3:10 that is an heretick after the *f*
Titus *s* ordained the *f* bishop of the
Heb 2:3 which at the *f* began to be spoken
Heb 4:6 they to whom it was *f* preached
Heb 5:12 *f* principles of the oracles of
Heb 7:2 *f* being by interpretation King of
Heb 7:27 *f* for his own sins, and then for
Heb 8:7 For if that *f* covenant had been
Heb 8:13 covenant, he hath made the *f* old
Heb 9:1 Then verily the *f* covenant had
Heb 9:2 the *f*, wherein was the
Heb 9:6 went always into the *f* tabernacle
Heb 9:8 while as the *f* tabernacle was yet
Heb 9:15 that were under the *f* testament
Heb 9:18 Whereupon neither the *f* testament
Heb 10:9 He taketh away the *f*, that he may
Jas 3:17 that is from above is *f* pure
1Pet 4:17 if it *f* begin at us, what shall
2Pet 1:20 Knowing this *f*, that no prophecy
2Pet 3:3 Knowing this *f*, that there shall
1Jn 4:19 love him, because he *f* loved us
Jude 6 which kept not their *f* estate
Rev 1:5 the *f* begotten of the dead, and
Rev 1:11 I am Alpha and Omega, the *f*
Rev 1:17 I am the *f* and the last
Rev 2:4 because thou hast left thy *f* love
Rev 2:5 and repent, and do the *f* works
Rev 2:8 These things saith the *f* and the
Rev 2:19 and the last to be more than the *f*
Rev 4:1 the *f* voice which I heard was as
Rev 4:7 the *f* beast was like a lion, and
Rev 8:7 The *f* angel sounded, and there
Rev 13:12 power of the *f* beast before him
Rev 13:12 therein to worship the *f* beast
Rev 16:2 the *f* went, and poured out his
Rev 20:5 This is the *f* resurrection
Rev 20:6 hath part in the *f* resurrection
Rev 21:1 *f* heaven and the *f* earth
Rev 21:19 The *f* foundation was jasper
Rev 22:13 the beginning and the end, the *f*

## FIRSTBORN

Gen 10:15 And Canaan begat Sidon his *f*
Gen 19:31 the *f* said unto the younger, Our
Gen 19:33 the *f* went in, and lay with her
Gen 19:34 that the *f* said unto the younger,
Gen 19:37 the *f* bare a son, and called his
Gen 22:21 Huz his *f*, and Buz his brother, and
Gen 25:13 the *f* of Ishmael, Nebajoth
Gen 27:19 unto his father, I am Esau thy *f*
Gen 27:32 he said, I am thy son, thy *f* Esau
Gen 29:26 to give the younger before the *f*
Gen 35:23 Reuben, Jacob's *f*, and Simeon, and
Gen 36:15 sons of Eliphaz the *f* son of Esau
Gen 38:6 And Judah took a wife for Er his *f*
Gen 38:7 And Er, Judah's *f*, was wicked in
Gen 41:51 called the name of the *f* Manasseh
Gen 43:33 the *f* according to his birthright
Gen 46:8 Reuben, Jacob's *f*
Gen 48:14 for Manasseh was the *f*
Gen 48:18 for this is the *f*
Gen 49:3 Reuben, thou art my *f*, my might,
Ex 4:22 LORD, Israel is my son, even my *f*
Ex 4:23 I will slay thy son, even thy *f*
Ex 6:14 sons of Reuben the *f* of Israel
Ex 11:5 all the *f* in the land of Egypt
Ex 11:5 from the *f* of Pharaoh that
Ex 11:5 throne, even unto the *f* of the
Ex 11:5 and all the *f* of beasts
Ex 12:12 will smite all the *f* in the land
Ex 12:29 all the *f* in the land of Egypt
Ex 12:29 from the *f* of Pharaoh that sat on
Ex 12:29 *f* of the captive that was in the
Ex 12:29 and all the *f* of cattle
Ex 13:2 Sanctify unto me all the *f*
Ex 13:13 all the *f* of man among thy
Ex 13:15 all the *f* in the land of Egypt
Ex 13:15 land of Egypt, both the *f* of man
Ex 13:15 of man, and the *f* of beast
Ex 13:15 but all the *f* of my children I
Ex 22:29 the *f* of thy sons shalt thou give
Ex 34:20 All the *f* of thy sons thou shalt
Num 3:2 Nadab the *f*, and Abihu, Eleazar,
Num 3:12 of Israel instead of all the *f*
Num 3:13 Because all the *f* are mine
Num 3:13 *f* in the land of Egypt I hallowed
Num 3:13 unto me all the *f* in Israel
Num 3:40 Number all the *f* of the males of
Num 3:41 *f* among the children of Israel
Num 3:42 all the *f* among the children of
Num 3:43 all the *f* males by the number of
Num 3:45 *f* among the children of Israel
Num 3:46 thirteen of the *f* of the children
Num 3:50 Of the *f* of the children of
Num 8:16 even instead of the *f* of all the
Num 8:17 For all the *f* of the children of
Num 8:17 every *f* in the land of Egypt I
Num 8:18 the *f* of the children of Israel
Num 18:15 nevertheless the *f* of man shalt
Num 33:4 the Egyptians buried all their *f*
Deut 21:15 if the *f* son be hers that was
Deut 21:16 *f* before the son of the hated
Deut 21:16 which is indeed the *f*
Deut 21:17 the son of the hated for the *f*
Deut 21:17 the right of the *f* is his
Deut 25:6 that the *f* which she beareth
Josh 6:26 the foundation thereof in his *f*
Josh 17:1 for he was the *f* of Joseph
Josh 17:1 wit, for Machir the *f* of Manasseh
Judg 8:20 And he said unto Jether his *f*
1Sa 8:2 Now the name of his *f* was Joel
1Sa 14:49 the name of the *f* Merab, and the
2Sa 3:2 his *f* was Amnon, of Ahinoam the
1Kin 16:34 thereof in Abiram his *f*, and set
1Chr 1:13 And Canaan begat Zidon his *f*
1Chr 1:29 The *f* of Ishmael, Nebaioth
1Chr 2:3 the *f* of Judah, was evil in the
1Chr 2:13 And Jesse begat his *f* Eliab
1Chr 2:25 of Jerahmeel the *f* of Hezron were
1Chr 2:25 Ram the *f*, and Bunah
1Chr 2:27 of Ram the *f* of Jerahmeel were
1Chr 2:42 of Jerahmeel were, Mesha his *f*
1Chr 2:50 the son of Hur, the *f* of Ephratah
1Chr 3:1 the *f* Amnon, of Ahinoam the
1Chr 3:15 the *f* Johanan, the second
1Chr 4:4 the *f* of Ephratah, the father of
1Chr 5:1 sons of Reuben the *f* of Israel
1Chr 5:1 (for he was the *f*;
1Chr 5:3 of Reuben the *f* of Israel were,
1Chr 6:28 the *f* Vashni, and Abiah
1Chr 8:1 Now Benjamin begat Bela his *f*
1Chr 8:30 his *f* son Abdon, and Zur, and Kish,
1Chr 8:39 his brother were, Ulam his *f*
1Chr 9:5 Asaiah the *f*, and his sons
1Chr 9:31 who was the *f* of Shallum the
1Chr 9:36 his *f* son Abdon, then Zur, and
1Chr 26:2 Meshelemiah were, Zechariah the *f*
1Chr 26:4 of Obed-edom were, Shemaiah the *f*
1Chr 26:10 (for though he was not the *f*
2Chr 21:3 because he was the *f*

Neh 10:36 Also the *f* of our sons, and of our
Job 18:13 even the *f* of death shall devour
Ps 78:51 And smote all the *f* in Egypt
Ps 89:27 Also I will make him my *f*
Ps 105:36 also all the *f* in their land
Ps 135:8 Who smote the *f* of Egypt, both of
Ps 136:10 him that smote Egypt in their *f*
Is 14:30 the *f* of the poor shall feed, and
Jer 31:9 to Israel, and Ephraim is my *f*
Mic 6:7 shall I give my *f* for my
Zec 12:10 that is in bitterness for his *f*
Mt 1:25 she had brought forth her *f* son
Lk 2:7 And she brought forth her *f* son
Rom 8:29 be the *f* among many brethren
Col 1:15 God, the *f* of every creature
Col 1:18 beginning, the *f* from the dead
Heb 11:28 destroyed the *f* should touch them
Heb 12:23 assembly and church of the *f*

**FIRSTFRUITS**

Ex 23:16 the *f* of thy labours, which thou
Ex 23:19 The first of the *f* of thy land
Ex 34:22 of the *f* of wheat harvest, and the
Ex 34:26 The first of the *f* of thy land
Lev 2:12 As for the oblation of the *f*
Lev 2:14 offering of thy *f* unto the LORD
Lev 2:14 for the meat offering of thy *f*
Lev 23:10 ye shall bring a sheaf of the *f*
Lev 23:17 they are the *f* unto the LORD
Num 18:12 the *f* of them which they shall
Num 28:26 Also in the day of the *f*, when ye
Deut 26:10 I have brought the *f* of the land
2Kin 4:42 the man of God bread of the *f*
2Chr 31:5 in abundance the *f* of corn
Neh 10:35 to bring the *f* of our ground, and
Neh 10:35 the *f* of all fruit of all trees,
Neh 10:37 should bring the *f* of our dough
Neh 12:44 for the offerings, for the *f*
Neh 13:31 at times appointed, and for the *f*
Prov 3:9 with the *f* of all thine increase
Jer 2:3 LORD, and the *f* of his increase
Eze 20:40 the *f* of your oblations, with all
Eze 44:30 first of all the *f* of all things
Eze 48:14 nor alienate the *f* of the land
Rom 8:23 which have the *f* of the Spirit
Rom 16:5 who is the *f* of Achaia unto
1Cor 15:20 become the *f* of them that slept
1Cor 15:23 Christ the *f*
1Cor 16:15 that it is the *f* of Achaia
Jas 1:18 be a kind of *f* of his creatures
Rev 14:4 among men, being the *f* unto God

**FIRSTLING**

Ex 13:12 every *f* that cometh of a beast
Ex 13:13 every *f* of an ass thou shalt
Ex 34:19 every *f* among thy cattle, whether
Ex 34:20 But the *f* of an ass thou shalt
Lev 27:26 Only the *f* of the beasts, which
Lev 27:26 which should be the LORD's *f*
Num 18:15 the *f* of unclean beasts shalt
Num 18:17 *f* of a cow, or the *f*
Num 18:17 or the *f* of a goat, thou shalt
Deut 15:19 All the *f* males that come of thy
Deut 15:19 no work with the *f* of thy bullock
Deut 15:19 nor shear the *f* of thy sheep
Deut 33:17 is like the *f* of his bullock

**FIRSTLINGS**

Gen 4:4 brought of the *f* of his flock
Num 3:41 all the *f* among the cattle of the
Deut 12:6 the *f* of your herds and of your
Deut 12:17 or the *f* of thy herds or of thy
Deut 14:23 the *f* of thy herds and of thy
Neh 10:36 the *f* of our herds and of our

**FISH**

Gen 1:26 dominion over the *f* of the sea
Gen 1:28 dominion over the *f* of the sea
Ex 7:18 the *f* that is in the river shall
Ex 7:21 the *f* that was in the river died
Num 11:5 We remember the *f*, which we did
Num 11:22 or shall all the *f* of the sea be
Deut 4:18 the likeness of any *f* that is in
2Chr 33:14 to the entering in at the *f* gate
Neh 3:3 But the *f* gate did the sons of
Neh 12:39 the old gate, and above the *f* gate
Neh 13:16 also therein, which brought *f*
Job 41:7 or his head with *f* spears
Ps 8:8 the *f* of the sea, and whatsoever
Ps 105:29 into blood, and slew their *f*
Is 19:10 that make sluices and ponds for *f*
Is 50:2 their *f* stinketh, because there
Jer 16:16 the LORD, and they shall *f* them
Eze 29:4 I will cause the *f* of thy rivers
Eze 29:4 all the *f* of thy rivers shall
Eze 29:5 thee and all the *f* of thy rivers
Eze 47:9 be a very great multitude of *f*
Eze 47:10 their *f* shall be according to
Eze 47:10 as the *f* of the great sea,
Jonah 1:17 a great *f* to swallow up Jonah
Jonah 1:17 in the belly of the *f* three days
Jonah 2:10 And the LORD spake unto the *f*
Zeph 1:10 noise of a cry from the *f* gate
Mt 7:10 Or if he ask a *f*, will he give
Mt 17:27 take up the *f* that first cometh
Lk 11:11 or if he ask a *f*
Lk 11:11 will he for a *f* give him a
Lk 24:42 gave him a piece of a broiled *f*
Jn 21:9 and *f* laid thereon, and bread
Jn 21:10 Bring of the *f* which ye have now
Jn 21:13 and giveth them, and *f* likewise

**FISHERS**

Is 19:8 The *f* also shall mourn, and all
Jer 16:16 Behold, I will send for many *f*
Eze 47:10 that the *f* shall stand upon it
Mt 4:18 for they were *f*
Mt 4:19 me, and I will make you *f* of men
Mk 1:16 for they were *f*
Mk 1:17 will make you to become *f* of men

**FISHES**

Gen 9:2 and upon all the *f* of the sea
1Kin 4:33 and of creeping things, and of *f*
Job 12:8 the *f* of the sea shall declare
Eccl 9:12 as the *f* that are taken in an
Eze 38:20 So that the *f* of the sea, and the
Hos 4:3 the *f* of the sea also shall be
Hab 1:14 And makest men as the *f* of the sea
Zeph 1:3 and the *f* of the sea, and the
Mt 14:17 here but five loaves, and two *f*
Mt 14:19 the five loaves, and the two *f*
Mt 15:34 said, Seven, and a few little *f*
Mt 15:36 he took the seven loaves and the *f*
Mk 6:38 knew, they say, Five, and two *f*
Mk 6:41 the five loaves and the two *f*
Mk 6:41 the two *f* divided he among them
Mk 6:43 of the fragments, and of the *f*
Mk 8:7 And they had a few small *f*
Lk 5:6 inclosed a great multitude of *f*
Lk 5:9 of the *f* which they had taken
Lk 9:13 no more but five loaves and two *f*
Lk 9:16 took the five loaves and the two *f*
Jn 6:9 barley loaves, and two small *f*
Jn 6:11 likewise of the *f* as much as they
Jn 21:6 to draw it for the multitude of *f*
Jn 21:8 cubits,) dragging the net with *f*
Jn 21:11 the net to land full of great *f*
1Cor 15:39 flesh of beasts, another of *f*

**FIT**

Lev 16:21 of a *f* man into the wilderness
1Chr 7:11 *f* to go out for war and battle
1Chr 12:8 men of war *f* for the battle, that
Job 34:18 Is it *f* to say to a king, Thou
Prov 24:27 make it *f* for thyself in the
Lk 9:62 is *f* for the kingdom of God
Lk 14:35 It is neither *f* for the land
Acts 22:22 for it is not *f* that he should
Col 3:18 husbands, as it is *f* in the Lord

**FIVE**

Gen 5:6 hundred and *f* years, and begat Enos
Gen 5:11 Enos were nine hundred and *f* years
Gen 5:15 sixty and *f* years, and begat Jared
Gen 5:17 eight hundred ninety and *f* years
Gen 5:21 *f* years, and begat Methuselah
Gen 5:23 three hundred sixty and *f* years
Gen 5:30 he begat Noah *f* hundred ninety
Gen 5:30 *f* years, and begat sons and
Gen 5:32 Noah was *f* hundred years old
Gen 11:11 he begat Arphaxad *f* hundred years
Gen 11:12 And Arphaxad lived *f* and thirty
Gen 11:32 Terah were two hundred and *f* years
Gen 12:4 *f* years old when he departed out
Gen 14:9 Ellasar; four kings with *f*
Gen 18:28 lack *f* of the fifty righteous
Gen 18:28 all the city for lack of *f*
Gen 18:28 said, If I find there forty and *f*
Gen 43:34 but Benjamin's mess was *f* times
Gen 45:6 and yet there are *f* years, in the
Gen 45:11 yet there are *f* years of famine
Gen 45:22 silver, and *f* changes of raiment
Gen 47:2 some of his brethren, even *f* men
Ex 22:1 he shall restore *f* oxen for an ox
Ex 26:3 The *f* curtains shall be coupled
Ex 26:3 other *f* curtains shall be coupled
Ex 26:9 thou shalt couple *f* curtains by
Ex 26:26 *f* for the boards of the one side
Ex 26:27 *f* bars for the boards of the
Ex 26:27 *f* bars for the boards of the side
Ex 26:37 hanging *f* pillars of shittim wood
Ex 26:37 thou shalt cast *f* sockets of
Ex 27:1 *f* cubits long, and *f* cubits
Ex 27:18 the height *f* cubits of fine
Ex 30:23 of pure myrrh *f* hundred shekels
Ex 30:24 of cassia *f* hundred shekels,
Ex 36:10 he coupled the *f* curtains one
Ex 36:10 the other *f* curtains he coupled
Ex 36:16 And he coupled *f* curtains by
Ex 36:31 *f* for the boards of the one side
Ex 36:32 *f* bars for the boards of the
Ex 36:32 *f* bars for the boards of the
Ex 36:38 the *f* pillars of it with their
Ex 36:38 but their *f* sockets were of brass
Ex 38:1 *f* cubits was the length thereof,
Ex 38:1 *f* cubits the breadth thereof
Ex 38:18 in the breadth was *f* cubits
Ex 38:26 and *f* hundred and fifty men
Ex 38:28 *f* shekels he made hooks for the
Lev 26:8 *f* of you shall chase an hundred,
Lev 27:5 if it be from *f* years old even
Lev 27:6 a month old even unto *f* years old
Lev 27:6 of the male *f* shekels of silver
Num 1:21 and six thousand and *f* hundred
Num 1:25 *f* thousand six hundred and fifty
Num 1:33 were forty thousand and *f* hundred
Num 1:37 *f* thousand and four hundred
Num 1:41 and one thousand and *f* hundred
Num 1:46 thousand and *f* hundred and fifty
Num 2:11 and six thousand and *f* hundred
Num 2:15 *f* thousand and six hundred and
Num 2:19 were forty thousand and *f* hundred
Num 2:23 *f* thousand and four hundred
Num 2:28 and one thousand and *f* hundred
Num 2:32 thousand and *f* hundred and fifty
Num 3:22 were seven thousand and *f* hundred
Num 3:47 Thou shalt even take *f* shekels
Num 3:50 *f* shekels, after the shekel of
Num 4:48 and *f* hundred and fourscore
Num 7:17 *f* rams, *f* he goats, *f* lambs
Num 7:23 *f* rams, *f* he goats, *f* lambs
Num 7:29 *f* rams, *f* he goats, *f* lambs
Num 7:35 *f* rams, *f* he goats, *f* lambs
Num 7:41 *f* rams, *f* he goats, *f* lambs
Num 7:47 *f* rams, *f* he goats, *f* lambs
Num 7:53 *f* rams, *f* he goats, *f* lambs
Num 7:59 *f* rams, *f* he goats, *f* lambs
Num 7:65 *f* rams, *f* he goats, *f* lambs
Num 7:71 *f* rams, *f* he goats, *f* lambs
Num 7:71 *f* he goats, *f* lambs of the
Num 7:77 *f* rams, *f* he goats, *f* lambs
Num 7:83 *f* rams, *f* he goats, *f* lambs
Num 8:24 *f* years old and upward they shall
Num 11:19 nor *f* days, neither ten days, nor
Num 18:16 for the money of *f* shekels
Num 26:18 them, forty thousand and *f* hundred
Num 26:22 and sixteen thousand and *f* hundred
Num 26:27 threescore thousand and *f* hundred
Num 26:37 and two thousand and *f* hundred
Num 26:41 *f* thousand and six hundred
Num 26:50 *f* thousand and four hundred
Num 31:8 Hur, and Reba, *f* kings of Midian
Num 31:28 one soul of *f* hundred, both of
Num 31:32 thousand and *f* thousand sheep,
Num 31:36 thousand and *f* hundred sheep
Num 31:39 were thirty thousand and *f* hundred
Num 31:43 thousand and *f* hundred sheep,
Num 31:45 thousand asses and *f* hundred,
Josh 8:12 And he took about *f* thousand men
Josh 10:5 Therefore the *f* kings of the
Josh 10:16 But these *f* kings fled, and hid
Josh 10:17 The *f* kings are found hid in a
Josh 10:22 bring out those *f* kings unto me
Josh 10:23 brought forth those *f* kings unto
Josh 10:26 them, and hanged them on *f* trees
Josh 13:3 *f* lords of the Philistines
Josh 14:10 *f* years, even since the LORD
Josh 14:10 this day fourscore and *f* years old
Judg 3:3 *f* lords of the Philistines, and
Judg 18:2 family *f* men from their coasts
Judg 18:7 Then the *f* men departed, and came
Judg 18:14 Then answered the *f* men that went
Judg 18:17 the *f* men that went to spy out

Judg 20:35 f thousand and an hundred men
Judg 20:45 in the highways f thousand men
Judg 20:46 f thousand men that drew the
1Sa 6:4 F golden emerods, and f golden
1Sa 6:4 f golden mice, according to the
1Sa 6:16 And when the f lords of the
1Sa 6:18 belonging to the f lords, both of
1Sa 17:5 was f thousand shekels of brass
1Sa 17:40 chose him f smooth stones out of
1Sa 21:3 give me f loaves of bread in mine
1Sa 22:18 f persons that did wear a linen
1Sa 25:18 f sheep ready dressed, and
1Sa 25:18 f measures of parched corn, and an
1Sa 25:42 with f damsels of hers that went
2Sa 4:4 He was f years old when the
2Sa 21:8 the f sons of Michal the daughter
2Sa 24:9 Judah were f hundred thousand men
1Kin 4:32 and his songs were a thousand and f
1Kin 6:6 chamber was f cubits broad
1Kin 6:10 all the house, f cubits high
1Kin 6:24 f cubits was the one wing of the
1Kin 6:24 f cubits the other wing of the
1Kin 7:3 that lay on forty f pillars
1Kin 7:16 of the one chapiter was f cubits
1Kin 7:16 the other chapiter was f cubits
1Kin 7:23 about, and his height was f cubits
1Kin 7:39 he put f bases on the right side
1Kin 7:39 f on the left side of the house
1Kin 7:49 f on the right side, and f on
1Kin 7:49 f on the left, before the oracle,
1Kin 9:23 f hundred and fifty, which bare
1Kin 22:42 f years old when he began to
1Kin 22:42 twenty and f years in Jerusalem
2Kin 6:25 dung for f pieces of silver
2Kin 7:13 f of the horses that remain,
2Kin 13:19 have smitten f or six times
2Kin 14:2 f years old when he began to
2Kin 15:33 F and twenty years old was he when
2Kin 18:2 f years old was he when he began
2Kin 19:35 hundred fourscore and f thousand
2Kin 21:1 fifty and f years in Jerusalem
2Kin 23:36 f years old when he began to
2Kin 25:19 f men of them that were in the
1Chr 2:4 All the sons of Judah were f
1Chr 2:6 f of them in all
1Chr 3:20 and Hasadiah, Jushab-hesed, f
1Chr 4:32 and Tochen, and Ashan, f cities
1Chr 4:42 f hundred men, went to mount Seir
1Chr 7:3 and Obadiah, and Joel, Ishiah, f
1Chr 7:7 and Uzziel, and Jerimoth, and Iri, f
1Chr 11:23 of great stature, f cubits high
1Chr 29:7 of God of gold f thousand talents
2Chr 3:11 of the one cherub was f cubits
2Chr 3:11 other wing was likewise f cubits
2Chr 3:12 of the other cherub was f cubits
2Chr 3:12 the other wing was f cubits also
2Chr 3:15 f cubits high, and the chapiter
2Chr 3:15 top of each of them was f cubits
2Chr 4:2 f cubits the height thereof
2Chr 4:6 put f on the right hand, and
2Chr 4:6 f on the left, to wash in them
2Chr 4:7 f on the right hand, and f on
2Chr 4:8 f on the right side, and f on
2Chr 6:13 of f cubits long, and f cubits
2Chr 13:17 f hundred thousand chosen men
2Chr 15:19 there was no more war unto the f
2Chr 20:31 f years old when he began to
2Chr 20:31 twenty and f years in Jerusalem
2Chr 25:1 f years old when he began to
2Chr 26:13 f hundred, that made war with
2Chr 27:1 f years old when he began to
2Chr 27:8 He was f and twenty years old when
2Chr 29:1 began to reign when he was f
2Chr 33:1 fifty and f years in Jerusalem
2Chr 35:9 offerings f thousand small cattle
2Chr 35:9 small cattle, and f hundred oxen
2Chr 36:5 f years old when he began to
Ezr 1:11 gold and of silver were f thousand
Ezr 2:5 Arah, seven hundred seventy and f
Ezr 2:8 of Zattu, nine hundred forty and f
Ezr 2:20 children of Gibbar, ninety and f
Ezr 2:33 and Ono, seven hundred twenty and f
Ezr 2:34 Jericho, three hundred forty and f
Ezr 2:66 mules, two hundred forty and f
Ezr 2:67 camels, four hundred thirty and f
Ezr 2:69 f thousand pound of silver, and
Neh 7:13 Zattu, eight hundred forty and f
Neh 7:20 of Adin, six hundred fifty and f
Neh 7:25 children of Gibeon, ninety and f
Neh 7:36 Jericho, three hundred forty and f
Neh 7:67 f singing men and singing women
Neh 7:68 mules, two hundred forty and f
Neh 7:69 camels, four hundred thirty and f
Neh 7:70 f hundred and thirty priests'
Est 9:6 slew and destroyed f hundred men
Est 9:12 destroyed f hundred men in
Est 9:16 f thousand, but they laid not
Job 1:3 f hundred yoke of oxen, and f
Job 1:3 f hundred she asses, and a very
Is 7:8 f years shall Ephraim be broken,
Is 17:6 four or f in the outmost fruitful
Is 19:18 In that day shall f cities in the
Is 30:17 at the rebuke of f shall ye flee
Is 37:36 and fourscore and f thousand
Jer 52:22 of one chapiter was f cubits
Jer 52:30 seven hundred forty and f persons
Jer 52:31 in the twelfth month, in the f
Eze 8:16 porch and the altar, were about f
Eze 11:1 behold at the door of the gate f
Eze 40:1 In the f and twentieth year of our
Eze 40:7 the little chambers were f cubits
Eze 40:13 the breadth was f and twenty
Eze 40:21 fifty cubits, and the breadth f
Eze 40:25 fifty cubits, and the breadth f
Eze 40:29 it was fifty cubits long, and f
Eze 40:30 And the arches round about were f
Eze 40:30 cubits long, and f cubits broad
Eze 40:33 it was fifty cubits long, and f
Eze 40:36 fifty cubits, and the breadth f
Eze 40:48 f cubits on this side
Eze 40:48 and f cubits on that side
Eze 41:2 were f cubits on the one side
Eze 41:2 f cubits on the other side
Eze 41:9 chamber without, was f cubits
Eze 41:11 was left was f cubits round about
Eze 41:12 was f cubits thick round about
Eze 42:16 f hundred reeds, with the
Eze 42:17 f hundred reeds, with the
Eze 42:18 f hundred reeds, with the
Eze 42:19 measured f hundred reeds with the
Eze 42:20 f hundred reeds long, and
Eze 42:20 f hundred broad, to make a
Eze 45:1 length shall be the length of f
Eze 45:2 the sanctuary f hundred in length
Eze 45:2 with f hundred in breadth, square
Eze 45:3 thou measure the length of f
Eze 45:5 And the f and twenty thousand of
Eze 45:6 city f thousand broad, and f
Eze 45:12 twenty shekels, f and twenty
Eze 48:8 which ye shall offer of f
Eze 48:9 offer unto the LORD shall be of f
Eze 48:10 toward the north f and twenty
Eze 48:10 in breadth, and toward the south f
Eze 48:13 priests the Levites shall have f
Eze 48:13 all the length shall be f
Eze 48:15 the f thousand, that are left in
Eze 48:15 in the breadth over against the f
Eze 48:16 f hundred, and the south side four
Eze 48:16 f hundred, and on the east side
Eze 48:16 f hundred, and the west side four
Eze 48:16 side four thousand and f hundred
Eze 48:20 be f and twenty thousand by f
Eze 48:21 of the city, over against the f
Eze 48:21 and westward over against the f
Eze 48:30 thousand and f hundred measures
Eze 48:32 side four thousand and f hundred
Eze 48:33 thousand and f hundred measures
Eze 48:34 f hundred, with their three gates
Dan 12:12 the thousand three hundred and f
Mt 14:17 him, We have here but f loaves
Mt 14:19 the grass, and took the f loaves
Mt 14:21 eaten were about f thousand men
Mt 16:9 neither remember the f loaves of
Mt 16:9 the f thousand, and how many baskets
Mt 25:2 f of them were wise, and f were
Mt 25:15 And unto one he gave f talents
Mt 25:16 had received the f talents went
Mt 25:16 and made them other f talents
Mt 25:20 that had received f talents came
Mt 25:20 came and brought other f talents
Mt 25:20 deliveredst unto me f talents
Mt 25:20 gained beside them f talents more
Mk 6:38 And when they knew, they say, F
Mk 6:41 And when he had taken the f loaves
Mk 6:44 loaves were about f thousand men
Mk 8:19 When I brake the f loaves among
Mk 8:19 f thousand, how many baskets
Lk 1:24 and hid herself f months, saying,
Lk 7:41 the one owed f hundred pence, and
Lk 9:13 We have no more but f loaves
Lk 9:14 they were about f thousand men
Lk 9:16 Then he took the f loaves
Lk 12:6 Are not f sparrows sold for two
Lk 12:52 shall be f in one house divided
Lk 14:19 I have bought f yoke of oxen
Lk 16:28 For I have f brethren
Lk 19:18 thy pound hath gained f pounds
Lk 19:19 him, Be thou also over f cities
Jn 4:18 For thou hast had f husbands
Jn 5:2 tongue Bethesda, having f porches
Jn 6:9 which hath f barley loaves, and
Jn 6:10 down, in number about f thousand
Jn 6:13 fragments of the f barley loaves
Jn 6:19 So when they had rowed about f
Acts 4:4 of the men was about f thousand
Acts 20:6 came unto them to Troas in f days
Acts 24:1 after f days Ananias the high
1Cor 14:19 f words with my understanding
1Cor 15:6 he was seen of above f hundred
2Cor 11:24 Of the Jews f times received I
Rev 9:5 they should be tormented f months
Rev 9:10 power was to hurt men f months
Rev 17:10 f are fallen, and one is, and the

## FIXED

Ps 57:7 My heart is f, O God, my heart is
Ps 57:7 is f, O God, my heart is f
Ps 108:1 O God, my heart is f
Ps 112:7 his heart is f, trusting in the
Lk 16:26 us and you there is a great gulf f

## FLAME

Ex 3:2 a f of fire out of the midst of a
Num 21:28 a f from the city of Sihon
Judg 13:20 when the f went up toward heaven
Judg 13:20 ascended in the f of the altar
Judg 20:38 f with smoke rise up out of the
Judg 20:40 But when the f began to arise up
Judg 20:40 the f of the city ascended up to
Job 15:30 the f shall dry up his branches,
Job 41:21 a f goeth out of his mouth
Ps 83:14 as the f setteth the mountains on
Ps 106:18 the f burned up the wicked
Song 8:6 which hath a most vehement f
Is 5:24 the f consumeth the chaff, so
Is 10:17 a fire, and his Holy One for a f
Is 29:6 and the f of devouring fire
Is 30:30 with the f of a devouring fire,
Is 43:2 shall the f kindle upon thee
Is 47:14 from the power of the f
Jer 48:45 a f from the midst of Sihon, and
Eze 20:47 the flaming f shall not be
Dan 3:22 the f of the fire slew those men
Dan 7:9 his throne was like the fiery f
Dan 7:11 and given to the burning f
Dan 11:33 shall fall by the sword, and by f
Joel 1:19 the f hath burned all the trees
Joel 2:3 and behind them a f burneth
Joel 2:5 like the noise of a f of fire
Obad 18 fire, and the house of Joseph a f
Lk 16:24 for I am tormented in this f
Acts 7:30 the Lord in a f of fire in a bush
Heb 1:7 and his ministers a f of fire
Rev 1:14 and his eyes were as a f of fire
Rev 2:18 his eyes like unto a f of fire
Rev 19:12 His eyes were as a f of fire

## FLAMING

Gen 3:24 a f sword which turned every way,
Ps 104:4 his ministers a f fire
Ps 105:32 for rain, and f fire in their land
Is 4:5 the shining of a f fire by night
Lam 2:3 against Jacob like a f fire
Eze 20:47 the f flame shall not be quenched
Hos 7:6 morning it burneth as a f fire
Nah 2:3 with f torches in the day of his
2Th 1:8 In f fire taking vengeance on

## FLAT

Lev 21:18 a lame, or he that hath a f nose
Num 22:31 his head, and fell f on his face
Josh 6:5 of the city shall fall down f
Josh 6:20 shout, that the wall fell down f

## FLATTERETH

Ps 36:2 For he f himself in his own eyes,
Prov 2:16 stranger which f with her words
Prov 7:5 stranger which f with her words
Prov 20:19 not with him that f with his lips
Prov 28:23 than he that f with the tongue
Prov 29:5 A man that f his neighbour

### FLATTERING
Job 32:21 let me give *f* titles unto man
Job 32:22 For I know not to give *f* titles
Ps 12:2 with *f* lips and with a double
Ps 12:3 The LORD shall cut off all *f* lips
Prov 7:21 with the *f* of her lips she forced
Prov 26:28 and a *f* mouth worketh ruin
Eze 12:24 *f* divination within the house of
1Th 2:5 at any time used we *f* words

### FLAX
Ex 9:31 And the *f* and the barley was
Ex 9:31 in the ear, and the *f* was bolled
Josh 2:6 and hid them with the stalks of *f*
Judg 15:14 as *f* that was burnt with fire
Prov 31:13 She seeketh wool, and *f*, and
Is 19:9 Moreover they that work in fine *f*
Is 42:3 the smoking *f* shall he not quench
Eze 40:3 with a line of *f* in his hand
Hos 2:5 and my water, my wool and my *f*
Hos 2:9 my *f* given to cover her nakedness
Mt 12:20 smoking *f* shall he not quench,

### FLED
Gen 14:10 the kings of Sodom and Gomorrah *f*
Gen 14:10 that remained *f* to the mountain
Gen 16:6 with her, she *f* from her face
Gen 31:20 in that he told him not that he *f*
Gen 31:21 So he *f* with all that he had
Gen 31:22 on the third day that Jacob was *f*
Gen 35:7 when he *f* from the face of his
Gen 39:12 his garment in her hand, and *f*
Gen 39:13 in her hand, and was *f* forth,
Gen 39:15 he left his garment with me, and *f*
Gen 39:18 his garment with me, and *f* out
Ex 2:15 But Moses *f* from the face of
Ex 4:3 and Moses *f* from before it
Ex 14:5 king of Egypt that the people *f*
Ex 14:27 and the Egyptians *f* against it
Num 16:34 about them *f* at the cry of them
Num 35:25 of his refuge, whither he was *f*
Num 35:26 of his refuge, whither he was *f*
Num 35:32 is *f* to the city of his refuge
Josh 7:4 they *f* before the men of Ai
Josh 8:15 *f* by the way of the wilderness
Josh 8:20 and the people that *f* to the
Josh 10:11 as they *f* from before Israel, and
Josh 10:16 But these five kings *f*, and hid
Josh 20:6 unto the city from whence he *f*
Judg 1:6 But Adoni-bezek *f*
Judg 4:15 chariot, and *f* away on his feet
Judg 4:17 Howbeit Sisera *f* away on his feet
Judg 7:21 all the host ran, and cried, and *f*
Judg 7:22 the host *f* to Beth-shittah in
Judg 8:12 And when Zebah and Zalmunna *f*
Judg 9:21 And Jotham ran away, and *f*, and went
Judg 9:40 he *f* before him, and many were
Judg 9:51 thither *f* all the men and women,
Judg 11:3 Then Jephthah *f* from his brethren
Judg 20:45 *f* toward the wilderness unto the
Judg 20:47 *f* to the wilderness unto the rock
1Sa 4:10 they *f* every man into his tent
1Sa 4:16 I *f* to day out of the army
1Sa 4:17 and said, Israel is *f* before the
1Sa 14:22 they heard that the Philistines *f*
1Sa 17:24 *f* from him, and were sore afraid
1Sa 17:51 their champion was dead, they *f*
1Sa 19:8 and they *f* from him
1Sa 19:10 and David *f*, and escaped that night
1Sa 19:12 and he went, and *f*, and escaped
1Sa 19:18 So David *f*, and escaped, and came
1Sa 20:1 David *f* from Naioth in Ramah, and
1Sa 21:10 *f* that day for fear of Saul, and
1Sa 22:17 and because they knew when he *f*
1Sa 22:20 escaped, and *f* after David
1Sa 23:6 of Ahimelech *f* to David to Keilah
1Sa 27:4 Saul that David was *f* to Gath
1Sa 30:17 men, which rode upon camels, and *f*
1Sa 31:1 the men of Israel *f* from before
1Sa 31:7 saw that the men of Israel *f*
1Sa 31:7 they forsook the cities, and *f*
2Sa 1:4 the people are *f* from the battle
2Sa 4:3 And the Beerothites *f* to Gittaim
2Sa 4:4 and his nurse took him up, and *f*
2Sa 10:13 and they *f* before him
2Sa 10:14 Ammon saw that the Syrians were *f*
2Sa 10:14 then *f* they also before Abishai,
2Sa 10:18 the Syrians *f* before Israel
2Sa 13:29 gat him up upon his mule, and *f*
2Sa 13:34 But Absalom *f*. And the young man
2Sa 13:37 But Absalom *f*, and went to Talmai,
2Sa 13:38 So Absalom *f*, and went to Geshur,
2Sa 18:17 all Israel *f* every one to his
2Sa 19:8 for Israel had *f* every man to his
2Sa 19:9 now he is *f* out of the land for
2Sa 23:11 the people *f* from the Philistines
1Kin 2:7 for so they came to me when I *f*
1Kin 2:28 Joab *f* unto the tabernacle of the
1Kin 2:29 *f* unto the tabernacle of the LORD
1Kin 11:17 That Hadad *f*, he and certain
1Kin 11:23 which *f* from his lord Hadadezer
1Kin 11:40 *f* into Egypt, unto Shishak king
1Kin 12:2 (for he was *f* from the presence
1Kin 20:20 and the Syrians *f*
1Kin 20:30 But the rest *f* to Aphek, into the
1Kin 20:30 And Ben-hadad *f*, and came into the
2Kin 3:24 so that they *f* before them
2Kin 7:7 *f* in the twilight, and left their
2Kin 7:7 as it was, and *f* for their life
2Kin 8:21 the people *f* into their tents
2Kin 9:10 And he opened the door, and *f*
2Kin 9:23 And Joram turned his hands, and *f*
2Kin 9:27 he *f* by the way of the garden
2Kin 9:27 he *f* to Megiddo, and died there
2Kin 14:12 they *f* every man to their tents
2Kin 14:19 and he *f* to Lachish
2Kin 25:4 all the men of war *f* by night by
1Chr 10:1 the men of Israel *f* from before
1Chr 10:7 in the valley saw that they *f*
1Chr 10:7 they forsook their cities, and *f*
1Chr 11:13 the people *f* from before the
1Chr 19:14 and they *f* before him
1Chr 19:15 Ammon saw that the Syrians were *f*
1Chr 19:15 they likewise *f* before Abishai
1Chr 19:18 But the Syrians *f* before Israel
2Chr 10:2 whither he had *f* from the
2Chr 13:16 children of Israel *f* before Judah
2Chr 14:12 and the Ethiopians *f*
2Chr 25:22 they *f* every man to his tent
2Chr 25:27 and he *f* to Lachish
Neh 13:10 were *f* every one to his field
Ps 3:*t* when he *f* from Absalom his son
Ps 31:11 that did see me without *f* from me
Ps 57:*t* when he *f* from Saul in the cave
Ps 104:7 At thy rebuke they *f*
Ps 114:3 The sea saw it, and *f*
Is 10:29 Gibeah of Saul is *f*
Is 21:14 with their bread him that *f*
Is 21:15 For they *f* from the swords, from
Is 22:3 All thy rulers are *f* together
Is 22:3 together, which have *f* from far
Is 33:3 noise of the tumult the people *f*
Jer 4:25 the birds of the heavens were *f*
Jer 9:10 of the heavens and the beast are *f*
Jer 26:21 heard it, he was afraid, and *f*
Jer 39:4 all the men of war, then they *f*
Jer 46:5 are *f* apace, and look not back
Jer 46:21 back, and are *f* away together
Jer 48:45 They that *f* stood under the
Jer 52:7 up, and all the men of war *f*
Lam 4:15 when they *f* away and wandered,
Dan 10:7 so that they *f* to hide themselves
Hos 7:13 for they have *f* from me
Hos 12:12 Jacob *f* into the country of Syria
Jonah 1:10 For the men knew that he *f* from
Jonah 4:2 Therefore I *f* before unto
Zec 14:5 like as ye *f* from before the
Mt 8:33 And they that kept them *f*, and went
Mt 26:56 the disciples forsook him, and *f*
Mk 5:14 And they that fed the swine *f*
Mk 14:50 And they all forsook him, and *f*
Mk 14:52 linen cloth, and *f* from them naked
Mk 16:8 quickly, and *f* from the sepulchre
Lk 8:34 them saw what was done, they *f*
Acts 7:29 Then *f* Moses at this saying, and
Acts 14:6 *f* unto Lystra and Derbe, cities of
Acts 16:27 that the prisoners had been *f*
Acts 19:16 so that they *f* out of that house
Heb 6:18 who have *f* for refuge to lay hold
Rev 12:6 the woman *f* into the wilderness,
Rev 16:20 And every island *f* away, and the
Rev 20:11 the earth and the heaven *f* away

### FLEE
Gen 16:8 I *f* from the face of my mistress
Gen 19:20 now, this city is near to *f* unto
Gen 27:43 *f* thou to Laban my brother to
Gen 31:27 didst thou *f* away secretly
Ex 9:20 his cattle *f* into the houses
Ex 14:25 Let us *f* from the face of Israel
Ex 21:13 thee a place whither he shall *f*
Lev 26:17 ye shall *f* when none pursueth you
Lev 26:36 and they shall *f*, as fleeing from
Num 10:35 them that hate thee *f* before thee
Num 24:11 Therefore now *f* thou to thy place
Num 35:6 manslayer, that he may *f* thither
Num 35:11 that the slayer may *f* thither
Num 35:15 any person unawares may *f* thither
Deut 4:42 That the slayer might *f* thither
Deut 19:3 that every slayer may *f* thither
Deut 19:4 the slayer, which shall *f* thither
Deut 19:5 he shall *f* unto one of those
Deut 28:7 way, and *f* before thee seven ways
Deut 28:25 them, and *f* seven ways before them
Josh 8:5 first, that we will *f* before them
Josh 8:6 They *f* before us, as at the first
Josh 8:6 therefore we will *f* before them
Josh 8:20 power to *f* this way or that way
Josh 20:3 and unwittingly may *f* thither
Josh 20:4 when he that doth *f* unto one of
Josh 20:9 at unawares might *f* thither
Judg 20:32 children of Israel said, Let us *f*
2Sa 4:4 to pass, as she made haste to *f*
2Sa 15:14 at Jerusalem, Arise, and let us *f*
2Sa 17:2 people that are with him shall *f*
2Sa 18:3 for if we *f* away, they will not
2Sa 19:3 steal away when they *f* in battle
2Sa 24:13 or wilt thou *f* three months
1Kin 12:18 to his chariot, to *f* to Jerusalem
2Kin 9:3 Then open the door, and *f*, and
2Chr 10:18 to his chariot, to *f* to Jerusalem
Neh 6:11 I said, Should such a man as I *f*
Job 9:25 they *f* away, they see no good
Job 20:24 He shall *f* from the iron weapon,
Job 27:22 he would fain *f* out of his hand
Job 30:10 they *f* far from me, and spare not
Job 41:28 The arrow cannot make him *f*
Ps 11:1 *F* as a bird to your mountain
Ps 64:8 all that see them shall *f* away
Ps 68:1 also that hate him *f* before him
Ps 68:12 Kings of armies did *f* apace
Ps 139:7 shall I *f* from thy presence
Ps 143:9 I *f* unto thee to hide me
Prov 28:1 The wicked *f* when no man pursueth
Prov 28:17 of any person shall *f* to the pit
Song 2:17 day break, and the shadows *f* away
Song 4:6 day break, and the shadows *f* away
Is 10:3 to whom will ye *f* for help
Is 10:31 of Gebim gather themselves to *f*
Is 13:14 *f* every one into his own land
Is 15:5 his fugitives shall *f* unto Zoar
Is 17:13 them, and they shall *f* far off
Is 20:6 whither we *f* for help to be
Is 30:16 for we will *f* upon horses
Is 30:16 therefore shall ye *f*
Is 30:17 One thousand shall *f* at the
Is 30:17 at the rebuke of five shall ye *f*
Is 31:8 but he shall *f* from the sword, and
Is 35:10 and sorrow and sighing shall *f* away
Is 48:20 *f* ye from the Chaldeans, with a
Is 51:11 sorrow and mourning shall *f* away
Jer 4:29 The whole city shall *f* for the
Jer 6:1 gather yourselves to *f* out of the
Jer 25:35 shepherds shall have no way to *f*
Jer 46:6 Let not the swift *f* away, nor the
Jer 48:6 *F*, save your lives, and be like
Jer 48:9 wings unto Moab, that it may *f*
Jer 49:8 *F* ye, turn back, dwell deep, O
Jer 49:24 feeble, and turneth herself to *f*
Jer 49:30 *F*, get you far off, dwell deep, O
Jer 50:16 they shall *f* every one to his own
Jer 50:28 The voice of them that *f* and
Jer 51:6 *F* out of the midst of Babylon, and
Amos 2:16 shall *f* away naked in that day
Amos 5:19 As if a man did *f* from a lion
Amos 7:12 *f* thee away into the land of
Amos 9:1 fleeth of them shall not *f* away
Jonah 1:3 But Jonah rose up to *f* unto
Nah 2:8 yet they shall *f* away
Nah 3:7 look upon thee shall *f* from thee
Nah 3:17 when the sun ariseth they *f* away
Zec 2:6 *f* from the land of the north,
Zec 14:5 ye shall *f* to the valley of the
Zec 14:5 yea, ye shall *f*, like as ye fled
Mt 2:13 *f* into Egypt, and be thou there
Mt 3:7 you to *f* from the wrath to come
Mt 10:23 in this city, *f* ye into another
Mt 24:16 be in Judaea *f* into the mountains
Mk 13:14 be in Judaea *f* to the mountains
Lk 3:7 you to *f* from the wrath to come
Lk 21:21 are in Judaea *f* to the mountains

Jn 10:5 not follow, but will *f* from him
Acts 27:30 were about to *f* out of the ship
1Cor 6:18 *F* fornication
1Cor 10:14 dearly beloved, *f* from idolatry
1Ti 6:11 O man of God, *f* these things
2Ti 2:22 *F* also youthful lusts
Jas 4:7 the devil, and he will *f* from you
Rev 9:6 die, and death shall *f* from them

**FLEECE**
Deut 18:4 the first of the *f* of thy sheep
Judg 6:37 I will put a *f* of wool in the
Judg 6:37 and if the dew be on the *f* only
Judg 6:38 morrow, and thrust the *f* together
Judg 6:38 and wringed the dew out of the *f*
Judg 6:39 thee, but this once with the *f*
Judg 6:39 let it now be dry only upon the *f*
Judg 6:40 for it was dry upon the *f* only
Job 31:20 not warmed with the *f* of my sheep

**FLEETH**
Deut 19:11 *f* into one of these cities
Job 14:2 he *f* also as a shadow, and
Is 24:18 that he who *f* from the noise of
Jer 48:19 ask him that *f*, and her that
Jer 48:44 He that *f* from the fear shall
Amos 9:1 he that *f* of them shall not flee
Nah 3:16 cankerworm spoileth, and *f* away
Jn 10:12 and leaveth the sheep, and *f*
Jn 10:13 The hireling *f*, because he is an

**FLESH**
Gen 2:21 closed up the *f* instead thereof
Gen 2:23 of my bones, and *f* of my *f*
Gen 2:24 and they shall be one *f*
Gen 6:3 with man, for that he also is *f*
Gen 6:12 for all *f* had corrupted his way
Gen 6:13 The end of all *f* is come before
Gen 6:17 upon the earth, to destroy all *f*
Gen 6:19 And of every living thing of all *f*
Gen 7:15 into the ark, two and two of all *f*
Gen 7:16 went in male and female of all *f*
Gen 7:21 all *f* died that moved upon the
Gen 8:17 thing that is with thee, of all *f*
Gen 9:4 But *f* with the life thereof,
Gen 9:11 neither shall all *f* be cut off
Gen 9:15 and every living creature of all *f*
Gen 9:15 become a flood to destroy all *f*
Gen 9:16 of all *f* that is upon the earth
Gen 9:17 all *f* that is upon the earth
Gen 17:11 circumcise the *f* of your foreskin
Gen 17:13 *f* for an everlasting covenant
Gen 17:14 whose *f* of his foreskin is not
Gen 17:23 circumcised the *f* of their
Gen 17:24 in the *f* of his foreskin
Gen 17:25 in the *f* of his foreskin
Gen 29:14 Surely thou art my bone and my *f*
Gen 37:27 for he is our brother and our *f*
Gen 40:19 shall eat thy *f* from off thee
Ex 4:7 was turned again as his other *f*
Ex 12:8 shall eat the *f* in that night
Ex 12:46 of the *f* abroad out of the house
Ex 16:3 Egypt, when we sat by the *f* pots
Ex 16:8 give you in the evening *f* to eat
Ex 16:12 saying, At even ye shall eat *f*
Ex 21:28 and his *f* shall not be eaten
Ex 22:31 neither shall ye eat any *f* that
Ex 29:14 But the *f* of the bullock, and his
Ex 29:31 seethe his *f* in the holy place
Ex 29:32 sons shall eat the *f* of the ram
Ex 29:34 And if ought of the *f* of the
Ex 30:32 Upon man's *f* shall it not be
Lev 4:11 skin of the bullock, and all his *f*
Lev 6:10 breeches shall he put upon his *f*
Lev 6:27 touch the *f* thereof shall be holy
Lev 7:15 the *f* of the sacrifice of his
Lev 7:17 But the remainder of the *f* of the
Lev 7:18 if any of the *f* of the sacrifice
Lev 7:19 the *f* that toucheth any unclean
Lev 7:19 and as for the *f*, all that be
Lev 7:20 the *f* of the sacrifice of peace
Lev 7:21 eat of the *f* of the sacrifice of
Lev 8:17 the bullock, and his hide, his *f*
Lev 8:31 Boil the *f* at the door of the
Lev 8:32 And that which remaineth of the *f*
Lev 9:11 And the *f* and the hide he burnt
Lev 11:8 Of their *f* shall ye not eat, and
Lev 11:11 ye shall not eat of their *f*
Lev 12:3 in the eighth day the *f* of his
Lev 13:2 in the skin of his *f* a rising
Lev 13:2 it be in the skin of his *f* like
Lev 13:3 the plague in the skin of the *f*
Lev 13:3 be deeper than the skin of his *f*
Lev 13:4 be white in the skin of his *f*
Lev 13:10 be quick raw *f* in the rising
Lev 13:11 old leprosy in the skin of his *f*
Lev 13:13 leprosy have covered all his *f*
Lev 13:14 But when raw *f* appeareth in him,
Lev 13:15 And the priest shall see the raw *f*
Lev 13:15 for the raw *f* is unclean
Lev 13:16 Or if the raw *f* turn again
Lev 13:18 The *f* also, in which, even in the
Lev 13:24 Or if there be any *f*, in the skin
Lev 13:24 the quick *f* that burneth have a
Lev 13:38 the skin of their *f* bright spots
Lev 13:39 skin of their *f* be darkish white
Lev 13:43 appeareth in the skin of the *f*
Lev 14:9 also he shall wash his *f* in water
Lev 15:2 hath a running issue out of his *f*
Lev 15:3 whether his *f* run with his issue,
Lev 15:3 or his *f* be stopped from his
Lev 15:7 he that toucheth the *f* of him
Lev 15:13 bathe his *f* in running water, and
Lev 15:16 he shall wash all his *f* in water
Lev 15:19 and her issue in her *f* be blood
Lev 16:4 the linen breeches upon his *f*
Lev 16:4 shall he wash his *f* in water
Lev 16:24 he shall wash his *f* with water in
Lev 16:26 clothes, and bathe his *f* in water
Lev 16:27 the fire their skins, and their *f*
Lev 16:28 clothes, and bathe his *f* in water
Lev 17:11 the life of the *f* is in the blood
Lev 17:14 For it is the life of all *f*
Lev 17:14 eat the blood of no manner of *f*
Lev 17:14 for the life of all *f* is the
Lev 17:16 he wash them not, nor bathe his *f*
Lev 19:28 cuttings in your *f* for the dead
Lev 21:5 nor make any cuttings in their *f*
Lev 22:6 unless he wash his *f* with water
Lev 26:29 ye shall eat the *f* of your sons
Lev 26:29 the *f* of your daughters shall ye
Num 8:7 and let them shave all their *f*
Num 11:4 said, Who shall give us *f* to eat
Num 11:13 Whence should I have *f* to give
Num 11:13 weep unto me, saying, Give us *f*
Num 11:18 to morrow, and ye shall eat *f*
Num 11:18 Who shall give us *f* to eat
Num 11:18 the LORD will give you *f*, and ye
Num 11:21 hast said, I will give them *f*
Num 11:33 while the *f* was yet between their
Num 12:12 of whom the *f* is half consumed
Num 16:22 the God of the spirits of all *f*
Num 18:15 that openeth the matrix in all *f*
Num 18:18 the *f* of them shall be thine, as
Num 19:5 her skin, and her *f*, and her blood,
Num 19:7 and he shall bathe his *f* in water
Num 19:8 in water, and bathe his *f* in water
Num 27:16 the God of the spirits of all *f*
Deut 5:26 For who is there of all *f*
Deut 12:15 kill and eat *f* in all thy gates,
Deut 12:20 and thou shalt say, I will eat *f*
Deut 12:20 because thy soul longeth to eat *f*
Deut 12:20 thou mayest eat *f*, whatsoever thy
Deut 12:23 not eat the life with the *f*
Deut 12:27 offer thy burnt offerings, the *f*
Deut 12:27 thy God, and thou shalt eat the *f*
Deut 14:8 ye shall not eat of their *f*
Deut 16:4 shall there any thing of the *f*
Deut 28:53 the *f* of thy sons and of thy
Deut 28:55 *f* of his children whom he shall
Deut 32:42 blood, and my sword shall devour *f*
Judg 6:19 the *f* he put in a basket, and he
Judg 6:20 of God said unto him, Take the *f*
Judg 6:21 was in his hand, and touched the *f*
Judg 6:21 of the rock, and consumed the *f*
Judg 8:7 then I will tear your *f* with the
Judg 9:2 that I am your bone and your *f*
1Sa 2:13 while the *f* was in seething, with
1Sa 2:15 Give *f* to roast for the priest
1Sa 2:15 he will not have sodden *f* of thee
1Sa 17:44 I will give thy *f* unto the fowls
1Sa 25:11 my *f* that I have killed for my
2Sa 5:1 Behold, we are thy bone and thy *f*
2Sa 6:19 of bread, and a good piece of *f*
2Sa 19:12 brethren, ye are my bones and my *f*
2Sa 19:13 thou not of my bone, and of my *f*
1Kin 17:6 *f* in the morning, and bread and
1Kin 17:6 and bread and *f* in the evening
1Kin 19:21 them, and boiled their *f* with the
1Kin 21:27 and put sackcloth upon his *f*
2Kin 4:34 the *f* of the child waxed warm
2Kin 5:10 thy *f* shall come again to thee,
2Kin 5:14 his *f* came again like unto the
2Kin 5:14 like unto the *f* of a little child
2Kin 6:30 had sackcloth within upon his *f*
2Kin 9:36 shall dogs eat the *f* of Jezebel
1Chr 11:1 Behold, we are thy bone and thy *f*
1Chr 16:3 of bread, and a good piece of *f*
2Chr 32:8 With his is an arm of *f*
Neh 5:5 *f* is as the *f* of our brethren
Job 2:5 now, and touch his bone and his *f*
Job 4:15 the hair of my *f* stood up
Job 6:12 or is my *f* of brass
Job 7:5 My *f* is clothed with worms and
Job 10:4 Hast thou eyes of *f*
Job 10:11 hast clothed me with skin and *f*
Job 13:14 do I take my *f* in my teeth
Job 14:22 But his *f* upon him shall have
Job 19:20 cleaveth to my skin and to my *f*
Job 19:22 and are not satisfied with my *f*
Job 19:26 yet in my *f* shall I see God
Job 21:6 and trembling taketh hold on my *f*
Job 31:31 said not, Oh that we had of his *f*
Job 33:21 His *f* is consumed away, that it
Job 33:25 His *f* shall be fresher than a
Job 34:15 All *f* shall perish together, and
Job 41:23 The flakes of his *f* are joined
Ps 16:9 my *f* also shall rest in hope
Ps 27:2 foes, came upon me to eat up my *f*
Ps 38:3 in my *f* because of thine anger
Ps 38:7 and there is no soundness in my *f*
Ps 50:13 Will I eat the *f* of bulls
Ps 56:4 not fear what *f* can do unto me
Ps 63:1 my *f* longeth for thee in a dry and
Ps 65:2 unto thee shall all *f* come
Ps 73:26 My *f* and my heart faileth
Ps 78:20 can he provide *f* for his people
Ps 78:27 He rained *f* also upon them as
Ps 78:39 remembered that they were but *f*
Ps 79:2 the *f* of thy saints unto the
Ps 84:2 my *f* crieth out for the living
Ps 109:24 and my *f* faileth of fatness
Ps 119:120 My *f* trembleth for fear of thee
Ps 136:25 Who giveth food to all *f*
Ps 145:21 let all *f* bless his holy name for
Prov 4:22 them, and health to all their *f*
Prov 5:11 mourn at the last, when thy *f*
Prov 11:17 that is cruel troubleth his own *f*
Prov 14:30 sound heart is the life of the *f*
Prov 23:20 among riotous eaters of *f*
Eccl 4:5 together, and eateth his own *f*
Eccl 5:6 thy mouth to cause thy *f* to sin
Eccl 11:10 and put away evil from thy *f*
Eccl 12:12 study is a weariness of the *f*
Is 9:20 every man the *f* of his own arm
Is 17:4 fatness of his *f* shall wax lean
Is 22:13 oxen, and killing sheep, eating *f*
Is 31:3 and their horses *f*, and not spirit
Is 40:5 all *f* shall see it together
Is 40:6 All *f* is grass, and all the
Is 44:16 with part thereof he eateth *f*
Is 44:19 I have roasted *f*, and eaten it
Is 49:26 oppress thee with their own *f*
Is 49:26 all *f* shall know that I the LORD
Is 58:7 hide not thyself from thine own *f*
Is 65:4 monuments, which eat swine's *f*
Is 66:16 will the LORD plead with all *f*
Is 66:17 in the midst, eating swine's *f*
Is 66:23 shall all *f* come to worship
Is 66:24 shall be an abhorring unto all *f*
Jer 7:21 unto your sacrifices, and eat *f*
Jer 11:15 the holy *f* is passed from thee
Jer 12:12 no *f* shall have peace
Jer 17:5 maketh *f* his arm, and whose heart
Jer 19:9 them to eat the *f* of their sons
Jer 19:9 the *f* of their daughters, and they
Jer 19:9 the *f* of his friend in the siege
Jer 25:31 nations, he will plead with all *f*
Jer 32:27 I am the LORD, the God of all *f*
Jer 45:5 I will bring evil upon all *f*
Jer 51:35 to my *f* be upon Babylon, shall
Lam 3:4 My *f* and my skin hath he made old
Eze 4:14 there abominable *f* into my mouth
Eze 11:3 is the caldron, and we be the *f*
Eze 11:7 the midst of it, they are the *f*
Eze 11:11 ye be the *f* in the midst thereof
Eze 11:19 the stony heart out of their *f*
Eze 11:19 and will give them an heart of *f*
Eze 16:26 thy neighbours, great of *f*
Eze 20:48 all *f* shall see that I the LORD
Eze 21:4 all *f* from the south to the north
Eze 21:5 That all *f* may know that I the

Eze 23:20 whose *f* is as the *f* of asses,
Eze 24:10 kindle the fire, consume the *f*
Eze 32:5 I will lay thy *f* upon the
Eze 36:26 the stony heart out of your *f*
Eze 36:26 and I will give you an heart of *f*
Eze 37:6 you, and will bring up *f* upon you
Eze 37:8 the *f* came up upon them, and the
Eze 39:17 of Israel, that ye may eat *f*
Eze 39:18 Ye shall eat the *f* of the mighty
Eze 40:43 tables was the *f* of the offering
Eze 44:7 in heart, and uncircumcised in *f*
Eze 44:9 in heart, nor uncircumcised in *f*
Dan 1:15 fatter in *f* than all the children
Dan 2:11 whose dwelling is not with *f*
Dan 4:12 thereof, and all *f* was fed of it
Dan 7:5 unto it, Arise, devour much *f*
Dan 10:3 neither came *f* nor wine in my
Hos 8:13 They sacrifice *f* for the
Joel 2:28 pour out my spirit upon all *f*
Mic 3:2 their *f* from off their bones
Mic 3:3 Who also eat the *f* of my people
Mic 3:3 pot, and as *f* within the caldron
Zeph 1:17 as dust, and their *f* as the dung
Hag 2:12 If one bear holy *f* in the skirt
Zec 2:13 Be silent, O all *f*, before the
Zec 11:9 eat every one the *f* of another
Zec 11:16 but he shall eat the *f* of the fat
Zec 14:12 Their *f* shall consume away while
Mt 16:17 for *f* and blood hath not revealed
Mt 19:5 and they twain shall be one *f*
Mt 19:6 they are no more twain, but one *f*
Mt 24:22 there should no *f* be saved
Mt 26:41 is willing, but the *f* is weak
Mk 10:8 And they twain shall be one *f*
Mk 10:8 they are no more twain, but one *f*
Mk 13:20 those days, no *f* should be saved
Mk 14:38 truly is ready, but the *f* is weak
Lk 3:6 all *f* shall see the salvation of
Lk 24:39 for a spirit hath not *f* and bones,
Jn 1:13 blood, nor of the will of the *f*
Jn 1:14 And the Word was made *f*, and dwelt
Jn 3:6 which is born of the *f* is *f*
Jn 3:6 which is born of the *f* is *f*
Jn 6:51 bread that I will give is my *f*
Jn 6:52 can this man give us his *f* to eat
Jn 6:53 ye eat the *f* of the Son of man
Jn 6:54 Whoso eateth my *f*, and drinketh my
Jn 6:55 For my *f* is meat indeed, and my
Jn 6:56 He that eateth my *f*, and drinketh
Jn 6:63 the *f* profiteth nothing
Jn 8:15 Ye judge after the *f*
Jn 17:2 hast given him power over all *f*
Acts 2:17 pour out of my Spirit upon all *f*
Acts 2:26 moreover also my *f* shall rest in
Acts 2:30 of his loins, according to the *f*
Acts 2:31 neither his *f* did see corruption
Rom 1:3 seed of David according to the *f*
Rom 2:28 which is outward in the *f*
Rom 3:20 no *f* be justified in his sight
Rom 4:1 father, as pertaining to the *f*
Rom 6:19 of the infirmity of your *f*
Rom 7:5 For when we were in the *f*
Rom 7:18 know that in me (that is, in my *f*
Rom 7:25 but with the *f* the law of sin
Rom 8:1 Jesus, who walk not after the *f*
Rom 8:3 in that it was weak through the *f*
Rom 8:3 Son in the likeness of sinful *f*
Rom 8:3 for sin, condemned sin in the *f*
Rom 8:4 in us, who walk not after the *f*
Rom 8:5 *f* do mind the things of the *f*
Rom 8:8 are in the *f* cannot please God
Rom 8:9 But ye are not in the *f*, but in
Rom 8:12 to the *f*, to live after the *f*
Rom 8:13 For if ye live after the *f*
Rom 9:3 my kinsmen according to the *f*
Rom 9:5 as concerning the *f* Christ came
Rom 9:8 which are the children of the *f*
Rom 11:14 to emulation them which are my *f*
Rom 13:14 and make not provision for the *f*
Rom 14:21 It is good neither to eat *f*
1Cor 1:26 not many wise men after the *f*
1Cor 1:29 That no *f* should glory in his
1Cor 5:5 for the destruction of the *f*
1Cor 6:16 for two, saith he, shall be one *f*
1Cor 7:28 such shall have trouble in the *f*
1Cor 8:13 I will eat no *f* while the world
1Cor 10:18 Behold Israel after the *f*
1Cor 15:39 All *f* is not the same *f*
1Cor 15:39 but there is one kind of *f* of men
1Cor 15:39 another *f* of beasts, another of
1Cor 15:50 Now this I say, brethren, that *f*
2Cor 1:17 do I purpose according to the *f*
2Cor 4:11 be made manifest in our mortal *f*
2Cor 5:16 know we no man after the *f*
2Cor 5:16 we have known Christ after the *f*
2Cor 7:1 from all filthiness of the *f*
2Cor 7:5 our *f* had no rest, but we were
2Cor 10:2 if we walked according to the *f*
2Cor 10:3 For though we walk in the *f*
2Cor 10:3 we do not war after the *f*
2Cor 11:18 that many glory after the *f*
2Cor 12:7 was given to me a thorn in the *f*
Gal 1:16 I conferred not with *f* and blood
Gal 2:16 the law shall no *f* be justified
Gal 2:20 life which I now live in the *f* I
Gal 3:3 are ye now made perfect by the *f*
Gal 4:13 how through infirmity of the *f* I
Gal 4:14 which was in my *f* ye despised not
Gal 4:23 bondwoman was born after the *f*
Gal 4:29 *f* persecuted him that was born
Gal 5:13 liberty for an occasion to the *f*
Gal 5:16 not fulfil the lust of the *f*
Gal 5:17 For the *f* lusteth against the
Gal 5:17 and the Spirit against the *f*
Gal 5:19 the works of the *f* are manifest
Gal 5:24 the *f* with the affections
Gal 6:8 to his *f* shall of the *f* reap
Gal 6:12 to make a fair shew in the *f*
Gal 6:13 that they may glory in your *f*
Eph 2:3 times past in the lusts of our *f*
Eph 2:3 fulfilling the desires of the *f*
Eph 2:11 in time past Gentiles in the *f*
Eph 2:11 in the *f* made by hands
Eph 2:15 abolished in his *f* the enmity
Eph 5:29 no man ever yet hated his own *f*
Eph 5:30 are members of his body, of his *f*
Eph 5:31 wife, and they two shall be one *f*
Eph 6:5 your masters according to the *f*
Eph 6:12 For we wrestle not against *f*
Phil 1:22 But if I live in the *f*, this is
Phil 1:24 in the *f* is more needful for you
Phil 3:3 and have no confidence in the *f*
Phil 3:4 also have confidence in the *f*
Phil 3:4 whereof he might trust in the *f*
Col 1:22 the body of his *f* through death
Col 1:24 in my *f* for his body's sake
Col 2:1 as have not seen my face in the *f*
Col 2:5 For though I be absent in the *f*
Col 2:11 *f* by the circumcision of Christ
Col 2:13 and the uncircumcision of your *f*
Col 2:23 honour to the satisfying of the *f*
Col 3:22 your masters according to the *f*
1Ti 3:16 God was manifest in the *f*
Philem 16 more unto thee, both in the *f*
Heb 2:14 the children are partakers of *f*
Heb 5:7 Who in the days of his *f*, when he
Heb 9:13 to the purifying of the *f*
Heb 10:20 the veil, that is to say, his *f*
Heb 12:9 of our *f* which corrected us
Jas 5:3 shall eat your *f* as it were fire
1Pet 1:24 For all *f* is as grass, and all the
1Pet 3:18 God, being put to death in the *f*
1Pet 3:21 away of the filth of the *f*
1Pet 4:1 hath suffered for us in the *f*
1Pet 4:1 in the *f* hath ceased from sin
1Pet 4:2 time in the *f* to the lusts of men
1Pet 4:6 judged according to men in the *f*
2Pet 2:10 them that walk after the *f* in the
2Pet 2:18 allure through the lusts of the *f*
1Jn 2:16 in the world, the lust of the *f*
1Jn 4:2 Christ is come in the *f* is of God
1Jn 4:3 is come in the *f* is not of God
2Jn 7 Jesus Christ is come in the *f*
Jude 7 and going after strange *f*
Jude 8 filthy dreamers defile the *f*
Jude 23 even the garment spotted by the *f*
Rev 17:16 and naked, and shall eat her *f*
Rev 19:18 That ye may eat the *f* of kings
Rev 19:18 the *f* of captains, and the *f*
Rev 19:18 the *f* of mighty men
Rev 19:18 the *f* of horses, and of them that
Rev 19:18 the *f* of all men, both free and
Rev 19:21 fowls were filled with their *f*

## FLESHHOOKS

Ex 27:3 shovels, and his basons, and his *f*
Ex 38:3 shovels, and the basons, and the *f*
Num 4:14 about it, even the censers, the *f*
1Chr 28:17 Also pure gold for the *f*, and the
2Chr 4:16 also, and the shovels, and the *f*

## FLIES

Ex 8:21 I will send swarms of *f* upon thee
Ex 8:21 shall be full of swarms of *f*
Ex 8:22 no swarms of *f* shall be there
Ex 8:24 of *f* into the house of Pharaoh
Ex 8:24 by reason of the swarm of *f*
Ex 8:29 of *f* may depart from Pharaoh
Ex 8:31 the swarms of *f* from Pharaoh
Ps 78:45 sent divers sorts of *f* among them
Ps 105:31 and there came divers sorts of *f*
Eccl 10:1 Dead *f* cause the ointment of the

## FLIGHT

Lev 26:8 you shall put ten thousand to *f*
Deut 32:30 and two put ten thousand to *f*
1Chr 12:15 they put to *f* all them of the
Is 52:12 go out with haste, nor go by *f*
Amos 2:14 Therefore the *f* shall perish from
Mt 24:20 that your *f* be not in the winter
Mk 13:18 pray ye that your *f* be not in the
Heb 11:34 turned to *f* the armies of the

## FLINT

Deut 8:15 forth water out of the rock of *f*
Ps 114:8 the *f* into a fountain of waters
Is 5:28 hoofs shall be counted like *f*
Is 50:7 have I set my face like a *f*
Eze 3:9 than *f* have I made thy forehead

## FLOCK

Gen 4:4 of the firstlings of his *f*
Gen 21:28 ewe lambs of the *f* by themselves
Gen 27:9 Go now to the *f*, and fetch me from
Gen 29:10 watered the *f* of Laban his
Gen 30:31 I will again feed and keep thy *f*
Gen 30:32 pass through all thy *f* to day
Gen 30:40 all the brown in the *f* of Laban
Gen 31:4 and Leah to the field unto his *f*
Gen 31:38 the rams of thy *f* have I not
Gen 33:13 them one day, all the *f* will die
Gen 37:2 was feeding the *f* with his
Gen 37:12 feed their father's *f* in Shechem
Gen 37:13 brethren feed the *f* in Shechem
Gen 38:17 I will send thee a kid from the *f*
Ex 2:16 troughs to water their father's *f*
Ex 2:17 helped them, and watered their *f*
Ex 2:19 enough for us, and watered the *f*
Ex 3:1 Now Moses kept the *f* of Jethro
Ex 3:1 he led the *f* to the backside of
Lev 1:2 even of the herd, and of the *f*
Lev 3:6 unto the LORD be of the *f*
Lev 5:6 hath sinned, a female from the *f*
Lev 5:18 ram without blemish out of the *f*
Lev 6:6 ram without blemish out of the *f*
Lev 27:32 tithe of the herd, or of the *f*
Num 15:3 LORD, of the herd, or of the *f*
Deut 12:17 of thy herds or of thy *f*, nor any
Deut 12:21 kill of thy herd and of thy *f*
Deut 15:14 him liberally out of thy *f*
Deut 15:19 of thy *f* thou shalt sanctify unto
Deut 16:2 unto the LORD thy God, of the *f*
1Sa 17:34 bear, and took a lamb out of the *f*
2Sa 12:4 and he spared to take of his own *f*
2Chr 35:7 gave to the people, of the *f*
Ezr 10:19 a ram of the *f* for their trespass
Job 21:11 forth their little ones like a *f*
Job 30:1 to have set with the dogs of my *f*
Ps 77:20 like a *f* by the hand of Moses
Ps 78:52 them in the wilderness like a *f*
Ps 80:1 thou that leadest Joseph like a *f*
Ps 107:41 and maketh him families like a *f*
Song 1:7 thou makest thy *f* to rest at noon
Song 1:8 forth by the footsteps of the *f*
Song 4:1 thy hair is as a *f* of goats
Song 4:2 Thy teeth are like a *f* of sheep
Song 6:5 thy hair is as a *f* of goats that
Song 6:6 Thy teeth are as a *f* of sheep
Is 40:11 shall feed his *f* like a shepherd
Is 63:11 sea with the shepherd of his *f*
Jer 13:17 because the LORD's *f* is carried
Jer 13:20 where is the *f* that was given
Jer 13:20 was given thee, thy beautiful *f*
Jer 23:2 Ye have scattered my *f*, and driven
Jer 23:3 *f* out of all countries whither I
Jer 25:34 the ashes, ye principal of the *f*
Jer 25:35 the principal of the *f* to escape
Jer 25:36 howling of the principal of the *f*
Jer 31:10 him, as a shepherd doth his *f*
Jer 31:12 oil, and for the young of the *f*
Jer 49:20 of the *f* shall draw them out
Jer 50:45 of the *f* shall draw them out
Jer 51:23 with thee the shepherd and his *f*

Eze 24:5 Take the choice of the f, and burn
Eze 34:3 but ye feed not the f
Eze 34:6 my f was scattered upon all the
Eze 34:8 surely because my f became a prey
Eze 34:8 my f became meat to every beast
Eze 34:8 did my shepherds search for my f
Eze 34:8 fed themselves, and fed not my f
Eze 34:10 I will require my f at their hand
Eze 34:10 them to cease from feeding the f
Eze 34:10 deliver my f from their mouth
Eze 34:12 As a shepherd seeketh out his f
Eze 34:15 I will feed my f, and I will cause
Eze 34:17 And as for you, O my f, thus saith
Eze 34:19 And as for my f, they eat that
Eze 34:22 Therefore will I save my f
Eze 34:31 And ye my f, the f of my
Eze 34:31 the f of my pasture, are men, and
Eze 36:37 increase them with men like a f
Eze 36:38 As the holy f, as the f of
Eze 43:23 ram out of the f without blemish
Eze 43:25 bullock, and a ram out of the f
Eze 45:15 And one lamb out of the f, out of
Amos 6:4 and eat the lambs out of the f
Amos 7:15 LORD took me as I followed the f
Jonah 3:7 neither man nor beast, herd nor f
Mic 2:12 as the f in the midst of their
Mic 4:8 And thou, O tower of the f
Mic 7:14 the f of thine heritage, which
Hab 3:17 the f shall be cut off from the
Zec 9:16 that day as the f of his people
Zec 10:2 they went their way as a f
Zec 10:3 visited his f the house of Judah
Zec 11:4 Feed the f of the slaughter
Zec 11:7 And I will feed the f of slaughter
Zec 11:7 even you, O poor of the f
Zec 11:7 and I fed the f
Zec 11:11 so the poor of the f that waited
Zec 11:17 idol shepherd that leaveth the f
Mal 1:14 which hath in his f a male
Mt 26:31 the sheep of the f shall be
Lk 2:8 watch over their f by night
Lk 12:32 Fear not, little f
Acts 20:28 unto yourselves, and to all the f
Acts 20:29 in among you, not sparing the f
1Cor 9:7 or who feedeth a f, and eateth not
1Cor 9:7 eateth not of the milk of the f
1Pet 5:2 Feed the f of God which is among
1Pet 5:3 but being ensamples to the f

## FLOCKS

Gen 13:5 which went with Abram, had f
Gen 24:35 and he hath given him f, and herds,
Gen 26:14 For he had possession of f
Gen 29:2 there were three f of sheep lying
Gen 29:2 of that well they watered the f
Gen 29:3 thither were all the f gathered
Gen 29:8 until all the f be gathered
Gen 30:36 Jacob fed the rest of Laban's f
Gen 30:38 f in the gutters in the watering
Gen 30:38 troughs when the f came to drink
Gen 30:39 the f conceived before the rods,
Gen 30:40 set the faces of the f toward the
Gen 30:40 and he put his own f by themselves
Gen 32:5 And I have oxen, and asses, f
Gen 32:7 that was with him, and the f
Gen 33:13 the children are tender, and the f
Gen 37:14 thy brethren, and well with the f
Gen 37:16 thee, where they feed their f
Gen 45:10 thy children's children, and thy f
Gen 46:32 and they have brought their f
Gen 47:1 father and my brethren, and their f
Gen 47:4 have no pasture for their f
Gen 47:17 exchange for horses, and for the f
Gen 50:8 their little ones, and their f
Ex 10:9 and with our daughters, with our f
Ex 10:24 only let your f and your herds be
Ex 12:32 Also take your f and your herds,
Ex 12:38 and f, and herds, even very much
Ex 34:3 neither let the f nor herds feed
Lev 1:10 And if his offering be of the f
Lev 5:15 ram without blemish out of the f
Num 11:22 Shall the f and the herds be slain
Num 31:9 all their cattle, and all their f
Num 31:30 beeves, of the asses, and of the f
Num 32:26 Our little ones, our wives, our f
Deut 7:13 the f of thy sheep, in the land
Deut 8:13 thy f multiply, and thy silver and
Deut 12:6 of your herds and of your f
Deut 14:23 of thy herds and of thy f
Deut 28:4 thy kine, and the f of thy sheep
Deut 28:18 thy kine, and the f of thy sheep
Deut 28:51 or f of thy sheep, until he have
Judg 5:16 to hear the bleatings of the f
1Sa 30:20 And David took all the f and the
2Sa 12:2 The rich man had exceeding many f
1Kin 20:27 them like two little f of kids
1Chr 4:39 to seek pasture for their f
1Chr 4:41 was pasture there for their f
1Chr 27:31 over the f was Jaziz the Hagerite
2Chr 17:11 and the Arabians brought him f
2Chr 32:28 manner of beasts, and cotes for f
2Chr 32:29 him cities, and possessions of f
Neh 10:36 of our herds and of our f, to
Job 24:2 they violently take away f
Ps 65:13 The pastures are clothed with f
Ps 78:48 their f to hot thunderbolts
Prov 27:23 to know the state of thy f
Song 1:7 aside by the f of thy companions
Is 17:2 they shall be for f, which shall
Is 32:14 joy of wild asses, a pasture of f
Is 60:7 All the f of Kedar shall be
Is 61:5 shall stand and feed your f
Is 65:10 And Sharon shall be a fold of f
Jer 3:24 their f and their herds, their
Jer 5:17 they shall eat up thy f and thine
Jer 6:3 with their f shall come unto her
Jer 10:21 all their f shall be scattered
Jer 31:24 and they that go forth with f
Jer 33:12 causing their f to lie down
Jer 33:13 shall the f pass again under the
Jer 49:29 their f shall they take away
Jer 50:8 be as the he goats before the f
Eze 25:5 Ammonites a couchingplace for f
Eze 34:2 not the shepherds feed the f
Eze 36:38 cities be filled with f of men
Hos 5:6 They shall go with their f
Joel 1:18 the f of sheep are made desolate
Mic 5:8 a young lion among the f of sheep
Zeph 2:6 for shepherds, and folds for f
Zeph 2:14 f shall lie down in the midst of

## FLOOD

Gen 6:17 do bring a f of waters upon the
Gen 7:6 f of waters was upon the earth
Gen 7:7 because of the waters of the f
Gen 7:10 of the f were upon the earth
Gen 7:17 the f was forty days upon the
Gen 9:11 off any more by the waters of a f
Gen 9:11 more be a f to destroy the earth
Gen 9:15 become a f to destroy all flesh
Gen 9:28 lived after the f three hundred
Gen 10:1 them were sons born after the f
Gen 10:32 divided in the earth after the f
Gen 11:10 Arphaxad two years after the f
Josh 24:2 other side of the f in old time
Josh 24:3 from the other side of the f
Josh 24:14 served on the other side of the f
Josh 24:15 were on the other side of the f
Job 14:11 the f decayeth and drieth up
Job 22:16 foundation was overflown with a f
Job 28:4 The f breaketh out from the
Ps 29:10 The LORD sitteth upon the f
Ps 66:6 they went through the f on foot
Ps 74:15 cleave the fountain and the f
Ps 90:5 carriest them away as with a f
Is 28:2 storm, as a f of mighty waters
Is 59:19 the enemy shall come in like a f
Jer 46:7 Who is this that cometh up as a f
Jer 46:8 Egypt riseth up like a f, and his
Jer 47:2 and shall be an overflowing f
Dan 9:26 the end thereof shall be with a f
Dan 11:22 with the arms of a f shall they
Amos 8:8 and it shall rise up wholly as a f
Amos 8:8 and drowned, as by the f of Egypt
Amos 9:5 it shall rise up wholly like a f
Amos 9:5 be drowned, as by the f of Egypt
Nah 1:8 But with an overrunning f he will
Mt 24:38 before the f they were eating
Mt 24:39 And knew not until the f came
Lk 6:48 and when the f arose, the stream
Lk 17:27 the f came, and destroyed them all
2Pet 2:5 bringing in the f upon the world
Rev 12:15 water as a f after the woman
Rev 12:15 her to be carried away of the f
Rev 12:16 swallowed up the f which the

## FLOODS

Ex 15:8 the f stood upright as an heap,
2Sa 22:5 the f of ungodly men made me
Job 20:17 shall not see the rivers, the f
Job 28:11 He bindeth the f from overflowing
Ps 18:4 the f of ungodly men made me
Ps 24:2 and established it upon the f
Ps 32:6 surely in the f of great waters
Ps 69:2 waters, where the f overflow me
Ps 78:44 and their f, that they could not
Ps 93:3 The f have lifted up, O LORD, the
Ps 93:3 the f have lifted up their voice
Ps 93:3 the f lift up their waves
Ps 98:8 Let the f clap their hands
Song 8:7 love, neither can the f drown it
Is 44:3 thirsty, and f upon the dry ground
Eze 31:15 and I restrained the f thereof
Jonah 2:3 and the f compassed me about
Mt 7:25 the f came, and the winds blew, and
Mt 7:27 the f came, and the winds blew, and

## FLOOR

Gen 50:11 saw the mourning in the f of Atad
Num 5:17 of the dust that is in the f of
Deut 15:14 out of thy flock, and out of thy f
Judg 6:37 put a fleece of wool in the f
Ruth 3:3 thee, and get thee down to the f
Ruth 3:6 And she went down unto the f
Ruth 3:14 that a woman came into the f
1Kin 6:15 both the f of the house, and the
1Kin 6:15 covered the f of the house with
1Kin 6:16 sides of the house, both the f
1Kin 6:30 the f of the house he overlaid
1Kin 7:7 one side of the f to the other
2Chr 34:11 to f the houses which the kings
Is 21:10 my threshing, and the corn of my f
Hos 9:2 The f and the winepress shall not
Hos 13:3 with the whirlwind out of the f
Mic 4:12 them as the sheaves into the f
Mt 3:12 and he will throughly purge his f
Lk 3:17 and he will throughly purge his f

## FLOUR

Ex 29:2 of wheaten f shalt thou make them
Ex 29:40 the one lamb a tenth deal of f
Lev 2:1 his offering shall be of fine f
Lev 2:2 his handful of the f thereof
Lev 2:4 cakes of fine f mingled with oil
Lev 2:5 it shall be of fine f unleavened
Lev 2:7 shall be made of fine f with oil
Lev 5:11 of fine f for a sin offering
Lev 6:15 of the f of the meat offering, and
Lev 6:20 f for a meat offering perpetual
Lev 7:12 cakes mingled with oil, of fine f
Lev 14:10 of fine f for a meat offering
Lev 14:21 one tenth deal of fine f mingled
Lev 23:13 deals of fine f mingled with oil
Lev 23:17 they shall be of fine f
Lev 24:5 And thou shalt take fine f
Num 6:15 cakes of fine f mingled with oil,
Num 7:13 f mingled with oil for a meat
Num 7:19 both of them full of fine f
Num 7:25 both of them full of fine f
Num 7:31 both of them full of fine f
Num 7:37 both of them full of fine f
Num 7:43 both of them full of fine f
Num 7:49 both of them full of fine f
Num 7:55 both of them full of fine f
Num 7:61 both of them full of fine f
Num 7:67 both of them full of fine f
Num 7:73 both of them full of fine f
Num 7:79 both of them full of fine f
Num 8:8 even fine f mingled with oil, and
Num 15:4 offering of a tenth deal of f
Num 15:6 offering two tenth deals of f
Num 15:9 of three tenth deals of f mingled
Num 28:5 an ephah of f for a meat offering
Num 28:9 two tenth deals of f for a meat
Num 28:12 deals of f for a meat offering
Num 28:12 two tenth deals of f for a meat
Num 28:13 a several tenth deal of f mingled
Num 28:20 shall be of f mingled with oil
Num 28:28 offering of f mingled with oil
Num 29:3 shall be of f mingled with oil
Num 29:9 shall be of f mingled with oil
Num 29:14 shall be of f mingled with oil
Judg 6:19 unleavened cakes of an ephah of f
1Sa 1:24 three bullocks, and one ephah of f
1Sa 28:24 hasted, and killed it, and took f
2Sa 13:8 And she took f, and kneaded it, and
2Sa 17:28 and wheat, and barley, and f
1Kin 4:22 day was thirty measures of fine f
2Kin 7:1 of fine f be sold for a shekel
2Kin 7:16 So a measure of fine f was sold
2Kin 7:18 a measure of fine f for a shekel
1Chr 9:29 of the sanctuary, and the fine f

1Chr 23:29 for the fine *f* for meat offering,
Eze 16:13 thou didst eat fine *f*, and honey,
Eze 16:19 also which I gave thee, fine *f*
Eze 46:14 of oil, to temper with the fine *f*
Rev 18:13 and wine, and oil, and fine *f*

## FLOURISH

Ps 72:7 In his days shall the righteous *f*
Ps 72:16 they of the city shall *f* like
Ps 92:7 all the workers of iniquity do *f*
Ps 92:12 shall *f* like the palm tree
Ps 92:13 shall *f* in the courts of our God
Ps 132:18 upon himself shall his crown *f*
Prov 11:28 the righteous shall *f* as a branch
Prov 14:11 tabernacle of the upright shall *f*
Eccl 12:5 way, and the almond tree shall *f*
Song 7:12 let us see if the vine *f*, whether
Is 17:11 shalt thou make thy seed to *f*
Is 66:14 your bones shall *f* like an herb
Eze 17:24 and have made the dry tree to *f*

## FLOW

Job 20:28 his goods shall *f* away in the day
Ps 147:18 his wind to blow, and the waters *f*
Song 4:16 that the spices thereof may *f* out
Is 2:2 and all nations shall *f* unto it
Is 48:21 he caused the waters to *f* out of
Is 60:5 *f* together, and thine heart shall
Is 64:1 might *f* down at thy presence
Jer 31:12 shall *f* together to the goodness
Jer 51:44 the nations shall not *f* together
Joel 3:18 and the hills shall *f* with milk
Joel 3:18 of Judah shall *f* with waters
Mic 4:1 and people shall *f* unto it
Jn 7:38 shall *f* rivers of living water

## FLOWER

Ex 25:33 with a knop and a *f* in one branch
Ex 25:33 other branch, with a knop and a *f*
Ex 37:19 in one branch, a knop and a *f*
Ex 37:19 in another branch, a knop and a *f*
1Sa 2:33 shall die in the *f* of their age
Job 14:2 He cometh forth like a *f*, and is
Job 15:33 shall cast off his *f* as the olive
Ps 103:15 as a *f* of the field, so he
Is 18:5 sour grape is ripening in the *f*
Is 28:1 glorious beauty is a fading *f*
Is 28:4 fat valley, shall be a fading *f*
Is 40:6 thereof is as the *f* of the field
Is 40:7 The grass withereth, the *f* fadeth
Is 40:8 The grass withereth, the *f* fadeth
Nah 1:4 the *f* of Lebanon languisheth
1Cor 7:36 if she pass the *f* of her age
Jas 1:10 because as the *f* of the grass he
Jas 1:11 the *f* thereof falleth, and the
1Pet 1:24 glory of man as the *f* of grass
1Pet 1:24 the *f* thereof falleth away

## FLOWERS

Ex 25:31 his bowls, his knops, and his *f*
Ex 25:34 with their knops and their *f*
Ex 37:17 his bowls, his knops, and his *f*
Ex 37:20 like almonds, his knops, and his *f*
Lev 15:24 her *f* be upon him, he shall be
Lev 15:33 And of her that is sick of her *f*
Num 8:4 shaft thereof, unto the *f* thereof
1Kin 6:18 was carved with knops and open *f*
1Kin 6:29 cherubims and palm trees and open *f*
1Kin 6:32 cherubims and palm trees and open *f*
1Kin 6:35 cherubims and palm trees and open *f*
1Kin 7:26 brim of a cup, with *f* of lilies
1Kin 7:49 before the oracle, with the *f*
2Chr 4:5 brim of a cup, with *f* of lilies
2Chr 4:21 And the *f*, and the lamps, and the
Song 2:12 The *f* appear on the earth
Song 5:13 as a bed of spices, as sweet *f*

## FLOWETH

Lev 20:24 it, a land that *f* with milk
Num 13:27 us, and surely it *f* with milk
Num 14:8 a land which *f* with milk and honey
Num 16:13 up out of a land that *f* with milk
Num 16:14 us into a land that *f* with milk
Deut 6:3 in the land that *f* with milk
Deut 11:9 seed, a land that *f* with milk
Deut 26:9 even a land that *f* with milk
Deut 26:15 fathers, a land that *f* with milk
Deut 27:3 thee, a land that *f* with milk
Deut 31:20 that *f* with milk and honey
Josh 5:6 give us, a land that *f* with milk

## FLOWING

Ex 3:8 a large, unto a land *f* with milk
Ex 3:17 unto a land *f* with milk and honey
Ex 13:5 a land *f* with milk and honey, that
Ex 33:3 Unto a land *f* with milk and honey
Prov 18:4 wellspring of wisdom as a *f* brook
Is 66:12 of the Gentiles like a *f* stream
Jer 11:5 to give them a land *f* with milk
Jer 18:14 or shall the cold *f* waters that
Jer 32:22 a land *f* with milk and honey
Jer 49:4 thy *f* valley, O backsliding
Eze 20:6 *f* with milk and honey, which is
Eze 20:15 *f* with milk and honey, which is

## FLY

Gen 1:20 fowl that may *f* above the earth
1Sa 15:19 but didst *f* upon the spoil, and
2Sa 22:11 he rode upon a cherub, and did *f*
Job 5:7 trouble, as the sparks *f* upward
Job 20:8 He shall *f* away as a dream, and
Job 39:26 Doth the hawk *f* by thy wisdom
Ps 18:10 he rode upon a cherub, and did *f*
Ps 18:10 he did *f* upon the wings of the
Ps 55:6 for then would I *f* away, and be at
Ps 90:10 it is soon cut off, and we *f* away
Prov 23:5 they *f* away as an eagle toward
Is 6:2 his feet, and with twain he did *f*
Is 7:18 the LORD shall hiss for the *f*
Is 11:14 But they shall *f* upon the
Is 60:8 Who are these that *f* as a cloud
Jer 48:40 he shall *f* as an eagle, and shall
Jer 49:22 *f* as the eagle, and spread his
Eze 13:20 hunt the souls to make them *f*
Eze 13:20 souls that ye hunt to make them *f*
Dan 9:21 being caused to *f* swiftly
Hos 9:11 glory shall *f* away like a bird
Hab 1:8 they shall *f* as the eagle that
Rev 12:14 that she might *f* into the
Rev 14:6 I saw another angel *f* in the
Rev 19:17 that *f* in the midst of heaven

## FLYING

Lev 11:21 Yet these may ye eat of every *f*
Lev 11:23 But all other *f* creeping things,
Ps 148:10 creeping things, and *f* fowl
Prov 26:2 by wandering, as the swallow by *f*
Is 14:29 fruit shall be a fiery *f* serpent
Is 30:6 fiery *f* serpent, they will carry
Is 31:5 As birds *f*, so will the LORD of
Zec 5:1 and looked, and behold a *f* roll
Zec 5:2 And I answered, I see a *f* roll
Rev 4:7 fourth beast was like a *f* eagle
Rev 8:13 heard an angel *f* through the

## FOAL

Gen 49:11 Binding his *f* unto the vine, and
Zec 9:9 and upon a colt the *f* of an ass
Mt 21:5 an ass, and a colt the *f* of an ass

## FOES

1Chr 21:12 to be destroyed before thy *f*
Est 9:16 and slew of their *f* seventy
Ps 27:2 wicked, even mine enemies and my *f*
Ps 30:1 hast not made my *f* to rejoice
Ps 89:23 beat down his *f* before his face
Mt 10:36 a man's *f* shall be they of his
Acts 2:35 Until I make thy *f* thy footstool

## FOLD

Is 13:20 the shepherds make their *f* there
Is 65:10 And Sharon shall be a *f* of flocks
Eze 34:14 of Israel shall their *f* be
Eze 34:14 there shall they lie in a good *f*
Mic 2:12 the flock in the midst of their *f*
Hab 3:17 flock shall be cut off from the *f*
Jn 10:16 I have, which are not of this *f*
Jn 10:16 and there shall be one *f*, and one
Heb 1:12 as a vesture shalt thou *f* them up

## FOLDING

1Kin 6:34 two leaves of the one door were *f*
1Kin 6:34 leaves of the other door were *f*
Prov 6:10 a little *f* of the hands to sleep
Prov 24:33 a little *f* of the hands to sleep

## FOLDS

Num 32:24 little ones, and *f* for your sheep
Num 32:36 and *f* of sheep
Ps 50:9 house, nor he goats out of thy *f*
Jer 23:3 will bring them again to their *f*
Zeph 2:6 for shepherds, and *f* for flocks

## FOLK

Gen 33:15 some of the *f* that are with me
Prov 30:26 The conies are but a feeble *f*
Jer 51:58 the *f* in the fire, and they shall
Mk 6:5 laid his hands upon a few sick *f*
Jn 5:3 a great multitude of impotent *f*

## FOLLOW

Gen 24:5 be willing to *f* me unto this land
Gen 24:8 will not be willing to *f* thee
Gen 24:39 the woman will not *f* me
Gen 44:4 his steward, Up, *f* after the men
Ex 11:8 and all the people that *f* thee
Ex 14:4 heart, that he shall *f* after them
Ex 14:17 Egyptians, and they shall *f* them
Ex 21:22 from her, and yet no mischief *f*
Ex 21:23 And if any mischief *f*, then thou
Ex 23:2 Thou shalt not *f* a multitude to
Deut 16:20 is altogether just shalt thou *f*
Deut 18:22 of the LORD, if the thing *f* not
Judg 3:28 And he said unto them, *F* after me
Judg 8:5 bread unto the people that *f* me
Judg 9:3 hearts inclined to *f* Abimelech
1Sa 25:27 unto the young men that *f* my lord
1Sa 30:21 faint that they could not *f* David
2Sa 17:9 among the people that *f* Absalom
1Kin 18:21 if the LORD be God, *f* him
1Kin 18:21 but if Baal, then *f* him
1Kin 19:20 my mother, and then I will *f* thee
1Kin 20:10 for all the people that *f* me
2Kin 6:19 *f* me, and I will bring you to the
Ps 23:6 mercy shall *f* me all the days of
Ps 38:20 because I *f* the thing that good
Ps 45:14 *f* her shall be brought unto thee
Ps 94:15 the upright in heart shall *f* it
Ps 119:150 draw nigh that *f* after mischief
Is 5:11 that they may *f* strong drink
Is 51:1 ye that *f* after righteousness, ye
Jer 17:16 from being a pastor to *f* thee
Jer 42:16 shall *f* close after you there in
Eze 13:3 that *f* their own spirit, and have
Hos 2:7 she shall *f* after her lovers, but
Hos 6:3 if we *f* on to know the LORD
Mt 4:19 *F* me, and I will make you fishers
Mt 8:19 I will *f* thee whithersoever thou
Mt 8:22 But Jesus said unto him, *F* me
Mt 9:9 and he saith unto him, *F* me
Mt 16:24 and take up his cross, and *f* me
Mt 19:21 and come and *f* me
Mk 2:14 of custom, and said unto him, *F* me
Mk 5:37 And he suffered no man to *f* him
Mk 6:1 and his disciples *f* him
Mk 8:34 and take up his cross, and *f* me
Mk 10:21 come, take up the cross, and *f* me
Mk 14:13 bearing a pitcher of water: *f* him
Mk 16:17 signs shall *f* them that believe
Lk 5:27 and he said unto him, *F* me
Lk 9:23 take up his cross daily, and *f* me
Lk 9:57 I will *f* thee whithersoever thou
Lk 9:59 And he said unto another, *F* me
Lk 9:61 also said, Lord, I will *f* thee
Lk 17:23 go not after them, nor *f* them
Lk 18:22 in heaven: and come, *f* me
Lk 22:10 *f* him into the house where he
Lk 22:49 were about him saw what would *f*
Jn 1:43 Philip, and saith unto him, *F* me
Jn 10:4 before them, and the sheep *f* him
Jn 10:5 And a stranger will they not *f*
Jn 10:27 and I know them, and they *f* me
Jn 12:26 If any man serve me, let him *f* me
Jn 13:36 I go, thou canst not *f* me now
Jn 13:36 but thou shalt *f* me afterwards
Jn 13:37 Lord, why cannot I *f* thee now
Jn 21:19 this, he saith unto him, *F* me
Jn 21:22 is that to thee? *f* thou me
Acts 3:24 from Samuel and those that *f* after
Acts 12:8 thy garment about thee, and *f* me
Rom 14:19 Let us therefore *f* after the
1Cor 14:1 *F* after charity, and desire
Phil 3:12 but I *f* after, if that I may
1Th 5:15 but ever *f* that which is good,
2Th 3:7 know how ye ought to *f* us
2Th 3:9 an ensample unto you to *f* us
1Ti 5:24 and some men they *f* after
1Ti 6:11 *f* after righteousness, godliness,
2Ti 2:22 but *f* righteousness, faith,
Heb 12:14 *F* peace with all men, and holiness
Heb 13:7 whose faith *f*, considering the
1Pet 1:11 and the glory that should *f*
1Pet 2:21 that ye should *f* his steps
2Pet 2:2 many shall *f* their pernicious
3Jn 11 *f* not that which is evil, but
Rev 14:4 These are they which *f* the Lamb
Rev 14:13 and their works do *f* them

## FOLLOWED

Gen 24:61 upon the camels, and f the man
Gen 32:19 all that f the droves, saying, On
Num 14:24 hath f me fully, him will I bring
Num 16:25 and the elders of Israel f him
Num 32:11 because they have not wholly f me
Num 32:12 for they have wholly f the LORD
Deut 1:36 because he hath wholly f the LORD
Deut 4:3 for all the men that f Baal-peor
Josh 6:8 the covenant of the LORD f them
Josh 14:8 but I wholly f the LORD my God
Josh 14:9 hast wholly f the LORD my God
Josh 14:14 wholly f the LORD God of Israel
Judg 2:12 f other gods, of the gods of the
Judg 9:4 and light persons, which f him
Judg 9:49 f Abimelech, and put them to the
1Sa 13:7 and all the people f him trembling
1Sa 14:22 even they also f hard after them
1Sa 17:13 went and f Saul to the battle
1Sa 17:14 and the three eldest f Saul
1Sa 31:2 the Philistines f hard upon Saul
2Sa 1:6 horsemen f hard after him
2Sa 2:10 But the house of Judah f David
2Sa 3:31 And king David himself f the bier
2Sa 11:8 there f him a mess of meat from
2Sa 17:23 saw that his counsel was not f
2Sa 20:2 f Sheba the son of Bichri
1Kin 12:20 none that f the house of David
1Kin 14:8 who f me with all his heart, to
1Kin 16:21 half of the people f Tibni the
1Kin 16:21 and half f Omri
1Kin 16:22 But the people that f Omri
1Kin 16:22 that f Tibni the son of Ginath
1Kin 18:18 the LORD, and thou hast f Baalim
1Kin 20:19 city, and the army which f them
2Kin 3:9 and for the cattle that f them
2Kin 4:30 And he arose, and f her
2Kin 5:21 So Gehazi f after Naaman
2Kin 9:27 Jehu f after him, and said, Smite
2Kin 13:2 f the sins of Jeroboam the son of
2Kin 17:15 they f vanity, and became vain,
1Chr 10:2 the Philistines f hard after Saul
Neh 4:23 the men of the guard which f me
Ps 68:25 players on instruments f after
Eze 10:11 whither the head looked they f it
Amos 7:15 the LORD took me as I f the flock
Mt 4:20 left their nets, and f him
Mt 4:22 ship and their father, and f him
Mt 4:25 there f him great multitudes of
Mt 8:1 mountain, great multitudes f him
Mt 8:10 marvelled, and said to them that f
Mt 8:23 into a ship, his disciples f him
Mt 9:9 And he arose, and f him
Mt 9:19 f him, and so did his disciples
Mt 9:27 thence, two blind men f him
Mt 12:15 and great multitudes f him
Mt 14:13 they f him on foot out of the
Mt 19:2 And great multitudes f him
Mt 19:27 we have forsaken all, and f thee
Mt 19:28 unto you, That ye which have f me
Mt 20:29 Jericho, a great multitude f him
Mt 20:34 received sight, and they f him
Mt 21:9 that went before, and that f
Mt 26:58 But Peter f him afar off unto the
Mt 27:55 which f Jesus from Galilee,
Mt 27:62 that f the day of the preparation
Mk 1:18 they forsook their nets, and f him
Mk 1:36 that were with him f after him
Mk 2:14 And he arose and f him
Mk 2:15 there were many, and they f him
Mk 3:7 multitude from Galilee f him
Mk 5:24 and much people f him, and thronged
Mk 10:28 we have left all, and have f thee
Mk 10:32 and as they f, they were afraid
Mk 10:52 his sight, and f Jesus in the way
Mk 11:9 that went before, and they that f
Mk 14:51 there f him a certain young man,
Mk 14:54 Peter f him afar off, even into
Mk 15:41 f him, and ministered unto him
Lk 5:11 land, they forsook all, and f him
Lk 5:28 And he left all, rose up, and f him
Lk 7:9 said unto the people that f him
Lk 9:11 people, when they knew it, f him
Lk 18:28 Lo, we have left all, and f thee
Lk 18:43 sight, and f him, glorifying God
Lk 22:39 and his disciples also f him
Lk 22:54 And Peter f afar off
Lk 23:27 there f him a great company of
Lk 23:49 the women that f him from Galilee
Lk 23:55 f after, and beheld the sepulchre,
Jn 1:37 heard him speak, and they f Jesus
Jn 1:40 f him, was Andrew, Simon Peter's
Jn 6:2 And a great multitude f him
Jn 11:31 f her, saying, She goeth unto the
Jn 18:15 And Simon Peter f Jesus, and so did
Acts 12:9 And he went out, and f him
Acts 13:43 and religious proselytes f Paul
Acts 16:17 The same f Paul and us, and cried,
Acts 21:36 multitude of the people f after
Rom 9:30 which f not after righteousness,
Rom 9:31 Israel, which f after the law of
1Cor 10:4 that spiritual Rock that f them
1Ti 5:10 have diligently f every good work
2Pet 1:16 For we have not f cunningly
Rev 6:8 him was Death, and Hell f with him
Rev 8:7 angel sounded, and there f hail
Rev 14:8 there f another angel, saying,
Rev 14:9 And the third angel f them
Rev 19:14 in heaven f him upon white horses

## FOLLOWERS

1Cor 4:16 I beseech you, be ye f of me
1Cor 11:1 Be ye f of me, even as I also am
Eph 5:1 Be ye therefore f of God, as dear
Phil 3:17 be f together of me, and mark them
1Th 1:6 And ye became f of us, and of the
1Th 2:14 became f of the churches of God
Heb 6:12 but f of them who through faith
1Pet 3:13 if ye be f of that which is good

## FOLLOWETH

2Kin 11:15 him that f her kill with the
2Chr 23:14 and whoso f her, let him be slain
Ps 63:8 My soul f hard after thee
Prov 12:11 but he that f vain persons is
Prov 15:9 him that f after righteousness
Prov 21:21 He that f after righteousness and
Prov 28:19 but he that f after vain persons
Is 1:23 loveth gifts, and f after rewards
Eze 16:34 whereas none f thee to commit
Hos 12:1 on wind, and f after the east wind
Mt 10:38 f after me, is not worthy of me
Mk 9:38 in thy name, and he f not us
Mk 9:38 forbad him, because he f not us
Lk 9:49 him, because he f not with us
Jn 8:12 he that f me shall not walk in

## FOLLOWING

Gen 41:31 land by reason of that famine f
Deut 7:4 will turn away thy son from f me
Deut 12:30 that thou be not snared by f them
Josh 22:16 away this day from f the LORD
Josh 22:18 away this day from f the LORD
Josh 22:23 an altar to turn from f the LORD
Josh 22:29 and turn this day from f the LORD
Judg 2:19 in f other gods to serve them, and
Ruth 1:16 or to return from f after thee
1Sa 12:14 you continue f the LORD your God
1Sa 12:20 turn not aside from f the LORD
1Sa 14:46 went up from f the Philistines
1Sa 15:11 for he is turned back from f me
1Sa 24:1 returned from f the Philistines
2Sa 2:19 hand nor to the left from f Abner
2Sa 2:21 not turn aside from f of him
2Sa 2:22 Asahel, Turn thee aside from f me
2Sa 2:26 return from f their brethren
2Sa 2:27 up every one from f his brother
2Sa 2:30 And Joab returned from f Abner
2Sa 7:8 from f the sheep, to be ruler
1Kin 1:7 they f Adonijah helped him
1Kin 9:6 if ye shall at all turn from f me
1Kin 21:26 he did very abominably in f idols
2Kin 17:21 drave Israel from f the LORD
2Kin 18:6 LORD, and departed not from f him
1Chr 17:7 sheepcote, even from f the sheep
2Chr 25:27 f the LORD they made a conspiracy
2Chr 34:33 they departed not from f the LORD
Ps 48:13 may tell it to the generation f
Ps 78:71 From f the ewes great with young
Ps 109:13 in the generation f let their
Mk 16:20 confirming the word with signs f
Lk 13:33 day, and to morrow, and the day f
Jn 1:38 Then Jesus turned, and saw them f
Jn 1:43 The day f Jesus would go forth
Jn 6:22 The day f, when the people which
Jn 20:6 Then cometh Simon Peter f him
Jn 21:20 the disciple whom Jesus loved f
Acts 21:1 the day f unto Rhodes, and from
Acts 21:18 the day f Paul went in with us
Acts 23:11 the night f the Lord stood by him
2Pet 2:15 f the way of Balaam the son of

## FOLLY

Gen 34:7 because he had wrought f in
Deut 22:21 she hath wrought f in Israel
Josh 7:15 he hath wrought f in Israel
Judg 19:23 into mine house, do not this f
Judg 20:6 committed lewdness and f in Israel
Judg 20:10 according to all the f that they
1Sa 25:25 is his name, and f is with him
2Sa 13:12 do not thou this f
Job 4:18 and his angels he charged with f
Job 24:12 yet God layeth not f to them
Job 42:8 lest I deal with you after your f
Ps 49:13 This their way is their f
Ps 85:8 but let them not turn again to f
Prov 5:23 of his f he shall go astray
Prov 13:16 but a fool layeth open his f
Prov 14:8 but the f of fools is deceit
Prov 14:18 The simple inherit f
Prov 14:24 but the foolishness of fools is f
Prov 14:29 is hasty of spirit exalteth f
Prov 15:21 F is joy to him that is destitute
Prov 16:22 but the instruction of fools is f
Prov 17:12 man, rather than a fool in his f
Prov 18:13 before he heareth it, it is f
Prov 26:4 not a fool according to his f
Prov 26:5 Answer a fool according to his f
Prov 26:11 so a fool returneth to his f
Eccl 1:17 wisdom, and to know madness and f
Eccl 2:3 and to lay hold on f, till I might
Eccl 2:12 behold wisdom, and madness, and f
Eccl 2:13 I saw that wisdom excelleth f
Eccl 7:25 and to know the wickedness of f
Eccl 10:1 so doth a little f him that is in
Eccl 10:6 F is set in great dignity, and the
Is 9:17 and every mouth speaketh f
Jer 23:13 I have seen f in the prophets of
2Cor 11:1 bear with me a little in my f
2Ti 3:9 for their f shall be manifest

## FOOD

Gen 2:9 to the sight, and good for f
Gen 3:6 saw that the tree was good for f
Gen 6:21 unto thee of all f that is eaten
Gen 6:21 and it shall be for f for thee
Gen 41:35 let them gather all the f of
Gen 41:35 and let them keep f in the cities
Gen 41:36 that f shall be for store to the
Gen 41:48 up all the f of the seven years
Gen 41:48 laid up the f in the cities
Gen 41:48 the f of the field, which was
Gen 42:7 From the land of Canaan to buy f
Gen 42:10 but to buy f are thy servants
Gen 42:33 take f for the famine of your
Gen 43:2 them, Go again, buy us a little f
Gen 43:4 us, we will go down and buy thee f
Gen 43:20 down at the first time to buy f
Gen 43:22 down in our hands to buy f
Gen 44:1 Fill the men's sacks with f
Gen 44:25 Go again, and buy us a little f
Gen 47:24 seed of the field, and for your f
Gen 47:24 for f for your little ones
Ex 21:10 her f, her raiment, and her duty
Lev 3:11 it is the f of the offering made
Lev 3:16 it is the f of the offering made
Lev 19:23 planted all manner of trees for f
Lev 22:7 because it is his f
Deut 10:18 the stranger, in giving him f
1Sa 14:24 that eateth any f until evening
1Sa 14:24 none of the people tasted any f
1Sa 14:28 man that eateth any f this day
2Sa 9:10 master's son may have f to eat
1Kin 5:9 in giving f for my household
1Kin 5:11 of wheat for f to his household
Job 23:12 mouth more than my necessary f
Job 24:5 wilderness yieldeth f for them
Job 38:41 Who provideth for the raven his f
Job 40:20 the mountains bring him forth f
Ps 78:25 Man did eat angels' f
Ps 104:14 bring forth f out of the earth
Ps 136:25 Who giveth f to all flesh
Ps 146:7 which giveth f to the hungry
Ps 147:9 He giveth to the beast his f
Prov 6:8 gathereth her f in the harvest
Prov 13:23 Much f is in the tillage of the
Prov 27:27 have goats' milk enough for thy f
Prov 27:27 for the f of thy household, and
Prov 28:3 sweeping rain which leaveth no f
Prov 30:8 feed me with f convenient for me
Prov 31:14 she bringeth her f from afar
Eze 16:27 have diminished thine ordinary f

Eze 48:18 f unto them that serve the city
Acts 14:17 filling our hearts with f
2Cor 9:10 both minister bread for your f
1Ti 6:8 And having f and raiment let us be
Jas 2:15 be naked, and destitute of daily f

## FOOL

1Sa 26:21 behold, I have played the f
2Sa 3:33 and said, Died Abner as a f dieth
Ps 14:1 The f hath said in his heart,
Ps 49:10 that wise men die, likewise the f
Ps 53:1 The f hath said in his heart,
Ps 92:6 neither doth a f understand this
Prov 7:22 or as a f to the correction of
Prov 10:8 but a prating f shall fall
Prov 10:10 but a prating f shall fall
Prov 10:18 that uttereth a slander, is a f
Prov 10:23 is as sport to a f to do mischief
Prov 11:29 the f shall be servant to the
Prov 12:15 The way of a f is right in his
Prov 13:16 but a f layeth open his folly
Prov 14:16 but the f rageth, and is confident
Prov 15:5 A f despiseth his father's
Prov 17:7 Excellent speech becometh not a f
Prov 17:10 than an hundred stripes into a f
Prov 17:12 man, rather than a f in his folly
Prov 17:16 in the hand of a f to get wisdom
Prov 17:21 He that begetteth a f doeth it to
Prov 17:21 and the father of a f hath no joy
Prov 17:24 but the eyes of a f are in the
Prov 17:28 Even a f, when he holdeth his
Prov 18:2 A f hath no delight in
Prov 19:1 perverse in his lips, and is a f
Prov 19:10 Delight is not seemly for a f
Prov 20:3 but every f will be meddling
Prov 23:9 Speak not in the ears of a f
Prov 24:7 Wisdom is too high for a f
Prov 26:1 so honour is not seemly for a f
Prov 26:4 Answer not a f according to his
Prov 26:5 Answer a f according to his folly
Prov 26:6 hand of a f cutteth off the feet
Prov 26:8 is he that giveth honour to a f
Prov 26:10 all things both rewardeth the f
Prov 26:11 so a f returneth to his folly
Prov 26:12 is more hope of a f than of him
Prov 27:22 Though thou shouldest bray a f in
Prov 28:26 trusteth in his own heart is a f
Prov 29:11 A f uttereth all his mind
Prov 29:20 is more hope of a f than of him
Prov 30:22 a f when he is filled with meat
Eccl 2:14 but the f walketh in darkness
Eccl 2:15 heart, As it happeneth to the f
Eccl 2:16 wise more than of the f for ever
Eccl 2:16 the wise man? as the f
Eccl 2:19 he shall be a wise man or a f
Eccl 4:5 The f foldeth his hands together,
Eccl 6:8 hath the wise more than the f
Eccl 7:6 pot, so is the laughter of the f
Eccl 10:3 when he that is a f walketh by
Eccl 10:3 saith to every one that he is a f
Eccl 10:12 but the lips of a f will swallow
Eccl 10:14 A f also is full of words
Jer 17:11 days, and at his end shall be a f
Hos 9:7 the prophet is a f, the spiritual
Mt 5:22 but whosoever shall say, Thou f
Lk 12:20 But God said unto him, Thou f
1Cor 3:18 in this world, let him become a f
1Cor 15:36 Thou f, that which thou sowest is
2Cor 11:16 again, Let no man think me a f
2Cor 11:16 yet as a f receive me, that I may
2Cor 11:23 (I speak as a f) I am more
2Cor 12:6 to glory, I shall not be a f
2Cor 12:11 I am become a f in glorying

## FOOLISH

Deut 32:6 the LORD, O f people and unwise
Deut 32:21 them to anger with a f nation
Job 2:10 as one of the f women speaketh
Job 5:2 For wrath killeth the f man
Job 5:3 I have seen the f taking root
Ps 5:5 The f shall not stand in thy
Ps 39:8 make me not the reproach of the f
Ps 73:3 For I was envious at the f
Ps 73:22 So f was I, and ignorant
Ps 74:18 that the f people have blasphemed
Ps 74:22 remember how the f man
Prov 9:6 Forsake the f, and live
Prov 9:13 A f woman is clamorous
Prov 10:1 but a f son is the heaviness of
Prov 10:14 of the f is near destruction
Prov 14:1 but the f plucketh it down with
Prov 14:3 mouth of the f is a rod of pride
Prov 14:7 Go from the presence of a f man
Prov 15:7 the heart of the f doeth not so
Prov 15:20 but a f man despiseth his mother
Prov 17:25 A f son is a grief to his father,
Prov 19:13 A f son is the calamity of his
Prov 21:20 but a f man spendeth it up
Prov 29:9 wise man contendeth with a f man
Eccl 4:13 f king, who will no more be
Eccl 7:17 much wicked, neither be thou f
Eccl 10:15 The labour of the f wearieth
Is 44:25 and maketh their knowledge f
Jer 4:22 For my people is f, they have not
Jer 5:4 these are poor; they are f
Jer 5:21 now this, O f people, and without
Jer 10:8 they are altogether brutish and f
Lam 2:14 seen vain and f things for thee
Eze 13:3 Woe unto the f prophets, that
Zec 11:15 the instruments of a f shepherd
Mt 7:26 shall be likened unto a f man
Mt 25:2 of them were wise, and five were f
Mt 25:3 They that were f took their lamps
Mt 25:8 the f said unto the wise, Give us
Rom 1:21 their f heart was darkened
Rom 2:20 An instructor of the f, a teacher
Rom 10:19 by a f nation I will anger you
1Cor 1:20 hath not God made f the wisdom of
1Cor 1:27 But God hath chosen the f things
Gal 3:1 O f Galatians, who hath bewitched
Gal 3:3 Are ye so f?
Eph 5:4 nor f talking, nor jesting, which
1Ti 6:9 and a snare, and into many f
2Ti 2:23 But f and unlearned questions
Titus 3:3 ourselves also were sometimes f
Titus 3:9 But avoid f questions, and
1Pet 2:15 to silence the ignorance of f men

## FOOLISHLY

Gen 31:28 thou hast now done f in so doing
Num 12:11 upon us, wherein we have done f
1Sa 13:13 said to Saul, Thou hast done f
2Sa 24:10 for I have done very f
1Chr 21:8 for I have done very f
2Chr 16:9 Herein thou hast done f
Job 1:22 Job sinned not, nor charged God f
Ps 75:4 I said unto the fools, Deal not f
Prov 14:17 He that is soon angry dealeth f
Prov 30:32 If thou hast done f in lifting up
2Cor 11:17 after the Lord, but as it were f
2Cor 11:21 any is bold, (I speak f,) I am

## FOOLISHNESS

2Sa 15:31 the counsel of Ahithophel into f
Ps 38:5 and are corrupt because of my f
Ps 69:5 O God, thou knowest my f
Prov 12:23 the heart of fools proclaimeth f
Prov 14:24 but the f of fools is folly
Prov 15:2 the mouth of fools poureth out f
Prov 15:14 the mouth of fools feedeth on f
Prov 19:3 The f of man perverteth his way
Prov 22:15 F is bound in the heart of a
Prov 24:9 The thought of f is sin
Prov 27:22 will not his f depart from him
Eccl 7:25 wickedness of folly, even of f
Eccl 10:13 of the words of his mouth is f
Mk 7:22 an evil eye, blasphemy, pride, f
1Cor 1:18 cross is to them that perish f
1Cor 1:21 it pleased God by the f of
1Cor 1:23 and unto the Greeks f
1Cor 1:25 Because the f of God is wiser
1Cor 2:14 for they are f unto him
1Cor 3:19 of this world is f with God

## FOOL'S

Prov 12:16 A f wrath is presently known
Prov 18:6 A f lips enter into contention,
Prov 18:7 A f mouth is his destruction, and
Prov 26:3 the ass, and a rod for the f back
Prov 27:3 but a f wrath is heavier than
Eccl 5:3 a f voice is known by multitude
Eccl 10:2 but a f heart at his left

## FOOLS

2Sa 13:13 be as one of the f in Israel
Job 12:17 spoiled, and maketh the judges f
Job 30:8 They were children of f, yea,
Ps 75:4 I said unto the f, Deal not
Ps 94:8 and ye f, when will ye be wise
Ps 107:17 F, because of their transgression
Prov 1:7 but f despise wisdom and
Prov 1:22 scorning, and f hate knowledge
Prov 1:32 the prosperity of f shall destroy
Prov 3:35 shame shall be the promotion of f
Prov 8:5 and, ye f, be ye of an
Prov 10:21 but f die for want of wisdom
Prov 12:23 but the heart of f proclaimeth
Prov 13:19 to f to depart from evil
Prov 13:20 companion of f shall be destroyed
Prov 14:8 but the folly of f is deceit
Prov 14:9 F make a mock at sin
Prov 14:24 but the foolishness of f is folly
Prov 14:33 in the midst of f is made known
Prov 15:2 but the mouth of f poureth out
Prov 15:14 but the mouth of f feedeth on
Prov 16:22 but the instruction of f is folly
Prov 19:29 and stripes for the back of f
Prov 26:7 so is a parable in the mouth of f
Prov 26:9 so is a parable in the mouth of f
Eccl 5:1 than to give the sacrifice of f
Eccl 5:4 for he hath no pleasure in f
Eccl 7:4 but the heart of f is in the
Eccl 7:5 for a man to hear the song of f
Eccl 7:9 anger resteth in the bosom of f
Eccl 9:17 cry of him that ruleth among f
Is 19:11 Surely the princes of Zoan are f
Is 19:13 The princes of Zoan are become f
Is 35:8 the wayfaring men, though f
Mt 23:17 Ye f and blind
Mt 23:19 Ye f and blind
Lk 11:40 Ye f, did not he that made that
Lk 24:25 Then he said unto them, O f
Rom 1:22 to be wise, they became f
1Cor 4:10 We are f for Christ's sake, but
2Cor 11:19 For ye suffer f gladly, seeing ye
Eph 5:15 ye walk circumspectly, not as f

## FOOT

Gen 8:9 no rest for the sole of her f
Gen 41:44 or f in all the land of Egypt
Ex 12:37 thousand on f that were men
Ex 21:24 tooth, hand for hand, f for f,
Ex 29:20 the great toe of their right f
Ex 30:18 his f also of brass, to wash
Ex 30:28 vessels, and the laver and his f
Ex 31:9 furniture, and the laver and his f
Ex 35:16 his vessels, the laver and his f
Ex 38:8 the f of it of brass, of the
Ex 39:39 his vessels, the laver and his f
Ex 40:11 shalt anoint the laver and his f
Lev 8:11 vessels, both the laver and his f
Lev 8:23 upon the great toe of his right f
Lev 13:12 from his head even to his f
Lev 14:14 upon the great toe of his right f
Lev 14:17 upon the great toe of his right f
Lev 14:25 upon the great toe of his right f
Lev 14:28 upon the great toe of his right f
Num 22:25 Balaam's f against the wall
Deut 8:4 thee, neither did thy f swell
Deut 11:10 seed, and wateredst it with thy f
Deut 19:21 tooth, hand for hand, f for f
Deut 25:9 and loose his shoe from off his f
Deut 28:35 from the sole of thy f unto the
Deut 28:56 sole of her f upon the ground for
Deut 28:65 shall the sole of thy f have rest
Deut 29:5 shoe is not waxen old upon thy f
Deut 32:35 their f shall slide in due time
Deut 33:24 and let him dip his f in oil
Josh 1:3 sole of your f shall tread upon
Josh 5:15 Loose thy shoe from off thy f
Judg 5:15 he was sent on f into the valley
2Sa 2:18 was as light of f as a wild roe
2Sa 14:25 from the sole of his f even to
2Sa 21:20 fingers, and on every f six toes
2Kin 9:33 and he trode her under f
1Chr 20:6 on each hand, and six on each f
2Chr 33:8 will I any more remove the f of
Job 2:7 the sole of his f unto his crown
Job 23:11 My f hath held his steps, his way
Job 28:4 the waters forgotten of the f
Job 31:5 or if my f hath hasted to deceit
Job 39:15 that the f may crush them
Ps 9:15 they hid is their own f taken
Ps 26:12 My f standeth in an even place
Ps 36:11 Let not the f of pride come
Ps 38:16 when my f slippeth, they magnify
Ps 66:6 they went through the flood on f
Ps 68:23 That thy f may be dipped in the
Ps 91:12 thou dash thy f against a stone
Ps 94:18 When I said, My f slippeth
Ps 121:3 will not suffer thy f to be moved
Prov 1:15 refrain thy f from their path
Prov 3:23 and thy f shall not stumble

Prov 3:26 shall keep thy f from being taken
Prov 4:27 remove thy f from evil
Prov 25:17 Withdraw thy f from thy
Prov 25:19 broken tooth, and a f out of joint
Eccl 5:1 Keep thy f when thou goest to the
Is 1:6 From the sole of the f even unto
Is 14:25 my mountains tread him under f
Is 18:7 meted out and trodden under f
Is 20:2 and put off thy shoe from thy f
Is 26:6 The f shall tread it down, even
Is 41:2 the east, called him to his f
Is 58:13 turn away thy f from the sabbath
Jer 2:25 Withhold thy f from being unshod,
Jer 12:10 have trodden my portion under f
Lam 1:15 The Lord hath trodden under f all
Eze 1:7 was like the sole of a calf's f
Eze 6:11 thine hand, and stamp with thy f
Eze 29:11 No f of man shall pass through it
Eze 29:11 nor f of beast shall pass through
Eze 32:13 neither shall the f of man
Dan 8:13 and the host to be trodden under f
Amos 2:15 he that is swift of f shall not
Mt 4:6 thou dash thy f against a stone
Mt 5:13 and to be trodden under f of men
Mt 14:13 him on f out of the cities
Mt 18:8 if thy hand or thy f offend thee
Mt 22:13 the servants, Bind him hand and f
Mk 9:45 if thy f offend thee, cut it off
Lk 4:11 thou dash thy f against a stone
Jn 11:44 bound hand and f with graveclothes
Acts 7:5 not so much as to set his f on
1Cor 12:15 If the f shall say, Because I am
Heb 10:29 trodden under f the Son of God
Rev 1:13 with a garment down to the f
Rev 10:2 he set his right f upon the sea
Rev 10:2 and his left f on the earth
Rev 11:2 shall they tread under f forty

### FOOTMEN

Num 11:21 I am, are six hundred thousand f
Judg 20:2 thousand f that drew sword
1Sa 4:10 fell of Israel thirty thousand f
1Sa 15:4 in Telaim, two hundred thousand f
1Sa 22:17 unto the f that stood about him
2Sa 8:4 horsemen, and twenty thousand f
2Sa 10:6 of Zoba, twenty thousand f
1Kin 20:29 an hundred thousand f in one day
2Kin 13:7 ten chariots, and ten thousand f
1Chr 18:4 horsemen, and twenty thousand f
1Chr 19:18 in chariots, and forty thousand f
Jer 12:5 If thou hast run with the f

### FOOTSTEPS

Ps 17:5 in thy paths, that my f slip not
Ps 77:19 waters, and thy f are not known
Ps 89:51 the f of thine anointed
Song 1:8 way forth by the f of the flock

### FOOTSTOOL

1Chr 28:2 for the f of our God, and had made
2Chr 9:18 with a f of gold, which were
Ps 99:5 our God, and worship at his f
Ps 110:1 until I make thine enemies thy f
Ps 132:7 we will worship at his f
Is 66:1 my throne, and the earth is my f
Lam 2:1 remembered not his f in the day
Mt 5:35 for it is his f
Mt 22:44 till I make thine enemies thy f
Mk 12:36 till I make thine enemies thy f
Lk 20:43 Till I make thine enemies thy f
Acts 2:35 Until I make thy foes thy f
Acts 7:49 my throne, and earth is my f
Heb 1:13 I make thine enemies thy f
Heb 10:13 till his enemies be made his f
Jas 2:3 there, or sit here under my f

### FORASMUCH

Gen 41:39 F as God hath shewed thee all
Num 10:31 f as thou knowest how we are
Deut 12:12 f as he hath no part nor
Deut 17:16 f as the LORD hath said unto you,
Josh 17:14 f as the LORD hath blessed me
Judg 11:36 f as the LORD hath taken
1Sa 20:42 f as we have sworn both of us in
1Sa 24:18 f as when the LORD had delivered
2Sa 19:30 f as my lord the king is come
1Kin 11:11 F as this is done of thee, and
1Kin 13:21 F as thou hast disobeyed the
1Kin 14:7 F as I exalted thee from among
1Kin 16:2 F as I exalted thee out of the
2Kin 1:16 F as thou hast sent messengers to
1Chr 5:1 f as he defiled his father's bed,
2Chr 6:8 F as it was in thine heart to
Ezr 7:14 F as thou art sent of the king,
Is 8:6 F as this people refuseth the
Is 29:13 F as this people draw near me
Jer 10:6 F as there is none like unto thee
Jer 10:7 f as among all the wise men of
Dan 2:40 f as iron breaketh in pieces
Dan 2:41 f as thou sawest the iron
Dan 2:45 F as thou sawest that the
Dan 4:18 f as all the wise men of my
Dan 5:12 F as an excellent spirit, and
Dan 6:4 f as he was faithful, neither
Dan 6:22 f as before him innocency was
Amos 5:11 F therefore as your treading is
Mt 18:25 But f as he had not to pay, his
Lk 1:1 F as many have taken in hand to
Acts 9:38 f as Lydda was nigh to Joppa, and
Acts 11:17 F then as God gave them the like
Acts 15:24 F as we have heard, that certain
Acts 17:29 F then as we are the offspring of
Acts 24:10 F as I know that thou hast been
1Cor 11:7 f as he is the image and glory of
1Cor 14:12 f as ye are zealous of spiritual
1Cor 15:58 f as ye know that your labour is
2Cor 3:3 F as ye are manifestly declared
Heb 2:14 F then as the children are
1Pet 1:18 F as ye know that ye were not
1Pet 4:1 F then as Christ hath suffered

### FORBAD

Deut 2:37 whatsoever the LORD our God f us
Mt 3:14 But John f him, saying, I have
Mk 9:38 we f him, because he followeth
Lk 9:49 we f him, because he followeth
2Pet 2:16 f the madness of the prophet

### FORBEAR

Ex 23:5 wouldest f to help him, thou
Deut 23:22 But if thou shalt f to vow
1Kin 22:6 to battle, or shall I f
1Kin 22:15 to battle, or shall we f
2Chr 18:5 to battle, or shall I f
2Chr 18:14 to battle, or shall I f
2Chr 25:16 f; why shouldest thou be smitten
2Chr 35:21 f thee from meddling with God,
Neh 9:30 Yet many years didst thou f them
Job 16:6 and though I f, what am I eased
Prov 24:11 If thou f to deliver them that
Jer 40:4 to come with me into Babylon, f
Eze 2:5 will hear, or whether they will f
Eze 2:7 will hear, or whether they will f
Eze 3:11 will hear, or whether they will f
Eze 3:27 and he that forbeareth, let him f
Eze 24:17 F to cry, make no mourning for
Zec 11:12 my price; and if not, f
1Cor 9:6 have not we power to f working
2Cor 12:6 but now I f, lest any man should
1Th 3:1 when we could no longer f
1Th 3:5 cause, when I could no longer f

### FORBEARING

Prov 25:15 By long f is a prince persuaded,
Jer 20:9 my bones, and I was weary with f
Eph 4:2 f one another in love
Eph 6:9 things unto them, f threatening
Col 3:13 F one another, and forgiving one

### FORBID

Gen 44:7 God f that thy servants should do
Gen 44:17 God f that I should do so
Num 11:28 and said, My lord Moses, f them
Josh 22:29 God f that we should rebel
Josh 24:16 God f that we should forsake the
1Sa 12:23 God f that I should sin against
1Sa 14:45 God f: as the LORD liveth
1Sa 20:2 And he said unto him, God f
1Sa 24:6 The LORD f that I should do this
1Sa 26:11 The LORD f that I should stretch
1Kin 21:3 said to Ahab, The LORD f it me
1Chr 11:19 And said, My God f it me, that I
Job 27:5 God f that I should justify you
Mt 19:14 f them not, to come unto me
Mk 9:39 But Jesus said, F him not
Mk 10:14 to come unto me, and f them not
Lk 6:29 cloke f not to take thy coat also
Lk 9:50 And Jesus said unto him, F him not
Lk 18:16 to come unto me, and f them not
Lk 20:16 they heard it, they said, God f
Acts 10:47 Can any man f water, that these
Acts 24:23 that he should f none of his
Rom 3:4 God f: yea, let God be true
Rom 3:6 God f: for then how shall God
Rom 3:31 God f: yea, we establish the law
Rom 6:2 God f. How shall we
Rom 6:15 but under grace? God f
Rom 7:7 Is the law sin? God f
Rom 7:13 good made death unto me? God f
Rom 9:14 unrighteousness with God? God f
Rom 11:1 God cast away his people? God f
Rom 11:11 that they should fall? God f
1Cor 6:15 members of an harlot? God f
1Cor 14:39 f not to speak with tongues
Gal 2:17 the minister of sin? God f
Gal 3:21 the promises of God? God f
Gal 6:14 But God f that I should glory,

### FORCE

Gen 31:31 take by f thy daughters from me
Deut 22:25 in the field, and the man f her
Deut 34:7 not dim, nor his natural f abated
1Sa 2:16 and if not, I will take it by f
2Sa 13:12 him, Nay, my brother, do not f me
Ezr 4:23 Jews, and made them to cease by f
Est 7:8 Will he f the queen also before
Job 30:18 By the great f of my disease is
Job 40:16 his f is in the navel of his
Jer 18:21 their blood by the f of the sword
Jer 23:10 is evil, and their f is not right
Jer 48:45 of Heshbon because of the f
Eze 34:4 but with f and with cruelty have
Eze 35:5 the f of the sword in the time of
Amos 2:14 strong shall not strengthen his f
Mt 11:12 and the violent take it by f
Jn 6:15 they would come and take him by f
Acts 23:10 to take him by f from among them,
Heb 9:17 is of f after men are dead

### FORCED

Judg 1:34 the Amorites f the children of
Judg 20:5 and my concubine have they f
1Sa 13:12 I f myself therefore, and offered
2Sa 13:14 than she, f her, and lay with her
2Sa 13:22 because he had f his sister Tamar
2Sa 13:32 day that he f his sister Tamar
Prov 7:21 flattering of her lips she f him

### FORCES

2Chr 17:2 he placed f in all the fenced
Job 36:19 gold, nor all the f of strength
Is 60:5 the f of the Gentiles shall come
Is 60:11 unto thee the f of the Gentiles
Jer 40:7 of the f which were in the fields
Jer 40:13 of the f that were in the fields
Jer 41:11 of the f that were with him
Jer 41:13 of the f that were with him
Jer 41:16 of the f that were with him
Jer 42:1 Then all the captains of the f
Jer 42:8 of the f which were with him
Jer 43:4 and all the captains of the f
Jer 43:5 and all the captains of the f
Dan 11:10 assemble a multitude of great f
Dan 11:38 shall he honour the God of f
Obad 11 carried away captive his f

### FOREFRONT

Ex 26:9 in the f of the tabernacle
Ex 28:37 upon the f of the mitre it shall
Lev 8:9 upon the mitre, even upon his f
1Sa 14:5 The f of the one was situate
2Sa 11:15 Set ye Uriah in the f of the
2Kin 16:14 from the f of the house, from
2Chr 20:27 and Jehoshaphat in the f of them
Eze 40:19 the f of the lower gate unto the
Eze 40:19 the f of the inner court without
Eze 47:1 for the f of the house stood

### FOREHEAD

Ex 28:38 And it shall be upon Aaron's f
Ex 28:38 and it shall be always upon his f
Lev 13:41 toward his face, he is f bald
Lev 13:42 be in the bald head, or bald f
Lev 13:42 in his bald head, or his bald f
Lev 13:43 his bald head, or in his bald f
1Sa 17:49 and smote the Philistine in his f
1Sa 17:49 that the stone sunk into his f
2Chr 26:19 f before the priests in the house
2Chr 26:20 behold, he was leprous in his f
Jer 3:3 and thou hadst a whore's f
Eze 3:8 thy f strong against their
Eze 3:9 than flint have I made thy f
Eze 16:12 And I put a jewel on thy f
Rev 14:9 and receive his mark in his f
Rev 17:5 upon her f was a name written,

**FOREHEADS**
Eze 3:8 forehead strong against their *f*
Eze 9:4 set a mark upon the *f* of the men
Rev 7:3 servants of our God in their *f*
Rev 9:4 not the seal of God in their *f*
Rev 13:16 their right hand, or in their *f*
Rev 14:1 Father's name written in their *f*
Rev 20:4 received his mark upon their *f*
Rev 22:4 and his name shall be in their *f*

**FOREKNEW**
Rom 11:2 cast away his people which he *f*

**FOREKNOW**
Rom 8:29 For whom he did *f*, he also did

**FOREKNOWLEDGE**
Acts 2:23 *f* of God, ye have taken, and by
1Pet 1:2 to the *f* of God the Father

**FOREORDAINED**
1Pet 1:20 Who verily was *f* before the

**FOREPART**
Ex 28:27 underneath, toward the *f* thereof
Ex 39:20 underneath, toward the *f* of it
1Kin 6:20 the oracle in the *f* was twenty
Eze 42:7 court on the *f* of the chambers
Acts 27:41 the *f* stuck fast, and remained

**FORESKIN**
Gen 17:11 circumcise the flesh of your *f*
Gen 17:14 flesh of his *f* is not circumcised
Gen 17:23 of their *f* in the selfsame day
Gen 17:24 circumcised in the flesh of his *f*
Gen 17:25 circumcised in the flesh of his *f*
Ex 4:25 and cut off the *f* of her son
Lev 12:3 of his *f* shall be circumcised
Deut 10:16 therefore the *f* of your heart
Hab 2:16 also, and let thy *f* be uncovered

**FORESKINS**
Josh 5:3 of Israel at the hill of the *f*
1Sa 18:25 dowry, but an hundred *f* of the
1Sa 18:27 and David brought their *f*, and they
2Sa 3:14 an hundred *f* of the Philistines
Jer 4:4 and take away the *f* of your heart

**FOREST**
1Sa 22:5 and came into the *f* of Hareth
1Kin 7:2 the house of the *f* of Lebanon
1Kin 10:17 in the house of the *f* of Lebanon
1Kin 10:21 *f* of Lebanon were of pure gold
2Kin 19:23 and into the *f* of his Carmel
2Chr 9:16 in the house of the *f* of Lebanon
2Chr 9:20 *f* of Lebanon were of pure gold
Neh 2:8 Asaph the keeper of the king's *f*
Ps 50:10 For every beast of the *f* is mine
Ps 104:20 beasts of the *f* do creep forth
Is 9:18 kindle in the thickets of the *f*
Is 10:18 shall consume the glory of his *f*
Is 10:19 the trees of his *f* shall be few
Is 10:34 the thickets of the *f* with iron
Is 21:13 In the *f* in Arabia shall ye lodge
Is 22:8 the armour of the house of the *f*
Is 29:17 field shall be esteemed as a *f*
Is 32:15 fruitful field be counted for a *f*
Is 32:19 shall hail, coming down on the *f*
Is 37:24 border, and the *f* of his Carmel
Is 44:14 himself among the trees of the *f*
Is 44:23 into singing, ye mountains, O *f*
Is 56:9 yea, all ye beasts in the *f*
Jer 5:6 lion out of the *f* shall slay them
Jer 10:3 one cutteth a tree out of the *f*
Jer 12:8 is unto me as a lion in the *f*
Jer 21:14 kindle a fire in the *f* thereof
Jer 26:18 house as the high places of a *f*
Jer 46:23 They shall cut down her *f*
Eze 15:2 which is among the trees of the *f*
Eze 15:6 tree among the trees of the *f*
Eze 20:46 against the *f* of the south field
Eze 20:47 say to the *f* of the south, Hear
Hos 2:12 and I will make them a *f*, and the
Amos 3:4 Will a lion roar in the *f*
Mic 3:12 house as the high places of the *f*
Mic 5:8 a lion among the beasts of the *f*
Zec 11:2 for the *f* of the vintage is come

**FORETELL**
2Cor 13:2 *f* you, as if I were present, the

**FORETOLD**
Mk 13:23 behold, I have *f* you all things
Acts 3:24 have likewise *f* of these days

**FOREWARN**
Lk 12:5 But I will *f* you whom ye shall

**FOREWARNED**
1Th 4:6 all such, as we also have *f* you

**FORGAT**
Gen 40:23 butler remember Joseph, but *f* him
Judg 3:7 *f* the LORD their God, and served
1Sa 12:9 when they *f* the LORD their God,
Ps 78:11 *f* his works, and his wonders that
Ps 106:13 They soon *f* his works
Ps 106:21 They *f* God their saviour, which
Lam 3:17 I *f* prosperity
Hos 2:13 lovers, and *f* me, saith the LORD

**FORGAVE**
Ps 78:38 *f* their iniquity, and destroyed
Mt 18:27 and loosed him, and *f* him the debt
Mt 18:32 I *f* thee all that debt, because
Lk 7:42 to pay, he frankly *f* them both
Lk 7:43 that he, to whom he *f* most
2Cor 2:10 *f* any thing, to whom I *f* it
2Cor 2:10 for your sakes *f* I it in the
Col 3:13 even as Christ *f* you, so also do

**FORGET**
Gen 27:45 he *f* that which thou hast done to
Gen 41:51 he, hath made me *f* all my toil
Deut 4:9 lest thou *f* the things which
Deut 4:23 lest ye *f* the covenant of the
Deut 4:31 nor *f* the covenant of thy fathers
Deut 6:12 Then beware lest thou *f* the LORD
Deut 8:11 Beware that thou *f* not the LORD
Deut 8:14 thou *f* the LORD thy God, which
Deut 8:19 thou do at all *f* the LORD thy God
Deut 9:7 *f* not, how thou provokedst the
Deut 25:19 thou shalt not *f* it
1Sa 1:11 not *f* thine handmaid, but wilt
2Kin 17:38 have made with you ye shall not *f*
Job 8:13 are the paths of all that *f* God
Job 9:27 I will *f* my complaint, I will
Job 11:16 Because thou shalt *f* thy misery
Job 24:20 The womb shall *f* him
Ps 9:17 and all the nations that *f* God
Ps 10:12 *f* not the humble
Ps 13:1 How long wilt thou *f* me, O LORD
Ps 45:10 *f* also thine own people, and thy
Ps 50:22 Now consider this, ye that *f* God
Ps 59:11 Slay them not, lest my people *f*
Ps 74:19 *f* not the congregation of thy
Ps 74:23 *F* not the voice of thine enemies
Ps 78:7 not *f* the works of God, but keep
Ps 102:4 so that I *f* to eat my bread
Ps 103:2 soul, and *f* not all his benefits
Ps 119:16 I will not *f* thy word
Ps 119:83 yet do I not *f* thy statutes
Ps 119:93 I will never *f* thy precepts
Ps 119:109 yet do I not *f* thy law
Ps 119:141 yet do not I *f* thy precepts
Ps 119:153 for I do not *f* thy law
Ps 119:176 for I do not *f* thy commandments
Ps 137:5 If I *f* thee, O Jerusalem
Ps 137:5 let my right hand *f* her cunning
Prov 3:1 My son, *f* not my law
Prov 4:5 get understanding: *f* it not
Prov 31:5 *f* the law, and pervert the
Prov 31:7 *f* his poverty, and remember his
Is 49:15 Can a woman *f* her sucking child,
Is 49:15 yea, they may *f*, yet will I not
Is 49:15 may *f*, yet will I not *f* thee
Is 54:4 for thou shalt *f* the shame of thy
Is 65:11 that *f* my holy mountain, that
Jer 2:32 Can a maid *f* her ornaments, or a
Jer 23:27 think to cause my people to *f* my
Jer 23:39 I, even I, will utterly *f* you
Lam 5:20 Wherefore dost thou *f* us for ever
Hos 4:6 I will also *f* thy children
Amos 8:7 I will never *f* any of their works
Heb 6:10 is not unrighteous to *f* your work
Heb 13:16 do good and to communicate *f* not

**FORGIVE**
Gen 50:17 So shall ye say unto Joseph, *F*
Gen 50:17 *f* the trespass of the servants of
Ex 10:17 Now therefore *f*, I pray thee, my
Ex 32:32 Yet now, if thou wilt *f* their sin
Num 30:5 and the LORD shall *f* her, because
Num 30:8 and the LORD shall *f* her
Num 30:12 and the LORD shall *f* her
Josh 24:19 he will not *f* your transgressions
1Sa 25:28 *f* the trespass of thine handmaid
1Kin 8:30 and when thou hearest, *f*
1Kin 8:34 *f* the sin of thy people Israel,
1Kin 8:36 *f* the sin of thy servants, and of
1Kin 8:39 heaven thy dwelling place, and *f*
1Kin 8:50 *f* thy people that have sinned
2Chr 6:21 and when thou hearest, *f*
2Chr 6:25 *f* the sin of thy people Israel,
2Chr 6:27 *f* the sin of thy servants, and of
2Chr 6:30 heaven thy dwelling place, and *f*
2Chr 6:39 *f* thy people which have sinned
2Chr 7:14 will *f* their sin, and will heal
Ps 25:18 and *f* all my sins
Ps 86:5 Lord, art good, and ready to *f*
Is 2:9 therefore *f* them not
Jer 18:23 *f* not their iniquity, neither
Jer 31:34 for I will *f* their iniquity, and I
Jer 36:3 that I may *f* their iniquity and
Dan 9:19 O Lord, hear; O Lord, *f*
Amos 7:2 land, then I said, O Lord GOD, *f*
Mt 6:12 *f* us our debts, as we *f* our
Mt 6:14 For if ye *f* men their trespasses,
Mt 6:14 heavenly Father will also *f* you
Mt 6:15 But if ye *f* not men their
Mt 6:15 your Father *f* your trespasses
Mt 9:6 man hath power on earth to *f* sins
Mt 18:21 sin against me, and I *f* him
Mt 18:35 if ye from your hearts *f* not
Mk 2:7 who can *f* sins but God only
Mk 2:10 man hath power on earth to *f* sins
Mk 11:25 And when ye stand praying, *f*
Mk 11:25 heaven may *f* you your trespasses
Mk 11:26 But if ye do not *f*, neither will
Mk 11:26 is in heaven *f* your trespasses
Lk 5:21 Who can *f* sins, but God alone
Lk 5:24 hath power upon earth to *f* sins
Lk 6:37 *f*, and ye shall be forgiven
Lk 11:4 And *f* us our sins
Lk 11:4 for we also *f* every one that is
Lk 17:3 and if he repent, *f* him
Lk 17:4 thou shalt *f* him
Lk 23:34 Then said Jesus, Father, *f* them
2Cor 2:7 ye ought rather to *f* him, and
2Cor 2:10 ye *f* any thing, I *f* also
2Cor 12:13 *f* me this wrong
1Jn 1:9 just to *f* us our sins, and to

**FORGIVEN**
Lev 4:20 for them, and it shall be *f* them
Lev 4:26 his sin, and it shall be *f* him
Lev 4:31 for him, and it shall be *f* him
Lev 4:35 committed, and it shall be *f* him
Lev 5:10 hath sinned, and it shall be *f* him
Lev 5:13 of these, and it shall be *f* him
Lev 5:16 offering, and it shall be *f* him
Lev 5:18 wist it not, and it shall be *f* him
Lev 6:7 it shall be *f* him for any thing
Lev 19:22 which he hath done shall be *f* him
Num 14:19 and as thou hast *f* this people
Num 15:25 of Israel, and it shall be *f* them
Num 15:26 And it shall be *f* all the
Num 15:28 and it shall be *f* him
Deut 21:8 And the blood shall be *f* them
Ps 32:1 is he whose transgression is *f*
Ps 85:2 Thou hast *f* the iniquity of thy
Is 33:24 therein shall be *f* their iniquity
Mt 9:2 thy sins be *f* thee
Mt 9:5 to say, Thy sins be *f* thee
Mt 12:31 and blasphemy shall be *f* unto men
Mt 12:31 Ghost shall not be *f* unto men
Mt 12:32 the Son of man, it shall be *f* him
Mt 12:32 Holy Ghost, it shall not be *f* him
Mk 2:5 palsy, Son, thy sins be *f* thee
Mk 2:9 of the palsy, Thy sins be *f* thee
Mk 3:28 All sins shall be *f* unto the sons
Mk 4:12 and their sins should be *f* them
Lk 5:20 him, Man, thy sins are *f* thee
Lk 5:23 to say, Thy sins be *f* thee
Lk 6:37 forgive, and ye shall be *f*
Lk 7:47 Her sins, which are many, are *f*
Lk 7:47 but to whom little is *f*, the same
Lk 7:48 he said unto her, Thy sins are *f*
Lk 12:10 the Son of man, it shall be *f* him
Lk 12:10 the Holy Ghost it shall not be *f*
Acts 8:22 of thine heart may be *f* thee
Rom 4:7 are they whose iniquities are *f*
Eph 4:32 God for Christ's sake hath *f* you
Col 2:13 having *f* you all trespasses
Jas 5:15 sins, they shall be *f* him
1Jn 2:12 because your sins are *f* you for

**FORGIVENESS**
Ps 130:4 But there is *f* with thee, that
Mk 3:29 the Holy Ghost hath never *f*
Acts 5:31 to Israel, and *f* of sins

Acts 13:38 preached unto you the *f* of sins
Acts 26:18 that they may receive *f* of sins
Eph 1:7 the *f* of sins, according to the
Col 1:14 his blood, even the *f* of sins

## FORGIVING
Ex 34:7 *f* iniquity and transgression and
Num 14:18 *f* iniquity and transgression, and
Eph 4:32 *f* one another, even as God for
Col 3:13 *f* one another, if any man have a

## FORGOTTEN
Gen 41:30 shall be *f* in the land of Egypt
Deut 26:13 neither have I *f* them
Deut 31:21 for it shall not be *f* out of the
Deut 32:18 hast *f* God that formed thee
Job 19:14 and my familiar friends have *f* me
Job 28:4 even the waters *f* of the foot
Ps 9:18 the needy shall not alway be *f*
Ps 10:11 said in his heart, God hath *f*
Ps 31:12 I am *f* as a dead man out of mind
Ps 42:9 God my rock, Why hast thou *f* me
Ps 44:17 yet have we not *f* thee, neither
Ps 44:20 If we have *f* the name of our God,
Ps 77:9 Hath God *f* to be gracious
Ps 119:61 but I have not *f* thy law
Ps 119:139 mine enemies have *f* thy words
Eccl 2:16 the days to come shall all be *f*
Eccl 8:10 they were *f* in the city where
Eccl 9:5 for the memory of them is *f*
Is 17:10 Because thou hast *f* the God of
Is 23:15 Tyre shall be *f* seventy years
Is 23:16 thou harlot that hast been *f*
Is 44:21 Israel, thou shalt not be *f* of me
Is 49:14 forsaken me, and my Lord hath *f* me
Is 65:16 because the former troubles are *f*
Jer 2:32 yet my people have *f* me days
Jer 3:21 they have *f* the LORD their God
Jer 13:25 because thou hast *f* me, and
Jer 18:15 Because my people hath *f* me
Jer 20:11 confusion shall never be *f*
Jer 23:27 fathers have *f* my name for Baal
Jer 23:40 shame, which shall not be *f*
Jer 30:14 All thy lovers have *f* thee
Jer 44:9 Have ye *f* the wickedness of your
Jer 50:5 covenant that shall not be *f*
Jer 50:6 they have *f* their restingplace
Lam 2:6 and sabbaths to be *f* in Zion
Eze 22:12 by extortion, and hast *f* me
Eze 23:35 Because thou hast *f* me, and cast
Hos 4:6 seeing thou hast *f* the law of thy
Hos 8:14 For Israel hath *f* his Maker
Hos 13:6 therefore have they *f* me
Mt 16:5 side, they had *f* to take bread
Mk 8:14 the disciples had *f* to take bread
Lk 12:6 not one of them is *f* before God
Heb 12:5 ye have *f* the exhortation which
2Pet 1:9 hath *f* that he was purged from

## FORM
Gen 1:2 And the earth was without *f*
1Sa 28:14 he said unto her, What *f* is he of
2Sa 14:20 To fetch about this *f* of speech
2Chr 4:7 of gold according to their *f*
Job 4:16 I could not discern the *f* thereof
Is 45:7 I *f* the light, and create darkness
Is 52:14 his *f* more than the sons of men
Is 53:2 he hath no *f* nor comeliness
Jer 4:23 earth, and, lo, it was without *f*
Eze 8:3 And he put forth the *f* of an hand
Eze 8:10 behold every *f* of creeping things
Eze 10:8 the *f* of a man's hand under their
Eze 43:11 shew them the *f* of the house
Eze 43:11 they may keep the whole *f* thereof
Dan 2:31 the *f* thereof was terrible
Dan 3:19 the *f* of his visage was changed
Dan 3:25 the *f* of the fourth is like the
Mk 16:12 in another *f* unto two of them
Rom 2:20 which hast the *f* of knowledge
Rom 6:17 *f* of doctrine which was delivered
Phil 2:6 Who, being in the *f* of God
Phil 2:7 took upon him the *f* of a servant
2Ti 1:13 Hold fast the *f* of sound words,
2Ti 3:5 Having a *f* of godliness, but

## FORMED
Gen 2:7 the LORD God *f* man of the dust of
Gen 2:8 he put the man whom he had *f*
Gen 2:19 God *f* every beast of the field
Deut 32:18 and hast forgotten God that *f* thee
2Kin 19:25 of ancient times that I have *f* it
Job 26:5 Dead things are *f* from under the
Job 26:13 his hand hath *f* the crooked
Job 33:6 I also am *f* out of the clay
Ps 90:2 or ever thou hadst *f* the earth
Ps 94:9 he that *f* the eye, shall he not
Ps 95:5 and his hands *f* the dry land
Prov 26:10 The great God that *f* all things
Is 27:11 he that *f* them will shew them no
Is 37:26 ancient times, that I have *f* it
Is 43:1 thee, O Jacob, and he that *f* thee
Is 43:7 him for my glory, I have *f* him
Is 43:10 before me there was no God *f*
Is 43:21 This people have I *f* for myself
Is 44:2 *f* thee from the womb, which will
Is 44:10 Who hath *f* a god, or molten a
Is 44:21 I have *f* thee
Is 44:24 he that *f* thee from the womb, I
Is 45:18 God himself that *f* the earth
Is 45:18 in vain, he *f* it to be inhabited
Is 49:5 saith the LORD that *f* me from the
Is 54:17 No weapon that is *f* against thee
Jer 1:5 Before I *f* thee in the belly I
Jer 33:2 maker thereof, the LORD that *f* it
Amos 7:1 behold, he *f* grasshoppers in the
Rom 9:20 Shall the thing *f* say to him that
Rom 9:20 thing *f* say to him that *f* it
Gal 4:19 again until Christ be *f* in you
1Ti 2:13 For Adam was first *f*, then Eve

## FORMER
Gen 40:13 after the *f* manner when thou wast
Num 21:26 fought against the *f* king of Moab
Deut 24:4 Her *f* husband, which sent her
Ruth 4:7 in *f* time in Israel concerning
1Sa 17:30 him again after the *f* manner
2Kin 1:14 the *f* fifties with their fifties
2Kin 17:34 day they do after the *f* manners
2Kin 17:40 but they did after their *f* manner
Neh 5:15 But the *f* governors that had been
Job 8:8 I pray thee, of the *f* age
Job 30:3 the wilderness in *f* time desolate
Ps 79:8 not against us *f* iniquities
Ps 89:49 where are thy *f* lovingkindnesses,
Eccl 1:11 is no remembrance of *f* things
Eccl 7:10 What is the cause that the *f* days
Is 41:22 let them shew the *f* things
Is 42:9 the *f* things are come to pass, and
Is 43:9 declare this, and shew us *f* things
Is 43:18 Remember ye not the *f* things
Is 46:9 Remember the *f* things of old
Is 48:3 I have declared the *f* things from
Is 61:4 shall raise up the *f* desolations
Is 65:7 their *f* work into their bosom
Is 65:16 because the *f* troubles are
Is 65:17 the *f* shall not be remembered,
Jer 5:24 God, that giveth rain, both the *f*
Jer 10:16 for he is the *f* of all things
Jer 34:5 the *f* kings which were before
Jer 36:28 write in it all the *f* words that
Jer 51:19 for he is the *f* of all things
Eze 16:55 shall return to their *f* estate
Eze 16:55 shall return to their *f* estate
Eze 16:55 shall return to your *f* estate
Dan 11:13 a multitude greater than the *f*
Dan 11:29 but it shall not be as the *f*
Hos 6:3 latter and *f* rain unto the earth
Joel 2:23 given you the *f* rain moderately
Joel 2:23 the *f* rain, and the latter rain in
Hag 2:9 shall be greater than of the *f*
Zec 1:4 unto whom the *f* prophets have
Zec 7:7 LORD hath cried by the *f* prophets
Zec 7:12 in his spirit by the *f* prophets
Zec 8:11 of this people as in the *f* days
Zec 14:8 half of them toward the *f* sea
Mal 3:4 the days of old, and as in *f* years
Acts 1:1 The *f* treatise have I made, O
Eph 4:22 the *f* conversation the old man
Heb 10:32 call to remembrance the *f* days
1Pet 1:14 to the *f* lusts in your ignorance
Rev 21:4 for the *f* things are passed away

## FORNICATION
2Chr 21:11 of Jerusalem to commit *f*, and
Is 23:17 shall commit *f* with all the
Eze 16:26 *f* with the Egyptians thy
Eze 16:29 thy *f* in the land of Canaan unto
Mt 5:32 wife, saving for the cause of *f*
Mt 19:9 away his wife, except it be for *f*
Jn 8:41 they to him, We be not born of *f*
Acts 15:20 pollutions of idols, and from *f*
Acts 15:29 from things strangled, and from *f*
Acts 21:25 and from strangled, and from *f*
Rom 1:29 with all unrighteousness, *f*
1Cor 5:1 that there is *f* among you
1Cor 5:1 such *f* as is not so much as named
1Cor 6:13 Now the body is not for *f*
1Cor 6:18 Flee *f*. Every sin that
1Cor 6:18 but he that committeth *f* sinneth
1Cor 7:2 Nevertheless, to avoid *f*, let
1Cor 10:8 Neither let us commit *f*, as some
2Cor 12:21 repented of the uncleanness and *f*
Gal 5:19 Adultery, *f*, uncleanness,
Eph 5:3 But *f*, and all uncleanness, or
Col 3:5 *f*, uncleanness, inordinate
1Th 4:3 that ye should abstain from *f*
Jude 7 giving themselves over to *f*
Rev 2:14 unto idols, and to commit *f*
Rev 2:20 to seduce my servants to commit *f*
Rev 2:21 gave her space to repent of her *f*
Rev 9:21 their sorceries, nor of their *f*
Rev 14:8 of the wine of the wrath of her *f*
Rev 17:2 of the earth have committed *f*
Rev 17:2 made drunk with the wine of her *f*
Rev 17:4 and filthiness of her *f*
Rev 18:3 of the wine of the wrath of her *f*
Rev 18:3 earth have committed *f* with her
Rev 18:9 the earth, who have committed *f*
Rev 19:2 did corrupt the earth with her *f*

## FORNICATIONS
Eze 16:15 pouredst out thy *f* on every one
Mt 15:19 thoughts, murders, adulteries, *f*
Mk 7:21 evil thoughts, adulteries, *f*

## FORNICATOR
1Cor 5:11 that is called a brother be a *f*
Heb 12:16 Lest there be any *f*, or profane

## FORNICATORS
1Cor 5:9 an epistle not to company with *f*
1Cor 5:10 with the *f* of this world, or with
1Cor 6:9 neither *f*, nor idolaters, nor

## FORSAKE
Deut 4:31 he will not *f* thee, neither
Deut 12:19 *f* not the Levite as long as thou
Deut 14:27 thou shalt not *f* him
Deut 31:6 he will not fail thee, nor *f* thee
Deut 31:8 not fail thee, neither *f* thee
Deut 31:16 go to be among them, and will *f* me
Deut 31:17 in that day, and I will *f* them
Josh 1:5 I will not fail thee, nor *f* thee
Josh 24:16 forbid that we should *f* the LORD
Josh 24:20 If ye *f* the LORD, and serve
Judg 9:11 Should I *f* my sweetness, and my
1Sa 12:22 For the LORD will not *f* his
1Kin 6:13 will not *f* my people Israel
1Kin 8:57 let him not leave us, nor *f* us
2Kin 21:14 I will *f* the remnant of mine
1Chr 28:9 but if thou *f* him, he will cast
1Chr 28:20 nor *f* thee, until thou hast
2Chr 7:19 *f* my statutes and my commandments,
2Chr 15:2 if ye *f* him, he will *f* you
Ezr 8:22 is against all them that *f* him
Neh 9:31 utterly consume them, nor *f* them
Neh 10:39 we will not *f* the house of our
Job 20:13 *f* it not, but keep it still
Ps 27:9 leave me not, neither *f* me
Ps 27:10 When my father and my mother *f* me
Ps 37:8 Cease from anger, and *f* wrath
Ps 38:21 *F* me not, O LORD
Ps 71:9 *f* me not when my strength faileth
Ps 71:18 and greyheaded, O God, *f* me not
Ps 89:30 If his children *f* my law, and walk
Ps 94:14 neither will he *f* his inheritance
Ps 119:8 O *f* me not utterly
Ps 119:53 of the wicked that *f* thy law
Ps 138:8 *f* not the works of thine own
Prov 1:8 *f* not the law of thy mother
Prov 3:3 Let not mercy and truth *f* thee
Prov 4:2 good doctrine, *f* ye not my law
Prov 4:6 *F* her not, and she shall preserve
Prov 6:20 *f* not the law of thy mother
Prov 9:6 *F* the foolish, and live
Prov 27:10 and thy father's friend, *f* not
Prov 28:4 They that *f* the law praise the
Is 1:28 they that *f* the LORD shall be
Is 41:17 the God of Israel will not *f* them
Is 42:16 I do unto them, and not *f* them
Is 55:7 Let the wicked *f* his way, and the
Is 65:11 But ye are they that *f* the LORD
Jer 17:13 all that *f* thee shall be ashamed,
Jer 23:33 I will even *f* you, saith the LORD
Jer 23:39 forget you, and I will *f* you

Jer 51:9 *f* her, and let us go every one
Lam 5:20 us for ever, and *f* us so long time
Eze 20:8 neither did they *f* the idols of
Dan 11:30 them that *f* the holy covenant
Jonah 2:8 lying vanities *f* their own mercy
Acts 21:21 are among the Gentiles to *f* Moses
Heb 13:5 will never leave thee, nor *f* thee

**FORSAKEN**

Deut 28:20 doings, whereby thou hast *f* me
Deut 29:25 Because they have *f* the covenant
Judg 6:13 but now the LORD hath *f* us
Judg 10:10 both because we have *f* our God
Judg 10:13 Yet ye have *f* me, and served other
1Sa 8:8 day, wherewith they have *f* me
1Sa 12:10 because we have *f* the LORD
1Kin 11:33 Because that they have *f* me
1Kin 18:18 house, in that ye have *f* the
1Kin 19:10 of Israel have *f* thy covenant
1Kin 19:14 of Israel have *f* thy covenant
2Kin 22:17 Because they have *f* me, and have
2Chr 12:5 Thus saith the LORD, Ye have *f* me
2Chr 13:10 is our God, and we have not *f* him
2Chr 13:11 but ye have *f* him
2Chr 21:10 because he had *f* the LORD God of
2Chr 24:20 because ye have *f* the LORD
2Chr 24:20 he hath also *f* you
2Chr 24:24 because they had *f* the LORD God
2Chr 28:6 because they had *f* the LORD God
2Chr 29:6 the LORD our God, and have *f* him
2Chr 34:25 Because they have *f* me, and have
Ezr 9:9 God hath not *f* us in our bondage
Ezr 9:10 for we have *f* thy commandments,
Neh 13:11 said, Why is the house of God *f*
Job 18:4 shall the earth be *f* for thee
Job 20:19 hath oppressed and hath *f* the poor
Ps 9:10 hast not *f* them that seek thee
Ps 22:1 God, my God, why hast thou *f* me
Ps 37:25 have I not seen the righteous *f*
Ps 71:11 Saying, God hath *f* him
Is 1:4 they have *f* the LORD, they have
Is 2:6 Therefore thou hast *f* thy people
Is 7:16 shall be *f* of both her kings
Is 17:2 The cities of Aroer are *f*
Is 17:9 his strong cities be as a *f* bough
Is 27:10 be desolate, and the habitation *f*
Is 32:14 Because the palaces shall be *f*
Is 49:14 But Zion said, The LORD hath *f* me
Is 54:6 hath called thee as a woman *f*
Is 54:7 For a small moment have I *f* thee
Is 60:15 Whereas thou hast been *f* and hated
Is 62:4 Thou shalt no more be termed *F*
Is 62:12 called, Sought out, A city not *f*
Jer 1:16 their wickedness, who have *f* me
Jer 2:13 they have *f* me the fountain of
Jer 2:17 that thou hast *f* the LORD thy God
Jer 2:19 that thou hast *f* the LORD thy God
Jer 4:29 every city shall be *f*, and not a
Jer 5:7 thy children have *f* me, and sworn
Jer 5:19 answer them, Like as ye have *f* me
Jer 7:29 *f* the generation of his wrath
Jer 9:13 Because they have *f* my law which
Jer 9:19 because we have *f* the land
Jer 12:7 I have *f* mine house, I have left
Jer 15:6 Thou hast *f* me, saith the LORD,
Jer 16:11 Because your fathers have *f* me
Jer 16:11 worshipped them, and have *f* me
Jer 17:13 because they have *f* the LORD
Jer 18:14 that come from another place be *f*
Jer 19:4 Because they have *f* me, and have
Jer 22:9 Because they have *f* the covenant
Jer 25:38 He hath *f* his covert, as the lion
Jer 51:5 For Israel hath not been *f*
Eze 8:12 the LORD hath *f* the earth
Eze 9:9 say, The LORD hath *f* the earth
Eze 36:4 and to the cities that are *f*
Amos 5:2 she is *f* upon her land
Zeph 2:4 For Gaza shall be *f*, and Ashkelon
Mt 19:27 unto him, Behold, we have *f* all
Mt 19:29 And every one that hath *f* houses
Mt 27:46 God, my God, why hast thou *f* me
Mk 15:34 God, my God, why hast thou *f* me
2Cor 4:9 Persecuted, but not *f*
2Ti 4:10 For Demas hath *f* me, having loved
2Pet 2:15 Which have *f* the right way, and

**FORSAKETH**

Job 6:14 but he *f* the fear of the Almighty
Ps 37:28 judgment, and *f* not his saints
Prov 2:17 Which *f* the guide of her youth,
Prov 15:10 grievous unto him that *f* the way
Prov 28:13 and *f* them shall have mercy
Lk 14:33 you that *f* not all that he hath

**FORSAKING**

Is 6:12 there be a great *f* in the midst
Heb 10:25 Not *f* the assembling of ourselves

**FORSOOK**

Deut 32:15 then he *f* God which made him, and
Judg 2:12 they *f* the LORD God of their
Judg 2:13 they *f* the LORD, and served Baal
Judg 10:6 *f* the LORD, and served not him
1Sa 31:7 they *f* the cities, and fled
1Kin 9:9 Because they *f* the LORD their God
1Kin 12:8 But he *f* the counsel of the old
1Kin 12:13 *f* the old men's counsel that they
2Kin 21:22 he *f* the LORD God of his fathers,
1Chr 10:7 then they *f* their cities, and fled
2Chr 7:22 Because they *f* the LORD God of
2Chr 10:8 But he *f* the counsel which the
2Chr 10:13 king Rehoboam *f* the counsel of
2Chr 12:1 he *f* the law of the LORD, and all
Ps 78:60 So that he *f* the tabernacle of
Ps 119:87 but I *f* not thy precepts
Is 58:2 *f* not the ordinance of their God
Jer 14:5 *f* it, because there was no grass
Mt 26:56 Then all the disciples *f* him
Mk 1:18 And straightway they *f* their nets
Mk 14:50 And they all *f* him, and fled
Lk 5:11 their ships to land, they *f* all
2Ti 4:16 stood with me, but all men *f* me
Heb 11:27 By faith he *f* Egypt, not fearing

**FORT**

2Sa 5:9 So David dwelt in the *f*, and
Is 25:12 the fortress of the high *f* of thy
Eze 4:2 build a *f* against it, and cast a
Eze 21:22 to cast a mount, and to build a *f*
Eze 26:8 and he shall make a *f* against thee
Dan 11:19 face toward the *f* of his own land

**FORTHWITH**

Ezr 6:8 *f* expences be given unto these
Mt 13:5 *f* they sprung up, because they
Mt 26:49 *f* he came to Jesus, and said, Hail
Mk 1:29 *f*, when they were come out of the
Mk 1:43 charged him, and *f* sent him away
Mk 5:13 And *f* Jesus gave them leave
Jn 19:34 *f* came there out blood and water
Acts 9:18 and he received sight *f*, and arose,
Acts 12:10 *f* the angel departed from him
Acts 21:30 and *f* the doors were shut

**FORTIETH**

Num 33:38 in the *f* year after the children
Deut 1:3 And it came to pass in the *f* year
1Chr 26:31 In the *f* year of the reign of
2Chr 16:13 in the one and *f* year of his reign

**FORTIFIED**

2Chr 11:11 he *f* the strong holds, and put
2Chr 26:9 turning of the wall, and *f* them
Neh 3:8 they *f* Jerusalem unto the broad
Mic 7:12 Assyria, and from the *f* cities

**FORTIFY**

Judg 9:31 they *f* the city against thee
Neh 4:2 will they *f* themselves
Is 22:10 have ye broken down to *f* the wall
Jer 51:53 though she should *f* the height of
Nah 2:1 strong, *f* thy power mightily
Nah 3:14 for the siege, *f* thy strong holds

**FORTRESS**

2Sa 22:2 The LORD is my rock, and my *f*
Ps 18:2 The LORD is my rock, and my *f*
Ps 31:3 For thou art my rock and my *f*
Ps 71:3 me, for thou art my rock and my *f*
Ps 91:2 the LORD, He is my refuge and my *f*
Ps 144:2 My goodness, and my *f*
Is 17:3 The *f* also shall cease from
Is 25:12 the *f* of the high fort of thy
Jer 6:27 a *f* among my people, that thou
Jer 10:17 the land, O inhabitant of the *f*
Jer 16:19 O LORD, my strength, and my *f*
Dan 11:7 shall enter into the *f* of the
Dan 11:10 and be stirred up, even to his *f*
Amos 5:9 spoiled shall come against the *f*
Mic 7:12 from the *f* even to the river, and

**FORTS**

2Kin 25:1 they built *f* against it round
Is 29:3 and I will raise *f* against thee
Is 32:14 the *f* and towers shall be for dens
Jer 52:4 built *f* against it round about
Eze 17:17 casting up mounts, and building *f*
Eze 33:27 and they that be in the *f*

**FORTUNATUS** *(for-chu-na'-tus) A Christian acquaintance of Paul.*

1Cor 16:17 of the coming of Stephanas and *F*
1Cor *s* from Philippi by Stephanus, and *F*

**FORTY**

Gen 5:13 *f* years, and begat sons and
Gen 7:4 it to rain upon the earth *f* days
Gen 7:4 the earth *f* days and *f* nights
Gen 7:12 the earth *f* days and *f* nights
Gen 7:17 the flood was *f* days upon the
Gen 8:6 came to pass at the end of *f* days
Gen 18:28 And he said, If I find there *f*
Gen 18:29 there shall be *f* found there
Gen 25:20 Isaac was *f* years old when he
Gen 26:34 Esau was *f* years old when he took
Gen 32:15 *f* kine, and ten bulls, twenty she
Gen 47:28 age of Jacob was an hundred *f*
Gen 50:3 *f* days were fulfilled for him
Ex 16:35 of Israel did eat manna *f* years
Ex 24:18 the mount *f* days and *f* nights
Ex 26:19 thou shalt make *f* sockets of
Ex 26:21 their *f* sockets of silver
Ex 34:28 the LORD *f* days and *f* nights
Ex 36:24 *f* sockets of silver he made under
Ex 36:26 their *f* sockets of silver
Lev 25:8 of years shall be unto thee *f*
Num 1:21 of the tribe of Reuben, were *f*
Num 1:25 even of the tribe of Gad, were *f*
Num 1:33 were *f* thousand and five hundred
Num 1:41 of the tribe of Asher, were *f*
Num 2:11 were numbered thereof, were *f*
Num 2:15 were numbered of them, were *f*
Num 2:19 were *f* thousand and five hundred
Num 2:28 were numbered of them, were *f*
Num 13:25 of the land after *f* days
Num 14:33 wander in the wilderness *f* years
Num 14:34 ye searched the land, even *f* days
Num 14:34 even *f* years, and ye shall know my
Num 26:7 that were numbered of them were *f*
Num 26:18 *f* thousand and five hundred
Num 26:41 that were numbered of them were *f*
Num 26:50 that were numbered of them were *f*
Num 32:13 wander in the wilderness *f* years
Num 35:6 and to them ye shall add *f*
Num 35:7 give to the Levites shall be *f*
Deut 2:7 these *f* years the LORD thy God
Deut 8:2 these *f* years in the wilderness
Deut 8:4 did thy foot swell, these *f* years
Deut 9:9 then I abode in the mount *f* days
Deut 9:9 *f* nights, I neither did eat bread
Deut 9:11 came to pass at the end of *f* days
Deut 9:11 *f* nights, that the LORD gave me
Deut 9:18 the first, *f* days and *f* nights
Deut 9:25 fell down before the LORD *f* days
Deut 9:25 *f* nights, as I fell down at the
Deut 10:10 time, *f* days and *f* nights
Deut 25:3 *F* stripes he may give him, and not
Deut 29:5 I have led you *f* years in the
Josh 4:13 About *f* thousand prepared for war
Josh 5:6 walked *f* years in the wilderness
Josh 14:7 *F* years old was I when Moses the
Josh 14:10 me alive, as he said, these *f*
Josh 21:41 of the children of Israel were *f*
Judg 3:11 And the land had rest *f* years
Judg 5:8 seen among *f* thousand in Israel
Judg 5:31 And the land had rest *f* years
Judg 8:28 *f* years in the days of Gideon
Judg 12:6 at that time of the Ephraimites *f*
Judg 12:14 And he had *f* sons and thirty
Judg 13:1 hand of the Philistines *f* years
1Sa 4:18 And he had judged Israel *f* years
1Sa 17:16 and presented himself *f* days
2Sa 2:10 was *f* years old when he began to
2Sa 5:4 to reign, and he reigned *f* years
2Sa 10:18 *f* thousand horsemen, and smote
2Sa 15:7 And it came to pass after *f* years
1Kin 2:11 reigned over Israel were *f* years
1Kin 4:26 Solomon had *f* thousand stalls of
1Kin 6:17 before it, was *f* cubits long
1Kin 7:3 that lay on *f* five pillars,
1Kin 7:38 one laver contained *f* baths
1Kin 11:42 over all Israel was *f* years
1Kin 14:21 Rehoboam was *f* and one years old
1Kin 15:10 And *f* and one years reigned he in
1Kin 19:8 the strength of that meat *f* days
1Kin 19:8 *f* nights unto Horeb the mount of
2Kin 2:24 bears out of the wood, and tare *f*

2Kin 8:9 *f* camels' burden, and came and
2Kin 10:14 shearing house, even two and *f* men
2Kin 12:1 *f* years reigned he in Jerusalem
2Kin 14:23 to reign in Samaria, and reigned *f*
1Chr 5:18 *f* thousand seven hundred and
1Chr 12:36 battle, expert in war, *f* thousand
1Chr 19:18 *f* thousand footmen, and killed
1Chr 29:27 reigned over Israel was *f* years
2Chr 9:30 Jerusalem over all Israel *f* years
2Chr 12:13 *f* years old when he began to
2Chr 22:2 *F* and two years old was Ahaziah
2Chr 24:1 he reigned *f* years in Jerusalem
Ezr 2:8 children of Zattu, nine hundred *f*
Ezr 2:10 children of Bani, six hundred *f*
Ezr 2:24 The children of Azmaveth, *f*
Ezr 2:25 and Beeroth, seven hundred and *f*
Ezr 2:34 of Jericho, three hundred *f*
Ezr 2:38 Pashur, a thousand two hundred *f*
Ezr 2:64 whole congregation together was *f*
Ezr 2:66 their mules, two hundred *f*
Neh 5:15 beside *f* shekels of silver
Neh 7:13 of Zattu, eight hundred *f*
Neh 7:15 children of Binnui, six hundred *f*
Neh 7:28 The men of Beth-azmaveth, *f*
Neh 7:29 and Beeroth, seven hundred *f*
Neh 7:36 of Jericho, three hundred *f*
Neh 7:41 Pashur, a thousand two hundred *f*
Neh 7:44 children of Asaph, an hundred *f*
Neh 7:62 children of Nekoda, six hundred *f*
Neh 7:66 whole congregation together was *f*
Neh 7:67 and they had two hundred *f*
Neh 7:68 their mules, two hundred *f*
Neh 9:21 *f* years didst thou sustain them
Neh 11:13 of the fathers, two hundred *f*
Job 42:16 *f* years, and saw his sons, and his
Ps 95:10 *F* years long was I grieved with
Jer 52:30 of the Jews seven hundred *f*
Eze 4:6 of the house of Judah *f* days
Eze 29:11 shall it be inhabited *f* years
Eze 29:12 waste shall be desolate *f* years
Eze 29:13 At the end of *f* years will I
Eze 41:2 the length thereof, *f* cubits
Eze 46:22 courts joined of *f* cubits long
Amos 2:10 led you *f* years through the
Amos 5:25 in the wilderness *f* years
Jonah 3:4 Yet *f* days, and Nineveh shall be
Mt 4:2 And when he had fasted *f* days
Mt 4:2 *f* nights, he was afterward an
Mk 1:13 there in the wilderness *f* days
Lk 4:2 Being *f* days tempted of the devil
Jn 2:20 Then said the Jews, *F* and six
Acts 1:3 proofs, being seen of them *f* days
Acts 4:22 For the man was above *f* years old
Acts 7:23 And when he was full *f* years old
Acts 7:30 when *f* years were expired, there
Acts 7:36 sea, and in the wilderness *f* years
Acts 7:42 of *f* years in the wilderness
Acts 13:18 about the time of *f* years
Acts 13:21 Benjamin, by the space of *f* years
Acts 23:13 they were more than *f* which had
Acts 23:21 for him of them more than *f* men
2Cor 11:24 received I *f* stripes save one
Heb 3:9 me, and saw my works *f* years
Heb 3:17 with whom was he grieved *f* years
Rev 7:4 there were sealed an hundred and *f*
Rev 11:2 shall they tread under foot *f*
Rev 13:5 was given unto him to continue *f*
Rev 14:1 Sion, and with him an hundred *f*
Rev 14:3 that song but the hundred and *f*
Rev 21:17 the wall thereof, an hundred and *f*

## FORWARD

Gen 26:13 And the man waxed great, and went *f*
Ex 14:15 of Israel, that they go *f*
Num 1:51 And when the tabernacle setteth *f*
Num 2:17 of the congregation shall set *f*
Num 2:17 they encamp, so shall they set *f*
Num 2:24 they shall go *f* in the third rank
Num 2:34 their standards, and so they set *f*
Num 4:5 And when the camp setteth *f*
Num 4:15 as the camp is to set *f*
Num 10:5 lie on the east parts shall go *f*
Num 10:17 and the sons of Merari set *f*
Num 10:18 set *f* according to their armies
Num 10:21 And the Kohathites set *f*, bearing
Num 10:22 set *f* according to their armies
Num 10:25 camp of the children of Dan set *f*
Num 10:28 to their armies, when they set *f*
Num 10:35 came to pass, when the ark set *f*
Num 21:10 And the children of Israel set *f*
Num 22:1 And the children of Israel set *f*
Num 32:19 them on yonder side Jordan, or *f*
Judg 9:44 that was with him, rushed *f*
1Sa 10:3 shalt thou go on *f* from thence
1Sa 16:13 came upon David from that day *f*
1Sa 18:9 eyed David from that day and *f*
1Sa 30:25 And it was so from that day *f*
2Kin 3:24 but they went *f* smiting the
2Kin 4:24 to her servant, Drive, and go *f*
2Kin 20:9 shall the shadow go *f* ten degrees
1Chr 23:4 four thousand were to set *f* the
2Chr 34:12 of the Kohathites, to set it *f*
Ezr 3:8 to set *f* the work of the house of
Ezr 3:9 to set *f* the workmen in the house
Job 23:8 Behold, I go *f*, but he is not
Job 30:13 they set *f* my calamity, they have
Jer 7:24 heart, and went backward, and not *f*
Eze 1:9 they went every one straight *f*
Eze 1:12 And they went every one straight *f*
Eze 10:22 they went every one straight *f*
Eze 39:22 LORD their God from that day and *f*
Eze 43:27 that upon the eighth day, and so *f*
Zec 1:15 they helped *f* the affliction
Mk 14:35 he went *f* a little, and fell on
Acts 19:33 multitude, the Jews putting him *f*
2Cor 8:10 do, but also to be *f* a year ago
2Cor 8:17 but being more *f*, of his own
Gal 2:10 the same which I also was *f* to do
3Jn 6 whom if thou bring *f* on their

## FOUGHT

Ex 17:8 *f* with Israel in Rephidim
Ex 17:10 had said to him, and *f* with Amalek
Num 21:1 then he *f* against Israel, and took
Num 21:23 to Jahaz, and *f* against Israel
Num 21:26 who had *f* against the former king
Josh 10:14 for the LORD *f* for Israel
Josh 10:29 unto Libnah, and *f* against Libnah
Josh 10:31 against it, and *f* against it
Josh 10:34 against it, and *f* against it
Josh 10:36 and they *f* against it
Josh 10:38 to Debir; and *f* against it
Josh 10:42 LORD God of Israel *f* for Israel
Josh 23:3 God is he that hath *f* for you
Josh 24:8 and they *f* with you
Josh 24:11 the men of Jericho *f* against you
Judg 1:5 they *f* against him, and they slew
Judg 1:8 of Judah had *f* against Jerusalem
Judg 5:19 The kings came and *f*
Judg 5:19 then *f* the kings of Canaan in
Judg 5:20 They *f* from heaven
Judg 5:20 in their courses *f* against Sisera
Judg 9:17 (For my father *f* for you, and
Judg 9:39 of Shechem, and *f* with Abimelech
Judg 9:45 Abimelech *f* against the city all
Judg 9:52 *f* against it, and went hard unto
Judg 11:20 in Jahaz, and *f* against Israel
Judg 12:4 men of Gilead, and *f* with Ephraim
1Sa 4:10 And the Philistines *f*, and Israel
1Sa 12:9 of Moab, and they *f* against them
1Sa 14:47 *f* against all his enemies on
1Sa 19:8 *f* with the Philistines, and slew
1Sa 23:5 *f* with the Philistines, and
1Sa 31:1 the Philistines *f* against Israel
2Sa 2:28 no more, neither *f* they any more
2Sa 8:10 him, because he had *f* against
2Sa 10:17 against David, and *f* with him
2Sa 11:17 the city went out, and *f* with Joab
2Sa 12:26 Joab *f* against Rabbah of the
2Sa 12:27 I have *f* against Rabbah, and have
2Sa 12:29 and *f* against it, and took it
2Sa 21:15 *f* against the Philistines
2Kin 8:29 when he *f* against Hazael king of
2Kin 9:15 when he *f* with Hazael king of
2Kin 12:17 *f* against Gath, and took it
2Kin 13:12 his might wherewith he *f* against
2Kin 14:15 how he *f* with Amaziah king of
1Chr 10:1 the Philistines *f* against Israel
1Chr 18:10 him, because he had *f* against
1Chr 19:17 the Syrians, they *f* with him
1Chr 19:18 thousand men which *f* in chariots
2Chr 20:29 they had heard that the LORD *f*
2Chr 22:6 when he *f* with Hazael king of
2Chr 27:5 He *f* also with the king of the
Ps 109:3 *f* against me without a cause
Is 20:1 *f* against Ashdod, and took it
Is 63:10 their enemy, and he *f* against them
Jer 34:1 *f* against Jerusalem, and against
Jer 34:7 army *f* against Jerusalem, and
Zec 14:3 as when he *f* in the day of battle
Zec 14:12 that have *f* against Jerusalem
1Cor 15:32 I have *f* with beasts at Ephesus
2Ti 4:7 I have *f* a good fight, I have
Rev 12:7 his angels *f* against the dragon
Rev 12:7 and the dragon *f* and his angels,

## FOUL

Job 16:16 My face is *f* with weeping, and on
Eze 34:18 but ye must *f* the residue with
Mt 16:3 It will be *f* weather to day
Mk 9:25 together, he rebuked the *f* spirit
Rev 18:2 and the hold of every *f* spirit

## FOUND

Gen 2:20 was not *f* an help meet for him
Gen 6:8 But Noah *f* grace in the eyes of
Gen 8:9 But the dove *f* no rest for the
Gen 11:2 that they *f* a plain in the land
Gen 16:7 the angel of the LORD *f* her by a
Gen 18:3 if now I have *f* favour in thy
Gen 18:29 there shall be forty *f* there
Gen 18:30 there shall thirty be *f* there
Gen 18:31 there shall be twenty *f* there
Gen 18:32 Peradventure ten shall be *f* there
Gen 19:19 thy servant hath *f* grace in thy
Gen 26:19 *f* there a well of springing water
Gen 26:32 and said unto him, We have *f* water
Gen 27:20 it that thou hast *f* it so quickly
Gen 30:14 *f* mandrakes in the field, and
Gen 30:27 if I have *f* favour in thine eyes,
Gen 31:33 but he *f* them not
Gen 31:34 all the tent, but *f* them not
Gen 31:35 he searched, but *f* not the images
Gen 31:37 what hast thou *f* of all thy
Gen 33:10 if now I have *f* grace in thy
Gen 36:24 this was that Anah that *f* the
Gen 37:15 And a certain man *f* him, and,
Gen 37:17 his brethren, and *f* them in Dothan
Gen 37:32 and said, This have we *f*
Gen 38:20 but he *f* her not
Gen 38:23 this kid, and thou hast not *f* her
Gen 39:4 Joseph *f* grace in his sight, and
Gen 44:8 which we *f* in our sacks' mouths,
Gen 44:9 of thy servants it be *f*, both let
Gen 44:10 he with whom it is *f* shall be my
Gen 44:12 the cup was *f* in Benjamin's sack
Gen 44:16 God hath *f* out the iniquity of
Gen 44:16 and he also with whom the cup is *f*
Gen 44:17 man in whose hand the cup is *f*
Gen 47:14 that was *f* in the land of Egypt
Gen 47:29 If now I have *f* grace in thy
Gen 50:4 If now I have *f* grace in your
Ex 9:19 which shall be *f* in the field
Ex 12:19 be no leaven *f* in your houses
Ex 15:22 in the wilderness, and *f* no water
Ex 16:27 day for to gather, and they *f* none
Ex 21:16 him, or if he be *f* in his hand
Ex 22:2 If a thief be *f* breaking up
Ex 22:4 be certainly *f* in his hand alive
Ex 22:7 if the thief be *f*, let him pay
Ex 22:8 If the thief be not *f*, then the
Ex 33:12 thou hast also *f* grace in my
Ex 33:13 if I have *f* grace in thy sight,
Ex 33:16 thy people have *f* grace in thy
Ex 33:17 for thou hast *f* grace in my sight
Ex 34:9 If now I have *f* grace in thy
Ex 35:23 every man, with whom was *f* blue
Ex 35:24 with whom was *f* shittim wood for
Lev 6:3 Or have *f* that which was lost, and
Lev 6:4 or the lost thing which he *f*
Num 11:11 have I not *f* favour in thy sight
Num 11:15 if I have *f* favour in thy sight
Num 15:32 they *f* a man that gathered sticks
Num 15:33 they that *f* him gathering sticks
Num 32:5 if we have *f* grace in thy sight,
Deut 17:2 If there be *f* among you, within
Deut 18:10 There shall not be *f* among you
Deut 20:11 that all the people that is *f*
Deut 21:1 If one be *f* slain in the land
Deut 22:3 he hath lost, and thou hast *f*
Deut 22:14 I came to her, I *f* her not a maid
Deut 22:17 I *f* not thy daughter a maid
Deut 22:20 virginity be not *f* for the damsel
Deut 22:22 If a man be *f* lying with a woman
Deut 22:27 For he *f* her in the field, and the
Deut 22:28 and lie with her, and they be *f*
Deut 24:1 his eyes, because he hath *f* some
Deut 24:7 If a man be *f* stealing any of his
Deut 32:10 He *f* him in a desert land, and in
Deut 33:29 shall be *f* liars unto thee
Josh 2:22 all the way, but *f* them not

Josh 10:17 The five kings are *f* hid in a
Judg 1:5 they *f* Adoni-bezek in Bezek
Judg 6:17 If now I have *f* grace in thy
Judg 14:18 ye had not *f* out my riddle
Judg 15:15 he *f* a new jawbone of an ass, and
Judg 21:12 they *f* among the inhabitants of
Ruth 2:10 Why have I *f* grace in thine eyes,
1Sa 9:4 of Shalisha, but they *f* them not
1Sa 9:4 Benjamites, but they *f* them not
1Sa 9:11 they *f* young maidens going out to
1Sa 9:20 for they are *f*
1Sa 10:2 which thou wentest to seek are *f*
1Sa 10:16 us plainly that the asses were *f*
1Sa 10:21 sought him, he could not be *f*
1Sa 12:5 ye have not *f* ought in my hand
1Sa 13:19 Now there was no smith *f*
1Sa 13:22 spear *f* in the hand of any of the
1Sa 13:22 with Jonathan his son was there *f*
1Sa 14:30 of their enemies which they *f*
1Sa 16:22 for he hath *f* favour in my sight
1Sa 20:3 that I have *f* grace in thine eyes
1Sa 20:29 if I have *f* favour in thine eyes,
1Sa 25:28 evil hath not been *f* in thee all
1Sa 27:5 If I have now *f* grace in thine
1Sa 29:3 I have *f* no fault in him since he
1Sa 29:6 for I have not *f* evil in thee
1Sa 29:8 what hast thou *f* in thy servant
1Sa 30:11 they *f* an Egyptian in the field,
1Sa 31:8 strip the slain, that they *f* Saul
2Sa 7:27 *f* in his heart to pray this
2Sa 14:22 that I have *f* grace in thy sight
2Sa 17:12 in some place where he shall be *f*
2Sa 17:13 be not one small stone *f* there
1Kin 1:3 *f* Abishag a Shunammite, and
1Kin 1:52 if wickedness shall be *f* in him
1Kin 7:47 was the weight of the brass *f* out
1Kin 11:19 Hadad *f* great favour in the sight
1Kin 11:29 the Shilonite *f* him in the way
1Kin 13:14 *f* him sitting under an oak
1Kin 13:28 *f* his carcase cast in the way, and
1Kin 14:13 because in him there is *f* some
1Kin 18:10 and nation, that they *f* thee not
1Kin 19:19 *f* Elisha the son of Shaphat, who
1Kin 20:36 departed from him, a lion *f* him
1Kin 20:37 Then he *f* another man, and said,
1Kin 21:20 said to Elijah, Hast thou *f* me
1Kin 21:20 And he answered, I have *f* thee
2Kin 2:17 sought three days, but *f* him not
2Kin 4:39 *f* a wild vine, and gathered
2Kin 9:35 but they *f* no more of her than
2Kin 12:5 wheresoever any breach shall be *f*
2Kin 12:10 told the money that was *f* in the
2Kin 12:18 all the gold that was *f* in the
2Kin 14:14 were *f* in the house of the LORD
2Kin 16:8 gold that was *f* in the house of
2Kin 17:4 the king of Assyria *f* conspiracy
2Kin 18:15 was *f* in the house of the LORD
2Kin 19:8 *f* the king of Assyria warring
2Kin 20:13 all that was *f* in his treasures
2Kin 22:8 I have *f* the book of the law in
2Kin 22:9 the money that was *f* in the house
2Kin 22:13 the words of this book that is *f*
2Kin 23:2 was *f* in the house of the LORD
2Kin 23:24 priest *f* in the house of the LORD
2Kin 25:19 which were *f* in the city, and the
2Kin 25:19 the land that were *f* in the city
1Chr 4:40 they *f* fat pasture and good, and
1Chr 4:41 the habitations that were *f* there
1Chr 10:8 strip the slain, that they *f* Saul
1Chr 17:25 therefore thy servant hath *f* in
1Chr 20:2 *f* it to weigh a talent of gold,
1Chr 24:4 there were more chief men *f* of
1Chr 26:31 there were *f* among them mighty
1Chr 28:9 seek him, he will be *f* of thee
1Chr 29:8 *f* gave them to the treasure of
2Chr 2:17 they were *f* an hundred and fifty
2Chr 4:18 of the brass could not be *f* out
2Chr 15:2 ye seek him, he will be *f* of you
2Chr 15:4 and sought him, he was *f* of them
2Chr 15:15 and he was *f* of them
2Chr 19:3 there are good things *f* in thee
2Chr 20:25 they *f* among them in abundance
2Chr 21:17 that was *f* in the king's house
2Chr 22:8 *f* the princes of Judah, and the
2Chr 25:5 *f* them three hundred thousand
2Chr 25:24 were *f* in the house of God with
2Chr 29:16 all the uncleanness that they *f*
2Chr 34:14 Hilkiah the priest *f* a book of
2Chr 34:15 I have *f* the book of the law in
2Chr 34:17 was *f* in the house of the LORD
2Chr 34:21 the words of the book that is *f*
2Chr 34:30 was *f* in the house of the LORD
2Chr 36:8 did, and that which was *f* in him
Ezr 2:62 by genealogy, but they were not *f*
Ezr 4:19 it is *f* that this city of old
Ezr 6:2 there was *f* at Achmetha, in the
Ezr 8:15 *f* there none of the sons of Levi
Ezr 10:18 *f* that had taken strange wives
Neh 2:5 have *f* favour in thy sight
Neh 5:8 peace, and *f* nothing to answer
Neh 7:5 I *f* a register of the genealogy
Neh 7:5 the first, and *f* written therein,
Neh 7:64 by genealogy, but it was not *f*
Neh 8:14 they *f* written in the law which
Neh 13:1 and therein was *f* written, that
Est 2:23 made of the matter, it was *f* out
Est 5:8 If I have *f* favour in the sight
Est 6:2 it was *f* written, that Mordecai
Est 7:3 If I have *f* favour in thy sight,
Est 8:5 if I have *f* favour in his sight,
Job 19:28 the root of the matter is *f* in me
Job 20:8 as a dream, and shall not be *f*
Job 28:12 But where shall wisdom be *f*
Job 28:13 neither is it *f* in the land of
Job 31:29 lifted up myself when evil *f* him
Job 32:3 because they had *f* no answer
Job 32:13 should say, We have *f* out wisdom
Job 33:24 I have *f* a ransom
Job 42:15 in all the land were no women *f*
Ps 32:6 in a time when thou mayest be *f*
Ps 36:2 his iniquity be *f* to be hateful
Ps 37:36 sought him, but he could not be *f*
Ps 69:20 and for comforters, but I *f* none
Ps 76:5 men of might have *f* their hands
Ps 84:3 Yea, the sparrow hath *f* an house
Ps 89:20 I have *f* David my servant
Ps 107:4 they *f* no city to dwell in
Ps 116:3 I *f* trouble and sorrow
Ps 132:6 we *f* it in the fields of the wood
Prov 6:31 But if he be *f*, he shall restore
Prov 7:15 seek thy face, and I have *f* thee
Prov 10:13 hath understanding wisdom is *f*
Prov 16:31 glory, if it be *f* in the way of
Prov 24:14 when thou hast *f* it, then there
Prov 25:16 Hast thou *f* honey
Prov 30:6 reprove thee, and thou be *f* a liar
Prov 30:10 curse thee, and thou be *f* guilty
Eccl 7:27 Behold, this have I *f*, saith the
Eccl 7:28 one man among a thousand have I *f*
Eccl 7:28 among all those have I not *f*
Eccl 7:29 Lo, this only have I *f*, that God
Eccl 9:15 Now there was *f* in it a poor wise
Song 3:1 I sought him, but I *f* him not
Song 3:2 I sought him, but I *f* him not
Song 3:3 that go about the city *f* me
Song 3:4 but I *f* him whom my soul loveth
Song 5:7 that went about the city *f* me
Song 8:10 in his eyes as one that *f* favour
Is 10:10 As my hand hath *f* the kingdoms of
Is 10:14 my hand hath *f* as a nest the
Is 13:15 Every one that is *f* shall be
Is 22:3 all that are *f* in thee are bound
Is 30:14 so that there shall not be *f* in
Is 35:9 thereon, it shall not be *f* there
Is 37:8 *f* the king of Assyria warring
Is 39:2 all that was *f* in his treasures
Is 51:3 and gladness shall be *f* therein
Is 55:6 ye the LORD while he may be *f*
Is 57:10 thou hast *f* the life of thine
Is 65:1 I am *f* of them that sought me not
Is 65:8 the new wine is *f* in the cluster
Jer 2:5 have your fathers *f* in me
Jer 2:26 the thief is ashamed when he is *f*
Jer 2:34 Also in thy skirts is *f* the blood
Jer 2:34 I have not *f* it by secret search,
Jer 5:26 among my people are *f* wicked men
Jer 11:9 A conspiracy is *f* among the men
Jer 14:3 came to the pits, and *f* no water
Jer 15:16 Thy words were *f*, and I did eat
Jer 23:11 house have I *f* their wickedness
Jer 29:14 And I will be *f* of you, saith the
Jer 31:2 sword *f* grace in the wilderness
Jer 41:3 the Chaldeans that were *f* there
Jer 41:8 But ten men were *f* among them
Jer 41:12 *f* him by the great waters that
Jer 48:27 was he *f* among thieves
Jer 50:7 All that *f* them have devoured
Jer 50:20 of Judah, and they shall not be *f*
Jer 50:24 thou art *f*, and also caught,
Jer 52:25 person, which were *f* in the city
Jer 52:25 that were *f* in the midst of the
Lam 2:16 we have *f*, we have seen it
Eze 22:30 not destroy it: but I *f* none
Eze 26:21 yet shalt thou never be *f* again
Eze 28:15 till iniquity was *f* in thee
Dan 1:19 them all was *f* none like Daniel
Dan 1:20 he *f* them ten times better than
Dan 2:25 I have *f* a man of the captives of
Dan 2:35 that no place was *f* for them
Dan 5:11 wisdom of the gods, was *f* in him
Dan 5:12 were *f* in the same Daniel, whom
Dan 5:14 and excellent wisdom is *f* in thee
Dan 5:27 in the balances, and art *f* wanting
Dan 6:4 there any error or fault *f* in him
Dan 6:11 *f* Daniel praying and making
Dan 6:22 before him innocency was *f* in me
Dan 6:23 no manner of hurt was *f* upon him
Dan 11:19 stumble and fall, and not be *f*
Dan 12:1 shall be *f* written in the book
Hos 9:10 I *f* Israel like grapes in the
Hos 10:2 now shall they be *f* faulty
Hos 12:4 he *f* him in Beth-el, and there he
Hos 12:8 I have *f* me out substance
Hos 14:8 From me is thy fruit *f*
Jonah 1:3 he *f* a ship going to Tarshish
Mic 1:13 of Israel were *f* in thee
Zeph 3:13 tongue be *f* in their mouth
Zec 10:10 and place shall not be *f* for them
Mal 2:6 and iniquity was not *f* in his lips
Mt 1:18 she was *f* with child of the Holy
Mt 2:8 and when ye have *f* him, bring me
Mt 8:10 I have not *f* so great faith, no,
Mt 13:44 the which when a man hath *f*
Mt 13:46 when he had *f* one pearl of great
Mt 18:28 *f* one of his fellowservants,
Mt 20:6 *f* others standing idle, and saith
Mt 21:19 *f* nothing thereon, but leaves
Mt 22:10 together all as many as they *f*
Mt 26:43 And he came and *f* them asleep again
Mt 26:60 But *f* none: yea, though
Mt 26:60 witnesses came, yet *f* they none
Mt 27:32 they *f* a man of Cyrene, Simon by
Mk 1:37 And when they had *f* him, they said
Mk 7:2 unwashen, hands, they *f* fault
Mk 7:30 she *f* the devil gone out, and her
Mk 11:4 *f* the colt tied by the door
Mk 11:13 to it, he *f* nothing but leaves
Mk 14:16 *f* as he had said unto them
Mk 14:40 he *f* them asleep again, (for
Mk 14:55 and *f* none.
Lk 1:30 for thou hast *f* favour with God
Lk 2:16 *f* Mary, and Joseph, and the babe
Lk 2:45 And when they *f* him not, they
Lk 2:46 days they *f* him in the temple
Lk 4:17 he *f* the place where it was
Lk 7:9 I have not *f* so great faith, no,
Lk 7:10 *f* the servant whole that had been
Lk 8:35 *f* the man, out of whom the devils
Lk 9:36 voice was past, Jesus was *f* alone
Lk 13:6 sought fruit thereon, and *f* none
Lk 15:5 And when he hath *f* it, he layeth
Lk 15:6 for I have *f* my sheep which was
Lk 15:9 And when she hath *f* it, she
Lk 15:9 for I have *f* the piece which I
Lk 15:24 he was lost, and is *f*
Lk 15:32 and was lost, and is *f*
Lk 17:18 There are not *f* that returned to
Lk 19:32 *f* even as he had said unto them
Lk 22:13 *f* as he had said unto them
Lk 22:45 he *f* them sleeping for sorrow,
Lk 23:2 We *f* this fellow perverting the
Lk 23:14 have *f* no fault in this man
Lk 23:22 I have *f* no cause of death in him
Lk 24:2 they *f* the stone rolled away from
Lk 24:3 *f* not the body of the Lord Jesus
Lk 24:23 when they *f* not his body, they
Lk 24:24 *f* it even so as the women had
Lk 24:33 *f* the eleven gathered together,
Jn 1:41 We have *f* the Messias, which is,
Jn 1:45 and saith unto him, We have *f* him
Jn 2:14 *f* in the temple those that sold
Jn 6:25 when they had *f* him on the other
Jn 9:35 and when he had *f* him, he said
Jn 11:17 he *f* that he had lain in the
Jn 12:14 Jesus, when he had *f* a young ass
Acts 5:10 *f* her dead, and, carrying her
Acts 5:22 *f* them not in the prison, they
Acts 5:23 The prison truly *f* we shut with
Acts 5:23 we had opened, we *f* no man within
Acts 5:39 lest haply ye be *f* even to fight

Acts 7:11 our fathers *f* no sustenance
Acts 7:46 Who *f* favour before God, and
Acts 8:40 But Philip was *f* at Azotus
Acts 9:2 that if he *f* any of this way,
Acts 9:33 there he *f* a certain man named
Acts 10:27 *f* many that were come together
Acts 11:26 And when he had *f* him, he brought
Acts 12:19 *f* him not, he examined the
Acts 13:6 they *f* a certain sorcerer, a
Acts 13:22 I have *f* David the son of Jesse,
Acts 13:28 though they *f* no cause of death
Acts 17:6 And when they *f* them not, they
Acts 17:23 devotions, I *f* an altar with this
Acts 18:2 *f* a certain Jew named Aquila,
Acts 19:19 *f* it fifty thousand pieces of
Acts 24:5 For we have *f* this man a
Acts 24:12 they neither *f* me in the temple
Acts 24:18 certain Jews from Asia *f* me
Acts 24:20 if they have *f* any evil doing in
Acts 25:25 But when I *f* that he had
Acts 27:6 there the centurion *f* a ship of
Acts 27:28 sounded, and *f* it twenty fathoms
Acts 27:28 again, and *f* it fifteen fathoms
Acts 28:14 Where we *f* brethren, and were
Rom 4:1 pertaining to the flesh, hath *f*
Rom 7:10 to life, I *f* to be unto death
Rom 10:20 I was *f* of them that sought me
1Cor 4:2 that a man be *f* faithful
1Cor 15:15 we are *f* false witnesses of God
2Cor 2:13 because I *f* not Titus my brother
2Cor 5:3 clothed we shall not be *f* naked
2Cor 7:14 I made before Titus, is *f* a truth
2Cor 11:12 glory, they may be *f* even as we
2Cor 12:20 that I shall be *f* unto you such
Gal 2:17 we ourselves also are *f* sinners
Phil 2:8 being *f* in fashion as a man, he
Phil 3:9 be *f* in him, not having mine own
1Ti 3:10 of a deacon, being *f* blameless
2Ti 1:17 me out very diligently, and *f* me
Heb 11:5 and was not *f*, because God had
Heb 12:17 for he *f* no place of repentance,
1Pet 1:7 might be *f* unto praise and honour
1Pet 2:22 neither was guile *f* in his mouth
2Pet 3:14 that ye may be *f* of him in peace
2Jn 4 I rejoiced greatly that I *f* of
Rev 2:2 and are not, and hast *f* them liars
Rev 3:2 for I have not *f* thy works
Rev 5:4 no man was *f* worthy to open
Rev 12:8 their place *f* any more in heaven
Rev 14:5 And in their mouth was *f* no guile
Rev 16:20 away, and the mountains were not *f*
Rev 18:21 shall be *f* no more at all
Rev 18:22 shall be *f* any more in thee
Rev 18:24 in her was *f* the blood of
Rev 20:11 there was *f* no place for them
Rev 20:15 whosoever was not *f* written in

## FOUNDATION

Ex 9:18 the *f* thereof even until now
Josh 6:26 he shall lay the *f* thereof in his
1Kin 5:17 to lay the *f* of the house
1Kin 6:37 In the fourth year was the *f* of
1Kin 7:9 even from the *f* unto the coping,
1Kin 7:10 the *f* was of costly stones, even
1Kin 16:34 he laid the *f* thereof in Abiram
2Chr 8:16 of the *f* of the house of the LORD
2Chr 23:5 a third part at the gate of the *f*
2Chr 31:7 began to lay the *f* of the heaps
Ezr 3:6 But the *f* of the temple of the
Ezr 3:10 the *f* of the temple of the LORD
Ezr 3:11 because the *f* of the house of the
Ezr 3:12 when the *f* of this house was laid
Ezr 5:16 laid the *f* of the house of God
Job 4:19 whose *f* is in the dust, which are
Job 22:16 whose *f* was overflown with a
Ps 87:1 His *f* is in the holy mountains
Ps 102:25 hast thou laid the *f* of the earth
Ps 137:7 rase it, even to the *f* thereof
Prov 10:25 the righteous is an everlasting *f*
Is 28:16 I lay in Zion for a *f* a stone
Is 28:16 a precious corner stone, a sure *f*
Is 44:28 the temple, Thy *f* shall be laid
Is 48:13 also hath laid the *f* of the earth
Eze 13:14 so that the *f* thereof shall be
Hab 3:13 discovering the *f* unto the neck
Hag 2:18 even from the day that the *f* of
Zec 4:9 have laid the *f* of this house
Zec 8:9 the *f* of the house of the LORD of
Zec 12:1 layeth the *f* of the earth, and
Mt 13:35 secret from the *f* of the world
Mt 25:34 for you from the *f* of the world
Lk 6:48 deep, and laid the *f* on a rock
Lk 6:49 is like a man that without a *f*
Lk 11:50 was shed from the *f* of the world
Lk 14:29 haply, after he hath laid the *f*
Jn 17:24 me before the *f* of the world
Rom 15:20 should build upon another man's *f*
1Cor 3:10 masterbuilder, I have laid the *f*
1Cor 3:11 For other *f* can no man lay than
1Cor 3:12 if any man build upon this *f* gold
Eph 1:4 in him before the *f* of the world
Eph 2:20 built upon the *f* of the apostles
1Ti 6:19 a good *f* against the time to come
2Ti 2:19 Nevertheless the *f* of God
Heb 1:10 hast laid the *f* of the earth
Heb 4:3 finished from the *f* of the world
Heb 6:1 not laying again the *f* of
Heb 9:26 suffered since the *f* of the world
1Pet 1:20 before the *f* of the world
Rev 13:8 slain from the *f* of the world
Rev 17:8 of life from the *f* of the world
Rev 21:19 The first *f* was jasper

## FOUNDATIONS

Deut 32:22 and set on fire the *f* of the
2Sa 22:8 the *f* of heaven moved and shook,
2Sa 22:16 appeared, the *f* of the world were
Ezr 4:12 walls thereof, and joined the *f*
Ezr 6:3 let the *f* thereof be strongly
Job 38:4 when I laid the *f* of the earth
Job 38:6 are the *f* thereof fastened
Ps 11:3 If the *f* be destroyed, what can
Ps 18:7 the *f* also of the hills moved and
Ps 18:15 seen, and the *f* of the world were
Ps 82:5 all the *f* of the earth are out of
Ps 104:5 Who laid the *f* of the earth
Prov 8:29 he appointed the *f* of the earth
Is 16:7 for the *f* of Kir-hareseth shall
Is 24:18 the *f* of the earth do shake
Is 40:21 from the *f* of the earth
Is 51:13 and laid the *f* of the earth
Is 51:16 lay the *f* of the earth, and say
Is 54:11 and lay thy *f* with sapphires
Is 58:12 up the *f* of many generations
Jer 31:37 the *f* of the earth searched out
Jer 50:15 her *f* are fallen, her walls are
Jer 51:26 for a corner, nor a stone for *f*
Lam 4:11 and it hath devoured the *f* thereof
Eze 30:4 her *f* shall be broken down
Eze 41:8 the *f* of the side chambers were a
Mic 1:6 and I will discover the *f* thereof
Mic 6:2 and ye strong *f* of the earth
Acts 16:26 so that the *f* of the prison were
Heb 11:10 he looked for a city which hath *f*
Rev 21:14 the wall of the city had twelve *f*
Rev 21:19 the *f* of the wall of the city

## FOUNDED

Ps 24:2 For he hath *f* it upon the seas,
Ps 89:11 fulness thereof, thou hast *f* them
Ps 104:8 place which thou hast *f* for them
Ps 119:152 that thou hast *f* them for ever
Prov 3:19 LORD by wisdom hath *f* the earth
Is 14:32 That the LORD hath *f* Zion
Is 23:13 til the Assyrian *f* it for them
Amos 9:6 hath *f* his troop in the earth
Mt 7:25 for it was *f* upon a rock
Lk 6:48 for it was *f* upon a rock

## FOUNDER

Judg 17:4 of silver, and gave them to the *f*
Jer 6:29 the *f* melteth in vain
Jer 10:9 workman, and of the hands of the *f*
Jer 10:14 every *f* is confounded by the
Jer 51:17 every *f* is confounded by the

## FOUNTAIN

Gen 16:7 by a *f* of water in the wilderness
Gen 16:7 by the *f* in the way to Shur
Lev 11:36 Nevertheless a *f* or pit, wherein
Lev 20:18 he hath discovered her *f*, and she
Lev 20:18 hath uncovered the *f* of her blood
Deut 33:28 the *f* of Jacob shall be upon a
Josh 15:9 the *f* of the water of Nephtoah
1Sa 29:1 by a *f* which is in Jezreel
Neh 2:14 I went on to the gate of the *f*
Neh 3:15 But the gate of the *f* repaired
Neh 12:37 And at the *f* gate, which was over
Ps 36:9 For with thee is the *f* of life
Ps 68:26 the Lord, from the *f* of Israel
Ps 74:15 Thou didst cleave the *f* and the
Ps 114:8 the flint into a *f* of waters
Prov 5:18 Let thy *f* be blessed
Prov 13:14 law of the wise is a *f* of life
Prov 14:27 fear of the LORD is a *f* of life
Prov 25:26 the wicked is as a troubled *f*
Eccl 12:6 or the pitcher be broken at the *f*
Song 4:12 a spring shut up, a *f* sealed
Song 4:15 A *f* of gardens, a well of living
Jer 2:13 me the *f* of living waters
Jer 6:7 As a *f* casteth out her waters, so
Jer 9:1 waters, and mine eyes a *f* of tears
Jer 17:13 the LORD, the *f* of living waters
Hos 13:15 dry, and his *f* shall be dried up
Joel 3:18 a *f* shall come forth of the house
Zec 13:1 a *f* opened to the house of David
Mk 5:29 straightway the *f* of her blood
Jas 3:11 Doth a *f* send forth at the same
Jas 3:12 so can no *f* both yield salt water
Rev 21:6 the *f* of the water of life freely

## FOUNTAINS

Gen 7:11 the same day were all the *f* of
Gen 8:2 The *f* also of the deep and the
Num 33:9 and in Elim were twelve *f* of water
Deut 8:7 a land of brooks of water, of *f*
1Kin 18:5 the land, unto all *f* of water
2Chr 32:3 the *f* which were without the city
2Chr 32:4 together, who stopped all the *f*
Prov 5:16 Let thy *f* be dispersed abroad, and
Prov 8:24 when there were no *f* abounding
Prov 8:28 he strengthened the *f* of the deep
Is 41:18 *f* in the midst of the valleys
Rev 7:17 lead them unto living *f* of waters
Rev 8:10 rivers, and upon the *f* of waters
Rev 14:7 and the sea, and the *f* of waters
Rev 16:4 upon the rivers and *f* of waters

## FOUR

Gen 2:10 parted, and became into *f* heads
Gen 11:13 after he begat Salah *f* hundred
Gen 11:15 after he begat Eber *f* hundred
Gen 11:16 And Eber lived *f* and thirty years,
Gen 11:17 after he begat Peleg *f* hundred
Gen 14:9 *f* kings with five
Gen 15:13 afflict them *f* hundred years
Gen 23:15 the land is worth *f* hundred
Gen 23:16 *f* hundred shekels of silver,
Gen 32:6 thee, and *f* hundred men with him
Gen 33:1 came, and with him *f* hundred men
Gen 47:24 *f* parts shall be your own, for
Ex 12:40 was *f* hundred and thirty years
Ex 12:41 pass at the end of the *f* hundred
Ex 22:1 for an ox, and *f* sheep for a sheep
Ex 25:12 thou shalt cast *f* rings of gold
Ex 25:12 put them in the *f* corners thereof
Ex 25:26 shalt make for it *f* rings of gold
Ex 25:26 put the rings in the *f* corners
Ex 25:26 that are on the *f* feet thereof
Ex 25:34 in the candlestick shall be *f*
Ex 26:2 breadth of one curtain *f* cubits
Ex 26:8 breadth of one curtain *f* cubits
Ex 26:32 it upon *f* pillars of shittim wood
Ex 26:32 upon the *f* sockets of silver
Ex 27:2 of it upon the *f* corners thereof
Ex 27:4 make *f* brasen rings in the *f*
Ex 27:16 shall be *f*, and their sockets *f*
Ex 28:17 of stones, even *f* rows of stones
Ex 36:9 breadth of one curtain *f* cubits
Ex 36:15 *f* cubits was the breadth of one
Ex 36:36 he made thereunto *f* pillars of
Ex 36:36 he cast for them *f* sockets of
Ex 37:3 And he cast for it *f* rings of gold
Ex 37:3 to be set by the *f* corners of it
Ex 37:13 And he cast for it *f* rings of gold
Ex 37:13 put the rings upon the *f* corners
Ex 37:13 that were in the *f* feet thereof
Ex 37:20 were *f* bowls made like almonds
Ex 38:2 thereof on the *f* corners of it
Ex 38:5 he cast *f* rings for the *f* ends
Ex 38:19 And their pillars were *f*
Ex 38:19 and their sockets of brass *f*
Ex 38:29 two thousand and *f* hundred shekels
Ex 39:10 they set in it *f* rows of stones
Lev 11:20 that creep, going upon all *f*
Lev 11:21 thing that goeth upon all *f*
Lev 11:23 things, which have *f* feet
Lev 11:27 manner of beasts that go on all *f*
Lev 11:42 and whatsoever goeth upon all *f*
Num 1:29 and *f* thousand and *f* hundred
Num 1:31 and seven thousand and *f* hundred
Num 1:37 and five thousand and *f* hundred
Num 1:43 and three thousand and *f* hundred

Num 2:6 and *f* thousand and *f* hundred
Num 2:8 and seven thousand and *f* hundred
Num 2:9 *f* hundred, throughout their
Num 2:16 *f* hundred and fifty, throughout
Num 2:23 and five thousand and *f* hundred
Num 2:30 and three thousand and *f* hundred
Num 7:7 *f* oxen he gave unto the sons of
Num 7:8 *f* wagons and eight oxen he gave
Num 7:85 *f* hundred shekels, after the
Num 7:88 *f* bullocks, the rams sixty, the
Num 25:9 plague were twenty and *f* thousand
Num 26:25 *f* thousand and three hundred
Num 26:43 and *f* thousand and *f* hundred
Num 26:47 and three thousand and *f* hundred
Num 26:50 and five thousand and *f* hundred
Deut 3:11 *f* cubits the breadth of it, after
Deut 22:12 the *f* quarters of thy vesture
Josh 19:7 *f* cities and their villages
Josh 21:18 Almon with her suburbs; *f* cities
Josh 21:22 Beth-horon with her suburbs; *f* cities
Josh 21:24 with her suburbs; *f* cities
Josh 21:29 with her suburbs; *f* cities
Josh 21:31 Rehob with her suburbs; *f* cities
Josh 21:35 with her suburbs; *f* cities
Josh 21:37 with her suburbs; *f* cities
Josh 21:39 Jazer with her suburbs; *f* cities
Judg 9:34 against Shechem in *f* companies
Judg 11:40 the Gileadite *f* days in a year
Judg 19:2 and was there *f* whole months
Judg 20:2 *f* hundred thousand footmen that
Judg 20:17 were numbered *f* hundred thousand
Judg 20:47 abode in the rock Rimmon *f* months
Judg 21:12 *f* hundred young virgins, that had
1Sa 4:2 in the field about *f* thousand men
1Sa 22:2 were with him about *f* hundred men
1Sa 25:13 after David about *f* hundred men
1Sa 27:7 was a full year and *f* months
1Sa 30:10 pursued, he and *f* hundred men
1Sa 30:17 save *f* hundred young men, which
2Sa 21:20 and on every foot six toes, *f*
2Sa 21:22 These *f* were born to the giant in
1Kin 6:1 it came to pass in the *f* hundred
1Kin 7:2 upon *f* rows of cedar pillars,
1Kin 7:19 lily work in the porch, *f* cubits
1Kin 7:27 *f* cubits was the length of one
1Kin 7:27 *f* cubits the breadth thereof, and
1Kin 7:30 And every base had *f* brasen wheels
1Kin 7:30 the *f* corners thereof had
1Kin 7:32 under the borders were *f* wheels
1Kin 7:34 there were *f* undersetters to the
1Kin 7:34 to the *f* corners of one base
1Kin 7:38 and every laver was *f* cubits
1Kin 7:42 *f* hundred pomegranates for the
1Kin 9:28 *f* hundred and twenty talents, and
1Kin 10:26 *f* hundred chariots, and twelve
1Kin 15:33 in Tirzah, twenty and *f* years
1Kin 18:19 and the prophets of Baal *f* hundred
1Kin 18:19 prophets of the groves *f* hundred
1Kin 18:22 but Baal's prophets are *f* hundred
1Kin 18:33 Fill *f* barrels with water, and
1Kin 22:6 about *f* hundred men, and said unto
2Kin 7:3 there were *f* leprous men at the
2Kin 14:13 the corner gate, *f* hundred cubits
1Chr 3:5 Shobab, and Nathan, and Solomon, *f*
1Chr 5:18 bow, and skilful in war, were *f*
1Chr 7:1 and Puah, Jashub, and Shimrom, *f*
1Chr 7:7 and two thousand and thirty and *f*
1Chr 9:24 In *f* quarters were the porters,
1Chr 9:26 the *f* chief porters, were in
1Chr 12:26 the children of Levi *f* thousand
1Chr 20:6 whose fingers and toes were *f*
1Chr 21:5 Judah was *f* hundred threescore and
1Chr 21:20 and his *f* sons with him hid
1Chr 23:4 *f* thousand were to set forward
1Chr 23:5 Moreover *f* thousand were porters
1Chr 23:5 *f* thousand praised the LORD with
1Chr 23:10 These *f* were the sons of Shimei
1Chr 23:12 Izhar, Hebron, and Uzziel, *f*
1Chr 24:18 and twentieth to Delaiah, the *f*
1Chr 25:31 The *f* and twentieth to
1Chr 26:17 *f* a day, southward *f* a day
1Chr 26:18 *f* at the causeway, and two at
1Chr 27:1 course were twenty and *f* thousand
1Chr 27:2 course were twenty and *f* thousand
1Chr 27:4 were twenty and *f* thousand
1Chr 27:5 course were twenty and *f* thousand
1Chr 27:7 course were twenty and *f* thousand
1Chr 27:8 course were twenty and *f* thousand
1Chr 27:9 course were twenty and *f* thousand
1Chr 27:10 course were twenty and *f* thousand
1Chr 27:11 course were twenty and *f* thousand
1Chr 27:12 course were twenty and *f* thousand
1Chr 27:13 course were twenty and *f* thousand
1Chr 27:14 course were twenty and *f* thousand
1Chr 27:15 course were twenty and *f* thousand
2Chr 1:14 *f* hundred chariots, and twelve
2Chr 4:13 *f* hundred pomegranates on the two
2Chr 8:18 Ophir, and took thence *f* hundred
2Chr 9:25 Solomon had *f* thousand stalls for
2Chr 13:3 even *f* hundred thousand chosen
2Chr 18:5 of prophets *f* hundred men
2Chr 25:23 the corner gate, *f* hundred cubits
Ezr 1:10 basons of a second sort *f* hundred
Ezr 1:11 were five thousand and *f* hundred
Ezr 2:7 a thousand two hundred fifty and *f*
Ezr 2:15 of Adin, *f* hundred fifty and *f*
Ezr 2:31 a thousand two hundred fifty and *f*
Ezr 2:40 of Hodaviah, seventy and *f*
Ezr 2:67 camels, *f* hundred thirty and five
Ezr 6:17 two hundred rams, *f* hundred lambs
Neh 6:4 unto me *f* times after this sort
Neh 7:12 a thousand two hundred fifty and *f*
Neh 7:23 Bezai, three hundred twenty and *f*
Neh 7:34 a thousand two hundred fifty and *f*
Neh 7:43 children of Hodevah, seventy and *f*
Neh 7:69 camels, *f* hundred thirty and five
Neh 11:6 were *f* hundred threescore
Neh 11:18 were two hundred fourscore and *f*
Job 1:19 smote the *f* corners of the house,
Job 42:16 sons' sons, even *f* generations
Prov 30:15 *f* things say not, It is enough
Prov 30:18 for me, yea, *f* which I know not
Prov 30:21 for *f* which it cannot bear
Prov 30:24 There be *f* things which are
Prov 30:29 well, yea, *f* are comely in going
Is 11:12 from the *f* corners of the earth
Is 17:6 *f* or five in the outmost fruitful
Jer 15:3 I will appoint over them *f* kinds
Jer 36:23 Jehudi had read three or *f* leaves
Jer 49:36 upon Elam will I bring the *f*
Jer 49:36 from the *f* quarters of heaven
Jer 52:21 thickness thereof was *f* fingers
Jer 52:30 all the persons were *f* thousand
Eze 1:5 likeness of *f* living creatures
Eze 1:6 And every one had *f* faces
Eze 1:6 and every one had *f* wings
Eze 1:8 their wings on their *f* sides
Eze 1:8 they *f* had their faces and their
Eze 1:10 they *f* had the face of a man, and
Eze 1:10 they *f* had the face of an ox on
Eze 1:10 they *f* also had the face of an
Eze 1:15 creatures, with his *f* faces
Eze 1:16 and they *f* had one likeness
Eze 1:17 they went upon their *f* sides
Eze 1:18 full of eyes round about them *f*
Eze 7:2 upon the *f* corners of the land
Eze 10:9 behold the *f* wheels by the
Eze 10:10 they *f* had one likeness, as if a
Eze 10:11 they went upon their *f* sides
Eze 10:12 even the wheels that they *f* had
Eze 10:14 And every one had *f* faces
Eze 10:21 Every one had *f* faces apiece
Eze 10:21 and every one *f* wings
Eze 14:21 How much more when I send my *f*
Eze 37:9 Come from the *f* winds, O breath,
Eze 40:41 *F* tables were on this side, and
Eze 40:41 *f* tables on that side, by the
Eze 40:42 the *f* tables were of hewn stone
Eze 41:5 *f* cubits, round about the house
Eze 42:20 He measured it by the *f* sides
Eze 43:14 greater settle shall be *f* cubits
Eze 43:15 So the altar shall be *f* cubits
Eze 43:15 altar and upward shall be *f* horns
Eze 43:16 square in the *f* squares thereof
Eze 43:17 broad in the *f* squares thereof
Eze 43:20 and put it on the *f* horns of it
Eze 43:20 on the *f* corners of the settle,
Eze 45:19 upon the *f* corners of the settle
Eze 46:21 by the *f* corners of the court
Eze 46:22 In the *f* corners of the court
Eze 46:22 these *f* corners were of one
Eze 46:23 about in them, round about them *f*
Eze 48:16 the north side *f* thousand
Eze 48:16 and the south side *f* thousand
Eze 48:16 and on the east side *f* thousand
Eze 48:16 and the west side *f* thousand
Eze 48:30 *f* thousand and five hundred
Eze 48:32 And at the east side *f* thousand
Eze 48:33 And at the south side *f* thousand
Eze 48:34 At the west side *f* thousand
Dan 1:17 As for these *f* children, God gave
Dan 3:25 I see *f* men loose, walking in the
Dan 7:2 the *f* winds of the heaven strove
Dan 7:3 *f* great beasts came up from the
Dan 7:6 the back of it *f* wings of a fowl
Dan 7:6 the beast had also *f* heads
Dan 7:17 These great beasts, which are *f*
Dan 7:17 are *f* kings, which shall arise
Dan 8:8 for it came up *f* notable ones
Dan 8:8 ones toward the *f* winds of heaven
Dan 8:22 whereas *f* stood up for it
Dan 8:22 *f* kingdoms shall stand up out of
Dan 10:4 And in the *f* and twentieth day of
Dan 11:4 toward the *f* winds of heaven
Amos 1:3 of Damascus, and for *f*, I will not
Amos 1:6 transgressions of Gaza, and for *f*
Amos 1:9 transgressions of Tyrus, and for *f*
Amos 1:11 transgressions of Edom, and for *f*
Amos 1:13 the children of Ammon, and for *f*
Amos 2:1 transgressions of Moab, and for *f*
Amos 2:4 transgressions of Judah, and for *f*
Amos 2:6 of Israel, and for *f*, I will not
Hag 1:15 In the *f* and twentieth day of the
Hag 2:10 In the *f* and twentieth day of the
Hag 2:18 this day and upward, from the *f*
Hag 2:20 LORD came unto Haggai in the *f*
Zec 1:7 Upon the *f* and twentieth day of
Zec 1:18 eyes, and saw, and behold *f* horns
Zec 1:20 the LORD shewed me *f* carpenters
Zec 2:6 as the *f* winds of the heaven
Zec 6:1 there came *f* chariots out from
Zec 6:5 These are the *f* spirits of the
Mt 15:38 that did eat were *f* thousand men
Mt 16:10 seven loaves of the *f* thousand
Mt 24:31 his elect from the *f* winds
Mk 2:3 the palsy, which was borne of *f*
Mk 8:9 had eaten were about *f* thousand
Mk 8:20 when the seven among *f* thousand
Mk 13:27 his elect from the *f* winds
Lk 2:37 *f* years, which departed not from
Jn 4:35 not ye, There are yet *f* months
Jn 11:17 lain in the grave *f* days already
Jn 11:39 for he hath been dead *f* days
Jn 19:23 made *f* parts, to every soldier a
Acts 5:36 of men, about *f* hundred, joined
Acts 7:6 entreat them evil *f* hundred years
Acts 10:11 great sheet knit at the *f* corners
Acts 10:30 *F* days ago I was fasting until
Acts 11:5 let down from heaven by *f* corners
Acts 12:4 delivered him to *f* quaternions of
Acts 13:20 about the space of *f* hundred
Acts 21:9 And the same man had *f* daughters
Acts 21:23 We have *f* men which have a vow on
Acts 21:38 *f* thousand men that were
Acts 27:29 they cast *f* anchors out of the
Gal 3:17 the law, which was *f* hundred
Rev 4:4 And round about the throne were *f*
Rev 4:4 and upon the seats I saw *f*
Rev 4:6 were *f* beasts full of eyes before
Rev 4:8 the *f* beasts had each of them six
Rev 4:10 The *f* and twenty elders fall down
Rev 5:6 of the throne and of the *f* beasts
Rev 5:8 the *f* beasts and *f* and twenty
Rev 5:14 And the *f* beasts said, Amen
Rev 5:14 And the *f* and twenty elders fell
Rev 6:1 one of the *f* beasts saying, Come
Rev 6:6 in the midst of the *f* beasts say
Rev 7:1 after these things I saw *f* angels
Rev 7:1 on the *f* corners of the earth
Rev 7:1 holding the *f* winds of the earth,
Rev 7:2 with a loud voice to the *f* angels
Rev 7:4 *f* thousand of all the tribes of
Rev 7:11 the *f* beasts, and fell before the
Rev 9:13 I heard a voice from the *f* horns
Rev 9:14 Loose the *f* angels which are
Rev 9:15 the *f* angels were loosed, which
Rev 11:16 And the *f* and twenty elders, which
Rev 14:1 *f* thousand, having his Father's
Rev 14:3 throne, and before the *f* beasts
Rev 14:3 *f* thousand, which were redeemed
Rev 15:7 one of the *f* beasts gave unto the
Rev 19:4 And the *f* and twenty elders and the
Rev 19:4 the *f* beasts fell down and
Rev 20:8 in the *f* quarters of the earth
Rev 21:17 *f* cubits, according to the

## FOURSCORE

Gen 16:16 And Abram was *f* and six years old,
Gen 35:28 Isaac were an hundred and *f* years
Ex 7:7 And Moses was *f* years old, and

Ex 7:7 *f* years old, and Aaron *f*
Num 2:9 *f* thousand and six thousand and
Num 4:48 thousand and five hundred and *f*
Josh 14:10 and now, lo, I am this day *f*
Judg 3:30 And the land had rest *f* years
1Sa 22:18 priests, and slew on that day *f*
2Sa 19:32 a very aged man, even *f* years old
2Sa 19:35 I am this day *f* years old
1Kin 5:15 and *f* thousand hewers in the
1Kin 12:21 *f* thousand chosen men, which were
2Kin 6:25 was sold for *f* pieces of silver
2Kin 10:24 Jehu appointed *f* men without
2Kin 19:35 of the Assyrians an hundred *f*
1Chr 7:5 in all by their genealogies *f*
1Chr 15:9 the chief, and his brethren *f*
1Chr 25:7 were cunning, was two hundred *f*
2Chr 2:2 *f* thousand to hew in the mountain
2Chr 2:18 *f* thousand to be hewers in the
2Chr 11:1 *f* thousand chosen men, which were
2Chr 14:8 bows, two hundred and *f* thousand
2Chr 17:15 him two hundred and *f* thousand
2Chr 17:18 *f* thousand ready prepared for the
2Chr 26:17 with him *f* priests of the LORD,
Ezr 8:8 of Michael, and with him *f* males
Neh 7:26 and Netophah, an hundred *f*
Neh 11:18 the holy city were two hundred *f*
Est 1:4 days, even an hundred and *f* days
Ps 90:10 of strength they be *f* years
Song 6:8 *f* concubines, and virgins without
Is 37:36 of the Assyrians an hundred and *f*
Jer 41:5 and from Samaria, even *f* men
Lk 2:37 And she was a widow of about *f*
Lk 16:7 him, Take thy bill, and write *f*

## FOURSQUARE

Ex 27:1 the altar shall be *f*
Ex 28:16 *F* it shall be being doubled
Ex 30:2 breadth thereof; *f* shall it be
Ex 37:25 of it a cubit; it was *f*
Ex 38:1 the breadth thereof; it was *f*
Ex 39:9 It was *f*; they made the
1Kin 7:31 gravings with their borders, *f*
Eze 40:47 and an hundred cubits broad, *f*
Eze 48:20 shall offer the holy oblation *f*
Rev 21:16 And the city lieth *f*, and the

## FOURTEEN

Gen 31:41 I served thee *f* years for thy two
Gen 46:22 all the souls were *f*
Num 1:27 *f* thousand and six hundred
Num 2:4 *f* thousand and six hundred
Num 16:49 in the plague were *f* thousand
Num 29:13 *f* lambs of the first year
Num 29:15 deal to each lamb of the *f* lambs
Num 29:17 *f* lambs of the first year without
Num 29:20 *f* lambs of the first year without
Num 29:23 *f* lambs of the first year without
Num 29:26 *f* lambs of the first year without
Num 29:29 *f* lambs of the first year without
Num 29:32 *f* lambs of the first year without
Josh 15:36 *f* cities with their villages
Josh 18:28 *f* cities with their villages
1Kin 8:65 days and seven days, even *f* days
1Chr 25:5 And God gave to Heman *f* sons
2Chr 13:21 waxed mighty, and married *f* wives
Job 42:12 for he had *f* thousand sheep, and
Eze 43:17 the settle shall be *f* cubits long
Eze 43:17 *f* broad in the four squares
Mt 1:17 to David are *f* generations
Mt 1:17 into Babylon are *f* generations
Mt 1:17 unto Christ are *f* generations
2Cor 12:2 a man in Christ above *f* years ago
Gal 2:1 Then *f* years after I went up

## FOURTEENTH

Gen 14:5 in the *f* year came Chedorlaomer,
Ex 12:6 until the *f* day of the same month
Ex 12:18 on the *f* day of the month at even
Lev 23:5 In the *f* day of the first month
Num 9:3 In the *f* day of this month, at
Num 9:5 they kept the passover on the *f*
Num 9:11 The *f* day of the second month at
Num 28:16 in the *f* day of the first month
Josh 5:10 kept the passover on the *f* day of
2Kin 18:13 Now in the *f* year of king
1Chr 24:13 to Huppah, the *f* to Jeshebeab,
1Chr 25:21 The *f* to Mattithiah, he, his sons
2Chr 30:15 on the *f* day of the second month
2Chr 35:1 on the *f* day of the first month
Ezr 6:19 upon the *f* day of the first month
Est 9:15 the *f* day also of the month Adar
Est 9:17 on the *f* day of the same rested
Est 9:18 day thereof, and on the *f* thereof
Est 9:19 made the *f* day of the month Adar
Est 9:21 keep the *f* day of the month Adar
Is 36:1 in the *f* year of king Hezekiah
Eze 40:1 in the *f* year after that the city
Eze 45:21 in the *f* day of the month, ye
Acts 27:27 But when the *f* night was come, as
Acts 27:33 This day is the *f* day that ye

## FOURTH

Gen 1:19 and the morning were the *f* day
Gen 2:14 And the *f* river is Euphrates
Gen 15:16 But in the *f* generation they
Ex 20:5 *f* generation of them that hate me
Ex 28:20 the *f* row a beryl, and an onyx, and
Ex 29:40 *f* part of an hin of beaten oil
Ex 29:40 the *f* part of an hin of wine for
Ex 34:7 the third and to the *f* generation
Ex 39:13 And the *f* row, a beryl, an onyx,
Lev 19:24 But in the *f* year all the fruit
Lev 23:13 be of wine, the *f* part of a hin
Num 7:30 On the *f* day Elizur the son of
Num 14:18 unto the third and *f* generation
Num 15:4 with the *f* part of an hin of oil
Num 15:5 the *f* part of an hin of wine for
Num 23:10 number of the *f* part of Israel
Num 28:5 mingled with the *f* part of an hin
Num 28:7 offering thereof shall be the *f*
Num 28:14 a *f* part of an hin unto a lamb
Num 29:23 on the *f* day ten bullocks, two
Deut 5:9 *f* generation of them that hate me
Josh 19:17 the *f* lot came out to Issachar,
Judg 19:5 And it came to pass on the *f* day
1Sa 9:8 I have here at hand the *f* part of
2Sa 3:4 And the *f*, Adonijah the son of
1Kin 6:1 in the *f* year of Solomon's reign
1Kin 6:33 olive tree, a *f* part of the wall
1Kin 6:37 In the *f* year was the foundation
1Kin 22:41 to reign over Judah in the *f* year
2Kin 6:25 the *f* part of a cab of dove's
2Kin 10:30 thy children of the *f* generation
2Kin 15:12 of Israel unto the *f* generation
2Kin 18:9 in the *f* year of king Hezekiah
2Kin 25:3 on the ninth day of the *f* month
1Chr 2:14 Nethaneel the *f*, Raddai the fifth
1Chr 3:2 the *f*, Adonijah the son of
1Chr 3:15 the third Zedekiah, the *f* Shallum
1Chr 8:2 Nohah the *f*, and Rapha the fifth
1Chr 12:10 Mishmannah the *f*, Jeremiah the
1Chr 23:19 the third, and Jekameam the *f*
1Chr 24:8 third to Harim, the *f* to Seorim,
1Chr 24:23 the third, Jekameam the *f*
1Chr 25:11 The *f* to Izri, he, his sons, and
1Chr 26:2 the third, Jathniel the *f*
1Chr 26:4 Joah the third, and Sacar the *f*
1Chr 26:11 the third, Zechariah the *f*
1Chr 27:7 The *f* captain for the *f*
1Chr 27:7 The *f* captain for the *f*
2Chr 3:2 in the *f* year of his reign
2Chr 20:26 on the *f* day they assembled
Ezr 8:33 Now on the *f* day was the silver
Neh 9:1 *f* day of this month the children
Neh 9:3 their God one *f* part of the day
Neh 9:3 another *f* part they confessed, and
Jer 25:1 *f* year of Jehoiakim the son of
Jer 28:1 king of Judah, in the *f* year
Jer 36:1 it came to pass in the *f* year of
Jer 39:2 year of Zedekiah, in the *f* month
Jer 45:1 in the *f* year of Jehoiakim the
Jer 46:2 *f* year of Jehoiakim the son of
Jer 51:59 in the *f* year of his reign
Jer 52:6 And in the *f* month, in the ninth
Eze 1:1 thirtieth year, in the *f* month
Eze 10:14 the *f* the face of an eagle
Dan 2:40 the *f* kingdom shall be strong as
Dan 3:25 the form of the *f* is like the Son
Dan 7:7 visions, and behold a *f* beast
Dan 7:19 know the truth of the *f* beast
Dan 7:23 The *f* beast shall be the *f*
Dan 11:2 the *f* shall be far richer than
Zec 6:3 in the *f* chariot grisled and bay
Zec 7:1 pass in the *f* year of king Darius
Zec 7:1 in the *f* day of the ninth month
Zec 8:19 The fast of the *f* month, and the
Mt 14:25 in the *f* watch of the night Jesus
Mk 6:48 about the *f* watch of the night he
Rev 4:7 the *f* beast was like a flying
Rev 6:7 And when he had opened the *f* seal
Rev 6:7 the voice of the *f* beast say
Rev 6:8 them over the *f* part of the earth
Rev 8:12 the *f* angel sounded, and the third
Rev 16:8 the *f* angel poured out his vial
Rev 21:19 the *f*, an emerald

## FOWL

Gen 1:20 *f* that may fly above the earth in
Gen 1:21 every winged *f* after his kind
Gen 1:22 let *f* multiply in the earth
Gen 1:26 over the *f* of the air, and over
Gen 1:28 over the *f* of the air, and over
Gen 1:30 to every *f* of the air, and to
Gen 2:19 the field, and every *f* of the air
Gen 2:20 to the *f* of the air, and to every
Gen 7:14 every *f* after his kind, every
Gen 7:21 moved upon the earth, both of *f*
Gen 7:23 things, and the *f* of the heaven
Gen 8:17 thee, of all flesh, both of *f*
Gen 8:19 every creeping thing, and every *f*
Gen 8:20 clean beast, and of every clean *f*
Gen 9:2 earth, and upon every *f* of the air
Gen 9:10 that is with you, of the *f*
Lev 7:26 whether it be of *f* or of beast
Lev 11:46 law of the beasts, and of the *f*
Lev 17:13 any beast or *f* that may be eaten
Lev 20:25 abominable by beast, or by *f*
Deut 4:17 winged *f* that flieth in the air
1Kin 4:23 and fallowdeer, and fatted *f*
1Kin 4:33 he spake also of beasts, and of *f*
Job 28:7 is a path which no *f* knoweth
Ps 8:8 The *f* of the air, and the fish of
Ps 148:10 creeping things, and flying *f*
Jer 9:10 both the *f* of the heavens and the
Eze 17:23 shall dwell all *f* of every wing
Eze 39:17 Speak unto every feathered *f*
Eze 44:31 or torn, whether it be *f* or beast
Dan 7:6 the back of it four wings of a *f*

## FOWLS

Gen 6:7 thing, and the *f* of the air
Gen 6:20 Of *f* after their kind, and of
Gen 7:3 Of *f* also of the air by sevens,
Gen 7:8 that are not clean, and of *f*
Gen 15:11 when the *f* came down upon the
Lev 1:14 his offering to the LORD be of *f*
Lev 11:13 have in abomination among the *f*
Lev 11:20 All *f* that creep, going upon all
Lev 20:25 and unclean, and between unclean *f*
Deut 14:20 But of all clean *f* ye may eat
Deut 28:26 be meat unto all *f* of the air
1Sa 17:44 thy flesh unto the *f* of the air
1Sa 17:46 this day unto the *f* of the air
1Kin 14:11 field shall the *f* of the air eat
1Kin 16:4 fields shall the *f* of the air eat
1Kin 21:24 field shall the *f* of the air eat
Neh 5:18 also *f* were prepared for me, and
Job 12:7 the *f* of the air, and they shall
Job 28:21 kept close from the *f* of the air
Job 35:11 us wiser than the *f* of heaven
Ps 50:11 I know all the *f* of the mountains
Ps 78:27 feathered *f* like as the sand of
Ps 79:2 be meat unto the *f* of the heaven
Ps 104:12 By them shall the *f* of the heaven
Is 18:6 unto the *f* of the mountains
Is 18:6 the *f* shall summer upon them, and
Jer 7:33 be meat for the *f* of the heaven
Jer 15:3 the *f* of the heaven, and the
Jer 16:4 shall be meat for the *f* of heaven
Jer 19:7 be meat for the *f* of the heaven
Jer 34:20 for meat unto the *f* of the heaven
Eze 29:5 field and to the *f* of the heaven
Eze 31:6 All the *f* of heaven made their
Eze 31:13 all the *f* of the heaven remain
Eze 32:4 will cause all the *f* of the
Eze 38:20 the *f* of the heaven, and the
Dan 2:38 the *f* of the heaven hath he given
Dan 4:12 the *f* of the heaven dwelt in the
Dan 4:14 it, and the *f* from his branches
Dan 4:21 the *f* of the heaven had their
Hos 2:18 with the *f* of heaven, and with the
Hos 4:3 field, and with the *f* of heaven
Hos 7:12 them down as the *f* of the heaven
Zeph 1:3 will consume the *f* of the heaven
Mt 6:26 Behold the *f* of the air
Mt 13:4 the *f* came and devoured them up
Mk 4:4 the *f* of the air came and devoured
Mk 4:32 so that the *f* of the air may
Lk 8:5 the *f* of the air devoured it
Lk 12:24 more are ye better than the *f*
Lk 13:19 the *f* of the air lodged in the
Acts 10:12 creeping things, and *f* of the air
Acts 11:6 creeping things, and *f* of the air

Rev 19:17 saying to all the *f* that fly in
Rev 19:21 all the *f* were filled with their

**FOXES**
Judg 15:4 went and caught three hundred *f*
Ps 63:10 they shall be a portion for *f*
Song 2:15 Take us the *f*, the little *f*,
Song 2:15 Take us the *f*, the little *f*
Lam 5:18 is desolate, the *f* walk upon it
Eze 13:4 are like the *f* in the deserts
Mt 8:20 The *f* have holes, and the birds of
Lk 9:58 *F* have holes, and birds of the air

**FRAGMENTS**
Mt 14:20 they took up of the *f* that
Mk 6:43 up twelve baskets full of the *f*
Mk 8:19 many baskets full of *f* took ye up
Mk 8:20 many baskets full of *f* took ye up
Lk 9:17 there was taken up of *f* that
Jn 6:12 Gather up the *f* that remain
Jn 6:13 the *f* of the five barley loaves

**FRAME**
Judg 12:6 for he could not *f* to pronounce
Ps 103:14 For he knoweth our *f*
Jer 18:11 I *f* evil against you, and devise a
Eze 40:2 by which was as the *f* of a city
Hos 5:4 They will not *f* their doings to

**FRAMED**
Is 29:16 or shall the thing *f* say of him
Is 29:16 thing *f* say of him that *f* it
Eph 2:21 *f* together groweth unto an holy
Heb 11:3 worlds were *f* by the word of God

**FRANKINCENSE**
Ex 30:34 these sweet spices with pure *f*
Lev 2:1 oil upon it, and put *f* thereon
Lev 2:2 thereof, with all the *f* thereof
Lev 2:15 put oil upon it, and lay *f* thereon
Lev 2:16 thereof, with all the *f* thereof
Lev 5:11 shall he put any *f* thereon
Lev 6:15 all the *f* which is upon the meat
Lev 24:7 shalt put pure *f* upon each row
Num 5:15 no oil upon it, nor put *f* thereon
1Chr 9:29 and the wine, and the oil, and the *f*
Neh 13:5 laid the meat offerings, the *f*
Neh 13:9 with the meat offering and the *f*
Song 3:6 smoke, perfumed with myrrh and *f*
Song 4:6 of myrrh, and to the hill of *f*
Song 4:14 and cinnamon, with all trees of *f*
Mt 2:11 gold, and *f*, and myrrh
Rev 18:13 and odours, and ointments, and *f*

**FREE**
Ex 21:2 he shall go out *f* for nothing
Ex 21:5 I will not go out *f*
Ex 21:11 shall she go out *f* without money
Ex 21:26 let him go *f* for his eye's sake
Ex 21:27 he shall let him go *f* for his
Ex 36:3 him *f* offerings every morning
Lev 19:20 to death, because she was not *f*
Num 5:19 be thou *f* from this bitter water
Num 5:28 then she shall be *f*, and shall
Deut 15:12 thou shalt let him go *f* from thee
Deut 15:13 thou sendest him out *f* from thee
Deut 15:18 thou sendest him away *f* from thee
Deut 24:5 but he shall be *f* at home one
1Sa 17:25 his father's house *f* in Israel
1Chr 9:33 remaining in the chambers were *f*
2Chr 29:31 as many as were of a *f* heart
Job 3:19 the servant is *f* from his master
Job 39:5 Who hath sent out the wild ass *f*
Ps 51:12 and uphold me with thy *f* spirit
Ps 88:5 *F* among the dead, like the slain
Ps 105:20 of the people, and let him go *f*
Is 58:6 and to let the oppressed go *f*
Jer 34:9 an Hebrew or an Hebrewess, go *f*
Jer 34:10 every one his maidservant, go *f*
Jer 34:11 handmaids, whom they had let go *f*
Jer 34:14 thou shalt let him go *f* from thee
Amos 4:5 and publish the *f* offerings
Mt 15:6 or his mother, he shall be *f*
Mt 17:26 unto him, Then are the children *f*
Mk 7:11 he shall be *f*
Jn 8:32 and the truth shall make you *f*
Jn 8:33 sayest thou, Ye shall be made *f*
Jn 8:36 Son therefore shall make you *f*
Jn 8:36 ye shall be *f* indeed
Acts 22:28 And Paul said, But I was *f* born
Rom 5:15 offence, so also is the *f* gift
Rom 5:16 but the *f* gift is of many
Rom 5:18 the *f* gift came upon all men unto
Rom 6:18 Being then made *f* from sin
Rom 6:20 ye were *f* from righteousness
Rom 6:22 But now being made *f* from sin
Rom 7:3 be dead, she is *f* from that law
Rom 8:2 made me *f* from the law of sin
1Cor 7:21 but if thou mayest be made *f*
1Cor 7:22 also he that is called, being *f*
1Cor 9:1 am I not *f*?
1Cor 9:19 For though I be *f* from all men
1Cor 12:13 Gentiles, whether we be bond or *f*
Gal 3:28 there is neither bond nor *f*
Gal 4:26 But Jerusalem which is above is *f*
Gal 4:30 heir with the son of the *f* woman
Gal 4:31 of the bondwoman, but of the *f*
Gal 5:1 wherewith Christ hath made us *f*
Eph 6:8 the Lord, whether he be bond or *f*
Col 3:11 Barbarian, Scythian, bond nor *f*
2Th 3:1 of the Lord may have *f* course
1Pet 2:16 As *f*, and not using your liberty
Rev 6:15 and every bondman, and every *f* man
Rev 13:16 small and great, rich and poor, *f*
Rev 19:18 and the flesh of all men, both *f*

**FREED**
Josh 9:23 of you be *f* from being bondmen
Rom 6:7 For he that is dead is *f* from sin

**FREELY**
Gen 2:16 of the garden thou mayest *f* eat
Num 11:5 fish, which we did eat in Egypt *f*
1Sa 14:30 *f* to day of the spoil of their
Ezr 2:68 offered *f* for the house of God to
Ezr 7:15 his counsellors have *f* offered
Ps 54:6 I will *f* sacrifice unto thee
Hos 14:4 backsliding, I will love them *f*
Mt 10:8 *f* ye have received, *f* give
Mt 10:8 *f* ye have received, *f* give
Acts 2:29 let me *f* speak unto you of the
Acts 26:26 before whom also I speak *f*
Rom 3:24 Being justified *f* by his grace
Rom 8:32 him also *f* give us all things
1Cor 2:12 that are *f* given to us of God
2Cor 11:7 to you the gospel of God *f*
Rev 21:6 fountain of the water of life *f*
Rev 22:17 let him take the water of life *f*

**FREEWILL**
Lev 22:18 vows, and for all his *f* offerings
Lev 22:21 or a *f* offering in beeves or
Lev 22:23 thou offer for a *f* offering
Lev 23:38 and beside all your *f* offerings
Num 15:3 or in a *f* offering, or in your
Num 29:39 your *f* offerings, for your burnt
Deut 12:6 vows, and your *f* offerings, and the
Deut 12:17 nor thy *f* offerings, or heave
Deut 16:10 of a *f* offering of thine hand
Deut 23:23 even a *f* offering, according as
2Chr 31:14 was over the *f* offerings of God,
Ezr 1:4 beside the *f* offering for the
Ezr 3:5 a *f* offering unto the LORD
Ezr 7:13 their own *f* to go up to Jerusalem
Ezr 7:16 with the *f* offering of the people
Ezr 8:28 the gold are a *f* offering unto
Ps 119:108 the *f* offerings of my mouth, O

**FRESH**
Num 11:8 of it was as the taste of *f* oil
Job 29:20 My glory was *f* in me, and my bow
Ps 92:10 I shall be anointed with *f* oil
Jas 3:12 both yield salt water and *f*

**FRET**
Lev 13:55 it is *f* inward, whether it be
1Sa 1:6 her sore, for to make her *f*
Ps 37:1 *F* not thyself because of
Ps 37:7 *f* not thyself because of him who
Ps 37:8 *f* not thyself in any wise to do
Prov 24:19 *F* not thyself because of evil men
Is 8:21 hungry, they shall *f* themselves

**FRIEND**
Gen 38:12 his *f* Hirah the Adullamite
Gen 38:20 the hand of his *f* the Adullamite
Ex 33:11 as a man speaketh unto his *f*
Deut 13:6 the wife of thy bosom, or thy *f*
Judg 14:20 whom he had used as his *f*
2Sa 13:3 But Amnon had a *f*, whose name was
2Sa 15:37 So Hushai David's *f* came into the
2Sa 16:16 Hushai the Archite, David's *f*
2Sa 16:17 Is this thy kindness to thy *f*
2Sa 16:17 why wentest thou not with thy *f*
1Kin 4:5 officer, and the king's *f*
2Chr 20:7 seed of Abraham thy *f* for ever
Job 6:14 pity should be shewed from his *f*
Job 6:27 and ye dig a pit for your *f*
Ps 35:14 he had been my *f* or brother
Ps 41:9 Yea, mine own familiar *f*, in whom
Ps 88:18 *f* hast thou put far from me, and
Prov 6:1 son, if thou be surety for thy *f*
Prov 6:3 art come into the hand of thy *f*
Prov 6:3 thyself, and make sure thy *f*
Prov 17:17 A *f* loveth at all times, and a
Prov 17:18 surety in the presence of his *f*
Prov 18:24 there is a *f* that sticketh closer
Prov 19:6 every man is a *f* to him that
Prov 22:11 his lips the king shall be his *f*
Prov 27:6 Faithful are the wounds of a *f*
Prov 27:9 of a man's *f* by hearty counsel
Prov 27:10 Thine own *f*, and thy father's
Prov 27:10 own *f*, and thy father's *f*
Prov 27:14 blesseth his *f* with a loud voice
Prov 27:17 the countenance of his *f*
Song 5:16 is my beloved, and this is my *f*
Is 41:8 chosen, the seed of Abraham my *f*
Jer 6:21 neighbour and his *f* shall perish
Jer 19:9 the flesh of his *f* in the siege
Hos 3:1 love a woman beloved of her *f*
Mic 7:5 Trust ye not in a *f*, put ye not
Mt 11:19 a *f* of publicans and sinners
Mt 20:13 answered one of them, and said, *F*
Mt 22:12 And he saith unto him, *F*, how
Mt 26:50 And Jesus said unto him, *F*
Lk 7:34 a *f* of publicans and sinners
Lk 11:5 them, Which of you shall have a *f*
Lk 11:5 at midnight, and say unto him, *F*
Lk 11:6 For a *f* of mine in his journey is
Lk 11:8 and give him, because he is his *f*
Lk 14:10 cometh, he may say unto thee, *F*
Jn 3:29 but the *f* of the bridegroom,
Jn 11:11 unto them, Our *f* Lazarus sleepeth
Jn 19:12 man go, thou art not Caesar's *f*
Acts 12:20 the king's chamberlain their *f*
Jas 2:23 and he was called the *F* of God
Jas 4:4 a *f* of the world is the enemy of

**FRIENDS**
Gen 26:26 Gerar, and Ahuzzath one of his *f*
1Sa 30:26 elders of Judah, even to his *f*
2Sa 3:8 to his brethren, and to his *f*
2Sa 19:6 thine enemies, and hatest thy *f*
1Kin 16:11 of his kinsfolks, nor of his *f*
Est 5:10 home, he sent and called for his *f*
Est 5:14 all his *f* unto him, Let a gallows
Est 6:13 all his *f* every thing that had
Job 2:11 Now when Job's three *f* heard of
Job 16:20 My *f* scorn me
Job 17:5 that speaketh flattery to his *f*
Job 19:14 my familiar *f* have forgotten me
Job 19:19 All my inward *f* abhorred me
Job 19:21 me, have pity upon me, O ye my *f*
Job 32:3 his three *f* was his wrath kindled
Job 42:7 thee, and against thy two *f*
Job 42:10 of Job, when he prayed for his *f*
Ps 38:11 my *f* stand aloof from my sore
Prov 14:20 but the rich hath many *f*
Prov 16:28 and a whisperer separateth chief *f*
Prov 17:9 a matter separateth very *f*
Prov 18:24 A man that hath *f* must shew
Prov 19:4 Wealth maketh many *f*
Prov 19:7 more do his *f* go far from him
Song 5:1 eat, O *f*; drink, yea
Jer 20:4 to thyself, and to all thy *f*
Jer 20:6 buried there, thou, and all thy *f*
Jer 38:22 Thy *f* have set thee on, and have
Lam 1:2 all her *f* have dealt
Zec 13:6 was wounded in the house of my *f*
Mk 3:21 when his *f* heard of it, they went
Mk 5:19 saith unto him, Go home to thy *f*
Lk 7:6 the centurion sent *f* to him
Lk 12:4 And I say unto you my *f*, Be not
Lk 14:12 or a supper, call not thy *f*
Lk 15:6 home, he calleth together his *f*
Lk 15:9 hath found it, she calleth her *f*
Lk 15:29 that I might make merry with my *f*
Lk 16:9 to yourselves *f* of the mammon of
Lk 21:16 and brethren, and kinsfolks, and *f*
Lk 23:12 and Herod were made *f* together
Jn 15:13 a man lay down his life for his *f*
Jn 15:14 Ye are my *f*, if ye do whatsoever
Jn 15:15 but I have called you *f*
Acts 10:24 together his kinsmen and near *f*
Acts 19:31 chief of Asia, which were his *f*
Acts 27:3 go unto his *f* to refresh himself
3Jn 14 Our *f* salute thee
3Jn 14 Greet the *f* by name

**FROGS**
Ex 8:2 will smite all thy borders with *f*
Ex 8:3 shall bring forth *f* abundantly
Ex 8:4 the *f* shall come up both on thee,
Ex 8:5 cause *f* to come up upon the land
Ex 8:6 the *f* came up, and covered the
Ex 8:7 brought up *f* upon the land of
Ex 8:8 he may take away the *f* from me
Ex 8:9 to destroy the *f* from thee
Ex 8:11 the *f* shall depart from thee, and
Ex 8:12 *f* which he had brought against
Ex 8:13 the *f* died out of the houses, out
Ps 78:45 and *f*, which destroyed them
Ps 105:30 land brought forth *f* in abundance
Rev 16:13 *f* come out of the mouth of the

**FROST**
Gen 31:40 consumed me, and the *f* by night
Ex 16:14 small as the hoar *f* on the ground
Job 37:10 By the breath of God *f* is given
Job 38:29 and the hoary *f* of heaven, who
Ps 78:47 and their sycomore trees with *f*
Ps 147:16 scattereth the hoar *f* like ashes
Jer 36:30 heat, and in the night to the *f*

**FRUIT**
Gen 1:11 the *f* tree yielding *f* after
Gen 1:12 his kind, and the tree yielding *f*
Gen 1:29 in the which is the *f* of a tree
Gen 3:2 We may eat of the *f* of the trees
Gen 3:3 But of the *f* of the tree which is
Gen 3:6 wise, she took of the *f* thereof
Gen 4:3 that Cain brought of the *f* of the
Gen 30:2 from thee the *f* of the womb
Ex 10:15 all the *f* of the trees which the
Ex 21:22 so that her *f* depart from her, and
Lev 19:23 then ye shall count the *f* thereof
Lev 19:24 But in the fourth year all the *f*
Lev 19:25 shall ye eat of the *f* thereof
Lev 23:39 gathered in the *f* of the land
Lev 25:3 and gather in the *f* thereof
Lev 25:19 And the land shall yield her *f*
Lev 25:21 bring forth *f* for three years
Lev 25:22 eat yet of old *f* until the ninth
Lev 26:4 of the field shall yield their *f*
Lev 27:30 or of the *f* of the tree, is the
Num 13:20 and bring of the *f* of the land
Num 13:26 and shewed them the *f* of the land
Num 13:27 and this is the *f* of it
Deut 1:25 they took of the *f* of the land in
Deut 7:13 will also bless the *f* of thy womb
Deut 7:13 the *f* of thy land, thy corn, and
Deut 11:17 and that the land yield not her *f*
Deut 22:9 lest the *f* of thy seed which thou
Deut 22:9 the *f* of thy vineyard, be defiled
Deut 26:2 first of all the *f* of the earth
Deut 28:4 shall be the *f* of thy body
Deut 28:4 the *f* of thy ground, and the *f*
Deut 28:4 the *f* of thy cattle, the increase
Deut 28:11 in the *f* of thy body, and in the
Deut 28:11 in the *f* of thy cattle, and in the
Deut 28:11 in the *f* of thy ground, in the
Deut 28:18 Cursed shall be the *f* of thy body
Deut 28:18 the *f* of thy land, the increase
Deut 28:33 The *f* of thy land, and all thy
Deut 28:40 for thine olive shall cast his *f*
Deut 28:42 *f* of thy land shall the locust
Deut 28:51 he shall eat the *f* of thy cattle
Deut 28:51 the *f* of thy land, until thou be
Deut 28:53 shalt eat the *f* of thine own body
Deut 30:9 in the *f* of thy body
Deut 30:9 in the *f* of thy cattle
Deut 30:9 in the *f* of thy land, for good
Josh 5:12 but they did eat of the *f* of the
Judg 9:11 my sweetness, and my good *f*
2Sa 16:2 summer *f* for the young men to eat
2Kin 19:30 root downward, and bear *f* upward
Neh 9:25 and *f* trees in abundance
Neh 9:36 our fathers to eat the *f* thereof
Neh 10:35 firstfruits of all *f* of all trees
Neh 10:37 the *f* of all manner of trees, of
Ps 1:3 forth his *f* in his season
Ps 21:10 Their *f* shalt thou destroy from
Ps 72:16 the *f* thereof shall shake like
Ps 92:14 still bring forth *f* in old age
Ps 104:13 satisfied with the *f* of thy works
Ps 105:35 devoured the *f* of their ground
Ps 127:3 the *f* of the womb is his reward
Ps 132:11 Of the *f* of thy body will I set
Prov 1:31 eat of the *f* of their own way
Prov 8:19 My *f* is better than gold, yea,
Prov 10:16 the *f* of the wicked to sin
Prov 11:30 The *f* of the righteous is a tree
Prov 12:12 root of the righteous yieldeth *f*
Prov 12:14 with good by the *f* of his mouth
Prov 13:2 eat good by the *f* of his mouth
Prov 18:20 satisfied with the *f* of his mouth
Prov 18:21 love it shall eat the *f* thereof
Prov 27:18 fig tree shall eat the *f* thereof
Prov 31:16 with the *f* of her hands she
Prov 31:31 Give her of the *f* of her hands
Song 2:3 his *f* was sweet to my taste
Song 8:11 every one for the *f* thereof was
Song 8:12 keep the *f* thereof two hundred
Is 3:10 shall eat the *f* of their doings
Is 4:2 the *f* of the earth shall be
Is 10:12 I will punish the *f* of the stout
Is 13:18 have no pity on the *f* of the womb
Is 14:29 his *f* shall be a fiery flying
Is 27:6 fill the face of the world with *f*
Is 27:9 this is all the *f* to take away
Is 28:4 as the hasty *f* before the summer
Is 37:30 vineyards, and eat the *f* thereof
Is 37:31 root downward, and bear *f* upward
Is 57:19 I create the *f* of the lips
Is 65:21 vineyards, and eat the *f* of them
Jer 2:7 country, to eat the *f* thereof
Jer 6:19 even the *f* of their thoughts,
Jer 7:20 and upon the *f* of the ground
Jer 11:16 olive tree, fair, and of goodly *f*
Jer 11:19 the tree with the *f* thereof
Jer 12:2 grow, yea, they bring forth *f*
Jer 17:8 shall cease from yielding *f*
Jer 17:10 according to the *f* of his doings
Jer 21:14 according to the *f* of your doings
Jer 29:5 gardens, and eat the *f* of them
Jer 29:28 gardens, and eat the *f* of them
Jer 32:19 according to the *f* of his doings
Lam 2:20 Shall the women eat their *f*
Eze 17:8 branches, and that it might bear *f*
Eze 17:9 thereof, and cut off the *f* thereof
Eze 17:23 bring forth boughs, and bear *f*
Eze 19:12 and the east wind dried up her *f*
Eze 19:14 which hath devoured her *f*
Eze 25:4 they shall eat thy *f*, and they
Eze 34:27 of the field shall yield her *f*
Eze 36:8 yield your *f* to my people of
Eze 36:11 and they shall increase and bring *f*
Eze 36:30 I will multiply the *f* of the tree
Eze 47:12 neither shall the *f* thereof be
Eze 47:12 new *f* according to his months
Eze 47:12 the *f* thereof shall be for meat,
Dan 4:12 the *f* thereof much, and in it was
Dan 4:14 off his leaves, and scatter his *f*
Dan 4:21 the *f* thereof much, and in it was
Hos 9:16 is dried up, they shall bear no *f*
Hos 9:16 even the beloved *f* of their womb
Hos 10:1 he bringeth forth *f* unto himself
Hos 10:1 to the multitude of his *f* he hath
Hos 10:13 ye have eaten the *f* of lies
Hos 14:8 From me is thy *f* found
Joel 2:22 for the tree beareth her *f*
Amos 2:9 yet I destroyed his *f* from above
Amos 6:12 the *f* of righteousness into
Amos 7:14 and a gatherer of sycomore *f*
Amos 8:1 and behold a basket of summer *f*
Amos 8:2 And I said, A basket of summer *f*
Amos 9:14 gardens, and eat the *f* of them
Mic 6:7 the *f* of my body for the sin of
Mic 7:1 my soul desired the firstripe *f*
Mic 7:13 for the *f* of their doings
Hab 3:17 neither shall *f* be in the vines
Hag 1:10 and the earth is stayed from her *f*
Zec 8:12 the vine shall give her *f*
Mal 1:12 the *f* thereof, even his meat, is
Mal 3:11 shall your vine cast her *f* before
Mt 3:10 not forth good *f* is hewn down
Mt 7:17 good tree bringeth forth good *f*
Mt 7:17 tree bringeth forth evil *f*
Mt 7:18 tree cannot bring forth evil *f*
Mt 7:18 a corrupt tree bring forth good *f*
Mt 7:19 not forth good *f* is hewn down
Mt 12:33 make the tree good, and his *f* good
Mt 12:33 tree corrupt, and his *f* corrupt
Mt 12:33 for the tree is known by his *f*
Mt 13:8 good ground, and brought forth *f*
Mt 13:23 which also beareth *f*, and bringeth
Mt 13:26 was sprung up, and brought forth *f*
Mt 21:19 unto it, Let no *f* grow on thee
Mt 21:34 when the time of the *f* drew near
Mt 26:29 henceforth of this *f* of the vine
Mk 4:7 and choked it, and it yielded no *f*
Mk 4:8 did yield *f* that sprang up and
Mk 4:20 and receive it, and bring forth *f*
Mk 4:28 earth bringeth forth *f* of herself
Mk 4:29 But when the *f* is brought forth,
Mk 11:14 No man eat *f* of thee hereafter
Mk 12:2 of the *f* of the vineyard
Mk 14:25 no more of the *f* of the vine
Lk 1:42 and blessed is the *f* of thy womb
Lk 3:9 not forth good *f* is hewn down
Lk 6:43 tree bringeth not forth corrupt *f*
Lk 6:43 a corrupt tree bring forth good *f*
Lk 6:44 every tree is known by his own *f*
Lk 8:8 up, and bare *f* an hundredfold
Lk 8:14 life, and bring no *f* to perfection
Lk 8:15 bring forth *f* with patience
Lk 13:6 sought *f* thereon, and found none
Lk 13:7 I come seeking *f* on this fig tree
Lk 13:9 And if it bear *f*, well
Lk 20:10 give him of the *f* of the vineyard
Lk 22:18 not drink of the *f* of the vine
Jn 4:36 gathereth *f* unto life eternal
Jn 12:24 it die, it bringeth forth much *f*
Jn 15:2 that beareth not *f* he taketh away
Jn 15:2 and every branch that beareth *f*
Jn 15:2 that it may bring forth more *f*
Jn 15:4 branch cannot bear *f* of itself
Jn 15:5 the same bringeth forth much *f*
Jn 15:8 glorified, that ye bear much *f*
Jn 15:16 ye should go and bring forth *f*
Jn 15:16 that your *f* should remain
Acts 2:30 that of the *f* of his loins,
Rom 1:13 might have some *f* among you also
Rom 6:21 What *f* had ye then in those
Rom 6:22 ye have your *f* unto holiness, and
Rom 7:4 we should bring forth *f* unto God
Rom 7:5 to bring forth *f* unto death
Rom 15:28 and have sealed to them this *f*
1Cor 9:7 and eateth not of the *f* thereof
Gal 5:22 But the *f* of the Spirit is love,
Eph 5:9 (For the *f* of the Spirit is in
Phil 1:22 this is the *f* of my labour
Phil 4:17 but I desire *f* that may abound to
Col 1:6 and bringeth forth *f*, as it doth
Heb 12:11 it yieldeth the peaceable *f* of
Heb 13:15 the *f* of our lips giving thanks
Jas 3:18 the *f* of righteousness is sown in
Jas 5:7 for the precious *f* of the earth
Jas 5:18 and the earth brought forth her *f*
Jude 12 trees whose *f* withereth, without
Jude 12 whose *f* withereth, without *f*
Rev 22:2 and yielded her *f* every month

**FRUITFUL**
Gen 1:22 And God blessed them, saying, Be *f*
Gen 1:28 them, and God said unto them, Be *f*
Gen 8:17 abundantly in the earth, and be *f*
Gen 9:1 his sons, and said unto them, Be *f*
Gen 9:7 And you, be ye *f*, and multiply
Gen 17:6 And I will make thee exceeding *f*
Gen 17:20 blessed him, and will make him *f*
Gen 26:22 us, and we shall be *f* in the land
Gen 28:3 bless thee, and make thee *f*
Gen 35:11 be *f* and multiply
Gen 41:52 be *f* in the land of my affliction
Gen 48:4 me, Behold, I will make thee *f*
Gen 49:22 Joseph is a *f* bough
Gen 49:22 even a *f* bough by a well
Ex 1:7 And the children of Israel were *f*
Lev 26:9 respect unto you, and make you *f*
Ps 107:34 A *f* land into barrenness, for the
Ps 128:3 Thy wife shall be as a *f* vine by
Ps 148:9 *f* trees, and all cedars
Is 5:1 hath a vineyard in a very *f* hill
Is 10:18 of his forest, and of his *f* field
Is 17:6 in the outmost *f* branches thereof
Is 29:17 shall be turned into a *f* field
Is 29:17 the *f* field shall be esteemed as
Is 32:12 pleasant fields, for the *f* vine
Is 32:15 and the wilderness be a *f* field
Is 32:15 the *f* field be counted for a
Is 32:16 remain in the *f* field
Jer 4:26 the *f* place was a wilderness, and
Jer 23:3 and they shall be *f* and increase
Eze 17:5 land, and planted it in a *f* field
Eze 19:10 she was *f* and full of branches by
Hos 13:15 Though he be *f* among his brethren
Acts 14:17 *f* seasons, filling our hearts
Col 1:10 being *f* in every good work, and

## FRUITS

Gen 43:11 take of the best *f* in the land in
Ex 22:29 to offer the first of thy ripe *f*
Ex 23:10 and shalt gather in the *f* thereof
Lev 23:20 with the bread of the first *f* for
Lev 25:15 of the *f* he shall sell unto thee
Lev 25:16 of the *f* doth he sell unto thee
Lev 25:22 until her *f* come in ye shall eat
Lev 26:20 trees of the land yield their *f*
Deut 33:14 for the precious *f* brought forth
2Sa 9:10 him, and thou shalt bring in the *f*
2Sa 16:1 and an hundred of summer *f*
2Kin 8:6 all the *f* of the field since the
2Kin 19:29 vineyards, and eat the *f* thereof
Job 31:39 If I have eaten the *f* thereof
Ps 107:37 which may yield *f* of increase
Eccl 2:5 trees in them of all kind of *f*
Song 4:13 of pomegranates, with pleasant *f*
Song 4:16 his garden, and eat his pleasant *f*
Song 6:11 nuts to see the *f* of the valley
Song 7:13 are all manner of pleasant *f*
Is 16:9 for the shouting for thy summer *f*
Is 33:9 and Carmel shake off their *f*
Jer 40:10 ye, gather ye wine, and summer *f*
Jer 40:12 wine and summer *f* very much
Jer 48:32 is fallen upon thy summer *f*
Lam 4:9 for want of the *f* of the field
Mic 7:1 they have gathered the summer *f*
Mal 3:11 not destroy the *f* of your ground
Mt 3:8 therefore *f* meet for repentance
Mt 7:16 Ye shall know them by their *f*
Mt 7:20 by their *f* ye shall know them
Mt 21:34 they might receive the *f* of it
Mt 21:41 render him the *f* in their seasons
Mt 21:43 bringing forth the *f* thereof
Lk 3:8 therefore *f* worthy of repentance
Lk 12:17 have no room where to bestow my *f*
Lk 12:18 and there will I bestow all my *f*
2Cor 9:10 sown, and increase the *f* of your
Phil 1:11 with the *f* of righteousness
2Ti 2:6 must be first partaker of the *f*
Jas 3:17 full of mercy and good *f*, without
Rev 18:14 the *f* that thy soul lusted after
Rev 22:2 which bare twelve manner of *f*

## FUEL

Is 9:5 be with burning and *f* of fire
Is 9:19 shall be as the *f* of the fire
Eze 15:4 it is cast into the fire for *f*
Eze 15:6 I have given to the fire for *f*
Eze 21:32 Thou shalt be for *f* to the fire

## FUGITIVE

Gen 4:12 a *f* and a vagabond shalt thou be
Gen 4:14 and I shall be a *f* and a vagabond

## FUGITIVES

Judg 12:4 Ye Gileadites are *f* of Ephraim
2Kin 25:11 the *f* that fell away to the king
Is 15:5 his *f* shall flee unto Zoar, an
Eze 17:21 all his *f* with all his bands

## FULFIL

Gen 29:27 *F* her week, and we will give thee
Ex 5:13 *F* your works, your daily tasks,
Ex 23:26 the number of thy days I will *f*
1Kin 2:27 that he might *f* the word of the
1Chr 22:13 takest heed to *f* the statutes
2Chr 36:21 To *f* the word of the LORD by the
2Chr 36:21 to *f* threescore and ten years
Job 39:2 number the months that they *f*
Ps 20:4 own heart, and *f* all thy counsel
Ps 20:5 the LORD *f* all thy petitions
Ps 145:19 He will *f* the desire of them that
Mt 3:15 us to *f* all righteousness
Mt 5:17 am not come to destroy, but to *f*
Acts 13:22 heart, which shall *f* all my will
Rom 2:27 if it *f* the law, judge thee, who
Rom 13:14 the flesh, to *f* the lusts thereof
Gal 5:16 ye shall not *f* the lust of the
Gal 6:2 and so *f* the law of Christ
Phil 2:2 *F* ye my joy, that ye be
Col 1:25 me for you, to *f* the word of God
Col 4:17 in the Lord, that thou *f* it
2Th 1:11 *f* all the good pleasure of his
Jas 2:8 If ye *f* the royal law according
Rev 17:17 put in their hearts to *f* his will

## FULFILLED

Gen 25:24 her days to be delivered were *f*
Gen 29:21 me my wife, for my days are *f*
Gen 29:28 And Jacob did so, and *f* her week
Gen 50:3 And forty days were *f* for him
Gen 50:3 for so are *f* the days of those
Ex 5:14 Wherefore have ye not *f* your task
Ex 7:25 And seven days were *f*, after that
Lev 12:4 the days of her purifying be *f*
Lev 12:6 the days of her purifying are *f*
Num 6:5 until the days be *f*, in the which
Num 6:13 the days of his separation are *f*
2Sa 7:12 And when thy days be *f*, and thou
2Sa 14:22 in that the king hath *f* the
1Kin 8:15 and hath with his hand *f* it
1Kin 8:24 hast *f* it with thine hand, as it
2Chr 6:4 who hath with his hands *f* that
2Chr 6:15 hast *f* it with thine hand, as it
Ezr 1:1 the mouth of Jeremiah might be *f*
Job 36:17 But thou hast *f* the judgment of
Jer 44:25 *f* with your hand, saying, We will
Lam 2:17 he hath *f* his word that he had
Lam 4:18 our end is near, our days are *f*
Eze 5:2 when the days of the siege are *f*
Dan 4:33 the thing *f* upon Nebuchadnezzar
Dan 10:3 till three whole weeks were *f*
Mt 1:22 that it might be *f* which was
Mt 2:15 that it might be *f* which was
Mt 2:17 Then was *f* that which was spoken
Mt 2:23 that it might be *f* which was
Mt 4:14 That it might be *f* which was
Mt 5:18 pass from the law, till all be *f*
Mt 8:17 That it might be *f* which was
Mt 12:17 That it might be *f* which was
Mt 13:14 in them is *f* the prophecy of
Mt 13:35 That it might be *f* which was
Mt 21:4 that it might be *f* which was
Mt 24:34 pass, till all these things be *f*
Mt 26:54 then shall the scriptures be *f*
Mt 26:56 of the prophets might be *f*
Mt 27:9 Then was *f* that which was spoken
Mt 27:35 that it might be *f* which was
Mk 1:15 And saying, The time is *f*, and the
Mk 13:4 when all these things shall be *f*
Mk 14:49 but the scriptures must be *f*
Mk 15:28 And the scripture was *f*, which
Lk 1:20 which shall be *f* in their season
Lk 2:43 And when they had *f* the days
Lk 4:21 is this scripture *f* in your ears
Lk 21:22 things which are written may be *f*
Lk 21:24 the times of the Gentiles be *f*
Lk 21:32 not pass away, till all be *f*
Lk 22:16 until it be *f* in the kingdom of
Lk 24:44 you, that all things must be *f*
Jn 3:29 this my joy therefore is *f*
Jn 12:38 of Esaias the prophet might be *f*
Jn 13:18 but that the scripture may be *f*
Jn 15:25 that the word might be *f* that is
Jn 17:12 that the scripture might be *f*
Jn 17:13 might have my joy *f* in themselves
Jn 18:9 That the saying might be *f*
Jn 18:32 the saying of Jesus might be *f*
Jn 19:24 that the scripture might be *f*
Jn 19:28 that the scripture might be *f*
Jn 19:36 that the scripture should be *f*
Acts 1:16 scripture must needs have been *f*
Acts 3:18 should suffer, he hath so *f*
Acts 9:23 And after that many days were *f*
Acts 12:25 when they had *f* their ministry,
Acts 13:25 as John *f* his course, he said,
Acts 13:27 they have *f* them in condemning
Acts 13:29 when they had *f* all that was
Acts 13:33 God hath *f* the same unto us their
Acts 14:26 of God for the work which they *f*
Rom 8:4 of the law might be *f* in us
Rom 13:8 loveth another hath *f* the law
2Cor 10:6 when your obedience is *f*
Gal 5:14 For all the law is *f* in one word
Jas 2:23 the scripture was *f* which saith
Rev 6:11 killed as they were, should be *f*
Rev 15:8 of the seven angels were *f*
Rev 17:17 until the words of God shall be *f*
Rev 20:3 the thousand years should be *f*

## FULL

Gen 14:10 vale of Siddim was *f* of slimepits
Gen 15:16 of the Amorites is not yet *f*
Gen 25:8 age, an old man, and *f* of years
Gen 35:29 people, being old and *f* of days
Gen 41:1 to pass at the end of two *f* years
Gen 41:7 devoured the seven rank and *f* ears
Gen 41:22 ears came up in one stalk, *f*
Gen 43:21 his sack, our money in *f* weight
Ex 8:21 shall be *f* of swarms of flies
Ex 16:3 and when we did eat bread to the *f*
Ex 16:8 and in the morning bread to the *f*
Ex 16:33 put an omer *f* of manna therein,
Ex 22:3 for he should make *f* restitution
Lev 2:14 even corn beaten out of *f* ears
Lev 16:12 he shall take a censer *f* of
Lev 16:12 his hands *f* of sweet incense
Lev 19:29 the land become *f* of wickedness
Lev 25:29 within a *f* year may he redeem it
Lev 25:30 within the space of a *f* year
Lev 26:5 ye shall eat your bread to the *f*
Num 7:13 both of them were *f* of fine flour
Num 7:14 ten shekels of gold, *f* of incense
Num 7:19 both of them *f* of fine flour
Num 7:20 gold of ten shekels, *f* of incense
Num 7:25 both of them *f* of fine flour
Num 7:26 of ten shekels, *f* of incense
Num 7:31 both of them *f* of fine flour
Num 7:32 of ten shekels, *f* of incense
Num 7:37 both of them *f* of fine flour
Num 7:38 of ten shekels, *f* of incense
Num 7:43 both of them *f* of fine flour
Num 7:44 of ten shekels, *f* of incense
Num 7:49 both of them *f* of fine flour
Num 7:50 of ten shekels, *f* of incense
Num 7:55 both of them *f* of fine flour
Num 7:56 of ten shekels, *f* of incense
Num 7:61 both of them *f* of fine flour
Num 7:62 of ten shekels, *f* of incense
Num 7:67 both of them *f* of fine flour
Num 7:68 of ten shekels, *f* of incense
Num 7:73 both of them *f* of fine flour
Num 7:74 of ten shekels, *f* of incense
Num 7:79 both of them *f* of fine flour
Num 7:80 of ten shekels, *f* of incense
Num 7:86 *f* of incense, weighing ten
Num 22:18 give me his house *f* of silver
Num 24:13 give me his house *f* of silver
Deut 6:11 houses *f* of all good things,
Deut 6:11 thou shalt have eaten and be *f*
Deut 8:10 When thou hast eaten and art *f*
Deut 8:12 when thou hast eaten and art *f*
Deut 11:15 that thou mayest eat and be *f*
Deut 21:13 father and her mother a *f* month
Deut 33:23 *f* with the blessing of the LORD,
Deut 34:9 Nun was *f* of the spirit of wisdom
Judg 6:38 of the fleece, a bowl *f* of water
Judg 16:27 Now the house was *f* of men
Ruth 1:21 I went out *f*, and the LORD hath
Ruth 2:12 a *f* reward be given thee of the
1Sa 2:5 They that were *f* have hired out
1Sa 18:27 gave them in *f* tale to the king
1Sa 27:7 of the Philistines was a *f* year
2Sa 8:2 with one *f* line to keep alive
2Sa 13:23 it came to pass after two *f* years
2Sa 14:28 dwelt two *f* years in Jerusalem
2Sa 23:11 a piece of ground *f* of lentiles
2Kin 3:16 Make this valley *f* of ditches
2Kin 4:4 shalt set aside that which is *f*
2Kin 4:6 to pass, when the vessels were *f*
2Kin 4:39 thereof wild gourds his lap *f*
2Kin 4:42 *f* ears of corn in the husk
2Kin 6:17 the mountain was *f* of horses
2Kin 7:15 lo, all the way was *f* of garments
2Kin 9:24 drew a bow with his *f* strength
2Kin 10:21 the house of Baal was *f* from one
2Kin 15:13 he reigned a *f* month in Samaria
1Chr 11:13 a parcel of ground *f* of barley
1Chr 21:22 shalt grant it me for the *f* price
1Chr 21:24 verily buy it for the *f* price
1Chr 23:1 *f* of days, he made Solomon his
1Chr 29:28 *f* of days, riches, and honour
2Chr 24:15 was *f* of days when he died
Neh 9:25 possessed houses *f* of all goods
Est 3:5 then was Haman *f* of wrath
Est 5:9 he was *f* of indignation against
Job 5:26 come to thy grave in a *f* age
Job 7:4 I am *f* of tossings to and fro unto
Job 10:15 I am *f* of confusion
Job 11:2 should a man *f* of talk be
Job 14:1 is of few days, and *f* of trouble
Job 20:11 His bones are *f* of the sin of his
Job 21:23 One dieth in his *f* strength
Job 21:24 His breasts are *f* of milk
Job 32:18 For I am *f* of matter
Job 36:16 thy table should be *f* of fatness
Job 42:17 Job died, being old and *f* of days
Ps 10:7 His mouth is *f* of cursing
Ps 17:14 they are *f* of children, and leave
Ps 26:10 their right hand is *f* of bribes
Ps 29:4 voice of the LORD is *f* of majesty

Ps 33:5 the earth is *f* of the goodness of
Ps 48:10 right hand is *f* of righteousness
Ps 65:9 river of God, which is *f* of water
Ps 69:20 and I am *f* of heaviness
Ps 73:10 waters of a *f* cup are wrung out
Ps 74:20 dark places of the earth are *f* of
Ps 75:8 it is *f* of mixture
Ps 78:25 he sent them meat to the *f*
Ps 78:38 being *f* of compassion, forgave
Ps 86:15 art a God *f* of compassion, and
Ps 88:3 For my soul is *f* of troubles
Ps 104:16 trees of the LORD are *f* of sap
Ps 104:24 the earth is *f* of thy riches
Ps 111:4 is gracious and *f* of compassion
Ps 112:4 *f* of compassion, and righteous
Ps 119:64 earth, O LORD, is *f* of thy mercy
Ps 127:5 that hath his quiver *f* of them
Ps 144:13 That our garners may be *f*
Ps 145:8 is gracious, and *f* of compassion
Prov 17:1 than an house *f* of sacrifices
Prov 27:7 The *f* soul loatheth an honeycomb
Prov 27:20 Hell and destruction are never *f*
Prov 30:9 Lest I be *f*, and deny thee, and say
Eccl 1:7 yet the sea is not *f*
Eccl 1:8 All things are *f* of labour
Eccl 4:6 both the hands *f* with travail
Eccl 9:3 of the sons of men is *f* of evil
Eccl 10:14 A fool also is *f* of words
Eccl 11:3 If the clouds be *f* of rain
Is 1:11 I am *f* of the burnt offerings of
Is 1:15 your hands are *f* of blood
Is 1:21 it was *f* of judgment
Is 2:7 Their land also is *f* of silver
Is 2:7 their land is also *f* of horses
Is 2:8 Their land also is *f* of idols
Is 6:3 the whole earth is *f* of his glory
Is 11:9 for the earth shall be *f* of the
Is 13:21 shall be *f* of doleful creatures
Is 15:9 of Dimon shall be *f* of blood
Is 22:2 Thou that art *f* of stirs, a
Is 22:7 valleys shall be *f* of chariots
Is 25:6 lees, of fat things *f* of marrow
Is 28:8 For all tables are *f* of vomit
Is 30:27 his lips are *f* of indignation, and
Is 51:20 they are *f* of the fury of the
Jer 4:12 Even a *f* wind from those places
Jer 4:27 yet will I not make a *f* end
Jer 5:7 when I had fed them to the *f*
Jer 5:10 but make not a *f* end
Jer 5:18 I will not make a *f* end with you
Jer 5:27 As a cage is *f* of birds, so are
Jer 5:27 so are their houses *f* of deceit
Jer 6:11 Therefore I am *f* of the fury of
Jer 6:11 aged with him that is *f* of days
Jer 23:10 For the land is *f* of adulterers
Jer 28:3 Within two *f* years will I bring
Jer 28:11 within the space of two *f* years
Jer 30:11 though I make a *f* end of all
Jer 30:11 will I not make a *f* end of thee
Jer 35:5 of the Rechabites pots *f* of wine
Jer 46:28 for I will make a *f* end of all
Jer 46:28 I will not make a *f* end of thee
Lam 1:1 solitary, that was *f* of people
Lam 3:30 he is filled *f* with reproach
Eze 1:18 their rings were *f* of eyes round
Eze 7:23 for the land is *f* of bloody
Eze 7:23 and the city is *f* of violence
Eze 9:9 great, and the land is *f* of blood
Eze 9:9 the city *f* of perverseness
Eze 10:4 the court was *f* of the brightness
Eze 10:12 were *f* of eyes round about, even
Eze 11:13 wilt thou make a *f* end of the
Eze 17:3 *f* of feathers, which had divers
Eze 19:10 *f* of branches by reason of many
Eze 28:12 *f* of wisdom, and perfect in beauty
Eze 32:6 and the rivers shall be *f* of thee
Eze 32:15 of that whereof it was *f*, when I
Eze 37:1 the valley which was *f* of bones
Eze 39:19 And ye shall eat fat till ye be *f*
Eze 41:8 were a *f* reed of six great cubits
Dan 3:19 Then was Nebuchadnezzar *f* of fury
Dan 8:23 transgressors are come to the *f*
Dan 10:2 Daniel was mourning three *f* weeks
Joel 2:24 And the floors shall be *f* of wheat
Joel 3:13 for the press is *f*, the fats
Amos 2:13 is pressed that is *f* of sheaves
Mic 3:8 But truly I am *f* of power by the
Mic 6:12 men thereof are *f* of violence
Nah 3:1 it is all *f* of lies and robbery
Hab 3:3 and the earth was *f* of his praise
Zec 8:5 of the city shall be *f* of boys
Mt 6:22 whole body shall be *f* of light
Mt 6:23 whole body shall be *f* of darkness
Mt 13:48 Which, when it was *f*, they drew
Mt 14:20 that remained twelve baskets *f*
Mt 15:37 that was left seven baskets *f*
Mt 23:25 within they are *f* of extortion
Mt 23:27 but are within *f* of dead men's
Mt 23:28 but within ye are *f* of hypocrisy
Mk 4:28 after that the *f* corn in the ear
Mk 4:37 the ship, so that it was now *f*
Mk 6:43 twelve baskets *f* of the fragments
Mk 7:9 *F* well ye reject the commandment
Mk 8:19 how many baskets *f* of fragments
Mk 8:20 how many baskets *f* of fragments
Mk 15:36 and filled a spunge *f* of vinegar
Lk 1:57 Now Elisabeth's *f* time came that
Lk 4:1 Jesus being *f* of the Holy Ghost
Lk 5:12 city, behold a man *f* of leprosy
Lk 6:25 Woe unto you that are *f*
Lk 11:34 thy whole body also is *f* of light
Lk 11:34 thy body also is *f* of darkness
Lk 11:36 body therefore be *f* of light
Lk 11:36 the whole shall be *f* of light
Lk 11:39 your inward part is *f* of ravening
Lk 16:20 was laid at his gate, *f* of sores,
Jn 1:14 the Father,) *f* of grace and truth
Jn 7:8 for my time is not yet *f* come
Jn 15:11 you, and that your joy might be *f*
Jn 16:24 receive, that your joy may be *f*
Jn 19:29 was set a vessel *f* of vinegar
Jn 21:11 the net to land *f* of great fishes
Acts 2:13 said, These men are *f* of new wine
Acts 2:28 thou shalt make me *f* of joy with
Acts 6:3 *f* of the Holy Ghost and wisdom,
Acts 6:5 a man *f* of faith and of the Holy
Acts 6:8 *f* of faith and power, did great
Acts 7:23 when he was *f* forty years old, it
Acts 7:55 being *f* of the Holy Ghost, looked
Acts 9:36 this woman was *f* of good works
Acts 11:24 *f* of the Holy Ghost and of faith
Acts 13:10 O *f* of all subtilty and all
Acts 19:28 sayings, they were *f* of wrath
Rom 1:29 *f* of envy, murder, debate, deceit
Rom 3:14 Whose mouth is *f* of cursing
Rom 15:14 that ye also are *f* of goodness
1Cor 4:8 Now ye are *f*, now ye are rich, ye
Phil 2:26 was *f* of heaviness, because that
Phil 4:12 I am instructed both to be *f*
Phil 4:18 I am *f*, having received of
Col 2:2 love, and unto all riches of the *f*
2Ti 4:5 make *f* proof of thy ministry
Heb 5:14 to them that are of *f* age
Heb 6:11 *f* assurance of hope unto the end
Heb 10:22 heart in *f* assurance of faith
Jas 3:8 unruly evil, *f* of deadly poison
Jas 3:17 *f* of mercy and good fruits,
1Pet 1:8 joy unspeakable and *f* of glory
2Pet 2:14 Having eyes *f* of adultery
1Jn 1:4 unto you, that your joy may be *f*
2Jn 8 but that we receive a *f* reward
2Jn 12 to face, that our joy may be *f*
Rev 4:6 were four beasts *f* of eyes before
Rev 4:8 they were *f* of eyes within
Rev 5:8 and golden vials *f* of odours
Rev 15:7 vials *f* of the wrath of God
Rev 16:10 and his kingdom was *f* of darkness
Rev 17:3 *f* of names of blasphemy, having
Rev 17:4 cup in her hand *f* of abominations
Rev 21:9 vials *f* of the seven last plagues

## FULLY

Num 7:1 Moses had *f* set up the tabernacle
Num 14:24 with him, and hath followed me *f*
Ruth 2:11 It hath *f* been shewed me, all
1Kin 11:6 went not *f* after the LORD, as did
Eccl 8:11 men is *f* set in them to do evil
Nah 1:10 be devoured as stubble *f* dry
Acts 2:1 the day of Pentecost was *f* come
Rom 4:21 being *f* persuaded that, what he
Rom 14:5 Let every man be *f* persuaded in
Rom 15:19 I have *f* preached the gospel of
2Ti 3:10 But thou hast *f* known my doctrine
2Ti 4:17 me the preaching might be *f* known
Rev 14:18 for her grapes are *f* ripe

## FULNESS

Num 18:27 as the *f* of the winepress
Deut 33:16 *f* thereof, and for the good will
1Chr 16:32 the sea roar, and the *f* thereof
Job 20:22 In the *f* of his sufficiency he
Ps 16:11 in thy presence is *f* of joy
Ps 24:1 is the LORD's, and the *f* thereof
Ps 50:12 world is mine, and the *f* thereof
Ps 89:11 the *f* thereof, thou hast founded
Ps 96:11 the sea roar, and the *f* thereof
Ps 98:7 the sea roar, and the *f* thereof
Eze 16:49 *f* of bread, and abundance of
Eze 19:7 the *f* thereof, by the noise of
Jn 1:16 of his *f* have all we received, and
Rom 11:12 how much more their *f*
Rom 11:25 until the *f* of the Gentiles be
Rom 15:29 I shall come in the *f* of the
1Cor 10:26 is the Lord's, and the *f* thereof
1Cor 10:28 is the Lord's, and the *f* thereof
Gal 4:4 But when the *f* of the time was
Eph 1:10 of the *f* of times he might gather
Eph 1:23 the *f* of him that filleth all in
Eph 3:19 be filled with all the *f* of God
Eph 4:13 of the stature of the *f* of Christ
Col 1:19 that in him should all *f* dwell
Col 2:9 all the *f* of the Godhead bodily

## FURBISHED

Eze 21:9 a sword is sharpened, and also *f*
Eze 21:10 it is *f* that it may glitter
Eze 21:11 And he hath given it to be *f*
Eze 21:11 sword is sharpened, and it is *f*
Eze 21:28 for the slaughter it is *f*

## FURIOUS

Prov 22:24 with a *f* man thou shalt not go
Prov 29:22 strife, and a *f* man aboundeth in
Eze 5:15 anger and in fury and in *f* rebukes
Eze 25:17 upon them with *f* rebukes
Dan 2:12 the king was angry and very *f*
Nah 1:2 the LORD revengeth, and is *f*

## FURLONGS

Lk 24:13 from Jerusalem about threescore *f*
Jn 6:19 about five and twenty or thirty *f*
Jn 11:18 Jerusalem, about fifteen *f* off
Rev 14:20 of a thousand and six hundred *f*
Rev 21:16 with the reed, twelve thousand *f*

## FURNACE

Gen 15:17 it was dark, behold a smoking *f*
Gen 19:28 went up as the smoke of a *f*
Ex 9:8 to you handfuls of ashes of the *f*
Ex 9:10 And they took ashes of the *f*
Ex 19:18 ascended as the smoke of a *f*
Deut 4:20 you forth out of the iron *f*
1Kin 8:51 from the midst of the *f* of iron
Ps 12:6 as silver tried in a *f* of earth
Prov 17:3 is for silver, and the *f* for gold
Prov 27:21 pot for silver, and the *f* for gold
Is 31:9 is in Zion, and his *f* in Jerusalem
Is 48:10 thee in the *f* of affliction
Jer 11:4 land of Egypt, from the iron *f*
Eze 22:18 and lead, in the midst of the *f*
Eze 22:20 and tin, into the midst of the *f*
Eze 22:22 is melted in the midst of the *f*
Dan 3:6 the midst of a burning fiery *f*
Dan 3:11 the midst of a burning fiery *f*
Dan 3:15 the midst of a burning fiery *f*
Dan 3:17 us from the burning fiery *f*
Dan 3:19 that they should heat the *f* one
Dan 3:20 them into the burning fiery *f*
Dan 3:21 the midst of the burning fiery *f*
Dan 3:22 the *f* exceeding hot, the flame of
Dan 3:23 the midst of the burning fiery *f*
Dan 3:26 the mouth of the burning fiery *f*
Mt 13:42 shall cast them into a *f* of fire
Mt 13:50 cast them into the *f* of fire
Rev 1:15 brass, as if they burned in a *f*
Rev 9:2 pit, as the smoke of a great *f*

## FURNISH

Deut 15:14 Thou shalt *f* him liberally out of
Ps 78:19 said, Can God *f* a table in the
Is 65:11 that *f* the drink offering unto
Jer 46:19 *f* thyself to go into captivity

## FURNISHED

1Kin 9:11 had *f* Solomon with cedar trees
Prov 9:2 she hath also *f* her table
Mt 22:10 and the wedding was *f* with guests
Mk 14:15 shew you a large upper room *f*
Lk 22:12 shew you a large upper room *f*
2Ti 3:17 throughly *f* unto all good works

## FURNITURE

Gen 31:34 and put them in the camel's *f*
Ex 31:7 all the *f* of the tabernacle,
Ex 31:8 And the table and his *f*, and the

Ex 31:8 pure candlestick with all his *f*
Ex 31:9 of burnt offering with all his *f*
Ex 35:14 also for the light, and his *f*
Ex 39:33 Moses, the tent, and all his *f*
Nah 2:9 glory out of all the pleasant *f*

**FURROWS**
Job 31:38 or that the *f* likewise thereof
Ps 65:10 thou settlest the *f* thereof
Ps 129:3 they made long their *f*
Eze 17:7 it by the *f* of her plantation
Eze 17:10 wither in the *f* where it grew
Hos 10:4 as hemlock in the *f* of the field
Hos 10:10 bind themselves in their two *f*
Hos 12:11 as heaps in the *f* of the fields

**FURY**
Gen 27:44 until thy brother's *f* turn away
Lev 26:28 walk contrary unto you also in *f*
Job 20:23 God shall cast the *f* of his wrath
Is 27:4 *F* is not in me
Is 34:2 his *f* upon all their armies
Is 42:25 upon him the *f* of his anger
Is 51:13 because of the *f* of the oppressor
Is 51:13 where is the *f* of the oppressor
Is 51:17 hand of the LORD the cup of his *f*
Is 51:20 are full of the *f* of the LORD
Is 51:22 even the dregs of the cup of my *f*
Is 59:18 *f* to his adversaries, recompence
Is 63:3 anger, and trample them in my *f*
Is 63:5 and my *f*, it upheld me
Is 63:6 anger, and make them drunk in my *f*
Is 66:15 to render his anger with *f*
Jer 4:4 lest my *f* come forth like fire,
Jer 6:11 I am full of the *f* of the LORD
Jer 7:20 my *f* shall be poured out upon
Jer 10:25 Pour out thy *f* upon the heathen
Jer 21:5 arm, even in anger, and in *f*
Jer 21:12 lest my *f* go out like fire, and
Jer 23:19 of the LORD is gone forth in *f*
Jer 25:15 the wine cup of this *f* at my hand
Jer 30:23 of the LORD goeth forth with *f*
Jer 32:31 of my *f* from the day that they
Jer 32:37 them in mine anger, and in my *f*
Jer 33:5 slain in mine anger and in my *f*
Jer 36:7 anger and the *f* that the LORD hath
Jer 42:18 my *f* hath been poured forth upon
Jer 42:18 so shall my *f* be poured forth
Jer 44:6 Wherefore my *f* and mine anger was
Lam 2:4 he poured out his *f* like fire
Lam 4:11 The LORD hath accomplished his *f*
Eze 5:13 I will cause my *f* to rest upon
Eze 5:13 I have accomplished my *f* in them
Eze 5:15 in thee in anger and in *f* and in
Eze 6:12 will I accomplish my *f* upon them
Eze 7:8 I shortly pour out my *f* upon thee
Eze 8:18 Therefore will I also deal in *f*
Eze 9:8 out of thy *f* upon Jerusalem
Eze 13:13 it with a stormy wind in my *f*
Eze 13:13 hailstones in my *f* to consume it
Eze 14:19 pour out my *f* upon it in blood,
Eze 16:38 and I will give thee blood in *f*
Eze 16:42 So will I make my *f* toward thee
Eze 19:12 But she was plucked up in *f*
Eze 20:8 I will pour out my *f* upon them
Eze 20:13 I would pour out my *f* upon them
Eze 20:21 I would pour out my *f* upon them
Eze 20:33 with *f* poured out, will I rule
Eze 20:34 out arm, and with *f* poured out
Eze 21:17 and I will cause my *f* to rest
Eze 22:20 you in mine anger and in my *f*
Eze 22:22 have poured out my *f* upon you
Eze 24:8 That it might cause *f* to come up
Eze 24:13 caused my *f* to rest upon thee
Eze 25:14 mine anger and according to my *f*
Eze 30:15 And I will pour my *f* upon Sin
Eze 36:6 spoken in my jealousy and in my *f*
Eze 36:18 Wherefore I poured my *f* upon them
Eze 38:18 that my *f* shall come up in my
Dan 3:13 *f* commanded to bring Shadrach,
Dan 3:19 Then was Nebuchadnezzar full of *f*
Dan 8:6 unto him in the *f* of his power
Dan 9:16 thy *f* be turned away from thy
Dan 11:44 go forth with great *f* to destroy
Mic 5:15 *f* upon the heathen, such as they
Nah 1:6 his *f* is poured out like fire, and
Zec 8:2 was jealous for her with great *f*

# G

**GAAL** *(ga'-al) A son of Ebed.*
Judg 9:26 G the son of Ebed came with his
Judg 9:28 G the son of Ebed said, Who is
Judg 9:30 the words of G the son of Ebed
Judg 9:31 G the son of Ebed and his brethren
Judg 9:35 G the son of Ebed went out, and
Judg 9:36 when G saw the people, he said to
Judg 9:37 G spake again and said, See there
Judg 9:39 G went out before the men of
Judg 9:41 and Zebul thrust out G and his

**GAASH** *(ga'-ash) A mountain near Mt. Ephraim.*
Josh 24:30 the north side of the hill of G
Judg 2:9 on the north side of the hill G
2Sa 23:30 Hiddai of the brooks of G
1Chr 11:32 Hurai of the brooks of G, Abiel

**GABA** *(ga'-bah)* See GEBA. *A Levitical city in Benjamin.*
Josh 18:24 and Ophni, and G
Ezr 2:26 The children of Ramah and G
Neh 7:30 The men of Ramah and G, six

**GABBAI** *(gab'-bahee) A family of exiles.*
Neh 11:8 And after him G, Sallai, nine

**GABBATHA** *(gab'-ba-thah) Place where Pilate judged.*
Jn 19:13 Pavement, but in the Hebrew, G

**GABRIEL** *(ga'-bre-el) An angel.*
Dan 8:16 of Ulai, which called, and said, G
Dan 9:21 in prayer, even the man G
Lk 1:19 answering said unto him, I am G
Lk 1:26 in the sixth month the angel G

**GAD** *(gad)*
*1. A son of Jacob.*
Gen 30:11 and she called his name G
Gen 35:26 Leah's handmaid; G, and Asher
Gen 46:16 And the sons of G
Gen 49:19 G, a troop shall overcome him
Ex 1:4 Dan, and Naphtali, G, and Asher
1Chr 5:11 the children of G dwelt over
*2. The tribe descended from Gad 1.*
Num 1:14 Of G; Eliasaph the son
Num 1:24 Of the children of G, by their
Num 1:25 of them, even of the tribe of G
Num 2:14 Then the tribe of G
Num 2:14 the captain of the sons of G
Num 7:42 prince of the children of G
Num 10:20 G was Eliasaph the son of Deuel
Num 13:15 Of the tribe of G, Geuel the son
Num 26:15 The children of G after their
Num 26:18 of G according to those that were
Num 32:1 the children of G had a very
Num 32:2 The children of G and the children
Num 32:6 Moses said unto the children of G
Num 32:25 And the children of G and the
Num 32:29 unto them, If the children of G
Num 32:31 And the children of G and the
Num 32:33 them, even to the children of G
Num 32:34 And the children of G built Dibon
Num 34:14 the tribe of the children of G
Deut 27:13 Reuben, G, and Asher, and Zebulun,
Deut 33:20 of G he said, Blessed be he that
Deut 33:20 Blessed be he that enlargeth G
Josh 4:12 of Reuben, and the children of G
Josh 13:24 inheritance unto the tribe of G
Josh 13:24 of G according their families
Josh 13:28 of G after their families
Josh 18:7 and G, and Reuben, and half the
Josh 20:8 in Gilead out of the tribe of G
Josh 21:7 Reuben, and out of the tribe of G
Josh 21:38 And out of the tribe of G, Ramoth
Josh 22:9 of Reuben and the children of G
Josh 22:10 of Reuben and the children of G
Josh 22:11 of Reuben and the children of G
Josh 22:13 Reuben, and to the children of G
Josh 22:15 Reuben, and to the children of G
Josh 22:21 of Reuben and the children of G
Josh 22:25 of Reuben and children of G
Josh 22:30 of Reuben and the children of G
Josh 22:31 Reuben, and to the children of G
Josh 22:32 Reuben, and from the children of G
Josh 22:33 the children of Reuben and G dwelt
Josh 22:34 the children of G called the
1Sa 13:7 went over Jordan to the land of G
2Sa 24:5 in the midst of the river of G
1Chr 2:2 Joseph, and Benjamin, Naphtali, G
1Chr 6:63 Reuben, and out of the tribe of G
1Chr 6:80 And out of the tribe of G
1Chr 12:14 These were of the sons of G
Jer 49:1 then doth their king inherit G
Eze 48:27 unto the west side, G a portion
Eze 48:28 And by the border of G, at the
Eze 48:34 one gate of G, one gate of Asher,
Rev 7:5 Of the tribe of G were sealed
*3. A prophet who assisted David.*
1Sa 22:5 the prophet G said unto David,
2Sa 24:11 the LORD came unto the prophet G
2Sa 24:13 So G came to David, and told him,
2Sa 24:14 And David said unto G, I am in a
2Sa 24:18 G came that day to David, and said
2Sa 24:19 according to the saying of G
1Chr 21:9 And the LORD spake unto G, David's
1Chr 21:11 So G came to David, and said unto
1Chr 21:13 And David said unto G, I am in a
1Chr 21:18 LORD commanded G to say to David
1Chr 21:19 David went up at the saying of G
1Chr 29:29 and in the book of G the seer
2Chr 29:25 of G the king's seer, and Nathan

**GADARENES** *(gad-a-renes') Inhabitants of Gadara.*
Mk 5:1 sea, into the country of the G
Lk 8:26 arrived at the country of the G
Lk 8:37 the G round about besought him to

**GADDI** *(gad'-di) One of the twelve spies.*
Num 13:11 of Manasseh, G the son of Susi

**GADDIEL** *(gad'-de-el) One of the twelve spies.*
Num 13:10 of Zebulun, G the son of Sodi

**GADI** *(ga'-di) Father of Menahem.*
2Kin 15:14 the son of G went up from Tirzah
2Kin 15:17 the son of G to reign over Israel

**GADITE** *(gad'-ite)* See GADITES. *A member of the tribe of Dan.*
2Sa 23:36 of Nathan of Zobah, Bani the G

**GADITES** *(gad'-ites)*
Deut 3:12 I unto the Reubenites and to the G
Deut 3:16 unto the G I gave from Gilead
Deut 4:43 and Ramoth in Gilead, of the G
Deut 29:8 unto the Reubenites, and to the G
Josh 1:12 And to the Reubenites, and to the G
Josh 12:6 unto the Reubenites, and the G
Josh 13:8 the G have received their
Josh 22:1 called the Reubenites, and the G
2Kin 10:33 all the land of Gilead, the G
1Chr 5:18 The sons of Reuben, and the G
1Chr 5:26 even the Reubenites, and the G
1Chr 12:8 And of the G there separated
1Chr 12:37 of the Reubenites, and the G
1Chr 26:32 rulers over the Reubenites, the G

**GAHAM** *(ga'-ham) A son of Nahor.*
Gen 22:24 Reumah, she bare also Tebah, and G

**GAHAR** *(ga'-har) A family of exiles.*
Ezr 2:47 of Giddel, the children of G
Neh 7:49 of Giddel, the children of G

**GAIN**
Judg 5:19 they took no *g* of money
Job 22:3 or is it *g* to him, that thou
Prov 1:19 of every one that is greedy of *g*
Prov 3:14 the *g* thereof than fine gold
Prov 15:27 He that is greedy of *g* troubleth
Prov 28:8 unjust *g* increaseth his substance
Is 33:15 despiseth the *g* of oppressions

Is 56:11 own way, every one for his *g*
Eze 22:13 dishonest *g* which thou hast made
Eze 22:27 destroy souls, to get dishonest *g*
Dan 2:8 that ye would *g* the time, because
Dan 11:39 and shall divide the land for *g*
Mic 4:13 consecrate their *g* unto the LORD
Mt 16:26 if he shall *g* the whole world, and
Mk 8:36 if he shall *g* the whole world, and
Lk 9:25 if he *g* the whole world, and lose
Acts 16:16 her masters much *g* by soothsaying
Acts 19:24 brought no small *g* unto the
1Cor 9:19 unto all, that I might *g* the more
1Cor 9:20 as a Jew, that I might *g* the Jews
1Cor 9:20 that I might *g* them that are
1Cor 9:21 that I might *g* them that are
1Cor 9:22 as weak, that I might *g* the weak
2Cor 12:17 Did I make a *g* of you by any of
2Cor 12:18 Did Titus make a *g* of you
Phil 1:21 to live is Christ, and to die is *g*
Phil 3:7 But what things were *g* to me
1Ti 6:5 supposing that *g* is godliness
1Ti 6:6 with contentment is great *g*
Jas 4:13 a year, and buy and sell, and get *g*

**GAINED**
Job 27:8 the hypocrite, though he hath *g*
Eze 22:12 thou hast greedily *g* of thy
Mt 18:15 thee, thou hast *g* thy brother
Mt 25:17 received two, he also *g* other two
Mt 25:20 I have *g* beside them five talents
Mt 25:22 I have *g* two other talents beside
Lk 19:15 much every man had *g* by trading
Lk 19:16 Lord, thy pound hath *g* ten pounds
Lk 19:18 thy pound hath *g* five pounds
Acts 27:21 to have *g* this harm and loss

**GAIUS** *(gah'-yus)*
*1. A native of Macedonia.*
Acts 19:29 and having caught G and Aristarchus
*2. A native of Derbe.*
Acts 20:4 and G of Derbe, and Timotheus
*3. A native of Corinth.*
Rom 16:23 G mine host, and of the whole
1Cor 1:14 none of you, but Crispus and G
*4. Addressee of John's third epistle.*
3Jn 1 The elder unto the wellbeloved G

**GALAL** *(ga'-lal)*
*1. Son of Jeduthun.*
1Chr 9:15 And Bakbakkar, Heresh, and G
*2. A Levite exile.*
1Chr 9:16 the son of Shemaiah, the son of G
Neh 11:17 the son of Shammua, the son of G

**GALATIA** *(ga-la'-she-ah)* See GALATIANS. *A Roman province in Asia Minor.*
Acts 16:6 Phrygia and the region of G
Acts 18:23 and went over all the country of G
1Cor 16:1 given order to the churches of G
Gal 1:2 with me, unto the churches of G
2Ti 4:10 Crescens to G, Titus unto
1Pet 1:1 scattered throughout Pontus, G

**GALATIANS** *(ga-la'-she-uns) Inhabitants of Galatia.*
Gal 3:1 O foolish G, who hath bewitched
Gal *s* Unto the G written from Rome

**GALBANUM**
Ex 30:34 spices, stacte, and onycha, and *g*

**GALEED** *(ga'-le-ed)* See JAGAR-SAHADUTHA. *A memorial mound of stones.*
Gen 31:47 but Jacob called it G
Gen 31:48 was the name of it called G

**GALILAEAN** *(gal-i-le'-un)* See GALILAEANS. *An inhabitant of Galilee.*
Mk 14:70 for thou art a G, and thy speech
Lk 22:59 for he is a G
Lk 23:6 he asked whether the man were a G

**GALILAEANS** *(gal-i-le'-uns)*
Lk 13:1 some that told him of the G
Lk 13:2 Suppose ye that these G were
Lk 13:2 were sinners above all the G
Jn 4:45 the G received him, having seen
Acts 2:7 are not all these which speak G

**GALILEE** *(gal'-i-lee)* See GALILAEAN. *A district north of Samaria.*
Josh 20:7 Kedesh in G in mount Naphtali
Josh 21:32 Kedesh in G with her suburbs, to
1Kin 9:11 twenty cities in the land of G
2Kin 15:29 Kedesh, and Hazor, and Gilead, and G
1Chr 6:76 Kedesh in G with her suburbs, and
Is 9:1 Jordan, in G of the nations
Mt 2:22 turned aside into the parts of G
Mt 3:13 Jesus from G to Jordan unto John
Mt 4:12 into prison, he departed into G
Mt 4:15 beyond Jordan, G of the Gentiles
Mt 4:18 And Jesus, walking by the sea of G
Mt 4:23 And Jesus went about all G
Mt 4:25 great multitudes of people from G
Mt 15:29 and came nigh unto the sea of G
Mt 17:22 And while they abode in G, Jesus
Mt 19:1 these sayings, he departed from G
Mt 21:11 the prophet of Nazareth of G
Mt 26:32 I will go before you into G
Mt 26:69 Thou also wast with Jesus of G
Mt 27:55 off, which followed Jesus from G
Mt 28:7 he goeth before you into G
Mt 28:10 my brethren that they go into G
Mt 28:16 eleven disciples went away into G
Mk 1:9 Jesus came from Nazareth of G
Mk 1:14 put in prison, Jesus came into G
Mk 1:16 Now as he walked by the sea of G
Mk 1:28 all the region round about G
Mk 1:39 their synagogues throughout all G
Mk 3:7 multitude from G followed him
Mk 6:21 captains, and chief estates of G
Mk 7:31 Sidon, he came unto the sea of G
Mk 9:30 thence, and passed through G
Mk 14:28 I will go before you into G
Mk 15:41 (Who also, when he was in G
Mk 16:7 that he goeth before you into G
Lk 1:26 sent from God unto a city of G
Lk 2:4 And Joseph also went up from G
Lk 2:39 of the Lord, they returned into G
Lk 3:1 and Herod being tetrarch of G
Lk 4:14 in the power of the Spirit into G
Lk 4:31 down to Capernaum, a city of G
Lk 4:44 preached in the synagogues of G
Lk 5:17 were come out of every town of G
Lk 8:26 which is over against G
Lk 17:11 through the midst of Samaria and G
Lk 23:5 beginning from G to this place
Lk 23:6 When Pilate heard of G, he asked
Lk 23:49 women that followed him from G
Lk 23:55 also, which came with him from G
Lk 24:6 unto you when he was yet in G
Jn 1:43 Jesus would go forth into G
Jn 2:1 there was a marriage in Cana of G
Jn 2:11 miracles did Jesus in Cana of G
Jn 4:3 Judaea, and departed again into G
Jn 4:43 departed thence, and went into G
Jn 4:45 Then when he was come into G
Jn 4:46 Jesus came again into Cana of G
Jn 4:47 was come out of Judaea into G
Jn 4:54 he was come out of Judaea into G
Jn 6:1 Jesus went over the sea of G
Jn 7:1 these things Jesus walked in G
Jn 7:9 unto them, he abode still in G
Jn 7:41 said, Shall Christ come out of G
Jn 7:52 said unto him, Art thou also of G
Jn 7:52 for out of G ariseth no prophet
Jn 12:21 which was of Bethsaida of G
Jn 21:2 and Nathanael of Cana in G
Acts 1:11 Which also said, Ye men of G
Acts 5:37 of G in the days of the taxing
Acts 9:31 rest throughout all Judaea and G
Acts 10:37 all Judaea, and began from G
Acts 13:31 up with him from G to Jerusalem

**GALL**
Deut 29:18 among you a root that beareth *g*
Deut 32:32 their grapes are grapes of *g*
Job 16:13 poureth out my *g* upon the ground
Job 20:14 it is the *g* of asps within him
Job 20:25 sword cometh out of his *g*
Ps 69:21 They gave me also *g* for my meat
Jer 8:14 and given us water of *g* to drink
Jer 9:15 and give them water of *g* to drink
Jer 23:15 and make them drink the water of *g*
Lam 3:5 me, and compassed me with *g*
Lam 3:19 my misery, the wormwood and the *g*
Amos 6:12 ye have turned judgment into *g*
Mt 27:34 vinegar to drink mingled with *g*
Acts 8:23 thou art in the *g* of bitterness

**GALLERIES**
Song 7:5 the king is held in the *g*
Eze 41:15 the *g* thereof on the one side and
Eze 41:16 the *g* round about on their three
Eze 42:5 for the *g* were higher than these,

**GALLIM** *(gal'-lim) A city in Benjamin.*
1Sa 25:44 the son of Laish, which was of G
Is 10:30 up thy voice, O daughter of G

**GALLIO** *(gal'-le-o) A Roman proconsul of Achaia.*
Acts 18:12 when G was the deputy of Achaia,
Acts 18:14 G said unto the Jews, If it were
Acts 18:17 G cared for none of those things

**GALLOWS**
Est 5:14 Let a *g* be made of fifty cubits
Est 5:14 and he caused the *g* to be made
Est 6:4 *g* that he had prepared for him
Est 7:9 the *g* fifty cubits high, which
Est 7:10 on the *g* that he had prepared for
Est 8:7 him they have hanged upon the *g*
Est 9:13 ten sons be hanged upon the *g*
Est 9:25 sons should be hanged on the *g*

**GAMALIEL** *(gam-a'-le-el)*
*1. A chief of Manasseh.*
Num 1:10 G the son of Pedahzur
Num 2:20 shall be G the son of Pedahzur
Num 7:54 day offered G the son of Pedahzur
Num 7:59 offering of G the son of Pedahzur
Num 10:23 was G the son of Pedahzur
*2. A noted Rabbinic teacher.*
Acts 5:34 the council, a Pharisee, named G
Acts 22:3 up in this city at the feet of G

**GAMMADIMS** *(gam'-ma-dims) Defenders of Tyre.*
Eze 27:11 and the G were in thy towers

**GAMUL** *(ga'-mul)* See BETH-GAMUL. *A sanctuary servant in David's time.*
1Chr 24:17 Jachin, the two and twentieth to G

**GARDEN**
Gen 2:8 God planted a *g* eastward in Eden
Gen 2:9 life also in the midst of the *g*
Gen 2:10 went out of Eden to water the *g*
Gen 2:15 put him into the *g* of Eden to
Gen 2:16 Of every tree of the *g* thou
Gen 3:1 not eat of every tree of the *g*
Gen 3:2 the fruit of the trees of the *g*
Gen 3:3 which is in the midst of the *g*
Gen 3:8 in the *g* in the cool of the day
Gen 3:8 God amongst the trees of the *g*
Gen 3:10 said, I heard thy voice in the *g*
Gen 3:23 sent him forth from the *g* of Eden
Gen 3:24 east of the *g* of Eden Cherubim
Gen 13:10 even as the *g* of the LORD
Deut 11:10 it with thy foot, as a *g* of herbs
1Kin 21:2 I may have it for a *g* of herbs
2Kin 9:27 he fled by the way of the *g* house
2Kin 21:18 buried in the *g* of his own house
2Kin 21:18 his own house, in the *g* of Uzza
2Kin 21:26 in his sepulchre in the *g* of Uzza
2Kin 25:4 walls, which is by the king's *g*
Neh 3:15 pool of Siloah by the king's *g*
Est 1:5 in the court of the *g* of the
Est 7:7 his wrath went into the palace *g*
Est 7:8 *g* into the place of the banquet
Job 8:16 branch shooteth forth in his *g*
Song 4:12 A *g* inclosed is my sister, my
Song 4:16 blow upon my *g*, that the spices
Song 4:16 Let my beloved come into his *g*
Song 5:1 I am come into my *g*, my sister,
Song 6:2 beloved is gone down into his *g*
Song 6:11 I went down into the *g* of nuts to
Is 1:8 as a lodge in a *g* of cucumbers
Is 1:30 as a *g* that hath no water
Is 51:3 her desert like the *g* of the LORD
Is 58:11 and thou shalt be like a watered *g*
Is 61:11 as the *g* causeth the things that
Jer 31:12 soul shall be as a watered *g*
Jer 39:4 night, by the way of the king's *g*
Jer 52:7 walls, which was by the king's *g*
Lam 2:6 tabernacle, as if it were of a *g*
Eze 28:13 hast been in Eden the *g* of God
Eze 31:8 The cedars in the *g* of God could
Eze 31:8 nor any tree in the *g* of God was
Eze 31:9 Eden, that were in the *g* of God
Eze 36:35 is become like the *g* of Eden
Joel 2:3 the land is as the *g* of Eden
Lk 13:19 a man took, and cast into his *g*
Jn 18:1 the brook Cedron, where was a *g*
Jn 18:26 not I see thee in the *g* with him
Jn 19:41 he was crucified there was a *g*
Jn 19:41 in the *g* a new sepulchre, wherein

**GARDENER**
Jn 20:15 She, supposing him to be the *g*

**GARDENS**
Num 24:6 as *g* by the river's side, as the
Eccl 2:5 I made me *g* and orchards, and I
Song 4:15 A fountain of *g*, a well of living
Song 6:2 beds of spices, to feed in the *g*
Song 8:13 Thou that dwellest in the *g*
Is 1:29 for the *g* that ye have chosen
Is 65:3 that sacrificeth in *g*, and burneth
Is 66:17 purify themselves in the *g* behind
Jer 29:5 and plant *g*, and eat the fruit of
Jer 29:28 and plant *g*, and eat the fruit of
Amos 4:9 when your *g* and your vineyards and
Amos 9:14 they shall also make *g*, and eat

**GAREB** *(ga'-reb)*
*1. A "mighty man" of David.*
2Sa 23:38 Ira an Ithrite, *G* an Ithrite,
1Chr 11:40 Ira the Ithrite, *G* the Ithrite,
*2. A hill near Jerusalem.*
Jer 31:39 over against it upon the hill G

**GARMENT**
Gen 9:23 And Shem and Japheth took a *g*
Gen 25:25 out red, all over like an hairy *g*
Gen 39:12 And she caught him by his *g*
Gen 39:12 and he left his *g* in her hand
Gen 39:13 he had left his *g* in her hand
Gen 39:15 cried, that he left his *g* with me
Gen 39:16 And she laid up his *g* by her
Gen 39:18 cried, that he left his *g* with me
Lev 6:10 priest shall put on his linen *g*
Lev 6:27 of the blood thereof upon any *g*
Lev 13:47 The *g* also that the plague of
Lev 13:47 a woollen *g*, or a linen *g*
Lev 13:49 be greenish or reddish in the *g*
Lev 13:51 if the plague be spread in the *g*
Lev 13:52 He shall therefore burn that *g*
Lev 13:53 the plague be not spread in the *g*
Lev 13:56 he shall rend it out of the *g*
Lev 13:57 And if it appear still in the *g*
Lev 13:58 And the *g*, either warp, or woof,
Lev 13:59 in a *g* of woollen or linen
Lev 14:55 And for the leprosy of a *g*
Lev 15:17 And every *g*, and every skin,
Lev 19:19 neither shall a *g* mingled of
Deut 22:5 shall a man put on a woman's *g*
Deut 22:11 not wear a *g* of divers sorts
Josh 7:21 the spoils a goodly Babylonish *g*
Josh 7:24 of Zerah, and the silver, and the *g*
Judg 8:25 And they spread a *g*, and did cast
2Sa 13:18 she had a *g* of divers colours
2Sa 13:19 rent her *g* of divers colours that
2Sa 20:8 Joab's *g* that he had put on was
1Kin 11:29 he had clad himself with a new *g*
1Kin 11:30 caught the new *g* that was on him
2Kin 9:13 hasted, and took every man his *g*
Ezr 9:3 I heard this thing, I rent my *g*
Ezr 9:5 and having rent my *g* and my mantle,
Est 8:15 with a *g* of fine linen and purple
Job 13:28 as a *g* that is moth eaten
Job 30:18 of my disease is my *g* changed
Job 38:9 I made the cloud the *g* thereof
Job 38:14 and they stand as a *g*
Job 41:13 can discover the face of his *g*
Ps 69:11 I made sackcloth also my *g*
Ps 73:6 violence covereth them as a *g*
Ps 102:26 of them shall wax old like a *g*
Ps 104:2 thyself with light as with a *g*
Ps 104:6 it with the deep as with a *g*
Ps 109:18 with cursing like as with his *g*
Ps 109:19 him as the *g* which covereth him
Prov 20:16 Take his *g* that is surety for a
Prov 25:20 taketh away a *g* in cold weather
Prov 27:13 Take his *g* that is surety for a
Prov 30:4 who hath bound the waters in a *g*
Is 50:9 lo, they all shall wax old as a *g*
Is 51:6 the earth shall wax old like a *g*
Is 51:8 moth shall eat them up like a *g*
Is 61:3 the *g* of praise for the spirit of
Jer 43:12 as a shepherd putteth on his *g*
Eze 18:7 hath covered the naked with a *g*
Eze 18:16 hath covered the naked with a *g*
Dan 7:9 whose *g* was white as snow, and the
Mic 2:8 ye pull off the robe with the *g*
Hag 2:12 holy flesh in the skirt of his *g*
Zec 13:4 they wear a rough *g* to deceive
Mal 2:16 one covereth violence with his *g*
Mt 9:16 piece of new cloth unto an old *g*
Mt 9:16 to fill it up taketh from the *g*
Mt 9:20 him, and touched the hem of his *g*
Mt 9:21 herself, If I may but touch his *g*
Mt 14:36 might only touch the hem of his *g*
Mt 22:11 man which had not on a wedding *g*
Mt 22:12 in hither not having a wedding *g*
Mk 2:21 a piece of new cloth on an old *g*
Mk 5:27 press behind, and touched his *g*
Mk 6:56 it were but the border of his *g*
Mk 10:50 And he, casting away his *g*
Mk 13:16 back again for to take up his *g*
Mk 16:5 side, clothed in a long white *g*
Lk 5:36 a piece of a new *g* upon an old
Lk 8:44 and touched the border of his *g*
Lk 22:36 hath no sword, let him sell his *g*
Acts 12:8 Cast thy *g* about thee, and follow
Heb 1:11 all shall wax old as doth a *g*
Jude 23 hating even the *g* spotted by the
Rev 1:13 clothed with a *g* down to the foot

**GARMENTS**
Gen 35:2 and be clean, and change your *g*
Gen 38:14 put her widow's *g* off from her
Gen 38:19 put on the *g* of her widowhood
Gen 49:11 he washed his *g* in wine, and his
Ex 28:2 thou shalt make holy *g* for Aaron
Ex 28:3 make Aaron's *g* to consecrate him
Ex 28:4 these are the *g* which they shall
Ex 28:4 they shall make holy *g* for Aaron
Ex 29:5 And thou shalt take the *g*, and put
Ex 29:21 it upon Aaron, and upon his *g*
Ex 29:21 upon the *g* of his sons with him
Ex 29:21 and he shall be hallowed, and his *g*
Ex 29:21 his sons, and his sons' *g* with him
Ex 29:29 the holy *g* of Aaron shall be his
Ex 31:10 the holy *g* for Aaron the priest,
Ex 31:10 the *g* of his sons, to minister in
Ex 35:19 the holy *g* for Aaron the priest,
Ex 35:19 the *g* of his sons, to minister in
Ex 35:21 his service, and for the holy *g*
Ex 39:1 and made the holy *g* for Aaron
Ex 39:41 the holy *g* for Aaron the priest,
Ex 39:41 Aaron the priest, and his sons' *g*
Ex 40:13 shalt put upon Aaron the holy *g*
Lev 6:11 his *g*, and put on other *g*
Lev 8:2 and his sons with him, and the *g*
Lev 8:30 it upon Aaron, and upon his *g*
Lev 8:30 and upon his sons' *g* with him
Lev 8:30 and sanctified Aaron, and his *g*
Lev 8:30 his sons, and his sons' *g* with him
Lev 16:4 these are holy *g*
Lev 16:23 and shall put off the linen *g*
Lev 16:24 the holy place, and put on his *g*
Lev 16:32 linen clothes, even the holy *g*
Lev 21:10 is consecrated to put on the *g*
Num 15:38 *g* throughout their generations
Num 20:26 And strip Aaron of his *g*, and put
Num 20:28 And Moses stripped Aaron of his *g*
Josh 9:5 their feet, and old *g* upon them
Josh 9:13 and these our *g* and our shoes are
Judg 14:12 sheets and thirty change of *g*
Judg 14:13 sheets and thirty change of *g*
Judg 14:19 gave change of *g* unto them which
1Sa 18:4 and gave it to David, and his *g*
2Sa 10:4 and cut off their *g* in the middle
2Sa 13:31 the king arose, and tare his *g*
1Kin 10:25 silver, and vessels of gold, and *g*
2Kin 5:22 of silver, and two changes of *g*
2Kin 5:23 two bags, with two changes of *g*
2Kin 5:26 to receive money, and to receive *g*
2Kin 7:15 and, lo, all the way was full of *g*
2Kin 25:29 And changed his prison *g*
1Chr 19:4 cut off their *g* in the midst hard
Ezr 2:69 silver, and one hundred priests' *g*
Neh 7:70 five hundred and thirty priests' *g*
Neh 7:72 and threescore and seven priests' *g*
Job 37:17 How thy *g* are warm, when he
Ps 22:18 They part my *g* among them
Ps 45:8 All thy *g* smell of myrrh, and
Ps 133:2 went down to the skirts of his *g*
Eccl 9:8 Let thy *g* be always white
Song 4:11 the smell of thy *g* is like the
Is 9:5 noise, and *g* rolled in blood
Is 52:1 put on thy beautiful *g*, O
Is 59:6 Their webs shall not become *g*
Is 59:17 he put on the *g* of vengeance for
Is 61:10 me with the *g* of salvation
Is 63:1 Edom, with dyed *g* from Bozrah
Is 63:2 thy *g* like him that treadeth in
Is 63:3 shall be sprinkled upon my *g*
Jer 36:24 were not afraid, nor rent their *g*
Jer 52:33 And changed his prison *g*
Lam 4:14 that men could not touch their *g*
Eze 16:16 of thy *g* thou didst take, and
Eze 16:18 And tookest thy broidered *g*
Eze 26:16 and put off their broidered *g*
Eze 42:14 lay their *g* wherein they minister
Eze 42:14 and shall put on other *g*, and shall
Eze 44:17 shall be clothed with linen *g*
Eze 44:19 their *g* wherein they ministered
Eze 44:19 and they shall put on other *g*
Eze 44:19 sanctify the people with their *g*
Dan 3:21 and their hats, and their other *g*
Joel 2:13 And rend your heart, and not your *g*
Zec 3:3 Joshua was clothed with filthy *g*
Zec 3:4 Take away the filthy *g* from him
Zec 3:5 his head, and clothed him with *g*
Mt 21:8 spread their *g* in the way
Mt 23:5 and enlarge the borders of their *g*
Mt 27:35 crucified him, and parted his *g*
Mt 27:35 They parted my *g* among them
Mk 11:7 to Jesus, and cast their *g* on him
Mk 11:8 And many spread their *g* in the way
Mk 15:24 crucified him, they parted his *g*
Lk 19:35 they cast their *g* upon the colt
Lk 24:4 men stood by them in shining *g*
Jn 13:4 from supper, and laid aside his *g*
Jn 13:12 their feet, and had taken his *g*
Jn 19:23 had crucified Jesus, took his *g*
Acts 9:39 *g* which Dorcas made, while she
Jas 5:2 and your *g* are motheaten
Rev 3:4 which have not defiled their *g*
Rev 16:15 that watcheth, and keepeth his *g*

**GARMITE** *(gar'-mite) A descendant of Judah.*
1Chr 4:19 Naham, the father of Keilah the G

**GARNISHED**
2Chr 3:6 he *g* the house with precious
Job 26:13 his spirit he hath *g* the heavens
Mt 12:44 he findeth it empty, swept, and *g*
Lk 11:25 cometh, he findeth it swept and *g*
Rev 21:19 *g* with all manner of precious

**GARRISON**
1Sa 10:5 where is the *g* of the Philistines
1Sa 13:3 Jonathan smote the *g* of the
1Sa 13:4 smitten a *g* of the Philistines
1Sa 13:23 the *g* of the Philistines went out
1Sa 14:1 us go over to the Philistines' *g*
1Sa 14:4 go over unto the Philistines' *g*
1Sa 14:6 unto the *g* of these uncircumcised
1Sa 14:11 unto the *g* of the Philistines
1Sa 14:12 the men of the *g* answered
1Sa 14:15 the *g*, and the spoilers, they also
2Sa 23:14 the *g* of the Philistines was then
1Chr 11:16 the Philistines' *g* was then at
2Cor 11:32 city of the Damascenes with a *g*

**GARRISONS**
2Sa 8:6 Then David put *g* in Syria of
2Sa 8:14 And he put *g* in Edom
2Sa 8:14 throughout all Edom put he *g*
1Chr 18:6 Then David put *g* in
1Chr 18:13 And he put *g* in Edom
2Chr 17:2 set *g* in the land of Judah, and in
Eze 26:11 thy strong *g* shall go down to the

**GASHMU** *(gash'-mu)* See GESHEM. *A Samaritan in Nehemiah's time.*
Neh 6:6 *G* saith it, that thou and the Jews

**GAT**
Gen 19:27 Abraham *g* up early in the morning
Ex 24:18 cloud, and *g* him up into the mount
Num 11:30 Moses *g* him into the camp, he and
Num 14:40 *g* them up into the top of the
Num 16:27 So they *g* up from the tabernacle
Judg 9:48 Abimelech *g* him up to mount
Judg 9:51 *g* them up to the top of the tower
Judg 19:28 rose up, and *g* him unto his place
1Sa 13:15 *g* him up from Gilgal unto Gibeah
1Sa 24:22 his men *g* them up unto the hold
1Sa 26:12 they *g* them away, and no man saw
2Sa 4:7 *g* them away through the plain all
2Sa 8:13 David *g* him a name when he
2Sa 13:29 every man *g* him up upon his mule,
2Sa 17:23 *g* him home to his house, to his
2Sa 19:3 the people *g* them by stealth that
1Kin 1:1 with clothes, but he *g* no heat
Ps 116:3 the pains of hell *g* hold upon me
Eccl 2:8 I *g* me men singers and women
Lam 5:9 We *g* our bread with the peril of

**GATAM** *(ga'-tam) A son of Eliphaz.*
Gen 36:11 were Teman, Omar, Zepho, and G
Gen 36:16 Duke Korah, duke G, and duke
1Chr 1:36 Teman, and Omar, Zephi, and G

**GATH** *(gath)* See GATH-HEPHER, GATH-RIMMON, GITTITE, MORESHETH-GATH. *A royal Philistine city.*
Josh 11:22 only in Gaza, in G, and in Ashdod,
1Sa 5:8 of Israel be carried about unto G
1Sa 6:17 one, for Askelon one, for G one
1Sa 7:14 to Israel, from Ekron even unto G
1Sa 17:4 Philistines, named Goliath, of G
1Sa 17:23 the champion, the Philistine of G
1Sa 17:52 the way to Shaaraim, even unto G
1Sa 21:10 and went to Achish the king of G
1Sa 21:12 afraid of Achish the king of G
1Sa 27:2 the son of Maoch, king of G
1Sa 27:3 And David dwelt with Achish at G
1Sa 27:4 Saul that David was fled to G
1Sa 27:11 alive, to bring tidings to G
2Sa 1:20 Tell it not in G, publish it not
2Sa 15:18 men which came after him from G
2Sa 21:20 And there was yet a battle in G
2Sa 21:22 four were born to the giant in G
1Kin 2:39 Achish son of Maachah king of G
1Kin 2:39 Behold, thy servants be in G
1Kin 2:40 went to G to Achish to seek his
1Kin 2:40 and brought his servants from G
1Kin 2:41 had gone from Jerusalem to G
2Kin 12:17 went up, and fought against G
1Chr 7:21 whom the men of G that were born
1Chr 8:13 drove away the inhabitants of G
1Chr 18:1 and subdued them, and took G
1Chr 20:6 And yet again there was war at G
1Chr 20:8 were born unto the giant in G
2Chr 11:8 And G, and Mareshah, and Ziph,
2Chr 26:6 and brake down the wall of G
Ps 56:*t* the Philistines took him in G
Amos 6:2 then go down to G of the
Mic 1:10 Declare ye it not at G, weep ye

**GATHER**
Gen 6:21 eaten, and thou shalt *g* it to thee
Gen 31:46 said unto his brethren, G stones
Gen 34:30 they shall *g* themselves together
Gen 41:35 let them *g* all the food of those
Gen 49:1 G yourselves together, that I may
Gen 49:2 G yourselves together, and hear,
Ex 3:16 *g* the elders of Israel together,
Ex 5:7 them go and *g* straw for themselves
Ex 5:12 to *g* stubble instead of straw
Ex 9:19 *g* thy cattle, and all that thou
Ex 16:4 *g* a certain rate every day, that
Ex 16:5 be twice as much as they *g* daily
Ex 16:16 G of it every man according to
Ex 16:26 Six days ye shall *g* it
Ex 16:27 on the seventh day for to *g*
Ex 23:10 shalt *g* in the fruits thereof
Lev 8:3 *g* thou all the congregation
Lev 19:9 field, neither shalt thou *g* the
Lev 19:10 neither shalt thou *g* every grape
Lev 23:22 neither shalt thou *g* any gleaning
Lev 25:3 and *g* in the fruit thereof
Lev 25:5 neither *g* the grapes of thy vine
Lev 25:11 nor *g* the grapes in it of thy
Lev 25:20 not sow, nor *g* in our increase
Num 8:9 thou shalt *g* the whole assembly
Num 10:4 shall *g* themselves unto thee
Num 11:16 G unto me seventy men of the
Num 19:9 a man that is clean shall *g* up
Num 20:8 *g* thou the assembly together,
Num 21:16 G the people together, and I will
Deut 4:10 G me the people together, and I
Deut 11:14 that thou mayest *g* in thy corn
Deut 13:16 thou shalt *g* all the spoil of it
Deut 28:30 shalt not *g* the grapes thereof
Deut 28:38 field, and shalt *g* but little in
Deut 28:39 of the wine, nor *g* the grapes
Deut 30:3 *g* thee from all the nations,
Deut 30:4 will the LORD thy God *g* thee
Deut 31:12 G the people together, men, and
Deut 31:28 G unto me all the elders of your
Ruth 2:7 *g* after the reapers among the
1Sa 7:5 G all Israel to Mizpeh, and I will
2Sa 3:21 will *g* all Israel unto my lord
2Sa 12:28 Now therefore *g* the rest of the
1Kin 18:19 *g* to me all Israel unto mount
2Kin 4:39 out into the field to *g* herbs
2Kin 22:20 I will *g* thee unto thy fathers,
1Chr 13:2 that they may *g* themselves unto
1Chr 16:35 *g* us together, and deliver us from
1Chr 22:2 David commanded to *g* together the
2Chr 24:5 *g* of all Israel money to repair
2Chr 34:28 I will *g* thee to thy fathers, and
Ezr 10:7 that they should *g* themselves
Neh 1:9 yet will I *g* them from thence, and
Neh 7:5 heart to *g* together the nobles
Neh 12:44 to *g* into them out of the fields
Est 2:3 that they may *g* together all the
Est 4:16 *g* together all the Jews that are
Est 8:11 city to *g* themselves together
Job 11:10 or *g* together, then who can
Job 24:6 they *g* the vintage of the wicked
Job 34:14 if he *g* unto himself his spirit
Job 39:12 thy seed, and *g* it into thy barn
Ps 26:9 G not my soul with sinners, nor
Ps 39:6 and knoweth not who shall *g* them
Ps 50:5 G my saints together unto me
Ps 56:6 They *g* themselves together, they
Ps 94:21 They *g* themselves together
Ps 104:22 they *g* themselves together, and
Ps 104:28 That thou givest them they *g*
Ps 106:47 *g* us from among the heathen, to
Prov 28:8 he shall *g* it for him that will
Eccl 2:26 sinner he giveth travail, to *g*
Eccl 3:5 a time to *g* stones together
Song 6:2 in the gardens, and to *g* lilies
Is 10:31 of Gebim *g* themselves to flee
Is 11:12 *g* together the dispersed of Judah
Is 34:15 and hatch, and *g* under her shadow
Is 40:11 he shall *g* the lambs with his arm
Is 43:5 the east, and *g* thee from the west
Is 49:18 all these *g* themselves together,
Is 54:7 with great mercies will I *g* thee
Is 54:15 they shall surely *g* together
Is 54:15 whosoever shall *g* together
Is 56:8 Yet will I *g* others to him,
Is 60:4 all they *g* themselves together,
Is 62:10 *g* out the stones
Is 66:18 come, that I will *g* all nations
Jer 4:5 *g* together, and say, Assemble
Jer 6:1 *g* yourselves to flee out of the
Jer 7:18 The children *g* wood, and the
Jer 9:22 harvestman, and none shall *g* them
Jer 10:17 G up thy wares out of the land, O
Jer 23:3 I will *g* the remnant of my flock
Jer 29:14 I will *g* you from all the nations
Jer 31:8 *g* them from the coasts of the
Jer 31:10 that scattered Israel will *g* him
Jer 32:37 Behold, I will *g* them out of all
Jer 40:10 *g* ye wine, and summer fruits, and
Jer 49:5 and none shall *g* up him that
Jer 49:14 G ye together, and come against
Jer 51:11 bright the arrows; *g* the shields
Eze 11:17 I will even *g* you from the people
Eze 16:37 therefore I will *g* all thy lovers
Eze 16:37 I will even *g* them round about
Eze 20:34 will *g* you out of the countries
Eze 20:41 *g* you out of the countries
Eze 22:19 therefore I will *g* you into the
Eze 22:20 As they *g* silver, and brass, and
Eze 22:20 so will I *g* you in mine anger and
Eze 22:21 Yea, I will *g* you, and blow upon
Eze 24:4 G the pieces thereof into it,
Eze 29:13 I *g* the Egyptians from the people
Eze 34:13 *g* them from the countries, and
Eze 36:24 *g* you out of all countries, and
Eze 37:21 will *g* them on every side, and
Eze 39:17 *g* yourselves on every side to my
Dan 3:2 sent to *g* together the princes
Hos 8:10 the nations, now will I *g* them
Hos 9:6 Egypt shall *g* them up, Memphis
Joel 1:14 assembly, *g* the elders and all the
Joel 2:6 all faces shall *g* blackness
Joel 2:16 G the people, sanctify the
Joel 2:16 *g* the children, and those that
Joel 3:2 I will also *g* all nations
Joel 3:11 *g* yourselves together round about
Mic 2:12 I will surely *g* the remnant of
Mic 4:6 I will *g* her that is driven out,
Mic 4:12 for he shall *g* them as the
Mic 5:1 Now *g* thyself in troops, O
Nah 2:10 the faces of them all *g* blackness
Hab 1:9 they shall *g* the captivity as the
Hab 1:15 net, and *g* them in their drag
Zeph 2:1 G yourselves together, yea,
Zeph 2:1 *g* together, O nation not desired
Zeph 3:8 determination is to *g* the nations
Zeph 3:18 I will *g* them that are sorrowful
Zeph 3:19 *g* her that was driven out
Zeph 3:20 even in the time that I *g* you
Zec 10:8 I will hiss for them, and *g* them
Zec 10:10 Egypt, and *g* them out of Assyria
Zec 14:2 For I will *g* all nations against
Mt 3:12 *g* his wheat into the garner
Mt 6:26 do they reap, nor *g* into barns
Mt 7:16 Do men *g* grapes of thorns, or
Mt 13:28 thou then that we go and *g* them up
Mt 13:29 lest while ye *g* up the tares
Mt 13:30 G ye together first the tares, and
Mt 13:30 but *g* the wheat into my barn
Mt 13:41 they shall *g* out of his kingdom
Mt 24:31 they shall *g* together his elect
Mt 25:26 *g* where I have not strawed
Mk 13:27 shall *g* together his elect from
Lk 3:17 will *g* the wheat into his garner
Lk 6:44 For of thorns men do not *g* figs
Lk 6:44 of a bramble bush *g* they grapes
Lk 13:34 as a hen doth *g* her brood under
Jn 6:12 G up the fragments that remain,
Jn 11:52 but that also he should *g*
Jn 15:6 men *g* them, and cast them into the
Eph 1:10 *g* together in one all things in
Rev 14:18 *g* the clusters of the vine of the
Rev 16:14 to *g* them to the battle of that
Rev 19:17 *g* yourselves together unto the
Rev 20:8 to *g* them together to battle

**GATHERED**
Gen 1:9 be *g* together unto one place
Gen 12:5 their substance that they had *g*
Gen 25:8 and was *g* to his people
Gen 25:17 and was *g* unto his people
Gen 29:3 And thither were all the flocks *g*
Gen 29:7 the cattle should be *g* together
Gen 29:8 all the flocks be *g* together
Gen 29:22 Laban *g* together all the men of
Gen 35:29 was *g* unto his people, being old
Gen 41:48 he *g* up all the food of the seven
Gen 41:49 Joseph *g* corn as the sand of the
Gen 47:14 Joseph *g* up all the money that
Gen 49:29 I am to be *g* unto my people
Gen 49:33 he *g* up his feet into the bed, and
Gen 49:33 ghost, and was *g* unto his people
Ex 4:29 *g* together all the elders of the
Ex 8:14 they *g* them together upon heaps
Ex 15:8 the waters were *g* together
Ex 16:17 children of Israel did so, and *g*
Ex 16:18 he that *g* much had nothing over,
Ex 16:18 he that *g* little had no lack
Ex 16:18 they *g* every man according to his
Ex 16:21 they *g* it every morning, every
Ex 16:22 day they *g* twice as much bread
Ex 23:16 when thou hast *g* in thy labours
Ex 32:1 the people *g* themselves together
Ex 32:26 all the sons of Levi *g* themselves
Ex 35:1 Moses *g* all the congregation of
Lev 8:4 the assembly was *g* together unto
Lev 23:39 when ye have *g* in the fruit of
Lev 26:25 when ye are *g* together within
Num 10:7 congregation is to be *g* together
Num 11:8 *g* it, and ground it in mills, or
Num 11:22 of the sea be *g* together for them
Num 11:24 *g* the seventy men of the elders
Num 11:32 next day, and they *g* the quails
Num 11:32 that *g* least *g* ten homers
Num 14:35 that are *g* together against me
Num 15:32 they found a man that *g* sticks
Num 16:3 they *g* themselves together
Num 16:11 all thy company are *g* together
Num 16:19 Korah *g* all the congregation
Num 16:42 congregation was *g* against Moses
Num 20:2 they *g* themselves together
Num 20:10 Aaron *g* the congregation together
Num 20:24 Aaron shall be *g* unto his people
Num 20:26 Aaron shall be *g* unto his people,
Num 21:23 but Sihon *g* all his people
Num 27:3 *g* themselves together against the
Num 27:13 also shalt be *g* unto thy people
Num 27:13 as Aaron thy brother was *g*
Num 31:2 shalt thou be *g* unto thy people
Deut 16:13 that thou hast *g* in thy corn
Deut 32:50 goest up, and be *g* unto thy people
Deut 32:50 Hor, and was *g* unto his people
Deut 33:5 tribes of Israel were *g* together
Josh 9:2 That they *g* themselves together,
Josh 10:5 *g* themselves together, and went up
Josh 10:6 are *g* together against us
Josh 22:12 of the children of Israel *g*
Josh 24:1 Joshua *g* all the tribes of Israel

Judg 1:7 *g* their meat under my table
Judg 2:10 were *g* unto their fathers
Judg 3:13 he *g* unto him the children of
Judg 4:13 Sisera *g* together all his
Judg 6:33 of the east were *g* together
Judg 6:34 and Abi-ezer was *g* after him
Judg 6:35 who also was *g* after him
Judg 7:23 the men of Israel *g* themselves
Judg 7:24 of Ephraim *g* themselves together
Judg 9:6 all the men of Shechem *g* together
Judg 9:27 *g* their vineyards, and trode the
Judg 9:47 tower of Shechem were *g* together
Judg 10:17 children of Ammon were *g* together
Judg 11:3 there were *g* vain men to Jephthah
Judg 11:20 but Sihon *g* all his people
Judg 12:1 the men of Ephraim *g* themselves
Judg 12:4 Then Jephthah *g* together all the
Judg 16:23 *g* them together for to offer a
Judg 18:22 to Micah's house were *g* together
Judg 20:1 was *g* together as one man
Judg 20:11 of Israel were *g* against the city
Judg 20:14 But the children of Benjamin *g*
1Sa 5:8 and *g* all the lords of the
1Sa 5:11 *g* together all the lords of the
1Sa 7:6 they *g* together to Mizpeh, and
1Sa 7:7 Israel were *g* together to Mizpeh
1Sa 8:4 of Israel *g* themselves together
1Sa 13:5 the Philistines *g* themselves
1Sa 13:11 that the Philistines *g* themselves
1Sa 14:48 he *g* an host, and smote the
1Sa 15:4 Saul *g* the people together, and
1Sa 17:1 Now the Philistines *g* together
1Sa 17:1 were *g* together at Shochoh, which
1Sa 17:2 the men of Israel were *g* together
1Sa 20:38 And Jonathan's lad *g* up the arrows
1Sa 22:2 *g* themselves unto him
1Sa 25:1 the Israelites were *g* together
1Sa 28:1 that the Philistines *g* their
1Sa 28:4 the Philistines *g* themselves
1Sa 28:4 Saul *g* all Israel together, and
1Sa 29:1 Now the Philistines *g* together
2Sa 2:25 the children of Benjamin *g*
2Sa 2:30 when he had *g* all the people
2Sa 6:1 David *g* together all the chosen
2Sa 10:15 they *g* themselves together
2Sa 10:17 he *g* all Israel together, and
2Sa 12:29 David *g* all the people together,
2Sa 14:14 which cannot be *g* up again
2Sa 17:11 Israel be generally *g* unto thee
2Sa 20:14 and they were *g* together, and went
2Sa 21:13 they *g* the bones of them that
2Sa 23:9 were there *g* together to battle
2Sa 23:11 the Philistines were *g* together
1Kin 10:26 Solomon *g* together chariots and
1Kin 11:24 he *g* men unto him, and became
1Kin 18:20 *g* the prophets together unto
1Kin 20:1 of Syria *g* all his host together
1Kin 22:6 of Israel *g* the prophets together
2Kin 3:21 they *g* all that were able to put
2Kin 4:39 *g* thereof wild gourds his lap
2Kin 6:24 king of Syria *g* all his host
2Kin 10:18 Jehu *g* all the people together,
2Kin 22:4 of the door have *g* of the people
2Kin 22:9 Thy servants have *g* the money
2Kin 22:20 thou shalt be *g* into thy grave in
2Kin 23:1 they *g* unto him all the elders of
1Chr 11:1 Then all Israel *g* themselves to
1Chr 11:13 were *g* together to battle
1Chr 13:5 So David *g* all Israel together,
1Chr 15:3 David *g* all Israel together to
1Chr 19:7 And the children of Ammon *g*
1Chr 19:17 he *g* all Israel, and passed over
1Chr 23:2 he *g* together all the princes of
2Chr 1:14 Solomon *g* chariots and horsemen
2Chr 11:1 he *g* of the house of Judah and
2Chr 12:5 that were *g* together to Jerusalem
2Chr 13:7 there are *g* unto him vain men,
2Chr 15:9 he *g* all Judah and Benjamin, and
2Chr 15:10 So they *g* themselves together at
2Chr 18:5 *g* together of prophets four
2Chr 20:4 Judah *g* themselves together, to
2Chr 23:2 *g* the Levites out of all the
2Chr 24:5 he *g* together the priests and the
2Chr 24:11 by day, and *g* money in abundance
2Chr 25:5 Moreover Amaziah *g* Judah together
2Chr 28:24 Ahaz *g* together the vessels of
2Chr 29:4 *g* them together into the east
2Chr 29:15 they *g* their brethren, and
2Chr 29:20 *g* the rulers of the city, and went
2Chr 30:3 people *g* themselves together to
2Chr 32:4 So there was *g* much people
2Chr 32:6 *g* them together to him in the
2Chr 34:9 had *g* of the hand of Manasseh
2Chr 34:17 they have *g* together the money
2Chr 34:28 thou shalt be *g* to thy grave in
2Chr 34:29 *g* together all the elders of
Ezr 3:1 the people *g* themselves together
Ezr 7:28 I *g* together out of Israel chief
Ezr 8:15 I *g* them together to the river
Ezr 10:9 Benjamin *g* themselves together
Neh 5:16 all my servants were *g* thither
Neh 8:1 all the people *g* themselves
Neh 8:13 on the second day were *g* together
Neh 12:28 the singers *g* themselves together
Neh 13:11 I *g* them together, and set them in
Est 2:8 when many maidens were *g* together
Est 2:19 when the virgins were *g* together
Est 9:2 The Jews *g* themselves together in
Est 9:15 *g* themselves together on the
Est 9:16 provinces *g* themselves together
Job 16:10 they have *g* themselves together
Job 27:19 lie down, but he shall not be *g*
Job 30:7 the nettles they were *g* together
Ps 35:15 and *g* themselves together
Ps 35:15 the abjects *g* themselves together
Ps 47:9 of the people are *g* together
Ps 59:3 the mighty are *g* against me
Ps 102:22 When the people are *g* together
Ps 107:3 *g* them out of the lands, from the
Ps 140:2 are they *g* together for war
Prov 27:25 and herbs of the mountains are *g*
Prov 30:4 who hath *g* the wind in his fists
Eccl 2:8 I *g* me also silver and gold, and
Song 5:1 I have *g* my myrrh with my spice
Is 5:2 *g* out the stones thereof, and
Is 10:14 are left, have I *g* all the earth
Is 13:4 kingdoms of nations *g* together
Is 22:9 ye *g* together the waters of the
Is 24:22 And they shall be *g* together
Is 24:22 as prisoners are *g* in the pit
Is 27:12 and ye shall be *g* one by one
Is 33:4 your spoil shall be *g* like the
Is 34:15 shall the vultures also be *g*
Is 34:16 and his spirit it hath *g* them
Is 43:9 Let all the nations be *g* together
Is 44:11 let them all be *g* together
Is 49:5 to him, Though Israel be not *g*
Is 56:8 beside those that are *g* unto him
Is 60:7 shall be *g* together unto thee
Is 62:9 they that have *g* it shall eat it
Jer 3:17 the nations shall be *g* unto it
Jer 8:2 they shall not be *g*, nor be
Jer 25:33 shall not be lamented, neither *g*
Jer 26:9 all the people were *g* against
Jer 40:12 *g* wine and summer fruits very much
Jer 40:15 that all the Jews which are *g*
Eze 28:25 When I shall have *g* the house of
Eze 29:5 not be brought together, nor *g*
Eze 38:8 is *g* out of many people, against
Eze 38:12 that are *g* out of the nations
Eze 38:13 hast thou *g* thy company to take a
Eze 39:27 *g* them out of their enemies'
Eze 39:28 but I have *g* them unto their own
Dan 3:3 were *g* together unto the
Dan 3:27 being *g* together, saw these men,
Hos 1:11 children of Israel be *g* together
Hos 10:10 people shall be *g* against them
Mic 1:7 for she *g* it of the hire of an
Mic 4:11 many nations are *g* against thee
Mic 7:1 they have *g* the summer fruits
Zec 12:3 earth be *g* together against it
Zec 14:14 round about shall be *g* together
Mt 2:4 when he had *g* all the chief
Mt 13:2 were *g* together unto him, so that
Mt 13:40 As therefore the tares are *g*
Mt 13:47 into the sea, and *g* of every kind
Mt 13:48 *g* the good into vessels, but cast
Mt 18:20 three are *g* together in my name
Mt 22:10 *g* together all as many as they
Mt 22:34 to silence, they were *g* together
Mt 22:41 the Pharisees were *g* together
Mt 23:37 I have *g* thy children together
Mt 24:28 will the eagles be *g* together
Mt 25:32 before him shall be *g* all nations
Mt 27:17 when they were *g* together
Mt 27:27 *g* unto him the whole band of
Mk 1:33 all the city was *g* together at
Mk 2:2 straightway many were *g* together
Mk 4:1 there was *g* unto him a great
Mk 5:21 side, much people *g* unto him
Mk 6:30 the apostles *g* themselves
Lk 8:4 when much people were *g* together
Lk 11:29 the people were *g* thick together
Lk 12:1 when there were *g* together an
Lk 13:34 I have *g* thy children together
Lk 15:13 the younger son *g* all together
Lk 17:37 will the eagles be *g* together
Lk 24:33 and found the eleven *g* together
Jn 6:13 Therefore they *g* them together
Jn 11:47 Then *g* the chief priests and the
Acts 4:6 were *g* together at Jerusalem
Acts 4:26 the rulers were *g* together
Acts 4:27 of Israel, were *g* together,
Acts 12:12 where many were *g* together
Acts 14:27 had *g* the church together, they
Acts 15:30 when they had *g* the multitude
Acts 17:5 *g* a company, and set all the city
Acts 20:8 where they were *g* together
Acts 28:3 when Paul had *g* a bundle of
1Cor 5:4 Christ, when ye are *g* together
2Cor 8:15 He that had *g* much had nothing
2Cor 8:15 he that had *g* little had no lack
Rev 14:19 *g* the vine of the earth, and cast
Rev 16:16 he *g* them together into a place
Rev 19:19 *g* together to make war against

**GATHERETH**

Num 19:10 he that *g* the ashes of the heifer
Ps 33:7 He *g* the waters of the sea
Ps 41:6 his heart *g* iniquity to itself
Ps 147:2 he *g* together the outcasts of
Prov 6:8 *g* her food in the harvest
Prov 10:5 He that *g* in summer is a wise son
Prov 13:11 but he that *g* by labour shall
Is 10:14 as one *g* eggs that are left, have
Is 17:5 as when the harvestman *g* the corn
Is 17:5 it shall be as he that *g* ears in
Is 56:8 The Lord GOD which *g* the outcasts
Nah 3:18 the mountains, and no man *g* them
Hab 2:5 but *g* unto him all nations, and
Mt 12:30 he that *g* not with me scattereth
Mt 23:37 even as a hen *g* her chickens
Lk 11:23 he that *g* not with me scattereth
Jn 4:36 *g* fruit unto life eternal

**GATHERING**

Gen 1:10 the *g* together of the waters
Gen 49:10 him shall the *g* of the people be
Num 15:33 they that found him *g* sticks
1Kin 17:10 widow woman was there *g* of sticks
1Kin 17:12 I am *g* two sticks, that I may go
2Chr 20:25 were three days in *g* of the spoil
Is 32:10 shall fail, the *g* shall not come
Is 33:4 like the *g* of the caterpiller
Mt 25:24 *g* where thou hast not strawed
Acts 16:10 assuredly *g* that the Lord had
2Th 2:1 by our *g* together unto him,

**GATH-HEPHER** *(gath-he'-fer)* See GITTAH-HEPHER. *A town in Zebulun.*

2Kin 14:25 the prophet, which was of G

**GATH-RIMMON** *(gath-rim'-mon)*

*1. A Levitical town in Dan.*
Josh 19:45 And Jehud, and Bene-berak, and G
*2. A Levitical town in Manasseh.*
Josh 21:24 her suburbs, G with her suburbs
Josh 21:25 suburbs, and G with her suburbs
1Chr 6:69 suburbs, and G with her suburbs

**GAZA** *(ga'-zah)* See AZZAH, GAZITES.

*1. A royal Philistine city.*
Gen 10:19 as thou comest to Gerar, unto G
Josh 10:41 from Kadesh-barnea even unto G
Josh 11:22 only in G, in Gath, and in Ashdod,
Josh 15:47 G with her towns and her villages,
Judg 1:18 Also Judah took G with the coast
Judg 16:1 Then went Samson to G, and saw
Judg 16:21 eyes, and brought him down to G
1Sa 6:17 for Ashdod one, for G one
2Kin 18:8 the Philistines, even unto G
Jer 47:1 before that Pharaoh smote G
Jer 47:5 Baldness is come upon G
Amos 1:6 For three transgressions of G
Amos 1:7 will send a fire on the wall of G
Zeph 2:4 For G shall be forsaken, and
Zec 9:5 G also shall see it, and be very
Zec 9:5 and the king shall perish from G
Acts 8:26 goeth down from Jerusalem unto G
*2. A city in Ephraim.*
Judg 6:4 the earth, till thou come unto G
1Chr 7:28 also and the towns thereof, unto G

**GAZATHITES** *(ga'-zath-ites)* See GAZITES. *Inhabitants of Gaza.*
Josh 13:3 the G, and the Ashdothites, the

**GAZER** *(ga'-zur)* See GEZER. *A Canaanite city.*
2Sa 5:25 from Geba until thou come to G
1Chr 14:16 Philistines from Gibeon even to G

**GAZEZ** *(ga'-zez)* *A son of Caleb.*
1Chr 2:46 bare Haran, and Moza, and G
1Chr 2:46 and Haran begat G

**GAZITES** *(ga'-zites)* See GAZATHITES. *Inhabitants of Gaza.*
Judg 16:2 And it was told the G, saying,

**GAZZAM** *(gaz'-zam)* *A family of exiles.*
Ezr 2:48 of Nekoda, the children of G
Neh 7:51 The children of G, the children

**GEBA** *(ghe'-bah)* See GABA, GIBEAH, GIBEON. *A Levitical city in Benjamin.*
Josh 21:17 her suburbs, G with her suburbs,
1Sa 13:3 of the Philistines that was in G
2Sa 5:25 from G until thou come to Gazer
1Kin 15:22 Asa built with them G of Benjamin
2Kin 23:8 from G to Beer-sheba, and brake
1Chr 6:60 G with her suburbs, and Alemeth
1Chr 8:6 fathers of the inhabitants of G
2Chr 16:6 and he built therewith G and Mizpah
Neh 11:31 Benjamin from G dwelt at Michmash
Neh 12:29 Gilgal, and out of the fields of G
Is 10:29 have taken up their lodging at G
Zec 14:10 G to Rimmon south of Jerusalem

**GEBAL** *(ghe'-bal)* See GIBLITES.
*1. An Edomite territory.*
Ps 83:7 G, and Ammon, and Amalek
*2. A Phoenician trade city.*
Eze 27:9 The ancients of G and the wise men

**GEBER** See EZION-GEBER.
*1. Father of an officer of Solomon.*
1Kin 4:13 The son of G, in Ramoth-gilead
*2. The son of Uri.*
1Kin 4:19 G the son of Uri was in the

**GEBIM** *(ghe'-bim)* *A city in Benjamin.*
Is 10:31 the inhabitants of G gather

**GEDALIAH** *(ghed-a-li'-ah)*
*1. Son of Ahikam.*
2Kin 25:22 them he made G the son of Ahikam
2Kin 25:23 of Babylon had made G governor
2Kin 25:23 there came to G to Mizpah
2Kin 25:24 G sware to them, and to their men,
2Kin 25:25 and ten men with him, and smote G
Jer 39:14 committed him unto G the son of
Jer 40:5 Go back also to G the son of
Jer 40:6 Then went Jeremiah unto G the son
Jer 40:7 the king of Babylon had made G
Jer 40:8 Then they came to G to Mizpah
Jer 40:9 G the son of Ahikam the son of
Jer 40:11 that he had set over them G the
Jer 40:12 came to the land of Judah, to G
Jer 40:13 the fields, came to G to Mizpah,
Jer 40:14 But G the son of Ahikam believed
Jer 40:15 spake to G in Mizpah secretly
Jer 40:16 But G the son of Ahikam said unto
Jer 41:1 came unto G the son of Ahikam to
Jer 41:2 smote G the son of Ahikam the son
Jer 41:3 that were with him, even with G
Jer 41:4 second day after he had slain G
Jer 41:6 Come to G the son of Ahikam
Jer 41:9 whom he had slain because of G
Jer 41:10 committed to G the son of Ahikam
Jer 41:16 he had slain G the son of Ahikam
Jer 41:18 had slain G the son of Ahikam
Jer 43:6 of the guard had left with G the
*2. A son of Jeduthun.*
1Chr 25:3 G, and Zeri, and Jeshaiah,
1Chr 25:9 the second to G, who with his
*3. Priest who married a foreigner.*
Ezr 10:18 and Eliezer, and Jarib, and G
*4. Grandfather of Zephaniah.*
Zeph 1:1 the son of Cushi, the son of G
*5. A prince who had Jeremiah imprisoned.*
Jer 38:1 G the son of Pashur, and Jucal the

**GEDEON** *(ghed'-e-on)* See GIDEON. *Greek form of Gideon.*
Heb 11:32 time would fail me to tell of G

**GEDER** *(ghe'-dur)* See BETH-GADER, GEDERITE, GEDOR. *A Canaanite city.*
Josh 12:13 the king of G, one

**GEDERAH** *(ghed'-e-rah)* See GEDERATHITE. *A city in Judah.*
Josh 15:36 And Sharaim, and Adithaim, and G

**GEDERATHITE** *(ghed'-e-rath-ite)* *An inhabitant of Gederah.*
1Chr 12:4 and Johanan, and Josabad the G

**GEDERITE** *(ghed'-e-rite)* *An inhabitant of Geder.*
1Chr 27:28 low plains was Baal-hanan the G

**GEDEROTH** *(ghed'-e-roth)* *A town in Judah.*
Josh 15:41 And G, Beth-dagon, and Naamah, and
2Chr 28:18 Beth-shemesh, and Ajalon, and G

**GEDEROTHAIM** *(ghed-e-ro-tha'-im)* *A town in Judah.*
Josh 15:36 and Adithaim, and Gederah, and G

**GEDOR** *(ghe'-dor)* See GEDER.
*1. A city in Judah.*
Josh 15:58 Halhul, Beth-zur, and G,
*2. Hometown of Jeroham.*
1Chr 12:7 the sons of Jeroham of G
*3. Son of Jehiel.*
1Chr 8:31 And G, and Ahio, and Zacher
1Chr 9:37 And G, and Ahio, and Zechariah, and
*4. A descendant of Judah.*
1Chr 4:4 And Penuel the father of G
1Chr 4:18 bare Jered the father of G
*5. A place in Judah.*
1Chr 4:39 And they went to the entrance of G

**GEHAZI** *(ghe-ha'-zi)* *A servant of Elijah.*
2Kin 4:12 he said to G his servant, Call
2Kin 4:14 G answered, Verily she hath no
2Kin 4:25 that he said to G his servant
2Kin 4:27 but G came near to thrust her
2Kin 4:29 Then he said to G, Gird up thy
2Kin 4:31 G passed on before them, and laid
2Kin 4:36 And he called G, and said, Call
2Kin 5:20 But G, the servant of Elisha the
2Kin 5:21 So G followed after Naaman
2Kin 5:25 unto him, Whence comest thou, G
2Kin 8:4 the king talked with G the
2Kin 8:5 G said, My lord, O king, this is

**GELILOTH** *(ghel'-il-oth)* *Place on boundary of Benjamin and Judah.*
Josh 18:17 and went forth toward G, which is

**GEMALLI** *(ghe-mal'-li)* *One of the twelve spies.*
Num 13:12 tribe of Dan, Ammiel the son of G

**GEMARIAH** *(ghem-a-ri'-ah)*
*1. Son of Shaphan.*
Jer 36:10 in the chamber of G the son of
Jer 36:11 When Michaiah the son of G
Jer 36:12 G the son of Shaphan, and Zedekiah
Jer 36:25 G had made intercession to the
*2. Son of Hilkiah.*
Jer 29:3 G the son of Hilkiah, (whom

**GENEALOGIES**
1Chr 5:17 All these were reckoned by *g* in
1Chr 7:5 in all by their *g* fourscore
1Chr 7:7 were reckoned by their *g* twenty
1Chr 9:1 So all Israel were reckoned by *g*
2Chr 12:15 and of Iddo the seer concerning *g*
2Chr 31:19 reckoned by *g* among the Levites
1Ti 1:4 give heed to fables and endless *g*
Titus 3:9 But avoid foolish questions, and *g*

**GENEALOGY**
1Chr 4:33 their habitations, and their *g*
1Chr 5:1 the *g* is not to be reckoned after
1Chr 5:7 when the *g* of their generations
1Chr 7:9 of them, after their *g* by their
1Chr 7:40 the number throughout the *g* of
1Chr 9:22 by their *g* in their villages
2Chr 31:16 Beside their *g* of males, from
2Chr 31:17 Both to the *g* of the priests by
2Chr 31:18 to the *g* of all their little ones
Ezr 2:62 those that were reckoned by *g*
Ezr 8:1 this is the *g* of them that went
Ezr 8:3 by *g* of the males an hundred
Neh 7:5 that they might be reckoned by *g*
Neh 7:5 I found a register of the *g* of
Neh 7:64 those that were reckoned by *g*

**GENERATION**
Gen 7:1 righteous before me in this *g*
Gen 15:16 But in the fourth *g* they shall
Gen 50:23 Ephraim's children of the third *g*
Ex 1:6 all his brethren, and all that *g*
Ex 17:16 with Amalek from *g* to *g*
Ex 20:5 fourth *g* of them that hate me
Ex 34:7 unto the third and to the fourth *g*
Num 14:18 unto the third and fourth *g*
Num 32:13 forty years, until all the *g*
Deut 1:35 of this evil *g* see that good land
Deut 2:14 until all the *g* of the men of war
Deut 5:9 fourth *g* of them that hate me,
Deut 23:2 even to his tenth *g* shall he not
Deut 23:3 even to their tenth *g* shall they
Deut 23:8 of the LORD in their third *g*
Deut 29:22 So that the *g* to come of your
Deut 32:5 they are a perverse and crooked *g*
Deut 32:20 for they are a very froward *g*
Judg 2:10 also all that *g* were gathered
Judg 2:10 there arose another *g* after them
2Kin 10:30 *g* shall sit on the throne of
2Kin 15:12 of Israel unto the fourth *g*
Est 9:28 and kept throughout every *g*
Ps 12:7 them from this *g* for ever
Ps 14:5 God is in the *g* of the righteous
Ps 22:30 be accounted to the Lord for a *g*
Ps 24:6 This is the *g* of them that seek
Ps 48:13 ye may tell it to the *g* following
Ps 49:19 shall go to the *g* of his fathers
Ps 71:18 shewed thy strength unto this *g*
Ps 73:15 against the *g* of thy children
Ps 78:4 shewing to the *g* to come the
Ps 78:6 That the *g* to come might know
Ps 78:8 a stubborn and rebellious *g*
Ps 78:8 a *g* that set not their heart
Ps 95:10 long was I grieved with this *g*
Ps 102:18 be written for the *g* to come
Ps 109:13 in the *g* following let their name
Ps 112:2 the *g* of the upright shall be
Ps 145:4 One *g* shall praise thy works to
Prov 27:24 doth the crown endure to every *g*
Prov 30:11 There is a *g* that curseth their
Prov 30:12 There is a *g* that are pure in
Prov 30:13 There is a *g*, O how lofty are
Prov 30:14 There is a *g*, whose teeth are as
Eccl 1:4 passeth away, and another *g* cometh
Is 13:20 be dwelt in from *g* to *g*
Is 34:10 from *g* to *g* it shall lie
Is 34:17 from *g* to *g* shall they
Is 51:8 my salvation from *g* to *g*
Is 53:8 and who shall declare his *g*
Jer 2:31 O *g*, see ye the word of the LORD
Jer 7:29 and forsaken the *g* of his wrath
Jer 50:39 be dwelt in from *g* to *g*
Lam 5:19 thy throne from *g* to *g*
Dan 4:3 dominion is from *g* to *g*
Dan 4:34 kingdom is from *g* to *g*
Joel 1:3 and their children another *g*
Joel 3:20 and Jerusalem from *g* to *g*
Mt 1:1 The book of the *g* of Jesus Christ
Mt 3:7 O *g* of vipers, who hath warned
Mt 11:16 whereunto shall I liken this *g*
Mt 12:34 O *g* of vipers, how can ye, being
Mt 12:39 adulterous *g* seeketh after a sign
Mt 12:41 rise in judgment with this *g*
Mt 12:42 up in the judgment with this *g*
Mt 12:45 it be also unto this wicked *g*
Mt 16:4 adulterous *g* seeketh after a sign
Mt 17:17 said, O faithless and perverse *g*
Mt 23:33 ye *g* of vipers, how can ye escape
Mt 23:36 things shall come upon this *g*
Mt 24:34 This *g* shall not pass, till all
Mk 8:12 Why doth this *g* seek after a sign
Mk 8:12 no sign be given unto this *g*
Mk 8:38 in this adulterous and sinful *g*
Mk 9:19 him, and saith, O faithless *g*
Mk 13:30 that this *g* shall not pass, till
Lk 1:50 fear him from *g* to *g*
Lk 3:7 O *g* of vipers, who hath warned
Lk 7:31 shall I liken the men of this *g*
Lk 9:41 said, O faithless and perverse *g*
Lk 11:29 began to say, This is an evil *g*
Lk 11:30 also the Son of man be to this *g*
Lk 11:31 judgment with the men of this *g*
Lk 11:32 up in the judgment with this *g*
Lk 11:50 world, may be required of this *g*
Lk 11:51 It shall be required of this *g*
Lk 16:8 *g* wiser than the children of
Lk 17:25 things, and be rejected of this *g*
Lk 21:32 This *g* shall not pass away, till
Acts 2:40 yourselves from this untoward *g*
Acts 8:33 and who shall declare his *g*
Acts 13:36 his own *g* by the will of God

Heb 3:10 I was grieved with that *g*
1Pet 2:9 But ye are a chosen *g*, a royal

## GENERATIONS

Gen 2:4 These are the *g* of the heavens and
Gen 5:1 This is the book of the *g* of Adam
Gen 6:9 These are the *g* of Noah
Gen 6:9 a just man and perfect in his *g*
Gen 9:12 that is with you, for perpetual *g*
Gen 10:1 Now these are the *g* of the sons
Gen 10:32 the sons of Noah, after their *g*
Gen 11:10 These are the *g* of Shem
Gen 11:27 Now these are the *g* of Terah
Gen 17:7 *g* for an everlasting covenant
Gen 17:9 and thy seed after thee in their *g*
Gen 17:12 you, every man child in your *g*
Gen 25:12 Now these are the *g* of Ishmael
Gen 25:13 their names, according to their *g*
Gen 25:19 And these are the *g* of Isaac
Gen 36:1 Now these are the *g* of Esau
Gen 36:9 these are the *g* of Esau the
Gen 37:2 These are the *g* of Jacob
Ex 3:15 and this is my memorial unto all *g*
Ex 6:16 sons of Levi according to their *g*
Ex 6:19 of Levi according to their *g*
Ex 12:14 to the LORD throughout your *g*
Ex 12:17 your *g* by an ordinance for ever
Ex 12:42 the children of Israel in their *g*
Ex 16:32 omer of it to be kept for your *g*
Ex 16:33 the LORD, to be kept for your *g*
Ex 27:21 *g* on the behalf of the children
Ex 29:42 *g* at the door of the tabernacle
Ex 30:8 before the LORD throughout your *g*
Ex 30:10 upon it throughout your *g*
Ex 30:21 and to his seed throughout their *g*
Ex 30:31 oil unto me throughout your *g*
Ex 31:13 me and you throughout your *g*
Ex 31:16 the sabbath throughout their *g*
Ex 40:15 priesthood throughout their *g*
Lev 3:17 *g* throughout all your dwellings
Lev 6:18 be a statute for ever in your *g*
Lev 7:36 for ever throughout their *g*
Lev 10:9 for ever throughout your *g*
Lev 17:7 ever unto them throughout their *g*
Lev 21:17 in their *g* that hath any blemish
Lev 22:3 be of all your seed among your *g*
Lev 23:14 your *g* in all your dwellings
Lev 23:21 your dwellings throughout your *g*
Lev 23:31 your *g* in all your dwellings
Lev 23:41 be a statute for ever in your *g*
Lev 23:43 That your *g* may know that I made
Lev 24:3 be a statute for ever in your *g*
Lev 25:30 that bought it throughout his *g*
Num 1:20 Israel's eldest son, by their *g*
Num 1:22 children of Simeon, by their *g*
Num 1:24 the children of Gad, by their *g*
Num 1:26 the children of Judah, by their *g*
Num 1:28 children of Issachar, by their *g*
Num 1:30 children of Zebulun, by their *g*
Num 1:32 children of Ephraim, by their *g*
Num 1:34 children of Manasseh, by their *g*
Num 1:36 children of Benjamin, by their *g*
Num 1:38 the children of Dan, by their *g*
Num 1:40 the children of Asher, by their *g*
Num 1:42 of Naphtali, throughout their *g*
Num 3:1 These also are the *g* of Aaron
Num 10:8 for ever throughout your *g*
Num 15:14 whosoever be among you in your *g*
Num 15:15 an ordinance for ever in your *g*
Num 15:21 LORD an heave offering in your *g*
Num 15:23 and henceforward among your *g*
Num 15:38 their garments throughout their *g*
Num 18:23 for ever throughout your *g*
Num 35:29 your *g* in all your dwellings
Deut 7:9 his commandments to a thousand *g*
Deut 32:7 old, consider the years of many *g*
Josh 22:27 our *g* after us, that we might do
Josh 22:28 to us or to our *g* in time to come
Judg 3:2 Only that the *g* of the children
Ruth 4:18 Now these are the *g* of Pharez
1Chr 1:29 These are their *g*
1Chr 5:7 genealogy of their *g* was reckoned
1Chr 7:2 valiant men of might in their *g*
1Chr 7:4 And with them, by their *g*, after
1Chr 7:9 after their genealogy by their *g*
1Chr 8:28 heads of the fathers, by their *g*
1Chr 9:9 brethren, according to their *g*
1Chr 9:34 were chief throughout their *g*
1Chr 16:15 he commanded to a thousand *g*
1Chr 26:31 according to the *g* of his fathers
Job 42:16 and his sons' sons, even four *g*
Ps 33:11 thoughts of his heart to all *g*
Ps 45:17 name to be remembered in all *g*
Ps 49:11 and their dwelling places to all *g*
Ps 61:6 and his years as many *g*
Ps 72:5 and moon endure, throughout all *g*
Ps 79:13 shew forth thy praise to all *g*
Ps 85:5 draw out thine anger to all *g*
Ps 89:1 known thy faithfulness to all *g*
Ps 89:4 and build up thy throne to all *g*
Ps 90:1 been our dwelling place in all *g*
Ps 100:5 and his truth endureth to all *g*
Ps 102:12 and thy remembrance unto all *g*
Ps 102:24 thy years are throughout all *g*
Ps 105:8 he commanded to a thousand *g*
Ps 106:31 unto all *g* for evermore
Ps 119:90 Thy faithfulness is unto all *g*
Ps 135:13 O LORD, throughout all *g*
Ps 145:13 endureth throughout all *g*
Ps 146:10 even thy God, O Zion, unto all *g*
Is 41:4 calling the *g* from the beginning
Is 51:9 the ancient days, in the *g* of old
Is 58:12 up the foundations of many *g*
Is 60:15 excellency, a joy of many *g*
Is 61:4 cities, the desolations of many *g*
Joel 2:2 it, even to the years of many *g*
Mt 1:17 So all the *g* from Abraham to
Mt 1:17 Abraham to David are fourteen *g*
Mt 1:17 away into Babylon are fourteen *g*
Mt 1:17 unto Christ are fourteen *g*
Lk 1:48 from henceforth all *g* shall call
Col 1:26 hath been hid from ages and from *g*

## GENNESARET *(ghen-nes'-a-ret)* See CHINNERETH. *Same as Galilee.*

Mt 14:34 they came into the land of *G*
Mk 6:53 they came into the land of *G*
Lk 5:1 of God, he stood by the lake of *G*

## GENTILE *(jen'-tile)* See GENTILES. *A non-Jew.*

Rom 2:9 the Jew first, and also of the *G*
Rom 2:10 the Jew first, and also to the *G*

## GENTILES

Gen 10:5 of the *G* divided in their lands
Judg 4:2 which dwelt in Harosheth of the *G*
Judg 4:13 from Harosheth of the *G* unto the
Judg 4:16 the host, unto Harosheth of the *G*
Is 11:10 to it shall the *G* seek
Is 42:1 bring forth judgment to the *G*
Is 42:6 the people, for a light of the *G*
Is 49:6 give thee for a light to the *G*
Is 49:22 I will lift up mine hand to the *G*
Is 54:3 and thy seed shall inherit the *G*
Is 60:3 the *G* shall come to thy light, and
Is 60:5 the forces of the *G* shall come
Is 60:11 unto thee the forces of the *G*
Is 60:16 shalt also suck the milk of the *G*
Is 61:6 ye shall eat the riches of the *G*
Is 61:9 seed shall be known among the *G*
Is 62:2 the *G* shall see thy righteousness
Is 66:12 the glory of the *G* like a flowing
Is 66:19 declare my glory among the *G*
Jer 4:7 destroyer of the *G* is on his way
Jer 14:22 of the *G* that can cause rain
Jer 16:19 the *G* shall come unto thee from
Jer 46:1 the prophet against the *G*
Lam 2:9 and her princes are among the *G*
Eze 4:13 their defiled bread among the *G*
Hos 8:8 the *G* as a vessel wherein is no
Joel 3:9 Proclaim ye this among the *G*
Mic 5:8 of Jacob shall be among the *G* in
Zec 1:21 to cast out the horns of the *G*
Mal 1:11 name shall be great among the *G*
Mt 4:15 beyond Jordan, Galilee of the *G*
Mt 6:32 all these things do the *G* seek
Mt 10:5 Go not into the way of the *G*
Mt 10:18 a testimony against them and the *G*
Mt 12:18 he shall shew judgment to the *G*
Mt 12:21 And in his name shall the *G* trust
Mt 20:19 deliver him to the *G* to mock
Mt 20:25 the *G* exercise dominion over them
Mk 10:33 and shall deliver him to the *G*
Mk 10:42 the *G* exercise lordship over them
Lk 2:32 A light to lighten the *G*, and the
Lk 18:32 he shall be delivered unto the *G*
Lk 21:24 shall be trodden down of the *G*
Lk 21:24 the times of the *G* be fulfilled
Lk 22:25 The kings of the *G* exercise
Jn 7:35 go unto the dispersed among the *G*
Jn 7:35 the *G*, and teach the *G*
Acts 4:27 and Pontius Pilate, with the *G*
Acts 7:45 into the possession of the *G*
Acts 9:15 me, to bear my name before the *G*
Acts 10:45 because that on the *G* also was
Acts 11:1 *G* had also received the word of
Acts 11:18 Then hath God also to the *G*
Acts 13:42 the *G* besought that these words
Acts 13:46 life, lo, we turn to the *G*
Acts 13:47 set thee to be a light of the *G*
Acts 13:48 when the *G* heard this, they were
Acts 14:2 unbelieving Jews stirred up the *G*
Acts 14:5 was an assault made both of the *G*
Acts 14:27 the door of faith unto the *G*
Acts 15:3 declaring the conversion of the *G*
Acts 15:7 that the *G* by my mouth should
Acts 15:12 had wrought among the *G* by them
Acts 15:14 God at the first did visit the *G*
Acts 15:17 seek after the Lord, and all the *G*
Acts 15:19 among the *G* are turned to God
Acts 15:23 which are of the *G* in Antioch
Acts 18:6 henceforth I will go unto the *G*
Acts 21:11 him into the hands of the *G*
Acts 21:19 among the *G* by his ministry
Acts 21:21 are among the *G* to forsake Moses
Acts 21:25 As touching the *G* which believe
Acts 22:21 send thee far hence unto the *G*
Acts 26:17 from the people, and from the *G*
Acts 26:20 of Judaea, and then to the *G*
Acts 26:23 unto the people, and to the *G*
Acts 28:28 of God is sent unto the *G*
Rom 1:13 you also, even as among other *G*
Rom 2:14 For when the *G*, which have not
Rom 2:24 among the *G* through you, as it is
Rom 3:9 have before proved both Jews and *G*
Rom 3:29 is he not also of the *G*
Rom 3:29 Yes, of the *G* also
Rom 9:24 the Jews only, but also of the *G*
Rom 9:30 That the *G*, which followed not
Rom 11:11 fall salvation is come unto the *G*
Rom 11:12 of them the riches of the *G*
Rom 11:13 For I speak to you *G*, inasmuch as
Rom 11:13 as I am the apostle of the *G*
Rom 11:25 the fulness of the *G* be come in
Rom 15:9 that the *G* might glorify God for
Rom 15:9 will confess to thee among the *G*
Rom 15:10 And again he saith, Rejoice, ye *G*
Rom 15:11 again, Praise the Lord, all ye *G*
Rom 15:12 shall rise to reign over the *G*
Rom 15:12 in him shall the *G* trust
Rom 15:16 minister of Jesus Christ to the *G*
Rom 15:16 up of the *G* might be acceptable
Rom 15:18 by me, to make the *G* obedient
Rom 15:27 For if the *G* have been made
Rom 16:4 also all the churches of the *G*
1Cor 5:1 not so much as named among the *G*
1Cor 10:20 the things which the *G* sacrifice
1Cor 10:32 neither to the Jews, nor to the *G*
1Cor 12:2 Ye know that ye were *G*, carried
1Cor 12:13 one body, whether we be Jews or *G*
Gal 2:2 gospel which I preach among the *G*
Gal 2:8 was mighty in me toward the *G*
Gal 2:12 from James, he did eat with the *G*
Gal 2:14 Jew, livest after the manner of *G*
Gal 2:14 thou the *G* to live as do the Jews
Gal 2:15 nature, and not sinners of the *G*
Gal 3:14 on the *G* through Jesus Christ
Eph 2:11 being in time past *G* in the flesh
Eph 3:1 of Jesus Christ for you *G*
Eph 3:6 That the *G* should be fellowheirs,
Eph 3:8 the *G* the unsearchable riches of
Eph 4:17 walk not as other *G* walk, in the
Col 1:27 glory of this mystery among the *G*
1Th 2:16 to the *G* that they might be saved
1Th 4:5 even as the *G* which know not God
1Ti 2:7 a teacher of the *G* in faith
1Ti 3:16 of angels, preached unto the *G*
2Ti 1:11 an apostle, and a teacher of the *G*
2Ti 4:17 and that all the *G* might hear
1Pet 2:12 conversation honest among the *G*
1Pet 4:3 to have wrought the will of the *G*
3Jn 7 forth, taking nothing of the *G*
Rev 11:2 for it is given unto the *G*

## GENTLE

1Th 2:7 But we were *g* among you, even as
2Ti 2:24 but be *g* unto all men, apt to
Titus 3:2 no man, to be no brawlers, but *g*
Jas 3:17 is first pure, then peaceable, *g*
1Pet 2:18 not only to the good and *g*

**GENTLENESS**
2Sa 22:36 and thy *g* hath made me great
Ps 18:35 up, and thy *g* hath made me great
2Cor 10:1 *g* of Christ, who in presence am
Gal 5:22 joy, peace, longsuffering, *g*

**GENUBATH** *(ghen'-u-bath) Son of Hadad.*
1Kin 11:20 of Tahpenes bare him G his son
1Kin 11:20 G was in Pharaoh's household

**GERA** *(ghe'-rah) A son of Bela.*
Gen 46:21 Belah, and Becher, and Ashbel, G
Judg 3:15 up a deliverer, Ehud the son of G
2Sa 16:5 name was Shimei, the son of G
2Sa 19:16 And Shimei the son of G, a
2Sa 19:18 Shimei the son of G fell down
1Kin 2:8 with thee Shimei the son of G
1Chr 8:3 sons of Bela were, Addar, and G
1Chr 8:5 And G, and Shephuphan, and Huram
1Chr 8:7 And Naaman, and Ahiah, and G

**GERAHS**
Ex 30:13 (a shekel is twenty *g*
Lev 27:25 twenty *g* shall be the shekel
Num 3:47 (the shekel is twenty *g*
Num 18:16 the sanctuary, which is twenty *g*
Eze 45:12 And the shekel shall be twenty *g*

**GERAR** *(ghe'-rar) A city in Gaza.*
Gen 10:19 from Sidon, as thou comest to G
Gen 20:1 Kadesh and Shur, and sojourned in G
Gen 20:2 and Abimelech king of G sent
Gen 26:1 king of the Philistines unto G
Gen 26:6 And Isaac dwelt in G
Gen 26:17 his tent in the valley of G
Gen 26:20 the herdmen of G did strive with
Gen 26:26 Then Abimelech went to him from G
2Chr 14:13 were with him pursued them unto G
2Chr 14:14 all the cities round about G

**GERGESENES** *(ghur'-ghes-enes') Inhabitants of an area near Sea of Galilee.*
Mt 8:28 side into the country of the G

**GERIZIM** *(gher'-iz-im) A mountain in central Palestine.*
Deut 11:29 put the blessing upon mount G
Deut 27:12 upon mount G to bless the people
Josh 8:33 half of them over against mount G
Judg 9:7 and stood in the top of mount G

**GERSHOM** *(ghur'-shom)* See GERSHON.
*1. Firstborn son of Moses.*
Ex 2:22 a son, and he called his name G
Ex 18:3 which the name of the one was G
1Chr 23:15 The sons of Moses were, G
1Chr 23:16 Of the sons of G, Shebuel was the
1Chr 26:24 And Shebuel the son of G, the son
*2. A son of Levi.*
1Chr 6:16 G, Kohath, and Merari
1Chr 6:17 be the names of the sons of G
1Chr 6:20 Of G
1Chr 6:43 The son of Jahath, the son of G
1Chr 6:62 to the sons of G throughout their
1Chr 6:71 Unto the sons of G were given out
1Chr 15:7 Of the sons of G
*3. A descendant of Phinehas.*
Ezr 8:2 of the sons of Phinehas; G
*4. Father of Jonathan.*
Judg 18:30 and Jonathan, the son of G

**GERSHON** *(ghur'-shon)* See GERSHOM, GERSHONITE. *A form of Gershom 2.*
Gen 46:11 G, Kohath, and Merari
Ex 6:16 G, and Kohath, and Merari
Ex 6:17 The sons of G
Num 3:17 G, and Kohath, and Merari
Num 3:18 the sons of G by their families
Num 3:21 Of G was the family of the
Num 3:25 of G in the tabernacle of the
Num 4:22 also the sum of the sons of G
Num 4:28 of G in the tabernacle of the
Num 4:38 were numbered of the sons of G
Num 4:41 of the families of the sons of G
Num 7:7 oxen he gave unto the sons of G
Num 10:17 and the sons of G and the sons of
Num 26:57 of G, the family of the
Josh 21:6 the children of G had by lot out
Josh 21:27 And unto the children of G
1Chr 6:1 G, Kohath, and Merari
1Chr 23:6 among the sons of Levi, namely, G

**GERSHONITE** *(ghur'-shon-ite)* See GERSHONITES. *Descendant of Gershom 2.*
1Chr 26:21 the sons of the G Laadan, chief
1Chr 26:21 fathers, even of Laadan the G
1Chr 29:8 LORD, by the hand of Jehiel the G

**GERSHONITES** *(ghur'-shon-ites)*
Num 3:21 these are the families of the G
Num 3:23 The families of the G shall pitch
Num 3:24 G shall be Eliasaph the son of
Num 4:24 service of the families of the G
Num 4:27 the service of the sons of the G
Num 26:57 of Gershon, the family of the G
Josh 21:33 All the cities of the G according
1Chr 23:7 Of the G were, Laadan, and Shimei
2Chr 29:12 and of the G

**GESHAM** *(ghe'-sham) A son of Jahdai.*
1Chr 2:47 Regem, and Jotham, and G, and Pelet,

**GESHEM** *(ghe'-shem)* See GASHMU. *An opponent of Nehemiah.*
Neh 2:19 G the Arabian, heard it, they
Neh 6:1 G the Arabian, and the rest of our
Neh 6:2 G sent unto me, saying, Come, let

**GESHUR** *(ghe'-shur)* See GESHURITES. *A kingdom in Bashan.*
2Sa 3:3 the daughter of Talmai king of G
2Sa 13:37 the son of Ammihud, king of G
2Sa 13:38 So Absalom fled, and went to G
2Sa 14:23 So Joab arose and went to G
2Sa 14:32 say, Wherefore am I come from G
2Sa 15:8 a vow while I abode at G in Syria
1Chr 2:23 And he took G, and Aram, with the
1Chr 3:2 the daughter of Talmai king of G

**GESHURI** *(ghesh'-u-ri)* See GESHURITES.
*1. Inhabitants of Geshur.*
Deut 3:14 of Argob unto the coasts of G
*2. A people dwelling between Arabia and Philistia.*
Josh 13:2 of the Philistines, and all G

**GESHURITES** *(ghesh'-u-rites)*
*1. Inhabitants of Geshur.*
Josh 12:5 Bashan, unto the border of the G
Josh 13:11 And Gilead, and the border of the G
Josh 13:13 of Israel expelled not the G
Josh 13:13 but the G and the Maachathites
*2. Same as Geshuri 2.*
1Sa 27:8 his men went up, and invaded the G

**GET**
Gen 12:1 G thee out of thy country, and
Gen 19:14 said, Up, *g* you out of this place
Gen 22:2 *g* thee into the land of Moriah
Gen 31:13 *g* thee out from this land, and
Gen 34:4 saying, G me this damsel to wife
Gen 34:10 *g* you possessions therein
Gen 42:2 *g* you down thither, and buy for us
Gen 44:17 *g* you up in peace unto your
Gen 45:17 *g* you unto the land of Canaan
Ex 1:10 so *g* them up out of the land
Ex 5:4 *g* you unto your burdens
Ex 5:11 *g* you straw where ye can find it
Ex 7:15 G thee unto Pharaoh in the
Ex 10:28 G thee from me, take heed to
Ex 11:8 G thee out, and all the people
Ex 12:31 *g* you forth from among my people,
Ex 14:17 I will *g* me honour upon Pharaoh,
Ex 19:24 *g* thee down, and thou shalt come
Ex 32:7 said unto Moses, Go, *g* thee down
Lev 14:21 he be poor, and cannot *g* so much
Lev 14:22 pigeons, such as he is able to *g*
Lev 14:30 young pigeons, such as he can *g*
Lev 14:31 Even such as he is able to *g*
Lev 14:32 whose hand is not able to *g* that
Num 6:21 beside that that his hand shall *g*
Num 13:17 G you up this way southward, and
Num 14:25 *g* you into the wilderness by the
Num 16:24 saying, G you up from about the
Num 16:45 G you up from among this
Num 22:13 of Balak, G you into your land
Num 22:34 thee, I will *g* me back again
Num 27:12 G thee up into this mount Abarim,
Deut 2:13 *g* you over the brook Zered
Deut 3:27 G thee up into the top of Pisgah,
Deut 5:30 G you into your tents again
Deut 8:18 giveth thee power to *g* wealth
Deut 9:12 *g* thee down quickly from hence
Deut 17:8 *g* thee up into the place which
Deut 28:43 shall *g* up above thee very high
Deut 32:49 G thee up into this mountain
Josh 2:16 G you to the mountain, lest the
Josh 7:10 LORD said unto Joshua, G thee up
Josh 17:15 then *g* thee up to the wood
Josh 22:4 *g* you unto your tents, and unto
Judg 7:9 *g* thee down unto the host
Judg 14:2 now therefore *g* her for me to
Judg 14:3 unto his father, G her for me
Judg 19:9 to morrow *g* you early on your way
Ruth 3:3 thee, and *g* thee down to the floor
1Sa 9:13 Now therefore *g* you up
1Sa 15:6 *g* you down from among the
1Sa 20:29 in thine eyes, let me *g* away
1Sa 22:5 *g* thee into the land of Judah
1Sa 23:26 David made haste to *g* away for
1Sa 25:5 G you up to Carmel, and go to
2Sa 20:6 lest he *g* him fenced cities, and
1Kin 1:2 that my lord the king may *g* heat
1Kin 1:13 *g* thee in unto king David, and say
1Kin 2:26 G thee to Anathoth, unto thine
1Kin 12:18 speed to *g* him up to his chariot
1Kin 14:2 and *g* thee to Shiloh
1Kin 14:12 *g* thee to thine own house
1Kin 17:3 G thee hence, and turn thee
1Kin 17:9 *g* thee to Zarephath, which
1Kin 18:41 Ahab, G thee up, eat and drink
1Kin 18:44 *g* thee down, that the rain stop
2Kin 3:13 *g* thee to the prophets of thy
2Kin 7:12 them alive, and *g* into the city
2Chr 10:18 speed to *g* him up to his chariot
Neh 9:10 So didst thou *g* thee a name
Ps 119:104 thy precepts I *g* understanding
Prov 4:5 G wisdom, *g* understanding
Prov 4:7 therefore *g* wisdom
Prov 4:7 all thy getting *g* understanding
Prov 6:33 A wound and dishonour shall he *g*
Prov 16:16 is it to *g* wisdom than gold
Prov 16:16 to *g* understanding rather to be
Prov 17:16 in the hand of a fool to *g* wisdom
Prov 22:25 ways, and *g* a snare to thy soul
Eccl 3:6 A time to *g*, and a time to lose
Song 4:6 I will *g* me to the mountain of
Song 7:12 Let us *g* up early to the
Is 22:15 *g* thee unto this treasurer, even
Is 30:11 G you out of the way, turn aside
Is 30:22 shalt say unto it, G thee hence
Is 40:9 *g* thee up into the high mountain
Is 47:5 *g* thee into darkness, O daughter
Jer 5:5 I will *g* me unto the great men,
Jer 13:1 *g* thee a linen girdle, and put it
Jer 19:1 *g* a potter's earthen bottle, and
Jer 46:4 *g* up, ye horsemen, and stand forth
Jer 48:9 Moab, that it may flee and *g* away
Jer 49:30 *g* you far off, dwell deep, O ye
Jer 49:31 *g* you up unto the wealthy nation,
Lam 3:7 me about, that I cannot *g* out
Eze 3:4 *g* thee unto the house of Israel,
Eze 3:11 *g* thee to them of the captivity,
Eze 11:15 said, G you far from the LORD
Eze 22:27 souls, to *g* dishonest gain
Dan 4:14 let the beasts *g* away from under
Joel 3:13 come, *g* you down
Zeph 3:19 I will *g* them praise and fame in
Zec 6:7 G you hence, walk to and fro
Mt 4:10 unto him, G thee hence, Satan
Mt 14:22 his disciples to *g* into a ship
Mt 16:23 Peter, G thee behind me, Satan
Mk 6:45 his disciples to *g* into the ship
Mk 8:33 saying, G thee behind me, Satan
Lk 4:8 unto him, G thee behind me, Satan
Lk 9:12 about, and lodge, and *g* victuals
Lk 13:31 G thee out, and depart hence
Acts 7:3 G thee out of thy country, and
Acts 10:20 *g* thee down, and go with them,
Acts 22:18 *g* thee quickly out of Jerusalem
Acts 27:43 first into the sea, and *g* to land
2Cor 2:11 Lest Satan should *g* an advantage
Jas 4:13 a year, and buy and sell, and *g* gain

**GETHER** *(ghe'-ther) A son of Aram.*
Gen 10:23 Uz, and Hul, and G, and Mash
1Chr 1:17 Aram, and Uz, and Hul, and G

**GETHSEMANE** *(gheth-sem'-a-ne) A garden near Jerusalem.*
Mt 26:36 with them unto a place called G
Mk 14:32 came to a place which was named G

**GETTETH**
2Sa 5:8 Whosoever *g* up to the gutter, and
Prov 3:13 the man that *g* understanding
Prov 9:7 a scorner *g* to himself shame
Prov 9:7 a wicked man *g* himself a blot

Prov 15:32 heareth reproof *g* understanding
Prov 18:15 heart of the prudent *g* knowledge
Prov 19:8 He that *g* wisdom loveth his own
Jer 17:11 so he that *g* riches, and not by
Jer 48:44 he that *g* up out of the pit shall

**GETTING**
Gen 31:18 had gotten, the cattle of his *g*
Prov 4:7 with all thy *g* get understanding
Prov 21:6 The *g* of treasures by a lying

**GEUEL** *(ghe-u'-el) A son of Machri.*
Num 13:15 tribe of Gad, G the son of Machi

**GEZER** *(ghe'-zur)* See GAZER, GEZRITES. *A Canaanite city.*
Josh 10:33 Then Horam king of G came up to
Josh 12:12 the king of G, one
Josh 16:3 of Beth-horon the nether, and to G
Josh 16:10 the Canaanites that dwelt in G
Josh 21:21 and G with her suburbs,
Judg 1:29 the Canaanites that dwelt in G
Judg 1:29 Canaanites dwelt in G among them
1Kin 9:15 and Hazor, and Megiddo, and G
1Kin 9:16 of Egypt had gone up, and taken G
1Kin 9:17 And Solomon built G, and Beth-horon
1Chr 6:67 they gave also G with her suburbs
1Chr 7:28 Naaran, and westward G
1Chr 20:4 war at G with the Philistines

**GEZRITES** *(ghez'-rites) Inhabitants of Gezer.*
1Sa 27:8 invaded the Geshurites, and the G

**GHOST**
Gen 25:8 Then Abraham gave up the *g*
Gen 25:17 and he gave up the *g* and died
Gen 35:29 And Isaac gave up the *g*, and died,
Gen 49:33 into the bed, and yielded up the *g*
Job 3:11 why did I not give up the *g* when
Job 10:18 Oh that I had given up the *g*
Job 11:20 be as the giving up of the *g*
Job 13:19 my tongue, I shall give up the *g*
Job 14:10 yea, man giveth up the *g*, and
Jer 15:9 she hath given up the *g*
Lam 1:19 elders gave up the *g* in the city
Mt 1:18 found with child of the Holy G
Mt 1:20 conceived in her is of the Holy G
Mt 3:11 shall baptize you with the Holy G
Mt 12:31 G shall not be forgiven unto men
Mt 12:32 speaketh against the Holy G
Mt 27:50 a loud voice, yielded up the *g*
Mt 28:19 and of the Son, and of the Holy G
Mk 1:8 shall baptize you with the Holy G
Mk 3:29 the Holy G hath never forgiveness
Mk 12:36 David himself said by the Holy G
Mk 13:11 not ye that speak, but the Holy G
Mk 15:37 a loud voice, and gave up the *g*
Mk 15:39 he so cried out, and gave up the *g*
Lk 1:15 shall be filled with the Holy G
Lk 1:35 The Holy G shall come upon thee,
Lk 1:41 was filled with the Holy G
Lk 1:67 was filled with the Holy G
Lk 2:25 and the Holy G was upon him
Lk 2:26 revealed unto him by the Holy G
Lk 3:16 shall baptize you with the Holy G
Lk 3:22 the Holy G descended in a bodily
Lk 4:1 the Holy G returned from Jordan
Lk 12:10 Holy G it shall not be forgiven
Lk 12:12 For the Holy G shall teach you in
Lk 23:46 said thus, he gave up the *g*
Jn 1:33 which baptizeth with the Holy G
Jn 7:39 for the Holy G was not yet given
Jn 14:26 Comforter, which is the Holy G
Jn 19:30 bowed his head, and gave up the *g*
Jn 20:22 unto them, Receive ye the Holy G
Acts 1:2 after that he through the Holy G
Acts 1:5 the Holy G not many days hence
Acts 1:8 that the Holy G is come upon you
Acts 1:16 which the Holy G by the mouth of
Acts 2:4 were all filled with the Holy G
Acts 2:33 Father the promise of the Holy G
Acts 2:38 receive the gift of the Holy G
Acts 4:8 Peter, filled with the Holy G
Acts 4:31 were all filled with the Holy G
Acts 5:3 thine heart to lie to the Holy G
Acts 5:5 words fell down, and gave up the *g*
Acts 5:10 at his feet, and yielded up the *g*
Acts 5:32 and so is also the Holy G, whom
Acts 6:3 honest report, full of the Holy G
Acts 6:5 full of faith and of the Holy G
Acts 7:51 ye do always resist the Holy G
Acts 7:55 But he, being full of the Holy G
Acts 8:15 they might receive the Holy G
Acts 8:17 them, and they received the Holy G
Acts 8:18 hands the Holy G was given
Acts 8:19 hands, he may receive the Holy G
Acts 9:17 and be filled with the Holy G
Acts 9:31 and in the comfort of the Holy G
Acts 10:38 Jesus of Nazareth with the Holy G
Acts 10:44 the Holy G fell on all them which
Acts 10:45 poured out the gift of the Holy G
Acts 10:47 received the Holy G as well as we
Acts 11:15 the Holy G fell on them, as on us
Acts 11:16 shall be baptized with the Holy G
Acts 11:24 a good man, and full of the Holy G
Acts 12:23 eaten of worms, and gave up the *g*
Acts 13:2 Lord, and fasted, the Holy G said
Acts 13:4 being sent forth by the Holy G
Acts 13:9 Paul,) filled with the Holy G
Acts 13:52 with joy, and with the Holy G
Acts 15:8 witness, giving them the Holy G
Acts 15:28 For it seemed good to the Holy G
Acts 16:6 Holy G to preach the word in Asia
Acts 19:2 the Holy G since ye believed
Acts 19:2 heard whether there be any Holy G
Acts 19:6 them, the Holy G came on them
Acts 20:23 Save that the Holy G witnesseth
Acts 20:28 Holy G hath made you overseers
Acts 21:11 and said, Thus saith the Holy G
Acts 28:25 Well spake the Holy G by Esaias
Rom 5:5 the Holy G which is given unto us
Rom 9:1 bearing me witness in the Holy G
Rom 14:17 and peace, and joy in the Holy G
Rom 15:13 through the power of the Holy G
Rom 15:16 being sanctified by the Holy G
1Cor 2:13 but which the Holy G teacheth
1Cor 6:19 of the Holy G which is in you
1Cor 12:3 is the Lord, but by the Holy G
2Cor 6:6 by kindness, by the Holy G
2Cor 13:14 and the communion of the Holy G
1Th 1:5 also in power, and in the Holy G
1Th 1:6 with joy of the Holy G
2Ti 1:14 the Holy G which dwelleth in us
Titus 3:5 and renewing of the Holy G
Heb 2:4 miracles, and gifts of the Holy G
Heb 3:7 Wherefore (as the Holy G saith
Heb 6:4 were made partakers of the Holy G
Heb 9:8 The Holy G this signifying, that
Heb 10:15 Whereof the Holy G also is a
1Pet 1:12 the Holy G sent down from heaven
2Pet 1:21 as they were moved by the Holy G
1Jn 5:7 Father, the Word, and the Holy G
Jude 20 holy faith, praying in the Holy G

**GIAH** *(ghi'-ah) A place near the wilderness of Gibeon.*
2Sa 2:24 that lieth before G by the way of

**GIANT**
2Sa 21:16 which was of the sons of the *g*
2Sa 21:18 which was of the sons of the *g*
2Sa 21:20 and he also was born to the *g*
2Sa 21:22 four were born to the *g* in Gath
1Chr 20:4 that was of the children of the *g*
1Chr 20:6 and he also was the son of the *g*
1Chr 20:8 were born unto the *g* in Gath
Job 16:14 he runneth upon me like a *g*

**GIANTS**
Gen 6:4 There were *g* in the earth in
Num 13:33 And there we saw the *g*
Num 13:33 sons of Anak, which come of the *g*
Deut 2:11 Which also were accounted *g*
Deut 2:20 also was accounted a land of *g*
Deut 2:20 *g* dwelt therein in old time
Deut 3:11 remained of the remnant of *g*
Deut 3:13 which was called the land of *g*
Josh 12:4 which was of the remnant of the *g*
Josh 13:12 remained of the remnant of the *g*
Josh 15:8 of the valley of the *g* northward
Josh 17:15 of the Perizzites and of the *g*
Josh 18:16 the valley of the *g* on the north

**GIBBAR** *(ghib'-bar)* See GIBEON. *A family of exiles.*
Ezr 2:20 The children of G, ninety and five

**GIBBETHON** *(ghib'-be-thon) A town in Dan.*
Josh 19:44 And Eltekeh, and G, and Baalath,
Josh 21:23 her suburbs, G with her suburbs,
1Kin 15:27 and Baasha smote him at G, which
1Kin 15:27 and all Israel laid siege to G
1Kin 16:15 people were encamped against G
1Kin 16:17 And Omri went up from G, and all

**GIBEA** *(ghib'-e-ah)* See GIBEAH. *Son of Sheva.*
1Chr 2:49 of Machbenah, and the father of G

**GIBEAH** *(ghib'-e-ah) A city in Judah.*
Josh 15:57 Cain, G, and Timnah
Judg 19:12 we will pass over to G
Judg 19:13 places to lodge all night, in G
Judg 19:14 upon them when they were by G
Judg 19:15 to go in and to lodge in G
Judg 19:16 and he sojourned in G
Judg 20:4 I came into G that belongeth to
Judg 20:5 the men of G rose against me, and
Judg 20:9 the thing which we will do to G
Judg 20:10 when they come to G of Benjamin
Judg 20:13 of Belial, which are in G
Judg 20:14 together out of the cities unto G
Judg 20:15 beside the inhabitants of G
Judg 20:19 morning, and encamped against G
Judg 20:20 array to fight against them at G
Judg 20:21 of Benjamin came forth out of G
Judg 20:25 them out of G the second day
Judg 20:29 set liers in wait round about G
Judg 20:30 put themselves in array against G
Judg 20:31 and the other to G in the field
Judg 20:33 even out of the meadows of G
Judg 20:34 there came against G ten thousand
Judg 20:36 wait which they had set beside G
Judg 20:37 in wait hasted, and rushed upon G
Judg 20:43 against G toward the sunrising
1Sa 10:26 And Saul also went home to G
1Sa 11:4 came the messengers to G of Saul
1Sa 13:2 with Jonathan in G of Benjamin
1Sa 13:15 up from Gilgal unto G of Benjamin
1Sa 13:16 with them, abode in G of Benjamin
1Sa 14:2 in the uttermost part of G under
1Sa 14:5 other southward over against G
1Sa 14:16 of Saul in G of Benjamin looked
1Sa 15:34 went up to his house to G of Saul
1Sa 22:6 (now Saul abode in G under a tree
1Sa 23:19 came up the Ziphites to Saul to G
1Sa 26:1 the Ziphites came unto Saul to G
2Sa 6:3 house of Abinadab that was in G
2Sa 6:4 house of Abinadab which was at G
2Sa 21:6 up unto the LORD in G of Saul
2Sa 23:29 of G of the children of Benjamin
1Chr 11:31 Ithai the son of Ribai of G
2Chr 13:2 the daughter of Uriel of G
Is 10:29 G of Saul is fled
Hos 5:8 Blow ye the cornet in G, and the
Hos 9:9 themselves, as in the days of G
Hos 10:9 hast sinned from the days of G
Hos 10:9 the battle in G against the

**GIBEATH** *(ghib'-e-ath)* See GIBEAH, GIBEATHITE. *Same as Gibeah.*
Josh 18:28 and Jebusi, which is Jerusalem, G

**GIBEATH-HAARALOTH** See FORESKINS.

**GIBEATHITE** *(ghib'-e-ath-ite) An inhabitant of Gibeah.*
1Chr 12:3 Joash, the sons of Shemaah the G

**GIBEON** *(ghib'-e-on)* See GEBA, GIBEAH, GIBEONITE.

*1. A Hivite city.*
Josh 9:3 when the inhabitants of G heard
Josh 9:17 Now their cities were G, and
Josh 10:1 how the inhabitants of G had made
Josh 10:2 because G was a great city, as
Josh 10:4 and help me, that we may smite G
Josh 10:5 their hosts, and encamped before G
Josh 10:6 the men of G sent unto Joshua to
Josh 10:10 them with a great slaughter at G
Josh 10:12 Sun, stand thou still upon G
Josh 10:41 country of Goshen, even unto G
Josh 11:19 the Hivites the inhabitants of G

*2. A city in Benjamin.*
Josh 18:25 G, and Ramah, and Beeroth,
Josh 21:17 G with her suburbs, Geba with her
2Sa 2:12 Saul, went out from Mahanaim to G
2Sa 2:13 and met together by the pool of G
2Sa 2:16 Helkath-hazzurim, which is in G
2Sa 2:24 by the way of the wilderness of G
2Sa 3:30 brother Asahel at G in the battle
2Sa 20:8 at the great stone which is in G
1Kin 3:4 the king went to G to sacrifice
1Kin 3:5 In G the LORD appeared to Solomon
1Kin 9:2 as he had appeared unto him at G
1Chr 8:29 at G dwelt the father of Gibeon
1Chr 9:35 in G dwelt the father of Gibeon,

1Chr 14:16 Philistines from G even to Gazer
1Chr 16:39 in the high place that was at G
1Chr 21:29 season in the high place at G
2Chr 1:3 to the high place that was at G
2Chr 1:13 place that was at G to Jerusalem
Neh 3:7 the Meronothite, the men of G
Neh 7:25 The children of G, ninety and five
Is 28:21 be wroth as in the valley of G
Jer 28:1 Azur the prophet, which was of G
Jer 41:12 by the great waters that are in G
Jer 41:16 whom he had brought again from G

**GIBEONITE** *(ghib'-e-on-ite)* See GIBEONITES. *An inhabitant of Gibeon.*
1Chr 12:4 And Ismaiah the G, a mighty man
Neh 3:7 unto them repaired Melatiah the G

**GIBEONITES** *(ghib'-e-on-ites)*
2Sa 21:1 house, because he slew the G
2Sa 21:2 And the king called the G, and said
2Sa 21:2 (now the G were not of the
2Sa 21:3 Wherefore David said unto the G
2Sa 21:4 the G said unto him, We will have
2Sa 21:9 them into the hands of the G

**GIBLITES** *(ghib'-lites) Inhabitants of Gebal.*
Josh 13:5 And the land of the G, and all

**GIDDALTI** *(ghid-dal'-ti) A son of Heman.*
1Chr 25:4 Hananiah, Hanani, Eliathah, G
1Chr 25:29 The two and twentieth to G

**GIDDEL** *(ghid'-del)*
*1. A family of exiles.*
Ezr 2:47 The children of G, the children
Neh 7:49 of Hanan, the children of G
*2. Servants of Solomon.*
Ezr 2:56 of Darkon, the children of G
Neh 7:58 of Darkon, the children of G

**GIDEON** *(ghid'-e-on)* See GEDEON, JERUBBAAL. *A judge of Israel.*
Judg 6:11 his son G threshed wheat by the
Judg 6:13 G said unto him, Oh my Lord, if
Judg 6:19 G went in, and made ready a kid,
Judg 6:22 when G perceived that he was an
Judg 6:22 LORD, G said, Alas, O Lord GOD
Judg 6:24 Then G built an altar there unto
Judg 6:27 Then G took ten men of his
Judg 6:29 G the son of Joash hath done this
Judg 6:34 Spirit of the LORD came upon G
Judg 6:36 G said unto God, If thou wilt
Judg 6:39 G said unto God, Let not thine
Judg 7:1 Then Jerubbaal, who is G, and all
Judg 7:2 And the LORD said unto G, The
Judg 7:4 And the LORD said unto G, The
Judg 7:5 and the LORD said unto G, Every
Judg 7:7 And the LORD said unto G, By the
Judg 7:13 when G was come, behold, there
Judg 7:14 the sword of G the son of Joash
Judg 7:15 when G heard the telling of the
Judg 7:18 The sword of the LORD, and of G
Judg 7:19 So G, and the hundred men that
Judg 7:20 The sword of the LORD, and of G
Judg 7:24 G sent messengers throughout all
Judg 7:25 Zeeb to G on the other side
Judg 8:4 G came to Jordan, and passed over,
Judg 8:7 G said, Therefore when the LORD
Judg 8:11 G went up by the way of them that
Judg 8:13 G the son of Joash returned from
Judg 8:21 G arose, and slew Zebah and
Judg 8:22 the men of Israel said unto G
Judg 8:23 G said unto them, I will not rule
Judg 8:24 G said unto them, I would desire
Judg 8:27 G made an ephod thereof, and put
Judg 8:27 which thing became a snare unto G
Judg 8:28 forty years in the days of G
Judg 8:30 G had threescore and ten sons of
Judg 8:32 G the son of Joash died in a good
Judg 8:33 to pass, as soon as G was dead
Judg 8:35 the house of Jerubbaal, namely, G

**GIDEONI** *(ghid-e-o'-ni) A Benjamite who counted the people.*
Num 1:11 Abidan the son of G
Num 2:22 shall be Abidan the son of G
Num 7:60 the ninth day Abidan the son of G
Num 7:65 offering of Abidan the son of G
Num 10:24 Benjamin was Abidan the son of G

**GIDOM** *(ghi'-dom) A place near Bethel.*
Judg 20:45 and pursued hard after them unto G

**GIFT**
Gen 34:12 Ask me never so much dowry and *g*
Ex 23:8 And thou shalt take no *g*
Ex 23:8 for the *g* blindeth the wise, and
Num 8:19 given the Levites as a *g* to Aaron
Num 18:6 are given as a *g* for the LORD
Num 18:7 office unto you as a service of *g*
Num 18:11 the heave offering of their *g*
Deut 16:19 respect persons, neither take a *g*
Deut 16:19 for a *g* doth blind the eyes of
2Sa 19:42 or hath he given us any *g*
Ps 45:12 of Tyre shall be there with a *g*
Prov 17:8 A *g* is as a precious stone in the
Prov 17:23 A wicked man taketh a *g* out of
Prov 18:16 A man's *g* maketh room for him, and
Prov 21:14 A *g* in secret pacifieth anger
Prov 25:14 of a false *g* is like clouds
Eccl 3:13 his labour, it is the *g* of God
Eccl 5:19 this is the *g* of God
Eccl 7:7 and a *g* destroyeth the heart
Eze 46:16 give a *g* unto any of his sons
Eze 46:17 But if he give a *g* of his
Mt 5:23 if thou bring thy *g* to the altar
Mt 5:24 Leave there thy *g* before the
Mt 5:24 and then come and offer thy *g*
Mt 8:4 offer the *g* that Moses commanded,
Mt 15:5 father or his mother, It is a *g*
Mt 23:18 sweareth by the *g* that is upon it
Mt 23:19 for whether is greater, the *g*
Mt 23:19 the altar that sanctifieth the *g*
Mk 7:11 It is Corban, that is to say, a *g*
Jn 4:10 her, If thou knewest the *g* of God
Acts 2:38 receive the *g* of the Holy Ghost
Acts 8:20 thou hast thought that the *g* of
Acts 10:45 out the *g* of the Holy Ghost
Acts 11:17 them the like *g* as he did unto us
Rom 1:11 impart unto you some spiritual *g*
Rom 5:15 offence, so also is the free *g*
Rom 5:15 the *g* by grace, which is by one
Rom 5:16 by one that sinned, so is the *g*
Rom 5:16 but the free *g* is of many
Rom 5:17 of the *g* of righteousness shall
Rom 5:18 the free *g* came upon all men unto
Rom 6:23 but the *g* of God is eternal life
1Cor 1:7 So that ye come behind in no *g*
1Cor 7:7 man hath his proper *g* of God
1Cor 13:2 though I have the *g* of prophecy
2Cor 1:11 that for the *g* bestowed upon us
2Cor 8:4 that we would receive the *g*
2Cor 9:15 be unto God for his unspeakable *g*
Eph 2:8 it is the *g* of God
Eph 3:7 according to the *g* of the grace
Eph 4:7 to the measure of the *g* of Christ
Phil 4:17 Not because I desire a *g*
1Ti 4:14 Neglect not the *g* that is in thee
2Ti 1:6 that thou stir up the *g* of God
Heb 6:4 and have tasted of the heavenly *g*
Jas 1:17 good *g* and every perfect *g*
1Pet 4:10 As every man hath received the *g*

**GIFTS**
Gen 25:6 which Abraham had, Abraham gave *g*
Ex 28:38 shall hallow in all their holy *g*
Lev 23:38 of the LORD, and beside your *g*
Num 18:29 Out of all your *g* ye shall offer
2Sa 8:2 David's servants, and brought *g*
2Sa 8:6 servants to David, and brought *g*
1Chr 18:2 David's servants, and brought *g*
1Chr 18:6 David's servants, and brought *g*
2Chr 19:7 of persons, nor taking of *g*
2Chr 21:3 gave them great *g* of silver
2Chr 26:8 And the Ammonites gave *g* to Uzziah
2Chr 32:23 many brought *g* unto the LORD to
Est 2:18 to the provinces, and gave *g*
Est 9:22 one to another, and *g* to the poor
Ps 68:18 thou hast received *g* for men
Ps 72:10 of Sheba and Seba shall offer *g*
Prov 6:35 though thou givest many *g*
Prov 15:27 but he that hateth *g* shall live
Prov 19:6 is a friend to him that giveth *g*
Prov 29:4 that receiveth *g* overthroweth it
Is 1:23 every one loveth *g*, and followeth
Eze 16:33 They give *g* to all whores
Eze 16:33 givest thy *g* to all thy lovers
Eze 20:26 And I polluted them in their own *g*
Eze 20:31 For when ye offer your *g*, when ye
Eze 20:39 my holy name no more with your *g*
Eze 22:12 have they taken *g* to shed blood
Dan 2:6 thereof, ye shall receive of me *g*
Dan 2:48 man, and gave him many great *g*
Dan 5:17 Let thy *g* be to thyself, and give
Mt 2:11 they presented unto him *g*
Mt 7:11 to give good *g* unto your children
Lk 11:13 to give good *g* unto your children
Lk 21:1 casting their *g* into the treasury
Lk 21:5 adorned with goodly stones and *g*
Rom 11:29 For the *g* and calling of God are
Rom 12:6 Having then *g* differing according
1Cor 12:1 Now concerning spiritual *g*
1Cor 12:4 Now there are diversities of *g*
1Cor 12:9 to another the *g* of healing by
1Cor 12:28 then *g* of healings, helps,
1Cor 12:30 Have all the *g* of healing
1Cor 12:31 But covet earnestly the best *g*
1Cor 14:1 charity, and desire spiritual *g*
1Cor 14:12 as ye are zealous of spiritual *g*
Eph 4:8 captive, and gave *g* unto men
Heb 2:4 *g* of the Holy Ghost, according to
Heb 5:1 to God, that he may offer both *g*
Heb 8:3 priest is ordained to offer *g*
Heb 8:4 that offer *g* according to the law
Heb 9:9 in which were offered both *g*
Heb 11:4 God testifying of his *g*
Rev 11:10 shall send *g* one to another

**GIHON** *(ghi'-hon)*
*1. A river in the Garden of Eden.*
Gen 2:13 the name of the second river is G
*2. A place near Jerusalem.*
1Kin 1:33 own mule, and bring him down to G
1Kin 1:38 David's mule, and brought him to G
1Kin 1:45 have anointed him king in G
2Chr 32:30 the upper watercourse of G
2Chr 33:14 of David, on the west side of G

**GILALAI** *(ghil'-a-lahee) A priest who dedicated the wall.*
Neh 12:36 Shemaiah, and Azarael, Milalai, G

**GILBOA** *(ghil-bo'-ah)*
*1. A district in Manasseh.*
1Sa 28:4 together, and they pitched in G
2Sa 21:12 Philistines had slain Saul in G
*2. A mountain near the valley Jezreel.*
1Sa 31:1 and fell down slain in mount G
1Sa 31:8 his three sons fallen in mount G
2Sa 1:6 I happened by chance upon mount G
2Sa 1:21 Ye mountains of G, let there be
1Chr 10:1 and fell down slain in mount G
1Chr 10:8 and his sons fallen in mount G

**GILEAD** *(ghil'-e-ad)* See GILEADITE, GILEAD'S, JABESH-GILEAD, RAMOTH-GILEAD.
*1. District east of the Jordan River.*
Gen 37:25 of Ishmeelites came from G with
Num 32:1 land of Jazer, and the land of G
Num 32:26 shall be there in the cities of G
Num 32:29 the land of G for a possession
Num 32:39 the son of Manasseh went to G
Num 32:40 Moses gave G unto Machir the son
Deut 2:36 that is by the river, even unto G
Deut 3:10 the cities of the plain, and all G
Deut 3:13 And the rest of G, and all Bashan,
Deut 3:15 And I gave G unto Machir
Deut 3:16 unto the Gadites I gave from G
Deut 4:43 and Ramoth in G, of the Gadites
Deut 34:1 LORD shewed him all the land of G
Josh 12:2 of the river, and from half G
Josh 12:5 and the Maachathites, and half G
Josh 13:11 And G, and the border of the
Josh 13:25 was Jazer, and all the cities of G
Josh 13:31 And half G, and Ashtaroth, and Edrei
Josh 17:1 a man of war, therefore he had G
Josh 17:5 to Manasseh, beside the land of G
Josh 17:6 Manasseh's sons had the land of G
Josh 20:8 Ramoth in G out of the tribe of
Josh 21:38 Ramoth in G with her suburbs, to
Josh 22:9 to go unto the country of G
Josh 22:13 of Manasseh, into the land of G
Josh 22:15 of Manasseh, unto the land of G
Josh 22:32 of Gad, out of the land of G
Judg 5:17 G abode beyond Jordan
Judg 10:4 day, which are in the land of G
Judg 10:8 of the Amorites, which is in G
Judg 10:17 together, and encamped in G
Judg 10:18 princes of G said one to another,
Judg 10:18 over all the inhabitants of G
Judg 11:5 the elders of G went to fetch
Judg 11:7 said unto the elders of G
Judg 11:8 the elders of G said unto
Judg 11:8 over all the inhabitants of G

Judg 11:9 said unto the elders of *G*
Judg 11:10 the elders of *G* said unto
Judg 11:11 went with the elders of *G*
Judg 11:29 Jephthah, and he passed over *G*
Judg 11:29 and passed over Mizpeh of *G*
Judg 11:29 from Mizpeh of *G* he passed over
Judg 12:4 together all the men of *G*
Judg 12:4 the men of *G* smote Ephraim,
Judg 12:5 that the men of *G* said unto him
Judg 12:7 buried in one of the cities of *G*
Judg 20:1 to Beer-sheba, with the land of *G*
1Sa 13:7 Jordan to the land of Gad and *G*
2Sa 2:9 And made him king over *G*, and over
2Sa 17:26 Absalom pitched in the land of *G*
2Sa 24:6 Then they came to *G*, and to the
1Kin 4:13 son of Manasseh, which are in *G*
1Kin 4:19 of Uri was in the country of *G*
1Kin 17:1 who was of the inhabitants of *G*
1Kin 22:3 Know ye that Ramoth in *G* is ours
2Kin 10:33 eastward, all the land of *G*
2Kin 10:33 is by the river Arnon, even *G*
2Kin 15:29 and Kedesh, and Hazor, and *G*
1Chr 2:22 and twenty cities in the land of *G*
1Chr 5:9 were multiplied in the land of *G*
1Chr 5:10 throughout all the east land of *G*
1Chr 5:16 And they dwelt in *G* in Bashan
1Chr 6:80 Ramoth in *G* with her suburbs, and
1Chr 26:31 men of valour at Jazer of *G*
1Chr 27:21 the half tribe of Manasseh in *G*
Ps 60:7 *G* is mine, and Manasseh is mine
Ps 108:8 *G* is mine
Song 6:5 flock of goats that appear from *G*
Jer 8:22 Is there no balm in *G*
Jer 22:6 Thou art *G* unto me, and the head
Jer 46:11 Go up into *G*, and take balm, O
Jer 50:19 satisfied upon mount Ephraim and *G*
Eze 47:18 and from Damascus, and from *G*
Hos 6:8 *G* is a city of them that work
Hos 12:11 Is there iniquity in *G*
Amos 1:3 because they have threshed *G* with
Amos 1:13 the women with child of *G*
Obad 19 and Benjamin shall possess *G*
Mic 7:14 let them feed in Bashan and *G*
Zec 10:10 bring them into the land of *G*

*2. A mountain range in Gilead 1.*

Gen 31:21 set his face toward the mount *G*
Gen 31:23 they overtook him in the mount *G*
Gen 31:25 pitched in the mount of *G*
Deut 3:12 the river Arnon, and half mount *G*
Judg 7:3 and depart early from mount *G*
Song 4:1 goats, that appear from mount *G*

*3. Son of Machir.*

Num 26:29 and Machir begat *G*
Num 26:29 of *G* come the family of the
Num 26:30 These are the sons of *G*
Num 27:1 the son of Hepher, the son of *G*
Num 36:1 the families of the children of *G*
Josh 17:1 of Manasseh, the father of *G*
Josh 17:3 the son of Hepher, the son of *G*
1Chr 2:21 of Machir the father of *G*
1Chr 2:23 sons of Machir the father of *G*
1Chr 7:14 bare Machir the father of *G*
1Chr 7:17 These were the sons of *G*, the son

*4. Father of Jephthah.*

Judg 11:1 and *G* begat Jephthah

*5. A chief of Gad.*

1Chr 5:14 the son of Jaroah, the son of *G*

**GILEADITE** *(ghil'-e-ad-ite)* See GILEADITES. *A descendant of Gilead.*

Judg 10:3 And after him arose Jair, a *G*
Judg 11:1 Now Jephthah the *G* was a mighty
Judg 11:40 the *G* four days in a year
Judg 12:7 Then died Jephthah the *G*, and was
2Sa 17:27 and Barzillai the *G* of Rogelim
2Sa 19:31 Barzillai the *G* came down from
1Kin 2:7 unto the sons of Barzillai the *G*
Ezr 2:61 the daughters of Barzillai the *G*
Neh 7:63 of Barzillai the *G* to wife

**GILEADITES** *(ghil'-e-ad-ites)*

Num 26:29 Gilead come the family of the *G*
Judg 12:4 Ye *G* are fugitives of Ephraim
Judg 12:5 the *G* took the passages of Jordan
2Kin 15:25 and with him fifty men of the *G*

**GILEAD'S** *(ghil'-e-ads) Refers to Gilead 4.*

Judg 11:2 And *G* wife bare him sons

**GILGAL** *(ghil'-gal)*

*1. A place near Jericho.*

Deut 11:30 in the champaign over against *G*
Josh 4:19 the first month, and encamped in *G*
Josh 4:20 of Jordan, did Joshua pitch in *G*
Josh 5:9 place is called *G* unto this day
Josh 5:10 children of Israel encamped in *G*
Josh 10:6 sent unto Joshua to the camp to *G*
Josh 10:7 So Joshua ascended from *G*
Josh 10:9 and went up from *G* all night
Josh 10:15 with him, unto the camp to *G*
Josh 10:43 with him, unto the camp to *G*
Josh 14:6 of Judah came unto Joshua in *G*
Josh 15:7 and so northward, looking toward *G*
Judg 2:1 the LORD came up from *G* to Bochim
Judg 3:19 from the quarries that were by *G*
1Sa 7:16 year in circuit to Beth-el, and *G*
1Sa 10:8 thou shalt go down before me to *G*
1Sa 11:14 people, Come, and let us go to *G*
1Sa 11:15 And all the people went to *G*
1Sa 11:15 Saul king before the LORD in *G*
1Sa 13:4 called together after Saul to *G*
1Sa 13:7 As for Saul, he was yet in *G*
1Sa 13:8 but Samuel came not to *G*
1Sa 13:12 will come down now upon me to *G*
1Sa 13:15 gat him up from *G* unto Gibeah of
1Sa 15:12 and passed on, and gone down to *G*
1Sa 15:21 unto the LORD thy God in *G*
1Sa 15:33 in pieces before the LORD in *G*
2Sa 19:15 And Judah came to *G*, to go to meet
2Sa 19:40 Then the king went on to *G*
Neh 12:29 Also from the house of *G*, and out
Hos 4:15 and come not ye unto *G*, neither go
Hos 9:15 All their wickedness is in *G*
Hos 12:11 they sacrifice bullocks in *G*
Amos 4:4 at *G* multiply transgression
Amos 5:5 not Beth-el, nor enter into *G*
Amos 5:5 for *G* shall surely go into
Mic 6:5 answered him from Shittim unto *G*

*2. A city between Dor and Tirsa.*

Josh 12:23 the king of the nations of *G*

*3. A city north of Joppa.*

Josh 9:6 went to Joshua unto the camp at *G*

*4. A place south of Ebal and Gerizim.*

2Kin 2:1 Elijah went with Elisha from *G*
2Kin 4:38 And Elisha came again to *G*

**GILOH** *(ghi'-loh)* See GILONITE. *A town in Judah.*

Josh 15:51 And Goshen, and Holon, and *G*
2Sa 15:12 from his city, even from *G*

**GILONITE** *(ghi'-lo-nite) An inhabitant of Giloh.*

2Sa 15:12 Absalom sent for Ahithophel the *G*
2Sa 23:34 Eliam the son of Ahithophel the *G*

**GIMZO** *(ghim'-zo) A city in Judah.*

2Chr 28:18 *G* also and the villages thereof

**GINATH** *(ghi'-nath) Father of Tibni.*

1Kin 16:21 followed Tibni the son of *G*
1Kin 16:22 that followed Tibni the son of *G*

**GINNETHO** *(ghin'-ne-tho)* See GINNETHON. *A priest who renewed the covenant.*

Neh 12:4 Iddo, *G*, Abijah,

**GINNETHON** *(ghin'-ne-thon)* See GINNETHO. *Same as Ginnetho.*

Neh 10:6 Daniel, *G*, Baruch,
Neh 12:16 of *G*, Meshullam

**GIRD**

Ex 29:5 *g* him with the curious girdle of
Ex 29:9 thou shalt *g* them with girdles,
Judg 3:16 he did *g* it under his raiment
1Sa 25:13 *G* ye on every man his sword
2Sa 3:31 *g* you with sackcloth, and mourn
2Kin 4:29 *G* up thy loins, and take my staff
2Kin 9:1 *G* up thy loins, and take this box
Job 38:3 *G* up now thy loins like a man
Job 40:7 *G* up thy loins now like a man
Ps 45:3 *G* thy sword upon thy thigh, O
Is 8:9 *g* yourselves, and ye shall be
Is 8:9 *g* yourselves, and ye shall be
Is 15:3 shall *g* themselves with sackcloth
Is 32:11 *g* sackcloth upon your loins
Jer 1:17 Thou therefore *g* up thy loins
Jer 4:8 For this *g* you with sackcloth,
Jer 6:26 *g* thee with sackcloth, and wallow
Jer 49:3 of Rabbah, *g* you with sackcloth
Eze 7:18 They shall also *g* themselves with
Eze 27:31 *g* them with sackcloth, and they
Eze 44:18 they shall not *g* themselves with
Joel 1:13 *G* yourselves, and lament, ye
Lk 12:37 unto you, that he shall *g* himself
Lk 17:8 *g* thyself, and serve me, till I
Jn 21:18 hands, and another shall *g* thee
Acts 12:8 *G* thyself, and bind on thy sandals
1Pet 1:13 Wherefore *g* up the loins of your

**GIRDED**

Ex 12:11 with your loins *g*, your shoes on
Lev 8:7 *g* him with the girdle, and clothed
Lev 8:7 he *g* him with the curious girdle
Lev 8:13 *g* them with girdles, and put
Lev 16:4 shall be *g* with a linen girdle,
Deut 1:41 when ye had *g* on every man his
1Sa 2:4 that stumbled are *g* with strength
1Sa 2:18 a child, *g* with a linen ephod
1Sa 17:39 David *g* his sword upon his armour
1Sa 25:13 they *g* on every man his sword
1Sa 25:13 David also *g* on his sword
2Sa 6:14 David was *g* with a linen ephod
2Sa 20:8 that he had put on was *g* unto him
2Sa 21:16 he being *g* with a new sword,
2Sa 22:40 For thou hast *g* me with strength
1Kin 18:46 he *g* up his loins, and ran before
1Kin 20:32 So they *g* sackcloth on their
Neh 4:18 one had his sword *g* by his side
Ps 18:39 For thou hast *g* me with strength
Ps 30:11 sackcloth, and *g* me with gladness
Ps 65:6 being *g* with power
Ps 93:1 wherewith he hath *g* himself
Ps 109:19 wherewith he is *g* continually
Is 45:5 I *g* thee, though thou hast not
Lam 2:10 they have *g* themselves with
Eze 16:10 I *g* thee about with fine linen,
Eze 23:15 *G* with girdles upon their loins,
Dan 10:5 whose loins were *g* with fine gold
Joel 1:8 Lament like a virgin *g* with
Lk 12:35 Let your loins be *g* about
Jn 13:4 and took a towel, and *g* himself
Jn 13:5 with the towel wherewith he was *g*
Rev 15:6 breasts *g* with golden girdles

**GIRDLE**

Ex 28:4 a broidered coat, a mitre, and a *g*
Ex 28:8 the curious *g* of the ephod, which
Ex 28:27 above the curious *g* of the ephod
Ex 28:28 above the curious *g* of the ephod
Ex 28:39 shalt make the *g* of needlework
Ex 29:5 with the curious *g* of the ephod
Ex 39:5 the curious *g* of his ephod, that
Ex 39:20 above the curious *g* of the ephod
Ex 39:21 above the curious *g* of the ephod
Ex 39:29 a *g* of fine twined linen, and blue
Lev 8:7 coat, and girded him with the *g*
Lev 8:7 with the curious *g* of the ephod
Lev 16:4 and shall be girded with a linen *g*
1Sa 18:4 sword, and to his bow, and to his *g*
2Sa 18:11 ten shekels of silver, and a *g*
2Sa 20:8 upon it a *g* with a sword fastened
1Kin 2:5 his *g* that was about his loins
2Kin 1:8 girt with a *g* of leather about
Job 12:18 and girdeth their loins with a *g*
Ps 109:19 for a *g* wherewith he is girded
Is 3:24 and instead of a *g* a rent
Is 5:27 neither shall the *g* of their
Is 11:5 shall be the *g* of his loins
Is 11:5 faithfulness the *g* of his reins
Is 22:21 and strengthen him with thy *g*
Jer 13:1 unto me, Go and get thee a linen *g*
Jer 13:2 So I got a *g* according to the
Jer 13:4 Take the *g* that thou hast got,
Jer 13:6 take the *g* from thence, which I
Jer 13:7 took the *g* from the place where I
Jer 13:7 behold, the *g* was marred, it was
Jer 13:10 them, shall even be as this *g*
Jer 13:11 For as the *g* cleaveth to the
Mt 3:4 a leathern *g* about his loins
Mk 1:6 with a *g* of a skin about his
Acts 21:11 come unto us, he took Paul's *g*
Acts 21:11 bind the man that owneth this *g*
Rev 1:13 about the paps with a golden *g*

**GIRDLES**

Ex 28:40 and thou shalt make for them *g*
Ex 29:9 And thou shalt gird them with *g*
Lev 8:13 upon them, and girded them with *g*
Prov 31:24 delivereth *g* unto the merchant
Eze 23:15 Girded with *g* upon their loins,
Rev 15:6 breasts girded with golden *g*

**GIRGASHITE** *(ghur'-gash-ite)* See GIRGASHITES, GIRGASITE. *A Canaanite tribe.*
1Chr 1:14 also, and the Amorite, and the *G*

**GIRGASHITES** *(ghur'-gash-ites)*
Gen 15:21 and the Canaanites, and the *G*
Deut 7:1 thee, the Hittites, and the *G*
Josh 3:10 and the Perizzites, and the *G*
Josh 24:11 and the Hittites, and the *G*
Neh 9:8 and the Jebusites, and the *G*

**GIRGASITE** *(ghur'-ga-site)* See GIRGASHITE. *Same as Girgashite.*
Gen 10:16 and the Amorite, and the *G*

**GISPA** *(ghis'-pah) An overseer of the Nethinim.*
Neh 11:21 *G* were over the Nethinims

**GITTAH-HEPHER** *(ghit'-tah-he'-fer)* See GATH-HEPHER. *A town in Zebulun.*
Josh 19:13 passeth on along on the east to *G*

**GITTAIM** *(ghit-ta'-im)*
*1. A city of refuge.*
2Sa 4:3 And the Beerothites fled to *G*
*2. A Benjamite city.*
Neh 11:33 Hazor, Ramah, *G*,

**GITTITE** *(ghit'-tite)* See GITTITES, GITTITH. *An inhabitant of Gath.*
2Sa 6:10 into the house of Obed-edom the *G*
2Sa 6:11 of Obed-edom the *G* three months
2Sa 15:19 Then said the king to Ittai the *G*
2Sa 15:22 Ittai the *G* passed over, and all
2Sa 18:2 under the hand of Ittai the *G*
2Sa 21:19 slew the brother of Goliath the *G*
1Chr 13:13 into the house of Obed-edom the *G*
1Chr 20:5 the brother of Goliath the *G*

**GITTITES**
Josh 13:3 the Eshkalonites, the *G*, and the
2Sa 15:18 all the Pelethites, and all the *G*

**GIVING**
Gen 24:19 And when she had done *g* him drink
Deut 10:18 in *g* him food and raiment
Deut 21:17 by *g* him a double portion of all
Ruth 1:6 his people in *g* them bread
1Kin 5:9 in *g* food for my household
2Chr 6:23 by *g* him according to his
Ezr 3:11 and *g* thanks unto the LORD
Job 11:20 shall be as the *g* up of the ghost
Mt 24:38 *g* in marriage, until the day that
Lk 17:16 face at his feet, *g* him thanks
Acts 8:9 *g* out that himself was some great
Acts 15:8 *g* them the Holy Ghost, even as he
Rom 4:20 strong in faith, *g* glory to God
Rom 9:4 the *g* of the law, and the service
1Cor 14:7 even things without life *g* sound
1Cor 14:16 say Amen at thy *g* of thanks
2Cor 6:3 *G* no offence in any thing, that
Eph 5:4 but rather *g* of thanks
Eph 5:20 *G* thanks always for all things
Phil 4:15 with me as concerning *g* and
Col 1:12 *G* thanks unto the Father, which
Col 3:17 *g* thanks to God and the Father by
1Ti 2:1 *g* of thanks, be made for all men
1Ti 4:1 *g* heed to seducing spirits, and
Titus 1:14 Not *g* heed to Jewish fables, and
Heb 13:15 of our lips *g* thanks to his name
1Pet 3:7 *g* honour unto the wife, as unto
2Pet 1:5 *g* all diligence, add to your
Jude 7 *g* themselves over to fornication,

**GIZONITE** *(ghi'-zo-nite) A bodyguard of David.*
1Chr 11:34 The sons of Hashem the *G*,

**GLAD**
Ex 4:14 he will be *g* in his heart
Judg 18:20 And the priest's heart was *g*
1Sa 11:9 and they were *g*
1Kin 8:66 *g* of heart for all the goodness
1Chr 16:31 Let the heavens be *g*, and let the
2Chr 7:10 people away into their tents, *g*
Est 5:9 that day joyful and with a *g* heart
Est 8:15 city of Shushan rejoiced and was *g*
Job 3:22 rejoice exceedingly, and are *g*
Job 22:19 The righteous see it, and are *g*
Ps 9:2 I will be *g* and rejoice in thee
Ps 14:7 rejoice, and Israel shall be *g*
Ps 16:9 Therefore my heart is *g*, and my
Ps 21:6 exceeding *g* with thy countenance
Ps 31:7 I will be *g* and rejoice in thy
Ps 32:11 Be *g* in the LORD, and rejoice, ye
Ps 34:2 shall hear thereof, and be *g*
Ps 35:27 Let them shout for joy, and be *g*
Ps 40:16 seek thee rejoice and be *g* in thee
Ps 45:8 whereby they have made thee *g*
Ps 46:4 shall make *g* the city of God
Ps 48:11 let the daughters of Judah be *g*
Ps 53:6 rejoice, and Israel shall be *g*
Ps 64:10 righteous shall be *g* in the LORD
Ps 67:4 O let the nations be *g* and sing
Ps 68:3 But let the righteous be *g*
Ps 69:32 humble shall see this, and be *g*
Ps 70:4 seek thee rejoice and be *g* in thee
Ps 90:14 may rejoice and be *g* all our days
Ps 90:15 Make us *g* according to the days
Ps 92:4 hast made me *g* through thy work
Ps 96:11 rejoice, and let the earth be *g*
Ps 97:1 multitude of isles be *g* thereof
Ps 97:8 Zion heard, and was *g*
Ps 104:15 that maketh *g* the heart of man
Ps 104:34 I will be *g* in the LORD
Ps 105:38 Egypt was *g* when they departed
Ps 107:30 Then are they *g* because they be
Ps 118:24 we will rejoice and be *g* in it
Ps 119:74 thee will be *g* when they see me
Ps 122:1 I was *g* when they said unto me,
Ps 126:3 whereof we are *g*
Prov 10:1 A wise son maketh a *g* father
Prov 12:25 but a good word maketh it *g*
Prov 15:20 A wise son maketh a *g* father
Prov 17:5 he that is *g* at calamities shall
Prov 23:25 father and thy mother shall be *g*
Prov 24:17 heart be *g* when he stumbleth
Prov 27:11 son, be wise, and make my heart *g*
Song 1:4 we will be *g* and rejoice in thee,
Is 25:9 have waited for him, we will be *g*
Is 35:1 place shall be *g* for them
Is 39:2 And Hezekiah was *g* of them
Is 65:18 But be ye *g* and rejoice for ever
Is 66:10 be *g* with her, all ye that love
Jer 20:15 making him very *g*
Jer 41:13 were with him, then they were *g*
Jer 50:11 Because ye were *g*, because ye
Lam 1:21 they are *g* that thou hast done it
Lam 4:21 Rejoice and be *g*, O daughter of
Dan 6:23 was the king exceeding *g* for him
Hos 7:3 They make the king *g* with their
Joel 2:21 be *g* and rejoice
Joel 2:23 Be *g* then, ye children of Zion,
Jonah 4:6 was exceeding *g* of the gourd
Hab 1:15 therefore they rejoice and are *g*
Zeph 3:14 be *g* and rejoice with all the
Zec 10:7 children shall see it, and be *g*
Mt 5:12 Rejoice, and be exceeding *g*
Mk 14:11 when they heard it, they were *g*
Lk 1:19 and to shew thee these *g* tidings
Lk 8:1 shewing the *g* tidings of the
Lk 15:32 we should make merry, and be *g*
Lk 22:5 And they were *g*, and covenanted to
Lk 23:8 saw Jesus, he was exceeding *g*
Jn 8:56 and he saw it, and was *g*
Jn 11:15 I am *g* for your sakes that I was
Jn 20:20 Then were the disciples *g*
Acts 2:26 heart rejoice, and my tongue was *g*
Acts 11:23 had seen the grace of God, was *g*
Acts 13:32 And we declare unto you *g* tidings
Acts 13:48 Gentiles heard this, they were *g*
Rom 10:15 bring *g* tidings of good things
Rom 16:19 I am *g* therefore on your behalf
1Cor 16:17 I am *g* of the coming of Stephanas
2Cor 2:2 who is he then that maketh me *g*
2Cor 13:9 For we are *g*, when we are weak,
1Pet 4:13 ye may be *g* also with exceeding
Rev 19:7 Let us be *g* and rejoice, and give

**GLADLY**
Mk 6:20 did many things, and heard him *g*
Mk 12:37 And the common people heard him *g*
Lk 8:40 the people *g* received him
Acts 2:41 Then they that *g* received his
Acts 21:17 the brethren received us *g*
2Cor 11:19 For ye suffer fools *g*, seeing ye
2Cor 12:9 Most *g* therefore will I rather
2Cor 12:15 And I will very *g* spend and be

**GLADNESS**
Num 10:10 Also in the day of your *g*
Deut 28:47 and with *g* of heart, for the
2Sa 6:12 into the city of David with *g*
1Chr 16:27 strength and *g* are in his place
1Chr 29:22 the LORD on that day with great *g*
2Chr 29:30 And they sang praises with *g*
2Chr 30:21 bread seven days with great *g*
2Chr 30:23 they kept other seven days with *g*
Neh 8:17 And there was very great *g*
Neh 12:27 to keep the dedication with *g*
Est 8:16 The Jews had light, and *g*, and joy,
Est 8:17 came, the Jews had joy and *g*
Est 9:17 and made it a day of feasting and *g*
Est 9:18 and made it a day of feasting and *g*
Est 9:19 day of the month Adar a day of *g*
Ps 4:7 Thou hast put *g* in my heart
Ps 30:11 my sackcloth, and girded me with *g*
Ps 45:7 the oil of *g* above thy fellows
Ps 45:15 With *g* and rejoicing shall they be
Ps 51:8 Make me to hear joy and *g*
Ps 97:11 *g* for the upright in heart
Ps 100:2 Serve the LORD with *g*
Ps 105:43 with joy, and his chosen with *g*
Ps 106:5 rejoice in the *g* of thy nation
Prov 10:28 hope of the righteous shall be *g*
Song 3:11 in the day of the *g* of his heart
Is 16:10 *g* is taken away, and joy out of
Is 22:13 And behold joy and *g*, slaying oxen,
Is 30:29 *g* of heart, as when one goeth
Is 35:10 they shall obtain joy and *g*
Is 51:3 *g* shall be found therein,
Is 51:11 they shall obtain *g* and joy
Jer 7:34 voice of mirth, and the voice of *g*
Jer 16:9 voice of mirth, and the voice of *g*
Jer 25:10 voice of mirth, and the voice of *g*
Jer 31:7 Sing with *g* for Jacob, and shout
Jer 33:11 voice of joy, and the voice of *g*
Jer 48:33 *g* is taken from the plentiful
Joel 1:16 *g* from the house of our God
Zec 8:19 be to the house of Judah joy and *g*
Mk 4:16 immediately receive it with *g*
Lk 1:14 And thou shalt have joy and *g*
Acts 2:46 house, did eat their meat with *g*
Acts 12:14 she opened not the gate for *g*
Acts 14:17 filling our hearts with food and *g*
Phil 2:29 therefore in the Lord with all *g*
Heb 1:9 the oil of *g* above thy fellows

**GLASS**
Job 37:18 strong, and as a molten looking *g*
1Cor 13:12 For now we see through a *g*
2Cor 3:18 as in a *g* the glory of the Lord
Jas 1:23 beholding his natural face in a *g*
Rev 4:6 was a sea of *g* like unto crystal
Rev 15:2 were a sea of *g* mingled with fire
Rev 15:2 his name, stand on the sea of *g*
Rev 21:18 was pure gold, like unto clear *g*
Rev 21:21 gold, as it were transparent *g*

**GLEAN**
Lev 19:10 And thou shalt not *g* thy vineyard
Deut 24:21 thou shalt not *g* it afterward
Ruth 2:2 *g* ears of corn after him in whose
Ruth 2:7 And she said, I pray you, let me *g*
Ruth 2:8 Go not to *g* in another field,
Ruth 2:15 And when she was risen up to *g*
Ruth 2:15 Let her *g* even among the sheaves,
Ruth 2:16 leave them, that she may *g* them
Ruth 2:23 *g* unto the end of barley harvest
Jer 6:9 They shall throughly *g* the

**GLEANED**
Judg 20:45 they *g* of them in the highways
Ruth 2:3 *g* in the field after the reapers
Ruth 2:17 So she *g* in the field until even,
Ruth 2:17 even, and beat out that she had *g*
Ruth 2:18 mother in law saw what she had *g*
Ruth 2:19 her, Where hast thou *g* to day

**GLEANING**
Lev 23:22 thou gather any *g* of thy harvest
Judg 8:2 Is not the *g* of the grapes of
Is 17:6 Yet *g* grapes shall be left in it,
Is 24:13 as the *g* grapes when the vintage
Jer 49:9 they not leave some *g* grapes

**GLITTERING**
Deut 32:41 If I whet my *g* sword, and mine
Job 20:25 the *g* sword cometh out of his
Job 39:23 the *g* spear and the shield
Eze 21:28 to consume because of the *g*
Nah 3:3 the bright sword and the *g* spear
Hab 3:11 and at the shining of thy *g* spear

**GLORIFIED**
Lev 10:3 before all the people I will be *g*
Is 26:15 thou art *g*
Is 44:23 Jacob, and *g* himself in Israel
Is 49:3 O Israel, in whom I will be *g*
Is 55:5 for he hath *g* thee

Is 60:9 of Israel, because he hath *g* thee
Is 60:21 work of my hands, that I may be *g*
Is 61:3 of the LORD, that he might be *g*
Is 66:5 sake, said, Let the LORD be *g*
Eze 28:22 I will be *g* in the midst of thee
Eze 39:13 renown the day that I shall be *g*
Dan 5:23 are all thy ways, hast thou not *g*
Hag 1:8 pleasure in it, and I will be *g*
Mt 9:8 *g* God, which had given such power
Mt 15:31 and they *g* the God of Israel
Mk 2:12 *g* God, saying, We never saw it on
Lk 4:15 their synagogues, being *g* of all
Lk 5:26 were all amazed, and they *g* God
Lk 7:16 and they *g* God, saying, That a
Lk 13:13 she was made straight, and *g* God
Lk 17:15 back, and with a loud voice *g* God
Lk 23:47 he *g* God, saying, Certainly this
Jn 7:39 because that Jesus was not yet *g*
Jn 11:4 the Son of God might be *g* thereby
Jn 12:16 but when Jesus was *g*, then
Jn 12:23 that the Son of man should be *g*
Jn 12:28 heaven, saying, I have both *g* it
Jn 13:31 said, Now is the Son of man *g*
Jn 13:31 man *g*, and God is *g* in him
Jn 13:32 If God be *g* in him, God shall
Jn 14:13 the Father may be *g* in the Son
Jn 15:8 Herein is my Father *g*, that ye
Jn 17:4 I have *g* thee on the earth
Jn 17:10 and I am *g* in them
Acts 3:13 our fathers, hath *g* his Son Jesus
Acts 4:21 for all men *g* God for that which
Acts 11:18 *g* God, saying, Then hath God also
Acts 13:48 glad, and *g* the word of the Lord
Acts 21:20 they *g* the Lord, and said unto him
Rom 1:21 they *g* him not as God, neither
Rom 8:17 that we may be also *g* together
Rom 8:30 whom he justified, them he also *g*
Gal 1:24 And they *g* God in me
2Th 1:10 shall come to be *g* in his saints
2Th 1:12 Lord Jesus Christ may be *g* in you
2Th 3:1 may have free course, and be *g*
Heb 5:5 So also Christ *g* not himself to
1Pet 4:11 may be *g* through Jesus Christ
1Pet 4:14 of, but on your part he is *g*
Rev 18:7 How much she hath *g* herself

## GLORIFY

Ps 22:23 all ye the seed of Jacob, *g* him
Ps 50:15 deliver thee, and thou shalt *g* me
Ps 86:9 and shall *g* thy name
Ps 86:12 I will *g* thy name for evermore
Is 24:15 Wherefore *g* ye the LORD in the
Is 25:3 shall the strong people *g* thee
Is 60:7 I will *g* the house of my glory
Jer 30:19 I will also *g* them, and they shall
Mt 5:16 *g* your Father which is in heaven
Jn 12:28 Father, *g* thy name
Jn 12:28 glorified it, and will *g* it again
Jn 13:32 God shall also *g* him in himself
Jn 13:32 and shall straightway *g* him
Jn 16:14 He shall *g* me
Jn 17:1 the hour is come; *g* thy Son
Jn 17:1 that thy Son also may *g* thee
Jn 17:5 *g* thou me with thine own self
Jn 21:19 by what death he should *g* God
Rom 15:6 with one mind and one mouth *g* God
Rom 15:9 might *g* God for his mercy
1Cor 6:20 therefore *g* God in your body, and
2Cor 9:13 they *g* God for your professed
1Pet 2:12 *g* God in the day of visitation
1Pet 4:16 but let him *g* God on this behalf
Rev 15:4 fear thee, O Lord, and *g* thy name

## GLORIFYING

Lk 2:20 And the shepherds returned, *g*
Lk 5:25 departed to his own house, *g* God
Lk 18:43 his sight, and followed him, *g* God

## GLORIOUS

Ex 15:6 O LORD, is become *g* in power
Ex 15:11 *g* in holiness, fearful in praises
Deut 28:58 that thou mayest fear this *g*
2Sa 6:20 How *g* was the king of Israel
1Chr 29:13 thank thee, and praise thy *g* name
Neh 9:5 and blessed be thy *g* name, which
Est 1:4 the riches of his *g* kingdom
Ps 45:13 king's daughter is all *g* within
Ps 66:2 make his praise *g*
Ps 72:19 And blessed be his *g* name for ever
Ps 76:4 Thou art more *g* and excellent than
Ps 87:3 *G* things are spoken of thee, O
Ps 111:3 His work is honourable and *g*
Ps 145:5 I will speak of the *g* honour of
Ps 145:12 the *g* majesty of his kingdom
Is 4:2 of the LORD be beautiful and *g*
Is 11:10 and his rest shall be *g*
Is 22:23 he shall be for a *g* throne to his
Is 28:1 whose *g* beauty is a fading flower
Is 28:4 the *g* beauty, which is on the
Is 30:30 cause his *g* voice to be heard
Is 33:21 But there the *g* LORD will be unto
Is 49:5 yet shall I be *g* in the eyes of
Is 60:13 will make the place of my feet *g*
Is 63:1 this that is *g* in his apparel,
Is 63:12 hand of Moses with his *g* arm
Is 63:14 people, to make thyself a *g* name
Jer 17:12 A *g* high throne from the
Eze 27:25 made very *g* in the midst of the
Dan 11:16 and he shall stand in the *g* land
Dan 11:41 shall enter also into the *g* land
Dan 11:45 the seas in the *g* holy mountain
Lk 13:17 *g* things that were done by him
Rom 8:21 *g* liberty of the children of God
2Cor 3:7 and engraven in stones, was *g*
2Cor 3:8 of the spirit be rather *g*
2Cor 3:10 *g* had no glory in this respect
2Cor 3:11 if that which is done away was *g*
2Cor 3:11 more that which remaineth is *g*
2Cor 4:4 light of the *g* gospel of Christ
Eph 5:27 present it to himself a *g* church
Phil 3:21 be fashioned like unto his *g* body
Col 1:11 might, according to his *g* power
1Ti 1:11 According to the *g* gospel of the
Titus 2:13 the *g* appearing of the great God

## GLORYING

1Cor 5:6 Your *g* is not good
1Cor 9:15 any man should make my *g* void
2Cor 7:4 toward you, great is my *g* of you
2Cor 12:11 I am become a fool in *g*

## GNASHING

Mt 8:12 shall be weeping and *g* of teeth
Mt 13:42 shall be wailing and *g* of teeth
Mt 13:50 shall be wailing and *g* of teeth
Mt 22:13 shall be weeping and *g* of teeth
Mt 24:51 shall be weeping and *g* of teeth
Mt 25:30 shall be weeping and *g* of teeth
Lk 13:28 *g* of teeth, when ye shall see

## GOAT

Gen 15:9 a she *g* of three years old, and a
Lev 3:12 And if his offering be a *g*
Lev 4:24 his hand upon the head of the *g*
Lev 7:23 fat, of ox, or of sheep, or of *g*
Lev 9:15 people's offering, and took the *g*
Lev 10:16 sought the *g* of the sin offering
Lev 16:9 Aaron shall bring the *g* upon
Lev 16:10 But the *g*, on which the lot fell
Lev 16:15 he kill the *g* of the sin offering
Lev 16:18 bullock, and of the blood of the *g*
Lev 16:20 altar, he shall bring the live *g*
Lev 16:21 hands upon the head of the live *g*
Lev 16:21 them upon the head of the *g*
Lev 16:22 the *g* shall bear upon him all
Lev 16:22 let go the *g* in the wilderness
Lev 16:26 he that let go the *g* for the
Lev 16:27 the *g* for the sin offering, whose
Lev 17:3 that killeth an ox, or lamb, or *g*
Lev 22:27 a bullock, or a sheep, or a *g*
Num 15:27 then he shall bring a she *g* of
Num 18:17 a sheep, or the firstling of a *g*
Num 28:22 one *g* for a sin offering, to make
Num 29:22 And one *g* for a sin offering
Num 29:28 And one *g* for a sin offering
Num 29:31 And one *g* for a sin offering
Num 29:34 And one *g* for a sin offering
Num 29:38 And one *g* for a sin offering
Deut 14:4 the ox, the sheep, and the *g*
Deut 14:5 and the fallow deer, and the wild *g*
Prov 30:31 an he *g* also
Eze 43:25 every day a *g* for a sin offering
Dan 8:5 an he *g* came from the west on the
Dan 8:5 the *g* had a notable horn between
Dan 8:8 the he *g* waxed very great
Dan 8:21 the rough *g* is the king of Grecia

## GOATH *(go'-ath) A place near Jerusalem.*

Jer 31:39 and shall compass about to G

## GOATS

Gen 27:9 thence two good kids of the *g*
Gen 27:16 the kids of the *g* upon his hands
Gen 30:32 spotted and speckled among the *g*
Gen 30:33 speckled and spotted among the *g*
Gen 30:35 the he *g* that were ringstraked
Gen 30:35 all the she *g* that were speckled
Gen 31:38 thy she *g* have not cast their
Gen 32:14 Two hundred she *g*
Gen 32:14 and twenty he *g*
Gen 37:31 coat, and killed a kid of the *g*
Ex 12:5 out from the sheep, or from the *g*
Lev 1:10 namely, of the sheep, or of the *g*
Lev 4:23 his offering, a kid of the *g*
Lev 4:28 his offering, a kid of the *g*
Lev 5:6 flock, a lamb or a kid of the *g*
Lev 9:3 a kid of the *g* for a sin offering
Lev 16:5 kids of the *g* for a sin offering
Lev 16:7 And he shall take the two *g*
Lev 16:8 shall cast lots upon the two *g*
Lev 22:19 beeves, of the sheep, or of the *g*
Lev 23:19 kid of the *g* for a sin offering
Num 7:16 One kid of the *g* for a sin
Num 7:17 two oxen, five rams, five he *g*
Num 7:22 One kid of the *g* for a sin
Num 7:23 two oxen, five rams, five he *g*
Num 7:28 One kid of the *g* for a sin
Num 7:29 two oxen, five rams, five he *g*
Num 7:34 One kid of the *g* for a sin
Num 7:35 two oxen, five rams, five he *g*
Num 7:40 One kid of the *g* for a sin
Num 7:41 two oxen, five rams, five he *g*
Num 7:46 One kid of the *g* for a sin
Num 7:47 two oxen, five rams, five he *g*
Num 7:52 One kid of the *g* for a sin
Num 7:53 two oxen, five rams, five he *g*
Num 7:58 One kid of the *g* for a sin
Num 7:59 two oxen, five rams, five he *g*
Num 7:64 One kid of the *g* for a sin
Num 7:65 two oxen, five rams, five he *g*
Num 7:70 One kid of the *g* for a sin
Num 7:71 two oxen, five rams, five he *g*
Num 7:76 One kid of the *g* for a sin
Num 7:77 two oxen, five rams, five he *g*
Num 7:82 One kid of the *g* for a sin
Num 7:83 two oxen, five rams, five he *g*
Num 7:87 the kids of the *g* for sin
Num 7:88 the rams sixty, the he *g* sixty
Num 15:24 one kid of the *g* for a sin
Num 28:15 one kid of the *g* for a sin
Num 28:30 And one kid of the *g*, to make an
Num 29:5 one kid of the *g* for a sin
Num 29:11 One kid of the *g* for a sin
Num 29:16 one kid of the *g* for a sin
Num 29:19 one kid of the *g* for a sin
Num 29:25 one kid of the *g* for a sin
Deut 32:14 rams of the breed of Bashan, and *g*
1Sa 24:2 men upon the rocks of the wild *g*
1Sa 25:2 thousand sheep, and a thousand *g*
2Chr 17:11 thousand and seven hundred he *g*
2Chr 29:21 and seven lambs, and seven he *g*
2Chr 29:23 they brought forth the he *g* for
Ezr 6:17 for all Israel, twelve he *g*
Ezr 8:35 twelve he *g* for a sin offering
Job 39:1 wild *g* of the rock bring forth
Ps 50:9 nor he *g* out of thy folds
Ps 50:13 of bulls, or drink the blood of *g*
Ps 66:15 I will offer bullocks with *g*
Ps 104:18 hills are a refuge for the wild *g*
Prov 27:26 the *g* are the price of the field
Song 4:1 thy hair is as a flock of *g*
Song 6:5 of *g* that appear from Gilead
Is 1:11 bullocks, or of lambs, or of he *g*
Is 34:6 and with the blood of lambs and *g*
Jer 50:8 be as the he *g* before the flocks
Jer 51:40 slaughter, like rams with he *g*
Eze 27:21 with thee in lambs, and rams, and *g*
Eze 34:17 between the rams and the he *g*
Eze 39:18 earth, of rams, of lambs, and of *g*
Eze 43:22 the *g* without blemish for a sin
Eze 45:23 a kid of the *g* daily for a sin
Zec 10:3 shepherds, and I punished the *g*
Mt 25:32 divideth his sheep from the *g*
Mt 25:33 right hand, but the *g* on the left
Heb 9:12 Neither by the blood of *g*
Heb 9:13 For if the blood of bulls and of *g*
Heb 9:19 took the blood of calves and of *g*
Heb 10:4 of *g* should take away sins

## GOATS'

Ex 25:4 and fine linen, and *g* hair,
Ex 26:7 thou shalt make curtains of *g*
Ex 35:6 and fine linen, and *g* hair,
Ex 35:23 *g* hair, and red skins of rams, and
Ex 35:26 them up in wisdom spun *g* hair

Ex 36:14 he made curtains of *g* hair for
Num 31:20 of skins, and all work of *g* hair
1Sa 19:13 put a pillow of *g* hair for his
1Sa 19:16 with a pillow of *g* hair for his
Prov 27:27 thou shalt have *g* milk enough for

**GOB** *(gob) A place where David battled the Philistines.*
2Sa 21:18 battle with the Philistines at *G*
2Sa 21:19 battle in *G* with the Philistines

**GOD** *(god)* See GODDESS, GODHEAD, GOD'S, GODS, GOD-WARD.
1. *Creator and Ruler of the world, Israel, and the church.*
Gen 1:1 In the beginning *G* created the
Gen 1:2 the Spirit of *G* moved upon the
Gen 1:3 *G* said, Let there be light
Gen 1:4 *G* saw the light, that it was good
Gen 1:4 *G* divided the light from the
Gen 1:5 *G* called the light Day, and the
Gen 1:6 *G* said, Let there be a firmament
Gen 1:7 *G* made the firmament, and divided
Gen 1:8 *G* called the firmament Heaven
Gen 1:9 *G* said, Let the waters under the
Gen 1:10 *G* called the dry land Earth
Gen 1:10 and *G* saw that it was good
Gen 1:11 *G* said, Let the earth bring forth
Gen 1:12 and *G* saw that it was good
Gen 1:14 *G* said, Let there be lights in
Gen 1:16 And *G* made two great lights
Gen 1:17 *G* set them in the firmament of
Gen 1:18 and *G* saw that it was good
Gen 1:20 *G* said, Let the waters bring
Gen 1:21 *G* created great whales, and every
Gen 1:21 and *G* saw that it was good
Gen 1:22 *G* blessed them, saying, Be
Gen 1:24 *G* said, Let the earth bring forth
Gen 1:25 *G* made the beast of the earth
Gen 1:25 and *G* saw that it was good
Gen 1:26 *G* said, Let us make man in our
Gen 1:27 So *G* created man in his own image
Gen 1:27 in the image of *G* created he him
Gen 1:28 *G* blessed them, and *G* said unto
Gen 1:28 *G* said unto them, Be fruitful, and
Gen 1:29 *G* said, Behold, I have given you
Gen 1:31 *G* saw every thing that he had
Gen 2:2 on the seventh day *G* ended his
Gen 2:3 *G* blessed the seventh day, and
Gen 2:3 from all his work which *G* created
Gen 2:4 that the LORD *G* made the earth
Gen 2:5 for the LORD *G* had not caused it
Gen 2:7 the LORD *G* formed man of the dust
Gen 2:8 the LORD *G* planted a garden
Gen 2:9 LORD *G* to grow every tree that is
Gen 2:15 the LORD *G* took the man, and put
Gen 2:16 the LORD *G* commanded the man,
Gen 2:18 And the LORD *G* said, It is not
Gen 2:19 out of the ground the LORD *G*
Gen 2:21 the LORD *G* caused a deep sleep to
Gen 2:22 which the LORD *G* had taken from
Gen 3:1 field which the LORD *G* had made
Gen 3:1 unto the woman, Yea, hath *G* said
Gen 3:3 *G* hath said, Ye shall not eat of
Gen 3:5 For *G* doth know that in the day
Gen 3:8 heard the voice of the LORD *G*
Gen 3:8 from the presence of the LORD *G*
Gen 3:9 the LORD *G* called unto Adam, and
Gen 3:13 the LORD *G* said unto the woman,
Gen 3:14 the LORD *G* said unto the serpent,
Gen 3:21 the LORD *G* make coats of skins
Gen 3:22 And the LORD *G* said, Behold, the
Gen 3:23 Therefore the LORD *G* sent him
Gen 4:25 For *G*, said she, hath appointed
Gen 5:1 In the day that *G* created man
Gen 5:1 in the likeness of *G* made he him
Gen 5:22 Enoch walked with *G* after he
Gen 5:24 And Enoch walked with *G*
Gen 5:24 for *G* took him
Gen 6:2 That the sons of *G* saw the
Gen 6:4 when the sons of *G* came in unto
Gen 6:5 *G* saw that the wickedness of man
Gen 6:9 and Noah walked with *G*
Gen 6:11 earth also was corrupt before *G*
Gen 6:12 *G* looked upon the earth, and,
Gen 6:13 *G* said unto Noah, The end of all
Gen 6:22 to all that *G* commanded him
Gen 7:9 female, as *G* had commanded Noah
Gen 7:16 all flesh, as *G* had commanded him
Gen 8:1 *G* remembered Noah, and every
Gen 8:1 *G* made a wind to pass over the
Gen 8:15 *G* spake unto Noah, saying,
Gen 9:1 *G* blessed Noah and his sons, and
Gen 9:6 for in the image of *G* made he man
Gen 9:8 *G* spake unto Noah, and to his sons
Gen 9:12 *G* said, This is the token of the
Gen 9:16 everlasting covenant between *G*
Gen 9:17 *G* said unto Noah, This is the
Gen 9:26 Blessed be the LORD *G* of Shem
Gen 9:27 *G* shall enlarge Japheth, and he
Gen 14:18 was the priest of the most high *G*
Gen 14:19 be Abram of the most high *G*
Gen 14:20 And blessed be the most high *G*
Gen 14:22 unto the LORD, the most high *G*
Gen 15:2 And Abram said, Lord *G*, what wilt
Gen 15:8 And he said, Lord *G*, whereby shall
Gen 16:13 spake unto her, Thou *G* seest me
Gen 17:1 unto him, I am the Almighty *G*
Gen 17:3 *G* talked with him, saying,
Gen 17:7 to be a *G* unto thee, and to thy
Gen 17:8 and I will be their *G*
Gen 17:9 *G* said unto Abraham, Thou shalt
Gen 17:15 *G* said unto Abraham, As for Sarai
Gen 17:18 And Abraham said unto *G*, O that
Gen 17:19 *G* said, Sarah thy wife shall bear
Gen 17:22 him, and *G* went up from Abraham
Gen 17:23 day, as *G* had said unto him
Gen 19:29 when *G* destroyed the cities of
Gen 19:29 that *G* remembered Abraham, and
Gen 20:3 But *G* came to Abimelech in a
Gen 20:6 *G* said unto him in a dream, Yea,
Gen 20:11 Surely the fear of *G* is not in
Gen 20:13 when *G* caused me to wander from
Gen 20:17 So Abraham prayed unto *G*
Gen 20:17 *G* healed Abimelech, and his wife,
Gen 21:2 time of which *G* had spoken to him
Gen 21:4 days old, as *G* had commanded him
Gen 21:6 *G* hath made me to laugh, so that
Gen 21:12 *G* said unto Abraham, Let it not
Gen 21:17 *G* heard the voice of the lad
Gen 21:17 the angel of *G* called to Hagar
Gen 21:17 for *G* hath heard the voice of the
Gen 21:19 *G* opened her eyes, and she saw a
Gen 21:20 And *G* was with the lad
Gen 21:22 *G* is with thee in all that thou
Gen 21:23 *G* that thou wilt not deal falsely
Gen 21:33 of the LORD, the everlasting *G*
Gen 22:1 that *G* did tempt Abraham, and said
Gen 22:3 the place of which *G* had told him
Gen 22:8 *G* will provide himself a lamb for
Gen 22:9 the place which *G* had told him of
Gen 22:12 now I know that thou fearest *G*
Gen 24:3 the *G* of heaven
Gen 24:3 the *G* of the earth
Gen 24:7 The LORD *G* of heaven, which took
Gen 24:12 O LORD *G* of my master Abraham, I
Gen 24:27 Blessed be the LORD *G* of my
Gen 24:42 O LORD *G* of my master Abraham, if
Gen 24:48 blessed the LORD *G* of my master
Gen 25:11 that *G* blessed his son Isaac
Gen 26:24 I am the *G* of Abraham thy father
Gen 27:20 the LORD thy *G* brought it to me
Gen 27:28 Therefore *G* give thee of the dew
Gen 28:3 *G* Almighty bless thee, and make
Gen 28:4 which *G* gave unto Abraham
Gen 28:12 behold the angels of *G* ascending
Gen 28:13 I am the LORD *G* of Abraham thy
Gen 28:13 thy father, and the *G* of Isaac
Gen 28:17 is none other but the house of *G*
Gen 28:20 If *G* will be with me, and will
Gen 28:21 then shall the LORD be my *G*
Gen 30:6 *G* hath judged me, and hath also
Gen 30:17 *G* hearkened unto Leah, and she
Gen 30:18 *G* hath given me my hire, because
Gen 30:20 *G* hath endued me with a good
Gen 30:22 *G* remembered Rachel
Gen 30:22 *G* hearkened to her, and opened her
Gen 30:23 *G* hath taken away my reproach
Gen 31:5 but the *G* of my father hath been
Gen 31:7 but *G* suffered him not to hurt me
Gen 31:9 Thus *G* hath taken away the cattle
Gen 31:11 the angel of *G* spake unto me in a
Gen 31:13 I am the *G* of Beth-el, where thou
Gen 31:16 For all the riches which *G* hath
Gen 31:16 whatsoever *G* hath said unto thee,
Gen 31:24 *G* came to Laban the Syrian in a
Gen 31:29 but the *G* of your father spake
Gen 31:42 Except the *G* of my father
Gen 31:42 the *G* of Abraham, and the fear of
Gen 31:42 *G* hath seen mine affliction and
Gen 31:50 *G* is witness betwixt me and thee
Gen 31:53 The *G* of Abraham
Gen 31:53 the *G* of Nahor
Gen 31:53 the *G* of their father, judge
Gen 32:1 way, and the angels of *G* met him
Gen 32:9 O *G* of my father Abraham
Gen 32:9 *G* of my father Isaac, the LORD
Gen 32:28 a prince hast thou power with *G*
Gen 32:30 for I have seen *G* face to face
Gen 33:5 The children which *G* hath
Gen 33:10 though I had seen the face of *G*
Gen 33:11 because *G* hath dealt graciously
Gen 35:1 *G* said unto Jacob, Arise, go up
Gen 35:1 and make there an altar unto *G*
Gen 35:3 I will make there an altar unto *G*
Gen 35:5 the terror of *G* was upon the
Gen 35:7 because there *G* appeared unto him
Gen 35:9 *G* appeared unto Jacob again, when
Gen 35:10 *G* said unto him, Thy name is
Gen 35:11 And *G* said unto him
Gen 35:11 I am *G* Almighty
Gen 35:13 *G* went up from him in the place
Gen 35:15 the place where *G* spake with him
Gen 39:9 wickedness, and sin against *G*
Gen 40:8 not interpretations belong to *G*
Gen 41:16 *G* shall give Pharaoh an answer of
Gen 41:25 *G* hath shewed Pharaoh what he is
Gen 41:28 What *G* is about to do he sheweth
Gen 41:32 the thing is established by *G*
Gen 41:32 *G* will shortly bring it to pass
Gen 41:38 a man in whom the Spirit of *G* is
Gen 41:39 Forasmuch as *G* hath shewed thee
Gen 41:51 For *G*, said he, hath made me
Gen 41:52 For *G* hath caused me to be
Gen 42:18 for I fear *G*
Gen 42:28 is this that *G* hath done unto us
Gen 43:14 *G* Almighty give you mercy before
Gen 43:23 your *G*, and the *G* of your father
Gen 43:29 *G* be gracious unto thee, my son
Gen 44:7 *G* forbid that thy servants should
Gen 44:16 *G* hath found out the iniquity of
Gen 44:17 *G* forbid that I should do so
Gen 45:5 for *G* did send me before you to
Gen 45:7 *G* sent me before you to preserve
Gen 45:8 you that sent me hither, but *G*
Gen 45:9 *G* hath made me lord of all Egypt
Gen 46:1 unto the *G* of his father Isaac
Gen 46:2 *G* spake unto Israel in the
Gen 46:3 I am *G*, the *G* of thy father
Gen 48:3 *G* Almighty appeared unto me at
Gen 48:9 whom *G* hath given me in this
Gen 48:11 *G* hath shewed me also thy seed
Gen 48:15 And he blessed Joseph, and said, *G*
Gen 48:15 the *G* which fed me all my life
Gen 48:20 *G* make thee as Ephraim and as
Gen 48:21 but *G* shall be with you, and bring
Gen 49:24 hands of the mighty *G* of Jacob
Gen 49:25 Even by the *G* of thy father, who
Gen 50:17 servants of the *G* of thy father
Gen 50:19 for am I in the place of *G*
Gen 50:20 but *G* meant it unto good, to
Gen 50:24 *G* will surely visit you, and bring
Gen 50:25 *G* will surely visit you, and ye
Ex 1:17 But the midwives feared *G*
Ex 1:20 Therefore *G* dealt well with the
Ex 1:21 because the midwives feared *G*
Ex 2:23 their cry came up unto *G* by
Ex 2:24 *G* heard their groaning
Ex 2:24 *G* remembered his covenant with
Ex 2:25 *G* looked upon the children of
Ex 2:25 and *G* had respect unto them
Ex 3:1 and came to the mountain of *G*
Ex 3:4 *G* called unto him out of the
Ex 3:6 I am the *G* of thy father
Ex 3:6 the *G* of Abraham
Ex 3:6 *G* of Isaac, and the *G* of Jacob
Ex 3:6 for he was afraid to look upon *G*
Ex 3:11 And Moses said unto *G*, Who am I,
Ex 3:12 ye shall serve *G* upon this
Ex 3:13 And Moses said unto *G*, Behold,
Ex 3:13 The *G* of your fathers hath sent
Ex 3:14 *G* said unto Moses, I AM THAT I AM
Ex 3:15 *G* said moreover unto Moses, Thus
Ex 3:15 The LORD *G* of your fathers
Ex 3:15 the *G* of Abraham
Ex 3:15 the *G* of Isaac
Ex 3:15 the *G* of Jacob
Ex 3:16 The LORD *G* of your fathers
Ex 3:16 the *G* of Abraham, of Isaac, and of
Ex 3:18 The LORD *G* of the Hebrews hath
Ex 3:18 may sacrifice to the LORD our *G*

Ex 4:5 that the LORD G of their fathers
Ex 4:5 the G of Abraham
Ex 4:5 the G of Isaac
Ex 4:5 the G of Jacob
Ex 4:16 thou shalt be to him instead of G
Ex 4:20 took the rod of G in his hand
Ex 4:27 and met him in the mount of G
Ex 5:1 Thus saith the LORD G of Israel
Ex 5:3 The G of the Hebrews hath met
Ex 5:3 and sacrifice unto the LORD our G
Ex 5:8 Let us go and sacrifice to our G
Ex 6:2 G spake unto Moses, and said unto
Ex 6:3 Jacob, by the name of G Almighty
Ex 6:7 a people, and I will be to you a G
Ex 6:7 know that I am the LORD your G
Ex 7:16 The LORD G of the Hebrews hath
Ex 8:10 is none like unto the LORD our G
Ex 8:19 Pharaoh, This is the finger of G
Ex 8:25 sacrifice to your G in the land
Ex 8:26 the Egyptians to the LORD our G
Ex 8:27 and sacrifice to the LORD our G
Ex 8:28 the LORD your G in the wilderness
Ex 9:1 saith the LORD G of the Hebrews
Ex 9:13 saith the LORD G of the Hebrews
Ex 9:30 ye will not yet fear the LORD G
Ex 10:3 saith the LORD G of the Hebrews
Ex 10:7 they may serve the LORD their G
Ex 10:8 them, Go, serve the LORD your G
Ex 10:16 sinned against the LORD your G
Ex 10:17 once, and intreat the LORD your G
Ex 10:25 may sacrifice unto the LORD our G
Ex 10:26 we take to serve the LORD our G
Ex 13:17 that G led them not through the
Ex 13:17 for G said, Lest peradventure the
Ex 13:18 But G led the people about,
Ex 13:19 saying, G will surely visit you
Ex 14:19 And the angel of G, which went
Ex 15:2 he is my G, and I will prepare him
Ex 15:2 my father's G, and I will exalt
Ex 15:26 to the voice of the LORD thy G
Ex 16:3 Would to G we had died by the
Ex 16:12 know that I am the LORD your G
Ex 17:9 with the rod of G in mine hand
Ex 18:1 heard of all that G had done for
Ex 18:4 for the G of my father, said he,
Ex 18:5 he encamped at the mount of G
Ex 18:12 offering and sacrifices for G
Ex 18:12 Moses' father in law before G
Ex 18:15 come unto me to enquire of G
Ex 18:16 make them know the statutes of G
Ex 18:19 counsel, and G shall be with thee
Ex 18:19 mayest bring the causes unto G
Ex 18:21 people able men, such as fear G
Ex 18:23 G command thee so, then thou
Ex 19:3 And Moses went up unto G, and the
Ex 19:17 out of the camp to meet with G
Ex 19:19 G answered him by a voice
Ex 20:1 G spake all these words, saying,
Ex 20:2 I am the LORD thy G, which have
Ex 20:5 I the LORD thy G am a jealous G
Ex 20:5 I the LORD thy G am a jealous G
Ex 20:7 name of the LORD thy G in vain
Ex 20:10 is the sabbath of the LORD thy G
Ex 20:12 which the LORD thy G giveth thee
Ex 20:19 but let not G speak with us, lest
Ex 20:20 for G is come to prove you, and
Ex 20:21 the thick darkness where G was
Ex 21:13 but G deliver him into his hand
Ex 23:17 shall appear before the Lord G
Ex 23:19 into the house of the LORD thy G
Ex 23:25 And ye shall serve the LORD your G
Ex 24:10 And they saw the G of Israel
Ex 24:11 also they saw G, and did eat and
Ex 24:13 Moses went up into the mount of G
Ex 29:45 of Israel, and will be their G
Ex 29:46 know that I am the LORD their G
Ex 29:46 I am the LORD their G
Ex 31:3 filled him with the spirit of G
Ex 31:18 written with the finger of G
Ex 32:11 And Moses besought the LORD his G
Ex 32:16 And the tables were the work of G
Ex 32:16 the writing was the writing of G
Ex 32:27 Thus saith the LORD G of Israel
Ex 34:6 proclaimed, The LORD, The LORD G
Ex 34:14 name is Jealous, is a jealous G
Ex 34:23 children appear before the Lord G
Ex 34:23 the G of Israel
Ex 34:24 the LORD thy G thrice in the year
Ex 34:26 unto the house of the LORD thy G
Ex 35:31 filled him with the spirit of G

Lev 2:13 thy G to be lacking from thy meat
Lev 4:22 commandments of the LORD his G
Lev 10:17 G hath given it you to bear the
Lev 11:44 For I am the LORD your G
Lev 11:45 the land of Egypt, to be your G
Lev 18:2 unto them, I am the LORD your G
Lev 18:4 I am the LORD your G
Lev 18:21 thou profane the name of thy G
Lev 18:30 I am the LORD your G
Lev 19:2 for I the LORD your G am holy
Lev 19:3 I am the LORD your G
Lev 19:4 I am the LORD your G
Lev 19:10 I am the LORD your G
Lev 19:12 thou profane the name of thy G
Lev 19:14 the blind, but shalt fear thy G
Lev 19:25 I am the LORD your G
Lev 19:31 I am the LORD your G
Lev 19:32 of the old man, and fear thy G
Lev 19:34 I am the LORD your G
Lev 19:36 I am the LORD your G, which
Lev 20:7 for I am the LORD your G
Lev 20:24 I am the LORD your G, which have
Lev 21:6 They shall be holy unto their G
Lev 21:6 not profane the name of their G
Lev 21:6 by fire, and the bread of their G
Lev 21:7 for he is holy unto his G
Lev 21:8 he offereth the bread of thy G
Lev 21:12 profane the sanctuary of his G
Lev 21:12 oil of his G is upon him
Lev 21:17 to offer the bread of his G
Lev 21:21 nigh to offer the bread of his G
Lev 21:22 He shall eat the bread of his G
Lev 22:25 bread of your G of any of these
Lev 22:33 the land of Egypt, to be your G
Lev 23:14 brought an offering unto your G
Lev 23:22 I am the LORD your G
Lev 23:28 for you before the LORD your G
Lev 23:40 before the LORD your G seven days
Lev 23:43 I am the LORD your G
Lev 24:15 curseth his G shall bear his sin
Lev 24:22 for I am the LORD your G
Lev 25:17 but thou shalt fear thy G
Lev 25:17 for I am the LORD your G
Lev 25:36 but fear thy G
Lev 25:38 I am the LORD your G, which
Lev 25:38 land of Canaan, and to be your G
Lev 25:43 but shalt fear thy G
Lev 25:55 I am the LORD your G
Lev 26:1 for I am the LORD your G
Lev 26:12 walk among you, and will be your G
Lev 26:13 I am the LORD your G, which
Lev 26:44 for I am the LORD their G
Lev 26:45 heathen, that I might be their G
Num 6:7 of his G is upon his head
Num 10:9 remembered before the LORD your G
Num 10:10 you for a memorial before your G
Num 10:10 I am the LORD your G
Num 11:29 would G that all the LORD's
Num 12:13 LORD, saying, Heal her now, O G
Num 14:2 Would G that we had died in the
Num 14:2 or would G we had died in this
Num 15:40 and be holy unto your G
Num 15:41 I am the LORD your G, which
Num 15:41 the land of Egypt, to be your G
Num 15:41 I am the LORD your G
Num 16:9 that the G of Israel hath
Num 16:22 upon their faces, and said, O G
Num 16:22 the G of the spirits of all flesh
Num 20:3 Would G that we had died when our
Num 21:5 And the people spake against G
Num 22:9 G came unto Balaam, and said, What
Num 22:10 And Balaam said unto G, Balak the
Num 22:12 G said unto Balaam, Thou shalt
Num 22:18 beyond the word of the LORD my G
Num 22:20 G came unto Balaam at night, and
Num 22:38 the word that G putteth in my
Num 23:4 And G met Balaam
Num 23:8 I curse, whom G hath not cursed
Num 23:19 G is not a man, that he should
Num 23:21 the LORD his G is with him
Num 23:22 G brought them out of Egypt
Num 23:23 and of Israel, What hath G wrought
Num 23:27 peradventure it will please G
Num 24:2 and the spirit of G came upon him
Num 24:4 said, which heard the words of G
Num 24:8 G brought him forth out of Egypt
Num 24:16 said, which heard the words of G
Num 24:23 who shall live when G doeth this
Num 25:13 because he was zealous for his G
Num 27:16 the G of the spirits of all flesh

Deut 1:6 The LORD our G spake unto us in
Deut 1:10 The LORD your G hath multiplied
Deut 1:11 (The LORD G of your fathers make
Deut 1:19 as the LORD our G commanded us
Deut 1:20 the LORD our G doth give unto us
Deut 1:21 the LORD thy G hath set the land
Deut 1:21 as the LORD G of thy fathers hath
Deut 1:25 which the LORD our G doth give us
Deut 1:26 commandment of the LORD your G
Deut 1:30 The LORD your G which goeth
Deut 1:31 how that the LORD thy G bare thee
Deut 1:32 did not believe the LORD your G
Deut 1:41 that the LORD our G commanded us
Deut 2:7 For the LORD thy G hath blessed
Deut 2:7 LORD thy G hath been with thee
Deut 2:29 which the LORD our G giveth us
Deut 2:30 for the LORD thy G hardened his
Deut 2:33 the LORD our G delivered him
Deut 2:36 the LORD our G delivered all unto
Deut 2:37 the LORD our G forbad us
Deut 3:3 So the LORD our G delivered into
Deut 3:18 The LORD your G hath given you
Deut 3:20 the land which the LORD your G
Deut 3:21 seen all that the LORD your G
Deut 3:22 for the LORD your G he shall
Deut 3:24 O Lord G, thou hast begun to shew
Deut 3:24 for what G is there in heaven or
Deut 4:1 LORD G of your fathers giveth you
Deut 4:2 LORD your G which I command you
Deut 4:3 the LORD thy G hath destroyed
Deut 4:4 did cleave unto the LORD your G
Deut 4:5 as the LORD my G commanded me
Deut 4:7 who hath G so nigh unto them
Deut 4:7 as the LORD our G is in all
Deut 4:10 before the LORD thy G in Horeb
Deut 4:19 which the LORD thy G hath divided
Deut 4:21 which the LORD thy G giveth thee
Deut 4:23 the covenant of the LORD your G
Deut 4:23 which the LORD thy G hath
Deut 4:24 For the LORD thy G is a consuming
Deut 4:24 consuming fire, even a jealous G
Deut 4:25 in the sight of the LORD thy G
Deut 4:29 thou shalt seek the LORD thy G
Deut 4:30 if thou turn to the LORD thy G
Deut 4:31 the LORD thy G is a merciful G
Deut 4:31 the LORD thy G is a merciful G
Deut 4:32 since the day that G created man
Deut 4:33 of G speaking out of the midst of
Deut 4:34 Or hath G assayed to go and take
Deut 4:34 to all that the LORD your G did
Deut 4:35 know that the LORD he is G
Deut 4:39 the LORD he is G in heaven above
Deut 4:40 which the LORD thy G giveth thee
Deut 5:2 The LORD our G made a covenant
Deut 5:6 I am the LORD thy G, which
Deut 5:9 I the LORD thy G am a jealous G
Deut 5:9 I the LORD thy G am a jealous G
Deut 5:11 name of the LORD thy G in vain
Deut 5:12 as the LORD thy G hath commanded
Deut 5:14 is the sabbath of the LORD thy G
Deut 5:15 that the LORD thy G brought thee
Deut 5:15 therefore the LORD thy G
Deut 5:16 as the LORD thy G hath commanded
Deut 5:16 which the LORD thy G giveth thee
Deut 5:24 the LORD our G hath shewed us his
Deut 5:24 day that G doth talk with man
Deut 5:25 voice of the LORD our G any more
Deut 5:26 G speaking out of the midst of
Deut 5:27 all that the LORD our G shall say
Deut 5:27 LORD our G shall speak unto thee
Deut 5:32 LORD your G hath commanded you
Deut 5:33 LORD your G hath commanded you
Deut 6:1 which the LORD your G commanded
Deut 6:2 thou mightest fear the LORD thy G
Deut 6:3 as the LORD G of thy fathers hath
Deut 6:4 The LORD our G is one LORD
Deut 6:5 LORD thy G with all thine heart
Deut 6:10 when the LORD thy G shall have
Deut 6:13 Thou shalt fear the LORD thy G
Deut 6:15 (For the LORD thy G is a jealous
Deut 6:15 G among you) lest the anger of
Deut 6:15 thy G be kindled against thee
Deut 6:16 shall not tempt the LORD your G
Deut 6:17 commandments of the LORD your G
Deut 6:20 the LORD our G hath commanded you
Deut 6:24 statutes, to fear the LORD our G
Deut 6:25 before the LORD our G, as he hath
Deut 7:1 When the LORD thy G shall bring
Deut 7:2 when the LORD thy G shall deliver
Deut 7:6 holy people unto the LORD thy G

Deut 7:6 the LORD thy G hath chosen thee
Deut 7:9 that the LORD thy G, he is G
Deut 7:9 the faithful G, which keepeth covenant
Deut 7:12 that the LORD thy G shall keep
Deut 7:16 the LORD thy G shall deliver thee
Deut 7:18 the LORD thy G did unto Pharaoh
Deut 7:19 the LORD thy G brought thee out
Deut 7:19 so shall the LORD thy G do unto
Deut 7:20 Moreover the LORD thy G will send
Deut 7:21 for the LORD thy G is among you
Deut 7:21 a mighty G and terrible
Deut 7:22 the LORD thy G will put out those
Deut 7:23 But the LORD thy G shall deliver
Deut 7:25 an abomination to the LORD thy G
Deut 8:2 G led thee these forty years in
Deut 8:5 so the LORD thy G chasteneth thee
Deut 8:6 commandments of the LORD thy G
Deut 8:7 For the LORD thy G bringeth thee
Deut 8:10 thou shalt bless the LORD thy G
Deut 8:11 thou forget not the LORD thy G
Deut 8:14 up, and thou forget the LORD thy G
Deut 8:18 shalt remember the LORD thy G
Deut 8:19 do at all forget the LORD thy G
Deut 8:20 unto the voice of the LORD your G
Deut 9:3 that the LORD thy G is he which
Deut 9:4 after that the LORD thy G hath
Deut 9:5 of these nations the LORD thy G
Deut 9:6 that the LORD thy G giveth thee
Deut 9:7 thy G to wrath in the wilderness
Deut 9:10 written with the finger of G
Deut 9:16 sinned against the LORD your G
Deut 9:23 commandment of the LORD your G
Deut 9:26 unto the LORD, and said, O Lord G
Deut 10:9 as the LORD thy G promised him
Deut 10:12 the LORD thy G require of thee
Deut 10:12 but to fear the LORD thy G
Deut 10:12 the LORD thy G with all thy heart
Deut 10:14 of heavens is the LORD's thy G
Deut 10:17 the LORD your G is G of gods
Deut 10:17 gods, and Lord of lords, a great G
Deut 10:20 Thou shalt fear the LORD thy G
Deut 10:21 He is thy praise, and he is thy G
Deut 10:22 now the LORD thy G hath made thee
Deut 11:1 thou shalt love the LORD thy G
Deut 11:2 chastisement of the LORD your G
Deut 11:12 which the LORD thy G careth for
Deut 11:12 the LORD thy G are always upon it
Deut 11:13 this day, to love the LORD your G
Deut 11:22 do them, to love the LORD your G
Deut 11:25 for the LORD your G shall lay the
Deut 11:27 commandments of the LORD your G
Deut 11:28 commandments of the LORD your G
Deut 11:29 when the LORD thy G hath brought
Deut 11:31 which the LORD your G giveth you
Deut 12:1 which the LORD G of thy fathers
Deut 12:4 not do so unto the LORD your G
Deut 12:5 G shall choose out of all your
Deut 12:7 shall eat before the LORD your G
Deut 12:7 the LORD thy G hath blessed thee
Deut 12:9 which the LORD your G giveth you
Deut 12:10 LORD your G giveth you to inherit
Deut 12:11 G shall choose to cause his name
Deut 12:12 rejoice before the LORD your G
Deut 12:15 thy G which he hath given thee
Deut 12:18 eat them before the LORD thy G in
Deut 12:18 which the LORD thy G shall choose
Deut 12:18 rejoice before the LORD thy G in
Deut 12:20 When the LORD thy G shall enlarge
Deut 12:21 thy G hath chosen to put his name
Deut 12:27 upon the altar of the LORD thy G
Deut 12:27 upon the altar of the LORD thy G
Deut 12:28 in the sight of the LORD thy G
Deut 12:29 When the LORD thy G shall cut off
Deut 12:31 not do so unto the LORD thy G
Deut 13:3 for the LORD your G proveth you
Deut 13:3 LORD your G with all your heart
Deut 13:4 shall walk after the LORD your G
Deut 13:5 you away from the LORD your G
Deut 13:5 thy G commanded thee to walk in
Deut 13:10 thee away from the LORD thy G
Deut 13:12 which the LORD thy G hath given
Deut 13:16 every whit, for the LORD thy G
Deut 13:18 to the voice of the LORD thy G
Deut 13:18 in the eyes of the LORD thy G
Deut 14:1 the children of the LORD your G
Deut 14:2 holy people unto the LORD thy G
Deut 14:21 holy people unto the LORD thy G
Deut 14:23 shalt eat before the LORD thy G
Deut 14:23 to fear the LORD thy G always
Deut 14:24 which the LORD thy G shall choose
Deut 14:24 the LORD thy G hath blessed thee
Deut 14:25 which the LORD thy G shall choose
Deut 14:26 eat there before the LORD thy G
Deut 14:29 that the LORD thy G may bless
Deut 15:4 G giveth thee for an inheritance
Deut 15:5 unto the voice of the LORD thy G
Deut 15:6 For the LORD thy G blesseth thee
Deut 15:7 which the LORD thy G giveth thee
Deut 15:10 thy G shall bless thee in all thy
Deut 15:14 G hath blessed thee thou shalt
Deut 15:15 the LORD thy G redeemed thee
Deut 15:18 the LORD thy G shall bless thee
Deut 15:19 sanctify unto the LORD thy G
Deut 15:20 eat it before the LORD thy G year
Deut 15:21 sacrifice it unto the LORD thy G
Deut 16:1 the passover unto the LORD thy G
Deut 16:1 the month of Abib the LORD thy G
Deut 16:2 the passover unto the LORD thy G
Deut 16:5 which the LORD thy G giveth thee
Deut 16:6 G shall choose to place his name
Deut 16:7 which the LORD thy G shall choose
Deut 16:8 solemn assembly to the LORD thy G
Deut 16:10 of weeks unto the LORD thy G with
Deut 16:10 shalt give unto the LORD thy G
Deut 16:10 the LORD thy G hath blessed thee
Deut 16:11 rejoice before the LORD thy G
Deut 16:11 G hath chosen to place his name
Deut 16:15 thy G in the place which the LORD
Deut 16:15 because the LORD thy G shall
Deut 16:16 appear before the LORD thy G in
Deut 16:17 thy G which he hath given thee
Deut 16:18 which the LORD thy G giveth thee
Deut 16:20 which the LORD thy G giveth thee
Deut 16:21 unto the altar of the LORD thy G
Deut 16:22 which the LORD thy G hateth
Deut 17:1 unto the LORD thy G any bullock
Deut 17:1 abomination unto the LORD thy G
Deut 17:2 which the LORD thy G giveth thee
Deut 17:2 in the sight of the LORD thy G
Deut 17:8 which the LORD thy G shall choose
Deut 17:12 there before the LORD thy G
Deut 17:14 which the LORD thy G giveth thee
Deut 17:15 whom the LORD thy G shall choose
Deut 17:19 may learn to fear the LORD his G
Deut 18:5 For the LORD thy G hath chosen
Deut 18:7 in the name of the LORD his G
Deut 18:9 which the LORD thy G giveth thee
Deut 18:12 G doth drive them out from before
Deut 18:13 be perfect with the LORD thy G
Deut 18:14 the LORD thy G hath not suffered
Deut 18:15 The LORD thy G will raise up unto
Deut 18:16 thy G in Horeb in the day of the
Deut 18:16 again the voice of the LORD my G
Deut 19:1 When the LORD thy G hath cut off
Deut 19:1 land the LORD thy G giveth thee
Deut 19:2 which the LORD thy G giveth thee
Deut 19:3 which the LORD thy G giveth thee
Deut 19:8 if the LORD thy G enlarge thy
Deut 19:9 this day, to love the LORD thy G
Deut 19:10 which the LORD thy G giveth thee
Deut 19:14 thy G giveth thee to possess it
Deut 20:1 for the LORD thy G is with thee
Deut 20:4 For the LORD your G is he that
Deut 20:13 And when the LORD thy G hath
Deut 20:14 the LORD thy G hath given thee
Deut 20:16 which the LORD thy G doth give
Deut 20:17 as the LORD thy G hath commanded
Deut 20:18 ye sin against the LORD your G
Deut 21:1 thy G giveth thee to possess it
Deut 21:5 for them the LORD thy G hath
Deut 21:10 the LORD thy G hath delivered
Deut 21:23 that is hanged is accursed of G
Deut 21:23 which the LORD thy G giveth thee
Deut 22:5 abomination unto the LORD thy G
Deut 23:5 Nevertheless the LORD thy G would
Deut 23:5 but the LORD thy G turned the
Deut 23:5 because the LORD thy G loved thee
Deut 23:14 For the LORD thy G walketh in the
Deut 23:18 of the LORD thy G for any vow
Deut 23:18 abomination unto the LORD thy G
Deut 23:20 that the LORD thy G may bless
Deut 23:21 vow a vow unto the LORD thy G
Deut 23:21 for the LORD thy G will surely
Deut 23:23 hast vowed unto the LORD thy G
Deut 24:4 which the LORD thy G giveth thee
Deut 24:9 thy G did unto Miriam by the way
Deut 24:13 unto thee before the LORD thy G
Deut 24:18 the LORD thy G redeemed thee
Deut 24:19 that the LORD thy G may bless
Deut 25:15 which the LORD thy G giveth thee
Deut 25:16 abomination unto the LORD thy G
Deut 25:18 and he feared not G
Deut 25:19 when the LORD thy G hath given
Deut 25:19 G giveth thee for an inheritance
Deut 26:1 the land which the LORD thy G
Deut 26:2 that the LORD thy G giveth thee
Deut 26:2 the place which the LORD thy G
Deut 26:3 this day unto the LORD thy G
Deut 26:4 the altar of the LORD thy G
Deut 26:5 and say before the LORD thy G
Deut 26:7 unto the LORD G of our fathers
Deut 26:10 set it before the LORD thy G
Deut 26:10 and worship before the LORD thy G
Deut 26:11 LORD thy G hath given unto thee
Deut 26:13 shalt say before the LORD thy G
Deut 26:14 to the voice of the LORD my G
Deut 26:16 This day the LORD thy G hath
Deut 26:17 the LORD this day to be thy G
Deut 26:19 holy people unto the LORD thy G
Deut 27:2 which the LORD thy G giveth thee
Deut 27:3 which the LORD thy G giveth thee
Deut 27:3 as the LORD G of thy fathers hath
Deut 27:5 an altar unto the LORD thy G
Deut 27:6 of the LORD thy G of whole stones
Deut 27:6 thereon unto the LORD thy G
Deut 27:7 and rejoice before the LORD thy G
Deut 27:9 the people of the LORD thy G
Deut 27:10 obey the voice of the LORD thy G
Deut 28:1 unto the voice of the LORD thy G
Deut 28:1 that the LORD thy G will set thee
Deut 28:2 unto the voice of the LORD thy G
Deut 28:8 which the LORD thy G giveth thee
Deut 28:9 commandments of the LORD thy G
Deut 28:13 commandments of the LORD thy G
Deut 28:15 unto the voice of the LORD thy G
Deut 28:45 unto the voice of the LORD thy G
Deut 28:47 the LORD thy G with joyfulness
Deut 28:52 the LORD thy G hath given thee
Deut 28:53 the LORD thy G hath given thee
Deut 28:58 and fearful name, THE LORD THY G
Deut 28:62 obey the voice of the LORD thy G
Deut 28:67 shalt say, Would G it were even
Deut 28:67 say, Would G it were morning
Deut 29:6 know that I am the LORD your G
Deut 29:10 all of you before the LORD your G
Deut 29:12 into covenant with the LORD thy G
Deut 29:12 which the LORD thy G maketh with
Deut 29:13 and that he may be unto thee a G
Deut 29:15 us this day before the LORD our G
Deut 29:18 away this day from the LORD our G
Deut 29:25 of the LORD G of their fathers
Deut 29:29 things belong unto the LORD our G
Deut 30:1 the LORD thy G hath driven thee
Deut 30:2 shalt return unto the LORD thy G
Deut 30:3 That then the LORD thy G will
Deut 30:3 LORD thy G hath scattered thee
Deut 30:4 will the LORD thy G gather thee
Deut 30:5 the LORD thy G will bring thee
Deut 30:6 the LORD thy G will circumcise
Deut 30:6 LORD thy G with all thine heart
Deut 30:7 the LORD thy G will put all these
Deut 30:9 the LORD thy G will make thee
Deut 30:10 unto the voice of the LORD thy G
Deut 30:10 LORD thy G with all thine heart
Deut 30:16 this day to love the LORD thy G
Deut 30:16 the LORD thy G shall bless thee
Deut 30:20 thou mayest love the LORD thy G
Deut 31:3 The LORD thy G, he will go over
Deut 31:6 for the LORD thy G, he it is that
Deut 31:11 thy G in the place which he shall
Deut 31:12 learn, and fear the LORD your G
Deut 31:13 and learn to fear the LORD your G
Deut 31:17 because our G is not among us
Deut 31:26 the covenant of the LORD your G
Deut 32:3 ascribe ye greatness unto our G
Deut 32:4 a G of truth and without iniquity,
Deut 32:15 then he forsook G which made him
Deut 32:17 sacrificed unto devils, not to G
Deut 32:18 hast forgotten G that formed thee
Deut 32:21 jealousy with that which is not G
Deut 33:1 wherewith Moses the man of G
Deut 33:26 none like unto the G of Jeshurun
Deut 33:27 The eternal G is thy refuge, and
Josh 1:9 for the LORD thy G is with thee
Josh 1:11 which the LORD your G giveth you
Josh 1:13 The LORD your G hath given you
Josh 1:15 which the LORD your G giveth them
Josh 1:17 only the LORD thy G be with thee
Josh 2:11 for the LORD your G, he is G in
Josh 3:3 the covenant of the LORD your G

Josh 3:9 hear the words of the LORD your G
Josh 3:10 that the living G is among you
Josh 4:5 your G into the midst of Jordan
Josh 4:23 For the LORD your G dried up the
Josh 4:23 as the LORD your G did to the Red
Josh 4:24 fear the LORD your G for ever
Josh 7:7 And Joshua said, Alas, O Lord G
Josh 7:7 would to G we had been content,
Josh 7:13 thus saith the LORD G of Israel
Josh 7:19 glory to the LORD G of Israel
Josh 7:20 against the LORD G of Israel
Josh 8:7 for the LORD your G will deliver
Josh 8:30 LORD G of Israel in mount Ebal
Josh 9:9 of the name of the LORD thy G
Josh 9:18 unto them by the LORD G of Israel
Josh 9:19 unto them by the LORD G of Israel
Josh 9:23 of water for the house of my G
Josh 9:24 how that the LORD thy G commanded
Josh 10:19 for the LORD your G hath
Josh 10:40 as the LORD G of Israel commanded
Josh 10:42 because the LORD G of Israel
Josh 13:14 LORD G of Israel made by fire are
Josh 13:33 the LORD G of Israel was their
Josh 14:6 Moses the man of G concerning me
Josh 14:8 I wholly followed the LORD my G
Josh 14:9 wholly followed the LORD my G
Josh 14:14 followed the LORD G of Israel
Josh 18:3 which the LORD G of your fathers
Josh 18:6 you here before the LORD our G
Josh 22:3 commandment of the LORD your G
Josh 22:4 now the LORD your G hath given
Josh 22:5 you, to love the LORD your G
Josh 22:16 committed against the G of Israel
Josh 22:19 the altar of the LORD our G
Josh 22:22 The LORD G of gods, the LORD G
Josh 22:24 to do with the LORD G of Israel
Josh 22:29 G forbid that we should rebel
Josh 22:29 the altar of the LORD our G that
Josh 22:33 the children of Israel blessed G
Josh 22:34 between us that the LORD is G
Josh 23:3 your G hath done unto all these
Josh 23:3 for the LORD your G is he that
Josh 23:5 And the LORD your G, he shall
Josh 23:5 as the LORD your G hath promised
Josh 23:8 But cleave unto the LORD your G
Josh 23:10 for the LORD your G, he it is
Josh 23:11 that ye love the LORD your G
Josh 23:13 G will no more drive out any of
Josh 23:13 the LORD your G hath given you
Josh 23:14 LORD your G spake concerning you
Josh 23:15 the LORD your G promised you
Josh 23:15 the LORD your G hath given you
Josh 23:16 the covenant of the LORD your G
Josh 24:1 presented themselves before G
Josh 24:2 Thus saith the LORD G of Israel
Josh 24:16 G forbid that we should forsake
Josh 24:17 For the LORD our G, he it is that
Josh 24:18 for he is our G
Josh 24:19 for he is an holy G
Josh 24:19 he is a jealous G
Josh 24:23 heart unto the LORD G of Israel
Josh 24:24 The LORD our G will we serve, and
Josh 24:26 words in the book of the law of G
Josh 24:27 unto you, lest ye deny your G
Judg 1:7 have done, so G hath requited me
Judg 2:12 the LORD G of their fathers
Judg 3:7 LORD, and forgat the LORD their G
Judg 3:20 I have a message from G unto thee
Judg 4:6 Hath not the LORD G of Israel
Judg 4:23 So G subdued on that day Jabin
Judg 5:3 praise to the LORD G of Israel
Judg 5:5 from before the LORD G of Israel
Judg 6:8 Thus saith the LORD G of Israel
Judg 6:10 unto you, I am the LORD your G
Judg 6:20 the angel of G said unto him,
Judg 6:22 LORD, Gideon said, Alas, O Lord G
Judg 6:26 thy G upon the top of this rock
Judg 6:36 And Gideon said unto G, If thou
Judg 6:39 And Gideon said unto G, Let not
Judg 6:40 And G did so that night
Judg 7:14 his hand hath G delivered Midian
Judg 8:3 G hath delivered into your hands
Judg 8:34 remembered not the LORD their G
Judg 9:7 that G may hearken unto you
Judg 9:9 wherewith by me they honour G
Judg 9:13 I leave my wine, which cheereth G
Judg 9:23 Then G sent an evil spirit
Judg 9:29 would to G this people were under
Judg 9:56 Thus G rendered the wickedness of
Judg 9:57 did G render upon their heads
Judg 10:10 because we have forsaken our G
Judg 11:21 the LORD G of Israel delivered
Judg 11:23 So now the LORD G of Israel hath
Judg 11:24 So whomsoever the LORD our G
Judg 13:5 a Nazarite unto G from the womb
Judg 13:6 A man of G came unto me, and his
Judg 13:6 the countenance of an angel of G
Judg 13:7 child shall be a Nazarite to G
Judg 13:8 let the man of G which thou didst
Judg 13:9 G hearkened to the voice of
Judg 13:9 the angel of G came again unto
Judg 13:22 die, because we have seen G
Judg 15:19 But G clave an hollow place that
Judg 16:17 unto G from my mother's womb
Judg 16:28 unto the LORD, and said, O Lord G
Judg 16:28 I pray thee, only this once, O G
Judg 18:5 Ask counsel, we pray thee, of G
Judg 18:10 for G hath given it into your
Judg 18:31 that the house of G was in Shiloh
Judg 20:2 the assembly of the people of G
Judg 20:18 and went up to the house of G
Judg 20:18 and asked counsel of G
Judg 20:26 up, and came unto the house of G
Judg 20:27 of G was there in those days
Judg 20:31 one goeth up to the house of G
Judg 21:2 the people came to the house of G
Judg 21:2 and abode there till even before G
Judg 21:3 O LORD G of Israel, why is this
Ruth 2:12 thee of the LORD G of Israel
1Sa 1:17 the G of Israel grant thee thy
1Sa 2:2 is there any rock like our G
1Sa 2:3 for the LORD is a G of knowledge
1Sa 2:27 And there came a man of G unto Eli
1Sa 2:30 the LORD G of Israel saith
1Sa 2:32 wealth which G shall give Israel
1Sa 3:3 ere the lamp of G went out in the
1Sa 3:3 the LORD, where the ark of G was
1Sa 3:17 G do so to thee, and more also, if
1Sa 4:4 with the ark of the covenant of G
1Sa 4:7 said, G is come into the camp
1Sa 4:11 And the ark of G was taken
1Sa 4:13 heart trembled for the ark of G
1Sa 4:17 dead, and the ark of G is taken
1Sa 4:18 he made mention of the ark of G
1Sa 4:19 that the ark of G was taken
1Sa 4:21 because the ark of G was taken
1Sa 4:22 for the ark of G is taken
1Sa 5:1 the Philistines took the ark of G
1Sa 5:2 the Philistines took the ark of G
1Sa 5:7 The ark of the G of Israel shall
1Sa 5:8 with the ark of the G of Israel
1Sa 5:8 Let the ark of the G of Israel be
1Sa 5:8 of the G of Israel about thither
1Sa 5:10 they sent the ark of G to Ekron
1Sa 5:10 as the ark of G came to Ekron
1Sa 5:10 the ark of the G of Israel to us
1Sa 5:11 away the ark of the G of Israel
1Sa 5:11 the hand of G was very heavy
1Sa 6:3 away the ark of the G of Israel
1Sa 6:5 give glory unto the G of Israel
1Sa 6:20 to stand before this holy LORD G
1Sa 7:8 to cry unto the LORD our G for us
1Sa 9:6 there is in this city a man of G
1Sa 9:7 present to bring to the man of G
1Sa 9:8 that will I give to the man of G
1Sa 9:9 when a man went to enquire of G
1Sa 9:10 the city where the man of G was
1Sa 9:27 I may shew thee the word of G
1Sa 10:3 men going up to G to Beth-el
1Sa 10:5 thou shalt come to the hill of G
1Sa 10:7 for G is with thee
1Sa 10:9 Samuel, G gave him another heart
1Sa 10:10 and the Spirit of G came upon him
1Sa 10:18 Thus saith the LORD G of Israel
1Sa 10:19 ye have this day rejected your G
1Sa 10:24 shouted, and said, G save the king
1Sa 10:26 men, whose hearts G had touched
1Sa 11:6 the Spirit of G came upon Saul
1Sa 12:9 when they forgat the LORD their G
1Sa 12:12 the LORD your G was your king
1Sa 12:14 following the LORD your G
1Sa 12:19 thy servants unto the LORD thy G
1Sa 12:23 G forbid that I should sin
1Sa 13:13 the commandment of the LORD thy G
1Sa 14:18 Ahiah, Bring hither the ark of G
1Sa 14:18 For the ark of G was at that time
1Sa 14:36 Let us draw near hither unto G
1Sa 14:37 And Saul asked counsel of G
1Sa 14:41 said unto the LORD G of Israel
1Sa 14:44 answered, G do so and more also
1Sa 14:45 G forbid: as the LORD liveth
1Sa 14:45 he hath wrought with G this day
1Sa 15:15 to sacrifice unto the LORD thy G
1Sa 15:21 unto the LORD thy G in Gilgal
1Sa 15:30 that I may worship the LORD thy G
1Sa 16:15 evil spirit from G troubleth thee
1Sa 16:16 evil spirit from G is upon thee
1Sa 16:23 evil spirit from G was upon Saul
1Sa 17:26 defy the armies of the living G
1Sa 17:36 defied the armies of the living G
1Sa 17:45 the G of the armies of Israel,
1Sa 17:46 know that there is a G in Israel
1Sa 18:10 evil spirit from G came upon Saul
1Sa 19:20 the Spirit of G was upon the
1Sa 19:23 the Spirit of G was upon him also
1Sa 20:2 And he said unto him, G forbid
1Sa 20:12 O LORD G of Israel, when I have
1Sa 22:3 till I know what G will do for me
1Sa 22:13 and hast enquired of G for him
1Sa 22:15 begin to enquire of G for him
1Sa 23:7 G hath delivered him into mine
1Sa 23:10 O LORD G of Israel, thy servant
1Sa 23:11 O LORD G of Israel, I beseech
1Sa 23:14 but G delivered him not into his
1Sa 23:16 and strengthened his hand in G
1Sa 25:22 more also do G unto the enemies
1Sa 25:29 of life with the LORD thy G
1Sa 25:32 Blessed be the LORD G of Israel
1Sa 25:34 as the LORD G of Israel liveth,
1Sa 26:8 G hath delivered thine enemy into
1Sa 28:15 G is departed from me, and
1Sa 29:9 in my sight, as an angel of G
1Sa 30:6 himself in the LORD his G
1Sa 30:15 And he said, Swear unto me by G
2Sa 2:27 As G liveth, unless thou hadst
2Sa 3:9 So do G to Abner, and more also,
2Sa 3:35 sware, saying, So do G to me
2Sa 5:10 the LORD G of hosts was with him
2Sa 6:2 bring up from thence the ark of G
2Sa 6:3 set the ark of G upon a new cart
2Sa 6:4 Gibeah, accompanying the ark of G
2Sa 6:6 forth his hand to the ark of G
2Sa 6:7 G smote him there for his error
2Sa 6:7 and there he died by the ark of G
2Sa 6:12 unto him, because of the ark of G
2Sa 6:12 brought up the ark of G from the
2Sa 7:2 but the ark of G dwelleth within
2Sa 7:18 and he said, Who am I, O Lord G
2Sa 7:19 thing in thy sight, O Lord G
2Sa 7:19 this the manner of man, O Lord G
2Sa 7:20 for thou, Lord G, knowest thy
2Sa 7:22 thou art great, O LORD G
2Sa 7:22 is there any G beside thee
2Sa 7:23 whom G went to redeem for a
2Sa 7:24 and thou, LORD, art become their G
2Sa 7:25 And now, O LORD G, the word that
2Sa 7:26 of hosts is the G over Israel
2Sa 7:27 G of Israel, hast revealed to thy
2Sa 7:28 And now, O Lord G
2Sa 7:28 thou art that G
2Sa 7:29 for thou, O Lord G, hast spoken
2Sa 9:3 shew the kindness of G unto him
2Sa 10:12 and for the cities of our G
2Sa 12:7 Thus saith the LORD G of Israel
2Sa 12:16 besought G for the child
2Sa 12:22 Who can tell whether G will be
2Sa 14:11 the king remember the LORD thy G
2Sa 14:13 a thing against the people of G
2Sa 14:14 neither doth G respect any person
2Sa 14:16 out of the inheritance of G
2Sa 14:17 for as an angel of G, so is my
2Sa 14:17 the LORD thy G will be with thee
2Sa 14:20 to the wisdom of an angel of G
2Sa 15:24 the ark of the covenant of G
2Sa 15:24 and they set down the ark of G
2Sa 15:25 back the ark of G into the city
2Sa 15:29 the ark of G again to Jerusalem
2Sa 15:32 the mount, where he worshipped G
2Sa 16:16 G save the king, G save the
2Sa 16:23 had enquired at the oracle of G
2Sa 18:28 said, Blessed be the LORD thy G
2Sa 18:33 would G I had died for thee, O
2Sa 19:13 G do so to me, and more also, if
2Sa 19:27 lord the king is as an angel of G
2Sa 21:14 after that G was intreated for
2Sa 22:3 The G of my rock
2Sa 22:7 upon the LORD, and cried to my G
2Sa 22:22 not wickedly departed from my G
2Sa 22:30 by my G have I leaped over a wall
2Sa 22:31 As for G, his way is perfect

2Sa 22:32 For who is G, save the LORD
2Sa 22:32 and who is a rock, save our G
2Sa 22:33 G is my strength and power
2Sa 22:47 exalted be the G of the rock of
2Sa 22:48 It is G that avengeth me, and that
2Sa 23:1 the anointed of the G of Jacob
2Sa 23:3 The G of Israel said, the Rock of
2Sa 23:3 be just, ruling in the fear of G
2Sa 23:5 my house be not so with G
2Sa 24:3 Now the LORD thy G add unto the
2Sa 24:23 king, The LORD thy G accept thee
2Sa 24:24 my G of that which doth cost me
1Kin 1:17 LORD thy G unto thine handmaid
1Kin 1:25 him, and say, G save king Adonijah
1Kin 1:30 unto thee by the LORD G of Israel
1Kin 1:34 and say, G save king Solomon
1Kin 1:36 the LORD G of my lord the king
1Kin 1:39 people said, G save king Solomon
1Kin 1:47 G make the name of Solomon better
1Kin 1:48 Blessed be the LORD G of Israel
1Kin 2:3 keep the charge of the LORD thy G
1Kin 2:23 G do so to me, and more also, if
1Kin 2:26 the Lord G before David my father
1Kin 3:5 G said, Ask what I shall give
1Kin 3:7 And now, O LORD my G, thou hast
1Kin 3:11 G said unto him, Because thou
1Kin 3:28 that the wisdom of G was in him
1Kin 4:29 And G gave Solomon wisdom and
1Kin 5:3 G for the wars which were about
1Kin 5:4 But now the LORD my G hath given
1Kin 5:5 unto the name of the LORD my G
1Kin 8:15 Blessed be the LORD G of Israel
1Kin 8:17 the name of the LORD G of Israel
1Kin 8:20 the name of the LORD G of Israel
1Kin 8:23 LORD G of Israel, there is no G
1Kin 8:25 LORD G of Israel, keep with thy
1Kin 8:26 O G of Israel, let thy word, I
1Kin 8:27 But will G indeed dwell on the
1Kin 8:28 to his supplication, O LORD my G
1Kin 8:53 fathers out of Egypt, O Lord G
1Kin 8:57 The LORD our G be with us
1Kin 8:59 be nigh unto the LORD our G day
1Kin 8:60 earth may know that the LORD is G
1Kin 8:61 be perfect with the LORD our G
1Kin 8:65 of Egypt, before the LORD our G
1Kin 9:9 they forsook the LORD their G
1Kin 10:9 Blessed be the LORD thy G
1Kin 10:24 which G had put in his heart
1Kin 11:4 not perfect with the LORD his G
1Kin 11:9 turned from the LORD G of Israel
1Kin 11:23 And G stirred him up another
1Kin 11:31 the G of Israel, Behold, I will
1Kin 12:22 But the word of G came unto
1Kin 12:22 came unto Shemaiah the man of G
1Kin 13:1 there came a man of G out of
1Kin 13:4 heard the saying of the man of G
1Kin 13:5 of G had given by the word of the
1Kin 13:6 and said unto the man of G
1Kin 13:6 now the face of the LORD thy G
1Kin 13:6 the man of G besought the LORD,
1Kin 13:7 the king said unto the man of G
1Kin 13:8 the man of G said unto the king,
1Kin 13:11 of G had done that day in Beth-el
1Kin 13:12 seen what way the man of G went
1Kin 13:14 And went after the man of G
1Kin 13:14 Art thou the man of G that camest
1Kin 13:21 the man of G that came from Judah
1Kin 13:21 the LORD thy G commanded thee
1Kin 13:26 he said, It is the man of G
1Kin 13:29 up the carcase of the man of G
1Kin 13:31 wherein the man of G is buried
1Kin 14:7 Thus saith the LORD G of Israel
1Kin 14:13 LORD G of Israel in the house of
1Kin 15:3 not perfect with the LORD his G
1Kin 15:4 G give him a lamp in Jerusalem
1Kin 15:30 the LORD G of Israel to anger
1Kin 16:13 in provoking the LORD G of Israel
1Kin 16:26 to provoke the LORD G of Israel
1Kin 16:33 did more to provoke the LORD G of
1Kin 17:1 As the LORD G of Israel liveth,
1Kin 17:12 said, As the LORD thy G liveth
1Kin 17:14 thus saith the LORD G of Israel
1Kin 17:18 to do with thee, O thou man of G
1Kin 17:20 the LORD, and said, O LORD my G
1Kin 17:21 the LORD, and said, O LORD my G
1Kin 17:24 I know that thou art a man of G
1Kin 18:10 As the LORD thy G liveth, there
1Kin 18:21 if the LORD be G, follow him
1Kin 18:24 the G that answereth by fire, let
1Kin 18:24 answereth by fire, let him be G
1Kin 18:36 LORD G of Abraham, Isaac, and of
1Kin 18:36 day that thou art G in Israel
1Kin 18:37 may know that thou art the LORD G
1Kin 18:39 they said, The LORD, he is the G
1Kin 18:39 the LORD, he is the G
1Kin 19:8 nights unto Horeb the mount of G
1Kin 19:10 jealous for the LORD G of hosts
1Kin 19:14 jealous for the LORD G of hosts
1Kin 20:28 And there came a man of G, and
1Kin 20:28 The LORD is G of the hills
1Kin 20:28 but he is not G of the valleys,
1Kin 21:10 saying, Thou didst blaspheme G
1Kin 21:13 saying, Naboth did blaspheme G
1Kin 22:53 to anger the LORD G of Israel
2Kin 1:3 there is not a G in Israel
2Kin 1:6 there is not a G in Israel
2Kin 1:9 he spake unto him, Thou man of G
2Kin 1:10 of fifty, If I be a man of G
2Kin 1:11 and said unto him, O man of G
2Kin 1:12 unto them, If I be a man of G
2Kin 1:12 the fire of G came down from
2Kin 1:13 him, and said unto him, O man of G
2Kin 1:16 no G in Israel to enquire of his
2Kin 2:14 Where is the LORD G of Elijah
2Kin 4:7 she came and told the man of G
2Kin 4:9 that this is an holy man of G
2Kin 4:16 said, Nay, my lord, thou man of G
2Kin 4:21 him on the bed of the man of G
2Kin 4:22 that I may run to the man of G
2Kin 4:25 unto the man of G to mount Carmel
2Kin 4:25 when the man of G saw her afar
2Kin 4:27 came to the man of G to the hill
2Kin 4:27 And the man of G said, Let her
2Kin 4:40 out, and said, O thou man of G
2Kin 4:42 brought the man of G bread of the
2Kin 5:3 Would G my lord were with the
2Kin 5:7 rent his clothes, and said, Am I G
2Kin 5:8 when Elisha the man of G had
2Kin 5:11 on the name of the LORD his G
2Kin 5:14 to the saying of the man of G
2Kin 5:15 And he returned to the man of G
2Kin 5:15 there is no G in all the earth
2Kin 5:20 servant of Elisha the man of G
2Kin 6:6 And the man of G said, Where fell
2Kin 6:9 the man of G sent unto the king
2Kin 6:10 place which the man of G told him
2Kin 6:15 of the man of G was risen early
2Kin 6:31 G do so and more also to me, if
2Kin 7:2 king leaned answered the man of G
2Kin 7:17 he died, as the man of G had said
2Kin 7:18 man of G had spoken to the king
2Kin 7:19 that lord answered the man of G
2Kin 8:2 after the saying of the man of G
2Kin 8:4 the servant of the man of G
2Kin 8:7 The man of G is come hither
2Kin 8:8 hand, and go, meet the man of G
2Kin 8:11 and the man of G wept
2Kin 9:6 Thus saith the LORD G of Israel
2Kin 10:31 G of Israel with all his heart
2Kin 11:12 hands, and said, G save the king
2Kin 13:19 the man of G was wroth with him,
2Kin 14:25 the word of the LORD G of Israel
2Kin 16:2 in the sight of the LORD his G
2Kin 17:7 sinned against the LORD their G
2Kin 17:9 right against the LORD their G
2Kin 17:14 not believe in the LORD their G
2Kin 17:16 commandments of the LORD their G
2Kin 17:19 commandments of the LORD their G
2Kin 17:26 the manner of the G of the land
2Kin 17:26 the manner of the G of the land
2Kin 17:27 the manner of the G of the land
2Kin 17:39 But the LORD your G ye shall fear
2Kin 18:5 trusted in the LORD G of Israel
2Kin 18:12 not the voice of the LORD their G
2Kin 18:22 me, We trust in the LORD our G
2Kin 19:4 It may be the LORD thy G will
2Kin 19:4 sent to reproach the living G
2Kin 19:4 which the LORD thy G hath heard
2Kin 19:10 Let not thy G in whom thou
2Kin 19:15 O LORD G of Israel, which
2Kin 19:15 the cherubims, thou art the G
2Kin 19:16 sent him to reproach the living G
2Kin 19:19 Now therefore, O LORD our G
2Kin 19:19 may know that thou art the LORD G
2Kin 19:20 Thus saith the LORD G of Israel
2Kin 20:5 the G of David thy father, I have
2Kin 21:12 thus saith the LORD G of Israel
2Kin 21:22 forsook the LORD G of his fathers
2Kin 22:15 Thus saith the LORD G of Israel
2Kin 22:18 Thus saith the LORD G of Israel
2Kin 23:16 which the man of G proclaimed
2Kin 23:17 is the sepulchre of the man of G
2Kin 23:21 the passover unto the LORD your G
1Chr 4:10 Jabez called on the G of Israel
1Chr 4:10 G granted him that which he
1Chr 5:20 for they cried to G in the battle
1Chr 5:22 slain, because the war was of G
1Chr 5:25 against the G of their fathers
1Chr 5:25 whom G destroyed before them
1Chr 5:26 the G of Israel stirred up the
1Chr 6:48 the tabernacle of the house of G
1Chr 6:49 the servant of G had commanded
1Chr 9:11 the ruler of the house of G
1Chr 9:13 of the service of the house of G
1Chr 9:26 and treasuries of the house of G
1Chr 9:27 lodged round about the house of G
1Chr 11:2 the LORD thy G said unto thee,
1Chr 11:19 My G forbid it me, that I should
1Chr 12:17 the G of our fathers look thereon
1Chr 12:18 for thy G helpeth thee
1Chr 12:22 a great host, like the host of G
1Chr 13:2 and that it be of the LORD our G
1Chr 13:3 again the ark of our G to us
1Chr 13:5 the ark of G from Kirjath-jearim
1Chr 13:6 up thence the ark of G the LORD
1Chr 13:7 they carried the ark of G in a
1Chr 13:8 before G with all their might
1Chr 13:10 and there he died before G
1Chr 13:12 And David was afraid of G that day
1Chr 13:12 I bring the ark of G home to me
1Chr 13:14 the ark of G remained with the
1Chr 14:10 And David enquired of G, saying,
1Chr 14:11 G hath broken in upon mine
1Chr 14:14 David enquired again of G
1Chr 14:14 G said unto him, Go not up after
1Chr 14:15 for G is gone forth before thee
1Chr 14:16 therefore did as G commanded him
1Chr 15:1 prepared a place for the ark of G
1Chr 15:2 the ark of G but the Levites
1Chr 15:2 LORD chosen to carry the ark of G
1Chr 15:12 bring up the ark of the LORD G of
1Chr 15:13 the LORD our G made a breach upon
1Chr 15:14 the ark of the LORD G of Israel
1Chr 15:15 G upon their shoulders with the
1Chr 15:24 the trumpets before the ark of G
1Chr 15:26 when G helped the Levites that
1Chr 16:1 So they brought the ark of G
1Chr 16:1 and peace offerings before G
1Chr 16:4 and praise the LORD G of Israel
1Chr 16:6 the ark of the covenant of G
1Chr 16:14 He is the LORD our G
1Chr 16:35 O G of our salvation, and gather
1Chr 16:36 be the LORD G of Israel for ever
1Chr 16:42 and with musical instruments of G
1Chr 17:2 for G is with thee
1Chr 17:3 that the word of G came to Nathan
1Chr 17:16 LORD, and said, Who am I, O LORD G
1Chr 17:17 a small thing in thine eyes, O G
1Chr 17:17 of a man of high degree, O LORD G
1Chr 17:20 is there any G beside thee
1Chr 17:21 whom G went to redeem to be his
1Chr 17:22 and thou, LORD, becamest their G
1Chr 17:24 G of Israel, even a G to Israel
1Chr 17:25 For thou, O my G, hast told thy
1Chr 17:26 And now, LORD, thou art G, and hast
1Chr 19:13 and for the cities of our G
1Chr 21:7 G was displeased with this thing
1Chr 21:8 And David said unto G, I have
1Chr 21:15 G sent an angel unto Jerusalem to
1Chr 21:17 And David said unto G, Is it not I
1Chr 21:17 hand, I pray thee, O LORD my G
1Chr 21:30 not go before it to enquire of G
1Chr 22:1 This is the house of the LORD G
1Chr 22:2 stones to build the house of G
1Chr 22:6 an house for the LORD G of Israel
1Chr 22:7 unto the name of the LORD my G
1Chr 22:11 build the house of the LORD thy G
1Chr 22:12 keep the law of the LORD thy G
1Chr 22:18 Is not the LORD your G with you
1Chr 22:19 your soul to seek the LORD your G
1Chr 22:19 ye the sanctuary of the LORD G
1Chr 22:19 LORD, and the holy vessels of G
1Chr 23:14 Now concerning Moses the man of G
1Chr 23:25 The LORD G of Israel hath given
1Chr 23:28 of the service of the house of G
1Chr 24:5 and governors of the house of G
1Chr 24:19 as the LORD G of Israel had
1Chr 25:5 the king's seer in the words of G
1Chr 25:5 G gave to Heman fourteen sons and

1Chr 25:6 for the service of the house of G
1Chr 26:5 for G blessed him
1Chr 26:20 the treasures of the house of G
1Chr 26:32 for every matter pertaining to G
1Chr 28:2 and for the footstool of our G
1Chr 28:3 But G said unto me, Thou shalt
1Chr 28:4 Howbeit the LORD G of Israel
1Chr 28:8 LORD, and in the audience of our G
1Chr 28:8 commandments of the LORD your G
1Chr 28:9 know thou the G of thy father
1Chr 28:12 the treasuries of the house of G
1Chr 28:20 for the LORD G, even my G
1Chr 28:21 all the service of the house of G
1Chr 29:1 whom alone G hath chosen, is yet
1Chr 29:1 not for man, but for the LORD G
1Chr 29:2 my might for the house of my G
1Chr 29:3 my affection to the house of my G
1Chr 29:3 I have given to the house of my G
1Chr 29:7 G of gold five thousand talents
1Chr 29:10 LORD G of Israel our father, for
1Chr 29:13 Now therefore, our G, we thank
1Chr 29:16 O LORD our G, all this store that
1Chr 29:17 I know also, my G, that thou
1Chr 29:18 O LORD G of Abraham, Isaac, and of
1Chr 29:20 Now bless the LORD your G
1Chr 29:20 the LORD G of their fathers
2Chr 1:1 and the LORD his G was with him
2Chr 1:3 of the congregation of G, which
2Chr 1:4 But the ark of G had David
2Chr 1:7 In that night did G appear unto
2Chr 1:8 And Solomon said unto G, Thou hast
2Chr 1:9 Now, O LORD G, let thy promise
2Chr 1:11 G said to Solomon, Because this
2Chr 2:4 to the name of the LORD my G
2Chr 2:4 solemn feasts of the LORD our G
2Chr 2:5 for great is our G above all gods
2Chr 2:12 Blessed be the LORD G of Israel
2Chr 3:3 the building of the house of G
2Chr 4:11 king Solomon for the house of G
2Chr 4:19 that were for the house of G
2Chr 5:1 the treasures of the house of G
2Chr 5:14 LORD had filled the house of G
2Chr 6:4 Blessed be the LORD G of Israel
2Chr 6:7 the name of the LORD G of Israel
2Chr 6:10 the name of the LORD G of Israel
2Chr 6:14 O LORD G of Israel
2Chr 6:14 there is no G like thee in the
2Chr 6:16 O LORD G of Israel, keep with thy
2Chr 6:17 O LORD G of Israel, let thy word
2Chr 6:18 But will G in very deed dwell
2Chr 6:19 to his supplication, O LORD my G
2Chr 6:40 Now, my G, let, I beseech thee,
2Chr 6:41 Now therefore arise, O LORD G
2Chr 6:41 let thy priests, O LORD G
2Chr 6:42 O LORD G, turn not away the face
2Chr 7:5 people dedicated the house of G
2Chr 7:22 the LORD G of their fathers
2Chr 8:14 had David the man of G commanded
2Chr 9:8 Blessed be the LORD thy G
2Chr 9:8 to be king for the LORD thy G
2Chr 9:8 because thy G loved Israel, to
2Chr 9:23 that G had put in his heart
2Chr 10:15 for the cause was of G, that the
2Chr 11:2 came to Shemaiah the man of G
2Chr 11:16 G of Israel came to Jerusalem
2Chr 11:16 unto the LORD G of their fathers
2Chr 13:5 ye not to know that the LORD G of
2Chr 13:10 But as for us, the LORD is our G
2Chr 13:11 keep the charge of the LORD our G
2Chr 13:12 G himself is with us for our
2Chr 13:12 the LORD G of your fathers
2Chr 13:15 that G smote Jeroboam and all
2Chr 13:16 G delivered them into their hand
2Chr 13:18 upon the LORD G of their fathers
2Chr 14:2 in the eyes of the LORD his G
2Chr 14:4 seek the LORD G of their fathers
2Chr 14:7 we have sought the LORD our G
2Chr 14:11 And Asa cried unto the LORD his G
2Chr 14:11 help us, O LORD our G
2Chr 14:11 O LORD, thou art our G
2Chr 15:1 the Spirit of G came upon Azariah
2Chr 15:3 hath been without the true G
2Chr 15:4 turn unto the LORD G of Israel
2Chr 15:6 for G did vex them with all
2Chr 15:9 that the LORD his G was with him
2Chr 15:12 a covenant to seek the LORD G of
2Chr 15:13 would not seek the LORD G of
2Chr 15:18 he brought into the house of G
2Chr 16:7 and not relied on the LORD thy G
2Chr 17:4 to the LORD G of his father
2Chr 18:5 for G will deliver it into the
2Chr 18:13 LORD liveth, even what my G saith
2Chr 18:31 G moved them to depart from him
2Chr 19:3 prepared thine heart to seek G
2Chr 19:4 unto the LORD G of their fathers
2Chr 19:7 no iniquity with the LORD our G
2Chr 20:6 O LORD G of our fathers
2Chr 20:6 art not thou G in heaven
2Chr 20:7 Art not thou our G, who didst
2Chr 20:12 O our G, wilt thou not judge them
2Chr 20:19 stood up to praise the LORD G of
2Chr 20:20 Believe in the LORD your G
2Chr 20:29 the fear of G was on all the
2Chr 20:30 for his G gave him rest round
2Chr 20:33 unto the G of their fathers
2Chr 21:10 the LORD G of his fathers
2Chr 21:12 the LORD G of David thy father
2Chr 22:7 was of G by coming to Joram
2Chr 22:12 hid in the house of G six years
2Chr 23:3 with the king in the house of G
2Chr 23:9 which were in the house of G
2Chr 23:11 him, and said, G save the king
2Chr 24:5 house of your G from year to year
2Chr 24:7 had broken up the house of G
2Chr 24:9 of G laid upon Israel in the
2Chr 24:13 set the house of G in his state
2Chr 24:16 good in Israel, both toward G
2Chr 24:18 of the LORD G of their fathers
2Chr 24:20 the Spirit of G came upon
2Chr 24:20 and said unto them, Thus saith G
2Chr 24:24 the LORD G of their fathers
2Chr 24:27 the repairing of the house of G
2Chr 25:7 But there came a man of G to him
2Chr 25:8 G shall make thee fall before the
2Chr 25:8 for G hath power to help, and to
2Chr 25:9 And Amaziah said to the man of G
2Chr 25:9 And the man of G answered, The
2Chr 25:16 I know that G hath determined to
2Chr 25:20 for it came of G, that he might
2Chr 25:24 in the house of G with Obed-edom
2Chr 26:5 he sought G in the days of
2Chr 26:5 understanding in the visions of G
2Chr 26:5 the LORD, G made him to prosper
2Chr 26:7 And G helped him against the
2Chr 26:16 against the LORD his G, and went
2Chr 26:18 for thine honour from the LORD G
2Chr 27:6 his ways before the LORD his G
2Chr 28:5 Wherefore the LORD his G
2Chr 28:6 the LORD G of their fathers
2Chr 28:9 because the LORD G of your
2Chr 28:10 you, sins against the LORD your G
2Chr 28:24 the vessels of the house of G
2Chr 28:24 the vessels of the house of G
2Chr 28:25 anger the LORD G of his fathers
2Chr 29:5 of the LORD G of your fathers
2Chr 29:6 in the eyes of the LORD our G
2Chr 29:7 holy place unto the G of Israel
2Chr 29:10 with the LORD G of Israel
2Chr 29:36 that G had prepared the people
2Chr 30:1 unto the LORD G of Israel
2Chr 30:5 the LORD G of Israel at Jerusalem
2Chr 30:6 again unto the LORD G of Abraham
2Chr 30:7 the LORD G of their fathers
2Chr 30:8 and serve the LORD your G, that
2Chr 30:9 for the LORD your G is gracious
2Chr 30:12 Also in Judah the hand of G was
2Chr 30:16 to the law of Moses the man of G
2Chr 30:19 prepareth his heart to seek G
2Chr 30:19 the LORD G of his fathers, though
2Chr 30:22 to the LORD G of their fathers
2Chr 31:6 consecrated unto the LORD their G
2Chr 31:13 the ruler of the house of G
2Chr 31:14 over the freewill offerings of G
2Chr 31:20 and truth before the LORD his G
2Chr 31:21 in the service of the house of G
2Chr 31:21 the commandments, to seek his G
2Chr 32:8 us is the LORD our G to help us
2Chr 32:11 The LORD our G shall deliver us
2Chr 32:14 that your G should be able to
2Chr 32:15 how much less shall your G
2Chr 32:16 spake yet more against the LORD G
2Chr 32:17 to rail on the LORD G of Israel
2Chr 32:17 so shall not the G of Hezekiah
2Chr 32:19 spake against the G of Jerusalem
2Chr 32:29 for G had given him substance
2Chr 32:31 G left him, to try him, that he
2Chr 33:7 he had made, in the house of G
2Chr 33:7 of which G had said to David and
2Chr 33:12 he besought the LORD his G
2Chr 33:12 before the G of his fathers
2Chr 33:13 knew that the LORD he was G
2Chr 33:16 to serve the LORD G of Israel
2Chr 33:17 yet unto the LORD their G only
2Chr 33:18 and his prayer unto his G
2Chr 33:18 the name of the LORD G of Israel
2Chr 33:19 how G was intreated of him, and
2Chr 34:3 after the G of David his father
2Chr 34:8 the house of the LORD his G
2Chr 34:9 was brought into the house of G
2Chr 34:23 Thus saith the LORD G of Israel
2Chr 34:26 Thus saith the LORD G of Israel
2Chr 34:27 didst humble thyself before G
2Chr 34:32 according to the covenant of G
2Chr 34:32 the G of their fathers
2Chr 34:33 even to serve the LORD their G
2Chr 34:33 the LORD, the G of their fathers
2Chr 35:3 serve now the LORD your G
2Chr 35:8 Jehiel, rulers of the house of G
2Chr 35:21 for G commanded me to make haste
2Chr 35:21 forbear thee from meddling with G
2Chr 35:22 of Necho from the mouth of G
2Chr 36:5 in the sight of the LORD his G
2Chr 36:12 in the sight of the LORD his G
2Chr 36:13 who had made him swear by G
2Chr 36:13 turning unto the LORD G of Israel
2Chr 36:15 the LORD G of their fathers sent
2Chr 36:16 they mocked the messengers of G
2Chr 36:18 all the vessels of the house of G
2Chr 36:19 And they burnt the house of G
2Chr 36:23 the LORD G of heaven given me
2Chr 36:23 The LORD his G be with him
Ezr 1:2 The LORD G of heaven hath given
Ezr 1:3 his G be with him, and let him go
Ezr 1:3 LORD G of Israel, (he is the G
Ezr 1:4 house of G that is in Jerusalem
Ezr 1:5 them whose spirit G had raised
Ezr 2:68 of G to set it up in his place
Ezr 3:2 the altar of the G of Israel
Ezr 3:2 in the law of Moses the man of G
Ezr 3:8 unto the house of G at Jerusalem
Ezr 3:9 the workmen in the house of G
Ezr 4:1 temple unto the LORD G of Israel
Ezr 4:2 for we seek your G, as ye do
Ezr 4:3 us to build an house unto our G
Ezr 4:3 build unto the LORD G of Israel
Ezr 4:24 house of G which is at Jerusalem
Ezr 5:1 in the name of the G of Israel
Ezr 5:2 house of G which is at Jerusalem
Ezr 5:2 the prophets of G helping them
Ezr 5:5 But the eye of their G was upon
Ezr 5:8 to the house of the great G
Ezr 5:11 the servants of the G of heaven
Ezr 5:12 the G of heaven unto wrath
Ezr 5:13 a decree to build this house of G
Ezr 5:14 gold and silver of the house of G
Ezr 5:15 let the house of G be builded in
Ezr 5:16 house of G which is in Jerusalem
Ezr 5:17 this house of G at Jerusalem
Ezr 6:3 the house of G at Jerusalem
Ezr 6:5 silver vessels of the house of G
Ezr 6:5 and place them in the house of G
Ezr 6:7 the work of this house of G alone
Ezr 6:7 this house of G in his place
Ezr 6:8 the building of this house of G
Ezr 6:9 offerings of the G of heaven
Ezr 6:10 savours unto the G of heaven
Ezr 6:12 the G that hath caused his name
Ezr 6:12 house of G which is at Jerusalem
Ezr 6:14 commandment of the G of Israel
Ezr 6:16 of this house of G with joy
Ezr 6:17 house of G an hundred bullocks
Ezr 6:18 courses, for the service of G
Ezr 6:21 to seek the LORD G of Israel
Ezr 6:22 the house of G, the G of Israel
Ezr 7:6 which the LORD G of Israel had
Ezr 7:6 hand of the LORD his G upon him
Ezr 7:9 the good hand of his G upon him
Ezr 7:12 of the law of the G of heaven
Ezr 7:14 of thy G which is in thine hand
Ezr 7:15 offered unto the G of Israel
Ezr 7:16 of their G which is in Jerusalem
Ezr 7:17 of your G which is in Jerusalem
Ezr 7:18 that do after the will of your G
Ezr 7:19 the service of the house of thy G
Ezr 7:19 thou before the G of Jerusalem
Ezr 7:20 be needful for the house of thy G
Ezr 7:21 of the law of the G of heaven
Ezr 7:23 is commanded by the G of heaven
Ezr 7:23 for the house of the G of heaven
Ezr 7:24 or ministers of this house of G

| | |
|---|---|
| Ezr 7:25 | Ezra, after the wisdom of thy G |
| Ezr 7:25 | such as know the laws of thy G |
| Ezr 7:26 | will not do the law of thy G |
| Ezr 7:27 | be the LORD G of our fathers |
| Ezr 7:28 | hand of the LORD my G was upon me |
| Ezr 8:17 | ministers for the house of our G |
| Ezr 8:18 | by the good hand of our G upon us |
| Ezr 8:21 | afflict ourselves before our G |
| Ezr 8:22 | The hand of our G is upon all |
| Ezr 8:23 | fasted and besought our G for this |
| Ezr 8:25 | offering of the house of our G |
| Ezr 8:28 | unto the LORD G of your fathers |
| Ezr 8:30 | Jerusalem unto the house of our G |
| Ezr 8:31 | and the hand of our G was upon us |
| Ezr 8:33 | weighed in the house of our G by |
| Ezr 8:35 | offerings unto the G of Israel |
| Ezr 8:36 | the people, and the house of G |
| Ezr 9:4 | at the words of the G of Israel |
| Ezr 9:5 | out my hands unto the LORD my G |
| Ezr 9:6 | And said, O my G, I am ashamed and |
| Ezr 9:6 | to lift up my face to thee, my G |
| Ezr 9:8 | been shewed from the LORD our G |
| Ezr 9:8 | that our G may lighten our eyes, |
| Ezr 9:9 | yet our G hath not forsaken us in |
| Ezr 9:9 | to set up the house of our G |
| Ezr 9:10 | And now, O our G, what shall we |
| Ezr 9:13 | seeing that thou our G hast |
| Ezr 9:15 | O LORD G of Israel, thou art |
| Ezr 10:1 | down before the house of G |
| Ezr 10:2 | We have trespassed against our G |
| Ezr 10:3 | our G to put away all the wives |
| Ezr 10:3 | at the commandment of our G |
| Ezr 10:6 | up from before the house of G |
| Ezr 10:9 | in the street of the house of G |
| Ezr 10:11 | unto the LORD G of your fathers |
| Ezr 10:14 | until the fierce wrath of our G |
| Neh 1:4 | and prayed before the G of heaven |
| Neh 1:5 | O LORD G of heaven |
| Neh 1:5 | the great and terrible G |
| Neh 2:4 | So I prayed to the G of heaven |
| Neh 2:8 | to the good hand of my G upon me |
| Neh 2:12 | my G had put in my heart to do at |
| Neh 2:18 | of my G which was good upon me |
| Neh 2:20 | The G of heaven, he will prosper |
| Neh 4:4 | Hear, O our G |
| Neh 4:9 | we made our prayer unto our G |
| Neh 4:15 | G had brought their counsel to |
| Neh 4:20 | our G shall fight for us |
| Neh 5:9 | G because of the reproach of the |
| Neh 5:13 | So G shake out every man from his |
| Neh 5:15 | not I, because of the fear of G |
| Neh 5:19 | Think upon me, my G, for good, |
| Neh 6:9 | Now therefore, O G, strengthen my |
| Neh 6:10 | meet together in the house of G |
| Neh 6:12 | perceived that G had not sent him |
| Neh 6:14 | My G, think thou upon Tobiah and |
| Neh 6:16 | this work was wrought of our G |
| Neh 7:2 | man, and feared G above many |
| Neh 7:5 | my G put into mine heart to |
| Neh 8:6 | blessed the LORD, the great G |
| Neh 8:8 | book in the law of G distinctly |
| Neh 8:9 | day is holy unto the LORD your G |
| Neh 8:16 | in the courts of the house of G |
| Neh 8:18 | read in the book of the law of G |
| Neh 9:3 | G one fourth part of the day |
| Neh 9:3 | and worshipped the LORD their G |
| Neh 9:4 | loud voice unto the LORD their G |
| Neh 9:5 | and bless the LORD your G for ever |
| Neh 9:7 | Thou art the LORD the G, who |
| Neh 9:17 | but thou art a G ready to pardon, |
| Neh 9:18 | This is thy G that brought thee |
| Neh 9:31 | thou art a gracious and merciful G |
| Neh 9:32 | Now therefore, our G, the great, |
| Neh 9:32 | the mighty, and the terrible G |
| Neh 10:28 | of the lands unto the law of G |
| Neh 10:29 | given by Moses the servant of G |
| Neh 10:32 | the service of the house of our G |
| Neh 10:33 | the work of the house of our G |
| Neh 10:34 | bring it into the house of our G |
| Neh 10:34 | upon the altar of the LORD our G |
| Neh 10:36 | to bring to the house of our G |
| Neh 10:36 | minister in the house of our G |
| Neh 10:37 | chambers of the house of our G |
| Neh 10:38 | tithes unto the house of our G |
| Neh 10:39 | not forsake the house of our G |
| Neh 11:11 | was the ruler of the house of G |
| Neh 11:16 | business of the house of G |
| Neh 11:22 | the business of the house of G |
| Neh 12:24 | commandment of David the man of G |
| Neh 12:36 | instruments of David the man of G |
| Neh 12:40 | gave thanks in the house of G |
| Neh 12:43 | for G had made them rejoice with |
| Neh 12:45 | porters kept the ward of their G |
| Neh 12:46 | of praise and thanskgiving unto G |
| Neh 13:1 | the congregation of G for ever |
| Neh 13:2 | howbeit our G turned the curse |
| Neh 13:4 | the chamber of the house of our G |
| Neh 13:7 | in the courts of the house of G |
| Neh 13:9 | the vessels of the house of G |
| Neh 13:11 | Why is the house of G forsaken |
| Neh 13:14 | Remember me, O my G, concerning |
| Neh 13:14 | I have done for the house of my G |
| Neh 13:18 | did not our G bring all this evil |
| Neh 13:22 | Remember me, O my G, concerning |
| Neh 13:25 | hair, and made them swear by G |
| Neh 13:26 | him, who was beloved of his G |
| Neh 13:26 | G made him king over all Israel |
| Neh 13:27 | our G in marrying strange wives |
| Neh 13:29 | Remember them, O my G, because |
| Neh 13:31 | Remember me, O my G, for good |
| Job 1:1 | and upright, and one that feared G |
| Job 1:5 | and cursed G in their hearts |
| Job 1:6 | of G came to present themselves |
| Job 1:8 | upright man, one that feareth G |
| Job 1:9 | said, Doth Job fear G for nought |
| Job 1:16 | The fire of G is fallen from |
| Job 1:22 | not, nor charged G foolishly |
| Job 2:1 | of G came to present themselves |
| Job 2:3 | upright man, one that feareth G |
| Job 2:9 | curse G, and die |
| Job 2:10 | we receive good at the hand of G |
| Job 3:4 | let not G regard it from above, |
| Job 3:23 | is hid, and whom G hath hedged in |
| Job 4:9 | By the blast of G they perish |
| Job 4:17 | mortal man be more just than G |
| Job 5:8 | I would seek unto G |
| Job 5:8 | unto G would I commit my cause |
| Job 5:17 | is the man whom G correcteth |
| Job 6:4 | the terrors of G do set |
| Job 6:8 | that G would grant me the thing |
| Job 6:9 | it would please G to destroy me |
| Job 8:3 | Doth G pervert judgment |
| Job 8:5 | thou wouldest seek unto G betimes |
| Job 8:13 | the paths of all that forget G |
| Job 8:20 | G will not cast away a perfect |
| Job 9:2 | but how should man be just with G |
| Job 9:13 | If G will not withdraw his anger, |
| Job 10:2 | I will say unto G, Do not condemn |
| Job 11:5 | But oh that G would speak |
| Job 11:6 | Know therefore that G exacteth of |
| Job 11:7 | thou by searching find out G |
| Job 12:4 | his neighbour, who calleth upon G |
| Job 12:6 | and they that provoke G are secure |
| Job 12:6 | into whose hand G bringeth |
| Job 13:3 | and I desire to reason with G |
| Job 13:7 | Will ye speak wickedly for G |
| Job 13:8 | will ye contend for G |
| Job 15:4 | and restrainest prayer before G |
| Job 15:8 | Hast thou heard the secret of G |
| Job 15:11 | consolations of G small with thee |
| Job 15:13 | thou turnest thy spirit against G |
| Job 15:25 | stretcheth out his hand against G |
| Job 16:11 | G hath delivered me to the |
| Job 16:20 | mine eye poureth out tears unto G |
| Job 16:21 | one might plead for a man with G |
| Job 18:21 | place of him that knoweth not G |
| Job 19:6 | Know now that G hath overthrown |
| Job 19:21 | for the hand of G hath touched me |
| Job 19:22 | Why do ye persecute me as G |
| Job 19:26 | yet in my flesh shall I see G |
| Job 20:15 | G shall cast them out of his |
| Job 20:23 | G shall cast the fury of his |
| Job 20:29 | portion of a wicked man from G |
| Job 20:29 | heritage appointed unto him by G |
| Job 21:9 | neither is the rod of G upon them |
| Job 21:14 | Therefore they say unto G |
| Job 21:17 | G distributeth sorrows in his |
| Job 21:19 | G layeth up his iniquity for his |
| Job 21:22 | Shall any teach G knowledge |
| Job 22:2 | Can a man be profitable unto G |
| Job 22:12 | Is not G in the height of heaven |
| Job 22:13 | And thou sayest, How doth G know |
| Job 22:17 | Which said unto G, Depart from us |
| Job 22:26 | and shalt lift up thy face unto G |
| Job 23:16 | For G maketh my heart soft, and |
| Job 24:12 | yet G layeth not folly to them |
| Job 25:4 | then can man be justified with G |
| Job 27:2 | As G liveth, who hath taken away |
| Job 27:3 | the spirit of G is in my nostrils |
| Job 27:5 | G forbid that I should justify |
| Job 27:8 | when G taketh away his soul |
| Job 27:9 | Will G hear his cry when trouble |
| Job 27:10 | will he always call upon G |
| Job 27:11 | I will teach you by the hand of G |
| Job 27:13 | portion of a wicked man with G |
| Job 27:22 | For G shall cast upon him, and not |
| Job 28:23 | G understandeth the way thereof, |
| Job 29:2 | in the days when G preserved me |
| Job 29:4 | when the secret of G was upon my |
| Job 31:2 | portion of G is there from above |
| Job 31:6 | that G may know mine integrity |
| Job 31:14 | then shall I do when G riseth up |
| Job 31:23 | from G was a terror to me |
| Job 31:28 | have denied the G that is above |
| Job 32:2 | justified himself rather than G |
| Job 32:13 | G thrusteth him down, not man |
| Job 33:4 | The spirit of G hath made me |
| Job 33:12 | that G is greater than man |
| Job 33:14 | For G speaketh once, yea twice, |
| Job 33:26 | He shall pray unto G, and he will |
| Job 33:29 | worketh G oftentimes with man |
| Job 34:5 | G hath taken away my judgment |
| Job 34:9 | he should delight himself with G |
| Job 34:10 | far be it from G, that he should |
| Job 34:12 | surely G will not do wickedly, |
| Job 34:23 | should enter into judgment with G |
| Job 34:31 | it is meet to be said unto G |
| Job 34:37 | multiplieth his words against G |
| Job 35:10 | none saith, Where is G my maker |
| Job 35:13 | Surely G will not hear vanity, |
| Job 36:5 | G is mighty, and despiseth not any |
| Job 36:22 | Behold, G exalteth by his power |
| Job 36:26 | G is great, and we know him not, |
| Job 37:5 | G thundereth marvellously with |
| Job 37:10 | By the breath of G frost is given |
| Job 37:14 | consider the wondrous works of G |
| Job 37:15 | thou know when G disposed them |
| Job 37:22 | with G is terrible majesty |
| Job 38:7 | all the sons of G shouted for joy |
| Job 38:41 | when his young ones cry unto G |
| Job 39:17 | Because G hath deprived her of |
| Job 40:2 | he that reproveth G, let him |
| Job 40:9 | Hast thou an arm like G |
| Job 40:19 | He is the chief of the ways of G |
| Ps 3:2 | There is no help for him in G |
| Ps 3:7 | save me, O my G |
| Ps 4:1 | I call, O G of my righteousness |
| Ps 5:2 | voice of my cry, my King, and my G |
| Ps 5:4 | For thou art not a G that hath |
| Ps 5:10 | Destroy thou them, O G |
| Ps 7:1 | O lord my G, in thee do I put my |
| Ps 7:3 | O LORD my G, if I have done this |
| Ps 7:9 | the righteous G trieth the hearts |
| Ps 7:10 | My defence is of G, which saveth |
| Ps 7:11 | G judgeth the righteous |
| Ps 7:11 | G is angry with the wicked every |
| Ps 9:17 | and all the nations that forget G |
| Ps 10:4 | will not seek after G |
| Ps 10:4 | G is not in all his thoughts |
| Ps 10:11 | in his heart, G hath forgotten |
| Ps 10:12 | O G, lift up thine hand |
| Ps 10:13 | doth the wicked contemn G |
| Ps 13:3 | Consider and hear me, O LORD my G |
| Ps 14:1 | said in his heart, There is no G |
| Ps 14:2 | that did understand, and seek G |
| Ps 14:5 | for G is in the generation of the |
| Ps 16:1 | Preserve me, O G |
| Ps 17:6 | thee, for thou wilt hear me, O G |
| Ps 18:2 | my G, my strength, in whom I will |
| Ps 18:6 | upon the LORD, and cried unto my G |
| Ps 18:21 | not wickedly departed from my G |
| Ps 18:28 | the LORD my G will enlighten my |
| Ps 18:29 | by my G have I leaped over a wall |
| Ps 18:30 | As for G, his way is perfect |
| Ps 18:31 | For who is G save the LORD |
| Ps 18:31 | or who is a rock save our G |
| Ps 18:32 | It is G that girdeth me with |
| Ps 18:46 | let the G of my salvation be |
| Ps 18:47 | It is G that avengeth me, and |
| Ps 19:1 | heavens declare the glory of G |
| Ps 20:1 | the name of the G of Jacob defend |
| Ps 20:5 | in the name of our G we will set |
| Ps 20:7 | the name of the LORD our G |
| Ps 22:1 | My G, my G, why hast thou |
| Ps 22:2 | O my G, I cry in the daytime, but |
| Ps 22:10 | thou art my G from my mother's |
| Ps 24:5 | from the G of his salvation |
| Ps 25:2 | O my G, I trust in thee |
| Ps 25:5 | thou art the G of my salvation |
| Ps 25:22 | Redeem Israel, O G, out of all |

Ps 27:9 forsake me, O G of my salvation
Ps 29:3 the G of glory thundereth
Ps 30:2 O LORD my G, I cried unto thee,
Ps 30:12 O LORD my G, I will give thanks
Ps 31:5 redeemed me, O LORD G of truth
Ps 31:14 I said, Thou art my G
Ps 33:12 is the nation whose G is the LORD
Ps 35:23 even unto my cause, my G
Ps 35:24 Judge me, O LORD my G, according
Ps 36:1 is no fear of G before his eyes
Ps 36:7 is thy lovingkindness, O G
Ps 37:31 The law of his G is in his heart
Ps 38:15 thou wilt hear, O Lord my G
Ps 38:21 O my G, be not far from me
Ps 40:3 my mouth, even praise unto our G
Ps 40:5 Many, O LORD my G, are thy
Ps 40:8 I delight to do thy will, O my G
Ps 40:17 make no tarrying, O my G
Ps 41:13 Blessed be the LORD G of Israel
Ps 42:1 panteth my soul after thee, O G
Ps 42:2 My soul thirsteth for G
Ps 42:2 for the living G
Ps 42:2 shall I come and appear before G
Ps 42:3 say unto me, Where is thy G
Ps 42:4 went with them to the house of G
Ps 42:5 hope thou in G
Ps 42:6 O my G, my soul is cast down
Ps 42:8 my prayer unto the G of my life
Ps 42:9 I will say unto G my rock
Ps 42:10 say daily unto me, Where is thy G
Ps 42:11 hope thou in G
Ps 42:11 health of my countenance, and my G
Ps 43:1 Judge me, O G, and plead my cause
Ps 43:2 For thou art the G of my strength
Ps 43:4 will I go unto the altar of G
Ps 43:4 of G, unto G my exceeding joy
Ps 43:4 will I praise thee, O G my G
Ps 43:5 hope in G: for I shall yet praise
Ps 43:5 health of my countenance, and my G
Ps 44:1 We have heard with our ears, O G
Ps 44:4 Thou art my King, O G
Ps 44:8 In G we boast all the day long,
Ps 44:20 have forgotten the name of our G
Ps 44:21 Shall not G search this out
Ps 45:2 therefore G hath blessed thee for
Ps 45:6 Thy throne, O G, is for ever and
Ps 45:7 therefore G, thy G, hath
Ps 46:1 G is our refuge and strength, a
Ps 46:4 shall make glad the city of G
Ps 46:5 G is in the midst of her
Ps 46:5 G shall help her, and that right
Ps 46:7 the G of Jacob is our refuge
Ps 46:10 Be still, and know that I am G
Ps 46:11 the G of Jacob is our refuge
Ps 47:1 shout unto G with the voice of
Ps 47:5 G is gone up with a shout, the
Ps 47:6 Sing praises to G, sing praises
Ps 47:7 For G is the King of all the
Ps 47:8 G reigneth over the heathen
Ps 47:8 G sitteth upon the throne of his
Ps 47:9 the people of the G of Abraham
Ps 47:9 of the earth belong unto G
Ps 48:1 be praised in the city of our G
Ps 48:3 G is known in her palaces for a
Ps 48:8 of hosts, in the city of our G
Ps 48:8 G will establish it for ever
Ps 48:9 of thy lovingkindness, O G
Ps 48:10 According to thy name, O G
Ps 48:14 For this G is our G for ever
Ps 49:7 nor give to G a ransom for him
Ps 49:15 But G will redeem my soul from
Ps 50:1 The mighty G, even the LORD, hath
Ps 50:2 of beauty, G hath shined
Ps 50:3 Our G shall come, and shall not
Ps 50:6 for G is judge himself
Ps 50:7 I am G, even thy G
Ps 50:14 Offer unto G thanksgiving
Ps 50:16 But unto the wicked G saith
Ps 50:22 consider this, ye that forget G
Ps 50:23 will I shew the salvation of G
Ps 51:1 Have mercy upon me, O G,
Ps 51:10 Create in me a clean heart, O G
Ps 51:14 O G, thou G of my salvation
Ps 51:17 The sacrifices of G are a broken
Ps 51:17 a broken and a contrite heart, O G
Ps 52:1 the goodness of G endureth
Ps 52:5 G shall likewise destroy thee for
Ps 52:7 man that made not G his strength
Ps 52:8 olive tree in the house of G
Ps 52:8 trust in the mercy of G for ever
Ps 53:1 said in his heart, There is no G
Ps 53:2 G looked down from heaven upon
Ps 53:2 did understand, that did seek G
Ps 53:4 they have not called upon G
Ps 53:5 for G hath scattered the bones of
Ps 53:5 because G hath despised them
Ps 53:6 When G bringeth back the
Ps 54:1 Save me, O G, by thy name, and
Ps 54:2 Hear my prayer, O G
Ps 54:3 they have not set G before them
Ps 54:4 Behold, G is mine helper
Ps 55:1 Give ear to my prayer, O G
Ps 55:14 unto the house of G in company
Ps 55:16 As for me, I will call upon G
Ps 55:19 G shall hear, and afflict them,
Ps 55:19 therefore they fear not G
Ps 55:23 But thou, O G, shalt bring them
Ps 56:1 Be merciful unto me, O G
Ps 56:4 In G I will praise his word
Ps 56:4 in G I have put my trust
Ps 56:7 anger cast down the people, O G
Ps 56:9 for G is for me
Ps 56:10 In G will I praise his word
Ps 56:11 In G have I put my trust
Ps 56:12 Thy vows are upon me, O G
Ps 56:13 that I may walk before G in the
Ps 57:1 Be merciful unto me, O G, be
Ps 57:2 I will cry unto G most high
Ps 57:2 unto G that performeth all things
Ps 57:3 G shall send forth his mercy and
Ps 57:5 Be thou exalted, O G, above the
Ps 57:7 My heart is fixed, O G, my heart
Ps 57:11 Be thou exalted, O G, above the
Ps 58:6 Break their teeth, O G, in their
Ps 58:11 verily he is a G that judgeth in
Ps 59:1 me from mine enemies, O my G
Ps 59:5 O LORD G of hosts, the G of
Ps 59:9 for G is my defence
Ps 59:10 The G of my mercy shall prevent
Ps 59:10 G shall let me see my desire upon
Ps 59:13 let them know that G ruleth in
Ps 59:17 for G is my defence, and the G
Ps 60:1 O G, thou hast cast us off, thou
Ps 60:6 G hath spoken in his holiness
Ps 60:10 Wilt not thou, O G, which hadst
Ps 60:10 and thou, O G, which didst not go
Ps 60:12 Through G we shall do valiantly
Ps 61:1 Hear my cry, O G
Ps 61:5 For thou, O G, hast heard my vows
Ps 61:7 He shall abide before G for ever
Ps 62:1 Truly my soul waiteth upon G
Ps 62:5 My soul, wait thou only upon G
Ps 62:7 In G is my salvation and my glory
Ps 62:7 strength, and my refuge, is in G
Ps 62:8 G is a refuge for us
Ps 62:11 G hath spoken once
Ps 62:11 that power belongeth unto G
Ps 63:1 O g, thou art
Ps 63:1 thou art my G
Ps 63:11 But the king shall rejoice in G
Ps 64:1 Hear my voice, O G, in my prayer
Ps 64:7 But G shall shoot at them with an
Ps 64:9 and shall declare the work of G
Ps 65:1 waiteth for thee, O G in Sion
Ps 65:5 answer us, O G of our salvation
Ps 65:9 enrichest it with the river of G
Ps 66:1 Make a joyful noise unto G
Ps 66:3 Say unto G, How terrible art thou
Ps 66:5 Come and see the works of G
Ps 66:8 O bless our G, ye people, and make
Ps 66:10 For thou, O G, hast proved us
Ps 66:16 Come and hear, all ye that fear G
Ps 66:19 But verily G hath heard me
Ps 66:20 Blessed be G, which hath not
Ps 67:1 G be merciful unto us, and bless
Ps 67:3 Let the people praise thee, O G
Ps 67:5 Let the people praise thee, O G
Ps 67:6 and G, even our own G, shall
Ps 67:7 G shall bless us
Ps 68:1 Let G arise, let his enemies be
Ps 68:2 perish at the presence of G
Ps 68:3 let them rejoice before G
Ps 68:4 Sing unto G, sing praises to his
Ps 68:5 is G in his holy habitation
Ps 68:6 G setteth the solitary in
Ps 68:7 O G, when thou wentest forth
Ps 68:8 also dropped at the presence of G
Ps 68:8 presence of G, the G of Israel
Ps 68:9 Thou, O G, didst send a plentiful
Ps 68:10 thou, O G, hast prepared of thy
Ps 68:15 The hill of G is as the hill of
Ps 68:16 hill which G desireth to dwell in
Ps 68:17 The chariots of G are twenty
Ps 68:18 that the LORD G might dwell among
Ps 68:19 even the G of our salvation
Ps 68:20 is our G is the G of salvation
Ps 68:20 unto G the Lord belong the issues
Ps 68:21 But G shall wound the head of his
Ps 68:24 They have seen thy goings, O G
Ps 68:24 even the goings of my G, my King,
Ps 68:26 Bless ye G in the congregations,
Ps 68:28 Thy G hath commanded thy strength
Ps 68:28 strengthen, O G, that which thou
Ps 68:31 soon stretch out her hands unto G
Ps 68:32 Sing unto G, ye kingdoms of the
Ps 68:34 Ascribe ye strength unto G
Ps 68:35 O G, thou art terrible out of thy
Ps 68:35 the G of Israel is he that giveth
Ps 68:35 Blessed be G
Ps 69:1 Save me, O G
Ps 69:3 eyes fail while I wait for my G
Ps 69:5 O G, thou knowest my foolishness
Ps 69:6 O Lord G of hosts, be ashamed for
Ps 69:6 for my sake, O G of Israel
Ps 69:13 O G, in the multitude of thy
Ps 69:29 let thy salvation, O G, set me up
Ps 69:30 praise the name of G with a song
Ps 69:32 your heart shall live that seek G
Ps 69:35 For G will save Zion, and will
Ps 70:1 Make haste, O G, to deliver me
Ps 70:4 continually, Let G be magnified
Ps 70:5 make haste unto me, O G
Ps 71:4 Deliver me, O my G, out of the
Ps 71:5 For thou art my hope, O Lord G
Ps 71:11 Saying, G hath forsaken him
Ps 71:12 O G, be not far from me
Ps 71:12 O my G, make haste for my help
Ps 71:16 go in the strength of the Lord G
Ps 71:17 O G, thou hast taught me from my
Ps 71:18 when I am old and greyheaded, O G
Ps 71:19 Thy righteousness also, O G
Ps 71:19 O G, who is like unto thee
Ps 71:22 psaltery, even thy truth, O my G
Ps 72:1 Give the king thy judgments, O G
Ps 72:18 Blessed be the LORD G
Ps 72:18 the G of Israel, who only doeth
Ps 73:1 Truly G is good to Israel, even
Ps 73:11 And they say, How doth G know
Ps 73:17 I went into the sanctuary of G
Ps 73:26 but G is the strength of my heart
Ps 73:28 is good for me to draw near to G
Ps 73:28 I have put my trust in the Lord G
Ps 74:1 O G, why hast thou cast us off
Ps 74:8 the synagogues of G in the land
Ps 74:10 O G, how long shall the adversary
Ps 74:12 For G is my King of old, working
Ps 74:22 Arise, O G, plead thine own cause
Ps 75:1 Unto thee, O G, do we give thanks
Ps 75:7 But G is the judge
Ps 75:9 sing praises to the G of Jacob
Ps 76:1 In Judah is G known
Ps 76:6 O G of Jacob, both the chariot and
Ps 76:9 When G arose to judgment, to save
Ps 76:11 Vow, and pay unto the LORD your G
Ps 77:1 I cried unto G with my voice,
Ps 77:1 even unto G with my voice
Ps 77:3 I remembered G, and was troubled
Ps 77:9 Hath G forgotten to be gracious
Ps 77:13 Thy way, O G, is in the sanctuary
Ps 77:13 who is so great a G
Ps 77:13 as our G
Ps 77:14 Thou art the G that doest wonders
Ps 77:16 The waters saw thee, O G, the
Ps 78:7 they might set their hope in G
Ps 78:7 and not forget the works of G
Ps 78:8 spirit was not stedfast with G
Ps 78:10 They kept not the covenant of G
Ps 78:18 they tempted G in their heart by
Ps 78:19 Yea, they spake against G
Ps 78:19 Can G furnish a table in the
Ps 78:22 Because they believed not in G
Ps 78:31 The wrath of G came upon them, and
Ps 78:34 and enquired early after G
Ps 78:35 remembered that G was their rock
Ps 78:35 the high G their redeemer
Ps 78:41 they turned back and tempted G
Ps 78:56 and provoked the most high G
Ps 78:59 When G heard this, he was wroth,
Ps 79:1 O g, the heathen are come into
Ps 79:9 O G of our salvation, for the

Ps 79:10 the heathen say, Where is their G
Ps 80:3 Turn us again, O G, and cause thy
Ps 80:4 O LORD G of hosts, how long wilt
Ps 80:7 O G of hosts, and cause thy face
Ps 80:14 we beseech thee, O G of hosts
Ps 80:19 O LORD G of hosts, cause thy face
Ps 81:1 Sing aloud unto G our strength
Ps 81:1 joyful noise unto the G of Jacob
Ps 81:4 and a law of the G of Jacob
Ps 81:10 I am the LORD thy G, which
Ps 82:1 G standeth in the congregation of
Ps 82:8 Arise, O G, judge the earth
Ps 83:1 Keep not thou silence, O G
Ps 83:1 thy peace, and be not still, O G
Ps 83:12 the houses of G in possession
Ps 83:13 O my G, make them like a wheel
Ps 84:2 flesh crieth out for the living G
Ps 84:3 O LORD of hosts, my King, and my G
Ps 84:7 them in Zion appeareth before G
Ps 84:8 O LORD G of hosts, hear my prayer
Ps 84:8 give ear, O G of Jacob
Ps 84:9 O G our shield, and look upon the
Ps 84:10 a doorkeeper in the house of my G
Ps 84:11 For the LORD G is a sun and shield
Ps 85:4 O G of our salvation, and cause
Ps 85:8 I will hear what G the LORD will
Ps 86:2 O thou my G, save thy servant
Ps 86:10 thou art G alone
Ps 86:12 I will praise thee, O Lord my G
Ps 86:14 O G, the proud are risen against
Ps 86:15 art a G full of compassion, and
Ps 87:3 are spoken of thee, O city of G
Ps 88:1 O lord G of my salvation, I have
Ps 89:7 G is greatly to be feared in the
Ps 89:8 O LORD G of hosts, who is a
Ps 89:26 unto me, Thou art my father, my G
Ps 90:*t* A Prayer of Moses, the man of G
Ps 90:2 to everlasting, thou art G
Ps 90:17 of the LORD our G be upon us
Ps 91:2 refuge and my fortress: my G
Ps 92:13 flourish in the courts of our G
Ps 94:1 O LORD G, to whom vengeance
Ps 94:1 O G, to whom vengeance belongeth,
Ps 94:7 neither shall the G of Jacob
Ps 94:22 my G is the rock of my refuge
Ps 94:23 the LORD our G shall cut them off
Ps 95:3 For the LORD is a great G
Ps 95:7 For he is our G
Ps 98:3 have seen the salvation of our G
Ps 99:5 Exalt ye the LORD our G, and
Ps 99:8 answeredst them, O LORD our G
Ps 99:8 thou wast a G that forgavest them
Ps 99:9 Exalt the LORD our G, and worship
Ps 99:9 for the LORD our G is holy
Ps 100:3 Know ye that the LORD he is G
Ps 102:24 I said, O my G, take me not away
Ps 104:1 O LORD my G, thou art very great
Ps 104:21 prey, and seek their meat from G
Ps 104:33 to my G while I have my being
Ps 105:7 He is the LORD our G
Ps 106:14 and tempted G in the desert
Ps 106:21 They forgat G their saviour,
Ps 106:47 Save us, O LORD our G, and gather
Ps 106:48 Blessed be the LORD G of Israel
Ps 107:11 rebelled against the words of G
Ps 108:1 O G, my heart is fixed
Ps 108:5 Be thou exalted, O G, above the
Ps 108:7 G hath spoken in his holiness
Ps 108:11 Wilt not thou, O G, who hast cast
Ps 108:11 and wilt not thou, O G, go forth
Ps 108:13 Through G we shall do valiantly
Ps 109:1 not thy peace, O G of my praise
Ps 109:21 O G the Lord, for thy name's sake
Ps 109:26 Help me, O LORD my G
Ps 113:5 Who is like unto the LORD our G
Ps 114:7 at the presence of the G of Jacob
Ps 115:2 heathen say, Where is now their G
Ps 115:3 But our G is in the heavens
Ps 116:5 yea, our G is merciful
Ps 118:27 G is the LORD, which hath shewed
Ps 118:28 Thou art my G, and I will praise
Ps 118:28 thou art my G, I will exalt thee
Ps 119:115 keep the commandments of my G
Ps 122:9 LORD our G I will seek thy good
Ps 123:2 our eyes wait upon the LORD our G
Ps 132:2 vowed unto the mighty G of Jacob
Ps 132:5 for the mighty G of Jacob
Ps 135:2 the courts of the house of our G
Ps 136:2 O give thanks unto the G of gods
Ps 136:26 give thanks unto the G of heaven
Ps 139:17 are thy thoughts unto me, O G
Ps 139:19 thou wilt slay the wicked, O G
Ps 139:23 Search me, O G, and know my heart
Ps 140:6 said unto the LORD, Thou art my G
Ps 140:7 O G the Lord, the strength of my
Ps 141:8 eyes are unto thee, O G the Lord
Ps 143:10 for thou art my G
Ps 144:9 sing a new song unto thee, O G
Ps 144:15 that people, whose G is the LORD
Ps 145:1 I will extol thee, my G, O king
Ps 146:2 unto my G while I have any being
Ps 146:5 hath the G of Jacob for his help
Ps 146:5 whose hope is in the LORD his G
Ps 146:10 shall reign for ever, even thy G
Ps 147:1 good to sing praises unto our G
Ps 147:7 praise upon the harp unto our G
Ps 147:12 praise thy G, O Zion
Ps 149:6 praises of G be in their mouth
Ps 150:1 Praise G in his sanctuary
Prov 2:5 LORD, and find the knowledge of G
Prov 2:17 forgetteth the covenant of her G
Prov 3:4 understanding in the sight of G
Prov 21:12 but G overthroweth the wicked for
Prov 25:2 the glory of G to conceal a thing
Prov 26:10 The great G that formed all
Prov 30:5 Every word of G is pure
Prov 30:9 and take the name of my G in vain
Eccl 1:13 this sore travail hath G given to
Eccl 2:24 that it was from the hand of G
Eccl 2:26 For G giveth to a man that is
Eccl 2:26 give to him that is good before G
Eccl 3:10 which G hath given to the sons of
Eccl 3:11 G maketh from the beginning to
Eccl 3:13 his labour, it is the gift of G
Eccl 3:14 I know that, whatsoever G doeth
Eccl 3:14 G doeth it, that men should fear
Eccl 3:15 G requireth that which is past
Eccl 3:17 G shall judge the righteous and
Eccl 3:18 that G might manifest them, and
Eccl 5:1 when thou goest to the house of G
Eccl 5:2 hasty to utter any thing before G
Eccl 5:2 for G is in heaven, and thou upon
Eccl 5:4 When thou vowest a vow unto G
Eccl 5:6 wherefore should G be angry at
Eccl 5:7 but fear thou G
Eccl 5:18 of his life, which G giveth him
Eccl 5:19 also to whom G hath given riches
Eccl 5:19 this is the gift of G
Eccl 5:20 because G answereth him in the
Eccl 6:2 A man to whom G hath given riches
Eccl 6:2 yet G giveth him not power to eat
Eccl 7:13 Consider the work of G
Eccl 7:14 G also hath set the one over
Eccl 7:18 for he that feareth G shall come
Eccl 7:26 whoso pleaseth G shall escape
Eccl 7:29 that G hath made man upright
Eccl 8:2 that in regard of the oath of G
Eccl 8:12 be well with them that fear G
Eccl 8:13 because he feareth not before G
Eccl 8:15 which G giveth him under the sun
Eccl 8:17 Then I beheld all the work of G
Eccl 9:1 their works, are in the hand of G
Eccl 9:7 for G now accepteth thy works
Eccl 11:5 not the works of G who maketh all
Eccl 11:9 that for all these things G will
Eccl 12:7 shall return unto G who gave it
Eccl 12:13 Fear G, and keep his commandments
Eccl 12:14 For G shall bring every work into
Is 1:10 give ear unto the law of our G
Is 2:3 to the house of the G of Jacob
Is 3:15 saith the Lord G of hosts
Is 5:16 and G that is holy shall be
Is 7:7 Thus saith the Lord G, It shall
Is 7:11 Ask thee a sign of the LORD thy G
Is 7:13 men, but will ye weary my G also
Is 8:10 for G is with us
Is 8:19 not a people seek unto their G
Is 8:21 and curse their king and their G
Is 9:6 Counsellor, The mighty G
Is 10:21 of Jacob, unto the mighty G
Is 10:23 For the Lord G of hosts shall
Is 10:24 thus saith the Lord G of hosts
Is 12:2 Behold, G is my salvation
Is 13:19 be as when G overthrew Sodom
Is 14:13 my throne above the stars of G
Is 17:6 saith the LORD G of Israel
Is 17:10 forgotten the G of thy salvation
Is 17:13 but G shall rebuke them, and they
Is 21:10 the G of Israel, have I declared
Is 21:17 for the LORD G of Israel hath
Is 22:5 Lord G of hosts in the valley of
Is 22:12 Lord G of hosts call to weeping
Is 22:14 ye die, saith the Lord G of hosts
Is 22:15 Thus saith the Lord G of hosts
Is 24:15 even the name of the LORD G of
Is 25:1 O lord, thou art my G
Is 25:8 the Lord G will wipe away tears
Is 25:9 in that day, Lo, this is our G
Is 26:1 salvation will G appoint for
Is 26:13 O LORD our G, other lords besides
Is 28:16 Therefore thus saith the Lord G
Is 28:22 the Lord G of hosts a consumption
Is 28:26 For his G doth instruct him to
Is 29:23 and shall fear the G of Israel
Is 30:15 For thus saith the Lord G
Is 30:18 for the LORD is a G of judgment
Is 31:3 the Egyptians are men, and not G
Is 35:2 LORD, and the excellency of our G
Is 35:4 your G will come with vengeance,
Is 35:4 even G with a recompence
Is 36:7 to me, We trust in the LORD our G
Is 37:4 LORD thy G will hear the words of
Is 37:4 sent to reproach the living G
Is 37:4 which the LORD thy G hath heard
Is 37:10 of Judah, saying, Let not thy G
Is 37:16 G of Israel, that dwellest
Is 37:16 the cherubims, thou art the G
Is 37:17 sent to reproach the living G
Is 37:20 Now therefore, O LORD our G
Is 37:21 Thus saith the LORD G of Israel
Is 37:38 in the house of Nisroch his *g*
Is 38:5 the G of David thy father, I have
Is 40:1 ye my people, saith your G
Is 40:3 in the desert a highway for our G
Is 40:8 but the word of our G shall stand
Is 40:9 cities of Judah, Behold your G
Is 40:10 the Lord G will come with strong
Is 40:18 To whom then will ye liken G
Is 40:27 judgment is passed over from my G
Is 40:28 not heard, that the everlasting G
Is 41:10 for I am thy G
Is 41:13 For I the LORD thy G will hold
Is 41:17 I the G of Israel will not
Is 42:5 Thus saith G the LORD, he that
Is 43:3 For I am the LORD thy G, the Holy
Is 43:10 before me there was no G formed
Is 43:12 saith the LORD, that I am G
Is 44:6 and beside me there is no G
Is 44:8 Is there a G beside me
Is 44:8 yea, there is no G
Is 45:3 by thy name, am the G of Israel
Is 45:5 else, there is no G beside me
Is 45:14 thee, saying, Surely G is in thee
Is 45:14 there is none else, there is no G
Is 45:15 Verily thou art a G that hidest
Is 45:15 O G of Israel, the Saviour
Is 45:18 G himself that formed the earth
Is 45:21 there is no G else beside me
Is 45:21 a just G and a Saviour
Is 45:22 for I am G, and there is none else
Is 46:9 for I am G, and there is none else
Is 46:9 I am G, and there is none like me,
Is 48:1 make mention of the G of Israel
Is 48:2 themselves upon the G of Israel
Is 48:16 and now the Lord G, and his Spirit,
Is 48:17 I am the LORD thy G which
Is 49:4 the LORD, and my work with my G
Is 49:5 my G shall be my strength
Is 49:22 Thus saith the Lord G, Behold, I
Is 50:4 The Lord G hath given me the
Is 50:5 The Lord G hath opened mine ear,
Is 50:7 For the Lord G will help me
Is 50:9 Behold, the Lord G will help me
Is 50:10 of the LORD, and stay upon his G
Is 51:15 But I am the LORD thy G, that
Is 51:20 of the LORD, the rebuke of thy G
Is 51:22 thy G that pleadeth the cause of
Is 52:4 For thus saith the Lord G
Is 52:7 saith unto Zion, Thy G reigneth
Is 52:10 shall see the salvation of our G
Is 52:12 the G of Israel will be your
Is 53:4 esteem him stricken, smitten of G
Is 54:5 The G of the whole earth shall he
Is 54:6 thou wast refused, saith thy G
Is 55:5 thee because of the LORD thy G
Is 55:7 and to our G, for he will
Is 56:8 The Lord G which gathereth the
Is 57:21 There is no peace, saith my G
Is 58:2 not the ordinance of their G
Is 58:2 take delight in approaching to G

Is 59:2 separated between you and your G
Is 59:13 and departing away from our G
Is 60:9 unto the name of the LORD thy G
Is 60:19 light, and thy G thy glory
Is 61:1 Spirit of the Lord G is upon me
Is 61:2 and the day of vengeance of our G
Is 61:6 call you the Ministers of our G
Is 61:10 my soul shall be joyful in my G
Is 61:11 so the Lord G will cause
Is 62:3 royal diadem in the hand of thy G
Is 62:5 so shall thy G rejoice over thee
Is 64:4 neither hath the eye seen, O G
Is 65:13 Therefore thus saith the Lord G
Is 65:15 for the Lord G shall slay thee,
Is 65:16 bless himself in the G of truth
Is 65:16 shall swear by the G of truth
Is 66:9 saith thy G
Jer 1:6 Then said I, Ah, Lord G
Jer 2:17 thou hast forsaken the LORD thy G
Jer 2:19 thou hast forsaken the LORD thy G
Jer 2:19 thee, saith the Lord G of hosts
Jer 2:22 before me, saith the Lord G
Jer 3:13 against the LORD thy G, and hast
Jer 3:21 have forgotten the LORD their G
Jer 3:22 for thou art the LORD our G
Jer 3:23 truly in the LORD our G is the
Jer 3:25 sinned against the LORD our G
Jer 3:25 the voice of the LORD our G
Jer 4:10 Then said I, Ah, Lord G
Jer 5:4 LORD, nor the judgment of their G
Jer 5:5 LORD, and the judgment of their G
Jer 5:14 thus saith the LORD G of hosts
Jer 5:19 our G all these things unto us
Jer 5:24 Let us now fear the LORD our G
Jer 7:3 the G of Israel, Amend your ways
Jer 7:20 Therefore thus saith the Lord G
Jer 7:21 LORD of hosts, the G of Israel
Jer 7:23 my voice, and I will be your G
Jer 7:28 not the voice of the LORD their G
Jer 8:14 for the LORD our G hath put us to
Jer 9:15 LORD of hosts, the G of Israel
Jer 10:10 the true G, he is the living G
Jer 11:3 Thus saith the LORD G of Israel
Jer 11:4 be my people, and I will be your G
Jer 13:12 Thus saith the LORD G of Israel
Jer 13:16 Give glory to the LORD your G
Jer 14:13 Then said I, Ah, Lord G
Jer 14:22 art not thou he, O LORD our G
Jer 15:16 by thy name, O LORD G of hosts
Jer 16:9 LORD of hosts, the G of Israel
Jer 16:10 committed against the LORD our G
Jer 19:3 LORD of hosts, the G of Israel
Jer 19:15 LORD of hosts, the G of Israel
Jer 21:4 Thus saith the LORD G of Israel
Jer 22:9 the covenant of the LORD their G
Jer 23:2 G of Israel against the pastors
Jer 23:23 Am I a G at hand, saith the LORD,
Jer 23:23 and not a G afar off
Jer 23:36 the words of the living G
Jer 23:36 of the LORD of hosts our G
Jer 24:5 saith the LORD, the G of Israel
Jer 24:7 my people, and I will be their G
Jer 25:15 the LORD G of Israel unto me
Jer 25:27 LORD of hosts, the G of Israel
Jer 26:13 obey the voice of the LORD your G
Jer 26:16 us in the name of the LORD our G
Jer 27:4 LORD of hosts, the G of Israel
Jer 27:21 the G of Israel, concerning the
Jer 28:2 the G of Israel, saying, I have
Jer 28:14 LORD of hosts, the G of Israel
Jer 29:4 the G of Israel, unto all that
Jer 29:8 LORD of hosts, the G of Israel
Jer 29:21 the G of Israel, of Ahab the son
Jer 29:25 the G of Israel, saying, Because
Jer 30:2 speaketh the LORD G of Israel
Jer 30:9 they shall serve the LORD their G
Jer 30:22 be my people, and I will be your G
Jer 31:1 will I be the G of all the
Jer 31:6 go up to Zion unto the LORD our G
Jer 31:18 for thou art the LORD my G
Jer 31:23 LORD of hosts, the G of Israel
Jer 31:33 and will be their G, and they shall
Jer 32:14 LORD of hosts, the G of Israel
Jer 32:15 LORD of hosts, the G of Israel
Jer 32:17 Ah Lord G!
Jer 32:18 the Great, the Mighty G, the LORD
Jer 32:25 thou hast said unto me, O Lord G
Jer 32:27 I am the LORD, the G of all flesh
Jer 32:36 the G of Israel, concerning this
Jer 32:38 my people, and I will be their G

Jer 33:4 the G of Israel, concerning the
Jer 34:2 saith the LORD, the G of Israel
Jer 34:13 saith the LORD, the G of Israel
Jer 35:4 the son of Igdaliah, a man of G
Jer 35:13 LORD of hosts, the G of Israel
Jer 35:17 G of hosts, the G of Israel
Jer 35:18 LORD of hosts, the G of Israel
Jer 35:19 LORD of hosts, the G of Israel
Jer 37:3 now unto the LORD our G for us
Jer 37:7 saith the LORD, the G of Israel
Jer 38:17 the G of hosts, the G of Israel
Jer 39:16 LORD of hosts, the G of Israel
Jer 40:2 The LORD thy G hath pronounced
Jer 42:2 pray for us unto the LORD thy G
Jer 42:3 That the LORD thy G may shew us
Jer 42:4 your G according to your words
Jer 42:5 LORD thy G shall send thee to us
Jer 42:6 obey the voice of the LORD our G
Jer 42:6 obey the voice of the LORD our G
Jer 42:9 the G of Israel, unto whom ye
Jer 42:13 obey the voice of the LORD your G
Jer 42:15 LORD of hosts, the G of Israel
Jer 42:18 LORD of hosts, the G of Israel
Jer 42:20 ye sent me unto the LORD your G
Jer 42:20 Pray for us unto the LORD our G
Jer 42:20 all that the LORD our G shall say
Jer 42:21 the voice of the LORD your G
Jer 43:1 all the words of the LORD their G
Jer 43:1 LORD their G had sent him to them
Jer 43:2 the LORD our G hath not sent thee
Jer 43:10 LORD of hosts, the G of Israel
Jer 44:2 LORD of hosts, the G of Israel
Jer 44:7 the G of hosts, the G of Israel
Jer 44:11 LORD of hosts, the G of Israel
Jer 44:25 of hosts, the G of Israel, saying
Jer 44:26 Egypt, saying, The Lord G liveth
Jer 45:2 the G of Israel, unto thee, O
Jer 46:10 is the day of the Lord G of hosts
Jer 46:10 for the Lord G of hosts hath a
Jer 46:25 of hosts, the G of Israel, saith
Jer 48:1 LORD of hosts, the G of Israel
Jer 49:5 thee, saith the Lord G of hosts
Jer 50:4 go, and seek the LORD their G
Jer 50:18 LORD of hosts, the G of Israel
Jer 50:25 G of hosts in the land of the
Jer 50:28 the vengeance of the LORD our G
Jer 50:31 proud, saith the Lord G of hosts
Jer 50:40 As G overthrew Sodom and Gomorrah
Jer 51:5 been forsaken, nor Judah of his G
Jer 51:10 Zion the work of the LORD our G
Jer 51:33 LORD of hosts, the G of Israel
Jer 51:56 for the LORD G of recompences
Lam 3:41 our hands unto G in the heavens
Eze 1:1 opened, and I saw visions of G
Eze 2:4 unto them, Thus saith the Lord G
Eze 3:11 tell them, Thus saith the Lord G
Eze 3:27 unto them, Thus saith the Lord G
Eze 4:14 Then said I, Ah Lord G
Eze 5:5 Thus saith the Lord G
Eze 5:7 Therefore thus saith the Lord G
Eze 5:8 Therefore thus saith the Lord G
Eze 5:11 as I live, saith the Lord G
Eze 6:3 hear the word of the Lord G
Eze 6:3 saith the Lord G to the mountains
Eze 6:11 Thus saith the Lord G
Eze 7:2 thus saith the Lord G unto the
Eze 7:5 Thus saith the Lord G
Eze 8:1 of the Lord G fell there upon me
Eze 8:3 in the visions of G to Jerusalem
Eze 8:4 the glory of the G of Israel was
Eze 9:3 the glory of the G of Israel was
Eze 9:8 and cried, and said, Ah Lord G
Eze 10:5 the Almighty G when he speaketh
Eze 10:19 the glory of the G of Israel was
Eze 10:20 the G of Israel by the river of
Eze 11:7 Therefore thus saith the Lord G
Eze 11:8 sword upon you, saith the Lord G
Eze 11:13 a loud voice, and said, Ah Lord G
Eze 11:16 say, Thus saith the Lord G
Eze 11:17 say, Thus saith the Lord G
Eze 11:20 my people, and I will be their G
Eze 11:21 their own heads, saith the Lord G
Eze 11:22 the glory of the G of Israel was
Eze 11:24 by the Spirit of G into Chaldea
Eze 12:10 unto them, Thus saith the Lord G
Eze 12:19 Thus saith the Lord G of the
Eze 12:23 therefore, Thus saith the Lord G
Eze 12:25 will perform it, saith the Lord G
Eze 12:28 unto them, Thus saith the Lord G
Eze 12:28 shall be done, saith the Lord G

Eze 13:3 Thus saith the Lord G
Eze 13:8 Therefore thus saith the Lord G
Eze 13:8 am against you, saith the Lord G
Eze 13:9 shall know that I am the Lord G
Eze 13:13 Therefore thus saith the Lord G
Eze 13:16 is no peace, saith the Lord G
Eze 13:18 And say, Thus saith the Lord G
Eze 13:20 Wherefore thus saith the Lord G
Eze 14:4 unto them, Thus saith the Lord G
Eze 14:6 of Israel, Thus saith the Lord G
Eze 14:11 be my people, and I may be their G
Eze 14:11 saith the Lord G
Eze 14:14 righteousness, saith the Lord G
Eze 14:16 it, as I live, saith the Lord G
Eze 14:18 it, as I live, saith the Lord G
Eze 14:20 it, as I live, saith the Lord G
Eze 14:21 For thus saith the Lord G
Eze 14:23 have done in it, saith the Lord G
Eze 15:6 Therefore thus saith the Lord G
Eze 15:8 a trespass, saith the Lord G
Eze 16:3 saith the Lord G unto Jerusalem
Eze 16:8 with thee, saith the Lord G
Eze 16:14 put upon thee, saith the Lord G
Eze 16:19 and thus it was, saith the Lord G
Eze 16:23 saith the Lord G
Eze 16:30 is thine heart, saith the Lord G
Eze 16:36 Thus saith the Lord G
Eze 16:43 upon thine head, saith the Lord G
Eze 16:48 As I live, saith the Lord G
Eze 16:59 For thus saith the Lord G
Eze 16:63 thou hast done, saith the Lord G
Eze 17:3 And say, Thus saith the Lord G
Eze 17:9 Say thou, Thus saith the Lord G
Eze 17:16 As I live, saith the Lord G
Eze 17:19 Therefore thus saith the Lord G
Eze 17:22 Thus saith the Lord G
Eze 18:3 As I live, saith the Lord G
Eze 18:9 surely live, saith the Lord G
Eze 18:23 saith the Lord G
Eze 18:30 to his ways, saith the Lord G
Eze 18:32 him that dieth, saith the Lord G
Eze 20:3 unto them, Thus saith the Lord G
Eze 20:3 As I live, saith the Lord G
Eze 20:5 unto them, Thus saith the Lord G
Eze 20:5 saying, I am the LORD your G
Eze 20:7 I am the LORD your G
Eze 20:19 I am the LORD your G
Eze 20:20 know that I am the LORD your G
Eze 20:27 unto them, Thus saith the Lord G
Eze 20:30 of Israel, Thus saith the Lord G
Eze 20:31 As I live, saith the Lord G
Eze 20:33 As I live, saith the Lord G
Eze 20:36 plead with you, saith the Lord G
Eze 20:39 of Israel, thus saith the Lord G
Eze 20:40 of Israel, saith the Lord G
Eze 20:44 house of Israel, saith the Lord G
Eze 20:47 Thus saith the Lord G
Eze 20:49 Then said I, Ah Lord G
Eze 21:7 brought to pass, saith the Lord G
Eze 21:13 be no more, saith the Lord G
Eze 21:24 Therefore thus saith the Lord G
Eze 21:26 Thus saith the Lord G
Eze 21:28 Thus saith the Lord G concerning
Eze 22:3 say thou, Thus saith the Lord G
Eze 22:12 forgotten me, saith the Lord G
Eze 22:19 Therefore thus saith the Lord G
Eze 22:28 saying, Thus saith the Lord G
Eze 22:31 their heads, saith the Lord G
Eze 23:22 O Aholibah, thus saith the Lord G
Eze 23:28 For thus saith the Lord G
Eze 23:32 Thus saith the Lord G
Eze 23:34 have spoken it, saith the Lord G
Eze 23:35 Therefore thus saith the Lord G
Eze 23:46 For thus saith the Lord G
Eze 23:49 shall know that I am the Lord G
Eze 24:3 unto them, Thus saith the Lord G
Eze 24:6 Wherefore thus saith the Lord G
Eze 24:9 Therefore thus saith the Lord G
Eze 24:14 they judge thee, saith the Lord G
Eze 24:21 of Israel, Thus saith the Lord G
Eze 24:24 shall know that I am the Lord G
Eze 25:3 Hear the word of the Lord G
Eze 25:3 Thus saith the Lord G
Eze 25:6 For thus saith the Lord G
Eze 25:8 Thus saith the Lord G
Eze 25:12 Thus saith the Lord G
Eze 25:13 Therefore thus saith the Lord G
Eze 25:14 my vengeance, saith the Lord G
Eze 25:15 Thus saith the Lord G
Eze 25:16 Therefore thus saith the Lord G

| | |
|---|---|
| Eze 26:3 | Therefore thus saith the Lord G |
| Eze 26:5 | have spoken it, saith the Lord G |
| Eze 26:7 | For thus saith the Lord G |
| Eze 26:14 | have spoken it, saith the Lord G |
| Eze 26:15 | Thus saith the Lord G to Tyrus |
| Eze 26:19 | For thus saith the Lord G |
| Eze 26:21 | be found again, saith the Lord G |
| Eze 27:3 | many isles, Thus saith the Lord G |
| Eze 28:2 | of Tyrus, Thus saith the Lord G |
| Eze 28:2 | up, and thou hast said, I am a G |
| Eze 28:2 | I sit in the seat of G |
| Eze 28:2 | yet thou art a man, and not G |
| Eze 28:2 | set thine heart as the heart of G |
| Eze 28:6 | Therefore thus saith the Lord G |
| Eze 28:6 | set thine heart as the heart of G |
| Eze 28:9 | him that slayeth thee, I am G |
| Eze 28:9 | but thou shalt be a man, and no G |
| Eze 28:10 | have spoken it, saith the Lord G |
| Eze 28:12 | unto him, Thus saith the Lord G |
| Eze 28:13 | hast been in Eden the garden of G |
| Eze 28:14 | wast upon the holy mountain of G |
| Eze 28:16 | profane out of the mountain of G |
| Eze 28:22 | And say, Thus saith the Lord G |
| Eze 28:24 | shall know that I am the Lord G |
| Eze 28:25 | Thus saith the Lord G |
| Eze 28:26 | know that I am the LORD their G |
| Eze 29:3 | and say, Thus saith the Lord G |
| Eze 29:8 | Therefore thus saith the Lord G |
| Eze 29:13 | Yet thus saith the Lord G |
| Eze 29:16 | shall know that I am the Lord G |
| Eze 29:19 | Therefore thus saith the Lord G |
| Eze 29:20 | wrought for me, saith the Lord G |
| Eze 30:2 | and say, Thus saith the Lord G |
| Eze 30:6 | it by the sword, saith the Lord G |
| Eze 30:10 | Thus saith the Lord G |
| Eze 30:13 | Thus saith the Lord G |
| Eze 30:22 | Therefore thus saith the Lord G |
| Eze 31:8 | garden of G could not hide him |
| Eze 31:8 | nor any tree in the garden of G |
| Eze 31:9 | that were in the garden of G |
| Eze 31:10 | Therefore thus saith the Lord G |
| Eze 31:15 | Thus saith the Lord G |
| Eze 31:18 | his multitude, saith the Lord G |
| Eze 32:3 | Thus saith the Lord G |
| Eze 32:8 | upon thy land, saith the Lord G |
| Eze 32:11 | For thus saith the Lord G |
| Eze 32:14 | to run like oil, saith the Lord G |
| Eze 32:16 | her multitude, saith the Lord G |
| Eze 32:31 | by the sword, saith the Lord G |
| Eze 32:32 | his multitude, saith the Lord G |
| Eze 33:11 | them, As I live, saith the Lord G |
| Eze 33:25 | unto them, Thus saith the Lord G |
| Eze 33:27 | unto them, Thus saith the Lord G |
| Eze 34:2 | the Lord G unto the shepherds |
| Eze 34:8 | As I live saith the Lord G |
| Eze 34:10 | Thus saith the Lord G |
| Eze 34:11 | For thus saith the Lord G |
| Eze 34:15 | to lie down, saith the Lord G |
| Eze 34:17 | O my flock, thus saith the Lord G |
| Eze 34:20 | thus saith the Lord G unto them |
| Eze 34:24 | And I the LORD will be their G |
| Eze 34:30 | I the LORD their G am with them |
| Eze 34:30 | are my people, saith the Lord G |
| Eze 34:31 | pasture, are men, and I am your G |
| Eze 34:31 | saith the Lord G |
| Eze 35:3 | unto it, Thus saith the Lord G |
| Eze 35:6 | as I live, saith the Lord G |
| Eze 35:11 | as I live, saith the Lord G |
| Eze 35:14 | Thus saith the Lord G |
| Eze 36:2 | Thus saith the Lord G |
| Eze 36:3 | and say, Thus saith the Lord G |
| Eze 36:4 | hear the word of the Lord G |
| Eze 36:4 | saith the Lord G to the mountains |
| Eze 36:5 | Therefore thus saith the Lord G |
| Eze 36:6 | valleys, Thus saith the Lord G |
| Eze 36:7 | Therefore thus saith the Lord G |
| Eze 36:13 | Thus saith the Lord G |
| Eze 36:14 | any more, saith the Lord G |
| Eze 36:15 | fall any more, saith the Lord G |
| Eze 36:22 | of Israel, Thus saith the Lord G |
| Eze 36:23 | I am the LORD, saith the Lord G |
| Eze 36:28 | be my people, and I will be your G |
| Eze 36:32 | sakes do I this, saith the Lord G |
| Eze 36:33 | Thus saith the Lord G |
| Eze 36:37 | Thus saith the Lord G |
| Eze 37:3 | And I answered, O Lord G, thou |
| Eze 37:5 | saith the Lord G unto these bones |
| Eze 37:9 | the wind, Thus saith the Lord G |
| Eze 37:12 | unto them, Thus saith the Lord G |
| Eze 37:19 | unto them, Thus saith the Lord G |

| | |
|---|---|
| Eze 37:21 | unto them, Thus saith the Lord G |
| Eze 37:23 | my people, and I will be their G |
| Eze 37:27 | yea, I will be their G, and they |
| Eze 38:3 | And say, Thus saith the Lord G |
| Eze 38:10 | Thus saith the Lord G |
| Eze 38:14 | unto Gog, Thus saith the Lord G |
| Eze 38:17 | Thus saith the Lord G |
| Eze 38:18 | land of Israel, saith the Lord G |
| Eze 38:21 | my mountains, saith the Lord G |
| Eze 39:1 | and say, Thus saith the Lord G |
| Eze 39:5 | have spoken it, saith the Lord G |
| Eze 39:8 | and it is done, saith the Lord G |
| Eze 39:10 | robbed them, saith the Lord G |
| Eze 39:13 | be glorified, saith the Lord G |
| Eze 39:17 | son of man, thus saith the Lord G |
| Eze 39:20 | all men of war, saith the Lord G |
| Eze 39:22 | am the LORD their G from that day |
| Eze 39:25 | Therefore thus saith the Lord G |
| Eze 39:28 | know that I am the LORD their G |
| Eze 39:29 | house of Israel, saith the Lord G |
| Eze 40:2 | In the visions of G brought he me |
| Eze 43:2 | the glory of the G of Israel came |
| Eze 43:18 | Son of man, thus saith the Lord G |
| Eze 43:19 | unto me, saith the Lord G |
| Eze 43:27 | will accept you, saith the Lord G |
| Eze 44:2 | the G of Israel, hath entered in |
| Eze 44:6 | of Israel, Thus saith the Lord G |
| Eze 44:9 | Thus saith the Lord G |
| Eze 44:12 | against them, saith the Lord G |
| Eze 44:15 | and the blood, saith the Lord G |
| Eze 44:27 | sin offering, saith the Lord G |
| Eze 45:9 | Thus saith the Lord G |
| Eze 45:9 | from my people, saith the Lord G |
| Eze 45:15 | for them, saith the Lord G |
| Eze 45:18 | Thus saith the Lord G |
| Eze 46:1 | Thus saith the Lord G |
| Eze 46:16 | Thus saith the Lord G |
| Eze 47:13 | Thus saith the Lord G |
| Eze 47:23 | his inheritance, saith the Lord G |
| Eze 48:29 | their portions, saith the Lord G |
| Dan 1:2 | of the vessels of the house of G |
| Dan 1:9 | Now G had brought Daniel into |
| Dan 1:17 | G gave them knowledge and skill in |
| Dan 2:18 | the G of heaven concerning this |
| Dan 2:19 | Daniel blessed the G of heaven |
| Dan 2:20 | Blessed be the name of G for ever |
| Dan 2:23 | O thou G of my fathers, who hast |
| Dan 2:28 | But there is a G in heaven that |
| Dan 2:37 | for the G of heaven hath given |
| Dan 2:44 | the G of heaven set up a kingdom |
| Dan 2:45 | the great G hath made known to |
| Dan 2:47 | is, that your G is a G of gods |
| Dan 3:15 | who is that G that shall deliver |
| Dan 3:17 | our G whom we serve is able to |
| Dan 3:25 | the fourth is like the Son of G |
| Dan 3:26 | ye servants of the most high G |
| Dan 3:28 | Blessed be the G of Shadrach |
| Dan 3:28 | except their own G |
| Dan 3:29 | amiss against the G of Shadrach |
| Dan 3:29 | because there is no other G that |
| Dan 4:2 | wonders that the high G hath |
| Dan 5:3 | house of G which was at Jerusalem |
| Dan 5:18 | O thou king, the most high G gave |
| Dan 5:21 | G ruled in the kingdom of men |
| Dan 5:23 | the G in whose hand thy breath is |
| Dan 5:26 | G hath numbered thy kingdom, and |
| Dan 6:5 | him concerning the law of his G |
| Dan 6:7 | of any G or man for thirty days |
| Dan 6:10 | and gave thanks before his G |
| Dan 6:11 | making supplication before his G |
| Dan 6:12 | any G or man within thirty days |
| Dan 6:16 | Daniel, Thy G whom thou servest |
| Dan 6:20 | of the living G, is thy G |
| Dan 6:22 | My G hath sent his angel, and hath |
| Dan 6:23 | him, because he believed in his G |
| Dan 6:26 | and fear before the G of Daniel |
| Dan 6:26 | for he is the living G, and |
| Dan 9:3 | And I set my face unto the Lord G |
| Dan 9:4 | And I prayed unto the LORD my G |
| Dan 9:4 | O Lord, the great and dreadful G |
| Dan 9:9 | To the Lord our G belong mercies |
| Dan 9:10 | the voice of the LORD our G |
| Dan 9:11 | the law of Moses the servant of G |
| Dan 9:13 | our prayer before the LORD our G |
| Dan 9:14 | for the LORD our G is righteous |
| Dan 9:15 | And now, O Lord our G, that hast |
| Dan 9:17 | Now therefore, O our G, hear the |
| Dan 9:18 | O my G, incline thine ear, and |
| Dan 9:19 | not, for thine own sake, O my G |
| Dan 9:20 | G for the holy mountain of my G |

| | |
|---|---|
| Dan 10:12 | to chasten thyself before thy G |
| Dan 11:32 | do know their G shall be strong |
| Dan 11:36 | things against the G of gods |
| Dan 11:37 | he regard the G of his fathers |
| Dan 11:38 | shall he honour the G of forces |
| Hos 1:6 | G said unto him, Call her name |
| Hos 1:7 | save them by the LORD their G |
| Hos 1:9 | Then said G, Call his name |
| Hos 1:9 | people, and I will not be your G |
| Hos 1:10 | Ye are the sons of the living G |
| Hos 2:23 | and they shall say, Thou art my G |
| Hos 3:5 | return, and seek the LORD their G |
| Hos 4:1 | nor knowledge of G in the land |
| Hos 4:6 | hast forgotten the law of thy G |
| Hos 4:12 | gone a whoring from under their G |
| Hos 5:4 | their doings to turn unto their G |
| Hos 6:6 | the knowledge of G more than |
| Hos 7:10 | do not return to the LORD their G |
| Hos 8:2 | Israel shall cry unto me, My G |
| Hos 8:6 | therefore it is not G |
| Hos 9:1 | hast gone a whoring from thy G |
| Hos 9:8 | watchman of Ephraim was with my G |
| Hos 9:8 | and hatred in the house of his G |
| Hos 9:17 | My G will cast them away, because |
| Hos 11:9 | for I am G, and not man |
| Hos 11:12 | but Judah yet ruleth with G |
| Hos 12:3 | his strength he had power with G |
| Hos 12:5 | Even the LORD G of hosts |
| Hos 12:6 | Therefore turn thou to thy G |
| Hos 12:6 | and wait on thy G continually |
| Hos 12:9 | I that am the LORD thy G from the |
| Hos 13:4 | Yet I am the LORD thy G from the |
| Hos 13:16 | she hath rebelled against her G |
| Hos 14:1 | return unto the LORD thy G |
| Joel 1:13 | sackcloth, ye ministers of my G |
| Joel 1:13 | from the house of your G |
| Joel 1:14 | into the house of the LORD your G |
| Joel 1:16 | gladness from the house of our G |
| Joel 2:13 | and turn unto the LORD your G |
| Joel 2:14 | offering unto the LORD your G |
| Joel 2:17 | the people, Where is their G |
| Joel 2:23 | and rejoice in the LORD your G |
| Joel 2:26 | the name of the LORD your G |
| Joel 2:27 | and that I am the LORD your G |
| Joel 3:17 | the LORD your G dwelling in Zion |
| Amos 1:8 | shall perish, saith the Lord G |
| Amos 3:7 | Surely the Lord G will do nothing |
| Amos 3:8 | the Lord G hath spoken, who can |
| Amos 3:11 | Therefore thus saith the Lord G |
| Amos 3:13 | house of Jacob, saith the Lord G |
| Amos 3:13 | the G of hosts, |
| Amos 4:2 | The Lord G hath sworn by his |
| Amos 4:5 | of Israel, saith the Lord G |
| Amos 4:11 | as G overthrew Sodom and Gomorrah, |
| Amos 4:12 | unto thee, prepare to meet thy G |
| Amos 4:13 | The G of hosts, is his name |
| Amos 5:3 | For thus saith the Lord G |
| Amos 5:14 | the G of hosts, shall be with you |
| Amos 5:15 | it may be that the LORD G of |
| Amos 5:16 | the G of hosts, the Lord, saith |
| Amos 5:27 | whose name is The G of hosts |
| Amos 6:8 | The Lord G hath sworn by himself, |
| Amos 6:8 | saith the LORD the G of hosts |
| Amos 6:14 | saith the LORD the G of hosts |
| Amos 7:1 | hath the Lord G shewed unto me |
| Amos 7:2 | the land, then I said, O Lord G |
| Amos 7:4 | hath the Lord G shewed unto me |
| Amos 7:4 | the Lord G called to contend by |
| Amos 7:5 | Then said I, O Lord G, cease, I |
| Amos 7:6 | shall not be, saith the Lord G |
| Amos 8:1 | hath the Lord G shewed unto me |
| Amos 8:3 | in that day, saith the Lord G |
| Amos 8:9 | in that day, saith the Lord G |
| Amos 8:11 | the days come, saith the Lord G |
| Amos 9:5 | the Lord G of hosts is he that |
| Amos 9:8 | the eyes of the Lord G are upon |
| Amos 9:15 | given them, saith the LORD thy G |
| Obad 1 | saith the Lord G concerning Edom |
| Jonah 1:6 | arise, call upon thy G |
| Jonah 1:6 | if so be that G will think upon |
| Jonah 1:9 | the G of heaven, which hath made |
| Jonah 2:1 | his G out of the fish's belly |
| Jonah 2:6 | life from corruption, O LORD my G |
| Jonah 3:5 | the people of Nineveh believed G |
| Jonah 3:8 | sackcloth, and cry mightily unto G |
| Jonah 3:9 | Who can tell if G will turn |
| Jonah 3:10 | G saw their works, that they |
| Jonah 3:10 | G repented of the evil, that he |
| Jonah 4:2 | I knew that thou art a gracious G |
| Jonah 4:6 | the LORD G prepared a gourd, and |

| | |
|---|---|
| Jonah 4:7 | But G prepared a worm when the |
| Jonah 4:8 | that G prepared a vehement east |
| Jonah 4:9 | G said to Jonah, Doest thou well |
| Mic 1:2 | let the Lord G be witness against |
| Mic 3:7 | for there is no answer of G |
| Mic 4:2 | and to the house of the G of Jacob |
| Mic 4:5 | name of the LORD our G for ever |
| Mic 5:4 | of the name of the LORD his G |
| Mic 6:6 | and bow myself before the high G |
| Mic 6:8 | and to walk humbly with thy G |
| Mic 7:7 | wait for the G of my salvation |
| Mic 7:7 | my G will hear me |
| Mic 7:10 | unto me, Where is the LORD thy G |
| Mic 7:17 | shall be afraid of the LORD our G |
| Mic 7:18 | Who is a G like unto thee, that |
| Nah 1:2 | G is jealous, and the LORD |
| Hab 1:12 | not from everlasting, O LORD my G |
| Hab 1:12 | and, O mighty G, thou hast |
| Hab 3:3 | G came from Teman, and the Holy |
| Hab 3:18 | will joy in the G of my salvation |
| Hab 3:19 | The LORD G is my strength, and he |
| Zeph 1:7 | at the presence of the Lord G |
| Zeph 2:7 | the LORD their G shall visit them |
| Zeph 2:9 | the G of Israel, Surely Moab |
| Zeph 3:2 | she drew not near to her G |
| Zeph 3:17 | The LORD thy G in the midst of |
| Hag 1:12 | the voice of the LORD their G |
| Hag 1:12 | as the LORD their G had sent him |
| Hag 1:14 | of the LORD of hosts, their G |
| Zec 6:15 | obey the voice of the LORD your G |
| Zec 7:2 | sent unto the house of G Sherezer |
| Zec 8:8 | my people, and I will be their G |
| Zec 8:23 | we have heard that G is with you |
| Zec 9:7 | even he, shall be for our G |
| Zec 9:14 | the Lord G shall blow the trumpet |
| Zec 9:16 | the LORD their G shall save them |
| Zec 10:6 | for I am the LORD their G |
| Zec 11:4 | Thus saith the LORD my G |
| Zec 12:5 | in the LORD of hosts their G |
| Zec 12:8 | the house of David shall be as G |
| Zec 13:9 | they shall say, The LORD is my G |
| Zec 14:5 | and the LORD my G shall come |
| Mal 1:9 | beseech G that he will be |
| Mal 2:10 | hath not one G created us |
| Mal 2:16 | the G of Israel, saith that he |
| Mal 2:17 | or, Where is the G of judgment |
| Mal 3:8 | Will a man rob G |
| Mal 3:14 | have said, It is vain to serve G |
| Mal 3:15 | they that tempt G are even |
| Mal 3:18 | between him that serveth G |
| Mt 1:23 | being interpreted is, G with us |
| Mt 2:12 | being warned of G in a dream that |
| Mt 2:22 | being warned of G in a dream |
| Mt 3:9 | that G is able of these stones to |
| Mt 3:16 | he saw the Spirit of G descending |
| Mt 4:3 | he said, If thou be the Son of G |
| Mt 4:4 | proceedeth out of the mouth of G |
| Mt 4:6 | unto him, If thou be the Son of G |
| Mt 4:7 | shalt not tempt the Lord thy G |
| Mt 4:10 | Thou shalt worship the Lord thy G |
| Mt 5:8 | for they shall see G |
| Mt 5:9 | shall be called the children of G |
| Mt 6:24 | Ye cannot serve G and mammon |
| Mt 6:30 | if G so clothe the grass of the |
| Mt 6:33 | seek ye first the kingdom of G |
| Mt 8:29 | with thee, Jesus, thou Son of G |
| Mt 9:8 | they marvelled, and glorified G |
| Mt 12:4 | he entered into the house of G |
| Mt 12:28 | out devils by the Spirit of G |
| Mt 12:28 | the kingdom of G is come unto you |
| Mt 14:33 | Of a truth thou art the Son of G |
| Mt 15:3 | of G by your tradition |
| Mt 15:4 | For G commanded, saying, Honour |
| Mt 15:6 | of G of none effect by your |
| Mt 15:31 | and they glorified the G of Israel |
| Mt 16:16 | Christ, the Son of the living G |
| Mt 16:23 | not the things that be of G |
| Mt 19:6 | What therefore G hath joined |
| Mt 19:17 | is none good but one, that is, G |
| Mt 19:24 | to enter into the kingdom of G |
| Mt 19:26 | but with G all things are |
| Mt 21:12 | Jesus went into the temple of G |
| Mt 21:31 | into the kingdom of G before you |
| Mt 21:43 | The kingdom of G shall be taken |
| Mt 22:16 | and teachest the way of G in truth |
| Mt 22:21 | unto G the things that are God's |
| Mt 22:29 | scriptures, nor the power of G |
| Mt 22:30 | are as the angels of G in heaven |
| Mt 22:31 | which was spoken unto you by G |
| Mt 22:32 | I am the G of Abraham |
| Mt 22:32 | G of Isaac, and the G of Jacob |
| Mt 22:32 | G is not the G of the dead |
| Mt 22:37 | the Lord thy G with all thy heart |
| Mt 23:22 | sweareth by the throne of G |
| Mt 26:61 | able to destroy the temple of G |
| Mt 26:63 | I adjure thee by the living G |
| Mt 26:63 | thou be the Christ, the Son of G |
| Mt 27:40 | If thou be the Son of G, come |
| Mt 27:43 | He trusted in G |
| Mt 27:43 | for he said, I am the Son of G |
| Mt 27:46 | that is to say, My G, my G |
| Mt 27:54 | Truly this was the Son of G |
| Mk 1:1 | of Jesus Christ, the Son of G |
| Mk 1:14 | the gospel of the kingdom of G |
| Mk 1:15 | and the kingdom of G is at hand |
| Mk 1:24 | who thou art, the Holy One of G |
| Mk 2:7 | who can forgive sins but G only |
| Mk 2:12 | were all amazed, and glorified G |
| Mk 2:26 | of G in the days of Abiathar the |
| Mk 3:11 | saying, Thou art the Son of G |
| Mk 3:35 | whosoever shall do the will of G |
| Mk 4:11 | the mystery of the kingdom of G |
| Mk 4:26 | he said, So is the kingdom of G |
| Mk 4:30 | shall we liken the kingdom of G |
| Mk 5:7 | thou Son of the most high G |
| Mk 5:7 | I adjure thee by G, that thou |
| Mk 7:8 | laying aside the commandment of G |
| Mk 7:9 | ye reject the commandment of G |
| Mk 7:13 | Making the word of G of none |
| Mk 8:33 | not the things that be of G |
| Mk 9:1 | the kingdom of G come with power |
| Mk 9:47 | the kingdom of G with one eye |
| Mk 10:6 | of the creation G made them male |
| Mk 10:9 | What therefore G hath joined |
| Mk 10:14 | for of such is the kingdom of G |
| Mk 10:15 | kingdom of G as a little child |
| Mk 10:18 | is none good but one, that is, G |
| Mk 10:23 | enter into the kingdom of G |
| Mk 10:24 | to enter into the kingdom of G |
| Mk 10:25 | to enter into the kingdom of G |
| Mk 10:27 | it is impossible, but not with G |
| Mk 10:27 | for with G all things are |
| Mk 11:22 | saith unto them, Have faith in G |
| Mk 12:14 | teachest the way of G in truth |
| Mk 12:17 | to G the things that are God's |
| Mk 12:24 | neither the power of G |
| Mk 12:26 | how in the bush G spake unto him |
| Mk 12:26 | I am the G of Abraham |
| Mk 12:26 | G of Isaac, and the G of Jacob |
| Mk 12:27 | He is not the G of the dead |
| Mk 12:27 | but the G of the living |
| Mk 12:29 | The Lord our G is one Lord |
| Mk 12:30 | the Lord thy G with all thy heart |
| Mk 12:32 | for there is one G |
| Mk 12:34 | art not far from the kingdom of G |
| Mk 13:19 | which G created unto this time |
| Mk 14:25 | drink it new in the kingdom of G |
| Mk 15:34 | being interpreted, My G, my G |
| Mk 15:39 | Truly this man was the Son of G |
| Mk 15:43 | also waited for the kingdom of G |
| Mk 16:19 | and sat on the right hand of G |
| Lk 1:6 | they were both righteous before G |
| Lk 1:8 | G in the order of his course |
| Lk 1:16 | shall he turn to the Lord their G |
| Lk 1:19 | that stand in the presence of G |
| Lk 1:26 | from G unto a city of Galilee |
| Lk 1:30 | for thou hast found favour with G |
| Lk 1:32 | the Lord G shall give unto him |
| Lk 1:35 | thee shall be called the Son of G |
| Lk 1:37 | For with G nothing shall be |
| Lk 1:47 | hath rejoiced in G my Saviour |
| Lk 1:64 | loosed, and he spake, and praised G |
| Lk 1:68 | Blessed be the Lord G of Israel |
| Lk 1:78 | Through the tender mercy of our G |
| Lk 2:13 | of the heavenly host praising G |
| Lk 2:14 | Glory to G in the highest, and on |
| Lk 2:20 | praising G for all the things |
| Lk 2:28 | him up in his arms, and blessed G |
| Lk 2:37 | but served G with fastings and |
| Lk 2:40 | and the grace of G was upon him |
| Lk 2:52 | and stature, and in favour with G |
| Lk 3:2 | the word of G came unto John the |
| Lk 3:6 | shall see the salvation of G |
| Lk 3:8 | That G is able of these stones to |
| Lk 3:38 | of Adam, which was the son of G |
| Lk 4:3 | unto him, If thou be the Son of G |
| Lk 4:4 | alone, but by every word of G |
| Lk 4:8 | Thou shalt worship the Lord thy G |
| Lk 4:9 | unto him, If thou be the Son of G |
| Lk 4:12 | shalt not tempt the Lord thy G |
| Lk 4:34 | the Holy One of G |
| Lk 4:41 | Thou art Christ the Son of G |
| Lk 4:43 | kingdom of G to other cities also |
| Lk 5:1 | upon him to hear the word of G |
| Lk 5:21 | Who can forgive sins, but G alone |
| Lk 5:25 | to his own house, glorifying G |
| Lk 5:26 | all amazed, and they glorified G |
| Lk 6:4 | How he went into the house of G |
| Lk 6:12 | all night in prayer to G |
| Lk 6:20 | for yours is the kingdom of G |
| Lk 7:16 | and they glorified G, saying, That |
| Lk 7:16 | That G hath visited his people |
| Lk 7:28 | kingdom of G is greater than he |
| Lk 7:29 | and the publicans, justified G |
| Lk 7:30 | counsel of G against themselves |
| Lk 8:1 | glad tidings of the kingdom of G |
| Lk 8:10 | the mysteries of the kingdom of G |
| Lk 8:11 | The seed is the word of G |
| Lk 8:21 | these which hear the word of G |
| Lk 8:28 | Jesus, thou Son of G most high |
| Lk 8:39 | things G hath done unto thee |
| Lk 9:2 | them to preach the kingdom of G |
| Lk 9:11 | unto them of the kingdom of G |
| Lk 9:20 | answering said, The Christ of G |
| Lk 9:27 | till they see the kingdom of G |
| Lk 9:43 | amazed at the mighty power of G |
| Lk 9:60 | thou and preach the kingdom of G |
| Lk 9:62 | back, is fit for the kingdom of G |
| Lk 10:9 | The kingdom of G is come nigh |
| Lk 10:11 | that the kingdom of G is come |
| Lk 10:27 | the Lord thy G with all thy heart |
| Lk 11:20 | the finger of G cast out devils |
| Lk 11:20 | the kingdom of G is come upon you |
| Lk 11:28 | are they that hear the word of G |
| Lk 11:42 | over judgment and the love of G |
| Lk 11:49 | also said the wisdom of G |
| Lk 12:6 | one of them is forgotten before G |
| Lk 12:8 | confess before the angels of G |
| Lk 12:9 | be denied before the angels of G |
| Lk 12:20 | But G said unto him, Thou fool, |
| Lk 12:21 | himself, and is not rich toward G |
| Lk 12:24 | and G feedeth them |
| Lk 12:28 | If then G so clothe the grass, |
| Lk 12:31 | rather seek ye the kingdom of G |
| Lk 13:13 | was made straight, and glorified G |
| Lk 13:18 | what is the kingdom of G like |
| Lk 13:20 | shall I liken the kingdom of G |
| Lk 13:28 | the prophets, in the kingdom of G |
| Lk 13:29 | sit down in the kingdom of G |
| Lk 14:15 | eat bread in the kingdom of G |
| Lk 15:10 | the presence of the angels of G |
| Lk 16:13 | Ye cannot serve G and mammon |
| Lk 16:15 | but G knoweth your hearts |
| Lk 16:15 | is abomination in the sight of G |
| Lk 16:16 | time the kingdom of G is preached |
| Lk 17:15 | and with a loud voice glorified G |
| Lk 17:18 | that returned to give glory to G |
| Lk 17:20 | when the kingdom of G should come |
| Lk 17:20 | The kingdom of G cometh not with |
| Lk 17:21 | the kingdom of G is within you |
| Lk 18:2 | city a judge, which feared not G |
| Lk 18:4 | himself, Though I fear not G |
| Lk 18:7 | shall not G avenge his own elect, |
| Lk 18:11 | and prayed thus with himself, G |
| Lk 18:13 | G be merciful to me a sinner |
| Lk 18:16 | for of such is the kingdom of G |
| Lk 18:17 | not receive the kingdom of G as a |
| Lk 18:19 | is good, save one, that is, G |
| Lk 18:24 | enter into the kingdom of G |
| Lk 18:25 | to enter into the kingdom of G |
| Lk 18:27 | with men are possible with G |
| Lk 18:43 | and followed him, glorifying G |
| Lk 18:43 | they saw it, gave praise unto G |
| Lk 19:11 | of G should immediately appear |
| Lk 19:37 | praise G with a loud voice for |
| Lk 20:16 | heard it, they said, G forbid |
| Lk 20:21 | but teachest the way of G truly |
| Lk 20:25 | unto G the things which be God's |
| Lk 20:36 | and are the children of G, being |
| Lk 20:37 | calleth the Lord the G of Abraham |
| Lk 20:37 | G of Isaac, and the G of Jacob |
| Lk 20:38 | For he is not a G of the dead |
| Lk 21:4 | cast in unto the offerings of G |
| Lk 21:31 | the kingdom of G is nigh at hand |
| Lk 22:16 | be fulfilled in the kingdom of G |
| Lk 22:18 | until the kingdom of G shall come |
| Lk 22:69 | the right hand of the power of G |
| Lk 22:70 | all, Art thou then the Son of G |
| Lk 23:35 | if he be Christ, the chosen of G |
| Lk 23:40 | him, saying, Dost not thou fear G |

Lk 23:47 saw what was done, he glorified G
Lk 23:51 waited for the kingdom of G
Lk 24:19 mighty in deed and word before G
Lk 24:53 temple, praising and blessing G
Jn 1:1 was with G, and the Word was G
Jn 1:2 same was in the beginning with G
Jn 1:6 There was a man sent from G
Jn 1:12 he power to become the sons of G
Jn 1:13 nor of the will of man, but of G
Jn 1:18 No man hath seen G at any time
Jn 1:29 and saith, Behold the Lamb of G
Jn 1:34 record that this is the Son of G
Jn 1:36 he saith, Behold the Lamb of G
Jn 1:49 him, Rabbi, thou art the Son of G
Jn 1:51 and the angels of G ascending
Jn 3:2 thou art a teacher come from G
Jn 3:2 thou doest, except G be with him
Jn 3:3 he cannot see the kingdom of G
Jn 3:5 enter into the kingdom of G
Jn 3:16 For G so loved the world, that he
Jn 3:17 For G sent not his Son into the
Jn 3:18 of the only begotten Son of G
Jn 3:21 that they are wrought in G
Jn 3:33 set to his seal that G is true
Jn 3:34 For he whom G hath sent speaketh
Jn 3:34 hath sent speaketh the words of G
Jn 3:34 for G giveth not the Spirit by
Jn 3:36 but the wrath of G abideth on him
Jn 4:10 If thou knewest the gift of G
Jn 4:24 G is a Spirit
Jn 5:18 said also that G was his Father
Jn 5:18 making himself equal with G
Jn 5:25 hear the voice of the Son of G
Jn 5:42 ye have not the love of G in you
Jn 5:44 honour that cometh from G only
Jn 6:27 for him hath G the Father sealed
Jn 6:28 that we might work the works of G
Jn 6:29 unto them, This is the work of G
Jn 6:33 For the bread of G is he which
Jn 6:45 And they shall be all taught of G
Jn 6:46 the Father, save he which is of G
Jn 6:69 Christ, the Son of the living G
Jn 7:17 the doctrine, whether it be of G
Jn 8:40 truth, which I have heard of G
Jn 8:41 we have one Father, even G
Jn 8:42 If G were your Father, ye would
Jn 8:42 I proceeded forth and came from G
Jn 8:47 He that is of G heareth God's
Jn 8:47 them not, because ye are not of G
Jn 8:54 of whom ye say, that he is your G
Jn 9:3 but that the works of G should be
Jn 9:16 Pharisees, This man is not of G
Jn 9:24 said unto him, Give G the praise
Jn 9:29 We know that G spake unto Moses
Jn 9:31 Now we know that G heareth not
Jn 9:31 if any man be a worshipper of G
Jn 9:33 If this man were not of G
Jn 9:35 Dost thou believe on the Son of G
Jn 10:33 being a man, makest thyself G
Jn 10:35 unto whom the word of G came
Jn 10:36 because I said, I am the Son of G
Jn 11:4 death, but for the glory of G
Jn 11:4 that the Son of G might be
Jn 11:22 ask of G, G will give it thee
Jn 11:27 thou art the Christ, the Son of G
Jn 11:40 thou shouldest see the glory of G
Jn 11:52 of G that were scattered abroad
Jn 12:43 of men more than the praise of G
Jn 13:3 was come from G, and went to G
Jn 13:31 and G is glorified in him
Jn 13:32 If G be glorified in him
Jn 13:32 G shall also glorify him in
Jn 14:1 ye believe in G, believe also in
Jn 16:2 think that he doeth G service
Jn 16:27 believed that I came out from G
Jn 16:30 that thou camest forth from G
Jn 17:3 might know thee the only true G
Jn 19:7 he made himself the Son of G
Jn 20:17 and to my G, and your G
Jn 20:28 and said unto him, My Lord and my G
Jn 20:31 Jesus is the Christ, the Son of G
Jn 21:19 by what death he should glorify G
Acts 1:3 pertaining to the kingdom of G
Acts 2:11 tongues the wonderful works of G
Acts 2:17 to pass in the last days, saith G
Acts 2:22 a man approved of G among you by
Acts 2:22 which G did by him in the midst
Acts 2:23 counsel and foreknowledge of G
Acts 2:24 Whom G hath raised up, having
Acts 2:30 knowing that G had sworn with an
Acts 2:32 This Jesus hath G raised up
Acts 2:33 by the right hand of G exalted
Acts 2:36 that G hath made that same Jesus,
Acts 2:39 many as the Lord our G shall call
Acts 2:47 Praising G, and having favour with
Acts 3:8 and leaping, and praising G
Acts 3:9 saw him walking and praising G
Acts 3:13 The G of Abraham, and of Isaac, and
Acts 3:13 the G of our fathers, hath
Acts 3:15 whom G hath raised from the dead
Acts 3:18 which G before had shewed by the
Acts 3:21 which G hath spoken by the mouth
Acts 3:22 your G raise up unto you of your
Acts 3:25 which G made with our fathers
Acts 3:26 Unto you first G, having raised
Acts 4:10 whom G raised from the dead, even
Acts 4:19 it be right in the sight of G to
Acts 4:19 hearken unto you more than unto G
Acts 4:21 for all men glorified G for that
Acts 4:24 their voice to G with one accord
Acts 4:24 and said, Lord, thou art G
Acts 4:31 spake the word of G with boldness
Acts 5:4 not lied unto men, but unto G
Acts 5:29 ought to obey G rather than men
Acts 5:30 The G of our fathers raised up
Acts 5:31 Him hath G exalted with his right
Acts 5:32 whom G hath given to them that
Acts 5:39 But if it be of G, ye cannot
Acts 5:39 be found even to fight against G
Acts 6:2 we should leave the word of G
Acts 6:7 And the word of G increased
Acts 6:11 words against Moses, and against G
Acts 7:2 The G of glory appeared unto our
Acts 7:6 G spake on this wise, That his
Acts 7:7 in bondage will I judge, said G
Acts 7:9 but G was with him,
Acts 7:17 which G had sworn to Abraham, the
Acts 7:25 G by his hand would deliver them
Acts 7:32 I am the G of thy fathers
Acts 7:32 the G of Abraham
Acts 7:32 G of Isaac, and the G of Jacob
Acts 7:35 the same did G send to be a ruler
Acts 7:37 your G raise up unto you of your
Acts 7:42 Then G turned, and gave them up to
Acts 7:45 whom G drave out before the face
Acts 7:46 Who found favour before G
Acts 7:46 a tabernacle for the G of Jacob
Acts 7:55 heaven, and saw the glory of G
Acts 7:55 standing on the right hand of G
Acts 7:56 standing on the right hand of G
Acts 7:59 stoned Stephen, calling upon G
Acts 8:10 This man is the great power of G
Acts 8:12 concerning the kingdom of G
Acts 8:14 had received the word of G
Acts 8:20 of G may be purchased with money
Acts 8:21 is not right in the sight of G
Acts 8:22 of this thy wickedness, and pray G
Acts 8:37 that Jesus Christ is the Son of G
Acts 9:20 that he is the Son of G
Acts 10:2 one that feared G with all his
Acts 10:2 the people, and prayed to G alway
Acts 10:3 an angel of G coming in to him
Acts 10:4 come up for a memorial before G
Acts 10:15 What G hath cleansed, that call
Acts 10:22 a just man, and one that feareth G
Acts 10:22 was warned from G by an holy
Acts 10:28 but G hath shewed me that I
Acts 10:31 in remembrance in the sight of G
Acts 10:33 are we all here present before G
Acts 10:33 that are commanded thee of G
Acts 10:34 that G is no respecter of persons
Acts 10:36 The word which G sent unto the
Acts 10:38 How G anointed Jesus of Nazareth
Acts 10:38 for G was with him
Acts 10:40 Him G raised up the third day, and
Acts 10:41 unto witnesses chosen before of G
Acts 10:42 of G to be the Judge of quick
Acts 10:46 speak with tongues, and magnify G
Acts 11:1 had also received the word of G
Acts 11:9 What G hath cleansed, that call
Acts 11:17 Forasmuch then as G gave them the
Acts 11:17 was I, that I could withstand G
Acts 11:18 held their peace, and glorified G
Acts 11:18 Then hath G also to the Gentiles
Acts 11:23 came, and had seen the grace of G
Acts 12:5 of the church unto G for him
Acts 12:23 because he gave not G the glory
Acts 12:24 But the word of G grew and
Acts 13:5 they preached the word of G in
Acts 13:7 and desired to hear the word of G
Acts 13:16 Men of Israel, and ye that fear G
Acts 13:17 The G of this people of Israel
Acts 13:21 G gave unto them Saul the son of
Acts 13:23 Of this man's seed hath G
Acts 13:26 and whosoever among you feareth G
Acts 13:30 But G raised him from the dead
Acts 13:33 G hath fulfilled the same unto us
Acts 13:36 own generation by the will of G
Acts 13:37 whom G raised again, saw no
Acts 13:43 to continue in the grace of G
Acts 13:44 together to hear the word of G
Acts 13:46 G should first have been spoken
Acts 14:15 these vanities unto the living G
Acts 14:22 enter into the kingdom of G
Acts 14:26 of G for the work which they
Acts 14:27 all that G had done with them
Acts 15:4 things that G had done with them
Acts 15:7 while ago G made choice among us
Acts 15:8 And G, which knoweth the hearts,
Acts 15:10 Now therefore why tempt ye G
Acts 15:12 wonders G had wrought among the
Acts 15:14 Simeon hath declared how G at the
Acts 15:18 Known unto G are all his works
Acts 15:19 the Gentiles are turned to G
Acts 15:40 the brethren unto the grace of G
Acts 16:14 of Thyatira, which worshipped G
Acts 16:17 the servants of the most high G
Acts 16:25 prayed, and sang praises unto G
Acts 16:34 believing in G with all his house
Acts 17:13 G was preached of Paul at Berea
Acts 17:23 inscription, TO THE UNKNOWN G
Acts 17:24 G that made the world and all
Acts 17:29 then as we are the offspring of G
Acts 17:30 of this ignorance G winked at
Acts 18:7 Justus, one that worshipped G
Acts 18:11 teaching the word of G among them
Acts 18:13 to worship G contrary to the law
Acts 18:21 return again unto you, if G will
Acts 18:26 him the way of G more perfectly
Acts 19:8 concerning the kingdom of G
Acts 19:11 G wrought special miracles by the
Acts 19:20 So mightily grew the word of G
Acts 20:21 the Greeks, repentance toward G
Acts 20:24 the gospel of the grace of G
Acts 20:25 gone preaching the kingdom of G
Acts 20:27 unto you all the counsel of G
Acts 20:28 to feed the church of G, which
Acts 20:32 now, brethren, I commend you to G
Acts 21:19 particularly what things G had
Acts 22:3 fathers, and was zealous toward G
Acts 22:14 The G of our fathers hath chosen
Acts 23:1 before G until this day
Acts 23:3 G shall smite thee, thou whited
Acts 23:9 him, let us not fight against G
Acts 24:14 so worship I the G of my fathers
Acts 24:15 And have hope toward G, which they
Acts 24:16 void of offence toward G, and
Acts 26:6 made of G unto our fathers
Acts 26:7 tribes, instantly serving G day
Acts 26:8 that G should raise the dead
Acts 26:18 and from the power of Satan unto G
Acts 26:20 they should repent and turn to G
Acts 26:22 therefore obtained help of G
Acts 26:29 And Paul said, I would to G
Acts 27:23 by me this night the angel of G
Acts 27:24 G hath given thee all them that
Acts 27:25 for I believe G, that it shall be
Acts 27:35 gave thanks to G in presence of
Acts 28:15 whom when Paul saw, he thanked G
Acts 28:23 and testified the kingdom of G
Acts 28:28 that the salvation of G is sent
Acts 28:31 Preaching the kingdom of G
Rom 1:1 separated unto the gospel of G
Rom 1:4 to be the Son of G with power
Rom 1:7 all that be in Rome, beloved of G
Rom 1:7 to you and peace from G our Father
Rom 1:8 I thank my G through Jesus Christ
Rom 1:9 For G is my witness, whom I serve
Rom 1:10 by the will of G to come unto you
Rom 1:16 for it is the power of G unto
Rom 1:17 of G revealed from faith to faith
Rom 1:18 For the wrath of G is revealed
Rom 1:19 be known of G is manifest in them
Rom 1:19 for G hath shewed it unto them
Rom 1:21 Because that, when they knew G
Rom 1:21 they glorified him not as G
Rom 1:23 G into an image made like to
Rom 1:24 Wherefore G also gave them up to
Rom 1:25 changed the truth of G into a lie
Rom 1:26 For this cause G gave them up

Rom 1:28 to retain G in their knowledge
Rom 1:28 G gave them over to a reprobate
Rom 1:30 Backbiters, haters of G,
Rom 1:32 Who knowing the judgment of G
Rom 2:2 G is according to truth against
Rom 2:3 shalt escape the judgment of G
Rom 2:4 of G leadeth thee to repentance
Rom 2:5 of the righteous judgment of G
Rom 2:11 is no respect of persons with G
Rom 2:13 of the law are just before G
Rom 2:16 In the day when G shall judge the
Rom 2:17 the law, and makest thy boast of G
Rom 2:23 the law dishonourest thou G
Rom 2:24 For the name of G is blasphemed
Rom 2:29 praise is not of men, but of G
Rom 3:2 were committed the oracles of G
Rom 3:3 the faith of G without effect
Rom 3:4 G forbid: yea,
Rom 3:4 let G be true, but every man a
Rom 3:5 commend the righteousness of G
Rom 3:5 Is G unrighteous who taketh
Rom 3:6 G forbid: for then how
Rom 3:6 then how shall G judge the world
Rom 3:7 For if the truth of G hath more
Rom 3:11 is none that seeketh after G
Rom 3:18 is no fear of G before their eyes
Rom 3:19 world may become guilty before G
Rom 3:21 But now the righteousness of G
Rom 3:22 Even the righteousness of G which
Rom 3:23 and come short of the glory of G
Rom 3:25 Whom G hath set forth to be a
Rom 3:25 through the forbearance of G
Rom 3:29 Is he the G of the Jews only
Rom 3:30 Seeing it is one G, which shall
Rom 3:31 G forbid: yea, we establish
Rom 4:2 but not before G
Rom 4:3 Abraham believed G, and it was
Rom 4:6 of the man, unto whom G imputeth
Rom 4:17 him whom he believed, even G
Rom 4:20 the promise of G through unbelief
Rom 4:20 in faith, giving glory to G
Rom 5:1 we have peace with G through our
Rom 5:2 rejoice in hope of the glory of G
Rom 5:5 because the love of G is shed
Rom 5:8 But G commendeth his love toward
Rom 5:10 we were reconciled to G by the
Rom 5:11 but we also joy in G through our
Rom 5:15 be dead, much more the grace of G
Rom 6:2 G forbid. How shall we
Rom 6:10 that he liveth, he liveth unto G
Rom 6:11 but alive unto G through Jesus
Rom 6:13 but yield yourselves unto G
Rom 6:13 of righteousness unto G
Rom 6:15 but under grace? G forbid
Rom 6:17 But G be thanked, that ye were
Rom 6:22 from sin, and become servants to G
Rom 6:23 but the gift of G is eternal life
Rom 7:4 should bring forth fruit unto G
Rom 7:7 Is the law sin? G forbid
Rom 7:13 made death unto me? G forbid
Rom 7:22 the law of G after the inward man
Rom 7:25 I thank G through Jesus Christ
Rom 7:25 mind I myself serve the law of G
Rom 8:3 G sending his own Son in the
Rom 8:7 carnal mind is enmity against G
Rom 8:7 it is not subject to the law of G
Rom 8:8 are in the flesh cannot please G
Rom 8:9 that the Spirit of G dwell in you
Rom 8:14 as are led by the Spirit of G
Rom 8:14 they are the sons of G
Rom 8:16 that we are the children of G
Rom 8:17 heirs of G, and joint-heirs with
Rom 8:19 manifestation of the sons of G
Rom 8:21 liberty of the children of G
Rom 8:27 saints according to the will of G
Rom 8:28 for good to them that love G
Rom 8:31 If G be for us, who can be
Rom 8:33 It is G that justifieth
Rom 8:34 is even at the right hand of G
Rom 8:39 to separate us from the love of G
Rom 9:4 of the law, and the service of G
Rom 9:5 is over all, G blessed for ever
Rom 9:6 word of G hath taken none effect
Rom 9:8 these are not the children of G
Rom 9:11 that the purpose of G according
Rom 9:14 Is there unrighteousness with G?
Rom 9:14 G forbid
Rom 9:16 but of G that sheweth mercy
Rom 9:20 art thou that repliest against G
Rom 9:22 What if G, willing to shew his
Rom 9:26 the children of the living G
Rom 10:1 prayer to G for Israel is, that
Rom 10:2 record that they have a zeal of G
Rom 10:3 unto the righteousness of G
Rom 10:9 believe in thine heart that G
Rom 10:17 and hearing by the word of G
Rom 11:1 Hath G cast away his people
Rom 11:1 cast away his people? G forbid
Rom 11:2 G hath not cast away his people
Rom 11:2 intercession to G against Israel
Rom 11:4 saith the answer of G unto him
Rom 11:8 G hath given them the spirit of
Rom 11:11 that they should fall? G forbid
Rom 11:21 For if G spared not the natural
Rom 11:22 the goodness and severity of G
Rom 11:23 for G is able to graff them in
Rom 11:29 gifts and calling of G are without
Rom 11:30 in times past have not believed G
Rom 11:32 For G hath concluded them all in
Rom 11:33 of the wisdom and knowledge of G
Rom 12:1 brethren, by the mercies of G
Rom 12:1 holy, acceptable unto G, which
Rom 12:2 acceptable, and perfect, will of G
Rom 12:3 according as G hath dealt to
Rom 13:1 For there is no power but of G
Rom 13:1 powers that be are ordained of G
Rom 13:2 resisteth the ordinance of G
Rom 13:4 minister of G to thee for good
Rom 13:4 for he is the minister of G
Rom 14:3 for G hath received him
Rom 14:4 for G is able to make him stand
Rom 14:6 the Lord, for he giveth G thanks
Rom 14:6 he eateth not, and giveth G thanks
Rom 14:11 every tongue shall confess to G
Rom 14:12 give account of himself to G
Rom 14:17 For the kingdom of G is not meat
Rom 14:18 serveth Christ is acceptable to G
Rom 14:20 meat destroy not the work of G
Rom 14:22 have it to thyself before G
Rom 15:5 Now the G of patience and
Rom 15:6 one mind and one mouth glorify G
Rom 15:7 received us to the glory of G
Rom 15:8 circumcision for the truth of G
Rom 15:9 might glorify G for his mercy
Rom 15:13 Now the G of hope fill you with
Rom 15:15 grace that is given to me of G
Rom 15:16 ministering the gospel of G
Rom 15:17 those things which pertain to G
Rom 15:19 by the power of the Spirit of G
Rom 15:30 me in your prayers to G for me
Rom 15:32 you with joy by the will of G
Rom 15:33 Now the G of peace be with you
Rom 16:20 the G of peace shall bruise Satan
Rom 16:26 commandment of the everlasting G
Rom 16:27 To G only wise, be glory through
1Cor 1:1 Christ through the will of G
1Cor 1:2 Unto the church of G which is at
1Cor 1:3 from G our Father, and from the
1Cor 1:4 I thank my G always on your
1Cor 1:4 for the grace of G which is given
1Cor 1:9 G is faithful, by whom ye were
1Cor 1:14 I thank G that I baptized none of
1Cor 1:18 are saved it is the power of G
1Cor 1:20 hath not G made foolish the
1Cor 1:21 that in the wisdom of G
1Cor 1:21 the world by wisdom knew not G
1Cor 1:21 it pleased G by the foolishness
1Cor 1:24 power of G, and the wisdom of G
1Cor 1:25 of G is wiser than men
1Cor 1:25 the weakness of G is stronger
1Cor 1:27 But G hath chosen the foolish
1Cor 1:27 G hath chosen the weak things of
1Cor 1:28 hath G chosen, yea, and things
1Cor 1:30 who of G is made unto us wisdom,
1Cor 2:1 unto you the testimony of G
1Cor 2:5 of men, but in the power of G
1Cor 2:7 the wisdom of G in a mystery
1Cor 2:7 which G ordained before the world
1Cor 2:9 the things which G hath prepared
1Cor 2:10 But G hath revealed them unto us
1Cor 2:10 things, yea, the deep things of G
1Cor 2:11 so the things of G knoweth no man
1Cor 2:11 but the Spirit of G
1Cor 2:12 but the spirit which is of G
1Cor 2:12 that are freely given to us of G
1Cor 2:14 not the things of the Spirit of G
1Cor 3:6 but G gave the increase
1Cor 3:7 but G that giveth the increase
1Cor 3:9 we are labourers together with G
1Cor 3:10 grace of G which is given unto me
1Cor 3:16 not that ye are the temple of G
1Cor 3:16 the Spirit of G dwelleth in you
1Cor 3:17 If any man defile the temple of G
1Cor 3:17 him shall G destroy
1Cor 3:17 for the temple of G is holy
1Cor 3:19 this world is foolishness with G
1Cor 4:1 and stewards of the mysteries of G
1Cor 4:5 shall every man have praise of G
1Cor 4:8 I would to G ye did reign, that
1Cor 4:9 For I think that G hath set forth
1Cor 4:20 the kingdom of G is not in word
1Cor 5:13 them that are without G judgeth
1Cor 6:9 not inherit the kingdom of G
1Cor 6:10 shall inherit the kingdom of G
1Cor 6:11 Jesus, and by the Spirit of our G
1Cor 6:13 but G shall destroy both it and
1Cor 6:14 G hath both raised up the Lord,
1Cor 6:15 members of an harlot? G forbid
1Cor 6:19 is in you, which ye have of G
1Cor 6:20 therefore glorify G in your body
1Cor 7:7 man hath his proper gift of G
1Cor 7:15 but G hath called us to peace
1Cor 7:17 But as G hath distributed to
1Cor 7:19 keeping of the commandments of G
1Cor 7:24 is called, therein abide with G
1Cor 7:40 also that I have the Spirit of G
1Cor 8:3 But if any man love G, the same
1Cor 8:4 there is none other G but one
1Cor 8:6 But to us there is but one G
1Cor 8:8 But meat commendeth us not to G
1Cor 9:9 Doth G take care for oxen
1Cor 9:21 law, (being not without law to G
1Cor 10:5 of them G was not well pleased
1Cor 10:13 but G is faithful, who will not
1Cor 10:20 sacrifice to devils, and not to G
1Cor 10:31 ye do, do all to the glory of G
1Cor 10:32 Gentiles, nor to the church of G
1Cor 11:3 and the head of Christ is G
1Cor 11:7 as he is the image and glory of G
1Cor 11:12 but all things of G
1Cor 11:13 a woman pray unto G uncovered
1Cor 11:16 custom, neither the churches of G
1Cor 11:22 or despise ye the church of G
1Cor 12:3 of G calleth Jesus accursed
1Cor 12:6 but it is the same G which
1Cor 12:18 But now hath G set the members
1Cor 12:24 but G hath tempered the body
1Cor 12:28 G hath set some in the church,
1Cor 14:2 speaketh not unto men, but unto G
1Cor 14:18 I thank my G, I speak with
1Cor 14:25 on his face he will worship G
1Cor 14:25 report that G is in you of a
1Cor 14:28 let him speak to himself, and to G
1Cor 14:33 For G is not the author of
1Cor 14:36 came the word of G out from you
1Cor 15:9 I persecuted the church of G
1Cor 15:10 by the grace of G I am what I am
1Cor 15:10 but the grace of G which was with
1Cor 15:15 we are found false witnesses of G
1Cor 15:15 of G that he raised up Christ
1Cor 15:24 delivered up the kingdom to G
1Cor 15:28 him, that G may be all in all
1Cor 15:34 some have not the knowledge of G
1Cor 15:38 But G giveth it a body as it hath
1Cor 15:50 cannot inherit the kingdom of G
1Cor 15:57 But thanks be to G, which giveth
1Cor 16:2 as G hath prospered him, that
2Cor 1:1 of Jesus Christ by the will of G
2Cor 1:1 unto the church of G which is at
2Cor 1:2 to you and peace from G our Father
2Cor 1:3 Blessed be G, even the Father of
2Cor 1:3 mercies, and the G of all comfort
2Cor 1:4 we ourselves are comforted of G
2Cor 1:9 but in G which raiseth the dead
2Cor 1:12 wisdom, but by the grace of G
2Cor 1:18 But as G is true, our word toward
2Cor 1:19 For the Son of G, Jesus Christ,
2Cor 1:20 the promises of G in him are yea
2Cor 1:20 Amen, unto the glory of G by us
2Cor 1:21 Christ, and hath anointed us, is G
2Cor 1:23 Moreover I call G for a record
2Cor 2:14 Now thanks be unto G, which
2Cor 2:15 For we are unto G a sweet savour
2Cor 2:17 many, which corrupt the word of G
2Cor 2:17 but as of sincerity, but as of G
2Cor 2:17 in the sight of G speak we in
2Cor 3:3 with the Spirit of the living G
2Cor 3:5 but our sufficiency is of G
2Cor 4:2 the word of G deceitfully
2Cor 4:2 conscience in the sight of G

2Cor 4:4 of Christ, who is the image of G
2Cor 4:6 For G, who commanded the light to
2Cor 4:6 of G in the face of Jesus Christ
2Cor 4:7 of the power may be of G, and not
2Cor 4:15 of many redound to the glory of G
2Cor 5:1 we have a building of G, an
2Cor 5:5 us for the selfsame thing is G
2Cor 5:11 but we are made manifest unto G
2Cor 5:13 be beside ourselves, it is to G
2Cor 5:18 And all things are of G, who hath
2Cor 5:19 that G was in Christ, reconciling
2Cor 5:20 as though G did beseech you by us
2Cor 5:20 stead, be ye reconciled to G
2Cor 5:21 the righteousness of G in him
2Cor 6:1 not the grace of G in vain
2Cor 6:4 ourselves as the ministers of G
2Cor 6:7 word of truth, by the power of G
2Cor 6:16 hath the temple of G with idols
2Cor 6:16 ye are the temple of the living G
2Cor 6:16 as G hath said, I will dwell in
2Cor 6:16 and I will be their G, and they
2Cor 7:1 holiness in the fear of G
2Cor 7:6 Nevertheless G, that comforteth
2Cor 7:12 sight of G might appear unto you
2Cor 8:1 of G bestowed on the churches of
2Cor 8:5 Lord, and unto us by the will of G
2Cor 8:16 But thanks be to G, which put the
2Cor 9:7 for G loveth a cheerful giver
2Cor 9:8 G is able to make all grace
2Cor 9:11 through us thanksgiving to G
2Cor 9:12 also by many thanksgivings unto G
2Cor 9:13 G for your professed subjection
2Cor 9:14 the exceeding grace of G in you
2Cor 9:15 Thanks be unto G for his
2Cor 10:4 but mighty through G to the
2Cor 10:5 itself against the knowledge of G
2Cor 10:13 which G hath distributed to us
2Cor 11:1 Would to G ye could bear with me
2Cor 11:7 to you the gospel of G freely
2Cor 11:11 I love you not? G knoweth
2Cor 11:31 The G and Father of our Lord Jesus
2Cor 12:2 body, I cannot tell: G knoweth
2Cor 12:3 I cannot tell: G knoweth
2Cor 12:19 we speak before G in Christ
2Cor 12:21 my G will humble me among you, and
2Cor 13:4 yet he liveth by the power of G
2Cor 13:4 him by the power of G toward you
2Cor 13:7 Now I pray to G that ye do no
2Cor 13:11 the G of love and peace shall be
2Cor 13:14 Jesus Christ, and the love of G
Gal 1:1 G the Father, who raised him from
Gal 1:3 to you and peace from G the Father
Gal 1:4 world, according to the will of G
Gal 1:10 For do I now persuade men, or G
Gal 1:13 I persecuted the church of G
Gal 1:15 But when it pleased G, who
Gal 1:20 write unto you, behold, before G
Gal 1:24 And they glorified G in me
Gal 2:6 G accepteth no man's person
Gal 2:17 minister of sin? G forbid
Gal 2:19 the law, that I might live unto G
Gal 2:20 live by the faith of the Son of G
Gal 2:21 I do not frustrate the grace of G
Gal 3:6 Even as Abraham believed G
Gal 3:8 foreseeing that G would justify
Gal 3:11 by the law in the sight of G
Gal 3:17 confirmed before of G in Christ
Gal 3:18 but G gave it to Abraham by
Gal 3:20 a mediator of one, but G is one
Gal 3:21 then against the promises of G
Gal 3:21 G forbid for if there had
Gal 3:26 of G by faith in Christ Jesus
Gal 4:4 G sent forth his Son, made of a
Gal 4:6 G hath sent forth the Spirit of
Gal 4:7 then an heir of G through Christ
Gal 4:8 Howbeit then, when ye knew not G
Gal 4:9 now, after that ye have known G
Gal 4:9 or rather are known of G
Gal 4:14 but received me as an angel of G
Gal 5:21 not inherit the kingdom of G
Gal 6:7 G is not mocked
Gal 6:14 But G forbid that I should glory,
Gal 6:16 and mercy, and upon the Israel of G
Eph 1:1 of Jesus Christ by the will of G
Eph 1:2 from G our Father, and from the
Eph 1:3 Blessed be the G and Father of our
Eph 1:17 That the G of our Lord Jesus
Eph 2:4 But G, who is rich in mercy, for
Eph 2:8 it is the gift of G
Eph 2:10 which G hath before ordained that
Eph 2:12 hope, and without G in the world
Eph 2:16 unto G in one body by the cross
Eph 2:19 saints, and of the household of G
Eph 2:22 of G through the Spirit
Eph 3:2 dispensation of the grace of G
Eph 3:7 to the gift of the grace of G
Eph 3:9 of the world hath been hid in G
Eph 3:10 church the manifold wisdom of G
Eph 3:19 filled with all the fulness of G
Eph 4:6 One G and Father of all, who is
Eph 4:13 of the knowledge of the Son of G
Eph 4:18 alienated from the life of G
Eph 4:24 which after G is created in
Eph 4:30 grieve not the holy Spirit of G
Eph 4:32 even as G for Christ's sake hath
Eph 5:1 Be ye therefore followers of G
Eph 5:2 and a sacrifice to G for a
Eph 5:5 in the kingdom of Christ and of G
Eph 5:6 wrath of G upon the children of
Eph 5:20 always for all things unto G
Eph 5:21 one to another in the fear of G
Eph 6:6 the will of G from the heart
Eph 6:11 Put on the whole armour of G
Eph 6:13 unto you the whole armour of G
Eph 6:17 Spirit, which is the word of G
Eph 6:23 from G the Father and the Lord
Phil 1:2 from G our Father, and from the
Phil 1:3 I thank my G upon every
Phil 1:8 For G is my record, how greatly I
Phil 1:11 unto the glory and praise of G
Phil 1:28 to you of salvation, and that of G
Phil 2:6 Who, being in the form of G
Phil 2:6 it not robbery to be equal with G
Phil 2:9 Wherefore G also hath highly
Phil 2:11 to the glory of G the Father
Phil 2:13 For it is G which worketh in you
Phil 2:15 and harmless, the sons of G
Phil 2:27 but G had mercy on him
Phil 3:3 which worship G in the spirit
Phil 3:9 which is of G by faith
Phil 3:14 high calling of G in Christ Jesus
Phil 3:15 G shall reveal even this unto you
Phil 3:19 whose G is their belly, and whose
Phil 4:6 requests be made known unto G
Phil 4:7 And the peace of G, which passeth
Phil 4:9 the G of peace shall be with you
Phil 4:18 acceptable, wellpleasing to G
Phil 4:19 But my G shall supply all your
Phil 4:20 Now unto G and our Father be glory
Col 1:1 of Jesus Christ by the will of G
Col 1:2 from G our Father and the Lord
Col 1:3 We give thanks to G and the Father
Col 1:6 and knew the grace of G in truth
Col 1:10 increasing in the knowledge of G
Col 1:15 is the image of the invisible G
Col 1:25 to the dispensation of G which is
Col 1:25 for you, to fulfil the word of G
Col 1:27 To whom G would make known what
Col 2:2 of the mystery of G, and of the
Col 2:12 the faith of the operation of G
Col 2:19 increaseth with the increase of G
Col 3:1 sitteth on the right hand of G
Col 3:3 your life is hid with Christ in G
Col 3:6 of G cometh on the children of
Col 3:12 on therefore, as the elect of G
Col 3:15 let the peace of G rule in your
Col 3:17 Lord Jesus, giving thanks to G
Col 3:22 in singleness of heart, fearing G
Col 4:3 that G would open unto us a door
Col 4:11 workers unto the kingdom of G
Col 4:12 and complete in all the will of G
1Th 1:1 which is in G the Father and in
1Th 1:1 from G our Father, and the Lord
1Th 1:2 We give thanks to G always for
1Th 1:3 Jesus Christ, in the sight of G
1Th 1:4 beloved, your election of G
1Th 1:9 how ye turned to G from idols to
1Th 1:9 to serve the living and true G
1Th 2:2 we were bold in our G to speak
1Th 2:2 gospel of G with much contention
1Th 2:4 But as we were allowed of G to be
1Th 2:4 not as pleasing men, but G
1Th 2:5 cloke of covetousness; G is witness
1Th 2:8 you, not the gospel of G only
1Th 2:9 preached unto you the gospel of G
1Th 2:10 G also, how holily and justly and
1Th 2:12 That ye would walk worthy of G
1Th 2:13 also thank we G without ceasing
1Th 2:13 word of G which ye heard of us
1Th 2:13 as it is in truth, the word of G
1Th 2:14 followers of the churches of G
1Th 2:15 and they please not G, and are
1Th 3:2 our brother, and minister of G
1Th 3:9 can we render to G again for you
1Th 3:9 joy for your sakes before our G
1Th 3:11 Now G himself and our Father, and
1Th 3:13 unblameable in holiness before G
1Th 4:1 ye ought to walk and to please G
1Th 4:3 For this is the will of G
1Th 4:5 as the Gentiles which know not G
1Th 4:7 For G hath not called us unto
1Th 4:8 despiseth not man, but G
1Th 4:9 taught of G to love one another
1Th 4:14 in Jesus will G bring with him
1Th 4:16 archangel, and with the trump of G
1Th 5:9 For G hath not appointed us to
1Th 5:18 for this is the will of G in
1Th 5:23 the very G of peace sanctify you
1Th 5:23 I pray G your whole spirit and
2Th 1:1 the Thessalonians in G our Father
2Th 1:2 from G our Father and the Lord
2Th 1:3 bound to thank G always for you
2Th 1:4 churches of G for your patience
2Th 1:5 of the righteous judgment of G
2Th 1:5 worthy of the kingdom of G
2Th 1:6 G to recompense tribulation to
2Th 1:8 vengeance on them that know not G
2Th 1:11 that our G would count you worthy
2Th 1:12 according to the grace of our G
2Th 2:4 above all that is called G
2Th 2:4 as G sitteth in the temple of G
2Th 2:4 shewing himself that he is G
2Th 2:11 for this cause G shall send them
2Th 2:13 to give thanks alway to G for you
2Th 2:13 because G hath from the beginning
2Th 2:16 Lord Jesus Christ himself, and G
2Th 3:5 your hearts into the love of G
1Ti 1:1 the commandment of G our Saviour
1Ti 1:2 from G our Father and Jesus Christ
1Ti 1:11 glorious gospel of the blessed G
1Ti 1:17 invisible, the only wise G
1Ti 2:3 in the sight of G our Saviour
1Ti 2:5 For there is one G
1Ti 2:5 and one mediator between G
1Ti 3:5 he take care of the church of G
1Ti 3:15 behave thyself in the house of G
1Ti 3:15 is the church of the living G
1Ti 3:16 G was manifest in the flesh,
1Ti 4:3 which G hath created to be
1Ti 4:4 For every creature of G is good
1Ti 4:5 it is sanctified by the word of G
1Ti 4:10 because we trust in the living G
1Ti 5:4 is good and acceptable before G
1Ti 5:5 and desolate, trusteth in G
1Ti 5:21 I charge thee before G, and the
1Ti 6:1 of all honour, that the name of G
1Ti 6:11 But thou, O man of G, flee these
1Ti 6:13 thee charge in the sight of G
1Ti 6:17 riches, but in the living G
2Ti 1:1 of Jesus Christ by the will of G
2Ti 1:2 from G the Father and Christ Jesus
2Ti 1:3 I thank G, whom I serve from my
2Ti 1:6 that thou stir up the gift of G
2Ti 1:7 For G hath not given us the
2Ti 1:8 according to the power of G
2Ti 2:9 but the word of G is not bound
2Ti 2:15 to shew thyself approved unto G
2Ti 2:19 the foundation of G standeth sure
2Ti 2:25 if G peradventure will give them
2Ti 3:4 pleasures more than lovers of G
2Ti 3:16 is given by inspiration of G
2Ti 3:17 That the man of G may be perfect
2Ti 4:1 I charge thee therefore before G
2Ti 4:16 I pray G that it may not be laid
Titus 1:1 Paul, a servant of G, and an
Titus 1:2 In hope of eternal life, which G
Titus 1:3 the commandment of G our Saviour
Titus 1:4 from G the Father and the Lord
Titus 1:7 be blameless, as the steward of G
Titus 1:16 They profess that they know G
Titus 2:5 that the word of G be not
Titus 2:10 of G our Saviour in all things
Titus 2:11 For the grace of G that bringeth
Titus 2:13 glorious appearing of the great G
Titus 3:4 love of G our Saviour toward man
Titus 3:8 they which have believed in G
Philem 3 from G our Father and the Lord
Philem 4 I thank my G, making mention of
Heb 1:1 G, who at sundry times and in
Heb 1:6 all the angels of G worship him

| | |
|---|---|
| Heb 1:8 | the Son he saith, Thy throne, O G |
| Heb 1:9 | therefore G, even thy G |
| Heb 2:4 | G also bearing them witness, both |
| Heb 2:9 | that he by the grace of G should |
| Heb 2:13 | children which G hath given me |
| Heb 2:17 | priest in things pertaining to G |
| Heb 3:4 | but he that built all things is G |
| Heb 3:12 | in departing from the living G |
| Heb 4:4 | G did rest the seventh day from |
| Heb 4:9 | a rest to the people of G |
| Heb 4:10 | his own works, as G did from his |
| Heb 4:12 | For the word of G is quick |
| Heb 4:14 | the heavens, Jesus the Son of G |
| Heb 5:1 | for men in things pertaining to G |
| Heb 5:4 | but he that is called of G |
| Heb 5:10 | Called of G an high priest after |
| Heb 5:12 | principles of the oracles of G |
| Heb 6:1 | dead works, and of faith toward G |
| Heb 6:3 | And this will we do, if G permit |
| Heb 6:5 | And have tasted the good word of G |
| Heb 6:6 | to themselves the Son of G afresh |
| Heb 6:7 | receiveth blessing from G |
| Heb 6:10 | For G is not unrighteous to |
| Heb 6:13 | For when G made promise to |
| Heb 6:17 | Wherein G, willing more |
| Heb 6:18 | it was impossible for G to lie |
| Heb 7:1 | Salem, priest of the most high G |
| Heb 7:3 | but made like unto the Son of G |
| Heb 7:19 | by the which we draw nigh unto G |
| Heb 7:25 | uttermost that come unto G by him |
| Heb 8:5 | as Moses was admonished of G when |
| Heb 8:10 | and I will be to them a G, and they |
| Heb 9:6 | accomplishing the service of G |
| Heb 9:14 | offered himself without spot to G |
| Heb 9:14 | dead works to serve the living G |
| Heb 9:20 | which G hath enjoined unto you |
| Heb 9:24 | in the presence of G for us |
| Heb 10:7 | of me,) to do thy will, O G |
| Heb 10:9 | Lo, I come to do thy will, O G |
| Heb 10:12 | sat down on the right hand of G |
| Heb 10:21 | high priest over the house of G |
| Heb 10:29 | trodden under foot the Son of G |
| Heb 10:31 | into the hands of the living G |
| Heb 10:36 | after ye have done the will of G |
| Heb 11:3 | were framed by the word of G |
| Heb 11:4 | By faith Abel offered unto G a |
| Heb 11:4 | G testifying of his gifts |
| Heb 11:5 | because G had translated him |
| Heb 11:5 | this testimony, that he pleased G |
| Heb 11:6 | for he that cometh to G must |
| Heb 11:7 | being warned of G of things not |
| Heb 11:10 | whose builder and maker is G |
| Heb 11:16 | wherefore G is not ashamed to be |
| Heb 11:16 | not ashamed to be called their G |
| Heb 11:19 | Accounting that G was able to |
| Heb 11:25 | affliction with the people of G |
| Heb 11:40 | G having provided some better |
| Heb 12:2 | the right hand of the throne of G |
| Heb 12:7 | G dealeth with you as with sons |
| Heb 12:15 | any man fail of the grace of G |
| Heb 12:22 | and unto the city of the living G |
| Heb 12:23 | to G the Judge of all, and to the |
| Heb 12:28 | whereby we may serve G acceptably |
| Heb 12:29 | For our G is a consuming fire |
| Heb 13:4 | and adulterers G will judge |
| Heb 13:7 | spoken unto you the word of G |
| Heb 13:15 | of praise to G continually |
| Heb 13:16 | such sacrifices G is well pleased |
| Heb 13:20 | Now the G of peace, that brought |
| Jas 1:1 | James, a servant of G and of the |
| Jas 1:5 | you lack wisdom, let him ask of G |
| Jas 1:13 | he is tempted, I am tempted of G |
| Jas 1:13 | for G cannot be tempted with evil |
| Jas 1:20 | not the righteousness of G |
| Jas 1:27 | religion and undefiled before G |
| Jas 2:5 | Hath not G chosen the poor of |
| Jas 2:19 | believest that there is one G |
| Jas 2:23 | which saith, Abraham believed G |
| Jas 2:23 | and he was called the Friend of G |
| Jas 3:9 | Therewith bless we G, even the |
| Jas 3:9 | made after the similitude of G |
| Jas 4:4 | of the world is enmity with G |
| Jas 4:4 | of the world is the enemy of G |
| Jas 4:6 | G resisteth the proud, but giveth |
| Jas 4:7 | Submit yourselves therefore to G |
| Jas 4:8 | Draw nigh to G, and he will draw |
| 1Pet 1:2 | the foreknowledge of G the Father |
| 1Pet 1:3 | Blessed be the G and Father of our |
| 1Pet 1:5 | of G through faith unto salvation |
| 1Pet 1:21 | Who by him do believe in G |
| 1Pet 1:21 | your faith and hope might be in G |
| 1Pet 1:23 | incorruptible, by the word of G |
| 1Pet 2:4 | indeed of men, but chosen of G |
| 1Pet 2:5 | acceptable to G by Jesus Christ |
| 1Pet 2:10 | but are now the people of G |
| 1Pet 2:12 | behold, glorify G in the day of |
| 1Pet 2:15 | For so is the will of G, that |
| 1Pet 2:16 | but as the servants of G |
| 1Pet 2:17 | Fear G. Honour the king. |
| 1Pet 2:19 | conscience toward G endure grief |
| 1Pet 2:20 | this is acceptable with G |
| 1Pet 3:4 | in the sight of G of great price |
| 1Pet 3:5 | holy women also, who trusted in G |
| 1Pet 3:15 | the Lord G in your hearts |
| 1Pet 3:17 | is better, if the will of G be so |
| 1Pet 3:18 | that he might bring us to G |
| 1Pet 3:20 | of G waited in the days of Noah |
| 1Pet 3:21 | of a good conscience toward G |
| 1Pet 3:22 | and is on the right hand of G |
| 1Pet 4:2 | of men, but to the will of G |
| 1Pet 4:6 | live according to G in the spirit |
| 1Pet 4:10 | of the manifold grace of G |
| 1Pet 4:11 | let him speak as the oracles of G |
| 1Pet 4:11 | as of the ability which G giveth |
| 1Pet 4:11 | that G in all things may be |
| 1Pet 4:14 | of glory and of G resteth upon you |
| 1Pet 4:16 | let him glorify G on this behalf |
| 1Pet 4:17 | must begin at the house of G |
| 1Pet 4:17 | that obey not the gospel of G |
| 1Pet 4:19 | of G commit the keeping of their |
| 1Pet 5:2 | Feed the flock of G which is |
| 1Pet 5:5 | for G resisteth the proud, and |
| 1Pet 5:6 | under the mighty hand of G |
| 1Pet 5:10 | But the G of all grace, who hath |
| 1Pet 5:12 | true grace of G wherein ye stand |
| 2Pet 1:1 | us through the righteousness of G |
| 2Pet 1:2 | you through the knowledge of G |
| 2Pet 1:17 | received from G the Father honour |
| 2Pet 1:21 | but holy men of G spake as they |
| 2Pet 2:4 | For if G spared not the angels |
| 2Pet 3:5 | that by the word of G the heavens |
| 2Pet 3:12 | unto the coming of the day of G |
| 1Jn 1:5 | that G is light, and in him is no |
| 1Jn 2:5 | verily is the love of G perfected |
| 1Jn 2:14 | the word of G abideth in you, and |
| 1Jn 2:17 | the will of G abideth for ever |
| 1Jn 3:1 | we should be called the sons of G |
| 1Jn 3:2 | Beloved, now are we the sons of G |
| 1Jn 3:8 | the Son of G was manifested |
| 1Jn 3:9 | is born of G doth not commit sin |
| 1Jn 3:9 | sin, because he is born of G |
| 1Jn 3:10 | the children of G are manifest |
| 1Jn 3:10 | not righteousness is not of G |
| 1Jn 3:16 | Hereby perceive we the love of G |
| 1Jn 3:17 | how dwelleth the love of G in him |
| 1Jn 3:20 | G is greater than our heart, and |
| 1Jn 3:21 | then have we confidence toward G |
| 1Jn 4:1 | the spirits whether they are of G |
| 1Jn 4:2 | Hereby know ye the Spirit of G |
| 1Jn 4:2 | is come in the flesh is of G |
| 1Jn 4:3 | is come in the flesh is not of G |
| 1Jn 4:4 | Ye are of G, little children, and |
| 1Jn 4:6 | We are of G |
| 1Jn 4:6 | he that knoweth G heareth us |
| 1Jn 4:6 | that is not of G heareth not us |
| 1Jn 4:7 | for love is of G |
| 1Jn 4:7 | is born of G, and knoweth G |
| 1Jn 4:8 | He that loveth not knoweth not G |
| 1Jn 4:8 | for G is love |
| 1Jn 4:9 | the love of G toward us, because |
| 1Jn 4:9 | because that G sent his only |
| 1Jn 4:10 | is love, not that we loved G |
| 1Jn 4:11 | if G so loved us, we ought also |
| 1Jn 4:12 | No man hath seen G at any time |
| 1Jn 4:12 | G dwelleth in us, and his love is |
| 1Jn 4:15 | that Jesus is the Son of G |
| 1Jn 4:15 | G dwelleth in him, and he in G |
| 1Jn 4:16 | the love that G hath to us |
| 1Jn 4:16 | G is love |
| 1Jn 4:16 | love dwelleth in G, and G in him |
| 1Jn 4:20 | If a man say, I love G, and hateth |
| 1Jn 4:20 | how can he love G whom he hath |
| 1Jn 4:21 | That he who loveth G love his |
| 1Jn 5:1 | Jesus is the Christ is born of G |
| 1Jn 5:2 | children of G, when we love G |
| 1Jn 5:3 | For this is the love of G |
| 1Jn 5:4 | is born of G overcometh the world |
| 1Jn 5:5 | that Jesus is the Son of G |
| 1Jn 5:9 | men, the witness of G is greater |
| 1Jn 5:9 | for this is the witness of G |
| 1Jn 5:10 | of G hath the witness in himself |
| 1Jn 5:10 | not G hath made him a liar |
| 1Jn 5:10 | the record that G gave of his Son |
| 1Jn 5:11 | that G hath given to us eternal |
| 1Jn 5:12 | not the Son of G hath not life |
| 1Jn 5:13 | on the name of the Son of G |
| 1Jn 5:13 | on the name of the Son of G |
| 1Jn 5:18 | is born of G sinneth not |
| 1Jn 5:18 | is begotten of G keepeth himself |
| 1Jn 5:19 | And we know that we are of G |
| 1Jn 5:20 | we know that the Son of G is come |
| 1Jn 5:20 | This is the true G, and eternal |
| 2Jn 3 | from G the Father, and from the |
| 2Jn 9 | doctrine of Christ, hath not G |
| 2Jn 10 | house, neither bid him G speed |
| 2Jn 11 | For he that biddeth him G speed |
| 3Jn 11 | He that doeth good is of G |
| 3Jn 11 | that doeth evil hath not seen G |
| Jude 1 | are sanctified by G the Father |
| Jude 4 | of our G into lasciviousness |
| Jude 4 | and denying the only Lord G |
| Jude 21 | Keep yourselves in the love of G |
| Jude 25 | To the only wise G our Saviour |
| Rev 1:1 | which G gave unto him, to shew |
| Rev 1:2 | Who bare record of the word of G |
| Rev 1:6 | made us kings and priests unto G |
| Rev 1:9 | called Patmos, for the word of G |
| Rev 2:7 | in the midst of the paradise of G |
| Rev 2:18 | These things saith the Son of G |
| Rev 3:1 | that hath the seven Spirits of G |
| Rev 3:2 | found thy works perfect before G |
| Rev 3:12 | a pillar in the temple of my G |
| Rev 3:12 | write upon him the name of my G |
| Rev 3:12 | and the name of the city of my G |
| Rev 3:12 | down out of heaven from my G |
| Rev 3:14 | beginning of the creation of G |
| Rev 4:5 | which are the seven Spirits of G |
| Rev 4:8 | Lord G Almighty, which was, and is |
| Rev 5:6 | G sent forth into all the earth |
| Rev 5:9 | hast redeemed us to G by thy |
| Rev 5:10 | And hast made us unto our G kings |
| Rev 6:9 | that were slain for the word of G |
| Rev 7:2 | having the seal of the living G |
| Rev 7:3 | of our G in their foreheads |
| Rev 7:10 | Salvation to our G which sitteth |
| Rev 7:11 | on their faces, and worshipped G |
| Rev 7:12 | and might, be unto our G for ever |
| Rev 7:15 | are they before the throne of G |
| Rev 7:17 | G shall wipe away all tears from |
| Rev 8:2 | seven angels which stood before G |
| Rev 8:4 | ascended up before G out of the |
| Rev 9:4 | the seal of G in their foreheads |
| Rev 9:13 | golden altar which is before G |
| Rev 10:7 | the mystery of G should be |
| Rev 11:1 | Rise, and measure the temple of G |
| Rev 11:4 | before the G of the earth |
| Rev 11:11 | of life from G entered into them |
| Rev 11:13 | and gave glory to the G of heaven |
| Rev 11:16 | which sat before G on their seats |
| Rev 11:16 | upon their faces, and worshipped G |
| Rev 11:17 | O Lord G Almighty, which art, and |
| Rev 11:19 | the temple of G was opened in |
| Rev 12:5 | and her child was caught up unto G |
| Rev 12:6 | she hath a place prepared of G |
| Rev 12:10 | strength, and the kingdom of our G |
| Rev 12:10 | accused them before our G day |
| Rev 12:17 | which keep the commandments of G |
| Rev 13:6 | his mouth in blasphemy against G |
| Rev 14:4 | men, being the firstfruits unto G |
| Rev 14:5 | fault before the throne of G |
| Rev 14:7 | Saying with a loud voice, Fear G |
| Rev 14:10 | of the wine of the wrath of G |
| Rev 14:12 | that keep the commandments of G |
| Rev 14:19 | great winepress of the wrath of G |
| Rev 15:1 | them is filled up the wrath of G |
| Rev 15:2 | of glass, having the harps of G |
| Rev 15:3 | song of Moses the servant of G |
| Rev 15:3 | are thy works, Lord G Almighty |
| Rev 15:7 | vials full of the wrath of G |
| Rev 15:8 | with smoke from the glory of G |
| Rev 16:1 | of the wrath of G upon the earth |
| Rev 16:7 | Even so, Lord G Almighty, true and |
| Rev 16:9 | heat, and blasphemed the name of G |
| Rev 16:11 | blasphemed the G of heaven |
| Rev 16:14 | of that great day of G Almighty |
| Rev 16:19 | came in remembrance before G |
| Rev 16:21 | men blasphemed G because of the |
| Rev 17:17 | For G hath put in their hearts to |
| Rev 17:17 | the words of G shall be fulfilled |
| Rev 18:5 | G hath remembered her iniquities |

Rev 18:8 is the Lord *G* who judgeth her
Rev 18:20 for *G* hath avenged you on her
Rev 19:1 and power, unto the Lord our *G*
Rev 19:4 worshipped *G* that sat on the
Rev 19:5 the throne, saying, Praise our *G*
Rev 19:6 for the Lord *G* omnipotent
Rev 19:9 These are the true sayings of *G*
Rev 19:10 worship *G*
Rev 19:13 his name is called The Word of *G*
Rev 19:15 fierceness and wrath of Almighty *G*
Rev 19:17 unto the supper of the great *G*
Rev 20:4 of Jesus, and for the word of *G*
Rev 20:6 but they shall be priests of *G*
Rev 20:9 came down from *G* out of heaven
Rev 20:12 small and great, stand before *G*
Rev 21:2 coming down from *G* out of heaven
Rev 21:3 the tabernacle of *G* is with men
Rev 21:3 *G* himself shall be with them
Rev 21:3 and be their *G*
Rev 21:4 *G* shall wipe away all tears from
Rev 21:7 and I will be his *G*, and he shall
Rev 21:10 descending out of heaven from *G*
Rev 21:11 Having the glory of *G*
Rev 21:22 for the Lord *G* Almighty and the
Rev 21:23 for the glory of *G* did lighten it
Rev 22:1 proceeding out of the throne of *G*
Rev 22:3 but the throne of *G* and of the
Rev 22:5 for the Lord *G* giveth them light
Rev 22:6 the Lord *G* of the holy prophets
Rev 22:9 worship *G*
Rev 22:18 *G* shall add unto him the plagues
Rev 22:19 *G* shall take away his part out of

*2. Any deity other than God 1.*

Ex 7:1 I have made thee a *g* to Pharaoh
Ex 22:20 He that sacrificeth unto any *g*
Ex 34:14 For thou shalt worship no other *g*
Deut 32:12 there was no strange *g* with him
Deut 32:39 am he, and there is no *g* with me
Judg 6:31 if he be a *g*, let him plead for
Judg 8:33 and made Baal-berith their *g*
Judg 9:27 and went into the house of their *g*
Judg 9:46 hold of the house of the *g* Berith
Judg 11:24 thy *g* giveth thee to possess
Judg 16:23 sacrifice unto Dagon their *g*
Judg 16:23 Our *g* hath delivered Samson our
Judg 16:24 saw him, they praised their *g*
Judg 16:24 Our *g* hath delivered into our
1Sa 5:7 sore upon us, and upon Dagon our *g*
1Kin 11:33 Chemosh the *g* of the Moabites, and
1Kin 11:33 Milcom the *g* of the children of
1Kin 18:27 for he is a *g*
2Kin 1:2 the *g* of Ekron whether I shall
2Kin 1:3 of Baal-zebub the *g* of Ekron
2Kin 1:6 of Baal-zebub the *g* of Ekron
2Kin 1:16 of Baal-zebub the *g* of Ekron
2Kin 19:37 in the house of Nisroch his *g*
2Chr 32:15 for no *g* of any nation or kingdom
2Chr 32:21 was come into the house of his *g*
Ps 16:4 that hasten after another *g*
Ps 44:20 out our hands to a strange *g*
Ps 81:9 shall no strange *g* be in thee
Ps 81:9 shalt thou worship any strange *g*
Is 43:12 there was no strange *g* among you
Is 44:10 Who hath formed a *g*, or molten a
Is 44:15 yea, he maketh a *g*, and
Is 44:17 the residue thereof he maketh a *g*
Is 44:17 for thou art my *g*
Is 45:20 pray unto a *g* that cannot save
Is 46:6 and he maketh it a *g*
Dan 1:2 of Shinar to the house of his *g*
Dan 1:2 into the treasure house of his *g*
Dan 3:28 might not serve nor worship any *g*
Dan 4:8 according to the name of my *g*
Dan 11:36 and magnify himself above every *g*
Dan 11:37 desire of women, nor regard any *g*
Dan 11:38 a *g* whom his fathers knew not
Dan 11:39 strong holds with a strange *g*
Hos 13:4 and thou shalt know no *g* but me
Amos 2:8 condemned in the house of their *g*
Amos 5:26 your images, the star of your *g*
Amos 8:14 the sin of Samaria, and say, Thy *g*
Jonah 1:5 and cried every man unto his *g*
Mic 4:5 every one in the name of his *g*
Hab 1:11 this his power unto his *g*
Mal 2:11 the daughter of a strange *g*
Acts 7:43 and the star of your *g* Remphan
Acts 12:22 saying, It is the voice of a *g*
Acts 28:6 minds, and said that he was a *g*
2Cor 4:4 In whom the *g* of this world hath

## GODDESS

1Kin 11:5 Ashtoreth the *g* of the Zidonians
1Kin 11:33 Ashtoreth the *g* of the Zidonians
Acts 19:27 great *g* Diana should be despised
Acts 19:35 a worshipper of the great *g* Diana
Acts 19:37 nor yet blasphemers of your *g*

## GODHEAD *That which is divine.*

Acts 17:29 that the *G* is like unto gold
Rom 1:20 made, even his eternal power and *G*
Col 2:9 all the fulness of the *G* bodily

## GODLINESS

1Ti 2:2 quiet and peaceable life in all *g*
1Ti 2:10 professing *g*) with good works
1Ti 3:16 great is the mystery of *g*
1Ti 4:7 and exercise thyself rather unto *g*
1Ti 4:8 but *g* is profitable unto all
1Ti 6:3 doctrine which is according to *g*
1Ti 6:5 truth, supposing that gain is *g*
1Ti 6:6 But *g* with contentment is great
1Ti 6:11 and follow after righteousness, *g*
2Ti 3:5 Having a form of *g*, but denying
Titus 1:1 of the truth which is after *g*
2Pet 1:3 that pertain unto life and *g*
2Pet 1:6 and to patience *g*
2Pet 1:7 And to *g* brotherly kindness
2Pet 3:11 be in all holy conversation and *g*

## GODLY

Ps 4:3 apart him that is *g* for himself
Ps 12:1 for the *g* man ceaseth
Ps 32:6 this shall every one that is *g*
Mal 2:15 That he might seek a *g* seed
2Cor 1:12 *g* sincerity, not with fleshly
2Cor 7:9 were made sorry after a *g* manner
2Cor 7:10 For *g* sorrow worketh repentance
2Cor 7:11 that ye sorrowed after a *g* sort
2Cor 11:2 jealous over you with *g* jealousy
1Ti 1:4 rather than *g* edifying which is
2Ti 3:12 all that will live *g* in Christ
Titus 2:12 live soberly, righteously, and *g*
Heb 12:28 with reverence and *g* fear
2Pet 2:9 deliver the *g* out of temptations
3Jn 6 on their journey after a *g* sort

## GOD'S *Refers to God 1.*

Gen 28:22 for a pillar, shall be *G* house
Gen 30:2 and he said, Am I in *G* stead
Gen 32:2 saw them, he said, This is *G* host
Num 22:22 *G* anger was kindled because he
Deut 1:17 for the judgment is *G*
2Chr 20:15 the battle is not yours, but *G*
Neh 10:29 and into an oath, to walk in *G* law
Job 33:6 according to thy wish in *G* stead
Job 35:2 My righteousness is more than *G*
Job 36:2 I have yet to speak on *G* behalf
Mt 5:34 for it is *G* throne
Mt 22:21 and unto God the things that are *G*
Mk 12:17 and to God the things that are *G*
Lk 18:29 for the kingdom of *G* sake
Lk 20:25 and unto God the things which be *G*
Jn 8:47 He that is of God heareth *G* words
Acts 23:4 said, Revilest thou *G* high priest
Rom 8:33 thing to the charge of *G* elect
Rom 10:3 being ignorant of *G* righteousness
Rom 13:6 for they are *G* ministers,
1Cor 3:9 ye are *G* husbandry, ye are *G*
1Cor 3:23 and Christ is *G*
1Cor 6:20 and in your spirit, which are *G*
Titus 1:1 according to the faith of *G* elect
1Pet 5:3 as being lords over *G* heritage

## GODS *Refers to God 2.*

Gen 3:5 be opened, and ye shall be as *g*
Gen 31:30 wherefore hast thou stolen my *g*
Gen 31:32 whomsoever thou findest thy *g*
Gen 35:2 the strange *g* that are among you
Gen 35:4 *g* which were in their hand
Ex 12:12 against all the *g* of Egypt I will
Ex 15:11 unto thee, O LORD, among the *g*
Ex 18:11 the LORD is greater than all *g*
Ex 20:3 shalt have no other *g* before me
Ex 20:23 not make with me *g* of silver
Ex 20:23 shall ye make unto you *g* of gold
Ex 22:28 Thou shalt not revile the *g*
Ex 23:13 no mention of the name of other *g*
Ex 23:24 shalt not bow down to their *g*
Ex 23:32 with them, nor with their *g*
Ex 23:33 for if thou serve their *g*
Ex 32:1 and said unto him, Up, make us *g*
Ex 32:4 and they said, These be thy *g*
Ex 32:8 and said, These be thy *g*, O
Ex 32:23 For they said unto me, Make us *g*
Ex 32:31 sin, and have made them *g* of gold
Ex 34:15 they go a whoring after their *g*
Ex 34:15 and do sacrifice unto their *g*
Ex 34:16 go a whoring after their *g*
Ex 34:16 sons go a whoring after their *g*
Ex 34:17 Thou shalt make thee no molten *g*
Lev 19:4 nor make to yourselves molten *g*
Num 25:2 unto the sacrifices of their *g*
Num 25:2 did eat, and bowed down to their *g*
Num 33:4 upon their *g* also the LORD
Deut 4:28 And there ye shall serve *g*
Deut 5:7 shalt have none other *g* before me
Deut 6:14 Ye shall not go after other *g*
Deut 6:14 of the *g* of the people which are
Deut 7:4 me, that they may serve other *g*
Deut 7:16 neither shalt thou serve their *g*
Deut 7:25 their *g* shall ye burn with fire
Deut 8:19 thy God, and walk after other *g*
Deut 10:17 For the LORD your God is God of *g*
Deut 11:16 ye turn aside, and serve other *g*
Deut 11:28 you this day, to go after other *g*
Deut 12:2 ye shall possess served their *g*
Deut 12:3 down the graven images of their *g*
Deut 12:30 thou enquire not after their *g*
Deut 12:30 did these nations serve their *g*
Deut 12:31 have they done unto their *g*
Deut 12:31 have burnt in the fire to their *g*
Deut 13:2 saying, Let us go after other *g*
Deut 13:6 Let us go and serve other *g*
Deut 13:7 of the *g* of the people which are
Deut 13:13 Let us go and serve other *g*
Deut 17:3 And hath gone and served other *g*
Deut 18:20 speak in the name of other *g*
Deut 20:18 which they have done unto their *g*
Deut 28:14 to go after other *g* to serve them
Deut 28:36 and there shalt thou serve other *g*
Deut 28:64 and there thou shalt serve other *g*
Deut 29:18 serve the *g* of these nations
Deut 29:26 For they went and served other *g*
Deut 29:26 *g* whom they knew not, and whom he
Deut 30:17 be drawn away, and worship other *g*
Deut 31:16 go a whoring after the *g* of the
Deut 31:18 that they are turned unto other *g*
Deut 31:20 then will they turn unto other *g*
Deut 32:16 him to jealousy with strange *g*
Deut 32:17 to *g* whom they knew not
Deut 32:17 to new *g* that came newly up, whom
Deut 32:37 he shall say, Where are their *g*
Josh 22:22 God of *g*, the LORD God of *g*
Josh 23:7 mention of the names of their *g*
Josh 23:16 and have gone and served other *g*
Josh 24:2 and they served other *g*
Josh 24:14 put away the *g* which your fathers
Josh 24:15 whether the *g* which your fathers
Josh 24:15 or the *g* of the Amorites, in
Josh 24:16 the LORD, to serve other *g*
Josh 24:20 the LORD, and serve strange *g*
Josh 24:23 the strange *g* which are among you
Judg 2:3 their *g* shall be a snare unto you
Judg 2:12 of Egypt, and followed other *g*
Judg 2:12 of the *g* of the people that were
Judg 2:17 they went a whoring after other *g*
Judg 2:19 following other *g* to serve them
Judg 3:6 to their sons, and served their *g*
Judg 5:8 They chose new *g*
Judg 6:10 fear not the *g* of the Amorites,
Judg 10:6 the *g* of Syria
Judg 10:6 the *g* of Zidon
Judg 10:6 the *g* of Moab
Judg 10:6 the *g* of the children of Ammon
Judg 10:6 the *g* of the Philistines, and
Judg 10:13 forsaken me, and served other *g*
Judg 10:14 cry unto the *g* which ye have
Judg 10:16 the strange *g* from among them
Judg 17:5 the man Micah had an house of *g*
Judg 18:24 have taken away my *g* which I made
Ruth 1:15 unto her people, and unto her *g*
1Sa 4:8 out of the hand of these mighty *G*
1Sa 4:8 these are the *G* that smote the
1Sa 6:5 from off you, and from off your *g*
1Sa 7:3 then put away the strange *g*
1Sa 8:8 forsaken me, and served other *g*
1Sa 17:43 Philistine cursed David by his *g*
1Sa 26:19 LORD, saying, Go, serve other *g*
1Sa 28:13 I saw *g* ascending out of the
2Sa 7:23 from the nations and their *g*
1Kin 9:6 you, but go and serve other *g*
1Kin 9:9 and have taken hold upon other *g*
1Kin 11:2 away your heart after their *g*

1Kin 11:4 away his heart after other *g*
1Kin 11:8 and sacrificed unto their *g*
1Kin 11:10 he should not go after other *g*
1Kin 12:28 behold thy *g*, O Israel, which
1Kin 14:9 hast gone and made thee other *g*
1Kin 18:24 And call ye on the name of your *g*
1Kin 18:25 and call on the name of your *g*
1Kin 19:2 saying, So let the *g* do to me
1Kin 20:10 The *g* do so unto me, and more also
1Kin 20:23 Their *g* are *g* of the hills
1Kin 20:23 Their *g* are *g* of the hills
2Kin 5:17 nor sacrifice unto other *g*
2Kin 17:7 of Egypt, and had feared other *g*
2Kin 17:29 every nation made *g* of their own
2Kin 17:31 Anammelech, the *g* of Sepharvaim
2Kin 17:33 the LORD, and served their own *g*
2Kin 17:35 saying, Ye shall not fear other *g*
2Kin 17:37 and ye shall not fear other *g*
2Kin 17:38 neither shall ye fear other *g*
2Kin 18:33 Hath any of the *g* of the nations
2Kin 18:34 Where are the *g* of Hamath
2Kin 18:34 where are the *g* of Sepharvaim
2Kin 18:35 among all the *g* of the countries
2Kin 19:12 Have the *g* of the nations
2Kin 19:18 have cast their *g* into the fire
2Kin 19:18 for they were no *g*, but the work
2Kin 22:17 have burned incense unto other *g*
1Chr 5:25 went a whoring after the *g* of the
1Chr 10:10 armour in the house of their *g*
1Chr 14:12 when they had left their *g* there
1Chr 16:25 also is to be feared above all *g*
1Chr 16:26 For all the *g* of the people are
2Chr 2:5 for great is our God above all *g*
2Chr 7:19 you, and shall go and serve other *g*
2Chr 7:22 of Egypt, and laid hold on other *g*
2Chr 13:8 which Jeroboam made you for *g*
2Chr 13:9 be a priest of them that are no *g*
2Chr 14:3 away the altars of the strange *g*
2Chr 25:14 that he brought the *g* of the
2Chr 25:14 Seir, and set them up to be his *g*
2Chr 25:15 sought after the *g* of the people
2Chr 25:20 they sought after the *g* of Edom
2Chr 28:23 sacrificed unto the *g* of Damascus
2Chr 28:23 Because the *g* of the kings of
2Chr 28:25 to burn incense unto other *g*
2Chr 32:13 were the *g* of the nations of
2Chr 32:14 the *g* of those nations that my
2Chr 32:17 As the *g* of the nations of other
2Chr 32:19 as against the *g* of the people of
2Chr 33:15 And he took away the strange *g*
2Chr 34:25 have burned incense unto other *g*
Ezr 1:7 put them in the house of his *g*
Ps 82:1 he judgeth among the *g*
Ps 82:6 I have said, Ye are *g*
Ps 86:8 Among the *g* there is none like
Ps 95:3 God, and a great King above all *g*
Ps 96:4 he is to be feared above all *g*
Ps 96:5 For all the *g* of the nations are
Ps 97:7 worship him, all ye *g*
Ps 97:9 thou art exalted far above all *g*
Ps 135:5 and that our Lord is above all *g*
Ps 136:2 O give thanks unto the God of *g*
Ps 138:1 before the *g* will I sing praise
Is 21:9 all the graven images of her *g* he
Is 36:18 Hath any of the *g* of the nations
Is 36:19 Where are the *g* of Hamath
Is 36:19 where are the *g* of Sepharvaim
Is 36:20 among all the *g* of these lands
Is 37:12 Have the *g* of the nations
Is 37:19 have cast their *g* into the fire
Is 37:19 for they were no *g*, but the work
Is 41:23 that we may know that ye are *g*
Is 42:17 the molten images, Ye are our *g*
Jer 1:16 have burned incense unto other *g*
Jer 2:11 their *g*, which are yet no *g*
Jer 2:28 But where are thy *g* that thou
Jer 2:28 number of thy cities are thy *g*
Jer 5:7 and sworn by them that are no *g*
Jer 5:19 and served strange *g* in your land
Jer 7:6 walk after other *g* to your hurt
Jer 7:9 after other *g* whom ye know not
Jer 7:18 out drink offerings unto other *g*
Jer 10:11 The *g* that have not made the
Jer 11:10 went after other *g* to serve them
Jer 11:12 cry unto the *g* unto whom they
Jer 11:13 number of thy cities were thy *g*
Jer 13:10 heart, and walk after other *g*
Jer 16:11 and have walked after other *g*
Jer 16:13 there shall ye serve other *g* day
Jer 16:20 Shall a man make *g* unto himself
Jer 16:20 and they are no *g*
Jer 19:4 burned incense in it unto other *g*
Jer 19:13 out drink offerings unto other *g*
Jer 22:9 their God, and worshipped other *g*
Jer 25:6 not after other *g* to serve them
Jer 32:29 out drink offerings unto other *g*
Jer 35:15 not after other *g* to serve them
Jer 43:12 in the houses of the *g* of Egypt
Jer 43:13 the houses of the *g* of the
Jer 44:3 burn incense, and to serve other *g*
Jer 44:5 to burn no incense unto other *g*
Jer 44:8 unto other *g* in the land of Egypt
Jer 44:15 had burned incense unto other *g*
Jer 46:25 Pharaoh, and Egypt, with their *g*
Jer 48:35 him that burneth incense to his *g*
Dan 2:11 it before the king, except the *g*
Dan 2:47 is, that your God is a God of *g*
Dan 3:12 they serve not thy *g*, nor worship
Dan 3:14 Abed-nego, do not ye serve my *g*
Dan 3:18 that we will not serve thy *g*
Dan 4:8 whom is the spirit of the holy *g*
Dan 4:9 spirit of the holy *g* is in thee
Dan 4:18 spirit of the holy *g* is in thee
Dan 5:4 wine, and praised the *g* of gold
Dan 5:11 whom is the spirit of the holy *g*
Dan 5:11 wisdom, like the wisdom of the *g*
Dan 5:14 the spirit of the *g* is in thee
Dan 5:23 thou hast praised the *g* of silver
Dan 11:8 carry captives into Egypt their *g*
Dan 11:36 things against the God of *g*
Hos 3:1 of Israel, who look to other *g*
Hos 14:3 work of our hands, Ye are our *g*
Nah 1:14 out of the house of thy *g* will I
Zeph 2:11 famish all the *g* of the earth
Jn 10:34 in your law, I said, Ye are *g*
Jn 10:35 If he called them *g*, unto whom
Acts 7:40 Make us *g* to go before us
Acts 14:11 The *g* are come down to us in the
Acts 17:18 to be a setter forth of strange *g*
Acts 19:26 people, saying that they be no *g*
1Cor 8:5 though there be that are called *g*
1Cor 8:5 or in earth, (as there be *g* many
Gal 4:8 them which by nature are no *g*

**GOG** See HAMON-GOG, MAGOG.

*1. Son of Shemarah.*

1Chr 5:4 G his son, Shimei his son,

*2. A prince of Scythia.*

Eze 38:2 of man, set thy face against G
Eze 38:3 Behold, I am against thee, O G
Eze 38:14 of man, prophesy and say unto G
Eze 38:16 shall be sanctified in thee, O G
Eze 38:18 to pass at the same time when G
Eze 39:1 son of man, prophesy against G
Eze 39:1 Behold, I am against thee, O G
Eze 39:11 that I will give unto G a place
Eze 39:11 and there shall they bury G
Rev 20:8 the four quarters of the earth, G

**GOLAN** *(go'-lan) A Levitical city in Manasseh.*

Deut 4:43 G in Bashan, of the Manassites
Josh 20:8 G in Bashan out of the tribe of
Josh 21:27 gave G in Bashan with her suburbs
1Chr 6:71 G in Bashan with her suburbs, and

**GOLD**

Gen 2:11 land of Havilah, where there is *g*
Gen 2:12 the *g* of that land is good
Gen 13:2 in cattle, in silver, and in *g*
Gen 24:22 hands of ten shekels weight of *g*
Gen 24:35 flocks, and herds, and silver, and *g*
Gen 24:53 jewels of silver, and jewels of *g*
Gen 41:42 put a *g* chain about his neck
Gen 44:8 of thy lord's house silver or *g*
Ex 3:22 jewels of silver, and jewels of *g*
Ex 11:2 jewels of silver, and jewels of *g*
Ex 12:35 jewels of silver, and jewels of *g*
Ex 20:23 shall ye make unto you gods of *g*
Ex 25:3 *g*, and silver, and brass,
Ex 25:11 thou shalt overlay it with pure *g*
Ex 25:11 upon it a crown of *g* round about
Ex 25:12 shalt cast four rings of *g* for it
Ex 25:13 wood, and overlay them with *g*
Ex 25:17 shalt make a mercy seat of pure *g*
Ex 25:18 shalt make two cherubims of *g*
Ex 25:24 thou shalt overlay it with pure *g*
Ex 25:24 thereto a crown of *g* round about
Ex 25:26 shalt make for it four rings of *g*
Ex 25:28 wood, and overlay them with *g*
Ex 25:29 of pure *g* shalt thou make them
Ex 25:31 make a candlestick of pure *g*
Ex 25:36 be one beaten work of pure *g*
Ex 25:38 thereof, shall be of pure *g*
Ex 25:39 talent of pure *g* shall he make it
Ex 26:6 thou shalt make fifty taches of *g*
Ex 26:29 shalt overlay the boards with *g*
Ex 26:29 make their rings of *g* for places
Ex 26:29 shalt overlay the bars with *g*
Ex 26:32 of shittim wood overlaid with *g*
Ex 26:32 their hooks shall be of *g*
Ex 26:37 wood, and overlay them with *g*
Ex 26:37 and their hooks shall be of *g*
Ex 28:5 And they shall take *g*, and blue, and
Ex 28:6 And they shall make the ephod of *g*
Ex 28:8 even of *g*, of blue, and purple, and
Ex 28:11 them to be set in ouches of *g*
Ex 28:13 And thou shalt make ouches of *g*
Ex 28:14 two chains of pure *g* at the ends
Ex 28:15 of *g*, of blue, and of purple, and
Ex 28:20 be set in *g* in their inclosings
Ex 28:22 ends of wreathen work of pure *g*
Ex 28:23 the breastplate two rings of *g*
Ex 28:24 *g* in the two rings which are on
Ex 28:26 And thou shalt make two rings of *g*
Ex 28:27 other rings of *g* thou shalt make
Ex 28:33 bells of *g* between them round
Ex 28:36 thou shalt make a plate of pure *g*
Ex 30:3 thou shalt overlay it with pure *g*
Ex 30:3 unto it a crown of *g* round about
Ex 30:5 wood, and overlay them with *g*
Ex 31:4 cunning works, to work in *g*
Ex 32:24 unto them, Whosoever hath any *g*
Ex 32:31 sin, and have made them gods of *g*
Ex 35:5 *g*, and silver, and brass,
Ex 35:22 and tablets, all jewels of *g*
Ex 35:22 an offering of *g* unto the LORD
Ex 35:32 curious works, to work in *g*
Ex 36:13 And he made fifty taches of *g*
Ex 36:34 And he overlaid the boards with *g*
Ex 36:34 made their rings of *g* to be
Ex 36:34 bars, and overlaid the bars with *g*
Ex 36:36 wood, and overlaid them with *g*
Ex 36:36 their hooks were of *g*
Ex 36:38 chapiters and their fillets with *g*
Ex 37:2 he overlaid it with pure *g* within
Ex 37:2 made a crown of *g* to it round
Ex 37:3 And he cast for it four rings of *g*
Ex 37:4 wood, and overlaid them with *g*
Ex 37:6 he made the mercy seat of pure *g*
Ex 37:7 And he made two cherubims of *g*
Ex 37:11 And he overlaid it with pure *g*
Ex 37:11 a crown of *g* round about
Ex 37:12 made a crown of *g* for the border
Ex 37:13 And he cast for it four rings of *g*
Ex 37:15 wood, and overlaid them with *g*
Ex 37:16 covers to cover withal, of pure *g*
Ex 37:17 he made the candlestick of pure *g*
Ex 37:22 it was one beaten work of pure *g*
Ex 37:23 and his snuffdishes, of pure *g*
Ex 37:24 Of a talent of pure *g* made he it
Ex 37:26 And he overlaid it with pure *g*
Ex 37:26 unto it a crown of *g* round about
Ex 37:27 he made two rings of *g* for it
Ex 37:28 wood, and overlaid them with *g*
Ex 38:24 All the *g* that was occupied for
Ex 38:24 even the *g* of the offering, was
Ex 39:2 And he made the ephod of *g*
Ex 39:3 did beat the *g* into thin plates
Ex 39:5 of *g*, blue, and purple, and scarlet
Ex 39:6 stones inclosed in ouches of *g*
Ex 39:8 of *g*, blue, and purple, and scarlet
Ex 39:13 ouches of *g* in their inclosings
Ex 39:15 ends, of wreathen work of pure *g*
Ex 39:16 And they made two ouches of *g*
Ex 39:16 ouches of *g*, and two *g* rings
Ex 39:17 put the two wreathen chains of *g*
Ex 39:19 And they made two rings of *g*
Ex 39:25 And they made bells of pure *g*
Ex 39:30 plate of the holy crown of pure *g*
Ex 40:5 thou shalt set the altar of *g* for
Num 7:14 One spoon of ten shekels of *g*
Num 7:20 One spoon of *g* of ten shekels,
Num 7:84 silver bowls, twelve spoons of *g*
Num 7:86 all the *g* of the spoons was an
Num 8:4 the candlestick was of beaten *g*
Num 22:18 me his house full of silver and *g*
Num 24:13 me his house full of silver and *g*
Num 31:22 Only the *g*, and the silver, the
Num 31:50 man hath gotten, of jewels of *g*
Num 31:51 the priest took the *g* of them
Num 31:52 all the *g* of the offering that

| | |
|---|---|
| Num 31:54 | Eleazar the priest took the *g* of |
| Deut 7:25 | the silver or *g* that is on them |
| Deut 8:13 | thy *g* is multiplied, and all that |
| Deut 17:17 | multiply to himself silver and *g* |
| Deut 29:17 | idols, wood and stone, silver and *g* |
| Josh 6:19 | But all the silver, and *g*, and |
| Josh 6:24 | only the silver, and the *g* |
| Josh 7:21 | a wedge of *g* of fifty shekels |
| Josh 7:24 | and the garment, and the wedge of *g* |
| Josh 22:8 | cattle, with silver, and with *g* |
| Judg 8:26 | and seven hundred shekels of *g* |
| 1Sa 6:8 | and put the jewels of *g*, which ye |
| 1Sa 6:11 | and the coffer with the mice of *g* |
| 1Sa 6:15 | it, wherein the jewels of *g* were |
| 2Sa 1:24 | ornaments of *g* upon your apparel |
| 2Sa 8:7 | David took the shields of *g* that |
| 2Sa 8:10 | of silver, and vessels of *g* |
| 2Sa 8:11 | *g* that he had dedicated of all |
| 2Sa 12:30 | of *g* with the precious stones |
| 2Sa 21:4 | will have no silver nor *g* of Saul |
| 1Kin 6:20 | and he overlaid it with pure *g* |
| 1Kin 6:21 | the house within with pure *g* |
| 1Kin 6:21 | the chains of *g* before the oracle |
| 1Kin 6:21 | and he overlaid it with *g* |
| 1Kin 6:22 | whole house he overlaid with *g* |
| 1Kin 6:22 | by the oracle he overlaid with *g* |
| 1Kin 6:28 | he overlaid the cherubims with *g* |
| 1Kin 6:30 | of the house he overlaid with *g* |
| 1Kin 6:32 | flowers, and overlaid them with *g* |
| 1Kin 6:32 | spread *g* upon the cherubims, and |
| 1Kin 6:35 | covered them with *g* fitted upon |
| 1Kin 7:48 | altar of *g*, and the table of *g* |
| 1Kin 7:49 | And the candlesticks of pure *g* |
| 1Kin 7:49 | and the lamps, and the tongs of *g* |
| 1Kin 7:50 | spoons, and the censers of pure *g* |
| 1Kin 7:50 | and the hinges of *g*, both for the |
| 1Kin 7:51 | even the silver, and the *g* |
| 1Kin 9:11 | trees and fir trees, and with *g* |
| 1Kin 9:14 | to the king sixscore talents of *g* |
| 1Kin 9:28 | Ophir, and fetched from thence *g* |
| 1Kin 10:2 | that bare spices, and very much *g* |
| 1Kin 10:10 | an hundred and twenty talents of *g* |
| 1Kin 10:11 | Hiram, that brought *g* from Ophir |
| 1Kin 10:14 | Now the weight of *g* that came to |
| 1Kin 10:14 | threescore and six talents of *g* |
| 1Kin 10:16 | two hundred targets of beaten *g* |
| 1Kin 10:16 | shekels of *g* went to one target |
| 1Kin 10:17 | three hundred shields of beaten *g* |
| 1Kin 10:17 | three pound of *g* went to one |
| 1Kin 10:18 | and overlaid it with the best *g* |
| 1Kin 10:21 | drinking vessels were of *g* |
| 1Kin 10:21 | forest of Lebanon were of pure *g* |
| 1Kin 10:22 | the navy of Tharshish, bringing *g* |
| 1Kin 10:25 | of silver, and vessels of *g* |
| 1Kin 12:28 | counsel, and made two calves of *g* |
| 1Kin 14:26 | of *g* which Solomon had made |
| 1Kin 15:15 | house of the LORD, silver, and *g* |
| 1Kin 15:18 | the *g* that were left in the |
| 1Kin 15:19 | thee a present of silver and *g* |
| 1Kin 20:3 | Thy silver and thy *g* is mine |
| 1Kin 20:5 | deliver me thy silver, and thy *g* |
| 1Kin 20:7 | and for my silver, and for my *g* |
| 1Kin 22:48 | of Tharshish to go to Ophir for *g* |
| 2Kin 5:5 | and six thousand pieces of *g* |
| 2Kin 7:8 | and carried thence silver, and *g* |
| 2Kin 12:13 | trumpets, any vessels of *g* |
| 2Kin 12:18 | all the *g* that was found in the |
| 2Kin 14:14 | And he took all the *g* and silver, |
| 2Kin 16:8 | *g* that was found in the house of |
| 2Kin 18:14 | of silver and thirty talents of *g* |
| 2Kin 18:16 | time did Hezekiah cut off the *g* |
| 2Kin 20:13 | things, the silver, and the *g* |
| 2Kin 23:33 | of silver, and a talent of *g* |
| 2Kin 23:35 | the silver and the *g* to Pharaoh |
| 2Kin 23:35 | the *g* of the people of the land, |
| 2Kin 24:13 | of *g* which Solomon king of Israel |
| 2Kin 25:15 | such things as were of *g*, in *g* |
| 1Chr 18:7 | David took the shields of *g* that |
| 1Chr 18:10 | him all manner of vessels of *g* |
| 1Chr 18:11 | the *g* that he brought from all |
| 1Chr 20:2 | found it to weigh a talent of *g* |
| 1Chr 21:25 | hundred shekels of *g* by weight |
| 1Chr 22:14 | an hundred thousand talents of *g* |
| 1Chr 22:16 | Of the *g*, the silver, and the |
| 1Chr 28:14 | of *g* by weight for things of *g* |
| 1Chr 28:15 | weight for the candlesticks of *g* |
| 1Chr 28:15 | and for their lamps of *g* |
| 1Chr 28:16 | by weight he gave *g* for the |
| 1Chr 28:17 | Also pure *g* for the fleshhooks, |
| 1Chr 28:17 | gave *g* by weight for every bason |
| 1Chr 28:18 | of incense refined *g* by weight |
| 1Chr 28:18 | *g* for the pattern of the chariot |
| 1Chr 29:2 | *g* for things to be made of *g* |
| 1Chr 29:3 | of mine own proper good, of *g* |
| 1Chr 29:4 | Even three thousand talents of *g* |
| 1Chr 29:4 | of the *g* of Ophir, and seven |
| 1Chr 29:5 | The *g* for things of *g*, and the |
| 1Chr 29:7 | of God of *g* five thousand talents |
| 2Chr 1:15 | *g* at Jerusalem as plenteous as |
| 2Chr 2:7 | a man cunning to work in *g* |
| 2Chr 2:14 | man of Tyre, skilful to work in *g* |
| 2Chr 3:4 | he overlaid it within with pure *g* |
| 2Chr 3:5 | which he overlaid with fine *g* |
| 2Chr 3:6 | and the *g* was *g* of Parvaim |
| 2Chr 3:7 | and the doors thereof, with *g* |
| 2Chr 3:8 | and he overlaid it with fine *g* |
| 2Chr 3:9 | the nails was fifty shekels of *g* |
| 2Chr 3:9 | the upper chambers with *g* |
| 2Chr 3:10 | work, and overlaid them with *g* |
| 2Chr 4:7 | of *g* according to their form |
| 2Chr 4:8 | And he made an hundred basons of *g* |
| 2Chr 4:20 | before the oracle, of pure *g* |
| 2Chr 4:21 | he of *g*, and that perfect *g* |
| 2Chr 4:22 | spoons, and the censers, of pure *g* |
| 2Chr 4:22 | house of the temple, were of *g* |
| 2Chr 5:1 | and the silver, and the *g*, and all |
| 2Chr 8:18 | hundred and fifty talents of *g* |
| 2Chr 9:1 | *g* in abundance, and precious |
| 2Chr 9:9 | an hundred and twenty talents of *g* |
| 2Chr 9:10 | which brought *g* from Ophir |
| 2Chr 9:13 | Now the weight of *g* that came to |
| 2Chr 9:13 | and threescore and six talents of *g* |
| 2Chr 9:14 | of the country brought *g* and |
| 2Chr 9:15 | two hundred targets of beaten *g* |
| 2Chr 9:15 | of beaten *g* went to one target |
| 2Chr 9:16 | shields made he of beaten *g* |
| 2Chr 9:16 | shekels of *g* went to one shield |
| 2Chr 9:17 | ivory, and overlaid it with pure *g* |
| 2Chr 9:18 | the throne, with a footstool of *g* |
| 2Chr 9:20 | vessels of king Solomon were of *g* |
| 2Chr 9:20 | forest of Lebanon were of pure *g* |
| 2Chr 9:21 | the ships of Tarshish bringing *g* |
| 2Chr 9:24 | of silver, and vessels of *g* |
| 2Chr 12:9 | of *g* which Solomon had made |
| 2Chr 13:11 | the candlestick of *g* with the |
| 2Chr 15:18 | had dedicated, silver, and *g* |
| 2Chr 16:2 | *g* out of the treasures of the |
| 2Chr 16:3 | I have sent thee silver and *g* |
| 2Chr 21:3 | great gifts of silver, and of *g* |
| 2Chr 24:14 | and spoons, and vessels of *g* |
| 2Chr 25:24 | And he took all the *g* and the |
| 2Chr 32:27 | treasuries for silver, and for *g* |
| 2Chr 36:3 | of silver and a talent of *g* |
| Ezr 1:4 | help him with silver, and with *g* |
| Ezr 1:6 | with vessels of silver, with *g* |
| Ezr 1:9 | thirty chargers of *g*, a thousand |
| Ezr 1:10 | Thirty basons of *g*, silver basons |
| Ezr 1:11 | All the vessels of *g* and of silver |
| Ezr 2:69 | and one thousand drams of *g* |
| Ezr 5:14 | And the vessels also of *g* and |
| Ezr 7:15 | And to carry the silver and *g* |
| Ezr 7:16 | *g* that thou canst find in all the |
| Ezr 7:18 | the rest of the silver and the *g* |
| Ezr 8:25 | unto them the silver, and the *g* |
| Ezr 8:26 | and of *g* an hundred talents |
| Ezr 8:27 | Also twenty basons of *g*, of a |
| Ezr 8:27 | of fine copper, precious as *g* |
| Ezr 8:28 | the *g* are a freewill offering |
| Ezr 8:30 | weight of the silver, and the *g* |
| Ezr 8:33 | day was the silver and the *g* |
| Neh 7:70 | treasure a thousand drams of *g* |
| Neh 7:71 | work twenty thousand drams of *g* |
| Neh 7:72 | was twenty thousand drams of *g* |
| Est 1:6 | the beds were of *g* and silver, |
| Est 1:7 | gave them drink in vessels of *g* |
| Est 8:15 | white, and with a great crown of *g* |
| Job 3:15 | Or with princes that had *g* |
| Job 22:24 | Then shalt thou lay up *g* as dust |
| Job 22:24 | the *g* of Ophir as the stones of |
| Job 23:10 | tried me, I shall come forth as *g* |
| Job 28:1 | a place for *g* where they fine it |
| Job 28:6 | and it hath dust of *g* |
| Job 28:15 | It cannot be gotten for *g* |
| Job 28:16 | be valued with the *g* of Ophir |
| Job 28:17 | The *g* and the crystal cannot equal |
| Job 28:17 | shall not be for jewels of fine *g* |
| Job 28:19 | shall it be valued with pure *g* |
| Job 31:24 | If I have made *g* my hope |
| Job 31:24 | or have said to the fine *g* |
| Job 36:19 | no, not *g*, nor all the forces of |
| Job 42:11 | and every one an earring of *g* |
| Ps 19:10 | to be desired are they than *g* |
| Ps 19:10 | yea, than much fine *g* |
| Ps 21:3 | a crown of pure *g* on his head |
| Ps 45:9 | did stand the queen in *g* of Ophir |
| Ps 45:13 | her clothing is of wrought *g* |
| Ps 68:13 | and her feathers with yellow *g* |
| Ps 72:15 | shall be given of the *g* of Sheba |
| Ps 105:37 | them forth also with silver and *g* |
| Ps 115:4 | Their idols are silver and *g* |
| Ps 119:72 | unto me than thousands of *g* |
| Ps 119:127 | I love thy commandments above *g* |
| Ps 119:127 | yea, above fine *g* |
| Ps 135:15 | of the heathen are silver and *g* |
| Prov 3:14 | and the gain thereof than fine *g* |
| Prov 8:10 | and knowledge rather than choice *g* |
| Prov 8:19 | My fruit is better than *g* |
| Prov 8:19 | yea, than fine *g* |
| Prov 11:22 | As a jewel of *g* in a swine's |
| Prov 16:16 | better is it to get wisdom than *g* |
| Prov 17:3 | for silver, and the furnace for *g* |
| Prov 20:15 | There is *g*, and a multitude of |
| Prov 22:1 | favour rather than silver and *g* |
| Prov 25:11 | apples of *g* in pictures of silver |
| Prov 25:12 | As an earring of *g*, and an |
| Prov 25:12 | of *g*, and an ornament of fine *g* |
| Prov 27:21 | for silver, and the furnace for *g* |
| Eccl 2:8 | I gathered me also silver and *g* |
| Song 1:10 | jewels, thy neck with chains of *g* |
| Song 1:11 | borders of *g* with studs of silver |
| Song 3:10 | silver, the bottom thereof of *g* |
| Song 5:11 | His head is as the most fine *g* |
| Song 5:14 | His hands are as *g* rings set with |
| Song 5:15 | set upon sockets of fine *g* |
| Is 2:7 | land also is full of silver and *g* |
| Is 2:20 | of silver, and his idols of *g* |
| Is 13:12 | a man more precious than fine *g* |
| Is 13:17 | and as for *g*, they shall not |
| Is 30:22 | of thy molten images of *g* |
| Is 31:7 | of silver, and his idols of *g* |
| Is 39:2 | things, the silver, and the *g* |
| Is 40:19 | spreadeth it over with *g*, and |
| Is 46:6 | They lavish *g* out of the bag, and |
| Is 60:6 | they shall bring *g* and incense |
| Is 60:9 | their *g* with them, unto the name |
| Is 60:17 | For brass I will bring *g*, and for |
| Jer 4:30 | deckest thee with ornaments of *g* |
| Jer 10:4 | deck it with silver and with *g* |
| Jer 10:9 | *g* from Uphaz, the work of the |
| Jer 52:19 | that which was of *g* in *g* |
| Lam 4:1 | How is the *g* become dim |
| Lam 4:1 | how is the most fine *g* changed |
| Lam 4:2 | of Zion, comparable to fine *g* |
| Eze 7:19 | and their *g* shall be removed |
| Eze 7:19 | their *g* shall not be able to |
| Eze 16:13 | Thus wast thou decked with *g* |
| Eze 16:17 | taken thy fair jewels of my *g* |
| Eze 27:22 | and with all precious stones, and *g* |
| Eze 28:4 | thee riches, and hast gotten *g* |
| Eze 28:13 | emerald, and the carbuncle, and *g* |
| Eze 38:13 | to carry away silver and *g* |
| Dan 2:32 | This image's head was of fine *g* |
| Dan 2:35 | the brass, the silver, and the *g* |
| Dan 2:38 | Thou art this head of *g* |
| Dan 2:45 | the clay, the silver, and the *g* |
| Dan 3:1 | the king made an image of *g* |
| Dan 5:4 | wine, and praised the gods of *g* |
| Dan 5:7 | have a chain of *g* about his neck |
| Dan 5:16 | have a chain of *g* about thy neck |
| Dan 5:23 | praised the gods of silver, and *g* |
| Dan 5:29 | put a chain of *g* about his neck |
| Dan 10:5 | were girded with fine *g* of Uphaz |
| Dan 11:8 | vessels of silver and of *g* |
| Dan 11:38 | knew not shall he honour with *g* |
| Dan 11:43 | power over the treasures of *g* |
| Hos 2:8 | and multiplied her silver and *g* |
| Hos 8:4 | their *g* have they made them idols |
| Joel 3:5 | ye have taken my silver and my *g* |
| Nah 2:9 | of silver, take the spoil of *g* |
| Hab 2:19 | Behold, it is laid over with *g* |
| Zeph 1:18 | *g* shall be able to deliver them |
| Hag 2:8 | the *g* is mine, saith the LORD of |
| Zec 4:2 | and behold a candlestick all of *g* |
| Zec 6:11 | Then take silver and *g*, and make |
| Zec 9:3 | fine *g* as the mire of the streets |
| Zec 13:9 | and will try them as *g* is tried |
| Zec 14:14 | shall be gathered together, *g* |
| Mal 3:3 | sons of Levi, and purge them as *g* |
| Mt 2:11 | *g*, and frankincense, and myrrh |
| Mt 10:9 | Provide neither *g*, nor silver, |

Mt 23:16 swear by the *g* of the temple
Mt 23:17 for whether is greater, the *g*
Mt 23:17 the temple that sanctifieth the *g*
Acts 3:6 said, Silver and *g* have I none
Acts 17:29 that the Godhead is like unto *g*
Acts 20:33 coveted no man's silver, or *g*
1Cor 3:12 man build upon this foundation *g*
1Ti 2:9 not with broided hair, or *g*
2Ti 2:20 there are not only vessels of *g*
Heb 9:4 overlaid round about with *g*
Jas 2:2 your assembly a man with a *g* ring
Jas 5:3 Your *g* and silver is cankered
1Pet 1:7 precious than of *g* that perisheth
1Pet 1:18 things, as silver and *g*, from your
1Pet 3:3 the hair, and of wearing of *g*
Rev 3:18 to buy of me *g* tried in the fire
Rev 4:4 had on their heads crowns of *g*
Rev 9:7 were as it were crowns like *g*
Rev 9:20 not worship devils, and idols of *g*
Rev 17:4 scarlet colour, and decked with *g*
Rev 18:12 The merchandise of *g*, and silver,
Rev 18:16 and scarlet, and decked with *g*
Rev 21:18 and the city was pure *g*, like unto
Rev 21:21 the street of the city was pure *g*

### GOLDEN

Gen 24:22 that the man took a *g* earring of
Ex 25:25 thou shalt make a *g* crown to the
Ex 28:34 A *g* bell and a pomegranate
Ex 28:34 a *g* bell and a pomegranate, upon
Ex 30:4 two *g* rings shalt thou make to it
Ex 32:2 them, Break off the *g* earrings
Ex 32:3 *g* earrings which were in their
Ex 39:20 And they made two other *g* rings
Ex 39:38 the *g* altar, and the anointing oil
Ex 40:26 he put the *g* altar in the tent of
Lev 8:9 forefront, did he put the *g* plate
Num 4:11 upon the *g* altar they shall
Num 7:26 One *g* spoon of ten shekels, full
Num 7:32 One *g* spoon of ten shekels, full
Num 7:38 One *g* spoon of ten shekels, full
Num 7:44 One *g* spoon of ten shekels, full
Num 7:50 One *g* spoon of ten shekels, full
Num 7:56 One *g* spoon of ten shekels, full
Num 7:62 One *g* spoon of ten shekels, full
Num 7:68 One *g* spoon of ten shekels, full
Num 7:74 One *g* spoon of ten shekels, full
Num 7:80 One *g* spoon of ten shekels, full
Num 7:86 The *g* spoons were twelve, full of
Judg 8:24 (For they had *g* earrings, because
Judg 8:26 the weight of the *g* earrings that
1Sa 6:4 *g* emerods, and five *g* mice
1Sa 6:17 these are the *g* emerods which the
1Sa 6:18 the *g* mice, according to the
2Kin 10:29 the *g* calves that were in Beth-el
1Chr 28:17 for the *g* basons he gave gold by
2Chr 4:19 the *g* altar also, and the tables
2Chr 13:8 and there are with you *g* calves
Ezr 6:5 And also let the *g* and silver
Est 4:11 king shall hold out the *g* sceptre
Est 5:2 *g* sceptre that was in his hand
Est 8:4 out the *g* sceptre toward Esther
Eccl 12:6 or the *g* bowl be broken, or the
Is 13:12 a man than the *g* wedge of Ophir
Is 14:4 the *g* city ceased
Jer 51:7 Babylon hath been a *g* cup in the
Dan 3:5 down and worship the *g* image that
Dan 3:7 worshipped the *g* image that
Dan 3:10 fall down and worship the *g* image
Dan 3:12 nor worship the *g* image which
Dan 3:14 nor worship the *g* image which I
Dan 3:18 nor worship the *g* image which
Dan 5:2 wine, commanded to bring the *g*
Dan 5:3 Then they brought the *g* vessels
Zec 4:12 *g* pipes empty the *g* oil out
Heb 9:4 Which had the *g* censer, and the
Heb 9:4 wherein was the *g* pot that had
Rev 1:12 I saw seven *g* candlesticks
Rev 1:13 about the paps with a *g* girdle
Rev 1:20 hand, and the seven *g* candlesticks
Rev 2:1 midst of the seven *g* candlesticks
Rev 5:8 *g* vials full of odours, which are
Rev 8:3 at the altar, having a *g* censer
Rev 8:3 the *g* altar which was before the
Rev 9:13 the *g* altar which is before God
Rev 14:14 man, having on his head a *g* crown
Rev 15:6 breasts girded with *g* girdles
Rev 15:7 unto the seven angels seven *g*
Rev 17:4 having a *g* cup in her hand full
Rev 21:15 had a *g* reed to measure the city

### GOLGOTHA *(gol'-go-thah)* See CALVARY. *Hill where Jesus was crucified.*

Mt 27:33 were come unto a place called G
Mk 15:22 they bring him unto the place G
Jn 19:17 which is called in the Hebrew G

### GOLIATH *(go-li'-ath) Philistine warrior killed by David.*

1Sa 17:4 camp of the Philistines, named G
1Sa 17:23 G by name, out of the armies of
1Sa 21:9 The sword of G the Philistine,
1Sa 22:10 him the sword of G the Philistine
2Sa 21:19 slew the brother of G the Gittite
1Chr 20:5 the brother of G the Gittite

### GOMER *(go'-mer)*

*1. Son of Japheth.*

Gen 10:2 G, and Magog, and Madai, and Javan,
Gen 10:3 And the sons of G
1Chr 1:5 G, and Magog, and Madai, and Javan,
1Chr 1:6 And the sons of G

*2. Descendants of Gomer 1.*

Eze 38:6 G, and all his bands

*3. Wife of Hosea.*

Hos 1:3 took G the daughter of Diblaim

### GOMORRAH *(go-mor'-rah)* See GOMORRHA. *City destroyed by God.*

Gen 10:19 as thou goest, unto Sodom, and G
Gen 13:10 the LORD destroyed Sodom and G
Gen 14:2 Sodom, and with Birsha king of G
Gen 14:8 king of Sodom, and the king of G
Gen 14:10 of Sodom and G fled, and fell there
Gen 14:11 took all the goods of Sodom and G
Gen 18:20 G is great, and because their sin
Gen 19:24 upon G brimstone and fire from the
Gen 19:28 And he looked toward Sodom and G
Deut 29:23 like the overthrow of Sodom, and G
Deut 32:32 of Sodom, and of the fields of G
Is 1:9 we should have been like unto G
Is 1:10 law of our God, ye people of G
Is 13:19 as when God overthrew Sodom and G
Jer 23:14 and the inhabitants thereof as G
Jer 49:18 As in the overthrow of Sodom and G
Jer 50:40 As God overthrew Sodom and G
Amos 4:11 you, as God overthrew Sodom and G
Zeph 2:9 and the children of Ammon as G
2Pet 2:6 G into ashes condemned them with

### GOMORRHA *(go-mor'-rah)* See GOMORRAH. *Greek form of Gomorrah.*

Mt 10:15 G in the day of judgment, than
Mk 6:11 G in the day of judgment, than
Rom 9:29 Sodoma, and been made like unto G
Jude 7 Even as Sodom and G, and the cities

### GOODMAN

Prov 7:19 For the *g* is not at home, he is
Mt 20:11 against the *g* of the house
Mt 24:43 that if the *g* of the house had
Mk 14:14 in, say ye to the *g* of the house
Lk 12:39 that if the *g* of the house had
Lk 22:11 shall say unto the *g* of the house

### GOODS

Gen 14:11 And they took all the *g* of Sodom
Gen 14:12 son, who dwelt in Sodom, and his *g*
Gen 14:16 And he brought back all the *g*
Gen 14:16 again his brother Lot, and his *g*
Gen 14:21 persons, and take the *g* to thyself
Gen 24:10 for all the *g* of his master were
Gen 31:18 all his *g* which he had gotten,
Gen 46:6 took their cattle, and their *g*
Ex 22:8 his hand unto his neighbour's *g*
Ex 22:11 his hand unto his neighbour's *g*
Num 16:32 unto Korah, and all their *g*
Num 31:9 all their flocks, and all their *g*
Num 35:3 for their cattle, and for their *g*
Deut 28:11 shall make thee plenteous in *g*
2Chr 21:14 and thy wives, and all thy *g*
Ezr 1:4 silver, and with gold, and with *g*
Ezr 1:6 of silver, with gold, with *g*
Ezr 6:8 that of the king's *g*, even of the
Ezr 7:26 or to confiscation of *g*, or to
Neh 9:25 and possessed houses full of all *g*
Job 20:10 his hands shall restore their *g*
Job 20:21 shall no man look for his *g*
Job 20:28 his *g* shall flow away in the day
Eccl 5:11 When *g* increase, they are
Eze 38:12 which have gotten cattle and *g*
Eze 38:13 and gold, to take away cattle and *g*
Zeph 1:13 Therefore their *g* shall become a
Mt 12:29 man's house, and spoil his *g*
Mt 24:47 make him ruler over all his *g*
Mt 25:14 and delivered unto them his *g*
Mk 3:27 man's house, and spoil his *g*
Lk 6:30 away thy *g* ask them not again
Lk 11:21 his palace, his *g* are in peace
Lk 12:18 I bestow all my fruits and my *g*
Lk 12:19 thou hast much *g* laid up for many
Lk 15:12 portion of *g* that falleth to me
Lk 16:1 unto him that he had wasted his *g*
Lk 19:8 the half of my *g* I give to the
Acts 2:45 And sold their possessions and *g*
1Cor 13:3 bestow all my *g* to feed the poor
Heb 10:34 joyfully the spoiling of your *g*
Rev 3:17 I am rich, and increased with *g*

### GOSHEN *(go'-shen)*

*1. A district of Egypt.*

Gen 45:10 thou shalt dwell in the land of G
Gen 46:28 Joseph, to direct his face unto G
Gen 46:28 and they came into the land of G
Gen 46:29 to meet Israel his father, to G
Gen 46:34 ye may dwell in the land of G
Gen 47:1 behold, they are in the land of G
Gen 47:4 servants dwell in the land of G
Gen 47:6 in the land of G let them dwell
Gen 47:27 of Egypt, in the country of G
Gen 50:8 herds, they left in the land of G
Ex 8:22 sever in that day the land of G
Ex 9:26 Only in the land of G, where the

*2. A district in southern Palestine.*

Josh 10:41 Gaza, and all the country of G
Josh 11:16 country, and all the land of G

*3. A town in Judea.*

Josh 15:51 And G, and Holon, and Giloh

### GOSPEL

Mt 4:23 preaching the *g* of the kingdom,
Mt 9:35 preaching the *g* of the kingdom,
Mt 11:5 poor have the *g* preached to them
Mt 24:14 this *g* of the kingdom shall be
Mt 26:13 Wheresoever this *g* shall be
Mk 1:1 of the *g* of Jesus Christ, the Son
Mk 1:14 preaching the *g* of the kingdom of
Mk 1:15 repent ye, and believe the *g*
Mk 13:10 the *g* must first be published
Mk 14:9 Wheresoever this *g* shall be
Mk 16:15 preach the *g* to every creature
Lk 4:18 me to preach the *g* to the poor
Lk 7:22 to the poor the *g* is preached
Lk 9:6 the towns, preaching the *g*
Lk 20:1 in the temple, and preached the *g*
Acts 8:25 preached the *g* in many villages
Acts 14:7 And there they preached the *g*
Acts 14:21 had preached the *g* to that city
Acts 15:7 should hear the word of the *g*
Acts 16:10 us for to preach the *g* unto them
Acts 20:24 to testify the *g* of the grace of
Rom 1:1 separated unto the *g* of God
Rom 1:9 my spirit in the *g* of his Son
Rom 1:15 I am ready to preach the *g* to you
Rom 1:16 am not ashamed of the *g* of Christ
Rom 2:16 by Jesus Christ according to my *g*
Rom 10:15 them that preach the *g* of peace
Rom 10:16 they have not all obeyed the *g*
Rom 11:28 As concerning the *g*, they are
Rom 15:16 ministering the *g* of God
Rom 15:19 fully preached the *g* of Christ
Rom 15:20 so have I strived to preach the *g*
Rom 15:29 the blessing of the *g* of Christ
Rom 16:25 to stablish you according to my *g*
1Cor 1:17 to baptize, but to preach the *g*
1Cor 4:15 I have begotten you through the *g*
1Cor 9:12 we should hinder the *g* of Christ
1Cor 9:14 the *g* should live of the *g*
1Cor 9:16 For though I preach the *g*
1Cor 9:16 is unto me, if I preach not the *g*
1Cor 9:17 of the *g* is committed unto me
1Cor 9:18 Verily that, when I preach the *g*
1Cor 9:18 I may make the *g* of Christ
1Cor 9:18 I abuse not my power in the *g*
1Cor 15:1 I declare unto you the *g* which I
2Cor 2:12 to Troas to preach Christ's *g*
2Cor 4:3 But if our *g* be hid, it is hid to
2Cor 4:4 light of the glorious *g* of Christ
2Cor 8:18 brother, whose praise is in the *g*
2Cor 9:13 subjection into the *g* of Christ
2Cor 10:14 also in preaching the *g* of Christ
2Cor 10:16 To preach the *g* in the regions
2Cor 11:4 have not received, or another *g*
2Cor 11:7 to you the *g* of God freely
Gal 1:6 grace of Christ unto another *g*
Gal 1:7 and would pervert the *g* of Christ

Gal 1:8 preach any other *g* unto you than
Gal 1:9 *g* unto you than that ye have
Gal 1:11 that the *g* which was preached of
Gal 2:2 that *g* which I preach among the
Gal 2:5 that the truth of the *g* might
Gal 2:7 when they saw that the *g* of the
Gal 2:7 as the *g* of the circumcision was
Gal 2:14 according to the truth of the *g*
Gal 3:8 before the *g* unto Abraham
Gal 4:13 the *g* unto you at the first
Eph 1:13 of truth, the *g* of your salvation
Eph 3:6 of his promise in Christ by the *g*
Eph 6:15 the preparation of the *g* of peace
Eph 6:19 make known the mystery of the *g*
Phil 1:5 For your fellowship in the *g* from
Phil 1:7 defence and comfirmation of the *g*
Phil 1:12 unto the furtherance of the *g*
Phil 1:17 I am set for the defence of the *g*
Phil 1:27 be as it becometh the *g* of Christ
Phil 1:27 together for the faith of the *g*
Phil 2:22 he hath served with me in the *g*
Phil 4:3 which laboured with me in the *g*
Phil 4:15 that in the beginning of the *g*
Col 1:5 in the word of the truth of the *g*
Col 1:23 moved away from the hope of the *g*
1Th 1:5 For our *g* came not unto you in
1Th 2:2 the *g* of God with much contention
1Th 2:4 God to be put in trust with the *g*
1Th 2:8 not the *g* of God only, but also
1Th 2:9 we preached unto you the *g* of God
1Th 3:2 fellowlabourer in the *g* of Christ
2Th 1:8 that obey not the *g* of our Lord
2Th 2:14 Whereunto he called you by our *g*
1Ti 1:11 the glorious *g* of the blessed God
2Ti 1:8 of the afflictions of the *g*
2Ti 1:10 to light through the *g*
2Ti 2:8 from the dead according to my *g*
Philem 13 unto me in the bonds of the *g*
Heb 4:2 For unto us was the *g* preached
1Pet 1:12 *g* unto you with the Holy Ghost
1Pet 1:25 by the *g* is preached unto you
1Pet 4:6 For for this cause was the *g*
1Pet 4:17 them that obey not the *g* of God
Rev 14:6 having the everlasting *g* to

**GOT**

Gen 36:6 which he had *g* in the land of
Gen 39:12 her hand, and fled, and *g* him out
Gen 39:15 with me, and fled, and *g* him out
Ps 44:3 For they *g* not the land in
Eccl 2:7 I *g* me servants and maidens, and
Jer 13:2 So I *g* a girdle according to the
Jer 13:4 Take the girdle that thou hast *g*

**GOURD**

Jonah 4:6 And the LORD God prepared a *g*
Jonah 4:6 Jonah was exceeding glad of the *g*
Jonah 4:7 it smote the *g* that it withered
Jonah 4:9 thou well to be angry for the *g*
Jonah 4:10 LORD, Thou hast had pity on the *g*

**GOVERNMENT**

Is 9:6 the *g* shall be upon his shoulder
Is 9:7 Of the increase of his *g* and peace
Is 22:21 I will commit thy *g* into his hand
2Pet 2:10 lust of uncleanness, and despise *g*

**GOVERNOR**

Gen 42:6 And Joseph was the *g* over the land
Gen 45:26 he is *g* over all the land of
1Kin 18:3 which was the *g* of his house
1Kin 22:26 back unto Amon the *g* of the city
2Kin 23:8 gate of Joshua the *g* of the city
2Kin 25:23 of Babylon had made Gedaliah *g*
1Chr 29:22 unto the LORD to be the chief *g*
2Chr 1:2 to every *g* in all Israel, the
2Chr 18:25 back to Amon the *g* of the city
2Chr 28:7 Azrikam the *g* of the house, and
2Chr 34:8 and Maaseiah the *g* of the city
Ezr 5:3 *g* on this side the river, and
Ezr 5:6 *g* on this side the river, and
Ezr 5:14 Sheshbazzar, whom he had made *g*
Ezr 6:6 Tatnai, *g* beyond the river,
Ezr 6:7 let the *g* of the Jews and the
Ezr 6:13 *g* on this side the river,
Neh 3:7 of the *g* on this side the river
Neh 5:14 be their *g* in the land of Judah
Neh 5:14 have not eaten the bread of the *g*
Neh 5:18 required not I the bread of the *g*
Neh 12:26 and in the days of Nehemiah the *g*
Ps 22:28 he is the *g* among the nations
Jer 20:1 who was also chief *g* in the house
Jer 30:21 their *g* shall proceed from the
Jer 40:5 made *g* over the cities of Judah
Jer 40:7 the son of Ahikam *g* in the land
Jer 41:2 Babylon had made *g* over the land
Jer 41:18 of Babylon made *g* in the land
Hag 1:1 *g* of Judah, and to Joshua the son
Hag 1:14 *g* of Judah, and the spirit of
Hag 2:2 *g* of Judah, and to Joshua the son
Hag 2:21 *g* of Judah, saying, I will shake
Zec 9:7 and he shall be as a *g* in Judah
Mal 1:8 offer it now unto thy *g*
Mt 2:6 for out of thee shall come a G
Mt 27:2 him to Pontius Pilate the *g*
Mt 27:11 And Jesus stood before the *g*
Mt 27:11 the *g* asked him, saying, Art thou
Mt 27:14 that the *g* marvelled greatly
Mt 27:15 Now at that feast the *g* was wont
Mt 27:21 The *g* answered and said unto them,
Mt 27:23 the *g* said, Why, what evil hath
Mt 27:27 Then the soldiers of the *g* took
Lk 2:2 made when Cyrenius was *g* of Syria
Lk 3:1 Pontius Pilate being *g* of Judaea
Lk 20:20 the power and authority of the *g*
Jn 2:8 and bear unto the *g* of the feast
Jn 2:9 the *g* of the feast called the
Acts 7:10 and he made him *g* over Egypt
Acts 23:24 bring him safe unto Felix the *g*
Acts 23:26 *g* Felix sendeth greeting
Acts 23:33 and delivered the epistle to the *g*
Acts 23:34 when the *g* had read the letter,
Acts 24:1 who informed the *g* against Paul
Acts 24:10 after that the *g* had beckoned
Acts 26:30 the king rose up, and the *g*
2Cor 11:32 In Damascus the *g* under Aretas
Jas 3:4 helm, whithersoever the *g* listeth

**GOVERNORS**

Judg 5:9 heart is toward the *g* of Israel
Judg 5:14 out of Machir came down *g*
1Kin 10:15 and of the *g* of the country
1Chr 24:5 for the *g* of the sanctuary, and
1Chr 24:5 *g* of the house of God, were of
2Chr 9:14 *g* of the country brought gold and
2Chr 23:20 the *g* of the people, and all the
Ezr 8:36 to the *g* on this side the river
Neh 2:7 me to the *g* beyond the river
Neh 2:9 I came to the *g* beyond the river
Neh 5:15 But the former *g* that had been
Est 3:12 to the *g* that were over every
Dan 2:48 chief of the *g* over all the wise
Dan 3:2 together the princes, the *g*
Dan 3:3 Then the princes, the *g*, and
Dan 3:27 And the princes, *g*, and captains,
Dan 6:7 presidents of the kingdom, the *g*
Zec 12:5 the *g* of Judah shall say in their
Zec 12:6 In that day will I make the *g* of
Mt 10:18 And ye shall be brought before *g*
Gal 4:2 *g* until the time appointed of the
1Pet 2:14 Or unto *g*, as unto them that are

**GOZAN** *(go'-zan) An Assyrian city.*

2Kin 17:6 and in Habor by the river of G
2Kin 18:11 and in Habor by the river of G
2Kin 19:12 as G, and Haran, and Rezeph, and the
1Chr 5:26 Habor, and Hara, and to the river G
Is 37:12 my fathers have destroyed, as G

**GRACE**

Gen 6:8 But Noah found *g* in the eyes of
Gen 19:19 servant hath found *g* in thy sight
Gen 32:5 that I may find *g* in thy sight
Gen 33:8 These are to find *g* in the sight
Gen 33:10 now I have found *g* in thy sight
Gen 33:15 let me find *g* in the sight of my
Gen 34:11 Let me find *g* in your eyes, and
Gen 39:4 And Joseph found *g* in his sight
Gen 47:25 let us find *g* in the sight of my
Gen 47:29 now I have found *g* in thy sight
Gen 50:4 now I have found *g* in your eyes
Ex 33:12 hast also found *g* in my sight
Ex 33:13 if I have found *g* in thy sight
Ex 33:13 that I may find *g* in thy sight
Ex 33:16 people have found *g* in thy sight
Ex 33:17 for thou hast found *g* in my sight
Ex 34:9 now I have found *g* in thy sight
Num 32:5 if we have found *g* in thy sight
Judg 6:17 now I have found *g* in thy sight
Ruth 2:2 him in whose sight I shall find *g*
Ruth 2:10 Why have I found *g* in thine eyes
1Sa 1:18 handmaid find *g* in thy sight
1Sa 20:3 that I have found *g* in thine eyes
1Sa 27:5 I have now found *g* in thine eyes
2Sa 14:22 that I have found *g* in thy sight
2Sa 16:4 that I may find *g* in thy sight
Ezr 9:8 now for a little space *g* hath
Est 2:17 all the women, and she obtained *g*
Ps 45:2 *g* is poured into thy lips
Ps 84:11 the LORD will give *g* and glory
Prov 1:9 be an ornament of *g* unto thy head
Prov 3:22 unto thy soul, and *g* to thy neck
Prov 3:34 but he giveth *g* unto the lowly
Prov 4:9 to thine head an ornament of *g*
Prov 22:11 for the *g* of his lips the king
Jer 31:2 sword found *g* in the wilderness
Zec 4:7 crying, G, *g* unto it
Zec 12:10 of Jerusalem, the spirit of *g*
Lk 2:40 the *g* of God was upon him
Jn 1:14 of the Father,) full of *g*
Jn 1:16 all we received, and *g* for *g*
Jn 1:17 the law was given by Moses, but *g*
Acts 4:33 great *g* was upon them all
Acts 11:23 he came, and had seen the *g* of God
Acts 13:43 them to continue in the *g* of God
Acts 14:3 testimony unto the word of his *g*
Acts 14:26 had been recommended to the *g* of
Acts 15:11 the *g* of the Lord Jesus Christ we
Acts 15:40 by the brethren unto the *g* of God
Acts 18:27 much which had believed through *g*
Acts 20:24 the gospel of the *g* of God
Acts 20:32 to God, and to the word of his *g*
Rom 1:5 By whom we have received *g*
Rom 1:7 G to you and peace from God our
Rom 3:24 Being justified freely by his *g*
Rom 4:4 is the reward not reckoned of *g*
Rom 4:16 of faith, that it might be by *g*
Rom 5:2 into this *g* wherein we stand
Rom 5:15 *g* of God, and the gift by *g*
Rom 5:17 they which receive abundance of *g*
Rom 5:20 abounded, *g* did much more abound
Rom 5:21 even so might *g* reign through
Rom 6:1 in sin, that *g* may abound
Rom 6:14 not under the law, but under *g*
Rom 6:15 not under the law, but under *g*
Rom 11:5 according to the election of *g*
Rom 11:6 And if by *g*, then is it no more of
Rom 11:6 otherwise *g* is no more *g*
Rom 11:6 be of works, then is it no more *g*
Rom 12:3 through the *g* given unto me, to
Rom 12:6 to the *g* that is given to us
Rom 15:15 because of the *g* that is given to
Rom 16:20 The *g* of our Lord Jesus Christ be
Rom 16:24 The *g* of our Lord Jesus Christ be
1Cor 1:3 G be unto you, and peace, from God
1Cor 1:4 for the *g* of God which is given
1Cor 3:10 According to the *g* of God which
1Cor 10:30 For if I by *g* be a partaker, why
1Cor 15:10 But by the *g* of God I am what I
1Cor 15:10 his *g* which was bestowed upon me
1Cor 15:10 but the *g* of God which was with
1Cor 16:23 The *g* of our Lord Jesus Christ be
2Cor 1:2 G be to you and peace from God our
2Cor 1:12 wisdom, but by the *g* of God
2Cor 4:15 that the abundant *g* might through
2Cor 6:1 receive not the *g* of God in vain
2Cor 8:1 we do you to wit of the *g* of God
2Cor 8:6 finish in you the same *g* also
2Cor 8:7 see that ye abound in this *g* also
2Cor 8:9 For ye know the *g* of our Lord
2Cor 8:19 to travel with us with this *g*
2Cor 9:8 to make all *g* abound toward you
2Cor 9:14 for the exceeding *g* of God in you
2Cor 12:9 My *g* is sufficient for thee
2Cor 13:14 The *g* of the Lord Jesus Christ,
Gal 1:3 G be to you and peace from God the
Gal 1:6 him that called you into the *g* of
Gal 1:15 womb, and called me by his *g*
Gal 2:9 perceived the *g* that was given
Gal 2:21 I do not frustrate the *g* of God
Gal 5:4 ye are fallen from *g*
Gal 6:18 the *g* of our Lord Jesus Christ be
Eph 1:2 G be to you, and peace, from God
Eph 1:6 the praise of the glory of his *g*
Eph 1:7 according to the riches of his *g*
Eph 2:5 with Christ, (by *g* ye are saved
Eph 2:7 his *g* in his kindness toward us
Eph 2:8 For by *g* are ye saved through
Eph 3:2 of the dispensation of the *g* of
Eph 3:7 the *g* of God given unto me by the
Eph 3:8 of all saints, is this *g* given
Eph 4:7 unto every one of us is given *g*
Eph 4:29 may minister *g* unto the hearers
Eph 6:24 G be with all them that love our

Phil 1:2 *G* be unto you, and peace, from God
Phil 1:7 ye all are partakers of my *g*
Phil 4:23 The *g* of our Lord Jesus Christ be
Col 1:2 *G* be unto you, and peace, from God
Col 1:6 knew the *g* of God in truth
Col 3:16 singing with *g* in your hearts to
Col 4:6 Let your speech be alway with *g*
Col 4:18 *G* be with you
1Th 1:1 *G* be unto you, and peace, from God
1Th 5:28 The *g* of our Lord Jesus Christ be
2Th 1:2 *G* unto you, and peace, from God
2Th 1:12 according to the *g* of our God
2Th 2:16 and good hope through *g*,
2Th 3:18 The *g* of our Lord Jesus Christ be
1Ti 1:2 *G*, mercy, and peace, from God our
1Ti 1:14 the *g* of our Lord was exceeding
1Ti 6:21 *G* be with thee
2Ti 1:2 *G*, mercy, and peace, from God the
2Ti 1:9 according to his own purpose and *g*
2Ti 2:1 be strong in the *g* that is in
2Ti 4:22 *G* be with you
Titus 1:4 *G*, mercy, and peace, from God the
Titus 2:11 For the *g* of God that bringeth
Titus 3:7 That being justified by his *g*
Titus 3:15 *G* be with you all
Philem 3 *G* to you, and peace, from God our
Philem 25 The *g* of our Lord Jesus Christ be
Heb 2:9 that he by the *g* of God should
Heb 4:16 come boldly unto the throne of *g*
Heb 4:16 find *g* to help in time of need
Heb 10:29 done despite unto the Spirit of *g*
Heb 12:15 lest any man fail of the *g* of God
Heb 12:28 cannot be moved, let us have *g*
Heb 13:9 the heart be established with *g*
Heb 13:25 *G* be with you all
Jas 1:11 the *g* of the fashion of it
Jas 4:6 But he giveth more *g*
Jas 4:6 but giveth *g* unto the humble
1Pet 1:2 *G* unto you, and peace, be
1Pet 1:10 who prophesied of the *g* that
1Pet 1:13 hope to the end for the *g* that is
1Pet 3:7 heirs together of the *g* of life
1Pet 4:10 stewards of the manifold *g* of God
1Pet 5:5 proud, and giveth *g* to the humble
1Pet 5:10 But the God of all *g*, who hath
1Pet 5:12 that this is the true *g* of God
2Pet 1:2 *G* and peace be multiplied unto you
2Pet 3:18 But grow in *g*, and in the
2Jn 3 *G* be with you, mercy, and peace,
Jude 4 turning the *g* of our God into
Rev 1:4 *G* be unto you, and peace, from him
Rev 22:21 The *g* of our Lord Jesus Christ be

## GRACIOUS

Gen 43:29 God be *g* unto thee, my son
Ex 22:27 for I am *g*
Ex 33:19 be *g* to whom I will be *g*
Ex 34:6 LORD, The LORD God, merciful and *g*
Num 6:25 upon thee, and be *g* unto thee
2Sa 12:22 tell whether GOD will be *g* to me
2Kin 13:23 And the LORD was *g* unto them
2Chr 30:9 for the LORD your God is *g*
Neh 9:17 thou art a God ready to pardon, *g*
Neh 9:31 for thou art a *g* and merciful God
Job 33:24 Then he is *g* unto him, and saith,
Ps 77:9 Hath God forgotten to be *g*
Ps 86:15 a God full of compassion, and *g*
Ps 103:8 The LORD is merciful and *g*
Ps 111:4 the LORD is *g* and full of
Ps 112:4 he is *g*, and full of compassion,
Ps 116:5 *G* is the LORD, and righteous
Ps 145:8 The LORD is *g*, and full of
Prov 11:16 A *g* woman retaineth honour
Eccl 10:12 words of a wise man's mouth are *g*
Is 30:18 wait, that he may be *g* unto you
Is 30:19 he will be very *g* unto thee at
Is 33:2 O LORD, be *g* unto us
Jer 22:23 how *g* shalt thou be when pangs
Joel 2:13 for he is *g* and merciful, slow to
Amos 5:15 be *g* unto the remnant of Joseph
Jonah 4:2 for I knew that thou art a *g* God
Mal 1:9 God that he will be *g* unto us
Lk 4:22 wondered at the *g* words which
1Pet 2:3 ye have tasted that the Lord is *g*

## GRACIOUSLY

Gen 33:5 God hath *g* given thy servant
Gen 33:11 because God hath dealt *g* with me
Ps 119:29 and grant me thy law *g*
Hos 14:2 all iniquity, and receive us *g*

## GRAFFED

Rom 11:17 wert *g* in among them, and with
Rom 11:19 broken off, that I might be *g* in
Rom 11:23 still in unbelief, shall be *g* in
Rom 11:24 wert *g* contrary to nature into a
Rom 11:24 be *g* into their own olive tree

## GRAIN

Amos 9:9 the least *g* fall upon the earth
Mt 13:31 is like to a *g* of mustard seed
Mt 17:20 have faith as a *g* of mustard seed
Mk 4:31 It is like a *g* of mustard seed,
Lk 13:19 It is like a *g* of mustard seed,
Lk 17:6 had faith as a *g* of mustard seed
1Cor 15:37 body that shall be, but bare *g*
1Cor 15:37 of wheat, or of some other *g*

## GRANT

Lev 25:24 shall *g* a redemption for the land
Ruth 1:9 The LORD *g* you that ye may find
1Sa 1:17 the God of Israel *g* thee thy
1Chr 21:22 to Ornan, *G* me the place of this
1Chr 21:22 thou shalt *g* it me for the full
2Chr 12:7 them, but I will *g* them some
Ezr 3:7 according to the *g* that they had
Neh 1:11 *g* him mercy in the sight of this
Est 5:8 please the king to *g* my petition
Job 6:8 that God would *g* me the thing
Ps 20:4 *G* thee according to thine own
Ps 85:7 O LORD, and *g* us thy salvation
Ps 119:29 and *g* me thy law graciously
Ps 140:8 *G* not, O LORD, the desires of the
Mt 20:21 *G* that these my two sons may sit,
Mk 10:37 *G* unto us that we may sit, one on
Lk 1:74 That he would *g* unto us, that we,
Acts 4:29 *g* unto thy servants, that with
Rom 15:5 and consolation *g* you to be
Eph 3:16 That he would *g* you, according to
2Ti 1:18 The Lord *g* unto him that he may
Rev 3:21 I *g* to sit with me in my throne

## GRANTED

1Chr 4:10 God *g* him that which he requested
2Chr 1:12 and knowledge is *g* unto thee
Ezr 7:6 the king *g* him all his request,
Neh 2:8 And the king *g* me, according to
Est 5:6 and it shall be *g* thee
Est 7:2 and it shall be *g* thee
Est 8:11 Wherein the king *g* the Jews which
Est 9:12 and it shall be *g* thee
Est 9:13 let it be *g* to the Jews which are
Job 10:12 Thou hast *g* me life and favour, and
Prov 10:24 of the righteous shall be *g*
Acts 3:14 a murderer to be *g* unto you
Acts 11:18 Gentiles *g* repentance unto life
Acts 14:3 *g* signs and wonders to be done by
Rev 19:8 to her was *g* that she should be

## GRAPE

Lev 19:10 gather every *g* of thy vineyard
Deut 32:14 drink the pure blood of the *g*
Job 15:33 off his unripe *g* as the vine
Song 2:13 the tender *g* give a good smell
Song 7:12 whether the tender *g* appear
Is 18:5 the sour *g* is ripening in the
Jer 31:29 The fathers have eaten a sour *g*
Jer 31:30 every man that eateth the sour *g*

## GRAPES

Gen 40:10 thereof brought forth ripe *g*
Gen 40:11 and I took the *g*, and pressed them
Gen 49:11 and his clothes in the blood of *g*
Lev 25:5 neither gather the *g* of thy vine
Lev 25:11 nor gather the *g* in it of thy
Num 6:3 liquor of *g*, nor eat moist *g*
Num 13:20 was the time of the firstripe *g*
Num 13:23 a branch with one cluster of *g*
Num 13:24 because of the cluster of *g* which
Deut 23:24 then thou mayest eat *g* thy fill
Deut 24:21 gatherest the *g* of thy vineyard
Deut 28:30 and shalt not gather the *g* thereof
Deut 28:39 of the wine, nor gather the *g*
Deut 32:32 their *g* are *g* of gall
Judg 8:2 the *g* of Ephraim better than the
Judg 9:27 their vineyards, and trode the *g*
Neh 13:15 as also wine, *g*, and figs, and all
Song 2:15 for our vines have tender *g*
Song 7:7 and thy breasts to clusters of *g*
Is 5:2 that it should bring forth *g*
Is 5:2 and it brought forth wild *g*
Is 5:4 that it should bring forth *g*
Is 5:4 brought it forth wild *g*
Is 17:6 Yet gleaning *g* shall be left in
Is 24:13 as the gleaning *g* when the
Jer 8:13 there shall be no *g* on the vine
Jer 25:30 a shout, as they that tread the *g*
Jer 49:9 they not leave some gleaning *g*
Eze 18:2 The fathers have eaten sour *g*
Hos 9:10 Israel like *g* in the wilderness
Amos 9:13 the treader of *g* him that soweth
Obad 5 thee, would they not leave some *g*
Mt 7:16 Do men gather *g* of thorns
Lk 6:44 of a bramble bush gather they *g*
Rev 14:18 for her *g* are fully ripe

## GRASS

Gen 1:11 said, Let the earth bring forth *g*
Gen 1:12 And the earth brought forth *g*
Num 22:4 ox licketh up the *g* of the field
Deut 11:15 I will send *g* in thy fields for
Deut 29:23 nor any *g* groweth therein, like
Deut 32:2 and as the showers upon the *g*
2Sa 23:4 as the tender *g* springing out of
1Kin 18:5 we may find *g* to save the horses
2Kin 19:26 they were as the *g* of the field
2Kin 19:26 as the *g* on the house tops, and as
Job 5:25 offspring as the *g* of the earth
Job 6:5 the wild ass bray when he hath *g*
Job 40:15 he eateth *g* as an ox
Ps 37:2 shall soon be cut down like the *g*
Ps 72:6 down like rain upon the mown *g*
Ps 72:16 flourish like *g* of the earth
Ps 90:5 they are like *g* which groweth up
Ps 92:7 When the wicked spring as the *g*
Ps 102:4 is smitten, and withered like *g*
Ps 102:11 and I am withered like *g*
Ps 103:15 As for man, his days are as *g*
Ps 104:14 He causeth the *g* to grow for the
Ps 106:20 similitude of an ox that eateth *g*
Ps 129:6 be as the *g* upon the housetops
Ps 147:8 who maketh *g* to grow upon the
Prov 19:12 his favour is as dew upon the *g*
Prov 27:25 the tender *g* sheweth itself, and
Is 15:6 the *g* faileth, there is no green
Is 35:7 shall be *g* with reeds and rushes
Is 37:27 they were as the *g* of the field
Is 37:27 as the *g* on the housetops, and as
Is 40:6 All flesh is *g*, and all the
Is 40:7 The *g* withereth, the flower
Is 40:7 surely the people is *g*
Is 40:8 The *g* withereth, the flower
Is 44:4 shall spring up as among the *g*
Is 51:12 of man which shall be made as *g*
Jer 14:5 it, because there was no *g*
Jer 14:6 did fail, because there was no *g*
Jer 50:11 are grown fat as the heifer at *g*
Dan 4:15 in the tender *g* of the field
Dan 4:15 the beasts in the *g* of the earth
Dan 4:23 in the tender *g* of the field
Dan 4:25 shall make thee to eat *g* as oxen
Dan 4:32 shall make thee to eat *g* as oxen
Dan 4:33 from men, and did eat *g* as oxen
Dan 5:21 they fed him with *g* like oxen
Amos 7:2 end of eating the *g* of the land
Mic 5:7 LORD, as the showers upon the *g*
Zec 10:1 rain, to every one *g* in the field
Mt 6:30 God so clothe the *g* of the field
Mt 14:19 multitude to sit down on the *g*
Mk 6:39 by companies upon the green *g*
Lk 12:28 If then God so clothe the *g*
Jn 6:10 Now there was much *g* in the place
Jas 1:10 of the *g* he shall pass away
Jas 1:11 heat, but it withereth the *g*
1Pet 1:24 For all flesh is as *g*, and all the
1Pet 1:24 glory of man as the flower of *g*
1Pet 1:24 The *g* withereth, and the flower
Rev 8:7 up, and all green *g* was burnt up
Rev 9:4 not hurt the *g* of the earth

## GRASSHOPPERS

Num 13:33 and we were in our own sight as *g*
Judg 6:5 they came as *g* for multitude
Judg 7:12 the valley like *g* for multitude
Is 40:22 the inhabitants thereof are as *g*
Jer 46:23 because they are more than the *g*
Amos 7:1 he formed *g* in the beginning of
Nah 3:17 and thy captains as the great *g*

## GRATE

Ex 27:4 for it a *g* of network of brass
Ex 35:16 burnt offering, with his brasen *g*
Ex 38:4 *g* of network under the compass
Ex 38:5 the four ends of the *g* of brass
Ex 38:30 altar, and the brasen *g* for it
Ex 39:39 his *g* of brass, his staves, and

### GRAVE
Gen 35:20 And Jacob set a pillar upon her *g*
Gen 35:20 of Rachel's *g* unto this day
Gen 37:35 into the *g* unto my son mourning
Gen 42:38 gray hairs with sorrow to the *g*
Gen 44:29 gray hairs with sorrow to the *g*
Gen 44:31 our father with sorrow to the *g*
Gen 50:5 in my *g* which I have digged for
Ex 28:9 *g* on them the names of the
Ex 28:36 *g* upon it, like the engravings of
Num 19:16 body, or a bone of a man, or a *g*
Num 19:18 or one slain, or one dead, or a *g*
1Sa 2:6 he bringeth down to the *g*
2Sa 3:32 voice, and wept at the *g* of Abner
2Sa 19:37 be buried by the *g* of my father
1Kin 2:6 head go down to the *g* in peace
1Kin 2:9 thou down to the *g* with blood
1Kin 13:30 he laid his carcase in his own *g*
1Kin 14:13 of Jeroboam shall come to the *g*
2Kin 22:20 be gathered into thy *g* in peace
2Chr 2:7 that can skill to *g* with the
2Chr 2:14 also to *g* any manner of graving,
2Chr 34:28 be gathered to thy *g* in peace
Job 3:22 glad, when they can find the *g*
Job 5:26 shalt come to thy *g* in a full age
Job 7:9 to the *g* shall come up no more
Job 10:19 carried from the womb to the *g*
Job 14:13 thou wouldest hide me in the *g*
Job 17:13 If I wait, the *g* is mine house
Job 21:13 and in a moment go down to the *g*
Job 21:32 Yet shall he be brought to the *g*
Job 24:19 so doth the *g* those which have
Job 30:24 not stretch out his hand to the *g*
Job 33:22 his soul draweth near unto the *g*
Ps 6:5 in the *g* who shall give thee
Ps 30:3 brought up my soul from the *g*
Ps 31:17 and let them be silent in the *g*
Ps 49:14 Like sheep they are laid in the *g*
Ps 49:14 in the *g* from their dwelling
Ps 49:15 my soul from the power of the *g*
Ps 88:3 my life draweth nigh unto the *g*
Ps 88:5 like the slain that lie in the *g*
Ps 88:11 be declared in the *g*
Ps 89:48 his soul from the hand of the *g*
Prov 1:12 us swallow them up alive as the *g*
Prov 30:16 The *g*; and the barren
Eccl 9:10 knowledge, nor wisdom, in the *g*
Song 8:6 jealousy is cruel as the *g*
Is 14:11 Thy pomp is brought down to the *g*
Is 14:19 thy *g* like an abominable branch
Is 38:10 I shall go to the gates of the *g*
Is 38:18 For the *g* cannot praise thee,
Is 53:9 he made his *g* with the wicked, and
Jer 20:17 my mother might have been my *g*
Eze 31:15 down to the *g* I caused a mourning
Eze 32:23 her company is round about her *g*
Eze 32:24 her multitude round about her *g*
Hos 13:14 them from the power of the *g*
Hos 13:14 O *g*, I will be thy destruction
Nah 1:14 I will make thy *g*
Jn 11:17 lain in the *g* four days already
Jn 11:31 goeth unto the *g* to weep there
Jn 11:38 in himself cometh to the *g*
Jn 12:17 he called Lazarus out of his *g*
1Cor 15:55 O *g*, where is thy victory
1Ti 3:8 Likewise must the deacons be *g*
1Ti 3:11 Even so must their wives be *g*
Titus 2:2 That the aged men be sober, *g*

### GRAVEN
Ex 20:4 not make unto thee any *g* image
Ex 32:16 writing of God, *g* upon the tables
Ex 39:6 inclosed in ouches of gold, *g*
Ex 39:6 of gold, *g*, as signets are *g*
Lev 26:1 make you no idols nor *g* image
Deut 4:16 yourselves, and make you a *g* image
Deut 4:23 with you, and make you a *g* image
Deut 4:25 yourselves, and make a *g* image
Deut 5:8 shalt not make thee any *g* image
Deut 7:5 burn their *g* images with fire
Deut 7:25 The *g* images of their gods shall
Deut 12:3 down the *g* images of their gods
Deut 27:15 that maketh any *g* or molten image
Judg 17:3 for my son, to make a *g* image
Judg 17:4 who made thereof a *g* image
Judg 18:14 a *g* image, and a molten image
Judg 18:17 in thither, and took the *g* image
Judg 18:20 the *g* image, and went in the midst
Judg 18:30 of Dan set up the *g* image
Judg 18:31 they set them up Micah's *g* image
2Kin 17:41 LORD, and served their *g* images
2Kin 21:7 he set a *g* image of the grove
2Chr 33:19 *g* images, before he was humbled
2Chr 34:7 had beaten the *g* images into
Job 19:24 That they were *g* with an iron pen
Ps 78:58 to jealousy with their *g* images
Ps 97:7 be all they that serve *g* images
Is 10:10 whose *g* images did excel them of
Is 21:9 all the *g* images of her gods he
Is 30:22 of thy *g* images of silver
Is 40:19 The workman melteth a *g* image
Is 40:20 workman to prepare a *g* image
Is 42:8 neither my praise to *g* images
Is 42:17 ashamed, that trust in *g* images
Is 44:9 They that make a *g* image are all
Is 44:10 or molten a *g* image that is
Is 44:15 he maketh it a *g* image, and
Is 44:17 he maketh a god, even his *g* image
Is 45:20 set up the wood of their *g* image
Is 48:5 my *g* image, and my molten image,
Is 49:16 I have *g* thee upon the palms of
Jer 8:19 me to anger with their *g* images
Jer 10:14 is confounded by the *g* image
Jer 17:1 it is *g* upon the table of their
Jer 50:38 for it is the land of *g* images
Jer 51:17 is confounded by the *g* image
Jer 51:47 upon the *g* images of Babylon
Jer 51:52 do judgment upon her *g* images
Hos 11:2 and burned incense to *g* images
Mic 1:7 all the *g* images thereof shall be
Mic 5:13 Thy *g* images also will I cut off,
Nah 1:14 gods will I cut off the *g* image
Hab 2:18 What profiteth the *g* image that
Hab 2:18 that the maker thereof hath *g* it
Acts 17:29 stone, *g* by art and man's device

### GRAVES
Ex 14:11 Because there were no *g* in Egypt
2Kin 23:6 the powder thereof upon the *g* of
2Chr 34:4 strowed it upon the *g* of them
Job 17:1 extinct, the *g* are ready for me
Is 65:4 Which remain among the *g*, and
Jer 8:1 of Jerusalem, out of their *g*
Jer 26:23 into the *g* of the common people
Eze 32:22 his *g* are about him
Eze 32:23 Whose *g* are set in the sides of
Eze 32:25 her *g* are round about him
Eze 32:26 her *g* are round about him
Eze 37:12 O my people, I will open your *g*
Eze 37:12 you to come up out of your *g*
Eze 37:13 LORD, when I have opened your *g*
Eze 37:13 and brought you up out of your *g*
Eze 39:11 Gog a place there of *g* in Israel
Mt 27:52 And the *g* were opened
Mt 27:53 came out of the *g* after his
Lk 11:44 for ye are as *g* which appear not,
Jn 5:28 are in the *g* shall hear his voice
Rev 11:9 their dead bodies to be put in *g*

### GRAY
Gen 42:38 then shall ye bring down my *g*
Gen 44:29 ye shall bring down my *g* hairs
Gen 44:31 servants shall bring down the *g*
Deut 32:25 also with the man of *g* hairs
Hos 7:9 *g* hairs are here and there upon

### GRECIA See GRECIANS, GREECE. *Latin form of Greece.*
Dan 8:21 the rough goat is the king of G
Dan 10:20 lo, the prince of G shall come
Dan 11:2 up all against the realm of G

### GRECIANS See GREEKS.
*1. Inhabitants of Greece.*
Joel 3:6 Jerusalem have ye sold unto the G
*2. Hellenistic Jews.*
Acts 6:1 of the G against the Hebrews
Acts 9:29 Jesus, and disputed against the G
Acts 11:20 come to Antioch, spake unto the G

### GREECE See GRECIA. *Peninsula south of the Balkans.*
Zec 9:13 O Zion, against thy sons, O G
Acts 20:2 much exhortation, he came into G

### GREEDY
Ps 17:12 as a lion that is *g* of his prey
Prov 1:19 of every one that is *g* of gain
Prov 15:27 He that is *g* of gain troubleth
Is 56:11 they are *g* dogs which can never
1Ti 3:3 no striker, not *g* of filthy lucre
1Ti 3:8 much wine, not *g* of filthy lucre

### GREEK See GREEKS.
*1. A native of Greece.*
Acts 16:1 but his father was a G
Acts 16:3 knew all that his father was a G
Rom 1:16 the Jew first, and also to the G
Rom 10:12 between the Jew and the G
Gal 2:3 Titus, who was with me, being a G
Gal 3:28 There is neither Jew nor G
Col 3:11 Where there is neither G nor Jew
*2. A language.*
Lk 23:38 written over him in letters of G
Jn 19:20 and it was written in Hebrew, and G
Acts 21:37 Who said, Canst thou speak G
Rev 9:11 but in the G tongue hath his name
*3. A female.*
Mk 7:26 The woman was a G, a

### GREEKS See GRECIANS. *Plural of Greek 1.*
Jn 12:20 there were certain G among them
Acts 14:1 Jews and also of the G believed
Acts 17:4 of the devout G a great multitude
Acts 17:12 of honourable women which were G
Acts 18:4 and persuaded the Jews and the G
Acts 18:17 Then all the G took Sosthenes,
Acts 19:10 of the Lord Jesus, both Jews and G
Acts 19:17 G also dwelling at Ephesus
Acts 20:21 to the Jews, and also to the G
Acts 21:28 further brought G also into the
Rom 1:14 I am debtor both to the G
1Cor 1:22 sign, and the G seek after wisdom
1Cor 1:23 and unto the G foolishness
1Cor 1:24 which are called, both Jews and G

### GREEN
Gen 1:30 have given every *g* herb for meat
Gen 9:3 even as the *g* herb have I given
Gen 30:37 Jacob took him rods of *g* poplar
Ex 10:15 not any *g* thing in the trees
Lev 2:14 offering of thy firstfruits *g*
Lev 23:14 nor *g* ears, until the selfsame
Deut 12:2 the hills, and under every *g* tree
Judg 16:7 If they bind me with seven *g*
Judg 16:8 brought up to her seven *g* withs
1Kin 14:23 high hill, and under every *g* tree
2Kin 16:4 the hills, and under every *g* tree
2Kin 17:10 high hill, and under every *g* tree
2Kin 19:26 of the field, and as the *g* herb
2Chr 28:4 the hills, and under every *g* tree
Est 1:6 Where were white, *g*, and blue,
Job 8:16 He is *g* before the sun, and his
Job 15:32 and his branch shall not be *g*
Job 39:8 he searcheth after every *g* thing
Ps 23:2 me to lie down in *g* pastures
Ps 37:2 grass, and wither as the *g* herb
Ps 37:35 himself like a *g* bay tree
Ps 52:8 But I am like a *g* olive tree in
Song 1:16 also our bed is *g*
Song 2:13 fig tree putteth forth her *g* figs
Is 15:6 faileth, there is no *g* thing
Is 37:27 of the field, and as the *g* herb
Is 57:5 with idols under every *g* tree
Jer 2:20 under every *g* tree thou wanderest
Jer 3:6 mountain and under every *g* tree
Jer 3:13 the strangers under every *g* tree
Jer 11:16 A *g* olive tree, fair, and of
Jer 17:2 their groves by the *g* trees upon
Jer 17:8 cometh, but her leaf shall be *g*
Eze 6:13 mountains, and under every *g* tree
Eze 17:24 tree, have dried up the *g* tree
Eze 20:47 shall devour every *g* tree in thee
Hos 14:8 I am like a *g* fir tree
Mk 6:39 by companies upon the *g* grass
Lk 23:31 they do these things in a *g* tree
Rev 8:7 up, and all *g* grass was burnt up
Rev 9:4 of the earth, neither any *g* thing

### GREET
1Sa 25:5 go to Nabal, and *g* him
Rom 16:3 G Priscilla and Aquila my helpers
Rom 16:5 Likewise *g* the church that is in
Rom 16:6 G Mary, who bestowed much labour
Rom 16:8 G Amplias my beloved in the Lord
Rom 16:11 G them that be of the household
1Cor 16:20 All the brethren *g* you
1Cor 16:20 G ye one another with an holy
2Cor 13:12 G one another with an holy kiss
Phil 4:21 brethren which are with me *g* you
Col 4:14 physician, and Demas, *g* you
1Th 5:26 G all the brethren with an holy
Titus 3:15 G them that love us in the faith
1Pet 5:14 G ye one another with a kiss of

2Jn 13 of thy elect sister *g* thee
3Jn 14 G the friends by name

## GREW

Gen 2:5 herb of the field before it *g*
Gen 19:25 that which *g* upon the ground
Gen 21:8 And the child *g*, and was weaned
Gen 21:20 and he *g*, and dwelt in the
Gen 25:27 And the boys *g*
Gen 26:13 *g* until he became very great
Gen 47:27 had possessions therein, and *g*
Ex 1:12 the more they multiplied and *g*
Ex 2:10 And the child *g*, and she brought
Judg 11:2 and his wife's sons *g* up, and they
Judg 13:24 and the child *g*, and the LORD
1Sa 2:21 child Samuel *g* before the LORD
1Sa 2:26 And the child Samuel *g* on, and was
1Sa 3:19 And Samuel *g*, and the LORD was with
2Sa 5:10 *g* great, and the LORD God of hosts
2Sa 12:3 it *g* up together with him, and
Eze 17:6 And it *g*, and became a spreading
Eze 17:10 wither in the furrows where it *g*
Dan 4:11 The tree *g*, and was strong, and the
Dan 4:20 tree that thou sawest, which *g*
Mk 4:7 among thorns, and the thorns *g* up
Mk 5:26 bettered, but rather *g* worse
Lk 1:80 And the child *g*, and waxed strong
Lk 2:40 And the child *g*, and waxed strong
Lk 13:19 and it *g*, and waxed a great tree
Acts 7:17 sworn to Abraham, the people *g*
Acts 12:24 But the word of God *g* and
Acts 19:20 So mightily *g* the word of God and

## GRIEF

Gen 26:35 Which were a *g* of mind unto Isaac
1Sa 1:16 and *g* have I spoken hitherto
1Sa 25:31 That this shall be no *g* unto thee
2Chr 6:29 know his own sore and his own *g*
Job 2:13 saw that his *g* was very great
Job 6:2 O that my *g* were throughly
Job 16:5 of my lips should asswage your *g*
Job 16:6 I speak, my *g* is not asswaged
Ps 6:7 Mine eye is consumed because of *g*
Ps 31:9 mine eye is consumed with *g*
Ps 31:10 For my life is spent with *g*
Ps 69:26 they talk to the *g* of those whom
Prov 17:25 foolish son is a *g* to his father
Eccl 1:18 For in much wisdom is much *g*
Eccl 2:23 are sorrows, and his travail *g*
Is 17:11 shall be a heap in the day of *g*
Is 53:3 of sorrows, and acquainted with *g*
Is 53:10 he hath put him to *g*
Jer 6:7 before me continually is *g*
Jer 10:19 but I said, Truly this is a *g*
Jer 45:3 LORD hath added *g* to my sorrow
Lam 3:32 But though he cause *g*, yet will
Jonah 4:6 head, to deliver him from his *g*
2Cor 2:5 But if any have caused *g*, he hath
Heb 13:17 may do it with joy, and not with *g*
1Pet 2:19 conscience toward God endure *g*

## GRIEVE

1Sa 2:33 thine eyes, and to *g* thine heart
1Chr 4:10 from evil, that it may not *g* me
Ps 78:40 and *g* him in the desert
Lam 3:33 nor *g* the children of men
Eph 4:30 *g* not the holy Spirit of God,

## GRIEVED

Gen 6:6 earth, and it *g* him at his heart
Gen 34:7 and the men were *g*, and they were
Gen 45:5 Now therefore be not *g*, nor angry
Gen 49:23 The archers have sorely *g* him
Ex 1:12 they were *g* because of the
Deut 15:10 thine heart shall not be *g* when
Judg 10:16 his soul was *g* for the misery of
1Sa 1:8 and why is thy heart *g*
1Sa 15:11 And it *g* Samuel
1Sa 20:3 Jonathan know this, lest he be *g*
1Sa 20:34 for he was *g* for David, because
1Sa 30:6 the soul of all the people was *g*
2Sa 19:2 how the king was *g* for his son
Neh 2:10 it *g* them exceedingly that there
Neh 8:11 neither be ye *g*
Neh 13:8 And it *g* me sore
Est 4:4 Then was the queen exceedingly *g*
Job 4:2 commune with thee, wilt thou be *g*
Job 30:25 was not my soul *g* for the poor
Ps 73:21 Thus my heart was *g*, and I was
Ps 95:10 long was I *g* with this generation
Ps 112:10 The wicked shall see it, and be *g*
Ps 119:158 the transgressors, and was *g*
Ps 139:21 am not I *g* with those that rise
Is 54:6 *g* in spirit, and a wife of youth,
Is 57:10 therefore thou wast not *g*
Jer 5:3 them, but they have not *g*
Dan 7:15 I Daniel was *g* in my spirit in
Dan 11:30 therefore he shall be *g*, and
Amos 6:6 but they are not *g* for the
Mk 3:5 being *g* for the hardness of their
Mk 10:22 at that saying, and went away *g*
Jn 21:17 Peter was *g* because he said unto
Acts 4:2 Being *g* that they taught the
Acts 16:18 But Paul, being *g*, turned and said
Rom 14:15 if thy brother be *g* with thy meat
2Cor 2:4 not that ye should be *g*, but that
2Cor 2:5 caused grief, he hath not *g* me
Heb 3:10 Wherefore I was *g* with that
Heb 3:17 with whom was he *g* forty years

## GRIEVOUS

Gen 12:10 for the famine was *g* in the land
Gen 18:20 and because their sin is very *g*
Gen 21:11 the thing was very *g* in Abraham's
Gen 21:12 Let it not be *g* in thy sight
Gen 41:31 for it shall be very *g*
Gen 50:11 This is a *g* mourning to the
Ex 8:24 there came a *g* swarm of flies
Ex 9:3 there shall be a very *g* murrain
Ex 9:18 cause it to rain a very *g* hail
Ex 9:24 mingled with the hail, very *g*
Ex 10:14 very *g* were they
1Kin 2:8 which cursed me with a *g* curse in
1Kin 12:4 Thy father made our yoke *g*
1Kin 12:4 thou the *g* service of thy father
2Chr 10:4 Thy father made our yoke *g*
2Chr 10:4 ease thou somewhat the *g*
Ps 10:5 His ways are always *g*
Ps 31:18 which speak *g* things proudly and
Prov 15:1 but *g* words stir up anger
Prov 15:10 Correction is *g* unto him that
Eccl 2:17 under the sun is *g* unto me
Is 15:4 his life shall be *g* unto him
Is 21:2 A *g* vision is declared unto me
Jer 6:28 They are all *g* revolters, walking
Jer 10:19 my wound is *g*
Jer 14:17 great breach, with a very *g* blow
Jer 16:4 They shall die of *g* deaths
Jer 23:19 forth in fury, even a *g* whirlwind
Jer 30:12 is incurable, and thy wound is *g*
Nah 3:19 thy wound is *g*
Mt 23:4 *g* to be borne, and lay them on
Lk 11:46 men with burdens *g* to be borne
Acts 20:29 shall *g* wolves enter in among you
Acts 25:7 *g* complaints against Paul, which
Phil 3:1 to you, to me indeed is not *g*
Heb 12:11 seemeth to be joyous, but *g*
1Jn 5:3 and his commandments are not *g*
Rev 16:2 *g* sore upon the men which had the

## GRIEVOUSLY

Is 9:1 afterward did more *g* afflict her
Jer 23:19 it shall fall *g* upon the head of
Lam 1:8 Jerusalem hath *g* sinned
Lam 1:20 for I have *g* rebelled
Eze 14:13 against me by trespassing *g*
Mt 8:6 sick of the palsy, *g* tormented
Mt 15:22 my daughter is *g* vexed with a

## GRIND

Judg 16:21 he did *g* in the prison house
Job 31:10 Then let my wife *g* unto another
Is 3:15 and *g* the faces of the poor
Is 47:2 Take the millstones, and *g* meal
Lam 5:13 They took the young men to *g*
Mt 21:44 fall, it will *g* him to powder
Lk 20:18 fall, it will *g* him to powder

## GRISLED

Gen 31:10 were ringstraked, speckled, and *g*
Gen 31:12 are ringstraked, speckled, and *g*
Zec 6:3 and in the fourth chariot *g*
Zec 6:6 the *g* go forth toward the south

## GROAN

Job 24:12 Men *g* from out of the city, and
Jer 51:52 all her land the wounded shall *g*
Eze 30:24 he shall *g* before him with the
Joel 1:18 How do the beasts *g*
Rom 8:23 we ourselves *g* within ourselves
2Cor 5:2 For in this we *g*, earnestly
2Cor 5:4 that are in this tabernacle do *g*

## GROANING

Ex 2:24 And God heard their *g*, and God
Ex 6:5 I have also heard the *g* of the
Job 23:2 my stroke is heavier than my *g*
Ps 6:6 I am weary with my *g*
Ps 38:9 my *g* is not hid from thee
Ps 102:5 my *g* my bones cleave to my skin
Ps 102:20 To hear the *g* of the prisoner
Jn 11:38 Jesus therefore again *g* in
Acts 7:34 in Egypt, and I have heard their *g*

## GROANINGS

Judg 2:18 of their *g* by reason of them that
Eze 30:24 the *g* of a deadly wounded man
Rom 8:26 us with *g* which cannot be uttered

## GROPE

Deut 28:29 And thou shalt *g* at noonday
Job 5:14 *g* in the noonday as in the night
Job 12:25 They *g* in the dark without light,
Is 59:10 We *g* for the wall like the blind,
Is 59:10 we *g* as if we had no eyes

## GROSS

Is 60:2 earth, and *g* darkness the people
Jer 13:16 of death, and make it *g* darkness
Mt 13:15 this people's heart is waxed *g*
Acts 28:27 heart of this people is waxed *g*

## GROUND

Gen 2:5 there was not a man to till the *g*
Gen 2:6 watered the whole face of the *g*
Gen 2:7 formed man of the dust of the *g*
Gen 2:9 out of the *g* made the LORD God to
Gen 2:19 out of the *g* the LORD God formed
Gen 3:17 cursed is the *g* for thy sake
Gen 3:19 till thou return unto the *g*
Gen 3:23 to till the *g* from whence he was
Gen 4:2 but Cain was a tiller of the *g*
Gen 4:3 the *g* an offering unto the LORD
Gen 4:10 blood crieth unto me from the *g*
Gen 4:12 When thou tillest the *g*, it shall
Gen 5:29 because of the *g* which the LORD
Gen 7:23 which was upon the face of the *g*
Gen 8:8 abated from off the face of the *g*
Gen 8:13 behold, the face of the *g* was dry
Gen 8:21 the *g* any more for man's sake
Gen 18:2 and bowed himself toward the *g*
Gen 19:1 with his face toward the *g*
Gen 19:25 and that which grew upon the *g*
Gen 33:3 himself to the *g* seven times
Gen 38:9 wife, that he spilled it on the *g*
Gen 44:11 down every man his sack to the *g*
Gen 44:14 and they fell before him on the *g*
Ex 3:5 whereon thou standest is holy *g*
Ex 4:3 And he said, Cast it on the *g*
Ex 4:3 And he cast it on the *g*, and it
Ex 8:21 also the *g* whereon they are
Ex 9:23 and the fire ran along upon the *g*
Ex 14:16 of Israel shall go on dry *g*
Ex 14:22 midst of the sea upon the dry *g*
Ex 16:14 small as the hoar frost on the *g*
Ex 32:20 *g* it to powder, and strawed it
Lev 20:25 thing that creepeth on the *g*
Num 11:8 *g* it in mills, or beat it in a
Num 16:31 that the *g* clave asunder that was
Deut 4:18 any thing that creepeth on the *g*
Deut 9:21 *g* it very small, even until it
Deut 15:23 shalt pour it upon the *g* as water
Deut 22:6 the way in any tree, or on the *g*
Deut 28:4 thy body, and the fruit of thy *g*
Deut 28:11 cattle, and in the fruit of thy *g*
Deut 28:56 foot upon the *g* for delicateness
Josh 3:17 on dry *g* in the midst of Jordan
Josh 3:17 Israelites passed over on dry *g*
Josh 24:32 in a parcel of *g* which Jacob
Judg 4:21 and fastened it into the *g*
Judg 6:39 upon all the *g* let there be dew
Judg 6:40 and there was dew on all the *g*
Judg 13:20 and fell on their faces to the *g*
Judg 20:21 destroyed down to the *g* of the
Judg 20:25 destroyed down to the *g* of the
Ruth 2:10 face, and bowed herself to the *g*
1Sa 3:19 none of his words fall to the *g*
1Sa 5:4 the *g* before the ark of the LORD
1Sa 8:12 and will set them to ear his *g*
1Sa 14:25 and there was honey upon the *g*
1Sa 14:32 and calves, and slew them on the *g*
1Sa 14:45 hair of his head fall to the *g*
1Sa 20:31 son of Jesse liveth upon the *g*
1Sa 20:41 and fell on his face to the *g*
1Sa 25:23 face, and bowed herself to the *g*

| | |
|---|---|
| 1Sa 26:7 | stuck in the *g* at his bolster |
| 1Sa 28:14 | he stooped with his face to the *g* |
| 2Sa 2:22 | should I smite thee to the *g* |
| 2Sa 8:2 | line, casting them down to the *g* |
| 2Sa 14:4 | she fell on her face to the *g* |
| 2Sa 14:14 | and are as water spilt on the *g* |
| 2Sa 14:22 | And Joab fell to the *g* on his face |
| 2Sa 14:33 | his face to the *g* before the king |
| 2Sa 17:12 | him as the dew falleth on the *g* |
| 2Sa 17:19 | mouth, and spread *g* corn thereon |
| 2Sa 18:11 | thou not smite him there to the *g* |
| 2Sa 20:10 | and shed out his bowels to the *g* |
| 2Sa 23:11 | was a piece of *g* full of lentiles |
| 2Sa 23:12 | he stood in the midst of the *g* |
| 2Sa 24:20 | the king on his face upon the *g* |
| 1Kin 1:23 | the king with his face to the *g* |
| 1Kin 7:46 | in the clay *g* between Succoth and |
| 2Kin 2:8 | that they two went over on dry *g* |
| 2Kin 2:15 | themselves to the *g* before him |
| 2Kin 2:19 | water is naught, and the *g* barren |
| 2Kin 4:37 | feet, and bowed herself to the *g* |
| 2Kin 9:26 | and cast him into the plat of *g* |
| 2Kin 13:18 | king of Israel, Smite upon the *g* |
| 1Chr 11:13 | was a parcel of *g* full of barley |
| 1Chr 21:21 | to David with his face to the *g* |
| 1Chr 27:26 | the *g* was Ezri the son of Chelub |
| 2Chr 4:17 | in the clay *g* between Succoth and |
| 2Chr 7:3 | faces to the *g* upon the pavement |
| 2Chr 20:18 | his head with his face to the *g* |
| Neh 8:6 | LORD with their faces to the *g* |
| Neh 10:35 | to bring the firstfruits of our *g* |
| Neh 10:37 | tithes of our *g* unto the Levites |
| Job 1:20 | his head, and fell down upon the *g* |
| Job 2:13 | with him upon the *g* seven days |
| Job 5:6 | doth trouble spring out of the *g* |
| Job 14:8 | and the stock thereof die in the *g* |
| Job 16:13 | he poureth out my gall upon the *g* |
| Job 18:10 | snare is laid for him in the *g* |
| Job 38:27 | satisfy the desolate and waste *g* |
| Job 39:24 | swalloweth the *g* with fierceness |
| Ps 74:7 | place of thy name to the *g* |
| Ps 89:39 | his crown by casting it to the *g* |
| Ps 89:44 | and cast his throne down to the *g* |
| Ps 105:35 | and devoured the fruit of their *g* |
| Ps 107:33 | and the watersprings into dry *g* |
| Ps 107:35 | water, and dry *g* into watersprings |
| Ps 143:3 | smitten my life down to the *g* |
| Ps 147:6 | casteth the wicked down to the *g* |
| Is 3:26 | desolate shall sit upon the *g* |
| Is 14:12 | how art thou cut down to the *g* |
| Is 21:9 | gods he hath broken unto the *g* |
| Is 25:12 | down, lay low, and bring to the *g* |
| Is 26:5 | he layeth it low, even to the *g* |
| Is 28:24 | open and break the clods of his *g* |
| Is 29:4 | down, and shalt speak out of the *g* |
| Is 29:4 | a familiar spirit, out of the *g* |
| Is 30:23 | that thou shalt sow the *g* withal |
| Is 30:24 | the *g* shall eat clean provender |
| Is 35:7 | the parched *g* shall become a pool |
| Is 44:3 | thirsty, and floods upon the dry *g* |
| Is 47:1 | daughter of Babylon, sit on the *g* |
| Is 51:23 | thou hast laid thy body as the *g* |
| Is 53:2 | and as a root out of a dry *g* |
| Jer 4:3 | Jerusalem, Break up your fallow *g* |
| Jer 7:20 | field, and upon the fruit of the *g* |
| Jer 14:2 | they are black unto the *g* |
| Jer 14:4 | Because the *g* is chapt, for there |
| Jer 25:33 | they shall be dung upon the *g* |
| Jer 27:5 | and the beast that are upon the *g* |
| Lam 2:2 | hath brought them down to the *g* |
| Lam 2:9 | Her gates are sunk into the *g* |
| Lam 2:10 | daughter of Zion sit upon the *g* |
| Lam 2:10 | hang down their heads to the *g* |
| Lam 2:21 | old lie on the *g* in the streets |
| Eze 12:6 | thy face, that thou see not the *g* |
| Eze 12:12 | he see not the *g* with his eyes |
| Eze 13:14 | morter, and bring it down to the *g* |
| Eze 19:12 | fury, she was cast down to the *g* |
| Eze 19:13 | wilderness, in a dry and thirsty *g* |
| Eze 24:7 | she poured it not upon the *g* |
| Eze 26:11 | garrisons shall go down to the *g* |
| Eze 26:16 | they shall sit upon the *g* |
| Eze 28:17 | I will cast thee to the *g* |
| Eze 38:20 | and every wall shall fall to the *g* |
| Eze 41:16 | from the *g* up to the windows, and |
| Eze 41:20 | From the *g* unto above the door |
| Eze 42:6 | and the middlemost from the *g* |
| Eze 43:14 | from the bottom upon the *g* even |
| Dan 8:5 | whole earth, and touched not the *g* |
| Dan 8:7 | but he cast him down to the *g* |
| Dan 8:10 | the host and of the stars to the *g* |
| Dan 8:12 | it cast down the truth to the *g* |
| Dan 8:18 | sleep on my face toward the *g* |
| Dan 10:9 | my face, and my face toward the *g* |
| Dan 10:15 | me, I set my face toward the *g* |
| Hos 2:18 | with the creeping things of the *g* |
| Hos 10:12 | break up your fallow *g* |
| Amos 3:14 | be cut off, and fall to the *g* |
| Obad 3 | Who shall bring me down to the *g* |
| Hag 1:11 | that which the *g* bringeth forth |
| Zec 8:12 | the *g* shall give her increase, and |
| Mal 3:11 | not destroy the fruits of your *g* |
| Mt 10:29 | fall on the *g* without your Father |
| Mt 13:8 | But other fell into good *g* |
| Mt 13:23 | *g* is he that heareth the word |
| Mt 15:35 | multitude to sit down on the *g* |
| Mk 4:5 | And some fell on stony *g*, where it |
| Mk 4:8 | And other fell on good *g*, and did |
| Mk 4:16 | which are sown on stony *g* |
| Mk 4:20 | are they which are sown on good *g* |
| Mk 4:26 | a man should cast seed into the *g* |
| Mk 8:6 | the people to sit down on the *g* |
| Mk 9:20 | and he fell on the *g*, and wallowed |
| Mk 14:35 | a little, and fell on the *g* |
| Lk 8:8 | And other fell on good *g*, and |
| Lk 8:15 | But that on the good *g* are they |
| Lk 12:16 | The *g* of a certain rich man |
| Lk 13:7 | why cumbereth it the *g* |
| Lk 14:18 | him, I have bought a piece of *g* |
| Lk 19:44 | And shall lay thee even with the *g* |
| Lk 22:44 | of blood falling down to the *g* |
| Jn 4:5 | near to the parcel of *g* that |
| Jn 8:6 | and with his finger wrote on the *g* |
| Jn 8:8 | stooped down, and wrote on the *g* |
| Jn 9:6 | had thus spoken, he spat on the *g* |
| Jn 12:24 | a corn of wheat fall into the *g* |
| Jn 18:6 | went backward, and fell to the *g* |
| Acts 7:33 | where thou standest is holy *g* |
| Acts 22:7 | And I fell unto the *g*, and heard a |
| 1Ti 3:15 | God, the pillar and *g* of the truth |

**GROVE**

| | |
|---|---|
| Gen 21:33 | Abraham planted a *g* in Beer-sheba |
| Deut 16:21 | a *g* of any trees near unto the |
| Judg 6:25 | cut down the *g* that is by it |
| Judg 6:26 | the *g* which thou shalt cut down |
| Judg 6:28 | the *g* was cut down that was by it |
| Judg 6:30 | cut down the *g* that was by it |
| 1Kin 15:13 | she had made an idol in a *g* |
| 1Kin 16:33 | And Ahab made a *g* |
| 2Kin 13:6 | remained the *g* also in Samaria |
| 2Kin 17:16 | even two calves, and made a *g* |
| 2Kin 21:3 | up altars for Baal, and made a *g* |
| 2Kin 21:7 | he set a graven image of the *g* |
| 2Kin 23:4 | were made for Baal, and for the *g* |
| 2Kin 23:6 | he brought out the *g* from the |
| 2Kin 23:7 | the women wove hangings for the *g* |
| 2Kin 23:15 | small to powder, and burned the *g* |
| 2Chr 15:16 | she had made an idol in a *g* |

**GROVES**

| | |
|---|---|
| Ex 34:13 | their images, and cut down their *g* |
| Deut 7:5 | their images, and cut down their *g* |
| Deut 12:3 | and burn their *g* with fire |
| Judg 3:7 | God, and served Baalim and the *g* |
| 1Kin 14:15 | because they have made their *g* |
| 1Kin 14:23 | them high places, and images, and *g* |
| 1Kin 18:19 | prophets of the *g* four hundred |
| 2Kin 17:10 | *g* in every high hill, and under |
| 2Kin 18:4 | the images, and cut down the *g* |
| 2Kin 23:14 | the images, and cut down the *g* |
| 2Chr 14:3 | the images, and cut down the *g* |
| 2Chr 17:6 | the high places and *g* out of Judah |
| 2Chr 19:3 | taken away the *g* out of the land |
| 2Chr 24:18 | God of their fathers, and served *g* |
| 2Chr 31:1 | in pieces, and cut down the *g* |
| 2Chr 33:3 | up altars for Baalim, and made *g* |
| 2Chr 33:19 | he built high places, and set up *g* |
| 2Chr 34:3 | from the high places, and the *g* |
| 2Chr 34:4 | and the *g*, and the carved images, |
| 2Chr 34:7 | broken down the altars and the *g* |
| Is 17:8 | fingers have made, either the *g* |
| Is 27:9 | that are beaten in sunder, the *g* |
| Jer 17:2 | their *g* by the green trees upon |
| Mic 5:14 | I will pluck up thy *g* out of the |

**GROW**

| | |
|---|---|
| Gen 2:9 | *g* every tree that is pleasant to |
| Gen 48:16 | let them *g* into a multitude in |
| Num 6:5 | locks of the hair of his head *g* |
| Judg 16:22 | to *g* again after he was shaven |
| 2Sa 23:5 | although he make it not to *g* |
| 2Kin 19:29 | such things as *g* of themselves |
| Ezr 4:22 | why should damage *g* to the hurt |
| Job 8:11 | Can the rush *g* up without mire |
| Job 8:11 | can the flag *g* without water |
| Job 8:19 | out of the earth shall others *g* |
| Job 14:19 | *g* out of the dust of the earth |
| Job 31:40 | Let thistles *g* instead of wheat, |
| Job 39:4 | good liking, they *g* up with corn |
| Ps 92:12 | he shall *g* like a cedar in |
| Ps 104:14 | the grass to *g* for the cattle |
| Ps 147:8 | grass to *g* upon the mountains |
| Eccl 11:5 | nor how the bones do *g* in the |
| Is 11:1 | a Branch shall *g* out of his roots |
| Is 17:11 | shalt thou make thy plant to *g* |
| Is 53:2 | For he shall *g* up before him as a |
| Jer 12:2 | they *g*, yea, they bring forth |
| Jer 33:15 | righteousness to *g* up unto David |
| Eze 44:20 | nor suffer their locks to *g* long |
| Eze 47:12 | shall *g* all trees for meat, whose |
| Hos 14:5 | he shall *g* as the lily, and cast |
| Hos 14:7 | as the corn, and *g* as the vine |
| Jonah 4:10 | not laboured, neither madest it *g* |
| Zec 6:12 | he shall *g* up out of his place, |
| Mal 4:2 | *g* up as calves of the stall |
| Mt 6:28 | lilies of the field, how they *g* |
| Mt 13:30 | Let both *g* together until the |
| Mt 21:19 | unto it, Let no fruit *g* on thee |
| Mk 4:27 | and *g* up, he knoweth not how |
| Lk 12:27 | Consider the lilies how they *g* |
| Acts 5:24 | of them whereunto this would *g* |
| Eph 4:15 | may *g* up into him in all things, |
| 1Pet 2:2 | the word, that ye may *g* thereby |
| 2Pet 3:18 | But *g* in grace, and in the |

**GROWETH**

| | |
|---|---|
| Ex 10:5 | which *g* for you out of the field |
| Lev 13:39 | freckled spot that *g* in the skin |
| Lev 25:5 | That which *g* of its own accord of |
| Lev 25:11 | reap that which *g* of itself in it |
| Deut 29:23 | beareth, nor any grass *g* therein |
| Judg 19:9 | the day *g* to an end, lodge here, |
| Job 38:38 | When the dust *g* into hardness |
| Ps 90:5 | they are like grass which *g* up |
| Ps 90:6 | morning it flourisheth, and *g* up |
| Ps 129:6 | which withereth afore it *g* up |
| Is 37:30 | eat this year such as *g* of itself |
| Mk 4:32 | But when it is sown, it *g* up |
| Eph 2:21 | building fitly framed together *g* |
| 2Th 1:3 | that your faith *g* exceedingly |

**GROWN**

| | |
|---|---|
| Gen 38:11 | house, till Shelah my son be *g* |
| Gen 38:14 | for she saw that Shelah was *g* |
| Ex 2:11 | in those days, when Moses was *g* |
| Ex 9:32 | for they were not *g* up |
| Lev 13:37 | there is black hair *g* up therein |
| Deut 32:15 | art waxen fat, thou art *g* thick |
| Ruth 1:13 | tarry for them till they were *g* |
| 2Sa 10:5 | at Jericho until your beards be *g* |
| 1Kin 12:8 | young men that were *g* up with him |
| 1Kin 12:10 | the young men that were *g* up with |
| 2Kin 4:18 | And when the child was *g*, it fell |
| 2Kin 19:26 | as corn blasted before it be *g* up |
| 1Chr 19:5 | at Jericho until your beards be *g* |
| Ezr 9:6 | our trespass is *g* up unto the |
| Ps 144:12 | be as plants *g* up in their youth |
| Prov 24:31 | it was all *g* over with thorns, and |
| Is 37:27 | as corn blasted before it be *g* up |
| Jer 50:11 | because ye are *g* fat as the |
| Eze 16:7 | are fashioned, and thine hair is *g* |
| Dan 4:22 | It is thou, O king, that art *g* |
| Dan 4:22 | for thy greatness is *g*, and |
| Dan 4:33 | till his hairs were *g* like |
| Mt 13:32 | but when it is *g*, it is the |

**GUARD**

| | |
|---|---|
| Gen 37:36 | of Pharaoh's, and captain of the *g* |
| Gen 39:1 | of Pharaoh, captain of the *g* |
| Gen 40:3 | the house of the captain of the *g* |
| Gen 40:4 | the captain of the *g* charged |
| Gen 41:12 | servant to the captain of the *g* |
| 2Sa 23:23 | And David set him over his *g* |
| 1Kin 14:27 | the hands of the chief of the *g* |
| 1Kin 14:28 | that the *g* bare them, and brought |
| 1Kin 14:28 | them back into the *g* chamber |
| 2Kin 10:25 | offering, that Jehu said to the *g* |
| 2Kin 10:25 | and the *g* and the captains cast |
| 2Kin 11:4 | with the captains and the *g* |
| 2Kin 11:6 | part at the gate behind the *g* |
| 2Kin 11:11 | the *g* stood, every man with his |
| 2Kin 11:13 | Athaliah heard the noise of the *g* |
| 2Kin 11:19 | and the captains, and the *g* |

2Kin 11:19 gate of the *g* to the king's house
2Kin 25:8 Nebuzar-adan, captain of the *g*
2Kin 25:10 were with the captain of the *g*
2Kin 25:11 the captain of the *g* carry away
2Kin 25:12 But the captain of the *g* left of
2Kin 25:15 the captain of the *g* took away
2Kin 25:18 the captain of the *g* took Seraiah
2Kin 25:20 captain of the *g* took these
1Chr 11:25 and David set him over his *g*
2Chr 12:10 the hands of the chief of the *g*
2Chr 12:11 the *g* came and fetched them, and
2Chr 12:11 them again into the *g* chamber
Neh 4:22 the night they may be a *g* to us
Neh 4:23 men of the *g* which followed me
Jer 39:9 the *g* carried away captive into
Jer 39:10 *g* left of the poor of the people
Jer 39:11 Nebuzar-adan the captain of the *g*
Jer 39:13 the captain of the *g* sent
Jer 40:1 the *g* had let him go from Ramah
Jer 40:2 captain of the *g* took Jeremiah
Jer 40:5 of the *g* gave him victuals
Jer 41:10 *g* had committed to Gedaliah the
Jer 43:6 *g* had left with Gedaliah the son
Jer 52:12 Nebuzar-adan, captain of the *g*
Jer 52:14 were with the captain of the *g*
Jer 52:15 *g* carried away captive certain of
Jer 52:16 *g* left certain of the poor of the
Jer 52:19 took the captain of the *g* away
Jer 52:24 the captain of the *g* took Seraiah
Jer 52:26 the captain of the *g* took them
Jer 52:30 the *g* carried away captive of the
Eze 38:7 thee, and be thou a *g* unto them
Dan 2:14 the captain of the king's *g*
Acts 28:16 prisoners to the captain of the *g*

**GUDGODAH** *(gud-go'-dah)* See HOR-HAGIDGAD. *A wilderness encampment of Israel.*
Deut 10:7 From thence they journeyed unto G
Deut 10:7 from G to Jotbath, a land of

**GUESTS**
1Kin 1:41 all the *g* that were with him
1Kin 1:49 all the *g* that were with Adonijah
Prov 9:18 that her *g* are in the depths of
Zeph 1:7 a sacrifice, he hath bid his *g*
Mt 22:10 the wedding was furnished with *g*
Mt 22:11 the king came in to see the *g*

**GUIDE**
Job 38:32 or canst thou *g* Arcturus with his
Ps 25:9 The meek will he *g* in judgment
Ps 31:3 thy name's sake lead me, and *g* me
Ps 32:8 I will *g* thee with mine eye
Ps 48:14 he will be our *g* even unto death
Ps 55:13 was thou, a man mine equal, my *g*
Ps 73:24 Thou shalt *g* me with thy counsel,
Ps 112:5 he will *g* his affairs with
Prov 2:17 forsaketh the *g* of her youth
Prov 6:7 Which having no *g*, overseer, or
Prov 11:3 of the upright shall *g* them
Prov 23:19 wise, and *g* thine heart in the way
Is 49:10 springs of water shall he *g* them
Is 51:18 There is none to *g* her among all
Is 58:11 the LORD shall *g* thee continually
Jer 3:4 thou art the *g* of my youth
Mic 7:5 put ye not confidence in a *g*
Lk 1:79 to *g* our feet into the way of
Jn 16:13 he will *g* you into all truth
Acts 1:16 which was *g* to them that took
Acts 8:31 I, except some man should *g* me
Rom 2:19 thou thyself art a *g* of the blind
1Ti 5:14 *g* the house, give none occasion

**GUIDED**
Ex 15:13 thou hast *g* them in thy strength
2Chr 32:22 other, and *g* them on every side
Job 31:18 I have *g* her from my mother's
Ps 78:52 *g* them in the wilderness like a
Ps 78:72 *g* them by the skilfulness of his

**GUILE**
Ex 21:14 his neighbour, to slay him with *g*
Ps 32:2 and in whose spirit there is no *g*
Ps 34:13 evil, and thy lips from speaking *g*
Ps 55:11 *g* depart not from her streets
Jn 1:47 Israelite indeed, in whom is no *g*
2Cor 12:16 being crafty, I caught you with *g*
1Th 2:3 nor of uncleanness, nor in *g*
1Pet 2:1 laying aside all malice, and all *g*
1Pet 2:22 neither was *g* found in his mouth
1Pet 3:10 and his lips that they speak no *g*
Rev 14:5 And in their mouth was found no *g*

**GUILTLESS**
Ex 20:7 *g* that taketh his name in vain
Num 5:31 shall the man be *g* from iniquity
Num 32:22 be *g* before the LORD, and before
Deut 5:11 *g* that taketh his name in vain
Josh 2:19 be upon his head, and we will be *g*
1Sa 26:9 the LORD's anointed, and be *g*
2Sa 3:28 my kingdom are *g* before the LORD
2Sa 14:9 and the king and his throne be *g*
1Kin 2:9 Now therefore hold him not *g*
Mt 12:7 ye would not have condemned the *g*

**GUILTY**
Gen 42:21 We are verily *g* concerning our
Ex 34:7 that will by no means clear the *g*
Lev 4:13 should not be done, and are *g*
Lev 4:22 which should not be done, and is *g*
Lev 4:27 ought not to be done, and be *g*
Lev 5:2 he also shall be unclean, and *g*
Lev 5:3 knoweth of it, then he shall be *g*
Lev 5:4 he shall be *g* in one of these
Lev 5:5 when he shall be *g* in one of
Lev 5:17 he wist it not, yet is he *g*
Lev 6:4 because he hath sinned, and is *g*
Num 5:6 the LORD, and that person be *g*
Num 14:18 and by no means clearing the *g*
Num 35:27 he shall not be *g* of blood
Num 35:31 a murderer, which is *g* of death
Judg 21:22 at this time, that ye should be *g*
Ezr 10:19 and being *g*, they offered a ram of
Prov 30:10 he curse thee, and thou be found *g*
Eze 22:4 Thou art become *g* in thy blood
Zec 11:5 them, and hold themselves not *g*
Mt 23:18 the gift that is upon it, he is *g*
Mt 26:66 and said, He is *g* of death
Mk 14:64 condemned him to be *g* of death
Rom 3:19 the world may become *g* before God
1Cor 11:27 shall be *g* of the body and blood
Jas 2:10 in one point, he is *g* of all

**GUNI** *(gu'-ni)* See GUNITES.
*1. A son of Naphtali.*
Gen 46:24 Jahzeel, and G, and Jezer, and
Num 26:48 of G, the family of the Gunites
1Chr 7:13 Jahziel, and G, and Jezer, and
*2. Father of Abdiel.*
1Chr 5:15 the son of Abdiel, the son of G

**GUNITES** *(gu'-nites) Descendants of Guni 1.*
Num 26:48 of Guni, the family of the G

**GUR** *(gur)* See GUR-BAAL. *A hill near Ibleam.*
2Kin 9:27 they did so at the going up to G

**GUR-BAAL** *(gur-ba'-al) Place in western Arabia.*
2Chr 26:7 the Arabians that dwelt in G

**GUSHED**
1Kin 18:28 till the blood *g* out upon them
Ps 78:20 the rock, that the waters *g* out
Ps 105:41 the rock, and the waters *g* out
Is 48:21 rock also, and the waters *g* out
Acts 1:18 midst, and all his bowels *g* out

# H

**HAAHASHTARI** *(ha-a-hash'-te-ri) A son of Naarah.*
1Chr 4:6 and Hepher, and Temeni, and *H*

**HABAIAH** *(hab-ah'-yah) A family of exiles.*
Ezr 2:61 the children of H, the children
Neh 7:63 the children of H, the children

**HABAKKUK** *(hab'-ak-kuk) A prophet of Judah.*
Hab 1:1 The burden which *H* the prophet
Hab 3:1 A prayer of *H* the prophet upon

**HABAZINIAH** *(hab-az-in-i'-ah) Head of a Rechabite family.*
Jer 35:3 the son of Jeremiah, the son of *H*

**HABITATION**
Ex 15:2 God, and I will prepare him an *h*
Ex 15:13 in thy strength unto thy holy *h*
Lev 13:46 without the camp shall his *h* be
Deut 12:5 even unto his *h* shall ye seek
Deut 26:15 Look down from thy holy *h*
1Sa 2:29 which I have commanded in my *h*
1Sa 2:32 thou shalt see an enemy in my *h*
2Sa 15:25 and shew me both it, and his *h*
2Chr 6:2 have built an house of *h* for thee
2Chr 29:6 faces from the *h* of the LORD
Ezr 7:15 Israel, whose *h* is in Jerusalem,
Job 5:3 but suddenly I cursed his *h*
Job 5:24 and thou shalt visit thy *h*
Job 8:6 make the *h* of thy righteousness
Job 18:15 shall be scattered upon his *h*
Ps 26:8 I have loved the *h* of thy house
Ps 33:14 From the place of his *h* he
Ps 68:5 the widows, is God in his holy *h*
Ps 69:25 Let their *h* be desolate
Ps 71:3 Be thou my strong *h*, whereunto I
Ps 89:14 judgment are the *h* of thy throne
Ps 91:9 refuge, even the most High, thy *h*
Ps 97:2 judgment are the *h* of his throne
Ps 104:12 fowls of the heaven have their *h*
Ps 107:7 that they might go to a city of *h*
Ps 107:36 they may prepare a city for *h*
Ps 132:5 an *h* for the mighty God of Jacob
Ps 132:13 he hath desired it for his *h*
Prov 3:33 but he blesseth the *h* of the just
Is 22:16 that graveth an *h* for himself in
Is 27:10 the *h* forsaken, and left like a
Is 32:18 shall dwell in a peaceable *h*
Is 33:20 shall see Jerusalem a quiet *h*
Is 34:13 and it shall be an *h* of dragons
Is 35:7 in the *h* of dragons, where each
Is 63:15 behold from the *h* of thy holiness
Jer 9:6 Thine *h* is in the midst of deceit
Jer 10:25 him, and have made his *h* desolate
Jer 25:30 utter his voice from his holy *h*
Jer 25:30 he shall mightily roar upon his *h*
Jer 31:23 O *h* of justice, and mountain of
Jer 33:12 shall be an *h* of shepherds
Jer 41:17 and dwelt in the *h* of Chimham
Jer 49:19 against the *h* of the strong
Jer 50:7 the *h* of justice, even the LORD,
Jer 50:19 will bring Israel again to his *h*
Jer 50:44 Jordan unto the *h* of the strong
Jer 50:45 make their *h* desolate with them
Eze 29:14 Pathros, into the land of their *h*
Dan 4:21 fowls of the heaven had their *h*
Obad 3 of the rock, whose *h* is high
Hab 3:11 and moon stood still in their *h*
Zec 2:13 he is raised up out of his holy *h*
Acts 1:20 Let his *h* be desolate, and let no
Acts 17:26 and the bounds of their *h*
Eph 2:22 an *h* of God through the Spirit
Jude 6 estate, but left their own *h*
Rev 18:2 and is become the *h* of devils

**HABITATIONS**
Gen 36:43 according to their *h* in the land
Gen 49:5 of cruelty are in their *h*
Ex 12:20 in all your *h* shall ye eat
Ex 35:3 your *h* upon the sabbath day
Lev 23:17 Ye shall bring out of your *h* two
Num 15:2 be come into the land of your *h*
1Chr 4:33 These were their *h*, and their
1Chr 4:41 the *h* that were found there, and
1Chr 7:28 *h* were, Beth-el and the towns

Ps 74:20 are full of the *h* of cruelty
Ps 78:28 their camp, round about their *h*
Is 54:2 forth the curtains of thine *h*
Jer 9:10 for the *h* of the wilderness a
Jer 21:13 or who shall enter into our *h*
Jer 25:37 the peaceable *h* are cut down
Jer 49:20 make their *h* desolate with them
Lam 2:2 swallowed up all the *h* of Jacob
Eze 6:14 toward Diblath, in all their *h*
Amos 1:2 the *h* of the shepherds shall
Lk 16:9 receive you into everlasting *h*

**HABOR** *(ha'-bor) A Mesopotamian district.*
2Kin 17:6 in *H* by the river of Gozan, and in
2Kin 18:11 in *H* by the river of Gozan, and in
1Chr 5:26 and brought them unto Halah, and *H*

**HACHALIAH** *(hak-a-li'-ah) Father of Nehemiah.*
Neh 1:1 words of Nehemiah the son of *H*
Neh 10:1 the Tirshatha, the son of *H*

**HACHILAH** *(hak'-i-lah) A hill in Judah.*
1Sa 23:19 in the wood, in the hill of *H*
1Sa 26:1 hide himself in the hill of *H*
1Sa 26:3 And Saul pitched in the hill of *H*

**HACHMONI** *(hak'-mo-ni)* See HACHMONITE. *Father of Jehiel.*
1Chr 27:32 Jehiel the son of *H* was with the

**HACHMONITE** *(hak'-mo-nite)* See TACHMONITE. *A descendant of Hachmoni.*
1Chr 11:11 Jashobeam, a *H*, the chief of the

**HADAD** *(ha'-dad)* See BEN-HADAD, HADADRIMMON, HADAR.
*1. A son of Bedad.*
Gen 36:35 *H* the son of Bedad, who smote
Gen 36:36 *H* died, and Samlah of Masrekah
1Chr 1:46 *H* the son of Bedad, which smote
1Chr 1:47 when *H* was dead, Samlah of
*2. A royal Edomite.*
1Kin 11:14 unto Solomon, *H* the Edomite
1Kin 11:17 That *H* fled, he and certain
1Kin 11:17 *H* being yet a little child
1Kin 11:19 *H* found great favour in the sight
1Kin 11:21 when *H* heard in Egypt that David
1Kin 11:21 *H* said to Pharaoh, Let me depart,
1Kin 11:25 beside the mischief that *H* did
*3. A son of Ishmael.*
1Chr 1:30 Mishma, and Dumah, Massa, *H*
*4. An early king of Edom.*
1Chr 1:50 was dead, *H* reigned in his stead
1Chr 1:51 *H* died also

**HADADEZER** *(had-a-de'-zer)* See HADAREZER. *King of Zobah.*
2Sa 8:3 David smote also *H*, the son of
2Sa 8:5 came to succour *H* king of Zobah
2Sa 8:7 that were on the servants of *H*
2Sa 8:8 and from Berothai, cities of *H*
2Sa 8:9 had smitten all the host of *H*
2Sa 8:10 because he had fought against *H*
2Sa 8:10 for *H* had wars with Toi
2Sa 8:12 of Amalek, and of the spoil of *H*
1Kin 11:23 from his lord *H* king of Zobah

**HADADRIMMON** *(ha'-dad-rim'-mon) A place in the valley of Megiddo.*
Zec 12:11 as the mourning of *H* in the

**HADAR** *(ha'-dar)* See HADAD.
*1. A son of Ishmael.*
Gen 25:15 *H*, and Tema, Jetur, Naphish, and
*2. An early king of Edom.*
Gen 36:39 died, and *H* reigned in his stead

**HADAREZER** *(had-a-re'-zer)* See HADADEZER. *Another name for Hadadezer.*
2Sa 10:16 *H* sent, and brought out the
2Sa 10:16 of the host of *H* went before them
2Sa 10:19 to *H* saw that they were smitten
1Chr 18:3 David smote *H* king of Zobah unto
1Chr 18:5 came to help *H* king of Zobah
1Chr 18:7 that were on the servants of *H*
1Chr 18:8 and from Chun, cities of *H*
1Chr 18:9 all the host of *H* king of Zobah
1Chr 18:10 because he had fought against *H*
1Chr 18:10 for *H* had war with Tou
1Chr 19:16 of the host of *H* went before them
1Chr 19:19 when the servants of *H* saw that

**HADASHAH** *(had'-a-shah) A town in Judah.*
Josh 15:37 Zenan, and *H*, and Migdal-gad,

**HADASSAH** *(ha-das'-sah)* See ESTHER. *Another name for Esther.*
Est 2:7 And he brought up *H*, that is,

**HADATTAH** *(ha-dat'-tah)* See HAZOR-=HADATTAH. *Another name for Hazor.*
Josh 15:25 And Hazor, *H*, and Kerioth, and

**HADID** *(ha'-did) A city in Benjamin.*
Ezr 2:33 The children of Lod, *H*, and Ono,
Neh 7:37 The children of Lod, *H*, and Ono,
Neh 11:34 *H*, Zeboim, Neballat,

**HADLAI** *(had'-la-i) Father of Amasa.*
2Chr 28:12 of Shallum, and Amasa the son of *H*

**HADORAM** *(ha-do'-ram)* See ADORAM.
*1. A son of Joktan.*
Gen 10:27 And *H*, and Uzal, and Diklah,
1Chr 1:21 *H* also, and Uzal, and Diklah,
*2. A son of Tou.*
1Chr 18:10 He sent *H* his son to king David,
*3. An officer of Rehoboam.*
2Chr 10:18 Then king Rehoboam sent *H* that

**HADRACH** *(ha'-drak) A district in Syria.*
Zec 9:1 word of the LORD in the land of *H*

**HADST**
Gen 30:30 little which thou *h* before I came
Gen 31:42 surely thou *h* sent me away now
Judg 15:2 that thou *h* utterly hated her
1Sa 25:34 thee, except thou *h* hasted
2Sa 2:27 God liveth, unless thou *h* spoken
2Kin 13:19 then *h* thou smitten Syria till
2Kin 13:19 Syria till thou *h* consumed it
Ezr 9:14 with us till thou *h* consumed us
Neh 9:15 which thou *h* sworn to give them
Neh 9:23 concerning which thou *h* promised
Ps 44:3 because thou *h* a favour unto them
Ps 60:10 thou, O God, which *h* cast us off
Ps 90:2 or ever thou *h* formed the earth
Is 26:15 thou *h* removed it far unto all
Is 48:18 O that thou *h* hearkened to my
Jer 3:3 thou *h* a whore's forehead, thou
Jonah 2:3 For thou *h* cast me into the deep,
Lk 19:42 Saying, If thou *h* known, even
Jn 11:21 if thou *h* been here, my brother
Jn 11:32 if thou *h* been here, my brother
1Cor 4:7 as if thou *h* not received it
Heb 10:8 neither *h* pleasure therein

**HAGAB** *(ha'-gab)* See HAGABA. *A family of exiles.*
Ezr 2:46 The children of *H*, the children

**HAGABA** *(hag'-a-bah) Same as Hagab.*
Neh 7:48 of Lebana, the children of *H*

**HAGABAH** *(hag'-a-bah)* See HAGABA. *Same as Hagab.*
Ezr 2:45 of Lebanah, the children of *H*

**HAGAR** *(ha'-gar) Sarah's handmaid.*
Gen 16:1 an Egyptian, whose name was *H*
Gen 16:3 wife took *H* her maid the Egyptian
Gen 16:4 And he went in unto *H*, and she
Gen 16:8 And he said, *H*, Sarai's maid,
Gen 16:15 And *H* bare Abram a son
Gen 16:15 his son's name, which *H* bare
Gen 16:16 when *H* bare Ishmael to Abram
Gen 21:9 saw the son of *H* the Egyptian
Gen 21:14 of water, and gave it unto *H*
Gen 21:17 of God called to *H* out of heaven
Gen 21:17 unto her, What aileth thee, *H*
Gen 25:12 whom *H* the Egyptian, Sarah's

**HAGARENES** *(hag-a-renes')* See HAGARITES. *A people east of the Jordan.*
Ps 83:6 of Moab, and the *H*

**HAGARITES** *(hag'-a-rites) Same as Hagarenes.*
1Chr 5:10 of Saul they made war with the *H*
1Chr 5:19 And they made war with the *H*
1Chr 5:20 the *H* were delivered into their

**HAGERITE** *(hag'-e-rite)* See HAGARITES, HAGGERI. *Family of David's herdsmen.*
1Chr 27:31 over the flocks was Jaziz the *H*

**HAGGAI** *(hag'-ga-i) A prophet.*
Ezr 5:1 *H* the prophet, and Zechariah the
Ezr 6:14 the prophesying of *H* the prophet
Hag 1:1 came the word of the LORD by *H*
Hag 1:3 word of the LORD by *H* the prophet
Hag 1:12 and the words of *H* the prophet
Hag 1:13 Then spake *H* the LORD's messenger
Hag 2:1 word of the LORD by the prophet *H*
Hag 2:10 word of the LORD by *H* the prophet
Hag 2:13 Then said *H*, If one that is
Hag 2:14 Then answered *H*, and said, So is
Hag 2:20 the LORD came unto *H* in the four

**HAGGERI** *(hag'-gher-i)* See HAGERITE. *Father of Mibhar.*
1Chr 11:38 of Nathan, Mibhar the son of *H*

**HAGGI** *(hag'-ghi)* See HAGGITES. *A son of Gad.*
Gen 46:16 Ziphion, and *H*, Shuni, and Ezbon,
Num 26:15 of *H*, the family of the Haggites

**HAGGIAH** *(hag-ghi'-ah) A descendant of Merari.*
1Chr 6:30 *H* his son, Asaiah his son

**HAGGITES** *(hag'-ghites)* See HAGGI. *Descendants of Haggi.*
Num 26:15 of Haggi, the family of the *H*

**HAGGITH** *(hag'-ghith) A wife of David.*
2Sa 3:4 the fourth, Adonijah the son of *H*
1Kin 1:5 the son of *H* exalted himself
1Kin 1:11 Adonijah the son of *H* doth reign
1Kin 2:13 Adonijah the son of *H* came to
1Chr 3:2 the fourth, Adonijah the son of *H*

**HAI** *(ha'-i)* See AI. *A form of Ai.*
Gen 12:8 on the west, and *H* on the east
Gen 13:3 beginning, between Beth-el and *H*

**HAIL**
Ex 9:18 it to rain a very grievous *h*
Ex 9:19 the *h* shall come down upon them,
Ex 9:22 that there may be *h* in all the
Ex 9:23 and the LORD sent thunder and *h*
Ex 9:23 the LORD rained *h* upon the land
Ex 9:24 *h*, and fire mingled with the *h*
Ex 9:25 the *h* smote throughout all the
Ex 9:25 the *h* smote every herb of the
Ex 9:26 of Israel were, was there no *h*
Ex 9:28 no more mighty thunderings and *h*
Ex 9:29 neither shall there be any more *h*
Ex 9:33 *h* ceased, and the rain was not
Ex 9:34 saw that the rain and the *h*
Ex 10:5 remaineth unto you from the *h*
Ex 10:12 even all that the *h* hath left
Ex 10:15 of the trees which the *h* had left
Job 38:22 thou seen the treasures of the *h*
Ps 18:12 *h* stones and coals of fire
Ps 18:13 *h* stones and coals of fire
Ps 78:47 He destroyed their vines with *h*
Ps 78:48 up their cattle also to the *h*
Ps 105:32 He gave them *h* for rain, and
Ps 148:8 Fire, and *h*; snow, and vapours
Is 28:2 one, which as a tempest of *h*
Is 28:17 the *h* shall sweep away the refuge
Is 32:19 When it shall *h*, coming down on
Hag 2:17 with *h* in all the labours of your
Mt 26:49 he came to Jesus, and said, *H*
Mt 27:29 him, and mocked him, saying, *H*
Mt 28:9 Jesus met them, saying, All *h*
Mk 15:18 And began to salute him, *H*
Lk 1:28 came in unto her, and said, *H*
Jn 19:3 And said, *H*, King of the Jews
Rev 8:7 sounded, and there followed *h*
Rev 11:19 and an earthquake, and great *h*
Rev 16:21 upon men a great *h* out of heaven
Rev 16:21 because of the plague of the *h*

**HAILSTONES**
Josh 10:11 *h* than they whom the children of
Is 30:30 scattering, and tempest, and *h*
Eze 13:11 and ye, O great *h*, shall fall
Eze 13:13 great *h* in my fury to consume it
Eze 38:22 and overflowing rain, and great *h*

**HAIR**
Ex 25:4 and fine linen, and goats' *h*
Ex 26:7 *h* to be a covering upon the
Ex 35:6 and fine linen, and goats' *h*
Ex 35:23 and fine linen, and goats' *h*
Ex 35:26 them up in wisdom spun goats' *h*
Ex 36:14 of goats' *h* for the tent over the
Lev 13:3 when the *h* in the plague is
Lev 13:4 the *h* thereof be not turned white
Lev 13:10 and it have turned the *h* white
Lev 13:20 the *h* thereof be turned white
Lev 13:25 if the *h* in the bright spot be
Lev 13:26 there be no white *h* in the bright
Lev 13:30 and there be in it a yellow thin *h*
Lev 13:31 and that there is no black *h* in it
Lev 13:32 and there be in it no yellow *h*
Lev 13:36 shall not seek for yellow *h*

Lev 13:37 there is black *h* grown up therein
Lev 13:40 the man whose *h* is fallen off his
Lev 13:41 he that hath his *h* fallen off
Lev 14:8 clothes, and shave off all his *h*
Lev 14:9 shave all his *h* off his head
Lev 14:9 even all his *h* he shall shave off
Num 6:5 locks of the *h* of his head grow
Num 6:18 shall take the *h* of the head of
Num 6:19 after the *h* of his separation is
Num 31:20 of skins, and all work of goats' *h*
Judg 16:22 Howbeit the *h* of his head began
Judg 20:16 sling stones at an *h* breadth
1Sa 14:45 there shall not one *h* of his head
1Sa 19:13 of goats' *h* for his bolster
1Sa 19:16 of goats' *h* for his bolster
2Sa 14:11 there shall not one *h* of thy son
2Sa 14:26 because the *h* was heavy on him,
2Sa 14:26 he weighed the *h* of his head at
1Kin 1:52 there shall not an *h* of him fall
Ezr 9:3 and plucked off the *h* of my head
Neh 13:25 of them, and plucked off their *h*
Job 4:15 the *h* of my flesh stood up
Song 4:1 thy *h* is as a flock of goats,
Song 6:5 thy *h* is as a flock of goats that
Song 7:5 the *h* of thine head like purple
Is 3:24 and instead of well set *h* baldness
Is 7:20 the head, and the *h* of the feet
Is 50:6 to them that plucked off the *h*
Jer 7:29 Cut off thine *h*, O Jerusalem, and
Eze 5:1 to weigh, and divide the *h*
Eze 16:7 thine *h* is grown, whereas thou
Dan 3:27 nor was an *h* of their head singed
Dan 7:9 the *h* of his head like the pure
Mt 3:4 John had his raiment of camel's *h*
Mt 5:36 not make one *h* white or black
Mk 1:6 John was clothed with camel's *h*
Lk 21:18 not an *h* of your head perish
Jn 11:2 and wiped his feet with her *h*
Jn 12:3 and wiped his feet with her *h*
Acts 27:34 for there shall not an *h* fall
1Cor 11:14 you, that, if a man have long *h*
1Cor 11:15 But if a woman have long *h*
1Cor 11:15 for her *h* is given her for a
1Ti 2:9 not with broided *h*, or gold, or
1Pet 3:3 adorning of plaiting the *h*
Rev 6:12 became black as sackcloth of *h*
Rev 9:8 they had *h* as the *h* of women,

**HAIRS**
Gen 42:38 gray *h* with sorrow to the grave
Gen 44:29 gray *h* with sorrow to the grave
Gen 44:31 shall bring down the gray *h* of
Lev 13:21 there be no white *h* therein
Deut 32:25 also with the man of gray *h*
Ps 40:12 are more than the *h* of mine head
Ps 69:4 are more than the *h* of mine head
Is 46:4 even to hoar *h* will I carry you
Dan 4:33 till his *h* were grown like
Hos 7:9 gray *h* are here and there upon him
Mt 10:30 But the very *h* of your head are
Lk 7:38 wipe them with the *h* of her head
Lk 7:44 wiped them with the *h* of her head
Lk 12:7 But even the very *h* of your head
Rev 1:14 his *h* were white like wool, as

**HAIRY**
Gen 25:25 red, all over like an *h* garment
Gen 27:11 Esau my brother is a *h* man
Gen 27:23 him not, because his hands were *h*
2Kin 1:8 answered him, He was an *h* man
Ps 68:21 the *h* scalp of such an one as

**HAKKATAN** *(hak'-ka-tan) A family of exiles.*
Ezr 8:12 Johanan the son of *H*, and with him

**HAKKOZ** *(hak'-koz)* See KOZ. *A sanctuary servant.*
1Chr 24:10 The seventh to *H*, the eighth to

**HAKUPHA** *(ha-ku'-fah) A family of exiles.*
Ezr 2:51 of Bakbuk, the children of *H*
Neh 7:53 of Bakbuk, the children of *H*

**HALAH** *(ha'-lah) An Assyrian district.*
2Kin 17:6 into Assyria, and placed them in *H*
2Kin 18:11 unto Assyria, and put them in *H*
1Chr 5:26 Manasseh, and brought them unto *H*

**HALAK** *(ha'-lak) A mountain in southern Canaan.*
Josh 11:17 Even from the mount *H*, that goeth
Josh 12:7 of Lebanon even unto the mount *H*

**HALF**
Gen 24:22 earring of *h* a shekel weight
Ex 24:6 Moses took *h* of the blood, and put
Ex 24:6 *h* of the blood he sprinkled on
Ex 25:10 a *h* shall be the length thereof,
Ex 25:10 a *h* the breadth thereof
Ex 25:10 a cubit and a *h* the height thereof
Ex 25:17 a *h* shall be the length thereof,
Ex 25:17 cubit and a *h* the breadth thereof
Ex 25:23 a cubit and a *h* the height thereof
Ex 26:12 the *h* curtain that remaineth,
Ex 26:16 a *h* shall be the breadth of one
Ex 30:13 *h* a shekel after the shekel of
Ex 30:13 an *h* shekel shall be the
Ex 30:15 not give less than *h* a shekel
Ex 30:23 and of sweet cinnamon *h* so much
Ex 36:21 of a board one cubit and a *h*
Ex 37:1 a *h* was the length of it, and a
Ex 37:1 a *h* the breadth of it
Ex 37:1 a cubit and a *h* the height of it
Ex 37:6 a *h* was the length thereof, and
Ex 37:6 cubit and a *h* the breadth thereof
Ex 37:10 a cubit and a *h* the height thereof
Ex 38:26 *h* a shekel, after the shekel of
Lev 6:20 *h* of it in the morning, and *h*
Num 12:12 of whom the flesh is *h* consumed
Num 15:9 mingled with *h* an hin of oil
Num 15:10 a drink offering *h* an hin of wine
Num 28:14 *h* an hin of wine unto a bullock
Num 31:29 Take it of their *h*, and give it
Num 31:30 And of the children of Israel's *h*
Num 31:36 And the *h*, which was the portion
Num 31:42 And of the children of Israel's *h*
Num 31:43 (Now the *h* that pertained unto
Num 31:47 of the children of Israel's *h*
Num 32:33 unto *h* the tribe of Manasseh the
Num 34:13 nine tribes, and to the *h* tribe
Num 34:14 *h* the tribe of Manasseh have
Num 34:15 the *h* tribe have received their
Deut 3:12 *h* mount Gilead, and the cities
Deut 3:13 gave I unto the *h* tribe of
Deut 3:16 unto the river Arnon *h* the valley
Deut 29:8 to the *h* tribe of Manasseh
Josh 1:12 to *h* the tribe of Manasseh, spake
Josh 4:12 *h* the tribe of Manasseh, passed
Josh 8:33 *h* of them over against mount
Josh 8:33 *h* of them over against mount Ebal
Josh 12:2 from *h* Gilead, even unto the
Josh 12:5 *h* Gilead, the border of Sihon
Josh 12:6 and the *h* tribe of Manasseh
Josh 13:7 and the *h* tribe of Manasseh,
Josh 13:25 *h* the land of the children of
Josh 13:29 unto the *h* tribe of Manasseh
Josh 13:29 of the *h* tribe of the children of
Josh 13:31 *h* Gilead, and Ashtaroth, and Edrei,
Josh 13:31 even to the one *h* of the children
Josh 14:2 nine tribes, and for the *h* tribe
Josh 14:3 an *h* tribe on the other side
Josh 18:7 *h* the tribe of Manasseh, have
Josh 21:5 out of the *h* tribe of Manasseh,
Josh 21:6 out of the *h* tribe of Manasseh in
Josh 21:25 out of the *h* tribe of Manasseh,
Josh 21:27 out of the other *h* tribe of
Josh 22:1 and the *h* tribe of Manasseh,
Josh 22:7 Now to the one *h* of the tribe of
Josh 22:7 but unto the other *h* thereof gave
Josh 22:9 the *h* tribe of Manasseh returned,
Josh 22:10 the *h* tribe of Manasseh built
Josh 22:11 the *h* tribe of Manasseh have
Josh 22:13 to the *h* tribe of Manasseh, into
Josh 22:15 to the *h* tribe of Manasseh, unto
Josh 22:21 the *h* tribe of Manasseh answered,
1Sa 14:14 as it were an *h* acre of land
2Sa 10:4 off the one *h* of their beards
2Sa 18:3 neither if *h* of us die, will they
2Sa 19:40 also *h* the people of Israel
1Kin 3:25 give *h* to the one, and *h* to the
1Kin 7:31 work of the base, a cubit and an *h*
1Kin 7:32 a wheel was a cubit and *h* a cubit
1Kin 7:35 a round compass of *h* a cubit high
1Kin 10:7 and, behold, the *h* was not told me
1Kin 13:8 thou wilt give me *h* thine house
1Kin 16:9 captain of *h* his chariots,
1Kin 16:21 *h* of the people followed Tibni
1Kin 16:21 and *h* followed Omri
1Chr 2:52 Haroeh, and *h* of the Manahethites
1Chr 2:54 *h* of the Manahethites, the
1Chr 5:18 *h* the tribe of Manasseh, of
1Chr 5:23 the children of the *h* tribe of
1Chr 5:26 the *h* tribe of Manasseh, and
1Chr 6:61 cities given out of the *h* tribe
1Chr 6:61 out of the *h* tribe of Manasseh,
1Chr 6:70 out of the *h* tribe of Manasseh
1Chr 6:71 family of the *h* tribe of Manasseh
1Chr 12:31 of the *h* tribe of Manasseh
1Chr 12:37 of the *h* tribe of Manasseh, with
1Chr 26:32 the *h* tribe of Manasseh, for
1Chr 27:20 of the *h* tribe of Manasseh, Joel
1Chr 27:21 Of the *h* tribe of Manasseh in
2Chr 9:6 the one *h* of the greatness of thy
Neh 3:9 the ruler of the *h* part of
Neh 3:12 the ruler of the *h* part of
Neh 3:16 ruler of the *h* part of Beth-zur
Neh 3:17 the ruler of the *h* part of Keilah
Neh 3:18 the ruler of the *h* part of Keilah
Neh 4:6 together unto the *h* thereof
Neh 4:16 that the *h* of my servants wrought
Neh 4:16 the other *h* of them held both the
Neh 4:21 *h* of them held the spears from
Neh 12:32 *h* of the princes of Judah,
Neh 12:38 the *h* of the people upon the wall
Neh 12:40 the *h* of the rulers with me
Neh 13:24 their children spake *h* in the
Est 5:3 thee to the *h* of the kingdom
Est 5:6 even to the *h* of the kingdom it
Est 7:2 even to the *h* of the kingdom
Ps 55:23 shall not live out *h* their days
Eze 16:51 Samaria committed *h* of thy sins
Eze 40:42 an *h* long, and a cubit and an *h*
Eze 43:17 about it shall be *h* a cubit
Dan 12:7 be for a time, times, and an *h*
Hos 3:2 barley, and an *h* homer of barley
Zec 14:2 *h* of the city shall go forth into
Zec 14:4 *h* of the mountain shall remove
Zec 14:4 and *h* of it toward the south
Zec 14:8 *h* of them toward the former sea,
Zec 14:8 *h* of them toward the hinder sea
Mk 6:23 it thee, unto the *h* of my kingdom
Lk 10:30 and departed, leaving him *h* dead
Lk 19:8 the *h* of my goods I give to the
Rev 8:1 about the space of *h* an hour
Rev 11:9 dead bodies three days and an *h*
Rev 11:11 an *h* the Spirit of life from God
Rev 12:14 *h* a time, from the face of the

**HALHUL** *(hal'-hul) A city in Judah.*
Josh 15:58 *H*, Beth-zur, and Gedor,

**HALI** *(ha'-li) A town in Asher.*
Josh 19:25 And their border was Helkath, and *H*

**HALL**
Mt 27:27 took Jesus into the common *h*
Mk 15:16 soldiers led him away into the *h*
Lk 22:55 a fire in the midst of the *h*
Jn 18:28 Caiaphas unto the *h* of judgment
Jn 18:28 went not into the judgment *h*
Jn 18:33 entered into the judgment *h* again
Jn 19:9 And went again into the judgment *h*
Acts 23:35 to be kept in Herod's judgment *h*

**HALLOHESH** *(hal-lo'-hesh)* See HALOHESH. *Father of Shallum.*
Neh 10:24 *H*, Pileha, Shobek,

**HALLOW**
Ex 28:38 shall *h* in all their holy gifts
Ex 29:1 thou shalt do unto them to *h* them
Ex 40:9 that is therein, and shalt *h* it
Lev 16:19 *h* it from the uncleanness of the
Lev 22:2 those things which they *h* unto me
Lev 22:3 of Israel *h* unto the LORD
Lev 22:32 I am the LORD which *h* you
Lev 25:10 ye shall *h* the fiftieth year, and
Num 6:11 shall *h* his head that same day
1Kin 8:64 The same day did the king *h* the
Jer 17:22 but *h* ye the sabbath day, as I
Jer 17:24 but *h* the sabbath day, to do no
Jer 17:27 unto me to *h* the sabbath day
Eze 20:20 And *h* my sabbaths
Eze 44:24 and they shall *h* my sabbaths

**HALLOWED**
Ex 20:11 blessed the sabbath day, and *h* it
Ex 29:21 and he shall be *h*, and his garments
Lev 12:4 she shall touch no *h* thing
Lev 19:8 profaned the *h* thing of the LORD
Lev 22:32 but I will be *h* among the
Num 3:13 in the land of Egypt I *h* unto me
Num 5:10 every man's *h* things shall be his
Num 16:37 for they are *h*
Num 16:38 the LORD, therefore they are *h*
Num 18:8 the *h* things of the children of
Num 18:29 even the *h* part thereof out of it

Deut 26:13 I have brought away the *h* things
1Sa 21:4 mine hand, but there is *h* bread
1Sa 21:6 So the priest gave him *h* bread
1Kin 9:3 I have *h* this house, which thou
1Kin 9:7 house, which I have *h* for my name
2Kin 12:18 all the *h* things that Jehoshaphat
2Kin 12:18 dedicated, and his own *h* things
2Chr 7:7 Moreover Solomon *h* the middle of
2Chr 36:14 LORD which he had *h* in Jerusalem
Mt 6:9 art in heaven, *H* be thy name
Lk 11:2 art in heaven, *H* be thy name

**HALOHESH** *(ha-lo'-hesh)* See HALLOHESH. *Same as Hallohesh.*
Neh 3:12 him repaired Shallum the son of *H*

**HALT**
1Kin 18:21 How long *h* ye between two
Ps 38:17 For I am ready to *h*, and my sorrow
Mt 18:8 to enter into life *h* or maimed
Mk 9:45 for thee to enter *h* into life
Lk 14:21 the poor, and the maimed, and the *h*
Jn 5:3 of impotent folk, of blind, *h*

**HAM** *(ham)*
*1. A son of Noah.*
Gen 5:32 and Noah begat Shem, *H*, and Japheth
Gen 6:10 And Noah begat three sons, Shem, *H*
Gen 7:13 day entered Noah, and Shem, and *H*
Gen 9:18 forth of the ark, were Shem, and *H*
Gen 9:18 *H* is the father of Canaan
Gen 9:22 And *H*, the father of Canaan, saw
Gen 10:1 of the sons of Noah, Shem, *H*
Gen 10:6 And the sons of *H*
Gen 10:20 These are the sons of *H*, after
Gen 14:5 Karnaim, and the Zuzims in *H*
1Chr 1:4 Noah, Shem, *H*, and Japheth
1Chr 1:8 The sons of *H*
*2. Descendants and land of Ham.*
1Chr 4:40 for they of *H* had dwelt there of
Ps 78:51 strength in the tabernacles of *H*
Ps 105:23 Jacob sojourned in the land of *H*
Ps 105:27 them, and wonders in the land of *H*
Ps 106:22 Wondrous works in the land of *H*

**HAMAN** *(ha'-man)* See HAMAN'S. *Prime minister under King Ahasuerus.*
Est 3:1 *H* the son of Hammedatha the
Est 3:2 gate, bowed, and reverenced *H*
Est 3:4 not unto them, that they told *H*
Est 3:5 when *H* saw that Mordecai bowed
Est 3:5 then was *H* full of wrath
Est 3:6 wherefore *H* sought to destroy all
Est 3:7 before *H* from day to day, and from
Est 3:8 *H* said unto king Ahasuerus, There
Est 3:10 gave it unto *H* the son of
Est 3:11 And the king said unto *H*, The
Est 3:12 *H* had commanded unto the king's
Est 3:15 the king and *H* sat down to drink
Est 4:7 that *H* had promised to pay to the
Est 5:4 *H* come this day unto the banquet
Est 5:5 Cause *H* to make haste, that he
Est 5:5 *H* came to the banquet that Esther
Est 5:8 *H* come to the banquet that I
Est 5:9 Then went *H* forth that day joyful
Est 5:9 but when *H* saw Mordecai in the
Est 5:10 Nevertheless *H* refrained himself
Est 5:11 *H* told them of the glory of his
Est 5:12 *H* said moreover, Yea, Esther the
Est 5:14 And the thing pleased *H*
Est 6:4 Now *H* was come into the outward
Est 6:5 Behold, *H* standeth in the court
Est 6:6 So *H* came in
Est 6:6 Now *H* thought in his heart, To
Est 6:7 *H* answered the king, For the man
Est 6:10 Then the king said to *H*, Make
Est 6:11 Then took *H* the apparel and the
Est 6:12 But *H* hasted to his house
Est 6:13 *H* told Zeresh his wife and all his
Est 6:14 hasted to bring *H* unto the
Est 7:1 *H* came to banquet with Esther the
Est 7:6 and enemy is this wicked *H*
Est 7:6 Then *H* was afraid before the king
Est 7:7 *H* stood up to make request for
Est 7:8 *H* was fallen upon the bed whereon
Est 7:9 which *H* had made for Mordecai,
Est 7:9 king, standeth in the house of *H*
Est 7:10 So they hanged *H* on the gallows
Est 8:1 Ahasuerus give the house of *H* the
Est 8:2 ring, which he had taken from *H*
Est 8:2 set Mordecai over the house of *H*
Est 8:3 the mischief of *H* the Agagite
Est 8:5 by *H* the son of Hammedatha the
Est 8:7 have given Esther the house of *H*
Est 9:10 The ten sons of *H* the son of
Est 9:12 the palace, and the ten sons of *H*
Est 9:24 Because *H* the son of Hammedatha,

**HAMAN'S** *(ha'-mans)*
Est 7:8 king's mouth, they covered *H* face
Est 9:13 let *H* ten sons be hanged upon the
Est 9:14 and they hanged *H* ten sons

**HAMATH** *(ha'-math)* See HAMATHITE, HAMATH-ZOBAH, HEMATH. *A capital of Syria.*
Num 13:21 Zin unto Rehob, as men come to *H*
Num 34:8 border unto the entrance of *H*
Josh 13:5 Hermon unto the entering into *H*
Judg 3:3 unto the entering in of *H*
2Sa 8:9 When Toi king of *H* heard that
1Kin 8:65 in of *H* unto the river of Egypt
2Kin 14:25 of *H* unto the sea of the plain
2Kin 14:28 how he recovered Damascus, and *H*
2Kin 17:24 Cuthah, and from Ava, and from *H*
2Kin 17:30 the men of *H* made Ashima,
2Kin 18:34 Where are the gods of *H*, and of
2Kin 19:13 Where is the king of *H*, and the
2Kin 23:33 bands at Riblah in the land of *H*
2Kin 25:21 them at Riblah in the land of *H*
1Chr 18:3 Hadarezer king of Zobah unto *H*
1Chr 18:9 Now when Tou king of *H* heard how
2Chr 7:8 in of *H* unto the river of Egypt
2Chr 8:4 store cities, which he built in *H*
Is 10:9 is not *H* as Arpad
Is 11:11 Elam, and from Shinar, and from *H*
Is 36:19 Where are the gods of *H* and Arphad
Is 37:13 Where is the king of *H*, and the
Jer 39:5 to Riblah in the land of *H*
Jer 49:23 *H* is confounded, and Arpad
Jer 52:9 to Riblah in the land of *H*
Jer 52:27 death in Riblah in the land of *H*
Eze 47:16 *H*, Berothah, Sibraim, which is
Eze 47:16 of Damascus and the border of *H*
Eze 47:17 northward, and the border of *H*
Eze 47:20 till a man come over against *H*
Eze 48:1 way of Hethlon, as one goeth to *H*
Eze 48:1 northward, to the coast of *H*
Amos 6:2 from thence go ye to *H* the great
Zec 9:2 *H* also shall border thereby

**HAMATHITE**
Gen 10:18 and the Zemarite, and the *H*
1Chr 1:16 and the Zemarite, and the *H*

**HAMATH-ZOBAH** *(ha'-math-zo'-bah) Full name of Hamath.*
2Chr 8:3 And Solomon went to *H*, and

**HAMMATH** *(ham'-math) A city in Naphtali.*
Josh 19:35 cities are Ziddim, Zer, and *H*

**HAMMEDATHA** *(ham-med'a-thah) Father of Haman.*
Est 3:1 Haman the son of *H* the Agagite
Est 3:10 Haman the son of *H* the Agagite
Est 8:5 by Haman the son of *H* the Agagite
Est 9:10 ten sons of Haman the son of *H*
Est 9:24 Because Haman the son of *H*

**HAMMELECH** *(ham'-me-lek) Father of Jerahmeel*
Jer 36:26 commanded Jerahmeel the son of *H*
Jer 38:6 dungeon of Malchiah the son of *H*

**HAMMER**
Judg 4:21 took an *h* in her hand, and went
Judg 5:26 her right hand to the workmen's *h*
Judg 5:26 with the *h* she smote Sisera, she
1Kin 6:7 so that there was neither *h* nor
Is 41:7 the *h* him that smote the anvil
Jer 23:29 like a *h* that breaketh the rock
Jer 50:23 How is the *h* of the whole earth

**HAMMOLEKETH** *(ham-mol'-e-keth) Daughter of Machir.*
1Chr 7:18 And his sister *H* bare Ishod

**HAMMON** *(ham'-mon)*
*1. A city in Asher.*
Josh 19:28 And Hebron, and Rehob, and *H*
*2. A city in Naphtali.*
1Chr 6:76 *H* with her suburbs, and Kirjathaim

**HAMMOTH-DOR** *(ham'-moth-dor') Same as Hammon 2.*
Josh 21:32 *H* with her suburbs, and Kartan

**HAMONAH** *(ha-mo'-nah) Place where Gog is buried.*
Eze 39:16 the name of the city shall be *H*

**HAMON-GOG** *(ha'-mon-gog) Same as Hamonah.*
Eze 39:11 shall call it The valley of *H*
Eze 39:15 have buried it in the valley of *H*

**HAMOR** *(ha'-mor)* See EMMOR, HAMOR'S. *Father of Shechem.*
Gen 33:19 at the hand of the children of *H*
Gen 34:2 Shechem the son of *H* the Hivite
Gen 34:4 Shechem spake unto his father *H*
Gen 34:6 *H* the father of Shechem went out
Gen 34:8 *H* communed with them, saying, The
Gen 34:13 *H* his father deceitfully, and said
Gen 34:18 And their words pleased *H*, and
Gen 34:20 And *H* and Shechem his son came unto
Gen 34:24 And unto *H* and unto Shechem his son
Gen 34:26 And they slew *H* and Shechem his son
Josh 24:32 Jacob bought of the sons of *H* the
Judg 9:28 serve the men of *H* the father of

**HAMOR'S** *(ha'-mors)*
Gen 34:18 pleased Hamor, and Shechem *H* son

**HAMUEL** *(ha-mu'-el) Son of Mishma.*
1Chr 4:26 *H* his son, Zacchur his son,

**HAMUL** *(ha'-mul)* See HAMULITES. *A son of Pharez.*
Gen 46:12 sons of Pharez were Hezron and *H*
Num 26:21 of *H*, the family of the Hamulites
1Chr 2:5 Hezron, and *H*.

**HAMULITES** *(ha'-mu-lites) Descendants of Hamul.*
Num 26:21 of Hamul, the family of the *H*

**HAMUTAL** *(ha-mu'-tal) Mother of King Jehoahaz.*
2Kin 23:31 And his mother's name was *H*
2Kin 24:18 And his mother's name was *H*
Jer 52:1 his mother's name was *H* the

**HANAMEEL** *(ha-nam'-e-el) Son of Shallum.*
Jer 32:7 *H* the son of Shallum thine uncle
Jer 32:8 So *H* mine uncle's son came to me
Jer 32:9 the field of *H* my uncle's son
Jer 32:12 in the sight of *H* mine uncle's

**HANAN** *(ha'-nan)* See BAAL-HANAN, BEN-HANAN, ELON-BETH-HANAN.
*1. A son of Shashak.*
1Chr 8:23 And Abdon, and Zichri, and *H*
*2. A son of Azel.*
1Chr 8:38 and Sheariah, and Obadiah, and *H*
1Chr 9:44 and Sheariah, and Obadiah, and *H*
*3. A "mighty man" of David.*
1Chr 11:43 *H* the son of Maachah, and
*4. Family of exiles.*
Ezr 2:46 of Shalmai, the children of *H*
Neh 7:49 The children of *H*, the children
*5. A priest who assisted Ezra.*
Neh 8:7 Kelita, Azariah, Jozabad, *H*
*6. A Levite who renewed the covenant.*
Neh 10:10 Hodijah, Kelita, Pelaiah, *H*
Neh 13:13 next to them was *H* the son of
*7. A chief who renewed the covenant.*
Neh 10:22 Pelatiah, *H*, Anaiah,
*8. Another chief who renewed the covenant.*
Neh 10:26 And Ahijah, *H*, Anan,
*9. Son of Igdaliah.*
Jer 35:4 into the chamber of the sons of *H*

**HANANEEL** *(ha-nan'-e-el) A tower on Jerusalem's wall.*
Neh 3:1 it, unto the tower of *H*
Neh 12:39 the fish gate, and the tower of *H*
Jer 31:38 of *H* unto the gate of the corner
Zec 14:10 from the tower of *H* unto the

**HANANI** *(ha-na'-ni)*
*1. A son of Heman.*
1Chr 25:4 Shebuel, and Jerimoth, Hananiah, *H*
1Chr 25:25 The eighteenth to *H*, he, his sons
*2. A prophet.*
2Chr 16:7 at that time *H* the seer came to
*3. Father of Jehu.*
1Kin 16:1 Jehu the son of *H* against Baasha
1Kin 16:7 of *H* came the word of the LORD
2Chr 19:2 Jehu the son of *H* the seer went
2Chr 20:34 in the book of Jehu the son of *H*

*4. Married a foreigner in exile.*
Ezr 10:20 of Immer; *H*, and Zebadiah
*5. Brother of Nehemiah.*
Neh 1:2 That *H*, one of my brethren, came,
Neh 7:2 That I gave my brother *H*, and
*6. A priest.*
Neh 12:36 Maai, Nethaneel, and Judah, *H*

**HANANIAH** *(han-a-ni'-ah)* See SHADRACH.
*1. A son of Heman.*
1Chr 25:4 Uzziel, Shebuel, and Jerimoth, *H*
1Chr 25:23 The sixteenth to *H*, he, his sons,
Neh 12:12 Meraiah; of Jeremiah, *H*
Jer 28:15 Hear now, *H*; The LORD hath
*2. A captain of King Uzziah.*
2Chr 26:11 the ruler, under the hand of *H*
*3. Father of Zedekiah.*
Jer 36:12 Shaphan, and Zedekiah the son of *H*
*4. A false prophet.*
Jer 28:1 that *H* the son of Azur the
Jer 28:5 *H* in the presence of the priests
Jer 28:10 Then *H* the prophet took the yoke
Jer 28:11 *H* spake in the presence of all
Jer 28:12 after that *H* the prophet had
Jer 28:13 Go and tell *H*, saying, Thus saith
Jer 28:15 Jeremiah unto *H* the prophet
Jer 28:17 So *H* the prophet died the same
*5. Grandfather of Irijah.*
Jer 37:13 son of Shelemiah, the son of *H*
*6. Son of Shashak.*
1Chr 8:24 And *H*, and Elam, and Antothijah,
*7. Hebrew form of Shadrach.*
Dan 1:6 the children of Judah, Daniel, *H*
Dan 1:7 and to *H*, of Shadrach
Dan 1:11 eunuchs had set over Daniel, *H*
Dan 1:19 all was found none like Daniel, *H*
Dan 2:17 and made the thing known to *H*
*8. A son of Zerubbabel.*
1Chr 3:19 Meshullam, and *H*, and Shelomith
1Chr 3:21 And the sons of *H*
*9. Married a foreigner in exile.*
Ezr 10:28 Jehohanan, *H*, Zabbai, and Athlai
*10. A rebuilder of Jerusalem's wall.*
Neh 3:8 repaired *H* the son of one of the
*11. Another rebuilder of Jerusalem's wall.*
Neh 3:30 After him repaired *H* the son of
*12. A palace servant of Nehemiah.*
Neh 7:2 *H* the ruler of the palace, charge
*13. An Israelite who renewed the covenant.*
Neh 10:23 Hoshea, *H*, Hashub,
*14. A priest.*
Neh 12:41 Elioenai, Zechariah, and *H*

**HAND**
Gen 3:22 and now, lest he put forth his *h*
Gen 4:11 thy brother's blood from thy *h*
Gen 8:9 then he put forth his *h*, and took
Gen 9:2 into your *h* are they delivered
Gen 9:5 at the *h* of every beast will I
Gen 9:5 I require it, and at the *h* of man
Gen 9:5 at the *h* of every man's brother
Gen 13:9 if thou wilt take the left *h*
Gen 13:9 or if thou depart to the right *h*
Gen 14:15 is on the left *h* of Damascus
Gen 14:20 thine enemies into thy *h*
Gen 14:22 have lift up mine *h* unto the LORD
Gen 16:6 Behold, thy maid is in thy *h*
Gen 16:12 his *h* will be against every man,
Gen 16:12 and every man's *h* against him
Gen 19:10 But the men put forth their *h*
Gen 19:16 the men laid hold upon his *h*
Gen 19:16 upon the *h* of his wife
Gen 19:16 upon the *h* of his two daughters
Gen 21:18 the lad, and hold him in thine *h*
Gen 21:30 ewe lambs shalt thou take of my *h*
Gen 22:6 and he took the fire in his *h*
Gen 22:10 And Abraham stretched forth his *h*
Gen 22:12 Lay not thine *h* upon the lad
Gen 24:2 I pray thee, thy *h* under my thigh
Gen 24:9 the servant put his *h* under the
Gen 24:10 goods of his master were in his *h*
Gen 24:18 let down her pitcher upon her *h*
Gen 24:49 that I may turn to the right *h*
Gen 25:26 his *h* took hold on Esau's heel
Gen 27:17 into the *h* of her son Jacob
Gen 27:41 mourning for my father are at *h*
Gen 30:35 gave them into the *h* of his sons
Gen 31:29 the power of my *h* to do you hurt
Gen 31:39 of my *h* didst thou require it,
Gen 32:11 from the *h* of my brother
Gen 32:11 from the *h* of Esau
Gen 32:13 *h* a present for Esau his brother
Gen 32:16 them into the *h* of his servants
Gen 33:10 then receive my present at my *h*
Gen 33:19 at the *h* of the children of Hamor
Gen 35:4 gods which were in their *h*
Gen 37:22 wilderness, and lay no *h* upon him
Gen 37:27 and let not our *h* be upon him
Gen 38:18 and thy staff that is in thine *h*
Gen 38:20 Judah sent the kid by the *h* of
Gen 38:20 his pledge from the woman's *h*
Gen 38:28 that the one put out his *h*
Gen 38:28 bound upon his *h* a scarlet thread
Gen 38:29 to pass, as he drew back his *h*
Gen 38:30 had the scarlet thread upon his *h*
Gen 39:3 that he did to prosper in his *h*
Gen 39:4 all that he had he put into his *h*
Gen 39:6 all that he had in Joseph's *h*
Gen 39:8 all that he hath to my *h*
Gen 39:12 and he left his garment in her *h*
Gen 39:13 he had left his garment in her *h*
Gen 39:22 prison committed to Joseph's *h*
Gen 39:23 to any thing that was under his *h*
Gen 40:11 And Pharaoh's cup was in my *h*
Gen 40:11 I gave the cup into Pharaoh's *h*
Gen 40:13 deliver Pharaoh's cup into his *h*
Gen 40:21 he gave the cup into Pharaoh's *h*
Gen 41:35 up corn under the *h* of Pharaoh
Gen 41:42 took off his ring from his *h*
Gen 41:42 *h*, and put it upon Joseph's *h*
Gen 41:44 his *h* or foot in all the land of
Gen 42:37 deliver him into my *h*, and I will
Gen 43:9 of my *h* shalt thou require him
Gen 43:12 And take double money in your *h*
Gen 43:12 sacks, carry it again in your *h*
Gen 43:15 they took double money in their *h*
Gen 43:21 we have brought it again in our *h*
Gen 43:26 was in their *h* into the house
Gen 44:17 man in whose *h* the cup is found
Gen 46:4 shall put his *h* upon thine eyes
Gen 47:29 thy *h* under my thigh, and deal
Gen 48:13 Ephraim in his right *h* toward
Gen 48:13 toward Israel's left *h*
Gen 48:13 Manasseh in his left *h* toward
Gen 48:13 toward Israel's right *h*
Gen 48:14 Israel stretched out his right *h*
Gen 48:14 his left *h* upon Manasseh's head,
Gen 48:17 right *h* upon the head of Ephraim
Gen 48:17 and he held up his father's *h*
Gen 48:18 put thy right *h* upon his head
Gen 48:22 which I took out of the *h* of the
Gen 49:8 thy *h* shall be in the neck of
Ex 2:19 us out of the *h* of the shepherds
Ex 3:8 out of the *h* of the Egyptians
Ex 3:19 let you go, no, not by a mighty *h*
Ex 3:20 And I will stretch out my *h*
Ex 4:2 unto him, What is that in thine *h*
Ex 4:4 unto Moses, Put forth thine *h*
Ex 4:4 And he put forth his *h*, and caught
Ex 4:4 it, and it became a rod in his *h*
Ex 4:6 Put now thine *h* into thy bosom
Ex 4:6 he put his *h* into his bosom
Ex 4:6 his *h* was leprous as snow
Ex 4:7 Put thine *h* into thy bosom again
Ex 4:7 he put his *h* into his bosom again
Ex 4:13 by the *h* of him whom thou wilt
Ex 4:17 shalt take this rod in thine *h*
Ex 4:20 took the rod of God in his *h*
Ex 4:21 which I have put in thine *h*
Ex 5:21 put a sword in their *h* to slay us
Ex 6:1 for with a strong *h* shall he let
Ex 6:1 with a strong *h* shall he drive
Ex 7:4 that I may lay my *h* upon Egypt
Ex 7:5 I stretch forth mine *h* upon Egypt
Ex 7:15 shalt thou take in thine *h*
Ex 7:17 *h* upon the waters which are in
Ex 7:19 stretch out thine *h* upon the
Ex 8:5 Stretch forth thine *h* with thy
Ex 8:6 Aaron stretched out his *h* over
Ex 8:17 stretched out his *h* with his rod
Ex 9:3 the *h* of the LORD is upon thy
Ex 9:15 For now I will stretch out my *h*
Ex 9:22 forth thine *h* toward heaven
Ex 10:12 Stretch out thine *h* over the land
Ex 10:21 Stretch out thine *h* toward heaven
Ex 10:22 forth his *h* toward heaven
Ex 12:11 feet, and your staff in your *h*
Ex 13:3 for by strength of *h* the LORD
Ex 13:9 for a sign unto thee upon thine *h*
Ex 13:9 for with a strong *h* hath the LORD
Ex 13:14 By strength of *h* the LORD brought
Ex 13:16 shall be for a token upon thine *h*
Ex 13:16 for by strength of *h* the LORD
Ex 14:8 of Israel went out with an high *h*
Ex 14:16 stretch out thine *h* over the sea
Ex 14:21 stretched out his *h* over the sea
Ex 14:22 a wall unto them on their right *h*
Ex 14:26 Stretch out thine *h* over the sea
Ex 14:27 forth his *h* over the sea, and the
Ex 14:29 a wall unto them on their right *h*
Ex 14:30 day out of the *h* of the Egyptians
Ex 15:6 Thy right *h*, O LORD, is become
Ex 15:6 thy right *h*, O LORD, hath dashed
Ex 15:9 my sword, my *h* shall destroy them
Ex 15:12 Thou stretchedst out thy right *h*
Ex 15:20 of Aaron, took a timbrel in her *h*
Ex 16:3 the *h* of the LORD in the land of
Ex 17:5 the river, take in thine *h*
Ex 17:9 with the rod of God in mine *h*
Ex 17:11 to pass, when Moses held up his *h*
Ex 17:11 and when he let down his *h*
Ex 18:9 out of the *h* of the Egyptians
Ex 18:10 you out of the *h* of the Egyptians
Ex 18:10 and out of the *h* of Pharaoh
Ex 18:10 from under the *h* of the Egyptians
Ex 19:13 There shall not an *h* touch it
Ex 21:13 but God deliver him into his *h*
Ex 21:16 him, or if he be found in his *h*
Ex 21:20 with a rod, and he die under his *h*
Ex 21:24 *h* for *h*, foot for foot,
Ex 22:4 be certainly found in his *h* alive
Ex 22:8 his *h* unto his neighbour's goods
Ex 22:11 that he hath not put his *h* unto
Ex 23:1 put not thine *h* with the wicked
Ex 23:31 of the land into your *h*
Ex 24:11 of Israel he laid not his *h*
Ex 25:25 of an *h* breadth round about
Ex 29:20 upon the thumb of their right *h*
Ex 32:4 And he received them at their *h*
Ex 32:11 great power, and with a mighty *h*
Ex 32:15 of the testimony were in his *h*
Ex 33:22 thee with my *h* while I pass by
Ex 33:23 And I will take away mine *h*
Ex 34:4 took in his *h* the two tables of
Ex 34:29 tables of testimony in Moses' *h*
Ex 35:29 to be made by the *h* of Moses
Ex 38:15 gate, on this *h* and that *h*
Ex 38:21 by the *h* of Ithamar, son to Aaron
Lev 1:4 he shall put his *h* upon the head
Lev 3:2 he shall lay his *h* upon the head
Lev 3:8 he shall lay his *h* upon the head
Lev 3:13 he shall lay his *h* upon the head
Lev 4:4 and shall lay his *h* upon the
Lev 4:24 he shall lay his *h* upon the head
Lev 4:29 he shall lay his *h* upon the head
Lev 4:33 he shall lay his *h* upon the head
Lev 8:23 and upon the thumb of his right *h*
Lev 8:36 LORD commanded by the *h* of Moses
Lev 9:22 lifted up his *h* toward the people
Lev 10:11 unto them by the *h* of Moses
Lev 14:14 and upon the thumb of his right *h*
Lev 14:15 into the palm of his own left *h*
Lev 14:16 in the oil that is in his left *h*
Lev 14:17 *h* shall the priest put upon the
Lev 14:17 and upon the thumb of his right *h*
Lev 14:18 *h* he shall pour upon the head of
Lev 14:25 and upon the thumb of his right *h*
Lev 14:26 into the palm of his own left *h*
Lev 14:27 *h* seven times before the LORD
Lev 14:28 *h* upon the tip of the right ear
Lev 14:28 and upon the thumb of his right *h*
Lev 14:29 *h* he shall put upon the head of
Lev 14:32 whose *h* is not able to get that
Lev 16:21 by the *h* of a fit man into the
Lev 22:25 Neither from a stranger's *h* shall
Lev 25:14 buyest ought of thy neighbour's *h*
Lev 25:28 the *h* of him that hath bought it
Lev 26:25 delivered into the *h* of the enemy
Lev 26:46 in mount Sinai by the *h* of Moses
Num 4:28 *h* of Ithamar the son of Aaron the
Num 4:33 under the *h* of Ithamar the son of
Num 4:37 of the LORD by the *h* of Moses
Num 4:45 of the LORD by the *h* of Moses
Num 4:49 were numbered by the *h* of Moses
Num 5:18 the priest shall have in his *h*
Num 5:25 offering out of the woman's *h*
Num 6:21 beside that that his *h* shall get
Num 7:8 under the *h* of Ithamar the son of
Num 9:23 of the LORD by the *h* of Moses
Num 10:13 of the LORD by the *h* of Moses

Num 11:15 kill me, I pray thee, out of *h*
Num 11:23 Is the LORD's *h* waxed short
Num 15:23 commanded you by the *h* of Moses
Num 16:40 said to him by the *h* of Moses
Num 20:11 And Moses lifted up his *h*, and with
Num 20:17 to the right *h* nor to the left
Num 20:20 much people, and with a strong *h*
Num 21:2 deliver this people into my *h*
Num 21:26 taken all his land out of his *h*
Num 21:34 I have delivered him into thy *h*
Num 22:7 rewards of divination in their *h*
Num 22:23 way, and his sword drawn in his *h*
Num 22:26 to the right *h* or to the left
Num 22:29 there were a sword in mine *h*
Num 22:31 way, and his sword drawn in his *h*
Num 25:7 and took a javelin in his *h*
Num 27:18 spirit, and lay thine *h* upon him
Num 27:23 LORD commanded by the *h* of Moses
Num 31:6 and the trumpets to blow in his *h*
Num 33:1 their armies under the *h* of Moses
Num 33:3 an high *h* in the sight of all the
Num 35:18 him with an *h* weapon of wood
Num 35:21 Or in enmity smite him with his *h*
Num 35:25 of the *h* of the revenger of blood
Num 36:13 *h* of Moses unto the children of
Deut 1:27 us into the *h* of the Amorites
Deut 2:7 thee in all the works of thy *h*
Deut 2:15 For indeed the *h* of the LORD was
Deut 2:24 into thine *h* Sihon the Amorite
Deut 2:27 unto the right *h* nor to the left
Deut 2:30 he might deliver him into thy *h*
Deut 3:2 people, and his land, into thy *h*
Deut 3:8 of the *h* of the two kings of the
Deut 3:24 thy greatness, and thy mighty *h*
Deut 4:34 and by war, and by a mighty *h*
Deut 5:15 out thence through a mighty *h*
Deut 5:32 to the right *h* or to the left
Deut 6:8 bind them for a sign upon thine *h*
Deut 6:21 us out of Egypt with a mighty *h*
Deut 7:8 brought you out with a mighty *h*
Deut 7:8 from the *h* of Pharaoh king of
Deut 7:19 and the wonders, and the mighty *h*
Deut 7:24 deliver their kings into thine *h*
Deut 8:17 the might of mine *h* hath gotten
Deut 9:26 out of Egypt with a mighty *h*
Deut 10:3 having the two tables in mine *h*
Deut 11:2 God, his greatness, his mighty *h*
Deut 11:18 bind them for a sign upon your *h*
Deut 12:6 and heave offerings of your *h*
Deut 12:7 in all that ye put your *h* unto
Deut 12:11 and the heave offering of your *h*
Deut 12:17 or heave offering of thine *h*
Deut 13:9 thine *h* shall be first upon him
Deut 13:9 afterwards the *h* of all the
Deut 13:17 of the cursed thing to thine *h*
Deut 14:25 and bind up the money in thine *h*
Deut 14:29 work of thine *h* which thou doest
Deut 15:3 thy brother thine *h* shall release
Deut 15:7 nor shut thine *h* from thy poor
Deut 15:8 shalt open thine *h* wide unto him
Deut 15:9 the year of release, is at *h*
Deut 15:10 that thou puttest thine *h* unto
Deut 15:11 thine *h* wide unto thy brother
Deut 16:10 of a freewill offering of thine *h*
Deut 17:11 shall shew thee, to the right *h*
Deut 17:20 the commandment, to the right *h*
Deut 19:5 his *h* fetcheth a stroke with the
Deut 19:12 deliver him into the *h* of the
Deut 19:21 *h* for *h*, foot for foot
Deut 23:20 *h* to in the land whither thou
Deut 23:25 pluck the ears with thine *h*
Deut 24:1 divorcement, and give it in her *h*
Deut 24:3 and giveth it in her *h*, and
Deut 25:11 of the *h* of him that smiteth him
Deut 25:11 and putteth forth her *h*
Deut 25:12 Then thou shalt cut off her *h*
Deut 26:4 take the basket out of thine *h*
Deut 26:8 out of Egypt with a mighty *h*
Deut 28:8 that thou settest thine *h* unto
Deut 28:12 to bless all the work of thine *h*
Deut 28:14 thee this day, to the right *h*
Deut 28:20 settest thine *h* unto for to do
Deut 28:32 shall be no might in thine *h*
Deut 30:9 in every work of thine *h*, in the
Deut 32:27 Our *h* is high, and the LORD hath
Deut 32:35 the day of their calamity is at *h*
Deut 32:39 any that can deliver out of my *h*
Deut 32:40 For I lift up my *h* to heaven
Deut 32:41 mine *h* take hold on judgment
Deut 33:2 from his right *h* went a fiery law
Deut 33:3 all his saints are in thy *h*
Deut 34:12 And in all that mighty *h*, and in
Josh 1:7 it to the right *h* or to the left
Josh 2:19 on our head, if any *h* be upon him
Josh 4:24 might know the *h* of the LORD
Josh 5:13 him with his sword drawn in his *h*
Josh 6:2 I have given into thine *h* Jericho
Josh 7:7 us into the *h* of the Amorites
Josh 8:1 given into thy *h* the king of Ai
Josh 8:7 God will deliver it into your *h*
Josh 8:18 spear that is in thy *h* toward Ai
Josh 8:18 for I will give it into thine *h*
Josh 8:18 he had in his *h* toward the city
Josh 8:19 as he had stretched out his *h*
Josh 8:26 For Joshua drew not his *h* back
Josh 9:25 And now, behold, we are in thine *h*
Josh 9:26 the *h* of the children of Israel
Josh 10:6 Slack not thy *h* from thy servants
Josh 10:8 have delivered them into thine *h*
Josh 10:19 hath delivered them into your *h*
Josh 10:30 thereof, into the *h* of Israel
Josh 10:32 Lachish into the *h* of Israel
Josh 11:8 them into the *h* of Israel
Josh 14:2 LORD commanded by the *h* of Moses
Josh 17:7 right *h* unto the inhabitants of
Josh 19:27 goeth out to Cabul on the left *h*
Josh 20:2 spake unto you by the *h* of Moses
Josh 20:5 deliver the slayer up into his *h*
Josh 20:9 not die by the *h* of the avenger
Josh 21:2 The LORD commanded by the *h* of
Josh 21:8 LORD commanded by the *h* of Moses
Josh 21:44 all their enemies into their *h*
Josh 22:9 of the LORD by the *h* of Moses
Josh 22:31 Israel out of the *h* of the LORD
Josh 23:6 to the right *h* or to the left
Josh 24:8 and I gave them into your *h*
Josh 24:10 so I delivered you out of his *h*
Josh 24:11 and I delivered them into your *h*
Judg 1:2 delivered the land into his *h*
Judg 1:4 and the Perizzites into their *h*
Judg 1:35 yet the *h* of the house of Joseph
Judg 2:15 the *h* of the LORD was against
Judg 2:16 the *h* of those that spoiled them
Judg 2:18 delivered them out of the *h* of
Judg 2:23 he them into the *h* of Joshua
Judg 3:4 their fathers by the *h* of Moses
Judg 3:8 he sold them into the *h* of
Judg 3:10 king of Mesopotamia into his *h*
Judg 3:10 and his *h* prevailed against
Judg 3:21 And Ehud put forth his left *h*
Judg 3:28 enemies the Moabites into your *h*
Judg 3:30 that day under the *h* of Israel
Judg 4:2 the *h* of Jabin king of Canaan
Judg 4:7 I will deliver him into thine *h*
Judg 4:9 sell Sisera into the *h* of a woman
Judg 4:14 delivered Sisera into thine *h*
Judg 4:21 tent, and took an hammer in her *h*
Judg 4:24 the *h* of the children of Israel
Judg 5:26 She put her *h* to the nail
Judg 5:26 her right *h* to the workmen's
Judg 6:1 into the *h* of Midian seven years
Judg 6:2 the *h* of Midian prevailed against
Judg 6:9 you out of the *h* of the Egyptians
Judg 6:9 and out of the *h* of all that
Judg 6:14 from the *h* of the Midianites
Judg 6:21 of the staff that was in his *h*
Judg 6:36 thou wilt save Israel by mine *h*
Judg 6:37 thou wilt save Israel by mine *h*
Judg 7:2 saying, Mine own *h* hath saved me
Judg 7:6 putting their *h* to their mouth,
Judg 7:7 the Midianites into thine *h*
Judg 7:8 people took victuals in their *h*
Judg 7:9 I have delivered it into thine *h*
Judg 7:14 for into his *h* hath God delivered
Judg 7:15 into your *h* the host of Midian
Judg 7:16 he put a trumpet in every man's *h*
Judg 8:6 Zebah and Zalmunna now in thine *h*
Judg 8:7 Zebah and Zalmunna into mine *h*
Judg 8:15 Zebah and Zalmunna now in thine *h*
Judg 8:22 delivered us from the *h* of Midian
Judg 9:17 you out of the *h* of Midian
Judg 9:29 God this people were under my *h*
Judg 9:48 and Abimelech took an axe in his *h*
Judg 10:12 and I delivered you out of their *h*
Judg 11:21 his people into the *h* of Israel
Judg 12:3 the LORD delivered them into my *h*
Judg 13:1 LORD delivered them into the *h* of
Judg 13:5 out of the *h* of the Philistines
Judg 14:6 a kid, and he had nothing in his *h*
Judg 15:12 into the *h* of the Philistines
Judg 15:13 and deliver thee into their *h*
Judg 15:15 of an ass, and put forth his *h*
Judg 15:17 away the jawbone out of his *h*
Judg 15:18 into the *h* of thy servant
Judg 15:18 thirst, and fall into the *h* of the
Judg 16:18 her, and brought money in their *h*
Judg 16:23 Samson our enemy into our *h*
Judg 16:26 the lad that held him by the *h*
Judg 16:29 up, of the one with his right *h*
Judg 17:3 the LORD from my *h* for my son
Judg 18:19 lay thine *h* upon thy mouth, and go
Judg 20:28 I will deliver them into thine *h*
Judg 20:48 the beast, and all that came to *h*
Ruth 1:13 *h* of the LORD is gone out against
Ruth 4:5 the field of the *h* of Naomi
Ruth 4:9 and Mahlon's, of the *h* of Naomi
1Sa 2:13 fleshhook of three teeth in his *h*
1Sa 4:3 us out of the *h* of our enemies
1Sa 4:8 out of the *h* of these mighty Gods
1Sa 5:6 But the *h* of the LORD was heavy
1Sa 5:7 for his *h* is sore upon us, and
1Sa 5:9 the *h* of the LORD was against the
1Sa 5:11 the *h* of God was very heavy there
1Sa 6:3 why his *h* is not removed from you
1Sa 6:5 will lighten his *h* from off you
1Sa 6:9 it is not his *h* that smote us
1Sa 6:12 to the right *h* or to the left
1Sa 7:3 out of the *h* of the Philistines
1Sa 7:8 out of the *h* of the Philistines
1Sa 7:13 the *h* of the LORD was against the
1Sa 9:8 I have here at *h* the fourth part
1Sa 9:16 out of the *h* of the Philistines
1Sa 10:18 you out of the *h* of the Egyptians
1Sa 10:18 out of the *h* of all kingdoms, and
1Sa 12:3 or of whose *h* have I received any
1Sa 12:4 thou taken ought of any man's *h*
1Sa 12:5 ye have not found ought in my *h*
1Sa 12:9 he sold them into the *h* of Sisera
1Sa 12:9 into the *h* of the Philistines, and
1Sa 12:9 into the *h* of the king of Moab,
1Sa 12:10 us out of the *h* of our enemies
1Sa 12:11 delivered you out of the *h* of
1Sa 12:15 then shall the *h* of the LORD be
1Sa 13:22 sword nor spear found in the *h* of
1Sa 14:10 hath delivered them into our *h*
1Sa 14:12 them into the *h* of Israel
1Sa 14:19 unto the priest, Withdraw thine *h*
1Sa 14:26 but no man put his *h* to his mouth
1Sa 14:27 end of the rod that was in his *h*
1Sa 14:27 and put his *h* to his mouth
1Sa 14:37 deliver them into the *h* of Israel
1Sa 14:43 end of the rod that was in mine *h*
1Sa 16:16 that he shall play with his *h*
1Sa 16:23 an harp, and played with his *h*
1Sa 17:22 *h* of the keeper of the carriage
1Sa 17:37 out of the *h* of this Philistine
1Sa 17:40 And he took his staff in his *h*
1Sa 17:40 and his sling was in his *h*
1Sa 17:46 the LORD deliver thee into mine *h*
1Sa 17:49 And David put his *h* in his bag
1Sa 17:50 was no sword in the *h* of David
1Sa 17:57 head of the Philistine in his *h*
1Sa 18:10 and David played with his *h*
1Sa 18:10 there was a javelin in Saul's *h*
1Sa 18:17 said, Let not mine *h* be upon him
1Sa 18:17 but let the *h* of the Philistines
1Sa 18:21 that the *h* of the Philistines may
1Sa 18:25 fall by the *h* of the Philistines
1Sa 19:5 For he did put his life in his *h*
1Sa 19:9 house with his javelin in his *h*
1Sa 19:9 and David played with his *h*
1Sa 20:16 it at the *h* of David's enemies
1Sa 20:19 when the business was in *h*
1Sa 21:3 therefore what is under thine *h*
1Sa 21:3 me five loaves of bread in mine *h*
1Sa 21:4 is no common bread under mine *h*
1Sa 21:8 here under thine *h* spear or sword
1Sa 22:6 Ramah, having his spear in his *h*
1Sa 22:17 because their *h* also is with
1Sa 22:17 king would not put forth their *h*
1Sa 23:4 the Philistines into thine *h*
1Sa 23:6 came down with an ephod in his *h*
1Sa 23:7 hath delivered him into mine *h*
1Sa 23:11 Keilah deliver me up into his *h*
1Sa 23:12 me and my men into the *h* of Saul
1Sa 23:14 God delivered him not into his *h*
1Sa 23:16 and strengthened his *h* in God
1Sa 23:17 for the *h* of Saul my father shall
1Sa 23:20 to deliver him into the king's *h*
1Sa 24:4 deliver thine enemy into thine *h*

1Sa 24:6 stretch forth mine *h* against him
1Sa 24:10 to day into mine *h* in the cave
1Sa 24:10 put forth mine *h* against my lord
1Sa 24:11 see the skirt of thy robe in my *h*
1Sa 24:11 evil nor transgression in mine *h*
1Sa 24:12 but mine *h* shall not be upon thee
1Sa 24:13 but mine *h* shall not be upon thee
1Sa 24:15 and deliver me out of thine *h*
1Sa 24:18 had delivered me into thine *h*
1Sa 24:20 shall be established in thine *h*
1Sa 25:8 to thine *h* unto thy servants
1Sa 25:26 avenging thyself with thine own *h*
1Sa 25:33 avenging myself with mine own *h*
1Sa 25:35 So David received of her *h* that
1Sa 25:39 my reproach from the *h* of Nabal
1Sa 26:8 thine enemy into thine *h* this day
1Sa 26:9 his *h* against the LORD's anointed
1Sa 26:11 *h* against the LORD's anointed
1Sa 26:18 or what evil is in mine *h*
1Sa 26:23 delivered thee into my *h* to day
1Sa 26:23 *h* against the LORD's anointed
1Sa 27:1 perish one day by the *h* of Saul
1Sa 27:1 so shall I escape out of his *h*
1Sa 28:17 rent the kingdom out of thine *h*
1Sa 28:19 into the *h* of the Philistines
1Sa 28:19 into the *h* of the Philistines
1Sa 28:21 and I have put my life in my *h*
1Sa 30:23 that came against us into our *h*
2Sa 1:14 afraid to stretch forth thine *h*
2Sa 2:19 he turned not to the right *h* nor
2Sa 2:21 to thy right *h* or to thy left
2Sa 3:8 thee into the *h* of David, that
2Sa 3:12 my *h* shall be with thee, to bring
2Sa 3:18 By the *h* of my servant David I
2Sa 3:18 out of the *h* of the Philistines
2Sa 3:18 out of the *h* of all their enemies
2Sa 4:11 now require his blood of your *h*
2Sa 5:19 thou deliver them into mine *h*
2Sa 5:19 the Philistines into thine *h*
2Sa 6:6 put forth his *h* to the ark of God
2Sa 8:1 out of the *h* of the Philistines
2Sa 10:2 sent to comfort him by the *h* of
2Sa 10:10 into the *h* of Abishai his brother
2Sa 11:14 and sent it by the *h* of Uriah
2Sa 12:7 thee out of the *h* of Saul
2Sa 12:25 he sent by the *h* of Nathan the
2Sa 13:5 I may see it, and eat it at her *h*
2Sa 13:6 my sight, that I may eat at her *h*
2Sa 13:10 that I may eat of thine *h*
2Sa 13:19 laid her *h* on her head, and went
2Sa 14:16 *h* of the man that would destroy
2Sa 14:19 Is not the *h* of Joab with thee in
2Sa 14:19 none can turn to the right *h* or
2Sa 15:5 him obeisance, he put forth his *h*
2Sa 16:6 mighty men were on his right *h*
2Sa 16:8 into the *h* of Absalom thy son
2Sa 18:2 of the people under the *h* of Joab
2Sa 18:2 a third part under the *h* of
2Sa 18:2 under the *h* of Ittai the Gittite
2Sa 18:12 shekels of silver in mine *h*
2Sa 18:12 mine *h* against the king's son
2Sa 18:14 And he took three darts in his *h*
2Sa 18:28 their *h* against my lord the king
2Sa 19:9 us out of the *h* of our enemies
2Sa 19:9 out of the *h* of the Philistines
2Sa 20:9 with the right *h* to kiss him
2Sa 20:10 to the sword that was in Joab's *h*
2Sa 20:21 lifted up his *h* against the king
2Sa 21:20 that had on every *h* six fingers
2Sa 21:22 Gath, and fell by the *h* of David
2Sa 21:22 and by the *h* of his servants
2Sa 22:1 out of the *h* of all his enemies
2Sa 22:1 enemies, and out of the *h* of Saul
2Sa 23:10 Philistines until his *h* was weary
2Sa 23:10 his *h* clave unto the sword
2Sa 23:21 the Egyptian had a spear in his *h*
2Sa 23:21 the spear out of the Egyptian's *h*
2Sa 24:14 fall now into the *h* of the LORD
2Sa 24:14 let me not fall into the *h* of man
2Sa 24:16 the angel stretched out his *h*
2Sa 24:16 stay now thine *h*
2Sa 24:17 let thine *h*, I pray thee, be
1Kin 2:19 and she sat on his right *h*
1Kin 2:25 king Solomon sent by the *h* of
1Kin 2:46 established in the *h* of Solomon
1Kin 7:26 it was an *h* breadth thick, and the
1Kin 8:15 and hath with his *h* fulfilled it
1Kin 8:24 and hast fulfilled it with thine *h*
1Kin 8:42 great name, and of thy strong *h*
1Kin 8:53 by the *h* of Moses thy servant
1Kin 8:56 by the *h* of Moses his servant
1Kin 11:12 rend it out of the *h* of thy son
1Kin 11:26 lifted up his *h* against the king
1Kin 11:27 lifted up his *h* against the king
1Kin 11:31 kingdom out of the *h* of Solomon
1Kin 11:34 the whole kingdom out of his *h*
1Kin 11:35 the kingdom out of his son's *h*
1Kin 13:4 he put forth his *h* from the altar
1Kin 13:4 And his *h*, which he put forth
1Kin 13:6 that my *h* may be restored me
1Kin 13:6 the king's *h* was restored him
1Kin 14:18 which he spake by the *h* of his
1Kin 15:18 them into the *h* of his servants
1Kin 16:7 also by the *h* of the prophet Jehu
1Kin 17:11 a morsel of bread in thine *h*
1Kin 18:9 thy servant into the *h* of Ahab
1Kin 18:44 out of the sea, like a man's *h*
1Kin 18:46 the *h* of the LORD was on Elijah
1Kin 20:6 they shall put it in their *h*
1Kin 20:13 deliver it into thine *h* this day
1Kin 20:28 this great multitude into thine *h*
1Kin 20:42 thou hast let go out of thy *h* a
1Kin 22:3 out of the *h* of the king of Syria
1Kin 22:6 deliver it into the *h* of the king
1Kin 22:12 deliver it into the king's *h*
1Kin 22:15 deliver it into the *h* of the king
1Kin 22:19 standing by him on his right *h*
1Kin 22:34 of his chariot, Turn thine *h*
2Kin 3:10 deliver them into the *h* of Moab
2Kin 3:13 deliver them into the *h* of Moab
2Kin 3:15 that the *h* of the LORD came upon
2Kin 3:18 the Moabites also into your *h*
2Kin 4:29 and take my staff in thine *h*
2Kin 5:11 strike his *h* over the place, and
2Kin 5:18 there, and he leaneth on my *h*
2Kin 5:24 tower, he took them from their *h*
2Kin 6:7 And he put out his *h*, and took it
2Kin 7:2 Then a lord on whose *h* the king
2Kin 7:17 appointed the lord on whose *h* he
2Kin 8:8 Hazael, Take a present in thine *h*
2Kin 8:20 from under the *h* of Judah
2Kin 8:22 the *h* of Judah unto this day
2Kin 9:1 take this box of oil in thine *h*
2Kin 9:7 of the LORD, at the *h* of Jezebel
2Kin 10:15 If it be, give me thine *h*
2Kin 10:15 And he gave him his *h*
2Kin 11:8 man with his weapons in his *h*
2Kin 11:11 man with his weapons in his *h*
2Kin 12:15 into whose *h* they delivered the
2Kin 13:3 the *h* of Hazael king of Syria
2Kin 13:3 into the *h* of Ben-hadad the son
2Kin 13:5 from under the *h* of the Syrians
2Kin 13:16 Israel, Put thine *h* upon the bow
2Kin 13:16 And he put his *h* upon it
2Kin 13:25 *h* of Ben-hadad the son of Hazael
2Kin 13:25 *h* of Jehoahaz his father by war
2Kin 14:5 kingdom was confirmed in his *h*
2Kin 14:25 by the *h* of his servant Jonah
2Kin 14:27 but he saved them by the *h* of
2Kin 15:19 that his *h* might be with him to
2Kin 15:19 to confirm the kingdom in his *h*
2Kin 16:7 save me out of the *h* of the king
2Kin 16:7 out of the *h* of the king of
2Kin 17:7 from under the *h* of Pharaoh king
2Kin 17:20 them into the *h* of spoilers
2Kin 17:39 out of the *h* of all your enemies
2Kin 18:21 a man lean, it will go into his *h*
2Kin 18:29 able to deliver you out of his *h*
2Kin 18:30 into the *h* of the king of Assyria
2Kin 18:33 of the *h* of the king of Assyria
2Kin 18:34 delivered Samaria out of mine *h*
2Kin 18:35 their country out of mine *h*
2Kin 18:35 deliver Jerusalem out of mine *h*
2Kin 19:10 into the *h* of the king of Assyria
2Kin 19:14 letter of the *h* of the messengers
2Kin 19:19 thee, save thou us out of his *h*
2Kin 20:6 this city out of the *h* of the
2Kin 21:14 them into the *h* of their enemies
2Kin 22:2 to the right *h* or to the left
2Kin 22:5 the *h* of the doers of the work
2Kin 22:7 that was delivered into their *h*
2Kin 22:9 the *h* of them that do the work
2Kin 23:8 left *h* at the gate of the city
2Kin 23:13 which were on the right *h* of the
1Chr 4:10 that thine *h* might be with me, and
1Chr 5:10 Hagarites, who fell by their *h*
1Chr 5:20 were delivered into their *h*
1Chr 6:15 Judah and Jerusalem by the *h* of
1Chr 6:39 Asaph, who stood on his right *h*
1Chr 6:44 of Merari stood on the left *h*
1Chr 11:23 in the Egyptian's *h* was a spear
1Chr 11:23 the spear out of the Egyptian's *h*
1Chr 12:2 and could use both the right *h*
1Chr 13:9 put forth his *h* to hold the ark
1Chr 13:10 because he put his *h* to the ark
1Chr 14:10 thou deliver them into mine *h*
1Chr 14:10 I will deliver them into thine *h*
1Chr 14:11 mine *h* like the breaking forth of
1Chr 16:7 the LORD into the *h* of Asaph
1Chr 18:1 out of the *h* of the Philistines
1Chr 19:11 unto the *h* of Abishai his brother
1Chr 20:6 four and twenty, six on each *h*
1Chr 20:8 and they fell by the *h* of David
1Chr 20:8 and by the *h* of his servants
1Chr 21:13 fall now into the *h* of the LORD
1Chr 21:13 let me not fall into the *h* of man
1Chr 21:15 It is enough, stay now thine *h*
1Chr 21:16 having a drawn sword in his *h*
1Chr 21:17 let thine *h*, I pray thee, O LORD
1Chr 22:18 of the land into mine *h*
1Chr 26:28 it was under the *h* of Shelomith
1Chr 28:19 in writing by his *h* upon me
1Chr 29:8 by the *h* of Jehiel the Gershonite
1Chr 29:12 and in thine *h* is power and might
1Chr 29:12 in thine *h* it is to make great,
1Chr 29:16 thine holy name cometh of thine *h*
2Chr 3:17 the temple, one on the right *h*
2Chr 3:17 of that on the right *h* Jachin
2Chr 4:6 and put five on the right *h*
2Chr 4:7 the temple, five on the right *h*
2Chr 6:15 and hast fulfilled it with thine *h*
2Chr 6:32 name's sake, and thy mighty *h*
2Chr 10:15 which he spake by the *h* of Ahijah
2Chr 12:5 also left you in the *h* of Shishak
2Chr 12:7 Jerusalem by the *h* of Shishak
2Chr 13:8 in the *h* of the sons of David
2Chr 13:16 God delivered them into their *h*
2Chr 16:7 of Syria escaped out of thine *h*
2Chr 16:8 he delivered them into thine *h*
2Chr 17:5 stablished the kingdom in his *h*
2Chr 18:5 will deliver it into the king's *h*
2Chr 18:11 deliver it into the *h* of the king
2Chr 18:14 shall be delivered into your *h*
2Chr 18:18 of heaven standing on his right *h*
2Chr 18:33 to his chariot man, Turn thine *h*
2Chr 20:6 in thine *h* is there not power and
2Chr 21:10 the *h* of Judah unto this day
2Chr 21:10 Libnah revolt from under his *h*
2Chr 23:7 man with his weapons in his *h*
2Chr 23:10 man having his weapon in his *h*
2Chr 23:18 the *h* of the priests the Levites
2Chr 24:11 office by the *h* of the Levites
2Chr 24:24 a very great host into their *h*
2Chr 25:15 their own people out of thine *h*
2Chr 25:20 them into the *h* of their enemies
2Chr 26:11 by the *h* of Jeiel the scribe
2Chr 26:11 under the *h* of Hananiah, one of
2Chr 26:13 And under their *h* was an army
2Chr 26:19 a censer in his *h* to burn incense
2Chr 28:5 into the *h* of the king of Syria
2Chr 28:5 into the *h* of the king of Israel
2Chr 28:9 hath delivered them into your *h*
2Chr 30:6 of the *h* of the kings of Assyria
2Chr 30:12 Also in Judah the *h* of God was to
2Chr 30:16 received of the *h* of the Levites
2Chr 31:13 overseers under the *h* of Cononiah
2Chr 32:11 of the *h* of the king of Assyria
2Chr 32:13 deliver their lands out of mine *h*
2Chr 32:14 deliver his people out of mine *h*
2Chr 32:14 able to deliver you out of mine *h*
2Chr 32:15 deliver his people out of mine *h*
2Chr 32:15 out of the *h* of my fathers
2Chr 32:15 God deliver you out of mine *h*
2Chr 32:17 their people out of mine *h*
2Chr 32:17 deliver his people out of mine *h*
2Chr 32:22 of Jerusalem from the *h* of
2Chr 32:22 from the *h* of all other, and
2Chr 33:8 the ordinances by the *h* of Moses
2Chr 34:2 declined neither to the right *h*
2Chr 34:9 had gathered of the *h* of Manasseh
2Chr 34:10 they put it in the *h* of the
2Chr 34:17 it into the *h* of the overseers
2Chr 34:17 and to the *h* of the workmen
2Chr 35:6 of the LORD by the *h* of Moses
2Chr 36:17 he gave them all into his *h*
Ezr 1:8 the *h* of Mithredath the treasurer
Ezr 5:12 he gave them into the *h* of
Ezr 6:12 shall put to their *h* to alter
Ezr 7:6 according to the *h* of the LORD
Ezr 7:9 to the good *h* of his God upon him

Ezr 7:14 of thy God which is in thine *h*
Ezr 7:25 of thy God, that is in thine *h*
Ezr 7:28 I was strengthened as the *h* of
Ezr 8:18 by the good *h* of our God upon us
Ezr 8:22 The *h* of our God is upon all them
Ezr 8:26 weighed unto their *h* six hundred
Ezr 8:31 the *h* of our God was upon us, and
Ezr 8:31 us from the *h* of the enemy
Ezr 8:33 *h* of Meremoth the son of Uriah
Ezr 9:2 the *h* of the princes and rulers
Ezr 9:7 been delivered into the *h* of the
Neh 1:10 great power, and by thy strong *h*
Neh 2:8 to the good *h* of my God upon me
Neh 2:18 Then I told them of the *h* of my
Neh 4:17 and with the other *h* held a weapon
Neh 6:5 time with an open letter in his *h*
Neh 8:4 and Maaseiah, on his right *h*
Neh 8:4 and on his left *h*, Pedaiah, and
Neh 9:14 by the *h* of Moses thy servant
Neh 9:27 them into the *h* of their enemies
Neh 9:27 out of the *h* of their enemies
Neh 9:28 them in the *h* of their enemies
Neh 9:30 gavest thou them into the *h* of
Neh 11:24 was at the king's *h* in all
Neh 12:31 *h* upon the wall toward the dung
Est 2:21 sought to lay *h* on the king
Est 3:10 the king took his ring from his *h*
Est 5:2 golden sceptre that was in his *h*
Est 6:2 who sought to lay *h* on the king
Est 6:9 horse be delivered to the *h* of
Est 8:7 he laid his *h* upon the Jews
Est 9:2 to lay *h* on such as sought their
Est 9:10 the spoil laid they not their *h*
Est 9:15 on the prey they laid not their *h*
Job 1:11 But put forth thine *h* now
Job 1:12 himself put not forth thine *h*
Job 2:5 But put forth thine *h* now
Job 2:6 Satan, Behold, he is in thine *h*
Job 2:10 we receive good at the *h* of God
Job 5:15 and from the *h* of the mighty
Job 6:9 that he would let loose his *h*
Job 6:23 Or, Deliver me from the enemy's *h*
Job 6:23 me from the *h* of the mighty
Job 9:24 is given into the *h* of the wicked
Job 9:33 that might lay his *h* upon us both
Job 10:7 that can deliver out of thine *h*
Job 11:14 If iniquity be in thine *h*
Job 12:6 into whose *h* God bringeth
Job 12:9 not in all these that the *h* of
Job 12:10 In whose *h* is the soul of every
Job 13:14 teeth, and put my life in mine *h*
Job 13:21 Withdraw thine *h* far from me
Job 15:23 day of darkness is ready at his *h*
Job 15:25 stretcheth out his *h* against God
Job 19:21 for the *h* of God hath touched me
Job 20:22 every *h* of the wicked shall come
Job 21:5 lay your *h* upon your mouth
Job 21:16 Lo, their good is not in their *h*
Job 23:9 On the left *h*, where he doth work
Job 23:9 he hideth himself on the right *h*
Job 26:13 his *h* hath formed the crooked
Job 27:11 I will teach you by the *h* of God
Job 27:22 he would fain flee out of his *h*
Job 28:9 putteth forth his *h* upon the rock
Job 29:9 laid their *h* on their mouth
Job 29:20 my bow was renewed in my *h*
Job 30:12 Upon my right *h* rise the youth
Job 30:21 with thy strong *h* thou opposest
Job 30:24 stretch out his *h* to the grave
Job 31:21 up my *h* against the fatherless
Job 31:25 because mine *h* had gotten much
Job 31:27 or my mouth hath kissed my *h*
Job 33:7 neither shall my *h* be heavy upon
Job 34:20 shall be taken away without *h*
Job 35:7 or what receiveth he of thine *h*
Job 37:7 He sealeth up the *h* of every man
Job 40:4 I will lay mine *h* upon my mouth
Job 40:14 thine own right *h* can save thee
Job 41:8 Lay thine *h* upon him, remember
Ps 10:12 O God, lift up thine *h*
Ps 10:14 spite, to requite it with thy *h*
Ps 16:8 because he is at my right *h*
Ps 16:11 at thy right *h* there are
Ps 17:7 *h* them which put their trust in
Ps 17:14 From men which are thy *h*, O LORD,
Ps 18:*t* him from the *h* of all his enemies
Ps 18:*t* and from the *h* of Saul
Ps 18:35 thy right *h* hath holden me up, and
Ps 20:6 saving strength of his right *h*
Ps 21:8 Thine *h* shall find out all thine
Ps 21:8 thy right *h* shall find out those
Ps 26:10 their right *h* is full of bribes
Ps 31:5 Into thine *h* I commit my spirit
Ps 31:8 me up into the *h* of the enemy
Ps 31:15 My times are in thy *h*
Ps 31:15 me from the *h* of mine enemies
Ps 32:4 night thy *h* was heavy upon me
Ps 36:11 let not the *h* of the wicked
Ps 37:24 the LORD upholdeth him with his *h*
Ps 37:33 LORD will not leave him in his *h*
Ps 38:2 in me, and thy *h* presseth me sore
Ps 39:10 consumed by the blow of thine *h*
Ps 44:2 drive out the heathen with thy *h*
Ps 44:3 but thy right *h*, and thine arm, and
Ps 45:4 thy right *h* shall teach thee
Ps 45:9 upon thy right *h* did stand the
Ps 48:10 thy right *h* is full of
Ps 60:5 save with thy right *h*, and hear me
Ps 63:8 thy right *h* upholdeth me
Ps 71:4 out of the *h* of the wicked
Ps 71:4 out of the *h* of the unrighteous
Ps 73:23 thou hast holden me by my right *h*
Ps 74:11 Why withdrawest thou thy *h*
Ps 74:11 even thy right *h*
Ps 75:8 For in the *h* of the LORD there is
Ps 77:10 of the right *h* of the most High
Ps 77:20 like a flock by the *h* of Moses
Ps 78:42 They remembered not his *h*
Ps 78:54 which his right *h* had purchased
Ps 78:61 and his glory into the enemy's *h*
Ps 80:15 which thy right *h* hath planted
Ps 80:17 Let thy *h* be upon the man of thy
Ps 80:17 be upon the man of thy right *h*
Ps 81:14 turned my *h* against their
Ps 82:4 them out of the *h* of the wicked
Ps 88:5 and they are cut off from thy *h*
Ps 89:13 thy *h*, and high is thy right *h*
Ps 89:21 With whom my *h* shall be
Ps 89:25 I will set his *h* also in the sea,
Ps 89:25 his right *h* in the rivers
Ps 89:42 up the right *h* of his adversaries
Ps 89:48 his soul from the *h* of the grave
Ps 91:7 and ten thousand at thy right *h*
Ps 95:4 In his *h* are the deep places of
Ps 95:7 pasture, and the sheep of his *h*
Ps 97:10 them out of the *h* of the wicked
Ps 98:1 his right *h*, and his holy arm,
Ps 104:28 thou openest thine *h*, they are
Ps 106:10 from the *h* of him that hated them
Ps 106:10 them from the *h* of the enemy
Ps 106:26 he lifted up his *h* against them
Ps 106:41 them into the *h* of the heathen
Ps 106:42 into subjection under their *h*
Ps 107:2 redeemed from the *h* of the enemy
Ps 108:6 save with thy right *h*, and answer
Ps 109:6 and let Satan stand at his right *h*
Ps 109:27 they may know that this is thy *h*
Ps 109:31 stand at the right *h* of the poor
Ps 110:1 my Lord, Sit thou at my right *h*
Ps 110:5 The LORD at thy right *h* shall
Ps 118:15 the right *h* of the LORD doeth
Ps 118:16 The right *h* of the LORD is
Ps 118:16 the right *h* of the LORD doeth
Ps 119:109 My soul is continually in my *h*
Ps 119:173 Let thine *h* help me
Ps 121:5 is thy shade upon thy right *h*
Ps 123:2 look unto the *h* of their masters
Ps 123:2 maiden unto the *h* of her mistress
Ps 127:4 are in the *h* of a mighty man
Ps 129:7 the mower filleth not his *h*
Ps 136:12 With a strong *h*, and with a
Ps 137:5 let my right *h* forget her cunning
Ps 138:7 thine *h* against the wrath of mine
Ps 138:7 thy right *h* shall save me
Ps 139:5 before, and laid thine *h* upon me
Ps 139:10 Even there shall thy *h* lead me
Ps 139:10 thy right *h* shall hold me
Ps 142:4 I looked on my right *h*, and beheld
Ps 144:7 Send thine *h* from above
Ps 144:7 from the *h* of strange children
Ps 144:8 their right *h* is a right *h* of
Ps 144:11 me from the *h* of strange children
Ps 144:11 their right *h* is a right *h* of
Ps 145:16 Thou openest thine *h*, and
Ps 149:6 and a twoedged sword in their *h*
Prov 1:24 I have stretched out my *h*
Prov 3:16 Length of days is in her right *h*
Prov 3:16 and in her left *h* riches and honour
Prov 3:27 in the power of thine *h* to do it
Prov 4:27 to the right *h* nor to the left
Prov 6:1 stricken thy *h* with a stranger
Prov 6:3 art come into the *h* of thy friend
Prov 6:5 as a roe from the *h* of the hunter
Prov 6:5 a bird from the *h* of the fowler
Prov 10:4 poor that dealeth with a slack *h*
Prov 10:4 but the *h* of the diligent maketh
Prov 11:21 Though *h* join in *h*, the wicked
Prov 12:24 The *h* of the diligent shall bear
Prov 16:5 though *h* join in *h*, he shall
Prov 17:16 in the *h* of a fool to get wisdom
Prov 19:24 man hideth his *h* in his bosom
Prov 21:1 heart is in the *h* of the LORD
Prov 26:6 that sendeth a message by the *h*
Prov 26:9 goeth up into the *h* of a drunkard
Prov 26:15 hideth his *h* in his bosom
Prov 27:16 and the ointment of his right *h*
Prov 30:32 lay thine *h* upon thy mouth
Prov 31:20 stretcheth out her *h* to the poor
Eccl 2:24 that it was from the *h* of God
Eccl 5:14 son, and there is nothing in his *h*
Eccl 5:15 which he may carry away in his *h*
Eccl 7:18 from this withdraw not thine *h*
Eccl 9:1 their works, are in the *h* of God
Eccl 9:10 Whatsoever thy *h* findeth to do
Eccl 10:2 man's heart is at his right *h*
Eccl 11:6 the evening withhold not thine *h*
Song 2:6 His left *h* is under my head, and
Song 2:6 his right *h* doth embrace me
Song 5:4 My beloved put in his *h* by the
Song 8:3 His left *h* should be under my
Song 8:3 his right *h* should embrace me
Is 1:12 who hath required this at your *h*
Is 1:25 And I will turn my *h* upon thee
Is 3:6 and let this ruin be under thy *h*
Is 5:25 forth his *h* against them, and hath
Is 5:25 but his *h* is stretched out still
Is 6:6 me, having a live coal in his *h*
Is 8:11 spake thus to me with a strong *h*
Is 9:12 but his *h* is stretched out still
Is 9:17 but his *h* is stretched out still
Is 9:20 And he shall snatch on the right *h*
Is 9:20 and he shall eat on the left *h*
Is 9:21 but his *h* is stretched out still
Is 10:4 but his *h* is stretched out still
Is 10:5 the staff in their *h* is mine
Is 10:10 As my *h* hath found the kingdoms
Is 10:13 strength of my *h* I have done it
Is 10:14 my *h* hath found as a nest the
Is 10:32 he shall shake his *h* against the
Is 11:8 put his *h* on the cockatrice' den
Is 11:11 his *h* again the second time to
Is 11:14 they shall lay their *h* upon Edom
Is 11:15 he shake his *h* over the river
Is 13:2 the voice unto them, shake the *h*
Is 13:6 for the day of the LORD is at *h*
Is 14:26 this is the *h* that is stretched
Is 14:27 his *h* is stretched out, and who
Is 19:4 over into the *h* of a cruel lord
Is 19:16 of the *h* of the LORD of hosts
Is 22:21 commit thy government into his *h*
Is 23:11 stretched out his *h* over the sea
Is 25:10 shall the *h* of the LORD rest
Is 26:11 when thy *h* is lifted up, they
Is 28:2 cast down to the earth with the *h*
Is 28:4 is yet in his *h* he eateth it up
Is 30:21 it, when ye turn to the right *h*
Is 31:3 the LORD shall stretch out his *h*
Is 34:17 his *h* hath divided it unto them
Is 36:6 a man lean, it will go into his *h*
Is 36:15 into the *h* of the king of Assyria
Is 36:18 of the *h* of the king of Assyria
Is 36:19 delivered Samaria out of my *h*
Is 36:20 delivered their land out of my *h*
Is 36:20 deliver Jerusalem out of my *h*
Is 37:10 into the *h* of the king of Assyria
Is 37:14 from the *h* of the messengers
Is 37:20 LORD our God, save us from his *h*
Is 38:6 this city out of the *h* of the
Is 40:2 LORD's *h* double for all her sins
Is 40:10 Lord GOD will come with strong *h*
Is 40:12 the waters in the hollow of his *h*
Is 41:10 the right *h* of my righteousness
Is 41:13 thy God will hold thy right *h*
Is 41:20 that the *h* of the LORD hath done
Is 42:6 and will hold thine *h*, and will
Is 43:13 none that can deliver out of my *h*
Is 44:5 with his *h* unto the LORD, and
Is 44:20 Is there not a lie in my right *h*
Is 45:1 whose right *h* I have holden, to
Is 47:6 and given them into thine *h*

Is 48:13 Mine *h* also hath laid the
Is 48:13 my right *h* hath spanned the
Is 49:2 shadow of his *h* hath he hid me
Is 49:22 lift up mine *h* to the Gentiles
Is 50:2 Is my *h* shortened at all, that it
Is 50:11 This shall ye have of mine *h*
Is 51:16 thee in the shadow of mine *h*
Is 51:17 which hast drunk at the *h* of the
Is 51:18 any that taketh her by the *h* of
Is 51:22 of thine *h* the cup of trembling
Is 51:23 the *h* of them that afflict thee
Is 53:10 the LORD shall prosper in his *h*
Is 54:3 shalt break forth on the right *h*
Is 56:2 keepeth his *h* from doing any evil
Is 57:10 hast found the life of thine *h*
Is 59:1 the LORD's *h* is not shortened,
Is 62:3 of glory in the *h* of the LORD
Is 62:3 royal diadem in the *h* of thy God
Is 62:8 LORD hath sworn by his right *h*
Is 63:12 That led them by the right *h* of
Is 64:8 and we all are the work of thy *h*
Is 66:2 all those things hath mine *h* made
Is 66:14 the *h* of the LORD shall be known
Jer 1:9 Then the LORD put forth his *h*
Jer 6:9 turn back thine *h* as a
Jer 6:12 for I will stretch out my *h* upon
Jer 11:21 LORD, that thou die not by our *h*
Jer 12:7 my soul into the *h* of her enemies
Jer 15:6 I stretch out my *h* against thee
Jer 15:17 I sat alone because of thy *h*
Jer 15:21 thee out of the *h* of the wicked
Jer 15:21 thee out of the *h* of the terrible
Jer 16:21 I will cause them to know mine *h*
Jer 18:4 was marred in the *h* of the potter
Jer 18:6 as the clay is in the potter's *h*
Jer 18:6 so are ye in mine *h*
Jer 20:4 into the *h* of the king of Babylon
Jer 20:5 give into the *h* of their enemies
Jer 20:13 the poor from the *h* of evildoers
Jer 21:5 you with an outstretched *h*
Jer 21:7 into the *h* of Nebuchadrezzar king
Jer 21:7 into the *h* of their enemies, and
Jer 21:7 into the *h* of those that seek
Jer 21:10 into the *h* of the king of Babylon
Jer 21:12 out of the *h* of the oppressor
Jer 22:3 out of the *h* of the oppressor
Jer 22:24 were the signet upon my right *h*
Jer 22:25 I will give thee into the *h* of
Jer 22:25 into the *h* of them whose face
Jer 22:25 even into the *h* of Nebuchadrezzar
Jer 22:25 into the *h* of the Chaldeans
Jer 23:23 Am I a God at *h*, saith the LORD,
Jer 25:15 the wine cup of this fury at my *h*
Jer 25:17 took I the cup at the LORD's *h*
Jer 25:28 take the cup at thine *h* to drink
Jer 26:14 As for me, behold, I am in your *h*
Jer 26:24 Nevertheless the *h* of Ahikam the
Jer 26:24 the *h* of the people to put him to
Jer 27:3 by the *h* of the messengers which
Jer 27:6 *h* of Nebuchadnezzar the king of
Jer 27:8 I have consumed them by his *h*
Jer 29:3 By the *h* of Elasah the son of
Jer 29:21 the *h* of Nebuchadrezzar king of
Jer 31:11 ransomed him from the *h* of him
Jer 31:32 *h* to bring them out of the land
Jer 32:3 into the *h* of the king of Babylon
Jer 32:4 out of the *h* of the Chaldeans
Jer 32:4 into the *h* of the king of Babylon
Jer 32:21 with wonders, and with a strong *h*
Jer 32:24 given into the *h* of the Chaldeans
Jer 32:25 given into the *h* of the Chaldeans
Jer 32:28 city into the *h* of the Chaldeans
Jer 32:28 into the *h* of Nebuchadrezzar king
Jer 32:36 *h* of the king of Babylon by the
Jer 32:43 given into the *h* of the Chaldeans
Jer 34:2 into the *h* of the king of Babylon
Jer 34:3 shalt not escape out of his *h*
Jer 34:3 be taken, and delivered into his *h*
Jer 34:20 them into the *h* of their enemies
Jer 34:20 into the *h* of them that seek
Jer 34:21 give into the *h* of their enemies
Jer 34:21 into the *h* of them that seek
Jer 34:21 into the *h* of the king of
Jer 36:14 Take in thine *h* the roll wherein
Jer 36:14 of Neriah took the roll in his *h*
Jer 37:17 into the *h* of the king of Babylon
Jer 38:3 *h* of the king of Babylon's army
Jer 38:5 said, Behold, he is in your *h*
Jer 38:16 will I give thee into the *h* of
Jer 38:18 given into the *h* of the Chaldeans
Jer 38:18 shalt not escape out of their *h*
Jer 38:19 lest they deliver me into their *h*
Jer 38:23 shalt not escape out of their *h*
Jer 38:23 by the *h* of the king of Babylon
Jer 39:17 the *h* of the men of whom thou art
Jer 40:4 chains which were upon thine *h*
Jer 41:5 offerings and incense in their *h*
Jer 42:11 you, and to deliver you from his *h*
Jer 43:3 us into the *h* of the Chaldeans
Jer 43:9 Take great stones in thine *h*
Jer 44:25 mouths, and fulfilled with your *h*
Jer 44:30 Egypt into the *h* of his enemies
Jer 44:30 into the *h* of them that seek his
Jer 44:30 the *h* of Nebuchadrezzar king of
Jer 46:24 the *h* of the people of the north
Jer 46:26 I will deliver them into the *h* of
Jer 46:26 into the *h* of Nebuchadrezzar king
Jer 46:26 into the *h* of his servants
Jer 50:15 she hath given her *h*
Jer 51:7 been a golden cup in the LORD's *h*
Jer 51:25 will stretch out mine *h* upon thee
Lam 1:7 fell into the *h* of the enemy
Lam 1:10 *h* upon all her pleasant things
Lam 1:14 transgressions is bound by his *h*
Lam 2:3 his right *h* from before the enemy
Lam 2:4 with his right *h* as an adversary
Lam 2:7 he hath given up into the *h* of
Lam 2:8 withdrawn his *h* from destroying
Lam 3:3 he turneth his *h* against me all
Lam 5:6 have given the *h* to the Egyptians
Lam 5:8 doth deliver us out of their *h*
Lam 5:12 Princes are hanged up by their *h*
Eze 1:3 the *h* of the LORD was there upon
Eze 2:9 behold, an *h* was sent unto me
Eze 3:14 but the *h* of the LORD was strong
Eze 3:18 blood will I require at thine *h*
Eze 3:20 blood will I require at thine *h*
Eze 3:22 the *h* of the LORD was there upon
Eze 6:11 Smite with thine *h*, and stamp with
Eze 6:14 will I stretch out my *h* upon them
Eze 8:1 that the *h* of the Lord GOD fell
Eze 8:3 And he put forth the form of an *h*
Eze 8:11 every man his censer in his *h*
Eze 9:1 his destroying weapon in his *h*
Eze 9:2 man a slaughter weapon in his *h*
Eze 10:2 fill thine *h* with coals of fire
Eze 10:7 one cherub stretched forth his *h*
Eze 10:8 of a man's *h* under their wings
Eze 12:7 through the wall with mine *h*
Eze 12:23 say unto them, The days are at *h*
Eze 13:9 mine *h* shall be upon the prophets
Eze 13:21 deliver my people out of your *h*
Eze 13:21 be no more in your *h* to be hunted
Eze 13:23 deliver my people out of your *h*
Eze 14:9 I will stretch out my *h* upon him
Eze 14:13 will I stretch out mine *h* upon it
Eze 16:27 have stretched out my *h* over thee
Eze 16:39 will also give thee into their *h*
Eze 16:46 that dwell at thy left *h*
Eze 16:46 that dwelleth at thy right *h*
Eze 16:49 she strengthen the *h* of the poor
Eze 17:18 when, lo, he had given his *h*
Eze 18:8 withdrawn his *h* from iniquity
Eze 18:17 taken off his *h* from the poor
Eze 20:5 lifted up mine *h* unto the seed of
Eze 20:5 when I lifted up mine *h* unto them
Eze 20:6 that I lifted up mine *h* unto them
Eze 20:15 Yet also I lifted up my *h* unto
Eze 20:22 Nevertheless I withdrew mine *h*
Eze 20:23 I lifted up mine *h* unto them also
Eze 20:28 up mine *h* to give it to them
Eze 20:33 Lord GOD, surely with a mighty *h*
Eze 20:34 ye are scattered, with a mighty *h*
Eze 20:42 mine *h* to give it to your fathers
Eze 21:11 give it into the *h* of the slayer
Eze 21:16 or other, either on the right *h*
Eze 21:22 At his right *h* was the divination
Eze 21:24 ye shall be taken with the *h*
Eze 21:31 thee into the *h* of brutish men
Eze 22:13 *h* at thy dishonest gain which
Eze 23:9 her into the *h* of her lovers
Eze 23:9 into the *h* of the Assyrians, upon
Eze 23:28 the *h* of them whom thou hatest
Eze 23:28 into the *h* of them from whom thy
Eze 23:31 will I give her cup into thine *h*
Eze 25:7 will stretch out mine *h* upon thee
Eze 25:13 also stretch out mine *h* upon Edom
Eze 25:14 Edom by the *h* of my people Israel
Eze 25:16 out mine *h* upon the Philistines
Eze 27:15 were the merchandise of thine *h*
Eze 28:9 in the *h* of him that slayeth thee
Eze 28:10 by the *h* of strangers
Eze 29:7 they took hold of thee by thy *h*
Eze 30:10 of Egypt to cease by the *h* of
Eze 30:12 the land into the *h* of the wicked
Eze 30:12 is therein, by the *h* of strangers
Eze 30:22 the sword to fall out of his *h*
Eze 30:24 Babylon, and put my sword in his *h*
Eze 30:25 into the *h* of the king of Babylon
Eze 31:11 delivered him into the *h* of the
Eze 33:6 I require at the watchman's *h*
Eze 33:8 blood will I require at thine *h*
Eze 33:22 Now the *h* of the LORD was upon me
Eze 34:10 will require my flock at their *h*
Eze 34:27 delivered them out of the *h* of
Eze 35:3 stretch out mine *h* against thee
Eze 36:7 I have lifted up mine *h*, Surely
Eze 36:8 for they are at *h* to come
Eze 37:1 The *h* of the LORD was upon me, and
Eze 37:17 they shall become one in thine *h*
Eze 37:19 which is in the *h* of Ephraim
Eze 37:19 and they shall be one in mine *h*
Eze 37:20 be in thine *h* before their eyes
Eze 38:12 to turn thine *h* upon the desolate
Eze 39:3 smite thy bow out of thy left *h*
Eze 39:3 arrows to fall out of thy right *h*
Eze 39:21 my *h* that I have laid upon them
Eze 39:23 them into the *h* of their enemies
Eze 40:1 day the *h* of the LORD was upon me
Eze 40:3 with a line of flax in his *h*
Eze 40:5 in the man's *h* a measuring reed
Eze 40:5 long by the cubit and an *h* breadth
Eze 40:43 an *h* broad, fastened round about
Eze 43:13 cubit is a cubit and an *h* breadth
Eze 44:12 I lifted up mine *h* against them
Eze 46:7 as his *h* shall attain unto
Eze 47:3 line in his *h* went forth eastward
Eze 47:14 the which I lifted up mine *h* to
Dan 1:2 king of Judah into his *h*, with
Dan 2:38 heaven hath he given into thine *h*
Dan 3:17 he will deliver us out of thine *h*
Dan 4:35 and none can stay his *h*, or say
Dan 5:5 came forth fingers of a man's *h*
Dan 5:5 saw the part of the *h* that wrote
Dan 5:23 the God in whose *h* thy breath is
Dan 5:24 the part of the *h* sent from him
Dan 7:25 be given into his *h* until a time
Dan 8:4 that could deliver out of his *h*
Dan 8:7 deliver the ram out of his *h*
Dan 8:25 cause craft to prosper in his *h*
Dan 8:25 but he shall be broken without *h*
Dan 9:15 the land of Egypt with a mighty *h*
Dan 10:10 an *h* touched me, which set me
Dan 11:11 shall be given into his *h*
Dan 11:16 which by his *h* shall be consumed
Dan 11:41 these shall escape out of his *h*
Dan 11:42 his *h* also upon the countries
Dan 12:7 when he held up his right *h*
Dan 12:7 his left *h* unto heaven, and sware
Hos 2:10 shall deliver her out of mine *h*
Hos 7:5 stretched out his *h* with scorners
Hos 12:7 balances of deceit are in his *h*
Joel 1:15 for the day of the LORD is at *h*
Joel 2:1 LORD cometh, for it is nigh at *h*
Joel 3:8 your daughters into the *h* of the
Amos 1:8 I will turn mine *h* against Ekron
Amos 5:19 leaned his *h* on the wall, and a
Amos 7:7 with a plumbline in his *h*
Amos 9:2 thence shall mine *h* take them
Jonah 4:11 discern between their right *h*
Jonah 4:11 their right *h* and their left *h*
Mic 2:1 it is in the power of their *h*
Mic 4:10 thee from the *h* of thine enemies
Mic 5:9 Thine *h* shall be lifted up upon
Mic 5:12 off witchcrafts out of thine *h*
Mic 7:16 lay their *h* upon their mouth
Hab 2:16 right *h* shall be turned unto thee
Hab 3:4 he had horns coming out of his *h*
Zeph 1:4 stretch out mine *h* upon Judah
Zeph 1:7 for the day of the LORD is at *h*
Zeph 2:13 out his *h* against the north
Zeph 2:15 by her shall hiss, and wag his *h*
Zec 2:1 with a measuring line in his *h*
Zec 2:9 I will shake mine *h* upon them
Zec 3:1 at his right *h* to resist him
Zec 4:10 shall see the plummet in the *h* of
Zec 8:4 his staff in his *h* for very age
Zec 11:6 every one into his neighbour's *h*
Zec 11:6 and into the *h* of his king
Zec 11:6 out of their *h* I will not deliver

Zec 12:6 round about, on the right *h*
Zec 13:7 I will turn mine *h* upon the
Zec 14:13 one on the *h* of his neighbour
Zec 14:13 his *h* shall rise up against the
Zec 14:13 up against the *h* of his neighbour
Mal 1:10 I accept an offering at your *h*
Mal 1:13 should I accept this of your *h*
Mal 2:13 it with good will at your *h*
Mt 3:2 for the kingdom of heaven is at *h*
Mt 3:12 Whose fan is in his *h*, and he will
Mt 4:17 for the kingdom of heaven is at *h*
Mt 5:30 And if thy right *h* offend thee
Mt 6:3 let not thy left *h* know what thy
Mt 6:3 know what thy right *h* doeth
Mt 8:3 And Jesus put forth his *h*, and
Mt 8:15 And he touched her *h*, and the fever
Mt 9:18 lay thy *h* upon her, and she shall
Mt 9:25 he went in, and took her by the *h*
Mt 10:7 The kingdom of heaven is at *h*
Mt 12:10 a man which had his *h* withered
Mt 12:13 to the man, Stretch forth thine *h*
Mt 12:49 forth his *h* toward his disciples
Mt 14:31 Jesus stretched forth his *h*
Mt 18:8 Wherefore if thy *h* or thy foot
Mt 20:21 may sit, the one on thy right *h*
Mt 20:23 but to sit on my right *h*, and on
Mt 22:13 king to the servants, Bind him *h*
Mt 22:44 my Lord, Sit thou on my right *h*
Mt 25:33 set the sheep on his right *h*
Mt 25:34 King say unto them on his right *h*
Mt 25:41 say also unto them on the left *h*
Mt 26:18 The Master saith, My time is at *h*
Mt 26:23 dippeth his *h* with me in the dish
Mt 26:45 behold, the hour is at *h*, and the
Mt 26:46 he is at *h* that doth betray me
Mt 26:51 with Jesus stretched out his *h*
Mt 26:64 sitting on the right *h* of power
Mt 27:29 head, and a reed in his right *h*
Mt 27:38 with him, one on the right *h*
Mk 1:15 and the kingdom of God is at *h*
Mk 1:31 And he came and took her by the *h*
Mk 1:41 with compassion, put forth his *h*
Mk 3:1 man there which had a withered *h*
Mk 3:3 the man which had the withered *h*
Mk 3:5 the man, Stretch forth thine *h*
Mk 3:5 his *h* was restored whole as the
Mk 5:41 And he took the damsel by the *h*
Mk 7:32 beseech him to put his *h* upon him
Mk 8:23 And he took the blind man by the *h*
Mk 9:27 But Jesus took him by the *h*
Mk 9:43 if thy *h* offend thee, cut it off
Mk 10:37 we may sit, one on thy right *h*
Mk 10:37 and the other on thy left *h*
Mk 10:40 But to sit on my right *h* and on my
Mk 10:40 on my left *h* is not mine to give
Mk 12:36 my Lord, Sit thou on my right *h*
Mk 14:42 lo, he that betrayeth me is at *h*
Mk 14:62 sitting on the right *h* of power
Mk 15:27 the one on his right *h*, and the
Mk 16:19 and sat on the right *h* of God
Lk 1:1 in *h* to set forth in order a
Lk 1:66 the *h* of the Lord was with him
Lk 1:71 from the *h* of all that hate us
Lk 1:74 being delivered out of the *h* of
Lk 3:17 Whose fan is in his *h*, and he will
Lk 5:13 And he put forth his *h*, and touched
Lk 6:6 a man whose right *h* was withered
Lk 6:8 the man which had the withered *h*
Lk 6:10 unto the man, Stretch forth thy *h*
Lk 6:10 his *h* was restored whole as the
Lk 8:54 all out, and took her by the *h*
Lk 9:62 having put his *h* to the plough
Lk 15:22 and put a ring on his *h*, and shoes
Lk 20:42 my Lord, Sit thou on my right *h*
Lk 21:30 that summer is now nigh at *h*
Lk 21:31 the kingdom of God is nigh at *h*
Lk 22:21 the *h* of him that betrayeth me is
Lk 22:69 the right *h* of the power of God
Lk 23:33 malefactors, one on the right *h*
Jn 2:13 And the Jews' passover was at *h*
Jn 3:35 hath given all things into his *h*
Jn 7:2 feast of tabernacles was at *h*
Jn 10:28 any man pluck them out of my *h*
Jn 10:29 pluck them out of my Father's *h*
Jn 10:39 but he escaped out of their *h*
Jn 11:44 that was dead came forth, bound *h*
Jn 11:55 the Jews' passover was nigh at *h*
Jn 18:22 Jesus with the palm of his *h*
Jn 19:42 for the sepulchre was nigh at *h*
Jn 20:25 thrust my *h* into his side, I will
Jn 20:27 and reach hither thy *h*, and thrust
Acts 2:25 my face, for he is on my right *h*
Acts 2:33 by the right *h* of God exalted
Acts 2:34 my Lord, Sit thou on my right *h*
Acts 3:7 And he took him by the right *h*
Acts 4:28 For to do whatsoever thy *h*
Acts 4:30 stretching forth thine *h* to heal
Acts 5:31 with his right *h* to be a Prince
Acts 7:25 God by his *h* would deliver them
Acts 7:35 a deliverer by the *h* of the angel
Acts 7:50 Hath not my *h* made all these
Acts 7:55 standing on the right *h* of God
Acts 7:56 standing on the right *h* of God
Acts 9:8 but they led him by the *h*
Acts 9:12 in, and putting his *h* on him
Acts 9:41 And he gave her his *h*, and lifted
Acts 11:21 the *h* of the Lord was with them
Acts 12:11 me out of the *h* of Herod, and from
Acts 12:17 with the *h* to hold their peace
Acts 13:11 the *h* of the Lord is upon thee,
Acts 13:11 seeking some to lead him by the *h*
Acts 13:16 up, and beckoning with his *h* said
Acts 19:33 And Alexander beckoned with the *h*
Acts 21:3 Cyprus, we left it on the left *h*
Acts 21:40 with the *h* unto the people
Acts 22:11 being led by the *h* of them that
Acts 23:19 chief captain took him by the *h*
Acts 26:1 Then Paul stretched forth the *h*
Acts 28:3 of the heat, and fastened on his *h*
Acts 28:4 the venomous beast hang on his *h*
Rom 8:34 who is even at the right *h* of God
Rom 13:12 is far spent, the day is at *h*
1Cor 12:15 shall say, Because I am not the *h*
1Cor 12:21 And the eye cannot say unto the *h*
1Cor 16:21 of me Paul with mine own *h*
2Cor 6:7 of righteousness on the right *h*
2Cor 10:16 of things made ready to our *h*
Gal 3:19 by angels in the *h* of a mediator
Gal 6:11 written unto you with mine own *h*
Eph 1:20 right *h* in the heavenly places
Phil 4:5 The Lord is at *h*
Col 3:1 sitteth on the right *h* of God
Col 4:18 salutation by the *h* of me Paul
2Th 2:2 as that the day of Christ is at *h*
2Th 3:17 of Paul with mine own *h*, which is
2Ti 4:6 the time of my departure is at *h*
Philem 19 have written it with mine own *h*
Heb 1:3 sat down on the right *h* of the
Heb 1:13 at any times, Sit on my right *h*
Heb 8:1 who is set on the right *h* of the
Heb 8:9 *h* to lead them out of the land of
Heb 10:12 sat down on the right *h* of God
Heb 12:2 the right *h* of the throne of God
1Pet 3:22 and is on the right *h* of God
1Pet 4:7 But the end of all things is at *h*
1Pet 5:6 under the mighty *h* of God
Rev 1:3 for the time is at *h*
Rev 1:16 he had in his right *h* seven stars
Rev 1:17 And he laid his right *h* upon me
Rev 1:20 which thou sawest in my right *h*
Rev 2:1 the seven stars in his right *h*
Rev 5:1 I saw in the right *h* of him that
Rev 5:7 took the book out of the right *h*
Rev 6:5 had a pair of balances in his *h*
Rev 8:4 before God out of the angel's *h*
Rev 10:2 he had in his *h* a little book
Rev 10:5 earth lifted up his *h* to heaven
Rev 10:8 book which is open in the *h* of
Rev 10:10 little book out of the angel's *h*
Rev 13:16 receive a mark in their right *h*
Rev 14:9 mark in his forehead, or in his *h*
Rev 14:14 crown, and in his *h* a sharp sickle
Rev 17:4 cup in her *h* full of abominations
Rev 19:2 blood of his servants at her *h*
Rev 20:1 pit and a great chain in his *h*
Rev 22:10 for the time is at *h*

**HANDFUL**

Lev 2:2 his *h* of the flour thereof
Lev 5:12 the priest shall take his *h* of it
Lev 6:15 And he shall take of it his *h*
Lev 9:17 offering, and took an *h* thereof
Num 5:26 shall take an *h* of the offering
1Kin 17:12 but an *h* of meal in a barrel, and
Ps 72:16 There shall be an *h* of corn in
Eccl 4:6 Better is an *h* with quietness,
Jer 9:22 as the *h* after the harvestman, and

**HANDFULS**

Gen 41:47 the earth brought forth by *h*
Ex 9:8 Take to you *h* of ashes of the
Ruth 2:16 some of the *h* of purpose for her
1Kin 20:10 of Samaria shall suffice for *h*
Eze 13:19 among my people for *h* of barley

**HANDLE**

Gen 4:21 father of all such as *h* the harp
Judg 5:14 they that *h* the pen of the writer
1Chr 12:8 the battle, that could *h* shield
2Chr 25:5 forth to war, that could *h* spear
Ps 115:7 They have hands, but they *h* not
Jer 2:8 they that *h* the law knew me not
Jer 46:9 and the Libyans, that *h* the shield
Jer 46:9 and the Lydians, that *h* and bend
Eze 27:29 And all that *h* the oar, the
Lk 24:39 *h* me, and see
Col 2:21 taste not; *h* not

**HANDMAID**

Gen 16:1 and she had an *h*, an Egyptian,
Gen 25:12 Hagar the Egyptian, Sarah's *h*
Gen 29:24 Leah Zilpah his maid for an *h*
Gen 29:29 Bilhah his *h* to be her maid
Gen 30:4 she gave him Bilhah her *h* to wife
Gen 35:25 And the sons of Bilhah, Rachel's *h*
Gen 35:26 And the sons of Zilpah, Leah's *h*
Ex 23:12 ass may rest, and the son of thy *h*
Judg 19:19 and wine also for me, and for thy *h*
Ruth 2:13 hast spoken friendly unto thine *h*
Ruth 3:9 she answered, I am Ruth thine *h*
Ruth 3:9 therefore thy skirt over thine *h*
1Sa 1:11 look on the affliction of thine *h*
1Sa 1:11 me, and not forget thine *h*
1Sa 1:11 give unto thine *h* a man child
1Sa 1:16 Count not thine *h* for a daughter
1Sa 1:18 Let thine *h* find grace in thy
1Sa 25:24 and let thine *h*, I pray thee,
1Sa 25:24 and hear the words of thine *h*
1Sa 25:25 but I thine *h* saw not the young
1Sa 25:27 thine *h* hath brought unto my lord
1Sa 25:28 forgive the trespass of thine *h*
1Sa 25:31 my lord, then remember thine *h*
1Sa 25:41 let thine *h* be a servant to wash
1Sa 28:21 thine *h* hath obeyed thy voice, and
1Sa 28:22 also unto the voice of thine *h*
2Sa 14:6 thy *h* had two sons, and they two
2Sa 14:7 family is risen against thine *h*
2Sa 14:12 Then the woman said, Let thine *h*
2Sa 14:15 thy *h* said, I will now speak unto
2Sa 14:15 will perform the request of his *h*
2Sa 14:16 to deliver his *h* out of the hand
2Sa 14:17 Then thine *h* said, The word of my
2Sa 14:19 words in the mouth of thine *h*
2Sa 20:17 him, Hear the words of thine *h*
1Kin 1:13 lord, O king, swear unto thine *h*
1Kin 1:17 by the LORD thy God unto thine *h*
1Kin 3:20 beside me, while thine *h* slept
2Kin 4:2 Thine *h* hath not any thing in the
2Kin 4:16 of God, do not lie unto thine *h*
Ps 86:16 and save the son of thine *h*
Ps 116:16 servant, and the son of thine *h*
Prov 30:23 an *h* that is heir to her mistress
Jer 34:16 his servant, and every man his *h*
Lk 1:38 said, Behold the *h* of the Lord

**HANDMAIDS**

Gen 33:1 and unto Rachel, and unto the two *h*
Gen 33:2 And he put the *h* and their children
2Sa 6:20 the eyes of the *h* of his servants
Is 14:2 of the LORD for servants and *h*
Jer 34:11 and caused the servants and the *h*
Jer 34:11 subjection for servants and for *h*
Jer 34:16 be unto you for servants and for *h*
Joel 2:29 upon the *h* in those days will I

**HANES** *(ha'-nees)* See TAHPANES. *A place in Egypt.*

Is 30:4 and his ambassadors came to *H*

**HANG**

Gen 40:19 thee, and shall *h* thee on a tree
Ex 26:12 shall *h* over the backside of the
Ex 26:13 it shall *h* over the sides of the
Ex 26:32 thou shalt *h* it upon four pillars
Ex 26:33 thou shalt *h* up the vail under
Ex 40:8 *h* up the hanging at the court
Num 25:4 *h* them up before the LORD against
Deut 21:22 to death, and thou *h* him on a tree
Deut 28:66 thy life shall *h* in doubt before
2Sa 21:6 we will *h* them up unto the LORD
Est 6:4 to speak unto the king to *h*
Est 7:9 Then the king said, *H* him thereon
Song 4:4 whereon there *h* a thousand
Is 22:24 they shall *h* upon him all the

Lam 2:10 the virgins of Jerusalem *h* down
Eze 15:3 pin of it to *h* any vessel thereon
Mt 22:40 two commandments *h* all the law
Acts 28:4 the venomous beast *h* on his hand
Heb 12:12 lift up the hands which *h* down

**HANGED**
Gen 40:22 But he *h* the chief baker
Gen 41:13 unto mine office, and him he *h*
Deut 21:23 (for he that is *h* is accursed of
Josh 8:29 the king of Ai he *h* on a tree
Josh 10:26 them, and *h* them on five trees
2Sa 4:12 *h* them up over the pool in Hebron
2Sa 17:23 *h* himself, and died, and was buried
2Sa 18:10 Behold, I saw Absalom *h* in an oak
2Sa 21:9 they *h* them in the hill before
2Sa 21:12 where the Philistines had *h* them
2Sa 21:13 the bones of them that were *h*
Ezr 6:11 set up, let him be *h* thereon
Est 2:23 they were both *h* on a tree
Est 5:14 that Mordecai may be *h* thereon
Est 7:10 So they *h* Haman on the gallows
Est 8:7 him they have *h* upon the gallows,
Est 9:13 ten sons be *h* upon the gallows
Est 9:14 and they *h* Haman's ten sons
Est 9:25 sons should be *h* on the gallows
Ps 137:2 We *h* our harps upon the willows
Lam 5:12 Princes are *h* up by their hand
Eze 27:10 they *h* the shield and helmet in
Eze 27:11 they *h* their shields upon thy
Mt 18:6 a millstone were *h* about his neck
Mt 27:5 and departed, and went and *h* himself
Mk 9:42 a millstone were *h* about his neck
Lk 17:2 a millstone were *h* about his neck
Lk 23:39 which were *h* railed on him
Acts 5:30 whom ye slew and *h* on a tree
Acts 10:39 whom they slew and *h* on a tree

**HANGING**
Ex 26:36 thou shalt make an *h* for the door
Ex 26:37 thou shalt make for the *h* five
Ex 27:16 shall be an *h* of twenty cubits
Ex 35:15 the *h* for the door at the
Ex 35:17 the *h* for the door of the court,
Ex 36:37 he made an *h* for the tabernacle
Ex 38:18 the *h* for the gate of the court
Ex 39:38 the *h* for the tabernacle door,
Ex 39:40 the *h* for the court gate, his
Ex 40:5 put the *h* of the door to the
Ex 40:8 hang up the *h* at the court gate
Ex 40:28 he set up the *h* at the door of
Ex 40:33 set up the *h* of the court gate
Num 3:25 the *h* for the door of the
Num 3:31 wherewith they minister, and the *h*
Num 4:25 the *h* for the door of the
Num 4:26 the *h* for the door of the gate of
Josh 10:26 they were *h* upon the trees until

**HANGINGS**
Ex 27:9 be *h* for the court of fine twined
Ex 27:11 be *h* of an hundred cubits long
Ex 27:12 side shall be *h* of fifty cubits
Ex 27:14 The *h* of one side of the gate
Ex 27:15 side shall be *h* fifteen cubits
Ex 35:17 The *h* of the court, his pillars,
Ex 38:9 the *h* of the court were of fine
Ex 38:11 side the *h* were an hundred cubits
Ex 38:12 west side were *h* of fifty cubits
Ex 38:14 The *h* of the one side of the gate
Ex 38:15 hand, were *h* of fifteen cubits
Ex 38:16 All the *h* of the court round
Ex 38:18 answerable to the *h* of the court
Ex 39:40 The *h* of the court, his pillars,
Num 3:26 the *h* of the court, and the
Num 4:26 the *h* of the court, and the
2Kin 23:7 the women wove *h* for the grove
Est 1:6 were white, green, and blue, *h*

**HANIEL** *(ha'-ne-el)* See HANNIEL. *A son of Ulla.*
1Chr 7:39 Arah, and *H*, and Rezia

**HANNAH** *(han'-nah) Mother of Samuel.*
1Sa 1:2 the name of the one was *H*
1Sa 1:2 children, but *H* had no children
1Sa 1:5 But unto *H* he gave a worthy
1Sa 1:5 for he loved *H*
1Sa 1:8 Elkanah her husband to her, *H*
1Sa 1:9 So *H* rose up after they had eaten
1Sa 1:13 Now *H*, she spake in her heart
1Sa 1:15 *H* answered and said, No, my lord,
1Sa 1:19 and Elkanah knew *H* his wife
1Sa 1:20 come about after *H* had conceived
1Sa 1:22 But *H* went not up
1Sa 2:1 *H* prayed, and said, My heart
1Sa 2:21 And the LORD visited *H*, so that

**HANNATHON** *(han'-na-thon) A city in Zebulun.*
Josh 19:14 it on the north side to *H*

**HANNIEL** *(han'-ne-el)* See HANIEL. *A prince of Manasseh.*
Num 34:23 of Manasseh, *H* the son of Ephod

**HANOCH** *(ha'-nok)* See HANOCHITES, HENOCH.
*1. A son of Midian.*
Gen 25:4 Ephah, and Epher, and *H*, and Abidah,
*2. A son of Reuben.*
Gen 46:9 *H*, and Phallu, and Hezron, and Carmi
Ex 6:14 *H*, and Pallu, Hezron, and Carmi
Num 26:5 *H*, of whom cometh the family of
1Chr 5:3 the firstborn of Israel were, *H*

**HANOCHITES** *(ha'-nok-ites) Descendants of Hanoch 2.*
Num 26:5 whom cometh the family of the *H*

**HANUN** *(ha'-nun)*
*1. A king of Ammon.*
2Sa 10:1 *H* his son reigned in his stead
2Sa 10:2 kindness unto *H* the son of Nahash
2Sa 10:3 of Ammon said unto *H* their lord
2Sa 10:4 Wherefore *H* took David's servants
1Chr 19:2 kindness unto *H* the son of Nahash
1Chr 19:2 of the children of Ammon to *H*
1Chr 19:3 the children of Ammon said to *H*
1Chr 19:4 Wherefore *H* took David's servants
1Chr 19:6 themselves odious to David, *H*
*2. A son of Zalaph.*
Neh 3:30 *H* the sixth son of Zalaph,
*3. A rebuilder of Jerusalem's wall.*
Neh 3:13 The valley gate repaired *H*

**HAP**
Ruth 2:3 her *h* was to light on a part of

**HAPHRAIM** *(haf-ra'-im) A city in Issachar.*
Josh 19:19 And *H*, and Shihon, and Anaharath,

**HAPLY**
1Sa 14:30 if *h* the people had eaten freely
Mk 11:13 if *h* he might find any thing
Lk 14:29 Lest *h*, after he hath laid the
Acts 5:39 lest *h* ye be found even to fight
Acts 17:27 if *h* they might feel after him,
2Cor 9:4 Lest *h* if they of Macedonia come

**HAPPY**
Gen 30:13 *H* am I, for the daughters will
Deut 33:29 *H* art thou, O Israel
1Kin 10:8 *H* are thy men, *h* are these
2Chr 9:7 *H* are thy men, and *h* are these
Job 5:17 *h* is the man whom God correcteth
Ps 127:5 *H* is the man that hath his quiver
Ps 128:2 *h* shalt thou be, and it shall be
Ps 137:8 *h* shall he be, that rewardeth
Ps 137:9 *H* shall he be, that taketh and
Ps 144:15 *H* is that people, that is in such
Ps 144:15 *h* is that people, whose God is
Ps 146:5 *H* is he that hath the God of
Prov 3:13 *H* is the man that findeth wisdom,
Prov 3:18 *h* is every one that retaineth her
Prov 14:21 hath mercy on the poor, *h* is he
Prov 16:20 trusteth in the LORD, *h* is he
Prov 28:14 *H* is the man that feareth alway
Prov 29:18 he that keepeth the law, *h* is he
Jer 12:1 wherefore are all they *h* that
Mal 3:15 And now we call the proud *h*
Jn 13:17 things, *h* are ye if ye do them
Acts 26:2 I think myself *h*, king Agrippa,
Rom 14:22 *H* is he that condemneth not
Jas 5:11 we count them *h* which endure
1Pet 3:14 for righteousness' sake, *h* are ye
1Pet 4:14 for the name of Christ, *h* are ye

**HARA** *(ha'-rah) An Assyrian province.*
1Chr 5:26 them unto Halah, and Habor, and *H*

**HARADAH** *(har'-a-dah) A Hebrew encampment in the wilderness.*
Num 33:24 mount Shapher, and encamped in *H*
Num 33:25 And they removed from *H*, and

**HARAN** *(ha'-ran)* See BETH-HARAN, CHARRAN.
*1. A son of Terah.*
Gen 11:26 and begat Abram, Nahor, and *H*
Gen 11:27 Terah begat Abram, Nahor, and *H*
Gen 11:27 and *H* begat Lot
Gen 11:28 *H* died before his father Terah in
Gen 11:29 wife, Milcah, the daughter of *H*
Gen 11:31 and Lot the son of *H* his son's son
*2. A Levite.*
1Chr 23:9 Shelomith, and Haziel, and *H*
*3. A son of Caleb.*
1Chr 2:46 Ephah, Caleb's concubine, bare *H*
1Chr 2:46 and *H* begat Gazez
*4. A city in northern Mesopotamia.*
Gen 11:31 and they came unto *H*, and dwelt
Gen 11:32 and Terah died in *H*
Gen 12:4 old when he departed out of *H*
Gen 12:5 souls that they had gotten in *H*
Gen 27:43 thou to Laban my brother to *H*
Gen 28:10 from Beer-sheba, and went toward *H*
Gen 29:4 And they said, Of *H* are we
2Kin 19:12 as Gozan, and *H*, and Rezeph, and the
Is 37:12 have destroyed, as Gozan, and *H*
Eze 27:23 *H*, and Canneh, and Eden, the

**HARARITE** *(har'-a-rite) Native of the hill country of Judah.*
2Sa 23:11 was Shammah the son of Agee the *H*
2Sa 23:33 Shammah the *H*, Ahiam the son of
2Sa 23:33 Ahiam the son of Sharar the *H*
1Chr 11:34 Jonathan the son of Shage the *H*
1Chr 11:35 Ahiam the son of Sacar the *H*

**HARBONA** *(har-bo'-nah)* See HARBONAH. *A servant of King Ahasuerus.*
Est 1:10 he commanded Mehuman, Biztha, *H*

**HARBONAH** *(har-bo'-nah)* See HARBONA. *Same as Harbona.*
Est 7:9 And *H*, one of the chamberlains,

**HARD**
Gen 18:14 Is any thing too *h* for the LORD
Gen 35:16 travailed, and she had *h* labour
Gen 35:17 to pass, when she was in *h* labour
Ex 1:14 their lives bitter with *h* bondage
Ex 18:26 the *h* causes they brought unto
Lev 3:9 he take off *h* by the backbone
Deut 1:17 the cause that is too *h* for you
Deut 15:18 It shall not seem *h* unto thee
Deut 17:8 matter too *h* for thee in judgment
Deut 26:6 us, and laid upon us *h* bondage
Judg 9:52 went *h* unto the door of the tower
Judg 20:45 pursued *h* after them unto Gidom,
1Sa 14:22 even they also followed *h* after
1Sa 31:2 Philistines followed *h* upon Saul
2Sa 1:6 and horsemen followed *h* after him
2Sa 3:39 sons of Zeruiah be too *h* for me
2Sa 13:2 Amnon thought it *h* for him to do
1Kin 10:1 to prove him with *h* questions
1Kin 21:1 *h* by the palace of Ahab king of
2Kin 2:10 said, Thou hast asked a *h* thing
1Chr 10:2 Philistines followed *h* after Saul
1Chr 19:4 in the midst *h* by their buttocks
2Chr 9:1 with *h* questions at Jerusalem
Job 41:24 as *h* as a piece of the nether
Ps 60:3 hast shewed thy people *h* things
Ps 63:8 My soul followeth *h* after thee
Ps 88:7 Thy wrath lieth *h* upon me
Ps 94:4 they utter and speak *h* things
Prov 13:15 but the way of transgressors is *h*
Is 14:3 from the *h* bondage wherein thou
Jer 32:17 there is nothing too *h* for thee
Jer 32:27 is there any thing too *h* for me
Eze 3:5 of an *h* language, but to the
Eze 3:6 of an *h* language, whose words
Dan 5:12 dreams, and shewing of *h* sentences
Jonah 1:13 rowed *h* to bring it to the land
Mt 25:24 knew thee that thou art an *h* man
Mk 10:24 how *h* is it for them that trust
Jn 6:60 this, said, This is an *h* saying
Acts 9:5 it is *h* for thee to kick against
Acts 18:7 house joined *h* to the synagogue
Acts 26:14 it is *h* for thee to kick against
Heb 5:11 *h* to be uttered, seeing ye are
2Pet 3:16 some things *h* to be understood
Jude 15 of all their *h* speeches which

**HARDEN**
Ex 4:21 but I will *h* his heart, that he
Ex 7:3 I will *h* Pharaoh's heart, and
Ex 14:4 I will *h* Pharaoh's heart, that he
Ex 14:17 I will *h* the hearts of the
Deut 15:7 thou shalt not *h* thine heart
Josh 11:20 was of the LORD to *h* their hearts
1Sa 6:6 then do ye *h* your hearts, as the
Job 6:10 I would *h* myself in sorrow

Ps 95:8 *H* not your heart, as in the
Heb 3:8 *H* not your hearts, as in the
Heb 3:15 *h* not your hearts, as in the
Heb 4:7 hear his voice, *h* not your hearts

**HARDENED**
Ex 7:13 he *h* Pharaoh's heart, that he
Ex 7:14 unto Moses, Pharaoh's heart is *h*
Ex 7:22 and Pharaoh's heart was *h*, neither
Ex 8:15 he *h* his heart, and hearkened not
Ex 8:19 and Pharaoh's heart was *h*, and he
Ex 8:32 Pharaoh *h* his heart at this time
Ex 9:7 And the heart of Pharaoh was *h*
Ex 9:12 the LORD *h* the heart of Pharaoh,
Ex 9:34 *h* his heart, he and his servants
Ex 9:35 And the heart of Pharaoh was *h*
Ex 10:1 for I have *h* his heart, and the
Ex 10:20 But the LORD *h* Pharaoh's heart,
Ex 10:27 But the LORD *h* Pharaoh's heart,
Ex 11:10 the LORD *h* Pharaoh's heart, so
Ex 14:8 the LORD *h* the heart of Pharaoh
Deut 2:30 for the LORD thy God *h* his spirit
1Sa 6:6 and Pharaoh *h* their hearts
2Kin 17:14 but *h* their necks, like to the
2Chr 36:13 *h* his heart from turning unto the
Neh 9:16 *h* their necks, and hearkened not
Neh 9:17 but *h* their necks, and in their
Neh 9:29 *h* their neck, and would not hear
Job 9:4 who hath *h* himself against him,
Job 39:16 She is *h* against her young ones,
Is 63:17 *h* our heart from thy fear
Jer 7:26 their ear, but *h* their neck
Jer 19:15 because they have *h* their necks
Dan 5:20 lifted up, and his mind *h* in pride
Mk 6:52 for their heart was *h*
Mk 8:17 have ye your heart yet *h*
Jn 12:40 their eyes, and *h* their heart
Acts 19:9 But when divers were *h*, and
Heb 3:13 lest any of you be *h* through the

**HARDENETH**
Prov 21:29 A wicked man *h* his face
Prov 28:14 but he that *h* his heart shall
Prov 29:1 being often reproved *h* his neck
Rom 9:18 have mercy, and whom he will he *h*

**HARDER**
Prov 18:19 A brother offended is *h* to be won
Jer 5:3 made their faces *h* than a rock
Eze 3:9 As an adamant *h* than flint have I

**HARDLY**
Gen 16:6 And when Sarai dealt *h* with her
Ex 13:15 when Pharaoh would *h* let us go
Is 8:21 through it, *h* bestead and hungry
Mt 19:23 That a rich man shall *h* enter
Mk 10:23 How *h* shall they that have riches
Lk 9:39 bruising him *h* departeth from him
Lk 18:24 How *h* shall they that have riches
Acts 27:8 *h* passing it, came unto a place

**HARDNESS**
Job 38:38 When the dust groweth into *h*
Mt 19:8 Moses because of the *h* of your
Mk 3:5 grieved for the *h* of their hearts
Mk 10:5 For the *h* of your heart he wrote
Mk 16:14 *h* of heart, because they believed
Rom 2:5 But after thy *h* and impenitent
2Ti 2:3 Thou therefore endure *h*, as a

**HAREPH** *(ha'-ref) A son of Caleb.*
1Chr 2:51 *H* the father of Beth-gader

**HARETH** *(ha'-reth) Forest land in Judah.*
1Sa 22:5 and came into the forest of *H*

**HARHAIAH** *(har-ha-i'-ah) Father of Uzziel.*
Neh 3:8 him repaired Uzziel the son of *H*

**HARHAS** *(har'-has)* See HASRAH. *Grandfather of Shallum.*
2Kin 22:14 the son of Tikvah, the son of *H*

**HARHUR** *(har'-hur) A family in exile.*
Ezr 2:51 of Hakupha, the children of *H*
Neh 7:53 of Hakupha, the children of *H*

**HARIM** *(ha'-rim)*
*1. A priest.*
1Chr 24:8 The third to *H*, the fourth to
Ezr 2:39 The children of *H*, a thousand and
Ezr 10:21 And of the sons of *H*
Neh 3:11 Malchijah the son of *H*, and Hashub
Neh 7:42 The children of *H*, a thousand and
Neh 12:15 Of *H*, Adna; of Meraioth
*2. A family in exile.*
Ezr 2:32 The children of *H*, three hundred
Neh 7:35 The children of *H*, three hundred
*3. Married a foreigner in exile.*
Ezr 10:31 And of the sons of *H*
*4. An Israelite who renewed the covenant.*
Neh 10:5 *H*, Meremoth, Obadiah,
*5. A family who renewed the covenant.*
Neh 10:27 Malluch, *H*, Baanah

**HARIPH** *(ha'-rif)* See JORAH.
*1. A family of exiles.*
Neh 7:24 The children of *H*, an hundred and
*2. A family who renewed the covenant.*
Neh 10:19 *H*, Anathoth, Nebai,

**HARLOT**
Gen 34:31 deal with our sister as with an *h*
Gen 38:15 her, he thought her to be an *h*
Gen 38:21 place, saying, Where is the *h*
Gen 38:21 There was no *h* in this place
Gen 38:22 that there was no *h* in this place
Gen 38:24 daughter in law hath played the *h*
Lev 21:14 woman, or profane, or an *h*
Josh 6:17 only Rahab the *h* shall live
Josh 6:25 And Joshua saved Rahab the *h* alive
Judg 11:1 valour, and he was the son of an *h*
Judg 16:1 Samson to Gaza, and saw there an *h*
Prov 7:10 a woman with the attire of an *h*
Is 1:21 is the faithful city become an *h*
Is 23:15 years shall Tyre sing as an *h*
Is 23:16 thou *h* that hast been forgotten
Jer 2:20 thou wanderest, playing the *h*
Jer 3:1 played the *h* with many lovers
Jer 3:6 tree, and there hath played the *h*
Jer 3:8 but went and played the *h* also
Eze 16:15 playedst the *h* because of thy
Eze 16:16 and playedst the *h* thereupon
Eze 16:28 thou hast played the *h* with them
Eze 16:31 and hast not been as an *h*, in that
Eze 16:35 Wherefore, O *h*, hear the word of
Eze 16:41 thee to cease from playing the *h*
Eze 23:5 played the *h* when she was mine
Eze 23:19 played the *h* in the land of Egypt
Eze 23:44 unto a woman that playeth the *h*
Hos 2:5 their mother hath played the *h*
Hos 3:3 thou shalt not play the *h*
Hos 4:15 Though thou, Israel, play the *h*
Joel 3:3 and have given a boy for an *h*
Amos 7:17 wife shall be an *h* in the city
Mic 1:7 gathered it of the hire of an *h*
Mic 1:7 shall return to the hire of an *h*
Nah 3:4 whoredoms of the wellfavoured *h*
1Cor 6:15 and make them the members of an *h*
1Cor 6:16 is joined to an *h* is one body
Heb 11:31 By faith the *h* Rahab perished not
Jas 2:25 Rahab the *h* justified by works

**HARLOTS**
1Kin 3:16 came there two women, that were *h*
Prov 29:3 with *h* spendeth his substance
Hos 4:14 whores, and they sacrifice with *h*
Mt 21:31 the *h* go into the kingdom of God
Mt 21:32 publicans and the *h* believed him
Lk 15:30 hath devoured thy living with *h*
Rev 17:5 THE GREAT, THE MOTHER OF *H*

**HARM**
Gen 31:52 and this pillar unto me, for *h*
Lev 5:16 he shall make amends for the *h*
Num 35:23 his enemy, neither sought his *h*
1Sa 26:21 for I will no more do thee *h*
2Sa 20:6 do us more *h* than did Absalom
2Kin 4:41 And there was no *h* in the pot
1Chr 16:22 anointed, and do my prophets no *h*
Ps 105:15 anointed, and do my prophets no *h*
Prov 3:30 cause, if he have done thee no *h*
Jer 39:12 look well to him, and do him no *h*
Acts 16:28 voice, saying, Do thyself no *h*
Acts 27:21 Crete, and to have gained this *h*
Acts 28:5 beast into the fire, and felt no *h*
Acts 28:6 saw no *h* come to him, they
Acts 28:21 shewed or spake any *h* of thee
1Pet 3:13 And who is he that will *h* you

**HARNEPHER** *(har-ne'-fur) A son of Zophah.*
1Chr 7:36 Suah, and *H*, and Shual, and Beri, and

**HARNESS**
1Kin 20:11 on his *h* boast himself as he that
1Kin 22:34 between the joints of the *h*
2Chr 9:24 and vessels of gold, and raiment, *h*
2Chr 18:33 between the joints of the *h*
Jer 46:4 *H* the horses

**HAROD** *(ha'-rod)* See HARODITE. *A spring of water.*
Judg 7:1 and pitched beside the well of *H*

**HARODITE** *(ha-ro'-dite)* See HARORITE. *Family name of two of David's "mighty men."*
2Sa 23:25 Shammah the *H*, Elika the *H*

**HAROEH** *(ha-ro'-eh)* See REAIAH. *A son of Shobal.*
1Chr 2:52 *H*, and half of the Manahethites

**HARORITE** *(ha'-ro-rite) Family name of a "mighty man."*
1Chr 11:27 Shammoth the *H*, Helez the

**HAROSHETH** *(har'-o-sheth) A city in Galilee.*
Judg 4:2 which dwelt in *H* of the Gentiles
Judg 4:13 from *H* of the Gentiles unto the
Judg 4:16 the host, unto *H* of the Gentiles

**HARP**
Gen 4:21 of all such as handle the *h*
Gen 31:27 songs, with tabret, and with *h*
1Sa 10:5 and a tabret, and a pipe, and a *h*
1Sa 16:16 who is a cunning player on an *h*
1Sa 16:23 upon Saul, that David took an *h*
1Chr 25:3 Jeduthun, who prophesied with a *h*
Job 21:12 They take the timbrel and *h*
Job 30:31 My *h* also is turned to mourning,
Ps 33:2 Praise the LORD with *h*
Ps 43:4 upon the *h* will I praise thee, O
Ps 49:4 open my dark saying upon the *h*
Ps 57:8 awake, psaltery and *h*
Ps 71:22 unto thee will I sing with the *h*
Ps 81:2 the pleasant *h* with the psaltery
Ps 92:3 upon the *h* with a solemn sound
Ps 98:5 Sing unto the LORD with the *h*
Ps 98:5 with the *h*, and the voice of a
Ps 108:2 Awake, psaltery and *h*
Ps 147:7 praise upon the *h* unto our God
Ps 149:3 unto him with the timbrel and *h*
Ps 150:3 praise him with the psaltery and *h*
Is 5:12 And the *h*, and the viol, the tabret
Is 16:11 shall sound like an *h* for Moab
Is 23:16 Take an *h*, go about the city,
Is 24:8 endeth, the joy of the *h* ceaseth
Dan 3:5 the sound of the cornet, flute, *h*
Dan 3:7 the sound of the cornet, flute, *h*
Dan 3:10 the sound of the cornet, flute, *h*
Dan 3:15 the sound of the cornet, flute, *h*
1Cor 14:7 giving sound, whether pipe or *h*

**HARPS**
2Sa 6:5 made of fir wood, even on *h*
1Kin 10:12 *h* also and psalteries for singers
1Chr 13:8 might, and with singing, and with *h*
1Chr 15:16 of musick, psalteries and *h*
1Chr 15:21 with *h* on the Sheminith to excel
1Chr 15:28 a noise with psalteries and *h*
1Chr 16:5 Jeiel with psalteries and with *h*
1Chr 25:1 who should prophesy with *h*
1Chr 25:6 with cymbals, psalteries, and *h*
2Chr 5:12 having cymbals and psalteries and *h*
2Chr 9:11 and to the king's palace, and *h*
2Chr 20:28 to Jerusalem with psalteries and *h*
2Chr 29:25 with psalteries, and with *h*
Neh 12:27 cymbals, psalteries, and with *h*
Ps 137:2 We hanged our *h* upon the willows
Is 30:32 it shall be with tabrets and *h*
Eze 26:13 the sound of thy *h* shall be no
Rev 5:8 Lamb, having every one of them *h*
Rev 14:2 of harpers harping with their *h*
Rev 15:2 sea of glass, having the *h* of God

**HARSHA** *(har'-shah) A family of exiles.*
Ezr 2:52 of Mehida, the children of *H*
Neh 7:54 of Mehida, the children of *H*

**HART**
Deut 12:15 as of the roebuck, and as of the *h*
Deut 12:22 the *h* is eaten, so thou shalt eat
Deut 14:5 The *h*, and the roebuck, and the
Deut 15:22 as the roebuck, and as the *h*
Ps 42:1 As the *h* panteth after the water
Song 2:9 is like a roe or a young *h*
Song 2:17 *h* upon the mountains of Bether
Song 8:14 like to a roe or to a young *h*
Is 35:6 shall the lame man leap as an *h*

**HARUM** *(ha'-rum) Father of Aharhel.*
1Chr 4:8 families of Aharhel the son of *H*

**HARUMAPH** *(ha-ru'-maf) Father of Jedaiah.*
Neh 3:10 repaired Jedaiah the son of *H*

**HARUPHITE** *(ha'-ru-fite) A Korhite soldier.*
1Chr 12:5 and Shemariah, and Shephatiah the *H*

**HARUZ** *(ha'-ruz) Father of Meshullemeth.*
2Kin 21:19 the daughter of *H* of Jotbah

**HARVEST**
Gen 8:22 earth remaineth, seedtime and *h*
Gen 30:14 went in the days of wheat *h*
Gen 45:6 shall neither be earing nor *h*
Ex 23:16 And the feast of *h*, the
Ex 34:21 time and in *h* thou shalt rest
Ex 34:22 of the firstfruits of wheat *h*
Lev 19:9 when ye reap the *h* of your land
Lev 19:9 gather the gleanings of thy *h*
Lev 23:10 you, and shall reap the *h* thereof
Lev 23:10 of your *h* unto the priest
Lev 23:22 when ye reap the *h* of your land
Lev 23:22 thou gather any gleaning of thy *h*
Lev 25:5 of thy *h* thou shalt not reap
Deut 24:19 cuttest down thine *h* in thy field
Josh 3:15 all his banks all the time of *h*
Judg 15:1 after, in the time of wheat *h*
Ruth 1:22 in the beginning of barley *h*
Ruth 2:21 until they have ended all my *h*
Ruth 2:23 of barley *h* and of wheat *h*
1Sa 6:13 their wheat *h* in the valley
1Sa 8:12 ear his ground, and to reap his *h*
1Sa 12:17 Is it not wheat *h* to day
2Sa 21:9 put to death in the days of *h*
2Sa 21:9 in the beginning of barley *h*
2Sa 21:10 from the beginning of *h* until
2Sa 23:13 came to David in the *h* time unto
Job 5:5 Whose *h* the hungry eateth up, and
Prov 6:8 and gathereth her food in the *h*
Prov 10:5 but he that sleepeth in *h* is a
Prov 20:4 therefore shall he beg in *h*
Prov 25:13 the cold of snow in the time of *h*
Prov 26:1 snow in summer, and as rain in *h*
Is 9:3 thee according to the joy in *h*
Is 16:9 fruits and for thy *h* is fallen
Is 17:11 but the *h* shall be a heap in the
Is 18:4 a cloud of dew in the heat of *h*
Is 18:5 For afore the *h*, when the bud is
Is 23:3 the *h* of the river, is her
Jer 5:17 And they shall eat up thine *h*
Jer 5:24 us the appointed weeks of the *h*
Jer 8:20 The *h* is past, the summer is
Jer 50:16 the sickle in the time of *h*
Jer 51:33 and the time of her *h* shall come
Hos 6:11 Judah, he hath set an *h* for thee
Joel 1:11 because the *h* of the field is
Joel 3:13 in the sickle, for the *h* is ripe
Amos 4:7 were yet three months to the *h*
Mt 9:37 The *h* truly is plenteous, but the
Mt 9:38 ye therefore the Lord of the *h*
Mt 9:38 send forth labourers into his *h*
Mt 13:30 both grow together until the *h*
Mt 13:30 in the time of *h* I will say to
Mt 13:39 the *h* is the end of the world
Mk 4:29 the sickle, because the *h* is come
Lk 10:2 The *h* truly is great, but the
Lk 10:2 ye therefore the Lord of the *h*
Lk 10:2 send forth labourers into his *h*
Jn 4:35 yet four months, and then cometh *h*
Jn 4:35 for they are white already to *h*
Rev 14:15 for the *h* of the earth is ripe

**HASADIAH** *(has-a-di'-ah) A son of Zerubbabel.*
1Chr 3:20 and Ohel, and Berechiah, and *H*

**HASENUAH** *(has-e-nu'-ah)* See SENUAH. *Father of Hodaviah.*
1Chr 9:7 the son of Hodaviah, the son of *H*

**HASHABIAH** *(hash-a-bi'-ah)*
*1. Son of Amaziah.*
1Chr 6:45 The son of *H*, the son of Amaziah,
*2. A Merarite Levite.*
1Chr 9:14 the son of Azrikam, the son of *H*
*3. A son of Jeduthun.*
1Chr 25:3 Gedaliah, and Zeri, and Jeshaiah, *H*
1Chr 25:19 The twelfth to *H*, he, his sons,
*4. A descendant of Hebron.*
1Chr 26:30 And of the Hebronites, *H* and his
*5. Son of Kemuel.*
1Chr 27:17 the Levites, *H* the son of Kemuel
*6. A Levite chief.*
2Chr 35:9 and Nethaneel, his brethren, and *H*
*7. A Levite in exile.*
Ezr 8:19 And *H*, and with him Jeshaiah of the
*8. A chief priest.*
Ezr 8:24 of the priests, Sherebiah, *H*
*9. A rebuilder of Jerusalem's wall.*
Neh 3:17 Next unto him repaired *H*, the
*10. A Levite who renewed the covenant.*
Neh 10:11 Micha, Rehob, *H*,
*11. Son of Bunni.*
Neh 11:15 the son of Azrikam, the son of *H*
*12. Another Levite.*
Neh 11:22 the son of Bani, the son of *H*
*13. A priest in Joiakim's time.*
Neh 12:21 Of Hilkiah, *H*
*14. A chief Levite.*
Neh 12:24 *H*, Sherebiah, and Jeshua the son

**HASHABNAH** *(hash-ab'-nah) A clan leader who renewed the covenant.*
Neh 10:25 Rehum, *H*, Maaseiah,

**HASHABNIAH** *(hash-ab-ni'-ah)*
*1. Father of Hattush.*
Neh 3:10 him repaired Hattush the son of *H*
*2. A Levite.*
Neh 9:5 Jeshua, and Kadmiel, Bani, *H*

**HASHBADANA** *(hash-bad'-a-nah) A priest.*
Neh 8:4 and Malchiah, and Hashum, and *H*

**HASHEM** *(ha'-shem) Father of several "mighty men."*
1Chr 11:34 The sons of *H* the Gizonite,

**HASHMONAH** *(hash-mo'-nah) A Hebrew encampment in the wilderness.*
Num 33:29 from Mithcah, and pitched in *H*
Num 33:30 And they departed from *H*, and

**HASHUB** *(ha'-shub)* See HASSHUB.
*1. Father of Shemaiah.*
Neh 11:15 Shemaiah the son of *H*, the son of
*2. Son of Pahath-moab.*
Neh 3:11 *H* the son of Pahath-moab,
*3. A rebuilder of Jerusalem's wall.*
Neh 3:23 *H* over against their house
*4. A clan leader who renewed the covenant.*
Neh 10:23 Hoshea, Hananiah, *H*,

**HASHUBAH** *(hash-u'-bah) A son of Zerubbabel.*
1Chr 3:20 And *H*, and Ohel, and Berechiah, and

**HASHUM** *(ha'-shum)*
*1. A family of exiles.*
Ezr 2:19 The children of *H*, two hundred
Ezr 10:33 Of the sons of *H*
Neh 7:22 The children of *H*, three hundred
*2. A priest.*
Neh 8:4 and Mishael, and Malchiah, and *H*
*3. A clan leader who renewed the covenant.*
Neh 10:18 Hodijah, *H*, Bezai,

**HASHUPHA** *(hash-u'-fah)* See HASUPHA. *A family of exiles.*
Neh 7:46 of Ziha, the children of *H*

**HASRAH** *(has'-rah)* See HARHAS. *Same as Harhas.*
2Chr 34:22 the son of Tikvath, the son of *H*

**HASSENAAH** *(has-se-na'-ah)* See SENAAH. *Father of some rebuilders of Jerusalem's wall.*
Neh 3:3 fish gate did the sons of *H* build

**HASSHUB** *(hash'-ub)* See HASHUB. *Father of Shemaiah.*
1Chr 9:14 Shemaiah the son of *H*, the son of

**HASTE**
Gen 19:22 *H* thee, escape thither
Gen 24:46 And she made *h*, and let down her
Gen 43:30 And Joseph made *h*
Gen 45:9 *H* ye, and go up to my father, and
Gen 45:13 and ye shall *h* and bring down my
Ex 10:16 called for Moses and Aaron in *h*
Ex 12:11 and ye shall eat it in *h*
Ex 12:33 send them out of the land in *h*
Ex 34:8 And Moses made *h*, and bowed his
Deut 16:3 out of the land of Egypt in *h*
Deut 32:35 that shall come upon them make *h*
Judg 9:48 What ye have seen me do, make *h*
Judg 13:10 And the woman made *h*, and ran, and
1Sa 9:12 make *h* now, for he came to day to
1Sa 20:38 after the lad, Make speed, *h*
1Sa 21:8 the king's business required *h*
1Sa 23:26 David made *h* to get away for fear
1Sa 23:27 Saul, saying, *H* thee, and come
1Sa 25:18 Then Abigail made *h*, and took two
2Sa 4:4 to pass, as she made *h* to flee
2Kin 7:15 Syrians had cast away in their *h*
2Chr 35:21 for God commanded me to make *h*
Ezr 4:23 they went up in *h* to Jerusalem
Est 5:5 king said, Cause Haman to make *h*
Est 6:10 the king said to Haman, Make *h*
Job 20:2 to answer, and for this I make *h*
Ps 22:19 O my strength, *h* thee to help me
Ps 31:22 For I said in my *h*, I am cut off
Ps 38:22 Make *h* to help me, O Lord my
Ps 40:13 O LORD, make *h* to help me
Ps 70:1 Make *h*, O God, to deliver me
Ps 70:1 make *h* to help me, O LORD
Ps 70:5 make *h* unto me, O God
Ps 71:12 O my God, make *h* for my help
Ps 116:11 I said in my *h*, All men are liars
Ps 119:60 I made *h*, and delayed not to keep
Ps 141:1 make *h* unto me
Prov 1:16 to evil, and make *h* to shed blood
Prov 28:20 but he that maketh *h* to be rich
Song 8:14 Make *h*, my beloved, and be thou
Is 28:16 that believeth shall not make *h*
Is 49:17 Thy children shall make *h*
Is 52:12 For ye shall not go out with *h*
Is 59:7 they make *h* to shed innocent
Jer 9:18 And let them make *h*, and take up a
Dan 2:25 in Daniel before the king in *h*
Dan 3:24 was astonied, and rose up in *h*
Dan 6:19 went in *h* unto the den of lions
Nah 2:5 they shall make *h* to the wall
Mk 6:25 straightway with *h* unto the king
Lk 1:39 went into the hill country with *h*
Lk 2:16 And they came with *h*, and found
Lk 19:5 said unto him, Zacchaeus, make *h*
Lk 19:6 And he made *h*, and came down, and
Acts 22:18 And saw him saying unto me, Make *h*

**HASTED**
Gen 18:7 and he *h* to dress it
Gen 24:18 and she *h*, and let down her pitcher
Gen 24:20 And she *h*, and emptied her pitcher
Ex 5:13 And the taskmasters *h* them
Josh 4:10 and the people *h* and passed over
Josh 8:14 king of Ai saw it, that they *h*
Josh 8:19 into the city, and took it, and *h*
Josh 10:13 *h* not to go down about a whole
Judg 20:37 And the liers in wait *h*, and rushed
1Sa 17:48 nigh to meet David, that David *h*
1Sa 25:23 And when Abigail saw David, she *h*
1Sa 25:34 hurting thee, except thou hadst *h*
1Sa 25:42 And Abigail *h*, and arose, and rode
1Sa 28:24 and she *h*, and killed it, and took
2Sa 19:16 which was of Bahurim, *h* and came
1Kin 20:41 And he *h*, and took the ashes away
2Kin 9:13 Then they *h*, and took every man
2Chr 26:20 himself *h* also to go out, because
Est 6:12 But Haman *h* to his house mourning
Est 6:14 *h* to bring Haman unto the banquet
Job 31:5 or if my foot hath *h* to deceit
Ps 48:5 they were troubled, and *h* away
Ps 104:7 voice of thy thunder they *h* away
Acts 20:16 for he *h*, if it were possible for

**HASTEN**
1Kin 22:9 *H* hither Micaiah the son of Imlah
2Chr 24:5 year, and see that ye *h* the matter
Ps 16:4 that *h* after another god
Ps 55:8 I would *h* my escape from the
Eccl 2:25 eat, or who else can *h* hereunto
Is 5:19 *h* his work, that we may see it
Is 60:22 I the LORD will *h* it in his time
Jer 1:12 for I will *h* my word to perform

**HASTENED**
Gen 18:6 Abraham *h* into the tent unto
Gen 19:15 arose, then the angels *h* Lot
2Chr 24:5 Howbeit the Levites *h* it not
Est 3:15 being *h* by the king's commandment
Est 8:14 mules and camels went out, being *h*
Jer 17:16 I have not *h* from being a pastor

**HASTETH**
Job 9:26 as the eagle that *h* to the prey
Job 40:23 he drinketh up a river, and *h* not
Prov 7:23 as a bird *h* to the snare, and
Prov 19:2 he that *h* with his feet sinneth

Prov 28:22 He that *h* to be rich hath an evil
Eccl 1:5 *h* to his place where he arose
Jer 48:16 to come, and his affliction *h* fast
Hab 1:8 fly as the eagle that *h* to eat
Zeph 1:14 *h* greatly, even the voice of the

**HASTILY**
Gen 41:14 they brought him *h* out of the
Judg 2:23 without driving them out *h*
Judg 9:54 Then he called *h* unto the young
1Sa 4:14 And the man came in *h*, and told Eli
1Kin 20:33 come from him, and did *h* catch it
Prov 20:21 may be gotten *h* at the beginning
Prov 25:8 Go not forth *h* to strive, lest
Jn 11:31 they saw Mary, that she rose up *h*

**HASTY**
Prov 14:29 but he that is *h* of spirit
Prov 21:5 every one that is *h* only to want
Prov 29:20 thou a man that is *h* in his words
Eccl 5:2 let not thine heart be *h* to utter
Eccl 7:9 Be not *h* in thy spirit to be
Eccl 8:3 Be not *h* to go out of his sight
Is 28:4 as the *h* fruit before the summer
Dan 2:15 is the decree so *h* from the king
Hab 1:6 *h* nation, which shall march

**HASUPHA** *(has-u'-fah) A family of exiles.*
Ezr 2:43 of Ziha, the children of *H*

**HATACH** *(ha'-tak) A servant of King Ahasuerus.*
Est 4:5 Then called Esther for *H*, one of
Est 4:6 So *H* went forth to Mordecai unto
Est 4:9 *H* came and told Esther the words
Est 4:10 Again Esther spake unto *H*

**HATE**
Gen 24:60 the gate of those which *h* them
Gen 26:27 come ye to me, seeing ye *h* me
Gen 50:15 Joseph will peradventure *h* us
Ex 20:5 generation of them that *h* me
Lev 19:17 Thou shalt not *h* thy brother in
Lev 26:17 they that *h* you shall reign over
Num 10:35 let them that *h* thee flee before
Deut 5:9 generation of them that *h* me
Deut 7:10 them that *h* him to their face
Deut 7:15 them upon all them that *h* thee
Deut 19:11 But if any man *h* his neighbour
Deut 22:13 and go in unto her, and *h* her,
Deut 24:3 And if the latter husband *h* her
Deut 30:7 enemies, and on them that *h* thee
Deut 32:41 and will reward them that *h* me
Deut 33:11 him, and of them that *h* him
Judg 11:7 elders of Gilead, Did not ye *h* me
Judg 14:16 him, and said, Thou dost but *h* me
2Sa 22:41 I might destroy them that *h* me
1Kin 22:8 but I *h* him
2Chr 18:7 but I *h* him
2Chr 19:2 and love them that *h* the LORD
Job 8:22 They that *h* thee shall be clothed
Ps 9:13 which I suffer of them that *h* me
Ps 18:40 I might destroy them that *h* me
Ps 21:8 shall find out those that *h* thee
Ps 25:19 they *h* me with cruel hatred
Ps 34:21 they that *h* the righteous shall
Ps 35:19 the eye that *h* me without a cause
Ps 38:19 they that *h* me wrongfully are
Ps 41:7 All that *h* me whisper together
Ps 44:10 they which *h* us spoil for
Ps 55:3 upon me, and in wrath they *h* me
Ps 68:1 let them also that *h* him flee
Ps 69:4 They that *h* me without a cause
Ps 69:14 be delivered from them that *h* me
Ps 83:2 they that *h* thee have lifted up
Ps 86:17 that they which *h* me may see it
Ps 89:23 face, and plague them that *h* him
Ps 97:10 Ye that love the LORD, *h* evil
Ps 101:3 I *h* the work of them that turn
Ps 105:25 their heart to *h* his people
Ps 118:7 see my desire upon them that *h* me
Ps 119:104 therefore I *h* every false way
Ps 119:113 I *h* vain thoughts
Ps 119:128 and I *h* every false way
Ps 119:163 I *h* and abhor lying
Ps 129:5 and turned back that *h* Zion
Ps 139:21 I *h* them, O LORD, that *h* thee
Ps 139:22 I *h* them with perfect hatred
Prov 1:22 scorning, and fools *h* knowledge
Prov 6:16 These six things doth the LORD *h*
Prov 8:13 The fear of the LORD is to *h* evil
Prov 8:13 way, and the froward mouth, do I *h*
Prov 8:36 all they that *h* me love death
Prov 9:8 not a scorner, lest he *h* thee
Prov 19:7 the brethren of the poor do *h* him
Prov 25:17 he be weary of thee, and so *h* thee
Prov 29:10 The bloodthirsty *h* the upright
Eccl 3:8 A time to love, and a time to *h*
Is 61:8 I *h* robbery for burnt offering
Jer 44:4 this abominable thing that I *h*
Eze 16:27 unto the will of them that *h* thee
Dan 4:19 the dream be to them that *h* thee
Amos 5:10 They *h* him that rebuketh in the
Amos 5:15 *H* the evil, and love the good, and
Amos 5:21 I *h*, I despise your feast days,
Amos 6:8 of Jacob, and *h* his palaces
Mic 3:2 Who *h* the good, and love the evil
Zec 8:17 for all these are things that I *h*
Mt 5:43 thy neighbour, and *h* thine enemy
Mt 5:44 you, do good to them that *h* you
Mt 6:24 for either he will *h* the one
Mt 24:10 another, and shall *h* one another
Lk 1:71 and from the hand of all that *h* us
Lk 6:22 are ye, when men shall *h* you
Lk 6:27 do good to them which *h* you
Lk 14:26 *h* not his father, and mother, and
Lk 16:13 for either he will *h* the one
Jn 7:7 The world cannot *h* you
Jn 15:18 If the world *h* you, ye know that
Rom 7:15 but what I *h*, that do I
1Jn 3:13 my brethren, if the world *h* you
Rev 2:6 the Nicolaitanes, which I also *h*
Rev 2:15 the Nicolaitanes, which thing I *h*
Rev 17:16 beast, these shall *h* the whore

**HATED**
Gen 27:41 Esau *h* Jacob because of the
Gen 29:31 when the LORD saw that Leah was *h*
Gen 29:33 the LORD hath heard that I was *h*
Gen 37:4 than all his brethren, they *h* him
Gen 37:5 and they *h* him yet the more
Gen 37:8 they *h* him yet the more for his
Gen 49:23 him, and shot at him, and *h* him
Deut 1:27 and said, Because the LORD *h* us
Deut 4:42 and *h* him not in times past
Deut 9:28 them, and because he *h* them
Deut 19:4 whom he *h* not in time past
Deut 19:6 inasmuch as he *h* him not in time
Deut 21:15 wives, one beloved, and another *h*
Deut 21:15 both the beloved and the *h*
Deut 21:15 firstborn son be hers that was *h*
Deut 21:16 firstborn before the son of the *h*
Deut 21:17 son of the *h* for the firstborn
Josh 20:5 and *h* him not beforetime
Judg 15:2 that thou hadst utterly *h* her
2Sa 5:8 that are *h* of David's soul, he
2Sa 13:15 Then Amnon *h* her exceedingly
2Sa 13:15 *h* her was greater than the love
2Sa 13:22 for Absalom *h* Amnon, because he
2Sa 22:18 enemy, and from them that *h* me
Est 9:1 had rule over them that *h* them
Est 9:5 they would unto those that *h* them
Job 31:29 the destruction of him that *h* me
Ps 18:17 enemy, and from them which *h* me
Ps 26:5 I have *h* the congregation of
Ps 31:6 I have *h* them that regard lying
Ps 44:7 hast put them to shame that *h* us
Ps 55:12 neither was it he that *h* me that
Ps 106:10 from the hand of him that *h* them
Ps 106:41 they that *h* them ruled over them
Prov 1:29 For that they *h* knowledge
Prov 5:12 How have I *h* instruction, and my
Prov 14:17 and a man of wicked devices is *h*
Prov 14:20 The poor is *h* even of his own
Eccl 2:17 Therefore I *h* life
Eccl 2:18 I *h* all my labour which I had
Is 60:15 thou hast been forsaken and *h*
Is 66:5 Your brethren that *h* you, that
Jer 12:8 therefore have I *h* it
Eze 16:37 with all them that thou hast *h*
Eze 35:6 sith thou hast not *h* blood
Hos 9:15 for there I *h* them
Mal 1:3 I *h* Esau, and laid his mountains
Mt 10:22 ye shall be *h* of all men for my
Mt 24:9 ye shall be *h* of all nations for
Mk 13:13 ye shall be *h* of all men for my
Lk 19:14 But his citizens *h* him, and sent a
Lk 21:17 ye shall be *h* of all men for my
Jn 15:18 ye know that it *h* me before it
Jn 15:18 me before it *h* you
Jn 15:24 seen and *h* both me and my Father
Jn 15:25 They *h* me without a cause
Jn 17:14 and the world hath *h* them, because
Rom 9:13 have I loved, but Esau have I *h*
Eph 5:29 no man ever yet *h* his own flesh
Heb 1:9 righteousness, and *h* iniquity

**HATEST**
2Sa 19:6 thine enemies, and *h* thy friends
Ps 5:5 thou *h* all workers of iniquity
Ps 45:7 righteousness, and *h* wickedness
Ps 50:17 Seeing thou *h* instruction
Eze 23:28 into the hand of them whom thou *h*
Rev 2:6 that thou *h* the deeds of the

**HATETH**
Ex 23:5 *h* thee lying under his burden
Deut 7:10 not be slack to him that *h* him
Deut 12:31 to the LORD, which he *h*, have
Deut 16:22 which the LORD thy God *h*
Deut 22:16 this man to wife, and he *h* her
Job 16:9 teareth me in his wrath, who *h* me
Job 34:17 Shall even he that *h* right govern
Ps 11:5 that loveth violence his soul *h*
Ps 120:6 long dwelt with him that *h* peace
Prov 11:15 he that *h* suretiship is sure
Prov 12:1 but he that *h* reproof is brutish
Prov 13:5 A righteous man *h* lying
Prov 13:24 He that spareth his rod *h* his son
Prov 15:10 he that *h* reproof shall die
Prov 15:27 but he that *h* gifts shall live
Prov 26:24 He that *h* dissembleth with his
Prov 26:28 A lying tongue *h* those that are
Prov 28:16 but he that *h* covetousness shall
Prov 29:24 with a thief *h* his own soul
Is 1:14 your appointed feasts my soul *h*
Mal 2:16 saith that he *h* putting away
Jn 3:20 one that doeth evil *h* the light
Jn 7:7 but me it *h*, because I testify of
Jn 12:25 he that *h* his life in this world
Jn 15:19 world, therefore the world *h* you
Jn 15:23 He that *h* me *h* my Father
1Jn 2:9 *h* his brother, is in darkness
1Jn 2:11 But he that *h* his brother is in
1Jn 3:15 Whosoever *h* his brother is a
1Jn 4:20 *h* his brother, he is a liar

**HATHATH** *(ha'-thath) Son of Othniel.*
1Chr 4:13 sons of Othniel; *H*

**HATIPHA** *(hat'-if-ah) A family of exiles.*
Ezr 2:54 of Neziah, the children of *H*
Neh 7:56 of Neziah, the children of *H*

**HATITA** *(hat'-it-ah) A family of exiles.*
Ezr 2:42 of Akkub, the children of *H*
Neh 7:45 of Akkub, the children of *H*

**HATRED**
Num 35:20 But if he thrust him of *h*
2Sa 13:15 so that the *h* wherewith he hated
Ps 25:19 and they hate me with cruel *h*
Ps 109:3 me about also with words of *h*
Ps 109:5 evil for good, and *h* for my love
Ps 139:22 I hate them with perfect *h*
Prov 10:12 *H* stirreth up strifes
Prov 10:18 He that hideth *h* with lying lips,
Prov 15:17 than a stalled ox and *h* therewith
Prov 26:26 Whose *h* is covered by deceit, his
Eccl 9:1 or *h* by all that is before them
Eccl 9:6 Also their love, and their *h*
Eze 25:15 to destroy it for the old *h*
Eze 35:5 thou hast had a perpetual *h*
Eze 35:11 used out of thy *h* against them
Hos 9:7 of thine iniquity, and the great *h*
Hos 9:8 *h* in the house of his God
Gal 5:20 Idolatry, witchcraft, *h*, variance

**HATTIL** *(hat'-til) A family of exiles.*
Ezr 2:57 of Shephatiah, the children of *H*
Neh 7:59 of Shephatiah, the children of *H*

**HATTUSH** *(hat'-tush)*
*1. A son of Shemaiah.*
1Chr 3:22 *H*, and Igeal, and Bariah, and
*2. A son of David.*
Ezr 8:2 the sons of David; *H*
*3. A priest.*
Neh 12:2 Amariah, Malluch, *H*,
*4. A rebuilder of Jerusalem's wall.*
Neh 3:10 repaired *H* the son of Hashabniah
*5. Renewed the covenant.*
Neh 10:4 *H*, Shebaniah, Malluch,

**HAUGHTINESS**
Is 2:11 the *h* of men shall be bowed down,
Is 2:17 the *h* of men shall be made low
Is 13:11 lay low the *h* of the terrible

Is 16:6 even of his *h*, and his pride, and
Jer 48:29 his pride, and the *h* of his heart

**HAUGHTY**
2Sa 22:28 but thine eyes are upon the *h*
Ps 131:1 Lord, my heart is not *h*, nor mine
Prov 16:18 an *h* spirit before a fall
Prov 18:12 destruction the heart of man is *h*
Prov 21:24 *h* scorner is his name, who
Is 3:16 the daughters of Zion are *h*
Is 10:33 down, and the *h* shall be humbled
Is 24:4 the *h* people of the earth do
Eze 16:50 And they were *h*, and committed
Zeph 3:11 thou shalt no more be *h* because

**HAURAN** *(hau'-ran) A province south of Damascus.*
Eze 47:16 which is by the coast of *H*
Eze 47:18 east side ye shall measure from *H*

**HAVILAH** *(hav'-il-ah)*
*1. A son of Cush.*
Gen 10:7 and *H*, and Sabtah, and Raamah,
1Chr 1:9 Seba, and *H*, and Sabta, and Raamah,
*2. A son of Joktan.*
Gen 10:29 And Ophir, and *H*, and Jobab
1Chr 1:23 And Ophir, and *H*, and Jobab
*3. A land west of Ural.*
Gen 2:11 compasseth the whole land of *H*
*4. A district east of Amalek.*
Gen 25:18 And they dwelt from *H* unto Shur
1Sa 15:7 from *H* until thou comest to Shur

**HAVOTH-JAIR** *(ha'-voth-ja'-ir)* See BASHAN-HAVOTH. *Villages in Gilead.*
Num 32:41 towns thereof, and called them *H*
Judg 10:4 which are called *H* unto this day

**HAZAEL** *(ha'-za-el) A king of Syria.*
1Kin 19:15 anoint *H* to be king over Syria
1Kin 19:17 the sword of *H* shall Jehu slay
2Kin 8:8 And the king said unto *H*, Take a
2Kin 8:9 So *H* went to meet him, and took a
2Kin 8:12 *H* said, Why weepeth my lord
2Kin 8:13 *H* said, But what, is thy servant
2Kin 8:15 and *H* reigned in his stead
2Kin 8:28 *H* king of Syria in Ramoth-gilead
2Kin 8:29 he fought against *H* king of Syria
2Kin 9:14 because of *H* king of Syria
2Kin 9:15 he fought with *H* king of Syria
2Kin 10:32 *H* smote them in all the coasts of
2Kin 12:17 Then *H* king of Syria went up, and
2Kin 12:17 *H* set his face to go up to
2Kin 12:18 sent it to *H* king of Syria
2Kin 13:3 into the hand of *H* king of Syria
2Kin 13:3 hand of Ben-hadad the son of *H*
2Kin 13:22 But *H* king of Syria oppressed
2Kin 13:24 So *H* king of Syria died
2Kin 13:25 Ben-hadad the son of *H* the cities
2Chr 22:5 king of Israel to war against *H*
2Chr 22:6 he fought with *H* king of Syria
Amos 1:4 send a fire into the house of *H*

**HAZAIAH** *(ha-za-i'-ah) Son of Adaiah.*
Neh 11:5 the son of Colhozeh, the son of *H*

**HAZAR-ADDAR** *(ha'-zar-ad'-dar)* See ADDAR. *A place in southern Palestine.*
Num 34:4 and shall go on to *H*, and pass on

**HAZAR-ENAN** *(ha'-zar-e'-nan) A village in northeastern Palestine.*
Num 34:9 goings out of it shall be at *H*
Num 34:10 east border from *H* to Shepham
Eze 47:17 border from the sea shall be *H*
Eze 48:1 as one goeth to Hamath, *H*

**HAZAR-GADDAH** *(ha'-zar-gad'-dah) A town in Judah.*
Josh 15:27 And *H*, and Heshmon, and Beth-palet,

**HAZAR-HATTICON** *(ha'-zar-hat'-ti-con) A place in Hauran.*
Eze 47:16 *H*, which is by the coast of

**HAZARMAVETH** *(ha-zar-ma'-veth) A son of Joktan.*
Gen 10:26 begat Almodad, and Sheleph, and *H*
1Chr 1:20 begat Almodad, and Sheleph, and *H*

**HAZAR-SHUAL** *(ha'-zar-shoo'-al) A town in Judah.*
Josh 15:28 And *H*, and Beer-sheba, and
Josh 19:3 And *H*, and Balah, and Azem,
1Chr 4:28 at Beer-sheba, and Moladah, and *H*
Neh 11:27 And at *H*, and at Beer-sheba, and in

**HAZAR-SUSAH** *(ha'-zar-soo'-sah)* See HAZAR-SUSIM. *A city in Judah.*
Josh 19:5 Ziklag, and Beth-marcaboth, and *H*

**HAZAR-SUSIM** *(ha'-zar-soo'-sim)* See HAZAR-SUSAH. *Same as Hazar-susah.*
1Chr 4:31 And at Beth-marcaboth, and *H*

**HAZAZON-TAMAR** *(haz'-a-zon-ta'-mar)* See HAZEZON-TAMAR. *A name for En-gedi.*
2Chr 20:2 and, behold, they be in *H*, which

**HAZELELPONI** *(haz-el-el-po'-ni) Sister of the sons of Etam.*
1Chr 4:3 and the name of their sister was *H*

**HAZER-HATTICON** See HAZAR-HATTICON.

**HAZERIM** *(haz'-e-rim) A district near Gaza.*
Deut 2:23 And the Avims which dwelt in *H*

**HAZEROTH** *(haz'-e-roth) A Hebrew encampment in the wilderness.*
Num 11:35 from Kibroth-hattaavah unto *H*
Num 11:35 and abode at *H*
Num 12:16 the people removed from *H*
Num 33:17 and encamped at *H*
Num 33:18 And they departed from *H*, and
Deut 1:1 Paran, and Tophel, and Laban, and *H*

**HAZEZON-TAMAR** *(haz'-e-zon-ta'-mar)* See EN-GEDI, HAZAZON-TAMAR. *Same as Hazazon-tamar.*
Gen 14:7 the Amorites, that dwelt in *H*

**HAZIEL** *(ha'-ze-el) A Levite.*
1Chr 23:9 Shelomith, and *H*, and Haran, three

**HAZO** *(ha'-zo) A son of Nahor.*
Gen 22:22 And Chesed, and *H*, and Pildash, and

**HAZOR** *(ha'-zor)* See BAAL-HAZOR, EN-HAZOR, HEZRON.
*1. A fortified city in Naphtali.*
Josh 11:1 when Jabin king of *H* had heard
Josh 11:10 that time turned back, and took *H*
Josh 11:10 for *H* beforetime was the head of
Josh 11:11 and he burnt *H* with fire
Josh 11:13 burned none of them, save *H* only
Josh 12:19 the king of *H*, one
Josh 19:36 And Adamah, and Ramah, and *H*
Judg 4:2 king of Canaan, that reigned in *H*
Judg 4:17 peace between Jabin the king of *H*
1Sa 12:9 Sisera, captain of the host of *H*
1Kin 9:15 and the wall of Jerusalem, and *H*
Neh 11:33 *H*, Ramah, Gittaim,
*2. A city in Judah.*
Josh 15:23 And Kedesh, and *H*, and Ithnan,
2Kin 15:29 and Janoah, and Kedesh, and *H*
*3. Another town in Judah.*
Josh 15:25 And *H*, Hadattah, and Kerioth, and
Josh 15:25 and Kerioth, and Hezron, which is *H*
*4. Where the Benjamites lived after the Exile.*
Jer 49:28 and concerning the kingdoms of *H*
*5. An area in eastern Arabia.*
Jer 49:30 dwell deep, O ye inhabitants of *H*
Jer 49:33 *H* shall be a dwelling for dragons

**HEAD**
Gen 3:15 it shall bruise thy *h*, and thou
Gen 24:26 And the man bowed down his *h*
Gen 24:48 And I bowed down my *h*, and
Gen 40:13 shall Pharaoh lift up thine *h*
Gen 40:16 I had three white baskets on my *h*
Gen 40:17 them out of the basket upon my *h*
Gen 40:19 lift up thy *h* from off thee
Gen 40:20 he lifted up the *h* of the chief
Gen 47:31 bowed himself upon the bed's *h*
Gen 48:14 hand, and laid it upon Ephraim's *h*
Gen 48:14 his left hand upon Manasseh's *h*
Gen 48:17 right hand upon the *h* of Ephraim
Gen 48:17 Ephraim's *h* unto Manasseh's *h*
Gen 48:18 put thy right hand upon his *h*
Gen 49:26 they shall be on the *h* of Joseph
Gen 49:26 on the crown of the *h* of him that
Ex 12:9 his *h* with his legs, and with the
Ex 12:27 And the people bowed the *h*
Ex 26:24 above the *h* of it unto one ring
Ex 29:6 shalt put the mitre upon his *h*
Ex 29:7 oil, and pour it upon his *h*
Ex 29:10 hands upon the *h* of the bullock
Ex 29:15 their hands upon the *h* of the ram
Ex 29:17 unto his pieces, and unto his *h*
Ex 29:19 their hands upon the *h* of the ram
Ex 34:8 bowed his *h* toward the earth, and
Ex 36:29 coupled together at the *h* thereof
Lev 1:4 upon the *h* of the burnt offering
Lev 1:8 sons, shall lay the parts, the *h*
Lev 1:12 it into his pieces, with his *h*
Lev 1:15 the altar, and wring off his *h*
Lev 3:2 hand upon the *h* of his offering
Lev 3:8 hand upon the *h* of his offering
Lev 3:13 lay his hand upon the *h* of it
Lev 4:4 lay his hand upon the bullock's *h*
Lev 4:11 and all his flesh, with his *h*
Lev 4:15 *h* of the bullock before the LORD
Lev 4:24 his hand upon the *h* of the goat
Lev 4:29 upon the *h* of the sin offering
Lev 4:33 upon the *h* of the sin offering
Lev 5:8 and wring off his *h* from his neck
Lev 8:9 And he put the mitre upon his *h*
Lev 8:12 the anointing oil upon Aaron's *h*
Lev 8:14 the *h* of the bullock for the sin
Lev 8:18 their hands upon the *h* of the ram
Lev 8:20 and Moses burnt the *h*, and the
Lev 8:22 their hands upon the *h* of the ram
Lev 9:13 with the pieces thereof, and the *h*
Lev 13:12 from his *h* even to his foot
Lev 13:29 a plague upon the *h* or the beard
Lev 13:30 a leprosy upon the *h* or beard
Lev 13:40 whose hair is fallen off his *h*
Lev 13:41 the part of his *h* toward his face
Lev 13:42 And if there be in the bald *h*
Lev 13:42 a leprosy sprung up in his bald *h*
Lev 13:43 be white reddish in his bald *h*
Lev 13:44 his plague is in his *h*
Lev 13:45 his *h* bare, and he shall put a
Lev 14:9 shave all his hair off his *h*
Lev 14:18 hand he shall pour upon the *h* of
Lev 14:29 hand he shall put upon the *h* of
Lev 16:21 hands upon the *h* of the live goat
Lev 16:21 them upon the *h* of the goat
Lev 19:32 shalt rise up before the hoary *h*
Lev 21:5 not make baldness upon their *h*
Lev 21:10 upon whose *h* the anointing oil
Lev 21:10 garments, shall not uncover his *h*
Lev 24:14 him lay their hands upon his *h*
Num 1:4 every one *h* of the house of his
Num 5:18 LORD, and uncover the woman's *h*
Num 6:5 shall no razor come upon his *h*
Num 6:5 locks of the hair of his *h* grow
Num 6:7 of his God is upon his *h*
Num 6:9 defiled the *h* of his consecration
Num 6:9 then he shall shave his *h* in the
Num 6:11 shall hallow his *h* that same day
Num 6:18 the Nazarite shall shave the *h* of
Num 6:18 hair of the *h* of his separation
Num 17:3 for one rod shall be for the *h* of
Num 22:31 and he bowed down his *h*, and fell
Num 25:15 he was *h* over a people, and of a
Deut 19:5 the *h* slippeth from the helve, and
Deut 21:12 and she shall shave her *h*, and pare
Deut 28:13 And the LORD shall make thee the *h*
Deut 28:23 that is over thy *h* shall be brass
Deut 28:35 of thy foot unto the top of thy *h*
Deut 28:44 he shall be the *h*, and thou shalt
Deut 33:16 come upon the *h* of Joseph
Deut 33:16 upon the top of the *h* of him that
Deut 33:20 the arm with the crown of the *h*
Josh 2:19 his blood shall be upon his *h*
Josh 2:19 his blood shall be on our *h*
Josh 11:10 was the *h* of all those kingdoms
Josh 22:14 each one was an *h* of the house of
Judg 5:26 smote Sisera, she smote off his *h*
Judg 9:53 of a millstone upon Abimelech's *h*
Judg 10:18 he shall be *h* over all the
Judg 11:8 be our *h* over all the inhabitants
Judg 11:9 them before me, shall I be your *h*
Judg 11:11 Gilead, and the people made him *h*
Judg 13:5 and no razor shall come on his *h*
Judg 16:13 seven locks of my *h* with the web
Judg 16:17 hath not come a razor upon mine *h*
Judg 16:19 off the seven locks of his *h*
Judg 16:22 Howbeit the hair of his *h* began
1Sa 1:11 shall no razor come upon his *h*
1Sa 4:12 rent, and with earth upon his *h*
1Sa 5:4 the *h* of Dagon and both the palms
1Sa 10:1 of oil, and poured it upon his *h*
1Sa 14:45 hair of his *h* fall to the ground
1Sa 15:17 wast thou not made the *h* of the
1Sa 17:5 had an helmet of brass upon his *h*
1Sa 17:7 his spear's *h* weighed six hundred
1Sa 17:38 put an helmet of brass upon his *h*
1Sa 17:46 thee, and take thine *h* from thee

1Sa 17:51 him, and cut off his *h* therewith
1Sa 17:54 And David took the *h* of the
1Sa 17:57 him before Saul with the *h* of the
1Sa 25:39 of Nabal upon his own *h*
1Sa 28:2 thee keeper of mine *h* for ever
1Sa 31:9 And they cut off his *h*, and
2Sa 1:2 clothes rent, and earth upon his *h*
2Sa 1:10 the crown that was upon his *h*
2Sa 1:16 unto him, Thy blood be upon thy *h*
2Sa 2:16 every one his fellow by the *h*
2Sa 3:8 and said, Am I a dog's *h*, which
2Sa 3:29 Let it rest on the *h* of Joab
2Sa 4:7 and beheaded him, and took his *h*
2Sa 4:8 they brought the *h* of Ish-bosheth
2Sa 4:8 Behold the *h* of Ish-bosheth the
2Sa 4:12 they took the *h* of Ish-bosheth
2Sa 12:30 their king's crown from off his *h*
2Sa 12:30 and it was set on David's *h*
2Sa 13:19 And Tamar put ashes on her *h*
2Sa 13:19 on her, and laid her hand on her *h*
2Sa 14:25 his *h* there was no blemish in him
2Sa 14:26 And when he polled his *h*, (for it
2Sa 14:26 he weighed the hair of his *h* at
2Sa 15:30 he went up, and had his *h* covered
2Sa 15:30 with him covered every man his *h*
2Sa 15:32 coat rent, and earth upon his *h*
2Sa 16:9 I pray thee, and take off his *h*
2Sa 18:9 his *h* caught hold of the oak, and
2Sa 20:21 his *h* shall be thrown to thee
2Sa 20:22 they cut off the *h* of Sheba the
2Sa 22:44 kept me to be *h* of the heathen
1Kin 2:6 let not his hoar *h* go down to the
1Kin 2:9 but his hoar *h* bring thou down to
1Kin 2:32 return his blood upon his own *h*
1Kin 2:33 return upon the *h* of Joab
1Kin 2:33 upon the *h* of his seed for ever
1Kin 2:37 blood shall be upon thine own *h*
1Kin 2:44 thy wickedness upon thine own *h*
1Kin 8:32 to bring his way upon his *h*
1Kin 19:6 and a cruse of water at his *h*
2Kin 2:3 away thy master from thy *h* to day
2Kin 2:5 away thy master from thy *h* to day
2Kin 2:23 said unto him, Go up, thou bald *h*
2Kin 2:23 go up, thou bald *h*
2Kin 4:19 unto his father, My *h*, my *h*
2Kin 6:5 the ax *h* fell into the water
2Kin 6:25 until an ass's *h* was sold for
2Kin 6:31 if the *h* of Elisha the son of
2Kin 6:32 hath sent to take away mine *h*
2Kin 9:3 box of oil, and pour it on his *h*
2Kin 9:6 and he poured the oil on his *h*
2Kin 9:30 painted her face, and tired her *h*
2Kin 19:21 hath shaken her *h* at thee
2Kin 25:27 began to reign did lift up the *h*
1Chr 10:9 had stripped him, they took his *h*
1Chr 10:10 fastened his *h* in the temple of
1Chr 20:2 of their king from off his *h*
1Chr 20:2 and it was set upon David's *h*
1Chr 29:11 thou art exalted as *h* above all
2Chr 6:23 his way upon his own *h*
2Chr 20:18 Jehoshaphat bowed his *h* with his
Ezr 9:3 and plucked off the hair of my *h*
Ezr 9:6 are increased over our *h*, and our
Neh 4:4 their reproach upon their own *h*
Est 2:17 he set the royal crown upon her *h*
Est 6:8 royal which is set upon his *h*
Est 6:12 mourning, and having his *h* covered
Est 9:25 should return upon his own *h*
Job 1:20 rent his mantle, and shaved his *h*
Job 10:15 yet will I not lift up my *h*
Job 16:4 you, and shake mine *h* at you
Job 19:9 and taken the crown from my *h*
Job 20:6 his *h* reach unto the clouds
Job 29:3 When his candle shined upon my *h*
Job 41:7 or his *h* with fish spears
Ps 3:3 glory, and the lifter up of mine *h*
Ps 7:16 shall return upon his own *h*
Ps 18:43 hast made me the *h* of the heathen
Ps 21:3 a crown of pure gold on his *h*
Ps 22:7 out the lip, they shake the *h*
Ps 23:5 thou anointest my *h* with oil
Ps 27:6 now shall mine *h* be lifted up
Ps 38:4 iniquities are gone over mine *h*
Ps 40:12 are more than the hairs of mine *h*
Ps 44:14 shaking of the *h* among the people
Ps 60:7 also is the strength of mine *h*
Ps 68:21 shall wound the *h* of his enemies
Ps 69:4 are more than the hairs of mine *h*
Ps 83:2 hate thee have lifted up the *h*
Ps 108:8 also is the strength of mine *h*
Ps 110:7 therefore shall he lift up the *h*
Ps 118:22 become the *h* stone of the corner
Ps 133:2 the precious ointment upon the *h*
Ps 140:7 covered my *h* in the day of battle
Ps 140:9 As for the *h* of those that
Ps 141:5 oil, which shall not break my *h*
Prov 1:9 an ornament of grace unto thy *h*
Prov 4:9 to thine *h* an ornament of grace
Prov 10:6 are upon the *h* of the just
Prov 11:26 upon the *h* of him that selleth it
Prov 16:31 The hoary *h* is a crown of glory,
Prov 20:29 beauty of old men is the grey *h*
Prov 25:22 heap coals of fire upon his *h*
Eccl 2:14 The wise man's eyes are in his *h*
Eccl 9:8 let thy *h* lack no ointment
Song 2:6 His left hand is under my *h*
Song 5:2 for my *h* is filled with dew, and
Song 5:11 His *h* is as the most fine gold,
Song 7:5 Thine *h* upon thee is like Carmel,
Song 7:5 the hair of thine *h* like purple
Song 8:3 left hand should be under my *h*
Is 1:5 the whole *h* is sick, and the whole
Is 1:6 the *h* there is no soundness in it
Is 3:17 of the *h* of the daughters of Zion
Is 7:8 For the *h* of Syria is Damascus,
Is 7:8 the *h* of Damascus is Rezin
Is 7:9 the *h* of Ephraim is Samaria, and
Is 7:9 the *h* of Samaria is Remaliah's
Is 7:20 by the king of Assyria, the *h*
Is 9:14 LORD will cut off from Israel *h*
Is 9:15 and honourable, he is the *h*
Is 19:15 for Egypt, which the *h* or tail
Is 28:1 which are on the *h* of the fat
Is 28:4 which is on the *h* of the fat
Is 37:22 hath shaken her *h* at thee
Is 51:11 joy shall be upon their *h*
Is 51:20 they lie at the *h* of all the
Is 58:5 it to bow down his *h* as a bulrush
Is 59:17 an helmet of salvation upon his *h*
Jer 2:16 have broken the crown of thy *h*
Jer 2:37 him, and thine hands upon thine *h*
Jer 9:1 Oh that my *h* were waters, and mine
Jer 18:16 shall be astonished, and wag his *h*
Jer 22:6 unto me, and the *h* of Lebanon
Jer 23:19 upon the *h* of the wicked
Jer 30:23 pain upon the *h* of the wicked
Jer 48:37 For every *h* shall be bald, and
Jer 48:45 the crown of the *h* of the
Jer 52:31 the *h* of Jehoiachin king of Judah
Lam 2:15 wag their *h* at the daughter of
Lam 3:54 Waters flowed over mine *h*
Lam 5:16 The crown is fallen from our *h*
Eze 5:1 and cause it to pass upon thine *h*
Eze 8:3 and took me by a lock of mine *h*
Eze 9:10 recompense their way upon their *h*
Eze 10:1 firmament that was above the *h* of
Eze 10:11 the *h* looked they followed it
Eze 13:18 make kerchiefs upon the *h* of
Eze 16:12 and a beautiful crown upon thine *h*
Eze 16:25 high place at every *h* of the way
Eze 16:31 place in the *h* of every way
Eze 16:43 recompense thy way upon thine *h*
Eze 17:19 will I recompense upon his own *h*
Eze 21:19 choose it at the *h* of the way to
Eze 21:21 at the *h* of the two ways, to use
Eze 24:17 the tire of thine *h* upon thee
Eze 29:18 every *h* was made bald, and every
Eze 33:4 his blood shall be upon his own *h*
Eze 42:12 was a door in the *h* of the way
Dan 1:10 make me endanger my *h* to the king
Dan 2:28 the visions of thy *h* upon thy bed
Dan 2:32 This image's *h* was of fine gold,
Dan 2:38 Thou art this *h* of gold
Dan 3:27 nor was an hair of their *h* singed
Dan 4:5 the visions of my *h* troubled me
Dan 4:10 the visions of mine *h* in my bed
Dan 4:13 the visions of my *h* upon my bed
Dan 7:1 and visions of his *h* upon his bed
Dan 7:9 the hair of his *h* like the pure
Dan 7:15 the visions of my *h* troubled me
Dan 7:20 the ten horns that were in his *h*
Hos 1:11 and appoint themselves one *h*
Joel 3:4 your recompence upon your own *h*
Joel 3:7 your recompence upon your own *h*
Amos 2:7 of the earth on the *h* of the poor
Amos 8:10 loins, and baldness upon every *h*
Amos 9:1 and cut them in the *h*, all of them
Obad 15 shall return upon thine own *h*
Jonah 2:5 the weeds were wrapped about my *h*
Jonah 4:6 it might be a shadow over his *h*
Jonah 4:8 the sun beat upon the *h* of Jonah
Mic 2:13 and the LORD on the *h* of them
Hab 3:13 thou woundedst the *h* out of the
Hab 3:14 his staves the *h* of his villages
Zec 1:21 so that no man did lift up his *h*
Zec 3:5 them set a fair mitre upon his *h*
Zec 3:5 they set a fair mitre upon his *h*
Zec 6:11 set them upon the *h* of Joshua the
Mt 5:36 Neither shalt thou swear by thy *h*
Mt 6:17 when thou fastest, anoint thine *h*
Mt 8:20 man hath not where to lay his *h*
Mt 10:30 hairs of your *h* are all numbered
Mt 14:8 John Baptist's *h* in a charger
Mt 14:11 his *h* was brought in a charger,
Mt 21:42 is become the *h* of the corner
Mt 26:7 ointment, and poured it on his *h*
Mt 27:29 of thorns, they put it upon his *h*
Mt 27:30 the reed, and smote him on the *h*
Mt 27:37 set up over his *h* his accusation
Mk 6:24 The *h* of John the Baptist
Mk 6:25 charger the *h* of John the Baptist
Mk 6:27 and commanded his *h* to be brought
Mk 6:28 brought his *h* in a charger, and
Mk 12:4 stones, and wounded him in the *h*
Mk 12:10 is become the *h* of the corner
Mk 14:3 the box, and poured it on his *h*
Mk 15:17 of thorns, and put it about his *h*
Mk 15:19 smote him on the *h* with a reed
Lk 7:38 wipe them with the hairs of her *h*
Lk 7:44 them with the hairs of her *h*
Lk 7:46 My *h* with oil thou didst not
Lk 9:58 man hath not where to lay his *h*
Lk 12:7 hairs of your *h* are all numbered
Lk 20:17 is become the *h* of the corner
Lk 21:18 not an hair of your *h* perish
Jn 13:9 only, but also my hands and my *h*
Jn 19:2 of thorns, and put it on his *h*
Jn 19:30 and he bowed his *h*, and gave up the
Jn 20:7 the napkin, that was about his *h*
Jn 20:12 white sitting, the one at the *h*
Acts 4:11 is become the *h* of the corner
Acts 18:18 having shorn his *h* in Cenchrea
Acts 27:34 fall from the *h* of any of you
Rom 12:20 shalt heap coals of fire on his *h*
1Cor 11:3 that the *h* of every man is Christ
1Cor 11:3 the *h* of the woman is the man
1Cor 11:3 and the *h* of Christ is God
1Cor 11:4 prophesying, having his *h* covered
1Cor 11:5 *h* uncovered dishonoureth her *h*
1Cor 11:7 indeed ought not to cover his *h*
1Cor 11:10 on her *h* because of the angels
1Cor 12:21 nor again the *h* to the feet
Eph 1:22 gave him to be the *h* over all
Eph 4:15 him in all things, which is the *h*
Eph 5:23 the husband is the *h* of the wife
Eph 5:23 as Christ is the *h* of the church
Col 1:18 he is the *h* of the body, the
Col 2:10 in him, which is the *h* of all
Col 2:19 And not holding the *H*, from which
1Pet 2:7 same is made the *h* of the corner
Rev 1:14 His *h* and his hairs were white
Rev 10:1 and a rainbow was upon his *h*
Rev 12:1 upon her *h* a crown of twelve
Rev 14:14 having on his *h* a golden crown,
Rev 19:12 on his *h* were many crowns

## HEADS

Gen 2:10 was parted, and became into four *h*
Gen 43:28 And they bowed down their *h*
Ex 4:31 then they bowed their *h* and
Ex 6:14 These be the *h* of their fathers'
Ex 6:25 these are the *h* of the fathers of
Ex 18:25 made them *h* over the people,
Lev 10:6 his sons, Uncover not your *h*
Lev 19:27 not round the corners of your *h*
Num 1:16 fathers, *h* of thousands in Israel
Num 7:2 *h* of the house of their fathers,
Num 8:12 hands upon the *h* of the bullocks
Num 10:4 which are *h* of the thousands of
Num 13:3 all those men were *h* of the
Num 25:4 Take all the *h* of the people, and
Num 30:1 Moses spake unto the *h* of the
Deut 1:15 and known, and made them *h* over you
Deut 5:23 even all the *h* of your tribes, and
Deut 33:5 when the *h* of the people and the
Deut 33:21 he came with the *h* of the people
Josh 7:6 Israel, and put dust upon their *h*
Josh 14:1 the *h* of the fathers of the
Josh 19:51 the *h* of the fathers of the
Josh 21:1 Then came near the *h* of the

Josh 21:1 unto the *h* of the fathers of the
Josh 22:21 said unto the *h* of the thousands
Josh 22:30 *h* of the thousands of Israel
Josh 23:2 for their elders, and for their *h*
Josh 24:1 elders of Israel, and for their *h*
Judg 7:25 Midian, and brought the *h* of Oreb
Judg 8:28 they lifted up their *h* no more
Judg 9:57 did God render upon their *h*
1Sa 29:4 it not be with the *h* of these men
1Kin 8:1 all the *h* of the tribes, the
1Kin 20:31 on our loins, and ropes upon our *h*
1Kin 20:32 loins, and put ropes on their *h*
2Kin 10:6 take ye the *h* of the men your
2Kin 10:7 put their *h* in baskets, and sent
2Kin 10:8 brought the *h* of the king's sons
1Chr 5:24 these were the *h* of the house of
1Chr 5:24 *h* of the house of their fathers
1Chr 7:2 *h* of their father's house, to wit
1Chr 7:7 *h* of the house of their fathers,
1Chr 7:9 *h* of the house of their fathers,
1Chr 7:11 by the *h* of their fathers, mighty
1Chr 7:40 *h* of their father's house, choice
1Chr 8:6 these are the *h* of the fathers of
1Chr 8:10 were his sons, *h* of the fathers
1Chr 8:13 who were *h* of the fathers of the
1Chr 8:28 These were *h* of the fathers, by
1Chr 9:13 *h* of the house of their fathers,
1Chr 12:19 Saul to the jeopardy of our *h*
1Chr 12:32 the *h* of them were two hundred
1Chr 29:20 fathers, and bowed down their *h*
2Chr 3:16 put them on the *h* of the pillars
2Chr 5:2 all the *h* of the tribes, the
2Chr 28:12 Then certain of the *h* of the
2Chr 29:30 gladness, and they bowed their *h*
Neh 8:6 and they bowed their *h*, and
Job 2:12 dust upon their *h* toward heaven
Ps 24:7 Lift up your *h*, O ye gates
Ps 24:9 Lift up your *h*, O ye gates
Ps 66:12 caused men to ride over our *h*
Ps 74:13 thou brakest the *h* of the dragons
Ps 74:14 Thou brakest the *h* of leviathan
Ps 109:25 upon me they shaked their *h*
Ps 110:6 he shall wound the *h* over many
Is 15:2 on all their *h* shall be baldness,
Is 35:10 and everlasting joy upon their *h*
Jer 14:3 and confounded, and covered their *h*
Jer 14:4 ashamed, they covered their *h*
Lam 2:10 have cast up dust upon their *h*
Lam 2:10 hang down their *h* to the ground
Eze 1:22 of the firmament upon the *h* of
Eze 1:22 forth over their *h* above
Eze 1:25 firmament that was over their *h*
Eze 1:26 *h* was the likeness of a throne
Eze 7:18 and baldness upon all their *h*
Eze 11:21 their way upon their own *h*
Eze 22:31 have I recompensed upon their *h*
Eze 23:15 in dyed attire upon their *h*
Eze 23:42 and beautiful crowns upon their *h*
Eze 24:23 your tires shall be upon your *h*
Eze 27:30 shall cast up dust upon their *h*
Eze 32:27 laid their swords under their *h*
Eze 44:18 have linen bonnets upon their *h*
Eze 44:20 Neither shall they shave their *h*
Eze 44:20 they shall only poll their *h*
Dan 7:6 the beast had also four *h*
Mic 3:1 O *h* of Jacob, and ye princes of
Mic 3:9 ye *h* of the house of Jacob, and
Mic 3:11 The *h* thereof judge for reward,
Mt 27:39 by reviled him, wagging their *h*
Mk 15:29 by railed on him, wagging their *h*
Lk 21:28 then look up, and lift up your *h*
Acts 18:6 Your blood be upon your own *h*
Acts 21:24 them, that they may shave their *h*
Rev 4:4 had on their *h* crowns of gold
Rev 9:7 on their *h* were as it were crowns
Rev 9:17 the *h* of the horses were as the
Rev 9:17 the horses were as the *h* of lions
Rev 9:19 were like unto serpents, and had *h*
Rev 12:3 great red dragon, having seven *h*
Rev 12:3 horns, and seven crowns upon his *h*
Rev 13:1 up out of the sea, having seven *h*
Rev 13:1 upon his *h* the name of blasphemy
Rev 13:3 I saw one of his *h* as it were
Rev 17:3 of blasphemy, having seven *h*
Rev 17:7 her, which hath the seven *h*
Rev 17:9 The seven *h* are seven mountains,
Rev 18:19 And they cast dust on their *h*

### HEAL

Num 12:13 *H* her now, O God, I beseech thee
Deut 32:39 I wound, and I *h*
2Kin 20:5 behold, I will *h* thee
2Kin 20:8 the sign that the LORD will *h* me
2Chr 7:14 their sin, and will *h* their land
Ps 6:2 O LORD, *h* me
Ps 41:4 *h* my soul
Ps 60:2 *h* the breaches thereof
Eccl 3:3 A time to kill, and a time to *h*
Is 19:22 he shall smite and *h* it
Is 19:22 of them, and shall *h* them
Is 57:18 have seen his ways, and will *h* him
Is 57:19 and I will *h* him
Jer 3:22 I will *h* your backslidings
Jer 17:14 *H* me, O LORD, and I shall be
Jer 30:17 I will *h* thee of thy wounds,
Lam 2:13 who can *h* thee?
Hos 5:13 yet could he not *h* you, nor cure
Hos 6:1 for he hath torn, and he will *h* us
Hos 14:4 I will *h* their backsliding, I
Zec 11:16 nor *h* that that is broken, nor
Mt 8:7 unto him, I will come and *h* him
Mt 10:1 to *h* all manner of sickness and
Mt 10:8 *H* the sick, cleanse the lepers,
Mt 12:10 Is it lawful to *h* on the sabbath
Mt 13:15 be converted, and I should *h* them
Mk 3:2 whether he would *h* him on the
Mk 3:15 And to have power to *h* sicknesses
Lk 4:18 sent me to *h* the brokenhearted
Lk 4:23 proverb, Physician, *h* thyself
Lk 5:17 of the Lord was present to *h* them
Lk 6:7 whether he would *h* on the sabbath
Lk 7:3 he would come and *h* his servant
Lk 9:2 kingdom of God, and to *h* the sick
Lk 10:9 *h* the sick that are therein, and
Lk 14:3 Is it lawful to *h* on the sabbath
Jn 4:47 he would come down, and *h* his son
Jn 12:40 be converted, and I should *h* them
Acts 4:30 stretching forth thine hand to *h*
Acts 28:27 be converted, and I should *h* them

### HEALED

Gen 20:17 God *h* Abimelech, and his wife, and
Ex 21:19 cause him to be thoroughly *h*
Lev 13:18 skin thereof, was a boil, and is *h*
Lev 13:37 the scall is *h*, he is clean
Lev 14:3 of leprosy be *h* in the leper
Lev 14:48 clean, because the plague is *h*
Deut 28:27 itch, whereof thou canst not be *h*
Deut 28:35 a sore botch that cannot be *h*
1Sa 6:3 then ye shall be *h*, and it shall
2Kin 2:21 the LORD, I have *h* these waters
2Kin 2:22 the waters were *h* unto this day
2Kin 8:29 king Joram went back to be *h* in
2Kin 9:15 king Joram was returned to be *h*
2Chr 22:6 he returned to be *h* in Jezreel
2Chr 30:20 to Hezekiah, and *h* the people
Ps 30:2 unto thee, and thou hast *h* me
Ps 107:20 *h* them, and delivered them from
Is 6:10 their heart, and convert, and be *h*
Is 53:5 and with his stripes we are *h*
Jer 6:14 They have *h* also the hurt of the
Jer 8:11 For they have *h* the hurt of the
Jer 15:18 incurable, which refuseth to be *h*
Jer 17:14 Heal me, O LORD, and I shall be *h*
Jer 51:8 her pain, if so be she may be *h*
Jer 51:9 *h* Babylon, but she is not *h*
Eze 30:21 it shall not be bound up to be *h*
Eze 34:4 neither have ye *h* that which was
Eze 47:8 the sea, the waters shall be *h*
Eze 47:9 for they shall be *h*
Eze 47:11 marishes thereof shall not be *h*
Hos 7:1 When I would have *h* Israel
Hos 11:3 but they knew not that I *h* them
Mt 4:24 and he *h* them
Mt 8:8 only, and my servant shall be *h*
Mt 8:13 his servant was *h* in the selfsame
Mt 8:16 his word, and *h* all that were sick
Mt 12:15 followed him, and he *h* them all
Mt 12:22 he *h* him, insomuch that the blind
Mt 14:14 toward them, and he *h* their sick
Mt 15:30 and he *h* them
Mt 19:2 and he *h* them there
Mt 21:14 and he *h* them
Mk 1:34 he *h* many that were sick of
Mk 3:10 For he had *h* many
Mk 5:23 hands on her, that she may be *h*
Mk 5:29 that she was *h* of that plague
Mk 6:5 upon a few sick folk, and *h* them
Mk 6:13 many that were sick, and *h* them
Lk 4:40 on every one of them, and *h* them
Lk 5:15 hear, and to be *h* by him of their
Lk 6:17 to be *h* of their diseases
Lk 6:18 and they were *h*
Lk 6:19 virtue out of him, and *h* them all
Lk 7:7 a word, and my servant shall be *h*
Lk 8:2 which had been *h* of evil spirits
Lk 8:36 was possessed of the devils was *h*
Lk 8:43 neither could be *h* of any
Lk 8:47 him, and how she was *h* immediately
Lk 9:11 *h* them that had need of healing
Lk 9:42 *h* the child, and delivered him
Lk 13:14 Jesus had *h* on the sabbath day
Lk 13:14 in them therefore come and be *h*
Lk 14:4 took him, and *h* him, and let him go
Lk 17:15 them, when he saw that he was *h*
Lk 22:51 And he touched his ear, and *h* him
Jn 5:13 he that was *h* wist not who it was
Acts 3:11 lame man which was *h* held Peter
Acts 4:14 which was *h* standing with them
Acts 5:16 and they were *h* every one
Acts 8:7 and that were lame, were *h*
Acts 14:9 that he had faith to be *h*
Acts 28:8 laid his hands on him, and *h* him
Acts 28:9 in the island, came, and were *h*
Heb 12:13 but let it rather be *h*
Jas 5:16 one for another, that ye may be *h*
1Pet 2:24 by whose stripes ye were *h*
Rev 13:3 and his deadly wound was *h*
Rev 13:12 beast, whose deadly wound was *h*

### HEALETH

Ex 15:26 for I am the LORD that *h* thee
Ps 103:3 who *h* all thy diseases
Ps 147:3 He *h* the broken in heart, and
Is 30:26 *h* the stroke of their wound

### HEALING

Jer 14:19 us, and there is no *h* for us
Jer 14:19 and for the time of *h*, and behold
Jer 30:13 thou hast no *h* medicines
Nah 3:19 There is no *h* of thy bruise
Mal 4:2 arise with *h* in his wings
Mt 4:23 *h* all manner of sickness and all
Mt 9:35 *h* every sickness and every disease
Lk 9:6 the gospel, and *h* every where
Lk 9:11 and healed them that had need of *h*
Acts 4:22 whom this miracle of *h* was shewed
Acts 10:38 *h* all that were oppressed of the
1Cor 12:9 the gifts of *h* by the same Spirit
1Cor 12:30 Have all the gifts of *h*
Rev 22:2 were for the *h* of the nations

### HEALTH

Gen 43:28 servant our father is in good *h*
2Sa 20:9 Joab said to Amasa, Art thou in *h*
Ps 42:11 who is the *h* of my countenance,
Ps 43:5 who is the *h* of my countenance,
Ps 67:2 thy saving *h* among all nations
Prov 3:8 It shall be *h* to thy navel, and
Prov 4:22 them, and *h* to all their flesh
Prov 12:18 but the tongue of the wise is *h*
Prov 13:17 but a faithful ambassador is *h*
Prov 16:24 to the soul, and *h* to the bones
Is 58:8 thine *h* shall spring forth
Jer 8:15 and for a time of *h*, and behold
Jer 8:22 why then is not the *h* of the
Jer 30:17 For I will restore *h* unto thee
Jer 33:6 Behold, I will bring it *h*
Acts 27:34 for this is for your *h*
3Jn 2 thou mayest prosper and be in *h*

### HEAP

Gen 31:46 and they took stones, and made an *h*
Gen 31:46 and they did eat there upon the *h*
Gen 31:48 This *h* is a witness between me and
Gen 31:51 said to Jacob, Behold this *h*
Gen 31:52 This *h* be witness, and this pillar
Gen 31:52 will not pass over this *h* to thee
Gen 31:52 thou shalt not pass over this *h*
Ex 15:8 the floods stood upright as an *h*
Deut 13:16 and it shall be an *h* for ever
Deut 32:23 I will *h* mischiefs upon them
Josh 3:13 and they shall stand upon an *h*
Josh 3:16 rose up upon an *h* very far from
Josh 7:26 a great *h* of stones unto this day
Josh 8:28 Ai, and made it an *h* for ever
Josh 8:29 raise thereon a great *h* of stones
Ruth 3:7 down at the end of the *h* of corn
2Sa 18:17 laid a very great *h* of stones
Job 8:17 His roots are wrapped about the *h*

Job 16:4 I could *h* up words against you,
Job 27:16 Though he *h* up silver as the dust
Job 36:13 hypocrites in heart *h* up wrath
Ps 33:7 of the sea together as an *h*
Ps 78:13 made the waters to stand as an *h*
Prov 25:22 For thou shalt *h* coals of fire
Eccl 2:26 travail, to gather and to *h* up
Song 7:2 thy belly is like an *h* of wheat
Is 17:1 city, and it shall be a ruinous *h*
Is 17:11 shall be a *h* in the day of grief
Is 25:2 For thou hast made of a city an *h*
Jer 30:18 shall be builded upon her own *h*
Jer 49:2 and it shall be a desolate *h*
Eze 24:10 *H* on wood, kindle the fire,
Mic 1:6 make Samaria as an *h* of the field
Hab 1:10 for they shall *h* dust, and take it
Hab 3:15 through the *h* of great waters
Hag 2:16 came to an *h* of twenty measures
Rom 12:20 shalt *h* coals of fire on his head
2Ti 4:3 they *h* to themselves teachers

**HEAPS**

Ex 8:14 gathered them together upon *h*
Judg 15:16 *h* upon *h*, with the jaw of an
2Kin 10:8 Lay ye them in two *h* at the
2Kin 19:25 fenced cities into ruinous *h*
2Chr 31:6 LORD their God, and laid them by *h*
2Chr 31:7 to lay the foundation of the *h*
2Chr 31:8 and the princes came and saw the *h*
2Chr 31:9 and the Levites concerning the *h*
Neh 4:2 revive the stones out of the *h* of
Job 15:28 which are ready to become *h*
Ps 79:1 they have laid Jerusalem on *h*
Is 37:26 defenced cities into ruinous *h*
Jer 9:11 And I will make Jerusalem *h*
Jer 26:18 and Jerusalem shall become *h*
Jer 31:21 up waymarks, make thee high *h*
Jer 50:26 cast her up as *h*, and destroy her
Jer 51:37 And Babylon shall become *h*
Hos 12:11 their altars are as *h* in the
Mic 3:12 and Jerusalem shall become *h*

**HEAR**

Gen 4:23 wives, Adah and Zillah, *H* my voice
Gen 21:6 so that all that *h* will laugh
Gen 23:6 *H* us, my lord
Gen 23:8 *h* me, and intreat for me to Ephron
Gen 23:11 Nay, my lord, *h* me
Gen 23:13 wilt give it, I pray thee, *h* me
Gen 37:6 And he said unto them, *H*, I pray
Gen 42:21 he besought us, and we would not *h*
Gen 42:22 and ye would not *h*
Gen 49:2 Gather yourselves together, and *h*
Ex 6:12 how then shall Pharaoh *h* me
Ex 7:16 hitherto thou wouldest not *h*
Ex 15:14 The people shall *h*, and be afraid
Ex 19:9 that the people may *h* when I
Ex 20:19 Speak thou with us, and we will *h*
Ex 22:23 me, I will surely *h* their cry
Ex 22:27 he crieth unto me, that I will *h*
Ex 32:18 noise of them that sing do I *h*
Lev 5:1 *h* the voice of swearing, and is a
Num 9:8 I will *h* what the LORD will
Num 12:6 And he said, *H* now my words
Num 14:13 Then the Egyptians shall *h* it
Num 16:8 And Moses said unto Korah, *H*
Num 20:10 said unto them, *H* now, ye rebels
Num 23:18 and said, Rise up, Balak, and *h*
Num 30:4 And her father *h* her vow, and her
Deut 1:16 *H* the causes between your
Deut 1:17 but ye shall *h* the small as well
Deut 1:17 bring it unto me, and I will *h* it
Deut 1:43 and ye would not *h*, but rebelled
Deut 2:25 who shall *h* report of thee, and
Deut 3:26 for your sakes, and would not *h* me
Deut 4:6 which shall *h* all these statutes,
Deut 4:10 and I will make them *h* my words
Deut 4:28 stone, which neither see, nor *h*
Deut 4:33 Did ever people *h* the voice of
Deut 4:36 he made thee to *h* his voice
Deut 5:1 all Israel, and said unto them, *H*
Deut 5:25 if we *h* the voice of the LORD our
Deut 5:27 *h* all that the LORD our God shall
Deut 5:27 and we will *h* it, and do it
Deut 6:3 *H* therefore, O Israel, and observe
Deut 6:4 *H*, O Israel
Deut 9:1 *H*, O Israel
Deut 12:28 *h* all these words which I command
Deut 13:11 And all Israel shall *h*, and fear,
Deut 13:12 If thou shalt *h* say in one of thy
Deut 17:13 And all the people shall *h*
Deut 18:16 Let me not *h* again the voice of
Deut 19:20 And those which remain shall *h*
Deut 20:3 And shall say unto them, *H*
Deut 21:21 and all Israel shall *h*, and fear
Deut 29:4 and eyes to see, and ears to *h*
Deut 30:12 it unto us, that we may *h* it
Deut 30:13 it unto us, that we may *h* it
Deut 30:17 away, so that thou wilt not *h*
Deut 31:12 within thy gates, that they may *h*
Deut 31:13 have not known any thing, may *h*
Deut 32:1 and *h*, O earth, the words of my
Deut 33:7 and he said, *H*, LORD, the voice of
Josh 3:9 *h* the words of the LORD your God
Josh 6:5 when ye *h* the sound of the
Josh 7:9 of the land shall *h* of it
Judg 5:3 *H*, O ye kings
Judg 5:16 to *h* the bleatings of the flocks
Judg 7:11 thou shalt *h* what they say
Judg 14:13 thy riddle, that we may *h* it
1Sa 2:23 for I *h* of your evil dealings by
1Sa 2:24 for it is no good report that I *h*
1Sa 8:18 LORD will not *h* you in that day
1Sa 13:3 land, saying, Let the Hebrews *h*
1Sa 15:14 the lowing of the oxen which I *h*
1Sa 16:2 if Saul *h* it, he will kill me
1Sa 22:7 about him, *H* now, ye Benjamites
1Sa 22:12 *H* now, thou son of Ahitub
1Sa 25:24 *h* the words of thine handmaid
1Sa 26:19 let my lord the king *h* the words
2Sa 14:16 For the king will *h*, to deliver
2Sa 15:3 man deputed of the king to *h* thee
2Sa 15:10 As soon as ye *h* the sound of the
2Sa 15:35 shalt *h* out of the king's house
2Sa 15:36 unto me every thing that ye can *h*
2Sa 16:21 all Israel shall *h* that thou art
2Sa 17:5 let us *h* likewise what he saith
2Sa 19:35 can I *h* any more the voice of
2Sa 20:16 woman out of the city, *H*, *h*
2Sa 20:17 *H* the words of thine handmaid
2Sa 20:17 And he answered, I do *h*
2Sa 22:7 he did *h* my voice out of his
2Sa 22:45 as soon as they *h*, they shall be
1Kin 4:34 people to *h* the wisdom of Solomon
1Kin 8:30 *h* thou in heaven thy dwelling
1Kin 8:32 Then *h* thou in heaven, and do, and
1Kin 8:34 Then *h* thou in heaven, and forgive
1Kin 8:36 Then *h* thou in heaven, and forgive
1Kin 8:39 Then *h* thou in heaven thy
1Kin 8:42 (For they shall *h* of thy great
1Kin 8:43 *H* thou in heaven thy dwelling
1Kin 8:45 Then *h* thou in heaven their
1Kin 8:49 Then *h* thou their prayer and their
1Kin 10:8 before thee, and that *h* thy wisdom
1Kin 10:24 to *h* his wisdom, which God had
1Kin 18:26 until noon, saying, O Baal, *h* us
1Kin 18:37 *H* me, O LORD, *h* me, that this
1Kin 22:19 *H* thou therefore the word of the
2Kin 7:1 *H* ye the word of the LORD
2Kin 7:6 Syrians to *h* a noise of chariots
2Kin 14:11 But Amaziah would not *h*
2Kin 17:14 Notwithstanding they would not *h*
2Kin 18:12 commanded, and would not *h* them
2Kin 18:28 *H* the word of the great king, the
2Kin 19:4 *h* all the words of Rab-shakeh
2Kin 19:7 upon him, and he shall *h* a rumour
2Kin 19:16 LORD, bow down thine ear, and *h*
2Kin 19:16 *h* the words of Sennacherib, which
2Kin 20:16 Hezekiah, *H* the word of the LORD
1Chr 14:15 when thou shalt *h* a sound of
1Chr 28:2 *H* me, my brethren, and my people
2Chr 6:21 *h* thou from thy dwelling place,
2Chr 6:23 Then *h* thou from heaven, and do,
2Chr 6:25 Then *h* thou from the heavens, and
2Chr 6:27 Then *h* thou from heaven, and
2Chr 6:30 Then *h* thou from heaven thy
2Chr 6:33 Then *h* thou from the heavens,
2Chr 6:35 Then *h* thou from the heavens
2Chr 6:39 Then *h* thou from the heavens,
2Chr 7:14 then will I *h* from heaven
2Chr 9:7 before thee, and *h* thy wisdom
2Chr 9:23 to *h* his wisdom, that God had put
2Chr 13:4 *H* me, thou Jeroboam, and all
2Chr 15:2 *H* ye me, Asa, and all Judah and
2Chr 18:18 Therefore *h* the word of the LORD
2Chr 20:9 our affliction, then thou wilt *h*
2Chr 20:20 *H* me, O Judah, and ye inhabitants
2Chr 25:20 But Amaziah would not *h*
2Chr 28:11 Now *h* me therefore, and deliver
2Chr 29:5 *H* me, ye Levites, sanctify now
Neh 1:6 that thou mayest *h* the prayer of
Neh 4:4 *H*, O our God
Neh 4:20 ye *h* the sound of the trumpet
Neh 8:2 women, and all that could *h* with
Neh 9:29 their neck, and would not *h*
Job 3:18 they *h* not the voice of the
Job 5:27 *h* it, and know thou it for thy
Job 13:6 *H* now my reasoning, and hearken to
Job 13:17 *H* diligently my speech, and my
Job 15:17 I will shew thee, *h* me
Job 21:2 *H* diligently my speech, and let
Job 22:27 unto him, and he shall *h* thee
Job 27:9 Will God *h* his cry when trouble
Job 30:20 unto thee, and thou dost not *h* me
Job 31:35 Oh that one would *h* me
Job 33:1 *h* my speeches, and hearken to all
Job 34:2 *H* my words, O ye wise men
Job 34:16 thou hast understanding, *h* this
Job 35:13 Surely God will not *h* vanity
Job 37:2 *H* attentively the noise of his
Job 42:4 *H*, I beseech thee, and I will
Ps 4:1 *H* me when I call, O God of my
Ps 4:1 mercy upon me, and *h* my prayer
Ps 4:3 the LORD will *h* when I call unto
Ps 5:3 voice shalt thou *h* in the morning
Ps 10:17 thou wilt cause thine ear to *h*
Ps 13:3 Consider and *h* me, O LORD my God
Ps 17:1 *H* the right, O LORD, attend unto
Ps 17:6 upon thee, for thou wilt *h* me
Ps 17:6 thine ear unto me, and *h* my speech
Ps 18:44 As soon as they *h* of me, they
Ps 20:1 The LORD *h* thee in the day of
Ps 20:6 he will *h* him from his holy
Ps 20:9 let the king *h* us when we call
Ps 27:7 *H*, O LORD, when I cry with my
Ps 28:2 *H* the voice of my supplications,
Ps 30:10 *H*, O LORD, and have mercy upon me
Ps 34:2 the humble shall *h* thereof
Ps 38:15 thou wilt *h*, O Lord my God
Ps 38:16 *H* me, lest otherwise they should
Ps 39:12 *H* my prayer, O LORD, and give ear
Ps 49:1 *H* this, all ye people
Ps 50:7 *H*, O my people, and I will speak
Ps 51:8 Make me to *h* joy and gladness
Ps 54:2 *H* my prayer, O God
Ps 55:2 Attend unto me, and *h* me
Ps 55:17 and he shall *h* my voice
Ps 55:19 God shall *h*, and afflict them,
Ps 59:7 for who, say they, doth *h*
Ps 60:5 save with thy right hand, and *h* me
Ps 61:1 *H* my cry, O God
Ps 64:1 *H* my voice, O God, in my prayer
Ps 66:16 Come and *h*, all ye that fear God,
Ps 66:18 my heart, the Lord will not *h* me
Ps 69:13 the multitude of thy mercy *h* me
Ps 69:16 *H* me, O LORD
Ps 69:17 *h* me speedily
Ps 81:8 *H*, O my people, and I will testify
Ps 84:8 O LORD God of hosts, *h* my prayer
Ps 85:8 I will *h* what God the LORD will
Ps 86:1 Bow down thine ear, O LORD, *h* me
Ps 92:11 mine ears shall *h* my desire of
Ps 94:9 planted the ear, shall he not *h*
Ps 95:7 To day if ye will *h* his voice
Ps 102:1 *H* my prayer, O LORD, and let my
Ps 102:20 To *h* the groaning of the prisoner
Ps 115:6 They have ears, but they *h* not
Ps 119:145 *h* me, O LORD
Ps 119:149 *H* my voice according unto thy
Ps 130:2 Lord, *h* my voice
Ps 135:17 They have ears, but they *h* not
Ps 138:4 when they *h* the words of thy
Ps 140:6 *h* the voice of my supplications,
Ps 141:6 places, they shall *h* my words
Ps 143:1 *H* my prayer, O LORD, give ear to
Ps 143:7 *H* me speedily, O LORD
Ps 143:8 Cause me to *h* thy lovingkindness
Ps 145:19 he also will *h* their cry, and will
Prov 1:5 A wise man will *h*, and will
Prov 1:8 *h* the instruction of thy father,
Prov 4:1 *H*, ye children, the instruction
Prov 4:10 *H*, O my son, and receive my
Prov 5:7 *H* me now therefore, O ye children
Prov 8:6 *H*; for I will speak
Prov 8:33 *H* instruction, and be wise, and
Prov 19:20 *H* counsel, and receive instruction
Prov 19:27 to *h* the instruction that causeth
Prov 22:17 *h* the words of the wise, and apply
Prov 23:19 *H* thou, my son, and be wise, and
Eccl 5:1 of God, and be more ready to *h*
Eccl 7:5 It is better to *h* the rebuke of

Eccl 7:5 for a man to *h* the song of fools
Eccl 7:21 lest thou *h* thy servant curse
Eccl 12:13 Let us *h* the conclusion of the
Song 2:14 countenance, let me *h* thy voice
Song 8:13 cause me to *h* it
Is 1:2 *H*, O heavens, and give ear, O
Is 1:10 *H* the word of the LORD, ye rulers
Is 1:15 make many prayers, I will not *h*
Is 6:9 *H* ye indeed, but understand not
Is 6:10 *h* with their ears, and understand
Is 7:13 *H* ye now, O house of David
Is 18:3 when he bloweth a trumpet, *h* ye
Is 28:12 yet they would not *h*
Is 28:14 Wherefore *h* the word of the LORD,
Is 28:23 Give ye ear, and *h* my voice
Is 28:23 hearken, and *h* my speech
Is 29:18 the deaf *h* the words of the book
Is 30:9 will not *h* the law of the LORD
Is 30:19 when he shall *h* it, he will
Is 30:21 thine ears shall *h* a word behind
Is 32:3 ears of them that *h* shall hearken
Is 32:9 *h* my voice, ye careless daughters
Is 33:13 *H*, ye that are far off, what I
Is 34:1 Come near, ye nations, to *h*
Is 34:1 let the earth *h*, and all that is
Is 36:13 *H* ye the words of the great king,
Is 37:4 God will *h* the words of Rabshakeh
Is 37:7 upon him, and he shall *h* a rumour
Is 37:17 Incline thine ear, O LORD, and *h*
Is 37:17 *h* all the words of Sennacherib,
Is 39:5 *H* the word of the LORD of hosts
Is 41:17 thirst, I the LORD will *h* them
Is 42:18 *H*, ye deaf
Is 42:23 hearken and *h* for the time to come
Is 43:9 or let them *h*, and say, It is
Is 44:1 Yet now *h*, O Jacob my servant
Is 47:8 Therefore *h* now this, thou that
Is 48:1 *H* ye this, O house of Jacob,
Is 48:14 All ye, assemble yourselves, and *h*
Is 48:16 Come ye near unto me, *h* ye this
Is 50:4 mine ear to *h* as the learned
Is 51:21 Therefore *h* now this, thou
Is 55:3 *h*, and your soul shall live
Is 59:1 his ear heavy, that it cannot *h*
Is 59:2 face from you, that he will not *h*
Is 65:12 when I spake, ye did not *h*
Is 65:24 they are yet speaking, I will *h*
Is 66:4 when I spake, they did not *h*
Is 66:5 *H* the word of the LORD, ye that
Jer 2:4 *H* ye the word of the LORD, O
Jer 4:21 *h* the sound of the trumpet
Jer 5:21 *H* now this, O foolish people, and
Jer 5:21 which have ears, and *h* not
Jer 6:10 and give warning, that they may *h*
Jer 6:18 Therefore *h*, ye nations, and know,
Jer 6:19 *H*, O earth
Jer 7:2 *H* the word of the LORD, all ye of
Jer 7:16 for I will not *h* thee
Jer 9:10 neither can men *h* the voice of
Jer 9:20 Yet *h* the word of the LORD, O ye
Jer 10:1 *H* ye the word which the LORD
Jer 11:2 *H* ye the words of this covenant,
Jer 11:6 *H* ye the words of this covenant,
Jer 11:10 which refused to *h* my words
Jer 11:14 for I will not *h* them in the time
Jer 13:10 which refuse to *h* my words
Jer 13:11 but they would not *h*
Jer 13:15 *H* ye, and give ear
Jer 13:17 But if ye will not *h* it, my soul
Jer 14:12 they fast, I will not *h* their cry
Jer 17:20 *H* ye the word of the LORD, ye
Jer 17:23 neck stiff, that they might not *h*
Jer 18:2 I will cause thee to *h* my words
Jer 19:3 *H* ye the word of the LORD, O
Jer 19:15 that they might not *h* my words
Jer 20:16 let him *h* the cry in the morning,
Jer 21:11 *H* ye the word of the LORD
Jer 22:2 *H* the word of the LORD, O king of
Jer 22:5 But if ye will not *h* these words
Jer 22:21 but thou saidst, I will not *h*
Jer 22:29 earth, *h* the word of the LORD
Jer 23:22 caused my people to *h* my words
Jer 25:4 nor inclined your ear to *h*
Jer 28:7 Nevertheless *h* thou now this word
Jer 28:15 the prophet, *H* now, Hananiah
Jer 29:19 but ye would not *h*, saith the
Jer 29:20 *H* ye therefore the word of the
Jer 31:10 *H* the word of the LORD, O ye
Jer 33:9 which shall *h* all the good that I
Jer 34:4 Yet *h* the word of the LORD, O
Jer 36:3 *h* all the evil which I purpose to
Jer 36:25 but he would not *h* them
Jer 37:20 Therefore *h* now, I pray thee, O
Jer 38:25 But if the princes *h* that I have
Jer 42:14 nor *h* the sound of the trumpet,
Jer 42:15 now therefore *h* the word of the
Jer 44:24 *H* the word of the LORD, all Judah
Jer 44:26 Therefore *h* ye the word of the
Jer 49:20 Therefore *h* the counsel of the
Jer 50:45 Therefore *h* ye the counsel of the
Lam 1:18 *h*, I pray you, all people, and
Eze 2:5 And they, whether they will *h*
Eze 2:7 unto them, whether they will *h*
Eze 2:8 of man, *h* what I say unto thee
Eze 3:10 thine heart, and *h* with thine ears
Eze 3:11 whether they will *h*, or whether
Eze 3:17 therefore *h* the word at my mouth,
Eze 3:27 He that heareth, let him *h*
Eze 6:3 *h* the word of the Lord GOD
Eze 8:18 loud voice, yet will I not *h* them
Eze 12:2 they have ears to *h*, and *h* not
Eze 13:2 *H* ye the word of the LORD
Eze 13:19 to my people that *h* your lies
Eze 16:35 O harlot, *h* the word of the LORD
Eze 18:25 *H* now, O house of Israel
Eze 20:47 the south, *H* the word of the LORD
Eze 24:26 to cause thee to *h* it with thine
Eze 25:3 *H* the word of the Lord GOD
Eze 33:7 thou shalt *h* the word at my mouth
Eze 33:30 *h* what is the word that cometh
Eze 33:31 they *h* thy words, but they will
Eze 33:32 for they *h* thy words, but they do
Eze 34:7 shepherds, *h* the word of the LORD
Eze 34:9 shepherds, *h* the word of the LORD
Eze 36:1 of Israel, *h* the word of the LORD
Eze 36:4 *h* the word of the Lord GOD
Eze 36:15 men to *h* in thee the shame of the
Eze 37:4 dry bones, *h* the word of the LORD
Eze 40:4 *h* with thine ears, and set thine
Eze 44:5 *h* with thine ears all that I say
Dan 3:5 That at what time ye *h* the sound
Dan 3:10 shall *h* the sound of the cornet
Dan 3:15 time ye *h* the sound of the cornet
Dan 5:23 and stone, which see not, nor *h*
Dan 9:17 *h* the prayer of thy servant, and
Dan 9:18 O my God, incline thine ear, and *h*
Dan 9:19 O Lord, *h*; O Lord
Hos 2:21 to pass in that day, I will *h*
Hos 2:21 I will *h* the heavens
Hos 2:21 and they shall *h* the earth
Hos 2:22 And the earth shall *h* the corn
Hos 2:22 and they shall *h* Jezreel
Hos 4:1 *H* the word of the LORD, ye
Hos 5:1 *H* ye this, O priests
Joel 1:2 *H* this, ye old men, and give ear,
Amos 3:1 *H* this word that the LORD hath
Amos 3:13 *H* ye, and testify in the house of
Amos 4:1 *H* this word, ye kine of Bashan,
Amos 5:1 *H* ye this word which I take up
Amos 5:23 for I will not *h* the melody of
Amos 7:16 Now therefore *h* thou the word of
Amos 8:4 *H* this, O ye that swallow up the
Mic 1:2 *H*, all ye people
Mic 3:1 And I said, *H*, I pray you, O heads
Mic 3:4 the LORD, but he will not *h* them
Mic 3:9 *H* this, I pray you, ye heads of
Mic 6:1 *H* ye now what the LORD saith
Mic 6:1 and let the hills *h* thy voice
Mic 6:2 *H* ye, O mountains, the LORD's
Mic 6:9 *h* ye the rod, and who hath
Mic 7:7 my God will *h* me
Nah 3:19 all that *h* the bruit of thee
Hab 1:2 shall I cry, and thou wilt not *h*
Zec 1:4 but they did not *h*, nor hearken
Zec 3:8 *H* now, O Joshua the high priest,
Zec 7:7 Should ye not *h* the words which
Zec 7:11 ears, that they should not *h*
Zec 7:12 stone, lest they should *h* the law
Zec 7:13 as he cried, and they would not *h*
Zec 7:13 so they cried, and I would not *h*
Zec 8:9 ye that *h* in these days these
Zec 10:6 LORD their God, and will *h* them
Zec 13:9 call on my name, and I will *h* them
Mal 2:2 If ye will not *h*, and if ye will
Mt 10:14 nor *h* your words, when ye depart
Mt 10:27 what ye *h* in the ear, that preach
Mt 11:4 again those things which ye do *h*
Mt 11:5 are cleansed, and the deaf *h*
Mt 11:15 that hath ears to *h*, let him *h*
Mt 12:19 neither shall any man *h* his voice
Mt 12:42 earth to *h* the wisdom of Solomon
Mt 13:9 Who hath ears to *h*, let him *h*
Mt 13:13 and hearing they *h* not, neither do
Mt 13:14 saith, By hearing ye shall *h*
Mt 13:15 *h* with their ears, and should
Mt 13:16 and your ears, for they *h*
Mt 13:17 to *h* those things which ye *h*,
Mt 13:18 *H* ye therefore the parable of the
Mt 13:43 Who hath ears to *h*, let him *h*
Mt 15:10 multitude, and said unto them, *H*
Mt 17:5 *h* ye him
Mt 18:15 if he shall *h* thee, thou hast
Mt 18:16 But if he will not *h* thee
Mt 18:17 And if he shall neglect to *h* them
Mt 18:17 but if he neglect to *h* the church
Mt 21:33 *H* another parable
Mt 24:6 And ye shall *h* of wars and rumours
Mk 4:9 that hath ears to *h*, let him *h*
Mk 4:12 and hearing they may *h*, and not
Mk 4:18 such as *h* the word,
Mk 4:20 such as *h* the word, and receive it
Mk 4:23 man have ears to *h*, let him *h*
Mk 4:24 unto them, Take heed what ye *h*
Mk 4:24 unto you that *h* shall more be
Mk 4:33 them, as they were able to *h* it
Mk 6:11 shall not receive you, nor *h* you
Mk 7:16 man have ears to *h*, let him *h*
Mk 7:37 he maketh both the deaf to *h*
Mk 8:18 and having ears, *h* ye not
Mk 9:7 *h* him
Mk 12:29 of all the commandments is, *H*
Mk 13:7 And when ye shall *h* of wars
Lk 5:1 upon him to *h* the word of God
Lk 5:15 multitudes came together to *h*
Lk 6:17 and Sidon, which came to *h* him
Lk 6:27 But I say unto you which *h*
Lk 7:22 lepers are cleansed, the deaf *h*
Lk 8:8 that hath ears to *h*, let him *h*
Lk 8:12 by the way side are they that *h*
Lk 8:13 rock are they, which, when they *h*
Lk 8:18 Take heed therefore how ye *h*
Lk 8:21 are these which *h* the word of God
Lk 9:9 is this, of whom I *h* such things
Lk 9:35 *h* him
Lk 10:24 to *h* those things which ye *h*,
Lk 11:28 are they that *h* the word of God
Lk 11:31 earth to *h* the wisdom of Solomon
Lk 14:35 that hath ears to *h*, let him *h*
Lk 15:1 publicans and sinners for to *h* him
Lk 16:2 How is it that I *h* this of thee
Lk 16:29 let them *h* them
Lk 16:31 If they *h* not Moses and the
Lk 18:6 *H* what the unjust judge saith
Lk 19:48 were very attentive to *h* him
Lk 21:9 But when ye shall *h* of wars
Lk 21:38 him in the temple, for to *h* him
Jn 5:25 when the dead shall *h* the voice
Jn 5:25 and they that *h* shall live
Jn 5:28 in the graves shall *h* his voice
Jn 5:30 as I *h*, I judge
Jn 6:60 who can *h* it?
Jn 7:51 judge any man, before it *h* him
Jn 8:43 even because ye cannot *h* my word
Jn 8:47 ye therefore *h* them not, because
Jn 9:27 told you already, and ye did not *h*
Jn 9:27 wherefore would ye *h* it again
Jn 10:3 and the sheep *h* his voice
Jn 10:8 but the sheep did not *h* them
Jn 10:16 bring, and they shall *h* my voice
Jn 10:20 why *h* ye him?
Jn 10:27 My sheep *h* my voice, and I know
Jn 12:47 And if any man *h* my words, and
Jn 14:24 the word which ye *h* is not mine
Jn 16:13 but whatsoever he shall *h*
Acts 2:8 how *h* we every man in our own
Acts 2:11 we do *h* them speak in our tongues
Acts 2:22 Ye men of Israel, *h* these words
Acts 2:33 forth this, which ye now see and *h*
Acts 3:22 him shall ye *h* in all things
Acts 3:23 which will not *h* that prophet
Acts 7:37 him shall ye *h*
Acts 10:22 his house, and to *h* words of thee
Acts 10:33 God, to *h* all things that are
Acts 13:7 desired to *h* the word of God
Acts 13:44 together to *h* the word of God
Acts 15:7 should *h* the word of the gospel
Acts 17:21 to tell, or to *h* some new thing
Acts 17:32 We will *h* thee again of this
Acts 19:26 Moreover ye see and *h*, that not
Acts 21:22 for they will *h* that thou art

Acts 22:1 *h* ye my defence which I make now
Acts 22:14 shouldest *h* the voice of his
Acts 23:35 I will *h* thee, said he, when
Acts 24:4 *h* us of thy clemency a few words
Acts 25:22 I would also *h* the man myself
Acts 25:22 morrow, said he, thou shalt *h* him
Acts 26:3 I beseech thee to *h* me patiently
Acts 26:29 but also all that *h* me this day
Acts 28:22 But we desire to *h* of thee what
Acts 28:26 and say, Hearing ye shall *h*
Acts 28:27 *h* with their ears, and understand
Acts 28:28 Gentiles, and that they will *h* it
Rom 10:14 how shall they *h* without a
Rom 11:8 and ears that they should not *h*
1Cor 11:18 I *h* that there be divisions among
1Cor 14:21 for all that will they not *h* me
Gal 4:21 the law, do ye not *h* the law
Phil 1:27 I may *h* of your affairs, that ye
Phil 1:30 saw in me, and now *h* to be in me
2Th 3:11 For we *h* that there are some
1Ti 4:16 save thyself, and them that *h* thee
2Ti 4:17 and that all the Gentiles might *h*
Heb 3:7 To day if ye will *h* his voice
Heb 3:15 To day if ye will *h* his voice
Heb 4:7 To day if ye will *h* his voice
Jas 1:19 let every man be swift to *h*
1Jn 5:15 And if we know that he *h* us
3Jn 4 I have no greater joy than to *h*
Rev 1:3 they that *h* the words of this
Rev 2:7 let him *h* what the Spirit saith
Rev 2:11 let him *h* what the Spirit saith
Rev 2:17 let him *h* what the Spirit saith
Rev 2:29 let him *h* what the Spirit saith
Rev 3:6 let him *h* what the Spirit saith
Rev 3:13 let him *h* what the Spirit saith
Rev 3:20 if any man *h* my voice, and open
Rev 3:22 let him *h* what the Spirit saith
Rev 9:20 which neither can see, nor *h*
Rev 13:9 If any man have an ear, let him *h*

## HEARD

Gen 3:8 they *h* the voice of the LORD God
Gen 3:10 I *h* thy voice in the garden, and I
Gen 14:14 when Abram *h* that his brother was
Gen 16:11 the LORD hath *h* thy affliction
Gen 17:20 And as for Ishmael, I have *h* thee
Gen 18:10 Sarah *h* it in the tent door,
Gen 21:17 God *h* the voice of the lad
Gen 21:17 for God hath *h* the voice of the
Gen 21:26 tell me, neither yet *h* I of it
Gen 24:30 when he *h* the words of Rebekah
Gen 24:52 Abraham's servant *h* their words
Gen 27:5 Rebekah *h* when Isaac spake to
Gen 27:6 I *h* thy father speak unto Esau
Gen 27:34 when Esau *h* the words of his
Gen 29:13 when Laban *h* the tidings of Jacob
Gen 29:33 the LORD hath *h* that I was hated
Gen 30:6 me, and hath also *h* my voice
Gen 31:1 he *h* the words of Laban's sons,
Gen 34:5 Jacob *h* that he had defiled Dinah
Gen 34:7 out of the field when they *h* it
Gen 35:22 and Israel *h* it
Gen 37:17 for I *h* them say, Let us go to
Gen 37:21 And Reuben *h* it, and he delivered
Gen 39:15 when he *h* that I lifted up my
Gen 39:19 when his master *h* the words of
Gen 41:15 I have *h* say of thee, that thou
Gen 42:2 I have *h* that there is corn in
Gen 43:25 for they *h* that they should eat
Gen 45:2 and the house of Pharaoh *h*
Gen 45:16 thereof was *h* in Pharaoh's house
Ex 2:15 Now when Pharaoh *h* this thing
Ex 2:24 God *h* their groaning, and God
Ex 3:7 have *h* their cry by reason of
Ex 4:31 when they *h* that the LORD had
Ex 6:5 I have also *h* the groaning of the
Ex 16:9 for he hath *h* your murmurings
Ex 16:12 I have *h* the murmurings of the
Ex 18:1 *h* of all that God had done for
Ex 23:13 let it be *h* out of thy mouth
Ex 28:35 his sound shall be *h* when he
Ex 32:17 when Joshua *h* the noise of the
Ex 33:4 when the people *h* these evil
Lev 10:20 And when Moses *h* that, he was
Lev 24:14 let all that *h* him lay their
Num 7:89 then he *h* the voice of one
Num 11:1 and the LORD *h* it
Num 11:10 Then Moses *h* the people weep
Num 12:2 And the LORD *h* it
Num 14:14 for they have *h* that thou LORD
Num 14:15 *h* the fame of thee will speak
Num 14:27 I have *h* the murmurings of the
Num 16:4 And when Moses *h* it, he fell upon
Num 20:16 he *h* our voice, and sent an angel,
Num 21:1 *h* tell that Israel came by the
Num 22:36 when Balak *h* that Balaam was come
Num 24:4 which *h* the words of God, which
Num 24:16 which *h* the words of God, and knew
Num 30:7 And her husband *h* it, and held his
Num 30:7 at her in the day that he *h* it
Num 30:8 her on the day that he *h* it
Num 30:11 And her husband *h* it, and held his
Num 30:12 them void on the day he *h* them
Num 30:14 at her in the day that he *h* them
Num 30:15 void after that he hath *h* them
Num 33:40 *h* of the coming of the children
Deut 1:34 the LORD *h* the voice of your
Deut 4:12 ye *h* the voice of the words, but
Deut 4:12 only ye *h* a voice
Deut 4:32 thing is, or hath been *h* like it
Deut 4:33 midst of the fire, as thou hast *h*
Deut 5:23 when ye *h* the voice out of the
Deut 5:24 we have *h* his voice out of the
Deut 5:26 that hath *h* the voice of the
Deut 5:28 the LORD *h* the voice of your
Deut 5:28 I have *h* the voice of the words
Deut 9:2 and of whom thou hast *h* say
Deut 17:4 told thee, and thou hast *h* of it
Deut 26:7 the LORD *h* our voice, and looked
Josh 2:10 For we have *h* how the LORD dried
Josh 2:11 as soon as we had *h* these things
Josh 5:1 *h* that the LORD had dried up the
Josh 6:20 when the people *h* the sound of
Josh 9:1 and the Jebusite, *h* thereof
Josh 9:3 *h* what Joshua had done unto
Josh 9:9 for we have *h* the fame of him, and
Josh 9:16 that they *h* that they were their
Josh 10:1 king of Jerusalem had *h* how
Josh 11:1 king of Hazor had *h* those things
Josh 22:11 And the children of Israel *h* say
Josh 22:12 the children of Israel *h* of it
Josh 22:30 *h* the words that the children of
Josh 24:27 for it hath *h* all the words of
Judg 7:15 when Gideon *h* the telling of the
Judg 9:30 Zebul the ruler of the city *h* the
Judg 9:46 of the tower of Shechem *h* that
Judg 18:25 Let not thy voice be *h* among us
Judg 20:3 *h* that the children of Israel
Ruth 1:6 for she had *h* in the country of
1Sa 1:13 moved, but her voice was not *h*
1Sa 2:22 *h* all that his sons did unto all
1Sa 4:6 when the Philistines *h* the noise
1Sa 4:14 when Eli *h* the noise of the
1Sa 4:19 when she *h* the tidings that the
1Sa 7:7 when the Philistines *h* that the
1Sa 7:7 when the children of Israel *h* it
1Sa 7:9 and the LORD *h* him
1Sa 8:21 Samuel *h* all the words of the
1Sa 11:6 upon Saul when he *h* those tidings
1Sa 13:3 Geba, and the Philistines *h* of it
1Sa 13:4 all Israel *h* say that Saul had
1Sa 14:22 when they *h* that the Philistines
1Sa 14:27 But Jonathan *h* not when his
1Sa 17:11 all Israel *h* those words of the
1Sa 17:23 and David *h* them
1Sa 17:28 Eliab his eldest brother *h* when
1Sa 17:31 words were *h* which David spake
1Sa 22:1 and all his father's house *h* it
1Sa 22:6 When Saul *h* that David was
1Sa 23:10 thy servant hath certainly *h* that
1Sa 23:11 come down, as thy servant hath *h*
1Sa 23:25 And when Saul *h* that, he pursued
1Sa 25:4 David *h* in the wilderness that
1Sa 25:7 now I have *h* that thou hast
1Sa 25:39 when David *h* that Nabal was dead,
1Sa 31:11 inhabitants of Jabesh-gilead *h* of
2Sa 3:28 And afterward when David *h* it
2Sa 4:1 when Saul's son *h* that Abner was
2Sa 5:17 But when the Philistines *h* that
2Sa 5:17 and David *h* of it, and went down to
2Sa 7:22 all that we have *h* with our ears
2Sa 8:9 When Toi king of Hamath *h* that
2Sa 10:7 And when David *h* of it, he sent
2Sa 11:26 when the wife of Uriah *h* that
2Sa 13:21 king David *h* of all these things
2Sa 18:5 all the people *h* when the king
2Sa 19:2 for the people *h* say that day how
1Kin 1:11 Hast thou not *h* that Adonijah the
1Kin 1:41 *h* it as they had made an end of
1Kin 1:41 when Joab *h* the sound of the
1Kin 1:45 This is the noise that ye have *h*
1Kin 2:42 The word that I have *h* is good
1Kin 3:28 all Israel *h* of the judgment
1Kin 4:34 which had *h* of his wisdom
1Kin 5:1 for he had *h* that they had
1Kin 5:7 when Hiram *h* the words of Solomon
1Kin 6:7 any tool of iron *h* in the house
1Kin 9:3 I have *h* thy prayer and thy
1Kin 10:1 of Sheba *h* of the fame of Solomon
1Kin 10:6 It was a true report that I *h* in
1Kin 10:7 exceedeth the fame which I *h*
1Kin 11:21 when Hadad *h* in Egypt that David
1Kin 12:2 *h* of it, (for he was fled from
1Kin 12:20 when all Israel *h* that Jeroboam
1Kin 13:4 when king Jeroboam *h* the saying
1Kin 13:26 him back from the way *h* thereof
1Kin 14:6 when Ahijah *h* the sound of her
1Kin 15:21 to pass, when Baasha *h* thereof
1Kin 16:16 people that were encamped *h* say
1Kin 17:22 the LORD *h* the voice of Elijah
1Kin 19:13 And it was so, when Elijah *h* it
1Kin 20:12 when Ben-hadad *h* this message
1Kin 20:31 we have *h* that the kings of the
1Kin 21:15 when Jezebel *h* that Naboth was
1Kin 21:16 when Ahab *h* that Naboth was dead,
1Kin 21:27 when Ahab *h* those words, that he
2Kin 3:21 when all the Moabites *h* that the
2Kin 5:8 had *h* that the king of Israel had
2Kin 6:30 when the king *h* the words of the
2Kin 9:30 come to Jezreel, Jezebel *h* of it
2Kin 11:13 when Athaliah *h* the noise of the
2Kin 19:1 to pass, when king Hezekiah *h* it
2Kin 19:4 which the LORD thy God hath *h*
2Kin 19:6 of the words which thou hast *h*
2Kin 19:8 for he had *h* that he was departed
2Kin 19:9 when he *h* say of Tirhakah king of
2Kin 19:11 thou hast *h* what the kings of
2Kin 19:20 king of Assyria I have *h*
2Kin 19:25 Hast thou not *h* long ago how I
2Kin 20:5 I have *h* thy prayer, I have seen
2Kin 20:12 for he had *h* that Hezekiah had
2Kin 22:11 when the king had *h* the words of
2Kin 22:18 the words which thou hast *h*
2Kin 22:19 I also have *h* thee, saith the
2Kin 25:23 *h* that the king of Babylon had
1Chr 10:11 when all Jabesh-gilead *h* all that
1Chr 14:8 when the Philistines *h* that David
1Chr 14:8 And David *h* of it, and went out
1Chr 17:20 all that we have *h* with our ears
1Chr 18:9 Now when Tou king of Hamath *h* how
1Chr 19:8 And when David *h* of it, he sent
2Chr 5:13 one sound to be *h* in praising
2Chr 7:12 I have *h* thy prayer, and have
2Chr 9:1 of Sheba *h* of the fame of Solomon
2Chr 9:5 It was a true report which I *h* in
2Chr 9:6 thou exceedest the fame that I *h*
2Chr 10:2 *h* it, that Jeroboam returned out
2Chr 15:8 when Asa *h* these words, and the
2Chr 16:5 it came to pass, when Baasha *h* it
2Chr 20:29 when they had *h* that the LORD
2Chr 23:12 Now when Athaliah *h* the noise of
2Chr 30:27 and their voice was *h*, and their
2Chr 33:13 *h* his supplication, and brought
2Chr 34:19 when the king had *h* the words of
2Chr 34:26 the words which thou hast *h*
2Chr 34:27 I have even *h* thee also, saith
Ezr 3:13 and the noise was *h* afar off
Ezr 4:1 Benjamin *h* that the children of
Ezr 9:3 when I *h* this thing, I rent my
Neh 1:4 when I *h* these words, that I sat
Neh 2:10 *h* of it, it grieved them
Neh 2:19 *h* it, they laughed us to scorn,
Neh 4:1 that when Sanballat *h* that we
Neh 4:7 *h* that the walls of Jerusalem
Neh 4:15 when our enemies *h* that it was
Neh 5:6 was very angry when I *h* their cry
Neh 6:1 *h* that I had builded the wall, and
Neh 6:16 when all our enemies *h* thereof
Neh 8:9 when they *h* the words of the law
Neh 12:43 of Jerusalem was *h* even afar off
Neh 13:3 to pass, when they had *h* the law
Est 1:18 which have *h* of the deed of the
Est 2:8 commandment and his decree was *h*
Job 2:11 Now when Job's three friends *h* of
Job 4:16 silence, and I *h* a voice, saying,
Job 13:1 seen all this, mine ear hath *h*
Job 15:8 Hast thou *h* the secret of God
Job 16:2 I have *h* many such things
Job 19:7 cry out of wrong, but I am not *h*
Job 20:3 I have *h* the check of my reproach

Job 26:14 how little a portion is *h* of him
Job 28:22 We have *h* the fame thereof with
Job 29:11 When the ear *h* me, then it
Job 33:8 I have *h* the voice of thy words,
Job 37:4 not stay them when his voice is *h*
Job 42:5 I have *h* of thee by the hearing
Ps 3:4 he *h* me out of his holy hill
Ps 6:8 for the LORD hath *h* the voice of
Ps 6:9 The LORD hath *h* my supplication
Ps 10:17 thou hast *h* the desire of the
Ps 18:6 he *h* my voice out of his temple,
Ps 19:3 where their voice is not *h*
Ps 22:21 for thou hast *h* me from the horns
Ps 22:24 but when he cried unto him, he *h*
Ps 28:6 because he hath *h* the voice of my
Ps 31:13 For I have *h* the slander of many
Ps 34:4 I sought the LORD, and he *h* me
Ps 34:6 poor man cried, and the LORD *h* him
Ps 38:13 But I, as a deaf man, *h* not
Ps 40:1 he inclined unto me, and *h* my cry
Ps 44:1 We have *h* with our ears, O God,
Ps 48:8 As we have *h*, so have we seen in
Ps 61:5 For thou, O God, hast *h* my vows
Ps 62:11 twice have I *h* this
Ps 66:8 the voice of his praise to be *h*
Ps 66:19 But verily God hath *h* me
Ps 76:8 judgment to be *h* from heaven
Ps 78:3 Which we have *h* and known, and our
Ps 78:21 Therefore the LORD *h* this
Ps 78:59 When God *h* this, he was wroth, and
Ps 81:5 where I *h* a language that I
Ps 97:8 Zion *h*, and was glad
Ps 106:44 affliction, when he *h* their cry
Ps 116:1 LORD, because he hath *h* my voice
Ps 118:21 for thou hast *h* me, and art become
Ps 120:1 I cried unto the LORD, and he *h* me
Ps 132:6 Lo, we *h* of it at Ephratah
Prov 21:13 cry himself, but shall not be *h*
Eccl 9:16 despised, and his words are not *h*
Eccl 9:17 The words of wise men are *h* in
Song 2:12 of the turtle is *h* in our land
Is 6:8 Also I *h* the voice of the Lord,
Is 10:30 cause it to be *h* unto Laish
Is 15:4 voice shall be *h* even unto Jahaz
Is 16:6 We have *h* of the pride of Moab
Is 21:10 that which I have *h* of the LORD
Is 24:16 part of the earth have we *h* songs
Is 28:22 for I have *h* from the Lord GOD of
Is 30:30 cause his glorious voice to be *h*
Is 37:1 to pass, when king Hezekiah *h* it
Is 37:4 which the LORD thy God hath *h*
Is 37:6 of the words that thou hast *h*
Is 37:8 for he had *h* that he was departed
Is 37:9 he *h* say concerning Tirhakah king
Is 37:9 And when he *h* it, he sent
Is 37:11 thou hast *h* what the kings of
Is 37:26 Hast thou not *h* long ago, how I
Is 38:5 I have *h* thy prayer, I have seen
Is 39:1 for he had *h* that he had been
Is 40:21 have ye not *h*?
Is 40:28 hast thou not *h*, that the
Is 42:2 his voice to be *h* in the street
Is 48:6 Thou hast *h*, see all this
Is 49:8 an acceptable time have I *h* thee
Is 52:15 had not *h* shall they consider
Is 58:4 make your voice to be *h* on high
Is 60:18 shall no more be *h* in thy land
Is 64:4 of the world men have not *h*
Is 65:19 weeping shall be no more *h* in her
Is 66:8 Who hath *h* such a thing
Is 66:19 afar off, that have not *h* my fame
Jer 3:21 A voice was *h* upon the high
Jer 4:19 my peace, because thou hast *h*
Jer 4:31 For I have *h* a voice as of a
Jer 6:7 violence and spoil is *h* in her
Jer 6:24 We have *h* the fame thereof
Jer 7:13 early and speaking, but ye *h* not
Jer 8:6 I hearkened and *h*, but they spake
Jer 8:16 of his horses was *h* from Dan
Jer 9:19 voice of wailing is *h* out of Zion
Jer 18:13 heathen, who hath *h* such things
Jer 18:22 Let a cry be *h* from their houses,
Jer 20:1 *h* that Jeremiah prophesied these
Jer 20:10 For I *h* the defaming of many,
Jer 23:18 and hath perceived and *h* his word
Jer 23:18 who hath marked his word, and *h* it
Jer 23:25 I have *h* what the prophets said,
Jer 25:8 Because ye have not *h* my words
Jer 25:36 of the flock, shall be *h*
Jer 26:7 all the people *h* Jeremiah
Jer 26:10 princes of Judah *h* these things
Jer 26:11 as ye have *h* with your ears
Jer 26:12 city all the words that ye have *h*
Jer 26:21 *h* his words, the king sought to
Jer 26:21 but when Urijah *h* it, he was
Jer 30:5 We have *h* a voice of trembling,
Jer 31:15 A voice was *h* in Ramah,
Jer 31:18 I have surely *h* Ephraim bemoaning
Jer 33:10 there shall be *h* in this place
Jer 34:10 *h* that every one should let his
Jer 35:17 unto them, but they have not *h*
Jer 36:11 had *h* out of the book all the
Jer 36:13 them all the words that he had *h*
Jer 36:16 when they had *h* all the words
Jer 36:24 servants that *h* all these words
Jer 37:5 Jerusalem *h* tidings of them
Jer 38:1 *h* the words that Jeremiah had
Jer 38:7 *h* that they had put Jeremiah in
Jer 40:7 *h* that the king of Babylon had
Jer 40:11 *h* that the king of Babylon had
Jer 41:11 *h* of all the evil that Ishmael
Jer 42:4 said unto them, I have *h* you
Jer 46:12 The nations have *h* of thy shame
Jer 48:4 ones have caused a cry to be *h*
Jer 48:5 have *h* a cry of destruction
Jer 48:29 We have *h* the pride of Moab, (he
Jer 49:2 be *h* in Rabbah of the Ammonites
Jer 49:14 I have *h* a rumour from the LORD,
Jer 49:21 thereof was *h* in the Red sea
Jer 49:23 for they have *h* evil tidings
Jer 50:43 Babylon hath *h* the report of them
Jer 50:46 the cry is *h* among the nations
Jer 51:46 that shall be *h* in the land
Jer 51:51 because we have *h* reproach
Lam 1:21 They have *h* that I sigh
Lam 1:21 mine enemies have *h* of my trouble
Lam 3:56 Thou hast *h* my voice
Lam 3:61 Thou hast *h* their reproach, O
Eze 1:24 I *h* the noise of their wings,
Eze 1:28 I *h* a voice of one that spake
Eze 2:2 that I *h* him that spake unto me
Eze 3:12 I *h* behind me a voice of a great
Eze 3:13 I *h* also the noise of the wings
Eze 10:5 was *h* even to the outer court
Eze 19:4 The nations also *h* of him
Eze 19:9 his voice should no more be *h*
Eze 26:13 of thy harps shall be no more *h*
Eze 27:30 their voice to be *h* against thee
Eze 33:5 He *h* the sound of the trumpet, and
Eze 35:12 that I have *h* all thy blasphemies
Eze 35:13 I have *h* them
Eze 43:6 I *h* him speaking unto me out of
Dan 3:7 when all the people *h* the sound
Dan 5:14 I have even *h* of thee, that the
Dan 5:16 I have *h* of thee, that thou canst
Dan 6:14 when he *h* these words, was sore
Dan 8:13 Then I *h* one saint speaking, and
Dan 8:16 I *h* a man's voice between the
Dan 10:9 Yet *h* I the voice of his words
Dan 10:9 when I *h* the voice of his words,
Dan 10:12 before thy God, thy words were *h*
Dan 12:7 I *h* the man clothed in linen,
Dan 12:8 And I *h*, but I understood not
Hos 7:12 as their congregation hath *h*
Hos 14:8 I have *h* him, and observed him
Obad 1 We have *h* a rumour from the LORD,
Jonah 2:2 unto the LORD, and he *h* me
Mic 5:15 heathen, such as they have not *h*
Nah 2:13 thy messengers shall no more be *h*
Hab 3:2 I have *h* thy speech, and was
Hab 3:16 When I *h*, my belly trembled
Zeph 2:8 I have *h* the reproach of Moab, and
Zec 8:23 for we have *h* that God is with
Mal 3:16 *h* it, and a book of remembrance
Mt 2:3 Herod the king had *h* these things
Mt 2:9 When they had *h* the king, they
Mt 2:18 In Rama was there a voice *h*
Mt 2:22 But when he *h* that Archelaus did
Mt 4:12 Now when Jesus had *h* that John
Mt 5:21 Ye have *h* that it was said by
Mt 5:27 Ye have *h* that it was said by
Mt 5:33 ye have *h* that it hath been said
Mt 5:38 Ye have *h* that it hath been said,
Mt 5:43 Ye have *h* that it hath been said,
Mt 6:7 be *h* for their much speaking
Mt 8:10 When Jesus *h* it, he marvelled, and
Mt 9:12 But when Jesus *h* that, he said
Mt 11:2 Now when John had *h* in the prison
Mt 12:24 But when the Pharisees *h* it
Mt 13:17 which ye hear, and have not *h* them
Mt 14:1 tetrarch *h* of the fame of Jesus
Mt 14:13 When Jesus *h* of it, he departed
Mt 14:13 and when the people had *h* thereof
Mt 15:12 after they *h* this saying
Mt 17:6 And when the disciples *h* it
Mt 19:22 when the young man *h* that saying
Mt 19:25 When his disciples *h* it, they
Mt 20:24 And when the ten *h* it, they were
Mt 20:30 when they *h* that Jesus passed by,
Mt 21:45 and Pharisees had *h* his parables
Mt 22:7 But when the king *h* thereof
Mt 22:22 When they had *h* these words
Mt 22:33 And when the multitude *h* this
Mt 22:34 But when the Pharisees had *h* that
Mt 26:65 now ye have *h* his blasphemy
Mt 27:47 stood there, when they *h* that
Mk 2:17 When Jesus *h* it, he saith unto
Mk 3:8 when they had *h* what great things
Mk 3:21 And when his friends *h* of it
Mk 4:15 but when they have *h*, Satan
Mk 4:16 who, when they have *h* the word
Mk 5:27 When she had *h* of Jesus, came in
Mk 5:36 As soon as Jesus *h* the word that
Mk 6:14 And king Herod *h* of him
Mk 6:16 But when Herod *h* thereof, he said
Mk 6:20 and when he *h* him, he did many
Mk 6:20 did many things, and *h* him gladly
Mk 6:29 And when his disciples *h* of it
Mk 6:55 were sick, where they *h* he was
Mk 7:25 *h* of him, and came and fell at his
Mk 10:41 And when the ten *h* it, they began
Mk 10:47 when he *h* that it was Jesus of
Mk 11:14 And his disciples *h* it
Mk 11:18 the scribes and chief priests *h* it
Mk 12:28 having *h* them reasoning together,
Mk 12:37 And the common people *h* him gladly
Mk 14:11 And when they *h* it, they were glad
Mk 14:58 We *h* him say, I will destroy this
Mk 14:64 Ye have *h* the blasphemy
Mk 15:35 stood by, when they *h* it said
Mk 16:11 when they had *h* that he was alive
Lk 1:13 for thy prayer is *h*
Lk 1:41 when Elisabeth *h* the salutation
Lk 1:58 her cousins *h* how the Lord had
Lk 1:66 all they that *h* them laid them up
Lk 2:18 all they that *h* it wondered at
Lk 2:20 all the things that they had *h*
Lk 2:47 all that *h* him were astonished at
Lk 4:23 we have *h* done in Capernaum
Lk 4:28 when they *h* these things, were
Lk 7:3 when he *h* of Jesus, he sent unto
Lk 7:9 When Jesus *h* these things, he
Lk 7:22 what things ye have seen and *h*
Lk 7:29 And all the people that *h* him
Lk 8:14 are they, which, when they have *h*
Lk 8:15 having *h* the word, keep it, and
Lk 8:50 But when Jesus *h* it, he answered
Lk 9:7 Now Herod the tetrarch *h* of all
Lk 10:24 which ye hear, and have not *h* them
Lk 10:39 sat at Jesus' feet, and *h* his word
Lk 12:3 darkness shall be *h* in the light
Lk 14:15 at meat with him *h* these things
Lk 15:25 the house, he *h* musick and dancing
Lk 16:14 were covetous, *h* all these things
Lk 18:22 Now when Jesus *h* these things
Lk 18:23 And when he *h* this, he was very
Lk 18:26 And they that *h* it said, Who then
Lk 19:11 as they *h* these things, he added
Lk 20:16 And when they *h* it, they said, God
Lk 22:71 ourselves have *h* of his own mouth
Lk 23:6 When Pilate *h* of Galilee, he
Lk 23:8 because he had *h* many things of
Jn 1:37 And the two disciples *h* him speak
Jn 1:40 One of the two which *h* John speak
Jn 3:32 And what he hath seen and *h*
Jn 4:1 Pharisees had *h* that Jesus made
Jn 4:42 for we have *h* him ourselves, and
Jn 4:47 When he *h* that Jesus was come out
Jn 5:37 Ye have neither *h* his voice at
Jn 6:45 Every man therefore that hath *h*
Jn 6:60 disciples, when they had *h* this
Jn 7:32 The Pharisees *h* that the people
Jn 7:40 when they *h* this saying, said, Of
Jn 8:6 ground, as though he *h* them not
Jn 8:9 And they which *h* it, being
Jn 8:26 things which I have *h* of him
Jn 8:40 the truth, which I have *h* of God
Jn 9:32 the world began was it not *h* that
Jn 9:35 Jesus *h* that they had cast him
Jn 9:40 which were with him *h* these words

Jn 11:4 When Jesus *h* that, he said, This
Jn 11:6 When he had *h* therefore that he
Jn 11:20 as soon as she *h* that Jesus was
Jn 11:29 As soon as she *h* that, she arose
Jn 11:41 I thank thee that thou hast *h* me
Jn 12:12 when they *h* that Jesus was coming
Jn 12:18 for that they *h* that he had done
Jn 12:29 *h* it, said that it thundered
Jn 12:34 We have *h* out of the law that
Jn 14:28 Ye have *h* how I said unto you, I
Jn 15:15 for all things that I have *h* of
Jn 18:21 ask them which *h* me, what I have
Jn 19:8 Pilate therefore *h* that saying
Jn 19:13 Pilate therefore *h* that saying
Jn 21:7 Peter *h* that it was the Lord
Acts 1:4 which, saith he, ye have *h* of me
Acts 2:6 because that every man *h* them
Acts 2:37 Now when they *h* this, they were
Acts 4:4 of them which *h* the word believed
Acts 4:20 things which we have seen and *h*
Acts 4:24 And when they *h* that, they lifted
Acts 5:5 on all them that *h* these things
Acts 5:11 and upon as many as *h* these things
Acts 5:21 And when they *h* that, they entered
Acts 5:24 the chief priests *h* these things
Acts 5:33 When they *h* that, they were cut
Acts 6:11 We have *h* him speak blasphemous
Acts 6:14 For we have *h* him say, that this
Acts 7:12 But when Jacob *h* that there was
Acts 7:34 I have *h* their groaning, and am
Acts 7:54 When they *h* these things, they
Acts 8:14 which were at Jerusalem *h* that
Acts 8:30 *h* him read the prophet Esaias, and
Acts 9:4 *h* a voice saying unto him, Saul,
Acts 9:13 I have *h* by many of this man, how
Acts 9:21 But all that *h* him were amazed,
Acts 9:38 the disciples had *h* that Peter
Acts 10:31 said, Cornelius, thy prayer is *h*
Acts 10:44 fell on all them which *h* the word
Acts 10:46 For they *h* them speak with
Acts 11:1 *h* that the Gentiles had also
Acts 11:7 I *h* a voice saying unto me, Arise
Acts 11:18 When they *h* these things, they
Acts 13:48 And when the Gentiles *h* this
Acts 14:9 The same *h* Paul speak
Acts 14:14 *h* of, they rent their clothes, and
Acts 15:24 Forasmuch as we have *h*, that
Acts 16:14 which worshipped God, *h* us
Acts 16:25 and the prisoners *h* them
Acts 16:38 when they *h* that they were Romans
Acts 17:8 city, when they *h* these things
Acts 17:32 when they *h* of the resurrection
Acts 18:26 when Aquila and Priscilla had *h*
Acts 19:2 We have not so much as *h* whether
Acts 19:5 When they *h* this, they were
Acts 19:10 Asia *h* the word of the Lord Jesus
Acts 19:28 when they *h* these sayings, they
Acts 21:12 when we *h* these things, both we,
Acts 21:20 And when they *h* it, they glorified
Acts 22:2 when they *h* that he spake in the
Acts 22:7 *h* a voice saying unto me, Saul,
Acts 22:9 but they *h* not the voice of him
Acts 22:15 men of what thou hast seen and *h*
Acts 22:26 When the centurion *h* that
Acts 23:16 son *h* of their lying in wait
Acts 24:22 when Felix *h* these things, having
Acts 24:24 *h* him concerning the faith in
Acts 26:14 I *h* a voice speaking unto me, and
Acts 28:15 thence, when the brethren *h* of us
Rom 10:14 in him of whom they have not *h*
Rom 10:18 But I say, Have they not *h*
Rom 15:21 that have not *h* shall understand
1Cor 2:9 Eye hath not seen, nor ear *h*
2Cor 6:2 I have *h* thee in a time accepted,
2Cor 12:4 *h* unspeakable words, which it is
Gal 1:13 For ye have *h* of my conversation
Gal 1:23 But they had *h* only, That he
Eph 1:13 after that ye *h* the word of truth
Eph 1:15 after I *h* of your faith in the
Eph 3:2 If ye have *h* of the dispensation
Eph 4:21 If so be that ye have *h* him
Phil 2:26 because that ye had *h* that he had
Phil 4:9 both learned, and received, and *h*
Col 1:4 Since we *h* of your faith in
Col 1:5 whereof ye *h* before in the word
Col 1:6 in you, since the day ye *h* of it
Col 1:9 we also, since the day we *h* it
Col 1:23 of the gospel, which ye have *h*
1Th 2:13 the word of God which ye *h* of us
2Ti 1:13 words, which thou hast *h* of me
2Ti 2:2 the things that thou hast *h* of me
Heb 2:1 to the things which we have *h*
Heb 2:3 unto us by them that *h* him
Heb 3:16 For some, when they had *h*
Heb 4:2 with faith in them that *h* it
Heb 5:7 death, and was *h* in that he feared
Heb 12:19 which voice they that *h* intreated
Jas 5:11 Ye have *h* of the patience of Job,
2Pet 1:18 voice which came from heaven we *h*
1Jn 1:1 the beginning, which we have *h*
1Jn 1:3 *h* declare we unto you, that ye
1Jn 1:5 message which we have *h* of him
1Jn 2:7 ye have *h* from the beginning
1Jn 2:18 as ye have *h* that antichrist
1Jn 2:24 in you, which ye have *h* from the
1Jn 2:24 If that which ye have *h* from the
1Jn 3:11 that ye *h* from the beginning
1Jn 4:3 whereof ye have *h* that it should
2Jn 6 as ye have *h* from the beginning,
Rev 1:10 *h* behind me a great voice, as of
Rev 3:3 how thou hast received and *h*
Rev 4:1 the first voice which I *h* was as
Rev 5:11 I *h* the voice of many angels
Rev 5:13 *h* I saying, Blessing, and honour,
Rev 6:1 opened one of the seals, and I *h*
Rev 6:3 I *h* the second beast say, Come and
Rev 6:5 I *h* the third beast say, Come and
Rev 6:6 I *h* a voice in the midst of the
Rev 6:7 I *h* the voice of the fourth beast
Rev 7:4 I *h* the number of them which were
Rev 8:13 *h* an angel flying through the
Rev 9:13 I *h* a voice from the four horns
Rev 9:16 and I *h* the number of them
Rev 10:4 I *h* a voice from heaven saying
Rev 10:8 the voice which I *h* from heaven
Rev 11:12 they *h* a great voice from heaven
Rev 12:10 I *h* a loud voice saying in heaven
Rev 14:2 I *h* a voice from heaven, as the
Rev 14:2 I *h* the voice of harpers harping
Rev 14:13 I *h* a voice from heaven saying
Rev 16:1 I *h* a great voice out of the
Rev 16:5 I *h* the angel of the waters say,
Rev 16:7 I *h* another out of the altar say,
Rev 18:4 I *h* another voice from heaven,
Rev 18:22 shall be *h* no more at all in thee
Rev 18:22 shall be *h* no more at all in thee
Rev 18:23 of the bride shall be *h* no more
Rev 19:1 after these things I *h* a great
Rev 19:6 I *h* as it were the voice of a
Rev 21:3 I *h* a great voice out of heaven
Rev 22:8 John saw these things, and *h* them
Rev 22:8 And when I had *h* and seen, I fell

## HEARDEST

Deut 4:36 thou *h* his words out of the midst
Josh 14:12 for thou *h* in that day how the
2Kin 22:19 when thou *h* what I spake against
2Chr 34:27 when thou *h* his words against
Neh 9:9 *h* their cry by the Red sea
Neh 9:27 thee, thou *h* them from heaven
Neh 9:28 thee, thou *h* them from heaven
Ps 31:22 nevertheless thou *h* the voice of
Ps 119:26 declared my ways, and thou *h* me
Is 48:7 the day when thou *h* them not
Is 48:8 Yea, thou *h* not
Jonah 2:2 hell cried I, and thou *h* my voice

## HEARERS

Rom 2:13 (For not the *h* of the law are
Eph 4:29 it may minister grace unto the *h*
2Ti 2:14 but to the subverting of the *h*
Jas 1:22 not *h* only, deceiving your own

## HEAREST

Ruth 2:8 Ruth, *H* thou not, my daughter
1Sa 24:9 Wherefore *h* thou men's words,
2Sa 5:24 when thou *h* the sound of a going
1Kin 8:30 and when thou *h*, forgive
2Chr 6:21 and when thou *h*, forgive
Ps 22:2 in the daytime, but thou *h* not
Ps 65:2 O thou that *h* prayer, unto thee
Mt 21:16 unto him, *H* thou what these say
Mt 27:13 *H* thou not how many things they
Jn 3:8 thou *h* the sound thereof, but
Jn 11:42 And I knew that thou *h* me always

## HEARETH

Ex 16:7 for that he *h* your murmurings
Ex 16:8 for that the LORD *h* your
Num 30:5 disallow her in the day that he *h*
Deut 29:19 when he *h* the words of this curse
1Sa 3:9 for thy servant *h*
1Sa 3:10 for thy servant *h*
1Sa 3:11 every one that *h* it shall tingle
2Sa 17:9 that whosoever *h* it will say
2Kin 21:12 and Judah, that whosoever *h* of it
Job 34:28 he *h* the cry of the afflicted
Ps 34:17 The righteous cry, and the LORD *h*
Ps 38:14 Thus I was as a man that *h* not
Ps 69:33 For the LORD *h* the poor, and
Prov 8:34 Blessed is the man that *h* me
Prov 13:1 A wise son *h* his father's
Prov 13:1 but a scorner *h* not rebuke
Prov 13:8 but the poor *h* not rebuke
Prov 15:29 but he *h* the prayer of the
Prov 15:31 The ear that *h* the reproof of
Prov 15:32 but he that *h* reproof getteth
Prov 18:13 answereth a matter before he *h* it
Prov 21:28 but the man that *h* speaketh
Prov 25:10 Lest he that *h* it put thee to
Prov 29:24 he *h* cursing, and bewrayeth it not
Is 41:26 there is none that *h* your words
Is 42:20 opening the ears, but he *h* not
Jer 19:3 this place, the which whosoever *h*
Eze 3:27 He that *h*, let him hear
Eze 33:4 Then whosoever *h* the sound of the
Mt 7:24 Therefore whosoever *h* these
Mt 7:26 every one that *h* these sayings of
Mt 13:19 When any one *h* the word of the
Mt 13:20 the same is he that *h* the word
Mt 13:22 the thorns is he that *h* the word
Mt 13:23 good ground is he that *h* the word
Lk 6:47 *h* my sayings, and doeth them, I
Lk 6:49 But he that *h*, and doeth not, is
Lk 10:16 He that *h* you *h* me
Jn 3:29 *h* him, rejoiceth greatly because
Jn 5:24 I say unto you, He that *h* my word
Jn 8:47 He that is of God *h* God's words
Jn 9:31 we know that God *h* not sinners
Jn 9:31 God, and doeth his will, him he *h*
Jn 18:37 that is of the truth *h* my voice
2Cor 12:6 me to be, or that he *h* of me
1Jn 4:5 of the world, and the world *h* them
1Jn 4:6 he that knoweth God *h* us
1Jn 4:6 he that is not of God *h* not us
1Jn 5:14 according to his will, he *h* us
Rev 22:17 And let him that *h* say, Come
Rev 22:18 *h* the words of the prophecy of

## HEARING

Deut 31:11 law before all Israel in their *h*
2Sa 18:12 for in our *h* the king charged
2Kin 4:31 there was neither voice, nor *h*
Job 33:8 Surely thou hast spoken in mine *h*
Job 42:5 heard of thee by the *h* of the ear
Prov 20:12 The *h* ear, and the seeing eye, the
Prov 28:9 away his ear from *h* the law
Eccl 1:8 seeing, nor the ear filled with *h*
Is 11:3 reprove after the *h* of his ears
Is 21:3 I was bowed down at the *h* of it
Is 33:15 stoppeth his ears from *h* of blood
Eze 9:5 to the others he said in mine *h*
Eze 10:13 it was cried unto them in my *h*
Amos 8:11 but of *h* the words of the LORD
Mt 13:13 *h* they hear not, neither do they
Mt 13:14 By *h* ye shall hear, and shall not
Mt 13:15 and their ears are dull of *h*
Mk 4:12 and *h* they may hear, and not
Mk 6:2 many *h* him were astonished,
Lk 2:46 midst of the doctors, both *h* them
Lk 8:10 *h* they might not understand
Lk 18:36 *h* the multitude pass by, he asked
Acts 5:5 Ananias *h* these words fell down,
Acts 8:6 things which Philip spake, *h*
Acts 9:7 *h* a voice, but seeing no man
Acts 18:8 of the Corinthians *h* believed
Acts 25:21 reserved unto the *h* of Augustus
Acts 25:23 was entered into the place of *h*
Acts 28:26 *H* ye shall hear, and shall not
Acts 28:27 and their ears are dull of *h*
Rom 10:17 So then faith cometh by *h*
Rom 10:17 and *h* by the word of God
1Cor 12:17 were an eye, where were the *h*
1Cor 12:17 If the whole were *h*, where were
Gal 3:2 of the law, or by the *h* of faith
Gal 3:5 of the law, or by the *h* of faith
Philem 5 *H* of thy love and faith, which
Heb 5:11 uttered, seeing ye are dull of *h*
2Pet 2:8 among them, in seeing and *h*

## HEARKEN

Gen 4:23 wives of Lamech, *h* unto my speech
Gen 21:12 said unto thee, *h* unto her voice

Gen 23:15 My lord, *h* unto me
Gen 34:17 But if ye will not *h* unto us
Gen 49:2 *h* unto Israel your father
Ex 3:18 they shall *h* to thy voice
Ex 4:1 believe me, nor *h* unto my voice
Ex 4:8 neither *h* to the voice of the
Ex 4:9 neither *h* unto thy voice, that
Ex 6:30 and how shall Pharaoh *h* unto me
Ex 7:4 But Pharaoh shall not *h* unto you
Ex 7:22 neither did he *h* unto them
Ex 11:9 Pharaoh shall not *h* unto you
Ex 15:26 If thou wilt diligently *h* to the
Ex 18:19 *H* now unto my voice, I will give
Lev 26:14 But if ye will not *h* unto me
Lev 26:18 not yet for all this *h* unto me
Lev 26:21 unto me, and will not *h* unto me
Lev 26:27 will not for all this *h* unto me
Num 23:18 *h* unto me, thou son of Zippor
Deut 1:45 LORD would not *h* to your voice
Deut 4:1 Now therefore *h*, O Israel, unto
Deut 7:12 if ye *h* to these judgments, and
Deut 11:13 if ye shall *h* diligently unto my
Deut 13:3 Thou shalt not *h* unto the words
Deut 13:8 consent unto him, nor *h* unto him
Deut 13:18 When thou shalt *h* to the voice of
Deut 15:5 Only if thou carefully *h* unto the
Deut 17:12 will not *h* unto the priest that
Deut 18:15 unto him ye shall *h*
Deut 18:19 that whosoever will not *h* unto my
Deut 21:18 him, will not *h* unto them
Deut 23:5 thy God would not *h* unto Balaam
Deut 26:17 judgments, and to *h* unto his voice
Deut 27:9 Israel, saying, Take heed, and *h*
Deut 28:1 if thou shalt *h* diligently unto
Deut 28:2 if thou shalt *h* unto the voice of
Deut 28:13 if that thou *h* unto the
Deut 28:15 if thou wilt not *h* unto the voice
Deut 30:10 If thou shalt *h* unto the voice of
Josh 1:17 things, so will we *h* unto thee
Josh 1:18 will not *h* unto thy words in all
Josh 24:10 But I would not *h* unto Balaam
Judg 2:17 would not *h* unto their judges
Judg 3:4 to know whether they would *h* unto
Judg 9:7 *H* unto me, ye men of Shechem,
Judg 9:7 that God may *h* unto you
Judg 11:17 king of Edom would not *h* thereto
Judg 19:25 But the men would not *h* to him
Judg 20:13 *h* to the voice of their brethren
1Sa 8:7 *H* unto the voice of the people in
1Sa 8:9 Now therefore *h* unto their voice
1Sa 8:22 *H* unto their voice, and make them
1Sa 15:1 now therefore *h* thou unto the
1Sa 15:22 to *h* than the fat of rams
1Sa 28:22 *h* thou also unto the voice of
1Sa 30:24 For who will *h* unto you in this
2Sa 12:18 he would not *h* unto our voice
2Sa 13:14 he would not *h* unto her voice
2Sa 13:16 But he would not *h* unto her
1Kin 8:28 to *h* unto the cry and to the
1Kin 8:29 that thou mayest *h* unto the
1Kin 8:30 *h* thou to the supplication of thy
1Kin 8:52 to *h* unto them in all that they
1Kin 11:38 if thou wilt *h* unto all that I
1Kin 20:8 *H* not unto him, nor consent
1Kin 22:28 And he said, *H*, O people, every
2Kin 10:6 if ye will *h* unto my voice, take
2Kin 17:40 Howbeit they did not *h*, but they
2Kin 18:31 *H* not to Hezekiah
2Kin 18:32 *h* not unto Hezekiah, when he
2Chr 6:19 to *h* unto the cry and the prayer
2Chr 6:20 to *h* unto the prayer which thy
2Chr 6:21 *H* therefore unto the
2Chr 10:16 the king would not *h* unto them
2Chr 18:27 And he said, *H*, all ye people
2Chr 20:15 he said, *H* ye, all Judah, and ye
2Chr 33:10 but they would not *h*
Neh 13:27 Shall we then *h* unto you to do
Job 13:6 *h* to the pleadings of my lips
Job 32:10 Therefore I said, *H* to me
Job 33:1 my speeches, and *h* to all my words
Job 33:31 Mark well, O Job, *h* unto me
Job 33:33 If not, *h* unto me
Job 34:10 Therefore *h* unto me, ye men of
Job 34:16 *h* to the voice of my words
Job 34:34 me, and let a wise man *h* unto me
Job 37:14 *H* unto this, O Job
Ps 5:2 *H* unto the voice of my cry, my
Ps 34:11 Come, ye children, *h* unto me
Ps 45:10 *H*, O daughter, and consider, and
Ps 58:5 Which will not *h* to the voice of
Ps 81:8 O Israel, if thou wilt *h* unto me
Ps 81:11 my people would not *h* to my voice
Prov 7:24 *H* unto me now therefore, O ye
Prov 8:32 Now therefore *h* unto me, O ye
Prov 23:22 *H* unto thy father that begat thee
Prov 29:12 If a ruler *h* to lies, all his
Song 8:13 the companions *h* to thy voice
Is 28:23 *h*, and hear my speech
Is 32:3 ears of them that hear shall *h*
Is 34:1 and *h*, ye people
Is 36:16 *H* not to Hezekiah
Is 42:23 who will *h* and hear for the time
Is 46:3 *H* unto me, O house of Jacob, and
Is 46:12 *H* unto me, ye stouthearted, that
Is 48:12 *H* unto me, O Jacob and Israel, my
Is 49:1 and *h*, ye people, from far
Is 51:1 *H* to me, ye that follow after
Is 51:4 *H* unto me, my people
Is 51:7 *H* unto me, ye that know
Is 55:2 *h* diligently unto me, and eat ye
Jer 6:10 uncircumcised, and they cannot *h*
Jer 6:17 *H* to the sound of the trumpet
Jer 6:17 But they said, We will not *h*
Jer 7:27 but they will not *h* to thee
Jer 11:11 unto me, I will not *h* unto them
Jer 16:12 that they may not *h* unto me
Jer 17:24 pass, if ye diligently *h* unto me
Jer 17:27 But if ye will not *h* unto me to
Jer 18:19 *h* to the voice of them that
Jer 23:16 *H* not unto the words of the
Jer 26:3 If so be they will *h*, and turn
Jer 26:4 If ye will not *h* to me, to walk
Jer 26:5 To *h* to the words of my servants
Jer 27:9 Therefore *h* not ye to your
Jer 27:14 Therefore *h* not unto the words of
Jer 27:16 *H* not to the words of your
Jer 27:17 *H* not unto them
Jer 29:8 neither *h* to your dreams which ye
Jer 29:12 unto me, and I will *h* unto you
Jer 35:13 instruction to *h* to my words
Jer 37:2 did *h* unto the words of the LORD,
Jer 38:15 counsel, wilt thou not *h* unto me
Jer 44:16 the LORD, we will not *h* unto thee
Eze 3:7 of Israel will not *h* unto thee
Eze 3:7 for they will not *h* unto me
Eze 20:8 me, and would not *h* unto me
Eze 20:39 also, if ye will not *h* unto me
Dan 9:19 O Lord, *h* and do
Hos 5:1 and *h*, ye house of Israel
Hos 9:17 because they did not *h* unto him
Mic 1:2 *h*, O earth, and all that therein
Zec 1:4 nor *h* unto me, saith the LORD
Zec 7:11 But they refused to *h*, and pulled
Mk 4:3 *H*; Behold, there went
Mk 7:14 *H* unto me every one of you, and
Acts 2:14 known unto you, and *h* to my words
Acts 4:19 to *h* unto you more than unto God
Acts 7:2 Men, brethren, and fathers, *h*
Acts 12:13 of the gate, a damsel came to *h*
Acts 15:13 Men and brethren, *h* unto me
Jas 2:5 *H*, my beloved brethren, Hath not

## HEARKENED

Gen 3:17 Because thou hast *h* unto the
Gen 16:2 Abram *h* to the voice of Sarai
Gen 23:16 And Abraham *h* unto Ephron
Gen 30:17 God *h* unto Leah, and she conceived
Gen 30:22 God *h* to her, and opened her womb
Gen 34:24 unto Shechem his son *h* all that
Gen 39:10 that he *h* not unto her, to lie by
Ex 6:9 but they *h* not unto Moses for
Ex 6:12 of Israel have not *h* unto me
Ex 7:13 heart, that he *h* not unto them
Ex 8:15 his heart, and *h* not unto them
Ex 8:19 hardened, and he *h* not unto them
Ex 9:12 of Pharaoh, and he *h* not unto them
Ex 16:20 they *h* not unto Moses
Ex 18:24 So Moses *h* to the voice of his
Num 14:22 times, and have not *h* to my voice
Num 21:3 the LORD *h* to the voice of Israel
Deut 9:19 But the LORD *h* unto me at that
Deut 9:23 him not, nor *h* to his voice
Deut 10:10 the LORD *h* unto me at that time
Deut 18:14 *h* unto observers of times, and
Deut 26:14 but I have *h* to the voice of the
Deut 34:9 the children of Israel *h* unto him
Josh 1:17 According as we *h* unto Moses in
Josh 10:14 that the LORD *h* unto the voice of
Judg 2:20 and have not *h* unto my voice
Judg 11:28 king of the children of Ammon *h*
Judg 13:9 God *h* to the voice of Manoah
1Sa 2:25 Notwithstanding they *h* not unto
1Sa 12:1 I have *h* unto your voice in all
1Sa 19:6 Saul *h* unto the voice of Jonathan
1Sa 25:35 I have *h* to thy voice, and have
1Sa 28:21 have *h* unto thy words which thou
1Sa 28:23 and he *h* unto their voice
1Kin 12:15 Wherefore the king *h* not unto the
1Kin 12:16 saw that the king *h* not unto them
1Kin 12:24 They *h* therefore to the word of
1Kin 15:20 So Ben-hadad *h* unto king Asa, and
1Kin 20:25 he *h* unto their voice, and did so
2Kin 13:4 the LORD, and the LORD *h* unto him
2Kin 16:9 And the king of Assyria *h* unto him
2Kin 20:13 Hezekiah *h* unto them, and shewed
2Kin 21:9 But they *h* not
2Kin 22:13 not *h* unto the words of this book
2Chr 10:15 So the king *h* not unto the people
2Chr 16:4 Ben-hadad *h* unto king Asa, and
2Chr 24:17 Then the king *h* unto them
2Chr 25:16 hast not *h* unto my counsel
2Chr 30:20 the LORD *h* to Hezekiah, and healed
2Chr 35:22 *h* not unto the words of Necho
Neh 9:16 *h* not to thy commandments,
Neh 9:29 *h* not unto thy commandments, but
Neh 9:34 nor *h* unto thy commandments and
Est 3:4 he *h* not unto them, that they
Job 9:16 that he had *h* unto my voice
Ps 81:13 Oh that my people had *h* unto me
Ps 106:25 *h* not unto the voice of the LORD
Is 21:7 he *h* diligently with much heed
Is 48:18 O that thou hadst *h* to my
Jer 6:19 they have not *h* unto my words
Jer 7:24 But they *h* not, nor inclined
Jer 7:26 Yet they *h* not unto me, nor
Jer 8:6 I *h* and heard, but they spake not
Jer 25:3 but ye have not *h*
Jer 25:4 but ye have not *h*, nor inclined
Jer 25:7 Yet ye have not *h* unto me
Jer 26:5 sending them, but ye have not *h*
Jer 29:19 they have not *h* to my words
Jer 32:33 yet they have not *h* to receive
Jer 34:14 but your fathers *h* not unto me
Jer 34:17 Ye have not *h* unto me, in
Jer 35:14 but ye *h* not unto me
Jer 35:15 inclined your ear, nor *h* unto me
Jer 35:16 this people hath not *h* unto me
Jer 36:31 but they *h* not
Jer 37:14 But he *h* not to him
Jer 44:5 But they *h* not, nor inclined
Eze 3:6 them, they would have *h* unto thee
Dan 9:6 Neither have we *h* unto thy
Mal 3:16 and the LORD *h*, and heard it, and a
Acts 27:21 Sirs, ye should have *h* unto me

## HEART

Gen 6:5 of the thoughts of his *h* was only
Gen 6:6 earth, and it grieved him at his *h*
Gen 8:21 and the LORD said in his *h*
Gen 8:21 of man's *h* is evil from his youth
Gen 17:17 and laughed, and said in his *h*
Gen 20:5 in the integrity of my *h* and
Gen 20:6 this in the integrity of thy *h*
Gen 24:45 I had done speaking in mine *h*
Gen 27:41 and Esau said in his *h*, The days
Gen 42:28 their *h* failed them, and they were
Gen 45:26 And Jacob's *h* fainted, for he
Ex 4:14 thee, he will be glad in his *h*
Ex 4:21 but I will harden his *h*, that he
Ex 7:3 And I will harden Pharaoh's *h*
Ex 7:13 And he hardened Pharaoh's *h*
Ex 7:14 Pharaoh's *h* is hardened, he
Ex 7:22 Pharaoh's *h* was hardened, neither
Ex 7:23 did he set his *h* to this also
Ex 8:15 was respite, he hardened his *h*
Ex 8:19 Pharaoh's *h* was hardened, and he
Ex 8:32 hardened his *h* at this time also
Ex 9:7 the *h* of Pharaoh was hardened, and
Ex 9:12 LORD hardened the *h* of Pharaoh
Ex 9:14 send all my plagues upon thine *h*
Ex 9:34 yet more, and hardened his *h*
Ex 9:35 the *h* of Pharaoh was hardened,
Ex 10:1 for I have hardened his *h*
Ex 10:1 the *h* of his servants, that I
Ex 10:20 But the LORD hardened Pharaoh's *h*
Ex 10:27 But the LORD hardened Pharaoh's *h*
Ex 11:10 and the LORD hardened Pharaoh's *h*
Ex 14:4 And I will harden Pharaoh's *h*
Ex 14:5 the *h* of Pharaoh and of his
Ex 14:8 the LORD hardened the *h* of

Ex 15:8 congealed in the *h* of the sea
Ex 23:9 for ye know the *h* of a stranger
Ex 25:2 his *h* ye shall take my offering
Ex 28:29 of judgment upon his *h*, when he
Ex 28:30 and they shall be upon Aaron's *h*
Ex 28:30 his *h* before the LORD continually
Ex 35:5 whosoever is of a willing *h*
Ex 35:21 every one whose *h* stirred him up
Ex 35:26 all the women whose *h* stirred
Ex 35:29 whose *h* made them willing to
Ex 35:34 put in his *h* that he may teach
Ex 35:35 hath he filled with wisdom of *h*
Ex 36:2 in whose *h* the LORD had put
Ex 36:2 even every one whose *h* stirred
Lev 19:17 not hate thy brother in thine *h*
Lev 26:16 the eyes, and cause sorrow of *h*
Num 15:39 that ye seek not after your own *h*
Num 32:7 wherefore discourage ye the *h* of
Num 32:9 they discouraged the *h* of the
Deut 1:28 brethren have discouraged our *h*
Deut 2:30 made his *h* obstinate, that he
Deut 4:9 thy *h* all the days of thy life
Deut 4:29 if thou seek him with all thy *h*
Deut 4:39 day, and consider it in thine *h*
Deut 5:29 that there were such an *h* in them
Deut 6:5 the LORD thy God with all thine *h*
Deut 6:6 this day, shall be in thine *h*
Deut 7:17 If thou shalt say in thine *h*
Deut 8:2 thee, to know what was in thine *h*
Deut 8:5 shalt also consider in thine *h*
Deut 8:14 Then thine *h* be lifted up, and
Deut 8:17 And thou say in thine *h*, My power
Deut 9:4 Speak not thou in thine *h*
Deut 9:5 or for the uprightness of thine *h*
Deut 10:12 the LORD thy God with all thy *h*
Deut 10:16 therefore the foreskin of your *h*
Deut 11:13 and to serve him with all your *h*
Deut 11:16 that your *h* be not deceived, and
Deut 11:18 lay up these my words in your *h*
Deut 13:3 the LORD your God with all your *h*
Deut 15:7 thou shalt not harden thine *h*
Deut 15:9 be not a thought in thy wicked *h*
Deut 15:10 thine *h* shall not be grieved when
Deut 17:17 himself, that his *h* turn not away
Deut 17:20 That his *h* be not lifted up above
Deut 18:21 And if thou say in thine *h*
Deut 19:6 the slayer, while his *h* is hot
Deut 20:8 *h* faint as well as his *h*
Deut 24:15 is poor, and setteth his *h* upon it
Deut 26:16 keep and do them with all thine *h*
Deut 28:28 blindness, and astonishment of *h*
Deut 28:47 joyfulness, and with gladness of *h*
Deut 28:65 give thee there a trembling *h*
Deut 28:67 for the fear of thine *h* wherewith
Deut 29:4 not given you an *h* to perceive
Deut 29:18 whose *h* turneth away this day
Deut 29:19 that he bless himself in his *h*
Deut 29:19 walk in the imagination of mine *h*
Deut 30:2 and thy children, with all thine *h*
Deut 30:6 thy God will circumcise thine *h*
Deut 30:6 the *h* of thy seed, to love the
Deut 30:6 the LORD thy God with all thine *h*
Deut 30:10 the LORD thy God with all thine *h*
Deut 30:14 thee, in thy mouth, and in thy *h*
Deut 30:17 But if thine *h* turn away, so that
Josh 5:1 passed over, that their *h* melted
Josh 14:7 word again as it was in mine *h*
Josh 14:8 me made the *h* of the people melt
Josh 22:5 and to serve him with all your *h*
Josh 24:23 incline your *h* unto the LORD God
Judg 5:9 My *h* is toward the governors of
Judg 5:15 there were great thoughts of *h*
Judg 5:16 there were great searchings of *h*
Judg 16:15 when thine *h* is not with me
Judg 16:17 That he told her all his *h*
Judg 16:18 that he had told her all his *h*
Judg 16:18 for he hath shewed me all his *h*
Judg 18:20 And the priest's *h* was glad
Judg 19:5 Comfort thine *h* with a morsel of
Judg 19:6 night, and let thine *h* be merry
Judg 19:8 father said, Comfort thine *h*
Judg 19:9 that thine *h* may be merry
Ruth 3:7 his *h* was merry, he went to lie
1Sa 1:8 and why is thy *h* grieved
1Sa 1:13 Now Hannah, she spake in her *h*
1Sa 2:1 My *h* rejoiceth in the LORD, mine
1Sa 2:33 thine eyes, and to grieve thine *h*
1Sa 2:35 to that which is in mine *h*
1Sa 4:13 for his *h* trembled for the ark of
1Sa 9:19 tell thee all that is in thine *h*
1Sa 10:9 Samuel, God gave him another *h*
1Sa 12:20 serve the LORD with all your *h*
1Sa 12:24 him in truth with all your *h*
1Sa 13:14 sought him a man after his own *h*
1Sa 14:7 him, Do all that is in thine *h*
1Sa 14:7 I am with thee according to thy *h*
1Sa 16:7 but the LORD looketh on the *h*
1Sa 17:28 and the naughtiness of thine *h*
1Sa 17:32 Let no man's *h* fail because of
1Sa 21:12 laid up these words in his *h*
1Sa 24:5 that David's *h* smote him
1Sa 25:31 nor offence of *h* unto my lord
1Sa 25:36 Nabal's *h* was merry within him
1Sa 25:37 that his *h* died within him, and he
1Sa 27:1 And David said in his *h*, I shall
1Sa 28:5 afraid, and his *h* greatly trembled
2Sa 3:21 over all that thine *h* desireth
2Sa 6:16 and she despised him in her *h*
2Sa 7:3 Go, do all that is in thine *h*
2Sa 7:21 sake, and according to thine own *h*
2Sa 7:27 *h* to pray this prayer unto thee
2Sa 13:28 when Amnon's *h* is merry with wine
2Sa 13:33 the king take the thing to his *h*
2Sa 14:1 the king's *h* was toward Absalom
2Sa 17:10 whose *h* is as the *h* of a lion
2Sa 18:14 them through the *h* of Absalom
2Sa 19:14 he bowed the *h* of all the men of
2Sa 19:14 Judah, even as the *h* of one man
2Sa 19:19 the king should take it to his *h*
2Sa 24:10 David's *h* smote him after that he
1Kin 2:4 me in truth with all their *h*
1Kin 2:44 which thine *h* is privy to
1Kin 3:6 and in uprightness of *h* with thee
1Kin 3:9 *h* to judge thy people, that I may
1Kin 3:12 thee a wise and an understanding *h*
1Kin 4:29 exceeding much, and largeness of *h*
1Kin 8:17 it was in the *h* of David my
1Kin 8:18 Whereas it was in thine *h* to
1Kin 8:18 didst well that it was in thine *h*
1Kin 8:23 walk before thee with all their *h*
1Kin 8:38 every man the plague of his own *h*
1Kin 8:39 to his ways, whose *h* thou knowest
1Kin 8:48 return unto thee with all their *h*
1Kin 8:61 Let your *h* therefore be perfect
1Kin 8:66 glad of *h* for all the goodness
1Kin 9:3 mine *h* shall be there perpetually
1Kin 9:4 father walked, in integrity of *h*
1Kin 10:2 with him of all that was in her *h*
1Kin 10:24 which God had put in his *h*
1Kin 11:2 turn away your *h* after their gods
1Kin 11:3 and his wives turned away his *h*
1Kin 11:4 away his *h* after other gods
1Kin 11:4 his *h* was not perfect with the
1Kin 11:4 as was the *h* of David his father
1Kin 11:9 because his *h* was turned from the
1Kin 12:26 And Jeroboam said in his *h*
1Kin 12:27 then shall the *h* of this people
1Kin 12:33 which he had devised of his own *h*
1Kin 14:8 and who followed me with all his *h*
1Kin 15:3 his *h* was not perfect with the
1Kin 15:3 as the *h* of David his father
1Kin 15:14 nevertheless Asa's *h* was perfect
1Kin 18:37 hast turned their *h* back again
1Kin 21:7 bread, and let thine *h* be merry
2Kin 5:26 him, Went not mine *h* with thee
2Kin 6:11 Therefore the *h* of the king of
2Kin 9:24 and the arrow went out at his *h*
2Kin 10:15 and said to him, Is thine *h* right
2Kin 10:15 as my *h* is with thy *h*
2Kin 10:30 to all that was in mine *h*
2Kin 10:31 LORD God of Israel with all his *h*
2Kin 12:4 that cometh into any man's *h* to
2Kin 14:10 thine *h* hath lifted thee up
2Kin 20:3 thee in truth and with a perfect *h*
2Kin 22:19 Because thine *h* was tender
2Kin 23:3 and his statutes with all their *h*
2Kin 23:25 turned to the LORD with all his *h*
1Chr 12:17 mine *h* shall be knit unto you
1Chr 12:33 they were not of double *h*
1Chr 12:38 came with a perfect *h* to Hebron
1Chr 12:38 were of one *h* to make David king
1Chr 15:29 and she despised him in her *h*
1Chr 16:10 let the *h* of them rejoice that
1Chr 17:2 David, Do all that is in thine *h*
1Chr 17:19 sake, and according to thine own *h*
1Chr 17:25 in his *h* to pray before thee
1Chr 22:19 Now set your *h* and your soul to
1Chr 28:2 I had in mine *h* to build an house
1Chr 28:9 and serve him with a perfect *h*
1Chr 29:9 because with perfect *h* they
1Chr 29:17 my God, that thou triest the *h*
1Chr 29:17 in the uprightness of mine *h* I
1Chr 29:18 thoughts of the *h* of thy people
1Chr 29:18 and prepare their *h* unto thee
1Chr 29:19 unto Solomon my son a perfect *h*
2Chr 1:11 Because this was in thine *h*
2Chr 6:7 Now it was in the *h* of David my
2Chr 6:8 Forasmuch as it was in thine *h* to
2Chr 6:8 well in that it was in thine *h*
2Chr 6:30 his ways, whose *h* thou knowest
2Chr 6:38 return to thee with all their *h*
2Chr 7:10 merry in *h* for the goodness that
2Chr 7:11 *h* to make in the house of the
2Chr 7:16 mine *h* shall be there perpetually
2Chr 9:1 with him of all that was in her *h*
2Chr 9:23 wisdom, that God had put in his *h*
2Chr 12:14 not his *h* to seek the LORD
2Chr 15:12 of their fathers with all their *h*
2Chr 15:15 they had sworn with all their *h*
2Chr 15:17 nevertheless the *h* of Asa was
2Chr 16:9 whose *h* is perfect toward him
2Chr 17:6 his *h* was lifted up in the ways
2Chr 19:3 hast prepared thine *h* to seek God
2Chr 19:9 faithfully, and with a perfect *h*
2Chr 22:9 sought the LORD with all his *h*
2Chr 25:2 LORD, but not with a perfect *h*
2Chr 25:19 thine *h* lifteth thee up to boast
2Chr 26:16 his *h* was lifted up to his
2Chr 29:10 Now it is in mine *h* to make a
2Chr 29:31 were of a free *h* burnt offerings
2Chr 29:34 Levites were more upright in *h* to
2Chr 30:12 of God was to give them one *h* to
2Chr 30:19 That prepareth his *h* to seek God
2Chr 31:21 his God, he did it with all his *h*
2Chr 32:25 for his *h* was lifted up
2Chr 32:26 himself for the pride of his *h*
2Chr 32:31 might know all that was in his *h*
2Chr 34:27 Because thine *h* was tender
2Chr 34:31 and his statutes, with all his *h*
2Chr 36:13 hardened his *h* from turning unto
Ezr 6:22 turned the *h* of the king of
Ezr 7:10 For Ezra had prepared his *h* to
Ezr 7:27 a thing as this in the king's *h*
Neh 2:2 is nothing else but sorrow of *h*
Neh 2:12 put in my *h* to do at Jerusalem
Neh 6:8 feignest them out of thine own *h*
Neh 7:5 my God put into mine *h* to gather
Neh 9:8 foundest his *h* faithful before
Est 1:10 when the *h* of the king was merry
Est 5:9 that day joyful and with a glad *h*
Est 6:6 Now Haman thought in his *h*
Est 7:5 durst presume in his *h* to do so
Job 7:17 shouldest set thine *h* upon him
Job 8:10 and utter words out of their *h*
Job 9:4 He is wise in *h*, and mighty in
Job 10:13 things hast thou hid in thine *h*
Job 11:13 If thou prepare thine *h*, and
Job 12:24 He taketh away the *h* of the chief
Job 15:12 Why doth thine *h* carry thee away
Job 17:4 hid their *h* from understanding
Job 17:11 off, even the thoughts of my *h*
Job 22:22 and lay up his words in thine *h*
Job 23:16 For God maketh my *h* soft, and the
Job 27:6 my *h* shall not reproach me so
Job 29:13 the widow's *h* to sing for joy
Job 31:7 mine *h* walked after mine eyes, and
Job 31:9 If mine *h* have been deceived by a
Job 31:27 my *h* hath been secretly enticed,
Job 33:3 be of the uprightness of my *h*
Job 34:14 If he set his *h* upon man, if he
Job 36:13 the hypocrites in *h* heap up wrath
Job 37:1 At this also my *h* trembleth
Job 37:24 not any that are wise of *h*
Job 38:36 hath given understanding to the *h*
Job 41:24 His *h* is as firm as a stone
Ps 4:4 with your own *h* upon your bed
Ps 4:7 Thou hast put gladness in my *h*
Ps 7:10 which saveth the upright in *h*
Ps 9:1 thee, O LORD, with my whole *h*
Ps 10:6 He hath said in his *h*, I shall
Ps 10:11 He hath said in his *h*, God hath
Ps 10:13 he hath said in his *h*, Thou wilt
Ps 10:17 thou wilt prepare their *h*
Ps 11:2 privily shoot at the upright in *h*
Ps 12:2 and with a double *h* do they speak
Ps 13:2 soul, having sorrow in my *h* daily
Ps 13:5 my *h* shall rejoice in thy
Ps 14:1 The fool hath said in his *h*
Ps 15:2 and speaketh the truth in his *h*
Ps 16:9 Therefore my *h* is glad, and my

Ps 17:3 Thou hast proved mine *h*
Ps 19:8 LORD are right, rejoicing the *h*
Ps 19:14 mouth, and the meditation of my *h*
Ps 20:4 thee according to thine own *h*
Ps 22:14 my *h* is like wax
Ps 22:26 your *h* shall live for ever
Ps 24:4 hath clean hands, and a pure *h*
Ps 25:17 The troubles of my *h* are enlarged
Ps 26:2 try my reins and my *h*
Ps 27:3 against me, my *h* shall not fear
Ps 27:8 my *h* said unto thee, Thy face,
Ps 27:14 and he shall strengthen thine *h*
Ps 28:7 my *h* trusted in him, and I am
Ps 28:7 therefore my *h* greatly rejoiceth
Ps 31:24 and he shall strengthen your *h*
Ps 32:11 joy, all ye that are upright in *h*
Ps 33:11 of his *h* to all generations
Ps 33:21 For our *h* shall rejoice in him,
Ps 34:18 unto them that are of a broken *h*
Ps 36:1 of the wicked saith within my *h*
Ps 36:10 righteousness to the upright in *h*
Ps 37:4 give thee the desires of thine *h*
Ps 37:15 shall enter into their own *h*
Ps 37:31 The law of his God is in his *h*
Ps 38:8 of the disquietness of my *h*
Ps 38:10 My *h* panteth, my strength faileth
Ps 39:3 My *h* was hot within me
Ps 40:8 yea, thy law is within my *h*
Ps 40:10 hid thy righteousness within my *h*
Ps 40:12 therefore my *h* faileth me
Ps 41:6 his *h* gathereth iniquity to
Ps 44:18 Our *h* is not turned back, neither
Ps 44:21 he knoweth the secrets of the *h*
Ps 45:1 My *h* is inditing a good matter
Ps 45:5 in the *h* of the king's enemies
Ps 49:3 the meditation of my *h* shall be
Ps 51:10 Create in me a clean *h*, O God
Ps 51:17 a broken and a contrite *h*, O God,
Ps 53:1 The fool hath said in his *h*
Ps 55:4 My *h* is sore pained within me
Ps 55:21 than butter, but war was in his *h*
Ps 57:7 My *h* is fixed, O God, my *h* is
Ps 58:2 Yea, in *h* ye work wickedness
Ps 61:2 thee, when my *h* is overwhelmed
Ps 62:8 pour out your *h* before him
Ps 62:10 set not your *h* upon them
Ps 64:6 of every one of them, and the *h*
Ps 64:10 all the upright in *h* shall glory
Ps 66:18 If I regard iniquity in my *h*
Ps 69:20 Reproach hath broken my *h*
Ps 69:32 your *h* shall live that seek God
Ps 73:1 even to such as are of a clean *h*
Ps 73:7 they have more than *h* could wish
Ps 73:13 I have cleansed my *h* in vain
Ps 73:21 Thus my *h* was grieved, and I was
Ps 73:26 My flesh and my *h* faileth
Ps 73:26 but God is the strength of my *h*
Ps 77:6 I commune with mine own *h*
Ps 78:8 that set not their *h* aright
Ps 78:18 they tempted God in their *h* by
Ps 78:37 For their *h* was not right with
Ps 78:72 to the integrity of his *h*
Ps 84:2 my *h* and my flesh crieth out for
Ps 84:5 in whose *h* are the ways of them
Ps 86:11 unite my *h* to fear thy name
Ps 86:12 O Lord my God, with all my *h*
Ps 94:15 the upright in *h* shall follow it
Ps 95:8 Harden not your *h*, as in the
Ps 95:10 a people that do err in their *h*
Ps 97:11 and gladness for the upright in *h*
Ps 101:2 within my house with a perfect *h*
Ps 101:4 A froward *h* shall depart from me
Ps 101:5 a proud *h* will not I suffer
Ps 102:4 My *h* is smitten, and withered like
Ps 104:15 that maketh glad the *h* of man
Ps 104:15 bread which strengtheneth man's *h*
Ps 105:3 let the *h* of them rejoice that
Ps 105:25 He turned their *h* to hate his
Ps 107:12 brought down their *h* with labour
Ps 108:1 O God, my *h* is fixed
Ps 109:16 might even slay the broken in *h*
Ps 109:22 my *h* is wounded within me
Ps 111:1 praise the LORD with my whole *h*
Ps 112:7 his *h* is fixed, trusting in the
Ps 112:8 His *h* is established, he shall
Ps 119:2 and that seek him with the whole *h*
Ps 119:7 praise thee with uprightness of *h*
Ps 119:10 With my whole *h* have I sought
Ps 119:11 Thy word have I hid in mine *h*
Ps 119:32 when thou shalt enlarge my *h*
Ps 119:34 shall observe it with my whole *h*
Ps 119:36 Incline my *h* unto thy testimonies
Ps 119:58 thy favour with my whole *h*
Ps 119:69 keep thy precepts with my whole *h*
Ps 119:70 Their *h* is as fat as grease
Ps 119:80 Let my *h* be sound in thy statutes
Ps 119:111 they are the rejoicing of my *h*
Ps 119:112 I have inclined mine *h* to perform
Ps 119:145 I cried with my whole *h*
Ps 119:161 but my *h* standeth in awe of thy
Ps 131:1 my *h* is not haughty, nor mine
Ps 138:1 will praise thee with my whole *h*
Ps 139:23 Search me, O God, and know my *h*
Ps 140:2 imagine mischiefs in their *h*
Ps 141:4 Incline not my *h* to any evil
Ps 143:4 my *h* within me is desolate
Ps 147:3 He healeth the broken in *h*
Prov 2:2 apply thine *h* to understanding
Prov 2:10 When wisdom entereth into thine *h*
Prov 3:1 but let thine *h* keep my
Prov 3:3 them upon the table of thine *h*
Prov 3:5 in the LORD with all thine *h*
Prov 4:4 Let thine *h* retain my words
Prov 4:21 keep them in the midst of thine *h*
Prov 4:23 Keep thy *h* with all diligence
Prov 5:12 and my *h* despised reproof
Prov 6:14 Frowardness is in his *h*, he
Prov 6:18 An *h* that deviseth wicked
Prov 6:21 them continually upon thine *h*
Prov 6:25 not after her beauty in thine *h*
Prov 7:3 them upon the table of thine *h*
Prov 7:10 of an harlot, and subtil of *h*
Prov 7:25 Let not thine *h* decline to her
Prov 8:5 be ye of an understanding *h*
Prov 10:8 The wise in *h* will receive
Prov 10:20 the *h* of the wicked is little
Prov 11:20 They that are of a froward *h* are
Prov 11:29 shall be servant to the wise of *h*
Prov 12:8 of a perverse *h* shall be despised
Prov 12:20 Deceit is in the *h* of them that
Prov 12:23 but the *h* of fools proclaimeth
Prov 12:25 Heaviness in the *h* of man maketh
Prov 13:12 Hope deferred maketh the *h* sick
Prov 14:10 The *h* knoweth his own bitterness
Prov 14:13 in laughter the *h* is sorrowful
Prov 14:14 The backslider in *h* shall be
Prov 14:30 A sound *h* is the life of the
Prov 14:33 Wisdom resteth in the *h* of him
Prov 15:7 but the *h* of the foolish doeth
Prov 15:13 A merry *h* maketh a cheerful
Prov 15:13 of the *h* the spirit is broken
Prov 15:14 The *h* of him that hath
Prov 15:15 a merry *h* hath a continual feast
Prov 15:28 The *h* of the righteous studieth
Prov 15:30 light of the eyes rejoiceth the *h*
Prov 16:1 The preparations of the *h* in man
Prov 16:5 Every one that is proud in *h* is
Prov 16:9 A man's *h* deviseth his way
Prov 16:21 The wise in *h* shall be called
Prov 16:23 The *h* of the wise teacheth his
Prov 17:16 wisdom, seeing he hath no *h* to it
Prov 17:20 hath a froward *h* findeth no good
Prov 17:22 A merry *h* doeth good like a
Prov 18:2 but that his *h* may discover
Prov 18:12 the *h* of man is haughty
Prov 18:15 The *h* of the prudent getteth
Prov 19:3 his *h* fretteth against the LORD
Prov 19:21 are many devices in a man's *h*
Prov 20:5 Counsel in the *h* of man is like
Prov 20:9 can say, I have made my *h* clean
Prov 21:1 The king's *h* is in the hand of
Prov 21:4 An high look, and a proud *h*
Prov 22:11 He that loveth pureness of *h*
Prov 22:15 is bound in the *h* of a child
Prov 22:17 apply thine *h* unto my knowledge
Prov 23:7 For as he thinketh in his *h*
Prov 23:7 but his *h* is not with thee
Prov 23:12 Apply thine *h* unto instruction,
Prov 23:15 My son, if thine *h* be wise
Prov 23:15 my *h* shall rejoice, even mine
Prov 23:17 Let not thine *h* envy sinners
Prov 23:19 wise, and guide thine *h* in the way
Prov 23:26 My son, give me thine *h*, and let
Prov 23:33 thine *h* shall utter perverse
Prov 24:2 For their *h* studieth destruction,
Prov 24:12 that pondereth the *h* consider it
Prov 24:17 let not thine *h* be glad when he
Prov 25:3 the *h* of kings is unsearchable
Prov 25:20 that singeth songs to an heavy *h*
Prov 26:23 a wicked *h* are like a potsherd
Prov 26:25 are seven abominations in his *h*
Prov 27:9 Ointment and perfume rejoice the *h*
Prov 27:11 son, be wise, and make my *h* glad
Prov 27:19 to face, so the *h* of man to man
Prov 28:14 his *h* shall fall into mischief
Prov 28:25 of a proud *h* stirreth up strife
Prov 28:26 trusteth in his own *h* is a fool
Prov 31:11 The *h* of her husband doth safely
Eccl 1:13 And I gave my *h* to seek and search
Eccl 1:16 I communed with mine own *h*
Eccl 1:16 my *h* had great experience of
Eccl 1:17 I gave my *h* to know wisdom, and to
Eccl 2:1 I said in mine *h*, Go to now, I
Eccl 2:3 I sought in mine *h* to give myself
Eccl 2:3 acquainting mine *h* with wisdom
Eccl 2:10 I withheld not my *h* from any joy
Eccl 2:10 for my *h* rejoiced in all my
Eccl 2:15 Then said I in my *h*, As it
Eccl 2:15 Then I said in my *h*, that this
Eccl 2:20 I went about to cause my *h* to
Eccl 2:22 and of the vexation of his *h*
Eccl 2:23 his *h* taketh not rest in the
Eccl 3:11 he hath set the world in their *h*
Eccl 3:17 I said in mine *h*, God shall judge
Eccl 3:18 I said in mine *h* concerning the
Eccl 5:2 let not thine *h* be hasty to utter
Eccl 5:20 answereth him in the joy of his *h*
Eccl 7:2 the living will lay it to his *h*
Eccl 7:3 countenance the *h* is made better
Eccl 7:4 The *h* of the wise is in the house
Eccl 7:4 but the *h* of fools is in the
Eccl 7:7 and a gift destroyeth the *h*
Eccl 7:22 own *h* knoweth that thou thyself
Eccl 7:25 I applied mine *h* to know, and to
Eccl 7:26 whose *h* is snares and nets, and her
Eccl 8:5 a wise man's *h* discerneth both
Eccl 8:9 applied my *h* unto every work that
Eccl 8:11 therefore the *h* of the sons of
Eccl 8:16 I applied mine *h* to know wisdom
Eccl 9:1 in my *h* even to declare all this
Eccl 9:3 also the *h* of the sons of men is
Eccl 9:3 is in their *h* while they live
Eccl 9:7 and drink thy wine with a merry *h*
Eccl 10:2 A wise man's *h* is at his right
Eccl 10:2 but a fool's *h* at his left
Eccl 11:9 let thy *h* cheer thee in the days
Eccl 11:9 and walk in the ways of thine *h*
Eccl 11:10 remove sorrow from thy *h*, and put
Song 3:11 the day of the gladness of his *h*
Song 4:9 Thou hast ravished my *h*, my
Song 4:9 thou hast ravished my *h* with one
Song 5:2 I sleep, but my *h* waketh
Song 8:6 Set me as a seal upon thine *h*
Is 1:5 is sick, and the whole *h* faint
Is 6:10 Make the *h* of this people fat, and
Is 6:10 ears, and understand with their *h*
Is 7:2 his *h* was moved, and the *h* of
Is 9:9 in the pride and stoutness of *h*
Is 10:7 so, neither doth his *h* think so
Is 10:7 but it is in his *h* to destroy
Is 10:12 stout *h* of the king of Assyria
Is 13:7 and every man's *h* shall melt
Is 14:13 For thou hast said in thine *h*
Is 15:5 My *h* shall cry out for Moab
Is 19:1 the *h* of Egypt shall melt in the
Is 21:4 My *h* panted, fearfulness
Is 29:13 have removed their *h* far from me
Is 30:29 and gladness of *h*, as when one
Is 32:4 The *h* also of the rash shall
Is 32:6 his *h* will work iniquity, to
Is 33:18 Thine *h* shall meditate terror
Is 35:4 to them that are of a fearful *h*
Is 38:3 thee in truth and with a perfect *h*
Is 42:25 him, yet he laid it not to *h*
Is 44:19 And none considereth in his *h*
Is 44:20 a deceived *h* hath turned him
Is 47:7 not lay these things to thy *h*
Is 47:8 that sayest in thine *h*, I am, and
Is 47:10 and thou hast said in thine *h*
Is 49:21 Then shalt thou say in thine *h*
Is 51:7 the people in whose *h* is my law
Is 57:1 and no man layeth it to *h*
Is 57:11 me, nor laid it to thy *h*
Is 57:15 to revive the *h* of the contrite
Is 57:17 on frowardly in the way of his *h*
Is 59:13 uttering from the *h* words of
Is 60:5 thine *h* shall fear, and be
Is 63:4 the day of vengeance is in mine *h*
Is 63:17 hardened our *h* from thy fear
Is 65:14 servants shall sing for joy of *h*

| | |
|---|---|
| Is 65:14 | but ye shall cry for sorrow of *h* |
| Is 66:14 | your *h* shall rejoice, and your |
| Jer 3:10 | turned unto me with her whole *h* |
| Jer 3:15 | you pastors according to mine *h* |
| Jer 3:17 | the imagination of their evil *h* |
| Jer 4:4 | take away the foreskins of your *h* |
| Jer 4:9 | that the *h* of the king shall |
| Jer 4:9 | perish, and the *h* of the princes |
| Jer 4:14 | wash thine *h* from wickedness, |
| Jer 4:18 | because it reacheth unto thine *h* |
| Jer 4:19 | I am pained at my very *h* |
| Jer 4:19 | my *h* maketh a noise in me |
| Jer 5:23 | a revolting and a rebellious *h* |
| Jer 5:24 | Neither say they in their *h* |
| Jer 7:24 | the imagination of their evil *h* |
| Jer 7:31 | not, neither came it into my *h* |
| Jer 8:18 | sorrow, my *h* is faint in me |
| Jer 9:8 | but in *h* he layeth his wait |
| Jer 9:14 | the imagination of their own *h* |
| Jer 9:26 | Israel are uncircumcised in the *h* |
| Jer 11:8 | the imagination of their evil *h* |
| Jer 11:20 | that triest the reins and the *h* |
| Jer 12:3 | me, and tried mine *h* toward thee |
| Jer 12:11 | because no man layeth it to *h* |
| Jer 13:10 | in the imagination of their *h* |
| Jer 13:22 | And if thou say in thine *h* |
| Jer 14:14 | nought, and the deceit of their *h* |
| Jer 15:16 | me the joy and rejoicing of mine *h* |
| Jer 16:12 | the imagination of his evil *h* |
| Jer 17:1 | graven upon the table of their *h* |
| Jer 17:5 | whose *h* departeth from the LORD |
| Jer 17:9 | The *h* is deceitful above all |
| Jer 17:10 | I the LORD search the *h*, I try |
| Jer 18:12 | do the imagination of his evil *h* |
| Jer 20:9 | But his word was in mine *h* as a |
| Jer 20:12 | and seest the reins and the *h* |
| Jer 22:17 | thine *h* are not but for thy |
| Jer 23:9 | Mine *h* within me is broken |
| Jer 23:16 | speak a vision of their own *h* |
| Jer 23:17 | the imagination of his own *h* |
| Jer 23:20 | performed the thoughts of his *h* |
| Jer 23:26 | *h* of the prophets that prophesy |
| Jer 23:26 | of the deceit of their own *h* |
| Jer 24:7 | I will give them an *h* to know me |
| Jer 24:7 | return unto me with their whole *h* |
| Jer 29:13 | search for me with all your *h* |
| Jer 30:21 | engaged his *h* to approach unto me |
| Jer 30:24 | performed the intents of his *h* |
| Jer 31:21 | set thine *h* toward the highway, |
| Jer 32:39 | And I will give them one *h* |
| Jer 32:41 | land assuredly with my whole *h* |
| Jer 48:29 | and the haughtiness of his *h* |
| Jer 48:31 | mine *h* shall mourn for the men of |
| Jer 48:36 | Therefore mine *h* shall sound for |
| Jer 48:36 | mine *h* shall sound like pipes for |
| Jer 48:41 | as the *h* of a woman in her pangs |
| Jer 49:16 | thee, and the pride of thine *h* |
| Jer 49:22 | at that day shall the *h* of the |
| Jer 49:22 | as the *h* of a woman in her pangs |
| Jer 51:46 | And lest your *h* faint, and ye fear |
| Lam 1:20 | mine *h* is turned within me |
| Lam 1:22 | sighs are many, and my *h* is faint |
| Lam 2:18 | Their *h* cried unto the Lord, O |
| Lam 2:19 | *h* like water before the face of |
| Lam 3:41 | Let us lift up our *h* with our |
| Lam 3:51 | Mine eye affecteth mine *h* because |
| Lam 3:65 | Give them sorrow of *h*, thy curse |
| Lam 5:15 | The joy of our *h* is ceased |
| Lam 5:17 | For this our *h* is faint |
| Eze 3:10 | unto thee receive in thine *h* |
| Eze 6:9 | I am broken with their whorish *h* |
| Eze 11:19 | And I will give them one *h* |
| Eze 11:19 | the stony *h* out of their flesh |
| Eze 11:19 | and will give them an *h* of flesh |
| Eze 11:21 | But as for them whose *h* walketh |
| Eze 11:21 | the *h* of their detestable things |
| Eze 13:17 | which prophesy out of their own *h* |
| Eze 13:22 | made the *h* of the righteous sad |
| Eze 14:3 | set up their idols in their *h* |
| Eze 14:4 | setteth up his idols in his *h* |
| Eze 14:5 | house of Israel in their own *h* |
| Eze 14:7 | and setteth up his idols in his *h* |
| Eze 16:30 | How weak is thine *h*, saith the |
| Eze 18:31 | and make you a new *h* and a new |
| Eze 20:16 | for their *h* went after their |
| Eze 21:7 | every *h* shall melt, and all hands |
| Eze 21:15 | gates, that their *h* may faint |
| Eze 22:14 | Can thine *h* endure, or can thine |
| Eze 25:6 | rejoiced in *h* with all thy |
| Eze 25:15 | vengeance with a despiteful *h* |
| Eze 27:31 | for thee with bitterness of *h* |
| Eze 28:2 | Because thine *h* is lifted up |
| Eze 28:2 | set thine *h* as the *h* of God |
| Eze 28:5 | thine *h* is lifted up because of |
| Eze 28:6 | set thine *h* as the *h* of God |
| Eze 28:17 | Thine *h* was lifted up because of |
| Eze 31:10 | his *h* is lifted up in his height |
| Eze 33:31 | but their *h* goeth after their |
| Eze 36:5 | with the joy of all their *h* |
| Eze 36:26 | A new *h* also will I give you, and |
| Eze 36:26 | the stony *h* out of your flesh |
| Eze 36:26 | and I will give you an *h* of flesh |
| Eze 40:4 | set thine *h* upon all that I shall |
| Eze 44:7 | strangers, uncircumcised in *h* |
| Eze 44:9 | No stranger, uncircumcised in *h* |
| Dan 1:8 | in his *h* that he would not defile |
| Dan 2:30 | know the thoughts of thy *h* |
| Dan 4:16 | Let his *h* be changed from man's, |
| Dan 4:16 | let a beast's *h* be given unto him |
| Dan 5:20 | But when his *h* was lifted up, and |
| Dan 5:21 | his *h* was made like the beasts, |
| Dan 5:22 | hast not humbled thine *h* |
| Dan 6:14 | set his *h* on Daniel to deliver |
| Dan 7:4 | a man's *h* was given to it |
| Dan 7:28 | but I kept the matter in my *h* |
| Dan 8:25 | he shall magnify himself in his *h* |
| Dan 10:12 | didst set thine *h* to understand |
| Dan 11:12 | his *h* shall be lifted up |
| Dan 11:28 | his *h* shall be against the holy |
| Hos 4:8 | they set their *h* on their |
| Hos 4:11 | wine and new wine take away the *h* |
| Hos 7:6 | made ready their *h* like an oven |
| Hos 7:11 | is like a silly dove without *h* |
| Hos 7:14 | not cried unto me with their *h* |
| Hos 10:2 | Their *h* is divided |
| Hos 11:8 | mine *h* is turned within me, my |
| Hos 13:6 | filled, and their *h* was exalted |
| Hos 13:8 | and will rend the caul of their *h* |
| Joel 2:12 | ye even to me with all your *h* |
| Joel 2:13 | And rend your *h*, and not your |
| Obad 3 | of thine *h* hath deceived thee |
| Obad 3 | that saith in his *h*, Who shall |
| Nah 2:10 | the *h* melteth, and the knees smite |
| Zeph 1:12 | that say in their *h*, The LORD |
| Zeph 2:15 | carelessly, that said in her *h* |
| Zeph 3:14 | be glad and rejoice with all the *h* |
| Zec 7:10 | against his brother in your *h* |
| Zec 10:7 | their *h* shall rejoice as through |
| Zec 10:7 | their *h* shall rejoice in the LORD |
| Zec 12:5 | of Judah shall say in their *h* |
| Mal 2:2 | and if ye will not lay it to *h* |
| Mal 2:2 | because ye do not lay it to *h* |
| Mal 4:6 | he shall turn the *h* of the |
| Mal 4:6 | the *h* of the children to their |
| Mt 5:8 | Blessed are the pure in *h* |
| Mt 5:28 | with her already in his *h* |
| Mt 6:21 | is, there will your *h* be also |
| Mt 11:29 | for I am meek and lowly in *h* |
| Mt 12:34 | of the *h* the mouth speaketh |
| Mt 12:35 | the *h* bringeth forth good things |
| Mt 12:40 | nights in the *h* of the earth |
| Mt 13:15 | this people's *h* is waxed gross |
| Mt 13:15 | and should understand with their *h* |
| Mt 13:19 | away that which was sown in his *h* |
| Mt 15:8 | but their *h* is far from me |
| Mt 15:18 | the mouth come forth from the *h* |
| Mt 15:19 | For out of the *h* proceed evil |
| Mt 22:37 | the Lord thy God with all thy *h* |
| Mt 24:48 | evil servant shall say in his *h* |
| Mk 6:52 | for their *h* was hardened |
| Mk 7:6 | but their *h* is far from me |
| Mk 7:19 | it entereth not into his *h* |
| Mk 7:21 | from within, out of the *h* of men |
| Mk 8:17 | have ye your *h* yet hardened |
| Mk 10:5 | For the hardness of your *h* he |
| Mk 11:23 | and shall not doubt in his *h* |
| Mk 12:30 | the Lord thy God with all thy *h* |
| Mk 12:33 | And to love him with all the *h* |
| Mk 16:14 | their unbelief and hardness of *h* |
| Lk 2:19 | things, and pondered them in her *h* |
| Lk 2:51 | kept all these sayings in her *h* |
| Lk 6:45 | *h* bringeth forth that which is |
| Lk 6:45 | *h* bringeth forth that which is |
| Lk 6:45 | of the *h* his mouth speaketh |
| Lk 8:15 | which in an honest and good *h* |
| Lk 9:47 | perceiving the thought of their *h* |
| Lk 10:27 | the Lord thy God with all thy *h* |
| Lk 12:34 | is, there will your *h* be also |
| Lk 12:45 | and if that servant say in his *h* |
| Lk 24:25 | slow of *h* to believe all that the |
| Lk 24:32 | Did not our *h* burn within us, |
| Jn 12:40 | their eyes, and hardened their *h* |
| Jn 12:40 | eyes, nor understand with their *h* |
| Jn 13:2 | put into the *h* of Judas Iscariot |
| Jn 14:1 | Let not your *h* be troubled |
| Jn 14:27 | Let not your *h* be troubled |
| Jn 16:6 | you, sorrow hath filled your *h* |
| Jn 16:22 | your *h* shall rejoice, and your joy |
| Acts 2:26 | Therefore did my *h* rejoice |
| Acts 2:37 | they were pricked in their *h* |
| Acts 2:46 | with gladness and singleness of *h* |
| Acts 4:32 | them that believed were of one *h* |
| Acts 5:3 | thine *h* to lie to the Holy Ghost |
| Acts 5:4 | conceived this thing in thine *h* |
| Acts 5:33 | that, they were cut to the *h* |
| Acts 7:23 | it came into his *h* to visit his |
| Acts 7:51 | stiffnecked and uncircumcised in *h* |
| Acts 7:54 | things, they were cut to the *h* |
| Acts 8:21 | for thy *h* is not right in the |
| Acts 8:22 | of thine *h* may be forgiven thee |
| Acts 8:37 | thou believest with all thine *h* |
| Acts 11:23 | that with purpose of *h* they would |
| Acts 13:22 | of Jesse, a man after mine own *h* |
| Acts 16:14 | whose *h* the Lord opened, that she |
| Acts 21:13 | ye to weep and to break mine *h* |
| Acts 28:27 | For the *h* of this people is waxed |
| Acts 28:27 | ears, and understand with their *h* |
| Rom 1:21 | and their foolish *h* was darkened |
| Rom 2:5 | impenitent *h* treasurest up unto |
| Rom 2:29 | and circumcision is that of the *h* |
| Rom 6:17 | but ye have obeyed from the *h* |
| Rom 9:2 | and continual sorrow in my *h* |
| Rom 10:6 | on this wise, Say not in thine *h* |
| Rom 10:8 | even in thy mouth, and in thy *h* |
| Rom 10:9 | shalt believe in thine *h* that God |
| Rom 10:10 | For with the *h* man believeth unto |
| 1Cor 2:9 | have entered into the *h* of man |
| 1Cor 7:37 | that standeth stedfast in his *h* |
| 1Cor 7:37 | hath so decreed in his *h* that he |
| 1Cor 14:25 | secrets of his *h* made manifest |
| 2Cor 2:4 | anguish of *h* I wrote unto you |
| 2Cor 3:3 | but in fleshly tables of the *h* |
| 2Cor 3:15 | is read, the vail is upon their *h* |
| 2Cor 5:12 | glory in appearance, and not in *h* |
| 2Cor 6:11 | open unto you, our *h* is enlarged |
| 2Cor 8:16 | care into the *h* of Titus for you |
| 2Cor 9:7 | as he purposeth in his *h*, so let |
| Eph 4:18 | of the blindness of their *h* |
| Eph 5:19 | melody in your *h* to the Lord |
| Eph 6:5 | in singleness of your *h*, as unto |
| Eph 6:6 | doing the will of God from the *h* |
| Phil 1:7 | all, because I have you in my *h* |
| Col 3:22 | but in singleness of *h*, fearing |
| 1Th 2:17 | short time in presence, not in *h* |
| 1Ti 1:5 | is charity out of a pure *h* |
| 2Ti 2:22 | call on the Lord out of a pure *h* |
| Heb 3:10 | They do alway err in their *h* |
| Heb 3:12 | any of you an evil *h* of unbelief |
| Heb 4:12 | the thoughts and intents of the *h* |
| Heb 10:22 | true *h* in full assurance of faith |
| Heb 13:9 | the *h* be established with grace |
| Jas 1:26 | tongue, but deceiveth his own *h* |
| 1Pet 1:22 | another with a pure *h* fervently |
| 1Pet 3:4 | let it be the hidden man of the *h* |
| 2Pet 2:14 | an *h* they have exercised with |
| 1Jn 3:20 | For if our *h* condemn |
| 1Jn 3:20 | God is greater than our *h* |
| 1Jn 3:21 | if our *h* condemn us not, then |
| Rev 18:7 | for she saith in her *h*, I sit a |

## HEARTED

| | |
|---|---|
| Ex 28:3 | speak unto all that are wise *h* |
| Ex 31:6 | that are wise *h* I have put wisdom |
| Ex 35:10 | every wise *h* among you shall come |
| Ex 35:22 | women, as many as were willing *h* |
| Ex 35:25 | wise *h* did spin with their hands |
| Ex 36:1 | and Aholiab, and every wise *h* man |
| Ex 36:2 | and Aholiab, and every wise *h* man |
| Ex 36:8 | every wise *h* man among them that |

## HEARTH

| | |
|---|---|
| Gen 18:6 | it, and make cakes upon the *h* |
| Ps 102:3 | and my bones are burned as an *h* |
| Is 30:14 | a sherd to take fire from the *h* |
| Jer 36:22 | fire on the *h* burning before him |
| Jer 36:23 | into the fire that was on the *h* |
| Jer 36:23 | in the fire that was on the *h* |
| Zec 12:6 | like an *h* of fire among the wood |

## HEARTS

| | |
|---|---|
| Gen 18:5 | of bread, and comfort ye your *h* |
| Ex 14:17 | harden the *h* of the Egyptians |

Ex 31:6 in the *h* of all that are wise
Lev 26:36 send a faintness into their *h* in
Lev 26:41 their uncircumcised *h* be humbled
Deut 20:3 let not your *h* faint, fear not,
Deut 32:46 Set your *h* unto all the words
Josh 2:11 our *h* did melt, neither did there
Josh 7:5 wherefore the *h* of the people
Josh 11:20 was of the LORD to harden their *h*
Josh 23:14 and ye know in all your *h* and in
Judg 9:3 their *h* inclined to follow
Judg 16:25 to pass, when their *h* were merry
Judg 19:22 as they were making their *h* merry
1Sa 6:6 then do ye harden your *h*, as the
1Sa 6:6 and Pharaoh hardened their *h*
1Sa 7:3 unto the LORD with all your *h*
1Sa 7:3 prepare your *h* unto the LORD, and
1Sa 10:26 of men, whose *h* God had touched
2Sa 15:6 stole the *h* of the men of Israel
2Sa 15:13 The *h* of the men of Israel are
1Kin 8:39 knowest the *h* of all the children
1Kin 8:58 he may incline our *h* unto him
1Chr 28:9 for the LORD searcheth all *h*
2Chr 6:14 walk before thee with all their *h*
2Chr 6:30 the *h* of the children of men
2Chr 11:16 of Israel such as set their *h* to
2Chr 20:33 *h* unto the God of their fathers
Job 1:5 sinned, and cursed God in their *h*
Ps 7:9 the righteous God trieth the *h*
Ps 28:3 but mischief is in their *h*
Ps 33:15 He fashioneth their *h* alike
Ps 35:25 Let them not say in their *h*
Ps 74:8 They said in their *h*, Let us
Ps 90:12 we may apply our *h* unto wisdom
Ps 125:4 them that are upright in their *h*
Prov 15:11 then the *h* of the children of men
Prov 17:3 but the LORD trieth the *h*
Prov 21:2 but the LORD pondereth the *h*
Prov 31:6 unto those that be of heavy *h*
Is 44:18 and their *h*, that they cannot
Jer 31:33 parts, and write it in their *h*
Jer 32:40 but I will put my fear in their *h*
Jer 42:20 For ye dissembled in your *h*
Jer 48:41 the mighty men's *h* in Moab at
Eze 13:2 that prophesy out of their own *h*
Eze 32:9 also vex the *h* of many people
Dan 11:27 both these kings' *h* shall be to
Hos 7:2 their *h* that I remember all their
Zec 7:12 they made their *h* as an adamant
Zec 8:17 in your *h* against his neighbour
Mt 9:4 Wherefore think ye evil in your *h*
Mt 18:35 if ye from your *h* forgive not
Mt 19:8 *h* suffered you to put away your
Mk 2:6 there, and reasoning in their *h*
Mk 2:8 reason ye these things in your *h*
Mk 3:5 for the hardness of their *h*
Mk 4:15 the word that was sown in their *h*
Lk 1:17 to turn the *h* of the fathers to
Lk 1:51 in the imagination of their *h*
Lk 1:66 them laid them up in their *h*
Lk 2:35 of many *h* may be revealed
Lk 3:15 all men mused in their *h* of John
Lk 5:22 them, What reason ye in your *h*
Lk 8:12 away the word out of their *h*
Lk 16:15 but God knoweth your *h*
Lk 21:14 Settle it therefore in your *h*
Lk 21:26 Men's *h* failing them for fear, and
Lk 21:34 lest at any time your *h* be
Lk 24:38 why do thoughts arise in your *h*
Acts 1:24 which knowest the *h* of all men
Acts 7:39 in their *h* turned back again into
Acts 14:17 seasons, filling our *h* with food
Acts 15:8 And God, which knoweth the *h*
Acts 15:9 them, purifying their *h* by faith
Rom 1:24 through the lusts of their own *h*
Rom 2:15 of the law written in their *h*
Rom 5:5 our *h* by the Holy Ghost which is
Rom 8:27 he that searcheth the *h* knoweth
Rom 16:18 deceive the *h* of the simple
1Cor 4:5 manifest the counsels of the *h*
2Cor 1:22 earnest of the Spirit in our *h*
2Cor 3:2 are our epistle written in our *h*
2Cor 4:6 of darkness, hath shined in our *h*
2Cor 7:3 that ye are in our *h* to die
Gal 4:6 the Spirit of his Son into your *h*
Eph 3:17 may dwell in your *h* by faith
Eph 6:22 and that he might comfort your *h*
Phil 4:7 understanding, shall keep your *h*
Col 2:2 That their *h* might be comforted,
Col 3:15 the peace of God rule in your *h*
Col 3:16 with grace in your *h* to the Lord
Col 4:8 your estate, and comfort your *h*
1Th 2:4 men, but God, which trieth our *h*
1Th 3:13 *h* unblameable in holiness before
2Th 2:17 Comfort your *h*, and stablish you
2Th 3:5 your *h* into the love of God
Heb 3:8 Harden not your *h*, as in the
Heb 3:15 hear his voice, harden not your *h*
Heb 4:7 hear his voice, harden not your *h*
Heb 8:10 mind, and write them in their *h*
Heb 10:16 I will put my laws into their *h*
Heb 10:22 having our *h* sprinkled from an
Jas 3:14 envying and strife in your *h*
Jas 4:8 and purify your *h*, ye double
Jas 5:5 ye have nourished your *h*, as in a
Jas 5:8 ye also patient; stablish your *h*
1Pet 3:15 sanctify the Lord God in your *h*
2Pet 1:19 and the day star arise in your *h*
1Jn 3:19 and shall assure our *h* before him
Rev 2:23 he which searcheth the reins and *h*
Rev 17:17 put in their *h* to fulfil his will

### HEAT

Gen 8:22 seedtime and harvest, and cold and *h*
Gen 18:1 the tent door in the *h* of the day
Deut 29:24 what meaneth the *h* of this great
Deut 32:24 and devoured with burning *h*
1Sa 11:11 Ammonites until the *h* of the day
2Sa 4:5 came about the *h* of the day to
1Kin 1:1 him with clothes, but he gat no *h*
1Kin 1:2 that my lord the king may get *h*
Job 24:19 *h* consume the snow waters
Job 30:30 me, and my bones are burned with *h*
Ps 19:6 is nothing hid from the *h* thereof
Eccl 4:11 lie together, then they have *h*
Is 4:6 shadow in the daytime from the *h*
Is 18:4 place like a clear *h* upon herbs
Is 18:4 cloud of dew in the *h* of harvest
Is 25:4 the storm, a shadow from the *h*
Is 25:5 as the *h* in a dry place
Is 25:5 even the *h* with the shadow of a
Is 49:10 neither shall the *h* nor sun smite
Jer 17:8 and shall not see when *h* cometh
Jer 36:30 be cast out in the day to the *h*
Jer 51:39 In their *h* I will make their
Eze 3:14 bitterness, in the *h* of my spirit
Dan 3:19 commanded that they should *h* the
Mt 20:12 borne the burden and *h* of the day
Lk 12:55 blow, ye say, There will be *h*
Acts 28:3 there came a viper out of the *h*
Jas 1:11 no sooner risen with a burning *h*
2Pet 3:10 shall melt with fervent *h*
2Pet 3:12 shall melt with fervent *h*
Rev 7:16 the sun light on them, nor any *h*
Rev 16:9 And men were scorched with great *h*

### HEATHEN

Lev 25:44 shall be of the *h* that are round
Lev 26:33 And I will scatter you among the *h*
Lev 26:38 And ye shall perish among the *h*
Lev 26:45 of Egypt in the sight of the *h*
Deut 4:27 be left few in number among the *h*
2Sa 22:44 hast kept me to be head of the *h*
2Sa 22:50 unto thee, O LORD, among the *h*
2Kin 16:3 to the abominations of the *h*
2Kin 17:8 walked in the statutes of the *h*
2Kin 17:11 as did the *h* whom the LORD
2Kin 17:15 went after the *h* that were round
2Kin 21:2 after the abominations of the *h*
1Chr 16:24 Declare his glory among the *h*
1Chr 16:35 and deliver us from the *h*
2Chr 20:6 over all the kingdoms of the *h*
2Chr 28:3 the *h* whom the LORD had cast out
2Chr 33:2 unto the abominations of the *h*
2Chr 33:9 to err, and to do worse than the *h*
2Chr 36:14 all the abominations of the *h*
Ezr 6:21 filthiness of the *h* of the land
Neh 5:8 Jews, which were sold unto the *h*
Neh 5:9 the reproach of the *h* our enemies
Neh 5:17 among the *h* that are about us
Neh 6:6 It is reported among the *h*
Neh 6:16 all the *h* that were about us saw
Ps 2:1 Why do the *h* rage, and the people
Ps 2:8 thee the *h* for thine inheritance
Ps 9:5 Thou hast rebuked the *h*, thou
Ps 9:15 The *h* are sunk down in the pit
Ps 9:19 let the *h* be judged in thy sight
Ps 10:16 the *h* are perished out of his
Ps 18:43 hast made me the head of the *h*
Ps 18:49 unto thee, O LORD, among the *h*
Ps 33:10 the counsel of the *h* to nought
Ps 44:2 drive out the *h* with thy hand
Ps 44:11 and hast scattered us among the *h*
Ps 44:14 makest us a byword among the *h*
Ps 46:6 The *h* raged, the kingdoms were
Ps 46:10 I will be exalted among the *h*
Ps 47:8 God reigneth over the *h*
Ps 59:5 Israel, awake to visit all the *h*
Ps 59:8 shalt have all the *h* in derision
Ps 78:55 He cast out the *h* also before
Ps 79:1 the *h* are come into thine
Ps 79:6 the *h* that have not known thee
Ps 79:10 Wherefore should the *h* say
Ps 79:10 let him be known among the *h* in
Ps 80:8 thou hast cast out the *h*, and
Ps 94:10 He that chastiseth the *h*, shall
Ps 96:3 Declare his glory among the *h*
Ps 96:10 Say among the *h* that the LORD
Ps 98:2 shewed in the sight of the *h*
Ps 102:15 So the *h* shall fear the name of
Ps 105:44 And gave them the lands of the *h*
Ps 106:35 But were mingled among the *h*
Ps 106:41 gave them into the hand of the *h*
Ps 106:47 and gather us from among the *h*
Ps 110:6 He shall judge among the *h*
Ps 111:6 give them the heritage of the *h*
Ps 115:2 Wherefore should the *h* say
Ps 126:2 then said they among the *h*
Ps 135:15 The idols of the *h* are silver
Ps 149:7 To execute vengeance upon the *h*
Is 16:8 the lords of the *h* have broken
Jer 9:16 scatter them also among the *h*
Jer 10:2 LORD, Learn not the way of the *h*
Jer 10:2 for the *h* are dismayed at them
Jer 10:25 upon the *h* that know thee not
Jer 18:13 Ask ye now among the *h*, who hath
Jer 49:14 an ambassador is sent unto the *h*
Jer 49:15 will make thee small among the *h*
Lam 1:3 she dwelleth among the *h*, she
Lam 1:10 the *h* entered into her sanctuary
Lam 4:15 wandered, they said among the *h*
Lam 4:20 shadow we shall live among the *h*
Eze 7:24 I will bring the worst of the *h*
Eze 11:12 of the *h* that are round about you
Eze 11:16 cast them far off among the *h*
Eze 12:16 among the *h* whither they come
Eze 16:14 forth among the *h* for thy beauty
Eze 20:9 not be polluted before the *h*
Eze 20:14 not be polluted before the *h*
Eze 20:22 be polluted in the sight of the *h*
Eze 20:23 I would scatter them among the *h*
Eze 20:32 that ye say, We will be as the *h*
Eze 20:41 be sanctified in you before the *h*
Eze 22:4 I made thee a reproach unto the *h*
Eze 22:15 I will scatter thee among the *h*
Eze 22:16 in thyself in the sight of the *h*
Eze 23:30 hast gone a whoring after the *h*
Eze 25:7 deliver thee for a spoil to the *h*
Eze 25:8 of Judah is like unto all the *h*
Eze 28:25 in them in the sight of the *h*
Eze 30:3 it shall be the time of the *h*
Eze 31:11 hand of the mighty one of the *h*
Eze 31:17 his shadow in the midst of the *h*
Eze 34:28 shall no more be a prey to the *h*
Eze 34:29 bear the shame of the *h* any more
Eze 36:3 unto the residue of the *h*
Eze 36:4 of the *h* that are round about
Eze 36:5 against the residue of the *h*
Eze 36:6 ye have borne the shame of the *h*
Eze 36:7 Surely the *h* that are about you,
Eze 36:15 thee the shame of the *h* any more
Eze 36:19 And I scattered them among the *h*
Eze 36:20 And when they entered unto the *h*
Eze 36:21 Israel had profaned among the *h*
Eze 36:22 ye have profaned among the *h*
Eze 36:23 which was profaned among the *h*
Eze 36:23 the *h* shall know that I am the
Eze 36:24 I will take you from among the *h*
Eze 36:30 reproach of famine among the *h*
Eze 36:36 Then the *h* that are left round
Eze 37:21 of Israel from among the *h*
Eze 37:28 the *h* shall know that I the LORD
Eze 38:16 that the *h* may know me, when I
Eze 39:7 the *h* shall know that I am the
Eze 39:21 I will set my glory among the *h*
Eze 39:21 all the *h* shall see my judgment
Eze 39:23 the *h* shall know that the house
Eze 39:28 be led into captivity among the *h*
Joel 2:17 that the *h* should rule over them
Joel 2:19 make you a reproach among the *h*
Joel 3:11 yourselves, and come, all ye *h*
Joel 3:12 Let the *h* be wakened, and come up

Joel 3:12 to judge all the *h* round about
Amos 9:12 remnant of Edom, and of all the *h*
Obad 1 an ambassador is sent among the *h*
Obad 2 have made thee small among the *h*
Obad 15 the LORD is near upon all the *h*
Obad 16 so shall all the *h* drink
Mic 5:15 in anger and fury upon the *h*
Hab 1:5 Behold ye among the *h*, and regard,
Hab 3:12 thou didst thresh the *h* in anger
Zeph 2:11 even all the isles of the *h*
Hag 2:22 strength of the kingdoms of the *h*
Zec 1:15 with the *h* that are at ease
Zec 8:13 as ye were a curse among the *h*
Zec 9:10 he shall speak peace unto the *h*
Zec 14:14 the wealth of all the *h* round
Zec 14:18 the LORD will smite the *h* that
Mal 1:11 name shall be great among the *h*
Mal 1:14 my name is dreadful among the *h*
Mt 6:7 not vain repetitions, as the *h* do
Mt 18:17 let him be unto thee as an *h* man
Acts 4:25 hast said, Why did the *h* rage
2Cor 11:26 countrymen, in perils by the *h*
Gal 1:16 I might preach him among the *h*
Gal 2:9 that we should go unto the *h*
Gal 3:8 would justify the *h* through faith

**HEAVE**

Ex 29:27 and the shoulder of the *h* offering
Ex 29:28 for it is an *h* offering
Ex 29:28 it shall be an *h* offering from
Ex 29:28 even their *h* offering unto the
Lev 7:14 for an *h* offering unto the LORD
Lev 7:32 *h* offering of the sacrifices of
Lev 7:34 the *h* shoulder have I taken of
Lev 10:14 *h* shoulder shall ye eat in a
Lev 10:15 The *h* shoulder and the wave breast
Num 6:20 the wave breast and *h* shoulder
Num 15:19 ye shall offer up an *h* offering
Num 15:20 of your dough for an *h* offering
Num 15:20 as ye do the *h* offering of the
Num 15:20 threshingfloor, so shall ye *h* it
Num 15:21 an *h* offering in your generations
Num 18:8 *h* offerings of all the hallowed
Num 18:11 the *h* offering of their gift,
Num 18:19 All the *h* offerings of the holy
Num 18:24 as an *h* offering unto the LORD
Num 18:26 then ye shall offer up an *h*
Num 18:27 this your *h* offering shall be
Num 18:28 Thus ye also shall offer an *h*
Num 18:28 *h* offering to Aaron the priest
Num 18:29 every *h* offering of the LORD
Num 31:29 for an *h* offering of the LORD
Num 31:41 which was the LORD's *h* offering
Deut 12:6 *h* offerings of your hand, and your
Deut 12:11 the *h* offering of your hand, and
Deut 12:17 or *h* offering of thine hand

**HEAVEN**

Gen 1:1 the beginning God created the *h*
Gen 1:8 And God called the firmament *H*
Gen 1:9 Let the waters under the *h* be
Gen 1:14 the *h* to divide the day from the
Gen 1:15 *h* to give light upon the earth
Gen 1:17 *h* to give light upon the earth
Gen 1:20 earth in the open firmament of *h*
Gen 6:17 the breath of life, from under *h*
Gen 7:11 and the windows of *h* were opened
Gen 7:19 that were under the whole *h*
Gen 7:23 things, and the fowl of the *h*
Gen 8:2 and the windows of *h* were stopped
Gen 8:2 the rain from *h* was restrained
Gen 11:4 tower, whose top may reach unto *h*
Gen 14:19 the most high God, possessor of *h*
Gen 14:22 most high God, the possessor of *h*
Gen 15:5 and said, Look now toward *h*
Gen 19:24 and fire from the LORD out of *h*
Gen 21:17 of God called to Hagar out of *h*
Gen 22:11 the LORD called unto him out of *h*
Gen 22:15 Abraham out of *h* the second time
Gen 22:17 thy seed as the stars of the *h*
Gen 24:3 swear by the LORD, the God of *h*
Gen 24:7 The LORD God of *h*, which took me
Gen 26:4 to multiply as the stars of *h*
Gen 27:28 God give thee of the dew of *h*
Gen 27:39 and of the dew of *h* from above
Gen 28:12 and the top of it reached to *h*
Gen 28:17 of God, and this is the gate of *h*
Gen 49:25 thee with blessings of *h* above
Ex 9:8 the *h* in the sight of Pharaoh
Ex 9:10 and Moses sprinkled it up toward *h*
Ex 9:22 Stretch forth thine hand toward *h*
Ex 9:23 stretched forth his rod toward *h*
Ex 10:21 Stretch out thine hand toward *h*
Ex 10:22 stretched forth his hand toward *h*
Ex 16:4 I will rain bread from *h* for you
Ex 17:14 of Amalek from under *h*
Ex 20:4 of any thing that is in *h* above
Ex 20:11 For in six days the LORD made *h*
Ex 20:22 I have talked with you from *h*
Ex 24:10 the body of *h* in his clearness
Ex 31:17 for in six days the LORD made *h*
Ex 32:13 your seed as the stars of *h*
Lev 26:19 and I will make your *h* as iron
Deut 1:10 as the stars of *h* for multitude
Deut 1:28 are great and walled up to *h*
Deut 2:25 that are under the whole *h*
Deut 3:24 God is there in *h* or in earth
Deut 4:11 with fire unto the midst of *h*
Deut 4:19 thou lift up thine eyes unto *h*
Deut 4:19 the stars, even all the host of *h*
Deut 4:19 all nations under the whole *h*
Deut 4:26 I call *h* and earth to witness
Deut 4:32 the one side of *h* unto the other
Deut 4:36 Out of *h* he made thee to hear his
Deut 4:39 the LORD he is God in *h* above
Deut 5:8 of any thing that is in *h* above
Deut 7:24 destroy their name from under *h*
Deut 9:1 cities great and fenced up to *h*
Deut 9:14 blot out their name from under *h*
Deut 10:14 Behold, the *h* and the *h* of
Deut 10:22 as the stars of *h* for multitude
Deut 11:11 drinketh water of the rain of *h*
Deut 11:17 against you, and he shut up the *h*
Deut 11:21 as the days of *h* upon the earth
Deut 17:3 or moon, or any of the host of *h*
Deut 25:19 of Amalek from under *h*
Deut 26:15 from thy holy habitation, from *h*
Deut 28:12 the *h* to give the rain unto thy
Deut 28:23 thy *h* that is over thy head shall
Deut 28:24 from *h* shall it come down upon
Deut 28:62 as the stars of *h* for multitude
Deut 29:20 blot out his name from under *h*
Deut 30:4 out unto the outmost parts of *h*
Deut 30:12 It is not in *h*, that thou
Deut 30:12 say, Who shall go up for us to *h*
Deut 30:19 I call *h* and earth to record this
Deut 31:28 words in their ears, and call *h*
Deut 32:40 For I lift up my hand to *h*
Deut 33:13 for the precious things of *h*
Deut 33:26 who rideth upon the *h* in thy help
Josh 2:11 your God, he is God in *h* above
Josh 8:20 of the city ascended up to *h*
Josh 10:11 from *h* upon them unto Azekah
Josh 10:13 sun stood still in the midst of *h*
Judg 5:20 They fought from *h*
Judg 13:20 up toward *h* from off the altar
Judg 20:40 of the city ascended up to *h*
1Sa 2:10 out of *h* shall he thunder upon
1Sa 5:12 the cry of the city went up to *h*
2Sa 18:9 and he was taken up between the *h*
2Sa 21:10 water dropped upon them out of *h*
2Sa 22:8 the foundations of *h* moved
2Sa 22:14 The LORD thundered from *h*
1Kin 8:22 spread forth his hands toward *h*
1Kin 8:23 in *h* above, or on earth beneath,
1Kin 8:27 behold, the *h* and *h* of
1Kin 8:30 hear thou in *h* thy dwelling place
1Kin 8:32 Then hear thou in *h*, and do, and
1Kin 8:34 Then hear thou in *h*, and forgive
1Kin 8:35 When *h* is shut up, and there is no
1Kin 8:36 Then hear thou in *h*, and forgive
1Kin 8:39 Then hear thou in *h* thy dwelling
1Kin 8:43 Hear thou in *h* thy dwelling place
1Kin 8:45 Then hear thou in *h* their prayer
1Kin 8:49 in *h* thy dwelling place, and
1Kin 8:54 with his hands spread up to *h*
1Kin 18:45 that the *h* was black with clouds
1Kin 22:19 all the host of *h* standing by him
2Kin 1:10 then let fire come down from *h*
2Kin 1:10 And there came down fire from *h*
2Kin 1:12 of God, let fire come down from *h*
2Kin 1:12 the fire of God came down from *h*
2Kin 1:14 there came fire down from *h*
2Kin 2:1 up Elijah into *h* by a whirlwind
2Kin 2:11 went up by a whirlwind into *h*
2Kin 7:2 the LORD would make windows in *h*
2Kin 7:19 the LORD should make windows in *h*
2Kin 14:27 the name of Israel from under *h*
2Kin 17:16 and worshipped all the host of *h*
2Kin 19:15 thou hast made *h* and earth
2Kin 21:3 and worshipped all the host of *h*
2Kin 21:5 altars for all the host of *h* in
2Kin 23:4 grove, and for all the host of *h*
2Kin 23:5 planets, and to all the host of *h*
1Chr 21:16 stand between the earth and the *h*
1Chr 21:26 he answered him from *h* by fire
1Chr 29:11 for all that is in the *h* and in
2Chr 2:6 build him an house, seeing the *h*
2Chr 2:6 *h* of heavens cannot contain him
2Chr 2:12 LORD God of Israel, that made *h*
2Chr 6:13 spread forth his hands toward *h*
2Chr 6:14 is no God like thee in the *h*
2Chr 6:18 behold, *h* and the *h* of
2Chr 6:21 thy dwelling place, even from *h*
2Chr 6:23 Then hear thou from *h*, and do, and
2Chr 6:26 When the *h* is shut up, and there
2Chr 6:27 Then hear thou from *h*, and forgive
2Chr 6:30 thou from *h* thy dwelling place
2Chr 7:1 the fire came down from *h*
2Chr 7:13 If I shut up *h* that there be no
2Chr 7:14 then will I hear from *h*, and will
2Chr 18:18 all the host of *h* standing on his
2Chr 20:6 fathers, art not thou God in *h*
2Chr 28:9 in a rage that reacheth up unto *h*
2Chr 30:27 holy dwelling place, even unto *h*
2Chr 32:20 son of Amoz, prayed and cried to *h*
2Chr 33:3 and worshipped all the host of *h*
2Chr 33:5 altars for all the host of *h* in
2Chr 36:23 hath the LORD God of *h* given me
Ezr 1:2 The LORD God of *h* hath given me
Ezr 5:11 are the servants of the God of *h*
Ezr 5:12 provoked the God of *h* unto wrath
Ezr 6:9 burnt offerings of the God of *h*
Ezr 6:10 sweet savours unto the God of *h*
Ezr 7:12 scribe of the law of the God of *h*
Ezr 7:21 scribe of the law of the God of *h*
Ezr 7:23 is commanded by the God of *h*
Ezr 7:23 for the house of the God of *h*
Neh 1:4 and prayed before the God of *h*
Neh 1:5 I beseech thee, O LORD God of *h*
Neh 1:9 unto the uttermost part of the *h*
Neh 2:4 So I prayed to the God of *h*
Neh 2:20 and said unto them, The God of *h*
Neh 9:6 thou hast made *h*, the *h* of
Neh 9:6 the host of *h* worshippeth thee
Neh 9:13 and spakest with them from *h*
Neh 9:15 bread from *h* for their hunger
Neh 9:23 thou as the stars of *h*, and
Neh 9:27 thee, thou heardest them from *h*
Neh 9:28 thee, thou heardest them from *h*
Job 1:16 The fire of God is fallen from *h*
Job 2:12 dust upon their heads toward *h*
Job 11:8 It is as high as *h*
Job 16:19 now, behold, my witness is in *h*
Job 20:27 The *h* shall reveal his iniquity
Job 22:12 Is not God in the height of *h*
Job 22:14 and he walketh in the circuit of *h*
Job 26:11 The pillars of *h* tremble, and are
Job 28:24 earth, and seeth under the whole *h*
Job 35:11 us wiser than the fowls of *h*
Job 37:3 He directeth it under the whole *h*
Job 38:29 and the hoary frost of *h*, who hath
Job 38:33 Knowest thou the ordinances of *h*
Job 38:37 or who can stay the bottles of *h*
Job 41:11 is under the whole *h* is mine
Ps 11:4 temple, the LORD's throne is in *h*
Ps 14:2 from *h* upon the children of men
Ps 19:6 forth is from the end of the *h*
Ps 20:6 he will hear him from his holy *h*
Ps 33:13 The LORD looketh from *h*
Ps 53:2 God looked down from *h* upon the
Ps 57:3 He shall send from *h*, and save me
Ps 69:34 Let the *h* and earth praise him,
Ps 73:25 Whom have I in *h* but thee
Ps 76:8 cause judgment to be heard from *h*
Ps 77:18 voice of thy thunder was in the *h*
Ps 78:23 above, and opened the doors of *h*
Ps 78:24 had given them of the corn of *h*
Ps 78:26 an east wind to blow in the *h*
Ps 79:2 be meat unto the fowls of the *h*
Ps 80:14 look down from *h*, and behold, and
Ps 85:11 shall look down from *h*
Ps 89:6 For who in the *h* can be compared
Ps 89:29 and his throne as the days of *h*
Ps 89:37 and as a faithful witness in *h*
Ps 102:19 from *h* did the LORD behold the
Ps 103:11 For as the *h* is high above the
Ps 104:12 of the *h* have their habitation
Ps 105:40 them with the bread of *h*
Ps 107:26 They mount up to the *h*, they go
Ps 113:6 behold the things that are in *h*

| | |
|---|---|
| Ps 115:15 | blessed of the LORD which made *h* |
| Ps 115:16 | The *h*, even the heavens, are the |
| Ps 119:89 | O LORD, thy word is settled in *h* |
| Ps 121:2 | from the LORD, which made *h* |
| Ps 124:8 | the name of the LORD, who made *h* |
| Ps 134:3 | The LORD that made *h* and earth |
| Ps 135:6 | LORD pleased, that did he in *h* |
| Ps 136:26 | O give thanks unto the God of *h* |
| Ps 139:8 | If I ascend up into *h*, thou art |
| Ps 146:6 | Which made *h*, and earth, the sea, |
| Ps 147:8 | Who covereth the *h* with clouds |
| Ps 148:13 | his glory is above the earth and *h* |
| Prov 23:5 | fly away as an eagle toward *h* |
| Prov 25:3 | The *h* for height, and the earth |
| Prov 30:4 | Who hath ascended up into *h* |
| Eccl 1:13 | all things that are done under *h* |
| Eccl 2:3 | the *h* all the days of their life |
| Eccl 3:1 | time to every purpose under the *h* |
| Eccl 5:2 | for God is in *h*, and thou upon |
| Is 13:5 | a far country, from the end of *h* |
| Is 13:10 | For the stars of *h* and the |
| Is 14:12 | How art thou fallen from *h* |
| Is 14:13 | thine heart, I will ascend into *h* |
| Is 34:4 | all the host of *h* shall be |
| Is 34:5 | For my sword shall be bathed in *h* |
| Is 37:16 | thou hast made *h* and earth |
| Is 40:12 | meted out *h* with the span, and |
| Is 55:10 | cometh down, and the snow from *h* |
| Is 63:15 | Look down from *h*, and behold from |
| Is 66:1 | The *h* is my throne, and the earth |
| Jer 7:18 | to make cakes to the queen of *h* |
| Jer 7:33 | be meat for the fowls of the *h* |
| Jer 8:2 | and the moon, and all the host of *h* |
| Jer 8:7 | the stork in the *h* knoweth her |
| Jer 10:2 | be not dismayed at the signs of *h* |
| Jer 15:3 | to tear, and the fowls of the *h* |
| Jer 16:4 | shall be meat for the fowls of *h* |
| Jer 19:7 | to be meat for the fowls of the *h* |
| Jer 19:13 | incense unto all the host of *h* |
| Jer 23:24 | Do not I fill *h* and earth |
| Jer 31:37 | If *h* above can be measured, and |
| Jer 32:17 | behold, thou hast made the *h* |
| Jer 33:22 | As the host of *h* cannot be |
| Jer 33:25 | not appointed the ordinances of *h* |
| Jer 34:20 | for meat unto the fowls of the *h* |
| Jer 44:17 | burn incense unto the queen of *h* |
| Jer 44:18 | to burn incense to the queen of *h* |
| Jer 44:19 | burned incense to the queen of *h* |
| Jer 44:25 | to burn incense to the queen of *h* |
| Jer 49:36 | winds from the four quarters of *h* |
| Jer 51:9 | for her judgment reacheth unto *h* |
| Jer 51:15 | out the *h* by his understanding |
| Jer 51:48 | Then the *h* and the earth, and all |
| Jer 51:53 | Babylon should mount up to *h* |
| Lam 2:1 | cast down from *h* unto the earth |
| Lam 3:50 | LORD look down, and behold from *h* |
| Lam 4:19 | swifter than the eagles of the *h* |
| Eze 8:3 | me up between the earth and the *h* |
| Eze 29:5 | field and to the fowls of the *h* |
| Eze 31:6 | All the fowls of *h* made their |
| Eze 31:13 | all the fowls of the *h* remain |
| Eze 32:4 | of the *h* to remain upon thee |
| Eze 32:7 | put thee out, I will cover the *h* |
| Eze 32:8 | All the bright lights of *h* will I |
| Eze 38:20 | of the sea, and the fowls of the *h* |
| Dan 2:18 | God of *h* concerning this secret |
| Dan 2:19 | Then Daniel blessed the God of *h* |
| Dan 2:28 | But there is a God in *h* that |
| Dan 2:37 | for the God of *h* hath given thee |
| Dan 2:38 | the fowls of the *h* hath he given |
| Dan 2:44 | the God of *h* set up a kingdom |
| Dan 4:11 | the height thereof reached unto *h* |
| Dan 4:12 | the fowls of the *h* dwelt in the |
| Dan 4:13 | and an holy one came down from *h* |
| Dan 4:15 | let it be wet with the dew of *h* |
| Dan 4:20 | whose height reached unto the *h* |
| Dan 4:21 | of the *h* had their habitation |
| Dan 4:22 | is grown, and reacheth unto *h* |
| Dan 4:23 | and an holy one coming down from *h* |
| Dan 4:23 | let it be wet with the dew of *h* |
| Dan 4:25 | shall wet thee with the dew of *h* |
| Dan 4:31 | mouth, there fell a voice from *h* |
| Dan 4:33 | body was wet with the dew of *h* |
| Dan 4:34 | lifted up mine eyes unto *h* |
| Dan 4:35 | to his will in the army of *h* |
| Dan 4:37 | and extol and honour the King of *h* |
| Dan 5:21 | body was wet with the dew of *h* |
| Dan 5:23 | up thyself against the Lord of *h* |
| Dan 6:27 | he worketh signs and wonders in *h* |
| Dan 7:2 | the four winds of the *h* strove |
| Dan 7:13 | of man came with the clouds of *h* |
| Dan 7:27 | of the kingdom under the whole *h* |
| Dan 8:8 | ones toward the four winds of *h* |
| Dan 8:10 | great, even to the host of *h* |
| Dan 9:12 | for under the whole *h* hath not |
| Dan 11:4 | toward the four winds of *h* |
| Dan 12:7 | hand and his left hand unto *h* |
| Hos 2:18 | the field, and with the fowls of *h* |
| Hos 4:3 | the field, and with the fowls of *h* |
| Hos 7:12 | them down as the fowls of the *h* |
| Amos 9:2 | though they climb up to *h* |
| Amos 9:6 | buildeth his stories in the *h* |
| Jonah 1:9 | and I fear the LORD, the God of *h* |
| Nah 3:16 | merchants above the stars of *h* |
| Zeph 1:3 | I will consume the fowls of the *h* |
| Zeph 1:5 | the host of *h* upon the housetops |
| Hag 1:10 | Therefore the *h* over you is |
| Zec 2:6 | abroad as the four winds of the *h* |
| Zec 5:9 | ephah between the earth and the *h* |
| Mal 3:10 | not open you the windows of *h* |
| Mt 3:2 | for the kingdom of *h* is at hand |
| Mt 3:17 | And lo a voice from *h*, saying, |
| Mt 4:17 | for the kingdom of *h* is at hand |
| Mt 5:3 | for theirs is the kingdom of *h* |
| Mt 5:10 | for theirs is the kingdom of *h* |
| Mt 5:12 | for great is your reward in *h* |
| Mt 5:16 | glorify your Father which is in *h* |
| Mt 5:18 | For verily I say unto you, Till *h* |
| Mt 5:19 | the least in the kingdom of *h* |
| Mt 5:19 | called great in the kingdom of *h* |
| Mt 5:20 | case enter into the kingdom of *h* |
| Mt 5:34 | Swear not at all; neither by *h* |
| Mt 5:45 | of your Father which is in *h* |
| Mt 5:48 | Father which is in *h* is perfect |
| Mt 6:1 | of your Father which is in *h* |
| Mt 6:9 | Our Father which art in *h* |
| Mt 6:10 | be done in earth, as it is in *h* |
| Mt 6:20 | up for yourselves treasures in *h* |
| Mt 7:11 | *h* give good things to them that |
| Mt 7:21 | shall enter into the kingdom of *h* |
| Mt 7:21 | will of my Father which is in *h* |
| Mt 8:11 | and Jacob, in the kingdom of *h* |
| Mt 10:7 | The kingdom of *h* is at hand |
| Mt 10:32 | before my Father which is in *h* |
| Mt 10:33 | before my Father which is in *h* |
| Mt 11:11 | kingdom of *h* is greater than he |
| Mt 11:12 | kingdom of *h* suffereth violence |
| Mt 11:23 | which art exalted unto *h* |
| Mt 11:25 | I thank thee, O Father, Lord of *h* |
| Mt 12:50 | will of my Father which is in *h* |
| Mt 13:11 | the mysteries of the kingdom of *h* |
| Mt 13:24 | The kingdom of *h* is likened unto |
| Mt 13:31 | The kingdom of *h* is like to a |
| Mt 13:33 | The kingdom of *h* is like unto |
| Mt 13:44 | the kingdom of *h* is like unto |
| Mt 13:45 | the kingdom of *h* is like unto a |
| Mt 13:47 | the kingdom of *h* is like unto a |
| Mt 13:52 | *h* is like unto a man that is an |
| Mt 14:19 | two fishes, and looking up to *h* |
| Mt 16:1 | he would shew them a sign from *h* |
| Mt 16:17 | thee, but my Father which is in *h* |
| Mt 16:19 | thee the keys of the kingdom of *h* |
| Mt 16:19 | bind on earth shall be bound in *h* |
| Mt 16:19 | on earth shall be loosed in *h* |
| Mt 18:1 | the greatest in the kingdom of *h* |
| Mt 18:3 | not enter into the kingdom of *h* |
| Mt 18:4 | is greatest in the kingdom of *h* |
| Mt 18:10 | That in *h* their angels do always |
| Mt 18:10 | face of my Father which is in *h* |
| Mt 18:14 | will of your Father which is in *h* |
| Mt 18:18 | bind on earth shall be bound in *h* |
| Mt 18:18 | on earth shall be loosed in *h* |
| Mt 18:19 | them of my Father which is in *h* |
| Mt 18:23 | of *h* likened unto a certain king |
| Mt 19:14 | for of such is the kingdom of *h* |
| Mt 19:21 | and thou shalt have treasure in *h* |
| Mt 19:23 | enter into the kingdom of *h* |
| Mt 20:1 | For the kingdom of *h* is like unto |
| Mt 21:25 | from *h*, or of men |
| Mt 21:25 | saying, If we shall say, From *h* |
| Mt 22:2 | The kingdom of *h* is like unto a |
| Mt 22:30 | but are as the angels of God in *h* |
| Mt 23:9 | one is your Father, which is in *h* |
| Mt 23:13 | up the kingdom of *h* against men |
| Mt 23:22 | And he that shall swear by *h* |
| Mt 24:29 | and the stars shall fall from *h* |
| Mt 24:30 | the sign of the Son of man in *h* |
| Mt 24:30 | in the clouds of *h* with power |
| Mt 24:31 | from one end of *h* to the other |
| Mt 24:35 | *H* and earth shall pass away, but |
| Mt 24:36 | no man, no, not the angels of *h* |
| Mt 25:1 | Then shall the kingdom of *h* be |
| Mt 25:14 | For the kingdom of *h* is as a man |
| Mt 26:64 | and coming in the clouds of *h* |
| Mt 28:2 | of the Lord descended from *h* |
| Mt 28:18 | All power is given unto me in *h* |
| Mk 1:11 | And there came a voice from *h* |
| Mk 6:41 | the two fishes, he looked up to *h* |
| Mk 7:34 | And looking up to *h*, he sighed, and |
| Mk 8:11 | him, seeking of him a sign from *h* |
| Mk 10:21 | and thou shalt have treasure in *h* |
| Mk 11:25 | your Father also which is in *h* |
| Mk 11:26 | is in *h* forgive your trespasses |
| Mk 11:30 | baptism of John, was it from *h* |
| Mk 11:31 | saying, If we shall say, From *h* |
| Mk 12:25 | are as the angels which are in *h* |
| Mk 13:25 | And the stars of *h* shall fall |
| Mk 13:25 | that are in *h* shall be shaken |
| Mk 13:27 | earth to the uttermost part of *h* |
| Mk 13:31 | *H* and earth shall pass away |
| Mk 13:32 | no, not the angels which are in *h* |
| Mk 14:62 | and coming in the clouds of *h* |
| Mk 16:19 | them, he was received up into *h* |
| Lk 2:15 | were gone away from them into *h* |
| Lk 3:21 | and praying, the *h* was opened, |
| Lk 3:22 | upon him, and a voice came from *h* |
| Lk 4:25 | when the *h* was shut up three |
| Lk 6:23 | behold, your reward is great in *h* |
| Lk 9:16 | two fishes, and looking up to *h* |
| Lk 9:54 | command fire to come down from *h* |
| Lk 10:15 | Capernaum, which art exalted to *h* |
| Lk 10:18 | Satan as lightning fall from *h* |
| Lk 10:20 | your names are written in *h* |
| Lk 10:21 | I thank thee, O Father, Lord of *h* |
| Lk 11:2 | say, Our Father which art in *h* |
| Lk 11:2 | Thy will be done, as in *h* |
| Lk 11:16 | him, sought of him a sign from *h* |
| Lk 15:7 | that likewise joy shall be in *h* |
| Lk 15:18 | Father, I have sinned against *h* |
| Lk 15:21 | Father, I have sinned against *h* |
| Lk 16:17 | And it is easier for *h* and earth to |
| Lk 17:24 | out of the one part under *h* |
| Lk 17:24 | unto the other part under *h* |
| Lk 17:29 | rained fire and brimstone from *h* |
| Lk 18:13 | up so much as his eyes unto *h* |
| Lk 18:22 | and thou shalt have treasure in *h* |
| Lk 19:38 | peace in *h*, and glory in the |
| Lk 20:4 | baptism of John, was it from *h* |
| Lk 20:5 | saying, If we shall say, From *h* |
| Lk 21:11 | great signs shall there be from *h* |
| Lk 21:26 | the powers of *h* shall be shaken |
| Lk 21:33 | *H* and earth shall pass away |
| Lk 22:43 | appeared an angel unto him from *h* |
| Lk 24:51 | from them, and carried up into *h* |
| Jn 1:32 | descending from *h* like a dove |
| Jn 1:51 | Hereafter ye shall see *h* open |
| Jn 3:13 | And no man hath ascended up to *h* |
| Jn 3:13 | but he that came down from *h* |
| Jn 3:13 | even the Son of man which is in *h* |
| Jn 3:27 | except it be given him from *h* |
| Jn 3:31 | that cometh from *h* is above all |
| Jn 6:31 | He gave them bread from *h* to eat |
| Jn 6:32 | gave you not that bread from *h* |
| Jn 6:32 | giveth you the true bread from *h* |
| Jn 6:33 | is he which cometh down from *h* |
| Jn 6:38 | For I came down from *h*, not to do |
| Jn 6:41 | the bread which came down from *h* |
| Jn 6:42 | that he saith, I came down from *h* |
| Jn 6:50 | bread which cometh down from *h* |
| Jn 6:51 | bread which came down from *h* |
| Jn 6:58 | that bread which came down from *h* |
| Jn 12:28 | Then came there a voice from *h* |
| Jn 17:1 | Jesus, and lifted up his eyes to *h* |
| Acts 1:10 | stedfastly toward *h* as he went up |
| Acts 1:11 | why stand ye gazing up into *h* |
| Acts 1:11 | which is taken up from you into *h* |
| Acts 1:11 | as ye have seen him go into *h* |
| Acts 2:2 | there came a sound from *h* as of a |
| Acts 2:5 | men, out of every nation under *h* |
| Acts 2:19 | And I will shew wonders in *h* above |
| Acts 3:21 | Whom the *h* must receive until the |
| Acts 4:12 | name under *h* given among men |
| Acts 4:24 | thou art God, which hast made *h* |
| Acts 7:42 | them up to worship the host of *h* |
| Acts 7:49 | *H* is my throne, and earth is my |
| Acts 7:55 | looked up stedfastly into *h* |
| Acts 9:3 | round about him a light from *h* |
| Acts 10:11 | saw *h* opened, and a certain vessel |
| Acts 10:16 | was received up again into *h* |
| Acts 11:5 | let down from *h* by four corners |

Acts 11:9 voice answered me again from *h*
Acts 11:10 and all were drawn up again into *h*
Acts 14:15 unto the living God, which made *h*
Acts 14:17 did good, and gave us rain from *h*
Acts 17:24 seeing that he is Lord of *h*
Acts 22:6 suddenly there shone from *h* a
Acts 26:13 I saw in the way a light from *h*
Rom 1:18 from *h* against all ungodliness
Rom 10:6 heart, Who shall ascend into *h*
1Cor 8:5 whether in *h* or in earth, (as
1Cor 15:47 the second man is the Lord from *h*
2Cor 5:2 with our house which is from *h*
2Cor 12:2 an one caught up to the third *h*
Gal 1:8 But though we, or an angel from *h*
Eph 1:10 in Christ, both which are in *h*
Eph 3:15 Of whom the whole family in *h*
Eph 6:9 that your Master also is in *h*
Phil 2:10 knee should bow, of things in *h*
Phil 3:20 For our conversation is in *h*
Col 1:5 which is laid up for you in *h*
Col 1:16 all things created, that are in *h*
Col 1:20 things in earth, or things in *h*
Col 1:23 every creature which is under *h*
Col 4:1 that ye also have a Master in *h*
1Th 1:10 And to wait for his Son from *h*
1Th 4:16 shall descend from *h* with a shout
2Th 1:7 from *h* with his mighty angels
Heb 9:24 but into *h* itself, now to appear
Heb 10:34 that ye have in *h* a better
Heb 12:23 firstborn, which are written in *h*
Heb 12:25 from him that speaketh from *h*
Heb 12:26 not the earth only, but also *h*
Jas 5:12 brethren, swear not, neither by *h*
Jas 5:18 the *h* gave rain, and the earth
1Pet 1:4 not away, reserved in *h* for you
1Pet 1:12 the Holy Ghost sent down from *h*
1Pet 3:22 Who is gone into *h*, and is on the
2Pet 1:18 voice which came from *h* we heard
1Jn 5:7 are three that bear record in *h*
Rev 3:12 cometh down out of *h* from my God
Rev 4:1 behold, a door was opened in *h*
Rev 4:2 and, behold, a throne was set in *h*
Rev 5:3 And no man in *h*, nor in earth,
Rev 5:13 And every creature which is in *h*
Rev 6:13 the stars of *h* fell unto the
Rev 6:14 the *h* departed as a scroll when
Rev 8:1 there was silence in *h* about the
Rev 8:10 and there fell a great star from *h*
Rev 8:13 flying through the midst of *h*
Rev 9:1 a star fall from *h* unto the earth
Rev 10:1 mighty angel come down from *h*
Rev 10:4 a voice from *h* saying unto me
Rev 10:5 the earth lifted up his hand to *h*
Rev 10:6 for ever and ever, who created *h*
Rev 10:8 heard from *h* spake unto me again
Rev 11:6 These have power to shut *h*
Rev 11:12 voice from *h* saying unto them
Rev 11:12 they ascended up to *h* in a cloud
Rev 11:13 and gave glory to the God of *h*
Rev 11:15 and there were great voices in *h*
Rev 11:19 the temple of God was opened in *h*
Rev 12:1 appeared a great wonder in *h*
Rev 12:3 appeared another wonder in *h*
Rev 12:4 the third part of the stars of *h*
Rev 12:7 And there was war in *h*
Rev 12:8 their place found any more in *h*
Rev 12:10 I heard a loud voice saying in *h*
Rev 13:6 and them that dwell in *h*
Rev 13:13 *h* on the earth in the sight of
Rev 14:2 And I heard a voice from *h*
Rev 14:6 angel fly in the midst of *h*
Rev 14:7 and worship him that made *h*
Rev 14:13 a voice from *h* saying unto me
Rev 14:17 out of the temple which is in *h*
Rev 15:1 And I saw another sign in *h*
Rev 15:5 of the testimony in *h* was opened
Rev 16:11 blasphemed the God of *h* because
Rev 16:17 voice out of the temple of *h*
Rev 16:21 upon men a great hail out of *h*
Rev 18:1 another angel come down from *h*
Rev 18:4 And I heard another voice from *h*
Rev 18:5 For her sins have reached unto *h*
Rev 18:20 Rejoice over her, thou *h*, and ye
Rev 19:1 a great voice of much people in *h*
Rev 19:11 I saw *h* opened, and behold a white
Rev 19:14 the armies which were in *h*
Rev 19:17 fowls that fly in the midst of *h*
Rev 20:1 I saw an angel come down from *h*
Rev 20:9 fire came down from God out of *h*
Rev 20:11 face the earth and the *h* fled away
Rev 21:1 And I saw a new *h* and a new earth
Rev 21:1 for the first *h* and the first
Rev 21:2 coming down from God out of *h*
Rev 21:3 a great voice out of *h* saying
Rev 21:10 descending out of *h* from God

## HEAVENLY

Mt 6:14 your *h* Father will also forgive
Mt 6:26 yet your *h* Father feedeth them
Mt 6:32 for your *h* Father knoweth that
Mt 15:13 which my *h* Father hath not
Mt 18:35 So likewise shall my *h* Father do
Lk 2:13 of the *h* host praising God
Lk 11:13 much more shall your *h* Father
Jn 3:12 if I tell you of *h* things
Acts 26:19 not disobedient unto the *h* vision
1Cor 15:48 and as is the *h*, such are they
1Cor 15:48 such are they also that are *h*
1Cor 15:49 also bear the image of the *h*
Eph 1:3 blessings in *h* places in Christ
Eph 1:20 own right hand in the *h* places
Eph 2:6 in *h* places in Christ Jesus
Eph 3:10 powers in *h* places might be known
2Ti 4:18 preserve me unto his *h* kingdom
Heb 3:1 partakers of the *h* calling
Heb 6:4 and have tasted of the *h* gift
Heb 8:5 the example and shadow of *h* things
Heb 9:23 but the *h* things themselves with
Heb 11:16 a better country, that is, an *h*
Heb 12:22 the *h* Jerusalem, and to an

## HEAVENS

Gen 2:1 Thus the *h* and the earth were
Gen 2:4 are the generations of the *h*
Gen 2:4 LORD God made the earth and the *h*
Deut 10:14 the heaven of *h* is the LORD's thy
Deut 32:1 Give ear, O ye *h*, and I will speak
Deut 33:28 also his *h* shall drop down dew
Judg 5:4 the *h* dropped, the clouds also
2Sa 22:10 He bowed the *h* also, and came down
1Kin 8:27 heaven of *h* cannot contain thee
1Chr 16:26 but the LORD made the *h*
1Chr 16:31 Let the *h* be glad, and let the
1Chr 27:23 Israel like to the stars of the *h*
2Chr 2:6 heaven of *h* cannot contain him
2Chr 6:18 the heaven of *h* cannot contain
2Chr 6:25 Then hear thou from the *h*
2Chr 6:33 Then hear thou from the *h*
2Chr 6:35 hear thou from the *h* their prayer
2Chr 6:39 Then hear thou from the *h*
Ezr 9:6 trespass is grown up unto the *h*
Neh 9:6 hast made heaven, the heaven of *h*
Job 9:8 Which alone spreadeth out the *h*
Job 14:12 till the *h* be no more, they shall
Job 15:15 the *h* are not clean in his sight
Job 20:6 his excellency mount up to the *h*
Job 26:13 spirit he hath garnished the *h*
Job 35:5 Look unto the *h*, and see
Ps 2:4 that sitteth in the *h* shall laugh
Ps 8:1 hast set thy glory above the *h*
Ps 8:3 When I consider thy *h*, the work
Ps 18:9 He bowed the *h* also, and came down
Ps 18:13 The LORD also thundered in the *h*
Ps 19:1 The *h* declare the glory of God
Ps 33:6 word of the LORD were the *h* made
Ps 36:5 Thy mercy, O LORD, is in the *h*
Ps 50:4 He shall call to the *h* from above
Ps 50:6 And the *h* shall declare his
Ps 57:5 thou exalted, O God, above the *h*
Ps 57:10 For thy mercy is great unto the *h*
Ps 57:11 thou exalted, O God, above the *h*
Ps 68:4 rideth upon the *h* by his name JAH
Ps 68:8 the *h* also dropped at the
Ps 68:33 that rideth upon the *h* of *h*
Ps 73:9 set their mouth against the *h*
Ps 89:2 thou establish in the very *h*
Ps 89:5 the *h* shall praise thy wonders, O
Ps 89:11 The *h* are thine, the earth also
Ps 96:5 but the LORD made the *h*
Ps 96:11 Let the *h* rejoice, and let the
Ps 97:6 The *h* declare his righteousness,
Ps 102:25 the *h* are the work of thy hands
Ps 103:19 hath prepared his throne in the *h*
Ps 104:2 out the *h* like a curtain
Ps 108:4 thy mercy is great above the *h*
Ps 108:5 thou exalted, O God, above the *h*
Ps 113:4 nations, and his glory above the *h*
Ps 115:3 But our God is in the *h*
Ps 115:16 The heaven, even the *h*, are the
Ps 123:1 O thou that dwellest in the *h*
Ps 136:5 To him that by wisdom made the *h*
Ps 144:5 Bow thy *h*, O LORD, and come down
Ps 148:1 Praise ye the LORD from the *h*
Ps 148:4 Praise him, ye *h* of *h*
Ps 148:4 and ye waters that be above the *h*
Prov 3:19 hath he established the *h*
Prov 8:27 When he prepared the *h*, I was
Is 1:2 Hear, O *h*, and give ear, O earth
Is 5:30 is darkened in the *h* thereof
Is 13:13 Therefore I will shake the *h*
Is 34:4 the *h* shall be rolled together as
Is 40:22 stretcheth out the *h* as a curtain
Is 42:5 the LORD, he that created the *h*
Is 44:23 Sing, O ye *h*
Is 44:24 that stretcheth forth the *h* alone
Is 45:8 Drop down, ye *h*, from above, and
Is 45:12 hands, have stretched out the *h*
Is 45:18 saith the LORD that created the *h*
Is 48:13 my right hand hath spanned the *h*
Is 49:13 Sing, O *h*
Is 50:3 I clothe the *h* with blackness, and
Is 51:6 Lift up your eyes to the *h*
Is 51:6 for the *h* shall vanish away like
Is 51:13 that hath stretched forth the *h*
Is 51:16 mine hand, that I may plant the *h*
Is 55:9 For as the *h* are higher than the
Is 64:1 Oh that thou wouldest rend the *h*
Is 65:17 For, behold, I create new *h*
Is 66:22 For as the new *h* and the new earth
Jer 2:12 Be astonished, O ye *h*, at this,
Jer 4:23 and the *h*, and they had no light
Jer 4:25 all the birds of the *h* were fled
Jer 4:28 mourn, and the *h* above be black
Jer 9:10 both the fowl of the *h* and the
Jer 10:11 The gods that have not made the *h*
Jer 10:11 the earth, and from under these *h*
Jer 10:12 out the *h* by his discretion
Jer 10:13 is a multitude of waters in the *h*
Jer 14:22 or can the *h* give showers
Jer 51:16 is a multitude of waters in the *h*
Lam 3:41 with our hands unto God in the *h*
Lam 3:66 from under the *h* of the LORD
Eze 1:1 that the *h* were opened, and I saw
Dan 4:26 have known that the *h* do rule
Hos 2:21 saith the LORD, I will hear the *h*
Joel 2:10 the *h* shall tremble
Joel 2:30 And I will shew wonders in the *h*
Joel 3:16 and the *h* and the earth shall shake
Hab 3:3 His glory covered the *h*, and the
Hag 2:6 while, and I will shake the *h*
Hag 2:21 Judah, saying, I will shake the *h*
Zec 6:5 are the four spirits of the *h*
Zec 8:12 the *h* shall give their dew
Zec 12:1 which stretcheth forth the *h*
Mt 3:16 the *h* were opened unto him, and he
Mt 24:29 powers of the *h* shall be shaken
Mk 1:10 of the water, he saw the *h* opened
Lk 12:33 in the *h* that faileth not
Acts 2:34 David is not ascended into the *h*
Acts 7:56 said, Behold, I see the *h* opened
2Cor 5:1 made with hands, eternal in the *h*
Eph 4:10 that ascended up far above all *h*
Heb 1:10 the *h* are the works of thine
Heb 4:14 priest, that is passed into the *h*
Heb 7:26 and made higher than the *h*
Heb 8:1 throne of the Majesty in the *h*
Heb 9:23 *h* should be purified with these
2Pet 3:5 the word of God the *h* were of old
2Pet 3:7 But the *h* and the earth, which are
2Pet 3:10 in the which the *h* shall pass
2Pet 3:12 wherein the *h* being on fire shall
2Pet 3:13 to his promise, look for new *h*
Rev 12:12 Therefore rejoice, ye *h*, and ye

## HEAVINESS

Ezr 9:5 sacrifice I arose up from my *h*
Job 9:27 complaint, I will leave off my *h*
Ps 69:20 and I am full of *h*
Ps 119:28 My soul melteth for *h*
Prov 10:1 son is the *h* of his mother
Prov 12:25 *H* in the heart of man maketh it
Prov 14:13 and the end of that mirth is *h*
Is 29:2 Ariel, and there shall be *h*
Is 61:3 of praise for the spirit of *h*
Rom 9:2 That I have great *h* and continual
2Cor 2:1 would not come again to you in *h*
Phil 2:26 after you all, and was full of *h*
Jas 4:9 to mourning, and your joy to *h*
1Pet 1:6 ye are in *h* through manifold

**HEAVY**
Ex 17:12 But Moses' hands were *h*
Ex 18:18 for this thing is too *h* for thee
Num 11:14 alone, because it is too *h* for me
1Sa 4:18 for he was an old man, and *h*
1Sa 5:6 LORD was *h* upon them of Ashdod
1Sa 5:11 the hand of God was very *h* there
2Sa 14:26 because the hair was *h* on him
1Kin 12:4 his *h* yoke which he put upon us,
1Kin 12:10 Thy father made our yoke *h*
1Kin 12:11 father did lade you with a *h* yoke
1Kin 12:14 My father made your yoke *h*
1Kin 14:6 I am sent to thee with *h* tidings
1Kin 20:43 of Israel went to his house *h*
1Kin 21:4 And Ahab came into his house *h*
2Chr 10:4 his *h* yoke that he put upon us,
2Chr 10:10 Thy father made our yoke *h*
2Chr 10:11 my father put a *h* yoke upon you
2Chr 10:14 My father made your yoke *h*
Neh 5:18 bondage was *h* upon this people
Job 33:7 shall my hand be *h* upon thee
Ps 32:4 and night thy hand was *h* upon me
Ps 38:4 as an *h* burden they are too *h*
Ps 38:4 burden they are too *h* for me
Prov 25:20 that singeth songs to an *h* heart
Prov 27:3 A stone is *h*, and the sand weighty
Prov 31:6 unto those that be of *h* hearts
Is 6:10 people fat, and make their ears *h*
Is 24:20 thereof shall be *h* upon it
Is 30:27 anger, and the burden thereof is *h*
Is 46:1 your carriages were *h* loaden
Is 58:6 wickedness, to undo the *h* burdens
Is 59:1 neither his ear *h*, that it cannot
Lam 3:7 he hath made my chain *h*
Mt 11:28 are *h* laden, and I will give you
Mt 23:4 For they bind *h* burdens and
Mt 26:37 began to be sorrowful and very *h*
Mt 26:43 for their eyes were *h*
Mk 14:33 be sore amazed, and to be very *h*
Mk 14:40 again, (for their eyes were *h*
Lk 9:32 were with him were *h* with sleep

**HEBER** *(he'-bur)* See EBER, HEBER'S, HEBERITES.
*1. A son of Beriah.*
Gen 46:17 *H*, and Malchiel
Num 26:45 of *H*, the family of the Heberites
1Chr 7:31 *H*, and Malchiel, who is the father
1Chr 7:32 *H* begat Japhlet, and Shomer, and
Lk 3:35 of Phalec, which was the son of *H*
*2. Husband of Jael.*
Judg 4:11 Now *H* the Kenite, which was of
Judg 4:17 of Jael the wife of *H* the Kenite
Judg 4:17 and the house of *H* the Kenite
Judg 5:24 Jael the wife of *H* the Kenite be
*3. A son of Ezra.*
1Chr 4:18 *H* the father of Socho, and
*4. A son of Elpaal.*
1Chr 8:17 and Meshullam, and Hezeki, and *H*
*5. A head of a Gadite family.*
1Chr 5:13 and Jorai, and Jachan, and Zia, and *H*
*6. A son of Shashak.*
1Chr 8:22 And Ishpan, and *H*, and Eliel,

**HEBERITES** *(he'-bur-ites) Descendants of Heber.*
Num 26:45 of Heber, the family of the *H*

**HEBER'S** *(he'-burs) Refers to Heber 2.*
Judg 4:21 Then Jael *H* wife took a nail of

**HEBREW** *(he'-broo)* See HEBREWESS, HEBREWS.
*1. Descendants of Jacob.*
Gen 14:13 had escaped, and told Abram the *H*
Gen 39:14 in an *H* unto us to mock us
Gen 39:17 The *H* servant, which thou hast
Gen 41:12 there with us a young man, an *H*
Ex 1:15 of Egypt spake to the *H* midwives
Ex 1:16 of a midwife to the *H* women
Ex 1:19 Because the *H* women are not as
Ex 2:7 to thee a nurse of the *H* women
Ex 2:11 he spied an Egyptian smiting an *H*
Ex 21:2 If thou buy an *H* servant, six
Deut 15:12 an *H* man, or an *H* woman, be
Jer 34:9 being an *H* or an Hebrewess, go
Jer 34:14 ye go every man his brother an *H*
Jonah 1:9 And he said unto them, I am an *H*
Phil 3:5 of Benjamin, an *H* of the Hebrews
*2. A language.*
Lk 23:38 letters of Greek, and Latin, and *H*
Jn 5:2 called in the *H* tongue Bethesda
Jn 19:13 called the Pavement, but in the *H*
Jn 19:17 which is called in the *H* Golgotha
Jn 19:20 and it was written in *H*, and Greek,
Acts 21:40 spake unto them in the *H* tongue
Acts 22:2 he spake in the *H* tongue to them
Acts 26:14 me, and saying in the *H* tongue
Rev 9:11 name in the *H* tongue is Abaddon
Rev 16:16 called in the *H* tongue Armageddon

**HEBREWESS** *(he'-broo-ess)*
Jer 34:9 being an Hebrew or an *H*, go free

**HEBREWS** *(he'-brooz)* See HEBREWS'.
Gen 40:15 away out of the land of the *H*
Gen 43:32 might not eat bread with the *H*
Ex 2:13 two men of the *H* strove together
Ex 3:18 God of the *H* hath met with us
Ex 5:3 The God of the *H* hath met with us
Ex 7:16 The LORD God of the *H* hath sent
Ex 9:1 Thus saith the LORD God of the *H*
Ex 9:13 Thus saith the LORD God of the *H*
Ex 10:3 Thus saith the LORD God of the *H*
1Sa 4:6 great shout in the camp of the *H*
1Sa 4:9 ye be not servants unto the *H*
1Sa 13:3 the land, saying, Let the *H* hear
1Sa 13:7 some of the *H* went over Jordan to
1Sa 13:19 Lest the *H* make them swords or
1Sa 14:11 the *H* come forth out of the holes
1Sa 14:21 Moreover the *H* that were with the
1Sa 29:3 Philistines, What do these *H* here
Acts 6:1 of the Grecians against the *H*
2Cor 11:22 Are they *H*
Phil 3:5 of Benjamin, an Hebrew of the *H*
Heb *s* Written to the *H* from Italy by

**HEBREWS'** *(he'-brooz)*
Ex 2:6 This is one of the *H* children

**HEBRON** *(he'-brun)* See HEBRONITES.
*1. A city in Asher.*
Josh 19:28 And *H*, and Rehob, and Hammon, and
*2. A city in Judah.*
Gen 13:18 the plain of Mamre, which is in *H*
Gen 23:2 the same is *H* in the land of
Gen 23:19 the same is *H* in the land of
Gen 35:27 the city of Arbah, which is *H*
Gen 37:14 he sent him out of the vale of *H*
Num 13:22 by the south, and came unto *H*
Num 13:22 (Now *H* was built seven years
Josh 10:3 sent unto Hoham king of *H*
Josh 10:5 king of Jerusalem, the king of *H*
Josh 10:23 king of Jerusalem, the king of *H*
Josh 10:36 and all Israel with him, unto *H*
Josh 10:39 as he had done to *H*, so he did to
Josh 11:21 from the mountains, from *H*
Josh 12:10 the king of *H*, one
Josh 14:13 of Jephunneh *H* for an inheritance
Josh 14:14 *H* therefore became the
Josh 14:15 And the name of *H* before was
Josh 15:13 father of Anak, which city is *H*
Josh 15:54 and Kirjath-arba, which is *H*
Josh 20:7 and Kirjath-arba, which is *H*
Josh 21:11 father of Anak, which city is *H*
Josh 21:13 the priest *H* with her suburbs
Judg 1:10 the Canaanites that dwelt in *H*
Judg 1:10 (now the name of *H* before was
Judg 1:20 they gave *H* unto Caleb, as Moses
Judg 16:3 top of an hill that is before *H*
1Sa 30:31 And to them which were in *H*
2Sa 2:1 And he said, Unto *H*
2Sa 2:3 and they dwelt in the cities of *H*
2Sa 2:11 in *H* over the house of Judah was
2Sa 2:32 they came to *H* at break of day
2Sa 3:2 And unto David were sons born in *H*
2Sa 3:5 These were born to David in *H*
2Sa 3:19 speak in the ears of David in *H*
2Sa 3:20 So Abner came to David to *H*
2Sa 3:22 but Abner was not with David in *H*
2Sa 3:27 And when Abner was returned to *H*
2Sa 3:32 And they buried Abner in *H*
2Sa 4:1 heard that Abner was dead in *H*
2Sa 4:8 of Ish-bosheth unto David to *H*
2Sa 4:12 hanged them up over the pool in *H*
2Sa 4:12 it in the sepulchre of Abner in *H*
2Sa 5:1 tribes of Israel to David unto *H*
2Sa 5:3 of Israel came to the king to *H*
2Sa 5:3 with them in *H* before the LORD
2Sa 5:5 In *H* he reigned over Judah seven
2Sa 5:13 after he was come from *H*
2Sa 15:7 I have vowed unto the LORD, in *H*
2Sa 15:9 So he arose, and went to *H*
2Sa 15:10 shall say, Absalom reigneth in *H*
1Kin 2:11 seven years reigned he in *H*
1Chr 3:1 which were born unto him in *H*
1Chr 3:4 These six were born unto him in *H*
1Chr 6:55 they gave them *H* in the land of
1Chr 6:57 the cities of Judah, namely, *H*
1Chr 11:1 themselves to David unto *H*
1Chr 11:3 elders of Israel to the king to *H*
1Chr 11:3 with them in *H* before the LORD
1Chr 12:23 to the war, and came to David to *H*
1Chr 12:38 came with a perfect heart to *H*
1Chr 29:27 seven years reigned he in *H*
2Chr 11:10 And Zorah, and Aijalon, and *H*
*3. A son of Kohath.*
Ex 6:18 Amram, and Izhar, and *H*, and Uzziel
Num 3:19 Amram, and Izehar, *H*, and Uzziel
1Chr 6:2 Amram, Izhar, and *H*, and Uzziel
1Chr 6:18 were, Amram, and Izhar, and *H*
1Chr 23:12 Amram, Izhar, *H*, and Uzziel, four
1Chr 23:19 Of the sons of *H*
1Chr 24:23 And the sons of *H*
*4. A son of Mareshah.*
1Chr 2:42 sons of Mareshah the father of *H*
1Chr 2:43 And the sons of *H*
1Chr 15:9 Of the sons of *H*

**HEBRONITES** *(he'-brun-ites) Descendants of Hebron 3.*
Num 3:27 and the family of the *H*, and the
Num 26:58 the Libnites, the family of the *H*
1Chr 26:23 and the Izharites, the *H*, and the
1Chr 26:30 And of the *H*, Hashabiah and his
1Chr 26:31 Among the *H* was Jerijah the chief
1Chr 26:31 even among the *H*, according to the

**HEDGE**
Job 1:10 Hast not thou made an *h* about him
Prov 15:19 slothful man is as an *h* of thorns
Eccl 10:8 and whoso breaketh an *h*, a serpent
Is 5:5 I will take away the *h* thereof
Eze 13:5 neither made up the *h* for the
Eze 22:30 them, that should make up the *h*
Hos 2:6 I will *h* up thy way with thorns,
Mic 7:4 upright is sharper than a thorn *h*
Mk 12:1 set an *h* about it, and digged a

**HEDGES**
1Chr 4:23 that dwelt among plants and *h*
Ps 80:12 hast thou then broken down her *h*
Ps 89:40 Thou hast broken down all his *h*
Jer 49:3 lament, and run to and fro by the *h*
Nah 3:17 camp in the *h* in the cold day
Lk 14:23 Go out into the highways and *h*

**HEED**
Gen 31:24 Take *h* that thou speak not to
Gen 31:29 Take thou *h* that thou speak not
Ex 10:28 take *h* to thyself, see my face no
Ex 19:12 Take *h* to yourselves, that ye go
Ex 34:12 Take *h* to thyself, lest thou make
Num 23:12 Must I not take *h* to speak that
Deut 2:4 take ye good *h* unto yourselves
Deut 4:9 Only take *h* to thyself, and keep
Deut 4:15 therefore good *h* unto yourselves
Deut 4:23 Take *h* unto yourselves, lest ye
Deut 11:16 Take *h* to yourselves, that your
Deut 12:13 Take *h* to thyself that thou offer
Deut 12:19 Take *h* to thyself that thou
Deut 12:30 Take *h* to thyself that thou be
Deut 24:8 Take *h* in the plague of leprosy,
Deut 27:9 unto all Israel, saying, Take *h*
Josh 22:5 But take diligent *h* to do the
Josh 23:11 Take good *h* therefore unto
1Sa 19:2 take *h* to thyself until the
2Sa 20:10 But Amasa took no *h* to the sword
1Kin 2:4 thy children take *h* to their way
1Kin 8:25 thy children take *h* to their way
2Kin 10:31 But Jehu took no *h* to walk in the
1Chr 22:13 if thou takest *h* to fulfil the
1Chr 28:10 Take *h* now
2Chr 6:16 yet so that thy children take *h*
2Chr 19:6 to the judges, Take *h* what ye do
2Chr 19:7 take *h* and do it
2Chr 33:8 so that they will take *h* to do
Ezr 4:22 Take *h* now that ye fail not to do
Job 36:21 Take *h*, regard not iniquity
Ps 39:1 I said, I will take *h* to my ways
Ps 119:9 by taking *h* thereto according to
Prov 17:4 doer giveth *h* to false lips
Eccl 7:21 Also take no *h* unto all words
Eccl 12:9 yea, he gave good *h*, and sought
Is 7:4 And say unto him, Take *h*, and be
Is 21:7 hearkened diligently with much *h*

Jer 9:4 Take ye *h* every one of his
Jer 17:21 Take *h* to yourselves, and bear no
Jer 18:18 let us not give *h* to any of his
Jer 18:19 Give *h* to me, O LORD, and hearken
Hos 4:10 left off to take *h* to the LORD
Mal 2:15 Therefore take *h* to your spirit
Mal 2:16 therefore take *h* to your spirit
Mt 6:1 Take *h* that ye do not your alms
Mt 16:6 Then Jesus said unto them, Take *h*
Mt 18:10 Take *h* that ye despise not one of
Mt 24:4 Take *h* that no man deceive you
Mk 4:24 unto them, Take *h* what ye hear
Mk 8:15 he charged them, saying, Take *h*
Mk 13:5 Take *h* lest any man deceive you
Mk 13:9 But take *h* to yourselves
Mk 13:23 But take ye *h*
Mk 13:33 Take ye *h*, watch and pray
Lk 8:18 Take *h* therefore how ye hear
Lk 11:35 Take *h* therefore that the light
Lk 12:15 And he said unto them, Take *h*
Lk 17:3 Take *h* to yourselves
Lk 21:8 Take *h* that ye be not deceived
Lk 21:34 take *h* to yourselves, lest at any
Acts 3:5 he gave *h* unto them, expecting to
Acts 5:35 take *h* to yourselves what ye
Acts 8:6 *h* unto those things which Philip
Acts 8:10 To whom they all gave *h*, from the
Acts 20:28 Take *h* therefore unto yourselves,
Acts 22:26 saying, Take *h* what thou doest
Rom 11:21 take *h* lest he also spare not
1Cor 3:10 But let every man take *h* how he
1Cor 8:9 But take *h* lest by any means this
1Cor 10:12 he standeth take *h* lest he fall
Gal 5:15 take *h* that ye be not consumed
Col 4:17 Take *h* to the ministry which thou
1Ti 1:4 Neither give *h* to fables and
1Ti 4:1 giving *h* to seducing spirits, and
1Ti 4:16 Take *h* unto thyself, and unto the
Titus 1:14 Not giving *h* to Jewish fables, and
Heb 2:1 *h* to the things which we have
Heb 3:12 Take *h*, brethren, lest there be
2Pet 1:19 ye do well that ye take *h*

**HEEL**
Gen 3:15 head, and thou shalt bruise his *h*
Gen 25:26 and his hand took hold on Esau's *h*
Job 18:9 The gin shall take him by the *h*
Ps 41:9 hath lifted up his *h* against me
Hos 12:3 his brother by the *h* in the womb
Jn 13:18 hath lifted up his *h* against me

**HEELS**
Gen 49:17 the path, that biteth the horse *h*
Job 13:27 a print upon the *h* of my feet
Ps 49:5 of my *h* shall compass me about
Jer 13:22 discovered, and thy *h* made bare

**HEGAI** *(he'-gahee)* See HEGE. *Servant of King Ahasuerus.*
Est 2:8 the palace, to the custody of *H*
Est 2:8 king's house, to the custody of *H*
Est 2:15 but what *H* the king's chamberlain

**HEGE** *(he'-ghe)* See HEGAI. *Same as Hegai.*
Est 2:3 unto the custody of *H* the king's

**HEIFER**
Gen 15:9 Take me an *h* of three years old,
Num 19:2 bring thee a red *h* without spot
Num 19:5 one shall burn the *h* in his sight
Num 19:6 the midst of the burning of the *h*
Num 19:9 gather up the ashes of the *h*
Num 19:10 of the *h* shall wash his clothes
Num 19:17 burnt *h* of purification for sin
Deut 21:3 of that city shall take an *h*
Deut 21:4 down the *h* unto a rough valley
Deut 21:6 *h* that is beheaded in the valley
Judg 14:18 If ye had not plowed with my *h*
1Sa 16:2 Take an *h* with thee, and say, I am
Is 15:5 Zoar, an *h* of three years old
Jer 46:20 Egypt is like a very fair *h*
Jer 48:34 as an *h* of three years old
Jer 50:11 are grown fat as the *h* at grass
Hos 4:16 slideth back as a backsliding *h*
Hos 10:11 Ephraim is as an *h* that is taught
Heb 9:13 the ashes of an *h* sprinkling the

**HEIGHT**
Gen 6:15 the *h* of it thirty cubits
Ex 25:10 a cubit and a half the *h* thereof
Ex 25:23 a cubit and a half the *h* thereof
Ex 27:1 the *h* thereof shall be three
Ex 27:18 the *h* five cubits of fine twined
Ex 30:2 two cubits shall be the *h* thereof
Ex 37:1 and a cubit and a half the *h* of it
Ex 37:10 a cubit and a half the *h* thereof
Ex 37:25 and two cubits was the *h* of it
Ex 38:1 and three cubits the *h* thereof
Ex 38:18 the *h* in the breadth was five
1Sa 16:7 or on the *h* of his stature
1Sa 17:4 whose *h* was six cubits and a span
1Kin 6:2 the *h* thereof thirty cubits
1Kin 6:20 and twenty cubits in the *h* thereof
1Kin 6:26 The *h* of the one cherub was ten
1Kin 7:2 the *h* thereof thirty cubits, upon
1Kin 7:16 the *h* of the one chapiter was
1Kin 7:16 the *h* of the other chapiter was
1Kin 7:23 about, and his *h* was five cubits
1Kin 7:27 and three cubits the *h* of it
1Kin 7:32 the *h* of a wheel was a cubit and
2Kin 19:23 come up to the *h* of the mountains
2Kin 25:17 The *h* of the one pillar was
2Kin 25:17 the *h* of the chapiter three
2Chr 3:4 the *h* was an hundred and twenty
2Chr 4:1 and ten cubits the *h* thereof
2Chr 4:2 and five cubits the *h* thereof
2Chr 33:14 and raised it up a very great *h*
Ezr 6:3 the *h* thereof threescore cubits,
Job 22:12 Is not God in the *h* of heaven
Job 22:12 behold the *h* of the stars, how
Ps 102:19 down from the *h* of his sanctuary
Prov 25:3 The heaven for *h*, and the earth
Is 7:11 in the depth, or in the *h* above
Is 37:24 come up to the *h* of the mountains
Is 37:24 enter into the *h* of his border
Jer 31:12 come and sing in the *h* of Zion
Jer 49:16 that holdest the *h* of the hill
Jer 51:53 fortify the *h* of her strength
Jer 52:21 the *h* of one pillar was eighteen
Jer 52:22 the *h* of one chapiter was five
Eze 17:23 In the mountain of the *h* of
Eze 19:11 she appeared in her *h* with the
Eze 20:40 the mountain of the *h* of Israel
Eze 31:5 Therefore his *h* was exalted above
Eze 31:10 thou hast lifted up thyself in *h*
Eze 31:10 his heart is lifted up in his *h*
Eze 31:14 exalt themselves for their *h*
Eze 31:14 their trees stand up in their *h*
Eze 32:5 and fill the valleys with thy *h*
Eze 40:5 and the *h*, one reed
Eze 41:8 I saw also the *h* of the house
Dan 3:1 whose *h* was threescore cubits, and
Dan 4:10 earth, and the *h* thereof was great
Dan 4:11 the *h* thereof reached unto heaven
Dan 4:20 whose *h* reached unto the heaven,
Amos 2:9 whose *h* was like the *h* of
Amos 2:9 was like the *h* of the cedars
Rom 8:39 Nor *h*, nor depth, nor any other
Eph 3:18 and length, and depth, and *h*
Rev 21:16 breadth and the *h* of it are equal

**HEIR**
Gen 15:3 one born in my house is mine *h*
Gen 15:4 saying, This shall not be thine *h*
Gen 15:4 thine own bowels shall be thine *h*
Gen 21:10 shall not be *h* with my son
2Sa 14:7 and we will destroy the *h* also
Prov 30:23 that is *h* to her mistress
Jer 49:1 hath he no *h*?
Jer 49:2 then shall Israel be *h* unto them
Mic 1:15 Yet will I bring an *h* unto thee
Mt 21:38 among themselves, This is the *h*
Mk 12:7 among themselves, This is the *h*
Lk 20:14 themselves, saying, This is the *h*
Rom 4:13 he should be the *h* of the world
Gal 4:1 Now I say, That the *h*, as long as
Gal 4:7 then an *h* of God through Christ
Gal 4:30 of the bondwoman shall not be *h*
Heb 1:2 he hath appointed *h* of all things
Heb 11:7 became *h* of the righteousness

**HEIRS**
Jer 49:2 be heir unto them that were his *h*
Rom 4:14 if they which are of the law be *h*
Rom 8:17 And if children, then *h*
Rom 8:17 *h* of God, and joint-heirs with
Gal 3:29 *h* according to the promise
Titus 3:7 we should be made *h* according to
Heb 1:14 them who shall be *h* of salvation
Heb 6:17 abundantly to shew unto the *h* of
Heb 11:9 the *h* with him of the same
Jas 2:5 *h* of the kingdom which he hath
1Pet 3:7 as being *h* together of the grace

**HELAH** *(he'-lah) A wife of Asher.*
1Chr 4:5 father of Tekoa had two wives, *H*
1Chr 4:7 And the sons of *H* were, Zereth, and

**HELAM** *(he'-lam) A place east of the Jordan.*
2Sa 10:16 and they came to *H*
2Sa 10:17 passed over Jordan, and came to *H*

**HELBAH** *(hel'-bah) A town in Asher.*
Judg 1:31 of Ahlab, nor of Achzib, nor of *H*

**HELBON** *(hel'-bon) A city near Damascus.*
Eze 27:18 in the wine of *H*, and white wool

**HELD**
Gen 24:21 man wondering at her *h* his peace
Gen 34:5 Jacob *h* his peace until they were
Gen 48:17 he *h* up his father's hand, to
Ex 17:11 when Moses *h* up his hand, that
Ex 36:12 the loops *h* one curtain to
Lev 10:3 And Aaron *h* his peace
Num 30:7 *h* his peace at her in the day
Num 30:11 *h* his peace at her, and disallowed
Num 30:14 because he *h* his peace at her in
Judg 7:20 *h* the lamps in their left hands,
Judg 16:26 the lad that *h* him by the hand
Ruth 3:15 And when she *h* it, he measured six
1Sa 10:27 But he *h* his peace
1Sa 25:36 he *h* a feast in his house, like
2Sa 18:16 for Joab *h* back the people
1Kin 8:65 And at that time Solomon *h* a feast
2Kin 18:36 But the people *h* their peace
2Chr 4:5 and *h* three thousand baths
Neh 4:16 half of them *h* both the spears
Neh 4:17 and with the other hand *h* a weapon
Neh 4:21 half of them *h* the spears from
Neh 5:8 Then *h* they their peace, and found
Est 5:2 the king *h* out to Esther the
Est 7:4 I had *h* my tongue, although the
Est 8:4 Then the king *h* out the golden
Job 23:11 My foot hath *h* his steps, his way
Job 29:10 The nobles *h* their peace, and
Ps 32:9 whose mouth must be *h* in with bit
Ps 39:2 I *h* my peace, even from good
Ps 94:18 thy mercy, O LORD, *h* me up
Song 3:4 I *h* him, and would not let him go,
Song 7:5 the king is *h* in the galleries
Is 36:21 But they *h* their peace, and
Is 57:11 have not I *h* my peace even of old
Jer 50:33 took them captives *h* them fast
Dan 12:7 when he *h* up his right hand and
Mt 12:14 *h* a council against him, how they
Mt 26:63 But Jesus *h* his peace
Mt 28:9 *h* him by the feet, and worshipped
Mk 3:4 But they *h* their peace
Mk 9:34 But they *h* their peace
Mk 14:61 But he *h* his peace, and answered
Mk 15:1 the morning the chief priests *h* a
Lk 14:4 And they *h* their peace
Lk 20:26 at his answer, and *h* their peace
Lk 22:63 the men that *h* Jesus mocked him,
Acts 3:11 lame man which was healed *h* Peter
Acts 11:18 they *h* their peace, and glorified
Acts 14:4 part *h* with the Jews, and part
Acts 15:13 And after they had *h* their peace
Rom 7:6 that being dead wherein we were *h*
Rev 6:9 and for the testimony which they *h*

**HELDAI** *(hel'-dahee)* See HELED, HELEM.
*1. A sanctuary servant.*
1Chr 27:15 month was *H* the Netophathite
*2. An honored exile.*
Zec 6:10 them of the captivity, even of *H*

**HELEB** *(he'-leb)* See HELED. *A "mighty man" of David.*
2Sa 23:29 *H* the son of Baanah, a

**HELED** *(he'-led)* See HELEB, HELDAI. *Same as Heleb.*
1Chr 11:30 *H* the son of Baanah the

**HELEK** *(he'-lek)* See HELEKITES. *A son of Gilead.*
Num 26:30 of *H*, the family of the Helekites
Josh 17:2 Abiezer, and for the children of *H*

**HELEKITES** *(he'-lek-ites) Descendants of Helek.*
Num 26:30 of Helek, the family of the *H*

**HELEM** *(he'-lem)*
*1. A descendant of Asher.*
1Chr 7:35 And the sons of his brother *H*

*2. Same as Heldai 2.*
Zec 6:14 And the crowns shall be to *H*

**HELEPH** *(he'-lef) A town in Naphtali.*
Josh 19:33 And their coast was from *H*

**HELEZ** *(he'-lez)*
*1. A "mighty man" of David.*
2Sa 23:26 *H* the Paltite, Ira the son of
1Chr 11:27 the Harorite, *H* the Pelonite,
1Chr 27:10 seventh month was *H* the Pelonite
*2. A son of Azariah.*
1Chr 2:39 And Azariah begat *H*, and Helez
1Chr 2:39 begat Helez, and *H* begat Eleasah,

**HELI** *(he'-li)* See ELI. *Father of Joseph; ancestor of Jesus.*
Lk 3:23 of Joseph, which was the son of *H*

**HELKAI** *(hel'-kahee) A priest.*
Neh 12:15 Adna; of Meraioth, *H*

**HELKATH** *(hel'-kath)* See HELKATH-HAZZURIM, HUKOK. *A town in Asher.*
Josh 19:25 And their border was *H*, and Hali,
Josh 21:31 *H* with her suburbs, and Rehob with

**HELKATH-HAZZURIM** *(hel'-kath-haz'-zu-rim) A plain near the pool of Gibeon.*
2Sa 2:16 wherefore that place was called *H*

**HELL**
Deut 32:22 and shall burn unto the lowest *h*
2Sa 22:6 The sorrows of *h* compassed me
Job 11:8 deeper than *h*
Job 26:6 *H* is naked before him, and
Ps 9:17 The wicked shall be turned into *h*
Ps 16:10 thou wilt not leave my soul in *h*
Ps 18:5 The sorrows of *h* compassed me
Ps 55:15 and let them go down quick into *h*
Ps 86:13 my soul from the lowest *h*
Ps 116:3 the pains of *h* gat hold upon me
Ps 139:8 if I make my bed in *h*, behold,
Prov 5:5 her steps take hold on *h*
Prov 7:27 Her house is the way to *h*
Prov 9:18 her guests are in the depths of *h*
Prov 15:11 *H* and destruction are before the
Prov 15:24 that he may depart from *h* beneath
Prov 23:14 and shalt deliver his soul from *h*
Prov 27:20 *H* and destruction are never full
Is 5:14 Therefore *h* hath enlarged herself
Is 14:9 *H* from beneath is moved for thee
Is 14:15 thou shalt be brought down to *h*
Is 28:15 with *h* are we at agreement
Is 28:18 agreement with *h* shall not stand
Is 57:9 didst debase thyself even unto *h*
Eze 31:16 when I cast him down to *h* with
Eze 31:17 They also went down into *h* with
Eze 32:21 of *h* with them that help him
Eze 32:27 which are gone down to *h* with
Amos 9:2 Though they dig into *h*, thence
Jonah 2:2 out of the belly of *h* cried I
Hab 2:5 who enlargeth his desire as *h*
Mt 5:22 shall be in danger of *h* fire
Mt 5:29 whole body should be cast into *h*
Mt 5:30 whole body should be cast into *h*
Mt 10:28 to destroy both soul and body in *h*
Mt 11:23 shalt be brought down to *h*
Mt 16:18 the gates of *h* shall not prevail
Mt 18:9 two eyes to be cast into *h* fire
Mt 23:15 the child of *h* than yourselves
Mt 23:33 can ye escape the damnation of *h*
Mk 9:43 having two hands to go into *h*
Mk 9:45 having two feet to be cast into *h*
Mk 9:47 two eyes to be cast into *h* fire
Lk 10:15 heaven, shalt be thrust down to *h*
Lk 12:5 killed hath power to cast into *h*
Lk 16:23 in *h* he lift up his eyes, being
Acts 2:27 thou wilt not leave my soul in *h*
Acts 2:31 that his soul was not left in *h*
Jas 3:6 and it is set on fire of *h*
2Pet 2:4 sinned, but cast them down to *h*
Rev 1:18 and have the keys of *h* and of death
Rev 6:8 was Death, and *H* followed with him
Rev 20:13 *h* delivered up the dead which
Rev 20:14 *h* were cast into the lake of fire

**HELMET**
1Sa 17:5 he had an *h* of brass upon his
1Sa 17:38 he put an *h* of brass upon his
Is 59:17 an *h* of salvation upon his head
Eze 23:24 and shield and *h* round about
Eze 27:10 hanged the shield and *h* in thee
Eze 38:5 all of them with shield and *h*
Eph 6:17 take the *h* of salvation, and the
1Th 5:8 and for an *h*, the hope of

**HELON** *(he'-lon) Father of Eliab.*
Num 1:9 Eliab the son of *H*
Num 2:7 Eliab the son of *H* shall be
Num 7:24 the third day Eliab the son of *H*
Num 7:29 offering of Eliab the son of *H*
Num 10:16 of Zebulun was Eliab the son of *H*

**HELP**
Gen 2:18 I will make him an *h* meet for him
Gen 2:20 was not found an *h* meet for him
Gen 49:25 of thy father, who shall *h* thee
Ex 18:4 of my father, said he, was mine *h*
Ex 23:5 and wouldest forbear to *h* him
Ex 23:5 thou shalt surely *h* with him
Deut 22:4 thou shalt surely *h* him to lift
Deut 32:38 *h* you, and be your protection
Deut 33:7 be thou an *h* to him from his
Deut 33:26 rideth upon the heaven in thy *h*
Deut 33:29 by the LORD, the shield of thy *h*
Josh 1:14 mighty men of valour, and *h* them
Josh 10:4 *h* me, that we may smite Gibeon
Josh 10:6 us quickly, and save us, and *h* us
Josh 10:33 of Gezer came up to *h* Lachish
Judg 5:23 came not to the *h* of the LORD
Judg 5:23 to the *h* of the LORD against the
1Sa 11:9 the sun be hot, ye shall have *h*
2Sa 10:11 for me, then thou shalt *h* me
2Sa 10:11 thee, then I will come and *h* thee
2Sa 10:19 So the Syrians feared to *h* the
2Sa 14:4 and did obeisance, and said, *H*
2Kin 6:26 cried a woman unto him, saying, *H*
2Kin 6:27 *h* thee, whence shall I *h* thee
1Chr 12:17 be come peaceably unto me to *h* me
1Chr 12:22 day there came to David to *h* him
1Chr 18:5 came to *h* Hadarezer king of Zobah
1Chr 19:12 for me, then thou shalt *h* me
1Chr 19:12 for thee, then I will *h* thee
1Chr 19:19 neither would the Syrians *h* the
1Chr 22:17 of Israel to *h* Solomon his son
2Chr 14:11 it is nothing with thee to *h*
2Chr 14:11 *h* us, O LORD our God
2Chr 19:2 Shouldest thou *h* the ungodly
2Chr 20:4 together, to ask *h* of the LORD
2Chr 20:9 then thou wilt hear and *h*
2Chr 25:8 for God hath power to *h*, and to
2Chr 26:13 to *h* the king against the enemy
2Chr 28:16 the kings of Assyria to *h* him
2Chr 28:23 gods of the kings of Syria *h* them
2Chr 28:23 to them, that they may *h* me
2Chr 29:34 brethren the Levites did *h* them
2Chr 32:3 and they did *h* him
2Chr 32:8 us is the LORD our God to *h* us
Ezr 1:4 of his place *h* him with silver
Ezr 8:22 horsemen to *h* us against the
Job 6:13 Is not my *h* in me
Job 8:20 neither will he *h* the evil doers
Job 29:12 and him that had none to *h* him
Job 31:21 when I saw my *h* in the gate
Ps 3:2 There is no *h* for him in God
Ps 12:1 *H*, LORD; for the godly
Ps 20:2 Send thee *h* from the sanctuary,
Ps 22:11 for there is none to *h*
Ps 22:19 O my strength, haste thee to *h* me
Ps 27:9 thou hast been my *h*
Ps 33:20 he is our *h* and our shield
Ps 35:2 buckler, and stand up for mine *h*
Ps 37:40 And the LORD shall *h* them, and
Ps 38:22 Make haste to *h* me, O Lord my
Ps 40:13 O LORD, make haste to *h* me
Ps 40:17 thou art my *h* and my deliverer
Ps 42:5 him for the *h* of his countenance
Ps 44:26 Arise for our *h*, and redeem us for
Ps 46:1 a very present *h* in trouble
Ps 46:5 God shall *h* her, and that right
Ps 59:4 awake to *h* me, and behold
Ps 60:11 Give us *h* from trouble
Ps 60:11 for vain is the *h* of man
Ps 63:7 Because thou hast been my *h*
Ps 70:1 make haste to *h* me, O LORD
Ps 70:5 thou art my *h* and my deliverer
Ps 71:12 O my God, make haste for my *h*
Ps 79:9 *H* us, O God of our salvation, for
Ps 89:19 I have laid *h* upon one that is
Ps 94:17 Unless the LORD had been my *h*
Ps 107:12 fell down, and there was none to *h*
Ps 108:12 Give us *h* from trouble
Ps 108:12 for vain is the *h* of man
Ps 109:26 *H* me, O LORD my God
Ps 115:9 he is their *h* and their shield
Ps 115:10 he is their *h* and their shield
Ps 115:11 he is their *h* and their shield
Ps 118:7 my part with them that *h* me
Ps 119:86 *h* thou me
Ps 119:173 Let thine hand *h* me
Ps 119:175 and let thy judgments *h* me
Ps 121:1 hills, from whence cometh my *h*
Ps 121:2 My *h* cometh from the LORD, which
Ps 124:8 Our *h* is in the name of the LORD,
Ps 146:3 son of man, in whom there is no *h*
Ps 146:5 hath the God of Jacob for his *h*
Eccl 4:10 he hath not another to *h* him up
Is 10:3 to whom will ye flee for *h*
Is 20:6 whither we flee for *h* to be
Is 30:5 nor be an *h* nor profit, but a
Is 30:7 For the Egyptians shall *h* in vain
Is 31:1 them that go down to Egypt for *h*
Is 31:2 against the *h* of them that work
Is 41:10 yea, I will *h* thee
Is 41:13 I will *h* thee
Is 41:14 I will *h* thee, saith the LORD, and
Is 44:2 from the womb, which will *h* thee
Is 50:7 For the Lord GOD will *h* me
Is 50:9 Behold, the Lord GOD will *h* me
Is 63:5 I looked, and there was none to *h*
Jer 37:7 which is come forth to *h* you
Lam 1:7 of the enemy, and none did *h* her
Lam 4:17 eyes as yet failed for our vain *h*
Eze 12:14 all that are about him to *h* him
Eze 32:21 of hell with them that *h* him
Dan 10:13 the chief princes, came to *h* me
Dan 11:34 shall be holpen with a little *h*
Dan 11:45 to his end, and none shall *h* him
Hos 13:9 but in me is thine *h*
Mt 15:25 him, saying, Lord, *h* me
Mk 9:22 have compassion on us, and *h* us
Mk 9:24 *h* thou mine unbelief
Lk 5:7 that they should come and *h* them
Lk 10:40 bid her therefore that she *h* me
Acts 16:9 Come over into Macedonia, and *h* us
Acts 21:28 Crying out, Men of Israel, *h*
Acts 26:22 therefore obtained *h* of God
Phil 4:3 *h* those women which laboured with
Heb 4:16 find grace to *h* in time of need

**HELPED**
Ex 2:17 *h* them, and watered their flock
1Sa 7:12 Hitherto hath the LORD *h* us
1Kin 1:7 and they following Adonijah *h* him
1Kin 20:16 thirty and two kings that *h* him
1Chr 5:20 they were *h* against them, and the
1Chr 12:19 but they *h* them not
1Chr 12:21 they *h* David against the band of
1Chr 15:26 when God *h* the Levites that bare
2Chr 18:31 cried out, and the LORD *h* him
2Chr 20:23 every one *h* to destroy another
2Chr 26:7 God *h* him against the Philistines
2Chr 26:15 for he was marvellously *h*
2Chr 28:21 but he *h* him not
Ezr 10:15 and Shabbethai the Levite *h* them
Est 9:3 officers of the king, *h* the Jews
Job 26:2 How hast thou *h* him that is
Ps 28:7 heart trusted in him, and I am *h*
Ps 116:6 I was brought low, and he *h* me
Ps 118:13 but the LORD *h* me
Is 41:6 They *h* every one his neighbour
Is 49:8 a day of salvation have I *h* thee
Zec 1:15 they *h* forward the affliction
Acts 18:27 *h* them much which had believed
Rev 12:16 And the earth *h* the woman, and the

**HELPER**
2Kin 14:26 any left, nor any *h* for Israel
Job 30:13 my calamity, they have no *h*
Ps 10:14 thou art the *h* of the fatherless
Ps 30:10 LORD, be thou my *h*
Ps 54:4 Behold, God is mine *h*
Ps 72:12 poor also, and him that hath no *h*
Jer 47:4 Zidon every *h* that remaineth
Rom 16:9 our *h* in Christ, and Stachys my
Heb 13:6 may boldly say, The Lord is my *h*

**HELPERS**
1Chr 12:1 the mighty men, *h* of the war
1Chr 12:18 unto thee, and peace be to thine *h*
Job 9:13 the proud *h* do stoop under him
Eze 30:8 when all her *h* shall be destroyed
Nah 3:9 Put and Lubim were thy *h*
Rom 16:3 Aquila my *h* in Christ Jesus
2Cor 1:24 your faith, but are *h* of your joy

**HELPETH**
1Chr 12:18 for thy God *h* thee
Is 31:3 hand, both he that *h* shall fall
Rom 8:26 the Spirit also *h* our infirmities
1Cor 16:16 and to every one that *h* with us

**HEM**
Ex 28:33 beneath upon the *h* of it thou
Ex 28:33 round about the *h* thereof
Ex 28:34 upon the *h* of the robe round
Ex 39:25 upon the *h* of the robe, round
Ex 39:26 round about the *h* of the robe to
Mt 9:20 touched the *h* of his garment
Mt 14:36 only touch the *h* of his garment

**HEMAM** *(he'-mam)* See HOMAM. *A son of Lotan.*
Gen 36:22 children of Lotan were Hori and *H*

**HEMAN** *(he'-man)*
*1. A son of Zerah.*
1Kin 4:31 than Ethan the Ezrahite, and *H*
1Chr 2:6 Zimri, and Ethan, and *H*, and Calcol,
1Chr 25:4 Of *H*: the sons of *H*
*2. A son of Joel.*
1Chr 6:33 *H* a singer, the son of Joel, the
1Chr 15:17 appointed *H* the son of Joel
1Chr 15:19 So the singers, *H*, Asaph, and
1Chr 16:41 And with them *H* and Jeduthun, and
1Chr 16:42 And with them *H* and Jeduthun with
1Chr 25:1 of the sons of Asaph, and of *H*
1Chr 25:5 All these were the sons of *H* the
1Chr 25:5 God gave to *H* fourteen sons and
1Chr 25:6 order to Asaph, Jeduthun, and *H*
2Chr 5:12 all of them of Asaph, of *H*
2Chr 29:14 And of the sons of *H*
2Chr 35:15 of David, and Asaph, and *H*, and
Ps 88:*t* Maschil of *H* the Ezrahite

**HEMATH** *(he'-math)* See HAMATH.
*1. Same as Hamath.*
1Chr 13:5 Egypt even unto the entering of *H*
Amos 6:14 in of *H* unto the river of the
*2. Father of the Kenites and Rechabites.*
1Chr 2:55 are the Kenites that came of *H*

**HEMDAN** *(hem'-dan)* See AMRAM. *Son of Dishon.*
Gen 36:26 *H*, and Eshban, and Ithran, and

**HEMLOCK**
Hos 10:4 as *h* in the furrows of the field
Amos 6:12 the fruit of righteousness into *h*

**HEN** *(hen) A son of Zephaniah.*
Zec 6:14 to *H* the son of Zephaniah, for a
Mt 23:37 even as a *h* gathereth her
Lk 13:34 as a *h* doth gather her brood

**HENA** *(he'-nah) A city on the Euphrates.*
2Kin 18:34 are the gods of Sepharvaim, *H*
2Kin 19:13 of the city of Sepharvaim, of *H*
Is 37:13 king of the city of Sepharvaim, *H*

**HENADAD** *(hen'-a-dad) A Levite.*
Ezr 3:9 the sons of *H*, with their sons and
Neh 3:18 brethren, Bavai the son of *H*
Neh 3:24 Binnui the son of *H* another piece
Neh 10:9 Azaniah, Binnui of the sons of *H*

**HENCE**
Gen 37:17 the man said, They are departed *h*
Gen 42:15 Pharaoh ye shall not go forth *h*
Gen 50:25 ye shall carry up my bones from *h*
Ex 11:1 afterwards he will let you go *h*
Ex 11:1 thrust you out *h* altogether
Ex 13:19 carry up my bones away *h* with you
Ex 33:1 unto Moses, Depart, and go up *h*
Ex 33:15 go not with me, carry us not up *h*
Deut 9:12 get thee down quickly from *h*
Josh 4:3 Take you *h* out of the midst of
Judg 6:18 Depart not *h*, I pray thee, until
Ruth 2:8 another field, neither go from *h*
1Kin 17:3 Get thee *h*, and turn thee eastward
Ps 39:13 recover strength, before I go *h*
Is 30:22 shalt say unto it, Get thee *h*
Jer 38:10 Take from *h* thirty men with thee,
Zec 6:7 and he said, Get you *h*, walk to and
Mt 4:10 saith Jesus unto him, Get thee *h*
Mt 17:20 Remove *h* to yonder place
Lk 4:9 of God, cast thyself down from *h*
Lk 13:31 him, Get thee out, and depart *h*
Lk 16:26 would pass from *h* to you cannot
Jn 2:16 sold doves, Take these things *h*
Jn 7:3 therefore said unto him, Depart *h*
Jn 14:31 Arise, let us go *h*
Jn 18:36 but now is my kingdom not from *h*
Jn 20:15 Sir, if thou have borne him *h*
Acts 1:5 the Holy Ghost not many days *h*
Acts 22:21 send thee far *h* unto the Gentiles
Jas 4:1 come they not *h*, even of your

**HENCEFORTH**
Gen 4:12 it shall not *h* yield unto thee
Num 18:22 must the children of Israel *h*
Deut 17:16 Ye shall *h* return no more that
Deut 19:20 shall *h* commit no more any such
Judg 2:21 I also will not *h* drive out any
2Kin 5:17 for thy servant will *h* offer
2Chr 16:9 therefore from *h* thou shalt have
Ps 125:2 his people from *h* even for ever
Ps 131:3 Israel hope in the LORD from *h*
Is 9:7 with justice from *h* even for ever
Is 52:1 for *h* there shall no more come
Is 59:21 seed, saith the LORD, from *h*
Eze 36:12 thou shalt no more *h* bereave them
Mic 4:7 over them in mount Zion from *h*
Mt 23:39 unto you, Ye shall not see me *h*
Mt 26:29 I will not drink *h* of this fruit
Lk 1:48 from *h* all generations shall call
Lk 5:10 from *h* thou shalt catch men
Lk 12:52 For from *h* there shall be five in
Jn 14:7 from *h* ye know him, and have seen
Jn 15:15 *H* I call you not servants
Acts 4:17 that they speak *h* to no man in
Acts 18:6 from *h* I will go unto the
Rom 6:6 that *h* we should not serve sin
2Cor 5:15 should not *h* live unto themselves
2Cor 5:16 *h* know we no man after
2Cor 5:16 yet now *h* know we him no more
Gal 6:17 From *h* let no man trouble me
Eph 4:14 That we *h* be no more children,
Eph 4:17 that ye *h* walk not as other
2Ti 4:8 *H* there is laid up for me a crown
Heb 10:13 From *h* expecting till his enemies
Rev 14:13 dead which die in the Lord from *h*

**HENOCH** *(he'-nok)* See ENOCH. *Same as Enoch.*
1Chr 1:3 *H*, Methuselah, Lamech,
1Chr 1:33 Ephah, and Epher, and *H*, and Abida,

**HEPHER** *(he'-fer)* See GATH-HEPHER, HEPHERITES.
*1. A son of Gilead.*
Num 26:32 and of *H*, the family of the
Num 26:33 the son of *H* had no sons, but
Num 27:1 of Zelophehad, the son of *H*
Josh 17:2 Shechem, and for the children of *H*
Josh 17:3 But Zelophehad, the son of *H*
*2. A son of Naarah.*
1Chr 4:6 And Naarah bare him Ahuzam, and *H*
*3. A "mighty man" of David.*
1Chr 11:36 *H* the Mecherathite, Ahijah the
*4. A Canaanite city.*
Josh 12:17 the king of *H*, one
1Kin 4:10 Sochoh, and all the land of *H*

**HEPHERITES** *(he'-fer-ites) Descendants of Hepher 1.*
Num 26:32 and of Hepher, the family of the *H*

**HEPHZI-BAH** *(hef'-zi-bah)*
*1. Wife of King Hezekiah.*
2Kin 21:1 And his mother's name was *H*
*2. A symbolic name for Jerusalem.*
Is 62:4 but thou shalt be called *H*

**HERB**
Gen 1:11 the *h* yielding seed, and the fruit
Gen 1:12 *h* yielding seed after his kind,
Gen 1:29 given you every *h* bearing seed
Gen 1:30 have given every green *h* for meat
Gen 2:5 every *h* of the field before it
Gen 3:18 thou shalt eat the *h* of the field
Gen 9:3 even as the green *h* have I given
Ex 9:22 upon every *h* of the field,
Ex 9:25 hail smote every *h* of the field
Ex 10:12 eat every *h* of the land, even all
Ex 10:15 they did eat every *h* of the land
Deut 32:2 the small rain upon the tender *h*
2Kin 19:26 of the field, and as the green *h*
Job 8:12 it withereth before any other *h*
Job 38:27 of the tender *h* to spring forth
Ps 37:2 grass, and wither as the green *h*
Ps 104:14 and *h* for the service of man
Is 37:27 of the field, and as the green *h*
Is 66:14 bones shall flourish like an *h*

**HERBS**
Ex 10:15 or in the *h* of the field, through
Ex 12:8 with bitter *h* they shall eat it
Num 9:11 with unleavened bread and bitter *h*
Deut 11:10 with thy foot, as a garden of *h*
1Kin 21:2 I may have it for a garden of *h*
2Kin 4:39 out into the field to gather *h*
Ps 105:35 eat up all the *h* in their land
Prov 15:17 is a dinner of *h* where love is
Prov 27:25 *h* of the mountains are gathered
Is 18:4 place like a clear heat upon *h*
Is 26:19 for thy dew is as the dew of *h*
Is 42:15 and hills, and dry up all their *h*
Jer 12:4 the *h* of every field wither, for
Mt 13:32 grown, it is the greatest among *h*
Mk 4:32 and becometh greater than all *h*
Lk 11:42 mint and rue and all manner of *h*
Rom 14:2 another, who is weak, eateth *h*
Heb 6:7 bringeth forth *h* meet for them by

**HERD**
Gen 18:7 And Abraham ran unto the *h*
Lev 1:2 of the cattle, even of the *h*
Lev 1:3 be a burnt sacrifice of the *h*
Lev 3:1 offering, if he offer it of the *h*
Lev 27:32 And concerning the tithe of the *h*
Num 15:3 savour unto the LORD, of the *h*
Deut 12:21 then thou shalt kill of thy *h*
Deut 15:19 males that come of thy *h* and of
Deut 16:2 thy God, of the flock and the *h*
1Sa 11:5 came after the *h* out of the field
2Sa 12:4 of his own flock and of his own *h*
Jer 31:12 young of the flock and of the *h*
Jonah 3:7 *h* nor flock, taste any thing
Hab 3:17 there shall be no *h* in the stalls
Mt 8:30 them an *h* of many swine feeding
Mt 8:31 us to go away into the *h* of swine
Mt 8:32 they went into the *h* of swine
Mt 8:32 behold, the whole *h* of swine ran
Mk 5:11 a great *h* of swine feeding
Mk 5:13 the *h* ran violently down a steep
Lk 8:32 there was there an *h* of many
Lk 8:33 the *h* ran violently down a steep

**HERDMEN**
Gen 13:7 between the *h* of Abram's cattle
Gen 13:7 cattle and the *h* of Lot's cattle
Gen 13:8 and between my *h* and thy *h*
Gen 26:20 the *h* of Gerar did strive with
Gen 26:20 Gerar did strive with Isaac's *h*
1Sa 21:7 the chiefest of the *h* that
Amos 1:1 who was among the *h* of Tekoa

**HERDS**
Gen 13:5 went with Abram, had flocks, and *h*
Gen 24:35 and he hath given him flocks, and *h*
Gen 26:14 of flocks, and possession of *h*
Gen 32:7 was with him, and the flocks, and *h*
Gen 33:13 and *h* with young are with me
Gen 45:10 children, and thy flocks, and thy *h*
Gen 46:32 brought their flocks, and their *h*
Gen 47:1 and their flocks, and their *h*
Gen 47:17 and for the cattle of the *h*
Gen 47:18 my lord also hath our *h* of cattle
Gen 50:8 ones, and their flocks, and their *h*
Ex 10:9 flocks and with our *h* will we go
Ex 10:24 your flocks and your *h* be stayed
Ex 12:32 Also take your flocks and your *h*
Ex 12:38 and flocks, and *h*, even very much
Ex 34:3 nor *h* feed before that mount
Num 11:22 the *h* be slain for them, to
Deut 8:13 And when thy *h* and thy flocks
Deut 12:6 and the firstlings of your *h*
Deut 12:17 of thy *h* or of thy flock, nor any
Deut 14:23 oil, and the firstlings of thy *h*
1Sa 30:20 took all the flocks and the *h*
2Sa 12:2 had exceeding many flocks and *h*
1Chr 27:29 over the *h* that fed in Sharon was
1Chr 27:29 over the *h* that were in the
2Chr 32:29 of flocks and *h* in abundance
Neh 10:36 law, and the firstlings of our *h*
Prov 27:23 thy flocks, and look well to thy *h*
Is 65:10 a place for the *h* to lie down in
Jer 3:24 their flocks and their *h*, their
Jer 5:17 eat up thy flocks and thine *h*
Hos 5:6 with their *h* to seek the LORD
Joel 1:18 the *h* of cattle are perplexed,

**HERES** *(he'-res)* See KIR-HERES, TIMMATH-HERES. *A mountain in Judah.*
Judg 1:35 would dwell in mount *H* in Aijalon

**HERESH** *(he'-resh) A Levite.*
1Chr 9:15 And Bakbakkar, *H*, and Galal, and

**HERITAGE**
Ex 6:8 and I will give it you for an *h*
Job 20:29 the *h* appointed unto him by God
Job 27:13 the *h* of oppressors, which they
Ps 16:6 yea, I have a goodly *h*
Ps 61:5 thou hast given me the *h* of those
Ps 94:5 O LORD, and afflict thine *h*
Ps 111:6 give them the *h* of the heathen
Ps 119:111 have I taken as an *h* for ever
Ps 127:3 Lo, children are an *h* of the LORD
Ps 135:12 And gave their land for an *h*
Ps 135:12 an *h* unto Israel his people
Ps 136:21 And gave their land for an *h*
Ps 136:22 Even an *h* unto Israel his servant
Is 54:17 This is the *h* of the servants of
Is 58:14 feed thee with the *h* of Jacob thy
Jer 2:7 made mine *h* an abomination
Jer 3:19 a goodly *h* of the hosts of
Jer 12:7 mine house, I have left mine *h*
Jer 12:8 Mine *h* is unto me as a lion in
Jer 12:9 Mine *h* is unto me as a speckled
Jer 12:15 them again, every man to his *h*
Jer 17:4 from thine *h* that I gave thee
Jer 50:11 O ye destroyers of mine *h*
Joel 2:17 and give not thine *h* to reproach
Joel 3:2 for my people and for my *h* Israel
Mic 2:2 and his house, even a man and his *h*
Mic 7:14 thy rod, the flock of thine *h*
Mic 7:18 of the remnant of his *h*
Mal 1:3 his *h* waste for the dragons of
1Pet 5:3 as being lords over God's *h*

**HERMAS** *(her'-mas) A Christian acquaintance of Paul.*
Rom 16:14 Salute Asyncritus, Phlegon, *H*

**HERMES** *(her'-mees) A Christian acquaintance of Paul.*
Rom 16:14 Phlegon, Hermas, Patrobas, *H*

**HERMOGENES** *(her-mog'-e-nees) A false Christian teacher.*
2Ti 1:15 of whom are Phygellus and *H*

**HERMON**
Deut 3:8 the river of Arnon unto mount *H*
Deut 3:9 (Which *H* the Sidonians call
Deut 4:48 even unto mount Sion which is *H*
Josh 11:3 to the Hivite under *H* in the land
Josh 11:17 valley of Lebanon under mount *H*
Josh 12:1 from the river Arnon unto mount *H*
Josh 12:5 And reigned in mount *H*, and in
Josh 13:5 from Baal-gad under mount *H* unto
Josh 13:11 and Maachathites, and all mount *H*
1Chr 5:23 and Senir, and unto mount *H*
Ps 89:12 *H* shall rejoice in thy name
Ps 133:3 As the dew of *H*, and as the dew
Song 4:8 from the top of Shenir and *H*

**HERMONITES** *(her'-mon-ites)* See HERMON. *Inhabitants of Mt. Hermon.*
Ps 42:6 the land of Jordan, and of the *H*

**HEROD** *(her'-od)* See HERODIANS, HEROD'S.
*1. Herod the Great.*
Mt 2:1 Judaea in the days of *H* the king
Mt 2:3 When *H* the king had heard these
Mt 2:7 Then *H*, when he had privily
Mt 2:12 that they should not return to *H*
Mt 2:13 for *H* will seek the young child
Mt 2:15 And was there until the death of *H*
Mt 2:16 Then *H*, when he saw that he was
Mt 2:19 But when *H* was dead, behold, an
Mt 2:22 in the room of his father *H*
Lk 1:5 There was in the days of *H*
Lk 23:15 No, nor yet *H*: for I sent
*2. Herod Antipas.*
Mt 14:1 At that time *H* the tetrarch heard
Mt 14:3 For *H* had laid hold on John, and
Mt 14:6 danced before them, and pleased *H*
Mk 6:14 And king *H* heard of him
Mk 6:16 But when *H* heard thereof, he said
Mk 6:17 For *H* himself had sent forth and
Mk 6:18 For John had said unto *H*, It is
Mk 6:20 For *H* feared John, knowing that
Mk 6:21 that *H* on his birthday made a
Mk 6:22 came in, and danced, and pleased *H*
Mk 8:15 Pharisees, and of the leaven of *H*
Lk 3:1 *H* being tetrarch of Galilee, and
Lk 3:19 But *H* the tetrarch, being
Lk 3:19 all the evils which *H* had done
Lk 9:7 Now *H* the tetrarch heard of all
Lk 9:9 *H* said, John have I beheaded
Lk 13:31 for *H* will kill thee
Lk 23:7 jurisdiction, he sent him to *H*
Lk 23:8 And when *H* saw Jesus, he was
Lk 23:11 *H* with his men of war set him at
Lk 23:12 *H* were made friends together
Acts 4:27 whom thou hast anointed, both *H*
Acts 13:1 brought up with *H* the tetrarch
*3. Herod Agrippa I.*
Acts 12:1 Now about that time *H* the king
Acts 12:6 when *H* would have brought him
Acts 12:11 delivered me out of the hand of *H*
Acts 12:19 when *H* had sought for him, and
Acts 12:20 *H* was highly displeased with them
Acts 12:21 And upon a set day *H*, arrayed in

**HERODIANS** *(he-ro'-de-uns) Hellenizing Jews.*
Mt 22:16 him their disciples with the *H*
Mk 3:6 counsel with the *H* against him
Mk 12:13 of the Pharisees and of the *H*

**HERODIAS** *(he-ro'-de-as)* See HERODIAS'. *Granddaughter of Herod 1.*
Mt 14:6 the daughter of *H* danced before
Mk 6:19 Therefore *H* had a quarrel against
Mk 6:22 daughter of the said *H* came in
Lk 3:19 for *H* his brother Philip's wife

**HERODIAS'** *(he-ro'-de-as)*
Mt 14:3 and put him in prison for *H* sake
Mk 6:17 and bound him in prison for *H* sake

**HERODION** *(he-ro'-de-on) A relative of Paul.*
Rom 16:11 Salute *H* my kinsman

**HEROD'S** *(her'-ods)*
*1. Refers to Herod 2.*
Mt 14:6 But when *H* birthday was kept, the
Lk 8:3 the wife of Chuza *H* steward
Lk 23:7 he belonged unto *H* jurisdiction
*2. Refers to Herod 3.*
Acts 23:35 him to be kept in *H* judgment hall

**HESED** *(he'-sed)* See JUSHAB-HESED. *Father of an officer of Solomon.*
1Kin 4:10 The son of *H*, in Aruboth

**HESHBON** *(hesh'-bon) A Levitical city in Reuben and Gad.*
Num 21:25 the cities of the Amorites, in *H*
Num 21:26 For *H* was the city of Sihon the
Num 21:27 in proverbs say, Come into *H*
Num 21:28 For there is a fire gone out of *H*
Num 21:30 *H* is perished even unto Dibon, and
Num 21:34 of the Amorites, which dwelt at *H*
Num 32:3 Dibon, and Jazer, and Nimrah, and *H*
Num 32:37 And the children of Reuben built *H*
Deut 1:4 of the Amorites, which dwelt in *H*
Deut 2:24 hand Sihon the Amorite, king of *H*
Deut 2:26 king of *H* with words of peace
Deut 2:30 But Sihon king of *H* would not let
Deut 3:2 of the Amorites, which dwelt at *H*
Deut 3:6 as we did unto Sihon king of *H*
Deut 4:46 of the Amorites, who dwelt at *H*
Deut 29:7 this place, Sihon the king of *H*
Josh 9:10 beyond Jordan, to Sihon king of *H*
Josh 12:2 of the Amorites, who dwelt in *H*
Josh 12:5 the border of Sihon king of *H*
Josh 13:10 the Amorites, which reigned in *H*
Josh 13:17 *H*, and all her cities that are in
Josh 13:21 the Amorites, which reigned in *H*
Josh 13:26 from *H* unto Ramath-mizpeh, and
Josh 13:27 of the kingdom of Sihon king of *H*
Josh 21:39 *H* with her suburbs, Jazer with
Judg 11:19 of the Amorites, the king of *H*
Judg 11:26 While Israel dwelt in *H* and her
1Chr 6:81 *H* with her suburbs, and Jazer with
Neh 9:22 and the land of the king of *H*
Song 7:4 eyes like the fishpools in *H*
Is 15:4 And *H* shall cry, and Elealeh
Is 16:8 For the fields of *H* languish
Is 16:9 water thee with my tears, O *H*
Jer 48:2 in *H* they have devised evil
Jer 48:34 From the cry of *H* even unto
Jer 48:45 shadow of *H* because of the force
Jer 48:45 a fire shall come forth out of *H*
Jer 49:3 Howl, O *H*, for Ai is spoiled

**HESHMON** *(hesh'-mon)* See AZMON. *A town in Judah.*
Josh 15:27 And Hazar-gaddah, and *H*, and

**HETH** *(heth) Son of Canaan.*
Gen 10:15 begat Sidon his firstborn, and *H*
Gen 23:3 dead, and spake unto the sons of *H*
Gen 23:5 the children of *H* answered
Gen 23:7 land, even to the children of *H*
Gen 23:10 dwelt among the children of *H*
Gen 23:10 the audience of the children of *H*
Gen 23:16 in the audience of the sons of *H*
Gen 23:18 the presence of the children of *H*
Gen 23:20 a buryingplace by the sons of *H*
Gen 25:10 purchased of the sons of *H*
Gen 27:46 because of the daughters of *H*
Gen 27:46 take a wife of the daughters of *H*
Gen 49:32 was from the children of *H*
1Chr 1:13 begat Zidon his firstborn, and *H*

**HETHLON** *(heth'-lon) A place in northern Palestine.*
Eze 47:15 from the great sea, the way of *H*
Eze 48:1 end to the coast of the way of *H*

**HEW**
Ex 34:1 *H* thee two tables of stone like
Deut 10:1 *H* thee two tables of stone like
Deut 12:3 ye shall *h* down the graven images
Deut 19:5 wood with his neighbour to *h* wood
1Kin 5:6 command thou that they *h* me cedar
1Kin 5:6 *h* timber like unto the Sidonians
1Kin 5:18 and Hiram's builders did *h* them
1Chr 22:2 he set masons to *h* wrought stones
2Chr 2:2 thousand to *h* in the mountain
Jer 6:6 *H* ye down trees, and cast a mount
Dan 4:14 *H* down the tree, and cut off his
Dan 4:23 *H* the tree down, and destroy it

**HEWED**
Ex 34:4 he *h* two tables of stone like
Deut 10:3 *h* two tables of stone like unto
1Sa 11:7 *h* them in pieces, and sent them
1Sa 15:33 Samuel *h* Agag in pieces before
1Kin 5:17 *h* stones, to lay the foundation
1Kin 6:36 court with three rows of *h* stone
1Kin 7:9 to the measures of *h* stones
1Kin 7:11 after the measures of *h* stones
1Kin 7:12 was with three rows of *h* stones
2Kin 12:12 *h* stone to repair the breaches of
Is 22:16 that thou hast *h* thee out a
Jer 2:13 *h* them out cisterns, broken
Hos 6:5 Therefore have I *h* them by the

**HEWERS**
Josh 9:21 but let them be *h* of wood
Josh 9:23 *h* of wood and drawers of water for
Josh 9:27 made them that day *h* of wood
1Kin 5:15 thousand *h* in the mountains
2Kin 12:12 *h* of stone, and to buy timber and
1Chr 22:15 workmen with thee in abundance, *h*
2Chr 2:10 the *h* that cut timber, twenty
2Chr 2:18 thousand to be *h* in the mountain
Jer 46:22 her with axes, as *h* of wood

**HEWN**
Ex 20:25 shalt not build it of *h* stone
2Kin 22:6 *h* stone to repair the house
2Chr 34:11 gave they it, to buy *h* stone
Prov 9:1 she hath *h* out her seven pillars
Is 9:10 but we will build with *h* stones
Is 10:33 ones of stature shall be *h* down
Is 33:9 Lebanon is ashamed and *h* down
Is 51:1 unto the rock whence ye are *h*
Lam 3:9 inclosed my ways with *h* stone
Eze 40:42 the four tables were of *h* stone
Amos 5:11 ye have built houses of *h* stone
Mt 3:10 not forth good fruit is *h* down
Mt 7:19 not forth good fruit is *h* down
Mt 27:60 which he had *h* out in the rock
Mk 15:46 which was *h* out of a rock
Lk 3:9 not forth good fruit is *h* down
Lk 23:53 a sepulchre that was *h* in stone

**HEZEKI** *(hez'-e-ki) A Benjamite.*
1Chr 8:17 And Zebadiah, and Meshullam, and *H*

**HEZEKIAH** *(hez-e-ki'-ah)* See EZEKIAS, HIZKIAH.
*1. Son of King Ahaz.*
2Kin 16:20 *H* his son reigned in his stead
2Kin 18:1 that *H* the son of Ahaz king of
2Kin 18:9 pass in the fourth year of king *H*
2Kin 18:10 even in the sixth year of *H*
2Kin 18:13 in the fourteenth year of king *H*
2Kin 18:14 *H* king of Judah sent to the king
2Kin 18:14 *H* king of Judah three hundred
2Kin 18:15 *H* gave him all the silver that

2Kin 18:16 At that time did *H* cut off the
2Kin 18:16 from the pillars which *H* king of
2Kin 18:17 king *H* with a great host against
2Kin 18:19 said unto them, Speak ye now to *H*
2Kin 18:22 whose altars *H* hath taken away,
2Kin 18:29 the king, Let not *H* deceive you
2Kin 18:30 Neither let *H* make you trust in
2Kin 18:31 Hearken not to *H*
2Kin 18:32 and hearken not unto *H*, when he
2Kin 18:37 to *H* with their clothes rent, and
2Kin 19:1 to pass, when king *H* heard it
2Kin 19:3 they said unto him, Thus saith *H*
2Kin 19:5 servants of king *H* came to Isaiah
2Kin 19:9 he sent messengers again unto *H*
2Kin 19:10 shall ye speak to *H* king of Judah
2Kin 19:14 *H* received the letter of the hand
2Kin 19:14 *H* went up into the house of the
2Kin 19:15 *H* prayed before the LORD, and said
2Kin 19:20 Isaiah the son of Amoz sent to *H*
2Kin 20:1 those days was *H* sick unto death
2Kin 20:3 And *H* wept sore
2Kin 20:5 tell *H* the captain of my people,
2Kin 20:8 *H* said unto Isaiah, What shall be
2Kin 20:10 *H* answered, It is a light thing
2Kin 20:12 sent letters and a present unto *H*
2Kin 20:12 he had heard that *H* had been sick
2Kin 20:13 *H* hearkened unto them, and shewed
2Kin 20:13 dominion, that *H* shewed them not
2Kin 20:14 Isaiah the prophet unto king *H*
2Kin 20:14 *H* said, They are come from a far
2Kin 20:15 *H* answered, All the things that
2Kin 20:16 And Isaiah said unto *H*, Hear the
2Kin 20:19 Then said *H* unto Isaiah, Good is
2Kin 20:20 And the rest of the acts of *H*
2Kin 20:21 And *H* slept with his fathers
2Kin 21:3 which *H* his father had destroyed
1Chr 3:13 *H* his son, Manasseh his son,
1Chr 4:41 in the days of *H* king of Judah
2Chr 28:27 *H* his son reigned in his stead
2Chr 29:1 *H* began to reign when he was five
2Chr 29:18 Then they went in to *H* the king
2Chr 29:20 Then *H* the king rose early, and
2Chr 29:27 *H* commanded to offer the burnt
2Chr 29:30 Moreover *H* the king and the
2Chr 29:31 Then *H* answered and said, Now ye
2Chr 29:36 *H* rejoiced, and all the people,
2Chr 30:1 *H* sent to all Israel and Judah, and
2Chr 30:18 But *H* prayed for them, saying,
2Chr 30:20 And the LORD hearkened to *H*
2Chr 30:22 *H* spake comfortably unto all the
2Chr 30:24 For *H* king of Judah did give to
2Chr 31:2 *H* appointed the courses of the
2Chr 31:8 And when *H* and the princes came and
2Chr 31:9 Then *H* questioned with the
2Chr 31:11 Then *H* commanded to prepare
2Chr 31:13 at the commandment of *H* the king
2Chr 31:20 thus did *H* throughout all Judah,
2Chr 32:2 when *H* saw that Sennacherib was
2Chr 32:8 upon the words of *H* king of Judah
2Chr 32:9 unto *H* king of Judah, and unto
2Chr 32:11 Doth not *H* persuade you to give
2Chr 32:12 Hath not the same *H* taken away
2Chr 32:15 therefore let not *H* deceive you
2Chr 32:16 God, and against his servant *H*
2Chr 32:17 so shall not the God of *H* deliver
2Chr 32:20 And for this cause *H* the king
2Chr 32:22 Thus the LORD saved *H* and the
2Chr 32:23 presents to *H* king of Judah
2Chr 32:24 In those days *H* was sick to the
2Chr 32:25 But *H* rendered not again
2Chr 32:26 Notwithstanding *H* humbled himself
2Chr 32:26 not upon them in the days of *H*
2Chr 32:27 *H* had exceeding much riches and
2Chr 32:30 This same *H* also stopped the
2Chr 32:30 *H* prospered in all his works
2Chr 32:32 Now the rest of the acts of *H*
2Chr 32:33 *H* slept with his fathers, and they
2Chr 33:3 *H* his father had broken down
Prov 25:1 which the men of *H* king of Judah
Is 1:1 of Uzziah, Jotham, Ahaz, and *H*
Is 36:1 in the fourteenth year of king *H*
Is 36:2 unto king *H* with a great army
Is 36:4 said unto them, Say ye now to *H*
Is 36:7 whose altars *H* hath taken away,
Is 36:14 the king, Let not *H* deceive you
Is 36:15 Neither let *H* make you trust in
Is 36:16 Hearken not to *H*
Is 36:18 Beware lest *H* persuade you,
Is 36:22 to *H* with their clothes rent, and
Is 37:1 to pass, when king *H* heard it
Is 37:3 they said unto him, Thus saith *H*
Is 37:5 servants of king *H* came to Isaiah
Is 37:9 heard it, he sent messengers to *H*
Is 37:10 shall ye speak to *H* king of Judah
Is 37:14 *H* received the letter from the
Is 37:14 *H* went up unto the house of the
Is 37:15 *H* prayed unto the LORD, saying,
Is 37:21 the son of Amoz sent unto *H*
Is 38:1 those days was *H* sick unto death
Is 38:2 Then *H* turned his face toward the
Is 38:3 And *H* wept sore
Is 38:5 Go, and say to *H*, Thus saith the
Is 38:9 The writing of *H* king of Judah
Is 38:22 *H* also had said, What is the sign
Is 39:1 sent letters and a present to *H*
Is 39:2 *H* was glad of them, and shewed
Is 39:2 dominion, that *H* shewed them not
Is 39:3 Isaiah the prophet unto king *H*
Is 39:3 *H* said, They are come from a far
Is 39:4 *H* answered, All that is in mine
Is 39:5 Then said Isaiah to *H*, Hear the
Is 39:8 Then said *H* to Isaiah, Good is
Jer 15:4 the son of *H* king of Judah
Jer 26:18 in the days of *H* king of Judah
Jer 26:19 Did *H* king of Judah and all Judah
Hos 1:1 of Uzziah, Jotham, Ahaz, and *H*
Mic 1:1 in the days of Jotham, Ahaz, and *H*

*2. A son of Neariah.*
1Chr 3:23 Elioenai, and *H*, and Azrikam, three

*3. A family of exiles.*
Ezr 2:16 The children of Ater of *H*
Neh 7:21 The children of Ater of *H*

**HEZION** *(he'-zi-on) Grandfather of King Ben-hadad of Syria.*
1Kin 15:18 the son of Tabrimon, the son of *H*

**HEZIR** *(he'-zir)*

*1. A sanctuary servant.*
1Chr 24:15 The seventeenth to *H*, the

*2. An Israelite who renewed the covenant.*
Neh 10:20 Magpiash, Meshullam, *H*,

**HEZRAI** *(hez'-rahee)* See HEZRO. *A "mighty man" of David.*
2Sa 23:35 *H* the Carmelite, Paarai the

**HEZRO** *(hez'-ro)* See HEZRAI. *Same as Hezrai.*
1Chr 11:37 *H* the Carmelite, Naarai the son

**HEZRON** *(hez'-ron)* See HAZOR, HEZRONITES, HEZBON'S.

*1. Son of Pharez.*
Gen 46:12 And the sons of Pharez were *H*
Num 26:6 Of *H*, the family of the
Num 26:21 of *H*, the family of the
Ruth 4:18 Pharez begat *H*,
Ruth 4:19 *H* begat Ram, and Ram begat
1Chr 2:5 of Pharez; *H*, and Hamul
1Chr 2:9 The sons also of *H*, that were
1Chr 2:18 Caleb the son of *H* begat children
1Chr 2:21 afterward *H* went in to the
1Chr 2:24 And after that *H* was dead in
1Chr 2:25 Jerahmeel the firstborn of *H* were
1Chr 4:1 Pharez, *H*, and Carmi, and Hur, and

*2. A son of Reuben.*
Gen 46:9 and Phallu, and *H*, and Carmi
Ex 6:14 Hanoch, and Pallu, *H*, and Carmi
1Chr 5:3 Israel were, Hanoch, and Pallu, *H*

*3. A town in Judah.*
Josh 15:3 and passed along to *H*, and went up
Josh 15:25 Hazor, Hadattah, and Kerioth, and *H*

**HEZRONITES** *(hez'-ron-ites) Descendants of Hezron 2.*
Num 26:6 Of Hezron, the family of the *H*
Num 26:21 of Hezron, the family of the *H*

**HEZRON'S** *(hez'-ronz) Refers to Hezron 2.*
1Chr 2:24 then Abiah *H* wife bare him Ashur

**HID**
Gen 3:8 his wife *h* themselves from the
Gen 3:10 and I *h* myself
Gen 4:14 and from thy face shall I be *h*
Gen 35:4 Jacob *h* them under the oak which
Ex 2:2 child, she *h* him three months
Ex 2:12 Egyptian, and *h* him in the sand
Ex 3:6 And Moses *h* his face
Lev 4:13 the thing be *h* from the eyes of
Lev 5:3 withal, and it be *h* from him
Lev 5:4 with an oath, and it be *h* from him
Num 5:13 it be *h* from the eyes of her
Deut 33:19 and of treasures *h* in the sand
Josh 2:4 *h* them, and said thus, There came
Josh 2:6 *h* them with the stalks of flax,
Josh 6:17 because she *h* the messengers that
Josh 6:25 because she *h* the messengers,
Josh 7:21 they are *h* in the earth in the
Josh 7:22 it was *h* in his tent, and the
Josh 10:16 *h* themselves in a cave at
Josh 10:17 are found *h* in a cave at Makkedah
Josh 10:27 the cave wherein they had been *h*
Judg 9:5 for he *h* himself
1Sa 3:18 every whit, and *h* nothing from him
1Sa 10:22 he hath *h* himself among the stuff
1Sa 14:11 holes where they had *h* themselves
1Sa 14:22 had *h* themselves in mount Ephraim
1Sa 20:24 So David *h* himself in the field
2Sa 17:9 he is *h* now in some pit, or in
2Sa 18:13 is no matter *h* from the king
1Kin 10:3 was not any thing *h* from the king
1Kin 18:4 *h* them by fifty in a cave, and fed
1Kin 18:13 how I *h* an hundred men of the
2Kin 4:27 and the LORD hath *h* it from me
2Kin 6:29 and she hath *h* her son
2Kin 7:8 gold, and raiment, and went and *h* it
2Kin 7:8 thence also, and went and *h* it
2Kin 11:2 and they *h* him, even him and his
2Kin 11:3 he was with her *h* in the house of
1Chr 21:20 four sons with him *h* themselves
2Chr 9:2 there was nothing *h* from Solomon
2Chr 22:9 him, (for he was *h* in Samaria
2Chr 22:11 *h* him from Athaliah, so that she
2Chr 22:12 he was with them *h* in the house
Job 3:10 nor *h* sorrow from mine eyes
Job 3:21 for it more than for *h* treasures
Job 3:23 given to a man whose way is *h*
Job 5:21 Thou shalt be *h* from the scourge
Job 6:16 the ice, and wherein the snow is *h*
Job 10:13 things hast thou *h* in thine heart
Job 15:18 their fathers, and have not *h* it
Job 17:4 For thou hast *h* their heart from
Job 20:26 shall be *h* in his secret places
Job 28:11 the thing that is *h* bringeth he
Job 28:21 Seeing it is *h* from the eyes of
Job 29:8 young men saw me, and *h* themselves
Job 38:30 The waters are *h* as with a stone,
Ps 9:15 in the net which they *h* is their
Ps 17:14 thou fillest with thy *h* treasure
Ps 19:6 there is nothing *h* from the heat
Ps 22:24 neither hath he *h* his face from
Ps 32:5 and mine iniquity have I not *h*
Ps 35:7 they *h* for me their net in a pit
Ps 35:8 net that he hath *h* catch himself
Ps 38:9 and my groaning is not *h* from thee
Ps 40:10 I have not *h* thy righteousness
Ps 55:12 I would have *h* myself from him
Ps 69:5 and my sins are not *h* from thee
Ps 119:11 Thy word have I *h* in mine heart
Ps 139:15 My substance was not *h* from thee
Ps 140:5 The proud have *h* a snare for me
Prov 2:4 for her as for *h* treasures
Is 28:15 falsehood have we *h* ourselves
Is 29:14 of their prudent men shall be *h*
Is 40:27 My way is *h* from the LORD, and my
Is 42:22 they are *h* in prison houses
Is 49:2 shadow of his hand hath he *h* me
Is 49:2 in his quiver hath he *h* me
Is 50:6 I *h* not my face from shame and
Is 53:3 we *h* as it were our faces from
Is 54:8 In a little wrath I *h* my face
Is 57:17 I *h* me, and was wroth, and he went
Is 59:2 your sins have *h* his face from
Is 64:7 for thou hast *h* thy face from us,
Is 65:16 because they are *h* from mine eyes
Jer 13:5 *h* it by Euphrates, as the LORD
Jer 13:7 from the place where I had *h* it
Jer 16:17 they are not *h* from my face
Jer 16:17 their iniquity *h* from mine eyes
Jer 18:22 take me, and *h* snares for my feet
Jer 33:5 I have *h* my face from this city
Jer 36:26 but the LORD *h* them
Jer 43:10 upon these stones that I have *h*
Eze 22:26 have *h* their eyes from my
Eze 39:23 therefore *h* I my face from them,
Eze 39:24 unto them, and *h* my face from them
Hos 5:3 and Israel is not *h* from me
Hos 13:12 his sin is *h*
Hos 13:14 shall be *h* from mine eyes
Amos 9:3 though they be *h* from my sight in
Nah 3:11 thou shalt be *h*, thou also shalt
Zeph 2:3 it may be ye shall be *h* in the

Mt 5:14 is set on an hill cannot be *h*
Mt 10:26 and *h*, that shall not be known
Mt 11:25 because thou hast *h* these things
Mt 13:33 *h* in three measures of meal, till
Mt 13:44 like unto treasure *h* in a field
Mt 25:18 the earth, and *h* his lord's money
Mt 25:25 *h* thy talent in the earth
Mk 4:22 For there is nothing *h*, which
Mk 7:24 but he could not be *h*
Lk 1:24 *h* herself five months, saying,
Lk 8:17 neither any thing *h*, that shall
Lk 8:47 the woman saw that she was not *h*
Lk 9:45 it was *h* from them, that they
Lk 10:21 that thou hast *h* these things
Lk 12:2 neither *h*, that shall not be
Lk 13:21 *h* in three measures of meal, till
Lk 18:34 and this saying was *h* from them
Lk 19:42 now they are *h* from thine eyes
Jn 8:59 but Jesus *h* himself, and went out
2Cor 4:3 But if our gospel be *h*, it is *h*
Eph 3:9 of the world hath been *h* in God
Col 1:26 which hath been *h* from ages
Col 2:3 In whom are *h* all the treasures
Col 3:3 your life is *h* with Christ in God
1Ti 5:25 that are otherwise cannot be *h*
Heb 11:23 was *h* three months of his parents
Rev 6:15 *h* themselves in the dens and in

**HIDDAI** *(hid'-dahee)* See HURAI. *A "mighty man" of David.*
2Sa 23:30 *H* of the brooks of Gaash,

**HIDDEKEL** *(hid'-de-kel) A name for the Tigris River.*
Gen 2:14 the name of the third river is *H*
Dan 10:4 of the great river, which is *H*

**HIDDEN**
Lev 5:2 things, and if it be *h* from him
Deut 30:11 this day, it is not *h* from thee
Job 3:16 Or as an *h* untimely birth I had
Job 15:20 of years is *h* to the oppressor
Job 24:1 times are not *h* from the Almighty
Ps 51:6 in the *h* part thou shalt make me
Ps 83:3 and consulted against thy *h* ones
Prov 28:12 when the wicked rise, a man is *h*
Is 45:3 *h* riches of secret places, that
Is 48:6 even *h* things, and thou didst not
Obad 6 how are his *h* things sought up
Acts 26:26 of these things are *h* from him
1Cor 2:7 in a mystery, even the *h* wisdom
1Cor 4:5 to light the *h* things of darkness
2Cor 4:2 the *h* things of dishonesty
1Pet 3:4 let it be the *h* man of the heart
Rev 2:17 will I give to eat of the *h* manna

**HIDE**
Gen 18:17 Shall I *h* from Abraham that thing
Gen 47:18 We will not *h* it from my lord,
Ex 2:3 when she could not longer *h* him
Lev 8:17 But the bullock, and his *h*
Lev 9:11 the *h* he burnt with fire without
Lev 20:4 ways *h* their eyes from the man
Deut 7:20 *h* themselves from thee, be
Deut 22:1 go astray, and *h* thyself from them
Deut 22:3 thou mayest not *h* thyself
Deut 22:4 the way, and *h* thyself from them
Deut 31:17 I will *h* my face from them, and
Deut 31:18 I will surely *h* my face in that
Deut 32:20 I will *h* my face from them, I
Josh 2:16 *h* yourselves there three days,
Josh 7:19 *h* it not from me
Judg 6:11 to *h* it from the Midianites
1Sa 3:17 I pray thee *h* it not from me
1Sa 3:17 if thou *h* any thing from me of
1Sa 13:6 people did *h* themselves in caves
1Sa 19:2 in a secret place, and *h* thyself
1Sa 20:2 my father *h* this thing from me
1Sa 20:5 that I may *h* myself in the field
1Sa 20:19 *h* thyself when the business was
1Sa 23:19 Doth not David *h* himself with us
1Sa 26:1 Doth not David *h* himself in the
2Sa 14:18 *H* not from me, I pray thee, the
1Kin 17:3 *h* thyself by the brook Cherith,
1Kin 22:25 an inner chamber to *h* thyself
2Kin 7:12 camp to *h* themselves in the field
2Chr 18:24 an inner chamber to *h* thyself
Job 13:20 then I will not *h* myself from
Job 14:13 thou wouldest *h* me in the grave
Job 20:12 though he *h* it under his tongue
Job 24:4 the earth *h* themselves together
Job 33:17 his purpose, and *h* pride from man
Job 34:22 of iniquity may *h* themselves
Job 40:13 *H* them in the dust together
Ps 13:1 long wilt thou *h* thy face from me
Ps 17:8 *h* me under the shadow of thy
Ps 27:5 he shall *h* me in his pavilion
Ps 27:5 of his tabernacle shall he *h* me
Ps 27:9 *H* not thy face far from me
Ps 30:7 thou didst *h* thy face, and I was
Ps 31:20 Thou shalt *h* them in the secret
Ps 51:9 *H* thy face from my sins, and blot
Ps 54:*t* Doth not David *h* himself with us
Ps 55:1 and *h* not thyself from my
Ps 56:6 they *h* themselves, they mark my
Ps 64:2 *H* me from the secret counsel of
Ps 69:17 *h* not thy face from thy servant
Ps 78:4 We will not *h* them from their
Ps 89:46 wilt thou *h* thyself for ever
Ps 102:2 *H* not thy face from me in the day
Ps 119:19 *h* not thy commandments from me
Ps 143:7 *h* not thy face from me, lest I be
Ps 143:9 I flee unto thee to *h* me
Prov 2:1 *h* my commandments with thee
Prov 28:28 the wicked rise, men *h* themselves
Is 1:15 I will *h* mine eyes from you
Is 2:10 *h* thee in the dust, for fear of
Is 3:9 their sin as Sodom, they *h* it not
Is 16:3 *h* the outcasts
Is 26:20 *h* thyself as it were for a little
Is 29:15 to *h* their counsel from the LORD
Is 58:7 that thou *h* not thyself from
Jer 13:4 *h* it there in a hole of the rock
Jer 13:6 which I commanded thee to *h* there
Jer 23:24 Can any *h* himself in secret
Jer 36:19 Go, *h* thee, thou and Jeremiah
Jer 38:14 *h* nothing from me
Jer 38:25 *h* it not from us, and we will not
Jer 43:9 *h* them in the clay in the
Jer 49:10 he shall not be able to *h* himself
Lam 3:56 *h* not thine ear at my breathing,
Eze 28:3 secret that they can *h* from thee
Eze 31:8 the garden of God could not *h* him
Eze 39:29 Neither will I *h* my face any more
Dan 10:7 so that they fled to *h* themselves
Amos 9:3 though they *h* themselves in the
Mic 3:4 he will even *h* his face from them
Jn 12:36 and did *h* himself from them
Jas 5:20 shall *h* a multitude of sins
Rev 6:16 *h* us from the face of him that

**HIDEST**
Job 13:24 Wherefore *h* thou thy face, and
Ps 10:1 why *h* thou thyself in times of
Ps 44:24 Wherefore *h* thou thy face, and
Ps 88:14 why *h* thou thy face from me
Ps 104:29 Thou *h* thy face, they are
Is 45:15 thou art a God that *h* thyself

**HIDETH**
1Sa 23:23 lurking places where he *h* himself
Job 23:9 he *h* himself on the right hand,
Job 34:29 when he *h* his face, who then can
Job 42:3 Who is he that *h* counsel without
Ps 10:11 he *h* his face
Ps 139:12 the darkness *h* not from thee
Prov 10:18 He that *h* hatred with lying lips,
Prov 19:24 A slothful man *h* his hand in his
Prov 22:3 foreseeth the evil, and *h* himself
Prov 26:15 The slothful *h* his hand in his
Prov 27:12 foreseeth the evil, and *h* himself
Prov 27:16 Whosoever *h* her *h* the wind,
Prov 28:27 but he that *h* his eyes shall have
Is 8:17 that *h* his face from the house of
Mt 13:44 which when a man hath found, he *h*

**HIDING**
Job 31:33 by *h* mine iniquity in my bosom
Ps 32:7 Thou art my *h* place
Ps 119:114 Thou art my *h* place and my shield
Is 28:17 waters shall overflow the *h* place
Is 32:2 be as an *h* place from the wind
Hab 3:4 and there was the *h* of his power

**HIEL** *(hi'-el) A Bethelite.*
1Kin 16:34 In his days did *H* the Beth-elite

**HIERAPOLIS** *(hi-e-rap'-o-lis) A city in Phrygia.*
Col 4:13 are in Laodicea, and them in *H*

**HIGHER**
Num 24:7 and his king shall be *h* than Agag
1Sa 9:2 upward he was *h* than any of the
1Sa 10:23 he was *h* than any of the people
2Kin 15:35 He built the *h* gate of the house
Neh 4:13 the wall, and on the *h* places
Job 35:5 the clouds which are *h* than thou
Ps 61:2 me to the rock that is *h* than I
Ps 89:27 *h* than the kings of the earth
Eccl 5:8 for he that is *h* than the highest
Eccl 5:8 and there be *h* than they
Is 55:9 the heavens are *h* than the earth
Is 55:9 so are my ways *h* than your ways
Jer 36:10 the scribe, in the *h* court
Eze 9:2 came from the way of the *h* gate
Eze 42:5 the galleries were *h* than these
Eze 43:13 this shall be the *h* place of the
Dan 8:3 but one was *h* than the other
Dan 8:3 and the *h* came up last
Lk 14:10 say unto thee, Friend, go up *h*
Rom 13:1 soul be subject unto the *h* powers
Heb 7:26 and made *h* than the heavens

**HIGHEST**
Ps 18:13 heavens, and the *H* gave his voice
Ps 87:5 the *h* himself shall establish her
Prov 8:26 nor the *h* part of the dust of the
Prov 9:3 upon the *h* places of the city
Eccl 5:8 is higher than the *h* regardeth
Eze 17:3 took the *h* branch of the cedar
Eze 17:22 I will also take of the *h* branch
Eze 41:7 chamber to the *h* by the midst
Mt 21:9 Hosanna in the *h*
Mk 11:10 Hosanna in the *h*
Lk 1:32 shall be called the Son of the *H*
Lk 1:35 thee, and the power of the *H* shall
Lk 1:76 be called the prophet of the *H*
Lk 2:14 Glory to God in the *h*, and on
Lk 6:35 ye shall be the children of the *H*
Lk 14:8 sit not down in the *h* room
Lk 19:38 in heaven, and glory in the *h*
Lk 20:46 the *h* seats in the synagogues, and

**HIGHLY**
Lk 1:28 Hail, thou that art *h* favoured
Lk 16:15 for that which is *h* esteemed
Acts 12:20 Herod was *h* displeased with them
Rom 12:3 more *h* than he ought to think
Phil 2:9 God also hath *h* exalted him
1Th 5:13 to esteem them very *h* in love for

**HIGHWAY**
Judg 21:19 on the east side of the *h* that
1Sa 6:12 Beth-shemesh, and went along the *h*
2Sa 20:12 in blood in the midst of the *h*
2Sa 20:12 Amasa out of the *h* into the field
2Sa 20:13 When he was removed out of the *h*
2Kin 18:17 which is in the *h* of the fuller's
Prov 16:17 The *h* of the upright is to depart
Is 7:3 in the *h* of the fuller's field
Is 11:16 there shall be an *h* for the
Is 19:23 be a *h* out of Egypt to Assyria
Is 35:8 an *h* shall be there, and a way, and
Is 36:2 in the *h* of the fuller's field
Is 40:3 in the desert a *h* for our God
Jer 31:21 set thine heart toward the *h*
Mk 10:46 sat by the *h* side begging

**HIGHWAYS**
Judg 5:6 the *h* were unoccupied, and the
Judg 20:31 kill, as at other times, in the *h*
Judg 20:32 them from the city unto the *h*
Judg 20:45 them in the *h* five thousand men
Is 33:8 The *h* lie waste, the wayfaring
Is 49:11 a way, and my *h* shall be exalted
Is 62:10 cast up, cast up the *h*
Amos 5:16 and they shall say in all the *h*
Mt 22:9 Go ye therefore into the *h*
Mt 22:10 servants went out into the *h*
Lk 14:23 the servant, Go out into the *h*

**HILEN** *(hi'-len)* See HOLON. *A Levitical city in Judah.*
1Chr 6:58 *H* with her suburbs, Debir with

**HILKIAH** *(hil-ki'-ah)* See HELKAI, HILKIAH'S.
*1. Father of Eliakim.*
2Kin 18:18 out to them Eliakim the son of *H*
2Kin 18:26 Then said Eliakim the son of *H*
2Kin 18:37 Then came Eliakim the son of *H*
1Chr 6:13 And Shallum begat *H*
1Chr 6:13 and *H* begat Azariah
Neh 12:21 Of *H*, Hashabiah; of Jedaiah
Is 22:20 my servant Eliakim the son of *H*
Is 36:22 Then came Eliakim, the son of *H*
*2. A high priest.*
2Kin 22:4 Go up to *H* the high priest, that
2Kin 22:8 *H* the high priest said unto

2Kin 22:8 *H* gave the book to Shaphan, and he
2Kin 22:10 *H* the priest hath delivered me a
2Kin 22:12 the king commanded *H* the priest
2Kin 22:14 So *H* the priest, and Ahikam, and
2Kin 23:4 king commanded *H* the high priest
2Kin 23:24 *H* the priest found in the house
1Chr 9:11 And Azariah the son of *H*, the son
2Chr 34:9 they came to *H* the high priest
2Chr 34:14 *H* the priest found a book of the
2Chr 34:15 *H* answered and said to Shaphan the
2Chr 34:15 *H* delivered the book to Shaphan
2Chr 34:18 *H* the priest hath given me a book
2Chr 34:20 And the king commanded *H*, and
2Chr 34:22 And *H*, and they that the king had
2Chr 35:8 *H* and Zechariah and Jehiel, rulers
Ezr 7:1 the son of Azariah, the son of *H*
Jer 29:3 Shaphan, and Gemariah the son of *H*

*3. A descendant of Merari.*
1Chr 6:45 the son of Amaziah, the son of *H*

*4. A son of Hosah.*
1Chr 26:11 *H* the second, Tebaliah the third,

*5. A priest who assisted Ezra.*
Neh 8:4 Anaiah, and Urijah, and *H*
Neh 11:11 Seraiah the son of *H*, the son of
Neh 12:7 Sallu, Amok, *H*, Jedaiah

*6. Father of Jeremiah.*
Jer 1:1 words of Jeremiah the son of *H*

**HILKIAH'S** *(hil-ki'-ahs) Refers to Hilkiah 1.*
Is 36:3 *H* son, which was over the house,

**HILL**
Ex 17:9 the *h* with the rod of God in mine
Ex 17:10 Hur went up to the top of the *h*
Ex 24:4 and builded an altar under the *h*
Num 14:44 presumed to go up unto the *h* top
Num 14:45 Canaanites which dwelt in that *h*
Deut 1:41 ye were ready to go up into the *h*
Deut 1:43 went presumptuously up into the *h*
Josh 5:3 Israel at the *h* of the foreskins
Josh 13:6 the *h* country from Lebanon unto
Josh 15:9 was drawn from the top of the *h*
Josh 17:16 The *h* is not enough for us
Josh 18:13 near the *h* that lieth on the
Josh 18:14 from the *h* that lieth before
Josh 21:11 in the *h* country of Judah, with
Josh 24:30 the north side of the *h* of Gaash
Josh 24:33 they buried him in a *h* that
Judg 2:9 on the north side of the *h* Gaash
Judg 7:1 by the *h* of Moreh, in the valley
Judg 16:3 top of an *h* that is before Hebron
1Sa 7:1 the house of Abinadab in the *h*
1Sa 9:11 as they went up the *h* to the city
1Sa 10:5 thou shalt come to the *h* of God
1Sa 10:10 when they came thither to the *h*
1Sa 23:19 in the *h* of Hachilah, which is on
1Sa 25:20 came down by the covert of the *h*
1Sa 26:1 hide himself in the *h* of Hachilah
1Sa 26:3 Saul pitched in the *h* of Hachilah
1Sa 26:13 stood on the top of an *h* afar off
2Sa 2:24 they were come to the *h* of Ammah
2Sa 2:25 and stood on the top of an *h*
2Sa 13:34 the way of the *h* side behind him
2Sa 16:1 a little past the top of the *h*
2Sa 21:9 them in the *h* before the LORD
1Kin 11:7 in the *h* that is before Jerusalem
1Kin 14:23 and groves, on every high *h*
1Kin 16:24 he bought the *h* Samaria of Shemer
1Kin 16:24 of silver, and built on the *h*
1Kin 16:24 name of Shemer, owner of the *h*
2Kin 1:9 behold, he sat on the top of an *h*
2Kin 4:27 came to the man of God to the *h*
2Kin 17:10 images and groves in every high *h*
Ps 2:6 my king upon my holy *h* of Zion
Ps 3:4 and he heard me out of his holy *h*
Ps 15:1 who shall dwell in thy holy *h*
Ps 24:3 ascend into the *h* of the LORD
Ps 42:6 the Hermonites, from the *h* Mizar
Ps 43:3 let them bring me unto thy holy *h*
Ps 68:15 *h* of God is as the *h* of Bashan
Ps 68:15 an high *h* as the *h* of Bashan
Ps 68:16 this is the *h* which God desireth
Ps 99:9 our God, and worship at his holy *h*
Song 4:6 and to the *h* of frankincense
Is 5:1 a vineyard in a very fruitful *h*
Is 10:32 of Zion, the *h* of Jerusalem
Is 30:17 mountain, and as an ensign on an *h*
Is 30:25 mountain, and upon every high *h*
Is 31:4 mount Zion, and for the *h* thereof
Is 40:4 mountain and *h* shall be made low
Jer 2:20 when upon every high *h* and under
Jer 16:16 every mountain, and from every *h*
Jer 31:39 over against it upon the *h* Gareb
Jer 49:16 that holdest the height of the *h*
Jer 50:6 they have gone from mountain to *h*
Eze 6:13 their altars, upon every high *h*
Eze 20:28 them, then they saw every high *h*
Eze 34:6 mountains, and upon every high *h*
Eze 34:26 round about my *h* a blessing
Mt 5:14 that is set on an *h* cannot be hid
Lk 1:39 went into the *h* country with
Lk 1:65 all the *h* country of Judaea
Lk 3:5 and *h* shall be brought low
Lk 4:29 *h* whereon their city was built
Lk 9:37 they were come down from the *h*
Acts 17:22 stood in the midst of Mars' *h*

**HILLEL** *(hil'-lel) Father of Abdon.*
Judg 12:13 And after him Abdon the son of *H*
Judg 12:15 And Abdon the son of *H* the

**HILLS**
Gen 7:19 and all the high *h*, that were
Gen 49:26 utmost bound of the everlasting *h*
Num 23:9 him, and from the *h* I behold him
Deut 1:7 thereunto, in the plain, in the *h*
Deut 8:7 that spring out of valleys and *h*
Deut 8:9 out of whose *h* thou mayest dig
Deut 11:11 go to possess it, is a land of *h*
Deut 12:2 the high mountains, and upon the *h*
Deut 33:15 precious things of the lasting *h*
Josh 9:1 on this side Jordan, in the *h*
Josh 10:40 smote all the country of the *h*
Josh 11:16 Joshua took all that land, the *h*
1Kin 20:23 him, Their gods are gods of the *h*
1Kin 20:28 said, The LORD is God of the *h*
1Kin 22:17 all Israel scattered upon the *h*
2Kin 16:4 in the high places, and on the *h*
2Chr 28:4 in the high places, and on the *h*
Job 15:7 or wast thou made before the *h*
Ps 18:7 foundations also of the *h* moved
Ps 50:10 and the cattle upon a thousand *h*
Ps 65:12 the little *h* rejoice on every
Ps 68:16 Why leap ye, ye high *h*
Ps 72:3 to the people, and the little *h*
Ps 80:10 The *h* were covered with the
Ps 95:4 the strength of the *h* is his also
Ps 97:5 The *h* melted like wax at the
Ps 98:8 let the *h* be joyful together
Ps 104:10 valleys, which run among the *h*
Ps 104:13 He watereth the *h* from his
Ps 104:18 The high *h* are a refuge for the
Ps 104:32 he toucheth the *h*, and they smoke
Ps 114:4 rams, and the little *h* like lambs
Ps 114:6 and ye little *h*, like lambs
Ps 121:1 will lift up mine eyes unto the *h*
Ps 148:9 Mountains, and all *h*
Prov 8:25 before the *h* was I brought forth
Song 2:8 mountains, skipping upon the *h*
Is 2:2 and shall be exalted above the *h*
Is 2:14 upon all the *h* that are lifted up
Is 5:25 the *h* did tremble, and their
Is 7:25 on all *h* that shall be digged
Is 40:12 in scales, and the *h* in a balance
Is 41:15 and shalt make the *h* as chaff
Is 42:15 I will make waste mountains and *h*
Is 54:10 shall depart, and the *h* be removed
Is 55:12 the *h* shall break forth before
Is 65:7 and blasphemed me upon the *h*
Jer 3:23 is salvation hoped for from the *h*
Jer 4:24 and all the *h* moved lightly
Jer 13:27 on the *h* in the fields
Jer 17:2 the green trees upon the high *h*
Eze 6:3 GOD to the mountains, and to the *h*
Eze 35:8 in thy *h*, and in thy valleys, and
Eze 36:4 GOD to the mountains, and to the *h*
Eze 36:6 unto the mountains, and to the *h*
Hos 4:13 and burn incense upon the *h*
Hos 10:8 and to the *h*, Fall on us
Joel 3:18 the *h* shall flow with milk, and
Amos 9:13 wine, and all the *h* shall melt
Mic 4:1 it shall be exalted above the *h*
Mic 6:1 and let the *h* hear thy voice
Nah 1:5 the *h* melt, and the earth is
Hab 3:6 the perpetual *h* did bow
Zeph 1:10 and a great crashing from the *h*
Lk 23:30 and to the *h*, Cover us

**HIN**
Ex 29:40 fourth part of an *h* of beaten oil
Ex 29:40 the fourth part of an *h* of wine
Ex 30:24 sanctuary, and of oil olive an *h*
Lev 19:36 a just ephah, and a just *h*
Lev 23:13 of wine, the fourth part of a *h*
Num 15:4 the fourth part of an *h* of oil
Num 15:5 the fourth part of an *h* of wine
Num 15:6 the third part of an *h* of oil
Num 15:7 the third part of an *h* of wine
Num 15:9 mingled with half an *h* of oil
Num 15:10 drink offering half an *h* of wine
Num 28:5 fourth part of an *h* of beaten oil
Num 28:7 part of an *h* for the one lamb
Num 28:14 half an *h* of wine unto a bullock
Num 28:14 the third part of an *h* unto a ram
Num 28:14 a fourth part of an *h* unto a lamb
Eze 4:11 measure, the sixth part of an *h*
Eze 45:24 ram, and an *h* of oil for an ephah
Eze 46:5 give, and an *h* of oil to an ephah
Eze 46:7 unto, and an *h* of oil to an ephah
Eze 46:11 give, and an *h* of oil to an ephah
Eze 46:14 and the third part of an *h* of oil

**HINDER**
Gen 24:56 *H* me not, seeing the LORD hath
Num 22:16 *h* thee from coming unto me
2Sa 2:23 wherefore Abner with the *h* end of
1Kin 7:25 all their *h* parts were inward
2Chr 4:4 all their *h* parts were inward
Neh 4:8 against Jerusalem, and to *h* it
Job 9:12 he taketh away, who can *h* him
Job 11:10 together, then who can *h* him
Ps 78:66 smote his enemies in the *h* parts
Joel 2:20 his *h* part toward the utmost sea,
Zec 14:8 and half of them toward the *h* sea
Mk 4:38 he was in the *h* part of the ship,
Acts 8:36 what doth *h* me to be baptized
Acts 27:41 the *h* part was broken with
1Cor 9:12 lest we should *h* the gospel of
Gal 5:7 who did *h* you that ye should not

**HINDERED**
Ezr 6:8 these men, that they be not *h*
Lk 11:52 them that were entering in ye *h*
Rom 15:22 been much *h* from coming to you
1Th 2:18 but Satan *h* us
1Pet 3:7 that your prayers be not *h*

**HINNOM** *(hin'-nom) A valley near Jerusalem.*
Josh 15:8 of *H* unto the south side of the
Josh 15:8 before the valley of *H* westward
Josh 18:16 before the valley of the son of *H*
Josh 18:16 and descended to the valley of *H*
2Kin 23:10 the valley of the children of *H*
2Chr 28:3 in the valley of the son of *H*
2Chr 33:6 in the valley of the son of *H*
Neh 11:30 Beer-sheba unto the valley of *H*
Jer 7:31 is in the valley of the son of *H*
Jer 7:32 nor the valley of the son of *H*
Jer 19:2 unto the valley of the son of *H*
Jer 19:6 nor The valley of the son of *H*
Jer 32:35 are in the valley of the son of *H*

**HIRAH** *(hi'-rah) A friend of Judah.*
Gen 38:1 Adullamite, whose name was *H*
Gen 38:12 his friend *H* the Adullamite

**HIRAM** *(hi'-ram)* See HIRAM'S, HURAM.

*1. A king of Tyre.*
2Sa 5:11 *H* king of Tyre sent messengers to
1Kin 5:1 *H* king of Tyre sent his servants
1Kin 5:1 for *H* was ever a lover of David
1Kin 5:2 And Solomon sent to *H*, saying,
1Kin 5:7 when *H* heard the words of Solomon
1Kin 5:8 *H* sent to Solomon, saying, I have
1Kin 5:10 So *H* gave Solomon cedar trees and
1Kin 5:11 Solomon gave *H* twenty thousand
1Kin 5:11 gave Solomon to *H* year by year
1Kin 5:12 and there was peace between *H*
1Kin 9:11 (Now *H* the king of Tyre had
1Kin 9:11 *H* twenty cities in the land of
1Kin 9:12 *H* came out from Tyre to see the
1Kin 9:14 *H* sent to the king sixscore
1Kin 9:27 *H* sent in the navy his servants,
1Kin 10:11 And the navy also of *H*, that
1Kin 10:22 of Tharshish with the navy of *H*
1Chr 14:1 Now *H* king of Tyre sent

*2. An architect.*
1Kin 7:13 sent and fetched *H* out of Tyre
1Kin 7:40 *H* made the lavers, and the shovels
1Kin 7:40 So *H* made an end of doing all the
1Kin 7:45 which *H* made to king Solomon for

**HIRAM'S** *(hi'-rams) Refers to Hiram 1.*
1Kin 5:18 *H* builders did hew them, and the

### HIRE
Gen 30:18 Leah said, God hath given me my *h*
Gen 30:32 and of such shall be my *h*
Gen 30:33 come for my *h* before thy face
Gen 31:8 The ringstraked shall be thy *h*
Ex 22:15 an hired thing, it came for his *h*
Deut 23:18 shalt not bring the *h* of a whore
Deut 24:15 his day thou shalt give him his *h*
1Kin 5:6 unto thee will I give *h* for thy
1Chr 19:6 of silver to *h* them chariots
Is 23:17 Tyre, and she shall turn to her *h*
Is 23:18 her *h* shall be holiness to the
Is 46:6 in the balance, and *h* a goldsmith
Eze 16:31 harlot, in that thou scornest *h*
Eze 16:41 also shalt give no *h* any more
Mic 1:7 gathered it of the *h* of an harlot
Mic 1:7 return to the *h* of an harlot
Mic 3:11 the priests thereof teach for *h*
Zec 8:10 *h* for man, nor any *h* for beast
Mt 20:1 to *h* labourers into his vineyard
Mt 20:8 labourers, and give them their *h*
Lk 10:7 the labourer is worthy of his *h*
Jas 5:4 the *h* of the labourers who have

### HIRED
Gen 30:16 for surely I have *h* thee with my
Ex 12:45 an *h* servant shall not eat
Ex 22:15 if it be an *h* thing, it came for
Lev 19:13 the wages of him that is *h* shall
Lev 22:10 or an *h* servant, shall not eat of
Lev 25:6 thy maid, and for thy *h* servant
Lev 25:40 But as an *h* servant, and as a
Lev 25:50 according to the time of an *h*
Lev 25:53 as a yearly *h* servant shall he be
Deut 15:18 worth a double *h* servant to thee
Deut 23:4 because they *h* against thee
Deut 24:14 oppress an *h* servant that is poor
Judg 9:4 wherewith Abimelech *h* vain
Judg 18:4 Micah with me, and hath *h* me
1Sa 2:5 have *h* out themselves for bread
2Sa 10:6 *h* the Syrians of Beth-rehob, and
2Kin 7:6 the king of Israel hath *h* against
1Chr 19:7 So they *h* thirty and two thousand
2Chr 24:12 *h* masons and carpenters to repair
2Chr 25:6 He *h* also an hundred thousand
Ezr 4:5 *h* counsellors against them, to
Neh 6:12 for Tobiah and Sanballat had *h* him
Neh 6:13 Therefore was he *h*, that I should
Neh 13:2 but *h* Balaam against them, that
Is 7:20 Lord shave with a razor that is *h*
Jer 46:21 Also her *h* men are in the midst
Hos 8:9 Ephraim hath *h* lovers
Hos 8:10 though they have *h* among the
Mt 20:7 him, Because no man hath *h* us
Mt 20:9 were *h* about the eleventh hour
Mk 1:20 in the ship with the *h* servants
Lk 15:17 How many *h* servants of my
Lk 15:19 make me as one of thy *h* servants
Acts 28:30 whole years in his own *h* house

### HIRELING
Job 7:1 days also like the days of a *h*
Job 7:2 as a *h* looketh for the reward of
Job 14:6 till he shall accomplish, as an *h*
Is 16:14 three years, as the years of an *h*
Is 21:16 according to the years of an *h*
Mal 3:5 that oppress the *h* in his wages
Jn 10:12 But he that is an *h*, and not the
Jn 10:13 *h* fleeth, because he is an *h*

### HISS
1Kin 9:8 shall be astonished, and shall *h*
Job 27:23 shall *h* him out of his place
Is 5:26 will *h* unto them from the end of
Is 7:18 that the LORD shall *h* for the fly
Jer 19:8 *h* because of all the plagues
Jer 49:17 shall *h* at all the plagues
Jer 50:13 and *h* at all her plagues
Lam 2:15 they *h* and wag their head at the
Lam 2:16 they *h* and gnash the teeth
Eze 27:36 among the people shall *h* at thee
Zeph 2:15 one that passeth by her shall *h*
Zec 10:8 I will *h* for them, and gather them

### HISSING
2Chr 29:8 trouble, to astonishment, and to *h*
Jer 18:16 land desolate, and a perpetual *h*
Jer 19:8 make this city desolate, and an *h*
Jer 25:9 them an astonishment, and an *h*
Jer 25:18 desolation, an astonishment, an *h*
Jer 29:18 and an astonishment, and an *h*
Jer 51:37 dragons, an astonishment, and an *h*
Mic 6:16 and the inhabitants thereof an *h*

### HITHER
Gen 15:16 they shall come *h* again
Gen 42:15 your youngest brother come *h*
Gen 45:5 yourselves, that ye sold me *h*
Gen 45:8 now it was not you that sent me *h*
Gen 45:13 haste and bring down my father *h*
Ex 3:5 And he said, Draw not nigh *h*
Josh 2:2 there came men in *h* to night of
Josh 3:9 the children of Israel, Come *h*
Josh 18:6 and bring the description *h* to me
Judg 16:2 Gazites, saying, Samson is come *h*
Judg 18:3 said unto him, Who brought thee *h*
Judg 19:12 We will not turn aside *h* into the
Ruth 2:14 unto her, At mealtime come thou *h*
1Sa 13:9 Bring *h* a burnt offering to me,
1Sa 14:18 Ahiah, Bring *h* the ark of God
1Sa 14:34 Bring me *h* every man his ox, and
1Sa 14:36 Let us draw near *h* unto God
1Sa 14:38 And Saul said, Draw ye near *h*
1Sa 15:32 Bring ye *h* to me Agag the king of
1Sa 16:11 will not sit down till he come *h*
1Sa 17:28 he said, Why camest thou down *h*
1Sa 23:9 the priest, Bring *h* the ephod
1Sa 30:7 I pray thee, bring me *h* the ephod
2Sa 1:10 have brought them *h* unto my lord
2Sa 5:6 lame, thou shalt not come in *h*
2Sa 14:32 I sent unto thee, saying, Come *h*
2Sa 20:16 pray you, unto Joab, Come near *h*
1Kin 22:9 Hasten *h* Micaiah the son of Imlah
2Kin 2:8 waters, and they were divided *h*
2Kin 2:14 smitten the waters, they parted *h*
2Kin 8:7 saying, The man of God is come *h*
1Chr 11:5 to David, Thou shalt not come *h*
2Chr 28:13 shall not bring in the captives *h*
Ezr 4:2 of Assur, which brought us up *h*
Ps 73:10 Therefore his people return *h*
Ps 81:2 bring *h* the timbrel, the pleasant
Prov 9:4 is simple, let him turn in *h*
Prov 9:16 is simple, let him turn in *h*
Prov 25:7 it be said unto thee, Come up *h*
Is 57:3 But draw near *h*, ye sons of the
Eze 40:4 them unto thee art thou brought *h*
Dan 3:26 high God, come forth, and come *h*
Mt 8:29 art thou come *h* to torment us
Mt 14:18 He said, Bring them *h* to me
Mt 17:17 bring him *h* to me
Mt 22:12 how camest thou in *h* not having a
Mk 11:3 and straightway he will send him *h*
Lk 9:41 Bring thy son *h*
Lk 14:21 the city, and bring in *h* the poor
Lk 15:23 bring *h* the fatted calf, and kill
Lk 19:27 I should reign over them, bring *h*
Lk 19:30 loose him, and bring him *h*
Jn 4:15 not, neither come *h* to draw
Jn 4:16 Go, call thy husband, and come *h*
Jn 6:25 him, Rabbi, when camest thou *h*
Jn 20:27 Reach *h* thy finger, and behold my
Jn 20:27 reach *h* thy hand, and thrust it
Acts 9:21 came *h* for that intent, that he
Acts 10:32 call *h* Simon, whose surname is
Acts 17:6 world upside down are come *h* also
Acts 19:37 For ye have brought *h* these men
Acts 25:17 Therefore, when they were come *h*
Rev 4:1 which said, Come up *h*, and I will
Rev 11:12 saying unto them, Come up *h*
Rev 17:1 with me, saying unto me, Come *h*
Rev 21:9 and talked with me, saying, Come *h*

### HITHERTO
Ex 7:16 behold, *h* thou wouldest not hear
Josh 17:14 as the LORD hath blessed me *h*
Judg 16:13 *H* thou hast mocked me, and told
1Sa 1:16 and grief have I spoken *h*
1Sa 7:12 *H* hath the LORD helped us
2Sa 7:18 that thou hast brought me *h*
2Sa 15:34 have been thy father's servant *h*
1Chr 9:18 Who *h* waited in the king's gate
1Chr 12:29 for *h* the greatest part of them
1Chr 17:16 that thou hast brought me *h*
Job 38:11 *H* shalt thou come, but no further
Ps 71:17 *h* have I declared thy wondrous
Is 18:2 terrible from their beginning *h*
Is 18:7 terrible from their beginning *h*
Dan 7:28 *H* is the end of the matter
Jn 5:17 them, My Father worketh *h*
Jn 16:24 *H* have ye asked nothing in my
Rom 1:13 to come unto you, (but was let *h*
1Cor 3:2 for *h* ye were not able to bear it

### HITTITE *(hit'-tite)* See HITTITES. *A descendant of Heth.*
Gen 23:10 Ephron the *H* answered Abraham in
Gen 25:9 of Ephron the son of Zohar the *H*
Gen 26:34 the daughter of Beeri the *H*
Gen 26:34 the daughter of Elon the *H*
Gen 36:2 Adah the daughter of Elon the *H*
Gen 49:29 is in the field of Ephron the *H*
Gen 49:30 the *H* for a possession of a
Gen 50:13 of a buryingplace of Ephron the *H*
Ex 23:28 Hivite, the Canaanite, and the *H*
Ex 33:2 Canaanite, the Amorite, and the *H*
Ex 34:11 and the Canaanite, and the *H*
Josh 9:1 sea over against Lebanon, the *H*
Josh 11:3 west, and to the Amorite, and the *H*
1Sa 26:6 David and said to Ahimelech the *H*
2Sa 11:3 of Eliam, the wife of Uriah the *H*
2Sa 11:6 Joab, saying, Send me Uriah the *H*
2Sa 11:17 and Uriah the *H* died also
2Sa 11:21 servant Uriah the *H* is dead also
2Sa 11:24 servant Uriah the *H* is dead also
2Sa 12:9 killed Uriah the *H* with the sword
2Sa 12:10 of Uriah the *H* to be thy wife
2Sa 23:39 Uriah the *H*: thirty and seven
1Kin 15:5 only in the matter of Uriah the *H*
1Chr 11:41 Uriah the *H*, Zabad the son of
Eze 16:3 an Amorite, and thy mother an *H*
Eze 16:45 your mother was an *H*, and your

### HITTITES *(hit'-tites)*
Gen 15:20 And the *H*, and the Perizzites, and
Ex 3:8 place of the Canaanites, and the *H*
Ex 3:17 land of the Canaanites, and the *H*
Ex 13:5 land of the Canaanites, and the *H*
Ex 23:23 in unto the Amorites, and the *H*
Num 13:29 and the *H*, and the Jebusites, and
Deut 7:1 many nations before thee, the *H*
Deut 20:17 namely, the *H*, and the Amorites,
Josh 1:4 Euphrates, all the land of the *H*
Josh 3:10 you the Canaanites, and the *H*
Josh 12:8 the *H*, the Amorites, and the
Josh 24:11 and the Canaanites, and the *H*
Judg 1:26 man went into the land of the *H*
Judg 3:5 dwelt among the Canaanites, *H*
1Kin 9:20 that were left of the Amorites, *H*
1Kin 10:29 and so for all the kings of the *H*
1Kin 11:1 Edomites, Zidonians, and *H*
2Kin 7:6 against us the kings of the *H*
2Chr 1:17 horses for all the kings of the *H*
2Chr 8:7 people that were left of the *H*
Ezr 9:1 even of the Canaanites, the *H*
Neh 9:8 the land of the Canaanites, the *H*

### HIVITE *(hi'-vite) A descendant of Canaan.*
Gen 10:17 And the *H*, and the Arkite, and the
Gen 34:2 Shechem the son of Hamor the *H*
Gen 36:2 Anah the daughter of Zibeon the *H*
Ex 23:28 thee, which shall drive out the *H*
Ex 33:2 Hittite, and the Perizzite, the *H*
Ex 34:11 and the Perizzite, and the *H*
Josh 9:1 Canaanite, the Perizzite, the *H*
Josh 11:3 to the *H* under Hermon in the land
1Chr 1:15 And the *H*, and the Arkite, and the

### HIVITES *(hi'-vites)*
Ex 3:8 and the Perizzites, and the *H*
Ex 3:17 and the Perizzites, and the *H*
Ex 13:5 and the Amorites, and the *H*
Ex 23:23 and the Canaanites, the *H*
Deut 7:1 and the Perizzites, and the *H*
Deut 20:17 and the Perizzites, the *H*
Josh 3:10 and the Hittites, and the *H*
Josh 9:7 the men of Israel said unto the *H*
Josh 11:19 save the *H* the inhabitants of
Josh 12:8 Canaanites, the Perizzites, the *H*
Josh 24:11 and the Girgashites, the *H*
Judg 3:3 the *H* that dwelt in mount Lebanon
Judg 3:5 and Amorites, and Perizzites, and *H*
2Sa 24:7 and to all the cities of the *H*
1Kin 9:20 Amorites, Hittites, Perizzites, *H*
2Chr 8:7 and the Perizzites, and the *H*

### HIZKIAH *(hiz-ki'-ah)* See HEZEKIAH, HIZKIJAH. *An ancestor of Zephaniah.*
Zeph 1:1 the son of Amariah, the son of *H*

### HIZKIJAH *(hiz-ki'-jah)* See HIZKIAH. *An Israelite who renewed the covenant.*
Neh 10:17 Ater, *H*, Azzur,

### HOAR
Ex 16:14 as small as the *h* frost on the
1Kin 2:6 let not his *h* head go down to the
1Kin 2:9 but his *h* head bring thou down to

Ps 147:16 scattereth the *h* frost like ashes
Is 46:4 even to *h* hairs will I carry you

**HOARY**
Lev 19:32 shalt rise up before the *h* head
Job 38:29 the *h* frost of heaven, who hath
Job 41:32 one would think the deep to be *h*
Prov 16:31 The *h* head is a crown of glory,

**HOBAB** *(ho'-bab)* See JETHRO. *Another name for Jethro.*
Num 10:29 And Moses said unto *H*, the son of
Judg 4:11 of *H* the father in law of Moses

**HOBAH** *(ho'-bah) Place where Abraham pursued the five kings.*
Gen 14:15 them, and pursued them unto *H*

**HOD** *(hod) A son of Zophah.*
1Chr 7:37 Bezer, and *H*, and Shamma, and

**HODAIAH** *(ho-da-i'-ah)* See HODAVIAH. *A royal descendant of Judah.*
1Chr 3:24 And the sons of Elioenai were, *H*

**HODAVIAH** *(ho-da-vi'-ah)* See HODAIAH, HODEVAH.
*1. A chief of Manasseh.*
1Chr 5:24 and Azriel, and Jeremiah, and *H*
*2. Son of Hassenuah.*
1Chr 9:7 son of Meshullam, the son of *H*
*3. A family of exiles.*
Ezr 2:40 and Kadmiel, of the children of *H*

**HODESH** *(ho'-desh) Wife of Shaharaim.*
1Chr 8:9 And he begat of *H* his wife

**HODEVAH** *(ho-de'-vah)* See HODAVIAH. *A family of exiles.*
Neh 7:43 Kadmiel, and of the children of *H*

**HODIAH** *(ho-di'-ah)* See HODIJAH. *A wife of Mered.*
1Chr 4:19 of his wife *H* the sister of Naham

**HODIJAH** *(ho-di'-jah)* See HODIAH.
*1. A Levite.*
Neh 8:7 Jamin, Akkub, Shabbethai, *H*
Neh 9:5 Bani, Hashabniah, Sherebiah, *H*
Neh 10:10 And their brethren, Shebaniah, *H*
Neh 10:13 *H*, Bani, Beninu
*2. A leader of the people.*
Neh 10:18 *H*, Hashum, Bezai,

**HOGLAH** *(hog'-lah)* See BETH-HOGLAH. *A daughter of Zelophehad.*
Num 26:33 were Mahlah, and Noah, *H*, Milcah,
Num 27:1 Mahlah, Noah, and *H*, and Milcah,
Num 36:11 For Mahlah, Tirzah, and *H*, and
Josh 17:3 his daughters, Mahlah, and Noah, *H*

**HOHAM** *(ho'-ham) An Amorite king.*
Josh 10:3 sent unto *H* king of Hebron

**HOLD**
Gen 19:16 the men laid *h* upon his hand, and
Gen 21:18 the lad, and *h* him in thine hand
Gen 25:26 his hand took *h* on Esau's heel
Ex 5:1 that they may *h* a feast unto me
Ex 9:2 them go, and wilt *h* them still,
Ex 10:9 for we must *h* a feast unto the
Ex 14:14 for you, and ye shall *h* your peace
Ex 15:14 sorrow shall take *h* on the
Ex 15:15 trembling shall take *h* upon them
Ex 20:7 for the LORD will not *h* him
Ex 26:5 loops may take *h* one of another
Num 30:4 father shall *h* his peace at her
Num 30:14 *h* his peace at her from day to
Deut 5:11 for the LORD will not *h* him
Deut 21:19 father and his mother lay *h* on him
Deut 22:28 lay *h* on her, and lie with her, and
Deut 32:41 and mine hand take *h* on judgment
Judg 9:46 they entered into an *h* of the
Judg 9:49 Abimelech, and put them to the *h*
Judg 9:49 set the *h* on fire upon them
Judg 16:29 Samson took *h* of the two middle
Judg 18:19 *H* thy peace, lay thine hand upon
Judg 19:29 laid *h* on his concubine, and
Ruth 3:15 that thou hast upon thee, and *h* it
1Sa 15:27 he laid *h* upon the skirt of his
1Sa 22:4 the while that David was in the *h*
1Sa 22:5 unto David, Abide not in the *h*
1Sa 24:22 and his men gat them up unto the *h*
2Sa 1:11 Then David took *h* on his clothes
2Sa 2:21 lay thee *h* on one of the young
2Sa 2:22 how then should I *h* up my face to
2Sa 4:10 good tidings, I took *h* of him
2Sa 5:7 David took the strong *h* of Zion
2Sa 5:17 of it, and went down to the *h*
2Sa 6:6 the ark of God, and took *h* of it
2Sa 13:11 unto him to eat, he took *h* of her
2Sa 13:20 but *h* now thy peace, my sister
2Sa 18:9 and his head caught *h* of the oak
2Sa 23:14 And David was then in an *h*
2Sa 24:7 And came to the strong *h* of Tyre
1Kin 1:50 caught *h* on the horns of the
1Kin 1:51 he hath caught *h* on the horns of
1Kin 2:9 Now therefore *h* him not guiltless
1Kin 2:28 caught *h* on the horns of the
1Kin 9:9 have taken *h* upon other gods, and
1Kin 13:4 the altar, saying, Lay *h* on him
2Kin 2:3 *h* ye your peace
2Kin 2:5 *h* ye your peace
2Kin 2:12 he took *h* of his own clothes, and
2Kin 6:32 door, and *h* him fast at the door
2Kin 7:9 good tidings, and we *h* our peace
1Chr 11:16 And David was then in the *h*
1Chr 12:8 *h* to the wilderness men of might
1Chr 12:16 and Judah to the *h* unto David
1Chr 13:9 put forth his hand to *h* the ark
2Chr 7:22 and laid *h* on other gods, and
Neh 8:11 *H* your peace, for the day is holy
Est 4:11 shall *h* out the golden sceptre
Job 6:24 Teach me, and I will *h* my tongue
Job 8:15 he shall *h* it fast, but it shall
Job 9:28 that thou wilt not *h* me innocent
Job 11:3 thy lies make men *h* their peace
Job 13:5 ye would altogether *h* your peace
Job 13:13 *H* your peace, let me alone, that
Job 13:19 if I *h* my tongue, I shall give up
Job 17:9 righteous also shall *h* on his way
Job 21:6 and trembling taketh *h* on my flesh
Job 27:6 My righteousness I *h* fast
Job 27:20 Terrors take *h* on him as waters,
Job 30:16 affliction have taken *h* upon me
Job 33:31 *h* thy peace, and I will speak
Job 33:33 *h* thy peace, and I shall teach
Job 36:17 and justice take *h* on thee
Job 38:13 That it might take *h* of the ends
Job 41:26 him that layeth at him cannot *h*
Ps 17:5 *H* up my goings in thy paths, that
Ps 35:2 Take *h* of shield and buckler, and
Ps 39:12 *h* not thy peace at my tears
Ps 40:12 iniquities have taken *h* upon me
Ps 48:6 Fear took *h* upon them there, and
Ps 69:24 thy wrathful anger take *h* of them
Ps 83:1 *h* not thy peace, and be not still,
Ps 109:1 *H* not thy peace, O God of my
Ps 116:3 the pains of hell gat *h* upon me
Ps 119:53 Horror hath taken *h* upon me
Ps 119:117 *H* thou me up, and I shall be safe
Ps 119:143 and anguish have taken *h* on me
Ps 139:10 me, and thy right hand shall *h* me
Prov 2:19 neither take they *h* of the paths
Prov 3:18 life to them that lay *h* upon her
Prov 4:13 Take fast *h* of instruction
Prov 5:5 her steps take *h* on hell
Prov 30:28 spider taketh *h* with her hands
Prov 31:19 and her hands *h* the distaff
Eccl 2:3 to lay *h* on folly, till I might
Eccl 7:18 thou shouldest take *h* of this
Song 3:8 They all *h* swords, being expert
Song 7:8 I will take *h* of the boughs
Is 3:6 When a man shall take *h* of his
Is 4:1 women shall take *h* of one man
Is 5:29 lay *h* of the prey, and shall carry
Is 13:8 and sorrows shall take *h* of them
Is 21:3 pangs have taken *h* upon me
Is 27:5 Or let him take *h* of my strength
Is 31:9 over to his strong *h* for fear
Is 41:13 thy God will *h* thy right hand
Is 42:6 will *h* thine hand, and will keep
Is 56:2 son of man that layeth *h* on it
Is 56:4 me, and take *h* of my covenant
Is 56:6 it, and taketh *h* of my covenant
Is 62:1 Zion's sake will I not *h* my peace
Is 62:6 which shall never *h* their peace
Is 64:7 up himself to take *h* of thee
Is 64:12 wilt thou *h* thy peace, and afflict
Jer 2:13 cisterns, that can *h* no water
Jer 4:19 I cannot *h* my peace, because thou
Jer 6:23 They shall lay *h* on bow and spear
Jer 6:24 anguish hath taken *h* of us
Jer 8:5 they *h* fast deceit, they refuse
Jer 8:21 astonishment hath taken *h* on me
Jer 50:42 They shall *h* the bow and the lance
Jer 50:43 anguish took *h* of him, and pangs
Eze 29:7 When they took *h* of thee by thy
Eze 30:21 to make it strong to *h* the sword
Eze 41:6 about, that they might have *h*
Eze 41:6 but they had not *h* in the wall of
Amos 6:10 Then shall he say, *H* thy tongue
Mic 4:8 the strong *h* of the daughter of
Mic 6:14 and thou shalt take *h*, but shalt
Nah 1:7 a strong *h* in the day of trouble
Hab 1:10 they shall deride every strong *h*
Zeph 1:7 *H* thy peace at the presence of
Zec 1:6 they not take *h* of your fathers
Zec 8:23 that ten men shall take *h* out of
Zec 8:23 even shall take *h* of the skirt of
Zec 9:3 did build herself a strong *h*
Zec 9:12 Turn you to the strong *h*, ye
Zec 11:5 them, and *h* themselves not guilty
Zec 14:13 they shall lay *h* every one on the
Mt 6:24 or else he will *h* to the one
Mt 12:11 day, will he not lay *h* on it
Mt 14:3 For Herod had laid *h* on John
Mt 20:31 because they should *h* their peace
Mt 21:26 for all *h* John as a prophet
Mt 26:48 same is he: *h* him fast
Mt 26:55 the temple, and ye laid no *h* on me
Mt 26:57 they that had laid *h* on Jesus led
Mk 1:25 *H* thy peace, and come out of him
Mk 3:21 it, they went out to lay *h* on him
Mk 6:17 laid *h* upon John, and bound him in
Mk 7:4 be, which they have received to *h*
Mk 7:8 ye *h* the tradition of men, as the
Mk 10:48 him that he should *h* his peace
Mk 12:12 And they sought to lay *h* on him
Mk 14:51 and the young men laid *h* on him
Lk 4:35 *H* thy peace, and come out of him
Lk 16:13 or else he will *h* to the one
Lk 18:39 him, that he should *h* his peace
Lk 19:40 if these should *h* their peace
Lk 20:20 they might take *h* of his words
Lk 20:26 they could not take *h* of his
Lk 23:26 they laid *h* upon one Simon, a
Acts 4:3 put them in *h* unto the next day
Acts 12:17 with the hand to *h* their peace
Acts 18:9 but speak, and *h* not thy peace
Rom 1:18 of men, who *h* the truth in
1Cor 14:30 by, let the first *h* his peace
Phil 2:29 and *h* such in reputation
1Th 5:21 *h* fast that which is good
2Th 2:15 *h* the traditions which ye have
1Ti 6:12 lay *h* on eternal life, whereunto
1Ti 6:19 they may lay *h* on eternal life
2Ti 1:13 *H* fast the form of sound words,
Heb 3:6 if we *h* fast the confidence and
Heb 3:14 if we *h* the beginning of our
Heb 4:14 let us *h* fast our profession
Heb 6:18 lay *h* upon the hope set before us
Heb 10:23 Let us *h* fast the profession of
Rev 2:14 that *h* the doctrine of Balaam
Rev 2:15 them that *h* the doctrine of the
Rev 2:25 have already *h* fast till I come
Rev 3:3 and heard, and *h* fast, and repent
Rev 3:11 *h* that fast which thou hast, that
Rev 18:2 the *h* of every foul spirit, and a
Rev 20:2 he laid *h* on the dragon, that old

**HOLDEN**
2Kin 23:22 Surely there was not *h* such a
2Kin 23:23 was *h* to the LORD in Jerusalem
Job 36:8 be *h* in cords of affliction
Ps 18:35 and thy right hand hath *h* me up
Ps 71:6 have I been *h* up from the womb
Ps 73:23 thou hast *h* me by my right hand
Prov 5:22 he shall be *h* with the cords of
Is 42:14 I have long time *h* my peace
Is 45:1 Cyrus, whose right hand I have *h*
Lk 24:16 But their eyes were *h* that they
Acts 2:24 that he should be *h* of it
Rom 14:4 Yea, he shall be *h* up

**HOLDEST**
Est 4:14 *h* thy peace at this time, then
Job 13:24 thy face, and *h* me for thine enemy
Ps 77:4 Thou *h* mine eyes waking
Jer 49:16 that *h* the height of the hill
Hab 1:13 *h* thy tongue when the wicked
Rev 2:13 thou *h* fast my name, and hast not

**HOLDETH**
Job 2:3 still he *h* fast his integrity,
Job 26:9 He *h* back the face of his throne,
Ps 66:9 Which *h* our soul in life, and
Prov 11:12 man of understanding *h* his peace
Prov 17:28 when he *h* his peace, is counted
Dan 10:21 there is none that *h* with me in
Amos 1:5 him that *h* the sceptre from the

Amos 1:8 him that *h* the sceptre from
Rev 2:1 These things saith he that *h* the

## HOLDING
Is 33:15 his hands from *h* of bribes
Jer 6:11 I am weary with *h* in
Mk 7:3 *h* the tradition of the elders
Phil 2:16 *H* forth the word of life
Col 2:19 not *h* the Head, from which all
1Ti 1:19 *H* faith, and a good conscience
1Ti 3:9 *H* the mystery of the faith in a
Titus 1:9 *H* fast the faithful word as he
Rev 7:1 *h* the four winds of the earth,

## HOLDS
Num 13:19 whether in tents, or in strong *h*
Judg 6:2 mountains, and caves, and strong *h*
1Sa 23:14 in the wilderness in strong *h*
1Sa 23:19 with us in strong *h* in the wood
1Sa 23:29 and dwelt in strong *h* at En-gedi
2Kin 8:12 their strong *h* wilt thou set on
2Chr 11:11 And he fortified the strong *h*
Ps 89:40 hast brought his strong *h* to ruin
Is 23:11 to destroy the strong *h* thereof
Jer 48:18 and he shall destroy thy strong *h*
Jer 48:41 the strong *h* are surprised, and
Jer 51:30 they have remained in their *h*
Lam 2:2 strong *h* of the daughter of Judah
Lam 2:5 he hath destroyed his strong *h*
Eze 19:9 they brought him into *h*, that his
Dan 11:24 his devices against the strong *h*
Dan 11:39 most strong *h* with a strange god
Mic 5:11 and throw down all thy strong *h*
Nah 3:12 All thy strong *h* shall be like
Nah 3:14 the siege, fortify thy strong *h*
2Cor 10:4 to the pulling down of strong *h*

## HOLE
Ex 28:32 shall be an *h* in the top of it
Ex 28:32 work round about the *h* of it
Ex 28:32 as it were the *h* of an habergeon,
Ex 39:23 there was an *h* in the midst of
Ex 39:23 as the *h* of an habergeon, with a
Ex 39:23 with a band round about the *h*
2Kin 12:9 bored a *h* in the lid of it, and
Song 5:4 in his hand by the *h* of the door
Is 11:8 shall play on the *h* of the asp
Is 51:1 to the *h* of the pit whence ye are
Jer 13:4 hide it there in a *h* of the rock
Eze 8:7 I looked, behold a *h* in the wall

## HOLES
1Sa 14:11 *h* where they had hid themselves
Is 2:19 shall go into the *h* of the rocks
Is 7:19 in the *h* of the rocks, and upon
Is 42:22 they are all of them snared in *h*
Jer 16:16 out of the *h* of the rocks
Mic 7:17 their *h* like worms of the earth
Nah 2:12 and filled his *h* with prey
Hag 1:6 wages to put it into a bag with *h*
Zec 14:12 shall consume away in their *h*
Mt 8:20 saith unto him, The foxes have *h*
Lk 9:58 Jesus said unto him, Foxes have *h*

## HOLINESS
Ex 15:11 Who is like thee, glorious in *h*
Ex 28:36 of a signet, *H* TO THE LORD
Ex 39:30 of a signet, *H* TO THE LORD
1Chr 16:29 the LORD in the beauty of *h*
2Chr 20:21 should praise the beauty of *h*
2Chr 31:18 they sanctified themselves in *h*
Ps 29:2 the LORD in the beauty of *h*
Ps 30:4 at the remembrance of his *h*
Ps 47:8 sitteth upon the throne of his *h*
Ps 48:1 our God, in the mountain of his *h*
Ps 60:6 God hath spoken in his *h*
Ps 89:35 Once have I sworn by my *h* that I
Ps 93:5 *h* becometh thine house, O LORD,
Ps 96:9 the LORD in the beauty of *h*
Ps 97:12 at the remembrance of his *h*
Ps 108:7 God hath spoken in his *h*
Ps 110:3 in the beauties of *h* from the
Is 23:18 her hire shall be *h* to the LORD
Is 35:8 it shall be called The way of *h*
Is 62:9 drink it in the courts of my *h*
Is 63:15 from the habitation of thy *h*
Is 63:18 The people of thy *h* have
Jer 2:3 Israel was *h* unto the LORD, and
Jer 23:9 and because of the words of his *h*
Jer 31:23 of justice, and mountain of *h*
Amos 4:2 The Lord GOD hath sworn by his *h*
Obad 17 deliverance, and there shall be *h*
Zec 14:20 of the horses, *H* UNTO THE LORD
Zec 14:21 in Judah shall be *h* unto the LORD
Mal 2:11 the *h* of the LORD which he loved
Lk 1:75 In *h* and righteousness before him,
Acts 3:12 or *h* we had made this man to walk
Rom 1:4 according to the spirit of *h*
Rom 6:19 servants to righteousness unto *h*
Rom 6:22 to God, ye have your fruit unto *h*
2Cor 7:1 perfecting *h* in the fear of God
Eph 4:24 in righteousness and true *h*
1Th 3:13 unblameable in *h* before God
1Th 4:7 us unto uncleanness, but unto *h*
1Ti 2:15 and charity and *h* with sobriety
Titus 2:3 be in behaviour as becometh *h*
Heb 12:10 we might be partakers of his *h*
Heb 12:14 Follow peace with all men, and *h*

## HOLLOW
Gen 32:25 he touched the *h* of his thigh
Gen 32:25 the *h* of Jacob's thigh was out of
Gen 32:32 which is upon the *h* of the thigh
Gen 32:32 because he touched the *h* of
Ex 27:8 *H* with boards shalt thou make it
Ex 38:7 he made the altar *h* with boards
Lev 14:37 walls of the house with *h* strakes
Judg 15:19 But God clave an *h* place that was
Is 40:12 the waters in the *h* of his hand
Jer 52:21 was four fingers: it was *h*

## HOLON *(ho'-lon)* See HILEN.
*1. A Levitical city in Judah.*
Josh 15:51 And Goshen, and *H*, and Giloh
Josh 21:15 *H* with her suburbs, and Debir with
*2. A Moabite city.*
Jer 48:21 upon *H*, and upon Jahazah, and upon

## HOMAM *(ho'-mam)* See HEMAM. *A son of Lotan.*
1Chr 1:39 of Lotan; Hori, and *H*

## HOME
Gen 39:16 by her, until his lord came *h*
Gen 43:16 of his house, Bring these men *h*
Gen 43:26 And when Joseph came *h*, they
Ex 9:19 field, and shall not be brought *h*
Lev 18:9 mother, whether she be born at *h*
Deut 21:12 shalt bring her *h* to thine house
Deut 24:5 he shall be free at *h* one year
Josh 2:18 father's household, *h* unto thee
Judg 11:9 If ye bring me *h* again to fight
Judg 19:9 your way, that thou mayest go *h*
Ruth 1:21 hath brought me *h* again empty
1Sa 2:20 And they went unto their own *h*
1Sa 6:7 and bring their calves *h* from them
1Sa 6:10 and shut up their calves at *h*
1Sa 10:26 And Saul also went *h* to Gibeah
1Sa 18:2 no more *h* to his father's house
1Sa 24:22 And Saul went *h*
2Sa 13:7 Then David sent *h* to Tamar
2Sa 14:13 not fetch *h* again his banished
2Sa 17:23 gat him *h* to his house, to his
1Kin 5:14 in Lebanon, and two months at *h*
1Kin 13:7 Come *h* with me, and refresh
1Kin 13:15 Come *h* with me, and eat bread
2Kin 14:10 glory of this, and tarry at *h*
1Chr 13:12 I bring the ark of God *h* to me
1Chr 13:13 So David brought not the ark *h* to
2Chr 25:10 him out of Ephraim, to go *h* again
2Chr 25:10 they returned *h* in great anger
2Chr 25:19 abide now at *h*
Est 5:10 and when he came *h*, he sent and
Job 39:12 that he will bring *h* thy seed
Ps 68:12 tarried at *h* divided the spoil
Prov 7:19 For the goodman is not at *h*
Prov 7:20 will come *h* at the day appointed
Eccl 12:5 because man goeth to his long *h*
Jer 39:14 that he should carry him *h*
Lam 1:20 bereaveth, at *h* there is as death
Hab 2:5 a proud man, neither keepeth at *h*
Hag 1:9 and when ye brought it *h*, I did
Mt 8:6 lieth at *h* sick of the palsy
Mk 5:19 Go *h* to thy friends, and tell them
Lk 9:61 which are at *h* at my house
Lk 15:6 And when he cometh *h*, he calleth
Jn 19:27 disciple took her unto his own *h*
Jn 20:10 went away again unto their own *h*
Acts 21:6 and they returned *h* again
1Cor 11:34 any man hunger, let him eat at *h*
1Cor 14:35 let them ask their husbands at *h*
2Cor 5:6 whilst we are at *h* in the body
1Ti 5:4 learn first to shew piety at *h*
Titus 2:5 be discreet, chaste, keepers at *h*

## HOMER
Lev 27:16 a *h* of barley seed shall be
Is 5:10 the seed of an *h* shall yield an
Eze 45:11 contain the tenth part of an *h*
Eze 45:11 the ephah the tenth part of an *h*
Eze 45:11 thereof shall be after the *h*
Eze 45:13 part of an ephah of an *h* of wheat
Eze 45:13 of an ephah of an *h* of barley
Eze 45:14 which is an *h* of ten baths
Eze 45:14 for ten baths are an *h*
Hos 3:2 an *h* of barley, and an half *h*

## HONEST
Lk 8:15 ground are they, which in an *h*
Acts 6:3 among you seven men of *h* report
Rom 12:17 Provide things *h* in the sight of
2Cor 8:21 Providing for *h* things, not only
2Cor 13:7 that ye should do that which is *h*
Phil 4:8 are true, whatsoever things are *h*
1Pet 2:12 conversation *h* among the Gentiles

## HONESTLY
Rom 13:13 Let us walk *h*, as in the day
1Th 4:12 That ye may walk *h* toward them
Heb 13:18 in all things willing to live *h*

## HONEY
Gen 43:11 a little balm, and a little *h*
Ex 3:8 a land flowing with milk and *h*
Ex 3:17 a land flowing with milk and *h*
Ex 13:5 a land flowing with milk and *h*
Ex 16:31 of it was like wafers made with *h*
Ex 33:3 a land flowing with milk and *h*
Lev 2:11 shall burn no leaven, nor any *h*
Lev 20:24 land that floweth with milk and *h*
Num 13:27 surely it floweth with milk and *h*
Num 14:8 land which floweth with milk and *h*
Num 16:13 land that floweth with milk and *h*
Num 16:14 land that floweth with milk and *h*
Deut 6:3 land that floweth with milk and *h*
Deut 8:8 a land of oil olive, and *h*
Deut 11:9 land that floweth with milk and *h*
Deut 26:9 land that floweth with milk and *h*
Deut 26:15 land that floweth with milk and *h*
Deut 27:3 land that floweth with milk and *h*
Deut 31:20 that floweth with milk and *h*
Deut 32:13 him to suck *h* out of the rock
Josh 5:6 land that floweth with milk and *h*
Judg 14:8 *h* in the carcase of the lion
Judg 14:9 *h* out of the carcase of the lion
Judg 14:18 went down, What is sweeter than *h*
1Sa 14:25 there was *h* upon the ground
1Sa 14:26 the wood, behold, the *h* dropped
1Sa 14:29 I tasted a little of this *h*
1Sa 14:43 I did but taste a little *h* with
2Sa 17:29 And *h*, and butter, and sheep, and
1Kin 14:3 and cracknels, and a cruse of *h*
2Kin 18:32 a land of oil olive and of *h*
2Chr 31:5 of corn, wine, and oil, and *h*
Job 20:17 the floods, the brooks of *h*
Ps 19:10 sweeter also than *h* and the
Ps 81:16 with *h* out of the rock should I
Ps 119:103 yea, sweeter than *h* to my mouth
Prov 24:13 My son, eat thou *h*, because it is
Prov 25:16 Hast thou found *h*?
Prov 25:27 It is not good to eat much *h*
Song 4:11 *h* and milk are under thy tongue
Song 5:1 have eaten my honeycomb with my *h*
Is 7:15 *h* shall he eat, that he may know
Is 7:22 *h* shall every one eat that is
Jer 11:5 a land flowing with milk and *h*
Jer 32:22 a land flowing with milk and *h*
Jer 41:8 and of barley, and of oil, and of *h*
Eze 3:3 in my mouth as *h* for sweetness
Eze 16:13 thou didst eat fine flour, and *h*
Eze 16:19 thee, fine flour, and oil, and *h*
Eze 20:6 for them, flowing with milk and *h*
Eze 20:15 them, flowing with milk and *h*
Eze 27:17 wheat of Minnith, and Pannag, and *h*
Mt 3:4 and his meat was locusts and wild *h*
Mk 1:6 and he did eat locusts and wild *h*
Rev 10:9 shall be in thy mouth sweet as *h*
Rev 10:10 and it was in my mouth sweet as *h*

## HONEYCOMB
1Sa 14:27 in his hand, and dipped it in an *h*
Ps 19:10 sweeter also than honey and the *h*
Prov 5:3 of a strange woman drop as an *h*
Prov 16:24 Pleasant words are as an *h*
Prov 24:13 and the *h*, which is sweet to thy
Prov 27:7 The full soul loatheth an *h*
Song 4:11 lips, O my spouse, drop as the *h*

Song 5:1 I have eaten my *h* with my honey
Lk 24:42 of a broiled fish, and of an *h*

### HONOUR

Gen 49:6 unto their assembly, mine *h*
Ex 14:17 and I will get me *h* upon Pharaoh
Ex 14:18 I have gotten me *h* upon Pharaoh
Ex 20:12 *H* thy father and thy mother
Lev 19:15 nor *h* the person of the mighty
Lev 19:32 *h* the face of the old man, and
Num 22:17 promote thee unto very great *h*
Num 22:37 able indeed to promote thee to *h*
Num 24:11 to promote thee unto great *h*
Num 24:11 LORD hath kept thee back from *h*
Num 27:20 put some of thine *h* upon him
Deut 5:16 *H* thy father and thy mother, as
Deut 26:19 in praise, and in name, and in *h*
Judg 4:9 takest shall not be for thine *h*
Judg 9:9 wherewith by me they *h* God
Judg 13:17 come to pass we may do thee *h*
1Sa 2:30 for them that *h* me I will *h*,
1Sa 15:30 yet *h* me now, I pray thee, before
2Sa 6:22 of, of them shall I be had in *h*
2Sa 10:3 thou that David doth *h* thy father
1Kin 3:13 hast not asked, both riches, and *h*
1Chr 16:27 Glory and *h* are in his presence
1Chr 17:18 to thee for the *h* of thy servant
1Chr 19:3 thou that David doth *h* thy father
1Chr 29:12 *h* come of thee, and thou reignest
1Chr 29:28 age, full of days, riches, and *h*
2Chr 1:11 not asked riches, wealth, or *h*
2Chr 1:12 give thee riches, and wealth, and *h*
2Chr 17:5 he had riches and *h* in abundance
2Chr 18:1 *h* in abundance, and joined
2Chr 26:18 be for thine *h* from the LORD God
2Chr 32:27 had exceeding much riches and *h*
2Chr 32:33 Jerusalem did him *h* at his death
Est 1:4 the *h* of his excellent majesty
Est 1:20 shall give to their husbands *h*
Est 6:3 And the king said, What *h* and
Est 6:6 man whom the king delighteth to *h*
Est 6:6 to do *h* more than to myself
Est 6:7 man whom the king delighteth to *h*
Est 6:9 whom the king delighteth to *h*
Est 6:9 man whom the king delighteth to *h*
Est 6:11 man whom the king delighteth to *h*
Est 8:16 light, and gladness, and joy, and *h*
Job 14:21 His sons come to *h*, and he knoweth
Ps 7:5 earth, and lay mine *h* in the dust
Ps 8:5 hast crowned him with glory and *h*
Ps 21:5 *h* and majesty hast thou laid upon
Ps 26:8 the place where thine *h* dwelleth
Ps 49:12 man being in *h* abideth not
Ps 49:20 Man that is in *h*, and
Ps 66:2 Sing forth the *h* of his name
Ps 71:8 praise and with thy *h* all the day
Ps 91:15 I will deliver him, and *h* him
Ps 96:6 *H* and majesty are before him
Ps 104:1 thou art clothed with *h* and
Ps 112:9 his horn shall be exalted with *h*
Ps 145:5 of the glorious *h* of thy majesty
Ps 149:9 this *h* have all his saints
Prov 3:9 *H* the LORD with thy substance, and
Prov 3:16 and in her left hand riches and *h*
Prov 4:8 she shall bring thee to *h*
Prov 5:9 thou give thine *h* unto others
Prov 8:18 Riches and *h* are with me
Prov 11:16 A gracious woman retaineth *h*
Prov 14:28 of people is the king's *h*
Prov 15:33 and before *h* is humility
Prov 18:12 and before *h* is humility
Prov 20:3 It is an *h* for a man to cease
Prov 21:21 findeth life, righteousness, and *h*
Prov 22:4 fear of the LORD are riches, and *h*
Prov 25:2 but the *h* of kings is to search
Prov 26:1 so *h* is not seemly for a fool
Prov 26:8 so is he that giveth *h* to a fool
Prov 29:23 but *h* shall uphold the humble in
Prov 31:25 Strength and *h* are her clothing
Eccl 6:2 hath given riches, wealth, and *h*
Eccl 10:1 is in reputation for wisdom and *h*
Is 29:13 mouth, and with their lips do *h* me
Is 43:20 The beast of the field shall *h* me
Is 58:13 and shalt *h* him, not doing thine
Jer 33:9 an *h* before all the nations of
Dan 2:6 of me gifts and rewards and great *h*
Dan 4:30 power, and for the *h* of my majesty
Dan 4:36 the glory of my kingdom, mine *h*
Dan 4:37 *h* the King of heaven, all whose
Dan 5:18 and majesty, and glory, and *h*
Dan 11:21 not give the *h* of the kingdom
Dan 11:38 shall he *h* the God of forces
Dan 11:38 knew not shall he *h* with gold
Mal 1:6 I be a father, where is mine *h*
Mt 13:57 them, A prophet is not without *h*
Mt 15:4 saying, *H* thy father and mother
Mt 15:6 *h* not his father or his mother,
Mt 19:19 *H* thy father and thy mother
Mk 6:4 them, A prophet is not without *h*
Mk 7:10 *H* thy father and thy mother
Mk 10:19 not, *H* thy father and mother
Lk 18:20 *H* thy father and thy mother
Jn 4:44 hath no *h* in his own country
Jn 5:23 That all men should *h* the Son
Jn 5:23 even as they *h* the Father
Jn 5:41 I receive not *h* from men
Jn 5:44 which receive *h* one of another,
Jn 5:44 seek not the *h* that cometh from
Jn 8:49 but I *h* my Father, and ye do
Jn 8:54 I *h* myself, my *h* is nothing
Jn 12:26 serve me, him will my Father *h*
Rom 2:7 in well doing seek for glory and *h*
Rom 2:10 But glory, *h*, and peace, to every
Rom 9:21 lump to make one vessel unto *h*
Rom 12:10 in *h* preferring one another
Rom 13:7 to whom fear; *h* to whom *h*
1Cor 12:23 these we bestow more abundant *h*
1Cor 12:24 *h* to that part which lacked
2Cor 6:8 By *h* and dishonour, by evil report
Eph 6:2 *H* thy father and mother
Col 2:23 not in any *h* to the satisfying of
1Th 4:4 his vessel in sanctification and *h*
1Ti 1:17 the only wise God, be *h* and glory
1Ti 5:3 *H* widows that are widows indeed
1Ti 5:17 be counted worthy of double *h*
1Ti 6:1 their own masters worthy of all *h*
1Ti 6:16 to whom be *h* and power everlasting
2Ti 2:20 and some to *h*, and some to
2Ti 2:21 he shall be a vessel unto *h*
Heb 2:7 crownedst him with glory and *h*
Heb 2:9 of death, crowned with glory and *h*
Heb 3:3 house hath more *h* than the house
Heb 5:4 no man taketh this *h* unto himself
1Pet 1:7 might be found unto praise and *h*
1Pet 2:17 *H* all men
1Pet 2:17 *H* the king
1Pet 3:7 giving *h* unto the wife, as unto
2Pet 1:17 he received from God the Father *h*
Rev 4:9 when those beasts give glory and *h*
Rev 4:11 O Lord, to receive glory and *h*
Rev 5:12 and wisdom, and strength, and *h*
Rev 5:13 heard I saying, Blessing, and *h*
Rev 7:12 and wisdom, and thanksgiving, and *h*
Rev 19:1 Salvation, and glory, and *h*
Rev 19:7 glad and rejoice, and give *h* to him
Rev 21:24 do bring their glory and *h* into it
Rev 21:26 glory and *h* of the nations into it

### HONOURABLE

Gen 34:19 he was more *h* than all the house
Num 22:15 more, and more *h* than they
1Sa 9:6 a man of God, and he is an *h* man
1Sa 22:14 bidding, and is *h* in thine house
2Sa 23:19 Was he not most *h* of three
2Sa 23:23 He was more *h* than the thirty,
2Kin 5:1 great man with his master, and *h*
1Chr 4:9 Jabez was more *h* than his
1Chr 11:21 he was more *h* than the two
1Chr 11:25 he was *h* among the thirty, but
Job 22:8 and the *h* man dwelt in it
Ps 45:9 daughters were among thy *h* women
Ps 111:3 His work is *h* and glorious
Is 3:3 captain of fifty, and the *h* man
Is 3:5 and the base against the *h*
Is 5:13 their *h* men are famished, and
Is 9:15 The ancient and *h*, he is the head
Is 23:8 are the *h* of the earth
Is 23:9 contempt all the *h* of the earth
Is 42:21 magnify the law, and make it *h*
Is 43:4 in my sight, thou hast been *h*
Is 58:13 delight, the holy of the LORD, *h*
Nah 3:10 and they cast lots for her *h* men
Mk 15:43 an *h* counsellor, which also
Lk 14:8 lest a more *h* man than thou be
Acts 13:50 *h* women, and the chief men of the
Acts 17:12 also of *h* women which were Greeks
1Cor 4:10 ye are *h*, but we are despised
1Cor 12:23 body, which we think to be less *h*
Heb 13:4 Marriage is *h* in all, and the bed

### HONOURED

Ex 14:4 I will be *h* upon Pharaoh, and upon
Prov 13:18 that regardeth reproof shall be *h*
Prov 27:18 waiteth on his master shall be *h*
Is 43:23 neither hast thou *h* me with thy
Lam 1:8 all that *h* her despise her,
Lam 5:12 the faces of elders were not *h*
Dan 4:34 *h* him that liveth for ever, whose
Acts 28:10 Who also *h* us with many honours
1Cor 12:26 or one member be *h*, all the

### HONOURETH

Ps 15:4 but he *h* them that fear the LORD
Prov 12:9 is better than he that *h* himself
Prov 14:31 but he that *h* him hath mercy on
Mal 1:6 A son *h* his father, and a servant
Mt 15:8 mouth, and *h* me with their lips
Mk 7:6 This people *h* me with their lips,
Jn 5:23 He that *h* not the Son *h* not
Jn 8:54 it is my Father that *h* me

### HOOF

Ex 10:26 shall not an *h* be left behind
Lev 11:3 Whatsoever parteth the *h*, and is
Lev 11:4 cud, or of them that divide the *h*
Lev 11:4 the cud, but divideth not the *h*
Lev 11:5 the cud, but divideth not the *h*
Lev 11:6 the cud, but divideth not the *h*
Lev 11:7 the swine, though he divide the *h*
Lev 11:26 every beast which divideth the *h*
Deut 14:6 And every beast that parteth the *h*
Deut 14:7 of them that divide the cloven *h*
Deut 14:7 the cud, but divide not the *h*
Deut 14:8 swine, because it divideth the *h*

### HOOFS

Ps 69:31 or bullock that hath horns and *h*
Is 5:28 their horses' *h* shall be counted
Jer 47:3 of the *h* of his strong horses
Eze 26:11 With the *h* of his horses shall he
Eze 32:13 nor the *h* of beasts trouble them
Mic 4:13 iron, and I will make thy *h* brass

### HOOK

2Kin 19:28 I will put my *h* in thy nose
Job 41:1 thou draw out leviathan with an *h*
Job 41:2 Canst thou put an *h* into his nose
Is 37:29 will I put my *h* in thy nose
Mt 17:27 go thou to the sea, and cast an *h*

### HOOKS

Ex 26:32 their *h* shall be of gold, upon
Ex 26:37 gold, and their *h* shall be of gold
Ex 27:10 the *h* of the pillars and their
Ex 27:11 the *h* of the pillars and their
Ex 27:17 their *h* shall be of silver, and
Ex 36:36 their *h* were of gold
Ex 36:38 five pillars of it with their *h*
Ex 38:10 the *h* of the pillars and their
Ex 38:11 the *h* of the pillars and their
Ex 38:12 the *h* of the pillars and their
Ex 38:17 the *h* of the pillars and their
Ex 38:19 their *h* of silver, and the
Ex 38:28 shekels he made *h* for the pillars
Eze 29:4 But I will put *h* in thy jaws
Eze 38:4 put *h* into thy jaws, and I will
Eze 40:43 And within were *h*, an hand broad,
Amos 4:2 that he will take you away with *h*

### HOPE

Ruth 1:12 If I should say, I have *h*
Ezr 10:2 yet now there is *h* in Israel
Job 4:6 thy fear, thy confidence, thy *h*
Job 5:16 So the poor hath *h*, and iniquity
Job 6:11 is my strength, that I should *h*
Job 7:6 shuttle, and are spent without *h*
Job 8:13 and the hypocrite's *h* shall perish
Job 8:14 Whose *h* shall be cut off, and
Job 11:18 be secure, because there is *h*
Job 11:20 their *h* shall be as the giving up
Job 14:7 For there is *h* of a tree, if it
Job 14:19 and thou destroyest the *h* of man
Job 17:15 And where is now my *h*
Job 17:15 as for my *h*, who shall see it
Job 19:10 mine *h* hath he removed like a
Job 27:8 For what is the *h* of the
Job 31:24 If I have made gold my *h*, or have
Job 41:9 Behold, the *h* of him is in vain
Ps 16:9 my flesh also shall rest in *h*
Ps 22:9 thou didst make me *h* when I was
Ps 31:24 heart, all ye that *h* in the LORD
Ps 33:18 upon them that *h* in his mercy
Ps 33:22 us, according as we *h* in thee
Ps 38:15 For in thee, O LORD, do I *h*

Ps 39:7 my *h* is in thee
Ps 42:5 *h* thou in God
Ps 42:11 *h* thou in God
Ps 43:5 *h* in God
Ps 71:5 For thou art my *h*, O Lord GOD
Ps 71:14 But I will *h* continually, and will
Ps 78:7 they might set their *h* in God
Ps 119:49 which thou hast caused me to *h*
Ps 119:81 but I *h* in thy word
Ps 119:114 I *h* in thy word
Ps 119:116 and let me not be ashamed of my *h*
Ps 130:5 doth wait, and in his word do I *h*
Ps 130:7 Let Israel *h* in the LORD
Ps 131:3 Let Israel *h* in the LORD from
Ps 146:5 whose *h* is in the LORD his God
Ps 147:11 him, in those that *h* in his mercy
Prov 10:28 The *h* of the righteous shall be
Prov 11:7 the *h* of unjust men perisheth
Prov 13:12 *H* deferred maketh the heart sick,
Prov 14:32 the righteous hath *h* in his death
Prov 19:18 Chasten thy son while there is *h*
Prov 26:12 there is more *h* of a fool than of
Prov 29:20 there is more *h* of a fool than of
Eccl 9:4 to all the living there is *h*
Is 38:18 the pit cannot *h* for thy truth
Is 57:10 saidst thou not, There is no *h*
Jer 2:25 but thou saidst, There is no *h*
Jer 14:8 O the *h* of Israel, the saviour
Jer 17:7 the LORD, and whose *h* the LORD is
Jer 17:13 the *h* of Israel, all that forsake
Jer 17:17 thou art my *h* in the day of evil
Jer 18:12 And they said, There is no *h*
Jer 31:17 there is *h* in thine end, saith
Jer 50:7 the LORD, the *h* of their fathers
Lam 3:18 my *h* is perished from the LORD
Lam 3:21 to my mind, therefore have I *h*
Lam 3:24 therefore will I *h* in him
Lam 3:26 is good that a man should both *h*
Lam 3:29 if so be there may be *h*
Eze 13:6 they have made others to *h* that
Eze 19:5 her *h* was lost, then she took
Eze 37:11 bones are dried, and our *h* is lost
Hos 2:15 valley of Achor for a door of *h*
Joel 3:16 LORD will be the *h* of his people
Zec 9:12 strong hold, ye prisoners of *h*
Lk 6:34 to them of whom ye *h* to receive
Acts 2:26 also my flesh shall rest in *h*
Acts 16:19 the *h* of their gains was gone
Acts 23:6 of the *h* and resurrection of the
Acts 24:15 have *h* toward God, which they
Acts 26:6 am judged for the *h* of the
Acts 26:7 God day and night, *h* to come
Acts 27:20 all *h* that we should be saved was
Acts 28:20 because that for the *h* of Israel
Rom 4:18 Who against *h* believed in *h*,
Rom 4:18 Who against *h* believed in *h*
Rom 5:2 rejoice in *h* of the glory of God
Rom 5:4 experience; and experience, *h*
Rom 5:5 And *h* maketh not ashamed
Rom 8:20 who hath subjected the same in *h*
Rom 8:24 For we are saved by *h*
Rom 8:24 but *h* that is seen is not *h*
Rom 8:24 man seeth, why doth he yet *h* for
Rom 8:25 But if we *h* for that we see not,
Rom 12:12 Rejoicing in *h*
Rom 15:4 of the scriptures might have *h*
Rom 15:13 Now the God of *h* fill you with
Rom 15:13 that ye may abound in *h*, through
1Cor 9:10 he that ploweth should plow in *h*
1Cor 9:10 that he that thresheth in *h*
1Cor 9:10 *h* should be partaker of his *h*
1Cor 13:13 And now abideth faith, *h*, charity,
1Cor 15:19 life only we have *h* in Christ
2Cor 1:7 our *h* of you is stedfast, knowing
2Cor 3:12 Seeing then that we have such *h*
2Cor 10:15 but having *h*, when your faith is
Gal 5:5 the *h* of righteousness by faith
Eph 1:18 know what is the *h* of his calling
Eph 2:12 covenants of promise, having no *h*
Eph 4:4 called in one *h* of your calling
Phil 1:20 to my earnest expectation and my *h*
Phil 2:23 Him therefore I *h* to send
Col 1:5 For the *h* which is laid up for
Col 1:23 away from the *h* of the gospel
Col 1:27 is Christ in you, the *h* of glory
1Th 1:3 patience of *h* in our Lord Jesus
1Th 2:19 For what is our *h*, or joy, or
1Th 4:13 even as others which have no *h*
1Th 5:8 for an helmet, the *h* of salvation
2Th 2:16 and good *h* through grace,
1Ti 1:1 Lord Jesus Christ, which is our *h*
Titus 1:2 In *h* of eternal life, which God,
Titus 2:13 Looking for that blessed *h*
Titus 3:7 to the *h* of eternal life
Heb 3:6 of the *h* firm unto the end
Heb 6:11 full assurance of *h* unto the end
Heb 6:18 lay hold upon the *h* set before us
Heb 6:19 Which *h* we have as an anchor of
Heb 7:19 the bringing in of a better *h* did
1Pet 1:3 *h* by the resurrection of Jesus
1Pet 1:13 *h* to the end for the grace that
1Pet 1:21 your faith and *h* might be in God
1Pet 3:15 *h* that is in you with meekness
1Jn 3:3 this *h* in him purifieth himself

**HOPED**
Est 9:1 Jews *h* to have power over them
Job 6:20 confounded because they had *h*
Ps 119:43 for I have *h* in thy judgments
Ps 119:74 because I have *h* in thy word
Ps 119:147 I *h* in thy word
Ps 119:166 I have *h* for thy salvation, and
Jer 3:23 is salvation *h* for from the hills
Lk 23:8 he *h* to have seen some miracle
Acts 24:26 He *h* also that money should have
2Cor 8:5 And this they did, not as we *h*
Heb 11:1 is the substance of things *h* for

**HOPHNI** *(hof'-ni) A son of Eli.*
1Sa 1:3 And the two sons of Eli, *H*
1Sa 2:34 come upon thy two sons, on *H*
1Sa 4:4 and the two sons of Eli, *H*
1Sa 4:11 and the two sons of Eli, *H*
1Sa 4:17 people, and thy two sons also, *H*

**HOR** *(hor)* See HOR-HAGIDGAD.
*1. A mountain in Moab.*
Num 20:22 from Kadesh, and came unto mount *H*
Num 20:23 unto Moses and Aaron in mount *H*
Num 20:25 and bring them up unto mount *H*
Num 20:27 mount *H* in the sight of all the
Num 21:4 mount *H* by the way of the Red sea
Num 33:37 Kadesh, and pitched in mount *H*
Num 33:38 the priest went up into mount *H*
Num 33:39 years old when he died in mount *H*
Num 33:41 And they departed from mount *H*
Deut 32:50 Aaron thy brother died in mount *H*
*2. A hill in northern Israel.*
Num 34:7 shall point out for you mount *H*
Num 34:8 From mount *H* ye shall point out

**HORAM** *(ho'-ram) A Canaanite king.*
Josh 10:33 Then *H* king of Gezer came up to

**HOREB** *(ho'-reb)* See SINAI. *A mountain range in Sinai.*
Ex 3:1 to the mountain of God, even to *H*
Ex 17:6 thee there upon the rock in *H*
Ex 33:6 of their ornaments by the mount *H*
Deut 1:2 *H* by the way of mount Seir unto
Deut 1:6 LORD our God spake unto us in *H*
Deut 1:19 And when we departed from *H*
Deut 4:10 before the LORD thy God in *H*
Deut 4:15 in *H* out of the midst of the fire
Deut 5:2 God made a covenant with us in *H*
Deut 9:8 Also in *H* ye provoked the LORD to
Deut 18:16 of the LORD thy God in *H* in the
Deut 29:1 which he made with them in *H*
1Kin 8:9 stone, which Moses put there at *H*
1Kin 19:8 nights unto *H* the mount of God
2Chr 5:10 which Moses put therein at *H*
Ps 106:19 They made a calf in *H*, and
Mal 4:4 unto him in *H* for all Israel

**HOREM** *(ho'-rem) A city in Naphtali.*
Josh 19:38 And Iron, and Migdal-el, *H*, and

**HOR-HAGIDGAD** *(hor-hag-id'-gad) An encampment of Israel in the wilderness.*
Num 33:32 Bene-jaakan, and encamped at *H*
Num 33:33 And they went from *H*, and pitched

**HORI** *(ho'-ri)* See HORITE.
*1. Son of Lotan.*
Gen 36:22 And the children of Lotan were *H*
Gen 36:30 are the dukes that came of *H*
1Chr 1:39 *H*, and Homam
*2. Father of Shapat.*
Num 13:5 of Simeon, Shaphat the son of *H*

**HORIMS** *(ho'-rims)* See HORITES. *Inhabitants of Mt. Seir.*
Deut 2:12 The *H* also dwelt in Seir
Deut 2:22 destroyed the *H* from before them

**HORITE** *(ho'-rite)* See HORI, HORITES. *An inhabitant of Mt. Seir.*
Gen 36:20 These are the sons of Seir the *H*

**HORITES** *(ho'-rites)* See HORIMS. *Same as Horims.*
Gen 14:6 the *H* in their mount Seir, unto
Gen 36:21 these are the dukes of the *H*
Gen 36:29 are the dukes that came of the *H*

**HORMAH** *(hor'-mah)* See ZEPHATH. *A Canaanite royal town.*
Num 14:45 and discomfited them, even unto *H*
Num 21:3 he called the name of the place *H*
Deut 1:44 you in Seir, even unto *H*
Josh 12:14 The king of *H*, one
Josh 15:30 And Eltolad, and Chesil, and *H*
Josh 19:4 And Eltolad, and Bethul, and *H*
Judg 1:17 the name of the city was called *H*
1Sa 30:30 And to them which were in *H*
1Chr 4:30 And at Bethuel, and at *H*, and at

**HORN**
Ex 21:29 to push with his *h* in time past
Josh 6:5 a long blast with the ram's *h*
1Sa 2:1 mine *h* is exalted in the LORD
1Sa 2:10 exalt the *h* of his anointed
1Sa 16:1 fill thine *h* with oil, and go, I
1Sa 16:13 Then Samuel took the *h* of oil
2Sa 22:3 the *h* of my salvation, my high
1Kin 1:39 Zadok the priest took an *h* of oil
1Chr 25:5 words of God, to lift up the *h*
Job 16:15 skin, and defiled my *h* in the dust
Ps 18:2 the *h* of my salvation, and my high
Ps 75:4 to the wicked, Lift not up the *h*
Ps 75:5 Lift not up your *h* on high
Ps 89:17 thy favour our *h* shall be exalted
Ps 89:24 in my name shall his *h* be exalted
Ps 92:10 But my *h* shalt thou exalt like
Ps 92:10 exalt like the *h* of an unicorn
Ps 112:9 his *h* shall be exalted with
Ps 132:17 will I make the *h* of David to bud
Ps 148:14 also exalteth the *h* of his people
Jer 48:25 The *h* of Moab is cut off, and his
Lam 2:3 fierce anger all the *h* of Israel
Lam 2:17 he hath set up the *h* of thine
Eze 29:21 In that day will I cause the *h* of
Dan 7:8 up among them another little *h*
Dan 7:8 in this *h* were eyes like the eyes
Dan 7:11 the great words which the *h* spake
Dan 7:20 even of that *h* that had eyes, and
Dan 7:21 the same *h* made war with the
Dan 8:5 had a notable *h* between his eyes
Dan 8:8 strong, the great *h* was broken
Dan 8:9 one of them came forth a little *h*
Dan 8:21 the great *h* that is between his
Mic 4:13 for I will make thine *h* iron
Zec 1:21 which lifted up their *h* over the
Lk 1:69 hath raised up an *h* of salvation

**HORNS**
Gen 22:13 ram caught in a thicket by his *h*
Ex 27:2 thou shalt make the *h* of it upon
Ex 27:2 his *h* shall be of the same
Ex 29:12 put it upon the *h* of the altar
Ex 30:2 the *h* thereof shall be of the
Ex 30:3 round about, and the *h* thereof
Ex 30:10 make an atonement upon the *h* of
Ex 37:25 the *h* thereof were of the same
Ex 37:26 round about, and the *h* of it
Ex 38:2 he made the *h* thereof on the four
Ex 38:2 the *h* thereof were of the same
Lev 4:7 *h* of the altar of sweet incense
Lev 4:18 *h* of the altar which is before
Lev 4:25 put it upon the *h* of the altar of
Lev 4:30 put it upon the *h* of the altar of
Lev 4:34 put it upon the *h* of the altar of
Lev 8:15 put it upon the *h* of the altar
Lev 9:9 and put it upon the *h* of the altar
Lev 16:18 put it upon the *h* of the altar
Deut 33:17 *h* are like the *h* of unicorns
Josh 6:4 the ark seven trumpets of rams' *h*
Josh 6:6 *h* before the ark of the LORD
Josh 6:8 rams' *h* passed on before the LORD
Josh 6:13 *h* before the ark of the LORD went
1Kin 1:50 caught hold on the *h* of the altar
1Kin 1:51 caught hold on the *h* of the altar
1Kin 2:28 caught hold on the *h* of the altar
1Kin 22:11 of Chenaanah made him *h* of iron
2Chr 18:10 Chenaanah had made him *h* of iron
Ps 22:21 me from the *h* of the unicorns
Ps 69:31 than an ox or bullock that hath *h*

Ps 75:10 All the *h* of the wicked also will
Ps 75:10 but the *h* of the righteous shall
Ps 118:27 even unto the *h* of the altar
Jer 17:1 upon the *h* of your altars
Eze 27:15 thee for a present *h* of ivory
Eze 34:21 all the diseased with your *h*
Eze 43:15 altar and upward shall be four *h*
Eze 43:20 and put it on the four *h* of it
Dan 7:7 and it had ten *h*
Dan 7:8 I considered the *h*, and, behold,
Dan 7:8 first *h* plucked up by the roots
Dan 7:20 of the ten *h* that were in his
Dan 7:24 the ten *h* out of this kingdom are
Dan 8:3 the river a ram which had two *h*
Dan 8:3 and the two *h* were high
Dan 8:6 he came to the ram that had two *h*
Dan 8:7 smote the ram, and brake his two *h*
Dan 8:20 two *h* are the kings of Media
Amos 3:14 the *h* of the altar shall be cut
Amos 6:13 taken to us *h* by our own strength
Hab 3:4 he had *h* coming out of his hand
Zec 1:18 eyes, and saw, and behold four *h*
Zec 1:19 These are the *h* which have
Zec 1:21 These are the *h* which have
Zec 1:21 to cast out the *h* of the Gentiles
Rev 5:6 it had been slain, having seven *h*
Rev 9:13 *h* of the golden altar which is
Rev 12:3 having seven heads and ten *h*
Rev 13:1 sea, having seven heads and ten *h*
Rev 13:1 upon his *h* ten crowns, and upon
Rev 13:11 he had two *h* like a lamb, and he
Rev 17:3 having seven heads and ten *h*
Rev 17:7 hath the seven heads and ten *h*
Rev 17:12 the ten *h* which thou sawest are
Rev 17:16 the ten *h* which thou sawest upon

**HORONAIM** *(hor-o-na'-im)* See HOLON. *A Moabite city.*
Is 15:5 for in the way of *H* they shall
Jer 48:3 A voice of crying shall be from *H*
Jer 48:5 for in the going down of *H* the
Jer 48:34 voice, from Zoar even unto *H*

**HORONITE** *(ho'-ron-ite) A native of Horonaim.*
Neh 2:10 When Sanballat the *H*, and Tobiah
Neh 2:19 But when Sanballat the *H*, and
Neh 13:28 was son in law to Sanballat the *H*

**HORRIBLE**
Ps 11:6 and brimstone, and an *h* tempest
Ps 40:2 me up also out of an *h* pit
Jer 5:30 *h* thing is committed in the land
Jer 18:13 Israel hath done a very *h* thing
Jer 23:14 prophets of Jerusalem an *h* thing
Hos 6:10 I have seen an *h* thing in the

**HORROR**
Gen 15:12 an *h* of great darkness fell upon
Ps 55:5 upon me, and *h* hath overwhelmed me
Ps 119:53 *H* hath taken hold upon me because
Eze 7:18 sackcloth, and *h* shall cover them

**HORSE**
Gen 49:17 the path, that biteth the *h* heels
Ex 15:1 the *h* and his rider hath he thrown
Ex 15:19 For the *h* of Pharaoh went in with
Ex 15:21 the *h* and his rider hath he thrown
1Kin 10:29 an *h* for an hundred and fifty
1Kin 20:20 escaped on an *h* with the horsemen
1Kin 20:25 *h* for *h*, and chariot for
1Kin 20:25 that thou hast lost, *h* for *h*
2Chr 1:17 an *h* for an hundred and fifty
2Chr 23:15 of the *h* gate by the king's house
Neh 3:28 From above the *h* gate repaired
Est 6:8 the *h* that the king rideth upon,
Est 6:9 *h* be delivered to the hand of one
Est 6:10 and take the apparel and the *h*
Est 6:11 took Haman the apparel and the *h*
Job 39:18 on high, she scorneth the *h*
Job 39:19 Hath thou given the *h* strength
Ps 32:9 Be ye not as the *h*, or as the
Ps 33:17 An *h* is a vain thing for safety
Ps 76:6 *h* are cast into a dead sleep
Ps 147:10 not in the strength of the *h*
Prov 21:31 The *h* is prepared against the day
Prov 26:3 A whip for the *h*, a bridle for
Is 43:17 bringeth forth the chariot and *h*
Is 63:13 as an *h* in the wilderness, that
Jer 8:6 as the *h* rusheth into the battle
Jer 31:40 of the *h* gate toward the east
Jer 51:21 thee will I break in pieces the *h*
Amos 2:15 that rideth the *h* deliver himself
Zec 1:8 behold a man riding upon a red *h*
Zec 9:10 the *h* from Jerusalem, and the
Zec 10:3 as his goodly *h* in the battle
Zec 12:4 smite every *h* with astonishment
Zec 12:4 will smite every *h* of the people
Zec 14:15 so shall be the plague of the *h*
Rev 6:2 And I saw, and behold a white *h*
Rev 6:4 went out another *h* that was red
Rev 6:5 And I beheld, and lo a black *h*
Rev 6:8 And I looked, and behold a pale *h*
Rev 14:20 even unto the *h* bridles, by the
Rev 19:11 opened, and behold a white *h*
Rev 19:19 war against him that sat on the *h*
Rev 19:21 sword of him that sat upon the *h*

**HORSEBACK**
2Kin 9:18 there went one on *h* to meet him
2Kin 9:19 Then he sent out a second on *h*
Est 6:9 bring him on *h* through the street
Est 6:11 brought him on *h* through the
Est 8:10 and sent letters by posts on *h*

**HORSEMEN**
Gen 50:9 up with him both chariots and *h*
Ex 14:9 and chariots of Pharaoh, and his *h*
Ex 14:17 upon his chariots, and upon his *h*
Ex 14:18 upon his chariots, and upon his *h*
Ex 14:23 horses, his chariots, and his *h*
Ex 14:26 their chariots, and upon their *h*
Ex 14:28 and covered the chariots, and the *h*
Ex 15:19 with his *h* into the sea, and the
Josh 24:6 chariots and *h* unto the Red sea
1Sa 8:11 for his chariots, and to be his *h*
1Sa 13:5 chariots, and six thousand *h*
2Sa 1:6 *h* followed hard after him
2Sa 8:4 chariots, and seven hundred *h*
2Sa 10:18 the Syrians, and forty thousand *h*
1Kin 1:5 and he prepared him chariots and *h*
1Kin 4:26 chariots, and twelve thousand *h*
1Kin 9:19 his chariots, and cities for his *h*
1Kin 9:22 rulers of his chariots, and his *h*
1Kin 10:26 gathered together chariots and *h*
1Kin 10:26 chariots, and twelve thousand *h*
1Kin 20:20 escaped on an horse with the *h*
2Kin 2:12 of Israel, and the *h* thereof
2Kin 13:7 people to Jehoahaz but fifty *h*
2Kin 13:14 of Israel, and the *h* thereof
2Kin 18:24 on Egypt for chariots and for *h*
1Chr 18:4 chariots, and seven thousand *h*
1Chr 19:6 *h* out of Mesopotamia, and out of
2Chr 1:14 And Solomon gathered chariots and *h*
2Chr 1:14 chariots, and twelve thousand *h*
2Chr 8:6 cities, and the cities of the *h*
2Chr 8:9 and captains of his chariots and *h*
2Chr 9:25 and chariots, and twelve thousand *h*
2Chr 12:3 and threescore thousand *h*
2Chr 16:8 with very many chariots and *h*
Ezr 8:22 *h* to help us against the enemy in
Neh 2:9 captains of the army and *h* with me
Is 21:7 saw a chariot with a couple of *h*
Is 21:9 of men, with a couple of *h*
Is 22:6 quiver with chariots of men and *h*
Is 22:7 the *h* shall set themselves in
Is 28:28 cart, nor bruise it with his *h*
Is 31:1 and in *h*, because they are very
Is 36:9 on Egypt for chariots and for *h*
Jer 4:29 shall flee for the noise of the *h*
Jer 46:4 and get up, ye *h*, and stand forth
Eze 23:6 young men, *h* riding upon horses
Eze 23:12 *h* riding upon horses, all of them
Eze 26:7 and with chariots, and with *h*
Eze 26:10 shall shake at the noise of the *h*
Eze 27:14 in thy fairs with horses and *h*
Eze 38:4 and all thine army, horses and *h*
Dan 11:40 with chariots, and with *h*
Hos 1:7 by battle, by horses, nor by *h*
Joel 2:4 and as *h*, so shall they run
Hab 1:8 their *h* shall spread themselves,
Hab 1:8 their *h* shall come from far
Acts 23:23 *h* threescore and ten, and spearmen
Acts 23:32 they left the *h* to go with him
Rev 9:16 the *h* were two hundred thousand

**HORSES**
Gen 47:17 gave them bread in exchange for *h*
Ex 9:3 which is in the field, upon the *h*
Ex 14:9 pursued after them, all the *h*
Ex 14:23 of the sea, even all Pharaoh's *h*
Deut 11:4 the army of Egypt, unto their *h*
Deut 17:16 shall not multiply *h* to himself
Deut 17:16 the end that he should multiply *h*
Deut 20:1 against thine enemies, and seest *h*
Josh 11:4 sea shore in multitude, with *h*
Josh 11:6 thou shalt hough their *h*, and burn
Josh 11:9 he houghed their *h*, and burnt
2Sa 8:4 David houghed all the chariot *h*
2Sa 15:1 prepared him chariots and *h*
1Kin 4:26 stalls of *h* for his chariots
1Kin 4:28 Barley also and straw for the *h*
1Kin 10:25 garments, and armour, and spices, *h*
1Kin 10:28 Solomon had *h* brought out of
1Kin 18:5 we may find grass to save the *h*
1Kin 20:1 and two kings with him, and *h*
1Kin 20:21 Israel went out, and smote the *h*
1Kin 22:4 as thy people, my *h* as thy *h*
2Kin 2:11 *h* of fire, and parted them both
2Kin 3:7 thy people, and my *h* as thy *h*
2Kin 5:9 So Naaman came with his *h*
2Kin 6:14 Therefore sent he thither *h*
2Kin 6:15 compassed the city both with *h*
2Kin 6:17 the mountain was full of *h*
2Kin 7:6 of chariots, and a noise of *h*
2Kin 7:7 and left their tents, and their *h*
2Kin 7:10 but *h* tied, and asses tied, and the
2Kin 7:13 thee, five of the *h* that remain
2Kin 7:14 They took therefore two chariot *h*
2Kin 9:33 on the wall, and on the *h*
2Kin 10:2 there are with you chariots and *h*
2Kin 11:16 the *h* came into the king's house
2Kin 14:20 And they brought him on *h*
2Kin 18:23 will deliver thee two thousand *h*
2Kin 23:11 he took away the *h* that the kings
1Chr 18:4 also houghed all the chariot *h*
2Chr 1:16 Solomon had *h* brought out of
2Chr 1:17 so brought they out *h* for all the
2Chr 9:24 and raiment, harness, and spices, *h*
2Chr 9:25 had four thousand stalls for *h*
2Chr 9:28 unto Solomon *h* out of Egypt
2Chr 25:28 And they brought him upon *h*
Ezr 2:66 Their *h* were seven hundred thirty
Neh 7:68 Their *h*, seven hundred thirty and
Ps 20:7 trust in chariots, and some in *h*
Eccl 10:7 I have seen servants upon *h*
Song 1:9 to a company of *h* in Pharaoh's
Is 2:7 their land is also full of *h*
Is 30:16 for we will flee upon *h*
Is 31:1 and stay on *h*, and trust in
Is 31:3 and their *h* flesh, and not spirit
Is 36:8 I will give thee two thousand *h*
Is 66:20 LORD out of all nations upon *h*
Jer 4:13 his *h* are swifter than eagles
Jer 5:8 They were as fed *h* in the morning
Jer 6:23 and they ride upon *h*, set in array
Jer 8:16 of his *h* was heard from Dan
Jer 12:5 how canst thou contend with *h*
Jer 17:25 David, riding in chariots and on *h*
Jer 22:4 David, riding in chariots and on *h*
Jer 46:4 Harness the *h*
Jer 46:9 Come up, ye *h*
Jer 47:3 of the hoofs of his strong *h*
Jer 50:37 A sword is upon their *h*, and upon
Jer 50:42 sea, and they shall ride upon *h*
Jer 51:27 cause the *h* to come up as the
Eze 17:15 Egypt, that they might give him *h*
Eze 23:6 young men, horsemen riding upon *h*
Eze 23:12 horsemen riding upon *h*, all of
Eze 23:20 issue is like the issue of *h*
Eze 23:23 all of them riding upon *h*
Eze 26:7 of kings, from the north, with *h*
Eze 26:10 his *h* their dust shall cover thee
Eze 26:11 With the hoofs of his *h* shall he
Eze 27:14 traded in thy fairs with *h*
Eze 38:4 thee forth, and all thine army, *h*
Eze 38:15 thee, all of them riding upon *h*
Eze 39:20 be filled at my table with *h*
Hos 1:7 nor by sword, nor by battle, by *h*
Hos 14:3 we will not ride upon *h*
Joel 2:4 of them is as the appearance of *h*
Amos 4:10 sword, and have taken away your *h*
Amos 6:12 Shall *h* run upon the rock
Mic 5:10 that I will cut off thy *h* out of
Nah 3:2 the wheels, and of the pransing *h*
Hab 1:8 Their *h* also are swifter than the
Hab 3:8 that thou didst ride upon thine *h*
Hab 3:15 walk through the sea with thine *h*
Hag 2:22 and the *h* and their riders shall
Zec 1:8 and behind him were there red *h*
Zec 6:2 In the first chariot were red *h*
Zec 6:2 and in the second chariot black *h*
Zec 6:3 And in the third chariot white *h*
Zec 6:3 fourth chariot grisled and bay *h*
Zec 6:6 The black *h* which are therein go

Zec 10:5 them, and the riders on *h* shall be
Zec 14:20 there be upon the bells of the *h*
Rev 9:7 like unto *h* prepared unto battle
Rev 9:9 of many *h* running to battle
Rev 9:17 And thus I saw the *h* in the vision
Rev 9:17 the heads of the *h* were as the
Rev 18:13 wheat, and beasts, and sheep, and *h*
Rev 19:14 heaven followed him upon white *h*
Rev 19:18 of mighty men, and the flesh of *h*

**HOSAH** *(ho'-sah)*
*1. A city in Asher.*
Josh 19:29 and the coast turneth to *H*
*2. A Levite.*
1Chr 16:38 of Jeduthun and *H* to be porters
1Chr 26:10 Also *H*, of the children of Merari
1Chr 26:11 brethren of *H* were thirteen
1Chr 26:16 *H* the lot came forth westward,

**HOSANNA**
Mt 21:9 saying, *H* to the son of David
Mt 21:9 *H* in the highest
Mt 21:15 and saying, *H* to the son of David
Mk 11:9 that followed, cried, saying, *H*
Mk 11:10 *H* in the highest
Jn 12:13 forth to meet him, and cried, *H*

**HOSEA** *(ho-se'-ah)* See HOSHEA, OSEE, OSHEA. *A prophet.*
Hos 1:1 word of the LORD that came unto *H*
Hos 1:2 of the word of the LORD by *H*
Hos 1:2 And the LORD said to *H*, Go, take

**HOSHAIAH** *(ho-sha-i'-ah)*
*1. Helped dedicate the wall.*
Neh 12:32 And after them went *H*, and half of
*2. Father of Jezaniah.*
Jer 42:1 Kareah, and Jezaniah the son of *H*
Jer 43:2 Then spake Azariah the son of *H*

**HOSHAMA** *(ho-sha'-mah) Father of Jeconiah.*
1Chr 3:18 Pedaiah, and Shenazar, Jecamiah, *H*

**HOSHEA** *(ho-she'-ah)* See HOSEA.
*1. Original name of Joshua.*
Deut 32:44 people, he, and *H* the son of Nun
*2. An Ephramite ruler.*
1Chr 27:20 of Ephraim, *H* the son of Azaziah
*3. Last king of Israel.*
2Kin 15:30 And *H* the son of Elah made a
2Kin 17:1 *H* the son of Elah to reign in
2Kin 17:3 *H* became his servant, and gave him
2Kin 17:4 of Assyria found conspiracy in *H*
2Kin 17:6 In the ninth year of *H* the king
2Kin 18:1 of *H* son of Elah king of Israel
2Kin 18:9 of *H* son of Elah king of Israel
2Kin 18:10 ninth year of *H* king of Israel
*4. An Israelite who renewed the covenant.*
Neh 10:23 *H*, Hananiah, Hashub,

**HOSPITALITY**
Rom 12:13 given to *h*
1Ti 3:2 of good behaviour, given to *h*
Titus 1:8 But a lover of *h*, a lover of good
1Pet 4:9 Use *h* one to another without

**HOST**
Gen 2:1 finished, and all the *h* of them
Gen 21:22 of his *h* spake unto Abraham
Gen 21:32 the chief captain of his *h*
Gen 32:2 them, he said, This is God's *h*
Ex 14:4 upon Pharaoh, and upon all his *h*
Ex 14:17 upon Pharaoh, and upon all his *h*
Ex 14:24 *h* of the Egyptians through the
Ex 14:24 troubled the *h* of the Egyptians,
Ex 14:28 all the *h* of Pharaoh that came
Ex 15:4 his *h* hath he cast into the sea
Ex 16:13 the dew lay round about the *h*
Num 2:4 And his *h*, and those that were
Num 2:6 And his *h*, and those that were
Num 2:8 And his *h*, and those that were
Num 2:11 And his *h*, and those that were
Num 2:13 And his *h*, and those that were
Num 2:15 And his *h*, and those that were
Num 2:19 And his *h*, and those that were
Num 2:21 And his *h*, and those that were
Num 2:23 And his *h*, and those that were
Num 2:26 And his *h*, and those that were
Num 2:28 And his *h*, and those that were
Num 2:30 And his *h*, and those that were
Num 4:3 old, all that enter into the *h*
Num 10:14 over his *h* was Nahshon the son of
Num 10:15 over the *h* of the tribe of the
Num 10:16 over the *h* of the tribe of the
Num 10:18 over his *h* was Elizur the son of
Num 10:19 over the *h* of the tribe of the
Num 10:20 over the *h* of the tribe of the
Num 10:22 over his *h* was Elishama the son
Num 10:23 over the *h* of the tribe of the
Num 10:24 over the *h* of the tribe of the
Num 10:25 over his *h* was Ahiezer the son of
Num 10:26 over the *h* of the tribe of the
Num 10:27 over the *h* of the tribe of the
Num 31:14 wroth with the officers of the *h*
Num 31:48 were over thousands of the *h*
Deut 2:14 were wasted out from among the *h*
Deut 2:15 to destroy them from among the *h*
Deut 4:19 stars, even all the *h* of heaven
Deut 17:3 moon, or any of the *h* of heaven
Deut 23:9 When the *h* goeth forth against
Josh 1:11 Pass through the *h*, and command
Josh 3:2 the officers went through the *h*
Josh 5:14 but as captain of the *h* of the
Josh 5:15 of the LORD's *h* said unto Joshua
Josh 8:13 even all the *h* that was on the
Josh 18:9 to Joshua to the *h* at Shiloh
Judg 4:2 the captain of whose *h* was Sisera
Judg 4:15 and all his chariots, and all his *h*
Judg 4:16 the chariots, and after the *h*
Judg 4:16 all the *h* of Sisera fell upon the
Judg 7:1 so that the *h* of the Midianites
Judg 7:8 the *h* of Midian was beneath him
Judg 7:9 Arise, get thee down unto the *h*
Judg 7:10 Phurah thy servant down to the *h*
Judg 7:11 to go down unto the *h*
Judg 7:11 the armed men that were in the *h*
Judg 7:13 tumbled into the *h* of Midian
Judg 7:14 delivered Midian, and all the *h*
Judg 7:15 and returned into the *h* of Israel
Judg 7:15 into your hand the *h* of Midian
Judg 7:21 and all the *h* ran, and cried, and
Judg 7:22 fellow, even throughout all the *h*
Judg 7:22 the *h* fled to Beth-shittah in
Judg 8:11 Nobah and Jogbehah, and smote the *h*
Judg 8:11 for the *h* was secure
Judg 8:12 and discomfited all the *h*
1Sa 11:11 of the *h* in the morning watch
1Sa 12:9 Sisera, captain of the *h* of Hazor
1Sa 14:15 And there was trembling in the *h*
1Sa 14:19 the *h* of the Philistines went on
1Sa 14:48 And he gathered an *h*, and smote the
1Sa 14:50 of the captain of his *h* was Abner
1Sa 17:20 as the *h* was going forth to the
1Sa 17:46 the *h* of the Philistines this day
1Sa 17:55 unto Abner, the captain of the *h*
1Sa 26:5 son of Ner, the captain of his *h*
1Sa 28:5 when Saul saw the *h* of the
1Sa 28:19 *h* of Israel into the hand of the
1Sa 29:6 me in the *h* is good in my sight
2Sa 2:8 son of Ner, captain of Saul's *h*
2Sa 3:23 all the *h* that was with him were
2Sa 5:24 to smite the *h* of the Philistines
2Sa 8:9 smitten all the *h* of Hadadezer
2Sa 8:16 the son of Zeruiah was over the *h*
2Sa 10:7 all the *h* of the mighty men
2Sa 10:16 Shobach the captain of the *h* of
2Sa 10:18 Shobach the captain of their *h*
2Sa 17:25 captain of the *h* instead of Joab
2Sa 19:13 *h* before me continually in the
2Sa 20:23 Joab was over all the *h* of Israel
2Sa 23:16 through the *h* of the Philistines
2Sa 24:2 said to Joab the captain of the *h*
2Sa 24:4 and against the captains of the *h*
2Sa 24:4 the captains of the *h* went out
1Kin 1:19 and Joab the captain of the *h*
1Kin 1:25 sons, and the captains of the *h*
1Kin 2:32 Ner, captain of the *h* of Israel
1Kin 2:32 Jether, captain of the *h* of Judah
1Kin 2:35 Jehoiada in his room over the *h*
1Kin 4:4 son of Jehoiada was over the *h*
1Kin 11:15 Joab the captain of the *h* was
1Kin 11:21 the captain of the *h* was dead
1Kin 16:16 made Omri, the captain of the *h*
1Kin 20:1 Syria gathered all his *h* together
1Kin 22:19 all the *h* of heaven standing by
1Kin 22:34 hand, and carry me out of the *h*
1Kin 22:36 a proclamation throughout the *h*
2Kin 3:9 and there was no water for the *h*
2Kin 4:13 king, or to the captain of the *h*
2Kin 5:1 captain of the *h* of the king of
2Kin 6:14 horses, and chariots, and a great *h*
2Kin 6:15 an *h* compassed the city both with
2Kin 6:24 king of Syria gathered all his *h*
2Kin 7:4 us fall unto the *h* of the Syrians
2Kin 7:6 For the LORD had made the *h* of
2Kin 7:6 even the noise of a great *h*
2Kin 7:14 sent after the *h* of the Syrians
2Kin 9:5 captains of the *h* were sitting
2Kin 11:15 hundreds, the officers of the *h*
2Kin 17:16 and worshipped all the *h* of heaven
2Kin 18:17 with a great *h* against Jerusalem
2Kin 21:3 and worshipped all the *h* of heaven
2Kin 21:5 he built altars for all the *h* of
2Kin 23:4 grove, and for all the *h* of heaven
2Kin 23:5 and to all the *h* of heaven
2Kin 25:1 of Babylon came, he, and all his *h*
2Kin 25:19 and the principal scribe of the *h*
1Chr 9:19 being over the *h* of the LORD
1Chr 11:15 the *h* of the Philistines encamped
1Chr 11:18 through the *h* of the Philistines
1Chr 12:14 sons of Gad, captains of the *h*
1Chr 12:21 valour, and were captains in the *h*
1Chr 12:22 a great *h*, like the *h* of God
1Chr 14:15 to smite the *h* of the Philistines
1Chr 14:16 and they smote the *h* of the
1Chr 18:9 the *h* of Hadarezer king of Zobah
1Chr 18:15 the son of Zeruiah was over the *h*
1Chr 19:8 all the *h* of the mighty men
1Chr 19:16 Shophach the captain of the *h* of
1Chr 19:18 Shophach the captain of the *h*
1Chr 25:1 the captains of the *h* separated
1Chr 26:26 and the captains of the *h*
1Chr 27:3 of the *h* for the first month
1Chr 27:5 The third captain of the *h* for
2Chr 14:9 with an *h* of a thousand thousand
2Chr 14:13 before the LORD, and before his *h*
2Chr 16:7 therefore is the *h* of the king of
2Chr 16:8 Ethiopians and the Lubims a huge *h*
2Chr 18:18 all the *h* of heaven standing on
2Chr 18:33 thou mayest carry me out of the *h*
2Chr 23:14 hundreds that were set over the *h*
2Chr 24:23 that the *h* of Syria came up
2Chr 24:24 a very great *h* into their hand
2Chr 26:11 Uzziah had an *h* of fighting men
2Chr 26:14 them throughout all the *h* shields
2Chr 28:9 before the *h* that came to Samaria
2Chr 33:3 and worshipped all the *h* of heaven
2Chr 33:5 he built altars for all the *h* of
2Chr 33:11 of the *h* of the king of Assyria
Neh 9:6 of heavens, with all their *h*
Neh 9:6 the *h* of heaven worshippeth thee
Ps 27:3 Though an *h* should encamp against
Ps 33:6 all the *h* of them by the breath
Ps 33:16 saved by the multitude of an *h*
Ps 136:15 Pharaoh and his *h* in the Red sea
Is 13:4 mustereth the *h* of the battle
Is 24:21 *h* of the high ones that are on
Is 34:4 all the *h* of heaven shall be
Is 34:4 all their *h* shall fall down, as
Is 40:26 bringeth out their *h* by number
Is 45:12 all their *h* have I commanded
Jer 8:2 all the *h* of heaven, whom they
Jer 19:13 incense unto all the *h* of heaven
Jer 33:22 As the *h* of heaven cannot be
Jer 51:3 destroy ye utterly all her *h*
Jer 52:25 and the principal scribe of the *h*
Eze 1:24 of speech, as the noise of an *h*
Dan 8:10 great, even to the *h* of heaven
Dan 8:10 and it cast down some of the *h*
Dan 8:11 even to the prince of the *h*
Dan 8:12 an *h* was given him against the
Dan 8:13 the *h* to be trodden under foot
Obad 20 the captivity of this *h* of the
Zeph 1:5 them that worship the *h* of heaven
Lk 2:13 of the heavenly *h* praising God
Lk 10:35 two pence, and gave them to the *h*
Acts 7:42 up to worship the *h* of heaven
Rom 16:23 Gaius mine *h*, and of the whole

**HOSTS**
Ex 12:41 that all the *h* of the LORD went
Num 1:52 own standard, throughout their *h*
Num 2:32 their *h* were six hundred thousand
Num 10:25 all the camps throughout their *h*
Josh 10:5 and went up, they and all their *h*
Josh 11:4 they and all their *h* with them
Judg 8:10 their *h* with them, about fifteen
Judg 8:10 the *h* of the children of the east
1Sa 1:3 unto the LORD of *h* in Shiloh
1Sa 1:11 vowed a vow, and said, O LORD of *h*
1Sa 4:4 of the covenant of the LORD of *h*
1Sa 15:2 Thus saith the LORD of *h*, I
1Sa 17:45 thee in the name of the LORD of *h*
2Sa 5:10 and the LORD God of *h* was with him

2Sa 6:2 of *h* that dwelleth between the
2Sa 6:18 in the name of the LORD of *h*
2Sa 7:8 David, Thus saith the LORD of *h*
2Sa 7:26 The LORD of *h* is the God over
2Sa 7:27 For thou, O LORD of *h*, God of
1Kin 2:5 two captains of the *h* of Israel
1Kin 15:20 sent the captains of the *h* which
1Kin 18:15 said, As the LORD of *h* liveth
1Kin 19:10 jealous for the LORD God of *h*
1Kin 19:14 jealous for the LORD God of *h*
2Kin 3:14 said, As the LORD of *h* liveth
2Kin 19:31 of the LORD of *h* shall do this
1Chr 11:9 for the LORD of *h* was with him
1Chr 17:7 David, Thus saith the LORD of *h*
1Chr 17:24 The LORD of *h* is the God of
Ps 24:10 The LORD of *h*, he is the King of
Ps 46:7 The LORD of *h* is with us
Ps 46:11 The LORD of *h* is with us
Ps 48:8 seen in the city of the LORD of *h*
Ps 59:5 Thou therefore, O LORD God of *h*
Ps 69:6 wait on thee, O Lord GOD of *h*
Ps 80:4 O LORD God of *h*, how long wilt
Ps 80:7 Turn us again, O God of *h*
Ps 80:14 we beseech thee, O God of *h*
Ps 80:19 Turn us again, O LORD God of *h*
Ps 84:1 are thy tabernacles, O LORD of *h*
Ps 84:3 even thine altars, O LORD of *h*
Ps 84:8 O LORD God of *h*, hear my prayer
Ps 84:12 O LORD of *h*, blessed is the man
Ps 89:8 O LORD God of *h*, who is a strong
Ps 103:21 Bless ye the LORD, all ye his *h*
Ps 108:11 thou, O God, go forth with our *h*
Ps 148:2 praise ye him, all his *h*
Is 1:9 Except the LORD of *h* had left
Is 1:24 saith the Lord, the LORD of *h*
Is 2:12 For the day of the LORD of *h*
Is 3:1 behold, the Lord, the LORD of *h*
Is 3:15 saith the Lord GOD of *h*
Is 5:7 LORD of *h* is the house of Israel
Is 5:9 In mine ears said the LORD of *h*
Is 5:16 But the LORD of *h* shall be
Is 5:24 away the law of the LORD of *h*
Is 6:3 holy, holy, is the LORD of *h*
Is 6:5 have seen the King, the LORD of *h*
Is 8:13 Sanctify the LORD of *h* himself
Is 8:18 in Israel from the LORD of *h*
Is 9:7 the LORD of *h* will perform this
Is 9:13 do they seek the LORD of *h*
Is 9:19 LORD of *h* is the land darkened
Is 10:16 shall the Lord, the Lord of *h*
Is 10:23 For the Lord GOD of *h* shall make
Is 10:24 thus saith the Lord GOD of *h*
Is 10:26 the LORD of *h* shall stir up a
Is 10:33 Behold, the Lord, the LORD of *h*
Is 13:4 the LORD of *h* mustereth the host
Is 13:13 in the wrath of the LORD of *h*
Is 14:22 against them, saith the LORD of *h*
Is 14:23 destruction, saith the LORD of *h*
Is 14:24 The LORD of *h* hath sworn, saying,
Is 14:27 For the LORD of *h* hath purposed
Is 17:3 of Israel, saith the LORD of *h*
Is 18:7 LORD of *h* of a people scattered
Is 18:7 of the name of the LORD of *h*
Is 19:4 saith the Lord, the LORD of *h*
Is 19:12 of *h* hath purposed upon Egypt
Is 19:16 of the hand of the LORD of *h*
Is 19:17 of the counsel of the LORD of *h*
Is 19:18 Canaan, and swear to the LORD of *h*
Is 19:20 LORD of *h* in the land of Egypt
Is 19:25 Whom the LORD of *h* shall bless
Is 21:10 I have heard of the LORD of *h*
Is 22:5 GOD of *h* in the valley of vision
Is 22:12 the Lord GOD of *h* call to weeping
Is 22:14 in mine ears by the LORD of *h*
Is 22:14 ye die, saith the Lord GOD of *h*
Is 22:15 Thus saith the Lord GOD of *h*
Is 22:25 In that day, saith the LORD of *h*
Is 23:9 The LORD of *h* hath purposed it,
Is 24:23 when the LORD of *h* shall reign in
Is 25:6 *h* make unto all people a feast of
Is 28:5 LORD of *h* be for a crown of glory
Is 28:22 the Lord GOD of *h* a consumption
Is 28:29 cometh forth from the LORD of *h*
Is 29:6 of the LORD of *h* with thunder
Is 31:4 so shall the LORD of *h* come down
Is 31:5 the LORD of *h* defend Jerusalem
Is 37:16 O LORD of *h*, God of Israel, that
Is 37:32 of the LORD of *h* shall do this
Is 39:5 Hear the word of the LORD of *h*
Is 44:6 and his redeemer the LORD of *h*

Is 45:13 nor reward, saith the LORD of *h*
Is 47:4 the LORD of *h* is his name
Is 48:2 The LORD of *h* is his name
Is 51:15 The LORD of *h* is his name
Is 54:5 the LORD of *h* is his name
Jer 2:19 in thee, saith the Lord GOD of *h*
Jer 3:19 heritage of the *h* of nations
Jer 5:14 thus saith the LORD God of *h*
Jer 6:6 For thus hath the LORD of *h* said
Jer 6:9 Thus saith the LORD of *h*, They
Jer 7:3 Thus saith the LORD of *h*, the God
Jer 7:21 Thus saith the LORD of *h*, the God
Jer 8:3 driven them, saith the LORD of *h*
Jer 9:7 thus saith the LORD of *h*, Behold,
Jer 9:15 thus saith the LORD of *h*, the God
Jer 9:17 Thus saith the LORD of *h*,
Jer 10:16 The LORD of *h* is his name
Jer 11:17 For the LORD of *h*, that planted
Jer 11:20 But, O LORD of *h*, that judgest
Jer 11:22 thus saith the LORD of *h*, Behold,
Jer 15:16 by thy name, O LORD God of *h*
Jer 16:9 For thus saith the LORD of *h*
Jer 19:3 Thus saith the LORD of *h*, the God
Jer 19:11 them, Thus saith the LORD of *h*
Jer 19:15 Thus saith the LORD of *h*, the God
Jer 20:12 But, O LORD of *h*, that triest the
Jer 23:15 thus saith the LORD of *h*
Jer 23:16 Thus saith the LORD of *h*, Hearken
Jer 23:36 God, of the LORD of *h* our God
Jer 25:8 thus saith the LORD of *h*
Jer 25:27 them, Thus saith the LORD of *h*
Jer 25:28 them, Thus saith the LORD of *h*
Jer 25:29 of the earth, saith the LORD of *h*
Jer 25:32 Thus saith the LORD of *h*, Behold,
Jer 26:18 saying, Thus saith the LORD of *h*
Jer 27:4 masters, Thus saith the LORD of *h*
Jer 27:18 intercession to the LORD of *h*
Jer 27:19 LORD of *h* concerning the pillars
Jer 27:21 Yea, thus saith the LORD of *h*
Jer 28:2 Thus speaketh the LORD of *h*
Jer 28:14 For thus saith the LORD of *h*
Jer 29:4 Thus saith the LORD of *h*, the God
Jer 29:8 For thus saith the LORD of *h*
Jer 29:17 Thus saith the LORD of *h*
Jer 29:21 Thus saith the LORD of *h*, the God
Jer 29:25 Thus speaketh the LORD of *h*
Jer 30:8 in that day, saith the LORD of *h*
Jer 31:23 Thus saith the LORD of *h*, the God
Jer 31:35 The LORD of *h* is his name
Jer 32:14 Thus saith the LORD of *h*, the God
Jer 32:15 For thus saith the LORD of *h*
Jer 32:18 the Mighty God, the LORD of *h*
Jer 33:11 shall say, Praise the LORD of *h*
Jer 33:12 Thus saith the LORD of *h*
Jer 35:13 Thus saith the LORD of *h*, the God
Jer 35:17 thus saith the LORD God of *h*
Jer 35:18 Thus saith the LORD of *h*
Jer 35:19 thus saith the LORD of *h*, the God
Jer 38:17 Thus saith the LORD, the God of *h*
Jer 39:16 saying, Thus saith the LORD of *h*
Jer 42:15 Thus saith the LORD of *h*, the God
Jer 42:18 For thus saith the LORD of *h*
Jer 43:10 them, Thus saith the LORD of *h*
Jer 44:2 Thus saith the LORD of *h*, the God
Jer 44:7 thus saith the LORD, the God of *h*
Jer 44:11 thus saith the LORD of *h*, the God
Jer 44:25 Thus saith the LORD of *h*, the God
Jer 46:10 is the day of the Lord GOD of *h*
Jer 46:10 for the Lord GOD of *h* hath a
Jer 46:18 King, whose name is the LORD of *h*
Jer 46:25 The LORD of *h*, the God of Israel,
Jer 48:1 Moab thus saith the LORD of *h*
Jer 48:15 King, whose name is the LORD of *h*
Jer 49:5 thee, saith the Lord GOD of *h*
Jer 49:7 Edom, thus saith the LORD of *h*
Jer 49:26 in that day, saith the LORD of *h*
Jer 49:35 Thus saith the LORD of *h*
Jer 50:18 thus saith the LORD of *h*, the God
Jer 50:25 of *h* in the land of the Chaldeans
Jer 50:31 proud, saith the Lord GOD of *h*
Jer 50:33 Thus saith the LORD of *h*
Jer 50:34 the LORD of *h* is his name
Jer 51:5 of his God, of the LORD of *h*
Jer 51:14 The LORD of *h* hath sworn by
Jer 51:19 the LORD of *h* is his name
Jer 51:33 For thus saith the LORD of *h*
Jer 51:57 King, whose name is the LORD of *h*
Jer 51:58 Thus saith the LORD of *h*
Hos 12:5 Even the LORD God of *h*
Amos 3:13 saith the Lord GOD, the God of *h*

Amos 4:13 the earth, The LORD, The God of *h*
Amos 5:14 and so the LORD, the God of *h*
Amos 5:15 of *h* will be gracious unto the
Amos 5:16 Therefore the LORD, the God of *h*
Amos 5:27 LORD, whose name is The God of *h*
Amos 6:8 saith the LORD the God of *h*
Amos 6:14 saith the LORD the God of *h*
Amos 9:5 the Lord GOD of *h* is he that
Mic 4:4 of the LORD of *h* hath spoken it
Nah 2:13 against thee, saith the LORD of *h*
Nah 3:5 against thee, saith the LORD of *h*
Hab 2:13 is it not of the LORD of *h* that
Zeph 2:9 as I live, saith the LORD of *h*
Zeph 2:10 the people of the LORD of *h*
Hag 1:2 Thus speaketh the LORD of *h*
Hag 1:5 thus saith the LORD of *h*
Hag 1:7 Thus saith the LORD of *h*
Hag 1:9 saith the LORD of *h*
Hag 1:14 in the house of the LORD of *h*
Hag 2:4 am with you, saith the LORD of *h*
Hag 2:6 For thus saith the LORD of *h*
Hag 2:7 with glory, saith the LORD of *h*
Hag 2:8 gold is mine, saith the LORD of *h*
Hag 2:9 the former, saith the LORD of *h*
Hag 2:9 I give peace, saith the LORD of *h*
Hag 2:11 Thus saith the LORD of *h*
Hag 2:23 In that day, saith the LORD of *h*
Hag 2:23 chosen thee, saith the LORD of *h*
Zec 1:3 them, Thus saith the LORD of *h*
Zec 1:3 ye unto me, saith the LORD of *h*
Zec 1:3 unto you, saith the LORD of *h*
Zec 1:4 saying, Thus saith the LORD of *h*
Zec 1:6 Like as the LORD of *h* thought to
Zec 1:12 answered and said, O LORD of *h*
Zec 1:14 saying, Thus saith the LORD of *h*
Zec 1:16 built in it, saith the LORD of *h*
Zec 1:17 saying, Thus saith the LORD of *h*
Zec 2:8 For thus saith the LORD of *h*
Zec 2:9 that the LORD of *h* hath sent me
Zec 2:11 LORD of *h* hath sent me unto thee
Zec 3:7 Thus saith the LORD of *h*
Zec 3:9 thereof, saith the LORD of *h*
Zec 3:10 In that day, saith the LORD of *h*
Zec 4:6 by my spirit, saith the LORD of *h*
Zec 4:9 LORD of *h* hath sent me unto you
Zec 5:4 it forth, saith the LORD of *h*
Zec 6:12 Thus speaketh the LORD of *h*
Zec 6:15 LORD of *h* hath sent me unto you
Zec 7:3 in the house of the LORD of *h*
Zec 7:4 the word of the LORD of *h* unto me
Zec 7:9 Thus speaketh the LORD of *h*
Zec 7:12 the words which the LORD of *h*
Zec 7:12 a great wrath from the LORD of *h*
Zec 7:13 not hear, saith the LORD of *h*
Zec 8:1 word of the LORD of *h* came to me
Zec 8:2 Thus saith the LORD of *h*
Zec 8:3 the LORD of *h* the holy mountain
Zec 8:4 Thus saith the LORD of *h*
Zec 8:6 Thus saith the LORD of *h*
Zec 8:6 saith the LORD of *h*
Zec 8:7 Thus saith the LORD of *h*
Zec 8:9 Thus saith the LORD of *h*
Zec 8:9 house of the LORD of *h* was laid
Zec 8:11 former days, saith the LORD of *h*
Zec 8:14 For thus saith the LORD of *h*
Zec 8:14 me to wrath, saith the LORD of *h*
Zec 8:18 of the LORD of *h* came unto me
Zec 8:19 Thus saith the LORD of *h*
Zec 8:20 Thus saith the LORD of *h*
Zec 8:21 LORD, and to seek the LORD of *h*
Zec 8:22 seek the LORD of *h* in Jerusalem
Zec 8:23 Thus saith the LORD of *h*
Zec 9:15 The LORD of *h* shall defend them
Zec 10:3 for the LORD of *h* hath visited
Zec 12:5 in the LORD of *h* their God
Zec 13:2 in that day, saith the LORD of *h*
Zec 13:7 is my fellow, saith the LORD of *h*
Zec 14:16 worship the King, the LORD of *h*
Zec 14:17 worship the King, the LORD of *h*
Zec 14:21 be holiness unto the LORD of *h*
Zec 14:21 in the house of the LORD of *h*
Mal 1:4 thus saith the LORD of *h*, They
Mal 1:6 saith the LORD of *h* unto you
Mal 1:8 saith the LORD of *h*
Mal 1:9 saith the LORD of *h*
Mal 1:10 in you, saith the LORD of *h*
Mal 1:11 the heathen, saith the LORD of *h*
Mal 1:13 at it, saith the LORD of *h*
Mal 1:14 a great King, saith the LORD of *h*
Mal 2:2 unto my name, saith the LORD of *h*

Mal 2:4 be with Levi, saith the LORD of *h*
Mal 2:7 is the messenger of the LORD of *h*
Mal 2:8 of Levi, saith the LORD of *h*
Mal 2:12 an offering unto the LORD of *h*
Mal 2:16 his garment, saith the LORD of *h*
Mal 3:1 shall come, saith the LORD of *h*
Mal 3:5 fear not me, saith the LORD of *h*
Mal 3:7 unto you, saith the LORD of *h*
Mal 3:10 now herewith, saith the LORD of *h*
Mal 3:11 in the field, saith the LORD of *h*
Mal 3:12 land, saith the LORD of *h*
Mal 3:14 mournfully before the LORD of *h*
Mal 3:17 be mine, saith the LORD of *h*
Mal 4:1 burn them up, saith the LORD of *h*
Mal 4:3 do this, saith the LORD of *h*

**HOT**
Ex 16:21 and when the sun waxed *h*, it
Ex 22:24 And my wrath shall wax *h*, and I
Ex 32:10 my wrath may wax *h* against them
Ex 32:11 wrath wax *h* against thy people
Ex 32:19 and Moses' anger waxed *h*, and he
Ex 32:22 not the anger of my lord wax *h*
Lev 13:24 skin whereof there is a *h* burning
Deut 9:19 *h* displeasure, wherewith the LORD
Deut 19:6 the slayer, while his heart is *h*
Josh 9:12 This our bread we took *h* for our
Judg 2:14 of the LORD was *h* against Israel
Judg 2:20 of the LORD was *h* against Israel
Judg 3:8 of the LORD was *h* against Israel
Judg 6:39 not thine anger be *h* against me
Judg 10:7 of the LORD was *h* against Israel
1Sa 11:9 morrow, by that time the sun be *h*
1Sa 21:6 to put *h* bread in the day when it
Neh 7:3 be opened until the sun be *h*
Job 6:17 when it is *h*, they are consumed
Ps 6:1 chasten me in thy *h* displeasure
Ps 38:1 chasten me in thy *h* displeasure
Ps 39:3 My heart was *h* within me
Ps 78:48 and their flocks to *h* thunderbolts
Prov 6:28 Can one go upon *h* coals, and his
Eze 24:11 that the brass of it may be *h*
Dan 3:22 and the furnace exceeding *h*
Hos 7:7 They are all *h* as an oven
1Ti 4:2 conscience seared with a *h* iron
Rev 3:15 that thou art neither cold nor *h*
Rev 3:15 I would thou wert cold or *h*
Rev 3:16 lukewarm, and neither cold nor *h*

**HOTHAM** *(ho'-tham)* See HOTHAN. *A son of Heber.*
1Chr 7:32 begat Japhlet, and Shomer, and *H*

**HOTHAN** *(ho'-than)* See HOTHAM. *Father of Shama and Jehiel.*
1Chr 11:44 Jehiel the sons of *H* the Aroerite

**HOTHIR** *(ho'-thir) A son of Heman.*
1Chr 25:4 Joshbekashah, Mallothi, *H*
1Chr 25:28 The one and twentieth to *H*

**HOUR**
Dan 3:6 worshippeth shall the same *h* be
Dan 3:15 ye shall be cast the same *h* into
Dan 4:19 was astonied for one *h*, and his
Dan 4:33 The same *h* was the thing
Dan 5:5 In the same *h* came forth fingers
Mt 8:13 was healed in the selfsame *h*
Mt 9:22 woman was made whole from that *h*
Mt 10:19 that same *h* what ye shall speak
Mt 15:28 was made whole from that very *h*
Mt 17:18 child was cured from that very *h*
Mt 20:3 And he went out about the third *h*
Mt 20:5 out about the sixth and ninth *h*
Mt 20:6 about the eleventh *h* he went out
Mt 20:9 were hired about the eleventh *h*
Mt 20:12 These last have wrought but one *h*
Mt 24:36 *h* knoweth no man, no, not the
Mt 24:42 not what *h* your Lord doth come
Mt 24:44 for in such an *h* as ye think not
Mt 24:50 in an *h* that he is not aware of,
Mt 25:13 *h* wherein the Son of man cometh
Mt 26:40 could ye not watch with me one *h*
Mt 26:45 the *h* is at hand, and the Son of
Mt 26:55 In that same *h* said Jesus to the
Mt 27:45 Now from the sixth *h* there was
Mt 27:45 all the land unto the ninth *h*
Mt 27:46 about the ninth *h* Jesus cried
Mk 13:11 shall be given you in that *h*
Mk 13:32 that *h* knoweth no man, no, not
Mk 14:35 the *h* might pass from him
Mk 14:37 couldest not thou watch one *h*
Mk 14:41 it is enough, the *h* is come
Mk 15:25 And it was the third *h*, and they
Mk 15:33 And when the sixth *h* was come
Mk 15:33 the whole land until the ninth *h*
Mk 15:34 at the ninth *h* Jesus cried with a
Lk 7:21 in that same *h* he cured many of
Lk 10:21 In that *h* Jesus rejoiced in
Lk 12:12 the same *h* what ye ought to say
Lk 12:39 known what *h* the thief would come
Lk 12:40 cometh at an *h* when ye think not
Lk 12:46 at an *h* when he is not aware, and
Lk 20:19 the scribes the same *h* sought to
Lk 22:14 And when the *h* was come, he sat
Lk 22:53 but this is your *h*, and the power
Lk 22:59 about the space of one *h* after
Lk 23:44 And it was about the sixth *h*
Lk 23:44 all the earth until the ninth *h*
Lk 24:33 And they rose up the same *h*
Jn 1:39 for it was about the tenth *h*
Jn 2:4 mine *h* is not yet come
Jn 4:6 and it was about the sixth *h*
Jn 4:21 the *h* cometh, when ye shall
Jn 4:23 But the *h* cometh, and now is, when
Jn 4:52 them the *h* when he began to amend
Jn 4:52 the seventh *h* the fever left him
Jn 4:53 knew that it was at the same *h*
Jn 5:25 The *h* is coming, and now is, when
Jn 5:28 for the *h* is coming, in the which
Jn 7:30 because his *h* was not yet come
Jn 8:20 for his *h* was not yet come
Jn 12:23 The *h* is come, that the Son of
Jn 12:27 Father, save me from this *h*
Jn 12:27 for this cause came I unto this *h*
Jn 13:1 when Jesus knew that his *h* was
Jn 16:21 sorrow, because her *h* is come
Jn 16:32 the *h* cometh, yea, is now come,
Jn 17:1 and said, Father, the *h* is come
Jn 19:14 passover, and about the sixth *h*
Jn 19:27 from that *h* that disciple took
Acts 2:15 it is but the third *h* of the day
Acts 3:1 *h* of prayer, being the ninth *h*
Acts 10:3 evidently about the ninth *h* of
Acts 10:9 to pray about the sixth *h*
Acts 10:30 ago I was fasting until this *h*
Acts 10:30 at the ninth *h* I prayed in my
Acts 16:18 And he came out the same *h*
Acts 16:33 took them the same *h* of the night
Acts 22:13 the same *h* I looked up upon him
Acts 23:23 at the third *h* of the night
1Cor 4:11 this present *h* we both hunger
1Cor 8:7 of the idol unto this *h* eat it as
1Cor 15:30 why stand we in jeopardy every *h*
Gal 2:5 by subjection, no, not for an *h*
Rev 3:3 know what *h* I will come upon thee
Rev 3:10 thee from the *h* of temptation
Rev 8:1 about the space of half an *h*
Rev 9:15 which were prepared for an *h*
Rev 11:13 the same *h* was there a great
Rev 14:7 for the *h* of his judgment is come
Rev 17:12 as kings one *h* with the beast
Rev 18:10 for in one *h* is thy judgment come
Rev 18:17 For in one *h* so great riches is
Rev 18:19 for in one *h* is she made desolate

**HOUSEHOLD**
Gen 18:19 his *h* after him, and they shall
Gen 31:37 thou found of all thy *h* stuff
Gen 35:2 Then Jacob said unto his *h*
Gen 45:11 lest thou, and thy *h*, and all that
Gen 47:12 brethren, and all his father's *h*
Ex 1:1 man and his *h* came with Jacob
Ex 12:4 if the *h* be too little for the
Lev 16:17 for himself, and for his *h*
Deut 6:22 upon Pharaoh, and upon all his *h*
Deut 14:26 shalt rejoice, thou, and thine *h*
Deut 15:20 LORD shall choose, thou and thy *h*
Josh 2:18 brethren, and all thy father's *h*
Josh 6:25 harlot alive, and her father's *h*
Josh 7:14 the *h* which the LORD shall take
Josh 7:18 And he brought his *h* man by man
Judg 6:27 because he feared his father's *h*
Judg 18:25 thy life, with the lives of thy *h*
1Sa 25:17 our master, and against all his *h*
1Sa 27:3 and his men, every man with his *h*
2Sa 2:3 bring up, every man with his *h*
2Sa 6:11 blessed Obed-edom, and all his *h*
2Sa 6:20 David returned to bless his *h*
2Sa 15:16 forth, and all his *h* after him
2Sa 16:2 be for the king's *h* to ride on
2Sa 17:23 put his *h* in order, and hanged
2Sa 19:18 boat to carry over the king's *h*
2Sa 19:41 have brought the king, and his *h*
1Kin 4:6 And Ahishar was over the *h*
1Kin 4:7 victuals for the king and his *h*
1Kin 5:9 desire, in giving food for my *h*
1Kin 5:11 of wheat for food to his *h*
1Kin 11:20 *h* among the sons of Pharaoh
2Kin 7:9 we may go and tell the king's *h*
2Kin 8:1 Arise, and go thou and thine *h*
2Kin 8:2 and she went with her *h*, and
2Kin 18:18 of Hilkiah, which was over the *h*
2Kin 18:37 of Hilkiah, which was over the *h*
2Kin 19:2 Eliakim, which was over the *h*
1Chr 24:6 one principal *h* being taken for
Neh 13:8 the *h* stuff of Tobiah out of the
Job 1:3 she asses, and a very great *h*
Prov 27:27 thy food, for the food of thy *h*
Prov 31:15 night, and giveth meat to her *h*
Prov 31:21 not afraid of the snow for her *h*
Prov 31:21 for all her *h* are clothed with
Prov 31:27 looketh well to the ways of her *h*
Is 36:22 of Hilkiah, that was over the *h*
Is 37:2 sent Eliakim, who was over the *h*
Mt 10:25 shall they call them of his *h*
Mt 10:36 foes shall be they of his own *h*
Mt 24:45 lord hath made ruler over his *h*
Lk 12:42 lord shall make ruler over his *h*
Acts 10:7 he called two of his *h* servants
Acts 16:15 when she was baptized, and her *h*
Rom 16:10 them which are of Aristobulus' *h*
Rom 16:11 that be of the *h* of Narcissus
1Cor 1:16 baptized also the *h* of Stephanas
Gal 6:10 them who are of the *h* of faith
Eph 2:19 the saints, and of the *h* of God
Phil 4:22 they that are of Caesar's *h*
2Ti 4:19 Aquila, and the *h* of Onesiphorus

**HOUSEHOLDER**
Mt 13:27 So the servants of the *h* came
Mt 13:52 is like unto a man that is an *h*
Mt 20:1 is like unto a man that is an *h*
Mt 21:33 There was a certain *h*, which

**HOUSEHOLDS**
Gen 42:33 food for the famine of your *h*
Gen 45:18 And take your father and your *h*
Gen 47:24 your food, and for them of your *h*
Num 18:31 it in every place, ye and your *h*
Deut 11:6 and swallowed them up, and their *h*
Deut 12:7 put your hand unto, ye and your *h*
Josh 7:14 LORD shall take shall come by *h*

**HOUSES**
Gen 42:19 corn for the famine of your *h*
Ex 1:21 feared God, that he made them *h*
Ex 6:14 be the heads of their fathers' *h*
Ex 8:9 the frogs from thee and thy *h*
Ex 8:11 depart from thee, and from thy *h*
Ex 8:13 and the frogs died out of the *h*
Ex 8:21 and upon thy people, and into thy *h*
Ex 8:21 the *h* of the Egyptians shall be
Ex 8:24 Pharaoh, and into his servants' *h*
Ex 9:20 and his cattle flee into the *h*
Ex 10:6 And they shall fill thy *h*
Ex 10:6 the *h* of all thy servants
Ex 10:6 the *h* of all the Egyptians
Ex 12:7 on the upper door post of the *h*
Ex 12:13 a token upon the *h* where ye are
Ex 12:15 put away leaven out of your *h*
Ex 12:19 be no leaven found in your *h*
Ex 12:23 come in unto your *h* to smite you
Ex 12:27 who passed over the *h* of the
Ex 12:27 the Egyptians, and delivered our *h*
Lev 25:31 But the *h* of the villages which
Lev 25:32 the *h* of the cities of their
Lev 25:33 for the *h* of the cities of their
Num 4:22 throughout the *h* of their fathers
Num 16:32 and swallowed them up, and their *h*
Num 17:6 according to their fathers' *h*
Num 32:18 We will not return unto our *h*
Deut 6:11 *h* full of all good things, which
Deut 8:12 art full, and hast built goodly *h*
Deut 19:1 in their cities, and in their *h*
Josh 9:12 for our provision out of our *h* on
Judg 18:14 that there is in these *h* an ephod
Judg 18:22 the men that were in the *h* near
1Kin 9:10 when Solomon had built the two *h*
1Kin 13:32 against all the *h* of the high
1Kin 20:6 house, and the *h* of thy servants
2Kin 17:29 put them in the *h* of the high
2Kin 17:32 them in the *h* of the high places
2Kin 23:7 brake down the *h* of the sodomites
2Kin 23:19 all the *h* also of the high places

2Kin 25:9 all the *h* of Jerusalem, and every
1Chr 15:1 David made him *h* in the city of
1Chr 28:11 of the *h* thereof, and of the
1Chr 29:4 overlay the walls of the *h* withal
2Chr 25:5 to the *h* of their fathers
2Chr 34:11 to floor the *h* which the kings of
2Chr 35:4 by the *h* of your fathers, after
Neh 4:14 daughters, your wives, and your *h*
Neh 5:3 our lands, vineyards, and *h*
Neh 5:11 their oliveyards, and their *h*
Neh 7:4 and the *h* were not builded
Neh 9:25 possessed *h* full of all goods,
Neh 10:34 after the *h* of our fathers, at
Job 1:4 sons went and feasted in their *h*
Job 3:15 who filled their *h* with silver
Job 4:19 in them that dwell in *h* of clay
Job 15:28 in *h* which no man inhabiteth,
Job 21:9 Their *h* are safe from fear,
Job 22:18 filled their *h* with good things
Job 24:16 In the dark they dig through *h*
Ps 49:11 that their *h* shall continue for
Ps 83:12 the *h* of God in possession
Prov 1:13 we shall fill our *h* with spoil
Prov 30:26 make they their *h* in the rocks
Eccl 2:4 I builded me *h*
Is 3:14 spoil of the poor is in your *h*
Is 5:9 Of a truth many *h* shall be
Is 6:11 the *h* without man, and the land be
Is 8:14 offence to both the *h* of Israel
Is 13:16 their *h* shall be spoiled, and
Is 13:21 their *h* shall be full of doleful
Is 13:22 shall cry in their desolate *h*
Is 15:3 on the tops of their *h*, and in
Is 22:10 have numbered the *h* of Jerusalem
Is 22:10 the *h* have ye broken down to
Is 32:13 upon all the *h* of joy in the
Is 42:22 and they are hid in prison *h*
Is 65:21 And they shall build *h*, and inhabit
Jer 5:7 by troops in the harlots' *h*
Jer 5:27 so are their *h* full of deceit
Jer 6:12 their *h* shall be turned unto
Jer 17:22 out of your *h* on the sabbath day
Jer 18:22 Let a cry be heard from their *h*
Jer 19:13 the *h* of Jerusalem
Jer 19:13 the *h* of the kings of Judah,
Jer 19:13 because of all the *h* upon whose
Jer 29:5 Build ye *h*, and dwell in them
Jer 29:28 build ye *h*, and dwell in them
Jer 32:15 *H* and fields and vineyards shall be
Jer 32:29 this city, and burn it with the *h*
Jer 33:4 concerning the *h* of this city
Jer 33:4 concerning the *h* of the kings of
Jer 35:9 Nor to build *h* for us to dwell in
Jer 39:8 the *h* of the people, with fire,
Jer 43:12 in the *h* of the gods of Egypt
Jer 43:13 and the *h* of the gods of the
Jer 52:13 all the *h* of Jerusalem, and all
Jer 52:13 all the *h* of the great men,
Lam 5:2 to strangers, our *h* to aliens
Eze 7:24 and they shall possess their *h*
Eze 11:3 let us build *h*
Eze 16:41 they shall burn thine *h* with fire
Eze 23:47 and burn up their *h* with fire
Eze 26:12 walls, and destroy thy pleasant *h*
Eze 28:26 safely therein, and shall build *h*
Eze 33:30 walls and in the doors of the *h*
Eze 45:4 it shall be a place for their *h*
Dan 2:5 your *h* shall be made a dunghill
Dan 3:29 their *h* shall be made a dunghill
Hos 11:11 and I will place them in their *h*
Joel 2:9 they shall climb up upon the *h*
Amos 3:15 the *h* of ivory shall perish, and
Amos 3:15 the great *h* shall have an end,
Amos 5:11 ye have built *h* of hewn stone
Mic 1:14 the *h* of Achzib shall be a lie to
Mic 2:2 and *h*, and take them away
Mic 2:9 ye cast out from their pleasant *h*
Zeph 1:9 their masters' *h* with violence
Zeph 1:13 a booty, and their *h* a desolation
Zeph 1:13 they shall also build *h*, but not
Zeph 2:7 in the *h* of Ashkelon shall they
Hag 1:4 O ye, to dwell in your cieled *h*
Zec 14:2 the *h* rifled, and the women
Mt 11:8 soft clothing are in kings' *h*
Mt 19:29 And every one that hath forsaken *h*
Mt 23:14 for ye devour widows' *h*, and for a
Mk 8:3 them away fasting to their own *h*
Mk 10:30 hundredfold now in this time, *h*
Mk 12:40 Which devour widows' *h*, and for a
Lk 16:4 they may receive me into their *h*
Lk 20:47 Which devour widows' *h*, and for a
Acts 4:34 of lands or *h* sold them, and
1Cor 11:22 have ye not *h* to eat and to drink
1Ti 3:12 children and their own *h* well
2Ti 3:6 sort are they which creep into *h*
Titus 1:11 be stopped, who subvert whole *h*

**HOUSETOP**
Prov 21:9 to dwell in a corner of the *h*
Prov 25:24 to dwell in the corner of the *h*
Mt 24:17 Let him which is on the *h* not
Mk 13:15 let him that is on the *h* not go
Lk 5:19 multitude, they went upon the *h*
Lk 17:31 day, he which shall be upon the *h*
Acts 10:9 Peter went up upon the *h* to pray

**HOUSETOPS**
Ps 129:6 them be as the grass upon the *h*
Is 22:1 thou art wholly gone up to the *h*
Is 37:27 green herb, as the grass on the *h*
Jer 48:38 generally upon all the *h* of Moab
Zeph 1:5 the host of heaven upon the *h*
Mt 10:27 ear, that preach ye upon the *h*
Lk 12:3 shall be proclaimed upon the *h*

**HOWL**
Is 13:6 *H* ye; for the day of the LORD
Is 14:31 *H*, O gate
Is 15:2 Moab shall *h* over Nebo, and over
Is 15:3 their streets, every one shall *h*
Is 16:7 *h* for Moab, every one shall *h*
Is 23:1 *H*, ye ships of Tarshish
Is 23:6 *h*, ye inhabitants of the isle
Is 23:14 *H*, ye ships of Tarshish
Is 52:5 rule over them make them to *h*
Is 65:14 shall *h* for vexation of spirit
Jer 4:8 you with sackcloth, lament and *h*
Jer 25:34 *H*, ye shepherds, and cry
Jer 47:2 inhabitants of the land shall *h*
Jer 48:20 *h* and cry; tell ye it
Jer 48:31 Therefore will I *h* for Moab
Jer 48:39 They shall *h*, saying, How is it
Jer 49:3 *H*, O Heshbon, for Ai is spoiled
Jer 51:8 *h* for her; take balm
Eze 21:12 Cry and *h*, son of man
Eze 30:2 *H* ye, Woe worth the day
Joel 1:5 and *h*, all ye drinkers of wine,
Joel 1:11 *h*, O ye vinedressers, for the
Joel 1:13 *h*, ye ministers of the altar
Mic 1:8 Therefore I will wail and *h*
Zeph 1:11 *H*, ye inhabitants of Maktesh, for
Zec 11:2 *H*, fir tree; for the cedar
Zec 11:2 *h*, O ye oaks of Bashan
Jas 5:1 *h* for your miseries that shall

**HOWLING**
Deut 32:10 and in the waste *h* wilderness
Is 15:8 the *h* thereof unto Eglaim, and the
Is 15:8 the *h* thereof unto Beer-elim
Jer 25:36 an *h* of the principal of the
Zeph 1:10 an *h* from the second, and a great
Zec 11:3 a voice of the *h* of the shepherds

**HOWSOEVER**
Judg 19:20 *h* let all thy wants lie upon me
2Sa 18:22 of Zadok yet again to Joab, But *h*
2Sa 18:23 But *h*, said he, let me run
Zeph 3:7 not be cut off, *h* I punished them

**HUKKOK** *(huk'-kok)* See HELKATH, HUKOK. *A place in Naphtali.*
Josh 19:34 and goeth out from thence to *H*

**HUKOK** *(hu'-kok)* See HUKKOK. *A city in Asher.*
1Chr 6:75 *H* with her suburbs, and Rehob with

**HUL** *(hul) A son of Aram.*
Gen 10:23 Uz, and *H*, and Gether, and Mash
1Chr 1:17 and Lud, and Aram, and Uz, and *H*

**HULDAH** *(hul'-dah) A prophetess.*
2Kin 22:14 went unto *H* the prophetess, the
2Chr 34:22 went to *H* the prophetess, the

**HUMBLE**
Ex 10:3 refuse to *h* thyself before me
Deut 8:2 to *h* thee, and to prove thee, to
Deut 8:16 knew not, that he might *h* thee
Judg 19:24 *h* ye them, and do with them what
2Chr 7:14 shall *h* themselves, and pray, and
2Chr 34:27 thou didst *h* thyself before God,
Job 22:29 and he shall save the *h* person
Ps 9:12 forgetteth not the cry of the *h*
Ps 10:12 forget not the *h*
Ps 10:17 hast heard the desire of the *h*
Ps 34:2 the *h* shall hear thereof, and be
Ps 69:32 The *h* shall see this, and be glad
Prov 6:3 *h* thyself, and make sure thy
Prov 16:19 be of an *h* spirit with the lowly
Prov 29:23 shall uphold the *h* in spirit
Is 57:15 that is of a contrite and *h* spirit
Is 57:15 to revive the spirit of the *h*
Jer 13:18 the queen, *H* yourselves, sit down
Mt 18:4 Whosoever therefore shall *h*
Mt 23:12 he that shall *h* himself shall be
2Cor 12:21 my God will *h* me among you, and
Jas 4:6 but giveth grace unto the *h*
Jas 4:10 *H* yourselves in the sight of the
1Pet 5:5 proud, and giveth grace to the *h*
1Pet 5:6 *H* yourselves therefore under the

**HUMBLED**
Lev 26:41 their uncircumcised hearts be *h*
Deut 8:3 he *h* thee, and suffered thee to
Deut 21:14 of her, because thou hast *h* her
Deut 22:24 because he hath *h* his neighbour's
Deut 22:29 because he hath *h* her, he may not
2Kin 22:19 thou hast *h* thyself before the
2Chr 12:6 Israel and the king *h* themselves
2Chr 12:7 LORD saw that they *h* themselves
2Chr 12:7 saying, They have *h* themselves
2Chr 12:12 And when he *h* himself, the wrath
2Chr 30:11 and of Zebulun *h* themselves
2Chr 32:26 Notwithstanding Hezekiah *h*
2Chr 33:12 *h* himself greatly before the God
2Chr 33:19 and graven images, before he was *h*
2Chr 33:23 *h* not himself before the LORD, as
2Chr 33:23 Manasseh his father had *h* himself
2Chr 36:12 *h* not himself before Jeremiah the
Ps 35:13 I *h* my soul with fasting
Is 2:11 The lofty looks of man shall be *h*
Is 5:15 and the mighty man shall be *h*
Is 5:15 the eyes of the lofty shall be *h*
Is 10:33 down, and the haughty shall be *h*
Jer 44:10 They are not *h* even unto this day
Lam 3:20 in remembrance, and is *h* in me
Eze 22:10 in thee have they *h* her that was
Eze 22:11 another in thee hath *h* his sister
Dan 5:22 hast not *h* thine heart, though
Phil 2:8 he *h* himself, and became obedient

**HUMBLETH**
1Kin 21:29 thou how Ahab *h* himself before me
1Kin 21:29 because he *h* himself before me, I
Ps 10:10 *h* himself, that the poor may fall
Ps 113:6 Who *h* himself to behold the
Is 2:9 down, and the great man *h* himself
Lk 14:11 he that *h* himself shall be
Lk 18:14 he that *h* himself shall be

**HUMILITY**
Prov 15:33 and before honour is *h*
Prov 18:12 and before honour is *h*
Prov 22:4 By *h* and the fear of the LORD are
Acts 20:19 the Lord with all *h* of mind
Col 2:18 of your reward in a voluntary *h*
Col 2:23 of wisdom in will worship, and *h*
1Pet 5:5 to another, and be clothed with *h*

**HUMTAH** *(hum'-tah) A city in Judah.*
Josh 15:54 And *H*, and Kirjath-arba, which is

**HUNDREDFOLD**
Gen 26:12 received in the same year an *h*
2Sa 24:3 how many soever they be, an *h*
Mt 13:8 and brought forth fruit, some an *h*
Mt 13:23 and bringeth forth, some an *h*
Mt 19:29 name's sake, shall receive an *h*
Mk 10:30 receive an *h* now in this time
Lk 8:8 and sprang up, and bare fruit an *h*

**HUNDREDS**
Ex 18:21 of thousands, and rulers of *h*
Ex 18:25 rulers of thousands, rulers of *h*
Num 31:14 thousands, and captains over *h*
Num 31:48 of thousands, and captains of *h*
Num 31:52 and of the captains of *h*, was
Num 31:54 the captains of thousands and of *h*
Deut 1:15 thousands, and captains over *h*
1Sa 22:7 of thousands, and captains of *h*
1Sa 29:2 of the Philistines passed on by *h*
2Sa 18:1 and captains of *h* over them
2Sa 18:4 and all the people came out by *h*
2Kin 11:4 sent and fetched the rulers over *h*
2Kin 11:9 the captains over the *h* did
2Kin 11:10 to the captains over *h* did the
2Kin 11:15 commanded the captains of the *h*
2Kin 11:19 And he took the rulers over *h*
1Chr 13:1 the captains of thousands and *h*

1Chr 26:26 the captains over thousands and *h*
1Chr 27:1 and captains of thousands and *h*
1Chr 28:1 thousands, and captains over the *h*
1Chr 29:6 the captains of thousands and of *h*
2Chr 1:2 the captains of thousands and of *h*
2Chr 23:1 and took the captains of *h*
2Chr 23:9 to the captains of *h* spears
2Chr 23:14 of *h* that were set over the host
2Chr 23:20 And he took the captains of *h*
2Chr 25:5 thousands, and captains over *h*
Mk 6:40 And they sat down in ranks, by *h*

**HUNGER**
Ex 16:3 kill this whole assembly with *h*
Deut 8:3 thee, and suffered thee to *h*
Deut 28:48 shall send against thee, in *h*
Deut 32:24 They shall be burnt with *h*
Neh 9:15 bread from heaven for their *h*
Ps 34:10 young lions do lack, and suffer *h*
Prov 19:15 and an idle soul shall suffer *h*
Is 49:10 They shall not *h* nor thirst
Jer 38:9 he is like to die for *h* in the
Jer 42:14 the trumpet, nor have *h* of bread
Lam 2:19 that faint for *h* in the top of
Lam 4:9 than they that be slain with *h*
Eze 34:29 more consumed with *h* in the land
Mt 5:6 Blessed are they which do *h*
Lk 6:21 Blessed are ye that *h* now
Lk 6:25 for ye shall *h*
Lk 15:17 and to spare, and I perish with *h*
Jn 6:35 that cometh to me shall never *h*
Rom 12:20 Therefore if thine enemy *h*
1Cor 4:11 unto this present hour we both *h*
1Cor 11:34 And if any man *h*, let him eat at
2Cor 11:27 in watchings often, in *h*
Rev 6:8 to kill with sword, and with *h*
Rev 7:16 They shall *h* no more, neither

**HUNGRED**
Mt 4:2 nights, he was afterward an *h*
Mt 12:1 and his disciples were an *h*
Mt 12:3 what David did, when he was an *h*
Mt 25:35 For I was an *h*, and ye gave me
Mt 25:37 Lord, when saw we thee an *h*
Mt 25:42 For I was an *h*, and ye gave me no
Mt 25:44 Lord, when saw we thee an *h*
Mk 2:25 when he had need, and was an *h*
Lk 6:3 David did, when himself was an *h*

**HUNGRY**
1Sa 2:5 and they that were *h* ceased
2Sa 17:29 for they said, The people is *h*
2Kin 7:12 They know that we be *h*
Job 5:5 Whose harvest the *h* eateth up
Job 22:7 hast withholden bread from the *h*
Job 24:10 take away the sheaf from the *h*
Ps 50:12 If I were *h*, I would not tell
Ps 107:5 *H* and thirsty, their soul fainted
Ps 107:9 filleth the *h* soul with goodness
Ps 107:36 And there he maketh the *h* to dwell
Ps 146:7 which giveth food to the *h*
Prov 6:30 to satisfy his soul when he is *h*
Prov 25:21 If thine enemy be *h*, give him
Prov 27:7 but to the *h* soul every bitter
Is 8:21 through it, hardly bestead and *h*
Is 8:21 pass, that when they shall be *h*
Is 9:20 snatch on the right hand, and be *h*
Is 29:8 even be as when an *h* man dreameth
Is 32:6 to make empty the soul of the *h*
Is 44:12 yea, he is *h*, and his strength
Is 58:7 it not to deal thy bread to the *h*
Is 58:10 thou draw out thy soul to the *h*
Is 65:13 shall eat, but ye shall be *h*
Eze 18:7 hath given his bread to the *h*
Eze 18:16 but hath given his bread to the *h*
Mk 11:12 were come from Bethany, he was *h*
Lk 1:53 filled the *h* with good things
Acts 10:10 And he became very *h*, and would
1Cor 11:21 and one is *h*, and another is
Phil 4:12 both to be full and to be *h*

**HUNT**
Gen 27:5 to the field to *h* for venison
1Sa 26:20 as when one doth *h* a partridge in
Job 38:39 Wilt thou *h* the prey for the lion
Ps 140:11 evil shall *h* the violent man to
Prov 6:26 the adulteress will *h* for the
Jer 16:16 they shall *h* them from every
Lam 4:18 They *h* our steps, that we cannot
Eze 13:18 head of every stature to *h* souls
Eze 13:18 Will ye *h* the souls of my people,
Eze 13:20 wherewith ye there *h* the souls to
Eze 13:20 souls that ye *h* to make them fly
Mic 7:2 they *h* every man his brother with

**HUPHAM** *(hu'-fam)* See HUPPIM, HUPHAMITES. *A son of Benjamin.*
Num 26:39 of *H*, the family of the

**HUPHAMITES** *(hu'-fam-ites) Descendants of Hupham.*
Num 26:39 of Hupham, the family of the *H*

**HUPPAH** *(hup'-pah) A priest.*
1Chr 24:13 The thirteenth to *H*, the

**HUPPIM** *(hup'-pim)* See HUPHAM. *Head of a Benjamite family.*
Gen 46:21 Ehi, and Rosh, Muppim, and *H*
1Chr 7:12 Shuppim also, and *H*, the children
1Chr 7:15 took to wife the sister of *H*

**HUR** *(hur)*
*1. Assisted Moses at Rephidim.*
Ex 17:10 *H* went up to the top of the hill
Ex 17:12 *H* stayed up his hands, the one on
Ex 24:14 behold, Aaron and *H* are with you
*2. A son of Caleb.*
Ex 31:2 the son of Uri, the son of *H*
Ex 35:30 the son of Uri, the son of *H*
Ex 38:22 the son of Uri, the son of *H*
1Chr 2:19 him Ephrath, which bare him *H*
1Chr 2:20 *H* begat Uri, and Uri begat
2Chr 1:5 the son of Uri, the son of *H*
*3. A Midianite king.*
Num 31:8 Evi, and Rekem, and Zur, and *H*
Josh 13:21 Evi, and Rekem, and Zur, and *H*
*4. An officer of Solomon.*
1Kin 4:8 The son of *H*, in mount Ephraim
*5. Father of Caleb.*
1Chr 2:50 the sons of Caleb the son of *H*
1Chr 4:4 These are the sons of *H*, the
*6. A descendant of Judah.*
1Chr 4:1 Pharez, Hezron, and Carmi, and *H*
*7. A rebuilder of Jerusalem's wall.*
Neh 3:9 repaired Rephaiah the son of *H*

**HURAI** *(hu'-rahee)* See HIDDAI. *A "mighty man" of David.*
1Chr 11:32 *H* of the brooks of Gaash, Abiel

**HURAM** *(hu'-ram)* See HIRAM.
*1. Son of Bela.*
1Chr 8:5 And Gera, and Shephuphan, and *H*
*2. Same as Hiram 1.*
2Chr 2:3 Solomon sent to *H* the king of
2Chr 2:11 Then *H* the king of Tyre answered
2Chr 2:12 *H* said moreover, Blessed be the
2Chr 2:13 understanding, of *H* my father's,
2Chr 8:2 That the cities which *H* had
2Chr 8:18 *H* sent him by the hands of his
2Chr 9:10 And the servants also of *H*
2Chr 9:21 Tarshish with the servants of *H*
*3. Same as Hiram 2.*
2Chr 4:11 *H* made the pots, and the shovels,
2Chr 4:11 *H* finished the work that he was
2Chr 4:16 did *H* his father make to king

**HURI** *(hu'-ri) Father of Abihail.*
1Chr 5:14 children of Abihail the son of *H*

**HURT**
Gen 4:23 wounding, and a young man to my *h*
Gen 26:29 That thou wilt do us no *h*
Gen 31:7 but God suffered him not to *h* me
Gen 31:29 the power of my hand to do you *h*
Ex 21:22 *h* a woman with child, so that her
Ex 21:35 And if one man's ox *h* another's
Ex 22:10 and it die, or be *h*, or driven
Ex 22:14 of his neighbour, and it be *h*
Num 16:15 neither have I *h* one of them
Josh 24:20 then he will turn and do you *h*
1Sa 20:21 there is peace to thee, and no *h*
1Sa 24:9 Behold, David seeketh thy *h*
1Sa 25:7 we *h* them not, neither was there
1Sa 25:15 good unto us, and we were not *h*
2Sa 18:32 rise against thee to do thee *h*
2Kin 14:10 shouldest thou meddle to thy *h*
2Chr 25:19 shouldest thou meddle to thine *h*
Ezr 4:22 damage grow to the *h* of the kings
Est 9:2 hand on such as sought their *h*
Job 35:8 may *h* a man as thou art
Ps 15:4 He that sweareth to his own *h*
Ps 35:4 to confusion that devise my *h*
Ps 35:26 together that rejoice at mine *h*
Ps 38:12 they that seek my *h* speak
Ps 41:7 against me do they devise my *h*
Ps 70:2 to confusion, that desire my *h*
Ps 71:13 and dishonour that seek my *h*
Ps 71:24 unto shame, that seek my *h*
Ps 105:18 Whose feet they *h* with fetters
Eccl 5:13 for the owners thereof to their *h*
Eccl 8:9 ruleth over another to his own *h*
Eccl 10:9 stones shall be *h* therewith
Is 11:9 They shall not *h* nor destroy in
Is 27:3 lest any *h* it, I will keep it
Is 65:25 They shall not *h* nor destroy in
Jer 6:14 They have healed also the *h* of
Jer 7:6 walk after other gods to your *h*
Jer 8:11 For they have healed the *h* of the
Jer 8:21 For the *h* of the daughter of my
Jer 8:21 the daughter of my people am I *h*
Jer 10:19 Woe is me for my *h*
Jer 24:9 kingdoms of the earth for their *h*
Jer 25:6 and I will do you no *h*
Jer 25:7 works of your hands to your own *h*
Jer 38:4 welfare of this people, but the *h*
Dan 3:25 of the fire, and they have no *h*
Dan 6:22 mouths, that they have not *h* me
Dan 6:22 thee, O king, have I done no *h*
Dan 6:23 no manner of *h* was found upon him
Mk 16:18 deadly thing, it shall not *h* them
Lk 4:35 he came out of him, and *h* him not
Lk 10:19 nothing shall by any means *h* you
Acts 18:10 man shall set on thee to *h* thee
Acts 27:10 that this voyage will be with *h*
Rev 2:11 not be *h* of the second death
Rev 6:6 see thou *h* not the oil and the
Rev 7:2 whom it was given to *h* the earth
Rev 7:3 *H* not the earth, neither the sea,
Rev 9:4 not *h* the grass of the earth
Rev 9:10 power was to *h* men five months
Rev 9:19 had heads, and with them they do *h*
Rev 11:5 And if any man will *h* them
Rev 11:5 and if any man will *h* them

**HUSBAND**
Gen 3:6 and gave also unto her *h* with her
Gen 3:16 and thy desire shall be to thy *h*
Gen 16:3 gave her to her *h* Abram to be his
Gen 29:32 now therefore my *h* will love me
Gen 29:34 time will my *h* be joined unto me
Gen 30:15 matter that thou hast taken my *h*
Gen 30:18 I have given my maiden to my *h*
Gen 30:20 now will my *h* dwell with me,
Ex 4:25 Surely a bloody *h* art thou to me
Ex 4:26 she said, A bloody *h* thou art
Ex 21:22 the woman's *h* will lay upon him
Lev 19:20 is a bondmaid, betrothed to an *h*
Lev 21:3 unto him, which hath had no *h*
Lev 21:7 take a woman put away from her *h*
Num 5:13 it be hid from the eyes of her *h*
Num 5:19 with another instead of thy *h*
Num 5:20 aside to another instead of thy *h*
Num 5:20 lain with thee beside thine *h*
Num 5:27 have done trespass against her *h*
Num 5:29 aside to another instead of her *h*
Num 30:6 And if she had at all an *h*
Num 30:7 her *h* heard it, and held his peace
Num 30:8 But if her *h* disallowed her on
Num 30:11 her *h* heard it, and held his peace
Num 30:12 But if her *h* hath utterly made
Num 30:12 her *h* hath made them void
Num 30:13 her *h* may establish it
Num 30:13 or her *h* may make it void
Num 30:14 But if her *h* altogether hold his
Deut 21:13 shalt go in unto her, and be her *h*
Deut 22:22 with a woman married to an *h*
Deut 22:23 a virgin be betrothed unto an *h*
Deut 24:3 And if the latter *h* hate her
Deut 24:3 or if the latter *h* die, which
Deut 24:4 Her former *h*, which sent her away
Deut 25:11 her *h* out of the hand of him that
Deut 28:56 be evil toward the *h* of her bosom
Judg 13:6 Then the woman came and told her *h*
Judg 13:9 but Manoah her *h* was not with her
Judg 13:10 haste, and ran, and shewed her *h*
Judg 14:15 unto Samson's wife, Entice thy *h*
Judg 19:3 her *h* arose, and went after her,
Judg 20:4 the *h* of the woman that was slain
Ruth 1:3 And Elimelech Naomi's *h* died
Ruth 1:5 was left of her two sons and her *h*
Ruth 1:9 each of you in the house of her *h*
Ruth 1:12 for I am too old to have an *h*
Ruth 1:12 I should have an *h* also to night
Ruth 2:11 in law since the death of thine *h*
1Sa 1:8 Then said Elkanah her *h* to her
1Sa 1:22 for she said unto her *h*, I will

1Sa 1:23 Elkanah her *h* said unto her, Do
1Sa 2:19 when she came up with her *h* to
1Sa 4:19 her *h* were dead, she bowed
1Sa 4:21 of her father in law and her *h*
1Sa 25:19 But she told not her *h* Nabal
2Sa 3:15 sent, and took her from her *h*
2Sa 3:16 her *h* went with her along weeping
2Sa 11:26 heard that Uriah her *h* was dead
2Sa 11:26 she mourned for her *h*
2Sa 14:5 a widow woman, and mine *h* is dead
2Sa 14:7 shall not leave to my *h* neither
2Kin 4:1 saying, Thy servant my *h* is dead
2Kin 4:9 And she said unto her *h*, Behold
2Kin 4:14 hath no child, and her *h* is old
2Kin 4:22 And she called unto her *h*, and said
2Kin 4:26 is it well with thy *h*
Prov 12:4 woman is a crown to her *h*
Prov 31:11 The heart of her *h* doth safely
Prov 31:23 Her *h* is known in the gates, when
Prov 31:28 her *h* also, and he praiseth her
Is 54:5 For thy Maker is thine *h*
Jer 3:20 departeth from her *h*, so have ye
Jer 6:11 for even the *h* with the wife
Jer 31:32 although I was an *h* unto them
Eze 16:32 taketh strangers instead of her *h*
Eze 16:45 daughter, that lotheth her *h*
Eze 44:25 or for sister that hath had no *h*
Hos 2:2 not my wife, neither am I her *h*
Hos 2:7 I will go and return to my first *h*
Joel 1:8 sackcloth for the *h* of her youth
Mt 1:16 Jacob begat Joseph the *h* of Mary
Mt 1:19 Then Joseph her *h*, being a just
Mk 10:12 if a woman shall put away her *h*
Lk 2:36 had lived with an *h* seven years
Lk 16:18 from her *h* committeth adultery
Jn 4:16 saith unto her, Go, call thy *h*
Jn 4:17 answered and said, I have no *h*
Jn 4:17 Thou hast well said, I have no *h*
Jn 4:18 whom thou now hast is not thy *h*
Acts 5:9 have buried thy *h* are at the door
Acts 5:10 her forth, buried her by her *h*
Rom 7:2 an *h* is bound by the law to her
Rom 7:2 law to her *h* so long as he liveth
Rom 7:2 but if the *h* be dead, she is
Rom 7:2 is loosed from the law of her *h*
Rom 7:3 So then if, while her *h* liveth
Rom 7:3 but if her *h* be dead, she is free
1Cor 7:2 and let every woman have her own *h*
1Cor 7:3 Let the *h* render unto the wife
1Cor 7:3 likewise also the wife unto the *h*
1Cor 7:4 power of her own body, but the *h*
1Cor 7:4 likewise also the *h* hath not
1Cor 7:10 not the wife depart from her *h*
1Cor 7:11 or be reconciled to her *h*
1Cor 7:11 let not the *h* put away his wife
1Cor 7:13 hath an *h* that believeth not
1Cor 7:14 For the unbelieving *h* is
1Cor 7:14 wife is sanctified by the *h*
1Cor 7:16 whether thou shalt save thy *h*
1Cor 7:34 world, how she may please her *h*
1Cor 7:39 the law as long as her *h* liveth
1Cor 7:39 but if her *h* be dead, she is at
2Cor 11:2 for I have espoused you to one *h*
Gal 4:27 children than she which hath a *h*
Eph 5:23 For the *h* is the head of the wife
Eph 5:33 wife see that she reverence her *h*
1Ti 3:2 the *h* of one wife, vigilant,
Titus 1:6 the *h* of one wife, having
Rev 21:2 as a bride adorned for her *h*

**HUSBANDMAN**
Gen 9:20 Noah began to be an *h*, and he
Jer 51:23 thee will I break in pieces the *h*
Amos 5:16 they shall call the *h* to mourning
Zec 13:5 say, I am no prophet, I am an *h*
Jn 15:1 true vine, and my Father is the *h*
2Ti 2:6 The *h* that laboureth must be
Jas 5:7 the *h* waiteth for the precious

**HUSBANDMEN**
2Kin 25:12 the land to be vinedressers and *h*
2Chr 26:10 *h* also, and vine dressers in the
Jer 31:24 the cities thereof together, *h*
Jer 52:16 land for vinedressers and for *h*
Joel 1:11 Be ye ashamed, O ye *h*
Mt 21:33 built a tower, and let it out to *h*
Mt 21:34 he sent his servants to the *h*
Mt 21:35 the *h* took his servants, and beat
Mt 21:38 But when the *h* saw the son
Mt 21:40 what will he do unto those *h*
Mt 21:41 let out his vineyard unto other *h*
Mk 12:1 built a tower, and let it out to *h*
Mk 12:2 season he sent to the *h* a servant
Mk 12:2 *h* of the fruit of the vineyard
Mk 12:7 But those *h* said among themselves
Mk 12:9 he will come and destroy the *h*
Lk 20:9 a vineyard, and let it forth to *h*
Lk 20:10 season he sent a servant to the *h*
Lk 20:10 but the *h* beat him, and sent him
Lk 20:14 But when the *h* saw him, they
Lk 20:16 He shall come and destroy these *h*

**HUSBANDS**
Ruth 1:11 my womb, that they may be your *h*
Ruth 1:13 ye stay for them from having *h*
Est 1:17 despise their *h* in their eyes
Est 1:20 shall give to their *h* honour
Jer 29:6 sons, and give your daughters to *h*
Eze 16:45 thy sisters, which lothed their *h*
Jn 4:18 For thou hast had five *h*
1Cor 14:35 let them ask their *h* at home
Eph 5:22 submit yourselves unto your own *h*
Eph 5:24 be to their own *h* in every thing
Eph 5:25 *H*, love your wives, even as
Col 3:18 submit yourselves unto your own *h*
Col 3:19 *H*, love your wives, and be not
1Ti 3:12 the deacons be the *h* of one wife
Titus 2:4 to be sober, to love their *h*
Titus 2:5 good, obedient to their own *h*
1Pet 3:1 be in subjection to your own *h*
1Pet 3:5 in subjection unto their own *h*
1Pet 3:7 Likewise, ye *h*, dwell with them

**HUSHAH** *(hu'-shah)* See HUSHATHITE, SHUAH. *A son of Ezer.*
1Chr 4:4 of Gedor, and Ezer the father of *H*

**HUSHAI** *(hu'-shahee) Friend and advisor of David.*
2Sa 15:32 *H* the Archite came to meet him
2Sa 15:37 So *H* David's friend came into the
2Sa 16:16 when *H* the Archite, David's
2Sa 16:16 that *H* said unto Absalom, God
2Sa 16:17 And Absalom said to *H*, Is this thy
2Sa 16:18 And *H* said unto Absalom, Nay
2Sa 17:5 Call now *H* the Archite also, and
2Sa 17:6 when *H* was come to Absalom,
2Sa 17:7 *H* said unto Absalom, The counsel
2Sa 17:8 For, said *H*, thou knowest thy
2Sa 17:14 The counsel of *H* the Archite is
2Sa 17:15 Then said *H* unto Zadok and to
1Kin 4:16 Baanah the son of *H* was in Asher
1Chr 27:33 *H* the Archite was the king's

**HUSHAM** *(hu'-sham) A king of Edom.*
Gen 36:34 *H* of the land of Temani reigned
Gen 36:35 *H* died, and Hadad the son of Bedad
1Chr 1:45 *H* of the land of the Temanites
1Chr 1:46 when *H* was dead, Hadad the son of

**HUSHATHITE** *(hu'-shath-ite) A descendant of Hushah.*
2Sa 21:18 then Sibbechai the *H* slew Saph
2Sa 23:27 the Anethothite, Mebunnai the *H*
1Chr 11:29 Sibbecai the *H*, Ilai the Ahohite,
1Chr 20:4 time Sibbechai the *H* slew Sippai
1Chr 27:11 eighth month was Sibbecai the *H*

**HUSHIM** *(hu'-shim)* See SHUHAM.
*1. A son of Dan.*
Gen 46:23 the sons of Dan; *H*
*2. Son of Aher.*
1Chr 7:12 Huppim, the children of Ir, and *H*
*3. A wife of Shaharaim.*
1Chr 8:8 *H* and Baara were his wives
1Chr 8:11 of *H* he begat Abitub, and Elpaal

**HUZ** *(huz) A son of Nabor.*
Gen 22:21 *H* his firstborn, and Buz his

**HUZZAB** *(huz'-zab) A region in Assyria.*
Nah 2:7 *H* shall be led away captive, she

**HYMENAEUS** *(hy-men-e'-us) A false Christian teacher.*
1Ti 1:20 Of whom is *H* and Alexander
2Ti 2:17 of whom is *H* and Philetus

**HYPOCRISY**
Is 32:6 will work iniquity, to practise *h*
Mt 23:28 men, but within ye are full of *h*
Mk 12:15 But he, knowing their *h*, said
Lk 12:1 of the Pharisees, which is *h*
1Ti 4:2 Speaking lies in *h*
Jas 3:17 without partiality, and without *h*

**HYPOCRITE**
Job 13:16 for an *h* shall not come before
Job 17:8 stir up himself against the *h*
Job 20:5 the joy of the *h* but for a moment
Job 27:8 For what is the hope of the *h*
Job 34:30 That the *h* reign not, lest the
Prov 11:9 An *h* with his mouth destroyeth
Is 9:17 for every one is an *h* and an
Mt 7:5 Thou *h*, first cast out the beam
Lk 6:42 Thou *h*, cast out first the beam
Lk 13:15 answered him, and said, Thou *h*

**HYPOCRITES**
Job 15:34 of *h* shall be desolate, and fire
Job 36:13 But the *h* in heart heap up wrath
Is 33:14 fearfulness hath surprised the *h*
Mt 6:2 as the *h* do in the synagogues and
Mt 6:5 thou shalt not be as the *h* are
Mt 6:16 when ye fast, be not, as the *h*
Mt 15:7 Ye *h*, well did Esaias prophesy of
Mt 16:3 O ye *h*, ye can discern the face
Mt 22:18 and said, Why tempt ye me, ye *h*
Mt 23:13 unto you, scribes and Pharisees, *h*
Mt 23:14 unto you, scribes and Pharisees, *h*
Mt 23:15 unto you, scribes and Pharisees, *h*
Mt 23:23 unto you, scribes and Pharisees, *h*
Mt 23:25 unto you, scribes and Pharisees, *h*
Mt 23:27 unto you, scribes and Pharisees, *h*
Mt 23:29 unto you, scribes and Pharisees, *h*
Mt 24:51 him his portion with the *h*
Mk 7:6 hath Esaias prophesied of you *h*
Lk 11:44 unto you, scribes and Pharisees, *h*
Lk 12:56 Ye *h*, ye can discern the face of

**HYSSOP**
Ex 12:22 And ye shall take a bunch of *h*
Lev 14:4 and cedar wood, and scarlet, and *h*
Lev 14:6 wood, and the scarlet, and the *h*
Lev 14:49 and cedar wood, and scarlet, and *h*
Lev 14:51 take the cedar wood, and the *h*
Lev 14:52 the cedar wood, and with the *h*
Num 19:6 shall take cedar wood, and *h*
Num 19:18 And a clean person shall take *h*
1Kin 4:33 is in Lebanon even unto the *h*
Ps 51:7 Purge me with *h*, and I shall be
Jn 19:29 with vinegar, and put it upon *h*
Heb 9:19 with water, and scarlet wool, and *h*

# I

**IBHAR** *(ib'-har) A son of David.*
2Sa 5:15 *I* also, and Elishua, and Nepheg, and
1Chr 3:6 *I* also, and Elishama, and Eliphelet
1Chr 14:5 And *I*, and Elishua, and Elpalet,

**IBLEAM** *(ib'-le-am) A city in Asher.*
Josh 17:11 Beth-shean and her towns, and *I*
Judg 1:27 towns, nor the inhabitants of *I*
2Kin 9:27 going up to Gur, which is by *I*

**IBNEIAH** *(ib-ne-i'-ah) A son of Jeroham.*
1Chr 9:8 *I* the son of Jeroham, and Elah the

**IBNIJAH** *(ib-ni'-jah) A family of exiles.*
1Chr 9:8 the son of Reuel, the son of *I*

**IBRI** *(ib'-ri) A descendant of Levi.*
1Chr 24:27 Beno, and Shoham, and Zaccur, and *I*

**IBZAN** *(ib'-zan) A judge of Israel.*
Judg 12:8 after him *I* of Beth-lehem judged
Judg 12:10 Then died *I*, and was buried at

**ICE**
Job 6:16 are blackish by reason of the *i*
Job 38:29 Out of whose womb came the *i*
Ps 147:17 casteth forth his *i* like morsels

**I-CHABOD** *(ik'-a-bod)* See I-CHABOD'S. *Son of Phinehas.*
1Sa 4:21 And she named the child *I*, saying,

**I-CHABOD'S** *(ik'-a-bods)*
1Sa 14:3 *I* brother, the son of Phinehas,

**ICONIUM** *(i-co'-ne-um) A city in Asia Minor.*
Acts 13:51 feet against them, and came unto *I*
Acts 14:1 And it came to pass in *I*, that
Acts 14:19 certain Jews from Antioch and *I*
Acts 14:21 returned again to Lystra, and to *I*
Acts 16:2 brethren that were at Lystra and *I*
2Ti 3:11 came unto me at Antioch, at *I*

**IDALAH** *(id'-a-lah) A town in Zebulun.*
Josh 19:15 and Nahallal, and Shimron, and *I*

**IDBASH** *(id'-bash) A son of Abi-etam.*
1Chr 4:3 Jezreel, and Ishma, and *I*

**IDDO** *(id'-do)*
*1. Father of Ahinadab.*
1Kin 4:14 the son of *I* had Mahanaim
*2. A descendant of Gershom.*
1Chr 6:21 *I* his son, Zerah his son,
*3. A son of Zechariah.*
1Chr 27:21 in Gilead, *I* the son of Zechariah
*4. A seer.*
2Chr 9:29 in the visions of *I* the seer
2Chr 12:15 and of *I* the seer concerning
2Chr 13:22 in the story of the prophet *I*
*5. An ancestor of Zechariah.*
Ezr 5:1 and Zechariah the son of *I*
Ezr 6:14 prophet and Zechariah the son of *I*
Zec 1:1 the son of *I* the prophet, saying,
Zec 1:7 the son of *I* the prophet, saying,
*6. A Nethinim chief in exile.*
Ezr 8:17 *I* the chief at the place Casiphia
Ezr 8:17 them what they should say unto *I*
*7. A priest.*
Neh 12:4 *I*, Ginnetho, Abijah,
Neh 12:16 Of *I*, Zechariah

**IDLE**
Ex 5:8 for they be *i*
Ex 5:17 he said, Ye are *i*, ye are *i*
Prov 19:15 an *i* soul shall suffer hunger
Mt 12:36 That every *i* word that men shall
Mt 20:3 standing *i* in the marketplace
Mt 20:6 out, and found others standing *i*
Mt 20:6 Why stand ye here all the day *i*
Lk 24:11 words seemed to them as *i* tales
1Ti 5:13 And withal they learn to be *i*
1Ti 5:13 and not only *i*, but tattlers also

**IDLENESS**
Prov 31:27 and eateth not the bread of *i*
Eccl 10:18 through *i* of the hands the house
Eze 16:49 and abundance of *i* was in her

**IDOL**
1Kin 15:13 she had made an *i* in a grove
1Kin 15:13 and Asa destroyed her *i*, and burnt
2Chr 15:16 she had made an *i* in a grove
2Chr 15:16 and Asa cut down her *i*, and stamped
2Chr 33:7 the *i* which he had made, in the
2Chr 33:15 the *i* out of the house of the
Is 48:5 Mine *i* hath done them, and my
Is 66:3 incense, as if he blessed an *i*
Jer 22:28 man Coniah a despised broken *i*
Zec 11:17 Woe to the *i* shepherd that
Acts 7:41 and offered sacrifice unto the *i*
1Cor 8:4 we know that an *i* is nothing in
1Cor 8:7 the *i* unto this hour eat it as a
1Cor 8:7 it as a thing offered unto an *i*
1Cor 10:19 that the *i* is any thing, or that

**IDOLATERS**
1Cor 5:10 or extortioners, or with *i*
1Cor 6:9 neither fornicators, nor *i*
1Cor 10:7 Neither be ye *i*, as were some of
Rev 21:8 whoremongers, and sorcerers, and *i*
Rev 22:15 whoremongers, and murderers, and *i*

**IDOLATRY**
1Sa 15:23 stubbornness is as iniquity and *i*
Acts 17:16 he saw the city wholly given to *i*
1Cor 10:14 my dearly beloved, flee from *i*
Gal 5:20 *I*, witchcraft, hatred, variance,
Col 3:5 and covetousness, which is *i*

**IDOLS**
Lev 19:4 Turn ye not unto *i*, nor make to
Lev 26:1 make you no *i* nor graven image
Lev 26:30 upon the carcases of your *i*
Deut 29:17 their abominations, and their *i*
1Sa 31:9 it in the house of their *i*
1Kin 15:12 removed all the *i* that his
1Kin 21:26 very abominably in following *i*
2Kin 17:12 For they served *i*, whereof the
2Kin 21:11 made Judah also to sin with his *i*
2Kin 21:21 served the *i* that his father
2Kin 23:24 wizards, and the images, and the *i*
1Chr 10:9 to carry tidings unto their *i*
1Chr 16:26 all the gods of the people are *i*
2Chr 15:8 put away the abominable *i* out of
2Chr 24:18 fathers, and served groves and *i*
2Chr 34:7 cut down all the *i* throughout all
Ps 96:5 all the gods of the nations are *i*
Ps 97:7 that boast themselves of *i*
Ps 106:36 And they served their *i*
Ps 106:38 sacrificed unto the *i* of Canaan
Ps 115:4 Their *i* are silver and gold, the
Ps 135:15 The *i* of the heathen are silver
Is 2:8 Their land also is full of *i*
Is 2:18 the *i* he shall utterly abolish
Is 2:20 a man shall cast his *i* of silver
Is 2:20 his *i* of gold, which they made
Is 10:10 hath found the kingdoms of the *i*
Is 10:11 I have done unto Samaria and her *i*
Is 10:11 so do to Jerusalem and her *i*
Is 19:1 the *i* of Egypt shall be moved at
Is 19:3 and they shall seek to the *i*
Is 31:7 shall cast away his *i* of silver
Is 31:7 his *i* of gold, which your own
Is 45:16 together that are makers of *i*
Is 46:1 their *i* were upon the beasts, and
Is 57:5 with *i* under every green tree
Jer 50:2 her *i* are confounded, her images
Jer 50:38 and they are mad upon their *i*
Eze 6:4 down your slain men before your *i*
Eze 6:5 children of Israel before their *i*
Eze 6:6 your *i* may be broken and cease, and
Eze 6:9 which go a whoring after their *i*
Eze 6:13 their *i* round about their altars
Eze 6:13 offer sweet savour to all their *i*
Eze 8:10 all the *i* of the house of Israel,
Eze 14:3 set up their *i* in their heart
Eze 14:4 setteth up his *i* in his heart
Eze 14:4 to the multitude of his *i*
Eze 14:5 estranged from me through their *i*
Eze 14:6 and turn yourselves from your *i*
Eze 14:7 and setteth up his *i* in his heart
Eze 16:36 lovers, and with all the *i* of thy
Eze 18:6 to the *i* of the house of Israel
Eze 18:12 hath lifted up his eyes to the *i*
Eze 18:15 to the *i* of the house of Israel
Eze 20:7 yourselves with the *i* of Egypt
Eze 20:8 did they forsake the *i* of Egypt
Eze 20:16 their heart went after their *i*
Eze 20:18 defile yourselves with their *i*
Eze 20:24 eyes were after their fathers' *i*
Eze 20:31 yourselves with all your *i*
Eze 20:39 Go ye, serve ye every one his *i*
Eze 20:39 with your gifts, and with your *i*
Eze 22:3 maketh *i* against herself to
Eze 22:4 in thine *i* which thou hast made
Eze 23:7 with all their *i* she defiled
Eze 23:30 thou art polluted with their *i*
Eze 23:37 with their *i* have they committed
Eze 23:39 slain their children to their *i*
Eze 23:49 ye shall bear the sins of your *i*
Eze 30:13 I will also destroy the *i*
Eze 33:25 lift up your eyes toward your *i*
Eze 36:18 for their *i* wherewith they had
Eze 36:25 filthiness, and from all your *i*
Eze 37:23 themselves any more with their *i*
Eze 44:10 astray away from me after their *i*
Eze 44:12 unto them before their *i*, and
Hos 4:17 Ephraim is joined to *i*
Hos 8:4 their gold have they made them *i*
Hos 13:2 and *i* according to their own
Hos 14:8 What have I to do any more with *i*
Mic 1:7 all the *i* thereof will I lay
Hab 2:18 trusteth therein, to make dumb *i*
Zec 10:2 For the *i* have spoken vanity, and
Zec 13:2 names of the *i* out of the land
Acts 15:20 they abstain from pollutions of *i*
Acts 15:29 abstain from meats offered to *i*
Acts 21:25 from things offered to *i*, and from
Rom 2:22 thou that abhorrest *i*, dost thou
1Cor 8:1 as touching things offered unto *i*
1Cor 8:4 are offered in sacrifice unto *i*
1Cor 8:10 things which are offered to *i*
1Cor 10:19 in sacrifice to *i* is any thing
1Cor 10:28 is offered in sacrifice unto *i*
1Cor 12:2 carried away unto these dumb *i*
2Cor 6:16 hath the temple of God with *i*
1Th 1:9 to God from *i* to serve the living
1Jn 5:21 children, keep yourselves from *i*
Rev 2:14 to eat things sacrificed unto *i*
Rev 2:20 to eat things sacrificed unto *i*
Rev 9:20 *i* of gold, and silver, and brass,

**IDUMAEA** *(i-doo-me'-ah)* See IDUMEA. *Greek form of Edom.*
Mk 3:8 And from Jerusalem, and from *I*

**IDUMEA** *(i-doo-me'-ah)* See EDOM, IDUMAEA. *Same as Edom.*
Is 34:5 behold, it shall come down upon *I*
Is 34:6 great slaughter in the land of *I*
Eze 35:15 desolate, O mount Seir, and all *I*
Eze 36:5 of the heathen, and against all *I*

**IGAL** *(i'-gal)* See IGEAL.
*1. One of the twelve spies.*
Num 13:7 of Issachar, *I* the son of Joseph
*2. A "mighty man" of David.*
2Sa 23:36 *I* the son of Nathan of Zobah,

**IGDALIAH** *(ig-da-li'-ah) Father of Hanan.*
Jer 35:4 the sons of Hanan, the son of *I*

**IGEAL** *(ig'-e-al)* See IGAL. *A royal descendant of Judah.*
1Chr 3:22 Hattush, and *I*, and Bariah, and

**IGNORANCE**
Lev 4:2 If a soul shall sin through *i*
Lev 4:13 of Israel sin through *i*, and the
Lev 4:22 done somewhat through *i* against
Lev 4:27 the common people sin through *i*
Lev 5:15 a trespass, and sin through *i*
Lev 5:18 concerning his *i* wherein he erred
Num 15:24 if ought be committed by *i*
Num 15:25 for it is *i*
Num 15:25 before the LORD, for their *i*
Num 15:26 seeing all the people were in *i*
Num 15:27 And if any soul sin through *i*
Num 15:28 he sinneth by *i* before the LORD
Num 15:29 for him that sinneth through *i*
Acts 3:17 I wot that through *i* ye did it
Acts 17:30 the times of this *i* God winked at
Eph 4:18 God through the *i* that is in them
1Pet 1:14 to the former lusts in your *i*
1Pet 2:15 to silence the *i* of foolish men

**IGNORANT**
Ps 73:22 So foolish was I, and *i*
Is 56:10 they are all *i*, they are all dumb
Is 63:16 father, though Abraham be *i* of us

Acts 4:13 and *i* men, they marvelled
Rom 1:13 Now I would not have you *i*
Rom 10:3 For they being *i* of God's
Rom 11:25 ye should be *i* of this mystery
1Cor 10:1 I would not that ye should be *i*
1Cor 12:1 brethren, I would not have you *i*
1Cor 14:38 any man be *i*, let him be *i*
2Cor 1:8 have you *i* of our trouble which
2Cor 2:11 for we are not *i* of his devices
1Th 4:13 But I would not have you to be *i*
Heb 5:2 Who can have compassion on the *i*
2Pet 3:5 For this they willingly are *i* of
2Pet 3:8 be not *i* of this one thing, that

**IGNORANTLY**
Num 15:28 for the soul that sinneth *i*
Deut 19:4 Whoso killeth his neighbour *i*
Acts 17:23 Whom therefore ye *i* worship
1Ti 1:13 because I did it *i* in unbelief

**IIM** *(i'-im)* See IJE-ABARIM.
*1. A Hebrew encampment in the wilderness.*
Num 33:45 And they departed from I, and
*2. A town in Judah.*
Josh 15:29 Baalah, and I, and Azem,

**IJE-ABARIM** *(i'-je-ab'-a-rim)* See IIM. *Same as Iim 1.*
Num 21:11 from Oboth, and pitched at *I*
Num 33:44 from Oboth, and pitched in *I*

**IJON** *(i'-jon) A town in Naphtali.*
1Kin 15:20 the cities of Israel, and smote *I*
2Kin 15:29 king of Assyria, and took *I*
2Chr 16:4 and they smote *I*, and Dan, and

**IKKESH** *(ik'-kesh) Father of Ira.*
2Sa 23:26 Ira the son of *I* the Tekoite
1Chr 11:28 Ira the son of *I* the Tekoite
1Chr 27:9 was Ira the son of *I* the Tekoite

**ILAI** *(i'-lahee)* See ZALMON. *A "mighty man" of David.*
1Chr 11:29 the Hushathite, *I* the Ahohite,

**ILL**
Gen 41:3 *i* favoured and leanfleshed
Gen 41:4 the *i* favoured and leanfleshed
Gen 41:19 very *i* favoured and leanfleshed,
Gen 41:20 the *i* favoured kine did eat up
Gen 41:21 but they were still *i* favoured
Gen 41:27 *i* favoured kine that came up
Gen 43:6 Wherefore dealt ye so *i* with me
Deut 15:21 or blind, or have any *i* blemish
Job 20:26 it shall go *i* with him that is
Ps 106:32 so that it went *i* with Moses for
Is 3:11 it shall be *i* with him
Jer 40:4 but if it seem *i* unto thee to
Joel 2:20 his *i* savour shall come up,
Mic 3:4 themselves *i* in their doings
Rom 13:10 Love worketh no *i* to his

**ILLYRICUM** *(il-lir'-ic-um) A Roman Adriatic province.*
Rom 15:19 Jerusalem, and round about unto *I*

**IMAGE**
Gen 1:26 said, Let us make man in our *i*
Gen 1:27 So God created man in his own *i*
Gen 1:27 in the *i* of God created he him
Gen 5:3 in his own likeness, after his *i*
Gen 9:6 for in the *i* of God made he man
Ex 20:4 not make unto thee any graven *i*
Lev 26:1 make you no idols nor graven *i*
Lev 26:1 neither rear you up a standing *i*
Lev 26:1 up any *i* of stone in your land
Deut 4:16 and make you a graven *i*, the
Deut 4:23 with you, and make you a graven *i*
Deut 4:25 yourselves, and make a graven *i*
Deut 5:8 shalt not make thee any graven *i*
Deut 9:12 they have made them a molten *i*
Deut 16:22 shalt thou set thee up any *i*
Deut 27:15 maketh any graven or molten *i*
Judg 17:3 make a graven *i* and a molten *i*
Judg 17:4 a graven *i* and a molten *i*
Judg 18:14 and a graven *i*, and a molten *i*
Judg 18:17 in thither, and took the graven *i*
Judg 18:17 and the teraphim, and the molten *i*
Judg 18:18 house, and fetched the carved *i*
Judg 18:18 and the teraphim, and the molten *i*
Judg 18:20 and the teraphim, and the graven *i*
Judg 18:30 of Dan set up the graven *i*
Judg 18:31 they set them up Micah's graven *i*
1Sa 19:13 And Michal took an *i*, and laid it
1Sa 19:16 behold, there was an *i* in the bed
2Kin 3:2 for he put away the *i* of Baal
2Kin 10:27 And they brake down the *i* of Baal
2Kin 21:7 he set a graven *i* of the grove
2Chr 3:10 he made two cherubims of *i* work
2Chr 33:7 And he set a carved *i*, the idol
Job 4:16 an *i* was before mine eyes, there
Ps 73:20 thou shalt despise their *i*
Ps 106:19 Horeb, and worshipped the molten *i*
Is 40:19 The workman melteth a graven *i*
Is 40:20 workman to prepare a graven *i*
Is 44:9 a graven *i* are all of them vanity
Is 44:10 or molten a graven *i* that is
Is 44:15 he maketh it a graven *i*, and
Is 44:17 maketh a god, even his graven *i*
Is 45:20 set up the wood of their graven *i*
Is 48:5 hath done them, and my graven *i*
Is 48:5 my graven *i*, and my molten *i*
Jer 10:14 is confounded by the graven *i*
Jer 10:14 for his molten *i* is falsehood
Jer 51:17 is confounded by the graven *i*
Jer 51:17 for his molten *i* is falsehood
Eze 8:3 was the seat of the *i* of jealousy
Eze 8:5 this *i* of jealousy in the entry
Dan 2:31 king, sawest, and behold a great *i*
Dan 2:31 This great *i*, whose brightness
Dan 2:34 which smote the *i* upon his feet
Dan 2:35 the *i* became a great mountain
Dan 3:1 the king made an *i* of gold
Dan 3:2 *i* which Nebuchadnezzar the king
Dan 3:3 unto the dedication of the *i* that
Dan 3:3 they stood before the *i* that
Dan 3:5 worship the golden *i* that
Dan 3:7 worshipped the golden *i* that
Dan 3:10 fall down and worship the golden *i*
Dan 3:12 golden *i* which thou hast set up
Dan 3:14 the golden *i* which I have set up
Dan 3:15 worship the *i* which I have made
Dan 3:18 golden *i* which thou hast set up
Hos 3:4 a sacrifice, and without an *i*
Nah 1:14 gods will I cut off the graven *i*
Nah 1:14 the graven *i* and the molten *i*
Hab 2:18 What profiteth the graven *i* that
Hab 2:18 the molten *i*, and a teacher of
Mt 22:20 saith unto them, Whose is this *i*
Mk 12:16 saith unto them, Whose is this *i*
Lk 20:24 Whose *i* and superscription hath it
Acts 19:35 of the *i* which fell down from
Rom 1:23 an *i* made like to corruptible man
Rom 8:29 be conformed to the *i* of his Son
Rom 11:4 bowed the knee to the *i* of Baal
1Cor 11:7 head, forasmuch as he is the *i*
1Cor 15:49 we have borne the *i* of the earthy
1Cor 15:49 also bear the *i* of the heavenly
2Cor 3:18 the same *i* from glory to glory
2Cor 4:4 of Christ, who is the *i* of God
Col 1:15 Who is the *i* of the invisible God
Col 3:10 the *i* of him that created him
Heb 1:3 the express *i* of his person, and
Heb 10:1 not the very *i* of the things, can
Rev 13:14 should make an *i* to the beast
Rev 13:15 give life unto the *i* of the beast
Rev 13:15 that the *i* of the beast should
Rev 13:15 *i* of the beast should be killed
Rev 14:9 man worship the beast and his *i*
Rev 14:11 who worship the beast and his *i*
Rev 15:2 over the beast, and over his *i*
Rev 16:2 upon them which worshipped his *i*
Rev 19:20 and them that worshipped his *i*
Rev 20:4 the beast, neither his *i*, neither

**IMAGES**
Gen 31:19 Rachel had stolen the *i* that were
Gen 31:34 Now Rachel had taken the *i*
Gen 31:35 he searched, but found not the *i*
Ex 23:24 them, and quite break down their *i*
Ex 34:13 their altars, break their *i*
Lev 26:30 high places, and cut down your *i*
Num 33:52 and destroy all their molten *i*
Deut 7:5 altars, and break down their *i*
Deut 7:5 and burn their graven *i* with fire
Deut 7:25 The graven *i* of their gods shall
Deut 12:3 down the graven *i* of their gods
1Sa 6:5 ye shall make *i* of your emerods
1Sa 6:5 *i* of your mice that mar the land
1Sa 6:11 of gold and the *i* of their emerods
2Sa 5:21 And there they left their *i*
1Kin 14:9 made thee other gods, and molten *i*
1Kin 14:23 also built them high places, and *i*
2Kin 10:26 they brought forth the *i* out of
2Kin 11:18 his *i* brake they in pieces
2Kin 17:10 And they set them up *i* and groves
2Kin 17:16 their God, and made them molten *i*
2Kin 17:41 LORD, and served their graven *i*
2Kin 18:4 the high places, and brake the *i*
2Kin 23:14 And he brake in pieces the *i*
2Kin 23:24 spirits, and the wizards, and the *i*
2Chr 14:3 high places, and brake down the *i*
2Chr 14:5 of Judah the high places and the *i*
2Chr 23:17 his *i* in pieces, and slew Mattan
2Chr 28:2 and made also molten *i* for Baalim
2Chr 31:1 Judah, and brake the *i* in pieces
2Chr 33:19 and set up groves and graven *i*
2Chr 33:22 *i* which Manasseh his father had
2Chr 34:3 carved *i*, and the molten *i*
2Chr 34:4 and the *i*, that were on high above
2Chr 34:4 carved *i*, and the molten *i*
2Chr 34:7 beaten the graven *i* into powder
Ps 78:58 to jealousy with their graven *i*
Ps 97:7 be all they that serve graven *i*
Is 10:10 whose graven *i* did excel them of
Is 17:8 made, either the groves, or the *i*
Is 21:9 all the graven *i* of her gods he
Is 27:9 groves and *i* shall not stand up
Is 30:22 of thy graven *i* of silver
Is 30:22 ornament of thy molten *i* of gold
Is 41:29 their molten *i* are wind and
Is 42:8 neither my praise to graven *i*
Is 42:17 ashamed, that trust in graven *i*
Is 42:17 *i*, that say to the molten *i*
Jer 8:19 me to anger with their graven *i*
Jer 43:13 break also the *i* of Beth-shemesh
Jer 50:2 her *i* are broken in pieces
Jer 50:38 for it is the land of graven *i*
Jer 51:47 upon the graven *i* of Babylon
Jer 51:52 do judgment upon her graven *i*
Eze 6:4 and your *i* shall be broken
Eze 6:6 your *i* may be cut down, and your
Eze 7:20 but they made the *i* of their
Eze 16:17 and madest to thyself *i* of men
Eze 21:21 bright, he consulted with *i*
Eze 23:14 the *i* of the Chaldeans pourtrayed
Eze 30:13 I will cause their *i* to cease out
Hos 10:1 his land they have made goodly *i*
Hos 10:2 altars, he shall spoil their *i*
Hos 11:2 and burned incense to graven *i*
Hos 13:2 them molten *i* of their silver
Amos 5:26 of your Moloch and Chiun your *i*
Mic 1:7 all the graven *i* thereof shall be
Mic 5:13 Thy graven *i* also will I cut off,
Mic 5:13 thy standing *i* out of the midst

**IMAGINATION**
Gen 6:5 that every *i* of the thoughts of
Gen 8:21 for the *i* of man's heart is evil
Deut 29:19 I walk in the *i* of mine heart
Deut 31:21 for I know their *i* which they go
1Chr 29:18 keep this for ever in the *i* of
Jer 3:17 after the *i* of their evil heart
Jer 7:24 in the *i* of their evil heart, and
Jer 9:14 after the *i* of their own heart
Jer 11:8 one in the *i* of their evil heart
Jer 13:10 walk in the *i* of their heart
Jer 16:12 one after the *i* of his evil heart
Jer 18:12 one do the *i* of his evil heart
Jer 23:17 after the *i* of his own heart
Lk 1:51 proud in the *i* of their hearts

**IMAGINATIONS**
1Chr 28:9 all the *i* of the thoughts
Prov 6:18 An heart that deviseth wicked *i*
Lam 3:60 and all their *i* against me
Lam 3:61 O LORD, and all their *i* against me
Rom 1:21 but became vain in their *i*
2Cor 10:5 Casting down *i*, and every high

**IMAGINE**
Job 6:26 Do ye *i* to reprove words, and the
Job 21:27 which ye wrongfully *i* against me
Ps 2:1 the people *i* a vain thing
Ps 38:12 *i* deceits all the day long
Ps 62:3 How long will ye *i* mischief
Ps 140:2 Which *i* mischiefs in their heart
Prov 12:20 in the heart of them that *i* evil
Hos 7:15 yet do they *i* mischief against me
Nah 1:9 What do ye *i* against the LORD
Zec 7:10 let none of you *i* evil against
Zec 8:17 let none of you *i* evil in your
Acts 4:25 rage, and the people *i* vain things

**IMAGINED**
Gen 11:6 them, which they have *i* to do
Ps 10:2 in the devices that they have *i*
Ps 21:11 they *i* a mischievous device,

**IMLA** *(im'-lah)* See IMLAH. *Father of Micaiah.*
2Chr 18:7 the same is Micaiah the son of *I*
2Chr 18:8 quickly Micaiah the son of *I*

**IMLAH** *(im'-lah)* See IMLA. *Same as Imla.*
1Kin 22:8 yet one man, Micaiah the son of *I*
1Kin 22:9 hither Micaiah the son of *I*

**IMMANUEL** *(im-man'-u-el)* See EMMANUEL. *A Messianic name.*
Is 7:14 a son, and shall call his name *I*
Is 8:8 fill the breadth of thy land, O *I*

**IMMEDIATELY**
Mt 4:22 they *i* left the ship and their
Mt 8:3 *i* his leprosy was cleansed
Mt 14:31 *i* Jesus stretched forth his hand,
Mt 20:34 *i* their eyes received sight, and
Mt 24:29 *I* after the tribulation of those
Mt 26:74 And *i* the cock crew
Mk 1:12 *i* the spirit driveth him into the
Mk 1:28 And *i* his fame spread abroad
Mk 1:31 *i* the fever left her, and she
Mk 1:42 *i* the leprosy departed from him,
Mk 2:8 *i* when Jesus perceived in his
Mk 2:12 *i* he arose, took up the bed, and
Mk 4:5 *i* it sprang up, because it had no
Mk 4:15 they have heard, Satan cometh *i*
Mk 4:16 *i* receive it with gladness
Mk 4:17 word's sake, *i* they are offended
Mk 4:29 *i* he putteth in the sickle,
Mk 5:2 *i* there met him out of the tombs
Mk 5:30 *i* knowing in himself that virtue
Mk 6:27 *i* the king sent an executioner,
Mk 6:50 *i* he talked with them, and saith
Mk 10:52 *i* he received his sight, and
Mk 14:43 And *i*, while he yet spake, cometh
Lk 1:64 And his mouth was opened *i*
Lk 4:39 *i* she arose and ministered unto
Lk 5:13 *i* the leprosy departed from him
Lk 5:25 *i* he rose up before them, and took
Lk 6:49 did beat vehemently, and *i* it fell
Lk 8:44 *i* her issue of blood stanched
Lk 8:47 him, and how she was healed *i*
Lk 12:36 they may open unto him *i*
Lk 13:13 *i* she was made straight, and
Lk 18:43 *i* he received his sight, and
Lk 19:11 kingdom of God should *i* appear
Lk 19:40 peace, the stones would *i* cry out
Lk 22:60 And *i*, while he yet spake, the
Jn 5:9 *i* the man was made whole, and took
Jn 6:21 *i* the ship was at the land
Jn 13:30 received the sop went *i* out
Jn 18:27 and *i* the cock crew
Jn 21:3 forth, and entered into a ship *i*
Acts 3:7 *i* his feet and ancle bones
Acts 9:18 *i* there fell from his eyes as it
Acts 9:34 And he arose *i*
Acts 10:33 *I* therefore I sent to thee
Acts 11:11 *i* there were three men already
Acts 12:23 *i* the angel of the Lord smote him
Acts 13:11 *i* there fell on him a mist and a
Acts 16:10 *i* we endeavoured to go into
Acts 16:26 *i* all the doors were opened, and
Acts 17:10 the brethren *i* sent away Paul and
Acts 17:14 then *i* the brethren sent away
Acts 21:32 Who *i* took soldiers and centurions
Gal 1:16 *i* I conferred not with flesh and
Rev 4:2 And *i* I was in the spirit

**IMMER** *(im'-mur)*
*1. Father of Meshillemeth.*
1Chr 9:12 son of Meshillemith, the son of *I*
Ezr 2:37 The children of *I*, a thousand
Ezr 10:20 And of the sons of *I*
Neh 7:40 The children of *I*, a thousand
Neh 11:13 son of Meshillemoth, the son of *I*
*2. A sanctuary servant.*
1Chr 24:14 to Bilgah, the sixteenth to *I*
*3. An exile.*
Ezr 2:59 Tel-harsa, Cherub, Addan, and *I*
Neh 7:61 Tel-haresha, Cherub, Addon, and *I*
*4. Father of Zadok.*
Neh 3:29 son of *I* over against his house
*5. A priest.*
Jer 20:1 Pashur the son of *I* the priest

**IMMORTALITY**
Rom 2:7 seek for glory and honour and *i*
1Cor 15:53 and this mortal must put on *i*
1Cor 15:54 this mortal shall have put on *i*
1Ti 6:16 Who only hath *i*, dwelling in the
2Ti 1:10 *i* to light through the gospel

**IMNA** *(im'-nah)* See IMNAH, JIMNA. *A son of Helem.*
1Chr 7:35 Zophah, and *I*, and Shelesh, and Amal

**IMNAH** *(im'-nah)* See IMNA, JIMNAH.
*1. Son of Asher.*
1Chr 7:30 *I*, and Isuah, and Ishuai, and Beriah
*2. Father of Kore.*
2Chr 31:14 And Kore the son of *I* the Levite

**IMPOSSIBLE**
Mt 17:20 and nothing shall be *i* unto you
Mt 19:26 unto them, With men this is *i*
Mk 10:27 upon them saith, With men it is *i*
Lk 1:37 For with God nothing shall be *i*
Lk 17:1 It is *i* but that offences will
Lk 18:27 The things which are *i* with men
Heb 6:4 For it is *i* for those who were
Heb 6:18 in which it was *i* for God to lie
Heb 11:6 faith it is *i* to please him

**IMPOTENT**
Jn 5:3 lay a great multitude of *i* folk
Jn 5:7 The *i* man answered him, Sir, I
Acts 4:9 the good deed done to the *i* man
Acts 14:8 *i* in his feet, being a cripple

**IMPUTED**
Lev 7:18 neither shall it be *i* unto him
Lev 17:4 blood shall be *i* unto that man
Rom 4:11 might be *i* unto them also
Rom 4:22 therefore it was *i* to him for
Rom 4:23 sake alone, that it was *i* to him
Rom 4:24 us also, to whom it shall be *i*
Rom 5:13 but sin is not *i* when there is no
Jas 2:23 God, and it was *i* unto him for

**IMRAH** *(im'-rah) A chief of Asher.*
1Chr 7:36 and Shual, and Beri, and *I*,

**IMRI** *(im'-ri)*
*1. Son of Bani.*
1Chr 9:4 the son of Omri, the son of *I*
*2. Father of Zaccur.*
Neh 3:2 them builded Zaccur the son of *I*

**INCENSE**
Ex 25:6 for anointing oil, and for sweet *i*
Ex 30:1 make an altar to burn *i* upon
Ex 30:7 thereon sweet *i* every morning
Ex 30:7 lamps, he shall burn *i* upon it
Ex 30:8 at even, he shall burn *i* upon it
Ex 30:8 a perpetual *i* before the LORD
Ex 30:9 shall offer no strange *i* thereon
Ex 30:27 and his vessels, and the altar of *i*
Ex 31:8 his furniture, and the altar of *i*
Ex 31:11 sweet *i* for the holy place
Ex 35:8 anointing oil, and for the sweet *i*
Ex 35:15 the *i* altar, and his staves, and
Ex 35:15 the anointing oil, and the sweet *i*
Ex 35:28 anointing oil, and for the sweet *i*
Ex 37:25 he made the *i* altar of shittim
Ex 37:29 the pure *i* of sweet spices,
Ex 39:38 the anointing oil, and the sweet *i*
Ex 40:5 set the altar of gold for the *i*
Ex 40:27 And he burnt sweet *i* thereon
Lev 4:7 altar of sweet *i* before the LORD
Lev 10:1 put *i* thereon, and offered strange
Lev 16:12 full of sweet *i* beaten small
Lev 16:13 he shall put the *i* upon the fire
Lev 16:13 that the cloud of the *i* may cover
Num 4:16 oil for the light, and the sweet *i*
Num 7:14 of ten shekels of gold, full of *i*
Num 7:20 of gold of ten shekels, full of *i*
Num 7:26 spoon of ten shekels, full of *i*
Num 7:32 spoon of ten shekels, full of *i*
Num 7:38 spoon of ten shekels, full of *i*
Num 7:44 spoon of ten shekels, full of *i*
Num 7:50 spoon of ten shekels, full of *i*
Num 7:56 spoon of ten shekels, full of *i*
Num 7:62 spoon of ten shekels, full of *i*
Num 7:68 spoon of ten shekels, full of *i*
Num 7:74 spoon of ten shekels, full of *i*
Num 7:80 spoon of ten shekels, full of *i*
Num 7:86 spoons were twelve, full of *i*
Num 16:7 put *i* in them before the LORD to
Num 16:17 put *i* in them, and bring ye before
Num 16:18 laid *i* thereon, and stood in the
Num 16:35 and fifty men that offered *i*
Num 16:40 near to offer *i* before the LORD
Num 16:46 from off the altar, and put on *i*
Num 16:47 and he put on *i*, and made an
Deut 33:10 they shall put *i* before thee
1Sa 2:28 offer upon mine altar, to burn *i*
1Kin 3:3 and burnt *i* in high places
1Kin 9:25 he burnt *i* upon the altar that
1Kin 11:8 his strange wives, which burnt *i*
1Kin 12:33 upon the altar, and burnt *i*
1Kin 13:1 stood by the altar to burn *i*
1Kin 13:2 high places that burn *i* upon thee
1Kin 22:43 burnt *i* yet in the high places
2Kin 12:3 burnt *i* in the high places
2Kin 14:4 burnt *i* on the high places
2Kin 15:4 burnt *i* still on the high places
2Kin 15:35 burned *i* still in the high places
2Kin 16:4 burnt *i* in the high places, and on
2Kin 17:11 there they burnt *i* in all the
2Kin 18:4 of Israel did burn *i* to it
2Kin 22:17 have burned *i* unto other gods,
2Kin 23:5 burn *i* in the high places in the
2Kin 23:5 them also that burned *i* unto Baal
2Kin 23:8 where the priests had burned *i*
1Chr 6:49 offering, and on the altar of *i*
1Chr 23:13 to burn *i* before the LORD, to
1Chr 28:18 for the altar of *i* refined gold
2Chr 2:4 and to burn before him sweet *i*
2Chr 13:11 burnt sacrifices and sweet *i*
2Chr 25:14 them, and burned *i* unto them
2Chr 26:16 burn *i* upon the altar of *i*
2Chr 26:18 to burn *i* unto the LORD, but to
2Chr 26:18 that are consecrated to burn *i*
2Chr 26:19 a censer in his hand to burn *i*
2Chr 26:19 the LORD, from beside the *i* altar
2Chr 28:3 Moreover he burnt *i* in the valley
2Chr 28:4 burnt *i* in the high places, and on
2Chr 28:25 places to burn *i* unto other gods
2Chr 29:7 have not burned *i* nor offered
2Chr 29:11 minister unto him, and burn *i*
2Chr 30:14 the altars for *i* took they away
2Chr 32:12 one altar, and burn *i* upon it
2Chr 34:25 have burned *i* unto other gods,
Ps 66:15 of fatlings, with the *i* of rams
Ps 141:2 be set forth before thee as *i*
Is 1:13 *i* is an abomination unto me
Is 43:23 offering, nor wearied thee with *i*
Is 60:6 they shall bring gold and *i*
Is 65:3 burneth *i* upon altars of brick
Is 65:7 which have burned *i* upon the
Is 66:3 he that burneth *i*, as if he
Jer 1:16 have burned *i* unto other gods, and
Jer 6:20 cometh there to me *i* from Sheba
Jer 7:9 burn *i* unto Baal, and walk after
Jer 11:12 the gods unto whom they offer *i*
Jer 11:13 even altars to burn *i* unto Baal
Jer 11:17 to anger in offering *i* unto Baal
Jer 17:26 and meat offerings, and *i*, and
Jer 18:15 me, they have burned *i* to vanity
Jer 19:4 have burned *i* in it unto other
Jer 19:13 *i* unto all the host of heaven
Jer 32:29 they have offered *i* unto Baal
Jer 41:5 *i* in their hand, to bring them to
Jer 44:3 in that they went to burn *i*
Jer 44:5 to burn no *i* unto other gods
Jer 44:8 burning *i* unto other gods in the
Jer 44:15 had burned *i* unto other gods
Jer 44:17 to burn *i* unto the queen of
Jer 44:18 to burn *i* to the queen of heaven
Jer 44:19 when we burned *i* to the queen of
Jer 44:21 The *i* that ye burned in the
Jer 44:23 Because ye have burned *i*, and
Jer 44:25 to burn *i* to the queen of heaven,
Jer 48:35 and him that burneth *i* to his gods
Eze 8:11 and a thick cloud of *i* went up
Eze 16:18 mine oil and mine *i* before them
Eze 23:41 whereupon thou hast set mine *i*
Hos 2:13 wherein she burned *i* to them
Hos 4:13 burn *i* upon the hills, under oaks
Hos 11:2 burned *i* to graven images
Hab 1:16 net, and burn *i* unto their drag
Mal 1:11 in every place *i* shall be offered
Lk 1:9 his lot was to burn *i* when he
Lk 1:10 praying without at the time of *i*
Lk 1:11 the right side of the altar of *i*
Rev 8:3 there was given unto him much *i*
Rev 8:4 And the smoke of the *i*, which came

**INCLINE**
Josh 24:23 *i* your heart unto the LORD God of
1Kin 8:58 That he may *i* our hearts unto him
Ps 17:6 *i* thine ear unto me, and hear my
Ps 45:10 and consider, and *i* thine ear
Ps 49:4 I will *i* mine ear to a parable

Ps 71:2 *i* thine ear unto me, and save me
Ps 78:1 *i* your ears to the words of my
Ps 88:2 *i* thine ear unto my cry
Ps 102:2 *i* thine ear unto me
Ps 119:36 *I* my heart unto thy testimonies,
Ps 141:4 *I* not my heart to any evil thing,
Prov 2:2 So that thou *i* thine ear unto
Prov 4:20 *i* thine ear unto my sayings
Is 37:17 *I* thine ear, O LORD, and hear
Is 55:3 *I* your ear, and come unto me
Dan 9:18 O my God, *i* thine ear, and hear

### INCLINED

Judg 9:3 and their hearts *i* to follow
Ps 40:1 he *i* unto me, and heard my cry
Ps 116:2 Because he hath *i* his ear unto me
Ps 119:112 I have *i* mine heart to perform
Prov 5:13 nor *i* mine ear to them that
Jer 7:24 nor *i* their ear, but walked in
Jer 7:26 nor *i* their ear, but hardened
Jer 11:8 nor *i* their ear, but walked every
Jer 17:23 neither *i* their ear, but made
Jer 25:4 hearkened, nor *i* your ear to hear
Jer 34:14 not unto me, neither *i* their ear
Jer 35:15 but ye have not *i* your ear
Jer 44:5 nor *i* their ear to turn from

### INCLOSED

Ex 39:6 onyx stones *i* in ouches of gold
Ex 39:13 they were *i* in ouches of gold in
Judg 20:43 Thus they *i* the Benjamites round
Ps 17:10 They are *i* in their own fat
Ps 22:16 assembly of the wicked have *i* me
Song 4:12 A garden *i* is my sister, my
Lam 3:9 He hath *i* my ways with hewn stone
Lk 5:6 they *i* a great multitude of

### INCORRUPTIBLE

1Cor 9:25 but we an *i*
1Cor 15:52 and the dead shall be raised *i*
1Pet 1:4 To an inheritance *i*, and undefiled
1Pet 1:23 not of corruptible seed, but of *i*

### INCORRUPTION

1Cor 15:42 it is raised in *i*
1Cor 15:50 neither doth corruption inherit *i*
1Cor 15:53 this corruptible must put on *i*
1Cor 15:54 corruptible shall have put on *i*

### INCREASE

Gen 47:24 And it shall come to pass in the *i*
Lev 19:25 may yield unto you the *i* thereof
Lev 25:7 shall all the *i* thereof be meat
Lev 25:12 ye shall eat the *i* thereof out of
Lev 25:16 thou shalt *i* the price thereof
Lev 25:20 not sow, nor gather in our *i*
Lev 25:36 Take thou no usury of him, or *i*
Lev 25:37 nor lend him thy victuals for *i*
Lev 26:4 and the land shall yield her *i*
Lev 26:20 your land shall not yield her *i*
Num 18:30 as the *i* of the threshingfloor
Num 18:30 as the *i* of the winepress
Num 32:14 an *i* of sinful men, to augment
Deut 6:3 thee, and that ye may *i* mightily
Deut 7:13 the *i* of thy kine, and the flocks
Deut 7:22 beasts of the field *i* upon thee
Deut 14:22 truly tithe all the *i* of thy seed
Deut 14:28 tithe of thine *i* the same year
Deut 16:15 shall bless thee in all thine *i*
Deut 26:12 tithes of thine *i* the third year
Deut 28:4 the *i* of thy kine, and the flocks
Deut 28:18 the *i* of thy kine, and the flocks
Deut 28:51 or the *i* of thy kine, or flocks
Deut 32:13 he might eat the *i* of the fields
Deut 32:22 consume the earth with her *i*
Judg 6:4 and destroyed the *i* of the earth
Judg 9:29 *I* thine army, and come out
1Sa 2:33 all the *i* of thine house shall
1Chr 27:23 the LORD had said he would *i*
1Chr 27:27 over the *i* of the vineyards for
2Chr 31:5 of all the *i* of the field
2Chr 32:28 also for the *i* of corn, and wine,
Ezr 10:10 to *i* the trespass of Israel
Neh 9:37 it yieldeth much *i* unto the kings
Job 8:7 thy latter end should greatly *i*
Job 20:28 The *i* of his house shall depart,
Job 31:12 and would root out all mine *i*
Ps 44:12 dost not *i* thy wealth by their
Ps 62:10 if riches *i*, set not your heart
Ps 67:6 Then shall the earth yield her *i*
Ps 71:21 Thou shalt *i* my greatness, and
Ps 73:12 they *i* in riches
Ps 78:46 He gave also their *i* unto the
Ps 85:12 and our land shall yield her *i*
Ps 107:37 which may yield fruits of *i*
Ps 115:14 The LORD shall *i* you more
Prov 1:5 man will hear, and will *i* learning
Prov 3:9 the firstfruits of all thine *i*
Prov 9:9 man, and he will *i* in learning
Prov 13:11 that gathereth by labour shall *i*
Prov 14:4 but much *i* is by the strength of
Prov 18:20 with the *i* of his lips shall he
Prov 22:16 the poor to *i* his riches, and he
Prov 28:28 when they perish, the righteous *i*
Eccl 5:10 he that loveth abundance with *i*
Eccl 5:11 When goods *i*, they are increased
Eccl 6:11 be many things that *i* vanity
Is 9:7 Of the *i* of his government and
Is 29:19 The meek also shall *i* their joy
Is 30:23 and bread of the *i* of the earth
Is 57:9 didst *i* thy perfumes, and didst
Jer 2:3 LORD, and the firstfruits of his *i*
Jer 23:3 and they shall be fruitful and *i*
Eze 5:16 I will *i* the famine upon you, and
Eze 18:8 usury, neither hath taken any *i*
Eze 18:13 forth upon usury, and hath taken *i*
Eze 18:17 hath not received usury nor *i*
Eze 22:12 thou hast taken usury and *i*
Eze 34:27 and the earth shall yield her *i*
Eze 36:11 and they shall *i* and bring fruit
Eze 36:29 call for the corn, and will *i* it
Eze 36:30 the *i* of the field, that ye shall
Eze 36:37 I will *i* them with men like a
Eze 48:18 the *i* thereof shall be for food
Dan 11:39 shall acknowledge and *i* with glory
Hos 4:10 commit whoredom, and shall not *i*
Zec 8:12 and the ground shall give her *i*
Zec 10:8 they shall *i* as they have
Lk 17:5 said unto the Lord, *I* our faith
Jn 3:30 He must *i*, but I must decrease
1Cor 3:6 but God gave the *i*
1Cor 3:7 but God that giveth the *i*
2Cor 9:10 sown, and *i* the fruits of your
Eph 4:16 maketh *i* of the body unto the
Col 2:19 increaseth with the *i* of God
1Th 3:12 And the Lord make you to *i*
1Th 4:10 you, brethren, that ye *i* more
2Ti 2:16 for they will *i* unto more

### INCREASED

Gen 7:17 and the waters *i*, and bare up the
Gen 7:18 were *i* greatly upon the earth
Gen 30:30 it is now *i* unto a multitude
Gen 30:43 the man *i* exceedingly, and had
Ex 1:7 *i* abundantly, and multiplied, and
Ex 23:30 from before thee, until thou be *i*
1Sa 14:19 of the Philistines went on and *i*
2Sa 15:12 for the people *i* continually with
1Kin 22:35 And the battle *i* that day
1Chr 4:38 house of their fathers *i* greatly
1Chr 5:23 they *i* from Bashan unto
2Chr 18:34 And the battle *i* that day
Ezr 9:6 iniquities are *i* over our head
Job 1:10 and his substance is *i* in the land
Ps 3:1 how are they *i* that trouble me
Ps 4:7 that their corn and their wine *i*
Ps 49:16 when the glory of his house is *i*
Ps 105:24 And he *i* his people greatly
Prov 9:11 the years of thy life shall be *i*
Eccl 2:9 *i* more than all that were before
Eccl 5:11 they are *i* that eat them
Is 9:3 the nation, and not *i* the joy
Is 26:15 Thou hast *i* the nation, O LORD,
Is 26:15 thou hast *i* the nation
Is 51:2 alone, and blessed him, and *i* him
Jer 3:16 *i* in the land, in those days,
Jer 5:6 many, and their backslidings are *i*
Jer 15:8 Their widows are *i* to me above
Jer 29:6 that ye may be *i* there, and not
Jer 30:14 because thy sins were *i*
Jer 30:15 because thy sins were *i*, I have
Lam 2:5 hath *i* in the daughter of Judah
Eze 16:7 bud of the field, and thou hast *i*
Eze 16:26 hast *i* thy whoredoms, to provoke
Eze 23:14 And that she *i* her whoredoms
Eze 28:5 traffick hast thou *i* thy riches
Eze 41:7 so *i* from the lowest chamber to
Dan 12:4 and fro, and knowledge shall be *i*
Hos 4:7 As they were *i*, so they sinned
Hos 10:1 of his fruit he hath *i* the altars
Amos 4:9 fig trees and your olive trees *i*
Zec 10:8 shall increase as they have *i*
Mk 4:8 yield fruit that sprang up and *i*
Lk 2:52 Jesus *i* in wisdom and stature, and
Acts 6:7 And the word of God *i*
Acts 9:22 But Saul *i* the more in strength,
Acts 16:5 the faith, and *i* in number daily
2Cor 10:15 having hope, when your faith is *i*
Rev 3:17 *i* with goods, and have need of

### INCREASETH

Job 10:16 For it *i*. Thou huntest me
Job 12:23 He *i* the nations, and destroyeth
Ps 74:23 up against thee *i* continually
Prov 11:24 is that scattereth, and yet *i*
Prov 16:21 sweetness of the lips *i* learning
Prov 23:28 *i* the transgressors among men
Prov 24:5 a man of knowledge *i* strength
Prov 28:8 unjust gain *i* his substance, he
Prov 29:16 are multiplied, transgression *i*
Eccl 1:18 he that *i* knowledge *i* sorrow
Is 40:29 that have no might he *i* strength
Hos 12:1 he daily *i* lies and desolation
Hab 2:6 Woe to him that *i* that which is
Col 2:19 *i* with the increase of God

### INCURABLE

2Chr 21:18 in his bowels with an *i* disease
Job 34:6 my wound is *i* without
Jer 15:18 my pain perpetual, and my wound *i*
Jer 30:12 saith the LORD, Thy bruise is *i*
Jer 30:15 thy sorrow is *i* for the multitude
Mic 1:9 For her wound is *i*

**INDIA** *(in'-de-ah) Eastern boundary of the Persian Empire.*

Est 1:1 reigned from *I* even unto Ethiopia
Est 8:9 which are from *I* unto Ethiopia

### INDIGNATION

Deut 29:28 anger, and in wrath, and in great *i*
2Kin 3:27 there was great *i* against Israel
Neh 4:1 he was wroth, and took great *i*
Est 5:9 he was full of *i* against Mordecai
Job 10:17 me, and increasest thine *i* upon me
Ps 69:24 Pour out thine *i* upon them
Ps 78:49 of his anger, wrath, and *i*
Ps 102:10 Because of thine *i* and thy wrath
Is 10:5 the staff in their hand is mine *i*
Is 10:25 the *i* shall cease, and mine anger
Is 13:5 the LORD, and the weapons of his *i*
Is 26:20 moment, until the *i* be overpast
Is 30:27 his lips are full of *i*, and his
Is 30:30 with the *i* of his anger, and with
Is 34:2 For the *i* of the LORD is upon all
Is 66:14 and his *i* toward his enemies
Jer 10:10 shall not be able to abide his *i*
Jer 15:17 for thou hast filled me with *i*
Jer 50:25 forth the weapons of his *i*
Lam 2:6 hath despised in the *i* of his
Eze 21:31 I will pour out mine *i* upon thee
Eze 22:24 nor rained upon in the day of *i*
Eze 22:31 I poured out mine *i* upon them
Dan 8:19 shall be in the last end of the *i*
Dan 11:30 have *i* against the holy covenant
Dan 11:36 till the *i* be accomplished
Mic 7:9 I will bear the *i* of the LORD
Nah 1:6 Who can stand before his *i*
Hab 3:12 didst march through the land in *i*
Zeph 3:8 to pour upon them mine *i*
Zec 1:12 thou hast had *i* these threescore
Mal 1:4 whom the LORD hath *i* for ever
Mt 20:24 they were moved with *i* against
Mt 26:8 his disciples saw it, they had *i*
Mk 14:4 some that had *i* within themselves
Lk 13:14 of the synagogue answered with *i*
Acts 5:17 Sadducees,) and were filled with *i*
Rom 2:8 but obey unrighteousness, *i*
2Cor 7:11 of yourselves, yea, what *i*
Heb 10:27 for of judgment and fiery *i*
Rev 14:10 mixture into the cup of his *i*

### INFIRMITIES

Mt 8:17 saying, Himself took our *i*
Lk 5:15 and to be healed by him of their *i*
Lk 7:21 hour he cured many of their *i*
Lk 8:2 been healed of evil spirits and *i*
Rom 8:26 the Spirit also helpeth our *i*
Rom 15:1 ought to bear the *i* of the weak
2Cor 11:30 the things which concern mine *i*
2Cor 12:5 I will not glory, but in mine *i*
2Cor 12:9 will I rather glory in my *i*
2Cor 12:10 Therefore I take pleasure in *i*
1Ti 5:23 stomach's sake and thine often *i*
Heb 4:15 touched with the feeling of our *i*

### INFIRMITY
Lev 12:2 for her *i* shall she be unclean
Ps 77:10 And I said, This is my *i*
Prov 18:14 of a man will sustain his *i*
Lk 13:11 had a spirit of *i* eighteen years
Lk 13:12 thou art loosed from thine *i*
Jn 5:5 was there, which had an *i* thirty
Rom 6:19 because of the *i* of your flesh
Gal 4:13 Ye know how through *i* of the
Heb 5:2 himself also is compassed with *i*
Heb 7:28 men high priests which have *i*

### INFORMED
Dan 9:22 And he *i* me, and talked with me, and
Acts 21:21 And they are *i* of thee, that thou
Acts 21:24 they were *i* concerning thee
Acts 24:1 who *i* the governor against Paul
Acts 25:2 of the Jews *i* him against Paul
Acts 25:15 and the elders of the Jews *i* me

### INHABIT
Num 35:34 the land which ye shall *i*
Prov 10:30 the wicked shall not *i* the earth
Is 42:11 the villages that Kedar doth *i*
Is 65:21 shall build houses, and *i* them
Is 65:22 shall not build, and another *i*
Jer 17:6 but shall *i* the parched places in
Jer 48:18 Thou daughter that dost *i* Dibon
Eze 33:24 they that *i* those wastes of the
Amos 9:14 build the waste cities, and *i* them
Zeph 1:13 also build houses, but not *i* them

### INHABITANT
Job 28:4 The flood breaketh out from the *i*
Is 5:9 even great and fair, without *i*
Is 6:11 the cities be wasted without *i*
Is 9:9 the *i* of Samaria, that say in the
Is 12:6 Cry out and shout, thou *i* of Zion
Is 20:6 the *i* of this isle shall say in
Is 24:17 are upon thee, O *i* of the earth
Is 33:24 the *i* shall not say, I am sick
Jer 2:15 his cities are burned without *i*
Jer 4:7 shall be laid waste, without an *i*
Jer 9:11 of Judah desolate, without an *i*
Jer 10:17 of the land, O *i* of the fortress
Jer 21:13 O *i* of the valley, and rock of the
Jer 22:23 O *i* of Lebanon, that makest thy
Jer 26:9 shall be desolate without an *i*
Jer 33:10 without man, and without *i*
Jer 34:22 Judah a desolation without an *i*
Jer 44:22 and a curse, without an *i*
Jer 46:19 be waste and desolate without an *i*
Jer 48:19 O *i* of Aroer, stand by the way,
Jer 48:43 O *i* of Moab, saith the LORD
Jer 51:29 Babylon a desolation without an *i*
Jer 51:35 Babylon, shall the *i* of Zion say
Jer 51:37 and an hissing, without an *i*
Amos 1:5 cut off the *i* from the plain of
Amos 1:8 I will cut off the *i* from Ashdod
Mic 1:11 thou *i* of Saphir, having thy
Mic 1:11 the *i* of Zaanan came not forth in
Mic 1:12 For the *i* of Maroth waited
Mic 1:13 O thou *i* of Lachish, bind the
Mic 1:15 heir unto thee, O *i* of Mareshah
Zeph 2:5 thee, that there shall be no *i*
Zeph 3:6 is no man, that there is none *i*

### INHABITANTS
Gen 19:25 all the *i* of the cities, and that
Gen 34:30 to stink among the *i* of the land
Gen 50:11 when the *i* of the land, the
Ex 15:14 take hold on the *i* of Palestina
Ex 15:15 all the *i* of Canaan shall melt
Ex 23:31 for I will deliver the *i* of the
Ex 34:12 thou make a covenant with the *i*
Ex 34:15 a covenant with the *i* of the land
Lev 18:25 land itself vomiteth out her *i*
Lev 25:10 the land unto all the *i* thereof
Num 13:32 land that eateth up the *i* thereof
Num 14:14 tell it to the *i* of this land
Num 32:17 because of the *i* of the land
Num 33:52 the *i* of the land from before you
Num 33:53 dispossess the *i* of the land
Num 33:55 the *i* of the land from before you
Deut 13:13 withdrawn the *i* of their city
Deut 13:15 Thou shalt surely smite the *i* of
Josh 2:9 that all the *i* of the land faint
Josh 2:24 for even all the *i* of the country
Josh 7:9 all the *i* of the land shall hear
Josh 8:24 all the *i* of Ai in the field
Josh 8:26 utterly destroyed all the *i* of Ai
Josh 9:3 when the *i* of Gibeon heard what
Josh 9:11 all the *i* of our country spake to
Josh 9:24 to destroy all the *i* of the land
Josh 10:1 how the *i* of Gibeon had made
Josh 11:19 save the Hivites the *i* of Gibeon
Josh 13:6 All the *i* of the hill country
Josh 15:15 went up thence to the *i* of Debir
Josh 15:63 the Jebusites the *i* of Jerusalem
Josh 17:7 hand unto the *i* of En-tappuah
Josh 17:11 the *i* of Dor and her towns
Josh 17:11 the *i* of En-dor and her towns, and
Josh 17:11 the *i* of Taanach and her towns, and
Josh 17:11 the *i* of Megiddo and her towns,
Josh 17:12 drive out the *i* of those cities
Judg 1:11 he went against the *i* of Debir
Judg 1:19 drave out the *i* of the mountain
Judg 1:19 not drive out the *i* of the valley
Judg 1:27 drive out the *i* of Beth-shean
Judg 1:27 and her towns, nor the *i* of Dor
Judg 1:27 nor the *i* of Ibleam and her towns,
Judg 1:27 nor the *i* of Megiddo and her towns
Judg 1:30 Zebulun drive out the *i* of Kitron
Judg 1:30 nor the *i* of Nahalol
Judg 1:31 Asher drive out the *i* of Accho
Judg 1:31 nor the *i* of Zidon, nor of Ahlab,
Judg 1:32 the Canaanites, the *i* of the land
Judg 1:33 drive out the *i* of Beth-shemesh
Judg 1:33 nor the *i* of Beth-anath
Judg 1:33 the Canaanites, the *i* of the land
Judg 1:33 the *i* of Beth-shemesh and of
Judg 2:2 no league with the *i* of this land
Judg 5:7 The *i* of the villages ceased,
Judg 5:11 the *i* of his villages in Israel
Judg 5:23 curse ye bitterly the *i* thereof
Judg 10:18 be head over all the *i* of Gilead
Judg 11:8 our head over all the *i* of Gilead
Judg 11:21 Amorites, the *i* of that country
Judg 20:15 sword, beside the *i* of Gibeah
Judg 21:9 of the *i* of Jabesh-gilead there
Judg 21:10 smite the *i* of Jabesh-gilead with
Judg 21:12 they found among the *i* of
Ruth 4:4 thee, saying, Buy it before the *i*
1Sa 6:21 to the *i* of Kirjath-jearim
1Sa 23:5 So David saved the *i* of Keilah
1Sa 27:8 were of old the *i* of the land
1Sa 31:11 when the *i* of Jabesh-gilead heard
2Sa 5:6 the Jebusites, the *i* of the land
1Kin 17:1 who was of the *i* of Gilead
1Kin 21:11 nobles who were the *i* in his city
2Kin 19:26 Therefore their *i* were of small
2Kin 22:16 this place, and upon the *i* thereof
2Kin 22:19 place, and against the *i* thereof
2Kin 23:2 all the *i* of Jerusalem with him,
1Chr 8:6 of the fathers of the *i* of Geba
1Chr 8:13 the fathers of the *i* of Aijalon
1Chr 8:13 who drove away the *i* of Gath
1Chr 9:2 Now the first *i* that dwelt in
1Chr 11:4 Jebusites were, the *i* of the land
1Chr 11:5 the *i* of Jebus said to David,
1Chr 22:18 for he hath given the *i* of the
2Chr 15:5 upon all the *i* of the countries
2Chr 20:7 who didst drive out the *i* of this
2Chr 20:15 ye *i* of Jerusalem, and thou king
2Chr 20:18 the *i* of Jerusalem fell before
2Chr 20:20 me, O Judah, and ye *i* of Jerusalem
2Chr 20:23 up against the *i* of mount Seir
2Chr 20:23 had made an end of the *i* of Seir
2Chr 21:11 caused the *i* of Jerusalem to
2Chr 21:13 the *i* of Jerusalem to go a
2Chr 22:1 the *i* of Jerusalem made Ahaziah
2Chr 32:22 the *i* of Jerusalem from the hand
2Chr 32:26 the *i* of Jerusalem, so that the
2Chr 32:33 the *i* of Jerusalem did him honour
2Chr 33:9 the *i* of Jerusalem to err, and to
2Chr 34:24 this place, and upon the *i* thereof
2Chr 34:27 place, and against the *i* thereof
2Chr 34:28 place, and upon the *i* of the same
2Chr 34:30 the *i* of Jerusalem, and the
2Chr 34:32 the *i* of Jerusalem did according
2Chr 35:18 present, and the *i* of Jerusalem
Ezr 4:6 accusation against the *i* of Judah
Neh 3:13 Hanun, and the *i* of Zanoah
Neh 7:3 watches of the *i* of Jerusalem
Neh 9:24 before them the *i* of the land
Job 26:5 the waters, and the *i* thereof
Ps 33:8 let all the *i* of the world stand
Ps 33:14 upon all the *i* of the earth
Ps 49:1 give ear, all ye *i* of the world
Ps 75:3 all the *i* thereof are dissolved
Ps 83:7 Philistines with the *i* of Tyre
Is 5:3 O *i* of Jerusalem, and men of Judah
Is 8:14 for a snare to the *i* of Jerusalem
Is 10:13 put down the *i* like a valiant man
Is 10:31 the *i* of Gebim gather themselves
Is 18:3 All ye *i* of the world, and
Is 21:14 The *i* of the land of Tema brought
Is 22:21 be a father to the *i* of Jerusalem
Is 23:2 Be still, ye *i* of the isle
Is 23:6 howl, ye *i* of the isle
Is 24:1 scattereth abroad the *i* thereof
Is 24:5 is defiled under the *i* thereof
Is 24:6 therefore the *i* of the earth are
Is 26:9 the *i* of the world will learn
Is 26:18 neither have the *i* of the world
Is 26:21 out of his place to punish the *i*
Is 37:27 Therefore their *i* were of small
Is 38:11 no more with the *i* of the world
Is 40:22 the *i* thereof are as grasshoppers
Is 42:10 the isles, and the *i* thereof
Is 42:11 let the *i* of the rock sing, let
Is 49:19 be too narrow by reason of the *i*
Jer 1:14 forth upon all the *i* of the land
Jer 4:4 ye men of Judah and *i* of Jerusalem
Jer 6:12 my hand upon the *i* of the land
Jer 8:1 the bones of the *i* of Jerusalem
Jer 10:18 I will sling out the *i* of the
Jer 11:2 Judah, and to the *i* of Jerusalem
Jer 11:9 and among the *i* of Jerusalem
Jer 11:12 *i* of Jerusalem go, and cry unto
Jer 13:13 will fill all the *i* of this land
Jer 13:13 all the *i* of Jerusalem, with
Jer 17:20 all the *i* of Jerusalem, that
Jer 17:25 of Judah, and the *i* of Jerusalem
Jer 18:11 to the *i* of Jerusalem, saying,
Jer 19:3 kings of Judah, and *i* of Jerusalem
Jer 19:12 to the *i* thereof, and even make
Jer 21:6 I will smite the *i* of this city
Jer 23:14 the *i* thereof as Gomorrah
Jer 25:2 to all the *i* of Jerusalem, saying
Jer 25:9 land, and against the *i* thereof
Jer 25:29 sword upon all the *i* of the earth
Jer 25:30 against all the *i* of the earth
Jer 26:15 this city, and upon the *i* thereof
Jer 32:32 of Judah, and the *i* of Jerusalem
Jer 35:13 the *i* of Jerusalem, Will ye not
Jer 35:17 upon all the *i* of Jerusalem all
Jer 36:31 upon the *i* of Jerusalem, and upon
Jer 42:18 forth upon the *i* of Jerusalem
Jer 46:8 destroy the city and the *i* thereof
Jer 47:2 all the *i* of the land shall howl
Jer 49:8 back, dwell deep, O *i* of Dedan
Jer 49:20 purposed against the *i* of Teman
Jer 49:30 O ye *i* of Hazor, saith the LORD
Jer 50:21 it, and against the *i* of Pekod
Jer 50:34 and disquiet the *i* of Babylon
Jer 50:35 upon the *i* of Babylon, and upon
Jer 51:12 he spake against the *i* of Babylon
Jer 51:24 to all the *i* of Chaldea all their
Jer 51:35 and my blood upon the *i* of Chaldea
Lam 4:12 all the *i* of the world, would not
Eze 11:15 whom the *i* of Jerusalem have said
Eze 12:19 Lord GOD of the *i* of Jerusalem
Eze 15:6 so will I give the *i* of Jerusalem
Eze 26:17 strong in the sea, she and her *i*
Eze 27:8 The *i* of Zidon and Arvad were thy
Eze 27:35 All the *i* of the isles shall be
Eze 29:6 all the *i* of Egypt shall know
Dan 4:35 all the *i* of the earth are
Dan 4:35 and among the *i* of the earth
Dan 9:7 to the *i* of Jerusalem, and unto
Hos 4:1 with the *i* of the land, because
Hos 10:5 The *i* of Samaria shall fear
Joel 1:2 and give ear, all ye *i* of the land
Joel 1:14 all the *i* of the land into the
Joel 2:1 let all the *i* of the land tremble
Mic 6:12 the *i* thereof have spoken lies,
Mic 6:16 and the *i* thereof an hissing
Zeph 1:4 and upon all the *i* of Jerusalem
Zeph 1:11 ye *i* of Maktesh, for all the
Zeph 2:5 Woe unto the *i* of the sea coast,
Zec 8:20 people, and the *i* of many cities
Zec 8:21 the *i* of one city shall go to
Zec 11:6 no more pity the *i* of the land
Zec 12:5 The *i* of Jerusalem shall be my
Zec 12:7 the glory of the *i* of Jerusalem
Zec 12:8 LORD defend the *i* of Jerusalem
Zec 12:10 upon the *i* of Jerusalem, the
Zec 13:1 to the *i* of Jerusalem for sin and
Rev 17:2 the *i* of the earth have been made

## INHABITED

Gen 36:20 Seir the Horite, who *i* the land
Ex 16:35 until they came to a land *i*
Lev 16:22 iniquities unto a land not *i*
Judg 1:17 the Canaanites that *i* Zephath
Judg 1:21 the Jebusites that *i* Jerusalem
1Chr 5:9 eastward he *i* unto the entering
Is 13:20 It shall never be *i*, neither
Is 44:26 to Jerusalem, Thou shalt be *i*
Is 45:18 not in vain, he formed it to be *i*
Is 54:3 make the desolate cities to be *i*
Jer 6:8 make thee desolate, a land not *i*
Jer 17:6 in a salt land and not *i*
Jer 22:6 and cities which are not *i*
Jer 46:26 and afterward it shall be *i*
Jer 50:13 of the LORD it shall not be *i*
Jer 50:39 and it shall be no more *i* for ever
Eze 12:20 that are *i* shall be laid waste
Eze 26:17 that wast *i* of seafaring men, the
Eze 26:19 like the cities that are not *i*
Eze 26:20 to the pit, that thou be not *i*
Eze 29:11 neither shall it be *i* forty years
Eze 34:13 in all the *i* places of the
Eze 36:10 and the cities shall be *i*, and the
Eze 36:35 are become fenced, and are *i*
Eze 38:12 desolate places that are now *i*
Zec 2:4 Jerusalem shall be *i* as towns
Zec 7:7 prophets, when Jerusalem was *i*
Zec 7:7 when men *i* the south and the plain
Zec 9:5 Gaza, and Ashkelon shall not be *i*
Zec 12:6 Jerusalem shall be *i* again in her
Zec 14:10 *i* in her place, from Benjamin's
Zec 14:11 but Jerusalem shall be safely *i*

## INHERIT

Gen 15:7 to give thee this land to *i* it
Gen 15:8 shall I know that I shall *i* it
Gen 28:4 that thou mayest *i* the land
Ex 23:30 thou be increased, and *i* the land
Ex 32:13 seed, and they shall *i* it for ever
Lev 20:24 Ye shall *i* their land, and I will
Lev 25:46 to *i* them for a possession
Num 18:24 I have given to the Levites to *i*
Num 26:55 of their fathers they shall *i*
Num 32:19 For we will not *i* with them on
Num 33:54 tribes of your fathers ye shall *i*
Num 34:13 the land which ye shall *i* by lot
Deut 1:38 for he shall cause Israel to *i* it
Deut 2:31 that thou mayest *i* his land
Deut 3:28 he shall cause them to *i* the land
Deut 12:10 the LORD your God giveth you to *i*
Deut 16:20 *i* the land which the LORD thy God
Deut 19:3 the LORD thy God giveth thee to *i*
Deut 19:14 which thou shalt *i* in the land
Deut 21:16 his sons to *i* that which he hath
Deut 31:7 and thou shalt cause them to *i* it
Josh 17:14 but one lot and one portion to *i*
Judg 11:2 Thou shalt not *i* in our father's
1Sa 2:8 to make them *i* the throne of
2Chr 20:11 which thou hast given us to *i*
Ps 25:13 and his seed shall *i* the earth
Ps 37:9 the LORD, they shall *i* the earth
Ps 37:11 But the meek shall *i* the earth
Ps 37:22 blessed of him shall *i* the earth
Ps 37:29 The righteous shall *i* the land
Ps 37:34 he shall exalt thee to *i* the land
Ps 69:36 also of his servants shall *i* it
Ps 82:8 for thou shalt *i* all nations
Prov 3:35 The wise shall *i* glory
Prov 8:21 those that love me to *i* substance
Prov 11:29 his own house shall *i* the wind
Prov 14:18 The simple *i* folly
Is 49:8 to cause to *i* the desolate
Is 54:3 and thy seed shall *i* the Gentiles
Is 57:13 land, and shall *i* my holy mountain
Is 60:21 they shall *i* the land for ever,
Is 65:9 and mine elect shall *i* it, and my
Jer 8:10 fields to them that shall *i* them
Jer 12:14 have caused my people Israel to *i*
Jer 49:1 why then doth their king *i* Gad
Eze 47:13 whereby ye shall *i* the land
Eze 47:14 And ye shall *i* it, one as well as
Zec 2:12 the LORD shall *i* Judah his
Mt 5:5 for they shall *i* the earth
Mt 19:29 and shall *i* everlasting life
Mt 25:34 *i* the kingdom prepared for you
Mk 10:17 I do that I may *i* eternal life
Lk 10:25 what shall I do to *i* eternal life
Lk 18:18 what shall I do to *i* eternal life
1Cor 6:9 shall not *i* the kingdom of God
1Cor 6:10 shall *i* the kingdom of God
1Cor 15:50 blood cannot *i* the kingdom of God
1Cor 15:50 doth corruption *i* incorruption
Gal 5:21 shall not *i* the kingdom of God
Heb 6:12 faith and patience *i* the promises
1Pet 3:9 that ye should *i* a blessing
Rev 21:7 overcometh shall *i* all things

## INHERITANCE

Gen 31:14 Is there yet any portion or *i* for
Gen 48:6 name of their brethren in their *i*
Ex 15:17 them in the mountain of thine *i*
Ex 34:9 our sin, and take us for thine *i*
Lev 25:46 ye shall take them as an *i* for
Num 16:14 and honey, or given us *i* of fields
Num 18:20 shalt have no *i* in their land
Num 18:20 thine *i* among the children of
Num 18:21 all the tenth in Israel for an *i*
Num 18:23 children of Israel they have no *i*
Num 18:24 of Israel they shall have no *i*
Num 18:26 given you from them for your *i*
Num 26:53 an *i* according to the number of
Num 26:54 many thou shalt give the more *i*
Num 26:54 to few thou shalt give the less *i*
Num 26:54 to every one shall his *i* be given
Num 26:62 because there was no *i* given them
Num 27:7 give them a possession of an *i*
Num 27:7 thou shalt cause the *i* of their
Num 27:8 then ye shall cause his *i* to pass
Num 27:9 give his *i* unto his brethren
Num 27:10 then ye shall give his *i* unto his
Num 27:11 then ye shall give his *i* unto his
Num 32:18 have inherited every man his *i*
Num 32:19 because our *i* is fallen to us on
Num 32:32 that the possession of our *i* on
Num 33:54 lot for an *i* among your families
Num 33:54 the more ye shall give the more *i*
Num 33:54 fewer ye shall give the less *i*
Num 33:54 every man's *i* shall be in the
Num 34:2 that shall fall unto you for an *i*
Num 34:14 fathers, have received their *i*
Num 34:14 of Manasseh have received their *i*
Num 34:15 their *i* on this side Jordan near
Num 34:18 tribe, to divide the land by *i*
Num 34:29 LORD commanded to divide the *i*
Num 35:2 give unto the Levites of the *i* of
Num 35:8 to his *i* which he inheriteth
Num 36:2 an *i* by lot to the children of
Num 36:2 by the LORD to give the *i* of
Num 36:3 then shall their *i* be taken from
Num 36:3 taken from the *i* of our fathers
Num 36:3 shall be put to the *i* of the
Num 36:3 it be taken from the lot of our *i*
Num 36:4 *i* be put unto the *i* of
Num 36:4 so shall their *i* be taken away
Num 36:4 be taken away from the *i* of the
Num 36:7 So shall not the *i* of the
Num 36:7 shall keep himself to the *i* of
Num 36:8 that possesseth an *i* in any tribe
Num 36:8 every man the *i* of his fathers
Num 36:9 Neither shall the *i* remove from
Num 36:9 shall keep himself to his own *i*
Num 36:12 their *i* remained in the tribe of
Deut 4:20 to be unto him a people of *i*
Deut 4:21 LORD thy God giveth thee for an *i*
Deut 4:38 to give thee their land for an *i*
Deut 9:26 destroy not thy people and thine *i*
Deut 9:29 they are thy people and thine *i*
Deut 10:9 no part nor *i* with his brethren
Deut 10:9 the LORD is his *i*, according as
Deut 12:9 yet come to the rest and to the *i*
Deut 12:12 as he hath no part nor *i* with you
Deut 14:27 he hath no part nor *i* with thee
Deut 14:29 he hath no part nor *i* with thee
Deut 15:4 thee for an *i* to possess it
Deut 18:1 have no part nor *i* with Israel
Deut 18:1 the LORD made by fire, and his *i*
Deut 18:2 have no *i* among their brethren
Deut 18:2 the LORD is their *i*, as he hath
Deut 19:10 LORD thy God giveth thee for an *i*
Deut 19:14 of old time have set in thine *i*
Deut 20:16 thy God doth give thee for an *i*
Deut 21:23 LORD thy God giveth thee for an *i*
Deut 24:4 LORD thy God giveth thee for an *i*
Deut 25:19 thee for an *i* to possess it
Deut 26:1 LORD thy God giveth thee for an *i*
Deut 29:8 gave it for an *i* unto the
Deut 32:8 divided to the nations their *i*
Deut 32:9 Jacob is the lot of his *i*
Deut 33:4 even the *i* of the congregation of
Josh 1:6 thou divide for an *i* the land
Josh 11:23 Joshua gave it for an *i* unto
Josh 13:6 lot unto the Israelites for an *i*
Josh 13:7 for an *i* unto the nine tribes
Josh 13:8 the Gadites have received their *i*
Josh 13:14 the tribe of Levi he gave none *i*
Josh 13:14 Israel made by fire are their *i*
Josh 13:15 *i* according to their families
Josh 13:23 This was the *i* of the children of
Josh 13:24 Moses gave *i* unto the tribe of
Josh 13:28 This is the *i* of the children of
Josh 13:29 Moses gave *i* unto the half tribe
Josh 13:32 for *i* in the plains of Moab
Josh 13:33 of Levi Moses gave not any *i*
Josh 13:33 LORD God of Israel was their *i*
Josh 14:1 Israel, distributed for *i* to them
Josh 14:2 By lot was their *i*, as the LORD
Josh 14:3 had given the *i* of two tribes
Josh 14:3 Levites he gave none *i* among them
Josh 14:9 have trodden shall be thine *i*
Josh 14:13 son of Jephunneh Hebron for an *i*
Josh 14:14 Hebron therefore became the *i* of
Josh 15:20 This is the *i* of the tribe of the
Josh 16:4 Manasseh and Ephraim, took their *i*
Josh 16:5 of their *i* on the east side was
Josh 16:8 This is the *i* of the tribe of the
Josh 16:9 of Ephraim were among the *i* of
Josh 17:4 give us an *i* among our brethren
Josh 17:4 an *i* among the brethren of their
Josh 17:6 Manasseh had an *i* among his sons
Josh 18:2 had not yet received their *i*
Josh 18:4 it according to the *i* of them
Josh 18:7 priesthood of the LORD is their *i*
Josh 18:7 have received their *i* beyond
Josh 18:20 This was the *i* of the children of
Josh 18:28 This is the *i* of the children of
Josh 19:1 and their *i* was within the
Josh 19:1 the *i* of the children of Judah
Josh 19:2 And they had in their *i* Beer-sheba
Josh 19:8 This is the *i* of the tribe of the
Josh 19:9 the *i* of the children of Simeon
Josh 19:9 *i* within the *i* of them
Josh 19:10 border of their *i* was unto Sarid
Josh 19:16 This is the *i* of the children of
Josh 19:23 This is the *i* of the tribe of the
Josh 19:31 This is the *i* of the tribe of the
Josh 19:39 This is the *i* of the tribe of the
Josh 19:41 And the coast of their *i* was Zorah
Josh 19:48 This is the *i* of the tribe of the
Josh 19:49 the land for *i* by their coasts
Josh 19:49 *i* to Joshua the son of Nun among
Josh 19:51 divided for an *i* by lot in Shiloh
Josh 21:3 unto the Levites out of their *i*
Josh 23:4 to be an *i* for your tribes, from
Josh 24:28 depart, every man unto his *i*
Josh 24:30 border of his *i* in Timnath-serah
Josh 24:32 it became the *i* of the children
Judg 2:6 unto his *i* to possess the land
Judg 2:9 border of his *i* in Timnath-heres
Judg 18:1 sought them an *i* to dwell in
Judg 18:1 for unto that day all their *i* had
Judg 20:6 the country of the *i* of Israel
Judg 21:17 There must be an *i* for them that
Judg 21:23 went and returned unto their *i*
Judg 21:24 from thence every man to his *i*
Ruth 4:5 the name of the dead upon his *i*
Ruth 4:6 for myself, lest I mar mine own *i*
Ruth 4:10 the name of the dead upon his *i*
1Sa 10:1 thee to be captain over his *i*
1Sa 26:19 from abiding in the *i* of the LORD
2Sa 14:16 son together out of the *i* of God
2Sa 20:1 neither have we *i* in the son of
2Sa 20:19 thou swallow up the *i* of the LORD
2Sa 21:3 ye may bless the *i* of the LORD
1Kin 8:36 hast given to thy people for an *i*
1Kin 8:51 they be thy people, and thine *i*
1Kin 8:53 of the earth, to be thine *i*
1Kin 12:16 neither have we *i* in the son of
1Kin 21:3 that I should give the *i* of my
1Kin 21:4 not give thee the *i* of my fathers
2Kin 21:14 forsake the remnant of mine *i*
1Chr 16:18 land of Canaan, the lot of your *i*
1Chr 28:8 leave it for an *i* for your
2Chr 6:27 given unto thy people for an *i*
2Chr 10:16 we have none *i* in the son of
Ezr 9:12 leave it for an *i* to your
Neh 11:20 of Judah, every one in his *i*
Job 31:2 what *i* of the Almighty from on
Job 42:15 gave them *i* among their brethren
Ps 2:8 give thee the heathen for thine *i*

Ps 16:5 The LORD is the portion of mine *i*
Ps 28:9 Save thy people, and bless thine *i*
Ps 33:12 whom he hath chosen for his own *i*
Ps 37:18 their *i* shall be for ever
Ps 47:4 He shall choose our *i* for us
Ps 68:9 thou didst confirm thine *i*
Ps 74:2 the rod of thine *i*, which thou
Ps 78:55 and divided them an *i* by line
Ps 78:62 and was wroth with his *i*
Ps 78:71 Jacob his people, and Israel his *i*
Ps 79:1 the heathen are come into thine *i*
Ps 94:14 neither will he forsake his *i*
Ps 105:11 land of Canaan, the lot of your *i*
Ps 106:5 that I may glory with thine *i*
Ps 106:40 that he abhorred his own *i*
Prov 13:22 A good man leaveth an *i* to his
Prov 17:2 part of the *i* among the brethren
Prov 19:14 and riches are the *i* of fathers
Prov 20:21 An *i* may be gotten hastily at the
Eccl 7:11 Wisdom is good with an *i*
Is 19:25 of my hands, and Israel mine *i*
Is 47:6 my people, I have polluted mine *i*
Is 63:17 sake, the tribes of thine *i*
Jer 3:18 given for an *i* unto your fathers
Jer 10:16 and Israel is the rod of his *i*
Jer 12:14 that touch the *i* which I have
Jer 16:18 they have filled mine *i* with the
Jer 32:8 for the right of *i* is thine
Jer 51:19 and Israel is the rod of his *i*
Lam 5:2 Our *i* is turned to strangers, our
Eze 22:16 thou shalt take thine *i* in
Eze 33:24 the land is given us for *i*
Eze 35:15 at the *i* of the house of Israel
Eze 36:12 thee, and thou shalt be their *i*
Eze 44:28 And it shall be unto them for an *i*
Eze 44:28 I am their *i*
Eze 45:1 divide by lot the land for *i*
Eze 46:16 the *i* thereof shall be his sons'
Eze 46:16 it shall be their possession by *i*
Eze 46:17 of his *i* to one of his servants
Eze 46:17 but his *i* shall be his sons' for
Eze 46:18 of the people's *i* by oppression
Eze 46:18 sons *i* out of his own possession
Eze 47:14 land shall fall unto you for *i*
Eze 47:22 it by lot for an *i* unto you
Eze 47:22 they shall have *i* with you among
Eze 47:23 there shall ye give him his *i*
Eze 48:29 unto the tribes of Israel for *i*
Mt 21:38 him, and let us seize on his *i*
Mk 12:7 kill him, and the *i* shall be ours
Lk 12:13 that he divide the *i* with me
Lk 20:14 kill him, that the *i* may be ours
Acts 7:5 And he gave him none *i* in it
Acts 20:32 to give you an *i* among all them
Acts 26:18 *i* among them which are sanctified
Gal 3:18 For if the *i* be of the law, it is
Eph 1:11 whom also we have obtained an *i*
Eph 1:14 our *i* until the redemption of the
Eph 1:18 the glory of his *i* in the saints
Eph 5:5 hath any *i* in the kingdom of
Col 1:12 of the *i* of the saints in light
Col 3:24 shall receive the reward of the *i*
Heb 1:4 as he hath by *i* obtained a more
Heb 9:15 receive the promise of eternal *i*
Heb 11:8 he should after receive for an *i*
1Pet 1:4 To an *i* incorruptible, and

## INHERITED

Num 32:18 have *i* every man his inheritance
Josh 14:1 of Israel *i* in the land of Canaan
Ps 105:44 they *i* the labour of the people
Jer 16:19 Surely our fathers have *i* lies
Eze 33:24 Abraham was one, and he *i* the land
Heb 12:17 when he would have *i* the blessing

## INIQUITIES

Lev 16:21 confess over him all the *i* of the
Lev 16:22 their *i* unto a land not inhabited
Lev 26:39 also in the *i* of their fathers
Num 14:34 for a year, shall ye bear your *i*
Ezr 9:6 for our *i* are increased over our
Ezr 9:7 and for our *i* have we, our kings,
Ezr 9:13 us less than our *i* deserve
Neh 9:2 sins, and the *i* of their fathers
Job 13:23 How many are mine *i* and sins
Job 13:26 me to possess the *i* of my youth
Job 22:5 and thine *i* infinite
Ps 38:4 For mine *i* are gone over mine
Ps 40:12 mine *i* have taken hold upon me,
Ps 51:9 my sins, and blot out all mine *i*
Ps 64:6 They search out *i*
Ps 65:3 *I* prevail against me
Ps 79:8 remember not against us former *i*
Ps 90:8 Thou hast set our *i* before thee
Ps 103:3 Who forgiveth all thine *i*
Ps 103:10 rewarded us according to our *i*
Ps 107:17 and because of their *i*, are
Ps 130:3 If thou, LORD, shouldest mark *i*
Ps 130:8 redeem Israel from all his *i*
Prov 5:22 His own *i* shall take the wicked
Is 43:24 thou hast wearied me with thine *i*
Is 50:1 Behold, for your *i* have ye sold
Is 53:5 he was bruised for our *i*
Is 53:11 for he shall bear their *i*
Is 59:2 But your *i* have separated between
Is 59:12 and as for our *i*, we know them
Is 64:6 and our *i*, like the wind, have
Is 64:7 consumed us, because of our *i*
Is 65:7 Your *i*, and the *i* of your
Jer 5:25 Your *i* have turned away these
Jer 11:10 to the *i* of their forefathers
Jer 14:7 though our *i* testify against us,
Jer 33:8 and I will pardon all their *i*
Lam 4:13 the *i* of her priests, that have
Lam 5:7 and we have borne their *i*
Eze 24:23 but ye shall pine away for your *i*
Eze 28:18 by the multitude of thine *i*
Eze 32:27 but their *i* shall be upon their
Eze 36:31 in your own sight for your *i*
Eze 36:33 *i* I will also cause you to dwell
Eze 43:10 they may be ashamed of their *i*
Dan 4:27 thine *i* by shewing mercy to the
Dan 9:13 that we might turn from our *i*
Dan 9:16 for the *i* of our fathers,
Amos 3:2 I will punish you for all your *i*
Mic 7:19 he will subdue our *i*
Acts 3:26 away every one of you from his *i*
Rom 4:7 are they whose *i* are forgiven
Heb 8:12 their *i* will I remember no more
Heb 10:17 *i* will I remember no more
Rev 18:5 and God hath remembered her *i*

## INIQUITY

Gen 15:16 for the *i* of the Amorites is not
Gen 19:15 be consumed in the *i* of the city
Gen 44:16 found out the *i* of thy servants
Ex 20:5 visiting the *i* of the fathers
Ex 28:38 may bear the *i* of the holy things
Ex 28:43 that they bear not *i*, and die
Ex 34:7 mercy for thousands, forgiving *i*
Ex 34:7 visiting the *i* of the fathers
Ex 34:9 and pardon our *i* and our sin, and
Lev 5:1 it, then he shall bear his *i*
Lev 5:17 is he guilty, and shall bear his *i*
Lev 7:18 eateth of it shall bear his *i*
Lev 10:17 to bear the *i* of the congregation
Lev 17:16 then he shall bear his *i*
Lev 18:25 I do visit the *i* thereof upon it
Lev 19:8 that eateth it shall bear his *i*
Lev 20:17 he shall bear his *i*
Lev 20:19 they shall bear their *i*
Lev 22:16 them to bear the *i* of trespass
Lev 26:39 in their *i* in your enemies' lands
Lev 26:40 If they shall confess their *i*
Lev 26:40 the *i* of their fathers, with
Lev 26:41 of the punishment of their *i*
Lev 26:43 of the punishment of their *i*
Num 5:15 bringing *i* to remembrance
Num 5:31 shall the man be guiltless from *i*
Num 5:31 and this woman shall bear her *i*
Num 14:18 and of great mercy, forgiving *i*
Num 14:18 visiting the *i* of the fathers
Num 14:19 the *i* of this people according
Num 15:31 his *i* shall be upon him
Num 18:1 shall bear the *i* of the sanctuary
Num 18:1 bear the *i* of your priesthood
Num 18:23 and they shall bear their *i*
Num 23:21 He hath not beheld *i* in Jacob
Num 30:15 then he shall bear her *i*
Deut 5:9 visiting the *i* of the fathers
Deut 19:15 rise up against a man for any *i*
Deut 32:4 a God of truth and without *i*
Josh 22:17 Is the *i* of Peor too little for
Josh 22:20 man perished not alone in his *i*
1Sa 3:13 ever for the *i* which he knoweth
1Sa 3:14 that the *i* of Eli's house shall
1Sa 15:23 and stubbornness is as *i* and
1Sa 20:1 what is mine *i*?
1Sa 20:8 if there be in me *i*, slay me
1Sa 25:24 my lord, upon me let this *i* be
2Sa 7:14 If he commit *i*, I will chasten
2Sa 14:9 the *i* be on me, and on my father's
2Sa 14:32 and if there be any *i* in me
2Sa 19:19 Let not my lord impute *i* unto me
2Sa 22:24 and have kept myself from mine *i*
2Sa 24:10 take away the *i* of thy servant
1Chr 21:8 do away the *i* of thy servant
2Chr 19:7 for there is no *i* with the LORD
Neh 4:5 And cover not their *i*, and let not
Job 4:8 as I have seen, they that plow *i*
Job 5:16 hope, and *i* stoppeth her mouth
Job 6:29 I pray you, let it not be *i*
Job 6:30 Is there *i* in my tongue
Job 7:21 and take away mine *i*
Job 10:6 That thou enquirest after mine *i*
Job 10:14 wilt not acquit me from mine *i*
Job 11:6 thee less than thine *i* deserveth
Job 11:14 If *i* be in thine hand, put it far
Job 14:17 a bag, and thou sewest up mine *i*
Job 15:5 For thy mouth uttereth thine *i*
Job 15:16 man, which drinketh *i* like water
Job 20:27 The heaven shall reveal his *i*
Job 21:19 layeth up his *i* for his children
Job 22:23 thou shalt put away *i* far from
Job 31:3 punishment to the workers of *i*
Job 31:11 it is an *i* to be punished by the
Job 31:28 This also were an *i* to be
Job 31:33 by hiding mine *i* in my bosom
Job 33:9 neither is there *i* in me
Job 34:8 in company with the workers of *i*
Job 34:10 Almighty, that he should commit *i*
Job 34:22 workers of *i* may hide themselves
Job 34:32 if I have done *i*, I will do no
Job 36:10 that they return from *i*
Job 36:21 Take heed, regard not *i*
Job 36:23 who can say, Thou hast wrought *i*
Ps 5:5 thou hatest all workers of *i*
Ps 6:8 from me, all ye workers of *i*
Ps 7:3 if there be *i* in my hands
Ps 7:14 Behold, he travaileth with *i*
Ps 14:4 all the workers of *i* no knowledge
Ps 18:23 him, and I kept myself from mine *i*
Ps 25:11 sake, O LORD, pardon mine *i*
Ps 28:3 wicked, and with the workers of *i*
Ps 31:10 faileth because of mine *i*
Ps 32:2 unto whom the LORD imputeth not *i*
Ps 32:5 thee, and mine *i* have I not hid
Ps 32:5 and thou forgavest the *i* of my sin
Ps 36:2 until his *i* be found to be
Ps 36:3 The words of his mouth are *i*
Ps 36:12 There are the workers of *i* fallen
Ps 37:1 envious against the workers of *i*
Ps 38:18 For I will declare mine *i*
Ps 39:11 rebukes dost correct man for *i*
Ps 41:6 his heart gathereth *i* to itself
Ps 49:5 when the *i* of my heels shall
Ps 51:2 Wash me throughly from mine *i*
Ps 51:5 Behold, I was shapen in *i*
Ps 53:1 they, and have done abominable *i*
Ps 53:4 the workers of *i* no knowledge
Ps 55:3 for they cast *i* upon me, and in
Ps 56:7 Shall they escape by *i*
Ps 59:2 Deliver me from the workers of *i*
Ps 64:2 insurrection of the workers of *i*
Ps 66:18 If I regard *i* in my heart
Ps 69:27 Add *i* unto their *i*
Ps 78:38 of compassion, forgave their *i*
Ps 85:2 hast forgiven the *i* of thy people
Ps 89:32 the rod, and their *i* with stripes
Ps 92:7 all the workers of *i* do flourish
Ps 92:9 workers of *i* shall be scattered
Ps 94:4 the workers of *i* boast themselves
Ps 94:16 for me against the workers of *i*
Ps 94:20 Shall the throne of *i* have
Ps 94:23 shall bring upon them their own *i*
Ps 106:6 our fathers, we have committed *i*
Ps 106:43 and were brought low for their *i*
Ps 107:42 all *i* shall stop her mouth
Ps 109:14 Let the *i* of his fathers be
Ps 119:3 They also do no *i*
Ps 119:133 let not any *i* have dominion over
Ps 125:3 put forth their hands unto *i*
Ps 125:5 them forth with the workers of *i*
Ps 141:4 wicked works with men that work *i*
Ps 141:9 and the gins of the workers of *i*
Prov 10:29 shall be to the workers of *i*
Prov 16:6 By mercy and truth *i* is purged
Prov 19:28 mouth of the wicked devoureth *i*
Prov 21:15 shall be to the workers of *i*
Prov 22:8 He that soweth *i* shall reap
Eccl 3:16 righteousness, that *i* was there

Is 1:4 nation, a people laden with *i*
Is 1:13 it is *i*, even the solemn meeting
Is 5:18 that draw *i* with cords of vanity
Is 6:7 thine *i* is taken away, and thy sin
Is 13:11 evil, and the wicked for their *i*
Is 14:21 for the *i* of their fathers
Is 22:14 Surely this *i* shall not be purged
Is 26:21 of the earth for their *i*
Is 27:9 shall the *i* of Jacob be purged
Is 29:20 all that watch for *i* are cut off
Is 30:13 Therefore this *i* shall be to you
Is 31:2 the help of them that work *i*
Is 32:6 villany, and his heart will work *i*
Is 33:24 therein shall be forgiven their *i*
Is 40:2 that her *i* is pardoned
Is 53:6 hath laid on him the *i* of us all
Is 57:17 For the *i* of his covetousness was
Is 59:3 blood, and your fingers with *i*
Is 59:4 mischief, and bring forth *i*
Is 59:6 their works are works of *i*
Is 59:7 their thoughts are thoughts of *i*
Is 64:9 LORD, neither remember *i* for ever
Jer 2:5 What *i* have your fathers found in
Jer 2:22 yet thine *i* is marked before me,
Jer 3:13 Only acknowledge thine *i*, that
Jer 9:5 and weary themselves to commit *i*
Jer 13:22 thine *i* are thy skirts discovered
Jer 14:10 he will now remember their *i*
Jer 14:20 and the *i* of our fathers
Jer 16:10 or what is our *i*
Jer 16:17 neither is their *i* hid from mine
Jer 16:18 first I will recompense their *i*
Jer 18:23 forgive not their *i*, neither blot
Jer 25:12 saith the LORD, for their *i*
Jer 30:14 one, for the multitude of thine *i*
Jer 30:15 for the multitude of thine *i*
Jer 31:30 every one shall die for his own *i*
Jer 31:34 for I will forgive their *i*
Jer 32:18 recompensest the *i* of the fathers
Jer 33:8 cleanse them from all their *i*
Jer 36:3 that I may forgive their *i*
Jer 36:31 seed and his servants for their *i*
Jer 50:20 the *i* of Israel shall be sought
Jer 51:6 be not cut off in her *i*
Lam 2:14 they have not discovered thine *i*
Lam 4:6 For the punishment of the *i* of
Lam 4:22 of thine *i* is accomplished
Lam 4:22 he will visit thine *i*, O daughter
Eze 3:18 wicked man shall die in his *i*
Eze 3:19 wicked way, he shall die in his *i*
Eze 3:20 his righteousness, and commit *i*
Eze 4:4 lay the *i* of the house of Israel
Eze 4:4 upon it thou shalt bear their *i*
Eze 4:5 upon thee the years of their *i*
Eze 4:5 bear the *i* of the house of Israel
Eze 4:6 thou shalt bear the *i* of the
Eze 4:17 and consume away for their *i*
Eze 7:13 himself in the *i* of his life
Eze 7:16 mourning, every one for his *i*
Eze 7:19 is the stumblingblock of their *i*
Eze 9:9 The *i* of the house of Israel and
Eze 14:3 of their *i* before their face
Eze 14:4 of his *i* before his face, and
Eze 14:7 of his *i* before his face, and
Eze 14:10 bear the punishment of their *i*
Eze 16:49 this was the *i* of thy sister
Eze 18:8 hath withdrawn his hand from *i*
Eze 18:17 not die for the *i* of his father
Eze 18:18 lo, even he shall die in his *i*
Eze 18:19 the son bear the *i* of the father
Eze 18:20 not bear the *i* of the father
Eze 18:20 the father bear the *i* of the son
Eze 18:24 righteousness, and committeth *i*
Eze 18:26 righteousness, and committeth *i*
Eze 18:26 for his *i* that he hath done shall
Eze 18:30 so *i* shall not be your ruin
Eze 21:23 he will call to remembrance the *i*
Eze 21:24 have made your *i* to be remembered
Eze 21:25 when *i* shall have an end,
Eze 21:29 when their *i* shall have an end
Eze 28:15 created, till *i* was found in thee
Eze 28:18 by the *i* of thy traffick
Eze 29:16 bringeth their *i* to remembrance
Eze 33:6 them, he is taken away in his *i*
Eze 33:8 wicked man shall die in his *i*
Eze 33:9 his way, he shall die in his *i*
Eze 33:13 own righteousness, and commit *i*
Eze 33:13 but for his *i* that he hath
Eze 33:15 of life, without committing *i*
Eze 33:18 righteousness, and committeth *i*
Eze 35:5 the time that their *i* had an end
Eze 39:23 went into captivity for their *i*
Eze 44:10 they shall even bear their *i*
Eze 44:12 house of Israel to fall into *i*
Eze 44:12 GOD, and they shall bear their *i*
Dan 9:5 have sinned, and have committed *i*
Dan 9:24 and to make reconciliation for *i*
Hos 4:8 they set their heart on their *i*
Hos 5:5 Israel and Ephraim fall in their *i*
Hos 6:8 is a city of them that work *i*
Hos 7:1 then the *i* of Ephraim was
Hos 8:13 now will he remember their *i*
Hos 9:7 mad, for the multitude of thine *i*
Hos 9:9 he will remember their *i*, he will
Hos 10:9 of *i* did not overtake them
Hos 10:13 wickedness, ye have reaped *i*
Hos 12:8 find none *i* in me that were sin
Hos 12:11 Is there *i* in Gilead
Hos 13:12 The *i* of Ephraim is bound up
Hos 14:1 for thou hast fallen by thine *i*
Hos 14:2 say unto him, Take away all *i*
Mic 2:1 Woe to them that devise *i*
Mic 3:10 with blood, and Jerusalem with *i*
Mic 7:18 like unto thee, that pardoneth *i*
Hab 1:3 Why dost thou shew me *i*, and cause
Hab 1:13 evil, and canst not look on *i*
Hab 2:12 blood, and stablisheth a city by *i*
Zeph 3:5 he will not do *i*
Zeph 3:13 remnant of Israel shall not do *i*
Zec 3:4 caused thine *i* to pass from thee
Zec 3:9 I will remove the *i* of that land
Mal 2:6 *i* was not found in his lips
Mal 2:6 and did turn many away from *i*
Mt 7:23 depart from me, ye that work *i*
Mt 13:41 that offend, and them which do *i*
Mt 23:28 ye are full of hypocrisy and *i*
Mt 24:12 because *i* shall abound, the love
Lk 13:27 from me, all ye workers of *i*
Acts 1:18 a field with the reward of *i*
Acts 8:23 bitterness, and in the bond of *i*
Rom 6:19 uncleanness and to *i* unto *i*
1Cor 13:6 Rejoiceth not in *i*, but rejoiceth
2Th 2:7 mystery of *i* doth already work
2Ti 2:19 the name of Christ depart from *i*
Titus 2:14 he might redeem us from all *i*
Heb 1:9 loved righteousness, and hated *i*
Jas 3:6 tongue is a fire, a world of *i*
2Pet 2:16 But was rebuked for his *i*

### INK
Jer 36:18 I wrote them with *i* in the book
2Cor 3:3 by us, written not with *i*
2Jn 12 I would not write with paper and *i*
3Jn 13 to write, but I will not with *i*

### INN
Gen 42:27 give his ass provender in the *i*
Gen 43:21 to pass, when we came to the *i*
Ex 4:24 came to pass by the way in the *i*
Lk 2:7 was no room for them in the *i*
Lk 10:34 own beast, and brought him to an *i*

### INNER
1Kin 6:27 the cherubims within the *i* house
1Kin 6:36 he built the *i* court with three
1Kin 7:12 both for the *i* court of the house
1Kin 7:50 both for the doors of the *i* house
1Kin 20:30 into the city, into an *i* chamber
1Kin 22:25 into an *i* chamber to hide thyself
2Kin 9:2 and carry him to an *i* chamber
1Chr 28:11 of the *i* parlours thereof, and of
2Chr 4:22 the *i* doors thereof for the most
2Chr 18:24 into an *i* chamber to hide thyself
2Chr 29:16 the priests went into the *i* part
Est 4:11 unto the king into the *i* court
Est 5:1 stood in the *i* court of the
Eze 8:3 to the door of the *i* gate
Eze 8:16 he brought me into the *i* court of
Eze 10:3 and the cloud filled the *i* court
Eze 40:15 of the *i* gate were fifty cubits
Eze 40:19 forefront of the *i* court without
Eze 40:23 the gate of the *i* court was over
Eze 40:27 in the *i* court toward the south
Eze 40:28 he brought me to the *i* court by
Eze 40:32 into the *i* court toward the east
Eze 40:44 without the *i* gate were the
Eze 40:44 of the singers in the *i* court
Eze 41:15 hundred cubits, with the *i* temple
Eze 41:17 the door, even unto the *i* house
Eze 42:3 cubits which were for the *i* court
Eze 42:15 an end of measuring the *i* house
Eze 43:5 and brought me into the *i* court
Eze 44:17 in at the gates of the *i* court
Eze 44:17 in the gates of the *i* court
Eze 44:21 when they enter into the *i* court
Eze 44:27 the sanctuary, unto the *i* court
Eze 45:19 posts of the gate of the *i* court
Eze 46:1 The gate of the *i* court that
Acts 16:24 thrust them into the *i* prison
Eph 3:16 might by his Spirit in the *i* man

### INNOCENT
Ex 23:7 and the *i* and righteous slay thou
Deut 19:10 That *i* blood be not shed in thy
Deut 19:13 the guilt of *i* blood from Israel
Deut 21:8 lay not *i* blood unto thy people
Deut 21:9 guilt of *i* blood from among you
Deut 27:25 taketh reward to slay an *i* person
1Sa 19:5 wilt thou sin against *i* blood
1Kin 2:31 thou mayest take away the *i* blood
2Kin 21:16 Manasseh shed *i* blood very much
2Kin 24:4 also for the *i* blood that he shed
2Kin 24:4 he filled Jerusalem with *i* blood
Job 4:7 thee, who ever perished, being *i*
Job 9:23 will laugh at the trial of the *i*
Job 9:28 know that thou wilt not hold me *i*
Job 17:8 the *i* shall stir up himself
Job 22:19 the *i* laugh them to scorn
Job 22:30 shall deliver the island of the *i*
Job 27:17 the *i* shall divide the silver
Job 33:9 without transgression, I am *i*
Ps 10:8 places doth he murder the *i*
Ps 15:5 nor taketh reward against the *i*
Ps 19:13 I shall be *i* from the great
Ps 94:21 righteous, and condemn the *i* blood
Ps 106:38 shed *i* blood, even the blood of
Prov 1:11 privily for the *i* without cause
Prov 6:17 and hands that shed *i* blood
Prov 6:29 toucheth her shall not be *i*
Prov 28:20 haste to be rich shall not be *i*
Is 59:7 they make haste to shed *i* blood
Jer 2:35 Yet thou sayest, Because I am *i*
Jer 7:6 shed not *i* blood in this place,
Jer 22:3 neither shed *i* blood in this
Jer 22:17 and for to shed *i* blood, and for
Jer 26:15 bring *i* blood upon yourselves
Joel 3:19 have shed *i* blood in their land
Jonah 1:14 life, and lay not upon us *i* blood
Mt 27:4 that I have betrayed the *i* blood
Mt 27:24 I am *i* of the blood of this just

### INNUMERABLE
Job 21:33 him, as there are *i* before him
Ps 40:12 For *i* evils have compassed me
Ps 104:25 wherein are things creeping *i*
Jer 46:23 than the grasshoppers, and are *i*
Lk 12:1 together an *i* multitude of people
Heb 11:12 sand which is by the sea shore *i*
Heb 12:22 to an *i* company of angels,

### INSPIRATION
Job 32:8 the *i* of the Almighty giveth them
2Ti 3:16 scripture is given by *i* of God

### INSTANT
Is 29:5 yea, it shall be at an *i* suddenly
Is 30:13 breaking cometh suddenly at an *i*
Jer 18:7 At what *i* I shall speak
Jer 18:9 And at what *i* I shall speak
Lk 2:38 she coming in that *i* gave thanks
Lk 23:23 they were *i* with loud voices,
Rom 12:12 continuing *i* in prayer
2Ti 4:2 be *i* in season, out of season

### INSTRUCT
Deut 4:36 his voice, that he might *i* thee
Neh 9:20 also thy good spirit to *i* them
Job 40:2 with the Almighty *i* him
Ps 16:7 my reins also *i* me in the night
Ps 32:8 I will *i* thee and teach thee in
Song 8:2 my mother's house, who would *i* me
Is 28:26 For his God doth *i* him to
Dan 11:33 among the people shall *i* many
1Cor 2:16 of the Lord, that he may *i* him

### INSTRUCTED
Deut 32:10 he *i* him, he kept him as the
2Kin 12:2 wherein Jehoiada the priest *i* him
1Chr 15:22 he *i* about the song, because he
1Chr 25:7 were *i* in the songs of the LORD
2Chr 3:3 *i* for the building of the house
Job 4:3 Behold, thou hast *i* many, and thou
Ps 2:10 be *i*, ye judges of the earth
Prov 5:13 mine ear to them that *i* me
Prov 21:11 and when the wise is *i*, he
Is 8:11 *i* me that I should not walk in

Is 40:14 took he counsel, and who *i* him
Jer 6:8 Be thou *i*, O Jerusalem, lest my
Jer 31:19 and after that I was *i*, I smote
Mt 13:52 *i* unto the kingdom of heaven is
Mt 14:8 being before *i* of her mother,
Lk 1:4 things, wherein thou hast been *i*
Acts 18:25 This man was *i* in the way of the
Rom 2:18 excellent, being *i* out of the law
Phil 4:12 all things I am *i* both to be full

## INSTRUCTION

Job 33:16 ears of men, and sealeth their *i*
Ps 50:17 Seeing thou hatest *i*, and castest
Prov 1:2 To know wisdom and *i*
Prov 1:3 To receive the *i* of wisdom
Prov 1:7 but fools despise wisdom and *i*
Prov 1:8 hear the *i* of thy father, and
Prov 4:1 the *i* of a father, and attend to
Prov 4:13 Take fast hold of *i*
Prov 5:12 And say, How have I hated *i*
Prov 5:23 He shall die without *i*
Prov 6:23 reproofs of *i* are the way of life
Prov 8:10 Receive my *i*, and not silver
Prov 8:33 Hear *i*, and be wise, and refuse it not
Prov 9:9 Give *i* to a wise man, and he will
Prov 10:17 in the way of life that keepeth *i*
Prov 12:1 Whoso loveth *i* loveth knowledge
Prov 13:1 A wise son heareth his father's *i*
Prov 13:18 shall be to him that refuseth *i*
Prov 15:5 A fool despiseth his father's *i*
Prov 15:32 He that refuseth *i* despiseth his
Prov 15:33 of the LORD is the *i* of wisdom
Prov 16:22 but the *i* of fools is folly
Prov 19:20 Hear counsel, and receive *i*
Prov 19:27 to hear the *i* that causeth to err
Prov 23:12 Apply thine heart unto *i*, and
Prov 23:23 also wisdom, and *i*, and
Prov 24:32 I looked upon it, and received *i*
Jer 17:23 might not hear, nor receive *i*
Jer 32:33 have not hearkened to receive *i*
Jer 35:13 Will ye not receive *i* to hearken
Eze 5:15 be a reproach and a taunt, an *i*
Zeph 3:7 wilt fear me, thou wilt receive *i*
2Ti 3:16 for *i* in righteousness

## INSTRUMENT

Num 35:16 if he smite him with an *i* of iron
Ps 33:2 psaltery and an *i* of ten strings
Ps 92:3 Upon an *i* of ten strings, and upon
Ps 144:9 an *i* of ten strings will I sing
Is 28:27 not threshed with a threshing *i*
Is 41:15 sharp threshing *i* having teeth
Is 54:16 bringeth forth an *i* for his work
Eze 33:32 voice, and can play well on an *i*

## INSTRUMENTS

Gen 49:5 *i* of cruelty are in their
Ex 25:9 the pattern of all the *i* thereof
Num 3:8 they shall keep all the *i* of the
Num 4:12 shall take all the *i* of ministry
Num 4:26 all the *i* of their service, and
Num 4:32 and their cords, with all their *i*
Num 4:32 by name ye shall reckon the *i* of
Num 7:1 it, and all the *i* thereof, both
Num 31:6 to the war, with the holy *i*
1Sa 8:12 harvest, and to make his *i* of war
1Sa 8:12 and *i* of his chariots
1Sa 18:6 with joy, and with *i* of musick
2Sa 6:5 all manner of *i* made of fir wood
2Sa 24:22 burnt sacrifice, and threshing *i*
2Sa 24:22 other *i* of the oxen for wood
1Kin 19:21 flesh with the *i* of the oxen
1Chr 9:29 all the *i* of the sanctuary, and
1Chr 12:33 expert in war, with all *i* of war
1Chr 12:37 with all manner of *i* of war for
1Chr 15:16 be the singers with *i* of musick
1Chr 16:42 a sound, and with musical *i* of God
1Chr 21:23 and the threshing *i* for wood
1Chr 23:5 the LORD with the *i* which I made
1Chr 28:14 for all *i* of all manner of
1Chr 28:14 for all *i* of silver by weight
1Chr 28:14 for all *i* of every kind of
2Chr 4:16 and the fleshhooks, and all their *i*
2Chr 5:1 silver, and the gold, and all the *i*
2Chr 5:13 *i* of musick, and praised the LORD,
2Chr 7:6 also with *i* of musick of the LORD
2Chr 23:13 also the singers with *i* of musick
2Chr 29:26 Levites stood with the *i* of David
2Chr 29:27 with the *i* ordained by David king
2Chr 30:21 singing with loud *i* unto the LORD
2Chr 34:12 that could skill of *i* of musick
Neh 12:36 with the musical *i* of David the
Ps 7:13 prepared for him the *i* of death
Ps 68:25 the players on *i* followed after
Ps 87:7 the players on *i* shall be there
Ps 150:4 praise him with stringed *i*
Eccl 2:8 of the sons of men, as musical *i*
Is 32:7 The *i* also of the churl are evil
Is 38:20 sing my songs to the stringed *i*
Eze 40:42 whereupon also they laid the *i*
Dan 6:18 neither were *i* of musick brought
Amos 1:3 Gilead with threshing *i* of iron
Amos 6:5 invent to themselves *i* of musick
Hab 3:19 the chief singer on my stringed *i*
Zec 11:15 yet the *i* of a foolish shepherd
Rom 6:13 yield ye your members as *i* of
Rom 6:13 the dead, and your members as *i* of

## INSURRECTION

Ezr 4:19 time hath made *i* against kings
Ps 64:2 from the *i* of the workers of
Mk 15:7 them that had made *i* with him
Mk 15:7 who had committed murder in the *i*
Acts 18:12 the Jews made *i* with one accord

## INTEGRITY

Gen 20:5 in the *i* of my heart and innocency
Gen 20:6 didst this in the *i* of thy heart
1Kin 9:4 in *i* of heart, and in uprightness,
Job 2:3 and still he holdeth fast his *i*
Job 2:9 Dost thou still retain thine *i*
Job 27:5 I will not remove mine *i* from me
Job 31:6 balance, that God may know mine *i*
Ps 7:8 according to mine *i* that is in me
Ps 25:21 Let *i* and uprightness preserve me
Ps 26:1 for I have walked in mine *i*
Ps 26:11 as for me, I will walk in mine *i*
Ps 41:12 me, thou upholdest me in mine *i*
Ps 78:72 according to the *i* of his heart
Prov 11:3 The *i* of the upright shall guide
Prov 19:1 is the poor that walketh in his *i*
Prov 20:7 The just man walketh in his *i*

## INTEND

Josh 22:33 did not *i* to go up against them
2Chr 28:13 ye *i* to add more to our sins and
Acts 5:28 *i* to bring this man's blood upon
Acts 5:35 ye *i* to do as touching these men

## INTENT

2Sa 17:14 to the *i* that the LORD might
2Kin 10:19 to the *i* that he might destroy
2Chr 16:1 to the *i* that he might let none
Eze 40:4 for to the *i* that I might shew
Dan 4:17 to the *i* that the living may know
Jn 11:15 there, to the *i* ye may believe
Jn 13:28 for what *i* he spake this unto him
Acts 9:21 and came hither for that *i*
Acts 10:29 for what *i* ye have sent for me
1Cor 10:6 to the *i* we should not lust after
Eph 3:10 To the *i* that now unto the

## INTERCESSION

Is 53:12 made *i* for the transgressors
Jer 7:16 for them, neither make *i* to me
Jer 27:18 let them now make *i* to the LORD
Jer 36:25 Gemariah had made *i* to the king
Rom 8:26 *i* for us with groanings which
Rom 8:27 because he maketh *i* for the
Rom 8:34 of God, who also maketh *i* for us
Rom 11:2 how he maketh *i* to God against
Heb 7:25 he ever liveth to make *i* for them

## INTERPRET

Gen 41:8 that could *i* them unto Pharaoh
Gen 41:12 according to his dream he did *i*
Gen 41:15 and there is none that can *i* it
Gen 41:15 canst understand a dream to *i* it
1Cor 12:30 do all *i*?
1Cor 14:5 with tongues, except he *i*
1Cor 14:13 unknown tongue pray that he may *i*
1Cor 14:27 and let one *i*

## INTERPRETATION

Gen 40:5 according to the *i* of his dream
Gen 40:12 unto him, This is the *i* of it
Gen 40:16 baker saw that the *i* was good
Gen 40:18 and said, This is the *i* thereof
Gen 41:11 according to the *i* of his dream
Judg 7:15 the *i* thereof, that he worshipped
Prov 1:6 To understand a proverb, and the *i*
Eccl 8:1 and who knoweth the *i* of a thing
Dan 2:4 the dream, and we will shew the *i*
Dan 2:5 me the dream, with the *i* thereof
Dan 2:6 the *i* thereof, ye shall receive
Dan 2:6 me the dream, and the *i* thereof
Dan 2:7 and we will shew the *i* of it
Dan 2:9 that ye can shew me the *i* thereof
Dan 2:16 that he would shew the king the *i*
Dan 2:24 I will shew unto the king the *i*
Dan 2:25 make known unto the king the *i*
Dan 2:26 I have seen, and the *i* thereof
Dan 2:30 make known the *i* to the king
Dan 2:36 we will tell the *i* thereof before
Dan 2:45 is certain, and the *i* thereof sure
Dan 4:6 known unto me the *i* of the dream
Dan 4:7 make known unto me the *i* thereof
Dan 4:9 I have seen, and the *i* thereof
Dan 4:18 declare the *i* thereof, forasmuch
Dan 4:18 able to make known unto me the *i*
Dan 4:19 or the *i* thereof, trouble thee
Dan 4:19 the *i* thereof to thine enemies
Dan 4:24 This is the *i*, O king, and this is
Dan 5:7 writing, and shew me the *i* thereof
Dan 5:8 known to the king the *i* thereof
Dan 5:12 be called, and he will shew the *i*
Dan 5:15 make known unto me the *i* thereof
Dan 5:15 could not shew the *i* of the thing
Dan 5:16 and make known to me the *i* thereof
Dan 5:17 king, and make known to him the *i*
Dan 5:26 This is the *i* of the thing
Dan 7:16 made me know the *i* of the things
Jn 1:42 be called Cephas, which is by *i*
Jn 9:7 pool of Siloam, (which is by *i*
Acts 9:36 which by *i* is called Dorcas
Acts 13:8 is his name by *i*) withstood them
1Cor 12:10 to another the *i* of tongues
1Cor 14:26 hath a revelation, hath an *i*
Heb 7:2 first being by *i* King of
2Pet 1:20 the scripture is of any private *i*

## INTERPRETED

Gen 40:22 as Joseph had *i* to them
Gen 41:12 him, and he *i* to us our dreams
Gen 41:13 And it came to pass, as he *i* to us
Ezr 4:7 tongue, and *i* in the Syrian tongue
Mt 1:23 name Emmanuel, which being *i* is
Mk 5:41 which is, being *i*, Damsel, I say
Mk 15:22 place Golgotha, which is, being *i*
Mk 15:34 which is, being *i*, My God, my God
Jn 1:38 Rabbi, (which is to say, being *i*
Jn 1:41 the Messias, which is, being *i*
Acts 4:36 Barnabas, (which is, being *i*

## INTERPRETER

Gen 40:8 a dream, and there is no *i* of it
Gen 42:23 for he spake unto them by an *i*
Job 33:23 be a messenger with him, an *i*
1Cor 14:28 But if there be no *i*, let him

## INTREAT

Gen 23:8 *i* for me to Ephron the son of
Ex 8:8 *I* the LORD, that he may take away
Ex 8:9 when shall I *i* for thee, and for
Ex 8:28 very far away: *i* for me
Ex 8:29 I will *i* the LORD that the swarms
Ex 9:28 *I* the LORD (for it is enough)
Ex 10:17 *i* the LORD your God, that he may
Ruth 1:16 *I* me not to leave thee, or to
1Sa 2:25 the LORD, who shall *i* for him
1Kin 13:6 *I* now the face of the LORD thy
Ps 45:12 the people shall *i* thy favour
Prov 19:6 Many will *i* the favour of the
1Cor 4:13 Being defamed, we *i*
Phil 4:3 I *i* thee also, true yokefellow,
1Ti 5:1 an elder, but *i* him as a father

## INTREATED

Gen 25:21 Isaac *i* the LORD for his wife,
Gen 25:21 and the LORD was *i* of him, and
Ex 8:30 out from Pharaoh, and *i* the LORD
Ex 10:18 out from Pharaoh, and *i* the LORD
Judg 13:8 Then Manoah *i* the LORD, and said,
2Sa 21:14 after that God was *i* for the land
2Sa 24:25 So the LORD was *i* for the land
1Chr 5:20 the battle, and he was *i* of them
2Chr 33:13 and he was *i* of him, and heard his
2Chr 33:19 also, and how God was *i* of him
Ezr 8:23 and he was *i* of us
Job 19:16 I *i* him with my mouth
Job 19:17 though I *i* for the children's
Ps 119:58 I *i* thy favour with my whole
Is 19:22 LORD, and he shall be *i* of them
Lk 15:28 came his father out, and *i* him
Heb 12:19 *i* that the word should not be
Jas 3:17 gentle, and easy to be *i*, full of

**INVADED**
1Sa 23:27 the Philistines have *i* the land
1Sa 27:8 *i* the Geshurites, and the Gezrites
1Sa 30:1 the Amalekites had *i* the south
2Kin 13:20 the bands of the Moabites *i* the
2Chr 28:18 The Philistines also had *i* the

**INVENTIONS**
Ps 99:8 thou tookest vengeance of their *i*
Ps 106:29 him to anger with their *i*
Ps 106:39 went a whoring with their own *i*
Prov 8:12 and find out knowledge of witty *i*
Eccl 7:29 but they have sought out many *i*

**INVISIBLE**
Rom 1:20 For the *i* things of him from the
Col 1:15 Who is the image of the *i* God
Col 1:16 that are in earth, visible and *i*
1Ti 1:17 the King eternal, immortal, *i*
Heb 11:27 endured, as seeing him who is *i*

**INWARD**
Ex 28:26 is in the side of the ephod *i*
Ex 39:19 was on the side of the ephod *i*
Lev 13:55 it is fret *i*, whether it be bare
2Sa 5:9 built round about from Millo and *i*
1Kin 7:25 and all their hinder parts were *i*
2Chr 3:13 their feet, and their faces were *i*
2Chr 4:4 and all their hinder parts were *i*
Job 19:19 All my *i* friends abhorred me
Job 38:36 hath put wisdom in the *i* parts
Ps 5:9 their *i* part is very wickedness
Ps 49:11 Their *i* thought is, that their
Ps 51:6 desirest truth in the *i* parts
Ps 64:6 both the *i* thought of every one
Prov 20:27 searching all the *i* parts of the
Prov 20:30 so do stripes the *i* parts of the
Is 16:11 mine *i* parts for Kir-haresh
Jer 31:33 will put my law in their *i* parts
Eze 40:9 and the porch of the gate was *i*
Eze 40:16 and windows were round about *i*
Eze 41:3 Then went he *i*, and measured the
Eze 42:4 a walk of ten cubits breadth *i*
Lk 11:39 but your *i* part is full of
Rom 7:22 in the law of God after the *i* man
2Cor 4:16 yet the *i* man is renewed day by
2Cor 7:15 his *i* affection is more abundant

**INWARDS**
Ex 29:13 all the fat that covereth the *i*
Ex 29:17 in pieces, and wash the *i* of him
Ex 29:22 and the fat that covereth the *i*
Lev 1:9 But his *i* and his legs shall he
Lev 1:13 But he shall wash the *i* and the
Lev 3:3 the fat that covereth the *i*
Lev 3:3 and all the fat that is upon the *i*
Lev 3:9 and the fat that covereth the *i*
Lev 3:9 and all the fat that is upon the *i*
Lev 3:14 the fat that covereth the *i*
Lev 3:14 and all the fat that is upon the *i*
Lev 4:8 the fat that covereth the *i*
Lev 4:8 and all the fat that is upon the *i*
Lev 4:11 head, and with his legs, and his *i*
Lev 7:3 and the fat that covereth the *i*
Lev 8:16 all the fat that was upon the *i*
Lev 8:21 And he washed the *i* and the legs in
Lev 8:25 all the fat that was upon the *i*
Lev 9:14 And he did wash the *i* and the legs,
Lev 9:19 and that which covereth the *i*

**IPHEDEIAH** *(if-e-di'-ah) A son of Shashak.*
1Chr 8:25 And *I*, and Penuel, the sons of

**IR** *(ur)* See IR-NAHASH, IR-SHEMESH. *Father of Machir.*
1Chr 7:12 and Huppim, the children of *I*

**IRA** *(i'-rah)*
*1. An officer of David.*
2Sa 20:26 *I* also the Jairite was a chief
*2. A mighty man of David.*
2Sa 23:26 *I* the son of Ikkesh the Tekoite,
2Sa 23:38 *I* an Ithrite, Gareb an Ithrite,
1Chr 11:28 *I* the son of Ikkesh the Tekoite,
1Chr 11:40 *I* the Ithrite, Gareb the Ithrite,
1Chr 27:9 *I* the son of Ikkesh the Tekoite

**IRAD** *(i'-rad) Son of Enoch.*
Gen 4:18 And unto Enoch was born *I*
Gen 4:18 and *I* begat Mehujael

**IRAM** *(i'-ram) An Edomite leader.*
Gen 36:43 Duke Magdiel, duke *I*
1Chr 1:54 Duke Magdiel, duke *I*

**IRI** *(i'-ri) A son of Bela.*
1Chr 7:7 and Uzziel, and Jerimoth, and *I*

**IRIJAH** *(i-ri'-jah) A captain of the guard.*
Jer 37:13 ward was there, whose name was *I*
Jer 37:14 so *I* took Jeremiah, and brought

**IR-NAHASH** *(ur-na'-hash) A descendant of Chelub.*
1Chr 4:12 and Tehinnah the father of *I*

**IRON** *(i'-ron) A city in Naphtali.*
Josh 19:38 And *I*, and Migdal-el, Horem, and
Gen 4:22 of every artificer in brass and *i*
Lev 26:19 and I will make your heaven as *i*
Num 31:22 and the silver, the brass, the *i*
Num 35:16 smite him with an instrument of *i*
Deut 3:11 his bedstead was a bedstead of *i*
Deut 4:20 you forth out of the *i* furnace
Deut 8:9 a land whose stones are *i*
Deut 27:5 not lift up any *i* tool upon them
Deut 28:23 that is under thee shall be *i*
Deut 28:48 put a yoke of *i* upon thy neck
Deut 33:25 Thy shoes shall be *i* and brass
Josh 6:19 and gold, and vessels of brass and *i*
Josh 6:24 and the vessels of brass and of *i*
Josh 8:31 which no man hath lift up any *i*
Josh 17:16 of the valley have chariots of *i*
Josh 17:18 though they have *i* chariots
Josh 22:8 gold, and with brass, and with *i*
Judg 1:19 because they had chariots of *i*
Judg 4:3 he had nine hundred chariots of *i*
Judg 4:13 even nine hundred chariots of *i*
1Sa 17:7 weighed six hundred shekels of *i*
2Sa 12:31 of iron, and under axes of *i*
2Sa 23:7 touch them must be fenced with *i*
1Kin 6:7 any tool of *i* heard in the house
1Kin 8:51 the midst of the furnace of *i*
1Kin 22:11 of Chenaanah made him horns of *i*
2Kin 6:6 and the *i* did swim
1Chr 20:3 with saws, and with harrows of *i*
1Chr 22:3 David prepared *i* in abundance for
1Chr 22:14 and of brass and *i* without weight
1Chr 22:16 silver, and the brass, and the *i*
1Chr 29:2 the *i* for things of iron, and wood
1Chr 29:2 brass, the iron for things of *i*
1Chr 29:7 one hundred thousand talents of *i*
2Chr 2:7 in silver, and in brass, and in *i*
2Chr 2:14 and in silver, in brass, in *i*
2Chr 18:10 Chenaanah had made him horns of *i*
2Chr 24:12 LORD, and also such as wrought *i*
Job 19:24 they were graven with an *i* pen
Job 20:24 He shall flee from the *i* weapon
Job 28:2 *I* is taken out of the earth, and
Job 40:18 his bones are like bars of *i*
Job 41:27 He esteemeth *i* as straw, and brass
Ps 2:9 shalt break them with a rod of *i*
Ps 105:18 he was laid in *i*
Ps 107:10 being bound in affliction and *i*
Ps 107:16 and cut the bars of *i* in sunder
Ps 149:8 and their nobles with fetters of *i*
Prov 27:17 *I* sharpeneth iron
Prov 27:17 Iron sharpeneth *i*
Eccl 10:10 If the *i* be blunt, and he do not
Is 10:34 the thickets of the forest with *i*
Is 45:2 and cut in sunder the bars of *i*
Is 48:4 and thy neck is an *i* sinew
Is 60:17 for *i* I will bring silver, and for
Is 60:17 for wood brass, and for stones *i*
Jer 1:18 an *i* pillar, and brasen walls
Jer 6:28 they are brass and *i*
Jer 11:4 land of Egypt, from the *i* furnace
Jer 15:12 Shall *i* break the northern iron
Jer 15:12 Shall iron break the northern *i*
Jer 17:1 Judah is written with a pen of *i*
Jer 28:13 shalt make for them yokes of *i*
Jer 28:14 I have put a yoke of *i* upon the
Eze 4:3 take thou unto thee an *i* pan
Eze 4:3 it for a wall of *i* between thee
Eze 22:18 all they are brass, and tin, and *i*
Eze 22:20 gather silver, and brass, and *i*
Eze 27:12 with silver, *i*, tin, and lead,
Eze 27:19 bright *i*, cassia, and calamus,
Dan 2:33 legs of iron, his feet part of *i*
Dan 2:34 upon his feet that were of *i*
Dan 2:35 Then was the *i*, the clay, the
Dan 2:40 kingdom shall be strong as *i*
Dan 2:40 forasmuch as *i* breaketh in pieces
Dan 2:40 as *i* that breaketh all these,
Dan 2:41 of potters' clay, and part of *i*
Dan 2:41 be in it of the strength of the *i*
Dan 2:41 sawest the *i* mixed with miry clay
Dan 2:42 toes of the feet were part of *i*
Dan 2:43 whereas thou sawest *i* mixed with
Dan 2:43 even as *i* is not mixed with clay
Dan 2:45 and that it brake in pieces the *i*
Dan 4:15 the earth, even with a band of *i*
Dan 4:23 the earth, even with a band of *i*
Dan 5:4 and of silver, of brass, of *i*
Dan 5:23 of silver, and gold, of brass, *i*
Dan 7:7 and it had great *i* teeth
Dan 7:19 dreadful, whose teeth were of *i*
Amos 1:3 with threshing instruments of *i*
Mic 4:13 for I will make thine horn *i*
Acts 12:10 they came unto the *i* gate that
1Ti 4:2 conscience seared with a hot *i*
Rev 2:27 shall rule them with a rod of *i*
Rev 9:9 as it were breastplates of *i*
Rev 12:5 rule all nations with a rod of *i*
Rev 18:12 precious wood, and of brass, and *i*
Rev 19:15 shall rule them with a rod of *i*

**IRPEEL** *(ur'-pe-el) A city in Benjamin.*
Josh 18:27 And Rekem, and *I*, and Taralah,

**IR-SHEMESH** *(ur-she'-mesh) A city in Dan.*
Josh 19:41 was Zorah, and Eshtaol, and *I*

**IRU** *(i'-ru) A son of Caleb.*
1Chr 4:15 *I*, Elah, and Naam

**ISAAC** *(i'-za-ak)* See ISAAC'S. *Son of Abraham and Sarah.*
Gen 17:19 and thou shalt call his name *I*
Gen 17:21 covenant will I establish with *I*
Gen 21:3 him, whom Sarah bare to him, *I*
Gen 21:4 his son *I* being eight days old
Gen 21:5 when his son *I* was born unto him
Gen 21:8 the same day that *I* was weaned
Gen 21:10 be heir with my son, even with *I*
Gen 21:12 for in *I* shall thy seed be called
Gen 22:2 now thy son, thine only son *I*
Gen 22:3 *I* his son, and clave the wood for
Gen 22:6 and laid it upon *I* his son
Gen 22:7 *I* spake unto Abraham his father,
Gen 22:9 bound *I* his son, and laid him on
Gen 24:4 and take a wife unto my son *I*
Gen 24:14 hast appointed for thy servant *I*
Gen 24:62 *I* came from the way of the well
Gen 24:63 *I* went out to meditate in the
Gen 24:64 up her eyes, and when she saw *I*
Gen 24:66 the servant told *I* all things
Gen 24:67 *I* brought her into his mother
Gen 24:67 *I* was comforted after his
Gen 25:5 gave all that he had unto *I*
Gen 25:6 and sent them away from *I* his son
Gen 25:9 And his sons *I* and Ishmael buried
Gen 25:11 that God blessed his son *I*
Gen 25:11 *I* dwelt by the well Lahai-roi
Gen 25:19 And these are the generations of *I*
Gen 25:19 Abraham begat *I*
Gen 25:20 *I* was forty years old when he
Gen 25:21 *I* intreated the LORD for his wife
Gen 25:26 *I* was threescore years old when
Gen 25:28 *I* loved Esau, because he did eat
Gen 26:1 *I* went unto Abimelech king of the
Gen 26:6 And *I* dwelt in Gerar
Gen 26:8 *I* was sporting with Rebekah his
Gen 26:9 And Abimelech called *I*, and said,
Gen 26:9 *I* said unto him, Because I said,
Gen 26:12 Then *I* sowed in that land, and
Gen 26:16 And Abimelech said unto *I*, Go from
Gen 26:17 *I* departed thence, and pitched his
Gen 26:18 *I* digged again the wells of water
Gen 26:27 *I* said unto them, Wherefore come
Gen 26:31 *I* sent them away, and they
Gen 26:35 Which were a grief of mind unto *I*
Gen 27:1 came to pass, that when *I* was old
Gen 27:5 Rebekah heard when *I* spake to
Gen 27:20 *I* said unto his son, How is it
Gen 27:21 *I* said unto Jacob, Come near, I
Gen 27:22 Jacob went near unto *I* his father
Gen 27:26 his father *I* said unto him, Come
Gen 27:30 as soon as *I* had made an end of
Gen 27:30 from the presence of *I* his father
Gen 27:32 *I* his father said unto him, Who
Gen 27:33 *I* trembled very exceedingly, and
Gen 27:37 *I* answered and said unto Esau,
Gen 27:39 *I* his father answered and said
Gen 27:46 And Rebekah said to *I*, I am weary
Gen 28:1 *I* called Jacob, and blessed him,
Gen 28:5 And *I* sent away Jacob
Gen 28:6 Esau saw that *I* had blessed Jacob

Gen 28:8 Canaan pleased not *I* his father
Gen 28:13 thy father, and the God of *I*
Gen 31:18 for to go to *I* his father in the
Gen 31:42 God of Abraham, and the fear of *I*
Gen 31:53 sware by the fear of his father *I*
Gen 32:9 Abraham, and God of my father *I*
Gen 35:12 land which I gave Abraham and *I*
Gen 35:27 Jacob came unto *I* his father unto
Gen 35:27 where Abraham and *I* sojourned
Gen 35:28 the days of *I* were an hundred and
Gen 35:29 *I* gave up the ghost, and died, and
Gen 46:1 unto the God of his father *I*
Gen 48:15 *I* did walk, the God which fed me
Gen 48:16 name of my fathers Abraham and *I*
Gen 49:31 there they buried *I* and Rebekah
Gen 50:24 which he sware to Abraham, to *I*
Ex 2:24 his covenant with Abraham, with *I*
Ex 3:6 the God of Abraham, the God of *I*
Ex 3:15 the God of Abraham, the God of *I*
Ex 3:16 fathers, the God of Abraham, of *I*
Ex 4:5 the God of Abraham, the God of *I*
Ex 6:3 I appeared unto Abraham, unto *I*
Ex 6:8 swear to give it to Abraham, to *I*
Ex 32:13 Remember Abraham, *I*, and Israel,
Ex 33:1 which I sware unto Abraham, to *I*
Lev 26:42 Jacob, and also my covenant with *I*
Num 32:11 I sware unto Abraham, unto *I*
Deut 1:8 unto your fathers, Abraham, *I*
Deut 6:10 thy fathers, to Abraham, to *I*
Deut 9:5 unto thy fathers, Abraham, *I*
Deut 9:27 Remember thy servants, Abraham, *I*
Deut 29:13 thy fathers, to Abraham, to *I*
Deut 30:20 thy fathers, to Abraham, to *I*
Deut 34:4 I sware unto Abraham, unto *I*
Josh 24:3 his seed, and gave him *I*
Josh 24:4 And I gave unto *I* Jacob and Esau
1Kin 18:36 and said, LORD God of Abraham, *I*
2Kin 13:23 of his covenant with Abraham, *I*
1Chr 1:28 *I*, and Ishmael
1Chr 1:34 And Abraham begat *I*
1Chr 1:34 The sons of *I*
1Chr 16:16 Abraham, and of his oath unto *I*
1Chr 29:18 O LORD God of Abraham, *I*, and of
2Chr 30:6 unto the LORD God of Abraham, *I*
Ps 105:9 with Abraham, and his oath unto *I*
Jer 33:26 over the seed of Abraham, *I*
Amos 7:9 places of *I* shall be desolate
Amos 7:16 thy word against the house of *I*
Mt 1:2 Abraham begat *I*
Mt 1:2 and *I* begat Jacob
Mt 8:11 shall sit down with Abraham, and *I*
Mt 22:32 God of Abraham, and the God of *I*
Mk 12:26 God of Abraham, and the God of *I*
Lk 3:34 of Jacob, which was the son of *I*
Lk 13:28 when ye shall see Abraham, and *I*
Lk 20:37 God of Abraham, and the God of *I*
Acts 3:13 The God of Abraham, and of *I*
Acts 7:8 and so Abraham begat *I*
Acts 7:8 and *I* begat Jacob
Acts 7:32 God of Abraham, and the God of *I*
Rom 9:7 In *I* shall thy seed be called
Rom 9:10 by one, even by our father *I*
Gal 4:28 as *I* was, are the children of
Heb 11:9 dwelling in tabernacles with *I*
Heb 11:17 when he was tried, offered up *I*
Heb 11:18 That in *I* shall thy seed be
Heb 11:20 By faith *I* blessed Jacob and Esau
Jas 2:21 when he had offered *I* his son

**ISAAC'S** *(i'-za-aks)*
Gen 26:19 *I* servants digged in the valley,
Gen 26:20 Gerar did strive with *I* herdmen
Gen 26:25 there *I* servants digged a well
Gen 26:32 that *I* servants came, and told him

**ISAIAH** *(i-za'-yah)* See ESAIAS. *A prophet.*
2Kin 19:2 to *I* the prophet the son of Amoz
2Kin 19:5 of king Hezekiah came to *I*
2Kin 19:6 *I* said unto them, Thus shall ye
2Kin 19:20 Then *I* the son of Amoz sent to
2Kin 20:1 the prophet *I* the son of Amoz
2Kin 20:4 afore *I* was gone out into the
2Kin 20:7 *I* said, Take a lump of figs
2Kin 20:8 And Hezekiah said unto *I*, What
2Kin 20:9 *I* said, This sign shalt thou have
2Kin 20:11 *I* the prophet cried unto the LORD
2Kin 20:14 Then came *I* the prophet unto king
2Kin 20:16 *I* said unto Hezekiah, Hear the
2Kin 20:19 Then said Hezekiah unto *I*
2Chr 26:22 did *I* the prophet, the son of
2Chr 32:20 the prophet *I* the son of Amoz,
2Chr 32:32 in the vision of *I* the prophet
Is 1:1 The vision of *I* the son of Amoz,
Is 2:1 The word that *I* the son of Amoz
Is 7:3 Then said the LORD unto *I*
Is 13:1 which *I* the son of Amoz did see
Is 20:2 the LORD by *I* the son of Amoz
Is 20:3 as my servant *I* hath walked naked
Is 37:2 unto *I* the prophet the son of
Is 37:5 of king Hezekiah came to *I*
Is 37:6 *I* said unto them, Thus shall ye
Is 37:21 Then *I* the son of Amoz sent unto
Is 38:1 *I* the prophet the son of Amoz
Is 38:4 came the word of the LORD to *I*
Is 38:21 For *I* had said, Let them take a
Is 39:3 Then came *I* the prophet unto king
Is 39:5 Then said *I* to Hezekiah, Hear the
Is 39:8 Then said Hezekiah to *I*, Good is

**ISCAH** *(is'-cah)* See SARAH. *A daughter of Haran.*
Gen 11:29 of Milcah, and the father of *I*

**ISCARIOT** *(is-car'-e-ot)* See JUDAS. *Disciple who betrayed Jesus.*
Mt 10:4 Simon the Canaanite, and Judas *I*
Mt 26:14 one of the twelve, called Judas *I*
Mk 3:19 And Judas *I*, which also betrayed
Mk 14:10 And Judas *I*, one of the twelve,
Lk 6:16 the brother of James, and Judas *I*
Lk 22:3 Satan into Judas surnamed *I*
Jn 6:71 spake of Judas *I* the son of Simon
Jn 12:4 one of his disciples, Judas *I*
Jn 13:2 now put into the heart of Judas *I*
Jn 13:26 the sop, he gave it to Judas *I*
Jn 14:22 Judas saith unto him, not *I*

**ISHBAH** *(ish'-bah) Father of Eshtemoa.*
1Chr 4:17 and *I* the father of Eshtemoa

**ISHBAK** *(ish'-bak) A son of Abraham.*
Gen 25:2 and Medan, and Midian, and *I*
1Chr 1:32 and Medan, and Midian, and *I*

**ISHBI-BENOB** *(ish'-bi-be'-nob) A Philistine giant.*
2Sa 21:16 And *I*, which was of the sons of

**ISH-BOSHETH** *(ish-bo'-sheth)* See ESH-BAAL. *Son of Saul.*
2Sa 2:8 took *I* the son of Saul, and
2Sa 2:10 *I* Saul's son was forty years old
2Sa 2:12 the servants of *I* the son of Saul
2Sa 2:15 pertained to *I* the son of Saul
2Sa 3:7 *I* said to Abner, Wherefore hast
2Sa 3:8 very wroth for the words of *I*
2Sa 3:14 sent messengers to *I* Saul's son
2Sa 3:15 *I* sent, and took her from her
2Sa 4:5 heat of the day to the house of *I*
2Sa 4:8 head of *I* unto David to Hebron
2Sa 4:8 Behold the head of *I* the son of
2Sa 4:12 But they took the head of *I*

**ISHI** *(i'-shi)*
*1. A descendant of Pharez.*
1Chr 2:31 sons of Appaim; *I*
1Chr 2:31 And the sons of *I*
*2. A descendant of Judah.*
1Chr 4:20 And the sons of *I* were, Zoheth, and
*3. A Simeonite.*
1Chr 4:42 and Uzziel, the sons of *I*
*4. A chief of Manasseh.*
1Chr 5:24 their fathers, even Epher, and *I*
*5. A symbolic name for Israel.*
Hos 2:16 LORD, that thou shalt call me *I*

**ISHIAH** *(i-shi'-ah)* See ISHIJAH, ISSHIAH. *A son of Izrahiah.*
1Chr 7:3 Michael, and Obadiah, and Joel, *I*

**ISHIJAH** *(i-shi'-jah)* See ISHIAH, JESIAH. *Married a foreigner in exile.*
Ezr 10:31 Eliezer, *I*, Malchiah, Shemaiah,

**ISHMA** *(ish'-mah) A descendant of Caleb.*
1Chr 4:3 Jezreel, and *I*, and Idbash

**ISHMAEL** *(ish'-ma-el)* See ISHMAELITE, ISHMAEL'S.
*1. Son of Abraham and Hagar.*
Gen 16:11 a son, and shalt call his name *I*
Gen 16:15 son's name, which Hagar bare, *I*
Gen 16:16 old, when Hagar bare *I* to Abram
Gen 17:18 O that *I* might live before thee
Gen 17:20 And as for *I*, I have heard thee
Gen 17:23 And Abraham took *I* his son
Gen 17:25 *I* his son was thirteen years old,
Gen 17:26 Abraham circumcised, and *I* his son
Gen 25:9 *I* buried him in the cave of
Gen 25:12 these are the generations of *I*
Gen 25:13 are the names of the sons of *I*
Gen 25:13 the firstborn of *I*, Nebajoth
Gen 25:16 These are the sons of *I*, and these
Gen 25:17 are the years of the life of *I*
Gen 28:9 Then went Esau unto *I*, and took
Gen 28:9 the daughter of *I* Abraham's son
1Chr 1:28 Isaac, and *I*
1Chr 1:29 The firstborn of *I*, Nebaioth
1Chr 1:31 These are the sons of *I*
*2. A ruler of Judah.*
2Chr 19:11 and Zebadiah the son of *I*, the
*3. Son of Azel.*
1Chr 8:38 are these, Azrikam, Bocheru, and *I*
1Chr 9:44 are these, Azrikam, Bocheru, and *I*
*4. A captain who aided Joash.*
2Chr 23:1 *I* the son of Jehohanan, and
*5. Married a foreigner in exile.*
Ezr 10:22 Elioenai, Maaseiah, *I*, Nethaneel,
*6. The son of Nethaniah.*
2Kin 25:23 even *I* the son of Nethaniah, and
2Kin 25:25 that *I* the son of Nethaniah, the
Jer 40:8 even *I* the son of Nethaniah, and
Jer 40:14 *I* the son of Nethaniah to slay
Jer 40:15 thee, and I will slay *I* the son of
Jer 40:16 for thou speakest falsely of *I*
Jer 41:1 that *I* the son of Nethaniah the
Jer 41:2 Then arose *I* the son of Nethaniah
Jer 41:3 *I* also slew all the Jews that
Jer 41:6 *I* the son of Nethaniah went forth
Jer 41:7 that *I* the son of Nethaniah slew
Jer 41:8 found among them that said unto *I*
Jer 41:9 Now the pit wherein *I* had cast
Jer 41:9 *I* the son of Nethaniah filled it
Jer 41:10 Then *I* carried away captive all
Jer 41:10 *I* the son of Nethaniah carried
Jer 41:11 heard of all the evil that *I* the
Jer 41:12 went to fight with *I* the son of
Jer 41:13 *I* saw Johanan the son of Kareah
Jer 41:14 So all the people that *I* had
Jer 41:15 But *I* the son of Nethaniah
Jer 41:16 from *I* the son of Nethaniah
Jer 41:18 because *I* the son of Nethaniah

**ISHMAELITE** *(ish'-ma-el-ite) Descendants of Ishmael 1.*
1Chr 27:30 the camels also was Obil the *I*

**ISHMAELITES** *(ish'-ma-el-lites)* See ISH-MEELITES.
Judg 8:24 earrings, because they were *I*
Ps 83:6 The tabernacles of Edom, and the *I*

**ISHMAEL'S** *(ish'-ma-els) Refers to Ishmael 1.*
Gen 36:3 And Bashemath *I* daughter, sister

**ISHMAIAH** *(ish-ma-i'-ah)* See ISMAIAH. *A prince of Zebulun.*
1Chr 27:19 Of Zebulun, *I* the son of Obadiah

**ISHMEELITE** *(ish'-me-el-ite)* See ISHMA-ELITE, ISHMEELITES. *Same as Ishmaelite.*
1Chr 2:17 father of Amasa was Jether the *I*

**ISHMEELITES** *(ish'-me-el-ites)* See ISH-MAELITES.
Gen 37:25 a company of *I* came from Gilead
Gen 37:27 Come, and let us sell him to the *I*
Gen 37:28 sold Joseph to the *I* for twenty
Gen 39:1 bought him of the hands of the *I*

**ISHMERAI** *(ish'-me-rahee) A chief of Benjamin.*
1Chr 8:18 *I* also, and Jezliah, and Jobab, the

**ISHOD** *(i'-shod) A son of Hammoleketh.*
1Chr 7:18 And his sister Hammoleketh bare *I*

**ISHPAN** *(ish'-pan) A son of Shashak.*
1Chr 8:22 And *I*, and Heber, and Eliel,

**ISH-TOB** *(ish'-tob) A district of Aram.*
2Sa 10:6 men, and of *I* twelve thousand men
2Sa 10:8 of Zoba, and of Rehob, and *I*

**ISHUAH** *(ish'-u-ah)* See ISUAH. *A son of Asher.*
Gen 46:17 Jimnah, and *I*, and Isui, and Beriah,

**ISHUAI**
1Chr 7:30 Imnah, and Isuah, and *I*, and Beriah,

**ISHUI** *(ish'-u-i)* See ISHUAI, JESUI. *A son of Saul.*
1Sa 14:49 sons of Saul were Jonathan, and *I*

## ISLAND
Job 22:30 deliver the *i* of the innocent
Is 34:14 with the wild beasts of the *i*
Acts 27:16 certain *i* which is called Clauda
Acts 27:26 we must be cast upon a certain *i*
Acts 28:1 knew that the *i* was called Melita
Acts 28:7 of the chief man of the *i*
Acts 28:9 also, which had diseases in the *i*
Rev 6:14 *i* were moved out of their places
Rev 16:20 every *i* fled away, and the

## ISLANDS
Is 11:11 Hamath, and from the *i* of the sea
Is 13:22 the wild beasts of the *i* shall
Is 41:1 Keep silence before me, O *i*
Is 42:12 and declare his praise in the *i*
Is 42:15 and I will make the rivers *i*
Is 59:18 to the *i* he will repay recompence
Jer 50:39 beasts of the *i* shall dwell there

## ISLE
Is 20:6 of this *i* shall say in that day
Is 23:2 Be still, ye inhabitants of the *i*
Is 23:6 howl, ye inhabitants of the *i*
Acts 13:6 gone through the *i* unto Paphos
Acts 28:11 which had wintered in the *i*
Rev 1:9 was in the *i* that is called

## ISLES
Gen 10:5 By these were the *i* of the
Est 10:1 land, and upon the *i* of the sea
Ps 72:10 of the *i* shall bring presents
Ps 97:1 multitude of *i* be glad thereof
Is 24:15 God of Israel in the *i* of the sea
Is 40:15 he taketh up the *i* as a very
Is 41:5 The *i* saw it, and feared
Is 42:4 the *i* shall wait for his law
Is 42:10 the *i*, and the inhabitants thereof
Is 49:1 Listen, O *i*, unto me
Is 51:5 the *i* shall wait upon me, and on
Is 60:9 Surely the *i* shall wait for me,
Is 66:19 to the *i* afar off, that have not
Jer 2:10 For pass over the *i* of Chittim
Jer 25:22 the kings of the *i* which are
Jer 31:10 and declare it in the *i* afar off
Eze 26:15 Shall not the *i* shake at the
Eze 26:18 Now shall the *i* tremble in the
Eze 26:18 the *i* that are in the sea shall
Eze 27:3 merchant of the people for many *i*
Eze 27:6 brought out of the *i* of Chittim
Eze 27:7 purple from the *i* of Elishah was
Eze 27:15 many *i* were the merchandise of
Eze 27:35 All the inhabitants of the *i*
Eze 39:6 that dwell carelessly in the *i*
Dan 11:18 shall he turn his face unto the *i*
Zeph 2:11 even all the *i* of the heathen

**ISMACHIAH** *(is-ma-ki'-ah) A temple servant.*
2Chr 31:13 and Jozabad, and Eliel, and *I*

**ISMAIAH** *(is-ma-i'-ah)* See ISHMAIAH. *A warrior in David's army.*
1Chr 12:4 *I* the Gibeonite, a mighty man

**ISPAH** *(is'-pah) A son of Beriah.*
1Chr 8:16 And Michael, and *I*, and Joha, the

**ISRAEL** *(iz'-ra-el)* See EL-ELOHE-ISRAEL, ISRAELITE, ISRAEL'S, JACOB, JESHURUN.

*1. Name given to Jacob.*
Gen 32:28 be called no more Jacob, but *I*
Gen 35:10 Jacob, but *I* shall be thy name
Gen 35:10 and he called his name *I*
Gen 35:21 *I* journeyed, and spread his tent
Gen 35:22 when *I* dwelt in that land, that
Gen 35:22 and *I* heard it
Gen 37:3 Now *I* loved Joseph more than all
Gen 37:13 *I* said unto Joseph, Do not thy
Gen 42:5 the sons of *I* came to buy corn
Gen 43:6 *I* said, Wherefore dealt ye so ill
Gen 43:8 And Judah said unto *I* his father
Gen 43:11 their father *I* said unto them, If
Gen 45:21 And the children of *I* did so
Gen 45:28 And *I* said, It is enough
Gen 46:1 *I* took his journey with all that
Gen 46:2 God spake unto *I* in the visions
Gen 46:5 the sons of *I* carried Jacob their
Gen 46:8 the names of the children of *I*
Gen 46:29 and went up to meet *I* his father
Gen 46:30 *I* said unto Joseph, Now let me
Gen 47:27 *I* dwelt in the land of Egypt, in
Gen 47:29 time drew nigh that *I* must die
Gen 47:31 *I* bowed himself upon the bed's
Gen 48:2 *I* strengthened himself, and sat
Gen 48:8 *I* beheld Joseph's sons, and said,
Gen 48:10 Now the eyes of *I* were dim for
Gen 48:11 *I* said unto Joseph, I had not
Gen 48:14 *I* stretched out his right hand,
Gen 48:20 saying, In thee shall *I* bless
Gen 48:21 *I* said unto Joseph, Behold, I die
Gen 49:2 and hearken unto *I* your father
Gen 50:2 and the physicians embalmed *I*
Ex 1:1 the names of the children of *I*
Ex 1:7 the children of *I* were fruitful
Ex 6:14 sons of Reuben the firstborn of *I*
Ex 32:13 Remember Abraham, Isaac, and *I*
Num 26:5 Reuben, the eldest son of *I*
Judg 18:29 their father, who was born unto *I*
1Kin 18:31 came, saying, *I* shall be thy name
1Kin 18:36 God of Abraham, Isaac, and of *I*
2Kin 17:34 of Jacob, whom he named *I*
1Chr 1:34 The sons of Isaac; Esau and *I*
1Chr 2:1 These are the sons of *I*
1Chr 5:1 sons of Reuben the firstborn of *I*
1Chr 5:1 the sons of Joseph the son of *I*
1Chr 5:3 of Reuben the firstborn of *I* were
1Chr 6:38 the son of Levi, the son of *I*
1Chr 7:29 children of Joseph the son of *I*
1Chr 29:10 be thou, LORD God of *I* our father
1Chr 29:18 God of Abraham, Isaac, and of *I*
2Chr 30:6 LORD God of Abraham, Isaac, and *I*
Ezr 8:18 the son of Levi, the son of *I*

*2. People descended from Jacob.*
Gen 32:32 Therefore the children of *I* eat
Gen 34:7 *I* in lying with Jacob's daughter
Gen 36:31 any king over the children of *I*
Gen 49:7 in Jacob, and scatter them in *I*
Gen 49:16 people, as one of the tribes of *I*
Gen 49:24 is the shepherd, the stone of *I*
Gen 49:28 these are the twelve tribes of *I*
Gen 50:25 took an oath of the children of *I*
Ex 1:9 of the children of *I* are more
Ex 1:12 because of the children of *I*
Ex 1:13 of *I* to serve with rigour
Ex 2:23 the children of *I* sighed by
Ex 2:25 God looked upon the children of *I*
Ex 3:9 the children of *I* is come unto me
Ex 3:10 the children of *I* out of Egypt
Ex 3:11 the children of *I* out of Egypt
Ex 3:13 I come unto the children of *I*
Ex 3:14 thou say unto the children of *I*
Ex 3:15 thou say unto the children of *I*
Ex 3:16 gather the elders of *I* together
Ex 3:18 come, thou and the elders of *I*
Ex 4:22 *I* is my son, even my firstborn
Ex 4:29 the elders of the children of *I*
Ex 4:31 had visited the children of *I*
Ex 5:1 Thus saith the LORD God of *I*
Ex 5:2 should obey his voice to let *I* go
Ex 5:2 the LORD, neither will I let *I* go
Ex 5:14 the officers of the children of *I*
Ex 5:15 of the children of *I* came
Ex 5:19 *I* did see that they were in evil
Ex 6:5 the groaning of the children of *I*
Ex 6:6 say unto the children of *I*
Ex 6:9 spake so unto the children of *I*
Ex 6:11 children of *I* go out of his land
Ex 6:12 the children of *I* have not
Ex 6:13 a charge unto the children of *I*
Ex 6:13 of *I* out of the land of Egypt
Ex 6:26 of *I* from the land of Egypt
Ex 6:27 out the children of *I* from Egypt
Ex 7:2 the children of *I* out of his land
Ex 7:4 and my people the children of *I*
Ex 7:5 the children of *I* from among them
Ex 9:4 sever between the cattle of *I*
Ex 9:4 all that is the children's of *I*
Ex 9:6 of the children of *I* died not one
Ex 9:26 where the children of *I* were
Ex 9:35 would he let the children of *I* go
Ex 10:20 not let the children of *I* go
Ex 10:23 but all the children of *I* had
Ex 11:7 against any of the children of *I*
Ex 11:7 between the Egyptians and *I*
Ex 11:10 children of *I* go out of his land
Ex 12:3 ye unto all the congregation of *I*
Ex 12:6 of *I* shall kill it in the evening
Ex 12:15 that soul shall be cut off from *I*
Ex 12:19 off from the congregation of *I*
Ex 12:21 called for all the elders of *I*
Ex 12:27 of the children of *I* in Egypt
Ex 12:28 And the children of *I* went away
Ex 12:31 both ye and the children of *I*
Ex 12:35 the children of *I* did according
Ex 12:37 the children of *I* journeyed from
Ex 12:40 sojourning of the children of *I*
Ex 12:42 of *I* in their generations
Ex 12:47 congregation of *I* shall keep it
Ex 12:50 Thus did all the children of *I*
Ex 12:51 of *I* out of the land of Egypt by
Ex 13:2 the womb among the children of *I*
Ex 13:18 the children of *I* went up
Ex 13:19 straitly sworn the children of *I*
Ex 14:2 Speak unto the children of *I*
Ex 14:3 will say of the children of *I*
Ex 14:5 that we have let *I* go from
Ex 14:8 pursued after the children of *I*
Ex 14:8 the children of *I* went out with
Ex 14:10 the children of *I* lifted up their
Ex 14:10 the children of *I* cried out unto
Ex 14:15 speak unto the children of *I*
Ex 14:16 the children of *I* shall go on dry
Ex 14:19 which went before the camp of *I*
Ex 14:20 of the Egyptians and the camp of *I*
Ex 14:22 the children of *I* went into the
Ex 14:25 Let us flee from the face of *I*
Ex 14:29 But the children of *I* walked upon
Ex 14:30 Thus the LORD saved *I* that day
Ex 14:30 *I* saw the Egyptians dead upon the
Ex 14:31 *I* saw that great work which the
Ex 15:1 the children of *I* this song unto
Ex 15:19 but the children of *I* went on dry
Ex 15:22 Moses brought *I* from the Red sea
Ex 16:1 *I* came unto the wilderness of Sin
Ex 16:2 of *I* murmured against Moses
Ex 16:3 the children of *I* said unto them
Ex 16:6 said unto all the children of *I*
Ex 16:9 congregation of the children of *I*
Ex 16:10 congregation of the children of *I*
Ex 16:12 murmurings of the children of *I*
Ex 16:15 And when the children of *I* saw it
Ex 16:17 And the children of *I* did so
Ex 16:31 the house of *I* called the name
Ex 16:35 the children of *I* did eat manna
Ex 17:1 *I* journeyed from the wilderness
Ex 17:5 take with thee of the elders of *I*
Ex 17:6 in the sight of the elders of *I*
Ex 17:7 the chiding of the children of *I*
Ex 17:8 and fought with *I* in Rephidim
Ex 17:11 up his hand, that *I* prevailed
Ex 18:1 for *I* his people, and that the
Ex 18:1 LORD had brought *I* out of Egypt
Ex 18:9 which the LORD had done to *I*
Ex 18:12 came, and all the elders of *I*
Ex 18:25 Moses chose able men out of all *I*
Ex 19:1 when the children of *I* were gone
Ex 19:2 there *I* camped before the mount
Ex 19:3 Jacob, and tell the children of *I*
Ex 19:6 speak unto the children of *I*
Ex 20:22 shalt say unto the children of *I*
Ex 24:1 and seventy of the elders of *I*
Ex 24:4 to the twelve tribes of *I*
Ex 24:5 young men of the children of *I*
Ex 24:9 and seventy of the elders of *I*
Ex 24:10 And they saw the God of *I*
Ex 24:11 of *I* he laid not his hand
Ex 24:17 in the eyes of the children of *I*
Ex 25:2 Speak unto the children of *I*
Ex 25:22 unto the children of *I*
Ex 27:20 shalt command the children of *I*
Ex 27:21 the behalf of the children of *I*
Ex 28:1 him, from among the children of *I*
Ex 28:9 the names of the children of *I*
Ex 28:11 the names of the children of *I*
Ex 28:12 memorial unto the children of *I*
Ex 28:21 the names of the children of *I*
Ex 28:29 the names of the children of *I* in
Ex 28:30 *I* upon his heart before the LORD
Ex 28:38 which the children of *I* shall
Ex 29:28 for ever from the children of *I*
Ex 29:28 offering from the children of *I*
Ex 29:43 will meet with the children of *I*
Ex 29:45 dwell among the children of *I*
Ex 30:12 children of *I* after their number
Ex 30:16 money of the children of *I*
Ex 30:16 the children of *I* before the LORD
Ex 30:31 speak unto the children of *I*
Ex 31:13 thou also unto the children of *I*
Ex 31:16 of *I* shall keep the sabbath
Ex 31:17 me and the children of *I* for ever
Ex 32:4 they said, These be thy gods, O *I*
Ex 32:8 and said, These be thy gods, O *I*

Ex 32:20 the children of *I* drink of it
Ex 32:27 Thus saith the LORD God of *I*
Ex 33:5 Moses, Say unto the children of *I*
Ex 33:6 the children of *I* stripped
Ex 34:23 before the Lord GOD, the God of *I*
Ex 34:27 a covenant with thee and with *I*
Ex 34:30 all the children of *I* saw Moses
Ex 34:32 all the children of *I* came nigh
Ex 34:34 spake unto the children of *I* that
Ex 34:35 the children of *I* saw the face of
Ex 35:1 of the children of *I* together
Ex 35:4 congregation of the children of *I*
Ex 35:20 *I* departed from the presence of
Ex 35:29 The children of *I* brought a
Ex 35:30 Moses said unto the children of *I*
Ex 36:3 which the children of *I* had
Ex 39:6 the names of the children of *I*
Ex 39:7 a memorial to the children of *I*
Ex 39:14 to the names of the children of *I*
Ex 39:32 the children of *I* did according
Ex 39:42 children of *I* made all the work
Ex 40:36 the children of *I* went onward in
Ex 40:38 the sight of all the house of *I*
Lev 1:2 Speak unto the children of *I*
Lev 4:2 Speak unto the children of *I*
Lev 4:13 of *I* sin through ignorance
Lev 7:23 Speak unto the children of *I*
Lev 7:29 Speak unto the children of *I*
Lev 7:34 of *I* from off the sacrifices of
Lev 7:34 ever from among the children of *I*
Lev 7:36 given them of the children of *I*
Lev 7:38 he commanded the children of *I* to
Lev 9:1 and his sons, and the elders of *I*
Lev 9:3 children of *I* thou shalt speak
Lev 10:6 brethren, the whole house of *I*
Lev 10:11 ye may teach the children of *I*
Lev 10:14 offerings of the children of *I*
Lev 11:2 Speak unto the children of *I*
Lev 12:2 Speak unto the children of *I*
Lev 15:2 Speak unto the children of *I*
Lev 15:31 of *I* from their uncleanness
Lev 16:5 *I* two kids of the goats for a sin
Lev 16:16 uncleanness of the children of *I*
Lev 16:17 and for all the congregation of *I*
Lev 16:19 uncleanness of the children of *I*
Lev 16:21 iniquities of the children of *I*
Lev 16:34 atonement for the children of *I*
Lev 17:2 and unto all the children of *I*
Lev 17:3 soever there be of the house of *I*
Lev 17:5 of *I* may bring their sacrifices
Lev 17:8 man there be of the house of *I*
Lev 17:10 man there be of the house of *I*
Lev 17:12 I said unto the children of *I*
Lev 17:13 man there be of the children of *I*
Lev 17:14 I said unto the children of *I*
Lev 18:2 Speak unto the children of *I*
Lev 19:2 congregation of the children of *I*
Lev 20:2 shalt say to the children of *I*
Lev 20:2 he be of the children of *I*
Lev 20:2 the strangers that sojourn in *I*
Lev 21:24 and unto all the children of *I*
Lev 22:2 holy things of the children of *I*
Lev 22:3 of *I* hallow unto the LORD
Lev 22:15 holy things of the children of *I*
Lev 22:18 and unto all the children of *I*
Lev 22:18 he be of the house of *I*
Lev 22:18 or of the strangers in *I*
Lev 22:32 hallowed among the children of *I*
Lev 23:2 Speak unto the children of *I*
Lev 23:10 Speak unto the children of *I*
Lev 23:24 Speak unto the children of *I*
Lev 23:34 Speak unto the children of *I*
Lev 23:43 children of *I* to dwell in booths
Lev 23:44 of *I* the feasts of the LORD
Lev 24:2 Command the children of *I*
Lev 24:8 of *I* by an everlasting covenant
Lev 24:10 went out among the children of *I*
Lev 24:10 a man of *I* strove together in the
Lev 24:15 speak unto the children of *I*
Lev 24:23 Moses spake to the children of *I*
Lev 24:23 the children of *I* did as the LORD
Lev 25:2 Speak unto the children of *I*
Lev 25:33 among the children of *I*
Lev 25:46 your brethren the children of *I*
Lev 25:55 me the children of *I* are servants
Lev 26:46 the children of *I* in mount Sinai
Lev 27:2 Speak unto the children of *I*
Lev 27:34 the children of *I* in mount Sinai
Num 1:2 congregation of the children of *I*
Num 1:3 are able to go forth to war in *I*
Num 1:16 fathers, heads of thousands in *I*
Num 1:44 numbered, and the princes of *I*
Num 1:45 numbered of the children of *I*
Num 1:45 were able to go forth to war in *I*
Num 1:49 of them among the children of *I*
Num 1:52 the children of *I* shall pitch
Num 1:53 congregation of the children of *I*
Num 1:54 the children of *I* did according
Num 2:2 Every man of the children of *I*
Num 2:32 numbered of the children of *I* by
Num 2:33 numbered among the children of *I*
Num 2:34 the children of *I* did according
Num 3:8 the charge of the children of *I*
Num 3:9 unto him out of the children of *I*
Num 3:12 from among the children of *I*
Num 3:12 matrix among the children of *I*
Num 3:13 unto me all the firstborn in *I*
Num 3:38 the charge of the children of *I*
Num 3:40 children of *I* from a month old
Num 3:41 firstborn among the children of *I*
Num 3:41 the cattle of the children of *I*
Num 3:42 firstborn among the children of *I*
Num 3:45 firstborn among the children of *I*
Num 3:46 firstborn of the children of *I*
Num 3:50 children of *I* took he the money
Num 4:46 Aaron and the chief of *I* numbered
Num 5:2 Command the children of *I*
Num 5:4 And the children of *I* did so
Num 5:4 Moses, so did the children of *I*
Num 5:6 Speak unto the children of *I*
Num 5:9 holy things of the children of *I*
Num 5:12 Speak unto the children of *I*
Num 6:2 Speak unto the children of *I*
Num 6:23 ye shall bless the children of *I*
Num 6:27 my name upon the children of *I*
Num 7:2 That the princes of *I*, heads of
Num 7:84 was anointed, by the princes of *I*
Num 8:6 from among the children of *I*
Num 8:9 of the children of *I* together
Num 8:10 the children of *I* shall put their
Num 8:11 an offering of the children of *I*
Num 8:14 from among the children of *I*
Num 8:16 me from among the children of *I*
Num 8:16 of all the children of *I*, have I
Num 8:17 of the children of *I* are mine
Num 8:18 firstborn of the children of *I*
Num 8:19 sons from among the children of *I*
Num 8:19 of *I* in the tabernacle of the
Num 8:19 atonement for the children of *I*
Num 8:19 no plague among the children of *I*
Num 8:19 when the children of *I* come nigh
Num 8:20 congregation of the children of *I*
Num 8:20 did the children of *I* unto them
Num 9:2 Let the children of *I* also keep
Num 9:4 spake unto the children of *I*
Num 9:5 Moses, so did the children of *I*
Num 9:7 season among the children of *I*
Num 9:10 Speak unto the children of *I*
Num 9:17 that the children of *I* journeyed
Num 9:17 children of *I* pitched their tents
Num 9:18 LORD the children of *I* journeyed
Num 9:19 then the children of *I* kept the
Num 9:22 the children of *I* abode in their
Num 10:4 are heads of the thousands of *I*
Num 10:12 the children of *I* took their
Num 10:28 of *I* according to their armies
Num 10:29 hath spoken good concerning *I*
Num 10:36 unto the many thousands of *I*
Num 11:4 the children of *I* also wept again
Num 11:16 me seventy men of the elders of *I*
Num 11:30 the camp, he and the elders of *I*
Num 13:2 I give unto the children of *I*
Num 13:3 were heads of the children of *I*
Num 13:24 of *I* cut down from thence
Num 13:26 congregation of the children of *I*
Num 13:32 searched unto the children of *I*
Num 14:2 all the children of *I* murmured
Num 14:5 congregation of the children of *I*
Num 14:7 the company of the children of *I*
Num 14:10 before all the children of *I*
Num 14:27 murmurings of the children of *I*
Num 14:39 unto all the children of *I*
Num 15:2 Speak unto the children of *I*
Num 15:18 Speak unto the children of *I*
Num 15:25 congregation of the children of *I*
Num 15:26 congregation of the children of *I*
Num 15:29 is born among the children of *I*
Num 15:32 while the children of *I* were in
Num 15:38 Speak unto the children of *I*
Num 16:2 with certain of the children of *I*
Num 16:9 that the God of *I* hath separated
Num 16:9 you from the congregation of *I*
Num 16:25 and the elders of *I* followed him
Num 16:34 all *I* that were round about them
Num 16:38 be a sign unto the children of *I*
Num 16:40 a memorial unto the children of *I*
Num 16:41 of *I* murmured against Moses
Num 17:2 Speak unto the children of *I*
Num 17:5 murmurings of the children of *I*
Num 17:6 spake unto the children of *I*
Num 17:9 LORD unto all the children of *I*
Num 17:12 the children of *I* spake unto
Num 18:5 any more upon the children of *I*
Num 18:6 from among the children of *I*
Num 18:8 things of the children of *I*
Num 18:11 offerings of the children of *I*
Num 18:14 thing devoted in *I* shall be thine
Num 18:19 children of *I* offer unto the LORD
Num 18:20 among the children of *I*
Num 18:21 the tenth in *I* for an inheritance
Num 18:22 of *I* henceforth come nigh the
Num 18:23 of *I* they have no inheritance
Num 18:24 the tithes of the children of *I*
Num 18:24 Among the children of *I* they
Num 18:26 *I* the tithes which I have given
Num 18:28 ye receive of the children of *I*
Num 18:32 holy things of the children of *I*
Num 19:2 Speak unto the children of *I*
Num 19:9 of *I* for a water of separation
Num 19:10 shall be unto the children of *I*
Num 19:13 that soul shall be cut off from *I*
Num 20:1 Then came the children of *I*
Num 20:12 in the eyes of the children of *I*
Num 20:13 of *I* strove with the LORD
Num 20:14 of Edom, Thus saith thy brother *I*
Num 20:19 the children of *I* said unto him
Num 20:21 Thus Edom refused to give *I*
Num 20:21 wherefore *I* turned away from him
Num 20:22 And the children of *I*, even the
Num 20:24 have given unto the children of *I*
Num 20:29 days, even all the house of *I*
Num 21:1 heard tell that *I* came by the way
Num 21:1 then he fought against *I*, and took
Num 21:2 *I* vowed a vow unto the LORD, and
Num 21:3 LORD hearkened to the voice of *I*
Num 21:6 and much people of *I* died
Num 21:10 And the children of *I* set forward
Num 21:17 Then *I* sang this song, Spring up,
Num 21:21 *I* sent messengers unto Sihon king
Num 21:23 Sihon would not suffer *I* to pass
Num 21:23 went out against *I* into the
Num 21:23 to Jahaz, and fought against *I*
Num 21:24 *I* smote him with the edge of the
Num 21:25 And *I* took all these cities
Num 21:25 *I* dwelt in all the cities of the
Num 21:31 Thus *I* dwelt in the land of the
Num 22:1 And the children of *I* set forward
Num 22:2 that *I* had done to the Amorites
Num 22:3 because of the children of *I*
Num 23:7 curse me Jacob, and come, defy *I*
Num 23:10 number of the fourth part of *I*
Num 23:21 hath he seen perverseness in *I*
Num 23:23 is there any divination against *I*
Num 23:23 it shall be said of Jacob and of *I*
Num 24:1 it pleased the LORD to bless *I*
Num 24:2 he saw *I* abiding in his tents
Num 24:5 O Jacob, and thy tabernacles, O *I*
Num 24:17 and a Sceptre shall rise out of *I*
Num 24:18 and *I* shall do valiantly
Num 25:1 *I* abode in Shittim, and the people
Num 25:3 *I* joined himself unto Baal-peor
Num 25:3 of the LORD was kindled against *I*
Num 25:4 LORD may be turned away from *I*
Num 25:5 Moses said unto the judges of *I*
Num 25:6 one of the children of *I* came
Num 25:6 congregation of the children of *I*
Num 25:8 after the man of *I* into the tent
Num 25:8 of them through, the man of *I*
Num 25:8 was stayed from the children of *I*
Num 25:11 wrath away from the children of *I*
Num 25:11 the children of *I* in my jealousy
Num 25:13 atonement for the children of *I*
Num 26:2 congregation of the children of *I*
Num 26:2 that are able to go to war in *I*
Num 26:4 Moses and the children of *I*
Num 26:51 the numbered of the children of *I*
Num 26:62 numbered among the children of *I*
Num 26:62 them among the children of *I*
Num 26:63 who numbered the children of *I* in
Num 26:64 of *I* in the wilderness of Sinai

Num 27:8 speak unto the children of *I*
Num 27:11 of *I* a statute of judgment
Num 27:12 have given unto the children of *I*
Num 27:20 the children of *I* may be obedient
Num 27:21 and all the children of *I* with him
Num 28:2 Command the children of *I*
Num 29:40 Moses told the children of *I*
Num 30:1 concerning the children of *I*
Num 31:2 children of *I* of the Midianites
Num 31:4 throughout all the tribes of *I*
Num 31:5 out of the thousands of *I*
Num 31:9 the children of *I* took all the
Num 31:12 congregation of the children of *I*
Num 31:16 these caused the children of *I*
Num 31:54 the children of *I* before the LORD
Num 32:4 before the congregation of *I*
Num 32:7 *I* from going over into the land
Num 32:9 the heart of the children of *I*
Num 32:13 anger was kindled against *I*
Num 32:14 fierce anger of the LORD toward *I*
Num 32:17 armed before the children of *I*
Num 32:18 until the children of *I* have
Num 32:22 before the LORD, and before *I*
Num 32:28 the tribes of the children of *I*
Num 33:1 the journeys of the children of *I*
Num 33:3 the passover the children of *I*
Num 33:5 the children of *I* removed from
Num 33:38 year after the children of *I* were
Num 33:40 the coming of the children of *I*
Num 33:51 Speak unto the children of *I*
Num 34:2 Command the children of *I*
Num 34:13 Moses commanded the children of *I*
Num 34:29 unto the children of *I* in the
Num 35:2 Command the children of *I*
Num 35:8 possession of the children of *I*
Num 35:10 Speak unto the children of *I*
Num 35:15 both for the children of *I*
Num 35:34 dwell among the children of *I*
Num 36:1 fathers of the children of *I*
Num 36:2 by lot to the children of *I*
Num 36:3 other tribes of the children of *I*
Num 36:4 of the children of *I* shall be
Num 36:5 of *I* according to the word of the
Num 36:7 of *I* remove from tribe to tribe
Num 36:7 of *I* shall keep himself to the
Num 36:8 in any tribe of the children of *I*
Num 36:8 that the children of *I* may enjoy
Num 36:9 *I* shall keep himself to his own
Num 36:13 of Moses unto the children of *I*
Deut 1:1 all *I* on this side Jordan in the
Deut 1:3 spake unto the children of *I*
Deut 1:38 he shall cause *I* to inherit it
Deut 2:12 as *I* did unto the land of his
Deut 3:18 your brethren the children of *I*
Deut 4:1 Now therefore hearken, O *I*
Deut 4:44 set before the children of *I*
Deut 4:45 spake unto the children of *I*
Deut 4:46 Moses and the children of *I* smote
Deut 5:1 And Moses called all *I*
Deut 5:1 and said unto them, Hear, O *I*
Deut 6:3 Hear therefore, O *I*, and observe
Deut 6:4 Hear, O *I*: The LORD our God
Deut 9:1 Hear, O *I*: Thou art to pass
Deut 10:6 the children of *I* took their
Deut 10:12 And now, *I*, what doth the LORD thy
Deut 11:6 possession, in the midst of all *I*
Deut 13:11 all *I* shall hear, and fear, and
Deut 17:4 such abomination is wrought in *I*
Deut 17:12 shalt put away the evil from *I*
Deut 17:20 his children, in the midst of *I*
Deut 18:1 no part nor inheritance with *I*
Deut 18:6 any of thy gates out of all *I*
Deut 19:13 guilt of innocent blood from *I*
Deut 20:3 And shall say unto them, Hear, O *I*
Deut 21:8 O LORD, unto thy people *I*
Deut 21:21 all *I* shall hear, and fear
Deut 22:19 an evil name upon a virgin of *I*
Deut 22:21 she hath wrought folly in *I*
Deut 22:22 shalt thou put away evil from *I*
Deut 23:17 be no whore of the daughters of *I*
Deut 23:17 nor a sodomite of the sons of *I*
Deut 24:7 his brethren of the children of *I*
Deut 25:6 that his name be not put out of *I*
Deut 25:7 up unto his brother a name in *I*
Deut 25:10 And his name shall be called in *I*
Deut 26:15 heaven, and bless thy people *I*
Deut 27:1 elders of *I* commanded the people
Deut 27:9 the Levites spake unto all *I*
Deut 27:9 Take heed, and hearken, O *I*
Deut 27:14 the men of *I* with a loud voice
Deut 29:1 children of *I* in the land of Moab
Deut 29:2 And Moses called unto all *I*
Deut 29:10 officers, with all the men of *I*
Deut 29:21 evil out of all the tribes of *I*
Deut 31:1 and spake these words unto all *I*
Deut 31:7 unto him in the sight of all *I*
Deut 31:9 LORD, and unto all the elders of *I*
Deut 31:11 When all *I* is come to appear
Deut 31:11 law before all *I* in their hearing
Deut 31:19 and teach it the children of *I*
Deut 31:19 for me against the children of *I*
Deut 31:22 and taught it the children of *I*
Deut 31:23 of *I* into the land which I sware
Deut 31:30 of *I* the words of this song
Deut 32:8 the number of the children of *I*
Deut 32:45 speaking all these words to all *I*
Deut 32:49 children of *I* for a possession
Deut 32:51 me among the children of *I* at the
Deut 32:51 in the midst of the children of *I*
Deut 32:52 which I give the children of *I*
Deut 33:1 children of *I* before his death
Deut 33:5 the tribes of *I* were gathered
Deut 33:10 Jacob thy judgments, and *I* thy law
Deut 33:21 the LORD, and his judgments with *I*
Deut 33:28 *I* then shall dwell in safety
Deut 33:29 Happy art thou, O *I*
Deut 34:8 the children of *I* wept for Moses
Deut 34:9 the children of *I* hearkened unto
Deut 34:10 since in *I* like unto Moses
Deut 34:12 shewed in the sight of all *I*
Josh 1:2 them, even to the children of *I*
Josh 2:2 of *I* to search out the country
Josh 3:1 he and all the children of *I*
Josh 3:7 thee in the sight of all *I*
Josh 3:9 said unto the children of *I*
Josh 3:12 twelve men out of the tribes of *I*
Josh 4:4 had prepared of the children of *I*
Josh 4:5 the tribes of the children of *I*
Josh 4:7 unto the children of *I* for ever
Josh 4:8 the children of *I* did so as
Josh 4:8 the tribes of the children of *I*
Josh 4:12 armed before the children of *I*
Josh 4:14 Joshua in the sight of all *I*
Josh 4:21 he spake unto the children of *I*
Josh 4:22 *I* came over this Jordan on dry
Josh 5:1 from before the children of *I*
Josh 5:1 because of the children of *I*
Josh 5:2 the children of *I* the second time
Josh 5:3 circumcised the children of *I* at
Josh 5:6 For the children of *I* walked
Josh 5:10 the children of *I* encamped in
Josh 5:12 the children of *I* manna any more
Josh 6:1 up because of the children of *I*
Josh 6:18 and make the camp of *I* a curse
Josh 6:23 left them without the camp of *I*
Josh 6:25 she dwelleth in *I* even unto this
Josh 7:1 But the children of *I* committed a
Josh 7:1 kindled against the children of *I*
Josh 7:6 eventide, he and the elders of *I*
Josh 7:8 when *I* turneth their backs before
Josh 7:11 *I* hath sinned, and they have also
Josh 7:12 Therefore the children of *I* could
Josh 7:13 for thus saith the LORD God of *I*
Josh 7:13 thing in the midst of thee, O *I*
Josh 7:15 he hath wrought folly in *I*
Josh 7:16 brought *I* by their tribes
Josh 7:19 thee, glory to the LORD God of *I*
Josh 7:20 sinned against the LORD God of *I*
Josh 7:23 and unto all the children of *I*
Josh 7:24 all *I* with him, took Achan the
Josh 7:25 all *I* stoned him with stones, and
Josh 8:10 and went up, he and the elders of *I*
Josh 8:14 city went out against *I* to battle
Josh 8:15 all *I* made as if they were beaten
Josh 8:17 that went not out after *I*
Josh 8:17 the city open, and pursued after *I*
Josh 8:21 all *I* saw that the ambush had
Josh 8:22 so they were in the midst of *I*
Josh 8:24 when *I* had made an end of slaying
Josh 8:27 the spoil of that city *I* took for
Josh 8:30 the LORD God of *I* in mount Ebal
Josh 8:31 LORD commanded the children of *I*
Josh 8:32 the presence of the children of *I*
Josh 8:33 And all *I*, and their elders, and
Josh 8:33 they should bless the people of *I*
Josh 8:35 before all the congregation of *I*
Josh 9:2 to fight with Joshua and with *I*
Josh 9:6 said unto him, and to the men of *I*
Josh 9:7 the men of *I* said unto the
Josh 9:17 And the children of *I* journeyed
Josh 9:18 the children of *I* smote them not
Josh 9:18 unto them by the LORD God of *I*
Josh 9:19 unto them by the LORD God of *I*
Josh 9:26 of the hand of the children of *I*
Josh 10:1 of Gibeon had made peace with *I*
Josh 10:4 Joshua and with the children of *I*
Josh 10:10 LORD discomfited them before *I*
Josh 10:11 pass, as they fled from before *I*
Josh 10:11 children of *I* slew with the sword
Josh 10:12 Amorites before the children of *I*
Josh 10:12 and he said in the sight of *I*
Josh 10:14 for the LORD fought for *I*
Josh 10:15 all *I* with him, unto the camp to
Josh 10:20 the children of *I* had made an end
Josh 10:21 against any of the children of *I*
Josh 10:24 called for all the men of *I*
Josh 10:29 all *I* with him, unto Libnah, and
Josh 10:30 king thereof, into the hand of *I*
Josh 10:31 all *I* with him, unto Lachish, and
Josh 10:32 Lachish into the hand of *I*
Josh 10:34 unto Eglon, and all *I* with him
Josh 10:36 all *I* with him, unto Hebron
Josh 10:38 and all *I* with him, to Debir
Josh 10:40 as the LORD God of *I* commanded
Josh 10:42 LORD God of *I* fought for Israel
Josh 10:42 LORD God of Israel fought for *I*
Josh 10:43 all *I* with him, unto the camp to
Josh 11:5 of Merom, to fight against *I*
Josh 11:6 them up all slain before *I*
Josh 11:8 delivered them into the hand of *I*
Josh 11:13 *I* burned none of them, save Hazor
Josh 11:14 the children of *I* took for a prey
Josh 11:16 the plain, and the mountain of *I*
Josh 11:19 made peace with the children of *I*
Josh 11:20 should come against *I* in battle
Josh 11:21 and from all the mountains of *I*
Josh 11:22 in the land of the children of *I*
Josh 11:23 *I* according to their divisions by
Josh 12:1 which the children of *I* smote
Josh 12:6 LORD and the children of *I* smite
Josh 12:7 the children of *I* smote on this
Josh 12:7 *I* for a possession according to
Josh 13:6 out from before the children of *I*
Josh 13:13 of *I* expelled not the Geshurites
Josh 13:14 God of *I* made by fire are their
Josh 13:22 did the children of *I* slay with
Josh 13:33 the LORD God of *I* was their
Josh 14:1 *I* inherited in the land of Canaan
Josh 14:1 the tribes of the children of *I*
Josh 14:5 Moses, so the children of *I* did
Josh 14:10 while the children of *I* wandered
Josh 14:14 wholly followed the LORD God of *I*
Josh 17:13 children of *I* were waxen strong
Josh 18:1 of *I* assembled together at Shiloh
Josh 18:2 the children of *I* seven tribes
Josh 18:3 said unto the children of *I*
Josh 18:10 of *I* according to their divisions
Josh 19:49 the children of *I* gave an
Josh 19:51 the tribes of the children of *I*
Josh 20:2 Speak to the children of *I*
Josh 20:9 for all the children of *I*
Josh 21:1 the tribes of the children of *I*
Josh 21:3 the children of *I* gave unto the
Josh 21:8 the children of *I* gave by lot
Josh 21:41 of the children of *I* were forty
Josh 21:43 the LORD gave unto *I* all the land
Josh 21:45 had spoken unto the house of *I*
Josh 22:9 the children of *I* out of Shiloh
Josh 22:11 And the children of *I* heard say
Josh 22:11 the passage of the children of *I*
Josh 22:12 the children of *I* heard of it
Josh 22:12 *I* gathered themselves together at
Josh 22:13 the children of *I* sent unto the
Josh 22:14 throughout all the tribes of *I*
Josh 22:14 fathers among the thousands of *I*
Josh 22:16 committed against the God of *I*
Josh 22:18 with the whole congregation of *I*
Josh 22:20 fell on all the congregation of *I*
Josh 22:21 the heads of the thousands of *I*
Josh 22:22 he knoweth, and *I* he shall know
Josh 22:24 ye to do with the LORD God of *I*
Josh 22:30 of *I* which were with him, heard
Josh 22:31 of *I* out of the hand of the LORD
Josh 22:32 of Canaan, to the children of *I*
Josh 22:33 thing pleased the children of *I*
Josh 22:33 and the children of *I* blessed God
Josh 23:1 *I* from all their enemies round
Josh 23:2 And Joshua called for all *I*
Josh 24:1 all the tribes of *I* to Shechem
Josh 24:1 and called for the elders of *I*

Josh 24:2 Thus saith the LORD God of I
Josh 24:9 Moab, arose and warred against I
Josh 24:23 your heart unto the LORD God of I
Josh 24:31 I served the LORD all the days of
Josh 24:31 the LORD, that he had done for I
Josh 24:32 which the children of I brought
Judg 1:1 the children of I asked the LORD
Judg 1:28 when I was strong, that they put
Judg 2:4 words unto all the children of I
Judg 2:6 the children of I went every man
Judg 2:7 of the LORD, that he did for I
Judg 2:10 the works which he had done for I
Judg 2:11 the children of I did evil in the
Judg 2:14 of the LORD was hot against I
Judg 2:20 of the LORD was hot against I
Judg 2:22 That through them I may prove I
Judg 3:1 the LORD left, to prove I by them
Judg 3:1 even as many of I as had not
Judg 3:2 of the children of I might know
Judg 3:4 And they were to prove I by them
Judg 3:5 the children of I dwelt among the
Judg 3:7 the children of I did evil in the
Judg 3:8 of the LORD was hot against I
Judg 3:8 and the children of I served
Judg 3:9 children of I cried unto the LORD
Judg 3:9 a deliverer to the children of I
Judg 3:10 came upon him, and he judged I
Judg 3:12 the children of I did evil again
Judg 3:12 Eglon the king of Moab against I
Judg 3:13 and Amalek, and went and smote I
Judg 3:14 So the children of I served Eglon
Judg 3:15 children of I cried unto the LORD
Judg 3:15 by him the children of I sent a
Judg 3:27 the children of I went down with
Judg 3:30 that day under the hand of I
Judg 3:31 and he also delivered I
Judg 4:1 the children of I again did evil
Judg 4:3 the children of I cried unto the
Judg 4:3 oppressed the children of I
Judg 4:4 she judged I at that time
Judg 4:5 the children of I came up to her
Judg 4:6 not the LORD God of I commanded
Judg 4:23 Canaan before the children of I
Judg 4:24 of the children of I prospered
Judg 5:2 ye the LORD for the avenging of I
Judg 5:3 sing praise to the LORD God of I
Judg 5:5 from before the LORD God of I
Judg 5:7 villages ceased, they ceased in I
Judg 5:7 arose, that I arose a mother in I
Judg 5:8 seen among forty thousand in I
Judg 5:9 is toward the governors of I
Judg 5:11 inhabitants of his villages in I
Judg 6:1 the children of I did evil in the
Judg 6:2 of Midian prevailed against I
Judg 6:2 the Midianites the children of I
Judg 6:3 when I had sown, that the
Judg 6:4 Gaza, and left no sustenance for I
Judg 6:6 I was greatly impoverished
Judg 6:6 the children of I cried unto the
Judg 6:7 when the children of I cried unto
Judg 6:8 a prophet unto the children of I
Judg 6:8 Thus saith the LORD God of I
Judg 6:14 thou shalt save I from the hand
Judg 6:15 my Lord, wherewith shall I save I
Judg 6:36 If thou wilt save I by mine hand
Judg 6:37 thou wilt save I by mine hand
Judg 7:2 lest I vaunt themselves against
Judg 7:8 rest of I every man unto his tent
Judg 7:14 the son of Joash, a man of I
Judg 7:15 and returned into the host of I
Judg 7:23 the men of I gathered themselves
Judg 8:22 Then the men of I said unto
Judg 8:27 all I went thither a whoring
Judg 8:28 subdued before the children of I
Judg 8:33 the children of I turned again
Judg 8:34 the children of I remembered not
Judg 8:35 which he had shewed unto I
Judg 9:22 had reigned three years over I
Judg 9:55 when the men of I saw that
Judg 10:1 to defend I Tola the son of Puah
Judg 10:2 And he judged I twenty and three
Judg 10:3 a Gileadite, and judged I twenty
Judg 10:6 the children of I did evil again
Judg 10:7 of the LORD was hot against I
Judg 10:8 and oppressed the children of I
Judg 10:8 all the children of I that were
Judg 10:9 so that I was sore distressed
Judg 10:10 the children of I cried unto the
Judg 10:11 LORD said unto the children of I
Judg 10:15 the children of I said unto the
Judg 10:16 was grieved for the misery of I
Judg 10:17 the children of I assembled
Judg 11:4 of Ammon made war against I
Judg 11:5 of Ammon made war against I
Judg 11:13 Because I took away my land, when
Judg 11:15 I took not away the land of Moab,
Judg 11:16 But when I came up from Egypt, and
Judg 11:17 Then I sent messengers unto the
Judg 11:17 and I abode in Kadesh
Judg 11:19 I sent messengers unto Sihon king
Judg 11:19 I said unto him, Let us pass, we
Judg 11:20 But Sihon trusted not I to pass
Judg 11:20 in Jahaz, and fought against I
Judg 11:21 the LORD God of I delivered Sihon
Judg 11:21 all his people into the hand of I
Judg 11:21 so I possessed all the land of
Judg 11:23 So now the LORD God of I hath
Judg 11:23 Amorites from before his people I
Judg 11:25 did he ever strive against I
Judg 11:26 While I dwelt in Heshbon and her
Judg 11:27 day between the children of I
Judg 11:33 subdued before the children of I
Judg 11:39 And it was a custom in I,
Judg 11:40 That the daughters of I went
Judg 12:7 And Jephthah judged I six years
Judg 12:8 him Ibzan of Beth-lehem judged I
Judg 12:9 And he judged I seven years
Judg 12:11 him Elon, a Zebulonite, judged I
Judg 12:11 and he judged I ten years
Judg 12:13 Hillel, a Pirathonite, judged I
Judg 12:14 and he judged I eight years
Judg 13:1 the children of I did evil again
Judg 13:5 deliver I out of the hand of the
Judg 14:4 Philistines had dominion over I
Judg 15:20 he judged I in the days of the
Judg 16:31 And he judged I twenty years
Judg 17:6 those days there was no king in I
Judg 18:1 those days there was no king in I
Judg 18:1 unto them among the tribes of I
Judg 18:19 unto a tribe and a family in I
Judg 19:1 days, when there was no king in I
Judg 19:12 that is not of the children of I
Judg 19:29 sent her into all the coasts of I
Judg 19:30 of I came up out of the land of
Judg 20:1 all the children of I went out
Judg 20:2 even of all the tribes of I
Judg 20:3 of I were gone up to Mizpeh
Judg 20:3 Then said the children of I
Judg 20:6 country of the inheritance of I
Judg 20:6 committed lewdness and folly in I
Judg 20:7 Behold, ye are all children of I
Judg 20:10 throughout all the tribes of I
Judg 20:10 folly that they have wrought in I
Judg 20:11 So all the men of I were gathered
Judg 20:12 the tribes of I sent men through
Judg 20:13 to death, and put away evil from I
Judg 20:13 their brethren the children of I
Judg 20:14 battle against the children of I
Judg 20:17 And the men of I, beside Benjamin,
Judg 20:18 And the children of I arose
Judg 20:19 the children of I rose up in the
Judg 20:20 the men of I went out to battle
Judg 20:20 the men of I put themselves in
Judg 20:22 men of I encouraged themselves
Judg 20:23 (And the children of I went up
Judg 20:24 the children of I came near
Judg 20:25 of I again eighteen thousand men
Judg 20:26 Then all the children of I
Judg 20:27 the children of I enquired of the
Judg 20:29 I set liers in wait round about
Judg 20:30 the children of I went up against
Judg 20:31 the field, about thirty men of I
Judg 20:32 But the children of I said
Judg 20:33 all the men of I rose up out of
Judg 20:33 the liers in wait of I came forth
Judg 20:34 thousand chosen men out of all I
Judg 20:35 the LORD smote Benjamin before I
Judg 20:35 the children of I destroyed of
Judg 20:36 for the men of I gave place to
Judg 20:38 sign between the men of I
Judg 20:39 when the men of I retired in the
Judg 20:39 kill of the men of I about thirty
Judg 20:41 And when the men of I turned again
Judg 20:42 their backs before the men of I
Judg 20:48 the men of I turned again upon
Judg 21:1 Now the men of I had sworn in
Judg 21:3 And said, O LORD God of I
Judg 21:3 why is this come to pass in I
Judg 21:3 be to day one tribe lacking in I
Judg 21:5 And the children of I said
Judg 21:5 of I that came not up with the
Judg 21:6 the children of I repented them
Judg 21:6 one tribe cut off from I this day
Judg 21:8 I that came not up to Mizpeh to
Judg 21:15 made a breach in the tribes of I
Judg 21:17 a tribe be not destroyed out of I
Judg 21:18 for the children of I have sworn
Judg 21:24 the children of I departed thence
Judg 21:25 those days there was no king in I
Ruth 2:12 given thee of the LORD God of I
Ruth 4:7 time in I concerning redeeming
Ruth 4:7 and this was a testimony in I
Ruth 4:11 two did build the house of I
Ruth 4:14 that his name may be famous in I
1Sa 1:17 the God of I grant thee thy
1Sa 2:22 all that his sons did unto all I
1Sa 2:28 the tribes of I to be my priest
1Sa 2:28 made by fire of the children of I
1Sa 2:29 all the offerings of I my people
1Sa 2:30 Wherefore the LORD God of I saith
1Sa 2:32 the wealth which God shall give I
1Sa 3:11 Behold, I will do a thing in I
1Sa 3:20 all I from Dan even to Beer-sheba
1Sa 4:1 the word of Samuel came to all I
1Sa 4:1 Now I went out against the
1Sa 4:2 put themselves in array against I
1Sa 4:2 battle, I was smitten before the
1Sa 4:3 the camp, the elders of I said
1Sa 4:5 all I shouted with a great shout,
1Sa 4:10 I was smitten, and they fled every
1Sa 4:10 for there fell of I thirty
1Sa 4:17 I is fled before the Philistines,
1Sa 4:18 And he had judged I forty years
1Sa 4:21 The glory is departed from I
1Sa 4:22 The glory is departed from I
1Sa 5:7 The ark of the God of I shall not
1Sa 5:8 do with the ark of the God of I
1Sa 5:8 Let the ark of the God of I be
1Sa 5:8 ark of the God of I about thither
1Sa 5:10 the ark of the God of I to us
1Sa 5:11 Send away the ark of the God of I
1Sa 6:3 send away the ark of the God of I
1Sa 6:5 give glory unto the God of I
1Sa 7:2 all the house of I lamented after
1Sa 7:3 spake unto all the house of I
1Sa 7:4 children of I did put away Baalim
1Sa 7:5 said, Gather all I to Mizpeh
1Sa 7:6 the children of I in Mizpeh
1Sa 7:7 of I were gathered together to
1Sa 7:7 the Philistines went up against I
1Sa 7:7 when the children of I heard it
1Sa 7:8 the children of I said to Samuel
1Sa 7:9 Samuel cried unto the LORD for I
1Sa 7:10 drew near to battle against I
1Sa 7:10 and they were smitten before I
1Sa 7:11 the men of I went out of Mizpeh,
1Sa 7:13 came no more into the coast of I
1Sa 7:14 from I were restored to Israel
1Sa 7:14 the coasts thereof did I deliver
1Sa 7:14 And there was peace between I
1Sa 7:15 Samuel judged I all the days of
1Sa 7:16 judged I in all those places
1Sa 7:17 and there he judged I
1Sa 8:1 he made his sons judges over I
1Sa 8:4 Then all the elders of I gathered
1Sa 8:22 And Samuel said unto the men of I
1Sa 9:2 of I a goodlier person than he
1Sa 9:9 (Beforetime in I, when a man went
1Sa 9:16 to be captain over my people I
1Sa 9:20 And on whom is all the desire of I
1Sa 9:21 the smallest of the tribes of I
1Sa 10:18 And said unto the children of I
1Sa 10:18 Thus saith the LORD God of I
1Sa 10:18 I brought up I out of Egypt
1Sa 10:20 all the tribes of I to come near
1Sa 11:2 lay it for a reproach upon all I
1Sa 11:3 unto all the coasts of I
1Sa 11:7 of I by the hands of messengers
1Sa 11:8 the children of I were three
1Sa 11:13 LORD hath wrought salvation in I
1Sa 11:15 all the men of I rejoiced greatly
1Sa 12:1 And Samuel said unto all I
1Sa 13:1 he had reigned two years over I
1Sa 13:2 chose him three thousand men of I
1Sa 13:4 all I heard say that Saul had
1Sa 13:4 and that I also was had in
1Sa 13:5 together to fight with I, thirty
1Sa 13:6 When the men of I saw that they
1Sa 13:13 thy kingdom upon I for ever
1Sa 13:19 throughout all the land of I

1Sa 14:12 delivered them into the hand of *I*
1Sa 14:18 that time with the children of *I*
1Sa 14:22 Likewise all the men of *I* which
1Sa 14:23 So the LORD saved *I* that day
1Sa 14:24 the men of *I* were distressed that
1Sa 14:37 deliver them into the hand of *I*
1Sa 14:39 the LORD liveth, which saveth *I*
1Sa 14:40 Then said he unto all *I*, Be ye on
1Sa 14:41 Saul said unto the LORD God of *I*
1Sa 14:45 wrought this great salvation in *I*
1Sa 14:47 So Saul took the kingdom over *I*
1Sa 14:48 delivered *I* out of the hands of
1Sa 15:1 be king over his people, over *I*
1Sa 15:2 that which Amalek did to *I*
1Sa 15:6 kindness to all the children of *I*
1Sa 15:17 made the head of the tribes of *I*
1Sa 15:17 LORD anointed thee king over *I*
1Sa 15:26 thee from being king over *I*
1Sa 15:28 kingdom of *I* from thee this day
1Sa 15:29 also the Strength of *I* will not
1Sa 15:30 elders of my people, and before *I*
1Sa 15:35 that he had made Saul king over *I*
1Sa 16:1 rejected him from reigning over *I*
1Sa 17:2 the men of *I* were gathered
1Sa 17:3 *I* stood on a mountain on the
1Sa 17:8 and cried unto the armies of *I*
1Sa 17:10 I defy the armies of *I* this day
1Sa 17:11 all *I* heard those words of the
1Sa 17:19 and they, and all the men of *I*
1Sa 17:21 For *I* and the Philistines had put
1Sa 17:24 And all the men of *I*, when they
1Sa 17:25 And the men of *I* said, Have ye
1Sa 17:25 surely to defy *I* is he come up
1Sa 17:25 make his father's house free in *I*
1Sa 17:26 taketh away the reproach from *I*
1Sa 17:45 hosts, the God of the armies of *I*
1Sa 17:46 may know that there is a God in *I*
1Sa 17:52 And the men of *I* and of Judah arose
1Sa 17:53 the children of *I* returned from
1Sa 18:6 women came out of all cities of *I*
1Sa 18:16 But all *I* and Judah loved David,
1Sa 18:18 life, or my father's family in *I*
1Sa 19:5 a great salvation for all *I*
1Sa 20:12 said unto David, O LORD God of *I*
1Sa 23:10 Then said David, O LORD God of *I*
1Sa 23:11 O LORD God of *I*, I beseech thee,
1Sa 23:17 and thou shalt be king over *I*
1Sa 24:2 thousand chosen men out of all *I*
1Sa 24:14 whom is the king of *I* come out
1Sa 24:20 that the kingdom of *I* shall be
1Sa 25:30 have appointed thee ruler over *I*
1Sa 25:32 Blessed be the LORD God of *I*
1Sa 25:34 deed, as the LORD God of *I* liveth
1Sa 26:2 thousand chosen men of *I* with him
1Sa 26:15 and who is like to thee in *I*
1Sa 26:20 for the king of *I* is come out to
1Sa 27:1 me any more in any coast of *I*
1Sa 27:12 his people *I* utterly to abhor him
1Sa 28:1 for warfare, to fight with *I*
1Sa 28:3 all *I* had lamented him, and buried
1Sa 28:4 and Saul gathered all *I* together
1Sa 28:19 the LORD will also deliver *I* with
1Sa 28:19 host of *I* into the hand of the
1Sa 29:3 the servant of Saul the king of *I*
1Sa 30:25 an ordinance for *I* unto this day
1Sa 31:1 the Philistines fought against *I*
1Sa 31:1 the men of *I* fled from before the
1Sa 31:7 when the men of *I* that were on
1Sa 31:7 saw that the men of *I* fled
2Sa 1:3 Out of the camp of *I* am I escaped
2Sa 1:12 the LORD, and for the house of *I*
2Sa 1:19 The beauty of *I* is slain upon thy
2Sa 1:24 Ye daughters of *I*, weep over Saul
2Sa 2:9 and over Benjamin, and over all *I*
2Sa 2:10 old when he began to reign over *I*
2Sa 2:17 Abner was beaten, and the men of *I*
2Sa 2:28 still, and pursued after *I* no more
2Sa 3:10 set up the throne of David over *I*
2Sa 3:12 to bring about all *I* unto thee
2Sa 3:17 with the elders of *I*, saying, Ye
2Sa 3:18 people *I* out of the hand of the
2Sa 3:19 Hebron all that seemed good to *I*
2Sa 3:21 will gather all *I* unto my lord
2Sa 3:37 all *I* understood that day that it
2Sa 3:38 a great man fallen this day in *I*
2Sa 5:1 tribes of *I* to David unto Hebron
2Sa 5:2 leddest out and broughtest in *I*
2Sa 5:2 thee, Thou shalt feed my people *I*
2Sa 5:2 and thou shalt be a captain over *I*
2Sa 5:3 So all the elders of *I* came to
2Sa 5:3 they anointed David king over *I*
2Sa 5:5 thirty and three years over all *I*
2Sa 5:12 had established him king over *I*
2Sa 5:17 had anointed David king over *I*
2Sa 6:1 together all the chosen men of *I*
2Sa 6:5 all the house of *I* played before
2Sa 6:15 all the house of *I* brought up the
2Sa 6:19 among the whole multitude of *I*
2Sa 6:20 glorious was the king of *I* today
2Sa 6:21 the people of the LORD, over *I*
2Sa 7:6 up the children of *I* out of Egypt
2Sa 7:7 *I* spake I a word with any of the
2Sa 7:7 word with any of the tribes of *I*
2Sa 7:7 I commanded to feed my people *I*
2Sa 7:8 be ruler over my people, over *I*
2Sa 7:10 appoint a place for my people *I*
2Sa 7:11 judges to be over my people *I*
2Sa 7:23 is like thy people, even like *I*
2Sa 7:24 *I* to be a people unto thee for
2Sa 7:26 LORD of hosts is the God over *I*
2Sa 7:27 thou, O LORD of hosts, God of *I*
2Sa 8:15 And David reigned over all *I*
2Sa 10:9 chose of all the choice men of *I*
2Sa 10:15 that they were smitten before *I*
2Sa 10:17 David, he gathered all *I* together
2Sa 10:18 And the Syrians fled before *I*
2Sa 10:19 that they were smitten before *I*
2Sa 10:19 Israel, they made peace with *I*
2Sa 11:1 his servants with him, and all *I*
2Sa 11:11 said unto David, The ark, and *I*
2Sa 12:7 Thus saith the LORD God of *I*
2Sa 12:7 I anointed thee king over *I*
2Sa 12:8 and gave thee the house of *I*
2Sa 12:12 I will do this thing before all *I*
2Sa 13:12 such thing ought to be done in *I*
2Sa 13:13 shalt be as one of the fools in *I*
2Sa 14:25 But in all *I* there was none to be
2Sa 15:2 is of one of the tribes of *I*
2Sa 15:6 all *I* that came to the king for
2Sa 15:6 stole the hearts of the men of *I*
2Sa 15:10 throughout all the tribes of *I*
2Sa 15:13 of the men of *I* are after Absalom
2Sa 16:3 Today shall the house of *I*
2Sa 16:15 and all the people the men of *I*
2Sa 16:18 this people, and all the men of *I*
2Sa 16:21 all *I* shall hear that thou art
2Sa 16:22 concubines in the sight of all *I*
2Sa 17:4 well, and all the elders of *I*
2Sa 17:10 for all *I* knoweth that thy father
2Sa 17:11 Therefore I counsel that all *I* be
2Sa 17:13 then shall all *I* bring ropes to
2Sa 17:14 Absalom and all the men of *I* said
2Sa 17:15 Absalom and the elders of *I*
2Sa 17:24 he and all the men of *I* with him
2Sa 17:26 So *I* and Absalom pitched in the
2Sa 18:6 went out into the field against *I*
2Sa 18:7 Where the people of *I* were slain
2Sa 18:16 returned from pursuing after *I*
2Sa 18:17 all *I* fled every one to his tent
2Sa 19:8 for *I* had fled every man to his
2Sa 19:9 throughout all the tribes of *I*
2Sa 19:11 of all *I* is come to the king
2Sa 19:22 man be put to death this day in *I*
2Sa 19:22 that I am this day king over *I*
2Sa 19:40 and also half the people of *I*
2Sa 19:41 all the men of *I* came to the king
2Sa 19:42 of Judah answered the men of *I*
2Sa 19:43 the men of *I* answered the men of
2Sa 19:43 than the words of the men of *I*
2Sa 20:1 every man to his tents, O *I*
2Sa 20:2 So every man of *I* went up from
2Sa 20:14 all the tribes of *I* unto Abel
2Sa 20:19 are peaceable and faithful in *I*
2Sa 20:19 destroy a city and a mother in *I*
2Sa 20:23 Joab was over all the host of *I*
2Sa 21:2 were not of the children of *I*
2Sa 21:2 the children of *I* had sworn unto
2Sa 21:2 in his zeal to the children of *I*
2Sa 21:4 us shalt thou kill any man in *I*
2Sa 21:5 in any of the coasts of *I*
2Sa 21:15 had yet war again with *I*
2Sa 21:17 thou quench not the light of *I*
2Sa 21:21 And when he defied *I*, Jonathan the
2Sa 23:1 Jacob, and the sweet psalmist of *I*
2Sa 23:3 The God of *I* said, the Rock of
2Sa 23:3 said, the Rock of *I* spake to me
2Sa 23:9 the men of *I* were gone away
2Sa 24:1 of the LORD was kindled against *I*
2Sa 24:1 against them to say, Go, number *I*
2Sa 24:2 now through all the tribes of *I*
2Sa 24:4 king, to number the people of *I*
2Sa 24:9 there were in *I* eight hundred
2Sa 24:15 *I* from the morning even to the
2Sa 24:25 and the plague was stayed from *I*
1Kin 1:3 throughout all the coasts of *I*
1Kin 1:20 the eyes of all *I* are upon thee
1Kin 1:30 unto thee by the LORD God of *I*
1Kin 1:34 anoint him there king over *I*
1Kin 1:35 appointed him to be ruler over *I*
1Kin 1:48 Blessed be the LORD God of *I*
1Kin 2:4 said he) a man on the throne of *I*
1Kin 2:5 two captains of the hosts of *I*
1Kin 2:11 reigned over *I* were forty years
1Kin 2:15 that all *I* set their faces on me,
1Kin 2:32 of Ner, captain of the host of *I*
1Kin 3:28 all *I* heard of the judgment which
1Kin 4:1 king Solomon was king over all *I*
1Kin 4:7 had twelve officers over all *I*
1Kin 5:13 raised a levy out of all *I*
1Kin 6:1 year after the children of *I* were
1Kin 6:1 year of Solomon's reign over *I*
1Kin 6:13 dwell among the children of *I*
1Kin 6:13 and will not forsake my people *I*
1Kin 8:1 Solomon assembled the elders of *I*
1Kin 8:1 the fathers of the children of *I*
1Kin 8:2 all the men of *I* assembled
1Kin 8:3 And all the elders of *I* came
1Kin 8:5 and all the congregation of *I*
1Kin 8:9 a covenant with the children of *I*
1Kin 8:14 blessed all the congregation of *I*
1Kin 8:14 all the congregation of *I* stood
1Kin 8:15 Blessed be the LORD God of *I*
1Kin 8:16 forth my people *I* out of Egypt
1Kin 8:16 the tribes of *I* to build an house
1Kin 8:16 David to be over my people *I*
1Kin 8:17 for the name of the LORD God of *I*
1Kin 8:20 father, and sit on the throne of *I*
1Kin 8:20 for the name of the LORD God of *I*
1Kin 8:22 of all the congregation of *I*
1Kin 8:23 And he said, LORD God of *I*
1Kin 8:25 Therefore now, LORD God of *I*
1Kin 8:25 sight to sit on the throne of *I*
1Kin 8:26 And now, O God of *I*, let thy word,
1Kin 8:30 thy servant, and of thy people *I*
1Kin 8:33 When thy people *I* be smitten down
1Kin 8:34 forgive the sin of thy people *I*
1Kin 8:36 thy servants, and of thy people *I*
1Kin 8:38 any man, or by all thy people *I*
1Kin 8:41 that is not of thy people *I*
1Kin 8:43 to fear thee, as do thy people *I*
1Kin 8:52 the supplication of thy people *I*
1Kin 8:55 of *I* with a loud voice, saying,
1Kin 8:56 hath given rest unto his people *I*
1Kin 8:59 of his people *I* at all times
1Kin 8:62 all *I* with him, offered sacrifice
1Kin 8:63 all the children of *I* dedicated
1Kin 8:65 feast, and all *I* with him, a great
1Kin 8:66 his servant, and for *I* his people
1Kin 9:5 of thy kingdom upon *I* for ever
1Kin 9:5 thee a man upon the throne of *I*
1Kin 9:7 Then will I cut off *I* out of the
1Kin 9:7 *I* shall be a proverb and a byword
1Kin 9:20 were not of the children of *I*
1Kin 9:21 whom the children of *I* also were
1Kin 9:22 But of the children of *I* did
1Kin 10:9 to set thee on the throne of *I*
1Kin 10:9 because the LORD loved *I* for ever
1Kin 11:2 LORD said unto the children of *I*
1Kin 11:9 was turned from the LORD God of *I*
1Kin 11:16 did Joab remain there with all *I*
1Kin 11:25 he was an adversary to *I* all the
1Kin 11:25 and he abhorred *I*, and reigned over
1Kin 11:31 thus saith the LORD, the God of *I*
1Kin 11:32 chosen out of all the tribes of *I*
1Kin 11:37 desireth, and shalt be king over *I*
1Kin 11:38 David, and will give *I* unto thee
1Kin 11:42 over all *I* was forty years
1Kin 12:1 for all *I* were come to Shechem to
1Kin 12:3 and all the congregation of *I* came
1Kin 12:16 So when all *I* saw that the king
1Kin 12:16 to your tents, O *I*
1Kin 12:16 So *I* departed unto their tents
1Kin 12:17 But as for the children of *I*
1Kin 14:7 Thus saith the LORD God of *I*
1Kin 14:7 made thee prince over my people *I*
1Kin 14:21 choose out of all the tribes of *I*
1Kin 14:24 cast out before the children of *I*
1Kin 15:34 sin wherewith he made *I* to sin
1Kin 16:33 *I* to anger than all the kings of
1Kin 17:1 Ahab, As the LORD God of *I* liveth

| | |
|---|---|
| 1Kin 17:14 | For thus saith the LORD God of *I* |
| 1Kin 18:36 | this day that thou art God in *I* |
| 1Kin 22:53 | to anger the LORD God of *I* |
| 2Kin 2:12 | my father, the chariot of *I* |
| 2Kin 9:6 | him, Thus saith the LORD God of *I* |
| 2Kin 10:31 | LORD God of *I* with all his heart |
| 2Kin 14:25 | He restored the coast of *I* from |
| 2Kin 14:25 | to the word of the LORD God of *I* |
| 2Kin 18:4 | of *I* did burn incense to it |
| 2Kin 18:5 | He trusted in the LORD God of *I* |
| 2Kin 19:15 | LORD, and said, O LORD God of *I* |
| 2Kin 19:20 | Thus saith the LORD God of *I* |
| 2Kin 19:22 | even against the Holy One of *I* |
| 2Kin 21:2 | cast out before the children of *I* |
| 2Kin 21:3 | a grove, as did Ahab king of *I* |
| 2Kin 21:7 | chosen out of all tribes of *I* |
| 2Kin 21:8 | *I* move any more out of the land |
| 2Kin 21:9 | before the children of *I* |
| 2Kin 21:12 | thus saith the LORD God of *I* |
| 2Kin 22:15 | Thus saith the LORD God of *I* |
| 2Kin 22:18 | him, Thus saith the LORD God of *I* |
| 2Kin 23:13 | which Solomon the king of *I* had |
| 2Kin 23:22 | days of the judges that judged *I* |
| 2Kin 24:13 | *I* had made in the temple of the |
| 1Chr 1:43 | reigned over the children of *I* |
| 1Chr 2:7 | Achar, the troubler of *I*, who |
| 1Chr 4:10 | And Jabez called on the God of *I* |
| 1Chr 5:26 | the God of *I* stirred up the |
| 1Chr 6:49 | and to make an atonement for *I* |
| 1Chr 6:64 | the children of *I* gave to the |
| 1Chr 9:1 | So all *I* were reckoned by |
| 1Chr 10:1 | the Philistines fought against *I* |
| 1Chr 10:1 | the men of *I* fled from before the |
| 1Chr 10:7 | when all the men of *I* that were |
| 1Chr 11:1 | Then all *I* gathered themselves to |
| 1Chr 11:2 | leddest out and broughtest in *I* |
| 1Chr 11:2 | thee, Thou shalt feed my people *I* |
| 1Chr 11:2 | shalt be ruler over my people *I* |
| 1Chr 11:3 | elders of *I* to the king to Hebron |
| 1Chr 11:3 | they anointed David king over *I* |
| 1Chr 11:4 | all *I* went to Jerusalem, which is |
| 1Chr 11:10 | him in his kingdom, and with all *I* |
| 1Chr 11:10 | the word of the LORD concerning *I* |
| 1Chr 12:32 | times, to know what *I* ought to do |
| 1Chr 12:38 | to make David king over all *I* |
| 1Chr 12:38 | all the rest also of *I* were of |
| 1Chr 12:40 | for there was joy in *I* |
| 1Chr 13:2 | unto all the congregation of *I* |
| 1Chr 13:2 | are left in all the land of *I* |
| 1Chr 13:5 | So David gathered all *I* together |
| 1Chr 13:6 | And David went up, and all *I* |
| 1Chr 13:8 | all *I* played before God with all |
| 1Chr 14:2 | had confirmed him king over *I* |
| 1Chr 14:2 | on high, because of his people *I* |
| 1Chr 14:8 | was anointed king over all *I* |
| 1Chr 15:3 | David gathered all *I* together to |
| 1Chr 15:12 | of *I* unto the place that I have |
| 1Chr 15:14 | up the ark of the LORD God of *I* |
| 1Chr 15:25 | So David, and the elders of *I* |
| 1Chr 15:28 | Thus all *I* brought up the ark of |
| 1Chr 16:3 | And he dealt to every one of *I* |
| 1Chr 16:4 | thank and praise the LORD God of *I* |
| 1Chr 16:13 | O ye seed of *I* his servant |
| 1Chr 16:17 | to *I* for an everlasting covenant, |
| 1Chr 16:36 | be the LORD God of *I* for ever |
| 1Chr 16:40 | of the LORD, which he commanded *I* |
| 1Chr 17:5 | that I brought up *I* unto this day |
| 1Chr 17:6 | I have walked with all *I*, spake I |
| 1Chr 17:6 | a word to any of the judges of *I* |
| 1Chr 17:7 | be ruler over my people *I* |
| 1Chr 17:9 | ordain a place for my people *I* |
| 1Chr 17:10 | judges to be over my people *I* |
| 1Chr 17:21 | in the earth is like thy people *I* |
| 1Chr 17:22 | For thy people *I* didst thou make |
| 1Chr 17:24 | God of Israel, even a God to *I* |
| 1Chr 18:14 | So David reigned over all *I* |
| 1Chr 19:10 | chose out of all the choice of *I* |
| 1Chr 19:16 | were put to the worse before *I* |
| 1Chr 19:17 | and he gathered all *I*, and passed |
| 1Chr 19:18 | But the Syrians fled before *I* |
| 1Chr 19:19 | were put to the worse before *I* |
| 1Chr 20:7 | But when he defied *I*, Jonathan |
| 1Chr 21:1 | And Satan stood up against *I* |
| 1Chr 21:1 | and provoked David to number *I* |
| 1Chr 21:2 | number *I* from Beer-sheba even to |
| 1Chr 21:3 | he be a cause of trespass to *I* |
| 1Chr 21:4 | and went throughout all *I* |
| 1Chr 21:5 | all they of *I* were a thousand |
| 1Chr 21:7 | therefore he smote *I* |
| 1Chr 21:12 | throughout all the coasts of *I* |
| 1Chr 21:14 | the LORD sent pestilence upon *I* |
| 1Chr 21:14 | there fell of *I* seventy thousand |
| 1Chr 21:16 | Then David and the elders of *I* |
| 1Chr 22:1 | altar of the burnt offering for *I* |
| 1Chr 22:2 | that were in the land of *I* |
| 1Chr 22:6 | an house for the LORD God of *I* |
| 1Chr 22:9 | and quietness unto *I* in his days |
| 1Chr 22:10 | of his kingdom over *I* for ever |
| 1Chr 22:12 | and give thee charge concerning *I* |
| 1Chr 22:13 | charged Moses with concerning *I* |
| 1Chr 22:17 | of *I* to help Solomon his son |
| 1Chr 23:1 | made Solomon his son king over *I* |
| 1Chr 23:2 | together all the princes of *I* |
| 1Chr 23:25 | The LORD God of *I* hath given rest |
| 1Chr 24:19 | LORD God of *I* had commanded him |
| 1Chr 26:29 | for the outward business over *I* |
| 1Chr 26:30 | were officers among them of *I* on |
| 1Chr 27:1 | children of *I* after their number |
| 1Chr 27:16 | Furthermore over the tribes of *I* |
| 1Chr 27:22 | the princes of the tribes of *I* |
| 1Chr 27:23 | *I* like to the stars of the |
| 1Chr 27:24 | there fell wrath for it against *I* |
| 1Chr 28:1 | assembled all the princes of *I* |
| 1Chr 28:4 | Howbeit the LORD God of *I* chose |
| 1Chr 28:4 | father to be king over *I* for ever |
| 1Chr 28:4 | me to make me king over all *I* |
| 1Chr 28:5 | of the kingdom of the LORD over *I* |
| 1Chr 28:8 | in the sight of all *I* the |
| 1Chr 29:6 | and princes of the tribes of *I* |
| 1Chr 29:21 | sacrifices in abundance for all *I* |
| 1Chr 29:23 | and all *I* obeyed him |
| 1Chr 29:25 | exceedingly in the sight of all *I* |
| 1Chr 29:25 | been on any king before him in *I* |
| 1Chr 29:26 | son of Jesse reigned over all *I* |
| 1Chr 29:27 | he reigned over *I* was forty years |
| 1Chr 29:30 | that went over him, and over *I* |
| 2Chr 1:2 | Then Solomon spake unto all *I* |
| 2Chr 1:2 | and to every governor in all *I* |
| 2Chr 1:13 | congregation, and reigned over *I* |
| 2Chr 2:4 | is an ordinance for ever to *I* |
| 2Chr 2:12 | Blessed be the LORD God of *I* |
| 2Chr 2:17 | that were in the land of *I* |
| 2Chr 5:2 | Solomon assembled the elders of *I* |
| 2Chr 5:2 | the fathers of the children of *I* |
| 2Chr 5:3 | Wherefore all the men of *I* |
| 2Chr 5:4 | And all the elders of *I* came |
| 2Chr 5:6 | all the congregation of *I* that |
| 2Chr 5:10 | a covenant with the children of *I* |
| 2Chr 6:3 | the whole congregation of *I* |
| 2Chr 6:3 | all the congregation of *I* stood |
| 2Chr 6:4 | Blessed be the LORD God of *I* |
| 2Chr 6:5 | tribes of *I* to build an house in |
| 2Chr 6:5 | to be a ruler over my people *I* |
| 2Chr 6:6 | David to be over my people *I* |
| 2Chr 6:7 | for the name of the LORD God of *I* |
| 2Chr 6:10 | and am set on the throne of *I* |
| 2Chr 6:10 | for the name of the LORD God of *I* |
| 2Chr 6:11 | he made with the children of *I* |
| 2Chr 6:12 | of all the congregation of *I* |
| 2Chr 6:13 | before all the congregation of *I* |
| 2Chr 6:14 | And said, O LORD God of *I*, there |
| 2Chr 6:16 | Now therefore, O LORD God of *I* |
| 2Chr 6:16 | sight to sit upon the throne of *I* |
| 2Chr 6:17 | Now then, O LORD God of *I* |
| 2Chr 6:21 | thy servant, and of thy people *I* |
| 2Chr 6:24 | if thy people *I* be put to the |
| 2Chr 6:25 | forgive the sin of thy people *I* |
| 2Chr 6:27 | thy servants, and of thy people *I* |
| 2Chr 6:29 | any man, or of all thy people *I* |
| 2Chr 6:32 | which is not of thy people *I* |
| 2Chr 6:33 | fear thee, as doth thy people *I* |
| 2Chr 7:3 | when all the children of *I* saw |
| 2Chr 7:6 | before them, and all *I* stood |
| 2Chr 7:8 | all *I* with him, a very great |
| 2Chr 7:10 | and to Solomon, and to *I* his people |
| 2Chr 7:18 | fail thee a man to be ruler in *I* |
| 2Chr 8:2 | the children of *I* to dwell there |
| 2Chr 8:7 | Jebusites, which were not of *I* |
| 2Chr 8:8 | the children of *I* consumed not |
| 2Chr 8:9 | But of the children of *I* did |
| 2Chr 8:11 | in the house of David king of *I* |
| 2Chr 9:8 | because thy God loved *I*, to |
| 2Chr 9:30 | Jerusalem over all *I* forty years |
| 2Chr 10:1 | were all *I* come to make him king |
| 2Chr 10:3 | all *I* came and spake to Rehoboam, |
| 2Chr 10:16 | when all *I* saw that the king |
| 2Chr 10:16 | every man to your tents, O *I* |
| 2Chr 10:16 | So all *I* went to their tents |
| 2Chr 10:17 | But as for the children of *I* that |
| 2Chr 11:3 | to all *I* in Judah and Benjamin, |
| 2Chr 11:16 | LORD God of *I* came to Jerusalem |
| 2Chr 12:1 | of the LORD, and all *I* with him |
| 2Chr 12:6 | Whereupon the princes of *I* |
| 2Chr 12:13 | chosen out of all the tribes of *I* |
| 2Chr 13:5 | to know that the LORD God of *I* |
| 2Chr 13:5 | kingdom over *I* to David for ever |
| 2Chr 15:3 | Now for a long season *I* hath been |
| 2Chr 15:4 | did turn unto the LORD God of *I* |
| 2Chr 15:13 | God of *I* should be put to death |
| 2Chr 19:8 | of the chief of the fathers of *I* |
| 2Chr 20:7 | of this land before thy people *I* |
| 2Chr 20:10 | thou wouldest not let *I* invade |
| 2Chr 20:19 | of *I* with a loud voice on high |
| 2Chr 20:29 | fought against the enemies of *I* |
| 2Chr 23:2 | and the chief of the fathers of *I* |
| 2Chr 24:5 | gather of all *I* money to repair |
| 2Chr 24:6 | LORD, and of the congregation of *I* |
| 2Chr 24:9 | God laid upon *I* in the wilderness |
| 2Chr 24:16 | because he had done good in *I* |
| 2Chr 28:3 | cast out before the children of *I* |
| 2Chr 28:23 | were the ruin of him, and of all *I* |
| 2Chr 28:26 | book of the kings of Judah and *I* |
| 2Chr 28:27 | the sepulchres of the kings of *I* |
| 2Chr 29:7 | the holy place unto the God of *I* |
| 2Chr 29:10 | a covenant with the LORD God of *I* |
| 2Chr 29:24 | to make an atonement for all *I* |
| 2Chr 29:24 | offering should be made for all *I* |
| 2Chr 29:27 | ordained by David king of *I* |
| 2Chr 30:1 | And Hezekiah sent to all *I* |
| 2Chr 30:1 | passover unto the LORD God of *I* |
| 2Chr 30:5 | proclamation throughout all *I* |
| 2Chr 30:5 | the LORD God of *I* at Jerusalem |
| 2Chr 30:6 | king, saying, Ye children of *I* |
| 2Chr 30:26 | the son of David king of *I* there |
| 2Chr 31:1 | all *I* that were present went out |
| 2Chr 31:1 | all the children of *I* returned |
| 2Chr 31:5 | the children of *I* brought in |
| 2Chr 31:8 | blessed the LORD, and his people *I* |
| 2Chr 32:17 | to rail on the LORD God of *I* |
| 2Chr 33:2 | cast out before the children of *I* |
| 2Chr 33:7 | chosen before all the tribes of *I* |
| 2Chr 33:8 | of *I* from out of the land which I |
| 2Chr 33:9 | before the children of *I* |
| 2Chr 33:16 | Judah to serve the LORD God of *I* |
| 2Chr 33:18 | in the name of the LORD God of *I* |
| 2Chr 33:18 | in the book of the kings of *I* |
| 2Chr 34:7 | throughout all the land of *I* |
| 2Chr 34:23 | Thus saith the LORD God of *I* |
| 2Chr 34:26 | Thus saith the LORD God of *I* |
| 2Chr 34:33 | pertained to the children of *I* |
| 2Chr 34:33 | that were present in *I* to serve |
| 2Chr 35:3 | the Levites that taught all *I* |
| 2Chr 35:3 | son of David king of *I* did build |
| 2Chr 35:3 | LORD your God, and his people *I* |
| 2Chr 35:4 | to the writing of David king of *I* |
| 2Chr 35:17 | the children of *I* that were |
| 2Chr 35:18 | in *I* from the days of Samuel the |
| 2Chr 35:25 | and made them an ordinance in *I* |
| 2Chr 36:13 | turning unto the LORD God of *I* |
| Ezr 1:3 | the house of the LORD God of *I* |
| Ezr 2:2 | of the men of the people of *I* |
| Ezr 2:59 | seed, whether they were of *I* |
| Ezr 2:70 | cities, and all *I* in their cities |
| Ezr 3:1 | the children of *I* were in the |
| Ezr 3:2 | builded the altar of the God of *I* |
| Ezr 3:10 | the ordinance of David king of *I* |
| Ezr 3:11 | mercy endureth for ever toward *I* |
| Ezr 4:1 | the temple unto the LORD God of *I* |
| Ezr 4:3 | of the chief of the fathers of *I* |
| Ezr 4:3 | will build unto the LORD God of *I* |
| Ezr 5:1 | in the name of the God of *I* |
| Ezr 5:11 | which a great king of *I* builded |
| Ezr 6:14 | the commandment of the God of *I* |
| Ezr 6:16 | And the children of *I*, the priests |
| Ezr 6:17 | and for a sin offering for all *I* |
| Ezr 6:17 | to the number of the tribes of *I* |
| Ezr 6:21 | And the children of *I*, which were |
| Ezr 6:21 | land, to seek the LORD God of *I* |
| Ezr 6:22 | of the house of God, the God of *I* |
| Ezr 7:6 | which the LORD God of *I* had given |
| Ezr 7:7 | went up some of the children of *I* |
| Ezr 7:10 | do it, and to teach in *I* statutes |
| Ezr 7:11 | the LORD, and of his statutes to *I* |
| Ezr 7:13 | that all they of the people of *I* |
| Ezr 7:15 | freely offered unto the God of *I* |
| Ezr 7:28 | of *I* chief men to go up with me |
| Ezr 8:25 | all *I* there present, had offered |
| Ezr 8:29 | and chief of the fathers of *I* |
| Ezr 8:35 | burnt offerings unto the God of *I* |
| Ezr 8:35 | twelve bullocks for all *I* |

Ezr 9:1 to me, saying, The people of *I*
Ezr 9:4 at the words of the God of *I*
Ezr 9:15 O LORD God of *I*, thou art
Ezr 10:1 of *I* a very great congregation of
Ezr 10:2 hope in *I* concerning this thing
Ezr 10:5 priests, the Levites, and all *I*
Ezr 10:10 to increase the trespass of *I*
Ezr 10:25 Moreover of *I*: of the sons of
Neh 1:6 the children of *I* thy servants
Neh 1:6 the sins of the children of *I*
Neh 2:10 the welfare of the children of *I*
Neh 7:7 men of the people of *I* was this
Neh 7:61 seed, whether they were of *I*
Neh 7:73 and the Nethinims, and all *I*
Neh 7:73 the children of *I* were in their
Neh 8:1 which the LORD had commanded to *I*
Neh 8:14 that the children of *I* should
Neh 8:17 had not the children of *I* done so
Neh 9:1 of *I* were assembled with fasting
Neh 9:2 And the seed of *I* separated
Neh 10:33 to make an atonement for *I*
Neh 10:39 For the children of *I* and the
Neh 11:3 in their cities, to wit, *I*
Neh 11:20 And the residue of *I*, of the
Neh 12:47 all *I* in the days of Zerubbabel,
Neh 13:2 not the children of *I* with bread
Neh 13:3 from *I* all the mixed multitude
Neh 13:18 upon *I* by profaning the sabbath
Neh 13:26 king of *I* sin by these things
Neh 13:26 and God made him king over all *I*
Ps 14:7 of *I* were come out of Zion
Ps 14:7 shall rejoice, and *I* shall be glad
Ps 22:3 that inhabitest the praises of *I*
Ps 22:23 and fear him, all ye the seed of *I*
Ps 25:22 Redeem *I*, O God, out of all his
Ps 41:13 LORD God of *I* from everlasting
Ps 50:7 O *I*, and I will testify against
Ps 53:6 of *I* were come out of Zion
Ps 53:6 shall rejoice, and *I* shall be glad
Ps 59:5 O LORD God of hosts, the God of *I*
Ps 68:8 the presence of God, the God of *I*
Ps 68:26 the Lord, from the fountain of *I*
Ps 68:34 his excellency is over *I*, and his
Ps 68:35 the God of *I* is he that giveth
Ps 69:6 for my sake, O God of *I*
Ps 71:22 the harp, O thou Holy One of *I*
Ps 72:18 be the LORD God, the God of *I*
Ps 73:1 Truly God is good to *I*, even to
Ps 76:1 his name is great in *I*
Ps 78:5 in Jacob, and appointed a law in *I*
Ps 78:21 and anger also came up against *I*
Ps 78:31 and smote down the chosen men of *I*
Ps 78:41 God, and limited the Holy One of *I*
Ps 78:55 made the tribes of *I* to dwell in
Ps 78:59 was wroth, and greatly abhorred *I*
Ps 78:71 his people, and *I* his inheritance
Ps 80:1 Give ear, O Shepherd of *I*
Ps 81:4 For this was a statute for *I*
Ps 81:8 O *I*, if thou wilt hearken unto me
Ps 81:11 and *I* would none of me
Ps 81:13 me, and *I* had walked in my ways
Ps 83:4 that the name of *I* may be no more
Ps 89:18 and the Holy One of *I* is our king
Ps 98:3 his truth toward the house of *I*
Ps 103:7 his acts unto the children of *I*
Ps 105:10 to *I* for an everlasting covenant
Ps 105:23 *I* also came into Egypt
Ps 106:48 Blessed be the LORD God of *I* from
Ps 114:1 When *I* went out of Egypt, the
Ps 114:2 his sanctuary, and *I* his dominion
Ps 115:9 O *I*, trust thou in the LORD
Ps 115:12 he will bless the house of *I*
Ps 118:2 Let *I* now say, that his mercy
Ps 121:4 he that keepeth *I* shall neither
Ps 122:4 the LORD, unto the testimony of *I*
Ps 124:1 was on our side, now may *I* say
Ps 125:5 but peace shall be upon *I*
Ps 128:6 children, and peace upon *I*
Ps 129:1 me from my youth, may *I* now say
Ps 130:7 Let *I* hope in the LORD
Ps 130:8 he shall redeem *I* from all his
Ps 131:3 Let *I* hope in the LORD from
Ps 135:4 *I* for his peculiar treasure
Ps 135:12 an heritage unto *I* his people
Ps 135:19 Bless the LORD, O house of *I*
Ps 136:11 brought out *I* from among them
Ps 136:14 made *I* to pass through the midst
Ps 136:22 an heritage unto *I* his servant
Ps 147:2 together the outcasts of *I*
Ps 147:19 statutes and his judgments unto *I*
Ps 148:14 even of the children of *I*
Ps 149:2 Let *I* rejoice in him that made
Prov 1:1 the son of David, king of *I*
Eccl 1:12 was king over *I* in Jerusalem
Song 3:7 are about it, of the valiant of *I*
Is 1:3 but *I* doth not know, my people
Is 1:4 the Holy One of *I* unto anger
Is 1:24 of hosts, the mighty One of *I*
Is 4:2 for them that are escaped of *I*
Is 5:7 LORD of hosts is the house of *I*
Is 5:19 of the Holy One of *I* draw nigh
Is 5:24 the word of the Holy One of *I*
Is 8:14 offence to both the houses of *I*
Is 8:18 for wonders in *I* from the LORD of
Is 9:8 Jacob, and it hath lighted upon *I*
Is 9:12 shall devour *I* with open mouth
Is 9:14 the LORD will cut off from *I* head
Is 10:17 the light of *I* shall be for a
Is 10:20 that day, that the remnant of *I*
Is 10:20 upon the LORD, the Holy One of *I*
Is 10:22 For though thy people *I* be as the
Is 11:12 shall assemble the outcasts of *I*
Is 11:16 like as it was to *I* in the day
Is 12:6 One of *I* in the midst of thee
Is 14:1 on Jacob, and will yet choose *I*
Is 14:2 the house of *I* shall possess them
Is 17:3 as the glory of the children of *I*
Is 17:6 thereof, saith the LORD God of *I*
Is 17:7 have respect to the Holy One of *I*
Is 17:9 left because of the children of *I*
Is 19:24 In that day shall *I* be the third
Is 19:25 my hands, and *I* mine inheritance
Is 21:10 the LORD of hosts, the God of *I*
Is 21:17 the LORD God of *I* hath spoken it
Is 24:15 God of *I* in the isles of the sea
Is 27:6 *I* shall blossom and bud, and fill
Is 27:12 one by one, O ye children of *I*
Is 29:19 rejoice in the Holy One of *I*
Is 29:23 Jacob, and shall fear the God of *I*
Is 30:11 cause the Holy One of *I* to cease
Is 30:12 thus saith the Holy One of *I*
Is 30:15 the Lord GOD, the Holy One of *I*
Is 30:29 the LORD, to the mighty One of *I*
Is 31:1 look not unto the Holy One of *I*
Is 31:6 of *I* have deeply revolted
Is 37:16 O LORD of hosts, God of *I*
Is 37:21 Thus saith the LORD God of *I*
Is 37:23 even against the Holy One of *I*
Is 40:27 thou, O Jacob, and speakest, O *I*
Is 41:8 But thou, *I*, art my servant,
Is 41:14 thou worm Jacob, and ye men of *I*
Is 41:14 thy redeemer, the Holy One of *I*
Is 41:16 shalt glory in the Holy One of *I*
Is 41:17 I the God of *I* will not forsake
Is 41:20 the Holy One of *I* hath created it
Is 42:24 for a spoil, and *I* to the robbers
Is 43:1 and he that formed thee, O *I*
Is 43:3 LORD thy God, the Holy One of *I*
Is 43:14 your redeemer, the Holy One of *I*
Is 43:15 your Holy One, the creator of *I*
Is 43:22 thou hast been weary of me, O *I*
Is 43:28 to the curse, and *I* to reproaches
Is 44:1 and *I*, whom I have chosen
Is 44:5 surname himself by the name of *I*
Is 44:6 Thus saith the LORD the King of *I*
Is 44:21 Remember these, O Jacob and *I*
Is 44:21 O *I*, thou shalt not be forgotten
Is 44:23 Jacob, and glorified himself in *I*
Is 45:3 thee by thy name, am the God of *I*
Is 45:4 *I* mine elect, I have even called
Is 45:11 saith the LORD, the Holy One of *I*
Is 45:15 that hidest thyself, O God of *I*
Is 45:17 But *I* shall be saved in the LORD
Is 45:25 all the seed of *I* be justified
Is 46:3 all the remnant of the house of *I*
Is 46:13 salvation in Zion for *I* my glory
Is 47:4 is his name, the Holy One of *I*
Is 48:1 which are called by the name of *I*
Is 48:1 and make mention of the God of *I*
Is 48:2 stay themselves upon the God of *I*
Is 48:12 Hearken unto me, O Jacob and *I*
Is 48:17 thy Redeemer, the Holy One of *I*
Is 49:3 unto me, Thou art my servant, O *I*
Is 49:5 Though *I* be not gathered, yet
Is 49:6 and to restore the preserved of *I*
Is 49:7 saith the LORD, the Redeemer of *I*
Is 49:7 is faithful, and the Holy One of *I*
Is 52:12 the God of *I* will be your
Is 54:5 and thy Redeemer the Holy One of *I*
Is 55:5 thy God, and for the Holy One of *I*
Is 56:8 gathereth the outcasts of *I* saith
Is 60:9 thy God, and to the Holy One of *I*
Is 60:14 The Zion of the Holy One of *I*
Is 63:7 goodness toward the house of *I*
Is 63:16 of us, and *I* acknowledge us not
Is 66:20 as the children of *I* bring an
Jer 2:3 *I* was holiness unto the LORD, and
Jer 2:4 the families of the house of *I*
Jer 2:14 Is *I* a servant?
Jer 3:20 with me, O house of *I*, saith the
Jer 3:21 of the children of *I*
Jer 3:23 our God is the salvation of *I*
Jer 4:1 If thou wilt return, O *I*, saith
Jer 5:15 upon you from far, O house of *I*
Jer 6:9 glean the remnant of *I* as a vine
Jer 7:3 the LORD of hosts, the God of *I*
Jer 7:12 for the wickedness of my people *I*
Jer 7:21 the LORD of hosts, the God of *I*
Jer 9:15 the LORD of hosts, the God of *I*
Jer 10:1 speaketh unto you, O house of *I*
Jer 10:16 *I* is the rod of his inheritance
Jer 11:3 Thus saith the LORD God of *I*
Jer 12:14 caused my people *I* to inherit
Jer 13:11 unto me the whole house of *I*
Jer 13:12 Thus saith the LORD God of *I*
Jer 14:8 O the hope of *I*, the saviour
Jer 16:9 the LORD of hosts, the God of *I*
Jer 16:14 of *I* out of the land of Egypt
Jer 16:15 of *I* from the land of the north
Jer 17:13 O LORD, the hope of *I*, all that
Jer 18:6 O house of *I*, cannot I do with
Jer 18:6 are ye in mine hand, O house of *I*
Jer 18:13 the virgin of *I* hath done a very
Jer 19:3 the LORD of hosts, the God of *I*
Jer 19:15 the LORD of hosts, the God of *I*
Jer 21:4 Thus saith the LORD God of *I*
Jer 23:2 thus saith the LORD God of *I*
Jer 23:7 of *I* out of the land of Egypt
Jer 23:8 of *I* out of the north country
Jer 23:13 and caused my people *I* to err
Jer 24:5 Thus saith the LORD, the God of *I*
Jer 25:15 saith the LORD God of *I* unto me
Jer 25:27 the LORD of hosts, the God of *I*
Jer 27:4 the LORD of hosts, the God of *I*
Jer 27:21 the LORD of hosts, the God of *I*
Jer 28:2 the LORD of hosts, the God of *I*
Jer 28:14 the LORD of hosts, the God of *I*
Jer 29:4 the LORD of hosts, the God of *I*
Jer 29:8 the LORD of hosts, the God of *I*
Jer 29:21 the LORD of hosts, the God of *I*
Jer 29:23 they have committed villany in *I*
Jer 29:25 the LORD of hosts, the God of *I*
Jer 30:2 Thus speaketh the LORD God of *I*
Jer 30:3 the captivity of my people *I*
Jer 30:4 that the LORD spake concerning *I*
Jer 30:10 neither be dismayed, O *I*
Jer 31:1 the God of all the families of *I*
Jer 31:2 even *I*, when I went to cause him
Jer 31:4 shalt be built, O virgin of *I*
Jer 31:7 save thy people, the remnant of *I*
Jer 31:9 for I am a father to *I*, and
Jer 31:10 that scattered *I* will gather him
Jer 31:21 turn again, O virgin of *I*
Jer 31:23 the LORD of hosts, the God of *I*
Jer 31:33 I will make with the house of *I*
Jer 31:36 then the seed of *I* also shall
Jer 31:37 of *I* for all that they have done
Jer 32:14 the LORD of hosts, the God of *I*
Jer 32:15 the LORD of hosts, the God of *I*
Jer 32:20 even unto this day, and in *I*
Jer 32:21 *I* out of the land of Egypt with
Jer 32:30 for the children of *I* have only
Jer 32:36 thus saith the LORD, the God of *I*
Jer 33:4 thus saith the LORD, the God of *I*
Jer 33:7 and the captivity of *I* to return
Jer 33:14 have promised unto the house of *I*
Jer 33:17 upon the throne of the house of *I*
Jer 34:2 Thus saith the LORD, the God of *I*
Jer 34:13 Thus saith the LORD, the God of *I*
Jer 35:13 the LORD of hosts, the God of *I*
Jer 35:17 LORD God of hosts, the God of *I*
Jer 35:18 the LORD of hosts, the God of *I*
Jer 35:19 the LORD of hosts, the God of *I*
Jer 36:2 I have spoken unto thee against *I*
Jer 37:7 Thus saith the LORD, the God of *I*
Jer 38:17 the God of hosts, the God of *I*
Jer 39:16 the LORD of hosts, the God of *I*
Jer 42:9 Thus saith the LORD, the God of *I*
Jer 42:15 the LORD of hosts, the God of *I*
Jer 42:18 the LORD of hosts, the God of *I*

| | |
|---|---|
| Jer 43:10 | the LORD of hosts, the God of *I* |
| Jer 44:2 | the LORD of hosts, the God of *I* |
| Jer 44:7 | the God of hosts, the God of *I* |
| Jer 44:11 | the LORD of hosts, the God of *I* |
| Jer 44:25 | the LORD of hosts, the God of *I* |
| Jer 45:2 | Thus saith the LORD, the God of *I* |
| Jer 46:25 | The LORD of hosts, the God of *I* |
| Jer 46:27 | Jacob, and be not dismayed, O *I* |
| Jer 48:1 | the LORD of hosts, the God of *I* |
| Jer 48:27 | For was not *I* a derision unto |
| Jer 49:1 | Hath *I* no sons? |
| Jer 49:2 | then shall *I* be heir unto them |
| Jer 50:4 | the children of *I* shall come |
| Jer 50:17 | *I* is a scattered sheep |
| Jer 50:18 | the LORD of hosts, the God of *I* |
| Jer 50:19 | I will bring *I* again to his |
| Jer 50:20 | the iniquity of *I* shall be sought |
| Jer 50:29 | LORD, against the Holy One of *I* |
| Jer 51:5 | For *I* hath not been forsaken, nor |
| Jer 51:5 | sin against the Holy One of *I* |
| Jer 51:19 | *I* is the rod of his inheritance |
| Jer 51:33 | the LORD of hosts, the God of *I* |
| Jer 51:49 | caused the slain of *I* to fall |
| Lam 2:1 | unto the earth the beauty of *I* |
| Lam 2:3 | fierce anger all the horn of *I* |
| Lam 2:5 | he hath swallowed up *I*, he hath |
| Eze 2:3 | I send thee to the children of *I* |
| Eze 3:1 | and go speak unto the house of *I* |
| Eze 3:4 | go, get thee unto the house of *I* |
| Eze 3:5 | language, but to the house of *I* |
| Eze 3:7 | But the house of *I* will not |
| Eze 3:7 | all the house of *I* are impudent |
| Eze 3:17 | a watchman unto the house of *I* |
| Eze 4:3 | shall be a sign to the house of *I* |
| Eze 4:13 | *I* eat their defiled bread among |
| Eze 5:4 | forth into all the house of *I* |
| Eze 6:2 | face toward the mountains of *I* |
| Eze 6:3 | And say, Ye mountains of *I* |
| Eze 6:5 | children of *I* before their idols |
| Eze 6:11 | abominations of the house of *I* |
| Eze 7:2 | the Lord GOD unto the land of *I* |
| Eze 8:4 | glory of the God of *I* was there |
| Eze 8:6 | the house of *I* committeth here |
| Eze 8:10 | all the idols of the house of *I* |
| Eze 8:11 | of the ancients of the house of *I* |
| Eze 8:12 | of the house of *I* do in the dark |
| Eze 9:3 | the glory of the God of *I* was |
| Eze 9:8 | *I* in thy pouring out of thy fury |
| Eze 10:19 | the God of *I* was over them above |
| Eze 10:20 | God of *I* by the river of Chebar |
| Eze 11:5 | Thus have ye said, O house of *I* |
| Eze 11:10 | will judge you in the border of *I* |
| Eze 11:11 | will judge you in the border of *I* |
| Eze 11:13 | a full end of the remnant of *I* |
| Eze 11:15 | and all the house of *I* wholly |
| Eze 11:17 | and I will give you the land of *I* |
| Eze 11:22 | the God of *I* was over them above |
| Eze 12:6 | for a sign unto the house of *I* |
| Eze 12:9 | of man, hath not the house of *I* |
| Eze 12:10 | all the house of *I* that are among |
| Eze 12:19 | of Jerusalem, and of the land of *I* |
| Eze 12:22 | that ye have in the land of *I* |
| Eze 12:23 | no more use it as a proverb in *I* |
| Eze 12:24 | divination within the house of *I* |
| Eze 12:27 | they of the house of *I* say |
| Eze 13:2 | the prophets of *I* that prophesy |
| Eze 13:4 | O *I*, thy prophets are like the |
| Eze 13:5 | *I* to stand in the battle in the |
| Eze 13:9 | in the writing of the house of *I* |
| Eze 13:9 | they enter into the land of *I* |
| Eze 13:16 | the prophets of *I* which prophesy |
| Eze 14:1 | of the elders of *I* unto me |
| Eze 14:4 | Every man of the house of *I* that |
| Eze 14:5 | the house of *I* in their own heart |
| Eze 14:6 | Therefore say unto the house of *I* |
| Eze 14:7 | For every one of the house of *I* |
| Eze 14:7 | the stranger that sojourneth in *I* |
| Eze 14:9 | him from the midst of my people *I* |
| Eze 14:11 | That the house of *I* may go no |
| Eze 17:2 | a parable unto the house of *I* |
| Eze 17:23 | the height of *I* will I plant it |
| Eze 18:2 | proverb concerning the land of *I* |
| Eze 18:3 | any more to use this proverb in *I* |
| Eze 18:6 | to the idols of the house of *I* |
| Eze 18:15 | to the idols of the house of *I* |
| Eze 18:25 | Hear now, O house of *I* |
| Eze 18:29 | Yet saith the house of *I*, The way |
| Eze 18:29 | O house of *I*, are not my ways |
| Eze 18:30 | I will judge you, O house of *I* |
| Eze 18:31 | for why will ye die, O house of *I* |
| Eze 19:1 | lamentation for the princes of *I* |
| Eze 19:9 | be heard upon the mountains of *I* |
| Eze 20:1 | of *I* came to enquire of the LORD |
| Eze 20:3 | man, speak unto the elders of *I* |
| Eze 20:5 | In the day when I chose *I* |
| Eze 20:13 | But the house of *I* rebelled |
| Eze 20:27 | of man, speak unto the house of *I* |
| Eze 20:30 | Wherefore say unto the house of *I* |
| Eze 20:31 | enquired of by you, O house of *I* |
| Eze 20:38 | not enter into the land of *I* |
| Eze 20:39 | As for you, O house of *I*, thus |
| Eze 20:40 | the mountain of the height of *I* |
| Eze 20:40 | there shall all the house of *I* |
| Eze 20:42 | bring you into the land of *I* |
| Eze 20:44 | corrupt doings, O ye house of *I* |
| Eze 21:2 | and prophesy against the land of *I* |
| Eze 21:3 | And say to the land of *I*, Thus |
| Eze 21:12 | be upon all the princes of *I* |
| Eze 21:25 | thou, profane wicked prince of *I* |
| Eze 22:6 | Behold, the princes of *I*, every |
| Eze 22:18 | the house of *I* is to me become |
| Eze 24:21 | Speak unto the house of *I* |
| Eze 25:3 | and against the land of *I*, when it |
| Eze 25:6 | thy despite against the land of *I* |
| Eze 25:14 | Edom by the hand of my people *I* |
| Eze 28:24 | brier unto the house of *I* |
| Eze 28:25 | have gathered the house of *I* from |
| Eze 29:6 | a staff of reed to the house of *I* |
| Eze 29:16 | the confidence of the house of *I* |
| Eze 29:21 | of the house of *I* to bud forth |
| Eze 33:7 | a watchman unto the house of *I* |
| Eze 33:10 | of man, speak unto the house of *I* |
| Eze 33:11 | for why will ye die, O house of *I* |
| Eze 33:20 | O ye house of *I*, I will judge you |
| Eze 33:24 | wastes of the land of *I* speak |
| Eze 33:28 | the mountains of *I* shall be |
| Eze 34:2 | against the shepherds of *I* |
| Eze 34:2 | of *I* that do feed themselves |
| Eze 34:13 | the mountains of *I* by the rivers |
| Eze 34:14 | of *I* shall their fold be |
| Eze 34:14 | they feed upon the mountains of *I* |
| Eze 34:30 | and that they, even the house of *I* |
| Eze 35:5 | of *I* by the force of the sword in |
| Eze 35:12 | spoken against the mountains of *I* |
| Eze 35:15 | the inheritance of the house of *I* |
| Eze 36:1 | prophesy unto the mountains of *I* |
| Eze 36:1 | and say, Ye mountains of *I* |
| Eze 36:4 | Therefore, ye mountains of *I* |
| Eze 36:6 | concerning the land of *I*, and say |
| Eze 36:8 | But ye, O mountains of *I*, ye |
| Eze 36:8 | your fruit to my people of *I* |
| Eze 36:10 | men upon you, all the house of *I* |
| Eze 36:12 | walk upon you, even my people *I* |
| Eze 36:17 | when the house of *I* dwelt in |
| Eze 36:21 | which the house of *I* had profaned |
| Eze 36:22 | Therefore say unto the house of *I* |
| Eze 36:22 | this for your sakes, O house of *I* |
| Eze 36:32 | for your own ways, O house of *I* |
| Eze 36:37 | be enquired of by the house of *I* |
| Eze 37:11 | bones are the whole house of *I* |
| Eze 37:12 | and bring you into the land of *I* |
| Eze 37:16 | all the house of *I* his companions |
| Eze 37:19 | and the tribes of *I* his fellows |
| Eze 37:21 | of *I* from among the heathen |
| Eze 37:22 | the land upon the mountains of *I* |
| Eze 37:28 | that I the LORD do sanctify *I* |
| Eze 38:8 | against the mountains of *I* |
| Eze 38:14 | my people of *I* dwelleth safely |
| Eze 38:16 | come up against my people of *I* |
| Eze 38:17 | by my servants the prophets of *I* |
| Eze 38:18 | shall come against the land of *I* |
| Eze 38:19 | a great shaking in the land of *I* |
| Eze 39:2 | thee upon the mountains of *I* |
| Eze 39:4 | fall upon the mountains of *I* |
| Eze 39:7 | known in the midst of my people *I* |
| Eze 39:7 | I am the LORD, the Holy One in *I* |
| Eze 39:9 | in the cities of *I* shall go forth |
| Eze 39:11 | Gog a place there of graves in *I* |
| Eze 39:12 | the house of *I* be burying of them |
| Eze 39:17 | sacrifice upon the mountains of *I* |
| Eze 39:22 | So the house of *I* shall know that |
| Eze 39:23 | shall know that the house of *I* |
| Eze 39:25 | mercy upon the whole house of *I* |
| Eze 39:29 | out my spirit upon the house of *I* |
| Eze 40:2 | brought he me into the land of *I* |
| Eze 40:4 | that thou seest to the house of *I* |
| Eze 43:2 | the glory of the God of *I* came |
| Eze 43:7 | of the children of *I* for ever |
| Eze 43:7 | the house of *I* no more defile |
| Eze 43:10 | shew the house to the house of *I* |
| Eze 44:2 | because the LORD, the God of *I* |
| Eze 44:6 | even to the house of *I*, Thus |
| Eze 44:6 | O ye house of *I*, let it suffice |
| Eze 44:9 | that is among the children of *I* |
| Eze 44:10 | when *I* went astray, which went |
| Eze 44:12 | caused the house of *I* to fall |
| Eze 44:22 | of the seed of the house of *I* |
| Eze 44:28 | give them no possession in *I* |
| Eze 44:29 | thing in *I* shall be their's |
| Eze 45:6 | shall be for the whole house of *I* |
| Eze 45:8 | land shall be his possession in *I* |
| Eze 45:8 | of *I* according to their tribes |
| Eze 45:9 | it suffice you, O princes of *I* |
| Eze 45:15 | out of the fat pastures of *I* |
| Eze 45:16 | this oblation for the prince in *I* |
| Eze 45:17 | all solemnities of the house of *I* |
| Eze 45:17 | reconciliation for the house of *I* |
| Eze 47:13 | to the twelve tribes of *I* |
| Eze 47:18 | and from the land of *I* by Jordan |
| Eze 47:21 | you according to the tribes of *I* |
| Eze 47:22 | country among the children of *I* |
| Eze 47:22 | with you among the tribes of *I* |
| Eze 48:11 | the children of *I* went astray |
| Eze 48:19 | it out of all the tribes of *I* |
| Eze 48:29 | the tribes of *I* for inheritance |
| Eze 48:31 | the names of the tribes of *I* |
| Dan 1:3 | certain of the children of *I* |
| Dan 9:7 | of Jerusalem, and unto all *I* |
| Dan 9:11 | all *I* have transgressed thy law, |
| Dan 9:20 | my sin and the sin of my people *I* |
| Hos 1:1 | the son of Joash, king of *I* |
| Hos 1:4 | the kingdom of the house of *I* |
| Hos 1:5 | bow of *I* in the valley of Jezreel |
| Hos 1:6 | have mercy upon the house of *I* |
| Hos 1:10 | the number of the children of *I* |
| Hos 1:11 | the children of *I* be gathered |
| Hos 3:1 | the LORD toward the children of *I* |
| Hos 3:4 | For the children of *I* shall abide |
| Hos 3:5 | shall the children of *I* return |
| Hos 4:1 | of the LORD, ye children of *I* |
| Hos 4:15 | Though thou, *I*, play the harlot, |
| Hos 4:16 | For *I* slideth back as a |
| Hos 5:1 | and hearken, ye house of *I* |
| Hos 5:3 | Ephraim, and *I* is not hid from me |
| Hos 5:3 | whoredom, and *I* is defiled |
| Hos 5:5 | the pride of *I* doth testify to |
| Hos 5:5 | therefore shall *I* and Ephraim fall |
| Hos 5:9 | among the tribes of *I* have I made |
| Hos 6:10 | horrible thing in the house of *I* |
| Hos 6:10 | whoredom of Ephraim, *I* is defiled |
| Hos 7:1 | When I would have healed *I* |
| Hos 7:10 | the pride of *I* testifieth to his |
| Hos 8:2 | *I* shall cry unto me, My God, we |
| Hos 8:3 | *I* hath cast off the thing that is |
| Hos 8:6 | For from *I* was it also |
| Hos 8:8 | *I* is swallowed up |
| Hos 8:14 | For *I* hath forgotten his Maker, |
| Hos 9:1 | Rejoice not, O *I*, for joy, as |
| Hos 9:7 | *I* shall know it |
| Hos 9:10 | I found *I* like grapes in the |
| Hos 10:1 | *I* is an empty vine, he bringeth |
| Hos 10:6 | *I* shall be ashamed of his own |
| Hos 10:8 | places also of Aven, the sin of *I* |
| Hos 10:9 | O *I*, thou hast sinned from the |
| Hos 10:15 | the king of *I* utterly be cut off |
| Hos 11:1 | When *I* was a child, then I loved |
| Hos 11:8 | how shall I deliver thee, *I* |
| Hos 11:12 | and the house of *I* with deceit |
| Hos 12:12 | *I* served for a wife, and for a |
| Hos 12:13 | the LORD brought *I* out of Egypt |
| Hos 13:1 | he exalted himself in *I* |
| Hos 13:9 | O *I*, thou hast destroyed thyself |
| Hos 14:1 | O *I*, return unto the LORD thy God |
| Hos 14:5 | I will be as the dew unto *I* |
| Joel 2:27 | know that I am in the midst of *I* |
| Joel 3:2 | my people and for my heritage *I* |
| Joel 3:16 | the strength of the children of *I* |
| Amos 1:1 | which he saw concerning *I* in the |
| Amos 1:1 | the son of Joash king of *I* |
| Amos 2:6 | For three transgressions of *I* |
| Amos 2:11 | not even thus, O ye children of *I* |
| Amos 3:1 | against you, O children of *I* |
| Amos 3:12 | so shall the children of *I* be |
| Amos 3:14 | visit the transgressions of *I* |
| Amos 4:5 | liketh you, O ye children of *I* |
| Amos 4:12 | thus will I do unto thee, O *I* |
| Amos 4:12 | prepare to meet thy God, O *I* |
| Amos 5:1 | even a lamentation, O house of *I* |
| Amos 5:2 | The virgin of *I* is fallen |
| Amos 5:3 | leave ten, to the house of *I* |

Amos 5:4 the LORD unto the house of *I*
Amos 5:25 forty years, O house of *I*
Amos 6:1 to whom the house of *I* came
Amos 6:14 you a nation, O house of *I*
Amos 7:8 in the midst of my people *I*
Amos 7:9 the sanctuaries of *I* shall be
Amos 7:10 sent to Jeroboam king of *I*
Amos 7:10 in the midst of the house of *I*
Amos 7:11 *I* shall surely be led away
Amos 7:15 me, Go, prophesy unto my people *I*
Amos 7:16 sayest, Prophesy not against *I*
Amos 7:17 *I* shall surely go into captivity
Amos 8:2 end is come upon my people of *I*
Amos 9:7 unto me, O children of *I*
Amos 9:7 Have not I brought up *I* out of
Amos 9:9 the house of *I* among all nations
Amos 9:14 the captivity of my people of *I*
Obad 20 of *I* shall possess that of the
Mic 1:5 and for the sins of the house of *I*
Mic 1:13 of *I* were found in thee
Mic 1:14 shall be a lie to the kings of *I*
Mic 1:15 come unto Adullam the glory of *I*
Mic 2:12 surely gather the remnant of *I*
Mic 3:1 and ye princes of the house of *I*
Mic 3:8 transgression, and to *I* his sin
Mic 3:9 and princes of the house of *I*
Mic 5:1 of *I* with a rod upon the cheek
Mic 5:2 unto me that is to be ruler in *I*
Mic 5:3 return unto the children of *I*
Mic 6:2 people, and he will plead with *I*
Nah 2:2 of Jacob, as the excellency of *I*
Zeph 2:9 the LORD of hosts, the God of *I*
Zeph 3:13 The remnant of *I* shall not do
Zeph 3:14 shout, O *I*
Zeph 3:15 the king of *I*, even the LORD, is
Zec 9:1 of man, as of all the tribes of *I*
Zec 12:1 of the word of the LORD for *I*
Mal 1:1 word of the LORD to *I* by Malachi
Mal 1:5 be magnified from the border of *I*
Mal 2:16 For the LORD, the God of *I*
Mal 4:4 unto him in Horeb for all *I*
Mt 2:6 that shall rule my people *I*
Mt 2:20 mother, and go into the land of *I*
Mt 2:21 and came into the land of *I*
Mt 8:10 so great faith, no, not in *I*
Mt 9:33 saying, It was never so seen in *I*
Mt 10:6 the lost sheep of the house of *I*
Mt 10:23 have gone over the cities of *I*
Mt 15:24 the lost sheep of the house of *I*
Mt 15:31 and they glorified the God of *I*
Mt 19:28 judging the twelve tribes of *I*
Mt 27:9 of the children of *I* did value
Mt 27:42 If he be the King of *I*, let him
Mk 12:29 the commandments is, Hear, O *I*
Mk 15:32 Let Christ the King of *I* descend
Lk 1:16 many of the children of *I* shall
Lk 1:54 He hath holpen his servant *I*
Lk 1:68 Blessed be the Lord God of *I*
Lk 1:80 the day of his shewing unto *I*
Lk 2:25 waiting for the consolation of *I*
Lk 2:32 and the glory of thy people *I*
Lk 2:34 fall and rising again of many in *I*
Lk 4:25 many widows were in *I* in the days
Lk 4:27 many lepers were in *I* in the time
Lk 7:9 so great faith, no, not in *I*
Lk 22:30 judging the twelve tribes of *I*
Lk 24:21 he which should have redeemed *I*
Jn 1:31 he should be made manifest to *I*
Jn 1:49 thou art the King of *I*
Jn 3:10 unto him, Art thou a master of *I*
Jn 12:13 Blessed is the King of *I* that
Acts 1:6 restore again the kingdom to *I*
Acts 2:22 Ye men of *I*, hear these words
Acts 2:36 all the house of *I* know assuredly
Acts 3:12 unto the people, Ye men of *I*
Acts 4:8 of the people, and elders of *I*
Acts 4:10 all, and to all the people of *I*
Acts 4:27 the Gentiles, and the people of *I*
Acts 5:21 the senate of the children of *I*
Acts 5:31 for to give repentance to *I*
Acts 5:35 And said unto them, Ye men of *I*
Acts 7:23 his brethren the children of *I*
Acts 7:37 which said unto the children of *I*
Acts 7:42 of the prophets, O ye house of *I*
Acts 9:15 and kings, and the children of *I*
Acts 10:36 God sent unto the children of *I*
Acts 13:16 with his hand said, Men of *I*
Acts 13:17 people of *I* chose our fathers
Acts 13:23 promise raised unto *I* a Saviour
Acts 13:24 repentance to all the people of *I*
Acts 21:28 Crying out, Men of *I*, help
Acts 28:20 of *I* I am bound with this chain
Rom 9:6 For they are not all *I*, which are
Rom 9:6 not all Israel, which are of *I*
Rom 9:27 Esaias also crieth concerning *I*
Rom 9:27 of *I* be as the sand of the sea
Rom 9:31 But *I*, which followed after the
Rom 10:1 desire and prayer to God for *I* is
Rom 10:19 But I say, Did not *I* know
Rom 10:21 But to *I* he saith, All day long I
Rom 11:2 intercession to God against *I*
Rom 11:7 *I* hath not obtained that which he
Rom 11:25 in part is happened to *I*, until
Rom 11:26 And so all *I* shall be saved
1Cor 10:18 Behold *I* after the flesh
2Cor 3:7 so that the children of *I* could
2Cor 3:13 that the children of *I* could not
Gal 6:16 and mercy, and upon the *I* of God
Eph 2:12 aliens from the commonwealth of *I*
Phil 3:5 the eighth day, of the stock of *I*
Heb 8:8 new covenant with the house of *I*
Heb 8:10 the house of *I* after those days
Heb 11:22 departing of the children of *I*
Rev 2:14 before the children of *I*, to eat
Rev 7:4 the tribes of the children of *I*
Rev 21:12 tribes of the children of *I*

*3. The ten northern tribes.*

1Kin 4:20 *I* were many, as the sand which is
1Kin 4:25 *I* dwelt safely, every man under
1Kin 12:18 all *I* stoned him with stones,
1Kin 12:19 So *I* rebelled against the house
1Kin 12:20 when all *I* heard that Jeroboam
1Kin 12:20 and made him king over all *I*
1Kin 12:21 to fight against the house of *I*
1Kin 12:24 your brethren the children of *I*
1Kin 12:28 behold thy gods, O *I*, which
1Kin 12:33 a feast unto the children of *I*
1Kin 14:10 him that is shut up and left in *I*
1Kin 14:13 all *I* shall mourn for him, and
1Kin 14:13 God of *I* in the house of Jeroboam
1Kin 14:14 shall raise him up a king over *I*
1Kin 14:15 For the LORD shall smite *I*
1Kin 14:15 he shall root up *I* out of this
1Kin 14:16 he shall give *I* up because of the
1Kin 14:16 who did sin, and who made *I* to sin
1Kin 14:18 all *I* mourned for him, according
1Kin 14:19 the chronicles of the kings of *I*
1Kin 15:9 king of *I* reigned Asa over Judah
1Kin 15:16 Baasha king of *I* all their days
1Kin 15:17 Baasha king of *I* went up against
1Kin 15:19 thy league with Baasha king of *I*
1Kin 15:20 he had against the cities of *I*
1Kin 15:25 *I* in the second year of Asa king
1Kin 15:25 and reigned over *I* two years
1Kin 15:26 sin wherewith he made *I* to sin
1Kin 15:27 all *I* laid siege to Gibbethon
1Kin 15:30 he sinned, and which he made *I* sin
1Kin 15:30 the LORD God of *I* to anger
1Kin 15:31 the chronicles of the kings of *I*
1Kin 15:32 Baasha king of *I* all their days
1Kin 15:33 to reign over all *I* in Tirzah
1Kin 16:2 made thee prince over my people *I*
1Kin 16:2 and hast made my people *I* to sin
1Kin 16:5 the chronicles of the kings of *I*
1Kin 16:8 Baasha to reign over *I* in Tirzah
1Kin 16:13 and by which they made *I* to sin
1Kin 16:13 of *I* to anger with their vanities
1Kin 16:14 the chronicles of the kings of *I*
1Kin 16:16 wherefore all *I* made Omri
1Kin 16:16 king over *I* that day in the camp
1Kin 16:17 all *I* with him, and they besieged
1Kin 16:19 which he did, to make *I* to sin
1Kin 16:20 the chronicles of the kings of *I*
1Kin 16:21 of *I* divided into two parts
1Kin 16:23 Judah began Omri to reign over *I*
1Kin 16:26 sin wherewith he made *I* to sin
1Kin 16:26 to provoke the LORD God of *I* to
1Kin 16:27 the chronicles of the kings of *I*
1Kin 16:29 the son of Omri to reign over *I*
1Kin 16:29 reigned over *I* in Samaria twenty
1Kin 16:33 kings of *I* that were before him
1Kin 18:17 him, Art thou he that troubleth *I*
1Kin 18:18 answered, I have not troubled *I*
1Kin 18:19 gather to me all *I* unto mount
1Kin 18:20 sent unto all the children of *I*
1Kin 19:10 for the children of *I* have
1Kin 19:14 because the children of *I* have
1Kin 19:16 thou anoint to be king over *I*
1Kin 19:18 have left me seven thousand in *I*
1Kin 20:2 to Ahab king of *I* into the city
1Kin 20:4 And the king of *I* answered
1Kin 20:7 Then the king of *I* called all the
1Kin 20:11 And the king of *I* answered
1Kin 20:13 a prophet unto Ahab king of *I*
1Kin 20:15 even all the children of *I*
1Kin 20:20 and *I* pursued them
1Kin 20:21 And the king of *I* went out
1Kin 20:22 the prophet came to the king of *I*
1Kin 20:26 up to Aphek, to fight against *I*
1Kin 20:27 the children of *I* were numbered
1Kin 20:27 the children of *I* pitched before
1Kin 20:28 God, and spake unto the king of *I*
1Kin 20:29 the children of *I* slew of the
1Kin 20:31 the house of *I* are merciful kings
1Kin 20:31 heads, and go out to the king of *I*
1Kin 20:32 heads, and came to the king of *I*
1Kin 20:40 the king of *I* said unto him, So
1Kin 20:41 the king of *I* discerned him that
1Kin 20:43 the king of *I* went to his house
1Kin 21:7 thou now govern the kingdom of *I*
1Kin 21:18 go down to meet Ahab king of *I*
1Kin 21:21 him that is shut up and left in *I*
1Kin 21:22 me to anger, and made *I* to sin
1Kin 21:26 cast out before the children of *I*
1Kin 22:1 without war between Syria and *I*
1Kin 22:2 Judah came down to the king of *I*
1Kin 22:3 the king of *I* said unto his
1Kin 22:4 Jehoshaphat said to the king of *I*
1Kin 22:5 said unto the king of *I*, Enquire,
1Kin 22:6 Then the king of *I* gathered the
1Kin 22:8 And the king of *I* said unto
1Kin 22:9 Then the king of *I* called an
1Kin 22:10 And the king of *I* and Jehoshaphat
1Kin 22:17 I saw all *I* scattered upon the
1Kin 22:18 And the king of *I* said unto
1Kin 22:26 And the king of *I* said, Take
1Kin 22:29 So the king of *I* and Jehoshaphat
1Kin 22:30 And the king of *I* said unto
1Kin 22:30 the king of *I* disguised himself,
1Kin 22:31 save only with the king of *I*
1Kin 22:32 said, Surely it is the king of *I*
1Kin 22:33 that it was not the king of *I*
1Kin 22:34 smote the king of *I* between the
1Kin 22:39 the chronicles of the kings of *I*
1Kin 22:41 the fourth year of Ahab king of *I*
1Kin 22:44 made peace with the king of *I*
1Kin 22:51 *I* in Samaria the seventeenth year
1Kin 22:51 and reigned two years over *I*
1Kin 22:52 son of Nebat, who made *I* to sin
2Kin 1:1 against *I* after the death of Ahab
2Kin 1:3 because there is not a God in *I*
2Kin 1:6 because there is not a God in *I*
2Kin 1:16 God in *I* to enquire of his word
2Kin 1:18 the chronicles of the kings of *I*
2Kin 3:1 *I* in Samaria the eighteenth year
2Kin 3:3 son of Nebat, which made *I* to sin
2Kin 3:4 of *I* an hundred thousand lambs
2Kin 3:5 rebelled against the king of *I*
2Kin 3:6 the same time, and numbered all *I*
2Kin 3:9 So the king of *I* went, and the
2Kin 3:10 And the king of *I* said, Alas
2Kin 3:12 So the king of *I* and Jehoshaphat
2Kin 3:13 And Elisha said unto the king of *I*
2Kin 3:13 the king of *I* said unto him, Nay
2Kin 3:24 when they came to the camp of *I*
2Kin 3:27 was great indignation against *I*
2Kin 5:2 of the land of *I* a little maid
2Kin 5:4 the maid that is of the land of *I*
2Kin 5:5 send a letter unto the king of *I*
2Kin 5:6 the letter to the king of *I*
2Kin 5:7 when the king of *I* had read the
2Kin 5:8 king of *I* had rent his clothes
2Kin 5:8 know that there is a prophet in *I*
2Kin 5:12 better than all the waters of *I*
2Kin 5:15 no God in all the earth, but in *I*
2Kin 6:8 king of Syria warred against *I*
2Kin 6:9 of God sent unto the king of *I*
2Kin 6:10 the king of *I* sent to the place
2Kin 6:11 which of us is for the king of *I*
2Kin 6:12 Elisha, the prophet that is in *I*
2Kin 6:12 telleth the king of *I* the words
2Kin 6:21 the king of *I* said unto Elisha,
2Kin 6:23 came no more into the land of *I*
2Kin 6:26 as the king of *I* was passing by
2Kin 7:6 the king of *I* hath hired against
2Kin 7:13 of *I* that are left in it
2Kin 8:12 wilt do unto the children of *I*
2Kin 8:16 Joram the son of Ahab king of *I*
2Kin 8:18 in the way of the kings of *I*
2Kin 8:25 Joram the son of Ahab king of *I*

2Kin 8:26 the daughter of Omri king of *I*
2Kin 9:3 I have anointed thee king over *I*
2Kin 9:6 people of the LORD, even over *I*
2Kin 9:8 him that is shut up and left in *I*
2Kin 9:12 I have anointed thee king over *I*
2Kin 9:14 kept Ramoth-gilead, he and all *I*
2Kin 9:21 And Joram king of *I* and Ahaziah
2Kin 10:21 And Jehu sent through all *I*
2Kin 10:28 Thus Jehu destroyed Baal out of *I*
2Kin 10:29 son of Nebat, who made *I* to sin
2Kin 10:30 shall sit on the throne of *I*
2Kin 10:31 of Jeroboam, which made *I* to sin
2Kin 10:32 the LORD began to cut *I* short
2Kin 10:32 smote them in all the coasts of *I*
2Kin 10:34 the chronicles of the kings of *I*
2Kin 10:36 over *I* in Samaria was twenty
2Kin 13:1 began to reign over *I* in Samaria
2Kin 13:2 son of Nebat, which made *I* to sin
2Kin 13:3 of the LORD was kindled against *I*
2Kin 13:4 for he saw the oppression of *I*
2Kin 13:5 (And the LORD gave *I* a saviour
2Kin 13:5 the children of *I* dwelt in their
2Kin 13:6 house of Jeroboam, who made *I* sin
2Kin 13:8 the chronicles of the kings of *I*
2Kin 13:10 to reign over *I* in Samaria
2Kin 13:11 the son of Nebat, who made *I* sin
2Kin 13:12 the chronicles of the kings of *I*
2Kin 13:13 in Samaria with the kings of *I*
2Kin 13:14 Joash the king of *I* came down
2Kin 13:14 my father, the chariot of *I*
2Kin 13:16 And he said to the king of *I*
2Kin 13:18 And he said unto the king of *I*
2Kin 13:22 *I* all the days of Jehoahaz
2Kin 13:25 him, and recovered the cities of *I*
2Kin 14:1 of *I* reigned Amaziah the son of
2Kin 14:8 Jehoahaz son of Jehu, king of *I*
2Kin 14:9 Jehoash the king of *I* sent to
2Kin 14:11 Jehoash king of *I* went up
2Kin 14:12 was put to the worse before *I*
2Kin 14:13 Jehoash king of *I* took Amaziah
2Kin 14:15 the chronicles of the kings of *I*
2Kin 14:16 in Samaria with the kings of *I*
2Kin 14:17 Jehoahaz king of *I* fifteen years
2Kin 14:23 the son of Joash king of *I* began
2Kin 14:24 son of Nebat, who made *I* to sin
2Kin 14:26 the LORD saw the affliction of *I*
2Kin 14:26 any left, nor any helper for *I*
2Kin 14:27 the name of *I* from under heaven
2Kin 14:28 which belonged to Judah, for *I*
2Kin 14:28 the chronicles of the kings of *I*
2Kin 14:29 fathers, even with the kings of *I*
2Kin 15:1 year of Jeroboam king of *I* began
2Kin 15:8 over *I* in Samaria six months
2Kin 15:9 son of Nebat, who made *I* to sin
2Kin 15:11 the chronicles of the kings of *I*
2Kin 15:12 of *I* unto the fourth generation
2Kin 15:15 the chronicles of the kings of *I*
2Kin 15:17 the son of Gadi to reign over *I*
2Kin 15:18 son of Nebat, who made *I* to sin
2Kin 15:20 And Menahem exacted the money of *I*
2Kin 15:21 the chronicles of the kings of *I*
2Kin 15:23 began to reign over *I* in Samaria
2Kin 15:24 son of Nebat, who made *I* to sin
2Kin 15:26 the chronicles of the kings of *I*
2Kin 15:27 began to reign over *I* in Samaria
2Kin 15:28 son of Nebat, who made *I* to sin
2Kin 15:29 of *I* came Tiglath-pileser king of
2Kin 15:31 the chronicles of the kings of *I*
2Kin 15:32 the son of Remaliah king of *I*
2Kin 16:3 in the way of the kings of *I*
2Kin 16:3 out from before the children of *I*
2Kin 16:5 of *I* came up to Jerusalem to war
2Kin 16:7 out of the hand of the king of *I*
2Kin 17:1 in Samaria over *I* nine years
2Kin 17:2 kings of *I* that were before him
2Kin 17:6 carried *I* away into Assyria, and
2Kin 17:7 that the children of *I* had sinned
2Kin 17:8 out from before the children of *I*
2Kin 17:8 and of the kings of *I*
2Kin 17:9 the children of *I* did secretly
2Kin 17:13 Yet the LORD testified against *I*
2Kin 17:18 the LORD was very angry with *I*
2Kin 17:19 the statutes of *I* which they made
2Kin 17:20 LORD rejected all the seed of *I*
2Kin 17:21 For he rent *I* from the house of
2Kin 17:21 Jeroboam drave *I* from following
2Kin 17:22 For the children of *I* walked in
2Kin 17:23 LORD removed *I* out of his sight
2Kin 17:23 So was *I* carried away out of
2Kin 17:24 instead of the children of *I*
2Kin 18:1 of Hoshea son of Elah king of *I*
2Kin 18:9 of Hoshea son of Elah king of *I*
2Kin 18:10 ninth year of Hoshea king of *I*
2Kin 18:11 did carry away *I* unto Assyria
2Kin 23:15 son of Nebat, who made *I* to sin
2Kin 23:19 which the kings of *I* had made to
2Kin 23:22 in all the days of the kings of *I*
2Kin 23:27 of my sight, as I have removed *I*
1Chr 5:17 in the days of Jeroboam king of *I*
1Chr 9:1 in the book of the kings of *I*
2Chr 10:18 the children of *I* stoned him with
2Chr 10:19 *I* rebelled against the house of
2Chr 11:1 were warriors, to fight against *I*
2Chr 11:13 all *I* resorted to him out of all
2Chr 11:16 of *I* such as set their hearts to
2Chr 13:4 Hear me, thou Jeroboam, and all *I*
2Chr 13:12 O children of *I*, fight ye not
2Chr 13:15 all *I* before Abijah and Judah
2Chr 13:16 the children of *I* fled before
2Chr 13:17 so there fell down slain of *I*
2Chr 13:18 Thus the children of *I* were
2Chr 15:9 fell to him out of *I* in abundance
2Chr 15:17 were not taken away out of *I*
2Chr 16:1 king of *I* came up against Judah
2Chr 16:3 thy league with Baasha king of *I*
2Chr 16:4 armies against the cities of *I*
2Chr 16:11 book of the kings of Judah and *I*
2Chr 17:1 and strengthened himself against *I*
2Chr 17:4 and not after the doings of *I*
2Chr 18:3 And Ahab king of *I* said unto
2Chr 18:4 said unto the king of *I*, Enquire,
2Chr 18:5 Therefore the king of *I* gathered
2Chr 18:7 And the king of *I* said unto
2Chr 18:8 the king of *I* called for one of
2Chr 18:9 And the king of *I* and Jehoshaphat
2Chr 18:16 I did see all *I* scattered upon
2Chr 18:17 the king of *I* said to Jehoshaphat
2Chr 18:19 Who shall entice Ahab king of *I*
2Chr 18:25 Then the king of *I* said, Take ye
2Chr 18:28 So the king of *I* and Jehoshaphat
2Chr 18:29 And the king of *I* said unto
2Chr 18:29 So the king of *I* disguised
2Chr 18:30 save only with the king of *I*
2Chr 18:31 they said, It is the king of *I*
2Chr 18:32 that it was not the king of *I*
2Chr 18:33 smote the king of *I* between the
2Chr 18:34 howbeit the king of *I* stayed
2Chr 20:34 in the book of the kings of *I*
2Chr 20:35 himself with Ahaziah king of *I*
2Chr 21:2 the sons of Jehoshaphat king of *I*
2Chr 21:4 divers also of the princes of *I*
2Chr 21:6 in the way of the kings of *I*
2Chr 21:13 in the way of the kings of *I*
2Chr 22:5 *I* to war against Hazael king of
2Chr 25:6 of *I* for an hundred talents of
2Chr 25:7 not the army of *I* go with thee
2Chr 25:7 for the LORD is not with *I*
2Chr 25:9 I have given to the army of *I*
2Chr 25:17 the son of Jehu, king of *I*
2Chr 25:18 Joash king of *I* sent to Amaziah
2Chr 25:21 So Joash the king of *I* went up
2Chr 25:22 was put to the worse before *I*
2Chr 25:23 Joash the king of *I* took Amaziah
2Chr 25:25 Jehoahaz king of *I* fifteen years
2Chr 25:26 book of the kings of Judah and *I*
2Chr 27:7 in the book of the kings of *I*
2Chr 28:2 in the ways of the kings of *I*
2Chr 28:5 into the hand of the king of *I*
2Chr 28:8 the children of *I* carried away
2Chr 28:13 there is fierce wrath against *I*
2Chr 28:19 low because of Ahaz king of *I*
2Chr 30:6 and his princes throughout all *I*
2Chr 30:21 the children of *I* that were
2Chr 30:25 congregation that came out of *I*
2Chr 30:25 that came out of the land of *I*
2Chr 31:6 And concerning the children of *I*
2Chr 32:32 book of the kings of Judah and *I*
2Chr 34:9 and of all the remnant of *I*
2Chr 34:21 and for them that are left in *I*
2Chr 35:18 neither did all the kings of *I*
2Chr 35:18 *I* that were present, and the
2Chr 35:27 in the book of the kings of *I*
2Chr 36:8 in the book of the kings of *I*
Is 7:1 the son of Remaliah, king of *I*
Jer 2:26 so is the house of *I* ashamed
Jer 2:31 Have I been a wilderness unto *I*
Jer 3:6 which backsliding *I* hath done
Jer 3:8 *I* committed adultery I had put
Jer 3:11 The backsliding *I* hath justified
Jer 3:12 say, Return, thou backsliding *I*
Jer 3:18 shall walk with the house of *I*
Jer 5:11 For the house of *I* and the house
Jer 9:26 and all the house of *I* are
Jer 11:10 the house of *I* and the house of
Jer 11:17 for the evil of the house of *I*
Jer 23:6 be saved, and *I* shall dwell safely
Jer 31:27 that I will sow the house of *I*
Jer 31:31 new covenant with the house of *I*
Jer 32:30 For the children of *I* and the
Jer 32:32 all the evil of the children of *I*
Jer 41:9 made for fear of Baasha king of *I*
Jer 48:13 as the house of *I* was ashamed of
Jer 50:33 The children of *I* and the children
Eze 4:4 of the house of *I* upon it
Eze 4:5 the iniquity of the house of *I*
Eze 9:9 The iniquity of the house of *I*
Eze 27:17 Judah, and the land of *I*, they
Eze 37:16 the children of *I* his companions
Eze 44:15 children of *I* went astray from me
Zec 1:19 which have scattered Judah, *I*
Zec 8:13 O house of Judah, and house of *I*
Zec 11:14 brotherhood between Judah and *I*
Mal 2:11 an abomination is committed in *I*

**ISRAELITE** *(iz'-ra-el-ite)* See ISRAELITES, ISRAELITISH. *A member of Israel 3.*
Num 25:14 the name of the *I* that was slain
2Sa 17:25 son, whose name was Ithra an *I*
Jn 1:47 saith of him, Behold an *I* indeed
Rom 11:1 For I also am an *I*, of the seed

**ISRAELITES** *(iz'-ra-el-ites)*
Ex 9:7 one of the cattle of the *I* dead
Lev 23:42 all that are *I* born shall dwell
Josh 3:17 all the *I* passed over on dry
Josh 8:24 that all the *I* returned unto Ai,
Josh 13:6 lot unto the *I* for an inheritance
Josh 13:13 dwell among the *I* until this day
Judg 20:21 ground of the *I* that day twenty
1Sa 2:14 unto all the *I* that came thither
1Sa 13:20 But all the *I* went down to the
1Sa 14:21 be with the *I* that were with Saul
1Sa 25:1 all the *I* were gathered together,
1Sa 29:1 the *I* pitched by a fountain which
2Sa 4:1 and all the *I* were troubled
2Kin 3:24 the *I* rose up and smote the
2Kin 7:13 of the *I* that are consumed
1Chr 9:2 in their cities were, the *I*
Rom 9:4 Who are *I*
2Cor 11:22 Are they *I*

**ISRAELITISH**
Lev 24:10 And the son of an *I* woman, whose
Lev 24:10 and this son of the *I* woman
Lev 24:11 the *I* woman's son blasphemed the

**ISRAEL'S** *(iz'-ra-els)*
*1. Refers to Israel 1.*
Gen 48:13 his right hand toward *I* left hand
Gen 48:13 his left hand toward *I* right hand
Num 1:20 of Reuben, *I* eldest son, by their
*2. Refers to Israel 2.*
Ex 18:8 and to the Egyptians for *I* sake
Num 31:30 And of the children of *I* half
Num 31:42 And of the children of *I* half
Num 31:47 Even of the children of *I* half
Deut 21:8 blood unto thy people of *I* charge
2Sa 5:12 his kingdom for his people *I* sake
*3. Refers to Israel 3.*
2Kin 3:11 the king of *I* servants answered

**ISSACHAR** *(is'-sa-kar)*
*1. A son of Jacob.*
Gen 30:18 and she called his name *I*
Gen 35:23 Simeon, and Levi, and Judah, and *I*
Gen 46:13 And the sons of *I*
Gen 49:14 *I* is a strong ass couching down
Ex 1:3 *I*, Zebulun, and Benjamin,
1Chr 2:1 Reuben, Simeon, Levi, and Judah, *I*
1Chr 7:1 Now the sons of *I* were, Tola, and
*2. Descendants of Issachar 1.*
Num 1:8 Of *I*
Num 1:28 Of the children of *I*, by their
Num 1:29 of them, even of the tribe of *I*
Num 2:5 unto him shall be the tribe of *I*
Num 2:5 be captain of the children of *I*
Num 7:18 the son of Zuar, prince of *I*
Num 10:15 *I* was Nethaneel the son of Zuar
Num 13:7 Of the tribe of *I*, Igal the son
Num 26:23 Of the sons of *I* after their
Num 26:25 These are the families of *I*
Num 34:26 of the tribe of the children of *I*
Deut 27:12 Simeon, and Levi, and Judah, and *I*

Deut 33:18 and, *I*, in thy tents
Josh 17:10 on the north, and in *I* on the east
Josh 17:11 And Manasseh had in *I* and in Asher
Josh 19:17 And the fourth lot came out to *I*
Josh 19:17 for the children of *I* according
Josh 19:23 of *I* according to their families
Josh 21:6 of the families of the tribe of *I*
Josh 21:28 And out of the tribe of *I*, Kishon
Judg 5:15 the princes of *I* were with
Judg 5:15 even *I*, and also Barak
Judg 10:1 Puah, the son of Dodo, a man of *I*
1Kin 4:17 the son of Paruah, in *I*
1Kin 15:27 son of Ahijah, of the house of *I*
1Chr 6:62 families out of the tribe of *I*
1Chr 6:72 And out of the tribe of *I*
1Chr 7:5 of *I* were valiant men of might
1Chr 12:32 And of the children of *I*, which
1Chr 12:40 that were nigh them, even unto *I*
1Chr 27:18 of *I*, Omri the son of Michael
2Chr 30:18 many of Ephraim, and Manasseh, *I*
Eze 48:25 unto the west side, *I* a portion
Eze 48:26 And by the border of *I*, from the
Eze 48:33 one gate of Simeon, one gate of *I*
Rev 7:7 Of the tribe of *I* were sealed

*3. A porter of the tabernacle.*

1Chr 26:5 *I* the seventh, Peulthai the

**ISSHIAH** *(is-shi'-ah)* See Isaiah, Jesiah.

*1. A descendant of Moses.*

1Chr 24:21 sons of Rehabiah, the first was *I*

*2. A Levite.*

1Chr 24:25 The brother of Michah was *I*
1Chr 24:25 of the sons of *I*

**ISSUE**

Gen 48:6 And thy *i*, which thou begettest
Lev 12:7 cleansed from the *i* of her blood
Lev 15:2 hath a running *i* out of his flesh
Lev 15:2 because of his *i* he is unclean
Lev 15:3 shall be his uncleanness in his *i*
Lev 15:3 whether his flesh run with his *i*
Lev 15:3 his flesh be stopped from his *i*
Lev 15:4 whereon he lieth that hath the *i*
Lev 15:6 hath the *i* shall wash his clothes
Lev 15:7 hath the *i* shall wash his clothes
Lev 15:8 if he that hath the *i* spit upon
Lev 15:9 that hath the *i* shall be unclean
Lev 15:11 he toucheth that hath the *i*
Lev 15:12 that he toucheth which hath the *i*
Lev 15:13 when he that hath an *i* is
Lev 15:13 an *i* is cleansed of his *i*
Lev 15:15 for him before the Lord for his *i*
Lev 15:19 And if a woman have an *i*
Lev 15:19 her *i* in her flesh be blood, she
Lev 15:25 if a woman have an *i* of her blood
Lev 15:25 all the days of the *i* of her
Lev 15:26 she lieth all the days of her *i*
Lev 15:28 But if she be cleansed of her *i*
Lev 15:30 Lord for the *i* of her uncleanness
Lev 15:32 is the law of him that hath an *i*
Lev 15:33 flowers, and of him that hath an *i*
Lev 22:4 is a leper, or hath a running *i*
Num 5:2 and every one that hath an *i*
2Sa 3:29 house of Joab one that hath an *i*
2Kin 20:18 thy sons that shall *i* from thee
Is 22:24 house, the offspring and the *i*
Is 39:7 thy sons that shall *i* from thee
Eze 23:20 *i* is like the *i* of horses
Eze 47:8 These waters *i* out toward the
Mt 9:20 with an *i* of blood twelve years
Mt 22:25 a wife, deceased, and, having no *i*
Mk 5:25 which had an *i* of blood twelve
Lk 8:43 a woman having an *i* of blood
Lk 8:44 immediately her *i* of blood

**ISSUED**

Josh 8:22 the other *i* out of the city
Job 38:8 as if it had *i* out of the womb
Eze 47:1 waters *i* out from under the
Eze 47:12 they they *i* out of the sanctuary
Dan 7:10 A fiery stream *i* and came forth
Rev 9:17 and out of their mouths *i* fire
Rev 9:18 which *i* out of their mouths

**ISUAH** *(is'-u-ah)* See Ishuah. *A son of Asher.*

1Chr 7:30 Imnah, and *I*, and Ishuai, and Beriah

**ISUI** *(is'-u-i)* See Ishui. *A son of Asher.*

Gen 46:17 Jimnah, and Ishuah, and *I*, and

**ITALIAN** *(it-al'-yan)*

Acts 10:1 of the band called the *I* band

**ITALY** *(it'-a-lee) Homeland of most Roman citizens.*

Acts 18:2 in Pontus, lately come from *I*
Acts 27:1 that we should sail into *I*
Acts 27:6 ship of Alexandria sailing into *I*
Heb 13:24 They of *I* salute you
Heb s to the Hebrews from *I* by Timothy

**ITHAI** *(ith'-a-i)* See Ittai. *A mighty man of David.*

1Chr 11:31 *I* the son of Ribai of Gibeah,

**ITHAMAR** *(ith'-a-mar) A son of Aaron.*

Ex 6:23 Nadab, and Abihu, Eleazar, and *I*
Ex 28:1 Nadab and Abihu, Eleazar and *I*
Ex 38:21 of the Levites, by the hand of *I*
Lev 10:6 Aaron, and unto Eleazar and unto *I*
Lev 10:12 Aaron, and unto Eleazar and unto *I*
Lev 10:16 and he was angry with Eleazar and *I*
Num 3:2 and Abihu, Eleazar, and *I*
Num 3:4 *I* ministered in the priest's
Num 4:28 shall be under the hand of *I* the
Num 4:33 under the hand of *I* the son of
Num 7:8 under the hand of *I* the son of
Num 26:60 Nadab, and Abihu, Eleazar, and *I*
1Chr 6:3 Nadab, and Abihu, Eleazar, and *I*
1Chr 24:1 Nadab, and Abihu, Eleazar, and *I*
1Chr 24:2 *I* executed the priest's office
1Chr 24:3 and Ahimelech of the sons of *I*
1Chr 24:4 of Eleazar than of the sons of *I*
1Chr 24:4 eight among the sons of *I*
1Chr 24:5 of Eleazar, and of the sons of *I*
1Chr 24:6 for Eleazar, and one taken for *I*
Ezr 8:2 of the sons of *I*

**ITHIEL** *(ith'-e-el)*

*1. Son of Jesaiah.*

Neh 11:7 the son of Maaseiah, the son of *I*

*2. Person mentioned in Proverbs.*

Prov 30:1 the man spake unto *I*, even unto
Prov 30:1 spake unto Ithiel, even unto *I*

**ITHMAH** *(ith'-mah) A mighty man of David.*

1Chr 11:46 sons of Elnaam, and *I* the Moabite,

**ITHNAN** *(ith'-nan) A town in Judah.*

Josh 15:23 And Kedesh, and Hazor, and *I*

**ITHRA** *(ith'-rah)* See Jether. *Father of Amasa.*

2Sa 17:25 whose name was *I* an Israelite

**ITHRAN** *(ith'-ran)*

*1. A son of Dishon.*

Gen 36:26 Hemdan, and Eshban, and *I*, and
1Chr 1:41 Amram, and Eshban, and *I*, and Cheran

*2. A son of Zophah.*

1Chr 7:37 Hod, and Shamma, and Shilshah, and *I*

**ITHREAM** *(ith'-re-am) A son of David.*

2Sa 3:5 And the sixth, *I*, by Eglah David's
1Chr 3:3 the sixth, *I* by Eglah his wife

**ITHRITE** *(ith'-rite)* See Ithrites. *A descendant of Jether.*

2Sa 23:38 Ira an *I*, Gareb an *I*,
2Sa 23:38 Ira an *I*, Gareb an *I*
1Chr 11:40 Ira the *I*, Gareb the *I*,
1Chr 11:40 Ira the *I*, Gareb the *I*

**ITHRITES** *(ith'-rites)*

1Chr 2:53 the *I*, and the Puhites, and the

**ITTAH-KAZIN** *(it'-tah-ka'-zin) A city in Zebulun.*

Josh 19:13 the east to Gittah-hepher, to *I*

**ITTAI** *(it'-ta-i)* See Ithai.

*1. A Philistine in David's army.*

2Sa 15:19 said the king to *I* the Gittite
2Sa 15:21 *I* answered the king, and said, As
2Sa 15:22 And David said to *I*, Go and pass
2Sa 15:22 *I* the Gittite passed over, and all
2Sa 18:2 under the hand of *I* the Gittite
2Sa 18:5 commanded Joab and Abishai and *I*
2Sa 18:12 king charged thee and Abishai and *I*

*2. A mighty man of David.*

2Sa 23:29 *I* the son of Ribai out of Gibeah

**ITURAEA** *(i-tu-re'-ah) A province near Mt. Hermon.*

Lk 3:1 his brother Philip tetrarch of *I*

**IVAH** *(i'-vah)* See Ahava, Ava. *A Mesopotamian district.*

2Kin 18:34 gods of Sepharvaim, Hena, and *I*
2Kin 19:13 city of Sepharvaim, of Hena, and *I*
Is 37:13 city of Sepharvaim, Hena, and *I*

**IVORY**

1Kin 10:18 the king made a great throne of *i*
1Kin 10:22 bringing gold, and silver, *i*
1Kin 22:39 the *i* house which he made, and all
2Chr 9:17 the king made a great throne of *i*
2Chr 9:21 bringing gold, and silver, *i*
Ps 45:8 and cassia, out of the *i* palaces
Song 5:14 his belly is as bright *i* overlaid
Song 7:4 Thy neck is as a tower of *i*
Eze 27:6 have made thy benches of *i*
Eze 27:15 thee for a present horns of *i*
Amos 3:15 and the houses of *i* shall perish
Amos 6:4 That lie upon beds of *i*, and
Rev 18:12 wood, and all manner vessels of *i*

**IZEHAR** *(iz'-e-har)* See Izeharites, Izhar. *A son of Kohath.*

Num 3:19 Amram, and *I*, Hebron, and Uzziel

**IZEHARITES** *(iz'-e-har-ites)* See Izharite. *Descendants of Izehar.*

Num 3:27 Amramites, and the family of the *I*

**IZHAR** *(iz'-har)* See Izehab, Izharites. *Same as Izehar.*

Ex 6:18 Amram, and *I*, and Hebron, and Uzziel
Ex 6:21 And the sons of *I*
Num 16:1 Now Korah, the son of *I*, the son
1Chr 6:2 Amram, *I*, and Hebron, and Uzziel
1Chr 6:18 sons of Kohath were, Amram, and *I*
1Chr 6:38 The son of *I*, the son of Kohath,
1Chr 23:12 Amram, *I*, Hebron, and Uzziel, four
1Chr 23:18 Of the sons of *I*

**IZHARITES** *(iz'-har-ites)* See Izeharites. *Same as Izeharites.*

1Chr 24:22 Of the *I*; Shelomoth
1Chr 26:23 Of the Amramites, and the *I*
1Chr 26:29 Of the *I*, Chenaniah and his sons

**IZRAHIAH** *(iz-ra-hi'-ah)* See Jezrahiah. *Grandson of Tola.*

1Chr 7:3 the sons of Uzzi; *I*
1Chr 7:3 and the sons of *I*

**IZRAHITE** *(iz'-ra-hite)* See Ezrahite. *Family name of Shamhuth.*

1Chr 27:8 fifth month was Shamhuth the *I*

**IZRI** *(iz'-ri)* See Zeri. *A sanctuary servant.*

1Chr 25:11 The fourth to *I*, he, his sons, and

# J

**JAAKAN** *(ja'-a-kan)* See AKAN, BENE-JAAKAN. *A son of Ezer.*
Deut 10:6 of the children of J to Mosera
**JAAKOBAH** *(ja-ak'-o-bah) A descendant of Simeon.*
1Chr 4:36 And Elioenai, and J, and Jeshohaiah,
**JAALA** *(ja'-a-lah)* See JAALAH. *A family of exiles.*
Neh 7:58 The children of J, the children
**JAALAH** *(ja'-a-lah)* See JAALA. *Same as Jaala.*
Ezr 2:56 The children of J, the children
**JAALAM** *(ja'-a-lam) A son of Esau.*
Gen 36:5 And Aholibamah bare Jeush, and J
Gen 36:14 and she bare to Esau Jeush, and J
Gen 36:18 duke Jeush, duke J, duke Korah
1Chr 1:35 Eliphaz, Reuel, and Jeush, and J
**JAANAI** *(ja'-a-nahee) A Gadite.*
1Chr 5:12 chief, and Shapham the next, and J
**JAARE-OREGIM** *(ja'-a-re-or'-eg-im)* See JAIR. *Father of Elhanan.*
2Sa 21:19 where Elhanan the son of J
**JAASAU** *(ja-a'-saw) Married a foreigner in exile.*
Ezr 10:37 Mattaniah, Mattenai, and J
**JAASIEL** *(ja-a'-se-el) A son of Abner.*
1Chr 27:21 of Benjamin, J the son of Abner
**JAAZANIAH** *(ja-az-a-ni'-ah)* See JEZANIAH.
*1. A son of a Maachathite.*
2Kin 25:23 J the son of a Maachathite, they
*2. A chief Rechabite.*
Jer 35:3 Then I took J the son of Jeremiah
*3. Son of Shaphan.*
Eze 8:11 them stood J the son of Shaphan
*4. Son of Azur.*
Eze 11:1 whom I saw J the son of Azur
**JAAZER** *(ja-a'-zer)* See JAZER. *A city in Gilead.*
Num 21:32 And Moses sent to spy out J
Num 32:35 And Atroth, Shophan, and J, and
**JAAZIAH** *(ja-a-zi'-ah) A descendant of Merari.*
1Chr 24:26 the sons of J; Beno.
1Chr 24:27 The sons of Merari by J
**JAAZIEL** *(ja-a'-ze-el)* See AZIEL. *A priest.*
1Chr 15:18 degree, Zechariah, Ben, and J
**JABAL** *(ja'-bal) A son of Adah.*
Gen 4:20 And Adah bare J
**JABBOK** *(jab'-bok) A brook in Bashan.*
Gen 32:22 sons, and passed over the ford J
Num 21:24 his land from Arnon unto J
Deut 2:37 nor unto any place of the river J
Deut 3:16 the border even unto the river J
Josh 12:2 Gilead, even unto the river J
Judg 11:13 of Egypt, from Arnon even unto J
Judg 11:22 Amorites, from Arnon even unto J
**JABESH** *(ja'-besh)* See JABESH-GILEAD.
*1. A city in Gad.*
1Sa 11:1 all the men of J said unto Nahash
1Sa 11:3 And the elders of J said unto him
1Sa 11:5 him the tidings of the men of J
1Sa 11:9 came and shewed it to the men of J
1Sa 11:10 Therefore the men of J said
1Sa 31:12 wall of Beth-shan, and came to J
1Sa 31:13 and buried them under a tree at J
1Chr 10:12 of his sons, and brought them to J
1Chr 10:12 their bones under the oak in J
*2. Father of Shallum.*
2Kin 15:10 Shallum the son of J conspired
2Kin 15:13 Shallum the son of J began to
2Kin 15:14 Shallum the son of J in Samaria
**JABESH-GILEAD** *(ja'-besh-ghil'-e-ad) Same as Jabesh 1.*
Judg 21:8 the camp from J to the assembly
Judg 21:9 of the inhabitants of J there
Judg 21:10 smite the inhabitants of J with
Judg 21:12 of J four hundred young virgins
Judg 21:14 had saved alive of the women of J
1Sa 11:1 came up, and encamped against J
1Sa 11:9 shall ye say unto the men of J
1Sa 31:11 of J heard of that which the
2Sa 2:4 That the men of J were they that
2Sa 2:5 sent messengers unto the men of J
2Sa 21:12 his son from the men of J
1Chr 10:11 when all J heard all that the
**JABEZ** *(ja'-bez)*
*1. A city in Judah.*
1Chr 2:55 of the scribes which dwelt at J
*2. Head of a family of Judah.*
1Chr 4:9 J was more honourable than his
1Chr 4:9 and his mother called his name J
1Chr 4:10 J called on the God of Israel,
**JABIN** *(ja'-bin)* See JABIN'S.
*1. A king of Hazor.*
Josh 11:1 when J king of Hazor had heard
*2. Another king of Hazor.*
Judg 4:2 into the hand of J king of Canaan
Judg 4:17 peace between J the king of Hazor
Judg 4:23 So God subdued on that day J the
Judg 4:24 prevailed against J the king of
Judg 4:24 had destroyed J king of Canaan
Ps 83:9 as to Sisera, as to J, at the
**JABIN'S**
Judg 4:7 Sisera, the captain of J army
**JABNEEL** *(jab'-ne-el)* See JABNEH.
*1. A city in Judah.*
Josh 15:11 mount Baalah, and went out unto J
*2. A city in Naphtali.*
Josh 19:33 Zaanannim, and Adami, Nekeb, and J
**JABNEH** *(jab'-neh)* See JABNEEL. *A Philistine city.*
2Chr 26:6 wall of Gath, and the wall of J
**JACHAN** *(ja'-kan)* See AKAN. *Head of a Gadite family.*
1Chr 5:13 and Sheba, and Jorai, and J
**JACHIN** *(ja'-kin)* See JACHINITES, JARIB.
*1. A son of Simeon.*
Gen 46:10 Jemuel, and Jamin, and Ohad, and J
Ex 6:15 Jemuel, and Jamin, and Ohad, and J
Num 26:12 of J, the family of the
*2. A pillar of Solomon's Temple.*
1Kin 7:21 and called the name thereof J
2Chr 3:17 name of that on the right hand J
*3. A family of exiles.*
1Chr 9:10 Jedaiah, and Jehoiarib, and J
Neh 11:10 Jedaiah the son of Joiarib, J
*4. A sanctuary servant.*
1Chr 24:17 The one and twentieth to J
**JACHINITES** *(ja'-kin-ites) Descendants of Jachin 1.*
Num 26:12 of Jachin, the family of the J
**JACOB** *(ja'-cub)* See ISRAEL, JACOB'S, JAMES.
*1. Son of Isaac and Rebekah.*
Gen 25:26 and his name was called J
Gen 25:27 J was a plain man, dwelling in
Gen 25:28 but Rebekah loved J
Gen 25:29 And J sod pottage
Gen 25:30 And Esau said to J, Feed me, I
Gen 25:31 J said, Sell me this day thy
Gen 25:33 J said, Swear to me this day
Gen 25:33 and he sold his birthright unto J
Gen 25:34 Then J gave Esau bread and pottage
Gen 27:6 And Rebekah spake unto J her son
Gen 27:11 J said to Rebekah his mother,
Gen 27:15 put them upon J her younger son
Gen 27:17 into the hand of her son J
Gen 27:19 J said unto his father, I am Esau
Gen 27:21 And Isaac said unto J, Come near,
Gen 27:22 J went near unto Isaac his father
Gen 27:30 had made an end of blessing J
Gen 27:30 J was yet scarce gone out from
Gen 27:36 said, Is not he rightly named J
Gen 27:41 Esau hated J because of the
Gen 27:41 then will I slay my brother J
Gen 27:42 called J her younger son, and said
Gen 27:46 if J take a wife of the daughters
Gen 28:1 And Isaac called J, and blessed him
Gen 28:5 And Isaac sent away J
Gen 28:6 Esau saw that Isaac had blessed J
Gen 28:7 that J obeyed his father and his
Gen 28:10 J went out from Beer-sheba, and
Gen 28:16 J awaked out of his sleep, and he
Gen 28:18 J rose up early in the morning,
Gen 28:20 J vowed a vow, saying, If God
Gen 29:1 Then J went on his journey, and
Gen 29:4 J said unto them, My brethren,
Gen 29:10 when J saw Rachel the daughter of
Gen 29:10 that J went near, and rolled the
Gen 29:11 J kissed Rachel, and lifted up his
Gen 29:12 J told Rachel that he was her
Gen 29:13 the tidings of J his sister's son
Gen 29:15 And Laban said unto J, Because
Gen 29:18 And J loved Rachel
Gen 29:20 J served seven years for Rachel
Gen 29:21 J said unto Laban, Give me my
Gen 29:28 J did so, and fulfilled her week
Gen 30:1 saw that she bare J no children
Gen 30:1 and said unto J, Give me children,
Gen 30:4 and J went in unto her
Gen 30:5 Bilhah conceived, and bare J a son
Gen 30:7 again, and bare J a second son
Gen 30:9 her maid, and gave her J to wife
Gen 30:10 Zilpah Leah's maid bare J a son
Gen 30:12 Leah's maid bare J a second son
Gen 30:16 J came out of the field in the
Gen 30:17 and bare J the fifth son
Gen 30:19 again, and bare J the sixth son
Gen 30:25 that J said unto Laban, Send me
Gen 30:31 J said, Thou shalt not give me
Gen 30:36 journey betwixt himself and J
Gen 30:36 J fed the rest of Laban's flocks
Gen 30:37 J took him rods of green poplar,
Gen 30:40 J did separate the lambs, and set
Gen 30:41 that J laid the rods before the
Gen 31:1 J hath taken away all that was
Gen 31:2 J beheld the countenance of Laban
Gen 31:3 And the LORD said unto J, Return
Gen 31:4 J sent and called Rachel and Leah
Gen 31:11 unto me in a dream, saying, J
Gen 31:17 Then J rose up, and set his sons
Gen 31:20 J stole away unawares to Laban
Gen 31:22 on the third day that J was fled
Gen 31:24 speak not to J either good or bad
Gen 31:25 Then Laban overtook J
Gen 31:25 Now J had pitched his tent in the
Gen 31:26 And Laban said to J, What hast
Gen 31:29 speak not to J either good or bad
Gen 31:31 J answered and said to Laban,
Gen 31:32 For J knew not that Rachel had
Gen 31:36 J was wroth, and chode with Laban
Gen 31:36 J answered and said to Laban, What
Gen 31:43 And Laban answered and said unto J
Gen 31:45 J took a stone, and set it up for
Gen 31:46 J said unto his brethren, Gather
Gen 31:47 but J called it Galeed
Gen 31:51 And Laban said to J, Behold this
Gen 31:53 J sware by the fear of his father
Gen 31:54 Then J offered sacrifice upon the
Gen 32:1 J went on his way, and the angels
Gen 32:2 when J saw them, he said, This is
Gen 32:3 J sent messengers before him to
Gen 32:4 Thy servant J saith thus, I have
Gen 32:6 And the messengers returned to J
Gen 32:7 Then J was greatly afraid and
Gen 32:9 J said, O God of my father
Gen 32:20 thy servant J is behind us
Gen 32:24 And J was left alone
Gen 32:27 And he said, J.
Gen 32:28 name shall be called no more J
Gen 32:29 J asked him, and said, Tell me, I
Gen 32:30 J called the name of the place
Gen 33:1 J lifted up his eyes, and looked,
Gen 33:10 J said, Nay, I pray thee, if now
Gen 33:17 J journeyed to Succoth, and built
Gen 33:18 J came to Shalem, a city of
Gen 34:1 of Leah, which she bare unto J
Gen 34:3 unto Dinah the daughter of J
Gen 34:5 J heard that he had defiled Dinah
Gen 34:5 J held his peace until they were
Gen 34:6 out unto J to commune with him
Gen 34:7 the sons of J came out of the field
Gen 34:13 the sons of J answered Shechem and
Gen 34:25 sore, that two of the sons of J
Gen 34:27 The sons of J came upon the slain
Gen 34:30 J said to Simeon and Levi, Ye have

Gen 35:1 And God said unto J, Arise, go up
Gen 35:2 Then J said unto his household,
Gen 35:4 they gave unto J all the strange
Gen 35:4 J hid them under the oak which
Gen 35:5 not pursue after the sons of J
Gen 35:6 So J came to Luz, which is in the
Gen 35:9 And God appeared unto J again
Gen 35:10 God said unto him, Thy name is J
Gen 35:10 shall not be called any more J
Gen 35:14 J set up a pillar in the place
Gen 35:15 J called the name of the place
Gen 35:20 J set a pillar upon her grave
Gen 35:22 Now the sons of J were twelve
Gen 35:26 these are the sons of J, which
Gen 35:27 J came unto Isaac his father unto
Gen 35:29 and his sons Esau and J buried him
Gen 36:6 from the face of his brother J
Gen 37:1 J dwelt in the land wherein his
Gen 37:2 These are the generations of J
Gen 37:34 J rent his clothes, and put
Gen 42:1 Now when J saw that there was
Gen 42:1 J said unto his sons, Why do ye
Gen 42:4 J sent not with his brethren
Gen 42:29 they came unto J their father
Gen 42:36 J their father said unto them, Me
Gen 45:25 of Canaan unto J their father
Gen 45:27 the spirit of J their father
Gen 46:2 of the night, and said, J, J
Gen 46:5 J rose up from Beer-sheba
Gen 46:5 of Israel carried J their father
Gen 46:6 of Canaan, and came into Egypt, J
Gen 46:8 Israel, which came into Egypt, J
Gen 46:15 she bare unto J in Padan-aram
Gen 46:18 and these she bare unto J
Gen 46:22 of Rachel, which were born to J
Gen 46:25 and she bare these unto J
Gen 46:26 souls that came with J into Egypt
Gen 46:27 all the souls of the house of J
Gen 47:7 And Joseph brought in J his father
Gen 47:7 and J blessed Pharaoh
Gen 47:8 And Pharaoh said unto J, How old
Gen 47:9 J said unto Pharaoh, The days of
Gen 47:10 J blessed Pharaoh, and went out
Gen 47:28 J lived in the land of Egypt
Gen 47:28 so the whole age of J was an
Gen 48:2 And one told J, and said, Behold,
Gen 48:3 J said unto Joseph, God Almighty
Gen 49:1 J called unto his sons, and said,
Gen 49:2 together, and hear, ye sons of J
Gen 49:7 I will divide them in J, and
Gen 49:24 the hands of the mighty God of J
Gen 49:33 when J had made an end of
Gen 50:24 to Abraham, to Isaac, and to J
Ex 1:1 man and his household came with J
Ex 1:5 the loins of J were seventy souls
Ex 2:24 Abraham, with Isaac, and with J
Ex 3:6 the God of Isaac, and the God of J
Ex 3:15 the God of Isaac, and the God of J
Ex 3:16 God of Abraham, of Isaac, and of J
Ex 4:5 the God of Isaac, and the God of J
Ex 6:3 Abraham, unto Isaac, and unto J
Ex 6:8 it to Abraham, to Isaac, and to J
Ex 19:3 shalt thou say to the house of J
Ex 33:1 unto Abraham, to Isaac, and to J
Lev 26:42 I remember my covenant with J
Num 32:11 Abraham, unto Isaac, and unto J
Deut 1:8 fathers, Abraham, Isaac, and J
Deut 6:10 to Abraham, to Isaac, and to J
Deut 9:5 thy fathers, Abraham, Isaac, and J
Deut 9:27 servants, Abraham, Isaac, and J
Deut 29:13 to Abraham, to Isaac, and to J
Deut 30:20 to Abraham, to Isaac, and to J
Deut 34:4 Abraham, unto Isaac, and unto J
Josh 24:4 And I gave unto Isaac J and Esau
Josh 24:4 but J and his children went down
Josh 24:32 in a parcel of ground which J
1Sa 12:8 When J was come into Egypt, and
2Kin 13:23 with Abraham, Isaac, and J
Mal 1:2 yet I loved J,
Mt 1:2 and Isaac begat J
Mt 1:2 J begat Judas and his brethren
Mt 8:11 down with Abraham, and Isaac, and J
Mt 22:32 the God of Isaac, and the God of J
Mk 12:26 the God of Isaac, and the God of J
Lk 1:33 over the house of J for ever
Lk 3:34 Which was the son of J, which was
Lk 13:28 shall see Abraham, and Isaac, and J
Lk 20:37 the God of Isaac, and the God of J
Jn 4:5 that J gave to his son Joseph
Jn 4:12 thou greater than our father J
Acts 3:13 of Abraham, and of Isaac, and of J
Acts 7:8 and Isaac begat J
Acts 7:8 J begat the twelve patriarchs
Acts 7:12 But when J heard that there was
Acts 7:14 and called his father J to him
Acts 7:15 So J went down into Egypt, and
Acts 7:32 the God of Isaac, and the God of J
Acts 7:46 a tabernacle for the God of J
Rom 9:13 J have I loved, but Esau have I
Rom 11:26 turn away ungodliness from J
Heb 11:9 in tabernacles with Isaac and J
Heb 11:20 By faith Isaac blessed J and Esau
Heb 11:21 By faith J, when he was a dying,

*2. Father of Joseph; ancestor of Jesus.*

Mt 1:15 and Matthan begat J
Mt 1:16 J begat Joseph the husband of

*3. Descendants of Jacob.*

Num 23:7 east, saying, Come, curse me J
Num 23:10 Who can count the dust of J
Num 23:21 He hath not beheld iniquity in J
Num 23:23 there is no enchantment against J
Num 23:23 this time it shall be said of J
Num 24:5 How goodly are thy tents, O J
Num 24:17 there shall come a Star out of J
Num 24:19 Out of J shall come he that shall
Deut 32:9 J is the lot of his inheritance
Deut 33:4 of the congregation of J
Deut 33:10 They shall teach J thy judgments
Deut 33:28 the fountain of J shall be upon a
2Sa 23:1 the anointed of the God of J
1Kin 18:31 of the tribes of the sons of J
2Kin 17:34 LORD commanded the children of J
1Chr 16:13 his servant, ye children of J
1Chr 16:17 confirmed the same to J for a law
Ps 14:7 J shall rejoice, and Israel shall
Ps 20:1 name of the God of J defend thee
Ps 22:23 all ye the seed of J, glorify him
Ps 24:6 seek him, that seek thy face, O J
Ps 44:4 command deliverances for J
Ps 46:7 the God of J is our refuge
Ps 46:11 the God of J is our refuge
Ps 47:4 the excellency of J whom he loved
Ps 53:6 J shall rejoice, and Israel shall
Ps 59:13 in J unto the ends of the earth
Ps 75:9 will sing praises to the God of J
Ps 76:6 At thy rebuke, O God of J
Ps 77:15 thy people, the sons of J
Ps 78:5 he established a testimony in J
Ps 78:21 so a fire was kindled against J
Ps 78:71 brought him to feed J his people
Ps 79:7 For they have devoured J, and laid
Ps 81:1 a joyful noise unto the God of J
Ps 81:4 Israel, and a law of the God of J
Ps 84:8 give ear, O God of J
Ps 85:1 brought back the captivity of J
Ps 87:2 more than all the dwellings of J
Ps 94:7 shall the God of J regard it
Ps 99:4 judgment and righteousness in J
Ps 105:6 ye children of J his chosen
Ps 105:10 the same unto J for a law
Ps 105:23 J sojourned in the land of Ham
Ps 114:1 the house of J from a people of
Ps 114:7 at the presence of the God of J
Ps 132:2 and vowed unto the mighty God of J
Ps 132:5 for the mighty God of J
Ps 135:4 LORD hath chosen J unto himself
Ps 146:5 hath the God of J for his help
Ps 147:19 He sheweth his word unto J
Is 2:3 to the house of the God of J
Is 2:5 O house of J, come ye, and let us
Is 2:6 thy people the house of J
Is 8:17 his face from the house of J
Is 9:8 The Lord sent a word into J
Is 10:20 as are escaped of the house of J
Is 10:21 return, even the remnant of J
Is 14:1 For the LORD will have mercy on J
Is 14:1 shall cleave to the house of J
Is 17:4 that the glory of J shall be made
Is 27:6 them that come of J to take root
Is 27:9 shall the iniquity of J be purged
Is 29:22 concerning the house of J
Is 29:22 J shall not now be ashamed,
Is 29:23 and sanctify the Holy One of J
Is 40:27 Why sayest thou, O J, and speakest
Is 41:8 J whom I have chosen, the seed of
Is 41:14 Fear not, thou worm J, and ye men
Is 41:21 reasons, saith the King of J
Is 42:24 Who gave J for a spoil, and Israel
Is 43:1 the LORD that created thee, O J
Is 43:22 thou hast not called upon me, O J
Is 43:28 have given J to the curse, and
Is 44:1 Yet now hear, O J my servant
Is 44:2 Fear not, O J, my servant
Is 44:5 call himself by the name of J
Is 44:21 Remember these, O J and Israel
Is 44:23 for the LORD hath redeemed J
Is 45:4 For J my servant's sake, and
Is 45:19 I said not unto the seed of J
Is 46:3 Hearken unto me, O house of J
Is 48:1 Hear ye this, O house of J
Is 48:12 Hearken unto me, O J and Israel,
Is 48:20 LORD hath redeemed his servant J
Is 49:5 to bring J again to him, Though
Is 49:6 to raise up the tribes of J
Is 49:26 thy Redeemer, the mighty One of J
Is 58:1 and the house of J their sins
Is 58:14 with the heritage of J thy father
Is 59:20 that turn from transgression in J
Is 60:16 thy Redeemer, the mighty One of J
Is 65:9 will bring forth a seed out of J
Jer 2:4 word of the LORD, O house of J
Jer 5:20 Declare this in the house of J
Jer 10:16 The portion of J is not like them
Jer 10:25 for they have eaten up J, and
Jer 30:10 fear thou not, O my servant J
Jer 30:10 J shall return, and shall be in
Jer 31:7 Sing with gladness for J, and
Jer 31:11 For the LORD hath redeemed J
Jer 33:26 will I cast away the seed of J
Jer 33:26 the seed of Abraham, Isaac, and J
Jer 46:27 But fear not thou, O my servant J
Jer 46:27 J shall return, and be in rest and
Jer 46:28 O J my servant, saith the LORD
Jer 51:19 The portion of J is not like them
Lam 1:17 LORD hath commanded concerning J
Lam 2:2 up all the habitations of J
Lam 2:3 he burned against J like a
Eze 20:5 unto the seed of the house of J
Eze 28:25 that I have given to my servant J
Eze 37:25 I have given unto J my servant
Eze 39:25 I bring again the captivity of J
Hos 10:11 plow, and J shall break his clods
Hos 12:2 will punish J according to his
Hos 12:12 J fled into the country of Syria,
Amos 3:13 ye, and testify in the house of J
Amos 6:8 I abhor the excellency of J
Amos 7:2 by whom shall J arise
Amos 7:5 by whom shall J arise
Amos 8:7 hath sworn by the excellency of J
Amos 9:8 utterly destroy the house of J
Obad 10 brother J shame shall cover thee
Obad 17 the house of J shall possess
Obad 18 the house of J shall be a fire,
Mic 1:5 transgression of J is all this
Mic 1:5 What is the transgression of J
Mic 2:7 that art named the house of J
Mic 2:12 I will surely assemble, O J
Mic 3:1 Hear, I pray you, O heads of J
Mic 3:8 of might, to declare unto J his
Mic 3:9 you, ye heads of the house of J
Mic 4:2 and to the house of the God of J
Mic 5:7 the remnant of J shall be in the
Mic 5:8 the remnant of J shall be among
Mic 7:20 Thou wilt perform the truth to J
Nah 2:2 turned away the excellency of J
Mal 2:12 out of the tabernacles of J
Mal 3:6 ye sons of J are not consumed

**JACOB'S** *(ja'-cubs)*

*1. Refers to Jacob 1.*

Gen 27:22 and said, The voice is J voice
Gen 28:5 Syrian, the brother of Rebekah, J
Gen 30:2 J anger was kindled against
Gen 30:42 were Laban's, and the stronger J
Gen 31:33 And Laban went into J tent
Gen 32:18 shalt say, They be thy servant J
Gen 32:25 the hollow of J thigh was out of
Gen 32:32 he touched the hollow of J thigh
Gen 34:7 Israel in lying with J daughter
Gen 34:19 he had delight in J daughter
Gen 35:23 J firstborn, and Simeon, and Levi,
Gen 45:26 J heart fainted, for he believed
Gen 46:8 Reuben, J firstborn
Gen 46:19 The sons of Rachel J wife
Gen 46:26 besides J sons' wives, all the
Mal 1:2 Was not Esau J brother
Jn 4:6 Now J well was there

*2. Refers to Jacob 3.*

Jer 30:7 it is even the time of J trouble
Jer 30:18 again the captivity of J tents

**JADA** *(ja'-dah) A grandson of Jerahmeel.*
1Chr 2:28 sons of Onam were, Shammai, and J
1Chr 2:32 the sons of J the brother of

**JADAU** *(ja'-daw) Married a foreigner in exile.*
Ezr 10:43 Mattithiah, Zabad, Zebina, J

**JADDUA** *(jad'-du-ah)*
*1. A Levite.*
Neh 10:21 Meshezabeel, Zadok, J,
*2. A priest.*
Neh 12:11 Jonathan, and Jonathan begat J
Neh 12:22 Joiada, and Johanan, and J

**JADON** *(ja'-don) A repairer of Jerusalem's wall.*
Neh 3:7 J the Meronothite, the men of

**JAEL** *(ja'-el) The wife of Heber.*
Judg 4:17 of J the wife of Heber the Kenite
Judg 4:18 J went out to meet Sisera, and
Judg 4:21 Then J Heber's wife took a nail
Judg 4:22 J came out to meet him, and said
Judg 5:6 son of Anath, in the days of J
Judg 5:24 Blessed above women shall J the

**JAGUR** *(ja'-gur) A town in Judah.*
Josh 15:21 were Kabzeel, and Eder, and J

**JAH** *(jah)* See JEHOVAH. *A shortened form of Jehovah.*
Ps 68:4 upon the heavens by his name J

**JAHATH** *(ja'-hath)*
*1. A descendant of Shobal.*
1Chr 4:2 Reaiah the son of Shobal begat J
1Chr 4:2 and J begat Ahumai, and Lahad
*2. A descendant of Gershom.*
1Chr 6:20 J his son, Zimmah his son,
1Chr 6:43 The son of J, the son of Gershom,
*3. Another descendant of Gershom.*
1Chr 23:10 And the sons of Shimei were, J
1Chr 23:11 J was the chief, and Zizah the
*4. A descendant of Kohath.*
1Chr 24:22 of the sons of Shelomoth; J
*5. A descendant of Merari.*
2Chr 34:12 and the overseers of them were J

**JAHAZ** *(ja'-haz)* See JAHAZA, JAHAZAH, JAHZAH. *A Levitical city in Reuben.*
Num 21:23 and he came to J, and fought
Deut 2:32 and all his people, to fight at J
Judg 11:20 people together, and pitched in J
Is 15:4 voice shall be heard even unto J
Jer 48:34 even unto Elealeh, and even unto J

**JAHAZA** *(ja-ha'-zah)* See JAHAZ. *Same as Jahaz.*
Josh 13:18 And J, and Kedemoth, and Mephaath,

**JAHAZAH** *(ja-ha'-zah)* See JAHAZ. *Same as Jahaz.*
Josh 21:36 suburbs, and J with her suburbs,
Jer 48:21 upon Holon, and upon J, and upon

**JAHAZIAH** *(ja-ha-zi'-ah) Son of Tikvah.*
Ezr 10:15 J the son of Tikvah were employed

**JAHAZIEL** *(ja-ha'-ze-el)*
*1. A captain in David's army.*
1Chr 12:4 Jeremiah, and J, and Johanan, and
*2. A priest.*
1Chr 16:6 J the priests with trumpets
*3. A son of Hebron.*
1Chr 23:19 J the third, and Jekameam the
1Chr 24:23 J the third, Jekameam the fourth
*4. A Levite.*
2Chr 20:14 Then upon J the son of Zechariah,
*5. A family of exiles.*
Ezr 8:5 the son of J, and with him three

**JAHDAI** *(jah'-dahee) A descendant of Caleb.*
1Chr 2:47 And the sons of J

**JAHDIEL** *(jah'-de-el) Head of a family of Manasseh.*
1Chr 5:24 and Jeremiah, and Hodaviah, and J

**JAHDO** *(jah'-do) Son of Buz.*
1Chr 5:14 son of Jeshishai, the son of J

**JAHLEEL** *(jah'-le-el)* See JAHLEELITES. *A son of Zebulun.*
Gen 46:14 Sered, and Elon, and J
Num 26:26 of J, the family of the

**JAHLEELITES** *(jah'-le-el-ites) Descendants of Jahleel.*
Num 26:26 of Jahleel, the family of the J

**JAHMAI** *(jah'-mahee) A son of Tola.*
1Chr 7:2 and Rephaiah, and Jeriel, and J

**JAHZAH** *(jah'-zah)* See JAHAZ. *A Levitical city in Reuben.*
1Chr 6:78 suburbs, and J with her suburbs,

**JAHZEEL** *(jah'-ze-el)* See JAHZEELITES, JAHZIEL. *A son of Naphtali.*
Gen 46:24 J, and Guni, and Jezer, and Shillem
Num 26:48 of J, the family of the

**JAHZEELITES** *(jah'-ze-el-ites) Descendants of Jahzeel.*
Num 26:48 of Jahzeel, the family of the J

**JAHZERAH** *(jah'-ze-rah)* See AHAZAI. *The son of Meshullam.*
1Chr 9:12 the son of Adiel, the son of J

**JAHZIEL** *(jah'-ze-el)* See JAHZEEL. *Same as Jahzeel.*
1Chr 7:13 J, and Guni, and Jezer, and Shallum,

**JAIR** *(ja'-ur)* See HAVOTH-JAIR, JAARE-OREGIM, JAIRITE.
*1. A descendant of Judah and Manasseh.*
Num 32:41 J the son of Manasseh went and
Deut 3:14 J the son of Manasseh took all
1Kin 4:13 towns of J the son of Manasseh
1Chr 2:22 And Segub begat J, who had three
*2. A judge.*
Judg 10:3 And after him arose J, a Gileadite
Judg 10:5 J died, and was buried in Camon
*3. A district in Bashan.*
Josh 13:30 of Bashan, and all the towns of J
1Chr 2:23 and Aram, with the towns of J
*4. Father of Mordecai.*
Est 2:5 name was Mordecai, the son of J
*5. Father of Elhanan.*
1Chr 20:5 Elhanan the son of J slew Lahmi

**JAIRITE** *(ja'-ur-ite) A descendant of Jair 1.*
2Sa 20:26 Ira also the J was a chief ruler

**JAIRUS** *(ja-i'-rus) A ruler of a synagogue.*
Mk 5:22 of the synagogue, J by name
Lk 8:41 behold, there came a man named J

**JAKAN** *(ja'-kan)* See AKAN, JAAKAN. *A son of Ezer.*
1Chr 1:42 Bilhan, and Zavan, and J

**JAKEH** *(ja'-keh) Father of Agur.*
Prov 30:1 The words of Agur the son of J

**JAKIM** *(ja'-kim)*
*1. Son of Shimhi.*
1Chr 8:19 And J, and Zichri, and Zabdi,
*2. A sanctuary servant.*
1Chr 24:12 to Eliashib, the twelfth to J

**JALON** *(ja'-lon) A son of Ezra.*
1Chr 4:17 Jether, and Mered, and Epher, and J

**JAMBRES** *(jam'-brees) An opponent of Moses.*
2Ti 3:8 J withstood Moses, so do these

**JAMES** *(james)* See JACOB.
*1. Son of Zebedee.*
Mt 4:21 J the son of Zebedee, and John his
Mt 10:2 J the son of Zebedee, and John his
Mt 17:1 six days Jesus taketh Peter, J
Mk 1:19 he saw J the son of Zebedee, and
Mk 1:29 house of Simon and Andrew, with J
Mk 3:17 And J the son of
Mk 3:17 and John the brother of J
Mk 5:37 J, and John the brother of J
Mk 9:2 Jesus taketh with him Peter, and J
Mk 10:35 And J and John, the sons of Zebedee
Mk 10:41 to be much displeased with J
Mk 13:3 against the temple, Peter and J
Mk 14:33 And he taketh with him Peter and J
Lk 5:10 And so was also J, and John, the
Lk 6:14 Peter,) and Andrew his brother, J
Lk 8:51 no man to go in, save Peter, and J
Lk 9:28 he took Peter and John and J
Lk 9:54 And when his disciples J and John
Acts 1:13 where abode both Peter, and J
Acts 12:2 he killed J the brother of John
*2. Son of Alphaeus.*
Mt 10:3 J the son of Alphaeus, and
Mk 3:18 J the son of Alphaeus, and
Lk 6:15 J the son of Alphaeus, and Simon
Acts 1:13 J the son of Alphaeus, and Simon
*3. Brother of Jesus.*
Mt 13:55 and his brethren, J, and Joses, and
Mt 27:56 and Mary the mother of J and Joses
Mk 6:3 the son of Mary, the brother of J
Mk 15:40 and Mary the mother of J the less
Mk 16:1 and Mary the mother of J, and
Lk 6:16 And Judas the brother of J
Lk 24:10 Joanna, and Mary the mother of J
Acts 1:13 and Judas the brother of J
Acts 12:17 said, Go shew these things unto J
Acts 15:13 J answered, saying, Men and
Acts 21:18 Paul went in with us unto J
1Cor 15:7 After that, he was seen of J
Gal 1:19 save J the Lord's brother
Gal 2:9 And when J, Cephas, and John, who
Gal 2:12 before that certain came from J
Jas 1:1 J, a servant of God and of the
Jude 1 of Jesus Christ, and brother of J

**JAMIN** *(ja'-min)* See JAMINITES.
*1. A son of Simeon.*
Gen 46:10 Jemuel, and J, and Ohad, and Jachin,
Ex 6:15 Jemuel, and J, and Ohad, and Jachin,
Num 26:12 of J, the family of the Jaminites
1Chr 4:24 sons of Simeon were, Nemuel, and J
*2. A descendant of Hezron.*
1Chr 2:27 of Jerahmeel were, Maaz, and J
*3. A priest.*
Neh 8:7 Jeshua, and Bani, and Sherebiah, J

**JAMINITES** *(ja'-min-ites) Descendants of Jamin.*
Num 26:12 of Jamin, the family of the J

**JAMLECH** *(jam'-lek) A royal descendant of Simeon.*
1Chr 4:34 And Meshobab, and J, and Joshah the

**JANNA** *(jan'-nah) Father of Melchi; ancestor of Jesus.*
Lk 3:24 of Melchi, which was the son of J

**JANNES** *(jan'-nees) An opponent of Moses.*
2Ti 3:8 Now as J and Jambres withstood

**JANOAH** *(ja-no'-ah)* See JANOHAH. *A city in Naphtali.*
2Kin 15:29 Ijon, and Abel-beth-maachah, and J

**JANOHAH** *(ja-no'-hah)* See JANOAH. *A city between Ephraim and Manasseh.*
Josh 16:6 and passed by it on the east to J
Josh 16:7 And it went down from J to Ataroth

**JANUM** *(ja'-num) A city in Judah.*
Josh 15:53 J, and Beth-tappuah, and Aphekah

**JAPHETH** *(ja'-feth) A son of Noah.*
Gen 5:32 and Noah begat Shem, Ham, and J
Gen 6:10 begat three sons, Shem, Ham, and J
Gen 7:13 Noah, and Shem, and Ham, and J
Gen 9:18 the ark, were Shem, and Ham, and J
Gen 9:23 J took a garment, and laid it upon
Gen 9:27 God shall enlarge J, and he shall
Gen 10:1 the sons of Noah, Shem, Ham, and J
Gen 10:2 The sons of J; Gomer
Gen 10:21 Eber, the brother of J the elder
1Chr 1:4 Noah, Shem, Ham, and J
1Chr 1:5 The sons of J; Gomer

**JAPHIA** *(ja-fi'-ah)*
*1. An Amorite king.*
Josh 10:3 unto J king of Lachish, and unto
*2. A town in Zebulun.*
Josh 19:12 out to Daberath, and goeth up to J
*3. A son of David.*
2Sa 5:15 also, and Elishua, and Nepheg, and J
1Chr 3:7 And Nogah, and Nepheg, and J
1Chr 14:6 And Nogah, and Nepheg, and J

**JAPHLET** *(jaf'-let)* See JAPHLETI. *A grandson of Beriah.*
1Chr 7:32 And Heber begat J, and Shomer, and
1Chr 7:33 And the sons of J
1Chr 7:33 These are the children of J

**JAPHLETI** *(jaf'-let-i)* See JAPHLET. *A landmark in Ephraim.*
Josh 16:3 down westward to the coast of J

**JAPHO** *(ja'-fo)* See JOPPA. *A city in Dan.*
Josh 19:46 Rakkon, with the border before J

**JARAH** *(ja'-rah)* See JEHOADAH. *A son of Ahaz.*
1Chr 9:42 And Ahaz begat J
1Chr 9:42 J begat Alemeth, and Azmaveth, and

**JAREB** *(ja'-reb) An Assyrian king.*
Hos 5:13 the Assyrian, and sent to king J
Hos 10:6 Assyria for a present to king J

**JARED** *(ja'-red)* See JERED.
*1. A descendant of Seth.*
Gen 5:15 sixty and five years, and begat J
Gen 5:16 after he begat J eight hundred
Gen 5:18 J lived an hundred sixty and two
Gen 5:19 J lived after he begat Enoch
Gen 5:20 all the days of J were nine
*2. Father of Enoch; ancestor of Jesus.*
Lk 3:37 of Enoch, which was the son of J

**JARESIAH** *(ja-re-si'-ah) A descendant of Benjamin.*
1Chr 8:27 And J, and Eliah, and Zichri, the

**JARHA** *(jar'-hah) An Egyptian servant.*
1Chr 2:34 an Egyptian, whose name was J
1Chr 2:35 daughter to J his servant to wife

**JARIB** *(ja'-rib)* See JACHIN.
*1. A son of Simeon.*
1Chr 4:24 Simeon were, Nemuel, and Jamin, J
*2. A family of exiles.*
Ezr 8:16 and for Elnathan, and for J
*3. Married a foreigner.*
Ezr 10:18 Maaseiah, and Eliezer, and J

**JARMUTH** *(jar'-muth)* See REMETH.
*1. A city in Judah.*
Josh 10:3 Hebron, and unto Piram king of J
Josh 10:5 the king of Hebron, the king of J
Josh 10:23 the king of Hebron, the king of J
Josh 12:11 The king of J, one
Josh 15:35 J, and Adullam, Socoh, and Azekah,
Josh 21:29 J with her suburbs, En-gannim
Neh 11:29 En-rimmon, and at Zareah, and at J

**JAROAH** *(ja-ro'-ah) A descendant of Gad.*
1Chr 5:14 the son of Huri, the son of J

**JASHEN** *(ja'-shen)* See HASHEM. *Father of several "mighty men" of David.*
2Sa 23:32 the Shaalbonite, of the sons of J

**JASHER** *(ja'-shur) A book of songs.*
Josh 10:13 not this written in the book of J
2Sa 1:18 it is written in the book of J

**JASHOBEAM** *(jash-o'-be-am)*
*1. A "mighty man" of David.*
1Chr 11:11 J, a Hachmonite, the chief of the
1Chr 27:2 month was J the son of Zabdiel
*2. Another "mighty man" of David.*
1Chr 12:6 and Azareel, and Joezer, and J

**JASHUB** *(ja'-shub)* See JASHUBI-LEHEM, JOB, JASHUBITES, SHEAR-JASHUB.
*1. A son of Issachar.*
Num 26:24 Of J, the family of the
1Chr 7:1 Issachar were, Tola, and Puah, J
*2. Married a foreigner in exile.*
Ezr 10:29 Meshullam, Malluch, and Adaiah, J

**JASHUBI-LEHEM** *(jash'-u-bi-le'-hem) A descendant of Shelah.*
1Chr 4:22 had the dominion in Moab, and J

**JASHUBITES** *(jash'-u-bites) Descendants of Jashub.*
Num 26:24 Of Jashub, the family of the J

**JASIEL** *(ja'-se-el) A "mighty man" of David.*
1Chr 11:47 and Obed, and J the Mesobaite

**JASON** *(ja'-sun)*
*1. A Christian in Thessalonica.*
Acts 17:5 and assaulted the house of J
Acts 17:6 they found them not, they drew J
Acts 17:7 Whom J hath received:
Acts 17:9 when they had taken security of J
*2. A relative of Paul.*
Rom 16:21 my workfellow, and Lucius, and J

**JASPER**
Ex 28:20 row a beryl, and an onyx, and a *j*
Ex 39:13 row, a beryl, an onyx, and a *j*
Eze 28:13 the beryl, the onyx, and the *j*
Rev 4:3 sat was to look upon like a *j*
Rev 21:11 precious, even like a *j* stone
Rev 21:18 of the wall of it was of *j*
Rev 21:19 The first foundation was *j*

**JATHNIEL** *(jath'-ne-el) A son of Meshelemiah.*
1Chr 26:2 Zebadiah the third, J the fourth,

**JATTIR** *(jat'-tur) A Levitical city in Judah.*
Josh 15:48 And in the mountains, Shamir, and J
Josh 21:14 J with her suburbs, and Eshtemoa
1Sa 30:27 and to them which were in J
1Chr 6:57 and Libnah with her suburbs, and J

**JAVAN** *(ja'-van)*
*1. A son of Joktan.*
Gen 10:2 Gomer, and Magog, and Madai, and J
Gen 10:4 And the sons of J
1Chr 1:5 Gomer, and Magog, and Madai, and J
1Chr 1:7 And the sons of J
*2. Descendants of Javan 1.*
Is 66:19 that draw the bow, to Tubal, and J
*3. A city in southern Arabia.*
Eze 27:13 J, Tubal, and Meshech, they were
Eze 27:19 J going to and fro occupied in thy

**JAVELIN**
Num 25:7 and took a *j* in his hand
1Sa 18:10 there was a *j* in Saul's hand
1Sa 18:11 And Saul cast the *j*
1Sa 19:9 his house with his *j* in his hand
1Sa 19:10 David even to the wall with the *j*
1Sa 19:10 he smote the *j* into the wall
1Sa 20:33 Saul cast a *j* at him to smite him

**JAW**
Judg 15:16 with the *j* of an ass have I slain
Judg 15:19 an hollow place that was in the *j*
Job 41:2 or bore his *j* through with a
Prov 30:14 their *j* teeth as knives, to

**JAWS**
Job 29:17 I brake the *j* of the wicked, and
Ps 22:15 and my tongue cleaveth to my *j*
Is 30:28 a bridle in the *j* of the people
Eze 29:4 But I will put hooks in thy *j*
Eze 38:4 back, and put hooks into thy *j*
Hos 11:4 that take off the yoke on their *j*

**JAZER** *(ja'-zur)* See JAAZER. *A Levitical city in Gad.*
Num 32:1 and when they saw the land of J
Num 32:3 Ataroth, and Dibon, and J, and
Josh 13:25 And their coast was J, and all the
Josh 21:39 her suburbs, J with her suburbs
2Sa 24:5 of the river of Gad, and toward J
1Chr 6:81 suburbs, and J with her suburbs
1Chr 26:31 men of valour at J of Gilead
Is 16:8 they are come even unto J
Is 16:9 weeping of J the vine of Sibmah
Jer 48:32 for thee with the weeping of J
Jer 48:32 they reach even to the sea of J

**JAZIZ** *(ja'-ziz) Overseer of David's flocks.*
1Chr 27:31 the flocks was J the Hagerite

**JEALOUS**
Ex 20:5 for I the LORD thy God am a *j* God
Ex 34:14 whose name is J, is a *j* God
Num 5:14 he be *j* of his wife, and she be
Num 5:14 he be *j* of his wife, and she be
Num 5:30 he be *j* over his wife, and shall
Deut 4:24 is a consuming fire, even a *j* God
Deut 5:9 for I the LORD thy God am a *j* God
Deut 6:15 (For the LORD thy God is a *j* God
Josh 24:19 he is a *j* God
1Kin 19:10 I have been very *j* for the LORD
1Kin 19:14 I have been very *j* for the LORD
Eze 39:25 will be *j* for my holy name
Joel 2:18 will the LORD be *j* for his land
Nah 1:2 God is *j*, and the LORD revengeth
Zec 1:14 I am *j* for Jerusalem and for Zion
Zec 8:2 I was *j* for Zion with great
Zec 8:2 I was *j* for her with great fury
2Cor 11:2 For I am *j* over you with godly

**JEALOUSY**
Num 5:14 And the spirit of *j* come upon him
Num 5:14 if the spirit of *j* come upon him
Num 5:15 for it is an offering of *j*
Num 5:18 hands, which is the *j* offering
Num 5:25 the *j* offering out of the woman's
Num 5:30 the spirit of *j* cometh upon him
Num 25:11 the children of Israel in my *j*
Deut 29:20 his *j* shall smoke against that
Deut 32:16 him to *j* with strange gods
Deut 32:21 They have moved me to *j* with that
Deut 32:21 I will move them to *j* with those
1Kin 14:22 they provoked him to *j* with their
Ps 78:58 moved him to *j* with their graven
Ps 79:5 shall thy *j* burn like fire
Prov 6:34 For *j* is the rage of a man
Song 8:6 *j* is cruel as the grave
Is 42:13 he shall stir up *j* like a man of
Eze 8:3 of *j*, which provoketh to *j*
Eze 8:5 this image of *j* in the entry
Eze 16:38 will give thee blood in fury and *j*
Eze 16:42 my *j* shall depart from thee, and I
Eze 23:25 And I will set my *j* against thee
Eze 36:5 Surely in the fire of my *j* have I
Eze 36:6 Behold, I have spoken in my *j*
Eze 38:19 For in my *j* and in the fire of my
Zeph 1:18 be devoured by the fire of his *j*
Zeph 3:8 be devoured with the fire of my *j*
Zec 1:14 and for Zion with a great *j*
Zec 8:2 was jealous for Zion with great *j*
Rom 10:19 I will provoke you to *j* by them
Rom 11:11 for to provoke them to *j*
1Cor 10:22 Do we provoke the Lord to *j*
2Cor 11:2 am jealous over you with godly *j*

**JEARIM** *(je'-a-rim)* See KIRJATH-JEARIM. *A mountain in Judah.*
Josh 15:10 along unto the side of mount J

**JEATERAI** *(je-at'-e-rahee) A descendant of Gershom.*
1Chr 6:21 his son, Zerah his son, J his son

**JEBERECHIAH** *(je-ber'-e-ki'-ah) Father of Zechariah.*
Is 8:2 priest, and Zechariah the son of J

**JEBEREKIAH** See JEBERECHIAH.

**JEBUS** *(je'-bus)* See JEBUSI, JEBUSITE, JERUSALEM. *Original name of Jerusalem.*
Judg 19:10 departed, and came over against J
Judg 19:11 And when they were by J, the day
1Chr 11:4 went to Jerusalem, which is J
1Chr 11:5 inhabitants of J said to David

**JEBUSI** *(jeb'-u-si)* See JEBUSITE. *Same as Jebus.*
Josh 18:16 to the side of J on the south
Josh 18:28 And Zelah, Eleph, and J, which is

**JEBUSITE** *(jeb'-u-site)* See JEBUSITES. *Descendant of Canaan.*
Gen 10:16 And the J, and the Amorite, and the
Ex 33:2 Perizzite, the Hivite, and the J
Ex 34:11 and the Hivite, and the J
Josh 9:1 Perizzite, the Hivite, and the J
Josh 11:3 the J in the mountains, and to the
Josh 15:8 unto the south side of the J
2Sa 24:16 threshingplace of Araunah the J
2Sa 24:18 threshingfloor of Araunah the J
1Chr 1:14 The J also, and the Amorite, and
1Chr 21:15 the threshingfloor of Ornan the J
1Chr 21:18 the threshingfloor of Ornan the J
1Chr 21:28 the threshingfloor of Ornan the J
2Chr 3:1 the threshingfloor of Ornan the J
Zec 9:7 in Judah, and Ekron as a J

**JEBUSITES** *(jeb'-u-sites)*
Gen 15:21 and the Girgashites, and the J
Ex 3:8 and the Hivites, and the J
Ex 3:17 and the Hivites, and the J
Ex 13:5 and the Hivites, and the J
Ex 23:23 Canaanites, the Hivites, and the J
Num 13:29 and the Hittites, and the J
Deut 7:1 and the Hivites, and the J
Deut 20:17 Perizzites, the Hivites, and the J
Josh 3:10 and the Amorites, and the J
Josh 12:8 Perizzites, the Hivites, and the J
Josh 15:63 As for the J the inhabitants of
Josh 15:63 but the J dwell with the children
Josh 24:11 the Hivites, and the J
Judg 1:21 the J that inhabited Jerusalem
Judg 1:21 but the J dwell with the children
Judg 3:5 and Perizzites, and Hivites, and J
Judg 19:11 turn in into this city of the J
2Sa 5:6 men went to Jerusalem unto the J
2Sa 5:8 to the gutter, and smiteth the J
1Kin 9:20 Perizzites, Hivites, and J
1Chr 11:4 where the J were, the inhabitants
1Chr 11:6 the J first shall be chief
2Chr 8:7 and the Hivites, and the J
Ezr 9:1 Hittites, the Perizzites, the J
Neh 9:8 and the Perizzites, and the J

**JECAMIAH** *(jek-a-mi'-ah)* See JEKAMIAH. *A son of Jeconiah.*
1Chr 3:18 also, and Pedaiah, and Shenazar, J

**JECHOLIAH** *(jek-o-li'-ah)* See JECOLIAH. *Mother of Uzziah.*
2Kin 15:2 mother's name was J of Jerusalem

**JECHONIAS** *(jek-o-ni'-as)* See JECONIAH. *Greek form of Jeconiah.*
Mt 1:11 And Josias begat J and his brethren
Mt 1:12 to Babylon, J begat Salathiel

**JECOLIAH** *(jek-o-li'-ah)* See JECHOLIAH. *Same as Jecholiah.*
2Chr 26:3 name also was J of Jerusalem

**JECONIAH** *(jek-o-ni'-ah)* See CONIAH, JECHONIAS, JEHOIACHIN. *A king of Judah.*
1Chr 3:16 J his son, Zedekiah his son
1Chr 3:17 And the sons of J
Est 2:6 carried away with J king of Judah
Jer 24:1 had carried away captive J the
Jer 27:20 J the son of Jehoiakim king of
Jer 28:4 J the son of Jehoiakim king of
Jer 29:2 (After that J the king, and the

**JEDAIAH** *(jed-a-i'-ah)*
*1. A descendant of Simeon.*
1Chr 4:37 the son of Allon, the son of J
*2. A rebuilder of Jerusalem's wall.*
Neh 3:10 repaired J the son of Harumaph
*3. A priest in Jerusalem.*
1Chr 9:10 J, and Jehoiarib, and Jachin,
1Chr 24:7 to Jehoiarib, the second to J
Ezr 2:36 the children of J, of the house
Neh 7:39 the children of J, of the house
*4. A family of exiles.*
Neh 11:10 J the son of Joiarib, Jachin
Neh 12:6 Shemaiah, and Joiarib, J,
Neh 12:19 Mattenai; of J, Uzzi
Zec 6:10 of Heldai, of Tobijah, and of J
Zec 6:14 to Helem, and to Tobijah, and to J
*5. A priest.*
Neh 12:7 Sallu, Amok, Hilkiah, J
Neh 12:21 of J, Nethaneel

**JEDIAEL** *(jed-e-a'-el)*
*1. A son of Benjamin.*
1Chr 7:6 Bela, and Becher, and J, three
1Chr 7:10 The sons also of J
1Chr 7:11 All these the sons of J, by the
*2. A "mighty man" of David.*
1Chr 11:45 J the son of Shimri, and Joha his
*3. A warrior in David's army.*
1Chr 12:20 Manasseh, Adnah, and Jozabad, and J
*4. Son of Meshelemiah.*
1Chr 26:2 J the second, Zebadiah the third,

**JEDIDAH** *(je-di'-dah) Mother of King Josiah.*
2Kin 22:1 And his mother's name was J

**JEDIDIAH** *(jed-id-i'-ah) Another name for Solomon.*
2Sa 12:25 and he called his name J, because

**JEDUTHUN** *(jed'-u-thun) A Levite.*
1Chr 9:16 the son of Galal, the son of J
1Chr 16:38 Obed-edom also the son of J
1Chr 16:41 And with them Heman and J, and the
1Chr 16:42 J with trumpets and cymbals for
1Chr 16:42 the sons of J were porters
1Chr 25:1 of Asaph, and of Heman, and of J
1Chr 25:3 Of J: the sons of J
1Chr 25:3 under the hands of their father J
1Chr 25:6 to the king's order to Asaph, J
2Chr 5:12 of them of Asaph, of Heman, of J
2Chr 29:14 and of the sons of J
2Chr 35:15 and Heman, and J the king's seer
Neh 11:17 the son of Galal, the son of J
Ps 39:t To the chief Musician, even to J
Ps 62:t To the chief Musician, to J
Ps 77:t To the chief Musician, to J

**JEEZER** *(je-e'-zur)* See ABIEZER, JEEZERITES. *A son of Gilead.*
Num 26:30 of J, the family of the

**JEEZERITES** *(je-e'-zur-ites) Descendants of Jeezer.*
Num 26:30 of Jeezer, the family of the J

**JEGAR-SAHADUTHA**
Gen 31:47 And Laban called it J

**JEHALELEEL** *(je-hal-e'-le-el)* See JEHALELEL. *A descendant of Judah.*
1Chr 4:16 And the sons of J

**JEHALELEL** *(je-hal'-e-lel)* See JEHALELEEL. *A descendant of Merari.*
2Chr 29:12 of Abdi, and Azariah the son of J

**JEHDEIAH** *(jeh-di'-ah)*
*1. A sanctuary servant.*
1Chr 24:20 the sons of Shubael; J
*2. A herdsman of David.*
1Chr 27:30 the asses was J the Meronothite

**JEHEZEKEL** *(je-hez'-e-kel)* See EZEKIEL. *A sanctuary servant.*
1Chr 24:16 to Pethahiah, the twentieth to J

**JEHIAH** *(je-hi'-ah)* See JEHIEL. *A priest.*
1Chr 15:24 J were doorkeepers for the ark

**JEHIEL** *(je-hi'-el)* See JEHIAH, JEIEL, JEHIELI.
*1. A Levite.*
1Chr 15:18 and Jaaziel, and Shemiramoth, and J
1Chr 15:20 and Aziel, and Shemiramoth, and J
1Chr 16:5 Jeiel, and Shemiramoth, and J
*2. A Gershonite.*
1Chr 23:8 the chief was J, and Zetham, and
1Chr 29:8 by the hand of J the Gershonite
*3. A friend of David's son.*
1Chr 27:32 J the son of Hachmoni was with
*4. Son of King Jehoshaphat.*
2Chr 21:2 of Jehoshaphat, Azariah, and J
*5. A son of Heman.*
2Chr 29:14 sons of Heman; J, and Shimei
*6. A Levite in Hezekiah's time.*
2Chr 31:13 And J, and Azaziah, and Nahath, and
*7. A chief priest.*
2Chr 35:8 Hilkiah and Zechariah and J
*8. A family of exiles.*
Ezr 8:9 Obadiah the son of J, and with him
*9. The father of Shechaniah.*
Ezr 10:2 And Shechaniah the son of J
*10. A son of Harim.*
Ezr 10:21 and Elijah, and Shemaiah, and J
*11. A man of Elam's family who married a foreigner.*
Ezr 10:26 Mattaniah, Zechariah, and J
*12. Father of Gibeon.*
1Chr 9:35 dwelt the father of Gibeon, J
*13. A "mighty man" of David.*
1Chr 11:44 J the sons of Hothan the Aroerite

**JEHIELI** *(je-hi'-el-i)* See JEHIEL. *A sanctuary servant.*
1Chr 26:21 of Laadan the Gershonite, were J
1Chr 26:22 The sons of J; Zetham, and

**JEHIZKIAH** *(je-hiz-ki'-ah)* See HEZEKIAH. *A son of Shallum.*
2Chr 28:12 J the son of Shallum, and Amasa

**JEHOADAH** *(je-ho'-a-dah)* See JARAH. *Son of Ahaz.*
1Chr 8:36 And Ahaz begat J
1Chr 8:36 J begat Alemeth, and Azmaveth, and

**JEHOADDAN** *(je-ho-ad'-dan) Mother of King Amaziah.*
2Kin 14:2 mother's name was J of Jerusalem
2Chr 25:1 mother's name was J of Jerusalem

**JEHOAHAZ** *(je-ho'-a-haz)* See AHAZIAH, JOAHAZ, SHALLUM.
*1. Son of King Jehu.*
2Kin 10:35 J his son reigned in his stead
2Kin 13:1 son of Ahaziah king of Judah J
2Kin 13:4 J besought the LORD, and the LORD
2Kin 13:7 people to J but fifty horsemen
2Kin 13:8 Now the rest of the acts of J
2Kin 13:9 And J slept with his fathers
2Kin 13:10 Judah began Jehoash the son of J
2Kin 13:22 Israel all the days of J
2Kin 13:25 Jehoash the son of J took again
2Kin 13:25 the hand of J his father by war
2Kin 14:1 J king of Israel reigned Amaziah
2Kin 14:8 the son of J son of Jehu, king of
2Kin 14:17 the death of Jehoash son of J
2Chr 25:17 and sent to Joash, the son of J
2Chr 25:25 of J king of Israel fifteen years
*2. Son of King Josiah.*
2Kin 23:30 the land took J the son of Josiah
2Kin 23:31 J was twenty and three years old
2Kin 23:34 name to Jehoiakim, and took J away
2Chr 36:2 J was twenty and three years old
2Chr 36:4 Necho took J his brother, and
*3. A son of King Jehoram.*
2Chr 21:17 was never a son left him, save J
2Chr 25:23 the son of Joash, the son of J

**JEHOASH** *(je-ho'-ash)* See JOASH.
*1. A king of Judah.*
2Kin 11:21 Seven years old was J when he
2Kin 12:1 year of Jehu J began to reign
2Kin 12:2 J did that which was right in the
2Kin 12:4 J said to the priests, All the
2Kin 12:6 twentieth year of king J the
2Kin 12:7 Then king J called for Jehoiada
2Kin 12:18 J king of Judah took all the
2Kin 14:13 the son of J the son of Ahaziah,
*2. A king of Israel.*
2Kin 13:10 J the son of Jehoahaz to reign
2Kin 13:25 J the son of Jehoahaz took again
2Kin 14:8 Then Amaziah sent messengers to J
2Kin 14:9 J the king of Israel sent to
2Kin 14:11 Therefore J king of Israel went
2Kin 14:13 J king of Israel took Amaziah
2Kin 14:15 of the acts of J which he did
2Kin 14:16 J slept with his fathers, and was
2Kin 14:17 J son of Jehoahaz king of Israel

**JEHOHANAN** *(je-ho'-ha-nan)*
*1. A sanctuary servant.*
1Chr 26:3 J the sixth, Elioenai the seventh
*2. A chief captain.*
2Chr 17:15 And next to him was J the captain
*3. Father of Ishmael.*
2Chr 23:1 Jeroham, and Ishmael the son of J
*4. Married a foreigner in exile.*
Ezr 10:28 J, Hananiah, Zabbai, and Athlai
*5. A priest in exile.*
Neh 12:13 Meshullam; of Amariah, J
*6. A priest who dedicated the wall.*
Neh 12:42 and Eleazar, and Uzzi, and J

**JEHOIACHIN** *(je-hoy'-a-kin)* See CONIAH, JECONIAH, JECONIAS, JEHOIACHIN'S. *A king of Judah.*
2Kin 24:6 J his son reigned in his stead
2Kin 24:8 J was eighteen years old when he
2Kin 24:12 J the king of Judah went out to
2Kin 24:15 And he carried away J to Babylon
2Kin 25:27 the captivity of J king of Judah
2Kin 25:27 of J king of Judah out of prison
2Chr 36:8 J his son reigned in his stead
2Chr 36:9 J was eight years old when he
Jer 52:31 the captivity of J king of Judah
Jer 52:31 up the head of J king of Judah

**JEHOIACHIN'S** *(je-hoy'-a-kins)*
Eze 1:2 fifth year of king J captivity

**JEHOIADA** *(je-hoy'-a-dah)* See BERECHIAS, JOIADA.
*1. Father of Benaiah.*
2Sa 8:18 Benaiah the son of J was over
2Sa 20:23 Benaiah the son of J was over the
2Sa 23:20 And Benaiah the son of J, the son
2Sa 23:22 things did Benaiah the son of J
1Kin 1:8 priest, and Benaiah the son of J
1Kin 1:26 priest, and Benaiah the son of J
1Kin 1:32 prophet, and Benaiah the son of J
1Kin 1:36 the son of J answered the king
1Kin 1:38 prophet, and Benaiah the son of J
1Kin 1:44 prophet, and Benaiah the son of J
1Kin 2:25 the hand of Benaiah the son of J
1Kin 2:29 Solomon sent Benaiah the son of J
1Kin 2:34 So Benaiah the son of J went up
1Kin 2:35 of J in his room over the host
1Kin 2:46 commanded Benaiah the son of J
1Kin 4:4 the son of J was over the host
1Chr 11:22 Benaiah the son of J, the son of
1Chr 11:24 things did Benaiah the son of J
1Chr 18:17 Benaiah the son of J was over the
1Chr 27:5 month was Benaiah the son of J
*2. A high priest.*
2Kin 11:4 And the seventh year J sent
2Kin 11:9 that J the priest commanded
2Kin 11:9 sabbath, and came to J the priest
2Kin 11:15 But J the priest commanded the
2Kin 11:17 J made a covenant between the
2Kin 12:2 J the priest instructed him
2Kin 12:7 Jehoash called for J the priest
2Kin 12:9 But J the priest took a chest, and
2Chr 22:11 Jehoram, the wife of J the priest
2Chr 23:1 And in the seventh year J
2Chr 23:8 that J the priest had commanded
2Chr 23:8 for J the priest dismissed not
2Chr 23:9 Moreover J the priest delivered
2Chr 23:11 And J and his sons anointed him, and
2Chr 23:14 Then J the priest brought out the
2Chr 23:16 J made a covenant between him, and
2Chr 23:18 Also J appointed the offices of
2Chr 24:2 LORD all the days of J the priest
2Chr 24:3 And J took for him two wives
2Chr 24:6 the king called for J the chief
2Chr 24:12 J gave it to such as did the work
2Chr 24:14 of the money before the king and J
2Chr 24:14 continually all the days of J
2Chr 24:15 But J waxed old, and was full of

2Chr 24:17 Now after the death of J came the
2Chr 24:20 Zechariah the son of J the priest
2Chr 24:22 not the kindness which J his
2Chr 24:25 blood of the sons of J the priest
*3. A captain in David's army.*
1Chr 12:27 J was the leader of the Aaronites
*4. Son of Benaiah.*
1Chr 27:34 was J the son of Benaiah, and
*5. A rebuilder of Jerusalem's wall.*
Neh 3:6 gate repaired J the son of Paseah
*6. A pre-exilic priest.*
Jer 29:26 in the stead of J the priest

**JEHOIAKIM** *(je-hoy'-a-kim)* See ELIAKIM, JOIAKIM. *A king of Judah.*
2Kin 23:34 father, and turned his name to J
2Kin 23:35 J gave the silver and the gold to
2Kin 23:36 J was twenty and five years old
2Kin 24:1 J became his servant three years
2Kin 24:5 Now the rest of the acts of J
2Kin 24:6 So J slept with his fathers
2Kin 24:19 according to all that J had done
1Chr 3:15 firstborn Johanan, the second J
1Chr 3:16 And the sons of J
2Chr 36:4 and turned his name to J
2Chr 36:5 J was twenty and five years old
2Chr 36:8 Now the rest of the acts of J
Jer 1:3 It came also in the days of J the
Jer 22:18 thus saith the LORD concerning J
Jer 22:24 though Coniah the son of J king
Jer 24:1 the son of J king of Judah
Jer 25:1 of Judah in the fourth year of J
Jer 26:1 the beginning of the reign of J
Jer 26:21 when J the king, with all his
Jer 26:22 J the king sent men into Egypt,
Jer 26:23 and brought him unto J the king
Jer 27:1 the beginning of the reign of J
Jer 27:20 captive Jeconiah the son of J
Jer 28:4 the son of J king of Judah
Jer 35:1 from the LORD in the days of J
Jer 36:1 to pass in the fourth year of J
Jer 36:9 to pass in the fifth year of J
Jer 36:28 which J the king of Judah hath
Jer 36:29 thou shalt say to J king of Judah
Jer 36:30 saith the LORD of J king of Judah
Jer 36:32 J king of Judah had burned in the
Jer 37:1 instead of Coniah the son of J
Jer 45:1 in the fourth year of J the son
Jer 46:2 smote in the fourth year of J the
Jer 52:2 according to all that J had done
Dan 1:1 the reign of J king of Judah came
Dan 1:2 the Lord gave J king of Judah

**JEHOIARIB** *(je-hoy'-a-rib)* See JOIARIB.
*1. A priest.*
1Chr 9:10 Jedaiah, and J, and Jachin,
*2. A sanctuary servant.*
1Chr 24:7 Now the first lot came forth to J

**JEHONADAB** *(je-hon'-a-dab)* See JONADAB. *A son of Rechab.*
2Kin 10:15 he lighted on J the son of Rechab
2Kin 10:15 And J answered, It is
2Kin 10:23 J the son of Rechab, into the

**JEHONATHAN** *(je-hon'-a-than)* See JONATHAN.
*1. A storehouse servant.*
1Chr 27:25 castles, was J the son of Uzziah
*2. A Levite teacher.*
2Chr 17:8 and Asahel, and Shemiramoth, and J
*3. A priest.*
Neh 12:18 of Shemaiah, J

**JEHORAM** *(je-ho'-ram)* See HADORAM, JORAM.
*1. A king of Judah.*
1Kin 22:50 J his son reigned in his stead
2Kin 1:17 J the son of Jehoshaphat king of
2Kin 8:16 J the son of Jehoshaphat king of
2Kin 8:25 of J king of Judah begin to reign
2Kin 8:29 Ahaziah the son of J king of
2Kin 12:18 things that Jehoshaphat, and J
2Chr 21:1 J his son reigned in his stead
2Chr 21:3 but the kingdom gave he to J
2Chr 21:4 Now when J was risen up to the
2Chr 21:5 J was thirty and two years old
2Chr 21:9 Then J went forth with his
2Chr 21:16 the LORD stirred up against J the
2Chr 22:1 son of J king of Judah reigned
2Chr 22:6 Azariah the son of J king of
2Chr 22:11 the daughter of king J, the wife
*2. A son of Ahab.*
2Kin 1:17 J reigned in his stead in the
2Kin 3:1 Now J the son of Ahab began to
2Kin 3:6 king J went out of Samaria the
2Kin 9:24 smote J between his arms, and the
2Chr 22:5 went with J the son of Ahab king
2Chr 22:6 see J the son of Ahab at Jezreel
2Chr 22:7 he went out with J against Jehu
*3. A priest.*
2Chr 17:8 and with them Elishama and J

**JEHOSHABEATH** *(je-ho-shab'-e-ath)* See JEHOSHEBA. *A daughter of King Jehoram.*
2Chr 22:11 But J, the daughter of the king,
2Chr 22:11 So J, the daughter of king

**JEHOSHAPHAT** *(je-hosh'-a-fat)* See JOSAPHAT, JOSHAPHAT.
*1. David's recorder.*
2Sa 8:16 J the son of Ahilud was recorder
2Sa 20:24 J the son of Ahilud was recorder
1Kin 4:3 J the son of Ahilud, the recorder
1Chr 18:15 J the son of Ahilud, recorder
*2. An officer of Solomon.*
1Kin 4:17 J the son of Paruah, in Issachar
*3. A king of Judah.*
1Kin 15:24 J his son reigned in his stead
1Kin 22:2 that J the king of Judah came
1Kin 22:4 And he said unto J, Wilt thou go
1Kin 22:4 J said to the king of Israel, I
1Kin 22:5 J said unto the king of Israel,
1Kin 22:7 J said, Is there not here a
1Kin 22:8 And the king of Israel said unto J
1Kin 22:8 J said, Let not the king say so
1Kin 22:10 J the king of Judah sat each on
1Kin 22:18 And the king of Israel said unto J
1Kin 22:29 J the king of Judah went up to
1Kin 22:30 And the king of Israel said unto J
1Kin 22:32 captains of the chariots saw J
1Kin 22:32 and J cried out
1Kin 22:41 J the son of Asa began to reign
1Kin 22:42 J was thirty and five years old
1Kin 22:44 J made peace with the king of
1Kin 22:45 Now the rest of the acts of J
1Kin 22:48 J made ships of Tharshish to go
1Kin 22:49 Ahaziah the son of Ahab unto J
1Kin 22:49 But J would not.
1Kin 22:50 J slept with his fathers, and was
1Kin 22:51 year of J king of Judah, and
2Kin 1:17 the son of J king of Judah
2Kin 3:1 year of J king of Judah, and
2Kin 3:7 sent to J the king of Judah,
2Kin 3:11 But J said, Is there not here a
2Kin 3:12 J said, The word of the LORD is
2Kin 3:12 So the king of Israel and J
2Kin 3:14 presence of J the king of Judah
2Kin 8:16 J being then king of Judah,
2Kin 8:16 Jehoram the son of J king of
2Kin 12:18 all the hallowed things that J
1Chr 3:10 his son, Asa his son, J his son,
2Chr 17:1 J his son reigned in his stead,
2Chr 17:3 And the LORD was with J, because
2Chr 17:5 all Judah brought to J presents
2Chr 17:10 that they made no war against J
2Chr 17:11 Philistines brought J presents
2Chr 17:12 J waxed great exceedingly
2Chr 18:1 Now J had riches and honour in
2Chr 18:3 Israel said unto J king of Judah
2Chr 18:4 J said unto the king of Israel,
2Chr 18:6 But J said, Is there not here a
2Chr 18:7 And the king of Israel said unto J
2Chr 18:7 J said, Let not the king say so
2Chr 18:9 J king of Judah sat either of
2Chr 18:17 And the king of Israel said to J
2Chr 18:28 J the king of Judah went up to
2Chr 18:29 And the king of Israel said unto J
2Chr 18:31 captains of the chariots saw J
2Chr 18:31 but J cried out, and the LORD
2Chr 19:1 J the king of Judah returned to
2Chr 19:2 to meet him, and said to king J
2Chr 19:4 And J dwelt at Jerusalem
2Chr 19:8 did J set of the Levites, and of
2Chr 20:1 came against J to battle
2Chr 20:2 Then there came some that told J
2Chr 20:3 J feared, and set himself to seek
2Chr 20:5 J stood in the congregation of
2Chr 20:15 of Jerusalem, and thou king J
2Chr 20:18 J bowed his head with his face to
2Chr 20:20 J stood and said, Hear me, O Judah
2Chr 20:25 And when J and his people came to
2Chr 20:27 J in the forefront of them, to go
2Chr 20:30 So the realm of J was quiet
2Chr 20:31 And J reigned over Judah
2Chr 20:34 Now the rest of the acts of J
2Chr 20:35 after this did J king of Judah
2Chr 20:37 of Mareshah prophesied against J
2Chr 21:1 Now J slept with his fathers, and
2Chr 21:2 And he had brethren the sons of J
2Chr 21:2 were the sons of J king of Israel
2Chr 21:12 in the ways of J thy father
2Chr 22:9 said they, he is the son of J
*4. Father of Jehu.*
2Kin 9:2 the son of J the son of Nimshi
2Kin 9:14 So Jehu the son of J the son of
*5. A priest.*
1Chr 15:24 And Shebaniah, and J, and Nethaneel,
*6. A valley near Jerusalem.*
Joel 3:2 them down into the valley of J
Joel 3:12 and come up to the valley of J

**JEHOSHEBA** *(je-hosh'-e-bah)* See JEHOSHABEATH. *Same as Jehoshabeath.*
2Kin 11:2 But J, the daughter of king Joram

**JEHOSHUA** *(je-hosh'-u-ah)* See JEHOSHUAH, JOSHUA. *Same as Joshua, son of Nun.*
Num 13:16 called Oshea the son of Nun J

**JEHOSHUAH** *(je-hosh'-u-ah) Same as Joshua, son of Nun.*
1Chr 7:27 Non his son, J his son

**JEHOVAH** *(je-ho'-vah)* See GOD, JAH, JEHOVAH-JIREH, JEHOVAH-NISSI, JEHOVAH-SHALOM, LORD. *A name for God.*
Ex 6:3 but by my name J was I not known
Ps 83:18 that thou, whose name alone is J
Is 12:2 for the LORD J is my strength and
Is 26:4 for in the LORD J is everlasting

**JEHOVAH-JIREH** *(je-ho'-vah-ji'-reh) Mt. Moriah.*
Gen 22:14 called the name of that place J

**JEHOVAH-NISSI** *(je-ho'-vah-nis'-si) An altar built by Moses.*
Ex 17:15 altar, and called the name of it J

**JEHOVAH-SHALOM** *(je-ho'-vah-sha'-lom) An altar built by Gideon.*
Judg 6:24 unto the LORD, and called it J

**JEHOZABAD** *(je-hoz'-a-bad)* See JOZABAD.
*1. Son of Shomer.*
2Kin 12:21 J the son of Shomer, his servants
2Chr 24:26 J the son of Shimrith a Moabitess
*2. A son of Obed-edom.*
1Chr 26:4 J the second, Joah the third, and
*3. A general of Jehoshaphat.*
2Chr 17:18 And next him was J, and with him an

**JEHOZADAK** *(je-hoz'-a-dak) Great-grandson of Hilkiah.*
1Chr 6:14 begat Seraiah, and Seraiah begat J
1Chr 6:15 J went into captivity, when the

**JEHU** *(je-hu)*
*1. A son of Hanani.*
1Kin 16:1 to J the son of Hanani against
1Kin 16:7 J the son of Hanani came the word
1Kin 16:12 against Baasha by J the prophet
2Chr 19:2 J the son of Hanani the seer went
2Chr 20:34 the book of J the son of Hanani
*2. A king of Israel.*
1Kin 19:16 J the son of Nimshi shalt thou
1Kin 19:17 the sword of Hazael shall J slay
1Kin 19:17 the sword of J shall Elisha slay
2Kin 9:2 look out there J the son of
2Kin 9:5 J said, Unto which of all us
2Kin 9:11 Then J came forth to the servants
2Kin 9:13 with trumpets, saying, J is king
2Kin 9:14 So J the son of Jehoshaphat the
2Kin 9:15 J said, If it be your minds, then
2Kin 9:16 So J rode in a chariot, and went
2Kin 9:17 spied the company of J as he came
2Kin 9:18 J said, What hast thou to do with
2Kin 9:19 J answered, What hast thou to do
2Kin 9:20 driving of J the son of Nimshi
2Kin 9:21 and they went out against J
2Kin 9:22 it came to pass, when Joram saw J
2Kin 9:22 that he said, Is it peace, J
2Kin 9:24 J drew a bow with his full
2Kin 9:25 Then said J to Bidkar his captain
2Kin 9:27 J followed after him, and said,

2Kin 9:30 when J was come to Jezreel,
2Kin 9:31 as J entered in at the gate, she
2Kin 10:1 J wrote letters, and sent to
2Kin 10:5 up of the children, sent to J
2Kin 10:11 So J slew all that remained of
2Kin 10:13 J met with the brethren of
2Kin 10:18 J gathered all the people
2Kin 10:18 but J shall serve him much
2Kin 10:19 But J did it in subtilty, to the
2Kin 10:20 J said, Proclaim a solemn
2Kin 10:21 J sent through all Israel
2Kin 10:23 J went, and Jehonadab the son of
2Kin 10:24 J appointed fourscore men without
2Kin 10:25 that J said to the guard and to
2Kin 10:28 Thus J destroyed Baal out of
2Kin 10:29 J departed not from after them,
2Kin 10:30 And the LORD said unto J, Because
2Kin 10:31 But J took no heed to walk in the
2Kin 10:34 Now the rest of the acts of J
2Kin 10:35 And J slept with his fathers
2Kin 10:36 the time that J reigned over
2Kin 12:1 year of J Jehoash began to reign
2Kin 13:1 of Judah Jehoahaz the son of J
2Kin 14:8 the son of Jehoahaz son of J
2Kin 15:12 of the LORD which he spake unto J
2Chr 22:7 against J the son of Nimshi
2Chr 22:8 when J was executing judgment
2Chr 22:9 in Samaria,) and brought him to J
2Chr 25:17 the son of Jehoahaz, the son of J
Hos 1:4 of Jezreel upon the house of J

*3. A son of Obed.*
1Chr 2:38 begat Jehu, and J begat Azariah,

*4. A son of Josibiah.*
1Chr 4:35 J the son of Josibiah, the son of

*5. A warrior in David's army.*
1Chr 12:3 and Berachah, and J the Antothite,

**JEHUBBAH** *(je-hub'-bah) A descendant of Shamer.*
1Chr 7:34 Ahi, and Rohgah, J, and Aram

**JEHUCAL** *(je-hu'-kal)* See JUCAL. *A son of Shelemiah.*
Jer 37:3 king sent J the son of Shelemiah

**JEHUD** *(je'-hud) A city in Dan.*
Josh 19:45 And J, and Bene-berak, and

**JEHUDI** *(je-hu'-di) Son of Nethaniah.*
Jer 36:14 sent J the son of Nethaniah
Jer 36:21 So the king sent J to fetch the
Jer 36:21 J read it in the ears of the king
Jer 36:23 that when J had read three or

**JEHUDIJAH** *(je-hu-di'-jah)* See HODIAH. *A descendant of Judah.*
1Chr 4:18 his wife J bare Jered the father

**JEHUSH** *(je'-hush)* See JEUSH. *A descendant of King Saul.*
1Chr 8:39 J the second, and Eliphelet the

**JEIEL** *(je-i'-el)* See JEHIEL, JEUEL.
*1. A chief Reubenite.*
1Chr 5:7 was reckoned, were the chief, J

*2. A Levite gatekeeper.*
1Chr 15:18 and Mikneiah, and Obed-edom, and J
1Chr 15:21 and Mikneiah, and Obed-edom, and J
1Chr 16:5 and next to him Zechariah, J
1Chr 16:5 J with psalteries and with harps

*3. A Levite of the Asaph family.*
2Chr 20:14 the son of Benaiah, the son of J

*4. A scribe.*
2Chr 26:11 by the hand of J the scribe

*5. A Levite in Hezekiah's time.*
2Chr 29:13 Shimri, and J: and of the sons

*6. A chief Levite.*
2Chr 35:9 his brethren, and Hashabiah and J

*7. An exile.*
Ezr 8:13 names are these, Eliphelet, J

*8. Married a foreigner in exile.*
Ezr 10:43 J, Mattithiah, Zabad, Zebina,

**JEKABZEEL** *(je-kab'-ze-el)* See KABZEEL. *A city in Judah.*
Neh 11:25 in the villages thereof, and at J

**JEKAMEAM** *(je-kam'-e-am) Son of Hebron.*
1Chr 23:19 the third, and J the fourth
1Chr 24:23 Jahaziel the third, J the fourth

**JEKAMIAH** *(jek-a-mi'-ah)* See JECAMIAH. *A descendant of Shallum.*
1Chr 2:41 And Shallum begat J
1Chr 2:41 and J begat Elishama

**JEKUTHIEL** *(je-ku'-the-el) A descendant of Ezra.*
1Chr 4:18 Socho, and J the father of Zanoah

**JEMIMA** *(je-mi'-mah) A daughter of Job.*
Job 42:14 called the name of the first, J

**JEMUEL** *(je-mu'-el)* See NEMUEL. *A son of Simeon.*
Gen 46:10 J, and Jamin, and Ohad, and Jachin,
Ex 6:15 J, and Jamin, and Ohad, and Jachin,

**JEOPARDY**
2Sa 23:17 men that went in j of their lives
1Chr 11:19 that have put their lives in j
1Chr 11:19 for with the j of their lives
1Chr 12:19 master Saul to the j of our heads
Lk 8:23 filled with water, and were in j
1Cor 15:30 And why stand we in j every hour

**JEPHTHAE** *(jef'-thah-e)* See JEPHTHAH. *Same as Jephthah.*
Heb 11:32 of Barak, and of Samson, and of J

**JEPHTHAH** *(jef'-thah)* See JEPHTHAE, JIPHTHAH-EL. *A judge.*
Judg 11:1 Now J the Gileadite was a mighty
Judg 11:1 and Gilead begat J
Judg 11:2 grew up, and they thrust out J
Judg 11:3 Then J fled from his brethren, and
Judg 11:3 there were gathered vain men to J
Judg 11:5 to fetch J out of the land of Tob
Judg 11:6 And they said unto J, Come, and be
Judg 11:7 J said unto the elders of Gilead,
Judg 11:8 the elders of Gilead said unto J
Judg 11:9 J said unto the elders of Gilead,
Judg 11:10 the elders of Gilead said unto J
Judg 11:11 Then J went with the elders of
Judg 11:11 J uttered all his words before
Judg 11:12 J sent messengers unto the king
Judg 11:13 answered unto the messengers of J
Judg 11:14 J sent messengers again unto the
Judg 11:15 And said unto him, Thus saith J
Judg 11:28 the words of J which he sent him
Judg 11:29 Spirit of the LORD came upon J
Judg 11:30 J vowed a vow unto the LORD, and
Judg 11:32 So J passed over unto the
Judg 11:34 J came to Mizpeh unto his house,
Judg 11:40 to lament the daughter of J the
Judg 12:1 and went northward, and said unto J
Judg 12:2 J said unto them, I and my people
Judg 12:4 Then J gathered together all the
Judg 12:7 J judged Israel six years
Judg 12:7 Then died J the Gileadite, and was
1Sa 12:11 sent Jerubbaal, and Bedan, and J

**JEPHUNNEH** *(je-fun'-neh)*
*1. Father of Caleb.*
Num 13:6 of Judah, Caleb the son of J
Num 14:6 son of Nun, and Caleb the son of J
Num 14:30 therein, save Caleb the son of J
Num 14:38 son of Nun, and Caleb the son of J
Num 26:65 of them, save Caleb the son of J
Num 32:12 Caleb the son of J the Kenezite
Num 34:19 of Judah, Caleb the son of J
Deut 1:36 Save Caleb the son of J
Josh 14:6 Caleb the son of J the Kenezite
Josh 14:13 of J Hebron for an inheritance
Josh 14:14 of J the Kenezite unto this day
Josh 15:13 unto Caleb the son of J he gave a
Josh 21:12 the son of J for his possession
1Chr 4:15 And the sons of Caleb the son of J
1Chr 6:56 they gave to Caleb the son of J

*2. Head of an Asherite family.*
1Chr 7:38 J, and Pispah, and Ara

**JERAH** *(je'-rah) A son of Joktan.*
Gen 10:26 and Sheleph, and Hazarmaveth, and J
1Chr 1:20 and Sheleph, and Hazarmaveth, and J

**JERAHMEEL** *(je-rah'-me-el)* See JERAHMEELITES.
*1. A son of Hezron.*
1Chr 2:9 J, and Ram, and Chelubai
1Chr 2:25 the sons of J the firstborn of
1Chr 2:26 J had also another wife, whose
1Chr 2:27 of Ram the firstborn of J were
1Chr 2:33 These were the sons of J
1Chr 2:42 of Caleb the brother of J were

*2. A son of Kish.*
1Chr 24:29 the son of Kish was J

*3. An officer of Jehoiakim.*
Jer 36:26 commanded J the son of Hammelech

**JERAHMEELITES** *(je-rah'-me-el-ites) Descendants of Jerahmeel.*
1Sa 27:10 and against the south of the J
1Sa 30:29 which were in the cities of the J

**JERED** *(je'-red)* See JARED.
*1. A descendant of Seth.*
1Chr 1:2 Kenan, Mahalaleel, J,

*2. A descendant of Ezra.*
1Chr 4:18 bare J the father of Gedor

**JEREMAI** *(jer'-e-mahee) Married a foreigner in exile.*
Ezr 10:33 Mattathah, Zabad, Eliphelet, J

**JEREMIAH** *(jer-e-mi'-ah)* See JEREMIAH'S, JEREMIAS, JEREMY.
*1. Father of Hamutal.*
2Kin 23:31 the daughter of J of Libnah
2Kin 24:18 the daughter of J of Libnah
Jer 52:1 the daughter of J of Libnah

*2. Head of a Manassite family.*
1Chr 5:24 Ishi, and Eliel, and Azriel, and J

*3. A warrior in David's army.*
1Chr 12:4 and J, and Jahaziel, and Johanan, and

*4. A Gadite warrior.*
1Chr 12:10 the fourth, J the fifth,

*5. Another Gadite warrior.*
1Chr 12:13 J the tenth, Machbanai the

*6. A prophet.*
2Chr 35:25 And J lamented for Josiah
2Chr 36:12 humbled not himself before J the
2Chr 36:21 of the LORD by the mouth of J
2Chr 36:22 mouth of J might be accomplished
Ezr 1:1 the mouth of J might be fulfilled
Jer 1:1 The words of J the son of Hilkiah
Jer 1:11 the LORD came unto me, saying, J
Jer 7:1 word that came to J from the LORD
Jer 11:1 word that came to J from the LORD
Jer 14:1 came to J concerning the dearth
Jer 18:1 which came to J from the LORD
Jer 18:18 let us devise devices against J
Jer 19:14 Then came J from Tophet, whither
Jer 20:1 heard that J prophesied these
Jer 20:2 Then Pashur smote J the prophet
Jer 20:3 brought forth J out of the stocks
Jer 20:3 Then said J unto him, The LORD
Jer 21:1 which came unto J from the LORD
Jer 21:3 Then said J unto them, Thus shall
Jer 24:3 LORD unto me, What seest thou, J
Jer 25:1 The word that came to J
Jer 25:2 The which J the prophet spake
Jer 25:13 which J hath prophesied against
Jer 26:7 all the people heard J speaking
Jer 26:8 when J had made an end of
Jer 26:9 J in the house of the LORD
Jer 26:12 Then spake J unto all the princes
Jer 26:20 according to all the words of J
Jer 26:24 the son of Shaphan was with J
Jer 27:1 this word unto J from the LORD
Jer 28:5 Then the prophet J said unto the
Jer 28:6 Even the prophet J said, Amen
Jer 28:11 the prophet J went his way
Jer 28:12 the LORD came unto J the prophet
Jer 28:12 off the neck of the prophet J
Jer 28:15 Then said the prophet J unto
Jer 29:1 the words of the letter that J
Jer 29:27 thou not reproved J of Anathoth
Jer 29:29 in the ears of J the prophet
Jer 29:30 came the word of the LORD unto J
Jer 30:1 word that came to J from the LORD
Jer 32:1 The word that came to J from the
Jer 32:2 J the prophet was shut up in the
Jer 32:6 J said, The word of the LORD came
Jer 32:26 came the word of the LORD unto J
Jer 33:1 LORD came unto J the second time
Jer 33:19 the word of the LORD came unto J
Jer 33:23 the word of the LORD came to J
Jer 34:1 which came unto J from the LORD
Jer 34:6 Then J the prophet spake all
Jer 34:8 that came unto J from the LORD
Jer 34:12 the LORD came to J from the LORD
Jer 35:1 The word which came unto J from
Jer 35:3 I took Jaazaniah the son of J
Jer 35:12 came the word of the LORD unto J
Jer 35:18 J said unto the house of the
Jer 36:1 word came unto J from the LORD
Jer 36:4 Then J called Baruch the son of
Jer 36:4 of J all the words of the LORD
Jer 36:5 J commanded Baruch, saying, I am
Jer 36:8 that J the prophet commanded him
Jer 36:10 of J in the house of the LORD

Jer 36:19 Baruch, Go, hide thee, thou and J
Jer 36:26 the scribe and J the prophet
Jer 36:27 the word of the LORD came to J
Jer 36:27 Baruch wrote at the mouth of J
Jer 36:32 Then took J another roll, and gave
Jer 36:32 J all the words of the book which
Jer 37:2 which he spake by the prophet J
Jer 37:3 the priest to the prophet J
Jer 37:4 Now J came in and went out among
Jer 37:6 of the LORD unto the prophet J
Jer 37:12 Then J went forth out of
Jer 37:13 he took J the prophet, saying,
Jer 37:14 Then said J, It is false
Jer 37:14 so Irijah took J, and brought him
Jer 37:15 the princes were wroth with J
Jer 37:16 When J was entered into the
Jer 37:16 J had remained there many days
Jer 37:17 And J said, There is
Jer 37:18 Moreover J said unto king
Jer 37:21 that they should commit J into
Jer 37:21 Thus J remained in the court of
Jer 38:1 heard the words that J had spoken
Jer 38:6 Then took they J, and cast him
Jer 38:6 and they let down J with cords
Jer 38:6 so J sunk in the mire
Jer 38:7 they had put J in the dungeon
Jer 38:9 they have done to J the prophet
Jer 38:10 take up J the prophet out of the
Jer 38:11 by cords into the dungeon to J
Jer 38:12 the Ethiopian said unto J
Jer 38:12 And J did so
Jer 38:13 So they drew up J with cords
Jer 38:13 J remained in the court of the
Jer 38:14 took J the prophet unto him into
Jer 38:14 and the king said unto J, I will
Jer 38:15 Then J said unto Zedekiah, If I
Jer 38:16 the king sware secretly unto J
Jer 38:17 Then said J unto Zedekiah, Thus
Jer 38:19 And Zedekiah the king said unto J
Jer 38:20 But J said, They shall not
Jer 38:24 Then said Zedekiah unto J
Jer 38:27 Then came all the princes unto J
Jer 38:28 So J abode in the court of the
Jer 39:11 J to Nebuzar-adan the captain of
Jer 39:14 took J out of the court of the
Jer 39:15 the word of the LORD came unto J
Jer 40:1 word that came to J from the LORD
Jer 40:2 the captain of the guard took J
Jer 40:6 Then went J unto Gedaliah the son
Jer 42:2 said unto J the prophet, Let, we
Jer 42:4 Then J the prophet said unto them
Jer 42:5 Then they said to J, The LORD be
Jer 42:7 the word of the LORD came unto J
Jer 43:1 that when J had made an end of
Jer 43:2 all the proud men, saying unto J
Jer 43:6 J the prophet, and Baruch the son
Jer 43:8 of the LORD unto J in Tahpanhes
Jer 44:1 The word that came to J
Jer 44:15 of Egypt, in Pathros, answered J
Jer 44:20 Then J said unto all the people,
Jer 44:24 Moreover J said unto all the
Jer 45:1 The word that J the prophet spake
Jer 45:1 words in a book at the mouth of J
Jer 46:1 came to J the prophet against the
Jer 46:13 the LORD spake to J the prophet
Jer 47:1 came to J the prophet against the
Jer 49:34 word of the LORD that came to J
Jer 50:1 of the Chaldeans by J the prophet
Jer 51:59 The word which J the prophet
Jer 51:60 So J wrote in a book all the evil
Jer 51:61 J said to Seraiah, When thou
Jer 51:64 Thus far are the words of J
Dan 9:2 of the LORD came to J the prophet

*7. A priest.*
Neh 10:2 Seraiah, Azariah, J,
Neh 12:1 Seraiah, J, Ezra,
Neh 12:12 of J, Hananiah
Neh 12:34 and Benjamin, and Shemaiah, and J

**JEREMIAH'S** *(jer-e-mi'-ahz) Refers to Jeremiah 6.*
Jer 28:10 yoke from off the prophet J neck

**JEREMIAS** *(jer-e-mi'-as)* See JEREMIAH. *Greek form of Jeremiah.*
Mt 16:14 and others, J, or one of the

**JEREMOTH** *(jer'-e-moth)* See JERIMOTH.
*1. A son of Beriah.*
1Chr 8:14 And Ahio, Shashak, and J,
*2. A son of Elam.*
Ezr 10:26 and Jehiel, and Abdi, and J
*3. Another who married a foreigner in exile.*
Ezr 10:27 Eliashib, Mattaniah, and J
*4. A son of Mushi.*
1Chr 23:23 Mahli, and Eder, and J, three
*5. A sanctuary servant.*
1Chr 25:22 The fifteenth to J, he, his sons,

**JEREMY** *(jer'-e-mee)* See JEREMIAH. *Latin form of Jeremiah.*
Mt 2:17 which was spoken by J the prophet
Mt 27:9 which was spoken by J the prophet

**JERIAH** *(je-ri'-ah)* See JERIJAH. *A descendant of Hebron.*
1Chr 23:19 J the first, Amariah the second,
1Chr 24:23 J the first, Amariah the second,

**JERIBAI** *(jer'-ib-ahee) A "mighty man" of David.*
1Chr 11:46 Eliel the Mahavite, and J, and

**JERICHO** *(jer'-ik-o) A city in Benjamin.*
Num 22:1 of Moab on this side Jordan by J
Num 26:3 plains of Moab by Jordan near J
Num 26:63 plains of Moab by Jordan near J
Num 31:12 Moab, which are by Jordan near J
Num 33:48 plains of Moab by Jordan near J
Num 33:50 plains of Moab by Jordan, near J
Num 34:15 this side Jordan near J eastward
Num 35:1 plains of Moab by Jordan near J
Num 36:13 plains of Moab by Jordan near J
Deut 32:49 of Moab, that is over against J
Deut 34:1 of Pisgah, that is over against J
Deut 34:3 and the plain of the valley of J
Josh 2:1 saying, Go view the land, even J
Josh 2:2 And it was told the king of J
Josh 2:3 the king of J sent unto Rahab,
Josh 3:16 passed over right against J
Josh 4:13 unto battle, to the plains of J
Josh 4:19 Gilgal, in the east border of J
Josh 5:10 month at even in the plains of J
Josh 5:13 to pass, when Joshua was by J
Josh 6:1 Now J was straitly shut up
Josh 6:2 I have given into thine hand J
Josh 6:25 which Joshua sent to spy out J
Josh 6:26 riseth up and buildeth this city J
Josh 7:2 And Joshua sent men from J to Ai
Josh 8:2 and her king as thou didst unto J
Josh 9:3 heard what Joshua had done unto J
Josh 10:1 as he had done to J and her king,
Josh 10:28 as he did unto the king of J
Josh 10:30 as he did unto the king of J
Josh 12:9 The king of J, one
Josh 13:32 on the other side Jordan, by J
Josh 16:1 of Joseph fell from Jordan by J
Josh 16:1 unto the water of J on the east
Josh 16:1 from J throughout mount Beth-el
Josh 16:7 and to Naarath, and came to J
Josh 18:12 the side of J on the north side
Josh 18:21 to their families were J, and
Josh 20:8 other side Jordan by J eastward
Josh 24:11 went over Jordan, and came unto J
Josh 24:11 the men of J fought against you,
2Sa 10:5 Tarry at J until your beards be
1Kin 16:34 did Hiel the Beth-elite build J
2Kin 2:4 for the LORD hath sent me to J
2Kin 2:4 So they came to J
2Kin 2:5 that were at J came to Elisha
2Kin 2:15 which were to view at J saw him
2Kin 2:18 to him, (for he tarried at J
2Kin 25:5 overtook him in the plains of J
1Chr 6:78 And on the other side Jordan by J
1Chr 19:5 Tarry at J until your beards be
2Chr 28:15 upon asses, and brought them to J
Ezr 2:34 The children of J, three hundred
Neh 3:2 unto him builded the men of J
Neh 7:36 The children of J, three hundred
Jer 39:5 Zedekiah in the plains of J
Jer 52:8 Zedekiah in the plains of J
Mt 20:29 And as they departed from J
Mk 10:46 And they came to J
Mk 10:46 as he went out of J with his
Lk 10:30 man went down from Jerusalem to J
Lk 18:35 that as he was come nigh unto J
Lk 19:1 Jesus entered and passed through J
Heb 11:30 By faith the walls of J fell down

**JERIEL** *(je-ri'-el) A son of Tola.*
1Chr 7:2 Uzzi, and Rephaiah, and J, and

**JERIJAH** *(je-ri'-jah) Same as Jeriah.*
1Chr 26:31 the Hebronites was J the chief

**JERIMOTH** *(jer'-im-oth)* See JEREMOTH.
*1. A son of Bela.*
1Chr 7:7 Ezbon, and Uzzi, and Uzziel, and J
*2. A son of Becher.*
1Chr 7:8 and Elioenai, and Omri, and J
*3. A warrior in David's army.*
1Chr 12:5 Eluzai, and J, and Bealiah, and
*4. A son of Mushi.*
1Chr 24:30 Mahli, and Eder, and J
*5. A sanctuary servant.*
1Chr 25:4 Mattaniah, Uzziel, Shebuel, and J
*6. A Naphtalite ruler.*
1Chr 27:19 of Naphtali, J the son of Azriel
*7. A son of David.*
2Chr 11:18 of J the son of David to wife
*8. A Temple servant.*
2Chr 31:13 and Nahath, and Asahel, and J

**JERIOTH** *(je'-re-oth) A wife of Caleb.*
1Chr 2:18 of Azubah his wife, and of J

**JEROBOAM** *(jer-o-bo'-am)* See JEROBOAM'S.
*1. A king of Israel.*
1Kin 11:26 J the son of Nebat, an Ephrathite
1Kin 11:28 the man J was a mighty man of
1Kin 11:29 time when J went out of Jerusalem
1Kin 11:31 And he said to J, Take thee ten
1Kin 11:40 sought therefore to kill J
1Kin 11:40 J arose, and fled into Egypt, unto
1Kin 12:2 when J the son of Nebat, who was
1Kin 12:2 king Solomon, and J dwelt in Egypt
1Kin 12:3 And J and all the congregation of
1Kin 12:12 So J and all the people came to
1Kin 12:15 Shilonite unto J the son of Nebat
1Kin 12:20 heard that J was come again
1Kin 12:25 Then J built Shechem in mount
1Kin 12:26 J said in his heart, Now shall
1Kin 12:32 J ordained a feast in the eighth
1Kin 13:1 J stood by the altar to burn
1Kin 13:4 when king J heard the saying of
1Kin 13:33 After this thing J returned not
1Kin 13:34 became sin unto the house of J
1Kin 14:1 Abijah the son of J fell sick
1Kin 14:2 J said to his wife, Arise, I pray
1Kin 14:2 be not known to be the wife of J
1Kin 14:5 the wife of J cometh to ask a
1Kin 14:6 he said, Come in, thou wife of J
1Kin 14:7 Go, tell J, Thus saith the LORD
1Kin 14:10 bring evil upon the house of J
1Kin 14:10 will cut off from J him that
1Kin 14:10 the remnant of the house of J
1Kin 14:11 Him that dieth of J in the city
1Kin 14:13 for he only of J shall come to
1Kin 14:13 God of Israel in the house of J
1Kin 14:14 cut off the house of J that day
1Kin 14:16 up because of the sins of J
1Kin 14:19 And the rest of the acts of J
1Kin 14:20 the days which J reigned were two
1Kin 14:30 Rehoboam and J all their days
1Kin 15:1 in the eighteenth year of king J
1Kin 15:6 J all the days of his life
1Kin 15:7 there was war between Abijam and J
1Kin 15:9 in the twentieth year of J king
1Kin 15:25 Nadab the son of J began to reign
1Kin 15:29 that he smote all the house of J
1Kin 15:29 he left not to J any that
1Kin 15:30 of the sins of J which he sinned
1Kin 15:34 LORD, and walked in the way of J
1Kin 16:2 thou hast walked in the way of J
1Kin 16:3 the house of J the son of Nebat
1Kin 16:7 in being like the house of J
1Kin 16:19 LORD, in walking in the way of J
1Kin 16:26 all the way of J the son of Nebat
1Kin 16:31 in the sins of J the son of Nebat
1Kin 21:22 the house of J the son of Nebat
1Kin 22:52 in the way of J the son of Nebat,
2Kin 3:3 the sins of J the son of Nebat
2Kin 9:9 the house of J the son of Nebat
2Kin 10:29 the sins of J the son of Nebat
2Kin 10:31 departed not from the sins of J
2Kin 13:2 the sins of J the son of Nebat
2Kin 13:6 from the sins of the house of J
2Kin 13:11 the sins of J the son of Nebat

2Kin 14:24 the sins of J the son of Nebat
2Kin 15:9 the sins of J the son of Nebat
2Kin 15:18 the sins of J the son of Nebat
2Kin 15:24 the sins of J the son of Nebat
2Kin 15:28 the sins of J the son of Nebat
2Kin 17:21 they made J the son of Nebat king
2Kin 17:21 J drave Israel from following the
2Kin 17:22 in all the sins of J which he did
2Kin 23:15 place which J the son of Nebat
2Chr 9:29 seer against J the son of Nebat
2Chr 10:2 when J the son of Nebat, who was
2Chr 10:2 that J returned out of Egypt
2Chr 10:3 So J and all Israel came and spake
2Chr 10:12 So J and all the people came to
2Chr 10:15 Shilonite to J the son of Nebat
2Chr 11:4 and returned from going against J
2Chr 11:14 for J and his sons had cast them
2Chr 12:15 between Rehoboam and J continually
2Chr 13:1 king J began Abijah to reign over
2Chr 13:2 there was war between Abijah and J
2Chr 13:3 J also set the battle in array
2Chr 13:4 Ephraim, and said, Hear me, thou J
2Chr 13:6 Yet J the son of Nebat, the
2Chr 13:8 which J made you for gods
2Chr 13:13 But J caused an ambushment to
2Chr 13:15 it came to pass, that God smote J
2Chr 13:19 And Abijah pursued after J
2Chr 13:20 Neither did J recover strength

*2. Another king of Israel, son of Jehoash.*

2Kin 13:13 and J sat upon his throne
2Kin 14:16 J his son reigned in his stead
2Kin 14:23 the son of Joash king of Judah J
2Kin 14:27 by the hand of J the son of Joash
2Kin 14:28 Now the rest of the acts of J
2Kin 14:29 J slept with his fathers, even
2Kin 15:1 seventh year of J king of Israel
2Kin 15:8 of J reign over Israel in Samaria
1Chr 5:17 in the days of J king of Israel
Hos 1:1 in the days of J the son of Joash
Amos 1:1 in the days of J the son of Joash
Amos 7:9 the house of J with the sword
Amos 7:10 Beth-el sent to J king of Israel
Amos 7:11 J shall die by the sword, and

**JEROBOAM'S** *(jer-o-bo'-ams) Refers to Jeroboam 1.*

1Kin 14:4 J wife did so, and arose, and went
1Kin 14:17 J wife arose, and departed, and

**JEROHAM** *(je-ro'-ham)*

*1. Grandfather of Samuel.*

1Sa 1:1 name was Elkanah, the son of J
1Chr 6:27 J his son, Elkanah his son
1Chr 6:34 The son of Elkanah, the son of J

*2. Head of a Benjamite family.*

1Chr 8:27 Eliah, and Zichri, the sons of J

*3. A descendant of Benjamin.*

1Chr 9:8 And Ibneiah the son of J, and Elah

*4. A family of exiles.*

1Chr 9:12 And Adaiah the son of J, the son
Neh 11:12 and Adaiah the son of J, the son

*5. A warrior in David's army.*

1Chr 12:7 Zebadiah, the sons of J of Gedor

*6. Father of Azareel.*

1Chr 27:22 Of Dan, Azareel the son of J

*7. Father of Azariah.*

2Chr 23:1 of hundreds, Azariah the son of J

**JERUBBAAL** *(je-rub'-ba-al)* See GIDEON, JERUBBESHETH. *Another name for Gideon.*

Judg 6:32 on that day he called him J
Judg 7:1 Then J, who is Gideon, and all the
Judg 8:29 J the son of Joash went and dwelt
Judg 8:35 they kindness to the house of J
Judg 9:1 Abimelech the son of J went to
Judg 9:2 either that all the sons of J
Judg 9:5 slew his brethren the sons of J
Judg 9:5 the youngest son of J was left
Judg 9:16 and if ye have dealt well with J
Judg 9:19 dealt truly and sincerely with J
Judg 9:24 and ten sons of J might come
Judg 9:28 is not he the son of J
Judg 9:57 the curse of Jotham the son of J
1Sa 12:11 And the LORD sent J, and Bedan, and

**JERUBBESHETH** *(je-rub'-be-sheth)* See JERUBBAAL. *Another name for Gideon.*

2Sa 11:21 Who smote Abimelech the son of J

**JERUEL** *(je-ru'-el) A wilderness in Judah.*

2Chr 20:16 brook, before the wilderness of J

**JERUSALEM** *(je-ru'-sa-lem)* See JERUSALEM'S, SALEM. *City where the Temple was located.*

Josh 10:1 when Adoni-zedek king of J had
Josh 10:3 Wherefore Adoni-zedek king of J
Josh 10:5 of the Amorites, the king of J
Josh 10:23 out of the cave, the king of J
Josh 12:10 The king of J, one
Josh 15:8 Jebusite; the same is J
Josh 15:63 Jebusites the inhabitants of J
Josh 15:63 of Judah at J unto this day
Josh 18:28 Eleph, and Jebusi, which is J
Judg 1:7 And they brought him to J, and
Judg 1:8 of Judah had fought against J
Judg 1:21 the Jebusites that inhabited J
Judg 1:21 of Benjamin in J unto this day
Judg 19:10 over against Jebus, which is J
1Sa 17:54 Philistine, and brought it to J
2Sa 5:5 in J he reigned thirty and three
2Sa 5:6 his men went to J unto the
2Sa 5:13 more concubines and wives out of J
2Sa 5:14 that were born unto him in J
2Sa 8:7 Hadadezer, and brought them to J
2Sa 9:13 So Mephibosheth dwelt in J
2Sa 10:14 children of Ammon, and came to J
2Sa 11:1 But David tarried still at J
2Sa 11:12 So Uriah abode in J that day
2Sa 12:31 and all the people returned unto J
2Sa 14:23 Geshur, and brought Absalom to J
2Sa 14:28 Absalom dwelt two full years in J
2Sa 15:8 shall bring me again indeed to J
2Sa 15:11 went two hundred men out of J
2Sa 15:14 servants that were with him at J
2Sa 15:29 carried the ark of God again to J
2Sa 15:37 the city, and Absalom came into J
2Sa 16:3 the king, Behold, he abideth at J
2Sa 16:15 the men of Israel, came to J
2Sa 17:20 not find them, they returned to J
2Sa 19:19 my lord the king went out of J
2Sa 19:25 he was come to J to meet the king
2Sa 19:33 and I will feed thee with me in J
2Sa 19:34 should go up with the king unto J
2Sa 20:2 their king, from Jordan even to J
2Sa 20:3 And David came to his house at J
2Sa 20:7 and they went out of J, to pursue
2Sa 20:22 Joab returned to J unto the king
2Sa 24:8 they came to J at the end of nine
2Sa 24:16 out his hand upon J to destroy it
1Kin 2:11 and three years reigned he in J
1Kin 2:36 him, Build thee an house in J
1Kin 2:38 And Shimei dwelt in J many days
1Kin 2:41 Shimei had gone from J to Gath
1Kin 3:1 and the wall of J round about
1Kin 3:15 And he came to J, and stood before
1Kin 8:1 of Israel, unto king Solomon in J
1Kin 9:15 house, and Millo, and the wall of J
1Kin 9:19 Solomon desired to build in J
1Kin 10:2 she came to J with a very great
1Kin 10:26 chariots, and with the king at J
1Kin 10:27 made silver to be in J as stones
1Kin 11:7 in the hill that is before J
1Kin 11:29 time when Jeroboam went out of J
1Kin 11:36 have a light alway before me in J
1Kin 11:42 time that Solomon reigned in J
1Kin 12:18 up to his chariot, to flee to J
1Kin 12:21 And when Rehoboam was come to J
1Kin 12:27 in the house of the LORD at J
1Kin 12:28 is too much for you to go up to J
1Kin 14:21 he reigned seventeen years in J
1Kin 14:25 king of Egypt came up against J
1Kin 15:2 Three years reigned he in J
1Kin 15:4 LORD his God give him a lamp in J
1Kin 15:4 son after him, and to establish J
1Kin 15:10 and one years reigned he in J
1Kin 22:42 reigned twenty and five years in J
2Kin 8:17 and he reigned eight years in J
2Kin 8:26 and he reigned one year in J
2Kin 9:28 carried him in a chariot to J
2Kin 12:1 and forty years reigned he in J
2Kin 12:17 Hazael set his face to go up to J
2Kin 12:18 and he went away from J
2Kin 14:2 reigned twenty and nine years in J
2Kin 14:2 mother's name was Jehoaddan of J
2Kin 14:13 at Beth-shemesh, and came to J
2Kin 14:13 brake down the wall of J from the
2Kin 14:19 a conspiracy against him in J
2Kin 14:20 he was buried at J with his
2Kin 15:2 reigned two and fifty years in J
2Kin 15:2 mother's name was Jecholiah of J
2Kin 15:33 and he reigned sixteen years in J
2Kin 16:2 and reigned sixteen years in J
2Kin 16:5 of Israel came up to J to war
2Kin 18:2 reigned twenty and nine years in J
2Kin 18:17 with a great host against J
2Kin 18:17 And they went up and came to J
2Kin 18:22 away, and hath said to Judah and J
2Kin 18:22 worship before this altar in J
2Kin 18:35 should deliver J out of mine hand
2Kin 19:10 J shall not be delivered into the
2Kin 19:21 the daughter of J hath shaken her
2Kin 19:31 For out of J shall go forth a
2Kin 21:1 reigned fifty and five years in J
2Kin 21:4 said, In J will I put my name
2Kin 21:7 his son, In this house, and in J
2Kin 21:12 I am bringing such evil upon J
2Kin 21:13 over J the line of Samaria
2Kin 21:13 I will wipe J as a man wipeth a
2Kin 21:16 till he had filled J from one end
2Kin 21:19 and he reigned two years in J
2Kin 22:1 reigned thirty and one years in J
2Kin 22:14 now she dwelt in J in the college
2Kin 23:1 all the elders of Judah and of J
2Kin 23:2 all the inhabitants of J with him
2Kin 23:4 he burned them without J in the
2Kin 23:5 and in the places round about J
2Kin 23:6 the house of the LORD, without J
2Kin 23:9 up to the altar of the LORD in J
2Kin 23:13 high places that were before J
2Kin 23:20 bones upon them, and returned to J
2Kin 23:23 was holden to the LORD in J
2Kin 23:24 in the land of Judah and in J
2Kin 23:27 this city J which I have chosen
2Kin 23:30 from Megiddo, and brought him to J
2Kin 23:31 and he reigned three months in J
2Kin 23:33 that he might not reign in J
2Kin 23:36 and he reigned eleven years in J
2Kin 24:4 for he filled J with innocent
2Kin 24:8 and he reigned in J three months
2Kin 24:8 the daughter of Elnathan of J
2Kin 24:10 king of Babylon came up against J
2Kin 24:14 And he carried away all J, and all
2Kin 24:15 into captivity from J to Babylon
2Kin 24:18 and he reigned eleven years in J
2Kin 24:20 of the LORD it came to pass in J
2Kin 25:1 he, and all his host, against J
2Kin 25:8 of the king of Babylon, unto J
2Kin 25:9 house, and all the houses of J
2Kin 25:10 down the walls of J round about
1Chr 3:4 in J he reigned thirty and three
1Chr 3:5 And these were born unto him in J
1Chr 6:10 temple that Solomon built in J
1Chr 6:15 J by the hand of Nebuchadnezzar
1Chr 6:32 built the house of the LORD in J
1Chr 8:28 These dwelt in J
1Chr 8:32 dwelt with their brethren in J
1Chr 9:3 in J dwelt of the children of
1Chr 9:34 these dwelt at J
1Chr 9:38 dwelt with their brethren at J
1Chr 11:4 And David and all Israel went to J
1Chr 14:3 And David took more wives at J
1Chr 14:4 of his children which he had in J
1Chr 15:3 gathered all Israel together to J
1Chr 18:7 Hadarezer, and brought them to J
1Chr 19:15 Then Joab came to J
1Chr 20:1 But David tarried at J
1Chr 20:3 and all the people returned to J
1Chr 21:4 all Israel, and came to J
1Chr 21:15 an angel unto J to destroy it
1Chr 21:16 in his hand stretched out over J
1Chr 23:25 that they may dwell in J for ever
1Chr 28:1 with all the valiant men, unto J
1Chr 29:27 and three years reigned he in J
2Chr 1:4 he had pitched a tent for it at J
2Chr 1:13 place that was at Gibeon to J
2Chr 1:14 cities, and with the king at J
2Chr 1:15 gold at J as plenteous as stones,
2Chr 2:7 that are with me in Judah and in J
2Chr 2:16 and thou shalt carry it up to J
2Chr 3:1 of the LORD at J in mount Moriah
2Chr 5:2 of the children of Israel, unto J
2Chr 6:6 But I have chosen J, that my name
2Chr 8:6 Solomon desired to build in J
2Chr 9:1 Solomon with hard questions at J
2Chr 9:25 cities, and with the king at J
2Chr 9:27 king made silver in J as stones
2Chr 9:30 Solomon reigned in J over all
2Chr 10:18 up to his chariot, to flee to J
2Chr 11:1 And when Rehoboam was come to J
2Chr 11:5 And Rehoboam dwelt in J, and built
2Chr 11:14 possession, and came to Judah and J

| | |
|---|---|
| 2Chr 11:16 | the LORD God of Israel came to J |
| 2Chr 12:2 | king of Egypt came up against J |
| 2Chr 12:4 | pertained to Judah, and came to J |
| 2Chr 12:5 | together to J because of Shishak |
| 2Chr 12:7 | out upon J by the hand of Shishak |
| 2Chr 12:9 | king of Egypt came up against J |
| 2Chr 12:13 | strengthened himself in J |
| 2Chr 12:13 | he reigned seventeen years in J |
| 2Chr 13:2 | He reigned three years in J |
| 2Chr 14:15 | in abundance, and returned to J |
| 2Chr 15:10 | together at J in the third month |
| 2Chr 17:13 | mighty men of valour, were in J |
| 2Chr 19:1 | to his house in peace to J |
| 2Chr 19:4 | And Jehoshaphat dwelt at J |
| 2Chr 19:8 | Moreover in J did Jehoshaphat set |
| 2Chr 19:8 | when they returned to J |
| 2Chr 20:5 | in the congregation of Judah and J |
| 2Chr 20:15 | all Judah, and ye inhabitants of J |
| 2Chr 20:17 | the LORD with you, O Judah and J |
| 2Chr 20:18 | the inhabitants of J fell before |
| 2Chr 20:20 | O Judah, and ye inhabitants of J |
| 2Chr 20:27 | returned, every man of Judah and J |
| 2Chr 20:27 | them, to go again to J with joy |
| 2Chr 20:28 | they came to J with psalteries and |
| 2Chr 20:31 | reigned twenty and five years in J |
| 2Chr 21:5 | and he reigned eight years in J |
| 2Chr 21:11 | of J to commit fornication |
| 2Chr 21:13 | inhabitants of J to go a whoring |
| 2Chr 21:20 | and he reigned in J eight years |
| 2Chr 22:1 | the inhabitants of J made Ahaziah |
| 2Chr 22:2 | and he reigned one year in J |
| 2Chr 23:2 | of Israel, and they came to J |
| 2Chr 24:1 | and he reigned forty years in J |
| 2Chr 24:6 | Judah and out of J the collection, |
| 2Chr 24:9 | a proclamation through Judah and J |
| 2Chr 24:18 | J for this their trespass |
| 2Chr 24:23 | and they came to Judah and J |
| 2Chr 25:1 | reigned twenty and nine years in J |
| 2Chr 25:1 | mother's name was Jehoaddan of J |
| 2Chr 25:23 | Beth-shemesh, and brought him to J |
| 2Chr 25:23 | brake down the wall of J from the |
| 2Chr 25:27 | a conspiracy against him in J |
| 2Chr 26:3 | reigned fifty and two years in J |
| 2Chr 26:3 | name also was Jecoliah of J |
| 2Chr 26:9 | towers in J at the corner gate |
| 2Chr 26:15 | And he made in J engines, invented |
| 2Chr 27:1 | and he reigned sixteen years in J |
| 2Chr 27:8 | and reigned sixteen years in J |
| 2Chr 28:1 | and he reigned sixteen years in J |
| 2Chr 28:10 | J for bondmen and bondwomen unto |
| 2Chr 28:24 | him altars in every corner of J |
| 2Chr 28:27 | buried him in the city, even in J |
| 2Chr 29:1 | reigned nine and twenty years in J |
| 2Chr 29:8 | of the LORD was upon Judah and J |
| 2Chr 30:1 | to the house of the LORD at J |
| 2Chr 30:2 | and all the congregation in J |
| 2Chr 30:3 | gathered themselves together to J |
| 2Chr 30:5 | unto the LORD God of Israel at J |
| 2Chr 30:11 | humbled themselves, and came to J |
| 2Chr 30:13 | there assembled at J much people |
| 2Chr 30:14 | away the altars that were in J |
| 2Chr 30:21 | at J kept the feast of unleavened |
| 2Chr 30:26 | So there was great joy in J |
| 2Chr 30:26 | there was not the like in J |
| 2Chr 31:4 | the people that dwelt in J to |
| 2Chr 32:2 | was purposed to fight against J |
| 2Chr 32:9 | of Assyria send his servants to J |
| 2Chr 32:9 | and unto all Judah that were at J |
| 2Chr 32:10 | that ye abide in the siege in J |
| 2Chr 32:12 | altars, and commanded Judah and J |
| 2Chr 32:18 | people of J that were on the wall |
| 2Chr 32:19 | they spake against the God of J |
| 2Chr 32:22 | the inhabitants of J from the |
| 2Chr 32:23 | brought gifts unto the LORD to J |
| 2Chr 32:25 | upon him, and upon Judah and J |
| 2Chr 32:26 | both he and the inhabitants of J |
| 2Chr 32:33 | the inhabitants of J did him |
| 2Chr 33:1 | reigned fifty and five years in J |
| 2Chr 33:4 | In J shall my name be for ever |
| 2Chr 33:7 | his son, In this house, and in J |
| 2Chr 33:9 | and the inhabitants of J to err |
| 2Chr 33:13 | him again to J into his kingdom |
| 2Chr 33:15 | of the house of the LORD, and in J |
| 2Chr 33:21 | reign, and reigned two years in J |
| 2Chr 34:1 | to reign, and he reigned in J one |
| 2Chr 34:3 | J from the high places, and the |
| 2Chr 34:5 | altars, and cleansed Judah and J |
| 2Chr 34:7 | land of Israel, he returned to J |
| 2Chr 34:9 | and they returned to J |
| 2Chr 34:22 | now she dwelt in J in the college |

| | |
|---|---|
| 2Chr 34:29 | all the elders of Judah and J |
| 2Chr 34:30 | of Judah, and the inhabitants of J |
| 2Chr 34:32 | caused all that were present in J |
| 2Chr 34:32 | And the inhabitants of J did |
| 2Chr 35:1 | a passover unto the LORD in J |
| 2Chr 35:18 | present, and the inhabitants of J |
| 2Chr 35:24 | and they brought him to J, and he |
| 2Chr 35:24 | all Judah and J mourned for Josiah |
| 2Chr 36:1 | king in his father's stead in J |
| 2Chr 36:2 | and he reigned three months in J |
| 2Chr 36:3 | king of Egypt put him down at J |
| 2Chr 36:4 | his brother king over Judah and J |
| 2Chr 36:5 | and he reigned eleven years in J |
| 2Chr 36:9 | three months and ten days in J |
| 2Chr 36:10 | his brother king over Judah and J |
| 2Chr 36:11 | and reigned eleven years in J |
| 2Chr 36:14 | LORD which he had hallowed in J |
| 2Chr 36:19 | God, and brake down the wall of J |
| 2Chr 36:23 | me to build him an house in J |
| Ezr 1:2 | me to build him an house at J |
| Ezr 1:3 | with him, and let him go up to J |
| Ezr 1:3 | (he is the God,) which is in J |
| Ezr 1:4 | for the house of God that is in J |
| Ezr 1:5 | house of the LORD which is in J |
| Ezr 1:7 | had brought forth out of J |
| Ezr 1:11 | brought up from Babylon unto J |
| Ezr 2:1 | Babylon, and came again unto J |
| Ezr 2:68 | house of the LORD which is at J |
| Ezr 3:1 | together as one man to J |
| Ezr 3:8 | coming unto the house of God at J |
| Ezr 3:8 | come out of the captivity unto J |
| Ezr 4:6 | the inhabitants of Judah and J |
| Ezr 4:8 | scribe wrote a letter against J |
| Ezr 4:12 | from thee to us are come unto J |
| Ezr 4:20 | been mighty kings also over J |
| Ezr 4:23 | up in haste to J unto the Jews |
| Ezr 4:24 | of the house of God which is at J |
| Ezr 5:1 | J in the name of the God of |
| Ezr 5:2 | the house of God which is at J |
| Ezr 5:14 | out of the temple that was in J |
| Ezr 5:15 | them into the temple that is in J |
| Ezr 5:16 | of the house of God which is in J |
| Ezr 5:17 | to build this house of God at J |
| Ezr 6:3 | concerning the house of God at J |
| Ezr 6:5 | out of the temple which is at J |
| Ezr 6:5 | unto the temple which is at J |
| Ezr 6:9 | of the priests which are at J |
| Ezr 6:12 | this house of God which is at J |
| Ezr 6:18 | the service of God, which is at J |
| Ezr 7:7 | porters, and the Nethinims, unto J |
| Ezr 7:8 | he came to J in the fifth month, |
| Ezr 7:9 | of the fifth month came he to J |
| Ezr 7:13 | their own freewill to go up to J |
| Ezr 7:14 | to enquire concerning Judah and J |
| Ezr 7:15 | Israel, whose habitation is in J |
| Ezr 7:16 | house of their God which is in J |
| Ezr 7:17 | house of your God which is in J |
| Ezr 7:19 | deliver thou before the God of J |
| Ezr 7:27 | house of the LORD which is in J |
| Ezr 8:29 | of the fathers of Israel, at J |
| Ezr 8:30 | to bring them to J unto the house |
| Ezr 8:31 | of the first month, to go unto J |
| Ezr 8:32 | And we came to J, and abode there |
| Ezr 9:9 | give us a wall in Judah and in J |
| Ezr 10:7 | J unto all the children of the |
| Ezr 10:7 | gather themselves together unto J |
| Ezr 10:9 | together unto J within three days |
| Neh 1:2 | of the captivity, and concerning J |
| Neh 1:3 | the wall of J also is broken down |
| Neh 2:11 | So I came to J, and was there |
| Neh 2:12 | had put in my heart to do at J |
| Neh 2:13 | port, and viewed the walls of J |
| Neh 2:17 | how J lieth waste, and the gates |
| Neh 2:17 | and let us build up the wall of J |
| Neh 2:20 | nor right, nor memorial, in J |
| Neh 3:8 | they fortified J unto the broad |
| Neh 3:9 | the ruler of the half part of J |
| Neh 3:12 | the ruler of the half part of J |
| Neh 4:7 | that the walls of J were made up |
| Neh 4:8 | to come and to fight against J |
| Neh 4:22 | with his servant lodge within J |
| Neh 6:7 | prophets to preach of thee at J |
| Neh 7:2 | of the palace, charge over J |
| Neh 7:3 | Let not the gates of J be opened |
| Neh 7:3 | watches of the inhabitants of J |
| Neh 7:6 | carried away, and came again to J |
| Neh 8:15 | in all their cities, and in J |
| Neh 11:1 | rulers of the people dwelt at J |
| Neh 11:1 | ten to dwell in J the holy city |
| Neh 11:2 | offered themselves to dwell at J |

| | |
|---|---|
| Neh 11:3 | of the province that dwelt in J |
| Neh 11:4 | at J dwelt certain of the |
| Neh 11:6 | at J were four hundred threescore |
| Neh 11:22 | at J was Uzzi the son of Bani |
| Neh 12:27 | the dedication of the wall of J |
| Neh 12:27 | their places, to bring them to J |
| Neh 12:28 | the plain country round about J |
| Neh 12:29 | them villages round about J |
| Neh 12:43 | so that the joy of J was heard |
| Neh 13:6 | in all this time was not I at J |
| Neh 13:7 | And I came to J, and understood of |
| Neh 13:15 | brought into J on the sabbath day |
| Neh 13:16 | the children of Judah, and in J |
| Neh 13:19 | that when the gates of J began to |
| Neh 13:20 | lodged without J once or twice |
| Est 2:6 | J with the captivity which had |
| Ps 51:18 | build thou the walls of J |
| Ps 68:29 | Because of thy temple at J shall |
| Ps 79:1 | they have laid J on heaps |
| Ps 79:3 | shed like water round about J |
| Ps 102:21 | LORD in Zion, and his praise in J |
| Ps 116:19 | house, in the midst of thee, O J |
| Ps 122:2 | shall stand within thy gates, O J |
| Ps 122:3 | J is builded as a city that is |
| Ps 122:6 | Pray for the peace of J |
| Ps 125:2 | the mountains are round about J |
| Ps 128:5 | of J all the days of thy life |
| Ps 135:21 | out of Zion, which dwelleth at J |
| Ps 137:5 | If I forget thee, O J, let my |
| Ps 137:6 | if I prefer not J above my chief |
| Ps 137:7 | children of Edom in the day of J |
| Ps 147:2 | The LORD doth build up J |
| Ps 147:12 | Praise the LORD, O J |
| Eccl 1:1 | the son of David, king in J |
| Eccl 1:12 | was king over Israel in J |
| Eccl 1:16 | that have been before me in J |
| Eccl 2:7 | all that were in J before me |
| Eccl 2:9 | than all that were before me in J |
| Song 1:5 | but comely, O ye daughters of J |
| Song 2:7 | I charge you, O ye daughters of J |
| Song 3:5 | I charge you, O ye daughters of J |
| Song 3:10 | with love, for the daughters of J |
| Song 5:8 | I charge you, O daughters of J |
| Song 5:16 | is my friend, O daughters of J |
| Song 6:4 | O my love, as Tirzah, comely as J |
| Song 8:4 | I charge you, O daughters of J |
| Is 1:1 | J in the days of Uzziah, Jotham, |
| Is 2:1 | of Amoz saw concerning Judah and J |
| Is 2:3 | and the word of the LORD from J |
| Is 3:1 | of hosts, doth take away from J |
| Is 3:8 | For J is ruined, and Judah is |
| Is 4:3 | Zion, and he that remaineth in J |
| Is 4:3 | is written among the living in J |
| Is 4:4 | J from the midst thereof by the |
| Is 5:3 | And now, O inhabitants of J |
| Is 7:1 | went up toward J to war against |
| Is 8:14 | a snare to the inhabitants of J |
| Is 10:10 | graven images did excel them of J |
| Is 10:11 | Samaria and her idols, so do to J |
| Is 10:12 | work upon mount Zion and on J |
| Is 10:32 | daughter of Zion, the hill of J |
| Is 22:10 | ye have numbered the houses of J |
| Is 22:21 | a father to the inhabitants of J |
| Is 24:23 | reign in mount Zion, and in J |
| Is 27:13 | the LORD in the holy mount at J |
| Is 28:14 | rule this people which is in J |
| Is 30:19 | people shall dwell in Zion at J |
| Is 31:5 | will the LORD of hosts defend J |
| Is 31:9 | is in Zion, and his furnace in J |
| Is 33:20 | shall see J a quiet habitation |
| Is 36:2 | sent Rabshakeh from Lachish to J |
| Is 36:7 | away, and said to Judah and to J |
| Is 36:20 | should deliver J out of my hand |
| Is 37:10 | J shall not be given into the |
| Is 37:22 | the daughter of J hath shaken her |
| Is 37:32 | For out of J shall go forth a |
| Is 40:2 | Speak ye comfortably to J |
| Is 40:9 | O J, that bringest good tidings, |
| Is 41:27 | I will give to J one that |
| Is 44:26 | that saith to J, Thou shalt be |
| Is 44:28 | even saying to J, Thou shalt be |
| Is 51:17 | Awake, awake, stand up, O J |
| Is 52:1 | on thy beautiful garments, O J |
| Is 52:2 | arise, and sit down, O J |
| Is 52:9 | together, ye waste places of J |
| Is 52:9 | his people, he hath redeemed J |
| Is 62:6 | set watchmen upon thy walls, O J |
| Is 62:7 | till he make J a praise in the |
| Is 64:10 | is a wilderness, J a desolation |
| Is 65:18 | I create J a rejoicing, and her |

| | |
|---|---|
| Is 65:19 | And I will rejoice in J, and joy in |
| Is 66:10 | Rejoice ye with J, and be glad |
| Is 66:13 | and ye shall be comforted in J |
| Is 66:20 | beasts, to my holy mountain J |
| Jer 1:3 | unto the carrying away of J |
| Jer 1:15 | at the entering of the gates of J |
| Jer 2:2 | Go and cry in the ears of J |
| Jer 3:17 | call J the throne of the LORD |
| Jer 3:17 | it, to the name of the LORD, to J |
| Jer 4:3 | the LORD to the men of Judah and J |
| Jer 4:4 | men of Judah and inhabitants of J |
| Jer 4:5 | ye in Judah, and publish in J |
| Jer 4:10 | greatly deceived this people and J |
| Jer 4:11 | it be said to this people and to J |
| Jer 4:14 | O J, wash thine heart from |
| Jer 4:16 | behold, publish against J |
| Jer 5:1 | and fro through the streets of J |
| Jer 6:1 | to flee out of the midst of J |
| Jer 6:6 | trees, and cast a mount against J |
| Jer 6:8 | Be thou instructed, O J, lest my |
| Jer 7:17 | of Judah and in the streets of J |
| Jer 7:29 | Cut off thine hair, O J, and cast |
| Jer 7:34 | Judah, and from the streets of J |
| Jer 8:1 | the bones of the inhabitants of J |
| Jer 8:5 | Why then is this people of J |
| Jer 9:11 | And I will make J heaps, and a den |
| Jer 11:2 | Judah, and to the inhabitants of J |
| Jer 11:6 | of Judah, and in the streets of J |
| Jer 11:9 | and among the inhabitants of J |
| Jer 11:12 | of Judah and inhabitants of J go |
| Jer 11:13 | J have ye set up altars to that |
| Jer 13:9 | of Judah, and the great pride of J |
| Jer 13:13 | and all the inhabitants of J |
| Jer 13:27 | Woe unto thee, O J |
| Jer 14:2 | and the cry of J is gone up |
| Jer 14:16 | of J because of the famine |
| Jer 15:4 | Judah, for that which he did in J |
| Jer 15:5 | shall have pity upon thee, O J |
| Jer 17:19 | go out, and in all the gates of J |
| Jer 17:20 | and all the inhabitants of J |
| Jer 17:21 | nor bring it in by the gates of J |
| Jer 17:25 | of Judah, and the inhabitants of J |
| Jer 17:26 | Judah, and from the places about J |
| Jer 17:27 | the gates of J on the sabbath day |
| Jer 17:27 | it shall devour the palaces of J |
| Jer 18:11 | Judah, and to the inhabitants of J |
| Jer 19:3 | of Judah, and inhabitants of J |
| Jer 19:7 | of Judah and J in this place |
| Jer 19:13 | And the houses of J, and the houses |
| Jer 22:19 | cast forth beyond the gates of J |
| Jer 23:14 | prophets of J an horrible thing |
| Jer 23:15 | for from the prophets of J is |
| Jer 24:1 | the carpenters and smiths, from J |
| Jer 24:8 | his princes, and the residue of J |
| Jer 25:2 | and to all the inhabitants of J |
| Jer 25:18 | To wit, J, and the cities of Judah |
| Jer 26:18 | J shall become heaps, and the |
| Jer 27:3 | to J unto Zedekiah king of Judah |
| Jer 27:18 | of the king of Judah, and at J |
| Jer 27:20 | king of Judah from J to Babylon |
| Jer 27:20 | and all the nobles of Judah and J |
| Jer 27:21 | of the king of Judah and of J |
| Jer 29:1 | J unto the residue of the elders |
| Jer 29:1 | away captive from J to Babylon |
| Jer 29:2 | the princes of Judah and J |
| Jer 29:2 | the smiths, were departed from J |
| Jer 29:4 | carried away from J unto Babylon |
| Jer 29:20 | I have sent from J to Babylon |
| Jer 29:25 | unto all the people that are at J |
| Jer 32:2 | king of Babylon's army besieged J |
| Jer 32:32 | of Judah, and the inhabitants of J |
| Jer 32:44 | and in the places about J |
| Jer 33:10 | of Judah, and in the streets of J |
| Jer 33:13 | and in the places about J |
| Jer 33:16 | be saved, and J shall dwell safely |
| Jer 34:1 | all the people, fought against J |
| Jer 34:6 | unto Zedekiah king of Judah in J |
| Jer 34:7 | Babylon's army fought against J |
| Jer 34:8 | all the people which were at J |
| Jer 34:19 | of Judah, and the princes of J |
| Jer 35:11 | let us go to J for fear of the |
| Jer 35:11 | so we dwell at J |
| Jer 35:13 | of Judah and the inhabitants of J |
| Jer 35:17 | of J all the evil that I have |
| Jer 36:9 | the LORD to all the people in J |
| Jer 36:9 | from the cities of Judah unto J |
| Jer 36:31 | and upon the inhabitants of J |
| Jer 37:5 | besieged J heard tidings of them |
| Jer 37:5 | of them, they departed from J |
| Jer 37:11 | from J for fear of Pharaoh's army |
| Jer 37:12 | J to go into the land of Benjamin |
| Jer 38:28 | until the day that J was taken |
| Jer 38:28 | and he was there when J was taken |
| Jer 39:1 | Babylon and all his army against J |
| Jer 39:8 | and brake down the walls of J |
| Jer 40:1 | were carried away captive of J |
| Jer 42:18 | forth upon the inhabitants of J |
| Jer 44:2 | evil that I have brought upon J |
| Jer 44:6 | of Judah and in the streets of J |
| Jer 44:9 | of Judah, and in the streets of J |
| Jer 44:13 | of Egypt, as I have punished J |
| Jer 44:17 | of Judah, and in the streets of J |
| Jer 44:21 | of Judah, and in the streets of J |
| Jer 51:35 | of Chaldea, shall J say |
| Jer 51:50 | let J come into your mind |
| Jer 52:1 | and he reigned eleven years in J |
| Jer 52:3 | of the LORD it came to pass in J |
| Jer 52:4 | he and all his army, against J |
| Jer 52:12 | the king of Babylon, into J |
| Jer 52:13 | and all the houses of J, and all |
| Jer 52:14 | all the walls of J round about |
| Jer 52:29 | from J eight hundred thirty |
| Lam 1:7 | J remembered in the days of her |
| Lam 1:8 | J hath grievously sinned |
| Lam 1:17 | J is as a menstruous woman among |
| Lam 2:10 | the virgins of J hang down their |
| Lam 2:13 | I liken to thee, O daughter of J |
| Lam 2:15 | their head at the daughter of J |
| Lam 4:12 | have entered into the gates of J |
| Eze 4:1 | pourtray upon it the city, even J |
| Eze 4:7 | thy face toward the siege of J |
| Eze 4:16 | break the staff of bread in J |
| Eze 5:5 | This is J |
| Eze 8:3 | me in the visions of God to J |
| Eze 9:4 | the city, through the midst of J |
| Eze 9:8 | pouring out of thy fury upon J |
| Eze 11:15 | the inhabitants of J have said |
| Eze 12:10 | burden concerneth the prince in J |
| Eze 12:19 | Lord GOD of the inhabitants of J |
| Eze 13:16 | which prophesy concerning J |
| Eze 14:21 | my four sore judgments upon J |
| Eze 14:22 | evil that I have brought upon J |
| Eze 15:6 | will I give the inhabitants of J |
| Eze 16:2 | cause J to know her abominations, |
| Eze 16:3 | Thus saith the Lord GOD unto J |
| Eze 17:12 | the king of Babylon is come to J |
| Eze 21:2 | Son of man, set thy face toward J |
| Eze 21:20 | to Judah in J the defenced |
| Eze 21:22 | hand was the divination for J |
| Eze 22:19 | gather you into the midst of J |
| Eze 23:4 | Samaria is Aholah, and J Aholibah |
| Eze 24:2 | himself against J this same day |
| Eze 26:2 | that Tyrus hath said against J |
| Eze 33:21 | had escaped out of J came unto me |
| Eze 36:38 | as the flock of J in her solemn |
| Dan 1:1 | king of Babylon unto J, and |
| Dan 5:2 | out of the temple which was in J |
| Dan 5:3 | the house of God which was at J |
| Dan 6:10 | open in his chamber toward J |
| Dan 9:2 | years in the desolations of J |
| Dan 9:7 | Judah, and to the inhabitants of J |
| Dan 9:12 | done as hath been done upon J |
| Dan 9:16 | be turned away from thy city J |
| Dan 9:16 | the iniquities of our fathers, J |
| Dan 9:25 | to build J unto the Messiah the |
| Joel 2:32 | in J shall be deliverance, as the |
| Joel 3:1 | again the captivity of Judah and J |
| Joel 3:6 | the children of J have ye sold |
| Joel 3:16 | Zion, and utter his voice from J |
| Joel 3:17 | then shall J be holy, and there |
| Joel 3:20 | J from generation to generation |
| Amos 1:2 | Zion, and utter his voice from J |
| Amos 2:5 | it shall devour the palaces of J |
| Obad 11 | his gates, and cast lots upon J |
| Obad 20 | and the captivity of J, which is |
| Mic 1:1 | he saw concerning Samaria and J |
| Mic 1:5 | are they not J? |
| Mic 1:9 | the gate of my people, even to J |
| Mic 1:12 | from the LORD unto the gate of J |
| Mic 3:10 | with blood, and J with iniquity |
| Mic 3:12 | J shall become heaps, and the |
| Mic 4:2 | and the word of the LORD from J |
| Mic 4:8 | shall come to the daughter of J |
| Zeph 1:4 | and upon all the inhabitants of J |
| Zeph 1:12 | that I will search J with candles |
| Zeph 3:14 | all the heart, O daughter of J |
| Zeph 3:16 | In that day it shall be said to J |
| Zec 1:12 | wilt thou not have mercy on J |
| Zec 1:14 | I am jealous for J and for Zion |
| Zec 1:16 | I am returned to J with mercies |
| Zec 1:16 | shall be stretched forth upon J |
| Zec 1:17 | Zion, and shall yet choose J |
| Zec 1:19 | scattered Judah, Israel, and J |
| Zec 2:2 | And he said unto me, To measure J |
| Zec 2:4 | J shall be inhabited as towns |
| Zec 2:12 | land, and shall choose J again |
| Zec 3:2 | that hath chosen J rebuke thee |
| Zec 7:7 | when J was inhabited and in |
| Zec 8:3 | and will dwell in the midst of J |
| Zec 8:3 | J shall be called a city of truth |
| Zec 8:4 | women dwell in the streets of J |
| Zec 8:8 | shall dwell in the midst of J |
| Zec 8:15 | in these days to do well unto J |
| Zec 8:22 | to seek the LORD of hosts in J |
| Zec 9:9 | shout, O daughter of J |
| Zec 9:10 | from Ephraim, and the horse from J |
| Zec 12:2 | I will make J a cup of trembling |
| Zec 12:2 | both against Judah and against J |
| Zec 12:3 | in that day will I make J a |
| Zec 12:5 | The inhabitants of J shall be my |
| Zec 12:6 | J shall be inhabited again in her |
| Zec 12:6 | again in her own place, even in J |
| Zec 12:7 | of J do not magnify themselves |
| Zec 12:8 | LORD defend the inhabitants of J |
| Zec 12:9 | the nations that come against J |
| Zec 12:10 | and upon the inhabitants of J |
| Zec 12:11 | there be a great mourning in J |
| Zec 13:1 | to the inhabitants of J for sin |
| Zec 14:2 | all nations against J to battle |
| Zec 14:4 | which is before J on the east |
| Zec 14:8 | living waters shall go out from J |
| Zec 14:10 | from Geba to Rimmon south of J |
| Zec 14:11 | but J shall be safely inhabited |
| Zec 14:12 | people that have fought against J |
| Zec 14:14 | And Judah also shall fight at J |
| Zec 14:16 | J shall even go up from year to |
| Zec 14:17 | earth unto J to worship the King |
| Zec 14:21 | Yea, every pot in J and in Judah |
| Mal 2:11 | is committed in Israel and in J |
| Mal 3:4 | J be pleasant unto the LORD, as |
| Mt 2:1 | came wise men from the east to J |
| Mt 2:3 | was troubled, and all J with him |
| Mt 3:5 | Then went out to him J, and all |
| Mt 4:25 | and from Decapolis, and from J |
| Mt 5:35 | neither by J; for it is the city |
| Mt 15:1 | and Pharisees, which were of J |
| Mt 16:21 | how that he must go unto J |
| Mt 20:17 | Jesus going up to J took the |
| Mt 20:18 | Behold, we go up to J |
| Mt 21:1 | And when they drew nigh unto J |
| Mt 21:10 | And when he was come into J |
| Mt 23:37 | O J, J, thou that killest |
| Mk 1:5 | the land of Judaea, and they of J |
| Mk 3:8 | And from J, and from Idumaea, and |
| Mk 3:22 | which came down from J said |
| Mk 7:1 | of the scribes, which came from J |
| Mk 10:32 | were in the way going up to J |
| Mk 10:33 | Saying, Behold, we go up to J |
| Mk 11:1 | And when they came nigh to J |
| Mk 11:11 | And Jesus entered into J, and into |
| Mk 11:15 | And they come to J |
| Mk 11:27 | And they come again to J |
| Mk 15:41 | which came up with him unto J |
| Lk 2:22 | they brought him to J, to |
| Lk 2:25 | And, behold, there was a man in J |
| Lk 2:38 | that looked for redemption in J |
| Lk 2:41 | Now his parents went to J every |
| Lk 2:42 | they went up to J after the |
| Lk 2:43 | child Jesus tarried behind in J |
| Lk 2:45 | not, they turned back again to J |
| Lk 4:9 | And he brought him to J, and set |
| Lk 5:17 | town of Galilee, and Judaea, and J |
| Lk 6:17 | of people out of all Judaea and J |
| Lk 9:31 | which he should accomplish at J |
| Lk 9:51 | set his face to go to J, |
| Lk 9:53 | was as though he would go to J |
| Lk 10:30 | man went down from J to Jericho |
| Lk 13:4 | above all men that dwelt in J |
| Lk 13:22 | teaching, and journeying toward J |
| Lk 13:33 | be that a prophet perish out of J |
| Lk 13:34 | O J, J, which killest the |
| Lk 17:11 | it came to pass, as he went to J |
| Lk 18:31 | unto them, Behold, we go up to J |
| Lk 19:11 | parable, because he was nigh to J |
| Lk 19:28 | he went before, ascending up to J |
| Lk 21:20 | when ye shall see J compassed |
| Lk 21:24 | J shall be trodden down of the |
| Lk 23:7 | also was at J at that time |
| Lk 23:28 | unto them said, Daughters of J |
| Lk 24:13 | which was from J about threescore |

Lk 24:18 Art thou only a stranger in J
Lk 24:33 the same hour, and returned to J
Lk 24:47 among all nations, beginning at J
Lk 24:49 but tarry ye in the city of J
Lk 24:52 returned to J with great joy
Jn 1:19 and Levites from J to ask him
Jn 2:13 at hand, and Jesus went up to J
Jn 2:23 when he was in J at the passover
Jn 4:20 that in J is the place where men
Jn 4:21 in this mountain, nor yet at J
Jn 4:45 that he did at J at the feast
Jn 5:1 and Jesus went up to J
Jn 5:2 Now there is at J by the sheep
Jn 7:25 Then said some of them of J
Jn 10:22 it was at J the feast of the
Jn 11:18 Now Bethany was nigh unto J
Jn 11:55 up to J before the passover
Jn 12:12 heard that Jesus was coming to J
Acts 1:4 they should not depart from J
Acts 1:8 be witnesses unto me both in J
Acts 1:12 Then returned they unto J from
Acts 1:12 which is from J a sabbath day's
Acts 1:19 known unto all the dwellers at J
Acts 2:5 And there were dwelling at J Jews
Acts 2:14 Judaea, and all ye that dwell at J
Acts 4:6 were gathered together at J
Acts 4:16 to all them that dwell in J
Acts 5:16 of the cities round about unto J
Acts 5:28 ye have filled J with your
Acts 6:7 disciples multiplied in J greatly
Acts 8:1 against the church which was at J
Acts 8:14 J heard that Samaria had received
Acts 8:25 word of the Lord, returned to J
Acts 8:26 that goeth down from J unto Gaza
Acts 8:27 had come to J for to worship,
Acts 9:2 he might bring them bound unto J
Acts 9:13 he hath done to thy saints at J
Acts 9:21 which called on this name in J
Acts 9:26 And when Saul was come to J
Acts 9:28 them coming in and going out at J
Acts 10:39 in the land of the Jews, and in J
Acts 11:2 And when Peter was come up to J
Acts 11:22 ears of the church which was in J
Acts 11:27 came prophets from J unto Antioch
Acts 12:25 Barnabas and Saul returned from J
Acts 13:13 departing from them returned to J
Acts 13:27 For they that dwell at J, and
Acts 13:31 up with him from Galilee to J
Acts 15:2 should go up to J unto the
Acts 15:4 And when they were come to J
Acts 16:4 and elders which were at J
Acts 18:21 keep this feast that cometh in J
Acts 19:21 Macedonia and Achaia, to go to J
Acts 20:16 to be at J the day of Pentecost
Acts 20:22 I go bound in the spirit unto J
Acts 21:4 that he should not go up to J
Acts 21:11 So shall the Jews at J bind the
Acts 21:12 besought him not to go up to J
Acts 21:13 but also to die at J for the name
Acts 21:15 up our carriages, and went up to J
Acts 21:17 And when we were come to J
Acts 21:31 that all J was in an uproar
Acts 22:5 which were there bound unto J
Acts 22:17 that, when I was come again to J
Acts 22:18 and get thee quickly out of J
Acts 23:11 as thou hast testified of me in J
Acts 24:11 I went up to J for to worship
Acts 25:1 he ascended from Caesarea to J
Acts 25:3 that he would send for him to J
Acts 25:7 down from J stood round about
Acts 25:9 and said, Wilt thou go up to J
Acts 25:15 About whom, when I was at J
Acts 25:20 him whether he would go to J
Acts 25:24 have dealt with me, both at J
Acts 26:4 first among mine own nation at J
Acts 26:10 Which thing I also did in J
Acts 26:20 unto them of Damascus, and at J
Acts 28:17 J into the hands of the Romans
Rom 15:19 so that from J, and round about
Rom 15:25 But now I go unto J to minister
Rom 15:26 the poor saints which are at J
Rom 15:31 my service which I have for J may
1Cor 16:3 to bring your liberality unto J
Gal 1:17 Neither went I up to J to them
Gal 1:18 years I went up to J to see Peter
Gal 2:1 went up again to J with Barnabas
Gal 4:25 and answereth to J which now is
Gal 4:26 But J which is above is free,
Heb 12:22 of the living God, the heavenly J
Rev 3:12 city of my God, which is new J
Rev 21:2 I John saw the holy city, new J
Rev 21:10 me that great city, the holy J

**JERUSHA** *(je-ru'-shah)* See JERUSHAH. *Mother of King Jotham of Judah.*
2Kin 15:33 And his mother's name was J

**JERUSHAH** *(je-ru'-shah)* See JERUSHA. *Same as Jerusha.*
2Chr 27:1 His mother's name also was J

**JESAIAH** *(jes-a-i'-ah)* See ISAIAH, JESHAIAH.
*1. Grandson of Zerubbabel.*
1Chr 3:21 Hananiah; Pelatiah, and J
*2. A family of exiles.*
Neh 11:7 the son of Ithiel, the son of J

**JESHAIAH** *(jesh-a-i'-ah)* See JESAIAH.
*1. A sanctuary servant.*
1Chr 25:3 Gedaliah, and Zeri, and J,
1Chr 25:15 The eighth to J, he, his sons, and
*2. A grandson of Eliezer.*
1Chr 26:25 J his son, and Joram his son, and
*3. An Elamite exile.*
Ezr 8:7 J the son of Athaliah, and with
*4. A Merarite exile.*
Ezr 8:19 with him J of the sons of Merari,

**JESHANAH** *(je-sha'-nah) A city near Bethel.*
2Chr 13:19 J with the towns thereof, and

**JESHARELAH** *(je-shar'-e-lah)* See ASARELAH. *A sanctuary servant.*
1Chr 25:14 The seventh to J, he, his sons,

**JESHEBEAB** *(je-sheb'-e-ab) A sanctuary servant.*
1Chr 24:13 to Huppah, the fourteenth to J

**JESHER** *(je'-shur) A son of Caleb.*
1Chr 2:18 J, and Shobab, and Ardon

**JESHIMON** *(jesh'-im-on)*
*1. A place in the Sinai.*
Num 21:20 of Pisgah, which looketh toward J
Num 23:28 of Peor, that looketh toward J
*2. A place in the wilderness of Judah.*
1Sa 23:19 which is on the south of J
1Sa 23:24 in the plain on the south of J
1Sa 26:1 of Hachilah, which is before J
1Sa 26:3 of Hachilah, which is before J

**JESHISHAI** *(jesh'-i-shahee) Ancestor of a Gadite family.*
1Chr 5:14 the son of Michael, the son of J

**JESHOHAIAH** *(je-sho-ha-i'-ah) A descendant of Simeon.*
1Chr 4:36 And Elioenai, and Jaakobah, and J

**JESHUA** *(jesh'-u-ah)* See JESHUAH, JOSHUA.
*1. A sanctuary servant.*
Ezr 2:36 of Jedaiah, of the house of J
Neh 7:39 of Jedaiah, of the house of J
*2. A Levite in Hezekiah's time.*
1Chr 24:11 The ninth to J, the tenth to
2Chr 31:15 him were Eden, and Miniamin, and J
Ezr 2:40 the children of J and Kadmiel, of
Neh 7:43 the children of J, of Kadmiel, and
*3. A priest in exile.*
Ezr 2:2 J, Nehemiah, Seraiah, Reelaiah,
Ezr 3:2 Then stood up J the son of
Ezr 3:8 J the son of Jozadak, and the
Ezr 3:9 Then stood J with his sons and his
Ezr 4:3 But Zerubbabel, and J, and the rest
Ezr 5:2 J the son of Jozadak, and began to
Ezr 10:18 of the sons of J the son of
Neh 7:7 Who came with Zerubbabel, J
Neh 12:1 the son of Shealtiel, and J
Neh 12:7 their brethren in the days of J
Neh 12:10 J begat Joiakim, Joiakim also
Neh 12:26 the days of Joiakim the son of J
*4. Father of Jozabad.*
Ezr 8:33 them was Jozabad the son of J
*5. A family of exiles.*
Ezr 2:6 Pahath-moab, of the children of J
Neh 7:11 Pahath-moab, of the children of J
*6. Father of Ezer.*
Neh 3:19 to him repaired Ezer the son of J
*7. A priest who assisted Ezra.*
Neh 8:7 Also J, and Bani, and Sherebiah,
Neh 9:4 the stairs, of the Levites, J
Neh 9:5 Then the Levites, J, and Kadmiel,
Neh 12:8 J, Binnui, Kadmiel, Sherebiah,
Neh 12:24 J the son of Kadmiel, with their
*8. Same as Joshua, son of Nun.*
Neh 8:17 for since the days of J the son
*9. A Levite who renewed the covenant.*
Neh 10:9 both J the son of Azaniah, Binnui
*10. A city in Benjamin.*
Neh 11:26 And at J, and at Moladah, and at

**JESHURUN** *(jesh'-u-run) Another name for the people Israel.*
Deut 32:15 But J waxed fat, and kicked
Deut 33:5 And he was king in J, when the
Deut 33:26 is none like unto the God of J

**JESIAH** *(je-si'-ah)* See ISHIAH.
*1. A warrior in David's army.*
1Chr 12:6 Elkanah, and J, and Azareel, and
*2. A descendant of Uzziel.*
1Chr 23:20 Micah the first, and J the second

**JESIMIEL** *(je-sim'-e-el) A descendant of Simeon.*
1Chr 4:36 and Asaiah, and Adiel, and J

**JESSE** *(jes'-se) Father of David.*
Ruth 4:17 he is the father of J, the father
Ruth 4:22 begat J, and J begat David
1Sa 16:1 send thee to J the Beth-lehemite
1Sa 16:3 call J to the sacrifice, and I
1Sa 16:5 And he sanctified J and his sons,
1Sa 16:8 Then J called Abinadab, and made
1Sa 16:9 Then J made Shammah to pass by
1Sa 16:10 J made seven of his sons to pass
1Sa 16:10 And Samuel said unto J, The LORD
1Sa 16:11 And Samuel said unto J, Are here
1Sa 16:11 And Samuel said unto J, Send and
1Sa 16:18 seen a son of J the Beth-lehemite
1Sa 16:19 Saul sent messengers unto J
1Sa 16:20 J took an ass laden with bread,
1Sa 16:22 And Saul sent to J, saying, Let
1Sa 17:12 whose name was J; and he had
1Sa 17:13 the three eldest sons of J went
1Sa 17:17 J said unto David his son, Take
1Sa 17:20 and went, as J had commanded him
1Sa 17:58 thy servant J the Beth-lehemite
1Sa 20:27 cometh not the son of J to meat
1Sa 20:30 son of J to thine own confusion
1Sa 20:31 son of J liveth upon the ground
1Sa 22:7 will the son of J give every one
1Sa 22:8 made a league with the son of J
1Sa 22:9 I saw the son of J coming to Nob
1Sa 22:13 against me, thou and the son of J
1Sa 25:10 and who is the son of J
2Sa 20:1 we inheritance in the son of J
2Sa 23:1 David the son of J said, and the
1Kin 12:16 we inheritance in the son of J
1Chr 2:12 Boaz begat Obed, and Obed begat J
1Chr 2:13 J begat his firstborn Eliab, and
1Chr 10:14 kingdom unto David the son of J
1Chr 12:18 and on thy side, thou son of J
1Chr 29:26 Thus David the son of J reigned
2Chr 10:16 none inheritance in the son of J
2Chr 11:18 daughter of Eliab the son of J
Ps 72:20 of David the son of J are ended
Is 11:1 forth a rod out of the stem of J
Is 11:10 day there shall be a root of J
Mt 1:5 and Obed begat J
Mt 1:6 And J begat David the king
Lk 3:32 Which was the son of J, which was
Acts 13:22 I have found David the son of J
Rom 15:12 saith, There shall be a root of J

**JESUI** *(jes'-u-i)* See ISHUI, JESUITES. *A descendant of Asher.*
Num 26:44 of J, the family of the Jesuites

**JESUITES** *(jes'-u-ites) Descendants of Jesui.*
Num 26:44 of Jesui, the family of the J

**JESURUN** *(jes'-u-run)* See JESHURUN. *Same as Jeshurun.*
Is 44:2 and thou, J, whom I have chosen

**JESUS** *(je'-zus)* See BAR-JESUS, CHRIST, JESUS', JOSHUA, JUSTUS.
*1. The Christ.*
Mt 1:1 of the generation of J Christ
Mt 1:16 of Mary, of whom was born J
Mt 1:18 Now the birth of J Christ was on
Mt 1:21 and thou shalt call his name J
Mt 1:25 and he called his name J
Mt 2:1 Now when J was born in Bethlehem
Mt 3:13 Then cometh J from Galilee to
Mt 3:15 J answering said unto him, Suffer
Mt 3:16 And J, when he was baptized, went

Mt 4:1 Then was J led up of the spirit
Mt 4:7 J said unto him, It is written
Mt 4:10 Then saith J unto him, Get thee
Mt 4:12 Now when J had heard that John
Mt 4:17 From that time J began to preach,
Mt 4:18 And J, walking by the sea of
Mt 4:23 J went about all Galilee,
Mt 7:28 when J had ended these sayings,
Mt 8:3 J put forth his hand, and touched
Mt 8:4 J saith unto him, See thou tell
Mt 8:5 when J was entered into Capernaum
Mt 8:7 J saith unto him, I will come and
Mt 8:10 When J heard it, he marvelled, and
Mt 8:13 J said unto the centurion, Go thy
Mt 8:14 when J was come into Peter's
Mt 8:18 Now when J saw great multitudes
Mt 8:20 J saith unto him, The foxes have
Mt 8:22 But J said unto him, Follow me
Mt 8:29 What have we to do with thee, J
Mt 8:34 the whole city came out to meet J
Mt 9:2 J seeing their faith said unto
Mt 9:4 J knowing their thoughts said,
Mt 9:9 as J passed forth from thence, he
Mt 9:10 as J sat at meat in the house,
Mt 9:12 But when J heard that, he said
Mt 9:15 J said unto them, Can the
Mt 9:19 J arose, and followed him, and so
Mt 9:22 But J turned him about, and when
Mt 9:23 when J came into the ruler's
Mt 9:27 when J departed thence, two blind
Mt 9:28 J saith unto them, Believe ye
Mt 9:30 J straitly charged them, saying,
Mt 9:35 J went about all the cities and
Mt 10:5 These twelve J sent forth
Mt 11:1 when J had made an end of
Mt 11:4 J answered and said unto them, Go
Mt 11:7 departed, J began to say unto the
Mt 11:25 At that time J answered and said,
Mt 12:1 At that time J went on the
Mt 12:15 But when J knew it, he withdrew
Mt 12:25 J knew their thoughts, and said
Mt 13:1 same day went J out of the house
Mt 13:34 All these things spake J unto the
Mt 13:36 Then J sent the multitude away,
Mt 13:51 J saith unto them, Have ye
Mt 13:53 that when J had finished these
Mt 13:57 But J said unto them, A prophet
Mt 14:1 tetrarch heard of the fame of J
Mt 14:12 and buried it, and went and told J
Mt 14:13 When J heard of it, he departed
Mt 14:14 J went forth, and saw a great
Mt 14:16 But J said unto them, They need
Mt 14:22 straightway J constrained his
Mt 14:25 of the night J went unto them
Mt 14:27 But straightway J spake unto them
Mt 14:29 walked on the water, to go to J
Mt 14:31 immediately J stretched forth his
Mt 15:1 Then came to J scribes and
Mt 15:16 J said, Are ye also yet without
Mt 15:21 Then J went thence, and departed
Mt 15:28 Then J answered and said unto her,
Mt 15:29 J departed from thence, and came
Mt 15:32 Then J called his disciples unto
Mt 15:34 J saith unto them, How many
Mt 16:6 Then J said unto them, Take heed
Mt 16:8 Which when J perceived, he said
Mt 16:13 When J came into the coasts of
Mt 16:17 J answered and said unto him,
Mt 16:20 no man that he was J the Christ
Mt 16:21 J to shew unto his disciples
Mt 16:24 Then said J unto his disciples,
Mt 17:1 And after six days J taketh Peter
Mt 17:4 answered Peter, and said unto J
Mt 17:7 J came and touched them, and said,
Mt 17:8 they saw no man, save J only
Mt 17:9 J charged them, saying, Tell the
Mt 17:11 J answered and said unto them,
Mt 17:17 Then J answered and said, O
Mt 17:18 And J rebuked the devil
Mt 17:19 came the disciples to J apart
Mt 17:20 J said unto them, Because of your
Mt 17:22 J said unto them, The Son of man
Mt 17:25 J prevented him, saying, What
Mt 17:26 J saith unto him, Then are the
Mt 18:1 time came the disciples unto J
Mt 18:2 J called a little child unto him,
Mt 18:22 J saith unto him, I say not unto
Mt 19:1 that when J had finished these
Mt 19:14 But J said, Suffer little
Mt 19:18 J said, Thou shalt do no murder,
Mt 19:21 J said unto him, If thou wilt be
Mt 19:23 Then said J unto his disciples,
Mt 19:26 But J beheld them, and said unto
Mt 19:28 J said unto them, Verily I say
Mt 20:17 J going up to Jerusalem took the
Mt 20:22 But J answered and said, Ye know
Mt 20:25 But J called them unto him, and
Mt 20:30 when they heard that J passed by
Mt 20:32 J stood still, and called them, and
Mt 20:34 So J had compassion on them, and
Mt 21:1 then sent J two disciples,
Mt 21:6 went, and did as J commanded them,
Mt 21:11 This is J the prophet of Nazareth
Mt 21:12 J went into the temple of God, and
Mt 21:16 And J saith unto them, Yea
Mt 21:21 J answered and said unto them,
Mt 21:24 J answered and said unto them, I
Mt 21:27 And they answered J, and said, We
Mt 21:31 J saith unto them, Verily I say
Mt 21:42 J saith unto them, Did ye never
Mt 22:1 J answered and spake unto them
Mt 22:18 But J perceived their wickedness,
Mt 22:29 J answered and said unto them, Ye
Mt 22:37 J said unto him, Thou shalt love
Mt 22:41 gathered together, J asked them,
Mt 23:1 Then spake J to the multitude, and
Mt 24:1 J went out, and departed from the
Mt 24:2 J said unto them, See ye not all
Mt 24:4 J answered and said unto them,
Mt 26:1 when J had finished all these
Mt 26:4 they might take J by subtilty
Mt 26:6 Now when J was in Bethany, in the
Mt 26:10 When J understood it, he said
Mt 26:17 bread the disciples came to J
Mt 26:19 did as J had appointed them
Mt 26:26 J took bread, and blessed it, and
Mt 26:31 Then saith J unto them, All ye
Mt 26:34 J said unto him, Verily I say
Mt 26:36 Then cometh J with them unto a
Mt 26:49 And forthwith he came to J
Mt 26:50 And J said unto him, Friend,
Mt 26:50 came they, and laid hands on J
Mt 26:51 with J stretched out his hand
Mt 26:52 Then said J unto him, Put up
Mt 26:55 hour said J to the multitudes
Mt 26:57 they that had laid hold on J led
Mt 26:59 sought false witness against J
Mt 26:63 But J held his peace
Mt 26:64 J saith unto him, Thou hast said
Mt 26:69 Thou also wast with J of Galilee
Mt 26:71 was also with J of Nazareth
Mt 26:75 And Peter remembered the word of J
Mt 27:1 against J to put him to death
Mt 27:11 J stood before the governor
Mt 27:11 J said unto him, Thou sayest
Mt 27:17 or J which is called Christ
Mt 27:20 should ask Barabbas, and destroy J
Mt 27:22 with J which is called Christ
Mt 27:26 and when he had scourged J
Mt 27:27 took J into the common hall
Mt 27:37 THIS IS J THE KING OF THE JEWS
Mt 27:46 about the ninth hour J cried with
Mt 27:50 J, when he had cried again with a
Mt 27:54 that were with him, watching J
Mt 27:55 which followed J from Galilee
Mt 27:58 Pilate, and begged the body of J
Mt 28:5 for I know that ye seek J
Mt 28:9 J met them, saying, All hail
Mt 28:10 Then said J unto them, Be not
Mt 28:16 where J had appointed them
Mt 28:18 J came and spake unto them, saying
Mk 1:1 of the gospel of J Christ
Mk 1:9 that J came from Nazareth of
Mk 1:14 J came into Galilee, preaching
Mk 1:17 J said unto them, Come ye after
Mk 1:24 do with thee, thou J of Nazareth
Mk 1:25 J rebuked him, saying, Hold thy
Mk 1:41 And J, moved with compassion, put
Mk 1:45 insomuch that J could no more
Mk 2:5 When J saw their faith, he said
Mk 2:8 immediately when J perceived in
Mk 2:15 as J sat at meat in his house,
Mk 2:15 sinners sat also together with J
Mk 2:17 When J heard it, he saith unto
Mk 2:19 J said unto them, Can the
Mk 3:7 But J withdrew himself with his
Mk 5:6 But when he saw J afar off
Mk 5:7 What have I to do with thee, J
Mk 5:13 forthwith J gave them leave
Mk 5:15 And they come to J, and see him
Mk 5:19 Howbeit J suffered him not, but
Mk 5:20 great things J had done for him
Mk 5:21 when J was passed over again by
Mk 5:24 And J went with him
Mk 5:27 When she had heard of J, came in
Mk 5:30 And J, immediately knowing in
Mk 5:36 As soon as J heard the word that
Mk 6:4 But J said unto them, A prophet
Mk 6:30 themselves together unto J
Mk 6:34 And J, when he came out, saw much
Mk 7:27 But J said unto her, Let the
Mk 8:1 J called his disciples unto him,
Mk 8:17 when J knew it, he saith unto
Mk 8:27 J went out, and his disciples,
Mk 9:2 after six days J taketh with him
Mk 9:4 and they were talking with J
Mk 9:5 And Peter answered and said to J
Mk 9:8 save J only with themselves
Mk 9:23 J said unto him, If thou canst
Mk 9:25 When J saw that the people came
Mk 9:27 But J took him by the hand, and
Mk 9:39 But J said, Forbid him not
Mk 10:5 J answered and said unto them, For
Mk 10:14 But when J saw it, he was much
Mk 10:18 J said unto him, Why callest thou
Mk 10:21 Then J beholding him loved him,
Mk 10:23 J looked round about, and saith
Mk 10:24 But J answereth again, and saith
Mk 10:27 J looking upon them saith, With
Mk 10:29 J answered and said, Verily I say
Mk 10:32 and J went before them
Mk 10:38 But J said unto them, Ye know not
Mk 10:39 J said unto them, Ye shall indeed
Mk 10:42 But J called them to him, and
Mk 10:47 heard that it was J of Nazareth
Mk 10:47 he began to cry out, and say, J
Mk 10:49 J stood still, and commanded him
Mk 10:50 his garment, rose, and came to J
Mk 10:51 J answered and said unto him, What
Mk 10:52 J said unto him, Go thy way
Mk 10:52 sight, and followed J in the way
Mk 11:6 unto them even as J had commanded
Mk 11:7 And they brought the colt to J
Mk 11:11 J entered into Jerusalem, and into
Mk 11:14 J answered and said unto it, No
Mk 11:15 J went into the temple, and began
Mk 11:22 J answering saith unto them, Have
Mk 11:29 J answered and said unto them, I
Mk 11:33 And they answered and said unto J
Mk 11:33 J answering saith unto them,
Mk 12:17 J answering said unto them,
Mk 12:24 J answering said unto them, Do ye
Mk 12:29 J answered him, The first of all
Mk 12:34 when J saw that he answered
Mk 12:35 J answered and said, while he
Mk 12:41 J sat over against the treasury,
Mk 13:2 J answering said unto him, Seest
Mk 13:5 J answering them began to say,
Mk 14:6 And J said, Let her alone
Mk 14:18 J said, Verily I say unto you,
Mk 14:22 J took bread, and blessed, and
Mk 14:27 J saith unto them, All ye shall
Mk 14:30 J saith unto him, Verily I say
Mk 14:48 J answered and said unto them, Are
Mk 14:53 they led J away to the high
Mk 14:55 against J to put him to death
Mk 14:60 stood up in the midst, and asked J
Mk 14:62 And J said, I am
Mk 14:67 thou also wast with J of Nazareth
Mk 14:72 the word that J said unto him
Mk 15:1 and the whole council, and bound J
Mk 15:5 But J yet answered nothing
Mk 15:15 unto them, and delivered J
Mk 15:34 at the ninth hour J cried with a
Mk 15:37 J cried with a loud voice, and
Mk 15:43 Pilate, and craved the body of J
Mk 16:6 Ye seek J of Nazareth, which was
Mk 16:9 Now when J was risen early the
Lk 1:31 a son, and shalt call his name J
Lk 2:21 the child, his name was called J
Lk 2:27 parents brought in the child J
Lk 2:43 the child J tarried behind in
Lk 2:52 J increased in wisdom and stature,
Lk 3:21 that J also being baptized, and
Lk 3:23 J himself began to be about
Lk 4:1 J being full of the Holy Ghost
Lk 4:4 J answered him, saying, It is
Lk 4:8 J answered and said unto him, Get
Lk 4:12 J answering said unto him, It is
Lk 4:14 J returned in the power of the

| | |
|---|---|
| Lk 4:34 | do with thee, thou J of Nazareth |
| Lk 4:35 | J rebuked him, saying, Hold thy |
| Lk 5:10 | J said unto Simon, Fear not |
| Lk 5:12 | who seeing J fell on his face, and |
| Lk 5:19 | his couch into the midst before J |
| Lk 5:22 | But when J perceived their |
| Lk 5:31 | J answering said unto them, They |
| Lk 6:3 | J answering them said, Have ye |
| Lk 6:9 | Then said J unto them, I will ask |
| Lk 6:11 | another what they might do to J |
| Lk 7:3 | And when he heard of J, he sent |
| Lk 7:4 | And when they came to J, they |
| Lk 7:6 | Then J went with them |
| Lk 7:9 | When J heard these things, he |
| Lk 7:19 | of his disciples sent them to J |
| Lk 7:22 | Then J answering said unto them, |
| Lk 7:37 | when she knew that J sat at meat |
| Lk 7:40 | J answering said unto him, Simon, |
| Lk 8:28 | When he saw J, he cried out, and |
| Lk 8:28 | What have I to do with thee, J |
| Lk 8:30 | J asked him, saying, What is thy |
| Lk 8:35 | and came to J, and found the man, |
| Lk 8:35 | sitting at the feet of J |
| Lk 8:38 | but J sent him away, saying, |
| Lk 8:39 | great things J had done unto him |
| Lk 8:40 | when J was returned, the people |
| Lk 8:45 | And J said, Who touched me |
| Lk 8:46 | J said, Somebody hath touched me |
| Lk 8:50 | But when J heard it, he answered |
| Lk 9:33 | from him, Peter said unto J |
| Lk 9:36 | voice was past, J was found alone |
| Lk 9:41 | J answering said, O faithless and |
| Lk 9:42 | J rebuked the unclean spirit, and |
| Lk 9:43 | one at all things which J did |
| Lk 9:47 | And J, perceiving the thought of |
| Lk 9:50 | J said unto him, Forbid him not |
| Lk 9:58 | J said unto him, Foxes have holes |
| Lk 9:60 | J said unto him, Let the dead |
| Lk 9:62 | J said unto him, No man, having |
| Lk 10:21 | In that hour J rejoiced in spirit |
| Lk 10:29 | to justify himself, said unto J |
| Lk 10:30 | J answering said, A certain man |
| Lk 10:37 | Then said J unto him, Go, and do |
| Lk 10:41 | J answered and said unto her, |
| Lk 13:2 | J answering said unto them, |
| Lk 13:12 | when J saw her, he called her to |
| Lk 13:14 | because that J had healed on the |
| Lk 14:3 | J answering spake unto the |
| Lk 17:13 | up their voices, and said, J |
| Lk 17:17 | J answering said, Were there not |
| Lk 18:16 | But J called them unto him, and |
| Lk 18:19 | J said unto him, Why callest thou |
| Lk 18:22 | Now when J heard these things, he |
| Lk 18:24 | when J saw that he was very |
| Lk 18:37 | that J of Nazareth passeth by |
| Lk 18:38 | And he cried, saying, J, thou son |
| Lk 18:40 | J stood, and commanded him to be |
| Lk 18:42 | J said unto him, Receive thy |
| Lk 19:1 | J entered and passed through |
| Lk 19:3 | And he sought to see J who he was |
| Lk 19:5 | when J came to the place, he |
| Lk 19:9 | J said unto him, This day is |
| Lk 19:35 | And they brought him to J |
| Lk 19:35 | the colt, and they set J thereon |
| Lk 20:8 | J said unto them, Neither tell I |
| Lk 20:34 | J answering said unto them, The |
| Lk 22:47 | and drew near unto J to kiss him |
| Lk 22:48 | But J said unto him, Judas, |
| Lk 22:51 | J answered and said, Suffer ye |
| Lk 22:52 | Then J said unto the chief |
| Lk 22:63 | And the men that held J mocked him |
| Lk 23:8 | And when Herod saw J, he was |
| Lk 23:20 | therefore, willing to release J |
| Lk 23:25 | but he delivered J to their will |
| Lk 23:26 | that he might bear it after J |
| Lk 23:28 | But J turning unto them said, |
| Lk 23:34 | Then said J, Father, forgive them |
| Lk 23:42 | And he said unto J, Lord, remember |
| Lk 23:43 | J said unto him, Verily I say |
| Lk 23:46 | when J had cried with a loud |
| Lk 23:52 | Pilate, and begged the body of J |
| Lk 24:3 | found not the body of the Lord J |
| Lk 24:15 | J himself drew near, and went with |
| Lk 24:19 | Concerning J of Nazareth, which |
| Lk 24:36 | J himself stood in the midst of |
| Jn 1:17 | grace and truth came by J Christ |
| Jn 1:29 | day John seeth J coming unto him |
| Jn 1:36 | And looking upon J as he walked |
| Jn 1:37 | him speak, and they followed J |
| Jn 1:38 | Then J turned, and saw them |
| Jn 1:42 | And he brought him to J |
| Jn 1:42 | when J beheld him, he said, Thou |
| Jn 1:43 | The day following J would go |
| Jn 1:45 | J of Nazareth, the son of Joseph |
| Jn 1:47 | J saw Nathanael coming to him, and |
| Jn 1:48 | J answered and said unto him, |
| Jn 1:50 | J answered and said unto him, |
| Jn 2:1 | and the mother of J was there |
| Jn 2:2 | both J was called, and his |
| Jn 2:3 | the mother of J saith unto him, |
| Jn 2:4 | J saith unto her, Woman, what |
| Jn 2:7 | J saith unto them, Fill the |
| Jn 2:11 | miracles did J in Cana of Galilee |
| Jn 2:13 | hand, and J went up to Jerusalem, |
| Jn 2:19 | J answered and said unto them, |
| Jn 2:22 | and the word which J had said |
| Jn 2:24 | But J did not commit himself unto |
| Jn 3:2 | The same came to J by night |
| Jn 3:3 | J answered and said unto him, |
| Jn 3:5 | J answered, Verily, verily, I say |
| Jn 3:10 | J answered and said unto him, Art |
| Jn 3:22 | After these things came J |
| Jn 4:1 | Pharisees had heard that J made |
| Jn 4:2 | (Though J himself baptized not, |
| Jn 4:6 | J therefore, being wearied with |
| Jn 4:7 | J saith unto her, Give me to |
| Jn 4:10 | J answered and said unto her, If |
| Jn 4:13 | J answered and said unto her, |
| Jn 4:16 | J saith unto her, Go, call thy |
| Jn 4:17 | J said unto her, Thou hast well |
| Jn 4:21 | J saith unto her, Woman, believe |
| Jn 4:26 | J saith unto her, I that speak |
| Jn 4:34 | J saith unto them, My meat is to |
| Jn 4:44 | For J himself testified, that a |
| Jn 4:46 | So J came again into Cana of |
| Jn 4:47 | When he heard that J was come out |
| Jn 4:48 | Then said J unto him, Except ye |
| Jn 4:50 | J saith unto him, Go thy way |
| Jn 4:50 | word that J had spoken unto him |
| Jn 4:53 | in the which J said unto him, Thy |
| Jn 4:54 | the second miracle that J did |
| Jn 5:1 | and J went up to Jerusalem |
| Jn 5:6 | When J saw him lie, and knew that |
| Jn 5:8 | J saith unto him, Rise, take up |
| Jn 5:13 | for J had conveyed himself away, |
| Jn 5:14 | Afterward J findeth him in the |
| Jn 5:15 | and told the Jews that it was J |
| Jn 5:16 | did the Jews persecute J, and |
| Jn 5:17 | But J answered them, My Father |
| Jn 5:19 | Then answered J and said unto them |
| Jn 6:1 | After these things J went over |
| Jn 6:3 | J went up into a mountain, and |
| Jn 6:5 | When J then lifted up his eyes, |
| Jn 6:10 | J said, Make the men sit down |
| Jn 6:11 | And J took the loaves |
| Jn 6:14 | had seen the miracle that J did |
| Jn 6:15 | When J therefore perceived that |
| Jn 6:17 | dark, and J was not come to them |
| Jn 6:19 | they see J walking on the sea, and |
| Jn 6:22 | and that J went not with his |
| Jn 6:24 | saw that J was not there, neither |
| Jn 6:24 | came to Capernaum, seeking for J |
| Jn 6:26 | J answered them and said, Verily, |
| Jn 6:29 | J answered and said unto them, |
| Jn 6:32 | Then J said unto them, Verily, |
| Jn 6:35 | J said unto them, I am the bread |
| Jn 6:42 | And they said, Is not this J |
| Jn 6:43 | J therefore answered and said unto |
| Jn 6:53 | Then J said unto them, Verily, |
| Jn 6:61 | When J knew in himself that his |
| Jn 6:64 | For J knew from the beginning who |
| Jn 6:67 | Then said J unto the twelve, Will |
| Jn 6:70 | J answered them, Have not I |
| Jn 7:1 | these things J walked in Galilee |
| Jn 7:6 | Then J said unto them, My time is |
| Jn 7:14 | feast J went up into the temple |
| Jn 7:16 | J answered them, and said, My |
| Jn 7:21 | J answered and said unto them, I |
| Jn 7:28 | Then cried J in the temple as he |
| Jn 7:33 | Then said J unto them, Yet a |
| Jn 7:37 | J stood and cried, saying, If any |
| Jn 7:39 | because that J was not yet |
| Jn 7:50 | them, (he that came to J by night |
| Jn 8:1 | J went unto the mount of Olives |
| Jn 8:6 | But J stooped down, and with his |
| Jn 8:9 | J was left alone, and the woman |
| Jn 8:10 | When J had lifted up himself, and |
| Jn 8:11 | J said unto her, Neither do I |
| Jn 8:12 | Then spake J again unto them, |
| Jn 8:14 | J answered and said unto them, |
| Jn 8:19 | J answered, Ye neither know me, |
| Jn 8:20 | words spake J in the treasury |
| Jn 8:21 | Then said J again unto them, I go |
| Jn 8:25 | J saith unto them, Even the same |
| Jn 8:28 | Then said J unto them, When ye |
| Jn 8:31 | Then said J to those Jews which |
| Jn 8:34 | J answered them, Verily, verily, |
| Jn 8:39 | J saith unto them, If ye were |
| Jn 8:42 | J said unto them, If God were |
| Jn 8:49 | J answered, I have not a devil |
| Jn 8:54 | J answered, If I honour myself, |
| Jn 8:58 | J said unto them, Verily, verily, |
| Jn 8:59 | but J hid himself, and went out of |
| Jn 9:1 | as J passed by, he saw a man |
| Jn 9:3 | J answered, Neither hath this man |
| Jn 9:11 | A man that is called J made clay |
| Jn 9:14 | sabbath day when J made the clay |
| Jn 9:35 | J heard that they had cast him |
| Jn 9:37 | J said unto him, Thou hast both |
| Jn 9:39 | J said, For judgment I am come |
| Jn 9:41 | J said unto them, If ye were |
| Jn 10:6 | This parable spake J unto them |
| Jn 10:7 | Then said J unto them again, |
| Jn 10:23 | J walked in the temple in |
| Jn 10:25 | J answered them, I told you, and |
| Jn 10:32 | J answered them, Many good works |
| Jn 10:34 | J answered them, Is it not |
| Jn 11:4 | When J heard that, he said, This |
| Jn 11:5 | Now J loved Martha, and her sister |
| Jn 11:9 | J answered, Are there not twelve |
| Jn 11:13 | Howbeit J spake of his death |
| Jn 11:14 | Then said J unto them plainly, |
| Jn 11:17 | Then when J came, he found that |
| Jn 11:20 | as she heard that J was coming |
| Jn 11:21 | Then said Martha unto J, Lord, if |
| Jn 11:23 | J saith unto her, Thy brother |
| Jn 11:25 | J said unto her, I am the |
| Jn 11:30 | Now J was not yet come into the |
| Jn 11:32 | when Mary was come where J was |
| Jn 11:33 | When J therefore saw her weeping, |
| Jn 11:35 | J wept |
| Jn 11:38 | J therefore again groaning in |
| Jn 11:39 | J said, Take ye away the stone |
| Jn 11:40 | J saith unto her, Said I not unto |
| Jn 11:41 | J lifted up his eyes, and said, |
| Jn 11:44 | J saith unto them, Loose him, and |
| Jn 11:45 | had seen the things which J did |
| Jn 11:46 | told them what things J had done |
| Jn 11:51 | he prophesied that J should die |
| Jn 11:54 | J therefore walked no more openly |
| Jn 11:56 | Then sought they for J, and spake |
| Jn 12:1 | Then J six days before the |
| Jn 12:3 | costly, and anointed the feet of J |
| Jn 12:7 | Then said J, Let her alone |
| Jn 12:11 | Jews went away, and believed on J |
| Jn 12:12 | when they heard that J was coming |
| Jn 12:14 | And J, when he had found a young |
| Jn 12:16 | but when J was glorified, then |
| Jn 12:21 | him, saying, Sir, we would see J |
| Jn 12:22 | and again Andrew and Philip tell J |
| Jn 12:23 | J answered them, saying, The hour |
| Jn 12:30 | J answered and said, This voice |
| Jn 12:35 | Then J said unto them, Yet a |
| Jn 12:36 | These things spake J, and departed |
| Jn 12:44 | J cried and said, He that |
| Jn 13:1 | when J knew that his hour was |
| Jn 13:3 | J knowing that the Father had |
| Jn 13:7 | J answered and said unto him, What |
| Jn 13:8 | J answered him, If I wash thee |
| Jn 13:10 | J saith to him, He that is washed |
| Jn 13:21 | When J had thus said, he was |
| Jn 13:23 | of his disciples, whom J loved |
| Jn 13:26 | J answered, He it is, to whom I |
| Jn 13:27 | Then said J unto him, That thou |
| Jn 13:29 | that J had said unto him, Buy |
| Jn 13:31 | J said, Now is the Son of man |
| Jn 13:36 | J answered him, Whither I go, |
| Jn 13:38 | J answered him, Wilt thou lay |
| Jn 14:6 | J saith unto him, I am the way, |
| Jn 14:9 | J saith unto him, Have I been so |
| Jn 14:23 | J answered and said unto him, If a |
| Jn 16:19 | Now J knew that they were |
| Jn 16:31 | J answered them, Do ye now |
| Jn 17:1 | These words spake J, and lifted up |
| Jn 17:3 | J Christ, whom thou hast sent |
| Jn 18:1 | When J had spoken these words, he |
| Jn 18:2 | for J ofttimes resorted thither |
| Jn 18:4 | J therefore, knowing all things |
| Jn 18:5 | They answered him, J of Nazareth |
| Jn 18:5 | J saith unto them, I am he |

| | |
|---|---|
| Jn 18:7 | And they said, J of Nazareth |
| Jn 18:8 | J answered, I have told you that |
| Jn 18:11 | Then said J unto Peter, Put up |
| Jn 18:12 | and officers of the Jews took J |
| Jn 18:15 | And Simon Peter followed J |
| Jn 18:15 | went in with J into the palace of |
| Jn 18:19 | then asked J of his disciples |
| Jn 18:20 | J answered him, I spake openly to |
| Jn 18:22 | J with the palm of his hand |
| Jn 18:23 | J answered him, If I have spoken |
| Jn 18:28 | Then led they J from Caiaphas |
| Jn 18:32 | saying of J might be fulfilled |
| Jn 18:33 | judgment hall again, and called J |
| Jn 18:34 | J answered him, Sayest thou this |
| Jn 18:36 | J answered, My kingdom is not of |
| Jn 18:37 | J answered, Thou sayest that I am |
| Jn 19:1 | Then Pilate therefore took J |
| Jn 19:5 | Then came J forth, wearing the |
| Jn 19:9 | judgment hall, and saith unto J |
| Jn 19:9 | But J gave him no answer |
| Jn 19:11 | J answered, Thou couldest have no |
| Jn 19:13 | that saying, he brought J forth |
| Jn 19:16 | And they took J, and led him away |
| Jn 19:18 | side one, and J in the midst |
| Jn 19:19 | J OF NAZARETH THE KING OF THE |
| Jn 19:20 | for the place where J was |
| Jn 19:23 | when they had crucified J |
| Jn 19:25 | by the cross of J his mother |
| Jn 19:26 | When J therefore saw his mother, |
| Jn 19:28 | J knowing that all things were |
| Jn 19:30 | When J therefore had received the |
| Jn 19:33 | But when they came to J, and saw |
| Jn 19:38 | Arimathaea, being a disciple of J |
| Jn 19:38 | he might take away the body of J |
| Jn 19:38 | therefore, and took the body of J |
| Jn 19:39 | at the first came to J by night |
| Jn 19:40 | Then took they the body of J |
| Jn 19:42 | There laid they J therefore |
| Jn 20:2 | whom J loved, and saith unto them, |
| Jn 20:12 | where the body of J had lain |
| Jn 20:14 | saw J standing, and knew not that |
| Jn 20:14 | and knew not that it was J |
| Jn 20:15 | J saith unto her, Woman, why |
| Jn 20:16 | J saith unto her, Mary |
| Jn 20:17 | J saith unto her, Touch me not |
| Jn 20:19 | for fear of the Jews, came J |
| Jn 20:21 | Then said J to them again, Peace |
| Jn 20:24 | was not with them when J came |
| Jn 20:26 | then came J, the doors being shut |
| Jn 20:29 | J saith unto him, Thomas, because |
| Jn 20:30 | did J in the presence of his |
| Jn 20:31 | believe that J is the Christ |
| Jn 21:1 | After these things J shewed |
| Jn 21:4 | now come, J stood on the shore |
| Jn 21:4 | disciples knew not that it was J |
| Jn 21:5 | Then J saith unto them, Children, |
| Jn 21:7 | whom J loved saith unto Peter |
| Jn 21:10 | J saith unto them, Bring of the |
| Jn 21:12 | J saith unto them, Come and dine |
| Jn 21:13 | J then cometh, and taketh bread, |
| Jn 21:14 | J shewed himself to his disciples |
| Jn 21:15 | J saith to Simon Peter, Simon, |
| Jn 21:17 | J saith unto him, Feed my sheep |
| Jn 21:20 | disciple whom J loved following |
| Jn 21:21 | Peter seeing him saith to J |
| Jn 21:22 | J saith unto him, If I will that |
| Jn 21:23 | yet J said not unto him, He shall |
| Jn 21:25 | many other things which J did |
| Acts 1:1 | of all that J began both to do and |
| Acts 1:11 | this same J, which is taken up |
| Acts 1:14 | women, and Mary the mother of J |
| Acts 1:16 | was guide to them that took J |
| Acts 1:21 | the time that the Lord J went in |
| Acts 2:22 | J of Nazareth, a man approved of |
| Acts 2:32 | This J hath God raised up, |
| Acts 2:36 | that God hath made that same J |
| Acts 2:38 | of J Christ for the remission of |
| Acts 3:6 | In the name of J Christ of |
| Acts 3:13 | fathers, hath glorified his Son J |
| Acts 3:20 | And he shall send J Christ |
| Acts 3:26 | God, having raised up his Son J |
| Acts 4:2 | people, and preached through J the |
| Acts 4:10 | the name of J Christ of Nazareth |
| Acts 4:13 | them, that they had been with J |
| Acts 4:18 | at all nor teach in the name of J |
| Acts 4:27 | a truth against thy holy child J |
| Acts 4:30 | by the name of thy holy child J |
| Acts 4:33 | of the resurrection of the Lord J |
| Acts 5:30 | God of our fathers raised up J |
| Acts 5:40 | should not speak in the name of J |
| Acts 5:42 | not to teach and preach J Christ |
| Acts 6:14 | that this J of Nazareth shall |
| Acts 7:45 | with J into the possession of the |
| Acts 7:55 | J standing on the right hand of |
| Acts 7:59 | upon God, and saying, Lord J |
| Acts 8:12 | of God, and the name of J Christ |
| Acts 8:16 | in the name of the Lord J |
| Acts 8:35 | scripture, and preached unto him J |
| Acts 8:37 | I believe that J Christ is the |
| Acts 9:5 | I am J whom thou persecutest |
| Acts 9:17 | Brother Saul, the Lord, even J |
| Acts 9:27 | at Damascus in the name of J |
| Acts 9:29 | boldly in the name of the Lord J |
| Acts 9:34 | J Christ maketh thee whole |
| Acts 10:36 | preaching peace by J Christ |
| Acts 10:38 | How God anointed J of Nazareth |
| Acts 11:17 | who believed on the Lord J Christ |
| Acts 11:20 | Grecians, preaching the Lord J |
| Acts 13:23 | raised unto Israel a Saviour, J |
| Acts 13:33 | in that he hath raised up J again |
| Acts 15:11 | Lord J Christ we shall be saved |
| Acts 15:26 | for the name of our Lord J Christ |
| Acts 16:18 | of J Christ to come out of her |
| Acts 16:31 | Believe on the Lord J Christ |
| Acts 17:3 | and that this J, whom I preach |
| Acts 17:7 | that there is another king, one J |
| Acts 17:18 | because he preached unto them J |
| Acts 18:5 | to the Jews that J was Christ |
| Acts 18:28 | the scriptures that J was Christ |
| Acts 19:4 | after him, that is, on Christ J |
| Acts 19:5 | in the name of the Lord J |
| Acts 19:10 | Asia heard the word of the Lord J |
| Acts 19:13 | spirits the name of the Lord J |
| Acts 19:13 | We adjure you by J whom Paul |
| Acts 19:15 | and said, J I know, and Paul I know |
| Acts 19:17 | name of the Lord J was magnified |
| Acts 20:21 | and faith toward our Lord J Christ |
| Acts 20:24 | I have received of the Lord J |
| Acts 20:35 | remember the words of the Lord J |
| Acts 21:13 | for the name of the Lord J |
| Acts 22:8 | I am J of Nazareth, whom thou |
| Acts 25:19 | own superstition, and of one J |
| Acts 26:9 | to the name of J of Nazareth |
| Acts 26:15 | I am J whom thou persecutest |
| Acts 28:23 | God, persuading them concerning J |
| Acts 28:31 | which concern the Lord J Christ |
| Rom 1:1 | Paul, a servant of J Christ |
| Rom 1:3 | his Son J Christ our Lord |
| Rom 1:6 | ye also the called of J Christ |
| Rom 1:7 | our Father, and the Lord J Christ |
| Rom 1:8 | God through J Christ for you all |
| Rom 2:16 | judge the secrets of men by J |
| Rom 3:22 | is by faith of J Christ unto all |
| Rom 3:24 | redemption that is in Christ J |
| Rom 3:26 | of him which believeth in J |
| Rom 4:24 | up J our Lord from the dead |
| Rom 5:1 | God through our Lord J Christ |
| Rom 5:11 | in God through our Lord J Christ |
| Rom 5:15 | J Christ, hath abounded unto many |
| Rom 5:17 | reign in life by one, J Christ |
| Rom 5:21 | eternal life by J Christ our Lord |
| Rom 6:3 | of us as were baptized into J |
| Rom 6:11 | God through J Christ our Lord |
| Rom 6:23 | life through J Christ our Lord |
| Rom 7:25 | God through J Christ our Lord |
| Rom 8:1 | to them which are in Christ J |
| Rom 8:2 | the Spirit of life in Christ J |
| Rom 8:11 | up J from the dead dwell in you |
| Rom 8:39 | which is in Christ J our Lord |
| Rom 10:9 | confess with thy mouth the Lord J |
| Rom 13:14 | But put ye on the Lord J Christ |
| Rom 14:14 | and am persuaded by the Lord J |
| Rom 15:5 | another according to Christ J |
| Rom 15:6 | the Father of our Lord J Christ |
| Rom 15:8 | Now I say that J Christ was a |
| Rom 15:16 | of J Christ to the Gentiles |
| Rom 15:17 | whereof I may glory through J |
| Rom 15:30 | for the Lord J Christ's sake, and |
| Rom 16:3 | and Aquila my helpers in Christ J |
| Rom 16:18 | such serve not our Lord J Christ |
| Rom 16:20 | of our Lord J Christ be with you |
| Rom 16:24 | The grace of our Lord J Christ be |
| Rom 16:25 | and the preaching of J Christ |
| Rom 16:27 | glory through J Christ for ever |
| 1Cor 1:1 | called to be an apostle of J |
| 1Cor 1:2 | that are sanctified in Christ J |
| 1Cor 1:2 | the name of J Christ our Lord |
| 1Cor 1:3 | Father, and from the Lord J Christ |
| 1Cor 1:4 | which is given you by J Christ |
| 1Cor 1:7 | the coming of our Lord J Christ |
| 1Cor 1:8 | in the day of our Lord J Christ |
| 1Cor 1:9 | of his Son J Christ our Lord |
| 1Cor 1:10 | by the name of our Lord J Christ |
| 1Cor 1:30 | But of him are ye in Christ J |
| 1Cor 2:2 | save J Christ, and him crucified |
| 1Cor 3:11 | that is laid, which is J Christ |
| 1Cor 4:15 | for in Christ J I have begotten |
| 1Cor 5:4 | In the name of our Lord J Christ |
| 1Cor 5:4 | the power of our Lord J Christ |
| 1Cor 5:5 | be saved in the day of the Lord J |
| 1Cor 6:11 | in the name of the Lord J |
| 1Cor 8:6 | and one Lord J Christ, by whom are |
| 1Cor 9:1 | have I not seen J Christ our Lord |
| 1Cor 11:23 | That the Lord J the same night in |
| 1Cor 12:3 | Spirit of God calleth J accursed |
| 1Cor 12:3 | no man can say that J is the Lord |
| 1Cor 15:31 | which I have in Christ J our Lord |
| 1Cor 15:57 | victory through our Lord J Christ |
| 1Cor 16:22 | man love not the Lord J Christ |
| 1Cor 16:23 | of our Lord J Christ be with you |
| 1Cor 16:24 | love be with you all in Christ J |
| 2Cor 1:1 | an apostle of J Christ by the |
| 2Cor 1:2 | Father, and from the Lord J Christ |
| 2Cor 1:3 | the Father of our Lord J Christ |
| 2Cor 1:14 | are ours in the day of the Lord J |
| 2Cor 1:19 | J Christ, who was preached among |
| 2Cor 4:5 | ourselves, but Christ J the Lord |
| 2Cor 4:6 | of God in the face of J Christ |
| 2Cor 4:10 | the body the dying of the Lord J |
| 2Cor 4:10 | that the life also of J might be |
| 2Cor 4:11 | that the life also of J might be |
| 2Cor 4:14 | he which raised up the Lord J |
| 2Cor 4:14 | shall raise up us also by J |
| 2Cor 5:18 | us to himself by J Christ |
| 2Cor 8:9 | the grace of our Lord J Christ |
| 2Cor 11:4 | that cometh preacheth another J |
| 2Cor 11:31 | and Father of our Lord J Christ |
| 2Cor 13:5 | how that J Christ is in you, |
| 2Cor 13:14 | The grace of the Lord J Christ |
| Gal 1:1 | neither by man, but by J Christ |
| Gal 1:3 | Father, and from our Lord J Christ |
| Gal 1:12 | but by the revelation of J Christ |
| Gal 2:4 | liberty which we have in Christ J |
| Gal 2:16 | law, but by the faith of J Christ |
| Gal 2:16 | even we have believed in J Christ |
| Gal 3:1 | before whose eyes J Christ hath |
| Gal 3:14 | on the Gentiles through J Christ |
| Gal 3:22 | that the promise by faith of J |
| Gal 3:26 | of God by faith in Christ J |
| Gal 3:28 | for ye are all one in Christ J |
| Gal 4:14 | an angel of God, even as Christ J |
| Gal 5:6 | For in J Christ neither |
| Gal 6:14 | in the cross of our Lord J Christ |
| Gal 6:15 | For in Christ J neither |
| Gal 6:17 | my body the marks of the Lord J |
| Gal 6:18 | the grace of our Lord J Christ be |
| Eph 1:1 | an apostle of J Christ by the |
| Eph 1:1 | and to the faithful in Christ J |
| Eph 1:2 | Father, and from the Lord J Christ |
| Eph 1:3 | and Father of our Lord J Christ |
| Eph 1:5 | children by J Christ to himself |
| Eph 1:15 | heard of your faith in the Lord J |
| Eph 1:17 | That the God of our Lord J Christ |
| Eph 2:6 | in heavenly places in Christ J |
| Eph 2:7 | toward us through Christ J |
| Eph 2:10 | in Christ J unto good works |
| Eph 2:13 | But now in Christ J ye who |
| Eph 2:20 | J Christ himself being the chief |
| Eph 3:1 | the prisoner of J Christ for you |
| Eph 3:9 | created all things by J Christ |
| Eph 3:11 | he purposed in Christ J our Lord |
| Eph 3:14 | the Father of our Lord J Christ |
| Eph 3:21 | by Christ J throughout all ages |
| Eph 4:21 | by him, as the truth is in J |
| Eph 5:20 | in the name of our Lord J Christ |
| Eph 6:23 | the Father and the Lord J Christ |
| Eph 6:24 | our Lord J Christ in sincerity |
| Phil 1:1 | the servants of J Christ |
| Phil 1:1 | in Christ J which are at Philippi |
| Phil 1:2 | Father, and from the Lord J Christ |
| Phil 1:6 | it until the day of J Christ |
| Phil 1:8 | you all in the bowels of J Christ |
| Phil 1:11 | which are by J Christ, unto the |
| Phil 1:19 | supply of the Spirit of J Christ |
| Phil 1:26 | may be more abundant in J Christ |
| Phil 2:5 | you, which was also in Christ J |
| Phil 2:10 | That at the name of J every knee |
| Phil 2:11 | confess that J Christ is Lord |
| Phil 2:19 | But I trust in the Lord J to send |
| Phil 2:21 | the things which are J Christ's |

Phil 3:3 spirit, and rejoice in Christ J
Phil 3:8 the knowledge of Christ J my Lord
Phil 3:12 also I am apprehended of Christ J
Phil 3:14 high calling of God in Christ J
Phil 3:20 the Saviour, the Lord J Christ
Phil 4:7 hearts and minds through Christ J
Phil 4:19 his riches in glory by Christ J
Phil 4:21 Salute every saint in Christ J
Phil 4:23 The grace of our Lord J Christ be
Col 1:1 an apostle of J Christ by the
Col 1:2 our Father and the Lord J Christ
Col 1:3 the Father of our Lord J Christ
Col 1:4 heard of your faith in Christ J
Col 1:28 every man perfect in Christ J
Col 2:6 received Christ J the Lord
Col 3:17 do all in the name of the Lord J
1Th 1:1 Father and in the Lord J Christ
1Th 1:1 our Father, and the Lord J Christ
1Th 1:3 of hope in our Lord J Christ
1Th 1:10 he raised from the dead, even J
1Th 2:14 which in Judaea are in Christ J
1Th 2:15 Who both killed the Lord J
1Th 2:19 our Lord J Christ at his coming
1Th 3:11 our Father, and our Lord J Christ
1Th 3:13 at the coming of our Lord J
1Th 4:1 and exhort you by the Lord J
1Th 4:2 we gave you by the Lord J
1Th 4:14 For if we believe that J died
1Th 4:14 in J will God bring with him
1Th 5:9 salvation by our Lord J Christ
1Th 5:18 of God in Christ J concerning you
1Th 5:23 the coming of our Lord J Christ
1Th 5:28 of our Lord J Christ be with you
2Th 1:1 our Father and the Lord J Christ
2Th 1:2 our Father and the Lord J Christ
2Th 1:7 when the Lord J shall be revealed
2Th 1:8 the gospel of our Lord J Christ
2Th 1:12 That the name of our Lord J
2Th 1:12 of our God and the Lord J Christ
2Th 2:1 the coming of our Lord J Christ
2Th 2:14 of the glory of our Lord J Christ
2Th 2:16 Now our Lord J Christ himself, and
2Th 3:6 in the name of our Lord J Christ
2Th 3:12 and exhort by our Lord J Christ
2Th 3:18 The grace of our Lord J Christ be
1Ti 1:1 an apostle of J Christ by the
1Ti 1:1 Lord J Christ, which is our hope
1Ti 1:2 our Father and J Christ our Lord
1Ti 1:12 And I thank Christ J our Lord
1Ti 1:14 and love which is in Christ J
1Ti 1:15 that Christ J came into the world
1Ti 1:16 that in me first J Christ might
1Ti 2:5 God and men, the man Christ J
1Ti 3:13 in the faith which is in Christ J
1Ti 4:6 be a good minister of J Christ
1Ti 5:21 before God, and the Lord J Christ
1Ti 6:3 the words of our Lord J Christ
1Ti 6:13 all things, and before Christ J
1Ti 6:14 appearing of our Lord J Christ
2Ti 1:1 an apostle of J Christ by the
2Ti 1:1 of life which is in Christ J
2Ti 1:2 the Father and Christ J our Lord
2Ti 1:9 Christ J before the world began
2Ti 1:10 appearing of our Saviour J Christ
2Ti 1:13 and love which is in Christ J
2Ti 2:1 in the grace that is in Christ J
2Ti 2:3 as a good soldier of J Christ
2Ti 2:8 Remember that J Christ of the
2Ti 2:10 is in Christ J with eternal glory
2Ti 3:12 Christ J shall suffer persecution
2Ti 3:15 faith which is in Christ J
2Ti 4:1 before God, and the Lord J Christ
2Ti 4:22 The Lord J Christ be with thy
Titus 1:1 of God, and an apostle of J Christ
Titus 1:4 the Lord J Christ our Saviour
Titus 2:13 great God and our Saviour J Christ
Titus 3:6 through J Christ our Saviour
Philem 1 Paul, a prisoner of J Christ
Philem 3 our Father and the Lord J Christ
Philem 5 which thou hast toward the Lord J
Philem 6 thing which is in you in Christ J
Philem 9 now also a prisoner of J Christ
Philem 23 my fellowprisoner in Christ J
Philem 25 The grace of our Lord J Christ be
Heb 2:9 But we see J, who was made a
Heb 3:1 of our profession, Christ J
Heb 4:14 J the Son of God, let us hold
Heb 6:20 is for us entered, even J
Heb 7:22 By so much was J made a surety of
Heb 10:10 the body of J Christ once for all
Heb 10:19 the holiest by the blood of J
Heb 12:2 Looking unto J the author
Heb 12:24 to J the mediator of the new
Heb 13:8 J Christ the same yesterday, and
Heb 13:12 Wherefore J also, that he might
Heb 13:20 again from the dead our Lord J
Heb 13:21 in his sight, through J Christ
Jas 1:1 of God and of the Lord J Christ
Jas 2:1 the faith of our Lord J Christ
1Pet 1:1 Peter, an apostle of J Christ
1Pet 1:2 of the blood of J Christ
1Pet 1:3 and Father of our Lord J Christ
1Pet 1:3 of J Christ from the dead
1Pet 1:7 at the appearing of J Christ
1Pet 1:13 you at the revelation of J Christ
1Pet 2:5 acceptable to God by J Christ
1Pet 3:21 by the resurrection of J Christ
1Pet 4:11 may be glorified through J Christ
1Pet 5:10 his eternal glory by Christ J
1Pet 5:14 with you all that are in Christ J
2Pet 1:1 servant and an apostle of J Christ
2Pet 1:1 of God and our Saviour J Christ
2Pet 1:2 of God, and of J our Lord,
2Pet 1:8 knowledge of our Lord J Christ
2Pet 1:11 of our Lord and Saviour J Christ
2Pet 1:14 even as our Lord J Christ hath
2Pet 1:16 and coming of our Lord J Christ
2Pet 2:20 of the Lord and Saviour J Christ
2Pet 3:18 of our Lord and Saviour J Christ
1Jn 1:3 Father, and with his Son J Christ
1Jn 1:7 the blood of J Christ his Son
1Jn 2:1 Father, J Christ the righteous
1Jn 2:22 that denieth that J is the Christ
1Jn 3:23 on the name of his Son J Christ
1Jn 4:2 spirit that confesseth that J
1Jn 4:3 J Christ is come in the flesh is
1Jn 4:15 confess that J is the Son of God
1Jn 5:1 Whosoever believeth that J is the
1Jn 5:5 that J is the Son of God
1Jn 5:6 by water and blood, even J Christ
1Jn 5:20 is true, even in his Son J Christ
2Jn 3 Father, and from the Lord J Christ
2Jn 7 who confess not that J Christ is
Jude 1 Jude, the servant of J Christ
Jude 1 Father, and preserved in J Christ
Jude 4 Lord God, and our Lord J Christ
Jude 17 the apostles of our Lord J Christ
Jude 21 Lord J Christ unto eternal life
Rev 1:1 The Revelation of J Christ
Rev 1:2 and of the testimony of J Christ
Rev 1:5 from J Christ, who is the
Rev 1:9 kingdom and patience of J Christ
Rev 1:9 and for the testimony of J Christ
Rev 12:17 and have the testimony of J Christ
Rev 14:12 of God, and the faith of J
Rev 17:6 the blood of the martyrs of J
Rev 19:10 that have the testimony of J
Rev 19:10 for the testimony of J is the
Rev 20:4 beheaded for the witness of J
Rev 22:16 I J have sent mine angel to
Rev 22:20 Even so, come, Lord J
Rev 22:21 The grace of our Lord J Christ be

*2. Joshua, son of Nun.*
Heb 4:8 For if J had given them rest,

*3. Justus, a Roman Christian.*
Col 4:11 And J, which is called Justus, who

**JESUS'** *(je'-zus) Refers to the Christ.*
Mt 15:30 and cast them down at J feet
Mt 27:57 who also himself was J disciple
Lk 5:8 saw it, he fell down at J knees
Lk 8:41 and he fell down at J feet
Lk 10:39 Mary, which also sat at J feet
Jn 12:9 and they came not for J sake only
Jn 13:23 Now there was leaning on J bosom
Jn 13:25 He then lying on J breast saith
2Cor 4:5 your servants for J sake
2Cor 4:11 delivered unto death for J sake

**JETHER** *(je'-thur)* See HOBAB, ITHRA, ITHRITES, JETHRO, RAGUEL.
*1. A son of Gideon.*
Judg 8:20 he said unto J his firstborn, Up,
*2. Father of Amasa.*
1Kin 2:5 Ner, and unto Amasa the son of J
1Kin 2:32 of Israel, and Amasa the son of J
1Chr 2:17 of Amasa was J the Ishmeelite
*3. A son of Jerahmeel.*
1Chr 2:32 J, and Jonathan
1Chr 2:32 and J died without children
*4. A son of Ezra.*
1Chr 4:17 And the sons of Ezra were, J
*5. A descendant of Asher.*
1Chr 7:38 And the sons of J

**JETHETH** *(je'-theth) A prince of Edom.*
Gen 36:40 duke Timnah, duke Alvah, duke J
1Chr 1:51 duke Timnah, duke Aliah, duke J

**JETHLAH** *(jeth'-lah) A city in Dan.*
Josh 19:42 And Shaalabbin, and Ajalon, and J

**JETHRO** *(je'-thro)* See JETHER. *Father-in-law of Moses.*
Ex 3:1 the flock of J his father in law
Ex 4:18 returned to J his father in law,
Ex 4:18 J said to Moses, Go in peace
Ex 18:1 When J, the priest of Midian,
Ex 18:2 Then J, Moses' father in law,
Ex 18:5 And J, Moses' father in law, came
Ex 18:6 father in law J am come unto thee
Ex 18:9 J rejoiced for all the goodness
Ex 18:10 J said, Blessed be the LORD, who
Ex 18:12 And J, Moses' father in law, took

**JETUR** *(je'-tur)*
*1. A son of Ishmael.*
Gen 25:15 Hadar, and Tema, J, Naphish, and
1Chr 1:31 J, Naphish, and Kedemah
*2. Descendants of Jetur.*
1Chr 5:19 war with the Hagarites, with J

**JEUEL** *(je-u'-el)* See JEIEL. *A descendant of Zerah.*
1Chr 9:6 J, and their brethren, six hundred

**JEUSH** *(je'-ush)* See JEHUSH.
*1. A son of Esau.*
Gen 36:5 And Aholibamah bare J, and Jaalam,
Gen 36:14 and she bare to Esau J, and Jaalam,
Gen 36:18 duke J, duke Jaalam, duke Korah
1Chr 1:35 Eliphaz, Reuel, and J, and Jaalam,
*2. Grandson of Jediael.*
1Chr 7:10 J, and Benjamin, and Ehud, and
*3. A sanctuary servant.*
1Chr 23:10 Shimei were, Jahath, Zina, and J
1Chr 23:11 but J and Beriah had not many sons
*4. A son of Rehoboam.*
2Chr 11:19 J, and Shamariah, and Zaham

**JEUZ** *(je'-uz) Son of Shaharaim.*
1Chr 8:10 And J, and Shachia, and Mirma

**JEW** *(jew)* See JEWESS, JEWISH, JEWS. *Post-exilic term for the Israelites.*
Est 2:5 the palace there was a certain J
Est 3:4 he had told them that he was a J
Est 5:13 the J sitting at the king's gate
Est 6:10 and do even so to Mordecai the J
Est 8:7 the queen and to Mordecai the J
Est 9:29 of Abihail, and Mordecai the J
Est 9:31 according as Mordecai the J
Est 10:3 For Mordecai the J was next unto
Jer 34:9 them, to wit, of a J his brother
Zec 8:23 of the skirt of him that is a J
Jn 4:9 How is it that thou, being a J
Jn 18:35 Pilate answered, Am I a J
Acts 10:28 a man that is a J to keep company
Acts 13:6 sorcerer, a false prophet, a J
Acts 18:2 And found a certain J named Aquila
Acts 18:24 a certain J named Apollos, born
Acts 19:14 were seven sons of one Sceva, a J
Acts 19:34 when they knew that he was a J
Acts 21:39 I am a man which am a J of Tarsus
Acts 22:3 I am verily a man which am a J
Rom 1:16 to the J first, and also to the
Rom 2:9 that doeth evil, of the J first
Rom 2:10 that worketh good, to the J first
Rom 2:17 Behold, thou art called a J
Rom 2:28 For he is not a J, which is one
Rom 2:29 But he is a J, which is one
Rom 3:1 What advantage then hath the J
Rom 10:12 is no difference between the J
1Cor 9:20 And unto the Jews I became as a J
Gal 2:14 them all, If thou, being a J
Gal 3:28 There is neither J nor Greek
Col 3:11 there is neither Greek nor J

**JEWEL**
Prov 11:22 As a *j* of gold in a swine's snout
Prov 20:15 of knowledge are a precious *j*
Eze 16:12 I put a *j* on thy forehead, and

**JEWELS**
Gen 24:53 servant brought forth *j* of silver
Gen 24:53 *j* of gold, and raiment, and gave

Ex 3:22 j of silver, and j of gold,
Ex 11:2 j of silver, and j of gold
Ex 12:35 of the Egyptians j of silver
Ex 12:35 and j of gold, and raiment
Ex 35:22 rings, and tablets, all j of gold
Num 31:50 gotten, of j of gold, chains, and
Num 31:51 gold of them, even all wrought j
1Sa 6:8 and put the j of gold, which ye
1Sa 6:15 wherein the j of gold were, and
2Chr 20:25 the dead bodies, and precious j
2Chr 32:27 and for all manner of pleasant j
Job 28:17 shall not be for j of fine gold
Song 1:10 cheeks are comely with rows of j
Song 7:1 joints of thy thighs are like j
Is 3:21 The rings, and nose j,
Is 61:10 bride adorneth herself with her j
Eze 16:17 also taken thy fair j of my gold
Eze 16:39 clothes, and shall take thy fair j
Eze 23:26 clothes, and take away thy fair j
Hos 2:13 with her earrings and her j
Mal 3:17 in that day when I make up my j

**JEWESS** *(jew'-ess) A female Jew.*

Acts 16:1 of a certain woman, which was a J
Acts 24:24 his wife Drusilla, which was a J

**JEWISH** *(jew'-ish) Of or relating to the Jews.*

Titus 1:14 Not giving heed to J fables

**JEWRY** *(jew'-ree)* See JUDEA. *Of or relating to the Jews.*

Dan 5:13 king my father brought out of J
Lk 23:5 people, teaching throughout all J
Jn 7:1 for he would not walk in J

**JEWS** *(jews)* See JEWS'.

2Kin 16:6 Syria, and drave the J from Elath
2Kin 25:25 Gedaliah, that he died, and the J
Ezr 4:12 that the J which came up from
Ezr 4:23 in haste to Jerusalem unto the J
Ezr 5:1 unto the J that were in Judah
Ezr 5:5 God was upon the elders of the J
Ezr 6:7 let the governor of the J
Ezr 6:7 the elders of the J build this
Ezr 6:8 J for the building of this house
Ezr 6:14 And the elders of the J builded
Neh 1:2 concerning the J that had escaped
Neh 2:16 had I as yet told it to the J
Neh 4:1 indignation, and mocked the J
Neh 4:2 and said, What do these feeble J
Neh 4:12 that when the J which dwelt by
Neh 5:1 against their brethren the J
Neh 5:8 have redeemed our brethren the J
Neh 5:17 an hundred and fifty of the J
Neh 6:6 that thou and the J think to rebel
Neh 13:23 In those days also saw I J that
Est 3:6 J that were throughout the whole
Est 3:13 and to cause to perish, all J
Est 4:3 was great mourning among the J
Est 4:7 the king's treasuries for the J
Est 4:13 king's house, more than all the J
Est 4:14 arise to the J from another place
Est 4:16 gather together all the J that
Est 6:13 Mordecai be of the seed of the J
Est 8:3 that he had devised against the J
Est 8:5 the J which are in all the king's
Est 8:7 he laid his hand upon the J
Est 8:8 Write ye also for the J, as it
Est 8:9 Mordecai commanded unto the J
Est 8:9 to the J according to their
Est 8:11 the J which were in every city to
Est 8:13 that the J should be ready
Est 8:16 The J had light, and gladness, and
Est 8:17 the J had joy and gladness, a
Est 8:17 the people of the land became J
Est 8:17 the fear of the J fell upon them
Est 9:1 J hoped to have power over them
Est 9:1 that the J had rule over them
Est 9:2 The J gathered themselves
Est 9:3 of the king, helped the J
Est 9:5 Thus the J smote all their
Est 9:6 in Shushan the palace the J slew
Est 9:10 of Hammedatha, the enemy of the J
Est 9:12 The J have slain and destroyed
Est 9:13 let it be granted to the J which
Est 9:15 For the J that were in Shushan
Est 9:16 But the other J that were in the
Est 9:18 But the J that were at Shushan
Est 9:19 Therefore the J of the villages,
Est 9:20 sent letters unto all the J that
Est 9:22 As the days wherein the J rested
Est 9:23 the J undertook to do as they had
Est 9:24 Agagite, the enemy of all the J
Est 9:24 against the J to destroy them
Est 9:25 which he devised against the J
Est 9:27 The J ordained, and took upon them
Est 9:28 should not fail from among the J
Est 9:30 sent the letters unto all the J
Est 10:3 Ahasuerus, and great among the J
Jer 32:12 before all the J that sat in the
Jer 38:19 I am afraid of the J that are
Jer 40:11 when all the J that were in Moab
Jer 40:12 Even all the J returned out of
Jer 40:15 that all the J which are gathered
Jer 41:3 slew all the J that were with him
Jer 44:1 the J which dwell in the land of
Jer 52:28 the seventh year three thousand J
Jer 52:30 of the J seven hundred forty
Dan 3:8 came near, and accused the J
Dan 3:12 There are certain J whom thou
Mt 2:2 is he that is born King of the J
Mt 27:11 Art thou the King of the J
Mt 27:29 him, saying, Hail, King of the J
Mt 27:37 THIS IS JESUS THE KING OF THE J
Mt 28:15 among the J until this day
Mk 7:3 For the Pharisees, and all the J
Mk 15:2 him, Art thou the King of the J
Mk 15:9 unto you the King of the J
Mk 15:12 whom ye call the King of the J
Mk 15:18 salute him, Hail, King of the J
Mk 15:26 written over, THE KING OF THE J
Lk 7:3 sent unto him the elders of the J
Lk 23:3 Art thou the King of the J
Lk 23:37 If thou be the king of the J
Lk 23:38 THIS IS THE KING OF THE J
Lk 23:51 of Arimathaea, a city of the J
Jn 1:19 when the J sent priests and
Jn 2:6 manner of the purifying of the J
Jn 2:18 Then answered the J and said unto
Jn 2:20 Then said the J, Forty and six
Jn 3:1 named Nicodemus, a ruler of the J
Jn 3:25 and the J about purifying
Jn 4:9 for the J have no dealings with
Jn 4:22 for salvation is of the J
Jn 5:1 this there was a feast of the J
Jn 5:10 The J therefore said unto him
Jn 5:15 told the J that it was Jesus,
Jn 5:16 did the J persecute Jesus
Jn 5:18 Therefore the J sought the more
Jn 6:4 And the passover, a feast of the J
Jn 6:41 The J then murmured at him,
Jn 6:52 The J therefore strove among
Jn 7:1 because the J sought to kill him
Jn 7:11 Then the J sought him at the
Jn 7:13 openly of him for fear of the J
Jn 7:15 the J marvelled, saying, How
Jn 7:35 Then said the J among themselves,
Jn 8:22 Then said the J, Will he kill
Jn 8:31 to those J which believed on him
Jn 8:48 Then answered the J, and said unto
Jn 8:52 Then said the J unto him, Now we
Jn 8:57 Then said the J unto him, Thou
Jn 9:18 But the J did not believe
Jn 9:22 because they feared the J
Jn 9:22 for the J had agreed already,
Jn 10:19 among the J for these sayings
Jn 10:24 Then came the J round about him,
Jn 10:31 Then the J took up stones again
Jn 10:33 The J answered him, saying, For a
Jn 11:8 the J of late sought to stone
Jn 11:19 many of the J came to Martha and
Jn 11:31 The J then which were with her in
Jn 11:33 the J also weeping which came
Jn 11:36 Then said the J, Behold how he
Jn 11:45 Then many of the J which came to
Jn 11:54 walked no more openly among the J
Jn 12:9 Much people of the J therefore
Jn 12:11 of him many of the J went away
Jn 13:33 and as I said unto the J, Whither
Jn 18:12 and officers of the J took Jesus
Jn 18:14 he, which gave counsel to the J
Jn 18:20 whither the J always resort
Jn 18:31 The J therefore said unto him, It
Jn 18:33 him, Art thou the King of the J
Jn 18:36 should not be delivered to the J
Jn 18:38 he went out again unto the J
Jn 18:39 unto you the King of the J
Jn 19:3 And said, Hail, King of the J
Jn 19:7 The J answered him, We have a law
Jn 19:12 but the J cried out, saying, If
Jn 19:14 and he saith unto the J, Behold
Jn 19:19 OF NAZARETH THE KING OF THE J
Jn 19:20 title then read many of the J
Jn 19:21 chief priests of the J to Pilate
Jn 19:21 Write not, The King of the J
Jn 19:21 that he said, I am King of the J
Jn 19:31 The J therefore, because it was
Jn 19:38 but secretly for fear of the J
Jn 19:40 as the manner of the J is to bury
Jn 20:19 were assembled for fear of the J
Acts 2:5 were dwelling at Jerusalem J
Acts 2:10 Cyrene, and strangers of Rome, J
Acts 9:22 confounded the J which dwelt at
Acts 9:23 the J took counsel to kill him
Acts 10:22 among all the nation of the J
Acts 10:39 he did both in the land of the J
Acts 11:19 word to none but unto the J only
Acts 12:3 because he saw it pleased the J
Acts 12:11 of the people of the J
Acts 13:5 of God in the synagogues of the J
Acts 13:42 when the J were gone out of the
Acts 13:43 was broken up, many of the J
Acts 13:45 But when the J saw the multitudes
Acts 13:50 But the J stirred up the devout
Acts 14:1 into the synagogue of the J
Acts 14:1 a great multitude both of the J
Acts 14:2 But the unbelieving J stirred up
Acts 14:4 and part held with the J, and part
Acts 14:5 also of the J with their rulers,
Acts 14:19 thither certain J from Antioch
Acts 16:3 J which were in those quarters
Acts 16:20 saying, These men, being J
Acts 17:1 where was a synagogue of the J
Acts 17:5 But the J which believed not,
Acts 17:10 went into the synagogue of the J
Acts 17:13 But when the J of Thessalonica
Acts 17:17 he in the synagogue with the J
Acts 18:2 all J to depart from Rome
Acts 18:4 every sabbath, and persuaded the J
Acts 18:5 testified to the J that Jesus was
Acts 18:12 the J made insurrection with one
Acts 18:14 his mouth, Gallio said unto the J
Acts 18:14 wrong or wicked lewdness, O ye J
Acts 18:19 synagogue, and reasoned with the J
Acts 18:28 For he mightily convinced the J
Acts 19:10 word of the Lord Jesus, both J
Acts 19:13 Then certain of the vagabond J
Acts 19:17 And this was known to all the J
Acts 19:33 the J putting him forward
Acts 20:3 when the J laid wait for him, as
Acts 20:19 me by the lying in wait of the J
Acts 20:21 Testifying both to the J, and also
Acts 21:11 So shall the J at Jerusalem bind
Acts 21:20 how many thousands of J there are
Acts 21:21 that thou teachest all the J
Acts 21:27 the J which were of Asia, when
Acts 22:12 of all the J which dwelt there
Acts 22:30 wherefore he was accused of the J
Acts 23:12 certain of the J banded together,
Acts 23:20 The J have agreed to desire thee
Acts 23:27 This man was taken of the J
Acts 23:30 that the J laid wait for the man
Acts 24:5 all the J throughout the world
Acts 24:9 the J also assented, saying that
Acts 24:18 Whereupon certain J from Asia
Acts 24:27 willing to shew the J a pleasure
Acts 25:2 the chief of the J informed him
Acts 25:7 the J which came down from
Acts 25:8 Neither against the law of the J
Acts 25:9 willing to do the J a pleasure
Acts 25:10 to the J have I done no wrong, as
Acts 25:15 the elders of the J informed me
Acts 25:24 of the J have dealt with me
Acts 26:2 whereof I am accused of the J
Acts 26:3 questions which are among the J
Acts 26:4 at Jerusalem, know all the J
Acts 26:7 Agrippa, I am accused of the J
Acts 26:21 For these causes the J caught me
Acts 28:17 the chief of the J together
Acts 28:19 But when the J spake against it,
Acts 28:29 the J departed, and had great
Rom 3:9 for we have before proved both J
Rom 3:29 Is he the God of the J only
Rom 9:24 he hath called, not of the J only
1Cor 1:22 For the J require a sign, and the
1Cor 1:23 unto the J a stumblingblock, and
1Cor 1:24 them which are called, both J
1Cor 9:20 unto the J I became as a Jew,
1Cor 9:20 as a Jew, that I might gain the J
1Cor 10:32 none offence, neither to the J
1Cor 12:13 body, whether we be J or Gentiles

2Cor 11:24 Of the J five times received I
Gal 2:13 the other J dissembled likewise
Gal 2:14 of Gentiles, and not as do the J
Gal 2:14 the Gentiles to live as do the J
Gal 2:15 We who are J by nature, and not
1Th 2:14 even as they have of the J
Rev 2:9 of them which say they are J
Rev 3:9 of Satan, which say they are J

**JEWS'** *(jews)*
2Kin 18:26 talk not with us in the J
2Kin 18:28 a loud voice in the J language
2Chr 32:18 the J speech unto the people of
Neh 13:24 could not speak in the J language
Est 3:10 the Agagite, the J enemy
Est 8:1 the J enemy unto Esther the queen
Is 36:11 speak not to us in the J language
Is 36:13 a loud voice in the J language
Jn 2:13 the J passover was at hand, and
Jn 7:2 Now the J feast of tabernacles
Jn 11:55 the J passover was nigh at hand
Jn 19:42 because of the J preparation day
Gal 1:13 in time past in the J religion
Gal 1:14 profited in the J religion above

**JEZANIAH** *(jez-a-ni'-ah)* See JAAZANIAH. *A Jewish captain.*
Jer 40:8 J the son of a Maachathite, they
Jer 42:1 J the son of Hoshaiah, and all the

**JEZEBEL** *(jez'-e-bel)* See JEZEBEL'S. *Wife of King Ahab.*
1Kin 16:31 that he took to wife J the
1Kin 18:4 when J cut off the prophets of
1Kin 18:13 told my lord what I did when J
1Kin 19:1 Ahab told J all that Elijah had
1Kin 19:2 Then J sent a messenger unto
1Kin 21:5 But J his wife came to him, and
1Kin 21:7 J his wife said unto him, Dost
1Kin 21:11 did as J had sent unto them, and
1Kin 21:14 Then they sent to J, saying,
1Kin 21:15 when J heard that Naboth was
1Kin 21:15 that J said to Ahab, Arise, take
1Kin 21:23 of J also spake the LORD, saying,
1Kin 21:23 The dogs shall eat J by the wall
1Kin 21:25 whom J his wife stirred up
2Kin 9:7 of the LORD, at the hand of J
2Kin 9:10 the dogs shall eat J in the
2Kin 9:22 as the whoredoms of thy mother J
2Kin 9:30 come to Jezreel, J heard of it
2Kin 9:36 shall dogs eat the flesh of J
2Kin 9:37 the carcase of J shall be as dung
2Kin 9:37 they shall not say, This is J
Rev 2:20 thou sufferest that woman J

**JEZEBEL'S** *(jez'-e-bels)*
1Kin 18:19 hundred, which eat at J table

**JEZER** *(je'-zur)* See JEZERITES. *A son of Naphtali.*
Gen 46:24 Jahzeel, and Guni, and J, and
Num 26:49 Of J, the family of the Jezerites
1Chr 7:13 Jahziel, and Guni, and J, and

**JEZERITES** *(je'-zur-ites) Descendants of Jezer.*
Num 26:49 Of Jezer, the family of the J

**JEZIAH** *(je-zi'-ah) Married a foreigner in exile.*
Ezr 10:25 Ramiah, and J, and Malchiah, and

**JEZIEL** *(je'-ze-el) A warrior in David's army.*
1Chr 12:3 and J, and Pelet, the sons of

**JEZLIAH** *(jez-li'-ah) A son of Elpaal.*
1Chr 8:18 Ishmerai also, and J, and Jobab,

**JEZOAR** *(je-zo'-ar)* See ZOAR. *A son of Helah.*
1Chr 4:7 sons of Helah were, Zereth, and J

**JEZRAHIAH** *(jez-ra-hi'-ah)* See IZRAHIAH. *A priest.*
Neh 12:42 sang loud, with J their overseer

**JEZREEL** *(jez'-re-el)* See JEZREELITE.
*1. A city in Judah.*
Josh 15:56 And J, and Jokdeam, and Zanoah,
Judg 6:33 and pitched in the valley of J
1Sa 25:43 David also took Ahinoam of J
1Sa 29:1 by a fountain which is in J
1Sa 29:11 And the Philistines went up to J
*2. A city in Issachar.*
Josh 19:18 And their border was toward J
2Sa 2:9 and over the Ashurites, and over J
2Sa 4:4 came of Saul and Jonathan out of J
1Kin 4:12 which is by Zartanah beneath J
1Kin 18:45 And Ahab rode, and went to J
1Kin 18:46 before Ahab to the entrance of J
1Kin 21:1 had a vineyard, which was in J
1Kin 21:23 eat Jezebel by the wall of J
2Kin 8:29 J of the wounds which the Syrians
2Kin 8:29 to see Joram the son of Ahab in J
2Kin 9:10 eat Jezebel in the portion of J
2Kin 9:15 was returned to be healed in J of
2Kin 9:15 of the city to go to tell it in J
2Kin 9:16 rode in a chariot, and went to J
2Kin 9:17 a watchman on the tower in J
2Kin 9:30 And when Jehu was come to J
2Kin 9:36 In the portion of J shall dogs
2Kin 9:37 of the field in the portion of J
2Kin 10:1 to Samaria, unto the rulers of J
2Kin 10:6 come to me to J by to morrow this
2Kin 10:7 in baskets, and sent him them to J
2Kin 10:11 of the house of Ahab in J
2Chr 22:6 in J because of the wounds which
2Chr 22:6 see Jehoram the son of Ahab at J
*3. A plain.*
Josh 17:16 they who are of the valley of J
Hos 1:5 bow of Israel in the valley of J
Hos 2:22 and they shall hear J
*4. A descendant of Etam.*
1Chr 4:3 J, and Ishma, and Idbash
*5. Symbolic name for Hosea's eldest son.*
Hos 1:4 said unto him, Call his name J
Hos 1:4 blood of J upon the house of Jehu
Hos 1:11 for great shall be the day of J

**JEZREELITE** *(jez'-re-el-ite)* See JEZREELITESS. *An inhabitant of Jezreel.*
1Kin 21:1 that Naboth the J had a vineyard
1Kin 21:4 Naboth the J had spoken to him
1Kin 21:6 Because I spake unto Naboth the J
1Kin 21:7 thee the vineyard of Naboth the J
1Kin 21:15 of the vineyard of Naboth the J
1Kin 21:16 to the vineyard of Naboth the J
2Kin 9:21 in the portion of Naboth the J
2Kin 9:25 of the field of Naboth the J

**JEZREELITESS** *(jez'-re-el-i-tess) A female Jezreelite.*
1Sa 27:3 with his two wives, Ahinoam the J
1Sa 30:5 taken captives, Ahinoam the J
2Sa 2:2 his two wives also, Ahinoam the J
2Sa 3:2 was Amnon, of Ahinoam the J
1Chr 3:1 firstborn Amnon, of Ahinoam the J

**JIBSAM** *(jib'-sam) A son of Tola.*
1Chr 7:2 and Jeriel, and Jahmai, and J

**JIDLAPH** *(jid'-laf) A son of Nahor.*
Gen 22:22 Chesed, and Hazo, and Pildash, and J

**JIMNA** *(jim'-nah)* See IMNA, JIMNAH, JIMNITES. *A son of Asher.*
Num 26:44 of J, the family of the Jimnites

**JIMNAH** *(jim'-nah)* See JIMNA. *Same as Jimna.*
Gen 46:17 J, and Ishuah, and Isui, and Beriah,

**JIMNITES** *(jim'-nites) Descendants of Jimna.*
Num 26:44 of Jimna, the family of the J

**JIPHTAH** *(jif'-tah)* See JEPHTHAH, JIPHTHAH-EL. *A city in Judah.*
Josh 15:43 And J, and Ashnah, and Nezib,

**JIPHTHAH-EL** *(jif'-thah-el) A valley in Zebulun.*
Josh 19:14 thereof are in the valley of J
Josh 19:27 to the valley of J toward the

**JOAB** *(jo'-ab)* See ATAROTH, HOUSE, JOAB'S.
*1. Commander of David's army.*
1Sa 26:6 the son of Zeruiah, brother to J
2Sa 2:13 J the son of Zeruiah, and the
2Sa 2:14 And Abner said to J, Let the young
2Sa 2:14 And J said, Let them arise
2Sa 2:18 three sons of Zeruiah there, J
2Sa 2:22 hold up my face to J thy brother
2Sa 2:24 J also and Abishai pursued after
2Sa 2:26 Then Abner called to J, and said,
2Sa 2:27 J said, As God liveth, unless
2Sa 2:28 So J blew a trumpet, and all the
2Sa 2:30 J returned from following Abner
2Sa 2:32 And J and his men went all night,
2Sa 3:22 J came from pursuing a troop, and
2Sa 3:23 When J and all the host that was
2Sa 3:23 with him were come, they told J
2Sa 3:24 Then J came to the king, and said,
2Sa 3:26 when J was come out from David,
2Sa 3:27 J took him aside in the gate to
2Sa 3:29 Let it rest on the head of J
2Sa 3:29 house of J one that hath an issue
2Sa 3:30 So J and Abishai his brother slew
2Sa 3:31 And David said to J, and to all the
2Sa 8:16 J the son of Zeruiah was over the
2Sa 10:7 when David heard of it, he sent J
2Sa 10:9 When J saw that the front of the
2Sa 10:13 J drew nigh, and the people that
2Sa 10:14 So J returned from the children
2Sa 11:1 to battle, that David sent J
2Sa 11:6 And David sent to J, saying, Send
2Sa 11:6 And J sent Uriah to David
2Sa 11:7 David demanded of him how J did
2Sa 11:11 and my lord J, and the servants of
2Sa 11:14 that David wrote a letter to J
2Sa 11:16 when J observed the city, that he
2Sa 11:17 city went out, and fought with J
2Sa 11:18 Then J sent and told David all the
2Sa 11:22 David all that J had sent him for
2Sa 11:25 Thus shalt thou say unto J
2Sa 12:26 J fought against Rabbah of the
2Sa 12:27 J sent messengers to David, and
2Sa 14:1 Now J the son of Zeruiah
2Sa 14:2 J sent to Tekoah, and fetched
2Sa 14:3 So J put the words in her mouth
2Sa 14:19 Is not the hand of J with thee in
2Sa 14:19 for thy servant J, he bade me, and
2Sa 14:20 thy servant J done this thing
2Sa 14:21 And the king said unto J, Behold
2Sa 14:22 J fell to the ground on his face,
2Sa 14:22 J said, Today thy servant knoweth
2Sa 14:23 So J arose and went to Geshur, and
2Sa 14:29 Therefore Absalom sent for J
2Sa 14:31 Then J arose, and came to Absalom
2Sa 14:32 And Absalom answered J, Behold, I
2Sa 14:33 So J came to the king, and told
2Sa 17:25 captain of the host instead of J
2Sa 18:2 of the people under the hand of J
2Sa 18:5 And the king commanded J and
2Sa 18:10 a certain man saw it, and told J
2Sa 18:11 J said unto the man that told him
2Sa 18:12 And the man said unto J, Though I
2Sa 18:14 Then said J, I may not tarry thus
2Sa 18:16 J blew the trumpet, and the people
2Sa 18:16 for J held back the people
2Sa 18:20 J said unto him, Thou shalt not
2Sa 18:21 Then said J to Cushi, Go tell the
2Sa 18:21 And Cushi bowed himself unto J
2Sa 18:22 the son of Zadok yet again to J
2Sa 18:22 J said, Wherefore wilt thou run,
2Sa 18:29 When J sent the king's servant,
2Sa 19:1 And it was told J, Behold, the
2Sa 19:5 J came into the house to the king
2Sa 19:13 me continually in the room of J
2Sa 20:9 J said to Amasa, Art thou in
2Sa 20:9 J took Amasa, by the beard with
2Sa 20:10 So J and Abishai his brother
2Sa 20:11 him, and said, He that favoureth J
2Sa 20:11 is for David, let him go after J
2Sa 20:13 all the people went on after J
2Sa 20:15 were with J battered the wall
2Sa 20:16 say, I pray you, unto J, Come
2Sa 20:17 her, the woman said, Art thou J
2Sa 20:20 J answered and said, Far be it,
2Sa 20:21 And the woman said unto J, Behold,
2Sa 20:22 of Bichri, and cast it out to J
2Sa 20:22 J returned to Jerusalem unto the
2Sa 20:23 Now J was over all the host of
2Sa 23:18 And Abishai, the brother of J
2Sa 23:24 of J was one of the thirty
2Sa 23:37 armourbearer to J the son of
2Sa 24:2 For the king said to J the
2Sa 24:3 J said unto the king, Now the
2Sa 24:4 king's word prevailed against J
2Sa 24:4 And J and the captains of the host
2Sa 24:9 J gave up the sum of the number
1Kin 1:7 he conferred with J the son of
1Kin 1:19 J the captain of the host
1Kin 1:41 when J heard the sound of the
1Kin 2:5 J the son of Zeruiah did to me
1Kin 2:22 and for J the son of Zeruiah
1Kin 2:28 Then tidings came to J
1Kin 2:28 for J had turned after Adonijah,
1Kin 2:28 J fled unto the tabernacle of the
1Kin 2:29 it was told king Solomon that J
1Kin 2:30 word again, saying, Thus said J
1Kin 2:31 the innocent blood, which J shed

1Kin 2:33 return upon the head of J
1Kin 11:15 J the captain of the host was
1Kin 11:16 (For six months did J remain
1Kin 11:21 that J the captain of the host
1Chr 2:16 Abishai, and J, and Asahel, three
1Chr 11:6 So J the son of Zeruiah went
1Chr 11:8 J repaired the rest of the city
1Chr 11:20 And Abishai the brother of J
1Chr 11:26 were, Asahel the brother of J
1Chr 11:39 of J the son of Zeruiah,
1Chr 18:15 J the son of Zeruiah was over the
1Chr 19:8 when David heard of it, he sent J
1Chr 19:10 Now when J saw that the battle
1Chr 19:14 So J and the people that were with
1Chr 19:15 Then J came to Jerusalem
1Chr 20:1 J led forth the power of the army
1Chr 20:1 J smote Rabbah, and destroyed it
1Chr 21:2 And David said to J and to the
1Chr 21:3 J answered, The LORD make his
1Chr 21:4 king's word prevailed against J
1Chr 21:4 Wherefore J departed, and went
1Chr 21:5 J gave the sum of the number of
1Chr 21:6 king's word was abominable to J
1Chr 26:28 J the son of Zeruiah, had
1Chr 27:7 month was Asahel the brother of J
1Chr 27:24 J the son of Zeruiah began to
1Chr 27:34 general of the king's army was J
Ps 60:*t* when J returned, and smote of Edom

*2. A descendant of Caleb.*

1Chr 2:54 Ataroth, the house of J, and half

*3. A grandson of Kenaz.*

1Chr 4:14 and Seraiah begat J, the father of

*4. A family of exiles with Zerubbabel.*

Ezr 2:6 of the children of Jeshua and J
Neh 7:11 of the children of Jeshua and J

*5. A family of exiles with Ezra.*

Ezr 8:9 Of the sons of J

**JOAB'S** *(jo'-abs) Refers to Joab 1.*

2Sa 14:30 J field is near mine, and he hath
2Sa 17:25 sister to Zeruiah J mother
2Sa 18:2 J brother, and a third part under
2Sa 18:15 bare J armour compassed about
2Sa 20:7 And there went out after him J men
2Sa 20:8 J garment that he had put on was
2Sa 20:10 to the sword that was in J hand
2Sa 20:11 one of J men stood by him, and

**JOAH** *(jo'-ah)* See ETHAN.

*1. A son of Asaph.*

2Kin 18:18 J the son of Asaph the recorder
2Kin 18:26 son of Hilkiah, and Shebna, and J
2Kin 18:37 J the son of Asaph the recorder,
Is 36:3 house, and Shebna the scribe, and J
Is 36:11 J unto Rabshakeh, Speak, I pray
Is 36:22 and Shebna the scribe, and J

*2. A descendant of Gershom.*

1Chr 6:21 J his son, Iddo his son, Zerah
2Chr 29:12 J the son of Zimmah
2Chr 29:12 and Eden the son of J

*3. A sanctuary servant.*

1Chr 26:4 J the third, and Sacar the fourth,

*4. A Levite.*

2Chr 34:8 J the son of Joahaz the recorder,

**JOAHAZ** *(jo'-a-haz)* See JEHOAHAZ. *Father of Joah.*

2Chr 34:8 and Joah the son of J the recorder

**JOANNA** *(jo-an'-nah)*

*1. A female disciple.*

Lk 8:3 J the wife of Chuza Herod's
Lk 24:10 It was Mary Magdalene, and J

*2. An ancestor of Jesus.*

Lk 3:27 Which was the son of J, which was

**JOASH** *(jo'-ash)* See JEHOASH.

*1. A son of Becher.*

1Chr 7:8 Zemira, and J, and Eliezer, and

*2. A sanctuary servant.*

1Chr 27:28 and over the cellars of oil was J

*3. Father of Gideon.*

Judg 6:11 pertained unto J the Abi-ezrite
Judg 6:29 Gideon the son of J hath done
Judg 6:30 the men of the city said unto J
Judg 6:31 J said unto all that stood
Judg 7:14 the sword of Gideon the son of J
Judg 8:13 Gideon the son of J returned from
Judg 8:29 And Jerubbaal the son of J went
Judg 8:32 Gideon the son of J died in a
Judg 8:32 in the sepulchre of J his father

*4. A son of King Ahab.*

1Kin 22:26 the city, and to J the king's son
2Chr 18:25 the city, and to J the king's son

*5. A son of King Ahaziah.*

2Kin 11:2 took J the son of Ahaziah, and
2Kin 12:19 And the rest of the acts of J
2Kin 12:20 slew J in the house of Millo,
2Kin 13:1 twentieth year of J the son of
2Kin 13:10 seventh year of J king of Judah
2Kin 14:1 the son of J king of Judah
2Kin 14:3 to all things as J his father did
2Kin 14:17 Amaziah the son of J king of
2Kin 14:23 year of Amaziah the son of J king
1Chr 3:11 son, Ahaziah his son, J his son,
2Chr 22:11 took J the son of Ahaziah, and
2Chr 24:1 J was seven years old when he
2Chr 24:2 J did that which was right in the
2Chr 24:4 that J was minded to repair the
2Chr 24:22 Thus J the king remembered not
2Chr 24:24 they executed judgment against J
2Chr 25:23 king of Judah, the son of J
2Chr 25:25 Amaziah the son of J king of

*6. A king of Israel.*

2Kin 13:9 J his son reigned in his stead
2Kin 13:12 And the rest of the acts of J
2Kin 13:13 And J slept with his fathers
2Kin 13:13 J was buried in Samaria with the
2Kin 13:14 J the king of Israel came down
2Kin 13:25 Three times did J beat him
2Kin 14:1 In the second year of J son of
2Kin 14:23 of Judah Jeroboam the son of J
2Kin 14:27 the hand of Jeroboam the son of J
2Chr 25:17 Judah took advice, and sent to J
2Chr 25:18 J king of Israel sent to Amaziah
2Chr 25:21 So J the king of Israel went up
2Chr 25:23 J the king of Israel took Amaziah
2Chr 25:25 J son of Jehoahaz king of Israel
Hos 1:1 the days of Jeroboam the son of J
Amos 1:1 the son of J king of Israel

*7. A descendant of Shelah.*

1Chr 4:22 and the men of Chozeba, and J

*8. A captain in David's army.*

1Chr 12:3 The chief was Ahiezer, then J

**JOATHAM** *(jo'-a-tham)* See JOTHAM. *Ancestor of Joseph, husband of Mary.*

Mt 1:9 And Ozias begat J
Mt 1:9 and J begat Achaz

**JOB** *(jobe)* See JASHUB, JOB'S.

*1. A descendant of Issachar.*

Gen 46:13 Tola, and Phuvah, and J, and Shimron

*2. A righteous sufferer.*

Job 1:1 the land of Uz, whose name was J
Job 1:5 were gone about, that J sent
Job 1:5 for J said, It may be that my
Job 1:5 Thus did J continually
Job 1:8 Hast thou considered my servant J
Job 1:9 Doth J fear God for nought
Job 1:14 And there came a messenger unto J
Job 1:20 Then J arose, and rent his mantle,
Job 1:22 In all this J sinned not, nor
Job 2:3 Hast thou considered my servant J
Job 2:7 smote J with sore boils from the
Job 2:10 this did not J sin with his lips
Job 3:1 After this opened J his mouth
Job 3:2 And J spake, and said,
Job 6:1 But J answered and said,
Job 9:1 Then J answered and said,
Job 12:1 And J answered and said,
Job 16:1 Then J answered and said,
Job 19:1 Then J answered and said,
Job 21:1 But J answered and said,
Job 23:1 Then J answered and said,
Job 26:1 But J answered and said,
Job 27:1 Moreover J continued his parable,
Job 29:1 Moreover J continued his parable,
Job 31:40 The words of J are ended
Job 32:1 three men ceased to answer J
Job 32:2 against J was his wrath kindled,
Job 32:3 no answer, and yet had condemned J
Job 32:4 had waited till J had spoken
Job 32:12 was none of you that convinced J
Job 33:1 Wherefore, J, I pray thee, hear
Job 33:31 Mark well, O J, hearken unto me
Job 34:5 For J hath said, I am righteous
Job 34:7 What man is like J, who drinketh
Job 34:35 J hath spoken without knowledge,
Job 34:36 My desire is that J may be tried
Job 35:16 Therefore doth J open his mouth
Job 37:14 Hearken unto this, O J
Job 38:1 answered J out of the whirlwind
Job 40:1 Moreover the LORD answered J
Job 40:3 Then J answered the LORD, and said
Job 40:6 LORD unto J out of the whirlwind
Job 42:1 Then J answered the LORD, and said
Job 42:7 had spoken these words unto J
Job 42:7 is right, as my servant J hath
Job 42:8 seven rams, and go to my servant J
Job 42:8 my servant J shall pray for you
Job 42:8 which is right, like my servant J
Job 42:9 the LORD also accepted J
Job 42:10 LORD turned the captivity of J
Job 42:10 also the LORD gave J twice as
Job 42:12 end of J more than his beginning
Job 42:15 so fair as the daughters of J
Job 42:16 After this lived J an hundred
Job 42:17 So J died, being old and full of
Eze 14:14 three men, Noah, Daniel, and J
Eze 14:20 Though Noah, Daniel, and J
Jas 5:11 have heard of the patience of J

**JOBAB** *(jo'-bab)*

*1. A son of Joktan.*

Gen 10:29 And Ophir, and Havilah, and J
1Chr 1:23 And Ophir, and Havilah, and J

*2. A king of Edom.*

Gen 36:33 J the son of Zerah of Bozrah
Gen 36:34 J died, and Husham of the land of
1Chr 1:44 J the son of Zerah of Bozrah
1Chr 1:45 when J was dead, Husham of the

*3. A Canaanite king.*

Josh 11:1 that he sent to J king of Madon

*4. A son of Shaharaim.*

1Chr 8:9 And he begat of Hodesh his wife, J

*5. A son of Elpaal.*

1Chr 8:18 Ishmerai also, and Jezliah, and J

**JOB'S** *(jobes) Refers to Job 2.*

Job 2:11 Now when J three friends heard of

**JOCHEBED** *(jok'-e-bed) Wife of Amram.*

Ex 6:20 Amram took him J his father's
Num 26:59 And the name of Amram's wife was J

**JOED** *(jo'-ed) A son of Pedaiah.*

Neh 11:7 son of Meshullam, the son of J

**JOEL** *(jo'-el)*

*1. A son of Samuel.*

1Sa 8:2 the name of his firstborn was J
1Chr 6:33 Heman a singer, the son of J
1Chr 15:17 appointed Heman the son of J

*2. A Simeonite.*

1Chr 4:35 And J, and Jehu the son of Josibiah

*3. Father of Shemaiah.*

1Chr 5:4 The sons of J
1Chr 5:8 the son of Shema, the son of J

*4. A chief Gadite.*

1Chr 5:12 J the chief, and Shapham the next,

*5. A Kohathite.*

1Chr 6:36 The son of Elkanah, the son of J

*6. A descendant of Tola.*

1Chr 7:3 Michael, and Obadiah, and J

*7. A "mighty man" of David.*

1Chr 11:38 J the brother of Nathan, Mibhar

*8. A Gershomite.*

1Chr 15:7 J the chief, and his brethren an
1Chr 15:11 Levites, for Uriel, Asaiah, and J
1Chr 23:8 chief was Jehiel, and Zetham, and J

*9. A treasurer of the Temple.*

1Chr 26:22 J his brother, which were over

*10. A prince of Manasseh.*

1Chr 27:20 of Manasseh, J the son of Pedaiah

*11. A Kohathite who cleansed the Temple.*

2Chr 29:12 J the son of Azariah, of the sons

*12. Married a foreigner in exile.*

Ezr 10:43 Zabad, Zebina, Jadau, and J

*13. An overseer of the Benjamites.*

Neh 11:9 J the son of Zichri was their

*14. A prophet.*

Joel 1:1 that came to J the son of Pethuel
Acts 2:16 which was spoken by the prophet J

**JOELAH** *(jo-e'-lah) A member of David's band.*

1Chr 12:7 And J, and Zebadiah, the sons of

**JOEZER** *(jo-e'-zer) A warrior in David's army.*

1Chr 12:6 and Jesiah, and Azareel, and J

**JOGBEHAH** *(jog'-be-hah) A place in Gad.*

Num 32:35 Atroth, Shophan, and Jaazer, and J
Judg 8:11 tents on the east of Nobah and J

**JOGLI** *(jog'-li) A Danite prince.*
Num 34:22 of Dan, Bukki the son of J

**JOHA** *(jo'-hah)*
*1. Son of Beriah.*
1Chr 8:16 And Michael, and Ispah, and J
*2. A "mighty man" of David.*
1Chr 11:45 J his brother, the Tizite,

**JOHANAN** *(jo-ha'-nan)* See JEHOHANAN, JOHN.
*1. A son of Kareah.*
2Kin 25:23 J the son of Careah, and Seraiah
Jer 40:8 the son of Nethaniah, and J
Jer 40:13 Moreover J the son of Kareah, and
Jer 40:15 Then J the son of Kareah spake to
Jer 40:16 said unto J the son of Kareah
Jer 41:11 But when J the son of Kareah, and
Jer 41:13 Ishmael saw J the son of Kareah
Jer 41:14 went unto J the son of Kareah
Jer 41:15 escaped from J with eight men
Jer 41:16 Then took J the son of Kareah, and
Jer 42:1 J the son of Kareah, and Jezaniah
Jer 42:8 Then called he J the son of
Jer 43:2 J the son of Kareah, and all the
Jer 43:4 So J the son of Kareah, and all
Jer 43:5 But J the son of Kareah, and all
*2. A son of King Josiah.*
1Chr 3:15 of Josiah were, the firstborn J
*3. A son of Elioenai.*
1Chr 3:24 and Pelaiah, and Akkub, and J
*4. A grandson of Ahimaaz.*
1Chr 6:9 begat Azariah, and Azariah begat J
1Chr 6:10 J begat Azariah, (he it is that
*5. A warrior in David's army.*
1Chr 12:4 and Jeremiah, and Jahaziel, and J
*6. A Gadite warrior in David's army.*
1Chr 12:12 J the eighth, Elzabad the ninth,
*7. An Ephraimite.*
2Chr 28:12 of Ephraim, Azariah the son of J
*8. An exile with Ezra.*
Ezr 8:12 J the son of Hakkatan, and with
*9. A priest in exile with Ezra.*
Ezr 10:6 chamber of J the son of Eliashib
*10. A son of Tobiah.*
Neh 6:18 his son J had taken the daughter
*11. A priest in exile with Zerubbabel.*
Neh 12:22 days of Eliashib, Joiada, and J
Neh 12:23 the days of J the son of Eliashib

**JOHN** *(jon)* See BAPTIST, JEHOHANAN, JOHN'S, MARK.
*1. The Baptizer.*
Mt 3:1 In those days came J the Baptist
Mt 3:4 the same J had his raiment of
Mt 3:13 from Galilee to Jordan unto J
Mt 3:14 But J forbad him, saying, I have
Mt 4:12 heard that J was cast into prison
Mt 9:14 came to him the disciples of J
Mt 11:2 Now when J had heard in the
Mt 11:4 shew J again those things which
Mt 11:7 unto the multitudes concerning J
Mt 11:11 a greater than J the Baptist
Mt 11:12 from the days of J the Baptist
Mt 11:13 and the law prophesied until J
Mt 11:18 For J came neither eating nor
Mt 14:2 servants, This is J the Baptist
Mt 14:3 For Herod had laid hold on J
Mt 14:4 For J said unto him, It is not
Mt 14:8 Give me here J Baptist's head in
Mt 14:10 sent, and beheaded J in the prison
Mt 16:14 say that thou art J the Baptist
Mt 17:13 spake unto them of J the Baptist
Mt 21:25 The baptism of J, whence was it
Mt 21:26 for all hold J as a prophet
Mt 21:32 For J came unto you in the way of
Mk 1:4 J did baptize in the wilderness,
Mk 1:6 J was clothed with camel's hair,
Mk 1:9 and was baptized of J in Jordan
Mk 1:14 Now after that J was put in
Mk 2:18 And the disciples of J and of the
Mk 2:18 him, Why do the disciples of J
Mk 6:14 That J the Baptist was risen from
Mk 6:16 heard thereof, he said, It is J
Mk 6:17 sent forth and laid hold upon J
Mk 6:18 For J had said unto Herod, It is
Mk 6:20 For Herod feared J, knowing that
Mk 6:24 said, The head of J the Baptist
Mk 6:25 charger the head of J the Baptist
Mk 8:28 And they answered, J the Baptist
Mk 11:30 The baptism of J, was it from
Mk 11:32 for all men counted J, that he
Lk 1:13 and thou shalt call his name J
Lk 1:60 but he shall be called J
Lk 1:63 and wrote, saying, His name is J
Lk 3:2 the word of God came unto J the
Lk 3:15 men mused in their hearts of J
Lk 3:16 J answered, saying unto them all,
Lk 3:20 all, that he shut up J in prison
Lk 5:33 do the disciples of J fast often
Lk 7:18 the disciples of J shewed him of
Lk 7:19 J calling unto him two of his
Lk 7:20 J Baptist hath sent us unto thee,
Lk 7:22 tell J what things ye have seen
Lk 7:24 the messengers of J were departed
Lk 7:24 unto the people concerning J
Lk 7:28 prophet than J the Baptist
Lk 7:29 baptized with the baptism of J
Lk 7:33 For J the Baptist came neither
Lk 9:7 that J was risen from the dead
Lk 9:9 And Herod said, J have I beheaded
Lk 9:19 answering said, J the Baptist
Lk 11:1 as J also taught his disciples
Lk 16:16 law and the prophets were until J
Lk 20:4 The baptism of J, was it from
Lk 20:6 be persuaded that J was a prophet
Jn 1:6 sent from God, whose name was J
Jn 1:15 J bare witness of him, and cried,
Jn 1:19 And this is the record of J
Jn 1:26 J answered them, saying, I
Jn 1:28 Jordan, where J was baptizing
Jn 1:29 The next day J seeth Jesus coming
Jn 1:32 J bare record, saying, I saw the
Jn 1:35 Again the next day after J stood
Jn 1:40 of the two which heard J speak
Jn 3:23 J also was baptizing in Aenon
Jn 3:24 For J was not yet cast into
Jn 3:26 And they came unto J, and said unto
Jn 3:27 J answered and said, A man can
Jn 4:1 and baptized more disciples than J
Jn 5:33 Ye sent unto J, and he bare
Jn 5:36 greater witness than that of J
Jn 10:40 place where J at first baptized
Jn 10:41 him, and said, J did no miracle
Jn 10:41 but all things that J spake of
Acts 1:5 For J truly baptized with water
Acts 1:22 Beginning from the baptism of J
Acts 10:37 the baptism which J preached
Acts 11:16 J indeed baptized with water
Acts 13:24 When J had first preached before
Acts 13:25 as J fulfilled his course, he
Acts 18:25 knowing only the baptism of J
Acts 19:4 J verily baptized with the
*2. Son of Zebedee.*
Mt 4:21 J his brother, in a ship with
Mt 10:2 son of Zebedee, and J his brother
Mt 17:1 J his brother, and bringeth them
Mk 1:19 J his brother, who also were in
Mk 1:29 Simon and Andrew, with James and J
Mk 3:17 and J the brother of James
Mk 5:37 James, and J the brother of James
Mk 9:2 with him Peter, and James, and J
Mk 9:38 J answered him, saying, Master,
Mk 10:35 And James and J, the sons of
Mk 10:41 much displeased with James and J
Mk 13:3 the temple, Peter and James and J
Mk 14:33 with him Peter and James and J
Lk 5:10 And so was also James, and J
Lk 6:14 and Andrew his brother, James and J
Lk 8:51 go in, save Peter, and James, and J
Lk 9:28 these sayings, he took Peter and J
Lk 9:49 J answered and said, Master, we
Lk 9:54 J saw this, they said, Lord, wilt
Lk 22:8 And he sent Peter and J, saying, Go
Acts 1:13 abode both Peter, and James, and J
Acts 3:1 J went up together into the
Acts 3:3 J about to go into the temple
Acts 3:4 his eyes upon him with J, said,
Acts 3:11 which was healed held Peter and J
Acts 4:13 saw the boldness of Peter and J
Acts 4:19 J answered and said unto them,
Acts 8:14 they sent unto them Peter and J
Acts 12:2 the brother of J with the sword
Gal 2:9 And when James, Cephas, and J
Rev 1:1 by his angel unto his servant J
Rev 1:4 J to the seven churches which are
Rev 1:9 I J, who also am your brother, and
Rev 21:2 I J saw the holy city, new
Rev 22:8 I J saw these things, and heard
*3. A relative of Annas the priest.*
Acts 4:6 high priest, and Caiaphas, and J
*4. Surnamed Mark.*
Acts 12:12 the house of Mary the mother of J
Acts 12:25 ministry, and took with them J
Acts 13:5 they had also J to their minister
Acts 13:13 J departing from them returned to
Acts 15:37 determined to take with them J

**JOHN'S** *(jonz) Refers to John 1.*
Jn 3:25 between some of J disciples
Acts 19:3 And they said, Unto J baptism

**JOIADA** *(joy'-a-dah)* See JEHOIADA. *A priest with Zerubbabel.*
Neh 12:10 Eliashib, and Eliashib begat J
Neh 12:11 J begat Jonathan, and Jonathan
Neh 12:22 in the days of Eliashib, J
Neh 13:28 And one of the sons of J, the son

**JOIAKIM** *(joy'-a-kim)* See JEHOIAKIM. *Another priest with Zerubbabel.*
Neh 12:10 And Jeshua begat J
Neh 12:10 J also begat Eliashib
Neh 12:12 And in the days of J were priests
Neh 12:26 the days of J the son of Jeshua

**JOIARIB** *(joy'-a-rib)* See JEHOIARIB.
*1. A messenger for Ezra.*
Ezr 8:16 also for J, and for Elnathan, men
*2. A descendant of Perez.*
Neh 11:5 the son of Adaiah, the son of J
*3. Father of Jedaiah.*
Neh 11:10 Jedaiah the son of J, Jachin
Neh 12:6 Shemaiah, and J, Jedaiah,
Neh 12:19 And of J, Mattenai

**JOIN**
Ex 1:10 they *j* also unto our enemies, and
2Chr 20:35 *j* himself with Ahaziah king of
Ezr 9:14 *j* in affinity with the people of
Prov 11:21 Though hand *j* in hand, the wicked
Prov 16:5 though hand *j* in hand, he shall
Is 5:8 unto them that *j* house to house
Is 9:11 him, and *j* his enemies together
Is 56:6 that *j* themselves to the LORD, to
Jer 50:5 let us *j* ourselves to the LORD in
Eze 37:17 *j* them one to another into one
Dan 11:6 they shall *j* themselves together
Acts 5:13 durst no man *j* himself to them
Acts 8:29 *j* thyself to this chariot
Acts 9:26 he assayed to *j* himself to the

**JOINED**
Gen 14:3 All these were *j* together in the
Gen 14:8 they *j* battle with them in the
Gen 29:34 time will my husband be *j* unto me
Ex 28:7 *j* at the two edges thereof
Ex 28:7 and so it shall be *j* together
Num 18:2 that they may be *j* unto thee
Num 18:4 And they shall be *j* unto thee
Num 25:3 Israel *j* himself unto Baal-peor
Num 25:5 men that were *j* unto Baal-peor
1Sa 4:2 and when they *j* battle, Israel was
1Kin 7:32 of the wheels were *j* to the base
1Kin 20:29 the seventh day the battle was *j*
2Chr 18:1 and *j* affinity with Ahab
2Chr 20:36 he *j* himself with him to make
2Chr 20:37 Because thou hast *j* thyself with
Ezr 4:12 thereof, and *j* the foundations
Neh 4:6 all the wall was *j* together unto
Est 9:27 upon all such as *j* themselves
Job 3:6 let it not be *j* unto the days of
Job 41:17 They are *j* one to another, they
Job 41:23 of his flesh are *j* together
Ps 83:8 Assur also is *j* with them
Ps 106:28 They *j* themselves also unto
Eccl 9:4 For to him that is *j* to all the
Is 13:15 every one that is *j* unto them
Is 14:1 strangers shall be *j* with them
Is 14:20 Thou shalt not be *j* with them in
Is 56:3 that hath *j* himself to the LORD,
Eze 1:9 Their wings were *j* one to another
Eze 1:11 every one were *j* one to another
Eze 46:22 courts *j* of forty cubits long
Hos 4:17 Ephraim is *j* to idols
Zec 2:11 many nations shall be *j* to the
Mt 19:6 therefore God hath *j* together
Mk 10:9 therefore God hath *j* together
Lk 15:15 *j* himself to a citizen of that
Acts 5:36 about four hundred, *j* themselves
Acts 18:7 whose house *j* hard to the
1Cor 1:10 but that ye be perfectly *j*
1Cor 6:16 is *j* to an harlot is one body
1Cor 6:17 But he that is *j* unto the Lord is

Eph 4:16 the whole body fitly *j* together
Eph 5:31 shall be *j* unto his wife, and they

**JOINT**
Gen 32:25 of Jacob's thigh was out of *j*
Ps 22:14 and all my bones are out of *j*
Prov 25:19 broken tooth, and a foot out of *j*
Eph 4:16 by that which every *j* supplieth

**JOINTS**
1Kin 22:34 between the *j* of the harness
2Chr 18:33 between the *j* of the harness
Song 7:1 the *j* of thy thighs are like
Dan 5:6 so that the *j* of his loins were
Col 2:19 from which all the body by *j*
Heb 4:12 of soul and spirit, and of the *j*

**JOKDEAM** *(jok'-de-am) A city in Judah.*
Josh 15:56 And Jezreel, and J, and Zanoah,

**JOKIM** *(jo'-kim) A descendant of Shelah.*
1Chr 4:22 And J, and the men of Chozeba, and

**JOKMEAM** *(jok'-me-am)* See JOKNEAM. *A Levitical city in Ephraim.*
1Chr 6:68 J with her suburbs, and Beth-horon

**JOKNEAM** *(jok'-ne-am)* See JOKMEAM, KIBZAIM.
*1. A Levitical city in Zebulun.*
Josh 12:22 the king of J of Carmel, one
Josh 19:11 to the river that is before J
Josh 21:34 J with her suburbs, and Kartah
*2. A Levitical city in Ephraim.*
1Kin 4:12 unto the place that is beyond J

**JOKSHAN** *(jok'-shan) A son of Abraham.*
Gen 25:2 And she bare him Zimran, and J
Gen 25:3 And J begat Sheba, and Dedan
1Chr 1:32 she bare Zimran, and J, and Medan,
1Chr 1:32 And the sons of J

**JOKTAN** *(jok'-tan) A son of Eber.*
Gen 10:25 and his brother's name was J
Gen 10:26 J begat Almodad, and Sheleph, and
Gen 10:29 all these were the sons of J
1Chr 1:19 and his brother's name was J
1Chr 1:20 J begat Almodad, and Sheleph, and
1Chr 1:23 All these were the sons of J

**JOKTHEEL** *(jok'-the-el)* See SELAH.
*1. A city in Judah.*
Josh 15:38 And Dilean, and Mizpeh, and J
*2. Another name for Petra in Edom.*
2Kin 14:7 the name of it J unto this day

**JONA** *(jo'-nah)* See BAR-JONA, JONAH, JONAS. *Greek form of Jonah.*
Jn 1:42 said, Thou art Simon the son of J

**JONADAB** *(jon'-a-dab)* See JEHONADAB.
*1. A son of Shimeah.*
2Sa 13:3 had a friend, whose name was J
2Sa 13:3 and J was a very subtil man
2Sa 13:5 J said unto him, Lay thee down on
2Sa 13:32 And J, the son of Shimeah David's
2Sa 13:35 J said unto the king, Behold, the
*2. A son of Rechab.*
Jer 35:6 for J the son of Rechab our
Jer 35:8 have we obeyed the voice of J the
Jer 35:10 that J our father commanded us
Jer 35:14 The words of J the son of Rechab,
Jer 35:16 Because the sons of J the son of
Jer 35:18 the commandment of J your father
Jer 35:19 J the son of Rechab shall not

**JONAH** *(jo'-nah)* See JONA, JONAS. *A prophet.*
2Kin 14:25 by the hand of his servant J
Jonah 1:1 came unto J the son of Amittai
Jonah 1:3 But J rose up to flee unto
Jonah 1:5 But J was gone down into the
Jonah 1:7 cast lots, and the lot fell upon J
Jonah 1:15 So they took up J, and cast him
Jonah 1:17 a great fish to swallow up J
Jonah 1:17 J was in the belly of the fish
Jonah 2:1 Then J prayed unto the LORD his
Jonah 2:10 it vomited out J upon the dry
Jonah 3:1 LORD came unto J the second time
Jonah 3:3 So J arose, and went unto Nineveh,
Jonah 3:4 J began to enter into the city a
Jonah 4:1 But it displeased J exceedingly
Jonah 4:5 So J went out of the city, and sat
Jonah 4:6 and made it to come up over J
Jonah 4:6 So J was exceeding glad of the
Jonah 4:8 the sun beat upon the head of J
Jonah 4:9 And God said to J, Doest thou well

**JONAN** *(jo'-nan) Ancestor of Joseph, husband of Mary.*
Lk 3:30 of Joseph, which was the son of J

**JONAS** *(jo'-nas)* See JONA, JONAH.
*1. Same as Jonah.*
Mt 12:39 it, but the sign of the prophet J
Mt 12:40 For as J was three days and three
Mt 12:41 repented at the preaching of J
Mt 12:41 behold, a greater than J is here
Mt 16:4 it, but the sign of the prophet J
Lk 11:29 it, but the sign of J the prophet
Lk 11:30 For as J was a sign unto the
Lk 11:32 repented at the preaching of J
Lk 11:32 behold, a greater than J is here
*2. Father of Peter.*
Jn 21:15 to Simon Peter, Simon, son of J
Jn 21:16 the second time, Simon, son of J
Jn 21:17 the third time, Simon, son of J

**JONATHAN** *(jon'-a-than)* See JEHONATHAN, JONATHAN'S.
*1. A Levite.*
Judg 18:30 and J, the son of Gershom, the son
*2. Son of Saul.*
1Sa 13:2 a thousand were with J in Gibeah
1Sa 13:3 J smote the garrison of the
1Sa 13:16 J his son, and the people that
1Sa 13:22 people that were with Saul and J
1Sa 13:22 with J his son was there found
1Sa 14:1 that J the son of Saul said unto
1Sa 14:3 people knew not that J was gone
1Sa 14:4 by which J sought to go over unto
1Sa 14:6 J said to the young man that bare
1Sa 14:8 Then said J, Behold, we will pass
1Sa 14:12 men of the garrison answered J
1Sa 14:12 J said unto his armourbearer,
1Sa 14:13 J climbed up upon his hands and
1Sa 14:13 and they fell before J
1Sa 14:14 And that first slaughter, which J
1Sa 14:17 when they had numbered, behold, J
1Sa 14:21 that were with Saul and J
1Sa 14:27 But J heard not when his father
1Sa 14:29 Then said J, My father hath
1Sa 14:39 Israel, though it be in J my son
1Sa 14:40 J my son will be on the other
1Sa 14:41 And Saul and J were taken
1Sa 14:42 Cast lots between me and J my son
1Sa 14:42 And J was taken
1Sa 14:43 Then Saul said to J, Tell me what
1Sa 14:43 J told him, and said, I did but
1Sa 14:44 for thou shalt surely die, J
1Sa 14:45 said unto Saul, Shall J die
1Sa 14:45 So the people rescued J, that he
1Sa 14:49 Now the sons of Saul were J
1Sa 18:1 that the soul of J was knit with
1Sa 18:1 J loved him as his own soul
1Sa 18:3 Then J and David made a covenant,
1Sa 18:4 J stripped himself of the robe
1Sa 19:1 And Saul spake to J his son
1Sa 19:2 But J Saul's son delighted much
1Sa 19:2 J told David, saying, Saul my
1Sa 19:4 J spake good of David unto Saul
1Sa 19:6 hearkened unto the voice of J
1Sa 19:7 J called David, and Jonathan
1Sa 19:7 J shewed him all those things
1Sa 19:7 J brought David to Saul, and he
1Sa 20:1 Ramah, and came and said before J
1Sa 20:3 Let not J know this, lest he be
1Sa 20:4 Then said J unto David,
1Sa 20:5 And David said unto J, Behold, to
1Sa 20:9 J said, Far be it from thee
1Sa 20:10 Then said David to J, Who shall
1Sa 20:11 J said unto David, Come, and let
1Sa 20:12 J said unto David, O LORD God of
1Sa 20:13 The LORD do so and much more to J
1Sa 20:16 So J made a covenant with the
1Sa 20:17 J caused David to swear again,
1Sa 20:18 Then J said to David, To morrow
1Sa 20:25 J arose, and Abner sat by Saul's
1Sa 20:27 and Saul said unto J his son
1Sa 20:28 J answered Saul, David earnestly
1Sa 20:30 anger was kindled against J
1Sa 20:32 J answered Saul his father, and
1Sa 20:33 whereby J knew that it was
1Sa 20:34 So J arose from the table in
1Sa 20:35 that J went out into the field at
1Sa 20:37 of the arrow which J had shot
1Sa 20:37 J cried after the lad, and said,
1Sa 20:38 J cried after the lad, Make speed
1Sa 20:39 only J and David knew the matter
1Sa 20:40 J gave his artillery unto his lad
1Sa 20:42 J said to David, Go in peace,
1Sa 20:42 and J went into the city
1Sa 23:16 J Saul's son arose, and went to
1Sa 23:18 the wood, and J went to his house
1Sa 31:2 and the Philistines slew J
2Sa 1:4 Saul and J his son are dead also
2Sa 1:5 that Saul and J his son be dead
2Sa 1:12 for J his son, and for the people
2Sa 1:17 over Saul and over J his son
2Sa 1:22 the bow of J turned not back, and
2Sa 1:23 J were lovely and pleasant in
2Sa 1:25 O J, thou wast slain in thine
2Sa 1:26 distressed for thee, my brother J
2Sa 4:4 And J, Saul's son, had a son that
2Sa 4:4 J out of Jezreel, and his nurse
2Sa 9:3 J hath yet a son, which is lame
2Sa 9:6 when Mephibosheth, the son of J
2Sa 9:7 kindness for J thy father's sake
2Sa 21:7 the son of J the son of Saul,
2Sa 21:7 David and J the son of Saul
2Sa 21:12 the bones of J his son from the
2Sa 21:13 of Saul and the bones of J his son
2Sa 21:14 J his son buried they in the
1Chr 8:33 Kish begat Saul, and Saul begat J
1Chr 8:34 the son of J was Merib-baal
1Chr 9:39 and Saul begat J, and Malchi-shua,
1Chr 9:40 the son of J was Merib-baal
1Chr 10:2 and the Philistines slew J
*3. A son of Abiathar.*
2Sa 15:27 thy son, and J the son of Abiathar
2Sa 15:36 Zadok's son, and J Abiathar's son
2Sa 17:17 Now J and Ahimaaz stayed by
2Sa 17:20 they said, Where is Ahimaaz and J
1Kin 1:42 J the son of Abiathar the priest
1Kin 1:43 J answered and said to Adonijah,
*4. A son of Shimea.*
2Sa 21:21 J the son of Shimeah the brother
1Chr 20:7 J the son of Shimea David's
*5. A "mighty man" of David.*
2Sa 23:32 of the sons of Jashen, J
1Chr 11:34 J the son of Shage the Hararite,
*6. A son of Jada.*
1Chr 2:32 Shammai; Jether, and J
1Chr 2:33 And the sons of J
*7. An uncle of David.*
1Chr 27:32 Also J David's uncle was a
*8. A family of exiles.*
Ezr 8:6 Ebed the son of J, and with him
*9. Son of Asahel.*
Ezr 10:15 Only J the son of Asahel and
*10. A descendant of Jeshua.*
Neh 12:11 And Joiada begat J
Neh 12:11 and J begat Jaddua
*11. A priest descended from Melicu.*
Neh 12:14 Of Melicu, J
*12. A priest descended from Shemaiah.*
Neh 12:35 namely, Zechariah the son of J
*13. A scribe.*
Jer 37:15 in the house of J the scribe
Jer 37:20 to the house of J the scribe
*14. A son of Kareah.*
Jer 40:8 J the sons of Kareah, and Seraiah

**JONATHAN'S** *(jon'-a-thans) Refers to Jonathan 2.*
1Sa 20:38 J lad gathered up the arrows, and
2Sa 9:1 may shew him kindness for J sake
Jer 38:26 not cause me to return to J house

**JONATH-ELEM-RECHOKIM** *(jo'-nath-e'-lem-re-ko'-kim) A musical notation.*
Ps 56:*t* To the chief Musician upon J

**JOPPA** *(jop'-pah) A seaport in Dan.*
2Chr 2:16 it to thee in flotes by sea to J
Ezr 3:7 from Lebanon to the sea of J
Jonah 1:3 of the LORD, and went down to J
Acts 9:36 Now there was at J a certain
Acts 9:38 forasmuch as Lydda was nigh to J
Acts 9:42 And it was known throughout all J
Acts 9:43 days in J with one Simon a tanner
Acts 10:5 And now send men to J, and call for
Acts 10:8 unto them, he sent them to J
Acts 10:23 brethren from J accompanied him
Acts 10:32 Send therefore to J, and call
Acts 11:5 I was in the city of J praying
Acts 11:13 and said unto him, Send men to J

**JORAH** *(jo'-rah)* See HARIPH. *A family of exiles.*
Ezr 2:18 The children of J, an hundred and

**JORAI** *(jo'-rahee) Head of a Gadite family.*
1Chr 5:13 and Meshullam, and Sheba, and J

**JORAM** *(jo'-ram)* See JEHORAM.
*1. A son of Toi.*
2Sa 8:10 Then Toi sent J his son unto king
2Sa 8:10 J brought with him vessels of
*2. Same as Jehoram.*
2Kin 8:21 So J went over to Zair, and all
2Kin 8:23 And the rest of the acts of J
2Kin 8:24 J slept with his fathers, and was
2Kin 11:2 Jehosheba, the daughter of king J
1Chr 3:11 J his son, Ahaziah his son, Joash
Mt 1:8 and Josaphat begat J
Mt 1:8 and J begat Ozias
*3. A son of Ahab.*
2Kin 8:16 in the fifth year of J the son of
2Kin 8:25 In the twelfth year of J the son
2Kin 8:28 he went with J the son of Ahab to
2Kin 8:28 and the Syrians wounded J
2Kin 8:29 king J went back to be healed in
2Kin 8:29 see J the son of Ahab in Jezreel
2Kin 9:14 son of Nimshi conspired against J
2Kin 9:14 (Now J had kept Ramoth-gilead, he
2Kin 9:15 But king J was returned to be
2Kin 9:16 for J lay there
2Kin 9:16 of Judah was come down to see J
2Kin 9:17 J said, Take an horseman, and send
2Kin 9:21 And J said, Make ready
2Kin 9:21 J king of Israel and Ahaziah king
2Kin 9:22 when J saw Jehu, that he said, Is
2Kin 9:23 J turned his hands, and fled, and
2Kin 9:29 in the eleventh year of J the son
2Chr 22:5 and the Syrians smote J
2Chr 22:7 Ahaziah was of God by coming to J
*4. A descendant of Eliezer.*
1Chr 26:25 J his son, and Zichri his son, and

**JORDAN** *(jor'-dan) A river that runs from the Sea of Galilee to the Dead Sea.*
Gen 13:10 and beheld all the plain of J
Gen 13:11 Lot chose him all the plain of J
Gen 32:10 my staff I passed over this J
Gen 50:10 of Atad, which is beyond J
Gen 50:11 Abel-mizraim, which is beyond J
Num 13:29 by the sea, and by the coast of J
Num 22:1 of Moab on this side J by Jericho
Num 26:3 plains of Moab by J near Jericho
Num 26:63 plains of Moab by J near Jericho
Num 31:12 Moab, which are by J near Jericho
Num 32:5 and bring us not over J
Num 32:19 with them on yonder side J
Num 32:19 to us on this side J eastward
Num 32:21 you armed over J before the LORD
Num 32:29 Reuben will pass with you over J
Num 32:32 on this side J may be ours
Num 33:48 plains of Moab by J near Jericho
Num 33:49 And they pitched by J, from
Num 33:50 Moses in the plains of Moab by J
Num 33:51 over J into the land of Canaan
Num 34:12 And the border shall go down to J
Num 34:15 this side J near Jericho eastward
Num 35:1 plains of Moab by J near Jericho
Num 35:10 When ye be come over J into the
Num 35:14 give three cities on this side J
Num 36:13 plains of Moab by J near Jericho
Deut 1:1 on this side J in the wilderness
Deut 1:5 On this side J, in the land of
Deut 2:29 until I shall pass over J into
Deut 3:8 the land that was on this side J
Deut 3:17 The plain also, and J, and the
Deut 3:20 your God hath given them beyond J
Deut 3:25 the good land that is beyond J
Deut 3:27 for thou shalt not go over this J
Deut 4:21 sware that I should not go over J
Deut 4:22 this land, I must not go over J
Deut 4:26 ye go over J to possess it
Deut 4:41 this side J toward the sunrising
Deut 4:46 On this side J, in the valley
Deut 4:47 this side J toward the sunrising
Deut 4:49 the plain on this side J eastward
Deut 9:1 Thou art to pass over J this day
Deut 11:30 Are they not on the other side J
Deut 11:31 For ye shall pass over J to go in
Deut 12:10 But when ye go over J, and dwell
Deut 27:2 J unto the land which the LORD
Deut 27:4 shall be when ye be gone over J
Deut 27:12 people, when ye are come over J
Deut 30:18 over J to go to possess it
Deut 31:2 me, Thou shalt not go over this J
Deut 31:13 ye go over J to possess it
Deut 32:47 ye go over J to possess it
Josh 1:2 therefore arise, go over this J
Josh 1:11 days ye shall pass over this J
Josh 1:14 Moses gave you on this side J
Josh 1:15 this side J toward the sunrising
Josh 2:7 them the way to J unto the fords
Josh 2:10 that were on the other side J
Josh 3:1 from Shittim, and came to J
Josh 3:8 to the brink of the water of J
Josh 3:8 J, ye shall stand still in J
Josh 3:11 passeth over before you into J
Josh 3:13 shall rest in the waters of J
Josh 3:13 that the waters of J shall be cut
Josh 3:14 from their tents, to pass over J
Josh 3:15 bare the ark were come unto J
Josh 3:15 (for J overfloweth all his banks
Josh 3:17 on dry ground in the midst of J
Josh 3:17 people were passed clean over J
Josh 4:1 people were clean passed over J
Josh 4:3 you hence out of the midst of J
Josh 4:5 LORD your God into the midst of J
Josh 4:7 That the waters of J were cut off
Josh 4:7 when it passed over J
Josh 4:7 the waters of J were cut off
Josh 4:8 stones out of the midst of J
Josh 4:9 twelve stones in the midst of J
Josh 4:10 the ark stood in the midst of J
Josh 4:16 that they come up out of J
Josh 4:17 saying, Come ye up out of J
Josh 4:18 come up out of the midst of J
Josh 4:18 that the waters of J returned
Josh 4:19 the people came up out of J on
Josh 4:20 stones, which they took out of J
Josh 4:22 came over this J on dry land
Josh 4:23 the waters of J from before you
Josh 5:1 were on the side of J westward
Josh 5:1 of J from before the children of
Josh 7:7 at all brought this people over J
Josh 7:7 and dwelt on the other side J
Josh 9:1 kings which were on this side J
Josh 9:10 the Amorites, that were beyond J
Josh 12:1 J toward the rising of the sun
Josh 12:7 smote on this side J on the west
Josh 13:8 beyond J eastward, even as Moses
Josh 13:23 of the children of Reuben was J
Josh 13:27 of Sihon king of Heshbon, J
Josh 13:27 on the other side J eastward
Josh 13:32 of Moab, on the other side J
Josh 14:3 an half tribe on the other side J
Josh 15:5 salt sea, even unto the end of J
Josh 15:5 sea at the uttermost part of J
Josh 16:1 of Joseph fell from J by Jericho
Josh 16:7 came to Jericho, and went out at J
Josh 17:5 which were on the other side J
Josh 18:7 inheritance beyond J on the east
Josh 18:12 on the north side was from J
Josh 18:19 salt sea at the south end of J
Josh 18:20 J was the border of it on the
Josh 19:22 of their border were at J
Josh 19:33 the outgoings thereof were at J
Josh 19:34 to Judah upon J toward the
Josh 20:8 on the other side J by Jericho
Josh 22:4 LORD gave you on the other side J
Josh 22:7 brethren on this side J westward
Josh 22:10 they came unto the borders of J
Josh 22:10 built there an altar by J
Josh 22:11 of Canaan, in the borders of J
Josh 22:25 hath made J a border between us
Josh 23:4 for your tribes, from J, with all
Josh 24:8 which dwelt on the other side J
Josh 24:11 And ye went over J, and came unto
Judg 3:28 took the fords of J toward Moab
Judg 5:17 Gilead abode beyond J
Judg 7:24 the waters unto Beth-barah and J
Judg 7:24 the waters unto Beth-barah and J
Judg 7:25 to Gideon on the other side J
Judg 8:4 And Gideon came to J, and passed
Judg 10:8 J in the land of the Amorites
Judg 10:9 J to fight also against Judah
Judg 11:13 Arnon even unto Jabbok, and unto J
Judg 11:22 from the wilderness even unto J
Judg 12:5 of J before the Ephraimites
Judg 12:6 and slew him at the passages of J
1Sa 13:7 went over J to the land of Gad
1Sa 31:7 that were on the other side J
2Sa 2:29 the plain, and passed over J
2Sa 10:17 Israel together, and passed over J
2Sa 17:22 with him, and they passed over J
2Sa 17:22 of them that was not gone over J
2Sa 17:24 And Absalom passed over J, he and
2Sa 19:15 the king returned, and came to J
2Sa 19:15 king, to conduct the king over J
2Sa 19:17 they went over J before the king
2Sa 19:18 the king, as he was come over J
2Sa 19:31 went over J with the king
2Sa 19:31 to conduct him over J
2Sa 19:36 a little way over J with the king
2Sa 19:39 And all the people went over J
2Sa 19:41 all David's men with him, over J
2Sa 20:2 king, from J even to Jerusalem
2Sa 24:5 And they passed over J, and pitched
1Kin 2:8 but he came down to meet me at J
1Kin 7:46 In the plain of J did the king
1Kin 17:3 brook Cherith, that is before J
1Kin 17:5 brook Cherith, that is before J
2Kin 2:6 for the LORD hath sent me to J
2Kin 2:7 and they two stood by J
2Kin 2:13 back, and stood by the bank of J
2Kin 5:10 wash in J seven times, and thy
2Kin 5:14 dipped himself seven times in J
2Kin 6:2 Let us go, we pray thee, unto J
2Kin 6:4 And when they came to J, they cut
2Kin 7:15 And they went after them unto J
2Kin 10:33 From J eastward, all the land of
1Chr 6:78 And on the other side J by Jericho
1Chr 6:78 on the east side of J
1Chr 12:15 went over J in the first month
1Chr 12:37 And on the other side of J
1Chr 19:17 all Israel, and passed over J
1Chr 26:30 them of Israel on this side J
2Chr 4:17 In the plain of J did the king
Job 40:23 he can draw up J into his mouth
Ps 42:6 remember thee from the land of J
Ps 114:3 J was driven back
Ps 114:5 thou J, that thou wast driven
Is 9:1 by the way of the sea, beyond J
Jer 12:5 wilt thou do in the swelling of J
Jer 49:19 a lion from the swelling of J
Jer 50:44 of J unto the habitation of the
Eze 47:18 and from the land of Israel by J
Zec 11:3 for the pride of J is spoiled
Mt 3:5 and all the region round about J
Mt 3:6 And were baptized of him in J
Mt 3:13 Jesus from Galilee to J unto John
Mt 4:15 by the way of the sea, beyond J
Mt 4:25 and from Judaea, and from beyond J
Mt 19:1 the coasts of Judaea beyond J
Mk 1:5 baptized of him in the river of J
Mk 1:9 and was baptized of John in J
Mk 3:8 and from Idumaea, and from beyond J
Mk 10:1 Judaea by the farther side of J
Lk 3:3 came into all the country about J
Lk 4:1 of the Holy Ghost returned from J
Jn 1:28 were done in Bethabara beyond J
Jn 3:26 he that was with thee beyond J
Jn 10:40 went away again beyond J into the

**JORIM** *(jo'-rim) Son of Matthat; ancestor of Jesus.*
Lk 3:29 Eliezer, which was the son of J

**JORKOAM** *(jor'-ko-am) A descendant of Hebron.*
1Chr 2:44 begat Raham, the father of J

**JOSABAD** *(jos'-a-bad)* See JOZABAD. *A warrior in David's army.*
1Chr 12:4 and Johanan, and J the Gederathite,

**JOSAPHAT** *(jos'-a-fat)* See JEHOSHAPHAT. *Son of Asa; ancestor of Jesus.*
Mt 1:8 And Asa begat J
Mt 1:8 and J begat Joram

**JOSE** *(jo'-ze)* See JOSES. *Son of Eliezer; ancestor of Jesus.*
Lk 3:29 Which was the son of J, which was

**JOSEDECH** *(jos'-e-dek)* See JOZADAK. *Father of Joshua, the priest.*
Hag 1:1 Judah, and to Joshua the son of J
Hag 1:12 Shealtiel, and Joshua the son of J
Hag 1:14 the spirit of Joshua the son of J
Hag 2:2 Judah, and to Joshua the son of J
Hag 2:4 and be strong, O Joshua, son of J
Zec 6:11 the head of Joshua the son of J

**JOSEPH** *(jo'-zef)* See BARSABAS, JOSEPH'S.
*1. Son of Jacob and Rachel.*
Gen 30:24 And she called his name J
Gen 30:25 to pass, when Rachel had born J
Gen 33:2 after, and Rachel and J hindermost
Gen 33:7 and after came J near and Rachel,

Gen 35:24 sons of Rachel; J, and Benjamin
Gen 37:2 J, being seventeen years old, was
Gen 37:2 J brought unto his father their
Gen 37:3 Now Israel loved J more than all
Gen 37:5 J dreamed a dream, and he told it
Gen 37:13 And Israel said unto J, Do not thy
Gen 37:17 J went after his brethren, and
Gen 37:23 when J was come unto his brethren
Gen 37:23 they stript J out of his coat
Gen 37:28 lifted up J out of the pit, and
Gen 37:28 sold J to the Ishmeelites for
Gen 37:28 and they brought J into Egypt
Gen 37:29 and, behold, J was not in the pit
Gen 37:33 J is without doubt rent in pieces
Gen 39:1 J was brought down to Egypt
Gen 39:2 And the LORD was with J, and he was
Gen 39:4 J found grace in his sight, and he
Gen 39:6 J was a goodly person, and well
Gen 39:7 wife cast her eyes upon J
Gen 39:10 as she spake to J day by day
Gen 39:11 that J went into the house to do
Gen 39:21 But the LORD was with J, and
Gen 40:3 the place where J was bound
Gen 40:4 of the guard charged J with them
Gen 40:6 J came in unto them in the
Gen 40:8 And J said unto them, Do not
Gen 40:9 chief butler told his dream to J
Gen 40:12 J said unto him, This is the
Gen 40:16 was good, he said unto J, I also
Gen 40:18 J answered and said, This is the
Gen 40:22 as J had interpreted to them
Gen 40:23 not the chief butler remember J
Gen 41:14 Then Pharaoh sent and called J
Gen 41:15 And Pharaoh said unto J, I have
Gen 41:16 J answered Pharaoh, saying, It is
Gen 41:17 And Pharaoh said unto J, In my
Gen 41:25 J said unto Pharaoh, The dream of
Gen 41:39 And Pharaoh said unto J, Forasmuch
Gen 41:41 And Pharaoh said unto J, See, I
Gen 41:44 And Pharaoh said unto J, I am
Gen 41:45 J went out over all the land of
Gen 41:46 J was thirty years old when he
Gen 41:46 J went out from the presence of
Gen 41:49 J gathered corn as the sand of
Gen 41:50 unto J were born two sons before
Gen 41:51 And J called the name of the
Gen 41:54 to come, according as J had said
Gen 41:55 unto all the Egyptians, Go unto J
Gen 41:56 J opened all the storehouses, and
Gen 41:57 into Egypt to J for to buy corn
Gen 42:6 J was the governor over the land,
Gen 42:7 J saw his brethren, and he knew
Gen 42:8 J knew his brethren, but they
Gen 42:9 J remembered the dreams which he
Gen 42:14 J said unto them, That is it that
Gen 42:18 J said unto them the third day,
Gen 42:23 knew not that J understood them
Gen 42:25 Then J commanded to fill their
Gen 42:36 J is not, and Simeon is not, and ye
Gen 43:15 down to Egypt, and stood before J
Gen 43:16 when J saw Benjamin with them, he
Gen 43:17 And the man did as J bade
Gen 43:25 present against J came at noon
Gen 43:26 when J came home, they brought
Gen 43:30 And J made haste
Gen 44:2 to the word that J had spoken
Gen 44:4 J said unto his steward, Up,
Gen 44:15 J said unto them, What deed is
Gen 45:1 Then J could not refrain himself
Gen 45:1 while J made himself known unto
Gen 45:3 J said unto his brethren
Gen 45:3 I am J; doth my father yet
Gen 45:4 J said unto his brethren, Come
Gen 45:4 I am J your brother, whom ye sold
Gen 45:9 unto him, Thus saith thy son J
Gen 45:17 And Pharaoh said unto J, Say unto
Gen 45:21 J gave them wagons, according to
Gen 45:26 J is yet alive, and he is governor
Gen 45:27 they told him all the words of J
Gen 45:27 which J had sent to carry him
Gen 45:28 J my son is yet alive
Gen 46:4 J shall put his hand upon thine
Gen 46:19 Jacob's wife; J, and Benjamin
Gen 46:20 unto J in the land of Egypt were
Gen 46:27 And the sons of J, which were born
Gen 46:28 he sent Judah before him unto J
Gen 46:29 J made ready his chariot, and went
Gen 46:30 And Israel said unto J, Now let me
Gen 46:31 J said unto his brethren, and unto
Gen 47:1 Then J came and told Pharaoh, and
Gen 47:5 And Pharaoh spake unto J, saying,
Gen 47:7 J brought in Jacob his father, and
Gen 47:11 J placed his father and his
Gen 47:12 J nourished his father, and his
Gen 47:14 J gathered up all the money that
Gen 47:14 and J brought the money into
Gen 47:15 all the Egyptians came unto J
Gen 47:16 And J said, Give your cattle
Gen 47:17 they brought their cattle unto J
Gen 47:17 J gave them bread in exchange for
Gen 47:20 J bought all the land of Egypt
Gen 47:23 Then J said unto the people,
Gen 47:26 J made it a law over the land of
Gen 47:29 and he called his son J, and said
Gen 48:1 these things, that one told J
Gen 48:2 thy son J cometh unto thee
Gen 48:3 And Jacob said unto J, God
Gen 48:9 J said unto his father, They are
Gen 48:11 And Israel said unto J, I had not
Gen 48:12 J brought them out from between
Gen 48:13 J took them both, Ephraim in his
Gen 48:15 And he blessed J, and said, God,
Gen 48:17 when J saw that his father laid
Gen 48:18 J said unto his father, Not so,
Gen 48:21 And Israel said unto J, Behold, I
Gen 49:22 J is a fruitful bough, even a
Gen 49:26 they shall be on the head of J
Gen 50:1 J fell upon his father's face, and
Gen 50:2 J commanded his servants the
Gen 50:4 J spake unto the house of Pharaoh
Gen 50:7 J went up to bury his father
Gen 50:8 And all the house of J, and his
Gen 50:14 J returned into Egypt, he, and his
Gen 50:15 J will peradventure hate us, and
Gen 50:16 And they sent a messenger unto J
Gen 50:17 So shall ye say unto J, Forgive,
Gen 50:17 J wept when they spake unto him
Gen 50:19 J said unto them, Fear not
Gen 50:22 J dwelt in Egypt, he, and his
Gen 50:22 J lived an hundred and ten years
Gen 50:23 J saw Ephraim's children of the
Gen 50:24 J said unto his brethren, I die
Gen 50:25 J took an oath of the children of
Gen 50:26 So J died, being an hundred and
Ex 1:5 for J was in Egypt already
Ex 1:6 J died, and all his brethren, and
Ex 1:8 king over Egypt, which knew not J
Ex 13:19 took the bones of J with him
Num 27:1 families of Manasseh the son of J
Num 32:33 tribe of Manasseh the son of J
Num 34:23 The prince of the children of J
Num 36:12 the sons of Manasseh the son of J
Deut 27:12 Levi, and Judah, and Issachar, and J
Josh 14:4 the children of J were two tribes
Josh 16:1 the lot of the children of J fell
Josh 16:4 So the children of J, Manasseh and
Josh 17:1 for he was the firstborn of J
Josh 17:2 the son of J by their families
Josh 17:14 the children of J spake unto
Josh 17:16 And the children of J said
Josh 24:32 And the bones of J, which the
1Chr 2:2 Dan, J, and Benjamin, Naphtali,
Ps 105:17 He sent a man before them, even J
Jn 4:5 that Jacob gave to his son J
Acts 7:9 with envy, sold J into Egypt
Acts 7:13 at the second time J was made
Acts 7:14 Then sent J, and called his father
Acts 7:18 king arose, which knew not J
Heb 11:21 dying, blessed both the sons of J
Heb 11:22 By faith J, when he died, made

*2. Descendants of Joseph 1.*

Num 1:10 Of the children of J
Num 1:32 Of the children of J, namely, of
Num 13:11 Of the tribe of J, namely, of the
Num 26:28 The sons of J after their
Num 26:37 sons of J after their families
Num 36:1 of the families of the sons of J
Num 36:5 of the sons of J hath said well
Deut 33:13 of J he said, Blessed of the LORD
Deut 33:16 blessing come upon the head of J
Josh 17:17 Joshua spake unto the house of J
Josh 18:5 the house of J shall abide in
Josh 18:11 of Judah and the children of J
Josh 24:32 inheritance of the children of J
Judg 1:22 And the house of J, they also went
Judg 1:23 the house of J sent to descry
Judg 1:35 hand of the house of J prevailed
2Sa 19:20 this day of all the house of J to
1Kin 11:28 all the charge of the house of J
1Chr 5:1 the sons of J the son of Israel
1Chr 7:29 children of J the son of Israel
Ps 77:15 people, the sons of Jacob and J
Ps 78:67 he refused the tabernacle of J
Ps 80:1 thou that leadest J like a flock
Ps 81:5 he ordained in J for a testimony
Eze 37:16 stick, and write upon it, For J
Eze 37:19 I will take the stick of J
Eze 47:13 J shall have two portions
Eze 48:32 and one gate of J, one gate of
Amos 5:6 out like fire in the house of J
Amos 5:15 be gracious unto the remnant of J
Amos 6:6 grieved for the affliction of J
Obad 18 a fire, and the house of J a flame
Zec 10:6 and I will save the house of J
Rev 7:8 Of the tribe of J were sealed

*3. A spy sent to the Promised Land.*

Num 13:7 of Issachar, Igal the son of J

*4. A son of Asaph.*

1Chr 25:2 Zaccur, and J, and Nethaniah, and
1Chr 25:9 lot came forth for Asaph to J

*5. Married a foreigner in exile.*

Ezr 10:42 Shallum, Amariah, and J

*6. A priest.*

Neh 12:14 Jonathan; of Shebaniah, J

*7. Husband of Mary, the mother of Jesus.*

Mt 1:16 Jacob begat J the husband of Mary
Mt 1:18 his mother Mary was espoused to J
Mt 1:19 Then J her husband, being a just
Mt 1:20 unto him in a dream, saying, J
Mt 1:24 Then J being raised from sleep
Mt 2:13 Lord appeareth to J in a dream
Mt 2:19 in a dream to J in Egypt,
Lk 1:27 to a man whose name was J
Lk 2:4 J also went up from Galilee, out
Lk 2:16 with haste, and found Mary, and J
Lk 2:33 And J and his mother marvelled at
Lk 2:43 and J and his mother knew not of it
Lk 3:23 (as was supposed) the son of J
Jn 1:45 Jesus of Nazareth, the son of J
Jn 6:42 Is not this Jesus, the son of J

*8. A disciple of Jesus.*

Mt 27:57 a rich man of Arimathaea, named J
Mt 27:59 when J had taken the body, he
Mk 15:43 J of Arimathaea, an honourable
Mk 15:45 centurion, he gave the body to J
Lk 23:50 behold, there was a man named J
Jn 19:38 after this J of Arimathaea, being

*9. Son of Mattathias; ancestor of Jesus.*

Lk 3:24 of Janna, which was the son of J

*10. Son of Juda; ancestor of Jesus.*

Lk 3:26 of Semei, which was the son of J

*11. Son of Jonan; ancestor of Jesus.*

Lk 3:30 of Juda, which was the son of J

*12. A nominee for Judas' apostleship.*

Acts 1:23 J called Barsabas, who was

**JOSEPH'S** *(jo'-zefs)*

*1. Refers to Joseph 1.*

Gen 37:31 And they took J coat, and killed a
Gen 39:5 the Egyptian's house for J sake
Gen 39:6 he left all that he had in J hand
Gen 39:20 J master took him, and put him
Gen 39:22 of the prison committed to J hand
Gen 41:42 his hand, and put it upon J hand
Gen 41:45 And Pharaoh called J name
Gen 42:3 J ten brethren went down to buy
Gen 42:4 J brother, Jacob sent not with
Gen 42:6 J brethren came, and bowed down
Gen 43:17 man brought the men into J house
Gen 43:18 they were brought into J house
Gen 43:19 near to the steward of J house
Gen 43:24 man brought the men into J house
Gen 44:14 and his brethren came to J house
Gen 45:16 saying, J brethren are come
Gen 48:8 And Israel beheld J sons, and said,
Gen 50:15 when J brethren saw that their
Gen 50:23 were brought up upon J knees
1Chr 5:2 but the birthright was J
Acts 7:13 J kindred was made known unto

*2. Refers to Joseph 7.*

Lk 4:22 And they said, Is not this J son

**JOSES** *(jo'-zez)* See JOSE.

*1. A brother of Jesus.*

Mt 13:55 and his brethren, James, and J
Mk 6:3 Mary, the brother of James, and J

*2. Brother of James the younger.*

Mt 27:56 and Mary the mother of James and J
Mk 15:40 mother of James the less and of J
Mk 15:47 Mary the mother of J beheld where

3. *Same as Barnabas.*
Acts 4:36 And J, who by the apostles was

**JOSHAH** *(jo'-shah) A descendant of Simeon.*
1Chr 4:34 Jamlech, and J the son of Amaziah,

**JOSHAPHAT** *(josh'-a-fat)* See JEHOSHAPHAT, JOSAPHAT. *A "mighty man" of David.*
1Chr 11:43 of Maachah, and J the Mithnite,

**JOSHAVIAH** *(josh-a-vi'-ah) A "mighty man" of David.*
1Chr 11:46 the Mahavite, and Jeribai, and J

**JOSHBEKASHAH** *(josh-bek'-a-shah) A sanctuary servant.*
1Chr 25:4 Giddalti, and Romamti-ezer, J
1Chr 25:24 The seventeenth to J, he, his

**JOSHUA** *(josh'-u-ah)* See HOSEA, HOSHEA, JEHOSHUAH, JESHUA, JESHUAH, JESUS, OSEA, OSHEA.
1. *Son of Nun.*
Ex 17:9 And Moses said unto J, Choose us
Ex 17:10 So J did as Moses had said to him
Ex 17:13 J discomfited Amalek and his
Ex 17:14 and rehearse it in the ears of J
Ex 24:13 Moses rose up, and his minister J
Ex 32:17 when J heard the noise of the
Ex 33:11 but his servant J, the son of Nun
Num 11:28 J the son of Nun, the servant of
Num 14:6 J the son of Nun, and Caleb the
Num 14:30 of Jephunneh, and J the son of Nun
Num 14:38 But J the son of Nun, and Caleb
Num 26:65 of Jephunneh, and J the son of Nun
Num 27:18 Take thee J the son of Nun, a man
Num 27:22 and he took J, and set him before
Num 32:12 the Kenezite, and J the son of Nun
Num 32:28 J the son of Nun, and the chief
Num 34:17 the priest, and J the son of Nun
Deut 1:38 But J the son of Nun, which
Deut 3:21 I commanded J at that time,
Deut 3:28 But charge J, and encourage him,
Deut 31:3 and J, he shall go over before
Deut 31:7 And Moses called unto J, and said
Deut 31:14 call J, and present yourselves in
Deut 31:14 J went, and presented themselves
Deut 31:23 he gave J the son of Nun a charge
Deut 34:9 J the son of Nun was full of the
Josh 1:1 LORD spake unto J the son of Nun
Josh 1:10 Then J commanded the officers of
Josh 1:12 the tribe of Manasseh, spake J
Josh 1:16 And they answered J, saying, All
Josh 2:1 J the son of Nun sent out of
Josh 2:23 came to J the son of Nun, and told
Josh 2:24 And they said unto J, Truly the
Josh 3:1 J rose early in the morning
Josh 3:5 J said unto the people, Sanctify
Josh 3:6 J spake unto the priests, saying,
Josh 3:7 And the LORD said unto J, This day
Josh 3:9 J said unto the children of
Josh 3:10 J said, Hereby ye shall know that
Josh 4:1 that the LORD spake unto J
Josh 4:4 Then J called the twelve men,
Josh 4:5 J said unto them, Pass over
Josh 4:8 of Israel did so as J commanded
Josh 4:8 Jordan, as the LORD spake unto J
Josh 4:9 J set up twelve stones in the
Josh 4:10 that the LORD commanded J to
Josh 4:10 to all that Moses commanded J
Josh 4:14 J in the sight of all Israel
Josh 4:15 And the LORD spake unto J, saying,
Josh 4:17 J therefore commanded the priests
Josh 4:20 of Jordan, did J pitch in Gilgal
Josh 5:2 At that time the LORD said unto J
Josh 5:3 J made him sharp knives, and
Josh 5:4 is the cause why J did circumcise
Josh 5:7 their stead, them J circumcised
Josh 5:9 And the LORD said unto J, This day
Josh 5:13 when J was by Jericho, that he
Josh 5:13 J went unto him, and said unto him
Josh 5:14 J fell on his face to the earth,
Josh 5:15 of the LORD's host said unto J
Josh 5:15 And J did so
Josh 6:2 And the LORD said unto J, See, I
Josh 6:6 J the son of Nun called the
Josh 6:8 when J had spoken unto the people
Josh 6:10 J had commanded the people,
Josh 6:12 J rose early in the morning, and
Josh 6:16 J said unto the people, Shout
Josh 6:22 But J had said unto the two men
Josh 6:25 J saved Rahab the harlot alive,
Josh 6:25 which J sent to spy out Jericho
Josh 6:26 J adjured them at that time,
Josh 6:27 So the LORD was with J
Josh 7:2 J sent men from Jericho to Ai,
Josh 7:3 And they returned to J, and said
Josh 7:6 J rent his clothes, and fell to
Josh 7:7 J said, Alas, O Lord GOD,
Josh 7:10 And the LORD said unto J, Get thee
Josh 7:16 So J rose up early in the morning
Josh 7:19 J said unto Achan, My son, give,
Josh 7:20 And Achan answered J, and said,
Josh 7:22 So J sent messengers, and they ran
Josh 7:23 the tent, and brought them unto J
Josh 7:24 And J, and all Israel with him,
Josh 7:25 J said, Why hast thou troubled us
Josh 8:1 And the LORD said unto J, Fear not
Josh 8:3 So J arose, and all the people of
Josh 8:3 J chose out thirty thousand
Josh 8:9 J therefore sent them forth
Josh 8:9 but J lodged that night among the
Josh 8:10 J rose up early in the morning,
Josh 8:13 J went that night into the midst
Josh 8:15 And J and all Israel made as if
Josh 8:16 and they pursued after J, and were
Josh 8:18 And the LORD said unto J, Stretch
Josh 8:18 J stretched out the spear that he
Josh 8:21 And when J and all Israel saw that
Josh 8:23 took alive, and brought him to J
Josh 8:26 For J drew not his hand back,
Josh 8:27 of the LORD which he commanded J
Josh 8:28 J burnt Ai, and made it an heap
Josh 8:29 J commanded that they should take
Josh 8:30 Then J built an altar unto the
Josh 8:35 which J read not before all the
Josh 9:2 together, to fight with J
Josh 9:3 of Gibeon heard what J had done
Josh 9:6 they went to J unto the camp at
Josh 9:8 And they said unto J, We are thy
Josh 9:8 J said unto them, Who are ye
Josh 9:15 J made peace with them, and made a
Josh 9:22 J called for them, and he spake
Josh 9:24 And they answered J, and said,
Josh 9:27 J made them that day hewers of
Josh 10:1 had heard how J had taken Ai
Josh 10:4 for it hath made peace with J
Josh 10:6 sent unto J to the camp to Gilgal
Josh 10:7 So J ascended from Gilgal, he, and
Josh 10:8 And the LORD said unto J, Fear
Josh 10:9 J therefore came unto them
Josh 10:12 Then spake J to the LORD in the
Josh 10:15 J returned, and all Israel with
Josh 10:17 And it was told J, saying, The
Josh 10:18 J said, Roll great stones upon
Josh 10:20 And it came to pass, when J
Josh 10:21 camp to J at Makkedah in peace
Josh 10:22 Then said J, Open the mouth of
Josh 10:24 brought out those kings unto J
Josh 10:24 that J called for all the men of
Josh 10:25 J said unto them, Fear not, nor
Josh 10:26 afterward J smote them, and slew
Josh 10:27 that J commanded, and they took
Josh 10:28 that day J took Makkedah, and
Josh 10:29 Then J passed from Makkedah, and
Josh 10:31 J passed from Libnah, and all
Josh 10:33 J smote him and his people, until
Josh 10:34 from Lachish J passed unto Eglon,
Josh 10:36 J went up from Eglon, and all
Josh 10:38 J returned, and all Israel with
Josh 10:40 So J smote all the country of the
Josh 10:41 J smote them from Kadesh-barnea
Josh 10:42 their land did J take at one time
Josh 10:43 J returned, and all Israel with
Josh 11:6 And the LORD said unto J, Be not
Josh 11:7 So J came, and all the people of
Josh 11:9 J did unto them as the LORD bade
Josh 11:10 J at that time turned back, and
Josh 11:12 did J take, and smote them with
Josh 11:13 that did J burn
Josh 11:15 Moses command J, and so did J
Josh 11:16 So J took all that land, the
Josh 11:18 J made war a long time with all
Josh 11:21 And at that time came J, and cut
Josh 11:21 J destroyed them utterly with
Josh 11:23 So J took the whole land,
Josh 11:23 J gave it for an inheritance unto
Josh 12:7 the kings of the country which J
Josh 12:7 which J gave unto the tribes of
Josh 13:1 Now J was old and stricken in
Josh 14:1 J the son of Nun, and the heads of
Josh 14:6 of Judah came unto J in Gilgal
Josh 14:13 J blessed him, and gave unto Caleb
Josh 15:13 the commandment of the LORD to J
Josh 17:4 before J the son of Nun, and
Josh 17:14 children of Joseph spake unto J
Josh 17:15 J answered them, If thou be a
Josh 17:17 J spake unto the house of Joseph,
Josh 18:3 J said unto the children of
Josh 18:8 J charged them that went to
Josh 18:9 came again to J to the host at
Josh 18:10 J cast lots for them in Shiloh
Josh 18:10 there J divided the land unto the
Josh 19:49 to J the son of Nun among them
Josh 19:51 J the son of Nun, and the heads of
Josh 20:1 The LORD also spake unto J
Josh 21:1 unto J the son of Nun, and unto
Josh 22:1 Then J called the Reubenites, and
Josh 22:6 So J blessed them, and sent them
Josh 22:7 the other half thereof gave J
Josh 22:7 when J sent them away also unto
Josh 23:1 that J waxed old and stricken in
Josh 23:2 J called for all Israel, and for
Josh 24:1 J gathered all the tribes of
Josh 24:2 J said unto all the people, Thus
Josh 24:19 J said unto the people, Ye cannot
Josh 24:21 And the people said unto J
Josh 24:22 J said unto the people, Ye are
Josh 24:24 And the people said unto J
Josh 24:25 So J made a covenant with the
Josh 24:26 J wrote these words in the book
Josh 24:27 J said unto all the people,
Josh 24:28 So J let the people depart, every
Josh 24:29 that J the son of Nun, the
Josh 24:31 served the LORD all the days of J
Josh 24:31 of the elders that overlived J
Judg 1:1 the death of J it came to pass
Judg 2:6 when J had let the people go, the
Judg 2:7 served the LORD all the days of J
Judg 2:7 of the elders that outlived J
Judg 2:8 J the son of Nun, the servant of
Judg 2:21 nations which J left when he died
Judg 2:23 he them into the hand of J
1Kin 16:34 he spake by J the son of Nun
2. *A Bethshemite.*
1Sa 6:14 the cart came into the field of J
1Sa 6:18 unto this day in the field of J
3. *A governor of Jerusalem.*
2Kin 23:8 of J the governor of the city
4. *A High Priest.*
Hag 1:1 to J the son of Josedech, the
Hag 1:12 J the son of Josedech, the high
Hag 1:14 the spirit of J the son of
Hag 2:2 to J the son of Josedech, the
Hag 2:4 and be strong, O J, son of
Zec 3:1 he shewed me J the high priest
Zec 3:3 Now J was clothed with filthy
Zec 3:6 of the LORD protested unto J
Zec 3:8 O J the high priest, thou, and thy
Zec 3:9 stone that I have laid before J
Zec 6:11 the head of J the son of Josedech

**JOSIAH** *(jo-si'-ah)* See JOSIAS.
1. *A king of Judah.*
1Kin 13:2 the house of David, J by name
2Kin 21:24 made J his son king in his stead
2Kin 21:26 J his son reigned in his stead
2Kin 22:1 J was eight years old when he
2Kin 22:3 in the eighteenth year of king J
2Kin 23:16 as J turned himself, he spied the
2Kin 23:19 J took away, and did to them
2Kin 23:23 in the eighteenth year of king J
2Kin 23:24 did J put away, that he might
2Kin 23:28 Now the rest of the acts of J
2Kin 23:29 and king J went against him
2Kin 23:30 land took Jehoahaz the son of J
2Kin 23:34 made Eliakim the son of J king in
2Kin 23:34 king in the room of J his father
1Chr 3:14 Amon his son, J his son
1Chr 3:15 And the sons of J were, the
2Chr 33:25 made J his son king in his stead
2Chr 34:1 J was eight years old when he
2Chr 34:33 J took away all the abominations
2Chr 35:1 Moreover J kept a passover unto
2Chr 35:7 J gave to the people, of the
2Chr 35:16 to the commandment of king J
2Chr 35:18 keep such a passover as J kept
2Chr 35:19 reign of J was this passover kept
2Chr 35:20 when J had prepared the temple,
2Chr 35:20 and J went out against him
2Chr 35:22 Nevertheless J would not turn his

2Chr 35:23 And the archers shot at king *J*
2Chr 35:24 Judah and Jerusalem mourned for *J*
2Chr 35:25 And Jeremiah lamented for *J*
2Chr 35:25 the singing women spake of *J* in
2Chr 35:26 Now the rest of the acts of *J*
2Chr 36:1 land took Jehoahaz the son of *J*
Jer 1:2 *J* the son of Amon king of Judah
Jer 1:3 the son of *J* king of Judah
Jer 1:3 the son of *J* king of Judah
Jer 3:6 unto me in the days of *J* the king
Jer 22:11 the son of *J* king of Judah
Jer 22:11 reigned instead of *J* his father
Jer 22:18 the son of *J* king of Judah
Jer 25:1 the son of *J* king of Judah
Jer 25:3 From the thirteenth year of *J* the
Jer 26:1 of *J* king of Judah came this word
Jer 27:1 of *J* king of Judah came this word
Jer 35:1 the son of *J* king of Judah
Jer 36:1 the son of *J* king of Judah
Jer 36:2 unto thee, from the days of *J*
Jer 36:9 the son of *J* king of Judah
Jer 37:1 king Zedekiah the son of *J*
Jer 45:1 the son of *J* king of Judah
Jer 46:2 the son of *J* king of Judah
Zeph 1:1 in the days of *J* the son of Amon,

*2. A son of Zephaniah.*
Zec 6:10 house of *J* the son of Zephaniah

**JOSIAS** *(jo-si'-as)* See JOSIAH. *Son of Amon; ancestor of Jesus.*
Mt 1:10 and Amon begat *J*
Mt 1:11 *J* begat Jechonias and his brethren

**JOSIBIAH** *(jos-ib-i'-ah) A Simeonite.*
1Chr 4:35 And Joel, and Jehu the son of *J*

**JOSIPHIAH** *(jos-if-i'-ah) A family of exiles.*
Ezr 8:10 the son of *J*, and with him an

**JOT**
Mt 5:18 one *j* or one tittle shall in no

**JOTBAH** *(jot'-bah) A place near Hebron.*
2Kin 21:19 the daughter of Haruz of *J*

**JOTBATH** *(jot'-bath)* See JOTBATHAH. *An encampment during the Exodus.*
Deut 10:7 and from Gudgodah to *J*, a land of

**JOTBATHAH** *(jot'-ba-thah)* See JOTBATH. *Same as Jotbath.*
Num 33:33 Hor-hagidgad, and pitched in *J*
Num 33:34 And they removed from *J*, and

**JOTHAM** *(jo'-tham)* See JOATHAM.
*1. A son of Gideon.*
Judg 9:5 notwithstanding yet *J* the
Judg 9:7 And when they told it to *J*
Judg 9:21 *J* ran away, and fled, and went to
Judg 9:57 curse of *J* the son of Jerubbaal

*2. Father of King Ahaz.*
2Kin 15:5 *J* the king's son was over the
2Kin 15:7 *J* his son reigned in his stead
2Kin 15:30 year of *J* the son of Uzziah
2Kin 15:32 Remaliah king of Israel began *J*
2Kin 15:36 Now the rest of the acts of *J*
2Kin 15:38 *J* slept with his fathers, and was
2Kin 16:1 of *J* king of Judah began to reign
1Chr 3:12 son, Azariah his son, *J* his son,
1Chr 5:17 in the days of *J* king of Judah
2Chr 26:21 *J* his son was over the king's
2Chr 26:23 *J* his son reigned in his stead
2Chr 27:1 *J* was twenty and five years old
2Chr 27:6 So *J* became mighty, because he
2Chr 27:7 Now the rest of the acts of *J*
2Chr 27:9 *J* slept with his fathers, and they
Is 1:1 in the days of Uzziah, *J*, Ahaz,
Is 7:1 in the days of Ahaz the son of *J*
Hos 1:1 Beeri, in the days of Uzziah, *J*
Mic 1:1 the Morasthite in the days of *J*

*3. A descendant of Caleb.*
1Chr 2:47 Regem, and *J*, and Gesham, and Pelet,

**JOURNEY**
Gen 24:21 had made his *j* prosperous or not
Gen 29:1 Jacob went on his *j*, and came
Gen 30:36 set three days' *j* betwixt himself
Gen 31:23 pursued after him seven days' *j*
Gen 33:12 And he said, Let us take our *j*
Gen 46:1 Israel took his *j* with all that
Ex 3:18 three days' *j* into the wilderness
Ex 5:3 three days' *j* into the desert, and
Ex 8:27 three days' *j* into the wilderness
Ex 13:20 And they took their *j* from Succoth
Ex 16:1 And they took their *j* from Elim
Num 9:10 dead body, or be in a *j* afar off
Num 9:13 that is clean, and is not in a *j*
Num 10:6 the south side shall take their *j*
Num 10:13 they first took their *j* according
Num 10:33 mount of the LORD three days' *j*
Num 10:33 before them in the three days' *j*
Num 11:31 as it were a day's *j* on this side
Num 11:31 were a day's *j* on the other side
Num 33:8 went three days' *j* in the
Num 33:12 they took their *j* out of the
Deut 1:2 (There are eleven days' *j* from
Deut 1:7 Turn you, and take your *j*, and go
Deut 1:40 take your *j* into the wilderness
Deut 2:1 took our *j* into the wilderness by
Deut 2:24 Rise ye up, take your *j*, and pass
Deut 10:6 children of Israel took their *j*
Deut 10:11 take thy *j* before the people,
Josh 9:11 Take victuals with you for the *j*
Josh 9:13 old by reason of the very long *j*
Judg 4:9 notwithstanding the *j* that thou
1Sa 15:18 And the LORD sent thee on a *j*
2Sa 11:10 Uriah, Camest thou not from thy *j*
1Kin 18:27 he is pursuing, or he is in a *j*
1Kin 19:4 a day's *j* into the wilderness
1Kin 19:7 because the *j* is too great for
2Kin 3:9 a compass of seven days' *j*
2Chr 1:13 Then Solomon came from his *j* to
Neh 2:6 him,) For how long shall thy *j* be
Prov 7:19 not at home, he is gone a long *j*
Jonah 3:3 great city of three days' *j*
Jonah 3:4 to enter into the city a day's *j*
Mt 10:10 Nor scrip for your *j*, neither two
Mt 25:15 and straightway took his *j*
Mk 6:8 should take nothing for their *j*
Mk 13:34 of man is as a man taking a far *j*
Lk 2:44 in the company, went a day's *j*
Lk 9:3 them, Take nothing for your *j*
Lk 11:6 of mine in his *j* is come to me
Lk 15:13 took his *j* into a far country, and
Jn 4:6 being wearied with his *j*
Acts 1:12 from Jerusalem a sabbath day's *j*
Acts 10:9 morrow, as they went on their *j*
Acts 22:6 to pass, that, as I made my *j*
Rom 1:10 I might have a prosperous *j* by
Rom 15:24 Whensoever I take my *j* into Spain
Rom 15:24 for I trust to see you in my *j*
1Cor 16:6 me on my *j* whithersoever I go
Titus 3:13 and Apollos on their *j* diligently
3Jn 6 on their *j* after a godly sort

**JOURNEYED**
Gen 11:2 as they *j* from the east, that
Gen 12:9 And Abram *j*, going on still toward
Gen 13:11 and Lot *j* east
Gen 20:1 Abraham *j* from thence toward the
Gen 33:17 Jacob *j* to Succoth, and built him
Gen 35:5 And they *j*: and the terror
Gen 35:16 And they *j* from Beth-el
Gen 35:21 And Israel *j*, and spread his tent
Ex 12:37 the children of Israel *j* from
Ex 17:1 of the children of Israel *j* from
Ex 40:37 then they *j* not till the day that
Num 9:17 that the children of Israel *j*
Num 9:18 the LORD the children of Israel *j*
Num 9:19 the charge of the LORD, and *j* not
Num 9:20 commandment of the LORD they *j*
Num 9:21 up in the morning, then they *j*
Num 9:21 the cloud was taken up, they *j*
Num 9:22 abode in their tents, and *j* not
Num 9:22 but when it was taken up, they *j*
Num 9:23 commandment of the LORD they *j*
Num 11:35 And the people *j* from
Num 12:15 the people *j* not till Miriam was
Num 20:22 *j* from Kadesh, and came unto mount
Num 21:4 they *j* from mount Hor by the way
Num 21:11 they *j* from Oboth, and pitched at
Num 33:22 they *j* from Rissah, and pitched in
Deut 10:7 From thence they *j* unto Gudgodah
Josh 9:17 And the children of Israel *j*
Judg 17:8 to the house of Micah, as he *j*
Lk 10:33 But a certain Samaritan, as he *j*
Acts 9:3 And as he *j*, he came near Damascus
Acts 9:7 the men which *j* with him stood
Acts 26:13 about me and them which *j* with me

**JOURNEYS**
Gen 13:3 he went on his *j* from the south
Ex 17:1 wilderness of Sin, after their *j*
Ex 40:36 Israel went onward in all their *j*
Ex 40:38 of Israel, throughout all their *j*
Num 10:6 shall blow an alarm for their *j*
Num 10:12 children of Israel took their *j*
Num 33:1 These are the *j* of the children
Num 33:2 goings out according to their *j*
Num 33:2 these are their *j* according to

**JOY**
1Sa 18:6 king Saul, with tabrets, with *j*
1Kin 1:40 pipes, and rejoiced with great *j*
1Chr 12:40 for there was *j* in Israel
1Chr 15:16 by lifting up the voice with *j*
1Chr 15:25 of the house of Obed-edom with *j*
1Chr 29:9 king also rejoiced with great *j*
1Chr 29:17 now have I seen with *j* thy people
2Chr 20:27 to go again to Jerusalem with *j*
2Chr 30:26 So there was great *j* in Jerusalem
Ezr 3:12 and many shouted aloud for *j*
Ezr 3:13 the noise of the shout of *j* from
Ezr 6:16 of this house of God with *j*
Ezr 6:22 bread seven days with *j*
Neh 8:10 for the *j* of the LORD is your
Neh 12:43 made them rejoice with great *j*
Neh 12:43 so that the *j* of Jerusalem was
Est 8:16 Jews had light, and gladness, and *j*
Est 8:17 his decree came, the Jews had *j*
Est 9:22 turned unto them from sorrow to *j*
Est 9:22 make them days of feasting and *j*
Job 8:19 Behold, this is the *j* of his way
Job 20:5 the *j* of the hypocrite but for a
Job 29:13 the widow's heart to sing for *j*
Job 33:26 and he shall see his face with *j*
Job 38:7 all the sons of God shouted for *j*
Job 41:22 is turned into *j* before him
Ps 5:11 let them ever shout for *j*
Ps 16:11 in thy presence is fulness of *j*
Ps 21:1 The king shall *j* in thy strength,
Ps 27:6 in his tabernacle sacrifices of *j*
Ps 30:5 but *j* cometh in the morning
Ps 32:11 and shout for *j*, all ye that are
Ps 35:27 Let them shout for *j*, and be glad,
Ps 42:4 house of God, with the voice of *j*
Ps 43:4 of God, unto God my exceeding *j*
Ps 48:2 the *j* of the whole earth, is
Ps 51:8 Make me to hear *j* and gladness
Ps 51:12 unto me the *j* of thy salvation
Ps 65:13 they shout for *j*, they also sing
Ps 67:4 the nations be glad and sing for *j*
Ps 105:43 brought forth his people with *j*
Ps 126:5 that sow in tears shall reap in *j*
Ps 132:9 and let thy saints shout for *j*
Ps 132:16 saints shall shout aloud for *j*
Ps 137:6 not Jerusalem above my chief *j*
Prov 12:20 to the counsellors of peace is *j*
Prov 14:10 doth not intermeddle with his *j*
Prov 15:21 Folly is *j* to him that is
Prov 15:23 A man hath *j* by the answer of his
Prov 17:21 and the father of a fool hath no *j*
Prov 21:15 It is *j* to the just to do
Prov 23:24 a wise child shall have *j* of him
Eccl 2:10 withheld not my heart from any *j*
Eccl 2:26 sight wisdom, and knowledge, and *j*
Eccl 5:20 him in the *j* of his heart
Eccl 9:7 Go thy way, eat thy bread with *j*
Is 9:3 nation, and not increased the *j*
Is 9:3 they *j* before thee according to
Is 9:3 according to the *j* in harvest
Is 9:17 have no *j* in their young men
Is 12:3 Therefore with *j* shall ye draw
Is 16:10 *j* out of the plentiful field
Is 22:13 And behold *j* and gladness, slaying
Is 24:8 the *j* of the harp ceaseth
Is 24:11 all *j* is darkened, the mirth of
Is 29:19 increase their *j* in the LORD
Is 32:13 houses of *j* in the joyous city
Is 32:14 a *j* of wild asses, a pasture of
Is 35:2 and rejoice even with *j* and
Is 35:10 everlasting *j* upon their heads
Is 35:10 they shall obtain *j* and gladness,
Is 51:3 *j* and gladness shall be found
Is 51:11 everlasting *j* shall be upon their
Is 51:11 they shall obtain gladness and *j*
Is 52:9 Break forth into *j*, sing together
Is 55:12 For ye shall go out with *j*
Is 60:15 a *j* of many generations
Is 61:3 the oil of *j* for mourning, the
Is 61:7 everlasting *j* shall be unto them
Is 65:14 shall sing for *j* of heart
Is 65:18 a rejoicing, and her people a *j*
Is 65:19 in Jerusalem, and *j* in my people
Is 66:5 but he shall appear to your *j*
Is 66:10 rejoice for *j* with her, all ye

Jer 15:16 and thy word was unto me the *j*
Jer 31:13 I will turn their mourning into *j*
Jer 33:9 And it shall be to me a name of *j*
Jer 33:11 The voice of *j*, and the voice of
Jer 48:27 of him, thou skippedst for *j*
Jer 48:33 And *j* and gladness is taken from
Jer 49:25 praise not left, the city of my *j*
Lam 2:15 beauty, The *j* of the whole earth
Lam 5:15 The *j* of our heart is ceased
Eze 24:25 the *j* of their glory, the desire
Eze 36:5 with the *j* of all their heart
Hos 9:1 Rejoice not, O Israel, for *j*
Joel 1:12 because *j* is withered away from
Joel 1:16 cut off before our eyes, yea, *j*
Hab 3:18 I will *j* in the God of my
Zeph 3:17 he will rejoice over thee with *j*
Zeph 3:17 he will *j* over thee with singing
Zec 8:19 shall be to the house of Judah *j*
Mt 2:10 rejoiced with exceeding great *j*
Mt 13:20 word, and anon with *j* receiveth it
Mt 13:44 for *j* thereof goeth and selleth
Mt 25:21 enter thou into the *j* of thy lord
Mt 25:23 enter thou into the *j* of thy lord
Mt 28:8 sepulchre with fear and great *j*
Lk 1:14 And thou shalt have *j* and gladness
Lk 1:44 the babe leaped in my womb for *j*
Lk 2:10 bring you good tidings of great *j*
Lk 6:23 ye in that day, and leap for *j*
Lk 8:13 hear, receive the word with *j*
Lk 10:17 the seventy returned again with *j*
Lk 15:7 that likewise *j* shall be in
Lk 15:10 there is *j* in the presence of the
Lk 24:41 while they yet believed not for *j*
Lk 24:52 to Jerusalem with great *j*
Jn 3:29 this my *j* therefore is fulfilled
Jn 15:11 that my *j* might remain in you, and
Jn 15:11 that your *j* might be full
Jn 16:20 sorrow shall be turned into *j*
Jn 16:21 for *j* that a man is born into the
Jn 16:22 your *j* no man taketh from you
Jn 16:24 receive, that your *j* may be full
Jn 17:13 have my *j* fulfilled in themselves
Acts 2:28 me full of *j* with thy countenance
Acts 8:8 And there was great *j* in that city
Acts 13:52 the disciples were filled with *j*
Acts 15:3 they caused great *j* unto all the
Acts 20:24 I might finish my course with *j*
Rom 5:11 but we also *j* in God through our
Rom 14:17 and peace, and *j* in the Holy Ghost
Rom 15:13 God of hope fill you with all *j*
Rom 15:32 you with *j* by the will of God
2Cor 1:24 faith, but are helpers of your *j*
2Cor 2:3 that my *j* is the *j* of you all
2Cor 2:3 that my *j* is the *j* of you all
2Cor 7:13 more joyed we for the *j* of Titus
2Cor 8:2 the abundance of their *j* and their
Gal 5:22 fruit of the Spirit is love, *j*
Phil 1:4 for you all making request with *j*
Phil 1:25 your furtherance and *j* of faith
Phil 2:2 Fulfil ye my *j*, that ye be
Phil 2:17 and service of your faith, I *j*
Phil 2:18 For the same cause also do ye *j*
Phil 4:1 beloved and longed for, my *j*
1Th 1:6 with *j* of the Holy Ghost
1Th 2:19 For what is our hope, or *j*
1Th 2:20 For ye are our glory and *j*
1Th 3:9 for all the *j* wherewith we *j*
1Th 3:9 for all the *j* wherewith we *j*
2Ti 1:4 that I may be filled with *j*
Philem 7 For we have great *j* and
Philem 20 let me have *j* of thee in the Lord
Heb 12:2 who for the *j* that was set before
Heb 13:17 that they may do it with *j*
Jas 1:2 count it all *j* when ye fall into
Jas 4:9 mourning, and your *j* to heaviness
1Pet 1:8 ye rejoice with *j* unspeakable
1Pet 4:13 may be glad also with exceeding *j*
1Jn 1:4 unto you, that your *j* may be full
2Jn 12 to face, that our *j* may be full
3Jn 4 I have no greater *j* than to hear
Jude 24 of his glory with exceeding *j*

**JOYFUL**
1Kin 8:66 king, and went unto their tents *j*
Ezr 6:22 for the LORD had made them *j*
Est 5:9 Then went Haman forth that day *j*
Job 3:7 let no *j* voice come therein
Ps 5:11 that love thy name be *j* in thee
Ps 35:9 And my soul shall be *j* in the LORD
Ps 63:5 shall praise thee with *j* lips
Ps 66:1 Make a *j* noise unto God, all ye
Ps 81:1 make a *j* noise unto the God of
Ps 89:15 the people that know the *j* sound
Ps 95:1 let us make a *j* noise to the rock
Ps 95:2 make a *j* noise unto him with
Ps 96:12 Let the field be *j*, and all that
Ps 98:4 Make a *j* noise unto the LORD, all
Ps 98:6 make a *j* noise before the LORD
Ps 98:8 let the hills be *j* together
Ps 100:1 Make a *j* noise unto the LORD, all
Ps 113:9 to be a *j* mother of children
Ps 149:2 of Zion be *j* in their King
Ps 149:5 Let the saints be *j* in glory
Eccl 7:14 In the day of prosperity be *j*
Is 49:13 and be *j*, O earth
Is 56:7 make them *j* in my house of prayer
Is 61:10 my soul shall be *j* in my God
2Cor 7:4 I am exceeding *j* in all our

**JOYOUS**
Is 22:2 a tumultuous city, a *j* city
Is 23:7 Is this your *j* city, whose
Is 32:13 the houses of joy in the *j* city
Heb 12:11 for the present seemeth to be *j*

**JOZABAD** *(joz'-a-bad)*
*1. Another warrior in David's army.*
1Chr 12:20 to him of Manasseh, Adnah, and *J*
1Chr 12:20 and Jediael, and Michael, and *J*
*2. A Chief Levite in Josiah's time.*
2Chr 31:13 and Asahel, and Jerimoth, and *J*
*3. An exile with Ezra.*
2Chr 35:9 and Hashabiah and Jeiel and *J*
*4. A priest.*
Ezr 8:33 with them was *J* the son of Jeshua
*5. A Levite.*
Ezr 10:22 Maaseiah, Ishmael, Nethaneel, *J*
*6. A priest who helped Ezra.*
Ezr 10:23 *J*, and Shimei, and Kelaiah, (the
*7. A chief Levite in exile.*
Neh 8:7 Maaseiah, Kelita, Azariah, *J*
*8. A chief Levite in exile.*
Neh 11:16 And Shabbethai and *J*, of the chief

**JOZACHAR** *(joz'-a-kar)* See ZABAD. *Son of Shimeath.*
2Kin 12:21 For *J* the son of Shimeath, and

**JOZADAK** *(joz'-a-dak)* See JEHOZADAK, JOSEDECH. *A priest with Zerubbabel.*
Ezr 3:2 Then stood up Jeshua the son of *J*
Ezr 3:8 Shealtiel, and Jeshua the son of *J*
Ezr 5:2 Shealtiel, and Jeshua the son of *J*
Ezr 10:18 the sons of Jeshua the son of *J*
Neh 12:26 the son of Jeshua, the son of *J*

**JUBAL** *(ju'-bal) Son of Adah.*
Gen 4:21 And his brother's name was *J*

**JUBILE**
Lev 25:9 *j* to sound on the tenth day of
Lev 25:10 it shall be a *j* unto you
Lev 25:11 A *j* shall that fiftieth year be
Lev 25:12 For it is the *j*
Lev 25:13 In the year of this *j* ye shall
Lev 25:15 the number of years after the *j*
Lev 25:28 bought it until the year of *j*
Lev 25:28 in the *j* it shall go out, and he
Lev 25:30 it shall not go out in the *j*
Lev 25:31 and they shall go out in the *j*
Lev 25:33 shall go out in the year of *j*
Lev 25:40 serve thee unto the year of *j*
Lev 25:50 sold to him unto the year of *j*
Lev 25:52 but few years unto the year of *j*
Lev 25:54 he shall go out in the year of *j*
Lev 27:17 his field from the year of *j*
Lev 27:18 he sanctify his field after the *j*
Lev 27:18 even unto the year of the *j*
Lev 27:21 field, when it goeth out in the *j*
Lev 27:23 even unto the year of the *j*
Lev 27:24 In the year of the *j* the field
Num 36:4 when the *j* of the children of

**JUCAL** *(ju'-kal)* See JEHUCAL. *An enemy of Jeremiah.*
Jer 38:1 *J* the son of Shelemiah, and Pashur

**JUDA** *(ju'-dah)* See JUDAH.
*1. Greek form of Judah, the tribe.*
Mt 2:6 thou Bethlehem, in the land of *J*
Mt 2:6 the least among the princes of *J*
Lk 1:39 with haste, into a city of *J*
Heb 7:14 that our Lord sprang out of *J*
Rev 5:5 the Lion of the tribe of *J*
Rev 7:5 Of the tribe of *J* were sealed
*2. A brother of Jesus.*
Mk 6:3 of James, and Joses, and of *J*
*3. An ancestor of Jesus.*
Lk 3:26 of Joseph, which was the son of *J*
Lk 3:33 of Phares, which was the son of *J*

**JUDAEA** *A Roman province.*
Mt 2:1 *J* in the days of Herod the king
Mt 2:5 said unto him, In Bethlehem of *J*
Mt 2:22 that Archelaus did reign in *J* in
Mt 3:1 preaching in the wilderness of *J*
Mt 3:5 out to him Jerusalem, and all *J*
Mt 4:25 and from Jerusalem, and from *J*
Mt 19:1 the coasts of *J* beyond Jordan
Mt 24:16 be in *J* flee into the mountains
Mk 1:5 out unto him all the land of *J*
Mk 3:7 Galilee followed him, and from *J*
Mk 10:1 cometh into the coasts of *J* by
Mk 13:14 be in *J* flee to the mountains
Lk 1:5 the days of Herod, the king of *J*
Lk 1:65 all the hill country of *J*
Lk 2:4 of the city of Nazareth, into *J*
Lk 3:1 Pilate being governor of *J*
Lk 5:17 of every town of Galilee, and *J*
Lk 6:17 multitude of people out of all *J*
Lk 7:17 him went forth throughout all *J*
Lk 21:21 are in *J* flee to the mountains
Jn 3:22 his disciples into the land of *J*
Jn 4:3 He left *J*, and departed again into
Jn 4:47 was come out of *J* into Galilee
Jn 4:54 he was come out of *J* into Galilee
Jn 7:3 him, Depart hence, and go into *J*
Jn 11:7 disciples, Let us go into *J* again
Acts 1:8 me both in Jerusalem, and in all *J*
Acts 2:9 dwellers in Mesopotamia, and in *J*
Acts 2:14 and said unto them, Ye men of *J*
Acts 8:1 throughout the regions of *J*
Acts 9:31 churches rest throughout all *J*
Acts 10:37 was published throughout all *J*
Acts 11:1 brethren that were in *J* heard
Acts 11:29 the brethren which dwelt in *J*
Acts 12:19 he went down from *J* to Caesarea
Acts 15:1 down from *J* taught the brethren
Acts 21:10 down from *J* a certain prophet
Acts 26:20 and throughout all the coasts of *J*
Acts 28:21 letters out of *J* concerning thee
Rom 15:31 them that do not believe in *J*
2Cor 1:16 to be brought on my way toward *J*
Gal 1:22 of *J* which were in Christ
1Th 2:14 which in *J* are in Christ Jesus

**JUDAH** *(ju'-dah)* See BETHLEHEM-JUDAH, JUDA, JUDAH'S, JUDAS, JUDEA, JUDE.
*1. Son of Jacob and Leah.*
Gen 29:35 therefore she called his name *J*
Gen 35:23 and Simeon, and Levi, and *J*
Gen 37:26 *J* said unto his brethren, What
Gen 38:1 that *J* went down from his
Gen 38:2 *J* saw there a daughter of a
Gen 38:6 And *J* took a wife for Er his
Gen 38:8 *J* said unto Onan, Go in unto thy
Gen 38:11 Then said *J* to Tamar his daughter
Gen 38:12 *J* was comforted, and went up unto
Gen 38:15 When *J* saw her, he thought her to
Gen 38:20 *J* sent the kid by the hand of his
Gen 38:22 And he returned to *J*, and said, I
Gen 38:23 *J* said, Let her take it to her,
Gen 38:24 months after, that it was told *J*
Gen 38:24 *J* said, Bring her forth, and let
Gen 38:26 *J* acknowledged them, and said, She
Gen 43:3 *J* spake unto him, saying, The man
Gen 43:8 *J* said unto Israel his father,
Gen 44:14 And *J* and his brethren came to
Gen 44:16 *J* said, What shall we say unto my
Gen 44:18 Then *J* came near unto him, and
Gen 46:12 And the sons of *J*
Gen 46:28 he sent *J* before him unto Joseph,
Gen 49:8 *J*, thou art he whom thy brethren
Gen 49:9 *J* is a lion's whelp
Ex 1:2 Reuben, Simeon, Levi, and *J*
Num 26:19 The sons of *J* were Er and Onan
Ruth 4:12 of Pharez, whom Tamar bare unto *J*
1Chr 2:1 Reuben, Simeon, Levi, and *J*
1Chr 2:3 The sons of *J*; Er, and
1Chr 2:3 And Er, the firstborn of *J*
1Chr 2:4 All the sons of *J* were five
1Chr 2:10 prince of the children of *J*
1Chr 4:1 The sons of *J*; Pharez
1Chr 4:21 sons of Shelah the son of *J* were
1Chr 4:27 like to the children of *J*
1Chr 5:2 For *J* prevailed above his

1Chr 9:4 children of Pharez the son of J
Neh 11:24 children of Zerah the son of J

*2. The tribe and its land.*

Gen 49:10 sceptre shall not depart from J
Ex 31:2 the son of Hur, of the tribe of J
Ex 35:30 the son of Hur, of the tribe of J
Ex 38:22 the son of Hur, of the tribe of J
Num 1:7 Of J; Nashon the son
Num 1:26 Of the children of J, by their
Num 1:27 of them, even of the tribe of J
Num 2:3 J pitch throughout their armies
Num 2:3 be captain of the children of J
Num 2:9 of J were an hundred thousand
Num 7:12 of Amminadab, of the tribe of J
Num 10:14 of J according to their armies
Num 13:6 Of the tribe of J, Caleb the son
Num 26:20 the sons of J after their
Num 26:22 These are the families of J
Num 34:19 Of the tribe of J, Caleb the son
Deut 27:12 Simeon, and Levi, and J, and
Deut 33:7 And this is the blessing of J
Deut 33:7 said, Hear, LORD, the voice of J
Deut 34:2 and Manasseh, and all the land of J
Josh 7:1 son of Zerah, of the tribe of J
Josh 7:16 and the tribe of J was taken
Josh 7:17 And he brought the family of J
Josh 7:18 son of Zerah, of the tribe of J
Josh 11:21 and from all the mountains of J
Josh 14:6 Then the children of J came unto
Josh 15:1 children of J by their families
Josh 15:12 J round about according to their
Josh 15:13 a part among the children of J
Josh 15:20 of J according to their families
Josh 15:21 of J toward the coast of Edom
Josh 15:63 the children of J could not drive
Josh 15:63 of J at Jerusalem unto this day
Josh 18:5 J shall abide in their coast on
Josh 18:11 forth between the children of J
Josh 18:14 a city of the children of J
Josh 19:1 inheritance of the children of J
Josh 19:9 of J was the inheritance of the
Josh 19:9 of J was too much for them
Josh 19:34 to J upon Jordan toward the
Josh 20:7 is Hebron, in the mountain of J
Josh 21:4 had by lot out of the tribe of J
Josh 21:9 of the tribe of the children of J
Josh 21:11 Hebron, in the hill country of J
Judg 1:2 And the LORD said, J shall go up
Judg 1:3 J said unto Simeon his brother,
Judg 1:4 And J went up
Judg 1:8 Now the children of J had fought
Judg 1:9 afterward the children of J went
Judg 1:10 J went against the Canaanites
Judg 1:16 of J into the wilderness of Judah
Judg 1:16 of Judah into the wilderness of J
Judg 1:17 J went with Simeon his brother,
Judg 1:18 Also J took Gaza with the coast
Judg 1:19 And the LORD was with J
Judg 10:9 Jordan to fight also against J
Judg 15:9 went up, and pitched in J, and
Judg 15:10 And the men of J said, Why are ye
Judg 15:11 Then three thousand men of J went
Judg 17:7 of the family of J, who was a
Judg 18:12 pitched in Kirjath-jearim, in J
Judg 20:18 LORD said, J shall go up first
Ruth 1:7 way to return unto the land of J
1Sa 11:8 the men of J thirty thousand
1Sa 15:4 footmen, and ten thousand men of J
1Sa 17:1 at Shochoh, which belongeth to J
1Sa 17:52 of J arose, and shouted, and
1Sa 18:16 J loved David, because he went
1Sa 22:5 and get thee into the land of J
1Sa 23:3 Behold, we be afraid here in J
1Sa 23:23 throughout all the thousands of J
1Sa 27:6 unto the kings of J unto this day
1Sa 27:10 said, Against the south of J
1Sa 30:14 the coast which belongeth to J
1Sa 30:16 and out of the land of J
1Sa 30:26 of the spoil unto the elders of J
2Sa 1:18 children of J the use of the bow
2Sa 2:1 go up into any of the cities of J
2Sa 2:4 And the men of J came, and there
2Sa 2:4 David king over the house of J
2Sa 2:7 also the house of J have anointed
2Sa 2:10 But the house of J followed David
2Sa 2:11 the house of J was seven years
2Sa 3:8 which against J do shew kindness
2Sa 3:10 of David over Israel and over J
2Sa 5:5 he reigned over J seven years
2Sa 5:5 three years over all Israel and J
2Sa 6:2 were with him from Baale of J
2Sa 11:11 David, The ark, and Israel, and J
2Sa 12:8 thee the house of Israel and of J
2Sa 19:11 Speak unto the elders of J
2Sa 19:14 the heart of all the men of J
2Sa 19:15 J came to Gilgal, to go to meet
2Sa 19:16 the men of J to meet king David
2Sa 19:40 all the people of J conducted the
2Sa 19:41 the men of J stolen thee away
2Sa 19:42 all the men of J answered the men
2Sa 19:43 of Israel answered the men of J
2Sa 19:43 the words of the men of J were
2Sa 20:2 but the men of J clave unto their
2Sa 20:4 me the men of J within three days
2Sa 20:5 went to assemble the men of J
2Sa 21:2 to the children of Israel and J
2Sa 24:1 to say, Go, number Israel and J
2Sa 24:7 they went out to the south of J
2Sa 24:9 the men of J were five hundred
1Kin 1:9 all the men of J the king's
1Kin 1:35 to be ruler over Israel and over J
1Kin 2:32 Jether, captain of the host of J
1Kin 4:20 J and Israel were many, as the
1Kin 4:25 And J and Israel dwelt safely,
1Chr 6:55 gave them Hebron in the land of J
1Chr 6:57 Aaron they gave the cities of J
1Chr 6:65 of the tribe of the children of J
1Chr 9:3 dwelt of the children of J
1Chr 12:16 and J to the hold unto David
1Chr 12:24 The children of J that bare
1Chr 13:6 which belonged to J, to bring up
1Chr 27:18 Of J, Elihu, one of the brethren
1Chr 28:4 he hath chosen J to be the ruler
1Chr 28:4 and of the house of J, the house
2Chr 2:7 cunning men that are with me in J
2Chr 9:11 such seen before in the land of J
Ezr 1:2 house at Jerusalem, which is in J
Ezr 1:3 go up to Jerusalem, which is in J
Ezr 1:5 up the chief of the fathers of J
Ezr 1:8 unto Sheshbazzar, the prince of J
Ezr 4:4 the hands of the people of J
Ezr 4:6 against the inhabitants of J
Ezr 5:1 unto the Jews that were in J
Ezr 7:14 to enquire concerning J and
Ezr 9:9 and to give us a wall in J
Ezr 10:7 made proclamation throughout J
Ezr 10:9 Then all the men of J and Benjamin
Neh 1:2 came, he and certain men of J
Neh 2:5 that thou wouldest send me unto J
Neh 2:7 convey me over till I come into J
Neh 4:10 J said, The strength of the
Neh 4:16 were behind all the house of J
Neh 5:14 their governor in the land of J
Neh 6:7 saying, There is a king in J
Neh 6:17 in those days the nobles of J
Neh 6:18 were many in J sworn unto him
Neh 7:6 came again to Jerusalem and to J
Neh 11:3 but in the cities of J dwelt
Neh 11:4 certain of the children of J
Neh 11:4 Of the children of J
Neh 11:20 were in all the cities of J
Neh 11:25 of J dwelt at Kirjath-arba
Neh 11:36 the Levites were divisions in J
Neh 12:31 up the princes of J upon the wall
Neh 12:32 and half of the princes of J
Neh 12:44 for J rejoiced for the priests and
Neh 13:12 Then brought all J the tithe of
Neh 13:15 In those days saw I in J some
Neh 13:16 sabbath unto the children of J
Neh 13:17 I contended with the nobles of J
Est 2:6 away with Jeconiah king of J
Ps 48:11 let the daughters of J be glad
Ps 60:7 J is my lawgiver
Ps 63:*t* he was in the wilderness of J
Ps 68:27 their ruler, the princes of J
Ps 69:35 and will build the cities of J
Ps 76:1 In J is God known
Ps 78:68 But chose the tribe of J, the
Ps 97:8 the daughters of J rejoiced
Ps 108:8 J is my lawgiver
Ps 114:2 J was his sanctuary, and Israel
Heb 8:8 of Israel and with the house of J

*3. The southern kingdom after the revolt of the ten northern tribes.*

1Kin 12:17 which dwelt in the cities of J
1Kin 12:20 of David, but the tribe of J only
1Kin 12:21 he assembled all the house of J
1Kin 12:23 the son of Solomon, king of J
1Kin 12:23 Judah, and unto all the house of J
1Kin 12:27 even unto Rehoboam king of J
1Kin 12:27 and go again to Rehoboam king of J
1Kin 12:32 like unto the feast that is in J
1Kin 13:1 of J by the word of the LORD unto
1Kin 13:12 of God went, which came from J
1Kin 13:14 the man of God that camest from J
1Kin 13:21 the man of God that came from J
1Kin 14:21 the son of Solomon reigned in J
1Kin 14:22 J did evil in the sight of the
1Kin 14:29 the chronicles of the kings of J
1Kin 15:1 of Nebat reigned Abijam over J
1Kin 15:7 the chronicles of the kings of J
1Kin 15:9 king of Israel reigned Asa over J
1Kin 15:17 king of Israel went up against J
1Kin 15:17 out or come in to Asa king of J
1Kin 15:22 a proclamation throughout all J
1Kin 15:23 the chronicles of the kings of J
1Kin 15:25 the second year of Asa king of J
1Kin 15:28 Asa king of J did Baasha slay him
1Kin 15:33 the third year of Asa king of J
1Kin 16:8 sixth year of Asa king of J began
1Kin 16:10 and seventh year of Asa king of J
1Kin 16:15 seventh year of Asa king of J did
1Kin 16:23 first year of Asa king of J began
1Kin 16:29 eighth year of Asa king of J
1Kin 19:3 Beer-sheba, which belongeth to J
1Kin 22:2 that Jehoshaphat the king of J
1Kin 22:10 king of J sat each on his throne
1Kin 22:29 Jehoshaphat the king of J went up
1Kin 22:41 son of Asa began to reign over J
1Kin 22:45 the chronicles of the kings of J
1Kin 22:51 year of Jehoshaphat king of J
2Kin 1:17 the son of Jehoshaphat king of J
2Kin 3:1 year of Jehoshaphat king of J
2Kin 3:7 sent to Jehoshaphat the king of J
2Kin 3:9 of Israel went, and the king of J
2Kin 3:14 of Jehoshaphat the king of J
2Kin 8:16 Jehoshaphat being then king of J
2Kin 8:16 king of J began to reign
2Kin 8:19 J for David his servant's sake
2Kin 8:20 revolted from under the hand of J
2Kin 8:22 under the hand of J unto this day
2Kin 8:23 the chronicles of the kings of J
2Kin 8:25 Jehoram king of J begin to reign
2Kin 8:29 the son of Jehoram king of J went
2Kin 9:16 Ahaziah king of J was come down
2Kin 9:21 and Ahaziah king of J went out
2Kin 9:27 Ahaziah the king of J saw this
2Kin 9:29 began Ahaziah to reign over J
2Kin 10:13 the brethren of Ahaziah king of J
2Kin 12:18 Jehoash king of J took all the
2Kin 12:18 Ahaziah, his fathers, kings of J
2Kin 12:19 the chronicles of the kings of J
2Kin 13:1 the son of Ahaziah king of J
2Kin 13:10 of J began Jehoash the son of
2Kin 13:12 fought against Amaziah king of J
2Kin 14:1 the son of Joash king of J
2Kin 14:9 Israel sent to Amaziah king of J
2Kin 14:10 fall, even thou, and J with thee
2Kin 14:11 Amaziah king of J looked one
2Kin 14:11 which belongeth to J
2Kin 14:12 J was put to the worse before
2Kin 14:13 of Israel took Amaziah king of J
2Kin 14:15 he fought with Amaziah king of J
2Kin 14:17 of J lived after the death of
2Kin 14:18 the chronicles of the kings of J
2Kin 14:21 all the people of J took Azariah
2Kin 14:22 built Elath, and restored it to J
2Kin 14:23 the son of Joash king of J
2Kin 14:28 and Hamath, which belonged to J
2Kin 15:1 son of Amaziah king of J to reign
2Kin 15:6 the chronicles of the kings of J
2Kin 15:8 of J did Zachariah the son of
2Kin 15:13 year of Uzziah king of J
2Kin 15:17 year of Azariah king of J began
2Kin 15:23 year of Azariah king of J
2Kin 15:27 year of Azariah king of J Pekah
2Kin 15:32 son of Uzziah king of J to reign
2Kin 15:36 the chronicles of the kings of J
2Kin 15:37 against J Rezin the king of Syria
2Kin 16:1 Jotham king of J began to reign
2Kin 16:19 the chronicles of the kings of J
2Kin 17:1 twelfth year of Ahaz king of J
2Kin 17:13 against Israel, and against J
2Kin 17:18 none left but the tribe of J only
2Kin 17:19 Also J kept not the commandments
2Kin 18:1 of Ahaz king of J began to reign
2Kin 18:5 like him among all the kings of J
2Kin 18:13 all the fenced cities of J
2Kin 18:14 Hezekiah king of J sent to the
2Kin 18:14 J three hundred talents of silver

2Kin 18:16 Hezekiah king of J had overlaid
2Kin 18:22 taken away, and hath said to J
2Kin 19:10 ye speak to Hezekiah king of J
2Kin 19:30 of J shall yet again take root
2Kin 20:20 the chronicles of the kings of J
2Kin 21:11 Because Manasseh king of J hath
2Kin 21:11 hath made J also to sin with his
2Kin 21:12 such evil upon Jerusalem and J
2Kin 21:16 sin wherewith he made J to sin
2Kin 21:17 the chronicles of the kings of J
2Kin 21:25 the chronicles of the kings of J
2Kin 22:13 and for the people, and for all J
2Kin 22:16 which the king of J hath read
2Kin 22:18 But to the king of J which sent
2Kin 23:1 unto him all the elders of J
2Kin 23:2 of the LORD, and all the men of J
2Kin 23:5 whom the kings of J had ordained
2Kin 23:5 high places in the cities of J
2Kin 23:8 priests out of the cities of J
2Kin 23:11 kings of J had given to the sun
2Kin 23:12 which the kings of J had made
2Kin 23:17 the man of God, which came from J
2Kin 23:22 of Israel, nor of the kings of J
2Kin 23:24 that were spied in the land of J
2Kin 23:26 his anger was kindled against J
2Kin 23:27 I will remove J also out of my
2Kin 23:28 the chronicles of the kings of J
2Kin 24:2 sent them against J to destroy it
2Kin 24:3 of the LORD came this upon J
2Kin 24:5 the chronicles of the kings of J
2Kin 24:12 Jehoiachin the king of J went out
2Kin 24:20 it came to pass in Jerusalem and J
2Kin 25:21 So J was carried away out of
2Kin 25:22 that remained in the land of J
2Kin 25:27 captivity of Jehoiachin king of J
2Kin 25:27 king of J out of prison
1Chr 4:41 in the days of Hezekiah king of J
1Chr 5:17 in the days of Jotham king of J
1Chr 6:15 when the LORD carried away J
1Chr 9:1 book of the kings of Israel and J
1Chr 21:5 J was four hundred threescore and
2Chr 10:17 that dwelt in the cities of J
2Chr 11:1 he gathered of the house of J
2Chr 11:3 the son of Solomon, king of J
2Chr 11:3 of Judah, and to all Israel in J
2Chr 11:5 and built cities for defence in J
2Chr 11:10 and Hebron, which are in J
2Chr 11:12 them exceeding strong, having J
2Chr 11:14 and their possession, and came to J
2Chr 11:17 strengthened the kingdom of J
2Chr 11:23 throughout all the countries of J
2Chr 12:4 cities which pertained to J
2Chr 12:5 Rehoboam, and to the princes of J
2Chr 12:12 also in J things went well
2Chr 13:1 began Abijah to reign over J
2Chr 13:13 so they were before J, and the
2Chr 13:14 when J looked back, behold, the
2Chr 13:15 Then the men of J gave a shout
2Chr 13:15 and as the men of J shouted
2Chr 13:15 and all Israel before Abijah and J
2Chr 13:16 children of Israel fled before J
2Chr 13:18 and the children of J prevailed
2Chr 14:4 commanded J to seek the LORD God
2Chr 14:5 the cities of J the high places
2Chr 14:6 And he built fenced cities in J
2Chr 14:7 Therefore he said unto J, Let us
2Chr 14:8 out of J three hundred thousand
2Chr 14:12 before Asa, and before J
2Chr 15:2 him, Hear ye me, Asa, and all J
2Chr 15:8 idols out of all the land of J
2Chr 15:9 And he gathered all J and Benjamin,
2Chr 15:15 all J rejoiced at the oath
2Chr 16:1 king of Israel came up against J
2Chr 16:1 out or come in to Asa king of J
2Chr 16:6 Then Asa the king took all J
2Chr 16:7 the seer came to Asa king of J
2Chr 16:11 in the book of the kings of J
2Chr 17:2 in all the fenced cities of J
2Chr 17:2 and set garrisons in the land of J
2Chr 17:5 all J brought to Jehoshaphat
2Chr 17:6 high places and groves out of J
2Chr 17:7 to teach in the cities of J
2Chr 17:9 And they taught in J, and had the
2Chr 17:9 throughout all the cities of J
2Chr 17:10 the lands that were round about J
2Chr 17:12 and he built in J castles, and
2Chr 17:13 much business in the cities of J
2Chr 17:14 Of J, the captains of thousands
2Chr 17:19 fenced cities throughout all J
2Chr 18:3 said unto Jehoshaphat king of J
2Chr 18:9 Jehoshaphat king of J sat either
2Chr 18:28 Jehoshaphat the king of J went up
2Chr 19:1 Jehoshaphat the king of J
2Chr 19:5 all the fenced cities of J
2Chr 19:11 the ruler of the house of J
2Chr 20:3 a fast throughout all J
2Chr 20:4 J gathered themselves together,
2Chr 20:4 of J they came to seek the LORD
2Chr 20:5 stood in the congregation of J
2Chr 20:13 all J stood before the LORD, with
2Chr 20:15 And he said, Hearken ye, all J
2Chr 20:17 of the LORD with you, O J
2Chr 20:18 and all J and the inhabitants of
2Chr 20:20 stood and said, Hear me, O J
2Chr 20:22 Seir, which were come against J
2Chr 20:24 when J came toward the watch
2Chr 20:27 they returned, every man of J
2Chr 20:31 And Jehoshaphat reigned over J
2Chr 20:35 this did Jehoshaphat king of J
2Chr 21:3 things, with fenced cities in J
2Chr 21:8 from under the dominion of J
2Chr 21:10 under the hand of J unto this day
2Chr 21:11 high places in the mountains of J
2Chr 21:11 and compelled J thereto
2Chr 21:12 nor in the ways of Asa king of J
2Chr 21:13 kings of Israel, and hast made J
2Chr 21:17 And they came up into J, and brake
2Chr 22:1 son of Jehoram king of J reigned
2Chr 22:6 the son of Jehoram king of J went
2Chr 22:8 Ahab, and found the princes of J
2Chr 22:10 the seed royal of the house of J
2Chr 23:2 And they went about in J, and
2Chr 23:2 out of all the cities of J
2Chr 23:8 all J did according to all things
2Chr 24:5 them, Go out unto the cities of J
2Chr 24:6 the Levites to bring in out of J
2Chr 24:9 made a proclamation through J
2Chr 24:17 of Jehoiada came the princes of J
2Chr 24:18 and wrath came upon J and Jerusalem
2Chr 24:23 and they came to J and Jerusalem,
2Chr 25:5 Amaziah gathered J together
2Chr 25:5 their fathers, throughout all J
2Chr 25:10 was greatly kindled against J
2Chr 25:12 children of J carry away captive
2Chr 25:13 battle, fell upon the cities of J
2Chr 25:17 Amaziah king of J took advice
2Chr 25:18 Israel sent to Amaziah king of J
2Chr 25:19 fall, even thou, and J with thee
2Chr 25:21 both he and Amaziah king of J
2Chr 25:21 which belongeth to J
2Chr 25:22 J was put to the worse before
2Chr 25:23 of Israel took Amaziah king of J
2Chr 25:25 the son of Joash king of J lived
2Chr 25:26 in the book of the kings of J
2Chr 25:28 with his fathers in the city of J
2Chr 26:1 all the people of J took Uzziah
2Chr 26:2 built Eloth, and restored it to J
2Chr 27:4 cities in the mountains of J
2Chr 27:7 book of the kings of Israel and J
2Chr 28:6 of Remaliah slew in J an hundred
2Chr 28:9 of your fathers was wroth with J
2Chr 28:10 to keep under the children of J
2Chr 28:17 Edomites had come and smitten J
2Chr 28:18 low country, and of the south of J
2Chr 28:19 For the LORD brought J low
2Chr 28:19 for he made J naked, and
2Chr 28:25 in every several city of J he
2Chr 28:26 in the book of the kings of J
2Chr 29:8 the wrath of the LORD was upon J
2Chr 29:21 and for the sanctuary, and for J
2Chr 30:1 Hezekiah sent to all Israel and J
2Chr 30:6 throughout all Israel and J
2Chr 30:12 Also in J the hand of God was to
2Chr 30:24 For Hezekiah king of J did give
2Chr 30:25 And all the congregation of J
2Chr 30:25 of Israel, and that dwelt in J
2Chr 31:1 went out to the cities of J
2Chr 31:1 places and the altars out of all J
2Chr 31:6 the children of Israel and J
2Chr 31:6 that dwelt in the cities of J
2Chr 31:20 did Hezekiah throughout all J
2Chr 32:1 Assyria came, and entered into J
2Chr 32:8 the words of Hezekiah king of J
2Chr 32:9 him,) unto Hezekiah king of J
2Chr 32:9 unto all J that were at Jerusalem
2Chr 32:12 and his altars, and commanded J
2Chr 32:23 and presents to Hezekiah king of J
2Chr 32:25 was wrath upon him, and upon J
2Chr 32:32 and in the book of the kings of J
2Chr 32:33 and all J and the inhabitants of
2Chr 33:9 So Manasseh made J and the
2Chr 33:14 war in all the fenced cities of J
2Chr 33:16 commanded J to serve the LORD God
2Chr 34:3 twelfth year he began to purge J
2Chr 34:5 upon their altars, and cleansed J
2Chr 34:9 remnant of Israel, and of all J
2Chr 34:11 the kings of J had destroyed
2Chr 34:21 that are left in Israel and in J
2Chr 34:24 have read before the king of J
2Chr 34:26 And as for the king of J, who sent
2Chr 34:29 together all the elders of J
2Chr 34:30 of the LORD, and all the men of J
2Chr 35:18 priests, and the Levites, and all J
2Chr 35:21 I to do with thee, thou king of J
2Chr 35:24 And all J and Jerusalem mourned for
2Chr 35:27 book of the kings of Israel and J
2Chr 36:4 Eliakim his brother king over J
2Chr 36:8 book of the kings of Israel and J
2Chr 36:10 Zedekiah his brother king over J
2Chr 36:23 house in Jerusalem, which is in J
Ezr 2:1 and came again unto Jerusalem and J
Ezr 4:1 Now when the adversaries of J
Prov 25:1 of Hezekiah king of J copied out
Is 1:1 Amoz, which he saw concerning J
Is 1:1 Ahaz, and Hezekiah, kings of J
Is 2:1 the son of Amoz saw concerning J
Is 3:1 from J the stay and the staff, the
Is 3:8 is ruined, and J is fallen
Is 5:3 of Jerusalem, and men of J
Is 5:7 the men of J his pleasant plant
Is 7:1 the son of Uzziah, king of J
Is 7:6 Let us go up against J, and vex it
Is 7:17 day that Ephraim departed from J
Is 8:8 And he shall pass through J
Is 9:21 they together shall be against J
Is 11:12 together the dispersed of J from
Is 11:13 adversaries of J shall be cut off
Is 11:13 Ephraim shall not envy J, and
Is 11:13 Judah, and J shall not vex Ephraim
Is 19:17 the land of J shall be a terror
Is 22:8 he discovered the covering of J
Is 22:21 Jerusalem, and to the house of J
Is 26:1 song be sung in the land of J
Is 36:1 all the defenced cities of J
Is 36:7 hath taken away, and said to J
Is 37:10 ye speak to Hezekiah king of J
Is 37:31 J shall again take root downward
Is 38:9 The writing of Hezekiah king of J
Is 40:9 say unto the cities of J, Behold
Is 44:26 and to the cities of J, Ye shall
Is 48:1 come forth out of the waters of J
Is 65:9 out of J an inheritor of my
Jer 1:2 Josiah the son of Amon king of J
Jer 1:3 the son of Josiah king of J
Jer 1:3 the son of Josiah king of J
Jer 1:15 and against all the cities of J
Jer 1:18 land, against the kings of J
Jer 2:28 of thy cities are thy gods, O J
Jer 3:7 her treacherous sister J saw it
Jer 3:8 treacherous sister J feared not
Jer 3:10 J hath not turned unto me with
Jer 3:11 herself more than treacherous J
Jer 3:18 In those days the house of J
Jer 4:3 saith the LORD to the men of J
Jer 4:4 of your heart, ye men of J
Jer 4:5 Declare ye in J, and publish in
Jer 4:16 voice against the cities of J
Jer 5:11 the house of J have dealt very
Jer 5:20 of Jacob, and publish it in J
Jer 7:2 the word of the LORD, all ye of J
Jer 7:17 what they do in the cities of J
Jer 7:30 For the children of J have done
Jer 7:34 to cease from the cities of J
Jer 8:1 out the bones of the kings of J
Jer 9:11 make the cities of J desolate
Jer 9:26 Egypt, and J, and Edom, and the
Jer 10:22 to make the cities of J desolate
Jer 11:2 and speak unto the men of J
Jer 11:6 these words in the cities of J
Jer 11:9 is found among the men of J
Jer 11:10 the house of J have broken my
Jer 11:12 Then shall the cities of J
Jer 11:13 of thy cities were thy gods, O J
Jer 11:17 of Israel and of the house of J
Jer 12:14 the house of J from among them
Jer 13:9 manner will I mar the pride of J
Jer 13:11 of Israel and the whole house of J
Jer 13:19 J shall be carried away captive
Jer 14:2 J mourneth, and the gates thereof
Jer 14:19 Hast thou utterly rejected J

Jer 15:4 the son of Hezekiah king of J
Jer 17:1 The sin of J is written with a
Jer 17:19 whereby the kings of J come in
Jer 17:20 word of the LORD, ye kings of J
Jer 17:20 LORD, ye kings of Judah, and all J
Jer 17:25 and their princes, the men of J
Jer 17:26 shall come from the cities of J
Jer 18:11 go to, speak to the men of J
Jer 19:3 word of the LORD, O kings of J
Jer 19:4 have known, nor the kings of J
Jer 19:7 I will make void the counsel of J
Jer 19:13 and the houses of the kings of J
Jer 20:4 I will give all J into the hand
Jer 20:5 of J will I give into the hand of
Jer 21:7 I will deliver Zedekiah king of J
Jer 21:11 the house of the king of J
Jer 22:1 to the house of the king of J
Jer 22:2 the word of the LORD, O king of J
Jer 22:6 LORD unto the king's house of J
Jer 22:11 the son of Josiah king of J
Jer 22:18 the son of Josiah king of J
Jer 22:24 the son of Jehoiakim king of J
Jer 22:30 of David, and ruling any more in J
Jer 23:6 In his days J shall be saved, and
Jer 24:1 the son of Jehoiakim king of J
Jer 24:1 and the princes of J
Jer 24:5 are carried away captive of J
Jer 24:8 I give Zedekiah the king of J
Jer 25:1 concerning all the people of J in
Jer 25:1 the son of Josiah king of J
Jer 25:2 spake unto all the people of J
Jer 25:3 Josiah the son of Amon king of J
Jer 25:18 Jerusalem, and the cities of J
Jer 26:1 the son of Josiah king of J came
Jer 26:2 and speak unto all the cities of J
Jer 26:10 princes of J heard these things
Jer 26:18 in the days of Hezekiah king of J
Jer 26:18 and spake to all the people of J
Jer 26:19 Did Hezekiah king of J and all
Jer 26:19 all J put him at all to death
Jer 27:1 the son of Josiah king of J came
Jer 27:3 Jerusalem unto Zedekiah king of J
Jer 27:12 of J according to all these words
Jer 27:18 and in the house of the king of J
Jer 27:20 of J from Jerusalem to Babylon
Jer 27:20 and all the nobles of J
Jer 27:21 and in the house of the king of J
Jer 28:1 the reign of Zedekiah king of J
Jer 28:4 the son of Jehoiakim king of J
Jer 28:4 Judah, with all the captives of J
Jer 29:2 and the eunuchs, the princes of J
Jer 29:3 king of J sent unto Babylon to
Jer 29:22 of J which are in Babylon
Jer 30:3 of my people Israel and J, saith
Jer 30:4 concerning Israel and concerning J
Jer 31:23 use this speech in the land of J
Jer 31:24 And there shall dwell in J itself
Jer 31:27 the house of J with the seed of
Jer 31:31 of Israel, and with the house of J
Jer 32:1 tenth year of Zedekiah king of J
Jer 32:3 king of J had shut him up
Jer 32:4 Zedekiah king of J shall not
Jer 32:30 the children of J have only done
Jer 32:32 of Israel and of the children of J
Jer 32:32 their prophets, and the men of J
Jer 32:35 abomination, to cause J to sin
Jer 32:44 Jerusalem, and in the cities of J
Jer 33:4 the houses of the kings of J
Jer 33:7 I will cause the captivity of J
Jer 33:10 beast, even in the cities of J
Jer 33:13 Jerusalem, and in the cities of J
Jer 33:14 of Israel and to the house of J
Jer 33:16 In those days shall J be saved
Jer 34:2 Go and speak to Zedekiah king of J
Jer 34:4 of the LORD, O Zedekiah king of J
Jer 34:6 Zedekiah king of J in Jerusalem
Jer 34:7 the cities of J that were left
Jer 34:7 remained of the cities of J
Jer 34:19 The princes of J, and the princes
Jer 34:21 And Zedekiah king of J and his
Jer 34:22 of J a desolation without an
Jer 35:1 the son of Josiah king of J
Jer 35:13 Go and tell the men of J and the
Jer 35:17 Behold, I will bring upon J
Jer 36:1 the son of Josiah king of J
Jer 36:2 thee against Israel, and against J
Jer 36:3 It may be that the house of J
Jer 36:6 read them in the ears of all J
Jer 36:9 the son of Josiah king of J
Jer 36:9 the cities of J unto Jerusalem
Jer 36:28 the king of J hath burned
Jer 36:29 shalt say to Jehoiakim king of J
Jer 36:30 the LORD of Jehoiakim king of J
Jer 36:31 Jerusalem, and upon the men of J
Jer 36:32 king of J had burned in the fire
Jer 37:1 made king in the land of J
Jer 37:7 shall ye say to the king of J
Jer 39:1 ninth year of Zedekiah king of J
Jer 39:4 Zedekiah the king of J saw them
Jer 39:6 Babylon slew all the nobles of J
Jer 39:10 had nothing, in the land of J
Jer 40:1 away captive of Jerusalem and J
Jer 40:5 governor over the cities of J
Jer 40:11 Babylon had left a remnant of J
Jer 40:12 driven, and came to the land of J
Jer 40:15 and the remnant in J perish
Jer 42:15 word of the LORD, ye remnant of J
Jer 42:19 concerning you, O ye remnant of J
Jer 43:4 LORD, to dwell in the land of J
Jer 43:5 forces, took all the remnant of J
Jer 43:5 driven, to dwell in the land of J
Jer 43:9 in the sight of the men of J
Jer 44:2 and upon all the cities of J
Jer 44:6 and was kindled in the cities of J
Jer 44:7 child and suckling, out of J
Jer 44:9 the wickedness of the kings of J
Jer 44:9 have committed in the land of J
Jer 44:11 you for evil, and to cut off all J
Jer 44:12 And I will take the remnant of J
Jer 44:14 So that none of the remnant of J
Jer 44:14 should return into the land of J
Jer 44:17 our princes, in the cities of J
Jer 44:21 that ye burned in the cities of J
Jer 44:24 all J that are in the land of
Jer 44:26 all J that dwell in the land of
Jer 44:26 man of J in all the land of Egypt
Jer 44:27 all the men of J that are in the
Jer 44:28 land of Egypt into the land of J
Jer 44:28 and all the remnant of J
Jer 44:30 as I gave Zedekiah king of J into
Jer 45:1 the son of Josiah king of J
Jer 46:2 the son of Josiah king of J
Jer 49:34 the reign of Zedekiah king of J
Jer 50:4 and the children of J together
Jer 50:20 and the sins of J, and they shall
Jer 50:33 the children of J were oppressed
Jer 51:5 nor J of his God, of the LORD of
Jer 51:59 went with Zedekiah the king of J
Jer 52:3 it came to pass in Jerusalem and J
Jer 52:10 all the princes of J in Riblah
Jer 52:27 Thus J was carried away captive
Jer 52:31 captivity of Jehoiachin king of J
Jer 52:31 the head of Jehoiachin king of J
Lam 1:3 J is gone into captivity because
Lam 1:15 the virgin, the daughter of J
Lam 2:2 strong holds of the daughter of J
Lam 2:5 in the daughter of J mourning
Lam 5:11 and the maids in the cities of J
Eze 4:6 of the house of J forty days
Eze 8:1 and the elders of J sat before me
Eze 8:17 house of J that they commit the
Eze 9:9 J is exceeding great, and the land
Eze 21:20 to J in Jerusalem the defenced
Eze 25:3 and against the house of J
Eze 25:8 the house of J is like unto all
Eze 25:12 house of J by taking vengeance
Eze 27:17 J, and the land of Israel, they
Eze 37:16 stick, and write upon it, For J
Eze 37:19 him, even with the stick of J
Eze 48:7 the west side, a portion for J
Eze 48:8 And by the border of J, from the
Eze 48:22 prince's, between the border of J
Eze 48:31 one gate of Reuben, one gate of J
Dan 1:1 of J came Nebuchadnezzar king of
Dan 1:2 Jehoiakim king of J into his hand
Dan 1:6 these were of the children of J
Dan 2:25 found a man of the captives of J
Dan 5:13 children of the captivity of J
Dan 6:13 children of the captivity of J
Dan 9:7 to the men of J, and to the
Hos 1:1 Ahaz, and Hezekiah, kings of J
Hos 1:7 have mercy upon the house of J
Hos 1:11 Then shall the children of J
Hos 4:15 the harlot, yet let not J offend
Hos 5:5 J also shall fall with them
Hos 5:10 The princes of J were like them
Hos 5:12 to the house of J as rottenness
Hos 5:13 J saw his wound, then went
Hos 5:14 as a young lion to the house of J
Hos 6:4 O J, what shall I do unto thee
Hos 6:11 Also, O J, he hath set an harvest
Hos 8:14 J hath multiplied fenced cities
Hos 10:11 J shall plow, and Jacob shall
Hos 11:12 but J yet ruleth with God, and is
Hos 12:2 hath also a controversy with J
Joel 3:1 bring again the captivity of J
Joel 3:6 The children also of J and the
Joel 3:8 the hand of the children of J
Joel 3:18 all the rivers of J shall flow
Joel 3:19 against the children of J
Joel 3:20 But J shall dwell for ever, and
Amos 1:1 in the days of Uzziah king of J
Amos 2:4 For three transgressions of J
Amos 2:5 But I will send a fire upon J
Amos 7:12 flee thee away into the land of J
Obad 12 rejoiced over the children of J
Mic 1:1 Ahaz, and Hezekiah, kings of J
Mic 1:5 and what are the high places of J
Mic 1:9 for it is come unto J
Mic 5:2 little among the thousands of J
Nah 1:15 O J, keep thy solemn feasts,
Zeph 1:1 Josiah the son of Amon, king of J
Zeph 1:4 also stretch out mine hand upon J
Zeph 2:7 for the remnant of the house of J
Hag 1:1 son of Shealtiel, governor of J
Hag 1:14 son of Shealtiel, governor of J
Hag 2:2 son of Shealtiel, governor of J
Hag 2:21 to Zerubbabel, governor of J
Zec 1:12 Jerusalem and on the cities of J
Zec 1:19 the horns which have scattered J
Zec 1:21 the horns which have scattered J
Zec 1:21 over the land of J to scatter it
Zec 2:12 the LORD shall inherit J his
Zec 8:13 among the heathen, O house of J
Zec 8:15 Jerusalem and to the house of J
Zec 8:19 shall be to the house of J joy
Zec 9:7 and he shall be as a governor in J
Zec 9:13 When I have bent J for me
Zec 10:3 visited his flock the house of J
Zec 10:6 I will strengthen the house of J
Zec 11:14 break the brotherhood between J
Zec 12:2 be in the siege both against J
Zec 12:4 mine eyes upon the house of J
Zec 12:5 the governors of J shall say in
Zec 12:6 of J like an hearth of fire among
Zec 12:7 shall save the tents of J first
Zec 12:7 not magnify themselves against J
Zec 14:5 in the days of Uzziah king of J
Zec 14:14 J also shall fight at Jerusalem
Zec 14:21 in J shall be holiness unto the
Mal 2:11 J hath dealt treacherously, and an
Mal 2:11 for J hath profaned the holiness
Mal 3:4 Then shall the offering of J

*4. A Levite.*
Ezr 3:9 and his sons, the sons of J

*5. A Levite who married a foreigner.*
Ezr 10:23 the same is Kelita,) Pethahiah, J

*6. An overseer.*
Neh 11:9 J the son of Senuah was second

*7. A Levite with Zerubbabel.*
Neh 12:8 Binnui, Kadmiel, Sherebiah, J

*8. An exile.*
Neh 12:34 J, and Benjamin, and Shemaiah, and

*9. A musician in exile.*
Neh 12:36 Gilalai, Maai, Nethaneel, and J

**JUDAH'S** *(ju'-dahs)*

*1. Refers to Judah 1.*
Gen 38:7 J firstborn, was wicked in the
Gen 38:12 the daughter of Shuah J wife died
Jer 32:2 which was in the king of J house
Jer 38:22 that are left in the king of J

**JUDAS** *(ju'-das)* See BARSABAS, ISCARIOT, JUDAH, JUDE, LEBBAEUS, THADDAEUS.

*1. Betrayer of Jesus.*
Mt 10:4 J Iscariot, who also betrayed him
Mt 26:14 called J Iscariot, went unto the
Mt 26:25 Then J, which betrayed him,
Mt 26:47 And while he yet spake, lo, J
Mt 27:3 Then J, which had betrayeth him,
Mk 3:19 J Iscariot, which also betrayed
Mk 14:10 J Iscariot, one of the twelve,
Mk 14:43 while he yet spake, cometh J
Lk 6:16 J Iscariot, which also was the
Lk 22:3 Satan into J surnamed Iscariot
Lk 22:47 and he that was called J, one of
Lk 22:48 But Jesus said unto him, J
Jn 6:71 He spake of J Iscariot the son of
Jn 12:4 J Iscariot, Simon's son, which

Jn 13:2 put into the heart of *J* Iscariot
Jn 13:26 the sop, he gave it to *J* Iscariot
Jn 13:29 because *J* had the bag, that Jesus
Jn 18:2 *J* also, which betrayed him, knew
Jn 18:3 *J* then, having received a band of
Jn 18:5 *J* also, which betrayed him, stood
Acts 1:16 David spake before concerning *J*
Acts 1:25 from which *J* by transgression

*2. A brother of Jesus.*

Mt 13:55 James, and Joses, and Simon, and *J*

*3. A disciple of Jesus.*

Lk 6:16 *J* the brother of James, and Judas
Jn 14:22 *J* saith unto him, not Iscariot,
Acts 1:13 and *J* the brother of James

*4. A seditious Galilean.*

Acts 5:37 After this man rose up *J* of

*5. Lodged Paul in Damascus.*

Acts 9:11 house of *J* for one called Saul

*6. Surnamed Barsabas.*

Acts 15:22 *J* surnamed Barsabas, and Silas,
Acts 15:27 We have sent therefore *J* and Silas
Acts 15:32 And *J* and Silas, being prophets

*7. A Greek form of Joseph.*

Mt 1:2 and Jacob begat *J* and his brethren
Mt 1:3 *J* begat Phares and Zara of Thamar

**JUDE** *(jood)* See JUDAS. *A brother of Jesus.*

Jude 1 *J*, the servant of Jesus Christ,

**JUDEA** *(ju-de'-ah)* See JEWRY, JUDAH. *Southern portion of Israel.*

Ezr 5:8 we went into the province of *J*

**JUDGE**

Gen 15:14 whom they shall serve, will I *j*
Gen 16:5 the LORD *j* between me and thee
Gen 18:25 Shall not the *J* of all the earth
Gen 19:9 sojourn, and he will needs be a *j*
Gen 31:37 that they may *j* betwixt us both
Gen 31:53 God of their father, *j* betwixt us
Gen 49:16 Dan shall *j* his people, as one of
Ex 2:14 made thee a prince and a *j* over us
Ex 5:21 The LORD look upon you, and *j*
Ex 18:13 that Moses sat to *j* the people
Ex 18:16 I *j* between one and another, and I
Ex 18:22 let them *j* the people at all
Ex 18:22 every small matter they shall *j*
Lev 19:15 shalt thou *j* thy neighbour
Num 35:24 shall *j* between the slayer
Deut 1:16 *j* righteously between every man
Deut 16:18 they shall *j* the people with just
Deut 17:9 unto the *j* that shall be in those
Deut 17:12 the LORD thy God, or unto the *j*
Deut 25:1 that the judges may *j* them
Deut 25:2 that the *j* shall cause him to lie
Deut 32:36 For the LORD shall *j* his people
Judg 2:18 then the LORD was with the *j*
Judg 2:18 enemies all the days of the *j*
Judg 2:19 came to pass, when the *j* was dead
Judg 11:27 the LORD the *J* be *j* this day
1Sa 2:10 the LORD shall *j* the ends of the
1Sa 2:25 another, the *j* shall *j* him
1Sa 3:13 will *j* his house for ever for the
1Sa 8:5 now make us a king to *j* us like
1Sa 8:6 they said, Give us a king to *j* us
1Sa 8:20 and that our king may *j* us
1Sa 24:12 The LORD *j* between me and thee, and
1Sa 24:15 The LORD therefore be *j*
1Sa 24:15 *j* between me and thee, and see, and
2Sa 15:4 Oh that I were made *j* in the land
1Kin 3:9 heart to *j* thy people, that I may
1Kin 3:9 for who is able to *j* this thy so
1Kin 7:7 for the throne where he might *j*
1Kin 8:32 *j* thy servants, condemning the
1Chr 16:33 because he cometh to *j* the earth
2Chr 1:10 for who can *j* this thy people,
2Chr 1:11 that thou mayest *j* my people
2Chr 6:23 *j* thy servants, by requiting the
2Chr 19:6 for ye *j* not for man, but for the
2Chr 20:12 O our God, wilt thou not *j* them
Ezr 7:25 which may *j* all the people that
Job 9:15 I would make supplication to my *j*
Job 22:13 can he *j* through the dark cloud
Job 23:7 I be delivered for ever from my *j*
Job 31:28 iniquity to be punished by the *j*
Ps 7:8 The LORD shall *j* the people
Ps 7:8 *j* me, O LORD, according to my
Ps 9:8 And he shall *j* the world in
Ps 10:18 To *j* the fatherless and the
Ps 26:1 *J* me, O LORD
Ps 35:24 *J* me, O LORD my God, according to
Ps 43:1 *J* me, O God, and plead my cause
Ps 50:4 earth, that he may *j* his people
Ps 50:6 for God is *j* himself
Ps 54:1 thy name, and *j* me by thy strength
Ps 58:1 do ye *j* uprightly, O ye sons of
Ps 67:4 for thou shalt *j* the people
Ps 68:5 a *j* of the widows, is God in his
Ps 72:2 He shall *j* thy people with
Ps 72:4 He shall *j* the poor of the people
Ps 75:2 congregation I will *j* uprightly
Ps 75:7 But God is the *j*
Ps 82:2 How long will ye *j* unjustly
Ps 82:8 Arise, O God, *j* the earth
Ps 94:2 up thyself, thou *j* of the earth
Ps 96:10 he shall *j* the people righteously
Ps 96:13 for he cometh to *j* the earth
Ps 96:13 he shall *j* the world with
Ps 98:9 for he cometh to *j* the earth
Ps 98:9 shall he *j* the world, and the
Ps 110:6 He shall *j* among the heathen, he
Ps 135:14 For the LORD will *j* his people
Prov 31:9 *j* righteously, and plead the cause
Eccl 3:17 God shall *j* the righteous and the
Is 1:17 *j* the fatherless, plead for the
Is 1:23 they *j* not the fatherless,
Is 2:4 he shall *j* among the nations, and
Is 3:2 man, and the man of war, the *j*
Is 3:13 and standeth to *j* the people
Is 5:3 of Jerusalem, and men of Judah, *j*
Is 11:3 he shall not *j* after the sight of
Is 11:4 righteousness shall he *j* the poor
Is 33:22 For the LORD is our *j*, the LORD
Is 51:5 and mine arms shall *j* the people
Jer 5:28 they *j* not the cause, the cause
Jer 5:28 right of the needy do they not *j*
Lam 3:59 *j* thou my cause
Eze 7:3 will *j* thee according to thy ways
Eze 7:8 I will *j* thee according to thy
Eze 7:27 to their deserts will I *j* them
Eze 11:10 I will *j* you in the border of
Eze 11:11 but I will *j* you in the border of
Eze 16:38 And I will *j* thee, as women that
Eze 18:30 Therefore I will *j* you, O house
Eze 20:4 Wilt thou *j* them, son of man,
Eze 20:4 son of man, wilt thou *j* them
Eze 21:30 I will *j* thee in the place where
Eze 22:2 Now, thou son of man, wilt thou *j*
Eze 22:2 wilt thou *j* the bloody city
Eze 23:24 they shall *j* thee according to
Eze 23:36 Son of man, wilt thou *j* Aholah
Eze 23:45 they shall *j* them after the
Eze 24:14 to thy doings, shall they *j* thee
Eze 33:20 I will *j* you every one after his
Eze 34:17 I *j* between cattle and cattle,
Eze 34:20 will *j* between the fat cattle and
Eze 34:22 I will *j* between cattle and cattle
Eze 44:24 they shall *j* it according to my
Joel 3:12 for there will I sit to *j* all the
Amos 2:3 I will cut off the *j* from the
Obad 21 mount Zion to *j* the mount of Esau
Mic 3:11 The heads thereof *j* for reward
Mic 4:3 he shall *j* among many people, and
Mic 5:1 they shall smite the *j* of Israel
Mic 7:3 the *j* asketh for a reward
Zec 3:7 then thou shalt also *j* my house
Mt 5:25 adversary deliver thee to the *j*
Mt 5:25 the *j* deliver thee to the officer
Mt 7:1 *J* not, that ye be not judged
Mt 7:2 For with what judgment ye *j*
Lk 6:37 *J* not, and ye shall not be judged
Lk 12:14 who made me a *j* or a divider over
Lk 12:57 yourselves *j* ye not what is right
Lk 12:58 lest he hale thee to the *j*
Lk 12:58 the *j* deliver thee to the officer
Lk 18:2 Saying, There was in a city a *j*
Lk 18:6 Hear what the unjust *j* saith
Lk 19:22 of thine own mouth will I *j* thee
Jn 5:30 as I hear, I *j*
Jn 7:24 *J* not according to the appearance
Jn 7:24 but *j* righteous judgment
Jn 7:51 Doth our law *j* any man, before it
Jn 8:15 Ye *j* after the flesh
Jn 8:15 I *j* no man
Jn 8:16 And yet if I *j*, my judgment is
Jn 8:26 many things to say and to *j* of you
Jn 12:47 and believe not, I *j* him not
Jn 12:47 for I came not to *j* the world
Jn 12:48 the same shall *j* him in the last
Jn 18:31 *j* him according to your law
Acts 4:19 unto you more than unto God, *j* ye
Acts 7:7 they shall be in bondage will I *j*
Acts 7:27 made thee a ruler and a *j* over us
Acts 7:35 Who made thee a ruler and a *j*
Acts 10:42 of God to be the *J* of quick
Acts 13:46 you, and *j* yourselves unworthy of
Acts 17:31 in the which he will *j* the world
Acts 18:15 I will be no *j* of such matters
Acts 23:3 thou to *j* me after the law
Acts 24:10 many years a *j* unto this nation
Rom 2:16 In the day when God shall *j* the
Rom 2:27 *j* thee, who by the letter and
Rom 3:6 then how shall God *j* the world
Rom 14:3 eateth not *j* him that eateth
Rom 14:10 But why dost thou *j* thy brother
Rom 14:13 therefore *j* one another any more
Rom 14:13 but *j* this rather, that no man
1Cor 4:3 yea, I *j* not mine own self
1Cor 4:5 Therefore *j* nothing before the
1Cor 5:12 For what have I to do to *j* them
1Cor 5:12 do not ye *j* them that are within
1Cor 6:2 that the saints shall *j* the world
1Cor 6:2 are ye unworthy to *j* the smallest
1Cor 6:3 ye not that we shall *j* angels
1Cor 6:4 set them to *j* who are least
1Cor 6:5 be able to *j* between his brethren
1Cor 10:15 *j* ye what I say
1Cor 11:13 *J* in yourselves
1Cor 11:31 For if we would *j* ourselves
1Cor 14:29 two or three, and let the other *j*
2Cor 5:14 because we thus *j*, that if one
Col 2:16 no man therefore *j* you in meat
2Ti 4:1 Christ, who shall *j* the quick
2Ti 4:8 which the Lord, the righteous *j*
Heb 10:30 The Lord shall *j* his people
Heb 12:23 in heaven, and to God the *J* of all
Heb 13:4 and adulterers God will *j*
Jas 4:11 but if thou *j* the law, thou art
Jas 4:11 not a doer of the law, but a *j*
Jas 5:9 the *j* standeth before the door
1Pet 4:5 him that is ready to *j* the quick
Rev 6:10 holy and true, dost thou not *j*
Rev 19:11 and in righteousness he doth *j*

**JUDGED**

Gen 30:6 And Rachel said, God hath *j* me
Ex 18:26 they *j* the people at all seasons
Ex 18:26 small matter they *j* themselves
Judg 3:10 he *j* Israel, and went out to war
Judg 4:4 she *j* Israel at that time
Judg 10:2 he *j* Israel twenty and three years
Judg 10:3 *j* Israel twenty and two years
Judg 12:7 Jephthah *j* Israel six years
Judg 12:8 him Ibzan of Beth-lehem *j* Israel
Judg 12:9 And he *j* Israel seven years
Judg 12:11 him Elon, a Zebulonite, *j* Israel
Judg 12:11 and he *j* Israel ten years
Judg 12:13 Hillel, a Pirathonite, *j* Israel
Judg 12:14 and he *j* Israel eight years
Judg 15:20 he *j* Israel in the days of the
Judg 16:31 And he *j* Israel twenty years
1Sa 4:18 he had *j* Israel forty years
1Sa 7:6 Samuel *j* the children of Israel
1Sa 7:15 Samuel *j* Israel all the days of
1Sa 7:16 *j* Israel in all those places
1Sa 7:17 and there he *j* Israel
1Kin 3:28 the judgment which the king had *j*
2Kin 23:22 days of the judges that *j* Israel
Ps 9:19 let the heathen be *j* in thy sight
Ps 37:33 nor condemn him when he is *j*
Ps 109:7 When he shall be *j*, let him be
Jer 22:16 He *j* the cause of the poor and
Eze 16:38 break wedlock and shed blood are *j*
Eze 16:52 which hast *j* thy sisters, bear
Eze 28:23 the wounded shall be *j* in the
Eze 35:11 among them, when I have *j* thee
Eze 36:19 to their doings I *j* them
Dan 9:12 and against our judges that *j* us
Mt 7:1 Judge not, that ye be not *j*
Mt 7:2 judgment ye judge, ye shall be *j*
Lk 6:37 Judge not, and ye shall not be *j*
Lk 7:43 unto him, Thou hast rightly *j*
Jn 16:11 the prince of this world is *j*
Acts 16:15 If ye have *j* me to be faithful to
Acts 24:6 would have *j* according to our law
Acts 25:9 there be *j* of these things before
Acts 25:10 seat, where I ought to be *j*
Acts 25:20 there be *j* of these matters
Acts 26:6 am *j* for the hope of the promise
Rom 2:12 in the law shall be *j* by the law
Rom 3:4 mightest overcome when thou art *j*

Rom 3:7 why yet am I also *j* as a sinner
1Cor 2:15 yet he himself is *j* of no man
1Cor 4:3 thing that I should be *j* of you
1Cor 5:3 have *j* already, as though I were
1Cor 6:2 and if the world shall be *j* by you
1Cor 10:29 for why is my liberty *j* of
1Cor 11:31 ourselves, we should not be *j*
1Cor 11:32 But when we are *j*, we are
1Cor 14:24 convinced of all, he is *j* of all
Heb 11:11 because she *j* him faithful who
Jas 2:12 shall be *j* by the law of liberty
1Pet 4:6 that they might be *j* according to
Rev 11:18 the dead, that they should be *j*
Rev 16:5 be, because thou hast *j* thus
Rev 19:2 for he hath *j* the great whore,
Rev 20:12 the dead were *j* out of those
Rev 20:13 they were *j* every man according

**JUDGES**

Ex 21:6 master shall bring him unto the *j*
Ex 21:22 he shall pay as the *j* determine
Ex 22:8 house shall be brought unto the *j*
Ex 22:9 parties shall come before the *j*
Ex 22:9 whom the *j* shall condemn, he
Num 25:5 Moses said unto the *j* of Israel
Deut 1:16 And I charged your *j* at that time
Deut 16:18 *J* and officers shalt thou make
Deut 19:17 LORD, before the priests and the *j*
Deut 19:18 the *j* shall make diligent
Deut 21:2 thy *j* shall come forth, and they
Deut 25:1 that the *j* may judge them
Deut 32:31 our enemies themselves being *j*
Josh 8:33 elders, and officers, and their *j*
Josh 23:2 for their heads, and for their *j*
Josh 24:1 for their heads, and for their *j*
Judg 2:16 Nevertheless the LORD raised up *j*
Judg 2:17 would not hearken unto their *j*
Judg 2:18 And when the LORD raised them up *j*
Ruth 1:1 pass in the days when the *j* ruled
1Sa 8:1 he made his sons *j* over Israel
1Sa 8:2 they were *j* in Beer-sheba
2Sa 7:11 *j* to be over my people Israel
2Kin 23:22 days of the *j* that judged Israel
1Chr 17:6 a word to any of the *j* of Israel
1Chr 17:10 *j* to be over my people Israel
1Chr 23:4 six thousand were officers and *j*
1Chr 26:29 over Israel, for officers and *j*
2Chr 1:2 and of hundreds, and to the *j*
2Chr 19:5 he set *j* in the land throughout
2Chr 19:6 And said to the *j*, Take heed what
Ezr 7:25 thine hand, set magistrates and *j*
Ezr 10:14 the *j* thereof, until the fierce
Job 9:24 the faces of the *j* thereof
Job 12:17 spoiled, and maketh the *j* fools
Job 31:11 iniquity to be punished by the *j*
Ps 2:10 be instructed, ye *j* of the earth
Ps 141:6 When their *j* are overthrown in
Ps 148:11 princes, and all *j* of the earth
Prov 8:16 even all the *j* of the earth
Is 1:26 restore thy *j* as at the first
Is 40:23 he maketh the *j* of the earth as
Dan 3:2 governors, and the captains, the *j*
Dan 3:3 the governors, and captains, the *j*
Dan 9:12 against our *j* that judged us, by
Hos 7:7 an oven, and have devoured their *j*
Hos 13:10 thy *j* of whom thou saidst, Give
Zeph 3:3 her *j* are evening wolves
Mt 12:27 therefore they shall be your *j*
Lk 11:19 therefore shall they be your *j*
Acts 13:20 after that he gave unto them *j*
Jas 2:4 are become *j* of evil thoughts

**JUDGEST**

Ps 51:4 speakest, and be clear when thou *j*
Jer 11:20 that *j* righteously, that triest
Rom 2:1 O man, whosoever thou art that *j*
Rom 2:1 for wherein thou *j* another
Rom 2:1 for thou that *j* doest the same
Rom 2:3 that *j* them which do such things,
Rom 14:4 Who art thou that *j* another man's
Jas 4:12 who art thou that *j* another

**JUDGETH**

Job 21:22 seeing he *j* those that are high
Job 36:31 For by them *j* he the people
Ps 7:11 God *j* the righteous, and God is
Ps 58:11 he is a God that *j* in the earth
Ps 82:1 he *j* among the gods
Prov 29:14 king that faithfully *j* the poor
Jn 5:22 For the Father *j* no man, but hath
Jn 8:50 there is one that seeketh and *j*
Jn 12:48 not my words, hath one that *j* him
1Cor 2:15 he that is spiritual *j* all things
1Cor 4:4 but he that *j* me is the Lord
1Cor 5:13 But them that are without God *j*
Jas 4:11 *j* his brother, speaketh evil of
Jas 4:11 evil of the law, and *j* the law
1Pet 1:17 *j* according to every man's work
1Pet 2:23 himself to him that *j* righteously
Rev 18:8 strong is the Lord God who *j* her

**JUDGING**

2Kin 15:5 house, *j* the people of the land
2Chr 26:21 house, *j* the people of the land
Ps 9:4 thou satest in the throne *j* right
Is 16:5 in the tabernacle of David, *j*
Mt 19:28 *j* the twelve tribes of Israel
Lk 22:30 sit on thrones *j* the twelve

**JUDGMENT**

Gen 18:19 of the LORD, to do justice and *j*
Ex 12:12 gods of Egypt I will execute *j*
Ex 21:31 according to this *j* shall it be
Ex 23:2 to decline after many to wrest *j*
Ex 23:6 the *j* of thy poor in his cause
Ex 28:15 of *j* with cunning work
Ex 28:29 breastplate of *j* upon his heart
Ex 28:30 in the breastplate of *j* the Urim
Ex 28:30 Aaron shall bear the *j* of the
Lev 19:15 shall do no unrighteousness in *j*
Lev 19:35 shall do no unrighteousness in *j*
Num 27:11 children of Israel a statute of *j*
Num 27:21 the *j* of Urim before the LORD
Num 35:12 before the congregation in *j*
Num 35:29 of *j* unto you throughout your
Deut 1:17 Ye shall not respect persons in *j*
Deut 1:17 for the *j* is God's
Deut 10:18 execute the *j* of the fatherless
Deut 16:18 judge the people with just *j*
Deut 16:19 Thou shalt not wrest *j*
Deut 17:8 a matter too hard for thee in *j*
Deut 17:9 shall shew thee the sentence of *j*
Deut 17:11 according to the *j* which they
Deut 24:17 not pervert the *j* of the stranger
Deut 25:1 between men, and they come unto *j*
Deut 27:19 perverteth the *j* of the stranger
Deut 32:4 for all his ways are *j*
Deut 32:41 and mine hand take hold on *j*
Josh 20:6 before the congregation for *j*
Judg 4:5 of Israel came up to her for *j*
Judg 5:10 on white asses, ye that sit in *j*
1Sa 8:3 and took bribes, and perverted *j*
2Sa 8:15 and David executed *j* and justice
2Sa 15:2 came to the king for *j*, then
2Sa 15:6 that came to the king for *j*
1Kin 3:11 understanding to discern *j*
1Kin 3:28 all Israel heard of the *j* which
1Kin 3:28 wisdom of God was in him, to do *j*
1Kin 7:7 might judge, even the porch of *j*
1Kin 10:9 made he thee king, to do *j*
1Kin 20:40 said unto him, So shall thy *j* be
2Kin 25:6 and they gave *j* upon him
1Chr 18:14 over all Israel, and executed *j*
2Chr 9:8 he thee king over them, to do *j*
2Chr 19:6 LORD, who is with you in the *j*
2Chr 19:8 for the *j* of the LORD, and for
2Chr 20:9 cometh upon us, as the sword, *j*
2Chr 22:8 *j* upon the house of Ahab, and
2Chr 24:24 So they executed *j* against Joash
Ezr 7:26 let *j* be executed speedily upon
Est 1:13 toward all that knew law and *j*
Job 8:3 Doth God pervert *j*?
Job 9:19 and if of *j*, who shall set me a
Job 9:32 and we should come together in *j*
Job 14:3 and bringest me into *j* with thee
Job 19:7 I cry aloud, but there is no *j*
Job 19:29 that ye may know there is a *j*
Job 22:4 will he enter with thee into *j*
Job 27:2 liveth, who hath taken away my *j*
Job 29:14 my *j* was as a robe and a diadem
Job 32:9 neither do the aged understand *j*
Job 34:4 Let us choose to us *j*
Job 34:5 and God hath taken away my *j*
Job 34:12 will the Almighty pervert *j*
Job 34:23 he should enter into *j* with God
Job 35:14 not see him, yet *j* is before him
Job 36:17 fulfilled the *j* of the wicked
Job 36:17 *j* and justice take hold on thee
Job 37:23 he is excellent in power, and in *j*
Job 40:8 Wilt thou also disannul my *j*
Ps 1:5 ungodly shall not stand in the *j*
Ps 7:6 awake for me to the *j* that thou
Ps 9:7 he hath prepared his throne for *j*
Ps 9:8 he shall minister *j* to the people
Ps 9:16 known by the *j* which he executeth
Ps 25:9 The meek will he guide in *j*
Ps 33:5 He loveth righteousness and *j*
Ps 35:23 Stir up thyself, and awake to my *j*
Ps 37:6 light, and thy *j* as the noonday
Ps 37:28 For the LORD loveth *j*, and
Ps 37:30 and his tongue talketh of *j*
Ps 72:2 righteousness and thy poor with *j*
Ps 76:8 Thou didst cause *j* to be heard
Ps 76:9 When God arose to *j*, to save all
Ps 89:14 *j* are the habitation of thy
Ps 94:15 But *j* shall return unto
Ps 97:2 *j* are the habitation of his
Ps 99:4 The king's strength also loveth *j*
Ps 99:4 equity, thou executest *j* and
Ps 101:1 I will sing of mercy and *j*
Ps 103:6 *j* for all that are oppressed
Ps 106:3 Blessed are they that keep *j*
Ps 106:30 stood up Phinehas, and executed *j*
Ps 111:7 of his hands are verity and *j*
Ps 119:66 Teach me good *j* and knowledge
Ps 119:84 when wilt thou execute *j* on them
Ps 119:121 I have done *j* and justice
Ps 119:149 quicken me according to thy *j*
Ps 122:5 For there are set thrones of *j*
Ps 143:2 enter not into *j* with thy servant
Ps 146:7 Which executeth *j* for the
Ps 149:9 execute upon them the *j* written
Prov 1:3 of wisdom, justice, and *j*, and
Prov 2:8 He keepeth the paths of *j*
Prov 2:9 understand righteousness, and *j*
Prov 8:20 in the midst of the paths of *j*
Prov 13:23 that is destroyed for want of *j*
Prov 16:10 his mouth transgresseth not in *j*
Prov 17:23 bosom to pervert the ways of *j*
Prov 18:5 to overthrow the righteous in *j*
Prov 19:28 An ungodly witness scorneth *j*
Prov 20:8 *j* scattereth away all evil with
Prov 21:3 *j* is more acceptable to the LORD
Prov 21:7 because they refuse to do *j*
Prov 21:15 It is joy to the just to do *j*
Prov 24:23 to have respect of persons in *j*
Prov 28:5 Evil men understand not *j*
Prov 29:4 The king by *j* establisheth the
Prov 29:26 but every man's *j* cometh from the
Prov 31:5 pervert the *j* of any of the
Eccl 3:16 saw under the sun the place of *j*
Eccl 5:8 poor, and violent perverting of *j*
Eccl 8:5 heart discerneth both time and *j*
Eccl 8:6 every purpose there is time and *j*
Eccl 11:9 things God will bring thee into *j*
Eccl 12:14 God shall bring every work into *j*
Is 1:17 seek *j*, relieve the oppressed,
Is 1:21 it was full of *j*
Is 1:27 Zion shall be redeemed with *j*
Is 3:14 The LORD will enter into *j* with
Is 4:4 midst thereof by the spirit of *j*
Is 5:7 and he looked for *j*, but behold
Is 5:16 of hosts shall be exalted in *j*
Is 9:7 it, and to establish it with *j*
Is 10:2 To turn aside the needy from *j*
Is 16:3 Take counsel, execute *j*
Is 16:5 of David, judging, and seeking *j*
Is 28:6 *j* to him that sitteth in *j*
Is 28:7 err in vision, they stumble in *j*
Is 28:17 *J* also will I lay to the line, and
Is 30:18 for the LORD is a God of *j*
Is 32:1 and princes shall rule in *j*
Is 32:16 Then *j* shall dwell in the
Is 33:5 he hath filled Zion with *j*
Is 34:5 upon the people of my curse, to *j*
Is 40:14 and taught him in the path of *j*
Is 40:27 my *j* is passed over from my God
Is 41:1 let us come near together to *j*
Is 42:1 bring forth *j* to the Gentiles
Is 42:3 he shall bring forth *j* unto truth
Is 42:4 till he have set *j* in the earth
Is 49:4 yet surely my *j* is with the LORD,
Is 51:4 I will make my *j* to rest for a
Is 53:8 was taken from prison and from *j*
Is 54:17 thee in *j* thou shalt condemn
Is 56:1 Thus saith the LORD, Keep ye *j*
Is 59:8 there is no *j* in their goings
Is 59:9 Therefore is *j* far from us
Is 59:11 we look for *j*, but there is none
Is 59:14 *j* is turned away backward, and
Is 59:15 him that there was no *j*
Is 61:8 For I the LORD love *j*, I hate
Jer 4:2 The LORD liveth, in truth, in *j*

Jer 5:1 if there be any that executeth *j*
Jer 5:4 the LORD, nor the *j* of their God
Jer 5:5 the LORD, and the *j* of their God
Jer 7:5 throughly execute *j* between a man
Jer 8:7 people know not the *j* of the LORD
Jer 9:24 which exercise lovingkindness, *j*
Jer 10:24 O LORD, correct me, but with *j*
Jer 21:12 Execute *j* in the morning, and
Jer 22:3 Execute ye *j* and righteousness, and
Jer 22:15 thy father eat and drink, and do *j*
Jer 23:5 and prosper, and shall execute *j*
Jer 33:15 and he shall execute *j* and
Jer 39:5 Hamath, where he gave *j* upon him
Jer 48:21 *j* is come upon the plain country
Jer 48:47 Thus far is the *j* of Moab
Jer 49:12 they whose *j* was not to drink of
Jer 51:9 for her *j* reacheth unto heaven,
Jer 51:47 that I will do *j* upon the graven
Jer 51:52 that I will do *j* upon her graven
Jer 52:9 where he gave *j* upon him
Eze 18:8 hath executed true *j* between man
Eze 23:10 for they had executed *j* upon her
Eze 23:24 I will set *j* before them, and they
Eze 34:16 I will feed them with *j*
Eze 39:21 see my *j* that I have executed
Eze 44:24 controversy they shall stand in *j*
Eze 45:9 violence and spoil, and execute *j*
Dan 4:37 works are truth, and his ways *j*
Dan 7:10 the *j* was set, and the books were
Dan 7:22 *j* was given to the saints of the
Dan 7:26 But the *j* shall sit, and they
Hos 2:19 unto me in righteousness, and in *j*
Hos 5:1 for *j* is toward you, because ye
Hos 5:11 is oppressed and broken in *j*
Hos 10:4 thus *j* springeth up as hemlock in
Hos 12:6 keep mercy and *j*, and wait on thy
Amos 5:7 Ye who turn *j* to wormwood
Amos 5:15 good, and establish *j* in the gate
Amos 5:24 But let *j* run down as waters, and
Amos 6:12 for ye have turned *j* into gall
Mic 3:1 Is it not for you to know *j*
Mic 3:8 the spirit of the LORD, and of *j*
Mic 3:9 the house of Israel, that abhor *j*
Mic 7:9 my cause, and execute *j* for me
Hab 1:4 slacked, and *j* doth never go forth
Hab 1:4 therefore wrong *j* proceedeth
Hab 1:7 their *j* and their dignity shall
Hab 1:12 thou hast ordained them for *j*
Zeph 2:3 earth, which have wrought his *j*
Zeph 3:5 doth he bring his *j* to light
Zec 7:9 of hosts, saying, Execute true *j*
Zec 8:16 execute the *j* of truth and peace
Mal 2:17 or, Where is the God of *j*
Mal 3:5 And I will come near to you to *j*
Mt 5:21 kill shall be in danger of the *j*
Mt 5:22 cause shall be in danger of the *j*
Mt 7:2 For with what *j* ye judge, ye
Mt 10:15 Sodom and Gomorrha in the day of *j*
Mt 11:22 for Tyre and Sidon at the day of *j*
Mt 11:24 the land of Sodom in the day of *j*
Mt 12:18 he shall shew *j* to the Gentiles
Mt 12:20 till he send forth *j* unto victory
Mt 12:36 account thereof in the day of *j*
Mt 12:41 rise in *j* with this generation
Mt 12:42 up in the *j* with this generation
Mt 23:23 weightier matters of the law, *j*
Mt 27:19 he was set down on the *j* seat
Mk 6:11 Sodom and Gomorrha in the day of *j*
Lk 10:14 for Tyre and Sidon at the *j*
Lk 11:31 the south shall rise up in the *j*
Lk 11:32 up in the *j* with this generation
Lk 11:42 manner of herbs, and pass over *j*
Jn 5:22 hath committed all *j* unto the Son
Jn 5:27 him authority to execute *j* also
Jn 5:30 and my *j* is just
Jn 7:24 appearance, but judge righteous *j*
Jn 8:16 And yet if I judge, my *j* is true
Jn 9:39 For *j* I am come into this world,
Jn 12:31 Now is the *j* of this world
Jn 16:8 sin, and of righteousness, and of *j*
Jn 16:11 Of *j*, because the prince of this
Jn 18:28 from Caiaphas unto the hall of *j*
Jn 18:28 went not into the *j* hall, lest
Jn 18:33 entered into the *j* hall again
Jn 19:9 And went again into the *j* hall
Jn 19:13 sat down in the *j* seat in a place
Acts 8:33 humiliation his *j* was taken away
Acts 18:12 and brought him to the *j* seat
Acts 18:16 And he drave them from the *j* seat
Acts 18:17 and beat him before the *j* seat
Acts 23:35 him to be kept in Herod's *j* hall
Acts 24:25 *j* to come, Felix trembled, and
Acts 25:6 the *j* seat commanded Paul to be
Acts 25:10 Paul, I stand at Caesar's *j* seat
Acts 25:15 desiring to have *j* against him
Acts 25:17 on the morrow I sat on the *j* seat
Rom 1:32 Who knowing the *j* of God, that
Rom 2:2 But we are sure that the *j* of God
Rom 2:3 thou shalt escape the *j* of God
Rom 2:5 of the righteous *j* of God
Rom 5:16 for the *j* was by one to
Rom 5:18 of one *j* came upon all men to
Rom 14:10 stand before the *j* seat of Christ
1Cor 1:10 in the same mind and in the same *j*
1Cor 4:3 be judged of you, or of man's *j*
1Cor 7:25 yet I give my *j*, as one that hath
1Cor 7:40 if she so abide, after my *j*
2Cor 5:10 before the *j* seat of Christ
Gal 5:10 troubleth you shall bear his *j*
Phil 1:9 and more in knowledge and in all *j*
2Th 1:5 token of the righteous *j* of God
1Ti 5:24 beforehand, going before to *j*
Heb 6:2 of the dead, and of eternal *j*
Heb 9:27 once to die, but after this the *j*
Heb 10:27 certain fearful looking for of *j*
Jas 2:6 and draw you before the *j* seats
Jas 2:13 For he shall have *j* without mercy
Jas 2:13 and mercy rejoiceth against *j*
1Pet 4:17 For the time is come that *j* must
2Pet 2:3 whose *j* now of a long time
2Pet 2:4 darkness, to be reserved unto *j*
2Pet 2:9 unto the day of *j* to be punished
2Pet 3:7 unto fire against the day of *j*
1Jn 4:17 may have boldness in the day of *j*
Jude 6 unto the *j* of the great day
Jude 15 To execute *j* upon all, and to
Rev 14:7 for the hour of his *j* is come
Rev 17:1 I will shew unto thee the *j* of
Rev 18:10 for in one hour is thy *j* come
Rev 20:4 them, and *j* was given unto them

**JUDGMENTS**

Ex 6:6 out arm, and with great *j*
Ex 7:4 of the land of Egypt by great *j*
Ex 21:1 Now these are the *j* which thou
Ex 24:3 words of the LORD, and all the *j*
Lev 18:4 Ye shall do my *j*, and keep mine
Lev 18:5 keep my statutes, and my *j*
Lev 18:26 keep my statutes and my *j*, and
Lev 19:37 all my statutes, and all my *j*
Lev 20:22 keep all my statutes, and all my *j*
Lev 25:18 do my statutes, and keep my *j*
Lev 26:15 or if your soul abhor my *j*
Lev 26:43 even because they despised my *j*
Lev 26:46 These are the statutes and *j*
Num 33:4 gods also the LORD executed *j*
Num 35:24 of blood according to these *j*
Num 36:13 are the commandments and the *j*
Deut 4:1 unto the statutes and unto the *j*
Deut 4:5 I have taught you statutes and *j*
Deut 4:8 *j* so righteous as all this law,
Deut 4:14 time to teach you statutes and *j*
Deut 4:45 and the statutes, and the *j*
Deut 5:1 *j* which I speak in your ears this
Deut 5:31 and the statutes, and the *j*
Deut 6:1 the statutes, and the *j*, which
Deut 6:20 and the statutes, and the *j*
Deut 7:11 and the statutes, and the *j*
Deut 7:12 to pass, if ye hearken to these *j*
Deut 8:11 his commandments, and his *j*
Deut 11:1 charge, and his statutes, and his *j*
Deut 11:32 *j* which I set before you this day
Deut 12:1 These are the statutes and *j*
Deut 26:16 thee to do these statutes and *j*
Deut 26:17 and his commandments, and his *j*
Deut 30:16 and his statutes and his *j*, that
Deut 33:10 They shall teach Jacob thy *j*
Deut 33:21 of the LORD, and his *j* with Israel
2Sa 22:23 For all his *j* were before me
1Kin 2:3 and his commandments, and his *j*
1Kin 6:12 in my statutes, and execute my *j*
1Kin 8:58 and his statutes, and his *j*
1Kin 9:4 and wilt keep my statutes and my *j*
1Kin 11:33 and to keep my statutes and my *j*
1Chr 16:12 wonders, and the *j* of his mouth
1Chr 16:14 his *j* are in all the earth
1Chr 22:13 *j* which the LORD charged Moses
1Chr 28:7 to do my commandments and my *j*
2Chr 7:17 shalt observe my statutes and my *j*
2Chr 19:10 law and commandment, statutes and *j*
Ezr 7:10 to teach in Israel statutes and *j*
Neh 1:7 nor the statutes, nor the *j*
Neh 9:13 heaven, and gavest them right *j*
Neh 9:29 but sinned against thy *j*
Neh 10:29 of the LORD our Lord, and his *j*
Ps 10:5 thy *j* are far above out of his
Ps 18:22 For all his *j* were before me, and
Ps 19:9 the *j* of the LORD are true and
Ps 36:6 thy *j* are a great deep
Ps 48:11 Judah be glad, because of thy *j*
Ps 72:1 Give the king thy *j*, O God, and
Ps 89:30 my law, and walk not in my *j*
Ps 97:8 Judah rejoiced because of thy *j*
Ps 105:5 wonders, and the *j* of his mouth
Ps 105:7 his *j* are in all the earth
Ps 119:7 have learned thy righteous *j*
Ps 119:13 I declared all the *j* of thy mouth
Ps 119:20 it hath unto thy *j* at all times
Ps 119:30 thy *j* have I laid before me
Ps 119:39 for thy *j* are good
Ps 119:43 for I have hoped in thy *j*
Ps 119:52 I remembered thy *j* of old
Ps 119:62 thee because of thy righteous *j*
Ps 119:75 that thy *j* are right, and that
Ps 119:102 I have not departed from thy *j*
Ps 119:106 that I will keep thy righteous *j*
Ps 119:108 mouth, O LORD, and teach me thy *j*
Ps 119:120 and I am afraid of thy *j*
Ps 119:137 O LORD, and upright are thy *j*
Ps 119:156 quicken me according to thy *j*
Ps 119:160 thy righteous *j* endureth for ever
Ps 119:164 thee because of thy righteous *j*
Ps 119:175 and let thy *j* help me
Ps 147:19 his statutes and his *j* unto Israel
Ps 147:20 and as for his *j*, they have not
Prov 19:29 *J* are prepared for scorners, and
Is 26:8 Yea, in the way of thy *j*, O LORD,
Is 26:9 for when thy *j* are in the earth,
Jer 1:16 I will utter my *j* against them
Jer 12:1 let me talk with thee of thy *j*
Eze 5:6 she hath changed my *j* into
Eze 5:6 for they have refused my *j*
Eze 5:7 statutes, neither have kept my *j*
Eze 5:7 have done according to the *j* of
Eze 5:8 will execute *j* in the midst of
Eze 5:10 and I will execute *j* in thee
Eze 5:15 shall execute *j* in thee in anger
Eze 11:9 and will execute *j* among you
Eze 11:12 statutes, neither executed my *j*
Eze 14:21 my four sore *j* upon Jerusalem
Eze 16:41 execute *j* upon thee in the sight
Eze 18:9 in my statutes, and hath kept my *j*
Eze 18:17 nor increase, hath executed my *j*
Eze 20:11 my statutes, and shewed them my *j*
Eze 20:13 statutes, and they despised my *j*
Eze 20:16 Because they despised my *j*
Eze 20:18 fathers, neither observe their *j*
Eze 20:19 walk in my statutes, and keep my *j*
Eze 20:21 neither kept my *j* to do them
Eze 20:24 they had not executed my *j*
Eze 20:25 *j* whereby they should not live
Eze 23:24 judge thee according to their *j*
Eze 25:11 And I will execute *j* upon Moab
Eze 28:22 I shall have executed *j* in her
Eze 28:26 when I have executed *j* upon all
Eze 30:14 in Zoan, and will execute *j* in No
Eze 30:19 Thus will I execute *j* in Egypt
Eze 36:27 statutes, and ye shall keep my *j*
Eze 37:24 they shall also walk in my *j*
Eze 44:24 shall judge it according to my *j*
Dan 9:5 from thy precepts and from thy *j*
Hos 6:5 thy *j* are as the light that goeth
Zeph 3:15 The LORD hath taken away thy *j*
Mal 4:4 Israel, with the statutes and *j*
Rom 11:33 how unsearchable are his *j*
1Cor 6:4 If then ye have *j* of things
Rev 15:4 for thy *j* are made manifest
Rev 16:7 true and righteous are thy *j*
Rev 19:2 For true and righteous are his *j*

**JUDITH** *(ju'-dith) A wife of Esau.*
Gen 26:34 wife *J* the daughter of Beeri the

**JULIA** *(ju'-le-ah) A Christian acquaintance of Paul.*
Rom 16:15 Salute Philologus, and *J*, Nereus,

**JULIUS** *(ju'-le-us) A Roman centurion.*
Acts 27:1 other prisoners unto one named *J*
Acts 27:3 *J* courteously entreated Paul, and

**JUNIA** *(ju'-ne-ah) A Christian acquaintance of Paul.*
Rom 16:7 Salute Andronicus and J, my

**JUNIPER**
1Kin 19:4 came and sat down under a *j* tree
1Kin 19:5 as he lay and slept under a *j* tree
Job 30:4 bushes, and *j* roots for their meat
Ps 120:4 of the mighty, with coals of *j*

**JUPITER** *(ju'-pit-ur) Chief god of the Romans.*
Acts 14:12 And they called Barnabas, J
Acts 14:13 Then the priest of J, which was
Acts 19:35 the image which fell down from J

**JUSHAB-HESED** *(ju'-shab-he'-sed) A son of Zerubbabel.*
1Chr 3:20 and Berechiah, and Hasadiah, J

**JUST**
Gen 6:9 Noah was a *j* man and perfect in
Lev 19:36 J balances, *j* weights
Lev 19:36 a *j* ephah, and a *j* hin, shall
Deut 16:18 judge the people with *j* judgment
Deut 16:20 is altogether *j* shalt thou follow
Deut 25:15 *j* weight, a perfect and
Deut 25:15 *j* measure shalt thou have
Deut 32:4 of truth and without iniquity, *j*
2Sa 23:3 He that ruleth over men must be *j*
Neh 9:33 Howbeit thou art *j* in all that is
Job 4:17 mortal man be more *j* than God
Job 9:2 but how should man be *j* with God
Job 12:4 the *j* upright man is laughed to
Job 27:17 but the *j* shall put it on, and the
Job 33:12 Behold, in this thou art not *j*
Job 34:17 thou condemn him that is most *j*
Ps 7:9 but establish the *j*
Ps 37:12 The wicked plotteth against the *j*
Prov 3:33 blesseth the habitation of the *j*
Prov 4:18 But the path of the *j* is as the
Prov 9:9 teach a *j* man, and he will
Prov 10:6 are upon the head of the *j*
Prov 10:7 The memory of the *j* is blessed
Prov 10:20 The tongue of the *j* is as choice
Prov 10:31 The mouth of the *j* bringeth forth
Prov 11:1 but a *j* weight is his delight
Prov 11:9 shall the *j* be delivered
Prov 12:13 but the *j* shall come out of
Prov 12:21 shall no evil happen to the *j*
Prov 13:22 the sinner is laid up for the *j*
Prov 16:11 A *j* weight and balance are the
Prov 17:15 and he that condemneth the *j*
Prov 17:26 Also to punish the *j* is not good
Prov 18:17 first in his own cause seemeth *j*
Prov 20:7 The *j* man walketh in his
Prov 21:15 It is joy to the *j* to do judgment
Prov 24:16 For a *j* man falleth seven times,
Prov 29:10 but the *j* seek his soul
Prov 29:27 man is an abomination to the *j*
Eccl 7:15 there is a *j* man that perisheth
Eccl 7:20 there is not a *j* man upon earth
Eccl 8:14 that there be *j* men, unto whom it
Is 26:7 The way of the *j* is uprightness
Is 26:7 dost weigh the path of the *j*
Is 29:21 turn aside the *j* for a thing of
Is 45:21 a *j* God and a Saviour
Lam 4:13 of the *j* in the midst of her
Eze 18:5 But if a man be *j*, and do that
Eze 18:9 he is *j*, he shall surely live,
Eze 45:10 Ye shall have *j* balances, and a
Eze 45:10 a *j* ephah, and a *j* bath
Hos 14:9 and the *j* shall walk in them
Amos 5:12 they afflict the *j*, they take a
Hab 2:4 but the *j* shall live by his faith
Zeph 3:5 The *j* LORD is in the midst
Zec 9:9 he is *j*, and having salvation
Mt 1:19 Joseph her husband, being a *j* man
Mt 5:45 good, and sendeth rain on the *j*
Mt 13:49 sever the wicked from among the *j*
Mt 27:19 nothing to do with that *j* man
Mt 27:24 of the blood of this *j* person
Mk 6:20 John, knowing that he was a *j* man
Lk 1:17 to the wisdom of the *j*
Lk 2:25 and the same man was *j* and devout,
Lk 14:14 at the resurrection of the *j*
Lk 15:7 nine *j* persons, which need no
Lk 20:20 should feign themselves *j* men
Lk 23:50 and he was a good man, and a *j*
Jn 5:30 and my judgment is *j*
Acts 3:14 ye denied the Holy One and the J
Acts 7:52 before of the coming of the J One
Acts 10:22 a *j* man, and one that feareth God,
Acts 22:14 know his will, and see that J One
Acts 24:15 of the dead, both of the *j*
Rom 1:17 The *j* shall live by faith
Rom 2:13 of the law are *j* before God
Rom 3:8 whose damnation is *j*
Rom 3:26 that he might be *j*, and the
Rom 7:12 and the commandment holy, and *j*
Gal 3:11 The *j* shall live by faith
Phil 4:8 honest, whatsoever things are *j*
Col 4:1 your servants that which is *j*
Titus 1:8 a lover of good men, sober, *j*
Heb 2:2 received a *j* recompence of reward
Heb 10:38 Now the *j* shall live by faith
Heb 12:23 the spirits of *j* men made perfect
Jas 5:6 Ye have condemned and killed the *j*
1Pet 3:18 the *j* for the unjust, that he
2Pet 2:7 And delivered *j* Lot, vexed with
1Jn 1:9 *j* to forgive us our sins, and to
Rev 15:3 *j* and true are thy ways, thou King

**JUSTICE**
Gen 18:19 keep the way of the LORD, to do *j*
Deut 33:21 he executed the *j* of the LORD
2Sa 8:15 judgment and *j* unto all his people
2Sa 15:4 come unto me, and I would do him *j*
1Kin 10:9 he thee king, to do judgment and *j*
1Chr 18:14 and *j* among all his people
2Chr 9:8 over them, to do judgment and *j*
Job 8:3 or doth the Almighty pervert *j*
Job 36:17 judgment and *j* take hold on thee
Job 37:23 and in judgment, and in plenty of *j*
Ps 82:3 do *j* to the afflicted and needy
Ps 89:14 J and judgment are the habitation
Ps 119:121 I have done judgment and *j*
Prov 1:3 the instruction of wisdom, *j*
Prov 8:15 kings reign, and princes decree *j*
Prov 21:3 To do *j* and judgment is more
Eccl 5:8 *j* in a province, marvel not at
Is 9:7 with *j* from henceforth even for
Is 56:1 LORD, Keep ye judgment, and do *j*
Is 58:2 ask of me the ordinances of *j*
Is 59:4 None calleth for *j*, nor any
Is 59:9 us, neither doth *j* overtake us
Is 59:14 backward, and *j* standeth afar off
Jer 22:15 eat and drink, and do judgment and *j*
Jer 23:5 judgment and *j* in the earth
Jer 31:23 bless thee, O habitation of *j*
Jer 50:7 the LORD, the habitation of *j*
Eze 45:9 spoil, and execute judgment and *j*

**JUSTIFICATION**
Rom 4:25 and was raised again for our *j*
Rom 5:16 gift is of many offences unto *j*
Rom 5:18 came upon all men unto *j* of life

**JUSTIFIED**
Job 11:2 and should a man full of talk be *j*
Job 13:18 I know that I shall be *j*
Job 25:4 How then can man be *j* with God
Job 32:2 because he *j* himself rather than
Ps 51:4 mightest be *j* when thou speakest
Ps 143:2 sight shall no man living be *j*
Is 43:9 witnesses, that they may be *j*
Is 43:26 thou, that thou mayest be *j*
Is 45:25 shall all the seed of Israel be *j*
Jer 3:11 The backsliding Israel hath *j*
Eze 16:51 hast *j* thy sisters in all thine
Eze 16:52 in that thou hast *j* thy sisters
Mt 11:19 But wisdom is *j* of her children
Mt 12:37 For by thy words thou shalt be *j*
Lk 7:29 *j* God, being baptized with the
Lk 7:35 But wisdom is *j* of all her
Lk 18:14 his house *j* rather than the other
Acts 13:39 believe are *j* from all things
Acts 13:39 not be *j* by the law of Moses
Rom 2:13 the doers of the law shall be *j*
Rom 3:4 thou mightest be *j* in thy sayings
Rom 3:20 shall no flesh be *j* in his sight
Rom 3:24 Being *j* freely by his grace
Rom 3:28 we conclude that a man is *j* by
Rom 4:2 For if Abraham were *j* by works
Rom 5:1 Therefore being *j* by faith
Rom 5:9 being now *j* by his blood, we
Rom 8:30 and whom he called, them he also *j*
Rom 8:30 and whom he *j*, them he also
1Cor 4:4 yet am I not hereby *j*
1Cor 6:11 but ye are *j* in the name of the
Gal 2:16 is not *j* by the works of the law
Gal 2:16 that we might be *j* by the faith
Gal 2:16 of the law shall no flesh be *j*
Gal 2:17 while we seek to be *j* by Christ
Gal 3:11 But that no man is *j* by the law
Gal 3:24 that we might be *j* by faith
Gal 5:4 whosoever of you are *j* by the law
1Ti 3:16 *j* in the Spirit, seen of angels,
Titus 3:7 That being *j* by his grace, we
Jas 2:21 not Abraham our father *j* by works
Jas 2:24 then how that by works a man is *j*
Jas 2:25 not Rahab the harlot *j* by works

**JUSTIFIETH**
Prov 17:15 He that *j* the wicked, and he that
Is 50:8 He is near that *j* me
Rom 4:5 on him that *j* the ungodly
Rom 8:33 It is God that *j*

**JUSTIFY**
Ex 23:7 for I will not *j* the wicked
Deut 25:1 then they shall *j* the righteous
Job 9:20 If I *j* myself, mine own mouth
Job 27:5 God forbid that I should *j* you
Job 33:32 speak, for I desire to *j* thee
Is 5:23 Which *j* the wicked for reward, and
Is 53:11 shall my righteous servant *j* many
Lk 10:29 But he, willing to *j* himself
Lk 16:15 Ye are they which *j* yourselves
Rom 3:30 which shall *j* the circumcision by
Gal 3:8 would *j* the heathen through faith

**JUSTUS** *(jus'-tus)* See BARSABAS, JESUS.
*1. Surname for Barsabas.*
Acts 1:23 Barsabas, who was surnamed J
*2. A Corinthian Christian.*
Acts 18:7 a certain man's house, named J
*3. A Christian acquaintance of Paul.*
Col 4:11 And Jesus, which is called J

**JUTTAH** *(jut'-tah) A city in Judah.*
Josh 15:55 Maon, Carmel, and Ziph, and J
Josh 21:16 and J with her suburbs, and

# K

**KABZEEL** *(kab'-ze-el)* See JEKABZEEL. *A city in Judah.*
Josh 15:21 coast of Edom southward were *K*
2Sa 23:20 the son of a valiant man, of *K*
1Chr 11:22 the son of a valiant man of *K*

**KADESH** *(ka'-desh)* See EN-MISHPAT, KADESH-BARNEA, KEDESH. *A place in the wilderness, south of Judah.*
Gen 14:7 and came to En=mishpat, which is *K*
Gen 16:14 behold, it is between *K* and Bered
Gen 20:1 country, and dwelled between *K*
Num 13:26 the wilderness of Paran, to *K*
Num 20:1 and the people abode in *K*
Num 20:14 from *K* unto the king of Edom
Num 20:16 and, behold, we are in *K*, a city
Num 20:22 congregation, journeyed from *K*
Num 27:14 in *K* in the wilderness of Zin
Num 33:36 the wilderness of Zin, which is *K*
Num 33:37 And they removed from *K*, and
Deut 1:46 So ye abode in *K* many days
Judg 11:16 unto the Red sea, and came to *K*
Judg 11:17 and Israel abode in *K*
Ps 29:8 LORD shaketh the wilderness of *K*
Eze 47:19 even to the waters of strife in *K*
Eze 48:28 unto the waters of strife in *K*

**KADESH-BARNEA** *(ka'-desh-bar'-ne-ah)* See KADESH. *Same as Kadesh.*
Num 32:8 sent them from *K* to see the land
Num 34:4 shall be from the south to *K*
Deut 1:2 by the way of mount Seir unto *K*

Deut 1:19 and we came to *K*
Deut 2:14 the space in which we came from *K*
Deut 9:23 when the LORD sent you from *K*
Josh 10:41 smote them from *K* even unto Gaza
Josh 14:6 of God concerning me and thee in *K*
Josh 14:7 me from *K* to espy out the land
Josh 15:3 up on the south side unto *K*

**KADMIEL** *(kad'-me-el)*
*1. An exile.*
Ezr 2:40 the children of Jeshua and *K*
Neh 7:43 the children of Jeshua, of *K*
*2. A rebuilder of the Temple.*
Ezr 3:9 with his sons and his brethren, *K*
*3. A Levite with Nehemiah.*
Neh 9:4 the Levites, Jeshua, and Bani, *K*
Neh 9:5 Then the Levites, Jeshua, and *K*
Neh 10:9 Binnui of the sons of Henadad, *K*
Neh 12:8 Jeshua, Binnui, *K*, Sherebiah,
Neh 12:24 Sherebiah, and Jeshua the son of *K*

**KADMONITES** *(kad'-mo-nites) A Phoenician tribe.*
Gen 15:19 and the Kenizzites, and the *K*

**KALLAI** *(kal'-la-i) A priest.*
Neh 12:20 Of Sallai, *K*; of Amok

**KANAH** *(ka'-nah)*
*1. A brook between Ephraim and Manasseh.*
Josh 16:8 Tappuah westward unto the river *K*
Josh 17:9 coast descended unto the river *K*
*2. A city in Asher.*
Josh 19:28 and Rehob, and Hammon, and *K*

**KAREAH** *(ka'-re-ah)* See CAREAH. *A captain of the Jews.*
Jer 40:8 Johanan and Jonathan the sons of *K*
Jer 40:13 Moreover Johanan the son of *K*
Jer 40:15 Then Johanan the son of *K* spake
Jer 40:16 said unto Johanan the son of *K*
Jer 41:11 But when Johanan the son of *K*
Jer 41:13 Ishmael saw Johanan the son of *K*
Jer 41:14 and went unto Johanan the son of *K*
Jer 41:16 Then took Johanan the son of *K*
Jer 42:1 forces, and Johanan the son of *K*
Jer 42:8 called he Johanan the son of *K*
Jer 43:2 Hoshaiah, and Johanan the son of *K*
Jer 43:4 So Johanan the son of *K*, and all
Jer 43:5 But Johanan the son of *K*, and all

**KARKAA** *(kar'-ka-ah) A city in Judah.*
Josh 15:3 Adar, and fetched a compass to *K*

**KARKOR** *(kar'-kor) A Gadite city.*
Judg 8:10 Now Zebah and Zalmunna were in *K*

**KARNAIM** *(kar'-na-im)* See ASHTEROTH. *A city in Og.*
Gen 14:5 smote the Rephaims in Ashteroth *K*

**KARTAH** *(kar'-tah)* See KATTATH. *A Levitical city in Zebulun.*
Josh 21:34 suburbs, and *K* with her suburbs,

**KARTAN** *(kar'-tan)* See KIRJATHAIM. *A Levitical city in Naphtali.*
Josh 21:32 suburbs, and *K* with her suburbs

**KATTATH** *(kat'-tath)* See KARTAH, KITRON. *A city in Zebulun.*
Josh 19:15 And *K*, and Nahallal, and Shimron,

**KEDAR** *(ke'-dar)*
*1. A son of Ishmael.*
Gen 25:13 and *K*, and Adbeel, and Mibsam,
1Chr 1:29 then *K*, and Adbeel, and Mibsam,
*2. The tribe.*
Ps 120:5 that I dwell in the tents of *K*
Song 1:5 of Jerusalem, as the tents of *K*
Is 21:16 and all the glory of *K* shall fail
Is 21:17 mighty men of the children of *K*
Is 42:11 the villages that *K* doth inhabit
Is 60:7 All the flocks of *K* shall be
Jer 2:10 and send unto *K*, and consider
Jer 49:28 Concerning *K*, and concerning the
Jer 49:28 Arise ye, go up to *K*, and spoil
Eze 27:21 Arabia, and all the princes of *K*

**KEDEMAH** *(ked'-e-mah) A son of Ishmael.*
Gen 25:15 and Tema, Jetur, Naphish, and *K*
1Chr 1:31 Jetur, Naphish, and *K*

**KEDEMOTH** *(ked'-e-moth)*
*1. A wilderness in Reuben.*
Deut 2:26 out of the wilderness of *K* unto
*2. A Levitical city in Reuben.*
Josh 13:18 And Jahaza, and *K*, and Mephaath,
Josh 21:37 *K* with her suburbs, and Mephaath
1Chr 6:79 *K* also with her suburbs, and

**KEDESH** *(ke'-desh)* See KADESH, KEDESH-NAPHTALI, KISHION.
*1. A Canaanite city.*
Josh 12:22 The king of *K*, one
Josh 19:37 And *K*, and Edrei, and En-hazor,
*2. A city of refuge in Naphtali.*
Josh 20:7 they appointed *K* in Galilee in
Josh 21:32 *K* in Galilee with her suburbs, to
Judg 4:9 arose, and went with Barak to *K*
Judg 4:10 called Zebulun and Naphtali to *K*
Judg 4:11 plain of Zaanaim, which is by *K*
2Kin 15:29 and Janoah, and *K*, and Hazor, and
1Chr 6:76 *K* in Galilee with her suburbs, and
*3. A Levitical city in Naphtali.*
1Chr 6:72 *K* with her suburbs, Daberath with
*4. A city in Judah.*
Josh 15:23 And *K*, and Hazor, and Ithnan,

**KEDESH-NAPHTALI** *(ke'-desh-naf'-ta-li) Same as Kedesh 2.*
Judg 4:6 Barak the son of Abinoam out of *K*

**KEEP**
Gen 2:15 of Eden to dress it and to *k* it
Gen 3:24 to *k* the way of the tree of life
Gen 6:19 to *k* them alive with thee
Gen 6:20 come unto thee, to *k* them alive
Gen 7:3 to *k* seed alive upon the face of
Gen 17:9 Abraham, Thou shalt *k* my covenant
Gen 17:10 is my covenant, which ye shall *k*
Gen 18:19 they shall *k* the way of the LORD,
Gen 28:15 will *k* thee in all places whither
Gen 28:20 will *k* me in this way that I go,
Gen 30:31 I will again feed and *k* thy flock
Gen 33:9 *k* that thou hast unto thyself
Gen 41:35 let them *k* food in the cities
Ex 6:5 whom the Egyptians *k* in bondage
Ex 12:6 ye shall *k* it up until the
Ex 12:14 ye shall *k* it a feast to the LORD
Ex 12:14 ye shall *k* it a feast by an
Ex 12:25 that ye shall *k* this service
Ex 12:47 congregation of Israel shall *k* it
Ex 12:48 will *k* the passover to the LORD,
Ex 12:48 and then let him come near and *k* it
Ex 13:5 that thou shalt *k* this service in
Ex 13:10 Thou shalt therefore *k* this
Ex 15:26 *k* all his statutes, I will put
Ex 16:28 refuse ye to *k* my commandments
Ex 19:5 *k* my covenant, then ye shall be a
Ex 20:6 love me, and *k* my commandments
Ex 20:8 the sabbath day, to *k* it holy
Ex 22:7 his neighbour money or stuff to *k*
Ex 22:10 or a sheep, or any beast, to *k*
Ex 23:7 *K* thee far from a false matter
Ex 23:14 Three times thou shalt *k* a feast
Ex 23:15 Thou shalt *k* the feast of
Ex 23:20 to *k* thee in the way, and to bring
Ex 31:13 Verily my sabbaths ye shall *k*
Ex 31:14 Ye shall *k* the sabbath therefore
Ex 31:16 of Israel shall *k* the sabbath
Ex 34:18 of unleavened bread shalt thou *k*
Lev 6:2 that which was delivered him to *k*
Lev 6:4 that which was delivered him to *k*
Lev 8:35 *k* the charge of the LORD, that ye
Lev 18:4 *k* mine ordinances, to walk
Lev 18:5 Ye shall therefore *k* my statutes
Lev 18:26 Ye shall therefore *k* my statutes
Lev 18:30 shall ye *k* mine ordinance
Lev 19:3 and his father, and *k* my sabbaths
Lev 19:19 Ye shall *k* my statutes
Lev 19:30 Ye shall *k* my sabbaths, and
Lev 20:8 ye shall *k* my statutes, and do
Lev 20:22 shall therefore *k* all my statutes
Lev 22:9 shall therefore *k* mine ordinance
Lev 22:31 shall ye *k* my commandments
Lev 23:39 ye shall *k* a feast unto the LORD
Lev 23:41 ye shall *k* it a feast unto the
Lev 25:2 then shall the land *k* a sabbath
Lev 25:18 *k* my judgments, and do them
Lev 26:2 Ye shall *k* my sabbaths, and
Lev 26:3 *k* my commandments, and do them
Num 1:53 the Levites shall *k* the charge of
Num 3:7 And they shall *k* his charge
Num 3:8 they shall *k* all the instruments
Num 3:32 *k* the charge of the sanctuary
Num 6:24 The LORD bless thee, and *k* thee
Num 8:26 to *k* the charge, and shall do no
Num 9:2 *k* the passover at his appointed
Num 9:3 ye shall *k* it in his appointed
Num 9:3 ceremonies thereof, shall ye *k* it
Num 9:4 that they should *k* the passover
Num 9:6 that they could not *k* the
Num 9:10 yet he shall *k* the passover unto
Num 9:11 month at even they shall *k* it
Num 9:12 of the passover they shall *k* it
Num 9:13 and forbeareth to *k* the passover
Num 9:14 will *k* the passover unto the LORD
Num 18:3 And they shall *k* thy charge
Num 18:4 *k* the charge of the tabernacle of
Num 18:5 ye shall *k* the charge of the
Num 18:7 thy sons with thee shall *k* your
Num 29:12 ye shall *k* a feast unto the LORD
Num 31:18 with him, *k* alive for yourselves
Num 31:30 which *k* the charge of the
Num 36:7 *k* himself to the inheritance of
Num 36:9 *k* himself to his own inheritance
Deut 4:2 that ye may *k* the commandments of
Deut 4:6 *K* therefore and do them
Deut 4:9 *k* thy soul diligently, lest thou
Deut 4:40 Thou shalt *k* therefore his
Deut 5:1 day, that ye may learn them, and *k*
Deut 5:10 that love me and *k* my commandments
Deut 5:12 *K* the sabbath day to sanctify it,
Deut 5:15 thee to *k* the sabbath day
Deut 5:29 *k* all my commandments always,
Deut 6:2 to *k* all his statutes and his
Deut 6:17 Ye shall diligently *k* the
Deut 7:8 because he would *k* the oath which
Deut 7:9 *k* his commandments to a thousand
Deut 7:11 therefore *k* the commandments
Deut 7:12 hearken to these judgments, and *k*
Deut 7:12 shall *k* unto thee the covenant
Deut 8:2 thou wouldest *k* his commandments
Deut 8:6 Therefore thou shalt *k* the
Deut 10:13 To *k* the commandments of the LORD
Deut 11:1 *k* his charge, and his statutes, and
Deut 11:8 Therefore shall ye *k* all the
Deut 11:22 For if ye shall diligently *k* all
Deut 13:4 *k* his commandments, and obey his
Deut 13:18 to *k* all his commandments which I
Deut 16:1 *k* the passover unto the LORD thy
Deut 16:10 thou shalt *k* the feast of weeks
Deut 16:15 Seven days shalt thou *k* a solemn
Deut 17:19 to *k* all the words of this law and
Deut 19:9 If thou shalt *k* all these
Deut 23:9 then *k* thee from every wicked
Deut 23:23 gone out of thy lips thou shalt *k*
Deut 26:16 thou shalt therefore *k* and do them
Deut 26:17 to *k* his statutes, and his
Deut 26:18 that thou shouldest *k* all his
Deut 27:1 *K* all the commandments which I
Deut 28:9 if thou shalt *k* the commandments
Deut 28:45 to *k* his commandments and his
Deut 29:9 *K* therefore the words of this
Deut 30:10 to *k* his commandments and his
Deut 30:16 to *k* his commandments and his
Josh 6:18 in any wise *k* yourselves from the
Josh 10:18 and set men by it for to *k* them
Josh 22:5 to *k* his commandments, and to
Josh 23:6 ye therefore very courageous to *k*
Judg 2:22 whether they will *k* the way of
Judg 2:22 as their fathers did *k* it
Judg 3:19 who said, *K* silence
Ruth 2:21 Thou shalt *k* fast by my young men
1Sa 2:9 He will *k* the feet of his saints,
1Sa 7:1 his son to *k* the ark of the LORD
2Sa 8:2 and with one full line to *k* alive
2Sa 15:16 were concubines, to *k* the house
2Sa 16:21 which he hath left to *k* the house
2Sa 18:18 I have no son to *k* my name in
2Sa 20:3 whom he had left to *k* the house
1Kin 2:3 *k* the charge of the LORD thy God,
1Kin 2:3 to *k* his statutes, and his
1Kin 3:14 my ways, to *k* my statutes and my
1Kin 6:12 *k* all my commandments to walk in
1Kin 8:25 *k* with thy servant David my
1Kin 8:58 to *k* his commandments, and his
1Kin 8:61 to *k* his commandments, as at this
1Kin 9:4 thee, and wilt *k* my statutes and my
1Kin 9:6 will not *k* my commandments and my
1Kin 11:33 to *k* my statutes and my judgments,
1Kin 11:38 my sight, to *k* my statutes and my
1Kin 20:39 man unto me, and said, *K* this man
2Kin 11:6 so shall ye *k* the watch of the
2Kin 11:7 even they shall *k* the watch of
2Kin 17:13 *k* my commandments and my statutes,
2Kin 23:3 to *k* his commandments and his

2Kin 23:21 *K* the passover unto the LORD your
1Chr 4:10 that thou wouldest *k* me from evil
1Chr 12:33 thousand, which could *k* rank
1Chr 12:38 men of war, that could *k* rank
1Chr 22:12 that thou mayest *k* the law of the
1Chr 23:32 that they should *k* the charge of
1Chr 28:8 and in the audience of our God, *k*
1Chr 29:18 fathers, *k* this for ever in the
1Chr 29:19 to *k* thy commandments, thy
2Chr 6:16 *k* with thy servant David my
2Chr 13:11 for we *k* the charge of the LORD
2Chr 22:9 no power to *k* still the kingdom
2Chr 23:6 shall *k* the watch of the LORD
2Chr 28:10 now ye purpose to *k* under the
2Chr 30:1 to *k* the passover unto the LORD
2Chr 30:2 to *k* the passover in the second
2Chr 30:3 they could not *k* it at that time
2Chr 30:5 that they should come to *k* the
2Chr 30:13 at Jerusalem much people to *k* the
2Chr 30:23 counsel to *k* other seven days
2Chr 34:31 to *k* his commandments, and his
2Chr 35:16 to *k* the passover, and to offer
2Chr 35:18 did all the kings of Israel *k*
Ezr 8:29 *k* them, until ye weigh them
Neh 1:9 *k* my commandments, and do them
Neh 12:27 to *k* the dedication with gladness
Neh 13:22 *k* the gates, to sanctify the
Est 3:8 neither *k* they the king's laws
Est 9:21 that they should *k* the fourteenth
Est 9:27 that they would *k* these two days
Job 14:13 that thou wouldest *k* me secret
Job 20:13 but *k* it still within his mouth
Ps 12:7 Thou shalt *k* them, O LORD, thou
Ps 17:8 *K* me as the apple of the eye
Ps 19:13 *K* back thy servant also from
Ps 22:29 none can *k* alive his own soul
Ps 25:10 truth unto such as *k* his covenant
Ps 25:20 O *k* my soul, and deliver me
Ps 31:20 thou shalt *k* them secretly in a
Ps 33:19 to *k* them alive in famine
Ps 34:13 *K* thy tongue from evil, and thy
Ps 35:22 *k* not silence
Ps 37:34 *k* his way, and he shall exalt thee
Ps 39:1 I will *k* my mouth with a bridle,
Ps 41:2 will preserve him, and *k* him alive
Ps 50:3 come, and shall not *k* silence
Ps 78:7 of God, but *k* his commandments
Ps 83:1 *K* not thou silence, O God
Ps 89:28 My mercy will I *k* for him for
Ps 89:31 and *k* not my commandments
Ps 91:11 to *k* thee in all thy ways
Ps 103:9 neither will he *k* his anger for
Ps 103:18 To such as *k* his covenant, and to
Ps 105:45 his statutes, and *k* his laws
Ps 106:3 Blessed are they that *k* judgment
Ps 113:9 the barren woman to *k* house
Ps 119:2 are they that *k* his testimonies
Ps 119:4 us to *k* thy precepts diligently
Ps 119:5 were directed to *k* thy statutes
Ps 119:8 I will *k* thy statutes
Ps 119:17 that I may live, and *k* thy word
Ps 119:33 I shall *k* it unto the end
Ps 119:34 and I shall *k* thy law
Ps 119:44 So shall I *k* thy law continually
Ps 119:57 said that I would *k* thy words
Ps 119:60 delayed not to *k* thy commandments
Ps 119:63 and of them that *k* thy precepts
Ps 119:69 but I will *k* thy precepts with my
Ps 119:88 so shall I *k* the testimony of thy
Ps 119:100 because I *k* thy precepts
Ps 119:101 evil way, that I might *k* thy word
Ps 119:106 that I will *k* thy righteous
Ps 119:115 for I will *k* the commandments of
Ps 119:129 therefore doth my soul *k* them
Ps 119:134 so will I *k* thy precepts
Ps 119:136 eyes, because they *k* not thy law
Ps 119:145 I will *k* thy statutes
Ps 119:146 I shall *k* thy testimonies
Ps 127:1 except the LORD *k* the city
Ps 132:12 thy children will *k* my covenant
Ps 140:4 *K* me, O LORD, from the hands of
Ps 141:3 *K* the door of my lips
Ps 141:9 *K* me from the snares which they
Prov 2:11 thee, understanding shall *k* thee
Prov 2:20 *k* the paths of the righteous
Prov 3:1 let thine heart *k* my commandments
Prov 3:21 *k* sound wisdom and discretion
Prov 3:26 shall *k* thy foot from being taken
Prov 4:4 *k* my commandments, and live
Prov 4:6 love her, and she shall *k* thee
Prov 4:13 let her not go: *k* her
Prov 4:21 *k* them in the midst of thine
Prov 4:23 *K* thy heart with all diligence
Prov 5:2 and that thy lips may *k* knowledge
Prov 6:20 *k* thy father's commandment, and
Prov 6:22 thou sleepest, it shall *k* thee
Prov 6:24 To *k* thee from the evil woman,
Prov 7:1 My son, *k* my words, and lay up my
Prov 7:2 *K* my commandments, and live
Prov 7:5 That they may *k* thee from the
Prov 8:32 blessed are they that *k* my ways
Prov 22:5 he that doth *k* his soul shall be
Prov 22:18 thing if thou *k* them within thee
Prov 28:4 but such as *k* the law contend
Eccl 3:6 a time to *k*, and a time to cast
Eccl 3:7 a time to *k* silence, and a time to
Eccl 5:1 *K* thy foot when thou goest to the
Eccl 8:2 I counsel thee to *k* the king's
Eccl 12:13 Fear God, and *k* his commandments
Song 8:12 those that *k* the fruit thereof
Is 26:3 Thou wilt *k* him in perfect peace,
Is 27:3 I the LORD do *k* it
Is 27:3 hurt it, I will *k* it night and day
Is 41:1 *K* silence before me, O islands
Is 42:6 hold thine hand, and will *k* thee
Is 43:6 and to the south, *K* not back
Is 56:1 *K* ye judgment, and do justice
Is 56:4 the eunuchs that *k* my sabbaths
Is 62:6 of the LORD, *k* not silence,
Is 65:6 I will not *k* silence, but will
Jer 3:5 will he *k* it to the end
Jer 3:12 I will not *k* anger for ever
Jer 31:10 *k* him, as a shepherd doth his
Jer 42:4 I will *k* nothing back from you
Lam 2:10 sit upon the ground, and *k* silence
Eze 11:20 *k* mine ordinances, and do them
Eze 18:21 *k* all my statutes, and do that
Eze 20:19 *k* my judgments, and do them
Eze 36:27 ye shall *k* my judgments, and do
Eze 43:11 that they may *k* the whole form
Eze 44:16 me, and they shall *k* my charge
Eze 44:24 and they shall *k* my laws and my
Dan 9:4 to them that *k* his commandments
Hos 12:6 *k* mercy and judgment, and wait on
Amos 5:13 shall *k* silence in that time
Mic 7:5 *k* the doors of thy mouth from her
Nah 1:15 *k* thy solemn feasts, perform thy
Nah 2:1 *k* the munition, watch the way,
Hab 2:20 let all the earth *k* silence
Zec 3:7 ways, and if thou wilt *k* my charge
Zec 3:7 house, and shalt also *k* my courts
Zec 13:5 me to *k* cattle from my youth
Zec 14:16 to *k* the feast of tabernacles
Zec 14:18 up to *k* the feast of tabernacles
Zec 14:19 up to *k* the feast of tabernacles
Mal 2:7 priest's lips should *k* knowledge
Mt 19:17 into life, *k* the commandments
Mt 26:18 I will *k* the passover at thy
Mk 7:9 that ye may *k* your own tradition
Lk 4:10 charge over thee, to *k* thee
Lk 8:15 *k* it, and bring forth fruit with
Lk 11:28 hear the word of God, and *k* it
Lk 19:43 and *k* thee in on every side,
Jn 8:51 If a man *k* my saying, he shall
Jn 8:52 If a man *k* my saying, he shall
Jn 8:55 but I know him, and *k* his saying
Jn 12:25 shall *k* it unto life eternal
Jn 14:15 If ye love me, *k* my commandments
Jn 14:23 a man love me, he will *k* my words
Jn 15:10 If ye *k* my commandments, ye shall
Jn 15:20 my saying, they will *k* yours also
Jn 17:11 *k* through thine own name those
Jn 17:15 shouldest *k* them from the evil
Acts 5:3 to *k* back part of the price of
Acts 10:28 a man that is a Jew to *k* company
Acts 12:4 quaternions of soldiers to *k* him
Acts 15:5 them to *k* the law of Moses
Acts 15:24 must be circumcised, and *k* the law
Acts 15:29 from which if ye *k* yourselves
Acts 16:4 them the decrees for to *k*
Acts 16:23 the jailer to *k* them safely
Acts 18:21 I must by all means *k* this feast
Acts 21:25 save only that they *k* themselves
Acts 24:23 commanded a centurion to *k* Paul
Rom 2:25 profiteth, if thou *k* the law
Rom 2:26 *k* the righteousness of the law
1Cor 5:8 Therefore let us *k* the feast
1Cor 5:11 written unto you not to *k* company
1Cor 7:37 heart that he will *k* his virgin
1Cor 9:27 But I *k* under my body, and bring
1Cor 11:2 *k* the ordinances, as I delivered
1Cor 14:28 let him *k* silence in the church
1Cor 14:34 Let your women *k* silence in the
1Cor 15:2 if ye *k* in memory what I preached
2Cor 11:9 unto you, and so will I *k* myself
Gal 6:13 who are circumcised *k* the law
Eph 4:3 Endeavouring to *k* the unity of
Phil 4:7 shall *k* your hearts and minds
2Th 3:3 stablish you, and *k* you from evil
1Ti 5:22 *k* thyself pure
1Ti 6:14 That thou *k* this commandment
1Ti 6:20 *k* that which is committed to thy
2Ti 1:12 to *k* that which I have committed
2Ti 1:14 thee *k* by the Holy Ghost which
Jas 1:27 to *k* himself unspotted from the
Jas 2:10 whosoever shall *k* the whole law
1Jn 2:3 him, if we *k* his commandments
1Jn 3:22 because we *k* his commandments, and
1Jn 5:2 love God, and *k* his commandments
1Jn 5:3 that we *k* his commandments
1Jn 5:21 children, *k* yourselves from idols
Jude 21 *K* yourselves in the love of God,
Jude 24 is able to *k* you from falling
Rev 1:3 *k* those things which are written
Rev 3:10 I also will *k* thee from the hour
Rev 12:17 which *k* the commandments of God,
Rev 14:12 here are they that *k* the
Rev 22:9 of them which *k* the sayings of

## KEEPER

Gen 4:2 And Abel was a *k* of sheep, but
Gen 4:9 Am I my brother's *k*
Gen 39:21 the sight of the *k* of the prison
Gen 39:22 the *k* of the prison committed to
Gen 39:23 The *k* of the prison looked not to
1Sa 17:20 and left the sheep with a *k*
1Sa 17:22 the hand of the *k* of the carriage
1Sa 28:2 make thee *k* of mine head for ever
2Kin 22:14 son of Harhas, *k* of the wardrobe
2Chr 34:22 son of Hasrah, *k* of the wardrobe
Neh 2:8 Asaph the *k* of the king's forest
Neh 3:29 the *k* of the east gate
Est 2:3 chamberlain, *k* of the women
Est 2:8 custody of Hegai, *k* of the women
Est 2:15 the *k* of the women, appointed
Job 27:18 and as a booth that the *k* maketh
Ps 121:5 The LORD is thy *k*
Song 1:6 made me the *k* of the vineyards
Jer 35:4 son of Shallum, the *k* of the door
Acts 16:27 the *k* of the prison awaking out
Acts 16:36 the *k* of the prison told this

## KEEPERS

2Kin 11:5 be *k* of the watch of the king's
2Kin 22:4 which the *k* of the door have
2Kin 23:4 the *k* of the door, to bring forth
2Kin 25:18 and the three *k* of the door
1Chr 9:19 *k* of the gates of the tabernacle
1Chr 9:19 of the LORD, were *k* of the entry
Est 6:2 the *k* of the door, who sought to
Eccl 12:3 In the day when the *k* of the
Song 5:7 the *k* of the walls took away my
Song 8:11 he let out the vineyard unto *k*
Jer 4:17 As *k* of a field, are they against
Jer 52:24 and the three *k* of the door
Eze 40:45 the *k* of the charge of the house
Eze 40:46 the *k* of the charge of the altar
Eze 44:8 but ye have set *k* of my charge in
Eze 44:14 But I will make them *k* of the
Mt 28:4 for fear of him the *k* did shake
Acts 5:23 the *k* standing without before the
Acts 12:6 the *k* before the door kept the
Acts 12:19 found him not, he examined the *k*
Titus 2:5 *k* at home, good, obedient to

## KEEPEST

1Kin 8:23 who *k* covenant and mercy with thy
2Chr 6:14 which *k* covenant, and shewest
Neh 9:32 who *k* covenant and mercy, let not
Acts 21:24 walkest orderly, and *k* the law

## KEEPETH

Ex 21:18 and he die not, but *k* his bed
Deut 7:9 which *k* covenant and mercy with
1Sa 16:11 and, behold, he *k* the sheep
Neh 1:5 that *k* covenant and mercy for them
Job 33:18 He *k* back his soul from the pit,
Ps 34:20 He *k* all his bones
Ps 121:3 he that *k* thee will not slumber
Ps 121:4 he that *k* Israel shall neither
Ps 146:6 which *k* truth for ever
Prov 2:8 He *k* the paths of judgment, and

Prov 10:17 way of life that *k* instruction
Prov 13:3 He that *k* his mouth *k* his
Prov 13:3 that *k* his mouth *k* his life
Prov 13:6 Righteousness *k* him that is
Prov 16:17 he that *k* his way preserveth his
Prov 19:8 he that *k* understanding shall
Prov 19:16 He that *k* the commandment *k*
Prov 21:23 Whoso *k* his mouth and his tongue
Prov 21:23 his tongue *k* his soul from
Prov 24:12 he that *k* thy soul, doth not he
Prov 27:18 Whoso *k* the fig tree shall eat
Prov 28:7 Whoso *k* the law is a wise son
Prov 29:3 but he that *k* company with
Prov 29:11 but a wise man *k* it in till
Prov 29:18 but he that *k* the law, happy is
Eccl 8:5 Whoso *k* the commandment shall
Is 26:2 which *k* the truth may enter in
Is 56:2 that *k* the sabbath from polluting
Is 56:2 *k* his hand from doing any evil
Is 56:6 every one that *k* the sabbath from
Jer 48:10 cursed be he that *k* back his
Lam 3:28 *k* silence, because he hath borne
Hab 2:5 is a proud man, neither *k* at home
Lk 11:21 a strong man armed *k* his palace
Jn 7:19 law, and yet none of you *k* the law
Jn 9:16 because he *k* not the sabbath day
Jn 14:21 *k* them, he it is that loveth me
Jn 14:24 loveth me not *k* not my sayings
1Jn 2:4 *k* not his commandments, is a liar
1Jn 2:5 But whoso *k* his word, in him
1Jn 3:24 he that *k* his commandments
1Jn 5:18 that is begotten of God *k* himself
Rev 2:26 *k* my works unto the end, to him
Rev 16:15 *k* his garments, lest he walk
Rev 22:7 blessed is he that *k* the sayings

**KEEPING**
Ex 34:7 *K* mercy for thousands, forgiving
Num 3:28 *k* the charge of the sanctuary
Num 3:38 *k* the charge of the sanctuary for
Deut 8:11 in not *k* his commandments, and his
1Sa 25:16 we were with them *k* the sheep
Neh 12:25 were porters *k* the ward at the
Ps 19:11 in *k* of them there is great
Eze 17:14 but that by *k* of his covenant it
Dan 9:4 *k* the covenant and mercy to them
Lk 2:8 *k* watch over their flock by night
1Cor 7:19 but the *k* of the commandments of
1Pet 4:19 *k* of their souls to him in well

**KEHELATHAH** *(ke-hel'-a-thah) An Israelite encampment in the wilderness.*
Num 33:22 from Rissah, and pitched in *K*
Num 33:23 And they went from *K*, and pitched

**KEILAH** *(ki'-lah)*
*1. A city in Judah.*
Josh 15:44 And *K*, and Achzib, and Mareshah
1Sa 23:1 the Philistines fight against *K*
1Sa 23:2 smite the Philistines, and save *K*
1Sa 23:3 to *K* against the armies of the
1Sa 23:4 him and said, Arise, go down to *K*
1Sa 23:5 So David and his men went to *K*
1Sa 23:5 David saved the inhabitants of *K*
1Sa 23:6 of Ahimelech fled to David to *K*
1Sa 23:7 Saul that David was come to *K*
1Sa 23:8 together to war, to go down to *K*
1Sa 23:10 that Saul seeketh to come to *K*
1Sa 23:11 Will the men of *K* deliver me up
1Sa 23:12 Will the men of *K* deliver me
1Sa 23:13 arose and departed out of *K*
1Sa 23:13 that David was escaped from *K*
Neh 3:17 the ruler of the half part of *K*
Neh 3:18 the ruler of the half part of *K*
*2. A descendant of Caleb.*
1Chr 4:19 the father of *K* the Garmite

**KELAIAH** *(kel-ah'-yah)* See KELITA. *Married a foreigner in exile.*
Ezr 10:23 Jozabad, and Shimei, and *K*, (the

**KELITA** *(kel'-i-tah)* See KELAIAH.
*1. Married a foreigner in exile.*
Ezr 10:23 and Kelaiah, (the same is *K*
*2. A priest who assisted Ezra.*
Neh 8:7 Shabbethai, Hodijah, Maaseiah, *K*
*3. A Levite who renewed the covenant.*
Neh 10:10 brethren, Shebaniah, Hodijah, *K*

**KEMUEL** *(kem-u'-el)*
*1. A son of Nahor.*
Gen 22:21 brother, and *K* the father of Aram,
*2. An Ephraimite prince.*
Num 34:24 of Ephraim, *K* the son of Shiphtan
*3. Father of Hashabiah.*
1Chr 27:17 Levites, Hashabiah the son of *K*

**KENAN** *(ke'-nan)* See CAINAN. *Son of Enosh.*
1Chr 1:2 *K*, Mahalaleel, Jered,

**KENATH** *(ke'-nath)* See NOBAH. *A city in Bashan.*
Num 32:42 And Nobah went and took *K*, and the
1Chr 2:23 towns of Jair, from them, with *K*

**KENAZ** *(ke'-naz)* See KENEZITE.
*1. A son of Eliphaz.*
Gen 36:11 Omar, Zepho, and Gatam, and *K*
Gen 36:15 duke Omar, duke Zepho, duke *K*
1Chr 1:36 and Omar, Zephi, and Gatam, *K*
*2. A duke of Edom.*
Gen 36:42 Duke *K*, duke Teman, duke Mibzar,
1Chr 1:53 Duke *K*, duke Teman, duke Mibzar,
*3. Brother of Caleb.*
Josh 15:17 And Othniel the son of *K*, the
Judg 1:13 And Othniel the son of *K*, Caleb's
Judg 3:9 them, even Othniel the son of *K*
Judg 3:11 And Othniel the son of *K* died
1Chr 4:13 And the sons of *K*
*4. A grandson of Caleb.*
1Chr 4:15 and the sons of Elah, even *K*

**KENEZITE** *(ken'-e-zite)* See KENIZZITES. *Descendants of Jephunneh.*
Num 32:12 Caleb the son of Jephunneh the *K*
Josh 14:6 of Jephunneh the *K* said unto him
Josh 14:14 of Jephunneh the *K* unto this day

**KENITE** *(ken'-ite)* See KENITES. *A member of a Canaanite tribe.*
Num 24:22 the *K* shall be wasted, until
Judg 1:16 And the children of the *K*, Moses'
Judg 4:11 Now Heber the *K*, which was of the
Judg 4:17 of Jael the wife of Heber the *K*
Judg 4:17 Hazor and the house of Heber the *K*
Judg 5:24 Jael the wife of Heber the *K* be

**KENITES** *(ken'-ites)* See MIDIANITES.
Gen 15:19 The *K*, and the Kenizzites, and the
Num 24:21 And he looked on the *K*, and took up
Judg 4:11 had severed himself from the *K*
1Sa 15:6 And Saul said unto the *K*, Go,
1Sa 15:6 So the *K* departed from among the
1Sa 27:10 and against the south of the *K*
1Sa 30:29 which were in the cities of the *K*
1Chr 2:55 These are the *K* that came of

**KENIZZITES** *(ken'-iz-zites)* See KENEZITE. *A Canaanite tribe in Abraham's time.*
Gen 15:19 The Kenites, and the *K*, and the

**KEPT**
Gen 26:5 *k* my charge, my commandments, my
Gen 29:9 father's sheep: for she *k* them
Gen 39:9 neither hath he *k* back any thing
Gen 42:16 and ye shall be *k* in prison
Ex 3:1 Now Moses *k* the flock of Jethro
Ex 16:23 for you to be *k* until the morning
Ex 16:32 it to be *k* for your generations
Ex 16:33 to be *k* for your generations
Ex 16:34 up before the Testimony, to be *k*
Ex 21:29 owner, and he hath not *k* him in
Ex 21:36 and his owner hath not *k* him in
Num 5:13 be *k* close, and she be defiled, and
Num 9:5 they *k* the passover on the
Num 9:7 wherefore are we *k* back, that we
Num 9:19 Israel *k* the charge of the LORD
Num 9:23 they *k* the charge of the LORD, at
Num 17:10 to be *k* for a token against the
Num 19:9 place, and it shall be *k* for the
Num 24:11 the LORD hath *k* thee back from
Num 31:47 which *k* the charge of the
Deut 32:10 he *k* him as the apple of his eye
Deut 33:9 thy word, and *k* thy covenant
Josh 5:10 *k* the passover on the fourteenth
Josh 14:10 behold, the LORD hath *k* me alive
Josh 22:2 Ye have *k* all that Moses the
Josh 22:3 but have *k* the charge of the
Ruth 2:23 So she *k* fast by the maidens of
1Sa 9:24 it been *k* for thee since I said
1Sa 13:13 thou hast not *k* the commandment
1Sa 13:14 because thou hast not *k* that
1Sa 17:34 Thy servant *k* his father's sheep,
1Sa 21:4 if the young men have *k*
1Sa 21:5 Of a truth women have been *k* from
1Sa 25:21 Surely in vain have I *k* all that
1Sa 25:33 which hast *k* me this day from
1Sa 25:34 which hath *k* me back from hurting
1Sa 25:39 hath *k* his servant from evil
1Sa 26:15 hast thou not *k* thy lord the king
1Sa 26:16 because ye have not *k* your master
2Sa 13:34 the young man that *k* the watch
2Sa 22:22 For I have *k* the ways of the LORD
2Sa 22:24 have *k* myself from mine iniquity
2Sa 22:44 thou hast *k* me to be head of the
1Kin 2:43 thou not *k* the oath of the LORD
1Kin 3:6 thou hast *k* for him this great
1Kin 8:24 Who hast *k* with thy servant David
1Kin 11:10 but he *k* not that which the LORD
1Kin 11:11 and thou hast not *k* my covenant
1Kin 11:34 because he *k* my commandments and
1Kin 13:21 hast not *k* the commandment which
1Kin 14:8 who *k* my commandments, and who
1Kin 14:27 which *k* the door of the king's
2Kin 9:14 (Now Joram had *k* Ramoth-gilead
2Kin 12:9 the priests that *k* the door put
2Kin 17:19 Also Judah *k* not the commandments
2Kin 18:6 but *k* his commandments, which the
1Chr 10:13 word of the LORD, which he *k* not
1Chr 12:1 while he yet *k* himself close
1Chr 12:29 *k* the ward of the house of Saul
2Chr 6:15 Thou which hast *k* with thy
2Chr 7:8 Solomon *k* the feast seven days
2Chr 7:9 for they *k* the dedication of the
2Chr 12:10 that *k* the entrance of the king's
2Chr 30:21 *k* the feast of unleavened bread
2Chr 30:23 they *k* other seven days with
2Chr 34:9 which the Levites that *k* the
2Chr 34:21 have not *k* the word of the LORD
2Chr 35:1 Moreover Josiah *k* a passover unto
2Chr 35:17 *k* the passover at that time
2Chr 35:18 that *k* in Israel from the days of
2Chr 35:18 keep such a passover as Josiah *k*
2Chr 35:19 of Josiah was this passover *k*
2Chr 36:21 as she lay desolate she *k* sabbath
Ezr 3:4 They *k* also the feast of
Ezr 6:16 *k* the dedication of this house of
Ezr 6:19 captivity *k* the passover upon the
Ezr 6:22 *k* the feast of unleavened bread
Neh 1:7 have not *k* the commandments, nor
Neh 8:18 they *k* the feast seven days
Neh 9:34 *k* thy law, nor hearkened unto thy
Neh 11:19 their brethren that *k* the gates
Neh 12:45 the porters *k* the ward of their
Est 2:14 which *k* the concubines
Est 2:21 Teresh, of those which *k* the door
Est 9:28 *k* throughout every generation,
Job 23:11 held his steps, his way have I *k*
Job 28:21 *k* close from the fowls of the air
Job 29:21 and *k* silence at my counsel
Job 31:34 that I *k* silence, and went not out
Ps 17:4 I have *k* me from the paths of the
Ps 18:21 For I have *k* the ways of the LORD
Ps 18:23 I *k* myself from mine iniquity
Ps 30:3 thou hast *k* me alive, that I
Ps 32:3 When I *k* silence, my bones waxed
Ps 42:4 with a multitude that *k* holyday
Ps 50:21 hast thou done, and I *k* silence
Ps 78:10 They *k* not the covenant of God,
Ps 78:56 God, and *k* not his testimonies
Ps 99:7 they *k* his testimonies, and the
Ps 119:22 for I have *k* thy testimonies
Ps 119:55 in the night, and have *k* thy law
Ps 119:56 I had, because I *k* thy precepts
Ps 119:67 but now have I *k* thy word
Ps 119:158 because they *k* not thy word
Ps 119:167 My soul hath *k* thy testimonies
Ps 119:168 I have *k* thy precepts and thy
Eccl 2:10 eyes desired I *k* not from them
Eccl 5:13 riches *k* for the owners thereof
Song 1:6 mine own vineyard have I not *k*
Is 30:29 night when a holy solemnity is *k*
Jer 16:11 forsaken me, and have not *k* my law
Jer 35:18 *k* all his precepts, and done
Eze 5:7 neither have *k* my judgments
Eze 18:9 hath *k* my judgments, to deal
Eze 18:19 hath *k* all my statutes, and hath
Eze 20:21 neither *k* my judgments to do them
Eze 44:8 ye have not *k* the charge of mine
Eze 44:15 that *k* the charge of my sanctuary
Eze 48:11 which have *k* my charge, which
Dan 5:19 and whom he would he *k* alive
Dan 7:28 but I *k* the matter in my heart
Hos 12:12 a wife, and for a wife he *k* sheep
Amos 1:11 and he *k* his wrath for ever
Amos 2:4 have not *k* his commandments, and
Mic 6:16 For the statutes of Omri are *k*

Mal 2:9 as ye have not *k* my ways, but
Mal 3:7 ordinances, and have not *k* them
Mal 3:14 it that we have *k* his ordinance
Mt 8:33 And they that *k* them fled, and went
Mt 13:35 utter things which have been *k*
Mt 14:6 But when Herod's birthday was *k*
Mt 19:20 things have I *k* from my youth up
Mk 4:22 neither was any thing *k* secret
Mk 9:10 And they *k* that saying with
Lk 2:19 But Mary *k* all these things, and
Lk 2:51 but his mother *k* all these
Lk 8:29 he was *k* bound with chains and in
Lk 9:36 they *k* it close, and told no man
Lk 18:21 these have I *k* from my youth up
Lk 19:20 which I have *k* laid up in a
Jn 2:10 but thou hast *k* the good wine
Jn 12:7 day of my burying hath she *k* this
Jn 15:10 even as I have *k* my Father's
Jn 15:20 if they have *k* my saying, they
Jn 17:6 and they have *k* thy word
Jn 17:12 the world, I *k* them in thy name
Jn 17:12 that thou gavest me I have *k*
Jn 18:16 and spake unto her that *k* the door
Jn 18:17 damsel that *k* the door unto Peter
Acts 5:2 *k* back part of the price, his
Acts 7:53 of angels, and have not *k* it
Acts 9:33 which had *k* his bed eight years,
Acts 12:5 Peter therefore was *k* in prison
Acts 12:6 before the door *k* the prison
Acts 15:12 Then all the multitude *k* silence
Acts 20:20 how I *k* back nothing that was
Acts 22:2 to them, they *k* the more silence
Acts 22:20 *k* the raiment of them that slew
Acts 23:35 he commanded him to be *k* in
Acts 25:4 that Paul should be *k* at Caesarea
Acts 25:21 I commanded him to be *k* till I
Acts 27:43 *k* them from their purpose
Acts 28:16 himself with a soldier that *k* him
Rom 16:25 which was *k* secret since the
2Cor 11:9 in all things I have *k* myself
2Cor 11:32 governor under Aretas the king *k*
Gal 3:23 we were *k* under the law, shut up
2Ti 4:7 my course, I have *k* the faith
Heb 11:28 Through faith he *k* the passover
Jas 5:4 which is of you *k* back by fraud
1Pet 1:5 Who are *k* by the power of God
2Pet 3:7 by the same word are *k* in store
Jude 6 the angels which *k* not their
Rev 3:8 hast *k* my word, and hast not
Rev 3:10 Because thou hast *k* the word of

**KERCHIEFS**

Eze 13:18 make *k* upon the head of every
Eze 13:21 Your *k* also will I tear, and

**KEREN-HAPPUCH** *(ke'-ren-hap'-puk) A daughter of Job.*

Job 42:14 and the name of the third, *K*

**KERIOTH** *(ke'-re-oth)* See ISCARIOT, KIRIOTH.

*1. A city in Judah.*
Josh 15:25 And Hazor, Hadattah, and *K*, and
*2. A city in Moab.*
Jer 48:24 And upon *K*, and upon Bozrah, and
Jer 48:41 *K* is taken, and the strong holds

**KERNELS**

Num 6:4 from the *k* even to the husk

**KEROS** *(ke'-ros) A family of exiles.*

Ezr 2:44 The children of *K*, the children
Neh 7:47 The children of *K*, the children

**KETTLE**

1Sa 2:14 he struck it into the pan, or *k*

**KETURAH** *(ket-u'-rah) A wife of Abraham.*

Gen 25:1 took a wife, and her name was *K*
Gen 25:4 All these were the children of *K*
1Chr 1:32 Now the sons of *K*, Abraham's
1Chr 1:33 All these are the sons of *K*

**KEY**

Judg 3:25 therefore they took a *k*, and
Is 22:22 the *k* of the house of David will
Lk 11:52 taken away the *k* of knowledge
Rev 3:7 true, he that hath the *k* of David
Rev 9:1 to him was given the *k* of the
Rev 20:1 having the *k* of the bottomless

**KEYS**

Mt 16:19 the *k* of the kingdom of heaven
Rev 1:18 and have the *k* of hell and of death

**KEZIA** *(ke-zi'-ah) A daughter of Job.*

Job 42:14 and the name of the second, *K*

**KEZIZ** *(ke'-ziz) A valley in Benjamin.*

Josh 18:21 Beth-hoglah, and the valley of *K*

**KIBROTH-HATTAAVAH** *(kib'-roth-hat-ta'-a-vah) A Hebrew encampment in the wilderness.*

Num 11:34 called the name of that place *K*
Num 11:35 journeyed from *K* unto Hazeroth
Num 33:16 desert of Sinai, and pitched at *K*
Num 33:17 And they departed from *K*, and
Deut 9:22 at Taberah, and at Massah, and at *K*

**KIBZAIM** *(kib-za'-im)* See JOKMEAM. *A Levitical city in Ephraim.*

Josh 21:22 *K* with her suburbs, and Beth-horon

**KID**

Gen 37:31 killed a *k* of the goats, and
Gen 38:17 will send thee a *k* from the flock
Gen 38:20 Judah sent the *k* by the hand of
Gen 38:23 behold, I sent this *k*, and thou
Ex 23:19 seethe a *k* in his mother's milk
Ex 34:26 seethe a *k* in his mother's milk
Lev 4:23 a *k* of the goats, a male without
Lev 4:28 a *k* of the goats, a female
Lev 5:6 a lamb or a *k* of the goats, for a
Lev 9:3 Take ye a *k* of the goats for a
Lev 23:19 Then ye shall sacrifice one *k* of
Num 7:16 One *k* of the goats for a sin
Num 7:22 One *k* of the goats for a sin
Num 7:28 One *k* of the goats for a sin
Num 7:34 One *k* of the goats for a sin
Num 7:40 One *k* of the goats for a sin
Num 7:46 One *k* of the goats for a sin
Num 7:52 One *k* of the goats for a sin
Num 7:58 One *k* of the goats for a sin
Num 7:64 One *k* of the goats for a sin
Num 7:70 One *k* of the goats for a sin
Num 7:76 One *k* of the goats for a sin
Num 7:82 One *k* of the goats for a sin
Num 15:11 one ram, or for a lamb, or a *k*
Num 15:24 one *k* of the goats for a sin
Num 28:15 one *k* of the goats for a sin
Num 28:30 one *k* of the goats, to make an
Num 29:5 one *k* of the goats for a sin
Num 29:11 One *k* of the goats for a sin
Num 29:16 one *k* of the goats for a sin
Num 29:19 one *k* of the goats for a sin
Num 29:25 one *k* of the goats for a sin
Deut 14:21 seethe a *k* in his mother's milk
Judg 6:19 went in, and made ready a *k*
Judg 13:15 have made ready a *k* for thee
Judg 13:19 So Manoah took a *k* with a meat
Judg 14:6 him as he would have rent a *k*
Judg 15:1 Samson visited his wife with a *k*
1Sa 16:20 and a bottle of wine, and a *k*
Is 11:6 leopard shall lie down with the *k*
Eze 43:22 a *k* of the goats without blemish
Eze 45:23 a *k* of the goats daily for a sin
Lk 15:29 and yet thou never gavest me a *k*

**KIDNEYS**

Ex 29:13 is above the liver, and the two *k*
Ex 29:22 above the liver, and the two *k*
Lev 3:4 And the two *k*, and the fat that is
Lev 3:4 caul above the liver, with the *k*
Lev 3:10 And the two *k*, and the fat that is
Lev 3:10 caul above the liver, with the *k*
Lev 3:15 And the two *k*, and the fat that is
Lev 3:15 caul above the liver, with the *k*
Lev 4:9 And the two *k*, and the fat that is
Lev 4:9 caul above the liver, with the *k*
Lev 7:4 And the two *k*, and the fat that is
Lev 7:4 is above the liver, with the *k*
Lev 8:16 above the liver, and the two *k*
Lev 8:25 above the liver, and the two *k*
Lev 9:10 But the fat, and the *k*, and the
Lev 9:19 covereth the inwards, and the *k*
Deut 32:14 goats, with the fat of *k* of wheat
Is 34:6 with the fat of the *k* of rams

**KIDRON** *(kid'-ron) A brook near Jerusalem.*

2Sa 15:23 himself passed over the brook *K*
1Kin 2:37 out, and passest over the brook *K*
1Kin 15:13 idol, and burnt it by the brook *K*
2Kin 23:4 Jerusalem in the fields of *K*
2Kin 23:6 Jerusalem, unto the brook *K*
2Kin 23:6 and burned it at the brook *K*
2Kin 23:12 the dust of them into the brook *K*
2Chr 15:16 it, and burnt it at the brook *K*
2Chr 29:16 it out abroad into the brook *K*
2Chr 30:14 and cast them into the brook *K*
Jer 31:40 the fields unto the brook of *K*

**KIDS**

Gen 27:9 thence two good *k* of the goats
Gen 27:16 she put the skins of the *k* of the
Lev 16:5 of the children of Israel two *k*
Num 7:87 the *k* of the goats for sin
1Sa 10:3 to Beth-el, one carrying three *k*
1Kin 20:27 them like two little flocks of *k*
2Chr 35:7 people, of the flock, lambs and *k*
Song 1:8 feed thy *k* beside the shepherds'

**KILL**

Gen 4:15 lest any finding him should *k* him
Gen 12:12 and they will *k* me, but they will
Gen 26:7 the place should *k* me for Rebekah
Gen 27:42 himself, purposing to *k* thee
Gen 37:21 and said, Let us not *k* him
Ex 1:16 it be a son, then ye shall *k* him
Ex 2:14 intendest thou to *k* me, as thou
Ex 4:24 LORD met him, and sought to *k* him
Ex 12:6 Israel shall *k* it in the evening
Ex 12:21 your families, and *k* the passover
Ex 16:3 to *k* this whole assembly with
Ex 17:3 us up out of Egypt, to *k* us
Ex 20:13 Thou shalt not *k*
Ex 22:1 or a sheep, and *k* it, or sell it
Ex 22:24 I will *k* you with the sword
Ex 29:11 thou shalt *k* the bullock before
Ex 29:20 Then shalt thou *k* the ram
Lev 1:5 he shall *k* the bullock before the
Lev 1:11 he shall *k* it on the side of the
Lev 3:2 and *k* it at the door of the
Lev 3:8 *k* it before the tabernacle of the
Lev 3:13 *k* it before the tabernacle of the
Lev 4:4 *k* the bullock before the LORD
Lev 4:24 *k* it in the place where they *k*
Lev 4:33 where they *k* the burnt offering
Lev 7:2 In the place where they *k* the
Lev 7:2 they *k* the trespass offering
Lev 14:13 where he shall *k* the sin offering
Lev 14:19 he shall *k* the burnt offering
Lev 14:25 he shall *k* the lamb of the
Lev 14:50 he shall *k* the one of the birds
Lev 16:11 shall *k* the bullock of the sin
Lev 16:15 Then shall he *k* the goat of the
Lev 20:4 seed unto Molech, and *k* him not
Lev 20:16 thereto, thou shalt *k* the woman
Lev 22:28 be cow or ewe, ye shall not *k* it
Num 11:15 *k* me, I pray thee, out of hand,
Num 14:15 Now if thou shalt *k* all this
Num 16:13 to *k* us in the wilderness, except
Num 22:29 mine hand, for now would I *k* thee
Num 31:17 Now therefore *k* every male among
Num 31:17 *k* every woman that hath known man
Num 35:27 revenger of blood *k* the slayer
Deut 4:42 which should *k* his neighbour
Deut 5:17 Thou shalt not *k*
Deut 12:15 Notwithstanding thou mayest *k*
Deut 12:21 then thou shalt *k* of thy herd
Deut 13:9 But thou shalt surely *k* him
Deut 32:39 I *k*, and I make alive
Judg 13:23 If the LORD were pleased to *k* us
Judg 15:13 but surely we will not *k* thee
Judg 16:2 when it is day, we shall *k* him
Judg 20:31 to smite of the people, and *k*
Judg 20:39 *k* of the men of Israel about
1Sa 16:2 if Saul hear it, he will *k* me
1Sa 17:9 able to fight with me, and to *k* me
1Sa 17:9 *k* him, then shall ye be our
1Sa 19:1 that they should *k* David
1Sa 19:2 Saul my father seeketh to *k* thee
1Sa 19:17 why should I *k* thee
1Sa 24:10 and some bade me *k* thee
1Sa 30:15 God, that thou wilt neither *k* me
2Sa 13:28 then *k* him, fear not
2Sa 14:7 his brother, that we may *k* him
2Sa 14:32 any iniquity in me, let him *k* me
2Sa 21:4 us shalt thou *k* any man in Israel
1Kin 11:40 sought therefore to *k* Jeroboam
1Kin 12:27 king of Judah, and they shall *k* me
2Kin 5:7 clothes, and said, Am I God, to *k*
2Kin 7:4 and if they *k* us, we shall but die
2Kin 11:15 followeth her *k* with the sword
2Chr 35:6 So *k* the passover, and sanctify
Est 3:13 provinces, to destroy, to *k*
Ps 59:*t* they watched the house to *k* him
Eccl 3:3 A time to *k*, and a time to heal
Is 14:30 I will *k* thy root with famine, and

Is 29:1 let them *k* sacrifices
Eze 34:3 the wool, ye *k* them that are fed
Mt 5:21 of old time, Thou shalt not *k*
Mt 5:21 whosoever shall *k* shall be in
Mt 10:28 And fear not them which *k* the body
Mt 10:28 but are not able to *k* the soul
Mt 17:23 And they shall *k* him, and the third
Mt 21:38 come, let us *k* him, and let us
Mt 23:34 and some of them ye shall *k*
Mt 24:9 to be afflicted, and shall *k* you
Mt 26:4 take Jesus by subtilty, and *k* him
Mk 3:4 to save life, or to *k*
Mk 9:31 hands of men, and they shall *k* him
Mk 10:19 Do not commit adultery, Do not *k*
Mk 10:34 spit upon him, and shall *k* him
Mk 12:7 come, let us *k* him, and the
Lk 12:4 afraid of them that *k* the body
Lk 13:31 for Herod will *k* thee
Lk 15:23 hither the fatted calf, and *k* it
Lk 18:20 Do not commit adultery, Do not *k*
Lk 20:14 come, let us *k* him, that the
Lk 22:2 sought how they might *k* him
Jn 5:18 the Jews sought the more to *k* him
Jn 7:1 because the Jews sought to *k* him
Jn 7:19 Why go ye about to *k* me
Jn 7:20 who goeth about to *k* thee
Jn 7:25 not this he, whom they seek to *k*
Jn 8:22 said the Jews, Will he *k* himself
Jn 8:37 but ye seek to *k* me, because my
Jn 8:40 But now ye seek to *k* me, a man
Jn 10:10 not, but for to steal, and to *k*
Acts 7:28 Wilt thou *k* me, as thou diddest
Acts 9:23 the Jews took counsel to *k* him
Acts 9:24 the gates day and night to *k* him
Acts 10:13 Rise, Peter; *k*, and eat
Acts 21:31 And as they went about to *k* him
Acts 23:15 he come near, are ready to *k* him
Acts 25:3 laying wait in the way to *k* him
Acts 26:21 the temple, and went about to *k* me
Acts 27:42 counsel was to *k* the prisoners
Rom 13:9 commit adultery, Thou shalt not *k*
Jas 2:11 adultery, said also, Do not *k*
Jas 2:11 commit no adultery, yet if thou *k*
Jas 4:2 ye *k*, and desire to have, and
Rev 2:23 I will *k* her children with death
Rev 6:4 and that they should *k* one another
Rev 6:8 to *k* with sword, and with hunger,
Rev 9:5 given that they should not *k* them
Rev 11:7 and shall overcome them, and *k* them

**KILLED**
Gen 37:31 *k* a kid of the goats, and dipped
Ex 21:29 that he hath *k* a man or a woman
Lev 4:15 shall be *k* before the LORD
Lev 6:25 is *k* shall the sin offering be
Lev 6:25 sin offering be *k* before the LORD
Lev 8:19 And he *k* it; and Moses
Lev 14:5 that one of the birds be *k* in an
Lev 14:6 that was *k* over the running water
Num 16:41 Ye have *k* the people of the LORD
Num 31:19 whosoever hath *k* any person
1Sa 24:11 *k* thee not, know thou and see that
1Sa 25:11 that I have *k* for my shearers
1Sa 28:24 *k* it, and took flour, and kneaded
2Sa 12:9 thou hast *k* Uriah the Hittite
2Sa 21:17 and smote the Philistine, and *k* him
1Kin 16:7 and because he *k* him
1Kin 16:10 *k* him, in the twenty and seventh
1Kin 21:19 Thus saith the LORD, Hast thou *k*
2Kin 15:25 he *k* him, and reigned in his room
1Chr 19:18 *k* Shophach the captain of the
2Chr 18:2 Ahab *k* sheep and oxen for him in
2Chr 25:3 that had *k* the king his father
2Chr 29:22 So they *k* the bullocks, and the
2Chr 29:22 when they had *k* the rams
2Chr 29:22 they *k* also the lambs, and they
2Chr 29:24 And the priests *k* them, and they
2Chr 30:15 Then they *k* the passover on the
2Chr 35:1 they *k* the passover on the
2Chr 35:11 they *k* the passover, and the
Ezr 6:20 *k* the passover for all the
Ps 44:22 sake are we *k* all the day long
Prov 9:2 She hath *k* her beasts
Lam 2:21 thou hast *k*, and not pitied
Mt 16:21 chief priests and scribes, and be *k*
Mt 21:35 *k* another, and stoned another
Mt 22:4 my oxen and my fatlings are *k*
Mt 23:31 of them which *k* the prophets
Mk 6:19 against him, and would have *k* him
Mk 8:31 priests, and scribes, and be *k*
Mk 9:31 and after that he is *k*, he shall
Mk 12:5 and him they *k*, and many others
Mk 12:8 *k* him, and cast him out of the
Mk 14:12 when they *k* the passover, his
Lk 11:47 prophets, and your fathers *k* them
Lk 11:48 for they indeed *k* them, and ye
Lk 12:5 which after he hath *k* hath power
Lk 15:27 thy father hath *k* the fatted calf
Lk 15:30 thou hast *k* for him the fatted
Lk 20:15 him out of the vineyard, and *k* him
Lk 22:7 when the passover must be *k*
Acts 3:15 *k* the Prince of life, whom God
Acts 12:2 he *k* James the brother of John
Acts 16:27 sword, and would have *k* himself
Acts 23:12 nor drink till they had *k* Paul
Acts 23:21 nor drink till they have *k* him
Acts 23:27 and should have been *k* of them
Rom 8:36 sake we are *k* all the day long
Rom 11:3 they have *k* thy prophets, and
2Cor 6:9 as chastened, and not *k*
1Th 2:15 Who both *k* the Lord Jesus, and
Jas 5:6 Ye have condemned and *k* the just
Rev 6:11 that should be *k* as they were
Rev 9:18 three was the third part of men *k*
Rev 9:20 *k* by these plagues yet repented
Rev 11:5 them, he must in this manner be *k*
Rev 13:10 sword must be *k* with the sword
Rev 13:15 image of the beast should be *k*

**KILLETH**
Lev 17:3 that *k* an ox, or lamb, or goat,
Lev 17:3 or that *k* it out of the camp,
Lev 24:17 he that *k* any man shall surely be
Lev 24:18 he that *k* a beast shall make it
Lev 24:21 And he that *k* a beast, he shall
Lev 24:21 and he that *k* a man, he shall be
Num 35:11 which *k* any person at unawares
Num 35:15 that every one that *k* any person
Num 35:30 Whoso *k* any person, the murderer
Deut 19:4 Whoso *k* his neighbour ignorantly,
Josh 20:3 slayer that *k* any person unawares
Josh 20:9 that whosoever *k* any person at
1Sa 2:6 The LORD *k*, and maketh alive
1Sa 17:25 shall be, that the man who *k* him
1Sa 17:26 to the man that *k* this Philistine
1Sa 17:27 it be done to the man that *k* him
Job 5:2 For wrath *k* the foolish man, and
Job 24:14 rising with the light *k* the poor
Prov 21:25 The desire of the slothful *k* him
Is 66:3 He that *k* an ox is as if he slew
Jn 16:2 that whosoever *k* you will think
2Cor 3:6 for the letter *k*, but the spirit
Rev 13:10 he that *k* with the sword must be

**KILLING**
Judg 9:24 him in the *k* of his brethren
2Chr 30:17 Levites had the charge of the *k*
Is 22:13 *k* sheep, eating flesh, and
Hos 4:2 By swearing, and lying, and *k*
Mk 12:5 beating some, and *k* some

**KIN**
Lev 18:6 to any that is near of *k* to him
Lev 20:19 for he uncovereth his near *k*
Lev 21:2 But for his *k*, that is near unto
Lev 25:25 if any of his *k* come to redeem it
Lev 25:49 or any that is nigh of *k* unto him
Ruth 2:20 her, The man is near of *k* unto us
2Sa 19:42 the king is near of *k* to us
Mk 6:4 own country, and among his own *k*

**KINAH** *(ki'-nah) A city in Judah.*
Josh 15:22 And K, and Dimonah, and Adadah,

**KIND**
Gen 1:11 tree yielding fruit after his *k*
Gen 1:12 and herb yielding seed after his *k*
Gen 1:12 seed was in itself, after his *k*
Gen 1:21 forth abundantly, after their *k*
Gen 1:21 and every winged fowl after his *k*
Gen 1:24 the living creature after his *k*
Gen 1:24 and beast of the earth after his *k*
Gen 1:25 his *k*, and cattle after their *k*
Gen 1:25 upon the earth after his *k*
Gen 6:20 Of fowls after their *k*
Gen 6:20 and of cattle after their *k*
Gen 6:20 thing of the earth after his *k*
Gen 7:14 They, and every beast after his *k*
Gen 7:14 and all the cattle after their *k*
Gen 7:14 upon the earth after his *k*
Gen 7:14 and every fowl after his *k*
Lev 11:14 vulture, and the kite after his *k*
Lev 11:15 Every raven after his *k*
Lev 11:16 cuckow, and the hawk after his *k*
Lev 11:19 the stork, the heron after her *k*
Lev 11:22 the locust after his *k*
Lev 11:22 and the bald locust after his *k*
Lev 11:22 and the beetle after his *k*
Lev 11:22 and the grasshopper after his *k*
Lev 11:29 and the tortoise after his *k*
Lev 19:19 cattle gender with a diverse *k*
Deut 14:13 kite, and the vulture after his *k*
Deut 14:14 And every raven after his *k*
Deut 14:15 cuckow, and the hawk after his *k*
Deut 14:18 stork, and the heron after her *k*
1Chr 28:14 instruments of every *k* of service
2Chr 10:7 If thou be *k* to this people, and
Neh 13:20 sellers of all *k* of ware lodged
Eccl 2:5 trees in them of all *k* of fruits
Eze 27:12 the multitude of all *k* of riches
Mt 13:47 the sea, and gathered of every *k*
Mt 17:21 Howbeit this *k* goeth not out but
Mk 9:29 This *k* can come forth by nothing,
Lk 6:35 for he is *k* unto the unthankful
1Cor 13:4 Charity suffereth long, and is *k*
1Cor 15:39 there is one *k* of flesh of men
Eph 4:32 And be ye *k* one to another,
Jas 1:18 truth, that we should be a *k* of
Jas 3:7 For every *k* of beasts, and of

**KINDLE**
Ex 35:3 Ye shall *k* no fire throughout
Prov 26:21 is a contentious man to *k* strife
Is 9:18 shall *k* in the thickets of the
Is 10:16 under his glory he shall *k* a
Is 30:33 a stream of brimstone, doth *k* it
Is 43:2 shall the flame *k* upon thee
Is 50:11 Behold, all ye that *k* a fire
Jer 7:18 wood, and the fathers *k* the fire
Jer 17:27 then will I *k* a fire in the gates
Jer 21:14 I will *k* a fire in the forest
Jer 33:18 to *k* meat offerings, and to do
Jer 43:12 I will *k* a fire in the houses of
Jer 49:27 I will *k* a fire in the wall of
Jer 50:32 I will *k* a fire in his cities, and
Eze 20:47 I will *k* a fire in thee, and it
Eze 24:10 *k* the fire, consume the flesh, and
Amos 1:14 But I will *k* a fire in the wall
Obad 18 stubble, and they shall *k* in them
Mal 1:10 neither do ye *k* fire on mine

**KINDLED**
Gen 30:2 anger was *k* against Rachel
Gen 39:19 that his wrath was *k*
Ex 4:14 of the LORD was *k* against Moses
Ex 22:6 he that *k* the fire shall surely
Lev 10:6 the burning which the LORD hath *k*
Num 11:1 and his anger was *k*
Num 11:10 anger of the LORD was *k* greatly
Num 11:33 the LORD was *k* against the people
Num 12:9 of the LORD was *k* against them
Num 22:22 God's anger was *k* because he went
Num 22:27 and Balaam's anger was *k*, and he
Num 24:10 anger was *k* against Balaam
Num 25:3 of the LORD was *k* against Israel
Num 32:10 LORD's anger was *k* the same time
Num 32:13 LORD's anger was *k* against Israel
Deut 6:15 LORD thy God be *k* against thee
Deut 7:4 of the LORD be *k* against you
Deut 11:17 the LORD's wrath be *k* against you
Deut 29:27 the LORD was *k* against this land
Deut 31:17 Then my anger shall be *k* against
Deut 32:22 For a fire is *k* in mine anger
Josh 7:1 the anger of the LORD was *k*
Josh 23:16 of the LORD be *k* against you
Judg 9:30 the son of Ebed, his anger was *k*
Judg 14:19 And his anger was *k*, and he went up
1Sa 11:6 and his anger was *k* greatly
1Sa 17:28 Eliab's anger was *k* against David
1Sa 20:30 anger was *k* against Jonathan
2Sa 6:7 of the LORD was *k* against Uzzah
2Sa 12:5 was greatly *k* against the man
2Sa 22:9 coals were *k* by it
2Sa 22:13 before him were coals of fire *k*
2Sa 24:1 of the LORD was *k* against Israel
2Kin 13:3 of the LORD was *k* against Israel
2Kin 22:13 of the LORD that is *k* against us
2Kin 22:17 shall be *k* against this place
2Kin 23:26 his anger was *k* against Judah
1Chr 13:10 of the LORD was *k* against Uzza
2Chr 25:10 anger was greatly *k* against Judah
2Chr 25:15 of the LORD was *k* against Amaziah
Job 19:11 He hath also *k* his wrath against
Job 32:2 Then was *k* the wrath of Elihu the

Job 32:2 against Job was his wrath *k*
Job 32:3 his three friends was his wrath *k*
Job 32:5 three men, then his wrath was *k*
Job 42:7 My wrath is *k* against thee, and
Ps 2:12 when his wrath is *k* but a little
Ps 18:8 coals were *k* by it
Ps 78:21 so a fire was *k* against Jacob
Ps 106:18 a fire was *k* in their company
Ps 106:40 of the LORD *k* against his people
Ps 124:3 when their wrath was *k* against us
Is 5:25 of the LORD *k* against his people
Is 50:11 and in the sparks that ye have *k*
Jer 11:16 tumult he hath *k* fire upon it
Jer 15:14 for a fire is *k* in mine anger
Jer 17:4 for ye have *k* a fire in mine
Jer 44:6 was *k* in the cities of Judah and
Lam 4:11 hath *k* a fire in Zion, and it hath
Eze 20:48 see that I the LORD have *k* it
Hos 8:5 mine anger is *k* against them
Hos 11:8 me, my repentings are *k* together
Zec 10:3 Mine anger was *k* against the
Lk 12:49 what will I, if it be already *k*
Lk 22:55 when they had *k* a fire in the
Acts 28:2 for they *k* a fire, and received us

**KINDLY**
Gen 24:49 And now if ye will deal *k* and truly
Gen 34:3 and spake *k* unto the damsel
Gen 47:29 hand under my thigh, and deal *k*
Gen 50:21 them, and spake *k* unto them
Josh 2:14 us the land, that we will deal *k*
Ruth 1:8 the LORD deal *k* with you, as ye
1Sa 20:8 shalt deal *k* with thy servant
2Kin 25:28 And he spake *k* to him, and set his
Jer 52:32 spake *k* unto him, and set his
Rom 12:10 Be *k* affectioned one to another

**KINDNESS**
Gen 20:13 This is thy *k* which thou shalt
Gen 21:23 but according to the *k* that I
Gen 24:12 shew *k* unto my master Abraham
Gen 24:14 thou hast shewed *k* unto my master
Gen 40:14 be well with thee, and shew *k*
Josh 2:12 LORD, since I have shewed you *k*
Josh 2:12 shew *k* unto my father's house
Judg 8:35 Neither shewed they *k* to the
Ruth 2:20 not left off his *k* to the living
Ruth 3:10 for thou hast shewed more *k* in
1Sa 15:6 for ye shewed *k* to all the
1Sa 20:14 I live shew me the *k* of the LORD
1Sa 20:15 off thy *k* from my house for ever
2Sa 2:5 have shewed this *k* unto your lord
2Sa 2:6 And now the LORD shew *k* and truth
2Sa 2:6 and I also will requite you this *k*
2Sa 3:8 which against Judah do shew *k*
2Sa 9:1 shew him *k* for Jonathan's sake
2Sa 9:3 I may shew the *k* of God unto him
2Sa 9:7 for I will surely shew thee *k* for
2Sa 10:2 I will shew *k* unto Hanun the son
2Sa 10:2 as his father shewed *k* unto me
2Sa 16:17 Is this thy *k* to thy friend
1Kin 2:7 But shew *k* unto the sons of
1Kin 3:6 hast kept for him this great *k*
1Chr 19:2 I will shew *k* unto Hanun the son
1Chr 19:2 because his father shewed *k* to me
2Chr 24:22 the king remembered not the *k*
Neh 9:17 slow to anger, and of great *k*
Est 2:9 him, and she obtained *k* of him
Ps 31:21 his marvellous *k* in a strong city
Ps 117:2 For his merciful *k* is great
Ps 119:76 thy merciful *k* be for my comfort,
Ps 141:5 it shall be a *k*
Prov 19:22 The desire of a man is his *k*
Prov 31:26 and in her tongue is the law of *k*
Is 54:8 but with everlasting *k* will I
Is 54:10 but my *k* shall not depart from
Jer 2:2 the *k* of thy youth, the love of
Joel 2:13 slow to anger, and of great *k*
Jonah 4:2 slow to anger, and of great *k*
Acts 28:2 people shewed us no little *k*
2Cor 6:6 knowledge, by longsuffering, by *k*
Eph 2:7 riches of his grace in his *k*
Col 3:12 and beloved, bowels of mercies, *k*
Titus 3:4 But after that the *k* and love of
2Pet 1:7 And to godliness brotherly *k*
2Pet 1:7 and to brotherly *k* charity

**KINDRED**
Gen 12:1 out of thy country, and from thy *k*
Gen 24:4 go unto my country, and to my *k*
Gen 24:7 house, and from the land of my *k*
Gen 24:38 my father's house, and to my *k*
Gen 24:40 take a wife for my son of my *k*
Gen 24:41 my oath, when thou comest to my *k*
Gen 31:3 land of thy fathers, and to thy *k*
Gen 31:13 and return unto the land of thy *k*
Gen 32:9 unto thy country, and to thy *k*
Gen 43:7 of our state, and of our *k*
Num 10:30 to mine own land, and to my *k*
Josh 6:23 and they brought out all her *k*
Ruth 2:3 who was of the *k* of Elimelech
Ruth 3:2 And now is not Boaz of our *k*
1Chr 12:29 the *k* of Saul, three thousand
Est 2:10 not shewed her people nor her *k*
Est 2:20 yet shewed her *k* nor her people
Est 8:6 to see the destruction of my *k*
Job 32:2 the Buzite, of the *k* of Ram
Eze 11:15 thy brethren, the men of thy *k*
Lk 1:61 There is none of thy *k* that is
Acts 4:6 were of the *k* of the high priest
Acts 7:3 out of thy country, and from thy *k*
Acts 7:13 Joseph's *k* was made known unto
Acts 7:14 father Jacob to him, and all his *k*
Acts 7:19 same dealt subtilly with our *k*
Rev 5:9 God by thy blood out of every *k*
Rev 14:6 earth, and to every nation, and *k*

**KINDREDS**
1Chr 16:28 ye *k* of the people, give unto the
Ps 22:27 all the *k* of the nations shall
Ps 96:7 O ye *k* of the people, give unto
Acts 3:25 all the *k* of the earth be blessed
Rev 1:7 all *k* of the earth shall wail
Rev 7:9 number, of all nations, and *k*
Rev 11:9 And they of the people and *k*
Rev 13:7 and power was given him over all *k*

**KINDS**
Gen 8:19 upon the earth, after their *k*
2Chr 16:14 divers *k* of spices prepared by
Jer 15:3 I will appoint over them four *k*
Eze 47:10 shall be according to their *k*
Dan 3:5 all *k* of musick, ye fall down and
Dan 3:7 all *k* of musick, all the people,
Dan 3:10 all *k* of musick, shall fall down
Dan 3:15 all *k* of musick, ye fall down and
1Cor 12:10 to another divers *k* of tongues
1Cor 14:10 so many *k* of voices in the world,

**KINE**
Gen 32:15 camels with their colts, forty *k*
Gen 41:2 the river seven well favoured *k*
Gen 41:3 seven other *k* came up after them
Gen 41:3 stood by the other *k* upon the
Gen 41:4 leanfleshed *k* did eat up the
Gen 41:4 the seven well favoured and fat *k*
Gen 41:18 came up out of the river seven *k*
Gen 41:19 seven other *k* came up after them,
Gen 41:20 the ill favoured *k* did eat up the
Gen 41:20 did eat up the first seven fat *k*
Gen 41:26 The seven good *k* are seven years
Gen 41:27 ill favoured *k* that came up after
Deut 7:13 thine oil, the increase of thy *k*
Deut 28:4 thy cattle, the increase of thy *k*
Deut 28:18 thy land, the increase of thy *k*
Deut 28:51 or oil, or the increase of thy *k*
Deut 32:14 Butter of *k*, and milk of sheep,
1Sa 6:7 a new cart, and take two milch *k*
1Sa 6:7 tie the *k* to the cart, and bring
1Sa 6:10 and took two milch *k*, and tied them
1Sa 6:12 the *k* took the straight way to
1Sa 6:14 offered the *k* a burnt offering
2Sa 17:29 butter, and sheep, and cheese of *k*
Amos 4:1 ye *k* of Bashan, that are in the

**KINSMAN**
Num 5:8 But if the man have no *k* to
Num 27:11 his *k* that is next to him of his
Ruth 2:1 Naomi had a *k* of her husband's, a
Ruth 3:9 for thou art a near *k*
Ruth 3:12 it is true that I am thy near *k*
Ruth 3:12 there is a *k* nearer than I
Ruth 3:13 perform unto thee the part of a *k*
Ruth 3:13 not do the part of a *k* to thee
Ruth 3:13 will I do the part of a *k* to thee
Ruth 4:1 the *k* of whom Boaz spake came by
Ruth 4:3 And he said unto the *k*, Naomi,
Ruth 4:6 the *k* said, I cannot redeem it
Ruth 4:8 Therefore the *k* said unto Boaz,
Ruth 4:14 left thee this day without a *k*
Jn 18:26 being his *k* whose ear Peter cut
Rom 16:11 Salute Herodion my *k*

**KINSMEN**
Ruth 2:20 of kin unto us, one of our next *k*
Ps 38:11 and my *k* stand afar off
Lk 14:12 nor thy brethren, neither thy *k*
Acts 10:24 and had called together his *k*
Rom 9:3 my *k* according to the flesh
Rom 16:7 Salute Andronicus and Junia, my *k*
Rom 16:21 and Jason, and Sosipater, my *k*

**KIR** *(kur)* See KIR-HARESH.
*1. An Assyrian district on the Kur River.*
2Kin 16:9 the people of it captive to *K*
Amos 1:5 shall go into captivity unto *K*
Amos 9:7 Caphtor, and the Syrians from *K*
*2. A Moabite city.*
Is 15:1 because in the night *K* of Moab is
*3. Inhabitants of Kir 1.*
Is 22:6 and *K* uncovered the shield

**KIR-HARASETH** *(kur-har'-a-seth)* See KIR-HARESETH. *A Moabite city.*
2Kin 3:25 only in *K* left they the stones

**KIR-HARESETH** *(kur-har'-e-seth)* See KIR-HARESH. *Same as Kir-haraseth.*
Is 16:7 foundations of *K* shall ye mourn

**KIR-HARESH** *(kur-ha'-resh)* See KIR-HARASETH, KIR-HARESETH, KIR-HERES. *Same as Kir-haraseth.*
Is 16:11 Moab, and mine inward parts for *K*

**KIR-HERES** *(kur-he'-res)* See KIR-HARESH. *Same as Kir-haraseth.*
Jer 48:31 shall mourn for the men of *K*
Jer 48:36 sound like pipes for the men of *K*

**KIRIATHAIM** *(kir-e-a-thay'-im)* See KIRJATHAIM.
*1. A town east of the Jordan.*
Gen 14:5 in Ham, and the Emims in Shaveh *K*
*2. A city in Reuben.*
Jer 48:1 *K* is confounded and taken
Jer 48:23 And upon *K*, and upon Beth-gamul,
Eze 25:9 Beth-jeshimoth, Baal-meon, and *K*

**KIRIOTH** *(kir'-e-oth)* See KERIOTH. *A Moabite city.*
Amos 2:2 it shall devour the palaces of *K*

**KIRJATH** *(kur'-jath)* See KIRJATH-ARIM, KIRJATH-BAAL, KIRJATH-JEARIM. *Short form of Kirjath-jearim.*
Josh 18:28 which is Jerusalem, Gibeath, and *K*

**KIRJATHAIM** *(jur'-jath-a'-im)*
*1. A city in Reuben.*
Num 32:37 built Heshbon, and Elealeh, and *K*
Josh 13:19 *K*, and Sibmah, and Zareth-shahar
*2. A Levitical city in Naphtali.*
1Chr 6:76 suburbs, and *K* with her suburbs

**KIRJATH-ARBA** *(kur'-jath-ar'-bah)* See HEBRON. *A city in Judah.*
Gen 23:2 And Sarah died in *K*
Josh 14:15 the name of Hebron before was *K*
Josh 15:54 And Humtah, and *K*, which is Hebron,
Josh 20:7 in mount Ephraim, and *K*
Judg 1:10 the name of Hebron before was *K*
Neh 11:25 the children of Judah dwelt at *K*

**KIRJATH-ARIM** *(kur'-jath-a'-rim)* See KIRJATH-JEARIM. *Same as Kirjath-jearim.*
Ezr 2:25 The children of *K*, Chephirah, and

**KIRJATH-BAAL** *(kur'-jath-ba'-al)* See BAALAH, KIRJATH-JEARIM. *Same as Kirjath-jearim.*
Josh 15:60 *K*, which is Kirjath-jearim, and
Josh 18:14 the goings out thereof were at *K*

**KIRJATH-HUZOTH** *(kur'-jath-hu'-zoth)* *Residence of Balak, king of Edom.*
Num 22:39 with Balak, and they came unto *K*

**KIRJATH-JEARIM** *(kur'-jath-je'-a-rim)* See KIRJATH, KIRJATH-ARIM, KIRJATH-BAAL.
*1. A city in Judah.*
Josh 9:17 and Chephirah, and Beeroth, and *K*
Josh 15:9 was drawn to Baalah, which is *K*
Josh 15:60 Kirjath-baal, which is *K*, and
Josh 18:14 were at Kirjath-baal, which is *K*
Josh 18:15 quarter was from the end of *K*
Judg 18:12 And they went up, and pitched in *K*
Judg 18:12 behold, it is behind *K*
1Sa 6:21 to the inhabitants of *K*, saying,
1Sa 7:1 And the men of *K* came, and brought

1Sa 7:2 to pass, while the ark abode in *K*
1Chr 13:5 to bring the ark of God from *K*
1Chr 13:6 Israel, to Baalah, that is, to *K*
2Chr 1:4 *K* to the place which David had
Neh 7:29 The men of *K*, Chephirah, and
Jer 26:20 Urijah the son of Shemaiah of *K*
*2. A descendant of Caleb.*
1Chr 2:50 Shobal the father of *K*,
1Chr 2:52 Shobal the father of *K* had sons
1Chr 2:53 And the families of *K*

**KIRJATH-SANNAH** *(kur'-jath-san'-nah) A city in Judah.*
Josh 15:49 And Dannah, and *K*, which is Debir,

**KIRJATH-SEPHER** *(kur'-jath-se'-fer)* See DEBIR, KIRJATH-SANNAH. *Same as Kirjath-sannah.*
Josh 15:15 and the name of Debir before was *K*
Josh 15:16 And Caleb said, He that smiteth *K*
Judg 1:11 and the name of Debir before was *K*
Judg 1:12 And Caleb said, He that smiteth *K*

**KISH** *(kish)*
*1. Father of King Saul.*
1Sa 9:1 man of Benjamin, whose name was *K*
1Sa 9:3 the asses of *K* Saul's father were
1Sa 9:3 *K* said to Saul his son, Take now
1Sa 10:11 that is come unto the son of *K*
1Sa 10:21 and Saul the son of *K* was taken
1Sa 14:51 And *K* was the father of Saul
2Sa 21:14 in the sepulchre of *K* his father
1Chr 8:33 And Ner begat *K*
1Chr 8:33 *K* begat Saul
1Chr 9:39 And Ner begat *K*
1Chr 9:39 and *K* begat Saul
1Chr 12:1 because of Saul the son of *K*
1Chr 26:28 the seer, and Saul the son of *K*
*2. Son of Abi-Gibeon.*
1Chr 8:30 firstborn son Abdon, and Zur, and *K*
1Chr 9:36 son Abdon, then Zur, and *K*
*3. A sanctuary servant.*
1Chr 23:21 of Mahli; Eleazar, and *K*
1Chr 23:22 brethren the sons of *K* took them
1Chr 24:29 Concerning *K*: the son of Kish
*4. A Levite.*
2Chr 29:12 *K* the son of Abdi, and Azariah the
*5. An ancestor of Mordecai.*
Est 2:5 the son of Shimei, the son of *K*

**KISHI** *(kish'-i)* See KUSHAIAH. *Father of Ethan.*
1Chr 6:44 Ethan the son of *K*, the son of

**KISHION** *(kish'-e-on)* See KEDESH, KISHON. *A Levitical city in Issachar.*
Josh 19:20 And Rabbith, and *K*, and Abez,

**KISHON** *(ki'-shon)* See KISHION, KISON.
*1. Same as Kishion.*
Josh 21:28 *K* with her suburbs, Dabareh with
Judg 4:13 the Gentiles unto the river of *K*
Judg 5:21 The river of *K* swept them away,
Judg 5:21 that ancient river, the river *K*
1Kin 18:40 brought them down to the brook *K*
*2. A brook near Mt. Tabor.*
Judg 4:7 draw unto thee to the river *K*

**KISON** *(ki'-son)* See KISHON. *Same as Kishon 2.*
Ps 83:9 as to Jabin, at the brook of *K*

**KISS**
Gen 27:26 Come near now, and *k* me, my son
Gen 31:28 hast not suffered me to *k* my sons
2Sa 20:9 with the right hand to *k* him
1Kin 19:20 *k* my father and my mother, and then
Ps 2:12 *K* the Son, lest he be angry, and
Prov 24:26 Every man shall *k* his lips that
Song 1:2 Let him *k* me with the kisses of
Song 8:1 find thee without, I would *k* thee
Hos 13:2 men that sacrifice *k* the calves
Mt 26:48 saying, Whomsoever I shall *k*
Mk 14:44 saying, Whomsoever I shall *k*
Lk 7:45 Thou gavest me no *k*
Lk 7:45 in hath not ceased to *k* my feet
Lk 22:47 and drew near unto Jesus to *k* him
Lk 22:48 thou the Son of man with a *k*
Rom 16:16 Salute one another with an holy *k*
1Cor 16:20 ye one another with an holy *k*
2Cor 13:12 Greet one another with an holy *k*
1Th 5:26 all the brethren with an holy *k*
1Pet 5:14 one another with a *k* of charity

**KISSED**
Gen 27:27 And he came near, and *k* him
Gen 29:11 Jacob *k* Rachel, and lifted up his
Gen 29:13 *k* him, and brought him to his
Gen 31:55 *k* his sons and his daughters, and
Gen 33:4 and fell on his neck, and *k* him
Gen 45:15 Moreover he *k* all his brethren,
Gen 48:10 he *k* them, and embraced them
Gen 50:1 face, and wept upon him, and *k* him
Ex 4:27 him in the mount of God, and *k* him
Ex 18:7 law, and did obeisance, and *k* him
Ruth 1:9 Then she *k* them
Ruth 1:14 Orpah *k* her mother in law
1Sa 10:1 *k* him, and said, Is it not because
1Sa 20:41 they *k* one another, and wept one
2Sa 14:33 and the king *k* Absalom
2Sa 15:5 his hand, and took him, and *k* him
2Sa 19:39 the king *k* Barzillai, and blessed
1Kin 19:18 every mouth which hath not *k* him
Job 31:27 or my mouth hath *k* my hand
Ps 85:10 and peace have *k* each other
Prov 7:13 *k* him, and with an impudent face
Mt 26:49 master; and *k* him
Mk 14:45 Master, master; and *k* him
Lk 7:38 *k* his feet, and anointed them with
Lk 15:20 and fell on his neck, and *k* him
Acts 20:37 and fell on Paul's neck, and *k* him,

**KITHLISH** *(kith'-lish) A city in Judah.*
Josh 15:40 And Cabbon, and Lahmam, and *K*

**KITRON** *(ki'-tron)* See KATTAH. *A city in Zebulun.*
Judg 1:30 drive out the inhabitants of *K*

**KITTIM** *(kit'-tim)* See CHITTIM. *A son of Javan.*
Gen 10:4 Elishah, and Tarshish, *K*, and
1Chr 1:7 Elishah, and Tarshish, *K*, and

**KNEE**
Gen 41:43 they cried before him, Bow the *k*
Is 45:23 That unto me every *k* shall bow
Mt 27:29 and they bowed the *k* before him
Rom 11:4 bowed the *k* to the image of Baal
Rom 14:11 every *k* shall bow to me, and every
Phil 2:10 name of Jesus every *k* should bow

**KNEELED**
2Chr 6:13 *k* down upon his knees before all
Dan 6:10 he *k* upon his knees three times a
Mk 10:17 *k* to him, and asked him, Good
Lk 22:41 cast, and *k* down, and prayed,
Acts 7:60 he *k* down, and cried with a loud
Acts 9:40 all forth, and *k* down, and prayed
Acts 20:36 he *k* down, and prayed with them
Acts 21:5 *k* down on the shore, and prayed

**KNEES**
Gen 30:3 and she shall bear upon my *k*
Gen 48:12 them out from between his *k*
Gen 50:23 were brought up upon Joseph's *k*
Deut 28:35 LORD shall smite thee in the *k*
Judg 7:5 boweth down upon his *k* to drink
Judg 7:6 down upon their *k* to drink water
Judg 16:19 And she made him sleep upon her *k*
1Kin 8:54 from kneeling on his *k* with his
1Kin 18:42 and put his face between his *k*
1Kin 19:18 all the *k* which have not bowed
2Kin 1:13 fell on his *k* before Elijah, and
2Kin 4:20 mother, he sat on her *k* till noon
2Chr 6:13 kneeled down upon his *k* before
Ezr 9:5 and my mantle, I fell upon my *k*
Job 3:12 Why did the *k* prevent me
Job 4:4 hast strengthened the feeble *k*
Ps 109:24 My *k* are weak through fasting
Is 35:3 hands, and confirm the feeble *k*
Is 66:12 sides, and be dandled upon her *k*
Eze 7:17 all *k* shall be weak as water
Eze 21:7 all *k* shall be weak as water
Eze 47:4 the waters were to the *k*
Dan 5:6 his *k* smote one against another
Dan 6:10 upon his *k* three times a day
Dan 10:10 me, which set me upon my *k*
Nah 2:10 the *k* smite together, and much
Mk 15:19 bowing their *k* worshipped him
Lk 5:8 saw it, he fell down at Jesus' *k*
Eph 3:14 For this cause I bow my *k* unto
Heb 12:12 which hang down, and the feeble *k*

**KNEW**
Gen 3:7 they *k* that they were naked
Gen 4:1 And Adam *k* Eve his wife
Gen 4:17 And Cain *k* his wife
Gen 4:25 And Adam *k* his wife again
Gen 8:11 so Noah *k* that the waters were
Gen 9:24 *k* what his younger son had done
Gen 28:16 and I *k* it not
Gen 31:32 For Jacob *k* not that Rachel had
Gen 37:33 And he *k* it, and said, It is my
Gen 38:9 Onan *k* that the seed should not
Gen 38:16 (for he *k* not that she was his
Gen 38:26 And he *k* her again no more
Gen 39:6 he *k* not ought he had, save the
Gen 42:7 he *k* them, but made himself
Gen 42:8 Joseph *k* his brethren
Gen 42:8 his brethren, but they *k* not him
Gen 42:23 they *k* not that Joseph understood
Ex 1:8 over Egypt, which *k* not Joseph
Num 22:34 for I *k* not that thou stoodest in
Num 24:16 *k* the knowledge of the most High,
Deut 8:16 manna, which thy fathers *k* not
Deut 9:24 LORD from the day that I *k* you
Deut 29:26 them, gods whom they *k* not
Deut 32:17 to gods whom they *k* not, to new
Deut 33:9 brethren, nor *k* his own children
Deut 34:10 whom the LORD *k* face to face
Judg 2:10 which *k* not the LORD, nor yet the
Judg 3:2 such as before *k* nothing thereof
Judg 11:39 and she *k* no man
Judg 13:16 For Manoah *k* not that he was an
Judg 13:21 Then Manoah *k* that he was an
Judg 14:4 his mother *k* not that it was of
Judg 18:3 they *k* the voice of the young man
Judg 19:25 and they *k* her, and abused her all
Judg 20:34 but they *k* not that evil was near
1Sa 1:19 Elkanah *k* Hannah his wife
1Sa 2:12 they *k* not the LORD
1Sa 3:20 from Dan even to Beer-sheba *k*
1Sa 10:11 when all that *k* him beforetime
1Sa 14:3 the people *k* not that Jonathan
1Sa 18:28 *k* that the LORD was with David,
1Sa 20:9 for if I *k* certainly that evil
1Sa 20:33 whereby Jonathan *k* that it was
1Sa 20:39 But the lad *k* not any thing
1Sa 20:39 Jonathan and David *k* the matter
1Sa 22:15 for thy servant *k* nothing of all
1Sa 22:17 and because they *k* when he fled
1Sa 22:22 I *k* it that day, when Doeg the
1Sa 23:9 David *k* that Saul secretly
1Sa 26:12 away, and no man saw it, nor *k* it
1Sa 26:17 Saul *k* David's voice, and said, Is
2Sa 3:26 but David *k* it not
2Sa 11:16 where he *k* that valiant men were
2Sa 11:20 *k* ye not that they would shoot
2Sa 15:11 and they *k* not any thing
2Sa 18:29 tumult, but I *k* not what it was
2Sa 22:44 a people which I *k* not shall
1Kin 1:4 but the king *k* her not
1Kin 18:7 he *k* him, and fell on his face, and
2Kin 4:39 for they *k* them not
2Chr 33:13 Then Manasseh *k* that the LORD he
Neh 2:16 the rulers *k* not whither I went,
Est 1:13 which *k* the times, (for so was
Est 1:13 manner toward all that *k* law
Job 2:12 *k* him not, they lifted up their
Job 23:3 Oh that I *k* where I might find
Job 29:16 the cause which I *k* not I
Job 42:3 wonderful for me, which I *k* not
Ps 35:11 to my charge things that I *k* not
Ps 35:15 against me, and I *k* it not
Prov 24:12 thou sayest, Behold, we *k* it not
Is 42:16 blind by a way that they *k* not
Is 42:25 on fire round about, yet he *k* not
Is 48:4 Because I *k* that thou art
Is 48:7 shouldest say, Behold, I *k* them
Is 48:8 for I *k* that thou wouldest deal
Is 55:5 nations that *k* not thee shall run
Jer 1:5 formed thee in the belly I *k* thee
Jer 2:8 they that handle the law *k* me not
Jer 11:19 I *k* not that they had devised
Jer 32:8 Then I *k* that this was the word
Jer 41:4 slain Gedaliah, and no man *k* it
Jer 44:3 serve other gods, whom they *k* not
Jer 44:15 Then all the men which *k* that
Eze 10:20 I *k* that they were the cherubims
Eze 19:7 he *k* their desolate palaces, and
Dan 5:21 till he *k* that the most high God
Dan 6:10 Now when Daniel *k* that the
Dan 11:38 a god whom his fathers *k* not
Hos 8:4 have made princes, and I *k* it not
Hos 11:3 but they *k* not that I healed them
Jonah 1:10 For the men *k* that he fled from
Jonah 4:2 for I *k* that thou art a gracious

Zec 7:14 all the nations whom they *k* not
Zec 11:11 me *k* that it was the word of the
Mt 1:25 *k* her not till she had brought
Mt 7:23 profess unto them, I never *k* you
Mt 12:15 But when Jesus *k* it, he withdrew
Mt 12:25 Jesus *k* their thoughts, and said
Mt 17:12 they *k* him not, but have done
Mt 24:39 *k* not until the flood came, and
Mt 25:24 I *k* thee that thou art an hard
Mt 27:18 For he *k* that for envy they had
Mk 1:34 to speak, because they *k* him
Mk 6:33 saw them departing, and many *k* him
Mk 6:38 And when they *k*, they say, Five,
Mk 6:54 the ship, straightway they *k* him
Mk 8:17 And when Jesus *k* it, he saith unto
Mk 12:12 for they *k* that he had spoken the
Mk 15:10 For he *k* that the chief priests
Mk 15:45 when he *k* it of the centurion, he
Lk 2:43 Joseph and his mother *k* not of it
Lk 4:41 for they *k* that he was Christ
Lk 6:8 But he *k* their thoughts, and said
Lk 7:37 when she *k* that Jesus sat at meat
Lk 9:11 And the people, when they *k* it
Lk 12:47 which *k* his lord's will, and
Lk 12:48 But he that *k* not, and did commit
Lk 18:34 neither *k* they the things which
Lk 23:7 as soon as he *k* that he belonged
Lk 24:31 eyes were opened, and they *k* him
Jn 1:10 by him, and the world *k* him not
Jn 1:31 And I *k* him not
Jn 1:33 And I *k* him not
Jn 2:9 made wine, and *k* not whence it was
Jn 2:9 servants which drew the water *k*
Jn 2:24 unto them, because he *k* all men
Jn 2:25 for he *k* what was in man
Jn 4:1 When therefore the Lord *k* how the
Jn 4:53 So the father *k* that it was at
Jn 5:6 *k* that he had been now a long
Jn 6:6 for he himself *k* what he would do
Jn 6:61 When Jesus *k* in himself that his
Jn 6:64 For Jesus *k* from the beginning
Jn 11:42 I *k* that thou hearest me always
Jn 11:57 if any man *k* where he were, he
Jn 12:9 therefore *k* that he was there
Jn 13:1 when Jesus *k* that his hour was
Jn 13:11 For he *k* who should betray him
Jn 13:28 Now no man at the table *k* for
Jn 16:19 Now Jesus *k* that they were
Jn 18:2 which betrayed him, *k* the place
Jn 20:9 For as yet they *k* not the
Jn 20:14 and *k* not that it was Jesus
Jn 21:4 but the disciples *k* not that it
Acts 3:10 they *k* that it was he which sat
Acts 7:18 king arose, which *k* not Joseph
Acts 9:30 Which when the brethren *k*
Acts 12:14 when she *k* Peter's voice, she
Acts 13:27 rulers, because they *k* him not
Acts 16:3 for they *k* all that his father
Acts 19:32 the more part *k* not wherefore
Acts 19:34 But when they *k* that he was a Jew
Acts 22:29 after he *k* that he was a Roman,
Acts 26:5 Which *k* me from the beginning, if
Acts 27:39 it was day, they *k* not the land
Acts 28:1 then they *k* that the island was
Rom 1:21 Because that, when they *k* God
1Cor 1:21 God the world by wisdom *k* not God
1Cor 2:8 of the princes of this world *k*
2Cor 5:21 to be sin for us, who *k* no sin
2Cor 12:2 I *k* a man in Christ above
2Cor 12:3 I *k* such a man, (whether in the
Gal 4:8 Howbeit then, when ye *k* not God
Col 1:6 *k* the grace of God in truth
Col 2:1 For I would that ye *k* what great
1Jn 3:1 us not, because it *k* him not
Jude 5 though ye once *k* this, how that
Rev 19:12 had a name written, that no man *k*

## KNIFE

Gen 22:6 took the fire in his hand, and a *k*
Gen 22:10 took the *k* to slay his son
Judg 19:29 come into his house, he took a *k*
Prov 23:2 put a *k* to thy throat, if thou be
Eze 5:1 son of man, take thee a sharp *k*
Eze 5:2 part, and smite about it with a *k*

## KNIT

Judg 20:11 the city, *k* together as one man
1Sa 18:1 was *k* with the soul of David
1Chr 12:17 mine heart shall be *k* unto you
Acts 10:11 great sheet *k* at the four corners
Col 2:2 being *k* together in love, and unto
Col 2:19 *k* together, increaseth with the

## KNIVES

Josh 5:2 unto Joshua, Make thee sharp *k*
Josh 5:3 And Joshua made him sharp *k*
1Kin 18:28 after their manner with *k*
Ezr 1:9 of silver, nine and twenty *k*
Prov 30:14 swords, and their jaw teeth as *k*

## KNOCK

Mt 7:7 *k*, and it shall be opened unto you
Lk 11:9 *k*, and it shall be opened unto you
Lk 13:25 to *k* at the door, saying, Lord,
Rev 3:20 Behold, I stand at the door, and *k*

## KNOCKETH

Song 5:2 is the voice of my beloved that *k*
Mt 7:8 to him that *k* it shall be opened
Lk 11:10 to him that *k* it shall be opened
Lk 12:36 that when he cometh and *k*, they

## KNOW

Gen 3:5 For God doth *k* that in the day ye
Gen 3:22 as one of us, to *k* good and evil
Gen 4:9 And he said, I *k* not
Gen 12:11 I *k* that thou art a fair woman to
Gen 15:8 whereby shall I *k* that I shall
Gen 15:13 *K* of a surety that thy seed shall
Gen 18:19 For I *k* him, that he will command
Gen 18:21 and if not, I will *k*
Gen 19:5 out unto us, that we may *k* them
Gen 20:6 I *k* that thou didst this in the
Gen 20:7 *k* thou that thou shalt surely die
Gen 22:12 for now I *k* that thou fearest God
Gen 24:14 thereby shall I *k* that thou hast
Gen 27:2 I *k* not the day of my death
Gen 29:5 *K* ye Laban the son of Nahor
Gen 29:5 And they said, We *k* him
Gen 31:6 ye *k* that with all my power I
Gen 37:32 *k* now whether it be thy son's
Gen 42:33 Hereby shall I *k* that ye are true
Gen 42:34 then shall I *k* that ye are no
Gen 43:7 we certainly *k* that he would say
Gen 44:27 Ye *k* that my wife bare me two
Gen 48:19 I *k* it, my son, I *k* it
Ex 3:7 for I *k* their sorrows
Ex 4:14 I *k* that he can speak well
Ex 5:2 I *k* not the LORD, neither will I
Ex 6:7 ye shall *k* that I am the LORD
Ex 7:5 shall *k* that I am the LORD
Ex 7:17 thou shalt *k* that I am the LORD
Ex 8:10 that thou mayest *k* that there is
Ex 8:22 to the end thou mayest *k* that I
Ex 9:14 that thou mayest *k* that there is
Ex 9:29 that thou mayest *k* how that the
Ex 9:30 I *k* that ye will not yet fear the
Ex 10:2 that ye may *k* how that I am the
Ex 10:26 we *k* not with what we must serve
Ex 11:7 that ye may *k* how that the LORD
Ex 14:4 may *k* that I am the LORD
Ex 14:18 shall *k* that I am the LORD
Ex 16:6 then ye shall *k* that the LORD
Ex 16:12 ye shall *k* that I am the LORD
Ex 18:11 Now I *k* that the LORD is greater
Ex 18:16 I do make them *k* the statutes of
Ex 23:9 for ye *k* the heart of a stranger,
Ex 29:46 they shall *k* that I am the LORD
Ex 31:13 that ye may *k* that I am the LORD
Ex 33:5 that I may *k* what to do unto thee
Ex 33:12 thou hast not let me *k* whom thou
Ex 33:12 I *k* thee by name, and thou hast
Ex 33:13 me now thy way, that I may *k* thee
Ex 33:17 in my sight, and I *k* thee by name
Ex 36:1 understanding to *k* how to work
Lev 23:43 That your generations may *k* that
Num 14:31 they shall *k* the land which ye
Num 14:34 ye shall *k* my breach of promise
Num 16:28 Hereby ye shall *k* that the LORD
Num 22:19 that I may *k* what the LORD will
Deut 3:19 (for I *k* that ye have much cattle
Deut 4:35 that thou mightest *k* that the
Deut 4:39 *K* therefore this day, and consider
Deut 7:9 *K* therefore that the LORD thy God
Deut 8:2 to *k* what was in thine heart,
Deut 8:3 not, neither did thy fathers *k*
Deut 8:3 that he might make thee *k* that
Deut 11:2 And *k* ye this day
Deut 13:3 to *k* whether ye love the LORD
Deut 18:21 How shall we *k* the word which the
Deut 22:2 unto thee, or if thou *k* him not
Deut 29:6 that ye might *k* that I am the
Deut 29:16 (For ye *k* how we have dwelt in
Deut 31:21 for I *k* their imagination which
Deut 31:27 For I *k* thy rebellion, and thy
Deut 31:29 For I *k* that after my death ye
Josh 2:9 I *k* that the LORD hath given you
Josh 3:4 that ye may *k* the way by which ye
Josh 3:7 all Israel, that they may *k* that
Josh 3:10 Hereby ye shall *k* that the living
Josh 4:22 Then ye shall let your children *k*
Josh 4:24 might *k* the hand of the LORD
Josh 22:22 he knoweth, and Israel he shall *k*
Josh 23:13 *K* for a certainty that the LORD
Josh 23:14 ye *k* in all your hearts and in all
Judg 3:2 of the children of Israel might *k*
Judg 3:4 to *k* whether they would hearken
Judg 6:37 then shall I *k* that thou wilt
Judg 17:13 Now *k* I that the LORD will do me
Judg 18:5 that we may *k* whether our way
Judg 18:14 Do ye *k* that there is in these
Judg 19:22 thine house, that we may *k* him
Ruth 3:11 *k* that thou art a virtuous woman
Ruth 3:14 up before one could *k* another
Ruth 3:18 until thou *k* how the matter will
Ruth 4:4 it, then tell me, that I may *k*
1Sa 3:7 Now Samuel did not yet *k* the LORD
1Sa 6:9 then we shall *k* that it is not
1Sa 14:38 and *k* and see wherein this sin hath
1Sa 17:28 I *k* thy pride, and the naughtiness
1Sa 17:46 that all the earth may *k* that
1Sa 17:47 all this assembly shall *k* that
1Sa 20:3 he saith, Let not Jonathan *k* this
1Sa 20:30 do not I *k* that thou hast chosen
1Sa 21:2 Let no man *k* any thing of the
1Sa 22:3 till I *k* what God will do for me
1Sa 23:22 Go, I pray you, prepare yet, and *k*
1Sa 24:11 *k* thou and see that there is
1Sa 24:20 I *k* well that thou shalt surely
1Sa 25:11 whom I *k* not whence they be
1Sa 25:17 Now therefore *k* and consider what
1Sa 28:1 *K* thou assuredly, that thou shalt
1Sa 28:2 Surely thou shalt *k* what thy
1Sa 29:9 I *k* that thou art good in my
2Sa 3:25 to *k* thy going out and thy coming
2Sa 3:25 in, and to *k* all that thou doest
2Sa 3:38 *K* ye not that there is a prince
2Sa 7:21 to make thy servant *k* them
2Sa 14:20 to *k* all things that are in the
2Sa 19:20 servant doth *k* that I have sinned
2Sa 19:22 for do not I *k* that I am this day
2Sa 24:2 that I may *k* the number of the
1Kin 2:37 thou shalt *k* for certain that
1Kin 2:42 *K* for a certain, on the day thou
1Kin 3:7 I *k* not how to go out or come in
1Kin 8:38 which shall *k* every man the
1Kin 8:43 of the earth may *k* thy name
1Kin 8:43 that they may *k* that this house,
1Kin 8:60 earth may *k* that the LORD is God
1Kin 17:24 Now by this I *k* that thou art a
1Kin 18:12 shall carry thee whither I *k* not
1Kin 18:37 that this people may *k* that thou
1Kin 20:13 thou shalt *k* that I am the LORD
1Kin 20:28 ye shall *k* that I am the LORD
1Kin 22:3 *K* ye that Ramoth in Gilead is
2Kin 2:3 And he said, Yea, I *k* it
2Kin 2:5 And he answered, Yea, I *k* it
2Kin 5:8 he shall *k* that there is a
2Kin 5:15 now I *k* that there is no God in
2Kin 7:12 They *k* that we be hungry
2Kin 8:12 Because I *k* the evil that thou
2Kin 9:11 unto them, Ye *k* the man, and his
2Kin 10:10 *K* now that there shall fall unto
2Kin 17:26 *k* not the manner of the God of
2Kin 17:26 because they *k* not the manner of
2Kin 19:19 may *k* that thou art the LORD God
2Kin 19:27 But I *k* thy abode, and thy going
1Chr 12:32 to *k* what Israel ought to do
1Chr 21:2 of them to me, that I may *k* it
1Chr 28:9 *k* thou the God of thy father, and
1Chr 29:17 I *k* also, my God, that thou
2Chr 2:8 for I *k* that thy servants can
2Chr 6:29 every one shall *k* his own sore
2Chr 6:33 of the earth may *k* thy name
2Chr 6:33 may *k* that this house which I
2Chr 12:8 that they may *k* my service
2Chr 13:5 Ought ye not to *k* that the LORD
2Chr 20:12 neither *k* we what to do
2Chr 25:16 I *k* that God hath determined to
2Chr 32:13 *K* ye not what I and my fathers
2Chr 32:31 that he might *k* all that was in
Ezr 4:15 *k* that this city is a rebellious

| | |
|---|---|
| Ezr 7:25 | all such as *k* the laws of thy God |
| Ezr 7:25 | and teach ye them that *k* them not |
| Neh 4:11 | said, They shall not *k*, neither |
| Est 2:11 | to *k* how Esther did, and what |
| Est 4:5 | to *k* what it was, and why it was |
| Est 4:11 | of the king's provinces, do *k* |
| Job 5:24 | thou shalt *k* that thy tabernacle |
| Job 5:25 | Thou shalt *k* also that thy seed |
| Job 5:27 | it, and *k* thou it for thy good |
| Job 7:10 | shall his place *k* him any more |
| Job 8:9 | *k* nothing, because our days upon |
| Job 9:2 | I *k* it is so of a truth |
| Job 9:5 | the mountains, and they *k* not |
| Job 9:21 | yet would I not *k* my soul |
| Job 9:28 | I *k* that thou wilt not hold me |
| Job 10:13 | I *k* that this is with thee |
| Job 11:6 | *K* therefore that God exacteth of |
| Job 11:8 | what canst thou *k* |
| Job 13:2 | What ye *k*, the same do I *k* |
| Job 13:2 | ye *k*, the same do I *k* also |
| Job 13:18 | I *k* that I shall be justified |
| Job 13:23 | make me to *k* my transgression and |
| Job 15:9 | What knowest thou, that we *k* not |
| Job 19:6 | *K* now that God hath overthrown me |
| Job 19:25 | For I *k* that my redeemer liveth, |
| Job 19:29 | that ye may *k* there is a judgment |
| Job 21:19 | rewardeth him, and he shall *k* it |
| Job 21:27 | I *k* your thoughts, and the devices |
| Job 21:29 | do ye not *k* their tokens, |
| Job 22:13 | And thou sayest, How doth God *k* |
| Job 23:5 | I would *k* the words which he |
| Job 24:1 | do they that *k* him not see his |
| Job 24:13 | they *k* not the ways thereof, nor |
| Job 24:16 | they *k* not the light |
| Job 24:17 | if one *k* them, they are in the |
| Job 30:23 | For I *k* that thou wilt bring me |
| Job 31:6 | that God may *k* mine integrity |
| Job 32:22 | For I *k* not to give flattering |
| Job 34:4 | let us *k* among ourselves what is |
| Job 36:26 | we *k* him not, neither can the |
| Job 37:7 | that all men may *k* his work |
| Job 37:15 | Dost thou *k* when God disposed |
| Job 37:16 | Dost thou *k* the balancings of the |
| Job 38:12 | the dayspring to *k* his place |
| Job 38:20 | that thou shouldest *k* the paths |
| Job 42:2 | I *k* that thou canst do every |
| Ps 4:3 | But *k* that the LORD hath set |
| Ps 9:10 | they that *k* thy name will put |
| Ps 9:20 | that the nations may *k* themselves |
| Ps 20:6 | Now *k* I that the LORD saveth his |
| Ps 36:10 | unto them that *k* thee |
| Ps 39:4 | LORD, make me to *k* mine end |
| Ps 39:4 | that I may *k* how frail I am |
| Ps 41:11 | By this I *k* that thou favourest |
| Ps 46:10 | Be still, and *k* that I am God |
| Ps 50:11 | I *k* all the fowls of the |
| Ps 51:6 | thou shalt make me to *k* wisdom |
| Ps 56:9 | enemies turn back: this I *k* |
| Ps 59:13 | let them *k* that God ruleth in |
| Ps 71:15 | for I *k* not the numbers thereof |
| Ps 73:11 | And they say, How doth God *k* |
| Ps 73:16 | When I thought to *k* this, it was |
| Ps 78:6 | generation to come might *k* them |
| Ps 82:5 | They *k* not, neither will they |
| Ps 83:18 | That men may *k* that thou, whose |
| Ps 87:4 | and Babylon to them that *k* me |
| Ps 89:15 | people that *k* the joyful sound |
| Ps 94:10 | man knowledge, shall not he *k* |
| Ps 100:3 | *K* ye that the LORD he is God |
| Ps 101:4 | I will not *k* a wicked person |
| Ps 103:16 | place thereof shall *k* it no more |
| Ps 109:27 | That they may *k* that this is thy |
| Ps 119:75 | I *k*, O LORD, that thy judgments |
| Ps 119:125 | that I may *k* thy testimonies |
| Ps 135:5 | For I *k* that the LORD is great, |
| Ps 139:23 | Search me, O God, and *k* my heart |
| Ps 139:23 | try me, and *k* my thoughts |
| Ps 140:12 | I *k* that the LORD will maintain |
| Ps 142:4 | there was no man that would *k* me |
| Ps 143:8 | cause me to *k* the way wherein I |
| Prov 1:2 | To *k* wisdom and instruction |
| Prov 4:1 | attend to *k* understanding |
| Prov 4:19 | they *k* not at what they stumble |
| Prov 5:6 | that thou canst not *k* them |
| Prov 10:32 | righteous *k* what is acceptable |
| Prov 22:21 | That I might make thee *k* the |
| Prov 24:12 | thy soul, doth not he *k* it |
| Prov 25:8 | lest thou *k* not what to do in the |
| Prov 27:23 | Be thou diligent to *k* the state |
| Prov 29:7 | the wicked regardeth not to *k* it |
| Prov 30:18 | for me, yea, four which I *k* not |
| Eccl 1:17 | And I gave my heart to *k* wisdom |
| Eccl 1:17 | and to *k* madness and folly |
| Eccl 3:12 | I *k* that there is no good in them |
| Eccl 3:14 | I *k* that, whatsoever God doeth, |
| Eccl 7:25 | I applied mine heart to *k* |
| Eccl 7:25 | to *k* the wickedness of folly, |
| Eccl 8:12 | yet surely I *k* that it shall be |
| Eccl 8:16 | I applied mine heart to *k* wisdom |
| Eccl 8:17 | though a wise man think to *k* it |
| Eccl 9:5 | For the living *k* that they shall |
| Eccl 9:5 | but the dead *k* not any thing, |
| Eccl 11:9 | but *k* thou, that for all these |
| Song 1:8 | If thou *k* not, O thou fairest |
| Is 1:3 | but Israel doth not *k*, my people |
| Is 5:19 | nigh and come, that we may *k* it |
| Is 7:15 | that he may *k* to refuse the evil, |
| Is 7:16 | child shall *k* to refuse the evil |
| Is 9:9 | And all the people shall *k* |
| Is 19:12 | let them *k* what the LORD of hosts |
| Is 19:21 | the Egyptians shall *k* the LORD in |
| Is 37:20 | may *k* that thou art the LORD |
| Is 37:28 | But I *k* thy abode, and thy going |
| Is 41:20 | That they may see, and *k*, and |
| Is 41:22 | them, and *k* the latter end of them |
| Is 41:23 | that we may *k* that ye are gods |
| Is 41:26 | from the beginning, that we may *k* |
| Is 43:10 | that ye may *k* and believe me, and |
| Is 43:19 | shall ye not *k* it |
| Is 44:8 | I *k* not any |
| Is 44:9 | they see not, nor *k* |
| Is 45:3 | places, that thou mayest *k* that I |
| Is 45:6 | That they may *k* from the rising |
| Is 47:8 | neither shall I *k* the loss of |
| Is 47:11 | thou shalt not *k* from whence it |
| Is 47:11 | suddenly, which thou shalt not *k* |
| Is 48:6 | things, and thou didst not *k* them |
| Is 49:23 | thou shalt *k* that I am the LORD |
| Is 49:26 | all flesh shall *k* that I the LORD |
| Is 50:4 | that I should *k* how to speak a |
| Is 50:7 | I *k* that I shall not be ashamed |
| Is 51:7 | ye that *k* righteousness, the |
| Is 52:6 | my people shall *k* my name |
| Is 52:6 | therefore they shall *k* in that |
| Is 58:2 | me daily, and delight to *k* my ways |
| Is 59:8 | The way of peace they *k* not |
| Is 59:8 | goeth therein shall not *k* peace |
| Is 59:12 | as for our iniquities, we *k* them |
| Is 60:16 | thou shalt *k* that I the LORD am |
| Is 66:18 | For I *k* their works and their |
| Jer 2:19 | *k* therefore and see that it is an |
| Jer 2:23 | the valley, *k* what thou hast done |
| Jer 5:1 | of Jerusalem, and see now, and *k* |
| Jer 5:4 | for they *k* not the way of the |
| Jer 6:18 | Therefore hear, ye nations, and *k* |
| Jer 6:27 | my people, that thou mayest *k* |
| Jer 7:9 | after other gods whom ye *k* not |
| Jer 8:7 | but my people *k* not the judgment |
| Jer 9:3 | they *k* not me, saith the LORD |
| Jer 9:6 | deceit they refuse to *k* me |
| Jer 10:23 | I *k* that the way of man is not in |
| Jer 10:25 | upon the heathen that *k* thee not |
| Jer 11:18 | me knowledge of it, and I *k* it |
| Jer 13:12 | Do we not certainly *k* that every |
| Jer 14:18 | about into a land that they *k* not |
| Jer 15:15 | *k* that for thy sake I have |
| Jer 16:13 | land into a land that ye *k* not |
| Jer 16:21 | I will this once cause them to *k* |
| Jer 16:21 | I will cause them to *k* mine hand |
| Jer 16:21 | they shall *k* that my name is The |
| Jer 17:9 | who can *k* it? |
| Jer 22:16 | was not this to *k* me |
| Jer 22:28 | cast into a land which they *k* not |
| Jer 24:7 | I will give them an heart to *k* me |
| Jer 26:15 | But *k* ye for certain, that if ye |
| Jer 29:11 | For I *k* the thoughts that I think |
| Jer 29:16 | *K* that thus saith the LORD of the |
| Jer 29:23 | even I *k*, and am a witness, saith |
| Jer 31:34 | his brother, saying, *K* the LORD |
| Jer 31:34 | for they shall all *k* me, from the |
| Jer 36:19 | and let no man *k* where ye be |
| Jer 38:24 | Let no man *k* of these words, and |
| Jer 40:14 | Dost thou certainly *k* that Baalis |
| Jer 40:15 | Nethaniah, and no man shall *k* it |
| Jer 42:19 | *k* certainly that I have |
| Jer 42:22 | Now therefore *k* certainly that ye |
| Jer 44:28 | shall *k* whose words shall stand, |
| Jer 44:29 | that ye may *k* that my words shall |
| Jer 48:17 | and all ye that *k* his name |
| Jer 48:30 | I *k* his wrath, saith the LORD |
| Eze 2:5 | yet shall *k* that there hath been |
| Eze 5:13 | they shall *k* that I the LORD have |
| Eze 6:7 | ye shall *k* that I am the LORD |
| Eze 6:10 | they shall *k* that I am the LORD, |
| Eze 6:13 | Then shall ye *k* that I am the |
| Eze 6:14 | they shall *k* that I am the LORD |
| Eze 7:4 | ye shall *k* that I am the LORD |
| Eze 7:9 | ye shall *k* that I am the LORD |
| Eze 7:27 | they shall *k* that I am the LORD |
| Eze 11:5 | for I *k* the things that come into |
| Eze 11:10 | ye shall *k* that I am the LORD |
| Eze 11:12 | ye shall *k* that I am the LORD |
| Eze 12:15 | they shall *k* that I am the LORD, |
| Eze 12:16 | they shall *k* that I am the LORD |
| Eze 12:20 | ye shall *k* that I am the LORD |
| Eze 13:9 | ye shall *k* that I am the Lord GOD |
| Eze 13:14 | ye shall *k* that I am the LORD |
| Eze 13:21 | ye shall *k* that I am the LORD |
| Eze 13:23 | ye shall *k* that I am the LORD |
| Eze 14:8 | ye shall *k* that I am the LORD |
| Eze 14:23 | ye shall *k* that I have not done |
| Eze 15:7 | ye shall *k* that I am the LORD, |
| Eze 16:2 | Jerusalem to *k* her abominations |
| Eze 16:62 | thou shalt *k* that I am the LORD |
| Eze 17:12 | *K* ye not what these things mean |
| Eze 17:21 | ye shall *k* that I the LORD have |
| Eze 17:24 | *k* that I the LORD have brought |
| Eze 20:4 | cause them to *k* the abominations |
| Eze 20:12 | that they might *k* that I am the |
| Eze 20:20 | that ye may *k* that I am the LORD |
| Eze 20:26 | they might *k* that I am the LORD |
| Eze 20:38 | ye shall *k* that I am the LORD |
| Eze 20:42 | ye shall *k* that I am the LORD, |
| Eze 20:44 | ye shall *k* that I am the LORD, |
| Eze 21:5 | That all flesh may *k* that I the |
| Eze 22:16 | thou shalt *k* that I am the LORD |
| Eze 22:22 | ye shall *k* that I the LORD have |
| Eze 23:49 | ye shall *k* that I am the Lord GOD |
| Eze 24:24 | ye shall *k* that I am the Lord GOD |
| Eze 24:27 | they shall *k* that I am the LORD |
| Eze 25:5 | ye shall *k* that I am the LORD |
| Eze 25:7 | thou shalt *k* that I am the LORD |
| Eze 25:11 | they shall *k* that I am the LORD |
| Eze 25:14 | they shall *k* my vengeance, saith |
| Eze 25:17 | they shall *k* that I am the LORD, |
| Eze 26:6 | they shall *k* that I am the LORD |
| Eze 28:19 | All they that *k* thee among the |
| Eze 28:22 | they shall *k* that I am the LORD, |
| Eze 28:23 | they shall *k* that I am the LORD |
| Eze 28:24 | they shall *k* that I am the Lord |
| Eze 28:26 | they shall *k* that I am the LORD |
| Eze 29:6 | Egypt shall *k* that I am the LORD |
| Eze 29:9 | they shall *k* that I am the LORD |
| Eze 29:16 | but they shall *k* that I am the |
| Eze 29:21 | they shall *k* that I am the LORD |
| Eze 30:8 | they shall *k* that I am the LORD, |
| Eze 30:19 | they shall *k* that I am the LORD |
| Eze 30:25 | they shall *k* that I am the LORD, |
| Eze 30:26 | they shall *k* that I am the LORD |
| Eze 32:15 | then shall they *k* that I am the |
| Eze 33:29 | Then shall they *k* that I am the |
| Eze 33:33 | then shall they *k* that a prophet |
| Eze 34:27 | shall *k* that I am the LORD, when |
| Eze 34:30 | Thus shall they *k* that I the LORD |
| Eze 35:4 | thou shalt *k* that I am the LORD |
| Eze 35:9 | ye shall *k* that I am the LORD |
| Eze 35:12 | thou shalt *k* that I am the LORD, |
| Eze 35:15 | they shall *k* that I am the LORD |
| Eze 36:11 | ye shall *k* that I am the Lord |
| Eze 36:23 | the heathen shall *k* that I am the |
| Eze 36:36 | shall *k* that I the LORD build the |
| Eze 36:38 | they shall *k* that I am the LORD |
| Eze 37:6 | ye shall *k* that I am the LORD |
| Eze 37:13 | ye shall *k* that I am the LORD, |
| Eze 37:14 | then shall ye *k* that I the LORD |
| Eze 37:28 | the heathen shall *k* that I the |
| Eze 38:14 | safely, shalt thou not *k* it |
| Eze 38:16 | land, that the heathen may *k* me |
| Eze 38:23 | they shall *k* that I am the LORD |
| Eze 39:6 | they shall *k* that I am the LORD |
| Eze 39:7 | the heathen shall *k* that I am the |
| Eze 39:22 | *k* that I am the LORD their God |
| Eze 39:23 | the heathen shall *k* that the |
| Eze 39:28 | Then shall they *k* that I am the |
| Dan 2:3 | was troubled to *k* the dream |
| Dan 2:8 | I *k* of certainty that ye would |
| Dan 2:9 | I shall *k* that ye can shew me the |
| Dan 2:21 | to them that *k* understanding |
| Dan 2:30 | that thou mightest *k* the thoughts |
| Dan 4:9 | because I *k* that the spirit of |

| | |
|---|---|
| Dan 4:17 | *k* that the most High ruleth in |
| Dan 4:25 | till thou *k* that the most High |
| Dan 4:32 | until thou *k* that the most High |
| Dan 5:23 | which see not, nor hear, nor *k* |
| Dan 6:15 | king, and said unto the king, *K* |
| Dan 7:16 | made me *k* the interpretation of |
| Dan 7:19 | Then I would *k* the truth of the |
| Dan 8:19 | I will make thee *k* what shall be |
| Dan 9:25 | *K* therefore and understand, that |
| Dan 11:32 | but the people that do *k* their |
| Hos 2:8 | For she did not *k* that I gave her |
| Hos 2:20 | and thou shalt *k* the LORD |
| Hos 5:3 | I *k* Ephraim, and Israel is not hid |
| Hos 6:3 | Then shall we *k*, if we follow on |
| Hos 6:3 | if we follow on to *k* the LORD |
| Hos 8:2 | cry unto me, My God, we *k* thee |
| Hos 9:7 | Israel shall *k* it |
| Hos 13:4 | thou shalt *k* no god but me |
| Hos 13:5 | I did *k* thee in the wilderness, |
| Hos 14:9 | prudent, and he shall *k* them |
| Joel 2:27 | ye shall *k* that I am in the midst |
| Joel 3:17 | So shall ye *k* that I am the LORD |
| Amos 3:10 | For they *k* not to do right, saith |
| Amos 5:12 | For I *k* your manifold |
| Jonah 1:7 | that we may *k* for whose cause |
| Jonah 1:12 | for I *k* that for my sake this |
| Mic 3:1 | Is it not for you to *k* judgment |
| Mic 4:12 | But they *k* not the thoughts of |
| Mic 6:5 | that ye may *k* the righteousness |
| Zec 2:9 | ye shall *k* that the LORD of hosts |
| Zec 2:11 | thou shalt *k* that the LORD of |
| Zec 4:9 | thou shalt *k* that the LORD of |
| Zec 6:15 | ye shall *k* that the LORD of hosts |
| Mal 2:4 | ye shall *k* that I have sent this |
| Mt 6:3 | let not thy left hand *k* what thy |
| Mt 7:11 | *k* how to give good gifts unto |
| Mt 7:16 | Ye shall *k* them by their fruits |
| Mt 7:20 | by their fruits ye shall *k* them |
| Mt 9:6 | But that ye may *k* that the Son of |
| Mt 9:30 | saying, See that no man *k* it |
| Mt 13:11 | *k* the mysteries of the kingdom of |
| Mt 20:22 | and said, Ye *k* not what ye ask |
| Mt 20:25 | Ye *k* that the princes of the |
| Mt 22:16 | we *k* that thou art true, and |
| Mt 24:32 | leaves, ye *k* that summer is nigh |
| Mt 24:33 | *k* that it is near, even at the |
| Mt 24:42 | for ye *k* not what hour your Lord |
| Mt 24:43 | But *k* this, that if the goodman |
| Mt 25:12 | I say unto you, I *k* you not |
| Mt 25:13 | for ye *k* neither the day nor the |
| Mt 26:2 | Ye *k* that after two days is the |
| Mt 26:70 | saying, I *k* not what thou sayest |
| Mt 26:72 | with an oath, I do not *k* the man |
| Mt 26:74 | to swear, saying, I *k* not the man |
| Mt 28:5 | for I *k* that ye seek Jesus, which |
| Mk 1:24 | I *k* thee who thou art, the Holy |
| Mk 2:10 | But that ye may *k* that the Son of |
| Mk 4:11 | Unto you it is given to *k* the |
| Mk 4:13 | unto them, *K* ye not this parable |
| Mk 4:13 | how then will ye *k* all parables |
| Mk 5:43 | straitly that no man should *k* it |
| Mk 7:24 | house, and would have no man *k* it |
| Mk 9:30 | not that any man should *k* it |
| Mk 10:38 | unto them, Ye *k* not what ye ask |
| Mk 10:42 | them, Ye *k* that they which are |
| Mk 12:14 | we *k* that thou art true, and |
| Mk 12:24 | because ye *k* not the scriptures, |
| Mk 13:28 | leaves, ye *k* that summer is near |
| Mk 13:29 | *k* that it is nigh, even at the |
| Mk 13:33 | for ye *k* not when the time is |
| Mk 13:35 | for ye *k* not when the master of |
| Mk 14:68 | I *k* not, neither understand I |
| Mk 14:71 | I *k* not this man of whom ye speak |
| Lk 1:4 | That thou mightest *k* the |
| Lk 1:18 | the angel, Whereby shall I *k* this |
| Lk 1:34 | this be, seeing I *k* not a man |
| Lk 4:34 | I *k* thee who thou art |
| Lk 5:24 | But that ye may *k* that the Son of |
| Lk 8:10 | Unto you it is given to *k* the |
| Lk 9:55 | Ye *k* not what manner of spirit ye |
| Lk 11:13 | *k* how to give good gifts unto |
| Lk 12:39 | And this *k*, that if the goodman of |
| Lk 13:25 | I *k* you not whence ye are |
| Lk 13:27 | I *k* you not whence ye are |
| Lk 19:15 | that he might *k* how much every |
| Lk 20:21 | we *k* that thou sayest and teachest |
| Lk 21:20 | then *k* that the desolation |
| Lk 21:30 | *k* of your own selves that summer |
| Lk 21:31 | *k* ye that the kingdom of God is |
| Lk 22:57 | him, saying, Woman, I *k* him not |

| | |
|---|---|
| Lk 22:60 | Man, I *k* not what thou sayest |
| Lk 23:34 | for they *k* not what they do |
| Lk 24:16 | holden that they should not *k* him |
| Jn 1:26 | one among you, whom ye *k* not |
| Jn 3:2 | we *k* that thou art a teacher come |
| Jn 3:11 | unto thee, We speak that we do *k* |
| Jn 4:22 | Ye worship ye *k* not what |
| Jn 4:22 | we *k* what we worship |
| Jn 4:25 | I *k* that Messias cometh, which is |
| Jn 4:32 | have meat to eat that ye *k* not of |
| Jn 4:42 | *k* that this is indeed the Christ, |
| Jn 5:32 | I *k* that the witness which he |
| Jn 5:42 | But I *k* you, that ye have not the |
| Jn 6:42 | whose father and mother we *k* |
| Jn 7:17 | he shall *k* of the doctrine, |
| Jn 7:26 | Do the rulers *k* indeed that this |
| Jn 7:27 | Howbeit we *k* this man whence he |
| Jn 7:28 | both *k* me, and ye *k* whence I am |
| Jn 7:28 | sent me is true, whom ye *k* not |
| Jn 7:29 | But I *k* him |
| Jn 7:51 | it hear him, and *k* what he doeth |
| Jn 8:14 | for I *k* whence I came, and whither |
| Jn 8:19 | Jesus answered, Ye neither *k* me |
| Jn 8:28 | man, then shall ye *k* that I am he |
| Jn 8:32 | ye shall *k* the truth, and the |
| Jn 8:37 | I *k* that ye are Abraham's seed |
| Jn 8:52 | Now we *k* that thou hast a devil |
| Jn 8:55 | but I *k* him |
| Jn 8:55 | I *k* him not, I shall be a liar |
| Jn 8:55 | but I *k* him, and keep his saying |
| Jn 9:12 | He said, I *k* not |
| Jn 9:20 | We *k* that this is our son, and |
| Jn 9:21 | what means he now seeth, we *k* not |
| Jn 9:21 | hath opened his eyes, we *k* not |
| Jn 9:24 | we *k* that this man is a sinner |
| Jn 9:25 | he be a sinner or no, I *k* not |
| Jn 9:25 | one thing I *k*, that, whereas I |
| Jn 9:29 | We *k* that God spake unto Moses |
| Jn 9:29 | we *k* not from whence he is |
| Jn 9:30 | that ye *k* not from whence he is, |
| Jn 9:31 | Now we *k* that God heareth not |
| Jn 10:4 | for they *k* his voice |
| Jn 10:5 | for they *k* not the voice of |
| Jn 10:14 | *k* my sheep, and am known of mine |
| Jn 10:15 | me, even so *k* I the Father |
| Jn 10:27 | I *k* them, and they follow me |
| Jn 10:38 | that ye may *k*, and believe, that |
| Jn 11:22 | But I *k*, that even now, |
| Jn 11:24 | I *k* that he shall rise again in |
| Jn 11:49 | unto them, Ye *k* nothing at all, |
| Jn 12:50 | I *k* that his commandment is life |
| Jn 13:7 | but thou shalt *k* hereafter |
| Jn 13:12 | *K* ye what I have done to you |
| Jn 13:17 | If ye *k* these things, happy are |
| Jn 13:18 | I *k* whom I have chosen |
| Jn 13:35 | By this shall all men *k* that ye |
| Jn 14:4 | I go ye *k*, and the way ye *k* |
| Jn 14:5 | we *k* not whither thou goest |
| Jn 14:5 | and how can we *k* the way |
| Jn 14:7 | and from henceforth ye *k* him |
| Jn 14:17 | but ye *k* him |
| Jn 14:20 | At that day ye shall *k* that I am |
| Jn 14:31 | may *k* that I love the Father |
| Jn 15:18 | ye *k* that it hated me before it |
| Jn 15:21 | because they *k* not him that sent |
| Jn 17:3 | that they might *k* thee the only |
| Jn 17:23 | that the world may *k* that thou |
| Jn 18:21 | behold, they *k* what I said |
| Jn 19:4 | that ye may *k* that I find no |
| Jn 20:2 | we *k* not where they have laid him |
| Jn 20:13 | I *k* not where they have laid him |
| Jn 21:24 | we *k* that his testimony is true |
| Acts 1:7 | It is not for you to *k* the times |
| Acts 2:22 | of you, as ye yourselves also *k* |
| Acts 2:36 | the house of Israel *k* assuredly |
| Acts 3:16 | this man strong, whom ye see and *k* |
| Acts 10:28 | Ye *k* how that it is an unlawful |
| Acts 10:37 | That word, I say, ye *k*, which was |
| Acts 12:11 | Now I *k* of a surety, that the |
| Acts 15:7 | ye *k* how that a good while ago |
| Acts 17:19 | May we *k* what this new doctrine, |
| Acts 17:20 | we would *k* therefore what these |
| Acts 19:15 | said, Jesus I *k*, and Paul I *k* |
| Acts 19:25 | ye *k* that by this craft we have |
| Acts 20:18 | to him, he said unto them, Ye *k* |
| Acts 20:25 | I *k* that ye all, among whom I |
| Acts 20:29 | For I *k* this, that after my |
| Acts 20:34 | Yea, ye yourselves *k*, that these |
| Acts 21:24 | all may *k* that those things, |
| Acts 21:34 | when he could not *k* the certainty |

| | |
|---|---|
| Acts 22:14 | that thou shouldest *k* his will |
| Acts 22:19 | they *k* that I imprisoned and beat |
| Acts 22:24 | that he might *k* wherefore they |
| Acts 24:10 | Forasmuch as I *k* that thou hast |
| Acts 24:22 | I will *k* the uttermost of your |
| Acts 26:3 | Especially because I *k* thee to be |
| Acts 26:4 | at Jerusalem, *k* all the Jews |
| Acts 26:27 | I *k* that thou believest |
| Acts 28:22 | we *k* that every where it is |
| Rom 3:19 | Now we *k* that what things soever |
| Rom 6:3 | *K* ye not, that so many of us as |
| Rom 6:16 | *K* ye not, that to whom ye yield |
| Rom 7:1 | *K* ye not, brethren, (for I speak |
| Rom 7:1 | I speak to them that *k* the law |
| Rom 7:14 | For we *k* that the law is |
| Rom 7:18 | For I *k* that in me (that is, in |
| Rom 8:22 | For we *k* that the whole creation |
| Rom 8:26 | for we *k* not what we should pray |
| Rom 8:28 | we *k* that all things work |
| Rom 10:19 | But I say, Did not Israel *k* |
| Rom 14:14 | I *k*, and am persuaded by the Lord |
| 1Cor 1:16 | I *k* not whether I baptized any |
| 1Cor 2:2 | not to *k* any thing among you |
| 1Cor 2:12 | that we might *k* the things that |
| 1Cor 2:14 | neither can he *k* them, because |
| 1Cor 3:16 | *K* ye not that ye are the temple |
| 1Cor 4:4 | For I *k* nothing by myself |
| 1Cor 4:19 | if the Lord will, and will *k* |
| 1Cor 5:6 | *K* ye not that a little leaven |
| 1Cor 6:2 | Do ye not *k* that the saints shall |
| 1Cor 6:3 | *K* ye not that we shall judge |
| 1Cor 6:9 | *K* ye not that the unrighteous |
| 1Cor 6:15 | *K* ye not that your bodies are the |
| 1Cor 6:16 | *k* ye not that he which is joined |
| 1Cor 6:19 | *k* ye not that your body is the |
| 1Cor 8:1 | we *k* that we all have knowledge |
| 1Cor 8:2 | nothing yet as he ought to *k* |
| 1Cor 8:4 | we *k* that an idol is nothing in |
| 1Cor 9:13 | Do ye not *k* that they which |
| 1Cor 9:24 | *K* ye not that they which run in a |
| 1Cor 11:3 | But I would have you *k*, that the |
| 1Cor 12:2 | Ye *k* that ye were Gentiles, |
| 1Cor 13:9 | For we *k* in part, and we prophesy |
| 1Cor 13:12 | now I *k* in part |
| 1Cor 13:12 | but then shall I *k* even as also I |
| 1Cor 14:11 | Therefore if I *k* not the meaning |
| 1Cor 15:58 | forasmuch as ye *k* that your |
| 1Cor 16:15 | (ye *k* the house of Stephanas, |
| 2Cor 2:4 | but that ye might *k* the love |
| 2Cor 2:9 | that I might *k* the proof of you, |
| 2Cor 5:1 | For we *k* that if our earthly |
| 2Cor 5:16 | Wherefore henceforth *k* we no man |
| 2Cor 5:16 | now henceforth *k* we him no more |
| 2Cor 8:9 | For ye *k* the grace of our Lord |
| 2Cor 9:2 | For I *k* the forwardness of your |
| 2Cor 13:5 | *K* ye not your own selves, how |
| 2Cor 13:6 | But I trust that ye shall *k* that |
| Gal 3:7 | *K* ye therefore that they which |
| Gal 4:13 | Ye *k* how through infirmity of the |
| Eph 1:18 | that ye may *k* what is the hope of |
| Eph 3:19 | to *k* the love of Christ, which |
| Eph 5:5 | For this ye *k*, that no |
| Eph 6:21 | But that ye also may *k* my affairs |
| Eph 6:22 | that ye might *k* our affairs |
| Phil 1:19 | For I *k* that this shall turn to |
| Phil 1:25 | I *k* that I shall abide and |
| Phil 2:19 | good comfort, when I *k* your state |
| Phil 2:22 | But ye *k* the proof of him, that, |
| Phil 3:10 | That I may *k* him, and the power of |
| Phil 4:12 | I *k* both how to be abased |
| Phil 4:12 | and I *k* how to abound |
| Phil 4:15 | Now ye Philippians *k* also |
| Col 4:6 | that ye may *k* how ye ought to |
| Col 4:8 | that he might *k* your estate |
| 1Th 1:5 | as ye *k* what manner of men we |
| 1Th 2:1 | *k* our entrance in unto you, that |
| 1Th 2:2 | shamefully entreated, as ye *k* |
| 1Th 2:5 | used we flattering words, as ye *k* |
| 1Th 2:11 | As ye *k* how we exhorted and |
| 1Th 3:3 | for yourselves *k* that we are |
| 1Th 3:4 | even as it came to pass, and ye *k* |
| 1Th 3:5 | I sent to *k* your faith, lest by |
| 1Th 4:2 | For ye *k* what commandments we |
| 1Th 4:4 | *k* how to possess his vessel in |
| 1Th 4:5 | as the Gentiles which *k* not God |
| 1Th 5:2 | For yourselves *k* perfectly that |
| 1Th 5:12 | to *k* them which labour among you, |
| 2Th 1:8 | vengeance on them that *k* not God |
| 2Th 2:6 | now ye *k* what withholdeth that he |
| 2Th 3:7 | For yourselves *k* how ye ought to |

1Ti 1:8 But we *k* that the law is good, if
1Ti 3:5 (For if a man *k* not how to rule
1Ti 3:15 that thou mayest *k* how thou
1Ti 4:3 them which believe and *k* the truth
2Ti 1:12 for I *k* whom I have believed, and
2Ti 3:1 This *k* also, that in the last
Titus 1:16 They profess that they *k* God
Heb 8:11 his brother, saying, *K* the Lord
Heb 8:11 for all shall *k* me, from the
Heb 10:30 For we *k* him that hath said,
Heb 12:17 For ye *k* how that afterward, when
Heb 13:23 *K* ye that our brother Timothy is
Jas 2:20 But wilt thou *k*, O vain man, that
Jas 4:4 *k* ye not that the friendship of
Jas 4:14 Whereas ye *k* not what shall be on
Jas 5:20 Let him *k*, that he which
1Pet 1:18 Forasmuch as ye *k* that ye were
2Pet 1:12 of these things, though ye *k* them
2Pet 3:17 seeing ye *k* these things before,
1Jn 2:3 hereby we do *k* that we *k* him,
1Jn 2:3 hereby we do *k* that we *k* him
1Jn 2:4 I *k* him, and keepeth not his
1Jn 2:5 hereby *k* we that we are in him
1Jn 2:18 whereby we *k* that it is the last
1Jn 2:20 the Holy One, and ye *k* all things
1Jn 2:21 you because ye *k* not the truth
1Jn 2:21 but because ye *k* it
1Jn 2:29 If ye *k* that he is righteous
1Jn 2:29 ye *k* that every one that doeth
1Jn 3:2 but we *k* that, when he shall
1Jn 3:5 ye *k* that he was manifested to
1Jn 3:14 We *k* that we have passed from
1Jn 3:15 ye *k* that no murderer hath
1Jn 3:19 hereby we *k* that we are of the
1Jn 3:24 hereby we *k* that he abideth in us
1Jn 4:2 Hereby *k* ye the Spirit of God
1Jn 4:6 Hereby *k* we the spirit of truth,
1Jn 4:13 Hereby *k* we that we dwell in him,
1Jn 5:2 By this we *k* that we love the
1Jn 5:13 that ye may *k* that ye have
1Jn 5:15 And if we *k* that he hear us,
1Jn 5:15 we *k* that we have the petitions
1Jn 5:18 We *k* that whosoever is born of
1Jn 5:19 we *k* that we are of God, and the
1Jn 5:20 we *k* that the Son of God is come,
1Jn 5:20 that we may *k* him that is true,
3Jn 12 ye *k* that our record is true
Jude 10 of those things which they *k* not
Jude 10 but what they *k* naturally
Rev 2:2 I *k* thy works, and thy labour, and
Rev 2:9 I *k* thy works, and tribulation, and
Rev 2:9 I *k* the blasphemy of them which
Rev 2:13 I *k* thy works, and where thou
Rev 2:19 I *k* thy works, and charity, and
Rev 2:23 all the churches shall *k* that I
Rev 3:1 I *k* thy works, that thou hast a
Rev 3:3 thou shalt not *k* what hour I will
Rev 3:8 I *k* thy works
Rev 3:9 to *k* that I have loved thee
Rev 3:15 I *k* thy works, that thou art

## KNOWEST

Gen 30:26 for thou *k* my service which I
Gen 30:29 Thou *k* how I have served thee, and
Gen 47:6 if thou *k* any men of activity
Ex 10:7 *k* thou not yet that Egypt is
Ex 32:22 thou *k* the people, that they are
Num 10:31 forasmuch as thou *k* how we are to
Num 11:16 whom thou *k* to be the elders of
Num 20:14 Thou *k* all the travel that hath
Deut 7:15 diseases of Egypt, which thou *k*
Deut 9:2 of the Anakims, whom thou *k*
Deut 20:20 Only the trees which thou *k* that
Deut 28:33 a nation which thou *k* not eat up
Josh 14:6 Thou *k* the thing that the LORD
Judg 15:11 *K* thou not that the Philistines
1Sa 28:9 thou *k* what Saul hath done, how
2Sa 1:5 How *k* thou that Saul and Jonathan
2Sa 2:26 *k* thou not that it will be
2Sa 3:25 Thou *k* Abner the son of Ner, that
2Sa 7:20 for thou, Lord GOD, *k* thy servant
2Sa 17:8 thou *k* thy father and his men,
1Kin 1:18 my lord the king, thou *k* it not
1Kin 2:5 Moreover thou *k* also what Joab
1Kin 2:9 *k* what thou oughtest to do unto
1Kin 2:15 Thou *k* that the kingdom was mine,
1Kin 2:44 Thou *k* all the wickedness which
1Kin 5:3 Thou *k* how that David my father
1Kin 5:6 for thou *k* that there is not
1Kin 8:39 to his ways, whose heart thou *k*
1Kin 8:39 *k* the hearts of all the children
2Kin 2:3 *K* thou that the LORD will take
2Kin 2:5 *K* thou that the LORD will take
2Kin 4:1 thou *k* that thy servant did fear
1Chr 17:18 for thou *k* thy servant
2Chr 6:30 all his ways, whose heart thou *k*
2Chr 6:30 (for thou only *k* the hearts of
Job 10:7 Thou *k* that I am not wicked
Job 15:9 What *k* thou, that we know not
Job 20:4 *K* thou not this of old, since man
Job 34:33 therefore speak what thou *k*
Job 38:5 the measures thereof, if thou *k*
Job 38:18 declare if thou *k* it all
Job 38:21 *K* thou it, because thou wast then
Job 38:33 *K* thou the ordinances of heaven
Job 39:1 *K* thou the time when the wild
Job 39:2 or *k* thou the time when they
Ps 40:9 refrained my lips, O LORD, thou *k*
Ps 69:5 O God, thou *k* my foolishness
Ps 139:2 Thou *k* my downsitting and mine
Ps 139:4 lo, O LORD, thou *k* it altogether
Prov 27:1 for thou *k* not what a day may
Eccl 11:2 for thou *k* not what evil shall be
Eccl 11:5 As thou *k* not what is the way of
Eccl 11:5 even so thou *k* not the works of
Eccl 11:6 for thou *k* not whether shall
Is 55:5 call a nation that thou *k* not
Jer 5:15 nation whose language thou *k* not
Jer 12:3 But thou, O LORD, *k* me
Jer 15:14 into a land which thou *k* not
Jer 15:15 O LORD, thou *k*
Jer 17:4 in the land which thou *k* not
Jer 17:16 thou *k*: that which came
Jer 18:23 thou *k* all their counsel against
Jer 33:3 mighty things, which thou *k* not
Eze 37:3 And I answered, O Lord GOD, thou *k*
Dan 10:20 *K* thou wherefore I come unto thee
Zec 4:5 unto me, *K* thou not what these be
Zec 4:13 and said, *K* thou not what these be
Mt 15:12 *K* thou that the Pharisees were
Mk 10:19 Thou *k* the commandments, Do not
Lk 18:20 Thou *k* the commandments, Do not
Lk 22:34 shalt thrice deny that thou *k* me
Jn 1:48 saith unto him, Whence *k* thou me
Jn 3:10 of Israel, and *k* not these things
Jn 13:7 him, What I do thou *k* not now
Jn 16:30 we sure that thou *k* all things
Jn 19:10 *k* thou not that I have power to
Jn 21:15 thou *k* that I love thee
Jn 21:16 thou *k* that I love thee
Jn 21:17 unto him, Lord, thou *k* all things
Jn 21:17 thou *k* that I love thee
Acts 1:24 which *k* the hearts of all men,
Acts 25:10 no wrong, as thou very well *k*
Rom 2:18 *k* his will, and approvest the
1Cor 7:16 For what *k* thou, O wife, whether
1Cor 7:16 or how *k* thou, O man, whether
2Ti 1:15 This thou *k*, that all they which
2Ti 1:18 me at Ephesus, thou *k* very well
Rev 3:17 *k* not that thou art wretched, and
Rev 7:14 And I said unto him, Sir, thou *k*

## KNOWETH

Gen 33:13 My lord *k* that the children are
Lev 5:3 when he *k* of it, then he shall be
Lev 5:4 when he *k* of it, then he shall be
Deut 2:7 he *k* thy walking through this
Deut 34:6 but no man *k* of his sepulchre
Josh 22:22 gods, the LORD God of gods, he *k*
1Sa 3:13 ever for the iniquity which he *k*
1Sa 20:3 Thy father certainly *k* that I
1Sa 23:17 and that also Saul my father *k*
2Sa 14:22 Today thy servant *k* that I have
2Sa 17:10 for all Israel *k* that thy father
1Kin 1:11 reign, and David our lord *k* it not
Est 4:14 who *k* whether thou art come to
Job 11:11 For he *k* vain men
Job 12:3 who *k* not such things as these
Job 12:9 Who *k* not in all these that the
Job 14:21 come to honour, and he *k* it not
Job 15:23 he *k* that the day of darkness is
Job 18:21 the place of him that *k* not God
Job 23:10 But he *k* the way that I take
Job 28:7 There is a path which no fowl *k*
Job 28:13 Man *k* not the price thereof
Job 28:23 and he *k* the place thereof
Job 34:25 Therefore he *k* their works
Job 35:15 yet he *k* it not in great
Ps 1:6 For the LORD *k* the way of the
Ps 37:18 The LORD *k* the days of the
Ps 39:6 *k* not who shall gather them
Ps 44:21 for he *k* the secrets of the heart
Ps 74:9 among us any that *k* how long
Ps 90:11 Who *k* the power of thine anger
Ps 92:6 A brutish man *k* not
Ps 94:11 The LORD *k* the thoughts of man,
Ps 103:14 For he *k* our frame
Ps 104:19 the sun *k* his going down
Ps 138:6 but the proud he *k* afar off
Ps 139:14 and that my soul *k* right well
Prov 7:23 *k* not that it is for his life
Prov 9:13 she is simple, and *k* nothing
Prov 9:18 But he *k* not that the dead are
Prov 14:10 The heart *k* his own bitterness
Prov 24:22 who *k* the ruin of them both
Eccl 2:19 who *k* whether he shall be a wise
Eccl 3:21 Who *k* the spirit of man that
Eccl 6:8 that *k* to walk before the living
Eccl 6:12 For who *k* what is good for man in
Eccl 7:22 *k* that thou thyself likewise hast
Eccl 8:1 who *k* the interpretation of a
Eccl 8:7 For he *k* not that which shall be
Eccl 9:1 no man *k* either love or hatred by
Eccl 9:12 For man also *k* not his time
Eccl 10:15 because he *k* not how to go to the
Is 1:3 The ox *k* his owner, and the ass
Is 29:15 and who *k* us?
Jer 8:7 the heaven *k* her appointed times
Jer 9:24 *k* me, that I am the LORD which
Dan 2:22 he *k* what is in the darkness, and
Hos 7:9 his strength, and he *k* it not
Hos 7:9 and there upon him, yet he *k* not
Joel 2:14 Who *k* if he will return and repent
Nah 1:7 he *k* them that trust in him
Zeph 3:5 but the unjust *k* no shame
Mt 6:8 for your Father *k* what things ye
Mt 6:32 for your heavenly Father *k* that
Mt 11:27 no man *k* the Son, but the Father
Mt 11:27 neither *k* any man the Father,
Mt 24:36 hour *k* no man, no, not the angels
Mk 4:27 spring and grow up, he *k* not how
Mk 13:32 of that day and that hour *k* no man
Lk 10:22 no man *k* who the Son is, but the
Lk 12:30 your Father *k* that ye have need
Lk 16:15 but God *k* your hearts
Jn 7:15 How *k* this man letters, having
Jn 7:27 cometh, no man *k* whence he is
Jn 7:49 But this people who *k* not the law
Jn 10:15 As the Father *k* me, even so know
Jn 12:35 darkness *k* not whither he goeth
Jn 14:17 it seeth him not, neither *k* him
Jn 15:15 for the servant *k* not what his
Jn 19:35 he *k* that he saith true, that ye
Acts 15:8 which *k* the hearts, bare them
Acts 19:35 what man is there that *k* not how
Acts 26:26 For the king *k* of these things,
Rom 8:27 he that searcheth the hearts *k*
1Cor 2:11 For what man *k* the things of a
1Cor 2:11 so the things of God *k* no man
1Cor 3:20 The Lord *k* the thoughts of the
1Cor 8:2 any man think that he *k* any thing
1Cor 8:2 he *k* nothing yet as he ought to
2Cor 11:11 I love you not? God *k*
2Cor 11:31 for evermore, *k* that I lie not
2Cor 12:2 I cannot tell: God *k*
2Cor 12:3 I cannot tell: God *k*
2Ti 2:19 The Lord *k* them that are his
Jas 4:17 to him that *k* to do good, and
2Pet 2:9 The Lord *k* how to deliver the
1Jn 2:11 *k* not whither he goeth, because
1Jn 3:1 therefore the world *k* us not
1Jn 3:20 than our heart, and *k* all things
1Jn 4:6 he that *k* God heareth us
1Jn 4:7 loveth is born of God, and *k* God
1Jn 4:8 He that loveth not *k* not God
Rev 2:17 which no man *k* saving he that
Rev 12:12 because he *k* that he hath but a

## KNOWING

Gen 3:5 shall be as gods, *k* good and evil
1Kin 2:32 my father David not *k* thereof
Mt 9:4 Jesus *k* their thoughts said,
Mt 22:29 not *k* the scriptures, nor the
Mk 5:30 immediately *k* in himself that
Mk 5:33 *k* what was done in her, came and
Mk 6:20 *k* that he was a just man and an
Mk 12:15 *k* their hypocrisy, said unto them
Lk 8:53 him to scorn, *k* that she was dead
Lk 9:33 not *k* what he said
Lk 11:17 *k* their thoughts, said unto them,

Jn 13:3 Jesus *k* that the Father had given
Jn 18:4 *k* all things that should come
Jn 19:28 Jesus *k* that all things were now
Jn 21:12 *k* that it was the Lord
Acts 2:30 *k* that God had sworn with an oath
Acts 5:7 not *k* what was done, came in
Acts 18:25 *k* only the baptism of John
Acts 20:22 not *k* the things that shall
Rom 1:32 Who *k* the judgment of God, that
Rom 2:4 not *k* that the goodness of God
Rom 5:3 *k* that tribulation worketh
Rom 6:6 *K* this, that our old man is
Rom 6:9 *K* that Christ being raised from
Rom 13:11 *k* the time, that now it is high
2Cor 1:7 And our hope of you is stedfast, *k*
2Cor 4:14 *K* that he which raised up the
2Cor 5:6 *k* that, whilst we are at home in
2Cor 5:11 *K* therefore the terror of the
Gal 2:16 *K* that a man is not justified by
Eph 6:8 *K* that whatsoever good thing any
Eph 6:9 *k* that your Master also is in
Phil 1:17 *k* that I am set for the defence
Col 3:24 *K* that of the Lord ye shall
Col 4:1 *k* that ye also have a Master in
1Th 1:4 *K*, brethren beloved, your
1Ti 1:9 *K* this, that the law is not made
1Ti 6:4 *k* nothing, but doting about
2Ti 2:23 *k* that they do gender strifes
2Ti 3:14 *k* of whom thou hast learned them
Titus 3:11 *K* that he that is such is
Philem 21 *k* that thou wilt also do more
Heb 10:34 *k* in yourselves that ye have in
Heb 11:8 went out, not *k* whither he went
Jas 1:3 *K* this, that the trying of your
Jas 3:1 *k* that we shall receive the
1Pet 3:9 *k* that ye are thereunto called,
1Pet 5:9 *k* that the same afflictions are
2Pet 1:14 *K* that shortly I must put off
2Pet 1:20 *K* this first, that no prophecy of
2Pet 3:3 *K* this first, that there shall

## KNOWLEDGE

Gen 2:9 garden, and the tree of *k* of good
Gen 2:17 But of the tree of the *k* of good
Ex 31:3 and in understanding, and in *k*
Ex 35:31 wisdom, in understanding, and in *k*
Lev 4:23 he hath sinned, come to his *k*
Lev 4:28 he hath sinned, come to his *k*
Num 15:24 without the *k* of the congregation
Num 24:16 knew the *k* of the most High,
Deut 1:39 in that day had no *k* between good
Ruth 2:10 that thou shouldest take *k* of me
Ruth 2:19 be he that did take *k* of thee
1Sa 2:3 for the LORD is a God of *k*
1Sa 23:23 take *k* of all the lurking places
1Kin 9:27 shipmen that had *k* of the sea
2Chr 1:10 Give me now wisdom and *k*, that I
2Chr 1:11 *k* for thyself, that thou mayest
2Chr 1:12 Wisdom and *k* is granted unto thee
2Chr 8:18 and servants that had *k* of the sea
2Chr 30:22 taught the good *k* of the LORD
Neh 10:28 daughters, every one having *k*
Job 15:2 Should a wise man utter vain *k*
Job 21:14 we desire not the *k* of thy ways
Job 21:22 Shall any teach God *k*
Job 33:3 and my lips shall utter *k* clearly
Job 34:2 give ear unto me, ye that have *k*
Job 34:35 Job hath spoken without *k*
Job 35:16 he multiplieth words without *k*
Job 36:3 I will fetch my *k* from afar
Job 36:4 that is perfect in *k* is with thee
Job 36:12 and they shall die without *k*
Job 37:16 of him which is perfect in *k*
Job 38:2 counsel by words without *k*
Job 42:3 he that hideth counsel without *k*
Ps 14:4 all the workers of iniquity no *k*
Ps 19:2 and night unto night sheweth *k*
Ps 53:4 Have the workers of iniquity no *k*
Ps 73:11 is there *k* in the most High
Ps 94:10 he that teacheth man *k*, shall not
Ps 119:66 Teach me good judgment and *k*
Ps 139:6 Such *k* is too wonderful for me
Ps 144:3 is man, that thou takest *k* of him
Prov 1:4 to the simple, to the young man *k*
Prov 1:7 of the LORD is the beginning of *k*
Prov 1:22 their scorning, and fools hate *k*
Prov 1:29 For that they hated *k*, and did not
Prov 2:3 Yea, if thou criest after *k*
Prov 2:5 of the LORD, and find the *k* of God
Prov 2:6 out of his mouth cometh *k*
Prov 2:10 *k* is pleasant unto thy soul
Prov 3:20 By his *k* the depths are broken up
Prov 5:2 and that thy lips may keep *k*
Prov 8:9 and right to them that find *k*
Prov 8:10 *k* rather than choice gold
Prov 8:12 find out *k* of witty inventions
Prov 9:10 and the *k* of the holy is
Prov 10:14 Wise men lay up *k*
Prov 11:9 but through *k* shall the just be
Prov 12:1 Whoso loveth instruction loveth *k*
Prov 12:23 A prudent man concealeth *k*
Prov 13:16 Every prudent man dealeth with *k*
Prov 14:6 but *k* is easy unto him that
Prov 14:7 not in him the lips of *k*
Prov 14:18 the prudent are crowned with *k*
Prov 15:2 tongue of the wise useth *k* aright
Prov 15:7 The lips of the wise disperse *k*
Prov 15:14 that hath understanding seeketh *k*
Prov 17:27 He that hath *k* spareth his words
Prov 18:15 heart of the prudent getteth *k*
Prov 18:15 and the ear of the wise seeketh *k*
Prov 19:2 Also, that the soul be without *k*
Prov 19:25 and he will understand *k*
Prov 19:27 to err from the words of *k*
Prov 20:15 but the lips of *k* are a precious
Prov 21:11 is instructed, he receiveth *k*
Prov 22:12 The eyes of the LORD preserve *k*
Prov 22:17 and apply thine heart unto my *k*
Prov 22:20 excellent things in counsels and *k*
Prov 23:12 and thine ears to the words of *k*
Prov 24:4 by *k* shall the chambers be filled
Prov 24:5 a man of *k* increaseth strength
Prov 24:14 So shall the *k* of wisdom be unto
Prov 28:2 *k* the state thereof shall be
Prov 30:3 nor have the *k* of the holy
Eccl 1:16 great experience of wisdom and *k*
Eccl 1:18 increaseth *k* increaseth sorrow
Eccl 2:21 labour is in wisdom, and in *k*
Eccl 2:26 is good in his sight wisdom, and *k*
Eccl 7:12 but the excellency of *k* is
Eccl 9:10 is no work, nor device, nor *k*
Eccl 12:9 he still taught the people *k*
Is 5:13 captivity, because they have no *k*
Is 8:4 the child shall have *k* to cry
Is 11:2 counsel and might, the spirit of *k*
Is 11:9 be full of the *k* of the LORD
Is 28:9 Whom shall he teach *k*
Is 32:4 of the rash shall understand *k*
Is 33:6 *k* shall be the stability of thy
Is 40:14 path of judgment, and taught him *k*
Is 44:19 his heart, neither is there *k* nor
Is 44:25 and maketh their *k* foolish
Is 45:20 they have no *k* that set up the
Is 47:10 Thy wisdom and thy *k*, it hath
Is 53:11 by his *k* shall my righteous
Is 58:3 our soul, and thou takest no *k*
Jer 3:15 which shall feed you with *k*
Jer 4:22 but to do good they have no *k*
Jer 10:14 Every man is brutish in his *k*
Jer 11:18 And the LORD hath given me *k* of it
Jer 51:17 Every man is brutish by his *k*
Dan 1:4 in all wisdom, and cunning in *k*
Dan 1:17 four children, God gave them *k*
Dan 2:21 *k* to them that know understanding
Dan 5:12 as an excellent spirit, and *k*
Dan 12:4 and fro, and *k* shall be increased
Hos 4:1 mercy, nor *k* of God in the land
Hos 4:6 are destroyed for lack of *k*
Hos 4:6 because thou hast rejected *k*
Hos 6:6 the *k* of God more than burnt
Hab 2:14 the *k* of the glory of the LORD
Mal 2:7 the priest's lips should keep *k*
Mt 14:35 men of that place had *k* of him
Lk 1:77 To give *k* of salvation unto his
Lk 11:52 ye have taken away the key of *k*
Acts 4:13 and they took *k* of them, that they
Acts 17:13 had *k* that the word of God was
Acts 24:8 mayest take *k* of all these things
Acts 24:22 having more perfect *k* of that way
Rom 1:28 not like to retain God in their *k*
Rom 2:20 babes, which hast the form of *k*
Rom 3:20 for by the law is the *k* of sin
Rom 10:2 of God, but not according to *k*
Rom 11:33 both of the wisdom and *k* of God
Rom 15:14 of goodness, filled with all *k*
1Cor 1:5 in all utterance, and in all *k*
1Cor 8:1 idols, we know that we all have *k*
1Cor 8:1 *K* puffeth up, but charity
1Cor 8:7 there is not in every man that *k*
1Cor 8:10 hast *k* sit at meat in the idol's
1Cor 8:11 through thy *k* shall the weak
1Cor 12:8 the word of *k* by the same Spirit
1Cor 13:2 all mysteries, and all *k*
1Cor 13:8 whether there be *k*, it shall
1Cor 14:6 you either by revelation, or by *k*
1Cor 15:34 for some have not the *k* of God
2Cor 2:14 of his *k* by us in every place
2Cor 4:6 to give the light of the *k* of the
2Cor 6:6 By pureness, by *k*, by
2Cor 8:7 in faith, and utterance, and *k*
2Cor 10:5 itself against the *k* of God
2Cor 11:6 I be rude in speech, yet not in *k*
Eph 1:17 and revelation in the *k* of him
Eph 3:4 ye may understand my *k* in the
Eph 3:19 love of Christ, which passeth *k*
Eph 4:13 of the *k* of the Son of God, unto
Phil 1:9 may abound yet more and more in *k*
Phil 3:8 of the *k* of Christ Jesus my Lord
Col 1:9 the *k* of his will in all wisdom
Col 1:10 and increasing in the *k* of God
Col 2:3 all the treasures of wisdom and *k*
Col 3:10 which is renewed in *k* after the
1Ti 2:4 to come unto the *k* of the truth
2Ti 3:7 to come to the *k* of the truth
Heb 10:26 have received the *k* of the truth
Jas 3:13 man and endued with *k* among you
1Pet 3:7 dwell with them according to *k*
2Pet 1:2 unto you through the *k* of God
2Pet 1:3 through the *k* of him that hath
2Pet 1:5 and to virtue *k*
2Pet 1:6 And to *k* temperance
2Pet 1:8 in the *k* of our Lord Jesus Christ
2Pet 2:20 world through the *k* of the Lord
2Pet 3:18 in the *k* of our Lord and Saviour

## KNOWN

Gen 19:8 daughters which have not *k* man
Gen 24:16 virgin, neither had any man *k* her
Gen 41:21 it could not be *k* that they had
Gen 41:31 the plenty shall not be *k* in the
Gen 45:1 made himself *k* unto his brethren
Ex 2:14 and said, Surely this thing is *k*
Ex 6:3 name JEHOVAH was I not *k* to them
Ex 21:36 Or if it be *k* that the ox hath
Ex 33:16 wherein shall it be *k* here that I
Lev 4:14 they have sinned against it, is *k*
Lev 5:1 whether he hath seen or *k* of it
Num 12:6 myself *k* unto him in a vision
Num 31:17 that hath *k* man by lying with him
Num 31:18 that have not *k* a man by lying
Num 31:35 had not *k* man by lying with him
Deut 1:13 *k* among your tribes, and I will
Deut 1:15 of your tribes, wise men, and *k*
Deut 11:2 your children which have not *k*
Deut 11:28 other gods, which ye have not *k*
Deut 13:2 other gods, which thou hast not *k*
Deut 13:6 other gods, which thou hast not *k*
Deut 13:13 other gods, which ye have not *k*
Deut 21:1 it be not *k* who hath slain him
Deut 28:36 thou nor thy fathers have *k*
Deut 28:64 thou nor thy fathers have *k*
Deut 31:13 which have not *k* any thing
Josh 24:31 which had *k* all the works of the
Judg 3:1 had not *k* all the wars of Canaan
Judg 16:9 So his strength was not *k*
Judg 21:12 that had *k* no man by lying with
Ruth 3:3 make not thyself *k* unto the man
Ruth 3:14 Let it not be *k* that a woman came
1Sa 6:3 it shall be *k* to you why his hand
1Sa 28:15 that thou mayest make *k* unto me
2Sa 17:19 and the thing was not *k*
1Kin 14:2 that thou be not *k* to be the wife
1Kin 18:36 let it be *k* this day that thou
1Chr 16:8 make *k* his deeds among the people
1Chr 17:19 in making *k* all these great
Ezr 4:12 Be it *k* unto the king, that the
Ezr 4:13 Be it *k* now unto the king, that,
Ezr 5:8 Be it *k* unto the king, that we
Neh 4:15 heard that it was *k* unto us
Neh 9:14 madest *k* unto them thy holy
Est 2:22 And the thing was *k* to Mordecai
Ps 9:16 The LORD is *k* by the judgment
Ps 18:43 whom I have not *k* shall serve me
Ps 31:7 thou hast *k* my soul in
Ps 48:3 God is *k* in her palaces for a
Ps 67:2 That thy way may be *k* upon earth
Ps 69:19 Thou hast *k* my reproach, and my

Ps 76:1 In Judah is God *k*
Ps 77:19 and thy footsteps are not *k*
Ps 78:3 Which we have heard and *k*, and our
Ps 78:5 make them *k* to their children
Ps 79:6 the heathen that have not *k* thee
Ps 79:10 let him be *k* among the heathen in
Ps 88:12 thy wonders be *k* in the dark
Ps 89:1 I make *k* thy faithfulness to all
Ps 91:14 high, because he hath *k* my name
Ps 95:10 heart, and they have not *k* my ways
Ps 98:2 LORD hath made *k* his salvation
Ps 103:7 He made *k* his ways unto Moses,
Ps 105:1 make *k* his deeds among the people
Ps 106:8 make his mighty power to be *k*
Ps 119:79 those that have *k* thy testimonies
Ps 119:152 I have *k* of old that thou hast
Ps 139:1 thou hast searched me, and *k* me
Ps 145:12 To make *k* to the sons of men his
Ps 147:20 judgments, they have not *k* them
Prov 1:23 I will make *k* my words unto you
Prov 10:9 perverteth his ways shall be *k*
Prov 12:16 A fool's wrath is presently *k*
Prov 14:33 in the midst of fools is made *k*
Prov 20:11 Even a child is *k* by his doings
Prov 22:19 I have made *k* to thee this day,
Prov 31:23 Her husband is *k* in the gates
Eccl 5:3 a fool's voice is *k* by multitude
Eccl 6:5 not seen the sun, nor *k* any thing
Eccl 6:10 and it is *k* that it is man
Is 12:5 this is *k* in all the earth
Is 19:21 And the LORD shall be *k* to Egypt
Is 38:19 children shall make *k* thy truth
Is 40:21 Have ye not *k*?
Is 40:28 Hast thou not *k*?
Is 42:16 in paths that they have not *k*
Is 44:18 They have not *k* nor understood
Is 45:4 thee, though thou hast not *k* me
Is 45:5 thee, though thou hast not *k* me
Is 61:9 shall be *k* among the Gentiles
Is 64:2 to make thy name *k* to thine
Is 66:14 shall be *k* toward his servants
Jer 4:22 is foolish, they have not *k* me
Jer 5:5 for they have *k* the way of the
Jer 9:16 they nor their fathers have *k*
Jer 19:4 they nor their fathers have *k*
Jer 28:9 pass, then shall the prophet be *k*
Lam 4:8 they are not *k* in the streets
Eze 20:5 made myself *k* unto them in the
Eze 20:9 sight I made myself *k* unto them
Eze 32:9 countries which thou hast not *k*
Eze 35:11 I will make myself *k* among them
Eze 36:32 the Lord GOD, be it *k* unto you
Eze 38:23 I will be *k* in the eyes of many
Eze 39:7 name *k* in the midst of my people
Dan 2:5 will not make *k* unto me the dream
Dan 2:9 will not make *k* unto me the dream
Dan 2:15 Arioch made the thing *k* to Daniel
Dan 2:17 and made the thing *k* to Hananiah
Dan 2:23 hast made *k* unto me now what we
Dan 2:23 for thou hast now made *k* unto us
Dan 2:25 that will make *k* unto the king
Dan 2:26 Art thou able to make *k* unto me
Dan 2:28 secrets, and maketh *k* to the king
Dan 2:29 that revealeth secrets maketh *k*
Dan 2:30 *k* the interpretation to the king
Dan 2:45 the great God hath made *k* to the
Dan 3:18 be it *k* unto thee, O king, that
Dan 4:6 that they might make *k* unto me
Dan 4:7 but they did not make *k* unto me
Dan 4:18 make *k* unto me the interpretation
Dan 4:26 have *k* that the heavens do rule
Dan 5:8 nor make *k* to the king the
Dan 5:15 make *k* unto me the interpretation
Dan 5:16 make *k* to me the interpretation
Dan 5:17 make *k* to him the interpretation
Hos 5:4 them, and they have not *k* the LORD
Hos 5:9 made *k* that which shall surely be
Amos 3:2 You only have I *k* of all the
Nah 3:17 place is not *k* where they are
Hab 3:2 in the midst of the years make *k*
Zec 14:7 day which shall be *k* to the LORD
Mt 10:26 and hid, that shall not be *k*
Mt 12:7 But if ye had *k* what this meaneth
Mt 12:16 that they should not make him *k*
Mt 12:33 for the tree is *k* by his fruit
Mt 24:43 *k* in what watch the thief would
Mk 3:12 that they should not make him *k*
Lk 2:15 the Lord hath made *k* unto us
Lk 2:17 they made *k* abroad the saying
Lk 6:44 every tree is *k* by his own fruit
Lk 7:39 were a prophet, would have *k* who
Lk 8:17 thing hid, that shall not be *k*
Lk 12:2 neither hid, that shall not be *k*
Lk 12:39 *k* what hour the thief would come
Lk 19:42 Saying, If thou hadst *k*, even
Lk 24:18 hast not *k* the things which are
Lk 24:35 how he was *k* of them in breaking
Jn 7:4 he himself seeketh to be *k* openly
Jn 8:19 if ye had *k* me, ye should have
Jn 8:19 ye should have *k* my Father also
Jn 8:55 Yet ye have not *k* him
Jn 10:14 my sheep, and am *k* of mine
Jn 14:7 If ye had *k* me, ye should have
Jn 14:7 ye should have *k* my Father also
Jn 14:9 you, and yet hast thou not *k* me
Jn 15:15 my Father I have made *k* unto you
Jn 16:3 they have not *k* the Father
Jn 17:7 Now they have *k* that all things
Jn 17:8 have *k* surely that I came out
Jn 17:25 Father, the world hath not *k* thee
Jn 17:25 but I have *k* thee, and these have
Jn 17:25 these have *k* that thou hast sent
Jn 18:15 that disciple was *k* unto the high
Jn 18:16 which was *k* unto the high priest,
Acts 1:19 it was *k* unto all the dwellers at
Acts 2:14 be this *k* unto you, and hearken to
Acts 2:28 Thou hast made *k* to me the ways
Acts 4:10 Be it *k* unto you all, and to all
Acts 7:13 Joseph was made *k* to his brethren
Acts 7:13 kindred was made *k* unto Pharaoh
Acts 9:24 their laying await was *k* of Saul
Acts 9:42 it was *k* throughout all Joppa
Acts 13:38 Be it *k* unto you therefore, men
Acts 15:18 *K* unto God are all his works from
Acts 19:17 this was *k* to all the Jews and
Acts 22:30 because he would have *k* the
Acts 23:28 when I would have *k* the cause
Acts 28:28 Be it *k* therefore unto you, that
Rom 1:19 Because that which may be *k* of
Rom 3:17 the way of peace have they not *k*
Rom 7:7 Nay, I had not *k* sin, but by the
Rom 7:7 for I had not *k* lust, except the
Rom 9:22 his wrath, and to make his power *k*
Rom 9:23 that he might make *k* the riches
Rom 11:34 For who hath *k* the mind of the
Rom 16:26 made *k* to all nations for the
1Cor 2:8 for had they *k* it, they would not
1Cor 2:16 For who hath *k* the mind of the
1Cor 8:3 love God, the same is *k* of him
1Cor 13:12 shall I know even as also I am *k*
1Cor 14:7 how shall it be *k* what is piped
1Cor 14:9 how shall it be *k* what is spoken
2Cor 3:2 epistle written in our hearts, *k*
2Cor 5:16 though we have *k* Christ after the
2Cor 6:9 As unknown, and yet well *k*
Gal 4:9 But now, after that ye have *k* God
Gal 4:9 or rather are *k* of God
Eph 1:9 Having made *k* unto us the mystery
Eph 3:3 he made *k* unto me the mystery
Eph 3:5 not made *k* unto the sons of men
Eph 3:10 be *k* by the church the manifold
Eph 6:19 to make *k* the mystery of the
Eph 6:21 shall make *k* to you all things
Phil 4:5 your moderation be *k* unto all men
Phil 4:6 your requests be made *k* unto God
Col 1:27 To whom God would make *k* what is
Col 4:9 They shall make *k* unto you all
2Ti 3:10 But thou hast fully *k* my doctrine
2Ti 3:15 thou hast *k* the holy scriptures
2Ti 4:17 me the preaching might be fully *k*
Heb 3:10 and they have not *k* my ways
2Pet 1:16 when we made *k* unto you the power
2Pet 2:21 have *k* the way of righteousness
2Pet 2:21 than, after they have *k* it
1Jn 2:13 because ye have *k* him that is
1Jn 2:13 because ye have *k* the Father
1Jn 2:14 because ye have *k* him that is
1Jn 3:6 hath not seen him, neither *k* him
1Jn 4:16 And we have *k* and believed the love
2Jn 1 all they that have *k* the truth
Rev 2:24 which have not *k* the depths of

**KOA** *(ko'-ah) An obscure tribe.*
Eze 23:23 Chaldeans, Pekod, and Shoa, and *K*

**KOHATH** *(ko'-hath)* See KOHATHITES. *A son of Levi.*
Gen 46:11 Gershon, *K*, and Merari
Ex 6:16 Gershon, and *K*, and Merari
Ex 6:18 And the sons of *K*
Ex 6:18 life of *K* were an hundred thirty
Num 3:17 Gershon, and *K*, and Merari
Num 3:19 the sons of *K* by their families
Num 3:27 of *K* was the family of the
Num 3:29 The families of the sons of *K*
Num 4:2 of *K* from among the sons of Levi
Num 4:4 of *K* in the tabernacle of the
Num 4:15 the sons of *K* shall come to bear
Num 4:15 of *K* in the tabernacle of the
Num 7:9 unto the sons of *K* he gave none
Num 16:1 the son of Izhar, the son of *K*
Num 26:57 of *K*, the family of the
Num 26:58 And *K* begat Amram
Josh 21:5 the rest of the children of *K* had
Josh 21:20 the families of the children of *K*
Josh 21:20 remained of the children of *K*
Josh 21:26 the children of *K* that remained
1Chr 6:1 Gershon, *K*, and Merari
1Chr 6:2 And the sons of *K*
1Chr 6:16 Gershom, *K*, and Merari
1Chr 6:18 And the sons of *K* were, Amram, and
1Chr 6:22 The sons of *K*
1Chr 6:38 The son of Izhar, the son of *K*
1Chr 6:61 And unto the sons of *K*, which were
1Chr 6:66 *K* had cities of their coasts out
1Chr 6:70 of the remnant of the sons of *K*
1Chr 15:5 Of the sons of *K*
1Chr 23:6 sons of Levi, namely, Gershon, *K*
1Chr 23:12 The sons of *K*

**KOHATHITES** *(ko'-hath-ites) Descendants of Kohath.*
Num 3:27 these are the families of the *K*
Num 3:30 *K* shall be Elizaphan the son of
Num 4:18 of the *K* from among the Levites
Num 4:34 of the *K* after their families
Num 4:37 numbered of the families of the *K*
Num 10:21 the *K* set forward, bearing the
Num 26:57 of Kohath, the family of the *K*
Josh 21:4 out for the families of the *K*
Josh 21:10 being of the families of the *K*
1Chr 6:33 Of the sons of the *K*
1Chr 6:54 Aaron, of the families of the *K*
1Chr 9:32 brethren, of the sons of the *K*
2Chr 20:19 Levites, of the children of the *K*
2Chr 29:12 of Azariah, of the sons of the *K*
2Chr 34:12 Meshullam, of the sons of the *K*

**KOLAIAH** *(ko-la-i'-ah)*
*1. A family of exiles.*
Neh 11:7 the son of Pedaiah, the son of *K*
*2. Father of Ahab.*
Jer 29:21 of Israel, of Ahab the son of *K*

**KORAH** *(ko'-rah)* See CORE, KORAHITE, KORE.
*1. A son of Esau.*
Gen 36:5 bare Jeush, and Jaalam, and *K*
Gen 36:14 to Esau Jeush, and Jaalam, and *K*
Gen 36:18 duke Jeush, duke Jaalam, duke *K*
1Chr 1:35 Reuel, and Jeush, and Jaalam, and *K*
*2. A son of Eliphaz.*
Gen 36:16 Duke *K*, duke Gatam, and duke
*3. A conspirator against Moses.*
Ex 6:21 *K*, and Nepheg, and Zichri
Ex 6:24 And the sons of *K*
Num 16:1 Now *K*, the son of Izhar, the son
Num 16:5 And he spake unto *K* and unto all
Num 16:6 Take you censers, *K*, and all his
Num 16:8 And Moses said unto *K*, Hear, I
Num 16:16 And Moses said unto *K*, Be thou and
Num 16:19 *K* gathered all the congregation
Num 16:24 up from about the tabernacle of *K*
Num 16:27 gat up from the tabernacle of *K*
Num 16:32 the men that appertained unto *K*
Num 16:40 that he be not as *K*, and as his
Num 16:49 that died about the matter of *K*
Num 26:9 against Aaron in the company of *K*
Num 26:10 swallowed them up together with *K*
Num 26:11 the children of *K* died not
Num 27:3 the LORD in the company of *K*

1Chr 6:37 the son of Ebiasaph, the son of *K*
1Chr 9:19 the son of Ebiasaph, the son of *K*
*4. A son of Hebron.*
1Chr 2:43 *K*, and Tappuah, and Rekem
*5. A grandson of Kohath.*
1Chr 6:22 *K* his son, Assir his son,
Ps 42:*t* Maschil, for the sons of *K*
Ps 44:*t* chief Musician for the sons of *K*
Ps 45:*t* Shoshannim, for the sons of *K*
Ps 46:*t* chief Musician for the sons of *K*
Ps 47:*t* A Psalm for the sons of *K*
Ps 48:*t* A Song and Psalm for the sons of *K*
Ps 49:*t* A Psalm for the sons of *K*
Ps 84:*t* A Psalm for the sons of *K*
Ps 85:*t* A Psalm for the sons of *K*
Ps 87:*t* A Psalm or Song for the sons of *K*
Ps 88:*t* of *K* to the chief Musician upon

**KORAHITE** *(ko'-ra-hite)* See KORAHITES, KORE. *A descendant of Korah.*
1Chr 9:31 the firstborn of Shallum the *K*

**KORAHITES** *(ko'-ra-hites)* See KORATHITES, KORHITES.
1Chr 9:19 of the house of his father, the *K*

**KORATHITES** *(ko'-ra-thites)* See KORAHITES. *Same as Korahites.*
Num 26:58 the Mushites, the family of the *K*

**KORE** *(ko'-re)* See KORAH, KORAHITE.
*1. Father of Shallum.*
1Chr 9:19 And Shallum the son of *K*, the son
1Chr 26:1 was Meshelemiah the son of *K*
1Chr 26:19 the porters among the sons of *K*
*2. A Temple servant.*
2Chr 31:14 *K* the son of Imnah the Levite,

**KORHITES** *(kor'-hites)* See KORAHITES. *Same as Korahites.*
Ex 6:24 these are the families of the *K*
1Chr 12:6 and Joezer, and Jashobeam, the *K*
1Chr 26:1 Of the *K* was Meshelemiah the son
2Chr 20:19 and of the children of the *K*

**KOZ** *(coz)* See HAKKOZ.
*1. A family of exiles.*
Ezr 2:61 of Habaiah, the children of *K*
Neh 7:63 of Habaiah, the children of *K*
*2. Father of two rebuilders of the wall.*
Neh 3:4 the son of Urijah, the son of *K*
Neh 3:21 Urijah the son of *K* another piece

**KUSHAIAH** *(cu-shah'-yah)* See KISHI. *Father of Ethan.*
1Chr 15:17 brethren, Ethan the son of *K*

# L

**LAADAH** *(la'-a-dah) Son of Shelah.*
1Chr 4:21 *L* the father of Mareshah, and the

**LAADAN** *(la'-a-dan)* See LIBNI.
*1. A descendant of Ephraim.*
1Chr 7:26 *L* his son, Ammihud his son,
*2. A descendant of Gershon.*
1Chr 23:7 Of the Gershonites were, *L*
1Chr 23:8 The sons of *L*
1Chr 23:9 the chief of the fathers of *L*
1Chr 26:21 As concerning the sons of *L*
1Chr 26:21 the sons of the Gershonite *L*
1Chr 26:21 even of *L* the Gershonite, were

**LABAN** *(la'-ban)* See LABAN'S, LIBNAH.
*1. Father of Rachel.*
Gen 24:29 had a brother, and his name was *L*
Gen 24:29 *L* ran out unto the man, unto the
Gen 24:50 Then *L* and Bethuel answered and
Gen 25:20 the sister to *L* the Syrian
Gen 27:43 flee thou to *L* my brother to
Gen 28:2 of *L* thy mother's brother
Gen 28:5 and he went to Padan-aram unto *L*
Gen 29:5 Know ye *L* the son of Nahor
Gen 29:10 of *L* his mother's brother
Gen 29:10 the sheep of *L* his mother's
Gen 29:10 flock of *L* his mother's brother
Gen 29:13 when *L* heard the tidings of Jacob
Gen 29:13 he told *L* all these things
Gen 29:14 *L* said to him, Surely thou art my
Gen 29:15 *L* said unto Jacob, Because thou
Gen 29:16 And *L* had two daughters
Gen 29:19 *L* said, It is better that I give
Gen 29:21 And Jacob said unto *L*, Give me my
Gen 29:22 *L* gathered together all the men
Gen 29:24 *L* gave unto his daughter Leah
Gen 29:25 and he said to *L*, What is this
Gen 29:26 *L* said, It must not be so done in
Gen 29:29 *L* gave to Rachel his daughter
Gen 30:25 Joseph, that Jacob said unto *L*
Gen 30:27 *L* said unto him, I pray thee, if
Gen 30:34 *L* said, Behold, I would it might
Gen 30:40 all the brown in the flock of *L*
Gen 31:2 Jacob beheld the countenance of *L*
Gen 31:12 seen all that *L* doeth unto thee
Gen 31:19 *L* went to shear his sheep
Gen 31:20 away unawares to *L* the Syrian
Gen 31:22 it was told *L* on the third day
Gen 31:24 God came to *L* the Syrian in a
Gen 31:25 Then *L* overtook Jacob
Gen 31:25 *L* with his brethren pitched in
Gen 31:26 *L* said to Jacob, What hast thou
Gen 31:31 And Jacob answered and said to *L*
Gen 31:33 *L* went into Jacob's tent, and into
Gen 31:34 *L* searched all the tent, but
Gen 31:36 Jacob was wroth, and chode with *L*
Gen 31:36 and Jacob answered and said to *L*
Gen 31:43 *L* answered and said unto Jacob,
Gen 31:47 *L* called it Jegar-sahadutha
Gen 31:48 *L* said, This heap is a witness
Gen 31:51 *L* said to Jacob, Behold this heap
Gen 31:55 And early in the morning *L* rose up
Gen 31:55 *L* departed, and returned unto his
Gen 32:4 thus, I have sojourned with *L*
Gen 46:18 whom *L* gave to Leah his daughter,
Gen 46:25 which *L* gave unto Rachel his

*2. A Hebrew encampment in the wilderness.*
Deut 1:1 between Paran, and Tophel, and *L*

**LABAN'S** *(la'-bans) Refers to Laban 1.*
Gen 30:36 and Jacob fed the rest of *L* flocks
Gen 30:40 and put them not unto *L* cattle
Gen 30:42 so the feebler were *L*, and the
Gen 31:1 And he heard the words of *L* sons

**LABOUR**
Gen 31:42 the *l* of my hands, and rebuked
Gen 35:16 travailed, and she had hard *l*
Gen 35:17 to pass, when she was in hard *l*
Ex 5:9 the men, that they may *l* therein
Ex 20:9 Six days shalt thou *l*, and do all
Deut 5:13 Six days thou shalt *l*, and do all
Deut 26:7 on our affliction, and our *l*
Josh 7:3 not all the people to *l* thither
Josh 24:13 you a land for which ye did not *l*
Neh 4:22 be a guard to us, and *l* on the day
Neh 5:13 man from his house, and from his *l*
Job 9:29 I be wicked, why then *l* I in vain
Job 39:11 or wilt thou leave thy *l* to him
Job 39:16 her *l* is in vain without fear
Ps 78:46 and their *l* unto the locust
Ps 90:10 years, yet is their strength *l*
Ps 104:23 to his *l* until the evening
Ps 105:44 inherited the *l* of the people
Ps 107:12 brought down their heart with *l*
Ps 109:11 and let the strangers spoil his *l*
Ps 127:1 they *l* in vain that build it
Ps 128:2 shalt eat the *l* of thine hands
Ps 144:14 That our oxen may be strong to *l*
Prov 10:16 The *l* of the righteous tendeth to
Prov 13:11 gathereth by *l* shall increase
Prov 14:23 In all *l* there is profit
Prov 21:25 for his hands refuse to *l*
Prov 23:4 *L* not to be rich
Eccl 1:3 profit hath a man of all his *l*
Eccl 1:8 All things are full of *l*
Eccl 2:10 for my heart rejoiced in all my *l*
Eccl 2:10 this was my portion of all my *l*
Eccl 2:11 on the *l* that I had laboured to
Eccl 2:18 I hated all my *l* which I had
Eccl 2:19 all my *l* wherein I have laboured
Eccl 2:20 the *l* which I took under the sun
Eccl 2:21 is a man whose *l* is in wisdom
Eccl 2:22 For what hath man of all his *l*
Eccl 2:24 make his soul enjoy good in his *l*
Eccl 3:13 and enjoy the good of all his *l*
Eccl 4:8 yet is there no end of all his *l*
Eccl 4:8 neither saith he, For whom do I *l*
Eccl 4:9 have a good reward for their *l*
Eccl 5:15 and shall take nothing of his *l*
Eccl 5:18 *l* that he taketh under the sun
Eccl 5:19 portion, and to rejoice in his *l*
Eccl 6:7 All the *l* of man is for his mouth
Eccl 8:15 him of his *l* the days of his life
Eccl 8:17 though a man *l* to seek it out
Eccl 9:9 in thy *l* This which thou takest under
Eccl 10:15 The *l* of the foolish wearieth
Is 22:4 *l* not to comfort me, because of
Is 45:14 The *l* of Egypt, and merchandise of
Is 55:2 your *l* for that which satisfieth
Is 65:23 They shall not *l* in vain, nor
Jer 3:24 For shame hath devoured the *l* of
Jer 20:18 I forth out of the womb to see *l*
Jer 51:58 and the people shall *l* in vain
Lam 5:5 we *l*, and have no rest
Eze 23:29 and shall take away all thy *l*
Eze 29:20 him the land of Egypt for his *l*
Mic 4:10 *l* to bring forth, O daughter of
Hab 2:13 people shall *l* in the very fire
Hab 3:17 the *l* of the olive shall fail, and
Hag 1:11 and upon all the *l* of the hands
Mt 11:28 Come unto me, all ye that *l*
Jn 4:38 that whereon ye bestowed no *l*
Jn 6:27 *L* not for the meat which
Rom 16:6 Mary, who bestowed much *l* on us
Rom 16:12 and Tryphosa, who *l* in the Lord
1Cor 3:8 own reward according to his own *l*
1Cor 4:12 And *l*, working with our own hands
1Cor 15:58 your *l* is not in vain in the Lord
2Cor 5:9 Wherefore we *l*, that, whether
Gal 4:11 have bestowed upon you *l* in vain
Eph 4:28 but rather let him *l*, working
Phil 1:22 flesh, this is the fruit of my *l*
Phil 2:25 my brother, and companion in *l*
Col 1:29 Whereunto I also *l*, striving
1Th 1:3 *l* of love, and patience of hope in
1Th 2:9 For ye remember, brethren, our *l*
1Th 3:5 tempted you, and our *l* be in vain
1Th 5:12 to know them which *l* among you
2Th 3:8 but wrought with *l* and travail
1Ti 4:10 For therefore we both *l* and suffer
1Ti 5:17 especially they who *l* in the word
Heb 4:11 Let us *l* therefore to enter into
Heb 6:10 *l* of love, which ye have shewed
Rev 2:2 I know thy works, and thy *l*

**LABOURED**
Neh 4:21 So we *l* in the work
Job 20:18 That which he *l* for shall he
Eccl 2:11 on the labour that I had *l* to do
Eccl 2:19 all my labour wherein I have *l*
Eccl 2:21 yet to a man that hath not *l*
Eccl 2:22 wherein he hath *l* under the sun
Eccl 5:16 hath he that hath *l* for the wind
Is 47:12 thou hast *l* from thy youth
Is 47:15 unto thee with whom thou hast *l*
Is 49:4 I have *l* in vain, I have spent my
Is 62:8 wine, for the which thou hast *l*
Dan 6:14 he *l* till the going down of the
Jonah 4:10 for the which thou hast not *l*
Jn 4:38 other men *l*, and ye are entered
Rom 16:12 Persis, which *l* much in the Lord
1Cor 15:10 but I *l* more abundantly than they
Phil 2:16 run in vain, neither *l* in vain
Phil 4:3 which *l* with me in the gospel
Rev 2:3 and for my name's sake hast *l*

**LABOURERS**
Mt 9:37 is plenteous, but the *l* are few
Mt 9:38 send forth *l* into his harvest
Mt 20:1 to hire *l* into his vineyard
Mt 20:2 with the *l* for a penny a day
Mt 20:8 unto his steward, Call the *l*
Lk 10:2 truly is great, but the *l* are few
Lk 10:2 send forth *l* into his harvest
1Cor 3:9 For we are *l* together with God
Jas 5:4 the hire of the *l* who have reaped

**LABOURETH**
Prov 16:26 He that l l for himself
Prov 16:26 He that l l for himself
Eccl 3:9 that worketh in that wherein he l
1Cor 16:16 one that helpeth with us, and l
2Ti 2:6 The husbandman that l must be

**LABOURS**
Ex 23:16 harvest, the firstfruits of thy l
Ex 23:16 in thy l out of the field
Deut 28:33 fruit of thy land, and all thy l
Prov 5:10 thy l be in the house of a
Is 58:3 pleasure, and exact all your l
Jer 20:5 this city, and all the l thereof
Hos 12:8 in all my l they shall find none
Hag 2:17 hail in all the l of your hands
Jn 4:38 and ye are entered into their l
2Cor 6:5 imprisonments, in tumults, in l
2Cor 10:15 that is, of other men's l
2Cor 11:23 in l more abundant, in stripes
Rev 14:13 that they may rest from their l

**LACE**
Ex 28:28 of the ephod with a l of blue
Ex 28:37 And thou shalt put it on a blue l
Ex 39:21 of the ephod with a l of blue
Ex 39:31 And they tied unto it a l of blue

**LACHISH** *(la'-kish) An Amorite city.*
Josh 10:3 Jarmuth, and unto Japhia king of L
Josh 10:5 king of Jarmuth, the king of L
Josh 10:23 king of Jarmuth, the king of L
Josh 10:31 and all Israel with him, unto L
Josh 10:32 the LORD delivered L into the
Josh 10:33 king of Gezer came up to help L
Josh 10:34 from L Joshua passed unto Eglon,
Josh 10:35 to all that he had done to L
Josh 12:11 the king of L, one
Josh 15:39 L, and Bozkath, and Eglon,
2Kin 14:19 and he fled to L
2Kin 14:19 but they sent after him to L
2Kin 18:14 sent to the king of Assyria to L
2Kin 18:17 Rab-shakeh from L to king
2Kin 19:8 heard that he was departed from L
2Chr 11:9 And Adoraim, and L, and Azekah,
2Chr 25:27 and he fled to L
2Chr 25:27 but they sent to L after him
2Chr 32:9 he himself laid siege against L
Neh 11:30 and in their villages, at L
Is 36:2 of Assyria sent Rabshakeh from L
Is 37:8 heard that he was departed from L
Jer 34:7 Judah that were left, against L
Mic 1:13 O thou inhabitant of L, bind the

**LACK**
Gen 18:28 Peradventure there shall l five
Gen 18:28 all the city for l of five
Ex 16:18 he that gathered little had no l
Deut 8:9 thou shalt not l any thing in it
Job 4:11 old lion perisheth for l of prey
Job 38:41 God, they wander for l of meat
Ps 34:10 The young lions do l, and suffer
Prov 28:27 giveth unto the poor shall not l
Eccl 9:8 and let thy head l no ointment
Hos 4:6 are destroyed for l of knowledge
Mt 19:20 what l I yet
2Cor 8:15 that had gathered little had no l
Phil 2:30 to supply your l of service
1Th 4:12 and that ye may have l of nothing
Jas 1:5 If any of you l wisdom, let him

**LACKED**
Deut 2:7 thou hast l nothing
2Sa 2:30 there l of David's servants
2Sa 17:22 by the morning light there l not
1Kin 4:27 they l nothing
1Kin 11:22 him, But what hast thou l with me
Neh 9:21 so that they l nothing
Lk 8:6 away, because it l moisture
Lk 22:35 scrip, and shoes, l ye any thing
Acts 4:34 was there any among them that l
1Cor 12:24 honour to that part which l
Phil 4:10 careful, but ye l opportunity

**LACKETH**
Num 31:49 there l not one man of us
2Sa 3:29 on the sword, or that l bread
Prov 6:32 with a woman l understanding
Prov 12:9 honoureth himself, and l bread
2Pet 1:9 But he that l these things is

**LACKING**
Lev 2:13 to be l from thy meat offering
Lev 22:23 superfluous or l in his parts
Judg 21:3 be to day one tribe l in Israel
1Sa 30:19 And there was nothing l to them
Jer 23:4 dismayed, neither shall they be l
1Cor 16:17 for that which was l on your part
2Cor 11:9 for that which was l to me the
1Th 3:10 that which is l in your faith

**LAD**
Gen 21:12 in thy sight because of the l
Gen 21:17 And God heard the voice of the l
Gen 21:17 the voice of the l where he is
Gen 21:18 Arise, lift up the l, and hold him
Gen 21:19 with water, and gave the l drink
Gen 21:20 And God was with the l
Gen 22:5 the l will go yonder and worship,
Gen 22:12 Lay not thine hand upon the l
Gen 37:2 the l was with the sons of Bilhah
Gen 43:8 his father, Send the l with me
Gen 44:22 The l cannot leave his father
Gen 44:30 father, and the l be not with us
Gen 44:31 seeth that the l is not with us
Gen 44:32 surety for the l unto my father
Gen 44:33 of the l a bondman to my lord
Gen 44:33 let the l go up with his brethren
Gen 44:34 father, and the l be not with me
Judg 16:26 Samson said unto the l that held
1Sa 20:21 And, behold, I will send a l
1Sa 20:21 If I expressly say unto the l
1Sa 20:35 David, and a little l with him
1Sa 20:36 And he said unto his l, Run, find
1Sa 20:36 And as the l ran, he shot an arrow
1Sa 20:37 when the l was come to the place
1Sa 20:37 shot, Jonathan cried after the l
1Sa 20:38 And Jonathan cried after the l
1Sa 20:38 Jonathan's l gathered up the
1Sa 20:39 But the l knew not any thing
1Sa 20:40 gave his artillery unto his l
1Sa 20:41 And as soon as the l was gone
2Sa 17:18 Nevertheless a l saw them
2Kin 4:19 And he said to a l, Carry him to
Jn 6:9 There is a l here, which hath

**LADEN**
Gen 45:23 ten asses l with the good things
Gen 45:23 and ten she asses l with corn
1Sa 16:20 And Jesse took an ass l with bread
Is 1:4 a people l with iniquity, a seed
Mt 11:28 all ye that labour and are heavy l
2Ti 3:6 captive silly women l with sins

**LAEL** *(la'-el) A Levite.*
Num 3:24 shall be Eliasaph the son of L

**LAHAD** *(la'-had) Great-grandson of Shobal.*
1Chr 4:2 and Jahath begat Ahumai, and L

**LAHAI-ROI** *(la-hah'-ee-roy)* See BEER-LAHAI-ROI. *A well in Paran.*
Gen 24:62 came from the way of the well L
Gen 25:11 and Isaac dwelt by the well L

**LAHMAM** *(lah'-mam) A city in Judah.*
Josh 15:40 And Cabbon, and L, and Kithlish,

**LAHMI** *(lah'-mi)* See BETHLEHEMITE. *A brother of Goliath.*
1Chr 20:5 slew L the brother of Goliath the

**LAID**
Gen 9:23 l it upon both their shoulders,
Gen 15:10 l each piece one against another
Gen 19:16 the men l hold upon his hand, and
Gen 22:6 and l it upon Isaac his son
Gen 22:9 l the wood in order, and bound
Gen 22:9 l him on the altar upon the wood
Gen 30:41 that Jacob l the rods before the
Gen 38:19 l by her vail from her, and put on
Gen 39:16 she l up his garment by her,
Gen 41:48 l up the food in the cities
Gen 41:48 every city, l he up in the same
Gen 48:14 l it upon Ephraim's head, who was
Gen 48:17 l his right hand upon the head of
Ex 2:3 she l it in the flags by the
Ex 5:9 there more work be l upon the men
Ex 16:24 they l it up till the morning, as
Ex 16:34 so Aaron l it up before the
Ex 19:7 l before their faces all these
Ex 21:30 If there be l on him a sum of
Ex 21:30 his life whatsoever is l upon him
Ex 24:11 of Israel he l not his hand
Lev 8:14 his sons l their hands upon the
Lev 8:18 his sons l their hands upon the
Lev 8:22 his sons l their hands upon the
Num 16:18 l incense thereon, and stood in
Num 17:7 Moses l up the rods before the
Num 21:30 we have l them waste even unto
Num 27:23 he l his hands upon him, and gave
Deut 26:6 us, and l upon us hard bondage
Deut 29:22 which the LORD hath l upon it
Deut 32:34 Is not this l up in store with me
Deut 34:9 for Moses had l his hands upon
Josh 2:6 which she had l in order upon the
Josh 2:8 And before they were l down
Josh 4:8 they lodged, and l them down there
Josh 7:23 l them out before the LORD
Josh 10:27 l great stones in the cave's
Judg 9:24 their blood be l upon Abimelech
Judg 9:34 they l wait against Shechem in
Judg 9:43 l wait in the field, and looked,
Judg 9:48 l it on his shoulder, and said
Judg 16:2 l wait for him all night in the
Judg 19:29 l hold on his concubine, and
Ruth 3:7 uncovered his feet, and l her down
Ruth 3:15 of barley, and l it on her
Ruth 4:16 l it in her bosom, and became
1Sa 3:2 when Eli was l down in his place,
1Sa 3:3 Samuel was l down to sleep
1Sa 6:11 they l the ark of the LORD upon
1Sa 10:25 book, and l it up before the LORD
1Sa 15:2 how he l wait for him in the way,
1Sa 15:5 Amalek, and l wait in the valley
1Sa 15:27 he l hold upon the skirt of his
1Sa 19:13 l it in the bed, and put a pillow
1Sa 21:12 David l up these words in his
1Sa 25:18 cakes of figs, and l them on asses
2Sa 13:8 and he was l down
2Sa 13:19 l her hand on her head, and went
2Sa 18:17 l a very great heap of stones
1Kin 3:20 l it in her bosom
1Kin 3:20 l her dead child in my bosom
1Kin 6:37 of the house of the LORD l
1Kin 8:31 an oath be l upon him to cause
1Kin 13:29 l it upon the ass, and brought it
1Kin 13:30 he l his carcase in his own grave
1Kin 15:27 all Israel l siege to Gibbethon
1Kin 16:34 he l the foundation thereof in
1Kin 17:19 abode, and l him upon his own bed
1Kin 18:33 l him on the wood, and said, Fill
1Kin 19:6 eat and drink, and l him down again
1Kin 21:4 he l him down upon his bed, and
2Kin 4:21 l him on the bed of the man of
2Kin 4:31 l the staff upon the face of the
2Kin 4:32 child was dead, and l upon his bed
2Kin 5:23 l them upon two of his servants
2Kin 9:25 the LORD l this burden upon him
2Kin 11:16 And they l hands on her
2Kin 12:11 they l it out to the carpenters
2Kin 12:12 for all that was l out for the
2Kin 20:7 l it on the boil, and he recovered
2Kin 20:17 have l up in store unto this day
2Chr 6:22 an oath be l upon him to make him
2Chr 7:22 and l hold on other gods, and
2Chr 16:14 l him in the bed which was filled
2Chr 23:15 So they l hands on her
2Chr 24:9 l upon Israel in the wilderness
2Chr 24:27 of the burdens l upon him
2Chr 29:23 they l their hands upon them
2Chr 31:6 their God, and l them by heaps
2Chr 32:9 (but he himself l siege against
Ezr 3:6 temple of the LORD was not yet l
Ezr 3:10 And when the builders l the
Ezr 3:11 of the house of the LORD was l
Ezr 3:12 house was l before their eyes
Ezr 5:8 timber is l in the walls, and this
Ezr 5:16 l the foundation of the house of
Ezr 6:1 treasures were l up in Babylon
Ezr 6:3 foundations thereof be strongly l
Neh 3:3 who also l the beams thereof, and
Neh 3:6 they l the beams thereof, and set
Neh 13:5 they l the meat offerings
Est 8:7 because he l his hand upon the
Est 9:10 but on the spoil l they not their
Est 9:15 on the prey they l not their hand
Est 9:16 but they l not their hands on the
Est 10:1 the king Ahasuerus l a tribute
Job 6:2 my calamity l in the balances
Job 18:10 The snare is l for him in the
Job 29:9 l their hand on their mouth
Job 31:9 or if I have l wait at my
Job 38:4 Where wast thou when I l the
Job 38:5 Who hath l the measures thereof,
Job 38:6 or who l the corner stone thereof
Ps 3:5 I l me down and slept
Ps 21:5 and majesty hast thou l upon him

Ps 31:4 that they have *l* privily for me
Ps 31:19 which thou hast *l* up for them
Ps 35:11 they *l* to my charge things that I
Ps 49:14 sheep they are *l* in the grave
Ps 62:9 to be *l* in the balance, they are
Ps 79:1 they have *l* Jerusalem on heaps
Ps 79:7 *l* waste his dwelling place
Ps 88:6 Thou hast *l* me in the lowest pit,
Ps 89:19 I have *l* help upon one that is
Ps 102:25 Of old hast thou *l* the foundation
Ps 104:5 Who *l* the foundations of the
Ps 105:18 he was *l* in iron
Ps 119:30 thy judgments have I *l* before me
Ps 119:110 The wicked have *l* a snare for me
Ps 139:5 before, and *l* thine hand upon me
Ps 141:9 snares which they have *l* for me
Ps 142:3 they privily *l* a snare for me
Prov 13:22 the sinner is *l* up for the just
Song 7:13 old, which I have *l* up for thee
Is 6:7 he *l* it upon my mouth, and said,
Is 10:28 he hath *l* up his carriages
Is 14:8 saying, Since thou art *l* down
Is 15:1 the night Ar of Moab is *l* waste
Is 15:1 the night Kir of Moab is *l* waste
Is 15:7 and that which they have *l* up
Is 23:1 for it is *l* waste, so that there
Is 23:14 for your strength is *l* waste
Is 23:18 shall not be treasured nor *l* up
Is 37:18 have *l* waste all the nations
Is 39:6 have *l* up in store until this day
Is 42:25 him, yet he *l* it not to heart
Is 44:28 temple, Thy foundation shall be *l*
Is 47:6 hast thou very heavily *l* thy yoke
Is 48:13 Mine hand also hath *l* the
Is 51:13 *l* the foundations of the earth
Is 51:23 thou hast *l* thy body as the
Is 53:6 the LORD hath *l* on him the
Is 57:11 me, nor *l* it to thy heart
Is 64:11 our pleasant things are *l* waste
Jer 4:7 and thy cities shall be *l* waste
Jer 27:17 should this city be *l* waste
Jer 36:20 but they *l* up the roll in the
Jer 50:24 I have *l* a snare for thee, and
Lam 4:19 they *l* wait for us in the
Eze 4:5 For I have *l* upon thee the years
Eze 6:6 the cities shall be *l* waste
Eze 6:6 that your altars may be *l* waste
Eze 11:7 whom ye have *l* in the midst of it
Eze 12:20 are inhabited shall be *l* waste
Eze 19:7 and he *l* waste their cities
Eze 26:2 replenished, now she is *l* waste
Eze 29:12 among the cities that are *l* waste
Eze 32:19 be thou *l* with the uncircumcised
Eze 32:27 they have *l* their swords under
Eze 32:29 which with their might are *l* by
Eze 32:32 he shall be *l* in the midst of the
Eze 33:29 when I have *l* the land most
Eze 35:12 saying, They are *l* desolate
Eze 39:21 my hand that I have *l* upon them
Eze 40:42 whereupon also they *l* the
Dan 6:17 *l* upon the mouth of the den
Hos 11:4 their jaws, and I *l* meat unto them
Joel 1:7 He hath *l* my vine waste, and
Joel 1:17 clods, the garners are *l* desolate
Amos 2:8 *l* to pledge by every altar
Amos 7:9 of Israel shall be *l* waste
Obad 7 bread have *l* a wound under thee
Obad 13 nor have *l* hands on their
Jonah 3:6 he *l* his robe from him, and
Mic 5:1 he hath *l* siege against us
Nah 3:7 thee, and say, Nineveh is *l* waste
Hab 2:19 it is *l* over with gold and silver,
Hag 2:15 from before a stone was *l* upon a
Hag 2:18 of the LORD's temple was *l*
Zec 3:9 stone that I have *l* before Joshua
Zec 4:9 *l* the foundation of this house
Zec 7:14 for they *l* the pleasant land
Zec 8:9 house of the LORD of hosts was *l*
Mal 1:3 *l* his mountains and his heritage
Mt 3:10 now also the ax is *l* unto the
Mt 8:14 house, he saw his wife's mother *l*
Mt 14:3 For Herod had *l* hold on John
Mt 18:28 he *l* hands on him, and took him by
Mt 19:15 he *l* his hands on them, and
Mt 26:50 *l* hands on Jesus, and took him
Mt 26:55 the temple, and ye *l* no hold on me
Mt 26:57 they that had *l* hold on Jesus led
Mt 27:60 *l* it in his own new tomb, which
Mk 6:5 save that he *l* his hands upon a
Mk 6:17 *l* hold upon John, and bound him in
Mk 6:29 up his corpse, and *l* it in a tomb
Mk 6:56 they *l* the sick in the streets,
Mk 7:30 and her daughter *l* upon the bed
Mk 14:46 they *l* their hands on him, and
Mk 14:51 and the young men *l* hold on him
Mk 15:46 *l* him in a sepulchre which was
Mk 15:47 of Joses beheld where he was *l*
Mk 16:6 behold the place where they *l* him
Lk 1:66 them *l* them up in their hearts
Lk 2:7 clothes, and *l* him in a manger
Lk 3:9 now also the axe is *l* unto the
Lk 4:40 he *l* his hands on every one of
Lk 6:48 *l* the foundation on a rock
Lk 12:19 much goods *l* up for many years
Lk 13:13 And he *l* his hands on her
Lk 14:29 after he hath *l* the foundation,
Lk 16:20 which was *l* at his gate, full of
Lk 19:20 I have kept *l* up in a napkin
Lk 19:22 man, taking up that I *l* not down
Lk 23:26 they *l* hold upon one Simon, a
Lk 23:26 and on him they *l* the cross
Lk 23:53 *l* it in a sepulchre that was hewn
Lk 23:53 wherein never man before was *l*
Lk 23:55 sepulchre, and how his body was *l*
Lk 24:12 the linen clothes *l* by themselves
Jn 7:30 but no man *l* hands on him,
Jn 7:44 but no man *l* hands on him
Jn 8:20 and no man *l* hands on him
Jn 11:34 And said, Where have ye *l* him
Jn 11:41 the place where the dead was *l*
Jn 13:4 supper, and *l* aside his garments
Jn 19:41 wherein was never man yet *l*
Jn 19:42 There *l* they Jesus therefore
Jn 20:2 we know not where they have *l* him
Jn 20:13 I know not where they have *l* him
Jn 20:15 tell me where thou hast *l* him
Jn 21:9 and fish *l* thereon, and bread
Acts 3:2 whom they *l* daily at the gate of
Acts 4:3 they *l* hands on them, and put them
Acts 4:35 *l* them down at the apostles' feet
Acts 4:37 *l* it at the apostles' feet
Acts 5:2 *l* it at the apostles' feet
Acts 5:15 *l* them on beds and couches, that
Acts 5:18 *l* their hands on the apostles, and
Acts 6:6 they *l* their hands on them
Acts 7:16 *l* in the sepulchre that Abraham
Acts 7:58 the witnesses *l* down their
Acts 8:17 Then *l* they their hands on them,
Acts 9:37 they *l* her in an upper chamber
Acts 13:3 *l* their hands on them, they sent
Acts 13:29 the tree, and *l* him in a sepulchre
Acts 13:36 was *l* unto his fathers, and saw
Acts 16:23 when they had *l* many stripes upon
Acts 19:6 when Paul had *l* his hands upon
Acts 20:3 And when the Jews *l* wait for him
Acts 21:27 the people, and *l* hands on him,
Acts 23:29 but to have nothing *l* to his
Acts 23:30 that the Jews *l* wait for the man
Acts 25:7 *l* many and grievous complaints
Acts 25:16 the crime *l* against him
Acts 25:27 signify the crimes *l* against him
Acts 28:3 *l* them on the fire, there came a
Acts 28:8 *l* his hands on him, and healed him
Rom 16:4 my life *l* down their own necks
1Cor 3:10 I have *l* the foundation, and
1Cor 3:11 can no man lay than that is *l*
1Cor 9:16 for necessity is *l* upon me
Col 1:5 which is *l* up for you in heaven
2Ti 4:8 Henceforth there is *l* up for me a
2Ti 4:16 it may not be *l* to their charge
Heb 1:10 in the beginning hast *l* the
1Jn 3:16 because he *l* down his life for us
Rev 1:17 he *l* his right hand upon me,
Rev 20:2 he *l* hold on the dragon, that old

**LAIN**
Num 5:19 woman, If no man have *l* with thee
Num 5:20 some man have *l* with thee beside
Judg 21:11 every woman that hath *l* by man
Job 3:13 For now should I have *l* still
Jn 11:17 he found that he had *l* in the
Jn 20:12 where the body of Jesus had *l*

**LAISH** *(la'-ish)* See DAN, LESHEM.
*1. Same as the city of Dan.*
Judg 18:7 five men departed, and came to *L*
Judg 18:14 went to spy out the country of *L*
Judg 18:27 which he had, and came unto *L*
Judg 18:29 of the city was *L* at the first
Is 10:30 cause it to be heard unto *L*
*2. Father of Phaltiel.*
1Sa 25:44 wife, to Phalti the son of *L*
2Sa 3:15 even from Phaltiel the son of *L*

**LAKE**
Lk 5:1 he stood by the *l* of Gennesaret
Lk 5:2 saw two ships standing by the *l*
Lk 8:22 over unto the other side of the *l*
Lk 8:23 down a storm of wind on the *l*
Lk 8:33 down a steep place into the *l*
Rev 19:20 both were cast alive into a *l* of
Rev 20:10 them was cast into the *l* of fire
Rev 20:14 hell were cast into the *l* of fire
Rev 20:15 life was cast into the *l* of fire
Rev 21:8 in the *l* which burneth with fire

**LAKUM** *(la'-kum) A city in Naphtali.*
Josh 19:33 Adami, Nekeb, and Jabneel, unto *L*

**LAMA**
Mt 27:46 saying, Eli, Eli, *l* sabachthani
Mk 15:34 saying, Eloi, Eloi, *l* sabachthani

**LAMB**
Gen 22:7 but where is the *l* for a burnt
Gen 22:8 himself a *l* for a burnt offering
Ex 12:3 shall take to them every man a *l*
Ex 12:3 their fathers, a *l* for an house
Ex 12:4 household be too little for the *l*
Ex 12:4 shall make your count for the *l*
Ex 12:5 Your *l* shall be without blemish,
Ex 12:21 take you a *l* according to your
Ex 13:13 an ass thou shalt redeem with a *l*
Ex 29:39 The one *l* thou shalt offer in the
Ex 29:39 the other *l* thou shalt offer at
Ex 29:40 with the one *l* a tenth deal of
Ex 29:41 the other *l* thou shalt offer at
Ex 34:20 an ass thou shalt redeem with a *l*
Lev 3:7 If he offer a *l* for his offering,
Lev 4:32 if he bring a *l* for a sin
Lev 4:35 as the fat of the *l* is taken away
Lev 5:6 a *l* or a kid of the goats, for a
Lev 5:7 And if he be not able to bring a *l*
Lev 9:3 and a calf and a *l*, both of the
Lev 12:6 she shall bring a *l* of the first
Lev 12:8 if she be not able to bring a *l*
Lev 14:10 one ewe *l* of the first year
Lev 14:12 And the priest shall take one he *l*
Lev 14:13 he shall slay the *l* in the place
Lev 14:21 then he shall take one *l* for a
Lev 14:24 the *l* of the trespass offering
Lev 14:25 he shall kill the *l* of the
Lev 17:3 Israel, that killeth an ox, or *l*
Lev 22:23 Either a bullock or a *l* that hath
Lev 23:12 he *l* without blemish of the first
Num 6:12 shall bring a *l* of the first year
Num 6:14 one he *l* of the first year
Num 6:14 one ewe *l* of the first year
Num 7:15 one *l* of the first year, for a
Num 7:21 one *l* of the first year, for a
Num 7:27 one *l* of the first year, for a
Num 7:33 one *l* of the first year, for a
Num 7:39 one *l* of the first year, for a
Num 7:45 one *l* of the first year, for a
Num 7:51 one *l* of the first year, for a
Num 7:57 one *l* of the first year, for a
Num 7:63 one *l* of the first year, for a
Num 7:69 one *l* of the first year, for a
Num 7:75 one *l* of the first year, for a
Num 7:81 one *l* of the first year, for a
Num 15:5 offering or sacrifice, for one *l*
Num 15:11 or for one ram, or for a *l*
Num 28:4 The one *l* shalt thou offer in the
Num 28:4 the other *l* shalt thou offer at
Num 28:7 part of an hin for the one *l*
Num 28:8 the other *l* shalt thou offer at
Num 28:13 for a meat offering unto one *l*
Num 28:14 a fourth part of an hin unto a *l*
Num 28:21 deal shalt thou offer for every *l*
Num 28:29 A several tenth deal unto one *l*
Num 29:4 And one tenth deal for one *l*
Num 29:10 A several tenth deal for one *l*
Num 29:15 to each *l* of the fourteen lambs
1Sa 7:9 And Samuel took a sucking *l*
1Sa 17:34 took a *l* out of the flock
2Sa 12:3 nothing, save one little ewe *l*
2Sa 12:4 but took the poor man's *l*
2Sa 12:6 he shall restore the *l* fourfold
Is 11:6 wolf also shall dwell with the *l*
Is 16:1 Send ye the *l* to the ruler of the
Is 53:7 brought as a *l* to the slaughter
Is 65:25 the *l* shall feed together, and the

Is 66:3 he that sacrificeth a *l*, as if he
Jer 11:19 But I was like a *l* or an ox that
Eze 45:15 one *l* out of the flock, out of
Eze 46:13 of a *l* of the first year without
Eze 46:15 Thus shall they prepare the *l*
Hos 4:16 feed them as a *l* in a large place
Jn 1:29 and saith, Behold the *L* of God
Jn 1:36 he saith, Behold the *L* of God
Acts 8:32 like a *l* dumb before his shearer,
1Pet 1:19 as of a *l* without blemish and
Rev 5:6 stood a *L* as it had been slain,
Rev 5:8 elders fell down before the *L*
Rev 5:12 Worthy is the *L* that was slain to
Rev 5:13 throne, and unto the *L* for ever
Rev 6:1 I saw when the *L* opened one of
Rev 6:16 and from the wrath of the *L*
Rev 7:9 the throne, and before the *L*
Rev 7:10 upon the throne, and unto the *L*
Rev 7:14 them white in the blood of the *L*
Rev 7:17 For the *L* which is in the midst
Rev 12:11 him by the blood of the *L*
Rev 13:8 in the book of life of the *L*
Rev 13:11 and he had two horns like a *l*
Rev 14:1 a *L* stood on the mount Sion, and
Rev 14:4 the *L* whithersoever he goeth
Rev 14:4 firstfruits unto God and to the *L*
Rev 14:10 and in the presence of the *L*
Rev 15:3 of God, and the song of the *L*
Rev 17:14 These shall make war with the *L*
Rev 17:14 the *L* shall overcome them
Rev 19:7 for the marriage of the *L* is come
Rev 19:9 unto the marriage supper of the *L*
Rev 21:14 of the twelve apostles of the *L*
Rev 21:22 the *L* are the temple of it
Rev 21:23 the *L* is the light thereof
Rev 22:1 of the throne of God and of the *L*
Rev 22:3 of God and of the *L* shall be in it

## LAMB'S

Rev 21:9 shew thee the bride, the *L* wife
Rev 21:27 are written in the *L* book of life

## LAMBS

Gen 21:28 Abraham set seven ewe *l* of the
Gen 21:29 ewe *l* which thou hast set by
Gen 21:30 For these seven ewe *l* shalt thou
Gen 30:40 And Jacob did separate the *l*
Ex 29:38 two *l* of the first year day by
Lev 14:10 take two he *l* without blemish
Lev 23:18 offer with the bread seven *l*
Lev 23:19 two *l* of the first year for a
Lev 23:20 before the LORD, with the two *l*
Num 7:17 goats, five *l* of the first year
Num 7:23 goats, five *l* of the first year
Num 7:29 goats, five *l* of the first year
Num 7:35 goats, five *l* of the first year
Num 7:41 goats, five *l* of the first year
Num 7:47 goats, five *l* of the first year
Num 7:53 goats, five *l* of the first year
Num 7:59 goats, five *l* of the first year
Num 7:65 goats, five *l* of the first year
Num 7:71 goats, five *l* of the first year
Num 7:77 goats, five *l* of the first year
Num 7:83 goats, five *l* of the first year
Num 7:87 the *l* of the first year twelve,
Num 7:88 the *l* of the first year sixty
Num 28:3 two *l* of the first year without
Num 28:9 on the sabbath day two *l* of the
Num 28:11 seven *l* of the first year without
Num 28:19 seven *l* of the first year
Num 28:21 lamb, throughout the seven *l*
Num 28:27 seven *l* of the first year
Num 28:29 one lamb, throughout the seven *l*
Num 29:2 seven *l* of the first year without
Num 29:4 one lamb, throughout the seven *l*
Num 29:8 seven *l* of the first year
Num 29:10 one lamb, throughout the seven *l*
Num 29:13 fourteen *l* of the first year
Num 29:15 to each lamb of the fourteen *l*
Num 29:17 fourteen *l* of the first year
Num 29:18 for the rams, and for the *l*
Num 29:20 fourteen *l* of the first year
Num 29:21 for the rams, and for the *l*
Num 29:23 fourteen *l* of the first year
Num 29:24 for the rams, and for the *l*
Num 29:26 fourteen *l* of the first year
Num 29:27 for the rams, and for the *l*
Num 29:29 fourteen *l* of the first year
Num 29:30 for the rams, and for the *l*
Num 29:32 fourteen *l* of the first year
Num 29:33 for the rams, and for the *l*
Num 29:36 seven *l* of the first year without
Num 29:37 for the ram, and for the *l*
Deut 32:14 and milk of sheep, with fat of *l*
1Sa 15:9 and of the fatlings, and the *l*
2Kin 3:4 of Israel an hundred thousand *l*
1Chr 29:21 a thousand rams, and a thousand *l*
2Chr 29:21 and seven rams, and seven *l*
2Chr 29:22 they killed also the *l*, and they
2Chr 29:32 an hundred rams, and two hundred *l*
2Chr 35:7 to the people, of the flock, *l*
Ezr 6:9 young bullocks, and rams, and *l*
Ezr 6:17 two hundred rams, four hundred *l*
Ezr 7:17 with this money bullocks, rams, *l*
Ezr 8:35 and six rams, seventy and seven *l*
Ps 37:20 the LORD shall be as the fat of *l*
Ps 114:4 rams, and the little hills like *l*
Ps 114:6 and ye little hills, like *l*
Prov 27:26 The *l* are for thy clothing, and
Is 1:11 in the blood of bullocks, or of *l*
Is 5:17 Then shall the *l* feed after their
Is 34:6 fatness, and with the blood of *l*
Is 40:11 shall gather the *l* with his arm
Jer 51:40 them down like *l* to the slaughter
Eze 27:21 they occupied with thee in *l*
Eze 39:18 of the earth, of rams, of *l*
Eze 46:4 shall be six *l* without blemish
Eze 46:5 the meat offering for the *l* as he
Eze 46:6 bullock without blemish, and six *l*
Eze 46:7 for the *l* according as his hand
Eze 46:11 to the *l* as he is able to give,
Amos 6:4 eat the *l* out of the flock, and
Lk 10:3 send you forth as *l* among wolves
Jn 21:15 He saith unto him, Feed my *l*

## LAME

Lev 21:18 a blind man, or a *l*, or he that
Deut 15:21 blemish therein, as if it be *l*
2Sa 4:4 had a son that was *l* of his feet
2Sa 4:4 flee, that he fell, and became *l*
2Sa 5:6 thou take away the blind and the *l*
2Sa 5:8 smiteth the Jebusites, and the *l*
2Sa 5:8 the *l* shall not come into the
2Sa 9:3 yet a son, which is *l* on his feet
2Sa 9:13 and was *l* on both his feet
2Sa 19:26 because thy servant is *l*
Job 29:15 the blind, and feet was I to the *l*
Prov 26:7 The legs of the *l* are not equal
Is 33:23 the *l* take the prey
Is 35:6 Then shall the *l* man leap as an
Jer 31:8 and with them the blind and the *l*
Mal 1:8 and if ye offer the *l* and sick, is
Mal 1:13 that which was torn, and the *l*
Mt 11:5 the *l* walk, the lepers are
Mt 15:30 with them those that were *l*
Mt 15:31 the *l* to walk, and the blind to
Mt 21:14 the *l* came to him in the temple
Lk 7:22 the *l* walk, the lepers are
Lk 14:13 call the poor, the maimed, the *l*
Acts 3:2 a certain man *l* from his mother's
Acts 3:11 as the *l* man which was healed
Acts 8:7 with palsies, and that were *l*
Heb 12:13 lest that which is *l* be turned

## LAMECH *(la'-mek) A son of Methuselah.*

Gen 4:18 and Methusael begat *L*
Gen 4:19 *L* took unto him two wives
Gen 4:23 *L* said unto his wives, Adah and
Gen 4:23 ye wives of *L*, hearken unto my
Gen 4:24 truly *L* seventy and sevenfold
Gen 5:25 eighty and seven years, and begat *L*
Gen 5:26 he begat *L* seven hundred eighty
Gen 5:28 *L* lived an hundred eighty and two
Gen 5:30 *L* lived after he begat Noah five
Gen 5:31 all the days of *L* were seven
1Chr 1:3 Henoch, Methuselah, *L*,
Lk 3:36 of Noe, which was the son of *L*

## LAMENT

Judg 11:40 of Israel went yearly to *l* the
Is 3:26 And her gates shall *l* and mourn
Is 19:8 angle into the brooks shall *l*
Is 32:12 They shall *l* for the teats, for
Jer 4:8 this gird you with sackcloth, *l*
Jer 16:5 neither go to *l* nor bemoan them
Jer 16:6 neither shall men *l* for them
Jer 22:18 They shall not *l* for him, saying,
Jer 22:18 they shall not *l* for him, saying,
Jer 34:5 and they will *l* thee, saying, Ah
Jer 49:3 *l*, and run to and fro by the hedges
Lam 2:8 made the rampart and the wall to *l*
Eze 27:32 *l* over thee, saying, What city is
Eze 32:16 wherewith they shall *l* her
Eze 32:16 of the nations shall *l* her
Eze 32:16 they shall *l* for her, even for
Joel 1:8 *L* like a virgin girded with
Joel 1:13 Gird yourselves, and *l*, ye priests
Mic 2:4 *l* with a doleful lamentation, and
Jn 16:20 unto you, That ye shall weep and *l*
Rev 18:9 *l* for her, when they shall see

## LAMENTATION

Gen 50:10 with a great and very sore *l*
2Sa 1:17 lamented with this *l* over Saul
Ps 78:64 and their widows made no *l*
Jer 6:26 as for an only son, most bitter *l*
Jer 7:29 take up a *l* on high places
Jer 9:10 habitations of the wilderness a *l*
Jer 9:20 and every one her neighbour *l*
Jer 31:15 A voice was heard in Ramah, *l*
Jer 48:38 There shall be *l* generally upon
Lam 2:5 daughter of Judah mourning and *l*
Eze 19:1 Moreover take thou up a *l* for the
Eze 19:14 is a *l*, and shall be for a *l*
Eze 26:17 they shall take up a *l* for thee
Eze 27:2 son of man, take up a *l* for Tyrus
Eze 27:32 they shall take up a *l* for thee
Eze 28:12 take up a *l* upon the king of
Eze 32:2 take up a *l* for Pharaoh king of
Eze 32:16 This is the *l* wherewith they
Amos 5:1 I take up against you, even a *l*
Amos 5:16 as are skilful of *l* to wailing
Amos 8:10 and all your songs into *l*
Mic 2:4 you, and lament with a doleful *l*
Mt 2:18 Rama was there a voice heard, *l*
Acts 8:2 burial, and made great *l* over him

## LAMENTATIONS

2Chr 35:25 of Josiah in their *l* to this day
2Chr 35:25 behold, they are written in the *l*
Eze 2:10 and there was written therein *l*

## LAMENTED

1Sa 6:19 and the people *l*, because the LORD
1Sa 7:2 house of Israel *l* after the LORD
1Sa 25:1 *l* him, and buried him in his house
1Sa 28:3 was dead, and all Israel had *l* him
2Sa 1:17 David *l* with this lamentation
2Sa 3:33 the king *l* over Abner, and said,
2Chr 35:25 And Jeremiah *l* for Josiah
Jer 16:4 they shall not be *l*
Jer 25:33 they shall not be *l*, neither
Mt 11:17 unto you, and ye have not *l*
Lk 23:27 which also bewailed and *l* him

## LAMP

Gen 15:17 a burning *l* that passed between
Ex 27:20 to cause the *l* to burn always
1Sa 3:3 ere the *l* of God went out in the
2Sa 22:29 For thou art my *l*, O LORD
1Kin 15:4 his God give him a *l* in Jerusalem
Job 12:5 to slip with his feet is as a *l*
Ps 119:105 Thy word is a *l* unto my feet
Ps 132:17 ordained a *l* for mine anointed
Prov 6:23 For the commandment is a *l*
Prov 13:9 but the *l* of the wicked shall be
Prov 20:20 his *l* shall be put out in obscure
Is 62:1 thereof as a *l* that burneth
Rev 8:10 heaven, burning as it were a *l*

## LAMPS

Ex 25:37 shalt make the seven *l* thereof
Ex 25:37 and they shall light the *l* thereof
Ex 30:7 when he dresseth the *l*, he shall
Ex 30:8 when Aaron lighteth the *l* at even
Ex 35:14 light, and his furniture, and his *l*
Ex 37:23 And he made his seven *l*, and his
Ex 39:37 candlestick, with the *l* thereof
Ex 39:37 even with the *l* to be set in
Ex 40:4 and light the *l* thereof
Ex 40:25 he lighted the *l* before the LORD
Lev 24:2 the light, to cause the *l* to burn
Lev 24:4 He shall order the *l* upon the
Num 4:9 of the light, and his *l*, and his
Num 8:2 him, When thou lightest the *l*
Num 8:2 the seven *l* shall give light over
Num 8:3 he lighted the *l* thereof over
Judg 7:16 and *l* within the pitchers
Judg 7:20 held the *l* in their left hands,
1Kin 7:49 with the flowers, and the *l*
1Chr 28:15 of gold, and for their *l* of gold
1Chr 28:15 candlestick, and for the *l* thereof
1Chr 28:15 and also for the *l* thereof
2Chr 4:20 the candlesticks with their *l*
2Chr 4:21 And the flowers, and the *l*, and the
2Chr 13:11 of gold with the *l* thereof

2Chr 29:7 of the porch, and put out the *l*
Job 41:19 Out of his mouth go burning *l*
Eze 1:13 fire, and like the appearance of *l*
Dan 10:6 and his eyes as *l* of fire
Zec 4:2 top of it, and his seven *l* thereon
Zec 4:2 and seven pipes to the seven *l*
Mt 25:1 ten virgins, which took their *l*
Mt 25:3 that were foolish took their *l*
Mt 25:4 oil in their vessels with their *l*
Mt 25:7 virgins arose, and trimmed their *l*
Mt 25:8 for our *l* are gone out
Rev 4:5 there were seven *l* of fire

**LANDMARK**
Deut 19:14 not remove thy neighbour's *l*
Deut 27:17 that removeth his neighbour's *l*
Prov 22:28 Remove not the ancient *l*, which
Prov 23:10 Remove not the old *l*

**LANGUAGE**
Gen 11:1 And the whole earth was of one *l*
Gen 11:6 is one, and they have all one *l*
Gen 11:7 down, and there confound their *l*
Gen 11:9 confound the *l* of all the earth
2Kin 18:26 to thy servants in the Syrian *l*
2Kin 18:26 talk not with us in the Jews' *l*
2Kin 18:28 with a loud voice in the Jews' *l*
Neh 13:24 and could not speak in the Jews' *l*
Neh 13:24 according to the *l* of each people
Est 1:22 and to every people after their *l*
Est 1:22 to the *l* of every people
Est 3:12 and to every people after their *l*
Est 8:9 unto every people after their *l*
Est 8:9 writing, and according to their *l*
Ps 19:3 There is no speech nor *l*, where
Ps 81:5 where I heard a *l* that I
Ps 114:1 Jacob from a people of strange *l*
Is 19:18 of Egypt speak the *l* of Canaan
Is 36:11 unto thy servants in the Syrian *l*
Is 36:11 and speak not to us in the Jews' *l*
Is 36:13 with a loud voice in the Jews' *l*
Jer 5:15 a nation whose *l* thou knowest not
Eze 3:5 a strange speech and of an hard *l*
Eze 3:6 a strange speech and of an hard *l*
Dan 3:29 That every people, nation, and *l*
Zeph 3:9 I turn to the people a pure *l*
Acts 2:6 man heard them speak in his own *l*

**LANGUAGES**
Dan 3:4 O people, nations, and *l*,
Dan 3:7 the people, the nations, and the *l*
Dan 4:1 unto all people, nations, and *l*
Dan 5:19 him, all people, nations, and *l*
Dan 6:25 unto all people, nations, and *l*
Dan 7:14 that all people, nations, and *l*
Zec 8:23 hold out of all *l* of the nations

**LANGUISH**
Is 16:8 For the fields of Heshbon *l*
Is 19:8 nets upon the waters shall *l*
Is 24:4 haughty people of the earth do *l*
Jer 14:2 mourneth, and the gates thereof *l*
Hos 4:3 one that dwelleth therein shall *l*

**LANGUISHETH**
Is 24:4 and fadeth away, the world *l*
Is 24:7 The new wine mourneth, the vine *l*
Is 33:9 The earth mourneth and *l*
Jer 15:9 She that hath borne seven *l*
Joel 1:10 new wine is dried up, the oil *l*
Joel 1:12 is dried up, and the fig tree *l*
Nah 1:4 Bashan *l*, and Carmel
Nah 1:4 and the flower of Lebanon *l*

**LAODICEA** *(la-od-i-se'-ah) Chief city of Phrygia.*
Col 2:1 I have for you, and for them at *L*
Col 4:13 for you, and them that are in *L*
Col 4:15 the brethren which are in *L*
Col 4:16 likewise read the epistle from *L*
1Ti *s* to Timothy was written from *L*
Rev 1:11 and unto Philadelphia, and unto *L*

**LAODICEANS** *(la-od-i-se'-uns) Inhabitants of Laodicea.*
Col 4:16 read also in the church of the *L*
Rev 3:14 of the church of the *L* write

**LAPIDOTH** *(lap'-i-doth) Husband of Deborah.*
Judg 4:4 a prophetess, the wife of *L*

**LASCIVIOUSNESS**
Mk 7:22 wickedness, deceit, *l*, an evil
2Cor 12:21 *l* which they have committed
Gal 5:19 fornication, uncleanness, *l*
Eph 4:19 have given themselves over unto *l*
1Pet 4:3 the Gentiles, when we walked in *l*
Jude 4 the grace of our God into *l*

**LASEA** *(la-se'-ah) A city on Crete.*
Acts 27:8 nigh whereunto was the city of *L*

**LASHA** *(la'-shah) A place in southern Canaan.*
Gen 10:19 and Admah, and Zeboim, even unto *L*

**LASHARON** *(lash'-ar-on) A Canaanite town.*
Josh 12:18 the king of *L*, one

**LAST**
Gen 49:1 shall befall you in the *l* days
Gen 49:19 but he shall overcome at the *l*
Num 23:10 and let my *l* end be like his
2Sa 19:11 Why are ye the *l* to bring the
2Sa 19:12 ye the *l* to bring back the king
2Sa 23:1 Now these be the *l* words of David
1Chr 23:27 For by the *l* words of David the
1Chr 29:29 of David the king, first and *l*
2Chr 9:29 the acts of Solomon, first and *l*
2Chr 12:15 the acts of Rehoboam, first and *l*
2Chr 16:11 the acts of Asa, first and *l*
2Chr 20:34 acts of Jehoshaphat, first and *l*
2Chr 25:26 the acts of Amaziah, first and *l*
2Chr 26:22 of the acts of Uzziah, first and *l*
2Chr 28:26 and of all his ways, first and *l*
2Chr 35:27 And his deeds, first and *l*, behold,
Ezr 8:13 of the *l* sons of Adonikam, whose
Neh 8:18 from the first day unto the *l* day
Prov 5:11 And thou mourn at the *l*, when thy
Prov 23:32 At the *l* it biteth like a serpent
Is 2:2 shall come to pass in the *l* days
Is 41:4 LORD, the first, and with the *l*
Is 44:6 I am the first, and I am the *l*
Is 48:12 I am the first, I also am the *l*
Jer 12:4 said, He shall not see our *l* end
Jer 50:17 *l* this Nebuchadrezzar king of
Lam 1:9 she remembereth not her *l* end
Dan 4:8 But at the *l* Daniel came in
Dan 8:3 other, and the higher came up *l*
Dan 8:19 in the *l* end of the indignation
Amos 9:1 I will slay the *l* of them with
Mic 4:1 But in the *l* days it shall come
Mt 12:45 the *l* state of that man is worse
Mt 19:30 many that are first shall be *l*
Mt 19:30 and the *l* shall be first
Mt 20:8 from the *l* unto the first
Mt 20:12 These *l* have wrought but one hour
Mt 20:14 I will give unto this *l*, even as
Mt 20:16 So the *l* shall be first
Mt 20:16 shall be first, and the first *l*
Mt 21:37 But *l* of all he sent unto them
Mt 22:27 *l* of all the woman died also
Mt 26:60 At the *l* came two false witnesses
Mt 27:64 so the *l* error shall be worse
Mk 9:35 first, the same shall be *l* of all
Mk 10:31 many that are first shall be *l*
Mk 10:31 and the *l* first
Mk 12:6 he sent him also *l* unto them
Mk 12:22 *l* of all the woman died also
Lk 11:26 the *l* state of that man is worse
Lk 12:59 thou hast paid the very *l* mite
Lk 13:30 there are *l* which shall be first,
Lk 13:30 there are first which shall be *l*
Lk 20:32 *L* of all the woman died also
Jn 6:39 raise it up again at the *l* day
Jn 6:40 I will raise him up at the *l* day
Jn 6:44 I will raise him up at the *l* day
Jn 6:54 I will raise him up at the *l* day
Jn 7:37 In the *l* day, that great day of
Jn 8:9 at the eldest, even unto the *l*
Jn 11:24 in the resurrection at the *l* day
Jn 12:48 same shall judge him in the *l* day
Acts 2:17 shall come to pass in the *l* days
1Cor 4:9 hath set forth us the apostles *l*
1Cor 15:8 *l* of all he was seen of me also,
1Cor 15:26 The *l* enemy that shall be
1Cor 15:45 the *l* Adam was made a quickening
1Cor 15:52 of an eye, at the *l* trump
Phil 4:10 that now at the *l* your care of me
2Ti 3:1 that in the *l* days perilous times
Heb 1:2 Hath in these *l* days spoken unto
Jas 5:3 treasure together for the *l* days
1Pet 1:5 to be revealed in the *l* time
1Pet 1:20 manifest in these *l* times for you
2Pet 3:3 shall come in the *l* days scoffers
1Jn 2:18 Little children, it is the *l* time
1Jn 2:18 we know that it is the *l* time
Jude 18 should be mockers in the *l* time
Rev 1:11 and Omega, the first and the *l*
Rev 1:17 I am the first and the *l*
Rev 2:8 things saith the first and the *l*
Rev 2:19 the *l* to be more than the first
Rev 15:1 angels having the seven *l* plagues
Rev 21:9 vials full of the seven *l* plagues
Rev 22:13 and the end, the first and the *l*

**LATCHET**
Is 5:27 nor the *l* of their shoes be
Mk 1:7 the *l* of whose shoes I am not
Lk 3:16 the *l* of whose shoes I am not
Jn 1:27 whose shoe's *l* I am not worthy to

**LATIN** *(lat'-in) Language spoken by the Romans.*
Lk 23:38 him in letters of Greek, and *L*
Jn 19:20 written in Hebrew, and Greek, and *L*

**LATTER**
Ex 4:8 believe the voice of the *l* sign
Num 24:14 do to thy people in the *l* days
Num 24:20 but his *l* end shall be that he
Deut 4:30 upon thee, even in the *l* days
Deut 8:16 to do thee good at thy *l* end
Deut 11:14 the *l* rain, that thou mayest
Deut 24:3 if the *l* husband hate her, and
Deut 24:3 or if the *l* husband die, which
Deut 31:29 will befall you in the *l* days
Deut 32:29 they would consider their *l* end
Ruth 3:10 the *l* end than at the beginning
2Sa 2:26 will be bitterness in the *l* end
Job 8:7 yet thy *l* end should greatly
Job 19:25 stand at the *l* day upon the earth
Job 29:23 mouth wide as for the *l* rain
Job 42:12 So the LORD blessed the *l* end of
Prov 16:15 is as a cloud of the *l* rain
Prov 19:20 thou mayest be wise in thy *l* end
Is 41:22 them, and know the *l* end of them
Is 47:7 didst remember the *l* end of it
Jer 3:3 and there hath been no *l* rain
Jer 5:24 rain, both the former and the *l*
Jer 23:20 in the *l* days ye shall consider
Jer 30:24 in the *l* days ye shall consider
Jer 48:47 captivity of Moab in the *l* days
Jer 49:39 shall come to pass in the *l* days
Eze 38:8 in the *l* years thou shalt come
Eze 38:16 it shall be in the *l* days
Dan 2:28 what shall be in the *l* days
Dan 8:23 in the *l* time of their kingdom,
Dan 10:14 befall thy people in the *l* days
Dan 11:29 not be as the former, or as the *l*
Hos 3:5 and his goodness in the *l* days
Hos 6:3 unto us as the rain, as the *l*
Joel 2:23 the *l* rain in the first month
Amos 7:1 the shooting up of the *l* growth
Amos 7:1 it was the *l* growth after the
Hag 2:9 The glory of this *l* house shall
Zec 10:1 rain in the time of the *l* rain
1Ti 4:1 that in the *l* times some shall
Jas 5:7 he receive the early and *l* rain
2Pet 2:20 the *l* end is worse with them than

**LAUGH**
Gen 18:13 Abraham, Wherefore did Sarah *l*
Gen 18:15 but thou didst *l*
Gen 21:6 Sarah said, God hath made me to *l*
Gen 21:6 that all that hear will *l* with me
Job 5:22 and famine thou shalt *l*
Job 9:23 he will *l* at the trial of the
Job 22:19 the innocent *l* them to scorn
Ps 2:4 sitteth in the heavens shall *l*
Ps 22:7 they that see me *l* me to scorn
Ps 37:13 The LORD shall *l* at him
Ps 52:6 see, and fear, and shall *l* at him
Ps 59:8 But thou, O LORD, shalt *l* at them
Ps 80:6 our enemies *l* among themselves
Prov 1:26 I also will *l* at your calamity
Prov 29:9 foolish man, whether he rage or *l*
Eccl 3:4 A time to weep, and a time to *l*
Lk 6:21 for ye shall *l*
Lk 6:25 Woe unto you that *l* now

**LAUGHED**
Gen 17:17 Abraham fell upon his face, and *l*
Gen 18:12 Therefore Sarah *l* within herself
Gen 18:15 Sarah denied, saying, I *l* not
2Kin 19:21 despised thee, and *l* thee to scorn
2Chr 30:10 but they *l* them to scorn, and
Neh 2:19 they *l* us to scorn, and despised
Job 12:4 just upright man is *l* to scorn

Job 29:24 If I *l* on them, they believed it
Is 37:22 despised thee, and *l* thee to scorn
Eze 23:32 thou shalt be *l* to scorn and had
Mt 9:24 And they *l* him to scorn
Mk 5:40 And they *l* him to scorn
Lk 8:53 they *l* him to scorn, knowing that

**LAUGHTER**
Ps 126:2 Then was our mouth filled with *l*
Prov 14:13 Even in *l* the heart is sorrowful
Eccl 2:2 I said of *l*, It is mad
Eccl 7:3 Sorrow is better than *l*
Eccl 7:6 a pot, so is the *l* of the fool
Eccl 10:19 A feast is made for *l*, and wine
Jas 4:9 let your *l* be turned to mourning,

**LAUNCHED**
Lk 8:22 And they *l* forth
Acts 21:1 were gotten from them, and had *l*
Acts 27:2 into a ship of Adramyttium, we *l*
Acts 27:4 And when we had *l* from thence

**LAVER**
Ex 30:18 Thou shalt also make a *l* of brass
Ex 30:28 with all his vessels, and the *l*
Ex 31:9 with all his furniture, and the *l*
Ex 35:16 staves, and all his vessels, the *l*
Ex 38:8 And he made the *l* of brass
Ex 39:39 staves, and all his vessels, the *l*
Ex 40:7 thou shalt set the *l* between the
Ex 40:11 And thou shalt anoint the *l*
Ex 40:30 he set the *l* between the tent of
Lev 8:11 and all his vessels, both the *l*
1Kin 7:30 under the *l* were undersetters
1Kin 7:38 one *l* contained forty baths
1Kin 7:38 and every *l* was four cubits
1Kin 7:38 every one of the ten bases one *l*
2Kin 16:17 removed the *l* from off them

**LAVERS**
1Kin 7:38 Then made he ten *l* of brass
1Kin 7:40 And Hiram made the *l*, and the
1Kin 7:43 ten bases, and ten *l* on the bases
2Chr 4:6 He made also ten *l*, and put five
2Chr 4:14 and *l* made he upon the bases

**LAW**
Gen 11:31 son, and Sarai his daughter in *l*
Gen 19:12 son in *l*, and thy sons, and thy
Gen 19:14 out, and spake unto his sons in *l*
Gen 19:14 that mocked unto his sons in *l*
Gen 38:11 Judah to Tamar his daughter in *l*
Gen 38:13 Behold thy father in *l* goeth up
Gen 38:16 that she was his daughter in *l*
Gen 38:24 Tamar thy daughter in *l* hath
Gen 38:25 she sent to her father in *l*
Gen 47:26 Joseph made it a *l* over the land
Ex 3:1 flock of Jethro his father in *l*
Ex 4:18 to Jethro his father in *l*
Ex 12:49 One *l* shall be to him that is
Ex 13:9 that the LORD's *l* may be in thy
Ex 16:4 whether they will walk in my *l*
Ex 18:1 of Midian, Moses' father in *l*
Ex 18:2 Then Jethro, Moses' father in *l*
Ex 18:5 And Jethro, Moses' father in *l*
Ex 18:6 I thy father in *l* Jethro am come
Ex 18:7 went out to meet his father in *l*
Ex 18:8 Moses told his father in *l* all
Ex 18:12 And Jethro, Moses' father in *l*
Ex 18:12 Moses' father in *l* before God
Ex 18:14 when Moses' father in *l* saw all
Ex 18:15 Moses said unto his father in *l*
Ex 18:17 Moses' father in *l* said unto him
Ex 18:24 to the voice of his father in *l*
Ex 18:27 Moses let his father in *l* depart
Ex 24:12 give thee tables of stone, and a *l*
Lev 6:9 This is the *l* of the burnt
Lev 6:14 this is the *l* of the meat
Lev 6:25 This is the *l* of the sin offering
Lev 7:1 Likewise this is the *l* of the
Lev 7:7 there is one *l* for them
Lev 7:11 this is the *l* of the sacrifice of
Lev 7:37 This is the *l* of the burnt
Lev 11:46 This is the *l* of the beasts, and
Lev 12:7 This is the *l* for her that hath
Lev 13:59 This is the *l* of the plague of
Lev 14:2 This shall be the *l* of the leper
Lev 14:32 This is the *l* of him in whom is
Lev 14:54 This is the *l* for all manner of
Lev 14:57 this is the *l* of leprosy
Lev 15:32 This is the *l* of him that hath an
Lev 18:15 nakedness of thy daughter in *l*
Lev 20:12 a man lie with his daughter in *l*
Lev 24:22 Ye shall have one manner of *l*
Num 5:29 This is the *l* of jealousies, when
Num 5:30 shall execute upon her all this *l*
Num 6:13 this is the *l* of the Nazarite,
Num 6:21 This is the *l* of the Nazarite who
Num 6:21 do after the *l* of his separation
Num 10:29 the Midianite, Moses' father in *l*
Num 15:16 One *l* and one manner shall be for
Num 15:29 Ye shall have one *l* for him that
Num 19:2 This is the ordinance of the *l*
Num 19:14 This is the *l*, when a man dieth
Num 31:21 This is the ordinance of the *l*
Deut 1:5 began Moses to declare this *l*
Deut 4:8 so righteous as all this *l*
Deut 4:44 this is the *l* which Moses set
Deut 17:11 to the sentence of the *l* which
Deut 17:18 *l* in a book out of that which is
Deut 17:19 to keep all the words of this *l*
Deut 27:3 upon them all the words of this *l*
Deut 27:8 the words of this *l* very plainly
Deut 27:23 that lieth with his mother in *l*
Deut 27:26 the words of this *l* to do them
Deut 28:58 to do all the words of this *l*
Deut 28:61 not written in the book of this *l*
Deut 29:21 are written in this book of the *l*
Deut 29:29 we may do all the words of this *l*
Deut 30:10 are written in this book of the *l*
Deut 31:9 And Moses wrote this *l*, and
Deut 31:11 thou shalt read this *l* before all
Deut 31:12 to do all the words of this *l*
Deut 31:24 the words of this *l* in a book
Deut 31:26 Take this book of the *l*, and put
Deut 32:46 to do, all the words of this *l*
Deut 33:2 hand went a fiery *l* for them
Deut 33:4 Moses commanded us a *l*, even the
Deut 33:10 thy judgments, and Israel thy *l*
Josh 1:7 to do according to all the *l*
Josh 1:8 This book of the *l* shall not
Josh 8:31 in the book of the *l* of Moses
Josh 8:32 stones a copy of the *l* of Moses
Josh 8:34 he read all the words of the *l*
Josh 8:34 is written in the book of the *l*
Josh 22:5 to do the commandment and the *l*
Josh 23:6 in the book of the *l* of Moses
Josh 24:26 words in the book of the *l* of God
Judg 1:16 of the Kenite, Moses' father in *l*
Judg 4:11 of Hobab the father in *l* of Moses
Judg 15:6 the son in *l* of the Timnite,
Judg 19:4 And his father in *l*, the damsel's
Judg 19:5 father said unto his son in *l*
Judg 19:7 depart, his father in *l* urged him
Judg 19:9 and his servant, his father in *l*
Ruth 1:6 she arose with her daughters in *l*
Ruth 1:7 her two daughters in *l* with her
Ruth 1:8 said unto her two daughters in *l*
Ruth 1:14 and Orpah kissed her mother in *l*
Ruth 1:15 thy sister in *l* is gone back unto
Ruth 1:15 return thou after thy sister in *l*
Ruth 1:22 the Moabitess, her daughter in *l*
Ruth 2:11 in *l* since the death of thine
Ruth 2:18 her mother in *l* saw what she had
Ruth 2:19 And her mother in *l* said unto her
Ruth 2:19 she shewed her mother in *l* with
Ruth 2:20 Naomi said unto her daughter in *l*
Ruth 2:22 said unto Ruth her daughter in *l*
Ruth 2:23 and dwelt with her mother in *l*
Ruth 3:1 her mother in *l* said unto her
Ruth 3:6 all that her mother in *l* bade her
Ruth 3:16 when she came to her mother in *l*
Ruth 3:17 Go not empty unto thy mother in *l*
Ruth 4:15 for thy daughter in *l*, which
1Sa 4:19 And his daughter in *l*, Phinehas'
1Sa 4:19 taken, and that her father in *l*
1Sa 4:21 and because of her father in *l*
1Sa 18:18 I should be son in *l* to the king
1Sa 18:21 son in *l* in the one of the twain
1Sa 18:22 therefore be the king's son in *l*
1Sa 18:23 thing to be a king's son in *l*
1Sa 18:26 well to be the king's son in *l*
1Sa 18:27 he might be the king's son in *l*
1Sa 22:14 which is the king's son in *l*
1Kin 2:3 it is written in the *l* of Moses
2Kin 8:27 the son in *l* of the house of Ahab
2Kin 10:31 took no heed to walk in the *l* of
2Kin 14:6 in the book of the *l* of Moses
2Kin 17:13 according to all the *l* which I
2Kin 17:34 their ordinances, or after the *l*
2Kin 17:37 and the ordinances, and the *l*
2Kin 21:8 according to all the *l* that my
2Kin 22:8 of the *l* in the house of the LORD
2Kin 22:11 the words of the book of the *l*
2Kin 23:24 *l* which were written in the book
2Kin 23:25 according to all the *l* of Moses
1Chr 2:4 his daughter in *l* bare him Pharez
1Chr 16:17 the same to Jacob for a *l*
1Chr 16:40 is written in the *l* of the LORD
1Chr 22:12 keep the *l* of the LORD thy God
2Chr 6:16 heed to their way to walk in my *l*
2Chr 12:1 he forsook the *l* of the LORD
2Chr 14:4 of their fathers, and to do the *l*
2Chr 15:3 a teaching priest, and without *l*
2Chr 17:9 had the book of the *l* of the LORD
2Chr 19:10 between blood and blood, between *l*
2Chr 23:18 it is written in the *l* of Moses
2Chr 25:4 in the *l* in the book of Moses
2Chr 30:16 according to the *l* of Moses the
2Chr 31:3 is written in the *l* of the LORD
2Chr 31:4 encouraged in the *l* of the LORD
2Chr 31:21 of the house of God, and in the *l*
2Chr 33:8 them, according to the whole *l*
2Chr 34:14 the *l* of the LORD given by Moses
2Chr 34:15 of the *l* in the house of the LORD
2Chr 34:19 king had heard the words of the *l*
2Chr 35:26 was written in the *l* of the LORD
Ezr 3:2 in the *l* of Moses the man of God
Ezr 7:6 a ready scribe in the *l* of Moses
Ezr 7:10 heart to seek the *l* of the LORD
Ezr 7:12 a scribe of the *l* of the God of
Ezr 7:14 according to the *l* of thy God
Ezr 7:21 the scribe of the *l* of the God of
Ezr 7:26 will not do the *l* of thy God
Ezr 7:26 the *l* of the king, let judgment
Ezr 10:3 let it be done according to the *l*
Neh 6:18 because he was the son in *l* of
Neh 8:1 bring the book of the *l* of Moses
Neh 8:2 Ezra the priest brought the *l*
Neh 8:3 attentive unto the book of the *l*
Neh 8:7 the people to understand the *l*
Neh 8:8 book in the *l* of God distinctly
Neh 8:9 they heard the words of the *l*
Neh 8:13 to understand the words of the *l*
Neh 8:14 they found written in the *l* which
Neh 8:18 read in the book of the *l* of God
Neh 9:3 read in the book of the *l* of the
Neh 9:26 cast thy *l* behind their backs, and
Neh 9:29 bring them again unto thy *l*
Neh 9:34 nor our fathers, kept thy *l*
Neh 10:28 of the lands unto the *l* of God
Neh 10:29 into an oath, to walk in God's *l*
Neh 10:34 God, as it is written in the *l*
Neh 10:36 cattle, as it is written in the *l*
Neh 12:44 portions of the *l* for the priests
Neh 13:3 pass, when they had heard the *l*
Neh 13:28 was son in *l* to Sanballat the
Est 1:8 drinking was according to the *l*
Est 1:13 manner toward all that knew *l*
Est 1:15 the queen Vashti according to *l*
Est 4:11 there is one *l* of his to put him
Est 4:16 which is not according to the *l*
Job 22:22 the *l* from his mouth, and lay up
Ps 1:2 delight is in the *l* of the LORD
Ps 1:2 in his *l* doth he meditate day and
Ps 19:7 The *l* of the LORD is perfect,
Ps 37:31 The *l* of his God is in his heart
Ps 40:8 yea, thy *l* is within my heart
Ps 78:1 Give ear, O my people, to my *l*
Ps 78:5 Jacob, and appointed a *l* in Israel
Ps 78:10 God, and refused to walk in his *l*
Ps 81:4 and a *l* of the God of Jacob
Ps 89:30 If his children forsake my *l*
Ps 94:12 and teachest him out of thy *l*
Ps 94:20 which frameth mischief by a *l*
Ps 105:10 the same unto Jacob for a *l*
Ps 119:1 who walk in the *l* of the LORD
Ps 119:18 wondrous things out of thy *l*
Ps 119:29 and grant me thy *l* graciously
Ps 119:34 and I shall keep thy *l*
Ps 119:44 So shall I keep thy *l* continually
Ps 119:51 have I not declined from thy *l*
Ps 119:53 of the wicked that forsake thy *l*
Ps 119:55 in the night, and have kept thy *l*
Ps 119:61 but I have not forgotten thy *l*
Ps 119:70 but I delight in thy *l*
Ps 119:72 The *l* of thy mouth is better unto
Ps 119:77 for thy *l* is my delight
Ps 119:85 for me, which are not after thy *l*
Ps 119:92 Unless thy *l* had been my delights
Ps 119:97 O how love I thy *l*
Ps 119:109 yet do I not forget thy *l*
Ps 119:113 but thy *l* do I love

Ps 119:126 for they have made void thy *l*
Ps 119:136 eyes, because they keep not thy *l*
Ps 119:142 and thy *l* is the truth
Ps 119:150 they are far from thy *l*
Ps 119:153 for I do not forget thy *l*
Ps 119:163 but thy *l* do I love
Ps 119:165 peace have they which love thy *l*
Ps 119:174 and thy *l* is my delight
Prov 1:8 forsake not the *l* of thy mother
Prov 3:1 My son, forget not my *l*
Prov 4:2 doctrine, forsake ye not my *l*
Prov 6:20 forsake not the *l* of thy mother
Prov 6:23 and the *l* is light
Prov 7:2 my *l* as the apple of thine eye
Prov 13:14 The *l* of the wise is a fountain
Prov 28:4 forsake the *l* praise the wicked
Prov 28:4 as keep the *l* contend with them
Prov 28:7 Whoso keepeth the *l* is a wise son
Prov 28:9 away his ear from hearing the *l*
Prov 29:18 but he that keepeth the *l*
Prov 31:5 Lest they drink, and forget the *l*
Prov 31:26 her tongue is the *l* of kindness
Is 1:10 give ear unto the *l* of our God
Is 2:3 out of Zion shall go forth the *l*
Is 5:24 away the *l* of the LORD of hosts
Is 8:16 seal the *l* among my disciples
Is 8:20 To the *l* and to the testimony
Is 30:9 will not hear the *l* of the LORD
Is 42:4 and the isles shall wait for his *l*
Is 42:21 he will magnify the *l*, and make it
Is 42:24 were they obedient unto his *l*
Is 51:4 for a *l* shall proceed from me, and
Is 51:7 the people in whose heart is my *l*
Jer 2:8 that handle the *l* knew me not
Jer 6:19 unto my words, nor to my *l*
Jer 8:8 the *l* of the LORD is with us
Jer 9:13 my *l* which I set before them
Jer 16:11 me, and have not kept my *l*
Jer 18:18 for the *l* shall not perish from
Jer 26:4 hearken to me, to walk in my *l*
Jer 31:33 I will put my *l* in their inward
Jer 32:11 was sealed according to the *l*
Jer 32:23 voice, neither walked in thy *l*
Jer 44:10 they feared, nor walked in my *l*
Jer 44:23 of the LORD, nor walked in his *l*
Lam 2:9 the *l* is no more
Eze 7:26 but the *l* shall perish from the
Eze 22:11 lewdly defiled his daughter in *l*
Eze 22:26 Her priests have violated my *l*
Eze 43:12 This is the *l* of the house
Eze 43:12 this is the *l* of the house
Dan 6:5 him concerning the *l* of his God
Dan 6:8 according to the *l* of the Medes
Dan 6:12 according to the *l* of the Medes
Dan 6:15 that the *l* of the Medes and
Dan 9:11 Israel have transgressed thy *l*
Dan 9:11 the *l* of Moses the servant of God
Dan 9:13 it is written in the *l* of Moses
Hos 4:6 hast forgotten the *l* of thy God
Hos 8:1 and trespassed against my *l*
Hos 8:12 to him the great things of my *l*
Amos 2:4 have despised the *l* of the LORD
Mic 4:2 for the *l* shall go forth of Zion,
Mic 7:6 the daughter in *l* against her
Mic 7:6 against her mother in *l*
Hab 1:4 Therefore the *l* is slacked
Zeph 3:4 they have done violence to the *l*
Hag 2:11 now the priests concerning the *l*
Zec 7:12 lest they should hear the *l*
Mal 2:6 The *l* of truth was in his mouth,
Mal 2:7 should seek the *l* at his mouth
Mal 2:8 caused many to stumble at the *l*
Mal 2:9 but have been partial in the *l*
Mal 4:4 Remember ye the *l* of Moses my
Mt 5:17 that I am come to destroy the *l*
Mt 5:18 shall in no wise pass from the *l*
Mt 5:40 if any man will sue thee at the *l*
Mt 7:12 for this is the *l* and the prophets
Mt 10:35 the daughter in *l* against her
Mt 10:35 against her mother in *l*
Mt 11:13 the *l* prophesied until John
Mt 12:5 Or have ye not read in the *l*
Mt 22:36 is the great commandment in the *l*
Mt 22:40 two commandments hang all the *l*
Mt 23:23 the weightier matters of the *l*
Lk 2:22 the *l* of Moses were accomplished
Lk 2:23 is written in the *l* of the Lord
Lk 2:24 is said in the *l* of the Lord
Lk 2:27 for him after the custom of the *l*
Lk 2:39 according to the *l* of the Lord
Lk 5:17 and doctors of the *l* sitting by
Lk 10:26 him, What is written in the *l*
Lk 12:53 the mother in *l* against her
Lk 12:53 against her daughter in *l*
Lk 12:53 the daughter in *l* against her
Lk 12:53 against her mother in *l*
Lk 16:16 The *l* and the prophets were until
Lk 16:17 than one tittle of the *l* to fail
Lk 24:44 were written in the *l* of Moses
Jn 1:17 For the *l* was given by Moses, but
Jn 1:45 found him, of whom Moses in the *l*
Jn 7:19 Did not Moses give you the *l*
Jn 7:19 and yet none of you keepeth the *l*
Jn 7:23 that the *l* of Moses should not be
Jn 7:49 who knoweth not the *l* are cursed
Jn 7:51 Doth our *l* judge any man, before
Jn 8:5 Now Moses in the *l* commanded us
Jn 8:17 It is also written in your *l*
Jn 10:34 them, Is it not written in your *l*
Jn 12:34 We have heard out of the *l* that
Jn 15:25 that is written in their *l*
Jn 18:13 he was father in *l* to Caiaphas
Jn 18:31 and judge him according to your *l*
Jn 19:7 Jews answered him, We have a *l*
Jn 19:7 by our *l* he ought to die, because
Acts 5:34 named Gamaliel, a doctor of the *l*
Acts 6:13 against this holy place, and the *l*
Acts 7:53 Who have received the *l* by the
Acts 13:15 And after the reading of the *l*
Acts 13:39 be justified by the *l* of Moses
Acts 15:5 them to keep the *l* of Moses
Acts 15:24 be circumcised, and keep the *l*
Acts 18:13 to worship God contrary to the *l*
Acts 18:15 of words and names, and of your *l*
Acts 19:38 the *l* is open, and there are
Acts 21:20 and they are all zealous of the *l*
Acts 21:24 walkest orderly, and keepest the *l*
Acts 21:28 against the people, and the *l*
Acts 22:3 manner of the *l* of the fathers
Acts 22:12 a devout man according to the *l*
Acts 23:3 thou to judge me after the *l*
Acts 23:3 to be smitten contrary to the *l*
Acts 23:29 accused of questions of their *l*
Acts 24:6 have judged according to our *l*
Acts 24:14 things which are written in the *l*
Acts 25:8 Neither against the *l* of the Jews
Acts 28:23 Jesus, both out of the *l* of Moses
Rom 2:12 *l* shall also perish without *l*
Rom 2:12 the *l* shall be judged by the *l*
Rom 2:13 of the *l* are just before God
Rom 2:13 doers of the *l* shall be justified
Rom 2:14 Gentiles, which have not the *l*
Rom 2:14 the things contained in the *l*
Rom 2:14 these, having not the *l*
Rom 2:14 the *l*, are a *l* unto themselves
Rom 2:15 of the *l* written in their hearts
Rom 2:17 called a Jew, and restest in the *l*
Rom 2:18 being instructed out of the *l*
Rom 2:20 and of the truth in the *l*
Rom 2:23 that makest thy boast of the *l*
Rom 2:23 through breaking the *l*
Rom 2:25 profiteth, if thou keep the *l*
Rom 2:25 but if thou be a breaker of the *l*
Rom 2:26 keep the righteousness of the *l*
Rom 2:27 is by nature, if it fulfil the *l*
Rom 2:27 dost transgress the *l*
Rom 3:19 what things soever the *l* saith
Rom 3:19 saith to them who are under the *l*
Rom 3:20 of the *l* there shall no flesh be
Rom 3:20 for by the *l* is the knowledge of
Rom 3:21 God without the *l* is manifested
Rom 3:21 being witnessed by the *l*
Rom 3:27 By what *l*?
Rom 3:27 but by the *l* of faith
Rom 3:28 faith without the deeds of the *l*
Rom 3:31 make void the *l* through faith
Rom 3:31 yea, we establish the *l*
Rom 4:13 or to his seed, through the *l*
Rom 4:14 they which are of the *l* be heirs
Rom 4:15 Because the *l* worketh wrath
Rom 4:15 for where no *l* is, there is no
Rom 4:16 to that only which is of the *l*
Rom 5:13 (For until the *l* sin was in the
Rom 5:13 is not imputed when there is no *l*
Rom 5:20 Moreover the *l* entered, that the
Rom 6:14 for ye are not under the *l*
Rom 6:15 because we are not under the *l*
Rom 7:1 I speak to them that know the *l*
Rom 7:1 how that the *l* hath dominion
Rom 7:2 *l* to her husband so long as he
Rom 7:2 loosed from the *l* of her husband
Rom 7:3 be dead, she is free from that *l*
Rom 7:4 to the *l* by the body of Christ
Rom 7:5 of sins, which were by the *l*
Rom 7:6 now we are delivered from the *l*
Rom 7:7 Is the *l* sin
Rom 7:7 I had not known sin, but by the *l*
Rom 7:7 known lust, except the *l* had said
Rom 7:8 For without the *l* sin was dead
Rom 7:9 I was alive without the *l* once
Rom 7:12 Wherefore the *l* is holy, and the
Rom 7:14 we know that the *l* is spiritual
Rom 7:16 unto the *l* that it is good
Rom 7:21 I find then a *l*, that, when I
Rom 7:22 For I delight in the *l* of God
Rom 7:23 But I see another *l* in my members
Rom 7:23 warring against the *l* of my mind
Rom 7:23 me into captivity to the *l* of sin
Rom 7:25 mind I myself serve the *l* of God
Rom 7:25 but with the flesh the *l* of sin
Rom 8:2 For the *l* of the Spirit of
Rom 8:2 made me free from the *l* of sin
Rom 8:3 For what the *l* could not do
Rom 8:4 of the *l* might be fulfilled in us
Rom 8:7 it is not subject to the *l* of God
Rom 9:4 covenants, and the giving of the *l*
Rom 9:31 after the *l* of righteousness
Rom 9:31 to the *l* of righteousness
Rom 9:32 as it were by the works of the *l*
Rom 10:4 For Christ is the end of the *l*
Rom 10:5 righteousness which is of the *l*
Rom 13:8 another hath fulfilled the *l*
Rom 13:10 love is the fulfilling of the *l*
1Cor 6:1 go to *l* before the unjust, and not
1Cor 6:6 brother goeth to *l* with brother
1Cor 6:7 ye go to *l* one with another
1Cor 7:39 The wife is bound by the *l* as
1Cor 9:8 or saith not the *l* the same also
1Cor 9:9 it is written in the *l* of Moses
1Cor 9:20 are under the *l*, as under the *l*
1Cor 9:20 gain them that are under the *l*
1Cor 9:21 are without *l*, as without *l*
1Cor 9:21 *l*, (being not without *l* to God
1Cor 9:21 but under the *l* to Christ
1Cor 9:21 gain them that are without *l*
1Cor 14:21 In the *l* it is written, With men
1Cor 14:34 obedience, as also saith the *l*
1Cor 15:56 and the strength of sin is the *l*
Gal 2:16 justified by the works of the *l*
Gal 2:16 and not by the works of the *l*
Gal 2:16 for by the works of the *l* shall
Gal 2:19 For I through the *l* am dead to
Gal 2:19 through the *l* am dead to the *l*
Gal 2:21 if righteousness come by the *l*
Gal 3:2 the Spirit by the works of the *l*
Gal 3:5 doeth he it by the works of the *l*
Gal 3:10 of the *l* are under the curse
Gal 3:10 in the book of the *l* to do them
Gal 3:11 by the *l* in the sight of God
Gal 3:12 And the *l* is not of faith
Gal 3:13 us from the curse of the *l*
Gal 3:17 before of God in Christ, the *l*
Gal 3:18 if the inheritance be of the *l*
Gal 3:19 Wherefore then serveth the *l*
Gal 3:21 Is the *l* then against the
Gal 3:21 for if there had been a *l* given
Gal 3:21 should have been by the *l*
Gal 3:23 came, we were kept under the *l*
Gal 3:24 Wherefore the *l* was our
Gal 4:4 made of a woman, made under the *l*
Gal 4:5 redeem them that were under the *l*
Gal 4:21 ye that desire to be under the *l*
Gal 4:21 do ye not hear the *l*
Gal 5:3 he is a debtor to do the whole *l*
Gal 5:4 of you are justified by the *l*
Gal 5:14 For all the *l* is fulfilled in one
Gal 5:18 Spirit, ye are not under the *l*
Gal 5:23 against such there is no *l*
Gal 6:2 and so fulfil the *l* of Christ
Gal 6:13 who are circumcised keep the *l*
Eph 2:15 even the *l* of commandments
Phil 3:5 as touching the *l*, a Pharisee
Phil 3:6 righteousness which is in the *l*
Phil 3:9 righteousness, which is of the *l*
1Ti 1:7 Desiring to be teachers of the *l*
1Ti 1:8 But we know that the *l* is good
1Ti 1:9 that the *l* is not made for a
Titus 3:9 and strivings about the *l*
Heb 7:5 of the people according to the *l*
Heb 7:11 it the people received the *l*

Heb 7:12 necessity a change also of the *l*
Heb 7:16 not after the *l* of a carnal
Heb 7:19 For the *l* made nothing perfect,
Heb 7:28 For the *l* maketh men high priests
Heb 7:28 the oath, which was since the *l*
Heb 8:4 offer gifts according to the *l*
Heb 9:19 all the people according to the *l*
Heb 9:22 are by the *l* purged with blood
Heb 10:1 For the *l* having a shadow of good
Heb 10:8 which are offered by the *l*
Heb 10:28 He that despised Moses' *l* died
Jas 1:25 into the perfect *l* of liberty
Jas 2:8 If ye fulfil the royal *l*
Jas 2:9 of the *l* as transgressors
Jas 2:10 whosoever shall keep the whole *l*
Jas 2:11 become a transgressor of the *l*
Jas 2:12 be judged by the *l* of liberty
Jas 4:11 evil of the *l*, and judgeth the *l*
Jas 4:11 but if thou judge the *l*
Jas 4:11 thou art not a doer of the *l*
1Jn 3:4 sin transgresseth also the *l*
1Jn 3:4 sin is the transgression of the *l*

## LAWFUL

Ezr 7:24 it shall not be *l* to impose toll
Is 49:24 or the *l* captive delivered
Eze 18:5 be just, and do that which is *l*
Eze 18:19 the son hath done that which is *l*
Eze 18:21 statutes, and do that which is *l*
Eze 18:27 and doeth that which is *l*
Eze 33:14 his sin, and do that which is *l*
Eze 33:16 he hath done that which is *l*
Eze 33:19 wickedness, and do that which is *l*
Mt 12:2 not *l* to do upon the sabbath day
Mt 12:4 which was not *l* for him to eat,
Mt 12:10 Is it *l* to heal on the sabbath
Mt 12:12 Wherefore it is *l* to do well on
Mt 14:4 It is not *l* for thee to have her
Mt 19:3 Is it *l* for a man to put away his
Mt 20:15 Is it not *l* for me to do what I
Mt 22:17 Is it *l* to give tribute unto
Mt 27:6 It is not *l* for to put them into
Mk 2:24 sabbath day that which is not *l*
Mk 2:26 which is not *l* to eat but for the
Mk 3:4 Is it *l* to do good on the sabbath
Mk 6:18 It is not *l* for thee to have thy
Mk 10:2 Is it *l* for a man to put away his
Mk 12:14 Is it *l* to give tribute to Caesar
Lk 6:2 not *l* to do on the sabbath days
Lk 6:4 which it is not *l* to eat but for
Lk 6:9 Is it *l* on the sabbath days to do
Lk 14:3 Is it *l* to heal on the sabbath
Lk 20:22 Is it *l* for us to give tribute
Jn 5:10 it is not *l* for thee to carry thy
Jn 18:31 It is not *l* for us to put any man
Acts 16:21 which are not *l* for us to receive
Acts 19:39 be determined in a *l* assembly
Acts 22:25 Is it *l* for you to scourge a man
1Cor 6:12 All things are *l* unto me, but all
1Cor 6:12 all things are *l* for me, but I
1Cor 10:23 All things are *l* for me, but all
1Cor 10:23 all things are *l* for me, but all
2Cor 12:4 which it is not *l* for a man to

## LAWGIVER

Gen 49:10 nor a *l* from between his feet,
Num 21:18 it, by the direction of the *l*
Deut 33:21 there, in a portion of the *l*
Ps 60:7 Judah is my *l*
Ps 108:8 Judah is my *l*
Is 33:22 is our judge, the LORD is our *l*
Jas 4:12 There is one *l*, who is able to

## LAWS

Gen 26:5 my statutes, and my *l*
Ex 16:28 to keep my commandments and my *l*
Ex 18:16 the statutes of God, and his *l*
Ex 18:20 shalt teach them ordinances and *l*
Lev 26:46 the statutes and judgments and *l*
Ezr 7:25 all such as know the *l* of thy God
Neh 9:13 them right judgments, and true *l*
Neh 9:14 them precepts, statutes, and *l*
Est 1:19 among the *l* of the Persians
Est 3:8 their *l* are diverse from all
Est 3:8 neither keep they the king's *l*
Ps 105:45 his statutes, and keep his *l*
Is 24:5 they have transgressed the *l*
Eze 43:11 thereof, and all the *l* thereof
Eze 44:5 of the LORD, and all the *l* thereof
Eze 44:24 and they shall keep my *l* and my
Dan 7:25 and think to change times and *l*
Dan 9:10 LORD our God, to walk in his *l*

Heb 8:10 I will put my *l* into their mind,
Heb 10:16 I will put my *l* into their hearts

## LAWYERS

Lk 7:30 *l* rejected the counsel of God
Lk 11:45 Then answered one of the *l*
Lk 11:46 he said, Woe unto you also, ye *l*
Lk 11:52 Woe unto you, *l*
Lk 14:3 Jesus answering spake unto the *l*

## LAY

Gen 19:4 But before they *l* down, the men
Gen 19:33 went in, and *l* with her father
Gen 19:33 he perceived not when she *l* down
Gen 19:34 I *l* yesternight with my father
Gen 19:35 the younger arose, and *l* with him
Gen 19:35 he perceived not when she *l* down
Gen 22:12 *L* not thine hand upon the lad,
Gen 28:11 *l* down in that place to sleep
Gen 30:16 And he *l* with her that night
Gen 34:2 *l* with her, and defiled her
Gen 35:22 *l* with Bilhah his father's
Gen 37:22 wilderness, and *l* no hand upon him
Gen 41:35 *l* up corn under the hand of
Ex 5:8 heretofore, ye shall *l* upon them
Ex 7:4 that I may *l* my hand upon Egypt,
Ex 16:13 the dew *l* round about the host
Ex 16:14 when the dew that *l* was gone up
Ex 16:14 there *l* a small round thing
Ex 16:23 that which remaineth over *l* up
Ex 16:33 *l* it up before the LORD, to be
Ex 21:22 woman's husband will *l* upon him
Ex 22:25 shalt thou *l* upon him usury
Lev 1:7 *l* the wood in order upon the fire
Lev 1:8 shall *l* the parts, the head, and
Lev 1:12 the priest shall *l* them in order
Lev 2:15 it, and *l* frankincense thereon
Lev 3:2 he shall *l* his hand upon the head
Lev 3:8 he shall *l* his hand upon the head
Lev 3:13 he shall *l* his hand upon the head
Lev 4:4 shall *l* his hand upon the
Lev 4:15 of the congregation shall *l* their
Lev 4:24 he shall *l* his hand upon the head
Lev 4:29 he shall *l* his hand upon the head
Lev 4:33 he shall *l* his hand upon the head
Lev 6:12 *l* the burnt offering in order
Lev 16:21 Aaron shall *l* both his hands upon
Lev 24:14 let all that heard him *l* their
Num 8:12 the Levites shall *l* their hands
Num 12:11 *l* not the sin upon us, wherein we
Num 17:4 thou shalt *l* them up in the
Num 19:9 *l* them up without the camp in a
Num 24:9 he *l* down as a lion, and as a
Num 27:18 spirit, and *l* thine hand upon him
Deut 7:15 but will *l* them upon all them
Deut 11:18 Therefore shall ye *l* up these my
Deut 11:25 your God shall *l* the fear of you
Deut 14:28 shalt *l* it up within thy gates
Deut 21:8 *l* not innocent blood unto thy
Deut 21:19 his mother *l* hold on him, and
Deut 22:22 the man that *l* with the woman
Deut 22:25 only that *l* with her shall die
Deut 22:28 *l* hold on her, and lie with her,
Deut 22:29 Then the man that *l* with her
Josh 6:26 he shall *l* the foundation thereof
Josh 8:2 *l* thee an ambush for the city
Josh 15:46 all that *l* near Ashdod, with
Judg 4:22 her tent, behold, Sisera *l* dead
Judg 5:27 feet he bowed, he fell, he *l* down
Judg 6:20 *l* them upon this rock, and pour
Judg 7:12 east *l* along in the valley like
Judg 7:13 it, that the tent *l* along
Judg 14:17 because she *l* sore upon him
Judg 16:3 Samson *l* till midnight, and arose
Judg 18:19 *l* thine hand upon thy mouth, and
Ruth 3:4 uncover his feet, and *l* thee down
Ruth 3:8 and, behold, a woman *l* at his feet
Ruth 3:14 she *l* at his feet until the
1Sa 2:22 how they *l* with the women that
1Sa 3:5 And he went and *l* down
1Sa 3:9 went and *l* down in his place
1Sa 3:15 Samuel *l* until the morning, and
1Sa 6:8 the LORD, and *l* it upon the cart
1Sa 11:2 *l* it for a reproach upon all
1Sa 19:24 *l* down naked all that day and all
1Sa 26:5 beheld the place where Saul *l*
1Sa 26:5 Saul *l* in the trench, and the
1Sa 26:7 Saul *l* sleeping within the trench
1Sa 26:7 the people *l* round about him
2Sa 2:21 *l* thee hold on one of the young
2Sa 4:5 who *l* on a bed at noon
2Sa 4:7 he *l* on his bed in his bedchamber
2Sa 11:4 in unto him, and he *l* with her
2Sa 12:3 *l* in his bosom, and was unto him
2Sa 12:16 *l* all night upon the earth
2Sa 12:24 went in unto her, and *l* with her
2Sa 13:5 *L* thee down on thy bed, and make
2Sa 13:6 So Amnon *l* down, and made himself
2Sa 13:14 she, forced her, and *l* with her
2Sa 13:31 his garments, and *l* on the earth
2Sa 19:32 sustenance while he *l* at Mahanaim
1Kin 5:17 to *l* the foundation of the house
1Kin 7:3 that *l* on forty-five pillars,
1Kin 13:4 the altar, saying, *L* hold on him
1Kin 13:31 *l* my bones beside his bones
1Kin 18:23 *l* it on wood, and put no fire
1Kin 18:23 *l* it on wood, and put no fire
1Kin 19:5 And as he *l* and slept under a
1Kin 21:27 *l* in sackcloth, and went softly
2Kin 4:11 into the chamber, and *l* there
2Kin 4:29 *l* my staff upon the face of the
2Kin 4:34 *l* upon the child, and put his
2Kin 9:16 for Joram *l* there
2Kin 10:8 *L* ye them in two heaps at the
2Kin 19:25 be to *l* waste fenced cities into
2Chr 31:7 to *l* the foundation of the heaps
2Chr 36:21 for as long as she *l* desolate she
Ezr 8:31 of such as *l* in wait by the way
Neh 13:21 so again, I will *l* hands on you
Est 2:21 sought to *l* hand on the king
Est 3:6 he thought scorn to *l* hands on
Est 4:3 many *l* in sackcloth and ashes
Est 6:2 who sought to *l* hand on the king
Est 9:2 to *l* hand on such as sought their
Job 9:33 that might *l* his hand upon us
Job 17:3 *L* down now, put me in a surety
Job 21:5 *l* your hand upon your mouth
Job 22:22 *l* up his words in thine heart
Job 22:24 Then shalt thou *l* up gold as dust
Job 29:19 the dew *l* all night upon my
Job 34:23 For he will not *l* upon man more
Job 40:4 I will *l* mine hand upon my mouth
Job 41:8 *L* thine hand upon him, remember
Ps 4:8 I will both *l* me down in peace,
Ps 7:5 *l* mine honour in the dust
Ps 38:12 after my life *l* snares for me
Ps 71:10 they that *l* wait for my soul take
Ps 84:3 where she may *l* her young
Ps 104:22 *l* them down in their dens
Prov 1:11 let us *l* wait for blood, let us
Prov 1:18 they *l* wait for their own blood
Prov 3:18 life to them that *l* hold upon her
Prov 7:1 *l* up my commandments with thee
Prov 10:14 Wise men *l* up knowledge
Prov 24:15 *L* not wait, O wicked man, against
Prov 30:32 *l* thine hand upon thy mouth
Eccl 2:3 to *l* hold on folly, till I might
Eccl 7:2 the living will *l* it to his heart
Is 5:6 And I will *l* it waste
Is 5:8 that *l* field to field, till there
Is 5:29 *l* hold of the prey, and shall
Is 11:14 they shall *l* their hand upon Edom
Is 13:9 anger, to *l* the land desolate
Is 13:11 will *l* low the haughtiness of the
Is 22:22 David will I *l* upon his shoulder
Is 25:12 *l* low, and bring to the ground,
Is 28:16 I *l* in Zion for a foundation a
Is 28:17 also will I *l* to the line
Is 29:3 will *l* siege against thee with a
Is 29:21 *l* a snare for him that reproveth
Is 30:32 which the LORD shall *l* upon him
Is 34:15 the great owl make her nest, and *l*
Is 35:7 of dragons, where each *l*, shall
Is 37:26 that thou shouldest be to *l* waste
Is 38:21 *l* it for a plaister upon the boil
Is 47:7 so that thou didst not *l* these
Is 51:16 *l* the foundations of the earth,
Is 54:11 I will *l* thy stones with fair
Is 54:11 *l* thy foundations with sapphires
Jer 5:26 they *l* wait, as he that setteth
Jer 6:21 I will *l* stumblingblocks before
Jer 6:23 They shall *l* hold on bow and spear
Eze 3:20 I *l* a stumblingblock before him,
Eze 4:1 *l* it before thee, and pourtray
Eze 4:2 *l* siege against it, and build a
Eze 4:3 thou shalt *l* siege against it
Eze 4:4 *l* the iniquity of the house of
Eze 4:8 I will *l* bands upon thee, and thou
Eze 6:5 I will *l* the dead carcases of the
Eze 19:2 she *l* down among lions, she
Eze 23:8 for in her youth they *l* with her

Eze 25:14 I will *l* my vengeance upon Edom
Eze 25:17 when I shall *l* my vengeance upon
Eze 26:12 and they shall *l* thy stones
Eze 26:16 *l* away their robes, and put off
Eze 28:17 I will *l* thee before kings, that
Eze 32:5 I will *l* thy flesh upon the
Eze 33:28 For I will *l* the land most
Eze 35:4 I will *l* thy cities waste, and
Eze 36:29 it, and *l* no famine upon you
Eze 36:34 whereas it *l* desolate in the
Eze 37:6 I will *l* sinews upon you, and will
Eze 42:13 there shall they *l* the most holy
Eze 42:14 but there they shall *l* their
Eze 44:19 *l* them in the holy chambers, and
Amos 2:8 they *l* themselves down upon
Jonah 1:5 and he *l*, and was fast asleep
Jonah 1:14 *l* not upon us innocent blood
Mic 1:7 idols thereof will I *l* desolate
Mic 7:16 they shall *l* their hand upon
Zec 14:13 they shall *l* hold every one on
Mal 2:2 and if ye will not *l* it to heart
Mal 2:2 because ye do not *l* it to heart
Mt 6:19 *L* not up for yourselves treasures
Mt 6:20 But *l* up for yourselves treasures
Mt 8:20 man hath not where to *l* his head
Mt 9:18 *l* thy hand upon her, and she shall
Mt 12:11 day, will he not *l* hold on it
Mt 21:46 they sought to *l* hands on him
Mt 23:4 *l* them on men's shoulders
Mt 28:6 see the place where the Lord *l*
Mk 1:30 wife's mother *l* sick of a fever
Mk 2:4 wherein the sick of the palsy *l*
Mk 3:21 they went out to *l* hold on him
Mk 5:23 *l* thy hands on her, that she may
Mk 12:12 And they sought to *l* hold on him
Mk 15:7 which *l* bound with them that had
Mk 16:18 they shall *l* hands on the sick,
Lk 5:18 him in, and to *l* him before him
Lk 5:25 and took up that whereon he *l*
Lk 8:42 years of age, and she *l* a dying
Lk 9:58 man hath not where to *l* his head
Lk 19:44 shall *l* thee even with the ground
Lk 20:19 hour sought to *l* hands on him
Lk 21:12 they shall *l* their hands on you,
Jn 5:3 In these *l* a great multitude of
Jn 10:15 I *l* down my life for the sheep
Jn 10:17 because I *l* down my life, that I
Jn 10:18 but I *l* it down of myself
Jn 10:18 I have power to *l* it down
Jn 11:38 was a cave, and a stone *l* upon it
Jn 13:37 I will *l* down my life for thy
Jn 13:38 Wilt thou *l* down thy life for my
Jn 15:13 that a man *l* down his life for
Acts 7:60 *l* not this sin to their charge
Acts 8:19 that on whomsoever I *l* hands
Acts 15:28 to *l* upon you no greater burden
Acts 27:20 and no small tempest *l* on us
Acts 28:8 of Publius *l* sick of a fever
Rom 8:33 Who shall *l* any thing to the
Rom 9:33 I *l* in Sion a stumblingstone and
1Cor 3:11 can no man *l* than that is laid
1Cor 16:2 one of you *l* by him in store
2Cor 12:14 ought not to *l* up for the parents
1Ti 5:22 *L* hands suddenly on no man,
1Ti 6:12 *l* hold on eternal life, whereunto
1Ti 6:19 that they may *l* hold on eternal
Heb 6:18 who have fled for refuge to *l*
Heb 12:1 let us *l* aside every weight, and
Jas 1:21 Wherefore *l* apart all filthiness
1Pet 2:6 I *l* in Sion a chief corner stone,
1Jn 3:16 we ought to *l* down our lives for

### LAYETH

Job 21:19 God *l* up his iniquity for his
Job 24:12 yet God *l* not folly to them
Job 41:26 of him that *l* at him cannot hold
Ps 33:7 he *l* up the depth in storehouses
Ps 104:3 Who *l* the beams of his chambers
Prov 2:7 He *l* up sound wisdom for the
Prov 13:16 but a fool *l* open his folly
Prov 26:24 lips, and *l* up deceit within him
Prov 31:19 She *l* her hands to the spindle,
Is 26:5 the lofty city, he *l* it low
Is 26:5 he *l* it low, even to the ground
Is 56:2 the son of man that *l* hold on it
Is 57:1 and no man *l* it to heart
Jer 9:8 mouth, but in heart he *l* his wait
Jer 12:11 because no man *l* it to heart
Zec 12:1 *l* the foundation of the earth, and
Lk 12:21 So is he that *l* up treasure for
Lk 15:5 he *l* it on his shoulders,

### LAYING

Num 35:20 or hurl at him by *l* of wait
Num 35:22 him any thing without *l* of wait
Ps 64:5 they commune of *l* snares privily
Mk 7:8 For *l* aside the commandment of
Lk 11:54 *L* wait for him, and seeking to
Acts 8:18 when Simon saw that through *l* on
Acts 9:24 But their *l* await was known of
Acts 25:3 *l* wait in the way to kill him
1Ti 4:14 with the *l* on of the hands of the
1Ti 6:19 *L* up in store for themselves a
Heb 6:1 not *l* again the foundation of
Heb 6:2 and of *l* on of hands, and of
1Pet 2:1 Wherefore *l* aside all malice, and

### LAZARUS *(laz'-a-rus)*

*1. Name for a beggar in a parable of Jesus.*
Lk 16:20 was a certain beggar named *L*
Lk 16:23 afar off, and *L* in his bosom
Lk 16:24 have mercy on me, and send *L*
Lk 16:25 things, and likewise *L* evil things
*2. Man raised from the dead by Jesus.*
Jn 11:1 a certain man was sick, named *L*
Jn 11:2 hair, whose brother *L* was sick
Jn 11:5 loved Martha, and her sister, and *L*
Jn 11:11 unto them, Our friend *L* sleepeth
Jn 11:14 unto them plainly, *L* is dead
Jn 11:43 he cried with a loud voice, *L*
Jn 12:1 where *L* was which had been dead,
Jn 12:2 but *L* was one of them that sat at
Jn 12:9 but that they might see *L* also
Jn 12:10 they might put *L* also to death
Jn 12:17 when he called *L* out of his grave

### LEAD

Gen 33:14 I will *l* on softly, according as
Ex 13:21 of a cloud, to *l* them the way
Ex 15:10 they sank as *l* in the mighty
Ex 32:34 *l* the people unto the place of
Num 27:17 them, and which may *l* them out
Num 31:22 the iron, the tin, and the *l*
Deut 4:27 whither the LORD shall *l* you
Deut 20:9 of the armies to *l* the people
Deut 28:37 whither the LORD shall *l* thee
Deut 32:12 So the LORD alone did *l* him
Judg 5:12 *l* thy captivity captive, thou son
1Sa 30:22 that they may *l* them away
2Chr 30:9 before them that *l* them captive
Neh 9:19 them by day, to *l* them in the way
Job 19:24 pen and *l* in the rock for ever
Ps 5:8 *L* me, O LORD, in thy
Ps 25:5 *L* me in thy truth, and teach me
Ps 27:11 *l* me in a plain path, because of
Ps 31:3 for thy name's sake *l* me, and
Ps 43:3 let them *l* me
Ps 60:9 who will *l* me into Edom
Ps 61:2 *l* me to the rock that is higher
Ps 108:10 who will *l* me into Edom
Ps 125:5 the LORD shall *l* them forth with
Ps 139:10 Even there shall thy hand *l* me
Ps 139:24 *l* me in the way everlasting
Ps 143:10 *l* me into the land of uprightness
Prov 6:22 When thou goest, it shall *l* thee
Prov 8:20 I *l* in the way of righteousness,
Song 8:2 I would *l* thee, and bring thee
Is 3:12 they which *l* thee cause thee to
Is 11:6 and a little child shall *l* them
Is 20:4 *l* away the Egyptians prisoners
Is 40:11 shall gently *l* those that are
Is 42:16 I will *l* them in paths that they
Is 49:10 hath mercy on them shall *l* them
Is 57:18 I will *l* him also, and restore
Is 63:14 so didst thou *l* thy people
Jer 6:29 the *l* is consumed of the fire
Jer 31:9 with supplications will I *l* them
Jer 32:5 he shall *l* Zedekiah to Babylon,
Eze 22:18 are brass, and tin, and iron, and *l*
Eze 22:20 silver, and brass, and iron, and *l*
Eze 27:12 with silver, iron, tin, and *l*
Nah 2:7 her maids shall *l* her as with the
Zec 5:7 there was lifted up a talent of *l*
Zec 5:8 he cast the weight of *l* upon the
Mt 6:13 *l* us not into temptation, but
Mt 15:14 And if the blind *l* the blind
Mk 13:11 But when they shall *l* you
Mk 14:44 take him, and *l* him away safely
Lk 6:39 them, Can the blind *l* the blind
Lk 11:4 And *l* us not into temptation
Lk 13:15 stall, and *l* him away to watering
Acts 13:11 seeking some to *l* him by the hand
1Cor 9:5 we not power to *l* about a sister
1Ti 2:2 that we may *l* a quiet and
2Ti 3:6 *l* captive silly women laden with
Heb 8:9 *l* them out of the land of Egypt
Rev 7:17 them, and shall *l* them unto living

### LEADETH

1Sa 13:17 unto the way that *l* to Ophrah
Job 12:17 He *l* counsellors away spoiled, and
Job 12:19 He *l* princes away spoiled, and
Ps 23:2 he *l* me beside the still waters
Ps 23:3 he *l* me in the paths of
Prov 16:29 *l* him into the way that is not
Is 48:17 which *l* thee by the way that thou
Mt 7:13 that *l* to destruction, and many
Mt 7:14 which *l* unto life, and few there
Mk 9:2 *l* them up into an high mountain
Jn 10:3 own sheep by name, and *l* them out
Acts 12:10 iron gate that *l* unto the city
Rom 2:4 of God *l* thee to repentance
Rev 13:10 He that *l* into captivity shall go

### LEAF

Gen 8:11 mouth was an olive *l* pluckt off
Lev 26:36 of a shaken *l* shall chase them
Job 13:25 Wilt thou break a *l* driven to
Ps 1:3 his *l* also shall not wither
Is 1:30 shall be as an oak whose *l* fadeth
Is 34:4 as the *l* falleth off from the
Is 64:6 and we all do fade as a *l*
Jer 8:13 the fig tree, and the *l* shall fade
Jer 17:8 cometh, but her *l* shall be green
Eze 47:12 whose *l* shall not fade, neither
Eze 47:12 the *l* thereof for medicine

### LEAGUE

Josh 9:6 now therefore make ye a *l* with us
Josh 9:7 and how shall we make a *l* with you
Josh 9:11 therefore now make ye a *l* with us
Josh 9:15 made a *l* with them, to let them
Josh 9:16 after they had made a *l* with them
Judg 2:2 ye shall make no *l* with the
1Sa 22:8 made a *l* with the son of Jesse
2Sa 3:12 saying also, Make thy *l* with me
2Sa 3:13 I will make a *l* with thee
2Sa 3:21 that they may make a *l* with thee
2Sa 5:3 king David made a *l* with them in
1Kin 5:12 and they two made a *l* together
1Kin 15:19 There is a *l* between me and thee,
1Kin 15:19 break thy *l* with Baasha king of
2Chr 16:3 There is a *l* between me and thee,
2Chr 16:3 break thy *l* with Baasha king of
Job 5:23 For thou shalt be in *l* with the
Eze 30:5 the men of the land that is in *l*
Dan 11:23 after the *l* made with him he

### LEAH *(le'-ah)* See LEAH'S. *Wife of Jacob.*

Gen 29:16 the name of the elder was *L*
Gen 29:17 *L* was tender eyed
Gen 29:23 that he took *L* his daughter
Gen 29:24 Laban gave unto his daughter *L*
Gen 29:25 in the morning, behold, it was *L*
Gen 29:30 he loved also Rachel more than *L*
Gen 29:31 the LORD saw that *L* was hated
Gen 29:32 *L* conceived, and bare a son, and
Gen 30:9 When *L* saw that she had left
Gen 30:11 And *L* said, A troop cometh
Gen 30:13 *L* said, Happy am I, for the
Gen 30:14 and brought them unto his mother *L*
Gen 30:14 Then Rachel said to *L*, Give me, I
Gen 30:16 *L* went out to meet him, and said,
Gen 30:17 And God hearkened unto *L*, and she
Gen 30:18 *L* said, God hath given me my hire
Gen 30:19 *L* conceived again, and bare Jacob
Gen 30:20 *L* said, God hath endued me with a
Gen 31:4 *L* to the field unto his flock,
Gen 31:14 *L* answered and said unto him, Is
Gen 33:1 And he divided the children unto *L*
Gen 33:2 and their children foremost, and *L*
Gen 33:7 *L* also with her children came
Gen 34:1 And Dinah the daughter of *L*
Gen 35:23 The sons of *L*; Reuben
Gen 46:15 These be the sons of *L*, which she
Gen 46:18 whom Laban gave to *L* his daughter
Gen 49:31 and there I buried *L*
Ruth 4:11 thine house like Rachel and like *L*

### LEAH'S *(le'-ahs)*

Gen 30:10 Zilpah *L* maid bare Jacob a son
Gen 30:12 Zilpah *L* maid bare Jacob a second
Gen 31:33 into Jacob's tent, and into *L* tent

Gen 31:33 Then went he out of *L* tent
Gen 35:26 And the sons of Zilpah, *L* handmaid

**LEAN**
Gen 41:20 And the *l* and the ill favoured kine
Num 13:20 land is, whether it be fat or *l*
Judg 16:26 standeth, that I may *l* upon them
2Sa 13:4 the king's son, *l* from day to day
2Kin 18:21 upon Egypt, on which if a man *l*
Job 8:15 He shall *l* upon his house, but it
Prov 3:5 and *l* not unto thine own
Is 17:4 fatness of his flesh shall wax *l*
Is 36:6 whereon if a man *l*, it will go
Eze 34:20 cattle and between the *l* cattle
Mic 3:11 yet will they *l* upon the LORD

**LEANED**
2Sa 1:6 behold, Saul *l* upon his spear
2Kin 7:2 king *l* answered the man of God
2Kin 7:17 the lord on whose hand he *l* to
Eze 29:7 and when they *l* upon thee, thou
Amos 5:19 *l* his hand on the wall, and a
Jn 21:20 which also *l* on his breast at

**LEANNESS**
Job 16:8 my *l* rising up in me beareth
Ps 106:15 but sent *l* into their soul
Is 10:16 hosts, send among his fat ones *l*
Is 24:16 But I said, My *l*, my *l*,

**LEANNOTH** *(le-an'-noth) A musical choir.*
Ps 88:*t* chief Musician upon Mahalath *L*

**LEAP**
Gen 31:12 all the rams which *l* upon the
Lev 11:21 to *l* withal upon the earth
Deut 33:22 he shall *l* from Bashan
Job 41:19 lamps, and sparks of fire *l* out
Ps 68:16 Why *l* ye, ye high hills
Is 35:6 shall the lame man *l* as an hart
Joel 2:5 tops of mountains shall they *l*
Zeph 1:9 all those that *l* on the threshold
Lk 6:23 ye in that day, and *l* for joy

**LEAPED**
Gen 31:10 the rams which *l* upon the cattle
2Sa 22:30 by my God have I *l* over a wall
1Kin 18:26 they *l* upon the altar which was
Ps 18:29 and by my God have I *l* over a wall
Lk 1:41 of Mary, the babe *l* in her womb
Lk 1:44 the babe *l* in my womb for joy
Acts 14:10 And he *l* and walked
Acts 19:16 the evil spirit was *l* on them

**LEAPING**
2Sa 6:16 a window, and saw king David *l*
Song 2:8 he cometh *l* upon the mountains,
Acts 3:8 he *l* up stood, and walked, and
Acts 3:8 into the temple, walking, and *l*

**LEARN**
Deut 4:10 that they may *l* to fear me all
Deut 5:1 ears this day, that ye may *l* them
Deut 14:23 that thou mayest *l* to fear the
Deut 17:19 that he may *l* to fear the LORD
Deut 18:9 thou shalt not *l* to do after the
Deut 31:12 they may hear, and that they may *l*
Deut 31:13 *l* to fear the LORD your God, as
Ps 119:71 that I might *l* thy statutes
Ps 119:73 that I may *l* thy commandments
Prov 22:25 Lest thou *l* his ways, and get a
Is 1:17 *L* to do well
Is 2:4 neither shall they *l* war any more
Is 26:9 of the world will *l* righteousness
Is 26:10 yet will he not *l* righteousness
Is 29:24 that murmured shall *l* doctrine
Jer 10:2 *L* not the way of the heathen, and
Jer 12:16 *l* the ways of my people, to swear
Mic 4:3 neither shall they *l* war any more
Mt 9:13 *l* what that meaneth, I will have
Mt 11:29 Take my yoke upon you, and *l* of me
Mt 24:32 Now *l* a parable of the fig tree
Mk 13:28 Now *l* a parable of the fig tree
1Cor 4:6 that ye might *l* in us not to
1Cor 14:31 one by one, that all may *l*
1Cor 14:35 And if they will *l* any thing
Gal 3:2 This only would I *l* of you
1Ti 1:20 that they may *l* not to blaspheme
1Ti 2:11 Let the woman *l* in silence with
1Ti 5:4 let them *l* first to shew piety at
1Ti 5:13 And withal they *l* to be idle
Titus 3:14 let ours also *l* to maintain good
Rev 14:3 no man could *l* that song but the

**LEARNED**
Gen 30:27 for I have *l* by experience that
Ps 106:35 the heathen, and *l* their works
Ps 119:7 when I shall have *l* thy righteous
Prov 30:3 I neither *l* wisdom, nor have the
Is 29:11 men deliver to one that is *l*
Is 29:12 is delivered to him that is not *l*
Is 29:12 and he saith, I am not *l*
Is 50:4 hath given me the tongue of the *l*
Is 50:4 mine ear to hear as the *l*
Eze 19:3 lion, and it *l* to catch the prey
Eze 19:6 *l* to catch the prey, and devoured
Jn 6:45 hath *l* of the Father, cometh unto
Jn 7:15 this man letters, having never *l*
Acts 7:22 Moses was *l* in all the wisdom of
Rom 16:17 to the doctrine which ye have *l*
Eph 4:20 But ye have not so *l* Christ
Phil 4:9 things, which ye have both *l*
Phil 4:11 for I have *l*, in whatsoever state
Col 1:7 As ye also *l* of Epaphras our dear
2Ti 3:14 in the things which thou hast *l*
2Ti 3:14 knowing of whom thou hast *l* them
Heb 5:8 yet *l* he obedience by the things

**LEARNING**
Prov 1:5 man will hear, and will increase *l*
Prov 9:9 man, and he will increase in *l*
Prov 16:21 of the lips increaseth *l*
Prov 16:23 mouth, and addeth *l* to his lips
Dan 1:4 and whom they might teach the *l*
Dan 1:17 them knowledge and skill in all *l*
Acts 26:24 much *l* doth make thee mad
Rom 15:4 aforetime were written for our *l*
2Ti 3:7 Ever *l*, and never able to come to

**LEAVEN**
Ex 12:15 put away *l* out of your houses
Ex 12:19 be no *l* found in your houses
Ex 13:7 neither shall there be *l* seen
Ex 34:25 the blood of my sacrifice with *l*
Lev 2:11 the LORD, shall be made with *l*
Lev 2:11 for ye shall burn no *l*, nor any
Lev 6:17 It shall not be baken with *l*
Lev 10:12 eat it without *l* beside the altar
Lev 23:17 they shall be baken with *l*
Amos 4:5 sacrifice of thanksgiving with *l*
Mt 13:33 kingdom of heaven is like unto *l*
Mt 16:6 beware of the *l* of the Pharisees
Mt 16:11 beware of the *l* of the Pharisees
Mt 16:12 them not beware of the *l* of bread
Mk 8:15 beware of the *l* of the Pharisees,
Mk 8:15 and of the *l* of Herod
Lk 12:1 ye of the *l* of the Pharisees
Lk 13:21 It is like *l*, which a woman took
1Cor 5:6 little *l* leaveneth the whole lump
1Cor 5:7 Purge out therefore the old *l*
1Cor 5:8 us keep the feast, not with old *l*
1Cor 5:8 neither with the *l* of malice
Gal 5:9 A little *l* leaveneth the whole

**LEAVENED**
Ex 12:15 for whosoever eateth *l* bread from
Ex 12:19 whosoever eateth that which is *l*
Ex 12:20 Ye shall eat nothing *l*
Ex 12:34 took their dough before it was *l*
Ex 12:39 out of Egypt, for it was not *l*
Ex 13:3 there shall no *l* bread be eaten
Ex 13:7 there shall no *l* bread be seen
Ex 23:18 of my sacrifice with *l* bread
Lev 7:13 *l* bread with the sacrifice of
Deut 16:3 Thou shalt eat no *l* bread with it
Deut 16:4 there shall be no *l* bread seen
Hos 7:4 kneaded the dough, until it be *l*
Mt 13:33 of meal, till the whole was *l*
Lk 13:21 of meal, till the whole was *l*

**LEAVES**
Gen 3:7 and they sewed fig *l* together
1Kin 6:34 the two *l* of the one door were
1Kin 6:34 the two *l* of the other door were
Is 6:13 in them, when they cast their *l*
Jer 36:23 Jehudi had read three or four *l*
Eze 17:9 wither in all the *l* of her spring
Eze 41:24 two *l* apiece, two turning *l*
Eze 41:24 two *l* for the one door
Eze 41:24 and two *l* for the other door
Dan 4:12 The *l* thereof were fair, and the
Dan 4:14 off his branches, shake off his *l*
Dan 4:21 Whose *l* were fair, and the fruit
Mt 21:19 but *l* only, and said unto it, Let
Mt 24:32 is yet tender, and putteth forth *l*
Mk 11:13 a fig tree afar off having *l*
Mk 11:13 to it, he found nothing but *l*
Mk 13:28 is yet tender, and putteth forth *l*
Rev 22:2 the *l* of the tree were for the

**LEBANA** *(leb'-a-nah)* See LEBANAH. *A family of exiles.*
Neh 7:48 The children of *L*, the children

**LEBANAH** *(leb'-a-nah) Same as Lebana.*
Ezr 2:45 The children of *L*, the children

**LEBANON** *(leb'-a-non) Chief mountain range in Syria.*
Deut 1:7 land of the Canaanites, and unto *L*
Deut 3:25 that goodly mountain, and *L*
Deut 11:24 from the wilderness and *L*, from
Josh 1:4 this *L* even unto the great river,
Josh 9:1 of the great sea over against *L*
Josh 11:17 valley of *L* under mount Hermon
Josh 12:7 of *L* even unto the mount Halak
Josh 13:5 land of the Giblites, and all *L*
Josh 13:6 from *L* unto Misrephoth-maim
Judg 3:3 the Hivites that dwelt in mount *L*
Judg 9:15 and devour the cedars of *L*
1Kin 4:33 is in *L* even unto the hyssop that
1Kin 5:6 they hew me cedar trees out of *L*
1Kin 5:9 them down from *L* unto the sea
1Kin 5:14 And he sent them to *L*, ten
1Kin 5:14 a month they were in *L*, and two
1Kin 7:2 also the house of the forest of *L*
1Kin 9:19 to build in Jerusalem, and in *L*
1Kin 10:17 in the house of the forest of *L*
1Kin 10:21 the forest of *L* were of pure gold
2Kin 14:9 The thistle that was in *L* sent to
2Kin 14:9 sent to the cedar that was in *L*
2Kin 14:9 by a wild beast that was in *L*
2Kin 19:23 the mountains, to the sides of *L*
2Chr 2:8 trees, and algum trees, out of *L*
2Chr 2:8 can skill to cut timber in *L*
2Chr 2:16 And we will cut wood out of *L*
2Chr 8:6 to build in Jerusalem, and in *L*
2Chr 9:16 in the house of the forest of *L*
2Chr 9:20 the forest of *L* were of pure gold
2Chr 25:18 The thistle that was in *L* sent to
2Chr 25:18 sent to the cedar that was in *L*
2Chr 25:18 by a wild beast that was in *L*
Ezr 3:7 trees from *L* to the sea of Joppa
Ps 29:5 the LORD breaketh the cedars of *L*
Ps 29:6 *L* and Sirion like a young unicorn
Ps 72:16 fruit thereof shall shake like *L*
Ps 92:12 he shall grow like a cedar in *L*
Ps 104:16 the cedars of *L*, which he hath
Song 3:9 a chariot of the wood of *L*
Song 4:8 Come with me from *L*, my spouse,
Song 4:8 with me from *L*
Song 4:11 garments is like the smell of *L*
Song 4:15 living waters, and streams from *L*
Song 5:15 his countenance is as *L*,
Song 7:4 thy nose is as the tower of *L*
Is 2:13 And upon all the cedars of *L*
Is 10:34 *L* shall fall by a mighty one
Is 14:8 at thee, and the cedars of *L*
Is 29:17 *L* shall be turned into a fruitful
Is 33:9 *L* is ashamed and hewn down
Is 35:2 the glory of *L* shall be given
Is 37:24 the mountains, to the sides of *L*
Is 40:16 *L* is not sufficient to burn, nor
Is 60:13 The glory of *L* shall come unto
Jer 18:14 Will a man leave the snow of *L*
Jer 22:6 Gilead unto me, and the head of *L*
Jer 22:20 Go up to *L*, and cry
Jer 22:23 O inhabitant of *L*, that makest
Eze 17:3 had divers colours, came unto *L*
Eze 27:5 from *L* to make masts for thee
Eze 31:3 a cedar in *L* with fair branches
Eze 31:15 I caused *L* to mourn for him, and
Eze 31:16 of Eden, the choice and best of *L*
Hos 14:5 and cast forth his roots as *L*
Hos 14:6 the olive tree, and his smell as *L*
Hos 14:7 thereof shall be as the wine of *L*
Nah 1:4 and the flower of *L* languisheth
Hab 2:17 violence of *L* shall cover thee
Zec 10:10 them into the land of Gilead and *L*
Zec 11:1 Open thy doors, O *L*, that the

**LEBAOTH** *(leb'-a-oth)* See BETH-LEBAOTH. *A city in Judah.*
Josh 15:32 And *L*, and Shilhim, and Ain, and

**LEBBAEUS** *(leb-be'-us)* See JUDAS, THADDAEUS. *Same as Thaddaeus.*
Mt 10:3 James the son of Alphaeus, and *L*

**LEBONAH** *(le-bo'-nah) A city in Ephraim.*
Judg 21:19 to Shechem, and on the south of L

**LECAH** *(le'-cah) Son of Er.*
1Chr 4:21 of Judah were, Er the father of L

**LED**
Gen 24:27 the LORD l me to the house of my
Gen 24:48 which had l me in the right way
Ex 3:1 he l the flock to the backside of
Ex 13:17 that God l them not through the
Ex 13:18 But God l the people about,
Ex 15:13 Thou in thy mercy hast l forth
Deut 8:2 l thee these forty years in the
Deut 8:15 Who l thee through that great and
Deut 29:5 I have l you forty years in the
Deut 32:10 he l him about, he instructed him
Josh 24:3 l him throughout all the land of
1Kin 8:48 which l them away captive, and
2Kin 6:19 But he l them to Samaria
1Chr 20:1 Joab l forth the power of the
2Chr 25:11 l forth his people, and went to
Ps 68:18 thou hast l captivity captive
Ps 78:14 also he l them with a cloud
Ps 78:53 he l them on safely, so that they
Ps 106:9 so he l them through the depths,
Ps 107:7 he l them forth by the right way,
Ps 136:16 To him which l his people through
Prov 4:11 I have l thee in right paths
Is 9:16 they that are l of them are
Is 48:21 he l them through the deserts
Is 55:12 joy, and be l forth with peace
Is 63:12 That l them by the right hand of
Is 63:13 That l them through the deep, as
Jer 2:6 that l us through the wilderness,
Jer 2:17 when he l thee by the way
Jer 22:12 whither they have l him captive
Jer 23:8 which l the seed of the house of
Lam 3:2 He hath l me, and brought me into
Eze 17:12 l them with him to Babylon
Eze 39:28 which caused them to be l into
Eze 47:2 l me about the way without unto
Amos 2:10 l you forty years through the
Amos 7:11 Israel shall surely be l away
Nah 2:7 And Huzzab shall be l away captive
Mt 4:1 Then was Jesus l up of the spirit
Mt 26:57 that had laid hold on Jesus l him
Mt 27:2 they l him away, and delivered him
Mt 27:31 l him away to crucify him
Mk 8:23 hand, and l him out of the town
Mk 14:53 they l Jesus away to the high
Mk 15:16 the soldiers l him away into the
Mk 15:20 him, and l him out to crucify him
Lk 4:1 was l by the Spirit into the
Lk 4:29 l him unto the brow of the hill
Lk 21:24 shall be l away captive into all
Lk 22:54 l him, and brought him into the
Lk 22:66 l him into their council, saying,
Lk 23:1 them arose, and l him unto Pilate
Lk 23:26 as they l him away, they laid
Lk 23:32 l with him to be put to death
Lk 24:50 he l them out as far as to
Jn 18:13 l him away to Annas first
Jn 18:28 Then l they Jesus from Caiaphas
Jn 19:16 And they took Jesus, and l him away
Acts 8:32 He was l as a sheep to the
Acts 9:8 but they l him by the hand, and
Acts 21:37 Paul was to be l into the castle
Acts 22:11 being l by the hand of them that
Rom 8:14 For as many as are l by the
1Cor 12:2 dumb idols, even as ye were l
Gal 5:18 But if ye be l of the Spirit, ye
Eph 4:8 he l captivity captive, and gave
2Ti 3:6 l away with divers lusts,
2Pet 3:17 being l away with the error of

**LEDDEST**
2Sa 5:2 over us, thou wast he that l out
1Chr 11:2 was king, thou wast he that l out
Neh 9:12 Moreover thou l them in the day
Ps 77:20 Thou l thy people like a flock by
Acts 21:38 l out into the wilderness four

**LEGION**
Mk 5:9 he answered, saying, My name is L
Mk 5:15 with the devil, and had the l
Lk 8:30 And he said, L

**LEGS**
Ex 12:9 his head with his l, and with the
Ex 29:17 wash the inwards of him, and his l
Lev 1:9 his l shall he wash in water
Lev 1:13 the inwards and the l with water
Lev 4:11 with his head, and with his l
Lev 8:21 the inwards and the l in water
Lev 9:14 he did wash the inwards and the l
Lev 11:21 which have l above their feet, to
Deut 28:35 thee in the knees, and in the l
1Sa 17:6 had greaves of brass upon his l
Ps 147:10 not pleasure in the l of a man
Prov 26:7 The l of the lame are not equal
Song 5:15 His l are as pillars of marble,
Is 3:20 and the ornaments of the l
Dan 2:33 His l of iron, his feet part of
Amos 3:12 of the mouth of the lion two l
Jn 19:31 that their l might be broken
Jn 19:32 brake the l of the first, and of
Jn 19:33 already, they brake not his l

**LEHABIM** *(le'-ha-bim) A son of Mizraim.*
Gen 10:13 begat Ludim, and Anamim, and L
1Chr 1:11 begat Ludim, and Anamim, and L

**LEHI** *(le'-hi)* See RAMATH-LEHI. *A district near Jerusalem.*
Judg 15:9 Judah, and spread themselves in L
Judg 15:14 And when he came unto L, the
Judg 15:19 which is in L unto this day

**LEMUEL** *(lem'-u-el) A king mentioned in Proverbs.*
Prov 31:1 The words of king L, the prophecy
Prov 31:4 It is not for kings, O L, it is

**LEND**
Ex 22:25 If thou l money to any of my
Lev 25:37 nor l him thy victuals for
Deut 15:6 thou shalt l unto many nations,
Deut 15:8 shalt surely l him sufficient for
Deut 23:19 Thou shalt not l upon usury to
Deut 23:20 stranger thou mayest l upon usury
Deut 23:20 thou shalt not l upon usury
Deut 24:10 When thou dost l thy brother any
Deut 24:11 the man to whom thou dost l shall
Deut 28:12 thou shalt l unto many nations,
Deut 28:44 He shall l to thee, and thou shalt
Deut 28:44 and thou shalt not l to him
Lk 6:34 if ye l to them of whom ye hope
Lk 6:34 for sinners also l to sinners
Lk 6:35 ye your enemies, and do good, and l
Lk 11:5 him, Friend, l me three loaves

**LENDETH**
Deut 15:2 Every creditor that l ought unto
Ps 37:26 He is ever merciful, and l
Ps 112:5 A good man sheweth favour, and l
Prov 19:17 upon the poor l unto the LORD

**LENGTH**
Gen 6:15 The l of the ark shall be three
Gen 13:17 through the land in the l of it
Ex 25:10 and a half shall be the l thereof
Ex 25:17 and a half shall be the l thereof
Ex 25:23 two cubits shall be the l thereof
Ex 26:2 The l of one curtain shall be
Ex 26:8 The l of one curtain shall be
Ex 26:13 the l of the curtains of the tent
Ex 26:16 cubits shall be the l of a board
Ex 27:11 l there shall be hangings of an
Ex 27:18 The l of the court shall be an
Ex 28:16 a span shall be the l thereof
Ex 30:2 A cubit shall be the l thereof
Ex 36:9 The l of one curtain was twenty
Ex 36:15 The l of one curtain was thirty
Ex 36:21 The l of a board was ten cubits,
Ex 37:1 cubits and a half was the l of it
Ex 37:6 and a half was the l thereof
Ex 37:10 two cubits was the l thereof
Ex 37:25 the l of it was a cubit, and the
Ex 38:1 five cubits was the l thereof
Ex 38:18 and twenty cubits was the l
Ex 39:9 a span was the l thereof, and a
Deut 3:11 nine cubits was the l thereof
Deut 30:20 is thy life, and the l of thy days
Judg 3:16 which had two edges, of a cubit l
1Kin 6:2 the l thereof was threescore
1Kin 6:3 twenty cubits was the l thereof
1Kin 6:20 forepart was twenty cubits in l
1Kin 7:2 the l thereof was an hundred
1Kin 7:6 the l thereof was fifty cubits,
1Kin 7:27 four cubits was the l of one base
2Chr 3:3 The l by cubits after the first
2Chr 3:4 the l of it was according to the
2Chr 3:8 the l whereof was according to
2Chr 4:1 twenty cubits the l thereof
Job 12:12 in l of days understanding
Ps 21:4 even l of days for ever and ever
Prov 3:2 For l of days, and long life, and
Prov 3:16 L of days is in her right hand
Prov 29:21 have him become his son at the l
Eze 31:7 in the l of his branches
Eze 40:11 the l of the gate, thirteen
Eze 40:18 the l of the gates was the lower
Eze 40:20 north, he measured the l thereof
Eze 40:21 the l thereof was fifty cubits,
Eze 40:25 the l was fifty cubits, and the
Eze 40:36 the l was fifty cubits, and the
Eze 40:49 The l of the porch was twenty
Eze 41:2 and he measured the l thereof
Eze 41:4 So he measured the l thereof
Eze 41:12 the l thereof ninety cubits
Eze 41:15 he measured the l of the building
Eze 41:22 high, and the l thereof two cubits
Eze 41:22 the l thereof, and the walls
Eze 42:2 Before the l of an hundred cubits
Eze 42:7 the l thereof was fifty cubits
Eze 42:8 For the l of the chambers that
Eze 45:1 the l shall be the l of five
Eze 45:2 the sanctuary five hundred in l
Eze 45:3 shalt thou measure the l of five
Eze 45:5 the five and twenty thousand of l
Eze 45:7 the l shall be over against one
Eze 48:8 in l as one of the other parts,
Eze 48:9 of five and twenty thousand in l
Eze 48:10 five and twenty thousand in l
Eze 48:10 five and twenty thousand in l
Eze 48:13 have five and twenty thousand in l
Eze 48:13 all the l shall be five and twenty
Eze 48:18 the residue in l over against the
Zec 2:2 thereof, and what is the l thereof
Zec 5:2 the l thereof is twenty cubits,
Rom 1:10 if by any means now at l I might
Eph 3:18 saints what is the breadth, and l
Rev 21:16 the l is as large as the breadth
Rev 21:16 The l and the breadth and the

**LENT**
Ex 12:36 so that they l unto them such
Deut 23:19 of any thing that is l upon usury
1Sa 1:28 also I have l him to the LORD
1Sa 1:28 liveth he shall be l to the LORD
1Sa 2:20 the loan which is l to the LORD
Jer 15:10 I have neither l on usury
Jer 15:10 nor men have l to me on usury

**LENTILES**
Gen 25:34 gave Esau bread and pottage of l
2Sa 17:28 and parched corn, and beans, and l
2Sa 23:11 was a piece of ground full of l
Eze 4:9 wheat, and barley, and beans, and l

**LEOPARD**
Is 11:6 the l shall lie down with the kid
Jer 5:6 a l shall watch over their cities
Jer 13:23 his skin, or the l his spots
Dan 7:6 I beheld, and lo another, like a l
Hos 13:7 as a l by the way will I observe
Rev 13:2 which I saw was like unto a l

**LEPER**
Lev 13:45 the l in whom the plague is, his
Lev 14:2 the l in the day of his cleansing
Lev 14:3 of leprosy be healed in the l
Lev 22:4 of the seed of Aaron is a l
Num 5:2 they put out of the camp every l
2Sa 3:29 hath an issue, or that is a l
2Kin 5:1 man in valour, but he was a l
2Kin 5:11 over the place, and recover the l
2Kin 5:27 his presence a l as white as snow
2Kin 15:5 so that he was a l unto the day
2Chr 26:21 Uzziah the king was a l unto the
2Chr 26:21 in a several house, being a l
2Chr 26:23 for they said, He is a l
Mt 8:2 And, behold, there came a l
Mt 26:6 in the house of Simon the l
Mk 1:40 And there came a l to him,
Mk 14:3 in the house of Simon the l

**LEPERS**
2Kin 7:8 And when these l came to the
Mt 10:8 Heal the sick, cleanse the l
Mt 11:5 the l are cleansed, and the deaf
Lk 4:27 many l were in Israel in the time
Lk 7:22 the l are cleansed, the deaf hear
Lk 17:12 there met him ten men that were l

**LEPROSY**
Lev 13:2 of his flesh like the plague of l
Lev 13:3 of his flesh, it is a plague of l
Lev 13:8 it is a l
Lev 13:9 When the plague of l is in a man

Lev 13:11 It is an old *l* in the skin of his
Lev 13:12 if a *l* break out abroad in the
Lev 13:12 the *l* cover all the skin of him
Lev 13:13 if the *l* have covered all his
Lev 13:15 it is a *l*
Lev 13:20 it is a plague of *l* broken out of
Lev 13:25 it is a *l* broken out of the
Lev 13:25 it is the plague of *l*
Lev 13:27 it is the plague of *l*
Lev 13:30 even a *l* upon the head or beard
Lev 13:42 it is a *l* sprung up in his bald
Lev 13:43 as the *l* appeareth in the skin of
Lev 13:47 also that the plague of *l* is in
Lev 13:49 it is a plague of *l*, and shall be
Lev 13:51 the plague is a fretting *l*
Lev 13:52 for it is a fretting *l*
Lev 13:59 of *l* in a garment of woollen or
Lev 14:3 if the plague of *l* be healed in
Lev 14:7 cleansed from the *l* seven times
Lev 14:32 of him in whom is the plague of *l*
Lev 14:34 I put the plague of *l* in a house
Lev 14:44 it is a fretting *l* in the house
Lev 14:54 law for all manner of plague of *l*
Lev 14:55 for the *l* of a garment, and of a
Lev 14:57 this is the law of *l*
Deut 24:8 Take heed in the plague of *l*
2Kin 5:3 for he would recover him of his *l*
2Kin 5:6 thou mayest recover him of his *l*
2Kin 5:7 unto me to recover a man of his *l*
2Kin 5:27 The *l* therefore of Naaman shall
2Chr 26:19 the *l* even rose up in his
Mt 8:3 And immediately his *l* was cleansed
Mk 1:42 immediately the *l* departed from
Lk 5:12 city, behold a man full of *l*
Lk 5:13 immediately the *l* departed from

**LEPROUS**

Ex 4:6 behold, his hand was *l* as snow
Lev 13:44 He is a *l* man, he is unclean
Num 12:10 and, behold, Miriam became *l*
Num 12:10 Miriam, and, behold, she was *l*
2Kin 7:3 there were four *l* men at the
2Chr 26:20 he was *l* in his forehead, and they

**LESHEM** *(le'-shem)* See LAISH. *Same as Laish.*

Josh 19:47 of Dan went up to fight against *L*
Josh 19:47 it, and dwelt therein, and called *L*

**LETTER**

2Sa 11:14 that David wrote a *l* to Joab
2Sa 11:15 And he wrote in the *l*, saying, Set
2Kin 5:5 I will send a *l* unto the king of
2Kin 5:6 he brought the *l* to the king of
2Kin 5:6 Now when this *l* is come unto thee
2Kin 5:7 the king of Israel had read the *l*
2Kin 10:2 as soon as this *l* cometh to you
2Kin 10:6 Then he wrote a *l* the second time
2Kin 10:7 when the *l* came to them, that
2Kin 19:14 Hezekiah received the *l* of the
Ezr 4:7 the writing of the *l* was written
Ezr 4:8 Shimshai the scribe wrote a *l*
Ezr 4:11 of the *l* that they sent unto him
Ezr 4:18 The *l* which ye sent unto us hath
Ezr 4:23 *l* was read before Rehum, and
Ezr 5:5 by *l* concerning this matter
Ezr 5:6 The copy of the *l* that Tatnai
Ezr 5:7 They sent a *l* unto him, wherein
Ezr 7:11 Now this is the copy of the *l*
Neh 2:8 a *l* unto Asaph the keeper of the
Neh 6:5 time with an open *l* in his hand
Est 9:26 for all the words of this *l*
Est 9:29 to confirm this second *l* of Purim
Is 37:14 Hezekiah received the *l* from the
Jer 29:1 *l* that Jeremiah the prophet sent
Jer 29:29 *l* in the ears of Jeremiah the
Acts 23:25 he wrote a *l* after this manner
Acts 23:34 when the governor had read the *l*
Rom 2:27 the law, judge thee, who by the *l*
Rom 2:29 in the spirit, and not in the *l*
Rom 7:6 and not in the oldness of the *l*
2Cor 3:6 not of the *l*, but of the spirit
2Cor 3:6 for the *l* killeth, but the spirit
2Cor 7:8 though I made you sorry with a *l*
Gal 6:11 Ye see how large a *l* I have
2Th 2:2 nor by *l* as from us, as that the
Heb 13:22 for I have written a *l* unto you

**LETTERS**

1Kin 21:8 So she wrote *l* in Ahab's name, and
1Kin 21:8 sent the *l* unto the elders and to
1Kin 21:9 And she wrote in the *l*, saying,
1Kin 21:11 as it was written in the *l* which
2Kin 10:1 And Jehu wrote *l*, and sent to
2Kin 20:12 Baladan, king of Babylon, sent *l*
2Chr 30:1 wrote *l* also to Ephraim and
2Chr 30:6 went with the *l* from the king
2Chr 32:17 He wrote also *l* to rail on the
Neh 2:7 king, let *l* be given me to the
Neh 2:9 river, and gave them the king's *l*
Neh 6:17 of Judah sent many *l* unto Tobiah
Neh 6:17 the *l* of Tobiah came unto them
Neh 6:19 Tobiah sent *l* to put me in fear
Est 1:22 For he sent *l* into all the king's
Est 3:13 the *l* were sent by posts into all
Est 8:5 the *l* devised by Haman the son of
Est 8:10 sent *l* by posts on horseback, and
Est 9:20 sent *l* unto all the Jews that
Est 9:25 he commanded by *l* that his wicked
Est 9:30 he sent the *l* unto all the Jews,
Is 39:1 Baladan, king of Babylon, sent *l*
Jer 29:25 Because thou hast sent *l* in thy
Lk 23:38 written over him in *l* of Greek
Jn 7:15 saying, How knoweth this man *l*
Acts 9:2 desired of him *l* to Damascus to
Acts 15:23 they wrote *l* by them after this
Acts 22:5 I received *l* unto the brethren
Acts 28:21 We neither received *l* out of
1Cor 16:3 ye shall approve by your *l*
2Cor 3:1 or *l* of commendation from you
2Cor 10:9 as if I would terrify you by *l*
2Cor 10:10 For his *l*, say they, are weighty
2Cor 10:11 in word by *l* when we are absent

**LETUSHIM** *(le-tu'-shim) A son of Dedan.*

Gen 25:3 sons of Dedan were Asshurim, and *L*

**LEUMMIM** *(le-um'-mim) A son of Dedan.*

Gen 25:3 were Asshurim, and Letushim, and *L*

**LEVI** *(le'-vi)* See LEVITE, LEVITICAL, MATTHEW.

*1. A son of Jacob.*

Gen 29:34 therefore was his name called *L*
Gen 34:25 of the sons of Jacob, Simeon and *L*
Gen 34:30 And Jacob said to Simeon and *L*
Gen 35:23 firstborn, and Simeon, and *L*
Gen 49:5 Simeon and *L* are brethren
Ex 1:2 Reuben, Simeon, *L*, and Judah,
Ex 6:16 are the names of the sons of *L*
Ex 6:16 life of *L* were an hundred thirty
Num 3:17 were the sons of *L* by their names
Num 16:1 the son of Kohath, the son of *L*
Num 26:59 was Jochebed, the daughter of *L*
Num 26:59 her mother bare to *L* in Egypt
1Chr 6:38 the son of Kohath, the son of *L*
1Chr 6:43 the son of Gershom, the son of *L*
1Chr 6:47 the son of Merari, the son of *L*
Ezr 8:18 the sons of Mahli, the son of *L*

*2. The tribe.*

Gen 46:11 And the sons of *L*
Ex 2:1 went a man of the house of *L*
Ex 2:1 and took to wife a daughter of *L*
Ex 6:19 these are the families of *L*
Ex 32:26 all the sons of *L* gathered
Ex 32:28 the children of *L* did according
Num 1:49 shalt not number the tribe of *L*
Num 3:6 Bring the tribe of *L* near
Num 3:15 Number the children of *L* after
Num 4:2 Kohath from among the sons of *L*
Num 16:7 too much upon you, ye sons of *L*
Num 16:8 Hear, I pray you, ye sons of *L*
Num 16:10 brethren the sons of *L* with thee
Num 17:3 Aaron's name upon the rod of *L*
Num 17:8 for the house of *L* was budded
Num 18:2 brethren also of the tribe of *L*
Num 18:21 I have given the children of *L*
Deut 10:8 the LORD separated the tribe of *L*
Deut 10:9 Wherefore *L* hath no part nor
Deut 18:1 Levites, and all the tribe of *L*
Deut 21:5 the sons of *L* shall come near
Deut 27:12 Simeon, and *L*, and Judah, and
Deut 31:9 it unto the priests the sons of *L*
Deut 33:8 of *L* he said, Let thy Thummim and
Josh 13:14 Only unto the tribe of *L* he gave
Josh 13:33 But unto the tribe of *L* Moses
Josh 21:10 who were of the children of *L*
1Kin 12:31 which were not of the sons of *L*
1Chr 2:1 Reuben, Simeon, *L*, and Judah,
1Chr 6:1 The sons of *L*; Gershon
1Chr 6:16 The sons of *L*; Gershom
1Chr 9:18 companies of the children of *L*
1Chr 12:26 the children of *L* four thousand
1Chr 21:6 But *L* and Benjamin counted he not
1Chr 23:6 into courses among the sons of *L*
1Chr 23:14 sons were named of the tribe of *L*
1Chr 23:24 These were the sons of *L* after
1Chr 24:20 rest of the sons of *L* were these
Ezr 8:15 found there none of the sons of *L*
Neh 10:39 the children of *L* shall bring the
Neh 12:23 The sons of *L*, the chief of the
Ps 135:20 Bless the LORD, O house of *L*
Eze 40:46 sons of Zadok among the sons of *L*
Eze 48:31 one gate of Judah, one gate of *L*
Zec 12:13 family of the house of *L* apart
Mal 2:4 that my covenant might be with *L*
Mal 2:8 have corrupted the covenant of *L*
Mal 3:3 and he shall purify the sons of *L*
Heb 7:5 they that are of the sons of *L*
Heb 7:9 *L* also, who receiveth tithes,
Rev 7:7 Of the tribe of *L* were sealed

*3. Same as Matthew the apostle.*

Mk 2:14 he saw *L* the son of Alphaeus
Lk 5:27 forth, and saw a publican, named *L*
Lk 5:29 *L* made him a great feast in his

*4. Father of Matthat; ancestor of Jesus.*

Lk 3:24 Matthat, which was the son of *L*

*5. Father of another Matthat; ancestor of Jesus.*

Lk 3:29 Matthat, which was the son of *L*

**LEVIATHAN**

Job 41:1 thou draw out *l* with an hook
Ps 74:14 brakest the heads of *l* in pieces
Ps 104:26 there is that *l*, whom thou hast
Is 27:1 punish *l* the piercing serpent
Is 27:1 even *l* that crooked serpent

**LEVITE** *(le'-vite)* See LEVITES, LEVITICAL. *A descendant of Levi.*

Ex 4:14 Is not Aaron the *L* thy brother
Deut 12:12 the *L* that is within your gates
Deut 12:18 the *L* that is within thy gates
Deut 12:19 that thou forsake not the *L* as
Deut 14:27 the *L* that is within thy gates
Deut 14:29 And the *L*, (because he hath no
Deut 16:11 the *L* that is within thy gates,
Deut 16:14 and thy maidservant, and the *L*
Deut 18:6 if a *L* come from any of thy gates
Deut 26:11 unto thine house, thou, and the *L*
Deut 26:12 and hast given it unto the *L*
Deut 26:13 also have given them unto the *L*
Judg 17:7 the family of Judah, who was a *L*
Judg 17:9 I am a *L* of Beth-lehem-judah, and
Judg 17:10 So the *L* went in
Judg 17:11 the *L* was content to dwell with
Judg 17:12 And Micah consecrated the *L*
Judg 17:13 seeing I have a *L* to my priest
Judg 18:3 the voice of the young man the *L*
Judg 18:15 the house of the young man the *L*
Judg 19:1 that there was a certain *L*
Judg 20:4 And the *L*, the husband of the
2Chr 20:14 a *L* of the sons of Asaph, came
2Chr 31:12 which Cononiah the *L* was ruler
2Chr 31:14 And Kore the son of Imnah the *L*
Ezr 10:15 and Shabbethai the *L* helped them
Lk 10:32 And likewise a *L*, when he was at
Acts 4:36 The son of consolation,) a *L*

**LEVITES**

Ex 6:25 the *L* according to their families
Ex 38:21 Moses, for the service of the *L*
Lev 25:32 the cities of the *L*, and the
Lev 25:32 may the *L* redeem at any time
Lev 25:33 And if a man purchase of the *L*
Lev 25:33 *L* are their possession among the
Num 1:47 But the *L* after the tribe of
Num 1:50 the *L* over the tabernacle of
Num 1:51 forward, the *L* shall take it down
Num 1:51 be pitched, the *L* shall set it up
Num 1:53 But the *L* shall pitch round about
Num 1:53 the *L* shall keep the charge of
Num 2:17 of the *L* in the midst of the camp
Num 2:33 But the *L* were not numbered among
Num 3:9 thou shalt give the *L* unto Aaron
Num 3:12 I have taken the *L* from among the
Num 3:12 therefore the *L* shall be mine
Num 3:20 These are the families of the *L*
Num 3:32 be chief over the chief of the *L*
Num 3:39 All that were numbered of the *L*
Num 3:41 thou shalt take the *L* for me (I
Num 3:41 the cattle of the *L* instead of
Num 3:45 Take the *L* instead of all the
Num 3:45 the cattle of the *L* instead of
Num 3:45 and the *L* shall be mine
Num 3:46 Israel, which are more than the *L*
Num 3:49 them that were redeemed by the *L*

Num 4:18 the Kohathites from among the *L*
Num 4:46 those that were numbered of the *L*
Num 7:5 thou shalt give them unto the *L*
Num 7:6 the oxen, and gave them unto the *L*
Num 8:6 Take the *L* from among the
Num 8:9 thou shalt bring the *L* before the
Num 8:10 shalt bring the *L* before the LORD
Num 8:10 shall put their hands upon the *L*
Num 8:11 Aaron shall offer the *L* before
Num 8:12 the *L* shall lay their hands upon
Num 8:12 to make an atonement for the *L*
Num 8:13 thou shalt set the *L* before Aaron
Num 8:14 the *L* from among the children of
Num 8:14 and the *L* shall be mine
Num 8:15 after that shall the *L* go in to
Num 8:18 I have taken the *L* for all the
Num 8:19 I have given the *L* as a gift to
Num 8:20 did to the *L* according unto all
Num 8:20 commanded Moses concerning the *L*
Num 8:21 the *L* were purified, and they
Num 8:22 after that went the *L* in to do
Num 8:22 commanded Moses concerning the *L*
Num 8:24 is it that belongeth unto the *L*
Num 8:26 unto the *L* touching their charge
Num 18:6 the *L* from among the children of
Num 18:23 But the *L* shall do the service of
Num 18:24 I have given to the *L* to inherit
Num 18:26 Thus speak unto the *L*, and say
Num 18:30 unto the *L* as the increase of the
Num 26:57 of the *L* after their families
Num 26:58 These are the families of the *L*
Num 31:30 beasts, and give them unto the *L*
Num 31:47 of beast, and gave them unto the *L*
Num 35:2 that they give unto the *L* of the
Num 35:2 ye shall give also unto the *L*
Num 35:4 which ye shall give unto the *L*
Num 35:6 which ye shall give unto the *L*
Num 35:7 give to the *L* shall be forty
Num 35:8 give of his cities unto the *L*
Deut 17:9 shalt come unto the priests the *L*
Deut 17:18 which is before the priests the *L*
Deut 18:1 The priests the *L*, and all the
Deut 18:7 God, as all his brethren the *L* do
Deut 24:8 the priests the *L* shall teach you
Deut 27:9 the priests the *L* spake unto all
Deut 27:14 the *L* shall speak, and say unto
Deut 31:25 That Moses commanded the *L*
Josh 3:3 and the priests the *L* bearing it
Josh 8:33 side before the priests the *L*
Josh 14:3 but unto the *L* he gave none
Josh 14:4 no part unto the *L* in the land
Josh 18:7 But the *L* have no part among you
Josh 21:1 of the *L* unto Eleazar the priest
Josh 21:3 of Israel gave unto the *L* out of
Josh 21:4 the priest, which were of the *L*
Josh 21:8 of Israel gave by lot unto the *L*
Josh 21:20 the *L* which remained of the
Josh 21:27 Gershon, of the families of the *L*
Josh 21:34 of Merari, the rest of the *L*
Josh 21:40 of the families of the *L*, were by
Josh 21:41 All the cities of the *L* within
1Sa 6:15 the *L* took down the ark of the
2Sa 15:24 all the *L* were with him, bearing
1Kin 8:4 did the priests and the *L* bring up
1Chr 6:19 the *L* according to their fathers
1Chr 6:48 Their brethren also the *L* were
1Chr 6:64 children of Israel gave to the *L*
1Chr 9:2 the Israelites, the priests, *L*
1Chr 9:14 And of the *L*
1Chr 9:26 For these *L*, the four chief
1Chr 9:31 And Mattithiah, one of the *L*
1Chr 9:33 chief of the fathers of the *L*
1Chr 9:34 These chief fathers of the *L* were
1Chr 13:2 *L* which are in their cities and
1Chr 15:2 to carry the ark of God but the *L*
1Chr 15:4 the children of Aaron, and the *L*
1Chr 15:11 the priests, and for the *L*
1Chr 15:12 the chief of the fathers of the *L*
1Chr 15:14 the *L* sanctified themselves to
1Chr 15:15 the children of the *L* bare the
1Chr 15:16 *L* to appoint their brethren to be
1Chr 15:17 So the *L* appointed Heman the son
1Chr 15:22 And Chenaniah, chief of the *L*
1Chr 15:26 when God helped the *L* that bare
1Chr 15:27 all the *L* that bare the ark, and
1Chr 16:4 he appointed certain of the *L* to
1Chr 23:2 Israel, with the priests and the *L*
1Chr 23:3 Now the *L* were numbered from the
1Chr 23:26 And also unto the *L*
1Chr 23:27 by the last words of David the *L*
1Chr 24:6 the scribe, one of the *L*, wrote
1Chr 24:6 the fathers of the priests and *L*
1Chr 24:30 of the *L* after the house of their
1Chr 24:31 the fathers of the priests and *L*
1Chr 26:17 Eastward were six *L*, northward
1Chr 26:20 And of the *L*, Ahijah was over the
1Chr 27:17 Of the *L*, Hashabiah the son of
1Chr 28:13 courses of the priests and the *L*
1Chr 28:21 courses of the priests and the *L*
2Chr 5:4 and the *L* took up the ark
2Chr 5:5 did the priests and the *L* bring up
2Chr 5:12 Also the *L* which were the singers
2Chr 7:6 the *L* also with instruments of
2Chr 8:14 the *L* to their charges, to praise
2Chr 8:15 *L* concerning any matter, or
2Chr 11:13 the *L* that were in all Israel
2Chr 11:14 For the *L* left their suburbs and
2Chr 13:9 LORD, the sons of Aaron, and the *L*
2Chr 13:10 the *L* wait upon their business
2Chr 17:8 And with them he sent *L*, even
2Chr 17:8 and Tobijah, and Tob-adonijah, *L*
2Chr 19:8 did Jehoshaphat set of the *L*
2Chr 19:11 also the *L* shall be officers
2Chr 20:19 And the *L*, of the children of the
2Chr 23:2 gathered the *L* out of all the
2Chr 23:4 of the priests and of the *L*
2Chr 23:6 and they that minister of the *L*
2Chr 23:7 the *L* shall compass the king
2Chr 23:8 So the *L* and all Judah did
2Chr 23:18 by the hand of the priests the *L*
2Chr 24:5 together the priests and the *L*
2Chr 24:5 Howbeit the *L* hastened it not
2Chr 24:6 of the *L* to bring in out of Judah
2Chr 24:11 office by the hand of the *L*
2Chr 29:4 brought in the priests and the *L*
2Chr 29:5 And said unto them, Hear me, ye *L*
2Chr 29:12 Then the *L* arose, Mahath the son
2Chr 29:16 the *L* took it, to carry it out
2Chr 29:25 he set the *L* in the house of the
2Chr 29:26 the *L* stood with the instruments
2Chr 29:30 the princes commanded the *L* to
2Chr 29:34 brethren the *L* did help them
2Chr 29:34 for the *L* were more upright in
2Chr 30:15 the *L* were ashamed, and sanctified
2Chr 30:16 received of the hand of the *L*
2Chr 30:17 therefore the *L* had the charge of
2Chr 30:21 and the *L* and the priests praised
2Chr 30:22 *L* that taught the good knowledge
2Chr 30:25 Judah, with the priests and the *L*
2Chr 30:27 Then the priests the *L* arose
2Chr 31:2 the *L* after their courses, every
2Chr 31:2 *L* for burnt offerings and for
2Chr 31:4 portion of the priests and the *L*
2Chr 31:9 the *L* concerning the heaps
2Chr 31:17 the *L* from twenty years old and
2Chr 31:19 by genealogies among the *L*
2Chr 34:9 which the *L* that kept the doors
2Chr 34:12 were Jahath and Obadiah, the *L*
2Chr 34:12 and other of the *L*, all that could
2Chr 34:13 of the *L* there were scribes, and
2Chr 34:30 and the priests, and the *L*
2Chr 35:3 said unto the *L* that taught all
2Chr 35:5 division of the families of the *L*
2Chr 35:8 to the priests, and to the *L*
2Chr 35:9 Jeiel and Jozabad, chief of the *L*
2Chr 35:9 gave unto the *L* for passover
2Chr 35:10 the *L* in their courses, according
2Chr 35:11 their hands, and the *L* flayed them
2Chr 35:14 therefore the *L* prepared for
2Chr 35:15 brethren the *L* prepared for them
2Chr 35:18 kept, and the priests, and the *L*
Ezr 1:5 and the priests, and the *L*
Ezr 2:40 The *L*: the children
Ezr 2:70 So the priests, and the *L*, and some
Ezr 3:8 brethren the priests and the *L*
Ezr 3:8 and appointed the *L*, from twenty
Ezr 3:9 sons and their brethren the *L*
Ezr 3:10 the *L* the sons of Asaph with
Ezr 3:12 But many of the priests and *L*
Ezr 6:16 of Israel, the priests, and the *L*
Ezr 6:18 the *L* in their courses, for the
Ezr 6:20 the *L* were purified together, all
Ezr 7:7 and of the priests, and the *L*
Ezr 7:13 of Israel, and of his priests and *L*
Ezr 7:24 touching any of the priests and *L*
Ezr 8:20 for the service of the *L*, two
Ezr 8:29 the chief of the priests and the *L*
Ezr 8:30 the *L* the weight of the silver,
Ezr 8:33 and Noadiah the son of Binnui, *L*
Ezr 9:1 Israel, and the priests, and the *L*
Ezr 10:5 and made the chief priests, the *L*
Ezr 10:23 Also of the *L*
Neh 3:17 After him repaired the *L*, Rehum
Neh 7:1 singers and the *L* were appointed,
Neh 7:43 The *L*: the children
Neh 7:73 So the priests, and the *L*, and the
Neh 8:7 Jozabad, Hanan, Pelaiah, and the *L*
Neh 8:9 the *L* that taught the people,
Neh 8:11 So the *L* stilled all the people,
Neh 8:13 the people, the priests, and the *L*
Neh 9:4 up upon the stairs, of the *L*
Neh 9:5 Then the *L*, Jeshua, and Kadmiel,
Neh 9:38 and our princes, *L*, and priests,
Neh 10:9 And the *L*: both Jeshua
Neh 10:28 of the people, the priests, the *L*
Neh 10:34 the lots among the priests, the *L*
Neh 10:37 tithes of our ground unto the *L*
Neh 10:37 that the same *L* might have the
Neh 10:38 son of Aaron shall be with the *L*
Neh 10:38 when the *L* take tithes
Neh 10:38 the *L* shall bring up the tithe of
Neh 11:3 Israel, the priests, and the *L*
Neh 11:15 Also of the *L*
Neh 11:16 and Jozabad, of the chief of the *L*
Neh 11:18 All the *L* in the holy city were
Neh 11:20 Israel, of the priests, and the *L*
Neh 11:22 The overseer also of the *L* at
Neh 11:36 of the *L* were divisions in Judah,
Neh 12:1 and the *L* that went up with
Neh 12:8 Moreover the *L*: Jeshua,
Neh 12:22 The *L* in the days of Eliashib,
Neh 12:24 And the chief of the *L*
Neh 12:27 the *L* out of all their places
Neh 12:30 the *L* purified themselves, and
Neh 12:44 of the law for the priests and *L*
Neh 12:44 priests and for the *L* that waited
Neh 12:47 sanctified holy things unto the *L*
Neh 12:47 the *L* sanctified them unto the
Neh 13:5 commanded to be given to the *L*
Neh 13:10 of the *L* had not been given them
Neh 13:10 for the *L* and the singers, that
Neh 13:13 and Zadok the scribe, and of the *L*
Neh 13:22 I commanded the *L* that they
Neh 13:29 of the priesthood, and of the *L*
Neh 13:30 the wards of the priests and the *L*
Is 66:21 take of them for priests and for *L*
Jer 33:18 *L* want a man before me to offer
Jer 33:21 with the *L* the priests, my
Jer 33:22 the *L* that minister unto me
Eze 43:19 *L* that be of the seed of Zadok
Eze 44:10 the *L* that are gone away far from
Eze 44:15 But the priests the *L*, the sons
Eze 45:5 of breadth, shall also the *L*
Eze 48:11 went astray, as the *L* went astray
Eze 48:12 most holy by the border of the *L*
Eze 48:13 the priests the *L* shall have five
Eze 48:22 from the possession of the *L*
Jn 1:19 *L* from Jerusalem to ask him, Who

**LEVITICAL** *(le-vit'-i-cal) Belonging to the Levites.*

Heb 7:11 were by the *L* priesthood, (for

**LEVY**

Num 31:28 *l* a tribute unto the LORD of the
1Kin 5:13 raised a *l* out of all Israel
1Kin 5:13 the *l* was thirty thousand men
1Kin 5:14 and Adoniram was over the *l*
1Kin 9:15 the *l* which king Solomon raised
1Kin 9:21 upon those did Solomon *l* a

**LEWDNESS**

Judg 20:6 for they have committed *l*
Jer 11:15 she hath wrought *l* with many
Jer 13:27 the *l* of thy whoredom, and thine
Eze 16:43 thou shalt not commit this *l*
Eze 16:58 Thou hast borne thy *l* and thine
Eze 22:9 the midst of thee they commit *l*
Eze 23:21 to remembrance the *l* of thy youth
Eze 23:27 I make thy *l* to cease from thee
Eze 23:29 shall be discovered, both thy *l*
Eze 23:35 therefore bear thou also thy *l*
Eze 23:48 Thus will I cause *l* to cease out
Eze 23:48 be taught not to do after your *l*
Eze 23:49 shall recompense your *l* upon you
Eze 24:13 In thy filthiness is *l*
Hos 2:10 now will I discover her *l* in the
Hos 6:9 for they commit *l*
Acts 18:14 a matter of wrong or wicked *l*

**LIAR**
Job 24:25 not so now, who will make me a *l*
Prov 17:4 a *l* giveth ear to a naughty
Prov 19:22 a poor man is better than a *l*
Prov 30:6 thee, and thou be found a *l*
Jer 15:18 thou be altogether unto me as a *l*
Jn 8:44 for he is a *l*, and the father of
Jn 8:55 I shall be a *l* like unto you
Rom 3:4 God be true, but every man a *l*
1Jn 1:10 have not sinned, we make him a *l*
1Jn 2:4 not his commandments, is a *l*
1Jn 2:22 Who is a *l* but he that denieth
1Jn 4:20 and hateth his brother, he is a *l*
1Jn 5:10 not God hath made him a *l*

**LIARS**
Deut 33:29 shall be found *l* unto thee
Ps 116:11 I said in my haste, All men are *l*
Is 44:25 frustrateth the tokens of the *l*
Jer 50:36 A sword is upon the *l*
1Ti 1:10 mankind, for menstealers, for *l*
Titus 1:12 said, The Cretians are alway *l*
Rev 2:2 and are not, and hast found them *l*
Rev 21:8 sorcerers, and idolaters, and all *l*

**LIBERAL**
Prov 11:25 The *l* soul shall be made fat
Is 32:5 person shall be no more called *l*
Is 32:8 But the *l* deviseth *l* things
Is 32:8 by *l* things shall he stand
2Cor 9:13 for your *l* distribution unto them

**LIBERTINES** *(lib'-ur-tins) Former Jewish slaves.*
Acts 6:9 is called the synagogue of the *L*

**LIBERTY**
Lev 25:10 proclaim *l* throughout all the
Ps 119:45 And I will walk at *l*
Is 61:1 to proclaim *l* to the captives, and
Jer 34:8 to proclaim *l* unto them
Jer 34:15 in proclaiming *l* every man to his
Jer 34:16 he had set at *l* at their pleasure
Jer 34:17 unto me, in proclaiming *l*
Jer 34:17 behold, I proclaim a *l* for you
Eze 46:17 it shall be his to the year of *l*
Lk 4:18 to set at *l* them that are bruised
Acts 24:23 keep Paul, and to let him have *l*
Acts 26:32 This man might have been set at *l*
Acts 27:3 gave him *l* to go unto his friends
Rom 8:21 glorious *l* of the children of God
1Cor 7:39 she is at *l* to be married to whom
1Cor 8:9 means this *l* of yours become a
1Cor 10:29 for why is my *l* judged of another
2Cor 3:17 Spirit of the Lord is, there is *l*
Gal 2:4 *l* which we have in Christ Jesus
Gal 5:1 Stand fast therefore in the *l*
Gal 5:13 ye have been called unto *l*
Gal 5:13 only use not *l* for an occasion to
Heb 13:23 our brother Timothy is set at *l*
Jas 1:25 looketh into the perfect law of *l*
Jas 2:12 shall be judged by the law of *l*
1Pet 2:16 not using your *l* for a cloke of
2Pet 2:19 While they promise them *l*

**LIBNAH** *(lib'-nah)* See LABAN.
*1. A Hebrew encampment in the wilderness.*
Num 33:20 Rimmon-parez, and pitched in *L*
Num 33:21 And they removed from *L*, and
*2. A Levitical city in Judah.*
Josh 10:29 and all Israel with him, unto *L*
Josh 10:29 unto Libnah, and fought against *L*
Josh 10:31 And Joshua passed from *L*, and all
Josh 10:32 to all that he had done to *L*
Josh 10:39 as he had done also to *L*, and to
Josh 12:15 The king of *L*, one
Josh 15:42 *L*, and Ether, and Ashan,
Josh 21:13 and *L* with her suburbs,
2Kin 8:22 Then *L* revolted at the same time
2Kin 19:8 king of Assyria warring against *L*
2Kin 23:31 the daughter of Jeremiah of *L*
2Kin 24:18 the daughter of Jeremiah of *L*
1Chr 6:57 *L* with her suburbs, and Jattir, and
2Chr 21:10 The same time also did *L* revolt
Is 37:8 king of Assyria warring against *L*
Jer 52:1 the daughter of Jeremiah of *L*

**LIBNI** *(lib'-ni)* See LAADAN, LIBNITES.
*1. Son of Gershon.*
Ex 6:17 *L*, and Shimi, according to their
Num 3:18 their families; *L*, and Shimei
1Chr 6:17 of Gershom; *L*, and Shimei
1Chr 6:20 *L* his son, Jahath his son, Zimmah
*2. Grandson of Merari.*
1Chr 6:29 *L* his son, Shimei his son, Uzza

**LIBNITES** *(lib'-nites) Descendants of Libni 1.*
Num 3:21 Gershon was the family of the *L*
Num 26:58 the family of the *L*, the family

**LIBYA** *(lib'-e-ah)* See LIBYANS. *A land in north Africa.*
Eze 30:5 Ethiopia, and *L*, and Lydia, and all
Eze 38:5 Persia, Ethiopia, and *L* with them
Acts 2:10 and in the parts of *L* about Cyrene

**LIBYANS** *(lib'-e-uns)* See LEHABIM. *Inhabitants of Libya.*
Jer 46:9 the Ethiopians and the *L*, that
Dan 11:43 and the *L* and the Ethiopians shall

**LICE**
Ex 8:16 that it may become *l* throughout
Ex 8:17 the earth, and it became *l* in man
Ex 8:17 *l* throughout all the land of
Ex 8:18 enchantments to bring forth *l*
Ex 8:18 so there were *l* upon man, and upon
Ps 105:31 flies, and *l* in all their coasts

**LICK**
Num 22:4 Now shall this company *l* up all
1Kin 21:19 of Naboth shall dogs *l* thy blood
Ps 72:9 and his enemies shall *l* the dust
Is 49:23 *l* up the dust of thy feet
Mic 7:17 They shall *l* the dust like a

**LICKED**
1Kin 18:38 *l* up the water that was in the
1Kin 21:19 In the place where dogs *l* the
1Kin 22:38 and the dogs *l* up his blood
Lk 16:21 the dogs came and *l* his sores

**LIE**
Gen 19:32 we will *l* with him, that we may
Gen 19:34 *l* with him, that we may preserve
Gen 30:15 Therefore he shall *l* with thee to
Gen 39:7 and she said, *L* with me
Gen 39:10 to *l* by her, or to be with her
Gen 39:12 by his garment, saying, *L* with me
Gen 39:14 he came in unto me to *l* with me
Gen 47:30 But I will *l* with my fathers, and
Ex 21:13 if a man *l* not in wait, but God
Ex 22:16 *l* with her, he shall surely endow
Ex 23:11 thou shalt let it rest and *l* still
Lev 6:2 *l* unto his neighbour in that
Lev 15:18 shall *l* with seed of copulation
Lev 15:24 if any man *l* with her at all, and
Lev 18:20 Moreover thou shalt not *l*
Lev 18:22 Thou shalt not *l* with mankind
Lev 18:23 Neither shalt thou *l* with any
Lev 18:23 before a beast to *l* down thereto
Lev 19:11 falsely, neither *l* one to another
Lev 20:12 if a man *l* with his daughter in
Lev 20:13 If a man also *l* with mankind
Lev 20:15 if a man *l* with a beast, he shall
Lev 20:16 *l* down thereto, thou shalt kill
Lev 20:18 if a man shall *l* with a woman
Lev 20:20 if a man shall *l* with his uncle's
Lev 26:6 in the land, and ye shall *l* down
Num 5:13 a man *l* with her carnally, and it
Num 10:5 then the camps that *l* on the east
Num 10:6 then the camps that *l* on the
Num 23:19 is not a man, that he should *l*
Num 23:24 he shall not *l* down until he eat
Deut 19:11 *l* in wait for him, and rise up
Deut 22:23 her in the city, and *l* with her
Deut 22:25 the man force her, and *l* with her
Deut 22:28 *l* with her, and they be found
Deut 25:2 judge shall cause him to *l* down
Deut 28:30 and another man shall *l* with her
Deut 29:20 in this book shall *l* upon him
Josh 8:4 ye shall *l* in wait against the
Josh 8:9 and they went to *l* in ambush
Josh 8:12 set them to *l* in ambush between
Judg 9:32 thee, and *l* in wait in the field
Judg 19:20 let all thy wants *l* upon me
Judg 21:20 *l* in wait in the vineyards
Ruth 3:4 mark the place where he shall *l*
Ruth 3:7 he went to *l* down at the end of
Ruth 3:13 *l* down until the morning
1Sa 3:5 *l* down again
1Sa 3:6 *l* down again
1Sa 3:9 Eli said unto Samuel, Go, *l* down
1Sa 15:29 of Israel will not *l* nor repent
1Sa 22:8 to *l* in wait, as at this day
1Sa 22:13 to *l* in wait, as at this day
2Sa 11:11 and to drink, and to *l* with my wife
2Sa 11:13 at even he went out to *l* on his
2Sa 12:11 he shall *l* with thy wives in the
2Sa 13:11 Come *l* with me, my sister
1Kin 1:2 let her *l* in thy bosom, that my
2Kin 4:16 do not *l* unto thine handmaid
Job 6:28 for it is evident unto you if I *l*
Job 7:4 When I *l* down, I say, When shall
Job 11:19 Also thou shalt *l* down, and none
Job 20:11 which shall *l* down with him in
Job 21:26 They shall *l* down alike in the
Job 27:19 The rich man shall *l* down
Job 34:6 Should I *l* against my right
Job 38:40 abide in the covert to *l* in wait
Ps 23:2 He maketh me to *l* down in green
Ps 57:4 I *l* even among them that are set
Ps 59:3 they *l* in wait for my soul
Ps 62:9 and men of high degree are a *l*
Ps 88:5 the slain that *l* in the grave
Ps 89:35 that I will not *l* unto David
Ps 119:69 proud have forged a *l* against me
Prov 3:24 yea, thou shalt *l* down, and thy
Prov 12:6 wicked are to *l* in wait for blood
Prov 14:5 A faithful witness will not *l*
Eccl 4:11 if two *l* together, then they have
Song 1:13 he shall *l* all night betwixt my
Is 11:6 leopard shall *l* down with the kid
Is 11:7 young ones shall *l* down together
Is 13:21 of the desert shall *l* there
Is 14:18 *l* in glory, every one in his own
Is 14:30 the needy shall *l* down in safety
Is 17:2 be for flocks, which shall *l* down
Is 27:10 feed, and there shall he *l* down
Is 33:8 The highways *l* waste, the
Is 34:10 to generation it shall *l* waste
Is 43:17 they shall *l* down together, they
Is 44:20 Is there not a *l* in my right hand
Is 50:11 ye shall *l* down in sorrow
Is 51:20 they *l* at the head of all the
Is 63:8 people, children that will not *l*
Is 65:10 place for the herds to *l* down in
Jer 3:25 We *l* down in our shame, and our
Jer 27:10 For they prophesy a *l* unto you
Jer 27:14 for they prophesy a *l* unto you
Jer 27:15 yet they prophesy a *l* in my name
Jer 27:16 for they prophesy a *l* unto you
Jer 28:15 this people to trust in a *l*
Jer 29:21 which prophesy a *l* unto you in my
Jer 29:31 and he caused you to trust in a *l*
Jer 33:12 causing their flocks to *l* down
Lam 2:21 the old *l* on the ground in the
Eze 4:4 *L* thou also upon thy left side,
Eze 4:4 of the days that thou shalt *l*
Eze 4:6 *l* again on thy right side, and
Eze 4:9 that thou shalt *l* upon thy side
Eze 21:29 whiles they divine a *l* unto thee
Eze 31:18 thou shalt *l* in the midst of the
Eze 32:21 they *l* uncircumcised, slain by
Eze 32:27 they shall not *l* with the mighty
Eze 32:28 shalt *l* with them that are slain
Eze 32:29 they shall *l* with the
Eze 32:30 they *l* uncircumcised with them
Eze 34:14 there shall they *l* in a good fold
Eze 34:15 and I will cause them to *l* down
Hos 2:18 will make them to *l* down safely
Hos 7:6 an oven, whiles they *l* in wait
Joel 1:13 *l* all night in sackcloth, ye
Amos 6:4 That *l* upon beds of ivory, and
Mic 1:14 be a *l* to the kings of Israel
Mic 2:11 in the spirit and falsehood do *l*
Mic 7:2 they all *l* in wait for blood
Hab 2:3 the end it shall speak, and not *l*
Zeph 2:7 shall they *l* down in the evening
Zeph 2:14 flocks shall *l* down in the midst
Zeph 2:15 a place for beasts to *l* down in
Zeph 3:13 *l* down, and none shall make them
Hag 1:4 houses, and this house *l* waste
Zec 10:2 and the diviners have seen a *l*
Jn 5:6 When Jesus saw him *l*, and knew
Jn 8:44 When he speaketh a *l*, he speaketh
Jn 20:6 and seeth the linen clothes *l*
Acts 5:3 heart to *l* to the Holy Ghost
Acts 23:21 for there *l* in wait for him of
Rom 1:25 changed the truth of God into a *l*
Rom 3:7 through my *l* unto his glory
Rom 9:1 I *l* not, my conscience also
2Cor 11:31 evermore, knoweth that I *l* not
Gal 1:20 you, behold, before God, I *l* not
Eph 4:14 whereby they *l* in wait to deceive
Col 3:9 *L* not one to another, seeing that

2Th 2:11 that they should believe a *l*
1Ti 2:7 the truth in Christ, and *l* not
Titus 1:2 life, which God, that cannot *l*
Heb 6:18 it was impossible for God to *l*
Jas 3:14 not, and *l* not against the truth
1Jn 1:6 him, and walk in darkness, we *l*
1Jn 2:21 that no *l* is of the truth
1Jn 2:27 things, and is truth, and is no *l*
Rev 3:9 are Jews, and are not, but do *l*
Rev 11:8 their dead bodies shall *l* in the
Rev 21:27 abomination, or maketh a *l*
Rev 22:15 and whosoever loveth and maketh a *l*

## LIED

1Kin 13:18 But he *l* unto him
Ps 78:36 they *l* unto him with their
Is 57:11 or feared, that thou hast *l*
Acts 5:4 thou hast not *l* unto men, but

## LIERS

Josh 8:13 their *l* in wait on the west of
Josh 8:14 *l* in ambush against him behind
Judg 9:25 the men of Shechem set *l* in wait
Judg 16:12 there were *l* in wait abiding in
Judg 20:29 Israel set *l* in wait round about
Judg 20:33 the *l* in wait of Israel came
Judg 20:36 the *l* in wait which they had set
Judg 20:37 the *l* in wait hasted, and rushed
Judg 20:37 the *l* in wait drew themselves
Judg 20:38 the *l* in wait, that they should

## LIES

Judg 16:10 thou hast mocked me, and told me *l*
Judg 16:13 thou hast mocked me, and told me *l*
Job 11:3 Should thy *l* make men hold their
Job 13:4 But ye are forgers of *l*, ye are
Ps 40:4 nor such as turn aside to *l*
Ps 58:3 soon as they be born, speaking *l*
Ps 62:4 they delight in *l*
Ps 63:11 that speak *l* shall be stopped
Ps 101:7 he that telleth *l* shall not tarry
Prov 6:19 A false witness that speaketh *l*
Prov 14:5 but a false witness will utter *l*
Prov 14:25 a deceitful witness speaketh *l*
Prov 19:5 that speaketh *l* shall not escape
Prov 19:9 he that speaketh *l* shall perish
Prov 29:12 If a ruler hearken to *l*, all his
Prov 30:8 Remove far from me vanity and *l*
Is 9:15 and the prophet that teacheth *l*
Is 16:6 but his *l* shall not be so
Is 28:15 for we have made *l* our refuge
Is 28:17 shall sweep away the refuge of *l*
Is 59:3 your lips have spoken *l*, your
Is 59:4 they trust in vanity, and speak *l*
Jer 9:3 tongues like their bow for *l*
Jer 9:5 taught their tongue to speak *l*
Jer 14:14 prophets prophesy *l* in my name
Jer 16:19 our fathers have inherited *l*
Jer 20:6 to whom thou hast prophesied *l*
Jer 23:14 commit adultery, and walk in *l*
Jer 23:25 said, that prophesy *l* in my name
Jer 23:26 of the prophets that prophesy *l*
Jer 23:32 cause my people to err by their *l*
Jer 48:30 his *l* shall not so effect it
Eze 13:8 ye have spoken vanity, and seen *l*
Eze 13:9 that see vanity, and that divine *l*
Eze 13:19 to my people that hear your *l*
Eze 13:22 Because with *l* ye have made the
Eze 22:28 divining *l* unto them, saying,
Eze 24:12 She hath wearied herself with *l*
Dan 11:27 they shall speak *l* at one table
Hos 7:3 and the princes with their *l*
Hos 7:13 yet they have spoken *l* against me
Hos 10:13 ye have eaten the fruit of *l*
Hos 11:12 compasseth me about with *l*
Hos 12:1 he daily increaseth *l* and
Amos 2:4 their *l* caused them to err, after
Mic 6:12 inhabitants thereof have spoken *l*
Nah 3:1 it is all full of *l* and robbery
Hab 2:18 molten image, and a teacher of *l*
Zeph 3:13 not do iniquity, nor speak *l*
Zec 13:3 for thou speakest *l* in the name
1Ti 4:2 Speaking *l* in hypocrisy

## LIETH

Gen 4:7 doest not well, sin *l* at the door
Gen 49:25 of the deep that *l* under,
Ex 22:19 Whosoever *l* with a beast shall
Lev 6:3 *l* concerning it, and sweareth
Lev 14:47 he that *l* in the house shall wash
Lev 15:4 whereon he *l* that hath the issue,
Lev 15:20 every thing that she *l* upon in
Lev 15:24 bed whereon he *l* shall be unclean
Lev 15:26 Every bed whereon she *l* all the
Lev 15:33 of him that *l* with her that is
Lev 19:20 whosoever *l* carnally with a woman
Lev 20:11 the man that *l* with his father's
Lev 20:13 as he *l* with a woman, both of
Lev 26:34 as long as it *l* desolate
Lev 26:35 As long as it *l* desolate it shall
Lev 26:43 while she *l* desolate without them
Num 21:15 *l* upon the border of Moab
Deut 27:20 Cursed be he that *l* with his
Deut 27:21 Cursed be he that *l* with any
Deut 27:22 be he that *l* with his sister
Deut 27:23 Cursed be he that *l* with his
Josh 15:8 *l* before the valley of Hinnom
Josh 17:7 Michmethah, that *l* before Shechem
Josh 18:13 near the hill that *l* on the south
Josh 18:14 from the hill that *l* before
Josh 18:16 *l* before the valley of the son of
Judg 1:16 which *l* in the south of Arad
Judg 16:5 see wherein his great strength *l*
Judg 16:6 wherein thy great strength *l*
Judg 16:15 me wherein thy great strength *l*
Judg 18:28 the valley that *l* by Beth-rehob
Ruth 3:4 And it shall be, when he *l* down
2Sa 2:24 that *l* before Giah by the way of
2Sa 24:5 *l* in the midst of the river of
Neh 2:3 *l* waste, and the gates thereof are
Neh 2:17 we are in, how Jerusalem *l* waste
Neh 3:25 the tower which *l* out from the
Neh 3:26 the east, and the tower that *l* out
Neh 3:27 the great tower that *l* out
Job 14:12 So man *l* down, and riseth not
Job 40:21 He *l* under the shady trees, in
Ps 10:9 He *l* in wait secretly as a lion
Ps 10:9 he *l* in wait to catch the poor
Ps 41:8 now that he *l* he shall rise up no
Ps 88:7 Thy wrath *l* hard upon me, and thou
Prov 7:12 *l* in wait at every corner
Prov 23:28 She also *l* in wait as for a prey,
Prov 23:34 thou shalt be as he that *l* down
Prov 23:34 or as he that *l* upon the top of a
Eze 9:2 which *l* toward the north, and
Eze 29:3 the great dragon that *l* in the
Mic 7:5 from her that *l* in thy bosom
Mt 8:6 my servant *l* at home sick of the
Mk 5:23 My little daughter *l* at the point
Acts 14:6 the region that *l* round about
Acts 27:12 *l* toward the south west and north
Rom 12:18 be possible, as much as *l* in you
1Jn 5:19 the whole world *l* in wickedness
Rev 21:16 the city *l* foursquare, and the

## LIFE

Gen 1:20 the moving creature that hath *l*
Gen 1:30 the earth, wherein there is *l*
Gen 2:7 into his nostrils the breath of *l*
Gen 2:9 the tree of *l* also in the midst
Gen 3:14 thou eat all the days of thy *l*
Gen 3:17 eat of it all the days of thy *l*
Gen 3:22 and take also of the tree of *l*
Gen 3:24 to keep the way of the tree of *l*
Gen 6:17 flesh, wherein is the breath of *l*
Gen 7:11 six hundredth year of Noah's *l*
Gen 7:15 flesh, wherein is the breath of *l*
Gen 7:22 nostrils was the breath of *l*
Gen 9:4 But flesh with the *l* thereof
Gen 9:5 will I require the *l* of man
Gen 18:10 thee according to the time of *l*
Gen 18:14 thee, according to the time of *l*
Gen 19:17 that he said, Escape for thy *l*
Gen 19:19 shewed unto me in saving my *l*
Gen 23:1 were the years of the *l* of Sarah
Gen 25:7 of Abraham's *l* which he lived
Gen 25:17 are the years of the *l* of Ishmael
Gen 27:46 I am weary of my *l* because of the
Gen 27:46 land, what good shall my *l* do me
Gen 32:30 to face, and my *l* is preserved
Gen 42:15 By the *l* of Pharaoh ye shall not
Gen 42:16 or else by the *l* of Pharaoh
Gen 44:30 seeing that his *l* is bound up in
Gen 44:30 is bound up in the lad's *l*
Gen 45:5 send me before you to preserve *l*
Gen 47:9 days of the years of my *l* been
Gen 47:9 *l* of my fathers in the days of
Gen 48:15 me all my *l* long unto this day
Ex 4:19 men are dead which sought thy *l*
Ex 6:16 the years of the *l* of Levi were
Ex 6:18 the years of the *l* of Kohath were
Ex 6:20 the years of the *l* of Amram were
Ex 21:23 then thou shalt give *l* for *l*
Ex 21:30 give for the ransom of his *l*
Lev 17:11 For the *l* of the flesh is in the
Lev 17:14 For it is the *l* of all flesh
Lev 17:14 blood of it is for the *l* thereof
Lev 17:14 for the *l* of all flesh is the
Lev 18:18 beside the other in her *l* time
Num 35:31 for the *l* of a murderer, which is
Deut 4:9 thy heart all the days of thy *l*
Deut 6:2 son's son, all the days of thy *l*
Deut 12:23 for the blood is the *l*
Deut 12:23 not eat the *l* with the flesh
Deut 16:3 of Egypt all the days of thy *l*
Deut 17:19 therein all the days of his *l*
Deut 19:21 but *l* shall go for *l*, eye for
Deut 20:19 *l*) to employ them in the siege
Deut 24:6 for he taketh a man's *l* to pledge
Deut 28:66 thy *l* shall hang in doubt before
Deut 28:66 have none assurance of thy *l*
Deut 30:15 I have set before thee this day *l*
Deut 30:19 you, that I have set before you *l*
Deut 30:19 therefore choose *l*, that both
Deut 30:20 for he is thy *l*, and the length of
Deut 32:47 because it is your *l*
Josh 1:5 before thee all the days of thy *l*
Josh 2:14 Our *l* for yours, if ye utter not
Josh 4:14 Moses, all the days of his *l*
Judg 9:17 for you, and adventured his *l* far
Judg 12:3 I put my *l* in my hands, and passed
Judg 16:30 than they which he slew in his *l*
Judg 18:25 run upon thee, and thou lose thy *l*
Ruth 4:15 be unto thee a restorer of thy *l*
1Sa 1:11 the LORD all the days of his *l*
1Sa 7:15 Israel all the days of his *l*
1Sa 18:18 and what is my *l*, or my father's
1Sa 19:5 For he did put his *l* in his hand
1Sa 20:1 thy father, that he seeketh my *l*
1Sa 22:23 seeketh my *l* seeketh thy *l*
1Sa 23:15 Saul was come out to seek his *l*
1Sa 25:29 bundle of *l* with the LORD thy God
1Sa 26:24 as thy *l* was much set by this day
1Sa 26:24 so let my *l* be much set by in the
1Sa 28:9 then layest thou a snare for my *l*
1Sa 28:21 and I have put my *l* in my hand
2Sa 1:9 because my *l* is yet whole in me
2Sa 4:8 thine enemy, which sought thy *l*
2Sa 14:7 for the *l* of his brother whom he
2Sa 15:21 shall be, whether in death or *l*
2Sa 16:11 forth of my bowels, seeketh my *l*
2Sa 18:13 falsehood against mine own *l*
2Sa 19:5 which this day have saved thy *l*
1Kin 1:12 that thou mayest save thine own *l*
1Kin 1:12 and the *l* of thy son Solomon
1Kin 2:23 this word against his own *l*
1Kin 3:11 hast not asked for thyself long *l*
1Kin 3:11 hast asked the *l* of thine enemies
1Kin 4:21 Solomon all the days of his *l*
1Kin 11:34 his *l* for David my servant's sake
1Kin 15:5 him all the days of his *l*
1Kin 15:6 and Jeroboam all the days of his *l*
1Kin 19:2 if I make not thy *l* as the *l*
1Kin 19:3 that, he arose, and went for his *l*
1Kin 19:4 now, O LORD, take away my *l*
1Kin 19:10 and they seek my *l*, to take it
1Kin 19:14 and they seek my *l*, to take it
1Kin 20:31 peradventure he will save thy *l*
1Kin 20:39 then shall thy *l* be for his *l*,
1Kin 20:42 thy *l* shall go for his *l*
2Kin 1:13 man of God, I pray thee, let my *l*
2Kin 1:13 the *l* of these fifty thy servants
2Kin 1:14 therefore let my *l* now be
2Kin 4:16 according to the time of *l*
2Kin 4:17 her, according to the time of *l*
2Kin 7:7 as it was, and fled for their *l*
2Kin 8:1 whose son he had restored to *l*
2Kin 8:5 he had restored a dead body to *l*
2Kin 8:5 whose son he had restored to *l*
2Kin 8:5 son, whom Elisha restored to *l*
2Kin 10:24 his *l* shall be for the *l* of
2Kin 10:24 *l* shall be for the *l* of him
2Kin 25:29 before him all the days of his *l*
2Kin 25:30 every day, all the days of his *l*
2Chr 1:11 nor the *l* of thine enemies,
2Chr 1:11 neither yet hast asked long *l*
Ezr 6:10 and pray for the *l* of the king
Neh 6:11 go into the temple to save his *l*
Est 7:3 let my *l* be given me at my
Est 7:7 for his *l* to Esther the queen
Est 8:11 together, and to stand for their *l*
Job 2:4 a man hath will he give for his *l*

| | |
|---|---|
| Job 2:6 | but save his *l* |
| Job 3:20 | *l* unto the bitter in soul |
| Job 6:11 | end, that I should prolong my *l* |
| Job 7:7 | O remember that my *l* is wind |
| Job 7:15 | and death rather than my *l* |
| Job 9:21 | I would despise my *l* |
| Job 10:1 | My soul is weary of my *l* |
| Job 10:12 | Thou hast granted me *l* and favour, |
| Job 13:14 | teeth, and put my *l* in mine hand |
| Job 24:22 | riseth up, and no man is sure of *l* |
| Job 31:39 | owners thereof to lose their *l* |
| Job 33:4 | of the Almighty hath given me *l* |
| Job 33:18 | his *l* from perishing by the sword |
| Job 33:20 | So that his *l* abhorreth bread, and |
| Job 33:22 | grave, and his *l* to the destroyers |
| Job 33:28 | his *l* shall see the light |
| Job 36:6 | not the *l* of the wicked |
| Job 36:14 | their *l* is among the unclean |
| Ps 7:5 | tread down my *l* upon the earth |
| Ps 16:11 | Thou wilt shew me the path of *l* |
| Ps 17:14 | have their portion in this *l* |
| Ps 21:4 | He asked *l* of thee, and thou |
| Ps 23:6 | follow me all the days of my *l* |
| Ps 26:9 | sinners, nor my *l* with bloody men |
| Ps 27:1 | the LORD is the strength of my *l* |
| Ps 27:4 | of the LORD all the days of my *l* |
| Ps 30:5 | in his favour is *l* |
| Ps 31:10 | For my *l* is spent with grief, and |
| Ps 31:13 | they devised to take away my *l* |
| Ps 34:12 | What man is he that desireth *l* |
| Ps 36:9 | with thee is the fountain of *l* |
| Ps 38:12 | seek after my *l* lay snares for me |
| Ps 42:8 | and my prayer unto the God of my *l* |
| Ps 61:6 | Thou wilt prolong the king's *l* |
| Ps 63:3 | lovingkindness is better than *l* |
| Ps 64:1 | preserve my *l* from fear of the |
| Ps 66:9 | Which holdeth our soul in *l* |
| Ps 78:50 | but gave their *l* over to the |
| Ps 88:3 | my *l* draweth nigh unto the grave |
| Ps 91:16 | With long *l* will I satisfy him, |
| Ps 103:4 | redeemeth thy *l* from destruction |
| Ps 128:5 | Jerusalem all the days of thy *l* |
| Ps 133:3 | the blessing, even *l* for evermore |
| Ps 143:3 | smitten my *l* down to the ground |
| Prov 1:19 | away the *l* of the owners thereof |
| Prov 2:19 | take they hold of the paths of *l* |
| Prov 3:2 | For length of days, and long *l* |
| Prov 3:18 | She is a tree of *l* to them that |
| Prov 3:22 | So shall they be *l* unto thy soul |
| Prov 4:10 | the years of thy *l* shall be many |
| Prov 4:13 | for she is thy *l* |
| Prov 4:22 | For they are *l* unto those that |
| Prov 4:23 | for out of it are the issues of *l* |
| Prov 5:6 | shouldest ponder the path of *l* |
| Prov 6:23 | of instruction are the way of *l* |
| Prov 6:26 | will hunt for the precious *l* |
| Prov 7:23 | knoweth not that it is for his *l* |
| Prov 8:35 | For whoso findeth me findeth *l* |
| Prov 9:11 | the years of thy *l* shall be |
| Prov 10:11 | of a righteous man is a well of *l* |
| Prov 10:16 | of the righteous tendeth to *l* |
| Prov 10:17 | He is in the way of *l* that |
| Prov 11:19 | As righteousness tendeth to *l* |
| Prov 11:30 | of the righteous is a tree of *l* |
| Prov 12:10 | man regardeth the *l* of his beast |
| Prov 12:28 | In the way of righteousness is *l* |
| Prov 13:3 | keepeth his mouth keepeth his *l* |
| Prov 13:8 | of a man's *l* are his riches |
| Prov 13:12 | desire cometh, it is a tree of *l* |
| Prov 13:14 | of the wise is a fountain of *l* |
| Prov 14:27 | of the LORD is a fountain of *l* |
| Prov 14:30 | sound heart is the *l* of the flesh |
| Prov 15:4 | A wholesome tongue is a tree of *l* |
| Prov 15:24 | The way of *l* is above to the wise |
| Prov 15:31 | of *l* abideth among the wise |
| Prov 16:15 | of the king's countenance is *l* |
| Prov 16:22 | is a wellspring of *l* unto him |
| Prov 18:21 | *l* are in the power of the tongue |
| Prov 19:23 | The fear of the LORD tendeth to *l* |
| Prov 21:21 | righteousness and mercy findeth *l* |
| Prov 22:4 | LORD are riches, and honour, and *l* |
| Prov 31:12 | and not evil all the days of her *l* |
| Eccl 2:3 | heaven all the days of their *l* |
| Eccl 2:17 | Therefore I hated *l* |
| Eccl 3:12 | rejoice, and to do good in his *l* |
| Eccl 5:18 | the sun all the days of his *l* |
| Eccl 5:20 | much remember the days of his *l* |
| Eccl 6:12 | what is good for man in this *l* |
| Eccl 6:12 | all the days of his vain *l* which |
| Eccl 7:12 | that wisdom giveth *l* to them that |
| Eccl 7:15 | his *l* in his wickedness |
| Eccl 8:15 | of his labour the days of his *l* |
| Eccl 9:9 | the days of the *l* of thy vanity |
| Eccl 9:9 | for that is thy portion in this *l* |
| Is 15:4 | his *l* shall be grievous unto him |
| Is 38:12 | I have cut off like a weaver my *l* |
| Is 38:16 | things is the *l* of my spirit |
| Is 38:20 | of our *l* in the house of the LORD |
| Is 43:4 | men for thee, and people for thy *l* |
| Is 57:10 | hast found the *l* of thine hand |
| Jer 4:30 | thee, they will seek thy *l* |
| Jer 8:3 | shall be chosen rather than *l* by |
| Jer 11:21 | men of Anathoth, that seek thy *l* |
| Jer 21:7 | hand of those that seek their *l* |
| Jer 21:8 | I set before you the way of *l* |
| Jer 21:9 | his *l* shall be unto him for a |
| Jer 22:25 | the hand of them that seek thy *l* |
| Jer 34:20 | hand of them that seek their *l* |
| Jer 34:21 | hand of them that seek their *l* |
| Jer 38:2 | he shall have his *l* for a prey |
| Jer 38:16 | hand of these men that seek thy *l* |
| Jer 39:18 | but thy *l* shall be for a prey |
| Jer 44:30 | the hand of them that seek his *l* |
| Jer 44:30 | his enemy, and that sought his *l* |
| Jer 45:5 | but thy *l* will I give unto thee |
| Jer 49:37 | and before them that seek their *l* |
| Jer 52:33 | before him all the days of his *l* |
| Jer 52:34 | his death, all the days of his *l* |
| Lam 2:19 | for the *l* of thy young children |
| Lam 3:53 | have cut off my *l* in the dungeon |
| Lam 3:58 | thou hast redeemed my *l* |
| Eze 3:18 | his wicked way, to save his *l* |
| Eze 7:13 | himself in the iniquity of his *l* |
| Eze 13:22 | wicked way, by promising him *l* |
| Eze 32:10 | moment, every man for his own *l* |
| Eze 33:15 | robbed, walk in the statutes of *l* |
| Dan 12:2 | awake, some to everlasting *l* |
| Jonah 1:14 | us not perish for this man's *l* |
| Jonah 2:6 | brought up my *l* from corruption |
| Jonah 4:3 | I beseech thee, my *l* from me |
| Mal 2:5 | My covenant was with him of *l* |
| Mt 2:20 | which sought the young child's *l* |
| Mt 6:25 | you, Take no thought for your *l* |
| Mt 6:25 | Is not the *l* more than meat, and |
| Mt 7:14 | is the way, which leadeth unto *l* |
| Mt 10:39 | that findeth his *l* shall lose it |
| Mt 10:39 | he that loseth his *l* for my sake |
| Mt 16:25 | will save his *l* shall lose it |
| Mt 16:25 | whosoever will lose his *l* for my |
| Mt 18:8 | to enter into *l* halt or maimed |
| Mt 18:9 | thee to enter into *l* with one eye |
| Mt 19:16 | I do, that I may have eternal *l* |
| Mt 19:17 | but if thou wilt enter into *l* |
| Mt 19:29 | and shall inherit everlasting *l* |
| Mt 20:28 | to give his *l* a ransom for many |
| Mt 25:46 | but the righteous into *l* eternal |
| Mk 3:4 | to save *l*, or to kill |
| Mk 8:35 | will save his *l* shall lose it |
| Mk 8:35 | shall lose his *l* for my sake |
| Mk 9:43 | for thee to enter into *l* maimed |
| Mk 9:45 | for thee to enter halt into *l* |
| Mk 10:17 | I do that I may inherit eternal *l* |
| Mk 10:30 | and in the world to come eternal *l* |
| Mk 10:45 | to give his *l* a ransom for many |
| Lk 1:75 | before him, all the days of our *l* |
| Lk 6:9 | to save *l*, or to destroy it |
| Lk 8:14 | and riches and pleasures of this *l* |
| Lk 9:24 | will save his *l* shall lose it |
| Lk 9:24 | will lose his *l* for my sake |
| Lk 10:25 | shall I do to inherit eternal *l* |
| Lk 12:15 | for a man's *l* consisteth not in |
| Lk 12:22 | you, Take no thought for your *l* |
| Lk 12:23 | The *l* is more than meat, and the |
| Lk 14:26 | sisters, yea, and his own *l* also |
| Lk 17:33 | seek to save his *l* shall lose it |
| Lk 17:33 | lose his *l* shall preserve it |
| Lk 18:18 | shall I do to inherit eternal *l* |
| Lk 18:30 | the world to come *l* everlasting |
| Lk 21:34 | drunkenness, and cares of this *l* |
| Jn 1:4 | In him was *l* |
| Jn 1:4 | the *l* was the light of men |
| Jn 3:15 | not perish, but have eternal *l* |
| Jn 3:16 | perish, but have everlasting *l* |
| Jn 3:36 | on the Son hath everlasting *l* |
| Jn 3:36 | not the Son shall not see *l* |
| Jn 4:14 | springing up into everlasting *l* |
| Jn 4:36 | and gathereth fruit unto *l* eternal |
| Jn 5:24 | that sent me, hath everlasting *l* |
| Jn 5:24 | but is passed from death unto *l* |
| Jn 5:26 | as the Father hath *l* in himself |
| Jn 5:26 | to the Son to have *l* in himself |
| Jn 5:29 | good, unto the resurrection of *l* |
| Jn 5:39 | them ye think ye have eternal *l* |
| Jn 5:40 | come to me, that ye might have *l* |
| Jn 6:27 | which endureth unto everlasting *l* |
| Jn 6:33 | and giveth *l* unto the world |
| Jn 6:35 | unto them, I am the bread of *l* |
| Jn 6:40 | on him, may have everlasting *l* |
| Jn 6:47 | on me hath everlasting *l* |
| Jn 6:48 | I am that bread of *l* |
| Jn 6:51 | will give for the *l* of the world |
| Jn 6:53 | his blood, ye have no *l* in you |
| Jn 6:54 | drinketh my blood, hath eternal *l* |
| Jn 6:63 | they are spirit, and they are *l* |
| Jn 6:68 | thou hast the words of eternal *l* |
| Jn 8:12 | but shall have the light of *l* |
| Jn 10:10 | I am come that they might have *l* |
| Jn 10:11 | giveth his *l* for the sheep |
| Jn 10:15 | and I lay down my *l* for the sheep |
| Jn 10:17 | love me, because I lay down my *l* |
| Jn 10:28 | And I give unto them eternal *l* |
| Jn 11:25 | I am the resurrection, and the *l* |
| Jn 12:25 | that loveth his *l* shall lose it |
| Jn 12:25 | he that hateth his *l* in this |
| Jn 12:25 | shall keep it unto *l* eternal |
| Jn 12:50 | his commandment is *l* everlasting |
| Jn 13:37 | I will lay down my *l* for thy sake |
| Jn 13:38 | thou lay down thy *l* for my sake |
| Jn 14:6 | I am the way, the truth, and the *l* |
| Jn 15:13 | lay down his *l* for his friends |
| Jn 17:2 | that he should give eternal *l* to |
| Jn 17:3 | And this is *l* eternal, that they |
| Jn 20:31 | ye might have *l* through his name |
| Acts 2:28 | made known to me the ways of *l* |
| Acts 3:15 | And killed the Prince of *l* |
| Acts 5:20 | people all the words of this *l* |
| Acts 8:33 | for his *l* is taken from the earth |
| Acts 11:18 | granted repentance unto *l* |
| Acts 13:46 | unworthy of everlasting *l* |
| Acts 13:48 | ordained to eternal *l* believed |
| Acts 17:25 | thing, seeing he giveth to all *l* |
| Acts 20:10 | for his *l* is in him |
| Acts 20:24 | count I my *l* dear unto myself |
| Acts 26:4 | My manner of *l* from my youth, |
| Acts 27:22 | no loss of any man's *l* among you |
| Rom 2:7 | honour and immortality, eternal *l* |
| Rom 5:10 | we shall be saved by his *l* |
| Rom 5:17 | shall reign in *l* by one, Jesus |
| Rom 5:18 | all men unto justification of *l* |
| Rom 5:21 | *l* by Jesus Christ our Lord |
| Rom 6:4 | also should walk in newness of *l* |
| Rom 6:22 | and the end everlasting *l* |
| Rom 6:23 | *l* through Jesus Christ our Lord |
| Rom 7:10 | which was ordained to *l*, I found |
| Rom 8:2 | of *l* in Christ Jesus hath made me |
| Rom 8:6 | but to be spiritually minded is *l* |
| Rom 8:10 | but the Spirit is *l* because of |
| Rom 8:38 | that neither death, nor *l* |
| Rom 11:3 | am left alone, and they seek my *l* |
| Rom 11:15 | of them be, but *l* from the dead |
| Rom 16:4 | Who have for my *l* laid down their |
| 1Cor 3:22 | or Cephas, or the world, or *l* |
| 1Cor 6:3 | things that pertain to this *l* |
| 1Cor 6:4 | of things pertaining to this *l* |
| 1Cor 14:7 | things without *l* giving sound |
| 1Cor 15:19 | If in this *l* only we have hope in |
| 2Cor 1:8 | that we despaired even of *l* |
| 2Cor 2:16 | other the savour of *l* unto *l* |
| 2Cor 3:6 | killeth, but the spirit giveth *l* |
| 2Cor 4:10 | that the *l* also of Jesus might be |
| 2Cor 4:11 | that the *l* also of Jesus might be |
| 2Cor 4:12 | death worketh in us, but *l* in you |
| 2Cor 5:4 | might be swallowed up of *l* |
| Gal 2:20 | the *l* which I now live in the |
| Gal 3:21 | given which could have given *l* |
| Gal 6:8 | of the Spirit reap *l* everlasting |
| Eph 4:18 | being alienated from the *l* of God |
| Phil 1:20 | in my body, whether it be by *l* |
| Phil 2:16 | Holding forth the word of *l* |
| Phil 2:30 | unto death, not regarding his *l* |
| Phil 4:3 | whose names are in the book of *l* |
| Col 3:3 | your *l* is hid with Christ in God |
| Col 3:4 | When Christ, who is our *l* |
| 1Ti 1:16 | believe on him to *l* everlasting |
| 1Ti 2:2 | peaceable *l* in all godliness and |
| 1Ti 4:8 | promise of the *l* that now is |
| 1Ti 6:12 | of faith, lay hold on eternal *l* |
| 1Ti 6:19 | they may lay hold on eternal *l* |
| 2Ti 1:1 | of *l* which is in Christ Jesus |
| 2Ti 1:10 | death, and hath brought *l* and |

2Ti 2:4 with the affairs of this *l*
2Ti 3:10 known my doctrine, manner of *l*
Titus 1:2 In hope of eternal *l*, which God,
Titus 3:7 to the hope of eternal *l*
Heb 7:3 beginning of days, nor end of *l*
Heb 7:16 after the power of an endless *l*
Heb 11:35 their dead raised to *l* again
Jas 1:12 he shall receive the crown of *l*
Jas 4:14 For what is your *l*
1Pet 3:7 heirs together of the grace of *l*
1Pet 3:10 For he that will love *l*, and see
1Pet 4:3 For the time past of our *l* may
2Pet 1:3 us all things that pertain unto *l*
1Jn 1:1 have handled, of the Word of *l*
1Jn 1:2 (For the *l* was manifested, and we
1Jn 1:2 and shew unto you that eternal *l*
1Jn 2:16 of the eyes, and the pride of *l*
1Jn 2:25 hath promised us, even eternal *l*
1Jn 3:14 we have passed from death unto *l*
1Jn 3:15 hath eternal *l* abiding in him
1Jn 3:16 because he laid down his *l* for us
1Jn 5:11 God hath given to us eternal *l*
1Jn 5:11 and this *l* is in his Son
1Jn 5:12 He that hath the Son hath *l*
1Jn 5:12 not the Son of God hath not *l*
1Jn 5:13 may know that ye have eternal *l*
1Jn 5:16 he shall give him *l* for them that
1Jn 5:20 is the true God, and eternal *l*
Jude 21 Lord Jesus Christ unto eternal *l*
Rev 2:7 I give to eat of the tree of *l*
Rev 2:10 and I will give thee a crown of *l*
Rev 3:5 out his name out of the book of *l*
Rev 8:9 which were in the sea, and had *l*
Rev 11:11 an half the Spirit of *l* from God
Rev 13:8 of *l* of the Lamb slain from the
Rev 13:15 he had power to give *l* unto the
Rev 17:8 of *l* from the foundation of the
Rev 20:12 opened, which is the book of *l*
Rev 20:15 found written in the book of *l*
Rev 21:6 fountain of the water of *l* freely
Rev 21:27 written in the Lamb's book of *l*
Rev 22:1 me a pure river of water of *l*
Rev 22:2 river, was there the tree of *l*
Rev 22:14 may have right to the tree of *l*
Rev 22:17 him take the water of *l* freely
Rev 22:19 his part out of the book of *l*

**LIFT**

Gen 7:17 it was *l* up above the earth
Gen 13:14 *L* up now thine eyes, and look from
Gen 14:22 I have *l* up mine hand unto the
Gen 18:2 he *l* up his eyes and looked, and,
Gen 21:16 him, and *l* up her voice, and wept
Gen 21:18 *l* up the lad, and hold him in
Gen 31:12 *L* up now thine eyes, and see, all
Gen 40:13 shall Pharaoh *l* up thine head
Gen 40:19 *l* up thy head from off thee
Gen 41:44 without thee shall no man *l* up
Ex 14:16 But *l* thou up thy rod, and stretch
Ex 20:25 for if thou *l* up thy tool upon it
Num 6:26 The LORD *l* up his countenance
Num 16:3 wherefore then *l* ye up yourselves
Num 23:24 *l* up himself as a young lion
Deut 3:27 *l* up thine eyes westward, and
Deut 4:19 lest thou *l* up thine eyes unto
Deut 22:4 help him to *l* them up again
Deut 27:5 thou shalt not *l* up any iron tool
Deut 32:40 For I *l* up my hand to heaven, and
Josh 8:31 which no man hath *l* up any iron
2Sa 23:8 he *l* up his spear against eight
2Kin 19:4 wherefore *l* up thy prayer for the
2Kin 25:27 *l* up the head of Jehoiachin king
1Chr 25:5 words of God, to *l* up the horn
Ezr 9:6 blush to *l* up my face to thee, my
Job 10:15 yet will I not *l* up my head
Job 11:15 For then shalt thou *l* up thy face
Job 22:26 shalt *l* up thy face unto God
Job 38:34 Canst thou *l* up thy voice to the
Ps 4:6 *l* thou up the light of thy
Ps 7:6 *l* up thyself because of the rage
Ps 10:12 O God, *l* up thine hand
Ps 24:7 *L* up your heads, O ye gates
Ps 24:9 *L* up your heads, O ye gates
Ps 24:9 even *l* them up, ye everlasting
Ps 25:1 thee, O LORD, do I *l* up my soul
Ps 28:2 when I *l* up my hands toward thy
Ps 28:9 them also, and *l* them up for ever
Ps 63:4 I will *l* up my hands in thy name
Ps 74:3 *L* up thy feet unto the perpetual
Ps 75:4 to the wicked, *L* not up the horn
Ps 75:5 *L* not up your horn on high
Ps 86:4 thee, O Lord, do I *l* up my soul
Ps 93:3 the floods *l* up their waves
Ps 94:2 *L* up thyself, thou judge of the
Ps 110:7 therefore shall he *l* up the head
Ps 119:48 My hands also will I *l* up unto
Ps 121:1 I will *l* up mine eyes unto the
Ps 123:1 Unto thee *l* I up mine eyes, O
Ps 134:2 *L* up your hands in the sanctuary,
Ps 143:8 for I *l* up my soul unto thee
Eccl 4:10 the one will *l* up his fellow
Is 2:4 nation shall not *l* up sword
Is 5:26 he will *l* up an ensign to the
Is 10:15 itself against them that *l* it up
Is 10:15 if the staff should *l* up itself
Is 10:24 shall *l* up his staff against thee
Is 10:26 so shall he *l* it up after the
Is 10:30 *L* up thy voice, O daughter of
Is 13:2 *L* ye up a banner upon the high
Is 24:14 They shall *l* up their voice, they
Is 33:10 now will I *l* up myself
Is 37:4 wherefore *l* up thy prayer for the
Is 40:9 *l* up thy voice with strength
Is 40:9 *l* it up, be not afraid
Is 40:26 *L* up your eyes on high, and behold
Is 42:2 He shall not cry, nor *l* up
Is 42:11 cities thereof *l* up their voice
Is 49:18 *L* up thine eyes round about, and
Is 49:22 I will *l* up mine hand to the
Is 51:6 *L* up your eyes to the heavens, and
Is 52:8 Thy watchmen shall *l* up the voice
Is 58:1 *l* up thy voice like a trumpet, and
Is 59:19 shall *l* up a standard against him
Is 60:4 *L* up thine eyes round about, and
Is 62:10 *l* up a standard for the people
Jer 3:2 *L* up thine eyes unto the high
Jer 7:16 neither *l* up cry nor prayer for
Jer 11:14 neither *l* up a cry or prayer for
Jer 13:20 *L* up your eyes, and behold them
Jer 22:20 *l* up thy voice in Bashan, and cry
Jer 51:14 they shall *l* up a shout against
Lam 2:19 *l* up thy hands toward him for the
Lam 3:41 Let us *l* up our heart with our
Eze 8:5 *l* up thine eyes now the way
Eze 11:22 the cherubims *l* up their wings
Eze 17:14 that it might not *l* itself up
Eze 21:22 to *l* up the voice with shouting,
Eze 23:27 so that thou shalt not *l* up thine
Eze 26:8 *l* up the buckler against thee
Eze 33:25 *l* up your eyes toward your idols,
Mic 4:3 nation shall not *l* up a sword
Zec 1:21 so that no man did *l* up his head
Zec 5:5 *L* up now thine eyes, and see what
Mt 12:11 not lay hold on it, and *l* it out
Lk 13:11 and could in no wise *l* up herself
Lk 16:23 in hell he *l* up his eyes, being
Lk 18:13 would not *l* up so much as his
Lk 21:28 then look up, and *l* up your heads
Jn 4:35 *L* up your eyes, and look on the
Heb 12:12 Wherefore *l* up the hands which
Jas 4:10 of the Lord, and he shall *l* you up

**LIFTED**

Gen 13:10 Lot *l* up his eyes, and beheld all
Gen 22:4 third day Abraham *l* up his eyes
Gen 22:13 Abraham *l* up his eyes, and looked,
Gen 24:63 he *l* up his eyes, and saw, and,
Gen 24:64 Rebekah *l* up her eyes, and when
Gen 27:38 Esau *l* up his voice, and wept
Gen 29:11 and *l* up his voice, and wept
Gen 31:10 that I *l* up mine eyes, and saw in
Gen 33:1 Jacob *l* up his eyes, and looked,
Gen 33:5 he *l* up his eyes, and saw the
Gen 37:25 they *l* up their eyes and looked,
Gen 37:28 *l* up Joseph out of the pit, and
Gen 39:15 he heard that I *l* up my voice
Gen 39:18 as I *l* up my voice and cried, that
Gen 40:20 he *l* up the head of the chief
Gen 43:29 he *l* up his eyes, and saw his
Ex 7:20 he *l* up the rod, and smote the
Ex 14:10 of Israel *l* up their eyes
Lev 9:22 Aaron *l* up his hand toward the
Num 14:1 the congregation *l* up their voice
Num 20:11 Moses *l* up his hand, and with his
Num 24:2 Balaam *l* up his eyes, and he saw
Deut 8:14 Then thine heart be *l* up, and thou
Deut 17:20 be not *l* up above his brethren
Josh 4:18 feet were *l* up unto the dry land
Josh 5:13 that he *l* up his eyes and looked,
Judg 2:4 that the people *l* up their voice
Judg 8:28 so that they *l* up their heads no
Judg 9:7 *l* up his voice, and cried, and said
Judg 19:17 And when he had *l* up his eyes
Judg 21:2 *l* up their voices, and wept sore
Ruth 1:9 they *l* up their voice, and wept
Ruth 1:14 they *l* up their voice, and wept
1Sa 6:13 they *l* up their eyes, and saw the
1Sa 11:4 all the people *l* up their voices,
1Sa 24:16 Saul *l* up his voice, and wept
1Sa 30:4 were with him *l* up their voice
2Sa 3:32 the king *l* up his voice, and wept
2Sa 13:34 that kept the watch *l* up his eyes
2Sa 13:36 came, and *l* up their voice and wept
2Sa 18:24 *l* up his eyes, and looked, and
2Sa 18:28 *l* up their hand against my lord
2Sa 20:21 hath *l* up his hand against the
2Sa 22:49 thou also hast *l* me up on high
2Sa 23:18 he *l* up his spear against three
1Kin 11:26 even he *l* up his hand against the
1Kin 11:27 this was the cause that he *l* up
2Kin 9:32 he *l* up his face to the window,
2Kin 14:10 and thine heart hath *l* thee up
2Kin 19:22 voice, and *l* up thine eyes on high
1Chr 11:11 he *l* up his spear against three
1Chr 14:2 for his kingdom was *l* up on high
1Chr 21:16 David *l* up his eyes, and saw the
2Chr 5:13 when they *l* up their voice with
2Chr 17:6 his heart was *l* up in the ways of
2Chr 26:16 his heart was *l* up to his
2Chr 32:25 for his heart was *l* up
Job 2:12 when they *l* up their eyes afar
Job 2:12 they *l* up their voice, and wept
Job 31:21 If I have *l* up my hand against
Job 31:29 or *l* up myself when evil found
Ps 24:4 who hath not *l* up his soul unto
Ps 24:7 and be ye *l* up, ye everlasting
Ps 27:6 now shall mine head be *l* up above
Ps 30:1 for thou hast *l* me up, and hast
Ps 41:9 hath *l* up his heel against me
Ps 74:5 *l* up axes upon the thick trees
Ps 83:2 that hate thee have *l* up the head
Ps 93:3 The floods have *l* up, O LORD, the
Ps 93:3 the floods have *l* up their voice
Ps 102:10 for thou hast *l* me up, and cast me
Ps 106:26 Therefore he *l* up his hand
Prov 30:13 and their eyelids are *l* up
Is 2:12 and upon every one that is *l* up
Is 2:13 *l* up, and upon all the oaks of
Is 2:14 upon all the hills that are *l* up
Is 6:1 *l* up, and his train filled the
Is 26:11 LORD, when thy hand is *l* up
Is 37:23 voice, and *l* up thine eyes on high
Jer 51:9 is *l* up even to the skies
Jer 52:31 *l* up the head of Jehoiachin king
Eze 1:19 were *l* up from the earth, the
Eze 1:19 the earth, the wheels were *l* up
Eze 1:20 the wheels were *l* up over against
Eze 1:21 when those were *l* up from the
Eze 1:21 the wheels were *l* up over against
Eze 3:14 So the spirit *l* me up, and took me
Eze 8:3 the spirit *l* me up between the
Eze 8:5 So I *l* up mine eyes the way
Eze 10:15 And the cherubims were *l* up
Eze 10:16 when the cherubims *l* up their
Eze 10:17 and when they were *l* up
Eze 10:17 these *l* up themselves also
Eze 10:19 the cherubims *l* up their wings,
Eze 11:1 Moreover the spirit *l* me up
Eze 18:6 neither hath *l* up his eyes to the
Eze 18:12 hath *l* up his eyes to the idols,
Eze 18:15 neither hath *l* up his eyes to the
Eze 20:5 *l* up mine hand unto the seed of
Eze 20:5 when I *l* up mine hand unto them,
Eze 20:6 In the day that I *l* up mine hand
Eze 20:15 Yet also I *l* up my hand unto them
Eze 20:23 I *l* up mine hand unto them also
Eze 20:28 for the which I *l* up mine hand to
Eze 20:42 the country for the which I *l* up
Eze 28:2 Because thine heart is *l* up
Eze 28:5 thine heart is *l* up because of
Eze 28:17 Thine heart was *l* up because of
Eze 31:10 Because thou hast *l* up thyself in
Eze 31:10 his heart is *l* up in his height
Eze 36:7 I have *l* up mine hand, Surely the
Eze 44:12 therefore have I *l* up mine hand
Eze 47:14 concerning the which I *l* up mine
Dan 4:34 *l* up mine eyes unto heaven
Dan 5:20 But when his heart was *l* up
Dan 5:23 But hast *l* up thyself against the
Dan 7:4 it was *l* up from the earth, and

Dan 8:3 Then I *l* up mine eyes, and saw, and
Dan 10:5 Then I *l* up mine eyes, and looked,
Dan 11:12 his heart shall be *l* up
Mic 5:9 Thine hand shall be *l* up upon
Hab 2:4 his soul which is *l* up is not
Hab 3:10 voice, and *l* up his hands on high
Zec 1:18 Then *l* I up mine eyes, and saw, and
Zec 1:21 which *l* up their horn over the
Zec 2:1 I *l* up mine eyes again, and looked
Zec 5:1 *l* up mine eyes, and looked, and
Zec 5:7 there was *l* up a talent of lead
Zec 5:9 Then *l* I up mine eyes, and looked,
Zec 5:9 they *l* up the ephah between the
Zec 6:1 *l* up mine eyes, and looked, and,
Zec 9:16 *l* up as an ensign upon his land
Zec 14:10 and it shall be *l* up, and inhabited
Mt 17:8 And when they had *l* up their eyes
Mk 1:31 took her by the hand, and *l* her up
Mk 9:27 took him by the hand, and *l* him up
Lk 6:20 he *l* up his eyes on his disciples
Lk 11:27 of the company *l* up her voice
Lk 17:13 they *l* up their voices, and said,
Lk 24:50 he *l* up his hands, and blessed
Jn 3:14 as Moses *l* up the serpent in the
Jn 3:14 so must the Son of man be *l* up
Jn 6:5 When Jesus then *l* up his eyes
Jn 8:7 he *l* up himself, and said unto
Jn 8:10 When Jesus had *l* up himself
Jn 8:28 When ye have *l* up the Son of man,
Jn 11:41 Jesus *l* up his eyes, and said,
Jn 12:32 if I be *l* up from the earth, will
Jn 12:34 thou, The Son of man must be *l* up
Jn 13:18 me hath *l* up his heel against me
Jn 17:1 *l* up his eyes to heaven, and said,
Acts 2:14 *l* up his voice, and said unto them
Acts 3:7 by the right hand, and *l* him up
Acts 4:24 they *l* up their voice to God with
Acts 9:41 *l* her up, and when he had called
Acts 14:11 they *l* up their voices, saying in
Acts 22:22 then *l* up their voices, and said,
1Ti 3:6 lest being *l* up with pride he
Rev 10:5 upon the earth *l* up his hand to

## LIFTETH

1Sa 2:7 he bringeth low, and *l* up
1Sa 2:8 *l* up the beggar from the dunghill
2Chr 25:19 thine heart *l* thee up to boast
Job 39:18 What time she *l* up herself on
Ps 107:25 which *l* up the waves thereof
Ps 113:7 *l* the needy out of the dunghill
Ps 147:6 The LORD *l* up the meek
Is 18:3 when he *l* up an ensign on the
Jer 51:3 against him that *l* himself up in
Nah 3:3 The horseman *l* up both the bright

## LIFTING

1Chr 11:20 for *l* up his spear against three
1Chr 15:16 by *l* up the voice with joy
Neh 8:6 Amen, Amen, with *l* up their hands
Job 22:29 thou shalt say, There is *l* up
Ps 141:2 the *l* up of my hands as the
Prov 30:32 done foolishly in *l* up thyself
Is 9:18 mount up like the *l* up of smoke
Is 33:3 at the *l* up of thyself the
1Ti 2:8 *l* up holy hands, without wrath and

## LIGHT

Gen 1:3 And God said, Let there be *l*
Gen 1:3 and there was *l*
Gen 1:4 And God saw the *l*, that it was
Gen 1:4 God divided the *l* from the
Gen 1:5 And God called the *l* Day, and the
Gen 1:15 heaven to give *l* upon the earth
Gen 1:16 the greater *l* to rule the day, and
Gen 1:16 the lesser *l* to rule the night
Gen 1:17 heaven to give *l* upon the earth
Gen 1:18 to divide the *l* from the darkness
Gen 44:3 As soon as the morning was *l*
Ex 10:23 Israel had *l* in their dwellings
Ex 13:21 a pillar of fire, to give them *l*
Ex 14:20 but it gave *l* by night to these
Ex 25:6 Oil for the *l*, spices for
Ex 25:37 they shall *l* the lamps thereof,
Ex 25:37 they may give *l* over against it
Ex 27:20 pure oil olive beaten for the *l*
Ex 35:8 And oil for the *l*, and spices for
Ex 35:14 The candlestick also for the *l*
Ex 35:14 his lamps, with the oil for the *l*
Ex 35:28 And spice, and oil for the *l*
Ex 39:37 vessels thereof, and the oil for *l*
Ex 40:4 and *l* the lamps thereof
Lev 24:2 pure oil olive beaten for the *l*
Num 4:9 and cover the candlestick of the *l*
Num 4:16 pertaineth the oil for the *l*
Num 8:2 the seven lamps shall give *l* over
Num 21:5 and our soul loatheth this *l* bread
Deut 27:16 Cursed be he that setteth *l* by
Judg 9:4 *l* persons, which followed him
Judg 19:26 where her lord was, till it was *l*
Ruth 2:3 her hap was to *l* on a part of the
1Sa 14:36 and spoil them until the morning *l*
1Sa 18:23 Seemeth it to you a *l* thing to be
1Sa 25:22 *l* any that pisseth against the
1Sa 25:34 *l* any that pisseth against the
1Sa 25:36 less or more, until the morning *l*
1Sa 29:10 early in the morning, and have *l*
2Sa 2:18 Asahel was as *l* of foot as a wild
2Sa 17:12 we will *l* upon him as the dew
2Sa 17:22 by the morning *l* there lacked not
2Sa 21:17 thou quench not the *l* of Israel
2Sa 23:4 shall be as the *l* of the morning
1Kin 7:4 *l* was against *l* in three
1Kin 7:5 *l* was against *l* in three
1Kin 7:5 was against *l* in three ranks
1Kin 11:36 David my servant may have a *l*
1Kin 16:31 as if it had been a *l* thing for
2Kin 3:18 this is but a *l* thing in the
2Kin 7:9 if we tarry till the morning *l*
2Kin 8:19 him to give him alway a *l*
2Kin 20:10 It is a *l* thing for the shadow to
2Chr 21:7 as he promised to give a *l* to him
Neh 9:12 to give them *l* in the way wherein
Neh 9:19 of fire by night, to shew them *l*
Est 8:16 The Jews had *l*, and gladness, and
Job 3:4 neither let the *l* shine upon it
Job 3:9 let it look for *l*, but have none
Job 3:16 as infants which never saw *l*
Job 3:20 Wherefore is *l* given to him that
Job 3:23 Why is *l* given to a man whose way
Job 10:22 where the *l* is as darkness
Job 12:22 bringeth out to *l* the shadow of
Job 12:25 They grope in the dark without *l*
Job 17:12 the *l* is short because of
Job 18:5 the *l* of the wicked shall be put
Job 18:6 The *l* shall be dark in his
Job 18:18 be driven from *l* into darkness
Job 22:28 the *l* shall shine upon thy ways
Job 24:13 of those that rebel against the *l*
Job 24:14 with the *l* killeth the poor
Job 24:16 they know not the *l*
Job 25:3 and upon whom doth not his *l* arise
Job 28:11 is hid bringeth he forth to *l*
Job 29:3 when by his *l* I walked through
Job 29:24 the *l* of my countenance they cast
Job 30:26 and when I waited for *l*, there
Job 33:28 pit, and his life shall see the *l*
Job 33:30 with the *l* of the living
Job 36:30 he spreadeth his *l* upon it
Job 36:32 With clouds he covereth the *l*
Job 37:15 caused the *l* of his cloud to
Job 37:21 bright *l* which is in the clouds
Job 38:15 the wicked their *l* is withholden
Job 38:19 Where is the way where *l* dwelleth
Job 38:24 By what way is the *l* parted
Job 41:18 By his neesings a *l* doth shine
Ps 4:6 lift thou up the *l* of thy
Ps 18:28 For thou wilt *l* my candle
Ps 27:1 The LORD is my *l* and my salvation
Ps 36:9 in thy *l* shall we see *l*
Ps 36:9 in thy *l* shall we see *l*
Ps 37:6 forth thy righteousness as the *l*
Ps 38:10 as for the *l* of mine eyes, it
Ps 43:3 O send out thy *l* and thy truth
Ps 44:3 the *l* of thy countenance, because
Ps 49:19 they shall never see *l*
Ps 56:13 before God in the *l* of the living
Ps 74:16 thou hast prepared the *l* and the
Ps 78:14 and all the night with a *l* of fire
Ps 89:15 in the *l* of thy countenance
Ps 90:8 sins in the *l* of thy countenance
Ps 97:11 *L* is sown for the righteous, and
Ps 104:2 thyself with *l* as with a garment
Ps 105:39 and fire to give *l* in the night
Ps 112:4 there ariseth *l* in the darkness
Ps 118:27 the LORD, which hath shewed us *l*
Ps 119:105 unto my feet, and a *l* unto my path
Ps 119:130 entrance of thy words giveth *l*
Ps 139:11 the night shall be *l* about me
Ps 139:12 the *l* are both alike to thee
Ps 148:3 praise him, all ye stars of *l*
Prov 4:18 of the just is as the shining *l*
Prov 6:23 and the law is *l*
Prov 13:9 The *l* of the righteous rejoiceth
Prov 15:30 The *l* of the eyes rejoiceth the
Prov 16:15 In the *l* of the king's
Eccl 2:13 as far as *l* excelleth darkness
Eccl 11:7 Truly the *l* is sweet, and a
Eccl 12:2 While the sun, or the *l*, or the
Is 2:5 let us walk in the *l* of the LORD
Is 5:20 for *l*, and *l* for darkness
Is 5:30 the *l* is darkened in the heavens
Is 8:20 is because there is no *l* in them
Is 9:2 in darkness have seen a great *l*
Is 9:2 upon them hath the *l* shined
Is 10:17 the *l* of Israel shall be for a
Is 13:10 thereof shall not give their *l*
Is 13:10 shall not cause her *l* to shine
Is 30:26 Moreover the *l* of the moon shall
Is 30:26 moon shall be as the *l* of the sun
Is 30:26 the *l* of the sun shall be
Is 30:26 as the *l* of seven days, in the
Is 42:6 people, for a *l* of the Gentiles
Is 42:16 will make darkness *l* before them
Is 45:7 I form the *l*, and create darkness
Is 49:6 It is a *l* thing that thou
Is 49:6 give thee for a *l* to the Gentiles
Is 50:10 walketh in darkness, and hath no *l*
Is 50:11 walk in the *l* of your fire, and in
Is 51:4 to rest for a *l* of the people
Is 58:8 Then shall thy *l* break forth as
Is 58:10 then shall thy *l* rise in
Is 59:9 we wait for *l*, but behold
Is 60:1 for thy *l* is come, and the glory
Is 60:3 the Gentiles shall come to thy *l*
Is 60:19 sun shall be no more thy *l* by day
Is 60:19 shall the moon give *l* unto thee
Is 60:19 be unto thee an everlasting *l*
Is 60:20 LORD shall be thine everlasting *l*
Jer 4:23 and the heavens, and they had no *l*
Jer 13:16 and, while ye look for *l*, he turn
Jer 25:10 and the *l* of the candle
Jer 31:35 giveth the sun for a *l* by day
Jer 31:35 and of the stars for a *l* by night
Lam 3:2 me into darkness, but not into *l*
Eze 8:17 Is it a *l* thing to the house of
Eze 22:7 In thee have they set *l* by father
Eze 32:7 and the moon shall not give her *l*
Dan 2:22 and the *l* dwelleth with him
Dan 5:11 and in the days of thy father *l*
Dan 5:14 of the gods is in thee, and that *l*
Hos 6:5 are as the *l* that goeth forth
Amos 5:18 of the LORD is darkness, and not *l*
Amos 5:20 of the LORD be darkness, and not *l*
Mic 2:1 when the morning is *l*, they
Mic 7:8 the LORD shall be a *l* unto me
Mic 7:9 he will bring me forth to the *l*
Hab 3:4 And his brightness was as the *l*
Hab 3:11 at the *l* of thine arrows they
Zeph 3:4 Her prophets are *l* and treacherous
Zeph 3:5 doth he bring his judgment to *l*
Zec 14:6 that the *l* shall not be clear,
Zec 14:7 at evening time it shall be *l*
Mt 4:16 which sat in darkness saw great *l*
Mt 4:16 and shadow of death *l* is sprung up
Mt 5:14 Ye are the *l* of the world
Mt 5:15 Neither do men *l* a candle
Mt 5:15 it giveth *l* unto all that are in
Mt 5:16 Let your *l* so shine before men,
Mt 6:22 The *l* of the body is the eye
Mt 6:22 thy whole body shall be full of *l*
Mt 6:23 If therefore the *l* that is in
Mt 10:27 in darkness, that speak ye in *l*
Mt 11:30 yoke is easy, and my burden is *l*
Mt 17:2 and his raiment was white as the *l*
Mt 22:5 But they made *l* of it, and went
Mt 24:29 and the moon shall not give her *l*
Mk 13:24 and the moon shall not give her *l*
Lk 1:79 To give *l* to them that sit in
Lk 2:32 A *l* to lighten the Gentiles, and
Lk 8:16 they which enter in may see the *l*
Lk 11:33 they which come in may see the *l*
Lk 11:34 The *l* of the body is the eye
Lk 11:34 thy whole body also is full of *l*
Lk 11:35 the *l* which is in thee be not
Lk 11:36 whole body therefore be full of *l*
Lk 11:36 the whole shall be full of *l*
Lk 11:36 of a candle doth give thee *l*
Lk 12:3 darkness shall be heard in the *l*
Lk 15:8 one piece, doth not *l* a candle
Lk 16:8 wiser than the children of *l*
Jn 1:4 and the life was the *l* of men
Jn 1:5 the *l* shineth in darkness

Jn 1:7 witness, to bear witness of the *L*
Jn 1:8 He was not that *L*, but was sent
Jn 1:8 sent to bear witness of that *L*
Jn 1:9 That was the true *L*, which
Jn 3:19 that *l* is come into the world, and
Jn 3:19 men loved darkness rather than *l*
Jn 3:20 one that doeth evil hateth the *l*
Jn 3:20 neither cometh to the *l*
Jn 3:21 that doeth truth cometh to the *l*
Jn 5:35 He was a burning and a shining *l*
Jn 5:35 for a season to rejoice in his *l*
Jn 8:12 saying, I am the *l* of the world
Jn 8:12 but shall have the *l* of life
Jn 9:5 world, I am the *l* of the world
Jn 11:9 he seeth the *l* of this world
Jn 11:10 because there is no *l* in him
Jn 12:35 a little while is the *l* with you
Jn 12:35 Walk while ye have the *l*, lest
Jn 12:36 ye have *l*, believe in the *l*
Jn 12:36 that ye may be the children of *l*
Jn 12:46 I am come a *l* into the world,
Acts 9:3 round about him a *l* from heaven
Acts 12:7 him, and a *l* shined in the prison
Acts 13:47 thee to be a *l* of the Gentiles
Acts 16:29 Then he called for a *l*, and sprang
Acts 22:6 heaven a great *l* round about me
Acts 22:9 were with me saw indeed the *l*
Acts 22:11 not see for the glory of that *l*
Acts 26:13 I saw in the way a *l* from heaven
Acts 26:18 to turn them from darkness to *l*
Acts 26:23 should shew *l* unto the people, and
Rom 2:19 a *l* of them which are in darkness
Rom 13:12 and let us put on the armour of *l*
1Cor 4:5 who both will bring to *l* the
2Cor 4:4 lest the *l* of the glorious gospel
2Cor 4:6 who commanded the *l* to shine out
2Cor 4:6 to give the *l* of the knowledge of
2Cor 4:17 For our *l* affliction, which is
2Cor 6:14 communion hath *l* with darkness
2Cor 11:14 is transformed into an angel of *l*
Eph 5:8 but now are ye *l* in the Lord
Eph 5:8 walk as children of *l*
Eph 5:13 are made manifest by the *l*
Eph 5:13 doth make manifest is *l*
Eph 5:14 dead, and Christ shall give thee *l*
Col 1:12 inheritance of the saints in *l*
1Th 5:5 Ye are all the children of *l*
1Ti 6:16 dwelling in the *l* which no man
2Ti 1:10 immortality to *l* through the
1Pet 2:9 of darkness into his marvellous *l*
2Pet 1:19 as unto a *l* that shineth in a
1Jn 1:5 declare unto you, that God is *l*
1Jn 1:7 in the *l*, as he is in the *l*
1Jn 2:8 past, and the true *l* now shineth
1Jn 2:9 He that saith he is in the *l*
1Jn 2:10 his brother abideth in the *l*
Rev 7:16 neither shall the sun *l* on them
Rev 18:23 the *l* of a candle shall shine no
Rev 21:11 her *l* was like unto a stone most
Rev 21:23 it, and the Lamb is the *l* thereof
Rev 21:24 saved shall walk in the *l* of it
Rev 22:5 no candle, neither *l* of the sun
Rev 22:5 for the Lord God giveth them *l*

**LIGHTED**
Gen 24:64 saw Isaac, she *l* off the camel
Gen 28:11 he *l* upon a certain place, and
Ex 40:25 he *l* the lamps before the LORD
Num 8:3 he *l* the lamps thereof over
Josh 15:18 and she *l* off her ass
Judg 1:14 and she *l* from off her ass
Judg 4:15 so that Sisera *l* down off his
1Sa 25:23 *l* off the ass, and fell before
2Kin 5:21 he *l* down from the chariot to
2Kin 10:15 he *l* on Jehonadab the son of
Is 9:8 Jacob, and it hath *l* upon Israel
Lk 8:16 No man, when he hath *l* a candle
Lk 11:33 No man, when he hath *l* a candle

**LIGHTEN**
1Sa 6:5 peradventure he will *l* his hand
2Sa 22:29 and the LORD will *l* my darkness
Ezr 9:8 that our God may *l* our eyes
Ps 13:3 *l* mine eyes, lest I sleep the
Jonah 1:5 into the sea, to *l* it of them
Lk 2:32 A light to *l* the Gentiles, and the
Rev 21:23 for the glory of God did *l* it

**LIGHTENED**
Ps 34:5 They looked unto him, and were *l*
Ps 77:18 the lightnings *l* the world
Acts 27:18 the next day they *l* the ship
Acts 27:38 they *l* the ship, and cast out the
Rev 18:1 the earth was *l* with his glory

**LIGHTLY**
Gen 26:10 might *l* have lien with thy wife
Deut 32:15 *l* esteemed the Rock of his
1Sa 2:30 despise me shall be *l* esteemed
1Sa 18:23 I am a poor man, and *l* esteemed
Is 9:1 when at the first he *l* afflicted
Jer 4:24 and all the hills moved *l*
Mk 9:39 that can *l* speak evil of me

**LIGHTNING**
2Sa 22:15 *l*, and discomfited them
Job 28:26 a way for the *l* of the thunder
Job 37:3 his *l* unto the ends of the earth
Job 38:25 or a way for the *l* of thunder
Ps 144:6 Cast forth *l*, and scatter them
Eze 1:13 and out of the fire went forth *l*
Eze 1:14 as the appearance of a flash of *l*
Dan 10:6 his face as the appearance of *l*
Zec 9:14 his arrow shall go forth as the *l*
Mt 24:27 For as the *l* cometh out of the
Mt 28:3 His countenance was like *l*
Lk 10:18 Satan as *l* fall from heaven
Lk 17:24 For as the *l*, that lighteneth out

**LIGHTNINGS**
Ex 19:16 that there were thunders and *l*
Ex 20:18 saw the thunderings, and the *l*
Job 38:35 Canst thou send *l*, that they may
Ps 18:14 and he shot out *l*, and discomfited
Ps 77:18 the *l* lightened the world
Ps 97:4 His *l* enlightened the world
Ps 135:7 he maketh *l* for the rain
Jer 10:13 he maketh *l* with rain, and
Jer 51:16 he maketh *l* with rain, and
Nah 2:4 they shall run like the *l*
Rev 4:5 And out of the throne proceeded *l*
Rev 8:5 were voices, and thunderings, and *l*
Rev 11:19 and there were *l*, and voices, and
Rev 16:18 were voices, and thunders, and *l*

**LIGHTS**
Gen 1:14 Let there be *l* in the firmament
Gen 1:15 And let them be for *l* in the
Gen 1:16 And God made two great *l*
1Kin 6:4 house he made windows of narrow *l*
Ps 136:7 To him that made great *l*
Eze 32:8 All the bright *l* of heaven will I
Lk 12:35 girded about, and your *l* burning
Acts 20:8 there were many *l* in the upper
Phil 2:15 whom ye shine as *l* in the world
Jas 1:17 cometh down from the Father of *l*

**LIKENESS**
Gen 1:26 man in our image, after our *l*
Gen 5:1 in the *l* of God made he him
Gen 5:3 and begat a son in his own *l*
Ex 20:4 or any *l* of any thing that is in
Deut 4:16 figure, the *l* of male or female,
Deut 4:17 The *l* of any beast that is on the
Deut 4:17 the *l* of any winged fowl that
Deut 4:18 The *l* of any thing that creepeth
Deut 4:18 the *l* of any fish that is in the
Deut 4:23 or the *l* of any thing, which the
Deut 4:25 or the *l* of any thing, and shall
Deut 5:8 or any *l* of any thing that is in
Ps 17:15 when I awake, with thy *l*
Is 40:18 or what *l* will ye compare unto
Eze 1:5 the *l* of four living creatures
Eze 1:5 they had the *l* of a man
Eze 1:10 As for the *l* of their faces, they
Eze 1:13 As for the *l* of the living
Eze 1:16 and they four had one *l*
Eze 1:22 the *l* of the firmament upon the
Eze 1:26 their heads was the *l* of a throne
Eze 1:26 upon the *l* of the throne was the
Eze 1:26 the *l* as the appearance of a man
Eze 1:28 of the *l* of the glory of the LORD
Eze 8:2 lo a *l* as the appearance of fire
Eze 10:1 appearance of the *l* of a throne
Eze 10:10 appearances, they four had one *l*
Eze 10:21 the *l* of the hands of a man was
Eze 10:22 the *l* of their faces was the same
Acts 14:11 come down to us in the *l* of men
Rom 6:5 together in the *l* of his death
Rom 6:5 also in the *l* of his resurrection
Rom 8:3 own Son in the *l* of sinful flesh
Phil 2:7 and was made in the *l* of men

**LIKHI** *(lik'-hi) Son of Shemidah.*
1Chr 7:19 were, Ahian, and Shechem, and *L*

**LILIES**
1Kin 7:26 brim of a cup, with flowers of *l*
2Chr 4:5 brim of a cup, with flowers of *l*
Song 2:16 he feedeth among the *l*
Song 4:5 are twins, which feed among the *l*
Song 5:13 his lips like *l*, dropping sweet
Song 6:2 in the gardens, and to gather *l*
Song 6:3 he feedeth among the *l*
Song 7:2 an heap of wheat set about with *l*
Mt 6:28 Consider the *l* of the field
Lk 12:27 Consider the *l* how they grow

**LILY**
1Kin 7:19 were of *l* work in the porch
1Kin 7:22 the top of the pillars was *l* work
Song 2:1 Sharon, and the *l* of the valleys
Song 2:2 As the *l* among thorns, so is my
Hos 14:5 he shall grow as the *l*, and cast

**LINE**
Josh 2:18 thou shalt bind this *l* of scarlet
Josh 2:21 bound the scarlet *l* in the window
2Sa 8:2 Moab, and measured them with a *l*
2Sa 8:2 and with one full *l* to keep alive
1Kin 7:15 a *l* of twelve cubits did compass
1Kin 7:23 a *l* of thirty cubits did compass
2Kin 21:13 over Jerusalem the *l* of Samaria
2Chr 4:2 a *l* of thirty cubits did compass
Job 38:5 who hath stretched the *l* upon it
Ps 19:4 Their *l* is gone out through all
Ps 78:55 divided them an inheritance by *l*
Is 28:10 *l* upon *l*, *l* upon *l*
Is 28:13 *l* upon *l*, *l* upon *l*
Is 28:17 Judgment also will I lay to the *l*
Is 34:11 out upon it the *l* of confusion
Is 34:17 hath divided it unto them by *l*
Is 44:13 he marketh it out with a *l*
Jer 31:39 the measuring *l* shall yet go
Lam 2:8 he hath stretched out a *l*
Eze 40:3 with a *l* of flax in his hand, and
Eze 47:3 when the man that had the *l* in
Amos 7:17 and thy land shall be divided by *l*
Zec 1:16 a *l* shall be stretched forth upon
Zec 2:1 with a measuring *l* in his hand
2Cor 10:16 *l* of things made ready to our

**LINEN**
Gen 41:42 arrayed him in vestures of fine *l*
Ex 25:4 and purple, and scarlet, and fine *l*
Ex 26:1 ten curtains of fine twined *l*
Ex 26:31 fine twined *l* of cunning work
Ex 26:36 and scarlet, and fine twined *l*
Ex 27:9 for the court of fine twined *l* of
Ex 27:16 and scarlet, and fine twined *l*
Ex 27:18 five cubits of fine twined *l*
Ex 28:5 and purple, and scarlet, and fine *l*
Ex 28:6 of scarlet, and fine twined *l*
Ex 28:8 and scarlet, and fine twined *l*
Ex 28:15 of scarlet, and of fine twined *l*
Ex 28:39 embroider the coat of fine *l*
Ex 28:39 shalt make the mitre of fine *l*
Ex 28:42 thou shalt make them *l* breeches
Ex 35:6 and purple, and scarlet, and fine *l*
Ex 35:23 and purple, and scarlet, and fine *l*
Ex 35:25 and of scarlet, and of fine *l*
Ex 35:35 purple, in scarlet, and in fine *l*
Ex 36:8 ten curtains of fine twined *l*
Ex 36:35 and scarlet, and fine twined *l*
Ex 36:37 and scarlet, and fine twined *l*
Ex 38:9 the court were of fine twined *l*
Ex 38:16 round about were of fine twined *l*
Ex 38:18 and scarlet, and fine twined *l*
Ex 38:23 purple, and in scarlet, and fine *l*
Ex 39:2 and scarlet, and fine twined *l*
Ex 39:3 in the scarlet, and in the fine *l*
Ex 39:5 and scarlet, and fine twined *l*
Ex 39:8 and scarlet, and fine twined *l*
Ex 39:24 purple, and scarlet, and twined *l*
Ex 39:27 of fine *l* of woven work for Aaron
Ex 39:28 And a mitre of fine *l*
Ex 39:28 and goodly bonnets of fine *l*
Ex 39:28 *l* breeches of fine twined *l*,
Ex 39:28 *l* breeches of fine twined *l*
Ex 39:29 And a girdle of fine twined *l*
Lev 6:10 priest shall put on his *l* garment
Lev 6:10 his *l* breeches shall he put upon
Lev 13:47 a woollen garment, or a *l* garment
Lev 13:48 of *l*, or of woollen
Lev 13:52 warp or woof, in woollen or in *l*
Lev 13:59 in a garment of woollen or *l*
Lev 16:4 He shall put on the holy *l* coat
Lev 16:4 he shall have the *l* breeches upon

Lev 16:4 shall be girded with a *l* girdle
Lev 16:4 with the *l* mitre shall he be
Lev 16:23 and shall put off the *l* garments
Lev 16:32 and shall put on the *l* clothes
Lev 19:19 shall a garment mingled of *l*
Deut 22:11 as of woollen and *l* together
1Sa 2:18 a child, girded with a *l* ephod
1Sa 22:18 persons that did wear a *l* ephod
2Sa 6:14 David was girded with a *l* ephod
1Kin 10:28 brought out of Egypt, and *l* yarn
1Kin 10:28 received the *l* yarn at a price
1Chr 4:21 house of them that wrought fine *l*
1Chr 15:27 was clothed with a robe of fine *l*
1Chr 15:27 also had upon him an ephod of *l*
2Chr 1:16 brought out of Egypt, and *l* yarn
2Chr 1:16 received the *l* yarn at a price
2Chr 2:14 in purple, in blue, and in fine *l*
2Chr 3:14 and purple, and crimson, and fine *l*
2Chr 5:12 being arrayed in white *l*
Est 1:6 fastened with cords of fine *l*
Est 8:15 gold, and with a garment of fine *l*
Prov 7:16 works, with fine *l* of Egypt
Prov 31:24 She maketh fine *l*, and selleth it
Is 3:23 The glasses, and the fine *l*
Jer 13:1 me, Go and get thee a *l* girdle
Eze 9:2 man among them was clothed with *l*
Eze 9:3 called to the man clothed with *l*
Eze 9:11 behold, the man clothed with *l*
Eze 10:2 spake unto the man clothed with *l*
Eze 10:6 commanded the man clothed with *l*
Eze 10:7 of him that was clothed with *l*
Eze 16:10 I girded thee about with fine *l*
Eze 16:13 and thy raiment was of fine *l*
Eze 27:7 Fine *l* with broidered work from
Eze 27:16 and broidered work, and fine *l*
Eze 44:17 shall be clothed with *l* garments
Eze 44:18 They shall have *l* bonnets upon
Eze 44:18 shall have *l* breeches upon their
Dan 10:5 behold a certain man clothed in *l*
Dan 12:6 one said to the man clothed in *l*
Dan 12:7 And I heard the man clothed in *l*
Mt 27:59 he wrapped it in a clean *l* cloth
Mk 14:51 having a *l* cloth cast about his
Mk 14:52 And he left the *l* cloth, and fled
Mk 15:46 And he bought fine *l*, and took him
Mk 15:46 him down, and wrapped him in the *l*
Lk 16:19 was clothed in purple and fine *l*
Lk 23:53 took it down, and wrapped it in *l*
Lk 24:12 he beheld the *l* clothes laid by
Jn 19:40 wound it in *l* clothes with the
Jn 20:5 in, saw the *l* clothes lying
Jn 20:6 and seeth the *l* clothes lie,
Jn 20:7 not lying with the *l* clothes
Rev 15:6 clothed in pure and white *l*
Rev 18:12 stones, and of pearls, and fine *l*
Rev 18:16 city, that was clothed in fine *l*
Rev 19:8 she should be arrayed in fine *l*
Rev 19:8 for the fine *l* is the
Rev 19:14 white horses, clothed in fine *l*

**LINTEL**
Ex 12:22 is in the bason, and strike the *l*
Ex 12:23 he seeth the blood upon the *l*
1Kin 6:31 the *l* and side posts were a fifth
Amos 9:1 Smite the *l* of the door, that the

**LINUS** *(li'-nus) A Christian at Rome.*
2Ti 4:21 greeteth thee, and Pudens, and *L*

**LION**
Gen 49:9 stooped down, he couched as a *l*
Gen 49:9 and as an old *l*
Num 23:24 people shall rise up as a great *l*
Num 23:24 and lift up himself as a young *l*
Num 24:9 He couched, he lay down as a *l*
Num 24:9 and as a great *l*
Deut 33:20 he dwelleth as a *l*, and teareth
Judg 14:5 a young *l* roared against him
Judg 14:8 aside to see the carcase of the *l*
Judg 14:8 and honey in the carcase of the *l*
Judg 14:9 honey out of the carcase of the *l*
Judg 14:18 And what is stronger than a *l*
1Sa 17:34 father's sheep, and there came a *l*
1Sa 17:36 Thy servant slew both the *l*
1Sa 17:37 me out of the paw of the *l*
2Sa 17:10 heart is as the heart of a *l*
2Sa 23:20 slew a *l* in the midst of a pit in
1Kin 13:24 a *l* met him by the way, and slew
1Kin 13:24 the *l* also stood by the carcase
1Kin 13:25 the *l* standing by the carcase
1Kin 13:26 hath delivered him unto the *l*
1Kin 13:28 the *l* standing by the carcase
1Kin 13:28 the *l* had not eaten the carcase,
1Kin 20:36 from me, a *l* shall slay thee
1Kin 20:36 a *l* found him, and slew him
1Chr 11:22 slew a *l* in a pit in a snowy day
Job 4:10 The roaring of the *l*
Job 4:10 and the voice of the fierce *l*
Job 4:11 The old *l* perisheth for lack of
Job 10:16 Thou huntest me as a fierce *l*
Job 28:8 it, nor the fierce *l* passed by it
Job 38:39 Wilt thou hunt the prey for the *l*
Ps 7:2 Lest he tear my soul like a *l*
Ps 10:9 wait secretly as a *l* in his den
Ps 17:12 Like as a *l* that is greedy of his
Ps 17:12 as it were a young *l* lurking in
Ps 22:13 as a ravening and a roaring *l*
Ps 91:13 Thou shalt tread upon the *l*
Ps 91:13 the young *l* and the dragon shalt
Prov 19:12 wrath is as the roaring of a *l*
Prov 20:2 a king is as the roaring of a *l*
Prov 22:13 man saith, There is a *l* without
Prov 26:13 saith, There is a *l* in the way
Prov 26:13 a *l* is in the streets
Prov 28:1 but the righteous are bold as a *l*
Prov 28:15 As a roaring *l*, and a ranging bear
Prov 30:30 A *l* which is strongest among
Eccl 9:4 dog is better than a dead *l*
Is 5:29 Their roaring shall be like a *l*
Is 11:6 and the calf and the young *l*
Is 11:7 the *l* shall eat straw like the ox
Is 21:8 And he cried, A *l*
Is 30:6 whence come the young and old *l*
Is 31:4 spoken unto me, Like as the *l*
Is 31:4 the young *l* roaring on his prey,
Is 35:9 No *l* shall be there, nor any
Is 38:13 till morning, that, as a *l*
Is 65:25 the *l* shall eat straw like the
Jer 2:30 prophets, like a destroying *l*
Jer 4:7 The *l* is come up from his thicket
Jer 5:6 Wherefore a *l* out of the forest
Jer 12:8 is unto me as a *l* in the forest
Jer 25:38 forsaken his covert, as the *l*
Jer 49:19 he shall come up like a *l* from
Jer 50:44 he shall come up like a *l* from
Lam 3:10 wait, and as a *l* in secret places
Eze 1:10 face of a man, and the face of a *l*
Eze 10:14 man, and the third the face of a *l*
Eze 19:3 it became a young *l*, and it
Eze 19:5 her whelps, and made him a young *l*
Eze 19:6 the lions, he became a young *l*
Eze 22:25 like a roaring *l* ravening the
Eze 32:2 art like a young *l* of the nations
Eze 41:19 the face of a young *l* toward the
Dan 7:4 The first was like a *l*, and had
Hos 5:14 For I will be unto Ephraim as a *l*
Hos 5:14 as a young *l* to the house of
Hos 11:10 he shall roar like a *l*
Hos 13:7 I will be unto them as a *l*
Hos 13:8 there will I devour them like a *l*
Joel 1:6 whose teeth are the teeth of a *l*
Joel 1:6 hath the cheek teeth of a great *l*
Amos 3:4 Will a *l* roar in the forest, when
Amos 3:4 will a young *l* cry out of his den
Amos 3:8 The *l* hath roared, who will not
Amos 3:12 of the mouth of the *l* two legs
Amos 5:19 As if a man did flee from a *l*
Mic 5:8 the midst of many people as a *l*
Mic 5:8 as a young *l* among the flocks of
Nah 2:11 of the young lions, where the *l*
Nah 2:11 even the old *l*
Nah 2:12 The *l* did tear in pieces enough
2Ti 4:17 out of the mouth of the *l*
1Pet 5:8 the devil, as a roaring *l*
Rev 4:7 And the first beast was like a *l*
Rev 5:5 the *L* of the tribe of Juda, the
Rev 10:3 a loud voice, as when a *l* roareth
Rev 13:2 and his mouth as the mouth of a *l*

**LION'S**
Gen 49:9 Judah is a *l* whelp
Deut 33:22 of Dan he said, Dan is a *l* whelp
Job 4:11 the stout *l* whelps are scattered
Job 28:8 The *l* whelps have not trodden it,
Ps 22:21 Save me from the *l* mouth
Nah 2:11 the *l* whelp, and none made them

**LIONS**
2Sa 1:23 eagles, they were stronger than *l*
1Kin 7:29 were between the ledges were *l*
1Kin 7:29 and beneath the *l* and oxen were
1Kin 7:36 thereof, he graved cherubims, *l*
1Kin 10:19 two *l* stood beside the stays
1Kin 10:20 twelve *l* stood there on the one
2Kin 17:25 the LORD sent *l* among them
2Kin 17:26 he hath sent *l* among them
1Chr 12:8 faces were like the faces of *l*
2Chr 9:18 two *l* standing by the stays
2Chr 9:19 twelve *l* stood there on the one
Job 4:10 lion, and the teeth of the young *l*
Job 38:39 fill the appetite of the young *l*
Ps 34:10 The young *l* do lack, and suffer
Ps 35:17 my darling from the *l*
Ps 57:4 My soul is among *l*
Ps 58:6 the great teeth of the young *l*
Ps 104:21 The young *l* roar after their prey
Is 5:29 they shall roar like young *l*
Is 15:9 *l* upon him that escapeth of Moab,
Jer 2:15 The young *l* roared upon him, and
Jer 50:17 the *l* have driven him away
Jer 51:38 They shall roar together like *l*
Eze 19:2 she lay down among *l*, she
Eze 19:2 her whelps among young *l*
Eze 19:6 And he went up and down among the *l*
Eze 38:13 with all the young *l* thereof
Dan 6:7 shall be cast into the den of *l*
Dan 6:12 shall be cast into the den of *l*
Dan 6:16 and cast him into the den of *l*
Dan 6:19 went in haste unto the den of *l*
Dan 6:20 able to deliver thee from the *l*
Dan 6:24 they cast them into the den of *l*
Dan 6:24 the *l* had the mastery of them, and
Dan 6:27 Daniel from the power of the *l*
Nah 2:11 Where is the dwelling of the *l*
Nah 2:11 the feeding place of the young *l*
Nah 2:13 sword shall devour thy young *l*
Zeph 3:3 princes within her are roaring *l*
Zec 11:3 a voice of the roaring of young *l*
Heb 11:33 promises, stopped the mouths of *l*
Rev 9:8 teeth were as the teeth of *l*
Rev 9:17 the horses were as the heads of *l*

**LIPS**
Ex 6:12 me, who am of uncircumcised *l*
Ex 6:30 Behold, I am of uncircumcised *l*
Lev 5:4 pronouncing with his *l* to do evil
Num 30:6 or uttered ought out of her *l*
Num 30:8 that which she uttered with her *l*
Num 30:12 out of her *l* concerning her vows
Deut 23:23 gone out of thy *l* thou shalt keep
1Sa 1:13 only her *l* moved, but her voice
2Kin 19:28 thy nose, and my bridle in thy *l*
Job 2:10 this did not Job sin with his *l*
Job 8:21 laughing, and thy *l* with rejoicing
Job 11:5 speak, and open his *l* against thee
Job 13:6 hearken to the pleadings of my *l*
Job 15:6 thine own *l* testify against thee
Job 16:5 the moving of my *l* should asswage
Job 23:12 from the commandment of his *l*
Job 27:4 My *l* shall not speak wickedness,
Job 32:20 I will open my *l* and answer
Job 33:3 my *l* shall utter knowledge
Ps 12:2 with flattering *l* and with a
Ps 12:3 shall cut off all flattering *l*
Ps 12:4 our *l* are our own
Ps 16:4 nor take up their names into my *l*
Ps 17:1 that goeth not out of feigned *l*
Ps 17:4 by the word of thy *l* I have kept
Ps 21:2 withholden the request of his *l*
Ps 31:18 Let the lying *l* be put to silence
Ps 34:13 thy *l* from speaking guile
Ps 40:9 lo, I have not refrained my *l*
Ps 45:2 grace is poured into thy *l*
Ps 51:15 O Lord, open thou my *l*
Ps 59:7 swords are in their *l*
Ps 59:12 the words of their *l* let them
Ps 63:3 than life, my *l* shall praise thee
Ps 63:5 shall praise thee with joyful *l*
Ps 66:14 Which my *l* have uttered, and my
Ps 71:23 My *l* shall greatly rejoice when I
Ps 89:34 thing that is gone out of my *l*
Ps 106:33 he spake unadvisedly with his *l*
Ps 119:13 With my *l* have I declared all the
Ps 119:171 My *l* shall utter praise, when
Ps 120:2 my soul, O LORD, from lying *l*
Ps 140:3 adders' poison is under their *l*
Ps 140:9 of their own *l* cover them
Ps 141:3 Keep the door of my *l*
Prov 4:24 perverse *l* put far from thee
Prov 5:2 that thy *l* may keep knowledge
Prov 5:3 For the *l* of a strange woman drop
Prov 7:21 of her *l* she forced him

Prov 8:6 the opening of my *l* shall be
Prov 8:7 is an abomination to my *l*
Prov 10:13 In the *l* of him that hath
Prov 10:18 that hideth hatred with lying *l*
Prov 10:19 he that refraineth his *l* is wise
Prov 10:21 The *l* of the righteous feed many
Prov 10:32 The *l* of the righteous know what
Prov 12:13 by the transgression of his *l*
Prov 12:22 Lying *l* are abomination to the
Prov 13:3 wide his *l* shall have destruction
Prov 14:3 but the *l* of the wise shall
Prov 14:7 not in him the *l* of knowledge
Prov 14:23 but the talk of the *l* tendeth
Prov 15:7 The *l* of the wise disperse
Prov 16:10 sentence is in the *l* of the king
Prov 16:13 Righteous *l* are the delight of
Prov 16:21 of the *l* increaseth learning
Prov 16:23 and addeth learning to his *l*
Prov 16:27 in his *l* there is as a burning
Prov 16:30 moving his *l* he bringeth evil to
Prov 17:4 doer giveth heed to false *l*
Prov 17:7 much less do lying *l* a prince
Prov 17:28 his *l* is esteemed a man of
Prov 18:6 A fool's *l* enter into contention,
Prov 18:7 his *l* are the snare of his soul
Prov 18:20 of his *l* shall he be filled
Prov 19:1 than he that is perverse in his *l*
Prov 20:15 but the *l* of knowledge are a
Prov 20:19 him that flattereth with his *l*
Prov 22:11 for the grace of his *l* the king
Prov 22:18 shall withal be fitted in thy *l*
Prov 23:16 when thy *l* speak right things
Prov 24:2 and their *l* talk of mischief
Prov 24:26 Every man shall kiss his *l* that
Prov 24:28 and deceive not with thy *l*
Prov 26:23 Burning *l* and a wicked heart are
Prov 26:24 hateth dissembleth with his *l*
Prov 27:2 a stranger, and not thine own *l*
Eccl 10:12 but the *l* of a fool will swallow
Song 4:3 Thy *l* are like a thread of
Song 4:11 Thy *l*, O my spouse, drop as the
Song 5:13 his *l* like lilies, dropping sweet
Song 7:9 causing the *l* of those that are
Is 6:5 because I am a man of unclean *l*
Is 6:5 midst of a people of unclean *l*
Is 6:7 said, Lo, this hath touched thy *l*
Is 11:4 with the breath of his *l* shall he
Is 28:11 For with stammering *l* and another
Is 29:13 with their *l* do honour me, but
Is 30:27 his *l* are full of indignation, and
Is 37:29 thy nose, and my bridle in thy *l*
Is 57:19 I create the fruit of the *l*
Is 59:3 your *l* have spoken lies, your
Jer 17:16 out of my *l* was right before thee
Lam 3:62 The *l* of those that rose up
Eze 24:17 upon thy feet, and cover not thy *l*
Eze 24:22 ye shall not cover your *l*
Eze 36:3 are taken up in the *l* of talkers
Dan 10:16 of the sons of men touched my *l*
Hos 14:2 we render the calves of our *l*
Mic 3:7 yea, they shall all cover their *l*
Hab 3:16 my *l* quivered at the voice
Mal 2:6 iniquity was not found in his *l*
Mal 2:7 For the priest's *l* should keep
Mt 15:8 and honoureth me with their *l*
Mk 7:6 people honoureth me with their *l*
Rom 3:13 poison of asps is under their *l*
1Cor 14:21 other *l* will I speak unto this
Heb 13:15 the fruit of our *l* giving thanks
1Pet 3:10 his *l* that they speak no guile

**LITTLE**

Gen 18:4 Let a *l* water, I pray you, be
Gen 19:20 to flee unto, and it is a *l* one
Gen 19:20 thither, (is it not a *l* one
Gen 24:17 drink a *l* water of thy pitcher
Gen 24:43 a *l* water of thy pitcher to drink
Gen 30:30 For it was *l* which thou hadst
Gen 34:29 their wealth, and all their *l* ones
Gen 35:16 there was but a *l* way to come to
Gen 43:2 them, Go again, buy us a *l* food
Gen 43:8 we, and thou, and also our *l* ones
Gen 43:11 a *l* balm, and a *l* honey,
Gen 44:20 a child of his old age, a *l* one
Gen 44:25 Go again, and buy us a *l* food
Gen 45:19 the land of Egypt for your *l* ones
Gen 46:5 their father, and their *l* ones
Gen 47:24 and for food for your *l* ones
Gen 48:7 but a *l* way to come unto Ephrath
Gen 50:8 only their *l* ones, and their
Gen 50:21 will nourish you, and your *l* ones
Ex 10:10 I will let you go, and your *l* ones
Ex 10:24 let your *l* ones also go with you
Ex 12:4 household be too *l* for the lamb
Ex 16:18 and he that gathered *l* had no lack
Ex 23:30 By *l* and *l* I will drive them
Lev 11:17 And the *l* owl, and the cormorant,
Num 14:31 But your *l* ones, which ye said
Num 16:27 their sons, and their *l* children
Num 31:9 Midian captives, and their *l* ones
Num 31:17 kill every male among the *l* ones
Num 32:16 cattle, and cities for our *l* ones
Num 32:17 our *l* ones shall dwell in the
Num 32:24 Build you cities for your *l* ones
Num 32:26 Our *l* ones, our wives, our flocks
Deut 1:39 Moreover your *l* ones, which ye
Deut 2:34 the *l* ones, of every city, we
Deut 3:19 But your wives, and your *l* ones
Deut 7:22 before thee by *l* and *l*
Deut 14:16 The *l* owl, and the great owl, and
Deut 20:14 the *l* ones, and the cattle, and all
Deut 28:38 field, and shalt gather but *l* in
Deut 29:11 Your *l* ones, your wives, and thy
Josh 1:14 Your wives, your *l* ones, and your
Josh 8:35 the *l* ones, and the strangers that
Josh 19:47 of Dan went out too *l* for them
Josh 22:17 the iniquity of Peor too *l* for us
Judg 4:19 I pray thee, a *l* water to drink
Judg 18:21 and departed, and put the *l* ones
Ruth 2:7 that she tarried a *l* in the house
1Sa 2:19 his mother made him a *l* coat
1Sa 14:29 I tasted a *l* of this honey
1Sa 14:43 I did but taste a *l* honey with
1Sa 15:17 When thou wast *l* in thine own
1Sa 20:35 with David, and a *l* lad with him
2Sa 12:3 had nothing, save one *l* ewe lamb
2Sa 12:8 and if that had been too *l*
2Sa 15:22 all the *l* ones that were with him
2Sa 16:1 when David was a *l* past the top
2Sa 19:36 Thy servant will go a *l* way over
1Kin 3:7 and I am but a *l* child
1Kin 8:64 was before the LORD was too *l* to
1Kin 11:17 Hadad being yet a *l* child
1Kin 12:10 My *l* finger shall be thicker than
1Kin 17:10 a *l* water in a vessel, that I may
1Kin 17:12 a barrel, and a *l* oil in a cruse
1Kin 17:13 make me thereof a *l* cake first
1Kin 18:44 there ariseth a *l* cloud out of
1Kin 20:27 them like two *l* flocks of kids
2Kin 2:23 there came forth *l* children out
2Kin 4:10 Let us make a *l* chamber, I pray
2Kin 5:2 of the land of Israel a *l* maid
2Kin 5:14 like unto the flesh of a *l* child
2Kin 5:19 So he departed from him a *l* way
2Kin 10:18 unto them, Ahab served Baal a *l*
2Chr 10:10 My *l* finger shall be thicker than
2Chr 20:13 the LORD, with their *l* ones
2Chr 31:18 the genealogy of all their *l* ones
Ezr 8:21 way for us, and for our *l* ones
Ezr 9:8 now for a *l* space grace hath been
Ezr 9:8 give us a *l* reviving in our
Neh 9:32 the trouble seem *l* before thee
Est 3:13 *l* children and women, in one day,
Est 8:11 would assault them, both *l* ones
Job 4:12 and mine ear received a *l* thereof
Job 10:20 that I may take comfort a *l*
Job 21:11 forth their *l* ones like a flock
Job 24:24 They are exalted for a *l* while
Job 26:14 but how *l* a portion is heard of
Job 36:2 Suffer me a *l*, and I will shew
Ps 2:12 when his wrath is kindled but a *l*
Ps 8:5 him a *l* lower than the angels
Ps 37:10 For yet a *l* while, and the wicked
Ps 37:16 A *l* that a righteous man hath is
Ps 65:12 the *l* hills rejoice on every side
Ps 68:27 There is *l* Benjamin with their
Ps 72:3 the *l* hills, by righteousness
Ps 114:4 rams, and the *l* hills like lambs
Ps 114:6 and ye *l* hills, like lambs
Ps 137:9 dasheth thy *l* ones against the
Prov 6:10 Yet a *l* sleep, a *l* slumber,
Prov 6:10 a *l* folding of the hands to sleep
Prov 10:20 heart of the wicked is *l* worth
Prov 15:16 Better is *l* with the fear of the
Prov 16:8 Better is a *l* with righteousness
Prov 24:33 Yet a *l* sleep, a *l* slumber,
Prov 24:33 a *l* folding of the hands to sleep
Prov 30:24 things which are *l* upon the earth
Eccl 5:12 sweet, whether he eat *l* or much
Eccl 9:14 There was a *l* city, and few men
Eccl 10:1 so doth a *l* folly him that is in
Song 2:15 the *l* foxes, that spoil the vines
Song 3:4 It was but a *l* that I passed from
Song 8:8 We have a *l* sister, and she hath
Is 10:25 For yet a very *l* while, and the
Is 11:6 a *l* child shall lead them
Is 26:20 thyself as it were for a *l* moment
Is 28:10 here a *l*, and there a *l*
Is 28:13 here a *l*, and there a *l*
Is 29:17 Is it not yet a very *l* while
Is 40:15 up the isles as a very *l* thing
Is 54:8 In a *l* wrath I hid my face from
Is 60:22 A *l* one shall become a thousand,
Is 63:18 have possessed it but a *l* while
Jer 14:3 sent their *l* ones to the waters
Jer 48:4 her *l* ones have caused a cry to
Jer 51:33 yet a *l* while, and the time of her
Eze 9:6 maids, and *l* children, and women
Eze 11:16 as a *l* sanctuary in the countries
Eze 16:47 as if that were a very *l* thing
Eze 31:4 sent out her *l* rivers unto all
Eze 40:7 every *l* chamber was one reed long
Eze 40:7 between the *l* chambers were five
Eze 40:10 the *l* chambers of the gate
Eze 40:12 The space also before the *l*
Eze 40:12 the *l* chambers were six cubits on
Eze 40:13 the gate from the roof of one *l*
Eze 40:16 narrow windows to the *l* chambers
Eze 40:21 the *l* chambers thereof were three
Eze 40:29 the *l* chambers thereof, and the
Eze 40:33 the *l* chambers thereof, and the
Eze 40:36 The *l* chambers thereof, the posts
Dan 7:8 came up among them another *l* horn
Dan 8:9 one of them came forth a *l* horn
Dan 11:34 shall be holpen with a *l* help
Hos 1:4 for yet a *l* while, and I will
Hos 8:10 they shall sorrow a *l* for the
Amos 6:11 and the *l* house with clefts
Mic 5:2 though thou be *l* among the
Hag 1:6 Ye have sown much, and bring in *l*
Hag 1:9 for much, and, lo, it came to *l*
Hag 2:6 Yet once, it is a *l* while
Zec 1:15 for I was but a *l* displeased
Zec 13:7 turn mine hand upon the *l* ones
Mt 6:30 more clothe you, O ye of *l* faith
Mt 8:26 are ye fearful, O ye of *l* faith
Mt 10:42 *l* ones a cup of cold water only
Mt 14:31 said unto him, O thou of *l* faith
Mt 15:34 said, Seven, and a few *l* fishes
Mt 16:8 said unto them, O ye of *l* faith
Mt 18:2 Jesus called a *l* child unto him
Mt 18:3 and become as *l* children, ye
Mt 18:4 humble himself as this *l* child
Mt 18:5 whoso shall receive one such *l*
Mt 18:6 these *l* ones which believe in me
Mt 18:10 despise not one of these *l* ones
Mt 18:14 that one of these *l* ones should
Mt 19:13 there brought unto him *l* children
Mt 19:14 Suffer *l* children, and forbid them
Mt 26:39 And he went a *l* farther, and fell
Mk 1:19 he had gone a *l* farther thence
Mk 4:36 were also with him other *l* ships
Mk 5:23 My *l* daughter lieth at the point
Mk 9:42 these *l* ones that believe in me
Mk 10:14 Suffer the *l* children to come
Mk 10:15 the kingdom of God as a *l* child
Mk 14:35 And he went forward a *l*, and fell
Mk 14:70 a *l* after, they that stood by
Lk 5:3 thrust out a *l* from the land
Lk 7:47 but to whom *l* is forgiven
Lk 7:47 is forgiven, the same loveth *l*
Lk 12:28 he clothe you, O ye of *l* faith
Lk 12:32 Fear not, *l* flock
Lk 17:2 should offend one of these *l* ones
Lk 18:16 Suffer *l* children to come unto me
Lk 18:17 a *l* child shall in no wise enter
Lk 19:3 because he was *l* of stature
Lk 19:17 hast been faithful in a very *l*
Lk 22:58 after a *l* while another saw him,
Jn 6:7 every one of them may take a *l*
Jn 7:33 Yet a *l* while am I with you, and
Jn 12:35 Yet a *l* while is the light with
Jn 13:33 *L* children, yet a *l* while I
Jn 14:19 Yet a *l* while, and the world seeth
Jn 16:16 A *l* while, and ye shall not see me
Jn 16:16 a *l* while, and ye shall see me,
Jn 16:17 A *l* while, and ye shall not see me
Jn 16:17 a *l* while, and ye shall see me
Jn 16:18 is this that he saith, A *l* while
Jn 16:19 A *l* while, and ye shall not see me

Jn 16:19 a *l* while, and ye shall see me
Jn 21:8 other disciples came in a *l* ship
Acts 5:34 put the apostles forth a *l* space
Acts 20:12 alive, and were not a *l* comforted
Acts 27:28 and when they had gone a *l* further
Acts 28:2 people shewed us no *l* kindness
1Cor 5:6 Know ye not that a *l* leaven
2Cor 8:15 that had gathered *l* had no lack
2Cor 11:1 bear with me a *l* in my folly
2Cor 11:16 me, that I may boast myself a *l*
Gal 4:19 My *l* children, of whom I travail
Gal 5:9 A *l* leaven leaveneth the whole
1Ti 4:8 For bodily exercise profiteth *l*
1Ti 5:23 water, but use a *l* wine for thy
Heb 2:7 Thou madest him a *l* lower than
Heb 2:9 who was made a *l* lower than the
Heb 10:37 For yet a *l* while, and he that
Jas 3:5 Even so the tongue is a *l* member
Jas 3:5 great a matter a *l* fire kindleth
Jas 4:14 that appeareth for a *l* time
1Jn 2:1 My *l* children, these things write
1Jn 2:12 *l* children, because your sins are
1Jn 2:13 *l* children, because ye have known
1Jn 2:18 *L* children, it is the last time
1Jn 2:28 And now, *l* children, abide in him
1Jn 3:7 *L* children, let no man deceive
1Jn 3:18 My *l* children, let us not love in
1Jn 4:4 *l* children, and have overcome them
1Jn 5:21 *L* children, keep yourselves from
Rev 3:8 for thou hast a *l* strength
Rev 6:11 should rest yet for a *l* season
Rev 10:2 he had in his hand a *l* book open
Rev 10:8 take the *l* book which is open in
Rev 10:9 said unto him, Give me the *l* book
Rev 10:10 I took the *l* book out of the
Rev 20:3 that he must be loosed a *l* season

**LIVE**

Gen 3:22 of life, and eat, and *l* for ever
Gen 12:13 my soul shall *l* because of thee
Gen 17:18 that Ishmael might *l* before thee
Gen 19:20 and my soul shall *l*
Gen 20:7 pray for thee, and thou shalt *l*
Gen 27:40 And by thy sword shalt thou *l*
Gen 31:32 findest thy gods, let him not *l*
Gen 42:2 that we may *l*, and not die
Gen 42:18 them the third day, This do, and *l*
Gen 43:8 that we may *l*, and not die, both
Gen 45:3 doth my father yet *l*
Gen 47:19 and give us seed, that we may *l*
Ex 1:16 be a daughter, then she shall *l*
Ex 19:13 be beast or man, it shall not *l*
Ex 21:35 then they shall sell the *l* ox
Ex 22:18 shalt not suffer a witch to *l*
Ex 33:20 there shall no man see me, and *l*
Lev 16:20 altar, he shall bring the *l* goat
Lev 16:21 hands upon the head of the *l* goat
Lev 18:5 if a man do, he shall *l* in them
Lev 25:35 that he may *l* with thee
Lev 25:36 that thy brother may *l* with thee
Num 4:19 do unto them, that they may *l*
Num 14:21 But as truly as I *l*, all the
Num 14:28 Say unto them, As truly as I *l*
Num 21:8 when he looketh upon it, shall *l*
Num 24:23 who shall *l* when God doeth this
Deut 4:1 for to do them, that ye may *l*
Deut 4:10 that they shall *l* upon the earth
Deut 4:33 fire, as thou hast heard, and *l*
Deut 4:42 one of these cities he might *l*
Deut 5:33 hath commanded you, that ye may *l*
Deut 8:1 ye observe to do, that ye may *l*
Deut 8:3 that man doth not *l* by bread only
Deut 8:3 the mouth of the LORD doth man *l*
Deut 12:1 the days that ye *l* upon the earth
Deut 16:20 thou follow, that thou mayest *l*
Deut 19:4 shall flee thither, that he may *l*
Deut 19:5 unto one of those cities, and *l*
Deut 30:6 all thy soul, that thou mayest *l*
Deut 30:16 his judgments, that thou mayest *l*
Deut 30:19 that both thou and thy seed may *l*
Deut 31:13 as long as ye *l* in the land
Deut 32:40 to heaven, and say, I *l* for ever
Deut 33:6 Let Reuben *l*, and not die
Josh 6:17 only Rahab the harlot shall *l*
Josh 9:15 a league with them, to let them *l*
Josh 9:20 we will even let them *l*, lest
Josh 9:21 said unto them, Let them *l*
1Sa 20:14 I *l* shew me the kindness of the
2Sa 1:10 not *l* after that he was fallen
2Sa 12:22 to me, that the child may *l*
2Sa 19:34 the king, How long have I to *l*
1Kin 1:31 Let my lord king David *l* for ever
1Kin 8:40 thee all the days that they *l* in
1Kin 20:32 saith, I pray thee, let me *l*
2Kin 4:7 *l* thou and thy children of the
2Kin 7:4 if they save us alive, we shall *l*
2Kin 10:19 shall be wanting, he shall not *l*
2Kin 18:32 olive and of honey, that ye may *l*
2Kin 20:1 for thou shalt die, and not *l*
2Chr 6:31 so long as they *l* in the land
Neh 2:3 the king, Let the king *l* for ever
Neh 5:2 for them, that we may eat, and *l*
Neh 9:29 if a man do, he shall *l* in them
Est 4:11 the golden sceptre, that he may *l*
Job 7:16 I would not *l* alway
Job 14:14 If a man die, shall he *l* again
Job 21:7 Wherefore do the wicked *l*
Job 27:6 not reproach me so long as I *l*
Ps 22:26 your heart shall *l* for ever
Ps 49:9 That he should still *l* for ever
Ps 55:23 shall not *l* out half their days
Ps 63:4 Thus will I bless thee while I *l*
Ps 69:32 your heart shall *l* that seek God
Ps 72:15 And he shall *l*, and to him shall be
Ps 104:33 sing unto the LORD as long as I *l*
Ps 116:2 I call upon him as long as I *l*
Ps 118:17 I shall not die, but *l*, and
Ps 119:17 with thy servant, that I may *l*
Ps 119:77 come unto me, that I may *l*
Ps 119:116 unto thy word, that I may *l*
Ps 119:144 me understanding, and I shall *l*
Ps 119:175 Let my soul *l*, and it shall praise
Ps 146:2 While I *l* will I praise the LORD
Prov 4:4 keep my commandments, and *l*
Prov 7:2 Keep my commandments, and *l*
Prov 9:6 Forsake the foolish, and *l*
Prov 15:27 but he that hateth gifts shall *l*
Eccl 6:3 *l* many years, so that the days of
Eccl 6:6 though he *l* a thousand years
Eccl 9:3 is in their heart while they *l*
Eccl 9:9 *L* joyfully with the wife whom
Eccl 11:8 But if a man *l* many years
Is 6:6 having a *l* coal in his hand,
Is 26:14 They are dead, they shall not *l*
Is 26:19 Thy dead men shall *l*, together
Is 38:1 for thou shalt die, and not *l*
Is 38:16 O Lord, by these things men *l*
Is 38:16 thou recover me, and make me to *l*
Is 49:18 As I *l*, saith the LORD, thou
Is 55:3 hear, and your soul shall *l*
Jer 21:9 that besiege you, he shall *l*
Jer 22:24 As I *l*, saith the LORD, though
Jer 27:12 and serve him and his people, and *l*
Jer 27:17 serve the king of Babylon, and *l*
Jer 35:7 that ye may *l* many days in the
Jer 38:2 forth to the Chaldeans shall *l*
Jer 38:2 his life for a prey, and shall *l*
Jer 38:17 princes, then thy soul shall *l*
Jer 38:17 and thou shalt *l*, and thine house
Jer 38:20 unto thee, and thy soul shall *l*
Jer 46:18 As I *l*, saith the King, whose
Lam 4:20 we shall *l* among the heathen
Eze 3:21 doth not sin, he shall surely *l*
Eze 5:11 Wherefore, as I *l*, saith the Lord
Eze 13:19 the souls alive that should not *l*
Eze 14:16 three men were in it, as I *l*
Eze 14:18 three men were in it, as I *l*
Eze 14:20 and Job, were in it, as I *l*
Eze 16:6 when thou wast in thy blood, *L*
Eze 16:6 when thou wast in thy blood, *L*
Eze 16:48 As I *l*, saith the Lord GOD, Sodom
Eze 17:16 As I *l*, saith the Lord GOD,
Eze 17:19 As I *l*, surely mine oath that he
Eze 18:3 As I *l*, saith the Lord GOD, ye
Eze 18:9 he is just, he shall surely *l*
Eze 18:13 shall he then *l*
Eze 18:13 he shall not *l*
Eze 18:17 of his father, he shall surely *l*
Eze 18:19 hath done them, he shall surely *l*
Eze 18:21 and right, he shall surely *l*
Eze 18:22 that he hath done he shall *l*
Eze 18:23 should return from his ways, and *l*
Eze 18:24 the wicked man doeth, shall he *l*
Eze 18:28 hath committed, he shall surely *l*
Eze 18:32 turn yourselves, and *l* ye
Eze 20:3 As I *l*, saith the Lord GOD, I
Eze 20:11 a man do, he shall even *l* in them
Eze 20:13 a man do, he shall even *l* in them
Eze 20:21 a man do, he shall even *l* in them
Eze 20:25 whereby they should not *l*
Eze 20:31 As I *l*, saith the Lord GOD, I
Eze 20:33 As I *l*, saith the Lord GOD,
Eze 33:10 in them, how should we then *l*
Eze 33:11 Say unto them, As I *l*, saith the
Eze 33:11 the wicked turn from his way and *l*
Eze 33:12 to *l* for his righteousness in the
Eze 33:13 righteous, that he shall surely *l*
Eze 33:15 he shall surely *l*, he shall not
Eze 33:16 he shall surely *l*
Eze 33:19 and right, he shall *l* thereby
Eze 33:27 As I *l*, surely they that are in
Eze 34:8 As I *l* saith the Lord GOD, surely
Eze 35:6 Therefore, as I *l*, saith the Lord
Eze 35:11 Therefore, as I *l*, saith the Lord
Eze 37:3 me, Son of man, can these bones *l*
Eze 37:5 to enter into you, and ye shall *l*
Eze 37:6 put breath in you, and ye shall *l*
Eze 37:9 upon these slain, that they may *l*
Eze 37:14 my spirit in you, and ye shall *l*
Eze 47:9 the rivers shall come, shall *l*
Eze 47:9 every thing shall *l* whither the
Dan 2:4 in Syriack, O king, *l* for ever
Dan 3:9 O king, *l* for ever
Dan 5:10 spake and said, O king, *l* for ever
Dan 6:6 unto him, King Darius, *l* for ever
Dan 6:21 unto the king, O king, *l* for ever
Hos 6:2 us up, and we shall *l* in his sight
Amos 5:4 Israel, Seek ye me, and ye shall *l*
Amos 5:6 Seek the LORD, and ye shall *l*
Amos 5:14 good, and not evil, that ye may *l*
Jonah 4:3 is better for me to die than to *l*
Jonah 4:8 is better for me to die than to *l*
Hab 2:4 but the just shall *l* by his faith
Zeph 2:9 Therefore as I *l*, saith the LORD
Zec 1:5 the prophets, do they *l* for ever
Zec 10:9 they shall *l* with their children,
Zec 13:3 say unto him, Thou shalt not *l*
Mt 4:4 Man shall not *l* by bread alone,
Mt 9:18 thy hand upon her, and she shall *l*
Mk 5:23 and she shall *l*
Lk 4:4 man shall not *l* by bread alone
Lk 7:25 *l* delicately, are in kings'
Lk 10:28 this do, and thou shalt *l*
Lk 20:38 for all *l* unto him
Jn 5:25 and they that hear shall *l*
Jn 6:51 this bread, he shall *l* for ever
Jn 6:57 sent me, and I *l* by the Father
Jn 6:57 eateth me, even he shall *l* by me
Jn 6:58 of this bread shall *l* for ever
Jn 11:25 he were dead, yet shall he *l*
Jn 14:19 because I *l*, ye shall *l* also
Acts 7:19 to the end they might not *l*
Acts 17:28 For in him we *l*, and move, and have
Acts 22:22 it is not fit that he should *l*
Acts 25:24 that he ought not to *l* any longer
Acts 28:4 yet vengeance suffereth not to *l*
Rom 1:17 The just shall *l* by faith
Rom 6:2 dead to sin, *l* any longer therein
Rom 6:8 that we shall also *l* with him
Rom 8:12 the flesh, to *l* after the flesh
Rom 8:13 For if ye *l* after the flesh, ye
Rom 8:13 the deeds of the body, ye shall *l*
Rom 10:5 those things shall *l* by them
Rom 12:18 in you, *l* peaceably with all men
Rom 14:8 we *l*, we *l* unto the Lord
Rom 14:8 whether we *l* therefore, or die,
Rom 14:11 For it is written, As I *l*
1Cor 9:13 minister about holy things *l* of
1Cor 9:14 the gospel should *l* of the gospel
2Cor 4:11 For we which *l* are alway
2Cor 5:15 that they which *l* should not
2Cor 5:15 not henceforth *l* unto themselves
2Cor 6:9 as dying, and, behold, we *l*
2Cor 7:3 our hearts to die and *l* with you
2Cor 13:4 but we shall *l* with him by the
2Cor 13:11 be of one mind, *l* in peace
Gal 2:14 the Gentiles to *l* as do the Jews
Gal 2:19 the law, that I might *l* unto God
Gal 2:20 nevertheless I *l*
Gal 2:20 the life which I now *l* in the
Gal 2:20 *l* by the faith of the Son of God
Gal 3:11 for, The just shall *l* by faith
Gal 3:12 that doeth them shall *l* in them
Gal 5:25 If we *l* in the Spirit, let us
Eph 6:3 thou mayest *l* long on the earth
Phil 1:21 For to me to *l* is Christ, and to
Phil 1:22 But if I *l* in the flesh, this is
1Th 3:8 For now we *l*, if ye stand fast in
1Th 5:10 we should *l* together with him
2Ti 2:11 him, we shall also *l* with him

2Ti 3:12 all that will *l* godly in Christ
Titus 2:12 lusts, we should *l* soberly
Heb 10:38 Now the just shall *l* by faith
Heb 12:9 unto the Father of spirits, and *l*
Heb 13:18 all things willing to *l* honestly
Jas 4:15 say, If the Lord will, we shall *l*
1Pet 2:24 should *l* unto righteousness
1Pet 4:2 That he no longer should *l* the
1Pet 4:6 but *l* according to God in the
2Pet 2:6 those that after should *l* ungodly
2Pet 2:18 escaped from them who *l* in error
1Jn 4:9 that we might *l* through him
Rev 13:14 the wound by a sword, and did *l*

### LIVED

Gen 5:3 Adam *l* an hundred and thirty years
Gen 5:5 that Adam *l* were nine hundred
Gen 5:6 Seth *l* an hundred and five years,
Gen 5:7 Seth *l* after he begat Enos eight
Gen 5:9 Enos *l* ninety years, and begat
Gen 5:10 Enos *l* after he begat Cainan
Gen 5:12 Cainan *l* seventy years, and begat
Gen 5:13 And Cainan *l* after he begat
Gen 5:15 And Mahalaleel *l* sixty and five
Gen 5:16 Mahalaleel *l* after he begat Jared
Gen 5:18 Jared *l* an hundred sixty and two
Gen 5:19 Jared *l* after he begat Enoch
Gen 5:21 And Enoch *l* sixty and five years,
Gen 5:25 Methuselah *l* an hundred eighty and
Gen 5:26 Methuselah *l* after he begat
Gen 5:28 Lamech *l* an hundred eighty and two
Gen 5:30 Lamech *l* after he begat Noah five
Gen 9:28 Noah *l* after the flood three
Gen 11:11 Shem *l* after he begat Arphaxad
Gen 11:12 And Arphaxad *l* five and thirty
Gen 11:13 Arphaxad *l* after he begat Salah
Gen 11:14 Salah *l* thirty years, and begat
Gen 11:15 Salah *l* after he begat Eber four
Gen 11:16 And Eber *l* four and thirty years,
Gen 11:17 Eber *l* after he begat Peleg four
Gen 11:18 Peleg *l* thirty years, and begat
Gen 11:19 Peleg *l* after he begat Reu two
Gen 11:20 And Reu *l* two and thirty years, and
Gen 11:21 Reu *l* after he begat Serug two
Gen 11:22 Serug *l* thirty years, and begat
Gen 11:23 Serug *l* after he begat Nahor two
Gen 11:24 And Nahor *l* nine and twenty years,
Gen 11:25 Nahor *l* after he begat Terah an
Gen 11:26 Terah *l* seventy years, and begat
Gen 25:6 Isaac his son, while he yet *l*
Gen 25:7 of Abraham's life which he *l*
Gen 47:28 Jacob *l* in the land of Egypt
Gen 50:22 Joseph *l* an hundred and ten years
Num 14:38 went to search the land, *l* still
Num 21:9 beheld the serpent of brass, he *l*
Deut 5:26 of the fire, as we have, and *l*
2Sa 19:6 I perceive, that if Absalom had *l*
1Kin 12:6 Solomon his father while he yet *l*
2Kin 14:17 *l* after the death of Jehoash son
2Chr 10:6 Solomon his father while he yet *l*
2Chr 25:25 the son of Joash king of Judah *l*
Job 42:16 After this *l* Job an hundred and
Ps 49:18 Though while he *l* he blessed his
Eze 37:10 breath came into them, and they *l*
Lk 2:36 had *l* with an husband seven years
Acts 23:1 I have *l* in all good conscience
Acts 26:5 of our religion I *l* a Pharisee
Col 3:7 some time, when ye *l* in them
Jas 5:5 Ye have *l* in pleasure on the
Rev 18:7 *l* deliciously, so much torment and
Rev 18:9 *l* deliciously with her, shall
Rev 20:4 and they *l* and reigned with Christ
Rev 20:5 But the rest of the dead *l* not

### LIVELY

Ex 1:19 for they are *l*, and are delivered
Ps 38:19 But mine enemies are *l*, and they
Acts 7:38 who received the *l* oracles to
1Pet 1:3 a *l* hope by the resurrection of
1Pet 2:5 as *l* stones, are built up a

### LIVER

Ex 29:13 and the caul that is above the *l*
Ex 29:22 inwards, and the caul above the *l*
Lev 3:4 flanks, and the caul above the *l*
Lev 3:10 flanks, and the caul above the *l*
Lev 3:15 flanks, and the caul above the *l*
Lev 4:9 flanks, and the caul above the *l*
Lev 7:4 and the caul that is above the *l*
Lev 8:16 inwards, and the caul above the *l*
Lev 8:25 inwards, and the caul above the *l*
Lev 9:10 the caul above the *l* of the sin
Lev 9:19 kidneys, and the caul above the *l*
Prov 7:23 Till a dart strike through his *l*
Lam 2:11 my *l* is poured upon the earth,
Eze 21:21 with images, he looked in the *l*

### LIVES

Gen 9:5 blood of your *l* will I require
Gen 45:7 to save your *l* by a great
Gen 47:25 they said, Thou hast saved our *l*
Ex 1:14 they made their *l* bitter with
Josh 2:13 have, and deliver our *l* from death
Josh 9:24 afraid of our *l* because of you
Judg 5:18 *l* unto the death in the high
Judg 18:25 with the *l* of thy household
2Sa 1:23 lovely and pleasant in their *l*
2Sa 19:5 the *l* of thy sons and of thy
2Sa 19:5 the *l* of thy wives
2Sa 19:5 and the *l* of thy concubines
2Sa 23:17 that went in jeopardy of their *l*
1Chr 11:19 that have put their *l* in jeopardy
1Chr 11:19 of their *l* they brought it
Est 9:16 together, and stood for their *l*
Prov 1:18 they lurk privily for their own *l*
Jer 19:7 hands of them that seek their *l*
Jer 19:9 and they that seek their *l*
Jer 46:26 hand of those that seek their *l*
Jer 48:6 Flee, save your *l*, and be like the
Lam 5:9 our *l* because of the sword of the
Dan 7:12 yet their *l* were prolonged for a
Lk 9:56 is not come to destroy men's *l*
Acts 15:26 Men that have hazarded their *l*
Acts 27:10 lading and ship, but also of our *l*
1Jn 3:16 lay down our *l* for the brethren
Rev 12:11 loved not their *l* unto the death

### LIVETH

Gen 9:3 that *l* shall be meat for you
Deut 5:24 God doth talk with man, and he *l*
Judg 8:19 as the LORD *l*, if ye had saved
Ruth 3:13 a kinsman to thee, as the LORD *l*
1Sa 1:26 said, Oh my lord, as thy soul *l*
1Sa 1:28 as long as he *l* he shall be lent
1Sa 14:39 For, as the LORD *l*, which saveth
1Sa 14:45 as the LORD *l*, there shall not
1Sa 17:55 And Abner said, As thy soul *l*
1Sa 19:6 and Saul sware, As the LORD *l*
1Sa 20:3 the LORD *l*, and as thy soul *l*
1Sa 20:21 as the LORD *l*
1Sa 20:31 son of Jesse *l* upon the ground
1Sa 25:6 say to him that *l* in prosperity
1Sa 25:26 the LORD *l*, and as thy soul *l*
1Sa 25:34 deed, as the LORD God of Israel *l*
1Sa 26:10 said furthermore, As the LORD *l*
1Sa 26:16 As the LORD *l*, ye are worthy to
1Sa 28:10 the LORD, saying, As the LORD *l*
1Sa 29:6 unto him, Surely, as the LORD *l*
2Sa 2:27 And Joab said, As God *l*, unless
2Sa 4:9 and said unto them, As the LORD *l*
2Sa 11:11 as thou livest, and as thy soul *l*
2Sa 12:5 he said to Nathan, As the LORD *l*
2Sa 14:11 And he said, As the LORD *l*
2Sa 14:19 answered and said, As thy soul *l*
2Sa 15:21 the king, and said, As the LORD *l*
2Sa 15:21 and as my lord the king *l*
2Sa 22:47 The LORD *l*
1Kin 1:29 sware, and said, As the LORD *l*
1Kin 2:24 Now therefore, as the LORD *l*
1Kin 3:23 one saith, This is my son that *l*
1Kin 17:1 Ahab, As the LORD God of Israel *l*
1Kin 17:12 she said, As the LORD thy God *l*
1Kin 17:23 and Elijah said, See, thy son *l*
1Kin 18:10 As the LORD thy God *l*, there is
1Kin 18:15 said, As the LORD of hosts *l*
1Kin 22:14 And Micaiah said, As the LORD *l*
2Kin 2:2 the LORD *l*, and as thy soul *l*
2Kin 2:4 the LORD *l*, and as thy soul *l*
2Kin 2:6 the LORD *l*, and as thy soul *l*
2Kin 3:14 said, As the LORD of hosts *l*
2Kin 4:30 the LORD *l*, and as thy soul *l*
2Kin 5:16 But he said, As the LORD *l*
2Kin 5:20 but, as the LORD *l*, I will run
2Chr 18:13 And Micaiah said, As the LORD *l*
Job 19:25 For I know that my redeemer *l*
Job 27:2 As God *l*, who hath taken away my
Ps 18:46 The LORD *l*
Ps 89:48 What man is he that *l*, and shall
Jer 4:2 And thou shalt swear, The LORD *l*
Jer 5:2 And though they say, The LORD *l*
Jer 12:16 to swear by my name, The LORD *l*
Jer 16:14 shall no more be said, The LORD *l*
Jer 16:15 But, The LORD *l*, that brought up
Jer 23:7 shall no more say, The LORD *l*
Jer 23:8 But, The LORD *l*, which brought up
Jer 38:16 Jeremiah, saying, As the LORD *l*
Jer 44:26 of Egypt, saying, The Lord GOD *l*
Eze 47:9 to pass, that every thing that *l*
Dan 4:34 and honoured him that *l* for ever
Dan 12:7 sware by him that *l* for ever that
Hos 4:15 Beth-aven, nor swear, The LORD *l*
Amos 8:14 and say, Thy god, O Dan, *l*
Amos 8:14 and, The manner of Beer-sheba *l*
Jn 4:50 thy son *l*
Jn 4:51 and told him, saying, Thy son *l*
Jn 4:53 Jesus said unto him, Thy son *l*
Jn 11:26 And whosoever *l* and believeth in me
Rom 6:10 in that he *l*, he *l* unto God
Rom 7:1 over a man as long as he *l*
Rom 7:2 to her husband so long as he *l*
Rom 7:3 So then if, while her husband *l*
Rom 14:7 For none of us *l* to himself
1Cor 7:39 the law as long as her husband *l*
2Cor 13:4 yet he *l* by the power of God
Gal 2:20 yet not I, but Christ *l* in me
1Ti 5:6 But she that *l* in pleasure is
1Ti 5:6 in pleasure is dead while she *l*
Heb 7:8 of whom it is witnessed that he *l*
Heb 7:25 by him, seeing he ever *l* to make
Heb 9:17 at all while the testator *l*
1Pet 1:23 by the word of God, which *l*
Rev 1:18 I am he that *l*, and was dead
Rev 4:9 throne, who *l* for ever and ever,
Rev 4:10 and worship him that *l* for ever
Rev 5:14 and worshipped him that *l* for ever
Rev 10:6 And sware by him that *l* for ever
Rev 15:7 of God, who *l* for ever and ever

### LIVING

Gen 1:21 every *l* creature that moveth,
Gen 1:24 the *l* creature after his kind
Gen 1:28 over every *l* thing that moveth
Gen 2:7 and man became a *l* soul
Gen 2:19 Adam called every *l* creature
Gen 3:20 she was the mother of all *l*
Gen 6:19 of every *l* thing of all flesh,
Gen 7:4 every *l* substance that I have
Gen 7:23 every *l* substance was destroyed
Gen 8:1 remembered Noah, and every *l* thing
Gen 8:17 every *l* thing that is with thee
Gen 8:21 smite any more every thing *l*
Gen 9:10 with every *l* creature that is
Gen 9:12 every *l* creature that is with you
Gen 9:15 every *l* creature of all flesh
Gen 9:16 every *l* creature of all flesh
Lev 11:10 of any *l* thing which is in the
Lev 11:46 of every *l* creature that moveth
Lev 14:6 As for the *l* bird, he shall take
Lev 14:6 the *l* bird in the blood of the
Lev 14:7 shall let the *l* bird loose into
Lev 14:51 the *l* bird, and dip them in the
Lev 14:52 running water, and with the *l* bird
Lev 14:53 But he shall let go the *l* bird
Lev 20:25 or by any manner of *l* thing that
Num 16:48 stood between the dead and the *l*
Deut 5:26 hath heard the voice of the *l* God
Josh 3:10 know that the *l* God is among you
Ruth 2:20 left off his kindness to the *l*
1Sa 17:26 defy the armies of the *l* God
1Sa 17:36 defied the armies of the *l* God
2Sa 20:3 of their death, *l* in widowhood
1Kin 3:22 but the *l* is my son, and the dead
1Kin 3:22 is thy son, and the *l* is my son
1Kin 3:23 is the dead, and my son is the *l*
1Kin 3:25 Divide the *l* child in two, and
1Kin 3:26 the *l* child was unto the king
1Kin 3:26 O my lord, give her the *l* child
1Kin 3:27 and said, Give her the *l* child
2Kin 19:4 hath sent to reproach the *l* God
2Kin 19:16 sent him to reproach the *l* God
Job 12:10 hand is the soul of every *l* thing
Job 28:13 is it found in the land of the *l*
Job 28:21 it is hid from the eyes of all *l*
Job 30:23 to the house appointed for all *l*
Job 33:30 with the light of the *l*
Ps 27:13 of the LORD in the land of the *l*
Ps 42:2 thirsteth for God, for the *l* God
Ps 52:5 thee out of the land of the *l*
Ps 56:13 before God in the light of the *l*
Ps 58:9 away as with a whirlwind, both *l*
Ps 69:28 blotted out of the book of the *l*
Ps 84:2 my flesh crieth out for the *l* God
Ps 116:9 the LORD in the land of the *l*

Ps 142:5 my portion in the land of the *l*
Ps 143:2 sight shall no man *l* be justified
Ps 145:16 the desire of every *l* thing
Eccl 4:2 than the *l* which are yet alive
Eccl 4:15 I considered all the *l* which walk
Eccl 6:8 that knoweth to walk before the *l*
Eccl 7:2 the *l* will lay it to his heart
Eccl 9:4 joined to all the *l* there is hope
Eccl 9:4 for a *l* dog is better than a dead
Eccl 9:5 For the *l* know that they shall
Song 4:15 of gardens, a well of *l* waters
Is 4:3 written among the *l* in Jerusalem
Is 8:19 for the *l* to the dead
Is 37:4 hath sent to reproach the *l* God
Is 37:17 hath sent to reproach the *l* God
Is 38:11 the LORD, in the land of the *l*
Is 38:19 The *l*, the *l*, he shall
Is 53:8 cut off out of the land of the *l*
Jer 2:13 me the fountain of *l* waters
Jer 10:10 is the true God, he is the *l* God
Jer 11:19 him off from the land of the *l*
Jer 17:13 LORD, the fountain of *l* waters
Jer 23:36 perverted the words of the *l* God
Lam 3:39 Wherefore doth a *l* man complain
Eze 1:5 the likeness of four *l* creatures
Eze 1:13 the likeness of the *l* creatures
Eze 1:13 up and down among the *l* creatures
Eze 1:14 the *l* creatures ran and returned
Eze 1:15 Now as I beheld the *l* creatures
Eze 1:15 upon the earth by the *l* creatures
Eze 1:19 when the *l* creatures went, the
Eze 1:19 when the *l* creatures were lifted
Eze 1:20 for the spirit of the *l* creature
Eze 1:21 for the spirit of the *l* creature
Eze 1:22 *l* creature was as the colour of
Eze 3:13 the *l* creatures that touched one
Eze 10:15 This is the *l* creature that I saw
Eze 10:17 of the *l* creature was in them
Eze 10:20 This is the *l* creature that I saw
Eze 26:20 set glory in the land of the *l*
Eze 32:23 terror in the land of the *l*
Eze 32:24 their terror in the land of the *l*
Eze 32:25 was caused in the land of the *l*
Eze 32:26 their terror in the land of the *l*
Eze 32:27 the mighty in the land of the *l*
Eze 32:32 my terror in the land of the *l*
Dan 2:30 that I have more than any *l*
Dan 4:17 to the intent that the *l* may know
Dan 6:20 O Daniel, servant of the *l* God
Dan 6:26 for he is the *l* God, and stedfast
Hos 1:10 Ye are the sons of the *l* God
Zec 14:8 that *l* waters shall go out from
Mt 16:16 the Christ, the Son of the *l* God
Mt 22:32 the God of the dead, but of the *l*
Mt 26:63 him, I adjure thee by the *l* God
Mk 12:27 of the dead, but the God of the *l*
Mk 12:44 all that she had, even all her *l*
Lk 8:43 spent all her *l* upon physicians
Lk 15:12 And he divided unto them his *l*
Lk 15:13 his substance with riotous *l*
Lk 15:30 hath devoured thy *l* with harlots
Lk 20:38 a God of the dead, but of the *l*
Lk 21:4 cast in all the *l* that she had
Lk 24:5 Why seek ye the *l* among the dead
Jn 4:10 he would have given thee *l* water
Jn 4:11 then hast thou that *l* water
Jn 6:51 I am the *l* bread which came down
Jn 6:57 As the *l* Father hath sent me, and
Jn 6:69 that Christ, the Son of the *l* God
Jn 7:38 shall flow rivers of *l* water
Acts 14:15 these vanities unto the *l* God
Rom 9:26 called the children of the *l* God
Rom 12:1 present your bodies a *l* sacrifice
Rom 14:9 be Lord both of the dead and *l*
1Cor 15:45 first man Adam was made a *l* soul
2Cor 3:3 but with the Spirit of the *l* God
2Cor 6:16 ye are the temple of the *l* God
Col 2:20 as though *l* in the world, are ye
1Th 1:9 to God from idols to serve the *l*
1Ti 3:15 which is the church of the *l* God
1Ti 4:10 because we trust in the *l* God
1Ti 6:17 riches, but in the *l* God, who
Titus 3:3 *l* in malice and envy, hateful, and
Heb 3:12 in departing from the *l* God
Heb 9:14 dead works to serve the *l* God
Heb 10:20 *l* way, which he hath consecrated
Heb 10:31 fall into the hands of the *l* God
Heb 12:22 and unto the city of the *l* God
1Pet 2:4 To whom coming, as unto a *l* stone
Rev 7:2 having the seal of the *l* God
Rev 7:17 them unto *l* fountains of waters
Rev 16:3 every *l* soul died in the sea

**LO-AMMI** *(lo-am'-mi) Symbolic name meaning "Not My People."*

Hos 1:9 Then said God, Call his name *L*

**LOATHSOME**

Num 11:20 nostrils, and it be *l* unto you
Job 7:5 my skin is broken, and become *l*
Ps 38:7 loins are filled with a *l* disease
Prov 13:5 but a wicked man is *l*, and cometh

**LOAVES**

Lev 23:17 two wave *l* of two tenth deals
Judg 8:5 *l* of bread unto the people that
1Sa 10:3 another carrying three *l* of bread
1Sa 10:4 thee, and give thee two *l* of bread
1Sa 17:17 this parched corn, and these ten *l*
1Sa 21:3 give me five *l* of bread in mine
1Sa 25:18 made haste, and took two hundred *l*
2Sa 16:1 upon them two hundred *l* of bread
1Kin 14:3 And take with thee ten *l*, and
2Kin 4:42 twenty *l* of barley, and full ears
Mt 14:17 unto him, We have here but five *l*
Mt 14:19 on the grass, and took the five *l*
Mt 14:19 gave the *l* to his disciples, and
Mt 15:34 unto them, How many *l* have ye
Mt 15:36 And he took the seven *l* and the
Mt 16:9 the five *l* of the five thousand
Mt 16:10 Neither the seven *l* of the four
Mk 6:38 unto them, How many *l* have ye
Mk 6:41 And when he had taken the five *l*
Mk 6:41 and blessed, and brake the *l*
Mk 6:44 they that did eat of the *l* were
Mk 6:52 not the miracle of the *l*
Mk 8:5 he asked them, How many *l* have ye
Mk 8:6 and he took the seven *l*, and gave
Mk 8:19 the five *l* among five thousand
Lk 9:13 said, We have no more but five *l*
Lk 9:16 Then he took the five *l* and the
Lk 11:5 unto him, Friend, lend me three *l*
Jn 6:9 here, which hath five barley *l*
Jn 6:11 And Jesus took the *l*
Jn 6:13 fragments of the five barley *l*
Jn 6:26 but because ye did eat of the *l*

**LOCKS**

Num 6:5 shall let the *l* of the hair of
Judg 16:13 seven *l* of my head with the web
Judg 16:19 shave off the seven *l* of his head
Neh 3:3 the *l* thereof, and the bars
Neh 3:6 the *l* thereof, and the bars
Neh 3:13 the *l* thereof, and the bars
Neh 3:14 the *l* thereof, and the bars
Neh 3:15 the *l* thereof, and the bars
Song 4:1 hast doves' eyes within thy *l*
Song 4:3 of a pomegranate within thy *l*
Song 5:2 my *l* with the drops of the night
Song 5:11 his *l* are bushy, and black as a
Song 6:7 are thy temples within thy *l*
Is 47:2 uncover thy *l*, make bare the leg,
Eze 44:20 nor suffer their *l* to grow long

**LOCUST**

Ex 10:19 there remained not one *l* in all
Lev 11:22 the *l* after his kind, and the bald
Lev 11:22 the bald *l* after his kind, and the
Deut 28:38 for the *l* shall consume it
Deut 28:42 of thy land shall the *l* consume
1Kin 8:37 pestilence, blasting, mildew, *l*
Ps 78:46 and their labour unto the *l*
Ps 109:23 I am tossed up and down as the *l*
Joel 1:4 hath left hath the *l* eaten
Joel 1:4 that which the *l* hath left hath
Joel 2:25 the years that the *l* hath eaten

**LOCUSTS**

Ex 10:4 will I bring the *l* into thy coast
Ex 10:12 over the land of Egypt for the *l*
Ex 10:13 the east wind brought the *l*
Ex 10:14 the *l* went up over all the land
Ex 10:14 them there were no such *l* as they
Ex 10:19 west wind, which took away the *l*
2Chr 6:28 there be blasting, or mildew, *l*
2Chr 7:13 command the *l* to devour the land
Ps 105:34 the *l* came, and caterpillers, and
Prov 30:27 The *l* have no king, yet go they
Is 33:4 fro of *l* shall he run upon them
Nah 3:15 make thyself many as the *l*
Nah 3:17 Thy crowned are as the *l*, and thy
Mt 3:4 and his meat was *l* and wild honey
Mk 1:6 and he did eat *l* and wild honey
Rev 9:3 out of the smoke *l* upon the earth
Rev 9:7 the shapes of the *l* were like

**LOD** *A city in Benjamin.*

1Chr 8:12 and Shamed, who built Ono, and *L*
Ezr 2:33 The children of *L*, Hadid, and Ono,
Neh 7:37 The children of *L*, Hadid, and Ono,
Neh 11:35 *L*, and Ono, the valley of

**LO-DEBAR** *(lo-de'-bar) A city in Manasseh.*

2Sa 9:4 Machir, the son of Ammiel, in *L*
2Sa 9:5 Machir, the son of Ammiel, from *L*
2Sa 17:27 and Machir the son of Ammiel of *L*

**LODGE**

Gen 24:23 thy father's house for us to *l* in
Gen 24:25 provender enough, and room to *l* in
Num 22:8 *L* here this night, and I will
Josh 4:3 where ye shall *l* this night
Judg 19:9 *l* here, that thine heart may be
Judg 19:11 city of the Jebusites, and *l* in it
Judg 19:13 of these places to *l* all night
Judg 19:15 to go in and to *l* in Gibeah
Judg 19:20 only *l* not in the street
Judg 20:4 Benjamin, I and my concubine, to *l*
Ruth 1:16 and where thou lodgest, I will *l*
2Sa 17:8 will not *l* with the people
2Sa 17:16 *L* not this night in the plains of
Neh 4:22 his servant *l* within Jerusalem
Neh 13:21 them, Why *l* ye about the wall
Job 24:7 the naked to *l* without clothing
Job 31:32 stranger did not *l* in the street
Song 7:11 let us *l* in the villages
Is 1:8 as a *l* in a garden of cucumbers,
Is 21:13 the forest in Arabia shall ye *l*
Is 65:4 *l* in the monuments, which eat
Jer 4:14 thy vain thoughts *l* within thee
Zeph 2:14 the bittern shall *l* in the upper
Mt 13:32 *l* in the branches thereof
Mk 4:32 air may *l* under the shadow of it
Lk 9:12 and country round about, and *l*
Acts 21:16 disciple, with whom we should *l*

**LODGED**

Gen 32:13 he *l* there that same night
Gen 32:21 himself *l* that night in the
Josh 2:1 house, named Rahab, and *l* there
Josh 3:1 *l* there before they passed over
Josh 4:8 them unto the place where they *l*
Josh 6:11 into the camp, and *l* in the camp
Josh 8:9 but Joshua *l* that night among the
Judg 18:2 the house of Micah, they *l* there
Judg 19:4 they did eat and drink, and *l* there
Judg 19:7 therefore he *l* there again
1Kin 19:9 thither unto a cave, and *l* there
1Chr 9:27 they *l* round about the house of
Neh 13:20 sellers of all kind of ware *l*
Is 1:21 righteousness *l* in it
Mt 21:17 and he *l* there
Lk 13:19 the fowls of the air *l* in the
Acts 10:18 was surnamed Peter, were *l* there
Acts 10:23 Then called he them in, and *l* them
Acts 10:32 he is *l* in the house of one Simon
Acts 28:7 *l* us three days courteously
1Ti 5:10 children, if she have *l* strangers

**LODGING**

Josh 4:3 you, and leave them in the *l* place
Judg 19:15 took them into his house to *l*
Is 10:29 have taken up their *l* at Geba
Jer 9:2 a *l* place of wayfaring men
Acts 28:23 there came many to him into his *l*
Philem 22 But withal prepare me also a *l*

**LOFTY**

Ps 131:1 is not haughty, nor mine eyes *l*
Prov 30:13 O how *l* are their eyes
Is 2:11 The *l* looks of man shall be
Is 2:12 upon every one that is proud and *l*
Is 5:15 the eyes of the *l* shall be
Is 26:5 the *l* city, he layeth it low
Is 57:7 Upon a *l* and high mountain hast
Is 57:15 *l* One that inhabiteth eternity,

**LOINS**

Gen 35:11 and kings shall come out of thy *l*
Gen 37:34 and put sackcloth upon his *l*
Gen 46:26 Egypt, which came out of his *l*
Ex 1:5 the *l* of Jacob were seventy souls
Ex 12:11 with your *l* girded, your shoes on
Ex 28:42 from the *l* even unto the thighs
Deut 33:11 smite through the *l* of them that
2Sa 20:8 upon his *l* in the sheath thereof

1Kin 2:5 his girdle that was about his *l*
1Kin 8:19 shall come forth out of thy *l*
1Kin 12:10 be thicker than my father's *l*
1Kin 18:46 and he girded up his *l*, and ran
1Kin 20:31 pray thee, put sackcloth on our *l*
1Kin 20:32 they girded sackcloth on their *l*
2Kin 1:8 a girdle of leather about his *l*
2Kin 4:29 he said to Gehazi, Gird up thy *l*
2Kin 9:1 and said unto him, Gird up thy *l*
2Chr 6:9 shall come forth out of thy *l*
2Chr 10:10 be thicker than my father's *l*
Job 12:18 and girdeth their *l* with a girdle
Job 31:20 If his *l* have not blessed me, and
Job 38:3 Gird up now thy *l* like a man
Job 40:7 Gird up thy *l* now like a man
Job 40:16 Lo now, his strength is in his *l*
Ps 38:7 For my *l* are filled with a
Ps 66:11 thou laidst affliction upon our *l*
Ps 69:23 make their *l* continually to shake
Prov 31:17 She girdeth her *l* with strength
Is 5:27 the girdle of their *l* be loosed
Is 11:5 shall be the girdle of his *l*
Is 20:2 the sackcloth from off thy *l*
Is 21:3 are my *l* filled with pain
Is 32:11 and gird sackcloth upon your *l*
Is 45:1 and I will loose the *l* of kings
Jer 1:17 Thou therefore gird up thy *l*
Jer 13:1 girdle, and put it upon thy *l*
Jer 13:2 of the LORD, and put it on my *l*
Jer 13:4 hast got, which is upon thy *l*
Jer 13:11 girdle cleaveth to the *l* of a man
Jer 30:6 every man with his hands on his *l*
Jer 48:37 cuttings, and upon the *l* sackcloth
Eze 1:27 appearance of his *l* even upward
Eze 1:27 appearance of his *l* even downward
Eze 8:2 appearance of his *l* even downward
Eze 8:2 from his *l* even upward, as the
Eze 21:6 man, with the breaking of thy *l*
Eze 23:15 Girded with girdles upon their *l*
Eze 29:7 all their *l* to be at a stand
Eze 44:18 have linen breeches upon their *l*
Eze 47:4 the waters were to the *l*
Dan 5:6 the joints of his *l* were loosed
Dan 10:5 whose *l* were girded with fine
Amos 8:10 bring up sackcloth upon all *l*
Nah 2:1 watch the way, make thy *l* strong
Nah 2:10 and much pain is in all *l*
Mt 3:4 and a leathern girdle about his *l*
Mk 1:6 a girdle of a skin about his *l*
Lk 12:35 Let your *l* be girded about, and
Acts 2:30 him, that of the fruit of his *l*
Eph 6:14 having your *l* girt about with
Heb 7:5 they come out of the *l* of Abraham
Heb 7:10 he was yet in the *l* of his father
1Pet 1:13 gird up the *l* of your mind

**LOIS** *(lo'-is) Grandmother of Timothy.*
2Ti 1:5 dwelt first in thy grandmother *L*

**LONG**
Gen 26:8 when he had been there a *l* time
Gen 48:15 me all my life *l* unto this day
Ex 10:3 How *l* wilt thou refuse to humble
Ex 10:7 How *l* shall this man be a snare
Ex 16:28 How *l* refuse ye to keep my
Ex 19:13 when the trumpet soundeth *l*
Ex 19:19 voice of the trumpet sounded *l*
Ex 20:12 that thy days may be *l* upon the
Ex 27:1 of shittim wood, five cubits *l*
Ex 27:9 an hundred cubits *l* for one side
Ex 27:11 hangings of an hundred cubits *l*
Lev 18:19 as *l* as she is put apart for her
Lev 26:34 as *l* as it lieth desolate, and ye
Lev 26:35 As *l* as it lieth desolate it
Num 9:18 as *l* as the cloud abode upon the
Num 9:19 when the cloud tarried *l* upon the
Num 14:11 How *l* will this people provoke me
Num 14:11 how *l* will it be ere they believe
Num 14:27 How *l* shall I bear with this evil
Num 20:15 we have dwelt in Egypt a *l* time
Deut 1:6 Ye have dwelt *l* enough in this
Deut 2:3 compassed this mountain *l* enough
Deut 4:25 shall have remained *l* in the land
Deut 12:19 *l* as thou livest upon the earth
Deut 14:24 And if the way be too *l* for thee
Deut 19:6 him, because the way is *l*
Deut 20:19 shalt besiege a city a *l* time
Deut 28:32 longing for them all the day *l*
Deut 28:59 of *l* continuance, and sore
Deut 28:59 sicknesses, and of *l* continuance
Deut 31:13 as *l* as ye live in the land
Deut 33:12 shall cover him all the day *l*
Josh 6:5 that when they make a *l* blast
Josh 9:13 by reason of the very *l* journey
Josh 11:18 Joshua made war a *l* time with all
Josh 18:3 How *l* are ye slack to go to
Josh 23:1 it came to pass a *l* time after
Josh 24:7 in the wilderness a *l* season
Judg 5:28 Why is his chariot so *l* in coming
1Sa 1:14 How *l* wilt thou be drunken
1Sa 1:28 as *l* as he liveth he shall be
1Sa 7:2 that the time was *l*
1Sa 16:1 How *l* wilt thou mourn for Saul,
1Sa 20:31 For as *l* as the son of Jesse
1Sa 25:15 as *l* as we were conversant with
1Sa 29:8 thou found in thy servant so *l* as
2Sa 2:26 how *l* shall it be then, ere thou
2Sa 3:1 Now there was *l* war between the
2Sa 14:2 had a *l* time mourned for the dead
2Sa 19:34 How *l* have I to live, that I
1Kin 3:11 hast not asked for thyself *l* life
1Kin 6:17 before it, was forty cubits *l*
1Kin 18:21 How *l* halt ye between two
2Kin 9:22 so *l* as the whoredoms of thy
2Kin 19:25 Hast thou not heard *l* ago how I
2Chr 1:11 neither yet hast asked *l* life
2Chr 3:11 cherubims were twenty cubits *l*
2Chr 6:13 brasen scaffold, of five cubits *l*
2Chr 6:31 so *l* as they live in the land
2Chr 15:3 Now for a *l* season Israel hath
2Chr 26:5 as *l* as he sought the LORD, God
2Chr 30:5 a *l* time in such sort as it was
2Chr 36:21 for as *l* as she lay desolate she
Neh 2:6 For how *l* shall thy journey be
Est 5:13 so *l* as I see Mordecai the Jew
Job 3:21 Which *l* for death, but it cometh
Job 6:8 grant me the thing that I *l* for
Job 7:19 How *l* wilt thou not depart from
Job 8:2 How *l* wilt thou speak these
Job 8:2 how *l* shall the words of thy
Job 18:2 How *l* will it be ere ye make an
Job 19:2 How *l* will ye vex my soul, and
Job 27:6 not reproach me so *l* as I live
Ps 4:2 how *l* will ye turn my glory into
Ps 4:2 how *l* will ye love vanity, and
Ps 6:3 but thou, O LORD, how *l*
Ps 13:1 How *l* wilt thou forget me, O LORD
Ps 13:1 how *l* wilt thou hide thy face
Ps 13:2 How *l* shall I take counsel in my
Ps 13:2 how *l* shall mine enemy be exalted
Ps 32:3 through my roaring all the day *l*
Ps 35:17 LORD, how *l* wilt thou look on
Ps 35:28 and of thy praise all the day *l*
Ps 38:6 I go mourning all the day *l*
Ps 38:12 and imagine deceits all the day *l*
Ps 44:8 In God we boast all the day *l*
Ps 44:22 sake are we killed all the day *l*
Ps 62:3 How *l* will ye imagine mischief
Ps 71:24 thy righteousness all the day *l*
Ps 72:5 shall fear thee as *l* as the sun
Ps 72:7 peace so *l* as the moon endureth
Ps 72:17 be continued as *l* as the sun
Ps 73:14 For all the day *l* have I been
Ps 74:9 among us any that knoweth how *l*
Ps 74:10 how *l* shall the adversary
Ps 79:5 How *l*, LORD
Ps 80:4 how *l* wilt thou be angry against
Ps 82:2 How *l* will ye judge unjustly, and
Ps 89:46 How *l*, LORD?
Ps 90:13 Return, O LORD, how *l*
Ps 91:16 With *l* life will I satisfy him,
Ps 94:3 how *l* shall the wicked
Ps 94:3 how *l* shall the wicked triumph
Ps 94:4 How *l* shall they utter and speak
Ps 95:10 Forty years *l* was I grieved with
Ps 104:33 sing unto the LORD as *l* as I live
Ps 116:2 I call upon him as *l* as I live
Ps 120:6 My soul hath *l* dwelt with him
Ps 129:3 they made *l* their furrows
Ps 143:3 as those that have been *l* dead
Prov 1:22 How *l*, ye simple ones, will ye
Prov 3:2 *l* life, and peace, shall they add
Prov 6:9 How *l* wilt thou sleep, O sluggard
Prov 7:19 at home, he is gone a *l* journey
Prov 21:26 coveteth greedily all the day *l*
Prov 23:17 fear of the LORD all the day *l*
Prov 23:30 They that tarry *l* at the wine
Prov 25:15 By *l* forbearing is a prince
Eccl 12:5 because man goeth to his *l* home
Is 6:11 Then said I, Lord, how *l*
Is 22:11 unto him that fashioned it *l* ago
Is 37:26 Hast thou not heard *l* ago
Is 42:14 I have *l* time holden my peace
Is 65:22 mine elect shall *l* enjoy the work
Jer 4:14 How *l* shall thy vain thoughts
Jer 4:21 How *l* shall I see the standard,
Jer 12:4 How *l* shall the land mourn, and
Jer 23:26 How *l* shall this be in the heart
Jer 29:28 saying, This captivity is *l*
Jer 31:22 How *l* wilt thou go about, O thou
Jer 47:5 how *l* wilt thou cut thyself
Jer 47:6 how *l* will it be ere thou be
Lam 2:20 fruit, and children of a span *l*
Lam 5:20 for ever, and forsake us so *l* time
Eze 31:5 his branches became *l* because of
Eze 40:5 reed of six cubits *l* by the cubit
Eze 40:7 little chamber was one reed *l*
Eze 40:29 it was fifty cubits *l*, and five and
Eze 40:30 were five and twenty cubits *l*
Eze 40:33 it was fifty cubits *l*, and five and
Eze 40:42 offering, of a cubit and an half *l*
Eze 40:47 the court, an hundred cubits *l*
Eze 41:13 the house, an hundred cubits *l*
Eze 41:13 thereof, an hundred cubits *l*
Eze 42:11 as *l* as they, and as broad as they
Eze 42:20 round about, five hundred reeds *l*
Eze 43:16 altar shall be twelve cubits *l*
Eze 43:17 settle shall be fourteen cubits *l*
Eze 44:20 nor suffer their locks to grow *l*
Eze 45:6 and five and twenty thousand *l*
Eze 46:22 courts joined of forty cubits *l*
Dan 8:13 How *l* shall be the vision
Dan 10:1 but the time appointed was *l*
Dan 12:6 How *l* shall it be to the end of
Hos 8:5 how *l* will it be ere they attain
Hos 13:13 for he should not stay *l* in the
Hab 1:2 how *l* shall I cry, and thou wilt
Hab 2:6 which is not his! how *l*?
Zec 1:12 how *l* wilt thou not have mercy on
Mt 9:15 as *l* as the bridegroom is with
Mt 11:21 have repented *l* ago in sackcloth
Mt 17:17 how *l* shall I be with you
Mt 17:17 how *l* shall I suffer you
Mt 23:14 and for a pretence make *l* prayer
Mt 25:19 After a *l* time the lord of those
Mk 2:19 as *l* as they have the bridegroom
Mk 9:19 how *l* shall I be with you
Mk 9:19 how *l* shall I suffer you
Mk 9:21 How *l* is it ago since this came
Mk 12:38 which love to go in *l* clothing
Mk 12:40 and for a pretence make *l* prayers
Mk 16:5 clothed in a *l* white garment
Lk 1:21 he tarried so *l* in the temple
Lk 8:27 man, which had devils *l* time
Lk 9:41 how *l* shall I be with you, and
Lk 18:7 him, though he bear *l* with them
Lk 20:9 into a far country for a *l* time
Lk 20:46 which desire to walk in *l* robes
Lk 20:47 and for a shew make *l* prayers
Lk 23:8 desirous to see him of a *l* season
Jn 5:6 been now a *l* time in that case
Jn 9:5 As *l* as I am in the world, I am
Jn 10:24 How *l* dost thou make us to doubt
Jn 14:9 Have I been so *l* time with you
Acts 8:11 because that of *l* time he had
Acts 14:3 *L* time therefore abode they
Acts 14:28 there they abode *l* time with the
Acts 20:9 and as Paul was *l* preaching
Acts 20:11 and eaten, and talked a *l* while
Acts 27:14 But not *l* after there arose
Acts 27:21 But after *l* abstinence Paul stood
Rom 1:11 For I *l* to see you, that I may
Rom 7:1 over a man as *l* as he liveth
Rom 7:2 to her husband so *l* as he liveth
Rom 8:36 sake we are killed all the day *l*
Rom 10:21 All day *l* I have stretched forth
1Cor 7:39 law as *l* as her husband liveth
1Cor 11:14 you, that, if a man have *l* hair
1Cor 11:15 But if a woman have *l* hair
1Cor 13:4 Charity suffereth *l*, and is kind
2Cor 9:14 which *l* after you for the
Gal 4:1 as *l* as he is a child, differeth
Eph 6:3 thou mayest live *l* on the earth
Phil 1:8 how greatly I *l* after you all in
1Ti 3:15 But if I tarry *l*, that thou
Heb 4:7 David, To day, after so *l* a time
Jas 5:7 hath *l* patience for it, until he
1Pet 3:6 as *l* as ye do well, and are not
2Pet 1:13 as *l* as I am in this tabernacle,
2Pet 2:3 now of a *l* time lingereth not
Rev 6:10 with a loud voice, saying, How *l*

## LONGED
2Sa 13:39 the soul of king David *l* to go
2Sa 23:15 And David *l*, and said, Oh that one
1Chr 11:17 And David *l*, and said, Oh that one
Ps 119:40 I have *l* after thy precepts
Ps 119:131 for I *l* for thy commandments
Ps 119:174 I have *l* for thy salvation, O
Phil 2:26 For he *l* after you all, and was
Phil 4:1 *l* for, my joy and crown, so stand

## LONGER
Ex 2:3 And when she could not *l* hide him
Ex 9:28 let you go, and ye shall stay no *l*
Judg 2:14 any *l* stand before their enemies
2Sa 20:5 but he tarried *l* than the set
2Kin 6:33 should I wait for the LORD any *l*
Job 11:9 thereof is *l* than the earth
Jer 44:22 So that the LORD could no *l* bear
Lk 16:2 for thou mayest be no *l* steward
Acts 18:20 him to tarry *l* time with them
Acts 25:24 that he ought not to live any *l*
Rom 6:2 dead to sin, live any *l* therein
Gal 3:25 we are no *l* under a schoolmaster
1Th 3:1 when we could no *l* forbear
1Th 3:5 cause, when I could no *l* forbear
1Ti 5:23 Drink no *l* water, but use a
1Pet 4:2 That he no *l* should live the rest
Rev 10:6 that there should be time no *l*

## LONGSUFFERING
Ex 34:6 God, merciful and gracious, *l*
Num 14:18 The LORD is *l*, and of great mercy,
Ps 86:15 of compassion, and gracious, *l*
Jer 15:15 take me not away in thy *l*
Rom 2:4 his goodness and forbearance and *l*
Rom 9:22 endured with much *l* the vessels
2Cor 6:6 By pureness, by knowledge, by *l*
Gal 5:22 the Spirit is love, joy, peace, *l*
Eph 4:2 all lowliness and meekness, with *l*
Col 1:11 all patience and *l* with joyfulness
Col 3:12 humbleness of mind, meekness, *l*
1Ti 1:16 Christ might shew forth all *l*
2Ti 3:10 manner of life, purpose, faith, *l*
2Ti 4:2 rebuke, exhort with all *l*
1Pet 3:20 when once the *l* of God waited in
2Pet 3:9 but is *l* to us-ward, not willing
2Pet 3:15 account that the *l* of our Lord is

## LOOK
Gen 9:16 I will *l* upon it, that I may
Gen 12:11 thou art a fair woman to *l* upon
Gen 13:14 *l* from the place where thou art
Gen 15:5 *L* now toward heaven, and tell the
Gen 19:17 *l* not behind thee, neither stay
Gen 24:16 damsel was very fair to *l* upon
Gen 26:7 because she was fair to *l* upon
Gen 40:7 Wherefore *l* ye so sadly to day
Gen 41:33 let Pharaoh *l* out a man discreet
Gen 42:1 Why do ye *l* one upon another
Ex 3:6 for he was afraid to *l* upon God
Ex 5:21 unto them, The LORD *l* upon you
Ex 10:10 *l* to it
Ex 25:20 faces shall *l* one to another
Ex 25:40 *l* that thou make them after their
Ex 39:43 Moses did *l* upon all the work, and
Lev 13:3 the priest shall *l* on the plague
Lev 13:3 and the priest shall *l* on him
Lev 13:5 the priest shall *l* on him the
Lev 13:6 the priest shall *l* on him again
Lev 13:21 But if the priest *l* on it
Lev 13:25 Then the priest shall *l* upon it
Lev 13:26 But if the priest *l* on it
Lev 13:27 the priest shall *l* upon him the
Lev 13:31 if the priest *l* on the plague of
Lev 13:32 the priest shall *l* on the plague
Lev 13:34 the priest shall *l* on the scall
Lev 13:36 Then the priest shall *l* on him
Lev 13:39 Then the priest shall *l*
Lev 13:43 Then the priest shall *l* upon it
Lev 13:50 priest shall *l* upon the plague
Lev 13:51 he shall *l* on the plague on the
Lev 13:53 And if the priest shall *l*, and,
Lev 13:55 the priest shall *l* on the plague
Lev 13:56 And if the priest *l*, and, behold,
Lev 14:3 and the priest shall *l*, and, behold
Lev 14:37 he shall *l* on the plague, and,
Lev 14:39 again the seventh day, and shall *l*
Lev 14:44 Then the priest shall come and *l*
Lev 14:48 *l* upon it, and, behold, the plague
Num 15:39 a fringe, that ye may *l* upon it
Deut 9:27 *l* not unto the stubbornness of
Deut 26:15 *L* down from thy holy habitation,
Deut 28:32 people, and thine eyes shall *l*
Judg 7:17 them, *L* on me, and do likewise
1Sa 1:11 if thou wilt indeed *l* on the
1Sa 16:7 *L* not on his countenance, or on
1Sa 16:12 countenance, and goodly to *l* to
1Sa 17:18 *l* how thy brethren fare, and take
2Sa 9:8 that thou shouldest *l* upon such a
2Sa 11:2 was very beautiful to *l* upon
2Sa 16:12 LORD will *l* on mine affliction
1Kin 18:43 Go up now, *l* toward the sea
2Kin 3:14 Judah, I would not *l* toward thee
2Kin 6:32 *l*, when the messenger cometh,
2Kin 9:2 *l* out there Jehu the son of
2Kin 10:3 *L* even out the best and meetest of
2Kin 10:23 *l* that there be here with you
2Kin 14:8 let us *l* one another in the face
1Chr 12:17 the God of our fathers *l* thereon
2Chr 24:22 died, he said, The LORD *l* upon it
Est 1:11 for she was fair to *l* on
Job 3:9 let it *l* for light, but have none
Job 6:28 therefore be content, *l* upon me
Job 20:21 shall no man *l* for his goods
Job 35:5 *L* unto the heavens, and see
Job 40:12 *L* on every one that is proud, and
Ps 5:3 my prayer unto thee, and will *l* up
Ps 22:17 they *l* and stare upon me
Ps 25:18 *L* upon mine affliction and my pain
Ps 35:17 LORD, how long wilt thou *l* on
Ps 40:12 me, so that I am not able to *l* up
Ps 80:14 *l* down from heaven, and behold, and
Ps 84:9 *l* upon the face of thine anointed
Ps 85:11 shall *l* down from heaven
Ps 101:5 him that hath an high *l* and a
Ps 119:132 *L* thou upon me, and be merciful
Ps 123:2 as the eyes of servants *l* unto
Prov 4:25 Let thine eyes *l* right on
Prov 4:25 let thine eyelids *l* straight
Prov 6:17 A proud *l*, a lying tongue, and
Prov 21:4 An high *l*, and a proud heart, and
Prov 23:31 *L* not thou upon the wine when it
Prov 27:23 flocks, and *l* well to thy herds
Eccl 12:3 those that *l* out of the windows
Song 1:6 *L* not upon me, because I am black
Song 4:8 *l* from the top of Amana, from the
Song 6:13 return, that we may *l* upon thee
Is 5:30 if one *l* unto the land, behold
Is 8:17 of Jacob, and I will *l* for him
Is 8:21 king and their God, and *l* upward
Is 8:22 they shall *l* unto the earth
Is 14:16 thee shall narrowly *l* upon thee
Is 17:7 day shall a man *l* to his Maker
Is 17:8 he shall not *l* to the altars, the
Is 22:4 Therefore said I, *L* away from me
Is 22:8 thou didst *l* in that day to the
Is 31:1 but they *l* not unto the Holy One
Is 33:20 *L* upon Zion, the city of our
Is 42:18 and *l*, ye blind, that ye may see
Is 45:22 *L* unto me, and be ye saved, all
Is 51:1 *l* unto the rock whence ye are
Is 51:2 *L* unto Abraham your father, and
Is 51:6 and *l* upon the earth beneath
Is 56:11 they all *l* to their own way,
Is 59:11 we *l* for judgment, but there is
Is 63:15 *L* down from heaven, and behold
Is 66:2 but to this man will I *l*, even to
Is 66:24 *l* upon the carcases of the men
Jer 13:16 while ye *l* for light, he turn it
Jer 39:12 *l* well to him, and do him no harm
Jer 40:4 and I will *l* well unto thee
Jer 46:5 and are fled apace, and *l* not back
Jer 47:3 the fathers shall not *l* back to
Lam 3:50 Till the LORD *l* down, and behold
Eze 23:15 all of them princes to *l* to
Eze 29:16 when they shall *l* after them
Eze 43:17 stairs shall *l* toward the east
Dan 7:20 whose *l* was more stout than his
Hos 3:1 who *l* to other gods, and love
Jonah 2:4 yet I will *l* again toward thy
Mic 4:11 and let our eye *l* upon Zion
Mic 7:7 Therefore I will *l* unto the LORD
Nah 2:8 but none shall *l* back
Nah 3:7 that all they that *l* upon thee
Hab 1:13 evil, and canst not *l* on iniquity
Hab 2:15 that thou mayest *l* on their
Zec 12:10 they shall *l* upon me whom they
Mt 11:3 come, or do we *l* for another
Mk 8:25 upon his eyes, and made him *l* up
Lk 7:19 or *l* we for another
Lk 7:20 or *l* we for another
Lk 9:38 I beseech thee, *l* upon my son
Lk 21:28 begin to come to pass, then *l* up
Jn 4:35 up your eyes, and *l* on the fields
Jn 7:52 Search, and *l*
Jn 19:37 They shall *l* on him whom they
Acts 3:4 upon him with John, said, *L* on us
Acts 3:12 or why *l* ye so earnestly on us,
Acts 6:3 *l* ye out among you seven men of
Acts 18:15 names, and of your law, *l* ye to it
1Cor 16:11 for I *l* for him with the brethren
2Cor 3:13 *l* to the end of that which is
2Cor 4:18 While we *l* not at the things
2Cor 10:7 Do ye *l* on things after the
Phil 2:4 *L* not every man on his own things
Phil 3:20 whence also we *l* for the Saviour
Heb 9:28 unto them that *l* for him shall he
1Pet 1:12 the angels desire to *l* into
2Pet 3:13 *l* for new heavens and a new earth,
2Pet 3:14 seeing that ye *l* for such things,
2Jn 8 *L* to yourselves, that we lose not
Rev 4:3 sat was to *l* upon like a jasper
Rev 5:3 the book, neither to *l* thereon
Rev 5:4 the book, neither to *l* thereon

## LOOKED
Gen 6:12 God *l* upon the earth, and, behold,
Gen 8:13 the covering of the ark, and *l*
Gen 16:13 Have I also here *l* after him that
Gen 18:2 And he lift up his eyes and *l*
Gen 18:16 up from thence, and *l* toward Sodom
Gen 19:26 But his wife *l* back from behind
Gen 19:28 he *l* toward Sodom and Gomorrah,
Gen 22:13 Abraham lifted up his eyes, and *l*
Gen 26:8 the Philistines *l* out at a window
Gen 29:2 And he *l*, and behold a well in the
Gen 29:32 LORD hath *l* upon my affliction
Gen 33:1 And Jacob lifted up his eyes, and *l*
Gen 37:25 and they lifted up their eyes and *l*
Gen 39:23 The keeper of the prison *l* not to
Gen 40:6 *l* upon them, and, behold, they
Ex 2:11 brethren, and *l* on their burdens
Ex 2:12 he *l* this way and that way, and
Ex 2:25 God *l* upon the children of Israel
Ex 3:2 and he *l*, and, behold, the bush
Ex 4:31 and that he had *l* upon their
Ex 14:24 in the morning watch the LORD *l*
Ex 16:10 that they *l* toward the wilderness
Ex 33:8 *l* after Moses, until he was gone
Num 12:10 Aaron *l* upon Miriam, and, behold,
Num 16:42 that they *l* toward the tabernacle
Num 17:9 and they *l*, and took every man his
Num 24:20 when he *l* on Amalek, he took up
Num 24:21 he *l* on the Kenites, and took up
Deut 9:16 And I *l*, and, behold, ye had sinned
Deut 26:7 *l* on our affliction, and our
Josh 5:13 that he lifted up his eyes and *l*
Josh 8:20 when the men of Ai *l* behind them
Judg 5:28 of Sisera *l* out at a window
Judg 6:14 And the LORD *l* upon him, and said,
Judg 9:43 and laid wait in the field, and *l*
Judg 13:19 and Manoah and his wife *l* on
Judg 13:20 And Manoah and his wife *l* on it
Judg 20:40 the Benjamites *l* behind them
1Sa 6:19 because they had *l* into the ark
1Sa 9:16 for I have *l* upon my people,
1Sa 14:16 of Saul in Gibeah of Benjamin *l*
1Sa 16:6 that he *l* on Eliab, and said,
1Sa 17:42 And when the Philistine *l* about
1Sa 24:8 when Saul *l* behind him, David
2Sa 1:7 when he *l* behind him, he saw me,
2Sa 2:20 Then Abner *l* behind him, and said,
2Sa 6:16 daughter *l* through a window
2Sa 13:34 watch lifted up his eyes, and *l*
2Sa 18:24 wall, and lifted up his eyes, and *l*
2Sa 22:42 They *l*, but there was none to
2Sa 24:20 And Araunah *l*, and saw the king and
1Kin 18:43 And he went up, and *l*, and said,
1Kin 19:6 And he *l*, and, behold, there was a
2Kin 2:24 *l* on them, and cursed them in the
2Kin 6:30 by upon the wall, and the people *l*
2Kin 9:30 her head, and *l* out at a window
2Kin 9:32 there *l* out to him two or three
2Kin 11:14 And when she *l*, behold, the king
2Kin 14:11 Amaziah king of Judah *l* one
1Chr 21:21 as David came to Ornan, Ornan *l*
2Chr 13:14 And when Judah *l* back, behold, the
2Chr 20:24 they *l* unto the multitude, and,
2Chr 23:13 And she *l*, and, behold, the king
2Chr 26:20 *l* upon him, and, behold, he was
Neh 4:14 And I *l*, and rose up, and said unto
Est 2:15 sight of all them that *l* upon her

Job 6:19 The troops of Tema *l*, the
Job 30:26 When I *l* for good, then evil came
Ps 14:2 The LORD *l* down from heaven upon
Ps 34:5 They *l* unto him, and were
Ps 53:2 God *l* down from heaven upon the
Ps 69:20 I *l* for some to take pity, but
Ps 102:19 For he hath *l* down from the
Ps 109:25 when they *l* upon me they shaked
Ps 142:4 I *l* on my right hand, and beheld,
Prov 7:6 my house I *l* through my casement
Prov 24:32 I *l* upon it, and received
Eccl 2:11 Then I *l* on all the works that my
Song 1:6 because the sun hath *l* upon me
Is 5:2 he *l* that it should bring forth
Is 5:4 when I *l* that it should bring
Is 5:7 he *l* for judgment, but behold
Is 22:11 but ye have not *l* unto the maker
Is 63:5 And I *l*, and there was none to help
Is 64:3 things which we *l* not for
Jer 8:15 We *l* for peace, but no good came
Jer 14:19 we *l* for peace, and there is no
Lam 2:16 this is the day that we *l* for
Eze 1:4 And I *l*, and, behold, a whirlwind
Eze 2:9 And when I *l*, behold, an hand was
Eze 8:7 and when I *l*, behold a hole in the
Eze 10:1 Then I *l*, and, behold, in the
Eze 10:9 And when I *l*, behold the four
Eze 10:11 the head *l* they followed it
Eze 16:8 *l* upon thee, behold, thy time was
Eze 21:21 with images, he *l* in the liver
Eze 40:20 court that *l* toward the north
Eze 44:4 and I *l*, and, behold, the glory of
Eze 46:19 priests, which *l* toward the north
Dan 1:13 be *l* upon before thee, and the
Dan 10:5 Then I lifted up mine eyes, and *l*
Dan 12:5 Then I Daniel *l*, and, behold,
Obad 12 But thou shouldest not have *l* on
Obad 13 thou shouldest not have *l* on
Hag 1:9 Ye *l* for much, and, lo, it came to
Zec 2:1 I lifted up mine eyes again, and *l*
Zec 4:2 And I said, I have *l*, and behold a
Zec 5:1 and lifted up mine eyes, and *l*
Zec 5:9 Then lifted I up mine eyes, and *l*
Zec 6:1 and lifted up mine eyes, and *l*
Mk 3:5 when he had *l* round about on them
Mk 3:34 he *l* round about on them which
Mk 5:32 he *l* round about to see her that
Mk 6:41 he *l* up to heaven, and blessed, and
Mk 8:24 And he *l* up, and said, I see men as
Mk 8:33 *l* on his disciples, he rebuked
Mk 9:8 when they had *l* round about
Mk 10:23 Jesus *l* round about, and saith
Mk 11:11 when he had *l* round about upon
Mk 14:67 she *l* upon him, and said, And thou
Mk 16:4 And when they *l*, they saw that the
Lk 1:25 me in the days wherein he *l* on me
Lk 2:38 *l* for redemption in Jerusalem
Lk 10:32 *l* on him, and passed by on the
Lk 19:5 Jesus came to the place, he *l* up
Lk 21:1 And he *l* up, and saw the rich men
Lk 22:56 the fire, and earnestly *l* upon him
Lk 22:61 the Lord turned, and *l* upon Peter
Jn 13:22 the disciples *l* one on another
Jn 20:11 down, and *l* into the sepulchre,
Acts 1:10 while they *l* stedfastly toward
Acts 7:55 *l* up stedfastly into heaven, and
Acts 10:4 And when he *l* on him, he was
Acts 22:13 And the same hour I *l* up upon him
Acts 28:6 Howbeit they *l* when he should
Acts 28:6 after they had *l* a great while
Heb 11:10 For he *l* for a city which hath
1Jn 1:1 our eyes, which we have *l* upon
Rev 4:1 After this I *l*, and, behold, a
Rev 6:8 And I *l*, and behold a pale horse
Rev 14:1 And I *l*, and, lo, a Lamb stood on
Rev 14:14 And I *l*, and behold a white cloud,
Rev 15:5 And after that I *l*, and, behold,

**LOOKETH**
Lev 13:12 foot, wheresoever the priest *l*
Num 21:8 that is bitten, when he *l* upon it
Num 21:20 Pisgah, which *l* toward Jeshimon
Num 23:28 of Peor, that *l* toward Jeshimon
Josh 15:2 from the bay that *l* southward
1Sa 13:18 to the way of the border that *l*
1Sa 16:7 for man *l* on the outward
1Sa 16:7 but the LORD *l* on the heart
Job 7:2 as a hireling *l* for the reward of
Job 28:24 For he *l* to the ends of the earth
Job 33:27 He *l* upon men, and if any say, I
Ps 33:13 The LORD *l* from heaven
Ps 33:14 the place of his habitation he *l*
Ps 104:32 He *l* on the earth, and it
Prov 14:15 prudent man *l* well to his going
Prov 31:27 She *l* well to the ways of her
Song 2:9 he *l* forth at the windows,
Song 6:10 Who is she that *l* forth as the
Song 7:4 Lebanon which *l* toward Damascus
Is 28:4 when he that *l* upon it seeth
Eze 8:3 gate, that *l* toward the north
Eze 11:1 LORD's house, which *l* eastward
Eze 40:6 the gate which *l* toward the east
Eze 40:22 the gate that *l* toward the east
Eze 43:1 the gate that *l* toward the east
Eze 44:1 sanctuary which *l* toward the east
Eze 46:1 gate of the inner court that *l*
Eze 46:12 the gate that *l* toward the east
Eze 47:2 gate by the way that *l* eastward
Mt 5:28 That whosoever *l* on a woman to
Mt 24:50 in a day when he *l* not for him
Lk 12:46 in a day when he *l* not for him
Jas 1:25 But whoso *l* into the perfect law

**LOOKING**
Josh 15:7 *l* toward Gilgal, that is before
1Kin 7:25 three *l* toward the north, and
1Kin 7:25 three *l* toward the west
1Kin 7:25 three *l* toward the south
1Kin 7:25 and three *l* toward the east
1Chr 15:29 Michal the daughter of Saul *l* out
2Chr 4:4 three *l* toward the north, and
2Chr 4:4 three *l* toward the west
2Chr 4:4 three *l* toward the south
2Chr 4:4 and three *l* toward the east
Job 37:18 is strong, and as a molten *l* glass
Is 38:14 mine eyes fail with *l* upward
Mt 14:19 *l* up to heaven, he blessed, and
Mk 7:34 *l* up to heaven, he sighed, and
Mk 10:27 Jesus *l* upon them saith, With men
Mk 15:40 were also women *l* on afar off
Lk 6:10 *l* round about upon them all, he
Lk 9:16 *l* up to heaven, he blessed them,
Lk 9:62 *l* back, is fit for the kingdom of
Lk 21:26 for *l* after those things which
Jn 1:36 *l* upon Jesus as he walked, he
Jn 20:5 *l* in, saw the linen clothes lying
Acts 6:15 *l* stedfastly on him, saw his face
Acts 23:21 *l* for a promise from thee
Titus 2:13 *L* for that blessed hope, and the
Heb 10:27 certain fearful *l* for of judgment
Heb 12:2 *L* unto Jesus the author and
Heb 12:15 *L* diligently lest any man fail of
2Pet 3:12 *L* for and hasting unto the coming
Jude 21 *l* for the mercy of our Lord Jesus

**LOOKS**
Ps 18:27 but wilt bring down high *l*
Is 2:11 The lofty *l* of man shall be
Is 10:12 and the glory of his high *l*
Eze 2:6 words, nor be dismayed at their *l*
Eze 3:9 neither be dismayed at their *l*

**LOOSE**
Gen 49:21 Naphtali is a hind let *l*
Lev 14:7 living bird *l* into the open field
Deut 25:9 *l* his shoe from off his foot, and
Josh 5:15 *L* thy shoe from off thy foot
Job 6:9 that he would let *l* his hand
Job 30:11 they have also let *l* the bridle
Job 38:31 Pleiades, or *l* the bands of Orion
Ps 102:20 to *l* those that are appointed to
Is 20:2 *l* the sackcloth from off thy
Is 45:1 I will *l* the loins of kings, to
Is 52:2 *l* thyself from the bands of thy
Is 58:6 to *l* the bands of wickedness, to
Jer 40:4 I *l* thee this day from the chains
Dan 3:25 and said, Lo, I see four men *l*
Mt 16:19 whatsoever thou shalt *l* on earth
Mt 18:18 whatsoever ye shall *l* on earth
Mt 21:2 *l* them, and bring them unto me
Mk 11:2 *l* him, and bring him
Mk 11:4 and they *l* him
Lk 13:15 *l* his ox or his ass from the
Lk 19:30 *l* him, and bring him hither
Lk 19:31 any man ask you, Why do ye *l* him
Lk 19:33 said unto them, Why *l* ye the colt
Jn 11:44 unto them, *L* him, and let him go
Acts 13:25 of his feet I am not worthy to *l*
Acts 24:26 him of Paul, that he might *l* him
Rev 5:2 book, and to *l* the seals thereof
Rev 5:5 to *l* the seven seals thereof
Rev 9:14 *L* the four angels which are bound

**LOOSED**
Ex 28:28 be not *l* from the ephod
Ex 39:21 might not be *l* from the ephod
Deut 25:10 house of him that hath his shoe *l*
Judg 15:14 his bands *l* from off his hands
Job 30:11 Because he hath *l* my cord
Job 39:5 or who hath *l* the bands of the
Ps 105:20 The king sent and *l* him
Ps 116:16 thou hast *l* my bonds
Eccl 12:6 Or ever the silver cord be *l*
Is 5:27 the girdle of their loins be *l*
Is 33:23 Thy tacklings are *l*
Is 51:14 exile hasteneth that he may be *l*
Dan 5:6 the joints of his loins were *l*
Mt 16:19 on earth shall be *l* in heaven
Mt 18:18 on earth shall be *l* in heaven
Mt 18:27 *l* him, and forgave him the debt
Mk 7:35 and the string of his tongue was *l*
Lk 1:64 immediately, and his tongue *l*
Lk 13:12 thou art *l* from thine infirmity
Lk 13:16 be *l* from this bond on the
Acts 2:24 having *l* the pains of death
Acts 13:13 Paul and his company *l* from Paphos
Acts 16:26 and every one's bands were *l*
Acts 22:30 he *l* him from his bands, and
Acts 27:21 not have *l* from Crete, and to have
Acts 27:40 *l* the rudder bands, and hoised up
Rom 7:2 she is *l* from the law of her
1Cor 7:27 seek not to be *l*
1Cor 7:27 Art thou *l* from a wife
Rev 9:15 And the four angels were *l*
Rev 20:3 that he must be *l* a little season
Rev 20:7 Satan shall be *l* out of his

**LO-RUHAMAH** *(lo-ru-ha'-mah) Symbolic name meaning "Not pitied."*
Hos 1:6 said unto him, Call her name *L*
Hos 1:8 Now when she had weaned *L*

**LOSE**
Judg 18:25 thou *l* thy life, with the lives
1Kin 18:5 that we *l* not all the beasts
Job 31:39 owners thereof to *l* their life
Prov 23:8 vomit up, and *l* thy sweet words
Eccl 3:6 A time to get, and a time to *l*
Mt 10:39 that findeth his life shall *l* it
Mt 10:42 he shall in no wise *l* his reward
Mt 16:25 will save his life shall *l* it
Mt 16:25 whosoever will *l* his life for my
Mt 16:26 whole world, and *l* his own soul
Mk 8:35 will save his life shall *l* it
Mk 8:35 but whosoever shall *l* his life
Mk 8:36 whole world, and *l* his own soul
Mk 9:41 you, he shall not *l* his reward
Lk 9:24 will save his life shall *l* it
Lk 9:24 but whosoever will *l* his life for
Lk 9:25 *l* himself, or be cast away
Lk 15:4 if he *l* one of them, doth not
Lk 15:8 if she *l* one piece, doth not
Lk 17:33 seek to save his life shall *l* it
Lk 17:33 whosoever shall *l* his life shall
Jn 6:39 hath given me I should *l* nothing
Jn 12:25 that loveth his life shall *l* it
2Jn 8 that we *l* not those things which

**LOSS**
Gen 31:39 I bare the *l* of it
Ex 21:19 shall pay for the *l* of his time
Is 47:8 shall I know the *l* of children
Is 47:9 the *l* of children, and widowhood
Acts 27:21 and to have gained this harm and *l*
Acts 27:22 for there shall be no *l* of any
1Cor 3:15 be burned, he shall suffer *l*
Phil 3:7 me, those I counted *l* for Christ
Phil 3:8 I count all things but *l* for the
Phil 3:8 have suffered the *l* of all things

**LOST**
Ex 22:9 or for any manner of *l* thing
Lev 6:3 Or have found that which was *l*
Lev 6:4 or the *l* thing which he found,
Num 6:12 days that were before shall be *l*
Deut 22:3 and with all *l* things of thy
Deut 22:3 of thy brother's, which he hath *l*
1Sa 9:3 of Kish Saul's father were *l*
1Sa 9:20 asses that were *l* three days ago
1Kin 20:25 like the army that thou hast *l*
Ps 119:176 I have gone astray like a *l* sheep
Is 49:20 have, after thou hast *l* the other
Is 49:21 seeing I have *l* my children
Jer 50:6 My people hath been *l* sheep
Eze 19:5 she had waited, and her hope was *l*

Eze 34:4 have ye sought that which was l
Eze 34:16 I will seek that which was l
Eze 37:11 bones are dried, and our hope is l
Mt 5:13 but if the salt have l his savour
Mt 10:6 But go rather to the l sheep of
Mt 15:24 I am not sent but unto the l
Mt 18:11 is come to save that which was l
Mk 9:50 if the salt have l his saltness
Lk 14:34 but if the salt have l his savour
Lk 15:4 and go after that which is l
Lk 15:6 I have found my sheep which was l
Lk 15:9 found the piece which I had l
Lk 15:24 he was l, and is found
Lk 15:32 and was l, and is found
Lk 19:10 seek and to save that which was l
Jn 6:12 that remain, that nothing be l
Jn 17:12 I have kept, and none of them is l
Jn 18:9 thou gavest me have I l none
2Cor 4:3 hid, it is hid to them that are l

**LOT** *(lot)* See LOT'S.
*1. Abraham's nephew.*
Gen 11:27 and Haran begat L
Gen 11:31 L the son of Haran his son's son,
Gen 12:4 and L went with him
Gen 12:5 L his brother's son, and all their
Gen 13:1 L with him, into the south
Gen 13:5 L also, which went with Abram,
Gen 13:8 And Abram said unto L, Let there
Gen 13:10 L lifted up his eyes, and beheld
Gen 13:11 Then L chose him all the plain of
Gen 13:11 and L journeyed east
Gen 13:12 L dwelled in the cities of the
Gen 13:14 after that L was separated from
Gen 14:12 And they took L, Abram's brother's
Gen 14:16 also brought again his brother L
Gen 19:1 L sat in the gate of Sodom
Gen 19:1 L seeing them rose up to meet
Gen 19:5 And they called unto L, and said
Gen 19:6 L went out at the door unto them,
Gen 19:9 pressed sore upon the man, even L
Gen 19:10 pulled L into the house to them,
Gen 19:12 And the men said unto L, Hast thou
Gen 19:14 L went out, and spake unto his
Gen 19:15 arose, then the angels hastened L
Gen 19:18 L said unto them, Oh, not so, my
Gen 19:23 earth when L entered into Zoar
Gen 19:29 sent L out of the midst of the
Gen 19:29 the cities in the which L dwelt
Gen 19:30 L went up out of Zoar, and dwelt
Gen 19:36 of L with child by their father
Deut 2:9 children of L for a possession
Deut 2:19 children of L for a possession
Ps 83:8 have holpen the children of L
Lk 17:28 also as it was in the days of L
Lk 17:29 But the same day that L went out
2Pet 2:7 And delivered just L, vexed with
*2. A die.*
Lev 16:8 one l for the LORD, and the other l
Lev 16:9 goat upon which the LORD's l fell
Lev 16:10 on which the l fell to be the
Num 26:55 the land shall be divided by l
Num 26:56 According to the l shall the
Num 33:54 ye shall divide the land by l for
Num 33:54 in the place where his l falleth
Num 34:13 land which ye shall inherit by l
Num 36:2 by l to the children of Israel
Num 36:3 from the l of our inheritance
Deut 32:9 Jacob is the l of his inheritance
Josh 13:6 only divide thou it by l unto the
Josh 14:2 By l was their inheritance, as
Josh 15:1 This then was the l of the tribe
Josh 16:1 the l of the children of Joseph
Josh 17:1 There was also a l for the tribe
Josh 17:2 There was also a l for the rest
Josh 17:14 Why hast thou given me but one l
Josh 17:17 thou shalt not have one l only
Josh 18:11 the l of the tribe of the
Josh 18:11 the coast of their l came forth
Josh 19:1 the second l came forth to Simeon
Josh 19:10 the third l came up for the
Josh 19:17 the fourth l came out to Issachar
Josh 19:24 the fifth l came out for the
Josh 19:32 The sixth l came out to the
Josh 19:40 the seventh l came out for the
Josh 19:51 by l in Shiloh before the LORD
Josh 21:4 the l came out for the families
Josh 21:4 had by l out of the tribe of
Josh 21:5 by l out of the families of the
Josh 21:6 by l out of the families of the
Josh 21:8 l unto the Levites these cities
Josh 21:10 for theirs was the first l
Josh 21:20 l out of the tribe of Ephraim
Josh 21:40 were by their l twelve cities
Josh 23:4 by l these nations that remain
Judg 1:3 Come up with me into my l
Judg 1:3 will go with thee into thy l
Judg 20:9 we will go up by l against it
1Sa 14:41 God of Israel, Give a perfect l
1Chr 6:54 for theirs was the l
1Chr 6:61 the half tribe of Manasseh, by l
1Chr 6:63 sons of Merari were given by l
1Chr 6:65 they gave by l out of the tribe
1Chr 16:18 the l of your inheritance
1Chr 24:5 Thus were they divided by l
1Chr 24:7 Now the first l came forth to
1Chr 25:9 Now the first l came forth for
1Chr 26:14 the l eastward fell to Shelemiah
1Chr 26:14 and his l came out northward
1Chr 26:16 Hosah the l came forth westward,
Est 3:7 they cast Pur, that is, the l
Est 9:24 and had cast Pur, that is, the l
Ps 16:5 thou maintainest my l
Ps 105:11 the l of your inheritance
Ps 125:3 rest upon the l of the righteous
Prov 1:14 Cast in thy l among us
Prov 16:33 The l is cast into the lap
Prov 18:18 The l causeth contentions to
Is 17:14 the l of them that rob us
Is 34:17 And he hath cast the l for them
Is 57:6 they, they are thy l
Jer 13:25 This is thy l, the portion of thy
Eze 24:6 let no l fall upon it
Eze 45:1 when ye shall divide by l the
Eze 47:22 that ye shall divide it by l for
Eze 48:29 l unto the tribes of Israel for
Dan 12:13 stand in thy l at the end of the
Jonah 1:7 lots, and the l fell upon Jonah
Mic 2:5 none that shall cast a cord by l
Lk 1:9 his l was to burn incense when he
Acts 1:26 and the l fell upon Matthias
Acts 8:21 neither part nor l in this matter
Acts 13:19 divided their land to them by l

**LOTAN** *(lo'-tan)* See LOTAN'S. *Son of Seir.*
Gen 36:20 L, and Shobal, and Zibeon, and Anah,
Gen 36:22 And the children of L were Hori
Gen 36:29 duke L, duke Shobal, duke Zibeon,
1Chr 1:38 L, and Shobal, and Zibeon, and Anah,
1Chr 1:39 And the sons of L

**LOTAN'S** *(lo'-tans)*
Gen 36:22 and L sister was Timna
1Chr 1:39 and Timna was L sister

**LOTHE**
Ex 7:18 the Egyptians shall l to drink of
Eze 6:9 they shall l themselves for the
Eze 20:43 ye shall l yourselves in your own
Eze 36:31 shall l yourselves in your own

**LOT'S** *(lots)*
Gen 13:7 cattle and the herdmen of L cattle
Lk 17:32 Remember L wife

**LOTS**
Lev 16:8 Aaron shall cast l upon the two
Josh 18:6 that I may cast l for you here
Josh 18:8 that I may here cast l for you
Josh 18:10 Joshua cast l for them in Shiloh
1Sa 14:42 Cast l between me and Jonathan my
1Chr 24:31 These likewise cast l over
1Chr 25:8 And they cast l, ward against ward
1Chr 26:13 And they cast l, as well the small
1Chr 26:14 a wise counsellor, they cast l
Neh 10:34 we cast the l among the priests,
Neh 11:1 rest of the people also cast l
Ps 22:18 them, and cast l upon my vesture
Joel 3:3 And they have cast l for my people
Obad 11 cast l upon Jerusalem, even thou
Jonah 1:7 fellow, Come, and let us cast l
Jonah 1:7 So they cast l, and the lot fell
Nah 3:10 they cast l for her honourable
Mt 27:35 and parted his garments, casting l
Mt 27:35 upon my vesture did they cast l
Mk 15:24 casting l upon them, what every
Lk 23:34 parted his raiment, and cast l
Jn 19:24 us not rend it, but cast l for it
Jn 19:24 and for my vesture they did cast l
Acts 1:26 And they gave forth their l

**LOUD**
Gen 39:14 me, and I cried with a l voice
Ex 19:16 voice of the trumpet exceeding l
Deut 27:14 the men of Israel with a l voice
1Sa 28:12 Samuel, she cried with a l voice
2Sa 15:23 the country wept with a l voice
2Sa 19:4 and the king cried with a l voice
1Kin 8:55 of Israel with a l voice, saying,
2Kin 18:28 cried with a l voice in the Jews'
2Chr 15:14 unto the LORD with a l voice
2Chr 20:19 of Israel with a l voice on high
2Chr 30:21 singing with l instruments unto
2Chr 32:18 Then they cried with a l voice in
Ezr 3:12 their eyes, wept with a l voice
Ezr 3:13 the people shouted with a l shout
Ezr 10:12 answered and said with a l voice
Neh 9:4 cried with a l voice unto the
Neh 12:42 And the singers sang l, with
Est 4:1 of the city, and cried with a l
Ps 33:3 play skilfully with a l noise
Ps 98:4 make a l noise, and rejoice, and
Ps 150:5 Praise him upon the l cymbals
Prov 7:11 (She is l and stubborn
Prov 27:14 his friend with a l voice
Is 36:13 cried with a l voice in the Jews'
Eze 8:18 cry in mine ears with a l voice
Eze 9:1 also in mine ears with a l voice
Eze 11:13 my face, and cried with a l voice
Mt 27:46 hour Jesus cried with a l voice
Mt 27:50 he had cried again with a l voice
Mk 1:26 torn him, and cried with a l voice
Mk 5:7 And cried with a l voice, and said,
Mk 15:34 hour Jesus cried with a l voice
Mk 15:37 And Jesus cried with a l voice
Lk 1:42 And she spake out with a l voice
Lk 4:33 and cried out with a l voice
Lk 8:28 with a l voice said, What have I
Lk 17:15 with a l voice glorified God,
Lk 19:37 praise God with a l voice for all
Lk 23:23 they were instant with l voices
Lk 23:46 Jesus had cried with a l voice
Jn 11:43 spoken, he cried with a l voice
Acts 7:57 they cried out with a l voice
Acts 7:60 down, and cried with a l voice
Acts 8:7 spirits, crying with l voice
Acts 14:10 Said with a l voice, Stand
Acts 16:28 But Paul cried with a l voice
Acts 26:24 Festus said with a l voice
Rev 5:2 angel proclaiming with a l voice
Rev 5:12 Saying with a l voice, Worthy is
Rev 6:10 And they cried with a l voice
Rev 7:2 he cried with a l voice to the
Rev 7:10 And cried with a l voice, saying,
Rev 8:13 of heaven, saying with a l voice
Rev 10:3 And cried with a l voice, as when
Rev 12:10 I heard a l voice saying in
Rev 14:7 Saying with a l voice, Fear God,
Rev 14:9 them, saying with a l voice
Rev 14:15 crying with a l voice to him that
Rev 14:18 cried with a l cry to him that
Rev 19:17 and he cried with a l voice

**LOVE**
Gen 27:4 make me savoury meat, such as I l
Gen 29:20 few days, for the l he had to her
Gen 29:32 therefore my husband will l me
Ex 20:6 unto thousands of them that l me
Ex 21:5 I l my master, my wife, and my
Lev 19:18 but thou shalt l thy neighbour as
Lev 19:34 thou shalt l him as thyself
Deut 5:10 unto thousands of them that l me
Deut 6:5 thou shalt l the LORD thy God
Deut 7:7 LORD did not set his l upon you
Deut 7:9 and mercy with them that l him
Deut 7:13 And he will l thee, and bless thee,
Deut 10:12 to l him, and to serve the LORD
Deut 10:15 delight in thy fathers to l them
Deut 10:19 L ye therefore the stranger
Deut 11:1 thou shalt l the LORD thy God
Deut 11:13 to l the LORD your God, and to
Deut 11:22 to l the LORD your God, to walk
Deut 13:3 to know whether ye l the LORD
Deut 19:9 to l the LORD thy God, and to walk
Deut 30:6 to l the LORD thy God with all
Deut 30:16 this day to l the LORD thy God
Deut 30:20 thou mayest l the LORD thy God
Josh 22:5 to l the LORD your God, and to
Josh 23:11 that ye l the LORD your God
Judg 5:31 but let them that l him be as the
Judg 16:15 I l thee, when thine heart is not
1Sa 18:22 thee, and all his servants l thee
2Sa 1:26 thy l to me was wonderful,
2Sa 1:26 passing the l of women

2Sa 13:4 I *l* Tamar, my brother Absalom's
2Sa 13:15 the *l* wherewith he had loved her
1Kin 11:2 Solomon clave unto these in *l*
2Chr 19:2 *l* them that hate the LORD
Neh 1:5 and mercy for them that *l* him
Ps 4:2 how long will ye *l* vanity
Ps 5:11 let them also that *l* thy name be
Ps 18:1 I will *l* thee, O LORD, my
Ps 31:23 O *l* the LORD, all ye his saints
Ps 40:16 let such as *l* thy salvation say
Ps 69:36 they that *l* his name shall dwell
Ps 70:4 let such as *l* thy salvation say
Ps 91:14 Because he hath set his *l* upon me
Ps 97:10 Ye that *l* the LORD, hate evil
Ps 109:4 For my *l* they are my adversaries
Ps 109:5 evil for good, and hatred for my *l*
Ps 116:1 I *l* the LORD, because he hath
Ps 119:97 O how *l* I thy law
Ps 119:113 but thy law do I *l*
Ps 119:119 therefore I *l* thy testimonies
Ps 119:127 Therefore I *l* thy commandments
Ps 119:132 to do unto those that *l* thy name
Ps 119:159 Consider how I *l* thy precepts
Ps 119:163 but thy law do I *l*
Ps 119:165 peace have they which *l* thy law
Ps 119:167 and I *l* them exceedingly
Ps 122:6 they shall prosper that *l* thee
Ps 145:20 preserveth all them that *l* him
Prov 1:22 simple ones, will ye *l* simplicity
Prov 4:6 *l* her, and she shall keep thee
Prov 5:19 thou ravished always with her *l*
Prov 7:18 our fill of *l* until the morning
Prov 8:17 I *l* them that *l* me
Prov 8:21 that *l* me to inherit substance
Prov 8:36 all they that hate me *l* death
Prov 9:8 a wise man, and he will *l* thee
Prov 10:12 but *l* covereth all sins
Prov 15:17 is a dinner of herbs where *l* is
Prov 16:13 they *l* him that speaketh right
Prov 17:9 a transgression seeketh *l*
Prov 18:21 they that *l* it shall eat the
Prov 20:13 *L* not sleep, lest thou come to
Prov 27:5 rebuke is better than secret *l*
Eccl 3:8 A time to *l*, and a time to hate
Eccl 9:1 no man knoweth either *l* or hatred
Eccl 9:6 Also their *l*, and their hatred, and
Song 1:2 for thy *l* is better than wine
Song 1:3 therefore do the virgins *l* thee
Song 1:4 remember thy *l* more than wine
Song 1:4 the upright *l* thee
Song 1:9 I have compared thee, O my *l*
Song 1:15 Behold, thou art fair, my *l*
Song 2:2 so is my *l* among the daughters
Song 2:4 and his banner over me was *l*
Song 2:5 for I am sick of *l*
Song 2:7 ye stir not up, nor awake my *l*
Song 2:10 and said unto me, Rise up, my *l*
Song 2:13 Arise, my *l*, my fair one, and come
Song 3:5 ye stir not up, nor awake my *l*
Song 3:10 midst thereof being paved with *l*
Song 4:1 Behold, thou art fair, my *l*
Song 4:7 Thou art all fair, my *l*
Song 4:10 How fair is thy *l*, my sister, my
Song 4:10 much better is thy *l* than wine
Song 5:2 Open to me, my sister, my *l*
Song 5:8 ye tell him, that I am sick of *l*
Song 6:4 Thou art beautiful, O my *l*
Song 7:6 and how pleasant art thou, O *l*
Song 8:4 ye stir not up, nor awake my *l*
Song 8:6 for *l* is strong as death
Song 8:7 Many waters cannot quench *l*
Song 8:7 the substance of his house for *l*
Is 38:17 but thou hast in *l* to my soul
Is 56:6 to *l* the name of the LORD, to be
Is 61:8 For I the LORD *l* judgment
Is 63:9 in his *l* and in his pity he
Is 66:10 glad with her, all ye that *l* her
Jer 2:2 the *l* of thine espousals, when
Jer 2:33 trimmest thou thy way to seek *l*
Jer 5:31 my people *l* to have it so
Jer 31:3 loved thee with an everlasting *l*
Eze 16:8 thy time was the time of *l*
Eze 23:11 in her inordinate *l* than she
Eze 23:17 came to her into the bed of *l*
Eze 33:31 with their mouth they shew much *l*
Dan 1:9 tender *l* with the prince of the
Dan 9:4 and mercy to them that *l* him
Hos 3:1 *l* a woman beloved of her friend,
Hos 3:1 according to the *l* of the LORD
Hos 3:1 other gods, and *l* flagons of wine
Hos 4:18 her rulers with shame do *l*
Hos 9:15 mine house, I will *l* them no more
Hos 11:4 cords of a man, with bands of *l*
Hos 14:4 backsliding, I will *l* them freely
Amos 5:15 *l* the good, and establish judgment
Mic 3:2 Who hate the good, and *l* the evil
Mic 6:8 to *l* mercy, and to walk humbly
Zeph 3:17 he will rest in his *l*, he will
Zec 8:17 and *l* no false oath
Zec 8:19 therefore *l* the truth and peace
Mt 5:43 Thou shalt *l* thy neighbour, and
Mt 5:44 *L* your enemies, bless them that
Mt 5:46 For if ye *l* them which *l* you,
Mt 6:5 for they *l* to pray standing in
Mt 6:24 will hate the one, and *l* the other
Mt 19:19 Thou shalt *l* thy neighbour as
Mt 22:37 Thou shalt *l* the Lord thy God
Mt 22:39 Thou shalt *l* thy neighbour as
Mt 23:6 *l* the uppermost rooms at feasts,
Mt 24:12 the *l* of many shall wax cold
Mk 12:30 thou shalt *l* the Lord thy God
Mk 12:31 Thou shalt *l* thy neighbour as
Mk 12:33 to *l* him with all the heart, and
Mk 12:33 to *l* his neighbour as himself, is
Mk 12:38 which *l* to go in long clothing,
Mk 12:38 *l* salutations in the marketplaces
Lk 6:27 *L* your enemies, do good to them
Lk 6:32 For if ye *l* them which *l* you
Lk 6:32 also *l* those that *l* them
Lk 6:35 But *l* ye your enemies, and do good
Lk 7:42 which of them will *l* him most
Lk 10:27 Thou shalt *l* the Lord thy God
Lk 11:42 over judgment and the *l* of God
Lk 11:43 for ye *l* the uppermost seats in
Lk 16:13 will hate the one, and *l* the other
Lk 20:46 *l* greetings in the markets, and
Jn 5:42 ye have not the *l* of God in you
Jn 8:42 were your Father, ye would *l* me
Jn 10:17 Therefore doth my Father *l* me
Jn 13:34 unto you, That ye *l* one another
Jn 13:34 you, that ye also *l* one another
Jn 13:35 if ye have *l* one to another
Jn 14:15 If ye *l* me, keep my commandments
Jn 14:21 of my Father, and I will *l* him
Jn 14:23 and said unto him, If a man *l* me
Jn 14:23 and my Father will *l* him, and we
Jn 14:31 may know that I *l* the Father
Jn 15:9 continue ye in my *l*
Jn 15:10 ye shall abide in my *l*
Jn 15:10 commandments, and abide in his *l*
Jn 15:12 That ye *l* one another, as I have
Jn 15:13 Greater *l* hath no man than this,
Jn 15:17 you, that ye *l* one another
Jn 15:19 world, the world would *l* his own
Jn 17:26 that the *l* wherewith thou hast
Jn 21:15 thou knowest that I *l* thee
Jn 21:16 thou knowest that I *l* thee
Jn 21:17 thou knowest that I *l* thee
Rom 5:5 because the *l* of God is shed
Rom 5:8 God commendeth his *l* toward us
Rom 8:28 for good to them that *l* God
Rom 8:35 separate us from the *l* of Christ
Rom 8:39 to separate us from the *l* of God
Rom 12:9 Let *l* be without dissimulation
Rom 12:10 one to another with brotherly *l*
Rom 13:8 any thing, but to *l* one another
Rom 13:9 Thou shalt *l* thy neighbour as
Rom 13:10 *L* worketh no ill to his neighbour
Rom 13:10 therefore *l* is the fulfilling of
Rom 15:30 for the *l* of the Spirit, that ye
1Cor 2:9 hath prepared for them that *l* him
1Cor 4:21 come unto you with a rod, or in *l*
1Cor 8:3 But if any man *l* God, the same is
1Cor 16:22 If any man *l* not the Lord Jesus
1Cor 16:24 My *l* be with you all in Christ
2Cor 2:4 but that ye might know the *l*
2Cor 2:8 would confirm your *l* toward him
2Cor 5:14 For the *l* of Christ constraineth
2Cor 6:6 the Holy Ghost, by *l* unfeigned,
2Cor 8:7 all diligence, and in your *l* to us
2Cor 8:8 to prove the sincerity of your *l*
2Cor 8:24 the churches, the proof of your *l*
2Cor 11:11 because I *l* you not
2Cor 12:15 the more abundantly I *l* you
2Cor 13:11 and the God of *l* and peace shall be
2Cor 13:14 the *l* of God, and the communion of
Gal 5:6 but faith which worketh by *l*
Gal 5:13 but by *l* serve one another
Gal 5:14 Thou shalt *l* thy neighbour as
Gal 5:22 But the fruit of the Spirit is *l*
Eph 1:4 and without blame before him in *l*
Eph 1:15 Jesus, and *l* unto all the saints,
Eph 2:4 for his great *l* wherewith he
Eph 3:17 ye, being rooted and grounded in *l*
Eph 3:19 And to know the *l* of Christ
Eph 4:2 forbearing one another in *l*
Eph 4:15 But speaking the truth in *l*
Eph 4:16 unto the edifying of itself in *l*
Eph 5:2 And walk in *l*, as Christ also hath
Eph 5:25 *l* your wives, even as Christ also
Eph 5:28 So ought men to *l* their wives as
Eph 5:33 so *l* his wife even as himself
Eph 6:23 *l* with faith, from God the Father
Eph 6:24 that *l* our Lord Jesus Christ in
Phil 1:9 that your *l* may abound yet more
Phil 1:17 But the other of *l*, knowing that
Phil 2:1 in Christ, if any comfort of *l*
Phil 2:2 be likeminded, having the same *l*
Col 1:4 of the *l* which ye have to all the
Col 1:8 unto us your *l* in the Spirit
Col 2:2 being knit together in *l*
Col 3:19 *l* your wives, and be not bitter
1Th 1:3 work of faith, and labour of *l*
1Th 3:12 abound in *l* one toward another,
1Th 4:9 But as touching brotherly *l* ye
1Th 4:9 taught of God to *l* one another
1Th 5:8 on the breastplate of faith and *l*
1Th 5:13 highly in *l* for their work's sake
2Th 2:10 received not the *l* of the truth
2Th 3:5 your hearts into the *l* of God
1Ti 1:14 *l* which is in Christ Jesus
1Ti 6:10 For the *l* of money is the root of
1Ti 6:11 godliness, faith, *l*, patience,
2Ti 1:7 but of power, and of *l*, and of a
2Ti 1:13 *l* which is in Christ Jesus
2Ti 4:8 them also that *l* his appearing
Titus 2:4 be sober, to *l* their husbands
Titus 2:4 to *l* their children
Titus 3:4 *l* of God our Saviour toward man
Titus 3:15 Greet them that *l* us in the faith
Philem 5 Hearing of thy *l* and faith, which
Philem 7 great joy and consolation in thy *l*
Heb 6:10 forget your work and labour of *l*
Heb 10:24 one another to provoke unto *l*
Heb 13:1 Let brotherly *l* continue
Jas 1:12 hath promised to them that *l* him
Jas 2:5 hath promised to them that *l* him
Jas 2:8 Thou shalt *l* thy neighbour as
1Pet 1:8 Whom having not seen, ye *l*
1Pet 1:22 unto unfeigned *l* of the brethren
1Pet 1:22 see that ye *l* one another with a
1Pet 2:17 *L* the brotherhood
1Pet 3:8 *l* as brethren, be pitiful, be
1Pet 3:10 For he that will *l* life, and see
1Jn 2:5 verily is the *l* of God perfected
1Jn 2:15 *L* not the world, neither the
1Jn 2:15 If any man *l* the world
1Jn 2:15 the *l* of the Father is not in him
1Jn 3:1 what manner of *l* the Father hath
1Jn 3:11 that we should *l* one another
1Jn 3:14 because we *l* the brethren
1Jn 3:16 Hereby perceive we the *l* of God
1Jn 3:17 how dwelleth the *l* of God in him
1Jn 3:18 children, let us not *l* in word
1Jn 3:23 *l* one another, as he gave us
1Jn 4:7 Beloved, let us *l* one another
1Jn 4:7 for *l* is of God
1Jn 4:8 for God is *l*
1Jn 4:9 manifested the *l* of God toward us
1Jn 4:10 Herein is *l*, not that we loved
1Jn 4:11 we ought also to *l* one another
1Jn 4:12 If we *l* one another, God dwelleth
1Jn 4:12 us, and his *l* is perfected in us
1Jn 4:16 believed the *l* that God hath to
1Jn 4:16 God is *l*
1Jn 4:16 dwelleth in *l* dwelleth in God
1Jn 4:17 Herein is our *l* made perfect
1Jn 4:18 There is no fear in *l*
1Jn 4:18 but perfect *l* casteth out fear
1Jn 4:18 feareth is not made perfect in *l*
1Jn 4:19 We *l* him, because he first loved
1Jn 4:20 I *l* God, and hateth his brother,
1Jn 4:20 how can he *l* God whom he hath not
1Jn 4:21 who loveth God *l* his brother also
1Jn 5:2 that we *l* the children of God
1Jn 5:2 children of God, when we *l* God
1Jn 5:3 For this is the *l* of God, that we
2Jn 1 children, whom I *l* in the truth
2Jn 3 Son of the Father, in truth and *l*
2Jn 5 beginning, that we *l* one another

2Jn 6 And this is *l*, that we walk after
3Jn 1 Gaius, whom I *l* in the truth
Jude 2 Mercy unto you, and peace, and *l*
Jude 21 Keep yourselves in the *l* of God
Rev 2:4 thou hast left thy first *l*
Rev 3:19 As many as I *l*, I rebuke and

## LOVED

Gen 24:67 his wife; and he *l* her
Gen 25:28 And Isaac *l* Esau, because he did
Gen 25:28 but Rebekah *l* Jacob
Gen 27:14 meat, such as his father *l*
Gen 29:18 And Jacob *l* Rachel
Gen 29:30 he *l* also Rachel more than Leah,
Gen 34:3 he *l* the damsel, and spake kindly
Gen 37:3 Now Israel *l* Joseph more than all
Gen 37:4 *l* him more than all his brethren
Deut 4:37 because he *l* thy fathers,
Deut 7:8 But because the LORD *l* you
Deut 23:5 because the LORD thy God *l* thee
Deut 33:3 Yea, he *l* the people
Judg 16:4 that he *l* a woman in the valley
1Sa 1:5 for he *l* Hannah
1Sa 16:21 and he *l* him greatly
1Sa 18:1 Jonathan *l* him as his own soul
1Sa 18:3 because he *l* him as his own soul
1Sa 18:16 But all Israel and Judah *l* David
1Sa 18:20 And Michal Saul's daughter *l* David
1Sa 18:28 that Michal Saul's daughter *l* him
1Sa 20:17 to swear again, because he *l* him
1Sa 20:17 for he *l* him as he
1Sa 20:17 him as he *l* his own soul
2Sa 12:24 and the LORD *l* him
2Sa 13:1 and Amnon the son of David *l* her
2Sa 13:15 the love wherewith he had *l* her
1Kin 3:3 Solomon *l* the LORD, walking in
1Kin 10:9 the LORD *l* Israel for ever
1Kin 11:1 But king Solomon *l* many strange
2Chr 2:11 the LORD hath *l* his people
2Chr 9:8 because thy God *l* Israel, to
2Chr 11:21 Rehoboam *l* Maachah the daughter
2Chr 26:10 for he *l* husbandry
Est 2:17 the king *l* Esther above all the
Job 19:19 they whom I *l* are turned against
Ps 26:8 I have *l* the habitation of thy
Ps 47:4 the excellency of Jacob whom he *l*
Ps 78:68 Judah, the mount Zion which he *l*
Ps 109:17 As he *l* cursing, so let it come
Ps 119:47 thy commandments, which I have *l*
Ps 119:48 thy commandments, which I have *l*
Is 43:4 been honourable, and I have *l* thee
Is 48:14 The LORD hath *l* him
Jer 2:25 for I have *l* strangers, and after
Jer 8:2 host of heaven, whom they have *l*
Jer 14:10 Thus have they *l* to wander
Jer 31:3 I have *l* thee with an everlasting
Eze 16:37 and all them that thou hast *l*
Hos 9:1 thou hast *l* a reward upon every
Hos 9:10 were according as they *l*
Hos 11:1 Israel was a child, then I *l* him
Mal 1:2 I have *l* you, saith the LORD
Mal 1:2 ye say, Wherein hast thou *l* us
Mal 1:2 yet I *l* Jacob,
Mal 2:11 holiness of the LORD which he *l*
Mk 10:21 Then Jesus beholding him *l* him
Lk 7:47 for she *l* much
Jn 3:16 For God so *l* the world, that he
Jn 3:19 men *l* darkness rather than light,
Jn 11:5 Now Jesus *l* Martha, and her sister
Jn 11:36 the Jews, Behold how he *l* him
Jn 12:43 For they *l* the praise of men more
Jn 13:1 having *l* his own which were in
Jn 13:1 the world, he *l* them unto the end
Jn 13:23 of his disciples, whom Jesus *l*
Jn 13:34 as I have *l* you, that ye also
Jn 14:21 loveth me shall be *l* of my Father
Jn 14:28 If ye *l* me, ye would rejoice,
Jn 15:9 hath *l* me, so have I *l* you
Jn 15:12 love one another, as I have *l* you
Jn 16:27 loveth you, because ye have *l* me
Jn 17:23 thou hast sent me, and hast *l* them
Jn 17:23 as thou hast *l* me
Jn 17:26 thou hast *l* me may be in them
Jn 19:26 disciple standing by, whom he *l*
Jn 20:2 the other disciple, whom Jesus *l*
Jn 21:7 whom Jesus *l* saith unto Peter
Jn 21:20 disciple whom Jesus *l* following
Rom 8:37 conquerors through him that *l* us
Rom 9:13 As it is written, Jacob have I *l*
2Cor 12:15 I love you, the less I be *l*
Gal 2:20 faith of the Son of God, who *l* me
Eph 2:4 his great love wherewith he *l* us
Eph 5:2 in love, as Christ also hath *l* us
Eph 5:25 even as Christ also *l* the church
2Th 2:16 even our Father, which hath *l* us
2Ti 4:10 having *l* this present world, and
Heb 1:9 Thou hast *l* righteousness, and
2Pet 2:15 son of Bosor, who *l* the wages of
1Jn 4:10 Herein is love, not that we *l* God
1Jn 4:10 but that he *l* us
1Jn 4:11 Beloved, if God so *l* us, we ought
1Jn 4:19 love him, because he first *l* us
Rev 1:5 Unto him that *l* us, and washed us
Rev 3:9 and to know that I have *l* thee
Rev 12:11 they *l* not their lives unto the

## LOVELY

2Sa 1:23 Saul and Jonathan were *l* and
Song 5:16 yea, he is altogether *l*
Eze 33:32 a very *l* song of one that hath a
Phil 4:8 are pure, whatsoever things are *l*

## LOVERS

Ps 38:11 My *l* and my friends stand aloof
Jer 3:1 played the harlot with many *l*
Jer 4:30 thy *l* will despise thee, they
Jer 22:20 for all thy *l* are destroyed
Jer 22:22 thy *l* shall go into captivity
Jer 30:14 All thy *l* have forgotten thee
Lam 1:2 among all her *l* she hath none to
Lam 1:19 I called for my *l*, but they
Eze 16:33 givest thy gifts to all thy *l*
Eze 16:36 through thy whoredoms with thy *l*
Eze 16:37 therefore I will gather all thy *l*
Eze 23:5 and she doted on her *l*, on the
Eze 23:9 her into the hand of her *l*
Eze 23:22 will raise up thy *l* against thee
Hos 2:5 she said, I will go after my *l*
Hos 2:7 And she shall follow after her *l*
Hos 2:10 lewdness in the sight of her *l*
Hos 2:12 rewards that my *l* have given me
Hos 2:13 jewels, and she went after her *l*
Hos 8:9 Ephraim hath hired *l*
2Ti 3:2 For men shall be *l* of their own
2Ti 3:4 *l* of pleasures more than
2Ti 3:4 of pleasures more than *l* of God

## LOVEST

Gen 22:2 thine only son Isaac, whom thou *l*
Judg 14:16 dost but hate me, and *l* me not
2Sa 19:6 In that thou *l* thine enemies, and
Ps 45:7 Thou *l* righteousness, and hatest
Ps 52:3 Thou *l* evil more than good
Ps 52:4 Thou *l* all devouring words, O
Eccl 9:9 with the wife whom thou *l* all the
Jn 11:3 behold, he whom thou *l* is sick
Jn 21:15 *l* thou me more than these
Jn 21:16 Simon, son of Jonas, *l* thou me
Jn 21:17 Simon, son of Jonas, *l* thou me
Jn 21:17 him the third time, *L* thou me

## LOVETH

Gen 27:9 meat for thy father, such as he *l*
Gen 44:20 his mother, and his father *l* him
Deut 10:18 *l* the stranger, in giving him
Deut 15:16 because he *l* thee and thine house,
Ruth 4:15 thy daughter in law, which *l* thee
Ps 11:5 him that *l* violence his soul
Ps 11:7 righteous LORD *l* righteousness
Ps 33:5 He *l* righteousness and judgment
Ps 34:12 *l* many days, that he may see good
Ps 37:28 For the LORD *l* judgment, and
Ps 87:2 The LORD *l* the gates of Zion more
Ps 99:4 king's strength also *l* judgment
Ps 119:140 therefore thy servant *l* it
Ps 146:8 the LORD *l* the righteous
Prov 3:12 For whom the LORD *l* he correcteth
Prov 12:1 *l* instruction *l* knowledge
Prov 13:24 but he that *l* him chasteneth him
Prov 15:9 but he *l* him that followeth after
Prov 15:12 A scorner *l* not one that
Prov 17:17 A friend *l* at all times, and a
Prov 17:19 He *l* transgression that
Prov 17:19 transgression that *l* strife
Prov 19:8 getteth wisdom *l* his own soul
Prov 21:17 He that *l* pleasure shall be a
Prov 21:17 he that *l* wine and oil shall not
Prov 22:11 He that *l* pureness of heart, for
Prov 29:3 Whoso *l* wisdom rejoiceth his
Eccl 5:10 He that *l* silver shall not be
Eccl 5:10 nor he that *l* abundance with
Song 1:7 Tell me, O thou whom my soul *l*
Song 3:1 bed I sought him whom my soul *l*
Song 3:2 I will seek him whom my soul *l*
Song 3:3 I said, Saw ye him whom my soul *l*
Song 3:4 but I found him whom my soul *l*
Is 1:23 every one *l* gifts, and followeth
Hos 10:11 and *l* to tread out the corn
Hos 12:7 he *l* to oppress
Mt 10:37 He that *l* father or mother more
Mt 10:37 he that *l* son or daughter more
Lk 7:5 For he *l* our nation, and he hath
Lk 7:47 is forgiven, the same *l* little
Jn 3:35 The Father *l* the Son, and hath
Jn 5:20 For the Father *l* the Son, and
Jn 12:25 He that *l* his life shall lose it
Jn 14:21 keepeth them, he it is that *l* me
Jn 14:21 he that *l* me shall be loved of my
Jn 14:24 He that *l* me not keepeth not my
Jn 16:27 For the Father himself *l* you
Rom 13:8 for he that *l* another hath
2Cor 9:7 for God *l* a cheerful giver
Eph 5:28 He that *l* his wife *l* himself
Heb 12:6 For whom the Lord *l* he chasteneth
1Jn 2:10 He that *l* his brother abideth in
1Jn 3:10 neither he that *l* not his brother
1Jn 3:14 He that *l* not his brother abideth
1Jn 4:7 every one that *l* is born of God
1Jn 4:8 He that *l* not knoweth not God
1Jn 4:20 for he that *l* not his brother
1Jn 4:21 That he who *l* God love his
1Jn 5:1 every one that *l* him that begat
1Jn 5:1 *l* him also that is begotten of
3Jn 9 who *l* to have the preeminence
Rev 22:15 and idolaters, and whosoever *l*

## LOVINGKINDNESS

Ps 17:7 Shew thy marvellous *l*, O thou
Ps 26:3 For thy *l* is before mine eyes
Ps 36:7 How excellent is thy *l*, O God
Ps 36:10 O continue thy *l* unto them that
Ps 40:10 I have not concealed thy *l*
Ps 40:11 let thy *l* and thy truth
Ps 42:8 will command his *l* in the daytime
Ps 48:9 We have thought of thy *l*, O God,
Ps 51:1 me, O God, according to thy *l*
Ps 63:3 Because thy *l* is better than life
Ps 69:16 for thy *l* is good
Ps 88:11 Shall thy *l* be declared in the
Ps 89:33 Nevertheless my *l* will I not
Ps 92:2 shew forth thy *l* in the morning
Ps 103:4 who crowneth thee with *l* and
Ps 107:43 understand the *l* of the LORD
Ps 119:88 Quicken me after thy *l*
Ps 119:149 my voice according unto thy *l*
Ps 119:159 me, O LORD, according to thy *l*
Ps 138:2 and praise thy name for thy *l*
Ps 143:8 me to hear thy *l* in the morning
Jer 9:24 I am the LORD which exercise *l*
Jer 16:5 people, saith the LORD, even *l*
Jer 31:3 therefore with *l* have I drawn
Jer 32:18 Thou shewest *l* unto thousands, and
Hos 2:19 and in judgment, and in *l*, and in

## LOWLY

Ps 138:6 yet hath he respect unto the *l*
Prov 3:34 but he giveth grace unto the *l*
Prov 11:2 but with the *l* is wisdom
Prov 16:19 be of an humble spirit with the *l*
Zec 9:9 *l*, and riding upon an ass, and upon
Mt 11:29 for I am meek and *l* in heart

**LUBIM** *(lu'-bim)* See LUBIMS. *An African race.*
2Chr 12:3 the *L*, the Sukkiims, and the
Nah 3:9 Put and *L* were thy helpers

**LUBIMS** *(lu'-bims)* See LEHABIM, LUBIM. *Same as Lubim.*
2Chr 16:8 the *L* a huge host, with very many

**LUCAS** *(lu'-cas)* See LUKE. *Same as Luke.*
2Cor *s* city of Macedonia, by Titus and *L*
Philem 24 Marcus, Aristarchus, Demas, *L*

**LUCIFER** *(lu'-sif-ur) Title applied to king of Babylon.*
Is 14:12 art thou fallen from heaven, O *L*

**LUCIUS** *(lu'-she-us)*
*1. A Christian from Cyrene.*
Acts 13:1 *L* of Cyrene, and Manaen, which had
*2. A relative of Paul.*
Rom 16:21 Timotheus my workfellow, and *L*

**LUCRE**
1Sa 8:3 ways, but turned aside after *l*
1Ti 3:3 striker, not greedy of filthy *l*
1Ti 3:8 much wine, not greedy of filthy *l*
Titus 1:7 no striker, not given to filthy *l*
1Pet 5:2 not for filthy *l*, but of a ready

**LUD** *(lud)* See LUDIM, LYDIA.
*1. Son of Shem.*
Gen 10:22 and Asshur, and Arphaxad, and *L*
1Chr 1:17 and Asshur, and Arphaxad, and *L*
*2. Descendants of Lud 1.*
Is 66:19 nations, to Tarshish, Pul, and *L*
Eze 27:10 They of Persia and of *L* and of Phut

**LUDIM** *(lu'-dim)* See LUD. *Son of Mizraim.*
Gen 10:13 Mizraim begat *L*, and Anamim, and
1Chr 1:11 And Mizraim begat *L*, and Anamim

**LUHITH** *(lu'-hith) A Moabite city.*
Is 15:5 for by the mounting up of *L* with
Jer 48:5 For in the going up of *L*

**LUKE** *(luke)* See LUCAS. *A companion of Paul.*
Col 4:14 *L*, the beloved physician, and
2Ti 4:11 Only *L* is with me

**LUMP**
2Kin 20:7 And Isaiah said, Take a *l* of figs
Is 38:21 said, Let them take a *l* of figs
Rom 9:21 of the same *l* to make one vessel
Rom 11:16 be holy, the *l* is also holy
1Cor 5:6 leaven leaveneth the whole *l*
1Cor 5:7 leaven, that ye may be a new *l*
Gal 5:9 leaven leaveneth the whole *l*

**LUST**
Ex 15:9 my *l* shall be satisfied upon them
Ps 78:18 heart by asking meat for their *l*
Ps 78:30 were not estranged from their *l*
Ps 81:12 them up unto their own hearts' *l*
Prov 6:25 *L* not after her beauty in thine
Mt 5:28 to *l* after her hath committed
Rom 1:27 burned in their *l* one toward
Rom 7:7 for I had not known *l*, except the
1Cor 10:6 we should not *l* after evil things
Gal 5:16 not fulfil the *l* of the flesh
1Th 4:5 Not in the *l* of concupiscence,
Jas 1:14 he is drawn away of his own *l*
Jas 1:15 Then when *l* hath conceived, it
Jas 4:2 Ye *l*, and have not
2Pet 1:4 that is in the world through *l*
2Pet 2:10 the flesh in the *l* of uncleanness
1Jn 2:16 the *l* of the flesh
1Jn 2:16 the *l* of the eyes, and the pride
1Jn 2:17 passeth away, and the *l* thereof

**LUSTED**
Num 11:34 they buried the people that *l*
Ps 106:14 But *l* exceedingly in the
1Cor 10:6 after evil things, as they also *l*
Rev 18:14 the fruits that thy soul *l* after

**LUSTETH**
Deut 12:15 whatsoever thy soul *l* after
Deut 12:20 whatsoever thy soul *l* after
Deut 12:21 gates whatsoever thy soul *l* after
Deut 14:26 for whatsoever thy soul *l* after
Gal 5:17 For the flesh *l* against the
Jas 4:5 that dwelleth in us *l* to envy

**LUSTS**
Mk 4:19 the *l* of other things entering in
Jn 8:44 the *l* of your father ye will do
Rom 1:24 through the *l* of their own hearts
Rom 6:12 should obey it in the *l* thereof
Rom 13:14 flesh, to fulfil the *l* thereof
Gal 5:24 flesh with the affections and *l*
Eph 2:3 times past in the *l* of our flesh
Eph 4:22 according to the deceitful *l*
1Ti 6:9 and into many foolish and hurtful *l*
2Ti 2:22 Flee also youthful *l*
2Ti 3:6 with sins, led away with divers *l*
2Ti 4:3 but after their own *l* shall they
Titus 2:12 denying ungodliness and worldly *l*
Titus 3:3 deceived, serving divers *l*
Jas 4:1 even of your *l* that war in your
Jas 4:3 ye may consume it upon your *l*
1Pet 1:14 to the former *l* in your ignorance
1Pet 2:11 pilgrims, abstain from fleshly *l*
1Pet 4:2 time in the flesh to the *l* of men
1Pet 4:3 we walked in lasciviousness, *l*
2Pet 2:18 allure through the *l* of the flesh
2Pet 3:3 walking after their own *l*
Jude 16 walking after their own *l*
Jude 18 walk after their own ungodly *l*

**LUZ** *(luz)* See BETH-EL.
*1. A Canaanite city.*
Gen 28:19 city was called *L* at the first
Gen 35:6 So Jacob came to *L*, which is in
Gen 48:3 me at *L* in the land of Canaan
Josh 16:2 And goeth out from Beth-el to *L*
Josh 18:13 toward *L*, to the side of *L*
Judg 1:23 the name of the city before was *L*
*2. A Hittite city.*
Judg 1:26 and called the name thereof *L*

**LYCAONIA** *(li-ca-o'-ne-ah) A Roman province in Asia Minor.*
Acts 14:6 unto Lystra and Derbe, cities of *L*
Acts 14:11 voices, saying in the speech of *L*

**LYCIA** *(lish'-e-ah) A Roman province in Asia Minor.*
Acts 27:5 we came to Myra, a city of *L*

**LYDDA** *(lid'-dah)* See LOD. *A city in Judea.*
Acts 9:32 to the saints which dwelt at *L*
Acts 9:35 And all that dwelt at *L* and Saron
Acts 9:38 forasmuch as *L* was nigh to Joppa,

**LYDIA** *(lid'-e-ah)* See LUDIM, LYDIANS.
*1. A people in North Africa.*
Eze 30:5 Ethiopia, and Libya, and *L*, and all
*2. A Christian woman.*
Acts 16:14 And a certain woman named *L*
Acts 16:40 and entered into the house of *L*

**LYDIANS** *(lid'-e-uns) Same as Lydia 1.*
Jer 46:9 and the *L*, that handle and bend the

**LYING**
Gen 29:2 three flocks of sheep *l* by it
Gen 34:7 Israel in *l* with Jacob's daughter
Ex 23:5 hateth thee *l* under his burden
Num 31:17 that hath known man by *l* with him
Num 31:18 not known a man by *l* with him
Num 31:35 had not known man by *l* with him
Deut 21:1 *l* in the field, and it be not
Deut 22:22 If a man be found *l* with a woman
Judg 9:35 were with him, from *l* in wait
Judg 16:9 Now there were men *l* in wait
Judg 21:12 known no man by *l* with any male
1Kin 22:22 I will be a *l* spirit in the mouth
1Kin 22:23 the LORD hath put a *l* spirit in
2Chr 18:21 be a *l* spirit in the mouth of all
2Chr 18:22 the LORD hath put a *l* spirit in
Ps 31:6 hated them that regard *l* vanities
Ps 31:18 Let the *l* lips be put to silence
Ps 52:3 and *l* rather than to speak
Ps 59:12 for cursing and *l* which they speak
Ps 109:2 spoken against me with a *l* tongue
Ps 119:29 Remove from me the way of *l*
Ps 119:163 I hate and abhor *l*
Ps 120:2 my soul, O LORD, from *l* lips
Ps 139:3 my *l* down, and art acquainted with
Prov 6:17 a *l* tongue, and hands that shed
Prov 10:18 He that hideth hatred with *l* lips
Prov 12:19 but a *l* tongue is but for a
Prov 12:22 *L* lips are abomination to the
Prov 13:5 A righteous man hateth *l*
Prov 17:7 much less do *l* lips a prince
Prov 21:6 a *l* tongue is a vanity tossed to
Prov 26:28 A *l* tongue hateth those that are
Is 30:9 *l* children, children that will
Is 32:7 to destroy the poor with *l* words
Is 56:10 *l* down, loving to slumber
Is 59:13 *l* against the LORD, and departing
Jer 7:4 Trust ye not in *l* words, saying,
Jer 7:8 Behold, ye trust in *l* words
Jer 29:23 have spoken *l* words in my name,
Lam 3:10 was unto me as a bear *l* in wait
Eze 13:6 *l* divination, saying, The LORD
Eze 13:7 have ye not spoken a *l* divination
Eze 13:19 by your *l* to my people that hear
Dan 2:9 for ye have prepared *l* and corrupt
Hos 4:2 By swearing, and *l*, and killing, and
Jonah 2:8 They that observe *l* vanities
Mt 9:2 man sick of the palsy, *l* on a bed
Mk 5:40 in where the damsel was *l*
Lk 2:12 swaddling clothes, *l* in a manger
Lk 2:16 Joseph, and the babe *l* in a manger
Jn 13:25 He then *l* on Jesus' breast saith
Jn 20:5 in, saw the linen clothes *l*
Jn 20:7 not *l* with the linen clothes, but
Acts 20:19 me by the *l* in wait of the Jews
Acts 23:16 son heard of their *l* in wait
Eph 4:25 Wherefore putting away *l*, speak
2Th 2:9 all power and signs and *l* wonders,

**LYSANIAS** *(li-sa'-ne-as) Governor of Abilene.*
Lk 3:1 *L* the tetrarch of Abilene,

**LYSIAS** *(lis'-e-as) A Roman commander.*
Acts 23:26 Claudius *L* unto the most
Acts 24:7 the chief captain *L* came upon us
Acts 24:22 When *L* the chief captain shall

**LYSTRA** *(lis'-trah) A city in Lycaonia.*
Acts 14:6 were ware of it, and fled unto *L*
Acts 14:8 And there sat a certain man at *L*
Acts 14:21 many, they returned again to *L*
Acts 16:1 Then came he to Derbe and *L*
Acts 16:2 of by the brethren that were at *L*
2Ti 3:11 me at Antioch, at Iconium, at *L*

# M

**MAACAH** *(ma'-a-kah)* See MAACHAH.
*1. A wife of David.*
2Sa 3:3 Absalom the son of *M* the daughter
*2. A king of Maacah 3.*
2Sa 10:6 of king *M* a thousand men, and of
*3. A district of Syria.*
2Sa 10:8 and of Rehob, and Ish-tob, and *M*

**MAACHAH** *(ma'-a-kah)* See BETH-MAACHAH, MAACAH, MAACHATHITE, SYRIA-MAACHAH.
*1. A son of Nahor.*
Gen 22:24 and Gaham, and Thahash, and *M*
*2. Father of Achish.*
1Kin 2:39 unto Achish son of *M* king of Gath
*3. Wife of King Rehoboam.*
1Kin 15:2 And his mother's name was *M*
1Kin 15:10 And his mother's name was *M*
2Chr 11:20 after her he took *M* the daughter
2Chr 11:21 Rehoboam loved *M* the daughter of
2Chr 11:22 Abijah the son of *M* the chief
*4. Mother of King Asa.*
1Kin 15:13 also *M* his mother, even her he
2Chr 15:16 also concerning *M* the mother of
*5. Concubine of Caleb.*
1Chr 2:48 *M*, Caleb's concubine, bare Sheber
*6. A wife of David.*
1Chr 3:2 Absalom the son of *M* the daughter
*7. A wife of Machir.*
1Chr 7:15 whose sister's name was *M*
1Chr 7:16 *M* the wife of Machir bare a son,
*8. Wife of Jehiel.*
1Chr 8:29 whose wife's name was *M*
1Chr 9:35 Jehiel, whose wife's name was *M*
*9. Father of Hanan.*
1Chr 11:43 Hanan the son of *M*, and Joshaphat
*10. A district of Syria.*
1Chr 19:7 chariots, and the king of *M*
*11. Father of Shephatiah.*
1Chr 27:16 Shephatiah the son of *M*

**MAACHATHI** *(ma-ak'-a-thi)* See MAd-c18ACHATHITE. *Inhabitants of Maachah 10.*
Deut 3:14 unto the coasts of Geshuri and *M*

**MAACHATHITE** *(ma-ak'-a-thite)* See MAACHATHI, MAACHATHITES. *Same as Maachathi.*
2Sa 23:34 son of Ahasbai, the son of the *M*
2Kin 25:23 and Jaazaniah the son of a *M*

1Chr 4:19 the Garmite, and Eshtemoa the *M*
Jer 40:8 and Jezaniah the son of a *M*

**MAACHATHITES**
Josh 12:5 border of the Geshurites and the *M*
Josh 13:11 the border of the Geshurites and *M*
Josh 13:13 not the Geshurites, nor the *M*
Josh 13:13 the *M* dwell among the Israelites

**MAADAI** *(ma'-a-dahee) Married a foreigner in exile.*
Ezr 10:34 *M*, Amram, and Uel,

**MAADIAH** *(ma-a-di'-ah)* See MOADIAH. *A priest with Zerubbabel.*
Neh 12:5 Miamin, *M*, Bilgah,

**MAAI** *(ma'-ahee) A priest.*
Neh 12:36 and Azarael, Milalai, Gilalai, *M*

**MAALEH-ACRABBIM** *(ma'-a-leh-ac-rab'-bim)* See AKRABBIM. *A pass on Judah's southern border.*
Josh 15:3 went out to the south side to *M*

**MAARATH** *(ma'-a-rath) A city in Judah.*
Josh 15:59 And *M*, and Beth-anoth, and Eltekon

**MAASEIAH** *(ma-a-si'-ah)*
*1. A priest who relocated the Ark.*
1Chr 15:18 and Unni, Eliab, and Benaiah, and *M*
1Chr 15:20 Jehiel, and Unni, and Eliab, and *M*
*2. Son of Adaiah.*
2Chr 23:1 Obed, and *M* the son of Adaiah, and
*3. An officer of King Uzziah.*
2Chr 26:11 *M* the ruler, under the hand of
*4. A son of King Ahaz.*
2Chr 28:7 slew *M* the king's son, and Azrikam
*5. A governor of Jerusalem.*
2Chr 34:8 *M* the governor of the city, and
*6. A priest who married a foreigner.*
Ezr 10:18 *M*, and Eliezer, and Jarib, and
*7. A priest of the Harim family.*
Ezr 10:21 *M*, and Elijah, and Shemaiah, and
*8. A priest of the Pashur family.*
Ezr 10:22 Elioenai, *M*, Ishmael, Nethaneel,
*9. A priest of the Pahath-moab family.*
Ezr 10:30 Adna, and Chelal, Benaiah, *M*
*10. Father of Azariah.*
Neh 3:23 *M* the son of Ananiah by his house
*11. A priest with Ezra.*
Neh 8:4 and Urijah, and Hilkiah, and *M*
*12. Another priest with Ezra.*
Neh 8:7 Akkub, Shabbethai, Hodijah, *M*
*13. An Israelite who renewed the covenant.*
Neh 10:25 Rehum, Hashabnah, *M*,
*14. A family of exiles.*
Neh 11:5 *M* the son of Baruch, the son of
*15. A descendant of Benjamin.*
Neh 11:7 the son of Kolaiah, the son of *M*
*16. A priest who dedicated the wall.*
Neh 12:41 Eliakim, *M*, Miniamin, Michaiah,
*17. Another priest who dedicated the wall.*
Neh 12:42 And *M*, and Shemaiah, and Eleazar
*18. Father of Zephaniah.*
Jer 21:1 Zephaniah the son of *M* the priest
Jer 29:25 Zephaniah the son of *M* the priest
Jer 37:3 Zephaniah the son of *M* the priest
*19. Father of Zedekiah.*
Jer 29:21 and of Zedekiah the son of *M*
*20. A Temple officer.*
Jer 35:4 chamber of *M* the son of Shallum
*21. Grandfather of Baruch.*
Jer 32:12 the son of Neriah, the son of *M*
Jer 51:59 the son of Neriah, the son of *M*

**MAASIAI** *(ma-a'-see-ahee) A family of exiles.*
1Chr 9:12 *M* the son of Adiel, the son of

**MAATH** *(ma'-ath) Father of Nagge; ancestor of Jesus.*
Lk 3:26 Which was the son of *M*, which was

**MAAZ** *(ma'-az) A son of Ram.*
1Chr 2:27 firstborn of Jerahmeel were, *M*

**MAAZIAH** *(ma-a-zi'-ah)*
*1. A sanctuary servant.*
1Chr 24:18 the four and twentieth to *M*
*2. A priest who renewed the covenant.*
Neh 10:8 *M*, Bilgai, Shemaiah

**MACEDONIA** *(mas-e-do'-nee-ah)* See MACEDONIAN. *A Roman province north of Greece.*
Acts 16:9 There stood a man of *M*, and prayed
Acts 16:9 him, saying, Come over into *M*
Acts 16:10 we endeavoured to go into *M*
Acts 16:12 the chief city of that part of *M*
Acts 18:5 and Timotheus were come from *M*
Acts 19:21 when he had passed through *M*
Acts 19:22 So he sent into *M* two of them
Acts 19:29 Gaius and Aristarchus, men of *M*
Acts 20:1 and departed for to go into *M*
Acts 20:3 he purposed to return through *M*
Rom 15:26 For it hath pleased them of *M*
1Cor 16:5 you, when I shall pass through *M*
1Cor 16:5 for I do pass through *M*
2Cor 1:16 And to pass by you into *M*
2Cor 1:16 to come again out of *M* unto you
2Cor 2:13 them, I went from thence into *M*
2Cor 7:5 For, when we were come into *M*
2Cor 8:1 God bestowed on the churches of *M*
2Cor 9:2 which I boast of you to them of *M*
2Cor 9:4 haply if they of *M* come with me
2Cor 11:9 which came from *M* supplied
2Cor s from Philippi, a city of *M*
Phil 4:15 gospel, when I departed from *M*
1Th 1:7 to all that believe in *M* and
1Th 1:8 word of the Lord not only in *M*
1Th 4:10 the brethren which are in all *M*
1Ti 1:3 at Ephesus, when I went into *M*
Titus s the Cretians, from Nicopolis of *M*

**MACEDONIAN** *(mas-e-do'-nee-an) An inhabitant of Macedonia.*
Acts 27:2 a *M* of Thessalonica, being with

**MACHBANAI** *(mak'-ba-nahee) A warrior in David's army.*
1Chr 12:13 the tenth, *M* the eleventh

**MACHBENAH** *(mak'-be-nah) A descendant of Caleb.*
1Chr 2:49 Madmannah, Sheva the father of *M*

**MACHI** *(ma'-ki) Father of Geuel.*
Num 13:15 tribe of Gad, Geuel the son of *M*

**MACHIR** *(ma'-kur)* See MACHIRITE.
*1. Son of Manasseh.*
Gen 50:23 the children also of *M* the son of
Num 26:29 of *M*, the family of the
Num 26:29 and *M* begat Gilead
Num 27:1 the son of Gilead, the son of *M*
Num 32:39 the children of *M* the son of
Num 32:40 Gilead unto *M* the son of Manasseh
Num 36:1 children of Gilead, the son of *M*
Deut 3:15 And I gave Gilead unto *M*
Josh 13:31 children of *M* the son of Manasseh
Josh 13:31 children of *M* by their families
Josh 17:1 for *M* the firstborn of Manasseh,
Josh 17:3 the son of Gilead, the son of *M*
Judg 5:14 out of *M* came down governors, and
1Chr 2:21 of *M* the father of Gilead
1Chr 2:23 sons of *M* the father of Gilead
1Chr 7:14 bare *M* the father of Gilead
1Chr 7:15 *M* took to wife the sister of
1Chr 7:16 Maachah the wife of *M* bare a son
1Chr 7:17 the sons of Gilead, the son of *M*
*2. Son of Ammiel.*
2Sa 9:4 Behold, he is in the house of *M*
2Sa 9:5 fetched him out of the house of *M*
2Sa 17:27 *M* the son of Ammiel of Lo-debar,

**MACHIRITES** *(ma'-kur-ites) Descendants of Machir 1.*
Num 26:29 of Machir, the family of the *M*

**MACHNADEBAI** *(mak-nad'-e-bahee) Married a foreigner in exile.*
Ezr 10:40 *M*, Shashai, Sharai,

**MACHPELAH** *(mak-pe'-lah) Burial place of Abraham.*
Gen 23:9 That he may give me the cave of *M*
Gen 23:17 field of Ephron, which was in *M*
Gen 23:19 of the field of *M* before Mamre
Gen 25:9 buried him in the cave of *M*
Gen 49:30 cave that is in the field of *M*
Gen 50:13 him in the cave of the field of *M*

**MAD**
Deut 28:34 So that thou shalt be *m* for the
1Sa 21:13 feigned himself *m* in their hands
1Sa 21:14 servants, Lo, ye see the man is *m*
1Sa 21:15 Have I need of *m* men, that ye
1Sa 21:15 to play the *m* man in my presence
2Kin 9:11 came this *m* fellow to thee
Ps 102:8 they that are *m* against me are
Prov 26:18 As a *m* man who casteth firebrands
Eccl 2:2 I said of laughter, It is *m*
Eccl 7:7 oppression maketh a wise man *m*
Is 44:25 the liars, and maketh diviners *m*
Jer 25:16 shall drink, and be moved, and be *m*
Jer 29:26 the LORD, for every man that is *m*
Jer 50:38 they are *m* upon their idols
Jer 51:7 therefore the nations are *m*
Hos 9:7 is a fool, the spiritual man is *m*
Jn 10:20 said, He hath a devil, and is *m*
Acts 12:15 And they said unto her, Thou art *m*
Acts 26:11 being exceedingly *m* against them
Acts 26:24 much learning doth make thee *m*
Acts 26:25 But he said, I am not *m*, most
1Cor 14:23 will they not say that ye are *m*

**MADAI** *(ma'-dahee)* See MEDE, MEDIA. *Son of Japheth.*
Gen 10:2 Gomer, and Magog, and *M*, and Javan,
1Chr 1:5 Gomer, and Magog, and *M*, and Javan,

**MADIAN** *(ma'-de-an)* See MIDIAN. *Same as Midian 2.*
Acts 7:29 was a stranger in the land of *M*

**MADMANNAH** *(mad-man'-nah)*
*1. A city in Judah.*
Josh 15:31 And Ziklag, and *M*, and Sansannah,
*2. Grandson of Caleb.*
1Chr 2:49 bare also Shaaph the father of *M*

**MADMEN** *(mad'-men)* See MADMENAH. *A Moabite city.*
Jer 48:2 Also thou shalt be cut down, O *M*

**MADMENAH** *(mad-me'-nah)* See MADMEN. *A city in Benjamin.*
Is 10:31 *M* is removed

**MADNESS**
Deut 28:28 The LORD shall smite thee with *m*
Eccl 1:17 to know wisdom, and to know *m*
Eccl 2:12 myself to behold wisdom, and *m*
Eccl 7:25 folly, even of foolishness and *m*
Eccl 9:3 *m* is in their heart while they
Eccl 10:13 end of his talk is mischievous *m*
Zec 12:4 astonishment, and his rider with *m*
Lk 6:11 And they were filled with *m*
2Pet 2:16 voice forbad the *m* of the prophet

**MADON** *(ma'-don) A Canaanite city.*
Josh 11:1 that he sent to Jobab king of *M*
Josh 12:19 The king of *M*, one

**MAGBISH** *(mag'-bish) A family of exiles.*
Ezr 2:30 The children of *M*, an hundred

**MAGDALA** *(mag'-da-lah)* See MAGDALENE. *A city in Galilee.*
Mt 15:39 and came into the coasts of *M*

**MAGDALENE** *(mag'-da-leen) A woman acquaintance of Jesus.*
Mt 27:56 Among which was Mary *M*, and Mary
Mt 27:61 And there was Mary *M*, and the other
Mt 28:1 day of the week, came Mary *M*
Mk 15:40 among whom was Mary *M*, and Mary
Mk 15:47 And Mary *M* and Mary the mother of
Mk 16:1 when the sabbath was past, Mary *M*
Mk 16:9 week, he appeared first to Mary *M*
Lk 8:2 and infirmities, Mary called *M*
Lk 24:10 It was Mary *M*, and Joanna, and Mary
Jn 19:25 the wife of Cleophas, and Mary *M*
Jn 20:1 of the week cometh Mary *M* early
Jn 20:18 Mary *M* came and told the disciples

**MAGDIEL** *(mag'-de-el) A duke of Edom.*
Gen 36:43 Duke *M*, duke Iram
1Chr 1:54 Duke *M*, duke Iram

**MAGICIANS**
Gen 41:8 and called for all the *m* of Egypt
Gen 41:24 and I told this unto the *m*
Ex 7:11 now the *m* of Egypt, they also did
Ex 7:22 the *m* of Egypt did so with their
Ex 8:7 And the *m* did so with their
Ex 8:18 And the *m* did so with their
Ex 8:19 Then the *m* said unto Pharaoh,
Ex 9:11 the *m* could not stand before
Ex 9:11 for the boil was upon the *m*
Dan 1:20 ten times better than all the *m*
Dan 2:2 the king commanded to call the *m*
Dan 2:27 wise men, the astrologers, the *m*
Dan 4:7 Then came in the *m*, the
Dan 4:9 O Belteshazzar, master of the *m*
Dan 5:11 thy father, made master of the *m*

**MAGISTRATES**
Ezr 7:25 God, that is in thine hand, set *m*
Lk 12:11 unto the synagogues, and unto *m*
Acts 16:20 And brought them to the *m*, saying,
Acts 16:22 the *m* rent off their clothes, and

Acts 16:35 the *m* sent the serjeants, saying,
Acts 16:36 The *m* have sent to let you go
Acts 16:38 told these words unto the *m*
Titus 3:1 and powers, to obey *m*, to be ready

**MAGNIFIED**
Gen 19:19 sight, and thou hast *m* thy mercy
Josh 4:14 On that day the LORD *m* Joshua in
2Sa 7:26 And let thy name be *m* for ever
1Chr 17:24 that thy name may be *m* for ever
1Chr 29:25 the LORD *m* Solomon exceedingly in
2Chr 1:1 with him, and *m* him exceedingly
2Chr 32:23 so that he was *m* in the sight of
Ps 35:27 continually, Let the LORD be *m*
Ps 40:16 say continually, The LORD be *m*
Ps 70:4 say continually, Let God be *m*
Ps 138:2 for thou hast *m* thy word above
Jer 48:26 for he *m* himself against the LORD
Jer 48:42 because he hath *m* himself against
Lam 1:9 for the enemy hath *m* himself
Dan 8:11 he *m* himself even to the prince
Zeph 2:8 *m* themselves against their border
Zeph 2:10 *m* themselves against the people
Mal 1:5 The LORD will be *m* from the
Acts 5:13 but the people *m* them
Acts 19:17 the name of the Lord Jesus was *m*
Phil 1:20 also Christ shall be *m* in my body

**MAGNIFY**
Josh 3:7 This day will I begin to *m* thee
Job 7:17 is man, that thou shouldest *m* him
Job 19:5 If indeed ye will *m* yourselves
Job 36:24 Remember that thou *m* his work
Ps 34:3 O *m* the LORD with me, and let us
Ps 35:26 dishonour that *m* themselves
Ps 38:16 they *m* themselves against me
Ps 55:12 me that did *m* himself against me
Ps 69:30 will *m* him with thanksgiving
Is 10:15 or shall the saw *m* itself against
Is 42:21 he will *m* the law, and make it
Eze 38:23 Thus will I *m* myself, and sanctify
Dan 8:25 he shall *m* himself in his heart,
Dan 11:36 *m* himself above every god, and
Dan 11:37 for he shall *m* himself above all
Zec 12:7 do not *m* themselves against Judah
Lk 1:46 said, My soul doth *m* the Lord
Acts 10:46 them speak with tongues, and *m* God
Rom 11:13 of the Gentiles, I *m* mine office

**MAGOG** *(ma'-gog)*
*1. A son of Japheth.*
Gen 10:2 Gomer, and *M*, and Madai, and Javan,
1Chr 1:5 Gomer, and *M*, and Madai, and Javan,
*2. Descendants of Magog.*
Eze 38:2 face against Gog, the land of *M*
Eze 39:6 And I will send a fire on *M*
Rev 20:8 quarters of the earth, Gog and *M*

**MAGOR-MISSABIB** *(ma'-gor-mis'-sa-bib) A symbolic name of Pashur.*
Jer 20:3 not called thy name Pashur, but *M*

**MAGPIASH** *(mag'-pe-ash) A chief Israelite who renewed the covenant.*
Neh 10:20 *M*, Meshullam, Hezir,

**MAHALAH** *(ma'-ha-lah)* See MAHLAH. *Great-grandson of Manasseh.*
1Chr 7:18 bare Ishod, and Abiezer, and *M*

**MAHALALEEL** *(ma-hal'-a-le-el)* See MALELEEL.
*1. Son of Cainan.*
Gen 5:12 lived seventy years, and begat *M*
Gen 5:13 after he begat *M* eight hundred
Gen 5:15 *M* lived sixty and five years, and
Gen 5:16 *M* lived after he begat Jared
Gen 5:17 all the days of *M* were eight
1Chr 1:2 Kenan, *M*, Jered,
*2. A family of exiles.*
Neh 11:4 son of Shephatiah, the son of *M*

**MAHALATH** *(ma'-ha-lath)* See BASHEMATH.
*1. A daughter of Ishmael.*
Gen 28:9 he had *M* the daughter of Ishmael
*2. A granddaughter of David.*
2Chr 11:18 Rehoboam took him *M* the daughter
*3. A musical choir.*
Ps 53:*t* To the chief Musician upon *M*
Ps 88:*t* chief Musician upon *M* Leannoth

**MAHALI** *(ma'-ha-li)* See MAHLI. *Same as Lahli 1.*
Ex 6:19 sons of Merari; *M* and Mushi

**MAHANAIM** *(ma-ha-na'-im) A town east of the Jordan.*
Gen 32:2 called the name of that place *M*
Josh 13:26 from *M* unto the border of Debir
Josh 13:30 And their coast was from *M*
Josh 21:38 and *M* with her suburbs,
2Sa 2:8 of Saul, and brought him over to *M*
2Sa 2:12 Saul, went out from *M* to Gibeon
2Sa 2:29 all Bithron, and they came to *M*
2Sa 17:24 Then David came to *M*
2Sa 17:27 to pass, when David was come to *M*
2Sa 19:32 of sustenance while he lay at *M*
1Kin 2:8 curse in the day when I went to *M*
1Kin 4:14 Ahinadab the son of Iddo had *M*
1Chr 6:80 suburbs, and *M* with her suburbs,

**MAHANEH-DAN** *(ma'-ha-neh-dan) A place in Judah.*
Judg 18:12 called that place *M* unto this day

**MAHARAI** *(ma'-ha-rahee) A warrior of David.*
2Sa 23:28 the Ahohite, *M* the Netophathite,
1Chr 11:30 *M* the Netophathite, Heled the son
1Chr 27:13 month was *M* the Netophathite

**MAHATH** *(ma'-hath)*
*1. A descendant of Kohath.*
1Chr 6:35 the son of Elkanah, the son of *M*
2Chr 29:12 *M* the son of Amasai, and Joel the
*2. A Temple servant.*
2Chr 31:13 and Eliel, and Ismachiah, and *M*

**MAHAVITE** *(ma'-ha-vite) Family name of Eliel.*
1Chr 11:46 Eliel the *M*, and Jeribai, and

**MAHAZIOTH** *(ma-ha'-ze-oth) A sanctuary servant.*
1Chr 25:4 Mallothi, Hothir, and *M*
1Chr 25:30 The three and twentieth to *M*

**MAHER-SHALAL-HASH-BAZ** *(ma'-=her-sha'-lal-hash'-baz) A son of Isaiah.*
Is 8:1 it with a man's pen concerning *M*
Is 8:3 the LORD to me, Call his name *M*

**MAHLAH** *(mah'-lah) A daughter of Zelophehad.*
Num 26:33 daughters of Zelophehad were *M*
Num 27:1 *M*, Noah, and Hoglah, and Milcah
Num 36:11 For *M*, Tirzah, and Hoglah, and
Josh 17:3 are the names of his daughters, *M*

**MAHLI** *(mah'-li)* See MAHALI, MAHLITES.
*1. Son of Merari.*
Num 3:20 their families; *M*, and Mushi
1Chr 6:19 of Merari; *M*, and Mushi
1Chr 6:29 *M*, Libni his son, Shimei his son,
1Chr 23:21 *M*, and Mushi. The sons of *M*
1Chr 24:26 The sons of Merari were *M*
1Chr 24:28 Of *M* came Eleazar, who had no
Ezr 8:18 understanding, of the sons of *M*
*2. Son of Mushi.*
1Chr 6:47 The son of *M*, the son of Mushi,
1Chr 23:23 *M*, and Eder, and Jeremoth, three
1Chr 24:30 *M*, and Eder, and Jerimoth

**MAHLITES** *(mah'-lites) Descendants of Mahli 1.*
Num 3:33 Of Merari was the family of the *M*
Num 26:58 Hebronites, the family of the *M*

**MAHLON** *(mah'-lon)* See MAHLON'S. *A son of Naomi.*
Ruth 1:2 and the name of his two sons *M*
Ruth 1:5 And *M* and Chilion died also both of
Ruth 4:10 Ruth the Moabitess, the wife of *M*

**MAHLON'S** *(mah'-lons)*
Ruth 4:9 and all that was Chilion's and *M*

**MAHOL** *(ma'-hol) Father of some wise men.*
1Kin 4:31 Chalcol, and Darda, the sons of *M*

**MAID**
Gen 16:2 I pray thee, go in unto my *m*
Gen 16:3 took Hagar her *m* the Egyptian
Gen 16:5 I have given my *m* into thy bosom
Gen 16:6 Behold, thy *m* is in thy hand
Gen 16:8 And he said, Hagar, Sarai's *m*
Gen 29:24 Leah Zilpah his *m* for an handmaid
Gen 29:29 Bilhah his handmaid to be her *m*
Gen 30:3 And she said, Behold my *m* Bilhah
Gen 30:7 Bilhah Rachel's *m* conceived again
Gen 30:9 bearing, she took Zilpah her *m*
Gen 30:10 Zilpah Leah's *m* bare Jacob a son
Gen 30:12 Zilpah Leah's *m* bare Jacob a
Ex 2:5 flags, she sent her *m* to fetch it
Ex 2:8 the *m* went and called the child's
Ex 21:20 a man smite his servant, or his *m*
Ex 21:26 his servant, or the eye of his *m*
Ex 22:16 if a man entice a *m* that is not
Lev 12:5 But if she bear a *m* child
Lev 25:6 and for thy servant, and for thy *m*
Deut 22:14 came to her, I found her not a *m*
Deut 22:17 I found not thy daughter a *m*
2Kin 5:2 of the land of Israel a little *m*
2Kin 5:4 thus said the *m* that is of the
Est 2:7 the *m* was fair and beautiful
Job 31:1 why then should I think upon a *m*
Prov 30:19 and the way of a man with a *m*
Is 24:2 as with the *m*, so with her
Jer 2:32 Can a *m* forget her ornaments, or
Jer 51:22 in pieces the young man and the *m*
Amos 2:7 father will go in unto the same *m*
Mt 9:24 for the *m* is not dead, but
Mt 9:25 her by the hand, and the *m* arose
Mt 26:71 into the porch, another *m* saw him
Mk 14:69 a *m* saw him again, and began to
Lk 8:54 by the hand, and called, saying, *M*
Lk 22:56 But a certain *m* beheld him as he

**MAIDEN**
Gen 30:18 I have given my *m* to my husband
Judg 19:24 Behold, here is my daughter a *m*
2Chr 36:17 no compassion upon young man or *m*
Est 2:4 let the *m* which pleaseth the king
Est 2:9 the *m* pleased him, and she
Est 2:13 thus came every *m* unto the king
Ps 123:2 as the eyes of a *m* unto the hand
Lk 8:51 the father and the mother of the *m*

**MAIDENS**
Ex 2:5 her *m* walked along by the river's
Ruth 2:8 but abide here fast by my *m*
Ruth 2:22 that thou go out with his *m*
Ruth 2:23 So she kept fast by the *m* of Boaz
Ruth 3:2 kindred, with whose *m* thou wast
1Sa 9:11 they found young *m* going out to
Est 2:8 when many *m* were gathered
Est 2:9 as belonged to her, and seven *m*
Est 4:16 I also and my *m* will fast likewise
Job 41:5 or wilt thou bind him for thy *m*
Ps 78:63 their *m* were not given to
Ps 148:12 Both young men, and *m*
Prov 9:3 She hath sent forth her *m*
Prov 27:27 and for the maintenance for thy *m*
Prov 31:15 household, and a portion to her *m*
Eccl 2:7 I got me servants and *m*, and had
Eze 44:22 but they shall take *m* of the seed
Lk 12:45 to beat the menservants and *m*

**MAIDS**
Ezr 2:65 Beside their servants and their *m*
Est 2:9 her *m* unto the best place of the
Est 4:4 So Esther's *m* and her chamberlains
Job 19:15 that dwell in mine house, and my *m*
Lam 5:11 the *m* in the cities of Judah
Eze 9:6 Slay utterly old and young, both *m*
Nah 2:7 her *m* shall lead her as with the
Zec 9:17 men cheerful, and new wine the *m*
Mk 14:66 one of the *m* of the high priest

**MAIDSERVANT**
Ex 11:5 of the *m* that is behind the mill
Ex 20:10 thy manservant, nor thy *m*
Ex 20:17 nor his manservant, nor his *m*
Ex 21:7 a man sell his daughter to be a *m*
Ex 21:32 ox shall push a manservant or a *m*
Deut 5:14 nor thy manservant, nor thy *m*
Deut 5:14 thy *m* may rest as well as thou
Deut 5:21 or his manservant, or his *m*
Deut 12:18 and thy manservant, and thy *m*
Deut 15:17 also unto thy *m* thou shalt do
Deut 16:11 and thy manservant, and thy *m*
Deut 16:14 and thy manservant, and thy *m*
Judg 9:18 made Abimelech, the son of his *m*
Job 31:13 cause of my manservant or of my *m*
Jer 34:9 manservant, and every man his *m*
Jer 34:10 manservant, and every one his *m*

**MAIDSERVANTS**
Gen 12:16 and he asses, and menservants, and *m*
Gen 20:17 Abimelech, and his wife, and his *m*
Gen 24:35 and gold, and menservants, and *m*
Gen 30:43 and had much cattle, and *m*
Deut 12:12 and your menservants, and your *m*
1Sa 8:16 take your menservants, and your *m*
2Sa 6:22 of the *m* which thou hast spoken

2Kin 5:26 and oxen, and menservants, and *m*
Neh 7:67 their manservants and their *m*

**MAIMED**
Lev 22:22 Blind, or broken, or *m*, or having
Mt 15:30 that were lame, blind, dumb, *m*
Mt 15:31 the *m* to be whole, the lame to
Mt 18:8 thee to enter into life halt or *m*
Mk 9:43 for thee to enter into life *m*
Lk 14:13 a feast, call the poor, the *m*
Lk 14:21 in hither the poor, and the *m*

**MAINTAIN**
1Kin 8:45 supplication, and *m* their cause
1Kin 8:49 dwelling place, and *m* their cause,
1Kin 8:59 that he *m* the cause of his
1Chr 26:27 to *m* the house of the LORD
2Chr 6:35 supplication, and *m* their cause
2Chr 6:39 *m* their cause, and forgive thy
Job 13:15 but I will *m* mine own ways before
Ps 140:12 I know that the LORD will *m* the
Titus 3:8 might be careful to *m* good works
Titus 3:14 let ours also learn to *m* good

**MAJESTY**
1Chr 29:11 glory, and the victory, and the *m*
1Chr 29:25 *m* as had not been on any king
Est 1:4 of his excellent *m* many days
Job 37:22 with God is terrible *m*
Job 40:10 Deck thyself now with *m* and
Ps 21:5 *m* hast thou laid upon him
Ps 29:4 voice of the LORD is full of *m*
Ps 45:3 mighty, with thy glory and thy *m*
Ps 45:4 in thy *m* ride prosperously
Ps 93:1 reigneth, he is clothed with *m*
Ps 96:6 Honour and *m* are before him
Ps 104:1 thou art clothed with honour and *m*
Ps 145:5 of the glorious honour of thy *m*
Ps 145:12 the glorious *m* of his kingdom
Is 2:10 LORD, and for the glory of his *m*
Is 2:19 LORD, and for the glory of his *m*
Is 2:21 LORD, and for the glory of his *m*
Is 24:14 shall sing for the *m* of the LORD
Is 26:10 will not behold the *m* of the LORD
Eze 7:20 of his ornament, he set it in *m*
Dan 4:30 power, and for the honour of my *m*
Dan 4:36 excellent *m* was added unto me
Dan 5:18 thy father a kingdom and *m*
Dan 5:19 for the *m* that he gave him, all
Mic 5:4 in the *m* of the name of the LORD
Heb 1:3 the right hand of the *M* on high
Heb 8:1 throne of the *M* in the heavens
2Pet 1:16 but were eyewitnesses of his *m*
Jude 25 God our Saviour, be glory and *m*

**MAKAZ** *(ma'-kaz) A town in Judah.*
1Kin 4:9 The son of Dekar, in *M*, and in

**MAKER**
Job 4:17 a man be more pure than his *m*
Job 32:22 in so doing my *m* would soon take
Job 35:10 But none saith, Where is God my *m*
Job 36:3 ascribe righteousness to my *M*
Ps 95:6 us kneel before the LORD our *m*
Prov 14:31 the poor reproacheth his *M*
Prov 17:5 the poor reproacheth his *M*
Prov 22:2 the LORD is the *m* of them all
Is 1:31 the *m* of it as a spark, and they
Is 17:7 day shall a man look to his *M*
Is 22:11 not looked unto the *m* thereof
Is 45:9 unto him that striveth with his *M*
Is 45:11 the Holy One of Israel, and his *M*
Is 51:13 And forgettest the LORD thy *m*
Is 54:5 For thy *M* is thine husband
Jer 33:2 Thus saith the LORD the *m* thereof
Hos 8:14 For Israel hath forgotten his *M*
Hab 2:18 that the *m* thereof hath graven it
Hab 2:18 that the *m* of his work trusteth
Heb 11:10 whose builder and *m* is God

**MAKHELOTH** *(mak'-he-loth) An Israelite encampment in the wilderness.*
Num 33:25 from Haradah, and pitched in *M*
Num 33:26 And they removed from *M*, and

**MAKING**
Ex 5:14 task in *m* brick both yesterday
Deut 20:19 in *m* war against it to take it,
Judg 19:22 Now as they were *m* their hearts
1Kin 4:20 eating and drinking, and *m* merry
1Chr 15:28 *m* a noise with psalteries and
1Chr 17:19 in *m* known all these great things
2Chr 30:22 *m* confession to the LORD God of
Ps 19:7 LORD is sure, *m* wise the simple
Eccl 12:12 of *m* many books there is no end
Is 3:16 *m* a tinkling with their feet
Jer 20:15 *m* him very glad
Eze 27:16 multitude of the wares of thy *m*
Eze 27:18 multitude of the wares of thy *m*
Dan 6:11 *m* supplication before his God
Hos 10:4 swearing falsely in *m* a covenant
Amos 8:5 *m* the ephah small, and the shekel
Mic 6:13 in *m* thee desolate because of thy
Mt 9:23 minstrels and the people *m* a noise
Mk 7:13 *M* the word of God of none effect
Jn 5:18 Father, *m* himself equal with God
Rom 1:10 *M* request, if by any means now at
2Cor 6:10 as poor, yet *m* many rich
Eph 1:16 *m* mention of you in my prayers
Eph 2:15 of twain one new man, so *m* peace
Eph 5:19 *m* melody in your heart to the
Phil 1:4 for you all *m* request with joy
1Th 1:2 *m* mention of you in our prayers
Philem 4 *m* mention of thee always in my
2Pet 2:6 *m* them an ensample unto those
Jude 22 have compassion, *m* a difference

**MAKKEDAH** *(mak'-ke-dah) A city in Judah.*
Josh 10:10 smote them to Azekah, and unto *M*
Josh 10:16 and hid themselves in a cave at *M*
Josh 10:17 are found hid in a cave at *M*
Josh 10:21 the camp to Joshua at *M* in peace
Josh 10:28 And that day Joshua took *M*
Josh 10:28 he did to the king of *M* as he did
Josh 10:29 Then Joshua passed from *M*
Josh 12:16 The king of *M*, one
Josh 15:41 Beth-dagon, and Naamah, and *M*

**MAKTESH** *(mak'-tesh) A district near Jerusalem.*
Zeph 1:11 Howl, ye inhabitants of *M*

**MALACHI** *(mal'-a-ki) A prophet.*
Mal 1:1 word of the LORD to Israel by *M*

**MALCHAM** *(mal'-kam)* See MILCOM.
*1. Son of Shaharaim.*
1Chr 8:9 Jobab, and Zibia, and Mesha, and *M*
*2. An Ammonite idol.*
Zeph 1:5 by the LORD, and that swear by *M*

**MALCHIAH** *(mal-ki'-ah)* See MALCHIJAH, MELCHIAH.
*1. Father of Baaseiah.*
1Chr 6:40 the son of Baaseiah, the son of *M*
*2. A descendant of Parosh.*
Ezr 10:25 Ramiah, and Jeziah, and *M*, and
Neh 11:12 the son of Pashur, the son of *M*
*3. Another descendant of Parosh.*
Ezr 10:31 Eliezer, Ishijah, *M*, Shemaiah,
*4. A repairer of Jerusalem's wall.*
Neh 3:14 gate repaired *M* the son of Rechab
*5. Another repairer of Jerusalem's wall.*
Neh 3:31 After him repaired *M* the
*6. A priest who aided Ezra.*
Neh 8:4 hand, Pedaiah, and Mishael, and *M*
*7. A priest who dedicated the wall.*
Jer 38:1 Shelemiah, and Pashur the son of *M*
Jer 38:6 dungeon of *M* the son of Hammelech

**MALCHIEL** *(mal'-ke-el)* See MALCHIELITES. *A son of Beriah.*
Gen 46:17 Heber, and *M*
Num 26:45 of *M*, the family of the
1Chr 7:31 Heber, and *M*, who is the father of

**MALCHIELITES** *(mal'-ke-el-ites) Descendants of Malchiel.*
Num 26:45 of Malchiel, the family of the *M*

**MALCHIJAH** *(mal-ki'-jah)* See MALCHIAH.
*1. A family of exiles.*
1Chr 9:12 the son of Pashur, the son of *M*
*2. A sanctuary servant.*
1Chr 24:9 The fifth to *M*, the sixth to
*3. Married a foreigner in exile.*
Ezr 10:25 and Miamin, and Eleazar, and *M*
*4. A rebuilder of Jerusalem's wall.*
Neh 3:11 *M* the son of Harim, and Hashub the
*5. A priest who dedicated the wall.*
Neh 10:3 Pashur, Amariah, *M*,
Neh 12:42 and Uzzi, and Jehohanan, and *M*

**MALCHIRAM** *(mal'-ki-ram) A descendant of King Jehoiakim.*
1Chr 3:18 *M* also, and Pedaiah, and Shenazar,

**MALCHI-SHUA** *(mal'-ki-shu'-ah)* See MELCHISHUA. *A son of King Saul.*
1Chr 8:33 and Saul begat Jonathan, and *M*
1Chr 9:39 and Saul begat Jonathan, and *M*
1Chr 10:2 slew Jonathan, and Abinadab, and *M*

**MALCHUS** *(mal'-kus) A servant wounded by Simon Peter.*
Jn 18:10 The servant's name was *M*

**MALE**
Gen 1:27 *m* and female created he them
Gen 5:2 *M* and female created he them
Gen 6:19 they shall be *m* and female
Gen 7:2 take to thee by sevens, the *m*
Gen 7:2 that are not clean by two, the *m*
Gen 7:3 also of the air by sevens, the *m*
Gen 7:9 two unto Noah into the ark, the *m*
Gen 7:16 And they that went in, went in *m*
Gen 17:23 money, every *m* among the men of
Gen 34:15 as we be, that every *m* of you be
Gen 34:22 people, if every *m* among us be
Gen 34:24 every *m* was circumcised, all that
Ex 12:5 blemish, a *m* of the first year
Ex 34:19 whether ox or sheep, that is *m*
Lev 1:3 let him offer a *m* without blemish
Lev 1:10 bring it a *m* without blemish
Lev 3:1 whether it be a *m* or female
Lev 3:6 *m* or female, he shall offer it
Lev 4:23 of the goats, a *m* without blemish
Lev 7:6 Every *m* among the priests shall
Lev 12:7 that hath born a *m* or a female
Lev 22:19 your own will a *m* without blemish
Lev 27:3 thy estimation shall be of the *m*
Lev 27:5 shall be of the *m* twenty shekels
Lev 27:6 of the *m* five shekels of silver
Lev 27:7 if it be a *m*, then thy estimation
Num 1:2 names, every *m* by their polls
Num 1:20 every *m* from twenty years old and
Num 1:22 every *m* from twenty years old and
Num 3:15 every *m* from a month old and
Num 5:3 Both *m* and female shall ye put out
Num 18:10 every *m* shall eat it
Num 31:17 every *m* among the little ones
Deut 4:16 the likeness of *m* or female
Deut 7:14 there shall not be *m* or female
Deut 20:13 thou shalt smite every *m* thereof
Josh 17:2 these were the *m* children of
Judg 21:11 Ye shall utterly destroy every *m*
Judg 21:12 known no man by lying with any *m*
1Kin 11:15 he had smitten every *m* in Edom
1Kin 11:16 he had cut off every *m* in Edom
Mal 1:14 which hath in his flock a *m*
Mt 19:4 them at the beginning made them *m*
Mk 10:6 of the creation God made them *m*
Lk 2:23 Every *m* that openeth the womb
Gal 3:28 there is neither *m* nor female

**MALELEEL** *(mal'-e-le-el)* See MAHALALEEL. *Son of Cainan; ancestor of Jesus.*
Lk 3:37 of Jared, which was the son of *M*

**MALES**
Gen 34:25 city boldly, and slew all the *m*
Ex 12:48 let all his *m* be circumcised, and
Ex 13:12 the *m* shall be the LORD's
Ex 13:15 that openeth the matrix, being *m*
Ex 23:17 *m* shall appear before the Lord
Lev 6:18 All the *m* among the children of
Lev 6:29 All the *m* among the priests shall
Num 3:22 to the number of all the *m*
Num 3:28 In the number of all the *m*
Num 3:34 to the number of all the *m*
Num 3:39 all the *m* from a month old and
Num 3:40 *m* of the children of Israel from
Num 3:43 all the firstborn *m* by the number
Num 26:62 all *m* from a month old and upward
Num 31:7 and they slew all the *m*
Deut 15:19 All the firstling *m* that come of
Deut 16:16 times in a year shall all thy *m*
Josh 5:4 came out of Egypt, that were *m*
2Chr 31:16 Beside their genealogy of *m*
2Chr 31:19 to all the *m* among the priests
Ezr 8:3 by genealogy of the *m* an hundred
Ezr 8:4 and with him two hundred *m*
Ezr 8:5 and with him three hundred *m*
Ezr 8:6 of Jonathan, and with him fifty *m*
Ezr 8:7 Athaliah, and with him seventy *m*
Ezr 8:8 Michael, and with him fourscore *m*
Ezr 8:9 him two hundred and eighteen *m*
Ezr 8:10 him an hundred and threescore *m*
Ezr 8:11 and with him twenty and eight *m*

Ezr 8:12 and with him an hundred and ten *m*
Ezr 8:13 and with them threescore *m*
Ezr 8:14 Zabbud, and with them seventy *m*

**MALICE**
1Cor 5:8 neither with the leaven of *m*
1Cor 14:20 howbeit in *m* be ye children, but
Eph 4:31 be put away from you, with all *m*
Col 3:8 anger, wrath, *m*, blasphemy,
Titus 3:3 lusts and pleasures, living in *m*
1Pet 2:1 Wherefore laying aside all *m*

**MALLOTHI** *(mal'-lo-thi) A son of Heman.*
1Chr 25:4 and Romamti-ezer, Joshbekashah, *M*
1Chr 25:26 The nineteenth to *M*, he, his sons

**MALLUCH** *(mal'-luk)* See MELICU.
*1. Ancestor of Ethan.*
1Chr 6:44 the son of Abdi, the son of *M*
*2. A son of Bani.*
Ezr 10:29 Meshullam, *M*, and Adaiah, Jashub,
*3. A descendant of Harim.*
Ezr 10:32 Benjamin, *M*, and Shemariah
*4. A priest who renewed the covenant.*
Neh 10:4 Hattush, Shebaniah, *M*,
Neh 12:2 Amariah, *M*, Hattush,
*5. A clan leader who renewed the covenant.*
Neh 10:27 *M*, Harim, Baanah

**MAMMON**
Mt 6:24 Ye cannot serve God and *m*
Lk 16:9 of the *m* of unrighteousness
Lk 16:11 faithful in the unrighteous *m*
Lk 16:13 Ye cannot serve God and *m*

**MAMRE** *(mam'-re)*
*1. A place near Hebron.*
Gen 13:18 came and dwelt in the plain of *M*
Gen 18:1 unto him in the plains of *M*
Gen 23:17 in Machpelah, which was before *M*
Gen 23:19 the field of Machpelah before *M*
Gen 25:9 the Hittite, which is before *M*
Gen 35:27 came unto Isaac his father unto *M*
Gen 49:30 of Machpelah, which is before *M*
Gen 50:13 of Ephron the Hittite, before *M*
*2. An Amorite ally of Abraham.*
Gen 14:13 in the plain of *M* the Amorite
Gen 14:24 went with me, Aner, Eshcol, and *M*

**MANAEN** *(man'-a-en) A Christian teacher at Antioch.*
Acts 13:1 Niger, and Lucius of Cyrene, and *M*

**MANAHATH** *(man'-a-hath)*
*1. A son of Shobal.*
Gen 36:23 Alvan, and *M*, and Ebal, Shepho, and
1Chr 1:40 Alian, and *M*, and Ebal, Shephi, and
*2. A city in Benjamin.*
1Chr 8:6 Geba, and they removed them to *M*

**MANAHETHITES** *(man'-a-heth-ites) Descendants of Shobal.*
1Chr 2:52 Haroeh, and half of the *M*
1Chr 2:54 house of Joab, and half of the *M*

**MANASSEH** *(ma-nas'-seh)* See MANASSEH'S, MANASSES, MANASSITES.
*1. A son of Joseph.*
Gen 41:51 the name of the firstborn *M*
Gen 46:20 in the land of Egypt were born *M*
Gen 48:1 he took with him his two sons, *M*
Gen 48:5 And now thy two sons, Ephraim and *M*
Gen 48:13 *M* in his left hand toward
Gen 48:14 for *M* was the firstborn
Gen 48:20 God make thee as Ephraim and as *M*
Gen 48:20 and he set Ephraim before *M*
Gen 50:23 also of Machir the son of *M* were
Num 26:28 after their families were *M*
Num 26:29 Of the sons of *M*
Num 27:1 the son of Machir, the son of *M*
Num 27:1 families of *M* the son of Joseph
Num 32:39 the son of *M* went to Gilead
Num 32:40 Gilead unto Machir the son of *M*
Num 32:41 And Jair the son of *M* went
Num 36:1 the son of Machir, the son of *M*
Deut 3:14 Jair the son of *M* took all the
Josh 13:31 children of Machir the son of *M*
Josh 17:1 for Machir the firstborn of *M*
Josh 17:2 of *M* the son of Joseph by their
Josh 17:3 the son of Machir, the son of *M*
1Kin 4:13 the towns of Jair the son of *M*
1Chr 7:14 The sons of *M*
1Chr 7:17 the son of Machir, the son of *M*
*2. Descendants and land of Manasseh 1.*
Num 1:10 of *M*; Gamaliel the son
Num 1:34 Of the children of *M*, by their
Num 1:35 of them, even of the tribe of *M*
Num 2:20 And by him shall be the tribe of *M*
Num 2:20 of *M* shall be Gamaliel the son of
Num 7:54 prince of the children of *M*
Num 10:23 of *M* was Gamaliel the son of
Num 13:11 Joseph, namely, of the tribe of *M*
Num 26:34 These are the families of *M*
Num 32:33 the tribe of *M* the son of Joseph
Num 34:14 half the tribe of *M* have received
Num 34:23 the tribe of the children of *M*
Num 36:12 the sons of *M* the son of Joseph
Deut 3:13 gave I unto the half tribe of *M*
Deut 29:8 and to the half tribe of *M*
Deut 33:17 and they are the thousands of *M*
Deut 34:2 and the land of Ephraim, and *M*
Josh 1:12 and to half the tribe of *M*
Josh 4:12 of Gad, and half the tribe of *M*
Josh 12:6 Gadites, and the half tribe of *M*
Josh 13:7 tribes, and the half tribe of *M*
Josh 13:29 unto the half tribe of *M*
Josh 13:29 children of *M* by their families
Josh 14:4 of Joseph were two tribes, *M*
Josh 16:4 So the children of Joseph, *M*
Josh 16:9 inheritance of the children of *M*
Josh 17:1 was also a lot for the tribe of *M*
Josh 17:2 children of *M* by their families
Josh 17:5 And there fell ten portions to *M*
Josh 17:6 Because the daughters of *M* had an
Josh 17:7 the coast of *M* was from Asher to
Josh 17:8 Now *M* had the land of Tappuah
Josh 17:8 of *M* belonged to the children of
Josh 17:9 Ephraim are among the cities of *M*
Josh 17:9 the coast of *M* also was on the
Josh 17:11 *M* had in Issachar and in Asher
Josh 17:12 Yet the children of *M* could not
Josh 17:17 Joseph, even to Ephraim and to *M*
Josh 18:7 and Reuben, and half the tribe of *M*
Josh 20:8 in Bashan out of the tribe of *M*
Josh 21:5 and out of the half tribe of *M*
Josh 21:6 of the half tribe of *M* in Bashan
Josh 21:25 And out of the half tribe of *M*
Josh 21:27 *M* they gave Golan in Bashan with
Josh 22:1 Gadites, and the half tribe of *M*
Josh 22:7 *M* Moses had given possession in
Josh 22:9 and the half tribe of *M* returned
Josh 22:10 the half tribe of *M* built there
Josh 22:11 the half tribe of *M* have built an
Josh 22:13 of Gad, and to the half tribe of *M*
Josh 22:15 of Gad, and to the half tribe of *M*
Josh 22:21 and the half tribe of *M* answered
Josh 22:30 of Gad and the children of *M* spake
Josh 22:31 of Gad, and to the children of *M*
Judg 1:27 Neither did *M* drive out the
Judg 6:15 behold, my family is poor in *M*
Judg 6:35 sent messengers throughout all *M*
Judg 7:23 and out of Asher, and out of all *M*
Judg 11:29 and he passed over Gilead, and *M*
1Chr 5:18 Gadites, and half the tribe of *M*
1Chr 5:23 half tribe of *M* dwelt in the land
1Chr 5:26 Gadites, and the half tribe of *M*
1Chr 6:61 out of the half tribe of *M*
1Chr 6:62 out of the tribe of *M* in Bashan
1Chr 6:70 And out of the half tribe of *M*
1Chr 6:71 the family of the half tribe of *M*
1Chr 7:29 the borders of the children of *M*
1Chr 9:3 of the children of Ephraim, and *M*
1Chr 12:19 And there fell some of *M* to David
1Chr 12:20 to Ziklag, there fell to him of *M*
1Chr 12:20 of the thousands that were of *M*
1Chr 12:31 half tribe of *M* eighteen thousand
1Chr 12:37 and of the half tribe of *M*
1Chr 26:32 Gadites, and the half tribe of *M*
1Chr 27:20 of the half tribe of *M*, Joel the
1Chr 27:21 Of the half tribe of *M* in Gilead
2Chr 15:9 with them out of Ephraim and *M*
2Chr 30:1 letters also to Ephraim and *M*
2Chr 30:10 of Ephraim and *M* even unto Zebulun
2Chr 30:11 Nevertheless divers of Asher and *M*
2Chr 30:18 even many of Ephraim, and *M*
2Chr 31:1 and Benjamin, in Ephraim also and *M*
2Chr 34:6 And so did he in the cities of *M*
2Chr 34:9 had gathered of the hand of *M*
Ps 60:7 Gilead is mine, and *M* is mine
Ps 80:2 *M* stir up thy strength, and come
Ps 108:8 *M* is mine
Is 9:21 *M*, Ephraim; and Ephraim
Is 9:21 and Ephraim, *M*
Eze 48:4 the west side, a portion for *M*
Eze 48:5 And by the border of *M*, from the
*3. Grandfather of Jonathan.*
Judg 18:30 the son of Gershom, the son of *M*
*4. Son of King Hezekiah.*
2Kin 20:21 *M* his son reigned in his stead
2Kin 21:1 *M* was twelve years old when he
2Kin 21:9 *M* seduced them to do more evil
2Kin 21:11 Because *M* king of Judah hath done
2Kin 21:16 Moreover *M* shed innocent blood
2Kin 21:17 Now the rest of the acts of *M*
2Kin 21:18 *M* slept with his fathers, and was
2Kin 21:20 of the LORD, as his father *M* did
2Kin 23:12 the altars which *M* had made in
2Kin 23:26 that *M* had provoked him withal
2Kin 24:3 of his sight, for the sins of *M*
1Chr 3:13 son, Hezekiah his son, *M* his son,
2Chr 32:33 *M* his son reigned in his stead
2Chr 33:1 *M* was twelve years old when he
2Chr 33:9 So *M* made Judah and the
2Chr 33:10 And the LORD spake to *M*, and to his
2Chr 33:11 which took *M* among the thorns, and
2Chr 33:13 Then *M* knew that the LORD he was
2Chr 33:18 Now the rest of the acts of *M*
2Chr 33:20 So *M* slept with his fathers, and
2Chr 33:22 of the LORD, as did *M* his father
2Chr 33:22 which *M* his father had made
2Chr 33:23 as *M* his father had humbled
Jer 15:4 because of *M* the son of Hezekiah
*5. Married a foreigner in exile.*
Ezr 10:30 Bezaleel, and Binnui, and *M*
*6. A descendant of Hashum.*
Ezr 10:33 Zabad, Eliphelet, Jeremai, *M*

**MANASSEH'S** *(ma-nas'-sez)*
*1. Refers to Manasseh 1.*
Gen 48:14 and his left hand upon *M* head
Gen 48:17 from Ephraim's head unto *M* head
Josh 17:6 the rest of *M* sons had the land
*2. Refers to Manasseh 2.*
Josh 17:10 Ephraim's, and northward it was *M*

**MANASSES** *(ma-nas'-seez)* See MANASSEH.
*1. Greek form of Manasseh; ancestor of Jesus.*
Mt 1:10 And Ezekias begat *M*
Mt 1:10 and *M* begat Amon
*2. Greek form of Manasseh 2.*
Rev 7:6 Of the tribe of *M* were sealed

**MANASSITES** *(ma-nas'-sites) Same as Manasseh 2.*
Deut 4:43 and Golan in Bashan, of the *M*
Judg 12:4 the Ephraimites, and among the *M*
2Kin 10:33 and the Reubenites, and the *M*

**MANDRAKES**
Gen 30:14 found *m* in the field, and brought
Gen 30:14 me, I pray thee, of thy son's *m*
Gen 30:15 thou take away my son's *m* also
Gen 30:15 thee to night for thy son's *m*
Gen 30:16 I have hired thee with my son's *m*
Song 7:13 The *m* give a smell, and at our

**MANIFEST**
Eccl 3:18 of men, that God might *m* them
Lk 8:17 secret, that shall not be made *m*
Jn 1:31 he should be made *m* to Israel
Jn 3:21 that his deeds may be made *m*
Jn 9:3 of God should be made *m* in him
Jn 14:21 love him, and will *m* myself to him
Jn 14:22 that thou wilt *m* thyself unto us
Acts 4:16 is *m* to all them that dwell in
Rom 1:19 may be known of God is *m* in them
Rom 10:20 I was made *m* unto them that asked
Rom 16:26 But now is made *m*, and by the
1Cor 3:13 Every man's work shall be made *m*
1Cor 4:5 will make *m* the counsels of the
1Cor 11:19 approved may be made *m* among you
1Cor 14:25 the secrets of his heart made *m*
1Cor 15:27 it is *m* that he is excepted,
2Cor 2:14 maketh *m* the savour of his
2Cor 4:10 Jesus might be made *m* in our body
2Cor 4:11 be made *m* in our mortal flesh
2Cor 5:11 but we are made *m* unto God
2Cor 5:11 are made *m* in your consciences
2Cor 11:6 made *m* among you in all things
Gal 5:19 Now the works of the flesh are *m*
Eph 5:13 reproved are made *m* by the light
Eph 5:13 whatsoever doth make *m* is light
Phil 1:13 in Christ are *m* in all the palace
Col 1:26 but now is made *m* to his saints
Col 4:4 That I may make it *m*, as I ought

2Th 1:5 Which is a *m* token of the
1Ti 3:16 God was *m* in the flesh, justified
1Ti 5:25 works of some are *m* beforehand
2Ti 1:10 But is now made *m* by the
2Ti 3:9 folly shall be *m* unto all men
Heb 4:13 that is not *m* in his sight
Heb 9:8 holiest of all was not yet made *m*
1Pet 1:20 but was *m* in these last times for
1Jn 2:19 that they might be made *m* that
1Jn 3:10 In this the children of God are *m*
Rev 15:4 for thy judgments are made *m*

**MANIFESTED**
Mk 4:22 nothing hid, which shall not be *m*
Jn 2:11 of Galilee, and *m* forth his glory
Jn 17:6 I have *m* thy name unto the men
Rom 3:21 of God without the law is *m*
Titus 1:3 But hath in due times *m* his word
1Jn 1:2 (For the life was *m*, and we have
1Jn 1:2 with the Father, and was *m* unto us
1Jn 3:5 ye know that he was *m* to take
1Jn 3:8 this purpose the Son of God was *m*
1Jn 4:9 In this was *m* the love of God

**MANIFOLD**
Neh 9:19 Yet thou in thy *m* mercies
Neh 9:27 according to thy *m* mercies thou
Ps 104:24 O LORD, how *m* are thy works
Amos 5:12 For I know your *m* transgressions
Lk 18:30 Who shall not receive *m* more in
Eph 3:10 by the church the *m* wisdom of God
1Pet 1:6 heaviness through *m* temptations
1Pet 4:10 stewards of the *m* grace of God

**MANKIND**
Lev 18:22 Thou shalt not lie with *m*
Lev 20:13 If a man also lie with *m*, as he
Job 12:10 thing, and the breath of all *m*
1Cor 6:9 nor abusers of themselves with *m*
1Ti 1:10 that defile themselves with *m*
Jas 3:7 and hath been tamed of *m*

**MANNA**
Ex 16:15 they said one to another, It is *m*
Ex 16:31 Israel called the name thereof *M*
Ex 16:33 and put an omer full of *m* therein
Ex 16:35 of Israel did eat *m* forty years
Ex 16:35 they did eat *m*, until they came
Num 11:6 is nothing at all, beside this *m*
Num 11:7 the *m* was as coriander seed, and
Num 11:9 in the night, the *m* fell upon it
Deut 8:3 to hunger, and fed thee with *m*
Deut 8:16 fed thee in the wilderness with *m*
Josh 5:12 the *m* ceased on the morrow after
Josh 5:12 the children of Israel *m* any more
Neh 9:20 not thy *m* from their mouth
Ps 78:24 had rained down *m* upon them to
Jn 6:31 fathers did eat *m* in the desert
Jn 6:49 did eat *m* in the wilderness
Jn 6:58 not as your fathers did eat *m*
Heb 9:4 was the golden pot that had *m*
Rev 2:17 I give to eat of the hidden *m*

**MANNER**
Gen 18:11 with Sarah after the *m* of women
Gen 18:25 far from thee to do after this *m*
Gen 19:31 us after the *m* of all the earth
Gen 25:23 womb, and two *m* of people shall be
Gen 32:19 On this *m* shall ye speak unto
Gen 39:19 After this *m* did thy servant to
Gen 40:13 after the former *m* when thou wast
Gen 40:17 basket there was of all *m* of
Gen 45:23 his father he sent after this *m*
Ex 1:14 in all *m* of service in the field
Ex 7:11 they also did in like *m* with
Ex 12:16 no *m* of work shall be done in
Ex 21:9 with her after the *m* of daughters
Ex 22:9 For all *m* of trespass, whether it
Ex 22:9 or for any *m* of lost thing, which
Ex 23:11 In like *m* thou shalt deal with
Ex 31:3 and in all *m* of workmanship,
Ex 31:5 to work in all *m* of workmanship
Ex 35:29 to bring for all *m* of work
Ex 35:31 and in all *m* of workmanship
Ex 35:33 to make any *m* of cunning work
Ex 35:35 of heart, to work all *m* of work
Ex 36:1 to know how to work all *m* of work
Lev 5:10 offering, according to the *m*
Lev 7:23 saying, Ye shall eat no *m* of fat
Lev 7:26 ye shall eat no *m* of blood
Lev 7:27 it be that eateth any *m* of blood
Lev 9:16 and offered it according to the *m*
Lev 11:27 among all *m* of beasts that go on
Lev 11:44 ye defile yourselves with any *m*
Lev 14:54 for all *m* of plague of leprosy
Lev 17:10 you, that eateth any *m* of blood
Lev 17:14 eat the blood of no *m* of flesh
Lev 19:23 planted all *m* of trees for food
Lev 20:25 or by any *m* of living thing that
Lev 23:31 Ye shall do no *m* of work
Lev 24:22 Ye shall have one *m* of law
Num 5:13 neither she be taken with the *m*
Num 9:14 and according to the *m* thereof
Num 15:13 do these things after this *m*
Num 15:16 one *m* shall be for you, and for
Num 15:24 offering, according to the *m*
Num 28:18 ye shall do no *m* of servile work
Num 28:24 After this *m* ye shall offer daily
Num 29:6 offerings, according unto their *m*
Num 29:18 to their number, after the *m*
Num 29:21 to their number, after the *m*
Num 29:24 to their number, after the *m*
Num 29:27 to their number, after the *m*
Num 29:30 to their number, after the *m*
Num 29:33 to their number, after the *m*
Num 29:37 to their number, after the *m*
Num 31:30 of all *m* of beasts, and give them
Deut 4:15 for ye saw no *m* of similitude on
Deut 15:2 this is the *m* of the release
Deut 22:3 In like *m* shalt thou do with his
Deut 27:21 he that lieth with any *m* of beast
Josh 6:15 city after the same *m* seven times
Judg 8:18 What *m* of men were they whom ye
Judg 11:17 in like *m* they sent unto the king
Judg 18:7 after the *m* of the Zidonians,
Ruth 4:7 Now this was the *m* in former time
1Sa 8:9 shew them the *m* of the king that
1Sa 8:11 This will be the *m* of the king
1Sa 10:25 the people the *m* of the kingdom
1Sa 17:27 people answered him after this *m*
1Sa 17:30 and spake after the same *m*
1Sa 17:30 him again after the former *m*
1Sa 18:24 saying, On this *m* spake David
1Sa 19:24 before Samuel in like *m*, and lay
1Sa 21:5 and the bread is in a *m* common
1Sa 27:11 so will be his *m* all the while he
2Sa 6:5 played before the LORD on all *m*
2Sa 7:19 And is this the *m* of man, O Lord
2Sa 14:3 king, and speak on this *m* unto him
2Sa 15:6 on this *m* did Absalom to all
2Sa 17:6 hath spoken after this *m*
1Kin 7:28 work of the bases was on this *m*
1Kin 7:37 After this *m* he made the ten
1Kin 18:28 after their *m* with knives
1Kin 22:20 And one said on this *m*
1Kin 22:20 and another said on that *m*
2Kin 1:7 What *m* of man was he which came
2Kin 11:14 stood by a pillar, as the *m* was
2Kin 17:26 know not the *m* of the God of the
2Kin 17:26 not the *m* of the God of the land
2Kin 17:27 them the *m* of the God of the land
2Kin 17:33 after the *m* of the nations whom
2Kin 17:40 but they did after their former *m*
1Chr 6:48 *m* of service of the tabernacle of
1Chr 12:37 with all *m* of instruments of war
1Chr 18:10 with him all *m* of vessels of gold
1Chr 22:15 all *m* of cunning men for every
1Chr 22:15 cunning men for every *m* of work
1Chr 23:29 for all *m* of measure and size
1Chr 24:19 of the LORD, according to their *m*
1Chr 28:14 instruments of all *m* of service
1Chr 28:21 shall be with thee for all *m* of
1Chr 28:21 skilful man, for any *m* of service
1Chr 29:2 all *m* of precious stones, and
1Chr 29:5 for all *m* of work to be made by
2Chr 2:14 also to grave any *m* of graving
2Chr 4:20 after the *m* before the oracle
2Chr 13:9 *m* of the nations of other lands
2Chr 18:19 And one spake saying after this *m*
2Chr 18:19 and another saying after that *m*
2Chr 30:16 in their place after their *m*
2Chr 32:15 you, nor persuade you on this *m*
2Chr 32:27 for all *m* of pleasant jewels
2Chr 32:28 and stalls for all *m* of beasts
2Chr 34:13 the work in any *m* of service
Ezr 5:4 said we unto them after this *m*
Neh 6:4 I answered them after the same *m*
Neh 6:5 *m* the fifth time with an open
Neh 8:18 assembly, according unto the *m*
Neh 10:37 and the fruit of all *m* of trees
Neh 13:15 all *m* of burdens, which they
Neh 13:16 all *m* of ware, and sold on the
Est 1:13 (for so was the king's *m* toward
Est 2:12 according to the *m* of the women
Ps 107:18 soul abhorreth all *m* of meat
Ps 144:13 be full, affording all *m* of store
Song 7:13 are all *m* of pleasant fruits
Is 5:17 the lambs feed after their *m*
Is 10:24 thee, after the *m* of Egypt
Is 10:26 lift it up after the *m* of Egypt
Is 51:6 dwell therein shall die in like *m*
Jer 13:9 After this *m* will I mar the pride
Jer 22:21 hath been thy *m* from thy youth
Jer 30:18 shall remain after the *m* thereof
Eze 20:30 after the *m* of your fathers
Eze 23:15 after the *m* of the Babylonians of
Eze 23:45 them after the *m* of adulteresses
Eze 23:45 after the *m* of women that shed
Dan 6:23 no *m* of hurt was found upon him,
Amos 4:10 pestilence after the *m* of Egypt
Amos 8:14 The *m* of Beer-sheba liveth
Mt 4:23 and healing all *m* of sickness
Mt 4:23 all *m* of disease among the people
Mt 5:11 shall say all *m* of evil against
Mt 6:9 After this *m* therefore pray ye
Mt 8:27 What *m* of man is this, that even
Mt 10:1 out, and to heal all *m* of sickness
Mt 10:1 of sickness and all *m* of disease
Mt 12:31 All *m* of sin and blasphemy shall
Mk 4:41 What *m* of man is this, that even
Mk 13:1 see what *m* of stones and what
Mk 13:29 So ye in like *m*, when ye shall
Lk 1:29 cast in her mind what *m* of
Lk 1:66 What *m* of child shall this be
Lk 6:23 for in the like *m* did their
Lk 7:39 what *m* of woman this is that
Lk 8:25 to another, What *m* of man is this
Lk 9:55 Ye know not what *m* of spirit ye
Lk 11:42 all *m* of herbs, and pass over
Lk 20:31 and in like *m* the seven also
Lk 24:17 What *m* of communications are
Jn 2:6 after the *m* of the purifying of
Jn 7:36 What *m* of saying is this that he
Jn 19:40 as the *m* of the Jews is to bury
Acts 1:11 shall so come in like *m* as ye
Acts 10:12 Wherein were all *m* of fourfooted
Acts 15:1 circumcised after the *m* of Moses
Acts 15:23 letters by them after this *m*
Acts 17:2 And Paul, as his *m* was, went in
Acts 20:18 after what *m* I have been with you
Acts 22:3 *m* of the law of the fathers
Acts 23:25 And he wrote a letter after this *m*
Acts 25:16 It is not the *m* of the Romans to
Acts 25:20 I doubted of such *m* of questions
Acts 26:4 My *m* of life from my youth, which
Rom 6:19 I speak after the *m* of men
Rom 7:8 in me all *m* of concupiscence
1Cor 7:7 gift of God, one after this *m*
1Cor 11:25 After the same *m* also he took the
1Cor 15:32 If after the *m* of men I have
2Cor 7:9 were made sorry after a godly *m*
Gal 2:14 livest after the *m* of Gentiles
Gal 3:15 I speak after the *m* of men
1Th 1:5 as ye know what *m* of men we were
1Th 1:9 *m* of entering in we had unto you
1Ti 2:9 In like *m* also, that women adorn
2Ti 3:10 *m* of life, purpose, faith,
Heb 10:25 together, as the *m* of some is
Jas 1:24 forgetteth what *m* of man he was
1Pet 1:11 or what *m* of time the Spirit of
1Pet 1:15 ye holy in all *m* of conversation
1Pet 3:5 For after this *m* in the old time
2Pet 3:11 what *m* of persons ought ye to be
1Jn 3:1 what *m* of love the Father hath
Jude 7 the cities about them in like *m*
Rev 11:5 them, he must in this *m* be killed
Rev 18:12 all *m* vessels of ivory
Rev 18:12 all *m* vessels of most precious
Rev 21:19 with all *m* of precious stones
Rev 22:2 which bare twelve *m* of fruits

**MANNERS**
Lev 20:23 not walk in the *m* of the nation
2Kin 17:34 day they do after the former *m*
Eze 11:12 but have done after the *m* of the
Acts 13:18 he their *m* in the wilderness
1Cor 15:33 communications corrupt good *m*
Heb 1:1 in divers *m* spake in time past

**MANOAH** *(ma-no'-ah) Father of Samson.*
Judg 13:2 of the Danites, whose name was *M*
Judg 13:8 Then *M* intreated the LORD, and
Judg 13:9 God hearkened to the voice of *M*
Judg 13:9 but *M* her husband was not with

Judg 13:11 *M* arose, and went after his wife,
Judg 13:12 *M* said, Now let thy words come to
Judg 13:13 the angel of the LORD said unto *M*
Judg 13:15 *M* said unto the angel of the LORD
Judg 13:16 the angel of the LORD said unto *M*
Judg 13:16 For *M* knew not that he was an
Judg 13:17 *M* said unto the angel of the LORD
Judg 13:19 So *M* took a kid with a meat
Judg 13:19 and *M* and his wife looked on
Judg 13:20 And *M* and his wife looked on it, and
Judg 13:21 the LORD did no more appear to *M*
Judg 13:21 Then *M* knew that he was an angel
Judg 13:22 *M* said unto his wife, We shall
Judg 16:31 the buryingplace of *M* his father

**MANSERVANT**
Ex 20:10 thy son, nor thy daughter, thy *m*
Ex 20:17 thy neighbour's wife, nor his *m*
Ex 21:32 shall push a *m* or a maidservant
Deut 5:14 son, nor thy daughter, nor thy *m*
Deut 5:14 that thy *m* and thy maidservant may
Deut 5:21 house, his field, or his *m*
Deut 12:18 son, and thy daughter, and thy *m*
Deut 16:11 son, and thy daughter, and thy *m*
Deut 16:14 son, and thy daughter, and thy *m*
Job 31:13 of my *m* or of my maidservant
Jer 34:9 That every man should let his *m*
Jer 34:10 that every one should let his *m*

**MANTLE**
Judg 4:18 tent, she covered him with a *m*
1Sa 15:27 laid hold upon the skirt of his *m*
1Sa 28:14 and he is covered with a *m*
1Kin 19:13 that he wrapped his face in his *m*
1Kin 19:19 by him, and cast his *m* upon him
2Kin 2:8 And Elijah took his *m*, and wrapped
2Kin 2:13 He took up also the *m* of Elijah
2Kin 2:14 he took the *m* of Elijah that fell
Ezr 9:3 thing, I rent my garment and my *m*
Ezr 9:5 having rent my garment and my *m*
Job 1:20 Then Job arose, and rent his *m*
Job 2:12 and they rent every one his *m*
Ps 109:29 their own confusion, as with a *m*

**MAOCH** *(ma'-ok) Father of Achish.*
1Sa 27:2 him unto Achish, the son of *M*

**MAON** *(ma'-on)* See MAONITES.
*1. A city in Judah.*
Josh 15:55 *M*, Carmel, and Ziph, and Juttah,
1Sa 25:2 And there was a man in *M*, whose
*2. A descendant of Caleb.*
1Chr 2:45 And the son of Shammai was *M*
1Chr 2:45 *M* was the father of Beth-zur
*3. A wilderness in Judah.*
1Sa 23:24 men were in the wilderness of *M*
1Sa 23:25 and abode in the wilderness of *M*
1Sa 23:25 David in the wilderness of *M*

**MAONITES** *(ma'-on-ites)* See MEHUNIM. *An enemy tribe of Israel.*
Judg 10:12 also, and the Amalekites, and the *M*

**MAR**
Lev 19:27 neither shalt thou *m* the corners
Ruth 4:6 lest I *m* mine own inheritance
1Sa 6:5 of your mice that *m* the land
2Kin 3:19 *m* every good piece of land with
Job 30:13 They *m* my path, they set forward
Jer 13:9 will I *m* the pride of Judah

**MARA** *(ma'-rah) Another name for Naomi.*
Ruth 1:20 Call me not Naomi, call me *M*

**MARAH** *(ma'-rah) An Israelite encampment in the wilderness.*
Ex 15:23 And when they came to *M*, they
Ex 15:23 not drink of the waters of *M*
Ex 15:23 the name of it was called *M*
Num 33:8 of Etham, and pitched in *M*
Num 33:9 And they removed from *M*, and came

**MARALAH** *(mar'-a-lah) A city in Zebulun.*
Josh 19:11 went up toward the sea, and *M*

**MARBLE**
1Chr 29:2 stones, and *m* stones in abundance
Est 1:6 to silver rings and pillars of *m*
Est 1:6 and blue, and white, and black, *m*
Song 5:15 His legs are as pillars of *m*
Rev 18:12 wood, and of brass, and iron, and *m*

**MARCH**
Ps 68:7 when thou didst *m* through the
Jer 46:22 for they shall *m* with an army
Joel 2:7 they shall *m* every one on his
Hab 1:6 which shall *m* through the breadth
Hab 3:12 Thou didst *m* through the land in

**MARCUS** *(mar'-cus)* See MARK. *Latin form of Mark.*
Col 4:10 fellowprisoner saluteth you, and *M*
Philem 24 *M*, Aristarchus, Demas, Lucas, my
1Pet 5:13 and so doth *M* my son

**MARDUK** See MERODACH.

**MAREAL** See MARALAH.

**MARESHAH**
*1. A city in Judah.*
Josh 15:44 And Keilah, and Achzib, and *M*
2Chr 11:8 And Gath, and *M*, and Ziph,
2Chr 14:9 and came unto *M*
2Chr 14:10 in the valley of Zephathah at *M*
2Chr 20:37 Eliezer the son of Dodavah of *M*
Mic 1:15 heir unto thee, O inhabitant of *M*
*2. Father of Hebron.*
1Chr 2:42 the sons of *M* the father of
*3. A descendant of Shelah.*
1Chr 4:21 Lecah, and Laadah the father of *M*

**MARINERS**
Eze 27:8 of Zidon and Arvad were thy *m*
Eze 27:9 *m* were in thee to occupy thy
Eze 27:27 thy fairs, thy merchandise, thy *m*
Eze 27:29 And all that handle the oar, the *m*
Jonah 1:5 Then the *m* were afraid, and cried

**MARK** See MARCUS.
Gen 4:15 And the LORD set a *m* upon Cain
Ruth 3:4 that thou shalt *m* the place where
1Sa 20:20 thereof, as though I shot at a *m*
2Sa 13:28 *M* ye now when Amnon's heart is
1Kin 20:7 elders of the land, and said, *M*
1Kin 20:22 him, Go, strengthen thyself, and *m*
Job 7:20 thou set me as a *m* against thee
Job 16:12 to pieces, and set me up for his *m*
Job 18:2 *m*, and afterwards we will speak
Job 21:5 *M* me, and be astonished, and lay
Job 33:31 *M* well, O Job, hearken unto me
Job 39:1 or canst thou *m* when the hinds do
Ps 37:37 *M* the perfect man, and behold the
Ps 48:13 *M* ye well her bulwarks, consider
Ps 56:6 they *m* my steps, when they wait
Ps 130:3 shouldest *m* iniquities, O Lord,
Lam 3:12 set me as a *m* for the arrow
Eze 9:4 set a *m* upon the foreheads of the
Eze 9:6 near any man upon whom is the *m*
Eze 44:5 *m* well, and behold with thine eyes
Eze 44:5 *m* well the entering in of the
Rom 16:17 *m* them which cause divisions and
Phil 3:14 I press toward the *m* for the
Phil 3:17 *m* them which walk so as ye have
Rev 13:16 to receive a *m* in their right
Rev 13:17 or sell, save he that had the *m*
Rev 14:9 receive his *m* in his forehead, or
Rev 14:11 receiveth the *m* of his name
Rev 15:2 and over his image, and over his *m*
Rev 16:2 men which had the *m* of the beast
Rev 19:20 had received the *m* of the beast
Rev 20:4 his *m* upon their foreheads
*Companion of Paul..*
Acts 12:12 of John, whose surname was *M*
Acts 12:25 them John, whose surname was *M*
Acts 15:37 them John, whose surname was *M*
Acts 15:39 and so Barnabas took *M*, and sailed
2Ti 4:11 Take *M*, and bring him with thee

**MARKED**
1Sa 1:12 the LORD, that Eli *m* her mouth
Job 22:15 Hast thou *m* the old way which
Job 24:16 which they had *m* for themselves
Jer 2:22 yet thine iniquity is *m* before me
Jer 23:18 who hath *m* his word, and heard it
Lk 14:7 when he *m* how they chose out the

**MARKET**
Eze 27:13 men and vessels of brass in thy *m*
Eze 27:17 traded in thy *m* wheat of Minnith
Eze 27:19 cassia, and calamus, were in thy *m*
Eze 27:25 did sing of thee in thy *m*
Mk 7:4 And when they come from the *m*
Jn 5:2 Jerusalem by the sheep *m* a pool
Acts 17:17 in the *m* daily with them that met

**MARKETS**
Mt 11:16 unto children sitting in the *m*
Mt 23:7 And greetings in the *m*, and to be
Lk 11:43 synagogues, and greetings in the *m*
Lk 20:46 robes, and love greetings in the *m*

**MAROTH** *(ma'-roth) A city in Judah.*
Mic 1:12 For the inhabitant of *M* waited

**MARRED**
Is 52:14 visage was so *m* more than any man
Jer 13:7 and, behold, the girdle was *m*
Jer 18:4 was *m* in the hand of the potter
Nah 2:2 out, and *m* their vine branches
Mk 2:22 spilled, and the bottles will be *m*

**MARRIAGE**
Ex 21:10 her raiment, and her duty of *m*
Ps 78:63 their maidens were not given to *m*
Mt 22:2 king, which made a *m* for his son
Mt 22:4 are ready: come unto the *m*
Mt 22:9 as ye shall find, bid to the *m*
Mt 22:30 neither marry, nor are given in *m*
Mt 24:38 drinking, marrying and giving in *m*
Mt 25:10 ready went in with him to the *m*
Mk 12:25 neither marry, nor are given in *m*
Lk 17:27 wives, they were given in *m*
Lk 20:34 world marry, and are given in *m*
Lk 20:35 neither marry, nor are given in *m*
Jn 2:1 there was a *m* in Cana of Galilee
Jn 2:2 and his disciples, to the *m*
1Cor 7:38 that giveth her in *m* doeth well
1Cor 7:38 giveth her not in *m* doeth better
Heb 13:4 *M* is honourable in all, and the
Rev 19:7 for the *m* of the Lamb is come, and
Rev 19:9 unto the *m* supper of the Lamb

**MARRIED**
Gen 19:14 which *m* his daughters, and said,
Ex 21:3 if he were *m*, then his wife shall
Lev 22:12 also be *m* unto a stranger
Num 12:1 the Ethiopian woman whom he had *m*
Num 12:1 for he had *m* an Ethiopian woman
Num 36:3 if they be *m* to any of the sons
Num 36:11 were *m* unto their father's
Num 36:12 they were *m* into the families of
Deut 22:22 with a woman *m* to an husband
Deut 24:1 *m* her, and it come to pass that
1Chr 2:21 whom he *m* when he was threescore
2Chr 13:21 *m* fourteen wives, and begat twenty
Neh 13:23 I Jews that had *m* wives of Ashdod
Prov 30:23 For an odious woman when she is *m*
Is 54:1 than the children of the *m* wife
Is 62:4 in thee, and thy land shall be *m*
Jer 3:14 for I am *m* unto you
Mal 2:11 hath *m* the daughter of a strange
Mt 22:25 the first, when he had *m* a wife
Mk 6:17 for he had *m* her
Mk 10:12 be *m* to another, she committeth
Lk 14:20 And another said, I have *m* a wife
Lk 17:27 they *m* wives, they were given in
Rom 7:3 she be *m* to another man, she
Rom 7:3 though she be *m* to another man
Rom 7:4 that ye should be *m* to another
1Cor 7:10 unto the *m* I command, yet not I,
1Cor 7:33 But he that is *m* careth for the
1Cor 7:34 but she that is *m* careth for the
1Cor 7:39 liberty to be *m* to whom she will

**MARRIETH**
Is 62:5 For as a young man *m* a virgin
Mt 19:9 whoso *m* her which is put away
Lk 16:18 *m* another, committeth adultery
Lk 16:18 whosoever *m* her that is put away

**MARROW**
Job 21:24 and his bones are moistened with *m*
Ps 63:5 soul shall be satisfied as with *m*
Prov 3:8 to thy navel, and *m* to thy bones
Is 25:6 the lees, of fat things full of *m*
Heb 4:12 and spirit, and of the joints and *m*

**MARRY**
Gen 38:8 *m* her, and raise up seed to thy
Num 36:6 Let them *m* to whom they think
Num 36:6 of their father shall they *m*
Deut 25:5 not *m* without unto a stranger
Is 62:5 virgin, so shall thy sons *m* thee
Mt 5:32 whosoever shall *m* her that is
Mt 19:9 shall *m* another, committeth
Mt 19:10 his wife, it is not good to *m*
Mt 22:24 his brother shall *m* his wife
Mt 22:30 the resurrection they neither *m*
Mk 10:11 *m* another, committeth adultery
Mk 12:25 from the dead, they neither *m*
Lk 20:34 The children of this world *m*
Lk 20:35 from the dead, neither *m*, nor are
1Cor 7:9 they cannot contain, let them *m*
1Cor 7:9 it is better to *m* than to burn
1Cor 7:28 But and if thou *m*, thou hast not

| | |
|---|---|
| 1Cor 7:28 | and if a virgin *m*, she hath not |
| 1Cor 7:36 | he sinneth not: let them *m* |
| 1Ti 4:3 | Forbidding to *m*, and commanding to |
| 1Ti 5:11 | against Christ, they will *m* |
| 1Ti 5:14 | that the younger women *m*, bear |

**MARS'** *(marz) Refers to a landmark in Athens.*

| | |
|---|---|
| Acts 17:22 | Paul stood in the midst of *M* hill |

**MARSENA** *(mar'-se-nah) A prince of Media and Persia.*

| | |
|---|---|
| Est 1:14 | Admatha, Tarshish, Meres, *M* |

**MARTHA** *(mar'-thah) Sister of Lazarus.*

| | |
|---|---|
| Lk 10:38 | a certain woman named *M* received |
| Lk 10:40 | But *M* was cumbered about much |
| Lk 10:41 | and said unto her, *M*, *M* |
| Jn 11:1 | the town of Mary and her sister *M* |
| Jn 11:5 | Now Jesus loved *M*, and her sister, |
| Jn 11:19 | And many of the Jews came to *M* |
| Jn 11:20 | Then *M*, as soon as she heard that |
| Jn 11:21 | Then said *M* unto Jesus, Lord, if |
| Jn 11:24 | *M* saith unto him, I know that he |
| Jn 11:30 | was in that place where *M* met him |
| Jn 11:39 | *M*, the sister of him that was |
| Jn 12:2 | a supper; and *M* served |

**MARVEL**

| | |
|---|---|
| Eccl 5:8 | a province, *m* not at the matter |
| Mk 5:20 | and all men did *m* |
| Jn 3:7 | *M* not that I said unto thee, Ye |
| Jn 5:20 | works than these, that ye may *m* |
| Jn 5:28 | *M* not at this |
| Jn 7:21 | I have done one work, and ye all *m* |
| Acts 3:12 | men of Israel, why *m* ye at this |
| 2Cor 11:14 | And no *m*; for Satan himself |
| Gal 1:6 | I *m* that ye are so soon removed |
| 1Jn 3:13 | *M* not, my brethren, if the world |
| Rev 17:7 | unto me, Wherefore didst thou *m* |

**MARVELLED**

| | |
|---|---|
| Gen 43:33 | and the men *m* one at another |
| Ps 48:5 | They saw it, and so they *m* |
| Mt 8:10 | When Jesus heard it, he *m* |
| Mt 8:27 | But the men *m*, saying, What |
| Mt 9:8 | the multitudes saw it, they *m* |
| Mt 9:33 | and the multitudes *m*, saying, It |
| Mt 21:20 | when the disciples saw it, they *m* |
| Mt 22:22 | had heard these words, they *m* |
| Mt 27:14 | that the governor *m* greatly |
| Mk 6:6 | he *m* because of their unbelief |
| Mk 12:17 | And they *m* at him |
| Mk 15:5 | so that Pilate *m* |
| Mk 15:44 | Pilate *m* if he were already dead |
| Lk 1:21 | *m* that he tarried so long in the |
| Lk 1:63 | And they *m* all |
| Lk 2:33 | his mother *m* at those things |
| Lk 7:9 | he *m* at him, and turned him about, |
| Lk 11:38 | he *m* that he had not first washed |
| Lk 20:26 | they *m* at his answer, and held |
| Jn 4:27 | *m* that he talked with the woman |
| Jn 7:15 | And the Jews *m*, saying, How |
| Acts 2:7 | And they were all amazed and *m* |
| Acts 4:13 | unlearned and ignorant men, they *m* |

**MARVELLOUS**

| | |
|---|---|
| 1Chr 16:12 | Remember his *m* works that he hath |
| 1Chr 16:24 | his *m* works among all nations |
| Job 5:9 | *m* things without number |
| Job 10:16 | thou shewest thyself *m* upon me |
| Ps 9:1 | I will shew forth all thy *m* works |
| Ps 17:7 | Shew thy *m* lovingkindness, O thou |
| Ps 31:21 | his *m* kindness in a strong city |
| Ps 78:12 | *M* things did he in the sight of |
| Ps 98:1 | for he hath done *m* things |
| Ps 105:5 | Remember his *m* works that he hath |
| Ps 118:23 | it is *m* in our eyes |
| Ps 139:14 | *m* are thy works |
| Is 29:14 | to do a *m* work among this people |
| Is 29:14 | among this people, even a *m* work |
| Dan 11:36 | shall speak *m* things against the |
| Mic 7:15 | will I shew unto him *m* things |
| Zec 8:6 | If it be *m* in the eyes of the |
| Zec 8:6 | should it also be *m* in mine eyes |
| Mt 21:42 | doing, and it is *m* in our eyes |
| Mk 12:11 | doing, and it is *m* in our eyes |
| Jn 9:30 | them, Why herein is a *m* thing |
| 1Pet 2:9 | out of darkness into his *m* light |
| Rev 15:1 | sign in heaven, great and *m* |
| Rev 15:3 | *m* are thy works, Lord God |

**MARY** *(ma'-ry)*

*1. Mother of Jesus.*

| | |
|---|---|
| Mt 1:16 | begat Joseph the husband of *M* |
| Mt 1:18 | When as his mother *M* was espoused |
| Mt 1:20 | not to take unto thee *M* thy wife |
| Mt 2:11 | the young child with *M* his mother |
| Mt 13:55 | is not his mother called *M* |
| Mk 6:3 | this the carpenter, the son of *M* |
| Lk 1:27 | and the virgin's name was *M* |
| Lk 1:30 | angel said unto her, Fear not, *M* |
| Lk 1:34 | Then said *M* unto the angel, How |
| Lk 1:38 | *M* said, Behold the handmaid of |
| Lk 1:39 | *M* arose in those days, and went |
| Lk 1:41 | heard the salutation of *M* |
| Lk 1:46 | *M* said, My soul doth magnify the |
| Lk 1:56 | *M* abode with her about three |
| Lk 2:5 | To be taxed with *M* his espoused |
| Lk 2:16 | they came with haste, and found *M* |
| Lk 2:19 | But *M* kept all these things, and |
| Lk 2:34 | said unto *M* his mother, Behold, |
| Acts 1:14 | *M* the mother of Jesus, and with |

*2. A woman of Magdala.*

| | |
|---|---|
| Mt 27:56 | Among which was *M* Magdalene |
| Mt 27:61 | And there was *M* Magdalene, and the |
| Mt 28:1 | came *M* Magdalene and the other |
| Mk 15:40 | among whom was *M* Magdalene |
| Mk 15:47 | *M* Magdalene and Mary the mother of |
| Mk 16:9 | he appeared first to *M* Magdalene |
| Lk 8:2 | *M* called Magdalene, out of whom |
| Lk 24:10 | It was *M* Magdalene, and Joanna, and |
| Jn 19:25 | wife of Cleophas, and *M* Magdalene |
| Jn 20:1 | the week cometh *M* Magdalene early |
| Jn 20:11 | But *M* stood without at the |
| Jn 20:16 | Jesus saith unto her, *M* |
| Jn 20:18 | *M* Magdalene came and told the |

*3. Mother of James and Joses.*

| | |
|---|---|
| Mt 27:56 | *M* the mother of James and Joses, |
| Mt 27:61 | Mary Magdalene, and the other *M* |
| Mt 28:1 | the other *M* to see the sepulchre |
| Mk 15:40 | *M* the mother of James the less and |
| Mk 15:47 | *M* the mother of Joses beheld |
| Mk 16:1 | *M* Magdalene, and Mary the mother |
| Mk 16:1 | *M* the mother of James, and Salome, |
| Lk 24:10 | *M* the mother of James, and other |

*4. Wife of Cleophas.*

| | |
|---|---|
| Jn 19:25 | *M* the wife of Cleophas, and Mary |

*5. Sister of Lazarus.*

| | |
|---|---|
| Lk 10:39 | And she had a sister called *M* |
| Lk 10:42 | *M* hath chosen that good part, |
| Jn 11:1 | of Bethany, the town of *M* |
| Jn 11:2 | (It was that *M* which anointed the |
| Jn 11:19 | of the Jews came to Martha and *M* |
| Jn 11:20 | but *M* sat still in the house |
| Jn 11:28 | called *M* her sister secretly, |
| Jn 11:31 | and comforted her, when they saw *M* |
| Jn 11:32 | Then when *M* was come where Jesus |
| Jn 11:45 | many of the Jews which came to *M* |
| Jn 12:3 | Then took *M* a pound of ointment |

*6. Mother of John Mark.*

| | |
|---|---|
| Acts 12:12 | the house of *M* the mother of John |

*7. A Christian in Rome.*

| | |
|---|---|
| Rom 16:6 | Greet *M*, who bestowed much labour |

**MASCHIL** *(mas'-kil) A didactic poem.*

| | |
|---|---|
| Ps 32:*t* | A Psalm of David, A *M* |
| Ps 42:*t* | To the chief Musician, *M*, for the |
| Ps 44:*t* | Musician for the sons of Korah, *M* |
| Ps 45:*t* | for the sons of Korah, A *M* |
| Ps 52:*t* | To the chief Musician, *M*, A Psalm |
| Ps 53:*t* | chief Musician upon Mahalath, *M* |
| Ps 54:*t* | the chief Musician on Neginoth, *M* |
| Ps 55:*t* | the chief Musician on Neginoth, *M* |
| Ps 74:*t* | *M* of Asaph |
| Ps 78:*t* | *M* of Asaph |
| Ps 88:*t* | Leannoth, *M* of Heman the Ezrahite |
| Ps 89:*t* | *M* of Ethan the Ezrahite |
| Ps 142:*t* | *M* of David |

**MASH** *(mash) A son of Aram.*

| | |
|---|---|
| Gen 10:23 | Uz, and Hul, and Gether, and *M* |

**MASHAL** *(ma'-shal) A Levitical city in Asher.*

| | |
|---|---|
| 1Chr 6:74 | *M* with her suburbs, and Abdon with |

**MASONS**

| | |
|---|---|
| 2Sa 5:11 | cedar trees, and carpenters, and *m* |
| 2Kin 12:12 | And to *m*, and hewers of stone, and |
| 2Kin 22:6 | carpenters, and builders, and *m* |
| 1Chr 14:1 | and timber of cedars, with *m* |
| 1Chr 22:2 | he set *m* to hew wrought stones to |
| 2Chr 24:12 | the house of the LORD, and hired *m* |
| Ezr 3:7 | They gave money also unto the *m* |

**MASREKAH** *(mas'-re-kah) A place in Edom.*

| | |
|---|---|
| Gen 36:36 | Samlah of *M* reigned in his stead |
| 1Chr 1:47 | Samlah of *M* reigned in his stead |

**MASSA** *(mas'-sah) A son of Ishmael.*

| | |
|---|---|
| Gen 25:14 | And Mishma, and Dumah, and *M* |
| 1Chr 1:30 | Mishma, and Dumah, *M*, Hadad, and |

**MASSAH** *(mas'-sah)* See MERIBAH. *A place in the wilderness where the Israelites murmured.*

| | |
|---|---|
| Ex 17:7 | he called the name of the place *M* |
| Deut 6:16 | your God, as ye tempted him in *M* |
| Deut 9:22 | And at Taberah, and at *M*, and at |
| Deut 33:8 | one, whom thou didst prove at *M* |

**MASTER**

| | |
|---|---|
| Gen 24:9 | under the thigh of Abraham his *m* |
| Gen 24:10 | ten camels of the camels of his *m* |
| Gen 24:10 | goods of his *m* were in his hand |
| Gen 24:12 | said, O LORD God of my *m* Abraham |
| Gen 24:12 | shew kindness unto my *m* Abraham |
| Gen 24:14 | hast shewed kindness unto my *m* |
| Gen 24:27 | be the LORD God of my *m* Abraham |
| Gen 24:27 | left destitute my *m* of his mercy |
| Gen 24:35 | LORD hath blessed my *m* greatly |
| Gen 24:36 | a son to my *m* when she was old |
| Gen 24:37 | my *m* made me swear, saying, Thou |
| Gen 24:39 | And I said unto my *m*, Peradventure |
| Gen 24:42 | said, O LORD God of my *m* Abraham |
| Gen 24:48 | the LORD God of my *m* Abraham |
| Gen 24:49 | deal kindly and truly with my *m* |
| Gen 24:54 | he said, Send me away unto my *m* |
| Gen 24:56 | me away that I may go to my *m* |
| Gen 24:65 | the servant had said, It is my *m* |
| Gen 39:2 | the house of his *m* the Egyptian |
| Gen 39:3 | his *m* saw that the LORD was with |
| Gen 39:8 | my *m* wotteth not what is with me |
| Gen 39:19 | when his *m* heard the words of his |
| Gen 39:20 | And Joseph's *m* took him, and put |
| Ex 21:4 | If his *m* have given him a wife, |
| Ex 21:5 | shall plainly say, I love my *m* |
| Ex 21:6 | Then his *m* shall bring him unto |
| Ex 21:6 | his *m* shall bore his ear through |
| Ex 21:8 | If she please not her *m*, who hath |
| Ex 21:32 | their *m* thirty shekels of silver |
| Ex 22:8 | then the *m* of the house shall be |
| Deut 23:15 | *m* the servant which is escaped |
| Deut 23:15 | is escaped from his *m* unto thee |
| Judg 19:11 | and the servant said unto his *m* |
| Judg 19:12 | his *m* said unto him, We will not |
| Judg 19:22 | and spake to the *m* of the house |
| Judg 19:23 | the *m* of the house, went out unto |
| 1Sa 20:38 | up the arrows, and came to his *m* |
| 1Sa 24:6 | I should do this thing unto my *m* |
| 1Sa 25:10 | break away every man from his *m* |
| 1Sa 25:14 | of the wilderness to salute our *m* |
| 1Sa 25:17 | evil is determined against our *m* |
| 1Sa 26:16 | because ye have not kept your *m* |
| 1Sa 29:4 | he reconcile himself unto his *m* |
| 1Sa 30:13 | my *m* left me, because three days |
| 1Sa 30:15 | deliver me into the hands of my *m* |
| 2Sa 2:7 | for your *m* Saul is dead, and also |
| 1Kin 22:17 | and the LORD said, These have no *m* |
| 2Kin 2:3 | away thy *m* from thy head to day |
| 2Kin 2:5 | away thy *m* from thy head to day |
| 2Kin 2:16 | go, we pray thee, and seek thy *m* |
| 2Kin 5:1 | Syria, was a great man with his *m* |
| 2Kin 5:18 | that when my *m* goeth into the |
| 2Kin 5:20 | my *m* hath spared Naaman this |
| 2Kin 5:22 | My *m* hath sent me, saying, Behold |
| 2Kin 5:25 | he went in, and stood before his *m* |
| 2Kin 6:5 | and he cried, and said, Alas, *m* |
| 2Kin 6:15 | servant said unto him, Alas, my *m* |
| 2Kin 6:22 | eat and drink, and go to their *m* |
| 2Kin 6:23 | away, and they went to their *m* |
| 2Kin 8:14 | from Elisha, and came to his *m* |
| 2Kin 9:7 | smite the house of Ahab thy *m* |
| 2Kin 9:31 | Had Zimri peace, who slew his *m* |
| 2Kin 10:9 | behold, I conspired against my *m* |
| 2Kin 18:27 | Hath my *m* sent me to thy *m*, |
| 2Kin 19:4 | his *m* hath sent to reproach the |
| 2Kin 19:6 | them, Thus shall ye say to your *m* |
| 1Chr 12:19 | He will fall to his *m* Saul to the |
| 1Chr 15:27 | Chenaniah the *m* of the song with |
| 2Chr 18:16 | and the LORD said, These have no *m* |
| Job 3:19 | and the servant is free from his *m* |
| Prov 27:18 | on his *m* shall be honoured |

Prov 30:10 Accuse not a servant unto his *m*
Is 24:2 with the servant, so with his *m*
Is 36:8 to my *m* the king of Assyria, and I
Is 36:12 Hath my *m* sent me to thy *m*
Is 37:4 his *m* hath sent to reproach the
Is 37:6 Thus shall ye say unto your *m*
Dan 1:3 Ashpenaz the *m* of his eunuchs
Dan 4:9 *m* of the magicians, because I
Dan 5:11 father, made *m* of the magicians,
Mal 1:6 his father, and a servant his *m*
Mal 1:6 and if I be a *m*, where is my fear
Mal 2:12 the man that doeth this, the *m*
Mt 8:19 scribe came, and said unto him, *M*
Mt 9:11 Why eateth your *M* with publicans
Mt 10:24 The disciple is not above his *m*
Mt 10:25 the disciple that he be as his *m*
Mt 10:25 the *m* of the house Beelzebub
Mt 12:38 the Pharisees answered, saying, *M*
Mt 17:24 said, Doth not your *m* pay tribute
Mt 19:16 one came and said unto him, Good *M*
Mt 22:16 with the Herodians, saying, *M*
Mt 22:24 Saying, *M*, Moses said, If a man
Mt 22:36 *M*, which is the great commandment
Mt 23:8 for one is your *M*, even Christ
Mt 23:10 for one is your *M*, even Christ
Mt 26:18 The *M* saith, My time is at hand
Mt 26:25 betrayed him, answered and said, *M*
Mt 26:49 came to Jesus, and said, Hail, *m*
Mk 4:38 awake him, and say unto him, *M*
Mk 5:35 troublest thou the *M* any further
Mk 9:5 answered and said to Jesus, *M*
Mk 9:17 the multitude answered and said, *M*
Mk 9:38 And John answered him, saying, *M*
Mk 10:17 to him, and asked him, Good *M*
Mk 10:20 he answered and said unto him, *M*
Mk 10:35 Zebedee, come unto him, saying, *M*
Mk 11:21 to remembrance saith unto him, *M*
Mk 12:14 were come, they say unto him, *M*
Mk 12:19 *M*, Moses wrote unto us, If a
Mk 12:32 the scribe said unto him, Well, *M*
Mk 13:1 his disciples saith unto him, *M*
Mk 13:35 when the *m* of the house cometh
Mk 14:14 The *M* saith, Where is the
Mk 14:45 to him, and saith, *M*, *m*
Lk 3:12 be baptized, and said unto him, *M*
Lk 5:5 Simon answering said unto him, *M*
Lk 6:40 The disciple is not above his *m*
Lk 6:40 that is perfect shall be as his *m*
Lk 7:40 And he saith, *M*, say on
Lk 8:24 and awoke him, saying, *M*, *m*
Lk 8:45 they that were with him said, *M*
Lk 8:49 trouble not the *M*
Lk 9:33 him, Peter said unto Jesus, *M*
Lk 9:38 the company cried out, saying, *M*
Lk 9:49 And John answered and said, *M*
Lk 10:25 up, and tempted him, saying, *M*
Lk 11:45 the lawyers, and said unto him, *M*
Lk 12:13 of the company said unto him, *M*
Lk 13:25 When once the *m* of the house is
Lk 14:21 Then the *m* of the house being
Lk 17:13 their voices, and said, Jesus, *M*
Lk 18:18 ruler asked him, saying, Good *M*
Lk 19:39 the multitude said unto him, *M*
Lk 20:21 And they asked him, saying, *M*
Lk 20:28 Saying, *M*, Moses wrote unto us,
Lk 20:39 of the scribes answering said, *M*
Lk 21:7 And they asked him, saying, *M*
Lk 22:11 The *M* saith unto thee, Where is
Jn 1:38 is to say, being interpreted, *M*
Jn 3:10 unto him, Art thou a *m* of Israel
Jn 4:31 disciples prayed him, saying, *M*
Jn 8:4 They say unto him, *M*, this woman
Jn 9:2 disciples asked him, saying, *M*
Jn 11:8 His disciples say unto him, *M*
Jn 11:28 The *M* is come, and calleth for
Jn 13:13 Ye call me *M* and Lord
Jn 13:14 If I then, your Lord and *M*
Jn 20:16 which is to say, *M*
Acts 27:11 the centurion believed the *m*
Rom 14:4 to his own *m* he standeth or
Eph 6:9 that your *M* also is in heaven
Col 4:1 that ye also have a *M* in heaven

**MASTER'S**
Gen 24:27 me to the house of my *m* brethren
Gen 24:36 Sarah my *m* wife bare a son to my
Gen 24:44 hath appointed out for my *m* son
Gen 24:48 me in the right way to take my *m*
Gen 24:51 and let her be thy *m* son's wife
Gen 39:7 that his *m* wife cast her eyes
Gen 39:8 refused, and said unto his *m* wife
Ex 21:4 and her children shall be her *m*
1Sa 29:10 thy *m* servants that are come with
2Sa 9:9 I have given unto thy *m* son all
2Sa 9:10 that thy *m* son may have food to
2Sa 9:10 but Mephibosheth thy *m* son shall
2Sa 12:8 And I gave thee thy *m* house
2Sa 12:8 thy *m* wives into thy bosom, and
2Sa 16:3 king said, And where is thy *m* son
2Kin 6:32 sound of his *m* feet behind him
2Kin 10:2 seeing your *m* sons are with you,
2Kin 10:3 best and meetest of your *m* sons
2Kin 10:3 throne, and fight for your *m* house
2Kin 10:6 the heads of the men your *m* sons
2Kin 18:24 of the least of my *m* servants
Is 1:3 his owner, and the ass his *m* crib
Is 36:9 of the least of my *m* servants
2Ti 2:21 sanctified, and meet for the *m* use

**MASTERS**
Ps 123:2 look unto the hand of their *m*
Prov 25:13 he refresheth the soul of his *m*
Eccl 12:11 fastened by the *m* of assemblies
Jer 27:4 command them to say unto their *m*
Jer 27:4 Thus shall ye say unto your *m*
Amos 4:1 the needy, which say to their *m*
Mt 6:24 No man can serve two *m*
Mt 23:10 Neither be ye called *m*
Lk 16:13 No servant can serve two *m*
Acts 16:16 which brought her *m* much gain by
Acts 16:19 when her *m* saw that the hope of
Eph 6:5 are your *m* according to the flesh
Eph 6:9 And, ye *m*, do the same things unto
Col 3:22 your *m* according to the flesh
Col 4:1 *M*, give unto your servants that
1Ti 6:1 their own *m* worthy of all honour
1Ti 6:2 And they that have believing *m*
Titus 2:9 to be obedient unto their own *m*
Jas 3:1 My brethren, be not many *m*
1Pet 2:18 subject to your *m* with all fear

**MATHUSALA** *(ma-thu'-sa-lah)* See METHUSALAH. *Son of Enoch; ancestor of Jesus.*
Lk 3:37 Which was the son of *M*, which was

**MATRED** *(ma'-tred) Mother of Mehetabel.*
Gen 36:39 was Mehetabel, the daughter of *M*
1Chr 1:50 was Mehetabel, the daughter of *M*

**MATRI** *(ma'-tri) An ancestoral family of King Saul.*
1Sa 10:21 the family of *M* was taken

**MATRIX**
Ex 13:12 the LORD all that openeth the *m*
Ex 13:15 the LORD all that openeth the *m*
Ex 34:19 All that openeth the *m* is mine
Num 3:12 *m* among the children of Israel
Num 18:15 that openeth the *m* in all flesh

**MATTAN** *(mat'-tan)*
*1. A priest of Baal.*
2Kin 11:18 slew *M* the priest of Baal before
2Chr 23:17 slew *M* the priest of Baal before
*2. Father of Shephatiah.*
Jer 38:1 Then Shephatiah the son of *M*

**MATTANAH** *(mat'-ta-nah) An encampment of Israel in the wilderness.*
Num 21:18 the wilderness they went to *M*
Num 21:19 And from *M* to Nahaliel

**MATTANIAH** *(mat-ta-ni'-ah)* See ZEDEKIAH.
*1. Same as Zedekiah, king of Judah.*
2Kin 24:17 the king of Babylon made *M* his
*2. A family of exiles.*
1Chr 9:15 *M* the son of Micah, the son of
2Chr 20:14 the son of Jeiel, the son of *M*
Neh 11:17 *M* the son of Micha, the son of
Neh 11:22 son of Hashabiah, the son of *M*
Neh 12:8 Kadmiel, Sherebiah, Judah, and *M*
Neh 12:25 *M*, and Bakbukiah, Obadiah,
Neh 12:35 the son of Shemaiah, the son of *M*
*3. A sanctuary servant.*
1Chr 25:4 Bukkiah, *M*, Uzziel, Shebuel, and
1Chr 25:16 The ninth to *M*, he, his sons, and
*4. A descendant of Asaph.*
2Chr 29:13 Zechariah, and *M*
*5. A descendant of Elam.*
Ezr 10:26 *M*, Zechariah, and Jehiel, and Abdi,
*6. A descendant of Zattu.*
Ezr 10:27 Elioenai, Eliashib, *M*, and
*7. A descendant of Pahath-Moab.*
Ezr 10:30 and Chelal, Benaiah, Maaseiah, *M*
*8. A descendant of Bani.*
Ezr 10:37 *M*, Mattenai, and Jaasau,
*9. Father of Zaccur.*
Neh 13:13 the son of Zaccur, the son of *M*

**MATTATHA** *(mat'-ta-thah)* See MATTATHAH. *A son of Nathan; ancestor of Jesus.*
Lk 3:31 of Menan, which was the son of *M*

**MATTATHAH** *(mat'-ta-thah)* See MATTATHA. *Married a foreigner in exile.*
Ezr 10:33 Mattenai, *M*, Zabad, Eliphelet,

**MATTATHIAS** *(mat-ta-thi'-as)* See MATTITHIAH.
*1. A son of Amos; ancestor of Jesus.*
Lk 3:25 Which was the son of *M*, which was
*2. A son of Semei; ancestor of Jesus.*
Lk 3:26 of Maath, which was the son of *M*

**MATTATTAH** See MATTATHAH.

**MATTENAI** *(mat'-te-nahee)*
*1. A descendant of Hashum.*
Ezr 10:33 *M*, Mattathah, Zabad, Eliphelet,
*2. A descendant of Bani.*
Ezr 10:37 Mattaniah, *M*, and Jaasau,
*3. A priest.*
Neh 12:19 And of Joiarib, *M*

**MATTHAN** *(mat'-than) Son of Eleazar; ancestor of Jesus.*
Mt 1:15 and Eleazar begat *M*
Mt 1:15 and *M* begat Jacob

**MATTHAT** *(mat'-that)*
*1. Son of Levi; an ancestor of Jesus.*
Lk 3:24 Which was the son of *M*, which was
*2. Father of Jorim; an ancestor of Jesus.*
Lk 3:29 of Jorim, which was the son of *M*

**MATTHEW** *(math'-ew)* See LEVI. *A disciple of Jesus.*
Mt 9:9 thence, he saw a man, named *M*
Mt 10:3 Thomas, and *M* the publican
Mk 3:18 and Philip, and Bartholomew, and *M*
Lk 6:15 *M* and Thomas, James the son of
Acts 1:13 and Thomas, Bartholomew, and *M*

**MATTHIAS** *(mat'-thias) Successor to Judas Iscariot as apostle.*
Acts 1:23 who was surnamed Justus, and *M*
Acts 1:26 and the lot fell upon *M*

**MATTITHIAH** *(mat-tith-i'-ah)* See MATTATHIAS.
*1. A son of Shallum.*
1Chr 9:31 And *M*, one of the Levites, who was
*2. A Levite gatekeeper.*
1Chr 15:18 and Benaiah, and Maaseiah, and *M*
1Chr 15:21 And *M*, and Elipheleh, and Mikneiah,
1Chr 16:5 and Shemiramoth, and Jehiel, and *M*
*3. Son of Jeduthun.*
1Chr 25:3 and Jeshaiah, Hashabiah, and *M*
1Chr 25:21 The fourteenth to *M*, he, his sons
*4. Married a foreigner in exile.*
Ezr 10:43 Jeiel, *M*, Zabad, Zebina, Jadau,
*5. A priest who aided Ezra.*
Neh 8:4 and beside him stood *M*, and Shema,

**MAZZAROTH** *(maz'-za-roth) The twelve signs of the Zodiac.*
Job 38:32 thou bring forth *M* in his season

**MEAH** *(me'-ah) A tower on Jerusalem's wall.*
Neh 3:1 the tower of *M* they sanctified it
Neh 12:39 of Hananeel, and the tower of *M*

**MEAL**
Gen 18:6 three measures of fine *m*
Num 5:15 part of an ephah of barley *m*
1Kin 4:22 and threescore measures of *m*
1Kin 17:12 but an handful of *m* in a barrel
1Kin 17:14 The barrel of *m* shall not waste,
1Kin 17:16 And the barrel of *m* wasted not
2Kin 4:41 But he said, Then bring *m*
1Chr 12:40 on mules, and on oxen, and meat, *m*
Is 47:2 Take the millstones, and grind *m*
Hos 8:7 the bud shall yield no *m*
Mt 13:33 and hid in three measures of *m*
Lk 13:21 and hid in three measures of *m*

**MEAN**
Gen 21:29 What *m* these seven ewe lambs
Ex 12:26 What *m* ye by this service

Deut 6:20 What *m* the testimonies, and the
Josh 4:6 What *m* ye by these stones
Josh 4:21 come, saying, What *m* these stones
1Kin 18:45 came to pass in the *m* while
Prov 22:29 he shall not stand before *m* men
Is 2:9 the *m* man boweth down, and the
Is 3:15 What *m* ye that ye beat my people
Is 5:15 the *m* man shall be brought down,
Is 31:8 and the sword, not of a *m* man
Eze 17:12 Know ye not what these things *m*
Eze 18:2 What *m* ye, that ye use this
Mk 9:10 the rising from the dead should *m*
Lk 12:1 In the *m* time, when there were
Jn 4:31 In the *m* while his disciples
Acts 10:17 vision which he had seen should *m*
Acts 17:20 what these things *m*
Acts 21:13 What *m* ye to weep and to break
Acts 21:39 Cilicia, a citizen of no *m* city
Rom 2:15 their thoughts the *m* while
2Cor 8:13 For I *m* not that other men be

## MEANEST

Gen 33:8 What *m* thou by all this drove
2Sa 16:2 unto Ziba, What *m* thou by these
Eze 37:18 not shew us what thou *m* by these
Jonah 1:6 and said unto him, What *m* thou

## MEANETH

Deut 29:24 what *m* the heat of this great
1Sa 4:6 What *m* the noise of this great
1Sa 4:14 What *m* the noise of this tumult
1Sa 15:14 What *m* then this bleating of the
Is 10:7 Howbeit he *m* not so, neither doth
Mt 9:13 But go ye and learn what that *m*
Mt 12:7 But if ye had known what this *m*
Acts 2:12 one to another, What *m* this

## MEANS

Ex 34:7 that will by no *m* clear the
Num 14:18 by no *m* clearing the guilty,
Judg 5:22 broken by the *m* of the pransings
Judg 16:5 by what *m* we may prevail against
2Sa 14:14 yet doth he devise *m*, that his
1Kin 10:29 they bring them out by their *m*
1Kin 20:39 if by any *m* he be missing, then
2Chr 1:17 the kings of Syria, by their *m*
Ezr 4:16 by this *m* thou shalt have no
Ps 49:7 can by any *m* redeem his brother
Prov 6:26 For by *m* of a whorish woman a man
Jer 5:31 the priests bear rule by their *m*
Mal 1:9 this hath been by your *m*
Mt 5:26 shalt by no *m* come out thence
Lk 5:18 they sought *m* to bring him in, and
Lk 8:36 *m* he that was possessed of the
Lk 10:19 nothing shall by any *m* hurt you
Jn 9:21 But by what *m* he now seeth, we
Acts 4:9 by what *m* he is made whole
Acts 18:21 I must by all *m* keep this feast
Acts 27:12 if by any *m* they might attain to
Rom 1:10 if by any *m* now at length I might
Rom 11:14 If by any *m* I may provoke to
1Cor 8:9 But take heed lest by any *m* this
1Cor 9:22 that I might by all *m* save some
1Cor 9:27 lest that by any *m*, when I have
2Cor 1:11 gift bestowed upon us by the *m* of
2Cor 11:3 But I fear, lest by any *m*
Gal 2:2 lest by any *m* I should run, or
Phil 3:11 If by any *m* I might attain unto
1Th 3:5 lest by some *m* the tempter have
2Th 2:3 Let no man deceive you by any *m*
2Th 3:16 give you peace always by all *m*
Heb 9:15 that by *m* of death, for the
Rev 13:14 *m* of those miracles which he had

## MEARAH *(me'-a-rah) A place near Sidon.*

Josh 13:4 *M* that is beside the Sidonians,

## MEASURE

Ex 26:2 of the curtains shall have one *m*
Ex 26:8 curtains shall be all of one *m*
Lev 19:35 in meteyard, in weight, or in *m*
Num 35:5 ye shall *m* from without the city
Deut 21:2 they shall *m* unto the cities
Deut 25:15 perfect and just *m* shalt thou have
Josh 3:4 about two thousand cubits by *m*
1Kin 6:25 both the cherubims were of one *m*
1Kin 7:37 of them had one casting, one *m*
2Kin 7:1 a *m* of fine flour be sold for a
2Kin 7:16 So a *m* of fine flour was sold for
2Kin 7:18 a *m* of fine flour for a shekel,
1Chr 23:29 is fried, and for all manner of *m*
2Chr 3:3 the first *m* was threescore cubits
Job 11:9 The *m* thereof is longer than the
Job 28:25 and he weigheth the waters by *m*
Ps 39:4 the *m* of my days, what it is
Ps 80:5 them tears to drink in great *m*
Is 5:14 and opened her mouth without *m*
Is 27:8 In *m*, when it shooteth forth,
Is 40:12 the dust of the earth in a *m*
Is 65:7 therefore will I *m* their former
Jer 30:11 but I will correct thee in *m*
Jer 46:28 of thee, but correct thee in *m*
Jer 51:13 the *m* of thy covetousness
Eze 4:11 Thou shalt drink also water by *m*
Eze 4:16 and they shall drink water by *m*
Eze 40:10 they three were of one *m*
Eze 40:10 the posts had one *m* on this side
Eze 40:21 after the *m* of the first gate
Eze 40:22 were after the *m* of the gate that
Eze 41:17 about within and without, by *m*
Eze 43:10 and let them *m* the pattern
Eze 45:3 of this *m* shalt thou
Eze 45:3 shalt thou *m* the length of five
Eze 45:11 and the bath shall be of one *m*
Eze 45:11 the *m* thereof shall be after the
Eze 46:22 these four corners were of one *m*
Eze 47:18 east side ye shall *m* from Hauran
Mic 6:10 the scant *m* that is abominable
Zec 2:2 To *m* Jerusalem, to see what is
Mt 7:2 and with what *m* ye mete, it shall
Mt 23:32 ye up then the *m* of your fathers
Mk 4:24 with what *m* ye mete, it shall be
Mk 6:51 amazed in themselves beyond *m*
Mk 7:37 And were beyond *m* astonished
Mk 10:26 And they were astonished out of *m*
Lk 6:38 good *m*, pressed down, and shaken
Lk 6:38 For with the same *m* that ye mete
Jn 3:34 not the Spirit by *m* unto him
Rom 12:3 dealt to every man the *m* of faith
2Cor 1:8 that we were pressed out of *m*
2Cor 10:13 not boast of things without our *m*
2Cor 10:13 but according to the *m* of the
2Cor 10:13 a *m* to reach even unto you
2Cor 10:14 not ourselves beyond our *m*
2Cor 10:15 boasting of things without our *m*
2Cor 11:23 more abundant, in stripes above *m*
2Cor 12:7 *m* through the abundance of the
2Cor 12:7 lest I should be exalted above *m*
Gal 1:13 how that beyond *m* I persecuted
Eph 4:7 to the *m* of the gift of Christ
Eph 4:13 unto the *m* of the stature of the
Eph 4:16 working in the *m* of every part
Rev 6:6 A *m* of wheat for a penny, and
Rev 11:1 *m* the temple of God, and the altar
Rev 11:2 the temple leave out, and *m* it not
Rev 21:15 had a golden reed to *m* the city
Rev 21:17 according to the *m* of a man

## MEASURED

Ruth 3:15 he *m* six measures of barley, and
2Sa 8:2 *m* them with a line, casting them
2Sa 8:2 two lines *m* he to put to death
Is 40:12 Who hath *m* the waters in the
Jer 31:37 If heaven above can be *m*, and the
Jer 33:22 neither the sand of the sea *m*
Eze 40:5 so he *m* the breadth of the
Eze 40:6 *m* the threshold of the gate,
Eze 40:8 He *m* also the porch of the gate
Eze 40:9 Then *m* he the porch of the gate,
Eze 40:11 he *m* the breadth of the entry of
Eze 40:13 He *m* then the gate from the roof
Eze 40:19 Then he *m* the breadth from the
Eze 40:20 he *m* the length thereof, and the
Eze 40:23 he *m* from gate to gate an hundred
Eze 40:24 he *m* the posts thereof and the
Eze 40:27 he *m* from gate to gate toward the
Eze 40:28 he *m* the south gate according to
Eze 40:32 he *m* the gate according to these
Eze 40:35 *m* it according to these measures
Eze 40:47 So he *m* the court, an hundred
Eze 40:48 *m* each post of the porch, five
Eze 41:1 *m* the posts, six cubits broad on
Eze 41:2 he *m* the length thereof, forty
Eze 41:3 *m* the post of the door, two
Eze 41:4 So he *m* the length thereof,
Eze 41:5 After he *m* the wall of the house,
Eze 41:13 So he *m* the house, an hundred
Eze 41:15 he *m* the length of the building
Eze 42:15 the east, and *m* it round about
Eze 42:16 He *m* the east side with the
Eze 42:17 He *m* the north side, five hundred
Eze 42:18 He *m* the south side, five hundred
Eze 42:19 *m* five hundred reeds with the
Eze 42:20 He *m* it by the four sides
Eze 47:3 he *m* a thousand cubits, and he
Eze 47:4 Again he *m* a thousand, and brought
Eze 47:4 Again he *m* a thousand, and brought
Eze 47:5 Afterward he *m* a thousand
Hos 1:10 which cannot be *m* nor numbered
Hab 3:6 He stood, and *m* the earth
Mt 7:2 it shall be *m* to you again
Mk 4:24 ye mete, it shall be *m* to you
Lk 6:38 withal it shall be *m* to you again
Rev 21:16 he *m* the city with the reed,
Rev 21:17 he *m* the wall thereof, an hundred

## MEASURES

Gen 18:6 quickly three *m* of fine meal
Deut 25:14 not have in thine house divers *m*
Ruth 3:15 it, he measured six *m* of barley
Ruth 3:17 These six *m* of barley gave he me
1Sa 25:18 five *m* of parched corn, and an
1Kin 4:22 day was thirty *m* of fine flour
1Kin 4:22 and threescore *m* of meal
1Kin 5:11 *m* of wheat for food to his
1Kin 5:11 and twenty *m* of pure oil
1Kin 7:9 to the *m* of hewed stones, sawed
1Kin 7:11 after the *m* of hewed stones, and
1Kin 18:32 as would contain two *m* of seed
2Kin 7:1 two *m* of barley for a shekel, in
2Kin 7:16 two *m* of barley for a shekel,
2Kin 7:18 Two *m* of barley for a shekel, and
2Chr 2:10 twenty thousand *m* of beaten wheat
2Chr 2:10 and twenty thousand *m* of barley
2Chr 27:5 and ten thousand *m* of wheat
Ezr 7:22 and to an hundred *m* of wheat
Job 38:5 Who hath laid the *m* thereof
Prov 20:10 Divers weights, and divers *m*
Jer 13:25 lot, the portion of thy *m* from me
Eze 40:24 thereof according to these *m*
Eze 40:28 south gate according to these *m*
Eze 40:29 thereof, according to these *m*
Eze 40:32 the gate according to these *m*
Eze 40:33 were according to these *m*
Eze 40:35 measured it according to these *m*
Eze 43:13 these are the *m* of the altar
Eze 48:16 And these shall be the *m* thereof
Eze 48:30 four thousand and five hundred *m*
Eze 48:33 four thousand and five hundred *m*
Eze 48:35 round about eighteen thousand *m*
Hag 2:16 one came to an heap of twenty *m*
Mt 13:33 took, and hid in three *m* of meal
Lk 13:21 took and hid in three *m* of meal
Lk 16:6 And he said, An hundred *m* of oil
Lk 16:7 And he said, An hundred *m* of wheat
Rev 6:6 three *m* of barley for a penny

## MEASURING

Jer 31:39 the *m* line shall yet go forth
Eze 40:3 of flax in his hand, and a *m* reed
Eze 40:5 in the man's hand a *m* reed of six
Eze 42:15 made an end of *m* the inner house
Eze 42:16 the east side with the *m* reed
Eze 42:16 with the *m* reed round about
Eze 42:17 with the *m* reed round about
Eze 42:18 hundred reeds, with the *m* reed
Eze 42:19 hundred reeds with the *m* reed
Zec 2:1 a man with a *m* line in his hand
2Cor 10:12 but they *m* themselves by

## MEAT

Gen 1:29 to you it shall be for *m*
Gen 1:30 have given every green herb for *m*
Gen 9:3 that liveth shall be *m* for you
Gen 24:33 there was set *m* before him to eat
Gen 27:4 And make me savoury *m*, such as I
Gen 27:7 me venison, and make me savoury *m*
Gen 27:9 them savoury *m* for thy father
Gen 27:14 and his mother made savoury *m*
Gen 27:17 And she gave the savoury *m*
Gen 27:31 And he also had made savoury *m*
Gen 45:23 *m* for his father by the way
Ex 29:41 to the *m* offering of the morning
Ex 30:9 burnt sacrifice, nor *m* offering
Ex 40:29 burnt offering and the *m* offering
Lev 2:1 when any will offer a *m* offering
Lev 2:3 the remnant of the *m* offerings
Lev 2:4 of a *m* offering baken in the oven
Lev 2:5 if thy oblation be a *m* offering
Lev 2:6 it is a *m* offering
Lev 2:7 if thy oblation be a *m* offering
Lev 2:8 thou shalt bring the *m* offering
Lev 2:9 the *m* offering a memorial thereof
Lev 2:10 the *m* offering shall be Aaron's
Lev 2:11 No *m* offering, which ye shall

Lev 2:13 every oblation of thy *m* offering
Lev 2:13 to be lacking from thy *m* offering
Lev 2:14 if thou offer a *m* offering of thy
Lev 2:14 thou shalt offer for the *m*
Lev 2:15 it is a *m* offering
Lev 5:13 be the priest's, as a *m* offering
Lev 6:14 this is the law of the *m* offering
Lev 6:15 of the flour of the *m* offering
Lev 6:15 which is upon the *m* offering
Lev 6:20 flour for a *m* offering perpetual
Lev 6:21 the baken pieces of the *m*
Lev 6:23 For every *m* offering for the
Lev 7:9 all the *m* offering that is baken
Lev 7:10 every *m* offering, mingled with
Lev 7:37 of the *m* offering, and of the sin
Lev 9:4 a *m* offering mingled with oil
Lev 9:17 And he brought the *m* offering
Lev 10:12 left, Take the *m* offering that
Lev 11:34 Of all *m* which may be eaten, that
Lev 14:10 of fine flour for a *m* offering
Lev 14:20 the *m* offering upon the altar
Lev 14:21 mingled with oil for a *m* offering
Lev 14:31 offering, with the *m* offering
Lev 22:11 they shall eat of his *m*
Lev 22:13 she shall eat of her father's *m*
Lev 23:13 the *m* offering thereof shall be
Lev 23:16 ye shall offer a new *m* offering
Lev 23:18 the LORD, with their *m* offering
Lev 23:37 a *m* offering, a sacrifice, and
Lev 25:6 of the land shall be *m* for you
Lev 25:7 all the increase thereof be *m*
Num 4:16 incense, and the daily *m* offering
Num 6:15 their *m* offering, and their drink
Num 6:17 shall offer also his *m* offering
Num 7:13 mingled with oil for a *m* offering
Num 7:19 mingled with oil for a *m* offering
Num 7:25 mingled with oil for a *m* offering
Num 7:31 mingled with oil for a *m* offering
Num 7:37 mingled with oil for a *m* offering
Num 7:43 mingled with oil for a *m* offering
Num 7:49 mingled with oil for a *m* offering
Num 7:55 mingled with oil for a *m* offering
Num 7:61 mingled with oil for a *m* offering
Num 7:67 mingled with oil for a *m* offering
Num 7:73 mingled with oil for a *m* offering
Num 7:79 mingled with oil for a *m* offering
Num 7:87 twelve, with their *m* offering
Num 8:8 young bullock with his *m* offering
Num 15:4 a *m* offering of a tenth deal of
Num 15:6 thou shalt prepare for a *m*
Num 15:9 a *m* offering of three tenth deals
Num 15:24 the LORD, with his *m* offering
Num 18:9 every *m* offering of theirs, and
Num 28:5 ephah of flour for a *m* offering
Num 28:8 as the *m* offering of the morning,
Num 28:9 deals of flour for a *m* offering
Num 28:12 deals of flour for a *m* offering
Num 28:12 deals of flour for a *m* offering
Num 28:13 for a *m* offering unto one lamb
Num 28:20 their *m* offering shall be of
Num 28:24 the *m* of the sacrifice made by
Num 28:26 when ye bring a new *m* offering
Num 28:28 their *m* offering of flour mingled
Num 28:31 his *m* offering, (they shall be
Num 29:3 their *m* offering shall be of
Num 29:6 his *m* offering, and the daily
Num 29:6 his *m* offering, and their drink
Num 29:9 their *m* offering shall be of
Num 29:11 the *m* offering of it, and their
Num 29:14 their *m* offering shall be of
Num 29:16 his *m* offering, and his drink
Num 29:18 their *m* offering and their drink
Num 29:19 the *m* offering thereof, and their
Num 29:21 their *m* offering and their drink
Num 29:22 his *m* offering, and his drink
Num 29:24 Their *m* offering and their drink
Num 29:25 his *m* offering, and his drink
Num 29:27 their *m* offering and their drink
Num 29:28 his *m* offering, and his drink
Num 29:30 their *m* offering and their drink
Num 29:31 his *m* offering, and his drink
Num 29:33 their *m* offering and their drink
Num 29:34 his *m* offering, and his drink
Num 29:37 Their *m* offering and their drink
Num 29:38 his *m* offering, and his drink
Num 29:39 for your *m* offerings, and for your
Deut 2:6 Ye shall buy *m* of them for money,
Deut 2:28 Thou shalt sell me *m* for money
Deut 20:20 that they be not trees for *m*
Deut 28:26 thy carcase shall be *m* unto all
Josh 22:23 burnt offering or *m* offering
Josh 22:29 for *m* offerings, or for
Judg 1:7 gathered their *m* under my table
Judg 13:19 took a kid with a *m* offering
Judg 13:23 a *m* offering at our hands,
Judg 14:14 Out of the eater came forth *m*
1Sa 20:5 fail to sit with the king at *m*
1Sa 20:24 the king sat him down to eat *m*
1Sa 20:27 cometh not the son of Jesse to *m*
1Sa 20:34 did eat no *m* the second day of
2Sa 3:35 to eat *m* while it was yet day
2Sa 11:8 him a mess of *m* from the king
2Sa 12:3 it did eat of his own *m*, and drank
2Sa 13:5 sister Tamar come, and give me *m*
2Sa 13:5 dress the *m* in my sight, that I
2Sa 13:7 Amnon's house, and dress him *m*
2Sa 13:10 Bring the *m* into the chamber,
1Kin 8:64 *m* offerings, and the fat of the
1Kin 8:64 *m* offerings, and the fat of the
1Kin 10:5 the *m* of his table, and the
1Kin 19:8 the strength of that *m* forty days
2Kin 3:20 when the *m* offering was offered,
2Kin 16:13 his *m* offering, and poured his
2Kin 16:15 and the evening *m* offering
2Kin 16:15 his *m* offering, with the burnt
2Kin 16:15 their *m* offering, and their drink
1Chr 12:40 and on mules, and on oxen, and *m*
1Chr 21:23 and the wheat for the *m* offering
1Chr 23:29 for the fine flour for *m* offering
2Chr 7:7 the *m* offerings, and the fat
2Chr 9:4 the *m* of his table, and the
Ezr 3:7 and *m*, and drink, and oil, unto them
Ezr 7:17 lambs, with their *m* offerings
Neh 10:33 and for the continual *m* offering
Neh 13:5 they laid the *m* offerings
Neh 13:9 house of God, with the *m* offering
Job 6:7 to touch are as my sorrowful *m*
Job 12:11 and the mouth taste his *m*
Job 20:14 Yet his *m* in his bowels is turned
Job 20:21 There shall none of his *m* be left
Job 30:4 and juniper roots for their *m*
Job 33:20 bread, and his soul dainty *m*
Job 34:3 words, as the mouth tasteth *m*
Job 36:31 he giveth *m* in abundance
Job 38:41 God, they wander for lack of *m*
Ps 42:3 My tears have been my *m* day
Ps 44:11 us like sheep appointed for *m*
Ps 59:15 Let them wander up and down for *m*
Ps 69:21 They gave me also gall for my *m*
Ps 74:14 gavest him to be *m* to the people
Ps 78:18 heart by asking *m* for their lust
Ps 78:25 he sent them *m* to the full
Ps 78:30 but while their *m* was yet in
Ps 79:2 be *m* unto the fowls of the heaven
Ps 104:21 prey, and seek their *m* from God
Ps 104:27 give them their *m* in due season
Ps 107:18 soul abhorreth all manner of *m*
Ps 111:5 He hath given *m* unto them that
Ps 145:15 givest them their *m* in due season
Prov 6:8 Provideth her *m* in the summer
Prov 23:3 for they are deceitful *m*
Prov 30:22 a fool when he is filled with *m*
Prov 30:25 prepare their *m* in the summer
Prov 31:15 giveth *m* to her household, and a
Is 57:6 thou hast offered a *m* offering
Is 62:8 corn to be *m* for thine enemies
Is 65:25 and dust shall be the serpent's *m*
Jer 7:33 of this people shall be *m* for the
Jer 16:4 be *m* for the fowls of heaven
Jer 17:26 *m* offerings, and incense, and
Jer 19:7 carcases will I give to be *m* for
Jer 33:18 and to kindle *m* offerings
Jer 34:20 *m* unto the fowls of the heaven
Lam 1:11 things for *m* to relieve the soul
Lam 1:19 their *m* to relieve their souls
Lam 4:10 they were their *m* in the
Eze 4:10 thy *m* which thou shalt eat shall
Eze 16:19 My *m* also which I gave thee, fine
Eze 29:5 I have given thee for *m* to the
Eze 34:5 they became *m* to all the beasts
Eze 34:8 my flock became *m* to every beast
Eze 34:10 that they may not be *m* for them
Eze 42:13 the *m* offering, and the sin
Eze 44:29 They shall eat the *m* offering
Eze 45:15 for a *m* offering, and for a burnt
Eze 45:17 *m* offerings, and drink offerings,
Eze 45:17 the *m* offering, and the burnt
Eze 45:24 he shall prepare a *m* offering of
Eze 45:25 and according to the *m* offering
Eze 46:5 the *m* offering shall be an ephah
Eze 46:5 the *m* offering for the lambs as
Eze 46:7 And he shall prepare a *m* offering
Eze 46:11 in the solemnities the *m* offering
Eze 46:14 thou shalt prepare a *m* offering
Eze 46:14 a *m* offering continually by a
Eze 46:15 the *m* offering, and the oil, every
Eze 46:20 they shall bake the *m* offering
Eze 47:12 side, shall grow all trees for *m*
Eze 47:12 the fruit thereof shall be for *m*
Dan 1:5 a daily provision of the king's *m*
Dan 1:8 with the portion of the king's *m*
Dan 1:10 king, who hath appointed your *m*
Dan 1:13 of the portion of the king's *m*
Dan 1:15 eat the portion of the king's *m*
Dan 1:16 took away the portion of their *m*
Dan 4:12 much, and in it was *m* for all
Dan 4:21 much, and in it was *m* for all
Dan 11:26 of his *m* shall destroy him
Hos 11:4 their jaws, and I laid *m* unto them
Joel 1:9 The *m* offering and the drink
Joel 1:13 for the *m* offering and the drink
Joel 1:16 Is not the *m* cut off before our
Joel 2:14 even a *m* offering and a drink
Amos 5:22 your *m* offerings, I will not
Hab 1:16 is fat, and their *m* plenteous
Hab 3:17 and the fields shall yield no *m*
Hag 2:12 or wine, or oil, or any *m*
Mal 1:12 and the fruit thereof, even his *m*
Mal 3:10 that there may be *m* in mine house
Mt 3:4 his *m* was locusts and wild honey
Mt 6:25 Is not the life more than *m*
Mt 9:10 as Jesus sat at *m* in the house
Mt 10:10 the workman is worthy of his *m*
Mt 14:9 and them which sat with him at *m*
Mt 15:37 they took up of the broken *m* that
Mt 24:45 to give them *m* in due season
Mt 25:35 I was an hungred, and ye gave me *m*
Mt 25:42 an hungred, and ye gave me no *m*
Mt 26:7 it on his head, as he sat at *m*
Mk 2:15 as Jesus sat at *m* in his house
Mk 8:8 they took up of the broken *m* that
Mk 14:3 Simon the leper, as he sat at *m*
Mk 16:14 unto the eleven as they sat at *m*
Lk 3:11 and he that hath *m*, let him do
Lk 7:36 house, and sat down to *m*
Lk 7:37 sat at *m* in the Pharisee's house
Lk 7:49 they that sat at *m* with him began
Lk 8:55 and he commanded to give her *m*
Lk 9:13 buy *m* for all this people
Lk 11:37 and he went in, and sat down to *m*
Lk 12:23 The life is more than *m*, and the
Lk 12:37 and make them to sit down to *m*
Lk 12:42 their portion of *m* in due season
Lk 14:10 of them that sit at *m* with thee
Lk 14:15 at *m* with him heard these things
Lk 17:7 the field, Go and sit down to *m*
Lk 22:27 is greater, he that sitteth at *m*
Lk 22:27 is not he that sitteth at *m*
Lk 24:30 to pass, as he sat at *m* with them
Lk 24:41 unto them, Have ye here any *m*
Jn 4:8 gone away unto the city to buy *m*
Jn 4:32 I have *m* to eat that ye know not
Jn 4:34 My *m* is to do the will of him
Jn 6:27 not for the *m* which perisheth
Jn 6:27 but for that *m* which endureth
Jn 6:55 For my flesh is *m* indeed, and my
Jn 21:5 them, Children, have ye any *m*
Acts 2:46 did eat their *m* with gladness
Acts 9:19 And when he had received *m*
Acts 16:34 he set *m* before them, and rejoiced
Acts 27:33 Paul besought them all to take *m*
Acts 27:34 I pray you to take some *m*
Acts 27:36 cheer, and they also took some *m*
Rom 14:15 thy brother be grieved with thy *m*
Rom 14:15 Destroy not him with thy *m*
Rom 14:17 For the kingdom of God is not *m*
Rom 14:20 For *m* destroy not the work of God
1Cor 3:2 fed you with milk, and not with *m*
1Cor 8:8 But *m* commendeth us not to God
1Cor 8:10 sit at *m* in the idol's temple
1Cor 8:13 if *m* make my brother to offend, I
1Cor 10:3 did all eat the same spiritual *m*
Col 2:16 no man therefore judge you in *m*
Heb 5:12 need of milk, and not of strong *m*
Heb 5:14 But strong *m* belongeth to them
Heb 12:16 morsel of *m* sold his birthright

**MEATS**

Prov 23:6 neither desire thou his dainty *m*
Mk 7:19 into the draught, purging all *m*

Acts 15:29 abstain from *m* offered to idols
1Cor 6:13 *M* for the belly, and the belly for
1Cor 6:13 for the belly, and the belly for *m*
1Ti 4:3 and commanding to abstain from *m*
Heb 9:10 Which stood only in *m* and drinks,
Heb 13:9 not with *m*, which have not

**MEBUNNAI** *(me-bun'-nahee)* See SIBBECHAI. *A "mighty man" of David.*
2Sa 23:27 Anethothite, *M* the Hushathite,

**MECHERATHITE** *(me-ker'-ath-ite) A family name of a "mighty man" of David.*
1Chr 11:36 Hepher the *M*, Ahijah the Pelonite

**MEDAD** *(me'-dad) An elder of Israel.*
Num 11:26 Eldad, and the name of the other *M*
Num 11:27 *M* do prophesy in the camp

**MEDAN** *(me'-dan) A son of Abraham.*
Gen 25:2 bare him Zimran, and Jokshan, and *M*
1Chr 1:32 she bare Zimran, and Jokshan, and *M*

**MEDDLE**
Deut 2:5 *M* not with them
Deut 2:19 them not, nor *m* with them
2Kin 14:10 why shouldest thou *m* to thy hurt
2Chr 25:19 shouldest thou *m* to thine hurt
Prov 20:19 therefore *m* not with him that
Prov 24:21 *m* not with them that are given to

**MEDE** *(meed)* See MEDES, MEDIAN. *An inhabitant of Media.*
Dan 11:1 in the first year of Darius the *M*

**MEDEBA** *(med'-e-bah) A city in Reuben.*
Num 21:30 Nophah, which reacheth unto *M*
Josh 13:9 and all the plain of *M* unto Dibon
Josh 13:16 the river, and all the plain by *M*
1Chr 19:7 who came and pitched before *M*
Is 15:2 shall howl over Nebo, and over *M*

**MEDES** *(meeds)*
2Kin 17:6 Gozan, and in the cities of the *M*
2Kin 18:11 Gozan, and in the cities of the *M*
Ezr 6:2 that is in the province of the *M*
Est 1:19 the laws of the Persians and the *M*
Is 13:17 I will stir up the *M* against them
Jer 25:25 Elam, and all the kings of the *M*
Jer 51:11 the spirit of the kings of the *M*
Jer 51:28 nations with the kings of the *M*
Dan 5:28 is divided, and given to the *M*
Dan 6:8 according to the law of the *M*
Dan 6:12 according to the law of the *M*
Dan 6:15 O king, that the law of the *M*
Dan 9:1 Ahasuerus, of the seed of the *M*
Acts 2:9 Parthians, and *M*, and Elamites, and

**MEDIA** *(me'-de-ah)* See MADAI, MEDE, MEDIAN. *A country north of Persia.*
Est 1:3 the power of Persia and *M*, the
Est 1:14 the seven princes of Persia and *M*
Est 1:18 *M* say this day unto all the
Est 10:2 the chronicles of the kings of *M*
Is 21:2 besiege, O *M*
Dan 8:20 two horns are the kings of *M*

**MEDIAN** *(me'-de-an)* See MEDE. *A native of Media.*
Dan 5:31 Darius the *M* took the kingdom,

**MEDIATOR**
Gal 3:19 by angels in the hand of a *m*
Gal 3:20 Now a *m* is not a
Gal 3:20 is not a *m* of one
1Ti 2:5 one *m* between God and men, the man
Heb 8:6 he is the *m* of a better covenant
Heb 9:15 he is the *m* of the new testament
Heb 12:24 to Jesus the *m* of the new

**MEDITATE**
Gen 24:63 Isaac went out to *m* in the field
Josh 1:8 but thou shalt *m* therein day
Ps 1:2 and in his law doth he *m* day
Ps 63:6 *m* on thee in the night watches
Ps 77:12 I will *m* also of all thy work, and
Ps 119:15 I will *m* in thy precepts, and have
Ps 119:23 thy servant did *m* in thy statutes
Ps 119:48 and I will *m* in thy statutes
Ps 119:78 but I will *m* in thy precepts
Ps 119:148 that I might *m* in thy word
Ps 143:5 I *m* on all thy works
Is 33:18 Thine heart shall *m* terror
Lk 21:14 not to *m* before what ye shall
1Ti 4:15 *M* upon these things

**MEDITATION**
Ps 5:1 consider my *m*
Ps 19:14 the *m* of my heart, be acceptable
Ps 49:3 the *m* of my heart shall be of
Ps 104:34 My *m* of him shall be sweet
Ps 119:97 it is my *m* all the day
Ps 119:99 for thy testimonies are my *m*

**MEEK**
Num 12:3 (Now the man Moses was very *m*
Ps 22:26 The *m* shall eat and be satisfied
Ps 25:9 The *m* will he guide in judgment
Ps 25:9 the *m* will he teach his way
Ps 37:11 But the *m* shall inherit the earth
Ps 76:9 to save all the *m* of the earth
Ps 147:6 The LORD lifteth up the *m*
Ps 149:4 beautify the *m* with salvation
Is 11:4 equity for the *m* of the earth
Is 29:19 The *m* also shall increase their
Is 61:1 to preach good tidings unto the *m*
Amos 2:7 and turn aside the way of the *m*
Zeph 2:3 all ye *m* of the earth, which have
Mt 5:5 Blessed are the *m*
Mt 11:29 for I am *m* and lowly in heart
Mt 21:5 thy King cometh unto thee, *m*
1Pet 3:4 even the ornament of a *m*

**MEEKNESS**
Ps 45:4 because of truth and *m* and
Zeph 2:3 seek righteousness, seek *m*
1Cor 4:21 or in love, and in the spirit of *m*
2Cor 10:1 Paul myself beseech you by the *m*
Gal 5:23 *M*, temperance
Gal 6:1 such an one in the spirit of *m*
Eph 4:2 With all lowliness and *m*, with
Col 3:12 kindness, humbleness of mind, *m*
1Ti 6:11 faith, love, patience, *m*
2Ti 2:25 In *m* instructing those that
Titus 3:2 shewing all *m* unto all men
Jas 1:21 receive with *m* the engrafted word
Jas 3:13 his works with *m* of wisdom
1Pet 3:15 of the hope that is in you with *m*

**MEET**
Gen 2:18 I will make him an help *m* for him
Gen 2:20 was not found an help *m* for him
Gen 14:17 *m* him after his return from the
Gen 18:2 he ran to *m* them from the tent
Gen 19:1 Lot seeing them rose up to *m* them
Gen 24:17 And the servant ran to *m* her
Gen 24:65 that walketh in the field to *m* us
Gen 29:13 son, that he ran to *m* him
Gen 30:16 and Leah went out to *m* him
Gen 32:6 Esau, and also he cometh to *m* thee
Gen 33:4 Esau ran to *m* him, and embraced
Gen 46:29 went up to *m* Israel his father,
Ex 4:14 behold, he cometh forth to *m* thee
Ex 4:27 Go into the wilderness to *m* Moses
Ex 8:26 Moses said, It is not *m* so to do
Ex 18:7 went out to *m* his father in law
Ex 19:17 out of the camp to *m* with God
Ex 23:4 If thou *m* thine enemy's ox or his
Ex 25:22 And there I will *m* with thee
Ex 29:42 where I will *m* you, to speak
Ex 29:43 there I will *m* with the children
Ex 30:6 where I will *m* with thee
Ex 30:36 where I will *m* with thee
Num 17:4 where I will *m* with you
Num 22:36 he went out to *m* him unto a city
Num 23:3 the LORD will come to *m* me
Num 23:15 while I *m* the LORD yonder
Num 31:13 went forth to *m* them without the
Deut 3:18 all that are *m* for the war
Josh 2:16 mountain, lest the pursuers *m* you
Josh 9:11 for the journey, and go to *m* them
Judg 4:18 And Jael went out to *m* Sisera
Judg 4:22 Sisera, Jael came out to *m* him
Judg 5:30 *m* for the necks of them that take
Judg 6:35 and they came up to *m* them
Judg 11:31 of the doors of my house to *m* me
Judg 11:34 came out to *m* him with timbrels
Judg 19:3 saw him, he rejoiced to *m* him
Ruth 2:22 that they *m* thee not in any other
1Sa 10:3 there shall *m* thee three men
1Sa 10:5 that thou shalt *m* a company of
1Sa 13:10 and Saul went out to *m* him
1Sa 15:12 early to *m* Saul in the morning
1Sa 17:48 and came and drew nigh to *m* David
1Sa 17:48 the army to *m* the Philistine
1Sa 18:6 to *m* king Saul, with tabrets,
1Sa 25:32 which sent thee this day to *m* me
1Sa 25:34 thou hadst hasted and come to *m* me
1Sa 30:21 and they went forth to *m* David
1Sa 30:21 to *m* the people that were with
2Sa 6:20 of Saul came out to *m* David
2Sa 10:5 it unto David, he sent to *m* them
2Sa 15:32 came to *m* him with his coat rent
2Sa 19:15 to Gilgal, to go to *m* the king
2Sa 19:16 the men of Judah to *m* king David
2Sa 19:20 to go down to *m* my lord the king
2Sa 19:24 of Saul came down to *m* the king
2Sa 19:25 come to Jerusalem to *m* the king
1Kin 2:8 he came down to *m* me at Jordan
1Kin 2:19 And the king rose up to *m* her
1Kin 18:16 So Obadiah went to *m* Ahab
1Kin 18:16 and Ahab went to *m* Elijah
1Kin 21:18 go down to *m* Ahab king of Israel,
2Kin 1:3 go up to *m* the messengers of the
2Kin 1:6 him, There came a man up to *m* us
2Kin 1:7 man was he which came up to *m* you
2Kin 2:15 And they came to *m* him, and bowed
2Kin 4:26 to *m* her, and say unto her, Is it
2Kin 4:29 if thou *m* any man, salute him not
2Kin 4:31 Wherefore he went again to *m* him
2Kin 5:21 down from the chariot to *m* him
2Kin 5:26 again from his chariot to *m* thee
2Kin 8:8 *m* the man of God, and enquire of
2Kin 8:9 So Hazael went to *m* him, and took
2Kin 9:17 an horseman, and send to *m* them
2Kin 9:18 went one on horseback to *m* him
2Kin 10:15 the son of Rechab coming to *m* him
2Kin 16:10 king Ahaz went to Damascus to *m*
1Chr 12:17 And David went out to *m* them
1Chr 19:5 And he sent to *m* them
2Chr 15:2 And he went out to *m* Asa, and said
2Chr 19:2 Hanani the seer went out to *m* him
Ezr 4:14 it was not *m* for us to see the
Neh 6:2 let us *m* together in some one of
Neh 6:10 Let us *m* together in the house of
Est 2:9 which were *m* to be given her, out
Job 5:14 They *m* with darkness in the
Job 34:31 Surely it is *m* to be said unto
Job 39:21 he goeth on to *m* the armed men
Prov 7:15 Therefore came I forth to *m* thee
Prov 11:24 that withholdeth more than is *m*
Prov 17:12 bear robbed of her whelps *m* a man
Prov 22:2 The rich and poor *m* together
Prov 29:13 and the deceitful man *m* together
Is 7:3 Isaiah, Go forth now to *m* Ahaz
Is 14:9 for thee to *m* thee at thy coming
Is 34:14 *m* with the wild beasts of the
Is 47:3 I will not *m* thee as a man
Jer 26:14 me as seemeth good and *m* unto you
Jer 27:5 it unto whom it seemed *m* unto me
Jer 41:6 went forth from Mizpah to *m* them
Jer 51:31 One post shall run to *m* another
Jer 51:31 and one messenger to *m* another
Eze 15:4 Is it *m* for any work
Eze 15:5 was whole, it was *m* for no work
Eze 15:5 shall it be *m* yet for any work
Hos 13:8 I will *m* them as a bear that is
Amos 4:12 unto thee, prepare to *m* thy God
Zec 2:3 another angel went out to *m* him
Mt 3:8 therefore fruits *m* for repentance
Mt 8:34 whole city came out to *m* Jesus
Mt 15:26 and said, It is not *m* to take the
Mt 25:1 went forth to *m* the bridegroom
Mt 25:6 go ye out to *m* him
Mk 7:27 for it is not *m* to take the
Mk 14:13 there shall *m* you a man bearing a
Lk 14:31 to *m* him that cometh against him
Lk 15:32 It was *m* that we should make
Lk 22:10 the city, there shall a man *m* you
Jn 12:13 trees, and went forth to *m* him
Acts 26:20 do works *m* for repentance
Acts 28:15 they came to *m* us as far as Appii
Rom 1:27 of their error which was *m*
1Cor 15:9 that am not *m* to be called an
1Cor 16:4 if it be *m* that I go also, they
Phil 1:7 Even as it is *m* for me to think
Col 1:12 which hath made us *m* to be
1Th 4:17 clouds, to *m* the Lord in the air
2Th 1:3 for you, brethren, as it is *m*
2Ti 2:21 *m* for the master's use, and
Heb 6:7 bringeth forth herbs *m* for them
2Pet 1:13 Yea, I think it *m*, as long as I

**MEGIDDO** *(me-ghid'-do)* See MEGIDDON. *A city on the plain of Jezreel.*
Josh 12:21 the king of *M*, one
Josh 17:11 towns, and the inhabitants of *M*
Judg 1:27 towns, nor the inhabitants of *M*

Judg 5:19 in Taanach by the waters of *M*
1Kin 4:12 to him pertained Taanach and *M*
1Kin 9:15 wall of Jerusalem, and Hazor, and *M*
2Kin 9:27 And he fled to *M*, and died there
2Kin 23:29 and he slew him at *M*, when he had
2Kin 23:30 him in a chariot dead from *M*
1Chr 7:29 towns, Taanach and her towns, *M*
2Chr 35:22 came to fight in the valley of *M*

**MEGIDDON** *(me-ghid'-don)* See ARMAGEDDON, MEGIDDO. *Same as Megiddo.*
Zec 12:11 of Hadadrimmon in the valley of *M*

**MEHETABEEL** *(me-het'-a-be-el)* See MEHETABEL. *Father of Delaiah.*
Neh 6:10 the son of Delaiah the son of *M*

**MEHETABEL** *(me-het'-a-bel)* See MEHETABEEL. *Wife of Hadar.*
Gen 36:39 and his wife's name was *M*, the
1Chr 1:50 and his wife's name was *M*, the

**MEHIDA** *(me-hi'-dah) A family of exiles.*
Ezr 2:52 of Bazluth, the children of *M*
Neh 7:54 of Bazlith, the children of *M*

**MEHIR** *(me'-hur) A son of Chelub.*
1Chr 4:11 the brother of Shuah begat *M*

**MEHOLATHITE** *(me-ho'-lath-ite) An inhabitant of a city in Issachar.*
1Sa 18:19 given unto Adriel the *M* to wife
2Sa 21:8 Adriel the son of Barzillai the *M*

**MEHUJAEL** *(me-hu'-ja-el) Son of Irad.*
Gen 4:18 and Irad begat *M*
Gen 4:18 and *M* begat Methusael

**MEHUMAN** *(me-hu'-man) A servant of King Ahasuerus.*
Est 1:10 merry with wine, he commanded *M*

**MEHUNIM** *(me-hu'-nim)* See MAONITE, MEHUNIMS, MEUNIM. *A family of exiles.*
Ezr 2:50 of Asnah, the children of *M*

**MEHUNIMS** *(me-hu'-nims)* See MEHUNIM. *A people who lived in Arabia.*
2Chr 26:7 that dwelt in Gur-baal, and the *M*

**ME-JARKON** *(me-jar'-kon) A city in Dan.*
Josh 19:46 And *M*, and Rakkon, with the border

**MEKONAH** *(me-ko'-nah) A city in Judah.*
Neh 11:28 And at Ziklag, and at *M*, and in the

**MELATIAH** *(mel-a-ti'-ah) A repairer of Jerusalem's wall.*
Neh 3:7 them repaired *M* the Gibeonite

**MELCHI** *(mel'-ki)* See MELCHI-SHUA, MELCHIZEDEK.
*1. Son of Janna; ancestor of Jesus.*
Lk 3:24 of Levi, which was the son of *M*
*2. Son of Addi; ancestor of Jesus.*
Lk 3:28 Which was the son of *M*, which was

**MELCHIAH** *(mel-ki'-ah)* See MALCHIAH. *Father of Pashur.*
Jer 21:1 sent unto him Pashur the son of *M*

**MELCHISEDEC** *(mel-kis'-e-dek)* See MELCHIZEDEK. *Greek form of Melchizedek.*
Heb 5:6 for ever after the order of *M*
Heb 5:10 high priest after the order of *M*
Heb 6:20 for ever after the order of *M*
Heb 7:1 For this *M*, king of Salem, priest
Heb 7:10 of his father, when *M* met him
Heb 7:11 should rise after the order of *M*
Heb 7:15 of *M* there ariseth another priest
Heb 7:17 for ever after the order of *M*
Heb 7:21 for ever after the order of *M*

**MELCHI-SHUA** *(mel'-ki-shu'-ah)* See MALCHISHUA. *A son of King Saul.*
1Sa 14:49 were Jonathan, and Ishui, and *M*
1Sa 31:2 slew Jonathan, and Abinadab, and *M*

**MELCHIZEDEK** *(mel-kiz'-e-dek)* See MELCHISEDEC. *King and priest of Salem.*
Gen 14:18 *M* king of Salem brought forth
Ps 110:4 for ever after the order of *M*

**MELEA** *(mel'-e-ah) Son of Menan; an ancestor of Jesus.*
Lk 3:31 Which was the son of *M*, which was

**MELECH** *(me'-lek)* See EBED-MELECH, HAM-MELECH, NATHAN-MELECH, REGEM-MELECH. *A son of Micah.*
1Chr 8:35 sons of Micah were, Pithon, and *M*
1Chr 9:41 sons of Micah were, Pithon, and *M*

**MELICU** *(mel'-i-cu)* See MALLUCH. *A priest.*
Neh 12:14 Of *M*, Jonathan

**MELITA** *(mel'-i-tah) A Mediterranean island.*
Acts 28:1 knew that the island was called *M*

**MELODY**
Is 23:16 make sweet *m*, sing many songs,
Is 51:3 thanksgiving, and the voice of *m*
Amos 5:23 will not hear the *m* of thy viols
Eph 5:19 making *m* in your heart to the

**MELT**
Ex 15:15 of Canaan shall *m* away
Josh 2:11 these things, our hearts did *m*
Josh 14:8 me made the heart of the people *m*
2Sa 17:10 heart of a lion, shall utterly *m*
Ps 58:7 Let them *m* away as waters which
Ps 112:10 gnash with his teeth, and *m* away
Is 13:7 and every man's heart shall *m*
Is 19:1 Egypt shall *m* in the midst of it
Jer 9:7 of hosts, Behold, I will *m* them
Eze 21:7 and every heart shall *m*, and all
Eze 22:20 to blow the fire upon it, to *m* it
Eze 22:20 I will leave you there, and *m* you
Amos 9:5 toucheth the land, and it shall *m*
Amos 9:13 wine, and all the hills shall *m*
Nah 1:5 quake at him, and the hills *m*
2Pet 3:10 shall *m* with fervent heat
2Pet 3:12 shall *m* with fervent heat

**MELTED**
Ex 16:21 and when the sun waxed hot, it *m*
Josh 5:1 passed over, that their heart *m*
Josh 7:5 the hearts of the people *m*
Judg 5:5 The mountains *m* from before the
1Sa 14:16 and, behold, the multitude *m* away
Ps 22:14 it is *m* in the midst of my bowels
Ps 46:6 he uttered his voice, the earth *m*
Ps 97:5 The hills *m* like wax at the
Ps 107:26 their soul is *m* because of
Is 34:3 shall be *m* with their blood
Eze 22:21 ye shall be *m* in the midst
Eze 22:22 As silver is *m* in the midst of
Eze 22:22 so shall ye be *m* in the midst

**MELTETH**
Ps 58:8 As a snail which *m*, let every one
Ps 68:2 as wax *m* before the fire, so let
Ps 119:28 My soul *m* for heaviness
Ps 147:18 sendeth out his word, and *m* them
Is 40:19 The workman *m* a graven image, and
Jer 6:29 the founder *m* in vain
Nah 2:10 and the heart *m*, and the knees

**MELZAR** *(mel'-zar) Babylonian officer charged with Daniel and his companions.*
Dan 1:11 Then said Daniel to *M*, whom the
Dan 1:16 Thus *M* took away the portion of

**MEMBER**
Deut 23:1 or hath his privy *m* cut off
1Cor 12:14 For the body is not one *m*
1Cor 12:19 And if they were all one *m*
1Cor 12:26 And whether one *m* suffer, all the
1Cor 12:26 or one *m* be honoured, all the
Jas 3:5 Even so the tongue is a little *m*

**MEMBERS**
Job 17:7 and all my *m* are as a shadow
Ps 139:16 in thy book all my *m* were written
Mt 5:29 that one of thy *m* should perish
Mt 5:30 that one of thy *m* should perish
Rom 6:13 yield ye your *m* as instruments of
Rom 6:13 dead, and your *m* as instruments of
Rom 6:19 your *m* servants to uncleanness
Rom 6:19 even so now yield your *m* servants
Rom 7:5 did work in our *m* to bring forth
Rom 7:23 But I see another law in my *m*
Rom 7:23 the law of sin which is in my *m*
Rom 12:4 For as we have many *m* in one body
Rom 12:4 all *m* have not the same office
Rom 12:5 every one *m* one of another
1Cor 6:15 your bodies are the *m* of Christ
1Cor 6:15 shall I then take the *m* of Christ
1Cor 6:15 and make them the *m* of an harlot
1Cor 12:12 the body is one, and hath many *m*
1Cor 12:12 all the *m* of that one body, being
1Cor 12:18 But now hath God set the *m* every
1Cor 12:20 But now are they many *m*, yet but
1Cor 12:22 much more those *m* of the body
1Cor 12:23 those *m* of the body, which we
1Cor 12:25 but that the *m* should have the
1Cor 12:26 suffer, all the *m* suffer with it
1Cor 12:26 all the *m* rejoice with it
1Cor 12:27 of Christ, and *m* in particular
Eph 4:25 for we are *m* one of another
Eph 5:30 For we are *m* of his body, of his
Col 3:5 Mortify therefore your *m* which
Jas 3:6 so is the tongue among our *m*
Jas 4:1 of your lusts that war in your *m*

**MEMORIAL**
Ex 3:15 this is my *m* unto all generations
Ex 12:14 day shall be unto you for a *m*
Ex 13:9 for a *m* between thine eyes, that
Ex 17:14 Write this for a *m* in a book
Ex 28:12 of the ephod for stones of *m* unto
Ex 28:12 upon his two shoulders for a *m*
Ex 28:29 place, for a *m* before the LORD
Ex 30:16 that it may be a *m* unto the
Ex 39:7 for a *m* to the children of Israel
Lev 2:2 burn the *m* of it upon the altar
Lev 2:9 the meat offering a *m* thereof
Lev 2:16 the priest shall burn the *m* of it
Lev 5:12 even a *m* thereof, and burn it on
Lev 6:15 a sweet savour, even the *m* of it
Lev 23:24 a *m* of blowing of trumpets, an
Lev 24:7 it may be on the bread for a *m*
Num 5:15 of jealousy, an offering of *m*
Num 5:18 the offering of *m* in her hands
Num 5:26 the offering, even the *m* thereof
Num 10:10 be to you for a *m* before your God
Num 16:40 To be a *m* unto the children of
Num 31:54 for a *m* for the children of
Josh 4:7 these stones shall be for a *m*
Neh 2:20 have no portion, nor right, nor *m*
Est 9:28 nor the *m* of them perish from
Ps 9:6 their *m* is perished with them
Ps 135:13 and thy *m*, O LORD, throughout all
Hos 12:5 the LORD is his *m*
Zec 6:14 for a *m* in the temple of the LORD
Mt 26:13 hath done, be told for a *m* of her
Mk 14:9 shall be spoken of for a *m* of her
Acts 10:4 are come up for a *m* before God

**MEMORY**
Ps 109:15 off the *m* of them from the earth
Ps 145:7 utter the *m* of thy great goodness
Prov 10:7 The *m* of the just is blessed
Eccl 9:5 for the *m* of them is forgotten
Is 26:14 and made all their *m* to perish
1Cor 15:2 if ye keep in *m* what I preached

**MEMPHIS** *(mem'-fis)* See NOPH. *A city in Egypt.*
Hos 9:6 gather them up, *M* shall bury them

**MEMUCAN** *(mem-u'-can) A prince of Media and Persia.*
Est 1:14 Tarshish, Meres, Marsena, and *M*
Est 1:16 *M* answered before the king and the
Est 1:21 did according to the word of *M*

**MENAHEM** *(men'-a-hem) Son of Gadi.*
2Kin 15:14 For *M* the son of Gadi went up
2Kin 15:16 Then *M* smote Tiphsah, and all that
2Kin 15:17 *M* the son of Gadi to reign over
2Kin 15:19 *M* gave Pul a thousand talents of
2Kin 15:20 *M* exacted the money of Israel,
2Kin 15:21 And the rest of the acts of *M*
2Kin 15:22 And *M* slept with his fathers
2Kin 15:23 of Judah Pekahiah the son of *M*

**MENAN** *(me'-nan) Father of Melea; ancestor of Jesus.*
Lk 3:31 of Melea, which was the son of *M*

**MENE** *(me'-ne) Part of "the handwriting on the wall".*
Dan 5:25 writing that was written, *M*, *M*
Dan 5:26 *M*; God hath numbered

**MENSERVANTS**
Gen 12:16 sheep, and oxen, and he asses, and *m*
Gen 20:14 took sheep, and oxen, and *m*
Gen 24:35 herds, and silver, and gold, and *m*
Gen 30:43 cattle, and maidservants, and *m*
Gen 32:5 have oxen, and asses, flocks, and *m*
Ex 21:7 she shall not go out as the *m* do
Deut 12:12 and your daughters, and your *m*
1Sa 8:16 And he will take your *m*, and your

2Kin 5:26 and sheep, and oxen, and *m*, and
Lk 12:45 and shall begin to beat the *m*

**MENTION**
Gen 40:14 make *m* of me unto Pharaoh, and
Ex 23:13 make no *m* of the name of other
Josh 23:7 neither make *m* of the names of
1Sa 4:18 when he made *m* of the ark of God,
Job 28:18 No *m* shall be made of coral, or
Ps 71:16 I will make *m* of thy
Ps 87:4 I will make *m* of Rahab and Babylon
Is 12:4 make *m* that his name is exalted
Is 19:17 every one that maketh *m* thereof
Is 26:13 only will we make *m* of thy name
Is 48:1 make *m* of the God of Israel, but
Is 49:1 mother hath he made *m* of my name
Is 62:6 ye that make *m* of the LORD
Is 63:7 I will *m* the lovingkindnesses of
Jer 4:16 Make ye *m* to the nations
Jer 20:9 I said, I will not make *m* of him
Jer 23:36 of the LORD shall ye *m* no more
Amos 6:10 for we may not make *m* of the name
Rom 1:9 *m* of you always in my prayers
Eph 1:16 making *m* of you in my prayers
1Th 1:2 making *m* of you in our prayers
Philem 4 making *m* of thee always in my
Heb 11:22 made *m* of the departing of the

**MENTIONED**
Josh 21:9 cities which are here *m* by name
1Chr 4:38 These *m* by their names were
2Chr 20:34 who is *m* in the book of the kings
Eze 16:56 For thy sister Sodom was not *m* by
Eze 18:22 they shall not be *m* unto him
Eze 18:24 that he hath done shall not be *m*
Eze 33:16 committed shall be *m* unto him

**MEONENIM** *(me-on'-e-nim) A place near Shechem.*
Judg 9:37 come along by the plain of *M*

**MEONOTHAI** *(me-on'-o-thahee) Descendant of Judah.*
1Chr 4:14 And *M* begat Ophrah

**MEPHAATH** *(mef'-a-ath) A Levitical city in Reuben.*
Josh 13:18 And Jahaza, and Kedemoth, and *M*
Josh 21:37 suburbs, and *M* with her suburbs
1Chr 6:79 suburbs, and *M* with her suburbs
Jer 48:21 Holon, and upon Jahazah, and upon *M*

**MEPHIBOSHETH** *(me-fib'-o-sheth)* See MERIBBAAL.
*1. Son of Jonathan.*
2Sa 4:4 And his name was *M*
2Sa 9:6 Now when *M*, the son of Jonathan,
2Sa 9:6 And David said, *M*
2Sa 9:10 but *M* thy master's son shall eat
2Sa 9:11 As for *M*, said the king, he shall
2Sa 9:12 *M* had a young son, whose name was
2Sa 9:12 of Ziba were servants unto *M*
2Sa 9:13 So *M* dwelt in Jerusalem
2Sa 16:1 Ziba the servant of *M* met him
2Sa 16:4 are all that pertained unto *M*
2Sa 19:24 *M* the son of Saul came down to
2Sa 19:25 wentest not thou with me, *M*
2Sa 19:30 *M* said unto the king, Yea, let
2Sa 21:7 But the king spared *M*, the son of
*2. Son of Rizpah.*
2Sa 21:8 she bare unto Saul, Armoni and *M*

**MERAB** *(me'-rab) Daughter of King Saul.*
1Sa 14:49 the name of the firstborn *M*
1Sa 18:17 David, Behold my elder daughter *M*
1Sa 18:19 *M* Saul's daughter should have

**MERAIAH** *(mer-a-i'-ah) A priest.*
Neh 12:12 fathers: of Seraiah, *M*

**MERAIOTH** *(me-rah'-yoth)* See MEREMOTH.
*1. An ancestor of Azariah.*
1Chr 6:6 Zerahiah, and Zerahiah begat *M*
1Chr 6:7 *M* begat Amariah, and Amariah begat
1Chr 6:52 *M* his son, Amariah his son,
Ezr 7:3 the son of Azariah, the son of *M*
*2. Another ancestor of Azariah.*
1Chr 9:11 the son of Zadok, the son of *M*
Neh 11:11 the son of Zadok, the son of *M*
*3. A priest in exile.*
Neh 12:15 of *M*, Helkai

**MERARI** *(me-ra'-ri)* See MERARITES. *A son of Levi.*
Gen 46:11 Gershon, Kohath, and *M*
Ex 6:16 Gershon, and Kohath, and *M*
Ex 6:19 And the sons of *M*
Num 3:17 Gershon, and Kohath, and *M*
Num 3:20 the sons of *M* by their families
Num 3:33 Of *M* was the family of the
Num 3:33 these are the families of *M*
Num 3:35 *M* was Zuriel the son of Abihail
Num 3:36 charge of the sons of *M* shall be
Num 4:29 As for the sons of *M*, thou shalt
Num 4:33 of the families of the sons of *M*
Num 4:42 of the families of the sons of *M*
Num 4:45 of the families of the sons of *M*
Num 7:8 oxen he gave unto the sons of *M*
Num 10:17 and the sons of *M* set forward
Num 26:57 of *M*, the family of the Merarites
Josh 21:7 The children of *M* by their
Josh 21:34 the families of the children of *M*
Josh 21:40 children of *M* by their families
1Chr 6:1 Gershon, Kohath, and *M*
1Chr 6:16 Gershom, Kohath, and *M*
1Chr 6:19 The sons of *M*; Mahli, and
1Chr 6:29 The sons of *M*; Mahli, Libni
1Chr 6:44 sons of *M* stood on the left hand
1Chr 6:47 the son of Mushi, the son of *M*
1Chr 6:63 Unto the sons of *M* were given by
1Chr 6:77 the rest of the children of *M*
1Chr 9:14 of Hashabiah, of the sons of *M*
1Chr 15:6 Of the sons of *M*
1Chr 15:17 of the sons of *M* their brethren
1Chr 23:6 namely, Gershon, Kohath, and *M*
1Chr 23:21 The sons of *M*; Mahli, and
1Chr 24:26 The sons of *M* were Mahli and Mushi
1Chr 24:27 The sons of *M* by Jaaziah
1Chr 26:10 Also Hosah, of the children of *M*
1Chr 26:19 of Kore, and among the sons of *M*
2Chr 29:12 and of the sons of *M*, Kish the son
2Chr 34:12 the Levites, of the sons of *M*
Ezr 8:19 him Jeshaiah of the sons of *M*

**MERARITES** *(me-ra'-rites) Descendants of Merari.*
Num 26:57 of Merari, the family of the *M*

**MERATHAIM** *(mer-a-tha'-im) A symbolic name for Babylon.*
Jer 50:21 Go up against the land of *M*

**MERCHANDISE**
Deut 21:14 thou shalt not make *m* of her
Deut 24:7 of Israel, and maketh *m* of him
Prov 3:14 For the *m* of it is better than
Prov 3:14 it is better than the *m* of silver
Prov 31:18 She perceiveth that her *m* is good
Is 23:18 And her *m* and her hire shall be
Is 23:18 for her *m* shall be for them that
Is 45:14 *m* of Ethiopia and of the Sabeans,
Eze 26:12 riches, and make a prey of thy *m*
Eze 27:9 were in thee to occupy thy *m*
Eze 27:15 isles were the *m* of thine hand
Eze 27:24 and made of cedar, among thy *m*
Eze 27:27 Thy riches, and thy fairs, thy *m*
Eze 27:27 and the occupiers of thy *m*
Eze 27:33 of thy riches and of thy *m*
Eze 27:34 in the depths of the waters thy *m*
Eze 28:16 By the multitude of thy *m* they
Mt 22:5 one to his farm, another to his *m*
Jn 2:16 my Father's house an house of *m*
2Pet 2:3 with feigned words make *m* of you
Rev 18:11 no man buyeth their *m* any more
Rev 18:12 The *m* of gold, and silver, and

**MERCHANT**
Gen 23:16 silver, current money with the *m*
Prov 31:24 and delivereth girdles unto the *m*
Song 3:6 with all powders of the *m*
Is 23:11 a commandment against the *m* city
Eze 27:3 which art a *m* of the people for
Eze 27:12 Tarshish was thy *m* by reason of
Eze 27:16 Syria was thy *m* by reason of the
Eze 27:18 Damascus was thy *m* in the
Eze 27:20 Dedan was thy *m* in precious
Hos 12:7 He is a *m*, the balances of deceit
Zeph 1:11 for all the *m* people are cut down
Mt 13:45 of heaven is like unto a *m* man

**MERCHANTS**
1Kin 10:15 and of the traffick of the spice *m*
1Kin 10:28 the king's *m* received the linen
2Chr 1:16 the king's *m* received the linen
2Chr 9:14 that which chapmen and *m* brought
Neh 3:31 of the Nethinims, and of the *m*
Neh 3:32 repaired the goldsmiths and the *m*
Neh 13:20 So the *m* and sellers of all kind
Job 41:6 shall they part him among the *m*
Is 23:2 thou whom the *m* of Zidon, that
Is 23:8 whose *m* are princes, whose
Is 47:15 thou hast laboured, even thy *m*
Eze 17:4 he set it in a city of *m*
Eze 27:13 and Meshech, they were thy *m*
Eze 27:15 The men of Dedan were thy *m*
Eze 27:17 land of Israel, they were thy *m*
Eze 27:21 in these were they thy *m*
Eze 27:22 The *m* of Sheba and Raamah
Eze 27:22 Sheba and Raamah, they were thy *m*
Eze 27:23 the *m* of Sheba, Asshur, and
Eze 27:23 and Chilmad, were thy *m*
Eze 27:24 These were thy *m* in all sorts of
Eze 27:36 The *m* among the people shall hiss
Eze 38:13 the *m* of Tarshish, with all the
Nah 3:16 Thou hast multiplied thy *m* above
Rev 18:3 the *m* of the earth are waxed rich
Rev 18:11 the *m* of the earth shall weep and
Rev 18:15 The *m* of these things, which were
Rev 18:23 for thy *m* were the great men of

**MERCIES**
Gen 32:10 worthy of the least of all the *m*
2Sa 24:14 for his *m* are great
1Chr 21:13 for very great are his *m*
2Chr 6:42 remember the *m* of David thy
Neh 9:19 Yet thou in thy manifold *m*
Neh 9:27 *m* thou gavest them saviours
Neh 9:28 deliver them according to thy *m*
Ps 25:6 Remember, O LORD, thy tender *m*
Ps 40:11 not thou thy tender *m* from me
Ps 51:1 *m* blot out my transgressions
Ps 69:16 to the multitude of thy tender *m*
Ps 77:9 he in anger shut up his tender *m*
Ps 79:8 let thy tender *m* speedily prevent
Ps 89:1 I will sing of the *m* of the LORD
Ps 103:4 with lovingkindness and tender *m*
Ps 106:7 not the multitude of thy *m*
Ps 106:45 to the multitude of his *m*
Ps 119:41 Let thy *m* come also unto me, O
Ps 119:77 Let thy tender *m* come unto me
Ps 119:156 Great are thy tender *m*, O LORD
Ps 145:9 his tender *m* are over all his
Prov 12:10 but the tender *m* of the wicked
Is 54:7 but with great *m* will I gather
Is 55:3 you, even the sure *m* of David
Is 63:7 on them according to his *m*
Is 63:15 thy bowels and of thy *m* toward me
Jer 16:5 LORD, even lovingkindness and *m*
Jer 42:12 And I will shew *m* unto you
Lam 3:22 It is of the LORD's *m* that we are
Lam 3:32 to the multitude of his *m*
Dan 2:18 That they would desire *m* of the
Dan 9:9 To the Lord our God belong *m*
Dan 9:18 but for thy great *m*
Hos 2:19 and in lovingkindness, and in *m*
Zec 1:16 I am returned to Jerusalem with *m*
Acts 13:34 will give you the sure *m* of David
Rom 12:1 brethren, by the *m* of God
2Cor 1:3 Jesus Christ, the Father of *m*
Phil 2:1 of the Spirit, if any bowels and *m*
Col 3:12 God, holy and beloved, bowels of *m*

**MERCIES'**
Neh 9:31 Nevertheless for thy great *m* sake
Ps 6:4 oh save me for thy *m* sake
Ps 31:16 save me for thy *m* sake
Ps 44:26 help, and redeem us for thy *m* sake

**MERCIFUL**
Gen 19:16 the LORD being *m* unto him
Ex 34:6 The LORD, The LORD God, *m*
Deut 4:31 (For the LORD thy God is a *m* God
Deut 21:8 Be *m*, O LORD, unto thy people
Deut 32:43 will be *m* unto his land, and to
2Sa 22:26 With the *m* thou wilt shew thyself
2Sa 22:26 thou wilt shew thyself *m*
1Kin 20:31 the house of Israel are *m* kings
2Chr 30:9 LORD your God is gracious and *m*
Neh 9:17 ready to pardon, gracious and *m*
Neh 9:31 for thou art a gracious and *m* God
Ps 18:25 With the *m* thou wilt shew thyself
Ps 18:25 thou wilt shew thyself *m*
Ps 26:11 redeem me, and be *m* unto me
Ps 37:26 He is ever *m*, and lendeth
Ps 41:4 I said, LORD, be *m* unto me
Ps 41:10 be *m* unto me, and raise me up,
Ps 56:1 Be *m* unto me, O God

Ps 57:1 Be *m* unto me, O God, be *m*
Ps 59:5 be not *m* to any wicked
Ps 67:1 God be *m* unto us, and bless us
Ps 86:3 Be *m* unto me, O Lord
Ps 103:8 The LORD is *m* and gracious, slow
Ps 116:5 yea, our God is *m*
Ps 117:2 For his *m* kindness is great
Ps 119:58 be *m* unto me according to thy
Ps 119:76 thy *m* kindness be for my comfort,
Ps 119:132 be *m* unto me, as thou usest to do
Prov 11:17 The *m* man doeth good to his own
Is 57:1 *m* men are taken away, none
Jer 3:12 for I am *m*, saith the LORD, and I
Joel 2:13 for he is gracious and *m*, slow to
Jonah 4:2 thou art a gracious God, and *m*
Mt 5:7 Blessed are the *m*
Lk 6:36 Be ye therefore *m*, as your Father
Lk 6:36 as your Father also is *m*
Lk 18:13 saying, God be *m* to me a sinner
Heb 2:17 brethren, that he might be a *m*
Heb 8:12 For I will be *m* to their

**MERCURIUS** *(mer-cu'-re-us) A Roman god.*
Acts 14:12 and Paul, *M*, because he was the

**MERCY**
Gen 19:19 and thou hast magnified thy *m*
Gen 24:27 left destitute my master of his *m*
Gen 39:21 was with Joseph, and shewed him *m*
Gen 43:14 give you *m* before the man
Ex 15:13 Thou in thy *m* hast led forth the
Ex 20:6 shewing *m* unto thousands of them
Ex 25:17 shalt make a *m* seat of pure gold
Ex 25:18 in the two ends of the *m* seat
Ex 25:19 even of the *m* seat shall ye make
Ex 25:20 covering the *m* seat with their
Ex 25:20 toward the *m* seat shall the faces
Ex 25:21 thou shalt put the *m* seat above
Ex 25:22 with thee from above the *m* seat
Ex 26:34 thou shalt put the *m* seat upon
Ex 30:6 before the *m* seat that is over
Ex 31:7 the *m* seat that is thereupon, and
Ex 33:19 shew *m* on whom I will shew *m*
Ex 34:7 Keeping *m* for thousands,
Ex 35:12 staves thereof, with the *m* seat
Ex 37:6 he made the *m* seat of pure gold
Ex 37:7 on the two ends of the *m* seat
Ex 37:8 out of the *m* seat made he the
Ex 37:9 with their wings over the *m* seat
Ex 37:9 even to the *m* seatward were the
Ex 39:35 staves thereof, and the *m* seat,
Ex 40:20 put the *m* seat above upon the ark
Lev 16:2 within the vail before the *m* seat
Lev 16:2 in the cloud upon the *m* seat
Lev 16:13 of the incense may cover the *m*
Lev 16:14 finger upon the *m* seat eastward
Lev 16:14 before the *m* seat shall he
Lev 16:15 and sprinkle it upon the *m* seat
Lev 16:15 and before the *m* seat
Num 7:89 *m* seat that was upon the ark of
Num 14:18 is longsuffering, and of great *m*
Num 14:19 unto the greatness of thy *m*
Deut 5:10 shewing *m* unto thousands of them
Deut 7:2 with them, nor shew *m* unto them
Deut 7:9 *m* with them that love him and keep
Deut 7:12 the *m* which he sware unto thy
Deut 13:17 of his anger, and shew thee *m*
Judg 1:24 the city, and we will shew thee *m*
2Sa 7:15 But my *m* shall not depart away
2Sa 15:20 *m* and truth be with thee
2Sa 22:51 sheweth *m* to his anointed, unto
1Kin 3:6 servant David my father great *m*
1Kin 8:23 *m* with thy servants that walk
1Chr 16:34 for his *m* endureth for ever
1Chr 16:41 because his *m* endureth for ever
1Chr 17:13 will not take my *m* away from him
1Chr 28:11 and of the place of the *m* seat
2Chr 1:8 great *m* unto David my father
2Chr 5:13 for his *m* endureth for ever
2Chr 6:14 shewest *m* unto thy servants, that
2Chr 7:3 for his *m* endureth for ever
2Chr 7:6 because his *m* endureth for ever,
2Chr 20:21 for his *m* endureth for ever
Ezr 3:11 for his *m* endureth for ever
Ezr 7:28 hath extended *m* unto me before
Ezr 9:9 but hath extended *m* unto us in
Neh 1:5 *m* for them that love him and
Neh 1:11 grant him *m* in the sight of this
Neh 9:32 God, who keepest covenant and *m*
Neh 13:22 to the greatness of thy *m*
Job 37:13 or for his land, or for *m*
Ps 4:1 have *m* upon me, and hear my prayer
Ps 5:7 house in the multitude of thy *m*
Ps 6:2 Have *m* upon me, O LORD
Ps 9:13 Have *m* upon me, O LORD
Ps 13:5 But I have trusted in thy *m*
Ps 18:50 sheweth *m* to his anointed, to
Ps 21:7 through the *m* of the most High he
Ps 23:6 *m* shall follow me all the days of
Ps 25:7 according to thy *m* remember thou
Ps 25:10 All the paths of the LORD are *m*
Ps 25:16 thee unto me, and have *m* upon me
Ps 27:7 have *m* also upon me, and answer me
Ps 30:10 Hear, O LORD, and have *m* upon me
Ps 31:7 will be glad and rejoice in thy *m*
Ps 31:9 Have *m* upon me, O LORD, for I am
Ps 32:10 *m* shall compass him about
Ps 33:18 him, upon them that hope in his *m*
Ps 33:22 Let thy *m*, O LORD, be upon us,
Ps 36:5 Thy *m*, O LORD, is in the heavens
Ps 37:21 but the righteous sheweth *m*
Ps 51:1 Have *m* upon me, O God, according
Ps 52:8 I trust in the *m* of God for ever
Ps 57:3 God shall send forth his *m*
Ps 57:10 For thy *m* is great unto the
Ps 59:10 The God of my *m* shall prevent me
Ps 59:16 aloud of thy *m* in the morning
Ps 59:17 is my defence, and the God of my *m*
Ps 61:7 O prepare *m* and truth, which may
Ps 62:12 unto thee, O Lord, belongeth *m*
Ps 66:20 away my prayer, nor his *m* from me
Ps 69:13 in the multitude of thy *m* hear me
Ps 77:8 Is his *m* clean gone for ever
Ps 85:7 Shew us thy *m*, O LORD, and grant
Ps 85:10 *M* and truth are met together
Ps 86:5 plenteous in *m* unto all them that
Ps 86:13 For great is thy *m* toward me
Ps 86:15 longsuffering, and plenteous in *m*
Ps 86:16 O turn unto me, and have *m* upon me
Ps 89:2 *M* shall be built up for ever
Ps 89:14 *m* and truth shall go before thy
Ps 89:24 and my *m* shall be with him
Ps 89:28 My *m* will I keep for him for
Ps 90:14 O satisfy us early with thy *m*
Ps 94:18 thy *m*, O LORD, held me up
Ps 98:3 He hath remembered his *m* and his
Ps 100:5 his *m* is everlasting
Ps 101:1 I will sing of *m* and judgment
Ps 102:13 shalt arise, and have *m* upon Zion
Ps 103:8 slow to anger, and plenteous in *m*
Ps 103:11 so great is his *m* toward them
Ps 103:17 But the *m* of the LORD is from
Ps 106:1 for his *m* endureth for ever
Ps 107:1 for his *m* endureth for ever
Ps 108:4 For thy *m* is great above the
Ps 109:12 be none to extend *m* unto him
Ps 109:16 that he remembered not to shew *m*
Ps 109:21 because thy *m* is good, deliver
Ps 109:26 O save me according to thy *m*
Ps 115:1 thy name give glory, for thy *m*
Ps 118:1 because his *m* endureth for ever
Ps 118:2 that his *m* endureth for ever
Ps 118:3 that his *m* endureth for ever
Ps 118:4 that his *m* endureth for ever
Ps 118:29 for his *m* endureth for ever
Ps 119:64 earth, O LORD, is full of thy *m*
Ps 119:124 thy servant according unto thy *m*
Ps 123:2 God, until that he have *m* upon us
Ps 123:3 Have *m* upon us, O LORD, have
Ps 123:3 upon us, O LORD, have *m* upon us
Ps 130:7 for with the LORD there is *m*
Ps 136:1 for his *m* endureth for ever
Ps 136:2 for his *m* endureth for ever
Ps 136:3 for his *m* endureth for ever
Ps 136:4 for his *m* endureth for ever
Ps 136:5 for his *m* endureth for ever
Ps 136:6 for his *m* endureth for ever
Ps 136:7 for his *m* endureth for ever
Ps 136:8 for his *m* endureth for ever
Ps 136:9 for his *m* endureth for ever
Ps 136:10 for his *m* endureth for ever
Ps 136:11 for his *m* endureth for ever
Ps 136:12 for his *m* endureth for ever
Ps 136:13 for his *m* endureth for ever
Ps 136:14 for his *m* endureth for ever
Ps 136:15 for his *m* endureth for ever
Ps 136:16 for his *m* endureth for ever
Ps 136:17 for his *m* endureth for ever
Ps 136:18 for his *m* endureth for ever
Ps 136:19 for his *m* endureth for ever
Ps 136:20 for his *m* endureth for ever
Ps 136:21 for his *m* endureth for ever
Ps 136:22 for his *m* endureth for ever
Ps 136:23 for his *m* endureth for ever
Ps 136:24 for his *m* endureth for ever
Ps 136:25 for his *m* endureth for ever
Ps 136:26 for his *m* endureth for ever
Ps 138:8 thy *m*, O LORD, endureth for ever
Ps 143:12 of thy *m* cut off mine enemies, and
Ps 145:8 slow to anger, and of great *m*
Ps 147:11 him, in those that hope in his *m*
Prov 3:3 Let not *m* and truth forsake thee
Prov 14:21 but he that hath *m* on the poor
Prov 14:22 but *m* and truth shall be to them
Prov 14:31 honoureth him hath *m* on the poor
Prov 16:6 By *m* and truth iniquity is purged
Prov 20:28 *M* and truth preserve the king
Prov 20:28 and his throne is upholden by *m*
Prov 21:21 *m* findeth life, righteousness, and
Prov 28:13 and forsaketh them shall have *m*
Is 9:17 neither shall have *m* on their
Is 14:1 For the LORD will have *m* on Jacob
Is 16:5 And in *m* shall the throne be
Is 27:11 made them will not have *m* on them
Is 30:18 that he may have *m* upon you
Is 47:6 thou didst shew them no *m*
Is 49:10 for he that hath *m* on them shall
Is 49:13 will have *m* upon his afflicted
Is 54:8 kindness will I have *m* on thee
Is 54:10 the LORD that hath *m* on thee
Is 55:7 LORD, and he will have *m* upon him
Is 60:10 in my favour have I had *m* on thee
Jer 6:23 they are cruel, and have no *m*
Jer 13:14 not pity, nor spare, nor have *m*
Jer 21:7 neither have pity, nor have *m*
Jer 30:18 have *m* on his dwellingplaces
Jer 31:20 I will surely have *m* upon him
Jer 33:11 for his *m* endureth for ever
Jer 33:26 to return, and have *m* on them
Jer 42:12 you, that he may have *m* upon you
Jer 50:42 are cruel, and will not shew *m*
Eze 39:25 have *m* upon the whole house of
Dan 4:27 by shewing *m* to the poor
Dan 9:4 *m* to them that love him, and to
Hos 1:6 for I will no more have *m* upon
Hos 1:7 But I will have *m* upon the house
Hos 2:4 I will not have *m* upon her
Hos 2:23 I will have *m* upon her that had
Hos 2:23 upon her that had not obtained *m*
Hos 4:1 because there is no truth, nor *m*
Hos 6:6 For I desired *m*, and not sacrifice
Hos 10:12 in righteousness, reap in *m*
Hos 12:6 keep *m* and judgment, and wait on
Hos 14:3 in thee the fatherless findeth *m*
Jonah 2:8 vanities forsake their own *m*
Mic 6:8 but to do justly, and to love *m*
Mic 7:18 ever, because he delighteth in *m*
Mic 7:20 the *m* to Abraham, which thou hast
Hab 3:2 in wrath remember *m*
Zec 1:12 wilt thou not have *m* on Jerusalem
Zec 7:9 Execute true judgment, and shew *m*
Zec 10:6 for I have *m* upon them
Mt 5:7 for they shall obtain *m*
Mt 9:13 what that meaneth, I will have *m*
Mt 9:27 Thou son of David, have *m* on us
Mt 12:7 what this meaneth, I will have *m*
Mt 15:22 Have *m* on me, O Lord, thou son of
Mt 17:15 Lord, have *m* on my son
Mt 20:30 Have *m* on us, O Lord, thou son of
Mt 20:31 Have *m* on us, O Lord, thou son of
Mt 23:23 matters of the law, judgment, *m*
Mk 10:47 thou son of David, have *m* on me
Mk 10:48 Thou son of David, have *m* on me
Lk 1:50 his *m* is on them that fear him
Lk 1:54 Israel, in remembrance of his *m*
Lk 1:58 Lord had shewed great *m* upon her
Lk 1:72 To perform the *m* promised to our
Lk 1:78 Through the tender *m* of our God
Lk 10:37 he said, He that shewed *m* on him
Lk 16:24 have *m* on me, and send Lazarus,
Lk 17:13 said, Jesus, Master, have *m* on us
Lk 18:38 thou son of David, have *m* on me
Lk 18:39 Thou son of David, have *m* on me
Rom 9:15 I will have *m* on whom I will have
Rom 9:15 have *m* on whom I will have *m*
Rom 9:16 but of God that sheweth *m*
Rom 9:18 Therefore hath he *m* on whom he
Rom 9:18 on whom he will have *m*
Rom 9:23 of his glory on the vessels of *m*
Rom 11:30 yet have now obtained *m* through

Rom 11:31 that through your *m* they also may
Rom 11:31 they also may obtain *m*
Rom 11:32 that he might have *m* upon all
Rom 12:8 he that sheweth *m*, with
Rom 15:9 might glorify God for his *m*
1Cor 7:25 as one that hath obtained *m* of
2Cor 4:1 ministry, as we have received *m*
Gal 6:16 this rule, peace be on them, and *m*
Eph 2:4 But God, who is rich in *m*
Phil 2:27 but God had *m* on him
1Ti 1:2 Grace, *m*, and peace, from God our
1Ti 1:13 but I obtained *m*, because I did
1Ti 1:16 for this cause I obtained *m*
2Ti 1:2 Grace, *m*, and peace, from God the
2Ti 1:16 The Lord give *m* unto the house of
2Ti 1:18 find *m* of the Lord in that day
Titus 1:4 Grace, *m*, and peace, from God the
Titus 3:5 according to his *m* he saved us
Heb 4:16 of grace, that we may obtain *m*
Heb 10:28 Moses' law died without *m* under
Jas 2:13 he shall have judgment without *m*
Jas 2:13 that hath shewed no *m*
Jas 2:13 *m* rejoiceth against judgment
Jas 3:17 easy to be intreated, full of *m*
Jas 5:11 is very pitiful, and of tender *m*
1Pet 1:3 *m* hath begotten us again unto a
1Pet 2:10 which had not obtained *m*
1Pet 2:10 but now have obtained *m*
2Jn 3 Grace be with you, *m*, and peace,
Jude 2 *M* unto you, and peace, and love, be
Jude 21 looking for the *m* of our Lord

**MERED** *(me'-red) A descendant of Judah.*
1Chr 4:17 sons of Ezra were, Jether, and *M*
1Chr 4:18 daughter of Pharaoh, which *M* took

**MEREMOTH** *(mer'-e-moth)* See MERAIOTH.
*1. Son of Uriah the priest.*
Ezr 8:33 of *M* the son of Uriah the priest
Neh 3:4 them repaired *M* the son of Urijah
Neh 3:21 After him repaired *M* the son of
*2. Married a foreigner in exile.*
Ezr 10:36 Vaniah, *M*, Eliashib,
*3. A priest who renewed the covenant.*
Neh 10:5 Harim, *M*, Obadiah,
Neh 12:3 Shechaniah, Rehum, *M*,

**MERES** *(me'-res) A prince of Media and Persia.*
Est 1:14 Shethar, Admatha, Tarshish, *M*

**MERIBAH** *(mer'-i-bah)* See MASSAH, MERIBAH-KADESH. *Same as Meribah-Kadesh.*
Ex 17:7 name of the place Massah, and *M*
Num 20:13 This is the water of *M*
Num 20:24 against my word at the water of *M*
Num 27:14 that is the water of *M* in Kadesh
Deut 33:8 didst strive at the waters of *M*
Ps 81:7 I proved thee at the waters of *M*

**MERIBAH-KADESH** *(mer'-i-bah-ka'-desh) A place between Zin and Sinai.*
Deut 32:51 of Israel at the waters of *M*

**MERIB-BAAL** *(me-rib'-ba-al)* See MEPHIBOSHETH. *Son of Jonathan.*
1Chr 8:34 And the son of Jonathan was *M*
1Chr 8:34 and *M* begat Micah
1Chr 9:40 And the son of Jonathan was *M*
1Chr 9:40 and *M* begat Micah

**MERODACH** *(mer'-o-dak)* See BERODACH, EVIL-MERODACH, MERODACH-BALADAN. *A Babylonian god of war.*
Jer 50:2 confounded, *M* is broken in pieces

**MERODACH-BALADAN** *(mer'-o-dak-bal'-a-dan)* See BERODACH-BALADAN. *A king of Babylon.*
Is 39:1 At that time *M*, the son of

**MEROM** *(me'-rom) A small lake north of the Sea of Chinneroth.*
Josh 11:5 together at the waters of *M*
Josh 11:7 them by the waters of *M* suddenly

**MERONOTHITE** *(me-ron'-o-thite) An inhabitant of a district of Zebulun.*
1Chr 27:30 over the asses was Jehdeiah the *M*
Neh 3:7 the Gibeonite, and Jadon the *M*

**MEROZ** *(me'-roz) A place near Lake Merom.*
Judg 5:23 Curse ye *M*, said the angel of the

**MERRY**
Gen 43:34 And they drank, and were *m* with him
Judg 9:27 and trode the grapes, and made *m*
Judg 16:25 to pass, when their hearts were *m*
Judg 19:6 night, and let thine heart be *m*
Judg 19:9 here, that thine heart may be *m*
Judg 19:22 they were making their hearts *m*
Ruth 3:7 and drunk, and his heart was *m*
1Sa 25:36 Nabal's heart was *m* within him
2Sa 13:28 when Amnon's heart is *m* with wine
1Kin 4:20 eating and drinking, and making *m*
1Kin 21:7 bread, and let thine heart be *m*
2Chr 7:10 *m* in heart for the goodness that
Est 1:10 heart of the king was *m* with wine
Prov 15:13 A *m* heart maketh a cheerful
Prov 15:15 but he that is of a *m* heart hath
Prov 17:22 A *m* heart doeth good like a
Eccl 8:15 to eat, and to drink, and to be *m*
Eccl 9:7 and drink thy wine with a *m* heart
Eccl 10:19 for laughter, and wine maketh *m*
Jer 30:19 and the voice of them that make *m*
Jer 31:4 in the dances of them that make *m*
Lk 12:19 thine ease, eat, drink, and be *m*
Lk 15:23 and let us eat, and be *m*
Lk 15:24 And they began to be *m*
Lk 15:29 I might make *m* with my friends
Lk 15:32 It was meet that we should make *m*
Jas 5:13 Is any *m*?
Rev 11:10 rejoice over them, and make *m*

**MESECH** *(me'-sek)* See MESHECH. *A tribe joined to Kedar.*
Ps 120:5 Woe is me, that I sojourn in *M*

**MESHA** *(me'-shah)*
*1. A place in southeastern Arabia.*
Gen 10:30 And their dwelling was from *M*
*2. A king of Moab.*
2Kin 3:4 *M* king of Moab was a sheepmaster,
*3. A son of Caleb.*
1Chr 2:42 *M* his firstborn, which was the
*4. A son of Shaharaim.*
1Chr 8:9 his wife, Jobab, and Zibia, and *M*

**MESHACH** *(me'-shak) A companion of Daniel.*
Dan 1:7 and to Mishael, of *M*
Dan 2:49 the king, and he set Shadrach, *M*
Dan 3:12 province of Babylon, Shadrach, *M*
Dan 3:13 commanded to bring Shadrach, *M*
Dan 3:14 them, Is it true, O Shadrach, *M*
Dan 3:16 Shadrach, *M*, and Abed-nego,
Dan 3:19 was changed against Shadrach, *M*
Dan 3:20 in his army to bind Shadrach, *M*
Dan 3:22 men that took up Shadrach, *M*
Dan 3:23 And these three men, Shadrach, *M*
Dan 3:26 and spake, and said, Shadrach, *M*
Dan 3:26 Then Shadrach, *M*, and Abed-nego,
Dan 3:28 Blessed be the God of Shadrach, *M*
Dan 3:29 against the God of Shadrach, *M*
Dan 3:30 the king promoted Shadrach, *M*

**MESHECH** *(me'-shek)* See MESECH.
*1. A son of Japheth.*
Gen 10:2 Madai, and Javan, and Tubal, and *M*
1Chr 1:5 Madai, and Javan, and Tubal, and *M*
*2. A son of Shem.*
1Chr 1:17 and Uz, and Hul, and Gether, and *M*
*3. Descendants of Meschech 1.*
Eze 27:13 Javan, Tubal, and *M*, they were thy
Eze 32:26 There is *M*, Tubal, and all her
Eze 38:2 of Magog, the chief prince of *M*
Eze 38:3 O Gog, the chief prince of *M*
Eze 39:1 O Gog, the chief prince of *M*

**MESHELEMIAH** *(me-shel-e-mi'-ah)* See MESHULLAM, SHELEMIAH, SHALLUM. *Father of Zechariah.*
1Chr 9:21 Zechariah the son of *M* was porter
1Chr 26:1 Korhites was *M* the son of Kore
1Chr 26:2 And the sons of *M* were, Zechariah
1Chr 26:9 *M* had sons and brethren, strong

**MESHEZABEEL** *(me-shez'-a-be-el)*
*1. Father of Berechiah.*
Neh 3:4 son of Berechiah, the son of *M*
*2. An Israelite who renewed the covenant.*
Neh 10:21 *M*, Zadok, Jaddua,
Neh 11:24 And Pethahiah the son of *M*

**MESHILLEMITH** *(me-shil'-le-mith)* See MESHILLEMOTH. *A family of exiles.*
1Chr 9:12 son of Meshullam, the son of *M*

**MESHILLEMOTH** *(me-shil'-le-moth)* See MESHILLEMITH.
*1. Father of Berechiah.*
2Chr 28:12 Johanan, Berechiah the son of *M*
*2. A family of exiles.*
Neh 11:13 the son of Ahasai, the son of *M*

**MESHOBAB** *(me-sho'-bab) A chief of Simeon.*
1Chr 4:34 And *M*, and Jamlech, and Joshah the

**MESHULLAM** *(me-shul'-lam)* See MESHELLEMIAH.
*1. A scribe in Josiah's time.*
2Kin 22:3 the son of Azaliah, the son of *M*
*2. A descendant of Jeconiah.*
1Chr 3:19 *M*, and Hananiah, and Shelomith
*3. Head of a Gadite family.*
1Chr 5:13 their fathers were, Michael, and *M*
*4. A Benjamite of the Elpaal family.*
1Chr 8:17 Zebadiah, and *M*, and Hezeki, and
*5. Father of Sallu.*
1Chr 9:7 Sallu the son of *M*, the son of
*6. Son of Shephathiah.*
1Chr 9:8 *M* the son of Shephatiah, the son
*7. Father of Hilkiah.*
1Chr 9:11 the son of Hilkiah, the son of *M*
Neh 11:11 the son of Hilkiah, the son of *M*
*8. Son of Meshillemith.*
1Chr 9:12 the son of Jahzerah, the son of *M*
*9. A Kohathite repairer of the wall.*
2Chr 34:12 and Zechariah and *M*, of the sons of
*10. A clan leader with Ezra.*
Ezr 8:16 and for Zechariah, and for *M*
*11. A priest who accounted for the foreign wives.*
Ezr 10:15 and *M* and Shabbethai the Levite
*12. A son of Bani.*
Ezr 10:29 *M*, Malluch, and Adaiah, Jashub, and
*13. A son of Berechiah.*
Neh 3:4 repaired *M* the son of Berechiah
Neh 3:30 After him repaired *M* the son of
Neh 6:18 of *M* the son of Berechiah
*14. A son of Besodeiah.*
Neh 3:6 Paseah, and *M* the son of Besodeiah
*15. A Levite who aided Ezra.*
Neh 8:4 and Hashbadana, Zechariah, and *M*
*16. A priest who renewed the covenant.*
Neh 10:7 *M*, Abijah, Mijamin,
*17. A clan leader who renewed the covenant.*
Neh 10:20 Magpiash, *M*, Hezir,
*18. A family of exiles.*
Neh 11:7 Sallu the son of *M*, the son of
*19. A priest who dedicated the wall.*
Neh 12:13 Of Ezra, *M*
Neh 12:33 And Azariah, Ezra, and *M*,
*20. A descendant of Ginnethon.*
Neh 12:16 of Ginnethon, *M*
*21. A Levite gatekeeper.*
Neh 12:25 and Bakbukiah, Obadiah, *M*

**MESHULLEMETH** *(me-shul'-le-meth) Mother of King Amon.*
2Kin 21:19 And his mother's name was *M*

**MESOBAITE** *(me-so'-ba-ite) Family name of Jasiel.*
1Chr 11:47 Eliel, and Obed, and Jasiel the *M*

**MESOPOTAMIA** *(mes-o-po-ta'-me-ah)* See ARAM, NAHARAIM. *Land between the Tigris and Euphrates Rivers.*
Gen 24:10 and he arose, and went to *M*
Deut 23:4 the son of Beor of Pethor of *M*
Judg 3:8 of Chushan-rishathaim king of *M*
Judg 3:10 king of *M* into his hand
1Chr 19:6 chariots and horsemen out of *M*
Acts 2:9 and Elamites, and the dwellers in *M*
Acts 7:2 father Abraham, when he was in *M*

**MESSAGE**
Judg 3:20 I have a *m* from God unto thee
1Kin 20:12 pass, when Ben-hadad heard this *m*
Prov 26:6 He that sendeth a *m* by the hand
Hag 1:13 in the LORD's *m* unto the people
Lk 19:14 sent a *m* after him, saying, We
1Jn 1:5 This then is the *m* which we have
1Jn 3:11 For this is the *m* that ye heard

**MESSENGER**
Gen 50:16 And they sent a *m* unto Joseph
1Sa 4:17 the *m* answered and said, Israel is
1Sa 23:27 But there came a *m* unto Saul
2Sa 11:19 And charged the *m*, saying, When

2Sa 11:22 So the *m* went, and came and shewed
2Sa 11:23 the *m* said unto David, Surely the
2Sa 11:25 Then David said unto the *m*
2Sa 15:13 And there came a *m* to David
1Kin 19:2 Then Jezebel sent a *m* unto Elijah
1Kin 22:13 the *m* that was gone to call
2Kin 5:10 And Elisha sent a *m* unto him
2Kin 6:32 but ere the *m* came to him
2Kin 6:32 look, when the *m* cometh, shut the
2Kin 6:33 behold, the *m* came down unto him
2Kin 9:18 The *m* came to them, but he cometh
2Kin 10:8 And there came a *m*, and told him,
2Chr 18:12 the *m* that went to call Micaiah
Job 1:14 And there came a *m* unto Job
Job 33:23 If there be a *m* with him, an
Prov 13:17 A wicked *m* falleth into mischief
Prov 17:11 therefore a cruel *m* shall be sent
Prov 25:13 so is a faithful *m* to them that
Is 42:19 or deaf, as my *m* that I sent
Jer 51:31 one *m* to meet another, to shew
Eze 23:40 from far, unto whom a *m* was sent
Hag 1:13 Then spake Haggai the LORD's *m* in
Mal 2:7 for he is the *m* of the LORD of
Mal 3:1 Behold, I will send my *m*, and he
Mal 3:1 even the *m* of the covenant, whom
Mt 11:10 I send my *m* before thy face,
Mk 1:2 I send my *m* before thy face,
Lk 7:27 I send my *m* before thy face,
2Cor 12:7 the *m* of Satan to buffet me, lest
Phil 2:25 and fellow soldier, but your *m*

**MESSENGERS**
Gen 32:3 Jacob sent *m* before him to Esau
Gen 32:6 the *m* returned to Jacob, saying,
Num 20:14 Moses sent *m* from Kadesh unto the
Num 21:21 Israel sent *m* unto Sihon king of
Num 22:5 He sent *m* therefore unto Balaam
Num 24:12 Spake I not also to thy *m* which
Deut 2:26 I sent *m* out of the wilderness of
Josh 6:17 she hid the *m* that we sent
Josh 6:25 because she hid the *m*, which
Josh 7:22 So Joshua sent *m*, and they ran
Judg 6:35 he sent *m* throughout all Manasseh
Judg 6:35 he sent *m* unto Asher, and unto
Judg 7:24 Gideon sent *m* throughout all
Judg 9:31 he sent *m* unto Abimelech privily,
Judg 11:12 Jephthah sent *m* unto the king of
Judg 11:13 answered unto the *m* of Jephthah
Judg 11:14 Jephthah sent *m* again unto the
Judg 11:17 Then Israel sent *m* unto the king
Judg 11:19 Israel sent *m* unto Sihon king of
1Sa 6:21 they sent *m* to the inhabitants of
1Sa 11:3 that we may send *m* unto all the
1Sa 11:4 Then came the *m* to Gibeah of Saul
1Sa 11:7 of Israel by the hands of *m*
1Sa 11:9 And they said unto the *m* that came
1Sa 11:9 the *m* came and shewed it to the
1Sa 16:19 Wherefore Saul sent *m* unto Jesse
1Sa 19:11 Saul also sent *m* unto David's
1Sa 19:14 And when Saul sent *m* to take David
1Sa 19:15 Saul sent the *m* again to see
1Sa 19:16 when the *m* were come in, behold,
1Sa 19:20 Saul sent *m* to take David
1Sa 19:20 of God was upon the *m* of Saul
1Sa 19:21 it was told Saul, he sent other *m*
1Sa 19:21 Saul sent *m* again the third time,
1Sa 25:14 Behold, David sent *m* out of the
1Sa 25:42 and she went after the *m* of David
2Sa 2:5 David sent *m* unto the men of
2Sa 3:12 Abner sent *m* to David on his
2Sa 3:14 David sent *m* to Ish-bosheth
2Sa 3:26 he sent *m* after Abner, which
2Sa 5:11 king of Tyre sent *m* to David
2Sa 11:4 And David sent *m*, and took her
2Sa 12:27 And Joab sent *m* to David, and said,
1Kin 20:2 he sent *m* to Ahab king of Israel
1Kin 20:5 the *m* came again, and said, Thus
1Kin 20:9 he said unto the *m* of Ben-hadad
1Kin 20:9 the *m* departed, and brought him
2Kin 1:2 and he sent *m*, and said unto them,
2Kin 1:3 go up to meet the *m* of the king
2Kin 1:5 when the *m* turned back unto him,
2Kin 1:16 Forasmuch as thou hast sent *m* to
2Kin 7:15 the *m* returned, and told the king
2Kin 14:8 Then Amaziah sent *m* to Jehoash
2Kin 16:7 So Ahaz sent *m* to Tiglath-pileser
2Kin 17:4 for he had sent *m* to So king of
2Kin 19:9 he sent *m* again unto Hezekiah,
2Kin 19:14 the letter of the hand of the *m*
2Kin 19:23 By thy *m* thou hast reproached the
1Chr 14:1 king of Tyre sent *m* to David
1Chr 19:2 David sent *m* to comfort him
1Chr 19:16 worse before Israel, they sent *m*
2Chr 36:15 fathers sent to them by his *m*
2Chr 36:16 But they mocked the *m* of God
Neh 6:3 I sent *m* unto them, saying, I am
Prov 16:14 wrath of a king is as *m* of death
Is 14:32 then answer the *m* of the nation
Is 18:2 waters, saying, Go, ye swift *m*
Is 37:9 he sent *m* to Hezekiah, saying,
Is 37:14 the letter from the hand of the *m*
Is 44:26 performeth the counsel of his *m*
Is 57:9 and didst send thy *m* far off
Jer 27:3 by the hand of the *m* which come
Eze 23:16 sent *m* unto them into Chaldea
Eze 30:9 In that day shall *m* go forth from
Nah 2:13 the voice of thy *m* shall no more
Lk 7:24 when the *m* of John were departed,
Lk 9:52 And sent *m* before his face
2Cor 8:23 they are the *m* of the churches,
Jas 2:25 when she had received the *m*

**MESSIAH** *(mes-si'-ah)* See MESSIAS. *The great Deliverer of Israel.*
Dan 9:25 to build Jerusalem unto the *M* the
Dan 9:26 and two weeks shall *M* be cut off

**MESSIAS** *(mes-si'-as)* See MESSIAH. *Greek form of Messiah.*
Jn 1:41 unto him, We have found the *M*
Jn 4:25 unto him, I know that *M* cometh

**MET**
Gen 32:1 way, and the angels of God *m* him
Gen 33:8 thou by all this drove which I *m*
Ex 3:18 God of the Hebrews hath *m* with us
Ex 4:24 in the inn, that the LORD *m* him
Ex 4:27 *m* him in the mount of God, and
Ex 5:3 God of the Hebrews hath *m* with us
Ex 5:20 they *m* Moses and Aaron, who stood
Num 23:4 And God *m* Balaam
Num 23:16 And the LORD *m* Balaam, and put a
Deut 23:4 Because they *m* you not with bread
Deut 25:18 How he *m* thee by the way, and
Josh 11:5 all these kings were *m* together
Josh 17:10 they *m* together in Asher on the
1Sa 10:10 a company of prophets *m* him
1Sa 25:20 and she *m* them
2Sa 2:13 *m* together by the pool of Gibeon
2Sa 16:1 the servant of Mephibosheth *m* him
2Sa 18:9 Absalom *m* the servants of David
1Kin 13:24 a lion *m* him by the way, and slew
1Kin 18:7 in the way, behold, Elijah *m* him
2Kin 9:21 *m* him in the portion of Naboth
2Kin 10:13 Jehu *m* with the brethren of
Neh 13:2 Because they *m* not the children
Ps 85:10 Mercy and truth are *m* together
Prov 7:10 there *m* him a woman with the
Jer 41:6 and it came to pass, as he *m* them
Amos 5:19 flee from a lion, and a bear *m* him
Mt 8:28 there *m* him two possessed with
Mt 28:9 disciples, behold, Jesus *m* them
Mk 5:2 immediately there *m* him out of
Mk 11:4 in a place where two ways *m*
Lk 8:27 there *m* him out of the city a
Lk 9:37 from the hill, much people *m* him
Lk 17:12 there *m* him ten men that were
Jn 4:51 going down, his servants *m* him
Jn 11:20 Jesus was coming, went and *m* him
Jn 11:30 in that place where Martha *m* him
Jn 12:18 this cause the people also *m* him
Acts 10:25 was coming in, Cornelius *m* him
Acts 16:16 with a spirit of divination *m* us
Acts 17:17 daily with them that *m* with him
Acts 20:14 when he *m* with us at Assos, we
Acts 27:41 into a place where two seas *m*
Heb 7:1 who *m* Abraham returning from the
Heb 7:10 father, when Melchisedec *m* him

**METE**
Ex 16:18 when they did *m* it with an omer,
Ps 60:6 *m* out the valley of Succoth
Ps 108:7 *m* out the valley of Succoth
Mt 7:2 and with what measure ye *m*
Mk 4:24 with what measure ye *m*, it shall
Lk 6:38 with the same measure that ye *m*

**METHEG-AMMAH** *(me'-theg-am'-mah) A place in Philistia.*
2Sa 8:1 David took *M* out of the hand of

**METHUSAEL** *(me-thu'-sa-el) A descendant of Cain.*
Gen 4:18 and Mehujael begat *M*
Gen 4:18 and *M* begat Lamech

**METHUSELAH** *(me-thu'-se-lah)* See MATHUSALA. *Son of Enoch.*
Gen 5:21 sixty and five years, and begat *M*
Gen 5:22 he begat *M* three hundred years
Gen 5:25 *M* lived an hundred eighty and
Gen 5:26 *M* lived after he begat Lamech
Gen 5:27 all the days of *M* were nine
1Chr 1:3 Henoch, *M*, Lamech,

**MEUNIM** *(me-u'-nim)* See MEHUNIM. *A family of exiles.*
Neh 7:52 of Besai, the children of *M*

**MEZAHAB** *(mez'-a-hab) Grandmother of Mehetabel.*
Gen 36:39 of Matred, the daughter of *M*
1Chr 1:50 of Matred, the daughter of *M*

**MIAMIN** *(mi'-a-min)* See MIJAMIN, MINIAMIN.
*1. Married a foreigner in exile.*
Ezr 10:25 and Jeziah, and Malchiah, and *M*
*2. A priest with Zerubbabel.*
Neh 12:5 *M*, Maadiah, Bilgah,

**MIBHAR** *(mib'-har) A "mighty man" of David.*
1Chr 11:38 of Nathan, *M* the son of Haggeri,

**MIBSAM** *(mib'-sam)*
*1. A son of Ishmael.*
Gen 25:13 and Kedar, and Adbeel, and *M*
1Chr 1:29 then Kedar, and Adbeel, and *M*
*2. A son of Simeon.*
1Chr 4:25 *M* his son, Mishma his son

**MIBZAR** *(mib'-zar) A descendant of Esau.*
Gen 36:42 Duke Kenaz, duke Teman, duke *M*
1Chr 1:53 Duke Kenaz, duke Teman, duke *M*

**MICAH** *(mi'-cah)* See MICAIAH, MICAH'S, MICHAH.
*1. An Ephraimite who set up idols.*
Judg 17:1 mount Ephraim, whose name was *M*
Judg 17:4 and they were in the house of *M*
Judg 17:5 the man *M* had an house of gods,
Judg 17:8 mount Ephraim to the house of *M*
Judg 17:9 *M* said unto him, Whence comest
Judg 17:10 *M* said unto him, Dwell with me,
Judg 17:12 And *M* consecrated the Levite
Judg 17:12 priest, and was in the house of *M*
Judg 17:13 Then said *M*, Now know I that the
Judg 18:2 mount Ephraim, to the house of *M*
Judg 18:3 When they were by the house of *M*
Judg 18:4 Thus and thus dealeth *M* with me
Judg 18:13 and came unto the house of *M*
Judg 18:15 Levite, even unto the house of *M*
Judg 18:22 a good way from the house of *M*
Judg 18:23 their faces, and said unto *M*
Judg 18:26 when *M* saw that they were too
Judg 18:27 took the things which *M* had made
*2. Head of a Reubenite family.*
1Chr 5:5 *M* his son, Reaia his son, Baal
*3. Son of Merib-baal.*
1Chr 8:34 and Merib-baal begat *M*
1Chr 8:35 And the sons of *M* were, Pithon, and
1Chr 9:40 and Merib-baal begat *M*
1Chr 9:41 And the sons of *M* were, Pithon, and
*4. A family of exiles.*
1Chr 9:15 Galal, and Mattaniah the son of *M*
*5. A sanctuary servant.*
1Chr 23:20 *M* the first, and Jesiah the second
*6. Father of Abdon.*
2Chr 34:20 of Shaphan, and Abdon the son of *M*
*7. A prophet.*
Jer 26:18 *M* the Morasthite prophesied in
Mic 1:1 *M* the Morasthite in the days of

**MICAH'S** *(mi'-cahs) Refers to Micah 1.*
Judg 18:18 And these went into *M* house
Judg 18:22 to *M* house were gathered together
Judg 18:31 they set them up *M* graven image

**MICAIAH** *(mi-ka-i'-ah)* See MICHA, MICHAIAH. *A prophet who foretold Ahab's fall.*
1Kin 22:8 *M* the son of Imlah, by whom we
1Kin 22:9 Hasten hither *M* the son of Imlah
1Kin 22:13 was gone to call *M* spake unto him
1Kin 22:14 *M* said, As the LORD liveth, what
1Kin 22:15 And the king said unto him, *M*

1Kin 22:24 smote *M* on the cheek, and said,
1Kin 22:25 *M* said, Behold, thou shalt see in
1Kin 22:26 the king of Israel said, Take *M*
1Kin 22:28 *M* said, If thou return at all in
2Chr 18:7 the same is *M* the son of Imla
2Chr 18:8 Fetch quickly *M* the son of Imla
2Chr 18:12 that went to call *M* spake to him
2Chr 18:13 *M* said, As the LORD liveth, even
2Chr 18:14 king, the king said unto him, *M*
2Chr 18:23 smote *M* upon the cheek, and said,
2Chr 18:24 *M* said, Behold, thou shalt see on
2Chr 18:25 king of Israel said, Take ye *M*
2Chr 18:27 *M* said, If thou certainly return

**MICHA** *(mi'-cah)* See MICAH, MICAIAH.
*1. Son of Mephibosheth.*
2Sa 9:12 had a young son, whose name was *M*
*2. A Levite who renewed the covenant.*
Neh 10:11 *M*, Rehob, Hashabiah,
*3. A family of exiles.*
Neh 11:17 And Mattaniah the son of *M*
Neh 11:22 son of Mattaniah, the son of *M*

**MICHAEL** *(mi'-ka-el)*
*1. Father of Sethur.*
Num 13:13 of Asher, Sethur the son of *M*
*2. A Gadite who settled in Bashan.*
1Chr 5:13 house of their fathers were, *M*
*3. Son of Jeshishai.*
1Chr 5:14 the son of Gilead, the son of *M*
*4. Son of Baaseiah.*
1Chr 6:40 The son of *M*, the son of Baaseiah
*5. A chief man of Issachar.*
1Chr 7:3 *M*, and Obadiah, and Joel, Ishiah,
*6. A Benjamite in Jerusalem.*
1Chr 8:16 And *M*, and Ispah, and Joha, the sons
*7. A warrior in David's army.*
1Chr 12:20 and Jozabad, and Jediael, and *M*
*8. Father of Omri.*
1Chr 27:18 of Issachar, Omri the son of *M*
*9. A son of Jehoshaphat.*
2Chr 21:2 and Zechariah, and Azariah, and *M*
*10. A family of exiles.*
Ezr 8:8 Zebadiah the son of *M*, and with
*11. Angelic messenger who came to Daniel.*
Dan 10:13 but, lo, *M*, one of the chief
Dan 10:21 these things, but *M* your prince
Dan 12:1 And at that time shall *M* stand up
Jude 9 Yet *M* the archangel, when
Rev 12:7 *M* and his angels fought against

**MICHAH** *(mi'-cah)* See MICAH, MICHAIAH. *A sanctuary servant.*
1Chr 24:24 sons of Uzziel; *M*
1Chr 24:24 of the sons of *M*
1Chr 24:25 The brother of *M* was Isshiah

**MICHAIAH** *(mi-ka-i'-ah)* See MICAH, MICAIAH.
*1. Father of Achbor.*
2Kin 22:12 Shaphan, and Achbor the son of *M*
*2. Wife of King Rehoboam.*
2Chr 13:2 His mother's name also was *M* the
*3. A prince of Judah.*
2Chr 17:7 and to Nethaneel, and to *M*
*4. A priest with Zerubbabel.*
Neh 12:35 son of Mattaniah, the son of *M*
Neh 12:41 Eliakim, Maaseiah, Miniamin, *M*
*5. Son of Gemariah.*
Jer 36:11 When *M* the son of Gemariah, the
Jer 36:13 Then *M* declared unto them all the

**MICHAL** *(mi'-kal)* See EGLAH. *A wife of David.*
1Sa 14:49 and the name of the younger *M*
1Sa 18:20 *M* Saul's daughter loved David
1Sa 18:27 Saul gave him *M* his daughter to
1Sa 18:28 that *M* Saul's daughter loved him
1Sa 19:11 *M* David's wife told him, saying,
1Sa 19:12 So *M* let David down through a
1Sa 19:13 *M* took an image, and laid it in
1Sa 19:17 And Saul said unto *M*, Why hast
1Sa 19:17 *M* answered Saul, He said unto me,
1Sa 25:44 But Saul had given *M* his daughter
2Sa 3:13 first bring *M* Saul's daughter
2Sa 3:14 son, saying, Deliver me my wife *M*
2Sa 6:16 *M* Saul's daughter looked through
2Sa 6:20 *M* the daughter of Saul came out
2Sa 6:21 And David said unto *M*, It was
2Sa 6:23 Therefore *M* the daughter of Saul
2Sa 21:8 the five sons of *M* the daughter
1Chr 15:29 that *M* the daughter of Saul

**MICHMAS** *(mik'-mas)* See MICHMASH. *Home of some exiles.*
Ezr 2:27 The men of *M*, an hundred twenty
Neh 7:31 The men of *M*, an hundred and

**MICHMASH** *(mik'-mash)* See MICHMAS. *A city near Jerusalem.*
1Sa 13:2 two thousand were with Saul in *M*
1Sa 13:5 and they came up, and pitched in *M*
1Sa 13:11 gathered themselves together at *M*
1Sa 13:16 but the Philistines encamped in *M*
1Sa 13:23 went out to the passage of *M*
1Sa 14:5 situate northward over against *M*
1Sa 14:31 that day from *M* to Aijalon
Neh 11:31 of Benjamin from Geba dwelt at *M*
Is 10:28 at *M* he hath laid up his

**MICHMETHAH** *(mik'-me-thah) A city between Ephraim and Manasseh.*
Josh 16:6 the sea to *M* on the north side
Josh 17:7 of Manasseh was from Asher to *M*

**MICHRI** *(mik'-ri) Father of Uzzi.*
1Chr 9:8 the son of Uzzi, the son of *M*

**MICHTAM** *(mik'-tam) A type of psalm.*
Ps 16:*t* *M* of David
Ps 56:*t* a *M* of David, when the
Ps 57:*t* *M* of David, when he fled from
Ps 58:*t* Musician, Altaschith, *M* of David
Ps 59:*t* Musician, Altaschith, *M* of David
Ps 60:*t* *M* of David, to teach

**MIDDAY**
1Kin 18:29 to pass, when *m* was past, and they
Neh 8:3 gate from the morning until *m*
Acts 26:13 At *m*, O king, I saw in the way a

**MIDDIN** *(mid'-din) A city in the wilderness south of Judah.*
Josh 15:61 In the wilderness, Beth-arabah, *M*

**MIDDLE**
Ex 26:28 the *m* bar in the midst of the
Ex 36:33 he made the *m* bar to shoot
Josh 12:2 from the *m* of the river, and from
Judg 7:19 in the beginning of the *m* watch
Judg 9:37 people down by the *m* of the land
Judg 16:29 Samson took hold of the two *m*
1Sa 25:29 out, as out of the *m* of a sling
2Sa 10:4 cut off their garments in the *m*
1Kin 6:6 the *m* was six cubits broad, and
1Kin 6:8 The door for the *m* chamber was in
1Kin 6:8 winding stairs into the *m* chamber
1Kin 6:8 out of the *m* into the third
1Kin 8:64 day did the king hallow the *m* of
2Kin 20:4 was gone out into the *m* court
2Chr 7:7 *m* of the court that was before
Jer 39:3 came in, and sat in the *m* gate
Eze 1:16 were a wheel in the *m* of a wheel
Eph 2:14 hath broken down the *m* wall of

**MIDIAN** *(mid'-e-an)* See MADIAN, MIDIANITE.
*1. A son of Abraham.*
Gen 25:2 and Jokshan, and Medan, and *M*
Gen 25:4 And the sons of *M*
1Chr 1:32 and Jokshan, and Medan, and *M*
1Chr 1:33 And the sons of *M*
*2. A nation on the southern border of Israel.*
Gen 36:35 who smote *M* in the field of Moab,
Ex 2:15 and dwelt in the land of *M*
Ex 2:16 Now the priest of *M* had seven
Ex 3:1 father in law, the priest of *M*
Ex 4:19 And the LORD said unto Moses in *M*
Ex 18:1 When Jethro, the priest of *M*
Num 22:4 And Moab said unto the elders of *M*
Num 22:7 the elders of *M* departed with the
Num 25:15 people, and of a chief house in *M*
Num 25:18 the daughter of a prince of *M*
Num 31:3 and avenge the LORD of *M*
Num 31:8 And they slew the kings of *M*
Num 31:8 and Hur, and Reba, five kings of *M*
Num 31:9 took all the women of *M* captives
Josh 13:21 Moses smote with the princes of *M*
Judg 6:1 into the hand of *M* seven years
Judg 6:2 the hand of *M* prevailed against
Judg 7:8 the host of *M* was beneath him in
Judg 7:13 bread tumbled into the host of *M*
Judg 7:14 his hand hath God delivered *M*
Judg 7:15 into your hand the host of *M*
Judg 7:25 winepress of Zeeb, and pursued *M*
Judg 8:3 into your hands the princes of *M*
Judg 8:5 Zebah and Zalmunna, kings of *M*
Judg 8:12 them, and took the two kings of *M*
Judg 8:22 delivered us from the hand of *M*
Judg 8:26 that was on the kings of *M*
Judg 8:28 Thus was *M* subdued before the
Judg 9:17 you out of the hand of *M*
1Kin 11:18 And they arose out of *M*, and came
1Chr 1:46 which smote *M* in the field of
Is 9:4 his oppressor, as in the day of *M*
Is 10:26 of *M* at the rock of Oreb
Is 60:6 cover thee, the dromedaries of *M*
Hab 3:7 of the land of *M* did tremble

**MIDIANITE** *(mid'-e-an-ite)* See MIDIANITES, MIDIANITISH. *A descendant of Midian.*
Num 10:29 Hobab, the son of Raguel the *M*

**MIDIANITES** *(mid'-e-an-ites)* See KENITES.
Gen 37:28 there passed by *M* merchantmen
Gen 37:36 the *M* sold him into Egypt unto
Num 25:17 Vex the *M*, and smite them
Num 31:2 the children of Israel of the *M*
Num 31:3 war, and let them go against the *M*
Num 31:7 And they warred against the *M*
Judg 6:2 because of the *M* the children of
Judg 6:3 had sown, that the *M* came up
Judg 6:6 impoverished because of the *M*
Judg 6:7 unto the LORD because of the *M*
Judg 6:11 winepress, to hide it from the *M*
Judg 6:13 us into the hands of the *M*
Judg 6:14 Israel from the hand of the *M*
Judg 6:16 thou shalt smite the *M* as one man
Judg 6:33 Then all the *M* and the Amalekites
Judg 7:1 so that the host of the *M* were on
Judg 7:2 me to give the *M* into their hands
Judg 7:7 deliver the *M* into thine hand
Judg 7:12 And the *M* and the Amalekites and all
Judg 7:23 Manasseh, and pursued after the *M*
Judg 7:24 saying, Come down against the *M*
Judg 7:25 And they took two princes of the *M*
Judg 8:1 thou wentest to fight with the *M*
Ps 83:9 Do unto them as unto the *M*

**MIDIANITISH** *(mid'-e-an-i'-tish) Belonging to the land of Midian.*
Num 25:6 a *M* woman in the sight of Moses
Num 25:14 that was slain with the *M* woman
Num 25:15 the name of the *M* woman that was

**MIDNIGHT**
Ex 11:4 About *m* will I go out into the
Ex 12:29 at *m* the LORD smote all the
Judg 16:3 lay till *m*, and arose at *m*
Ruth 3:8 it came to pass at *m*, that the
1Kin 3:20 arose at *m*, and took my son
Job 34:20 the people shall be troubled at *m*
Ps 119:62 At *m* I will rise to give thanks
Mt 25:6 *m* there was a cry made, Behold
Mk 13:35 house cometh, at even, or at *m*
Lk 11:5 and shall go unto him at *m*
Acts 16:25 at *m* Paul and Silas prayed, and
Acts 20:7 and continued his speech until *m*
Acts 27:27 about *m* the shipmen deemed

**MIDWIVES**
Ex 1:15 of Egypt spake to the Hebrew *m*
Ex 1:17 But the *m* feared God, and did not
Ex 1:18 king of Egypt called for the *m*
Ex 1:19 the *m* said unto Pharaoh, Because
Ex 1:19 ere the *m* come in unto them
Ex 1:20 God dealt well with the *m*
Ex 1:21 to pass, because the *m* feared God

**MIGDAL-EL** *(mig'-dal-el) A city in Naphtali.*
Josh 19:38 And Iron, and *M*, Horem, and

**MIGDAL-GAD** *(mig'-dal-gad) A city in Judah.*
Josh 15:37 Zenan, and Hadashah, and *M*,

**MIGDOL** *(mig'-dol)*
*1. A place west of the Red Sea.*
Ex 14:2 before Pi-hahiroth, between *M*
Num 33:7 and they pitched before *M*
*2. A place in northern Egypt.*
Jer 44:1 land of Egypt, which dwell at *M*
Jer 46:14 ye in Egypt, and publish in *M*

**MIGHTIER**
Gen 26:16 for thou art much *m* than we
Ex 1:9 of Israel are more and *m* than we
Num 14:12 a greater nation and *m* than they
Deut 4:38 *m* than thou art, to bring thee in
Deut 7:1 nations greater and *m* than thou
Deut 9:1 *m* than thyself, cities great and

Deut 9:14 and I will make of thee a nation *m*
Deut 11:23 nations and *m* than yourselves
Ps 93:4 The LORD on high is *m* than the
Eccl 6:10 with him that is *m* than he
Mt 3:11 that cometh after me is *m* than I
Mk 1:7 cometh one *m* than I after me
Lk 3:16 but one *m* than I cometh, the

## MIGHTILY

Deut 6:3 thee, and that ye may increase *m*
Judg 4:3 twenty years he *m* oppressed the
Judg 14:6 of the LORD came *m* upon him
Judg 15:14 of the LORD came *m* upon him
Jer 25:30 he shall *m* roar upon his
Jonah 3:8 with sackcloth, and cry *m* unto God
Nah 2:1 loins strong, fortify thy power *m*
Acts 18:28 For he *m* convinced the Jews, and
Acts 19:20 So *m* grew the word of God and
Col 1:29 which worketh in me *m*
Rev 18:2 he cried *m* with a strong voice,

## MIGHTY

Gen 6:4 the same became *m* men which were
Gen 10:8 began to be a *m* one in the earth
Gen 10:9 He was a *m* hunter before the LORD
Gen 10:9 Even as Nimrod the *m* hunter
Gen 18:18 *m* nation, and all the nations of
Gen 23:6 thou art a *m* prince among us
Gen 49:24 the hands of the *m* God of Jacob
Ex 1:7 multiplied, and waxed exceeding *m*
Ex 1:20 multiplied, and waxed very *m*
Ex 3:19 let you go, no, not by a *m* hand
Ex 9:28 there be no more *m* thunderings
Ex 10:19 LORD turned a *m* strong west wind
Ex 15:10 they sank as lead in the *m* waters
Ex 15:15 the *m* men of Moab, trembling
Ex 32:11 great power, and with a *m* hand
Lev 19:15 nor honour the person of the *m*
Num 22:6 for they are too *m* for me
Deut 3:24 thy greatness, and thy *m* hand
Deut 4:34 and by war, and by a *m* hand
Deut 4:37 with his *m* power out of Egypt
Deut 5:15 thee out thence through a *m* hand
Deut 6:21 us out of Egypt with a *m* hand
Deut 7:8 brought you out with a *m* hand
Deut 7:19 the *m* hand, and the stretched out
Deut 7:21 is among you, a *m* God and terrible
Deut 7:23 destroy them with a *m* destruction
Deut 9:26 forth out of Egypt with a *m* hand
Deut 9:29 broughtest out by thy *m* power
Deut 10:17 Lord of lords, a great God, a *m*
Deut 11:2 his *m* hand, and his stretched out
Deut 26:5 became there a nation, great, *m*
Deut 26:8 forth out of Egypt with a *m* hand
Deut 34:12 And in all that *m* hand, and in all
Josh 1:14 all the *m* men of valour, and help
Josh 4:24 hand of the LORD, that it is *m*
Josh 6:2 thereof, and the *m* men of valour
Josh 8:3 thirty thousand *m* men of valour
Josh 10:2 Ai, and all the men thereof were *m*
Josh 10:7 him, and all the *m* men of valour
Judg 5:13 made me have dominion over the *m*
Judg 5:22 the pransings of their *m* ones
Judg 5:23 help of the LORD against the *m*
Judg 6:12 with thee, thou *m* man of valour
Judg 11:1 Gileadite was a *m* man of valour
Ruth 2:1 a *m* man of wealth, of the family
1Sa 2:4 The bows of the *m* men are broken
1Sa 4:8 out of the hand of these *m* Gods
1Sa 9:1 a Benjamite, a *m* man of power
1Sa 16:18 a *m* valiant man, and a man of war,
2Sa 1:19 how are the *m* fallen
2Sa 1:21 of the *m* is vilely cast away
2Sa 1:22 the slain, from the fat of the *m*
2Sa 1:25 How are the *m* fallen in the midst
2Sa 1:27 How are the *m* fallen, and the
2Sa 10:7 and all the host of the *m* men
2Sa 16:6 all the *m* men were on his right
2Sa 17:8 and his men, that they be *m* men
2Sa 17:10 that thy father is a *m* man
2Sa 20:7 the Pelethites, and all the *m* men
2Sa 23:8 names of the *m* men whom David had
2Sa 23:9 one of the three *m* men with David
2Sa 23:16 the three *m* men brake through the
2Sa 23:17 things did these three *m* men
2Sa 23:22 had the name among three *m* men
1Kin 1:8 the *m* men which belonged to David
1Kin 1:10 prophet, and Benaiah, and the *m* men
1Kin 11:28 Jeroboam was a *m* man of valour
2Kin 5:1 he was also a *m* man in valour
2Kin 15:20 even of all the *m* men of wealth
2Kin 24:14 all the *m* men of valour, even ten
2Kin 24:15 the *m* of the land, those carried
1Chr 1:10 he began to be *m* upon the earth
1Chr 5:24 *m* men of valour, famous men, and
1Chr 7:7 of their fathers, *m* men of valour
1Chr 7:9 *m* men of valour, was twenty
1Chr 7:11 *m* men of valour, were seventeen
1Chr 7:40 *m* men of valour, chief of the
1Chr 8:40 sons of Ulam were *m* men of valour
1Chr 11:10 chief of the *m* men whom David had
1Chr 11:11 of the *m* men whom David had
1Chr 12:1 and they were among the *m* men
1Chr 12:4 a *m* man among the thirty, and over
1Chr 12:21 for they were all *m* men of valour
1Chr 12:25 *m* men of valour for the war,
1Chr 12:28 And Zadok, a young man *m* of valour
1Chr 12:30 hundred, *m* men of valour, famous
1Chr 19:8 and all the host of the *m* men
1Chr 26:6 for they were *m* men of valour
1Chr 26:31 them *m* men of valour at Jazer of
1Chr 27:6 who was *m* among the thirty, and
1Chr 28:1 the officers, and with the *m* men
1Chr 29:24 And all the princes, and the *m* men
2Chr 6:32 thy *m* hand, and thy stretched out
2Chr 13:3 chosen men, being *m* men of valour
2Chr 13:21 But Abijah waxed *m*, and married
2Chr 14:8 all these were *m* men of valour
2Chr 17:13 of war, *m* men of valour, were in
2Chr 17:14 with him *m* men of valour three
2Chr 17:16 hundred thousand *m* men of valour
2Chr 17:17 Eliada a *m* man of valour, and with
2Chr 25:6 hired also an hundred thousand *m*
2Chr 26:12 *m* men of valour were two thousand
2Chr 26:13 that made war with *m* power
2Chr 27:6 So Jotham became *m*, because he
2Chr 28:7 a *m* man of Ephraim, slew Maaseiah
2Chr 32:3 his *m* men to stop the waters of
2Chr 32:21 cut off all the *m* men of valour
Ezr 4:20 There have been *m* kings also over
Ezr 7:28 before all the king's *m* princes
Neh 3:16 made, and unto the house of the *m*
Neh 9:11 as a stone into the *m* waters
Neh 9:32 our God, the great, the *m*
Neh 11:14 *m* men of valour, an hundred
Job 5:15 mouth, and from the hand of the *m*
Job 6:23 Redeem me from the hand of the *m*
Job 9:4 wise in heart, and *m* in strength
Job 12:19 spoiled, and overthroweth the *m*
Job 12:21 weakeneth the strength of the *m*
Job 21:7 become old, yea, are *m* in power
Job 22:8 But as for the *m* man, he had the
Job 24:22 draweth also the *m* with his power
Job 34:20 the *m* shall be taken away without
Job 34:24 in pieces *m* men without number
Job 35:9 out by reason of the arm of the *m*
Job 36:5 Behold, God is *m*, and despiseth
Job 36:5 he is *m* in strength and wisdom
Job 41:25 up himself, the *m* are afraid
Ps 24:8 and *m*, the LORD *m* in battle
Ps 29:1 Give unto the LORD, O ye *m*
Ps 33:16 a *m* man is not delivered by much
Ps 45:3 sword upon thy thigh, O most *m*
Ps 50:1 The *m* God, even the LORD, hath
Ps 52:1 thou thyself in mischief, O *m* man
Ps 59:3 the *m* are gathered against me
Ps 68:33 out his voice, and that a *m* voice
Ps 69:4 mine enemies wrongfully, are *m*
Ps 74:15 thou driedst up *m* rivers
Ps 78:65 like a *m* man that shouteth by
Ps 82:1 in the congregation of the *m*
Ps 89:6 who among the sons of the *m* can
Ps 89:13 Thou hast a *m* arm
Ps 89:19 have laid help upon one that is *m*
Ps 89:50 the reproach of all the *m* people
Ps 93:4 than the *m* waves of the sea
Ps 106:2 can utter the *m* acts of the LORD
Ps 106:8 make his *m* power to be known
Ps 112:2 His seed shall be *m* upon earth
Ps 120:4 Sharp arrows of the *m*, with coals
Ps 127:4 arrows are in the hand of a *m* man
Ps 132:2 and vowed unto the *m* God of Jacob
Ps 132:5 habitation for the *m* God of Jacob
Ps 135:10 great nations, and slew *m* kings
Ps 145:4 and shall declare thy *m* acts
Ps 145:12 to the sons of men his *m* acts
Ps 150:2 Praise him for his *m* acts
Prov 16:32 to anger is better than the *m*
Prov 18:18 cease, and parteth between the *m*
Prov 21:22 man scaleth the city of the *m*
Prov 23:11 For their redeemer is *m*
Eccl 7:19 the wise more than ten *m* men
Song 4:4 bucklers, all shields of *m* men
Is 1:24 the *m* One of Israel, Ah, I will
Is 3:2 The *m* man, and the man of war, the
Is 3:25 by the sword, and thy *m* in the war
Is 5:15 the *m* man shall be humbled, and
Is 5:22 them that are *m* to drink wine
Is 9:6 Wonderful, Counsellor, The *m* God
Is 10:21 remnant of Jacob, unto the *m* God
Is 10:34 and Lebanon shall fall by a *m* one
Is 11:15 with his *m* wind shall he shake
Is 13:3 called my *m* ones for mine anger
Is 17:12 like the rushing of *m* waters
Is 21:17 the *m* men of the children of
Is 22:17 thee away with a *m* captivity
Is 28:2 Behold, the Lord hath a *m*
Is 28:2 storm, as a flood of *m* waters
Is 30:29 the LORD, to the *m* One of Israel
Is 31:8 with the sword, not of a *m* man
Is 42:13 LORD shall go forth as a *m* man
Is 43:16 sea, and a path in the *m* waters
Is 49:24 the prey be taken from the *m*
Is 49:25 of the *m* shall be taken away
Is 49:26 thy Redeemer, the *m* One of Jacob
Is 60:16 thy Redeemer, the *m* One of Jacob
Is 63:1 speak in righteousness, *m* to save
Jer 5:15 it is a *m* nation, it is an
Jer 5:16 sepulchre, they are all *m* men
Jer 9:23 neither let the *m* man glory in
Jer 14:9 as a *m* man that cannot save
Jer 20:11 is with me as a *m* terrible one
Jer 26:21 the king, with all his *m* men
Jer 32:18 the Great, the *M* God, the LORD of
Jer 32:19 Great in counsel, and *m* in work
Jer 33:3 *m* things, which thou knowest not
Jer 41:16 even *m* men of war, and the women,
Jer 46:5 their *m* ones are beaten down, and
Jer 46:6 flee away, nor the *m* man escape
Jer 46:9 and let the *m* men come forth
Jer 46:12 for the *m* man hath stumbled
Jer 46:12 man hath stumbled against the *m*
Jer 48:14 How say ye, We are *m* and strong
Jer 48:41 the *m* men's hearts in Moab at
Jer 49:22 *m* men of Edom be as the heart of
Jer 50:9 shall be as of a *m* expert man
Jer 50:36 a sword is upon her *m* men
Jer 51:30 The *m* men of Babylon have forborn
Jer 51:56 her *m* men are taken, every one of
Jer 51:57 and her rulers, and her *m* men
Lam 1:15 all my *m* men in the midst of me
Eze 17:13 hath also taken the *m* of the land
Eze 17:17 shall Pharaoh with his *m* army
Eze 20:33 Lord GOD, surely with a *m* hand
Eze 20:34 ye are scattered, with a *m* hand
Eze 31:11 hand of the *m* one of the heathen
Eze 32:12 By the swords of the *m* will I
Eze 32:21 The strong among the *m* shall
Eze 32:27 with the *m* that are fallen of the
Eze 32:27 the *m* in the land of the living
Eze 38:15 a great company, and a *m* army
Eze 39:18 Ye shall eat the flesh of the *m*
Eze 39:20 horses and chariots, with *m* men
Dan 3:20 he commanded the most *m* men that
Dan 4:3 and how *m* are his wonders
Dan 8:24 And his power shall be *m*, but not
Dan 8:24 practise, and shall destroy the *m*
Dan 9:15 the land of Egypt with a *m* hand
Dan 11:3 a *m* king shall stand up, that
Dan 11:25 with a very great and *m* army
Hos 10:13 in the multitude of thy *m* men
Joel 2:7 They shall run like *m* men
Joel 3:9 Prepare war, wake up the *m* men
Joel 3:11 cause thy *m* ones to come down
Amos 2:14 shall the *m* deliver himself
Amos 2:16 *m* shall flee away naked in that
Amos 5:12 transgressions and your *m* sins
Amos 5:24 and righteousness as a *m* stream
Obad 9 And thy *m* men, O Teman, shall be
Jonah 1:4 there was a *m* tempest in the sea,
Nah 2:3 shield of his *m* men is made red
Hab 1:12 O *m* God, thou hast established
Zeph 1:14 the *m* man shall cry there
Zeph 3:17 thy God in the midst of thee is *m*
Zec 9:13 made thee as the sword of a *m* man
Zec 10:5 And they shall be as *m* men
Zec 10:7 of Ephraim shall be like a *m* man
Zec 11:2 because the *m* are spoiled
Mt 11:20 most of his *m* works were done
Mt 11:21 for if the *m* works, which were
Mt 11:23 for if the *m* works, which have

Mt 13:54 man this wisdom, and these *m* works
Mt 13:58 he did not many *m* works there
Mt 14:2 therefore *m* works do shew forth
Mk 6:2 that even such *m* works are
Mk 6:5 And he could there do no *m* work
Mk 6:14 therefore *m* works do shew forth
Lk 1:49 For he that is *m* hath done to me
Lk 1:52 put down the *m* from their seats
Lk 9:43 all amazed at the *m* power of God
Lk 10:13 for if the *m* works had been done
Lk 15:14 there arose a *m* famine in that
Lk 19:37 the *m* works that they had seen
Lk 24:19 which was a prophet *m* in deed
Acts 2:2 heaven as of a rushing *m* wind
Acts 7:22 was *m* in words and in deeds
Acts 18:24 *m* in the scriptures, came to
Rom 15:19 Through *m* signs and wonders, by
1Cor 1:26 men after the flesh, not many *m*
1Cor 1:27 confound the things which are *m*
2Cor 10:4 but *m* through God to the pulling
2Cor 12:12 in signs, and wonders, and *m* deeds
2Cor 13:3 is not weak, but is *m* in you
Gal 2:8 the same was *m* in me toward the
Eph 1:19 to the working of his *m* power
2Th 1:7 from heaven with his *m* angels
1Pet 5:6 therefore under the *m* hand of God
Rev 6:13 when she is shaken of a *m* wind
Rev 6:15 the chief captains, and the *m* men
Rev 10:1 I saw another *m* angel come down
Rev 16:18 so *m* an earthquake, and so great
Rev 18:10 great city Babylon, that *m* city
Rev 18:21 a *m* angel took up a stone like a
Rev 19:6 and as the voice of *m* thunderings
Rev 19:18 captains, and the flesh of *m* men

**MIGRON** *(mi'-gron) A city in Benjamin.*
1Sa 14:2 a pomegranate tree which is in *M*
Is 10:28 come to Aiath, he is passed to *M*

**MIJAMIN** *(mij'-a-min)* See MIAMIN.
*1. A priest in David's time.*
1Chr 24:9 to Malchijah, the sixth to *M*
*2. A priest who renewed the covenant.*
Neh 10:7 Meshullam, Abijah, *M*,

**MIKLOTH** *(mik'-loth)*
*1. A Benjamite in Jerusalem.*
1Chr 8:32 And *M* begat Shimeah
1Chr 9:37 and Ahio, and Zechariah, and *M*
1Chr 9:38 And *M* begat Shimeam
*2. A ruler of David's guard.*
1Chr 27:4 his course was *M* also the ruler

**MIKNEIAH** *(mik-ne-i'-ah) A Levite musician.*
1Chr 15:18 and Mattithiah, and Elipheleh, and *M*
1Chr 15:21 And Mattithiah, and Elipheleh, and *M*

**MILALAI** *(mil'-a-lahee) A priest who purified the wall.*
Neh 12:36 brethren, Shemaiah, and Azarael, *M*

**MILCAH** *(mil'-cah)*
*1. Daughter of Haran.*
Gen 11:29 and the name of Nahor's wife, *M*
Gen 11:29 of Haran, the father of *M*
Gen 22:20 told Abraham, saying, Behold, *M*
Gen 22:23 these eight *M* did bear to Nahor,
Gen 24:15 who was born to Bethuel, son of *M*
Gen 24:24 daughter of Bethuel the son of *M*
Gen 24:47 Nahor's son, whom *M* bare unto him
*2. A daughter of Zelophehad.*
Num 26:33 were Mahlah, and Noah, Hoglah, *M*
Num 27:1 Mahlah, Noah, and Hoglah, and *M*
Num 36:11 Mahlah, Tirzah, and Hoglah, and *M*
Josh 17:3 Mahlah, and Noah, Hoglah, *M*

**MILCOM** *(mil'-com)* See MALCHAM, MOLECH. *Chief god of the Ammonites.*
1Kin 11:5 after *M* the abomination of the
1Kin 11:33 *M* the god of the children of
2Kin 23:13 for *M* the abomination of the

**MILETUM** *(mi-le'-tum)* See MILETUS. *A city in the Roman province of Caria.*
2Ti 4:20 Trophimus have I left at *M* sick

**MILETUS** *(mi-le-tus)* See MILETUM. *Same as Miletum.*
Acts 20:15 and the next day we came to *M*
Acts 20:17 from *M* he sent to Ephesus, and

**MILK**
Gen 18:8 And he took butter, and *m*, and the
Gen 49:12 wine, and his teeth white with *m*
Ex 3:8 large, unto a land flowing with *m*
Ex 3:17 unto a land flowing with *m*
Ex 13:5 give thee, a land flowing with *m*
Ex 23:19 seethe a kid in his mother's *m*
Ex 33:3 Unto a land flowing with *m*
Ex 34:26 seethe a kid in his mother's *m*
Lev 20:24 it, a land that floweth with *m*
Num 13:27 us, and surely it floweth with *m*
Num 14:8 a land which floweth with *m*
Num 16:13 out of a land that floweth with *m*
Num 16:14 into a land that floweth with *m*
Deut 6:3 in the land that floweth with *m*
Deut 11:9 seed, a land that floweth with *m*
Deut 14:21 seethe a kid in his mother's *m*
Deut 26:9 even a land that floweth with *m*
Deut 26:15 a land that floweth with *m*
Deut 27:3 thee, a land that floweth with *m*
Deut 31:20 fathers, that floweth with *m*
Deut 32:14 *m* of sheep, with fat of lambs, and
Josh 5:6 us, a land that floweth with *m*
Judg 4:19 And she opened a bottle of *m*
Judg 5:25 He asked water, and she gave him *m*
Job 10:10 Hast thou not poured me out as *m*
Job 21:24 His breasts are full of *m*
Prov 27:27 have goats' *m* enough for thy food
Prov 30:33 of *m* bringeth forth butter
Song 4:11 honey and *m* are under thy tongue
Song 5:1 I have drunk my wine with my *m*
Song 5:12 rivers of waters, washed with *m*
Is 7:22 of *m* that they shall give
Is 28:9 them that are weaned from the *m*
Is 55:1 *m* without money and without price
Is 60:16 also suck the *m* of the Gentiles
Is 66:11 that ye may *m* out, and be
Jer 11:5 give them a land flowing with *m*
Jer 32:22 give them, a land flowing with *m*
Lam 4:7 snow, they were whiter than *m*
Eze 20:6 espied for them, flowing with *m*
Eze 20:15 I had given them, flowing with *m*
Eze 25:4 fruit, and they shall drink thy *m*
Joel 3:18 and the hills shall flow with *m*
1Cor 3:2 I have fed you with *m*, and not
1Cor 9:7 eateth not of the *m* of the flock
Heb 5:12 are become such as have need of *m*
Heb 5:13 For every one that useth *m* is
1Pet 2:2 desire the sincere *m* of the word

**MILLO** *(mil'-lo)*
*1. A fort near Shechem.*
Judg 9:6 together, and all the house of *M*
Judg 9:20 men of Shechem, and the house of *M*
Judg 9:20 Shechem, and from the house of *M*
*2. A fort near Jerusalem.*
2Sa 5:9 And David built round about from *M*
1Kin 9:15 the LORD, and his own house, and *M*
1Kin 9:24 then did he build *M*
1Kin 11:27 Solomon built *M*, and repaired the
2Kin 12:20 and slew Joash in the house of *M*
1Chr 11:8 about, even from *M* round about
2Chr 32:5 repaired *M* in the city of David,

**MIND**
Gen 23:8 If it be your *m* that I should
Gen 26:35 were a grief of *m* unto Isaac
Lev 24:12 that the *m* of the LORD might be
Num 16:28 have not done them of mine own *m*
Num 24:13 either good or bad of mine own *m*
Deut 18:6 *m* unto the place which the LORD
Deut 28:65 failing of eyes, and sorrow of *m*
Deut 30:1 them to *m* among all the nations
1Sa 2:35 which is in mine heart and in my *m*
1Sa 9:20 days ago, set not thy *m* on them
1Chr 22:7 it was in my *m* to build an house
1Chr 28:9 perfect heart and with a willing *m*
Neh 4:6 for the people had a *m* to work
Job 23:13 But he is in one *m*, and who can
Job 34:33 Should it be according to thy *m*
Ps 31:12 forgotten as a dead man out of *m*
Prov 21:27 he bringeth it with a wicked *m*
Prov 29:11 A fool uttereth all his *m*
Is 26:3 whose *m* is stayed on thee
Is 46:8 bring it again to *m*, O ye
Is 65:17 be remembered, nor come into *m*
Jer 3:16 neither shall it come to *m*
Jer 15:1 yet my *m* could not be toward this
Jer 19:5 it, neither came it into my *m*
Jer 32:35 not, neither came it into my *m*
Jer 44:21 them, and came it not into his *m*
Jer 51:50 and let Jerusalem come into your *m*
Lam 3:21 This I recall to my *m*, therefore
Eze 11:5 the things that come into your *m*
Eze 20:32 into your *m* shall not be at all
Eze 23:17 her *m* was alienated from them
Eze 23:18 then my *m* was alienated from her,
Eze 23:18 like as my *m* was alienated from
Eze 23:22 from whom thy *m* is alienated
Eze 23:28 them from whom thy *m* is alienated
Eze 38:10 time shall things come into thy *m*
Dan 2:29 came into thy *m* upon thy bed
Dan 5:20 his *m* hardened in pride, he was
Hab 1:11 Then shall his *m* change, and he
Mt 22:37 all thy soul, and with all thy *m*
Mk 5:15 and clothed, and in his right *m*
Mk 12:30 all thy soul, and with all thy *m*
Mk 14:72 Peter called to *m* the word that
Lk 1:29 cast in her *m* what manner of
Lk 8:35 Jesus, clothed, and in his right *m*
Lk 10:27 thy strength, and with all thy *m*
Lk 12:29 neither be ye of doubtful *m*
Acts 17:11 the word with all readiness of *m*
Acts 20:19 the Lord with all humility of *m*
Rom 1:28 gave them over to a reprobate *m*
Rom 7:23 warring against the law of my *m*
Rom 7:25 So then with the *m* I myself serve
Rom 8:5 do *m* the things of the flesh
Rom 8:7 Because the carnal *m* is enmity
Rom 8:27 what is the *m* of the Spirit
Rom 11:34 who hath known the *m* of the Lord
Rom 12:2 by the renewing of your *m*
Rom 12:16 Be of the same *m* one toward
Rom 12:16 *M* not high things, but condescend
Rom 14:5 be fully persuaded in his own *m*
Rom 15:6 That ye may with one *m* and one
Rom 15:15 in some sort, as putting you in *m*
1Cor 1:10 joined together in the same *m*
1Cor 2:16 who hath known the *m* of the Lord
1Cor 2:16 But we have the *m* of Christ
2Cor 7:7 your fervent *m* toward me
2Cor 8:12 For if there be first a willing *m*
2Cor 8:19 and declaration of your ready *m*
2Cor 9:2 I know the forwardness of your *m*
2Cor 13:11 be of good comfort, be of one *m*
Eph 2:3 desires of the flesh and of the *m*
Eph 4:17 walk, in the vanity of their *m*
Eph 4:23 renewed in the spirit of your *m*
Phil 1:27 with one *m* striving together for
Phil 2:2 being of one accord, of one *m*
Phil 2:3 but in lowliness of *m* let each
Phil 2:5 Let this *m* be in you, which was
Phil 3:16 rule, let us *m* the same thing
Phil 3:19 their shame, who *m* earthly things
Phil 4:2 they be of the same *m* in the Lord
Col 1:21 enemies in your *m* by wicked works
Col 2:18 vainly puffed up by his fleshly *m*
Col 3:12 kindness, humbleness of *m*
2Th 2:2 That ye be not soon shaken in *m*
2Ti 1:7 and of love, and of a sound *m*
Titus 1:15 but even their *m* and conscience is
Titus 3:1 Put them in *m* to be subject to
Philem 14 But without thy *m* would I do
Heb 8:10 I will put my laws into their *m*
1Pet 1:13 gird up the loins of your *m*
1Pet 3:8 Finally, be ye all of one *m*
1Pet 4:1 likewise with the same *m*
1Pet 5:2 filthy lucre, but of a ready *m*
Rev 17:9 here is the *m* which hath wisdom
Rev 17:13 These have one *m*, and shall give

**MINDED**
Ruth 1:18 was stedfastly *m* to go with her
2Chr 24:4 Joash was *m* to repair the
Ezr 7:13 which are *m* of their own freewill
Mt 1:19 was *m* to put her away privily
Acts 27:39 shore, into the which they were *m*
Rom 8:6 For to be carnally *m* is death
Rom 8:6 but to be spiritually *m* is life
2Cor 1:15 I was *m* to come unto you before
2Cor 1:17 When I therefore was thus *m*
Gal 5:10 that ye will be none otherwise *m*
Phil 3:15 as many as be perfect, be thus *m*
Phil 3:15 if in any thing ye be otherwise *m*
Titus 2:6 men likewise exhort to be sober *m*
Jas 1:8 A double *m* man is unstable in all
Jas 4:8 purify your hearts, ye double *m*

**MINDFUL**
1Chr 16:15 Be ye *m* always of his covenant
Neh 9:17 neither were *m* of thy wonders
Ps 8:4 is man, that thou art *m* of him
Ps 111:5 he will ever be *m* of his covenant
Ps 115:12 The LORD hath been *m* of us
Is 17:10 hast not been *m* of the rock of
2Ti 1:4 being *m* of thy tears, that I may

Heb 2:6 is man, that thou art *m* of him
Heb 11:15 if they had been *m* of that
2Pet 3:2 That ye may be *m* of the words

**MINDS**
Judg 19:30 it, take advice, and speak your *m*
2Sa 17:8 men, and they be chafed in their *m*
2Kin 9:15 And Jehu said, If it be your *m*
Eze 24:25 that whereupon they set their *m*
Eze 36:5 their heart, with despiteful *m*
Acts 14:2 made their *m* evil affected
Acts 28:6 come to him, they changed their *m*
2Cor 3:14 But their *m* were blinded
2Cor 4:4 the *m* of them which believe not
2Cor 11:3 so your *m* should be corrupted
Phil 4:7 hearts and *m* through Christ Jesus
1Ti 6:5 disputings of men of corrupt *m*
2Ti 3:8 men of corrupt *m*, reprobate
Heb 10:16 in their *m* will I write them
Heb 12:3 ye be wearied and faint in your *m*
2Pet 3:1 your pure *m* by way of remembrance

**MINGLED**
Ex 9:24 fire *m* with the hail, very
Ex 29:40 *m* with the fourth part of an hin
Lev 2:4 cakes of fine flour *m* with oil
Lev 2:5 fine flour unleavened, *m* with oil
Lev 7:10 *m* with oil, and dry, shall all the
Lev 7:12 unleavened cakes *m* with oil
Lev 7:12 cakes *m* with oil, of fine flour,
Lev 9:4 and a meat offering *m* with oil
Lev 14:10 *m* with oil, and one log of oil
Lev 14:21 *m* with oil for a meat offering
Lev 19:19 not sow thy field with *m* seed
Lev 19:19 shall a garment *m* of linen
Lev 23:13 deals of fine flour *m* with oil
Num 6:15 cakes of fine flour *m* with oil
Num 7:13 *m* with oil for a meat offering
Num 7:19 *m* with oil for a meat offering
Num 7:25 *m* with oil for a meat offering
Num 7:31 *m* with oil for a meat offering
Num 7:37 *m* with oil for a meat offering
Num 7:43 *m* with oil for a meat offering
Num 7:49 *m* with oil for a meat offering
Num 7:55 *m* with oil for a meat offering
Num 7:61 *m* with oil for a meat offering
Num 7:67 *m* with oil for a meat offering
Num 7:73 *m* with oil for a meat offering
Num 7:79 *m* with oil for a meat offering
Num 8:8 even fine flour *m* with oil
Num 15:4 of a tenth deal of flour *m* with
Num 15:6 two tenth deals of flour *m* with
Num 15:9 flour *m* with half an hin of oil
Num 28:5 *m* with the fourth part of an hin
Num 28:9 *m* with oil, and the drink offering
Num 28:12 *m* with oil, for one bullock
Num 28:12 offering, *m* with oil, for one ram
Num 28:13 *m* with oil for a meat offering
Num 28:20 shall be of flour *m* with oil
Num 28:28 meat offering of flour *m* with oil
Num 29:3 shall be of flour *m* with oil
Num 29:9 shall be of flour *m* with oil
Num 29:14 shall be of flour *m* with oil
Ezr 9:2 so that the holy seed have *m*
Ps 102:9 and *m* my drink with weeping,
Ps 106:35 But were *m* among the heathen, and
Prov 9:2 she hath *m* her wine
Prov 9:5 drink of the wine which I have *m*
Is 19:14 The LORD hath *m* a perverse spirit
Jer 25:20 And all the *m* people, and all the
Jer 25:24 all the kings of the *m* people
Jer 50:37 upon all the *m* people that are in
Eze 30:5 and Lydia, and all the *m* people
Mt 27:34 him vinegar to drink *m* with gall
Mk 15:23 him to drink wine *m* with myrrh
Lk 13:1 had *m* with their sacrifices
Rev 8:7 fire *m* with blood, and they were
Rev 15:2 were a sea of glass *m* with fire

**MINIAMIN** *(min'-e-a-min)* See MIAMIN.
*1. A Levite.*
2Chr 31:15 And next him were Eden, and *M*
*2. A priest with Zerubbabel.*
Neh 12:17 of *M*, of Moadiah, Piltai
Neh 12:41 Eliakim, Maaseiah, *M*, Michaiah,

**MINISTER**
Ex 24:13 And Moses rose up, and his *m* Joshua
Ex 28:1 that he may *m* unto me in the
Ex 28:3 that he may *m* unto me in the
Ex 28:4 that he may *m* unto me in the
Ex 28:35 And it shall be upon Aaron to *m*
Ex 28:41 that they may *m* unto me in the
Ex 28:43 the altar to *m* in the holy place
Ex 29:1 to *m* unto me in the priest's
Ex 29:30 to *m* in the holy place
Ex 29:44 to *m* to me in the priest's office
Ex 30:20 they come near to the altar to *m*
Ex 30:30 that they may *m* unto me in the
Ex 31:10 to *m* in the priest's office,
Ex 35:19 to *m* in the priest's office
Ex 39:26 about the hem of the robe to *m* in
Ex 39:41 to *m* in the priest's office
Ex 40:13 that he may *m* unto me in the
Ex 40:15 that they may *m* unto me in the
Lev 7:35 *m* unto the LORD in the priest's
Lev 16:32 whom he shall consecrate to *m* in
Num 1:50 and they shall *m* unto it, and shall
Num 3:3 to *m* in the priest's office
Num 3:6 priest, that they may *m* unto him
Num 3:31 of the sanctuary wherewith they *m*
Num 4:9 thereof, wherewith they *m* unto it
Num 4:12 wherewith they *m* in the sanctuary
Num 4:14 wherewith they *m* about it
Num 8:26 But shall *m* with their brethren
Num 16:9 the congregation to *m* unto them
Num 18:2 joined unto thee, and *m* unto thee
Num 18:2 shall *m* before the tabernacle of
Deut 10:8 before the LORD to *m* unto him
Deut 17:12 the priest that standeth to *m*
Deut 18:5 to stand to *m* in the name of the
Deut 18:7 Then he shall *m* in the name of
Deut 21:5 thy God hath chosen to *m* unto him
Josh 1:1 Joshua the son of Nun, Moses' *m*
1Sa 2:11 the child did *m* unto the LORD
1Kin 8:11 stand to *m* because of the cloud
1Chr 15:2 of God, and to *m* unto him for ever
1Chr 16:4 certain of the Levites to *m*
1Chr 16:37 to *m* before the ark continually,
1Chr 23:13 to *m* unto him, and to bless in his
1Chr 26:12 to *m* in the house of the LORD
2Chr 5:14 stand to *m* by reason of the cloud
2Chr 8:14 *m* before the priests, as the duty
2Chr 13:10 which *m* unto the LORD, are the
2Chr 23:6 they that *m* of the Levites
2Chr 24:14 of the LORD, even vessels to *m*
2Chr 29:11 him, and that ye should *m* unto him
2Chr 31:2 and for peace offerings, to *m*
Neh 10:36 unto the priests that *m* in the
Neh 10:39 sanctuary, and the priests that *m*
Ps 9:8 he shall *m* judgment to the people
Is 60:7 of Nebaioth shall *m* unto thee
Is 60:10 and their kings shall *m* unto thee
Jer 33:22 and the Levites that *m* unto me
Eze 40:46 near to the LORD to *m* unto him
Eze 42:14 lay their garments wherein they *m*
Eze 43:19 to *m* unto me, saith the Lord GOD,
Eze 44:11 stand before them to *m* unto them
Eze 44:15 come near to me to *m* unto me
Eze 44:16 to *m* unto me, and they shall keep
Eze 44:17 whiles they *m* in the gates of the
Eze 44:27 to *m* in the sanctuary, he shall
Eze 45:4 come near to *m* unto the LORD
Mt 20:26 among you, let him be your *m*
Mt 20:28 to be ministered unto, but to *m*
Mt 25:44 in prison, and did not *m* unto thee
Mk 10:43 great among you, shall be your *m*
Mk 10:45 to be ministered unto, but to *m*
Lk 4:20 and he gave it again to the *m*
Acts 13:5 and they had also John to their *m*
Acts 24:23 to *m* or come unto him
Acts 26:16 this purpose, to make thee a *m*
Rom 13:4 For he is the *m* of God to thee
Rom 13:4 for he is the *m* of God, a
Rom 15:8 a *m* of the circumcision for the
Rom 15:16 That I should be the *m* of Jesus
Rom 15:25 Jerusalem to *m* unto the saints
Rom 15:27 their duty is also to *m* unto them
1Cor 9:13 *m* about holy things live of the
2Cor 9:10 sower both *m* bread for your food
Gal 2:17 is therefore Christ the *m* of sin
Eph 3:7 Whereof I was made a *m*, according
Eph 4:29 that it may *m* grace unto the
Eph 6:21 faithful *m* in the Lord, shall
Col 1:7 is for you a faithful *m* of Christ
Col 1:23 whereof I Paul am made a *m*
Col 1:25 Whereof I am made a *m*, according
Col 4:7 beloved brother, and a faithful *m*
1Th 3:2 *m* of God, and our fellowlabourer
1Ti 1:4 which *m* questions, rather than
1Ti 4:6 shalt be a good *m* of Jesus Christ
Heb 1:14 sent forth to *m* for them who
Heb 6:10 ministered to the saints, and do *m*
Heb 8:2 A *m* of the sanctuary, and of the
1Pet 1:12 but unto us they did *m* the things
1Pet 4:10 even so *m* the same one to another
1Pet 4:11 if any man *m*, let him do it as of

**MINISTERED**
Num 3:4 Ithamar *m* in the priest's office
Deut 10:6 Eleazar his son *m* in the priest's
1Sa 2:18 But Samuel *m* before the LORD,
1Sa 3:1 the child Samuel *m* unto the LORD
2Sa 13:17 his servant that *m* unto him
1Kin 1:4 cherished the king, and *m* to him
1Kin 1:15 the Shunammite *m* unto the king
1Kin 19:21 went after Elijah, and *m* unto him
2Kin 25:14 vessels of brass wherewith they *m*
1Chr 6:32 they *m* before the dwelling place
1Chr 28:1 that *m* to the king by course
2Chr 22:8 that *m* to Ahaziah, he slew them
Est 2:2 king's servants that *m* unto him
Est 6:3 king's servants that *m* unto him
Jer 52:18 vessels of brass wherewith they *m*
Eze 44:12 Because they *m* unto them before
Eze 44:19 off their garments wherein they *m*
Dan 7:10 thousand thousands *m* unto him
Mt 4:11 behold, angels came and *m* unto him
Mt 8:15 and she arose, and *m* unto them
Mt 20:28 Son of man came not to be *m* unto
Mk 1:13 and the angels *m* unto him
Mk 1:31 left her, and she *m* unto them
Mk 10:45 Son of man came not to be *m* unto
Mk 15:41 followed him, and *m* unto him
Lk 4:39 she arose and *m* unto them
Lk 8:3 which *m* unto him of their
Acts 13:2 As they *m* to the Lord, and fasted,
Acts 19:22 two of them that *m* unto him
Acts 20:34 hands have *m* unto my necessities
2Cor 3:3 be the epistle of Christ *m* by us
Phil 2:25 and he that *m* to my wants
Col 2:19 and bands having nourishment *m*
2Ti 1:18 things he *m* unto me at Ephesus
Philem 13 *m* unto me in the bonds of the
Heb 6:10 in that ye have *m* to the saints
2Pet 1:11 For so an entrance shall be *m*

**MINISTERING**
1Chr 9:28 had the charge of the *m* vessels
Eze 44:11 of the house, and *m* to the house
Mt 27:55 Jesus from Galilee, *m* unto him
Rom 12:7 Or ministry, let us wait on our *m*
Rom 15:16 *m* the gospel of God, that the
2Cor 8:4 fellowship of the *m* to the saints
2Cor 9:1 as touching the *m* to the saints
Heb 1:14 Are they not all *m* spirits
Heb 10:11 And every priest standeth daily *m*

**MINISTERS**
1Kin 10:5 and the attendance of his *m*
2Chr 9:4 and the attendance of his *m*
Ezr 7:24 or *m* of this house of God, it
Ezr 8:17 us *m* for the house of our God
Ps 103:21 ye *m* of his, that do his pleasure
Ps 104:4 his *m* a flaming fire
Is 61:6 shall call you the *M* of our God
Jer 33:21 the Levites the priests, my *m*
Eze 44:11 they shall be *m* in my sanctuary
Eze 45:4 priests the *m* of the sanctuary
Eze 45:5 the *m* of the house, have for
Eze 46:24 where the *m* of the house shall
Joel 1:9 the priests, the LORD's *m*
Joel 1:13 howl, ye *m* of the altar
Joel 1:13 in sackcloth, ye *m* of my God
Joel 2:17 the *m* of the LORD, weep between
Lk 1:2 eyewitnesses, and *m* of the word
Rom 13:6 for they are God's *m*, attending
1Cor 3:5 but *m* by whom ye believed, even
1Cor 4:1 of us, as of the *m* of Christ
2Cor 3:6 us able *m* of the new testament
2Cor 6:4 ourselves as the *m* of God
2Cor 11:15 his *m* also be transformed as the
2Cor 11:15 as the *m* of righteousness
2Cor 11:23 Are they *m* of Christ?
Heb 1:7 spirits, and his *m* a flame of fire

**MINISTRATION**
Lk 1:23 days of his *m* were accomplished
Acts 6:1 were neglected in the daily *m*
2Cor 3:7 But if the *m* of death, written and
2Cor 3:8 How shall not the *m* of the spirit
2Cor 3:9 For if the *m* of condemnation be
2Cor 3:9 be glory, much more doth the *m* of
2Cor 9:13 this *m* they glorify God for your

**MINISTRY**
Num 4:12 take all the instruments of *m*
Num 4:47 came to do the service of the *m*
2Chr 7:6 when David praised by their *m*
Hos 12:10 by the *m* of the prophets
Acts 1:17 and had obtained part of this *m*
Acts 1:25 That he may take part of this *m*
Acts 6:4 prayer, and to the *m* of the word
Acts 12:25 when they had fulfilled their *m*
Acts 20:24 my course with joy, and the *m*
Acts 21:19 among the Gentiles by his *m*
Rom 12:7 Or *m*, let us wait on our
1Cor 16:15 themselves to the *m* of the saints
2Cor 4:1 Therefore, seeing we have this *m*
2Cor 5:18 to us the *m* of reconciliation
2Cor 6:3 thing, that the *m* be not blamed
Eph 4:12 the saints, for the work of the *m*
Col 4:17 Take heed to the *m* which thou
1Ti 1:12 faithful, putting me into the *m*
2Ti 4:5 make full proof of thy *m*
2Ti 4:11 he is profitable to me for the *m*
Heb 8:6 he obtained a more excellent *m*
Heb 9:21 and all the vessels of the *m*

**MINNI** *(min'-ni) A district in Armenia.*
Jer 51:27 her the kingdoms of Ararat, *M*

**MINNITH** *(min'-nith) An Ammonite city.*
Judg 11:33 Aroer, even till thou come to *M*
Eze 27:17 traded in thy market wheat of *M*

**MIPHKAD** *(mif'-kad) A gate of Jerusalem.*
Neh 3:31 over against the gate *M*, and to

**MIRACLE**
Ex 7:9 you, saying, Shew a *m* for you
Mk 6:52 not the *m* of the loaves
Mk 9:39 man which shall do a *m* in my name
Lk 23:8 to have seen some *m* done by him
Jn 4:54 again the second *m* that Jesus did
Jn 6:14 had seen the *m* that Jesus did
Jn 10:41 unto him, and said, John did no *m*
Jn 12:18 heard that he had done this *m*
Acts 4:16 *m* hath been done by them is
Acts 4:22 on whom this *m* of healing was

**MIRACLES**
Num 14:22 which have seen my glory, and my *m*
Deut 11:3 And his *m*, and his acts, which he
Deut 29:3 seen, the signs, and those great *m*
Judg 6:13 where be all his *m* which our
Jn 2:11 This beginning of *m* did Jesus in
Jn 2:23 when they saw the *m* which he did
Jn 3:2 can do these *m* that thou doest
Jn 6:2 because they saw his *m* which he
Jn 6:26 seek me, not because ye saw the *m*
Jn 7:31 will he do more *m* than these
Jn 9:16 a man that is a sinner do such *m*
Jn 11:47 for this man doeth many *m*
Jn 12:37 he had done so many *m* before them
Acts 2:22 approved of God among you by *m*
Acts 6:8 wonders and *m* among the people
Acts 8:6 seeing the *m* which he did
Acts 8:13 and wondered, beholding the *m*
Acts 15:12 and Paul, declaring what *m*
Acts 19:11 God wrought special *m* by the
1Cor 12:10 To another the working of *m*
1Cor 12:28 thirdly teachers, after that *m*
1Cor 12:29 are all workers of *m*?
Gal 3:5 worketh *m* among you, doeth he it
Heb 2:4 and wonders, and with divers *m*
Rev 13:14 *m* which he had power to do in the
Rev 16:14 the spirits of devils, working *m*
Rev 19:20 prophet that wrought *m* before him

**MIRE**
2Sa 22:43 stamp them as the *m* of the street
Job 8:11 Can the rush grow up without *m*
Job 30:19 He hath cast me into the *m*
Job 41:30 sharp pointed things upon the *m*
Ps 69:2 I sink in deep *m*, where there is
Ps 69:14 Deliver me out of the *m*, and let
Is 10:6 down like the *m* of the streets
Is 57:20 rest, whose waters cast up *m*
Jer 38:6 dungeon there was no water, but *m*
Jer 38:6 so Jeremiah sunk in the *m*
Jer 38:22 thy feet are sunk in the *m*
Mic 7:10 down as the *m* of the streets
Zec 9:3 fine gold as the *m* of the streets
Zec 10:5 *m* of the streets in the battle
2Pet 2:22 washed to her wallowing in the *m*

**MIRIAM** *(mir'-e-am)* See MARY.
*1. Sister of Aaron.*
Ex 15:20 *M* the prophetess, the sister of
Ex 15:21 *M* answered them, Sing ye to the
Num 12:1 *M* and Aaron spake against Moses
Num 12:4 Moses, and unto Aaron, and unto *M*
Num 12:5 tabernacle, and called Aaron and *M*
Num 12:10 *M* became leprous, white as snow
Num 12:10 and Aaron looked upon *M*, and,
Num 12:15 *M* was shut out from the camp
Num 12:15 not till *M* was brought in again
Num 20:1 *M* died there, and was buried there
Num 26:59 Aaron and Moses, and *M* their sister
Deut 24:9 thy God did unto *M* by the way
1Chr 6:3 Aaron, and Moses, and *M*
Mic 6:4 before thee Moses, Aaron, and *M*
*2. A daughter of Ezra.*
1Chr 4:17 and she bare *M*, and Shammai, and

**MIRMA** *(mur'-mah) Son of Shaharaim.*
1Chr 8:10 And Jeuz, and Shachia, and *M*

**MIRTH**
Gen 31:27 might have sent thee away with *m*
Neh 8:12 send portions, and to make great *m*
Ps 137:3 that wasted us required of us *m*
Prov 14:13 and the end of that *m* is heaviness
Eccl 2:1 to now, I will prove thee with *m*
Eccl 2:2 and of *m*, What doeth it
Eccl 7:4 of fools is in the house of *m*
Eccl 8:15 Then I commended *m*, because a man
Is 24:8 The *m* of tabrets ceaseth, the
Is 24:11 the *m* of the land is gone
Jer 7:34 of Jerusalem, the voice of *m*
Jer 16:9 and in your days, the voice of *m*
Jer 25:10 take from them the voice of *m*
Eze 21:10 should we then make *m*?
Hos 2:11 also cause all her *m* to cease

**MIRY**
Ps 40:2 horrible pit, out of the *m* clay
Eze 47:11 But the *m* places thereof and the
Dan 2:41 sawest the iron mixed with *m* clay
Dan 2:43 sawest iron mixed with *m* clay

**MISCHIEF**
Gen 42:4 Lest peradventure *m* befall him
Gen 42:38 if *m* befall him by the way in the
Gen 44:29 *m* befall him, ye shall bring down
Ex 21:22 from her, and yet no *m* follow
Ex 21:23 And if any *m* follow, then thou
Ex 32:12 For *m* did he bring them out, to
Ex 32:22 people, that they are set on *m*
1Sa 23:9 secretly practised *m* against him
2Sa 16:8 behold, thou art taken in thy *m*
1Kin 11:25 beside the *m* that Hadad did
1Kin 20:7 and see how this man seeketh *m*
2Kin 7:9 light, some *m* will come upon us
Neh 6:2 But they thought to do me *m*
Est 8:3 away the *m* of Haman the Agagite
Job 15:35 They conceive *m*, and bring forth
Ps 7:14 iniquity, and hath conceived *m*
Ps 7:16 His *m* shall return upon his own
Ps 10:7 under his tongue is *m* and vanity
Ps 10:14 for thou beholdest *m* and spite, to
Ps 26:10 In whose hands is *m*, and their
Ps 28:3 but *m* is in their hearts
Ps 36:4 He deviseth *m* upon his bed
Ps 52:1 Why boastest thou thyself in *m*
Ps 55:10 *m* also and sorrow are in the midst
Ps 62:3 will ye imagine *m* against a man
Ps 94:20 thee, which frameth *m* by a law
Ps 119:150 draw nigh that follow after *m*
Ps 140:9 let the *m* of their own lips cover
Prov 4:16 not, except they have done *m*
Prov 6:14 heart, he deviseth *m* continually
Prov 6:18 that be swift in running to *m*
Prov 10:23 It is as sport to a fool to do *m*
Prov 11:27 but he that seeketh *m*, it shall
Prov 12:21 the wicked shall be filled with *m*
Prov 13:17 A wicked messenger falleth into *m*
Prov 17:20 a perverse tongue falleth into *m*
Prov 24:2 and their lips talk of *m*
Prov 24:16 but the wicked shall fall into *m*
Prov 28:14 his heart shall fall into *m*
Is 47:11 and *m* shall fall upon thee
Is 59:4 they conceive *m*, and bring forth
Eze 7:26 *M* shall come upon *m*
Eze 11:2 these are the men that devise *m*
Dan 11:27 kings' hearts shall be to do *m*
Hos 7:15 yet do they imagine *m* against me
Acts 13:10 O full of all subtilty and all *m*

**MISCHIEFS**
Deut 32:23 I will heap *m* upon them
Ps 52:2 Thy tongue deviseth *m*
Ps 140:2 Which imagine *m* in their heart

**MISCHIEVOUS**
Ps 21:11 they imagined a *m* device, which
Ps 38:12 that seek my hurt speak *m* things
Prov 24:8 evil shall be called a *m* person
Eccl 10:13 the end of his talk is *m* madness
Mic 7:3 man, he uttereth his *m* desire

**MISERABLE**
Job 16:2 *m* comforters are ye all
1Cor 15:19 Christ, we are of all men most *m*
Rev 3:17 not that thou art wretched, and *m*

**MISERY**
Judg 10:16 was grieved for the *m* of Israel
Job 3:20 light given to him that is in *m*
Job 11:16 Because thou shalt forget thy *m*
Prov 31:7 and remember his *m* no more
Eccl 8:6 therefore the *m* of man is great
Lam 3:19 mine affliction and my *m*, the
Rom 3:16 and *m* are in their ways

**MISGAB** *(mis'-gab) The mountainous area in Moab.*
Jer 48:1 *M* is confounded and dismayed

**MISHAEL** *(mish'-a-el)* See MISHAL.
*1. A son of Uzziel.*
Ex 6:22 *M*, and Elzaphan, and Zithri
Lev 10:4 Moses called *M* and Elzaphan, and
Dan 1:6 of Judah, Daniel, Hananiah, *M*
Dan 1:7 and to *M*, of Meshach
Dan 1:11 had set over Daniel, Hananiah, *M*
Dan 1:19 none like Daniel, Hananiah, *M*
Dan 2:17 the thing known to Hananiah, *M*
*2. A priest who aided Ezra.*
Neh 8:4 on his left hand, Pedaiah, and *M*

**MISHAL** *(mi'-shal)* See MISHAEL. *A Levitical city in Asher.*
Josh 21:30 *M* with her suburbs, Abdon with

**MISHAM** *(mi'-sham) Son of Elpaal.*
1Chr 8:12 Eber, and *M*, and Shamed, who built

**MISHEAL** *(mish'-e-al) Same as Mishal.*
Josh 19:26 And Alammelech, and Amad, and *M*

**MISHMA** *(mish'-mah) A son of Ishmeal.*
Gen 25:14 And *M*, and Dumah, and Massa,
1Chr 1:30 *M*, and Dumah, Massa, Hadad, and
1Chr 4:25 son, Mibsam his son, *M* his son
1Chr 4:26 And the sons of *M*

**MISHMANNAH** *(mish-man'-nah) A warrior in David's army.*
1Chr 12:10 *M* the fourth, Jeremiah the fifth,

**MISHRAITES** *(mish'-ra-ites) A family of Kirjath-jearim.*
1Chr 2:53 and the Shumathites, and the *M*

**MISPERETH** *(mis-pe'-reth)* See MIZPAR. *An exile with Ezra.*
Neh 7:7 Nahamani, Mordecai, Bilshan, *M*

**MISREPHOTH-MAIM** *Same as Zarephath.*
Josh 11:8 them unto great Zidon, and unto *M*
Josh 13:6 hill country from Lebanon unto *M*

**MISTRESS**
Gen 16:4 her *m* was despised in her eyes
Gen 16:8 flee from the face of my *m* Sarai
Gen 16:9 said unto her, Return to thy *m*
1Kin 17:17 the *m* of the house, fell sick
2Kin 5:3 And she said unto her *m*, Would God
Ps 123:2 a maiden unto the hand of her *m*
Prov 30:23 an handmaid that is heir to her *m*
Is 24:2 as with the maid, so with her *m*
Nah 3:4 the *m* of witchcrafts, that

**MITHCAH** *(mith'-cah) An Israelite encampment in the wilderness.*
Num 33:28 from Tarah, and pitched in *M*
Num 33:29 And they went from *M*, and pitched

**MITHNITE** *(mith'-nite) Family name of Joshaphat.*
1Chr 11:43 of Maachah, and Joshaphat the *M*

**MITHREDATH** *(mith'-re-dath) Treasurer for King Cyrus of Persia.*
Ezr 1:8 by the hand of *M* the treasurer
Ezr 4:7 of Artaxerxes wrote Bishlam, *M*

**MITRE**
Ex 28:4 a robe, and a broidered coat, a *m*
Ex 28:37 lace, that it may be upon the *m*
Ex 28:37 forefront of the *m* it shall be
Ex 28:39 shalt make the *m* of fine linen
Ex 29:6 shalt put the *m* upon his head
Ex 29:6 and put the holy crown upon the *m*
Ex 39:28 a *m* of fine linen, and goodly
Ex 39:31 to fasten it on high upon the *m*
Lev 8:9 he put the *m* upon his head
Lev 8:9 also upon the *m*, even upon his
Lev 16:4 with the linen *m* shall he be
Zec 3:5 them set a fair *m* upon his head
Zec 3:5 they set a fair *m* upon his head

**MITYLENE** *(mit-i-le'-ne) Major city of the island of Lesbos.*
Acts 20:14 we took him in, and came to *M*

**MIXED**
Ex 12:38 a *m* multitude went up also with
Neh 13:3 from Israel all the *m* multitude
Prov 23:30 they that go to seek *m* wine
Is 1:22 dross, thy wine *m* with water
Dan 2:41 sawest the iron *m* with miry clay
Dan 2:43 thou sawest iron *m* with miry clay
Dan 2:43 even as iron is not *m* with clay
Hos 7:8 he hath *m* himself among the
Heb 4:2 not being *m* with faith in them

**MIZAR** *(mi'-zar) A hill near Hermon.*
Ps 42:6 the Hermonites, from the hill *M*

**MIZPAH** *(miz'-pah)* See MIZPEH.
*1. A city in Gad.*
Gen 31:49 And *M*; for he said
*2. A city in Benjamin.*
1Kin 15:22 with them Geba of Benjamin, and *M*
Neh 3:7 the men of Gibeon, and of *M*
*3. A city in Judah.*
2Kin 25:23 there came to Gedaliah to *M*
2Kin 25:25 Chaldees that were with him at *M*
2Chr 16:6 and he built therewith Geba and *M*
Jer 40:6 Gedaliah the son of Ahikam to *M*
Jer 40:8 Then they came to Gedaliah to *M*
Jer 40:10 I will dwell at *M* to serve the
Jer 40:12 of Judah, to Gedaliah, unto *M*
Jer 40:13 the fields, came to Gedaliah to *M*
Jer 40:15 spake to Gedaliah in *M* secretly
Jer 41:1 Gedaliah the son of Ahikam to *M*
Jer 41:1 they did eat bread together in *M*
Jer 41:3 him, even with Gedaliah, at *M*
Jer 41:6 went forth from *M* to meet them
Jer 41:10 of the people that were in *M*
Jer 41:10 all the people that remained in *M*
Jer 41:14 away captive from *M* cast about
Jer 41:16 the son of Nethaniah, from *M*
Hos 5:1 because ye have been a snare on *M*
*4. A district ruled by Shallum.*
Neh 3:15 Colhozeh, the ruler of part of *M*
*5. A place ruled by Ezer.*
Neh 3:19 the son of Jeshua, the ruler of *M*

**MIZPAR** *(miz'-par)* See MISPERETH. *A clan leader with Zerubbabel.*
Ezr 2:2 Reelaiah, Mordecai, Bilshan, *M*

**MIZPEH** *(miz'-peh)* See MIZPAH, RAMATH-MIZPEH.
*1. A valley near Mt. Hermon.*
Josh 11:3 under Hermon in the land of *M*
Josh 11:8 and unto the valley of *M* eastward
*2. A city in Judah.*
Josh 15:38 And Dilean, and *M*, and Joktheel,
Judg 20:1 of Gilead, unto the LORD in *M*
Judg 20:3 of Israel were gone up to *M*
Judg 21:1 the men of Israel had sworn in *M*
Judg 21:5 that came not up to the LORD to *M*
Judg 21:8 that came not up to *M* to the LORD
1Sa 7:5 said, Gather all Israel to *M*
1Sa 7:6 And they gathered together to *M*
1Sa 7:6 the children of Israel in *M*
1Sa 7:7 were gathered together to *M*
1Sa 7:11 the men of Israel went out of *M*
1Sa 7:12 took a stone, and set it between *M*
1Sa 7:16 to Beth-el, and Gilgal, and *M*
1Sa 10:17 together unto the LORD to *M*
*3. A city in Benjamin.*
Josh 18:26 And *M*, and Chephirah, and Mozah,
*4. A city in Gad.*
Judg 10:17 together, and encamped in *M*
Judg 11:11 his words before the LORD in *M*
Judg 11:29 and passed over *M* of Gilead
Judg 11:29 from *M* of Gilead he passed over
Judg 11:34 Jephthah came to *M* unto his house
*5. A city in Moab.*
1Sa 22:3 And David went thence to *M* of Moab

**MIZRAIM** *(miz'-ra-im)* See ABEL-MIZRAIM. *Son of Ham.*
Gen 10:6 Cush, and *M*, and Phut, and Canaan
Gen 10:13 *M* begat Ludim, and Anamim, and
1Chr 1:8 Cush, and *M*, Put, and Canaan
1Chr 1:11 *M* begat Ludim, and Anamim, and

**MIZZAH** *(miz'-zah) Son of Reuel.*
Gen 36:13 Nahath, and Zerah, Shammah, and *M*
Gen 36:17 duke Zerah, duke Shammah, duke *M*
1Chr 1:37 Nahath, Zerah, Shammah, and *M*

**MNASON** *(na'-son) A Christian in Jerusalem.*
Acts 21:16 brought with them one *M* of Cyprus

**MOAB** *(mo'-ab)*
*1. A nation east of Israel.*
Gen 36:35 smote Midian in the field of *M*
Ex 15:15 the mighty men of *M*, trembling
Num 21:11 the wilderness which is before *M*
Num 21:13 is the border of *M*, between *M*
Num 21:15 Ar, and lieth upon the border of *M*
Num 21:20 that is in the country of *M*
Num 21:26 against the former king of *M*
Num 21:28 it hath consumed Ar of *M*, and the
Num 21:29 Woe to thee, *M*
Num 22:1 pitched in the plains of *M* on
Num 22:3 *M* was sore afraid of the people,
Num 22:3 *M* was distressed because of the
Num 22:4 *M* said unto the elders of Midian,
Num 22:7 And the elders of *M* and the elders
Num 22:8 the princes of *M* abode with
Num 22:10 the son of Zippor, king of *M*
Num 22:14 And the princes of *M* rose up
Num 22:21 and went with the princes of *M*
Num 22:36 out to meet him unto a city of *M*
Num 23:6 he, and all the princes of *M*
Num 23:7 Balak the king of *M* hath brought
Num 23:17 and the princes of *M* with him
Num 24:17 and shall smite the corners of *M*
Num 25:1 whoredom with the daughters of *M*
Num 26:3 of *M* by Jordan near Jericho
Num 26:63 of *M* by Jordan near Jericho
Num 31:12 unto the camp at the plains of *M*
Num 33:44 in Ije-abarim, in the border of *M*
Num 33:48 of *M* by Jordan near Jericho
Num 33:49 Abel-shittim in the plains of *M*
Num 33:50 in the plains of *M* by Jordan
Num 35:1 of *M* by Jordan near Jericho
Num 36:13 of *M* by Jordan near Jericho
Deut 1:5 side Jordan, in the land of *M*
Deut 2:8 by the way of the wilderness of *M*
Deut 2:18 over through Ar, the coast of *M*
Deut 29:1 of Israel in the land of *M*
Deut 32:49 Nebo, which is in the land of *M*
Deut 34:1 of *M* unto the mountain of Nebo
Deut 34:5 LORD died there in the land of *M*
Deut 34:6 him in a valley in the land of *M*
Deut 34:8 in the plains of *M* thirty days
Josh 13:32 inheritance in the plains of *M*
Josh 24:9 the son of Zippor, king of *M*
Judg 3:12 the king of *M* against Israel
Judg 3:14 the king of *M* eighteen years
Judg 3:15 present unto Eglon the king of *M*
Judg 3:17 the present unto Eglon king of *M*
Judg 3:28 took the fords of Jordan toward *M*
Judg 3:29 they slew of *M* at that time about
Judg 3:30 So *M* was subdued that day under
Judg 10:6 gods of Zidon, and the gods of *M*
Judg 11:15 took not away the land of *M*
Judg 11:17 they sent unto the king of *M*
Judg 11:18 land of Edom, and the land of *M*
Judg 11:18 by the east side of the land of *M*
Judg 11:18 came not within the border of *M*
Judg 11:18 for Arnon was the border of *M*
Judg 11:25 the son of Zippor, king of *M*
Ruth 1:1 to sojourn in the country of *M*
Ruth 1:2 they came into the country of *M*
Ruth 1:4 took them wives of the women of *M*
Ruth 1:6 return from the country of *M*
Ruth 1:6 *M* how that the LORD had visited
Ruth 1:22 returned out of the country of *M*
Ruth 2:6 Naomi out of the country of *M*
Ruth 4:3 again out of the country of *M*
1Sa 12:9 and into the hand of the king of *M*
1Sa 14:47 enemies on every side, against *M*
1Sa 22:3 David went thence to Mizpeh of *M*
1Sa 22:3 and he said unto the king of *M*
1Sa 22:4 brought them before the king of *M*
2Sa 8:2 And he smote *M*, and measured them
2Sa 8:12 Of Syria, and of *M*, and of the
2Sa 23:20 he slew two lionlike men of *M*
1Kin 11:7 for Chemosh, the abomination of *M*
2Kin 1:1 Then *M* rebelled against Israel
2Kin 3:4 Mesha king of *M* was a sheepmaster
2Kin 3:5 that the king of *M* rebelled
2Kin 3:7 The king of *M* hath rebelled
2Kin 3:7 go with me against *M* to battle
2Kin 3:10 deliver them into the hand of *M*
2Kin 3:13 deliver them into the hand of *M*
2Kin 3:23 now therefore, *M*, to the spoil
2Kin 3:26 when the king of *M* saw that the
1Chr 1:46 smote Midian in the field of *M*
1Chr 4:22 Saraph, who had the dominion in *M*
1Chr 8:8 children in the country of *M*
1Chr 11:22 he slew two lionlike men of *M*
1Chr 18:2 And he smote *M*
1Chr 18:11 from Edom, and from *M*, and from the
2Chr 20:1 this also, that the children of *M*
2Chr 20:10 the children of Ammon and *M*
2Chr 20:22 against the children of Ammon, *M*
2Chr 20:23 Ammon and *M* stood up against the
Neh 13:23 of Ashdod, of Ammon, and of *M*
Ps 60:8 *M* is my washpot
Ps 83:6 of *M*, and the Hagarenes
Ps 108:9 *M* is my washpot
Is 11:14 lay their hand upon Edom and *M*
Is 15:1 The burden of *M*.
Is 15:1 the night Ar of *M* is laid waste
Is 15:1 the night Kir of *M* is laid waste
Is 15:2 *M* shall howl over Nebo, and over
Is 15:4 armed soldiers of *M* shall cry out
Is 15:5 My heart shall cry out for *M*
Is 15:8 gone round about the borders of *M*
Is 15:9 lions upon him that escapeth of *M*
Is 16:2 so the daughters of *M* shall be at
Is 16:4 mine outcasts dwell with thee, *M*
Is 16:6 We have heard of the pride of *M*
Is 16:7 Therefore shall *M* howl for *M*
Is 16:7 Therefore shall *M* howl for *M*
Is 16:11 shall sound like an harp for *M*
Is 16:12 when it is seen that *M* is weary
Is 16:13 concerning *M* since that time
Is 16:14 the glory of *M* shall be contemned
Is 25:10 *M* shall be trodden down under him
Jer 9:26 and the children of Ammon, and *M*
Jer 25:21 Edom, and *M*, and the children of
Jer 27:3 king of Edom, and to the king of *M*
Jer 40:11 when all the Jews that were in *M*
Jer 48:1 Against *M* thus saith the LORD of
Jer 48:2 shall be no more praise of *M*
Jer 48:4 *M* is destroyed
Jer 48:9 Give wings unto *M*, that it may
Jer 48:11 *M* hath been at ease from his
Jer 48:13 *M* shall be ashamed of Chemosh, as
Jer 48:15 *M* is spoiled, and gone up out of
Jer 48:16 The calamity of *M* is near to come
Jer 48:18 for the spoiler of *M* shall come
Jer 48:20 *M* is confounded
Jer 48:20 it in Arnon, that *M* is spoiled,
Jer 48:24 all the cities of the land of *M*
Jer 48:25 The horn of *M* is cut off, and his
Jer 48:26 *M* also shall wallow in his vomit,
Jer 48:28 O ye that dwell in *M*, leave the
Jer 48:29 We have heard the pride of *M*
Jer 48:31 Therefore will I howl for *M*
Jer 48:31 and I will cry out for all *M*
Jer 48:33 field, and from the land of *M*
Jer 48:35 I will cause to cease in *M*
Jer 48:36 shall sound for *M* like pipes
Jer 48:38 upon all the housetops of *M*
Jer 48:38 for I have broken *M* like a vessel
Jer 48:39 how hath *M* turned the back with
Jer 48:39 so shall *M* be a derision and a
Jer 48:40 and shall spread his wings over *M*
Jer 48:41 the mighty men's hearts in *M* at
Jer 48:42 *M* shall be destroyed from being a
Jer 48:43 be upon thee, O inhabitant of *M*
Jer 48:44 I will bring upon it, even upon *M*
Jer 48:45 and shall devour the corner of *M*
Jer 48:46 Woe be unto thee, O *M*
Jer 48:47 captivity of *M* in the latter days
Jer 48:47 Thus far is the judgment of *M*
Eze 25:8 Because that *M* and Seir do say,
Eze 25:9 the side of *M* from the cities
Eze 25:11 I will execute judgments upon *M*

Dan 11:41 out of his hand, even Edom, and *M*
Amos 2:1 For three transgressions of *M*
Amos 2:2 But I will send a fire upon *M*
Amos 2:2 *M* shall die with tumult, with
Mic 6:5 what Balak king of *M* consulted
Zeph 2:8 I have heard the reproach of *M*
Zeph 2:9 Surely *M* shall be as Sodom, and
*2. Son of Lot.*
Gen 19:37 bare a son, and called his name *M*

**MOABITE** *(mo'-ab-ite)* See MOABITES, MOABITESS, MOABITISH. *An inhabitant of Moab.*
Deut 23:3 An Ammonite or *M* shall not enter
1Chr 11:46 sons of Elnaam, and Ithmah the *M*
Neh 13:1 the *M* should not come into the

**MOABITES** *(mo'-ab-ites)*
Gen 19:37 the father of the *M* unto this day
Num 22:4 was king of the *M* at that time
Deut 2:9 said unto me, Distress not the *M*
Deut 2:11 but the *M* call them Emims
Deut 2:29 the *M* which dwell in Ar, did unto
Judg 3:28 your enemies the *M* into your hand
2Sa 8:2 so the *M* became David's servants,
1Kin 11:1 of Pharaoh, women of the *M*
1Kin 11:33 Chemosh the god of the *M*
2Kin 3:18 deliver the *M* also into your hand
2Kin 3:21 when all the *M* heard that the
2Kin 3:22 the *M* saw the water on the other
2Kin 3:24 Israelites rose up and smote the *M*
2Kin 3:24 they went forward smiting the *M*
2Kin 13:20 the bands of the *M* invaded the
2Kin 23:13 Chemosh the abomination of the *M*
2Kin 24:2 of the Syrians, and bands of the *M*
1Chr 18:2 the *M* became David's servants, and
Ezr 9:1 Jebusites, the Ammonites, the *M*

**MOABITESS** *(mo'-ab-i-tess) A female Moabite.*
Ruth 1:22 So Naomi returned, and Ruth the *M*
Ruth 2:2 Ruth the *M* said unto Naomi, Let
Ruth 2:21 And Ruth the *M* said, He said unto
Ruth 4:5 must buy it also of Ruth the *M*
Ruth 4:10 Moreover Ruth the *M*, the wife of
2Chr 24:26 Jehozabad the son of Shimrith a *M*

**MOABITISH** *(mo'-ab-i-tish) Belonging to the Moabites.*
Ruth 2:6 It is the *M* damsel that came back

**MOADIAH** *(mo-ad-i'-ah)* See MAADIAH. *A priest.*
Neh 12:17 of Miniamin, of *M*, Piltai

**MOCK**
Gen 39:14 in an Hebrew unto us to *m* us
Gen 39:17 unto us, came in unto me to *m* me
Job 13:9 mocketh another, do ye so *m* him
Job 21:3 and after that I have spoken, *m* on
Prov 1:26 I will *m* when your fear cometh
Prov 14:9 Fools make a *m* at sin
Jer 38:19 me into their hand, and they *m* me
Lam 1:7 saw her, and did *m* at her sabbaths
Eze 22:5 be far from thee, shall *m* thee
Mt 20:19 deliver him to the Gentiles to *m*
Mk 10:34 And they shall *m* him, and shall
Lk 14:29 all that behold it begin to *m* him

**MOCKED**
Gen 19:14 one that *m* unto his sons in law
Num 22:29 the ass, Because thou hast *m* me
Judg 16:10 Samson, Behold, thou hast *m* me
Judg 16:13 Samson, Hitherto thou hast *m* me
Judg 16:15 thou hast *m* me these three times,
1Kin 18:27 pass at noon, that Elijah *m* them
2Kin 2:23 *m* him, and said unto him, Go up,
2Chr 30:10 laughed them to scorn, and *m* them
2Chr 36:16 But they *m* the messengers of God,
Neh 4:1 great indignation, and *m* the Jews
Job 12:4 I am as one *m* of his neighbour,
Mt 2:16 saw that he was *m* of the wise men
Mt 27:29 *m* him, saying, Hail, King of the
Mt 27:31 And after that they had *m* him
Mk 15:20 And when they had *m* him, they took
Lk 18:32 unto the Gentiles, and shall be *m*
Lk 22:63 And the men that held Jesus *m* him
Lk 23:11 *m* him, and arrayed him in a
Lk 23:36 And the soldiers also *m* him
Acts 17:32 resurrection of the dead, some *m*
Gal 6:7 God is not *m*

**MOCKERS**
Job 17:2 Are there not *m* with me
Ps 35:16 With hypocritical *m* in feasts
Is 28:22 Now therefore be ye not *m*
Jer 15:17 sat not in the assembly of the *m*
Jude 18 should be *m* in the last time

**MOCKETH**
Job 13:9 or as one man *m* another, do ye so
Job 39:22 He *m* at fear, and is not
Prov 17:5 Whoso *m* the poor reproacheth his
Prov 30:17 The eye that *m* at his father, and
Jer 20:7 in derision daily, every one *m* me

**MOCKING**
Gen 21:9 she had born unto Abraham, *m*
Eze 22:4 heathen, and a *m* to all countries
Mt 27:41 also the chief priests *m* him
Mk 15:31 *m* said among themselves with the
Acts 2:13 Others *m* said, These men are full

**MOLADAH** *(mo-la'-dah) A city in Judah.*
Josh 15:26 Amam, and Shema, and *M*,
Josh 19:2 Beer-sheba, or Sheba, and *M*
1Chr 4:28 And they dwelt at Beer-sheba, and *M*
Neh 11:26 And at Jeshua, and at *M*, and at

**MOLECH** *(mo'-lek)* See MALCHAM, MOLOCH. *An Ammonite god.*
Lev 18:21 seed pass through the fire to *M*
Lev 20:2 giveth any of his seed unto *M*
Lev 20:3 he hath given of his seed unto *M*
Lev 20:4 when he giveth of his seed unto *M*
Lev 20:5 him, to commit whoredom with *M*
1Kin 11:7 is before Jerusalem, and for *M*
2Kin 23:10 to pass through the fire to *M*
Jer 32:35 to pass through the fire unto *M*

**MOLID** *(mo'-lid) A descendant of Jerahmeel.*
1Chr 2:29 and she bare him Ahban, and *M*

**MOLOCH** *(mo'-loch)* See MILCHOM, MOLECH. *Same as Molech.*
Amos 5:26 borne the tabernacle of your *M*
Acts 7:43 ye took up the tabernacle of *M*

**MOLTEN**
Ex 32:4 after he had made it a *m* calf
Ex 32:8 they have made them a *m* calf
Ex 34:17 Thou shalt make thee no *m* gods
Lev 19:4 nor make to yourselves *m* gods
Num 33:52 and destroy all their *m* images
Deut 9:12 they have made them a *m* image
Deut 9:16 God, and had made you a *m* calf
Deut 27:15 that maketh any graven or *m* image
Judg 17:3 make a graven image and a *m* image
Judg 17:4 a graven image and a *m* image
Judg 18:14 and a graven image, and a *m* image
Judg 18:17 and the teraphim, and the *m* image
Judg 18:18 and the teraphim, and the *m* image
1Kin 7:16 he made two chapiters of *m* brass
1Kin 7:23 And he made a *m* sea, ten cubits
1Kin 7:30 the laver were undersetters *m*
1Kin 7:33 and their spokes, were all *m*
1Kin 14:9 *m* images, to provoke me to anger,
2Kin 17:16 their God, and made them *m* images
2Chr 4:2 Also he made a *m* sea of ten
2Chr 28:2 made also *m* images for Baalim
2Chr 34:3 carved images, and the *m* images
2Chr 34:4 the *m* images, he brake in pieces,
Neh 9:18 when they had made them a *m* calf
Job 28:2 brass is *m* out of the stone
Job 37:18 strong, and as a *m* looking glass
Ps 106:19 Horeb, and worshipped the *m* image
Is 30:22 ornament of thy *m* images of gold
Is 41:29 their *m* images are wind and
Is 42:17 images, that say to the *m* images
Is 44:10 or *m* a graven image that is
Is 48:5 my *m* image, hath commanded them
Jer 10:14 for his *m* image is falsehood, and
Jer 51:17 for his *m* image is falsehood, and
Eze 24:11 filthiness of it may be *m* in it
Hos 13:2 have made them *m* images of their
Mic 1:4 mountains shall be *m* under him
Nah 1:14 the graven image and the *m* image
Hab 2:18 the *m* image, and a teacher of lies

**MOMENT**
Ex 33:5 up into the midst of thee in a *m*
Num 16:21 that I may consume them in a *m*
Num 16:45 that I may consume them as in a *m*
Job 7:18 every morning, and try him every *m*
Job 20:5 joy of the hypocrite but for a *m*
Job 21:13 in a *m* go down to the grave
Job 34:20 In a *m* shall they die, and the
Ps 30:5 For his anger endureth but a *m*
Ps 73:19 into desolation, as in a *m*
Prov 12:19 but a lying tongue is but for a *m*
Is 26:20 thyself as it were for a little *m*
Is 27:3 I will water it every *m*
Is 47:9 come to thee in a *m* in one day
Is 54:7 For a small *m* have I forsaken
Is 54:8 I hid my face from thee for a *m*
Jer 4:20 spoiled, and my curtains in a *m*
Lam 4:6 that was overthrown as in a *m*
Eze 26:16 and shall tremble at every *m*
Eze 32:10 and they shall tremble at every *m*
Lk 4:5 of the world in a *m* of time
1Cor 15:52 In a *m*, in the twinkling of an
2Cor 4:17 affliction, which is but for a *m*

**MONEY**
Gen 17:12 or bought with *m* of any stranger,
Gen 17:13 and he that is bought with thy *m*
Gen 17:23 all that were bought with his *m*
Gen 17:27 bought with *m* of the stranger,
Gen 23:9 for as much *m* as it is worth he
Gen 23:13 I will give thee *m* for the field
Gen 23:16 current *m* with the merchant
Gen 31:15 and hath quite devoured also our *m*
Gen 33:19 for an hundred pieces of *m*
Gen 42:25 every man's *m* into his sack
Gen 42:27 in the inn, he espied his *m*
Gen 42:28 his brethren, My *m* is restored
Gen 42:35 man's bundle of *m* was in his sack
Gen 42:35 their father saw the bundles of *m*
Gen 43:12 take double *m* in your hand
Gen 43:12 the *m* that was brought again in
Gen 43:15 they took double *m* in their hand
Gen 43:18 Because of the *m* that was
Gen 43:21 every man's *m* was in the mouth of
Gen 43:21 of his sack, our *m* in full weight
Gen 43:22 other *m* have we brought down in
Gen 43:22 tell who put our *m* in our sacks
Gen 43:23 I had your *m*
Gen 44:1 put every man's *m* in his sack's
Gen 44:2 of the youngest, and his corn *m*
Gen 44:8 Behold, the *m*, which we found in
Gen 47:14 Joseph gathered up all the *m* that
Gen 47:14 Joseph brought the *m* into
Gen 47:15 when *m* failed in the land of
Gen 47:15 for the *m* faileth
Gen 47:16 you for your cattle, if *m* fail
Gen 47:18 my lord, how that our *m* is spent
Ex 12:44 servant that is bought for *m*
Ex 21:11 shall she go out free without *m*
Ex 21:21 for he is his *m*
Ex 21:30 there be laid on him a sum of *m*
Ex 21:34 give *m* unto the owner of them
Ex 21:35 live ox, and divide the *m* of it
Ex 22:7 his neighbour *m* or stuff to keep
Ex 22:17 he shall pay *m* according to the
Ex 22:25 If thou lend *m* to any of my
Ex 30:16 *m* of the children of Israel
Lev 22:11 priest buy any soul with his *m*
Lev 25:37 not give him thy *m* upon usury
Lev 25:51 of the *m* that he was bought for
Lev 27:15 the *m* of thy estimation unto it
Lev 27:18 shall reckon unto him the *m*
Lev 27:19 the *m* of thy estimation unto it
Num 3:48 And thou shalt give the *m*,
Num 3:49 *m* of them that were over and above
Num 3:50 children of Israel took he the *m*
Num 3:51 Moses gave the *m* of them that
Num 18:16 for the *m* of five shekels, after
Deut 2:6 Ye shall buy meat of them for *m*
Deut 2:6 also buy water of them for *m*
Deut 2:28 Thou shalt sell me meat for *m*
Deut 2:28 and give me water for *m*, that I
Deut 14:25 Then shalt thou turn it into *m*
Deut 14:25 bind up the *m* in thine hand, and
Deut 14:26 thou shalt bestow that *m* for
Deut 21:14 shalt not sell her at all for *m*
Deut 23:19 usury of *m*, usury of victuals,
Judg 5:19 they took no gain of *m*
Judg 16:18 her, and brought *m* in their hand
Judg 17:4 he restored the *m* unto his mother
1Kin 21:2 give thee the worth of it in *m*
1Kin 21:6 him, Give me thy vineyard for *m*
1Kin 21:15 he refused to give thee for *m*
2Kin 5:26 Is it a time to receive *m*
2Kin 12:4 All the *m* of the dedicated things
2Kin 12:4 even the *m* of every one that
2Kin 12:4 the *m* that every man is set at,
2Kin 12:4 all the *m* that cometh into any
2Kin 12:7 no more *m* of your acquaintance
2Kin 12:8 receive no more *m* of the people

2Kin 12:9 the door put therein all the *m*
2Kin 12:10 there was much *m* in the chest
2Kin 12:10 told the *m* that was found in the
2Kin 12:11 And they gave the *m*, being told,
2Kin 12:13 of the *m* that was brought into
2Kin 12:15 the *m* to be bestowed on workmen
2Kin 12:16 The trespass *m* and sin *m* was
2Kin 15:20 Menahem exacted the *m* of Israel
2Kin 22:7 *m* that was delivered into their
2Kin 22:9 the *m* that was found in the house
2Kin 23:35 he taxed the land to give the *m*
2Chr 24:5 gather of all Israel *m* to repair
2Chr 24:11 they saw that there was much *m*
2Chr 24:11 day, and gathered *m* in abundance
2Chr 24:14 the rest of the *m* before the king
2Chr 34:9 they delivered the *m* that was
2Chr 34:14 when they brought out the *m* that
2Chr 34:17 *m* that was found in the house of
Ezr 3:7 They gave *m* also unto the masons,
Ezr 7:17 buy speedily with this *m* bullocks
Neh 5:4 We have borrowed *m* for the king's
Neh 5:10 servants, might exact of them *m*
Neh 5:11 also the hundredth part of the *m*
Est 4:7 of the sum of the *m* that Haman
Job 31:39 the fruits thereof without *m*
Job 42:11 man also gave him a piece of *m*
Ps 15:5 putteth not out his *m* to usury
Prov 7:20 He hath taken a bag of *m* with him
Eccl 7:12 is a defence, and *m* is a defence
Eccl 10:19 but *m* answereth all things
Is 43:24 bought me no sweet cane with *m*
Is 52:3 and ye shall be redeemed without *m*
Is 55:1 the waters, and he that hath no *m*
Is 55:1 come, buy wine and milk without *m*
Is 55:2 Wherefore do ye spend *m* for that
Jer 32:9 in Anathoth, and weighed him the *m*
Jer 32:10 weighed him the *m* in the balances
Jer 32:25 GOD, Buy thee the field for *m*
Jer 32:44 Men shall buy fields for *m*
Lam 5:4 We have drunken our water for *m*
Mic 3:11 the prophets thereof divine for *m*
Mt 17:24 received tribute *m* came to Peter
Mt 17:27 thou shalt find a piece of *m*
Mt 22:19 Shew me the tribute *m*
Mt 25:18 in the earth, and hid his lord's *m*
Mt 25:27 have put my *m* to the exchangers
Mt 28:12 they gave large *m* unto the
Mt 28:15 So they took the *m*, and did as
Mk 6:8 no bread, no *m* in their purse
Mk 12:41 people cast *m* into the treasury
Mk 14:11 glad, and promised to give him *m*
Lk 9:3 scrip, neither bread, neither *m*
Lk 19:15 him, to whom he had given the *m*
Lk 19:23 not thou my *m* into the bank
Lk 22:5 glad, and covenanted to give him *m*
Jn 2:14 and the changers of *m* sitting
Jn 2:15 and poured out the changers' *m*
Acts 4:37 land, sold it, and brought the *m*
Acts 7:16 Abraham bought for a sum of *m* of
Acts 8:18 was given, he offered them *m*
Acts 8:20 Thy *m* perish with thee, because
Acts 8:20 of God may be purchased with *m*
Acts 24:26 He hoped also that *m* should have
1Ti 6:10 For the love of *m* is the root of

**MOON**
Gen 37:9 and, behold, the sun and the *m*
Deut 4:19 when thou seest the sun, and the *m*
Deut 17:3 them, either the sun, or *m*
Deut 33:14 things put forth by the *m*
Josh 10:12 and thou, *M*, in the valley of
Josh 10:13 the *m* stayed, until the people
1Sa 20:5 Behold, to morrow is the new *m*
1Sa 20:18 to David, To morrow is the new *m*
1Sa 20:24 and when the new *m* was come
2Kin 4:23 it is neither new *m*, nor sabbath
2Kin 23:5 Baal, to the sun, and to the *m*
Job 25:5 Behold even to the *m*, and it
Job 31:26 or the *m* walking in brightness
Ps 8:3 the work of thy fingers, the *m*
Ps 72:5 sun and *m* endure, throughout all
Ps 72:7 peace so long as the *m* endureth
Ps 81:3 Blow up the trumpet in the new *m*
Ps 89:37 be established for ever as the *m*
Ps 104:19 He appointed the *m* for seasons
Ps 121:6 thee by day, nor the *m* by night
Ps 136:9 The *m* and stars to rule by night
Ps 148:3 Praise ye him, sun and *m*
Eccl 12:2 the sun, or the light, or the *m*
Song 6:10 as the morning, fair as the *m*
Is 3:18 and their round tires like the *m*
Is 13:10 the *m* shall not cause her light
Is 24:23 Then the *m* shall be confounded,
Is 30:26 Moreover the light of the *m* shall
Is 60:19 shall the *m* give light unto thee
Is 60:20 shall thy *m* withdraw itself
Is 66:23 that from one new *m* to another
Jer 8:2 them before the sun, and the *m*
Jer 31:35 day, and the ordinances of the *m*
Eze 32:7 the *m* shall not give her light
Eze 46:1 of the new *m* it shall be opened
Eze 46:6 in the day of the new *m* it shall
Joel 2:10 the *m* shall be dark, and the stars
Joel 2:31 the *m* into blood, before the
Joel 3:15 the *m* shall be darkened, and the
Amos 8:5 When will the new *m* be gone
Hab 3:11 *m* stood still in their habitation
Mt 24:29 the *m* shall not give her light,
Mk 13:24 the *m* shall not give her light,
Lk 21:25 be signs in the sun, and in the *m*
Acts 2:20 the *m* into blood, before that
1Cor 15:41 sun, and another glory of the *m*
Col 2:16 of an holyday, or of the new *m*
Rev 6:12 of hair, and the *m* became as blood
Rev 8:12 and the third part of the *m*
Rev 12:1 the *m* under her feet, and upon her
Rev 21:23 need of the sun, neither of the *m*

**MOONS**
1Chr 23:31 in the sabbaths, in the new *m*
2Chr 2:4 on the sabbaths, and on the new *m*
2Chr 8:13 on the sabbaths, and on the new *m*
2Chr 31:3 the sabbaths, and for the new *m*
Ezr 3:5 burnt offering, both of the new *m*
Neh 10:33 of the sabbaths, of the new *m*
Is 1:13 the new *m* and sabbaths, the
Is 1:14 Your new *m* and your appointed
Eze 45:17 in the feasts, and in the new *m*
Eze 46:3 in the sabbaths and in the new *m*
Hos 2:11 cease, her feast days, her new *m*

**MORASTHITE** *(mo'-ras-thite) Family name of Micah the prophet.*
Jer 26:18 Micah the *M* prophesied in the
Mic 1:1 Micah the *M* in the days of Jotham

**MORDECAI** *(mor'-de-cahee)* See MORDECAI'S.
*1. A clan leader with Zerubbabel.*
Ezr 2:2 Nehemiah, Seraiah, Reelaiah, *M*
Neh 7:7 Azariah, Raamiah, Nahamani, *M*
*2. Cousin of Esther.*
Est 2:5 a certain Jew, whose name was *M*
Est 2:7 whom *M*, when her father and mother
Est 2:10 for *M* had charged her that she
Est 2:11 *M* walked every day before the
Est 2:15 of Abihail the uncle of *M*
Est 2:19 then *M* sat in the king's gate
Est 2:20 as *M* had charged her
Est 2:20 Esther did the commandment of *M*
Est 2:21 while *M* sat in the king's gate,
Est 2:22 And the thing was known to *M*
Est 3:2 But *M* bowed not, nor did him
Est 3:3 in the king's gate, said unto *M*
Est 3:5 when Haman saw that *M* bowed not
Est 3:6 scorn to lay hands on *M* alone
Est 3:6 had shewed him the people of *M*
Est 3:6 Ahasuerus, even the people of *M*
Est 4:1 When *M* perceived all that was
Est 4:1 *M* rent his clothes, and put on
Est 4:4 and she sent raiment to clothe *M*
Est 4:5 and gave him a commandment to *M*
Est 4:6 So Hatach went forth to *M* unto
Est 4:7 *M* told him of all that had
Est 4:9 and told Esther the words of *M*
Est 4:10 and gave him commandment unto *M*
Est 4:12 they told to *M* Esther's words
Est 4:13 Then *M* commanded to answer Esther
Est 4:15 bade them return *M* this answer
Est 4:17 So *M* went his way, and did
Est 5:9 Haman saw *M* in the king's gate
Est 5:9 was full of indignation against *M*
Est 5:13 so long as I see *M* the Jew
Est 5:14 king that *M* may be hanged thereon
Est 6:2 that *M* had told of Bigthana and
Est 6:3 hath been done to *M* for this
Est 6:4 hang *M* on the gallows that he had
Est 6:10 said, and do even so to *M* the Jew
Est 6:11 and the horse, and arrayed *M*
Est 6:12 *M* came again to the king's gate
Est 6:13 If *M* be of the seed of the Jews,
Est 7:9 high, which Haman had made for *M*
Est 7:10 that he had prepared for *M*
Est 8:1 And *M* came before the king
Est 8:2 from Haman, and gave it unto *M*
Est 8:2 Esther set *M* over the house of
Est 8:7 to *M* the Jew, Behold, I have
Est 8:9 that *M* commanded unto the Jews
Est 8:15 *M* went out from the presence of
Est 9:3 the fear of *M* fell upon them
Est 9:4 For *M* was great in the king's
Est 9:4 for this man *M* waxed greater and
Est 9:20 *M* wrote these things, and sent
Est 9:23 as *M* had written unto them
Est 9:29 *M* the Jew, wrote with all
Est 9:31 appointed, according as *M* the Jew
Est 10:2 declaration of the greatness of *M*
Est 10:3 For *M* the Jew was next unto king

**MORDECAI'S** *(mor'-de-cahees) Refers to Mordecai 2.*
Est 2:22 the king thereof in *M* name
Est 3:4 to see whether *M* matters would

**MOREH** *(mo'-reh)*
*1. A place in Ephraim.*
Gen 12:6 of Sichem, unto the plain of *M*
Deut 11:30 Gilgal, beside the plains of *M*
*2. A place in Issachar.*
Judg 7:1 side of them, by the hill of *M*

**MORESHETH-GATH** *(mor'-e-sheth-gath)* See MORASTHITE. *A city in Judah.*
Mic 1:14 shalt thou give presents to *M*

**MORIAH** *(mo-ri'-ah) The Temple Mount.*
Gen 22:2 and get thee into the land of *M*
2Chr 3:1 the LORD at Jerusalem in mount *M*

**MORNING**
Gen 1:5 and the *m* were the first day
Gen 1:8 the *m* were the second day
Gen 1:13 and the *m* were the third day
Gen 1:19 the *m* were the fourth day
Gen 1:23 and the *m* were the fifth day
Gen 1:31 and the *m* were the sixth day
Gen 19:15 And when the *m* arose, then the
Gen 19:27 the *m* to the place where he stood
Gen 20:8 Abimelech rose early in the *m*
Gen 21:14 And Abraham rose up early in the *m*
Gen 22:3 And Abraham rose up early in the *m*
Gen 24:54 and they rose up in the *m*, and he
Gen 26:31 And they rose up betimes in the *m*
Gen 28:18 And Jacob rose up early in the *m*
Gen 29:25 And it came to pass, that in the *m*
Gen 31:55 early in the *m* Laban rose up, and
Gen 40:6 Joseph came in unto them in the *m*
Gen 41:8 it came to pass in the *m* that his
Gen 44:3 As soon as the *m* was light
Gen 49:27 in the *m* he shall devour the prey
Ex 7:15 Get thee unto Pharaoh in the *m*
Ex 8:20 Moses, Rise up early in the *m*
Ex 9:13 Moses, Rise up early in the *m*
Ex 10:13 and when it was *m*, the east wind
Ex 12:10 nothing of it remain until the *m*
Ex 12:10 the *m* ye shall burn with fire
Ex 12:22 the door of his house until the *m*
Ex 14:24 that in the *m* watch the LORD
Ex 14:27 his strength when the *m* appeared
Ex 16:7 And in the *m*, then ye shall see
Ex 16:8 in the *m* bread to the full
Ex 16:12 in the *m* ye shall be filled with
Ex 16:13 in the *m* the dew lay round about
Ex 16:19 Let no man leave of it till the *m*
Ex 16:20 of them left of it until the *m*
Ex 16:21 And they gathered it every *m*
Ex 16:23 up for you to be kept until the *m*
Ex 16:24 And they laid it up till the *m*
Ex 18:13 Moses from the *m* unto the evening
Ex 18:14 stand by thee from *m* unto even
Ex 19:16 to pass on the third day in the *m*
Ex 23:18 my sacrifice remain until the *m*
Ex 24:4 LORD, and rose up early in the *m*
Ex 27:21 from evening to *m* before the LORD
Ex 29:34 of the bread, remain unto the *m*
Ex 29:39 lamb thou shalt offer in the *m*
Ex 29:41 to the meat offering of the *m*
Ex 30:7 thereon sweet incense every *m*
Ex 34:2 And be ready in the *m*, and come up
Ex 34:2 come up in the *m* unto mount Sinai
Ex 34:4 and Moses rose up early in the *m*
Ex 34:25 the passover be left unto the *m*
Ex 36:3 unto him free offerings every *m*
Lev 6:9 the altar all night unto the *m*

Lev 6:12 shall burn wood on it every *m*
Lev 6:20 perpetual, half of it in the *m*
Lev 7:15 not leave any of it until the *m*
Lev 9:17 the burnt sacrifice of the *m*
Lev 19:13 with thee all night until the *m*
Lev 24:3 the *m* before the LORD continually
Num 9:12 shall leave none of it unto the *m*
Num 9:15 appearance of fire, until the *m*
Num 9:21 cloud abode from even unto the *m*
Num 9:21 the cloud was taken up in the *m*
Num 14:40 And they rose up early in the *m*
Num 22:13 And Balaam rose up in the *m*
Num 22:21 And Balaam rose up in the *m*
Num 28:4 lamb shalt thou offer in the *m*
Num 28:8 as the meat offering of the *m*
Num 28:23 the burnt offering in the *m*
Deut 16:4 remain all night until the *m*
Deut 16:7 and thou shalt turn in the *m*
Deut 28:67 In the *m* thou shalt say, Would
Deut 28:67 shalt say, Would God it were *m*
Josh 3:1 And Joshua rose early in the *m*
Josh 6:12 And Joshua rose early in the *m*
Josh 7:14 In the *m* therefore ye shall be
Josh 7:16 So Joshua rose up early in the *m*
Josh 8:10 And Joshua rose up early in the *m*
Judg 6:28 of the city arose early in the *m*
Judg 6:31 put to death whilst it is yet *m*
Judg 9:33 And it shall be, that in the *m*
Judg 16:2 all the night, saying, In the *m*
Judg 19:5 when they arose early in the *m*
Judg 19:8 he arose early in the *m* on the
Judg 19:25 her all the night until the *m*
Judg 19:27 And her lord rose up in the *m*
Judg 20:19 of Israel rose up in the *m*
Ruth 2:7 even from the *m* until now
Ruth 3:13 night, and it shall be in the *m*
Ruth 3:13 lie down until the *m*
Ruth 3:14 she lay at his feet until the *m*
1Sa 1:19 And they rose up in the *m* early
1Sa 3:15 And Samuel lay until the *m*
1Sa 5:4 they arose early on the morrow *m*
1Sa 11:11 midst of the host in the *m* watch
1Sa 14:36 and spoil them until the *m* light
1Sa 15:12 rose early to meet Saul in the *m*
1Sa 17:16 And the Philistine drew near *m*
1Sa 17:20 And David rose up early in the *m*
1Sa 19:2 take heed to thyself until the *m*
1Sa 19:11 him, and to slay him in the *m*
1Sa 20:35 And it came to pass in the *m*
1Sa 25:22 *m* light any that pisseth against
1Sa 25:34 *m* light any that pisseth against
1Sa 25:36 less or more, until the *m* light
1Sa 25:37 But it came to pass in the *m*
1Sa 29:10 now rise up early in the *m* with
1Sa 29:10 soon as ye be up early in the *m*
1Sa 29:11 rose up early to depart in the *m*
2Sa 2:27 surely then in the *m* the people
2Sa 11:14 And it came to pass in the *m*
2Sa 17:22 by the *m* light there lacked not
2Sa 23:4 he shall be as the light of the *m*
2Sa 23:4 riseth, even a *m* without clouds
2Sa 24:11 For when David was up in the *m*
2Sa 24:15 the *m* even to the time appointed
1Kin 3:21 when I rose in the *m* to give my
1Kin 3:21 when I had considered it in the *m*
1Kin 17:6 him bread and flesh in the *m*
1Kin 18:26 of Baal from *m* even until noon
2Kin 3:20 And it came to pass in the *m*
2Kin 3:22 And they rose up early in the *m*
2Kin 7:9 if we tarry till the *m* light
2Kin 10:8 in of the gate until the *m*
2Kin 10:9 And it came to pass in the *m*
2Kin 16:15 altar burn the *m* burnt offering
2Kin 19:35 and when they arose early in the *m*
1Chr 9:27 thereof every *m* pertained to them
1Chr 16:40 the burnt offering continually *m*
1Chr 23:30 And to stand every *m* to thank
2Chr 2:4 and for the burnt offerings *m*
2Chr 13:11 they burn unto the LORD every *m*
2Chr 20:20 And they rose early in the *m*
2Chr 31:3 offerings, to wit, for the *m*
Ezr 3:3 the LORD, even burnt offerings *m*
Neh 4:21 of the *m* till the stars appeared
Neh 8:3 gate from the *m* until midday
Job 1:5 them, and rose up early in the *m*
Job 4:20 are destroyed from *m* to evening
Job 7:18 thou shouldest visit him every *m*
Job 7:21 and thou shalt seek me in the *m*
Job 11:17 forth, thou shalt be as the *m*
Job 24:17 For the *m* is to them even as the
Job 38:7 When the *m* stars sang together,
Job 38:12 commanded the *m* since thy days
Job 41:18 are like the eyelids of the *m*
Ps 5:3 My voice shalt thou hear in the *m*
Ps 5:3 in the *m* will I direct my prayer
Ps 30:5 a night, but joy cometh in the *m*
Ps 49:14 have dominion over them in the *m*
Ps 55:17 Evening, and *m*, and at noon, will I
Ps 59:16 sing aloud of thy mercy in the *m*
Ps 65:8 makest the outgoings of the *m*
Ps 73:14 plagued, and chastened every *m*
Ps 88:13 in the *m* shall my prayer prevent
Ps 90:5 in the *m* they are like grass
Ps 90:6 In the *m* it flourisheth, and
Ps 92:2 forth thy lovingkindness in the *m*
Ps 110:3 holiness from the womb of the *m*
Ps 119:147 I prevented the dawning of the *m*
Ps 130:6 than they that watch for the *m*
Ps 130:6 than they that watch for the *m*
Ps 139:9 If I take the wings of the *m*
Ps 143:8 hear thy lovingkindness in the *m*
Prov 7:18 take our fill of love until the *m*
Prov 27:14 loud voice, rising early in the *m*
Eccl 10:16 and thy princes eat in the *m*
Eccl 11:6 In the *m* sow thy seed, and in the
Song 6:10 she that looketh forth as the *m*
Is 5:11 them that rise up early in the *m*
Is 14:12 heaven, O Lucifer, son of the *m*
Is 17:11 in the *m* shalt thou make thy seed
Is 17:14 and before the *m* he is not
Is 21:12 The *m* cometh, and also the night
Is 28:19 for *m* by *m* shall it pass
Is 33:2 be thou their arm every *m*
Is 37:36 and when they arose early in the *m*
Is 38:13 I reckoned till *m*, that, as a
Is 50:4 he wakeneth *m* by *m*, he
Is 58:8 thy light break forth as the *m*
Jer 5:8 They were as fed horses in the *m*
Jer 20:16 and let him hear the cry in the *m*
Jer 21:12 Execute judgment in the *m*
Lam 3:23 They are new every *m*
Eze 7:7 The *m* is come unto thee, O thou
Eze 7:10 the *m* is gone forth
Eze 12:8 in the *m* came the word of the
Eze 24:18 I spake unto the people in the *m*
Eze 24:18 I did in the *m* as I was commanded
Eze 33:22 until he came to me in the *m*
Eze 46:13 thou shalt prepare it every *m*
Eze 46:14 a meat offering for it every *m*
Eze 46:15 every *m* for a continual burnt
Dan 6:19 king arose very early in the *m*
Dan 8:26 the *m* which was told is true
Hos 6:3 going forth is prepared as the *m*
Hos 6:4 for your goodness is as a *m* cloud
Hos 7:6 in the *m* it burneth as a flaming
Hos 10:15 in a *m* shall the king of Israel
Hos 13:3 they shall be as the *m* cloud
Joel 2:2 as the *m* spread upon the
Amos 4:4 and bring your sacrifices every *m*
Amos 4:13 that maketh the *m* darkness
Amos 5:8 the shadow of death into the *m*
Jonah 4:7 worm when the *m* rose the next day
Mic 2:1 when the *m* is light, they
Zeph 3:5 every *m* doth he bring his
Mt 16:3 And in the *m*, It will be foul
Mt 20:1 the *m* to hire labourers into his
Mt 21:18 Now in the *m* as he returned into
Mt 27:1 When the *m* was come, all the
Mk 1:35 And in the *m*, rising up a great
Mk 11:20 And in the *m*, as they passed by,
Mk 13:35 at the cockcrowing, or in the *m*
Mk 15:1 straightway in the *m* the chief
Mk 16:2 very early in the *m* the first day
Lk 21:38 in the *m* to him in the temple
Lk 24:1 of the week, very early in the *m*
Jn 8:1 And early in the *m* he came
Jn 8:2 early in the *m* he came again into
Jn 21:4 But when the *m* was now come
Acts 5:21 into the temple early in the *m*
Acts 28:23 the prophets, from *m* till evening
Rev 2:28 And I will give him the *m* star
Rev 22:16 of David, and the bright and *m* star

## MORROW

Gen 19:34 And it came to pass on the *m*
Ex 8:10 And he said, To *m*
Ex 8:23 to *m* shall this sign be
Ex 8:29 and from his people, to *m*
Ex 9:5 To *m* the LORD shall do this thing
Ex 9:6 the LORD did that thing on the *m*
Ex 9:18 to *m* about this time I will cause
Ex 10:4 to *m* will I bring the locusts
Ex 16:23 To *m* is the rest of the holy
Ex 17:9 to *m* I will stand on the top of
Ex 18:13 And it came to pass on the *m*
Ex 19:10 and sanctify them to day and to *m*
Ex 32:5 To *m* is a feast to the LORD
Ex 32:6 And they rose up early on the *m*
Ex 32:30 And it came to pass on the *m*
Lev 7:16 on the *m* also the remainder of it
Lev 19:6 same day ye offer it, and on the *m*
Lev 22:30 leave none of it until the *m*
Lev 23:11 on the *m* after the sabbath the
Lev 23:15 you from the *m* after the sabbath
Lev 23:16 Even unto the *m* after the seventh
Num 11:18 Sanctify yourselves against to *m*
Num 14:25 ) To *m* turn you, and get you into
Num 16:5 Even to *m* the LORD will shew who
Num 16:7 in them before the LORD to *m*
Num 16:16 thou, and they, and Aaron, to *m*
Num 16:41 But on the *m* all the congregation
Num 17:8 that on the *m* Moses went into the
Num 22:41 And it came to pass on the *m*
Num 33:3 on the *m* after the passover the
Josh 3:5 for to *m* the LORD will do wonders
Josh 5:11 land on the *m* after the passover
Josh 5:12 the manna ceased on the *m* after
Josh 7:13 Sanctify yourselves against to *m*
Josh 11:6 for to *m* about this time will I
Josh 22:18 that to *m* he will be wroth with
Judg 6:38 for he rose up early on the *m*
Judg 9:42 And it came to pass on the *m*
Judg 19:9 to *m* get you early on your way,
Judg 20:28 for to *m* I will deliver them into
Judg 21:4 And it came to pass on the *m*
1Sa 5:3 of Ashdod arose early on the *m*
1Sa 5:4 they arose early on the *m* morning
1Sa 9:16 To *m* about this time I will send
1Sa 9:19 to *m* I will let thee go, and will
1Sa 11:9 the men of Jabesh-gilead, To *m*
1Sa 11:10 To *m* we will come out unto you,
1Sa 11:11 And it was so on the *m*, that Saul
1Sa 18:10 And it came to pass on the *m*
1Sa 19:11 night, to *m* thou shalt be slain
1Sa 20:5 to *m* is the new moon, and I should
1Sa 20:12 my father about to *m* any time
1Sa 20:18 to David, To *m* is the new moon
1Sa 20:27 And it came to pass on the *m*
1Sa 28:19 to *m* shalt thou and thy sons be
1Sa 31:8 And it came to pass on the *m*
2Sa 11:12 to *m* I will let thee depart
2Sa 11:12 in Jerusalem that day, and the *m*
1Kin 19:2 of them by to *m* about this time
1Kin 20:6 unto thee to *m* about this time
2Kin 6:28 day, and we will eat my son to *m*
2Kin 7:1 To *m* about this time shall a
2Kin 7:18 shall be to *m* about this time in
2Kin 8:15 And it came to pass on the *m*
2Kin 10:6 me to Jezreel by to *m* this time
1Chr 10:8 And it came to pass on the *m*
1Chr 29:21 on the *m* after that day, even a
2Chr 20:16 To *m* go ye down against them
2Chr 20:17 to *m* go out against them
Est 2:14 on the *m* she returned into the
Est 5:8 I will do to *m* as the king hath
Est 5:12 to *m* am I invited unto her also
Est 5:14 to *m* speak thou unto the king
Est 9:13 which are in Shushan to do to *m*
Prov 3:28 come again, and to *m* I will give
Prov 27:1 Boast not thyself of to *m*
Is 22:13 for to *m* we shall die
Is 56:12 to *m* shall be as this day, and
Jer 20:3 And it came to pass on the *m*
Zeph 3:3 gnaw not the bones till the *m*
Mt 6:30 to *m* is cast into the oven, shall
Mt 6:34 therefore no thought for the *m*
Mt 6:34 for the *m* shall take thought for
Mk 11:12 And on the *m*, when they were come
Lk 10:35 on the *m* when he departed, he
Lk 12:28 to *m* is cast into the oven
Lk 13:32 and I do cures to day and to *m*
Lk 13:33 I must walk to day, and to *m*
Acts 4:5 And it came to pass on the *m*
Acts 10:9 On the *m*, as they went on their
Acts 10:23 on the *m* Peter went away with
Acts 10:24 the *m* after they entered into
Acts 20:7 them, ready to depart on the *m*
Acts 22:30 On the *m*, because he would have
Acts 23:15 he bring him down unto you to *m*
Acts 23:20 down Paul to *m* into the council

Acts 23:32 On the *m* they left the horsemen
Acts 25:17 without any delay on the *m* I sat
Acts 25:22 To *m*, said he, thou shalt hear
Acts 25:23 And on the *m*, when Agrippa was
1Cor 15:32 for to *m* we die
Jas 4:13 To day or to *m* we will go into
Jas 4:14 know not what shall be on the *m*

**MORSEL**
Gen 18:5 And I will fetch a *m* of bread
Judg 19:5 thine heart with a *m* of bread
Ruth 2:14 and dip thy *m* in the vinegar
1Sa 2:36 a *m* of bread, and shall say, Put
1Sa 28:22 let me set a *m* of bread before
1Kin 17:11 a *m* of bread in thine hand
Job 31:17 Or have eaten my *m* myself alone
Prov 17:1 Better is a dry *m*, and quietness
Prov 23:8 The *m* which thou hast eaten shalt
Heb 12:16 who for one *m* of meat sold his

**MORTAL**
Job 4:17 Shall *m* man be more just than God
Rom 6:12 therefore reign in your *m* body
Rom 8:11 your *m* bodies by his Spirit that
1Cor 15:53 this *m* must put on immortality
1Cor 15:54 and this *m* shall have put on
2Cor 4:11 be made manifest in our *m* flesh

**MORTER**
Gen 11:3 stone, and slime had they for *m*
Ex 1:14 bitter with hard bondage, in *m*
Lev 14:42 and he shall take other *m*, and
Lev 14:45 and all the *m* of the house
Is 41:25 shall come upon princes as upon *m*
Eze 13:10 daubed it with untempered *m*
Eze 13:11 which daub it with untempered *m*
Eze 13:14 ye have daubed with untempered *m*
Eze 13:15 have daubed it with untempered *m*
Eze 22:28 daubed them with untempered *m*
Nah 3:14 go into clay, and tread the *m*

**MOSERA** *(mo-se'-rah)* See MOSEROTH. *Where Aaron was buried.*
Deut 10:6 of the children of Jaakan to *M*

**MOSEROTH** *(mo-se'-roth)* See MOSERA. *An Israelite encampment in the wilderness.*
Num 33:30 from Hashmonah, and encamped at *M*
Num 33:31 And they departed from *M*, and

**MOSES** *(mo'-zez)* See MOSES'. *Led Israel out of Egypt.*
Ex 2:10 And she called his name *M*
Ex 2:11 when *M* was grown, that he went
Ex 2:14 *M* feared, and said, Surely this
Ex 2:15 this thing, he sought to slay *M*
Ex 2:15 But *M* fled from the face of
Ex 2:17 but *M* stood up and helped them, and
Ex 2:21 *M* was content to dwell with the
Ex 2:21 he gave *M* Zipporah his daughter
Ex 3:1 Now *M* kept the flock of Jethro
Ex 3:3 *M* said, I will now turn aside, and
Ex 3:4 of the bush, and said, *M*, *M*
Ex 3:6 And *M* hid his face
Ex 3:11 *M* said unto God, Who am I, that I
Ex 3:13 *M* said unto God, Behold, when I
Ex 3:14 And God said unto *M*, I AM THAT I
Ex 3:15 And God said moreover unto *M*
Ex 4:1 *M* answered and said, But, behold,
Ex 4:3 and *M* fled from before it
Ex 4:4 And the LORD said unto *M*, Put
Ex 4:10 *M* said unto the LORD, O my Lord,
Ex 4:14 of the LORD was kindled against *M*
Ex 4:18 *M* went and returned to Jethro his
Ex 4:18 And Jethro said to *M*, Go in peace
Ex 4:19 And the LORD said unto *M* in Midian
Ex 4:20 *M* took his wife and his sons, and
Ex 4:20 *M* took the rod of God in his hand
Ex 4:21 And the LORD said unto *M*, When
Ex 4:27 Go into the wilderness to meet *M*
Ex 4:28 *M* told Aaron all the words of the
Ex 4:29 And *M* and Aaron went and gathered
Ex 4:30 which the LORD had spoken unto *M*
Ex 5:1 And afterward *M* and Aaron went in,
Ex 5:4 unto them, Wherefore do ye, *M*
Ex 5:20 And they met *M* and Aaron, who stood
Ex 5:22 *M* returned unto the LORD, and said
Ex 6:1 Then the LORD said unto *M*
Ex 6:2 And God spake unto *M*, and said unto
Ex 6:9 *M* spake so unto the children of
Ex 6:9 not unto *M* for anguish of spirit
Ex 6:10 And the LORD spake unto *M*, saying,
Ex 6:12 *M* spake before the LORD, saying,
Ex 6:13 And the LORD spake unto *M* and unto
Ex 6:20 and she bare him Aaron and *M*
Ex 6:26 These are that Aaron and *M*
Ex 6:27 these are that *M* and Aaron
Ex 6:28 spake unto *M* in the land of Egypt
Ex 6:29 That the LORD spake unto *M*
Ex 6:30 *M* said before the LORD, Behold, I
Ex 7:1 And the LORD said unto *M*, See, I
Ex 7:6 And *M* and Aaron did as the LORD
Ex 7:7 *M* was fourscore years old, and
Ex 7:8 And the LORD spake unto *M* and unto
Ex 7:10 And *M* and Aaron went in unto
Ex 7:14 And the LORD said unto *M*,
Ex 7:19 And the LORD spake unto *M*, Say
Ex 7:20 And *M* and Aaron did so, as the LORD
Ex 8:1 And the LORD spake unto *M*, Go unto
Ex 8:5 And the LORD spake unto *M*, Say
Ex 8:8 Then Pharaoh called for *M*
Ex 8:9 *M* said unto Pharaoh, Glory over
Ex 8:12 And *M* and Aaron went out from
Ex 8:12 *M* cried unto the LORD because of
Ex 8:13 did according to the word of *M*
Ex 8:16 And the LORD said unto *M*, Say unto
Ex 8:20 And the LORD said unto *M*, Rise up
Ex 8:25 And Pharaoh called for *M* and for
Ex 8:26 *M* said, It is not meet so to do
Ex 8:29 *M* said, Behold, I go out from
Ex 8:30 *M* went out from Pharaoh, and
Ex 8:31 did according to the word of *M*
Ex 9:1 Then the LORD said unto *M*
Ex 9:8 And the LORD said unto *M* and unto
Ex 9:8 let *M* sprinkle it toward the
Ex 9:10 *M* sprinkled it up toward heaven
Ex 9:11 before *M* because of the boils
Ex 9:12 as the LORD had spoken unto *M*
Ex 9:13 And the LORD said unto *M*, Rise up
Ex 9:22 And the LORD said unto *M*, Stretch
Ex 9:23 *M* stretched forth his rod toward
Ex 9:27 And Pharaoh sent, and called for *M*
Ex 9:29 *M* said unto him, As soon as I am
Ex 9:33 *M* went out of the city from
Ex 9:35 as the LORD had spoken by *M*
Ex 10:1 And the LORD said unto *M*, Go in
Ex 10:3 And *M* and Aaron came in unto
Ex 10:8 And *M* and Aaron were brought again
Ex 10:9 *M* said, We will go with our young
Ex 10:12 And the LORD said unto *M*, Stretch
Ex 10:13 *M* stretched forth his rod over
Ex 10:16 Then Pharaoh called for *M*
Ex 10:21 And the LORD said unto *M*, Stretch
Ex 10:22 *M* stretched forth his hand toward
Ex 10:24 And Pharaoh called unto *M*, and said
Ex 10:25 *M* said, Thou must give us also
Ex 10:29 *M* said, Thou hast spoken well, I
Ex 11:1 And the LORD said unto *M*, Yet will
Ex 11:3 Moreover the man *M* was very great
Ex 11:4 *M* said, Thus saith the LORD,
Ex 11:9 And the LORD said unto *M*, Pharaoh
Ex 11:10 And *M* and Aaron did all these
Ex 12:1 the LORD spake unto *M* and Aaron
Ex 12:21 Then *M* called for all the elders
Ex 12:28 did as the LORD had commanded *M*
Ex 12:31 And he called for *M* and Aaron by
Ex 12:35 did according to the word of *M*
Ex 12:43 And the LORD said unto *M* and Aaron,
Ex 12:50 the LORD commanded *M* and Aaron,
Ex 13:1 And the LORD spake unto *M*, saying,
Ex 13:3 *M* said unto the people, Remember
Ex 13:19 *M* took the bones of Joseph with
Ex 14:1 And the LORD spake unto *M*, saying,
Ex 14:11 And they said unto *M*, Because
Ex 14:13 *M* said unto the people, Fear ye
Ex 14:15 And the LORD said unto *M*,
Ex 14:21 *M* stretched out his hand over the
Ex 14:26 And the LORD said unto *M*, Stretch
Ex 14:27 *M* stretched forth his hand over
Ex 14:31 the LORD, and his servant *M*
Ex 15:1 Then sang *M* and the children of
Ex 15:22 So *M* brought Israel from the Red
Ex 15:24 And the people murmured against *M*
Ex 16:2 of Israel murmured against *M*
Ex 16:4 Then said the LORD unto *M*
Ex 16:6 And *M* and Aaron said unto all the
Ex 16:8 *M* said, This shall be, when the
Ex 16:9 *M* spake unto Aaron, Say unto all
Ex 16:11 And the LORD spake unto *M*, saying,
Ex 16:15 *M* said unto them, This is the
Ex 16:19 *M* said, Let no man leave of it
Ex 16:20 they hearkened not unto *M*
Ex 16:20 and *M* was wroth with them
Ex 16:22 the congregation came and told *M*
Ex 16:24 it up till the morning, as *M* bade
Ex 16:25 And *M* said, Eat that to day
Ex 16:28 And the LORD said unto *M*, How long
Ex 16:32 *M* said, This is the thing which
Ex 16:33 *M* said unto Aaron, Take a pot, and
Ex 16:34 As the LORD commanded *M*, so Aaron
Ex 17:2 the people did chide with *M*
Ex 17:2 *M* said unto them, Why chide ye
Ex 17:3 and the people murmured against *M*
Ex 17:4 *M* cried unto the LORD, saying,
Ex 17:5 And the LORD said unto *M*, Go on
Ex 17:6 *M* did so in the sight of the
Ex 17:9 *M* said unto Joshua, Choose us out
Ex 17:10 Joshua did as *M* had said to him
Ex 17:10 and *M*, Aaron, and Hur went up to
Ex 17:11 when *M* held up his hand, that
Ex 17:14 And the LORD said unto *M*, Write
Ex 17:15 *M* built an altar, and called the
Ex 18:1 of all that God had done for *M*
Ex 18:5 sons and his wife unto *M* into the
Ex 18:6 And he said unto *M*, I thy father
Ex 18:7 *M* went out to meet his father in
Ex 18:8 *M* told his father in law all that
Ex 18:13 that *M* sat to judge the people
Ex 18:13 the people stood by *M* from the
Ex 18:15 *M* said unto his father in law,
Ex 18:24 So *M* hearkened to the voice of
Ex 18:25 *M* chose able men out of all
Ex 18:26 hard causes they brought unto *M*
Ex 18:27 *M* let his father in law depart
Ex 19:3 *M* went up unto God, and the LORD
Ex 19:7 *M* came and called for the elders
Ex 19:8 *M* returned the words of the
Ex 19:9 And the LORD said unto *M*, Lo, I
Ex 19:9 *M* told the words of the people
Ex 19:10 And the LORD said unto *M*, Go unto
Ex 19:14 *M* went down from the mount unto
Ex 19:17 *M* brought forth the people out of
Ex 19:19 *M* spake, and God answered him by a
Ex 19:20 the LORD called *M* up to the top
Ex 19:20 and *M* went up
Ex 19:21 And the LORD said unto *M*, Go down,
Ex 19:23 *M* said unto the LORD, The people
Ex 19:25 So *M* went down unto the people,
Ex 20:19 And they said unto *M*, Speak thou
Ex 20:20 *M* said unto the people, Fear not
Ex 20:21 *M* drew near unto the thick
Ex 20:22 And the LORD said unto *M*, Thus
Ex 24:1 And he said unto *M*, Come up unto
Ex 24:2 *M* alone shall come near the LORD
Ex 24:3 *M* came and told the people all the
Ex 24:4 *M* wrote all the words of the LORD
Ex 24:6 *M* took half of the blood, and put
Ex 24:8 *M* took the blood, and sprinkled it
Ex 24:9 Then went up *M*, and Aaron, Nadab,
Ex 24:12 And the LORD said unto *M*, Come up
Ex 24:13 *M* rose up, and his minister Joshua
Ex 24:13 *M* went up into the mount of God
Ex 24:15 *M* went up into the mount, and a
Ex 24:16 *M* out of the midst of the cloud
Ex 24:18 *M* went into the midst of the
Ex 24:18 *M* was in the mount forty days and
Ex 25:1 And the LORD spake unto *M*, saying,
Ex 30:11 And the LORD spake unto *M*, saying,
Ex 30:17 And the LORD spake unto *M*, saying,
Ex 30:22 Moreover the LORD spake unto *M*
Ex 30:34 And the LORD said unto *M*, Take
Ex 31:1 And the LORD spake unto *M*, saying,
Ex 31:12 And the LORD spake unto *M*, saying,
Ex 31:18 And he gave unto *M*, when he had
Ex 32:1 when the people saw that *M*
Ex 32:1 for as for this *M*, the man that
Ex 32:7 And the LORD said unto *M*, Go, get
Ex 32:9 And the LORD said unto *M*, I have
Ex 32:11 *M* besought the LORD his God, and
Ex 32:15 *M* turned, and went down from the
Ex 32:17 as they shouted, he said unto *M*
Ex 32:21 *M* said unto Aaron, What did this
Ex 32:23 for as for this *M*, the man that
Ex 32:25 when *M* saw that the people were
Ex 32:26 Then *M* stood in the gate of the
Ex 32:28 did according to the word of *M*
Ex 32:29 For *M* had said, Consecrate
Ex 32:30 that *M* said unto the people, Ye
Ex 32:31 *M* returned unto the LORD, and said
Ex 32:33 And the LORD said unto *M*,
Ex 33:1 And the LORD said unto *M*, Depart,
Ex 33:5 For the LORD had said unto *M*
Ex 33:7 *M* took the tabernacle, and pitched

| | |
|---|---|
| Ex 33:8 | to pass, when *M* went out unto the |
| Ex 33:8 | his tent door, and looked after *M* |
| Ex 33:9 | as *M* entered into the tabernacle, |
| Ex 33:9 | and the LORD talked with *M* |
| Ex 33:11 | LORD spake unto *M* face to face |
| Ex 33:12 | *M* said unto the LORD, See, thou |
| Ex 33:17 | And the LORD said unto *M*, I will |
| Ex 34:1 | And the LORD said unto *M*, Hew thee |
| Ex 34:4 | *M* rose up early in the morning, |
| Ex 34:8 | *M* made haste, and bowed his head |
| Ex 34:27 | And the LORD said unto *M*, Write |
| Ex 34:29 | when *M* came down from mount Sinai |
| Ex 34:29 | that *M* wist not that the skin of |
| Ex 34:30 | all the children of Israel saw *M* |
| Ex 34:31 | And *M* called unto them |
| Ex 34:31 | and *M* talked with them |
| Ex 34:33 | till *M* had done speaking with |
| Ex 34:34 | But when *M* went in before the |
| Ex 34:35 | of Israel saw the face of *M* |
| Ex 34:35 | *M* put the vail upon his face |
| Ex 35:1 | *M* gathered all the congregation |
| Ex 35:4 | *M* spake unto all the congregation |
| Ex 35:20 | departed from the presence of *M* |
| Ex 35:29 | to be made by the hand of *M* |
| Ex 35:30 | *M* said unto the children of |
| Ex 36:2 | *M* called Bezaleel and Aholiab, and |
| Ex 36:3 | received of *M* all the offering |
| Ex 36:5 | And they spake unto *M*, saying, The |
| Ex 36:6 | *M* gave commandment, and they |
| Ex 38:21 | according to the commandment of *M* |
| Ex 38:22 | all that the LORD commanded *M* |
| Ex 39:1 | as the LORD commanded *M* |
| Ex 39:5 | as the LORD commanded *M* |
| Ex 39:7 | as the LORD commanded *M* |
| Ex 39:21 | as the LORD commanded *M* |
| Ex 39:26 | as the LORD commanded *M* |
| Ex 39:29 | as the LORD commanded *M* |
| Ex 39:31 | as the LORD commanded *M* |
| Ex 39:32 | to all that the LORD commanded *M* |
| Ex 39:33 | brought the tabernacle unto *M* |
| Ex 39:42 | to all that the LORD commanded *M* |
| Ex 39:43 | *M* did look upon all the work |
| Ex 39:43 | and *M* blessed them |
| Ex 40:1 | And the LORD spake unto *M*, saying, |
| Ex 40:16 | Thus did *M* |
| Ex 40:18 | *M* reared up the tabernacle, and |
| Ex 40:19 | as the LORD commanded *M* |
| Ex 40:21 | as the LORD commanded *M* |
| Ex 40:23 | as the LORD had commanded *M* |
| Ex 40:25 | as the LORD commanded *M* |
| Ex 40:27 | as the LORD commanded *M* |
| Ex 40:29 | as the LORD commanded *M* |
| Ex 40:31 | *M* and Aaron and his sons washed |
| Ex 40:32 | as the LORD commanded *M* |
| Ex 40:33 | So *M* finished the work |
| Ex 40:35 | *M* was not able to enter into the |
| Lev 1:1 | And the LORD called unto *M* |
| Lev 4:1 | And the LORD spake unto *M*, saying, |
| Lev 5:14 | And the LORD spake unto *M*, saying, |
| Lev 6:1 | And the LORD spake unto *M*, saying, |
| Lev 6:8 | And the LORD spake unto *M*, saying, |
| Lev 6:19 | And the LORD spake unto *M*, saying, |
| Lev 6:24 | And the LORD spake unto *M*, saying, |
| Lev 7:22 | And the LORD spake unto *M*, saying, |
| Lev 7:28 | And the LORD spake unto *M*, saying, |
| Lev 7:38 | LORD commanded *M* in mount Sinai |
| Lev 8:1 | And the LORD spake unto *M*, saying, |
| Lev 8:4 | *M* did as the LORD commanded him |
| Lev 8:5 | *M* said unto the congregation, |
| Lev 8:6 | *M* brought Aaron and his sons, and |
| Lev 8:9 | as the LORD commanded *M* |
| Lev 8:10 | *M* took the anointing oil, and |
| Lev 8:13 | *M* brought Aaron's sons, and put |
| Lev 8:13 | as the LORD commanded *M* |
| Lev 8:15 | *M* took the blood, and put it upon |
| Lev 8:16 | *M* burned it upon the altar |
| Lev 8:17 | as the LORD commanded *M* |
| Lev 8:19 | *M* sprinkled the blood upon the |
| Lev 8:20 | *M* burnt the head, and the pieces, |
| Lev 8:21 | *M* burnt the whole ram upon the |
| Lev 8:21 | as the LORD commanded *M* |
| Lev 8:23 | *M* took of the blood of it, and put |
| Lev 8:24 | *M* put of the blood upon the tip |
| Lev 8:24 | *M* sprinkled the blood upon the |
| Lev 8:28 | *M* took them from off their hands, |
| Lev 8:29 | *M* took the breast, and waved it |
| Lev 8:29 | as the LORD commanded *M* |
| Lev 8:30 | *M* took of the anointing oil, and |
| Lev 8:31 | *M* said unto Aaron and to his sons, |
| Lev 8:36 | LORD commanded by the hand of *M* |
| Lev 9:1 | that *M* called Aaron and his sons, |
| Lev 9:5 | they brought that which *M* |
| Lev 9:6 | *M* said, This is the thing which |
| Lev 9:7 | *M* said unto Aaron, Go unto the |
| Lev 9:10 | as the LORD commanded *M* |
| Lev 9:21 | as *M* commanded |
| Lev 9:23 | And *M* and Aaron went into the |
| Lev 10:3 | Then *M* said unto Aaron, This is |
| Lev 10:4 | *M* called Mishael and Elzaphan, and |
| Lev 10:5 | as *M* had said |
| Lev 10:6 | *M* said unto Aaron, and unto |
| Lev 10:7 | did according to the word of *M* |
| Lev 10:11 | spoken unto them by the hand of *M* |
| Lev 10:12 | *M* spake unto Aaron, and unto |
| Lev 10:16 | *M* diligently sought the goat of |
| Lev 10:19 | And Aaron said unto *M*, Behold, |
| Lev 10:20 | when *M* heard that, he was content |
| Lev 11:1 | And the LORD spake unto *M* and to |
| Lev 12:1 | And the LORD spake unto *M*, saying, |
| Lev 13:1 | the LORD spake unto *M* and Aaron |
| Lev 14:1 | And the LORD spake unto *M*, saying, |
| Lev 14:33 | And the LORD spake unto *M* and unto |
| Lev 15:1 | And the LORD spake unto *M* and to |
| Lev 16:1 | the LORD spake unto *M* after the |
| Lev 16:2 | And the LORD said unto *M*, Speak |
| Lev 16:34 | he did as the LORD commanded *M* |
| Lev 17:1 | And the LORD spake unto *M*, saying, |
| Lev 18:1 | And the LORD spake unto *M*, saying, |
| Lev 19:1 | And the LORD spake unto *M*, saying, |
| Lev 20:1 | And the LORD spake unto *M*, saying, |
| Lev 21:1 | And the LORD said unto *M*, Speak |
| Lev 21:16 | And the LORD spake unto *M*, saying, |
| Lev 21:24 | *M* told it unto Aaron, and to his |
| Lev 22:1 | And the LORD spake unto *M*, saying, |
| Lev 22:17 | And the LORD spake unto *M*, saying, |
| Lev 22:26 | And the LORD spake unto *M*, saying, |
| Lev 23:1 | And the LORD spake unto *M*, saying, |
| Lev 23:9 | And the LORD spake unto *M*, saying, |
| Lev 23:23 | And the LORD spake unto *M*, saying, |
| Lev 23:26 | And the LORD spake unto *M*, saying, |
| Lev 23:33 | And the LORD spake unto *M*, saying, |
| Lev 23:44 | *M* declared unto the children of |
| Lev 24:1 | And the LORD spake unto *M*, saying, |
| Lev 24:11 | And they brought him unto *M* |
| Lev 24:13 | And the LORD spake unto *M*, saying, |
| Lev 24:23 | *M* spake to the children of Israel |
| Lev 24:23 | did as the LORD commanded *M* |
| Lev 25:1 | LORD spake unto *M* in mount Sinai |
| Lev 26:46 | in mount Sinai by the hand of *M* |
| Lev 27:1 | And the LORD spake unto *M*, saying, |
| Lev 27:34 | which the LORD commanded *M* for |
| Num 1:1 | the LORD spake unto *M* in the |
| Num 1:17 | And *M* and Aaron took these men |
| Num 1:19 | As the LORD commanded *M*, so he |
| Num 1:44 | those that were numbered, which *M* |
| Num 1:48 | For the LORD had spoken unto *M* |
| Num 1:54 | to all that the LORD commanded *M* |
| Num 2:1 | And the LORD spake unto *M* and unto |
| Num 2:33 | as the LORD commanded *M* |
| Num 2:34 | to all that the LORD commanded *M* |
| Num 3:1 | *M* in the day that the LORD spake |
| Num 3:1 | LORD spake with *M* in mount Sinai |
| Num 3:5 | And the LORD spake unto *M*, saying, |
| Num 3:11 | And the LORD spake unto *M*, saying, |
| Num 3:14 | the LORD spake unto *M* in the |
| Num 3:16 | *M* numbered them according to the |
| Num 3:38 | congregation eastward, shall be *M* |
| Num 3:39 | numbered of the Levites, which *M* |
| Num 3:40 | And the LORD said unto *M*, Number |
| Num 3:42 | *M* numbered, as the LORD commanded |
| Num 3:44 | And the LORD spake unto *M*, saying, |
| Num 3:49 | *M* took the redemption money of |
| Num 3:51 | *M* gave the money of them that |
| Num 3:51 | the LORD, as the LORD commanded *M* |
| Num 4:1 | And the LORD spake unto *M* and unto |
| Num 4:17 | And the LORD spake unto *M* and unto |
| Num 4:21 | And the LORD spake unto *M*, saying, |
| Num 4:34 | And *M* and Aaron and the chief of the |
| Num 4:37 | of the congregation, which *M* |
| Num 4:37 | of the LORD by the hand of *M* |
| Num 4:41 | of the congregation, whom *M* |
| Num 4:45 | of the sons of Merari, whom *M* |
| Num 4:45 | word of the LORD by the hand of *M* |
| Num 4:46 | numbered of the Levites, whom *M* |
| Num 4:49 | were numbered by the hand of *M* |
| Num 4:49 | of him, as the LORD commanded *M* |
| Num 5:1 | And the LORD spake unto *M*, saying, |
| Num 5:4 | as the LORD spake unto *M*, so did |
| Num 5:5 | And the LORD spake unto *M*, saying, |
| Num 5:11 | And the LORD spake unto *M*, saying, |
| Num 6:1 | And the LORD spake unto *M*, saying, |
| Num 6:22 | And the LORD spake unto *M*, saying, |
| Num 7:1 | *M* had fully set up the tabernacle |
| Num 7:4 | And the LORD spake unto *M*, saying, |
| Num 7:6 | *M* took the wagons and the oxen, and |
| Num 7:11 | And the LORD said unto *M*, They |
| Num 7:89 | And when *M* was gone into the |
| Num 8:1 | And the LORD spake unto *M*, saying, |
| Num 8:3 | as the LORD commanded *M* |
| Num 8:4 | which the LORD had shewed *M* |
| Num 8:5 | And the LORD spake unto *M*, saying, |
| Num 8:20 | And *M*, and Aaron, and all the |
| Num 8:20 | *M* concerning the Levites, so did |
| Num 8:22 | *M* concerning the Levites, so did |
| Num 8:23 | And the LORD spake unto *M*, saying, |
| Num 9:1 | the LORD spake unto *M* in the |
| Num 9:4 | *M* spake unto the children of |
| Num 9:5 | to all that the LORD commanded *M* |
| Num 9:6 | and they came before *M* and before |
| Num 9:8 | *M* said unto them, Stand still, and |
| Num 9:9 | And the LORD spake unto *M*, saying, |
| Num 9:23 | of the LORD by the hand of *M* |
| Num 10:1 | And the LORD spake unto *M*, saying, |
| Num 10:13 | of the LORD by the hand of *M* |
| Num 10:29 | *M* said unto Hobab, the son of |
| Num 10:35 | the ark set forward, that *M* said |
| Num 11:2 | And the people cried unto *M* |
| Num 11:2 | when *M* prayed unto the LORD, the |
| Num 11:10 | Then *M* heard the people weep |
| Num 11:10 | *M* also was displeased |
| Num 11:11 | *M* said unto the LORD, Wherefore |
| Num 11:16 | And the LORD said unto *M*, Gather |
| Num 11:21 | *M* said, The people, among whom I |
| Num 11:23 | And the LORD said unto *M*, Is the |
| Num 11:24 | *M* went out, and told the people |
| Num 11:27 | there ran a young man, and told *M* |
| Num 11:28 | the son of Nun, the servant of *M* |
| Num 11:28 | men, answered and said, My lord *M* |
| Num 11:29 | *M* said unto him, Enviest thou for |
| Num 11:30 | *M* gat him into the camp, he and |
| Num 12:1 | Aaron spake against *M* because of |
| Num 12:2 | the LORD indeed spoken only by *M* |
| Num 12:3 | (Now the man *M* was very meek, |
| Num 12:4 | And the LORD spake suddenly unto *M* |
| Num 12:7 | My servant *M* is not so, who is |
| Num 12:8 | to speak against my servant *M* |
| Num 12:11 | And Aaron said unto *M*, Alas, my |
| Num 12:13 | *M* cried unto the LORD, saying, |
| Num 12:14 | And the LORD said unto *M*, If her |
| Num 13:1 | And the LORD spake unto *M*, saying, |
| Num 13:3 | *M* by the commandment of the LORD |
| Num 13:16 | which *M* sent to spy out the land |
| Num 13:16 | *M* called Oshea the son of Nun |
| Num 13:17 | *M* sent them to spy out the land |
| Num 13:26 | And they went and came to *M* |
| Num 13:30 | Caleb stilled the people before *M* |
| Num 14:2 | of Israel murmured against *M* |
| Num 14:5 | Then *M* and Aaron fell on their |
| Num 14:11 | And the LORD said unto *M*, How long |
| Num 14:13 | *M* said unto the LORD, Then the |
| Num 14:26 | And the LORD spake unto *M* and unto |
| Num 14:36 | which *M* sent to search the land, |
| Num 14:39 | *M* told these sayings unto all the |
| Num 14:41 | *M* said, Wherefore now do ye |
| Num 14:44 | of the covenant of the LORD, and *M* |
| Num 15:1 | And the LORD spake unto *M*, saying, |
| Num 15:17 | And the LORD spake unto *M*, saying, |
| Num 15:22 | which the LORD hath spoken unto *M* |
| Num 15:23 | commanded you by the hand of *M* |
| Num 15:23 | the day that the LORD commanded *M* |
| Num 15:33 | sticks brought him unto *M* |
| Num 15:35 | And the LORD said unto *M*, The man |
| Num 15:36 | as the LORD commanded *M* |
| Num 15:37 | And the LORD spake unto *M*, saying, |
| Num 16:2 | And they rose up before *M*, with |
| Num 16:3 | themselves together against *M* |
| Num 16:4 | when *M* heard it, he fell upon his |
| Num 16:8 | *M* said unto Korah, Hear, I pray |
| Num 16:12 | *M* sent to call Dathan and Abiram, |
| Num 16:15 | *M* was very wroth, and said unto |
| Num 16:16 | *M* said unto Korah, Be thou and all |
| Num 16:18 | of the congregation with *M* |
| Num 16:20 | And the LORD spake unto *M* and unto |
| Num 16:23 | And the LORD spake unto *M*, saying, |
| Num 16:25 | *M* rose up and went unto Dathan and |
| Num 16:28 | *M* said, Hereby ye shall know that |
| Num 16:36 | And the LORD spake unto *M*, saying, |
| Num 16:40 | LORD said to him by the hand of *M* |

Num 16:41 of Israel murmured against *M*
Num 16:42 was gathered against *M* and against
Num 16:43 And *M* and Aaron came before the
Num 16:44 And the LORD spake unto *M*, saying,
Num 16:46 *M* said unto Aaron, Take a censer,
Num 16:47 And Aaron took as *M* commanded
Num 16:50 Aaron returned unto *M* unto the
Num 17:1 And the LORD spake unto *M*, saying,
Num 17:6 *M* spake unto the children of
Num 17:7 *M* laid up the rods before the
Num 17:8 that on the morrow *M* went into
Num 17:9 *M* brought out all the rods from
Num 17:10 And the LORD said unto *M*, Bring
Num 17:11 And *M* did so
Num 17:12 children of Israel spake unto *M*
Num 18:25 And the LORD spake unto *M*, saying,
Num 19:1 And the LORD spake unto *M* and unto
Num 20:2 themselves together against *M*
Num 20:3 And the people chode with *M*
Num 20:6 And *M* and Aaron went from the
Num 20:7 And the LORD spake unto *M*, saying,
Num 20:9 *M* took the rod from before the
Num 20:10 And *M* and Aaron gathered the
Num 20:11 *M* lifted up his hand, and with his
Num 20:12 the LORD spake unto *M* and Aaron
Num 20:14 *M* sent messengers from Kadesh
Num 20:23 the LORD spake unto *M* and Aaron
Num 20:27 *M* did as the LORD commanded
Num 20:28 *M* stripped Aaron of his garments,
Num 20:28 and *M* and Eleazar came down from
Num 21:5 spake against God, and against *M*
Num 21:7 Therefore the people came to *M*
Num 21:7 And *M* prayed for the people
Num 21:8 And the LORD said unto *M*, Make
Num 21:9 *M* made a serpent of brass, and put
Num 21:16 whereof the LORD spake unto *M*
Num 21:32 *M* sent to spy out Jaazer, and they
Num 21:34 And the LORD said unto *M*, Fear him
Num 25:4 And the LORD said unto *M*, Take all
Num 25:5 *M* said unto the judges of Israel,
Num 25:6 woman in the sight of *M*, and in
Num 25:10 And the LORD spake unto *M*, saying,
Num 25:16 And the LORD spake unto *M*, saying,
Num 26:1 that the LORD spake unto *M*
Num 26:3 And *M* and Eleazar the priest spake
Num 26:4 as the LORD commanded *M* and the
Num 26:9 who strove against *M* and against
Num 26:52 And the LORD spake unto *M*, saying,
Num 26:59 she bare unto Amram Aaron and *M*
Num 26:63 are they that were numbered by *M*
Num 26:64 was not a man of them whom *M*
Num 27:2 And they stood before *M*, and before
Num 27:5 *M* brought their cause before the
Num 27:6 And the LORD spake unto *M*, saying,
Num 27:11 judgment, as the LORD commanded *M*
Num 27:12 And the LORD said unto *M*, Get thee
Num 27:15 *M* spake unto the LORD, saying,
Num 27:18 And the LORD said unto *M*, Take
Num 27:22 *M* did as the LORD commanded him
Num 27:23 LORD commanded by the hand of *M*
Num 28:1 And the LORD spake unto *M*, saying,
Num 29:40 *M* told the children of Israel
Num 29:40 to all that the LORD commanded *M*
Num 30:1 *M* spake unto the heads of the
Num 30:16 which the LORD commanded *M*
Num 31:1 And the LORD spake unto *M*, saying,
Num 31:3 *M* spake unto the people, saying,
Num 31:6 *M* sent them to the war, a
Num 31:7 as the LORD commanded *M*
Num 31:12 and the prey, and the spoil, unto *M*
Num 31:13 And *M*, and Eleazar the priest, and
Num 31:14 *M* was wroth with the officers of
Num 31:15 *M* said unto them, Have ye saved
Num 31:21 law which the LORD commanded *M*
Num 31:25 And the LORD spake unto *M*, saying,
Num 31:31 And *M* and Eleazar the priest did as
Num 31:31 did as the LORD commanded *M*
Num 31:41 *M* gave the tribute, which was the
Num 31:41 priest, as the LORD commanded *M*
Num 31:42 which *M* divided from the men that
Num 31:47 *M* took one portion of fifty, both
Num 31:47 as the LORD commanded *M*
Num 31:48 of hundreds, came near unto *M*
Num 31:49 And they said unto *M*, Thy servants
Num 31:51 And *M* and Eleazar the priest took
Num 31:54 And *M* and Eleazar the priest took
Num 32:2 of Reuben came and spake unto *M*
Num 32:6 *M* said unto the children of Gad
Num 32:20 *M* said unto them, If ye will do
Num 32:25 children of Reuben spake unto *M*
Num 32:28 So concerning them *M* commanded
Num 32:29 *M* said unto them, If the children
Num 32:33 *M* gave unto them, even to the
Num 32:40 *M* gave Gilead unto Machir the son
Num 33:1 their armies under the hand of *M*
Num 33:2 And *M* wrote their goings out
Num 33:50 the LORD spake unto *M* in the
Num 34:1 And the LORD spake unto *M*, saying,
Num 34:13 *M* commanded the children of
Num 34:16 And the LORD spake unto *M*, saying,
Num 35:1 the LORD spake unto *M* in the
Num 35:9 And the LORD spake unto *M*, saying,
Num 36:1 came near, and spake before *M*
Num 36:5 *M* commanded the children of
Num 36:10 Even as the LORD commanded *M*
Num 36:13 LORD commanded by the hand of *M*
Deut 1:1 These be the words which *M* spake
Deut 1:3 that *M* spake unto the children of
Deut 1:5 began *M* to declare this law,
Deut 4:41 Then *M* severed three cities on
Deut 4:44 this is the law which *M* set
Deut 4:45 which *M* spake unto the children
Deut 4:46 who dwelt at Heshbon, whom *M*
Deut 5:1 *M* called all Israel, and said unto
Deut 27:1 *M* with the elders of Israel
Deut 27:9 And *M* and the priests the Levites
Deut 27:11 *M* charged the people the same day
Deut 29:1 which the LORD commanded *M* to
Deut 29:2 *M* called unto all Israel, and said
Deut 31:1 *M* went and spake these words unto
Deut 31:7 *M* called unto Joshua, and said
Deut 31:9 *M* wrote this law, and delivered it
Deut 31:10 *M* commanded them, saying, At the
Deut 31:14 And the LORD said unto *M*, Behold,
Deut 31:14 *M* and Joshua went, and presented
Deut 31:16 And the LORD said unto *M*, Behold,
Deut 31:22 *M* therefore wrote this song the
Deut 31:24 when *M* had made an end of writing
Deut 31:25 That *M* commanded the Levites,
Deut 31:30 *M* spake in the ears of all the
Deut 32:44 *M* came and spake all the words of
Deut 32:45 *M* made an end of speaking all
Deut 32:48 spake unto *M* that selfsame day
Deut 33:1 wherewith *M* the man of God
Deut 33:4 *M* commanded us a law, even the
Deut 34:1 *M* went up from the plains of Moab
Deut 34:5 So *M* the servant of the LORD died
Deut 34:7 *M* was an hundred and twenty years
Deut 34:8 *M* in the plains of Moab thirty
Deut 34:8 and mourning for *M* were ended
Deut 34:9 for *M* had laid his hands upon him
Deut 34:9 and did as the LORD commanded *M*
Deut 34:10 since in Israel like unto *M*
Deut 34:12 *M* shewed in the sight of all
Josh 1:1 Now after the death of *M* the
Josh 1:2 *M* my servant is dead
Josh 1:3 given unto you, as I said unto *M*
Josh 1:5 as I was with *M*, so I will be
Josh 1:7 which *M* my servant commanded thee
Josh 1:13 which *M* the servant of the LORD
Josh 1:14 *M* gave you on this side Jordan
Josh 1:15 which *M* the LORD's servant gave
Josh 1:17 we hearkened unto *M* in all things
Josh 1:17 be with thee, as he was with *M*
Josh 3:7 may know that, as I was with *M*
Josh 4:10 to all that *M* commanded Joshua
Josh 4:12 of Israel, as *M* spake unto them
Josh 4:14 they feared him, as they feared *M*
Josh 8:31 As *M* the servant of the LORD
Josh 8:31 in the book of the law of *M*
Josh 8:32 the stones a copy of the law of *M*
Josh 8:33 as *M* the servant of the LORD had
Josh 8:35 a word of all that *M* commanded
Josh 9:24 *M* to give you all the land
Josh 11:12 as *M* the servant of the LORD
Josh 11:15 the LORD commanded *M* his servant
Josh 11:15 so did *M* command Joshua, and so
Josh 11:15 of all that the LORD commanded *M*
Josh 11:20 them, as the LORD commanded *M*
Josh 11:23 to all that the LORD said unto *M*
Josh 12:6 Them did *M* the servant of the
Josh 12:6 *M* the servant of the LORD gave it
Josh 13:8 which *M* gave them, beyond Jordan
Josh 13:8 even as *M* the servant of the LORD
Josh 13:12 for these did *M* smite, and cast
Josh 13:15 *M* gave unto the tribe of the
Josh 13:21 whom *M* smote with the princes of
Josh 13:24 *M* gave inheritance unto the tribe
Josh 13:29 *M* gave inheritance unto the half
Josh 13:32 These are the countries which *M*
Josh 13:33 Levi *M* gave not any inheritance
Josh 14:2 LORD commanded by the hand of *M*
Josh 14:3 For *M* had given the inheritance
Josh 14:5 As the LORD commanded *M*, so the
Josh 14:6 *M* the man of God concerning me
Josh 14:7 Forty years old was I when *M* the
Josh 14:9 *M* sware on that day, saying,
Josh 14:10 the LORD spake this word unto *M*
Josh 14:11 I was in the day that *M* sent me
Josh 17:4 The LORD commanded *M* to give us
Josh 18:7 which *M* the servant of the LORD
Josh 20:2 I spake unto you by the hand of *M*
Josh 21:2 *M* to give us cities to dwell in
Josh 21:8 LORD commanded by the hand of *M*
Josh 22:2 Ye have kept all that *M* the
Josh 22:4 which *M* the servant of the LORD
Josh 22:5 which *M* the servant of the LORD
Josh 22:7 half of the tribe of Manasseh *M*
Josh 22:9 word of the LORD by the hand of *M*
Josh 23:6 in the book of the law of *M*
Josh 24:5 I sent *M* also and Aaron, and I
Judg 1:20 gave Hebron unto Caleb, as *M* said
Judg 3:4 their fathers by the hand of *M*
Judg 4:11 of Hobab the father in law of *M*
1Sa 12:6 It is the LORD that advanced *M*
1Sa 12:8 the LORD, then the LORD sent *M*
1Kin 2:3 as it is written in the law of *M*
1Kin 8:9 which *M* put there at Horeb, when
1Kin 8:53 by the hand of *M* thy servant
1Kin 8:56 by the hand of *M* his servant
2Kin 14:6 in the book of the law of *M*
2Kin 18:4 brasen serpent that *M* had made
2Kin 18:6 which the LORD commanded *M*
2Kin 18:12 all that *M* the servant of the
2Kin 21:8 that my servant *M* commanded them
2Kin 23:25 according to all the law of *M*
1Chr 6:3 Aaron, and *M*, and Miriam
1Chr 6:49 according to all that *M* the
1Chr 15:15 as *M* commanded according to the
1Chr 21:29 which *M* made in the wilderness,
1Chr 22:13 charged *M* with concerning Israel
1Chr 23:13 of Amram; Aaron and *M*
1Chr 23:14 Now concerning *M* the man of God
1Chr 23:15 The sons of *M* were, Gershom, and
1Chr 26:24 the son of Gershom, the son of *M*
2Chr 1:3 which *M* the servant of the LORD
2Chr 5:10 which *M* put therein at Horeb
2Chr 8:13 according to the commandment of *M*
2Chr 23:18 as it is written in the law of *M*
2Chr 24:6 of *M* the servant of the LORD
2Chr 24:9 *M* the servant of God laid upon
2Chr 25:4 in the law in the book of *M*
2Chr 30:16 to the law of *M* the man of God
2Chr 33:8 the ordinances by the hand of *M*
2Chr 34:14 of the law of the LORD given by *M*
2Chr 35:6 word of the LORD by the hand of *M*
2Chr 35:12 as it is written in the book of *M*
Ezr 3:2 in the law of *M* the man of God
Ezr 6:18 as it is written in the book of *M*
Ezr 7:6 a ready scribe in the law of *M*
Neh 1:7 thou commandedst thy servant *M*
Neh 1:8 thou commandedst thy servant *M*
Neh 8:1 to bring the book of the law of *M*
Neh 8:14 which the LORD had commanded by *M*
Neh 9:14 by the hand of *M* thy servant
Neh 10:29 was given by *M* the servant of God
Neh 13:1 day they read in the book of *M* in
Ps 77:20 like a flock by the hand of *M*
Ps 90:*t* A Prayer of *M*, the man of God
Ps 99:6 *M* and Aaron among his priests, and
Ps 103:7 He made known his ways unto *M*
Ps 105:26 He sent *M* his servant
Ps 106:16 They envied *M* also in the camp,
Ps 106:23 had not *M* his chosen stood before
Ps 106:32 went ill with *M* for their sakes
Is 63:11 he remembered the days of old, *M*
Is 63:12 hand of *M* with his glorious arm
Jer 15:1 said the LORD unto me, Though *M*
Dan 9:11 the law of *M* the servant of God
Dan 9:13 As it is written in the law of *M*
Mic 6:4 and I sent before thee *M*, Aaron,
Mal 4:4 ye the law of *M* my servant
Mt 8:4 offer the gift that *M* commanded
Mt 17:3 there appeared unto them *M*
Mt 17:4 one for thee, and one for *M*
Mt 19:7 Why did *M* then command to give a
Mt 19:8 *M* because of the hardness of your
Mt 22:24 *M* said, If a man die, having no

Mk 1:44 those things which *M* commanded
Mk 7:10 For *M* said, Honour thy father and
Mk 9:4 appeared unto them Elias with *M*
Mk 9:5 one for thee, and one for *M*
Mk 10:3 unto them, What did *M* command you
Mk 10:4 *M* suffered to write a bill of
Mk 12:19 *M* wrote unto us, If a man's
Mk 12:26 have ye not read in the book of *M*
Lk 2:22 to the law of *M* were accomplished
Lk 5:14 according as *M* commanded
Lk 9:30 with him two men, which were *M*
Lk 9:33 one for thee, and one for *M*
Lk 16:29 saith unto him, They have *M*
Lk 16:31 said unto him, If they hear not *M*
Lk 20:28 *M* wrote unto us, If any man's
Lk 20:37 even *M* shewed at the bush, when
Lk 24:27 And beginning at *M* and all the
Lk 24:44 were written in the law of *M*
Jn 1:17 For the law was given by *M*
Jn 1:45 of whom *M* in the law, and the
Jn 3:14 as *M* lifted up the serpent in the
Jn 5:45 is one that accuseth you, even *M*
Jn 5:46 For had ye believed *M*, ye would
Jn 6:32 *M* gave you not that bread from
Jn 7:19 Did not *M* give you the law, and
Jn 7:22 *M* therefore gave unto you
Jn 7:22 (not because it is of *M*, but of
Jn 7:23 that the law of *M* should not be
Jn 8:5 Now *M* in the law commanded us,
Jn 9:29 We know that God spake unto *M*
Acts 3:22 For *M* truly said unto the fathers
Acts 6:11 speak blasphemous words against *M*
Acts 6:14 the customs which *M* delivered us
Acts 7:20 In which time *M* was born, and was
Acts 7:22 *M* was learned in all the wisdom
Acts 7:29 Then fled *M* at this saying, and
Acts 7:31 When *M* saw it, he wondered at the
Acts 7:32 Then *M* trembled, and durst not
Acts 7:35 This *M* whom they refused, saying,
Acts 7:37 This is that *M*, which said unto
Acts 7:40 for as for this *M*, which brought
Acts 7:44 he had appointed, speaking unto *M*
Acts 13:39 not be justified by the law of *M*
Acts 15:1 circumcised after the manner of *M*
Acts 15:5 command them to keep the law of *M*
Acts 15:21 For *M* of old time hath in every
Acts 21:21 among the Gentiles to forsake *M*
Acts 26:22 prophets and *M* did say should come
Acts 28:23 Jesus, both out of the law of *M*
Rom 5:14 death reigned from Adam to *M*
Rom 9:15 For he saith to *M*, I will have
Rom 10:5 For *M* describeth the
Rom 10:19 First *M* saith, I will provoke you
1Cor 9:9 For it is written in the law of *M*
1Cor 10:2 all baptized unto *M* in the cloud
2Cor 3:7 face of *M* for the glory of his
2Cor 3:13 And not as *M*, which put a vail
2Cor 3:15 when *M* is read, the vail is upon
2Ti 3:8 as Jannes and Jambres withstood *M*
Heb 3:2 as also *M* was faithful in all his
Heb 3:3 worthy of more glory than *M*
Heb 3:5 *M* verily was faithful in all his
Heb 3:16 all that came out of Egypt by *M*
Heb 7:14 of which tribe *M* spake nothing
Heb 8:5 as *M* was admonished of God when
Heb 9:19 For when *M* had spoken every
Heb 11:23 By faith *M*, when he was born, was
Heb 11:24 By faith *M*, when he was come to
Heb 12:21 was the sight, that *M* said
Jude 9 he disputed about the body of *M*
Rev 15:3 the song of *M* the servant of God

## MOSES'

Ex 17:12 But *M* hands were heavy
Ex 18:1 *M* father in law, heard of all
Ex 18:2 *M* father in law, took Zipporah,
Ex 18:2 *M* wife, after he had sent her
Ex 18:5 *M* father in law, came with his
Ex 18:12 *M* father in law, took a burnt
Ex 18:12 to eat bread with *M* father in law
Ex 18:14 when *M* father in law saw all that
Ex 18:17 *M* father in law said unto him,
Ex 32:19 *M* anger waxed hot, and he cast the
Ex 34:29 two tables of testimony in *M* hand
Ex 34:35 that the skin of *M* face shone
Lev 8:29 ram of consecration it was *M* part
Num 10:29 *M* father in law, We are
Josh 1:1 son of Nun, *M* minister, saying,
Judg 1:16 *M* father in law, went up out of
Mt 23:2 and the Pharisees sit in *M* seat
Jn 9:28 but we are *M* disciples
Heb 10:28 He that despised *M* law died

## MOTE

Mt 7:3 why beholdest thou the *m* that is
Mt 7:4 pull out the *m* out of thine eye
Mt 7:5 the *m* out of thy brother's eye
Lk 6:41 why beholdest thou the *m* that is
Lk 6:42 let me pull out the *m* that is in
Lk 6:42 see clearly to pull out the *m*

## MOTH

Job 4:19 which are crushed before the *m*
Job 13:28 as a garment that is *m* eaten
Job 27:18 He buildeth his house as a *m*
Ps 39:11 beauty to consume away like a *m*
Is 50:9 the *m* shall eat them up
Is 51:8 For the *m* shall eat them up like
Hos 5:12 will I be unto Ephraim as a *m*
Mt 6:19 treasures upon earth, where *m*
Mt 6:20 where neither *m* nor rust doth
Lk 12:33 approacheth, neither *m* corrupteth

## MOTHER

Gen 2:24 a man leave his father and his *m*
Gen 3:20 she was the *m* of all living
Gen 17:16 and she shall be a *m* of nations
Gen 20:12 but not the daughter of my *m*
Gen 21:21 his *m* took him a wife out of the
Gen 24:53 and to her *m* precious things
Gen 24:55 her *m* said, Let the damsel abide
Gen 24:60 be thou the *m* of thousands of
Gen 24:67 her into his *m* Sarah's tent
Gen 27:11 And Jacob said to Rebekah his *m*
Gen 27:13 his *m* said unto him, Upon me be
Gen 27:14 fetched, and brought them to his *m*
Gen 27:14 his *m* made savoury meat, such as
Gen 28:5 of Rebekah, Jacob's and Esau's *m*
Gen 28:7 Jacob obeyed his father and his *m*
Gen 30:14 and brought them unto his *m* Leah
Gen 32:11 me, and the *m* with the children
Gen 37:10 Shall I and thy *m* and thy brethren
Gen 44:20 and he alone is left of his *m*
Ex 2:8 maid went and called the child's *m*
Ex 20:12 Honour thy father and thy *m*
Ex 21:15 that smiteth his father, or his *m*
Ex 21:17 that curseth his father, or his *m*
Lev 18:7 father, or the nakedness of thy *m*
Lev 18:7 she is thy *m*
Lev 18:9 thy father, or daughter of thy *m*
Lev 19:3 Ye shall fear every man his *m*
Lev 20:9 *m* shall be surely put to death
Lev 20:9 hath cursed his father or his *m*
Lev 20:14 And if a man take a wife and her *m*
Lev 21:2 near unto him, that is, for his *m*
Lev 21:11 for his father, or for his *m*
Num 6:7 for his father, or for his *m*
Num 26:59 whom her *m* bare to Levi in Egypt
Deut 5:16 Honour thy father and thy *m*
Deut 13:6 If thy brother, the son of thy *m*
Deut 21:13 her father and her *m* a full month
Deut 21:18 his father, or the voice of his *m*
Deut 21:19 his *m* lay hold on him, and bring
Deut 22:15 father of the damsel, and her *m*
Deut 27:16 light by his father or his *m*
Deut 27:22 father, or the daughter of his *m*
Deut 27:23 he that lieth with his *m* in law
Deut 33:9 said unto his father and to his *m*
Josh 2:13 save alive my father, and my *m*
Josh 2:18 shalt bring thy father, and thy *m*
Josh 6:23 Rahab, and her father, and her *m*
Judg 5:7 arose, that I arose a *m* in Israel
Judg 5:28 The *m* of Sisera looked out at a
Judg 8:19 brethren, even the sons of my *m*
Judg 14:2 up, and told his father and his *m*
Judg 14:3 his *m* said unto him, Is there
Judg 14:4 his *m* knew not that it was of the
Judg 14:5 down, and his father and his *m*
Judg 14:6 father or his *m* what he had done
Judg 14:9 and came to his father and *m*
Judg 14:16 not told it my father nor my *m*
Judg 17:2 And he said unto his *m*, The eleven
Judg 17:2 his *m* said, Blessed be thou of
Judg 17:3 shekels of silver to his *m*
Judg 17:3 his *m* said, I had wholly
Judg 17:4 he restored the money unto his *m*
Judg 17:4 his *m* took two hundred shekels of
Ruth 1:14 and Orpah kissed her *m* in law
Ruth 2:11 that thou hast done unto thy *m* in
Ruth 2:11 hast left thy father and thy *m*
Ruth 2:18 her *m* in law saw what she had
Ruth 2:19 her *m* in law said unto her, Where
Ruth 2:19 she shewed her *m* in law with whom
Ruth 2:23 and dwelt with her *m* in law
Ruth 3:1 Then Naomi her *m* in law said unto
Ruth 3:6 to all that her *m* in law bade her
Ruth 3:16 And when she came to her *m* in law
Ruth 3:17 Go not empty unto thy *m* in law
1Sa 2:19 Moreover his *m* made him a little
1Sa 15:33 so shall thy *m* be childless among
1Sa 22:3 of Moab, Let my father and my *m*
2Sa 17:25 sister to Zeruiah Joab's *m*
2Sa 19:37 the grave of my father and of my *m*
2Sa 20:19 destroy a city and a *m* in Israel
1Kin 1:6 his *m* bare him after Absalom
1Kin 1:11 unto Bath-sheba the *m* of Solomon
1Kin 2:13 to Bath-sheba the *m* of Solomon
1Kin 2:19 a seat to be set for the king's *m*
1Kin 2:20 king said unto her, Ask on, my *m*
1Kin 2:22 answered and said unto his *m*
1Kin 3:27 she is the *m* thereof
1Kin 15:13 And also Maachah his *m*, even her
1Kin 17:23 and delivered him unto his *m*
1Kin 19:20 pray thee, kiss my father and my *m*
1Kin 22:52 father, and in the way of his *m*
2Kin 3:2 like his father, and like his *m*
2Kin 3:13 and to the prophets of thy *m*
2Kin 4:19 said to a lad, Carry him to his *m*
2Kin 4:20 him, and brought him to his *m*
2Kin 4:30 the *m* of the child said, As the
2Kin 9:22 as the whoredoms of thy *m* Jezebel
2Kin 11:1 when Athaliah the *m* of Ahaziah
2Kin 24:12 the king of Babylon, he, and his *m*
2Kin 24:15 to Babylon, and the king's *m*
1Chr 2:26 she was the *m* of Onam
1Chr 4:9 his *m* called his name Jabez,
2Chr 15:16 Maachah the *m* of Asa the king
2Chr 22:3 for his *m* was his counsellor to
2Chr 22:10 But when Athaliah the *m* of
Est 2:7 for she had neither father nor *m*
Est 2:7 *m* were dead, took for his own
Job 17:14 to the worm, Thou art my *m*
Ps 27:10 my *m* forsake me, then the LORD
Ps 35:14 as one that mourneth for his *m*
Ps 51:5 and in sin did my *m* conceive me
Ps 109:14 the sin of his *m* be blotted out
Ps 113:9 and to be a joyful *m* of children
Ps 131:2 a child that is weaned of his *m*
Prov 1:8 and forsake not the law of thy *m*
Prov 4:3 only beloved in the sight of my *m*
Prov 6:20 and forsake not the law of thy *m*
Prov 10:1 son is the heaviness of his *m*
Prov 15:20 but a foolish man despiseth his *m*
Prov 19:26 his father, and chaseth away his *m*
Prov 20:20 Whoso curseth his father or his *m*
Prov 23:22 despise not thy *m* when she is old
Prov 23:25 thy *m* shall be glad, and she that
Prov 28:24 Whoso robbeth his father or his *m*
Prov 29:15 himself bringeth his *m* to shame
Prov 30:11 father, and doth not bless their *m*
Prov 30:17 and despiseth to obey his *m*
Prov 31:1 prophecy that his *m* taught him
Song 3:11 with the crown wherewith his *m*
Song 6:9 she is the only one of her *m*
Song 8:1 that sucked the breasts of my *m*
Song 8:5 there thy *m* brought thee forth
Is 8:4 to cry, My father, and my *m*
Is 49:1 from the bowels of my *m* hath he
Is 50:1 transgressions is your *m* put away
Is 66:13 As one whom his *m* comforteth
Jer 15:8 *m* of the young men a spoiler at
Jer 15:10 Woe is me, my *m*, that thou hast
Jer 16:7 for their father or for their *m*
Jer 20:14 wherein my *m* bare me be blessed
Jer 20:17 or that my *m* might have been my
Jer 22:26 thy *m* that bare thee, into
Jer 50:12 Your *m* shall be sore confounded
Eze 16:3 an Amorite, and thy *m* an Hittite
Eze 16:44 against thee, saying, As is the *m*
Eze 16:45 your *m* was an Hittite, and your
Eze 19:2 And say, What is thy *m*
Eze 19:10 Thy *m* is like a vine in thy blood
Eze 22:7 they set light by father and *m*
Eze 23:2 two women, the daughters of one *m*
Eze 44:25 but for father, or for *m*, or for
Hos 2:2 Plead with your *m*, plead
Hos 2:5 For their *m* hath played the
Hos 4:5 night, and I will destroy thy *m*
Hos 10:14 the *m* was dashed in pieces upon
Mic 7:6 daughter riseth up against her *m*
Mic 7:6 in law against her *m* in law
Zec 13:3 his *m* that begat him shall say

Zec 13:3 his *m* that begat him shall thrust
Mt 1:18 When as his *m* Mary was espoused
Mt 2:11 the young child with Mary his *m*
Mt 2:13 and take the young child and his *m*
Mt 2:14 his *m* by night, and departed into
Mt 2:20 and take the young child and his *m*
Mt 2:21 and took the young child and his *m*
Mt 8:14 house, he saw his wife's *m* laid
Mt 10:35 and the daughter against her *m*
Mt 10:35 in law against her *m* in law
Mt 10:37 He that loveth father or *m* more
Mt 12:46 to the people, behold, his *m*
Mt 12:47 one said unto him, Behold, thy *m*
Mt 12:48 him that told him, Who is my *m*
Mt 12:49 disciples, and said, Behold my *m*
Mt 12:50 is my brother, and sister, and *m*
Mt 13:55 is not his *m* called Mary
Mt 14:8 being before instructed of her *m*
Mt 14:11 and she brought it to her *m*
Mt 15:4 saying, Honour thy father and *m*
Mt 15:4 and, He that curseth father or *m*
Mt 15:5 shall say to his father or his *m*
Mt 15:6 And honour not his father or his *m*
Mt 19:5 shall a man leave father and *m*
Mt 19:19 Honour thy father and thy *m*
Mt 19:29 or sisters, or father, or *m*
Mt 20:20 Then came to him the *m* of
Mt 27:56 Magdalene, and Mary the *m* of James
Mt 27:56 the *m* of Zebedee's children
Mk 1:30 But Simon's wife's *m* lay sick of
Mk 3:31 came then his brethren and his *m*
Mk 3:32 they said unto him, Behold, thy *m*
Mk 3:33 them, saying, Who is my *m*
Mk 3:34 about him, and said, Behold my *m*
Mk 3:35 is my brother, and my sister, and *m*
Mk 5:40 the *m* of the damsel, and them that
Mk 6:24 went forth, and said unto her *m*
Mk 6:28 and the damsel gave it to her *m*
Mk 7:10 said, Honour thy father and thy *m*
Mk 7:10 and, Whoso curseth father or *m*
Mk 7:11 man shall say to his father or *m*
Mk 7:12 do ought for his father or his *m*
Mk 10:7 shall a man leave his father and *m*
Mk 10:19 not, Honour thy father and *m*
Mk 10:29 or sisters, or father, or *m*
Mk 15:40 Mary the *m* of James the less and
Mk 15:47 Mary the *m* of Joses beheld where
Mk 16:1 Magdalene, and Mary the *m* of James
Lk 1:43 that the *m* of my Lord should come
Lk 1:60 his *m* answered and said, Not so
Lk 2:33 his *m* marvelled at those things
Lk 2:34 them, and said unto Mary his *m*
Lk 2:43 and Joseph and his *m* knew not of it
Lk 2:48 his *m* said unto him, Son, why
Lk 2:51 but his *m* kept all these sayings
Lk 4:38 Simon's wife's *m* was taken with a
Lk 7:12 out, the only son of his *m*
Lk 7:15 And he delivered him to his *m*
Lk 8:19 Then came to him his *m* and his
Lk 8:20 him by certain which said, Thy *m*
Lk 8:21 answered and said unto them, My *m*
Lk 8:51 the father and the *m* of the maiden
Lk 12:53 the *m* against the daughter
Lk 12:53 and the daughter against the *m*
Lk 12:53 the *m* in law against her daughter
Lk 12:53 in law against her *m* in law
Lk 14:26 me, and hate not his father, and *m*
Lk 18:20 Honour thy father and thy *m*
Lk 24:10 and Joanna, and Mary the *m* of James
Jn 2:1 and the *m* of Jesus was there
Jn 2:3 the *m* of Jesus saith unto him,
Jn 2:5 His *m* saith unto the servants,
Jn 2:12 down to Capernaum, he, and his *m*
Jn 6:42 Joseph, whose father and *m* we know
Jn 19:25 stood by the cross of Jesus his *m*
Jn 19:26 When Jesus therefore saw his *m*
Jn 19:26 he loved, he saith unto his *m*
Jn 19:27 he to the disciple, Behold thy *m*
Acts 1:14 the women, and Mary the *m* of Jesus
Acts 12:12 the house of Mary the *m* of John
Rom 16:13 chosen in the Lord, and his *m*
Gal 4:26 is free, which is the *m* of us all
Eph 5:31 shall a man leave his father and *m*
Eph 6:2 Honour thy father and *m*
2Ti 1:5 grandmother Lois, and thy *m* Eunice
Heb 7:3 Without father, without *m*
Rev 17:5 THE *M* OF HARLOTS AND

### MOTHER'S

Gen 24:28 told them of her *m* house these
Gen 24:67 was comforted after his *m* death
Gen 27:29 let thy *m* sons bow down to thee
Gen 28:2 the house of Bethuel thy *m* father
Gen 28:2 daughters of Laban thy *m* brother
Gen 29:10 daughter of Laban his *m* brother
Gen 29:10 the sheep of Laban his *m* brother
Gen 29:10 the flock of Laban his *m* brother
Gen 43:29 his brother Benjamin, his *m* son
Ex 23:19 not seethe a kid in his *m* milk
Ex 34:26 not seethe a kid in his *m* milk
Lev 18:13 the nakedness of thy *m* sister
Lev 18:13 for she is thy *m* near kinswoman
Lev 20:17 or his *m* daughter, and see her
Lev 20:19 the nakedness of thy *m* sister
Lev 24:11 his *m* name was Shelomith, the
Num 12:12 when he cometh out of his *m* womb
Deut 14:21 not seethe a kid in his *m* milk
Judg 9:1 to Shechem unto his *m* brethren
Judg 9:1 of the house of his *m* father
Judg 9:3 his *m* brethren spake of him in
Judg 16:17 Nazarite unto God from my *m* womb
Ruth 1:8 Go, return each to her *m* house
1Sa 20:30 the confusion of thy *m* nakedness
1Kin 11:26 whose *m* name was Zeruah, a widow
1Kin 14:21 And his *m* name was Naamah an
1Kin 14:31 And his *m* name was Naamah an
1Kin 15:2 his *m* name was Maachah, the
1Kin 15:10 his *m* name was Maachah, the
1Kin 22:42 his *m* name was Azubah the
2Kin 8:26 his *m* name was Athaliah, the
2Kin 12:1 And his *m* name was Zibiah of
2Kin 14:2 his *m* name was Jehoaddan of
2Kin 15:2 his *m* name was Jecholiah of
2Kin 15:33 his *m* name was Jerusha, the
2Kin 18:2 His *m* name also was Abi, the
2Kin 21:1 his *m* name was Hephzi-bah
2Kin 21:19 his *m* name was Meshullemeth, the
2Kin 22:1 his *m* name was Jedidah, the
2Kin 23:31 his *m* name was Hamutal, the
2Kin 23:36 his *m* name was Zebudah, the
2Kin 24:8 his *m* name was Nehushta, the
2Kin 24:18 his *m* name was Hamutal, the
2Chr 12:13 And his *m* name was Naamah an
2Chr 13:2 His *m* name also was Michaiah the
2Chr 20:31 his *m* name was Azubah the
2Chr 22:2 His *m* name also was Athaliah the
2Chr 24:1 His *m* name also was Zibiah of
2Chr 25:1 his *m* name was Jehoaddan of
2Chr 26:3 His *m* name also was Jecoliah of
2Chr 27:1 His *m* name also was Jerushah, the
2Chr 29:1 his *m* name was Abijah, the
Job 1:21 Naked came I out of my *m* womb
Job 3:10 not up the doors of my *m* womb
Job 31:18 I have guided her from my *m* womb
Ps 22:9 hope when I was upon my *m* breasts
Ps 22:10 thou art my God from my *m* belly
Ps 50:20 thou slanderest thine own *m* son
Ps 69:8 and an alien unto my *m* children
Ps 71:6 that took me out of my *m* bowels
Ps 139:13 thou hast covered me in my *m* womb
Eccl 5:15 As he came forth of his *m* womb
Song 1:6 my *m* children were angry with me
Song 3:4 I had brought him into my *m* house
Song 8:2 and bring thee into my *m* house
Is 50:1 is the bill of your *m* divorcement
Jer 52:1 his *m* name was Hamutal the
Eze 16:45 Thou art thy *m* daughter, that
Mt 19:12 were so born from their *m* womb
Lk 1:15 Holy Ghost, even from his *m* womb
Jn 3:4 the second time into his *m* womb
Jn 19:25 his *m* sister, Mary the wife of
Acts 3:2 lame from his *m* womb was carried
Acts 14:8 being a cripple from his *m* womb
Gal 1:15 who separated me from my *m* womb

### MOTHERS

Is 49:23 and their queens thy nursing *m*
Jer 16:3 concerning their *m* that bare them
Lam 2:12 They say to their *m*, Where is
Lam 5:3 fatherless, our *m* are as widows
Mk 10:30 and brethren, and sisters, and *m*
1Ti 1:9 of fathers and murderers of *m*
1Ti 5:2 The elder women as *m*

### MOUNT

Gen 10:30 goest unto Sephar a *m* of the east
Gen 14:6 And the Horites in their *m* Seir
Gen 22:14 In the *m* of the LORD it shall be
Gen 31:21 set his face toward the *m* Gilead
Gen 31:23 they overtook him in the *m* Gilead
Gen 31:25 had pitched his tent in the *m*
Gen 31:25 pitched in the *m* of Gilead
Gen 31:54 offered sacrifice upon the *m*
Gen 31:54 and tarried all night in the *m*
Gen 36:8 Thus dwelt Esau in *m* Seir
Gen 36:9 father of the Edomites in *m* Seir
Ex 4:27 went, and met him in the *m* of God
Ex 18:5 where he encamped at the *m* of God
Ex 19:2 there Israel camped before the *m*
Ex 19:11 of all the people upon *m* Sinai
Ex 19:12 that ye go not up into the *m*
Ex 19:12 whosoever toucheth the *m* shall be
Ex 19:13 long, they shall come up to the *m*
Ex 19:14 down from the *m* unto the people
Ex 19:16 and a thick cloud upon the *m*
Ex 19:17 stood at the nether part of the *m*
Ex 19:18 *m* Sinai was altogether on a smoke
Ex 19:18 the whole *m* quaked greatly
Ex 19:20 *m* Sinai, on the top of the *m*
Ex 19:20 Moses up to the top of the *m*
Ex 19:23 people cannot come up to *m* Sinai
Ex 19:23 saying, Set bounds about the *m*
Ex 24:12 Moses, Come up to me into the *m*
Ex 24:13 Moses went up into the *m* of God
Ex 24:15 And Moses went up into the *m*
Ex 24:15 and a cloud covered the *m*
Ex 24:16 of the LORD abode upon *m* Sinai
Ex 24:17 fire on the top of the *m* in the
Ex 24:18 cloud, and gat him up into the *m*
Ex 24:18 and Moses was in the *m* forty days
Ex 25:40 which was shewed thee in the *m*
Ex 26:30 which was shewed thee in the *m*
Ex 27:8 as it was shewed thee in the *m*
Ex 31:18 communing with him upon *m* Sinai
Ex 32:1 delayed to come down out of the *m*
Ex 32:15 turned, and went down from the *m*
Ex 32:19 and brake them beneath the *m*
Ex 33:6 of their ornaments by the *m* Horeb
Ex 34:2 up in the morning unto *m* Sinai
Ex 34:2 there to me in the top of the *m*
Ex 34:3 man be seen throughout all the *m*
Ex 34:3 nor herds feed before that *m*
Ex 34:4 morning, and went up unto *m* Sinai
Ex 34:29 when Moses came down from *m* Sinai
Ex 34:29 when he came down from the *m*
Ex 34:32 had spoken with him in *m* Sinai
Lev 7:38 LORD commanded Moses in *m* Sinai
Lev 25:1 LORD spake unto Moses in *m* Sinai
Lev 26:46 the children of Israel in *m* Sinai
Lev 27:34 the children of Israel in *m* Sinai
Num 3:1 LORD spake with Moses in *m* Sinai
Num 10:33 they departed from the *m* of the
Num 20:22 from Kadesh, and came unto *m* Hor
Num 20:23 unto Moses and Aaron in *m* Hor
Num 20:25 son, and bring them up unto *m* Hor
Num 20:27 they went up into *m* Hor in the
Num 20:28 died there in the top of the *m*
Num 20:28 and Eleazar came down from the *m*
Num 21:4 they journeyed from *m* Hor by the
Num 27:12 Get thee up into this *m* Abarim
Num 28:6 which was ordained in *m* Sinai for
Num 33:23 and pitched in *m* Shapher
Num 33:24 And they removed from *m* Shapher
Num 33:37 from Kadesh, and pitched in *m* Hor
Num 33:38 *m* Hor at the commandment of the
Num 33:39 years old when he died in *m* Hor
Num 33:41 And they departed from *m* Hor
Num 34:7 ye shall point out for you *m* Hor
Num 34:8 From *m* Hor ye shall point out
Deut 1:2 way of *m* Seir unto Kadesh-barnea
Deut 1:6 have dwelt long enough in this *m*
Deut 1:7 go to the *m* of the Amorites, and
Deut 2:1 we compassed *m* Seir many days
Deut 2:5 because I have given *m* Seir unto
Deut 3:8 the river of Arnon unto *m* Hermon
Deut 3:12 half *m* Gilead, and the cities
Deut 4:48 even unto *m* Sion which is Hermon,
Deut 5:4 *m* out of the midst of the fire
Deut 5:5 fire, and went not up into the *m*
Deut 5:22 *m* out of the midst of the fire
Deut 9:9 When I was gone up into the *m* to
Deut 9:9 then I abode in the *m* forty days
Deut 9:10 the LORD spake with you in the *m*
Deut 9:15 I turned and came down from the *m*
Deut 9:15 and the *m* burned with fire
Deut 9:21 brook that descended out of the *m*
Deut 10:1 and come up unto me into the *m*
Deut 10:3 the first, and went up into the *m*
Deut 10:4 the LORD spake unto you in the *m*

Deut 10:5 myself and came down from the *m*
Deut 10:10 And I stayed in the *m*, according
Deut 11:29 put the blessing upon *m* Gerizim
Deut 11:29 and the curse upon *m* Ebal
Deut 27:4 in *m* Ebal, and thou shalt plaister
Deut 27:12 These shall stand upon *m* Gerizim
Deut 27:13 shall stand upon *m* Ebal to curse
Deut 32:49 this mountain Abarim, unto *m* Nebo
Deut 32:50 die in the *m* whither thou goest
Deut 32:50 Aaron thy brother died in *m* Hor
Deut 33:2 he shined forth from *m* Paran
Josh 8:30 the LORD God of Israel in *m* Ebal
Josh 8:33 of them over against *m* Gerizim
Josh 8:33 half of them over against *m* Ebal
Josh 11:17 Even from the *m* Halak, that goeth
Josh 11:17 valley of Lebanon under *m* Hermon
Josh 12:1 the river Arnon unto *m* Hermon
Josh 12:5 And reigned in *m* Hermon, and in
Josh 12:7 of Lebanon even unto the *m* Halak
Josh 13:5 from Baal-gad under *m* Hermon unto
Josh 13:11 all *m* Hermon, and all Bashan unto
Josh 13:19 in the *m* of the valley,
Josh 15:9 out to the cities of *m* Ephron
Josh 15:10 from Baalah westward unto *m* Seir
Josh 15:10 along unto the side of *m* Jearim
Josh 15:11 and passed along to *m* Baalah
Josh 16:1 from Jericho throughout *m* Beth-el
Josh 17:15 if *m* Ephraim be too narrow for
Josh 19:50 even Timnath-serah in *m* Ephraim
Josh 20:7 Kedesh in Galilee in *m* Naphtali
Josh 20:7 and Shechem in *m* Ephraim
Josh 21:21 with her suburbs in *m* Ephraim
Josh 24:4 and I gave unto Esau *m* Seir
Josh 24:30 which is in *m* Ephraim, on the
Josh 24:33 which was given him in *m* Ephraim
Judg 1:35 would dwell in *m* Heres in Aijalon
Judg 2:9 in the *m* of Ephraim, on the north
Judg 3:3 Hivites that dwelt in *m* Lebanon
Judg 3:3 from *m* Baal-hermon unto the
Judg 3:27 went down with him from the *m*
Judg 4:5 Ramah and Beth-el in *m* Ephraim
Judg 4:6 saying, Go and draw toward *m* Tabor
Judg 4:12 of Abinoam was gone up to *m* Tabor
Judg 4:14 So Barak went down from *m* Tabor
Judg 7:3 and depart early from *m* Gilead
Judg 7:24 throughout all *m* Ephraim, saying,
Judg 9:7 and stood in the top of *m* Gerizim
Judg 9:48 Abimelech gat him up to *m* Zalmon
Judg 10:1 he dwelt in Shamir in *m* Ephraim
Judg 12:15 in the *m* of the Amalekites
Judg 17:1 And there was a man of *m* Ephraim
Judg 17:8 he came to *m* Ephraim to the house
Judg 18:2 who when they came to *m* Ephraim
Judg 18:13 they passed thence unto *m* Ephraim
Judg 19:1 on the side of *m* Ephraim, who
Judg 19:16 even, which was also of *m* Ephraim
Judg 19:18 toward the side of *m* Ephraim
1Sa 1:1 of *m* Ephraim, and his name was
1Sa 9:4 And he passed through *m* Ephraim
1Sa 13:2 in *m* Beth-el, and a thousand were
1Sa 14:22 had hid themselves in *m* Ephraim
1Sa 31:1 and fell down slain in *m* Gilboa
1Sa 31:8 his three sons fallen in *m* Gilboa
2Sa 1:6 happened by chance upon *m* Gilboa
2Sa 15:30 went up by the ascent of *m* Olivet
2Sa 15:32 was come to the top of the *m*
2Sa 20:21 but a man of *m* Ephraim, Sheba the
1Kin 4:8 The son of Hur, in *m* Ephraim
1Kin 12:25 built Shechem in *m* Ephraim
1Kin 18:19 to me all Israel unto *m* Carmel
1Kin 18:20 prophets together unto *m* Carmel
1Kin 19:8 nights unto Horeb the *m* of God
1Kin 19:11 stand upon the *m* before the LORD
2Kin 2:25 he went from thence to *m* Carmel
2Kin 4:25 unto the man of God to *m* Carmel
2Kin 5:22 *m* Ephraim two young men of the
2Kin 19:31 and they that escape out of *m* Zion
2Kin 23:13 right hand of the *m* of corruption
2Kin 23:16 that were there in the *m*, and sent
1Chr 4:42 five hundred men, went to *m* Seir
1Chr 5:23 and Senir, and unto *m* Hermon
1Chr 6:67 Shechem in *m* Ephraim with her
1Chr 10:1 and fell down slain in *m* Gilboa
1Chr 10:8 and his sons fallen in *m* Gilboa
2Chr 3:1 the LORD at Jerusalem in *m* Moriah
2Chr 13:4 Abijah stood up upon *m* Zemaraim
2Chr 13:4 Zemaraim, which is in *m* Ephraim
2Chr 15:8 which he had taken from *m* Ephraim
2Chr 19:4 from Beer-sheba to *m* Ephraim
2Chr 20:10 *m* Seir, whom thou wouldest not
2Chr 20:22 *m* Seir, which were come against
2Chr 20:23 against the inhabitants of *m* Seir
2Chr 33:15 in the *m* of the house of the LORD
Neh 8:15 saying, Go forth unto the *m*
Neh 9:13 camest down also upon *m* Sinai
Job 20:6 excellency *m* up to the heavens
Job 39:27 Doth the eagle *m* up at thy
Ps 48:2 is *m* Zion, on the sides of the
Ps 48:11 Let *m* Zion rejoice, let the
Ps 74:2 this *m* Zion, wherein thou hast
Ps 78:68 the *m* Zion which he loved
Ps 107:26 They *m* up to the heaven, they go
Ps 125:1 in the LORD shall be as *m* Zion
Song 4:1 goats, that appear from *m* Gilead
Is 4:5 every dwelling place of *m* Zion
Is 8:18 hosts, which dwelleth in *m* Zion
Is 9:18 they shall *m* up like the lifting
Is 10:12 his whole work upon *m* Zion
Is 10:32 the *m* of the daughter of Zion
Is 14:13 upon the *m* of the congregation
Is 16:1 unto the *m* of the daughter of
Is 18:7 of the LORD of hosts, the *m* Zion
Is 24:23 of hosts shall reign in *m* Zion
Is 27:13 LORD in the holy *m* at Jerusalem
Is 28:21 shall rise up as in *m* Perazim
Is 29:3 lay siege against thee with a *m*
Is 29:8 be, that fight against *m* Zion
Is 31:4 come down to fight for *m* Zion
Is 37:32 and they that escape out of *m* Zion
Is 40:31 they shall *m* up with wings as
Jer 4:15 affliction from *m* Ephraim
Jer 6:6 cast a *m* against Jerusalem
Jer 31:6 upon the *m* Ephraim shall cry
Jer 50:19 shall be satisfied upon *m* Ephraim
Jer 51:53 Babylon should *m* up to heaven
Eze 4:2 it, and cast a *m* against it
Eze 10:16 wings to *m* up from the earth
Eze 21:22 against the gates, to cast a *m*
Eze 26:8 cast a *m* against thee, and lift up
Eze 35:2 man, set thy face against *m* Seir
Eze 35:3 O *m* Seir, I am against thee, and I
Eze 35:7 Thus will I make *m* Seir most
Eze 35:15 O *m* Seir, and all Idumea, even all
Dan 11:15 north shall come, and cast up a *m*
Joel 2:32 for in *m* Zion and in Jerusalem
Obad 8 out of the *m* of Esau
Obad 9 the *m* of Esau may be cut off by
Obad 17 But upon *m* Zion shall be
Obad 19 south shall possess the *m* of Esau
Obad 21 *m* Zion to judge the *m* of Esau
Mic 4:7 them in *m* Zion from henceforth
Hab 3:3 and the Holy One from *m* Paran
Zec 14:4 in that day upon the *m* of Olives
Zec 14:4 the *m* of Olives shall cleave in
Mt 21:1 unto the *m* of Olives, then sent
Mt 24:3 And as he sat upon the *m* of Olives
Mt 26:30 went out into the *m* of Olives
Mk 11:1 at the *m* of Olives, he sendeth
Mk 13:3 as he sat upon the *m* of Olives
Mk 14:26 went out into the *m* of Olives
Lk 19:29 at the *m* called the *m* of
Lk 19:29 called the *m* of Olives
Lk 19:37 at the descent of the *m* of Olives
Lk 21:37 abode in the *m* that is called the
Lk 21:37 that is called the *m* of Olives
Lk 22:39 he was wont, to the *m* of Olives
Jn 8:1 Jesus went unto the *m* of Olives
Acts 1:12 from the *m* called Olivet, which
Acts 7:30 to him in the wilderness of *m*
Acts 7:38 which spake to him in the *m* Sina
Gal 4:24 the one from the *m* Sinai, which
Gal 4:25 this Agar is *m* Sinai in Arabia
Heb 8:5 pattern shewed to thee in the *m*
Heb 12:18 unto the *m* that might be touched
Heb 12:22 But ye are come unto *m* Sion
2Pet 1:18 we were with him in the holy *m*
Rev 14:1 lo, a Lamb stood on the *m* Sion

**MOUNTAIN**

Gen 12:8 unto a *m* on the east of Beth-el
Gen 14:10 they that remained fled to the *m*
Gen 19:17 escape to the *m*, lest thou be
Gen 19:19 and I cannot escape to the *m*
Gen 19:30 up out of Zoar, and dwelt in the *m*
Ex 3:1 desert, and came to the *m* of God
Ex 3:12 ye shall serve God upon this *m*
Ex 15:17 plant them in the *m* of thine
Ex 19:3 LORD called unto him out of the *m*
Ex 20:18 of the trumpet, and the *m* smoking
Num 13:17 southward, and go up into the *m*
Num 14:40 gat them up into the top of the *m*
Deut 1:19 the way of the *m* of the Amorites
Deut 1:20 come unto the *m* of the Amorites
Deut 1:24 they turned and went up into the *m*
Deut 1:44 Amorites, which dwelt in that *m*
Deut 2:3 have compassed this *m* long enough
Deut 3:25 is beyond Jordan, that goodly *m*
Deut 4:11 ye came near and stood under the *m*
Deut 4:11 the *m* burned with fire unto the
Deut 5:23 (for the *m* did burn with fire,)
Deut 32:49 Get thee up into this *m* Abarim
Deut 33:19 shall call the people unto the *m*
Deut 34:1 plains of Moab unto the *m* of Nebo
Josh 2:16 said unto them, Get you to the *m*
Josh 2:22 And they went, and came unto the *m*
Josh 2:23 returned, and descended from the *m*
Josh 11:16 the *m* of Israel, and the valley of
Josh 14:12 Now therefore give me this *m*
Josh 15:8 went up to the top of the *m* that
Josh 17:18 But the *m* shall be thine
Josh 18:16 came down to the end of the *m*
Josh 20:7 is Hebron, in the *m* of Judah
Judg 1:9 Canaanites, that dwelt in the *m*
Judg 1:19 out the inhabitants of the *m*
Judg 1:34 the children of Dan into the *m*
Judg 3:27 a trumpet in the *m* of Ephraim
1Sa 17:3 stood on a *m* on the one side
1Sa 17:3 stood on a *m* on the other side
1Sa 23:14 remained in a *m* in the wilderness
1Sa 23:26 Saul went on this side of the *m*
1Sa 23:26 and his men on that side of the *m*
2Kin 2:16 him up, and cast him upon some *m*
2Kin 6:17 the *m* was full of horses and
2Chr 2:2 thousand to hew in the *m*, and
2Chr 2:18 thousand to be hewers in the *m*
Job 14:18 surely the *m* falling cometh to
Ps 11:1 my soul, Flee as a bird to your *m*
Ps 30:7 hast made my *m* to stand strong
Ps 48:1 our God, in the *m* of his holiness
Ps 78:54 of his sanctuary, even to this *m*
Song 4:6 I will get me to the *m* of myrrh
Is 2:2 that the *m* of the LORD's house
Is 2:3 let us go up to the *m* of the LORD
Is 11:9 hurt nor destroy in all my holy *m*
Is 13:2 ye up a banner upon the high *m*
Is 25:6 in this *m* shall the LORD of hosts
Is 25:7 he will destroy in this *m* the
Is 25:10 For in this *m* shall the hand of
Is 30:17 as a beacon upon the top of a *m*
Is 30:25 there shall be upon every high *m*
Is 30:29 to come into the *m* of the LORD
Is 40:4 shall be exalted, and every *m*
Is 40:9 get thee up into the high *m*
Is 56:7 them will I bring to my holy *m*
Is 57:7 high *m* hast thou set thy bed
Is 57:13 land, and shall inherit my holy *m*
Is 65:11 the LORD, that forget my holy *m*
Is 65:25 hurt nor destroy in all my holy *m*
Is 66:20 beasts, to my holy *m* Jerusalem
Jer 3:6 she is gone up upon every high *m*
Jer 16:16 they shall hunt them from every *m*
Jer 17:3 O my *m* in the field, I will give
Jer 26:18 the *m* of the house as the high
Jer 31:23 of justice, and *m* of holiness
Jer 50:6 they have gone from *m* to hill
Jer 51:25 I am against thee, O destroying *m*
Jer 51:25 and will make thee a burnt *m*
Lam 5:18 Because of the *m* of Zion, which
Eze 11:23 stood upon the *m* which is on the
Eze 17:22 and will plant it upon an high *m*
Eze 17:23 In the *m* of the height of Israel
Eze 20:40 For in mine holy *m*
Eze 20:40 in the *m* of the height of Israel,
Eze 28:14 thou wast upon the holy *m* of God
Eze 28:16 as profane out of the *m* of God
Eze 40:2 and set me upon a very high *m*
Eze 43:12 Upon the top of the *m* the whole
Dan 2:35 smote the image became a great *m*
Dan 2:45 cut out of the *m* without hands
Dan 9:16 thy city Jerusalem, thy holy *m*
Dan 9:20 my God for the holy *m* of my God
Dan 11:45 the seas in the glorious holy *m*
Joel 2:1 and sound an alarm in my holy *m*
Joel 3:17 God dwelling in Zion, my holy *m*
Amos 4:1 that are in the *m* of Samaria
Amos 6:1 and trust in the *m* of Samaria
Obad 16 as ye have drunk upon my holy *m*
Mic 3:12 the *m* of the house as the high
Mic 4:1 that the *m* of the house of the
Mic 4:2 let us go up to the *m* of the LORD

Mic 7:12 sea to sea, and from *m* to *m*
Zeph 3:11 be haughty because of my holy *m*
Hag 1:8 Go up to the *m*, and bring wood, and
Zec 4:7 Who art thou, O great *m*
Zec 8:3 the *m* of the LORD of hosts the
Zec 8:3 of the LORD of hosts the holy *m*
Zec 14:4 half of the *m* shall remove toward
Mt 4:8 him up into an exceeding high *m*
Mt 5:1 multitudes, he went up into a *m*
Mt 8:1 When he was come down from the *m*
Mt 14:23 he went up into a *m* apart to pray
Mt 15:29 and went up into a *m*, and sat down
Mt 17:1 them up into an high *m* apart
Mt 17:9 And as they came down from the *m*
Mt 17:20 seed, ye shall say unto this *m*
Mt 21:21 also if ye shall say unto this *m*
Mt 28:16 Galilee, into a *m* where Jesus had
Mk 3:13 And he goeth up into a *m*, and
Mk 6:46 he departed into a *m* to pray
Mk 9:2 an high *m* apart by themselves
Mk 9:9 And as they came down from the *m*
Mk 11:23 whosoever shall say unto this *m*
Lk 3:5 shall be filled, and every *m*
Lk 4:5 taking him up into an high *m*
Lk 6:12 that he went out into a *m* to pray
Lk 8:32 of many swine feeding on the *m*
Lk 9:28 and went up into a *m* to pray
Jn 4:20 Our fathers worshipped in this *m*
Jn 4:21 when ye shall neither in this *m*
Jn 6:3 And Jesus went up into a *m*
Jn 6:15 again into a *m* himself alone
Heb 12:20 if so much as a beast touch the *m*
Rev 6:14 and every *m* and island were moved
Rev 8:8 as it were a great *m* burning with
Rev 21:10 the spirit to a great and high *m*

## MOUNTAINS

Gen 7:20 and the *m* were covered
Gen 8:4 the month, upon the *m* of Ararat
Gen 8:5 were the tops of the *m* seen
Gen 22:2 the *m* which I will tell thee of
Ex 32:12 them out, to slay them in the *m*
Num 13:29 and the Amorites, dwell in the *m*
Num 23:7 out of the *m* of the east, saying,
Num 33:47 and pitched in the *m* of Abarim
Num 33:48 departed from the *m* of Abarim
Deut 2:37 nor unto the cities in the *m*
Deut 12:2 their gods, upon the high *m*
Deut 32:22 on fire the foundations of the *m*
Deut 33:15 the chief things of the ancient *m*
Josh 10:6 *m* are gathered together against
Josh 11:2 that were on the north of the *m*
Josh 11:3 and the Jebusite in the *m*
Josh 11:21 and cut off the Anakims from the *m*
Josh 11:21 Anab, and from all the *m* of Judah
Josh 11:21 and from all the *m* of Israel
Josh 12:8 In the *m*, and in the valleys, and
Josh 15:48 And in the *m*, Shamir, and Jattir,
Josh 18:12 and went up through the *m* westward
Judg 5:5 The *m* melted from before the LORD
Judg 6:2 them the dens which are in the *m*
Judg 9:25 wait for him in the top of the *m*
Judg 9:36 people down from the top of the *m*
Judg 9:36 of the *m* as if they were men
Judg 11:37 I may go up and down upon the *m*
Judg 11:38 bewailed her virginity upon the *m*
1Sa 26:20 doth hunt a partridge in the *m*
2Sa 1:21 Ye *m* of Gilboa, let there be no
1Kin 5:15 thousand hewers in the *m*
1Kin 19:11 a great and strong wind rent the *m*
2Kin 19:23 am come up to the height of the *m*
1Chr 12:8 as swift as the roes upon the *m*
2Chr 18:16 all Israel scattered upon the *m*
2Chr 21:11 high places in the *m* of Judah
2Chr 26:10 also, and vine dressers in the *m*
2Chr 27:4 he built cities in the *m* of Judah
Job 9:5 Which removeth the *m*, and they
Job 24:8 are wet with the showers of the *m*
Job 28:9 he overturneth the *m* by the roots
Job 39:8 The range of the *m* is his pasture
Job 40:20 Surely the *m* bring him forth food
Ps 36:6 righteousness is like the great *m*
Ps 46:2 though the *m* be carried into the
Ps 46:3 though the *m* shake with the
Ps 50:11 I know all the fowls of the *m*
Ps 65:6 his strength setteth fast the *m*
Ps 72:3 The *m* shall bring peace to the
Ps 72:16 the earth upon the top of the *m*
Ps 76:4 and excellent than the *m* of prey
Ps 83:14 the flame setteth the *m* on fire
Ps 87:1 His foundation is in the holy *m*
Ps 90:2 Before the *m* were brought forth,
Ps 104:6 the waters stood above the *m*
Ps 104:8 They go up by the *m*
Ps 114:4 The *m* skipped like rams, and the
Ps 114:6 Ye *m*, that ye skipped like rams
Ps 125:2 As the *m* are round about
Ps 133:3 that descended upon the *m* of Zion
Ps 144:5 touch the *m*, and they shall smoke
Ps 147:8 maketh grass to grow upon the *m*
Ps 148:9 *M*, and all hills
Prov 8:25 Before the *m* were settled, before
Prov 27:25 and herbs of the *m* are gathered
Song 2:8 he cometh leaping upon the *m*
Song 2:17 a young hart upon the *m* of Bether
Song 4:8 from the *m* of the leopards
Song 8:14 a young hart upon the *m* of spices
Is 2:2 established in the top of the *m*
Is 2:14 And upon all the high *m*, and upon
Is 13:4 The noise of a multitude in the *m*
Is 14:25 upon my *m* tread him under foot
Is 17:13 chaff of the *m* before the wind
Is 18:3 he lifteth up an ensign on the *m*
Is 18:6 together unto the fowls of the *m*
Is 22:5 the walls, and of crying to the *m*
Is 34:3 the *m* shall be melted with their
Is 37:24 I come up to the height of the *m*
Is 40:12 and weighed the *m* in scales
Is 41:15 thou shalt thresh the *m*, and beat
Is 42:11 them shout from the top of the *m*
Is 42:15 I will make waste *m* and hills, and
Is 44:23 break forth into singing, ye *m*
Is 49:11 And I will make all my *m* a way
Is 49:13 and break forth into singing, O *m*
Is 52:7 How beautiful upon the *m* are the
Is 54:10 For the *m* shall depart, and the
Is 55:12 the *m* and the hills shall break
Is 64:1 that the *m* might flow down at thy
Is 64:3 the *m* flowed down at thy presence
Is 65:7 have burned incense upon the *m*
Is 65:9 out of Judah an inheritor of my *m*
Jer 3:23 hills, and from the multitude of *m*
Jer 4:24 I beheld the *m*, and, lo, they
Jer 9:10 For the *m* will I take up a
Jer 13:16 your feet stumble upon the dark *m*
Jer 17:26 and from the plain, and from the *m*
Jer 31:5 plant vines upon the *m* of Samaria
Jer 32:44 Judah, and in the cities of the *m*
Jer 33:13 In the cities of the *m*, in the
Jer 46:18 Surely as Tabor is among the *m*
Jer 50:6 have turned them away on the *m*
Lam 4:19 they pursued us upon the *m*
Eze 6:2 thy face toward the *m* of Israel
Eze 6:3 Ye *m* of Israel, hear the word of
Eze 6:3 Thus saith the Lord GOD to the *m*
Eze 6:13 hill, in all the tops of the *m*
Eze 7:7 not the sounding again of the *m*
Eze 7:16 shall be on the *m* like doves of
Eze 18:6 And hath not eaten upon the *m*
Eze 18:11 but even hath eaten upon the *m*
Eze 18:15 That hath not eaten upon the *m*
Eze 19:9 be heard upon the *m* of Israel
Eze 22:9 and in thee they eat upon the *m*
Eze 31:12 upon the *m* and in all the valleys
Eze 32:5 I will lay thy flesh upon the *m*
Eze 32:6 thou swimmest, even to the *m*
Eze 33:28 the *m* of Israel shall be desolate
Eze 34:6 sheep wandered through all the *m*
Eze 34:13 feed them upon the *m* of Israel by
Eze 34:14 upon the high *m* of Israel shall
Eze 34:14 they feed upon the *m* of Israel
Eze 35:8 I will fill his *m* with his slain
Eze 35:12 spoken against the *m* of Israel
Eze 36:1 prophesy unto the *m* of Israel
Eze 36:1 Ye *m* of Israel, hear the word of
Eze 36:4 ye *m* of Israel, hear the word of
Eze 36:4 Thus saith the Lord GOD to the *m*
Eze 36:6 land of Israel, and say unto the *m*
Eze 36:8 O *m* of Israel, ye shall shoot
Eze 37:22 in the land upon the *m* of Israel
Eze 38:8 people, against the *m* of Israel
Eze 38:20 the *m* shall be thrown down, and
Eze 38:21 against him throughout all my *m*
Eze 39:2 bring thee upon the *m* of Israel
Eze 39:4 shalt fall upon the *m* of Israel
Eze 39:17 sacrifice upon the *m* of Israel
Hos 4:13 sacrifice upon the tops of the *m*
Hos 10:8 and they shall say to the *m*
Joel 2:2 as the morning spread upon the *m*
Joel 2:5 on the tops of *m* shall they leap
Joel 3:18 that the *m* shall drop down new
Amos 3:9 yourselves upon the *m* of Samaria
Amos 4:13 For, lo, he that formeth the *m*
Amos 9:13 the *m* shall drop sweet wine, and
Jonah 2:6 went down to the bottoms of the *m*
Mic 1:4 the *m* shall be molten under him,
Mic 4:1 established in the top of the *m*
Mic 6:1 Arise, contend thou before the *m*
Mic 6:2 Hear ye, O *m*, the LORD's
Nah 1:5 The *m* quake at him, and the hills
Nah 1:15 Behold upon the *m* the feet of him
Nah 3:18 people is scattered upon the *m*
Hab 3:6 the everlasting *m* were scattered
Hab 3:10 The *m* saw thee, and they trembled
Hag 1:11 upon the land, and upon the *m*
Zec 6:1 chariots out from between two *m*
Zec 6:1 and the *m* were *m* of brass
Zec 14:5 shall flee to the valley of the *m*
Zec 14:5 of the *m* shall reach unto Azal
Mal 1:3 And I hated Esau, and laid his *m*
Mt 18:12 and nine, and goeth into the *m*
Mt 24:16 be in Judaea flee into the *m*
Mk 5:5 night and day, he was in the *m*
Mk 5:11 *m* a great herd of swine feeding
Mk 13:14 that be in Judaea flee to the *m*
Lk 21:21 which are in Judaea flee to the *m*
Lk 23:30 shall they begin to say to the *m*
1Cor 13:2 faith, so that I could remove *m*
Heb 11:38 they wandered in deserts, and in *m*
Rev 6:15 the dens and in the rocks of the *m*
Rev 6:16 And said to the *m* and rocks, Fall
Rev 16:20 away, and the *m* were not found
Rev 17:9 The seven heads are seven *m*

## MOURN

Gen 23:2 and Abraham came to *m* for Sarah
1Sa 16:1 How long wilt thou *m* for Saul
2Sa 3:31 with sackcloth, and *m* before Abner
1Kin 13:29 prophet came to the city, to *m*
1Kin 14:13 And all Israel shall *m* for him
Neh 8:9 *m* not, nor weep
Job 2:11 together to come to *m* with him
Job 5:11 that those which *m* may be exalted
Job 14:22 and his soul within him shall *m*
Ps 55:2 I *m* in my complaint, and make a
Prov 5:11 thou *m* at the last, when thy
Prov 29:2 wicked beareth rule, the people *m*
Eccl 3:4 a time to *m*, and a time to dance
Is 3:26 And her gates shall lament and *m*
Is 16:7 of Kir-hareseth shall ye *m*
Is 19:8 The fishers also shall *m*, and all
Is 38:14 I did *m* as a dove
Is 59:11 like bears, and *m* sore like doves
Is 61:2 to comfort all that *m*
Is 61:3 appoint unto them that *m* in Zion
Is 66:10 with her, all ye that *m* for her
Jer 4:28 For this shall the earth *m*
Jer 12:4 How long shall the land *m*
Jer 48:31 mine heart shall *m* for the men of
Lam 1:4 The ways of Zion do *m*, because
Eze 7:12 buyer rejoice, nor the seller *m*
Eze 7:27 The king shall *m*, and the prince
Eze 24:16 yet neither shalt thou *m* nor weep
Eze 24:23 ye shall not *m* nor weep
Eze 24:23 and *m* one toward another
Eze 31:15 and I caused Lebanon to *m* for him
Hos 4:3 Therefore shall the land *m*
Hos 10:5 people thereof shall *m* over it
Joel 1:9 priests, the LORD's ministers, *m*
Amos 1:2 of the shepherds shall *m*, and the
Amos 8:8 every one *m* that dwelleth therein
Amos 9:5 and all that dwell therein shall *m*
Zec 12:10 pierced, and they shall *m* for him
Zec 12:12 And the land shall *m*, every family
Mt 5:4 Blessed are they that *m*
Mt 9:15 children of the bridechamber *m*
Mt 24:30 all the tribes of the earth *m*
Lk 6:25 for ye shall *m* and weep
Jas 4:9 Be afflicted, and *m*, and weep
Rev 18:11 earth shall weep and *m* over her

## MOURNED

Gen 37:34 loins, and *m* for his son many days
Gen 50:3 and the Egyptians *m* for him
Gen 50:10 there they *m* with a great and very
Ex 33:4 heard these evil tidings, they *m*
Num 14:39 and the people *m* greatly
Num 20:29 they *m* for Aaron thirty days,
1Sa 15:35 nevertheless Samuel *m* for Saul
2Sa 1:12 And they *m*, and wept, and fasted
2Sa 11:26 was dead, she *m* for her husband

2Sa 13:37 David *m* for his son every day
2Sa 14:2 had a long time *m* for the dead
1Kin 13:30 they *m* over him, saying, Alas, my
1Kin 14:18 and all Israel *m* for him,
1Chr 7:22 Ephraim their father *m* many days
2Chr 35:24 Judah and Jerusalem *m* for Josiah
Ezr 10:6 for he *m* because of the
Neh 1:4 *m* certain days, and fasted, and
Zec 7:5 *m* in the fifth and seventh month,
Mt 11:17 we have *m* unto you, and ye have
Mk 16:10 that had been with him, as they *m*
Lk 7:32 we have *m* to you, and ye have not
1Cor 5:2 puffed up, and have not rather *m*

## MOURNERS

Job 29:25 as one that comforteth the *m*
Eccl 12:5 the *m* go about the streets
Is 57:18 comforts unto him and to his *m*
Hos 9:4 be unto them as the bread of *m*

## MOURNETH

2Sa 19:1 the king weepeth and *m* for Absalom
Ps 35:14 as one that *m* for his mother
Ps 88:9 Mine eye *m* by reason of
Is 24:4 The earth *m* and fadeth away, the
Is 24:7 The new wine *m*, the vine
Is 33:9 The earth *m* and languisheth
Jer 12:11 and being desolate it *m* unto me
Jer 14:2 Judah *m*, and the gates thereof
Jer 23:10 because of swearing the land *m*
Joel 1:10 The field is wasted, the land *m*
Zec 12:10 as one *m* for his only son, and

## MOURNFULLY

Mal 3:14 that we have walked *m* before the

## MOURNING

Gen 27:41 The days of *m* for my father are
Gen 37:35 down into the grave unto my son *m*
Gen 50:4 when the days of his *m* were past
Gen 50:10 he made a *m* for his father seven
Gen 50:11 saw the *m* in the floor of Atad,
Gen 50:11 is a grievous *m* to the Egyptians
Deut 26:14 I have not eaten thereof in my *m*
Deut 34:8 weeping and *m* for Moses were ended
2Sa 11:27 And when the *m* was past, David
2Sa 14:2 mourner, and put on now *m* apparel
2Sa 19:2 turned into *m* unto all the people
Est 4:3 there was great *m* among the Jews
Est 6:12 But Haman hasted to his house *m*
Est 9:22 to joy, and from *m* into a good day
Job 3:8 who are ready to raise up their *m*
Job 30:28 I went *m* without the sun
Job 30:31 My harp also is turned to *m*
Ps 30:11 turned for me my *m* into dancing
Ps 38:6 I go *m* all the day long
Ps 42:9 why go I *m* because of the
Ps 43:2 Why go I *m* because of the
Eccl 7:2 is better to go to the house of *m*
Eccl 7:4 of the wise is in the house of *m*
Is 22:12 of hosts call to weeping, and to *m*
Is 51:11 and sorrow and *m* shall flee away
Is 60:20 the days of thy *m* shall be ended
Is 61:3 for ashes, the oil of joy for *m*
Jer 6:26 make thee *m*, as for an only son,
Jer 9:17 ye, and call for the *m* women
Jer 16:5 Enter not into the house of *m*
Jer 16:7 men tear themselves for them in *m*
Jer 31:13 for I will turn their *m* into joy
Lam 2:5 in the daughter of Judah *m*
Lam 5:15 our dance is turned into *m*
Eze 2:10 therein lamentations, and *m*
Eze 7:16 of the valleys, all of them *m*
Eze 24:17 make no *m* for the dead, bind the
Eze 31:15 down to the grave I caused a *m*
Dan 10:2 I Daniel was *m* three full weeks
Joel 2:12 and with weeping, and with *m*
Amos 5:16 shall call the husbandman to *m*
Amos 8:10 And I will turn your feasts into *m*
Amos 8:10 make it as the *m* of an only son
Mic 1:8 the dragons, and *m* as the owls
Mic 1:11 not forth in the *m* of Beth-ezel
Zec 12:11 there be a great *m* in Jerusalem
Zec 12:11 as the *m* of Hadadrimmon in the
Mt 2:18 and weeping, and great *m*, Rachel
2Cor 7:7 us your earnest desire, your *m*
Jas 4:9 let your laughter be turned to *m*
Rev 18:8 come in one day, death, and *m*

## MOUTH

Gen 4:11 which hath opened her *m* to
Gen 8:11 in her *m* was an olive leaf pluckt
Gen 24:57 the damsel, and enquire at her *m*
Gen 29:2 great stone was upon the well's *m*
Gen 29:3 the stone from the well's *m*
Gen 29:3 upon the well's *m* in his place
Gen 29:8 roll the stone from the well's *m*
Gen 29:10 the stone from the well's *m*
Gen 42:27 behold, it was in his sack's *m*
Gen 43:12 again in the *m* of your sacks
Gen 43:21 money was in the *m* of his sack
Gen 44:1 every man's money in his sack's *m*
Gen 44:2 in the sack's *m* of the youngest,
Gen 45:12 that it is my *m* that speaketh
Ex 4:11 unto him, Who hath made man's *m*
Ex 4:12 go, and I will be with thy *m*
Ex 4:15 unto him, and put words in his *m*
Ex 4:15 be with thy *m*, and with his *m*
Ex 4:16 shall be to thee instead of a *m*
Ex 13:9 the LORD's law may be in thy *m*
Ex 23:13 let it be heard out of thy *m*
Num 12:8 With him will I speak *m* to *m*
Num 12:8 With him will I speak *m* to *m*
Num 16:30 thing, and the earth open her *m*
Num 16:32 And the earth opened her *m*
Num 22:28 the LORD opened the *m* of the ass
Num 22:38 the word that God putteth in my *m*
Num 23:5 the LORD put a word in Balaam's *m*
Num 23:12 which the LORD hath put in my *m*
Num 23:16 Balaam, and put a word in his *m*
Num 26:10 And the earth opened her *m*
Num 30:2 all that proceedeth out of his *m*
Num 32:24 hath proceeded out of your *m*
Num 35:30 to death by the *m* of witnesses
Deut 8:3 the *m* of the LORD doth man live
Deut 11:6 how the earth opened her *m*
Deut 17:6 At the *m* of two witnesses, or
Deut 17:6 but at the *m* of one witness he
Deut 18:18 and will put my words in his *m*
Deut 19:15 at the *m* of two witnesses
Deut 19:15 or at the *m* of three witnesses,
Deut 23:23 thou hast promised with thy *m*
Deut 30:14 is very nigh unto thee, in thy *m*
Deut 32:1 hear, O earth, the words of my *m*
Josh 1:8 law shall not depart out of thy *m*
Josh 6:10 any word proceed out of your *m*
Josh 9:14 not counsel at the *m* of the LORD
Josh 10:18 stones upon the *m* of the cave
Josh 10:22 Open the *m* of the cave, and bring
Josh 10:27 laid great stones in the cave's *m*
Judg 7:6 putting their hand to their *m*
Judg 9:38 unto him, Where is now thy *m*
Judg 11:35 I have opened my *m* unto the LORD
Judg 11:36 hast opened thy *m* unto the LORD
Judg 11:36 which hath proceeded out of thy *m*
Judg 18:19 peace, lay thine hand upon thy *m*
1Sa 1:12 the LORD, that Eli marked her *m*
1Sa 2:1 my *m* is enlarged over mine
1Sa 2:3 not arrogancy come out of your *m*
1Sa 14:26 but no man put his hand to his *m*
1Sa 14:27 and put his hand to his *m*
1Sa 17:35 him, and delivered it out of his *m*
2Sa 1:16 for thy *m* hath testified against
2Sa 14:3 So Joab put the words in her *m*
2Sa 14:19 words in the *m* of thine handmaid
2Sa 17:19 a covering over the well's *m*
2Sa 18:25 alone, there is tidings in his *m*
2Sa 22:9 and fire out of his *m* devoured
1Kin 7:31 the *m* of it within the chapiter
1Kin 7:31 but the *m* thereof was round after
1Kin 7:31 also upon the *m* of it were
1Kin 8:15 with his *m* unto David my father
1Kin 8:24 thou spakest also with thy *m*
1Kin 13:21 hast disobeyed the *m* of the LORD
1Kin 17:24 of the LORD in thy *m* is truth
1Kin 19:18 every *m* which hath not kissed him
1Kin 22:13 good unto the king with one *m*
1Kin 22:22 in the *m* of all his prophets
1Kin 22:23 the *m* of all these thy prophets
2Kin 4:34 and put his *m* upon his *m*
1Chr 16:12 and the judgments of his *m*
2Chr 6:4 with his *m* to my father David
2Chr 6:15 and spakest with thy *m*, and hast
2Chr 18:21 in the *m* of all his prophets
2Chr 18:22 in the *m* of these thy prophets
2Chr 35:22 words of Necho from the *m* of God
2Chr 36:12 speaking from the *m* of the LORD
2Chr 36:21 of the LORD by the *m* of Jeremiah
2Chr 36:22 by the *m* of Jeremiah might be
Ezr 1:1 the word of the LORD by the *m* of
Neh 9:20 not thy manna from their *m*
Est 7:8 the word went out of the king's *m*
Job 3:1 After this opened Job his *m*
Job 5:15 poor from the sword, from their *m*
Job 5:16 hope, and iniquity stoppeth her *m*
Job 7:11 Therefore I will not refrain my *m*
Job 8:2 of thy *m* be like a strong wind
Job 8:21 Till he fill thy *m* with laughing
Job 9:20 mine own *m* shall condemn me
Job 12:11 and the *m* taste his meat
Job 15:5 For thy *m* uttereth thine iniquity
Job 15:6 Thine own *m* condemneth thee, and
Job 15:13 such words go out of thy *m*
Job 15:30 breath of his *m* shall he go away
Job 16:5 I would strengthen you with my *m*
Job 16:10 have gaped upon me with their *m*
Job 19:16 I intreated him with my *m*
Job 20:12 wickedness be sweet in his *m*
Job 20:13 but keep it still within his *m*
Job 21:5 and lay your hand upon your *m*
Job 22:22 I pray thee, the law from his *m*
Job 23:4 him, and fill my *m* with arguments
Job 23:12 his *m* more than my necessary food
Job 29:9 and laid their hand on their *m*
Job 29:10 cleaved to the roof of their *m*
Job 29:23 they opened their *m* wide as for
Job 31:27 or my *m* hath kissed my hand
Job 31:30 (Neither have I suffered my *m* to
Job 32:5 in the *m* of these three men
Job 33:2 Behold, now I have opened my *m*
Job 33:2 my tongue hath spoken in my *m*
Job 34:3 words, as the *m* tasteth meat
Job 35:16 doth Job open his *m* in vain
Job 37:2 the sound that goeth out of his *m*
Job 40:4 I will lay mine hand upon my *m*
Job 40:23 he can draw up Jordan into his *m*
Job 41:19 Out of his *m* go burning lamps, and
Job 41:21 and a flame goeth out of his *m*
Ps 5:9 is no faithfulness in their *m*
Ps 8:2 Out of the *m* of babes and
Ps 10:7 His *m* is full of cursing and
Ps 17:3 that my *m* shall not transgress
Ps 17:10 with their *m* they speak proudly
Ps 18:8 and fire out of his *m* devoured
Ps 19:14 Let the words of my *m*, and the
Ps 22:21 Save me from the lion's *m*
Ps 32:9 whose *m* must be held in with bit
Ps 33:6 of them by the breath of his *m*
Ps 34:1 shall continually be in my *m*
Ps 35:21 opened their *m* wide against me
Ps 36:3 The words of his *m* are iniquity
Ps 37:30 The *m* of the righteous speaketh
Ps 38:13 a dumb man that openeth not his *m*
Ps 38:14 in whose *m* are no reproofs
Ps 39:1 I will keep my *m* with a bridle
Ps 39:9 I was dumb, I opened not my *m*
Ps 40:3 And he hath put a new song in my *m*
Ps 49:3 My *m* shall speak of wisdom
Ps 50:16 take my covenant in thy *m*
Ps 50:19 Thou givest thy *m* to evil
Ps 51:15 my *m* shall shew forth thy praise
Ps 54:2 give ear to the words of my *m*
Ps 55:21 The words of his *m* were smoother
Ps 58:6 their teeth, O God, in their *m*
Ps 59:7 they belch out with their *m*
Ps 59:12 For the sin of their *m* and the
Ps 62:4 they bless with their *m*, but they
Ps 63:5 my *m* shall praise thee with
Ps 63:11 but the *m* of them that speak lies
Ps 66:14 my *m* hath spoken, when I was in
Ps 66:17 I cried unto him with my *m*
Ps 69:15 not the pit shut her *m* upon me
Ps 71:8 Let my *m* be filled with thy
Ps 71:15 My *m* shall shew forth thy
Ps 73:9 They set their *m* against the
Ps 78:1 your ears to the words of my *m*
Ps 78:2 I will open my *m* in a parable
Ps 78:36 they did flatter him with their *m*
Ps 81:10 open thy *m* wide, and I will fill
Ps 89:1 with my *m* will I make known thy
Ps 103:5 satisfieth thy *m* with good things
Ps 105:5 and the judgments of his *m*
Ps 107:42 and all iniquity shall stop her *m*
Ps 109:2 For the *m* of the wicked and the
Ps 109:2 the *m* of the deceitful are opened
Ps 109:30 greatly praise the LORD with my *m*
Ps 119:13 all the judgments of thy *m*
Ps 119:43 word of truth utterly out of my *m*
Ps 119:72 The law of thy *m* is better unto
Ps 119:88 I keep the testimony of thy *m*
Ps 119:103 yea, sweeter than honey to my *m*
Ps 119:108 the freewill offerings of my *m*
Ps 119:131 I opened my *m*, and panted

Ps 126:2 Then was our *m* filled with
Ps 137:6 tongue cleave to the roof of my *m*
Ps 138:4 when they hear the words of thy *m*
Ps 141:3 Set a watch, O LORD, before my *m*
Ps 141:7 are scattered at the grave's *m*
Ps 144:8 Whose *m* speaketh vanity, and their
Ps 144:11 whose *m* speaketh vanity, and their
Ps 145:21 My *m* shall speak the praise of
Ps 149:6 high praises of God be in their *m*
Prov 2:6 out of his *m* cometh knowledge and
Prov 4:5 decline from the words of my *m*
Prov 4:24 Put away from thee a froward *m*
Prov 5:3 her *m* is smoother than oil
Prov 5:7 depart not from the words of my *m*
Prov 6:2 snared with the words of thy *m*
Prov 6:2 art taken with the words of thy *m*
Prov 6:12 man, walketh with a froward *m*
Prov 7:24 and attend to the words of my *m*
Prov 8:7 For my *m* shall speak truth
Prov 8:8 All the words of my *m* are in
Prov 8:13 and the evil way, and the froward *m*
Prov 10:6 covereth the *m* of the wicked
Prov 10:11 The *m* of a righteous man is a
Prov 10:11 covereth the *m* of the wicked
Prov 10:14 but the *m* of the foolish is near
Prov 10:31 The *m* of the just bringeth forth
Prov 10:32 but the *m* of the wicked speaketh
Prov 11:9 An hypocrite with his *m*
Prov 11:11 overthrown by the *m* of the wicked
Prov 12:6 but the *m* of the upright shall
Prov 12:14 with good by the fruit of his *m*
Prov 13:2 eat good by the fruit of his *m*
Prov 13:3 keepeth his *m* keepeth his life
Prov 14:3 In the *m* of the foolish is a rod
Prov 15:2 but the *m* of fools poureth out
Prov 15:14 but the *m* of fools feedeth on
Prov 15:23 hath joy by the answer of his *m*
Prov 15:28 but the *m* of the wicked poureth
Prov 16:10 his *m* transgresseth not in
Prov 16:23 heart of the wise teacheth his *m*
Prov 16:26 for his *m* craveth it of him
Prov 18:4 of a man's *m* are as deep waters
Prov 18:6 his *m* calleth for strokes
Prov 18:7 A fool's *m* is his destruction, and
Prov 18:20 satisfied with the fruit of his *m*
Prov 19:24 much as bring it to his *m* again
Prov 19:28 the *m* of the wicked devoureth
Prov 20:17 but afterwards his *m* shall be
Prov 21:23 Whoso keepeth his *m* and his tongue
Prov 22:14 The *m* of strange women is a deep
Prov 24:7 he openeth not his *m* in the gate
Prov 26:7 so is a parable in the *m* of fools
Prov 26:9 so is a parable in the *m* of fools
Prov 26:15 him to bring it again to his *m*
Prov 26:28 and a flattering *m* worketh ruin
Prov 27:2 praise thee, and not thine own *m*
Prov 30:20 she eateth, and wipeth her *m*
Prov 30:32 evil, lay thine hand upon thy *m*
Prov 31:8 Open thy *m* for the dumb in the
Prov 31:9 Open thy *m*, judge righteously, and
Prov 31:26 She openeth her *m* with wisdom
Eccl 5:2 Be not rash with thy *m*, and let
Eccl 5:6 Suffer not thy *m* to cause thy
Eccl 6:7 the labour of man is for his *m*
Eccl 10:12 of a wise man's *m* are gracious
Eccl 10:13 the words of his *m* is foolishness
Song 1:2 kiss me with the kisses of his *m*
Song 5:16 His *m* is most sweet
Song 7:9 the roof of thy *m* like the best
Is 1:20 for the *m* of the LORD hath spoken
Is 5:14 opened her *m* without measure
Is 6:7 And he laid it upon my *m*, and said,
Is 9:12 shall devour Israel with open *m*
Is 9:17 and every *m* speaketh folly
Is 10:14 moved the wing, or opened the *m*
Is 11:4 the earth with the rod of his *m*
Is 19:7 by the *m* of the brooks, and every
Is 29:13 people draw near me with their *m*
Is 30:2 Egypt, and have not asked at my *m*
Is 34:16 for my *m* it hath commanded, and
Is 40:5 for the *m* of the LORD hath spoken
Is 45:23 gone out of my *m* in righteousness
Is 48:3 and they went forth out of my *m*
Is 49:2 he hath made my *m* like a sharp
Is 51:16 And I have put my words in thy *m*
Is 53:7 yet he opened not his *m*
Is 53:7 is dumb, so he openeth not his *m*
Is 53:9 neither was any deceit in his *m*
Is 55:11 be that goeth forth out of my *m*
Is 57:4 against whom make ye a wide *m*
Is 58:14 for the *m* of the LORD hath spoken
Is 59:21 words which I have put in thy *m*
Is 59:21 shall not depart out of thy *m*
Is 59:21 nor out of the *m* of thy seed
Is 59:21 nor out of the *m* of thy seed's
Is 62:2 which the *m* of the LORD shall
Jer 1:9 forth his hand, and touched my *m*
Jer 1:9 I have put my words in thy *m*
Jer 5:14 will make my words in thy *m* fire
Jer 7:28 and is cut off from their *m*
Jer 9:8 to his neighbour with his *m*
Jer 9:12 who is he to whom the *m* of the
Jer 9:20 ear receive the word of his *m*
Jer 12:2 thou art near in their *m*, and far
Jer 15:19 the vile, thou shalt be as my *m*
Jer 23:16 and not out of the *m* of the LORD
Jer 32:4 shall speak with him *m* to *m*
Jer 34:3 shall speak with thee *m* to *m*
Jer 36:4 Baruch wrote from the *m* of
Jer 36:6 which thou hast written from my *m*
Jer 36:17 write all these words at his *m*
Jer 36:18 these words unto me with his *m*
Jer 36:27 Baruch wrote at the *m* of Jeremiah
Jer 36:32 who wrote therein from the *m* of
Jer 44:17 goeth forth out of our own *m*
Jer 44:26 shall no more be named in the *m*
Jer 45:1 in a book at the *m* of Jeremiah
Jer 48:28 nest in the sides of the hole's *m*
Jer 51:44 I will bring forth out of his *m*
Lam 2:16 have opened their *m* against thee
Lam 3:29 He putteth his *m* in the dust
Lam 3:38 Out of the *m* of the most High
Lam 4:4 to the roof of his *m* for thirst
Eze 2:8 open thy *m*, and eat that I give
Eze 3:2 So I opened my *m*, and he caused me
Eze 3:3 it was in my *m* as honey for
Eze 3:17 therefore hear the word at my *m*
Eze 3:26 cleave to the roof of thy *m*
Eze 3:27 with thee, I will open thy *m*
Eze 4:14 there abominable flesh into my *m*
Eze 16:56 by thy *m* in the day of thy pride
Eze 16:63 never open thy *m* any more because
Eze 21:22 to open the *m* in the slaughter,
Eze 24:27 In that day shall thy *m* be opened
Eze 29:21 of the *m* in the midst of them
Eze 33:7 thou shalt hear the word at my *m*
Eze 33:22 and had opened my *m*, until he came
Eze 33:22 my *m* was opened, and I was no more
Eze 33:31 for with their *m* they shew much
Eze 34:10 deliver my flock from their *m*
Eze 35:13 Thus with your *m* ye have boasted
Dan 3:26 *m* of the burning fiery furnace
Dan 4:31 the word was in the king's *m*
Dan 6:17 and laid upon the *m* of the den
Dan 7:5 it had three ribs in the *m* of it
Dan 7:8 a *m* speaking great things
Dan 7:20 a *m* that spake very great things,
Dan 10:3 came flesh nor wine in my *m*
Dan 10:16 then I opened my *m*, and spake, and
Hos 2:17 the names of Baalim out of her *m*
Hos 6:5 slain them by the words of my *m*
Hos 8:1 Set the trumpet to thy *m*
Joel 1:5 for it is cut off from your *m*
Amos 3:12 out of the *m* of the lion two legs
Mic 4:4 for the *m* of the LORD of hosts
Mic 6:12 tongue is deceitful in their *m*
Mic 7:5 keep the doors of thy *m* from her
Mic 7:16 shall lay their hand upon their *m*
Nah 3:12 even fall into the *m* of the eater
Zeph 3:13 tongue be found in their *m*
Zec 5:8 weight of lead upon the *m* thereof
Zec 8:9 words by the *m* of the prophets
Zec 9:7 take away his blood out of his *m*
Zec 14:12 shall consume away in their *m*
Mal 2:6 The law of truth was in his *m*
Mal 2:7 they should seek the law at his *m*
Mt 4:4 proceedeth out of the *m* of God
Mt 5:2 And he opened his *m*, and taught
Mt 12:34 of the heart the *m* speaketh
Mt 13:35 I will open my *m* in parables
Mt 15:8 draweth nigh unto me with their *m*
Mt 15:11 goeth into the *m* defileth a man
Mt 15:11 that which cometh out of the *m*
Mt 15:17 in at the *m* goeth into the belly
Mt 15:18 the *m* come forth from the heart
Mt 17:27 and when thou hast opened his *m*
Mt 18:16 that in the *m* of two or three
Mt 21:16 never read, Out of the *m* of babes
Lk 1:64 his *m* was opened immediately, and
Lk 1:70 As he spake by the *m* of his holy
Lk 4:22 which proceeded out of his *m*
Lk 6:45 of the heart his *m* speaketh
Lk 11:54 to catch something out of his *m*
Lk 19:22 Out of thine own *m* will I judge
Lk 21:15 For I will give you a *m* and wisdom
Lk 22:71 ourselves have heard of his own *m*
Jn 19:29 upon hyssop, and put it to his *m*
Acts 1:16 by the *m* of David spake before
Acts 3:18 by the *m* of all his prophets
Acts 3:21 which God hath spoken by the *m* of
Acts 4:25 Who by the *m* of thy servant David
Acts 8:32 shearer, so opened he not his *m*
Acts 8:35 Then Philip opened his *m*, and
Acts 10:34 Then Peter opened his *m*, and said,
Acts 11:8 at any time entered into my *m*
Acts 15:7 that the Gentiles by my *m* should
Acts 15:27 tell you the same things by *m*
Acts 18:14 Paul was now about to open his *m*
Acts 22:14 shouldest hear the voice of his *m*
Acts 23:2 by him to smite him on the *m*
Rom 3:14 Whose *m* is full of cursing and
Rom 3:19 that every *m* may be stopped, and
Rom 10:8 word is nigh thee, even in thy *m*
Rom 10:9 confess with thy *m* the Lord Jesus
Rom 10:10 with the *m* confession is made
Rom 15:6 one *m* glorify God, even the
1Cor 9:9 Thou shalt not muzzle the *m* of
2Cor 6:11 our *m* is open unto you, our heart
2Cor 13:1 In the *m* of two or three
Eph 4:29 proceed out of your *m*, but that
Eph 6:19 me, that I may open my *m* boldly
Col 3:8 communication out of your *m*
2Th 2:8 consume with the spirit of his *m*
2Ti 4:17 out of the *m* of the lion
Jas 3:10 Out of the same *m* proceedeth
1Pet 2:22 neither was guile found in his *m*
Jude 16 their *m* speaketh great swelling
Rev 1:16 out of his *m* went a sharp
Rev 2:16 them with the sword of my *m*
Rev 3:16 hot, I will spue thee out of my *m*
Rev 9:19 For their power is in their *m*
Rev 10:9 shall be in thy *m* sweet as honey
Rev 10:10 it was in my *m* sweet as honey
Rev 11:5 fire proceedeth out of their *m*
Rev 12:15 his *m* water as a flood after the
Rev 12:16 woman, and the earth opened her *m*
Rev 12:16 the dragon cast out of his *m*
Rev 13:2 his *m* as the *m* of a lion
Rev 13:2 and his *m* as the *m* of a lion
Rev 13:5 him a *m* speaking great things
Rev 13:6 he opened his *m* in blasphemy
Rev 14:5 in their *m* was found no guile
Rev 16:13 come out of the *m* of the dragon
Rev 16:13 out of the *m* of the beast
Rev 16:13 out of the *m* of the false prophet
Rev 19:15 out of his *m* goeth a sharp sword,
Rev 19:21 sword proceeded out of his *m*

## MOUTHS

Gen 44:8 which we found in our sacks' *m*
Deut 31:19 put it in their *m*, that this song
Deut 31:21 out of the *m* of their seed
Ps 22:13 They gaped upon me with their *m*
Ps 78:30 their meat was yet in their *m*
Ps 115:5 They have *m*, but they speak not
Ps 135:16 They have *m*, but they speak not
Ps 135:17 is there any breath in their *m*
Is 52:15 kings shall shut their *m* at him
Jer 44:25 have both spoken with your *m*
Lam 3:46 have opened their *m* against us
Dan 6:22 angel, and hath shut the lions' *m*
Mic 3:5 he that putteth not into their *m*
Titus 1:11 Whose *m* must be stopped, who
Heb 11:33 promises, stopped the *m* of lions
Jas 3:3 we put bits in the horses' *m*
Rev 9:17 and out of their *m* issued fire
Rev 9:18 which issued out of their *m*

## MOVE

Ex 11:7 shall not a dog *m* his tongue
Lev 11:10 of all that *m* in the waters, and
Deut 23:25 but thou shalt not *m* a sickle
Deut 32:21 I will *m* them to jealousy with
Judg 13:25 *m* him at times in the camp of Dan
2Sa 7:10 place of their own, and *m* no more
2Kin 21:8 *m* any more out of the land which
2Kin 23:18 let no man *m* his bones
Jer 10:4 and with hammers, that it *m* not
Mic 7:17 they shall *m* out of their holes
Mt 23:4 but they themselves will not *m*

Acts 17:28 For in him we live, and *m*, and have
Acts 20:24 But none of these things *m* me

**MOVED**
Gen 1:2 the Spirit of God *m* upon the face
Gen 7:21 flesh died that *m* upon the earth
Deut 32:21 They have *m* me to jealousy with
Josh 10:21 none *m* his tongue against any of
Josh 15:18 that she *m* him to ask of her
Judg 1:14 that she *m* him to ask of her
Ruth 1:19 all the city was *m* about them
1Sa 1:13 only her lips *m*, but her voice
2Sa 18:33 And the king was much *m*, and went
2Sa 22:8 the foundations of heaven *m*
2Sa 24:1 he *m* David against them to say,
1Chr 16:30 shall be stable, that it be not *m*
1Chr 17:9 place, and shall be *m* no more
2Chr 18:31 God *m* them to depart from him
Ezr 4:15 that they have *m* sedition within
Est 5:9 nor *m* for him, he was full of
Job 37:1 and is *m* out of his place
Job 41:23 they cannot be *m*
Ps 10:6 in his heart, I shall not be *m*
Ps 13:4 trouble me rejoice when I am *m*
Ps 15:5 these things shall never be *m*
Ps 16:8 my right hand, I shall not be *m*
Ps 18:7 foundations also of the hills *m*
Ps 21:7 the most High he shall not be *m*
Ps 30:6 I said, I shall never be *m*
Ps 46:5 she shall not be *m*
Ps 46:6 raged, the kingdoms were *m*
Ps 55:22 suffer the righteous to be *m*
Ps 62:2 I shall not be greatly *m*
Ps 62:6 I shall not be *m*
Ps 66:9 and suffereth not our feet to be *m*
Ps 68:8 even Sinai itself was *m* at the
Ps 78:58 *m* him to jealousy with their
Ps 93:1 stablished, that it cannot be *m*
Ps 96:10 that it shall not be *m*
Ps 99:1 let the earth be *m*
Ps 112:6 Surely he shall not be *m* for ever
Ps 121:3 will not suffer thy foot to be *m*
Prov 12:3 of the righteous shall not be *m*
Song 5:4 door, and my bowels were *m* for him
Is 6:4 the posts of the door *m* at the
Is 7:2 And his heart was *m*, and the heart
Is 7:2 of the wood are *m* with the wind
Is 10:14 and there was none that *m* the wing
Is 14:9 Hell from beneath is *m* for thee
Is 19:1 Egypt shall be *m* at his presence
Is 24:19 the earth is *m* exceedingly
Is 40:20 graven image, that shall not be *m*
Is 41:7 nails, that it should not be *m*
Jer 4:24 and all the hills *m* lightly
Jer 25:16 And they shall drink, and be *m*
Jer 46:7 whose waters are *m* as the rivers
Jer 46:8 his waters are *m* like the rivers
Jer 49:21 The earth is *m* at the noise of
Jer 50:46 taking of Babylon the earth is *m*
Dan 8:7 he was *m* with choler against him,
Dan 11:11 the south shall be *m* with choler
Mt 9:36 he was *m* with compassion on them,
Mt 14:14 was *m* with compassion toward them
Mt 18:27 servant was *m* with compassion
Mt 20:24 they were *m* with indignation
Mt 21:10 Jerusalem, all the city was *m*
Mk 1:41 *m* with compassion, put forth his
Mk 6:34 was *m* with compassion toward them
Mk 15:11 the chief priests *m* the people
Acts 2:25 hand, that I should not be *m*
Acts 7:9 *m* with envy, sold Joseph into
Acts 17:5 *m* with envy, took unto them
Acts 21:30 And all the city was *m*, and the
Col 1:23 be not *m* away from the hope of
1Th 3:3 should be *m* by these afflictions
Heb 11:7 *m* with fear, prepared an ark to
Heb 12:28 a kingdom which cannot be *m*
2Pet 1:21 as they were *m* by the Holy Ghost
Rev 6:14 island were *m* out of their places

**MOVETH**
Gen 1:21 and every living creature that *m*
Gen 1:28 thing that *m* upon the earth
Gen 9:2 upon all that *m* upon the earth,
Lev 11:46 creature that *m* in the waters
Job 40:17 He *m* his tail like a cedar
Ps 69:34 and every thing that *m* therein
Prov 23:31 the cup, when it *m* itself aright
Eze 47:9 every thing that liveth, which *m*

**MOVING**
Gen 1:20 the *m* creature that hath life
Gen 9:3 Every *m* thing that liveth shall
Job 16:5 the *m* of my lips should asswage
Prov 16:30 *m* his lips he bringeth evil to
Jn 5:3 waiting for the *m* of the water

**MOZA** *(mo'-zah)*
*1. A son of Caleb.*
1Chr 2:46 concubine, bare Haran, and *M*
*2. Descendant of King Saul.*
1Chr 8:36 and Zimri begat *M*,
1Chr 8:37 And *M* begat Binea
1Chr 9:42 and Zimri begat *M*
1Chr 9:43 And *M* begat Binea

**MOZAH** *(mo'-zah) A city in Benjamin.*
Josh 18:26 And Mizpeh, and Chephirah, and *M*

**MULBERRY**
2Sa 5:23 them over against the *m* trees
2Sa 5:24 going in the tops of the *m* trees
1Chr 14:14 them over against the *m* trees
1Chr 14:15 going in the tops of the *m* trees

**MULE**
2Sa 13:29 every man gat him up upon his *m*
2Sa 18:9 And Absalom rode upon a *m*, and the
2Sa 18:9 the *m* went under the thick boughs
2Sa 18:9 the *m* that was under him went
1Kin 1:33 my son to ride upon mine own *m*
1Kin 1:38 to ride upon king David's *m*
1Kin 1:44 him to ride upon the king's *m*
Ps 32:9 ye not as the horse, or as the *m*
Zec 14:15 the plague of the horse, of the *m*

**MULES**
Gen 36:24 found the *m* in the wilderness
1Kin 10:25 armour, and spices, horses, and *m*
1Kin 18:5 *m* alive, that we lose not all the
1Chr 12:40 on asses, and on camels, and on *m*
2Chr 9:24 harness, and spices, horses, and *m*
Ezr 2:66 their *m*, two hundred forty and
Neh 7:68 their *m*, two hundred forty and
Est 8:10 on horseback, and riders on *m*
Est 8:14 So the posts that rode upon *m*
Is 66:20 and in litters, and upon *m*
Eze 27:14 with horses and horsemen and *m*

**MULTIPLIED**
Gen 47:27 and grew, and *m* exceedingly
Ex 1:7 and increased abundantly, and *m*
Ex 1:12 afflicted them, the more they *m*
Ex 1:20 and the people *m*, and waxed very
Ex 11:9 may be *m* in the land of Egypt
Deut 1:10 The LORD your God hath *m* you
Deut 8:13 and thy silver and thy gold is *m*
Deut 8:13 and all that thou hast is *m*
Deut 11:21 That your days may be *m*, and the
Josh 24:3 *m* his seed, and gave him Isaac
1Chr 5:9 were *m* in the land of Gilead
Job 27:14 If his children be *m*, it is for
Job 35:6 or if thy transgressions be *m*
Ps 16:4 Their sorrows shall be *m* that
Ps 38:19 that hate me wrongfully are *m*
Ps 107:38 also, so that they are *m* greatly
Prov 9:11 For by me thy days shall be *m*
Prov 29:16 When the wicked are *m*,
Is 9:3 Thou hast *m* the nation, and not
Is 59:12 transgressions are *m* before thee
Jer 3:16 shall come to pass, when ye be *m*
Eze 5:7 Because ye *m* more than the
Eze 11:6 Ye have *m* your slain in this city
Eze 16:25 passed by, and *m* thy whoredoms
Eze 16:29 Thou hast moreover *m* thy
Eze 16:51 but thou hast *m* thine
Eze 21:15 may faint, and their ruins be *m*
Eze 23:19 Yet she *m* her whoredoms, in
Eze 31:5 the field, and his boughs were *m*
Eze 35:13 have *m* your words against me
Dan 4:1 Peace be *m* unto you
Dan 6:25 Peace be *m* unto you
Hos 2:8 *m* her silver and gold, which they
Hos 8:14 Judah hath *m* fenced cities
Hos 12:10 I have *m* visions, and used
Nah 3:16 Thou hast *m* thy merchants above
Acts 6:1 the number of the disciples was *m*
Acts 6:7 disciples *m* in Jerusalem greatly
Acts 7:17 the people grew and *m* in Egypt,
Acts 9:31 comfort of the Holy Ghost, were *m*
Acts 12:24 But the word of God grew and *m*
1Pet 1:2 Grace unto you, and peace, be *m*
2Pet 1:2 peace be *m* unto you through the
Jude 2 unto you, and peace, and love, be *m*

**MULTIPLY**
Gen 1:22 them, saying, Be fruitful, and *m*
Gen 1:22 seas, and let fowl *m* in the earth
Gen 1:28 said unto them, Be fruitful, and *m*
Gen 3:16 said, I will greatly *m* thy sorrow
Gen 6:1 when men began to *m* on the face
Gen 8:17 be fruitful, and *m* upon the earth
Gen 9:1 said unto them, Be fruitful, and *m*
Gen 9:7 And you, be ye fruitful, and *m*
Gen 9:7 in the earth, and *m* therein
Gen 16:10 I will *m* thy seed exceedingly,
Gen 17:2 thee, and will *m* thee exceedingly
Gen 17:20 and will *m* him exceedingly
Gen 22:17 in multiplying I will *m* thy seed
Gen 26:4 seed to *m* as the stars of heaven
Gen 26:24 *m* thy seed for my servant
Gen 28:3 *m* thee, that thou mayest be a
Gen 35:11 be fruitful and *m*
Gen 48:4 *m* thee, and I will make of thee a
Ex 1:10 lest they *m*, and it come to pass,
Ex 7:3 *m* my signs and my wonders in the
Ex 23:29 beast of the field *m* against thee
Ex 32:13 I will *m* your seed as the stars
Lev 26:9 *m* you, and establish my covenant
Deut 7:13 thee, and bless thee, and *m* thee
Deut 8:1 to do, that ye may live, and *m*
Deut 8:13 And when thy herds and thy flocks *m*
Deut 13:17 *m* thee, as he hath sworn unto thy
Deut 17:16 But he shall not *m* horses to
Deut 17:16 the end that he should *m* horses
Deut 17:17 shall he *m* wives to himself
Deut 17:17 he greatly *m* to himself silver
Deut 28:63 you to do you good, and to *m* you
Deut 30:5 good, and *m* thee above thy fathers
Deut 30:16 that thou mayest live and *m*
1Chr 4:27 neither did all their family *m*
Job 29:18 I shall *m* my days as the sand
Jer 30:19 and I will *m* them, and they shall
Jer 33:22 so will I *m* the seed of David my
Eze 16:7 I have caused thee to *m* as the
Eze 36:10 I will *m* men upon you, all the
Eze 36:11 I will *m* upon you man and beast
Eze 36:30 I will *m* the fruit of the tree,
Eze 37:26 *m* them, and will set my sanctuary
Amos 4:4 at Gilgal *m* transgression
2Cor 9:10 *m* your seed sown, and increase the
Heb 6:14 and multiplying I will *m* thee

**MULTITUDE**
Gen 16:10 it shall not be numbered for *m*
Gen 28:3 that thou mayest be a *m* of people
Gen 30:30 and it is now increased unto a *m*
Gen 32:12 which cannot be numbered for *m*
Gen 48:4 I will make of thee a *m* of people
Gen 48:16 let them grow into a *m* in the
Gen 48:19 seed shall become a *m* of nations
Ex 12:38 a mixed *m* went up also with them
Ex 23:2 shalt not follow a *m* to do evil
Lev 25:16 According to the *m* of years thou
Num 11:4 the mixt *m* that was among them
Num 32:1 Gad had a very great *m* of cattle
Deut 1:10 day as the stars of heaven for *m*
Deut 10:22 thee as the stars of heaven for *m*
Deut 28:62 were as the stars of heaven for *m*
Josh 11:4 that is upon the sea shore in *m*
Judg 4:7 army, with his chariots and his *m*
Judg 6:5 they came as grasshoppers for *m*
Judg 7:12 valley like grasshoppers for *m*
Judg 7:12 as the sand by the sea side for *m*
1Sa 13:5 which is on the sea shore in *m*
1Sa 14:16 the *m* melted away, and they went
2Sa 6:19 even among the whole *m* of Israel
2Sa 17:11 the sand that is by the sea for *m*
1Kin 3:8 be numbered nor counted for *m*
1Kin 4:20 the sand which is by the sea in *m*
1Kin 8:5 not be told nor numbered for *m*
1Kin 20:13 Hast thou seen all this great *m*
1Kin 20:28 all this great *m* into thine hand
2Kin 7:13 they are as all the *m* of Israel
2Kin 7:13 they are even as all the *m* of the
2Kin 19:23 With the *m* of my chariots I am
2Kin 25:11 with the remnant of the *m*
2Chr 1:9 like the dust of the earth in *m*
2Chr 5:6 not be told nor numbered for *m*
2Chr 13:8 and ye be a great *m*, and there are
2Chr 14:11 in thy name we go against this *m*
2Chr 20:2 There cometh a great *m* against
2Chr 20:15 by reason of this great *m*
2Chr 20:24 they looked unto the *m*, and,
2Chr 28:5 away a great *m* of them captives

2Chr 30:18 For a *m* of the people, even many
2Chr 32:7 nor for all the *m* that is with
Neh 13:3 from Israel all the mixed *m*
Est 5:11 the *m* of his children, and all the
Est 10:3 accepted of the *m* of his brethren
Job 11:2 Should not the *m* of words be
Job 31:34 Did I fear a great *m*, or did the
Job 32:7 *m* of years should teach wisdom
Job 33:19 the *m* of his bones with strong
Job 35:9 By reason of the *m* of oppressions
Job 39:7 He scorneth the *m* of the city
Ps 5:7 thy house in the *m* of thy mercy
Ps 5:10 cast them out in the *m* of their
Ps 33:16 no king saved by the *m* of an host
Ps 42:4 for I had gone with the *m*
Ps 42:4 with a *m* that kept holyday
Ps 49:6 in the *m* of their riches
Ps 51:1 according unto the *m* of thy
Ps 68:30 the *m* of the bulls, with the
Ps 69:13 in the *m* of thy mercy hear me, in
Ps 69:16 to the *m* of thy tender mercies
Ps 74:19 unto the *m* of the wicked
Ps 94:19 In the *m* of my thoughts within me
Ps 97:1 let the *m* of isles be glad
Ps 106:7 not the *m* of thy mercies
Ps 106:45 according to the *m* of his mercies
Ps 109:30 I will praise him among the *m*
Prov 10:19 In the *m* of words there wanteth
Prov 11:14 but in the *m* of counsellors there
Prov 14:28 In the *m* of people is the king's
Prov 15:22 but in the *m* of counsellors they
Prov 20:15 There is gold, and a *m* of rubies
Prov 24:6 in *m* of counsellors there is
Eccl 5:3 cometh through the *m* of business
Eccl 5:3 voice is known by *m* of words
Eccl 5:7 For in the *m* of dreams and many
Is 1:11 To what purpose is the *m* of your
Is 5:13 their *m* dried up with thirst
Is 5:14 and their glory, and their *m*
Is 13:4 The noise of a *m* in the mountains
Is 16:14 contemned, with all that great *m*
Is 17:12 Woe to the *m* of many people,
Is 29:5 Moreover the *m* of thy strangers
Is 29:5 the *m* of the terrible ones shall
Is 29:7 the *m* of all the nations that
Is 29:8 so shall the *m* of all the nations
Is 31:4 when a *m* of shepherds is called
Is 32:14 the *m* of the city shall be left
Is 37:24 By the *m* of my chariots am I come
Is 47:9 for the *m* of thy sorceries
Is 47:12 with the *m* of thy sorceries,
Is 47:13 wearied in the *m* of thy counsels
Is 60:6 The *m* of camels shall cover thee,
Is 63:7 according to the *m* of his
Jer 3:23 hills, and from the *m* of mountains
Jer 10:13 there is a *m* of waters in the
Jer 12:6 they have called a *m* after thee
Jer 30:14 for the *m* of thine iniquity
Jer 30:15 for the *m* of thine iniquity
Jer 44:15 women that stood by, a great *m*
Jer 46:25 Behold, I will punish the *m* of No
Jer 49:32 the *m* of their cattle a spoil
Jer 51:16 there is a *m* of waters in the
Jer 51:42 with the *m* of the waves thereof
Jer 52:15 of Babylon, and the rest of the *m*
Lam 1:5 for the *m* of her transgressions
Lam 3:32 according to the *m* of his mercies
Eze 7:11 them shall remain, nor of their *m*
Eze 7:12 wrath is upon all the *m* thereof
Eze 7:13 is touching the whole *m* thereof
Eze 7:14 wrath is upon all the *m* thereof
Eze 14:4 according to the *m* of his idols
Eze 19:11 height with the *m* of her branches
Eze 23:42 a voice of a *m* being at ease was
Eze 27:12 of the *m* of all kind of riches
Eze 27:16 the *m* of the wares of thy making
Eze 27:18 was thy merchant in the *m* of the
Eze 27:18 making, for the *m* of all riches
Eze 27:33 earth with the *m* of thy riches
Eze 28:16 By the *m* of thy merchandise they
Eze 28:18 by the *m* of thine iniquities
Eze 29:19 and he shall take her *m*, and take
Eze 30:4 and they shall take away her *m*
Eze 30:10 I will also make the *m* of Egypt
Eze 30:15 and I will cut off the *m* of No
Eze 31:2 king of Egypt, and to his *m*
Eze 31:5 long because of the *m* of waters
Eze 31:9 him fair by the *m* of his branches
Eze 31:18 This is Pharaoh and all his *m*
Eze 32:12 mighty will I cause thy *m* to fall
Eze 32:12 all the *m* thereof shall be
Eze 32:16 even for Egypt, and for all her *m*
Eze 32:18 of man, wail for the *m* of Egypt
Eze 32:24 all her *m* round about her grave,
Eze 32:25 midst of the slain with all her *m*
Eze 32:26 is Meshech, Tubal, and all her *m*
Eze 32:31 shall be comforted over all his *m*
Eze 32:32 sword, even Pharaoh and all his *m*
Eze 39:11 shall they bury Gog and all his *m*
Eze 47:9 shall be a very great *m* of fish
Dan 10:6 his words like the voice of a *m*
Dan 11:10 assemble a *m* of great forces
Dan 11:11 and he shall set forth a great *m*
Dan 11:11 but the *m* shall be given into his
Dan 11:12 And when he hath taken away the *m*
Dan 11:13 shall set forth a *m* greater than
Hos 9:7 for the *m* of thine iniquity, and
Hos 10:1 according to the *m* of his fruit
Hos 10:13 in the *m* of thy mighty men
Mic 2:12 noise by reason of the *m* of men
Nah 3:3 and there is a *m* of slain, and a
Nah 3:4 Because of the *m* of the whoredoms
Zec 2:4 without walls for the *m* of men
Mt 13:2 the whole *m* stood on the shore
Mt 13:34 Jesus unto the *m* in parables
Mt 13:36 Then Jesus sent the *m* away
Mt 14:5 put him to death, he feared the *m*
Mt 14:14 went forth, and saw a great *m*
Mt 14:15 send the *m* away, that they may go
Mt 14:19 he commanded the *m* to sit down on
Mt 14:19 and the disciples to the *m*
Mt 15:10 And he called the *m*, and said unto
Mt 15:31 Insomuch that the *m* wondered
Mt 15:32 said, I have compassion on the *m*
Mt 15:33 as to fill so great a *m*
Mt 15:35 he commanded the *m* to sit down on
Mt 15:36 and the disciples to the *m*
Mt 15:39 And he sent away the *m*, and took
Mt 17:14 And when they were come to the *m*
Mt 20:29 Jericho, a great *m* followed him
Mt 20:31 the *m* rebuked them, because they
Mt 21:8 a very great *m* spread their
Mt 21:11 the *m* said, This is Jesus the
Mt 21:46 hands on him, they feared the *m*
Mt 22:33 when the *m* heard this, they were
Mt 23:1 Then spake Jesus to the *m*
Mt 26:47 and with him a great *m* with swords
Mt 27:20 elders persuaded the *m* that they
Mt 27:24 and washed his hands before the *m*
Mk 2:13 all the *m* resorted unto him, and
Mk 3:7 a great *m* from Galilee followed
Mk 3:8 about Tyre and Sidon, a great *m*
Mk 3:9 wait on him because of the *m*
Mk 3:20 the *m* cometh together again, so
Mk 3:32 the *m* sat about him, and they said
Mk 4:1 was gathered unto him a great *m*
Mk 4:1 the whole *m* was by the sea on the
Mk 4:36 And when they had sent away the *m*
Mk 5:31 Thou seest the *m* thronging thee
Mk 7:33 And he took him aside from the *m*
Mk 8:1 those days the *m* being very great
Mk 8:2 I have compassion on the *m*
Mk 9:14 he saw a great *m* about them
Mk 9:17 And one of the *m* answered and said,
Mk 14:43 and with him a great *m* with swords
Mk 15:8 the *m* crying aloud began to
Lk 1:10 the whole *m* of the people were
Lk 2:13 there was with the angel a *m* of
Lk 3:7 Then said he to the *m* that came
Lk 5:6 they inclosed a great *m* of fishes
Lk 5:19 bring him in because of the *m*
Lk 6:17 a great *m* of people out of all
Lk 6:19 the whole *m* sought to touch him
Lk 8:37 Then the whole *m* of the country
Lk 8:45 the *m* throng thee and press thee,
Lk 9:12 and said unto him, Send the *m* away
Lk 9:16 the disciples to set before the *m*
Lk 12:1 an innumerable *m* of people
Lk 18:36 And hearing the *m* pass by, he
Lk 19:37 the whole *m* of the disciples
Lk 19:39 from among the *m* said unto him
Lk 22:6 unto them in the absence of the *m*
Lk 22:47 And while he yet spake, behold a *m*
Lk 23:1 the whole *m* of them arose, and led
Jn 5:3 lay a great *m* of impotent folk
Jn 5:13 away, a *m* being in that place
Jn 6:2 a great *m* followed him, because
Jn 21:6 to draw it for the *m* of fishes
Acts 2:6 the *m* came together, and were
Acts 4:32 the *m* of them that believed were
Acts 5:16 There came also a *m* out of the
Acts 6:2 the *m* of the disciples unto them
Acts 6:5 And the saying pleased the whole *m*
Acts 14:1 that a great *m* both of the Jews
Acts 14:4 But the *m* of the city was divided
Acts 15:12 Then all the *m* kept silence
Acts 15:30 they had gathered the *m* together
Acts 16:22 the *m* rose up together against
Acts 17:4 and of the devout Greeks a great *m*
Acts 19:9 evil of that way before the *m*
Acts 19:33 they drew Alexander out of the *m*
Acts 21:22 the *m* must needs come together
Acts 21:34 thing, some another, among the *m*
Acts 21:36 For the *m* of the people followed
Acts 23:7 and the *m* was divided
Acts 24:18 in the temple, neither with *m*
Acts 25:24 about whom all the *m* of the Jews
Heb 11:12 many as the stars of the sky in *m*
Jas 5:20 death, and shall hide a *m* of sins
1Pet 4:8 charity shall cover the *m* of sins
Rev 7:9 this I beheld, and, lo, a great *m*
Rev 19:6 as it were the voice of a great *m*

**MULTITUDES**
Eze 32:20 draw her and all her *m*
Joel 3:14 *M*, *m* in the valley of
Mt 4:25 great *m* of people from Galilee
Mt 5:1 And seeing the *m*, he went up into
Mt 8:1 mountain, great *m* followed him
Mt 8:18 when Jesus saw great *m* about him
Mt 9:8 But when the *m* saw it, they
Mt 9:33 the *m* marvelled, saying, It was
Mt 9:36 But when he saw the *m*, he was
Mt 11:7 to say unto the *m* concerning John
Mt 12:15 great *m* followed him, and he
Mt 13:2 great *m* were gathered together
Mt 14:22 side, while he sent the *m* away
Mt 14:23 And when he had sent the *m* away
Mt 15:30 great *m* came unto him, having
Mt 19:2 And great *m* followed him
Mt 21:9 the *m* that went before, and that
Mt 26:55 same hour said Jesus to the *m*
Lk 5:15 great *m* came together to hear, and
Lk 14:25 And there went great *m* with him
Acts 5:14 the Lord, *m* both of men and women
Acts 13:45 But when the Jews saw the *m*
Rev 17:15 whore sitteth, are peoples, and *m*

**MUPPIM** *(mup'-pim)* See SHUPPIM. *A son of Benjamin.*
Gen 46:21 Gera, and Naaman, Ehi, and Rosh, *M*

**MURDER**
Ps 10:8 places doth he *m* the innocent
Ps 94:6 the stranger, and *m* the fatherless
Jer 7:9 Will ye steal, *m*, and commit
Hos 6:9 priests *m* in the way by consent
Mt 19:18 Jesus said, Thou shalt do no *m*
Mk 15:7 who had committed *m* in the
Lk 23:19 made in the city, and for *m*
Lk 23:25 *m* was cast into prison, whom they
Rom 1:29 full of envy, *m*, debate, deceit,

**MURDERER**
Num 35:16 iron, so that he die, he is a *m*
Num 35:16 the *m* shall surely be put to
Num 35:17 he may die, and he die, he is a *m*
Num 35:17 the *m* shall surely be put to
Num 35:18 he may die, and he die, he is a *m*
Num 35:18 the *m* shall surely be put to
Num 35:19 of blood himself shall slay the *m*
Num 35:21 for he is a *m*
Num 35:21 of blood shall slay the *m*
Num 35:30 the *m* shall be put to death by
Num 35:31 satisfaction for the life of a *m*
2Kin 6:32 See ye how this son of a *m* hath
Job 24:14 The *m* rising with the light
Hos 9:13 bring forth his children to the *m*
Jn 8:44 He was a *m* from the beginning, and
Acts 3:14 desired a *m* to be granted unto
Acts 28:4 No doubt this man is a *m*
1Pet 4:15 But let none of you suffer as a *m*
1Jn 3:15 hateth his brother is a *m*
1Jn 3:15 ye know that no *m* hath eternal

**MURDERERS**
2Kin 14:6 the children of the *m* he slew not
Is 1:21 lodged in it; but now *m*
Jer 4:31 my soul is wearied because of *m*
Mt 22:7 his armies, and destroyed those *m*
Acts 7:52 have been now the betrayers and *m*
Acts 21:38 four thousand men that were *m*
1Ti 1:9 for *m* of fathers and *m* of

1Ti 1:9 *m* of mothers, for manslayers,
Rev 21:8 and the abominable, and *m*, and
Rev 22:15 sorcerers, and whoremongers, and *m*

**MURDERS**
Mt 15:19 heart proceed evil thoughts, *m*
Mk 7:21 adulteries, fornications, *m*
Gal 5:21 Envyings, *m*, drunkenness,
Rev 9:21 Neither repented they of their *m*

**MURMUR**
Ex 16:7 what are we, that ye *m* against us
Ex 16:8 murmurings which ye *m* against him
Num 14:27 congregation, which *m* against me
Num 14:27 Israel, which they *m* against me
Num 14:36 the congregation to *m* against him
Num 16:11 is Aaron, that ye *m* against him
Num 17:5 whereby they *m* against you
Jn 6:43 unto them, *M* not among yourselves
1Cor 10:10 Neither *m* ye, as some of them

**MURMURED**
Ex 15:24 the people *m* against Moses,
Ex 16:2 of Israel *m* against Moses
Ex 17:3 the people *m* against Moses, and
Num 14:2 of Israel *m* against Moses
Num 14:29 upward, which have *m* against me
Num 16:41 of Israel *m* against Moses
Deut 1:27 ye *m* in your tents, and said,
Josh 9:18 *m* against the princes
Ps 106:25 But *m* in their tents, and
Is 29:24 they that *m* shall learn doctrine
Mt 20:11 they *m* against the goodman of the
Mk 14:5 And they *m* against her
Lk 5:30 Pharisees *m* against his disciples
Lk 15:2 And the Pharisees and scribes *m*
Lk 19:7 And when they saw it, they all *m*
Jn 6:41 The Jews then *m* at him, because
Jn 6:61 that his disciples *m* at it
Jn 7:32 *m* such things concerning him
1Cor 10:10 murmur ye, as some of them also *m*

**MURMURINGS**
Ex 16:7 heareth your *m* against the LORD
Ex 16:8 *m* which ye murmur against him
Ex 16:8 your *m* are not against us, but
Ex 16:9 for he hath heard your *m*
Ex 16:12 I have heard the *m* of the
Num 14:27 I have heard the *m* of the
Num 17:5 the *m* of the children of Israel
Num 17:10 quite take away their *m* from me
Phil 2:14 Do all things without *m* and

**MUSHI** *(mu'-shi)* See MUSHITES. *A son of Merari.*
Ex 6:19 of Merari; Mahali and *M*
Num 3:20 families; Mahli, and *M*
1Chr 6:19 Merari; Mahli, and *M*
1Chr 6:47 The son of Mahli, the son of *M*
1Chr 23:21 Merari; Mahli, and *M*
1Chr 23:23 The sons of *M*; Mahli
1Chr 24:26 sons of Merari were Mahli and *M*
1Chr 24:30 The sons also of *M*

**MUSHITES** *(mu'-shites) The family of Mushi.*
Num 3:33 Mahlites, and the family of the *M*
Num 26:58 the Mahlites, the family of the *M*

**MUSICK**
1Sa 18:6 joy, and with instruments of *m*
1Chr 15:16 the singers with instruments of *m*
2Chr 5:13 and cymbals and instruments of *m*
2Chr 7:6 with instruments of *m* of the LORD
2Chr 23:13 the singers with instruments of *m*
2Chr 34:12 could skill of instruments of *m*
Eccl 12:4 of *m* shall be brought low
Lam 3:63 I am their *m*
Lam 5:14 gate, the young men from their *m*
Dan 3:5 dulcimer, and all kinds of *m*
Dan 3:7 psaltery, and all kinds of *m*
Dan 3:10 and dulcimer, and all kinds of *m*
Dan 3:15 and dulcimer, and all kinds of *m*
Dan 6:18 of *m* brought before him
Amos 6:5 to themselves instruments of *m*
Lk 15:25 nigh to the house, he heard *m*

**MUST**
Gen 17:13 thy money, *m* needs be circumcised
Gen 24:5 *m* I needs bring thy son again
Gen 29:26 It *m* not be so done in our
Gen 30:16 and said, Thou *m* come in unto me
Gen 43:11 If it *m* be so now, do this
Gen 47:29 time drew nigh that Israel *m* die
Ex 10:9 for we *m* hold a feast unto the
Ex 10:25 Thou *m* give us also sacrifices and
Ex 10:26 for thereof *m* we take to serve
Ex 10:26 not with what we *m* serve the LORD
Ex 12:16 save that which every man *m* eat
Ex 18:20 them the way wherein they *m* walk
Ex 18:20 walk, and the work that they *m* do
Lev 11:32 it *m* be put into water, and it
Lev 23:6 seven days ye *m* eat unleavened
Num 6:21 so he *m* do after the law of his
Num 18:22 Neither *m* the children of Israel
Num 20:10 *m* we fetch you water out of this
Num 23:12 *M* I not take heed to speak that
Num 23:26 the LORD speaketh, that I *m* do
Deut 1:22 word again by what way we *m* go up
Deut 4:22 But I *m* die in this land, I *m*
Deut 12:18 But thou *m* eat them before the
Deut 31:7 for thou *m* go with this people
Deut 31:14 thy days approach that thou *m* die
Josh 3:4 may know the way by which ye *m* go
Josh 22:18 But that ye *m* turn away this day
Judg 13:16 thou *m* offer it unto the LORD
Judg 21:17 There *m* be an inheritance for
Ruth 4:5 thou *m* buy it also of Ruth the
1Sa 14:43 was in mine hand, and, lo, I *m* die
2Sa 14:14 For we *m* needs die, and are as
2Sa 23:3 He that ruleth over men *m* be just
2Sa 23:7 touch them *m* be fenced with iron
1Kin 18:27 he sleepeth, and *m* be awaked
1Chr 17:11 thou *m* go to be with thy fathers
1Chr 22:5 LORD *m* be exceeding magnifical
Ezr 10:12 As thou hast said, so *m* we do
Ps 32:9 whose mouth *m* be held in with bit
Prov 18:24 friends *m* shew himself friendly
Prov 19:19 him, yet thou *m* do it again
Eccl 10:10 then *m* he put to more strength
Song 8:12 *m* have a thousand, and those that
Is 28:10 For precept *m* be upon precept,
Jer 10:5 they *m* needs be borne, because
Jer 10:19 this is a grief, and I *m* bear it
Eze 34:18 but ye *m* tread down with your
Eze 34:18 but ye *m* foul the residue with
Mt 16:21 how that he *m* go unto Jerusalem,
Mt 17:10 scribes that Elias *m* first come
Mt 18:7 for it *m* needs be that offences
Mt 24:6 all these things *m* come to pass
Mt 26:54 be fulfilled, that thus it *m* be
Mk 2:22 but new wine *m* be put into new
Mk 8:31 Son of man *m* suffer many things
Mk 9:11 scribes that Elias *m* first come
Mk 9:12 that he *m* suffer many things, and
Mk 13:7 for such things *m* needs be
Mk 13:10 the gospel *m* first be published
Mk 14:49 but the scriptures *m* be fulfilled
Lk 2:49 wist ye not that I *m* be about my
Lk 4:43 I *m* preach the kingdom of God to
Lk 5:38 But new wine *m* be put into new
Lk 9:22 The Son of man *m* suffer many
Lk 13:33 Nevertheless I *m* walk to day
Lk 14:18 ground, and I *m* needs go and see it
Lk 17:25 But first *m* he suffer many things
Lk 19:5 for to day I *m* abide at thy house
Lk 21:9 for these things *m* first come to
Lk 22:7 when the passover *m* be killed
Lk 22:37 *m* yet be accomplished in me
Lk 23:17 (For of necessity he *m* release
Lk 24:7 The Son of man *m* be delivered
Lk 24:44 that all things *m* be fulfilled
Jn 3:7 unto thee, Ye *m* be born again
Jn 3:14 even so *m* the Son of man be
Jn 3:30 He *m* increase, but I
Jn 3:30 increase, but I *m* decrease
Jn 4:4 he *m* needs go through Samaria
Jn 4:24 him *m* worship him in spirit
Jn 9:4 I *m* work the works of him that
Jn 10:16 them also I *m* bring, and they
Jn 12:34 The Son of man *m* be lifted up
Jn 20:9 that he *m* rise again from the
Acts 1:16 this scripture *m* needs have been
Acts 1:22 *m* one be ordained to be a witness
Acts 3:21 Whom the heaven *m* receive until
Acts 4:12 among men, whereby we *m* be saved
Acts 9:6 shall be told thee what thou *m* do
Acts 9:16 he *m* suffer for my name's sake
Acts 14:22 faith, and that we *m* through much
Acts 15:24 Ye *m* be circumcised, and keep the
Acts 16:30 Sirs, what *m* I do to be saved
Acts 17:3 that Christ *m* needs have suffered
Acts 18:21 I *m* by all means keep this feast
Acts 19:21 been there, I *m* also see Rome
Acts 21:22 the multitude *m* needs come
Acts 23:11 so *m* thou bear witness also at
Acts 27:24 thou *m* be brought before Caesar
Acts 27:26 Howbeit we *m* be cast upon a
Rom 13:5 Wherefore ye *m* needs be subject,
1Cor 5:10 for then *m* ye needs go out of the
1Cor 11:19 For there *m* be also heresies
1Cor 15:25 For he *m* reign, till he hath put
1Cor 15:53 corruptible *m* put on incorruption
1Cor 15:53 this mortal *m* put on immortality
2Cor 5:10 For we *m* all appear before the
2Cor 11:30 If I *m* needs glory, I will glory
1Ti 3:2 A bishop then *m* be blameless
1Ti 3:7 Moreover he *m* have a good report
1Ti 3:8 Likewise *m* the deacons be grave,
1Ti 3:11 Even so *m* their wives be grave,
2Ti 2:6 The husbandman that laboureth *m*
2Ti 2:24 servant of the Lord *m* not strive
Titus 1:7 For a bishop *m* be blameless
Titus 1:11 Whose mouths *m* be stopped
Heb 4:6 that some *m* enter therein
Heb 9:16 there *m* also of necessity be the
Heb 9:26 For then *m* he often have suffered
Heb 11:6 to God *m* believe that he is
Heb 13:17 as they that *m* give account
1Pet 4:17 *m* begin at the house of God
2Pet 1:14 Knowing that shortly I *m* put off
Rev 1:1 which *m* shortly come to pass
Rev 4:1 thee things which *m* be hereafter
Rev 10:11 Thou *m* prophesy again before many
Rev 11:5 he *m* in this manner be killed
Rev 13:10 sword *m* be killed with the sword
Rev 17:10 he *m* continue a short space
Rev 20:3 after that he *m* be loosed a
Rev 22:6 things which *m* shortly be done

**MUSTARD**
Mt 13:31 is like to a grain of *m* seed
Mt 17:20 have faith as a grain of *m* seed
Mk 4:31 It is like a grain of *m* seed
Lk 13:19 It is like a grain of *m* seed
Lk 17:6 ye had faith as a grain of *m* seed

**MUTH-LABBEN** *(muth-lab'-ben) A musical notation.*
Ps 9:*t* To the chief Musician upon *M*

**MYRA** *(mi'-rah) A city in Lycia.*
Acts 27:5 and Pamphylia, we came to *M*

**MYRRH**
Gen 37:25 bearing spicery and balm and *m*
Gen 43:11 and a little honey, spices, and *m*
Ex 30:23 of pure *m* five hundred shekels
Est 2:12 to wit, six months with oil of *m*
Ps 45:8 All thy garments smell of *m*
Prov 7:17 I have perfumed my bed with *m*
Song 1:13 A bundle of *m* is my wellbeloved
Song 3:6 pillars of smoke, perfumed with *m*
Song 4:6 will get me to the mountain of *m*
Song 4:14 *m* and aloes, with all the chief
Song 5:1 have gathered my *m* with my spice
Song 5:5 and my hands dropped with *m*
Song 5:5 my fingers with sweet smelling *m*
Song 5:13 lilies, dropping sweet smelling *m*
Mt 2:11 gold, and frankincense, and *m*
Mk 15:23 him to drink wine mingled with *m*
Jn 19:39 night, and brought a mixture of *m*

**MYRTLE**
Neh 8:15 *m* branches, and palm branches, and
Is 41:19 cedar, the shittah tree, and the *m*
Is 55:13 brier shall come up the *m* tree
Zec 1:8 he stood among the *m* trees that
Zec 1:10 stood among the *m* trees answered
Zec 1:11 LORD that stood among the *m* trees

**MYSIA** *(miz'-ye-ah) A Roman province in Asia Minor.*
Acts 16:7 After they were come to *M*
Acts 16:8 they passing by *M* came down to

**MYSTERIES**
Mt 13:11 the *m* of the kingdom of heaven
Lk 8:10 know the *m* of the kingdom of God
1Cor 4:1 and stewards of the *m* of God
1Cor 13:2 of prophecy, and understand all *m*
1Cor 14:2 in the spirit he speaketh *m*

**MYSTERY**
Mk 4:11 know the *m* of the kingdom of God
Rom 11:25 ye should be ignorant of this *m*
Rom 16:25 to the revelation of the *m*
1Cor 2:7 we speak the wisdom of God in a *m*

1Cor 15:51 Behold, I shew you a *m*
Eph 1:9 known unto us the *m* of his will
Eph 3:3 he made known unto me the *m*
Eph 3:4 my knowledge in the *m* of Christ)
Eph 3:9 what is the fellowship of the *m*
Eph 5:32 This is a great *m*
Eph 6:19 to make known the *m* of the gospel
Col 1:26 Even the *m* which hath been hid
Col 1:27 of this *m* among the Gentiles
Col 2:2 acknowledgement of the *m* of God
Col 4:3 to speak the *m* of Christ
2Th 2:7 For the *m* of iniquity doth
1Ti 3:9 Holding the *m* of the faith in a
1Ti 3:16 great is the *m* of godliness
Rev 1:20 The *m* of the seven stars which
Rev 10:7 the *m* of God should be finished,
Rev 17:5 forehead was a name written, *M*
Rev 17:7 will tell thee the *m* of the woman

# N

**NAAM** *(na'-am) A son of Caleb.*
1Chr 4:15 Iru, Elah, and *N*

**NAAMAH** *(na'-a-mah)* See NAAMATHITE.
*1. Sister of Tubal-cain.*
Gen 4:22 and the sister of Tubal-cain was *N*
*2. Mother of King Rehoboam.*
1Kin 14:21 mother's name was *N* an Ammonitess
1Kin 14:31 mother's name was *N* an Ammonitess
2Chr 12:13 mother's name was *N* an Ammonitess
*3. A city in Judah.*
Josh 15:41 And Gederoth, Beth-dagon, and *N*

**NAAMAN** *(na'-a-man)* See NAAMAN'S, NAAMITES.
*1. A son of Benjamin.*
Gen 46:21 and Becher, and Ashbel, Gera, and *N*
*2. A son of Bela.*
Num 26:40 And the sons of Bela were Ard and *N*
Num 26:40 and of *N*, the family of the
1Chr 8:4 And Abishua, and *N*, and Ahoah,
*3. A son of Ehud.*
1Chr 8:7 And *N*, and Ahiah, and Gera, he
*4. A Syrian captain.*
2Kin 5:1 Now *N*, captain of the host of the
2Kin 5:6 sent *N* my servant to thee
2Kin 5:9 So *N* came with his horses and with
2Kin 5:11 But *N* was wroth, and went away, and
2Kin 5:17 *N* said, Shall there not then, I
2Kin 5:20 master hath spared *N* this Syrian
2Kin 5:21 So Gehazi followed after *N*
2Kin 5:21 when *N* saw him running after him,
2Kin 5:23 *N* said, Be content, take two
2Kin 5:27 of *N* shall cleave unto thee
Lk 4:27 was cleansed, saving *N* the Syrian

**NAAMAN'S** *(na'-a-mans) Refers to Naaman 4.*
2Kin 5:2 and she waited on *N* wife

**NAAMATHITE** *(na'-a-math-ite) Family name of Zophar.*
Job 2:11 the Shuhite, and Zophar the *N*
Job 11:1 Then answered Zophar the *N*
Job 20:1 Then answered Zophar the *N*
Job 42:9 the Shuhite and Zophar the *N* went

**NAAMITES** *(na'-a-mites) Descendants of Naaman 3.*
Num 26:40 and of Naaman, the family of the *N*

**NAARAH** *(na'-a-rah)* See NAARAN, NAARATH. *A wife of Ashur.*
1Chr 4:5 Tekoa had two wives, Helah and *N*
1Chr 4:6 *N* bare him Ahuzam, and Hepher, and
1Chr 4:6 These were the sons of *N*

**NAARAI** *(na'-a-rahee)* See PAARAI. *A "mighty man" of David.*
1Chr 11:37 Carmelite, *N* the son of Ezbai,

**NAARAN** *(na'-a-ran) A city in Ephraim.*
1Chr 7:28 the towns thereof, and eastward *N*

**NAARATH** *(na'-a-rath)* See NAARAH, NAARAN. *Same as Naaran.*
Josh 16:7 from Janohah to Ataroth, and to *N*

**NAASHON** *(na'-a-shon)* See NAHSHON. *Brother of Elisheba.*
Ex 6:23 of Amminadab, sister of *N*

**NAASSON** *(na'-as-son)* See NAASHON. *Father of Salmon.*
Mt 1:4 and Aminadab begat *N*
Mt 1:4 and *N* begat Salmon
Lk 3:32 of Salmon, which was the son of *N*

**NABAL** *(na'-bal)* See NABAL'S. *A wife of David.*
1Sa 25:3 Now the name of the man was *N*
1Sa 25:4 that *N* did shear his sheep
1Sa 25:5 Get you up to Carmel, and go to *N*
1Sa 25:9 they spake to *N* according to all
1Sa 25:10 *N* answered David's servants, and
1Sa 25:19 But she told not her husband *N*
1Sa 25:25 regard this man of Belial, even *N*
1Sa 25:25 *N* is his name, and folly is with
1Sa 25:26 seek evil to my lord, be as *N*
1Sa 25:34 there had not been left unto *N* by
1Sa 25:36 And Abigail came to *N*
1Sa 25:37 when the wine was gone out of *N*
1Sa 25:38 days after, that the LORD smote *N*
1Sa 25:39 when David heard that *N* was dead
1Sa 25:39 of my reproach from the hand of *N*
1Sa 25:39 wickedness of *N* upon his own head
1Sa 30:5 the wife of *N* the Carmelite
2Sa 3:3 the wife of *N* the Carmelite

**NABAL'S** *(na'-balz)*
1Sa 25:14 *N* wife, saying, Behold, David
1Sa 25:36 *N* heart was merry within him for
1Sa 27:3 Abigail the Carmelitess, *N* wife
2Sa 2:2 Abigail *N* wife the Carmelite

**NABOTH** *(na'-both) A Jezreelite of Issachar.*
1Kin 21:1 that *N* the Jezreelite had a
1Kin 21:2 And Ahab spake unto *N*, saying,
1Kin 21:3 *N* said to Ahab, The LORD forbid
1Kin 21:4 because of the word which *N* the
1Kin 21:6 I spake unto *N* the Jezreelite
1Kin 21:7 the vineyard of *N* the Jezreelite
1Kin 21:8 were in his city, dwelling with *N*
1Kin 21:9 set *N* on high among the people
1Kin 21:12 set *N* on high among the people
1Kin 21:13 against him, even against *N*
1Kin 21:13 *N* did blaspheme God and the king
1Kin 21:14 saying, *N* is stoned, and is dead
1Kin 21:15 Jezebel heard that *N* was stoned
1Kin 21:15 the vineyard of *N* the Jezreelite
1Kin 21:15 for *N* is not alive, but dead
1Kin 21:16 when Ahab heard that *N* was dead
1Kin 21:16 the vineyard of *N* the Jezreelite
1Kin 21:18 he is in the vineyard of *N*
1Kin 21:19 of *N* shall dogs lick thy blood
2Kin 9:21 the portion of *N* the Jezreelite
2Kin 9:25 of the field of *N* the Jezreelite
2Kin 9:26 seen yesterday the blood of *N*

**NACHON'S** *(na'-kons)*
2Sa 6:6 they came to *N* threshingfloor

**NACHOR** *(na'-kor)* See NAHOR.
*1. Brother of Abraham.*
Josh 24:2 of Abraham, and the father of *N*
*2. Father of Thara; ancestor of Jesus.*
Lk 3:34 of Thara, which was the son of *N*

**NADAB** *(na'-dab)*
*1. Son of Aaron.*
Ex 6:23 and she bare him *N*, and Abihu,
Ex 24:1 unto the LORD, thou, and Aaron, *N*
Ex 24:9 Then went up Moses, and Aaron, *N*
Ex 28:1 priest's office, even Aaron, *N*
Lev 10:1 And *N* and Abihu, the sons of Aaron,
Num 3:2 *N* the firstborn, and Abihu,
Num 3:4 And *N* and Abihu died before the
Num 26:60 And unto Aaron was born *N*, and
Num 26:61 And *N* and Abihu died, when they
1Chr 6:3 *N*, and Abihu, Eleazar, and Ithamar
1Chr 24:1 *N*, and Abihu, Eleazar, and Ithamar
1Chr 24:2 But *N* and Abihu died before their
*2. Son of King Jeroboam 1.*
1Kin 14:20 *N* his son reigned in his stead
1Kin 15:25 *N* the son of Jeroboam began to
1Kin 15:27 for *N* and all Israel laid siege to
1Kin 15:31 Now the rest of the acts of *N*
*3. Great-grandson of Jerahmeel.*
1Chr 2:28 Shammai; *N*, and
1Chr 2:30 And the sons of *N*
*4. A descendant of King Saul.*
1Chr 8:30 and Zur, and Kish, and Baal, and *N*
1Chr 9:36 and Kish, and Baal, and Ner, and *N*

**NAGGE** *(nag'-e)* See NEARIAH. *Father of Esli; ancestor of Jesus.*
Lk 3:25 of Esli, which was the son of *N*

**NAHALAL** *(na'-ha-lal) A Levitical city in Zebulun.*
Josh 21:35 her suburbs, *N* with her suburbs

**NAHALIEL** *(na-ha'-le-el) An Israelite encampment in the wilderness.*
Num 21:19 And from Mattanah to *N*
Num 21:19 and from *N* to Bamoth

**NAHALLAL** *(na'-hal-el)* See NAHALAL. *Same as Nahalal.*
Josh 19:15 And Kattath, and *N*, and Shimron, and

**NAHALOL** *(na'-ha-lol) Same as Nahalal.*
Judg 1:30 Kitron, nor the inhabitants of *N*

**NAHAM** *(na'-ham)* See ISHBAH. *A descendant of Caleb.*
1Chr 4:19 his wife Hodiah the sister of *N*

**NAHAMANI** *(na-ham'-a-ni) A clan chief with Zerubbabel.*
Neh 7:7 Nehemiah, Azariah, Raamiah, *N*

**NAHARAI** *(na'-ha-rahee)* See NAHARI. *A "mighty man" of David.*
1Chr 11:39 *N* the Berothite, the armourbearer

**NAHARI** *(na'-ha-ri)* See NAHARAI. *Same as Naharai.*
2Sa 23:37 *N* the Beerothite, armourbearer to

**NAHASH** *(na'-hash)* See IR-NAHASH.
*1. An Ammonite king.*
1Sa 11:1 Then *N* the Ammonite came up, and
1Sa 11:1 all the men of Jabesh said unto *N*
1Sa 11:2 *N* the Ammonite answered them, On
1Sa 12:12 when ye saw that *N* the king of
*2. Father of Shobi and Hanun.*
2Sa 10:2 kindness unto Hanun the son of *N*
2Sa 17:27 that Shobi the son of *N* of Rabbah
1Chr 19:1 that *N* the king of the children
1Chr 19:2 kindness unto Hanun the son of *N*
*3. Mother of Abigail.*
2Sa 17:25 in to Abigail the daughter of *N*

**NAHATH** *(na'-hath)* See TOHU.
*1. A son of Reuel.*
Gen 36:13 *N*, and Zerah, Shammah, and Mizzah
Gen 36:17 duke *N*, duke Zerah, duke Shammah,
1Chr 1:37 *N*, Zerah, Shammah, and Mizzah
*2. Son of Zophi.*
1Chr 6:26 Zophai his son, and *N* his son,
*3. A Temple servant.*
2Chr 31:13 And Jehiel, and Azaziah, and *N*

**NAHBI** *(nah'-bi) A spy sent to the Promised Land.*
Num 13:14 of Naphtali, *N* the son of Vophsi

**NAHOR** *(na'-hor)* See NACHOR, NAHOR'S.
*1. Grandfather of Abraham.*
Gen 11:22 lived thirty years, and begat *N*
Gen 11:23 he begat *N* two hundred years
Gen 11:24 *N* lived nine and twenty years, and
Gen 11:25 *N* lived after he begat Terah an
1Chr 1:26 Serug, *N*, Terah,
*2. Son of Terah.*
Gen 11:26 seventy years, and begat Abram, *N*
Gen 11:27 Terah begat Abram, *N*, and Haran
Gen 11:29 And Abram and *N* took them wives
Gen 22:20 born children unto thy brother *N*
Gen 22:23 these eight Milcah did bear to *N*
Gen 24:10 Mesopotamia, unto the city of *N*
Gen 24:15 son of Milcah, the wife of *N*
Gen 24:24 of Milcah, which she bare unto *N*

Gen 29:5 them, Know ye Laban the son of *N*
Gen 31:53 God of Abraham, and the God of *N*

**NAHOR'S** *(na'-hors) Refers to Nahor 2.*
Gen 11:29 and the name of *N* wife, Milcah,
Gen 24:47 *N* son, whom Milcah bare unto him

**NAHSHON** *(nah'-shon)* See NAASHON, NAASSON. *Son of Amminadab.*
Num 1:7 *N* the son of Amminadab
Num 2:3 *N* the son of Amminadab shall be
Num 7:12 day was *N* the son of Amminadab
Num 7:17 of *N* the son of Amminadab
Num 10:14 over his host was *N* the son of
Ruth 4:20 And Amminadab begat *N*, and *N*
Ruth 4:20 begat *N*, and *N* begat Salmon,
1Chr 2:10 and Amminadab begat *N*, prince of
1Chr 2:11 *N* begat Salma, and Salma begat

**NAHUM** *(na'-hum)* See NAUM. *A prophet who spoke against Nineveh.*
Nah 1:1 of the vision of *N* the Elkoshite

**NAIL**
Judg 4:21 Heber's wife took a *n* of the tent
Judg 4:21 smote the *n* into his temples, and
Judg 4:22 dead, and the *n* was in his temples
Judg 5:26 She put her hand to the *n*
Ezr 9:8 to give us a *n* in his holy place,
Is 22:23 fasten him as a *n* in a sure place
Is 22:25 shall the *n* that is fastened in
Zec 10:4 the corner, out of him the *n*

**NAILS**
Deut 21:12 shave her head, and pare her *n*
1Chr 22:3 iron in abundance for the *n* for
2Chr 3:9 the weight of the *n* was fifty
Eccl 12:11 as *n* fastened by the masters of
Is 41:7 and he fastened it with *n*, that it
Jer 10:4 they fasten it with *n* and with
Dan 4:33 and his *n* like birds' claws
Dan 7:19 were of iron, and his *n* of brass
Jn 20:25 in his hands the print of the *n*
Jn 20:25 my finger into the print of the *n*

**NAIN** *(nane) A city in Galilee.*
Lk 7:11 that he went into a city called *N*

**NAIOTH** *(nay'-yoth) A place in Ramah.*
1Sa 19:18 he and Samuel went and dwelt in *N*
1Sa 19:19 Behold, David is at *N* in Ramah
1Sa 19:22 Behold, they be at *N* in Ramah
1Sa 19:23 And he went thither to *N* in Ramah
1Sa 19:23 until he came to *N* in Ramah
1Sa 20:1 And David fled from *N* in Ramah

**NAKED**
Gen 2:25 And they were both *n*, the man and
Gen 3:7 and they knew that they were *n*
Gen 3:10 and I was afraid, because I was *n*
Gen 3:11 Who told thee that thou wast *n*
Ex 32:25 Moses saw that the people were *n*
Ex 32:25 (for Aaron had made them *n* unto
1Sa 19:24 lay down *n* all that day and all
2Chr 28:15 all that were *n* among them
2Chr 28:19 for he made Judah *n*, and
Job 1:21 *N* came I out of my mother's womb,
Job 1:21 and *n* shall I return thither
Job 22:6 stripped the *n* of their clothing
Job 24:7 They cause the *n* to lodge without
Job 24:10 him to go *n* without clothing
Job 26:6 Hell is *n* before him, and
Eccl 5:15 *n* shall he return to go as he
Is 20:2 And he did so, walking *n* and
Is 20:3 my servant Isaiah hath walked *n*
Is 20:4 captives, young and old, *n*
Is 58:7 when thou seest the *n*, that thou
Lam 4:21 drunken, and shalt make thyself *n*
Eze 16:7 is grown, whereas thou wast *n*
Eze 16:22 of thy youth, when thou wast *n*
Eze 16:39 thy fair jewels, and leave thee *n*
Eze 18:7 hath covered the *n* with a garment
Eze 18:16 hath covered the *n* with a garment
Eze 23:29 thy labour, and shall leave thee *n*
Hos 2:3 Lest I strip her *n*, and set her as
Amos 2:16 shall flee away *n* in that day
Mic 1:8 and howl, I will go stripped and *n*
Mic 1:11 of Saphir, having thy shame *n*
Hab 3:9 Thy bow was made quite *n*,
Mt 25:36 *N*, and ye clothed me
Mt 25:38 or *n*, and clothed thee
Mt 25:43 *n*, and ye clothed me not
Mt 25:44 or athirst, or a stranger, or *n*
Mk 14:51 linen cloth cast about his *n* body
Mk 14:52 linen cloth, and fled from them *n*
Jn 21:7 coat unto him, (for he was *n*
Acts 19:16 they fled out of that house *n*
1Cor 4:11 both hunger, and thirst, and are *n*
2Cor 5:3 clothed we shall not be found *n*
Heb 4:13 but all things are *n* and opened
Jas 2:15 If a brother or sister be *n*
Rev 3:17 and poor, and blind, and *n*
Rev 16:15 his garments, lest he walk *n*
Rev 17:16 and shall make her desolate and *n*

**NAKEDNESS**
Gen 9:22 saw the *n* of his father, and told
Gen 9:23 covered the *n* of their father
Gen 9:23 and they saw not their father's *n*
Gen 42:9 to see the *n* of the land ye are
Gen 42:12 but to see the *n* of the land ye
Ex 20:26 that thy *n* be not discovered
Ex 28:42 linen breeches to cover their *n*
Lev 18:6 of kin to him, to uncover their *n*
Lev 18:7 The *n* of thy father
Lev 18:7 or the *n* of thy mother, shalt
Lev 18:7 thou shalt not uncover her *n*
Lev 18:8 The *n* of thy father's wife shalt
Lev 18:8 it is thy father's *n*
Lev 18:9 The *n* of thy sister, the daughter
Lev 18:9 even their *n* thou shalt not
Lev 18:10 The *n* of thy son's daughter, or
Lev 18:10 even their *n* thou shalt not
Lev 18:10 for theirs is thine own *n*
Lev 18:11 The *n* of thy father's wife's
Lev 18:11 thou shalt not uncover her *n*
Lev 18:12 the *n* of thy father's sister
Lev 18:13 the *n* of thy mother's sister
Lev 18:14 the *n* of thy father's brother
Lev 18:15 the *n* of thy daughter in law
Lev 18:15 thou shalt not uncover her *n*
Lev 18:16 the *n* of thy brother's wife
Lev 18:16 it is thy brother's *n*
Lev 18:17 not uncover the *n* of a woman
Lev 18:17 daughter, to uncover her *n*
Lev 18:18 to vex her, to uncover her *n*
Lev 18:19 unto a woman to uncover her *n*
Lev 20:11 hath uncovered his father's *n*
Lev 20:17 her *n*, and she see his *n*
Lev 20:17 he hath uncovered his sister's *n*
Lev 20:18 sickness, and shall uncover her *n*
Lev 20:19 the *n* of thy mother's sister
Lev 20:20 he hath uncovered his uncle's *n*
Lev 20:21 he hath uncovered his brother's *n*
Deut 28:48 in hunger, and in thirst, and in *n*
1Sa 20:30 the confusion of thy mother's *n*
Is 47:3 Thy *n* shall be uncovered, yea,
Lam 1:8 her, because they have seen her *n*
Eze 16:8 skirt over thee, and covered thy *n*
Eze 16:36 thy *n* discovered through thy
Eze 16:37 and will discover thy *n* unto them
Eze 16:37 that they may see all thy *n*
Eze 22:10 they discovered their fathers' *n*
Eze 23:10 These discovered her *n*
Eze 23:18 whoredoms, and discovered her *n*
Eze 23:29 the *n* of thy whoredoms shall be
Hos 2:9 and my flax given to cover her *n*
Nah 3:5 and I will shew the nations thy *n*
Hab 2:15 that thou mayest look on their *n*
Rom 8:35 or persecution, or famine, or *n*
2Cor 11:27 in fastings often, in cold and *n*
Rev 3:18 the shame of thy *n* do not appear

**NAOMI** *(na'-o-mee)* See NAOMI'S. *Mother-in-law of Ruth.*
Ruth 1:2 and the name of his wife *N*
Ruth 1:8 *N* said unto her two daughters in
Ruth 1:11 *N* said, Turn again, my daughters
Ruth 1:19 them, and they said, Is this *N*
Ruth 1:20 she said unto them, Call me not *N*
Ruth 1:21 why then call ye me *N*, seeing the
Ruth 1:22 So *N* returned, and Ruth the
Ruth 2:1 *N* had a kinsman of her husband's,
Ruth 2:2 And Ruth the Moabitess said unto *N*
Ruth 2:6 with *N* out of the country of Moab
Ruth 2:20 *N* said unto her daughter in law,
Ruth 2:20 *N* said unto her, The man is near
Ruth 2:22 *N* said unto Ruth her daughter in
Ruth 3:1 Then *N* her mother in law said
Ruth 4:3 And he said unto the kinsman, *N*
Ruth 4:5 buyest the field of the hand of *N*
Ruth 4:9 and Mahlon's, of the hand of *N*
Ruth 4:14 And the women said unto *N*, Blessed
Ruth 4:16 *N* took the child, and laid it in
Ruth 4:17 saying, There is a son born to *N*

**NAOMI'S** *(na'-o-meze)*
Ruth 1:3 And Elimelech *N* husband died

**NAPHISH** *(na'-fish)* See NEPHISH. *A son of Ishmael.*
Gen 25:15 Hadar, and Tema, Jetur, *N*, and
1Chr 1:31 Jetur, *N*, and Kedemah

**NAPHTALI** *(naf'-ta-li)* See NEPHTHALIM.
*1. A son of Jacob.*
Gen 30:8 and she called his name *N*
Gen 35:25 handmaid; Dan, and *N*
Gen 46:24 And the sons of *N*
Gen 49:21 *N* is a hind let loose
Ex 1:4 Dan, and *N*, Gad, and Asher
1Chr 2:2 Dan, Joseph, and Benjamin, *N*
1Chr 7:13 The sons of *N*
Eze 48:34 one gate of Asher, one gate of *N*
*2. The tribe and land.*
Num 1:15 Of *N*; Ahira the son
Num 1:42 Of the children of *N*, throughout
Num 1:43 of them, even of the tribe of *N*
Num 2:29 Then the tribe of *N*
Num 2:29 *N* shall be Ahira the son of Enan
Num 7:78 Enan, prince of the children of *N*
Num 10:27 of *N* was Ahira the son of Enan
Num 13:14 Of the tribe of *N*, Nahbi the son
Num 26:48 Of the sons of *N* after their
Num 26:50 These are the families of *N*
Num 34:28 of the tribe of the children of *N*
Deut 27:13 and Asher, and Zebulun, Dan, and *N*
Deut 33:23 And of Naphtali he said, O *N*
Deut 34:2 And all *N*, and the land of Ephraim,
Josh 19:32 lot came out to the children of *N*
Josh 19:32 even for the children of *N*
Josh 19:39 of *N* according to their families
Josh 20:7 Kedesh in Galilee in mount *N*
Josh 21:6 Asher, and out of the tribe of *N*
Josh 21:32 And out of the tribe of *N*, Kedesh
Judg 1:33 Neither did *N* drive out the
Judg 4:6 thousand men of the children of *N*
Judg 4:10 called Zebulun and *N* to Kedesh
Judg 5:18 *N* were a people that jeoparded
Judg 6:35 Asher, and unto Zebulun, and unto *N*
Judg 7:23 themselves together out of *N*
1Kin 4:15 Ahimaaz was in *N*
1Kin 7:14 a widow's son of the tribe of *N*
1Kin 15:20 Cinneroth, with all the land of *N*
2Kin 15:29 and Galilee, all the land of *N*
1Chr 6:62 Asher, and out of the tribe of *N*
1Chr 6:76 And out of the tribe of *N*
1Chr 12:34 of *N* a thousand captains, and with
1Chr 12:40 unto Issachar and Zebulun and *N*
1Chr 27:19 of *N*, Jerimoth the son of Azriel
2Chr 16:4 and all the store cities of *N*
2Chr 34:6 Ephraim, and Simeon, even unto *N*
Ps 68:27 of Zebulun, and the princes of *N*
Is 9:1 land of Zebulun and the land of *N*
Eze 48:3 the west side, a portion for *N*
Eze 48:4 And by the border of *N*, from the

**NAPHTUHIM** *(naf'-too-him) Inhabitants of central Egypt.*
Gen 10:13 and Anamim, and Lehabim, and *N*

**NAPTHTUHIM**
1Chr 1:11 and Anamim, and Lehabim, and *N*

**NARCISSUS** *(nar-sis'-sus) A Christian in Rome.*
Rom 16:11 that be of the household of *N*

**NARROW**
Num 22:26 further, and stood in a *n* place
Josh 17:15 mount Ephraim be too *n* for thee
1Kin 6:4 house he made windows of *n* lights
Prov 23:27 and a strange woman is a *n* pit
Is 49:19 shall even now be too *n* by reason
Eze 40:16 there were *n* windows to the
Eze 41:16 the *n* windows, and the galleries
Eze 41:26 And there were *n* windows and palm
Mt 7:14 *n* is the way, which leadeth unto

**NATHAN** *(na'-than)* See NATHAN-MELECH.
*1. A son of David.*
2Sa 5:14 Shammuah, and Shobab, and *N*
1Chr 3:5 Shimea, and Shobab, and *N*, and
1Chr 14:4 and Shobab, *N*, and Solomon
Lk 3:31 Mattatha, which was the son of *N*
*2. A prophet in David's court.*
2Sa 7:2 the king said unto *N* the prophet
2Sa 7:3 *N* said to the king, Go, do all
2Sa 7:4 the word of the LORD came unto *N*

2Sa 7:17 so did *N* speak unto David
2Sa 12:1 And the LORD sent *N* unto David
2Sa 12:5 and he said to *N*, As the LORD
2Sa 12:7 *N* said to David, Thou art the man
2Sa 12:13 And David said unto *N*, I have
2Sa 12:13 *N* said unto David, The LORD also
2Sa 12:15 *N* departed unto his house
2Sa 12:25 sent by the hand of *N* the prophet
1Kin 1:8 *N* the prophet, and Shimei, and Rei,
1Kin 1:10 But *N* the prophet, and Benaiah, and
1Kin 1:11 Wherefore *N* spake unto Bath-sheba
1Kin 1:22 *N* the prophet also came in
1Kin 1:23 saying, Behold *N* the prophet
1Kin 1:24 *N* said, My lord, O king, hast
1Kin 1:32 *N* the prophet, and Benaiah the son
1Kin 1:34 *N* the prophet anoint him there
1Kin 1:38 *N* the prophet, and Benaiah the son
1Kin 1:44 *N* the prophet, and Benaiah the son
1Kin 1:45 *N* the prophet have anointed him
1Chr 17:1 that David said to *N* the prophet
1Chr 17:2 Then *N* said unto David, Do all
1Chr 17:3 that the word of God came to *N*
1Chr 17:15 so did *N* speak unto David
1Chr 29:29 and in the book of *N* the prophet
2Chr 9:29 in the book of *N* the prophet
2Chr 29:25 the king's seer, and *N* the prophet
Ps 51:*t* when *N* the prophet came unto him,

*3. Father of Igal.*

2Sa 23:36 Igal the son of *N* of Zobah

*4. Father of Azariah.*

1Kin 4:5 Azariah the son of *N* was over the

*5. Father of Zebud.*

1Kin 4:5 Zabud the son of *N* was principal

*6. Son of Attai.*

1Chr 2:36 And Attai begat *N*
1Chr 2:36 and *N* begat Zabad

*7. Brother of Joel.*

1Chr 11:38 Joel the brother of *N*, Mibhar the

*8. A clan leader with Ezra.*

Ezr 8:16 Jarib, and for Elnathan, and for *N*

*9. Married a foreigner in exile.*

Ezr 10:39 And Shelemiah, and *N*, and Adaiah,

*10. A family leader.*

Zec 12:12 family of the house of *N* apart

**NATHANAEL** *(na-than'-a-el)* See BARTHOLOMEW. *A disciple of Jesus.*

Jn 1:45 Philip findeth *N*, and saith unto
Jn 1:46 *N* said unto him, Can there any
Jn 1:47 Jesus saw *N* coming to him, and
Jn 1:48 *N* saith unto him, Whence knowest
Jn 1:49 *N* answered and saith unto him,
Jn 21:2 *N* of Cana in Galilee, and the sons

**NATHAN-MELECH** *(na'-than-me'-lek) A servant of King Josiah.*

2Kin 23:11 the chamber of *N* the chamberlain

**NATION**

Gen 12:2 And I will make of thee a great *n*
Gen 15:14 And also that *n*, whom they shall
Gen 17:20 and I will make him a great *n*
Gen 18:18 surely become a great and mighty *n*
Gen 20:4 wilt thou slay also a righteous *n*
Gen 21:13 of the bondwoman will I make a *n*
Gen 21:18 for I will make him a great *n*
Gen 35:11 a *n* and a company of nations shall
Gen 46:3 will there make of thee a great *n*
Ex 9:24 land of Egypt since it became a *n*
Ex 19:6 kingdom of priests, and an holy *n*
Ex 21:8 strange *n* he shall have no power
Ex 32:10 and I will make of thee a great *n*
Ex 33:13 that this *n* is thy people
Ex 34:10 in all the earth, nor in any *n*
Lev 18:26 neither any of your own *n*
Lev 20:23 not walk in the manners of the *n*
Num 14:12 and will make of thee a greater *n*
Deut 4:6 Surely this great *n* is a wise
Deut 4:7 For what *n* is there so great, who
Deut 4:8 what *n* is there so great, that
Deut 4:34 take him a *n* from the midst of
Deut 4:34 from the midst of another *n*
Deut 9:14 I will make of thee a *n* mightier
Deut 26:5 with a few, and became there a *n*
Deut 28:33 shall a *n* which thou knowest not
Deut 28:36 unto a *n* which neither thou nor
Deut 28:49 bring a *n* against thee from far
Deut 28:49 a *n* whose tongue thou shalt not
Deut 28:50 A *n* of fierce countenance, which
Deut 32:21 them to anger with a foolish *n*
Deut 32:28 For they are a *n* void of counsel,
2Sa 7:23 what one *n* in the earth is like
1Kin 18:10 liveth, there is no *n* or kingdom
1Kin 18:10 took an oath of the kingdom and *n*
2Kin 17:29 Howbeit every *n* made gods of
2Kin 17:29 every *n* in their cities wherein
1Chr 16:20 when they went from *n* to *n*
1Chr 17:21 what one *n* in the earth is like
2Chr 15:6 And *n* was destroyed of *n*
2Chr 32:15 for no god of any *n* or kingdom
Job 34:29 whether it be done against a *n*
Ps 33:12 Blessed is the *n* whose God is the
Ps 43:1 my cause against an ungodly *n*
Ps 83:4 us cut them off from being a *n*
Ps 105:13 they went from one *n* to another
Ps 106:5 rejoice in the gladness of thy *n*
Ps 147:20 He hath not dealt so with any *n*
Prov 14:34 Righteousness exalteth a *n*
Is 1:4 Ah sinful *n*, a people laden with
Is 2:4 *n* shall not lift up sword against
Is 2:4 shall not lift up sword against *n*
Is 9:3 Thou hast multiplied the *n*
Is 10:6 him against an hypocritical *n*
Is 14:32 answer the messengers of the *n*
Is 18:2 to a *n* scattered and peeled, to a
Is 18:2 a *n* meted out and trodden down,
Is 18:7 a *n* meted out and trodden under
Is 26:2 that the righteous *n* which
Is 26:15 Thou hast increased the *n*
Is 26:15 O LORD, thou hast increased the *n*
Is 49:7 to him whom the *n* abhorreth
Is 51:4 and give ear unto me, O my *n*
Is 55:5 thou shalt call a *n* that thou
Is 58:2 as a *n* that did righteousness, and
Is 60:12 For the *n* and kingdom that will
Is 60:22 and a small one a strong *n*
Is 65:1 unto a *n* that was not called by
Is 66:8 or shall a *n* be born at once
Jer 2:11 Hath a *n* changed their gods,
Jer 5:9 be avenged on such a *n* as this
Jer 5:15 I will bring a *n* upon you from
Jer 5:15 mighty *n*, it is an ancient *n*
Jer 5:15 a *n* whose language thou knowest
Jer 5:29 be avenged on such a *n* as this
Jer 6:22 a great *n* shall be raised from
Jer 7:28 This is a *n* that obeyeth not the
Jer 9:9 be avenged on such a *n* as this
Jer 12:17 pluck up and destroy that *n*
Jer 18:7 I shall speak concerning a *n*
Jer 18:8 If that *n*, against whom I have
Jer 18:9 I shall speak concerning a *n*
Jer 25:12 the king of Babylon, and that *n*
Jer 25:32 shall go forth from *n* to *n*
Jer 27:8 it shall come to pass, that the *n*
Jer 27:8 that *n* will I punish, saith the
Jer 27:13 LORD hath spoken against the *n*
Jer 31:36 from being a *n* before me for ever
Jer 33:24 should be no more a *n* before them
Jer 48:2 let us cut it off from being a *n*
Jer 49:31 get you up unto the wealthy *n*
Jer 49:36 there shall be no *n* whither the
Jer 50:3 there cometh up a *n* against her
Jer 50:41 come from the north, and a great *n*
Lam 4:17 for a *n* that could not save us
Eze 2:3 to a rebellious *n* that hath
Eze 37:22 I will make them one *n* in the
Dan 3:29 a decree, That every people, *n*
Dan 8:22 shall stand up out of the *n*
Dan 12:1 was a *n* even to that same time
Joel 1:6 For a *n* is come up upon my land,
Amos 6:14 I will raise up against you a *n*
Mic 4:3 *n* shall not lift up a sword
Mic 4:3 not lift up a sword against *n*
Mic 4:7 that was cast far off a strong *n*
Hab 1:6 Chaldeans, that bitter and hasty *n*
Zeph 2:1 gather together, O *n* not desired
Zeph 2:5 coast, the *n* of the Cherethites
Hag 2:14 people, and so is this *n* before me
Mal 3:9 have robbed me, even this whole *n*
Mt 21:43 given to a *n* bringing forth the
Mt 24:7 For *n* shall rise against *n*,
Mk 7:26 was a Greek, a Syrophenician by *n*
Mk 13:8 For *n* shall rise against *n*,
Lk 7:5 For he loveth our *n*, and he hath
Lk 21:10 *N* shall rise against *n*, and
Lk 23:2 this fellow perverting the *n*
Jn 11:48 and take away both our place and *n*
Jn 11:50 and that the whole *n* perish not
Jn 11:51 that Jesus should die for that *n*
Jn 11:52 And not for that *n* only, but that
Jn 18:35 Thine own *n* and the chief priests
Acts 2:5 men, out of every *n* under heaven
Acts 7:7 the *n* to whom they shall be in
Acts 10:22 among all the *n* of the Jews
Acts 10:28 or come unto one of another *n*
Acts 10:35 But in every *n* he that feareth
Acts 24:2 unto this *n* by thy providence
Acts 24:10 of many years a judge unto this *n*
Acts 24:17 I came to bring alms to my *n*
Acts 26:4 among mine own *n* at Jerusalem
Acts 28:19 I had ought to accuse my *n* of
Rom 10:19 by a foolish *n* I will anger you
Gal 1:14 many my equals in mine own *n*
Phil 2:15 midst of a crooked and perverse *n*
1Pet 2:9 a royal priesthood, an holy *n*
Rev 5:9 and tongue, and people, and *n*
Rev 14:6 dwell on the earth, and to every *n*

**NATIONS**

Gen 10:5 after their families, in their *n*
Gen 10:20 in their countries, and in their *n*
Gen 10:31 in their lands, after their *n*
Gen 10:32 their generations, in their *n*
Gen 10:32 by these were the *n* divided in
Gen 14:1 king of Elam, and Tidal king of *n*
Gen 14:9 of Elam, and with Tidal king of *n*
Gen 17:4 thou shalt be a father of many *n*
Gen 17:5 father of many *n* have I made thee
Gen 17:6 and I will make *n* of thee
Gen 17:16 and she shall be a mother of *n*
Gen 18:18 all the *n* of the earth shall be
Gen 22:18 all the *n* of the earth be blessed
Gen 25:16 princes according to their *n*
Gen 25:23 Two *n* are in thy womb, and two
Gen 26:4 all the *n* of the earth be blessed
Gen 27:29 serve thee, and *n* bow down to thee
Gen 35:11 a company of *n* shall be of thee,
Gen 48:19 shall become a multitude of *n*
Ex 34:24 I will cast out the *n* before thee
Lev 18:24 for in all these the *n* are
Lev 18:28 as it spued out the *n* that were
Num 14:15 then the *n* which have heard the
Num 23:9 shall not be reckoned among the *n*
Num 24:8 he shall eat up the *n* his enemies
Num 24:20 Amalek was the first of the *n*
Deut 2:25 the fear of thee upon the *n* that
Deut 4:6 in the sight of the *n*, which
Deut 4:19 unto all *n* under the whole heaven
Deut 4:27 shall scatter you among the *n*
Deut 4:38 To drive out *n* from before thee
Deut 7:1 hath cast out many *n* before thee
Deut 7:1 seven *n* greater and mightier than
Deut 7:17 heart, These *n* are more than I
Deut 7:22 out those *n* before thee by little
Deut 8:20 As the *n* which the LORD
Deut 9:1 to go in to possess *n* greater
Deut 9:4 *n* the LORD doth drive them out
Deut 9:5 *n* the LORD thy God doth drive
Deut 11:23 out all these *n* from before you
Deut 11:23 and ye shall possess greater *n*
Deut 12:2 wherein the *n* which ye shall
Deut 12:29 cut off the *n* from before thee
Deut 12:30 How did these *n* serve their gods
Deut 14:2 above all the *n* that are upon the
Deut 15:6 and thou shalt lend unto many *n*
Deut 15:6 and thou shalt reign over many *n*
Deut 17:14 like as all the *n* that are about
Deut 18:9 after the abominations of those *n*
Deut 18:14 For these *n*, which thou shalt
Deut 19:1 LORD thy God hath cut off the *n*
Deut 20:15 are not of the cities of these *n*
Deut 26:19 above all *n* which he hath made
Deut 28:1 on high above all *n* of the earth
Deut 28:12 and thou shalt lend unto many *n*
Deut 28:37 among all *n* whither the LORD
Deut 28:65 among these *n* shalt thou find no
Deut 29:16 through the *n* which ye passed by
Deut 29:18 go and serve the gods of these *n*
Deut 29:24 Even all *n* shall say, Wherefore
Deut 30:1 call them to mind among all the *n*
Deut 30:3 and gather thee from all the *n*
Deut 31:3 destroy these *n* from before thee
Deut 32:8 to the *n* their inheritance
Deut 32:43 Rejoice, O ye *n*, with his people
Josh 12:23 the king of the *n* of Gilgal
Josh 23:3 unto all these *n* because of you
Josh 23:4 you by lot these *n* that remain
Josh 23:4 with all the *n* that I have cut
Josh 23:7 That ye come not among these *n*
Josh 23:9 out from before you great *n*
Josh 23:12 unto the remnant of these *n*
Josh 23:13 any of these *n* from before you

Judg 2:21 *n* which Joshua left when he died
Judg 2:23 Therefore the LORD left those *n*
Judg 3:1 Now these are the *n* which the
1Sa 8:5 a king to judge us like all the *n*
1Sa 8:20 we also may be like all the *n*
1Sa 27:8 for those *n* were of old the
2Sa 7:23 to thee from Egypt, from the *n*
2Sa 8:11 of all *n* which he subdued
1Kin 4:31 his fame was in all *n* round about
1Kin 11:2 Of the *n* concerning which the
1Kin 14:24 *n* which the LORD cast out before
2Kin 17:26 The *n* which thou hast removed, and
2Kin 17:33 after the manner of the *n* whom
2Kin 17:41 So these *n* feared the LORD, and
2Kin 18:33 Hath any of the gods of the *n*
2Kin 19:12 Have the gods of the *n* delivered
2Kin 19:17 of Assyria have destroyed the *n*
2Kin 21:9 to do more evil than did the *n*
1Chr 14:17 the fear of him upon all *n*
1Chr 16:24 his marvellous works among all *n*
1Chr 16:31 and let men say among the *n*
1Chr 17:21 by driving out *n* from before thy
1Chr 18:11 that he brought from all these *n*
2Chr 7:20 a proverb and a byword among all *n*
2Chr 13:9 manner of the *n* of other lands
2Chr 32:13 were the gods of the *n* of those
2Chr 32:14 those *n* that my fathers utterly
2Chr 32:17 As the gods of the *n* of other
2Chr 32:23 sight of all *n* from thenceforth
Ezr 4:10 the rest of the *n* whom the great
Neh 1:8 scatter you abroad among the *n*
Neh 9:22 thou gavest them kingdoms and *n*
Neh 13:26 yet among many *n* was there no
Job 12:23 He increaseth the *n*, and
Job 12:23 he enlargeth the *n*, and
Ps 9:17 all the *n* that forget God
Ps 9:20 that the *n* may know themselves to
Ps 22:27 all the kindreds of the *n* shall
Ps 22:28 and he is the governor among the *n*
Ps 47:3 under us, and the *n* under our feet
Ps 57:9 I will sing unto thee among the *n*
Ps 66:7 his eyes behold the *n*
Ps 67:2 thy saving health among all *n*
Ps 67:4 O let the *n* be glad and sing for
Ps 67:4 and govern the *n* upon earth
Ps 72:11 all *n* shall serve him
Ps 72:17 all *n* shall call him blessed
Ps 82:8 for thou shalt inherit all *n*
Ps 86:9 All *n* whom thou hast made shall
Ps 96:5 all the gods of the *n* are idols
Ps 106:27 their seed also among the *n*
Ps 106:34 They did not destroy the *n*
Ps 108:3 praises unto thee among the *n*
Ps 113:4 The LORD is high above all *n*
Ps 117:1 O praise the LORD, all ye *n*
Ps 118:10 All *n* compassed me about
Ps 135:10 Who smote great *n*, and slew mighty
Prov 24:24 people curse, *n* shall abhor him
Is 2:2 and all *n* shall flow unto it
Is 2:4 And he shall judge among the *n*
Is 5:26 up an ensign to the *n* from far
Is 9:1 Jordan, in Galilee of the *n*
Is 10:7 to destroy and cut off *n* not a few
Is 11:12 shall set up an ensign for the *n*
Is 13:4 kingdoms of *n* gathered together
Is 14:6 he that ruled the *n* in anger
Is 14:9 thrones all the kings of the *n*
Is 14:12 ground, which didst weaken the *n*
Is 14:18 All the kings of the *n*, even all
Is 14:26 is stretched out upon all the *n*
Is 17:12 and to the rushing of *n*, that make
Is 17:13 The *n* shall rush like the rushing
Is 23:3 and she is a mart of *n*
Is 25:3 of the terrible *n* shall fear thee
Is 25:7 vail that is spread over all *n*
Is 29:7 the *n* that fight against Ariel
Is 29:8 the multitude of all the *n* be
Is 30:28 to sift the *n* with the sieve of
Is 33:3 of thyself the *n* were scattered
Is 34:1 Come near, ye *n*, to hear
Is 34:2 of the LORD is upon all *n*
Is 36:18 Hath any of the gods of the *n*
Is 37:12 Have the gods of the *n* delivered
Is 37:18 Assyria have laid waste all the *n*
Is 40:15 the *n* are as a drop of a bucket,
Is 40:17 All *n* before him are as nothing
Is 41:2 gave the *n* before him, and made
Is 43:9 Let all the *n* be gathered
Is 45:1 holden, to subdue *n* before him
Is 45:20 ye that are escaped of the *n*
Is 52:10 holy arm in the eyes of all the *n*
Is 52:15 So shall he sprinkle many *n*
Is 55:5 *n* that knew not thee shall run
Is 60:12 those *n* shall be utterly wasted
Is 61:11 to spring forth before all the *n*
Is 64:2 that the *n* may tremble at thy
Is 66:18 come, that I will gather all *n*
Is 66:19 that escape of them unto the *n*
Is 66:20 the LORD out of all *n* upon horses
Jer 1:5 thee a prophet unto the *n*
Jer 1:10 have this day set thee over the *n*
Jer 3:17 all the *n* shall be gathered unto
Jer 3:19 goodly heritage of the hosts of *n*
Jer 4:2 the *n* shall bless themselves in
Jer 4:16 Make ye mention to the *n*
Jer 6:18 Therefore hear, ye *n*, and know, O
Jer 9:26 for all these *n* are uncircumcised
Jer 10:7 would not fear thee, O King of *n*
Jer 10:7 among all the wise men of the *n*
Jer 10:10 the *n* shall not be able to abide
Jer 22:8 many *n* shall pass by this city,
Jer 25:9 against all these *n* round about
Jer 25:11 these *n* shall serve the king of
Jer 25:13 hath prophesied against all the *n*
Jer 25:14 For many *n* and great kings shall
Jer 25:15 at my hand, and cause all the *n*
Jer 25:17 hand, and made all the *n* to drink
Jer 25:31 hath a controversy with the *n*
Jer 26:6 a curse to all the *n* of the earth
Jer 27:7 all *n* shall serve him, and his son
Jer 27:7 and then many *n* and great kings
Jer 27:11 But the *n* that bring their neck
Jer 28:11 *n* within the space of two full
Jer 28:14 iron upon the neck of all these *n*
Jer 29:14 I will gather you from all the *n*
Jer 29:18 among all the *n* whither I have
Jer 30:11 *n* whither I have scattered thee
Jer 31:7 and shout among the chief of the *n*
Jer 31:10 Hear the word of the LORD, O ye *n*
Jer 33:9 before all the *n* of the earth
Jer 36:2 Judah, and against all the *n*
Jer 43:5 that were returned from all *n*
Jer 44:8 among all the *n* of the earth
Jer 46:12 The *n* have heard of thy shame, and
Jer 46:28 the *n* whither I have driven thee
Jer 50:2 Declare ye among the *n*, and
Jer 50:9 of great *n* from the north country
Jer 50:12 of the *n* shall be a wilderness
Jer 50:23 become a desolation among the *n*
Jer 50:46 and the cry is heard among the *n*
Jer 51:7 the *n* have drunken of her wine
Jer 51:7 therefore the *n* are mad
Jer 51:20 thee will I break in pieces the *n*
Jer 51:27 blow the trumpet among the *n*
Jer 51:27 prepare the *n* against her
Jer 51:28 Prepare against her the *n* with
Jer 51:41 an astonishment among the *n*
Jer 51:44 the *n* shall not flow together any
Lam 1:1 she that was great among the *n*
Eze 5:5 have set it in the midst of the *n*
Eze 5:6 into wickedness more than the *n*
Eze 5:7 the *n* that are round about you
Eze 5:7 to the judgments of the *n* that
Eze 5:8 of thee in the sight of the *n*
Eze 5:14 a reproach among the *n* that are
Eze 5:15 an astonishment unto the *n* that
Eze 6:8 escape the sword among the *n*
Eze 6:9 *n* whither they shall be carried
Eze 12:15 I shall scatter them among the *n*
Eze 19:4 The *n* also heard of him
Eze 19:8 Then the *n* set against him on
Eze 25:10 may not be remembered among the *n*
Eze 26:3 will cause many *n* to come up
Eze 26:5 it shall become a spoil to the *n*
Eze 28:7 upon thee, the terrible of the *n*
Eze 29:12 scatter the Egyptians among the *n*
Eze 29:15 exalt itself any more above the *n*
Eze 29:15 shall no more rule over the *n*
Eze 30:11 with him, the terrible of the *n*
Eze 30:23 scatter the Egyptians among the *n*
Eze 30:26 scatter the Egyptians among the *n*
Eze 31:6 his shadow dwelt all great *n*
Eze 31:12 strangers, the terrible of the *n*
Eze 31:16 I made the *n* to shake at the
Eze 32:2 art like a young lion of the *n*
Eze 32:9 bring thy destruction among the *n*
Eze 32:12 to fall, the terrible of the *n*
Eze 32:16 of the *n* shall lament her
Eze 32:18 and the daughters of the famous *n*
Eze 35:10 thou hast said, These two *n*
Eze 36:13 up men, and hast bereaved thy *n*
Eze 36:14 neither bereave thy *n* any more
Eze 36:15 thou cause thy *n* to fall any more
Eze 37:22 and they shall be no more two *n*
Eze 38:8 it is brought forth out of the *n*
Eze 38:12 that are gathered out of the *n*
Eze 38:23 be known in the eyes of many *n*
Eze 39:27 in them in the sight of many *n*
Dan 3:4 you it is commanded, O people, *n*
Dan 3:7 of musick, all the people, the *n*
Dan 4:1 the king, unto all people, *n*
Dan 5:19 that he gave him, all people, *n*
Dan 6:25 Darius wrote unto all people, *n*
Dan 7:14 and a kingdom, that all people, *n*
Hos 8:10 they have hired among the *n*
Hos 9:17 shall be wanderers among the *n*
Joel 3:2 I will also gather all *n*, and will
Joel 3:2 they have scattered among the *n*
Amos 6:1 which are named chief of the *n*
Amos 9:9 the house of Israel among all *n*
Mic 4:2 many *n* shall come, and say, Come,
Mic 4:3 and rebuke strong *n* afar off
Mic 4:11 Now also many *n* are gathered
Mic 7:16 The *n* shall see and be confounded
Nah 3:4 that selleth *n* through her
Nah 3:5 I will shew the *n* thy nakedness
Hab 1:17 spare continually to slay the *n*
Hab 2:5 but gathereth unto him all *n*
Hab 2:8 Because thou hast spoiled many *n*
Hab 3:6 he beheld, and drove asunder the *n*
Zeph 2:14 of her, all the beasts of the *n*
Zeph 3:6 I have cut off the *n*
Zeph 3:8 determination is to gather the *n*
Hag 2:7 I will shake all *n*
Hag 2:7 and the desire of all *n* shall come
Zec 2:8 me unto the *n* which spoiled you
Zec 2:11 many *n* shall be joined to the
Zec 7:14 all the *n* whom they knew not
Zec 8:22 strong *n* shall come to seek the
Zec 8:23 out of all languages of the *n*
Zec 12:9 the *n* that come against Jerusalem
Zec 14:2 For I will gather all *n* against
Zec 14:3 forth, and fight against those *n*
Zec 14:16 one that is left of all the *n*
Zec 14:19 the punishment of all *n* that come
Mal 3:12 all *n* shall call you blessed
Mt 24:9 hated of all *n* for my name's sake
Mt 24:14 world for a witness unto all *n*
Mt 25:32 him shall be gathered all *n*
Mt 28:19 Go ye therefore, and teach all *n*
Mk 11:17 of all *n* the house of prayer
Mk 13:10 first be published among all *n*
Lk 12:30 do the *n* of the world seek after
Lk 21:24 be led away captive into all *n*
Lk 21:25 and upon the earth distress of *n*
Lk 24:47 preached in his name among all *n*
Acts 13:19 seven *n* in the land of Chanaan
Acts 14:16 all *n* to walk in their own ways
Acts 17:26 hath made of one blood all *n* of
Rom 1:5 to the faith among all *n*, for his
Rom 4:17 have made thee a father of many *n*
Rom 4:18 might become the father of many *n*
Rom 16:26 made known to all *n* for the
Gal 3:8 In thee shall all *n* be blessed
Rev 2:26 him will I give power over the *n*
Rev 7:9 no man could number, of all *n*
Rev 10:11 again before many peoples, and *n*
Rev 11:9 *n* shall see their dead bodies
Rev 11:18 the *n* were angry, and thy wrath is
Rev 12:5 to rule all *n* with a rod of iron
Rev 13:7 all kindreds, and tongues, and *n*
Rev 14:8 because she made all *n* drink of
Rev 15:4 for all *n* shall come and worship
Rev 16:19 and the cities of the *n* fell
Rev 17:15 are peoples, and multitudes, and *n*
Rev 18:3 For all *n* have drunk of the wine
Rev 18:23 thy sorceries were all *n* deceived
Rev 19:15 with it he should smite the *n*
Rev 20:3 he should deceive the *n* no more
Rev 20:8 shall go out to deceive the *n*
Rev 21:24 the *n* of them which are saved
Rev 21:26 glory and honour of the *n* into it
Rev 22:2 were for the healing of the *n*

## NATIVITY

Gen 11:28 father Terah in the land of his *n*
Ruth 2:11 thy mother, and the land of thy *n*
Jer 46:16 people, and to the land of our *n*
Eze 16:3 thy *n* is of the land of Canaan
Eze 16:4 And as for thy *n*, in the day thou

Eze 21:30 created, in the land of thy *n*
Eze 23:15 of Chaldea, the land of their *n*

**NATURAL**
Deut 34:7 not dim, nor his *n* force abated
Rom 1:26 *n* use into that which is against
Rom 1:27 leaving the *n* use of the woman,
Rom 1:31 without *n* affection, implacable,
Rom 11:21 if God spared not the *n* branches
Rom 11:24 these, which be the *n* branches
1Cor 2:14 But the *n* man receiveth not the
1Cor 15:44 It is sown a *n* body
1Cor 15:44 There is a *n* body, and there is a
1Cor 15:46 is spiritual, but that which is *n*
2Ti 3:3 Without *n* affection,
Jas 1:23 beholding his *n* face in a glass
2Pet 2:12 as *n* brute beasts, made to be

**NATURE**
Rom 1:26 use into that which is against *n*
Rom 2:14 do by *n* the things contained in
Rom 2:27 not uncircumcision which is by *n*
Rom 11:24 the olive tree which is wild by *n*
Rom 11:24 to *n* into a good olive tree
1Cor 11:14 Doth not even *n* itself teach you,
Gal 2:15 We who are Jews by *n*, and not
Gal 4:8 unto them which by *n* are no gods
Eph 2:3 were by *n* the children of wrath,
Heb 2:16 took not on him the *n* of angels
Jas 3:6 setteth on fire the course of *n*
2Pet 1:4 be partakers of the divine *n*

**NAUGHTINESS**
1Sa 17:28 pride, and the *n* of thine heart
Prov 11:6 shall be taken in their own *n*
Jas 1:21 filthiness and superfluity of *n*

**NAUM** *(na'-um)* See NAHUM. *Father of Amos; ancestor of Jesus.*
Lk 3:25 of Amos, which was the son of *N*

**NAVEL**
Job 40:16 force is in the *n* of his belly
Prov 3:8 It shall be health to thy *n*
Song 7:2 Thy *n* is like a round goblet,
Eze 16:4 thou wast born thy *n* was not cut

**NAVY**
1Kin 9:26 king Solomon made a *n* of ships in
1Kin 9:27 Hiram sent in the *n* his servants
1Kin 10:11 the *n* also of Hiram, that brought
1Kin 10:22 For the king had at sea a *n* of
1Kin 10:22 of Tharshish with the *n* of Hiram
1Kin 10:22 years came the *n* of Tharshish

**NAY**
Gen 18:15 And he said, *N*; but thou didst
Gen 19:2 And they said, *N*; but we will
Gen 23:11 *N*, my lord, hear me
Gen 33:10 And Jacob said, *N*, I pray thee, if
Gen 42:10 And they said unto him, *N*, my lord
Gen 42:12 And he said unto them, *N*, but to
Num 22:30 And he said, *N*.
Josh 5:14 And he said, *N*; but as captain
Josh 24:21 And the people said unto Joshua, *N*
Judg 12:5 If he said, *N*
Judg 19:23 unto them, and said unto them, *N*
Judg 19:23 my brethren, *n*, I pray you
Ruth 1:13 *n*, my daughters; for it
1Sa 2:16 then he would answer him, *N*
1Sa 2:24 *N*, my sons; for it is
1Sa 8:19 and they said, *N*; but we will
1Sa 10:19 and ye have said unto him, *N*
1Sa 12:12 against you, ye said unto me, *N*
2Sa 13:12 And she answered him, *N*, my
2Sa 13:25 And the king said to Absalom, *N*
2Sa 16:18 And Hushai said unto Absalom, *N*
2Sa 24:24 And the king said unto Araunah, *N*
1Kin 2:17 king, (for he will not say thee *n*
1Kin 2:20 I pray thee, say me not *n*
1Kin 2:20 for I will not say thee *n*
1Kin 2:30 And he said, *N*; but I
1Kin 3:22 And the other woman said, *N*
1Kin 3:23 and the other saith, *N*
2Kin 3:13 king of Israel said unto him, *N*
2Kin 4:16 And she said, *N*, my lord, thou man
2Kin 20:10 *n*, but let the shadow return
1Chr 21:24 And king David said to Ornan, *N*
Jer 6:15 *n*, they were not at all ashamed,
Jer 8:12 *n*, they were not at all ashamed,
Mt 5:37 be, Yea, yea; *N*, *n*
Mt 13:29 But he said, *N*; lest while
Lk 12:51 I tell you, *N*; but rather
Lk 13:3 I tell you, *N*: but, except
Lk 13:5 I tell you, *N*: but, except
Lk 16:30 And he said, *N*, father Abraham
Jn 7:12 others said, *N*; but he
Acts 16:37 *n* verily; but let them
Rom 3:27 *N*: but by the law
Rom 7:7 *N*, I had not known sin, but by
Rom 8:37 *N*, in all these things we are
Rom 9:20 *N* but, O man, who art thou that
1Cor 6:8 *N*, ye do wrong, and defraud, and
1Cor 12:22 *N*, much more those members of the
2Cor 1:17 there should be yea yea, and *n n*
2Cor 1:18 word toward you was not yea and *n*
2Cor 1:19 and Timotheus, was not yea and *n*
Jas 5:12 be yea; and your *n*, *n*

**NAZARENE** *(naz-a-reen')* See NAZARENES. *Native to Nazareth.*
Mt 2:23 prophets, He shall be called a *N*

**NAZARENES** *(naz-a-reens')*
Acts 24:5 a ringleader of the sect of the *N*

**NAZARETH** *(naz'-a-reth)* See NAZARENE. *A city in Galilee.*
Mt 2:23 came and dwelt in a city called *N*
Mt 4:13 And leaving *N*, he came and dwelt in
Mt 21:11 Jesus the prophet of *N* of Galilee
Mt 26:71 fellow was also with Jesus of *N*
Mk 1:9 that Jesus came from *N* of Galilee
Mk 1:24 to do with thee, thou Jesus of *N*
Mk 10:47 he heard that it was Jesus of *N*
Mk 14:67 And thou also wast with Jesus of *N*
Mk 16:6 Ye seek Jesus of *N*, which was
Lk 1:26 unto a city of Galilee, named *N*
Lk 2:4 Galilee, out of the city of *N*
Lk 2:39 into Galilee, to their own city *N*
Lk 2:51 went down with them, and came to *N*
Lk 4:16 And he came to *N*, where he had
Lk 4:34 to do with thee, thou Jesus of *N*
Lk 18:37 him, that Jesus of *N* passeth by
Lk 24:19 unto him, Concerning Jesus of *N*
Jn 1:45 prophets, did write, Jesus of *N*
Jn 1:46 any good thing come out of *N*
Jn 18:5 They answered him, Jesus of *N*
Jn 18:7 And they said, Jesus of *N*
Jn 19:19 JESUS OF *N* THE KING OF THE
Acts 2:22 Jesus of *N*, a man approved of God
Acts 3:6 name of Jesus Christ of *N* rise up
Acts 4:10 by the name of Jesus Christ of *N*
Acts 6:14 that this Jesus of *N* shall
Acts 10:38 Jesus of *N* with the Holy Ghost
Acts 22:8 he said unto me, I am Jesus of *N*
Acts 26:9 to the name of Jesus of *N*

**NAZARITE** *(naz'-a-rite)* See NAZARITES. *Title applied to one making a special vow of abstention.*
Num 6:2 themselves to vow a vow of a *N*
Num 6:13 And this is the law of the *N*
Num 6:18 the *N* shall shave the head of his
Num 6:19 put them upon the hands of the *N*
Num 6:20 after that the *N* may drink wine
Num 6:21 the law of the *N* who hath vowed
Judg 13:5 be a *N* unto God from the womb
Judg 13:7 for the child shall be a *N* to God
Judg 16:17 for I have been a *N* unto God from

**NAZARITES** *(naz'-a-rites)*
Lam 4:7 Her *N* were purer than snow, they
Amos 2:11 and of your young men for *N*
Amos 2:12 But ye gave the *N* wine to drink

**NEAH** *(ne'-ah) A city in Zebulun.*
Josh 19:13 goeth out to Remmon-methoar to *N*

**NEAPOLIS** *(ne-ap'-o-lis) A Macedonian seaport.*
Acts 16:11 Samothracia, and the next day to *N*

**NEARIAH** *(ne-a-ri'-ah)* See NAGGE.
*1. A son of Shemiah.*
1Chr 3:22 and Igeal, and Bariah, and *N*
1Chr 3:23 And the sons of *N*
*2. A son of Ishi.*
1Chr 4:42 for their captains Pelatiah, and *N*

**NEBAI** *(ne'-bahee) A renewer of the covenant.*
Neh 10:19 Hariph, Anathoth, *N*,

**NEBAIOTH** *(ne-bah'-yoth)* See NEBAJOTH.
*1. A son of Ishmael.*
1Chr 1:29 The firstborn of Ishmael, *N*
*2. Descendants of Ishmael.*
Is 60:7 the rams of *N* shall minister unto

**NEBAJOTH** *(ne-ba'-joth)* See NEBAIOTH. *Same as Nebaioth 1.*
Gen 25:13 the firstborn of Ishmael, *N*
Gen 28:9 Abraham's son, the sister of *N*
Gen 36:3 Ishmael's daughter, sister of *N*

**NEBALLAT** *(ne-bal'-lat) A Benjamite city.*
Neh 11:34 Hadid, Zeboim, *N*,

**NEBAT** *(ne'-bat) Father of King Jeroboam.*
1Kin 11:26 And Jeroboam the son of *N*, an
1Kin 12:2 pass, when Jeroboam the son of *N*
1Kin 12:15 unto Jeroboam the son of *N*
1Kin 15:1 of *N* reigned Abijam over Judah
1Kin 16:3 house of Jeroboam the son of *N*
1Kin 16:26 the way of Jeroboam the son of *N*
1Kin 16:31 the sins of Jeroboam the son of *N*
1Kin 21:22 house of Jeroboam the son of *N*
1Kin 22:52 the way of Jeroboam the son of *N*
2Kin 3:3 the sins of Jeroboam the son of *N*
2Kin 9:9 house of Jeroboam the son of *N*
2Kin 10:29 the sins of Jeroboam the son of *N*
2Kin 13:2 the sins of Jeroboam the son of *N*
2Kin 13:11 the sins of Jeroboam the son of *N*
2Kin 14:24 the sins of Jeroboam the son of *N*
2Kin 15:9 the sins of Jeroboam the son of *N*
2Kin 15:18 the sins of Jeroboam the son of *N*
2Kin 15:24 the sins of Jeroboam the son of *N*
2Kin 15:28 the sins of Jeroboam the son of *N*
2Kin 17:21 made Jeroboam the son of *N* king
2Kin 23:15 place which Jeroboam the son of *N*
2Chr 9:29 against Jeroboam the son of *N*
2Chr 10:2 pass, when Jeroboam the son of *N*
2Chr 10:15 to Jeroboam the son of *N*
2Chr 13:6 Yet Jeroboam the son of *N*

**NEBO** *(ne'-bo)* See PISGAH, SAMGAR-NEBO.
*1. A city in Reuben.*
Num 32:3 and Elealeh, and Shebam, and *N*
Num 32:38 And *N*, and Baal-meon, (their names
Num 33:47 the mountains of Abarim, before *N*
1Chr 5:8 who dwelt in Aroer, even unto *N*
Is 15:2 Moab shall howl over *N*, and over
Jer 48:1 Woe unto *N*
Jer 48:22 And upon Dibon, and upon *N*,
*2. A mountain east of the Jordan.*
Deut 32:49 mountain Abarim, unto mount *N*
Deut 34:1 of Moab unto the mountain of *N*
*3. A city in Judah.*
Ezr 2:29 The children of *N*, fifty and two
Neh 7:33 The men of the other *N*, fifty and
*4. A Chaldean idol.*
Is 46:1 *N* stoopeth, their idols were upon
*5. Father of several who married foreigners.*
Ezr 10:43 Of the sons of *N*

**NEBUCHADNEZZAR** *(neb-u-kad-nez'-zar)* See NEBUCHADREZZAR. *King of Babylon.*
2Kin 24:1 In his days *N* king of Babylon
2Kin 24:10 At that time the servants of *N*
2Kin 24:11 *N* king of Babylon came against
2Kin 25:1 that *N* king of Babylon came, he,
2Kin 25:8 year of king *N* king of Babylon
2Kin 25:22 whom *N* king of Babylon had left,
1Chr 6:15 and Jerusalem by the hand of *N*
2Chr 36:6 him came up *N* king of Babylon
2Chr 36:7 *N* also carried of the vessels of
2Chr 36:10 the year was expired, king *N* sent
2Chr 36:13 he also rebelled against king *N*
Ezr 1:7 which *N* had brought forth out of
Ezr 2:1 whom *N* the king of Babylon had
Ezr 5:12 the hand of *N* the king of Babylon
Ezr 5:14 which *N* took out of the temple
Ezr 6:5 which *N* took forth out of the
Neh 7:6 whom *N* the king of Babylon had
Est 2:6 whom *N* the king of Babylon had
Jer 27:6 the hand of *N* the king of Babylon
Jer 27:8 the same *N* the king of Babylon
Jer 27:20 Which *N* king of Babylon took not,
Jer 28:3 that *N* king of Babylon took away
Jer 28:11 so will I break the yoke of *N*
Jer 28:14 they may serve *N* king of Babylon
Jer 29:1 to all the people whom *N* had
Jer 29:3 to *N* king of Babylon) saying
Jer 34:1 when *N* king of Babylon, and all
Jer 39:5 they brought him up to *N* king of
Dan 1:1 *N* king of Babylon unto Jerusalem
Dan 1:18 eunuchs brought them in before *N*
Dan 2:1 the second year of the reign of *N*
Dan 2:1 *N* dreamed dreams, wherewith his

Dan 2:28 maketh known to the king *N* what
Dan 2:46 Then the king *N* fell upon his
Dan 3:1 *N* the king made an image of gold,
Dan 3:2 Then *N* the king sent to gather
Dan 3:2 image which *N* the king had set up
Dan 3:3 image that *N* the king had set up
Dan 3:3 the image that *N* had set up
Dan 3:5 image that *N* the king hath set up
Dan 3:7 image that *N* the king had set up
Dan 3:9 They spake and said to the king *N*
Dan 3:13 Then *N* in his rage and fury
Dan 3:14 *N* spake and said unto them, Is it
Dan 3:16 answered and said to the king, O *N*
Dan 3:19 Then was *N* full of fury, and the
Dan 3:24 Then *N* the king was astonied, and
Dan 3:26 Then *N* came near to the mouth of
Dan 3:28 Then *N* spake, and said, Blessed be
Dan 4:1 *N* the king, unto all people,
Dan 4:4 I *N* was at rest in mine house, and
Dan 4:18 This dream I king *N* have seen
Dan 4:28 All this came upon the king *N*
Dan 4:31 from heaven, saying, O king *N*
Dan 4:33 was the thing fulfilled upon *N*
Dan 4:34 at the end of the days I *N* lifted
Dan 4:37 Now I *N* praise and extol and honour
Dan 5:2 *N* had taken out of the temple
Dan 5:11 whom the king *N* thy father
Dan 5:18 God gave *N* thy father a kingdom

**NEBUCHADREZZAR** *(neb-u-kad-rez'-zar)* See NEBUCHADNEZZAR. *Same as Nebuchadnezzar.*

Jer 21:2 for *N* king of Babylon maketh war
Jer 21:7 the hand of *N* king of Babylon
Jer 22:25 the hand of *N* king of Babylon
Jer 24:1 after that *N* king of Babylon had
Jer 25:1 first year of *N* king of Babylon
Jer 25:9 *N* the king of Babylon, my servant
Jer 29:21 the hand of *N* king of Babylon
Jer 32:1 was the eighteenth year of *N*
Jer 32:28 the hand of *N* king of Babylon
Jer 35:11 when *N* king of Babylon came up
Jer 37:1 whom *N* king of Babylon made king
Jer 39:1 came *N* king of Babylon and all his
Jer 39:11 Now *N* king of Babylon gave charge
Jer 43:10 take *N* the king of Babylon, my
Jer 44:30 the hand of *N* king of Babylon
Jer 46:2 which *N* king of Babylon smote in
Jer 46:13 how *N* king of Babylon should come
Jer 46:26 the hand of *N* king of Babylon
Jer 49:28 which *N* king of Babylon shall
Jer 49:30 for *N* king of Babylon hath taken
Jer 50:17 last this *N* king of Babylon hath
Jer 51:34 *N* the king of Babylon hath
Jer 52:4 that *N* king of Babylon came, he
Jer 52:12 year of *N* king of Babylon
Jer 52:28 whom *N* carried away captive
Jer 52:29 In the eighteenth year of *N* he
Jer 52:30 twentieth year of *N* Nebuzar-adan
Eze 26:7 upon Tyrus *N* king of Babylon
Eze 29:18 *N* king of Babylon caused his army
Eze 29:19 of Egypt unto *N* king of Babylon
Eze 30:10 by the hand of *N* king of Babylon

**NEBUSHASBAN** *(neb-u-shas'-ban) A Babylonian prince.*

Jer 39:13 captain of the guard sent, and *N*

**NEBUZAR-ADAN** *(neb-u-zar'-a-dan) Commander of Nebuchadnezzar's army.*

2Kin 25:8 king of Babylon, came *N*, captain
2Kin 25:11 did *N* the captain of the guard
2Kin 25:20 *N* captain of the guard took these
Jer 39:9 Then *N* the captain of the guard
Jer 39:10 But *N* the captain of the guard
Jer 39:11 to *N* the captain of the guard
Jer 39:13 So *N* the captain of the guard
Jer 40:1 after that *N* the captain of the
Jer 41:10 whom *N* the captain of the guard
Jer 43:6 every person that *N* the captain
Jer 52:12 king of Babylon, came *N*, captain
Jer 52:15 Then *N* the captain of the guard
Jer 52:16 But *N* the captain of the guard
Jer 52:26 So *N* the captain of the guard
Jer 52:30 year of Nebuchadrezzar *N* the

**NECESSARY**

Job 23:12 of his mouth more than my *n* food
Acts 13:46 It was *n* that the word of God
Acts 15:28 burden than these *n* things
Acts 28:10 us with such things as were *n*
1Cor 12:22 seem to be more feeble, are *n*
2Cor 9:5 it *n* to exhort the brethren
Phil 2:25 Yet I supposed it *n* to send to
Titus 3:14 to maintain good works for *n* uses
Heb 9:23 It was therefore *n* that the

**NECESSITY**

Lk 23:17 (For of *n* he must release one
Rom 12:13 Distributing to the *n* of saints
1Cor 7:37 in his heart, having no *n*
1Cor 9:16 for *n* is laid upon me
2Cor 9:7 not grudgingly, or of *n*
Phil 4:16 ye sent once and again unto my *n*
Philem 14 should not be as it were of *n*
Heb 7:12 there is made of *n* a change also
Heb 8:3 wherefore it is of *n* that this
Heb 9:16 there must also of *n* be the death

**NECHO** *(ne'-ko)* See PHARAOH-NECHOH. *A king of Egypt.*

2Chr 35:20 *N* king of Egypt came up to fight
2Chr 35:22 words of *N* from the mouth of God
2Chr 36:4 *N* took Jehoahaz his brother, and

**NECK**

Gen 27:16 and upon the smooth of his *n*
Gen 27:40 break his yoke from off thy *n*
Gen 33:4 and embraced him, and fell on his *n*
Gen 41:42 and put a gold chain about his *n*
Gen 45:14 upon his brother Benjamin's *n*
Gen 45:14 and Benjamin wept upon his *n*
Gen 46:29 and he fell on his *n*, and wept on
Gen 46:29 wept on his *n* a good while
Gen 49:8 be in the *n* of thine enemies
Ex 13:13 it, then thou shalt break his *n*
Ex 34:20 not, then shalt thou break his *n*
Lev 5:8 and wring off his head from his *n*
Deut 21:4 heifer's *n* there in the valley
Deut 28:48 put a yoke of iron upon thy *n*
Deut 31:27 thy rebellion, and thy stiff *n*
1Sa 4:18 gate, and his *n* brake, and he died
2Kin 17:14 like to the *n* of their fathers,
2Chr 36:13 but he stiffened his *n*, and
Neh 9:29 the shoulder, and hardened their *n*
Job 15:26 runneth upon him, even on his *n*
Job 16:12 he hath also taken me by my *n*
Job 39:19 thou clothed his *n* with thunder
Job 41:22 In his *n* remaineth strength, and
Ps 75:5 speak not with a stiff *n*
Prov 1:9 thy head, and chains about thy *n*
Prov 3:3 bind them about thy *n*
Prov 3:22 unto thy soul, and grace to thy *n*
Prov 6:21 heart, and tie them about thy *n*
Prov 29:1 often reproved hardeneth his *n*
Song 1:10 thy *n* with chains of gold
Song 4:4 Thy *n* is like the tower of David
Song 4:9 eyes, with one chain of thy *n*
Song 7:4 Thy *n* is as a tower of ivory
Is 8:8 he shall reach even to the *n*
Is 10:27 and his yoke from off thy *n*
Is 30:28 shall reach to the midst of the *n*
Is 48:4 thy *n* is an iron sinew, and thy
Is 52:2 thyself from the bands of thy *n*
Is 66:3 lamb, as if he cut off a dog's *n*
Jer 7:26 their ear, but hardened their *n*
Jer 17:23 their ear, but made their *n* stiff
Jer 27:2 and yokes, and put them upon thy *n*
Jer 27:8 that will not put their *n* under
Jer 27:11 the nations that bring their *n*
Jer 28:10 from off the prophet Jeremiah's *n*
Jer 28:11 king of Babylon from the *n* of all
Jer 28:12 off the *n* of the prophet Jeremiah
Jer 28:14 upon the *n* of all these nations
Jer 30:8 break his yoke from off thy *n*
Lam 1:14 wreathed, and come up upon my *n*
Eze 16:11 thy hands, and a chain on thy *n*
Dan 5:7 have a chain of gold about his *n*
Dan 5:16 have a chain of gold about thy *n*
Dan 5:29 put a chain of gold about his *n*
Hos 10:11 but I passed over upon her fair *n*
Hab 3:13 the foundation unto the *n*
Mt 18:6 millstone were hanged about his *n*
Mk 9:42 millstone were hanged about his *n*
Lk 15:20 and ran, and fell on his *n*
Lk 17:2 millstone were hanged about his *n*
Acts 15:10 yoke upon the *n* of the disciples
Acts 20:37 wept sore, and fell on Paul's *n*

**NECKS**

Josh 10:24 feet upon the *n* of these kings
Josh 10:24 put their feet upon the *n* of them
Judg 5:30 meet for the *n* of them that take
Judg 8:21 that were on their camels' *n*
Judg 8:26 that were about their camels' *n*
2Sa 22:41 given me the *n* of mine enemies
2Kin 17:14 not hear, but hardened their *n*
Neh 3:5 their *n* to the work of their Lord
Neh 9:16 proudly, and hardened their *n*
Neh 9:17 but hardened their *n*, and in their
Ps 18:40 given me the *n* of mine enemies
Is 3:16 and walk with stretched forth *n*
Jer 19:15 they have hardened their *n*
Jer 27:12 Bring your *n* under the yoke of
Lam 5:5 Our *n* are under persecution
Eze 21:29 upon the *n* of them that are slain
Mic 2:3 which ye shall not remove your *n*
Rom 16:4 for my life laid down their own *n*

**NEDABIAH** *(ned-a-bi'-ah) Son of Jeconiah.*

1Chr 3:18 Shenazar, Jecamiah, Hoshama, and *N*

**NEED**

Deut 15:8 lend him sufficient for his *n*
1Sa 21:15 Have I *n* of mad men, that ye have
2Chr 2:16 Lebanon, as much as thou shalt *n*
2Chr 20:17 Ye shall not *n* to fight in this
Ezr 6:9 And that which they have *n* of
Prov 31:11 that he shall have no *n* of spoil
Mt 3:14 I have *n* to be baptized of thee,
Mt 6:8 knoweth what things ye have *n* of
Mt 6:32 ye have *n* of all these things
Mt 9:12 that be whole *n* not a physician
Mt 14:16 said unto them, They *n* not depart
Mt 21:3 say, The Lord hath *n* of them
Mt 26:65 what further *n* have we of
Mk 2:17 whole have no *n* of the physician
Mk 2:25 what David did, when he had *n*
Mk 11:3 ye that the Lord hath *n* of him
Mk 14:63 What *n* we any further witnesses
Lk 5:31 that are whole *n* not a physician
Lk 9:11 healed them that had *n* of healing
Lk 12:30 that ye have *n* of these things
Lk 15:7 persons, which *n* no repentance
Lk 19:31 Because the Lord hath *n* of him
Lk 19:34 they said, The Lord hath *n* of him
Lk 22:71 What *n* we any further witness
Jn 13:29 we have *n* of against the feast
Acts 2:45 to all men, as every man had *n*
Acts 4:35 every man according as he had *n*
Rom 16:2 business she hath *n* of you
1Cor 7:36 *n* so require, let him do what he
1Cor 12:21 the hand, I have no *n* of thee
1Cor 12:21 to the feet, I have no *n* of you
1Cor 12:24 For our comely parts have no *n*
2Cor 3:1 or *n* we, as some others, epistles
Phil 4:12 both to abound and to suffer *n*
Phil 4:19 your *n* according to his riches in
1Th 1:8 so that we *n* not to speak any
1Th 4:9 ye *n* not that I write unto you
1Th 5:1 ye have no *n* that I write unto
Heb 4:16 find grace to help in time of *n*
Heb 5:12 ye have *n* that one teach you
Heb 5:12 are become such as have *n* of milk
Heb 7:11 what further *n* was there that
Heb 10:36 For ye have *n* of patience
1Pet 1:6 though now for a season, if *n* be
1Jn 2:27 ye *n* not that any man teach you
1Jn 3:17 good, and seeth his brother have *n*
Rev 3:17 with goods, and have *n* of nothing
Rev 21:23 And the city had no *n* of the sun
Rev 22:5 they *n* no candle, neither light

**NEEDETH**

Gen 33:15 And he said, What *n* it
Lk 11:8 rise and give him as many as he *n*
Jn 13:10 He that is washed *n* not save to
Eph 4:28 he may have to give to him that *n*
2Ti 2:15 a workman that *n* not to be
Heb 7:27 Who *n* not daily, as those high

**NEEDFUL**

Ezr 7:20 be *n* for the house of thy God
Lk 10:42 But one thing is *n*
Acts 15:5 That it was *n* to circumcise them,
Phil 1:24 in the flesh is more *n* for you
Jas 2:16 things which are *n* to the body
Jude 3 it was *n* for me to write unto you

**NEEDLEWORK**

Ex 26:36 fine twined linen, wrought with *n*
Ex 27:16 fine twined linen, wrought with *n*
Ex 28:39 thou shalt make the girdle of *n*
Ex 36:37 and fine twined linen, of *n*
Ex 38:18 for the gate of the court was *n*
Ex 39:29 blue, and purple, and scarlet, of *n*

Judg 5:30 a prey of divers colours of *n*
Judg 5:30 divers colours of *n* on both sides
Ps 45:14 unto the king in raiment of *n*

**NEEDS**
Gen 17:13 thy money, must *n* be circumcised
Gen 19:9 sojourn, and he will *n* be a judge
Gen 24:5 must I *n* bring thy son again unto
Gen 31:30 though thou wouldest *n* be gone
2Sa 14:14 For we must *n* die, and are as
Jer 10:5 they must *n* be borne, because
Mt 18:7 for it must *n* be that offences
Mk 13:7 for such things must *n* be
Lk 14:18 a piece of ground, and I must *n* go
Jn 4:4 he must *n* go through Samaria
Acts 1:16 must *n* have been fulfilled
Acts 17:3 that Christ must *n* have suffered
Acts 21:22 multitude must *n* come together
Rom 13:5 Wherefore ye must *n* be subject
1Cor 5:10 for then must ye *n* go out of the
2Cor 11:30 If I must *n* glory, I will glory

**NEEDY**
Deut 15:11 brother, to thy poor, and to thy *n*
Deut 24:14 hired servant that is poor and *n*
Job 24:4 They turn the *n* out of the way
Job 24:14 the light killeth the poor and *n*
Ps 9:18 For the *n* shall not alway be
Ps 12:5 poor, for the sighing of the *n*
Ps 35:10 the *n* from him that spoileth him
Ps 37:14 bow, to cast down the poor and *n*
Ps 40:17 But I am poor and *n*
Ps 70:5 But I am poor and *n*
Ps 72:4 shall save the children of the *n*
Ps 72:12 deliver the *n* when he crieth
Ps 72:13 He shall spare the poor and *n*
Ps 72:13 and shall save the souls of the *n*
Ps 74:21 let the poor and *n* praise thy name
Ps 82:3 do justice to the afflicted and *n*
Ps 82:4 Deliver the poor and *n*
Ps 86:1 for I am poor and *n*
Ps 109:16 *n* man, that he might even slay
Ps 109:22 For I am poor and *n*, and my heart
Ps 113:7 lifteth the *n* out of the dunghill
Prov 30:14 earth, and the *n* from among men
Prov 31:9 plead the cause of the poor and *n*
Prov 31:20 reacheth forth her hands to the *n*
Is 10:2 To turn aside the *n* from judgment
Is 14:30 the *n* shall lie down in safety
Is 25:4 strength to the *n* in his distress
Is 26:6 the poor, and the steps of the *n*
Is 32:7 even when the *n* speaketh right
Is 41:17 *n* seek water, and there is none,
Jer 5:28 the right of the *n* do they not
Jer 22:16 judged the cause of the poor and *n*
Eze 16:49 the hand of the poor and *n*
Eze 18:12 Hath oppressed the poor and *n*
Eze 22:29 and have vexed the poor and *n*
Amos 4:1 the poor, which crush the *n*
Amos 8:4 this, O ye that swallow up the *n*
Amos 8:6 the *n* for a pair of shoes

**NEGINAH** *(neg'-i-nah)* See NEGINOTH. *A stringed instrument.*
Ps 61:*t* To the chief Musician upon *N*

**NEGINOTH** *(neg'-i-noth)* See NEGINAH. *Same as Neginah.*
Ps 4:*t* To the chief Musician on *N*
Ps 6:*t* Musician on *N* upon Sheminith
Ps 54:*t* To the chief Musician on *N*
Ps 55:*t* To the chief Musician on *N*
Ps 67:*t* To the chief Musician on *N*
Ps 76:*t* To the chief Musician on *N*

**NEGLECT**
Mt 18:17 if he shall *n* to hear them, tell
Mt 18:17 but if he *n* to hear the church,
1Ti 4:14 *N* not the gift that is in thee,
Heb 2:3 if we *n* so great salvation

**NEHELAMITE** *(ne-hel'-am-ite) Family name of Shemaiah.*
Jer 29:24 thou also speak to Shemaiah the *N*
Jer 29:31 LORD concerning Shemaiah the *N*
Jer 29:32 I will punish Shemaiah the *N*

**NEHEMIAH** *(ne-he-mi'-ah)*
*1. A clan leader with Zerubbabel.*
Ezr 2:2 Jeshua, *N*, Seraiah, Reelaiah,
Neh 7:7 came with Zerubbabel, Jeshua, *N*
*2. Governor of Jerusalem.*
Neh 1:1 The words of *N* the son of
Neh 8:9 And *N*, which is the Tirshatha, and
Neh 10:1 Now those that sealed were, *N*
Neh 12:26 and in the days of *N* the governor
Neh 12:47 Zerubbabel, and in the days of *N*
*3. A rebuilder of Jerusalem's wall.*
Neh 3:16 him repaired *N* the son of Azbuk

**NEHILOTH** *(ne'-hi-loth) A musical choir or instrument.*
Ps 5:*t* To the chief Musician upon *N*

**NEHUM** *(ne'-hum)* See REHUM. *A clan leader with Zerubbabel.*
Neh 7:7 Bilshan, Mispereth, Bigvai, *N*

**NEHUSHTA** *(ne-hush'-tah) Mother of King Jehoiachin.*
2Kin 24:8 And his mother's name was *N*

**NEHUSHTAN** *(ne-hush'-tan) Name given to the brazen serpents.*
2Kin 18:4 and he called it *N*

**NEIEL** *(ne-i'-el) A city in Asher.*
Josh 19:27 the north side of Beth-emek, and *N*

**NEIGHBOUR**
Ex 3:22 every woman shall borrow of her *n*
Ex 11:2 and let every man borrow of his *n*
Ex 11:2 and every woman of her *n*, jewels
Ex 12:4 his *n* next unto his house take it
Ex 20:16 bear false witness against thy *n*
Ex 21:14 come presumptuously upon his *n*
Ex 22:7 unto his *n* money or stuff to keep
Ex 22:9 he shall pay double unto his *n*
Ex 22:10 a man deliver unto his *n* an ass
Ex 22:14 And if a man borrow ought of his *n*
Ex 32:27 his companion, and every man his *n*
Lev 6:2 lie unto his *n* in that which was
Lev 6:2 violence, or hath deceived his *n*
Lev 19:13 Thou shalt not defraud thy *n*
Lev 19:15 shalt thou judge thy *n*
Lev 19:16 stand against the blood of thy *n*
Lev 19:17 shalt in any wise rebuke thy *n*
Lev 19:18 thou shalt love thy *n* as thyself
Lev 24:19 if a man cause a blemish in his *n*
Lev 25:14 And if thou sell ought unto thy *n*
Lev 25:15 jubile thou shalt buy of thy *n*
Deut 4:42 which should kill his *n* unawares
Deut 5:20 bear false witness against thy *n*
Deut 15:2 ought unto his *n* shall release it
Deut 15:2 he shall not exact it of his *n*
Deut 19:4 Whoso killeth his *n* ignorantly
Deut 19:5 the wood with his *n* to hew wood
Deut 19:5 the helve, and lighteth upon his *n*
Deut 19:11 But if any man hate his *n*
Deut 22:26 when a man riseth against his *n*
Deut 23:25 into the standing corn of thy *n*
Deut 27:24 be he that smiteth his *n* secretly
Josh 20:5 he smote his *n* unwittingly
Ruth 4:7 off his shoe, and gave it to his *n*
1Sa 15:28 and hath given it to a *n* of thine
1Sa 28:17 thine hand, and given it to thy *n*
2Sa 12:11 eyes, and give them unto thy *n*
1Kin 8:31 If any man trespass against his *n*
1Kin 20:35 his *n* in the word of the LORD
2Chr 6:22 If a man sin against his *n*
Job 12:4 I am as one mocked of his *n*
Job 16:21 God, as a man pleadeth for his *n*
Ps 12:2 speak vanity every one with his *n*
Ps 15:3 tongue, nor doeth evil to his *n*
Ps 15:3 up a reproach against his *n*
Ps 101:5 Whoso privily slandereth his *n*
Prov 3:28 Say not unto thy *n*, Go, and come
Prov 3:29 Devise not evil against thy *n*
Prov 11:9 with his mouth destroyeth his *n*
Prov 11:12 is void of wisdom despiseth his *n*
Prov 12:26 is more excellent than his *n*
Prov 14:20 poor is hated even of his own *n*
Prov 14:21 He that despiseth his *n* sinneth
Prov 16:29 A violent man enticeth his *n*
Prov 18:17 but his *n* cometh and searcheth him
Prov 19:4 the poor is separated from his *n*
Prov 21:10 his *n* findeth no favour in his
Prov 24:28 against thy *n* without cause
Prov 25:8 when thy *n* hath put thee to shame
Prov 25:9 thy cause with thy *n* himself
Prov 25:18 witness against his *n* is a maul
Prov 26:19 is the man that deceiveth his *n*
Prov 27:10 for better is a *n* that is near
Prov 29:5 A man that flattereth his *n*
Eccl 4:4 for this a man is envied of his *n*
Is 3:5 by another, and every one by his *n*
Is 19:2 and every one against his *n*
Is 41:6 They helped every one his *n*
Jer 6:21 the *n* and his friend shall perish
Jer 7:5 judgment between a man and his *n*
Jer 9:4 Take ye heed every one of his *n*
Jer 9:4 every *n* will walk with slanders
Jer 9:5 they will deceive every one his *n*
Jer 9:8 peaceably to his *n* with his mouth
Jer 9:20 and every one her *n* lamentation
Jer 22:8 they shall say every man to his *n*
Jer 23:27 they tell every man to his *n*
Jer 23:30 my words every one from his *n*
Jer 23:35 shall ye say every one to his *n*
Jer 31:34 teach no more every man his *n*
Jer 34:15 liberty every man to his *n*
Jer 34:17 brother, and every man to his *n*
Jer 49:18 the *n* cities thereof, saith the
Jer 50:40 the *n* cities thereof, saith the
Hab 2:15 unto him that giveth his *n* drink
Zec 3:10 every man his *n* under the vine
Zec 8:10 all men every one against his *n*
Zec 8:16 ye every man the truth to his *n*
Zec 8:17 evil in your hearts against his *n*
Zec 14:13 every one on the hand of his *n*
Zec 14:13 rise up against the hand of his *n*
Mt 5:43 been said, Thou shalt love thy *n*
Mt 19:19 Thou shalt love thy *n* as thyself
Mt 22:39 Thou shalt love thy *n* as thyself
Mk 12:31 Thou shalt love thy *n* as thyself
Mk 12:33 and to love his *n* as himself
Lk 10:27 and thy *n* as thyself
Lk 10:29 said unto Jesus, And who is my *n*
Lk 10:36 was *n* unto him that fell among
Acts 7:27 But he that did his *n* wrong
Rom 13:9 Thou shalt love thy *n* as thyself
Rom 13:10 Love worketh no ill to his *n*
Rom 15:2 his *n* for his good to edification
Gal 5:14 Thou shalt love thy *n* as thyself
Eph 4:25 speak every man truth with his *n*
Heb 8:11 shall not teach every man his *n*
Jas 2:8 Thou shalt love thy *n* as thyself

**NEIGHBOUR'S**
Ex 20:17 Thou shalt not covet thy *n* house
Ex 20:17 thou shalt not covet thy *n* wife
Ex 20:17 ass, nor any thing that is thy *n*
Ex 22:8 put his hand unto his *n* goods
Ex 22:11 not put his hand unto his *n* goods
Ex 22:26 all take thy *n* raiment to pledge
Lev 18:20 not lie carnally with thy *n* wife
Lev 20:10 adultery with his *n* wife, the
Lev 25:14 or buyest ought of thy *n* hand
Deut 5:21 shalt thou desire thy *n* wife
Deut 5:21 shalt thou covet thy *n* house
Deut 5:21 ass, or any thing that is thy *n*
Deut 19:14 shalt not remove thy *n* landmark
Deut 22:24 he hath humbled his *n* wife
Deut 23:24 thou comest into thy *n* vineyard
Deut 23:25 a sickle unto thy *n* standing corn
Deut 27:17 he that removeth his *n* landmark
Job 31:9 if I have laid wait at my *n* door
Prov 6:29 So he that goeth in to his *n* wife
Prov 25:17 thy foot from thy *n* house
Jer 5:8 one neighed after his *n* wife
Jer 22:13 that useth his *n* service without
Eze 18:6 neither hath defiled his *n* wife
Eze 18:11 mountains, and defiled his *n* wife
Eze 18:15 hath not defiled his *n* wife
Eze 22:11 abomination with his *n* wife
Eze 33:26 and ye defile every one his *n* wife
Zec 11:6 the men every one into his *n* hand

**NEIGHBOURS**
Josh 9:16 they heard that they were their *n*
Ruth 4:17 the women her *n* gave it a name,
2Kin 4:3 thee vessels abroad of all thy *n*
Ps 28:3 which speak peace to their *n*
Ps 31:11 but especially among my *n*
Ps 44:13 makest us a reproach to our *n*
Ps 79:4 We are become a reproach to our *n*
Ps 79:12 render unto our *n* sevenfold into
Ps 80:6 makest us a strife unto our *n*
Ps 89:41 he is a reproach to his *n*
Jer 12:14 the LORD against all mine evil *n*
Jer 49:10 and his brethren, and his *n*
Eze 16:26 with the Egyptians thy *n*, great
Eze 22:12 gained of thy *n* by extortion
Eze 23:5 lovers, on the Assyrians her *n*
Eze 23:12 doted upon the Assyrians her *n*
Lk 1:58 And her *n* and her cousins heard how
Lk 14:12 thy kinsmen, nor thy rich *n*
Lk 15:6 calleth together his friends and *n*

Lk 15:9 her *n* together, saying, Rejoice
Jn 9:8 The *n* therefore, and they which

**NEKEB** *(ne'-keb) A city in Naphtali.*
Josh 19:33 Allon to Zaanannim, and Adami, *N*

**NEKODA** *(ne-ko'-dah)*
*1. A family of exiles.*
Ezr 2:48 of Rezin, the children of *N*
Neh 7:50 of Rezin, the children of *N*
*2. A family of uncertain origin.*
Ezr 2:60 of Tobiah, the children of *N*
Neh 7:62 of Tobiah, the children of *N*

**NEMUEL** *(ne-mu'-el)* See JEMUEL, NEMUELITES.
*1. Son of Eliab.*
Num 26:9 *N*, and Dathan, and Abiram
*2. A son of Simeon.*
Num 26:12 of *N*, the family of the
1Chr 4:24 The sons of Simeon were, *N*

**NEMUELITES** *(ne-mu'-el-ites) Descendants of Nemuel 2.*
Num 26:12 of Nemuel, the family of the *N*

**NEPHEG** *(ne'-feg)*
*1. A son of Izhar.*
Ex 6:21 Korah, and *N*, and Zichri
*2. A son of David.*
2Sa 5:15 Ibhar also, and Elishua, and *N*
1Chr 3:7 And Nogah, and *N*, and Japhia,
1Chr 14:6 And Nogah, and *N*, and Japhia,

**NEPHISH** *(ne'-fish)* See NAPHISH. *Descendants of Naphish.*
1Chr 5:19 the Hagarites, with Jetur, and *N*

**NEPHISHESIM** *(ne-fish'-e-sim)* See NEPHUSIM. *A family of exiles.*
Neh 7:52 of Meunim, the children of *N*

**NEPHTHALIM** *(nef'-tha-lim)* See NAPHTALI. *Country and tribe of Naphtali.*
Mt 4:13 in the borders of Zabulon and *N*
Mt 4:15 land of Zabulon, and the land of *N*

**NEPHTOAH** *(nef-to'-ah) A stream near Jerusalem.*
Josh 15:9 the fountain of the water of *N*
Josh 18:15 out to the well of waters of *N*

**NEPHUSIM** *(ne-fu'-sim)* See NEPHISHESIM. *A family of exiles.*
Ezr 2:50 of Mehunim, the children of *N*

**NEPTHALIM**
Rev 7:6 Of the tribe of *N* were sealed

**NER** *(nur) Grandfather of King Saul.*
1Sa 14:50 his host was Abner, the son of *N*
1Sa 14:51 *N* the father of Abner was the son
1Sa 26:5 Saul lay, and Abner the son of *N*
1Sa 26:14 people, and to Abner the son of *N*
2Sa 2:8 But Abner the son of *N*, captain
2Sa 2:12 And Abner the son of *N*, and the
2Sa 3:23 the son of *N* came to the king
2Sa 3:25 Thou knowest Abner the son of *N*
2Sa 3:28 the blood of Abner the son of *N*
2Sa 3:37 king to slay Abner the son of *N*
1Kin 2:5 Israel, unto Abner the son of *N*
1Kin 2:32 to wit, Abner the son of *N*
1Chr 8:33 *N* begat Kish, and Kish begat Saul,
1Chr 9:36 then Zur, and Kish, and Baal, and *N*
1Chr 9:39 And *N* begat Kish
1Chr 26:28 of Kish, and Abner the son of *N*

**NEREUS** *(ne'-re-us) A Christian acquaintance of Paul.*
Rom 16:15 Salute Philologus, and Julia, *N*

**NERGAL** *(nur'-gal)* See NERGAL-SHAREZER. *War god of Cuth.*
2Kin 17:30 and the men of Cuth made *N*

**NERGAL-SHAREZER** *(nur'-gal-sha-re'-zur)*
*1. A Babylonian prince.*
Jer 39:3 and sat in the middle gate, even *N*
*2. Another Babylonian prince.*
Jer 39:3 Sarsechim, Rab-saris, *N*, Rab-mag
Jer 39:13 and Nebushasban, Rab-saris, and *N*

**NERI** *(ne'-ri) Father of Salathiel; ancestor of Jesus.*
Lk 3:27 Salathiel, which was the son of *N*

**NERIAH** *(ne-ri'-ah) Father of Baruch.*
Jer 32:12 purchase unto Baruch the son of *N*
Jer 32:16 purchase unto Baruch the son of *N*
Jer 36:4 called Baruch the son of *N*
Jer 36:8 Baruch the son of *N* did according
Jer 36:14 So Baruch the son of *N* took the
Jer 36:32 Baruch the scribe, the son of *N*
Jer 43:3 But Baruch the son of *N* setteth
Jer 43:6 prophet, and Baruch the son of *N*
Jer 45:1 spake unto Baruch the son of *N*
Jer 51:59 commanded Seraiah the son of *N*

**NERO** *(ne'-ro) Emperor of Rome.*
2Ti *s* brought before *N* the second time

**NEST**
Num 24:21 and thou puttest thy *n* in a rock
Deut 22:6 If a bird's *n* chance to be before
Deut 32:11 As an eagle stirreth up her *n*
Job 29:18 Then I said, I shall die in my *n*
Job 39:27 command, and make her *n* on high
Ps 84:3 and the swallow a *n* for herself
Prov 27:8 a bird that wandereth from her *n*
Is 10:14 my hand hath found as a *n* the
Is 16:2 wandering bird cast out of the *n*
Is 34:15 shall the great owl make her *n*
Jer 22:23 that makest thy *n* in the cedars
Jer 48:28 her *n* in the sides of the hole's
Jer 49:16 make thy *n* as high as the eagle
Obad 4 thou set thy *n* among the stars
Hab 2:9 that he may set his *n* on high

**NESTS**
Ps 104:17 Where the birds make their *n*
Eze 31:6 heaven made their *n* in his boughs
Mt 8:20 and the birds of the air have *n*
Lk 9:58 holes, and birds of the air have *n*

**NET**
Ex 27:4 upon the *n* shalt thou make four
Ex 27:5 that the *n* may be even to the
Job 18:8 is cast into a *n* by his own feet
Job 19:6 and hath compassed me with his *n*
Ps 9:15 in the *n* which they hid is their
Ps 10:9 when he draweth him into his *n*
Ps 25:15 shall pluck my feet out of the *n*
Ps 31:4 Pull me out of the *n* that they
Ps 35:7 they hid for me their *n* in a pit
Ps 35:8 let his *n* that he hath hid catch
Ps 57:6 have prepared a *n* for my steps
Ps 66:11 Thou broughtest us into the *n*
Ps 140:5 have spread a *n* by the wayside
Prov 1:17 Surely in vain the *n* is spread in
Prov 12:12 wicked desireth the *n* of evil men
Prov 29:5 spreadeth a *n* for his feet
Eccl 9:12 that are taken in an evil *n*
Is 51:20 streets, as a wild bull in a *n*
Lam 1:13 he hath spread a *n* for my feet
Eze 12:13 My *n* also will I spread upon him,
Eze 17:20 And I will spread my *n* upon him
Eze 19:8 and spread their *n* over him
Eze 32:3 my *n* over thee with a company of
Eze 32:3 they shall bring thee up in my *n*
Hos 5:1 Mizpah, and a *n* spread upon Tabor
Hos 7:12 go, I will spread my *n* upon them
Mic 7:2 every man his brother with a *n*
Hab 1:15 angle, they catch them in their *n*
Hab 1:16 they sacrifice unto their *n*
Hab 1:17 they therefore empty their *n*
Mt 4:18 brother, casting a *n* into the sea
Mt 13:47 of heaven is like unto a *n*
Mk 1:16 brother casting a *n* into the sea
Lk 5:5 at thy word I will let down the *n*
Lk 5:6 and their *n* brake
Jn 21:6 Cast the *n* on the right side of
Jn 21:8 dragging the *n* with fishes
Jn 21:11 drew the *n* to land full of great
Jn 21:11 so many, yet was not the *n* broken

**NETHANEEL** *(ne-than'-e-el)*
*1. A son of Zuar.*
Num 1:8 *N* the son of Zuar
Num 2:5 *N* the son of Zuar shall be
Num 7:18 the second day *N* the son of Zuar
Num 7:23 the offering of *N* the son of Zuar
Num 10:15 of Issachar was *N* the son of Zuar
*2. A brother of David.*
1Chr 2:14 *N* the fourth, Raddai the fifth,
*3. A priest who relocated the Ark.*
1Chr 15:24 Shebaniah, and Jehoshaphat, and *N*
*4. A sanctuary servant.*
1Chr 24:6 Shemaiah the son of *N* the scribe
*5. A son of Obed-edom.*
1Chr 26:4 Sacar the fourth, and *N* the fifth,
*6. A prince of Judah.*
2Chr 17:7 Obadiah, and to Zechariah, and to *N*
*7. A chief Levite.*
2Chr 35:9 Conaniah also, and Shemaiah and *N*
*8. Married a foreigner in exile.*
Ezr 10:22 Elioenai, Maaseiah, Ishmael, *N*
*9. A priest with Zerubbabel.*
Neh 12:21 of Jedaiah, *N*
*10. A priest who dedicated the wall.*
Neh 12:36 Milalai, Gilalai, Maai, *N*

**NETHANIAH** *(neth-a-ni'-ah)*
*1. Father of Ishmael.*
2Kin 25:23 Mizpah, even Ishmael the son of *N*
2Kin 25:25 month, that Ishmael the son of *N*
Jer 40:8 Mizpah, even Ishmael the son of *N*
Jer 40:14 Ishmael the son of *N* to slay thee
Jer 40:15 I will slay Ishmael the son of *N*
Jer 41:1 the son of *N* the son of Elishama
Jer 41:2 Then arose Ishmael the son of *N*
Jer 41:6 Ishmael the son of *N* went forth
Jer 41:7 Ishmael the son of *N* slew them
Jer 41:9 Ishmael the son of *N* filled it
Jer 41:10 Ishmael the son of *N* carried them
Jer 41:11 Ishmael the son of *N* had done
Jer 41:12 fight with Ishmael the son of *N*
Jer 41:15 But Ishmael the son of *N* escaped
Jer 41:16 from Ishmael the son of *N*
Jer 41:18 because Ishmael the son of *N* had
*2. A sanctuary servant.*
1Chr 25:2 Zaccur, and Joseph, and *N*, and
1Chr 25:12 The fifth to *N*, he, his sons, and
*3. A Levite.*
2Chr 17:8 sent Levites, even Shemaiah, and *N*
*4. Father of Jehudi.*
Jer 36:14 princes sent Jehudi the son of *N*

**NETHER**
Ex 19:17 stood at the *n* part of the mount
Deut 24:6 No man shall take the *n* or the
Josh 15:19 upper springs, and the *n* springs
Josh 16:3 the coast of Beth-horon the *n*
Josh 18:13 south side of the *n* Beth-horon
Judg 1:15 upper springs and the *n* springs
1Kin 9:17 built Gezer, and Beth-horon the *n*
1Chr 7:24 who built Beth-horon the *n*
2Chr 8:5 the upper, and Beth-horon the *n*
Job 41:24 as a piece of the *n* millstone
Eze 31:14 to the *n* parts of the earth, in
Eze 31:16 in the *n* parts of the earth
Eze 31:18 unto the *n* parts of the earth
Eze 32:18 unto the *n* parts of the earth,
Eze 32:24 into the *n* parts of the earth

**NETHINIMS** *(neth'-in-ims) Assistants to the Levites.*
1Chr 9:2 the priests, Levites, and the *N*
Ezr 2:43 The *N*: the children of Ziha
Ezr 2:58 All the *N*, and the children of
Ezr 2:70 singers, and the porters, and the *N*
Ezr 7:7 singers, and the porters, and the *N*
Ezr 7:24 and Levites, singers, porters, *N*
Ezr 8:17 Iddo, and to his brethren the *N*
Ezr 8:20 Also of the *N*, whom David and the
Ezr 8:20 Levites, two hundred and twenty *N*
Neh 3:26 Moreover the *N* dwelt in Ophel,
Neh 3:31 son unto the place of the *N*
Neh 7:46 The *N*: the children of Ziha
Neh 7:60 All the *N*, and the children of
Neh 7:73 and some of the people, and the *N*
Neh 10:28 the porters, the singers, the *N*
Neh 11:3 priests, and the Levites, and the *N*
Neh 11:21 But the *N* dwelt in Ophel
Neh 11:21 and Ziha and Gispa were over the *N*

**NETOPHAH** *(ne-to'-fah)* See NETOPHATHITE. *A city in Judah.*
Ezr 2:22 The men of *N*, fifty and six
Neh 7:26 The men of Beth-lehem and *N*

**NETOPHATHI** *(ne-to'-fa-thi)* See NETOPHATHITE. *An inhabitant of Netophah.*
Neh 12:28 and from the villages of *N*

**NETOPHATHITE** *(ne-to'-fa-thite)* See NETOPHATHI, NETHOPHATHITES. *Same as Netophathi.*
2Sa 23:28 Zalmon the Ahohite, Maharai the *N*
2Sa 23:29 Heleb the son of Baanah, a *N*
2Kin 25:23 the son of Tanhumeth the *N*
1Chr 11:30 Maharai the *N*, Heled the son of
1Chr 11:30 Heled the son of Baanah the *N*
1Chr 27:13 the tenth month was Maharai the *N*
1Chr 27:15 twelfth month was Heldai the *N*
Jer 40:8 and the sons of Ephai the *N*

**NETOPHATHITES** *(ne-to'-fa-thites)*
1Chr 2:54 Beth-lehem, and the *N*, Ataroth,
1Chr 9:16 dwelt in the villages of the *N*

**NETS**
1Kin 7:17 *n* of checker work, and wreaths of
Ps 141:10 the wicked fall into their own *n*
Eccl 7:26 woman, whose heart is snares and *n*
Is 19:8 they that spread *n* upon the
Eze 26:5 of *n* in the midst of the sea
Eze 26:14 shalt be a place to spread *n* upon
Eze 47:10 be a place to spread forth *n*
Mt 4:20 And they straightway left their *n*
Mt 4:21 their father, mending their *n*
Mk 1:18 straightway they forsook their *n*
Mk 1:19 were in the ship mending their *n*
Lk 5:2 of them, and were washing their *n*
Lk 5:4 and let down your *n* for a draught

**NETTLES**
Job 30:7 under the *n* they were gathered
Prov 24:31 *n* had covered the face thereof,
Is 34:13 shall come up in her palaces, *n*
Hos 9:6 silver, *n* shall possess them
Zeph 2:9 Gomorrah, even the breeding of *n*

**NETWORK**
Ex 27:4 make for it a grate of *n* of brass
Ex 38:4 of *n* under the compass thereof
1Kin 7:18 rows round about upon the one *n*
1Kin 7:20 the belly which was by the *n*
1Kin 7:42 rows of pomegranates for one *n*
Jer 52:22 chapiter was five cubits, with *n*
Jer 52:23 the *n* were an hundred round about

**NEW**
Ex 1:8 arose up a *n* king over Egypt
Lev 23:16 ye shall offer a *n* meat offering
Lev 26:10 forth the old because of the *n*
Num 16:30 But if the LORD make a *n* thing
Num 28:26 when ye bring a *n* meat offering
Deut 20:5 there that hath built a *n* house
Deut 22:8 When thou buildest a *n* house
Deut 24:5 When a man hath taken a *n* wife
Deut 32:17 to *n* gods that came newly up,
Josh 9:13 of wine, which we filled, were *n*
Judg 5:8 They chose *n* gods
Judg 15:13 they bound him with two *n* cords
Judg 15:15 he found a *n* jawbone of an ass,
Judg 16:11 If they bind me fast with *n* ropes
Judg 16:12 Delilah therefore took *n* ropes
1Sa 6:7 Now therefore make a *n* cart
1Sa 20:5 Behold, to morrow is the *n* moon
1Sa 20:18 to David, To morrow is the *n* moon
1Sa 20:24 when the *n* moon was come, the
2Sa 6:3 set the ark of God upon a *n* cart
2Sa 6:3 of Abinadab, drave the *n* cart
2Sa 21:16 he being girded with a *n* sword
1Kin 11:29 had clad himself with a *n* garment
1Kin 11:30 Ahijah caught the *n* garment that
2Kin 2:20 And he said, Bring me a *n* cruse
2Kin 4:23 it is neither *n* moon, nor sabbath
1Chr 13:7 in a *n* cart out of the house of
1Chr 23:31 in the sabbaths, in the *n* moons
2Chr 2:4 the sabbaths, and on the *n* moons
2Chr 8:13 the sabbaths, and on the *n* moons
2Chr 20:5 of the LORD, before the *n* court
2Chr 31:3 the sabbaths, and for the *n* moons
Ezr 3:5 offering, both of the *n* moons
Ezr 6:4 stones, and a row of *n* timber
Neh 10:33 of the sabbaths, of the *n* moons
Neh 10:39 of the corn, of the *n* wine
Neh 13:5 the *n* wine, and the oil, which was
Neh 13:12 the *n* wine and the oil unto the
Job 32:19 is ready to burst like *n* bottles
Ps 33:3 Sing unto him a *n* song
Ps 40:3 he hath put a *n* song in my mouth,
Ps 81:3 Blow up the trumpet in the *n* moon
Ps 96:1 O sing unto the LORD a *n* song
Ps 98:1 O sing unto the LORD a *n* song
Ps 144:9 I will sing a *n* song unto thee, O
Ps 149:1 Sing unto the LORD a *n* song
Prov 3:10 shall burst out with *n* wine
Eccl 1:9 there is no *n* thing under the sun
Eccl 1:10 it may be said, See, this is *n*
Song 7:13 all manner of pleasant fruits, *n*
Is 1:13 the *n* moons and sabbaths, the
Is 1:14 Your *n* moons and your appointed
Is 24:7 The *n* wine mourneth, the vine
Is 41:15 I will make thee a *n* sharp
Is 42:9 to pass, and *n* things do I declare
Is 42:10 Sing unto the LORD a *n* song
Is 43:19 Behold, I will do a *n* thing
Is 48:6 I have shewed thee *n* things from
Is 62:2 thou shalt be called by a *n* name
Is 65:8 As the *n* wine is found in the
Is 65:17 I create *n* heavens and a *n* earth
Is 66:22 For as the *n* heavens
Is 66:22 the *n* earth, which I will make,
Is 66:23 that from one *n* moon to another,
Jer 26:10 of the *n* gate of the LORD's house
Jer 31:22 created a *n* thing in the earth
Jer 31:31 that I will make a *n* covenant
Jer 36:10 at the entry of the *n* gate of the
Lam 3:23 They are *n* every morning
Eze 11:19 I will put a *n* spirit within you
Eze 18:31 you a *n* heart and a *n* spirit
Eze 36:26 A *n* heart also will I give you,
Eze 36:26 a *n* spirit will I put within you
Eze 45:17 in the feasts, and in the *n* moons
Eze 46:1 in the day of the *n* moon it shall
Eze 46:3 in the sabbaths and in the *n* moons
Eze 46:6 in the day of the *n* moon it shall
Eze 47:12 it shall bring forth *n* fruit
Hos 2:11 her *n* moons, and her sabbaths, and
Hos 4:11 *n* wine take away the heart
Hos 9:2 the *n* wine shall fail in her
Joel 1:5 of wine, because of the *n* wine
Joel 1:10 the *n* wine is dried up, the oil
Joel 3:18 mountains shall drop down *n* wine
Amos 8:5 When will the *n* moon be gone
Hag 1:11 upon the corn, and upon the *n* wine
Zec 9:17 men cheerful, and *n* wine the maids
Mt 9:16 of *n* cloth unto an old garment
Mt 9:17 Neither do men put *n* wine into
Mt 9:17 but they put *n* wine into
Mt 9:17 wine into *n* bottles
Mt 13:52 out of his treasure things *n*
Mt 26:28 is my blood of the *n* testament
Mt 26:29 until that day when I drink it *n*
Mt 27:60 And laid it in his own *n* tomb
Mk 1:27 what *n* doctrine is this
Mk 2:21 of *n* cloth on an old garment
Mk 2:21 else the *n* piece that filled it
Mk 2:22 no man putteth *n* wine into old
Mk 2:22 else the *n* wine doth burst the
Mk 2:22 but *n* wine must be put into
Mk 2:22 wine must be put into *n* bottles
Mk 14:24 is my blood of the *n* testament
Mk 14:25 drink it *n* in the kingdom of God
Mk 16:17 they shall speak with *n* tongues
Lk 5:36 piece of a *n* garment upon an old
Lk 5:36 then both the *n* maketh a rent
Lk 5:36 of the *n* agreeth not with the old
Lk 5:37 no man putteth *n* wine into old
Lk 5:37 else the *n* wine will burst the
Lk 5:38 But *n* wine must be put into
Lk 5:38 wine must be put into *n* bottles
Lk 5:39 old wine straightway desireth *n*
Lk 22:20 This cup is the *n* testament in my
Jn 13:34 A *n* commandment I give unto you,
Jn 19:41 and in the garden a *n* sepulchre
Acts 2:13 These men are full of *n* wine
Acts 17:19 May we know what this *n* doctrine
Acts 17:21 to tell, or to hear some *n* thing
1Cor 5:7 leaven, that ye may be a *n* lump
1Cor 11:25 This cup is the *n* testament in my
2Cor 3:6 able ministers of the *n* testament
2Cor 5:17 be in Christ, he is a *n* creature
2Cor 5:17 behold, all things are become *n*
Gal 6:15 uncircumcision, but a *n* creature
Eph 2:15 in himself of twain one *n* man
Eph 4:24 And that ye put on the *n* man
Col 2:16 of an holyday, or of the *n* moon
Col 3:10 And have put on the *n* man, which
Heb 8:8 when I will make a *n* covenant
Heb 8:13 A *n* covenant, he hath made the
Heb 9:15 the mediator of the *n* testament
Heb 10:20 By a *n* and living way, which he
Heb 12:24 the mediator of the *n* covenant
2Pet 3:13 his promise, look for *n* heavens
2Pet 3:13 a *n* earth, wherein dwelleth
1Jn 2:7 I write no *n* commandment unto you
1Jn 2:8 a *n* commandment I write unto you,
2Jn 5 I wrote a *n* commandment unto thee
Rev 2:17 and in the stone a *n* name written
Rev 3:12 which is *n* Jerusalem, which
Rev 3:12 I will write upon him my *n* name
Rev 5:9 And they sung a *n* song, saying,
Rev 14:3 were a *n* song before the throne
Rev 21:1 I saw a *n* heaven and a *n* earth
Rev 21:2 *n* Jerusalem, coming down from God
Rev 21:5 said, Behold, I make all things *n*

**NEZIAH** *(ne-zi'-ah) A family of exiles.*
Ezr 2:54 The children of *N*, the children
Neh 7:56 The children of *N*, the children

**NEZIB** *(ne'-zib) A city in Judah.*
Josh 15:43 And Jiphtah, and Ashnah, and *N*

**NIBHAZ** *(nib'-haz) A god of the Avites.*
2Kin 17:31 And the Avites made *N* and Tartak,

**NIBSHAN** *(nib'-shan) A city in Judah.*
Josh 15:62 And *N*, and the city of Salt, and

**NICANOR** *(ni-ca'-nor) A leader in the Jerusalem church.*
Acts 6:5 and Philip, and Prochorus, and *N*

**NICODEMUS** *(nic-o-de'-mus) A Pharisee sympathetic to Jesus.*
Jn 3:1 a man of the Pharisees, named *N*
Jn 3:4 *N* saith unto him, How can a man
Jn 3:9 *N* answered and said unto him, How
Jn 7:50 *N* saith unto them, (he that came
Jn 19:39 And there came also *N*, which at

**NICOLAITANES** *(nic-o-la'-i-tans) A group condemned in Revelation.*
Rev 2:6 thou hatest the deeds of the *N*
Rev 2:15 that hold the doctrine of the *N*

**NICOLAS** *(nic'-o-las) A leader in the Jerusalem church.*
Acts 6:5 and *N* a proselyte of Antioch

**NICOPOLIS** *(ni-cop'-o-lis) A city in Thrace.*
Titus 3:12 be diligent to come unto me to *N*
Titus *s* the Cretians, from *N* of Macedonia

**NIGER** *(ni'-jur) See* SIMEON. *A Christian teacher and prophet at Antioch.*
Acts 13:1 and Simeon that was called *N*

**NIGH**
Gen 47:29 the time drew *n* that Israel must
Ex 3:5 And he said, Draw not *n* hither
Ex 14:10 And when Pharaoh drew *n*, the
Ex 24:2 but they shall not come *n*
Ex 32:19 soon as he came *n* unto the camp
Ex 34:30 and they were afraid to come *n* him
Ex 34:32 all the children of Israel came *n*
Lev 10:3 sanctified in them that come *n* me
Lev 21:3 that is *n* unto him, which hath
Lev 21:21 *n* to offer the offerings of the
Lev 21:21 he shall not come *n* to offer the
Lev 21:23 nor come *n* unto the altar,
Lev 25:49 or any that is *n* of kin unto him
Num 1:51 cometh *n* shall be put to death
Num 3:10 cometh *n* shall be put to death
Num 3:38 cometh *n* shall be put to death
Num 8:19 Israel come *n* unto the sanctuary
Num 18:3 only they shall not come *n* the
Num 18:4 shall not come *n* unto you
Num 18:7 cometh *n* shall be put to death
Num 18:22 come *n* the tabernacle of the
Num 24:17 I shall behold him, but not *n*
Deut 1:7 unto all the places *n* thereunto
Deut 2:19 when thou comest *n* over against
Deut 4:7 who hath God so *n* unto them
Deut 13:7 *n* unto thee, or far off from thee
Deut 20:2 ye are come *n* unto the battle
Deut 20:10 When thou comest *n* unto a city to
Deut 22:2 if thy brother be not *n* unto thee
Deut 30:14 But the word is very *n* unto thee
Josh 8:11 were with him, went up, and drew *n*
1Sa 17:48 drew *n* to meet David, that David
2Sa 10:13 And Joab drew *n*, and the people
2Sa 11:20 Wherefore approached ye so *n* unto
2Sa 11:21 why went ye *n* the wall
2Sa 15:5 that when any man came *n* to him
1Kin 2:1 David drew *n* that he should die
1Kin 8:59 be *n* unto the LORD our God day and
1Chr 12:40 Moreover they that were *n* them
1Chr 19:14 *n* before the Syrians unto the
Est 9:20 of the king Ahasuerus, both *n*
Ps 32:6 they shall not come *n* unto him
Ps 34:18 The LORD is *n* unto them that are
Ps 69:18 Draw *n* unto my soul, and redeem it
Ps 73:2 my steps had well *n* slipped
Ps 85:9 salvation is *n* them that fear him
Ps 88:3 my life draweth *n* unto the grave
Ps 91:7 but it shall not come *n* thee
Ps 91:10 any plague come *n* thy dwelling
Ps 119:150 They draw *n* that follow after

Ps 145:18 The LORD is *n* unto all them that
Prov 5:8 come not *n* the door of her house
Eccl 12:1 come not, nor the years draw *n*
Is 5:19 of the Holy One of Israel draw *n*
Joel 2:1 LORD cometh, for it is *n* at hand
Mt 15:8 This people draweth *n* unto me
Mt 15:29 came *n* unto the sea of Galilee
Mt 21:1 when they drew *n* unto Jerusalem
Mt 24:32 leaves, ye know that summer is *n*
Mk 2:4 not come *n* unto him for the press
Mk 5:11 Now there was there *n* unto the
Mk 5:21 and he was *n* unto the sea
Mk 11:1 And when they came *n* to Jerusalem
Mk 13:29 come to pass, know that it is *n*
Lk 7:12 Now when he came *n* to the gate of
Lk 10:9 kingdom of God is come *n* unto you
Lk 10:11 kingdom of God is come *n* unto you
Lk 15:25 drew *n* to the house, he heard
Lk 18:35 as he was come *n* unto Jericho
Lk 19:11 because he was *n* to Jerusalem
Lk 19:29 when he was come *n* to Bethphage
Lk 19:37 And when he was come *n*, even now
Lk 21:20 that the desolation thereof is *n*
Lk 21:28 for your redemption draweth *n*
Lk 21:30 that summer is now *n* at hand
Lk 21:31 the kingdom of God is *n* at hand
Lk 22:1 feast of unleavened bread drew *n*
Lk 24:28 they drew *n* unto the village,
Jn 6:4 a feast of the Jews, was *n*
Jn 6:19 sea, and drawing *n* unto the ship
Jn 6:23 *n* unto the place where they did
Jn 11:18 Now Bethany was *n* unto Jerusalem
Jn 11:55 the Jews' passover was *n* at hand
Jn 19:20 was crucified was *n* to the city
Jn 19:42 for the sepulchre was *n* at hand
Acts 7:17 the time of the promise drew *n*
Acts 9:38 forasmuch as Lydda was *n* to Joppa
Acts 10:9 drew *n* unto the city, Peter went
Acts 22:6 was come *n* unto Damascus about
Acts 27:8 *n* whereunto was the city of Lasea
Rom 10:8 The word is *n* thee, even in thy
Eph 2:13 are made *n* by the blood of Christ
Eph 2:17 afar off, and to them that were *n*
Phil 2:27 indeed he was sick *n* unto death
Phil 2:30 of Christ he was *n* unto death
Heb 6:8 is rejected, and is *n* unto cursing
Heb 7:19 by the which we draw *n* unto God
Jas 4:8 Draw *n* to God, and he will draw
Jas 4:8 to God, and he will draw *n* to you
Jas 5:8 the coming of the Lord draweth *n*

**NIGHT**

Gen 1:5 Day, and the darkness he called *N*
Gen 1:14 to divide the day from the *n*
Gen 1:16 and the lesser light to rule the *n*
Gen 1:18 rule over the day and over the *n*
Gen 8:22 and day and *n* shall not cease
Gen 14:15 them, he and his servants, by *n*
Gen 19:2 servant's house, and tarry all *n*
Gen 19:2 we will abide in the street all *n*
Gen 19:5 men which came in to thee this *n*
Gen 19:33 their father drink wine that *n*
Gen 19:34 make him drink wine this *n* also
Gen 19:35 father drink wine that *n* also
Gen 20:3 came to Abimelech in a dream by *n*
Gen 24:54 were with him, and tarried all *n*
Gen 26:24 LORD appeared unto him the same *n*
Gen 28:11 place, and tarried there all *n*
Gen 30:15 thee to *n* for thy son's mandrakes
Gen 30:16 And he lay with her that *n*
Gen 31:24 Laban the Syrian in a dream by *n*
Gen 31:39 stolen by day, or stolen by *n*
Gen 31:40 consumed me, and the frost by *n*
Gen 31:54 tarried all *n* in the mount
Gen 32:13 And he lodged there that same *n*
Gen 32:21 lodged that *n* in the company
Gen 32:22 And he rose up that *n*, and took his
Gen 40:5 them, each man his dream in one *n*
Gen 41:11 And we dreamed a dream in one *n*
Gen 46:2 Israel in the visions of the *n*
Gen 49:27 at *n* he shall divide the spoil
Ex 10:13 land all that day, and all that *n*
Ex 12:8 shall eat the flesh in that *n*
Ex 12:12 through the land of Egypt this *n*
Ex 12:30 And Pharaoh rose up in the *n*
Ex 12:31 he called for Moses and Aaron by *n*
Ex 12:42 It is a *n* to be much observed
Ex 12:42 this is that *n* of the LORD to be
Ex 13:21 by *n* in a pillar of fire, to give
Ex 13:21 to go by day and *n*
Ex 13:22 day, nor the pillar of fire by *n*
Ex 14:20 but it gave light by *n* to these
Ex 14:20 came not near the other all the *n*
Ex 14:21 by a strong east wind all that *n*
Ex 40:38 by day, and fire was on it by *n*
Lev 6:9 the altar all *n* unto the morning
Lev 6:20 the morning, and half thereof at *n*
Lev 8:35 *n* seven days, and keep the charge
Lev 11:16 the *n* hawk, and the cuckow, and the
Lev 19:13 with thee all *n* until the morning
Num 9:16 and the appearance of fire by *n*
Num 9:21 by *n* that the cloud was taken up
Num 11:9 dew fell upon the camp in the *n*
Num 11:32 up all that day, and all that *n*
Num 14:1 and the people wept that *n*
Num 14:14 and in a pillar of fire by *n*
Num 22:8 said unto them, Lodge here this *n*
Num 22:19 you, tarry ye also here this *n*
Num 22:20 And God came unto Balaam at *n*
Deut 1:33 pitch your tents in, in fire by *n*
Deut 14:15 the *n* hawk, and the cuckow, and the
Deut 16:1 thee forth out of Egypt by *n*
Deut 16:4 remain all *n* until the morning
Deut 21:23 not remain all *n* upon the tree
Deut 23:10 that chanceth him by *n*, then
Deut 28:66 and thou shalt fear day and *n*
Josh 1:8 shalt meditate therein day and *n*
Josh 2:2 there came men in hither to *n* of
Josh 4:3 where ye shall lodge this *n*
Josh 8:3 of valour, and sent them away by *n*
Josh 8:9 lodged that *n* among the people
Josh 8:13 Joshua went that *n* into the midst
Josh 10:9 and went up from Gilgal all *n*
Judg 6:25 And it came to pass the same *n*
Judg 6:27 do it by day, that he did it by *n*
Judg 6:40 And God did so that *n*
Judg 7:9 And it came to pass the same *n*
Judg 9:32 Now therefore up by *n*, thou and
Judg 9:34 people that were with him, by *n*
Judg 16:2 laid wait for him all *n* in the
Judg 16:2 the city, and were quiet all the *n*
Judg 19:6 I pray thee, and tarry all *n*
Judg 19:9 evening, I pray you tarry all *n*
Judg 19:10 the man would not tarry that *n*
Judg 19:13 of these places to lodge all *n*
Judg 19:25 her all the *n* until the morning
Judg 20:5 house round about upon me by *n*
Ruth 1:12 should have an husband also to *n*
Ruth 3:2 barley to *n* in the threshingfloor
Ruth 3:13 Tarry this *n*, and it shall be in
1Sa 14:34 every man his ox with him that *n*
1Sa 14:36 down after the Philistines by *n*
1Sa 15:11 and he cried unto the LORD all *n*
1Sa 15:16 the LORD hath said to me this *n*
1Sa 19:10 and David fled, and escaped that *n*
1Sa 19:11 saying, If thou save not thy to *n*
1Sa 19:24 naked all that day and all that *n*
1Sa 25:16 were a wall unto us both by *n*
1Sa 26:7 Abishai came to the people by *n*
1Sa 28:8 and they came to the woman by *n*
1Sa 28:20 bread all the day, nor all the *n*
1Sa 28:25 they rose up, and went away that *n*
1Sa 31:12 valiant men arose, and went all *n*
2Sa 2:29 all that *n* through the plain
2Sa 2:32 And Joab and his men went all *n*
2Sa 4:7 them away through the plain all *n*
2Sa 7:4 And it came to pass that *n*
2Sa 12:16 in, and lay all *n* upon the earth
2Sa 17:1 and pursue after David this *n*
2Sa 17:16 Lodge not this *n* in the plains of
2Sa 19:7 not tarry one with thee this *n*
2Sa 21:10 nor the beasts of the field by *n*
1Kin 3:5 to Solomon in a dream by *n*
1Kin 3:19 this woman's child died in the *n*
1Kin 8:29 may be open toward this house *n*
1Kin 8:59 unto the LORD our God day and *n*
2Kin 6:14 and they came by *n*, and compassed
2Kin 7:12 And the king arose in the *n*
2Kin 8:21 and he rose by *n*, and smote the
2Kin 19:35 And it came to pass that *n*
2Kin 25:4 all the men of war fled by *n* by
1Chr 9:33 employed in that work day and *n*
1Chr 17:3 And it came to pass the same *n*
2Chr 1:7 In that *n* did God appear unto
2Chr 6:20 be open upon this house day and *n*
2Chr 7:12 the LORD appeared to Solomon by *n*
2Chr 21:9 and he rose up by *n*, and smote the
2Chr 35:14 offerings and the fat until *n*
Neh 1:6 I pray before thee now, day and *n*
Neh 2:12 And I arose in the *n*, I and some
Neh 2:13 I went out by *n* by the gate of
Neh 2:15 went I up in the *n* by the brook
Neh 4:9 set a watch against them day and *n*
Neh 4:22 that in the *n* they may be a guard
Neh 6:10 in the *n* will they come to slay
Neh 9:12 in the *n* by a pillar of fire, to
Neh 9:19 neither the pillar of fire by *n*
Est 4:16 nor drink three days, *n* or day
Est 6:1 On that *n* could not the king
Job 3:3 the *n* in which it was said, There
Job 3:6 As for that *n*, let darkness seize
Job 3:7 Lo, let that *n* be solitary
Job 4:13 from the visions of the *n*
Job 5:14 grope in the noonday as in the *n*
Job 7:4 shall I arise, and the *n* be gone
Job 17:12 They change the *n* into day
Job 20:8 chased away as a vision of the *n*
Job 24:14 needy, and in the *n* is as a thief
Job 26:10 until the day and *n* come to an end
Job 27:20 stealeth him away in the *n*
Job 29:19 the dew lay all *n* upon my branch
Job 30:17 are pierced in me in the *n* season
Job 33:15 In a dream, in a vision of the *n*
Job 34:25 and he overturneth them in the *n*
Job 35:10 maker, who giveth songs in the *n*
Job 36:20 Desire not the *n*, when people are
Ps 1:2 his law doth he meditate day and *n*
Ps 6:6 all the *n* make I my bed to swim
Ps 16:7 also instruct me in the *n* seasons
Ps 17:3 thou hast visited me in the *n*
Ps 19:2 *n* unto *n* sheweth knowledge
Ps 22:2 and in the *n* season, and am not
Ps 30:5 weeping may endure for a *n*
Ps 32:4 *n* thy hand was heavy upon me
Ps 42:3 tears have been my meat day and *n*
Ps 42:8 in the *n* his song shall be with
Ps 55:10 *n* they go about it upon the walls
Ps 63:6 meditate on thee in the *n* watches
Ps 74:16 day is thine, the *n* also is thine
Ps 77:2 my sore ran in the *n*, and ceased
Ps 77:6 to remembrance my song in the *n*
Ps 78:14 all the *n* with a light of fire
Ps 88:1 I have cried day and *n* before thee
Ps 90:4 is past, and as a watch in the *n*
Ps 91:5 not be afraid for the terror by *n*
Ps 92:2 and thy faithfulness every *n*
Ps 104:20 Thou makest darkness, and it is *n*
Ps 105:39 and fire to give light in the *n*
Ps 119:55 thy name, O LORD, in the *n*
Ps 119:148 Mine eyes prevent the *n* watches
Ps 121:6 thee by day, nor the moon by *n*
Ps 134:1 which by *n* stand in the house of
Ps 136:9 The moon and stars to rule by *n*
Ps 139:11 even the *n* shall be light about
Ps 139:12 but the *n* shineth as the day
Prov 7:9 evening, in the black and dark *n*
Prov 31:15 She riseth also while it is yet *n*
Prov 31:18 her candle goeth not out by *n*
Eccl 2:23 heart taketh not rest in the *n*
Eccl 8:16 nor *n* seeth sleep with his eyes
Song 1:13 he shall lie all *n* betwixt my
Song 3:1 By *n* on my bed I sought him whom
Song 3:8 thigh because of fear in the *n*
Song 5:2 my locks with the drops of the *n*
Is 4:5 shining of a flaming fire by *n*
Is 5:11 that continue until *n*, till wine
Is 15:1 Because in the *n* Ar of Moab is
Is 15:1 because in the *n* Kir of Moab is
Is 16:3 make thy shadow as the *n* in the
Is 21:4 the *n* of my pleasure hath he
Is 21:11 of Seir, Watchman, what of the *n*
Is 21:11 Watchman, what of the *n*
Is 21:12 The morning cometh, and also the *n*
Is 26:9 soul have I desired thee in the *n*
Is 27:3 any hurt it, I will keep it *n*
Is 28:19 it pass over, by day and by *n*
Is 29:7 shall be as a dream of a *n* vision
Is 30:29 as in the *n* when a holy solemnity
Is 34:10 shall not be quenched *n* nor day
Is 38:12 from day even to *n* wilt thou make
Is 38:13 from day even to *n* wilt thou make
Is 59:10 we stumble at noonday as in the *n*
Is 60:11 they shall not be shut day nor *n*
Is 62:6 never hold their peace day nor *n*
Jer 6:5 Arise, and let us go by *n*, and let
Jer 9:1 *n* for the slain of the daughter
Jer 14:8 turneth aside to tarry for a *n*
Jer 14:17 mine eyes run down with tears *n*
Jer 16:13 ye serve other gods day and *n*
Jer 31:35 and of the stars for a light by *n*

Jer 33:20 the day, and my covenant of the *n*
Jer 33:20 not be day and *n* in their season
Jer 33:25 my covenant be not with day and *n*
Jer 36:30 heat, and in the *n* to the frost
Jer 39:4 went forth out of the city by *n*
Jer 49:9 if thieves by *n*, they will
Jer 52:7 went forth out of the city by *n*
Lam 1:2 She weepeth sore in the *n*
Lam 2:18 run down like a river day and *n*
Lam 2:19 Arise, cry out in the *n*
Dan 2:19 unto Daniel in a *n* vision
Dan 5:30 In that *n* was Belshazzar the king
Dan 6:18 palace, and passed the *n* fasting
Dan 7:2 and said, I saw in my vision by *n*
Dan 7:7 After this I saw in the *n* visions
Dan 7:13 I saw in the *n* visions, and,
Hos 4:5 shall fall with thee in the *n*
Hos 7:6 their baker sleepeth all the *n*
Joel 1:13 lie all *n* in sackcloth, ye
Amos 5:8 and maketh the day dark with *n*
Obad 5 came to thee, if robbers by *n*
Jonah 4:10 up in a *n*, and perished in a *n*
Mic 3:6 Therefore *n* shall be unto you,
Zec 1:8 I saw by *n*, and behold a man
Zec 14:7 known to the LORD, not day, nor *n*
Mt 2:14 young child and his mother by *n*
Mt 14:25 of the *n* Jesus went unto them
Mt 26:31 be offended because of me this *n*
Mt 26:34 I say unto thee, That this *n*
Mt 27:64 day, lest his disciples come by *n*
Mt 28:13 Say ye, His disciples came by *n*
Mk 4:27 And should sleep, and rise *n*
Mk 5:5 And always, *n* and day, he was in
Mk 6:48 of the *n* he cometh unto them
Mk 14:27 be offended because of me this *n*
Mk 14:30 That this day, even in this *n*
Lk 2:8 watch over their flock by *n*
Lk 2:37 God with fastings and prayers *n*
Lk 5:5 Master, we have toiled all the *n*
Lk 6:12 continued all *n* in prayer to God
Lk 12:20 this *n* thy soul shall be required
Lk 17:34 in that *n* there shall be two men
Lk 18:7 *n* unto him, though he bear long
Lk 21:37 at *n* he went out, and abode in the
Jn 3:2 The same came to Jesus by *n*
Jn 7:50 them, (he that came to Jesus by *n*
Jn 9:4 the *n* cometh, when no man can
Jn 11:10 But if a man walk in the *n*
Jn 13:30 and it was *n*
Jn 19:39 at the first came to Jesus by *n*
Jn 21:3 that *n* they caught nothing
Acts 5:19 Lord by *n* opened the prison doors
Acts 9:24 the gates day and *n* to kill him
Acts 9:25 Then the disciples took him by *n*
Acts 12:6 the same *n* Peter was sleeping
Acts 16:9 vision appeared to Paul in the *n*
Acts 16:33 took them the same hour of the *n*
Acts 17:10 Paul and Silas by *n* unto Berea
Acts 18:9 Lord to Paul in the *n* by a vision
Acts 20:31 I ceased not to warn every one *n*
Acts 23:11 the *n* following the Lord stood by
Acts 23:23 at the third hour of the *n*
Acts 23:31 and brought him by *n* to Antipatris
Acts 26:7 instantly serving God day and *n*
Acts 27:23 by me this *n* the angel of God
Acts 27:27 when the fourteenth *n* was come
Rom 13:12 The *n* is far spent, the day is at
1Cor 11:23 That the Lord Jesus the same *n* in
2Cor 11:25 thrice I suffered shipwreck, a *n*
1Th 2:9 for labouring *n* and day, because
1Th 3:10 *N* and day praying exceedingly that
1Th 5:2 so cometh as a thief in the *n*
1Th 5:5 we are not of the *n*, nor of
1Th 5:7 they that sleep sleep in the *n*
1Th 5:7 be drunken are drunken in the *n*
2Th 3:8 wrought with labour and travail *n*
1Ti 5:5 in supplications and prayers *n*
2Ti 1:3 of thee in my prayers *n* and day
2Pet 3:10 will come as a thief in the *n*
Rev 4:8 and they rest not day and *n*
Rev 7:15 serve him day and *n* in his temple
Rev 8:12 part of it, and the *n* likewise
Rev 12:10 them before our God day and *n*
Rev 14:11 and they have no rest day nor *n*
Rev 20:10 day and *n* for ever and ever
Rev 21:25 for there shall be no *n* there
Rev 22:5 And there shall be no *n* there

**NIGHTS**
Gen 7:4 the earth forty days and forty *n*
Gen 7:12 the earth forty days and forty *n*
Ex 24:18 the mount forty days and forty *n*
Ex 34:28 the LORD forty days and forty *n*
Deut 9:9 the mount forty days and forty *n*
Deut 9:11 the end of forty days and forty *n*
Deut 9:18 the first, forty days and forty *n*
Deut 9:25 the LORD forty days and forty *n*
Deut 10:10 first time, forty days and forty *n*
1Sa 30:12 any water, three days and three *n*
1Kin 19:8 forty *n* unto Horeb the mount of
Job 2:13 the ground seven days and seven *n*
Job 7:3 wearisome *n* are appointed to me
Is 21:8 and I am set in my ward whole *n*
Jonah 1:17 of the fish three days and three *n*
Mt 4:2 had fasted forty days and forty *n*
Mt 12:40 three *n* in the whale's belly
Mt 12:40 three *n* in the heart of the earth

**NIMRAH** *(nim'-rah)* See BETH-NIMRAH. *A city in Gad.*
Num 32:3 Ataroth, and Dibon, and Jazer, and *N*

**NIMRIM** *(nim'-rim) A body of water on the border of Gad.*
Is 15:6 the waters of *N* shall be desolate
Jer 48:34 also of *N* shall be desolate

**NIMROD** *(nim'-rod) Son of Cush.*
Gen 10:8 And Cush begat *N*
Gen 10:9 Even as *N* the mighty hunter
1Chr 1:10 And Cush begat *N*
Mic 5:6 the land of *N* in the entrances

**NIMSHI** *(nim'-shi) Grandfather of Jehu.*
1Kin 19:16 Jehu the son of *N* shalt thou
2Kin 9:2 son of Jehoshaphat the son of *N*
2Kin 9:14 son of *N* conspired against Joram
2Kin 9:20 the driving of Jehu the son of *N*
2Chr 22:7 Jehoram against Jehu the son of *N*

**NINE**
Gen 5:5 that Adam lived were *n* hundred
Gen 5:8 the days of Seth were *n* hundred
Gen 5:11 the days of Enos were *n* hundred
Gen 5:14 the days of Cainan were *n* hundred
Gen 5:20 of Jared were *n* hundred sixty
Gen 5:27 *n* hundred sixty and *n* years
Gen 9:29 the days of Noah were *n* hundred
Gen 11:19 *n* years, and begat sons and
Gen 11:24 And Nahor lived *n* and twenty years,
Gen 17:1 Abram was ninety years old and *n*
Gen 17:24 Abraham was ninety years old and *n*
Ex 38:24 *n* talents, and seven hundred and
Lev 25:8 be unto thee forty and *n* years
Num 1:23 *n* thousand and three hundred
Num 2:13 *n* thousand and three hundred
Num 29:26 And on the fifth day *n* bullocks
Num 34:13 to give unto the *n* tribes
Deut 3:11 *n* cubits was the length thereof,
Josh 13:7 an inheritance unto the *n* tribes
Josh 14:2 hand of Moses, for the *n* tribes
Josh 15:32 all the cities are twenty and *n*
Josh 15:44 *n* cities with their villages
Josh 15:54 *n* cities with their villages
Josh 21:16 *n* cities out of those two tribes
Judg 4:3 for he had *n* hundred chariots of
Judg 4:13 even *n* hundred chariots of iron,
2Sa 24:8 Jerusalem at the end of *n* months
2Kin 14:2 twenty and *n* years in Jerusalem
2Kin 15:13 of Jabesh began to reign in the *n*
2Kin 15:17 In the *n* and thirtieth year of
2Kin 17:1 in Samaria over Israel *n* years
2Kin 18:2 twenty and *n* years in Jerusalem
1Chr 3:8 and Eliada, and Eliphelet, *n*
1Chr 9:9 *n* hundred and fifty and six
2Chr 25:1 twenty and *n* years in Jerusalem
2Chr 29:1 twenty years old, and he reigned *n*
Ezr 1:9 a thousand chargers of silver, *n*
Ezr 2:8 of Zattu, *n* hundred forty and five
Ezr 2:36 *n* hundred seventy and three
Ezr 2:42 in all an hundred thirty and *n*
Neh 7:38 Senaah, three thousand *n* hundred
Neh 7:39 *n* hundred seventy and three
Neh 11:1 *n* parts to dwell in other cities
Neh 11:8 *n* hundred twenty and eight
Mt 18:12 doth he not leave the ninety and *n*
Mt 18:13 ninety and *n* which went not astray
Lk 15:4 *n* in the wilderness, and go after
Lk 15:7 *n* just persons, which need no
Lk 17:17 but where are the *n*

**NINETEENTH**
2Kin 25:8 which is the *n* year of king
1Chr 24:16 The *n* to Pethahiah, the twentieth
1Chr 25:26 The *n* to Mallothi, he, his sons,
Jer 52:12 month, which was the *n* year of

**NINETY**
Gen 5:9 And Enos lived *n* years, and begat
Gen 5:17 Mahalaleel were eight hundred *n*
Gen 5:30 he begat Noah five hundred *n*
Gen 17:1 And when Abram was *n* years old
Gen 17:17 that is *n* years old, bear
Gen 17:24 And Abraham was *n* years old
1Sa 4:15 Now Eli was *n* and eight years old
1Chr 9:6 their brethren, six hundred and *n*
Ezr 2:16 children of Ater of Hezekiah, *n*
Ezr 2:20 The children of Gibbar, *n*
Ezr 2:58 servants, were three hundred *n*
Ezr 8:35 twelve bullocks for all Israel, *n*
Neh 7:21 children of Ater of Hezekiah, *n*
Neh 7:25 The children of Gibeon, *n*
Neh 7:60 servants, were three hundred *n*
Jer 52:23 And there were *n* and six
Eze 4:5 the days, three hundred and *n* days
Eze 4:9 *n* days shalt thou eat thereof
Eze 41:12 and the length thereof *n* cubits
Dan 12:11 a thousand two hundred and *n* days
Mt 18:12 astray, doth he not leave the *n*
Mt 18:13 more of that sheep, than of the *n*
Lk 15:4 one of them, doth not leave the *n*
Lk 15:7 that repenteth, more than over *n*

**NINEVE** *(nen'-e-ve)* See NINEVEH, NINEVITES. *Same as Nineveh.*
Lk 11:32 The men of *N* shall rise up in the

**NINEVEH** *(nin'-e-veh)* See NINEVE. *Capital of Assyria.*
Gen 10:11 went forth Asshur, and builded *N*
Gen 10:12 And Resen between *N* and Calah
2Kin 19:36 went and returned, and dwelt at *N*
Is 37:37 went and returned, and dwelt at *N*
Jonah 1:2 Arise, go to *N*, that great city,
Jonah 3:2 Arise, go unto *N*, that great city
Jonah 3:3 So Jonah arose, and went unto *N*
Jonah 3:3 Now *N* was an exceeding great city
Jonah 3:4 days, and *N* shall be overthrown
Jonah 3:5 So the people of *N* believed God
Jonah 3:6 For word came unto the king of *N*
Jonah 3:7 published through *N* by the decree
Jonah 4:11 And should not I spare *N*, that
Nah 1:1 The burden of *N*
Nah 2:8 But *N* is of old like a pool of
Nah 3:7 thee, and say, *N* is laid waste
Zeph 2:13 will make *N* a desolation, and dry
Mt 12:41 The men of *N* shall rise in

**NINEVITES** *(nin'-e-vites) Inhabitants of Nineveh.*
Lk 11:30 as Jonas was a sign unto the *N*

**NINTH**
Lev 23:32 in the *n* day of the month at even
Lev 25:22 yet of old fruit until the *n* year
Num 7:60 On the *n* day Abidan the son of
2Kin 17:6 In the *n* year of Hoshea the king
2Kin 18:10 that is the *n* year of Hoshea king
2Kin 25:1 pass in the *n* year of his reign
2Kin 25:3 on the *n* day of the fourth month
1Chr 12:12 Johanan the eighth, Elzabad the *n*
1Chr 24:11 The *n* to Jeshua, the tenth to
1Chr 25:16 The *n* to Mattaniah, he, his sons,
1Chr 27:12 The *n* captain for the *n* month
1Chr 27:12 for the *n* month was Abiezer the
2Chr 16:12 *n* year of his reign was diseased
Ezr 10:9 It was the *n* month, on the
Jer 36:9 king of Judah, in the *n* month
Jer 36:22 in the winterhouse in the *n* month
Jer 39:1 In the *n* year of Zedekiah king of
Jer 39:2 the *n* day of the month, the city
Jer 52:4 pass in the *n* year of his reign
Jer 52:6 in the *n* day of the month, the
Eze 24:1 Again in the *n* year, in the tenth
Hag 2:10 and twentieth day of the *n* month
Hag 2:18 and twentieth day of the *n* month
Zec 7:1 in the fourth day of the *n* month
Mt 20:5 sixth and *n* hour, and did likewise
Mt 27:45 over all the land unto the *n* hour
Mt 27:46 about the *n* hour Jesus cried with
Mk 15:33 the whole land until the *n* hour
Mk 15:34 at the *n* hour Jesus cried with a
Lk 23:44 all the earth until the *n* hour
Acts 3:1 hour of prayer, being the *n* hour

Acts 10:3 *n* hour of the day an angel of God
Acts 10:30 at the *n* hour I prayed in my
Rev 21:20 the *n*, a topaz

**NISAN** *(ni'-san)* See ABIB. *First month of the Hebrew year.*
Neh 2:1 And it came to pass in the month *N*
Est 3:7 first month, that is, the month *N*

**NISROCH** *(nis'-rok) An Assyrian god.*
2Kin 19:37 in the house of *N* his god
Is 37:38 in the house of *N* his god

**NOADIAH** *(no-a-di'-ah)*
*1. Son of Binnui.*
Ezr 8:33 *N* the son of Binnui, Levites
*2. An opponent of Nehemiah.*
Neh 6:14 works, and on the prophetess *N*

**NOAH** *(no'-ah)* See NOAH'S, NOE.
*1. Son of Lamech; built the ark.*
Gen 5:29 And he called his name *N*, saying,
Gen 5:30 he begat *N* five hundred ninety
Gen 5:32 *N* was five hundred years old
Gen 5:32 *N* begat Shem, Ham, and Japheth
Gen 6:8 But *N* found grace in the eyes of
Gen 6:9 These are the generations of *N*
Gen 6:9 *N* was a just man and perfect in
Gen 6:9 generations, and *N* walked with God
Gen 6:10 *N* begat three sons, Shem, Ham, and
Gen 6:13 And God said unto *N*, The end of
Gen 6:22 Thus did *N*
Gen 7:1 And the LORD said unto *N*, Come
Gen 7:5 *N* did according unto all that the
Gen 7:6 *N* was six hundred years old when
Gen 7:7 *N* went in, and his sons, and his
Gen 7:9 two unto *N* into the ark, the male
Gen 7:9 female, as God had commanded *N*
Gen 7:13 In the selfsame day entered *N*
Gen 7:13 and Ham, and Japheth, the sons of *N*
Gen 7:15 they went in unto *N* into the ark
Gen 7:23 *N* only remained alive, and they
Gen 8:1 And God remembered *N*, and every
Gen 8:6 that *N* opened the window of the
Gen 8:11 so *N* knew that the waters were
Gen 8:13 *N* removed the covering of the ark
Gen 8:15 And God spake unto *N*, saying,
Gen 8:18 *N* went forth, and his sons, and his
Gen 8:20 *N* builded an altar unto the LORD
Gen 9:1 And God blessed *N* and his sons, and
Gen 9:8 And God spake unto *N*, and to his
Gen 9:17 And God said unto *N*, This is the
Gen 9:18 And the sons of *N*, that went forth
Gen 9:19 These are the three sons of *N*
Gen 9:20 *N* began to be an husbandman, and
Gen 9:24 *N* awoke from his wine, and knew
Gen 9:28 *N* lived after the flood three
Gen 9:29 all the days of *N* were nine
Gen 10:1 the generations of the sons of *N*
Gen 10:32 are the families of the sons of *N*
1Chr 1:4 *N*, Shem, Ham, and Japheth
Is 54:9 is as the waters of *N* unto me
Is 54:9 of *N* should no more go over the
Eze 14:14 Though these three men, *N*
Eze 14:20 Though *N*, Daniel, and Job, were in
Heb 11:7 By faith *N*, being warned of God
1Pet 3:20 of God waited in the days of *N*
2Pet 2:5 but saved *N* the eighth person, a
*2. A daughter of Zelophehad.*
Num 26:33 of Zelophehad were Mahlah, and *N*
Num 27:1 Mahlah, *N*, and Hoglah, and Milcah,
Num 36:11 and Hoglah, and Milcah, and *N*
Josh 17:3 of his daughters, Mahlah, and *N*

**NOAH'S** *(no'-ahz) Refers to Noah 1.*
Gen 7:11 the six hundredth year of *N* life
Gen 7:13 *N* wife, and the three wives of his

**NOB** *(nob) A Levitical city in Benjamin.*
1Sa 21:1 Then came David to *N* to Ahimelech
1Sa 22:9 saw the son of Jesse coming to *N*
1Sa 22:11 house, the priests that were in *N*
1Sa 22:19 And *N*, the city of the priests,
Neh 11:32 And at Anathoth, *N*, Ananiah,
Is 10:32 yet shall he remain at *N* that day

**NOBAH** *(no'-bah)* See KENAH, NOPHAH.
*1. A Manassite who captured an Amorite city.*
Num 32:42 *N* went and took Kenath, and the
Num 32:42 villages thereof, and called it *N*
*2. A city in the Trachonitis.*
Judg 8:11 dwelt in tents on the east of *N*

**NOBLE**
Ezr 4:10 *n* Asnapper brought over, and set
Est 6:9 one of the king's most *n* princes
Jer 2:21 Yet I had planted thee a *n* vine
Acts 17:11 These were more *n* than those in
Acts 24:3 places, most *n* Felix, with all
Acts 26:25 said, I am not mad, most *n* Festus
1Cor 1:26 not many mighty, not many *n*

**NOBLES**
Ex 24:11 upon the *n* of the children of
Num 21:18 the *n* of the people digged it, by
Judg 5:13 over the *n* among the people
1Kin 21:8 to the *n* that were in his city,
1Kin 21:11 the *n* who were the inhabitants in
2Chr 23:20 captains of hundreds, and the *n*
Neh 2:16 nor to the priests, nor to the *n*
Neh 3:5 but their *n* put not their necks
Neh 4:14 and rose up, and said unto the *n*
Neh 4:19 And I said unto the *n*, and to the
Neh 5:7 with myself, and I rebuked the *n*
Neh 6:17 Moreover in those days the *n* of
Neh 7:5 heart to gather together the *n*
Neh 10:29 clave to their brethren, their *n*
Neh 13:17 I contended with the *n* of Judah
Est 1:3 power of Persia and Media, the *n*
Job 29:10 The *n* held their peace, and their
Ps 83:11 Make their *n* like Oreb, and like
Ps 149:8 their *n* with fetters of iron
Prov 8:16 By me princes rule, and *n*, even
Eccl 10:17 when thy king is the son of *n*
Is 13:2 may go into the gates of the *n*
Is 34:12 They shall call the *n* thereof to
Is 43:14 and have brought down all their *n*
Jer 14:3 their *n* have sent their little
Jer 27:20 all the *n* of Judah and Jerusalem
Jer 30:21 their *n* shall be of themselves,
Jer 39:6 Babylon slew all the *n* of Judah
Jonah 3:7 the decree of the king and his *n*
Nah 3:18 thy *n* shall dwell in the dust

**NOD** *(nod) A land east of Eden.*
Gen 4:16 LORD, and dwelt in the land of *N*

**NODAB** *(no'-dab) Name of tribe east of the Jordan.*
1Chr 5:19 with Jetur, and Nephish, and *N*

**NOE** *(no'-e)* See NOAH. *Greek form of Noah.*
Mt 24:37 But as the days of *N* were
Mt 24:38 until the day that *N* entered into
Lk 3:36 of Sem, which was the son of *N*
Lk 17:26 And as it was in the days of *N*
Lk 17:27 until the day that *N* entered into

**NOGAH** *(no'-gah) A son of David.*
1Chr 3:7 And *N*, and Nepheg, and Japhia,
1Chr 14:6 And *N*, and Nepheg, and Japhia,

**NOHAH** *(no'-hah) A son of Benjamin.*
1Chr 8:2 *N* the fourth, and Rapha the fifth

**NOISE**
Ex 20:18 the *n* of the trumpet, and the
Ex 32:17 when Joshua heard the *n* of the
Ex 32:17 There is a *n* of war in the camp
Ex 32:18 but the *n* of them that sing do I
Josh 6:10 nor make any *n* with your voice,
Judg 5:11 the *n* of archers in the places of
1Sa 4:6 heard the *n* of the shout, they
1Sa 4:6 What meaneth the *n* of this great
1Sa 4:14 Eli heard the *n* of the crying
1Sa 4:14 What meaneth the *n* of this tumult
1Sa 14:19 that the *n* that was in the host
1Kin 1:41 Wherefore is this *n* of the city
1Kin 1:45 This is the *n* that ye have heard
2Kin 7:6 Syrians to hear a *n* of chariots
2Kin 7:6 a *n* of horses, even the *n* of
2Kin 11:13 Athaliah heard the *n* of the guard
1Chr 15:28 making a *n* with psalteries and
2Chr 23:12 heard the *n* of the people running
Ezr 3:13 *n* of the shout of joy from the
Ezr 3:13 *n* of the weeping of the people
Ezr 3:13 and the *n* was heard afar off
Job 36:29 or the *n* of his tabernacle
Job 36:33 The *n* thereof sheweth concerning
Job 37:2 attentively the *n* of his voice
Ps 33:3 play skilfully with a loud *n*
Ps 42:7 deep at the *n* of thy waterspouts
Ps 55:2 in my complaint, and make a *n*
Ps 59:6 they make a *n* like a dog, and go
Ps 59:14 and let them make a *n* like a dog
Ps 65:7 Which stilleth the *n* of the seas
Ps 65:7 the *n* of their waves, and the
Ps 66:1 Make a joyful *n* unto God, all ye
Ps 81:1 make a joyful *n* unto the God of
Ps 93:4 than the *n* of many waters
Ps 95:1 let us make a joyful *n* to the
Ps 95:2 make a joyful *n* unto him with
Ps 98:4 Make a joyful *n* unto the LORD
Ps 98:4 make a loud *n*, and rejoice, and
Ps 98:6 make a joyful *n* before the LORD
Ps 100:1 Make a joyful *n* unto the LORD
Is 9:5 of the warrior is with confused *n*
Is 13:4 The *n* of a multitude in the
Is 13:4 a tumultuous *n* of the kingdoms of
Is 14:11 the grave, and the *n* of thy viols
Is 17:12 a *n* like the *n* of the seas
Is 24:8 the *n* of them that rejoice endeth
Is 24:18 that he who fleeth from the *n* of
Is 25:5 bring down the *n* of strangers
Is 29:6 and with earthquake, and great *n*
Is 31:4 abase himself for the *n* of them
Is 33:3 At the *n* of the tumult the people
Is 66:6 A voice of *n* from the city, a
Jer 4:19 my heart maketh a *n* in me
Jer 4:29 flee for the *n* of the horsemen
Jer 10:22 the *n* of the bruit is come, and a
Jer 11:16 with the *n* of a great tumult he
Jer 25:31 A *n* shall come even to the ends
Jer 46:17 Pharaoh king of Egypt is but a *n*
Jer 47:3 At the *n* of the stamping of the
Jer 49:21 is moved at the *n* of their fall
Jer 49:21 at the cry the *n* thereof was
Jer 50:46 At the *n* of the taking of Babylon
Jer 51:55 a *n* of their voice is uttered
Lam 2:7 they have made a *n* in the house
Eze 1:24 I heard the *n* of their wings,
Eze 1:24 like the *n* of great waters, as
Eze 1:24 of speech, as the *n* of an host
Eze 3:13 I heard also the *n* of the wings
Eze 3:13 the *n* of the wheels over against
Eze 3:13 them, and a *n* of a great rushing
Eze 19:7 thereof, by the *n* of his roaring
Eze 26:10 shake at the *n* of the horsemen
Eze 26:13 I will cause the *n* of thy songs
Eze 37:7 and as I prophesied, there was a *n*
Eze 43:2 voice was like a *n* of many waters
Joel 2:5 Like the *n* of chariots on the
Joel 2:5 like the *n* of a flame of fire
Amos 5:23 away from me the *n* of thy songs
Mic 2:12 they shall make great *n* by reason
Nah 3:2 The *n* of a whip, and the *n* of
Zeph 1:10 that there shall be the *n* of a
Zec 9:15 and make a *n* as through wine
Mt 9:23 and the people making a *n*,
2Pet 3:10 shall pass away with a great *n*
Rev 6:1 as it were the *n* of thunder

**NOISED**
Josh 6:27 his fame was *n* throughout all the
Mk 2:1 it was *n* that he was in the house
Lk 1:65 all these sayings were *n* abroad
Acts 2:6 Now when this was *n* abroad

**NOISOME**
Ps 91:3 fowler, and from the *n* pestilence
Eze 14:15 If I cause *n* beasts to pass
Eze 14:21 the *n* beast, and the pestilence,
Rev 16:2 and there fell a *n* and grievous

**NON** *(non)* See NUN. *Son of Elishama.*
1Chr 7:27 *N* his son, Jehoshuah his son

**NOON**
Gen 43:16 these men shall dine with me at *n*
Gen 43:25 present against Joseph came at *n*
2Sa 4:5 who lay on a bed at *n*
1Kin 18:26 of Baal from morning even until *n*
1Kin 18:27 And it came to pass at *n*, that
1Kin 20:16 And they went out at *n*
2Kin 4:20 he sat on her knees till *n*
Ps 55:17 Evening, and morning, and at *n*
Song 1:7 makest thy flock to rest at *n*
Jer 6:4 arise, and let us go up at *n*
Amos 8:9 cause the sun to go down at *n*
Acts 22:6 come nigh unto Damascus about *n*

**NOONDAY**
Deut 28:29 And thou shalt grope at *n*, as the
Job 5:14 grope in the *n* as in the night
Job 11:17 age shall be clearer than the *n*
Ps 37:6 light, and thy judgment as the *n*
Ps 91:6 the destruction that wasteth at *n*
Is 16:3 the night in the midst of the *n*
Is 58:10 and thy darkness be as the *n*

Is 59:10 we stumble at *n* as in the night
Jer 15:8 of the young men a spoiler at *n*
Zeph 2:4 shall drive out Ashdod at the *n*

**NOPH** *(nof)* See MEMPHIS. *Same as Memphis.*
Is 19:13 the princes of *N* are deceived
Jer 2:16 Also the children of *N* and
Jer 44:1 Migdol, and at Tahpanhes, and at *N*
Jer 46:14 in Migdol, and publish in *N*
Jer 46:19 for *N* shall be waste and desolate
Eze 30:13 their images to cease out of *N*
Eze 30:16 *N* shall have distresses daily

**NOPHAH** *(no'-fah)* See NOBAH. *A city in Sihon.*
Num 21:30 have laid them waste even unto *N*

**NORTH**
Gen 28:14 west, and to the east, and to the *n*
Ex 26:20 the *n* side there shall be twenty
Ex 26:35 shalt put the table on the *n* side
Ex 27:11 likewise for the *n* side in length
Ex 36:25 which is toward the *n* corner
Ex 38:11 for the *n* side the hangings were
Num 2:25 be on the *n* side by their armies
Num 34:7 And this shall be your *n* border
Num 34:9 this shall be your *n* border
Num 35:5 on the *n* side two thousand cubits
Josh 8:11 and pitched on the *n* side of Ai
Josh 8:13 that was on the *n* of the city
Josh 11:2 were on the *n* of the mountains
Josh 15:5 their border in the *n* quarter was
Josh 15:6 along by the *n* of Beth-arabah
Josh 15:10 which is Chesalon, on the *n* side
Josh 16:6 sea to Michmethah on the *n* side
Josh 17:9 was on the *n* side of the river
Josh 17:10 met together in Asher on the *n*
Josh 18:5 abide in their coasts on the *n*
Josh 18:12 their border on the *n* side was
Josh 18:12 the side of Jericho on the *n* side
Josh 18:16 the valley of the giants on the *n*
Josh 18:17 And was drawn from the *n*, and went
Josh 18:19 of the border were at the *n* bay
Josh 19:14 it on the *n* side to Hannathon
Josh 19:27 toward the *n* side of Beth-emek
Josh 24:30 on the *n* side of the hill of
Judg 2:9 on the *n* side of the hill Gaash
Judg 7:1 were on the *n* side of them
Judg 21:19 which is on the *n* side of Beth-el
1Kin 7:25 oxen, three looking toward the *n*
2Kin 16:14 put it on the *n* side of the altar
1Chr 9:24 porters, toward the east, west, *n*
2Chr 4:4 oxen, three looking toward the *n*
Job 26:7 out the *n* over the empty place
Job 37:9 and cold out of the *n*
Job 37:22 Fair weather cometh out of the *n*
Ps 48:2 mount Zion, on the sides of the *n*
Ps 89:12 The *n* and the south thou hast
Ps 107:3 and from the west, from the *n*
Prov 25:23 The *n* wind driveth away rain
Eccl 1:6 and turneth about unto the *n*
Eccl 11:3 toward the south, or toward the *n*
Song 4:16 Awake, O *n* wind
Is 14:13 in the sides of the *n*
Is 14:31 shall come from the *n* a smoke
Is 41:25 I have raised up one from the *n*
Is 43:6 I will say to the *n*, Give up
Is 49:12 and, lo, these from the *n* and from
Jer 1:13 the face thereof is toward the *n*
Jer 1:14 Out of the *n* an evil shall break
Jer 1:15 families of the kingdoms of the *n*
Jer 3:12 proclaim these words toward the *n*
Jer 3:18 *n* to the land that I have given
Jer 4:6 for I will bring evil from the *n*
Jer 6:1 for evil appeareth out of the *n*
Jer 6:22 people cometh from the *n* country
Jer 10:22 commotion out of the *n* country
Jer 13:20 behold them that come from the *n*
Jer 16:15 of Israel from the land of the *n*
Jer 23:8 of Israel out of the *n* country
Jer 25:9 and take all the families of the *n*
Jer 25:26 And all the kings of the *n*
Jer 31:8 bring them from the *n* country
Jer 46:6 fall toward the *n* by the river
Jer 46:10 hosts hath a sacrifice in the *n*
Jer 46:20 it cometh out of the *n*
Jer 46:24 the hand of the people of the *n*
Jer 47:2 waters rise up out of the *n*
Jer 50:3 For out of the *n* there cometh up
Jer 50:9 great nations from the *n* country
Jer 50:41 a people shall come from the *n*
Jer 51:48 shall come unto her from the *n*
Eze 1:4 a whirlwind came out of the *n*
Eze 8:3 gate, that looketh toward the *n*
Eze 8:5 eyes now the way toward the *n*
Eze 8:5 up mine eyes the way toward the *n*
Eze 8:14 house which was toward the *n*
Eze 9:2 gate, which lieth toward the *n*
Eze 20:47 to the *n* shall be burned therein
Eze 21:4 all flesh from the south to the *n*
Eze 26:7 a king of kings, from the *n*
Eze 32:30 There be the princes of the *n*
Eze 38:6 of Togarmah of the *n* quarters
Eze 38:15 from thy place out of the *n* parts
Eze 39:2 thee to come up from the *n* parts
Eze 40:20 court that looked toward the *n*
Eze 40:23 against the gate toward the *n*
Eze 40:35 And he brought me to the *n* gate
Eze 40:40 up to the entry of the *n* gate
Eze 40:44 was at the side of the *n* gate
Eze 40:44 having the prospect toward the *n*
Eze 40:46 toward the *n* is for the priests
Eze 41:11 was left, one door toward the *n*
Eze 42:1 utter court, the way toward the *n*
Eze 42:1 before the building toward the *n*
Eze 42:2 an hundred cubits was the *n* door
Eze 42:4 and their doors toward the *n*
Eze 42:11 chambers which were toward the *n*
Eze 42:13 The *n* chambers and the south
Eze 42:17 He measured the *n* side, five
Eze 44:4 of the *n* gate before the house
Eze 46:9 entereth in by the way of the *n*
Eze 46:9 go forth by the way of the *n* gate
Eze 46:19 which looked toward the *n*
Eze 47:15 of the land toward the *n* side
Eze 47:17 the *n* northward, and the border of
Eze 47:17 And this is the *n* side
Eze 48:1 From the *n* end to the coast of
Eze 48:10 toward the *n* five and twenty
Eze 48:16 the *n* side four thousand and five
Eze 48:17 shall be toward the *n* two hundred
Eze 48:30 out of the city on the *n* side
Dan 11:6 of the *n* to make an agreement
Dan 11:7 the fortress of the king of the *n*
Dan 11:8 more years than the king of the *n*
Dan 11:11 him, even with the king of the *n*
Dan 11:13 the king of the *n* shall return
Dan 11:15 So the king of the *n* shall come
Dan 11:40 the king of the *n* shall come
Dan 11:44 out of the *n* shall trouble him
Amos 8:12 from the *n* even to the east, they
Zeph 2:13 out his hand against the *n*
Zec 2:6 and flee from the land of the *n*
Zec 6:6 go forth into the *n* country
Zec 6:8 these that go toward the *n*
Zec 6:8 my spirit in the *n* country
Zec 14:4 shall remove toward the *n*
Lk 13:29 and from the west, and from the *n*
Acts 27:12 toward the south west and *n* west
Rev 21:13 on the *n* three gates

**NORTHWARD**
Gen 13:14 from the place where thou art *n*
Ex 40:22 upon the side of the tabernacle *n*
Lev 1:11 of the altar *n* before the LORD
Num 3:35 on the side of the tabernacle *n*
Deut 2:3 turn you *n*
Deut 3:27 lift up thine eyes westward, and *n*
Josh 13:3 even unto the borders of Ekron *n*
Josh 15:7 from the valley of Achor, and so *n*
Josh 15:8 end of the valley of the giants *n*
Josh 15:11 went out unto the side of Ekron *n*
Josh 17:10 *n* it was Manasseh's, and the sea
Josh 18:18 the side over against Arabah *n*
Josh 18:19 to the side of Beth-hoglah *n*
Judg 12:1 themselves together, and went *n*
1Sa 14:5 situate *n* over against Michmash
1Chr 26:14 and his lot came out *n*
1Chr 26:17 *n* four a day, southward four a
Eze 8:5 behold *n* at the gate of the altar
Eze 40:19 an hundred cubits eastward and *n*
Eze 47:2 me out of the way of the gate *n*
Eze 47:17 of Damascus, and the north *n*
Eze 48:1 the border of Damascus *n*
Eze 48:31 three gates *n*; one gate
Dan 8:4 the ram pushing westward, and *n*

**NOSE**
Lev 21:18 a lame, or he that hath a flat *n*
2Kin 19:28 I will put my hook in thy *n*
Job 40:24 his *n* pierceth through snares
Job 41:2 Canst thou put an hook into his *n*
Prov 30:33 the wringing of the *n* bringeth
Song 7:4 thy *n* is as the tower of Lebanon
Song 7:8 and the smell of thy *n* like apples
Is 3:21 The rings, and *n* jewels,
Is 37:29 will I put my hook in thy *n*
Is 65:5 These are a smoke in my *n*
Eze 8:17 they put the branch to their *n*
Eze 23:25 they shall take away thy *n*

**NOSTRILS**
Gen 2:7 breathed into his *n* the breath of
Gen 7:22 All in whose *n* was the breath of
Ex 15:8 with the blast of thy *n* the
Num 11:20 until it come out at your *n*
2Sa 22:9 went up a smoke out of his *n*
2Sa 22:16 the blast of the breath of his *n*
Job 4:9 breath of his *n* are they consumed
Job 27:3 and the spirit of God is in my *n*
Job 39:20 the glory of his *n* is terrible
Job 41:20 Out of his *n* goeth smoke, as out
Ps 18:8 went up a smoke out of his *n*
Ps 18:15 the blast of the breath of thy *n*
Is 2:22 man, whose breath is in his *n*
Lam 4:20 The breath of our *n*, the anointed
Amos 4:10 your camps to come up unto your *n*

**NOTABLE**
Dan 8:5 the goat had a *n* horn between his
Dan 8:8 for it came up four *n* ones toward
Mt 27:16 And they had then a *n* prisoner
Acts 2:20 great and *n* day of the Lord come
Acts 4:16 for that indeed a *n* miracle hath

**NOTE**
Is 30:8 *n* it in a book, that it may be
Rom 16:7 who are of *n* among the apostles,
2Th 3:14 *n* that man, and have no company

**NOTWITHSTANDING**
Ex 16:20 *N* they hearkened not unto Moses
Ex 21:21 *N*, if he continue a day or two,
Lev 25:32 *N* the cities of the Levites, and
Lev 27:28 *N* no devoted thing, that a man
Num 26:11 *N* the children of Korah died not
Num 26:55 *N* the land shall be divided by
Deut 1:26 *N* ye would not go up, but
Deut 12:15 *N* thou mayest kill and eat flesh
Josh 22:19 *N*, if the land of your possession
Judg 4:9 *n* the journey that thou takest
Judg 9:5 *n* yet Jotham the youngest son of
1Sa 2:25 *N* they hearkened not unto the
1Sa 20:8 *n*, if there be in me iniquity,
1Sa 29:9 *n* the princes of the Philistines
2Sa 24:4 *N* the king's word prevailed
1Kin 11:12 *N* in thy days I will not do it
2Kin 17:14 *N* they would not hear, but
2Kin 23:26 *N* the LORD turned not from the
2Chr 6:9 *N* thou shalt not build the house
2Chr 32:26 *N* Hezekiah humbled himself for
Jer 35:14 *n* I have spoken unto you, rising
Eze 20:21 *N* the children rebelled against
Mic 7:13 *N* the land shall be desolate
Mt 2:22 *n*, being warned of God in a dream
Mt 11:11 *n* he that is least in the kingdom
Mt 17:27 *N*, lest we should offend them, go
Lk 10:11 *n* be ye sure of this, that the
Lk 10:20 *N* in this rejoice not, that the
Acts 15:34 *N* it pleased Silas to abide there
Acts 24:4 *N*, that I be not further tedious
Phil 1:18 *n*, every way, whether in pretence
Phil 4:14 *N* ye have well done, that ye did
1Ti 2:15 *N* she shall be saved in
2Ti 4:17 *N* the Lord stood with me, and
Jas 2:16 *n* ye give them not those things
Rev 2:20 *N* I have a few things against

**NOUGHT**
Gen 29:15 thou therefore serve me for *n*
Deut 13:17 there shall cleave *n* of the
Deut 15:9 brother, and thou givest him *n*
Deut 28:63 destroy you, and to bring you to *n*
Neh 4:15 had brought their counsel to *n*
Job 1:9 and said, Doth Job fear God for *n*
Job 8:22 of the wicked shall come to *n*
Job 14:18 the mountain falling cometh to *n*
Job 22:6 a pledge from thy brother for *n*
Ps 33:10 the counsel of the heathen to *n*
Ps 44:12 Thou sellest thy people for *n*
Prov 1:25 ye have set at *n* all my counsel
Is 8:10 together, and it shall come to *n*
Is 29:20 the terrible one is brought to *n*
Is 29:21 aside the just for a thing of *n*
Is 41:12 be as nothing, and as a thing of *n*

Is 41:24 are of nothing, and your work of *n*
Is 49:4 I have spent my strength for *n*
Is 52:3 Ye have sold yourselves for *n*
Is 52:5 my people is taken away for *n*
Jer 14:14 and divination, and a thing of *n*
Amos 5:5 and Beth-el shall come to *n*
Amos 6:13 Ye which rejoice in a thing of *n*
Mal 1:10 that would shut the doors for *n*
Mal 1:10 kindle fire on mine altar for *n*
Mk 9:12 many things, and be set at *n*
Lk 23:11 with his men of war set him at *n*
Acts 4:11 was set at *n* of you builders
Acts 5:36 were scattered, and brought to *n*
Acts 5:38 work be of men, it will come to *n*
Acts 19:27 craft is in danger to be set at *n*
Rom 14:10 dost thou set at *n* thy brother
1Cor 1:28 to bring to *n* things that are
1Cor 2:6 of this world, that come to *n*
2Th 3:8 did we eat any man's bread for *n*
Rev 18:17 hour so great riches is come to *n*

## NOURISH
Gen 45:11 And there will I *n* thee
Gen 50:21 I will *n* you, and your little ones
Is 7:21 that a man shall *n* a young cow
Is 23:4 neither do I *n* up young men
Is 44:14 an ash, and the rain doth *n* it

## NOURISHED
Gen 47:12 Joseph *n* his father, and his
2Sa 12:3 lamb, which he had bought and *n* up
Is 1:2 the LORD hath spoken, I have *n*
Eze 19:2 she *n* her whelps among young
Acts 7:20 *n* up in his father's house three
Acts 7:21 him up, and *n* him for her own son
Acts 12:20 was *n* by the king's country
1Ti 4:6 *n* up in the words of faith and of
Jas 5:5 ye have *n* your hearts, as in a
Rev 12:14 place, where she is *n* for a time

## NUMBER
Gen 13:16 so that if a man can *n* the dust
Gen 15:5 stars, if thou be able to *n* them
Gen 34:30 and I being few in *n*, they shall
Gen 41:49 for it was without *n*
Ex 12:4 according to the *n* of the souls
Ex 16:16 to the *n* of your persons
Ex 23:26 the *n* of thy days I will fulfil
Ex 30:12 children of Israel after their *n*
Lev 15:13 then he shall *n* to himself seven
Lev 15:28 then she shall *n* to herself seven
Lev 23:16 sabbath shall ye *n* fifty days
Lev 25:8 thou shalt *n* seven sabbaths of
Lev 25:15 According to the *n* of years after
Lev 25:15 according unto the *n* of years of
Lev 25:16 for according to the *n* of the
Lev 25:50 be according unto the *n* of years
Lev 26:22 your cattle, and make you few in *n*
Num 1:2 with the *n* of their names, every
Num 1:3 Aaron shall *n* them by their
Num 1:18 according to the *n* of the names
Num 1:20 according to the *n* of the names
Num 1:22 according to the *n* of the names
Num 1:24 according to the *n* of the names
Num 1:26 according to the *n* of the names
Num 1:28 according to the *n* of the names
Num 1:30 according to the *n* of the names
Num 1:32 according to the *n* of the names
Num 1:34 according to the *n* of the names
Num 1:36 according to the *n* of the names
Num 1:38 according to the *n* of the names
Num 1:40 according to the *n* of the names
Num 1:42 according to the *n* of the names
Num 1:49 shalt not *n* the tribe of Levi
Num 3:15 *N* the children of Levi after the
Num 3:15 old and upward shalt thou *n* them
Num 3:22 to the *n* of all the males
Num 3:28 In the *n* of all the males, from a
Num 3:34 to the *n* of all the males
Num 3:40 *N* all the firstborn of the males
Num 3:40 take the *n* of their names
Num 3:43 firstborn males by the *n* of names
Num 3:48 wherewith the odd *n* of them is to
Num 4:23 fifty years old shalt thou *n* them
Num 4:29 thou shalt *n* them after their
Num 4:30 fifty years old shalt thou *n* them
Num 4:37 Aaron did *n* according to the
Num 4:41 Aaron did *n* according to the
Num 14:29 of you, according to your whole *n*
Num 14:34 After the *n* of the days in which
Num 15:12 According to the *n* that ye shall
Num 15:12 to every one according to their *n*
Num 23:10 the *n* of the fourth part of
Num 26:53 according to the *n* of names
Num 29:18 shall be according to their *n*
Num 29:21 shall be according to their *n*
Num 29:24 shall be according to their *n*
Num 29:27 shall be according to their *n*
Num 29:30 shall be according to their *n*
Num 29:33 shall be according to their *n*
Num 29:37 shall be according to their *n*
Num 31:36 was in *n* three hundred thousand
Deut 4:27 left few in *n* among the heathen
Deut 7:7 ye were more in *n* than any people
Deut 16:9 weeks shalt thou *n* unto thee
Deut 16:9 begin to *n* the seven weeks from
Deut 25:2 to his fault, by a certain *n*
Deut 28:62 And ye shall be left few in *n*
Deut 32:8 the *n* of the children of Israel
Josh 4:5 according unto the *n* of the
Josh 4:8 according to the *n* of the tribes
Judg 6:5 and their camels were without *n*
Judg 7:6 the *n* of them that lapped,
Judg 7:12 and their camels were without *n*
Judg 21:23 them wives, according to their *n*
1Sa 6:4 according to the *n* of the lords
1Sa 6:18 according to the *n* of all the
1Sa 14:17 *N* now, and see who is gone from us
2Sa 2:15 went over by *n* twelve of Benjamin
2Sa 21:20 six toes, four and twenty in *n*
2Sa 24:1 to say, Go, *n* Israel and Judah
2Sa 24:2 *n* ye the people, that I may know
2Sa 24:2 I may know the *n* of the people
2Sa 24:4 to *n* the people of Israel
2Sa 24:9 the *n* of the people unto the king
1Kin 18:31 according to the *n* of the tribes
1Kin 20:25 *n* thee an army, like the army
1Chr 7:2 whose *n* was in the days of David
1Chr 7:9 the *n* of them, after their
1Chr 7:40 the *n* throughout the genealogy of
1Chr 11:11 this is the *n* of the mighty men
1Chr 21:1 and provoked David to *n* Israel
1Chr 21:2 *n* Israel from Beer-sheba even to
1Chr 21:2 bring the *n* of them to me, that I
1Chr 21:5 of the *n* of the people unto David
1Chr 22:16 brass, and the iron, there is no *n*
1Chr 23:3 their *n* by their polls, man by
1Chr 23:24 by *n* of names by their polls
1Chr 23:31 moons, and on the set feasts, by *n*
1Chr 25:1 the *n* of the workmen according to
1Chr 25:7 So the *n* of them, with their
1Chr 27:1 children of Israel after their *n*
1Chr 27:23 But David took not the *n* of them
1Chr 27:24 the son of Zeruiah began to *n*
1Chr 27:24 neither was the *n* put in the
2Chr 12:3 the people were without *n* that
2Chr 26:11 according to the *n* of their
2Chr 26:12 The whole *n* of the chief of the
2Chr 29:32 the *n* of the burnt offerings,
2Chr 30:24 a great *n* of priests sanctified
2Chr 35:7 to the *n* of thirty thousand, and
Ezr 1:9 And this is the *n* of them
Ezr 2:2 The *n* of the men of the people of
Ezr 3:4 the daily burnt offerings by *n*
Ezr 6:17 according to the *n* of the tribes
Ezr 8:34 By *n* and by weight of every one
Neh 7:7 The *n*, I say, of the men of the
Est 9:11 On that day the *n* of those that
Job 1:5 according to the *n* of them all
Job 3:6 not come into the *n* of the months
Job 5:9 marvellous things without *n*
Job 9:10 yea, and wonders without *n*
Job 14:5 the *n* of his months are with thee
Job 15:20 the *n* of years is hidden to the
Job 21:21 when the *n* of his months is cut
Job 25:3 Is there any *n* of his armies
Job 31:37 unto him the *n* of my steps
Job 34:24 in pieces mighty men without *n*
Job 36:26 neither can the *n* of his years be
Job 38:21 or because the *n* of thy days is
Job 38:37 Who can *n* the clouds in wisdom
Job 39:2 Canst thou *n* the months that they
Ps 90:12 So teach us to *n* our days
Ps 105:12 When they were but a few men in *n*
Ps 105:34 caterpillers, and that without *n*
Ps 139:18 they are more in *n* than the sand
Ps 147:4 He telleth the *n* of the stars
Song 6:8 concubines, and virgins without *n*
Is 21:17 the residue of the *n* of archers
Is 40:26 that bringeth out their host by *n*
Is 65:11 the drink offering unto that *n*
Is 65:12 will I *n* you to the sword
Jer 2:28 for according to the *n* of thy
Jer 2:32 have forgotten me days without *n*
Jer 11:13 For according to the *n* of thy
Jer 11:13 according to the *n* of the streets
Jer 44:28 Yet a small *n* that escape the
Eze 4:4 according to the *n* of the days
Eze 4:5 according to the *n* of the days
Eze 4:9 according to the *n* of the days
Eze 5:3 also take thereof a few in *n*
Dan 9:2 by books the *n* of the years
Hos 1:10 Yet the *n* of the children of
Joel 1:6 my land, strong, and without *n*
Nah 3:3 slain, and a great *n* of carcases
Mk 10:46 a great *n* of people, blind
Lk 22:3 being of the *n* of the twelve
Jn 6:10 down, in *n* about five thousand
Acts 1:15 (the *n* of names together were
Acts 4:4 the *n* of the men was about five
Acts 5:36 to whom a *n* of men, about four
Acts 6:1 when the *n* of the disciples was
Acts 6:7 the *n* of the disciples multiplied
Acts 11:21 a great *n* believed, and turned
Acts 16:5 faith, and increased in *n* daily
Rom 9:27 Though the *n* of the children of
2Cor 10:12 dare not make ourselves of the *n*
1Ti 5:9 the *n* under threescore years old
Rev 5:11 the *n* of them was ten thousand
Rev 7:4 I heard the *n* of them which were
Rev 7:9 multitude, which no man could *n*
Rev 9:16 the *n* of the army of the horsemen
Rev 9:16 and I heard the *n* of them
Rev 13:17 the beast, or the *n* of his name
Rev 13:18 count the *n* of the beast
Rev 13:18 for it is the *n* of a man
Rev 13:18 his *n* is six hundred threescore
Rev 15:2 over the *n* of his name, stand on
Rev 20:8 the *n* of whom is as the sand of

## NUMBERED
Gen 13:16 then shall thy seed also be *n*
Gen 16:10 it shall not be *n* for multitude
Gen 32:12 which cannot be *n* for multitude
Ex 30:13 passeth among them that are *n*
Ex 30:14 passeth among them that are *n*
Ex 38:25 were *n* of the congregation was an
Ex 38:26 for every one that went to be *n*
Num 1:19 so he *n* them in the wilderness of
Num 1:21 Those that were *n* of them
Num 1:22 those that were *n* of them
Num 1:23 Those that were *n* of them
Num 1:25 Those that were *n* of them
Num 1:27 Those that were *n* of them
Num 1:29 Those that were *n* of them
Num 1:31 Those that were *n* of them
Num 1:33 Those that were *n* of them
Num 1:35 Those that were *n* of them
Num 1:37 Those that were *n* of them
Num 1:39 Those that were *n* of them
Num 1:41 Those that were *n* of them
Num 1:43 Those that were *n* of them
Num 1:44 *n*, which Moses and Aaron *n*
Num 1:45 were *n* of the children of Israel
Num 1:46 Even all they that were *n* were
Num 1:47 fathers were not *n* among them
Num 2:4 and those that were *n* of them
Num 2:6 and those that were *n* thereof
Num 2:8 and those that were *n* thereof
Num 2:9 All that were *n* in the camp of
Num 2:11 and those that were *n* thereof
Num 2:13 and those that were *n* of them
Num 2:15 and those that were *n* of them
Num 2:16 All that were *n* in the camp of
Num 2:19 and those that were *n* of them
Num 2:21 and those that were *n* of them
Num 2:23 and those that were *n* of them
Num 2:24 All that were *n* of the camp of
Num 2:26 and those that were *n* of them
Num 2:28 and those that were *n* of them
Num 2:30 and those that were *n* of them
Num 2:31 All they that were *n* in the camp
Num 2:32 These are those which were *n* of
Num 2:32 all those that were *n* of the
Num 2:33 But the Levites were not *n* among
Num 3:16 Moses *n* them according to the
Num 3:22 Those that were *n* of them
Num 3:22 even those that were *n* of them
Num 3:34 And those that were *n* of them
Num 3:39 All that were *n* of the Levites,
Num 3:39 Aaron *n* at the commandment of the
Num 3:42 Moses *n*, as the LORD commanded

Num 3:43 of those that were *n* of them
Num 4:34 *n* the sons of the Kohathites
Num 4:36 those that were *n* of them by
Num 4:37 were *n* of the families of the
Num 4:38 those that were *n* of the sons of
Num 4:40 Even those that were *n* of them
Num 4:41 These are they that were *n* of the
Num 4:42 those that were *n* of the families
Num 4:44 Even those that were *n* of them
Num 4:45 These be those that were *n* of the
Num 4:45 Aaron *n* according to the word of
Num 4:46 those that were *n* of the Levites
Num 4:46 and Aaron and the chief of Israel *n*
Num 4:48 Even those that were *n* of them
Num 4:49 they were *n* by the hand of Moses
Num 4:49 thus were they *n* of him, as the
Num 7:2 and were over them that were *n*
Num 14:29 and all that were *n* of you
Num 26:7 they that were *n* of them were
Num 26:18 to those that were *n* of them
Num 26:22 to those that were *n* of them
Num 26:25 to those that were *n* of them
Num 26:27 to those that were *n* of them
Num 26:34 and those that were *n* of them
Num 26:37 to those that were *n* of them
Num 26:41 they that were *n* of them were
Num 26:43 to those that were *n* of them
Num 26:47 to those that were *n* of them
Num 26:50 they that were *n* of them were
Num 26:51 These were the *n* of the children
Num 26:54 to those that were *n* of him
Num 26:57 these are they that were *n* of the
Num 26:62 those that were *n* of them were
Num 26:62 for they were not *n* among the
Num 26:63 are they that were *n* by Moses
Num 26:63 who *n* the children of Israel in
Num 26:64 whom Moses and Aaron the priest *n*
Num 26:64 when they *n* the children of
Josh 8:10 *n* the people, and went up, he and
Judg 20:15 the children of Benjamin were *n*
Judg 20:15 which were *n* seven hundred chosen
Judg 20:17 were *n* four hundred thousand men
Judg 21:9 For the people were *n*, and, behold
1Sa 11:8 when he *n* them in Bezek, the
1Sa 13:15 Saul *n* the people that were
1Sa 14:17 And when they had *n*, behold,
1Sa 15:4 *n* them in Telaim, two hundred
2Sa 18:1 David *n* the people that were with
2Sa 24:10 after that he had *n* the people
1Kin 3:8 that cannot be *n* nor counted for
1Kin 8:5 not be told nor *n* for multitude
1Kin 20:15 Then he *n* the young men of the
1Kin 20:15 after them he *n* all the people,
1Kin 20:26 that Ben-hadad *n* the Syrians
1Kin 20:27 And the children of Israel were *n*
2Kin 3:6 the same time, and *n* all Israel
1Chr 21:17 that commanded the people to be *n*
1Chr 23:3 Now the Levites were *n* from the
1Chr 23:27 were *n* from twenty years old
2Chr 2:17 Solomon *n* all the strangers that
2Chr 2:17 David his father had *n* them
2Chr 5:6 not be told nor *n* for multitude
2Chr 25:5 he *n* them from twenty years old
Ezr 1:8 *n* them unto Sheshbazzar, the
Ps 40:5 them, they are more than can be *n*
Eccl 1:15 that which is wanting cannot be *n*
Is 22:10 ye have *n* the houses of Jerusalem
Is 53:12 he was *n* with the transgressors
Jer 33:22 As the host of heaven cannot be *n*
Dan 5:26 God hath *n* thy kingdom, and
Hos 1:10 which cannot be measured nor *n*
Mt 10:30 very hairs of your head are all *n*
Mk 15:28 he was *n* with the transgressors
Lk 12:7 very hairs of your head are all *n*
Acts 1:17 For he was *n* with us, and had
Acts 1:26 he was *n* with the eleven apostles

**NUN** *(nun)* See NON. *Father of Joshua.*
Ex 33:11 his servant Joshua, the son of *N*
Num 11:28 And Joshua the son of *N*, the
Num 13:8 of Ephraim, Oshea the son of *N*
Num 13:16 Oshea the son of *N* Jehoshua
Num 14:6 And Joshua the son of *N*, and Caleb
Num 14:30 Jephunneh, and Joshua the son of *N*
Num 14:38 But Joshua the son of *N*, and Caleb
Num 26:65 Jephunneh, and Joshua the son of *N*
Num 27:18 Take thee Joshua the son of *N*
Num 32:12 Kenezite, and Joshua the son of *N*
Num 32:28 priest, and Joshua the son of *N*
Num 34:17 priest, and Joshua the son of *N*
Deut 1:38 But Joshua the son of *N*, which
Deut 31:23 gave Joshua the son of *N* a charge
Deut 32:44 he, and Hoshea the son of *N*
Deut 34:9 Joshua the son of *N* was full of
Josh 1:1 spake unto Joshua the son of *N*
Josh 2:1 Joshua the son of *N* sent out of
Josh 2:23 and came to Joshua the son of *N*
Josh 6:6 Joshua the son of *N* called the
Josh 14:1 priest, and Joshua the son of *N*
Josh 17:4 and before Joshua the son of *N*
Josh 19:49 to Joshua the son of *N* among them
Josh 19:51 priest, and Joshua the son of *N*
Josh 21:1 and unto Joshua the son of *N*
Josh 24:29 things, that Joshua the son of *N*
Judg 2:8 And Joshua the son of *N*, the
1Kin 16:34 he spake by Joshua the son of *N*
Neh 8:17 of *N* unto that day had not the

**NURSE**
Gen 24:59 Rebekah their sister, and her *n*
Gen 35:8 But Deborah Rebekah's *n* died
Ex 2:7 call to thee a *n* of the Hebrew
Ex 2:7 that she may *n* the child for thee
Ex 2:9 *n* it for me, and I will give thee
Ruth 4:16 in her bosom, and became *n* unto it
2Sa 4:4 his *n* took him up, and fled
2Kin 11:2 they hid him, even him and his *n*
2Chr 22:11 put him and his *n* in a bedchamber
1Th 2:7 even as a *n* cherisheth her

**NYMPHAS** *(nim'-fas) A Christian at Colosse.*
Col 4:15 which are in Laodicea, and *N*

# O

**OAK**
Gen 35:4 under the *o* which was by Shechem
Gen 35:8 buried beneath Beth-el under an *o*
Josh 24:26 and set it up there under an *o*
Judg 6:11 sat under an *o* which was in
Judg 6:19 it out unto him under the *o*
2Sa 18:9 the thick boughs of a great *o*
2Sa 18:9 and his head caught hold of the *o*
2Sa 18:10 I saw Absalom hanged in an *o*
2Sa 18:14 yet alive in the midst of the *o*
1Kin 13:14 and found him sitting under an *o*
1Chr 10:12 their bones under the *o* in Jabesh
Is 1:30 be as an *o* whose leaf fadeth
Is 6:13 as a teil tree, and as an *o*
Is 44:14 and taketh the cypress and the *o*
Eze 6:13 tree, and under every thick *o*

**OAKS**
Is 1:29 of the *o* which ye have desired
Is 2:13 up, and upon all the *o* of Bashan
Eze 27:6 Of the *o* of Bashan have they made
Hos 4:13 incense upon the hills, under *o*
Amos 2:9 cedars, and he was strong as the *o*
Zec 11:2 howl, O ye *o* of Bashan

**OATH**
Gen 24:8 shalt be clear from this my *o*
Gen 24:41 thou be clear from this my *o*
Gen 24:41 thou shalt be clear from my *o*
Gen 26:3 I will perform the *o* which I
Gen 26:28 Let there be now an *o* betwixt us
Gen 50:25 Joseph took an *o* of the children
Ex 22:11 Then shall an *o* of the LORD be
Lev 5:4 a man shall pronounce with an *o*
Num 5:19 priest shall charge her by an *o*
Num 5:21 the woman with an *o* of cursing
Num 5:21 an *o* among thy people, when the
Num 30:2 or swear an *o* to bind his soul
Num 30:10 her soul by a bond with an *o*
Num 30:13 every binding *o* to afflict the
Deut 7:8 because he would keep the *o* which
Deut 29:12 the LORD thy God, and into his *o*
Deut 29:14 do I make this covenant and this *o*
Josh 2:17 *o* which thou hast made us swear
Josh 2:20 *o* which thou hast made us to
Josh 9:20 because of the *o* which we sware
Judg 21:5 For they had made a great *o*
1Sa 14:26 for the people feared the *o*
1Sa 14:27 charged the people with the *o*
1Sa 14:28 charged the people with an *o*
2Sa 21:7 LORD's *o* that was between them
1Kin 2:43 thou not kept the *o* of the LORD
1Kin 8:31 an *o* be laid upon him to cause
1Kin 8:31 the *o* come before thine altar in
1Kin 18:10 he took an *o* of the kingdom and
2Kin 11:4 took an *o* of them in the house of
1Chr 16:16 Abraham, and of his *o* unto Isaac
2Chr 6:22 an *o* be laid upon him to make him
2Chr 6:22 the *o* come before thine altar in
2Chr 15:15 And all Judah rejoiced at the *o*
Neh 5:12 the priests, and took an *o* of them
Neh 10:29 into a curse, and into an *o*
Ps 105:9 with Abraham, and his *o* unto Isaac
Eccl 8:2 and that in regard of the *o* of God
Eccl 9:2 sweareth, as he that feareth an *o*
Jer 11:5 That I may perform the *o* which I
Eze 16:59 which hast despised the *o* in
Eze 17:13 him, and hath taken an *o* of him
Eze 17:16 whose *o* he despised, and whose
Eze 17:18 Seeing he despised the *o* by
Eze 17:19 surely mine *o* that he hath
Dan 9:11 the *o* that is written in the law
Zec 8:17 and love no false *o*
Mt 14:7 an *o* to give her whatsoever she
Mt 26:72 And again he denied with an *o*
Lk 1:73 The *o* which he sware to our
Acts 2:30 God had sworn with an *o* to him
Acts 23:21 have bound themselves with an *o*
Heb 6:16 an *o* for confirmation is to them
Heb 6:17 his counsel, confirmed it by an *o*
Heb 7:20 without an *o* he was made priest
Heb 7:21 priests were made without an *o*
Heb 7:21 but this with an *o* by him that
Heb 7:28 but the word of the *o*, which was
Jas 5:12 the earth, neither by any other *o*

**OBADIAH** *(o-ba-di'-ah)*
*1. An officer in Ahab's court.*
1Kin 18:3 And Ahab called *O*, which was the
1Kin 18:3 (Now *O* feared the LORD greatly
1Kin 18:4 that *O* took an hundred prophets,
1Kin 18:5 And Ahab said unto *O*, Go into the
1Kin 18:6 *O* went another way by himself
1Kin 18:7 as *O* was in the way, behold,
1Kin 18:16 So *O* went to meet Ahab, and told
*2. A descendant of David.*
1Chr 3:21 the sons of Arnan, the sons of *O*
*3. A descendant of Tola.*
1Chr 7:3 Michael, and *O*, and Joel, Ishiah,
*4. Son of Azel.*
1Chr 8:38 and Ishmael, and Sheariah, and *O*
1Chr 9:44 and Ishmael, and Sheariah, and *O*
*5. Son of Shemaiah.*
1Chr 9:16 *O* the son of Shemaiah, the son of
*6. A warrior in David's army.*
1Chr 12:9 *O* the second, Eliab the third,
*7. A prince of Zebulun.*
1Chr 27:19 Of Zebulun, Ishmaiah the son of *O*
*8. A prince of Judah.*
2Chr 17:7 even to Ben-hail, and to *O*
*9. A Levite in Josiah's time.*
2Chr 34:12 of them were Jahath and *O*, the
*10. A clan leader with Ezra.*
Ezr 8:9 *O* the son of Jehiel, and with him
*11. A priest who renewed the covenant.*
Neh 10:5 Harim, Meremoth, *O*,
*12. A Temple gatekeeper.*
Neh 12:25 Mattaniah, and Bakbukiah, *O*
*13. A prophet.*
Obad 1 The vision of *O*

**OBAL** *(o'-bal) A son of Joktan.*
Gen 10:28 And *O*, and Abimael, and Sheba,

**OBED** *(o'-bed)* See OBED-EDOM.
*1. Father of Jesse.*
Ruth 4:17 and they called his name O
Ruth 4:21 begat Boaz, and Boaz begat O
Ruth 4:22 O begat Jesse, and Jesse begat
1Chr 2:12 And Boaz begat O, and O begat
Mt 1:5 and Booz begat O of Ruth
Mt 1:5 and O begat Jesse
Lk 3:32 of Jesse, which was the son of O
*2. A descendant of Judah.*
1Chr 2:37 begat Ephlal, and Ephlal begat O
1Chr 2:38 O begat Jehu, and Jehu begat
*3. A "mighty man" of David.*
1Chr 11:47 Eliel, and O, and Jasiel the
*4. A sanctuary servant.*
1Chr 26:7 Othni, and Rephael, and O, Elzabad,
*5. Father of Azariah.*
2Chr 23:1 and Azariah the son of O, and

**OBED-EDOM** *(o'-bed-e'-dom)*
*1. A Levite.*
2Sa 6:10 into the house of O the Gittite
2Sa 6:11 of O the Gittite three months
2Sa 6:11 and the LORD blessed O, and all his
2Sa 6:12 LORD hath blessed the house of O
2Sa 6:12 of O into the city of David with
1Chr 13:13 into the house of O the Gittite
1Chr 13:14 of O in his house three months
1Chr 13:14 the LORD blessed the house of O
1Chr 15:24 and O and Jehiah were doorkeepers
1Chr 15:25 out of the house of O with joy
*2. A priest who relocated the Ark.*
1Chr 15:18 and Elipheleh, and Mikneiah, and O
1Chr 15:21 and Elipheleh, and Mikneiah, and O
1Chr 26:4 Moreover the sons of O were
1Chr 26:8 All these of the sons of O
1Chr 26:8 were threescore and two of O
1Chr 26:15 To O southward
*3. Another priest who relocated the Ark.*
1Chr 16:5 and Eliab, and Benaiah, and O
1Chr 16:38 O with their brethren, threescore
*4. Son of Jeduthun.*
1Chr 16:38 O also the son of Jeduthun and
*5. A Temple servant.*
2Chr 25:24 found in the house of God with O

**OBEDIENCE**
Rom 1:5 for o to the faith among all
Rom 5:19 so by the o of one shall many be
Rom 6:16 or of o unto righteousness
Rom 16:19 For your o is come abroad unto
Rom 16:26 to all nations for the o of faith
1Cor 14:34 they are commanded to be under o
2Cor 7:15 he remembereth the o of you all
2Cor 10:5 every thought to the o of Christ
2Cor 10:6 when your o is fulfilled
Philem 21 in thy o I wrote unto thee
Heb 5:8 yet learned he o by the things
1Pet 1:2 of the Spirit, unto o and

**OBEDIENT**
Ex 24:7 hath said will we do, and be o
Num 27:20 the children of Israel may be o
Deut 4:30 shalt be o unto his voice
Deut 8:20 because ye would not be o unto
2Sa 22:45 hear, they shall be o unto me
Prov 25:12 is a wise reprover upon an o ear
Is 1:19 If ye be willing and o, ye shall
Is 42:24 neither were they o unto his law
Acts 6:7 the priests were o to the faith
Rom 15:18 by me, to make the Gentiles o
2Cor 2:9 whether ye be o in all things
Eph 6:5 be o to them that are your
Phil 2:8 became o unto death, even the
Titus 2:5 o to their own husbands, that the
Titus 2:9 Exhort servants to be o unto
1Pet 1:14 As o children, not fashioning

**OBEISANCE**
Gen 37:7 about, and made o to my sheaf
Gen 37:9 and the eleven stars made o to me
Gen 43:28 bowed down their heads, and made o
Ex 18:7 meet his father in law, and did o
2Sa 1:2 he fell to the earth, and did o
2Sa 14:4 her face to the ground, and did o
2Sa 15:5 man came nigh to him to do him o
1Kin 1:16 bowed, and did o unto the king
2Chr 24:17 of Judah, and made o to the king

**OBEY**
Gen 27:8 o my voice according to that
Gen 27:13 only o my voice, and go fetch me
Gen 27:43 Now therefore, my son, o my voice
Ex 5:2 that I should o his voice to let
Ex 19:5 if ye will o my voice indeed, and
Ex 23:21 o his voice, provoke him not
Ex 23:22 if thou shalt indeed o his voice
Deut 11:27 if ye o the commandments of the
Deut 11:28 if ye will not o the commandments
Deut 13:4 o his voice, and ye shall serve
Deut 21:18 which will not o the voice of his
Deut 21:20 he will not o our voice
Deut 27:10 Thou shalt therefore o the voice
Deut 28:62 because thou wouldest not o the
Deut 30:2 shalt o his voice according to
Deut 30:8 o the voice of the LORD, and do
Deut 30:20 and that thou mayest o his voice
Josh 24:24 we serve, and his voice will we o
1Sa 8:19 refused to o the voice of Samuel
1Sa 12:14 o his voice, and not rebel against
1Sa 12:15 But if ye will not o the voice of
1Sa 15:19 thou not o the voice of the LORD
1Sa 15:22 to o is better than sacrifice, and
Neh 9:17 And refused to o, neither were
Job 36:11 If they o and serve him, they
Job 36:12 But if they o not, they shall
Ps 18:44 they hear of me, they shall o me
Prov 30:17 and despiseth to o his mother
Is 11:14 children of Ammon shall o them
Jer 7:23 O my voice, and I will be your God
Jer 11:4 O my voice, and do them, according
Jer 11:7 and protesting, saying, O my voice
Jer 12:17 But if they will not o, I will
Jer 18:10 that it o not my voice, then I
Jer 26:13 o the voice of the LORD your God
Jer 35:14 but o their father's commandment
Jer 38:20 O, I beseech thee, the voice of
Jer 42:6 we will o the voice of the LORD
Jer 42:6 when we o the voice of the LORD
Jer 42:13 neither o the voice of the LORD
Dan 7:27 dominions shall serve and o him
Dan 9:11 that they might not o thy voice
Zec 6:15 if ye will diligently o the voice
Mt 8:27 even the winds and the sea o him
Mk 1:27 unclean spirits, and they do o him
Mk 4:41 even the wind and the sea o him
Lk 8:25 the winds and water, and they o him
Lk 17:6 and it should o you
Acts 5:29 We ought to o God rather than men
Acts 5:32 God hath given to them that o him
Acts 7:39 To whom our fathers would not o
Rom 2:8 do not o the truth
Rom 2:8 but o unrighteousness
Rom 6:12 that ye should o it in the lusts
Rom 6:16 ye yield yourselves servants to o
Rom 6:16 his servants ye are to whom ye o
Gal 3:1 that ye should not o the truth
Gal 5:7 that ye should not o the truth
Eph 6:1 o your parents in the Lord
Col 3:20 o your parents in all things
Col 3:22 o in all things your masters
2Th 1:8 that o not the gospel of our Lord
2Th 3:14 if any man o not our word by this
Titus 3:1 to o magistrates, to be ready to
Heb 5:9 unto all them that o him
Heb 13:17 O them that have the rule over
Jas 3:3 mouths, that they may o us
1Pet 3:1 if any o not the word, they also
1Pet 4:17 them that o not the gospel of God

**OBEYED**
Gen 22:18 because thou hast o my voice
Gen 26:5 Because that Abraham o my voice
Gen 28:7 And that Jacob o his father
Josh 5:6 because they o not the voice of
Josh 22:2 have o my voice in all that I
Judg 2:2 but ye have not o my voice
Judg 6:10 but ye have not o my voice
1Sa 15:20 I have o the voice of the LORD,
1Sa 15:24 the people, and o their voice
1Sa 28:21 thine handmaid hath o thy voice
1Kin 20:36 hast not o the voice of the LORD
2Kin 18:12 Because they o not the voice of
1Chr 29:23 and all Israel o him
2Chr 11:4 they o the words of the LORD, and
Prov 5:13 have not o the voice of my
Jer 3:13 tree, and ye have not o my voice
Jer 3:25 have not o the voice of the LORD
Jer 9:13 them, and have not o my voice
Jer 11:8 Yet they o not, nor inclined
Jer 17:23 But they o not, neither inclined
Jer 32:23 but they o not thy voice, neither
Jer 34:10 of them any more, then they o
Jer 35:8 Thus have we o the voice of
Jer 35:10 we have dwelt in tents, and have o
Jer 35:18 Because ye have o the commandment
Jer 40:3 have not o his voice, therefore
Jer 42:21 but ye have not o the voice of
Jer 43:4 o not the voice of the LORD, to
Jer 43:7 for they o not the voice of the
Jer 44:23 have not o the voice of the LORD,
Dan 9:10 Neither have we o the voice of
Dan 9:14 for we o not his voice
Zeph 3:2 She o not the voice
Hag 1:12 o the voice of the LORD their God
Acts 5:36 and all, as many as o him, were
Acts 5:37 and all, even as many as o him
Rom 6:17 but ye have o from the heart that
Rom 10:16 they have not all o the gospel
Phil 2:12 my beloved, as ye have always o
Heb 11:8 receive for an inheritance, o
1Pet 3:6 Even as Sarah o Abraham, calling

**OBIL** *(o'-bil) An Ishmaelite camel driver.*
1Chr 27:30 camels also was O the Ishmaelite

**OBLATION**
Lev 2:4 if thou bring an o of a meat
Lev 2:5 if thy o be a meat offering baken
Lev 2:7 if thy o be a meat offering baken
Lev 2:12 As for the o of the firstfruits,
Lev 2:13 every o of thy meat offering
Lev 3:1 if his o be a sacrifice of peace
Lev 7:14 offer one out of the whole o for
Lev 7:29 unto the LORD shall bring his o
Lev 22:18 will offer his o for all his vows
Num 18:9 every o of theirs, every meat
Num 31:50 brought an o for the LORD
Is 19:21 day, and shall do sacrifice and o
Is 40:20 o chooseth a tree that will not
Is 66:3 he that offereth an o, as if he
Jer 14:12 they offer burnt offering and an o
Eze 44:30 every o of all, of every sort of
Eze 45:1 ye shall offer an o unto the LORD
Eze 45:6 over against the o of the holy
Eze 45:7 side of the o of the holy portion
Eze 45:7 before the o of the holy portion,
Eze 45:13 This is the o that ye shall offer
Eze 45:16 this o for the prince in Israel
Eze 48:9 The o that ye shall offer unto
Eze 48:10 the priests, shall be this holy o
Eze 48:12 this o of the land that is
Eze 48:18 in length over against the o of
Eze 48:18 against the o of the holy portion
Eze 48:20 All the o shall be five and twenty
Eze 48:20 shall offer the holy o foursquare
Eze 48:21 and on the other of the holy o
Eze 48:21 of the o toward the east border
Eze 48:21 and it shall be the holy o
Dan 2:46 that they should offer an o
Dan 9:21 about the time of the evening o
Dan 9:27 the o to cease, and for the

**OBLATIONS**
Lev 7:38 to offer their o unto the LORD
2Chr 31:14 to distribute the o of the LORD
Is 1:13 Bring no more vain o
Eze 20:40 and the firstfruits of your o
Eze 44:30 of all, of every sort of your o

**OBOTH** *(o'-both) An Israelite encampment in the wilderness.*
Num 21:10 set forward, and pitched in O
Num 21:11 And they journeyed from O, and
Num 33:43 from Punon, and pitched in O
Num 33:44 And they departed from O, and

**OBSERVE**
Ex 12:17 And ye shall o the feast of
Ex 12:17 therefore shall ye o this day in
Ex 12:24 ye shall o this thing for an
Ex 31:16 to o the sabbath throughout their
Ex 34:11 O thou that which I command thee
Ex 34:22 thou shalt o the feast of weeks,
Lev 19:26 ye use enchantment, nor o times
Lev 19:37 shall ye o all my statutes
Num 28:2 shall ye o to offer unto me in
Deut 5:32 Ye shall o to do therefore as the
Deut 6:3 O Israel, and o to do it
Deut 6:25 if we o to do all these
Deut 8:1 thee this day shall ye o to do
Deut 11:32 ye shall o to do all the statutes
Deut 12:1 which ye shall o to do in the
Deut 12:28 O and hear all these words which I
Deut 12:32 soever I command you, o to do it
Deut 15:5 to o to do all these commandments

Deut 16:1 O the month of Abib, and keep the
Deut 16:12 and thou shalt o and do these
Deut 16:13 Thou shalt o the feast of
Deut 17:10 thou shalt o to do according to
Deut 24:8 that thou o diligently, and do
Deut 24:8 them, so ye shall o to do
Deut 28:1 voice of the LORD thy God, to o
Deut 28:13 I command thee this day, to o
Deut 28:15 to o to do all his commandments
Deut 28:58 If thou wilt not o to do all the
Deut 31:12 o to do all the words of this law
Deut 32:46 command your children to o to do
Josh 1:7 that thou mayest o to do
Josh 1:8 night, that thou mayest o to do
Judg 13:14 that I commanded her let her o
1Kin 20:33 Now the men did diligently o
2Kin 17:37 ye shall o to do for evermore
2Kin 21:8 only if they will o to do
2Chr 7:17 shalt o my statutes and my
Neh 1:5 love him and o his commandments
Neh 10:29 Moses the servant of God, and to o
Ps 105:45 That they might o his statutes
Ps 107:43 will o these things, even they
Ps 119:34 I shall o it with my whole heart
Prov 23:26 and let thine eyes o my ways
Jer 8:7 the swallow o the time of their
Eze 20:18 neither o their judgments, nor
Eze 37:24 o my statutes, and do them
Hos 13:7 leopard by the way will I o them
Jonah 2:8 They that o lying vanities
Mt 23:3 they bid you o, that o
Mt 28:20 Teaching them to o all things
Acts 16:21 for us to receive, neither to o
Acts 21:25 that they o no such thing
Gal 4:10 Ye o days, and months, and times,
1Ti 5:21 that thou o these things without

## OBSERVED
Gen 37:11 but his father o the saying
Ex 12:42 It is a night to be much o unto
Ex 12:42 o of all the children of Israel
Num 15:22 not o all these commandments,
Deut 33:9 for they have o thy word, and kept
2Sa 11:16 to pass, when Joab o the city
2Kin 21:6 o times, and used enchantments, and
2Chr 33:6 also he o times, and used
Hos 14:8 I have heard him, and o him
Mk 6:20 a just man and an holy, and o him
Mk 10:20 all these have I o from my youth

## OBSERVER
Deut 18:10 or an o of times, or an enchanter

## OBTAIN
Gen 16:2 be that I may o children by her
Prov 8:35 shall o favour of the LORD
Is 35:10 they shall o joy and gladness, and
Is 51:11 they shall o gladness and joy
Dan 11:21 o the kingdom by flatteries
Mt 5:7 for they shall o mercy
Lk 20:35 accounted worthy to o that world
Rom 11:31 your mercy they also may o mercy
1Cor 9:24 So run, that ye may o
1Cor 9:25 Now they do it to o a corruptible
1Th 5:9 but to o salvation by our Lord
2Ti 2:10 sakes, that they may also o the
Heb 4:16 of grace, that we may o mercy
Heb 11:35 that they might o a better
Jas 4:2 and desire to have, and cannot o

## OBTAINED
Neh 13:6 after certain days o I leave of
Est 2:9 him, and she o kindness of him
Est 2:15 Esther o favour in the sight of
Est 2:17 she o grace and favour in his
Est 5:2 that she o favour in his sight
Hos 2:23 upon her that had not o mercy
Acts 1:17 had o part of this ministry
Acts 22:28 With a great sum o I this freedom
Acts 26:22 Having therefore o help of God
Acts 27:13 that they had o their purpose
Rom 11:7 Israel hath not o that which he
Rom 11:7 but the election hath o it
Rom 11:30 yet have now o mercy through
1Cor 7:25 as one that hath o mercy of the
Eph 1:11 also we have o an inheritance
1Ti 1:13 but I o mercy, because I did it
1Ti 1:16 Howbeit for this cause I o mercy
Heb 1:4 as he hath by inheritance o a
Heb 6:15 endured, he o the promise
Heb 8:6 But now hath he o a more
Heb 9:12 having o eternal redemption for
Heb 11:2 by it the elders o a good report
Heb 11:4 by which he o witness that he was
Heb 11:33 o promises, stopped the mouths of
Heb 11:39 having o a good report through
1Pet 2:10 which had not o mercy
1Pet 2:10 but now have o mercy
2Pet 1:1 to them that have o like precious

## OCCASION
Gen 43:18 that he may seek o against us
Judg 9:33 do to them as thou shalt find o
Judg 14:4 that he sought an o against the
1Sa 10:7 that thou do as o serve thee
2Sa 12:14 o to the enemies of the LORD to
Ezr 7:20 which thou shalt have o to bestow
Jer 2:24 in her o who can turn her away
Eze 18:3 ye shall not have o any more to
Dan 6:4 princes sought to find o against
Dan 6:4 they could find none o nor fault
Dan 6:5 find any o against this Daniel
Rom 7:8 taking o by the commandment,
Rom 7:11 taking o by the commandment,
Rom 14:13 an o to fall in his brother's way
2Cor 5:12 but give you o to glory on our
2Cor 8:8 but by o of the forwardness of
2Cor 11:12 o from them which desire o
Gal 5:13 not liberty for an o to the flesh
1Ti 5:14 give none o to the adversary to
1Jn 2:10 there is none o of stumbling in

## OCCASIONS
Deut 22:14 give o of speech against her, and
Deut 22:17 he hath given o of speech against
Job 33:10 Behold, he findeth o against me

## OCCUPATION
Gen 46:33 you, and shall say, What is your o
Gen 47:3 unto his brethren, What is your o
Jonah 1:8 What is thine o
Acts 18:3 for by their o they were
Acts 19:25 with the workmen of like o

## OCCUPIED
Ex 38:24 All the gold that was o for the
Judg 16:11 with new ropes that never were o
Eze 27:16 they o in thy fairs with emeralds
Eze 27:19 going to and fro o in thy fairs
Eze 27:21 they o with thee in lambs, and
Eze 27:22 they o in thy fairs with chief of
Heb 13:9 them that have been o therein

## OCRAN *(o'-cran) An Asherite who counted the people.*
Num 1:13 Pagiel the son of O
Num 2:27 shall be Pagiel the son of O
Num 7:72 eleventh day Pagiel the son of O
Num 7:77 offering of Pagiel the son of O
Num 10:26 of Asher was Pagiel the son of O

## ODED *(o'-ded)*
*1. Father of Azariah.*
2Chr 15:1 came upon Azariah the son of O
2Chr 15:8 and the prophecy of O the prophet
*2. A prophet of Samaria.*
2Chr 28:9 LORD was there, whose name was O

## ODIOUS
1Chr 19:6 had made themselves o to David
Prov 30:23 For an o woman when she is

## ODOUR
Jn 12:3 filled with the o of the ointment
Phil 4:18 you, an o of a sweet smell, a

## ODOURS
Lev 26:31 smell the savour of your sweet o
2Chr 16:14 bed which was filled with sweet o
Est 2:12 myrrh, and six months with sweet o
Jer 34:5 so shall they burn o for thee
Dan 2:46 an oblation and sweet o unto him
Rev 5:8 harps, and golden vials full of o
Rev 18:13 And cinnamon, and o, and ointments,

## OFFENCE
1Sa 25:31 nor o of heart unto my lord,
Is 8:14 for a rock of o to both the
Hos 5:15 till they acknowledge their o
Mt 16:23 thou art an o unto me
Mt 18:7 to that man by whom the o cometh
Acts 24:16 a conscience void of o toward God
Rom 5:15 But not as the o, so also is the
Rom 5:15 For if through the o of one many
Rom 5:17 For if by one man's o death
Rom 5:18 Therefore as by the o of one
Rom 5:20 entered, that the o might abound
Rom 9:33 a stumblingstone and rock of o
Rom 14:20 for that man who eateth with o
1Cor 10:32 Give none o, neither to the Jews,
2Cor 6:3 Giving no o in any thing, that
2Cor 11:7 Have I committed an o in abasing
Gal 5:11 then is the o of the cross ceased
Phil 1:10 without o till the day of Christ
1Pet 2:8 of stumbling, and a rock of o

## OFFENCES
Eccl 10:4 for yielding pacifieth great o
Mt 18:7 Woe unto the world because of o
Mt 18:7 for it must needs be that o come
Lk 17:1 impossible but that o will come
Rom 4:25 Who was delivered for our o
Rom 5:16 is of many o unto justification
Rom 16:17 o contrary to the doctrine which

## OFFEND
Job 34:31 I will not o any more
Ps 73:15 I should o against the generation
Ps 119:165 and nothing shall o them
Jer 2:3 all that devour him shall o
Jer 50:7 We o not, because they have
Hos 4:15 the harlot, yet let not Judah o
Hab 1:11 and he shall pass over, and o
Mt 5:29 And if thy right eye o thee
Mt 5:30 And if thy right hand o thee
Mt 13:41 of his kingdom all things that o
Mt 17:27 lest we should o them, go thou
Mt 18:6 But whoso shall o one of these
Mt 18:8 if thy hand or thy foot o thee
Mt 18:9 And if thine eye o thee, pluck it
Mk 9:42 whosoever shall o one of these
Mk 9:43 And if thy hand o thee, cut it off
Mk 9:45 And if thy foot o thee, cut it off
Mk 9:47 And if thine eye o thee, pluck it
Lk 17:2 than that he should o one of
Jn 6:61 said unto them, Doth this o you
1Cor 8:13 if meat make my brother to o
1Cor 8:13 lest I make my brother to o
Jas 2:10 yet o in one point, he is guilty
Jas 3:2 For in many things we o all
Jas 3:2 If any man o not in word, the

## OFFENDED
Gen 20:9 and what have I o thee, that thou
Gen 40:1 his baker had o their lord the
2Kin 18:14 to Lachish, saying, I have o
2Chr 28:13 for whereas we have o against the
Prov 18:19 A brother o is harder to be won
Jer 37:18 What have I o against thee, or
Eze 25:12 vengeance, and hath greatly o
Hos 13:1 but when he o in Baal, he died
Mt 11:6 whosoever shall not be o in me
Mt 13:21 of the word, by and by he is o
Mt 13:57 And they were o in him
Mt 15:12 thou that the Pharisees were o
Mt 24:10 And then shall many be o, and shall
Mt 26:31 All ye shall be o because of me
Mt 26:33 men shall be o because of thee
Mt 26:33 yet will I never be o
Mk 4:17 sake, immediately they are o
Mk 6:3 And they were o at him
Mk 14:27 All ye shall be o because of me
Mk 14:29 unto him, Although all shall be o
Lk 7:23 whosoever shall not be o in me
Jn 16:1 unto you, that ye should not be o
Acts 25:8 have I o any thing at all
Rom 14:21 thy brother stumbleth, or is o
2Cor 11:29 who is o, and I burn not

## OFFER
Gen 22:2 o him there for a burnt offering
Ex 22:29 Thou shalt not delay to o the
Ex 23:18 Thou shalt not o the blood of my
Ex 29:36 thou shalt o every day a bullock
Ex 29:38 which thou shalt o upon the altar
Ex 29:39 lamb thou shalt o in the morning
Ex 29:39 other lamb thou shalt o at even
Ex 29:41 other lamb thou shalt o at even
Ex 30:9 Ye shall o no strange incense
Ex 34:25 Thou shalt not o the blood of my
Ex 35:24 Every one that did o an offering
Lev 1:3 let him o a male without blemish
Lev 1:3 he shall o it of his own
Lev 2:1 when any will o a meat offering
Lev 2:12 ye shall o them unto the LORD
Lev 2:13 thine offerings thou shalt o salt
Lev 2:14 if thou o a meat offering of thy
Lev 2:14 thou shalt o for the meat
Lev 3:1 offering, if he o it of the herd
Lev 3:1 he shall o it without blemish

Lev 3:3 he shall o of the sacrifice of
Lev 3:6 he shall o it without blemish
Lev 3:7 If he o a lamb for his offering,
Lev 3:7 then shall he o it before the
Lev 3:9 he shall o of the sacrifice of
Lev 3:12 then he shall o it before the
Lev 3:14 he shall o thereof his offering,
Lev 4:14 o a young bullock for the sin
Lev 5:8 who shall o that which is for the
Lev 5:10 he shall o the second for a burnt
Lev 6:14 Aaron shall o it before the LORD
Lev 6:20 which they shall o unto the LORD
Lev 6:21 o for a sweet savour unto the
Lev 6:22 anointed in his stead shall o it
Lev 7:3 he shall o of it all the fat
Lev 7:11 which he shall o unto the LORD
Lev 7:12 If he o it for a thanksgiving,
Lev 7:12 then he shall o with the
Lev 7:13 he shall o for his offering
Lev 7:14 of it he shall o one out of the
Lev 7:25 of which men o an offering made
Lev 7:38 the children of Israel to o their
Lev 9:2 and o them before the LORD
Lev 9:7 o thy sin offering, and thy burnt
Lev 9:7 o the offering of the people, and
Lev 12:7 Who shall o it before the LORD,
Lev 14:12 o him for a trespass offering, and
Lev 14:19 priest shall o the sin offering
Lev 14:20 the priest shall o the burnt
Lev 14:30 he shall o the one of the
Lev 15:15 And the priest shall o them
Lev 15:30 the priest shall o the one for a
Lev 16:6 Aaron shall o his bullock of the
Lev 16:9 fell, and o him for a sin offering
Lev 16:24 o his burnt offering, and the
Lev 17:4 to o an offering unto the LORD
Lev 17:5 which they o in the open field,
Lev 17:5 o them for peace offerings unto
Lev 17:7 they shall no more o their
Lev 17:9 to o it unto the LORD
Lev 19:5 if ye o a sacrifice of peace
Lev 19:5 ye shall o it at your own will
Lev 19:6 be eaten the same day ye o it
Lev 21:6 the bread of their God, they do o
Lev 21:17 to o the bread of his God
Lev 21:21 the priest shall come nigh to o
Lev 21:21 nigh to o the bread of his God
Lev 22:15 which they o unto the LORD
Lev 22:18 that will o his oblation for all
Lev 22:18 which they will o unto the LORD
Lev 22:19 Ye shall o at your own will a
Lev 22:20 a blemish, that shall ye not o
Lev 22:22 ye shall not o these unto the
Lev 22:23 that mayest thou o for a freewill
Lev 22:24 Ye shall not o unto the LORD that
Lev 22:25 o the bread of your God of any of
Lev 22:29 when ye will o a sacrifice of
Lev 22:29 the LORD, o it at your own will
Lev 23:8 But ye shall o an offering made
Lev 23:12 ye shall o that day when ye wave
Lev 23:16 ye shall o a new meat offering
Lev 23:18 ye shall o with the bread seven
Lev 23:25 but ye shall o an offering made
Lev 23:27 o an offering made by fire unto
Lev 23:36 Seven days ye shall o an offering
Lev 23:36 ye shall o an offering made by
Lev 23:37 to o an offering made by fire
Lev 27:11 beast, of which they do not o a
Num 5:25 the LORD, and o it upon the altar
Num 6:11 the priest shall o the one for a
Num 6:14 he shall o his offering unto the
Num 6:16 shall o his sin offering, and his
Num 6:17 And he shall o the ram for a
Num 6:17 the priest shall o also his meat
Num 7:11 They shall o their offering, each
Num 7:18 Zuar, prince of Issachar, did o
Num 7:24 of the children of Zebulun, did o
Num 7:30 of the children of Reuben, did o
Num 7:36 of the children of Simeon, did o
Num 8:11 Aaron shall o the Levites before
Num 8:12 thou shalt o the one for a sin
Num 8:13 o them for an offering unto the
Num 8:15 them, and o them for an offering
Num 9:7 that we may not o an offering of
Num 15:7 o the third part of an hin of
Num 15:14 will o an offering made by fire,
Num 15:19 ye shall o up an heave offering
Num 15:20 Ye shall o up a cake of the first
Num 15:24 o one young bullock for a burnt
Num 16:40 come near to o incense before the
Num 18:12 which they shall o unto the LORD
Num 18:19 of Israel o unto the LORD
Num 18:24 which they o as an heave offering
Num 18:26 then ye shall o up an heave
Num 18:28 Thus ye also shall o an heave
Num 18:29 o every heave offering of the
Num 28:2 shall ye observe to o unto me in
Num 28:3 which ye shall o unto the LORD
Num 28:4 lamb shalt thou o in the morning
Num 28:4 other lamb shalt thou o at even
Num 28:8 other lamb shalt thou o at even
Num 28:8 offering thereof, thou shalt o it
Num 28:11 of your months ye shall o a burnt
Num 28:19 But ye shall o a sacrifice made
Num 28:20 deals shall ye o for a bullock
Num 28:21 deal shalt thou o for every lamb
Num 28:23 Ye shall o these beside the burnt
Num 28:24 this manner ye shall o daily
Num 28:27 But ye shall o the burnt offering
Num 28:31 Ye shall o them beside the
Num 29:2 ye shall o a burnt offering for a
Num 29:8 But ye shall o a burnt offering
Num 29:13 ye shall o a burnt offering, a
Num 29:17 ye shall o twelve young bullocks
Num 29:36 But ye shall o a burnt offering,
Deut 12:13 thou o not thy burnt offerings in
Deut 12:14 there thou shalt o thy burnt
Deut 12:27 thou shalt o thy burnt offerings,
Deut 18:3 from them that o a sacrifice
Deut 27:6 thou shalt o burnt offerings
Deut 27:7 thou shalt o peace offerings, and
Deut 33:19 there they shall o sacrifices of
Josh 22:23 or if to o thereon burnt offering
Josh 22:23 or if to o peace offerings
Judg 3:18 had made an end to o the present
Judg 6:26 o a burnt sacrifice with the wood
Judg 11:31 I will o it up for a burnt
Judg 13:16 if thou wilt o a burnt offering,
Judg 13:16 thou must o it unto the LORD
Judg 16:23 to o a great sacrifice unto Dagon
1Sa 1:21 went up to o unto the LORD the
1Sa 2:19 husband to o the yearly sacrifice
1Sa 2:28 to o upon mine altar, to burn
1Sa 10:8 to o burnt offerings, and to
2Sa 24:12 the LORD, I o thee three things
2Sa 24:22 o up what seemeth good unto him
2Sa 24:24 neither will I o burnt offerings
1Kin 3:4 did Solomon o upon that altar
1Kin 9:25 did Solomon o burnt offerings
1Kin 13:2 upon thee shall he o the priests
2Kin 5:17 o neither burnt offering nor
2Kin 10:24 when they went in to o sacrifices
1Chr 16:40 To o burnt offerings unto the
1Chr 21:10 the LORD, I o thee three things
1Chr 21:24 nor o burnt offerings without
1Chr 23:31 to o all burnt sacrifices unto
1Chr 29:14 that we should be able to o so
1Chr 29:17 here, to o willingly unto thee
2Chr 23:18 to o the burnt offerings of the
2Chr 24:14 to o withal, and spoons, and
2Chr 29:21 priests the sons of Aaron to o
2Chr 29:27 Hezekiah commanded to o the burnt
2Chr 35:12 to o unto the LORD, as it is
2Chr 35:16 to o burnt offerings upon the
Ezr 3:2 to o burnt offerings thereon, as
Ezr 3:6 o burnt offerings unto the LORD
Ezr 6:10 That they may o sacrifices of
Ezr 7:17 o them upon the altar of the
Job 42:8 o up for yourselves a burnt
Ps 4:5 O the sacrifices of righteousness
Ps 16:4 offerings of blood will I not o
Ps 27:6 therefore will I o in his
Ps 50:14 O unto God thanksgiving
Ps 51:19 then shall they o bullocks upon
Ps 66:15 I will o unto thee burnt
Ps 66:15 I will o bullocks with goats
Ps 72:10 of Sheba and Seba shall o gifts
Ps 116:17 I will o to thee the sacrifice of
Is 57:7 wentest thou up to o sacrifice
Jer 11:12 the gods unto whom they o incense
Jer 14:12 when they o burnt offering and an
Jer 33:18 before me to o burnt offerings
Eze 6:13 the place where they did o sweet
Eze 20:31 For when ye o your gifts, when ye
Eze 43:18 to o burnt offerings thereon, and
Eze 43:22 o a kid of the goats without
Eze 43:23 thou shalt o a young bullock
Eze 43:24 thou shalt o them before the LORD
Eze 43:24 they shall o them up for a burnt
Eze 44:7 when ye o my bread, the fat and
Eze 44:15 before me to o unto me the fat
Eze 44:27 he shall o his sin offering,
Eze 45:1 ye shall o an oblation unto the
Eze 45:13 is the oblation that ye shall o
Eze 45:14 ye shall o the tenth part of a
Eze 46:4 o unto the LORD in the sabbath
Eze 48:8 offering which ye shall o of five
Eze 48:9 The oblation that ye shall o unto
Eze 48:20 ye shall o the holy oblation
Dan 2:46 that they should o an oblation
Hos 9:4 They shall not o wine offerings
Amos 4:5 o a sacrifice of thanksgiving
Amos 5:22 Though ye o me burnt offerings and
Hag 2:14 that which they o there is
Mal 1:7 Ye o polluted bread upon mine
Mal 1:8 if ye o the blind for sacrifice,
Mal 1:8 if ye o the lame and sick, is it
Mal 1:8 o it now unto thy governor
Mal 3:3 that they may o unto the LORD an
Mt 5:24 and then come and o thy gift
Mt 8:4 o the gift that Moses commanded,
Mk 1:44 o for thy cleansing those things
Lk 2:24 to o a sacrifice according to
Lk 5:14 o for thy cleansing, according as
Lk 6:29 on the one cheek o also the other
Lk 11:12 an egg, will he o him a scorpion
Heb 5:1 to God, that he may o both gifts
Heb 5:3 also for himself, to o for sins
Heb 7:27 to o up sacrifice, first for his
Heb 8:3 priest is ordained to o gifts
Heb 8:3 this man have somewhat also to o
Heb 8:4 that o gifts according to the law
Heb 9:25 that he should o himself often
Heb 13:15 By him therefore let us o the
1Pet 2:5 to o up spiritual sacrifices,
Rev 8:3 that he should o it with the

**OFFERED**

Gen 8:20 o burnt offerings on the altar
Gen 22:13 o him up for a burnt offering in
Gen 31:54 Then Jacob o sacrifice upon the
Gen 46:1 o sacrifices unto the God of his
Ex 24:5 which o burnt offerings, and
Ex 32:6 o burnt offerings, and brought
Ex 35:22 every man that o
Ex 35:22 o an offering of gold
Ex 40:29 o upon it the burnt offering and
Lev 7:8 burnt offering which he hath o
Lev 7:15 eaten the same day that it is o
Lev 9:15 o it for sin, as the first
Lev 9:16 o it according to the manner
Lev 10:1 o strange fire before the LORD,
Lev 10:19 have they o their sin offering
Lev 16:1 when they o before the LORD, and
Num 3:4 when they o strange fire before
Num 7:2 over them that were numbered, o
Num 7:10 the princes o for dedicating of
Num 7:10 even the princes o their offering
Num 7:12 he that o his offering the first
Num 7:19 He o for his offering one silver
Num 7:42 prince of the children of Gad, o
Num 7:48 of the children of Ephraim, o
Num 7:54 On the eighth day o Gamaliel the
Num 7:60 of the children of Benjamin, o
Num 7:66 prince of the children of Dan, o
Num 7:72 of the children of Asher, o
Num 7:78 of the children of Naphtali, o
Num 8:21 Aaron o them as an offering
Num 16:35 and fifty men that o incense
Num 16:38 for they o them before the LORD,
Num 16:39 they that were burnt had o
Num 22:40 And Balak o oxen and sheep, and sent
Num 23:2 Balaam o on every altar a bullock
Num 23:4 I have o upon every altar a
Num 23:14 o a bullock and a ram on every
Num 23:30 o a bullock and a ram on every
Num 26:61 when they o strange fire before
Num 28:15 offering unto the LORD shall be o
Num 28:24 it shall be o beside the
Num 31:52 that they o up to the LORD
Josh 8:31 they o thereon burnt offerings
Judg 5:2 the people willingly o themselves
Judg 5:9 that o themselves willingly among
Judg 6:28 the second bullock was o upon the
Judg 13:19 o it upon a rock unto the LORD
Judg 20:26 o burnt offerings and peace
Judg 21:4 o burnt offerings and peace
1Sa 1:4 when the time was that Elkanah o
1Sa 2:13 that, when any man o sacrifice
1Sa 6:14 o the kine a burnt offering unto

1Sa 6:15 of Beth-shemesh *o* burnt offerings
1Sa 7:9 *o* it for a burnt offering wholly
1Sa 13:9 And he *o* the burnt offering
1Sa 13:12 therefore, and *o* a burnt offering
2Sa 6:17 David *o* burnt offerings and peace
2Sa 15:12 from Giloh, while he *o* sacrifices
2Sa 24:25 *o* burnt offerings and peace
1Kin 3:15 *o* up burnt offerings
1Kin 3:15 *o* peace offerings, and made a
1Kin 8:62 *o* sacrifice before the LORD
1Kin 8:63 Solomon *o* a sacrifice of peace
1Kin 8:63 which he *o* unto the LORD, two and
1Kin 8:64 for there he *o* burnt offerings,
1Kin 12:32 in Judah, and he *o* upon the altar
1Kin 12:33 So he *o* upon the altar which he
1Kin 12:33 he *o* upon the altar, and burnt
1Kin 22:43 for the people *o* and burnt incense
2Kin 3:20 when the meat offering was *o*
2Kin 3:27 *o* him for a burnt offering upon
2Kin 16:12 to the altar, and *o* thereon
1Chr 6:49 his sons *o* upon the altar of the
1Chr 15:26 that they *o* seven bullocks and
1Chr 16:1 they *o* burnt sacrifices and peace
1Chr 21:26 *o* burnt offerings and peace
1Chr 29:6 of the king's work, *o* willingly,
1Chr 29:9 for that they *o* willingly
1Chr 29:9 they *o* willingly to the LORD
1Chr 29:17 have willingly *o* all these things
1Chr 29:21 *o* burnt offerings unto the LORD,
2Chr 1:6 *o* a thousand burnt offerings upon
2Chr 4:6 such things as they *o* for the
2Chr 7:4 all the people *o* sacrifices
2Chr 7:5 king Solomon *o* a sacrifice of
2Chr 7:7 for there he *o* burnt offerings,
2Chr 8:12 Then Solomon *o* burnt offerings
2Chr 15:11 they *o* unto the LORD the same
2Chr 17:16 who willingly *o* himself unto the
2Chr 24:14 they *o* burnt offerings in the
2Chr 29:7 nor *o* burnt offerings in the holy
Ezr 1:6 beside all that was willingly *o*
Ezr 2:68 *o* freely for the house of God to
Ezr 3:3 they *o* burnt offerings thereon
Ezr 3:4 *o* the daily burnt offerings by
Ezr 3:5 afterward *o* the continual burnt
Ezr 3:5 of every one that willingly *o* a
Ezr 6:3 the place where they *o* sacrifices
Ezr 6:17 *o* at the dedication of this house
Ezr 7:15 freely *o* unto the God of Israel
Ezr 8:25 all Israel there present, had *o*
Ezr 8:35 *o* burnt offerings unto the God of
Ezr 10:19 they *o* a ram of the flock for
Neh 11:2 that willingly *o* themselves to
Neh 12:43 that day they *o* great sacrifices
Job 1:5 *o* burnt offerings according to
Is 57:6 thou hast *o* a meat offering
Is 66:3 as if he *o* swine's blood
Jer 32:29 they have *o* incense unto Baal
Eze 20:28 they *o* there their sacrifices, and
Eze 48:12 oblation of the land that is *o*
Dan 11:18 the reproach *o* by him to cease
Amos 5:25 Have ye *o* unto me sacrifices and
Jonah 1:16 *o* a sacrifice unto the LORD, and
Mal 1:11 incense shall be *o* unto my name
Acts 7:41 *o* sacrifice unto the idol, and
Acts 7:42 have ye *o* to me slain beasts and
Acts 8:18 Ghost was given, he *o* them money,
Acts 15:29 ye abstain from meats *o* to idols
Acts 21:25 themselves from things *o* to idols
Acts 21:26 should be *o* for every one of them
1Cor 8:1 as touching things *o* unto idols
1Cor 8:4 are *o* in sacrifice unto idols
1Cor 8:7 eat it as a thing *o* unto an idol
1Cor 8:10 those things which are *o* to idols
1Cor 10:19 or that which is *o* in sacrifice
1Cor 10:28 This is *o* in sacrifice unto idols
Phil 2:17 if I be *o* upon the sacrifice and
2Ti 4:6 For I am now ready to be *o*
Heb 5:7 flesh, when he had *o* up prayers
Heb 7:27 he did once, when he *o* up himself
Heb 9:7 which he *o* for himself, and for
Heb 9:9 in which were *o* both gifts
Heb 9:14 *o* himself without spot to God
Heb 9:28 So Christ was once *o* to bear the
Heb 10:1 those sacrifices which they *o*
Heb 10:2 they not have ceased to be *o*
Heb 10:8 which are *o* by the law
Heb 10:12 after he had *o* one sacrifice for
Heb 11:4 By faith Abel *o* unto God a more
Heb 11:17 when he was tried, *o* up Isaac
Heb 11:17 *o* up his only begotten son
Jas 2:21 when he had *o* Isaac his son upon

**OFFERETH**
Lev 6:26 The priest that *o* it for sin
Lev 7:8 the priest that *o* any man's burnt
Lev 7:9 shall be the priest's that *o* it
Lev 7:16 same day that he *o* his sacrifice
Lev 7:18 it be imputed unto him that *o* it
Lev 7:29 He that *o* the sacrifice of his
Lev 7:33 that *o* the blood of the peace
Lev 17:8 that *o* a burnt offering or
Lev 21:8 for he *o* the bread of thy God
Lev 22:21 whosoever *o* a sacrifice of peace
Num 15:4 Then shall he that *o* his offering
Ps 50:23 Whoso *o* praise glorifieth me
Is 66:3 he that *o* an oblation, as if he
Jer 48:35 him that *o* in the high places, and
Mal 2:12 him that *o* an offering unto the

**OFFICE**
Gen 41:13 me he restored unto mine *o*
Ex 1:16 When ye do the *o* of a midwife to
Ex 28:1 unto me in the priest's *o*
Ex 28:3 unto me in the priest's *o*
Ex 28:4 unto me in the priest's *o*
Ex 28:41 unto me in the priest's *o*
Ex 29:1 unto me in the priest's *o*
Ex 29:9 the priest's *o* shall be theirs
Ex 29:44 minister to me in the priest's *o*
Ex 30:30 unto me in the priest's *o*
Ex 31:10 to minister in the priest's *o*
Ex 35:19 to minister in the priest's *o*
Ex 39:41 to minister in the priest's *o*
Ex 40:13 unto me in the priest's *o*
Ex 40:15 unto me in the priest's *o*
Lev 7:35 unto the LORD in the priest's *o*
Lev 16:32 priest's *o* in his father's stead
Num 3:3 to minister in the priest's *o*
Num 3:4 ministered in the priest's *o* in
Num 3:10 shall wait on their priest's *o*
Num 4:16 to the *o* of Eleazar the son of
Num 18:7 *o* for every thing of the altar
Num 18:7 I have given your priest's *o* unto
Deut 10:6 in the priest's *o* in his stead
1Chr 6:10 *o* in the temple that Solomon
1Chr 6:32 their *o* according to their order
1Chr 9:22 seer did ordain in their set *o*
1Chr 9:26 porters, were in their set *o*
1Chr 9:31 had the set *o* over the things
1Chr 23:28 Because their *o* was to wait on
1Chr 24:2 Ithamar executed the priest's *o*
2Chr 11:14 the priest's *o* unto the LORD
2Chr 24:11 *o* by the hand of the Levites
2Chr 31:15 of the priests, in their set *o*
2Chr 31:18 for in their set *o* they
Neh 13:13 their *o* was to distribute unto
Ps 109:8 and let another take his *o*
Eze 44:13 to do the *o* of a priest unto me,
Lk 1:8 *o* before God in the order of his
Lk 1:9 to the custom of the priest's *o*
Rom 11:13 of the Gentiles, I magnify mine *o*
Rom 12:4 all members have not the same *o*
1Ti 3:1 If a man desire the *o* of a bishop
1Ti 3:10 let them use the *o* of a deacon
1Ti 3:13 For they that have used the *o* of
Heb 7:5 of Levi, who receive the *o* of the

**OFFICER**
Gen 37:36 an *o* of Pharaoh's, and captain of
Gen 39:1 an *o* of Pharaoh, captain of the
Judg 9:28 and Zebul his *o*
1Kin 4:5 the son of Nathan was principal *o*
1Kin 4:19 he was the only *o* which was in
1Kin 22:9 the king of Israel called an *o*
2Kin 8:6 appointed unto her a certain *o*
2Kin 25:19 out of the city he took an *o* that
2Chr 24:11 and the high priest's *o* came
Mt 5:25 the judge deliver thee to the *o*
Lk 12:58 the judge deliver thee to the *o*
Lk 12:58 the *o* cast thee into prison

**OFFICERS**
Gen 40:2 was wroth against two of his *o*
Gen 40:7 he asked Pharaoh's *o* that were
Gen 41:34 let him appoint *o* over the land
Ex 5:6 of the people, and their *o*
Ex 5:10 the people went out, and their *o*
Ex 5:14 the *o* of the children of Israel,
Ex 5:15 Then the *o* of the children of
Ex 5:19 the *o* of the children of Israel
Num 11:16 of the people, and *o* over them
Num 31:14 was wroth with the *o* of the host
Num 31:48 the *o* which were over thousands
Deut 1:15 over tens, and *o* among your tribes
Deut 16:18 *o* shalt thou make thee in all thy
Deut 20:5 the *o* shall speak unto the people
Deut 20:8 the *o* shall speak further unto
Deut 20:9 when the *o* have made an end of
Deut 29:10 tribes, your elders, and your *o*
Deut 31:28 elders of your tribes, and your *o*
Josh 1:10 commanded the *o* of the people
Josh 3:2 that the *o* went through the host
Josh 8:33 all Israel, and their elders, and *o*
Josh 23:2 for their judges, and for their *o*
Josh 24:1 for their judges, and for their *o*
1Sa 8:15 your vineyards, and give to his *o*
1Kin 4:5 the son of Nathan was over the *o*
1Kin 4:7 had twelve *o* over all Israel
1Kin 4:27 those *o* provided victual for king
1Kin 4:28 unto the place where the *o* were
1Kin 5:16 *o* which were over the work
1Kin 9:23 These were the chief of the *o*
2Kin 11:15 the *o* of the host, and said unto
2Kin 11:18 the priest appointed *o* over the
2Kin 24:12 and his princes, and his *o*
2Kin 24:15 and the king's wives, and his *o*
1Chr 23:4 and six thousand were *o* and judges
1Chr 26:29 business over Israel, for *o*
1Chr 26:30 were *o* among them of Israel on
1Chr 27:1 their *o* that served the king in
1Chr 28:1 king, and of his sons, with the *o*
2Chr 8:10 the chief of king Solomon's *o*
2Chr 18:8 of Israel called for one of his *o*
2Chr 19:11 the Levites shall be *o* before you
2Chr 34:13 Levites there were scribes, and *o*
Est 1:8 to all the *o* of his house
Est 2:3 let the king appoint *o* in all the
Est 9:3 *o* of the king, helped the Jews
Is 60:17 I will also make thy *o* peace
Jer 29:26 that ye should be *o* in the house
Jn 7:32 chief priests sent *o* to take him
Jn 7:45 Then came the *o* to the chief
Jn 7:46 The *o* answered, Never man spake
Jn 18:3 *o* from the chief priests and
Jn 18:12 *o* of the Jews took Jesus, and
Jn 18:18 *o* stood there, who had made a
Jn 18:22 one of the *o* which stood by
Jn 19:6 *o* saw him, they cried out, saying
Acts 5:22 But when the *o* came, and found
Acts 5:26 Then went the captain with the *o*

**OFFICES**
1Sa 2:36 thee, into one of the priests' *o*
1Chr 24:3 to their *o* in their service
2Chr 7:6 And the priests waited on their *o*
2Chr 23:18 Also Jehoiada appointed the *o* of
Neh 13:14 of my God, and for the *o* thereof

**OFFSPRING**
Job 5:25 thine *o* as the grass of the earth
Job 21:8 their *o* before their eyes
Job 27:14 his *o* shall not be satisfied with
Job 31:8 yea, let my *o* be rooted out
Is 22:24 of his father's house, the *o*
Is 44:3 seed, and my blessing upon thine *o*
Is 48:19 the *o* of thy bowels like the
Is 61:9 and their *o* among the people
Is 65:23 of the LORD, and their *o* with them
Acts 17:28 have said, For we are also his *o*
Acts 17:29 then as we are the *o* of God
Rev 22:16 the *o* of David, and the bright and

**OFT**
2Kin 4:8 that as *o* as he passed by, he
Job 21:17 How *o* is the candle of the wicked
Job 21:17 how *o* cometh their destruction
Ps 78:40 How *o* did they provoke him in the
Mt 9:14 Why do we and the Pharisees fast *o*
Mt 17:15 the fire, and *o* into the water
Mt 18:21 how *o* shall my brother sin
Mk 7:3 except they wash their hands *o*
Acts 26:11 I punished them *o* in every
1Cor 11:25 do ye, as *o* as ye drink it, in
2Cor 11:23 more frequent, in deaths *o*
2Ti 1:16 for he *o* refreshed me, and was not
Heb 6:7 in the rain that cometh *o* upon it

**OG** *(og) An Amorite king.*
Num 21:33 *O* the king of Bashan went out
Num 32:33 the kingdom of *O* king of Bashan
Deut 1:4 *O* the king of Bashan, which dwelt
Deut 3:1 *O* the king of Bashan came out
Deut 3:3 delivered into our hands *O* also

Deut 3:4 Argob, the kingdom of *O* in Bashan
Deut 3:10 of the kingdom of *O* in Bashan
Deut 3:11 For only *O* king of Bashan
Deut 3:13 Bashan, being the kingdom of *O*
Deut 4:47 the land of *O* king of Bashan, two
Deut 29:7 *O* the king of Bashan, came out
Deut 31:4 them as he did to Sihon and to *O*
Josh 2:10 the other side Jordan, Sihon and *O*
Josh 9:10 to *O* king of Bashan, which was at
Josh 12:4 the coast of *O* king of Bashan,
Josh 13:12 All the kingdom of *O* in Bashan
Josh 13:30 the kingdom of *O* king of Bashan
Josh 13:31 of the kingdom of *O* in Bashan
1Kin 4:19 Amorites, and of *O* king of Bashan
Neh 9:22 the land of *O* king of Bashan
Ps 135:11 *O* king of Bashan, and all the
Ps 136:20 And *O* the king of Bashan

**OHAD** *(o'-had) A son of Simeon.*
Gen 46:10 Jemuel, and Jamin, and *O*, and Jachin
Ex 6:15 Jemuel, and Jamin, and *O*, and Jachin

**OHEL** *(o'-hel) A son of Zerubbabel.*
1Chr 3:20 And Hashubah, and *O*, and Berechiah,

**OIL**
Gen 28:18 poured *o* upon the top of it
Gen 35:14 thereon, and he poured *o* thereon
Ex 25:6 *O* for the light, spices for
Ex 25:6 the light, spices for anointing *o*
Ex 27:20 that they bring thee pure *o* olive
Ex 29:2 cakes unleavened tempered with *o*
Ex 29:2 wafers unleavened anointed with *o*
Ex 29:7 shalt thou take the anointing *o*
Ex 29:21 the altar, and of the anointing *o*
Ex 29:40 fourth part of an hin of beaten *o*
Ex 30:24 sanctuary, and of *o* olive an hin
Ex 30:25 make it an *o* of holy ointment
Ex 30:25 it shall be an holy anointing *o*
Ex 30:31 *o* unto me throughout your
Ex 31:11 And the anointing *o*, and sweet
Ex 35:8 *o* for the light, and spices for
Ex 35:8 light, and spices for anointing *o*
Ex 35:14 with the *o* for the light,
Ex 35:15 and his staves, and the anointing *o*
Ex 35:28 *o* for the light, and for the
Ex 35:28 the light, and for the anointing *o*
Ex 37:29 And he made the holy anointing *o*
Ex 39:37 thereof, and the *o* for light,
Ex 39:38 golden altar, and the anointing *o*
Ex 40:9 thou shalt take the anointing *o*
Lev 2:1 and he shall pour *o* upon it
Lev 2:2 of the *o* thereof, with all the
Lev 2:4 of fine flour mingled with *o*
Lev 2:4 unleavened wafers anointed with *o*
Lev 2:5 flour unleavened, mingled with *o*
Lev 2:6 it in pieces, and pour *o* thereon
Lev 2:7 be made of fine flour with *o*
Lev 2:15 And thou shalt put *o* upon it
Lev 2:16 thereof, and part of the *o* thereof
Lev 5:11 he shall put no *o* upon it
Lev 6:15 of the *o* thereof, and all the
Lev 6:21 In a pan it shall be made with *o*
Lev 7:10 meat offering, mingled with *o*
Lev 7:12 unleavened cakes mingled with *o*
Lev 7:12 with *o*, and cakes mingled with *o*
Lev 8:2 the garments, and the anointing *o*
Lev 8:10 And Moses took the anointing *o*
Lev 8:12 the anointing *o* upon Aaron's head
Lev 8:30 And Moses took of the anointing *o*
Lev 9:4 and a meat offering mingled with *o*
Lev 10:7 for the anointing *o* of the LORD
Lev 14:10 mingled with *o*, and one log of *o*
Lev 14:12 offering, and the log of *o*
Lev 14:15 shall take some of the log of *o*
Lev 14:16 in the *o* that is in his left hand
Lev 14:16 shall sprinkle of the *o* with his
Lev 14:17 of the rest of the *o* that is in
Lev 14:18 the remnant of the *o* that is in
Lev 14:21 with *o* for a meat offering
Lev 14:21 a meat offering, and a log of *o*
Lev 14:24 offering, and the log of *o*
Lev 14:26 the priest shall pour of the *o*
Lev 14:27 his right finger some of the *o*
Lev 14:28 the priest shall put of the *o*
Lev 14:29 the rest of the *o* that is in the
Lev 21:10 head the anointing *o* was poured
Lev 21:12 *o* of his God is upon him
Lev 23:13 of fine flour mingled with *o*
Lev 24:2 pure *o* olive beaten for the light
Num 4:9 all the *o* vessels thereof,
Num 4:16 pertaineth the *o* for the light
Num 4:16 meat offering, and the anointing *o*
Num 5:15 he shall pour no *o* upon it
Num 6:15 of fine flour mingled with *o*
Num 6:15 unleavened bread anointed with *o*
Num 7:13 with *o* for a meat offering
Num 7:19 with *o* for a meat offering
Num 7:25 with *o* for a meat offering
Num 7:31 with *o* for a meat offering
Num 7:37 with *o* for a meat offering
Num 7:43 with *o* for a meat offering
Num 7:49 with *o* for a meat offering
Num 7:55 with *o* for a meat offering
Num 7:61 with *o* for a meat offering
Num 7:67 with *o* for a meat offering
Num 7:73 with *o* for a meat offering
Num 7:79 with *o* for a meat offering
Num 8:8 even fine flour mingled with *o*
Num 11:8 of it was as the taste of fresh *o*
Num 15:4 the fourth part of an hin of *o*
Num 15:6 the third part of an hin of *o*
Num 15:9 mingled with half an hin of *o*
Num 18:12 All the best of the *o*, and all the
Num 28:5 fourth part of an hin of beaten *o*
Num 28:9 a meat offering, mingled with *o*
Num 28:12 a meat offering, mingled with *o*
Num 28:12 a meat offering, mingled with *o*
Num 28:13 deal of flour mingled with *o* for
Num 28:20 shall be of flour mingled with *o*
Num 28:28 offering of flour mingled with *o*
Num 29:3 shall be of flour mingled with *o*
Num 29:9 shall be of flour mingled with *o*
Num 29:14 shall be of flour mingled with *o*
Num 35:25 was anointed with the holy *o*
Deut 7:13 thy corn, and thy wine, and thine *o*
Deut 8:8 a land of *o* olive, and honey
Deut 11:14 thy corn, and thy wine, and thine *o*
Deut 12:17 corn, or of thy wine, or of thy *o*
Deut 14:23 corn, of thy wine, and of thine *o*
Deut 18:4 corn, of thy wine, and of thine *o*
Deut 28:40 not anoint thyself with the *o*
Deut 28:51 thee either corn, wine, or *o*
Deut 32:13 rock, and *o* out of the flinty rock
Deut 33:24 and let him dip his foot in *o*
1Sa 10:1 Then Samuel took a vial of *o*
1Sa 16:1 fill thine horn with *o*, and go, I
1Sa 16:13 Then Samuel took the horn of *o*
2Sa 1:21 he had not been anointed with *o*
2Sa 14:2 and anoint not thyself with *o*
1Kin 1:39 horn of *o* out of the tabernacle
1Kin 5:11 and twenty measures of pure *o*
1Kin 17:12 barrel, and a little *o* in a cruse
1Kin 17:14 neither shall the cruse of *o* fail
1Kin 17:16 neither did the cruse of *o* fail
2Kin 4:2 in the house, save a pot of *o*
2Kin 4:6 And the *o* stayed
2Kin 4:7 And he said, Go, sell the *o*
2Kin 9:1 take this box of *o* in thine hand
2Kin 9:3 Then take the box of *o*, and pour
2Kin 9:6 and he poured the *o* on his head
2Kin 18:32 and vineyards, a land of *o* olive
1Chr 9:29 fine flour, and the wine, and the *o*
1Chr 12:40 bunches of raisins, and wine, and *o*
1Chr 27:28 over the cellars of *o* was Joash
2Chr 2:10 and twenty thousand baths of *o*
2Chr 2:15 the wheat, and the barley, the *o*
2Chr 11:11 and store of victual, and of *o*
2Chr 31:5 firstfruits of corn, wine, and *o*
2Chr 32:28 increase of corn, and wine, and *o*
Ezr 3:7 and meat, and drink, and *o*, unto
Ezr 6:9 heaven, wheat, salt, wine, and *o*
Ezr 7:22 wine, and to an hundred baths of *o*
Neh 5:11 of the corn, the wine, and the *o*
Neh 10:37 manner of trees, of wine and of *o*
Neh 10:39 corn, of the new wine, and the *o*
Neh 13:5 the corn, the new wine, and the *o*
Neh 13:12 the *o* unto the treasuries
Est 2:12 wit, six months with *o* of myrrh
Job 24:11 Which make *o* within their walls,
Job 29:6 rock poured me out rivers of *o*
Ps 23:5 thou anointest my head with *o*
Ps 45:7 hath anointed thee with the *o* of
Ps 55:21 his words were softer than *o*
Ps 89:20 with my holy *o* have I anointed
Ps 92:10 I shall be anointed with fresh *o*
Ps 104:15 *o* to make his face to shine, and
Ps 109:18 water, and like *o* into his bones
Ps 141:5 it shall be an excellent *o*
Prov 5:3 and her mouth is smoother than *o*
Prov 21:17 wine and *o* shall not be rich
Prov 21:20 *o* in the dwelling of the wise
Is 41:19 and the myrtle, and the *o* tree
Is 61:3 the *o* of joy for mourning, the
Jer 31:12 for wheat, and for wine, and for *o*
Jer 40:10 ye wine, and summer fruits, and *o*
Jer 41:8 of wheat, and of barley, and of *o*
Eze 16:9 thee, and I anointed thee with *o*
Eze 16:13 eat fine flour, and honey, and *o*
Eze 16:18 and thou hast set mine *o* and mine
Eze 16:19 I gave thee, fine flour, and *o*
Eze 23:41 hast set mine incense and mine *o*
Eze 27:17 and Pannag, and honey, and *o*
Eze 32:14 cause their rivers to run like *o*
Eze 45:14 ordinance of *o*, the bath of *o*
Eze 45:24 ram, and an hin of *o* for an ephah
Eze 45:25 offering, and according to the *o*
Eze 46:5 give, and an hin of *o* to an ephah
Eze 46:7 unto, and an hin of *o* to an ephah
Eze 46:11 give, and an hin of *o* to an ephah
Eze 46:14 and the third part of an hin of *o*
Eze 46:15 and the meat offering, and the *o*
Hos 2:5 water, my wool and my flax, mine *o*
Hos 2:8 I gave her corn, and wine, and *o*
Hos 2:22 the corn, and the wine, and the *o*
Hos 12:1 and *o* is carried into Egypt
Joel 1:10 is dried up, the *o* languisheth
Joel 2:19 will send you corn, and wine, and *o*
Joel 2:24 shall overflow with wine and *o*
Mic 6:7 with ten thousands of rivers of *o*
Mic 6:15 thou shalt not anoint thee with *o*
Hag 1:11 upon the new wine, and upon the *o*
Hag 2:12 bread, or pottage, or wine, or *o*
Zec 4:12 the golden *o* out of themselves
Mt 25:3 lamps, and took no *o* with them
Mt 25:4 But the wise took *o* in their
Mt 25:8 unto the wise, Give us of your *o*
Mk 6:13 anointed with *o* many that were
Lk 7:46 My head with *o* thou didst not
Lk 10:34 bound up his wounds, pouring in *o*
Lk 16:6 he said, An hundred measures of *o*
Heb 1:9 hath anointed thee with the *o* of
Jas 5:14 anointing him with *o* in the name
Rev 6:6 and see thou hurt not the *o*
Rev 18:13 and frankincense, and wine, and *o*

**OINTMENT**
Ex 30:25 shalt make it an oil of holy *o*
Ex 30:25 an *o* compound after the art of
2Kin 20:13 and the spices, and the precious *o*
1Chr 9:30 priests made the *o* of the spices
Job 41:31 he maketh the sea like a pot of *o*
Ps 133:2 like the precious *o* upon the head
Prov 27:9 *O* and perfume rejoice the heart
Prov 27:16 the *o* of his right hand, which
Eccl 7:1 name is better than precious *o*
Eccl 9:8 and let thy head lack no *o*
Eccl 10:1 Dead flies cause the *o* of the
Song 1:3 thy name is as *o* poured forth
Is 1:6 up, neither mollified with *o*
Is 39:2 and the spices, and the precious *o*
Is 57:9 thou wentest to the king with *o*
Mt 26:7 alabaster box of very precious *o*
Mt 26:9 For this *o* might have been sold
Mt 26:12 she hath poured this *o* on my body
Mk 14:3 of *o* of spikenard very precious
Mk 14:4 Why was this waste of the *o* made
Lk 7:37 brought an alabaster box of *o*
Lk 7:38 feet, and anointed them with the *o*
Lk 7:46 hath anointed my feet with *o*
Jn 11:2 which anointed the Lord with *o*
Jn 12:3 Mary a pound of *o* of spikenard
Jn 12:3 filled with the odour of the *o*
Jn 12:5 Why was not this *o* sold for three

**OINTMENTS**
Song 1:3 of the savour of thy good *o* thy
Song 4:10 smell of thine *o* than all spices
Amos 6:6 themselves with the chief *o*
Lk 23:56 returned, and prepared spices and *o*
Rev 18:13 And cinnamon, and odours, and *o*

**OLIVE**
Gen 8:11 mouth was an *o* leaf pluckt off
Ex 27:20 pure oil *o* beaten for the light
Ex 30:24 the sanctuary, and of oil *o* an hin
Lev 24:2 pure oil *o* beaten for the light
Deut 6:11 *o* trees, which thou plantedst not
Deut 8:8 a land of oil *o*, and honey
Deut 24:20 When thou beatest thine *o* tree
Deut 28:40 Thou shalt have *o* trees
Deut 28:40 for thine *o* shall cast his fruit
Judg 9:8 and they said unto the *o* tree
Judg 9:9 But the *o* tree said unto them,

1Kin 6:23 he made two cherubims of *o* tree
1Kin 6:31 oracle he made doors of *o* tree
1Kin 6:32 The two doors also were of *o* tree
1Kin 6:33 of the temple posts of *o* tree
2Kin 18:32 and vineyards, a land of oil *o*
1Chr 27:28 And over the *o* trees and the
Neh 8:15 fetch *o* branches, and pine
Job 15:33 cast off his flower as the *o*
Ps 52:8 But I am like a green *o* tree in
Ps 128:3 thy children like *o* plants round
Is 17:6 it, as the shaking of an *o* tree
Is 24:13 be as the shaking of an *o* tree
Jer 11:16 called thy name, A green *o* tree
Hos 14:6 his beauty shall be as the *o* tree
Amos 4:9 your *o* trees increased, the
Hab 3:17 the labour of the *o* shall fail
Hag 2:19 the *o* tree, hath not brought
Zec 4:3 two *o* trees by it, one upon the
Zec 4:11 What are these two *o* trees upon
Zec 4:12 What be these two *o* branches
Rom 11:17 off, and thou, being a wild *o* tree
Rom 11:17 the root and fatness of the *o* tree
Rom 11:24 *o* tree which is wild by nature
Rom 11:24 to nature into a good *o* tree
Rom 11:24 be graffed into their own *o* tree
Jas 3:12 tree, my brethren, bear *o* berries
Rev 11:4 These are the two *o* trees

**OLIVES**
Judg 15:5 corn, with the vineyards and *o*
Mic 6:15 thou shalt tread the *o*, but thou
Zec 14:4 in that day upon the mount of *O*
Zec 14:4 the mount of *O* shall cleave in
Mt 21:1 to Bethphage, unto the mount of *O*
Mt 24:3 And as he sat upon the mount of *O*
Mt 26:30 they went out into the mount of *O*
Mk 11:1 and Bethany, at the mount of *O*
Mk 13:3 of *O* over against the temple
Mk 14:26 they went out into the mount of *O*
Lk 19:29 the mount called the mount of *O*
Lk 19:37 at the descent of the mount of *O*
Lk 21:37 that is called the mount of *O*
Lk 22:39 as he was wont, to the mount of *O*
Jn 8:1 Jesus went unto the mount of *O*

**OLIVET** See MOUNT, OLIVES. *Hills east of Jerusalem.*
2Sa 15:30 went up by the ascent of mount *O*
Acts 1:12 Jerusalem from the mount called *O*

**OLIVEYARDS**
Josh 24:13 *o* which ye planted not do ye eat
1Sa 8:14 and your vineyards, and your *o*
2Kin 5:26 and to receive garments, and *o*
Neh 5:11 lands, their vineyards, their *o*
Neh 9:25 wells digged, vineyards, and *o*

**OLYMPAS** *(o-lim'-pas) A Christian acquaintance of Paul.*
Rom 16:15 Nereus, and his sister, and *O*

**OMAR** *(o'-mar) A son of Eliphaz.*
Gen 36:11 the sons of Eliphaz were Teman, *O*
Gen 36:15 duke Teman, duke *O*, duke Zepho,
1Chr 1:36 Teman, and *O*, Zephi, and Gatam,

**OMEGA** *(o'-me-gah) Last letter of Greek alphabet; a title applied to Jesus.*
Rev 1:8 I am Alpha and *O*, the beginning and
Rev 1:11 Saying, I am Alpha and *O*, the
Rev 21:6 I am Alpha and *O*, the beginning and
Rev 22:13 I am Alpha and *O*, the beginning and

**OMRI** *(om'-ri)*
*1. A king of Israel.*
1Kin 16:16 wherefore all Israel made *O*
1Kin 16:17 *O* went up from Gibbethon, and all
1Kin 16:21 and half followed *O*
1Kin 16:22 *O* prevailed against the people
1Kin 16:22 so Tibni died, and *O* reigned
1Kin 16:23 began *O* to reign over Israel
1Kin 16:25 But *O* wrought evil in the eyes of
1Kin 16:27 of the acts of *O* which he did
1Kin 16:28 So *O* slept with his fathers, and
1Kin 16:29 the son of *O* to reign over Israel
1Kin 16:29 Ahab the son of *O* reigned over
1Kin 16:30 Ahab the son of *O* did evil in the
2Kin 8:26 the daughter of *O* king of Israel
2Chr 22:2 was Athaliah the daughter of *O*
Mic 6:16 For the statutes of *O* are kept
*2. Son of Becher.*
1Chr 7:8 and Eliezer, and Elioenai, and *O*
*3. A descendant of Pharez.*
1Chr 9:4 the son of Ammihud, the son of *O*
*4. A ruler of Issachar.*
1Chr 27:18 of Issachar, *O* the son of Michael

**ONAM** *(o'-nam)*
*1. A son of Shobal.*
Gen 36:23 Manahath, and Ebal, Shepho, and *O*
1Chr 1:40 Manahath, and Ebal, Shephi, and *O*
*2. A son of Jerahmeel.*
1Chr 2:26 she was the mother of *O*
1Chr 2:28 And the sons of *O* were, Shammai,

**ONAN** *(o'-nan) A son of Judah.*
Gen 38:4 and she called his name *O*
Gen 38:8 And Judah said unto *O*, Go in unto
Gen 38:9 *O* knew that the seed should not
Gen 46:12 Er, and *O*, and Shelah, and Pharez,
Gen 46:12 *O* died in the land of Canaan
Num 26:19 The sons of Judah were Er and *O*
Num 26:19 *O* died in the land of Canaan
1Chr 2:3 Er, and *O*, and Shelah

**ONCE**
Gen 18:32 and I will speak yet but this *o*
Ex 10:17 I pray thee, my sin only this *o*
Ex 30:10 atonement upon the horns of it *o*
Ex 30:10 *o* in the year shall he make
Lev 16:34 for all their sins *o* a year
Num 13:30 Moses, and said, Let us go up at *o*
Deut 7:22 thou mayest not consume them at *o*
Josh 6:3 war, and go round about the city *o*
Josh 6:11 the city, going about it *o*
Josh 6:14 day they compassed the city *o*
Judg 6:39 me, and I will speak but this *o*
Judg 6:39 but this *o* with the fleece
Judg 16:18 saying, Come up this *o*, for he
Judg 16:28 me, I pray thee, only this *o*
Judg 16:28 that I may be at *o* avenged of the
1Sa 26:8 the spear even to the earth at *o*
1Kin 10:22 *o* in three years came the navy of
2Kin 6:10 himself there, not *o* nor twice
2Chr 9:21 every three years *o* came the
Neh 5:18 *o* in ten days store of all sorts
Neh 13:20 without Jerusalem *o* or twice
Job 33:14 For God speaketh *o*, yea twice,
Job 40:5 *O* have I spoken
Ps 62:11 God hath spoken *o*
Ps 74:6 work thereof at *o* with axes
Ps 76:7 thy sight when *o* thou art angry
Ps 89:35 *O* have I sworn by my holiness
Prov 28:18 in his ways shall fall at *o*
Is 42:14 I will destroy and devour at *o*
Is 66:8 or shall a nation be born at *o*
Jer 10:18 inhabitants of the land at this *o*
Jer 13:27 when shall it *o* be
Jer 16:21 I will this *o* cause them to know,
Hag 2:6 Yet *o*, it is a little while, and I
Lk 13:25 When *o* the master of the house is
Lk 23:18 And they cried out all at *o*
Rom 6:10 that he died, he died unto sin *o*
Rom 7:9 For I was alive without the law *o*
1Cor 15:6 above five hundred brethren at *o*
2Cor 11:25 *o* was I stoned, thrice I suffered
Gal 1:23 the faith which *o* he destroyed
Eph 5:3 let it not be *o* named among you,
Phil 4:16 even in Thessalonica ye sent *o*
1Th 2:18 come unto you, even I Paul, *o*
Heb 6:4 for those who were *o* enlightened
Heb 7:27 for this he did *o*, when he
Heb 9:7 high priest alone *o* every year
Heb 9:12 entered in *o* into the holy place
Heb 9:26 but now *o* in the end of the world
Heb 9:27 it is appointed unto men *o* to die
Heb 9:28 So Christ was *o* offered to bear
Heb 10:2 because that the worshippers *o*
Heb 10:10 body of Jesus Christ *o* for all
Heb 12:26 Yet *o* more I shake not the earth
Heb 12:27 Yet *o* more, signifieth the
1Pet 3:18 also hath *o* suffered for sins
1Pet 3:20 when *o* the longsuffering of God
Jude 3 was *o* delivered unto the saints
Jude 5 though ye *o* knew this, how that

**ONESIMUS** *(o-nes'-i-mus) A Christian of Colosse.*
Col 4:9 With *O*, a faithful and beloved
Col *s* the Colossians by Tychicus and *O*
Philem 10 I beseech thee for my son *O*
Philem *s* from Rome to Philemon, by *O*

**ONESIPHORUS** *(o-ne-sif'-o-rus) A Christian of Ephesus.*
2Ti 1:16 give mercy unto the house of *O*
2Ti 4:19 and Aquila, and the household of *O*

**ONO** *(o'-no)*
*1. A city in Benjamin.*
1Chr 8:12 Misham, and Shamed, who built *O*
Ezr 2:33 The children of Lod, Hadid, and *O*
Neh 7:37 The children of Lod, Hadid, and *O*
Neh 11:35 Lod, and *O*, the valley of
*2. A valley near Jerusalem.*
Neh 6:2 of the villages in the plain of *O*

**ONYX**
Gen 2:12 there is bdellium and the *o* stone
Ex 25:7 *O* stones, and stones to be set in
Ex 28:9 And thou shalt take two *o* stones
Ex 28:20 the fourth row a beryl, and an *o*
Ex 35:9 *o* stones, and stones to be set for
Ex 35:27 And the rulers brought *o* stones
Ex 39:6 they wrought *o* stones inclosed in
Ex 39:13 And the fourth row, a beryl, an *o*
1Chr 29:2 *o* stones, and stones to be set,
Job 28:16 of Ophir, with the precious *o*
Eze 28:13 and the diamond, the beryl, the *o*

**OPEN**
Gen 1:20 in the *o* firmament of heaven
Gen 38:14 herself, and sat in an *o* place
Ex 21:33 And if a man shall *o* a pit
Lev 14:7 bird loose into the *o* field
Lev 14:53 out of the city into the *o* fields
Lev 17:5 which they offer in the *o* field
Num 8:16 instead of such as *o* every womb
Num 16:30 thing, and the earth *o* her mouth
Num 19:15 every *o* vessel, which hath no
Num 19:16 with a sword in the *o* fields
Num 24:3 man whose eyes are *o* hath said
Num 24:4 a trance, but having his eyes *o*
Num 24:15 man whose eyes are *o* hath said
Num 24:16 a trance, but having his eyes *o*
Deut 15:8 But thou shalt *o* thine hand wide
Deut 15:11 Thou shalt *o* thine hand wide unto
Deut 20:11 *o* unto thee, then it shall be,
Deut 28:12 The LORD shall *o* unto thee his
Josh 8:17 and they left the city *o*, and
Josh 10:22 *O* the mouth of the cave, and bring
1Sa 3:1 there was no *o* vision
2Sa 11:11 are encamped in the *o* fields
1Kin 6:18 carved with knops and *o* flowers
1Kin 6:29 *o* flowers, within and without
1Kin 6:32 *o* flowers, and overlaid them with
1Kin 6:35 and palm trees and *o* flowers
1Kin 8:29 That thine eyes may be *o* toward
1Kin 8:52 That thine eyes may be *o* unto the
2Kin 6:17 *o* his eyes, that he may see
2Kin 6:20 *o* the eyes of these men, that
2Kin 9:3 Then *o* the door, and flee, and
2Kin 13:17 And he said, *O* the window eastward
2Kin 19:16 *o*, LORD, thine eyes, and see
2Chr 6:20 eyes may be *o* upon this house day
2Chr 6:40 I beseech thee, thine eyes be *o*
2Chr 7:15 Now mine eyes shall be *o*, and mine
Neh 1:6 now be attentive, and thine eyes *o*
Neh 6:5 time with an *o* letter in his hand
Job 11:5 speak, and *o* his lips against thee
Job 14:3 dost thou *o* thine eyes upon such
Job 32:20 I will *o* my lips and answer
Job 34:26 men in the *o* sight of others
Job 35:16 doth Job *o* his mouth in vain
Job 41:14 Who can *o* the doors of his face
Ps 5:9 their throat is an *o* sepulchre
Ps 34:15 his ears are *o* unto their cry
Ps 49:4 I will *o* my dark saying upon the
Ps 51:15 O Lord, *o* thou my lips
Ps 78:2 I will *o* my mouth in a parable
Ps 81:10 *o* thy mouth wide, and I will fill
Ps 118:19 *O* to me the gates of
Ps 119:18 *O* thou mine eyes, that I may
Prov 13:16 but a fool layeth *o* his folly
Prov 20:13 *o* thine eyes, and thou shalt be
Prov 27:5 *O* rebuke is better than secret
Prov 31:8 *O* thy mouth for the dumb in the
Prov 31:9 *O* thy mouth, judge righteously,
Song 5:2 *O* to me, my sister, my love, my
Song 5:5 I rose up to *o* to my beloved
Is 9:12 shall devour Israel with *o* mouth
Is 22:22 so he shall *o*, and none shall shut
Is 22:22 and he shall shut, and none shall *o*
Is 24:18 the windows from on high are *o*
Is 26:2 *O* ye the gates, that the
Is 28:24 doth he *o* and break the clods of
Is 37:17 *o* thine eyes, O LORD, and see
Is 41:18 I will *o* rivers in high places,
Is 42:7 To *o* the blind eyes, to bring out

Is 45:1 to o before him the two leaved
Is 45:8 let the earth o, and let them
Is 60:11 thy gates shall be o continually
Jer 5:16 Their quiver is as an o sepulchre
Jer 9:22 fall as dung upon the o field
Jer 13:19 be shut up, and none shall o them
Jer 32:11 and custom, and that which was o
Jer 32:14 and this evidence which is o
Jer 32:19 for thine eyes are o upon all the
Jer 50:26 utmost border, o her storehouses
Eze 2:8 o thy mouth, and eat that I give
Eze 3:27 I will o thy mouth, and thou shalt
Eze 16:5 thou wast cast out in the o field
Eze 16:63 never o thy mouth any more
Eze 21:22 to o the mouth in the slaughter,
Eze 25:9 I will o the side of Moab from
Eze 29:5 thou shalt fall upon the o fields
Eze 32:4 cast thee forth upon the o field
Eze 33:27 him that is in the o field will I
Eze 37:2 were very many in the o valley
Eze 37:12 I will o your graves, and cause
Eze 39:5 Thou shalt fall upon the o field
Eze 46:12 one shall then o him the gate
Dan 6:10 his windows being o in his
Dan 9:18 o thine eyes, and behold our
Nah 3:13 be set wide o unto thine enemies
Zec 11:1 O thy doors, O Lebanon, that the
Zec 12:4 I will o mine eyes upon the house
Mal 3:10 if I will not o you the windows
Mt 13:35 I will o my mouth in parables
Mt 25:11 saying, Lord, Lord, o to us
Lk 12:36 they may o unto him immediately
Lk 13:25 saying, Lord, Lord, o unto us
Jn 1:51 Hereafter ye shall see heaven o
Jn 10:21 Can a devil o the eyes of the
Acts 16:27 and seeing the prison doors o
Acts 18:14 Paul was now about to o his mouth
Acts 19:38 against any man, the law is o
Acts 26:18 To o their eyes, and to turn them
Rom 3:13 Their throat is an o sepulchre
2Cor 3:18 with o face beholding as in a
2Cor 6:11 our mouth is o unto you, our
Eph 6:19 that I may o my mouth boldly, to
Col 4:3 that God would o unto us a door
1Ti 5:24 Some men's sins are o beforehand
Heb 6:6 afresh, and put him to an o shame
1Pet 3:12 his ears are o unto their prayers
Rev 3:8 I have set before thee an o door
Rev 3:20 o the door, I will come in to him
Rev 5:2 Who is worthy to o the book
Rev 5:3 the earth, was able to o the book
Rev 5:4 no man was found worthy to o
Rev 5:5 hath prevailed to o the book
Rev 5:9 book, and to o the seals thereof
Rev 10:2 had in his hand a little book o
Rev 10:8 take the little book which is o

## OPENED

Gen 3:5 then your eyes shall be o
Gen 3:7 And the eyes of them both were o
Gen 4:11 which hath o her mouth to receive
Gen 7:11 and the windows of heaven were o
Gen 8:6 that Noah o the window of the ark
Gen 21:19 God o her eyes, and she saw a well
Gen 29:31 Leah was hated, he o her womb
Gen 30:22 hearkened to her, and o her womb
Gen 41:56 Joseph o all the storehouses, and
Gen 42:27 as one of them o his sack to give
Gen 43:21 that we o our sacks, and, behold,
Gen 44:11 ground, and o every man his sack
Ex 2:6 And when she had o it, she saw the
Num 16:32 And the earth o her mouth, and
Num 22:28 the LORD o the mouth of the ass,
Num 22:31 Then the LORD o the eyes of
Num 26:10 And the earth o her mouth, and
Deut 11:6 how the earth o her mouth
Judg 3:25 he o not the doors of the parlour
Judg 3:25 they took a key, and o them
Judg 4:19 she o a bottle of milk, and gave
Judg 11:35 for I have o my mouth unto the
Judg 11:36 if thou hast o thy mouth unto the
Judg 19:27 o the doors of the house, and went
1Sa 3:15 o the doors of the house of the
2Kin 4:35 times, and the child o his eyes
2Kin 6:17 the LORD o the eyes of the young
2Kin 6:20 the LORD o their eyes, and they
2Kin 9:10 And he o the door, and fled
2Kin 13:17 And he o it
2Kin 15:16 because they o not to him
2Chr 29:3 o the doors of the house of the
Neh 7:3 be o until the sun be hot
Neh 8:5 Ezra o the book in the sight of
Neh 8:5 and when he o it, all the people
Neh 13:19 not be o till after the sabbath
Job 3:1 After this o Job his mouth, and
Job 29:23 they o their mouth wide as for
Job 31:32 but I o my doors to the traveller
Job 33:2 Behold, now I have o my mouth
Job 38:17 gates of death been o unto thee
Ps 35:21 they o their mouth wide against
Ps 39:9 I was dumb, I o not my mouth
Ps 40:6 mine ears hast thou o
Ps 78:23 above, and o the doors of heaven,
Ps 105:41 He o the rock, and the waters
Ps 106:17 The earth o and swallowed up
Ps 109:2 of the deceitful are o against me
Ps 119:131 I o my mouth, and panted
Song 5:6 I o to my beloved
Is 5:14 o her mouth without measure
Is 10:14 or o the mouth, or peeped
Is 14:17 that o not the house of his
Is 35:5 the eyes of the blind shall be o
Is 48:8 time that thine ear was not o
Is 50:5 The Lord GOD hath o mine ear
Is 53:7 afflicted, yet he o not his mouth
Jer 20:12 for unto thee have I o my cause
Jer 50:25 The LORD hath o his armoury
Lam 2:16 All thine enemies have o their
Lam 3:46 All our enemies have o their
Eze 1:1 Chebar, that the heavens were o
Eze 3:2 So I o my mouth, and he caused me
Eze 16:25 hast o thy feet to every one that
Eze 24:27 be o to him which is escaped
Eze 33:22 had o my mouth, until he came to
Eze 33:22 and my mouth was o, and I was no
Eze 37:13 LORD, when I have o your graves
Eze 44:2 shall be shut, it shall not be o
Eze 46:1 but on the sabbath it shall be o
Eze 46:1 day of the new moon it shall be o
Dan 7:10 was set, and the books were o
Dan 10:16 then I o my mouth, and spake, and
Nah 2:6 gates of the rivers shall be o
Zec 13:1 fountain o to the house of David
Mt 2:11 when they had o their treasures,
Mt 3:16 lo, the heavens were o unto him
Mt 5:2 he o his mouth, and taught them,
Mt 7:7 knock, and it shall be o unto you
Mt 7:8 him that knocketh it shall be o
Mt 9:30 And their eyes were o
Mt 17:27 and when thou hast o his mouth
Mt 20:33 him, Lord, that our eyes may be o
Mt 27:52 And the graves were o
Mk 1:10 the water, he saw the heavens o
Mk 7:34 him, Ephphatha, that is, Be o
Mk 7:35 And straightway his ears were o
Lk 1:64 And his mouth was o immediately
Lk 3:21 and praying, the heaven was o
Lk 4:17 And when he had o the book
Lk 11:9 knock, and it shall be o unto you
Lk 11:10 him that knocketh it shall be o
Lk 24:31 And their eyes were o, and they
Lk 24:32 while he o to us the scriptures
Lk 24:45 Then o he their understanding,
Jn 9:10 unto him, How were thine eyes o
Jn 9:14 made the clay, and o his eyes
Jn 9:17 of him, that he hath o thine eyes
Jn 9:21 or who hath o his eyes, we know
Jn 9:26 how o he thine eyes
Jn 9:30 he is, and yet he hath o mine eyes
Jn 9:32 o the eyes of one that was born
Jn 11:37 which o the eyes of the blind,
Acts 5:19 Lord by night o the prison doors
Acts 5:23 but when we had o, we found no
Acts 7:56 said, Behold, I see the heavens o
Acts 8:32 shearer, so o he not his mouth
Acts 8:35 Then Philip o his mouth, and began
Acts 9:8 and when his eyes were o, he saw
Acts 9:40 And she o her eyes
Acts 10:11 And saw heaven o, and a certain
Acts 10:34 Then Peter o his mouth, and said,
Acts 12:10 which o to them of his own accord
Acts 12:14 she o not the gate for gladness,
Acts 12:16 and when they had o the door
Acts 14:27 how he had o the door of faith
Acts 16:14 whose heart the Lord o, that she
Acts 16:26 immediately all the doors were o
1Cor 16:9 door and effectual is o unto me
2Cor 2:12 a door was o unto me of the Lord,
Heb 4:13 o unto the eyes of him with whom
Rev 4:1 behold, a door was o in heaven
Rev 6:1 when the Lamb o one of the seals
Rev 6:3 when he had o the second seal, I
Rev 6:5 when he had o the third seal, I
Rev 6:7 when he had o the fourth seal, I
Rev 6:9 when he had o the fifth seal, I
Rev 6:12 when he had o the sixth seal
Rev 8:1 when he had o the seventh seal,
Rev 9:2 And he o the bottomless pit
Rev 11:19 the temple of God was o in heaven
Rev 12:16 woman, and the earth o her mouth
Rev 13:6 he o his mouth in blasphemy
Rev 15:5 of the testimony in heaven was o
Rev 19:11 And I saw heaven o, and behold a
Rev 20:12 and the books were o
Rev 20:12 and another book was o, which is

## OPENETH

Ex 13:2 whatsoever o the womb among the
Ex 13:12 the LORD all that o the matrix
Ex 13:15 to the LORD all that o the matrix
Ex 34:19 All that o the matrix is mine
Num 3:12 of all the firstborn that o the
Num 18:15 Every thing that o the matrix in
Job 27:19 he o his eyes, and he is not
Job 33:16 Then he o the ears of men, and
Job 36:10 He o also their ear to discipline
Job 36:15 o their ears in oppression
Ps 38:13 a dumb man that o not his mouth
Ps 146:8 The LORD o the eyes of the blind
Prov 13:3 but he that o wide his lips shall
Prov 24:7 he o not his mouth in the gate
Prov 31:26 She o her mouth with wisdom
Is 53:7 is dumb, so he o not his mouth
Eze 20:26 the fire all that o the womb
Lk 2:23 Every male that o the womb shall
Jn 10:3 To him the porter o
Rev 3:7 hath the key of David, he that o
Rev 3:7 and shutteth, and no man o

## OPENING

1Chr 9:27 the o thereof every morning
Job 12:14 up a man, and there can be no o
Prov 8:6 the o of my lips shall be right
Is 42:20 o the ears, but he heareth not
Is 61:1 the o of the prison to them that
Eze 29:21 I will give thee the o of the
Acts 17:3 O and alleging, that Christ must

## OPENLY

Gen 38:21 that was o by the way side
Ps 98:2 his righteousness hath he o
Mt 6:4 himself shall reward thee o
Mt 6:6 in secret shall reward thee o
Mt 6:18 in secret, shall reward thee o
Mk 1:45 no more o enter into the city
Mk 8:32 And he spake that saying o
Jn 7:4 he himself seeketh to be known o
Jn 7:10 he also up unto the feast, not o
Jn 7:13 Howbeit no man spake o of him for
Jn 11:54 walked no more o among the Jews
Jn 18:20 him, I spake o to the world
Acts 10:40 up the third day, and shewed him o
Acts 16:37 They have beaten us o uncondemned
Col 2:15 powers, he made a shew of them o

## OPERATION

Ps 28:5 nor the o of his hands, he shall
Is 5:12 consider the o of his hands
Col 2:12 through the faith of the o of God

## OPHEL (o'-fel) *A fortified place near Jerusalem.*

2Chr 27:3 and on the wall of O he built much
2Chr 33:14 fish gate, and compassed about O
Neh 3:26 Moreover the Nethinims dwelt in O
Neh 3:27 out, even unto the wall of O
Neh 11:21 But the Nethinims dwelt in O

## OPHIR (o'-fur)

*1. A son of Joktan.*

Gen 10:29 And O, and Havilah, and Jobab
1Chr 1:23 And O, and Havilah, and Jobab

*2. A place in southern Arabia.*

1Kin 9:28 And they came to O, and fetched
1Kin 10:11 Hiram, that brought gold from O
1Kin 10:11 brought in from O great plenty of
1Kin 22:48 of Tharshish to go to O for gold
1Chr 29:4 talents of gold, of the gold of O
2Chr 8:18 with the servants of Solomon to O
2Chr 9:10 which brought gold from O
Job 22:24 the gold of O as the stones of
Job 28:16 be valued with the gold of O
Ps 45:9 did stand the queen in gold of O
Is 13:12 a man than the golden wedge of O

**OPHNI** *(of'-ni) A place in Benjamin.*
Josh 18:24 And Chephar-haammonai, and O

**OPHRAH** *(of'-rah)* See APHRAH.
*1. A city in Benjamin.*
Josh 18:23 And Avim, and Parah, and O,
1Sa 13:17 unto the way that leadeth to O
*2. A city in Manasseh.*
Judg 6:11 sat under an oak which was in O
Judg 6:24 it is yet in O of the Abi-ezrites
Judg 8:27 and put it in his city, even in O
Judg 8:32 father, in O of the Abi-ezrites
Judg 9:5 went unto his father's house at O
*3. Head of a family in Judah.*
1Chr 4:14 And Meonothai begat O

**OPPORTUNITY**
Mt 26:16 time he sought *o* to betray him
Lk 22:6 sought *o* to betray him unto them
Gal 6:10 As we have therefore *o*, let us do
Phil 4:10 also careful, but ye lacked *o*
Heb 11:15 might have had *o* to have returned

**OPPRESS**
Ex 3:9 wherewith the Egyptians *o* them
Ex 22:21 neither vex a stranger, nor *o* him
Ex 23:9 Also thou shalt not *o* a stranger
Lev 25:14 hand, ye shall not *o* one another
Lev 25:17 shall not therefore *o* one another
Deut 23:16 thou shalt not *o* him
Deut 24:14 Thou shalt not *o* an hired servant
Judg 10:12 and the Maonites, did *o* you
Job 10:3 unto thee that thou shouldest *o*
Ps 10:18 man of the earth may no more *o*
Ps 17:9 From the wicked that *o* me
Ps 119:122 let not the proud *o* me
Prov 22:22 neither *o* the afflicted in the
Is 49:26 I will feed them that *o* thee with
Jer 7:6 If ye *o* not the stranger, the
Jer 30:20 and I will punish all that *o* them
Eze 45:8 princes shall no more *o* my people
Hos 12:7 he loveth to *o*
Amos 4:1 which *o* the poor, which crush the
Mic 2:2 so they *o* a man and his house,
Zec 7:10 And *o* not the widow, nor the
Mal 3:5 against those that *o* the hireling
Jas 2:6 Do not rich men *o* you, and draw

**OPPRESSED**
Deut 28:29 and thou shalt be only *o* and
Deut 28:33 and thou shalt be only *o* and
Judg 2:18 by reason of them that *o* them
Judg 4:3 mightily *o* the children of Israel
Judg 6:9 out of the hand of all that *o* you
Judg 10:8 vexed and *o* the children of Israel
1Sa 10:18 kingdoms, and of them that *o* you
1Sa 12:3 whom have I *o*
1Sa 12:4 hast not defrauded us, nor *o* us
2Kin 13:4 because the king of Syria *o* them
2Kin 13:22 But Hazael king of Syria *o* Israel
2Chr 16:10 Asa *o* some of the people the same
Job 20:19 Because he hath *o* and hath
Job 35:9 they make the *o* to cry
Ps 9:9 also will be a refuge for the *o*
Ps 10:18 To judge the fatherless and the *o*
Ps 74:21 O let not the *o* return ashamed
Ps 103:6 and judgment for all that are *o*
Ps 106:42 Their enemies also *o* them
Ps 146:7 executeth judgment for the *o*
Eccl 4:1 the tears of such as were *o*
Is 1:17 seek judgment, relieve the *o*
Is 3:5 And the people shall be *o*, every
Is 23:12 no more rejoice, O thou *o* virgin
Is 38:14 O LORD, I am *o*
Is 52:4 the Assyrian *o* them without cause
Is 53:7 He was *o*, and he was afflicted,
Is 58:6 burdens, and to let the *o* go free
Jer 50:33 children of Judah were *o* together
Eze 18:7 And hath not *o* any, but hath
Eze 18:12 Hath *o* the poor and needy, hath
Eze 18:16 Neither hath *o* any, hath not
Eze 18:18 his father, because he cruelly *o*
Eze 22:29 yea, they have *o* the stranger
Hos 5:11 Ephraim is *o* and broken in
Amos 3:9 the *o* in the midst thereof
Acts 7:24 him, and avenged him that was *o*
Acts 10:38 all that were *o* of the devil

**OPPRESSETH**
Num 10:9 land against the enemy that *o* you
Ps 56:1 he fighting daily *o* me
Prov 14:31 He that *o* the poor reproacheth
Prov 22:16 He that *o* the poor to increase
Prov 28:3 A poor man that *o* the poor is

**OPPRESSION**
Ex 3:9 I have also seen the *o* wherewith
Deut 26:7 and our labour, and our *o*
2Kin 13:4 for he saw the *o* of Israel
Job 36:15 and openeth their ears in *o*
Ps 12:5 For the *o* of the poor, for the
Ps 42:9 because of the *o* of the enemy
Ps 43:2 because of the *o* of the enemy
Ps 44:24 our affliction and our *o*
Ps 55:3 because of the *o* of the wicked
Ps 62:10 Trust not in *o*, and become not
Ps 73:8 and speak wickedly concerning *o*
Ps 107:39 minished and brought low through *o*
Ps 119:134 Deliver me from the *o* of man
Eccl 5:8 If thou seest the *o* of the poor
Eccl 7:7 Surely *o* maketh a wise man mad
Is 5:7 looked for judgment, but behold *o*
Is 30:12 despise this word, and trust in *o*
Is 54:14 thou shalt be far from *o*
Is 59:13 away from our God, speaking *o*
Jer 6:6 she is wholly *o* in the midst of
Jer 22:17 to shed innocent blood, and for *o*
Eze 22:7 they dealt by *o* with the stranger
Eze 22:29 people of the land have used *o*
Eze 46:18 of the people's inheritance by *o*

**OPPRESSOR**
Job 3:18 they hear not the voice of the *o*
Job 15:20 of years is hidden to the *o*
Ps 72:4 and shall break in pieces the *o*
Prov 3:31 Envy thou not the *o*, and choose
Prov 28:16 understanding is also a great *o*
Is 9:4 of his shoulder, the rod of his *o*
Is 14:4 and say, How hath the *o* ceased
Is 51:13 day because of the fury of the *o*
Is 51:13 and where is the fury of the *o*
Jer 21:12 spoiled out of the hand of the *o*
Jer 22:3 spoiled out of the hand of the *o*
Jer 25:38 of the fierceness of the *o*
Zec 9:8 no *o* shall pass through them any
Zec 10:4 bow, out of him every *o* together

**OPPRESSORS**
Job 27:13 with God, and the heritage of *o*
Ps 54:3 me, and *o* seek after my soul
Ps 119:121 leave me not to mine *o*
Eccl 4:1 side of their *o* there was power
Is 3:12 my people, children are their *o*
Is 14:2 and they shall rule over their *o*
Is 16:4 the *o* are consumed out of the
Is 19:20 unto the LORD because of the *o*

**ORACLE**
2Sa 16:23 man had enquired at the *o* of God
1Kin 6:5 both of the temple and of the *o*
1Kin 6:16 for it within, even for the *o*
1Kin 6:19 the *o* he prepared in the house
1Kin 6:20 the *o* in the forepart was twenty
1Kin 6:21 the chains of gold before the *o*
1Kin 6:22 by the *o* he overlaid with gold
1Kin 6:23 And within the *o* he made two
1Kin 6:31 for the entering of the *o* he made
1Kin 7:49 and five on the left, before the *o*
1Kin 8:6 into the *o* of the house, to the
1Kin 8:8 in the holy place before the *o*
2Chr 3:16 And he made chains, as in the *o*
2Chr 4:20 after the manner before the *o*
2Chr 5:7 to the *o* of the house, into the
2Chr 5:9 seen from the ark before the *o*
Ps 28:2 up my hands toward thy holy *o*

**ORACLES**
Acts 7:38 the lively *o* to give unto us
Rom 3:2 them were committed the *o* of God
Heb 5:12 first principles of the *o* of God
1Pet 4:11 let him speak as the *o* of God

**ORDAIN**
1Chr 9:22 seer did *o* in their set office
1Chr 17:9 Also I will *o* a place for my
Is 26:12 LORD, thou wilt *o* peace for us
1Cor 7:17 And so *o* I in all churches
Titus 1:5 *o* elders in every city, as I had

**ORDAINED**
Num 28:6 which was *o* in mount Sinai for a
1Kin 12:32 Jeroboam *o* a feast in the eighth
1Kin 12:33 *o* a feast unto the children of
2Kin 23:5 had *o* to burn incense in the high
2Chr 11:15 he *o* him priests for the high
2Chr 23:18 singing, as it was *o* by David
2Chr 29:27 with the instruments *o* by David
Est 9:27 The Jews *o*, and took upon them, and
Ps 8:2 sucklings hast thou *o* strength
Ps 8:3 and the stars, which thou hast *o*
Ps 81:5 This he *o* in Joseph for a
Ps 132:17 I have *o* a lamp for mine anointed
Is 30:33 For Tophet is *o* of old
Jer 1:5 I *o* thee a prophet unto the
Dan 2:24 whom the king had *o* to destroy
Hab 1:12 thou hast *o* them for judgment
Mk 3:14 he *o* twelve, that they should be
Jn 15:16 *o* you, that ye should go and bring
Acts 1:22 must one be *o* to be a witness
Acts 10:42 *o* of God to be the Judge of quick
Acts 13:48 as many as were *o* to eternal life
Acts 14:23 when they had *o* them elders in
Acts 16:4 that were *o* of the apostles and
Acts 17:31 by that man whom he hath *o*
Rom 7:10 commandment, which was *o* to life
Rom 13:1 the powers that be are *o* of God
1Cor 2:7 which God *o* before the world unto
1Cor 9:14 Even so hath the Lord *o* that they
Gal 3:19 it was *o* by angels in the hand of
Eph 2:10 which God hath before *o* that we
1Ti 2:7 Whereunto I am *o* a preacher
2Ti *s* *o* the first bishop of the church
Titus *s* *o* the first bishop of the church
Heb 5:1 priest taken from among men is *o*
Heb 8:3 high priest is *o* to offer gifts
Heb 9:6 Now when these things were thus *o*
Jude 4 of old *o* to this condemnation

**ORDER**
Gen 22:9 there, and laid the wood in *o*
Ex 26:17 set in *o* one against another
Ex 27:21 his sons shall *o* it from evening
Ex 39:37 with the lamps to be set in *o*
Ex 40:4 set in *o* the things that are to
Ex 40:4 that are to be set in *o* upon it
Ex 40:23 he set the bread in *o* upon it
Lev 1:7 lay the wood in *o* upon the fire
Lev 1:8 in *o* upon the wood that is on the
Lev 1:12 the priest shall lay them in *o* on
Lev 6:12 the burnt offering in *o* upon it
Lev 24:3 shall Aaron *o* it from the evening
Lev 24:4 He shall *o* the lamps upon the
Lev 24:8 sabbath he shall set it in *o*
Josh 2:6 she had laid in *o* upon the roof
Judg 13:12 How shall we *o* the child, and how
2Sa 17:23 city, and put his household in *o*
1Kin 18:33 And he put the wood in *o*, and cut
1Kin 20:14 he said, Who shall *o* the battle
2Kin 20:1 the LORD, Set thine house in *o*
2Kin 23:4 and the priests of the second *o*
1Chr 6:32 their office according to their *o*
1Chr 15:13 we sought him not after the due *o*
1Chr 23:31 according to the *o* commanded unto
1Chr 25:2 according to the *o* of the king
1Chr 25:6 to the king's *o* to Asaph,
2Chr 8:14 according to the *o* of David his
2Chr 13:11 set they in *o* upon the pure table
2Chr 29:35 house of the LORD was set in *o*
Job 10:22 shadow of death, without any *o*
Job 23:4 I would *o* my cause before him, and
Job 33:5 me, set thy words in *o* before me
Job 37:19 for we cannot *o* our speech by
Ps 40:5 be reckoned up in *o* unto thee
Ps 50:21 set them in *o* before thine eyes
Ps 110:4 ever after the *o* of Melchizedek
Ps 119:133 O my steps in thy word
Eccl 12:9 out, and set in *o* many proverbs
Is 9:7 and upon his kingdom, to *o* it
Is 38:1 the LORD, Set thine house in *o*
Is 44:7 declare it, and set it in *o* for me
Jer 46:3 O ye the buckler and shield, and
Eze 41:6 one over another, and thirty in *o*
Lk 1:1 *o* a declaration of those things
Lk 1:3 first, to write unto thee in *o*
Lk 1:8 before God in the *o* of his course
Acts 11:4 and expounded it by *o* unto them
Acts 18:23 of Galatia and Phrygia in *o*
1Cor 11:34 rest will I set in *o* when I come
1Cor 14:40 things be done decently and in *o*
1Cor 15:23 But every man in his own *o*
1Cor 16:1 as I have given *o* to the churches
Col 2:5 joying and beholding your *o*
Titus 1:5 that thou shouldest set in *o* the
Heb 5:6 ever after the *o* of Melchisedec
Heb 5:10 priest after the *o* of Melchisedec
Heb 6:20 ever after the *o* of Melchisedec

Heb 7:11 rise after the o of Melchisedec
Heb 7:11 be called after the o of Aaron
Heb 7:17 ever after the o of Melchisedec
Heb 7:21 ever after the o of Melchisedec

**ORDERED**
Judg 6:26 top of this rock, in the o place
2Sa 23:5 o in all things, and sure
Job 13:18 Behold now, I have o my cause
Ps 37:23 of a good man are o by the LORD

**ORDINANCE**
Ex 12:14 keep it a feast by an o for ever
Ex 12:17 your generations by an o for ever
Ex 12:24 this thing for an o to thee
Ex 12:43 This is the o of the passover
Ex 13:10 Thou shalt therefore keep this o
Ex 15:25 made for them a statute and an o
Lev 18:30 Therefore shall ye keep mine o
Lev 22:9 They shall therefore keep mine o
Num 9:14 to the o of the passover, and
Num 9:14 ye shall have one o, both for the
Num 10:8 for an o for ever throughout your
Num 15:15 One o shall be both for you of
Num 15:15 an o for ever in your generations
Num 18:8 and to thy sons, by an o for ever
Num 19:2 This is the o of the law which
Num 31:21 This is the o of the law which
Josh 24:25 them a statute and an o in Shechem
1Sa 30:25 an o for Israel unto this day
2Chr 2:4 This is an o for ever to Israel
2Chr 35:13 with fire according to the o
2Chr 35:25 day, and made them an o in Israel
Ezr 3:10 after the o of David king of
Ps 99:7 and the o that he gave them
Is 24:5 the laws, changed the o, broken
Is 58:2 and forsook not the o of their God
Eze 45:14 Concerning the o of oil, the bath
Eze 46:14 by a perpetual o unto the LORD
Mal 3:14 is it that we have kept his o
Rom 13:2 the power, resisteth the o of God
1Pet 2:13 o of man for the Lord's sake

**ORDINANCES**
Ex 18:20 And thou shalt teach them o
Lev 18:3 neither shall ye walk in their o
Lev 18:4 do my judgments, and keep mine o
Num 9:12 according to all the o of the
2Kin 17:34 their statutes, or after their o
2Kin 17:37 And the statutes, and the o
2Chr 33:8 the o by the hand of Moses
Neh 10:32 Also we made o for us, to charge
Job 38:33 Knowest thou the o of heaven
Ps 119:91 this day according to thine o
Is 58:2 they ask of me the o of justice
Jer 31:35 the o of the moon and of the stars
Jer 31:36 If those o depart from before me,
Jer 33:25 not appointed the o of heaven
Eze 11:20 in my statutes, and keep mine o
Eze 43:11 thereof, and all the o thereof
Eze 43:11 thereof, and all the o thereof
Eze 43:18 These are the o of the altar in
Eze 44:5 the o of the house of the LORD
Mal 3:7 ye are gone away from mine o
Lk 1:6 and o of the Lord blameless
1Cor 11:2 me in all things, and keep the o
Eph 2:15 of commandments contained in o
Col 2:14 of o that was against us, which
Col 2:20 in the world, are ye subject to o
Heb 9:1 had also o of divine service
Heb 9:10 and divers washings, and carnal o

**OREB** *(o'-reb)*
*1. A prince of Midian.*
Judg 7:25 two princes of the Midianites, O
Judg 7:25 they slew O upon the rock O,
Judg 7:25 Midian, and brought the heads of O
Judg 8:3 hands the princes of Midian, O
Ps 83:11 Make their nobles like O, and like
*2. A rock east of the Jordan.*
Is 10:26 of Midian at the rock of O

**OREN** *(o'-ren) A son of Jerahmeel.*
1Chr 2:25 Ram the firstborn, and Bunah, and O

**ORION** *(o'-ri'-on) A constellation of stars.*
Job 9:9 Which maketh Arcturus, O, and
Job 38:31 Pleiades, or loose the bands of O
Amos 5:8 that maketh the seven stars and O

**ORNAMENT**
Prov 1:9 For they shall be an o of grace
Prov 4:9 give to thine head an o of grace
Prov 25:12 an o of fine gold, so is a wise
Is 30:22 the o of thy molten images of
Is 49:18 thee with them all, as with an o
Eze 7:20 As for the beauty of his o
1Pet 3:4 even the o of a meek and quiet

**ORNAMENTS**
Ex 33:4 and no man did put on him his o
Ex 33:5 now put off thy o from thee
Ex 33:6 of their o by the mount Horeb
Judg 8:21 took away the o that were on
Judg 8:26 beside o, and collars, and purple
2Sa 1:24 who put on o of gold upon your
Is 3:18 their tinkling o about their feet
Is 3:20 the o of the legs, and the
Is 61:10 bridegroom decketh himself with o
Jer 2:32 Can a maid forget her o, or a
Jer 4:30 thou deckest thee with o of gold
Eze 16:7 and thou art come to excellent o
Eze 16:11 I decked thee also with o
Eze 23:40 eyes, and deckedst thyself with o

**ORNAN** *(or'-nan)* See ARAUNAH. *A Jebusite prince.*
1Chr 21:15 threshingfloor of O the Jebusite
1Chr 21:18 threshingfloor of O the Jebusite
1Chr 21:20 O turned back, and saw the angel
1Chr 21:20 Now O was threshing wheat
1Chr 21:21 And as David came to O, O
1Chr 21:22 Then David said to O, Grant me
1Chr 21:23 O said unto David, Take it to
1Chr 21:24 And king David said to O, Nay
1Chr 21:25 So David gave to O for the place
1Chr 21:28 threshingfloor of O the Jebusite
2Chr 3:1 threshingfloor of O the Jebusite

**ORPAH** *(or'-pah) Daughter-in-law of Naomi.*
Ruth 1:4 the name of the one was O
Ruth 1:14 O kissed her mother in law

**OSEE** *(o'-see)* See HOSEA, JOSHUA, OSHEA. *Greek form of Hoshea.*
Rom 9:25 As he saith also in O, I will

**OSHEA** *(o-she'-ah)* See HOSHEA, OSEE. *Same as Joshua, son of Nun.*
Num 13:8 of Ephraim, O the son of Nun
Num 13:16 Moses called O the son of Nun

**OTHNI** *(oth'-ni) A son of Shemiah.*
1Chr 26:7 O, and Rephael, and Obed, Elzabad,

**OTHNIEL** *(oth'-ne-el)*
*1. A brother of Caleb.*
Josh 15:17 O the son of Kenaz, the brother
Judg 1:13 O the son of Kenaz, Caleb's
Judg 3:9 even O the son of Kenaz, Caleb's
Judg 3:11 And O the son of Kenaz died
1Chr 4:13 O, and Seraiah
1Chr 4:13 and the sons of O
*2. Tribe or family of Othniel 1.*
1Chr 27:15 was Heldai the Netophathite, of O

**OUCHES**
Ex 28:11 make them to be set in o of gold
Ex 28:13 And thou shalt make o of gold
Ex 28:14 the wreathen chains to the o
Ex 28:25 thou shalt fasten in the two o
Ex 39:6 onyx stones inclosed in o of gold
Ex 39:13 they were inclosed in o of gold
Ex 39:16 And they made two o of gold
Ex 39:18 chains they fastened in the two o

**OUTCASTS**
Ps 147:2 together the o of Israel
Is 11:12 and shall assemble the o of Israel
Is 16:3 hide the o
Is 16:4 Let mine o dwell with thee, Moab
Is 27:13 the o in the land of Egypt, and
Is 56:8 gathereth the o of Israel saith
Jer 49:36 the o of Elam shall not come

**OUTGOINGS**
Josh 17:9 the o of it were at the sea
Josh 17:18 the o of it shall be thine
Josh 18:19 the o of the border were at the
Josh 19:14 the o thereof are in the valley
Josh 19:22 the o of their border were at
Josh 19:29 the o thereof are at the sea from
Josh 19:33 the o thereof were at Jordan
Ps 65:8 thou makest the o of the morning

**OUTMOST**
Ex 26:10 curtain that is o in the coupling
Num 34:3 o coast of the salt sea eastward
Deut 30:4 out unto the o parts of heaven
Is 17:6 four or five in the o fruitful

**OUTWARD**
Num 35:4 o a thousand cubits round about
1Sa 16:7 man looketh on the o appearance
1Chr 26:29 for the o business over Israel
Neh 11:16 had the oversight of the o
Est 6:4 the o court of the king's house
Eze 40:17 brought he me into the o court
Eze 40:20 the gate of the o court that
Eze 40:34 thereof were toward the o court
Eze 44:1 o sanctuary which looketh toward
Mt 23:27 which indeed appear beautiful o
Rom 2:28 which is o in the flesh
2Cor 4:16 but though our o man perish
2Cor 10:7 on things after the o appearance
1Pet 3:3 adorning let it not be that o

**OVEN**
Lev 2:4 of a meat offering baken in the o
Lev 7:9 offering that is baken in the o
Lev 11:35 whether it be o, or ranges for
Lev 26:26 shall bake your bread in one o
Ps 21:9 o in the time of thine anger
Lam 5:10 Our skin was black like an o
Hos 7:4 as an o heated by the baker, who
Hos 7:6 made ready their heart like an o
Hos 7:7 They are all hot as an o, and have
Mal 4:1 cometh, that shall burn as an o
Mt 6:30 and to morrow is cast into the o
Lk 12:28 and to morrow is cast into the o

**OVERCOME**
Gen 49:19 Gad, a troop shall o him
Gen 49:19 but he shall o at the last
Ex 32:18 of them that cry for being o
Num 13:30 for we are well able to o it
Num 22:11 I shall be able to o them
2Kin 16:5 Ahaz, but could not o him
Song 6:5 eyes from me, for they have o me
Is 28:1 of them that are o with wine
Jer 23:9 and like a man whom wine hath o
Lk 11:22 o him, he taketh from him all his
Jn 16:33 I have o the world
Rom 3:4 mightest o when thou art judged
Rom 12:21 Be not o of evil, but o
2Pet 2:19 for of whom a man is o, of the
2Pet 2:20 are again entangled therein, and o
1Jn 2:13 because ye have o the wicked one
1Jn 2:14 you, and ye have o the wicked one
1Jn 4:4 little children, and have o them
Rev 11:7 war against them, and shall o them
Rev 13:7 war with the saints, and to o them
Rev 17:14 Lamb, and the Lamb shall o them

**OVERCOMETH**
1Jn 5:4 is born of God o the world
1Jn 5:4 is the victory that o the world
1Jn 5:5 Who is he that o the world
Rev 2:7 To him that o will I give to eat
Rev 2:11 He that o shall not be hurt of
Rev 2:17 To him that o will I give to eat
Rev 2:26 And he that o, and keepeth my works
Rev 3:5 He that o, the same shall be
Rev 3:12 Him that o will I make a pillar
Rev 3:21 To him that o will I grant to sit
Rev 21:7 He that o shall inherit all

**OVERFLOW**
Deut 11:4 the water of the Red sea to o
Ps 69:2 waters, where the floods o me
Ps 69:15 Let not the waterflood o me
Is 8:8 he shall o and go over, he shall
Is 10:22 shall o with righteousness
Is 28:17 waters shall o the hiding place
Is 43:2 the rivers, they shall not o thee
Jer 47:2 shall o the land, and all that is
Dan 11:10 and one shall certainly come, and o
Dan 11:26 destroy him, and his army shall o
Dan 11:40 into the countries, and shall o
Joel 2:24 and the fats shall o with wine
Joel 3:13 for the press is full, the fats o

**OVERFLOWING**
Job 28:11 He bindeth the floods from o
Job 38:25 a watercourse for the o of waters
Is 28:2 as a flood of mighty waters o
Is 28:15 when the o scourge shall pass
Is 28:18 when the o scourge shall pass
Is 30:28 as an o stream, shall reach to
Jer 47:2 the north, and shall be an o flood
Eze 13:11 there shall be an o shower
Eze 13:13 there shall be an o shower in
Eze 38:22 o rain, and great hailstones, fire
Hab 3:10 the o of the water passed by

### OVERLAID
Ex 26:32 of shittim wood *o* with gold
Ex 36:34 he *o* the boards with gold, and
Ex 36:34 the bars, and *o* the bars with gold
Ex 36:36 shittim wood, and *o* them with gold
Ex 36:38 he *o* their chapiters and their
Ex 37:2 he *o* it with pure gold within and
Ex 37:4 shittim wood, and *o* them with gold
Ex 37:11 he *o* it with pure gold, and made
Ex 37:15 *o* them with gold, to bear the
Ex 37:26 he *o* it with pure gold, both the
Ex 37:28 shittim wood, and *o* them with gold
Ex 38:2 and he *o* it with brass
Ex 38:6 wood, and *o* them with brass
Ex 38:28 *o* their chapiters, and filleted
1Kin 3:19 because she *o* it
1Kin 6:20 and he *o* it with pure gold
1Kin 6:21 So Solomon *o* the house within
1Kin 6:21 and he *o* it with gold
1Kin 6:22 And the whole house he *o* with gold
1Kin 6:22 was by the oracle he *o* with gold
1Kin 6:28 he *o* the cherubims with gold
1Kin 6:30 floor of the house he *o* with gold
1Kin 6:32 *o* them with gold, and spread gold
1Kin 10:18 ivory, and *o* it with the best gold
2Kin 18:16 Hezekiah king of Judah had *o*
2Chr 3:4 he *o* it within with pure gold
2Chr 3:5 which he *o* with fine gold, and set
2Chr 3:7 He *o* also the house, the beams,
2Chr 3:8 he *o* it with fine gold, amounting
2Chr 3:9 he *o* the upper chambers with gold
2Chr 3:10 image work, and *o* them with gold
2Chr 4:9 *o* the doors of them with brass
2Chr 9:17 of ivory, and *o* it with pure gold
Song 5:14 as bright ivory *o* with sapphires
Heb 9:4 covenant *o* round about with gold

### OVERLAY
Ex 25:11 thou shalt *o* it with pure gold,
Ex 25:11 within and without shalt thou *o* it
Ex 25:13 shittim wood, and *o* them with gold
Ex 25:24 thou shalt *o* it with pure gold,
Ex 25:28 *o* them with gold, that the table
Ex 26:29 thou shalt *o* the boards with gold
Ex 26:29 thou shalt *o* the bars with gold
Ex 26:37 *o* them with gold, and their hooks
Ex 27:2 thou shalt *o* it with brass
Ex 27:6 wood, and *o* them with brass
Ex 30:3 thou shalt *o* it with pure gold,
Ex 30:5 shittim wood, and *o* them with gold
1Chr 29:4 to *o* the walls of the houses

### OVERSEER
Gen 39:4 he made him *o* over his house, and
Gen 39:5 he had made him *o* in his house
Neh 11:9 the son of Zichri was their *o*
Neh 11:14 their *o* was Zabdiel, the son of
Neh 11:22 The *o* also of the Levites at
Neh 12:42 sang loud, with Jezrahiah their *o*
Prov 6:7 Which having no guide, *o*, or

### OVERSEERS
2Chr 2:18 six hundred *o* to set the people a
2Chr 31:13 were *o* under the hand of Cononiah
2Chr 34:12 the *o* of them were Jahath and
2Chr 34:13 were *o* of all that wrought the
2Chr 34:17 it into the hand of the *o*
Acts 20:28 the Holy Ghost hath made you *o*

### OVERSIGHT
Gen 43:12 peradventure it was an *o*
Num 3:32 have the *o* of them that keep the
Num 4:16 the *o* of all the tabernacle, and
2Kin 12:11 that had the *o* of the house of
2Kin 22:5 that have the *o* of the house of
2Kin 22:9 that have the *o* of the house of
1Chr 9:23 their children had the *o* of the
2Chr 34:10 the *o* of the house of the LORD
Neh 11:16 had the *o* of the outward business
Neh 13:4 having the *o* of the chamber of
1Pet 5:2 among you, taking the *o* thereof

### OVERTAKE
Gen 44:4 and when thou dost *o* them, say
Ex 15:9 said, I will pursue, I will *o*
Deut 19:6 *o* him, because the way is long,
Deut 28:2 *o* thee, if thou shalt hearken
Deut 28:15 shall come upon thee, and *o* thee
Deut 28:45 *o* thee, till thou be destroyed
Josh 2:5 for ye shall *o* them
1Sa 30:8 shall I *o* them
1Sa 30:8 for thou shalt surely *o* them
2Sa 15:14 lest he *o* us suddenly, and bring
Is 59:9 us, neither doth justice *o* us
Jer 42:16 shall *o* you there in the land of
Hos 2:7 lovers, but she shall not *o* them
Hos 10:9 of iniquity did not *o* them
Amos 9:10 evil shall not *o* nor prevent us
Amos 9:13 the plowman shall *o* the reaper
1Th 5:4 that day should *o* you as a thief

### OVERTHREW
Gen 19:25 he *o* those cities, and all the
Gen 19:29 when he *o* the cities in the which
Ex 14:27 the LORD *o* the Egyptians in the
Deut 29:23 which the LORD *o* in his anger
Ps 136:15 But *o* Pharaoh and his host in the
Is 13:19 shall be as when God *o* Sodom
Jer 20:16 be as the cities which the LORD *o*
Jer 50:40 As God *o* Sodom and Gomorrah
Amos 4:11 some of you, as God *o* Sodom
Mt 21:12 *o* the tables of the moneychangers
Mk 11:15 *o* the tables of the moneychangers
Jn 2:15 changers' money, and *o* the tables

### OVERTHROW
Gen 19:21 also, that I will not *o* this city
Gen 19:29 Lot out of the midst of the *o*
Ex 23:24 but thou shalt utterly *o* them
Deut 12:3 ye shall *o* their altars, and break
Deut 29:23 therein, like the *o* of Sodom
2Sa 10:3 and to spy it out, and to *o* it
2Sa 11:25 strong against the city, and *o* it
1Chr 19:3 unto thee for to search, and to *o*
Ps 106:26 to *o* them in the wilderness
Ps 106:27 To *o* their seed also among the
Ps 140:4 who have purposed to *o* my goings
Ps 140:11 hunt the violent man to *o* him
Prov 18:5 to *o* the righteous in judgment
Jer 49:18 As in the *o* of Sodom and Gomorrah
Hag 2:22 I will *o* the throne of kingdoms,
Hag 2:22 I will *o* the chariots, and those
Acts 5:39 if it be of God, ye cannot *o* it
2Ti 2:18 and *o* the faith of some
2Pet 2:6 ashes condemned them with an *o*

### OVERTHROWETH
Job 12:19 away spoiled, and *o* the mighty
Prov 13:6 but wickedness *o* the sinner
Prov 21:12 but God *o* the wicked for their
Prov 22:12 and he *o* the words of the
Prov 29:4 but he that receiveth gifts *o* it

### OVERTHROWN
Ex 15:7 of thine excellency thou hast *o*
Judg 9:40 fled before him, and many were *o*
2Sa 17:9 some of them be *o* at the first
2Chr 14:13 and the Ethiopians were *o*, that
Job 19:6 Know now that God hath *o* me
Ps 141:6 judges are *o* in stony places
Prov 11:11 but it is *o* by the mouth of the
Prov 12:7 The wicked are *o*, and are not
Prov 14:11 house of the wicked shall be *o*
Is 1:7 it is desolate, as *o* by strangers
Jer 18:23 but let them be *o* before thee
Lam 4:6 that was *o* as in a moment, and no
Dan 11:41 and many countries shall be *o*
Amos 4:11 I have *o* some of you, as God
Jonah 3:4 forty days, and Nineveh shall be *o*
1Cor 10:5 for they were *o* in the wilderness

### OVERTOOK
Gen 31:23 they *o* him in the mount Gilead
Gen 31:25 Then Laban *o* Jacob
Gen 44:6 he *o* them, and he spake unto them
Ex 14:9 *o* them encamping by the sea,
Judg 18:22 and *o* the children of Dan
Judg 20:42 but the battle *o* them
2Kin 25:5 *o* him in the plains of Jericho
Jer 39:5 *o* Zedekiah in the plains of
Jer 52:8 *o* Zedekiah in the plains of
Lam 1:3 all her persecutors *o* her between

### OVERWHELMED
Ps 55:5 come upon me, and horror hath *o* me
Ps 61:2 cry unto thee, when my heart is *o*
Ps 77:3 I complained, and my spirit was *o*
Ps 78:53 but the sea *o* their enemies
Ps 102:*t* of the afflicted, when he is *o*
Ps 124:4 Then the waters had *o* us, the
Ps 142:3 When my spirit was *o* within me
Ps 143:4 is my spirit *o* within me

### OWL
Lev 11:16 And the *o*, and the night hawk, and
Lev 11:17 And the little *o*, and the cormorant
Lev 11:17 and the cormorant, and the great *o*
Deut 14:15 And the *o*, and the night hawk
Deut 14:16 The little *o*, and the great
Deut 14:16 and the great *o*
Ps 102:6 I am like an *o* of the desert
Is 34:11 the *o* also and the raven shall
Is 34:14 the screech *o* also shall rest
Is 34:15 shall the great *o* make her nest

### OWLS
Job 30:29 to dragons, and a companion to *o*
Is 13:21 *o* shall dwell there, and satyrs
Is 34:13 of dragons, and a court for *o*
Is 43:20 honour me, the dragons and the *o*
Jer 50:39 the *o* shall dwell therein
Mic 1:8 dragons, and mourning as the *o*

### OWNER
Ex 21:28 but the *o* of the ox shall be quit
Ex 21:29 it hath been testified to his *o*
Ex 21:29 his *o* also shall be put to death
Ex 21:34 The *o* of the pit shall make it
Ex 21:34 and give money unto the *o* of them
Ex 21:36 his *o* hath not kept him in
Ex 22:11 the *o* of it shall accept thereof,
Ex 22:12 restitution unto the *o* thereof
Ex 22:14 the *o* thereof being not with it,
Ex 22:15 But if the *o* thereof be with it,
1Kin 16:24 of Shemer, *o* of the hill, Samaria
Is 1:3 The ox knoweth his *o*, and the ass
Acts 27:11 the *o* of the ship, more than

### OWNERS
Job 31:39 or have caused the *o* thereof to
Prov 1:19 away the life of the *o* thereof
Eccl 5:11 good is there to the *o* thereof
Eccl 5:13 riches kept for the *o* thereof to
Lk 19:33 the *o* thereof said unto them, Why

### OX
Ex 20:17 nor his maidservant, nor his *o*
Ex 21:28 If an *o* gore a man or a woman,
Ex 21:28 then the *o* shall be surely stoned
Ex 21:28 the owner of the *o* shall be quit
Ex 21:29 But if the *o* were wont to push
Ex 21:29 the *o* shall be stoned, and his
Ex 21:32 If the *o* shall push a manservant
Ex 21:32 silver, and the *o* shall be stoned
Ex 21:33 an *o* or an ass fall therein
Ex 21:35 if one man's *o* hurt another's,
Ex 21:35 then they shall sell the live *o*
Ex 21:35 the dead *o* also they shall divide
Ex 21:36 Or if it be known that the *o* hath
Ex 21:36 he shall surely pay *o* for *o*
Ex 22:1 If a man shall steal an *o*
Ex 22:1 shall restore five oxen for an *o*
Ex 22:4 his hand alive, whether it be *o*
Ex 22:9 of trespass, whether it be for *o*
Ex 22:10 his neighbour an ass, or an *o*
Ex 23:4 enemy's *o* or his ass going astray
Ex 23:12 that thine *o* and thine ass may
Ex 34:19 whether *o* or sheep, that is male
Lev 7:23 shall eat no manner of fat, of *o*
Lev 17:3 of Israel, that killeth an *o*
Lev 27:26 whether it be *o*, or sheep
Num 7:3 the princes, and for each one an *o*
Num 22:4 as the *o* licketh up the grass of
Deut 5:14 nor thy maidservant, nor thine *o*
Deut 5:21 or his maidservant, his *o*
Deut 14:4 the *o*, the sheep, and the goat,
Deut 14:5 and the pygarg, and the wild *o*
Deut 18:3 whether it be *o* or sheep
Deut 22:1 *o* or his sheep go astray, and hide
Deut 22:4 ass or his *o* fall down by the way
Deut 22:10 Thou shalt not plow with an *o*
Deut 25:4 Thou shalt not muzzle the *o* when
Deut 28:31 Thine *o* shall be slain before
Josh 6:21 man and woman, young and old, and *o*
Judg 3:31 six hundred men with an *o* goad
Judg 6:4 for Israel, neither sheep, nor *o*
1Sa 12:3 whose *o* have I taken
1Sa 14:34 Bring me hither every man his *o*
1Sa 14:34 man his *o* with him that night
1Sa 15:3 and woman, infant and suckling, *o*
Neh 5:18 prepared for me daily was one *o*
Job 6:5 or loweth the *o* over his fodder
Job 24:3 take the widow's *o* for a pledge
Job 40:15 he eateth grass as an *o*
Ps 69:31 an *o* or bullock that hath horns
Ps 106:20 of an *o* that eateth grass
Prov 7:22 as an *o* goeth to the slaughter,
Prov 14:4 is by the strength of the *o*

Prov 15:17 where love is, than a stalled o
Is 1:3 The o knoweth his owner, and the
Is 11:7 lion shall eat straw like the o
Is 32:20 forth thither the feet of the o
Is 66:3 He that killeth an o is as if he
Jer 11:19 or an o that is brought to the
Eze 1:10 the face of an o on the left side
Lk 13:15 his o or his ass from the stall
Lk 14:5 an ass or an o fallen into a pit
1Cor 9:9 the o that treadeth out the corn
1Ti 5:18 Thou shalt not muzzle the o that

**OXEN**
Gen 12:16 and he had sheep, and o, and he
Gen 20:14 And Abimelech took sheep, and o
Gen 21:27 And Abraham took sheep and o
Gen 32:5 And I have o, and asses, flocks, and
Gen 34:28 They took their sheep, and their o
Ex 9:3 upon the camels, upon the o
Ex 20:24 offerings, thy sheep, and thine o
Ex 22:1 he shall restore five o for an ox
Ex 22:30 shalt thou do with thine o
Ex 24:5 offerings of o unto the LORD
Num 7:3 six covered wagons, and twelve o
Num 7:6 And Moses took the wagons and the o
Num 7:7 four o he gave unto the sons of
Num 7:8 eight o he gave unto the sons of
Num 7:17 of peace offerings, two o
Num 7:23 of peace offerings, two o
Num 7:29 of peace offerings, two o
Num 7:35 of peace offerings, two o
Num 7:41 of peace offerings, two o
Num 7:47 of peace offerings, two o
Num 7:53 of peace offerings, two o
Num 7:59 of peace offerings, two o
Num 7:65 of peace offerings, two o
Num 7:71 of peace offerings, two o
Num 7:77 of peace offerings, two o
Num 7:83 of peace offerings, two o
Num 7:87 All the o for the burnt offering
Num 7:88 all the o for the sacrifice of
Num 22:40 And Balak offered o and sheep, and
Num 23:1 and prepare me here seven o
Deut 14:26 thy soul lusteth after, for o
Josh 7:24 sons, and his daughters, and his o
1Sa 11:7 And he took a yoke of o, and hewed
1Sa 11:7 so shall it be done unto his o
1Sa 14:14 which a yoke of o might plow
1Sa 14:32 the spoil, and took sheep, and o
1Sa 15:9 best of the sheep, and of the o
1Sa 15:14 the lowing of the o which I hear
1Sa 15:15 the best of the sheep and of the o
1Sa 15:21 took of the spoil, sheep and o
1Sa 22:19 children and sucklings, and o
1Sa 27:9 and took away the sheep, and the o
2Sa 6:6 for the o shook it
2Sa 6:13 gone six paces, he sacrificed o
2Sa 24:22 here be o for burnt sacrifice, and
2Sa 24:22 instruments of the o for wood
2Sa 24:24 the o for fifty shekels of silver
1Kin 1:9 And Adonijah slew sheep and o
1Kin 1:19 And he hath slain o and fat cattle
1Kin 1:25 down this day, and hath slain o
1Kin 4:23 Ten fat o, and twenty o out of
1Kin 7:25 It stood upon twelve o, three
1Kin 7:29 between the ledges were lions, o
1Kin 7:29 o were certain additions made of
1Kin 7:44 sea, and twelve o under the sea
1Kin 8:5 the ark, sacrificing sheep and o
1Kin 8:63 LORD, two and twenty thousand o
1Kin 19:19 with twelve yoke of o before him
1Kin 19:20 And he left the o, and ran after
1Kin 19:21 from him, and took a yoke of o
1Kin 19:21 with the instruments of the o
2Kin 5:26 and vineyards, and sheep, and o
2Kin 16:17 the brasen o that were under it
1Chr 12:40 on camels, and on mules, and on o
1Chr 12:40 of raisins, and wine, and oil, and o
1Chr 13:9 for the o stumbled
1Chr 21:23 I give thee the o also for burnt
2Chr 4:3 under it was the similitude of o
2Chr 4:3 Two rows of o were cast, when it
2Chr 4:4 It stood upon twelve o, three
2Chr 4:15 One sea, and twelve o under it
2Chr 5:6 the ark, sacrificed sheep and o
2Chr 7:5 of twenty and two thousand o
2Chr 15:11 they had brought, seven hundred o
2Chr 18:2 o for him in abundance, and for
2Chr 29:33 things were six hundred o
2Chr 31:6 also brought in the tithe of o
2Chr 35:8 small cattle, and three hundred o
2Chr 35:9 small cattle, and five hundred o
2Chr 35:12 And so did they with the o
Job 1:3 camels, and five hundred yoke of o
Job 1:14 The o were plowing, and the asses
Job 42:12 camels, and a thousand yoke of o
Ps 8:7 All sheep and o, yea, and the
Ps 144:14 That our o may be strong to
Prov 14:4 Where no o are, the crib is clean
Is 7:25 be for the sending forth of o
Is 22:13 behold joy and gladness, slaying o
Is 30:24 The o likewise and the young asses
Jer 51:23 the husbandman and his yoke of o
Dan 4:25 shall make thee to eat grass as o
Dan 4:32 shall make thee to eat grass as o
Dan 4:33 from men, and did eat grass as o
Dan 5:21 they fed him with grass like o
Amos 6:12 will one plow there with o
Mt 22:4 my o and my fatlings are killed,
Lk 14:19 I have bought five yoke of o
Jn 2:14 in the temple those that sold o
Jn 2:15 temple, and the sheep, and the o
Acts 14:13 was before their city, brought o
1Cor 9:9 Doth God take care for o

**OZEM** *(o'-zem)*
*1. Son of Jesse.*
1Chr 2:15 O the sixth, David the seventh
*2. Son of Jerahmeel.*
1Chr 2:25 and Bunah, and Oren, and O, and

**OZIAS** *(o-zi'-as)* See UZZIAH. *Son of Joram; ancestor of Jesus.*
Mt 1:8 and Joram begat O
Mt 1:9 And O begat Joatham

**OZNI** *(oz'-ni)* See OZNITES. *A son of Gad.*
Num 26:16 Of O, the family of the Oznites

**OZNITES** *(oz'-nites) Descendants of Ozni.*
Num 26:16 Of Ozni, the family of the O

# P

**PAARAI** *(pa'-ar-ahee)* See NOARAI. *A "mighty man" of David.*
2Sa 23:35 the Carmelite, P the Arbite,

**PACATIANA** *(pa-ca-she-a'-nah) A region of Phrygia in Asia Minor.*
1Ti s is the chiefest city of Phrygia P

**PADAN** *(pa'-dan)* See PADAN-ARAM. *Same as Padan-aram.*
Gen 48:7 And as for me, when I came from P

**PADAN-ARAM** *(pa'-dan-a'-ram) The plains of Mesopotamia.*
Gen 25:20 of Bethuel the Syrian of P
Gen 28:2 Arise, go to P, to the house of
Gen 28:5 and he went to P unto Laban
Gen 28:6 Jacob, and sent him away to P
Gen 28:7 and his mother, and was gone to P
Gen 31:18 getting, which he had gotten in P
Gen 33:18 of Canaan, when he came from P
Gen 35:9 again, when he came out of P
Gen 35:26 which were born to him in P
Gen 46:15 which she bare unto Jacob in P

**PADON** *(pa'-don) A family of exiles.*
Ezr 2:44 of Siaha, the children of P
Neh 7:47 of Sia, the children of P

**PAGIEL** *(pa'-ghe-el) An Asherite who counted the people.*
Num 1:13 P the son of Ocran
Num 2:27 Asher shall be P the son of Ocran
Num 7:72 eleventh day P the son of Ocran
Num 7:77 offering of P the son of Ocran
Num 10:26 of Asher was P the son of Ocran

**PAHATH-MOAB** *(pa'-hath-mo'-ab)*
*1. A family of exiles.*
Ezr 2:6 The children of P, of the
Ezr 10:30 And of the sons of P
Neh 3:11 of Harim, and Hashub the son of P
Neh 7:11 The children of P, of the
*2. Another family of exiles.*
Ezr 8:4 Of the sons of P
*3. A family who renewed the covenant.*
Neh 10:14 Parosh, P, Elam, Zatthu, Bani,

**PAI** *(pa'-i)* See PAU. *A city in Edom.*
1Chr 1:50 and the name of his city was P

**PAIN**
Job 14:22 his flesh upon him shall have p
Job 15:20 travaileth with p all his days
Job 33:19 also with p upon his bed, and the
Job 33:19 of his bones with strong p
Ps 25:18 Look upon mine affliction and my p
Ps 48:6 took hold upon them there, and p
Is 13:8 they shall be in p as a woman
Is 21:3 are my loins filled with p
Is 26:17 the time of her delivery, is in p
Is 26:18 with child, we have been in p
Is 66:7 before her p came, she was
Jer 6:24 hath taken hold of us, and p
Jer 12:13 they have put themselves to p
Jer 15:18 Why is my p perpetual, and my
Jer 22:23 the p as of a woman in travail
Jer 30:23 it shall fall with p upon the
Jer 51:8 take balm for her p, if so be she
Eze 30:4 great p shall be in Ethiopia,
Eze 30:9 great p shall come upon them, as
Eze 30:16 Sin shall have great p, and No
Mic 4:10 Be in p, and labour to bring forth
Nah 2:10 much p is in all loins, and the
Rom 8:22 travaileth in p together until
Rev 16:10 they gnawed their tongues for p
Rev 21:4 neither shall there be any more p

**PAINED**
Ps 55:4 My heart is sore p within me
Is 23:5 be sorely p at the report of Tyre
Jer 4:19 I am p at my very heart
Joel 2:6 face the people shall be much p
Rev 12:2 in birth, and p to be delivered

**PAINS**
1Sa 4:19 for her p came upon her
Ps 116:3 the p of hell gat hold upon me
Acts 2:24 up, having loosed the p of death
Rev 16:11 God of heaven because of their p

**PAIR**
Amos 2:6 and the poor for a p of shoes
Amos 8:6 and the needy for a p of shoes
Lk 2:24 A p of turtledoves, or two young
Rev 6:5 had a p of balances in his hand

**PALACE**
1Kin 16:18 into the p of the king's house
1Kin 21:1 hard by the p of Ahab king of
2Kin 15:25 in the p of the king's house,
2Kin 20:18 in the p of the king of Babylon
1Chr 29:1 for the p is not for man, but for
1Chr 29:19 these things, and to build the p
2Chr 9:11 of the LORD, and to the king's p
Ezr 4:14 maintenance from the king's p
Ezr 6:2 in the p that is in the province
Neh 1:1 year, as I was in Shushan the p
Neh 2:8 p which appertained to the house
Neh 7:2 and Hananiah the ruler of the p
Est 1:2 which was in Shushan the p
Est 1:5 were present in Shushan the p
Est 1:5 of the garden of the king's p
Est 2:3 young virgins unto Shushan the p
Est 2:5 Now in Shushan the p there was a
Est 2:8 together unto Shushan the p
Est 3:15 decree was given in Shushan the p
Est 7:7 his wrath went into the p garden
Est 7:8 p garden into the place of the
Est 8:14 decree was given at Shushan the p
Est 9:6 And in Shushan the p the Jews slew

Est 9:11 the *p* was brought before the king
Est 9:12 five hundred men in Shushan the *p*
Ps 45:15 shall enter into the king's *p*
Ps 144:12 after the similitude of a *p*
Song 8:9 will build upon her a *p* of silver
Is 25:2 a *p* of strangers to be no city
Is 39:7 in the *p* of the king of Babylon
Jer 30:18 the *p* shall remain after the
Dan 1:4 in them to stand in the king's *p*
Dan 4:4 house, and flourishing in my *p*
Dan 4:29 the *p* of the kingdom of Babylon
Dan 5:5 of the wall of the king's *p*
Dan 6:18 Then the king went to his *p*
Dan 8:2 that I was at Shushan in the *p*
Dan 11:45 of his *p* between the seas in the
Amos 4:3 and ye shall cast them into the *p*
Nah 2:6 and the *p* shall be dissolved
Mt 26:3 unto the *p* of the high priest,
Mt 26:58 afar off unto the high priest's *p*
Mt 26:69 Now Peter sat without in the *p*
Mk 14:54 even into the *p* of the high
Mk 14:66 And as Peter was beneath in the *p*
Lk 11:21 a strong man armed keepeth his *p*
Jn 18:15 into the *p* of the high priest
Phil 1:13 Christ are manifest in all the *p*

**PALACES**
2Chr 36:19 burnt all the *p* thereof with fire
Ps 45:8 and cassia, out of the ivory *p*
Ps 48:3 is known in her *p* for a refuge
Ps 48:13 well her bulwarks, consider her *p*
Ps 78:69 built his sanctuary like high *p*
Ps 122:7 walls, and prosperity within thy *p*
Prov 30:28 with her hands, and is in kings' *p*
Is 13:22 and dragons in their pleasant *p*
Is 23:13 they raised up the *p* thereof
Is 32:14 Because the *p* shall be forsaken
Is 34:13 And thorns shall come up in her *p*
Jer 6:5 by night, and let us destroy her *p*
Jer 9:21 windows, and is entered into our *p*
Jer 17:27 shall devour the *p* of Jerusalem
Jer 49:27 shall consume the *p* of Ben-hadad
Lam 2:5 he hath swallowed up all her *p*
Lam 2:7 of the enemy the walls of her *p*
Eze 19:7 And he knew their desolate *p*
Eze 25:4 and they shall set their *p* in thee
Hos 8:14 and it shall devour the *p* thereof
Amos 1:4 shall devour the *p* of Ben-hadad
Amos 1:7 which shall devour the *p* thereof
Amos 1:10 which shall devour the *p* thereof
Amos 1:12 shall devour the *p* of Bozrah
Amos 1:14 and it shall devour the *p* thereof
Amos 2:2 it shall devour the *p* of Kirioth
Amos 2:5 shall devour the *p* of Jerusalem
Amos 3:9 Publish in the *p* at Ashdod
Amos 3:9 in the *p* in the land of Egypt, and
Amos 3:10 up violence and robbery in their *p*
Amos 3:11 thee, and thy *p* shall be spoiled
Amos 6:8 of Jacob, and hate his *p*
Mic 5:5 and when he shall tread in our *p*

**PALAL** *(pa'-lal) A rebuilder of Jerusalem's wall.*
Neh 3:25 *P* the son of Uzai, over against

**PALESTINA** *(pal-es-ti'-nah)* See PALESTINE, PHILISTIA. *The west coast of Canaan.*
Ex 15:14 take hold on the inhabitants of *P*
Is 14:29 Rejoice not thou, whole *P*
Is 14:31 thou, whole *P*, art dissolved

**PALESTINE** *(pal'-es-tine)* See PALESTINA. *Same as Palestina.*
Joel 3:4 and Zidon, and all the coasts of *P*

**PALLU** *(pal'-lu)* See PALLUITES, PHALLU. *A son of Reuben.*
Ex 6:14 Hanoch, and *P*, Hezron, and Carmi
Num 26:5 of *P*, the family of the Palluites
Num 26:8 And the sons of *P*
1Chr 5:3 of Israel were, Hanoch, and *P*

**PALLUITES** *(pal'-lu-ites) Descendants of Pallu.*
Num 26:5 of Pallu, the family of the *P*

**PALM**
Ex 15:27 and threescore and ten *p* trees
Lev 14:15 pour it into the *p* of his own
Lev 14:26 into the *p* of his own left hand
Lev 23:40 goodly trees, branches of *p* trees
Num 33:9 and threescore and ten *p* trees
Deut 34:3 of Jericho, the city of *p* trees
Judg 1:16 of *p* trees with the children of
Judg 3:13 and possessed the city of *p* trees
Judg 4:5 she dwelt under the *p* tree of
1Kin 6:29 *p* trees and open flowers, within
1Kin 6:32 *p* trees and open flowers, and
1Kin 6:32 cherubims, and upon the *p* trees
1Kin 6:35 and *p* trees and open flowers
1Kin 7:36 *p* trees, according to the
2Chr 3:5 fine gold, and set thereon *p* trees
2Chr 28:15 to Jericho, the city of *p* trees
Neh 8:15 *p* branches, and branches of thick
Ps 92:12 shall flourish like the *p* tree
Song 7:7 thy stature is like to a *p* tree
Song 7:8 said, I will go up to the *p* tree
Jer 10:5 They are upright as the *p* tree
Eze 40:16 and upon each post were *p* trees
Eze 40:22 and their arches, and their *p* trees
Eze 40:26 and it had *p* trees, one on this
Eze 40:31 *p* trees were upon the posts
Eze 40:34 *p* trees were upon the posts
Eze 40:37 *p* trees were upon the posts
Eze 41:19 toward the *p* tree on the one side
Eze 41:19 the *p* tree on the other side
Eze 41:20 *p* trees made, and on the wall of
Eze 41:25 *p* trees, like as were made upon
Eze 41:26 *p* trees on the one side and on the
Joel 1:12 the *p* tree also, and the apple
Jn 12:13 Took branches of *p* trees, and went
Jn 18:22 Jesus with the *p* of his hand

**PALMS**
1Sa 5:4 both the *p* of his hands were cut
2Kin 9:35 the feet, and the *p* of her hands
Is 49:16 thee upon the *p* of my hands
Dan 10:10 knees and upon the *p* of my hands
Mt 26:67 him with the *p* of their hands
Mk 14:65 him with the *p* of their hands
Rev 7:9 white robes, and *p* in their hands

**PALSY**
Mt 4:24 lunatick, and those that had the *p*
Mt 8:6 lieth at home sick of the *p*
Mt 9:2 to him a man sick of the *p*
Mt 9:2 faith said unto the sick of the *p*
Mt 9:6 saith he to the sick of the *p*
Mk 2:3 him, bringing one sick of the *p*
Mk 2:4 bed wherein the sick of the *p* lay
Mk 2:5 he said unto the sick of the *p*
Mk 2:9 to say to the sick of the *p*
Mk 2:10 (he saith to the sick of the *p*
Lk 5:18 a man which was taken with a *p*
Lk 5:24 (he said unto the sick of the *p*
Acts 9:33 eight years, and was sick of the *p*

**PALTI** *(pal'-ti) A spy sent to the Promised Land.*
Num 13:9 of Benjamin, *P* the son of Raphu

**PALTIEL** *(pal'-te-el)* See PHALTIEL. *A chief of Issachar.*
Num 34:26 of Issachar, *P* the son of Azzan

**PALTITE** *(pal'-tite)* See PELONITE. *A resident of Beth-palet.*
2Sa 23:26 Helez the *P*, Ira the son of

**PAMPHYLIA** *(pam-fil'-e-ah) A province of Asia Minor.*
Acts 2:10 Phrygia, and *P*, in Egypt, and in
Acts 13:13 Paphos, they came to Perga in *P*
Acts 14:24 Pisidia, they came to *P*
Acts 15:38 who departed from them from *P*
Acts 27:5 over the sea of Cilicia and *P*

**PAN**
Lev 2:5 be a meat offering baken in a *p*
Lev 2:7 offering baken in the frying *p*
Lev 6:21 In a *p* it shall be made with oil
Lev 7:9 in the fryingpan, and in the *p*
1Sa 2:14 And he struck it into the *p*
2Sa 13:9 And she took a *p*, and poured them
1Chr 23:29 for that which is baked in the *p*
Eze 4:3 take thou unto thee an iron *p*

**PANGS**
Is 13:8 *p* and sorrows shall take hold of
Is 21:3 *p* have taken hold upon me, as the
Is 21:3 upon me, as the *p* of a woman that
Is 26:17 in pain, and crieth out in her *p*
Jer 22:23 thou be when *p* come upon thee
Jer 48:41 as the heart of a woman in her *p*
Jer 49:22 as the heart of a woman in her *p*
Jer 50:43 *p* as of a woman in travail
Mic 4:9 for *p* have taken thee as a woman

**PANNAG** *(pan'-nag) A place on the Damascus-Baalbeck road.*
Eze 27:17 thy market wheat of Minnith, and *P*

**PANS**
Ex 27:3 thou shalt make his *p* to receive
Num 11:8 it in a mortar, and baked it in *p*
1Chr 9:31 things that were made in the *p*
2Chr 35:13 in pots, and in caldrons, and in *p*

**PAPHOS** *(pa'-fos) Capital of Cyprus.*
Acts 13:6 had gone through the isle unto *P*
Acts 13:13 Paul and his company loosed from *P*

**PAPS**
Eze 23:21 Egyptians for the *p* of thy youth
Lk 11:27 the *p* which thou hast sucked
Lk 23:29 the *p* which never gave suck
Rev 1:13 girt about the *p* with a golden

**PARABLE**
Num 23:7 And he took up his *p*, and said,
Num 23:18 And he took up his *p*, and said,
Num 24:3 And he took up his *p*, and said,
Num 24:15 And he took up his *p*, and said,
Num 24:20 on Amalek, he took up his *p*
Num 24:21 on the Kenites, and took up his *p*
Num 24:23 And he took up his *p*, and said,
Job 27:1 Moreover Job continued his *p*
Job 29:1 Moreover Job continued his *p*
Ps 49:4 I will incline mine ear to a *p*
Ps 78:2 I will open my mouth in a *p*
Prov 26:7 so is a *p* in the mouth of fools
Prov 26:9 so is a *p* in the mouth of fools
Eze 17:2 speak a *p* unto the house of
Eze 24:3 utter a *p* unto the rebellious
Mic 2:4 shall one take up a *p* against you
Hab 2:6 all these take up a *p* against him
Mt 13:18 ye therefore the *p* of the sower
Mt 13:24 Another *p* put he forth unto them,
Mt 13:31 Another *p* put he forth unto them,
Mt 13:33 Another *p* spake he unto them
Mt 13:34 without a *p* spake he not unto
Mt 13:36 Declare unto us the *p* of the
Mt 15:15 unto him, Declare unto us this *p*
Mt 21:33 Hear another *p*
Mt 24:32 Now learn a *p* of the fig tree
Mk 4:10 the twelve asked of him the *p*
Mk 4:13 unto them, Know ye not this *p*
Mk 4:34 But without a *p* spake he not unto
Mk 7:17 asked him concerning the *p*
Mk 12:12 he had spoken the *p* against them
Mk 13:28 Now learn a *p* of the fig tree
Lk 5:36 And he spake also a *p* unto them
Lk 6:39 And he spake a *p* unto them
Lk 8:4 of every city, he spake by a *p*
Lk 8:9 him, saying, What might this *p* be
Lk 8:11 Now the *p* is this
Lk 12:16 And he spake a *p* unto them
Lk 12:41 speakest thou this *p* unto us
Lk 13:6 He spake also this *p*
Lk 14:7 he put forth a *p* to those which
Lk 15:3 And he spake this *p* unto them
Lk 18:1 he spake a *p* unto them to this
Lk 18:9 he spake this *p* unto certain
Lk 19:11 things, he added and spake a *p*
Lk 20:9 he to speak to the people this *p*
Lk 20:19 he had spoken this *p* against them
Lk 21:29 And he spake to them a *p*
Jn 10:6 This *p* spake Jesus unto them

**PARABLES**
Eze 20:49 say of me, Doth he not speak *p*
Mt 13:3 spake many things unto them in *p*
Mt 13:10 Why speakest thou unto them in *p*
Mt 13:13 Therefore speak I to them in *p*
Mt 13:34 Jesus unto the multitude in *p*
Mt 13:35 saying, I will open my mouth in *p*
Mt 13:53 when Jesus had finished these *p*
Mt 21:45 and Pharisees had heard his *p*
Mt 22:1 and spake unto them again by *p*
Mk 3:23 unto him, and said unto them in *p*
Mk 4:2 he taught them many things by *p*
Mk 4:11 all these things are done in *p*
Mk 4:13 and how then will ye know all *p*
Mk 4:33 with many such *p* spake he the
Mk 12:1 he began to speak unto them by *p*
Lk 8:10 but to others in *p*

**PARAH** *(pa'-rah) A city in Benjamin.*
Josh 18:23 And Avim, and *P*, and Ophrah,

**PARAN** *(pa'-ran) A wilderness south of Canaan.*
Gen 21:21 he dwelt in the wilderness of *P*
Num 10:12 rested in the wilderness of *P*
Num 12:16 and pitched in the wilderness of *P*
Num 13:3 them from the wilderness of *P*
Num 13:26 Israel, unto the wilderness of *P*
Deut 1:1 against the Red sea, between *P*
Deut 33:2 he shined forth from mount *P*
1Sa 25:1 went down to the wilderness of *P*
1Kin 11:18 arose out of Midian, and came to *P*
1Kin 11:18 they took men with them out of *P*
Hab 3:3 and the Holy One from mount *P*

**PARBAR** *(par'-bar) A place near the Temple in Jerusalem.*
1Chr 26:18 At *P* westward, four at the
1Chr 26:18 four at the causeway, and two at *P*

**PARCEL**
Gen 33:19 And he bought a *p* of a field
Josh 24:32 in a *p* of ground which Jacob
Ruth 4:3 of Moab, selleth a *p* of land
1Chr 11:13 where was a *p* of ground full of
1Chr 11:14 themselves in the midst of that *p*
Jn 4:5 near to the *p* of ground that

**PARCHED**
Lev 23:14 nor *p* corn, nor green ears, until
Josh 5:11 *p* corn in the selfsame day
Ruth 2:14 and he reached her *p* corn, and she
1Sa 17:17 brethren an ephah of this *p* corn
1Sa 25:18 and five measures of *p* corn
2Sa 17:28 *p* corn, and beans, and lentiles, and
2Sa 17:28 beans, and lentiles, and *p* pulse,
Is 35:7 the *p* ground shall become a pool,
Jer 17:6 but shall inhabit the *p* places in

**PARDON**
Ex 23:21 for he will not *p* your
Ex 34:9 *p* our iniquity and our sin, and
Num 14:19 *P*, I beseech thee, the iniquity
1Sa 15:25 *p* my sin, and turn again with me,
2Kin 5:18 this thing the LORD *p* thy servant
2Kin 5:18 the LORD *p* thy servant in this
2Kin 24:4 which the LORD would not *p*
2Chr 30:18 saying, The good LORD *p* every one
Neh 9:17 but thou art a God ready to *p*
Job 7:21 dost thou not *p* my transgression
Ps 25:11 sake, O LORD, *p* mine iniquity
Is 55:7 our God, for he will abundantly *p*
Jer 5:1 and I will *p* it
Jer 5:7 How shall I *p* thee for this
Jer 33:8 I will *p* all their iniquities,
Jer 50:20 for I will *p* them whom I reserve

**PARENTS**
Mt 10:21 shall rise up against their *p*
Mk 13:12 shall rise up against their *p*
Lk 2:27 when the *p* brought in the child
Lk 2:41 Now his *p* went to Jerusalem every
Lk 8:56 And her *p* were astonished
Lk 18:29 no man that hath left house, or *p*
Lk 21:16 And ye shall be betrayed both by *p*
Jn 9:2 who did sin, this man, or his *p*
Jn 9:3 hath this man sinned, nor his *p*
Jn 9:18 until they called the *p* of him
Jn 9:20 His *p* answered them and said, We
Jn 9:22 These words spake his *p*, because
Jn 9:23 Therefore said his *p*, He is of
Rom 1:30 of evil things, disobedient to *p*
2Cor 12:14 ought not to lay up for the *p*
2Cor 12:14 but the *p* for the children
Eph 6:1 Children, obey your *p* in the Lord
Col 3:20 obey your *p* in all things
1Ti 5:4 at home, and to requite their *p*
2Ti 3:2 blasphemers, disobedient to *p*
Heb 11:23 was hid three months of his *p*

**PARLOUR**
Judg 3:20 and he was sitting in a summer *p*
Judg 3:23 shut the doors of the *p* upon him
Judg 3:24 the doors of the *p* were locked
Judg 3:25 he opened not the doors of the *p*
1Sa 9:22 and brought them into the *p*

**PARMASHTA** *(par-mash'-tah) A son of Haman.*
Est 9:9 And *P*, and Arisai, and Aridai, and

**PARMENAS** *(par'-me-nas) A leader in the Jerusalem church.*
Acts 6:5 and Nicanor, and Timon, and *P*

**PARNACH** *(par'-nak) A Zebulunite who apportioned the Promised Land.*
Num 34:25 Zebulun, Elizaphan the son of *P*

**PAROSH** *(pa'-rosh)* See PHAROSH.
*1. A family of exiles.*
Ezr 2:3 The children of *P*, two thousand
Neh 7:8 The children of *P*, two thousand
*2. Married a foreigner in exile.*
Ezr 10:25 of the sons of *P*
*3. Father of Pedaiah.*
Neh 3:25 After him Pedaiah the son of *P*
*4. A family who renewed the covenant.*
Neh 10:14 *P*, Pahath-moab, Elam, Zatthu,

**PARSHANDATHA** *(par-shan'-da-thah) A son of Haman.*
Est 9:7 And *P*, and Dalphon, and Aspatha,

**PARTAKER**
Ps 50:18 hast been *p* with adulterers
1Cor 9:10 in hope should be *p* of his hope
1Cor 9:23 that I might be *p* thereof with
1Cor 10:30 For if I by grace be a *p*, why am
1Ti 5:22 neither be *p* of other men's sins
2Ti 1:8 but be thou *p* of the afflictions
2Ti 2:6 must be first *p* of the fruits
1Pet 5:1 also a *p* of the glory that shall
2Jn 11 God speed is *p* of his evil deeds

**PARTAKERS**
Mt 23:30 we would not have been *p* with
Rom 15:27 made *p* of their spiritual things
1Cor 9:12 If others be *p* of this power over
1Cor 9:13 at the altar are *p* with the altar
1Cor 10:17 for we are all *p* of that one
1Cor 10:18 of the sacrifices *p* of the altar
1Cor 10:21 ye cannot be *p* of the Lord's
2Cor 1:7 knowing, that as ye are *p* of the
Eph 3:6 *p* of his promise in Christ by the
Eph 5:7 Be not ye therefore *p* with them
Phil 1:7 gospel, ye all are *p* of my grace
Col 1:12 to be *p* of the inheritance of the
1Ti 6:2 and beloved, *p* of the benefit
Heb 2:14 as the children are *p* of flesh
Heb 3:1 *p* of the heavenly calling,
Heb 3:14 For we are made *p* of Christ
Heb 6:4 were made *p* of the Holy Ghost,
Heb 12:8 chastisement, whereof all are *p*
Heb 12:10 we might be *p* of his holiness
1Pet 4:13 inasmuch as ye are *p* of Christ's
2Pet 1:4 might be *p* of the divine nature
Rev 18:4 that ye be not *p* of her sins

**PARTED**
Gen 2:10 and from thence it was *p*, and
2Kin 2:11 of fire, and *p* them both asunder
2Kin 2:14 waters, they *p* hither and thither
Job 38:24 By what way is the light *p*
Joel 3:2 among the nations, and *p* my land
Mt 27:35 *p* his garments, casting lots
Mt 27:35 They *p* my garments among them, and
Mk 15:24 they *p* his garments, casting lots
Lk 23:34 they *p* his raiment, and cast lots
Lk 24:51 he was *p* from them, and carried up
Jn 19:24 They *p* my raiment among them, and
Acts 2:45 *p* them to all men, as every man

**PARTHIANS** *(par-the'-uns) Inhabitants of Parthia, now Iran.*
Acts 2:9 *P*, and Medes, and Elamites, and the

**PARUAH** *(par'-u-ah) Father of Jehoshaphat.*
1Kin 4:17 Jehoshaphat the son of *P*, in

**PARVAIM** *(par-va'-im) A place rich in gold.*
2Chr 3:6 and the gold was gold of *P*

**PASACH** *(pa'-sak) A son of Japhet.*
1Chr 7:33 *P*, and Bimhal, and Ashvath

**PAS-DAMMIM** *(pas-dam'-mim) A place in Judah.*
1Chr 11:13 He was with David at *P*, and there

**PASEAH** *(pa-se'-ah)* See PHASEAH.
*1. A son of Eshton.*
1Chr 4:12 And Eshton begat Beth-rapha, and *P*
*2. A family of exiles.*
Ezr 2:49 of Uzza, the children of *P*
*3. Father of Jehoiada.*
Neh 3:6 repaired Jehoiada the son of *P*

**PASHUR** *(pash'-ur)*
*1. Head of a priestly family.*
1Chr 9:12 the son of Jeroham, the son of *P*
Ezr 2:38 The children of *P*, a thousand two
Ezr 10:22 And of the sons of *P*
Neh 7:41 The children of *P*, a thousand two
Neh 11:12 son of Zechariah, the son of *P*
*2. A priest who renewed the covenant.*
Neh 10:3 *P*, Amariah, Malchijah,
*3. A son of Immer.*
Jer 20:1 Now *P* the son of Immer the priest
Jer 20:2 Then *P* smote Jeremiah the prophet
Jer 20:3 that *P* brought forth Jeremiah out
Jer 20:3 LORD hath not called thy name *P*
Jer 20:6 And thou, *P*, and all that dwell in
Jer 38:1 Mattan, and Gedaliah the son of *P*
*4. A son of Melchiah/Malchiah.*
Jer 21:1 unto him *P* the son of Melchiah
Jer 38:1 *P* the son of Malchiah, heard the

**PASSAGE**
Num 20:21 give Israel *p* through his border
Josh 22:11 at the *p* of the children of
1Sa 13:23 went out to the *p* of Michmash
Is 10:29 They are gone over the *p*

**PASSAGES**
Judg 12:5 took the *p* of Jordan before the
Judg 12:6 and slew him at the *p* of Jordan
1Sa 14:4 And between the *p*, by which
Jer 22:20 in Bashan, and cry from the *p*
Jer 51:32 that the *p* are stopped, and the

**PASSED**
Gen 12:6 Abram *p* through the land unto the
Gen 15:17 a burning lamp that *p* between
Gen 31:21 *p* over the river, and set his face
Gen 32:10 my staff I *p* over this Jordan
Gen 32:22 sons, and *p* over the ford Jabbok
Gen 32:31 as he *p* over Penuel the sun rose
Gen 33:3 he *p* over before them, and bowed
Gen 37:28 Then there *p* by Midianites
Ex 12:27 who *p* over the houses of the
Ex 34:6 the LORD *p* by before him, and
Num 14:7 which we *p* through to search it,
Num 20:17 left, until we have *p* thy borders
Num 33:8 *p* through the midst of the sea
Num 33:51 When ye are *p* over Jordan into
Deut 2:8 when we *p* by from our brethren
Deut 2:8 *p* by the way of the wilderness of
Deut 27:3 of this law, when thou art *p* over
Deut 29:16 through the nations which ye *p* by
Josh 2:23 *p* over, and came to Joshua the son
Josh 3:1 lodged there before they *p* over
Josh 3:4 for ye have not *p* this way
Josh 3:16 the people *p* over right against
Josh 3:17 Israelites *p* over on dry ground
Josh 3:17 people were *p* clean over Jordan
Josh 4:1 people were clean *p* over Jordan
Josh 4:7 when it *p* over Jordan, the waters
Josh 4:10 and the people hasted and *p* over
Josh 4:11 all the people were clean *p* over
Josh 4:11 that the ark of the LORD *p* over
Josh 4:12 *p* over armed before the children
Josh 4:13 war *p* over before the LORD unto
Josh 4:23 before you, until ye were *p* over
Josh 5:1 of Israel, until we were *p* over
Josh 6:8 rams' horns *p* on before the LORD
Josh 10:29 Then Joshua *p* from Makkedah, and
Josh 10:31 Joshua *p* from Libnah, and all
Josh 10:34 from Lachish Joshua *p* unto Eglon
Josh 15:3 *p* along to Zin, and ascended up on
Josh 15:3 *p* along to Hezron, and went up to
Josh 15:4 From thence it *p* toward Azmon
Josh 15:6 and *p* along by the north of
Josh 15:7 the border *p* toward the waters of
Josh 15:10 *p* along unto the side of mount
Josh 15:10 Beth-shemesh, and *p* on to Timnah
Josh 15:11 *p* along to mount Baalah, and went
Josh 16:6 *p* by it on the east to Janohah
Josh 18:9 *p* through the land, and described
Josh 18:18 *p* along toward the side over
Josh 18:19 the border *p* along to the side of
Josh 24:17 all the people through whom we *p*
Judg 3:26 *p* beyond the quarries, and escaped
Judg 8:4 *p* over, he, and the three hundred
Judg 10:9 Ammon *p* over Jordan to fight also
Judg 11:29 he *p* over Gilead, and Manasseh, and
Judg 11:29 *p* over Mizpeh of Gilead, and from
Judg 11:29 from Mizpeh of Gilead he *p* over
Judg 11:32 So Jephthah *p* over unto the
Judg 12:3 *p* over against the children of

Judg 18:13 they *p* thence unto mount Ephraim,
Judg 19:14 And they *p* on and went their way
1Sa 9:4 he *p* through mount Ephraim, and
1Sa 9:4 *p* through the land of Shalisha,
1Sa 9:4 then they *p* through the land of
1Sa 9:4 he *p* through the land of the
1Sa 9:27 pass on before us, (and he *p* on
1Sa 14:23 the battle *p* over unto Beth-aven
1Sa 15:12 *p* on, and gone down to Gilgal
1Sa 27:2 he *p* over with the six hundred
1Sa 29:2 the Philistines *p* on by hundreds
1Sa 29:2 his men *p* on in the rereward with
2Sa 2:29 *p* over Jordan, and went through
2Sa 10:17 *p* over Jordan, and came to Helam
2Sa 15:18 all his servants *p* on beside him
2Sa 15:18 from Gath, *p* on before the king
2Sa 15:22 And Ittai the Gittite *p* over
2Sa 15:23 voice, and all the people *p* over
2Sa 15:23 himself *p* over the brook Kidron
2Sa 15:23 and all the people *p* over
2Sa 17:22 with him, and they *p* over Jordan
2Sa 17:24 Absalom *p* over Jordan, he and all
2Sa 24:5 they *p* over Jordan, and pitched in
1Kin 13:25 And, behold, men *p* by, and saw the
1Kin 19:11 And, behold, the LORD *p* by
1Kin 19:19 and Elijah *p* by him, and cast his
1Kin 20:39 And as the king *p* by, he cried
2Kin 4:8 on a day, that Elisha *p* to Shunem
2Kin 4:8 so it was, that as oft as he *p* by
2Kin 4:31 Gehazi *p* on before them, and laid
2Kin 6:30 he *p* by upon the wall, and the
2Kin 14:9 there *p* by a wild beast that was
1Chr 19:17 *p* over Jordan, and came upon them,
2Chr 9:22 king Solomon *p* all the kings of
2Chr 25:18 there *p* by a wild beast that was
2Chr 30:10 So the posts *p* from city to city
Job 4:15 Then a spirit *p* before my face
Job 9:26 They are *p* away as the swift
Job 15:19 and no stranger *p* among them
Job 28:8 it, nor the fierce lion *p* by it
Ps 18:12 was before him his thick clouds *p*
Ps 37:36 Yet he *p* away, and, lo, he was not
Ps 48:4 assembled, they *p* by together
Ps 90:9 our days are *p* away in thy wrath
Song 3:4 but a little that I *p* from them
Is 10:28 come to Aiath, he is *p* to Migron
Is 40:27 my judgment is *p* over from my God
Is 41:3 He pursued them, and *p* safely
Jer 2:6 a land that no man *p* through
Jer 11:15 and the holy flesh is *p* from thee
Jer 34:18 *p* between the parts thereof,
Jer 34:19 which *p* between the parts of the
Jer 46:17 he hath *p* the time appointed
Eze 16:6 when I *p* by thee, and saw thee
Eze 16:8 Now when I *p* by thee, and looked
Eze 16:15 on every one that *p* by
Eze 16:25 thy feet to every one that *p* by
Eze 36:34 in the sight of all that *p* by
Eze 47:5 a river that could not be *p* over
Dan 3:27 the smell of fire had *p* on them
Dan 6:18 palace, and *p* the night fasting
Hos 10:11 but I *p* over upon her fair neck
Jonah 2:3 billows and thy waves *p* over me
Mic 2:13 have *p* through the gate, and are
Nah 3:19 not thy wickedness *p* continually
Hab 3:10 the overflowing of the water *p* by
Zec 7:14 that no man *p* through nor
Mt 9:1 *p* over, and came into his own city
Mt 9:9 as Jesus *p* forth from thence, he
Mt 20:30 when they heard that Jesus *p* by
Mt 27:39 they that *p* by reviled him,
Mk 2:14 And as he *p* by, he saw Levi the
Mk 5:21 when Jesus was *p* over again by
Mk 6:35 place, and now the time is far *p*
Mk 6:48 the sea, and would have *p* by them
Mk 6:53 And when they had *p* over, they
Mk 9:30 thence, and *p* through Galilee
Mk 11:20 And in the morning, as they *p* by
Mk 15:21 one Simon a Cyrenian, who *p* by
Mk 15:29 they that *p* by railed on him,
Lk 10:31 he *p* by on the other side
Lk 10:32 on him, and *p* by on the other side
Lk 17:11 that he *p* through the midst of
Lk 19:1 entered and *p* through Jericho
Jn 5:24 but is *p* from death unto life
Jn 8:59 the midst of them, and so *p* by
Jn 9:1 And as Jesus *p* by, he saw a man
Acts 9:32 as Peter *p* throughout all
Acts 12:10 out, and *p* on through one street
Acts 14:24 after they had *p* throughout
Acts 15:3 they *p* through Phenice and Samaria
Acts 17:1 Now when they had *p* through
Acts 17:23 For as I *p* by, and beheld your
Acts 19:1 Paul having *p* through the upper
Acts 19:21 when he had *p* through Macedonia
Rom 5:12 so death *p* upon all men, for that
1Cor 10:1 cloud, and all *p* through the sea
2Cor 5:17 old things are *p* away
Heb 4:14 that is *p* into the heavens, Jesus
Heb 11:29 By faith they *p* through the Red
1Jn 3:14 we have *p* from death unto life
Rev 21:1 and the first earth were *p* away
Rev 21:4 for the former things are *p* away

**PASSENGERS**

Prov 9:15 To call *p* who go right on their
Eze 39:11 the valley of the *p* on the east
Eze 39:11 it shall stop the noses of the *p*
Eze 39:14 the land to bury with the *p* those
Eze 39:15 the *p* that pass through the land,

**PASSEST**

Deut 3:21 all the kingdoms whither thou *p*
Deut 30:18 whither thou *p* over Jordan to go
2Sa 15:33 If thou *p* on with me, then thou
1Kin 2:37 *p* over the brook Kidron, thou
Is 43:2 When thou *p* through the waters, I

**PASSETH**

Ex 30:13 every one that *p* among them that
Ex 30:14 Every one that *p* among them that
Ex 33:22 come to pass, while my glory *p* by
Lev 27:32 of whatsoever *p* under the rod
Josh 3:11 *p* over before you into Jordan
Josh 16:2 *p* along unto the borders of Archi
Josh 19:13 from thence *p* on along on the
1Kin 9:8 every one that *p* by it shall be
2Kin 4:9 which *p* by us continually
2Kin 12:4 of every one that *p* the account
2Chr 7:21 to every one that *p* by it
Job 9:11 he *p* on also, but I perceive him
Job 14:20 for ever against him, and he *p*
Job 30:15 my welfare *p* away as a cloud
Job 37:21 but the wind *p*, and cleanseth them
Ps 8:8 whatsoever *p* through the paths of
Ps 78:39 a wind that *p* away, and cometh not
Ps 103:16 For the wind *p* over it, and it is
Ps 144:4 days are as a shadow that *p* away
Prov 10:25 As the whirlwind *p*, so is the
Prov 26:17 He that *p* by, and meddleth with
Eccl 1:4 One generation *p* away, and another
Is 29:5 shall be as chaff that *p* away
Jer 9:12 a wilderness, that none *p* through
Jer 13:24 that *p* away by the wind of the
Jer 18:16 every one that *p* thereby shall be
Jer 19:8 every one that *p* thereby shall be
Eze 35:7 and cut off from it him that *p* out
Hos 13:3 and as the early dew that *p* away
Mic 7:18 *p* by the transgression of the
Zeph 2:15 every one that *p* by her shall
Zeph 3:6 streets waste, that none *p* by
Zec 9:8 army, because of him that *p* by
Lk 18:37 him, that Jesus of Nazareth *p* by
1Cor 7:31 the fashion of this world *p* away
Eph 3:19 which *p* knowledge, that ye might
Phil 4:7 which *p* all understanding, shall
1Jn 2:17 And the world *p* away, and the lust

**PASSING**

Judg 19:18 We are *p* from Beth-lehem-judah
2Sa 1:26 wonderful, *p* the love of women
2Sa 15:24 people had done *p* out of the city
2Kin 6:26 of Israel was *p* by upon the wall
Ps 84:6 Who *p* through the valley of Baca
Prov 7:8 *P* through the street near her
Is 31:5 *p* over he will preserve it
Eze 39:14 *p* through the land to bury with
Lk 4:30 But he *p* through the midst of
Acts 5:15 *p* by might overshadow some of
Acts 8:40 *p* through he preached in all the
Acts 16:8 they *p* by Mysia came down to
Acts 27:8 And, hardly *p* it, came unto a

**PASSOVER**

Ex 12:11 it is the LORD's *p*
Ex 12:21 to your families, and kill the *p*
Ex 12:27 is the sacrifice of the LORD's *p*
Ex 12:43 This is the ordinance of the *p*
Ex 12:48 and will keep the *p* to the LORD
Ex 34:25 of the *p* be left unto the morning
Lev 23:5 month at even is the LORD's *p*
Num 9:2 the *p* at his appointed season
Num 9:4 that they should keep the *p*
Num 9:5 they kept the *p* on the fourteenth
Num 9:6 could not keep the *p* on that day
Num 9:10 he shall keep the *p* unto the LORD
Num 9:12 of the *p* they shall keep it
Num 9:13 and forbeareth to keep the *p*
Num 9:14 and will keep the *p* unto the LORD
Num 9:14 to the ordinance of the *p*
Num 28:16 first month is the *p* of the LORD
Num 33:3 on the morrow after the *p* the
Deut 16:1 keep the *p* unto the LORD thy God
Deut 16:2 the *p* unto the LORD thy God
Deut 16:5 the *p* within any of thy gates
Deut 16:6 shalt sacrifice the *p* at even
Josh 5:10 kept the *p* on the fourteenth day
Josh 5:11 land on the morrow after the *p*
2Kin 23:21 Keep the *p* unto the LORD your God
2Kin 23:22 a *p* from the days of the judges
2Kin 23:23 wherein this *p* was holden to the
2Chr 30:1 to keep the *p* unto the LORD God
2Chr 30:2 to keep the *p* in the second month
2Chr 30:5 they should come to keep the *p*
2Chr 30:15 Then they killed the *p* on the
2Chr 30:18 yet did they eat the *p* otherwise
2Chr 35:1 Moreover Josiah kept a *p* unto the
2Chr 35:1 and they killed the *p* on the
2Chr 35:6 So kill the *p*, and sanctify
2Chr 35:7 and kids, all for the *p* offerings
2Chr 35:8 for the *p* offerings two thousand
2Chr 35:9 gave unto the Levites for *p*
2Chr 35:11 And they killed the *p*, and the
2Chr 35:13 they roasted the *p* with fire
2Chr 35:16 the same day, to keep the *p*
2Chr 35:17 present kept the *p* at that time
2Chr 35:18 there was no *p* like to that kept
2Chr 35:18 keep such a *p* as Josiah kept
2Chr 35:19 reign of Josiah was this *p* kept
Ezr 6:19 of the captivity kept the *p* upon
Ezr 6:20 killed the *p* for all the children
Eze 45:21 of the month, ye shall have the *p*
Mt 26:2 two days is the feast of the *p*
Mt 26:17 we prepare for thee to eat the *p*
Mt 26:18 I will keep the *p* at thy house
Mt 26:19 and they made ready the *p*
Mk 14:1 two days was the feast of the *p*
Mk 14:12 bread, when they killed the *p*
Mk 14:12 that thou mayest eat the *p*
Mk 14:14 shall eat the *p* with my disciples
Mk 14:16 and they made ready the *p*
Lk 2:41 every year at the feast of the *p*
Lk 22:1 drew nigh, which is called the *P*
Lk 22:7 when the *p* must be killed
Lk 22:8 saying, Go and prepare us the *p*
Lk 22:11 shall eat the *p* with my disciples
Lk 22:13 and they made ready the *p*
Lk 22:15 this *p* with you before I suffer
Jn 2:13 the Jews' *p* was at hand, and Jesus
Jn 2:23 when he was in Jerusalem at the *p*
Jn 6:4 And the *p*, a feast of the Jews,
Jn 11:55 the Jews' *p* was nigh at hand
Jn 11:55 up to Jerusalem before the *p*
Jn 12:1 days before the *p* came to Bethany
Jn 13:1 Now before the feast of the *p*
Jn 18:28 but that they might eat the *p*
Jn 18:39 release unto you one at the *p*
Jn 19:14 it was the preparation of the *p*
1Cor 5:7 For even Christ our *p* is
Heb 11:28 Through faith he kept the *p*

**PAST**

Gen 50:4 the days of his mourning were *p*
Ex 21:29 to push with his horn in time *p*
Ex 21:36 ox hath used to push in time *p*
Num 21:22 way, until we be *p* thy borders
Deut 2:10 Emims dwelt therein in times *p*
Deut 4:32 ask now of the days that are *p*
Deut 4:42 and hated him not in times *p*
Deut 19:4 whom he hated not in time *p*
Deut 19:6 as he hated him not in time *p*
1Sa 15:32 the bitterness of death is *p*
1Sa 19:7 in his presence, as in times *p*
2Sa 3:17 in times *p* to be king over you
2Sa 5:2 Also in time *p*, when Saul was
2Sa 11:27 And when the mourning was *p*
2Sa 16:1 a little *p* the top of the hill
1Kin 18:29 came to pass, when midday was *p*
1Chr 9:20 was the ruler over them in time *p*
1Chr 11:2 And moreover in time *p*, even when
Job 9:10 doeth great things *p* finding out
Job 14:13 me secret, until thy wrath be *p*
Job 17:11 My days are *p*, my purposes are

Job 29:2 Oh that I were as in months *p*
Ps 90:4 are but as yesterday when it is *p*
Eccl 3:15 and God requireth that which is *p*
Song 2:11 For, lo, the winter is *p*, the
Jer 8:20 The harvest is *p*, the summer is
Mt 14:15 place, and the time is now *p*
Mk 16:1 And when the sabbath was *p*
Lk 9:36 And when the voice was *p*, Jesus
Acts 12:10 When they were *p* the first
Acts 14:16 Who in times *p* suffered all
Acts 27:9 the fast was now already *p*
Rom 3:25 the remission of sins that are *p*
Rom 11:30 For as ye in times *p* have not
Rom 11:33 and his ways *p* finding out
Gal 1:13 in time *p* in the Jews' religion
Gal 1:23 *p* now preacheth the faith which
Gal 5:21 as I have also told you in time *p*
Eph 2:2 Wherein in time *p* ye walked
Eph 2:3 times *p* in the lusts of our flesh
Eph 2:11 in time *p* Gentiles in the flesh
Eph 4:19 Who being *p* feeling have given
2Ti 2:18 the resurrection is *p* already
Philem 11 Which in time *p* was to thee
Heb 1:1 in time *p* unto the fathers by the
Heb 11:11 of a child when she was *p* age
1Pet 2:10 Which in time *p* were not a people
1Pet 4:3 For the time *p* of our life may
1Jn 2:8 because the darkness is *p*
Rev 9:12 One woe is *p*
Rev 11:14 The second woe is *p*

**PASTORS**
Jer 2:8 the *p* also transgressed against
Jer 3:15 I will give you *p* according to
Jer 10:21 For the *p* are become brutish, and
Jer 12:10 Many *p* have destroyed my vineyard
Jer 22:22 The wind shall eat up all thy *p*
Jer 23:1 Woe be unto the *p* that destroy
Jer 23:2 against the *p* that feed my people
Eph 4:11 and some, *p* and teachers

**PASTURE**
Gen 47:4 have no *p* for their flocks
1Chr 4:39 to seek *p* for their flocks
1Chr 4:40 And they found fat *p* and good, and
1Chr 4:41 because there was *p* there for
Job 39:8 range of the mountains is his *p*
Ps 74:1 smoke against the sheep of thy *p*
Ps 79:13 sheep of thy *p* will give thee
Ps 95:7 and we are the people of his *p*
Ps 100:3 his people, and the sheep of his *p*
Is 32:14 joy of wild asses, a *p* of flocks
Jer 23:1 and scatter the sheep of my *p*
Jer 25:36 for the LORD hath spoiled their *p*
Lam 1:6 become like harts that find no *p*
Eze 34:14 I will feed them in a good *p*
Eze 34:14 in a fat *p* shall they feed upon
Eze 34:18 you to have eaten up the good *p*
Eze 34:31 And ye my flock, the flock of my *p*
Hos 13:6 According to their *p*, so were
Joel 1:18 perplexed, because they have no *p*
Jn 10:9 and shall go in and out, and find *p*

**PASTURES**
1Kin 4:23 oxen, and twenty oxen out of the *p*
Ps 23:2 maketh me to lie down in green *p*
Ps 65:12 drop upon the *p* of the wilderness
Ps 65:13 The *p* are clothed with flocks
Is 30:23 shall thy cattle feed in large *p*
Is 49:9 their *p* shall be in all high
Eze 34:18 your feet the residue of your *p*
Eze 45:15 out of the fat *p* of Israel
Joel 1:19 devoured the *p* of the wilderness
Joel 1:20 devoured the *p* of the wilderness
Joel 2:22 for the *p* of the wilderness do

**PATARA** *(pat'-a-rah) A city in Lycia in Asia Minor.*
Acts 21:1 Rhodes, and from thence unto *P*

**PATH**
Gen 49:17 by the way, an adder in the *p*
Num 22:24 stood in a *p* of the vineyards
Job 28:7 There is a *p* which no fowl
Job 30:13 They mar my *p*, they set forward
Job 41:32 He maketh a *p* to shine after him
Ps 16:11 Thou wilt shew me the *p* of life
Ps 27:11 O LORD, and lead me in a plain *p*
Ps 77:19 thy *p* in the great waters, and thy
Ps 119:35 go in the *p* of thy commandments
Ps 119:105 my feet, and a light unto my *p*
Ps 139:3 Thou compassest my *p* and my lying
Ps 142:3 within me, then thou knewest my *p*
Prov 1:15 refrain thy foot from their *p*
Prov 2:9 yea, every good *p*
Prov 4:14 not into the *p* of the wicked
Prov 4:18 But the *p* of the just is as the
Prov 4:26 Ponder the *p* of thy feet, and let
Prov 5:6 shouldest ponder the *p* of life
Is 26:7 dost weigh the *p* of the just
Is 30:11 the way, turn aside out of the *p*
Is 40:14 taught him in the *p* of judgment
Is 43:16 sea, and a *p* in the mighty waters
Joel 2:8 shall walk every one in his *p*

**PATHROS** *(path'-ros)* See PATHRUSIM. *A name for Upper Egypt.*
Is 11:11 Assyria, and from Egypt, and from *P*
Jer 44:1 at Noph, and in the country of *P*
Jer 44:15 dwelt in the land of Egypt, in *P*
Eze 29:14 them to return into the land of *P*
Eze 30:14 And I will make *P* desolate

**PATHRUSIM** *(path-ru'-sim) A descendant of Mizraim.*
Gen 10:14 And *P*, and Casluhim, (out of whom
1Chr 1:12 And *P*, and Casluhim, (of whom came

**PATHS**
Job 6:18 The *p* of their way are turned
Job 8:13 So are the *p* of all that forget
Job 13:27 and lookest narrowly unto all my *p*
Job 19:8 and he hath set darkness in my *p*
Job 24:13 nor abide in the *p* thereof
Job 33:11 the stocks, he marketh all my *p*
Job 38:20 know the *p* to the house thereof
Ps 8:8 passeth through the *p* of the seas
Ps 17:4 me from the *p* of the destroyer
Ps 17:5 Hold up my goings in thy *p*
Ps 23:3 he leadeth me in the *p* of
Ps 25:4 teach me thy *p*
Ps 25:10 All the *p* of the LORD are mercy
Ps 65:11 and thy *p* drop fatness
Prov 2:8 He keepeth the *p* of judgment
Prov 2:13 Who leave the *p* of uprightness,
Prov 2:15 and they froward in their *p*
Prov 2:18 death, and her *p* unto the dead
Prov 2:19 take they hold of the *p* of life
Prov 2:20 keep the *p* of the righteous
Prov 3:6 him, and he shall direct thy *p*
Prov 3:17 and all her *p* are peace
Prov 4:11 I have led thee in right *p*
Prov 7:25 her ways, go not astray in her *p*
Prov 8:2 by the way in the places of the *p*
Prov 8:20 in the midst of the *p* of judgment
Is 2:3 ways, and we will walk in his *p*
Is 3:12 err, and destroy the way of thy *p*
Is 42:16 I will lead them in *p* that they
Is 58:12 The restorer of *p* to dwell in
Is 59:7 and destruction are in their *p*
Is 59:8 they have made them crooked *p*
Jer 6:16 and see, and ask for the old *p*
Jer 18:15 in their ways from the ancient *p*
Jer 18:15 the ancient *p*, to walk in *p*
Lam 3:9 stone, he hath made my *p* crooked
Hos 2:6 that she shall not find her *p*
Mic 4:2 ways, and we will walk in his *p*
Mt 3:3 of the Lord, make his *p* straight
Mk 1:3 of the Lord, make his *p* straight
Lk 3:4 of the Lord, make his *p* straight
Heb 12:13 And make straight *p* for your feet

**PATIENCE**
Mt 18:26 have *p* with me, and I will pay
Mt 18:29 Have *p* with me, and I will pay
Lk 8:15 it, and bring forth fruit with *p*
Lk 21:19 In your *p* possess ye your souls
Rom 5:3 that tribulation worketh *p*
Rom 5:4 And *p*, experience
Rom 8:25 then do we with *p* wait for it
Rom 15:4 our learning, that we through *p*
Rom 15:5 Now the God of *p* and consolation
2Cor 6:4 the ministers of God, in much *p*
2Cor 12:12 were wrought among you in all *p*
Col 1:11 to his glorious power, unto all *p*
1Th 1:3 *p* of hope in our Lord Jesus
2Th 1:4 in the churches of God for your *p*
1Ti 6:11 godliness, faith, love, *p*
2Ti 3:10 faith, longsuffering, charity, *p*
Titus 2:2 sound in faith, in charity, in *p*
Heb 6:12 faith and *p* inherit the promises
Heb 10:36 For ye have need of *p*, that,
Heb 12:1 let us run with *p* the race that
Jas 1:3 trying of your faith worketh *p*
Jas 1:4 But let *p* have her perfect work,
Jas 5:7 the earth, and hath long *p* for it
Jas 5:10 of suffering affliction, and of *p*
Jas 5:11 Ye have heard of the *p* of Job
2Pet 1:6 and to temperance *p*
2Pet 1:6 and to *p* godliness
Rev 1:9 *p* of Jesus Christ, was in the
Rev 2:2 works, and thy labour, and thy *p*
Rev 2:3 And hast borne, and hast *p*, and for
Rev 2:19 and service, and faith, and thy *p*
Rev 3:10 thou hast kept the word of my *p*
Rev 13:10 Here is the *p* and the faith of the
Rev 14:12 Here is the *p* of the saints

**PATIENT**
Eccl 7:8 the *p* in spirit is better than
Rom 2:7 To them who by *p* continuance in
Rom 12:12 *p* in tribulation
1Th 5:14 the weak, be *p* toward all men
2Th 3:5 into the *p* waiting for Christ
1Ti 3:3 but *p*, not a brawler, not
2Ti 2:24 unto all men, apt to teach, *p*
Jas 5:7 Be *p* therefore, brethren, unto
Jas 5:8 Be ye also *p*

**PATIENTLY**
Ps 37:7 in the LORD, and wait *p* for him
Ps 40:1 I waited *p* for the LORD
Acts 26:3 I beseech thee to hear me *p*
Heb 6:15 And so, after he had *p* endured
1Pet 2:20 your faults, ye shall take it *p*
1Pet 2:20 and suffer for it, ye take it *p*

**PATMOS** *(pat'-mos) An island off the west coast of Asia Minor.*
Rev 1:9 was in the isle that is called *P*

**PATROBAS** *(pat'-ro-bas) A Christian in Rome.*
Rom 16:14 Asyncritus, Phlegon, Hermas, *P*

**PATTERN**
Ex 25:9 after the *p* of the tabernacle, and
Ex 25:9 the *p* of all the instruments
Ex 25:40 that thou make them after their *p*
Num 8:4 according unto the *p* which the
Josh 22:28 Behold the *p* of the altar of the
2Kin 16:10 the *p* of it, according to all the
1Chr 28:11 his son the *p* of the porch
1Chr 28:12 the *p* of all that he had by the
1Chr 28:18 gold for the *p* of the chariot of
1Chr 28:19 me, even all the works of this *p*
Eze 43:10 and let them measure the *p*
1Ti 1:16 for a *p* to them which should
Titus 2:7 shewing thyself a *p* of good works
Heb 8:5 the *p* shewed to thee in the mount

**PAU** *(pa'-u)* See PAI. *City of King Hagar of Edom.*
Gen 36:39 and the name of his city was *P*

**PAUL** *(pawl)* See PAUL'S, PAULUS, SAUL. *The apostle to the Gentiles.*
Acts 13:9 Then Saul, (who also is called *P*
Acts 13:13 Now when *P* and his company loosed
Acts 13:16 Then *P* stood up, and beckoning
Acts 13:43 religious proselytes followed *P*
Acts 13:45 things which were spoken by *P*
Acts 13:46 Then *P* and Barnabas waxed bold, and
Acts 13:50 and raised persecution against *P*
Acts 14:9 The same heard *P* speak
Acts 14:11 the people saw what *P* had done
Acts 14:12 and *P*, Mercurius, because he was
Acts 14:14 when the apostles, Barnabas and *P*
Acts 14:19 the people, and, having stoned *P*
Acts 15:2 When therefore *P* and Barnabas had
Acts 15:2 with them, they determined that *P*
Acts 15:12 and gave audience to Barnabas and *P*
Acts 15:22 own company to Antioch with *P*
Acts 15:25 with our beloved Barnabas and *P*
Acts 15:35 *P* also and Barnabas continued in
Acts 15:36 some days after *P* said unto
Acts 15:38 But *P* thought not good to take
Acts 15:40 *P* chose Silas, and departed, being
Acts 16:3 Him would *P* have to go forth with
Acts 16:9 vision appeared to *P* in the night
Acts 16:14 the things which were spoken of *P*
Acts 16:17 The same followed *P* and us, and
Acts 16:18 But *P*, being grieved, turned and
Acts 16:19 gains was gone, they caught *P*
Acts 16:25 And at midnight *P* and Silas prayed,
Acts 16:28 But *P* cried with a loud voice,
Acts 16:29 trembling, and fell down before *P*
Acts 16:36 the prison told this saying to *P*
Acts 16:37 But *P* said unto them, They have

Acts 17:2 And P, as his manner was, went in
Acts 17:4 believed, and consorted with P
Acts 17:10 brethren immediately sent away P
Acts 17:13 of God was preached of P at Berea
Acts 17:14 the brethren sent away P to go as
Acts 17:15 they that conducted P brought him
Acts 17:16 Now while P waited for them at
Acts 17:22 Then P stood in the midst of
Acts 17:33 So P departed from among them
Acts 18:1 After these things P departed
Acts 18:5 P was pressed in the spirit, and
Acts 18:9 Then spake the Lord to P in the
Acts 18:12 with one accord against P
Acts 18:14 when P was now about to open his
Acts 18:18 P after this tarried there yet a
Acts 19:1 P having passed through the upper
Acts 19:4 Then said P, John verily baptized
Acts 19:6 when P had laid his hands upon
Acts 19:11 miracles by the hands of P
Acts 19:13 you by Jesus whom P preacheth
Acts 19:15 said, Jesus I know, and P I know
Acts 19:21 P purposed in the spirit, when he
Acts 19:26 this P hath persuaded and turned
Acts 19:30 when P would have entered in unto
Acts 20:1 P called unto him the disciples,
Acts 20:7 P preached unto them, ready to
Acts 20:9 as P was long preaching, he sunk
Acts 20:10 P went down, and fell on him, and
Acts 20:13 there intending to take in P
Acts 20:16 For P had determined to sail by
Acts 21:4 who said to P through the Spirit,
Acts 21:13 Then P answered, What mean ye to
Acts 21:18 the day following P went in with
Acts 21:26 Then P took the men, and the next
Acts 21:29 whom they supposed that P had
Acts 21:30 and they took P, and drew him out
Acts 21:32 soldiers, they left beating of P
Acts 21:37 as P was to be led into the
Acts 21:39 But P said, I am a man which am a
Acts 21:40 P stood on the stairs, and
Acts 22:25 P said unto the centurion that
Acts 22:28 P said, But I was free born
Acts 22:30 to appear, and brought P down
Acts 23:1 And P, earnestly beholding the
Acts 23:3 Then said P unto him, God shall
Acts 23:5 Then said P, I wist not, brethren
Acts 23:6 But when P perceived that the one
Acts 23:10 fearing lest P should have been
Acts 23:11 him, and said, Be of good cheer, P
Acts 23:12 nor drink till they had killed P
Acts 23:14 eat nothing until we have slain P
Acts 23:16 into the castle, and told P
Acts 23:17 Then P called one of the
Acts 23:18 P the prisoner called me unto him
Acts 23:20 down P to morrow into the council
Acts 23:24 beasts, that they may set P on
Acts 23:31 as it was commanded them, took P
Acts 23:33 presented P also before him
Acts 24:1 informed the governor against P
Acts 24:10 Then P, after that the governor
Acts 24:23 commanded a centurion to keep P
Acts 24:24 which was a Jewess, he sent for P
Acts 24:26 should have been given him of P
Acts 24:27 the Jews a pleasure, left P bound
Acts 25:2 the Jews informed him against P
Acts 25:4 that P should be kept at Caesarea
Acts 25:6 seat commanded P to be brought
Acts 25:7 and grievous complaints against P
Acts 25:9 the Jews a pleasure, answered P
Acts 25:10 Then said P, I stand at Caesar's
Acts 25:19 whom P affirmed to be alive
Acts 25:21 But when P had appealed to be
Acts 25:23 commandment P was brought forth
Acts 26:1 Then Agrippa said unto P, Thou
Acts 26:1 Then P stretched forth the hand,
Acts 26:24 Festus said with a loud voice, P
Acts 26:28 Then Agrippa said unto P, Almost
Acts 26:29 P said, I would to God, that not
Acts 27:1 sail into Italy, they delivered P
Acts 27:3 And Julius courteously entreated P
Acts 27:9 already past, P admonished them,
Acts 27:11 things which were spoken by P
Acts 27:21 But after long abstinence P stood
Acts 27:24 Saying, Fear not, P
Acts 27:31 P said to the centurion and to the
Acts 27:33 P besought them all to take meat,
Acts 27:43 the centurion, willing to save P
Acts 28:3 when P had gathered a bundle of
Acts 28:8 to whom P entered in, and prayed,
Acts 28:15 whom when P saw, he thanked God,
Acts 28:16 but P was suffered to dwell by
Acts 28:17 that after three days P called
Acts 28:25 after that P had spoken one word,
Acts 28:30 P dwelt two whole years in his
Rom 1:1 P, a servant of Jesus Christ,
1Cor 1:1 P, called to be an apostle of
1Cor 1:12 every one of you saith, I am of P
1Cor 1:13 was P crucified for you
1Cor 1:13 were ye baptized in the name of P
1Cor 3:4 For while one saith, I am of P
1Cor 3:5 Who then is P, and who is Apollos,
1Cor 3:22 Whether P, or Apollos, or Cephas,
1Cor 16:21 of me P with mine own hand
2Cor 1:1 P, an apostle of Jesus Christ by
2Cor 10:1 Now I P myself beseech you by the
Gal 1:1 P, an apostle, (not of men,
Gal 5:2 I P say unto you, that if ye be
Eph 1:1 P, an apostle of Jesus Christ by
Eph 3:1 For this cause I P, the prisoner
Phil 1:1 P and Timotheus, the servants of
Col 1:1 P, an apostle of Jesus Christ by
Col 1:23 whereof I P am made a minister
Col 4:18 salutation by the hand of me P
1Th 1:1 P, and Silvanus, and Timotheus,
1Th 2:18 have come unto you, even I P
2Th 1:1 P, and Silvanus, and Timotheus,
2Th 3:17 The salutation of P with mine own
1Ti 1:1 P, an apostle of Jesus Christ by
2Ti 1:1 P, an apostle of Jesus Christ by
2Ti *s* when P was brought before Nero
Titus 1:1 P, a servant of God, and an
Philem 1 P, a prisoner of Jesus Christ, and
Philem 9 being such an one as P the aged
Philem 19 I P have written it with mine own
2Pet 3:15 even as our beloved brother P

**PAUL'S** *(pawls)*
Acts 19:29 P companions in travel, they
Acts 20:37 all wept sore, and fell on P neck
Acts 21:8 that were of P company departed
Acts 21:11 come unto us, he took P girdle
Acts 23:16 when P sister's son heard of
Acts 25:14 Festus declared P cause unto the

**PAULUS** See PAUL. *A Roman proconsul.*
Acts 13:7 deputy of the country, Sergius P

**PAVEMENT**
2Kin 16:17 it, and put it upon a p of stones
2Chr 7:3 faces to the ground upon the p
Est 1:6 gold and silver, upon a p of red
Eze 40:17 a p made for the court round
Eze 40:17 thirty chambers were upon the p
Eze 40:18 the p by the side of the gates
Eze 40:18 of the gates was the lower p
Eze 42:3 over against the p which was for
Jn 19:13 in a place that is called the P

**PAVILION**
Ps 18:11 his p round about him were dark
Ps 27:5 trouble he shall hide me in his p
Ps 31:20 in a p from the strife of tongues
Jer 43:10 spread his royal p over them

**PAY**
Ex 21:19 only he shall p for the loss of
Ex 21:22 and he shall p as the judges
Ex 21:36 he shall surely p ox for ox
Ex 22:7 thief be found, let him p double
Ex 22:9 he shall p double unto his
Ex 22:17 he shall p money according to the
Num 20:19 thy water, then I will p for it
Deut 23:21 God, thou shalt not slack to p it
2Sa 15:7 p my vow, which I have vowed unto
1Kin 20:39 thou shalt p a talent of silver
2Kin 4:7 p thy debt, and live thou and thy
2Chr 8:8 make to p tribute until this day
2Chr 27:5 the children of Ammon p unto him
Ezr 4:13 again, then will they not p toll
Est 3:9 I will p ten thousand talents of
Est 4:7 that Haman had promised to p to
Job 22:27 thee, and thou shalt p thy vows
Ps 22:25 I will p my vows before them that
Ps 50:14 p thy vows unto the most High
Ps 66:13 I will p thee my vows,
Ps 76:11 Vow, and p unto the LORD your God
Ps 116:14 I will p my vows unto the LORD
Ps 116:18 I will p my vows unto the LORD
Prov 19:17 he hath given will he p him again
Prov 22:27 If thou hast nothing to p
Eccl 5:4 a vow unto God, defer not to p it
Eccl 5:4 p that which thou hast vowed
Eccl 5:5 that thou shouldest vow and not p
Jonah 2:9 I will p that that I have vowed
Mt 17:24 Doth not your master p tribute
Mt 18:25 But forasmuch as he had not to p
Mt 18:26 with me, and I will p thee all
Mt 18:28 saying, P me that thou owest
Mt 18:29 with me, and I will p thee all
Mt 18:30 prison, till he should p the debt
Mt 18:34 till he should p all that was due
Mt 23:23 for ye p tithe of mint and anise
Lk 7:42 And when they had nothing to p
Rom 13:6 for this cause p ye tribute also

**PEACE**
Gen 15:15 thou shalt go to thy fathers in p
Gen 24:21 man wondering at her held his p
Gen 26:29 good, and have sent thee away in p
Gen 26:31 and they departed from him in p
Gen 28:21 again to my father's house in p
Gen 34:5 Jacob held his p until they were
Gen 41:16 shall give Pharaoh an answer of p
Gen 43:23 And he said, P be to you, fear not
Gen 44:17 get you up in p unto your father
Ex 4:18 And Jethro said to Moses, Go in p
Ex 14:14 for you, and ye shall hold your p
Ex 18:23 shall also go to their place in p
Ex 20:24 thy p offerings, thy sheep, and
Ex 24:5 sacrificed p offerings of oxen
Ex 29:28 sacrifice of their p offerings
Ex 32:6 offerings, and brought p offerings
Lev 3:1 be a sacrifice of p offering
Lev 3:3 p offering an offering made by
Lev 3:6 of p offering unto the LORD be of
Lev 3:9 p offering an offering made by
Lev 4:10 of the sacrifice of p offerings
Lev 4:26 of the sacrifice of p offerings
Lev 4:31 off the sacrifice of p offerings
Lev 4:35 the sacrifice of the p offerings
Lev 6:12 the fat of the p offerings
Lev 7:11 of the sacrifice of p offerings
Lev 7:13 thanksgiving of his p offerings
Lev 7:14 the blood of the p offerings
Lev 7:15 his p offerings for thanksgiving
Lev 7:18 p offerings be eaten at all on
Lev 7:20 of the sacrifice of p offerings
Lev 7:21 of the sacrifice of p offerings
Lev 7:29 p offerings unto the LORD shall
Lev 7:29 the sacrifice of his p offerings
Lev 7:32 sacrifices of your p offerings
Lev 7:33 the blood of the p offerings
Lev 7:34 sacrifices of their p offerings
Lev 7:37 the sacrifice of the p offerings
Lev 9:4 bullock and a ram for p offerings
Lev 9:18 for a sacrifice of p offerings
Lev 9:22 burnt offering, and p offerings
Lev 10:3 And Aaron held his p
Lev 10:14 of p offerings of the children of
Lev 17:5 offer them for p offerings unto
Lev 19:5 of p offerings unto the LORD
Lev 22:21 offereth a sacrifice of p
Lev 23:19 for a sacrifice of p offerings
Lev 26:6 And I will give p in the land
Num 6:14 without blemish for p offerings
Num 6:17 of p offerings unto the LORD
Num 6:18 the sacrifice of the p offerings
Num 6:26 upon thee, and give thee p
Num 7:17 And for a sacrifice of p offerings
Num 7:23 And for a sacrifice of p offerings
Num 7:29 And for a sacrifice of p offerings
Num 7:35 And for a sacrifice of p offerings
Num 7:41 And for a sacrifice of p offerings
Num 7:47 And for a sacrifice of p offerings
Num 7:53 And for a sacrifice of p offerings
Num 7:59 And for a sacrifice of p offerings
Num 7:65 And for a sacrifice of p offerings
Num 7:71 And for a sacrifice of p offerings
Num 7:77 And for a sacrifice of p offerings
Num 7:83 And for a sacrifice of p offerings
Num 7:88 of the p offerings were twenty
Num 10:10 sacrifices of your p offerings
Num 15:8 or p offerings unto the LORD
Num 25:12 I give unto him my covenant of p
Num 29:39 and for your p offerings
Num 30:4 father shall hold his p at her
Num 30:7 held his p at her in the day that
Num 30:11 heard it, and held his p at her
Num 30:14 hold his p at her from day to day
Num 30:14 because he held his p at her in
Deut 2:26 king of Heshbon with words of p
Deut 20:10 it, then proclaim p unto it
Deut 20:11 be, if it make thee answer of p

Jn 20:19 and saith unto them, *P* be unto you
Jn 20:21 to them again, *P* be unto you
Jn 20:26 the midst, and said, *P* be unto you
Acts 10:36 preaching *p* by Jesus Christ
Acts 11:18 these things, they held their *p*
Acts 12:17 with the hand to hold their *p*
Acts 12:20 their friend, desired *p*
Acts 15:13 And after they had held their *p*
Acts 15:33 they were let go in *p* from the
Acts 16:36 now therefore depart, and go in *p*
Acts 18:9 but speak, and hold not thy *p*
Rom 1:7 *p* from God our Father, and the
Rom 2:10 But glory, honour, and *p*, to every
Rom 3:17 the way of *p* have they not known
Rom 5:1 we have *p* with God through our
Rom 8:6 spiritually minded is life and *p*
Rom 10:15 them that preach the gospel of *p*
Rom 14:17 but righteousness, and *p*, and joy
Rom 14:19 after the things which make for *p*
Rom 15:13 *p* in believing, that ye may
Rom 15:33 Now the God of *p* be with you all
Rom 16:20 the God of *p* shall bruise Satan
1Cor 1:3 Grace be unto you, and *p*, from God
1Cor 7:15 but God hath called us to *p*
1Cor 14:30 by, let the first hold his *p*
1Cor 14:33 the author of confusion, but of *p*
1Cor 16:11 but conduct him forth in *p*
2Cor 1:2 *p* from God our Father, and from
2Cor 13:11 be of one mind, live in *p*
2Cor 13:11 of love and *p* shall be with you
Gal 1:3 *p* from God the Father, and from
Gal 5:22 of the Spirit is love, joy, *p*
Gal 6:16 *p* be on them, and mercy, and upon
Eph 1:2 Grace be to you, and *p*, from God
Eph 2:14 For he is our *p*, who hath made
Eph 2:15 of twain one new man, so making *p*
Eph 2:17 preached *p* to you which were afar
Eph 4:3 of the Spirit in the bond of *p*
Eph 6:15 preparation of the gospel of *p*
Eph 6:23 *P* be to the brethren, and love
Phil 1:2 Grace be unto you, and *p*, from God
Phil 4:7 the *p* of God, which passeth all
Phil 4:9 the God of *p* shall be with you
Col 1:2 Grace be unto you, and *p*, from God
Col 1:20 having made *p* through the blood
Col 3:15 let the *p* of God rule in your
1Th 1:1 Grace be unto you, and *p*, from God
1Th 5:3 For when they shall say, *P*
1Th 5:13 And be at *p* among yourselves
1Th 5:23 the very God of *p* sanctify you
2Th 1:2 Grace unto you, and *p*, from God
2Th 3:16 Now the Lord of *p* himself give
2Th 3:16 give you *p* always by all means
1Ti 1:2 Grace, mercy, and *p*, from God our
2Ti 1:2 Grace, mercy, and *p*, from God the
2Ti 2:22 righteousness, faith, charity, *p*
Titus 1:4 Grace, mercy, and *p*, from God the
Philem 3 Grace to you, and *p*, from God our
Heb 7:2 of Salem, which is, King of *p*
Heb 11:31 she had received the spies with *p*
Heb 12:14 Follow *p* with all men, and
Heb 13:20 Now the God of *p*, that brought
Jas 2:16 of you say unto them, Depart in *p*
Jas 3:18 sown in *p* of them that make *p*
1Pet 1:2 Grace unto you, and *p*, be
1Pet 3:11 let him seek *p*, and ensue it
1Pet 5:14 *P* be with you all that are in
2Pet 1:2 *p* be multiplied unto you through
2Pet 3:14 that ye may be found of him in *p*
2Jn 3 Grace be with you, mercy, and *p*
3Jn 14 *P* be to thee
Jude 2 Mercy unto you, and *p*, and love, be
Rev 1:4 Grace be unto you, and *p*, from him
Rev 6:4 thereon to take *p* from the earth

**PEACEABLE**
Gen 34:21 These men are *p* with us
2Sa 20:19 I am one of them that are *p*
1Chr 4:40 the land was wide, and quiet, and *p*
Is 32:18 shall dwell in a *p* habitation
Jer 25:37 the *p* habitations are cut down
1Ti 2:2 *p* life in all godliness and
Heb 12:11 afterward it yieldeth the *p* fruit
Jas 3:17 from above is first pure, then *p*

**PEACEABLY**
Gen 37:4 and could not speak *p* unto him
Judg 11:13 restore those lands again *p*
Judg 21:13 Rimmon, and to call *p* unto them
1Sa 16:4 coming, and said, Comest thou *p*
1Sa 16:5 And he said, *P*
1Kin 2:13 And she said, Comest thou *p*
1Kin 2:13 And he said, *P*
1Chr 12:17 If ye be come *p* unto me to help
Jer 9:8 one speaketh *p* to his neighbour
Dan 11:21 but he shall come in *p*, and obtain
Dan 11:24 He shall enter *p* even upon the
Rom 12:18 lieth in you, live *p* with all men

**PEACOCKS**
1Kin 10:22 and silver, ivory, and apes, and *p*
2Chr 9:21 and silver, ivory, and apes, and *p*
Job 39:13 thou the goodly wings unto the *p*

**PEARLS**
Job 28:18 shall be made of coral, or of *p*
Mt 7:6 cast ye your *p* before swine
Mt 13:45 a merchant man, seeking goodly *p*
1Ti 2:9 with broided hair, or gold, or *p*
Rev 17:4 with gold and precious stones and *p*
Rev 18:12 and precious stones, and of *p*
Rev 18:16 gold, and precious stones, and *p*
Rev 21:21 And the twelve gates were twelve *p*

**PECULIAR**
Ex 19:5 then ye shall be a *p* treasure
Deut 14:2 to be a *p* people unto himself
Deut 26:18 thee this day to be his *p* people
Ps 135:4 and Israel for his *p* treasure
Eccl 2:8 the *p* treasure of kings and of the
Titus 2:14 and purify unto himself a *p* people
1Pet 2:9 an holy nation, a *p* people

**PEDAHEL** *(ped'-a-hel) A Naphtalite who apportioned the Promised Land.*
Num 34:28 of Naphtali, *P* the son of Ammihud

**PEDAHZUR** *(pe-dah'-zur) Father of Gamaliel.*
Num 1:10 Gamaliel the son of *P*
Num 2:20 shall be Gamaliel the son of *P*
Num 7:54 day offered Gamaliel the son of *P*
Num 7:59 offering of Gamaliel the son of *P*
Num 10:23 was Gamaliel the son of *P*

**PEDAIAH** *(pe-dah'-yah)*
*1. Grandfather of King Josiah.*
2Kin 23:36 the daughter of *P* of Rumah
*2. Descendant of Jeconiah.*
1Chr 3:18 Malchiram also, and *P*, and Shenazar
1Chr 3:19 And the sons of *P* were, Zerubbabel
*3. Father of Joel.*
1Chr 27:20 of Manasseh, Joel the son of *P*
*4. Son of Parosh.*
Neh 3:25 After him *P* the son of Parosh
*5. A priest who aided Ezra.*
Neh 8:4 and on his left hand, *P*, and
Neh 13:13 the scribe, and of the Levites, *P*
*6. A family of exiles.*
Neh 11:7 the son of Joed, the son of *P*

**PEKAH** *(pe'-kah) A king of Israel.*
2Kin 15:25 But *P* the son of Remaliah, a
2Kin 15:27 *P* the son of Remaliah began to
2Kin 15:29 In the days of *P* king of Israel
2Kin 15:30 against *P* the son of Remaliah
2Kin 15:31 And the rest of the acts of *P*
2Kin 15:32 In the second year of *P* the son
2Kin 15:37 Syria, and *P* the son of Remaliah
2Kin 16:1 In the seventeenth year of *P* the
2Kin 16:5 *P* son of Remaliah king of Israel
2Chr 28:6 For *P* the son of Remaliah slew in
Is 7:1 *P* the son of Remaliah, king of

**PEKAHIAH** *(pe-ka-hi'-ah) Son of King Menahem.*
2Kin 15:22 *P* his son reigned in his stead
2Kin 15:23 *P* the son of Menahem began to
2Kin 15:26 And the rest of the acts of *P*

**PEKOD** *(pe'-kod) Symbolic name for Chaldea.*
Jer 50:21 and against the inhabitants of *P*
Eze 23:23 and all the Chaldeans, *P*, and Shoa

**PELAIAH** *(pel-a-i'-ah)*
*1. A son of Elioenai.*
1Chr 3:24 were, Hodaiah, and Eliashib, and *P*
*2. A priest who aided Ezra.*
Neh 8:7 Azariah, Jozabad, Hanan, *P*
*3. A Levite who renewed the covenant.*
Neh 10:10 Shebaniah, Hodijah, Kelita, *P*

**PELALIAH** *(pel-a-li'-ah) A family of exiles.*
Neh 11:12 the son of Jeroham, the son of *P*

**PELATIAH** *(pel-a-ti'-ah)*
*1. Son of Hananiah.*
1Chr 3:21 of Hananiah; *P*, and Jesaiah
*2. A Simeonite captain.*
1Chr 4:42 Seir, having for their captains *P*
*3. A family who renewed the covenant.*
Neh 10:22 *P*, Hanan, Anaiah,
*4. Son of Benaiah.*
Eze 11:1 *P* the son of Benaiah, princes of
Eze 11:13 that *P* the son of Benaiah died

**PELEG** *(pe'-leg)* See PHALEC. *A son of Eber.*
Gen 10:25 the name of one was *P*
Gen 11:16 four and thirty years, and begat *P*
Gen 11:17 after he begat *P* four hundred
Gen 11:18 *P* lived thirty years, and begat
Gen 11:19 *P* lived after he begat Reu two
1Chr 1:19 the name of the one was *P*
1Chr 1:25 Eber, *P*, Reu,

**PELET** *(pe'-let)* See BETH-PALET.
*1. A son of Jahdai.*
1Chr 2:47 Jotham, and Gesham, and *P*
*2. A captain in David's army.*
1Chr 12:3 and Jeziel, and *P*, the sons of

**PELETH** *(pe'-leth)*
*1. Father of On.*
Num 16:1 of Eliab, and On, the son of *P*
1Chr 2:33 of Jonathan; *P*, and Zaza

**PELETHITES** *(pel'-e-thites) A company of David's bodyguards.*
2Sa 8:18 both the Cherethites and the *P*
2Sa 15:18 all the Cherethites, and all the *P*
2Sa 20:7 men, and the Cherethites, and the *P*
2Sa 20:23 the Cherethites and over the *P*
1Kin 1:38 and the Cherethites, and the *P*
1Kin 1:44 and the Cherethites, and the *P*
1Chr 18:17 was over the Cherethites and the *P*

**PELICAN**
Lev 11:18 And the swan, and the *p*, and the
Deut 14:17 And the *p*, and the gier eagle, and
Ps 102:6 I am like a *p* of the wilderness

**PELONITE** *(pel'-o-nite)* See PALTITE.
*1. Family name of Helez.*
1Chr 11:27 the Harorite, Helez the *P*
1Chr 27:10 the seventh month was Helez the *P*
*2. Family name of Ahijah.*
1Chr 11:36 the Mecherathite, Ahijah the *P*

**PEN**
Judg 5:14 that handle the *p* of the writer
Job 19:24 they were graven with an iron *p*
Ps 45:1 my tongue is the *p* of a ready
Is 8:1 in it with a man's *p* concerning
Jer 8:8 the *p* of the scribes is in vain
Jer 17:1 Judah is written with a *p* of iron
3Jn 13 not with ink and *p* write unto thee

**PENCE**
Mt 18:28 which owed him an hundred *p*
Mk 14:5 for more than three hundred *p*
Lk 7:41 the one owed five hundred *p*
Lk 10:35 he departed, he took out two *p*
Jn 12:5 ointment sold for three hundred *p*

**PENIEL** *(pe-ni'-el)* See PENUEL. *Same as Penuel.*
Gen 32:30 called the name of the place *P*

**PENINNAH** *(pe-nin'-nah) A wife of Elkanah.*
1Sa 1:2 and the name of the other *P*
1Sa 1:2 *P* had children, but Hannah had no
1Sa 1:4 offered, he gave to *P* his wife

**PENNY**
Mt 20:2 with the labourers for a *p* a day
Mt 20:9 hour, they received every man a *p*
Mt 20:10 likewise received every man a *p*
Mt 20:13 not thou agree with me for a *p*
Mt 22:19 And they brought unto him a *p*
Mk 12:15 bring me a *p*, that I may see it
Lk 20:24 Shew me a *p*
Rev 6:6 say, A measure of wheat for a *p*
Rev 6:6 three measures of barley for a *p*

**PENTECOST** *(pen'-te-cost) Greek name for Passover.*
Acts 2:1 when the day of *P* was fully come
Acts 20:16 to be at Jerusalem the day of *P*
1Cor 16:8 I will tarry at Ephesus until *P*

**PENUEL** *(pe-nu'-el)* See PENIEL.
*1. Where Jacob wrestled God.*
Gen 32:31 as he passed over *P* the sun rose
Judg 8:8 And he went up thence to *P*
Judg 8:8 the men of *P* answered him as the
Judg 8:9 he spake also unto the men of *P*
Judg 8:17 And he beat down the tower of *P*
*2. Father of Gedor.*
1Chr 4:4 *P* the father of Gedor, and Ezer
*3. A son of Shashak.*
1Chr 8:25 And Iphedeiah, and *P*, the sons of

**PEOR** *(pe'-or)* See BAAL-PEOR, BETH-PEOR, PEOR'S.
*1. A Moabite god.*
Num 25:18 beguiled you in the matter of *P*
Num 31:16 the LORD in the matter of *P*
Josh 22:17 iniquity of *P* too little for us
*2. A mountain.*
Num 23:28 brought Balaam unto the top of *P*

**PEOR'S**
Num 25:18 the day of the plague for *P* sake

**PERADVENTURE**
Gen 18:24 *P* there be fifty righteous within
Gen 18:28 *P* there shall lack five of the
Gen 18:29 *P* there shall be forty found
Gen 18:30 *P* there shall thirty be found
Gen 18:31 *P* there shall be twenty found
Gen 18:32 *P* ten shall be found there
Gen 24:5 *P* the woman will not be willing
Gen 24:39 *P* the woman will not follow me
Gen 27:12 My father *p* will feel me, and I
Gen 31:31 *P* thou wouldest take by force thy
Gen 32:20 *p* he will accept of me
Gen 38:11 Lest *p* he die also, as his
Gen 42:4 Lest *p* mischief befall him
Gen 43:12 *p* it was an oversight
Gen 44:34 lest *p* I see the evil that shall
Gen 50:15 they said, Joseph will *p* hate us
Ex 13:17 Lest *p* the people repent when
Ex 32:30 *p* I shall make an atonement for
Num 22:6 *p* I shall prevail, that we may
Num 22:11 *p* I shall be able to overcome
Num 23:3 *p* the LORD will come to meet me
Num 23:27 *p* it will please God that thou
Josh 9:7 the Hivites, *P* ye dwell among us
1Sa 6:5 *p* he will lighten his hand from
1Sa 9:6 *p* he can shew us our way that we
1Kin 18:5 *p* we may find grass to save the
1Kin 18:27 or *p* he sleepeth, and must be
1Kin 20:31 *p* he will save thy life
2Kin 2:16 lest *p* the Spirit of the LORD
Jer 20:10 *P* he will be enticed, and we shall
Rom 5:7 yet *p* for a good man some would
2Ti 2:25 if God *p* will give them

**PERAZIM** *(per'-a-zim) Where David defeated the Philistines.*
Is 28:21 LORD shall rise up as in mount *P*

**PERCEIVE**
Deut 29:4 hath not given you an heart to *p*
Josh 22:31 This day we *p* that the LORD is
1Sa 12:17 that ye may *p* and see that your
2Sa 19:6 for this day I *p*, that if Absalom
2Kin 4:9 I *p* that this is an holy man of
Job 9:11 passeth on also, but I *p* him not
Job 23:8 and backward, but I cannot *p* him
Prov 1:2 to *p* the words of understanding
Eccl 3:22 Wherefore I *p* that there is
Is 6:9 and see ye indeed, but *p* not
Is 33:19 a deeper speech than thou canst *p*
Mt 13:14 ye shall see, and shall not *p*
Mk 4:12 seeing they may see, and not *p*
Mk 7:18 Do ye not *p*, that whatsoever
Mk 8:17 *p* ye not yet, neither understand
Lk 8:46 for I *p* that virtue is gone out
Jn 4:19 I *p* that thou art a prophet
Jn 12:19 *P* ye how ye prevail nothing
Acts 8:23 For I *p* that thou art in the gall
Acts 10:34 Of a truth I *p* that God is no
Acts 17:22 I *p* that in all things ye are too
Acts 27:10 I *p* that this voyage will be with
Acts 28:26 and seeing ye shall see, and not *p*
2Cor 7:8 for I *p* that the same epistle
1Jn 3:16 Hereby *p* we the love of God,

**PERCEIVED**
Gen 19:33 he *p* not when she lay down, nor
Gen 19:35 he *p* not when she lay down, nor
Judg 6:22 when Gideon *p* that he was an
1Sa 3:8 Eli *p* that the LORD had called
1Sa 28:14 Saul *p* that it was Samuel, and he
2Sa 5:12 David *p* that the LORD had
2Sa 12:19 David *p* that the child was dead
2Sa 14:1 *p* that the king's heart was
1Kin 22:33 *p* that it was not the king of
1Chr 14:2 David *p* that the LORD had
2Chr 18:32 *p* that it was not the king of
Neh 6:12 I *p* that God had not sent him
Neh 6:16 for they *p* that this work was
Neh 13:10 I *p* that the portions of the
Est 4:1 When Mordecai *p* all that was done
Job 38:18 Hast thou *p* the breadth of the
Eccl 1:17 I *p* that this also is vexation of
Eccl 2:14 I myself *p* also that one event
Is 64:4 nor *p* by the ear, neither hath
Jer 23:18 counsel of the LORD, and hath *p*
Jer 38:27 for the matter was not *p*
Mt 16:8 Which when Jesus *p*, he said unto
Mt 21:45 they *p* that he spake of them
Mt 22:18 But Jesus *p* their wickedness, and
Mk 2:8 immediately when Jesus *p* in his
Lk 1:22 they *p* that he had seen a vision
Lk 5:22 But when Jesus *p* their thoughts
Lk 9:45 hid from them, that they *p* it not
Lk 20:19 for they *p* that he had spoken
Lk 20:23 But he *p* their craftiness, and
Jn 6:15 therefore *p* that they would come
Acts 4:13 *p* that they were unlearned and
Acts 23:6 But when Paul *p* that the one part
Acts 23:29 Whom I *p* to be accused of
Gal 2:9 *p* the grace that was given unto

**PERDITION**
Jn 17:12 of them is lost, but the son of *p*
Phil 1:28 is to them an evident token of *p*
2Th 2:3 of sin be revealed, the son of *p*
1Ti 6:9 drown men in destruction and *p*
Heb 10:39 not of them who draw back unto *p*
2Pet 3:7 of judgment and *p* of ungodly men
Rev 17:8 the bottomless pit, and go into *p*
Rev 17:11 is of the seven, and goeth into *p*

**PERES** *(pe'-res) Portion of "the handwriting on the wall."*
Dan 5:28 *P*; Thy kingdom is

**PERESH** *(pe'-resh) A son of Machir.*
1Chr 7:16 a son, and she called his name *P*

**PEREZ** *(pe'-rez)* See PEREZ-UZZAH, PHARES.
*1. An ancestor of Jashobeam.*
1Chr 27:3 Of the children of *P* was the
*2. A son of Judah; same as Pharez.*
Neh 11:4 Mahalaleel, of the children of *P*
Neh 11:6 All the sons of *P* that dwelt at

**PEREZ-UZZA** *(pe'-rez-uz'-zah)* See PEREZ-UZZAH. *Where Uzza died.*
1Chr 13:11 place is called *P* to this day

**PEREZ-UZZAH** *(pe'-rez-uz'-zah)* See PEREZ-UZZA. *Same as Perez-uzza.*
2Sa 6:8 name of the place *P* to this day

**PERFECT**
Gen 6:9 *p* in his generations, and Noah
Gen 17:1 walk before me, and be thou *p*
Lev 22:21 it shall be *p* to be accepted
Deut 18:13 Thou shalt be *p* with the LORD thy
Deut 25:15 a *p* and just weight, a *p*
Deut 32:4 He is the Rock, his work is *p*
1Sa 14:41 LORD God of Israel, Give a *p* lot
2Sa 22:31 As for God, his way is *p*
2Sa 22:33 and he maketh my way *p*
1Kin 8:61 be *p* with the LORD our God
1Kin 11:4 his heart was not *p* with the LORD
1Kin 15:3 his heart was not *p* with the LORD
1Kin 15:14 was *p* with the LORD all his days
2Kin 20:3 thee in truth and with a *p* heart
1Chr 12:38 came with a *p* heart to Hebron, to
1Chr 28:9 and serve him with a *p* heart
1Chr 29:9 because with *p* heart they offered
1Chr 29:19 unto Solomon my son a *p* heart
2Chr 4:21 made he of gold, and that *p* gold
2Chr 15:17 heart of Asa was *p* all his days
2Chr 16:9 them whose heart is *p* toward him
2Chr 19:9 faithfully, and with a *p* heart
2Chr 25:2 the LORD, but not with a *p* heart
Ezr 7:12 *p* peace, and at such a time
Job 1:1 and that man was *p* and upright, and
Job 1:8 none like him in the earth, a *p*
Job 2:3 none like him in the earth, a *p*
Job 8:20 God will not cast away a *p* man
Job 9:20 if I say, I am *p*, it shall also
Job 9:21 Though I were *p*, yet would I not
Job 9:22 I said it, He destroyeth the *p*
Job 22:3 him, that thou makest thy ways *p*
Job 36:4 he that is *p* in knowledge is with
Job 37:16 of him which is *p* in knowledge
Ps 18:30 As for God, his way is *p*
Ps 18:32 with strength, and maketh my way *p*
Ps 19:7 The law of the LORD is *p*,
Ps 37:37 Mark the *p* man, and behold the
Ps 64:4 they may shoot in secret at the *p*
Ps 101:2 behave myself wisely in a *p* way
Ps 101:2 within my house with a *p* heart
Ps 101:6 he that walketh in a *p* way
Ps 138:8 The LORD will *p* that which
Ps 139:22 I hate them with *p* hatred
Prov 2:21 land, and the *p* shall remain in it
Prov 4:18 more and more unto the *p* day
Prov 11:5 of the *p* shall direct his way
Is 18:5 the harvest, when the bud is *p*
Is 26:3 Thou wilt keep him in *p* peace
Is 38:3 thee in truth and with a *p* heart
Is 42:19 who is blind as he that is *p*
Eze 16:14 for it was *p* through my
Eze 27:3 thou hast said, I am of *p* beauty
Eze 27:11 they have made thy beauty *p*
Eze 28:12 full of wisdom, and *p* in beauty
Eze 28:15 Thou wast *p* in thy ways from the
Mt 5:48 Be ye therefore *p*, even as your
Mt 5:48 Father which is in heaven is *p*
Mt 19:21 said unto him, If thou wilt be *p*
Lk 1:3 having had *p* understanding of all
Lk 6:40 but every one that is *p* shall be
Jn 17:23 that they may be made *p* in one
Acts 3:16 *p* soundness in the presence of
Acts 22:3 taught according to the *p* manner
Acts 24:22 having more *p* knowledge of that
Rom 12:2 is that good, and acceptable, and *p*
1Cor 2:6 wisdom among them that are *p*
1Cor 13:10 But when that which is *p* is come
2Cor 12:9 my strength is made *p* in weakness
2Cor 13:11 Be *p*, be of good comfort, be of
Gal 3:3 are ye now made *p* by the flesh
Eph 4:13 of the Son of God, unto a *p* man
Phil 3:12 attained, either were already *p*
Phil 3:15 Let us therefore, as many as be *p*
Col 1:28 every man *p* in Christ Jesus
Col 4:12 in prayers, that ye may stand *p*
1Th 3:10 might *p* that which is lacking in
2Ti 3:17 That the man of God may be *p*
Heb 2:10 salvation *p* through sufferings
Heb 5:9 And being made *p*, he became the
Heb 7:19 For the law made nothing *p*
Heb 9:9 make him that did the service *p*
Heb 9:11 more *p* tabernacle, not made with
Heb 10:1 make the comers thereunto *p*
Heb 11:40 without us should not be made *p*
Heb 12:23 to the spirits of just men made *p*
Heb 13:21 Make you *p* in every good work to
Jas 1:4 But let patience have her *p* work
Jas 1:4 that ye may be *p*
Jas 1:17 every *p* gift is from above, and
Jas 1:25 looketh into the *p* law of liberty
Jas 2:22 and by works was faith made *p*
Jas 3:2 not in word, the same is a *p* man
1Pet 5:10 have suffered a while, make you *p*
1Jn 4:17 Herein is our love made *p*
1Jn 4:18 but *p* love casteth out fear
1Jn 4:18 feareth is not made *p* in love
Rev 3:2 not found thy works *p* before God

**PERFECTED**
2Chr 8:16 So the house of the LORD was *p*
2Chr 24:13 and the work was *p* by them
Eze 27:4 thy builders have *p* thy beauty
Mt 21:16 and sucklings thou hast *p* praise
Lk 13:32 and the third day I shall be *p*
Heb 10:14 he hath *p* for ever them that are
1Jn 2:5 him verily is the love of God *p*
1Jn 4:12 in us, and his love is *p* in us

**PERFECTION**
Job 11:7 thou find out the Almighty unto *p*
Job 15:29 the *p* thereof upon the earth
Job 28:3 darkness, and searcheth out all *p*
Ps 50:2 the *p* of beauty, God hath shined
Ps 119:96 I have seen an end of all *p*
Is 47:9 their *p* for the multitude of thy
Lam 2:15 that men call The *p* of beauty
Lk 8:14 this life, and bring no fruit to *p*
2Cor 13:9 and this also we wish, even your *p*

Heb 6:1 of Christ, let us go on unto *p*
Heb 7:11 If therefore *p* were by the

**PERFECTLY**
Jer 23:20 days ye shall consider it *p*
Mt 14:36 many as touched were made *p* whole
Acts 18:26 unto him the way of God more *p*
Acts 23:15 something more *p* concerning him
Acts 23:20 enquire somewhat of him more *p*
1Cor 1:10 but that ye be *p* joined together
1Th 5:2 For yourselves know *p* that the

**PERFORM**
Gen 26:3 I will *p* the oath which I sware
Ex 18:18 not able to *p* it thyself alone
Num 4:23 that enter in to *p* the service
Deut 4:13 which he commanded you to *p*
Deut 9:5 that he may *p* the word which the
Deut 23:23 of thy lips thou shalt keep and *p*
Deut 25:5 *p* the duty of an husband's
Deut 25:7 he will not *p* the duty of my
Ruth 3:13 that if he will *p* unto thee the
1Sa 3:12 In that day I will *p* against Eli
2Sa 14:15 *p* the request of his handmaid
1Kin 6:12 then will I *p* my word with thee,
1Kin 12:15 LORD, that he might *p* his saying
2Kin 23:3 to *p* the words of this covenant
2Kin 23:24 that he might *p* the words of the
2Chr 10:15 that the LORD might *p* his word
2Chr 34:31 to *p* the words of the covenant
Est 5:8 to *p* my request, let the king and
Job 5:12 hands cannot *p* their enterprise
Ps 21:11 which they are not able to *p*
Ps 61:8 ever, that I may daily *p* my vows
Ps 119:106 I have sworn, and I will *p* it
Ps 119:112 heart to *p* thy statutes alway
Is 9:7 of the LORD of hosts will *p* this
Is 19:21 vow a vow unto the LORD, and *p* it
Is 44:28 and shall *p* all my pleasure
Jer 1:12 for I will hasten my word to *p* it
Jer 11:5 That I may *p* the oath which I
Jer 28:6 the LORD *p* thy words which thou
Jer 29:10 *p* my good word toward you, in
Jer 33:14 that I will *p* that good thing
Jer 44:25 We will surely *p* our vows that we
Jer 44:25 your vows, and surely *p* your vows
Eze 12:25 will I say the word, and will *p* it
Mic 7:20 Thou wilt *p* the truth to Jacob,
Nah 1:15 thy solemn feasts, *p* thy vows
Mt 5:33 but shalt *p* unto the Lord thine
Lk 1:72 To *p* the mercy promised to our
Rom 4:21 promised, he was able also to *p*
Rom 7:18 but how to *p* that which is good I
2Cor 8:11 Now therefore *p* the doing of it
Phil 1:6 will *p* it until the day of Jesus

**PERFORMED**
1Sa 15:11 hath not *p* my commandments
1Sa 15:13 I have *p* the commandment of the
2Sa 21:14 and they *p* all that the king
1Kin 8:20 the LORD hath *p* his word that he
2Chr 6:10 The LORD therefore hath *p* his
Neh 9:8 to his seed, and hast *p* thy words
Est 1:15 because she hath not *p* the
Est 5:6 half of the kingdom it shall be *p*
Est 7:2 and it shall be *p*, even to the
Ps 65:1 and unto thee shall the vow be *p*
Is 10:12 that when the Lord hath *p* his
Jer 23:20 till he have *p* the thoughts of
Jer 30:24 until he have *p* the intents of
Jer 34:18 which have not *p* the words of the
Jer 35:14 his sons not to drink wine, are *p*
Jer 35:16 Jonadab the son of Rechab have *p*
Jer 51:29 LORD shall be *p* against Babylon
Eze 37:14 it, and *p* it, saith the LORD
Lk 1:20 day that these things shall be *p*
Lk 2:39 when they had *p* all things
Rom 15:28 When therefore I have *p* this

**PERFORMETH**
Neh 5:13 that *p* not this promise, even
Job 23:14 For he *p* the thing that is
Ps 57:2 unto God that *p* all things for me
Is 44:26 *p* the counsel of his messengers

**PERGA** *(pur'-gah) Capital of Pamphylia.*
Acts 13:13 they came to *P* in Pamphylia
Acts 13:14 But when they departed from *P*
Acts 14:25 they had preached the word in *P*

**PERGAMOS** *(pur'-ga-mos) A city in Mysia in Asia Minor.*
Rev 1:11 and unto Smyrna, and unto *P*
Rev 2:12 angel of the church in *P* write

**PERIDA** *(per-i'-dah) A family of exiles.*
Neh 7:57 of Sophereth, the children of *P*

**PERISH**
Gen 41:36 that the land *p* not through the
Ex 19:21 LORD to gaze, and many of them *p*
Ex 21:26 or the eye of his maid, that it *p*
Lev 26:38 ye shall *p* among the heathen, and
Num 17:12 we die, we *p*, we all *p*
Num 24:20 end shall be that he *p* for ever
Num 24:24 Eber, and he also shall *p* for ever
Deut 4:26 that ye shall soon utterly *p* from
Deut 8:19 this day that ye shall surely *p*
Deut 8:20 before your face, so shall ye *p*
Deut 11:17 lest ye *p* quickly from off the
Deut 26:5 A Syrian ready to *p* was my father
Deut 28:20 and until thou *p* quickly
Deut 28:22 shall pursue thee until thou *p*
Deut 30:18 this day, that ye shall surely *p*
Josh 23:13 until ye *p* from off this good
Josh 23:16 ye shall *p* quickly from off the
Judg 5:31 So let all thine enemies *p*
1Sa 26:10 shall descend into battle, and *p*
1Sa 27:1 I shall now *p* one day by the hand
2Kin 9:8 the whole house of Ahab shall *p*
Est 3:13 to kill, and to cause to *p*
Est 4:16 and if I *p*, I *p*
Est 7:4 destroyed, to be slain, and to *p*
Est 8:11 to slay, and to cause to *p*
Est 9:28 of them *p* from their seed
Job 3:3 Let the day *p* wherein I was born,
Job 4:9 By the blast of God they *p*
Job 4:20 they *p* for ever without any
Job 6:18 they go to nothing, and *p*
Job 8:13 and the hypocrite's hope shall *p*
Job 18:17 shall *p* from the earth, and he
Job 20:7 Yet he shall *p* for ever like his
Job 29:13 that was ready to *p* came upon me
Job 31:19 If I have seen any *p* for want of
Job 34:15 All flesh shall *p* together
Job 36:12 they shall *p* by the sword, and
Ps 1:6 the way of the ungodly shall *p*
Ps 2:12 ye *p* from the way, when his wrath
Ps 9:3 shall fall and *p* at thy presence
Ps 9:18 of the poor shall not *p* for ever
Ps 37:20 But the wicked shall *p*, and the
Ps 41:5 When shall he die, and his name *p*
Ps 49:10 the fool and the brutish person *p*
Ps 49:12 he is like the beasts that *p*
Ps 49:20 not, is like the beasts that *p*
Ps 68:2 so let the wicked *p* at the
Ps 73:27 that are far from thee shall *p*
Ps 80:16 they *p* at the rebuke of thy
Ps 83:17 let them be put to shame, and *p*
Ps 92:9 for, lo, thine enemies shall *p*
Ps 102:26 They shall *p*, but thou shalt
Ps 112:10 the desire of the wicked shall *p*
Ps 146:4 in that very day his thoughts *p*
Prov 10:28 expectation of the wicked shall *p*
Prov 11:7 dieth, his expectation shall *p*
Prov 11:10 and when the wicked *p*, there is
Prov 19:9 and he that speaketh lies shall *p*
Prov 21:28 A false witness shall *p*
Prov 28:28 but when they *p*, the righteous
Prov 29:18 there is no vision, the people *p*
Prov 31:6 drink unto him that is ready to *p*
Eccl 5:14 those riches *p* by evil travail
Is 26:14 and made all their memory to *p*
Is 27:13 ready to *p* in the land of Assyria
Is 29:14 wisdom of their wise men shall *p*
Is 41:11 that strive with thee shall *p*
Is 60:12 that will not serve thee shall *p*
Jer 4:9 the heart of the king shall *p*
Jer 6:21 neighbour and his friend shall *p*
Jer 10:11 even they shall *p* from the earth
Jer 10:15 of their visitation they shall *p*
Jer 18:18 law shall not *p* from the priest
Jer 27:10 drive you out, and ye should *p*
Jer 27:15 drive you out, and that ye might *p*
Jer 40:15 and the remnant in Judah *p*
Jer 48:8 the valley also shall *p*, and the
Jer 51:18 of their visitation they shall *p*
Eze 7:26 the law shall *p* from the priest
Eze 25:7 thee to *p* out of the countries
Dan 2:18 his fellows should not *p* with the
Amos 1:8 of the Philistines shall *p*
Amos 2:14 the flight shall *p* from the swift
Amos 3:15 and the houses of ivory shall *p*
Jonah 1:6 will think upon us, that we *p* not
Jonah 1:14 let us not *p* for this man's life,
Jonah 3:9 his fierce anger, that we *p* not
Zec 9:5 and the king shall *p* from Gaza
Mt 5:29 that one of thy members should *p*
Mt 5:30 that one of thy members should *p*
Mt 8:25 Lord, save us: we *p*
Mt 9:17 runneth out, and the bottles *p*
Mt 18:14 one of these little ones should *p*
Mt 26:52 the sword shall *p* with the sword
Mk 4:38 Master, carest thou not that we *p*
Lk 5:37 spilled, and the bottles shall *p*
Lk 8:24 him, saying, Master, master, we *p*
Lk 13:3 repent, ye shall all likewise *p*
Lk 13:5 repent, ye shall all likewise *p*
Lk 13:33 that a prophet *p* out of Jerusalem
Lk 15:17 and to spare, and I *p* with hunger
Lk 21:18 shall not an hair of your head *p*
Jn 3:15 believeth in him should not *p*
Jn 3:16 believeth in him should not *p*
Jn 10:28 and they shall never *p*, neither
Jn 11:50 and that the whole nation *p* not
Acts 8:20 him, Thy money *p* with thee
Acts 13:41 ye despisers, and wonder, and *p*
Rom 2:12 law shall also *p* without law
1Cor 1:18 is to them that *p* foolishness
1Cor 8:11 shall the weak brother *p*, for
2Cor 2:15 that are saved, and in them that *p*
2Cor 4:16 but though our outward man *p*
Col 2:22 Which all are to *p* with the using
2Th 2:10 of unrighteousness in them that *p*
Heb 1:11 They shall *p*; but thou
2Pet 2:12 shall utterly *p* in their own
2Pet 3:9 not willing that any should *p*

**PERISHED**
Num 16:33 and they *p* from among the
Num 21:30 Heshbon is *p* even unto Dibon, and
Josh 22:20 that man *p* not alone in his
2Sa 1:27 fallen, and the weapons of war *p*
Job 4:7 Remember, I pray thee, who ever *p*
Job 30:2 profit me, in whom old age was *p*
Ps 9:6 their memorial is *p* with them
Ps 10:16 the heathen are *p* out of his land
Ps 83:10 Which *p* at En-dor
Ps 119:92 then have *p* in mine affliction
Eccl 9:6 hatred, and their envy, is now *p*
Jer 7:28 truth is *p*, and is cut off from
Jer 48:36 riches that he hath gotten are *p*
Jer 49:7 is counsel *p* from the prudent
Lam 3:18 my hope is *p* from the LORD
Joel 1:11 the harvest of the field is *p*
Jonah 4:10 up in a night, and *p* in a night
Mic 4:9 is thy counsellor *p*
Mic 7:2 The good man is *p* out of the
Mt 8:32 into the sea, and *p* in the waters
Lk 11:51 which *p* between the altar and the
Acts 5:37 after him: he also *p*
1Cor 15:18 are fallen asleep in Christ are *p*
Heb 11:31 By faith the harlot Rahab *p* not
2Pet 3:6 being overflowed with water, *p*
Jude 11 *p* in the gainsaying of Core

**PERISHETH**
Job 4:11 The old lion *p* for lack of prey,
Prov 11:7 and the hope of unjust men *p*
Eccl 7:15 man that *p* in his righteousness
Is 57:1 The righteous *p*, and no man layeth
Jer 9:12 declare it, for what the land *p*
Jer 48:46 the people of Chemosh *p*
Jn 6:27 Labour not for the meat which *p*
Jas 1:11 the grace of the fashion of it *p*
1Pet 1:7 more precious than of gold that *p*

**PERIZZITE** *(per'-iz-zite)* See PERIZZITES. *A tribe in Judah.*
Gen 13:7 the *P* dwelled then in the land
Ex 33:2 Amorite, and the Hittite, and the *P*
Ex 34:11 and the Hittite, and the *P*
Josh 9:1 the Amorite, the Canaanite, the *P*
Josh 11:3 Amorite, and the Hittite, and the *P*

**PERIZZITES** *(per'-iz-zites)*
Gen 15:20 And the Hittites, and the *P*
Gen 34:30 among the Canaanites and the *P*
Ex 3:8 and the Amorites, and the *P*
Ex 3:17 and the Amorites, and the *P*
Ex 23:23 and the Hittites, and the *P*
Deut 7:1 and the Canaanites, and the *P*
Deut 20:17 the Canaanites, and the *P*
Josh 3:10 and the Hivites, and the *P*
Josh 12:8 and the Canaanites, the *P*
Josh 17:15 there in the land of the *P*
Josh 24:11 you, the Amorites, and the *P*

Judg 1:4 and the *P* into their hand
Judg 1:5 they slew the Canaanites and the *P*
Judg 3:5 Hittites, and Amorites, and *P*
1Kin 9:20 left of the Amorites, Hittites, *P*
2Chr 8:7 and the Amorites, and the *P*
Ezr 9:1 Canaanites, the Hittites, the *P*
Neh 9:8 Hittites, the Amorites, and the *P*

### PERPETUAL
Gen 9:12 is with you, for *p* generations
Ex 29:9 shall be theirs for a *p* statute
Ex 30:8 a *p* incense before the LORD
Ex 31:16 generations, for a *p* covenant
Lev 3:17 It shall be a *p* statute for your
Lev 6:20 fine flour for a meat offering *p*
Lev 24:9 LORD made by fire by a *p* statute
Lev 25:34 for it is their *p* possession
Num 19:21 it shall be a *p* statute unto them
Ps 9:6 destructions are come to a *p* end
Ps 74:3 thy feet unto the *p* desolations
Ps 78:66 he put them to a *p* reproach
Jer 5:22 bound of the sea by a *p* decree
Jer 8:5 slidden back by a *p* backsliding
Jer 15:18 Why is my pain *p*, and my wound
Jer 18:16 land desolate, and a *p* hissing
Jer 23:40 a *p* shame, which shall not be
Jer 25:9 and an hissing, and *p* desolations
Jer 25:12 and will make it *p* desolations
Jer 49:13 cities thereof shall be *p* wastes
Jer 50:5 in a *p* covenant that shall not be
Jer 51:39 may rejoice, and sleep a *p* sleep
Jer 51:57 and they shall sleep a *p* sleep
Eze 35:5 Because thou hast had a *p* hatred
Eze 35:9 I will make thee *p* desolations
Eze 46:14 by a *p* ordinance unto the LORD
Hab 3:6 scattered, the *p* hills did bow
Zeph 2:9 and saltpits, and a *p* desolation

### PERPETUALLY
1Kin 9:3 and mine heart shall be there *p*
2Chr 7:16 and mine heart shall be there *p*
Amos 1:11 all pity, and his anger did tear *p*

### PERPLEXED
Est 3:15 but the city Shushan was *p*
Joel 1:18 the herds of cattle are *p*
Lk 9:7 and he was *p*, because that it was
Lk 24:4 as they were much *p* thereabout
2Cor 4:8 we are *p*, but not in despair

### PERSECUTE
Job 19:22 Why do ye *p* me as God, and are not
Job 19:28 Why *p* we him, seeing the root of
Ps 7:1 save me from all them that *p* me
Ps 7:5 Let the enemy *p* my soul, and take
Ps 10:2 in his pride doth *p* the poor
Ps 31:15 enemies, and from them that *p* me
Ps 35:3 the way against them that *p* me
Ps 35:6 let the angel of the LORD *p* them
Ps 69:26 For they *p* him whom thou hast
Ps 71:11 *p* and take him
Ps 83:15 So *p* them with thy tempest, and
Ps 119:84 judgment on them that *p* me
Ps 119:86 they *p* me wrongfully
Jer 17:18 Let them be confounded that *p* me
Jer 29:18 I will *p* them with the sword,
Lam 3:66 *P* and destroy them in anger from
Mt 5:11 *p* you, and shall say all manner of
Mt 5:44 despitefully use you, and *p* you
Mt 10:23 But when they *p* you in this city,
Mt 23:34 and *p* them from city to city
Lk 11:49 some of them they shall slay and *p*
Lk 21:12 *p* you, delivering you up to the
Jn 5:16 And therefore did the Jews *p* Jesus
Jn 15:20 me, they will also *p* you
Rom 12:14 Bless them which *p* you

### PERSECUTED
Deut 30:7 them that hate thee, which *p* thee
Ps 109:16 but *p* the poor and needy man, that
Ps 119:161 Princes have *p* me without a cause
Ps 143:3 For the enemy hath *p* my soul
Is 14:6 ruled the nations in anger, is *p*
Lam 3:43 hast covered with anger, and *p* us
Mt 5:10 are *p* for righteousness' sake
Mt 5:12 for so *p* they the prophets which
Jn 15:20 If they have *p* me, they will also
Acts 7:52 prophets have not your fathers *p*
Acts 22:4 I *p* this way unto the death,
Acts 26:11 I *p* them even unto strange cities
1Cor 4:12 being *p*, we suffer it
1Cor 15:9 because I *p* the church of God
2Cor 4:9 *P*, but not forsaken
Gal 1:13 measure I *p* the church of God
Gal 1:23 That he which *p* us in times past
Gal 4:29 *p* him that was born after the
1Th 2:15 their own prophets, and have *p* us
Rev 12:13 he *p* the woman which brought

### PERSECUTEST
Acts 9:4 him, Saul, Saul, why *p* thou me
Acts 9:5 Lord said, I am Jesus whom thou *p*
Acts 22:7 me, Saul, Saul, why *p* thou me
Acts 22:8 am Jesus of Nazareth, whom thou *p*
Acts 26:14 tongue, Saul, Saul, why *p* thou me
Acts 26:15 he said, I am Jesus whom thou *p*

### PERSECUTION
Lam 5:5 Our necks are under *p*
Mt 13:21 for when tribulation or *p* ariseth
Mk 4:17 when affliction or *p* ariseth for
Acts 8:1 at that time there was a great *p*
Acts 11:19 the *p* that arose about Stephen
Acts 13:50 raised *p* against Paul and Barnabas
Rom 8:35 tribulation, or distress, or *p*
Gal 5:11 why do I yet suffer *p*
Gal 6:12 suffer *p* for the cross of Christ
2Ti 3:12 in Christ Jesus shall suffer *p*

### PERSECUTIONS
Mk 10:30 and children, and lands, with *p*
2Cor 12:10 reproaches, in necessities, in *p*
2Th 1:4 patience and faith in all your *p*
2Ti 3:11 *P*, afflictions, which came unto
2Ti 3:11 what *p* I endured

### PERSECUTORS
Neh 9:11 their *p* thou threwest into the
Ps 7:13 his arrows against the *p*
Ps 119:157 Many are my *p* and mine enemies
Ps 142:6 deliver me from my *p*
Jer 15:15 visit me, and revenge me of my *p*
Jer 20:11 therefore my *p* shall stumble, and
Lam 1:3 all her *p* overtook her between
Lam 4:19 Our *p* are swifter than the eagles

### PERSIA
(*per'-she-ah*) See ELAM, PERSIAN. *An ancient world power located in present-day Iran.*

2Chr 36:20 the reign of the kingdom of *P*
2Chr 36:22 the first year of Cyrus king of *P*
2Chr 36:22 up the spirit of Cyrus king of *P*
2Chr 36:23 Thus saith Cyrus king of *P*
Ezr 1:1 the first year of Cyrus king of *P*
Ezr 1:1 up the spirit of Cyrus king of *P*
Ezr 1:2 Thus saith Cyrus king of *P*
Ezr 1:8 of *P* bring forth by the hand of
Ezr 3:7 that they had of Cyrus king of *P*
Ezr 4:3 the king of *P* hath commanded us
Ezr 4:5 all the days of Cyrus king of *P*
Ezr 4:5 the reign of Darius king of *P*
Ezr 4:7 unto Artaxerxes king of *P*
Ezr 4:24 of the reign of Darius king of *P*
Ezr 6:14 Darius, and Artaxerxes king of *P*
Ezr 7:1 the reign of Artaxerxes king of *P*
Ezr 9:9 us in the sight of the kings of *P*
Est 1:3 the power of *P* and Media, the
Est 1:14 Memucan, the seven princes of *P*
Est 1:18 Likewise shall the ladies of *P*
Est 10:2 of the kings of Media and *P*
Eze 27:10 They of *P* and of Lud and of Phut
Eze 38:5 *P*, Ethiopia, and Libya with them
Dan 8:20 horns are the kings of Media and *P*
Dan 10:1 of *P* a thing was revealed unto
Dan 10:13 the kingdom of *P* withstood me one
Dan 10:13 there with the kings of *P*
Dan 10:20 to fight with the prince of *P*
Dan 11:2 stand up yet three kings in *P*

### PERSIAN
(*per'-she-un*) *A native of Persia.*

Neh 12:22 to the reign of Darius the *P*
Dan 6:28 and in the reign of Cyrus the *P*

### PERSIANS
(*per'-she-uns*) See ELAMITES.

Est 1:19 written among the laws of the *P*
Dan 5:28 and given to the Medes and *P*
Dan 6:8 to the law of the Medes and *P*
Dan 6:12 to the law of the Medes and *P*
Dan 6:15 *P* is, That no decree nor statute

### PERSIS
(*pur'-sis*) *A Christian in Rome.*

Rom 16:12 Salute the beloved *P*, which

### PERSON
Gen 39:6 And Joseph was a goodly *p*, and well
Ex 12:48 uncircumcised *p* shall eat thereof
Lev 19:15 not respect the *p* of the poor
Lev 19:15 nor honour the *p* of the mighty
Num 5:6 the LORD, and that *p* be guilty
Num 19:17 for an unclean *p* they shall take
Num 19:18 a clean *p* shall take hyssop, and
Num 19:19 the clean *p* shall sprinkle upon
Num 19:22 whatsoever the unclean *p* toucheth
Num 31:19 whosoever hath killed any *p*
Num 35:11 which killeth any *p* at unawares
Num 35:15 any *p* unawares may flee thither
Num 35:30 Whoso killeth any *p*, the murderer
Num 35:30 against any *p* to cause him to die
Deut 15:22 the clean *p* shall eat it alike,
Deut 27:25 reward to slay an innocent *p*
Deut 28:50 shall not regard the *p* of the old
Josh 20:3 that killeth any *p* unawares
Josh 20:9 that whosoever killeth any *p* at
1Sa 9:2 of Israel a goodlier *p* than he
1Sa 16:18 prudent in matters, and a comely *p*
1Sa 25:35 thy voice, and have accepted thy *p*
2Sa 4:11 men have slain a righteous *p* in
2Sa 14:14 neither doth God respect any *p*
2Sa 17:11 thou go to battle in thine own *p*
Job 13:8 Will ye accept his *p*
Job 22:29 and he shall save the humble *p*
Job 32:21 I pray you, accept any man's *p*
Ps 15:4 whose eyes a vile *p* is contemned
Ps 49:10 the fool and the brutish *p* perish
Ps 101:4 I will not know a wicked *p*
Ps 105:37 one feeble *p* among their tribes
Prov 6:12 A naughty *p*, a wicked man,
Prov 18:5 to accept the *p* of the wicked
Prov 24:8 shall be called a mischievous *p*
Prov 28:17 of any *p* shall flee to the pit
Is 32:5 The vile *p* shall be no more
Is 32:6 For the vile *p* will speak villany
Jer 43:6 every *p* that Nebuzar-adan the
Jer 52:25 them that were near the king's *p*
Eze 16:5 field, to the lothing of thy *p*
Eze 33:6 take any *p* from among them, he is
Eze 44:25 at no dead *p* to defile themselves
Dan 11:21 estate shall stand up a vile *p*
Mal 1:8 with thee, or accept thy *p*
Mt 22:16 thou regardest not the *p* of men
Mt 27:24 of the blood of this just *p*
Mk 12:14 thou regardest not the *p* of men
Lk 20:21 acceptest thou the *p* of any
1Cor 5:13 among yourselves that wicked *p*
2Cor 2:10 forgave I it in the *p* of Christ
Gal 2:6 God accepteth no man's *p*
Eph 5:5 no whoremonger, nor unclean *p*
Heb 1:3 and the express image of his *p*
Heb 12:16 be any fornicator, or profane *p*
2Pet 2:5 but saved Noah the eighth *p*

### PERSONS
Gen 14:21 said unto Abram, Give me the *p*
Gen 36:6 all the *p* of his house, and his
Ex 16:16 according to the number of your *p*
Lev 27:2 the *p* shall be for the LORD by
Num 19:18 upon the *p* that were there, and
Num 31:28 of five hundred, both of the *p*
Num 31:30 one portion of fifty, of the *p*
Num 31:35 thirty and two thousand *p* in all
Num 31:40 the *p* were sixteen thousand
Num 31:40 tribute was thirty and two *p*
Num 31:46 And sixteen thousand *p*
Deut 1:17 shall not respect *p* in judgment
Deut 10:17 a terrible, which regardeth not *p*
Deut 10:22 Egypt with threescore and ten *p*
Deut 16:19 thou shalt not respect *p*, neither
Judg 9:2 which are threescore and ten *p*
Judg 9:4 Abimelech hired vain and light *p*
Judg 9:5 being threescore and ten *p*
Judg 9:18 his sons, threescore and ten *p*
Judg 20:39 the men of Israel about thirty *p*
1Sa 9:22 bidden, which were about thirty *p*
1Sa 22:18 five *p* that did wear a linen
1Sa 22:22 all the *p* of thy father's house
2Kin 10:6 the king's sons, being seventy *p*
2Kin 10:7 king's sons, and slew seventy *p*
2Chr 19:7 LORD our God, nor respect of *p*
Job 13:10 you, if ye do secretly accept *p*
Job 34:19 accepteth not the *p* of princes
Ps 26:4 I have not sat with vain *p*
Ps 82:2 accept the *p* of the wicked
Prov 12:11 vain *p* is void of understanding
Prov 24:23 to have respect of *p* in judgment
Prov 28:19 vain *p* shall have poverty enough
Prov 28:21 To have respect of *p* is not good
Jer 52:29 eight hundred thirty and two *p*
Jer 52:30 seven hundred forty and five *p*
Jer 52:30 all the *p* were four thousand and

Lam 4:16 not the *p* of the priests, they
Eze 17:17 building forts, to cut off many *p*
Eze 27:13 they traded the *p* of men and
Jonah 4:11 *p* that cannot discern between
Zeph 3:4 are light and treacherous *p*
Mal 1:9 will he regard your *p*
Lk 15:7 than over ninety and nine just *p*
Acts 10:34 that God is no respecter of *p*
Acts 17:17 the Jews, and with the devout *p*
Rom 2:11 there is no respect of *p* with God
2Cor 1:11 upon us by the means of many *p*
Eph 6:9 is there respect of *p* with him
Col 3:25 and there is no respect of *p*
1Ti 1:10 for liars, for perjured *p*
Jas 2:1 Lord of glory, with respect of *p*
Jas 2:9 But if ye have respect to *p*
1Pet 1:17 who without respect of *p* judgeth
2Pet 3:11 what manner of *p* ought ye to be
Jude 16 having men's *p* in admiration

**PERSUADE**

1Kin 22:20 the LORD said, Who shall *p* Ahab
1Kin 22:21 the LORD, and said, I will *p* him
1Kin 22:22 And he said, Thou shalt *p* him
2Chr 32:11 Doth not Hezekiah *p* you to give
2Chr 32:15 nor *p* you on this manner, neither
Is 36:18 Beware lest Hezekiah *p* you
Mt 28:14 governor's ears, we will *p* him
2Cor 5:11 the terror of the Lord, we *p* men
Gal 1:10 For do I now *p* men, or God

**PERSUADED**

2Chr 18:2 *p* him to go up with him to
Prov 25:15 By long forbearing is a prince *p*
Mt 27:20 elders *p* the multitude that they
Lk 16:31 prophets, neither will they be *p*
Lk 20:6 for they be *p* that John was a
Acts 13:43 *p* them to continue in the grace
Acts 14:19 who *p* the people, and, having
Acts 18:4 and *p* the Jews and the Greeks
Acts 19:26 all Asia, this Paul hath *p*
Acts 21:14 And when he would not be *p*
Acts 26:26 for I am *p* that none of these
Rom 4:21 And being fully *p* that, what he
Rom 8:38 For I am *p*, that neither death,
Rom 14:5 man be fully *p* in his own mind
Rom 14:14 am *p* by the Lord Jesus, that
Rom 15:14 And I myself also am *p* of you
2Ti 1:5 and I am *p* that in thee also
2Ti 1:12 am *p* that he is able to keep that
Heb 6:9 we are *p* better things of you, and
Heb 11:13 were *p* of them, and embraced them,

**PERTAIN**

Lev 7:20 that *p* unto the LORD, having his
Lev 7:21 which *p* unto the LORD, even that
1Sa 25:22 if I leave of all that *p* to him
Rom 15:17 in those things which *p* to God
1Cor 6:3 more things that *p* to this life
2Pet 1:3 us all things that *p* unto life

**PERTAINED**

Num 31:43 (Now the half that *p* unto the
Josh 24:33 a hill that *p* to Phinehas his son
Judg 6:11 that *p* unto Joash the Abi-ezrite
1Sa 25:21 was missed of all that *p* unto him
2Sa 2:15 which *p* to Ish-bosheth the son of
2Sa 9:9 master's son all that *p* to Saul
2Sa 16:4 are all that *p* unto Mephibosheth
1Kin 4:10 to him *p* Sochoh, and all the land
1Kin 4:12 to him *p* Taanach and Megiddo, and
1Kin 4:13 to him *p* the towns of Jair the
1Kin 4:13 to him also *p* the region of Argob
1Kin 7:48 made all the vessels that *p* unto
2Kin 24:7 all that *p* to the king of Egypt
1Chr 9:27 thereof every morning *p* to them
1Chr 11:31 that *p* to the children of
2Chr 12:4 fenced cities which *p* to Judah
2Chr 34:33 that *p* to the children of Israel

**PERTAINETH**

Lev 14:32 get that which *p* to his cleansing
Num 4:16 priest *p* the oil for the light
Deut 22:5 not wear that which *p* unto a man
1Sa 27:6 wherefore Ziklag *p* unto the kings
2Sa 6:12 Obed-edom, and all that *p* unto him
Rom 9:4 to whom *p* the adoption, and the
Heb 7:13 are spoken *p* to another tribe

**PERTAINING**

Josh 13:31 were *p* unto the children of
1Chr 26:32 for every matter *p* to God
Acts 1:3 things *p* to the kingdom of God
Rom 4:1 as *p* to the flesh, hath found
1Cor 6:4 of things *p* to this life, set
Heb 2:17 high priest in things *p* to God
Heb 5:1 for men in things *p* to God
Heb 9:9 perfect, as *p* to the conscience

**PERUDA** *(per'-u-dah)* See PERIDA. *A family of exiles.*

Ezr 2:55 of Sophereth, the children of *P*

**PERVERSE**

Num 22:32 because thy way is *p* before me
Deut 32:5 they are a *p* and crooked
1Sa 20:30 Thou son of the *p* rebellious
Job 6:30 cannot my taste discern *p* things
Job 9:20 perfect, it shall also prove me *p*
Prov 4:24 and *p* lips put far from thee
Prov 8:8 is nothing froward or *p* in them
Prov 12:8 but he that is of a *p* heart shall
Prov 14:2 but he that is *p* in his ways
Prov 17:20 he that hath a *p* tongue falleth
Prov 19:1 than he that is *p* in his lips
Prov 23:33 thine heart shall utter *p* things
Prov 28:6 than he that is *p* in his ways
Prov 28:18 but he that is *p* in his ways
Is 19:14 The LORD hath mingled a *p* spirit
Mt 17:17 *p* generation, how long shall I be
Lk 9:41 *p* generation, how long shall I be
Acts 20:30 men arise, speaking *p* things
Phil 2:15 *p* nation, among whom ye shine as
1Ti 6:5 *P* disputings of men of corrupt

**PERVERSENESS**

Num 23:21 neither hath he seen *p* in Israel
Prov 11:3 but the *p* of transgressors shall
Prov 15:4 but *p* therein is a breach in the
Is 30:12 word, and trust in oppression and *p*
Is 59:3 lies, your tongue hath muttered *p*
Eze 9:9 of blood, and the city full of *p*

**PERVERT**

Deut 16:19 *p* the words of the righteous
Deut 24:17 Thou shalt not *p* the judgment of
Job 8:3 Doth God *p* judgment
Job 8:3 or doth the Almighty *p* justice
Job 34:12 will the Almighty *p* judgment
Prov 17:23 bosom to *p* the ways of judgment
Prov 31:5 *p* the judgment of any of the
Mic 3:9 abhor judgment, and *p* all equity
Acts 13:10 wilt thou not cease to *p* the
Gal 1:7 would *p* the gospel of Christ

**PERVERTED**

1Sa 8:3 and took bribes, and *p* judgment
Job 33:27 *p* that which was right, and it
Is 47:10 and thy knowledge, it hath *p* thee
Jer 3:21 for they have *p* their way
Jer 23:36 for ye have *p* the words of the

**PERVERTETH**

Ex 23:8 *p* the words of the righteous
Deut 27:19 Cursed be he that *p* the judgment
Prov 10:9 but he that *p* his ways shall be
Prov 19:3 The foolishness of man *p* his way
Lk 23:14 unto me, as one that *p* the people

**PESTILENCE**

Ex 5:3 lest he fall upon us with *p*
Ex 9:15 smite thee and thy people with *p*
Lev 26:25 I will send the *p* among you
Num 14:12 I will smite them with the *p*
Deut 28:21 shall make the *p* cleave unto thee
2Sa 24:13 be three days' *p* in thy land
2Sa 24:15 So the LORD sent a *p* upon Israel
1Kin 8:37 in the land famine, if there be *p*
1Chr 21:12 the sword of the LORD, even the *p*
1Chr 21:14 So the LORD sent *p* upon Israel
2Chr 6:28 dearth in the land, if there be *p*
2Chr 7:13 or if I send *p* among my people
2Chr 20:9 us, as the sword, judgment, or *p*
Ps 78:50 but gave their life over to the *p*
Ps 91:3 the fowler, and from the noisome *p*
Ps 91:6 Nor for the *p* that walketh in
Jer 14:12 and by the famine, and by the *p*
Jer 21:6 they shall die of a great *p*
Jer 21:7 are left in this city from the *p*
Jer 21:9 and by the famine, and by the *p*
Jer 24:10 the sword, the famine, and the *p*
Jer 27:8 and with the famine, and with the *p*
Jer 27:13 sword, by the famine, and by the *p*
Jer 28:8 of war, and of evil, and of *p*
Jer 29:17 the sword, the famine, and the *p*
Jer 29:18 with the famine, and with the *p*
Jer 32:24 and of the famine, and of the *p*
Jer 32:36 and by the famine, and by the *p*
Jer 34:17 the LORD, to the sword, to the *p*
Jer 38:2 sword, by the famine, and by the *p*
Jer 42:17 sword, by the famine, and by the *p*
Jer 42:22 sword, by the famine, and by the *p*
Jer 44:13 sword, by the famine, and by the *p*
Eze 5:12 part of thee shall die with the *p*
Eze 5:17 and *p* and blood shall pass through
Eze 6:11 sword, by the famine, and by the *p*
Eze 6:12 is far off shall die of the *p*
Eze 7:15 The sword is without, and the *p*
Eze 7:15 famine and *p* shall devour him
Eze 12:16 from the famine, and from the *p*
Eze 14:19 Or if I send a *p* into that land
Eze 14:21 and the noisome beast, and the *p*
Eze 28:23 For I will send into her *p*
Eze 33:27 in the caves shall die of the *p*
Eze 38:22 I will plead against him with *p*
Amos 4:10 the *p* after the manner of Egypt
Hab 3:5 Before him went the *p*, and burning

**PETER** *(pe'-tur)* See CEPHAS, PETER'S, SIMON. *A disciple of Jesus.*

Mt 4:18 saw two brethren, Simon called *P*
Mt 10:2 The first, Simon, who is called *P*
Mt 14:28 *P* answered him and said, Lord, if
Mt 14:29 when *P* was come down out of the
Mt 15:15 Then answered *P* and said unto him,
Mt 16:16 Simon *P* answered and said, Thou
Mt 16:18 also unto thee, That thou art *P*
Mt 16:22 Then *P* took him, and began to
Mt 16:23 But he turned, and said unto *P*
Mt 17:1 And after six days Jesus taketh *P*
Mt 17:4 Then answered *P*, and said unto
Mt 17:24 received tribute money came to *P*
Mt 17:26 *P* saith unto him, Of strangers
Mt 18:21 Then came *P* to him, and said, Lord
Mt 19:27 Then answered *P* and said unto him,
Mt 26:33 *P* answered and said unto him,
Mt 26:35 *P* said unto him, Though I should
Mt 26:37 And he took with him *P* and the two
Mt 26:40 them asleep, and saith unto *P*
Mt 26:58 But *P* followed him afar off unto
Mt 26:69 Now *P* sat without in the palace
Mt 26:73 they that stood by, and said to *P*
Mt 26:75 *P* remembered the word of Jesus,
Mk 3:16 And Simon he surnamed *P*
Mk 5:37 no man to follow him, save *P*
Mk 8:29 *P* answereth and saith unto him,
Mk 8:32 *P* took him, and began to rebuke
Mk 8:33 on his disciples, he rebuked *P*
Mk 9:2 six days Jesus taketh with him *P*
Mk 9:5 *P* answered and said to Jesus,
Mk 10:28 Then *P* began to say unto him, Lo,
Mk 11:21 *P* calling to remembrance saith
Mk 13:3 Olives over against the temple, *P*
Mk 14:29 But *P* said unto him, Although all
Mk 14:33 And he taketh with him *P* and James
Mk 14:37 them sleeping, and saith unto *P*
Mk 14:54 *P* followed him afar off, even
Mk 14:66 as *P* was beneath in the palace,
Mk 14:67 when she saw *P* warming himself,
Mk 14:70 that stood by said again to *P*
Mk 14:72 *P* called to mind the word that
Mk 16:7 *P* that he goeth before you into
Lk 5:8 When Simon *P* saw it, he fell down
Lk 6:14 Simon, (whom he also named *P*
Lk 8:45 When all denied, *P* and they that
Lk 8:51 suffered no man to go in, save *P*
Lk 9:20 *P* answering said, The Christ of
Lk 9:28 after these sayings, he took *P*
Lk 9:32 But *P* and they that were with him
Lk 9:33 *P* said unto Jesus, Master, it is
Lk 12:41 Then *P* said unto him, Lord,
Lk 18:28 Then *P* said, Lo, we have left all
Lk 22:8 And he sent *P* and John, saying, Go
Lk 22:34 And he said, I tell thee, *P*
Lk 22:54 And *P* followed afar off
Lk 22:55 together, *P* sat down among them
Lk 22:58 And *P* said, Man, I am not
Lk 22:60 *P* said, Man, I know not what thou
Lk 22:61 the Lord turned, and looked upon *P*
Lk 22:61 *P* remembered the word of the Lord
Lk 22:62 *P* went out, and wept bitterly
Lk 24:12 Then arose *P*, and ran unto the
Jn 1:44 the city of Andrew and *P*
Jn 6:68 Then Simon *P* answered him, Lord,
Jn 13:6 Then cometh he to Simon *P*
Jn 13:6 *P* saith unto him, Lord, dost thou
Jn 13:8 *P* saith unto him, Thou shalt
Jn 13:9 Simon *P* saith unto him, Lord, not

Jn 13:24 Simon *P* therefore beckoned to him
Jn 13:36 Simon *P* said unto him, Lord,
Jn 13:37 *P* said unto him, Lord, why cannot
Jn 18:10 Then Simon *P* having a sword drew
Jn 18:11 Then said Jesus unto *P*, Put up
Jn 18:15 Simon *P* followed Jesus, and so did
Jn 18:16 But *P* stood at the door without
Jn 18:16 kept the door, and brought in *P*
Jn 18:17 damsel that kept the door unto *P*
Jn 18:18 *P* stood with them, and warmed
Jn 18:25 And Simon *P* stood and warmed
Jn 18:26 his kinsman whose ear *P* cut off
Jn 18:27 *P* then denied again
Jn 20:2 she runneth, and cometh to Simon *P*
Jn 20:3 *P* therefore went forth, and that
Jn 20:4 the other disciple did outrun *P*
Jn 20:6 Then cometh Simon *P* following him
Jn 21:2 There were together Simon *P*
Jn 21:3 Simon *P* saith unto them, I go a
Jn 21:7 whom Jesus loved saith unto *P*
Jn 21:7 Now when Simon *P* heard that it
Jn 21:11 Simon *P* went up, and drew the net
Jn 21:15 had dined, Jesus saith to Simon *P*
Jn 21:17 *P* was grieved because he said
Jn 21:20 Then *P*, turning about, seeth the
Jn 21:21 *P* seeing him saith to Jesus, Lord
Acts 1:13 an upper room, where abode both *P*
Acts 1:15 in those days *P* stood up in the
Acts 2:14 But *P*, standing up with the
Acts 2:37 in their heart, and said unto *P*
Acts 2:38 Then *P* said unto them, Repent, and
Acts 3:1 Now *P* and John went up together
Acts 3:3 Who seeing *P* and John about to go
Acts 3:4 And *P*, fastening his eyes upon him
Acts 3:6 Then *P* said, Silver and gold have
Acts 3:11 lame man which was healed held *P*
Acts 3:12 when *P* saw it, he answered unto
Acts 4:8 Then *P*, filled with the Holy
Acts 4:13 when they saw the boldness of *P*
Acts 4:19 But *P* and John answered and said
Acts 5:3 But *P* said, Ananias, why hath
Acts 5:8 *P* answered unto her, Tell me
Acts 5:9 Then *P* said unto her, How is it
Acts 5:15 of *P* passing by might overshadow
Acts 5:29 Then *P* and the other apostles
Acts 8:14 of God, they sent unto them *P*
Acts 8:20 But *P* said unto him, Thy money
Acts 9:32 as *P* passed throughout all
Acts 9:34 *P* said unto him, Aeneas, Jesus
Acts 9:38 had heard that *P* was there
Acts 9:39 Then *P* arose and went with them
Acts 9:40 But *P* put them all forth, and
Acts 9:40 and when she saw *P*, she sat up
Acts 10:5 for one Simon, whose surname is *P*
Acts 10:9 *P* went up upon the housetop to
Acts 10:13 came a voice to him, Rise, *P*
Acts 10:14 But *P* said, Not so, Lord
Acts 10:17 Now while *P* doubted in himself
Acts 10:18 Simon, which was surnamed *P*
Acts 10:19 While *P* thought on the vision,
Acts 10:21 Then *P* went down to the men which
Acts 10:23 on the morrow *P* went away with
Acts 10:25 as *P* was coming in, Cornelius met
Acts 10:26 But *P* took him up, saying, Stand
Acts 10:32 hither Simon, whose surname is *P*
Acts 10:34 Then *P* opened his mouth, and said,
Acts 10:44 While *P* yet spake these words,
Acts 10:45 as many as came with *P*, because
Acts 10:46 Then answered *P*,
Acts 11:2 when *P* was come up to Jerusalem,
Acts 11:4 But *P* rehearsed the matter from
Acts 11:7 a voice saying unto me, Arise, *P*
Acts 11:13 for Simon, whose surname is *P*
Acts 12:3 proceeded further to take *P* also
Acts 12:5 *P* therefore was kept in prison
Acts 12:6 the same night *P* was sleeping
Acts 12:7 he smote *P* on the side, and raised
Acts 12:11 when *P* was come to himself, he
Acts 12:13 as *P* knocked at the door of the
Acts 12:14 told how *P* stood before the gate
Acts 12:16 But *P* continued knocking
Acts 12:18 soldiers, what was become of *P*
Acts 15:7 *P* rose up, and said unto them, Men
Gal 1:18 I went up to Jerusalem to see *P*
Gal 2:7 of the circumcision was unto *P*
Gal 2:8 in *P* to the apostleship of the
Gal 2:11 But when *P* was come to Antioch, I
Gal 2:14 I said unto *P* before them all, If
1Pet 1:1 *P*, an apostle of Jesus Christ, to
2Pet 1:1 Simon *P*, a servant and an apostle

**PETHAHIAH** *(peth-a-hi'-ah)*
*1. A sanctuary servant.*
1Chr 24:16 The nineteenth to *P*, the
*2. Married a foreigner.*
Ezr 10:23 Kelaiah, (the same is Kelita,) *P*
*3. A Levite who helped Ezra.*
Neh 9:5 Hodijah, Shebaniah, and *P*
*4. An aide to Nehemiah.*
Neh 11:24 *P* the son of Meshezabeel, of the

**PETHOR** *(pe'-thor) A city in Mesopotamia.*
Num 22:5 unto Balaam the son of Beor to *P*
Deut 23:4 son of Beor of *P* of Mesopotamia

**PETHUEL** *Father of Joel the prophet.*
Joel 1:1 that came to Joel the son of *P*

**PETITION**
1Sa 1:17 thy *p* that thou hast asked of him
1Sa 1:27 me my *p* which I asked of him
1Kin 2:16 And now I ask one *p* of thee
1Kin 2:20 I desire one small *p* of thee
Est 5:6 banquet of wine, What is thy *p*
Est 5:7 answered Esther, and said, My *p*
Est 5:8 it please the king to grant my *p*
Est 7:2 banquet of wine, What is thy *p*
Est 7:3 let my life be given me at my *p*
Est 9:12 now what is thy *p*
Dan 6:7 that whosoever shall ask a *p* of
Dan 6:12 *p* of any God or man within thirty
Dan 6:13 but maketh his *p* three times a

**PEULTHAI** *(pe-ul'-thahee) A sanctuary servant.*
1Chr 26:5 the seventh, *P* the eighth

**PHALEC** *(fa'-lek)* See PELEG. *Father of Ragau; ancestor of Jesus.*
Lk 3:35 of Ragau, which was the son of *P*

**PHALLU** *(fal'-lu) Son of Reuben.*
Gen 46:9 and *P*, and Hezron, and Carmi

**PHALTI** *(fal'-ti)* See PHALTIEL. *Son of Laish.*
1Sa 25:44 to *P* the son of Laish, which was

**PHALTIEL** *(fal'-te-el)* See PHALTI. *Same as Phalti.*
2Sa 3:15 even from *P* the son of Laish

**PHANUEL** *(fan-u'-el) Mother of Anna.*
Lk 2:36 a prophetess, the daughter of *P*

**PHARAOH** *(fa'-ra-o)* See PHARAOH'S, PHARAOH-HOPHRA, PHARAOH-NECHO.
*1. Ruler of Egypt in Abraham's time.*
Gen 12:15 The princes also of *P* saw her
Gen 12:15 and commended her before *P*
Gen 12:17 And the LORD plagued *P* and his
Gen 12:18 *P* called Abram, and said, What is
Gen 12:20 *P* commanded his men concerning
*2. Ruler of Egypt in Joseph's time.*
Gen 39:1 and Potiphar, an officer of *P*
Gen 40:2 *P* was wroth against two of his
Gen 40:13 days shall *P* lift up thine head
Gen 40:14 me, and make mention of me unto *P*
Gen 40:17 of all manner of bakemeats for *P*
Gen 40:19 Yet within three days shall *P*
Gen 41:1 of two full years, that *P* dreamed
Gen 41:4 So *P* awoke
Gen 41:7 *P* awoke, and, behold, it was a
Gen 41:8 and *P* told them his dream
Gen 41:8 that could interpret them unto *P*
Gen 41:9 spake the chief butler unto *P*
Gen 41:10 *P* was wroth with his servants, and
Gen 41:14 Then *P* sent and called Joseph, and
Gen 41:14 his raiment, and came in unto *P*
Gen 41:15 *P* said unto Joseph, I have
Gen 41:16 And Joseph answered *P*, saying, It
Gen 41:16 God shall give *P* an answer of
Gen 41:17 *P* said unto Joseph, In my dream,
Gen 41:25 And Joseph said unto *P*
Gen 41:25 The dream of *P* is one
Gen 41:25 God hath shewed *P* what he is
Gen 41:28 thing which I have spoken unto *P*
Gen 41:28 is about to do he sheweth unto *P*
Gen 41:32 dream was doubled unto *P* twice
Gen 41:33 Now therefore let *P* look out a
Gen 41:34 Let *P* do this, and let him appoint
Gen 41:35 lay up corn under the hand of *P*
Gen 41:37 thing was good in the eyes of *P*
Gen 41:38 *P* said unto his servants, Can we
Gen 41:39 *P* said unto Joseph, Forasmuch as
Gen 41:41 *P* said unto Joseph, See, I have
Gen 41:42 *P* took off his ring from his hand
Gen 41:44 *P* said unto Joseph, I am Pharaoh,
Gen 41:45 And *P* called Joseph's name
Gen 41:46 he stood before *P* king of Egypt
Gen 41:46 went out from the presence of *P*
Gen 41:55 the people cried to *P* for bread
Gen 41:55 *P* said unto all the Egyptians, Go
Gen 42:15 By the life of *P* ye shall not go
Gen 42:16 the life of *P* surely ye are spies
Gen 44:18 for thou art even as *P*
Gen 45:2 Egyptians and the house of *P* heard
Gen 45:8 and he hath made me a father to *P*
Gen 45:16 and it pleased *P* well, and his
Gen 45:17 *P* said unto Joseph, Say unto thy
Gen 45:21 according to the commandment of *P*
Gen 46:5 in the wagons which *P* had sent to
Gen 46:31 house, I will go up, and shew *P*
Gen 46:33 when *P* shall call you, and shall
Gen 47:1 Then Joseph came and told *P*
Gen 47:2 men, and presented them unto *P*
Gen 47:3 *P* said unto his brethren, What is
Gen 47:3 And they said unto *P*, Thy servants
Gen 47:4 They said moreover unto *P*
Gen 47:5 *P* spake unto Joseph, saying, Thy
Gen 47:7 his father, and set him before *P*
Gen 47:7 and Jacob blessed *P*
Gen 47:8 *P* said unto Jacob, How old art
Gen 47:9 And Jacob said unto *P*, The days of
Gen 47:10 And Jacob blessed *P*
Gen 47:10 and went out from before *P*
Gen 47:11 of Rameses, as *P* had commanded
Gen 47:19 our land will be servants unto *P*
Gen 47:20 all the land of Egypt for *P*
Gen 47:22 had a portion assigned them of *P*
Gen 47:22 their portion which *P* gave them
Gen 47:23 you this day and your land for *P*
Gen 47:24 shall give the fifth part unto *P*
Gen 47:26 that *P* should have the fifth part
Gen 50:4 Joseph spake unto the house of *P*
Gen 50:4 I pray you, in the ears of *P*
Gen 50:6 *P* said, Go up, and bury thy father
Gen 50:7 him went up all the servants of *P*
Acts 7:10 in the sight of *P* king of Egypt
Acts 7:13 kindred was made known unto *P*
*3. Ruler of Egypt during Moses' infancy.*
Ex 1:11 they built for *P* treasure cities,
Ex 1:19 And the midwives said unto *P*
Ex 1:22 *P* charged all his people, saying,
Ex 2:5 the daughter of *P* came down to
*4. Ruler of Egypt during Moses' adulthood.*
Ex 2:15 Now when *P* heard this thing, he
Ex 2:15 But Moses fled from the face of *P*
*5. Ruler of Egypt when Moses returned to Egypt.*
Ex 3:10 and I will send thee unto *P*
Ex 3:11 Who am I, that I should go unto *P*
Ex 4:21 do all those wonders before *P*
Ex 4:22 And thou shalt say unto *P*, Thus
Ex 5:1 Moses and Aaron went in, and told *P*
Ex 5:2 *P* said, Who is the LORD, that I
Ex 5:5 *P* said, Behold, the people of the
Ex 5:6 *P* commanded the same day the
Ex 5:10 the people, saying, Thus saith *P*
Ex 5:15 of Israel came and cried unto *P*
Ex 5:20 way, as they came forth from *P*
Ex 5:21 to be abhorred in the eyes of *P*
Ex 5:23 For since I came to *P* to speak in
Ex 6:1 thou see what I will do to *P*
Ex 6:11 speak unto *P* king of Egypt, that
Ex 6:12 how then shall *P* hear me, who am
Ex 6:13 unto *P* king of Egypt, to bring
Ex 6:27 which spake to *P* king of Egypt
Ex 6:29 speak thou unto *P* king of Egypt
Ex 6:30 how shall *P* hearken unto me
Ex 7:1 See, I have made thee a god to *P*
Ex 7:2 thy brother shall speak unto *P*
Ex 7:4 But *P* shall not hearken unto you,
Ex 7:7 years old, when they spake unto *P*
Ex 7:9 When *P* shall speak unto you,
Ex 7:9 Take thy rod, and cast it before *P*
Ex 7:10 And Moses and Aaron went in unto *P*
Ex 7:10 Aaron cast down his rod before *P*
Ex 7:11 Then *P* also called the wise men
Ex 7:15 Get thee unto *P* in the morning
Ex 7:20 in the river, in the sight of *P*
Ex 7:23 *P* turned and went into his house,
Ex 8:1 LORD spake unto Moses, Go unto *P*
Ex 8:8 Then *P* called for Moses and Aaron,
Ex 8:9 And Moses said unto *P*, Glory over

Ex 8:12 And Moses and Aaron went out from *P*
Ex 8:12 which he had brought against *P*
Ex 8:15 But when *P* saw that there was
Ex 8:19 Then the magicians said unto *P*
Ex 8:20 in the morning, and stand before *P*
Ex 8:24 of flies into the house of *P*
Ex 8:25 *P* called for Moses and for Aaron,
Ex 8:28 *P* said, I will let you go, that
Ex 8:29 swarms of flies may depart from *P*
Ex 8:29 but let not *P* deal deceitfully
Ex 8:30 And Moses went out from *P*, and
Ex 8:31 the swarms of flies from *P*
Ex 8:32 *P* hardened his heart at this time
Ex 9:1 said unto Moses, Go in unto *P*
Ex 9:7 *P* sent, and, behold, there was not
Ex 9:7 And the heart of *P* was hardened
Ex 9:8 the heaven in the sight of *P*
Ex 9:10 of the furnace, and stood before *P*
Ex 9:12 the LORD hardened the heart of *P*
Ex 9:13 in the morning, and stand before *P*
Ex 9:20 servants of *P* made his servants
Ex 9:27 *P* sent, and called for Moses and
Ex 9:33 Moses went out of the city from *P*
Ex 9:34 when *P* saw that the rain and the
Ex 9:35 And the heart of *P* was hardened
Ex 10:1 said unto Moses, Go in unto *P*
Ex 10:3 And Moses and Aaron came in unto *P*
Ex 10:6 himself, and went out from *P*
Ex 10:8 Aaron were brought again unto *P*
Ex 10:16 Then *P* called for Moses and Aaron
Ex 10:18 And he went out from *P*, and
Ex 10:24 *P* called unto Moses, and said, Go
Ex 10:28 *P* said unto him, Get thee from me
Ex 11:1 I bring one plague more upon *P*
Ex 11:5 from the firstborn of *P* that
Ex 11:8 went out from *P* in a great anger
Ex 11:9 *P* shall not hearken unto you
Ex 11:10 did all these wonders before *P*
Ex 12:29 from the firstborn of *P* that sat
Ex 12:30 *P* rose up in the night, he, and
Ex 13:15 when *P* would hardly let us go,
Ex 13:17 when *P* had let the people go,
Ex 14:3 For *P* will say of the children of
Ex 14:4 and I will be honoured upon *P*
Ex 14:5 and the heart of *P* and of his
Ex 14:8 the heart of *P* king of Egypt
Ex 14:9 all the horses and chariots of *P*
Ex 14:10 when *P* drew nigh, the children of
Ex 14:17 and I will get me honour upon *P*
Ex 14:18 I have gotten me honour upon *P*
Ex 14:28 all the host of *P* that came into
Ex 15:19 For the horse of *P* went in with
Ex 18:4 delivered me from the sword of *P*
Ex 18:8 all that the LORD had done unto *P*
Ex 18:10 and out of the hand of *P*, who
Deut 6:22 great and sore, upon Egypt, upon *P*
Deut 7:8 from the hand of *P* king of Egypt
Deut 7:18 what the LORD thy God did unto *P*
Deut 11:3 of Egypt unto *P* the king of Egypt
Deut 29:2 eyes in the land of Egypt unto *P*
Deut 34:11 to do in the land of Egypt to *P*
1Sa 6:6 and *P* hardened their hearts
2Kin 17:7 under the hand of *P* king of Egypt
Neh 9:10 shewedst signs and wonders upon *P*
Ps 135:9 midst of thee, O Egypt, upon *P*
Ps 136:15 But overthrew *P* and his host in
Rom 9:17 For the scripture saith unto *P*

*6. Ruler of Egypt in Solomon's time.*

1Kin 3:1 affinity with *P* king of Egypt
1Kin 9:16 For *P* king of Egypt had gone up,
1Kin 11:1 together with the daughter of *P*
1Kin 11:18 to Egypt, unto *P* king of Egypt
1Kin 11:19 great favour in the sight of *P*
1Kin 11:20 household among the sons of *P*
1Kin 11:21 host was dead, Hadad said to *P*
1Kin 11:22 Then *P* said unto him, But what
2Chr 8:11 brought up the daughter of *P* out

*7. Ruler of Egypt in Isaiah's time.*

Is 19:11 of *P* is become brutish
Is 19:11 how say ye unto *P*, I am the son
Is 30:2 themselves in the strength of *P*
Is 30:3 the strength of *P* be your shame
Is 36:6 so is *P* king of Egypt to all that

*8. Ruler of Egypt in Jeremiah's time.*

2Kin 18:21 so is *P* king of Egypt unto all
2Kin 23:35 gave the silver and the gold to *P*
2Kin 23:35 according to the commandment of *P*
1Chr 4:18 sons of Bithiah the daughter of *P*
Jer 25:19 *P* king of Egypt, and his servants,
Jer 46:17 *P* king of Egypt is but a noise
Jer 46:25 punish the multitude of No, and *P*
Jer 46:25 even *P*, and all them that trust in
Jer 47:1 before that *P* smote Gaza
Eze 17:17 Neither shall *P* with his mighty
Eze 29:2 thy face against *P* king of Egypt
Eze 29:3 *P* king of Egypt, the great dragon
Eze 30:21 broken the arm of *P* king of Egypt
Eze 30:22 I am against *P* king of Egypt, and
Eze 30:25 the arms of *P* shall fall down
Eze 31:2 speak unto *P* king of Egypt, and to
Eze 31:18 This is *P* and all his multitude,
Eze 32:2 a lamentation for *P* king of Egypt
Eze 32:31 *P* shall see them, and shall be
Eze 32:31 over all his multitude, even *P*
Eze 32:32 are slain with the sword, even *P*

**PHARAOH-HOPHRA** *(fa'-ra-o-hof'-rah)* *Same as Pharaoh 8.*

Jer 44:30 I will give *P* king of Egypt into

**PHARAOH-NECHO** *(fa'-ra-o-ne'-ko)* See PHARAOH-NECHOH. *Egyptian ruler during Josiah's time.*

Jer 46:2 the army of *P* king of Egypt

**PHARAOH-NECHOH** *(fa'-ra-o-ne'-ko)* See PHARAOH-NECHO. *Same as Pharaoh-necho.*

2Kin 23:29 In his days *P* king of Egypt went
2Kin 23:33 *P* put him in bands at Riblah in
2Kin 23:34 *P* made Eliakim the son of Josiah
2Kin 23:35 his taxation, to give it unto *P*

**PHARAOH'S** *(fa'-ra-oze)*

Gen 12:15 the woman was taken into *P* house
Gen 37:36 unto Potiphar, an officer of *P*
Gen 40:7 he asked *P* officers that were
Gen 40:11 And *P* cup was in my hand
Gen 40:11 and pressed them into *P* cup
Gen 40:11 and I gave the cup into *P* hand
Gen 40:13 shalt deliver *P* cup into his hand
Gen 40:20 third day, which was *P* birthday
Gen 40:21 and he gave the cup into *P* hand
Gen 45:16 fame thereof was heard in *P* house
Gen 47:14 brought the money into *P* house
Gen 47:20 so the land became *P*
Gen 47:25 my lord, and we will be *P* servants
Gen 47:26 priests only, which became not *P*
Ex 2:7 said his sister to *P* daughter
Ex 2:8 *P* daughter said to her, Go
Ex 2:9 *P* daughter said unto her, Take
Ex 2:10 she brought him unto *P* daughter
Ex 5:14 which *P* taskmasters had set over
Ex 7:3 And I will harden *P* heart, and
Ex 7:13 And he hardened *P* heart, that he
Ex 7:14 *P* heart is hardened, he refuseth
Ex 7:22 *P* heart was hardened, neither did
Ex 8:19 *P* heart was hardened, and he
Ex 10:7 *P* servants said unto him, How
Ex 10:11 were driven out from *P* presence
Ex 10:20 But the LORD hardened *P* heart
Ex 10:27 But the LORD hardened *P* heart
Ex 11:3 Egypt, in the sight of *P* servants
Ex 11:10 and the LORD hardened *P* heart
Ex 14:4 And I will harden *P* heart, that he
Ex 14:23 of the sea, even all *P* horses
Ex 15:4 *P* chariots and his host hath he
Deut 6:21 We were *P* bondmen in Egypt
1Sa 2:27 they were in Egypt in *P* house
1Kin 3:1 took *P* daughter, and brought her
1Kin 7:8 made also an house for *P* daughter
1Kin 9:24 But *P* daughter came up out of the
1Kin 11:20 whom Tahpenes weaned in *P* house
1Kin 11:20 Genubath was in *P* household among
Song 1:9 a company of horses in *P* chariots
Jer 37:5 Then *P* army was come forth out of
Jer 37:7 *P* army, which is come forth to
Jer 37:11 from Jerusalem for fear of *P* army
Jer 43:9 the entry of *P* house in Tahpanhes
Eze 30:24 but I will break *P* arms, and he
Acts 7:21 *P* daughter took him up, and
Heb 11:24 be called the son of *P* daughter

**PHARES** *(fa'-rez)* See PHAREZ. *Same as Pharez.*

Mt 1:3 And Judas begat *P* and Zara of
Mt 1:3 and *P* begat Esrom
Lk 3:33 of Esrom, which was the son of *P*

**PHAREZ** *(fa'-rez)* See PEREZ, PHARES, PHARZITES. *A son of Judah.*

Gen 38:29 therefore his name was called *P*
Gen 46:12 Er, and Onan, and Shelah, and *P*
Gen 46:12 And the sons of *P* were Hezron
Num 26:20 of *P*, the family of the Pharzites
Num 26:21 And the sons of *P* were
Ruth 4:12 thy house be like the house of *P*
Ruth 4:18 these are the generations of *P*
Ruth 4:18 *P* begat Hezron,
1Chr 2:4 his daughter in law bare him *P*
1Chr 2:5 The sons of *P*
1Chr 4:1 *P*, Hezron, and Carmi, and Hur, and
1Chr 9:4 children of *P* the son of Judah

**PHARISEE** *(far'-i-see)* See PHARISEE'S, PHARISEES. *A member of a Jewish sect.*

Mt 23:26 Thou blind *P*, cleanse first that
Lk 7:39 Now when the *P* which had bidden
Lk 11:37 a certain *P* besought him to dine
Lk 11:38 And when the *P* saw it, he
Lk 18:10 the one a *P*, and the other a
Lk 18:11 The *P* stood and prayed thus with
Acts 5:34 there up one in the council, a *P*
Acts 23:6 I am a *P*, the son of a *P*
Acts 26:5 sect of our religion I lived a *P*
Phil 3:5 as touching the law, a *P*

**PHARISEE'S** *(far'-i-seze)*

Lk 7:36 And he went into the *P* house
Lk 7:37 Jesus sat at meat in the *P* house

**PHARISEES** *(far'-i-seze)* See PHARISEES'. *A Jewish sect.*

Mt 3:7 But when he saw many of the *P*
Mt 5:20 righteousness of the scribes and *P*
Mt 9:11 And when the *P* saw it, they said
Mt 9:14 the *P* fast oft, but thy disciples
Mt 9:34 But the *P* said, He casteth out
Mt 12:2 But when the *P* saw it, they said
Mt 12:14 Then the *P* went out, and held a
Mt 12:24 But when the *P* heard it, they
Mt 12:38 of the *P* answered, saying, Master
Mt 15:1 Then came to Jesus scribes and *P*
Mt 15:12 thou that the *P* were offended
Mt 16:1 The *P* also with the Sadducees
Mt 16:6 and beware of the leaven of the *P*
Mt 16:11 beware of the leaven of the *P*
Mt 16:12 but of the doctrine of the *P*
Mt 19:3 The *P* also came unto him,
Mt 21:45 *P* had heard his parables, they
Mt 22:15 Then went the *P*, and took counsel
Mt 22:34 But when the *P* had heard that he
Mt 22:41 While the *P* were gathered
Mt 23:2 and the *P* sit in Moses' seat
Mt 23:13 But woe unto you, scribes and *P*
Mt 23:14 Woe unto you, scribes and *P*
Mt 23:15 Woe unto you, scribes and *P*
Mt 23:23 Woe unto you, scribes and *P*
Mt 23:25 Woe unto you, scribes and *P*
Mt 23:27 Woe unto you, scribes and *P*
Mt 23:29 Woe unto you, scribes and *P*
Mt 27:62 *P* came together unto Pilate,
Mk 2:16 *P* saw him eat with publicans and
Mk 2:18 of John and of the *P* used to fast
Mk 2:18 of John and of the *P* fast, but thy
Mk 2:24 the *P* said unto him, Behold, why
Mk 3:6 the *P* went forth, and straightway
Mk 7:1 Then came together unto him the *P*
Mk 7:3 For the *P*, and all the Jews,
Mk 7:5 Then the *P* and scribes asked him,
Mk 8:11 the *P* came forth, and began to
Mk 8:15 beware of the leaven of the *P*
Mk 10:2 the *P* came to him, and asked him,
Mk 12:13 send unto him certain of the *P*
Lk 5:17 was teaching, that there were *P*
Lk 5:21 the *P* began to reason, saying,
Lk 5:30 *P* murmured against his disciples,
Lk 5:33 likewise the disciples of the *P*
Lk 6:2 certain of the *P* said unto them
Lk 6:7 *P* watched him, whether he would
Lk 7:30 But the *P* and lawyers rejected the
Lk 7:36 one of the *P* desired him that he
Lk 11:39 Now do ye *P* make clean the
Lk 11:42 But woe unto you, *P*
Lk 11:43 Woe unto you, *P*
Lk 11:44 Woe unto you, scribes and *P*
Lk 11:53 and the *P* began to urge him
Lk 12:1 Beware ye of the leaven of the *P*
Lk 13:31 day there came certain of the *P*
Lk 14:1 the house of one of the chief *P*
Lk 14:3 spake unto the lawyers and *P*
Lk 15:2 And the *P* and scribes murmured,
Lk 16:14 the *P* also, who were covetous,
Lk 17:20 And when he was demanded of the *P*

Lk 19:39 some of the P from among the
Jn 1:24 which were sent were of the P
Jn 3:1 There was a man of the P, named
Jn 4:1 the P had heard that Jesus made
Jn 7:32 The P heard that the people
Jn 7:32 and the P and the chief priests
Jn 7:45 to the chief priests and P
Jn 7:47 Then answered them the P, Are ye
Jn 7:48 or of the P believed on him
Jn 8:3 P brought unto him a woman taken
Jn 8:13 The P therefore said unto him,
Jn 9:13 They brought to the P him that
Jn 9:15 Then again the P also asked him
Jn 9:16 Therefore said some of the P
Jn 9:40 some of the P which were with him
Jn 11:46 of them went their ways to the P
Jn 11:47 the P a council, and said, What do
Jn 11:57 the P had given a commandment,
Jn 12:19 The P therefore said among
Jn 12:42 but because of the P they did not
Jn 18:3 from the chief priests and P
Acts 15:5 the sect of the P which believed
Acts 23:6 were Sadducees, and the other P
Acts 23:7 arose a dissension between the P
Acts 23:8 but the P confess both

**PHARISEES'** *(far'-i-seez)*
Acts 23:9 that were of the P part arose

**PHAROSH** *(fa'-rosh) A family of exiles.*
Ezr 8:3 of Shechaniah, of the sons of P

**PHARPAR** *(far'-par) A river near Damascus.*
2Kin 5:12 Are not Abana and P, rivers of

**PHARZITES** *(far'-zites) Descendants of Pharez.*
Num 26:20 of Pharez, the family of the P

**PHASEAH** *(fa-se'-ah)* See PASEAH. *A family of exiles.*
Neh 7:51 of Uzza, the children of P

**PHEBE** *(fe'-be) A Christian acquaintance of Paul.*
Rom 16:1 I commend unto you P our sister
Rom s sent by P servant of the church

**PHENICE** *(fe-ni'-se)* See PHENICIA.
*1. Same as Phenecia.*
Acts 11:19 Stephen travelled as far as P
Acts 15:3 the church, they passed through P
*2. A harbor on Crete.*
Acts 27:12 any means they might attain to P

**PHENICIA** *(fe-nish'-e-ah)* See PHENICE. *Coastal region of northern Palestine.*
Acts 21:2 a ship sailing over unto P

**PHICHOL** *The commander of Abimelech's army.*
Gen 21:22 P the chief captain of his host
Gen 21:32 P the chief captain of his host,
Gen 26:26 P the chief captain of his army

**PHICOL** *(fi'-col)* See PHICHOL. *A Philistine commander.*

**PHILADELPHIA** *(fil-a-del'-fe-ah) A city in Lydia in Asia Minor.*
Rev 1:11 and unto Sardis, and unto P
Rev 3:7 angel of the church in P write

**PHILEMON** *(fi-le'-mon) A recipient of a New Testament epistle.*
Philem 1 unto P our dearly beloved, and
Philem s Written from Rome to P, by

**PHILETUS** *(fi-le'tus) A false Christian teacher.*
2Ti 2:17 of whom is Hymenaeus and P

**PHILIP** *(fil'-ip)* See PHILIP'S.
*1. An apostle.*
Mt 10:3 P, and Bartholomew
Mk 3:18 And Andrew, and P, and Bartholomew,
Lk 6:14 his brother, James and John, P
Jn 1:43 forth into Galilee, and findeth P
Jn 1:44 Now P was of Bethsaida, the city
Jn 1:45 P findeth Nathanael, and saith
Jn 1:46 P saith unto him, Come and see
Jn 1:48 him, Before that P called thee
Jn 6:5 come unto him, he saith unto P
Jn 6:7 P answered him, Two hundred
Jn 12:21 The same came therefore to P
Jn 12:22 P cometh and telleth Andrew
Jn 12:22 and again Andrew and P tell Jesus
Jn 14:8 P saith unto him, Lord, shew us
Jn 14:9 and yet hast thou not known me, P
Acts 1:13 and James, and John, and Andrew, P
*2. A son of Herod the Great.*
Lk 3:1 his brother P tetrarch of Ituraea
*3. The evangelist.*
Acts 6:5 faith and of the Holy Ghost, and P
Acts 8:5 Then P went down to the city of
Acts 8:6 unto those things which P spake
Acts 8:12 But when they believed P
Acts 8:13 was baptized, he continued with P
Acts 8:26 angel of the Lord spake unto P
Acts 8:29 Then the Spirit said unto P
Acts 8:30 P ran thither to him, and heard
Acts 8:31 he desired P that he would come
Acts 8:34 And the eunuch answered P, and said
Acts 8:35 Then P opened his mouth, and began
Acts 8:37 P said, If thou believest with
Acts 8:38 down both into the water, both P
Acts 8:39 Spirit of the Lord caught away P
Acts 8:40 But P was found at Azotus
Acts 21:8 the house of P the evangelist

**PHILIPPI** *(fil-ip'-pi)* See PHILIPPIANS.
*1. A town in northern Palestine.*
Mt 16:13 into the coasts of Caesarea P
Mk 8:27 into the towns of Caesarea P
*2. A Macedonian city.*
Acts 16:12 And from thence to P, which is the
Acts 20:6 we sailed away from P after the
1Cor s was written from P by Stephanus
2Cor s Corinthians was written from P
Phil 1:1 in Christ Jesus which are at P
1Th 2:2 entreated, as ye know, at P

**PHILIPPIANS** *(fil-ip'-pe-uns) Residents of Philippi 2.*
Phil 4:15 Now ye P know also, that in the
Phil s It was written to the P from Rome

**PHILIP'S** *(fil'-ips) Refers to Philip 2.*
Mt 14:3 sake, his brother P wife
Mk 6:17 sake, his brother P wife
Lk 3:19 for Herodias his brother P wife

**PHILISTIA** *(fil-is'-te-ah)* See PALESTINE, PHILISTINE. *Land of the Philistines.*
Ps 60:8 P, triumph thou because of me
Ps 87:4 behold P, and Tyre, with Ethiopia
Ps 108:9 over P will I triumph

**PHILISTIM** *(fil-is'-tim)* See PHILISTINES. *Descendents of Casluhim.*
Gen 10:14 and Casluhim, (out of whom came P

**PHILISTINE** *(fil-is'-tin)* See PHILISTINES. *An inhabitant of Philistia.*
1Sa 17:8 am not I a P, and ye servants to
1Sa 17:10 the P said, I defy the armies of
1Sa 17:11 Israel heard those words of the P
1Sa 17:16 the P drew near morning and
1Sa 17:23 the P of Gath, Goliath by name,
1Sa 17:26 to the man that killeth this P
1Sa 17:26 for who is this uncircumcised P
1Sa 17:32 will go and fight with this P
1Sa 17:33 against this P to fight with him
1Sa 17:36 this uncircumcised P shall be as
1Sa 17:37 me out of the hand of this P
1Sa 17:40 and he drew near to the P
1Sa 17:41 the P came on and drew near unto
1Sa 17:42 when the P looked about, and saw
1Sa 17:43 the P said unto David, Am I a dog
1Sa 17:43 the P cursed David by his gods
1Sa 17:44 the P said to David, Come to me,
1Sa 17:45 Then said David to the P, Thou
1Sa 17:48 it came to pass, when the P arose
1Sa 17:48 ran toward the army to meet the P
1Sa 17:49 smote the P in his forehead, that
1Sa 17:50 prevailed over the P with a sling
1Sa 17:50 and with a stone, and smote the P
1Sa 17:51 David ran, and stood upon the P
1Sa 17:54 And David took the head of the P
1Sa 17:55 saw David go forth against the P
1Sa 17:57 from the slaughter of the P
1Sa 17:57 the head of the P in his hand
1Sa 18:6 from the slaughter of the P
1Sa 19:5 life in his hand, and slew the P
1Sa 21:9 said, The sword of Goliath the P
1Sa 22:10 him the sword of Goliath the P
2Sa 21:17 succoured him, and smote the P

**PHILISTINES** *(fil-is'-tinz)* See PHILISTIM, PHILISTINES'.
Gen 21:32 returned into the land of the P
Gen 26:1 king of the P unto Gerar
Gen 26:8 of the P looked out at a window
Gen 26:14 and the P envied him
Gen 26:15 the P had stopped them, and filled
Gen 26:18 for the P had stopped them after
Ex 13:17 the way of the land of the P
Ex 23:31 sea even unto the sea of the P
Josh 13:2 all the borders of the P, and all
Josh 13:3 five lords of the P
Judg 3:3 Namely, five lords of the P
Judg 3:31 which slew of the P six hundred
Judg 10:6 of Ammon, and the gods of the P
Judg 10:7 sold them into the hands of the P
Judg 10:11 children of Ammon, and from the P
Judg 13:1 the hand of the P forty years
Judg 13:5 Israel out of the hand of the P
Judg 14:1 Timnath of the daughters of the P
Judg 14:2 Timnath of the daughters of the P
Judg 14:3 a wife of the uncircumcised P
Judg 14:4 sought an occasion against the P
Judg 14:4 for at that time the P had
Judg 15:3 I be more blameless than the P
Judg 15:5 into the standing corn of the P
Judg 15:6 Then the P said, Who hath done
Judg 15:6 the P came up, and burnt her and
Judg 15:9 Then the P went up, and pitched in
Judg 15:11 not that the P are rulers over us
Judg 15:12 thee into the hand of the P
Judg 15:14 the P shouted against him
Judg 15:20 in the days of the P twenty years
Judg 16:5 lords of the P came up unto her
Judg 16:8 Then the lords of the P brought
Judg 16:9 The P be upon thee, Samson
Judg 16:12 The P be upon thee, Samson
Judg 16:14 The P be upon thee, Samson
Judg 16:18 and called for the lords of the P
Judg 16:18 lords of the P came up unto her
Judg 16:20 The P be upon thee, Samson
Judg 16:21 But the P took him, and put out
Judg 16:23 Then the lords of the P gathered
Judg 16:27 all the lords of the P were there
Judg 16:28 avenged of the P for my two eyes
Judg 16:30 said, Let me die with the P
1Sa 4:1 went out against the P to battle
1Sa 4:1 and the P pitched in Aphek
1Sa 4:2 the P put themselves in array
1Sa 4:2 Israel was smitten before the P
1Sa 4:3 smitten us to day before the P
1Sa 4:6 when the P heard the noise of the
1Sa 4:7 the P were afraid, for they said,
1Sa 4:9 quit yourselves like men, O ye P
1Sa 4:10 the P fought, and Israel was
1Sa 4:17 said, Israel is fled before the P
1Sa 5:1 the P took the ark of God, and
1Sa 5:2 When the P took the ark of God,
1Sa 5:8 all the lords of the P unto them
1Sa 5:11 together all the lords of the P
1Sa 6:1 the country of the P seven months
1Sa 6:2 the P called for the priests and
1Sa 6:4 the number of the lords of the P
1Sa 6:12 the lords of the P went after
1Sa 6:16 five lords of the P had seen it
1Sa 6:17 the P returned for a trespass
1Sa 6:18 the P belonging to the five lords
1Sa 6:21 The P have brought again the ark
1Sa 7:3 you out of the hand of the P
1Sa 7:7 when the P heard that the
1Sa 7:7 the lords of the P went up
1Sa 7:7 it, they were afraid of the P
1Sa 7:8 save us out of the hand of the P
1Sa 7:10 the P drew near to battle against
1Sa 7:10 thunder on that day upon the P
1Sa 7:11 out of Mizpeh, and pursued the P
1Sa 7:13 So the P were subdued, and they
1Sa 7:13 the P all the days of Samuel
1Sa 7:14 the cities which the P had taken
1Sa 7:14 deliver out of the hands of the P
1Sa 9:16 people out of the hand of the P
1Sa 10:5 where is the garrison of the P
1Sa 12:9 Hazor, and into the hand of the P
1Sa 13:3 of the P that was in Geba
1Sa 13:3 and the P heard of it
1Sa 13:4 had smitten a garrison of the P
1Sa 13:4 was had in abomination with the P
1Sa 13:5 the P gathered themselves
1Sa 13:11 that the P gathered themselves
1Sa 13:12 The P will come down now upon me
1Sa 13:16 but the P encamped in Michmash
1Sa 13:17 camp of the P in three companies
1Sa 13:19 for the P said, Lest the Hebrews
1Sa 13:20 the Israelites went down to the P

1Sa 13:23 the garrison of the P went out to
1Sa 14:11 unto the garrison of the P
1Sa 14:11 the P said, Behold, the Hebrews
1Sa 14:19 was in the host of the P went on
1Sa 14:21 were with the P before that time
1Sa 14:22 when they heard that the P fled
1Sa 14:30 greater slaughter among the P
1Sa 14:31 they smote the P that day from
1Sa 14:36 us go down after the P by night
1Sa 14:37 God, Shall I go down after the P
1Sa 14:46 Saul went up from following the P
1Sa 14:46 the P went to their own place
1Sa 14:47 kings of Zobah, and against the P
1Sa 14:52 the P all the days of Saul
1Sa 17:1 Now the P gathered together their
1Sa 17:2 the battle in array against the P
1Sa 17:3 the P stood on a mountain on the
1Sa 17:4 champion out of the camp of the P
1Sa 17:19 of Elah, fighting with the P
1Sa 17:21 the P had put the battle in array
1Sa 17:23 name, out of the armies of the P
1Sa 17:46 P this day unto the fowls of the
1Sa 17:51 when the P saw their champion was
1Sa 17:52 and shouted, and pursued the P
1Sa 17:52 the wounded of the P fell down by
1Sa 17:53 returned from chasing after the P
1Sa 18:17 let the hand of the P be upon him
1Sa 18:21 hand of the P may be against him
1Sa 18:25 but an hundred foreskins of the P
1Sa 18:25 David fall by the hand of the P
1Sa 18:27 slew of the P two hundred men
1Sa 18:30 the princes of the P went forth
1Sa 19:8 went out, and fought with the P
1Sa 23:1 the P fight against Keilah, and
1Sa 23:2 Shall I go and smite these P
1Sa 23:2 unto David, Go, and smite the P
1Sa 23:3 against the armies of the P
1Sa 23:4 deliver the P into thine hand
1Sa 23:5 to Keilah, and fought with the P
1Sa 23:27 for the P have invaded the land
1Sa 23:28 David, and went against the P
1Sa 24:1 was returned from following the P
1Sa 27:1 escape into the land of the P
1Sa 27:7 country of the P was a full year
1Sa 27:11 dwelleth in the country of the P
1Sa 28:1 that the P gathered their armies
1Sa 28:4 the P gathered themselves
1Sa 28:5 when Saul saw the host of the P
1Sa 28:15 for the P make war against me, and
1Sa 28:19 with thee into the hand of the P
1Sa 28:19 of Israel into the hand of the P
1Sa 29:1 Now the P gathered together all
1Sa 29:2 the lords of the P passed on by
1Sa 29:3 Then said the princes of the P
1Sa 29:3 said unto the princes of the P
1Sa 29:4 the princes of the P were wroth
1Sa 29:4 princes of the P said unto him
1Sa 29:7 displease not the lords of the P
1Sa 29:9 the princes of the P have said
1Sa 29:11 to return into the land of the P
1Sa 29:11 And the P went up to Jezreel
1Sa 30:16 taken out of the land of the P
1Sa 31:1 Now the P fought against Israel
1Sa 31:1 of Israel fled from before the P
1Sa 31:2 the P followed hard upon Saul and
1Sa 31:2 the P slew Jonathan, and Abinadab,
1Sa 31:7 the P came and dwelt in them
1Sa 31:8 when the P came to strip the
1Sa 31:9 the land of the P round about
1Sa 31:11 that which the P had done to Saul
2Sa 1:20 the daughters of the P rejoice
2Sa 3:14 for an hundred foreskins of the P
2Sa 3:18 Israel out of the hand of the P
2Sa 5:17 But when the P heard that they
2Sa 5:17 all the P came up to seek David
2Sa 5:18 The P also came and spread
2Sa 5:19 saying, Shall I go up to the P
2Sa 5:19 deliver the P into thine hand
2Sa 5:22 the P came up yet again, and
2Sa 5:24 thee, to smite the host of the P
2Sa 5:25 smote the P from Geba until thou
2Sa 8:1 to pass, that David smote the P
2Sa 8:1 out of the hand of the P
2Sa 8:12 children of Ammon, and of the P
2Sa 19:9 us out of the hand of the P
2Sa 21:12 where the P had hanged them
2Sa 21:12 when the P had slain Saul in
2Sa 21:15 Moreover the P had yet war again
2Sa 21:15 with him, and fought against the P
2Sa 21:18 again a battle with the P at Gob
2Sa 21:19 again a battle in Gob with the P
2Sa 23:9 when they defied the P that were
2Sa 23:10 smote the P until his hand was
2Sa 23:11 the P were gathered together into
2Sa 23:11 and the people fled from the P
2Sa 23:12 and defended it, and slew the P
2Sa 23:13 the troop of the P pitched in the
2Sa 23:14 the garrison of the P was then in
2Sa 23:16 brake through the host of the P
1Kin 4:21 the river unto the land of the P
1Kin 15:27 which belonged to the P
1Kin 16:15 which belonged to the P
2Kin 8:2 in the land of the P seven years
2Kin 8:3 returned out of the land of the P
2Kin 18:8 He smote the P, even unto Gaza,
1Chr 1:12 and Casluhim, (of whom came the P
1Chr 10:1 Now the P fought against Israel
1Chr 10:1 of Israel fled from before the P
1Chr 10:2 the P followed hard after Saul,
1Chr 10:2 the P slew Jonathan, and Abinadab,
1Chr 10:7 the P came and dwelt in them
1Chr 10:8 when the P came to strip the
1Chr 10:9 the land of the P round about
1Chr 10:11 all that the P had done to Saul
1Chr 11:13 there the P were gathered
1Chr 11:13 the people fled from before the P
1Chr 11:14 and delivered it, and slew the P
1Chr 11:15 the host of the P encamped in the
1Chr 11:18 brake through the host of the P
1Chr 12:19 when he came with the P against
1Chr 12:19 for the lords of the P upon
1Chr 14:8 when the P heard that David was
1Chr 14:8 all the P went up to seek David
1Chr 14:9 the P came and spread themselves
1Chr 14:10 Shall I go up against the P
1Chr 14:13 the P yet again spread themselves
1Chr 14:15 thee to smite the host of the P
1Chr 14:16 the P from Gibeon even to Gazer
1Chr 18:1 to pass, that David smote the P
1Chr 18:1 towns out of the hand of the P
1Chr 18:11 children of Ammon, and from the P
1Chr 20:4 arose war at Gezer with the P
1Chr 20:5 And there was war again with the P
2Chr 9:26 river even unto the land of the P
2Chr 17:11 Also some of the P brought
2Chr 21:16 Jehoram the spirit of the P
2Chr 26:6 forth and warred against the P
2Chr 26:6 about Ashdod, and among the P
2Chr 26:7 And God helped him against the P
2Chr 28:18 The P also had invaded the cities
Ps 56:*t* when the P took him in Gath
Ps 83:7 the P with the inhabitants of
Is 2:6 and are soothsayers like the P
Is 9:12 Syrians before, and the P behind
Is 11:14 of the P toward the west
Jer 25:20 the kings of the land of the P
Jer 47:1 the prophet against the P
Jer 47:4 that cometh to spoil all the P
Jer 47:4 for the LORD will spoil the P
Eze 16:27 hate thee, the daughters of the P
Eze 16:57 about her, the daughters of the P
Eze 25:15 Because the P have dealt by
Eze 25:16 stretch out mine hand upon the P
Amos 1:8 the remnant of the P shall perish
Amos 6:2 then go down to Gath of the P
Amos 9:7 the P from Caphtor, and the
Obad 19 and they of the plain the P
Zeph 2:5 O Canaan, the land of the P
Zec 9:6 I will cut off the pride of the P

**PHILISTINES'** *(fil-is'-tinz)*
Gen 21:34 sojourned in the P land many days
1Sa 14:1 let us go over to the P garrison
1Sa 14:4 to go over unto the P garrison
1Chr 11:16 the P garrison was then at

**PHILOLOGUS** *(fil-ol'-o-gus) A Christian in Rome.*
Rom 16:15 Salute P, and Julia, Nereus, and

**PHINEHAS** *(fin'-e-has)* See PHINEHAS'.
*1. A son of Eleazar.*
Ex 6:25 and she bare him P
Num 25:7 And when P, the son of Eleazar,
Num 25:11 P, the son of Eleazar, the son of
Num 31:6 P the son of Eleazar the priest,
Josh 22:13 P the son of Eleazar the priest,
Josh 22:30 when P the priest, and the princes
Josh 22:31 P the son of Eleazar the priest
Josh 22:32 P the son of Eleazar the priest,
Josh 24:33 hill that pertained to P his son
Judg 20:28 And P, the son of Eleazar, the son
1Chr 6:4 Eleazar begat P
1Chr 6:4 P begat Abishua
1Chr 6:50 P his son, Abishua his son,
1Chr 9:20 P the son of Eleazar was the
Ezr 7:5 The son of Abishua, the son of P
Ezr 8:2 Of the sons of P
Ps 106:30 Then stood up P, and executed
*2. A son of Eli.*
1Sa 1:3 the two sons of Eli, Hophni and P
1Sa 2:34 upon thy two sons, on Hophni and P
1Sa 4:4 the two sons of Eli, Hophni and P
1Sa 4:11 the two sons of Eli, Hophni and P
1Sa 4:17 and thy two sons also, Hophni and P
1Sa 14:3 I-chabod's brother, the son of P
*3. Father of Eleazar.*
Ezr 8:33 with him was Eleazar the son of P

**PHINEHAS'** *(fin'-e-has) Refers to Phinehas 2.*
1Sa 4:19 P wife, was with child, near to

**PHLEGON** *(fle'-gon) A Christian in Rome.*
Rom 16:14 Salute Asyncritus, P, Hermas,

**PHRYGIA** *(frij'-e-ah) A Roman province in Asia Minor.*
Acts 2:10 P, and Pamphylia, in Egypt, and in
Acts 16:6 when they had gone throughout P
Acts 18:23 P in order, strengthening all the
1Ti s the chiefest city of P Pacatiana

**PHURAH** *(fu'-rah) A servant of Gideon.*
Judg 7:10 go thou with P thy servant down
Judg 7:11 Then went he down with P his

**PHUT** *(fut)* See PUT.
*1. A son of Ham.*
Gen 10:6 and Mizraim, and P, and Canaan
*2. Land of Phut's descendants.*
Eze 27:10 of P were in thine army, thy men

**PHUVAH** *(fu'-vah)* See PUAH. *A son of Issachar.*
Gen 46:13 Tola, and P, and Job, and Shimron

**PHYGELLUS** *(fi-jel'-lus) An unfaithful Christian.*
2Ti 1:15 of whom are P and Hermogenes

**PHYSICIAN**
Jer 8:22 is there no p there
Mt 9:12 They that be whole need not a p
Mk 2:17 are whole have no need of the p
Lk 4:23 say unto me this proverb, P
Lk 5:31 They that are whole need not a p
Col 4:14 Luke, the beloved p, and Demas,

**PHYSICIANS**
Gen 50:2 the p to embalm his father
Gen 50:2 and the p embalmed Israel
2Chr 16:12 not to the LORD, but to the p
Job 13:4 of lies, ye are all p of no value
Mk 5:26 suffered many things of many p
Lk 8:43 had spent all her living upon p

**PI-BESETH** A city in Egypt.
Eze 30:17 of P shall fall by the sword

**PIECE**
Gen 15:10 laid each p one against another
Ex 37:7 beaten out of one p made he them
Num 10:2 of a whole p shalt thou make them
Judg 9:53 a certain woman cast a p of a
1Sa 2:36 crouch to him for a p of silver
1Sa 2:36 that I may eat a p of bread
1Sa 30:12 they gave him a p of a cake of
2Sa 6:19 a good p of flesh, and a flagon of
2Sa 11:21 did not a woman cast a p of a
2Sa 23:11 where was a p of ground full of
2Kin 3:19 mar every good p of land with
2Kin 3:25 on every good p of land cast
1Chr 16:3 a good p of flesh, and a flagon of
Neh 3:11 Pahath-moab, repaired the other p
Neh 3:19 another p over against the going
Neh 3:20 earnestly repaired the other p
Neh 3:21 Urijah the son of Koz another p
Neh 3:24 the son of Henadad another p
Neh 3:27 the Tekoites repaired another p
Neh 3:30 sixth son of Zalaph, another p
Job 41:24 as hard as a p of the nether
Job 42:11 man also gave him a p of money
Prov 6:26 a man is brought to a p of bread
Prov 28:21 for for a p of bread that man
Song 4:3 thy temples are like a p of a
Song 6:7 As a p of a pomegranate are thy
Jer 37:21 a p of bread out of the bakers'
Eze 24:4 into it, even every good p

Eze 24:6 bring it out *p* by *p*
Amos 3:12 lion two legs, or a *p* of an ear
Amos 4:7 one *p* was rained upon
Amos 4:7 the *p* whereupon it rained not
Mt 9:16 No man putteth a *p* of new cloth
Mt 17:27 thou shalt find a *p* of money
Mk 2:21 No man also seweth a *p* of new
Mk 2:21 else the new *p* that filled it up
Lk 5:36 No man putteth a *p* of a new
Lk 5:36 the *p* that was taken out of the
Lk 14:18 him, I have bought a *p* of ground
Lk 15:8 of silver, if she lose one *p*
Lk 15:9 have found the *p* which I had lost
Lk 24:42 they gave him a *p* of a broiled

**PIECES**
Gen 15:17 lamp that passed between those *p*
Gen 20:16 brother a thousand *p* of silver
Gen 33:19 father, for an hundred *p* of money
Gen 37:28 for twenty *p* of silver
Gen 37:33 Joseph is without doubt rent in *p*
Gen 44:28 and I said, Surely he is torn in *p*
Gen 45:22 he gave three hundred *p* of silver
Ex 15:6 LORD, hath dashed in *p* the enemy
Ex 22:13 If it be torn in *p*, then let him
Ex 29:17 And thou shalt cut the ram in *p*
Ex 29:17 his legs, and put them unto his *p*
Lev 1:6 offering, and cut it into his *p*
Lev 1:12 And he shall cut it into his *p*
Lev 2:6 Thou shalt part it in *p*, and pour
Lev 6:21 the baken *p* of the meat offering
Lev 8:20 And he cut the ram into *p*
Lev 8:20 and Moses burnt the head, and the *p*
Lev 9:13 unto him, with the *p* thereof
Josh 24:32 for an hundred *p* of silver
Judg 9:4 ten *p* of silver out of the house
Judg 16:5 of us eleven hundred *p* of silver
Judg 19:29 with her bones, into twelve *p*
Judg 20:6 my concubine, and cut her in *p*
1Sa 2:10 of the LORD shall be broken to *p*
1Sa 11:7 yoke of oxen, and hewed them in *p*
1Sa 15:33 Samuel hewed Agag in *p* before the
1Kin 11:30 on him, and rent it in twelve *p*
1Kin 11:31 said to Jeroboam, Take thee ten *p*
1Kin 18:23 for themselves, and cut it in *p*
1Kin 18:33 in order, and cut the bullock in *p*
1Kin 19:11 brake in *p* the rocks before the
2Kin 2:12 clothes, and rent them in two *p*
2Kin 5:5 silver, and six thousand *p* of gold
2Kin 6:25 sold for fourscore *p* of silver
2Kin 6:25 dove's dung for five *p* of silver
2Kin 11:18 images brake they in *p* thoroughly
2Kin 18:4 brake in *p* the brasen serpent
2Kin 23:14 And he brake in *p* the images
2Kin 24:13 cut in *p* all the vessels of gold
2Kin 25:13 LORD, did the Chaldees break in *p*
2Chr 23:17 his altars and his images in *p*
2Chr 25:12 that they all were broken in *p*
2Chr 28:24 cut in *p* the vessels of the house
2Chr 31:1 Judah, and brake the images in *p*
2Chr 34:4 the molten images, he brake in *p*
Job 16:12 me by my neck, and shaken me to *p*
Job 19:2 soul, and break me in *p* with words
Job 34:24 He shall break in *p* mighty men
Job 40:18 bones are as strong *p* of brass
Ps 2:9 them in *p* like a potter's vessel
Ps 7:2 soul like a lion, rending it in *p*
Ps 50:22 forget God, lest I tear you in *p*
Ps 58:7 arrows, let them be as cut in *p*
Ps 68:30 submit himself with *p* of silver
Ps 72:4 and shall break in *p* the oppressor
Ps 74:14 the heads of leviathan in *p*
Ps 89:10 Thou hast broken Rahab in *p*
Ps 94:5 They break in *p* thy people
Song 8:11 to bring a thousand *p* of silver
Is 3:15 ye that ye beat my people to *p*
Is 8:9 and ye shall be broken in *p*
Is 8:9 and ye shall be broken in *p*
Is 8:9 and ye shall be broken in *p*
Is 13:16 be dashed to *p* before their eyes
Is 13:18 shall dash the young men to *p*
Is 30:14 vessel that is broken in *p*
Is 45:2 I will break in *p* the gates of
Jer 5:6 out thence shall be torn in *p*
Jer 23:29 that breaketh the rock in *p*
Jer 50:2 Merodach is broken in *p*
Jer 50:2 her images are broken in *p*
Jer 51:20 will I break in *p* the nations
Jer 51:21 thee will I break in *p* the horse
Jer 51:21 will I break in *p* the chariot
Jer 51:22 thee also will I break in *p* man
Jer 51:22 with thee will I break in *p* old
Jer 51:22 will I break in *p* the young man
Jer 51:23 I will also break in *p* with thee
Jer 51:23 will I break in *p* the husbandman
Jer 51:23 thee will I break in *p* captains
Lam 3:11 aside my ways, and pulled me in *p*
Eze 4:14 dieth of itself, or is torn in *p*
Eze 13:19 for *p* of bread, to slay the souls
Eze 24:4 Gather the *p* thereof into it,
Dan 2:5 thereof, ye shall be cut in *p*
Dan 2:34 iron and clay, and brake them to *p*
Dan 2:35 and the gold, broken to *p* together
Dan 2:40 forasmuch as iron breaketh in *p*
Dan 2:40 all these, shall it break in *p*
Dan 2:44 people, but it shall break in *p*
Dan 2:45 and that it brake in *p* the iron
Dan 3:29 and Abed-nego, shall be cut in *p*
Dan 6:24 brake all their bones in *p* or
Dan 7:7 it devoured and brake in *p*
Dan 7:19 which devoured, brake in *p*
Dan 7:23 tread it down, and break it in *p*
Hos 3:2 her to me for fifteen *p* of silver
Hos 8:6 of Samaria shall be broken in *p*
Hos 10:14 was dashed in *p* upon her children
Hos 13:16 infants shall be dashed in *p*
Mic 1:7 thereof shall be beaten to *p*
Mic 3:3 their bones, and chop them in *p*
Mic 4:13 thou shalt beat in *p* many people
Mic 5:8 treadeth down, and teareth in *p*
Nah 2:1 He that dasheth in *p* is come up
Nah 2:12 The lion did tear in *p* enough for
Nah 3:10 children also were dashed in *p* at
Zec 11:12 for my price thirty *p* of silver
Zec 11:13 And I took the thirty *p* of silver
Zec 11:16 the fat, and tear their claws in *p*
Zec 12:3 with it shall be cut in *p*
Mt 26:15 with him for thirty *p* of silver
Mt 27:3 brought again the thirty *p* of
Mt 27:5 he cast down the *p* of silver in
Mt 27:6 chief priests took the silver *p*
Mt 27:9 they took the thirty *p* of silver
Mk 5:4 him, and the fetters broken in *p*
Lk 15:8 what woman having ten *p* of silver
Acts 19:19 it fifty thousand *p* of silver
Acts 23:10 have been pulled in *p* of them
Acts 27:44 and some on broken *p* of the ship

**PIERCE**
Num 24:8 *p* them through with his arrows
2Kin 18:21 it will go into his hand, and *p* it
Is 36:6 it will go into his hand, and *p* it
Lk 2:35 a sword shall *p* through thy own

**PIERCED**
Judg 5:26 off his head, when she had *p*
Job 30:17 My bones are *p* in me in the night
Ps 22:16 they *p* my hands and my feet
Zec 12:10 look upon me whom they have *p*
Jn 19:34 soldiers with a spear *p* his side
Jn 19:37 shall look on him whom they *p*
1Ti 6:10 *p* themselves through with many
Rev 1:7 see him, and they also which *p* him

**PIGEONS**
Lev 1:14 of turtledoves, or of young *p*
Lev 5:7 two turtledoves, or two young *p*
Lev 5:11 two turtledoves, or two young *p*
Lev 12:8 bring two turtles, or two young *p*
Lev 14:22 two turtledoves, or two young *p*
Lev 14:30 turtledoves, or of the young *p*
Lev 15:14 two turtledoves, or two young *p*
Lev 15:29 her two turtles, or two young *p*
Num 6:10 bring two turtles, or two young *p*
Lk 2:24 of turtledoves, or two young *p*

**PI-HAHIROTH** *A wilderness encampment.*
Ex 14:2 that they turn and encamp before *P*
Ex 14:9 encamping by the sea, beside *P*
Num 33:7 Etham, and turned again unto *P*
Num 33:8 And they departed from before *P*

**PILATE** *(pi'-lut) A Roman procurator of Judea.*
Mt 27:2 him to Pontius *P* the governor
Mt 27:13 Then said *P* unto him, Hearest
Mt 27:17 *P* said unto them, Whom will ye
Mt 27:22 *P* saith unto them, What shall I
Mt 27:24 When *P* saw that he could prevail
Mt 27:58 He went to *P*, and begged the body
Mt 27:58 Then *P* commanded the body to be
Mt 27:62 and Pharisees came together unto *P*
Mt 27:65 *P* said unto them, Ye have a watch
Mk 15:1 him away, and delivered him to *P*
Mk 15:2 *P* asked him, Art thou the King of
Mk 15:4 *P* asked him again, saying,
Mk 15:5 so that *P* marvelled
Mk 15:9 But *P* answered them, saying, Will
Mk 15:12 *P* answered and said again unto
Mk 15:14 Then *P* said unto them, Why, what
Mk 15:15 And so *P*, willing to content the
Mk 15:43 came, and went in boldly unto *P*
Mk 15:44 *P* marvelled if he were already
Lk 3:1 Pontius *P* being governor of
Lk 13:1 whose blood *P* had mingled with
Lk 23:1 of them arose, and led him unto *P*
Lk 23:3 *P* asked him, saying, Art thou the
Lk 23:4 Then said *P* to the chief priests
Lk 23:6 When *P* heard of Galilee, he asked
Lk 23:11 robe, and sent him again to *P*
Lk 23:12 And the same day *P* and Herod were
Lk 23:13 And *P*, when he had called together
Lk 23:20 *P* therefore, willing to release
Lk 23:24 *P* gave sentence that it should be
Lk 23:52 This man went unto *P*, and begged
Jn 18:29 *P* then went out unto them, and
Jn 18:31 Then said *P* unto them, Take ye
Jn 18:33 Then *P* entered into the judgment
Jn 18:35 *P* answered, Am I a Jew
Jn 18:37 *P* therefore said unto him, Art
Jn 18:38 *P* saith unto him, What is truth
Jn 19:1 Then *P* therefore took Jesus, and
Jn 19:4 *P* therefore went forth again, and
Jn 19:5 *P* saith unto them, Behold the man
Jn 19:6 *P* saith unto them, Take ye him,
Jn 19:8 When *P* therefore heard that
Jn 19:10 Then saith *P* unto him, Speakest
Jn 19:12 from thenceforth *P* sought to
Jn 19:13 When *P* therefore heard that
Jn 19:15 *P* saith unto them, Shall I
Jn 19:19 *P* wrote a title, and put it on the
Jn 19:21 chief priests of the Jews to *P*
Jn 19:22 *P* answered, What I have written I
Jn 19:31 besought *P* that their legs might
Jn 19:38 besought *P* that he might take
Jn 19:38 and *P* gave him leave
Acts 3:13 denied him in the presence of *P*
Acts 4:27 both Herod, and Pontius *P*
Acts 13:28 yet desired they *P* that he should
1Ti 6:13 who before Pontius *P* witnessed a

**PILDASH** *(pil'-dash) A son of Nahor.*
Gen 22:22 And Chesed, and Hazo, and *P*, and

**PILEHA** *(pil'-e-hah) A renewer of the covenant.*
Neh 10:24 Hallohesh, *P*, Shobek,

**PILGRIMAGE**
Gen 47:9 the years of my *p* are an hundred
Gen 47:9 my fathers in the days of their *p*
Ex 6:4 of Canaan, the land of their *p*
Ps 119:54 my songs in the house of my *p*

**PILLAR**
Gen 19:26 him, and she became a *p* of salt
Gen 28:18 his pillows, and set it up for a *p*
Gen 28:22 stone, which I have set for a *p*
Gen 31:13 where thou anointedst the *p*
Gen 31:45 a stone, and set it up for a *p*
Gen 31:51 this heap, and behold this *p*
Gen 31:52 this *p* be witness, that I will
Gen 31:52 heap and this *p* unto me, for harm
Gen 35:14 Jacob set up a *p* in the place
Gen 35:14 with him, even a *p* of stone
Gen 35:20 Jacob set a *p* upon her grave
Gen 35:20 that is the *p* of Rachel's grave
Ex 13:21 them by day in a *p* of a cloud
Ex 13:21 and by night in a *p* of fire
Ex 13:22 away the *p* of the cloud by day
Ex 13:22 nor the *p* of fire by night, from
Ex 14:19 the *p* of the cloud went from
Ex 14:24 Egyptians through the *p* of fire
Ex 33:9 the cloudy *p* descended, and stood
Ex 33:10 *p* stand at the tabernacle door
Num 12:5 came down in the *p* of the cloud
Num 14:14 by daytime in a *p* of a cloud
Num 14:14 and in a *p* of fire by night
Deut 31:15 the tabernacle in a *p* of a cloud
Deut 31:15 the *p* of the cloud stood over the
Judg 9:6 of the *p* that was in Shechem
Judg 20:40 out of the city with a *p* of smoke
2Sa 18:18 and reared up for himself a *p*
2Sa 18:18 he called the *p* after his own

1Kin 7:21 and he set up the right *p*, and
1Kin 7:21 and he set up the left *p*, and
2Kin 11:14 behold, the king stood by a *p*
2Kin 23:3 And the king stood by a *p*, and made
2Kin 25:17 of the one *p* was eighteen cubits
2Kin 25:17 the second *p* with wreathen work
2Chr 23:13 stood at his *p* at the entering in
Neh 9:12 them in the day by a cloudy *p*
Neh 9:12 and in the night by a *p* of fire
Neh 9:19 the *p* of the cloud departed not
Neh 9:19 neither the *p* of fire by night,
Ps 99:7 spake unto them in the cloudy *p*
Is 19:19 a *p* at the border thereof to the
Jer 1:18 day a defenced city, and an iron *p*
Jer 52:21 the height of one *p* was eighteen
Jer 52:22 The second *p* also and the
1Ti 3:15 church of the living God, the *p*
Rev 3:12 make a *p* in the temple of my God

**PILLARS**
Ex 24:4 altar under the hill, and twelve *p*
Ex 26:32 thou shalt hang it upon four *p* of
Ex 26:37 hanging five *p* of shittim wood
Ex 27:10 And the twenty *p* thereof and their
Ex 27:10 the hooks of the *p* and their
Ex 27:11 cubits long, and his twenty *p*
Ex 27:11 the hooks of the *p* and their
Ex 27:12 their *p* ten, and their sockets ten
Ex 27:14 their *p* three, and their sockets
Ex 27:15 their *p* three, and their sockets
Ex 27:16 their *p* shall be four, and their
Ex 27:17 All the *p* round about the court
Ex 35:11 and his boards, his bars, his *p*
Ex 35:17 The hangings of the court, his *p*
Ex 36:36 thereunto four *p* of shittim wood
Ex 36:38 the five *p* of it with their hooks
Ex 38:10 Their *p* were twenty, and their
Ex 38:10 the hooks of the *p* and their
Ex 38:11 their *p* were twenty, and their
Ex 38:11 the hooks of the *p* and their
Ex 38:12 of fifty cubits, their *p* ten
Ex 38:12 the hooks of the *p* and their
Ex 38:14 their *p* three, and their sockets
Ex 38:15 their *p* three, and their sockets
Ex 38:17 sockets for the *p* were of brass
Ex 38:17 the hooks of the *p* and their
Ex 38:17 all the *p* of the court were
Ex 38:19 their *p* were four, and their
Ex 38:28 shekels he made hooks for the *p*
Ex 39:33 his boards, his bars, and his *p*
Ex 39:40 The hangings of the court, his *p*
Ex 40:18 bars thereof, and reared up his *p*
Num 3:36 the *p* thereof, and the sockets
Num 3:37 the *p* of the court round about,
Num 4:31 the *p* thereof, and sockets thereof
Num 4:32 the *p* of the court round about,
Deut 12:3 their altars, and break their *p*
Judg 16:25 and they set him between the *p*
Judg 16:26 *p* whereupon the house standeth
Judg 16:29 *p* upon which the house stood
1Sa 2:8 for the *p* of the earth are the
1Kin 7:2 cubits, upon four rows of cedar *p*
1Kin 7:2 with cedar beams upon the *p*
1Kin 7:3 beams, that lay on forty five *p*
1Kin 7:6 And he made a porch of *p*
1Kin 7:6 and the other *p* and the thick beam
1Kin 7:15 For he cast two *p* of brass
1Kin 7:16 to set upon the tops of the *p*
1Kin 7:17 which were upon the top of the *p*
1Kin 7:18 And he made the *p*, and two rows
1Kin 7:19 that were upon the top of the *p*
1Kin 7:20 the chapiters upon the two *p* had
1Kin 7:21 he set up the *p* in the porch of
1Kin 7:22 the top of the *p* was lily work
1Kin 7:22 so was the work of the *p* finished
1Kin 7:41 The two *p*, and the two bowls of
1Kin 7:41 that were on the top of the two *p*
1Kin 7:41 which were upon the top of the *p*
1Kin 7:42 chapiters that were upon the *p*
1Kin 10:12 trees *p* for the house of the LORD
2Kin 18:16 from the *p* which Hezekiah king of
2Kin 25:13 the *p* of brass that were in the
2Kin 25:16 The two *p*, one sea, and the bases
1Chr 18:8 made the brasen sea, and the *p*
2Chr 3:15 before the house two *p* of thirty
2Chr 3:16 and put them on the heads of the *p*
2Chr 3:17 he reared up the *p* before the
2Chr 4:12 To wit, the two *p*, and the pommels
2Chr 4:12 were on the top of the two *p*
2Chr 4:12 which were on the top of the *p*
2Chr 4:13 chapiters which were upon the *p*
Est 1:6 to silver rings and *p* of marble
Job 9:6 place, and the *p* thereof tremble
Job 26:11 The *p* of heaven tremble, and are
Ps 75:3 I bear up the *p* of it
Prov 9:1 she hath hewn out her seven *p*
Song 3:6 of the wilderness like *p* of smoke
Song 3:10 He made the *p* thereof of silver,
Song 5:15 His legs are as *p* of marble
Jer 27:19 LORD of hosts concerning the *p*
Jer 52:17 Also the *p* of brass that were in
Jer 52:20 The two *p*, one sea, and twelve
Jer 52:21 And concerning the *p*, the height
Eze 40:49 there were *p* by the posts, one on
Eze 42:6 *p* as the *p* of the courts
Joel 2:30 blood, and fire, and *p* of smoke
Gal 2:9 and John, who seemed to be *p*
Rev 10:1 the sun, and his feet as *p* of fire

**PILLOWS**
Gen 28:11 that place, and put them for his *p*
Gen 28:18 stone that he had put for his *p*
Eze 13:18 women that sew *p* to all armholes
Eze 13:20 Behold, I am against your *p*

**PILTAI** *(pil'-tahee) A priest.*
Neh 12:17 of Miniamin, of Moadiah, *P*

**PINE**
Lev 26:39 *p* away in their iniquity in your
Lev 26:39 shall they *p* away with them
Neh 8:15 *p* branches, and myrtle branches,
Is 41:19 the desert the fir tree, and the *p*
Is 60:13 the *p* tree, and the box together,
Lam 4:9 for these *p* away, stricken
Eze 24:23 but ye shall *p* away for your
Eze 33:10 we *p* away in them, how should we

**PINON**
Gen 36:41 Aholibamah, duke Elah, duke *P*
1Chr 1:52 Aholibamah, duke Elah, duke *P*

**PINS**
Ex 27:19 thereof, and all the *p* thereof
Ex 27:19 all the *p* of the court, shall be
Ex 35:18 The *p* of the tabernacle, and the
Ex 35:18 the *p* of the court, and their
Ex 38:20 all the *p* of the tabernacle, and
Ex 38:31 all the *p* of the tabernacle, and
Ex 38:31 all the *p* of the court round
Ex 39:40 court gate, his cords, and his *p*
Num 3:37 and their sockets, and their *p*
Num 4:32 and their sockets, and their *p*
Is 3:22 and the wimples, and the crisping *p*

**PIPE**
1Sa 10:5 a psaltery, and a tabret, and a *p*
Is 5:12 and the viol, the tabret, and *p*
Is 30:29 as when one goeth with a *p* to
1Cor 14:7 giving sound, whether *p* or harp

**PIPED**
1Kin 1:40 him, and the people *p* with pipes
Mt 11:17 We have *p* unto you, and ye have
Lk 7:32 We have *p* unto you, and ye have
1Cor 14:7 it be known what is *p* or harped

**PIPES**
1Kin 1:40 him, and the people piped with *p*
Jer 48:36 heart shall sound for Moab like *p*
Jer 48:36 like *p* for the men of Kir-heres
Eze 28:13 of thy *p* was prepared in thee in
Zec 4:2 seven *p* to the seven lamps, which
Zec 4:12 *p* empty the golden oil out of

**PIRAM** *(pi'-ram) An Amorite king.*
Josh 10:3 unto *P* king of Jarmuth, and unto

**PIRATHON** *(pir'-a-thon)* See PIRATHONITE. *A place in Ephraim.*
Judg 12:15 was buried in *P* in the land of

**PIRATHONITE** *(pir'-a-thon-ite) An inhabitant of Pirathon.*
Judg 12:13 him Abdon the son of Hillel, a *P*
Judg 12:15 the son of Hillel the *P* died
2Sa 23:30 Benaiah the *P*, Hiddai of the
1Chr 11:31 of Benjamin, Benaiah the *P*
1Chr 27:14 eleventh month was Benaiah the *P*

**PISGAH** *(piz'-gah) A mountain peak in Moab.*
Num 21:20 country of Moab, to the top of *P*
Num 23:14 field of Zophim, to the top of *P*
Deut 3:27 Get thee up into the top of *P*
Deut 4:49 the plain, under the springs of *P*
Deut 34:1 mountain of Nebo, to the top of *P*

**PISIDIA** *(pi-sid'-e-ah) A Roman province in Asia Minor.*
Acts 13:14 Perga, they came to Antioch in *P*
Acts 14:24 they had passed throughout *P*

**PISON** *(pi'-son) A river of Eden.*
Gen 2:11 The name of the first is *P*

**PISPAH** *(piz'-pah) A son of Jether.*
1Chr 7:38 Jephunneh, and *P*, and Ara

**PIT**
Gen 37:20 slay him, and cast him into some *p*
Gen 37:22 but cast him into this *p* that is
Gen 37:24 took him, and cast him into a *p*
Gen 37:24 the *p* was empty, there was no
Gen 37:28 and lifted up Joseph out of the *p*
Gen 37:29 And Reuben returned unto the *p*
Gen 37:29 behold, Joseph was not in the *p*
Ex 21:33 And if a man shall open a *p*
Ex 21:33 or if a man shall dig a *p*
Ex 21:34 The owner of the *p* shall make it
Lev 11:36 Nevertheless a fountain or *p*
Num 16:30 and they go down quick into the *p*
Num 16:33 them, went down alive into the *p*
2Sa 17:9 Behold, he is hid now in some *p*
2Sa 18:17 him into a great *p* in the wood
2Sa 23:20 the midst of a *p* in time of snow
2Kin 10:14 slew them at the *p* of the
1Chr 11:22 slew a lion in a *p* in a snowy day
Job 6:27 ye dig a *p* for your friend
Job 17:16 go down to the bars of the *p*
Job 33:18 keepeth back his soul from the *p*
Job 33:24 him from going down to the *p*
Job 33:28 his soul from going into the *p*
Job 33:30 To bring back his soul from the *p*
Ps 7:15 He made a *p*, and digged it, and is
Ps 9:15 sunk down in the *p* that they made
Ps 28:1 like them that go down into the *p*
Ps 30:3 I should not go down to the *p*
Ps 30:9 my blood, when I go down to the *p*
Ps 35:7 they hid for me their net in a *p*
Ps 40:2 me up also out of an horrible *p*
Ps 55:23 down into the *p* of destruction
Ps 57:6 they have digged a *p* before me
Ps 69:15 let not the *p* shut her mouth upon
Ps 88:4 with them that go down into the *p*
Ps 88:6 Thou hast laid me in the lowest *p*
Ps 94:13 until the *p* be digged for the
Ps 143:7 unto them that go down into the *p*
Prov 1:12 as those that go down into the *p*
Prov 22:14 of strange women is a deep *p*
Prov 23:27 and a strange woman is a narrow *p*
Prov 26:27 Whoso diggeth a *p* shall fall
Prov 28:10 shall fall himself into his own *p*
Prov 28:17 of any person shall flee to the *p*
Eccl 10:8 He that diggeth a *p* shall fall
Is 14:15 to hell, to the sides of the *p*
Is 14:19 go down to the stones of the *p*
Is 24:17 Fear, and the *p*, and the snare, are
Is 24:18 of the fear shall fall into the *p*
Is 24:18 up out of the midst of the *p*
Is 24:22 prisoners are gathered in the *p*
Is 30:14 to take water withal out of the *p*
Is 38:17 it from the *p* of corruption
Is 38:18 the *p* cannot hope for thy truth
Is 51:1 to the hole of the *p* whence ye
Is 51:14 that he should not die in the *p*
Jer 18:20 they have digged a *p* for my soul
Jer 18:22 they have digged a *p* to take me
Jer 41:7 cast them into the midst of the *p*
Jer 41:9 Now the *p* wherein Ishmael had
Jer 48:43 Fear, and the *p*, and the snare,
Jer 48:44 the fear shall fall into the *p*
Jer 48:44 the *p* shall be taken in the snare
Eze 19:4 he was taken in their *p*, and they
Eze 19:8 he was taken in their *p*
Eze 26:20 with them that descend into the *p*
Eze 26:20 with them that go down to the *p*
Eze 28:8 shall bring thee down to the *p*
Eze 31:14 with them that go down to the *p*
Eze 31:16 with them that descend into the *p*
Eze 32:18 with them that go down into the *p*
Eze 32:23 are set in the sides of the *p*
Eze 32:24 with them that go down to the *p*
Eze 32:25 with them that go down to the *p*
Eze 32:29 with them that go down to the *p*
Eze 32:30 with them that go down to the *p*
Zec 9:11 out of the *p* wherein is no water
Mt 12:11 if it fall into a *p* on the
Lk 14:5 an ass or an ox fallen into a *p*
Rev 9:1 given the key of the bottomless *p*

Rev 9:2 And he opened the bottomless *p*
Rev 9:2 there arose a smoke out of the *p*
Rev 9:2 by reason of the smoke of the *p*
Rev 9:11 is the angel of the bottomless *p*
Rev 11:7 *p* shall make war against them
Rev 17:8 ascend out of the bottomless *p*
Rev 20:1 the key of the bottomless *p*
Rev 20:3 And cast him into the bottomless *p*

**PITCH**
Gen 6:14 *p* it within and without with *p*
Ex 2:3 and daubed it with slime and with *p*
Num 1:52 of Israel shall *p* their tents
Num 1:53 But the Levites shall *p* round
Num 2:2 shall *p* by his own standard
Num 2:2 of the congregation shall they *p*
Num 2:3 Judah *p* throughout their armies
Num 2:5 those that do *p* next unto him
Num 2:12 those which *p* by him shall be the
Num 3:23 of the Gershonites shall *p* behind
Num 3:29 of the sons of Kohath shall *p* on
Num 3:35 these shall *p* on the side of the
Deut 1:33 out a place to *p* your tents in
Josh 4:20 of Jordan, did Joshua *p* in Gilgal
Is 13:20 shall the Arabian *p* tent there
Is 34:9 thereof shall be turned into *p*
Is 34:9 thereof shall become burning *p*
Jer 6:3 they shall *p* their tents against

**PITCHED**
Gen 12:8 *p* his tent, having Beth-el on the
Gen 13:12 plain, and *p* his tent toward Sodom
Gen 26:17 *p* his tent in the valley of Gerar
Gen 26:25 of the LORD, and *p* his tent there
Gen 31:25 Now Jacob had *p* his tent in the
Gen 31:25 brethren *p* in the mount of Gilead
Gen 33:18 *p* his tent before the city
Ex 17:1 of the LORD, and *p* in Rephidim
Ex 19:2 Sinai, and had *p* in the wilderness
Ex 33:7 *p* it without the camp, afar off
Num 1:51 and when the tabernacle is to be *p*
Num 2:34 so they *p* by their standards, and
Num 9:17 children of Israel *p* their tents
Num 9:18 commandment of the LORD they *p*
Num 12:16 *p* in the wilderness of Paran
Num 21:10 Israel set forward, and *p* in Oboth
Num 21:11 Oboth, and *p* at Ije-abarim, in the
Num 21:12 and *p* in the valley of Zared
Num 21:13 *p* on the other side of Arnon,
Num 22:1 *p* in the plains of Moab on this
Num 33:5 from Rameses, and *p* in Succoth
Num 33:6 *p* in Etham, which is in the edge
Num 33:7 and they *p* before Migdol
Num 33:8 of Etham, and *p* in Marah
Num 33:9 and they *p* there
Num 33:15 *p* in the wilderness of Sinai
Num 33:16 Sinai, and *p* at Kibroth-hattaavah
Num 33:18 from Hazeroth, and *p* in Rithmah
Num 33:19 Rithmah, and *p* at Rimmon-parez
Num 33:20 from Rimmon-parez, and *p* in Libnah
Num 33:21 from Libnah, and *p* at Rissah
Num 33:22 from Rissah, and *p* in Kehelathah
Num 33:23 Kehelathah, and *p* in mount Shapher
Num 33:25 from Haradah, and *p* in Makheloth
Num 33:27 from Tahath, and *p* at Tarah
Num 33:28 from Tarah, and *p* in Mithcah
Num 33:29 from Mithcah, and *p* in Hashmonah
Num 33:31 Moseroth, and *p* in Bene-jaakan
Num 33:33 Hor-hagidgad, and *p* in Jotbathah
Num 33:36 *p* in the wilderness of Zin, which
Num 33:37 *p* in mount Hor, in the edge of
Num 33:41 from mount Hor, and *p* in Zalmonah
Num 33:42 from Zalmonah, and *p* in Punon
Num 33:43 from Punon, and *p* in Oboth
Num 33:44 *p* in Ije-abarim, in the border of
Num 33:45 from Iim, and *p* in Dibon-gad
Num 33:47 *p* in the mountains of Abarim,
Num 33:48 *p* in the plains of Moab by Jordan
Num 33:49 And they *p* by Jordan, from
Josh 8:11 *p* on the north side of Ai
Josh 11:5 *p* together at the waters of Merom
Judg 4:11 *p* his tent unto the plain of
Judg 6:33 *p* in the valley of Jezreel
Judg 7:1 *p* beside the well of Harod
Judg 11:18 *p* on the other side of Arnon, but
Judg 11:20 *p* in Jahaz, and fought against
Judg 15:9 *p* in Judah, and spread themselves
Judg 18:12 *p* in Kirjath-jearim, in Judah
1Sa 4:1 to battle, and *p* beside Eben-ezer
1Sa 4:1 and the Philistines *p* in Aphek
1Sa 13:5 *p* in Michmash, eastward from
1Sa 17:1 *p* between Shochoh and Azekah, in
1Sa 17:2 *p* by the valley of Elah, and set
1Sa 26:3 Saul *p* in the hill of Hachilah,
1Sa 26:5 to the place where Saul had *p*
1Sa 26:5 the people *p* round about him
1Sa 28:4 together, and came and *p* in Shunem
1Sa 28:4 together, and they *p* in Gilboa
1Sa 29:1 the Israelites *p* by a fountain
2Sa 6:17 that David had *p* for it
2Sa 17:26 Absalom *p* in the land of Gilead
2Sa 23:13 *p* in the valley of Rephaim
2Sa 24:5 *p* in Aroer, on the right side of
1Kin 20:27 the children of Israel *p* before
1Kin 20:29 they *p* one over against the other
2Kin 25:1 Jerusalem, and *p* against it
1Chr 15:1 ark of God, and *p* for it a tent
1Chr 16:1 the tent that David had *p* for it
1Chr 19:7 who came and *p* before Medeba
2Chr 1:4 for he had *p* a tent for it at
Jer 52:4 *p* against it, and built forts
Heb 8:2 true tabernacle, which the Lord *p*

**PITCHER**
Gen 24:14 whom I shall say, Let down thy *p*
Gen 24:15 with her *p* upon her shoulder
Gen 24:16 down to the well, and filled her *p*
Gen 24:17 drink a little water of thy *p*
Gen 24:18 let down her *p* upon her hand, and
Gen 24:20 emptied her *p* into the trough, and
Gen 24:43 a little water of thy *p* to drink
Gen 24:45 forth with her *p* on her shoulder
Gen 24:46 let down her *p* from her shoulder,
Eccl 12:6 or the *p* be broken at the
Mk 14:13 you a man bearing a *p* of water
Lk 22:10 meet you, bearing a *p* of water

**PITCHERS**
Judg 7:16 in every man's hand, with empty *p*
Judg 7:16 and lamps within the *p*
Judg 7:19 brake the *p* that were in their
Judg 7:20 blew the trumpets, and brake the *p*
Lam 4:2 are they esteemed as earthen *p*

**PITHOM** *(pi'-thom) A city in Lower Egypt.*
Ex 1:11 for Pharaoh treasure cities, *P*

**PITHON** *(pi'-thon) A son of Micah.*
1Chr 8:35 And the sons of Micah were, *P*
1Chr 9:41 And the sons of Micah were, *P*

**PITIED**
Ps 106:46 He made them also to be *p* of all
Lam 2:2 of Jacob, and hath not *p*
Lam 2:17 hath thrown down, and hath not *p*
Lam 2:21 thou hast killed, and not *p*
Lam 3:43 thou hast slain, thou hast not *p*
Eze 16:5 None eye *p* thee, to do any of

**PITIETH**
Ps 103:13 Like as a father *p* his children
Ps 103:13 so the LORD *p* them that fear him
Eze 24:21 eyes, and that which your soul *p*

**PITS**
1Sa 13:6 rocks, and in high places, and in *p*
Ps 119:85 The proud have digged *p* for me
Ps 140:10 into deep *p*, that they rise not
Jer 2:6 through a land of deserts and of *p*
Jer 14:3 they came to the *p*, and found no
Lam 4:20 of the LORD, was taken in their *p*

**PITY**
Deut 7:16 eye shall have no *p* upon them
Deut 13:8 neither shall thine eye *p* him
Deut 19:13 Thine eye shall not *p* him
Deut 19:21 And thine eye shall not *p*
Deut 25:12 hand, thine eye shall not *p* her
2Sa 12:6 thing, and because he had no *p*
Job 6:14 To him that is afflicted *p* should
Job 19:21 Have *p* upon me, have *p* upon me
Ps 69:20 and I looked for some to take *p*
Prov 19:17 He that hath *p* upon the poor
Prov 28:8 it for him that will *p* the poor
Is 13:18 they shall have no *p* on the fruit
Is 63:9 in his *p* he redeemed them
Jer 13:14 I will not *p*, nor spare, nor have
Jer 15:5 For who shall have *p* upon thee
Jer 21:7 not spare them, neither have *p*
Eze 5:11 spare, neither will I have any *p*
Eze 7:4 spare thee, neither will I have *p*
Eze 7:9 not spare, neither will I have *p*
Eze 8:18 not spare, neither will I have *p*
Eze 9:5 your eye spare, neither have ye *p*
Eze 9:10 not spare, neither will I have *p*
Eze 36:21 But I had *p* for mine holy name,
Joel 2:18 for his land, and *p* his people
Amos 1:11 the sword, and did cast off all *p*
Jonah 4:10 Thou hast had *p* on the gourd
Zec 11:5 and their own shepherds *p* them not
Zec 11:6 For I will no more *p* the
Mt 18:33 even as I had *p* on thee

**PLAGUE**
Ex 11:1 I bring one *p* more upon Pharaoh
Ex 12:13 the *p* shall not be upon you to
Ex 30:12 that there be no *p* among them
Lev 13:2 his flesh like the *p* of leprosy
Lev 13:3 on the *p* in the skin of the flesh
Lev 13:3 the hair in the *p* is turned white
Lev 13:3 the *p* in sight be deeper than the
Lev 13:3 his flesh, it is a *p* of leprosy
Lev 13:4 up him that hath the *p* seven days
Lev 13:5 if the *p* in his sight be at a
Lev 13:5 the *p* spread not in the skin
Lev 13:6 if the *p* be somewhat dark
Lev 13:6 the *p* spread not in the skin
Lev 13:9 When the *p* of leprosy is in a man
Lev 13:12 the skin of him that hath the *p*
Lev 13:13 him clean that hath the *p*
Lev 13:17 if the *p* be turned into white
Lev 13:17 him clean that hath the *p*
Lev 13:20 it is a *p* of leprosy broken out
Lev 13:22 it is a *p*
Lev 13:25 it is the *p* of leprosy
Lev 13:27 it is the *p* of leprosy
Lev 13:29 If a man or woman have a *p* upon
Lev 13:30 Then the priest shall see the *p*
Lev 13:31 priest look on the *p* of the scall
Lev 13:31 the *p* of the scall seven days
Lev 13:32 the priest shall look on the *p*
Lev 13:44 his *p* is in his head
Lev 13:45 And the leper in whom the *p* is
Lev 13:46 All the days wherein the *p* shall
Lev 13:47 also that the *p* of leprosy is in
Lev 13:49 if the *p* be greenish or reddish
Lev 13:49 it is a *p* of leprosy, and shall be
Lev 13:50 the priest shall look upon the *p*
Lev 13:50 up it that hath the *p* seven days
Lev 13:51 look on the *p* on the seventh day
Lev 13:51 if the *p* be spread in the garment
Lev 13:51 the *p* is a fretting leprosy
Lev 13:52 thing of skin, wherein the *p* is
Lev 13:53 the *p* be not spread in the
Lev 13:54 wash the thing wherein the *p* is
Lev 13:55 And the priest shall look on the *p*
Lev 13:55 if the *p* have not changed his
Lev 13:55 colour, and the *p* be not spread
Lev 13:56 the *p* be somewhat dark after the
Lev 13:57 it is a spreading *p*
Lev 13:57 that wherein the *p* is with fire
Lev 13:58 if the *p* be departed from them,
Lev 13:59 This is the law of the *p* of
Lev 14:3 if the *p* of leprosy be healed in
Lev 14:32 him in whom is the *p* of leprosy
Lev 14:34 I put the *p* of leprosy in a house
Lev 14:35 is as it were a *p* in the house
Lev 14:36 priest go into it to see the *p*
Lev 14:37 And he shall look on the *p*
Lev 14:37 if the *p* be in the walls of the
Lev 14:39 if the *p* be spread in the walls
Lev 14:40 away the stones in which the *p* is
Lev 14:43 if the *p* come again, and break out
Lev 14:44 if the *p* be spread in the house,
Lev 14:48 the *p* hath not spread in the
Lev 14:48 clean, because the *p* is healed
Lev 14:54 for all manner of *p* of leprosy
Num 8:19 that there be no *p* among the
Num 11:33 the people with a very great *p*
Num 14:37 died by the *p* before the LORD
Num 16:46 the *p* is begun
Num 16:47 the *p* was begun among the people
Num 16:48 and the *p* was stayed
Num 16:49 in the *p* were fourteen thousand
Num 16:50 and the *p* was stayed
Num 25:8 So the *p* was stayed from the
Num 25:9 that died in the *p* were twenty
Num 25:18 the day of the *p* for Peor's sake
Num 26:1 And it came to pass after the *p*
Num 31:16 Peor, and there was a *p* among the
Deut 24:8 Take heed in the *p* of leprosy
Deut 28:61 Also every sickness, and every *p*
Josh 22:17 although there was a *p* in the
1Sa 6:4 for one *p* was on you all, and on
2Sa 24:21 that the *p* may be stayed from the
2Sa 24:25 the *p* was stayed from Israel

1Kin 8:37 whatsoever *p*, whatsoever sickness
1Kin 8:38 every man the *p* of his own heart
1Chr 21:22 that the *p* may be stayed from the
2Chr 21:14 with a great *p* will the LORD
Ps 89:23 his face, and *p* them that hate him
Ps 91:10 neither shall any *p* come nigh thy
Ps 106:29 and the *p* brake in upon them
Ps 106:30 and so the *p* was stayed
Zec 14:12 this shall be the *p* wherewith the
Zec 14:15 And so shall be the *p* of the horse
Zec 14:15 be in these tents, as this *p*
Zec 14:18 there shall be the *p*, wherewith
Mk 5:29 that she was healed of that *p*
Mk 5:34 go in peace, and be whole of thy *p*
Rev 16:21 God because of the *p* of the hail
Rev 16:21 for the *p* thereof was exceeding

**PLAGUED**
Gen 12:17 And the LORD *p* Pharaoh and his
Ex 32:35 the LORD *p* the people, because
Josh 24:5 I *p* Egypt, according to that
1Chr 21:17 thy people, that they should be *p*
Ps 73:5 neither are they *p* like other men
Ps 73:14 all the day long have I been *p*

**PLAGUES**
Gen 12:17 his house with great *p* because of
Ex 9:14 send all my *p* upon thine heart
Lev 26:21 I will bring seven times more *p*
Deut 28:59 LORD will make thy *p* wonderful
Deut 28:59 *p* of thy seed, even great *p*
Deut 29:22 when they see the *p* of that land
1Sa 4:8 with all the *p* in the wilderness
Jer 19:8 hiss because of all the *p* thereof
Jer 49:17 shall hiss at all the *p* thereof
Jer 50:13 astonished, and hiss at all her *p*
Hos 13:14 O death, I will be thy *p*
Mk 3:10 to touch him, as many as had *p*
Lk 7:21 many of their infirmities and *p*
Rev 9:20 *p* yet repented not of the works
Rev 11:6 and to smite the earth with all *p*
Rev 15:1 angels having the seven last *p*
Rev 15:6 of the temple, having the seven *p*
Rev 15:8 till the seven *p* of the seven
Rev 16:9 which hath power over these *p*
Rev 18:4 and that ye receive not of her *p*
Rev 18:8 shall her *p* come in one day
Rev 21:9 vials full of the seven last *p*
Rev 22:18 God shall add unto him the *p* that

**PLAIN**
Gen 11:2 that they found a *p* in the land
Gen 12:6 of Sichem, unto the *p* of Moreh
Gen 13:10 and beheld all the *p* of Jordan
Gen 13:11 Lot chose him all the *p* of Jordan
Gen 13:12 dwelled in the cities of the *p*
Gen 13:18 came and dwelt in the *p* of Mamre
Gen 14:13 for he dwelt in the *p* of Mamre
Gen 19:17 neither stay thou in all the *p*
Gen 19:25 those cities, and all the *p*
Gen 19:28 and toward all the land of the *p*
Gen 19:29 God destroyed the cities of the *p*
Gen 25:27 and Jacob was a *p* man, dwelling in
Deut 1:1 in the *p* over against the Red sea
Deut 1:7 places nigh thereunto, in the *p*
Deut 2:8 the way of the *p* from Elath
Deut 3:10 All the cities of the *p*, and all
Deut 3:17 The *p* also, and Jordan, and the
Deut 3:17 even unto the sea of the *p*
Deut 4:43 in the *p* country, of the
Deut 4:49 all the *p* on this side Jordan
Deut 4:49 even unto the sea of the *p*
Deut 34:3 the *p* of the valley of Jericho,
Josh 3:16 came down toward the sea of the *p*
Josh 8:14 at a time appointed, before the *p*
Josh 11:16 Goshen, and the valley, and the *p*
Josh 12:1 Hermon, and all the *p* on the east
Josh 12:3 And from the *p* to the sea of
Josh 12:3 east, and unto the sea of the *p*
Josh 13:9 all the *p* of Medeba unto Dibon
Josh 13:16 the river, and all the *p* by Medeba
Josh 13:17 all her cities that are in the *p*
Josh 13:21 And all the cities of the *p*
Josh 20:8 the *p* out of the tribe of Reuben
Judg 4:11 his tent unto the *p* of Zaanaim
Judg 9:6 by the *p* of the pillar that was
Judg 9:37 come along by the *p* of Meonenim
Judg 11:33 unto the *p* of the vineyards, with
1Sa 10:3 thou shalt come to the *p* of Tabor
1Sa 23:24 in the *p* on the south of Jeshimon
2Sa 2:29 all that night through the *p*
2Sa 4:7 them away through the *p* all night
2Sa 15:28 tarry in the *p* of the wilderness
2Sa 18:23 Ahimaaz ran by the way of the *p*
1Kin 7:46 In the *p* of Jordan did the king
1Kin 20:23 us fight against them in the *p*
1Kin 20:25 will fight against them in the *p*
2Kin 14:25 of Hamath unto the sea of the *p*
2Kin 25:4 king went the way toward the *p*
2Chr 4:17 In the *p* of Jordan did the king
Neh 3:22 the priests, the men of the *p*
Neh 6:2 of the villages in the *p* of Ono
Neh 12:28 both out of the *p* country round
Ps 27:11 O LORD, and lead me in a *p* path
Prov 8:9 They are all *p* to him that
Prov 15:19 way of the righteous is made *p*
Is 28:25 he hath made *p* the face thereof
Is 40:4 straight, and the rough places *p*
Jer 17:26 land of Benjamin, and from the *p*
Jer 21:13 of the valley, and rock of the *p*
Jer 39:4 and he went out the way of the *p*
Jer 48:8 the *p* shall be destroyed, as the
Jer 48:21 is come upon the *p* country
Jer 52:7 ) and they went by the way of the *p*
Eze 3:22 me, Arise, go forth into the *p*
Eze 3:23 I arose, and went forth into the *p*
Eze 8:4 to the vision that I saw in the *p*
Dan 3:1 he set it up in the *p* of Dura
Amos 1:5 the inhabitant from the *p* of Aven
Obad 19 they of the *p* the Philistines
Hab 2:2 make it *p* upon tables, that he
Zec 4:7 Zerubbabel thou shalt become a *p*
Zec 7:7 men inhabited the south and the *p*
Zec 14:10 a *p* from Geba to Rimmon south of
Mk 7:35 tongue was loosed, and he spake *p*
Lk 6:17 with them, and stood in the *p*

**PLAINLY**
Ex 21:5 And if the servant shall *p* say
Deut 27:8 all the words of this law very *p*
1Sa 2:27 Did I *p* appear unto the house of
1Sa 10:16 He told us *p* that the asses were
Ezr 4:18 us hath been *p* read before me
Is 32:4 shall be ready to speak *p*
Jn 10:24 If thou be the Christ, tell us *p*
Jn 11:14 Then said Jesus unto them *p*
Jn 16:25 I shall shew you *p* of the Father
Jn 16:29 unto him, Lo, now speakest thou *p*
Heb 11:14 *p* that they seek a country

**PLAINS**
Gen 18:1 unto him in the *p* of Mamre
Num 22:1 pitched in the *p* of Moab on this
Num 26:3 priest spake with them in the *p*
Num 26:63 the children of Israel in the *p*
Num 31:12 unto the camp at the *p* of Moab
Num 33:48 pitched in the *p* of Moab by
Num 33:49 Abel-shittim in the *p* of Moab
Num 33:50 Moses in the *p* of Moab by Jordan
Num 35:1 LORD spake unto Moses in the *p* of
Num 36:13 the children of Israel in the *p*
Deut 11:30 Gilgal, beside the *p* of Moreh
Deut 34:1 Moses went up from the *p* of Moab
Deut 34:8 in the *p* of Moab thirty days
Josh 4:13 unto battle, to the *p* of Jericho
Josh 5:10 month at even in the *p* of Jericho
Josh 11:2 of the *p* south of Chinneroth, and
Josh 12:8 and in the valleys, and in the *p*
Josh 13:32 for inheritance in the *p* of Moab
2Sa 17:16 night in the *p* of the wilderness
2Kin 25:5 overtook him in the *p* of Jericho
1Chr 27:28 trees that were in the low *p* was
2Chr 9:27 are in the low *p* in abundance
2Chr 26:10 in the low country, and in the *p*
Jer 39:5 Zedekiah in the *p* of Jericho
Jer 52:8 Zedekiah in the *p* of Jericho

**PLAISTER**
Lev 14:42 morter, and shall *p* the house
Deut 27:2 stones, and *p* them with *p*
Deut 27:4 thou shalt *p* them with *p*
Is 38:21 lay it for a *p* upon the boil, and
Dan 5:5 the candlestick upon the *p* of the

**PLANT**
Gen 2:5 every *p* of the field before it
Ex 15:17 *p* them in the mountain of thine
Deut 16:21 Thou shalt not *p* thee a grove of
Deut 28:30 thou shalt *p* a vineyard, and shalt
Deut 28:39 Thou shalt *p* vineyards, and dress
2Sa 7:10 my people Israel, and will *p* them
2Kin 19:29 *p* vineyards, and eat the fruits
1Chr 17:9 my people Israel, and will *p* them
Job 14:9 and bring forth boughs like a *p*
Ps 107:37 *p* vineyards, which may yield
Eccl 3:2 a time to *p*, and a time to pluck
Is 5:7 the men of Judah his pleasant *p*
Is 17:10 shalt thou *p* pleasant plants
Is 17:11 day shalt thou make thy *p* to grow
Is 37:30 *p* vineyards, and eat the fruit
Is 41:19 I will *p* in the wilderness the
Is 51:16 that I may *p* the heavens, and lay
Is 53:2 grow up before him as a tender *p*
Is 65:21 and they shall *p* vineyards
Is 65:22 they shall not *p*, and another eat
Jer 1:10 to throw down, to build, and to *p*
Jer 2:21 *p* of a strange vine unto me
Jer 18:9 a kingdom, to build and to *p* it
Jer 24:6 and I will *p* them, and not pluck
Jer 29:5 *p* gardens, and eat the fruit of
Jer 29:28 *p* gardens, and eat the fruit of
Jer 31:5 Thou shalt yet *p* vines upon the
Jer 31:5 the planters shall *p*, and shall
Jer 31:28 over them, to build, and to *p*
Jer 32:41 I will *p* them in this land
Jer 35:7 nor *p* vineyard, nor have any
Jer 42:10 pull you down, and I will *p* you
Eze 17:22 will *p* it upon an high mountain
Eze 17:23 the height of Israel will I *p* it
Eze 28:26 build houses, and *p* vineyards
Eze 34:29 raise up for them a *p* of renown
Eze 36:36 and *p* that that was desolate
Dan 11:45 he shall *p* the tabernacles of his
Amos 9:14 and they shall *p* vineyards
Amos 9:15 I will *p* them upon their land, and
Zeph 1:13 and they shall *p* vineyards
Mt 15:13 But he answered and said, Every *p*

**PLANTED**
Gen 2:8 the LORD God *p* a garden eastward
Gen 9:20 an husbandman, and he *p* a vineyard
Gen 21:33 Abraham *p* a grove in Beer-sheba,
Lev 19:23 shall have *p* all manner of trees
Num 24:6 lign aloes which the LORD hath *p*
Deut 20:6 man is he that hath *p* a vineyard
Josh 24:13 which ye *p* not do ye eat
Ps 1:3 a tree *p* by the rivers of water
Ps 80:8 cast out the heathen, and *p* it
Ps 80:15 which thy right hand hath *p*
Ps 92:13 Those that be *p* in the house of
Ps 94:9 He that *p* the ear, shall he not
Ps 104:16 of Lebanon, which he hath *p*
Eccl 2:4 I *p* me vineyards
Eccl 2:5 I *p* trees in them of all kind of
Eccl 3:2 time to pluck up that which is *p*
Is 5:2 *p* it with the choicest vine, and
Is 40:24 Yea, they shall not be *p*
Jer 2:21 Yet I had *p* thee a noble vine,
Jer 11:17 the LORD of hosts, that *p* thee
Jer 12:2 Thou hast *p* them, yea, they have
Jer 17:8 be as a tree *p* by the waters
Jer 45:4 which I have *p* I will pluck up
Eze 17:5 land, and *p* it in a fruitful field
Eze 17:8 It was *p* in a good soil by great
Eze 17:10 Yea, behold, being *p*, shall it
Eze 19:10 in thy blood, *p* by the waters
Eze 19:13 now she is *p* in the wilderness,
Hos 9:13 Tyrus, is *p* in a pleasant place
Amos 5:11 ye have *p* pleasant vineyards, but
Mt 15:13 my heavenly Father hath not *p*
Mt 21:33 which *p* a vineyard, and hedged it
Mk 12:1 A certain man *p* a vineyard
Lk 13:6 had a fig tree *p* in his vineyard
Lk 17:6 the root, and be thou *p* in the sea
Lk 17:28 they bought, they sold, they *p*
Lk 20:9 A certain man *p* a vineyard
Rom 6:5 For if we have been *p* together in
1Cor 3:6 I have *p*, Apollos watered

**PLANTETH**
Prov 31:16 of her hands she *p* a vineyard
Is 44:14 he *p* an ash, and the rain doth
1Cor 3:7 neither is he that *p* any thing
1Cor 3:8 Now he that *p* and he that watereth
1Cor 9:7 who *p* a vineyard, and eateth not

**PLANTS**
1Chr 4:23 and those that dwelt among *p*
Ps 128:3 olive *p* round about thy table
Ps 144:12 be as *p* grown up in their youth
Song 4:13 Thy *p* are an orchard of
Is 16:8 down the principal *p* thereof
Is 17:10 shalt thou plant pleasant *p*
Jer 48:32 thy *p* are gone over the sea, they
Eze 31:4 rivers running round about his *p*

## PLATES

Ex 39:3 did beat the gold into thin *p*
Num 16:38 let them make them broad *p* for a
Num 16:39 they were made broad *p* for a
1Kin 7:30 four brasen wheels, and *p* of brass
1Kin 7:36 For on the *p* of the ledges
Jer 10:9 Silver spread into *p* is brought

## PLAY

Ex 32:6 eat and to drink, and rose up to *p*
Deut 22:21 to *p* the whore in her father's
1Sa 16:16 that he shall *p* with his hand
1Sa 16:17 me now a man that can *p* well
1Sa 21:15 to *p* the mad man in my presence
2Sa 2:14 men now arise, and *p* before us
2Sa 6:21 will I *p* before the LORD
2Sa 10:12 let us *p* the men for our people,
Job 40:20 all the beasts of the field *p*
Job 41:5 Wilt thou *p* with him as with a
Ps 33:3 *p* skilfully with a loud noise
Ps 104:26 whom thou hast made to *p* therein
Is 11:8 shall *p* on the hole of the asp
Eze 33:32 can *p* well on an instrument
Hos 3:3 thou shalt not *p* the harlot
Hos 4:15 *p* the harlot, yet let not Judah
1Cor 10:7 to eat and drink, and rose up to *p*

## PLAYED

Gen 38:24 daughter in law hath *p* the harlot
Judg 19:2 his concubine *p* the whore against
1Sa 16:23 took an harp, and *p* with his hand
1Sa 18:7 answered one another as they *p*
1Sa 18:10 David *p* with his hand, as at
1Sa 19:9 and David *p* with his hand
1Sa 26:21 I have *p* the fool, and have erred
2Sa 6:5 all the house of Israel *p* before
2Kin 3:15 came to pass, when the minstrel *p*
1Chr 13:8 all Israel *p* before God with all
Jer 3:1 but thou hast *p* the harlot with
Jer 3:6 tree, and there hath *p* the harlot
Jer 3:8 but went and *p* the harlot also
Eze 16:28 Thou hast *p* the whore also with
Eze 16:28 thou hast *p* the harlot with them,
Eze 23:5 Aholah *p* the harlot when she was
Eze 23:19 wherein she had *p* the harlot in
Hos 2:5 their mother hath *p* the harlot

## PLAYING

Lev 21:9 profane herself by *p* the whore
1Sa 16:18 that is cunning in *p*, and a
1Chr 15:29 saw king David dancing and *p*
Ps 68:25 were the damsels *p* with timbrels
Jer 2:20 tree thou wanderest, *p* the harlot
Eze 16:41 thee to cease from *p* the harlot
Zec 8:5 girls *p* in the streets thereof

## PLEAD

Judg 6:31 against him, Will ye *p* for Baal
Judg 6:31 he that will *p* for him, let him
Judg 6:31 let him *p* for himself, because
Judg 6:32 Let Baal *p* against him, because
1Sa 24:15 *p* my cause, and deliver me out of
Job 9:19 who shall set me a time to *p*
Job 13:19 Who is he that will *p* with me
Job 16:21 Oh that one might *p* for a man
Job 19:5 me, and *p* against me my reproach
Job 23:6 Will he *p* against me with his
Ps 35:1 *P* my cause, O LORD, with them
Ps 43:1 *p* my cause against an ungodly
Ps 74:22 Arise, O God, *p* thine own cause
Ps 119:154 *P* my cause, and deliver me
Prov 22:23 For the LORD will *p* their cause
Prov 23:11 he shall *p* their cause with thee
Prov 31:9 *p* the cause of the poor and needy
Is 1:17 the fatherless, *p* for the widow
Is 3:13 The LORD standeth up to *p*
Is 43:26 let us *p* together
Is 66:16 will the LORD *p* with all flesh
Jer 2:9 Wherefore I will yet *p* with you
Jer 2:9 your children's children will I *p*
Jer 2:29 Wherefore will ye *p* with me
Jer 2:35 I will *p* with thee, because thou
Jer 12:1 thou, O LORD, when I *p* with thee
Jer 25:31 nations, he will *p* with all flesh
Jer 30:13 There is none to *p* thy cause
Jer 50:34 he shall throughly *p* their cause
Jer 51:36 I will *p* thy cause, and take
Eze 17:20 will *p* with him there for his
Eze 20:35 there will I *p* with you face to
Eze 20:36 of Egypt, so will I *p* with you
Eze 38:22 I will *p* against him with
Hos 2:2 *P* with your mother, *p*
Joel 3:2 will *p* with them there for my
Mic 6:2 people, and he will *p* with Israel
Mic 7:9 against him, until he *p* my cause

## PLEASANT

Gen 2:9 every tree that is *p* to the sight
Gen 3:6 and that it was *p* to the eyes
Gen 49:15 good, and the land that it was *p*
2Sa 1:23 *p* in their lives, and in their
2Sa 1:26 very *p* hast thou been unto me
1Kin 20:6 whatsoever is *p* in thine eyes
2Kin 2:19 the situation of this city is *p*
2Chr 32:27 and for all manner of *p* jewels
Ps 16:6 are fallen unto me in *p* places
Ps 81:2 the *p* harp with the psaltery
Ps 106:24 Yea, they despised the *p* land
Ps 133:1 how *p* it is for brethren to dwell
Ps 135:3 for it is *p*
Prov 2:10 knowledge is *p* unto thy soul
Prov 5:19 be as the loving hind and *p* roe
Prov 9:17 and bread eaten in secret is *p*
Prov 15:26 the words of the pure are *p* words
Prov 16:24 *P* words are as an honeycomb,
Prov 22:18 For it is a *p* thing if thou keep
Prov 24:4 with all precious and *p* riches
Eccl 11:7 a *p* thing it is for the eyes to
Song 1:16 thou art fair, my beloved, yea, *p*
Song 4:13 of pomegranates, with *p* fruits
Song 4:16 his garden, and eat his *p* fruits
Song 7:6 how *p* art thou, O love, for
Song 7:13 gates are all manner of *p* fruits
Is 2:16 Tarshish, and upon all *p* pictures
Is 5:7 and the men of Judah his *p* plant
Is 13:22 and dragons in their *p* palaces
Is 17:10 shalt thou plant *p* plants
Is 32:12 for the teats, for the *p* fields
Is 54:12 and all thy borders of *p* stones
Is 64:11 all our *p* things are laid waste
Jer 3:19 children, and give thee a *p* land
Jer 12:10 they have made my *p* portion a
Jer 23:10 the *p* places of the wilderness
Jer 25:34 and ye shall fall like a *p* vessel
Jer 31:20 is he a *p* child
Lam 1:7 of her miseries all her *p* things
Lam 1:10 his hand upon all her *p* things
Lam 1:11 they have given their *p* things
Lam 2:4 slew all that were *p* to the eye
Eze 26:12 walls, and destroy thy *p* houses
Eze 33:32 song of one that hath a *p* voice
Dan 8:9 the east, and toward the *p* land
Dan 10:3 I ate no *p* bread, neither came
Dan 11:38 with precious stones, and *p* things
Hos 9:6 the *p* places for their silver,
Hos 9:13 Tyrus, is planted in a *p* place
Hos 13:15 the treasure of all *p* vessels
Joel 3:5 your temples my goodly *p* things
Amos 5:11 ye have planted *p* vineyards
Mic 2:9 ye cast out from their *p* houses
Nah 2:9 glory out of all the *p* furniture
Zec 7:14 for they laid the *p* land desolate
Mal 3:4 Jerusalem be *p* unto the LORD, as

## PLEASE

Ex 21:8 If she *p* not her master, who hath
Num 23:27 peradventure it will *p* God that
1Sa 20:13 but if it *p* my father to do thee
2Sa 7:29 Therefore now let it *p* thee to
1Kin 21:6 or else, if it *p* thee, I will
1Chr 17:27 Now therefore let it *p* thee to
2Chr 10:7 *p* them, and speak good words to
Neh 2:5 If it *p* the king, and if thy
Neh 2:7 If it *p* the king, let letters be
Est 1:19 If it *p* the king, let there go a
Est 3:9 If it *p* the king, let it be
Est 5:8 if it *p* the king to grant my
Est 7:3 if it *p* the king, let my life be
Est 8:5 If it *p* the king, and if I have
Est 9:13 If it *p* the king, let it be
Job 6:9 that it would *p* God to destroy me
Job 20:10 children shall seek to *p* the poor
Ps 69:31 This also shall *p* the LORD better
Prov 16:7 When a man's ways *p* the LORD
Song 2:7 up, nor awake my love, till he *p*
Song 3:5 up, nor awake my love, till he *p*
Song 8:4 up, nor awake my love, until he *p*
Is 2:6 they *p* themselves in the children
Is 55:11 shall accomplish that which I *p*
Is 56:4 and choose the things that *p* me
Jn 8:29 do always those things that *p* him
Rom 8:8 are in the flesh cannot *p* God
Rom 15:1 the weak, and not to *p* ourselves
Rom 15:2 Let every one of us *p* his
1Cor 7:32 the Lord, how he may *p* the Lord
1Cor 7:33 the world, how he may *p* his wife
1Cor 7:34 world, how she may *p* her husband
1Cor 10:33 Even as I *p* all men in all things
Gal 1:10 or do I seek to *p* men
1Th 2:15 they *p* not God, and are contrary
1Th 4:1 to *p* God, so ye would abound more
2Ti 2:4 that he may *p* him who hath chosen
Titus 2:9 to *p* them well in all things
Heb 11:6 faith it is impossible to *p* him

## PLEASED

Gen 28:8 of Canaan *p* not Isaac his father
Gen 33:10 of God, and thou wast *p* with me
Gen 34:18 And their words *p* Hamor, and
Gen 45:16 it *p* Pharaoh well, and his
Num 24:1 when Balaam saw that it *p* the
Deut 1:23 And the saying *p* me well
Josh 22:30 of Manasseh spake, it *p* them
Josh 22:33 the thing *p* the children of
Judg 13:23 If the LORD were *p* to kill us
Judg 14:7 and she *p* Samson well
1Sa 12:22 because it hath *p* the LORD to
1Sa 18:20 told Saul, and the thing *p* him
1Sa 18:26 it *p* David well to be the king's
2Sa 3:36 took notice of it, and it *p* them
2Sa 3:36 the king did *p* all the people
2Sa 17:4 the saying *p* Absalom well, and all
2Sa 19:6 this day, then it had *p* thee well
1Kin 3:10 And the speech *p* the Lord, that
1Kin 9:1 desire which he was *p* to do
1Kin 9:12 and they *p* him not
2Chr 30:4 And the thing *p* the king and all
Neh 2:6 So it *p* the king to send me
Est 1:21 And the saying *p* the king and the
Est 2:4 And the thing *p* the king
Est 2:9 And the maiden *p* him, and she
Est 5:14 And the thing *p* Haman
Ps 40:13 Be *p*, O LORD, to deliver me
Ps 51:19 Then shalt thou be *p* with the
Ps 115:3 he hath done whatsoever he hath *p*
Ps 135:6 Whatsoever the LORD *p*, that did
Is 42:21 The LORD is well *p* for his
Is 53:10 Yet it *p* the LORD to bruise him
Dan 6:1 It *p* Darius to set over the
Jonah 1:14 O LORD, hast done as it *p* thee
Mic 6:7 Will the LORD be *p* with thousands
Mal 1:8 will he be *p* with thee, or accept
Mt 3:17 beloved Son, in whom I am well *p*
Mt 12:18 in whom my soul is well *p*
Mt 14:6 danced before them, and *p* Herod
Mt 17:5 beloved Son, in whom I am well *p*
Mk 1:11 beloved Son, in whom I am well *p*
Mk 6:22 *p* Herod and them that sat with him
Lk 3:22 in thee I am well *p*
Acts 6:5 the saying *p* the whole multitude
Acts 12:3 And because he saw it *p* the Jews
Acts 15:22 Then *p* it the apostles and elders,
Acts 15:34 Notwithstanding it *p* Silas to
Rom 15:3 For even Christ *p* not himself
Rom 15:26 For it hath *p* them of Macedonia
Rom 15:27 It hath *p* them verily
1Cor 1:21 it *p* God by the foolishness of
1Cor 7:12 she be *p* to dwell with him, let
1Cor 7:13 if he be *p* to dwell with her, let
1Cor 10:5 many of them God was not well *p*
1Cor 12:18 in the body, as it hath *p* him
1Cor 15:38 giveth it a body as it hath *p* him
Gal 1:10 for if I yet *p* men, I should not
Gal 1:15 But when it *p* God, who separated
Col 1:19 For it *p* the Father that in him
Heb 11:5 had this testimony, that he *p* God
Heb 13:16 such sacrifices God is well *p*
2Pet 1:17 beloved Son, in whom I am well *p*

## PLEASETH

Gen 16:6 do to her as it *p* thee
Gen 20:15 dwell where it *p* thee
Judg 14:3 for she *p* me well
Est 2:4 let the maiden which *p* the king
Eccl 7:26 *p* God shall escape from her
Eccl 8:3 for he doeth whatsoever *p* him

## PLEASING

Est 8:5 I be *p* in his eyes, let it be
Hos 9:4 neither shall they be *p* unto him
Col 1:10 worthy of the Lord unto all *p*
Col 3:20 for this is well *p* unto the Lord
1Th 2:4 not as *p* men, but God, which
1Jn 3:22 things that are *p* in his sight

### PLEASURE
Gen 18:12 I am waxed old shall I have *p*
Deut 23:24 grapes thy fill at thine own *p*
1Chr 29:17 heart, and hast *p* in uprightness
Ezr 5:17 let the king send his *p* to us
Ezr 10:11 God of your fathers, and do his *p*
Neh 9:37 and over our cattle, at their *p*
Est 1:8 do according to every man's *p*
Job 21:21 For what *p* hath he in his house
Job 21:25 his soul, and never eateth with *p*
Job 22:3 Is it any *p* to the Almighty, that
Ps 5:4 a God that hath *p* in wickedness
Ps 35:27 which hath *p* in the prosperity of
Ps 51:18 Do good in thy good *p* unto Zion
Ps 102:14 thy servants take *p* in her stones
Ps 103:21 ministers of his, that do his *p*
Ps 105:22 To bind his princes at his *p*
Ps 111:2 of all them that have *p* therein
Ps 147:10 he taketh not *p* in the legs of a
Ps 147:11 The LORD taketh *p* in them that
Ps 149:4 the LORD taketh *p* in his people
Prov 21:17 He that loveth *p* shall be a poor
Eccl 2:1 with mirth, therefore enjoy *p*
Eccl 5:4 for he hath no *p* in fools
Eccl 12:1 shalt say, I have no *p* in them
Is 21:4 the night of my *p* hath he turned
Is 44:28 and shall perform all my *p*
Is 46:10 stand, and I will do all my *p*
Is 48:14 he will do his *p* on Babylon
Is 53:10 the *p* of the LORD shall prosper
Is 58:3 in the day of your fast ye find *p*
Is 58:13 from doing thy *p* on my holy day
Is 58:13 own ways, nor finding thine own *p*
Jer 2:24 snuffeth up the wind at her *p*
Jer 22:28 is he a vessel wherein is no *p*
Jer 34:16 he had set at liberty at their *p*
Jer 48:38 like a vessel wherein is no *p*
Eze 16:37 with whom thou hast taken *p*
Eze 18:23 Have I any *p* at all that the
Eze 18:32 For I have no *p* in the death of
Eze 33:11 I have no *p* in the death of the
Hos 8:8 as a vessel wherein is no *p*
Hag 1:8 and I will take *p* in it, and I will
Mal 1:10 I have no *p* in you, saith the
Lk 12:32 good *p* to give you the kingdom
Acts 24:27 willing to shew the Jews a *p*
Acts 25:9 willing to do the Jews a *p*
Rom 1:32 but have *p* in them that do them
2Cor 12:10 Therefore I take *p* in infirmities
Eph 1:5 to the good *p* of his will
Eph 1:9 according to his good *p* which he
Phil 2:13 to will and to do of his good *p*
2Th 1:11 all the good *p* of his goodness
2Th 2:12 but had *p* in unrighteousness
1Ti 5:6 But she that liveth in *p* is dead
Heb 10:6 for sin thou hast had no *p*
Heb 10:8 not, neither hadst *p* therein
Heb 10:38 my soul shall have no *p* in him
Heb 12:10 chastened us after their own *p*
Jas 5:5 Ye have lived in *p* on the earth
2Pet 2:13 as they that count it *p* to riot
Rev 4:11 for thy *p* they are and were

### PLEASURES
Job 36:11 prosperity, and their years in *p*
Ps 16:11 hand there are *p* for evermore
Ps 36:8 them drink of the river of thy *p*
Is 47:8 this, thou that art given to *p*
Lk 8:14 *p* of this life, and bring no fruit
2Ti 3:4 lovers of *p* more than lovers of
Titus 3:3 serving divers lusts and *p*
Heb 11:25 than to enjoy the *p* of sin for a

### PLEDGE
Gen 38:17 she said, Wilt thou give me a *p*
Gen 38:18 he said, What *p* shall I give thee
Gen 38:20 to receive his *p* from the woman's
Ex 22:26 take thy neighbour's raiment to *p*
Deut 24:6 or the upper millstone to *p*
Deut 24:6 for he taketh a man's life to *p*
Deut 24:10 go into his house to fetch his *p*
Deut 24:11 bring out the *p* abroad unto thee
Deut 24:12 thou shalt not sleep with his *p*
Deut 24:13 *p* again when the sun goeth down
Deut 24:17 nor take a widow's raiment to *p*
1Sa 17:18 brethren fare, and take their *p*
Job 22:6 For thou hast taken a *p* from thy
Job 24:3 they take the widow's ox for a *p*
Job 24:9 breast, and take a *p* of the poor
Prov 20:16 take a *p* of him for a strange
Prov 27:13 take a *p* of him for a strange
Eze 18:7 hath restored to the debtor his *p*
Eze 18:12 violence, hath not restored the *p*
Eze 18:16 any, hath not withholden the *p*
Eze 33:15 If the wicked restore the *p*
Amos 2:8 clothes laid to *p* by every altar

### PLENTEOUS
Gen 41:34 of Egypt in the seven *p* years
Gen 41:47 in the seven *p* years the earth
Deut 28:11 LORD shall make thee *p* in goods
Deut 30:9 *p* in every work of thine hand
2Chr 1:15 gold at Jerusalem as *p* as stones
Ps 86:5 *p* in mercy unto all them that
Ps 86:15 and *p* in mercy and truth
Ps 103:8 slow to anger, and *p* in mercy
Ps 130:7 and with him is *p* redemption
Is 30:23 earth, and it shall be fat and *p*
Hab 1:16 portion is fat, and their meat *p*
Mt 9:37 disciples, The harvest truly is *p*

### PLENTIFUL
Ps 68:9 Thou, O God, didst send a *p* rain
Is 16:10 away, and joy out of the *p* field
Jer 2:7 And I brought you into a *p* country
Jer 48:33 is taken from the *p* field

### PLENTY
Gen 27:28 the earth, and *p* of corn and wine
Gen 41:29 *p* throughout all the land of
Gen 41:30 all the *p* shall be forgotten in
Gen 41:31 the *p* shall not be known in the
Lev 11:36 pit, wherein there is *p* of water
1Kin 10:11 from Ophir great *p* of almug trees
2Chr 31:10 had enough to eat, and have left *p*
Job 22:25 and thou shalt have *p* of silver
Job 37:23 in judgment, and in *p* of justice
Prov 3:10 shall thy barns be filled with *p*
Prov 28:19 his land shall have *p* of bread
Jer 44:17 for then had we *p* of victuals
Joel 2:26 And ye shall eat in *p*, and be

### PLOW
Deut 22:10 Thou shalt not *p* with an ox
1Sa 14:14 which a yoke of oxen might *p*
Job 4:8 I have seen, they that *p* iniquity
Prov 20:4 will not *p* by reason of the cold
Is 28:24 Doth the plowman *p* all day to sow
Hos 10:11 Judah shall *p*, and Jacob shall
Amos 6:12 will one *p* there with oxen
1Cor 9:10 he that ploweth should *p* in hope

### PLOWED
Judg 14:18 If ye had not *p* with my heifer,
Ps 129:3 The plowers *p* upon my back
Jer 26:18 Zion shall be *p* like a field
Hos 10:13 Ye have *p* wickedness, ye have
Mic 3:12 for your sake be *p* as a field

### PLOWING
1Kin 19:19 who was *p* with twelve yoke of
Job 1:14 Job, and said, The oxen were *p*
Prov 21:4 the *p* of the wicked, is sin
Lk 17:7 having a servant *p* or feeding

### PLUCK
Lev 1:16 he shall *p* away his crop with his
Num 33:52 quite *p* down all their high
Deut 23:25 then thou mayest *p* the ears with
2Chr 7:20 Then will I *p* them up by the
Job 24:9 They *p* the fatherless from the
Ps 25:15 for he shall *p* my feet out of the
Ps 52:5 *p* thee out of thy dwelling place,
Ps 74:11 *p* it out of thy bosom
Ps 80:12 which pass by the way do *p* her
Eccl 3:2 a time to *p* up that which is
Jer 12:14 I will *p* them out of their land,
Jer 12:14 *p* out the house of Judah from
Jer 12:17 not obey, I will utterly *p* up
Jer 18:7 and concerning a kingdom, to *p* up
Jer 22:24 hand, yet would I *p* thee thence
Jer 24:6 will plant them, and not *p* them up
Jer 31:28 I have watched over them, to *p* up
Jer 42:10 I will plant you, and not *p* you up
Jer 45:4 which I have planted I will *p* up
Eze 17:9 to *p* it up by the roots thereof
Eze 23:34 and *p* off thine own breasts
Mic 3:2 who *p* off their skin from off
Mic 5:14 I will *p* up thy groves out of the
Mt 5:29 *p* it out, and cast it from thee
Mt 12:1 began to *p* the ears of corn, and
Mt 18:9 *p* it out, and cast it from thee
Mk 2:23 they went, to *p* the ears of corn
Mk 9:47 thine eye offend thee, *p* it out
Jn 10:28 any man *p* them out of my hand
Jn 10:29 no man is able to *p* them out of

### PLUCKED
Ex 4:7 *p* it out of his bosom, and, behold
Deut 28:63 ye shall be *p* from off the land
Ruth 4:7 a man *p* off his shoe, and gave it
2Sa 23:21 *p* the spear out of the Egyptian's
1Chr 11:23 *p* the spear out of the Egyptian's
Ezr 9:3 *p* off the hair of my head and of
Neh 13:25 *p* off their hair, and made them
Job 29:17 *p* the spoil out of his teeth
Is 50:6 to them that *p* off the hair
Jer 6:29 for the wicked are not *p* away
Jer 12:15 after that I have *p* them out I
Jer 31:40 it shall not be *p* up, nor thrown
Eze 19:12 But she was *p* up in fury, she was
Dan 7:4 till the wings thereof were *p*
Dan 7:8 the first horns *p* up by the roots
Dan 11:4 for his kingdom shall be *p* up
Amos 4:11 a firebrand *p* out of the burning
Zec 3:2 this a brand *p* out of the fire
Mk 5:4 chains had been *p* asunder by him
Lk 6:1 his disciples *p* the ears of corn,
Lk 17:6 Be thou *p* up by the root, and be
Gal 4:15 ye would have *p* out your own eyes
Jude 12 twice dead, *p* up by the roots

### POCHERETH *(po-ke'-reth) A family of exiles.*
Ezr 2:57 the children of *P* of Zebaim
Neh 7:59 the children of *P* of Zebaim

### POINT
Gen 25:32 Behold, I am at the *p* to die
Num 34:7 ye shall *p* out for you mount Hor
Num 34:8 From mount Hor ye shall *p* out
Num 34:10 ye shall *p* out your east border
Jer 17:1 iron, and with the *p* of a diamond
Eze 21:15 I have set the *p* of the sword
Mk 5:23 daughter lieth at the *p* of death
Jn 4:47 for he was at the *p* of death
Jas 2:10 whole law, and yet offend in one *p*

### POISON
Deut 32:24 with the *p* of serpents of the
Deut 32:33 Their wine is the *p* of dragons
Job 6:4 the *p* whereof drinketh up my
Job 20:16 He shall suck the *p* of asps
Ps 58:4 *p* is like the *p* of a serpent
Ps 140:3 adders' *p* is under their lips
Rom 3:13 the *p* of asps is under their lips
Jas 3:8 an unruly evil, full of deadly *p*

### POLLS
Num 1:2 names, every male by their *p*
Num 1:18 years old and upward, by their *p*
Num 1:20 number of the names, by their *p*
Num 1:22 number of the names, by their *p*
1Chr 23:3 and their number by their *p*
1Chr 23:24 by number of names by their *p*

### POLLUTE
Num 18:32 neither shall ye *p* the holy
Num 35:33 So ye shall not *p* the land
Jer 7:30 is called by my name, to *p* it
Eze 7:21 and they shall *p* it
Eze 7:22 they shall *p* my secret place
Eze 13:19 will ye *p* me among my people for
Eze 20:31 ye *p* yourselves with all your
Eze 20:39 but *p* ye my holy name no more
Eze 39:7 I will not let them *p* my holy
Eze 44:7 to be in my sanctuary, to *p* it
Dan 11:31 they shall *p* the sanctuary of

### POLLUTED
Ex 20:25 thy tool upon it, thou hast *p* it
2Kin 23:16 *p* it, according to the word of
2Chr 36:14 *p* the house of the LORD which he
Ezr 2:62 therefore were they, as *p*
Neh 7:64 therefore were they, as *p*
Ps 106:38 and the land was *p* with blood
Is 47:6 I have *p* mine inheritance, and
Is 48:11 for how should my name be *p*
Jer 2:23 How canst thou say, I am not *p*
Jer 3:1 shall not that land be greatly *p*
Jer 3:2 thou hast *p* the land with thy
Jer 34:16 *p* my name, and caused every man
Lam 2:2 he hath *p* the kingdom and the
Lam 4:14 they have *p* themselves with blood
Eze 4:14 behold, my soul hath not been *p*
Eze 14:11 neither be *p* any more with all
Eze 16:6 saw thee *p* in thine own blood, I
Eze 16:22 and bare, and wast *p* in thy blood

Eze 20:9 not be *p* before the heathen
Eze 20:13 and my sabbaths they greatly *p*
Eze 20:14 not be *p* before the heathen
Eze 20:16 in my statutes, but *p* my sabbaths
Eze 20:21 they *p* my sabbaths
Eze 20:22 that it should not be *p* in the
Eze 20:24 had *p* my sabbaths, and their eyes
Eze 20:26 I *p* them in their own gifts, in
Eze 20:30 Are ye *p* after the manner of your
Eze 23:17 she was *p* with them, and her mind
Eze 23:30 thou art *p* with their idols
Eze 36:18 idols wherewith they had *p* it
Hos 6:8 work iniquity, and is *p* with blood
Hos 9:4 all that eat thereof shall be *p*
Amos 7:17 and thou shalt die in a *p* land
Mic 2:10 because it is *p*, it shall destroy
Zeph 3:1 Woe to her that is filthy and *p*
Zeph 3:4 her priests have *p* the sanctuary
Mal 1:7 Ye offer *p* bread upon mine altar
Mal 1:7 and ye say, Wherein have we *p* thee
Mal 1:12 say, The table of the LORD is *p*
Acts 21:28 temple, and hath *p* this holy place

**POLLUX** *A Roman god.*
Acts 28:11 isle, whose sign was Castor and *P*

**POMEGRANATE**
Ex 28:34 A golden bell and a *p*, a golden
Ex 28:34 *p*, a golden bell and a *p*
Ex 39:26 A bell and a *p*, a bell and a
Ex 39:26 and a *p*, a bell and a *p*
1Sa 14:2 part of Gibeah under a *p* tree
Song 4:3 a piece of a *p* within thy locks
Song 6:7 As a piece of a *p* are thy temples
Song 8:2 spiced wine of the juice of my *p*
Joel 1:12 the *p* tree, the palm tree also,
Hag 2:19 vine, and the fig tree, and the *p*

**POMEGRANATES**
Ex 28:33 of it thou shalt make *p* of blue
Ex 39:24 the hems of the robe *p* of blue
Ex 39:25 the *p* upon the hem of the robe
Ex 39:25 robe, round about between the *p*
Num 13:23 and they brought of the *p*, and of
Num 20:5 or of figs, or of vines, or of *p*
Deut 8:8 and vines, and fig trees, and *p*
1Kin 7:18 that were upon the top, with *p*
1Kin 7:20 the two pillars had *p* also above
1Kin 7:20 the *p* were two hundred in rows
1Kin 7:42 four hundred *p* for the two
1Kin 7:42 two rows of *p* for one network
2Kin 25:17 *p* upon the chapiter round about,
2Chr 3:16 and made an hundred *p*, and put them
2Chr 4:13 four hundred *p* on the two wreaths
2Chr 4:13 two rows of *p* on each wreath, to
Song 4:13 Thy plants are an orchard of *p*
Song 6:11 vine flourished, and the *p* budded
Song 7:12 grape appear, and the *p* bud forth
Jer 52:22 *p* upon the chapiters round about,
Jer 52:22 the *p* were like unto these
Jer 52:23 were ninety and six *p* on a side
Jer 52:23 all the *p* upon the network were

**POMP**
Is 5:14 and their multitude, and their *p*
Is 14:11 Thy *p* is brought down to the
Eze 7:24 I will also make the *p* of the
Eze 30:18 the *p* of her strength shall cease
Eze 32:12 they shall spoil the *p* of Egypt
Eze 33:28 the *p* of her strength shall cease
Acts 25:23 come, and Bernice, with great *p*

**PONTIUS** *(pon'-she-us) The family name of Pilate.*
Mt 27:2 delivered him to *P* Pilate the
Lk 3:1 *P* Pilate being governor of Judaea
Acts 4:27 *P* Pilate, with the Gentiles, and
1Ti 6:13 who before *P* Pilate witnessed a

**PONTUS** *(pon'-tus) A Roman province in Asia Minor.*
Acts 2:9 and in Judaea, and Cappadocia, in *P*
Acts 18:2 Jew named Aquila, born in *P*
1Pet 1:1 strangers scattered throughout *P*

**POOL**
2Sa 2:13 met together by the *p* of Gibeon
2Sa 2:13 the one on the one side of the *p*
2Sa 2:13 other on the other side of the *p*
2Sa 4:12 them up over the *p* in Hebron
1Kin 22:38 the chariot in the *p* of Samaria
2Kin 18:17 by the conduit of the upper *p*
2Kin 20:20 all his might, and how he made a *p*
Neh 2:14 the fountain, and to the king's *p*
Neh 3:15 the wall of the *p* of Siloah by
Neh 3:16 to the *p* that was made, and unto
Is 7:3 *p* in the highway of the fuller's
Is 22:9 the waters of the lower *p*
Is 22:11 walls for the water of the old *p*
Is 35:7 parched ground shall become a *p*
Is 36:2 by the conduit of the upper *p* in
Is 41:18 make the wilderness a *p* of water
Nah 2:8 is of old like a *p* of water
Jn 5:2 Jerusalem by the sheep market a *p*
Jn 5:4 at a certain season into the *p*
Jn 5:7 is troubled, to put me into the *p*
Jn 9:7 him, Go, wash in the *p* of Siloam
Jn 9:11 unto me, Go to the *p* of Siloam

**POOLS**
Ex 7:19 and upon all their *p* of water
Ps 84:6 the rain also filleth the *p*
Eccl 2:6 I made me *p* of water, to water
Is 14:23 for the bittern, and *p* of water
Is 42:15 islands, and I will dry up the *p*

**POOR**
Gen 41:19 other kine came up after them, *p*
Ex 22:25 of my people that is *p* by thee
Ex 23:3 countenance a *p* man in his cause
Ex 23:6 judgment of thy *p* in his cause
Ex 23:11 that the *p* of thy people may eat
Ex 30:15 the *p* shall not give less than
Lev 14:21 And if he be *p*, and cannot get so
Lev 19:10 thou shalt leave them for the *p*
Lev 19:15 not respect the person of the *p*
Lev 23:22 thou shalt leave them unto the *p*
Lev 25:25 If thy brother be waxen *p*
Lev 25:35 And if thy brother be waxen *p*
Lev 25:39 that dwelleth by thee be waxen *p*
Lev 25:47 that dwelleth by him wax *p*
Deut 15:4 there shall be no *p* among you
Deut 15:7 If there be among you a *p* man of
Deut 15:7 thine hand from thy *p* brother
Deut 15:9 eye be evil against thy *p* brother
Deut 15:11 For the *p* shall never cease out
Deut 15:11 wide unto thy brother, to thy *p*
Deut 24:12 And if the man be *p*, thou shalt
Deut 24:14 an hired servant that is *p*
Deut 24:15 for he is *p*, and setteth his heart
Judg 6:15 my family is *p* in Manasseh
Ruth 3:10 not young men, whether *p* or rich
1Sa 2:7 The LORD maketh *p*, and maketh rich
1Sa 2:8 raiseth up the *p* out of the dust
1Sa 18:23 in law, seeing that I am a *p* man
2Sa 12:1 the one rich, and the other *p*
2Sa 12:3 But the *p* man had nothing, save
2Sa 12:4 but took the *p* man's lamb
2Kin 25:12 of the guard left of the *p* of the
Est 9:22 one to another, and gifts to the *p*
Job 5:15 he saveth the *p* from the sword
Job 5:16 So the *p* hath hope, and iniquity
Job 20:10 shall seek to please the *p*
Job 20:19 oppressed and hath forsaken the *p*
Job 24:4 the *p* of the earth hide
Job 24:9 breast, and take a pledge of the *p*
Job 24:14 with the light killeth the *p*
Job 29:12 I delivered the *p* that cried
Job 29:16 I was a father to the *p*
Job 30:25 was not my soul grieved for the *p*
Job 31:16 withheld the *p* from their desire
Job 31:19 or any *p* without covering
Job 34:19 the rich more than the *p*
Job 34:28 the cry of the *p* to come unto him
Job 36:6 but giveth right to the *p*
Job 36:15 the *p* in his affliction, and
Ps 9:18 the expectation of the *p* shall
Ps 10:2 in his pride doth persecute the *p*
Ps 10:8 are privily set against the *p*
Ps 10:9 he lieth in wait to catch the *p*
Ps 10:9 he doth catch the *p*, when he
Ps 10:10 that the *p* may fall by his strong
Ps 10:14 the *p* committeth himself unto
Ps 12:5 For the oppression of the *p*
Ps 14:6 have shamed the counsel of the *p*
Ps 34:6 This *p* man cried, and the LORD
Ps 35:10 which deliverest the *p* from him
Ps 35:10 is too strong for him, yea, the *p*
Ps 37:14 their bow, to cast down the *p*
Ps 40:17 But I am *p* and needy
Ps 41:1 is he that considereth the *p*
Ps 49:2 Both low and high, rich and *p*
Ps 68:10 of thy goodness for the *p*
Ps 69:29 But I am *p* and sorrowful
Ps 69:33 For the LORD heareth the *p*
Ps 70:5 But I am *p* and needy
Ps 72:2 and thy *p* with judgment
Ps 72:4 shall judge the *p* of the people
Ps 72:12 the *p* also, and him that hath no
Ps 72:13 He shall spare the *p* and needy, and
Ps 74:19 congregation of thy *p* for ever
Ps 74:21 let the *p* and needy praise thy
Ps 82:3 Defend the *p* and fatherless
Ps 82:4 Deliver the *p* and needy
Ps 86:1 for I am *p* and needy
Ps 107:41 Yet setteth he the *p* on high from
Ps 109:16 shew mercy, but persecuted the *p*
Ps 109:22 For I am *p* and needy, and my heart
Ps 109:31 stand at the right hand of the *p*
Ps 112:9 dispersed, he hath given to the *p*
Ps 113:7 raiseth up the *p* out of the dust
Ps 132:15 I will satisfy her *p* with bread
Ps 140:12 afflicted, and the right of the *p*
Prov 10:4 He becometh *p* that dealeth with a
Prov 10:15 of the *p* is their poverty
Prov 13:7 there is that maketh himself *p*
Prov 13:8 but the *p* heareth not rebuke
Prov 13:23 food is in the tillage of the *p*
Prov 14:20 The *p* is hated even of his own
Prov 14:21 but he that hath mercy on the *p*
Prov 14:31 the *p* reproacheth his Maker
Prov 14:31 honoureth him hath mercy on the *p*
Prov 17:5 Whoso mocketh the *p* reproacheth
Prov 18:23 The *p* useth intreaties
Prov 19:1 Better is the *p* that walketh in
Prov 19:4 but the *p* is separated from his
Prov 19:7 the brethren of the *p* do hate him
Prov 19:17 upon the *p* lendeth unto the LORD
Prov 19:22 a *p* man is better than a liar
Prov 21:13 his ears at the cry of the *p*
Prov 21:17 loveth pleasure shall be a *p* man
Prov 22:2 The rich and *p* meet together
Prov 22:7 The rich ruleth over the *p*
Prov 22:9 he giveth of his bread to the *p*
Prov 22:16 the *p* to increase his riches
Prov 22:22 Rob not the *p*, because he is *p*
Prov 28:3 A *p* man that oppresseth the
Prov 28:3 *p* is like a sweeping rain which
Prov 28:6 Better is the *p* that walketh in
Prov 28:8 it for him that will pity the *p*
Prov 28:11 but the *p* that hath understanding
Prov 28:15 a wicked ruler over the *p* people
Prov 28:27 giveth unto the *p* shall not lack
Prov 29:7 considereth the cause of the *p*
Prov 29:13 The *p* and the deceitful man meet
Prov 29:14 that faithfully judgeth the *p*
Prov 30:9 or lest I be *p*, and steal, and take
Prov 30:14 to devour the *p* from off the
Prov 31:9 and plead the cause of the *p*
Prov 31:20 stretcheth out her hand to the *p*
Eccl 4:13 Better is a *p* and a wise child
Eccl 4:14 is born in his kingdom becometh *p*
Eccl 5:8 seest the oppression of the *p*
Eccl 6:8 what hath the *p*, that knoweth to
Eccl 9:15 was found in it a *p* wise man
Eccl 9:15 no man remembered that same *p* man
Eccl 9:16 nevertheless the *p* man's wisdom
Is 3:14 the spoil of the *p* is in your
Is 3:15 and grind the faces of the *p*
Is 10:2 the right from the *p* of my people
Is 10:30 be heard unto Laish, O *p* Anathoth
Is 11:4 shall he judge the *p*, and reprove
Is 14:30 the firstborn of the *p* shall feed
Is 14:32 the *p* of his people shall trust
Is 25:4 hast been a strength to the *p*
Is 26:6 it down, even the feet of the *p*
Is 29:19 the *p* among men shall rejoice in
Is 32:7 to destroy the *p* with lying words
Is 41:17 When the *p* and needy seek water,
Is 58:7 that thou bring the *p* that are
Is 66:2 I look, even to him that is *p*
Jer 2:34 of the souls of the *p* innocents
Jer 5:4 I said, Surely these are *p*
Jer 20:13 the *p* from the hand of evildoers
Jer 22:16 He judged the cause of the *p*
Jer 39:10 guard left of the *p* of the people
Jer 40:7 of the *p* of the land, of them
Jer 52:15 certain of the *p* of the people
Jer 52:16 *p* of the land for vinedressers
Eze 16:49 she strengthen the hand of the *p*
Eze 18:12 Hath oppressed the *p* and needy,
Eze 18:17 taken off his hand from the *p*
Eze 22:29 robbery, and have vexed the *p*
Dan 4:27 by shewing mercy to the *p*
Amos 2:6 the *p* for a pair of shoes

Amos 2:7 of the earth on the head of the *p*
Amos 4:1 of Samaria, which oppress the *p*
Amos 5:11 as your treading is upon the *p*
Amos 5:12 they turn aside the *p* in the gate
Amos 8:4 even to make the *p* of the land to
Amos 8:6 That we may buy the *p* for silver
Hab 3:14 was as to devour the *p* secretly
Zeph 3:12 *p* people, and they shall trust in
Zec 7:10 the stranger, nor the *p*
Zec 11:7 even you, O *p* of the flock
Zec 11:11 so the *p* of the flock that waited
Mt 5:3 Blessed are the *p* in spirit
Mt 11:5 the *p* have the gospel preached to
Mt 19:21 that thou hast, and give to the *p*
Mt 26:9 sold for much, and given to the *p*
Mt 26:11 For ye have the *p* always with you
Mk 10:21 thou hast, and give to the *p*
Mk 12:42 And there came a certain *p* widow
Mk 12:43 That this *p* widow hath cast more
Mk 14:5 and have been given to the *p*
Mk 14:7 For ye have the *p* with you always
Lk 4:18 me to preach the gospel to the *p*
Lk 6:20 and said, Blessed be ye *p*
Lk 7:22 to the *p* the gospel is preached
Lk 14:13 thou makest a feast, call the *p*
Lk 14:21 city, and bring in hither the *p*
Lk 18:22 hast, and distribute unto the *p*
Lk 19:8 half of my goods I give to the *p*
Lk 21:2 he saw also a certain *p* widow
Lk 21:3 that this *p* widow hath cast in
Jn 12:5 hundred pence, and given to the *p*
Jn 12:6 said, not that he cared for the *p*
Jn 12:8 For the *p* always ye have with you
Jn 13:29 he should give something to the *p*
Rom 15:26 *p* saints which are at Jerusalem
1Cor 13:3 bestow all my goods to feed the *p*
2Cor 6:10 as *p*, yet making many rich
2Cor 8:9 yet for your sakes he became *p*
2Cor 9:9 he hath given to the *p*
Gal 2:10 that we should remember the *p*
Jas 2:2 in also a *p* man in vile raiment
Jas 2:3 and say to the *p*, Stand thou there
Jas 2:5 Hath not God chosen the *p* of this
Jas 2:6 But ye have despised the *p*
Rev 3:17 art wretched, and miserable, and *p*
Rev 13:16 both small and great, rich and *p*

**PORATHA** *(por'-a-thah) A son of Haman.*
Est 9:8 And P, and Adalia, and Aridatha,

**PORCH**
Judg 3:23 Ehud went forth through the *p*
1Kin 6:3 the *p* before the temple of the
1Kin 7:6 And he made a *p* of pillars
1Kin 7:6 and the *p* was before them
1Kin 7:7 Then he made a *p* for the throne
1Kin 7:7 judge, even the *p* of judgment
1Kin 7:8 had another court within the *p*
1Kin 7:8 taken to wife, like unto this *p*
1Kin 7:12 LORD, and for the *p* of the house
1Kin 7:19 were of lily work in the *p*
1Kin 7:21 pillars in the *p* of the temple
1Chr 28:11 his son the pattern of the *p*
2Chr 3:4 the *p* that was in the front of
2Chr 8:12 which he had built before the *p*
2Chr 15:8 that was before the *p* of the LORD
2Chr 29:7 have shut up the doors of the *p*
2Chr 29:17 came they to the *p* of the LORD
Eze 8:16 temple of the LORD, between the *p*
Eze 40:7 threshold of the gate by the *p* of
Eze 40:8 also the *p* of the gate within
Eze 40:9 measured he the *p* of the gate
Eze 40:9 the *p* of the gate was inward
Eze 40:15 *p* of the inner gate were fifty
Eze 40:39 in the *p* of the gate were two
Eze 40:40 which was at the *p* of the gate
Eze 40:48 brought me to the *p* of the house
Eze 40:48 and measured each post of the *p*
Eze 40:49 length of the *p* was twenty cubits
Eze 41:25 upon the face of the *p* without
Eze 41:26 other side, on the sides of the *p*
Eze 44:3 by the way of the *p* of that gate
Eze 46:2 way of the *p* of that gate without
Eze 46:8 by the way of the *p* of that gate
Joel 2:17 of the LORD, weep between the *p*
Mt 26:71 when he was gone out into the *p*
Mk 14:68 And he went out into the *p*
Jn 10:23 in the temple in Solomon's *p*
Acts 3:11 in the *p* that is called Solomon's
Acts 5:12 with one accord in Solomon's *p*

**PORCIUS** *(por'-she-us) Family name of Festus.*
Acts 24:27 But after two years *P* Festus came

**PORTER**
2Sa 18:26 and the watchman called unto the *p*
2Kin 7:10 and called unto the *p* of the city
1Chr 9:21 the son of Meshelemiah was *p* of
2Chr 31:14 the *p* toward the east, was over
Mk 13:34 work, and commanded the *p* to watch
Jn 10:3 To him the *p* openeth

**PORTERS**
2Kin 7:11 And he called the *p*
1Chr 9:17 the *p* were, Shallum, and Akkub, and
1Chr 9:18 they were *p* in the companies of
1Chr 9:22 *p* in the gates were two hundred
1Chr 9:24 In four quarters were the *p*
1Chr 9:26 these Levites, the four chief *p*
1Chr 15:18 and Obed-edom, and Jeiel, the *p*
1Chr 16:38 son of Jeduthun and Hosah to be *p*
1Chr 16:42 And the sons of Jeduthun were *p*
1Chr 23:5 Moreover four thousand were *p*
1Chr 26:1 Concerning the divisions of the *p*
1Chr 26:12 these were the divisions of the *p*
1Chr 26:19 of the *p* among the sons of Kore
2Chr 8:14 the *p* also by their courses at
2Chr 23:4 Levites, shall be *p* of the doors
2Chr 23:19 he set the *p* at the gates of the
2Chr 34:13 were scribes, and officers, and *p*
2Chr 35:15 the *p* waited at every gate
Ezr 2:42 The children of the *p*
Ezr 2:70 people, and the singers, and the *p*
Ezr 7:7 Levites, and the singers, and the *p*
Ezr 7:24 priests and Levites, singers, *p*
Ezr 10:24 the *p*; Shallum, and Telem
Neh 7:1 I had set up the doors, and the *p*
Neh 7:45 The *p*: the children of Shallum
Neh 7:73 priests, and the Levites, and the *p*
Neh 10:28 the priests, the Levites, the *p*
Neh 10:39 priests that minister, and the *p*
Neh 11:19 Moreover the *p*, Akkub, Talmon, and
Neh 12:25 were *p* keeping the ward at the
Neh 12:45 the *p* kept the ward of their God,
Neh 12:47 portions of the singers and the *p*
Neh 13:5 Levites, and the singers, and the *p*

**PORTION**
Gen 14:24 the *p* of the men which went with
Gen 14:24 let them take their *p*
Gen 31:14 Is there yet any *p* or inheritance
Gen 47:22 for the priests had a *p* assigned
Gen 47:22 did eat their *p* which Pharaoh
Gen 48:22 to thee one *p* above thy brethren
Lev 6:17 *p* of my offerings made by fire
Lev 7:35 This is the *p* of the anointing of
Num 31:30 thou shalt take one *p* of fifty
Num 31:36 which was the *p* of them that went
Num 31:47 half, Moses took one *p* of fifty
Deut 21:17 a double *p* of all that he hath
Deut 32:9 For the LORD's *p* is his people
Deut 33:21 in a *p* of the lawgiver, was he
Josh 17:14 one *p* to inherit, seeing I am a
Josh 19:9 Out of the *p* of the children of
1Sa 1:5 unto Hannah he gave a worthy *p*
1Sa 9:23 Bring the *p* which I gave thee, of
1Kin 12:16 saying, What *p* have we in David
2Kin 2:9 let a double *p* of thy spirit be
2Kin 9:10 eat Jezebel in the *p* of Jezreel
2Kin 9:21 met him in the *p* of Naboth the
2Kin 9:25 cast him in the *p* of the field of
2Kin 9:36 In the *p* of Jezreel shall dogs
2Kin 9:37 of the field in the *p* of Jezreel
2Chr 10:16 saying, What *p* have we in David
2Chr 28:21 For Ahaz took away a *p* out of the
2Chr 31:3 He appointed also the king's *p* of
2Chr 31:4 to give the *p* of the priests
2Chr 31:16 his daily *p* for their service in
Ezr 4:16 have no *p* on this side the river
Neh 2:20 but ye have no *p*, nor right, nor
Neh 11:23 that a certain *p* should be for
Neh 12:47 and the porters, every day his *p*
Job 20:29 This is the *p* of a wicked man
Job 24:18 their *p* is cursed in the earth
Job 26:14 how little a *p* is heard of him
Job 27:13 This is the *p* of a wicked man
Job 31:2 For what *p* of God is there from
Ps 11:6 this shall be the *p* of their cup
Ps 16:5 The LORD is the *p* of mine
Ps 17:14 which have their *p* in this life
Ps 63:10 they shall be a *p* for foxes
Ps 73:26 of my heart, and my *p* for ever
Ps 119:57 Thou art my *p*, O LORD
Ps 142:5 my *p* in the land of the living
Prov 31:15 household, and a *p* to her maidens
Eccl 2:10 this was my *p* of all my labour
Eccl 2:21 shall he leave it for his *p*
Eccl 3:22 for that is his *p*
Eccl 5:18 for it is his *p*
Eccl 5:19 to eat thereof, and to take his *p*
Eccl 9:6 neither have they any more a *p*
Eccl 9:9 for that is thy *p* in this life
Eccl 11:2 Give a *p* to seven, and also to
Is 17:14 This is the *p* of them that spoil
Is 53:12 I divide him a *p* with the great
Is 57:6 stones of the stream is thy *p*
Is 61:7 they shall rejoice in their *p*
Jer 10:16 The *p* of Jacob is not like them
Jer 12:10 they have trodden my *p* under foot
Jer 12:10 pleasant *p* a desolate wilderness
Jer 13:25 the *p* of thy measures from me,
Jer 51:19 The *p* of Jacob is not like them
Jer 52:34 every day a *p* until the day of
Lam 3:24 The LORD is my *p*, saith my soul
Eze 45:1 the LORD, an holy *p* of the land
Eze 45:4 The holy *p* of the land shall be
Eze 45:6 the oblation of the holy *p*
Eze 45:7 a *p* shall be for the prince on
Eze 45:7 of the oblation of the holy *p*
Eze 45:7 before the oblation of the holy *p*
Eze 48:1 a *p* for Dan
Eze 48:2 unto the west side, a *p* for Asher
Eze 48:3 the west side, a *p* for Naphtali
Eze 48:4 the west side, a *p* for Manasseh
Eze 48:5 the west side, a *p* for Ephraim
Eze 48:6 the west side, a *p* for Reuben
Eze 48:7 unto the west side, a *p* for Judah
Eze 48:18 the oblation of the holy *p* shall
Eze 48:18 the oblation of the holy *p*
Eze 48:23 side, Benjamin shall have a *p*
Eze 48:24 west side, Simeon shall have a *p*
Eze 48:25 unto the west side, Issachar a *p*
Eze 48:26 unto the west side, Zebulun a *p*
Eze 48:27 side unto the west side, Gad a *p*
Dan 1:8 with the *p* of the king's meat
Dan 1:13 eat of the *p* of the king's meat
Dan 1:15 did eat the *p* of the king's meat
Dan 1:16 took away the *p* of their meat
Dan 4:15 let his *p* be with the beasts in
Dan 4:23 let his *p* be with the beasts of
Dan 11:26 they that feed of the *p* of his
Mic 2:4 hath changed the *p* of my people
Hab 1:16 because by them their *p* is fat
Zec 2:12 Judah his *p* in the holy land
Mt 24:51 appoint him his *p* with the
Lk 12:42 to give them their *p* of meat in
Lk 12:46 him his *p* with the unbelievers
Lk 15:12 give me the *p* of goods that

**PORTIONS**
Deut 18:8 They shall have like *p* to eat
Josh 17:5 And there fell ten *p* to Manasseh
1Sa 1:4 all her sons and her daughters, *p*
2Chr 31:19 to give *p* to all the males among
Neh 8:10 send *p* unto them for whom nothing
Neh 8:12 to eat, and to drink, and to send *p*
Neh 12:44 the *p* of the law for the priests
Neh 12:47 gave the *p* of the singers and the
Neh 13:10 I perceived that the *p* of the
Est 9:19 of sending *p* one to another
Est 9:22 of sending *p* one to another, and
Eze 45:7 be over against one of the *p*
Eze 47:13 Joseph shall have two *p*
Eze 48:21 over against the *p* for the prince
Eze 48:29 inheritance, and these are their *p*
Hos 5:7 a month devour them with their *p*

**POSSESS**
Gen 22:17 thy seed shall *p* the gate of his
Gen 24:60 let thy seed *p* the gate of those
Lev 20:24 I will give it unto you to *p* it
Num 13:30 Let us go up at once, and *p* it
Num 14:24 and his seed shall *p* it
Num 27:11 of his family, and he shall *p* it
Num 33:53 I have given you the land to *p* it
Deut 1:8 *p* the land which the LORD sware
Deut 1:21 *p* it, as the LORD God of thy
Deut 1:39 I give it, and they shall *p* it
Deut 2:24 begin to *p* it, and contend with
Deut 2:31 begin to *p*, that thou mayest
Deut 3:18 hath given you this land to *p* it
Deut 3:20 until they also *p* the land which
Deut 4:1 *p* the land which the LORD God of

Deut 4:5 in the land whither ye go to *p* it
Deut 4:14 land whither ye go over to *p* it
Deut 4:22 go over, and *p* that good land
Deut 4:26 ye go over Jordan to *p* it
Deut 5:31 land which I give them to *p* it
Deut 5:33 days in the land which ye shall *p*
Deut 6:1 in the land whither ye go to *p* it
Deut 6:18 *p* the good land which the LORD
Deut 7:1 land whither thou goest to *p* it
Deut 8:1 *p* the land which the LORD sware
Deut 9:1 to go in to *p* nations greater and
Deut 9:4 hath brought me in to *p* this land
Deut 9:5 dost thou go to *p* their land
Deut 9:6 to *p* it for thy righteousness
Deut 9:23 *p* the land which I have given you
Deut 10:11 *p* the land, which I sware unto
Deut 11:8 *p* the land, whither ye go to
Deut 11:8 the land, whither ye go to *p* it
Deut 11:10 whither thou goest in to *p* it
Deut 11:11 the land, whither ye go to *p* it
Deut 11:23 ye shall *p* greater nations and
Deut 11:29 land whither thou goest to *p* it
Deut 11:31 to *p* the land which the LORD your
Deut 11:31 God giveth you, and ye shall *p* it
Deut 12:1 thy fathers giveth thee to *p* it
Deut 12:2 ye shall *p* served their gods
Deut 12:29 whither thou goest to *p* them
Deut 15:4 thee for an inheritance to *p* it
Deut 17:14 God giveth thee, and shalt *p* it
Deut 18:14 these nations, which thou shalt *p*
Deut 19:2 LORD thy God giveth thee to *p* it
Deut 19:14 LORD thy God giveth thee to *p* it
Deut 21:1 LORD thy God giveth thee to *p* it
Deut 23:20 land whither thou goest to *p* it
Deut 25:19 thee for an inheritance to *p* it
Deut 28:21 land, whither thou goest to *p* it
Deut 28:63 land whither thou goest to *p* it
Deut 30:5 possessed, and thou shalt *p* it
Deut 30:16 land whither thou goest to *p* it
Deut 30:18 passest over Jordan to go to *p* it
Deut 31:3 before thee, and thou shalt *p* them
Deut 31:13 whither ye go over Jordan to *p* it
Deut 32:47 whither ye go over Jordan to *p* it
Deut 33:23 *p* thou the west and the south
Josh 1:11 Jordan, to go in to *p* the land
Josh 1:11 LORD your God giveth you to *p* it
Josh 18:3 are ye slack to go to *p* the land
Josh 23:5 ye shall *p* their land, as the
Josh 24:4 unto Esau mount Seir, to *p* it
Josh 24:8 hand, that ye might *p* their land
Judg 2:6 his inheritance to *p* the land
Judg 11:23 Israel, and shouldest thou *p* it
Judg 11:24 Wilt not thou *p* that which
Judg 11:24 Chemosh thy god giveth thee to *p*
Judg 11:24 from before us, them will we *p*
Judg 18:9 to go, and to enter to *p* the land
1Kin 21:18 whither he is gone down to *p* it
1Chr 28:8 that ye may *p* this good land, and
Ezr 9:11 land, unto which ye go to *p* it
Neh 9:15 them that they should go in to *p*
Neh 9:23 that they should go in to *p* it
Job 7:3 So am I made to *p* months of
Job 13:26 makest me to *p* the iniquities of
Is 14:2 the house of Israel shall *p* them
Is 14:21 nor *p* the land, nor fill the face
Is 34:11 and the bittern shall *p* it
Is 34:17 they shall *p* it for ever, from
Is 57:13 his trust in me shall *p* the land
Is 61:7 land they shall *p* the double
Jer 30:3 their fathers, and they shall *p* it
Eze 7:24 they shall *p* their houses
Eze 33:25 and shall ye *p* the land
Eze 33:26 and shall ye *p* the land
Eze 35:10 shall be mine, and we will *p* it
Eze 36:12 and they shall *p* thee, and thou
Dan 7:18 *p* the kingdom for ever, even for
Hos 9:6 silver, nettles shall *p* them
Amos 2:10 to *p* the land of the Amorite
Amos 9:12 That they may *p* the remnant of
Obad 17 Jacob shall *p* their possessions
Obad 19 south shall *p* the mount of Esau
Obad 19 they shall *p* the fields of
Obad 19 and Benjamin shall *p* Gilead
Obad 20 shall *p* that of the Canaanites
Obad 20 shall *p* the cities of the south
Hab 1:6 to *p* the dwellingplaces that are
Zeph 2:9 remnant of my people shall *p* them
Zec 8:12 this people to *p* all these things
Lk 18:12 I give tithes of all that I *p*
Lk 21:19 In your patience *p* ye your souls
1Th 4:4 to *p* his vessel in sanctification

## POSSESSED

Num 21:24 *p* his land from Arnon unto Jabbok
Num 21:35 and they *p* his land
Deut 3:12 which we *p* at that time, from
Deut 4:47 they *p* his land, and the land of
Deut 30:5 into the land which thy fathers *p*
Josh 1:15 they also have *p* the land which
Josh 12:1 *p* their land on the other side
Josh 13:1 yet very much land to be *p*
Josh 19:47 *p* it, and dwelt therein, and called
Josh 21:43 and they *p* it, and dwelt therein
Josh 22:9 possession, whereof they were *p*
Judg 3:13 and *p* the city of palm trees
Judg 11:21 so Israel *p* all the land of the
Judg 11:22 they *p* all the coasts of the
2Kin 17:24 they *p* Samaria, and dwelt in the
Neh 9:22 so they *p* the land of Sihon, and
Neh 9:24 *p* the land, and thou subduedst
Neh 9:25 *p* houses full of all goods, wells
Ps 139:13 For thou hast *p* my reins
Prov 8:22 The LORD *p* me in the beginning of
Is 63:18 have *p* it but a little while
Jer 32:15 shall be *p* again in this land
Jer 32:23 And they came in, and *p* it
Dan 7:22 that the saints *p* the kingdom
Mt 4:24 and those which were *p* with devils
Mt 8:16 him many that were *p* with devils
Mt 8:28 there met him two *p* with devils
Mt 8:33 befallen to the *p* of the devils
Mt 9:32 to him a dumb man *p* with a devil
Mt 12:22 unto him one *p* with a devil
Mk 1:32 and them that were *p* with devils
Mk 5:15 see him that was *p* with the devil
Mk 5:16 to him that was *p* with the devil
Mk 5:18 he that had been *p* with the devil
Lk 8:36 was *p* of the devils was healed
Acts 4:32 the things which he *p* was his own
Acts 8:7 out of many that were *p* with them
Acts 16:16 a certain damsel *p* with a spirit
1Cor 7:30 that buy, as though they *p* not

## POSSESSION

Gen 17:8 of Canaan, for an everlasting *p*
Gen 23:4 give me a *p* of a buryingplace
Gen 23:9 a *p* of a buryingplace amongst you
Gen 23:18 Unto Abraham for a *p* in the
Gen 23:20 made sure unto Abraham for a *p* of
Gen 26:14 For he had *p* of flocks, and
Gen 26:14 *p* of herds, and great store of
Gen 36:43 in the land of their *p*
Gen 47:11 gave them a *p* in the land of
Gen 48:4 after thee for an everlasting *p*
Gen 49:30 Hittite for a *p* of a buryingplace
Gen 50:13 bought with the field for a *p* of
Lev 14:34 which I give to you for a *p*
Lev 14:34 in a house of the land of your *p*
Lev 25:10 shall return every man unto his *p*
Lev 25:13 shall return every man unto his *p*
Lev 25:24 in all the land of your *p* ye
Lev 25:25 and hath sold away some of his *p*
Lev 25:27 that he may return unto his *p*
Lev 25:28 and he shall return unto his *p*
Lev 25:32 houses of the cities of their *p*
Lev 25:33 was sold, and the city of his *p*
Lev 25:33 *p* among the children of Israel
Lev 25:34 for it is their perpetual *p*
Lev 25:41 unto the *p* of his fathers shall
Lev 25:45 and they shall be your *p*
Lev 25:46 you, to inherit them for a *p*
Lev 27:16 some part of a field of his *p*
Lev 27:21 the *p* thereof shall be the
Lev 27:22 is not of the fields of his *p*
Lev 27:24 whom the *p* of the land did belong
Lev 27:28 beast, and of the field of his *p*
Num 24:18 And Edom shall be a *p*
Num 24:18 also shall be a *p* for his enemies
Num 26:56 According to the lot shall the *p*
Num 27:4 Give unto us therefore a *p* among
Num 27:7 a *p* of an inheritance among their
Num 32:5 given unto thy servants for a *p*
Num 32:22 shall be your *p* before the LORD
Num 32:29 them the land of Gilead for a *p*
Num 32:32 that the *p* of our inheritance on
Num 35:2 of their *p* cities to dwell in
Num 35:8 the *p* of the children of Israel
Num 35:28 return into the land of his *p*
Deut 2:5 mount Seir unto Esau for a *p*
Deut 2:9 give thee of their land for a *p*
Deut 2:9 unto the children of Lot for a *p*
Deut 2:12 Israel did unto the land of his *p*
Deut 2:19 of the children of Ammon any *p*
Deut 2:19 unto the children of Lot for a *p*
Deut 3:20 ye return every man unto his *p*
Deut 11:6 the substance that was in their *p*
Deut 32:49 the children of Israel for a *p*
Josh 1:15 return unto the land of your *p*
Josh 12:6 it for a *p* unto the Reubenites
Josh 12:7 a *p* according to their divisions
Josh 13:29 this was the *p* of the half tribe
Josh 21:12 the son of Jephunneh for his *p*
Josh 21:41 of the Levites within the *p* of
Josh 22:4 tents, and unto the land of your *p*
Josh 22:7 Moses had given *p* in Bashan
Josh 22:9 of Gilead, to the land of their *p*
Josh 22:19 if the land of your *p* be unclean
Josh 22:19 the land of the *p* of the LORD
Josh 22:19 dwelleth, and take *p* among us
1Kin 21:15 take *p* of the vineyard of Naboth
1Kin 21:16 the Jezreelite, to take *p* of it
1Kin 21:19 Hast thou killed, and also taken *p*
1Chr 28:1 *p* of the king, and of his sons,
2Chr 11:14 left their suburbs and their *p*
2Chr 20:11 to come to cast us out of thy *p*
2Chr 31:1 returned, every man to his *p*
Neh 11:3 one in his *p* in their cities
Ps 2:8 parts of the earth for thy *p*
Ps 44:3 the land in *p* by their own sword
Ps 69:35 may dwell there, and have it in *p*
Ps 83:12 ourselves the houses of God in *p*
Prov 28:10 shall have good things in *p*
Is 14:23 also make it a *p* for the bittern
Eze 11:15 unto us is this land given in *p*
Eze 25:4 to the men of the east for a *p*
Eze 25:10 Ammonites, and will give them in *p*
Eze 36:2 ancient high places are ours in *p*
Eze 36:3 that ye might be a *p* unto the
Eze 36:5 appointed my land into their *p*
Eze 44:28 ye shall give them no *p* in Israel
Eze 44:28 I am their *p*
Eze 45:5 for a *p* for twenty chambers
Eze 45:6 ye shall appoint the *p* of the
Eze 45:7 of the *p* of the city, before the
Eze 45:7 before the *p* of the city, from
Eze 45:8 the land shall be his *p* in Israel
Eze 46:16 shall be their *p* by inheritance
Eze 46:18 to thrust them out of their *p*
Eze 46:18 sons inheritance out of his own *p*
Eze 46:18 scattered every man from his *p*
Eze 48:20 with the *p* of the city
Eze 48:21 of the *p* of the city, over
Eze 48:22 from the *p* of the Levites
Eze 48:22 from the *p* of the city, being in
Acts 5:1 with Sapphira his wife, sold a *p*
Acts 7:5 he would give it to him for a *p*
Acts 7:45 Jesus into the *p* of the Gentiles
Eph 1:14 the redemption of the purchased *p*

## POSSESSIONS

Gen 34:10 ye therein, and get you *p* therein
Gen 47:27 and they had *p* therein, and grew,
Num 32:30 they shall have *p* among you in
1Sa 25:2 in Maon, whose *p* were in Carmel
1Chr 7:28 And their *p* and habitations were,
1Chr 9:2 in their *p* in their cities were
2Chr 32:29 *p* of flocks and herds in abundance
Eccl 2:7 also I had great *p* of great
Obad 17 of Jacob shall possess their *p*
Mt 19:22 for he had great *p*
Mk 10:22 for he had great *p*
Acts 2:45 And sold their *p* and goods, and
Acts 28:7 In the same quarters were *p* of

## POSSIBLE

Mt 19:26 but with God all things are *p*
Mt 24:24 insomuch that, if it were *p*
Mt 26:39 saying, O my Father, if it be *p*
Mk 9:23 all things are *p* to him that
Mk 10:27 for with God all things are *p*
Mk 13:22 wonders, to seduce, if it were *p*
Mk 14:35 and prayed that, if it were *p*
Mk 14:36 all things are *p* unto thee
Lk 18:27 with men are *p* with God
Acts 2:24 because it was not *p* that he
Acts 20:16 he hasted, if it were *p* for him
Acts 27:39 they were minded, if it were *p*
Rom 12:18 If it be *p*, as much as lieth in
Gal 4:15 record, that, if it had been *p*
Heb 10:4 For it is not *p* that the blood of

**POST**
Ex 12:7 on the upper door *p* of the houses
Ex 21:6 to the door, or unto the door *p*
1Sa 1:9 by a *p* of the temple of the LORD
Job 9:25 Now my days are swifter than a *p*
Jer 51:31 One *p* shall run to meet another,
Eze 40:14 even unto the *p* of the court
Eze 40:16 upon each *p* were palm trees
Eze 40:48 and measured each *p* of the porch
Eze 41:3 and measured the *p* of the door
Eze 43:8 their *p* by my posts, and the wall
Eze 46:2 shall stand by the *p* of the gate

**POSTERITY**
Gen 45:7 to preserve you a *p* in the earth
Num 9:10 If any man of you or of your *p*
1Kin 16:3 I will take away the *p* of Baasha
1Kin 16:3 of Baasha, and the *p* of his house
1Kin 21:21 thee, and will take away thy *p*
Ps 49:13 yet their *p* approve their sayings
Ps 109:13 Let his *p* be cut off
Dan 11:4 and not to his *p*, nor according to
Amos 4:2 hooks, and your *p* with fishhooks

**POSTS**
Ex 12:7 and strike it on the two side *p*
Ex 12:22 the two side *p* with the blood
Ex 12:23 the lintel, and on the two side *p*
Deut 6:9 them upon the *p* of thy house
Deut 11:20 upon the door *p* of thine house
Judg 16:3 gate of the city, and the two *p*
1Kin 6:31 side *p* were a fifth part of the
1Kin 6:33 of the temple *p* of olive tree
1Kin 7:5 *p* were square, with the windows
2Chr 3:7 also the house, the beams, the *p*
2Chr 30:6 So the *p* went with the letters
2Chr 30:10 So the *p* passed from city to city
Est 3:13 the letters were sent by *p* into
Est 3:15 The *p* went out, being hastened by
Est 8:10 and sent letters by *p* on horseback
Est 8:14 So the *p* that rode upon mules and
Prov 8:34 waiting at the *p* of my doors
Is 6:4 the *p* of the door moved at the
Is 57:8 the *p* hast thou set up thy
Eze 40:9 the *p* thereof, two cubits
Eze 40:10 the *p* had one measure on this
Eze 40:14 He made also *p* of threescore
Eze 40:16 to their *p* within the gate round
Eze 40:21 the *p* thereof and the arches
Eze 40:24 and he measured the *p* thereof
Eze 40:26 on that side, upon the *p* thereof
Eze 40:29 the *p* thereof, and the arches
Eze 40:31 trees were upon the *p* thereof
Eze 40:33 the *p* thereof, and the arches
Eze 40:34 trees were upon the *p* thereof
Eze 40:36 the *p* thereof, and the arches
Eze 40:37 the *p* thereof were toward the
Eze 40:37 trees were upon the *p* thereof
Eze 40:38 were by the *p* of the gates
Eze 40:49 and there were pillars by the *p*
Eze 41:1 to the temple, and measured the *p*
Eze 41:16 The door *p*, and the narrow windows
Eze 41:21 The *p* of the temple were squared,
Eze 43:8 thresholds, and their post by my *p*
Eze 45:19 and put it upon the *p* of the house
Eze 45:19 upon the *p* of the gate of the
Amos 9:1 of the door, that the *p* may shake

**POT**
Ex 16:33 Moses said unto Aaron, Take a *p*
Lev 6:28 and if it be sodden in a brasen *p*
Judg 6:19 and he put the broth in a *p*
1Sa 2:14 pan, or kettle, or caldron, or *p*
2Kin 4:2 in the house, save a *p* of oil
2Kin 4:38 his servant, Set on the great *p*
2Kin 4:39 shred them into the *p* of pottage
2Kin 4:40 of God, there is death in the *p*
2Kin 4:41 And he cast it into the *p*
2Kin 4:41 And there was no harm in the *p*
Job 41:20 as out of a seething *p* or caldron
Job 41:31 maketh the deep to boil like a *p*
Job 41:31 the sea like a *p* of ointment
Prov 17:3 The fining *p* is for silver, and
Prov 27:21 As the fining *p* for silver
Eccl 7:6 the crackling of thorns under a *p*
Jer 1:13 and I said, I see a seething *p*
Eze 24:3 Set on a *p*, set it on, and also
Eze 24:6 to the *p* whose scum is therein,
Mic 3:3 chop them in pieces, as for the *p*
Zec 14:21 every *p* in Jerusalem and in Judah
Heb 9:4 was the golden *p* that had manna

**POTIPHAR** *(pot'i-far) A captain of Pharaoh's guard.*
Gen 37:36 sold him into Egypt unto *P*
Gen 39:1 and *P*, an officer of Pharaoh,

**POTI-PHERAH** *Priest of On.*
Gen 41:45 the daughter of *P* priest of On
Gen 41:50 of *P* priest of On bare unto him
Gen 46:20 of *P* priest of On bare unto him

**POTS**
Ex 16:3 Egypt, when we sat by the flesh *p*
Ex 38:3 the vessels of the altar, the *p*
Lev 11:35 it be oven, or ranges for *p*
1Kin 7:45 And the *p*, and the shovels, and the
2Kin 25:14 And the *p*, and the shovels, and the
2Chr 4:11 And Huram made the *p*, and the
2Chr 4:16 The *p* also, and the shovels, and
2Chr 35:13 holy offerings sod they in *p*
Ps 58:9 Before your *p* can feel the thorns
Ps 68:13 Though ye have lien among the *p*
Ps 81:6 hands were delivered from the *p*
Jer 35:5 of the Rechabites *p* full of wine
Zec 14:20 the *p* in the LORD's house shall
Mk 7:4 as the washing of cups, and *p*
Mk 7:8 of men, as the washing of *p*

**POTSHERD**
Job 2:8 he took him a *p* to scrape himself
Ps 22:15 My strength is dried up like a *p*
Prov 26:23 a *p* covered with silver dross
Is 45:9 Let the *p* strive with the

**POTTAGE**
Gen 25:29 And Jacob sod *p*
Gen 25:30 I pray thee, with that same red *p*
Gen 25:34 gave Esau bread and *p* of lentiles
2Kin 4:38 seethe *p* for the sons of the
2Kin 4:39 and shred them into the pot of *p*
2Kin 4:40 as they were eating of the *p*
Hag 2:12 his skirt do touch bread, or *p*

**POTTER**
Is 41:25 morter, and as the *p* treadeth clay
Is 64:8 we are the clay, and thou our *p*
Jer 18:4 was marred in the hand of the *p*
Jer 18:4 seemed good to the *p* to make it
Jer 18:6 cannot I do with you as this *p*
Lam 4:2 the work of the hands of the *p*
Zec 11:13 said unto me, Cast it unto the *p*
Zec 11:13 cast them to the *p* in the house
Rom 9:21 Hath not the *p* power over the
Rev 2:27 as the vessels of a *p* shall they

**POTTER'S**
Ps 2:9 them in pieces like a *p* vessel
Is 29:16 shall be esteemed as the *p* clay
Jer 18:2 Arise, and go down to the *p* house
Jer 18:3 Then I went down to the *p* house
Jer 18:6 as the clay is in the *p* hand
Jer 19:1 get a *p* earthen bottle, and take
Jer 19:11 city, as one breaketh a *p* vessel
Mt 27:7 and bought with them the *p* field
Mt 27:10 And gave them for the *p* field

**POUND**
1Kin 10:17 three *p* of gold went to one
Ezr 2:69 and five thousand *p* of silver
Lk 19:16 thy *p* hath gained ten pounds
Lk 19:18 thy *p* hath gained five pounds
Lk 19:20 Lord, behold, here is thy *p*
Lk 19:24 stood by, Take from him the *p*
Jn 12:3 Then took Mary a *p* of ointment of
Jn 19:39 aloes, about an hundred *p* weight

**POUNDS**
Neh 7:71 and two hundred *p* of silver
Neh 7:72 gold, and two thousand *p* of silver
Lk 19:13 servants, and delivered them ten *p*
Lk 19:16 Lord, thy pound hath gained ten *p*
Lk 19:18 thy pound hath gained five *p*
Lk 19:24 and give it to him that hath ten *p*
Lk 19:25 unto him, Lord, he hath ten *p*

**POUR**
Ex 4:9 river, and *p* it upon the dry land
Ex 29:7 *p* it upon his head, and anoint him
Ex 29:12 *p* all the blood beside the bottom
Ex 30:9 neither shall ye *p* drink offering
Lev 2:1 he shall *p* oil upon it, and put
Lev 2:6 it in pieces, and *p* oil thereon
Lev 4:7 shall *p* all the blood of the
Lev 4:18 shall *p* out all the blood at the
Lev 4:25 shall *p* out his blood at the
Lev 4:30 shall *p* out all the blood thereof
Lev 4:34 shall *p* out all the blood thereof
Lev 14:15 *p* it into the palm of his own
Lev 14:18 in the priest's hand he shall *p*
Lev 14:26 the priest shall *p* of the oil
Lev 14:41 they shall *p* out the dust that
Lev 17:13 he shall even *p* out the blood
Num 5:15 he shall *p* no oil upon it, nor
Num 24:7 He shall *p* the water out of his
Deut 12:16 ye shall *p* it upon the earth as
Deut 12:24 thou shalt *p* it upon the earth as
Deut 15:23 thou shalt *p* it upon the ground
Judg 6:20 this rock, and *p* out the broth
1Kin 18:33 *p* it on the burnt sacrifice, and
2Kin 4:4 shalt *p* out into all those
2Kin 4:41 *P* out for the people, that they
2Kin 9:3 *p* it on his head, and say, Thus
Job 36:27 they *p* down rain according to the
Ps 42:4 things, I *p* out my soul in me
Ps 62:8 *p* out your heart before him
Ps 69:24 *P* out thine indignation upon them
Ps 79:6 *P* out thy wrath upon the heathen
Prov 1:23 I will *p* out my spirit unto you,
Is 44:3 For I will *p* water upon him that
Is 44:3 I will *p* my spirit upon thy seed,
Is 45:8 above, and let the skies *p* down
Jer 6:11 I will *p* it out upon the children
Jer 7:18 to *p* out drink offerings unto
Jer 10:25 *P* out thy fury upon the heathen
Jer 14:16 for I will *p* their wickedness
Jer 18:21 *p* out their blood by the force of
Jer 44:17 to *p* out drink offerings unto her
Jer 44:18 to *p* out drink offerings unto her
Jer 44:19 *p* out drink offerings unto her,
Jer 44:25 to *p* out drink offerings unto her
Lam 2:19 *p* out thine heart like water
Eze 7:8 Now will I shortly *p* out my fury
Eze 14:19 *p* out my fury upon it in blood,
Eze 20:8 I will *p* out my fury upon them,
Eze 20:13 I would *p* out my fury upon them
Eze 20:21 I would *p* out my fury upon them,
Eze 21:31 I will *p* out mine indignation
Eze 24:3 it on, and also *p* water into it
Eze 30:15 I will *p* my fury upon Sin, the
Hos 5:10 therefore I will *p* out my wrath
Joel 2:28 that I will *p* out my spirit upon
Joel 2:29 those days will I *p* out my spirit
Mic 1:6 I will *p* down the stones thereof
Zeph 3:8 to *p* upon them mine indignation,
Zec 12:10 I will *p* upon the house of David,
Mal 3:10 *p* you out a blessing, that there
Acts 2:17 I will *p* out of my Spirit upon
Acts 2:18 on my handmaidens I will *p* out in
Rev 16:1 *p* out the vials of the wrath of

**POURED**
Gen 28:18 and *p* oil upon the top of it
Gen 35:14 he *p* a drink offering thereon
Gen 35:14 and he *p* oil thereon
Ex 9:33 the rain was not *p* upon the earth
Ex 30:32 man's flesh shall it not be *p*
Lev 4:12 place, where the ashes are *p* out
Lev 4:12 where the ashes are *p* out shall
Lev 8:12 he *p* of the anointing oil upon
Lev 8:15 *p* the blood at the bottom of the
Lev 9:9 *p* out the blood at the bottom of
Lev 21:10 head the anointing oil was *p*
Num 28:7 to be *p* unto the LORD for a drink
Deut 12:27 of thy sacrifices shall be *p* out
1Sa 1:15 but have *p* out my soul before the
1Sa 7:6 *p* it out before the LORD, and
1Sa 10:1 *p* it upon his head, and kissed him
2Sa 13:9 a pan, and *p* them out before him
2Sa 23:16 but *p* it out unto the LORD
1Kin 13:3 that are upon it shall be *p* out
1Kin 13:5 the ashes *p* out from the altar,
2Kin 3:11 which *p* water on the hands of
2Kin 4:5 and she *p* out
2Kin 4:40 So they *p* out for the men to eat
2Kin 9:6 he *p* the oil on his head, and said
2Kin 16:13 and *p* his drink offering, and
1Chr 11:18 but *p* it out to the LORD,
2Chr 12:7 my wrath shall not be *p* out upon
2Chr 34:21 of the LORD that is *p* out upon us
2Chr 34:25 shall be *p* out upon this place
Job 3:24 my roarings are *p* out like the
Job 10:10 Hast thou not *p* me out as milk,
Job 29:6 the rock *p* me out rivers of oil
Job 30:16 And now my soul is *p* out upon me
Ps 22:14 I am *p* out like water, and all my
Ps 45:2 grace is *p* into thy lips
Ps 77:17 The clouds *p* out water

Ps 142:2 I *p* out my complaint before him
Song 1:3 thy name is as ointment *p* forth
Is 26:16 they *p* out a prayer when thy
Is 29:10 For the LORD hath *p* out upon you
Is 32:15 Until the spirit be *p* upon us
Is 42:25 Therefore he hath *p* upon him the
Is 53:12 because he hath *p* out his soul
Is 57:6 them hast thou *p* a drink offering
Jer 7:20 my fury shall be *p* out upon this
Jer 19:13 have *p* out drink offerings unto
Jer 32:29 *p* out drink offerings unto other
Jer 42:18 my fury hath been *p* forth upon
Jer 42:18 shall my fury be *p* forth upon you
Jer 44:6 my fury and mine anger was *p* forth
Jer 44:19 *p* out drink offerings unto her,
Lam 2:4 he *p* out his fury like fire
Lam 2:11 my liver is *p* upon the earth, for
Lam 2:12 when their soul was *p* out into
Lam 4:1 *p* out in the top of every street
Lam 4:11 he hath *p* out his fierce anger,
Eze 16:36 Because thy filthiness was *p* out
Eze 20:28 *p* out there their drink offerings
Eze 20:33 out arm, and with fury *p* out
Eze 20:34 out arm, and with fury *p* out
Eze 22:22 LORD have *p* out my fury upon you
Eze 22:31 Therefore have I *p* out mine
Eze 23:8 *p* their whoredom upon her
Eze 24:7 she *p* it not upon the ground, to
Eze 36:18 Wherefore I *p* my fury upon them
Eze 39:29 for I have *p* out my spirit upon
Dan 9:11 therefore the curse is *p* upon us
Dan 9:27 shall be *p* upon the desolate
Mic 1:4 that are *p* down a steep place
Nah 1:6 his fury is *p* out like fire, and
Zeph 1:17 blood shall be *p* out as dust
Mt 26:7 *p* it on his head, as he sat at
Mt 26:12 For in that she hath *p* this
Mk 14:3 the box, and *p* it on his head
Jn 2:15 *p* out the changers' money, and
Acts 10:45 that on the Gentiles also was *p*
Rev 14:10 which is *p* out without mixture
Rev 16:2 *p* out his vial upon the earth
Rev 16:3 the second angel *p* out his vial
Rev 16:4 the third angel *p* out his vial
Rev 16:8 the fourth angel *p* out his vial
Rev 16:10 the fifth angel *p* out his vial
Rev 16:12 the sixth angel *p* out his vial
Rev 16:17 the seventh angel *p* out his vial

## POURETH

Job 12:21 He *p* contempt upon princes, and
Job 16:13 he *p* out my gall upon the ground
Job 16:20 but mine eye *p* out tears unto God
Ps 75:8 and he *p* out of the same
Ps 102:*t* *p* out his complaint before the
Ps 107:40 He *p* contempt upon princes, and
Prov 15:2 mouth of fools *p* out foolishness
Prov 15:28 of the wicked *p* out evil things
Amos 5:8 *p* them out upon the face of the
Amos 9:6 *p* them out upon the face of the
Jn 13:5 After that he *p* water into a

## POURTRAYED

Eze 8:10 *p* upon the wall round about
Eze 23:14 when she saw men *p* upon the wall
Eze 23:14 of the Chaldeans *p* with vermilion

## POVERTY

Gen 45:11 and all that thou hast, come to *p*
Prov 6:11 So shall thy *p* come as one that
Prov 10:15 of the poor is their *p*
Prov 11:24 than is meet, but it tendeth to *p*
Prov 13:18 *P* and shame shall be to him that
Prov 20:13 not sleep, lest thou come to *p*
Prov 23:21 and the glutton shall come to *p*
Prov 24:34 So shall thy *p* come as one that
Prov 28:19 vain persons shall have *p* enough
Prov 28:22 not that *p* shall come upon him
Prov 30:8 give me neither *p* nor riches
Prov 31:7 Let him drink, and forget his *p*
2Cor 8:2 their deep *p* abounded unto the
2Cor 8:9 ye through his *p* might be rich
Rev 2:9 thy works, and tribulation, and *p*

## POWDER

Ex 32:20 it in the fire, and ground it to *p*
Deut 28:24 shall make the rain of thy land *p*
2Kin 23:6 Kidron, and stamped it small to *p*
2Kin 23:6 cast the *p* thereof upon the
2Kin 23:15 place, and stamped it small to *p*
2Chr 34:7 beaten the graven images into *p*
Mt 21:44 fall, it will grind him to *p*
Lk 20:18 fall, it will grind him to *p*

## POWER

Gen 31:6 ye know that with all my *p* I have
Gen 31:29 It is in the *p* of my hand to do
Gen 32:28 as a prince hast thou *p* with God
Gen 49:3 dignity, and the excellency of *p*
Ex 9:16 thee up, for to shew in thee my *p*
Ex 15:6 O LORD, is become glorious in *p*
Ex 21:8 strange nation he shall have no *p*
Ex 32:11 of the land of Egypt with great *p*
Lev 26:19 I will break the pride of your *p*
Lev 26:37 ye shall have no *p* to stand
Num 14:17 let the *p* of my LORD be great,
Num 22:38 have I now any *p* at all to say
Deut 4:37 with his mighty *p* out of Egypt
Deut 8:17 And thou say in thine heart, My *p*
Deut 8:18 that giveth thee *p* to get wealth
Deut 9:29 broughtest out by thy mighty *p*
Deut 32:36 he seeth that their *p* is gone
Josh 8:20 they had no *p* to flee this way or
Josh 17:17 a great people, and hast great *p*
1Sa 9:1 a Benjamite, a mighty man of *p*
1Sa 30:4 until they had no more *p* to weep
2Sa 22:33 God is my strength and *p*
2Kin 17:36 of the land of Egypt with great *p*
2Kin 19:26 their inhabitants were of small *p*
1Chr 20:1 Joab led forth the *p* of the army
1Chr 29:11 LORD, is the greatness, and the *p*
1Chr 29:12 and in thine hand is *p* and might
2Chr 14:11 many, or with them that have no *p*
2Chr 20:6 and in thine hand is there not *p*
2Chr 22:9 no *p* to keep still the kingdom
2Chr 25:8 for God hath *p* to help, and to
2Chr 26:13 that made war with mighty *p*
2Chr 32:9 all his *p* with him,) unto
Ezr 4:23 made them to cease by force and *p*
Ezr 8:22 but his *p* and his wrath is against
Neh 1:10 thou hast redeemed by thy great *p*
Neh 5:5 is it in our *p* to redeem them
Est 1:3 the *p* of Persia and Media, the
Est 8:11 all the *p* of the people and
Est 9:1 Jews hoped to have *p* over them
Est 10:2 And all the acts of his *p* and of
Job 1:12 all that he hath is in thy *p*
Job 5:20 and in war from the *p* of the sword
Job 21:7 become old, yea, are mighty in *p*
Job 23:6 plead against me with his great *p*
Job 24:22 also the mighty with his *p*
Job 26:2 thou helped him that is without *p*
Job 26:12 He divideth the sea with his *p*
Job 26:14 of his *p* who can understand
Job 36:22 Behold, God exalteth by his *p*
Job 37:23 he is excellent in *p*, and in
Job 41:12 not conceal his parts, nor his *p*
Ps 21:13 so will we sing and praise thy *p*
Ps 22:20 my darling from the *p* of the dog
Ps 37:35 I have seen the wicked in great *p*
Ps 49:15 my soul from the *p* of the grave
Ps 59:11 scatter them by thy *p*
Ps 59:16 But I will sing of thy *p*
Ps 62:11 that *p* belongeth unto God
Ps 63:2 To see thy *p* and thy glory, so as
Ps 65:6 being girded with *p*
Ps 66:3 thy *p* shall thine enemies submit
Ps 66:7 He ruleth by his *p* for ever
Ps 68:35 strength and *p* unto his people
Ps 71:18 thy *p* to every one that is to
Ps 78:26 by his *p* he brought in the south
Ps 79:11 to the greatness of thy *p*
Ps 90:11 Who knoweth the *p* of thine anger
Ps 106:8 make his mighty *p* to be known
Ps 110:3 be willing in the day of thy *p*
Ps 111:6 his people the *p* of his works
Ps 145:11 of thy kingdom, and talk of thy *p*
Ps 147:5 Great is our Lord, and of great *p*
Ps 150:1 him in the firmament of his *p*
Prov 3:27 when it is in the *p* of thine hand
Prov 18:21 life are in the *p* of the tongue
Eccl 4:1 of their oppressors there was *p*
Eccl 5:19 hath given him *p* to eat thereof
Eccl 6:2 giveth him not *p* to eat thereof
Eccl 8:4 the word of a king is, there is *p*
Eccl 8:8 There is no man that hath *p* over
Eccl 8:8 neither hath he *p* in the day of
Is 37:27 their inhabitants were of small *p*
Is 40:26 might, for that he is strong in *p*
Is 40:29 He giveth *p* to the faint
Is 43:17 and horse, the army and the *p*
Is 47:14 from the *p* of the flame
Is 50:2 or have I no *p* to deliver
Jer 10:12 He hath made the earth by his *p*
Jer 27:5 upon the ground, by my great *p*
Jer 32:17 and the earth by thy great *p*
Jer 51:15 He hath made the earth by his *p*
Eze 17:9 even without great *p* or many
Eze 22:6 in thee to their *p* to shed blood
Eze 30:6 pride of her *p* shall come down
Dan 2:37 hath given thee a kingdom, *p*
Dan 3:27 whose bodies the fire had no *p*
Dan 4:30 the kingdom by the might of my *p*
Dan 6:27 Daniel from the *p* of the lions
Dan 8:6 ran unto him in the fury of his *p*
Dan 8:7 there was no *p* in the ram to
Dan 8:22 of the nation, but not in his *p*
Dan 8:24 his *p* shall be mighty
Dan 8:24 but not by his own *p*
Dan 11:6 shall not retain the *p* of the arm
Dan 11:25 And he shall stir up his *p*
Dan 11:43 But he shall have *p* over the
Dan 12:7 scatter the *p* of the holy people
Hos 12:3 by his strength he had *p* with God
Hos 12:4 he had *p* over the angel, and
Hos 13:14 them from the *p* of the grave
Mic 2:1 it is in the *p* of their hand
Mic 3:8 But truly I am full of *p* by the
Nah 1:3 is slow to anger, and great in *p*
Nah 2:1 strong, fortify thy *p* mightily
Hab 1:11 imputing this his *p* unto his god
Hab 2:9 be delivered from the *p* of evil
Hab 3:4 and there was the hiding of his *p*
Zec 4:6 saying, Not by might, nor by *p*
Zec 9:4 and he will smite her *p* in the sea
Mt 6:13 thine is the kingdom, and the *p*
Mt 9:6 hath *p* on earth to forgive sins
Mt 9:8 which had given such *p* unto men
Mt 10:1 he gave them *p* against unclean
Mt 22:29 the scriptures, nor the *p* of God
Mt 24:30 in the clouds of heaven with *p*
Mt 26:64 sitting on the right hand of *p*
Mt 28:18 All *p* is given unto me in heaven
Mk 2:10 hath *p* on earth to forgive sins
Mk 3:15 to have *p* to heal sicknesses, and
Mk 6:7 gave them *p* over unclean spirits
Mk 9:1 the kingdom of God come with *p*
Mk 12:24 scriptures, neither the *p* of God
Mk 13:26 coming in the clouds with great *p*
Mk 14:62 sitting on the right hand of *p*
Lk 1:17 *p* of Elias, to turn the hearts of
Lk 1:35 the *p* of the Highest shall
Lk 4:6 All this *p* will I give thee, and
Lk 4:14 Jesus returned in the *p* of the
Lk 4:32 for his word was with *p*
Lk 4:36 *p* he commandeth the unclean
Lk 5:17 the *p* of the Lord was present to
Lk 5:24 hath *p* upon earth to forgive sins
Lk 9:1 together, and gave them *p* and
Lk 9:43 all amazed at the mighty *p* of God
Lk 10:19 I give unto you *p* to tread on
Lk 10:19 and over all the *p* of the enemy
Lk 12:5 killed hath *p* to cast into hell
Lk 20:20 they might deliver him unto the *p*
Lk 21:27 of man coming in a cloud with *p*
Lk 22:53 your hour, and the *p* of darkness
Lk 22:69 on the right hand of the *p* of God
Lk 24:49 ye be endued with *p* from on high
Jn 1:12 to them gave he *p* to become the
Jn 10:18 I have *p* to lay it down, and I
Jn 10:18 I have *p* to take it again
Jn 17:2 hast given him *p* over all flesh
Jn 19:10 not that I have *p* to crucify thee
Jn 19:10 and have *p* to release thee
Jn 19:11 have no *p* at all against me
Acts 1:7 the Father hath put in his own *p*
Acts 1:8 But ye shall receive *p*, after
Acts 3:12 as though by our own *p* or
Acts 4:7 the midst, they asked, By what *p*
Acts 4:33 with great *p* gave the apostles
Acts 5:4 sold, was it not in thine own *p*
Acts 6:8 And Stephen, full of faith and *p*
Acts 8:10 This man is the great *p* of God
Acts 8:19 Saying, Give me also this *p*
Acts 10:38 with the Holy Ghost and with *p*
Acts 26:18 from the *p* of Satan unto God,
Rom 1:4 to be the Son of God with *p*
Rom 1:16 for it is the *p* of God unto
Rom 1:20 that are made, even his eternal *p*
Rom 9:17 that I might shew my *p* in thee
Rom 9:21 not the potter *p* over the clay

Rom 9:22 his wrath, and to make his *p* known
Rom 13:1 For there is no *p* but of God
Rom 13:2 therefore resisteth the *p*
Rom 13:3 thou then not be afraid of the *p*
Rom 15:13 through the *p* of the Holy Ghost
Rom 15:19 by the *p* of the Spirit of God
Rom 16:25 Now to him that is of *p* to
1Cor 1:18 are saved it is the *p* of God
1Cor 1:24 and Greeks, Christ the *p* of God
1Cor 2:4 of the Spirit and of *p*
1Cor 2:5 of men, but in the *p* of God
1Cor 4:19 which are puffed up, but the *p*
1Cor 4:20 of God is not in word, but in *p*
1Cor 5:4 with the *p* of our Lord Jesus
1Cor 6:12 not be brought under the *p* of any
1Cor 6:14 also raise up us by his own *p*
1Cor 7:4 wife hath not *p* of her own body
1Cor 7:4 hath not *p* of his own body
1Cor 7:37 but hath *p* over his own will, and
1Cor 9:4 Have we not *p* to eat and to drink
1Cor 9:5 Have we not *p* to lead about a
1Cor 9:6 have not we *p* to forbear working
1Cor 9:12 be partakers of this *p* over you
1Cor 9:12 we have not used this *p*
1Cor 9:18 I abuse not my *p* in the gospel
1Cor 11:10 have *p* on her head because of the
1Cor 15:24 all rule and all authority and *p*
1Cor 15:43 it is raised in *p*
2Cor 4:7 excellency of the *p* may be of God
2Cor 6:7 word of truth, by the *p* of God
2Cor 8:3 For to their *p*, I bear record,
2Cor 8:3 beyond their *p* they were willing
2Cor 12:9 that the *p* of Christ may rest
2Cor 13:4 yet he liveth by the *p* of God
2Cor 13:4 him by the *p* of God toward you
2Cor 13:10 according to the *p* which the Lord
Eph 1:19 of his *p* to us-ward who believe
Eph 1:19 to the working of his mighty *p*
Eph 1:21 Far above all principality, and *p*
Eph 2:2 to the prince of the *p* of the air
Eph 3:7 by the effectual working of his *p*
Eph 3:20 according to the *p* that worketh
Eph 6:10 Lord, and in the *p* of his might
Phil 3:10 the *p* of his resurrection, and the
Col 1:11 according to his glorious *p*
Col 1:13 us from the *p* of darkness
Col 2:10 the head of all principality and *p*
1Th 1:5 you in word only, but also in *p*
2Th 1:9 Lord, and from the glory of his *p*
2Th 1:11 and the work of faith with *p*
2Th 2:9 the working of Satan with all *p*
2Th 3:9 Not because we have not *p*
1Ti 6:16 whom be honour and *p* everlasting
2Ti 1:7 but of *p*, and of love, and of a
2Ti 1:8 gospel according to the *p* of God
2Ti 3:5 but denying the *p* thereof
Heb 1:3 all things by the word of his *p*
Heb 2:14 him that had the *p* of death
Heb 7:16 but after the *p* of an endless
1Pet 1:5 Who are kept by the *p* of God
2Pet 1:3 According as his divine *p* hath
2Pet 1:16 when we made known unto you the *p*
2Pet 2:11 angels, which are greater in *p*
Jude 25 glory and majesty, dominion and *p*
Rev 2:26 will I give *p* over the nations
Rev 4:11 to receive glory and honour and *p*
Rev 5:12 Lamb that was slain to receive *p*
Rev 5:13 and honour, and glory, and *p*
Rev 6:4 *p* was given to him that sat
Rev 6:8 *p* was given unto them over the
Rev 7:12 and thanksgiving, and honour, and *p*
Rev 9:3 and unto them was given *p*, as the
Rev 9:3 the scorpions of the earth have *p*
Rev 9:10 their *p* was to hurt men five
Rev 9:19 For their *p* is in their mouth, and
Rev 11:3 I will give *p* unto my two
Rev 11:6 These have *p* to shut heaven, that
Rev 11:6 have *p* over waters to turn them
Rev 11:17 hast taken to thee thy great *p*
Rev 12:10 our God, and the *p* of his Christ
Rev 13:2 and the dragon gave him his *p*
Rev 13:4 which gave *p* unto the beast
Rev 13:5 *p* was given unto him to continue
Rev 13:7 *p* was given him over all kindreds
Rev 13:12 he exerciseth all the *p* of the
Rev 13:14 of those miracles which he had *p*
Rev 13:15 he had *p* to give life unto the
Rev 14:18 the altar, which had *p* over fire
Rev 15:8 the glory of God, and from his *p*
Rev 16:8 *p* was given unto him to scorch
Rev 16:9 which hath *p* over these plagues
Rev 17:12 but receive *p* as kings one hour
Rev 17:13 one mind, and shall give their *p*
Rev 18:1 down from heaven, having great *p*
Rev 19:1 and glory, and honour, and *p*
Rev 20:6 such the second death hath no *p*

**POWERS**

Mt 24:29 the *p* of the heavens shall be
Mk 13:25 the *p* that are in heaven shall be
Lk 12:11 and unto magistrates, and *p*
Lk 21:26 for the *p* of heaven shall be
Rom 8:38 angels, nor principalities, nor *p*
Rom 13:1 soul be subject unto the higher *p*
Rom 13:1 the *p* that be are ordained of God
Eph 3:10 *p* in heavenly places might be
Eph 6:12 against principalities, against *p*
Col 1:16 or principalities, or *p*
Col 2:15 spoiled principalities and *p*
Titus 3:1 be subject to principalities and *p*
Heb 6:5 the *p* of the world to come,
1Pet 3:22 *p* being made subject unto him

**PRACTISE**

Ps 141:4 to *p* wicked works with men that
Is 32:6 to *p* hypocrisy, and to utter error
Dan 8:24 and shall prosper, and *p*, and shall
Mic 2:1 the morning is light, they *p* it

**PRAETORIUM** *(pre-to'-re-um) Palace of the Roman procurator in Jerusalem.*

Mk 15:16 him away into the hall, called *P*

**PRAISE**

Gen 29:35 she said, Now will I *p* the LORD
Gen 49:8 art he whom thy brethren shall *p*
Lev 19:24 be holy to *p* the LORD withal
Deut 10:21 He is thy *p*, and he is thy God,
Deut 26:19 nations which he hath made, in *p*
Judg 5:2 *P* ye the LORD for the avenging of
Judg 5:3 I will sing *p* to the LORD God of
1Chr 16:4 thank and *p* the LORD God of Israel
1Chr 16:35 thy holy name, and glory in thy *p*
1Chr 23:5 made, said David, to *p* therewith
1Chr 23:30 *p* the LORD, and likewise at even
1Chr 25:3 to give thanks and to *p* the LORD
1Chr 29:13 thee, and *p* thy glorious name
2Chr 7:6 the king had made to *p* the LORD
2Chr 8:14 Levites to their charges, to *p*
2Chr 20:19 stood up to *p* the LORD God of
2Chr 20:21 that should *p* the beauty of
2Chr 20:21 the army, and to say, *P* the LORD
2Chr 20:22 when they began to sing and to *p*
2Chr 23:13 and such as taught to sing *p*
2Chr 29:30 commanded the Levites to sing *p*
2Chr 31:2 to *p* in the gates of the tents of
Ezr 3:10 cymbals, to *p* the LORD, after the
Neh 9:5 exalted above all blessing and *p*
Neh 12:24 brethren over against them, to *p*
Neh 12:46 of the singers, and songs of *p*
Ps 7:17 I will *p* the LORD according to
Ps 7:17 will sing *p* to the name of the
Ps 9:1 I will *p* thee, O LORD, with my
Ps 9:2 I will sing *p* to thy name
Ps 9:14 That I may shew forth all thy *p*
Ps 21:13 so will we sing and *p* thy power
Ps 22:22 of the congregation will I *p* thee
Ps 22:23 Ye that fear the LORD, *p* him
Ps 22:25 My *p* shall be of thee in the
Ps 22:26 they shall *p* the LORD that seek
Ps 28:7 and with my song will I *p* him
Ps 30:9 shall the dust *p* thee
Ps 30:12 that my glory may sing *p* to thee
Ps 33:1 for *p* is comely for the upright
Ps 33:2 *P* the LORD with harp
Ps 34:1 his *p* shall continually be in my
Ps 35:18 I will *p* thee among much people
Ps 35:28 of thy *p* all the day long
Ps 40:3 in my mouth, even *p* unto our God
Ps 42:4 God, with the voice of joy and *p*
Ps 42:5 for I shall yet *p* him for the
Ps 42:11 for I shall yet *p* him, who is the
Ps 43:4 yea, upon the harp will I *p* thee
Ps 43:5 for I shall yet *p* him, who is the
Ps 44:8 day long, and *p* thy name for ever
Ps 45:17 shall the people *p* thee for ever
Ps 48:10 so is thy *p* unto the ends of the
Ps 49:18 his soul, and men will *p* thee
Ps 50:23 Whoso offereth *p* glorifieth me
Ps 51:15 my mouth shall shew forth thy *p*
Ps 52:9 I will *p* thee for ever, because
Ps 54:6 I will *p* thy name, O LORD
Ps 56:4 In God I will *p* his word, in God
Ps 56:10 In God will I *p* his word
Ps 56:10 in the LORD will I *p* his word
Ps 57:7 I will sing and give *p*
Ps 57:9 I will *p* thee, O Lord, among the
Ps 61:8 So will I sing *p* unto thy name
Ps 63:3 than life, my lips shall *p* thee
Ps 63:5 my mouth shall *p* thee with joyful
Ps 65:1 *P* waiteth for thee, O God in Sion
Ps 66:2 make his *p* glorious
Ps 66:8 the voice of his *p* to be heard
Ps 67:3 Let the people *p* thee, O God
Ps 67:3 let all the people *p* thee
Ps 67:5 Let the people *p* thee, O God
Ps 67:5 let all the people *p* thee
Ps 69:30 I will *p* the name of God with a
Ps 69:34 Let the heaven and earth *p* him
Ps 71:6 my *p* shall be continually of thee
Ps 71:8 Let my mouth be filled with thy *p*
Ps 71:14 will yet *p* thee more and more
Ps 71:22 I will also *p* thee with the
Ps 74:21 let the poor and needy *p* thy name
Ps 76:10 the wrath of man shall *p* thee
Ps 79:13 forth thy *p* to all generations
Ps 86:12 I will *p* thee, O Lord my God,
Ps 88:10 shall the dead arise and *p* thee
Ps 89:5 the heavens shall *p* thy wonders
Ps 98:4 loud noise, and rejoice, and sing *p*
Ps 99:3 Let them *p* thy great and terrible
Ps 100:*t* A Psalm of *p*
Ps 100:4 and into his courts with *p*
Ps 102:18 shall be created shall *p* the LORD
Ps 102:21 in Zion, and his *p* in Jerusalem
Ps 104:33 I will sing *p* to my God while I
Ps 104:35 *P* ye the LORD
Ps 105:45 *P* ye the LORD
Ps 106:1 *P* ye the LORD
Ps 106:2 who can shew forth all his *p*
Ps 106:12 they sang his *p*
Ps 106:47 holy name, and to triumph in thy *p*
Ps 106:48 *P* ye the LORD
Ps 107:8 Oh that men would *p* the LORD for
Ps 107:15 Oh that men would *p* the LORD for
Ps 107:21 Oh that men would *p* the LORD for
Ps 107:31 Oh that men would *p* the LORD for
Ps 107:32 *p* him in the assembly of the
Ps 108:1 I will sing and give *p*, even with
Ps 108:3 I will *p* thee, O LORD, among the
Ps 109:1 Hold not thy peace, O God of my *p*
Ps 109:30 I will greatly *p* the LORD with my
Ps 109:30 I will *p* him among the multitude
Ps 111:1 *P* ye the LORD
Ps 111:1 I will *p* the LORD with my whole
Ps 111:10 his *p* endureth for ever
Ps 112:1 *P* ye the LORD
Ps 113:1 *P* ye the LORD
Ps 113:1 *P*, O ye servants of the LORD,
Ps 113:1 *p* the name of the LORD
Ps 113:9 *P* ye the LORD
Ps 115:17 The dead *p* not the LORD, neither
Ps 115:18 *P* the LORD
Ps 116:19 *P* ye the LORD
Ps 117:1 O *p* the LORD, all ye nations
Ps 117:1 *p* him, all ye people
Ps 117:2 *P* ye the LORD
Ps 118:19 into them, and I will *p* the LORD
Ps 118:21 I will *p* thee
Ps 118:28 Thou art my God, and I will *p* thee
Ps 119:7 I will *p* thee with uprightness of
Ps 119:164 Seven times a day do I *p* thee
Ps 119:171 My lips shall utter *p*, when thou
Ps 119:175 my soul live, and it shall *p* thee
Ps 135:1 *P* ye the LORD
Ps 135:1 *P* ye the name of the LORD
Ps 135:1 *p* him, O ye servants of the LORD
Ps 135:3 *P* the LORD
Ps 135:21 *P* ye the LORD
Ps 138:1 I will *p* thee with my whole heart
Ps 138:1 the gods will I sing *p* unto thee
Ps 138:2 *p* thy name for thy lovingkindness
Ps 138:4 kings of the earth shall *p* thee
Ps 139:14 I will *p* thee
Ps 142:7 of prison, that I may *p* thy name
Ps 145:*t* David's Psalm of *p*
Ps 145:2 I will *p* thy name for ever and
Ps 145:4 shall *p* thy works to another
Ps 145:10 All thy works shall *p* thee
Ps 145:21 shall speak the *p* of the LORD
Ps 146:1 *P* ye the LORD
Ps 146:1 *P* the LORD, O my soul

Ps 146:2 While I live will I *p* the LORD
Ps 146:10 *P* ye the LORD
Ps 147:1 *P* ye the LORD
Ps 147:1 and *p* is comely
Ps 147:7 sing *p* upon the harp unto our God
Ps 147:12 *P* the LORD, O Jerusalem
Ps 147:12 *p* thy God, O Zion
Ps 147:20 *P* ye the LORD
Ps 148:1 *P* ye the LORD
Ps 148:1 *P* ye the LORD from the heavens
Ps 148:1 *p* him in the heights
Ps 148:2 *P* ye him, all his angels
Ps 148:2 *p* ye him, all his hosts
Ps 148:3 *P* ye him, sun and moon
Ps 148:3 *p* him, all ye stars of light
Ps 148:4 *P* him, ye heavens of heavens, and
Ps 148:5 Let them *p* the name of the LORD
Ps 148:7 *P* the LORD from the earth, ye
Ps 148:13 Let them *p* the name of the LORD
Ps 148:14 people, the *p* of all his saints
Ps 148:14 *P* ye the LORD
Ps 149:1 *P* ye the LORD
Ps 149:1 his *p* in the congregation of
Ps 149:3 Let them *p* his name in the dance
Ps 149:9 *P* ye the LORD
Ps 150:1 *P* ye the LORD
Ps 150:1 *P* God in his sanctuary
Ps 150:1 *p* him in the firmament of his
Ps 150:2 *P* him for his mighty acts
Ps 150:2 *p* him according to his excellent
Ps 150:3 *P* him with the sound of the
Ps 150:3 *p* him with the psaltery and harp
Ps 150:4 *P* him with the timbrel and dance
Ps 150:4 *p* him with stringed instruments
Ps 150:5 *P* him upon the loud cymbals
Ps 150:5 *p* him upon the high sounding
Ps 150:6 thing that hath breath *p* the LORD
Ps 150:6 *P* ye the LORD
Prov 27:2 Let another man *p* thee, and not
Prov 27:21 so is a man to his *p*
Prov 28:4 that forsake the law *p* the wicked
Prov 31:31 her own works *p* her in the gates
Is 12:1 shalt say, O LORD, I will *p* thee
Is 12:4 *P* the LORD, call upon his name,
Is 25:1 exalt thee, I will *p* thy name
Is 38:18 For the grave cannot *p* thee
Is 38:19 the living, he shall *p* thee
Is 42:8 neither my *p* to graven images
Is 42:10 his *p* from the end of the earth,
Is 42:12 declare his *p* in the islands
Is 43:21 they shall shew forth my *p*
Is 48:9 for my *p* will I refrain for thee,
Is 60:18 walls Salvation, and thy gates *P*
Is 61:3 the garment of *p* for the spirit
Is 61:11 *p* to spring forth before all the
Is 62:7 make Jerusalem a *p* in the earth
Is 62:9 it shall eat it, and *p* the LORD
Jer 13:11 people, and for a name, and for a *p*
Jer 17:14 for thou art my *p*
Jer 17:26 and bringing sacrifices of *p*
Jer 20:13 Sing unto the LORD, *p* ye the LORD
Jer 31:7 *p* ye, and say, O LORD, save thy
Jer 33:9 shall be to me a name of joy, a *p*
Jer 33:11 shall say, *P* the LORD of hosts
Jer 33:11 of *p* into the house of the LORD
Jer 48:2 There shall be no more *p* of Moab
Jer 49:25 How is the city of *p* not left
Jer 51:41 how is the *p* of the whole earth
Dan 2:23 *p* thee, O thou God of my fathers,
Dan 4:37 Now I Nebuchadnezzar *p* and extol
Joel 2:26 *p* the name of the LORD your God,
Hab 3:3 and the earth was full of his *p*
Zeph 3:19 and I will get them *p* and fame in
Zeph 3:20 a *p* among all people of the earth
Mt 21:16 sucklings thou hast perfected *p*
Lk 18:43 when they saw it, gave *p* unto God
Lk 19:37 *p* God with a loud voice for all
Jn 9:24 and said unto him, Give God the *p*
Jn 12:43 For they loved the *p* of men more
Jn 12:43 of men more than the *p* of God
Rom 2:29 whose *p* is not of men, but of God
Rom 13:3 and thou shalt have *p* of the same
Rom 15:11 *P* the Lord, all ye Gentiles
1Cor 4:5 shall every man have *p* of God
1Cor 11:2 Now I *p* you, brethren, that ye
1Cor 11:17 I declare unto you I *p* you not
1Cor 11:22 shall I *p* you in this
1Cor 11:22 I *p* you not
2Cor 8:18 brother, whose *p* is in the gospel
Eph 1:6 To the *p* of the glory of his
Eph 1:12 should be to the *p* of his glory
Eph 1:14 unto the *p* of his glory
Phil 1:11 unto the glory and *p* of God
Phil 4:8 any virtue, and if there be any *p*
Heb 2:12 church will I sing *p* unto thee
Heb 13:15 sacrifice of *p* to God continually
1Pet 1:7 with fire, might be found unto *p*
1Pet 2:14 for the *p* of them that do well
1Pet 4:11 Jesus Christ, to whom be *p*
Rev 19:5 *P* our God, all ye his servants,

### PRAISED

Judg 16:24 people saw him, they *p* their god
2Sa 14:25 much *p* as Absalom for his beauty
2Sa 22:4 the LORD, who is worthy to be *p*
1Chr 16:25 is the LORD, and greatly to be *p*
1Chr 16:36 people said, Amen, and *p* the LORD
1Chr 23:5 four thousand *p* the LORD with the
2Chr 5:13 *p* the LORD, saying, For he is
2Chr 7:3 *p* the LORD, saying, For he is
2Chr 7:6 when David *p* by their ministry
2Chr 30:21 the priests *p* the LORD day by day
Ezr 3:11 great shout, when they *p* the LORD
Neh 5:13 said, Amen, and *p* the LORD
Ps 18:3 the LORD, who is worthy to be *p*
Ps 48:1 greatly to be *p* in the city of
Ps 72:15 and daily shall he be *p*
Ps 96:4 LORD is great, and greatly to be *p*
Ps 113:3 same the LORD's name is to be *p*
Ps 145:3 is the LORD, and greatly to be *p*
Prov 31:30 feareth the LORD, she shall be *p*
Eccl 4:2 Wherefore I *p* the dead which are
Song 6:9 and the concubines, and they *p* her
Is 64:11 house, where our fathers *p* thee
Dan 4:34 I blessed the most High, and I *p*
Dan 5:4 *p* the gods of gold, and of silver,
Dan 5:23 thou hast *p* the gods of silver,
Lk 1:64 loosed, and he spake, and *p* God

### PRAISES

Ex 15:11 in holiness, fearful in *p*
2Chr 29:30 they sang *p* with gladness, and
Ps 9:11 Sing *p* to the LORD, which
Ps 18:49 heathen, and sing *p* unto thy name
Ps 22:3 that inhabitest the *p* of Israel
Ps 27:6 I will sing *p* unto the LORD
Ps 47:6 Sing *p* to God, sing *p*
Ps 47:6 *p* unto our King, sing *p*
Ps 47:7 sing ye *p* with understanding
Ps 56:12 I will render *p* unto thee
Ps 68:4 Sing unto God, sing *p* to his name
Ps 68:32 O sing *p* unto the Lord
Ps 75:9 I will sing *p* to the God of Jacob
Ps 78:4 to come the *p* of the LORD
Ps 92:1 to sing *p* unto thy name, O most
Ps 108:3 I will sing *p* unto thee among the
Ps 135:3 sing *p* unto his name
Ps 144:9 strings will I sing *p* unto thee
Ps 146:2 I will sing *p* unto my God while I
Ps 147:1 it is good to sing *p* unto our God
Ps 149:3 let them sing *p* unto him with the
Ps 149:6 Let the high *p* of God be in their
Is 60:6 shew forth the *p* of the LORD
Is 63:7 the *p* of the LORD, according to
Acts 16:25 Silas prayed, and sang *p* unto God
1Pet 2:9 that ye should shew forth the *p*

### PRAISING

2Chr 5:13 make one sound to be heard in *p*
2Chr 23:12 *p* the king, she came to the
Ezr 3:11 they sang together by course in *p*
Ps 84:4 they will be still *p* thee
Lk 2:13 of the heavenly host *p* God
Lk 2:20 *p* God for all the things that
Lk 24:53 were continually in the temple, *p*
Acts 2:47 *P* God, and having favour with all
Acts 3:8 walking, and leaping, and *p* God
Acts 3:9 people saw him walking and *p* God

### PRAYED

Gen 20:17 So Abraham *p* unto God
Num 11:2 when Moses *p* unto the LORD, the
Num 21:7 And Moses *p* for the people
Deut 9:20 I *p* for Aaron also the same time
Deut 9:26 I *p* therefore unto the LORD, and
1Sa 1:10 *p* unto the LORD, and wept sore
1Sa 1:27 For this child I *p*
1Sa 2:1 And Hannah *p*, and said, My heart
1Sa 8:6 And Samuel *p* unto the LORD
2Kin 4:33 them twain, and *p* unto the LORD
2Kin 6:17 And Elisha *p*, and said, LORD, I
2Kin 6:18 Elisha *p* unto the LORD, and said,
2Kin 19:15 Hezekiah *p* before the LORD, and
2Kin 19:20 That which thou hast *p* to me
2Kin 20:2 wall, and *p* unto the LORD, saying,
2Chr 30:18 But Hezekiah *p* for them, saying,
2Chr 32:20 prophet Isaiah the son of Amoz, *p*
2Chr 32:24 to the death, and *p* unto the LORD
2Chr 33:13 And *p* unto him
Ezr 10:1 Now when Ezra had *p*, and when he
Neh 1:4 *p* before the God of heaven,
Neh 2:4 So I *p* to the God of heaven
Job 42:10 when he *p* for his friends
Is 37:15 Hezekiah *p* unto the LORD, saying,
Is 37:21 Whereas thou hast *p* to me against
Is 38:2 the wall, and *p* unto the LORD,
Jer 32:16 I *p* unto the LORD, saying,
Dan 6:10 his knees three times a day, and *p*
Dan 9:4 I *p* unto the LORD my God, and made
Jonah 2:1 Then Jonah *p* unto the LORD his
Jonah 4:2 he *p* unto the LORD, and said, I
Mt 26:39 and fell on his face, and *p*
Mt 26:42 away again the second time, and *p*
Mt 26:44 *p* the third time, saying the same
Mk 1:35 into a solitary place, and there *p*
Mk 5:18 *p* him that he might be with him
Mk 14:35 *p* that, if it were possible, the
Mk 14:39 And again he went away, and *p*
Lk 5:3 *p* him that he would thrust out a
Lk 5:16 himself into the wilderness, and *p*
Lk 9:29 And as he *p*, the fashion of his
Lk 18:11 *p* thus with himself, God, I thank
Lk 22:32 But I have *p* for thee, that thy
Lk 22:41 cast, and kneeled down, and *p*
Lk 22:44 in an agony he *p* more earnestly
Jn 4:31 mean while his disciples *p* him
Acts 1:24 And they *p*, and said, Thou, Lord,
Acts 4:31 And when they had *p*, the place was
Acts 6:6 and when they had *p*, they laid
Acts 8:15 *p* for them, that they might
Acts 9:40 all forth, and kneeled down, and *p*
Acts 10:2 to the people, and *p* to God alway
Acts 10:30 at the ninth hour I *p* in my house
Acts 10:48 Then *p* they him to tarry certain
Acts 13:3 And when they had fasted and *p*
Acts 14:23 and had *p* with fasting, they
Acts 16:9 *p* him, saying, Come over into
Acts 16:25 And at midnight Paul and Silas *p*
Acts 20:36 kneeled down, and *p* with them all
Acts 21:5 kneeled down on the shore, and *p*
Acts 22:17 even while I *p* in the temple, I
Acts 23:18 *p* me to bring this young man unto
Acts 28:8 to whom Paul entered in, and *p*
Jas 5:17 he *p* earnestly that it might not
Jas 5:18 he *p* again, and the heaven gave

### PRAYER

2Sa 7:27 heart to pray this *p* unto thee
1Kin 8:28 respect unto the *p* of thy servant
1Kin 8:28 hearken unto the cry and to the *p*
1Kin 8:29 *p* which thy servant shall make
1Kin 8:38 What *p* and supplication soever be
1Kin 8:45 Then hear thou in heaven their *p*
1Kin 8:49 Then hear thou their *p* and their
1Kin 8:54 made an end of praying all this *p*
1Kin 9:3 said unto him, I have heard thy *p*
2Kin 19:4 wherefore lift up thy *p* for the
2Kin 20:5 thy father, I have heard thy *p*
2Chr 6:19 therefore to the *p* of thy servant
2Chr 6:19 the *p* which thy servant prayeth
2Chr 6:20 to hearken unto the *p* which thy
2Chr 6:29 Then what *p* or what supplication
2Chr 6:35 thou from the heavens their *p*
2Chr 6:39 from thy dwelling place, their *p*
2Chr 6:40 the *p* that is made in this place
2Chr 7:12 said unto him, I have heard thy *p*
2Chr 7:15 mine ears attent unto the *p* that
2Chr 30:27 their *p* came up to his holy
2Chr 33:18 his *p* unto his God, and the words
2Chr 33:19 His *p* also, and how God was
Neh 1:6 mayest hear the *p* of thy servant
Neh 1:11 attentive to the *p* of thy servant
Neh 1:11 to the *p* of thy servants, who
Neh 4:9 we made our *p* unto our God
Neh 11:17 to begin the thanksgiving in *p*
Job 15:4 fear, and restrainest *p* before God
Job 16:17 also my *p* is pure
Job 22:27 Thou shalt make thy *p* unto him
Ps 4:1 have mercy upon me, and hear my *p*
Ps 5:3 will I direct my *p* unto thee
Ps 6:9 the LORD will receive my *p*
Ps 17:*t* A *P* of David

Ps 17:1 unto my cry, give ear unto my *p*
Ps 35:13 my *p* returned into mine own bosom
Ps 39:12 Hear my *p*, O LORD, and give ear
Ps 42:8 my *p* unto the God of my life
Ps 54:2 Hear my *p*, O God
Ps 55:1 Give ear to my *p*, O God
Ps 61:1 attend unto my *p*
Ps 64:1 Hear my voice, O God, in my *p*
Ps 65:2 O thou that hearest *p*, unto thee
Ps 66:19 attended to the voice of my *p*
Ps 66:20 which hath not turned away my *p*
Ps 69:13 my *p* is unto thee, O LORD, in an
Ps 72:15 *p* also shall be made for him
Ps 80:4 angry against the *p* of thy people
Ps 84:8 O LORD God of hosts, hear my *p*
Ps 86:*t* A *P* of David
Ps 86:6 Give ear, O LORD, unto my *p*
Ps 88:2 Let my *p* come before thee
Ps 88:13 morning shall my *p* prevent thee
Ps 90:*t* A *P* of Moses, the man of God
Ps 102:*t* A *P* of the afflicted, when he is
Ps 102:1 Hear my *p*, O LORD, and let my cry
Ps 102:17 regard the *p* of the destitute
Ps 102:17 and not despise their *p*
Ps 109:4 but I give myself unto *p*
Ps 109:7 and let his *p* become sin
Ps 141:2 Let my *p* be set forth before thee
Ps 141:5 for yet my *p* also shall be in
Ps 142:*t* A *P* when he was in the cave
Ps 143:1 Hear my *p*, O LORD, give ear to my
Prov 15:8 but the *p* of the upright is his
Prov 15:29 he heareth the *p* of the righteous
Prov 28:9 even his *p* shall be abomination
Is 26:16 they poured out a *p* when thy
Is 37:4 wherefore lift up thy *p* for the
Is 38:5 thy father, I have heard thy *p*
Is 56:7 make them joyful in my house of *p*
Is 56:7 an house of *p* for all people
Jer 7:16 lift up cry nor *p* for them
Jer 11:14 lift up a cry or *p* for them
Lam 3:8 and shout, he shutteth out my *p*
Lam 3:44 that our *p* should not pass
Dan 9:3 unto the Lord God, to seek by *p*
Dan 9:13 yet made we not our *p* before the
Dan 9:17 hear the *p* of thy servant, and his
Dan 9:21 Yea, whiles I was speaking in *p*
Jonah 2:7 my *p* came in unto thee, into
Hab 3:1 A *p* of Habakkuk the prophet upon
Mt 17:21 this kind goeth not out but by *p*
Mt 21:13 shall be called the house of *p*
Mt 21:22 whatsoever ye shall ask in *p*
Mt 23:14 and for a pretence make long *p*
Mk 9:29 come forth by nothing, but by *p*
Mk 11:17 of all nations the house of *p*
Lk 1:13 for thy *p* is heard
Lk 6:12 continued all night in *p* to God
Lk 19:46 My house is the house of *p*
Lk 22:45 And when he rose up from *p*
Acts 1:14 continued with one accord in *p*
Acts 3:1 into the temple at the hour of *p*
Acts 6:4 give ourselves continually to *p*
Acts 10:31 thy *p* is heard, and thine alms are
Acts 12:5 but *p* was made without ceasing of
Acts 16:13 where *p* was wont to be made
Acts 16:16 it came to pass, as we went to *p*
Rom 10:1 *p* to God for Israel is, that they
Rom 12:12 continuing instant in *p*
1Cor 7:5 give yourselves to fasting and *p*
2Cor 1:11 also helping together by *p* for us
2Cor 9:14 And by their *p* for you, which long
Eph 6:18 Praying always with all *p*
Phil 1:4 Always in every *p* of mine for you
Phil 1:19 to my salvation through your *p*
Phil 4:6 but in every thing by *p* and
Col 4:2 Continue in *p*, and watch in the
1Ti 4:5 by the word of God and *p*
Jas 5:15 the *p* of faith shall save the
Jas 5:16 The effectual fervent *p* of a
1Pet 4:7 therefore sober, and watch unto *p*

## PRAYERS

Ps 72:20 The *p* of David the son of Jesse
Is 1:15 yea, when ye make many *p*, I will
Mk 12:40 and for a pretence make long *p*
Lk 2:37 with fastings and *p* night and day
Lk 5:33 of John fast often, and make *p*
Lk 20:47 houses, and for a shew make long *p*
Acts 2:42 and in breaking of bread, and in *p*
Acts 10:4 And he said unto him, Thy *p*
Rom 1:9 mention of you always in my *p*
Rom 15:30 with me in your *p* to God for me
Eph 1:16 making mention of you in my *p*
Col 4:12 labouring fervently for you in *p*
1Th 1:2 making mention of you in our *p*
1Ti 2:1 first of all, supplications, *p*
1Ti 5:5 supplications and *p* night and day
2Ti 1:3 remembrance of thee in my *p* night
Philem 4 mention of thee always in my *p*
Philem 22 your *p* I shall be given unto you
Heb 5:7 flesh, when he had offered up *p*
1Pet 3:7 that your *p* be not hindered
1Pet 3:12 and his ears are open unto their *p*
Rev 5:8 odours, which are the *p* of saints
Rev 8:3 he should offer it with the *p* of
Rev 8:4 came with the *p* of the saints

## PRAYETH

1Kin 8:28 which thy servant *p* before thee
2Chr 6:19 which thy servant *p* before thee
2Chr 6:20 thy servant *p* toward this place
Is 44:17 *p* unto it, and saith, Deliver me
Acts 9:11 for, behold, he *p*,
1Cor 11:5 But every woman that *p* or
1Cor 14:14 in an unknown tongue, my spirit *p*

## PRAYING

1Sa 1:12 she continued *p* before the LORD
1Sa 1:26 by thee here, *p* unto the LORD
1Kin 8:54 made an end of *p* all this prayer
2Chr 7:1 when Solomon had made an end of *p*
Dan 6:11 men assembled, and found Daniel *p*
Dan 9:20 And whiles I was speaking, and *p*
Mk 11:25 And when ye stand *p*, forgive, if
Lk 1:10 multitude of the people were *p*
Lk 3:21 Jesus also being baptized, and *p*
Lk 9:18 came to pass, as he was alone *p*
Lk 11:1 as he was *p* in a certain place,
Acts 11:5 I was in the city of Joppa *p*
Acts 12:12 many were gathered together *p*
1Cor 11:4 Every man *p* or prophesying,
2Cor 8:4 *P* us with much intreaty that we
Eph 6:18 *P* always with all prayer and
Col 1:3 Jesus Christ, *p* always for you,
Col 4:3 Withal *p* also for us, that God
1Th 3:10 day *p* exceedingly that we might
Jude 20 holy faith, *p* in the Holy Ghost,

## PREACH

Neh 6:7 to *p* of thee at Jerusalem
Is 61:1 to *p* good tidings unto the meek
Jonah 3:2 *p* unto it the preaching that I
Mt 4:17 From that time Jesus began to *p*
Mt 10:7 And as ye go, *p*, saying, The
Mt 10:27 that *p* ye upon the housetops
Mt 11:1 to teach and to *p* in their cities
Mk 1:4 *p* the baptism of repentance for
Mk 1:38 towns, that I may *p* there also
Mk 3:14 he might send them forth to *p*
Mk 16:15 *p* the gospel to every creature
Lk 4:18 me to *p* the gospel to the poor
Lk 4:18 to *p* deliverance to the captives,
Lk 4:19 To *p* the acceptable year of the
Lk 4:43 I must *p* the kingdom of God to
Lk 9:2 he sent them to *p* the kingdom of
Lk 9:60 go thou and *p* the kingdom of God
Acts 5:42 not to teach and *p* Jesus Christ
Acts 10:42 commanded us to *p* unto the people
Acts 14:15 *p* unto you that ye should turn
Acts 15:21 in every city them that *p* him
Acts 16:6 Holy Ghost to *p* the word in Asia
Acts 16:10 us for to *p* the gospel unto them
Acts 17:3 whom I *p* unto you, is Christ
Rom 1:15 I am ready to *p* the gospel to you
Rom 10:8 is, the word of faith, which we *p*
Rom 10:15 And how shall they *p*, except they
Rom 10:15 them that *p* the gospel of peace
Rom 15:20 so have I strived to *p* the gospel
1Cor 1:17 to baptize, but to *p* the gospel
1Cor 1:23 But we *p* Christ crucified, unto
1Cor 9:14 *p* the gospel should live of the
1Cor 9:16 For though I *p* the gospel
1Cor 9:16 is unto me, if I *p* not the gospel
1Cor 9:18 when I *p* the gospel, I may make
1Cor 15:11 it were I or they, so we *p*
2Cor 2:12 to Troas to *p* Christ's gospel
2Cor 4:5 For we *p* not ourselves, but
2Cor 10:16 To *p* the gospel in the regions
Gal 1:8 *p* any other gospel unto you than
Gal 1:9 If any man *p* any other gospel
Gal 1:16 that I might *p* him among the
Gal 2:2 which I *p* among the Gentiles
Gal 5:11 if I yet *p* circumcision, why do I
Eph 3:8 that I should *p* among the
Phil 1:15 Some indeed *p* Christ even of envy
Phil 1:16 The one *p* Christ of contention,
Col 1:28 Whom we *p*, warning every man, and
2Ti 4:2 *P* the word
Rev 14:6 the everlasting gospel to *p* unto

## PREACHED

Ps 40:9 I have *p* righteousness in the
Mt 11:5 poor have the gospel *p* to them
Mt 24:14 *p* in all the world for a witness
Mt 26:13 shall be *p* in the whole world
Mk 1:7 And *p*, saying, There cometh one
Mk 1:39 And he *p* in their synagogues
Mk 2:2 and he *p* the word unto them
Mk 6:12 out, and *p* that men should repent
Mk 14:9 this gospel shall be *p* throughout
Mk 16:20 *p* every where, the Lord working
Lk 3:18 exhortation *p* he unto the people
Lk 4:44 he *p* in the synagogues of Galilee
Lk 7:22 to the poor the gospel is *p*
Lk 16:16 that time the kingdom of God is *p*
Lk 20:1 *p* the gospel, the chief priests
Lk 24:47 remission of sins should be *p* in
Acts 3:20 which before was *p* unto you
Acts 4:2 *p* through Jesus the resurrection
Acts 8:5 of Samaria, and *p* Christ unto them
Acts 8:25 *p* the word of the Lord, returned
Acts 8:25 *p* the gospel in many villages of
Acts 8:35 scripture, and *p* unto him Jesus
Acts 8:40 through he *p* in all the cities
Acts 9:20 straightway he *p* Christ in the
Acts 9:27 how he had *p* boldly at Damascus
Acts 10:37 after the baptism which John *p*
Acts 13:5 they *p* the word of God in the
Acts 13:24 When John had first *p* before his
Acts 13:38 that through this man is *p* unto
Acts 13:42 be *p* to them the next sabbath
Acts 14:7 And there they *p* the gospel
Acts 14:21 when they had *p* the gospel to
Acts 14:25 when they had *p* the word in Perga
Acts 15:36 we have *p* the word of the Lord
Acts 17:13 of God was *p* of Paul at Berea
Acts 17:18 because he *p* unto them Jesus, and
Acts 20:7 Paul *p* unto them, ready to depart
Rom 15:19 I have fully *p* the gospel of
1Cor 9:27 means, when I have *p* to others
1Cor 15:1 you the gospel which I *p* unto you
1Cor 15:2 keep in memory what I *p* unto you
1Cor 15:12 Now if Christ be *p* that he rose
2Cor 1:19 who was *p* among you by us, even
2Cor 11:4 another Jesus, whom we have not *p*
2Cor 11:7 because I have *p* to you the
Gal 1:8 that which we have *p* unto you
Gal 1:11 was *p* of me is not after man
Gal 3:8 *p* before the gospel unto Abraham,
Gal 4:13 infirmity of the flesh I *p* the
Eph 2:17 *p* peace to you which were afar
Phil 1:18 or in truth, Christ is *p*
Col 1:23 which was *p* to every creature
1Th 2:9 we *p* unto you the gospel of God
1Ti 3:16 *p* unto the Gentiles, believed on
Heb 4:2 For unto us was the gospel *p*
Heb 4:2 but the word *p* did not profit
Heb 4:6 first *p* entered not in because of
1Pet 1:12 unto you by them that have *p* the
1Pet 1:25 which by the gospel is *p* unto you
1Pet 3:19 *p* unto the spirits in prison
1Pet 4:6 *p* also to them that are dead

## PREACHER

Eccl 1:1 The words of the *P*, the son of
Eccl 1:2 Vanity of vanities, saith the *P*
Eccl 1:12 I the *P* was king over Israel in
Eccl 7:27 this have I found, saith the *p*
Eccl 12:8 Vanity of vanities, saith the *p*
Eccl 12:9 moreover, because the *p* was wise
Eccl 12:10 The *p* sought to find out
Rom 10:14 how shall they hear without a *p*
1Ti 2:7 Whereunto I am ordained a *p*
2Ti 1:11 Whereunto I am appointed a *p*
2Pet 2:5 a *p* of righteousness, bringing in

## PREACHING

Jonah 3:2 unto it the *p* that I bid thee
Mt 3:1 *p* in the wilderness of Judaea,
Mt 4:23 *p* the gospel of the kingdom, and
Mt 9:35 *p* the gospel of the kingdom, and
Mt 12:41 they repented at the *p* of Jonas
Mk 1:14 *p* the gospel of the kingdom of
Lk 3:3 *p* the baptism of repentance for
Lk 8:1 every city and village, *p* and

Lk 9:6 *p* the gospel, and healing every
Lk 11:32 they repented at the *p* of Jonas
Acts 8:4 went every where *p* the word
Acts 8:12 *p* the things concerning the
Acts 10:36 Israel, *p* peace by Jesus Christ
Acts 11:19 *p* the word to none but unto the
Acts 11:20 the Grecians, *p* the Lord Jesus
Acts 15:35 *p* the word of the Lord, with many
Acts 20:9 and as Paul was long *p*, he sunk
Acts 20:25 I have gone *p* the kingdom of God
Acts 28:31 *P* the kingdom of God, and teaching
Rom 16:25 the *p* of Jesus Christ, according
1Cor 1:18 For the *p* of the cross is to them
1Cor 1:21 of *p* to save them that believe
1Cor 2:4 my *p* was not with enticing words
1Cor 15:14 be not risen, then is our *p* vain
2Cor 10:14 also in *p* the gospel of Christ
2Ti 4:17 that by me the *p* might be fully
Titus 1:3 manifested his word through *p*

### PRECEPT

Is 28:10 For *p* must be upon *p*,
Is 28:10 *p* upon *p*; line upon line
Is 28:13 LORD was unto them *p* upon *p*
Is 28:13 *p* upon *p*; line upon line
Is 29:13 me is taught by the *p* of men
Mk 10:5 of your heart he wrote you this *p*
Heb 9:19 *p* to all the people according to

### PRECEPTS

Neh 9:14 sabbath, and commandedst them *p*
Ps 119:4 us to keep thy *p* diligently
Ps 119:15 I will meditate in thy *p*, and have
Ps 119:27 me to understand the way of thy *p*
Ps 119:40 Behold, I have longed after thy *p*
Ps 119:45 for I seek thy *p*
Ps 119:56 This I had, because I kept thy *p*
Ps 119:63 thee, and of them that keep thy *p*
Ps 119:69 keep thy *p* with my whole heart
Ps 119:78 but I will meditate in thy *p*
Ps 119:87 but I forsook not thy *p*
Ps 119:93 I will never forget thy *p*
Ps 119:94 for I have sought thy *p*
Ps 119:100 ancients, because I keep thy *p*
Ps 119:104 Through thy *p* I get understanding
Ps 119:110 yet I erred not from thy *p*
Ps 119:128 Therefore I esteem all thy *p*
Ps 119:134 so will I keep thy *p*
Ps 119:141 yet do not I forget thy *p*
Ps 119:159 Consider how I love thy *p*
Ps 119:168 I have kept thy *p* and thy
Ps 119:173 for I have chosen thy *p*
Jer 35:18 your father, and kept all his *p*
Dan 9:5 even by departing from thy *p*

### PRECIOUS

Gen 24:53 brother and to her mother *p* things
Deut 33:13 for the *p* things of heaven, for
Deut 33:14 for the *p* fruits brought forth by
Deut 33:14 for the *p* things put forth by the
Deut 33:15 for the *p* things of the lasting
Deut 33:16 for the *p* things of the earth and
1Sa 3:1 of the LORD was *p* in those days
1Sa 26:21 because my soul was *p* in thine
2Sa 12:30 talent of gold with the *p* stones
1Kin 10:2 and very much gold, and *p* stones
1Kin 10:10 very great store, and *p* stones
1Kin 10:11 of almug trees, and *p* stones
2Kin 1:13 thy servants, be *p* in thy sight
2Kin 1:14 let my life now be *p* in thy sight
2Kin 20:13 all the house of his *p* things
2Kin 20:13 the *p* ointment, and all the house
1Chr 20:2 there were *p* stones in it
1Chr 29:2 and all manner of *p* stones
1Chr 29:8 they with whom *p* stones were
2Chr 3:6 house with *p* stones for beauty
2Chr 9:1 and gold in abundance, and *p* stones
2Chr 9:9 great abundance, and *p* stones
2Chr 9:10 brought algum trees and *p* stones
2Chr 20:25 *p* jewels, which they stripped off
2Chr 21:3 of *p* things, with fenced cities
2Chr 32:27 for *p* stones, and for spices, and
Ezr 1:6 with *p* things, beside all that
Ezr 8:27 vessels of fine copper, *p* as gold
Job 28:10 and his eye seeth every *p* thing
Job 28:16 gold of Ophir, with the *p* onyx
Ps 49:8 the redemption of their soul is *p*
Ps 72:14 *p* shall their blood be in his
Ps 116:15 *P* in the sight of the LORD is the
Ps 126:6 forth and weepeth, bearing *p* seed
Ps 133:2 It is like the *p* ointment upon
Ps 139:17 How *p* also are thy thoughts unto
Prov 1:13 We shall find all *p* substance
Prov 3:15 She is more *p* than rubies
Prov 6:26 will hunt for the *p* life
Prov 12:27 substance of a diligent man is *p*
Prov 17:8 A gift is as a *p* stone in the
Prov 20:15 lips of knowledge are a *p* jewel
Prov 24:4 the chambers be filled with all *p*
Eccl 7:1 name is better than *p* ointment
Is 13:12 make a man more *p* than fine gold
Is 28:16 stone, a *p* corner stone, a sure
Is 39:2 them the house of his *p* things
Is 39:2 the *p* ointment, and all the house
Is 43:4 Since thou wast *p* in my sight
Jer 15:19 take forth the *p* from the vile
Jer 20:5 all the *p* things thereof, and all
Lam 4:2 The *p* sons of Zion, comparable to
Eze 22:25 taken the treasure and *p* things
Eze 27:20 in *p* clothes for chariots
Eze 27:22 all spices, and with all *p* stones
Eze 28:13 every *p* stone was thy covering,
Dan 11:8 with their *p* vessels of silver and
Dan 11:38 with *p* stones, and pleasant things
Dan 11:43 over all the *p* things of Egypt
Mt 26:7 alabaster box of very *p* ointment
Mk 14:3 of ointment of spikenard very *p*
1Cor 3:12 *p* stones, wood, hay, stubble
Jas 5:7 for the *p* fruit of the earth
1Pet 1:7 being much more *p* than of gold
1Pet 1:19 But with the *p* blood of Christ,
1Pet 2:4 of men, but chosen of God, and *p*
1Pet 2:6 a chief corner stone, elect, *p*
1Pet 2:7 therefore which believe he is *p*
2Pet 1:1 like *p* faith with us through the
2Pet 1:4 us exceeding great and *p* promises
Rev 17:4 *p* stones and pearls, having a
Rev 18:12 *p* stones, and of pearls, and fine
Rev 18:12 all manner vessels of most *p* wood
Rev 18:16 with gold, and *p* stones, and pearls
Rev 21:11 was like unto a stone most *p*
Rev 21:19 with all manner of *p* stones

### PREDESTINATE

Rom 8:29 he also did *p* to be conformed to
Rom 8:30 Moreover whom he did *p*, them he

### PREDESTINATED

Eph 1:5 Having *p* us unto the adoption of
Eph 1:11 being *p* according to the purpose

### PREEMINENCE

Eccl 3:19 a man hath no *p* above a beast
Col 1:18 in all things he might have the *p*
3Jn 9 loveth to have the *p* among them

### PREFER

Ps 137:6 if I *p* not Jerusalem above my

### PREFERRED

Est 2:9 he *p* her and her maids unto the
Dan 6:3 Daniel was *p* above the presidents
Jn 1:15 cometh after me is *p* before me
Jn 1:27 coming after me is *p* before me
Jn 1:30 cometh a man which is *p* before me

### PREPARATION

1Chr 22:5 will therefore now make *p* for it
Nah 2:3 torches in the day of his *p*
Mt 27:62 that followed the day of the *p*
Mk 15:42 was come, because it was the *p*
Lk 23:54 And that day was the *p*, and the
Jn 19:14 it was the *p* of the passover, and
Jn 19:31 therefore, because it was the *p*
Jn 19:42 because of the Jews' *p* day
Eph 6:15 with the *p* of the gospel of peace

### PREPARE

Ex 15:2 I will *p* him an habitation
Ex 16:5 shall *p* that which they bring in
Num 15:5 thou *p* with the burnt offering or
Num 15:6 thou shalt *p* for a meat offering
Num 15:12 to the number that ye shall *p*
Num 23:1 *p* me here seven oxen and seven
Num 23:29 *p* me here seven bullocks and seven
Deut 19:3 Thou shalt *p* thee a way, and
Josh 1:11 people, saying, *P* you victuals
Josh 22:26 Let us now *p* to build us an altar
1Sa 7:3 *p* your hearts unto the LORD, and
1Sa 23:22 *p* yet, and know and see his place
1Kin 18:44 *P* thy chariot, and get thee down,
1Chr 9:32 shewbread, to *p* it every sabbath
1Chr 29:18 and *p* their heart unto thee
2Chr 2:9 Even to *p* me timber in abundance
2Chr 31:11 Then Hezekiah commanded to *p*
2Chr 35:4 *p* yourselves by the houses of
2Chr 35:6 *p* your brethren, that they may do
Est 5:8 banquet that I shall *p* for them
Job 8:8 *p* thyself to the search of their
Job 11:13 If thou *p* thine heart, and stretch
Job 27:16 dust, and *p* raiment as the clay
Job 27:17 He may *p* it, but the just shall
Ps 10:17 thou wilt *p* their heart, thou
Ps 59:4 *p* themselves without my fault
Ps 61:7 O *p* mercy and truth, which may
Ps 107:36 that they may *p* a city for
Prov 24:27 *P* thy work without, and make it
Prov 30:25 yet they *p* their meat in the
Is 14:21 *P* slaughter for his children for
Is 21:5 *P* the table, watch in the
Is 40:3 *P* ye the way of the LORD, make
Is 40:20 workman to *p* a graven image
Is 57:14 ye up, *p* the way, take up the
Is 62:10 *p* ye the way of the people
Is 65:11 that *p* a table for that troop, and
Jer 6:4 *P* ye war against her
Jer 12:3 *p* them for the day of slaughter
Jer 22:7 I will *p* destroyers against thee,
Jer 46:14 say ye, Stand fast, and *p* thee
Jer 51:12 up the watchmen, *p* the ambushes
Jer 51:27 *p* the nations against her, call
Jer 51:28 *P* against her the nations with
Eze 4:15 thou shalt *p* thy bread therewith
Eze 12:3 *p* thee stuff for removing, and
Eze 35:6 I will *p* thee unto blood, and
Eze 38:7 *p* for thyself, thou, and all thy
Eze 43:25 Seven days shalt thou *p* every day
Eze 43:25 they shall also *p* a young bullock
Eze 45:17 he shall *p* the sin offering, and
Eze 45:22 shall the prince *p* for himself
Eze 45:23 days of the feast he shall *p* a
Eze 45:24 he shall *p* a meat offering of an
Eze 46:2 the priests shall *p* his burnt
Eze 46:7 he shall *p* a meat offering, an
Eze 46:12 Now when the prince shall *p* a
Eze 46:12 he shall *p* his burnt offering and
Eze 46:13 Thou shalt daily *p* a burnt
Eze 46:13 thou shalt *p* it every morning
Eze 46:14 thou shalt *p* a meat offering for
Eze 46:15 Thus shall they *p* the lamb
Joel 3:9 *P* war, wake up the mighty men,
Amos 4:12 *p* to meet thy God, O Israel
Mic 3:5 they even *p* war against him
Mal 3:1 he shall *p* the way before me
Mt 3:3 *P* ye the way of the Lord, make
Mt 11:10 which shall *p* thy way before thee
Mt 26:17 Where wilt thou that we *p* for
Mk 1:2 which shall *p* thy way before thee
Mk 1:3 *P* ye the way of the Lord, make
Mk 14:12 *p* that thou mayest eat the
Lk 1:76 face of the Lord to *p* his ways
Lk 3:4 *P* ye the way of the Lord, make
Lk 7:27 which shall *p* thy way before thee
Lk 22:8 *p* us the passover, that we may
Lk 22:9 him, Where wilt thou that we *p*
Jn 14:2 I go to *p* a place for you
Jn 14:3 *p* a place for you, I will come
1Cor 14:8 who shall *p* himself to the battle
Philem 22 But withal *p* me also a lodging

### PREPARED

Gen 24:31 for I have *p* the house, and room
Gen 27:17 and the bread, which she had *p*
Ex 12:39 neither had they *p* for themselves
Ex 23:20 into the place which I have *p*
Num 21:27 the city of Sihon be built and *p*
Num 23:4 I have *p* seven altars, and I have
Josh 4:4 whom he had *p* of the children of
Josh 4:13 About forty thousand *p* for war
2Sa 15:1 this, that Absalom *p* him chariots
1Kin 1:5 he *p* him chariots and horsemen, and
1Kin 5:18 so they *p* timber and stones to
1Kin 6:19 the oracle he *p* in the house
2Kin 6:23 he *p* great provision for them
1Chr 12:39 for their brethren had *p* for them
1Chr 15:1 *p* a place for the ark of God, and
1Chr 15:3 his place, which he had *p* for it
1Chr 15:12 the place that I have *p* for it
1Chr 22:3 David *p* iron in abundance for the
1Chr 22:5 So David *p* abundantly before his
1Chr 22:14 in my trouble I have *p* for the
1Chr 22:14 timber also and stone have I *p*
1Chr 29:2 Now I have *p* with all my might
1Chr 29:3 that I have *p* for the holy house
1Chr 29:16 have *p* to build thee an house for
2Chr 1:4 place which David had *p* for it

2Chr 3:1 in the place that David had *p* in
2Chr 8:16 *p* unto the day of the foundation
2Chr 12:14 because he *p* not his heart to
2Chr 16:14 divers kinds of spices *p* by the
2Chr 17:18 thousand ready *p* for the war
2Chr 19:3 hast *p* thine heart to seek God
2Chr 20:33 *p* their hearts unto the God of
2Chr 26:14 Uzziah *p* for them throughout all
2Chr 27:6 because he *p* his ways before the
2Chr 29:19 in his transgression, have we *p*
2Chr 29:36 people, that God had *p* the people
2Chr 31:11 and they *p* them,
2Chr 35:10 So the service was *p*, and the
2Chr 35:14 the Levites *p* for themselves
2Chr 35:15 brethren the Levites *p* for them
2Chr 35:16 of the LORD was *p* the same day
2Chr 35:20 when Josiah had *p* the temple
Ezr 7:10 For Ezra had *p* his heart to seek
Neh 5:18 Now that which was *p* for me daily
Neh 5:18 also fowls were *p* for me, and once
Neh 8:10 unto them for whom nothing is *p*
Neh 13:5 he had *p* for him a great chamber,
Est 5:4 the banquet that I have *p* for him
Est 5:5 to the banquet that Esther had *p*
Est 5:12 banquet that she had *p* but myself
Est 6:4 the gallows that he had *p* for him
Est 6:14 the banquet that Esther had *p*
Est 7:10 that he had *p* for Mordecai
Job 28:27 he *p* it, yea, and searched it out
Job 29:7 when I *p* my seat in the street
Ps 7:13 He hath also *p* for him the
Ps 9:7 he hath *p* his throne for judgment
Ps 57:6 They have *p* a net for my steps
Ps 68:10 hast *p* of thy goodness for the
Ps 74:16 thou hast *p* the light and the sun
Ps 103:19 The LORD hath *p* his throne in the
Prov 8:27 When he *p* the heavens, I was
Prov 19:29 Judgments are *p* for scorners
Prov 21:31 The horse is *p* against the day of
Is 30:33 yea, for the king it is *p*
Is 64:4 what he hath *p* for him that
Eze 23:41 a table *p* before it, whereupon
Eze 28:13 of thy pipes was *p* in thee in the
Eze 38:7 Be thou *p*, and prepare for thyself
Dan 2:9 for ye have *p* lying and corrupt
Hos 2:8 and gold, which they *p* for Baal
Hos 6:3 going forth is *p* as the morning
Jonah 1:17 Now the LORD had *p* a great fish
Jonah 4:6 And the LORD God *p* a gourd
Jonah 4:7 But God *p* a worm when the morning
Jonah 4:8 that God *p* a vehement east wind
Nah 2:5 and the defence shall be *p*
Zeph 1:7 for the LORD hath *p* a sacrifice
Mt 20:23 for whom it is *p* of my Father
Mt 22:4 Behold, I have *p* my dinner
Mt 25:34 inherit the kingdom *p* for you
Mt 25:41 *p* for the devil and his angels
Mk 10:40 be given to them for whom it is *p*
Mk 14:15 a large upper room furnished and *p*
Lk 1:17 ready a people *p* for the Lord
Lk 2:31 Which thou hast *p* before the face
Lk 12:47 *p* not himself, neither did
Lk 23:56 and *p* spices and ointments
Lk 24:1 the spices which they had *p*
Rom 9:23 which he had afore *p* unto glory
1Cor 2:9 God hath *p* for them that love him
2Ti 2:21 use, and *p* unto every good work
Heb 10:5 not, but a body hast thou *p* me
Heb 11:7 *p* an ark to the saving of his
Heb 11:16 for he hath *p* for them a city
Rev 8:6 trumpets *p* themselves to sound
Rev 9:7 like unto horses *p* unto battle
Rev 9:15 which were *p* for an hour, and a
Rev 12:6 where she hath a place *p* of God
Rev 16:12 the kings of the east might be *p*
Rev 21:2 *p* as a bride adorned for her

**PRESENCE**

Gen 3:8 the *p* of the LORD God amongst the
Gen 4:16 went out from the *p* of the LORD
Gen 16:12 in the *p* of all his brethren
Gen 23:11 in the *p* of the sons of my people
Gen 23:18 in the *p* of the children of Heth
Gen 25:18 he died in the *p* of all his
Gen 27:30 from the *p* of Isaac his father
Gen 41:46 went out from the *p* of Pharaoh
Gen 45:3 for they were troubled at his *p*
Gen 47:15 for why should we die in thy *p*
Ex 10:11 were driven out from Pharaoh's *p*
Ex 33:14 My *p* shall go with thee, and I
Ex 33:15 If thy *p* go not with me, carry us
Ex 35:20 departed from the *p* of Moses
Lev 22:3 soul shall be cut off from my *p*
Num 20:6 Aaron went from the *p* of the
Deut 25:9 unto him in the *p* of the elders
Josh 4:11 priests, in the *p* of the people
Josh 8:32 which he wrote in the *p* of the
1Sa 18:11 David avoided out of his *p* twice
1Sa 19:7 David to Saul, and he was in his *p*
1Sa 19:10 he slipped away out of Saul's *p*
1Sa 21:15 to play the mad man in my *p*
2Sa 16:19 I not serve in the *p* of his son
2Sa 16:19 I have served in thy father's *p*
2Sa 16:19 so will I be in thy *p*
2Sa 24:4 went out from the *p* of the king
1Kin 1:28 And she came into the king's *p*
1Kin 8:22 the *p* of all the congregation of
1Kin 12:2 fled from the *p* of king Solomon
1Kin 21:13 in the *p* of the people, saying,
2Kin 3:14 the *p* of Jehoshaphat the king of
2Kin 5:27 he went out from his *p* a leper as
2Kin 13:23 cast he them from his *p* as yet
2Kin 24:20 he had cast them out from his *p*
2Kin 25:19 of them that were in the king's *p*
1Chr 16:27 Glory and honour are in his *p*
1Chr 16:33 sing out at the *p* of the LORD
1Chr 24:31 Aaron in the *p* of David the king
2Chr 6:12 the *p* of all the congregation of
2Chr 9:23 the earth sought the *p* of Solomon
2Chr 10:2 from the *p* of Solomon the king
2Chr 20:9 before this house, and in thy *p*
2Chr 34:4 the altars of Baalim in his *p*
Neh 2:1 not been beforetime sad in his *p*
Est 1:10 in the *p* of Ahasuerus the king
Est 8:15 Mordecai went out from the *p* of
Job 1:12 went forth from the *p* of the LORD
Job 2:7 forth from the *p* of the LORD
Job 23:15 Therefore am I troubled at his *p*
Ps 9:3 shall fall and perish at thy *p*
Ps 16:11 in thy *p* is fulness of joy
Ps 17:2 my sentence come forth from thy *p*
Ps 23:5 me in the *p* of mine enemies
Ps 31:20 of thy *p* from the pride of man
Ps 51:11 Cast me not away from thy *p*
Ps 68:2 the wicked perish at the *p* of God
Ps 68:8 also dropped at the *p* of God
Ps 68:8 itself was moved at the *p* of God
Ps 95:2 before his *p* with thanksgiving
Ps 97:5 like wax at the *p* of the LORD
Ps 97:5 at the *p* of the LORD of the whole
Ps 100:2 come before his *p* with singing
Ps 114:7 at the *p* of the Lord
Ps 114:7 at the *p* of the God of Jacob
Ps 116:14 now in the *p* of all his people
Ps 116:18 now in the *p* of all his people
Ps 139:7 whither shall I flee from thy *p*
Ps 140:13 the upright shall dwell in thy *p*
Prov 14:7 Go from the *p* of a foolish man,
Prov 17:18 surety in the *p* of his friend
Prov 25:6 thyself in the *p* of the king
Prov 25:7 *p* of the prince whom thine eyes
Is 1:7 strangers devour it in your *p*
Is 19:1 of Egypt shall be moved at his *p*
Is 63:9 and the angel of his *p* saved them
Is 64:1 might flow down at thy *p*,
Is 64:2 the nations may tremble at thy *p*
Is 64:3 mountains flowed down at thy *p*
Jer 4:26 broken down at the *p* of the LORD
Jer 5:22 will ye not tremble at my *p*
Jer 23:39 fathers, and cast you out of my *p*
Jer 28:1 in the *p* of the priests and of all
Jer 28:5 Hananiah in the *p* of the priests
Jer 28:5 in the *p* of all the people that
Jer 28:11 spake in the *p* of all the people
Jer 32:12 in the *p* of the witnesses that
Jer 52:3 he had cast them out from his *p*
Eze 38:20 of the earth, shall shake at my *p*
Dan 2:27 answered in the *p* of the king
Jonah 1:3 Tarshish from the *p* of the LORD
Jonah 1:3 Tarshish from the *p* of the LORD
Jonah 1:10 he fled from the *p* of the LORD
Nah 1:5 and the earth is burned at his *p*
Zeph 1:7 peace at the *p* of the Lord GOD
Lk 1:19 that stand in the *p* of God
Lk 13:26 We have eaten and drunk in thy *p*
Lk 14:10 *p* of them that sit at meat with
Lk 15:10 there is joy in the *p* of the
Jn 20:30 Jesus in the *p* of his disciples
Acts 3:13 and denied him in the *p* of Pilate
Acts 3:16 soundness in the *p* of you all
Acts 3:19 shall come from the *p* of the Lord
Acts 5:41 from the *p* of the council
Acts 27:35 thanks to God in *p* of them all
1Cor 1:29 no flesh should glory in his *p*
2Cor 10:1 who in *p* am base among you, but
2Cor 10:10 but his bodily *p* is weak, and his
Phil 2:12 obeyed, not as in my *p* only
1Th 2:17 from you for a short time in *p*
1Th 2:19 Are not even ye in the *p* of our
2Th 1:9 from the *p* of the Lord, and from
Heb 9:24 to appear in the *p* of God for us
Jude 24 you faultless before the *p* of his
Rev 14:10 brimstone in the *p* of the holy
Rev 14:10 angels, and in the *p* of the Lamb

**PRESENT**

Gen 32:13 his hand a *p* for Esau his brother
Gen 32:18 it is a *p* sent unto my lord Esau
Gen 32:20 with the *p* that goeth before me
Gen 32:21 So went the *p* over before him
Gen 33:10 then receive my *p* at my hand
Gen 43:11 and carry down the man a *p*
Gen 43:15 And the men took that *p*, and they
Gen 43:25 they made ready the *p* against
Gen 43:26 they brought him the *p* which was
Ex 34:2 *p* thyself there to me in the top
Lev 14:11 *p* the man that is to be made
Lev 16:7 *p* them before the LORD at the
Lev 27:8 then he shall *p* himself before
Lev 27:11 then he shall *p* the beast before
Num 3:6 *p* them before Aaron the priest,
Deut 31:14 *p* yourselves in the tabernacle of
Judg 3:15 a *p* unto Eglon the king of Moab
Judg 3:17 he brought the *p* unto Eglon king
Judg 3:18 he had made an end to offer the *p*
Judg 3:18 away the people that bare the *p*
Judg 6:18 unto thee, and bring forth my *p*
1Sa 9:7 there is not a *p* to bring to the
1Sa 10:19 Now therefore *p* yourselves before
1Sa 13:15 the people that were *p* with him
1Sa 13:16 the people that were *p* with them
1Sa 21:3 in mine hand, or what there is *p*
1Sa 30:26 Behold a *p* for you of the spoil
2Sa 20:4 three days, and be thou here *p*
1Kin 9:16 given it for a *p* unto his
1Kin 10:25 And they brought every man his *p*
1Kin 15:19 have sent unto thee a *p* of silver
1Kin 20:27 were numbered, and were all *p*
2Kin 8:8 Take a *p* in thine hand, and go,
2Kin 8:9 took a *p* with him, even of every
2Kin 16:8 sent it for a *p* to the king of
2Kin 17:4 brought no *p* to the king of
2Kin 18:31 Make an agreement with me by a *p*
2Kin 20:12 sent letters and a *p* unto Hezekiah
1Chr 29:17 joy thy people, which are *p* here
2Chr 5:11 that were *p* were sanctified
2Chr 9:24 And they brought every man his *p*
2Chr 29:29 all that were *p* with him bowed
2Chr 30:21 children of Israel that were *p* at
2Chr 31:1 all Israel that were *p* went out
2Chr 34:32 all that were *p* in Jerusalem
2Chr 34:33 that were *p* in Israel to serve
2Chr 35:7 offerings, for all that were *p*
2Chr 35:17 children of Israel that were *p*
2Chr 35:18 all Judah and Israel that were *p*
Ezr 8:25 his lords, and all Israel there *p*
Est 1:5 that were *p* in Shushan the palace
Est 4:16 the Jews that are *p* in Shushan
Job 1:6 to *p* themselves before the LORD
Job 2:1 to *p* themselves before the LORD
Job 2:1 them to *p* himself before the LORD
Ps 46:1 a very *p* help in trouble
Is 18:7 In that time shall the *p* be
Is 36:16 Make an agreement with me by a *p*
Is 39:1 sent letters and a *p* to Hezekiah
Jer 36:7 It may be they will *p* their
Jer 42:9 unto whom ye sent me to *p* your
Eze 27:15 thee for a *p* horns of ivory
Dan 9:18 for we do not *p* our supplications
Hos 10:6 Assyria for a *p* to king Jareb
Lk 2:22 Jerusalem, to *p* him to the Lord
Lk 5:17 of the Lord was *p* to heal them
Lk 13:1 There were *p* at that season some
Lk 18:30 manifold more in this *p* time
Jn 14:25 unto you, being yet *p* with you
Acts 10:33 are we all here *p* before God
Acts 21:18 and all the elders were *p*
Acts 25:24 all men which are here *p* with us
Acts 28:2 every one, because of the *p* rain
Rom 7:18 for to will is *p* with me

Rom 7:21 would do good, evil is *p* with me
Rom 8:18 this *p* time are not worthy to be
Rom 8:38 nor powers, nor things *p*
Rom 11:5 Even so then at this *p* time also
Rom 12:1 that ye *p* your bodies a living
1Cor 3:22 or life, or death, or things *p*
1Cor 4:11 Even unto this *p* hour we both
1Cor 5:3 but *p* in spirit, have judged
1Cor 5:3 already, as though I were *p*
1Cor 7:26 this is good for the *p* distress
1Cor 15:6 greater part remain unto this *p*
2Cor 4:14 by Jesus, and shall *p* us with you
2Cor 5:8 body, and to be *p* with the Lord
2Cor 5:9 whether *p* or absent, we may be
2Cor 10:2 when I am *p* with that confidence
2Cor 10:11 we be also in deed when we are *p*
2Cor 11:2 that I may *p* you as a chaste
2Cor 11:9 And when I was *p* with you, and
2Cor 13:2 and foretell you, as if I were *p*
2Cor 13:10 lest being *p* I should use
Gal 1:4 deliver us from this *p* evil world
Gal 4:18 and not only when I am *p* with you
Gal 4:20 I desire to be *p* with you now
Eph 5:27 That he might *p* it to himself a
Col 1:22 to *p* you holy and unblameable and
Col 1:28 that we may *p* every man perfect
2Ti 4:10 me, having loved this *p* world
Titus 2:12 and godly, in this *p* world
Heb 9:9 was a figure for the time then *p*
Heb 12:11 for the *p* seemeth to be joyous
2Pet 1:12 and be established in the *p* truth
Jude 24 to *p* you faultless before the

## PRESENTED

Gen 46:29 to Goshen, and *p* himself unto him
Gen 47:2 five men, and *p* them unto Pharaoh
Lev 2:8 when it is *p* unto the priest, he
Lev 7:35 in the day when he *p* them to
Lev 9:12 Aaron's sons *p* unto him the blood
Lev 9:13 they *p* the burnt offering unto
Lev 9:18 Aaron's sons *p* unto him the blood
Lev 16:10 shall be *p* alive before the LORD,
Deut 31:14 *p* themselves in the tabernacle of
Josh 24:1 they *p* themselves before God
Judg 6:19 unto him under the oak, and *p* it
Judg 20:2 *p* themselves in the assembly of
1Sa 17:16 evening, and *p* himself forty days
Jer 38:26 I *p* my supplication before the
Eze 20:28 there they *p* the provocation of
Mt 2:11 treasures, they *p* unto him gifts
Acts 9:41 the saints and widows, *p* her alive
Acts 23:33 governor, *p* Paul also before him

## PRESENTLY

1Sa 2:16 them not fail to burn the fat *p*
Prov 12:16 A fool's wrath is *p* known
Mt 21:19 *p* the fig tree withered away
Mt 26:53 he shall *p* give me more than
Phil 2:23 Him therefore I hope to send *p*

## PRESENTS

1Sa 10:27 despised him, and brought him no *p*
1Kin 4:21 they brought *p*, and served Solomon
2Kin 17:3 became his servant, and gave him *p*
2Chr 17:5 Judah brought to Jehoshaphat *p*
2Chr 17:11 Philistines brought Jehoshaphat *p*
2Chr 32:23 *p* to Hezekiah king of Judah
Ps 68:29 shall kings bring *p* unto thee
Ps 72:10 and of the isles shall bring *p*
Ps 76:11 bring *p* unto him that ought to be
Mic 1:14 thou give *p* to Moresheth-gath

## PRESERVE

Gen 19:32 that we may *p* seed of our father
Gen 19:34 that we may *p* seed of our father
Gen 45:5 did send me before you to *p* life
Gen 45:7 God sent me before you to *p* you a
Deut 6:24 always, that he might *p* us alive
Ps 12:7 thou shalt *p* them from this
Ps 16:1 *P* me, O God
Ps 25:21 Let integrity and uprightness *p* me
Ps 32:7 thou shalt *p* me from trouble
Ps 40:11 and thy truth continually *p* me
Ps 41:2 The LORD will *p* him, and keep him
Ps 61:7 mercy and truth, which may *p* him
Ps 64:1 *p* my life from fear of the enemy
Ps 79:11 *p* thou those that are appointed
Ps 86:2 *P* my soul
Ps 121:7 The LORD shall *p* thee from all
Ps 121:7 he shall *p* thy soul
Ps 121:8 The LORD shall *p* thy going out
Ps 140:1 *p* me from the violent man
Ps 140:4 *p* me from the violent man
Prov 2:11 Discretion shall *p* thee,
Prov 4:6 her not, and she shall *p* thee
Prov 14:3 the lips of the wise shall *p* them
Prov 20:28 Mercy and truth *p* the king
Prov 22:12 The eyes of the LORD *p* knowledge
Is 31:5 and passing over he will *p* it
Is 49:8 and I will *p* thee, and give thee
Jer 49:11 children, I will *p* them alive
Lk 17:33 shall lose his life shall *p* it
2Ti 4:18 will *p* me unto his heavenly

## PRESERVED

Gen 32:30 God face to face, and my life is *p*
Josh 24:17 *p* us in all the way wherein we
1Sa 30:23 LORD hath given us, who hath *p* us
2Sa 8:6 the LORD *p* David whithersoever he
2Sa 8:14 the LORD *p* David whithersoever he
1Chr 18:6 Thus the LORD *p* David
1Chr 18:13 Thus the LORD *p* David
Job 10:12 thy visitation hath *p* my spirit
Job 29:2 as in the days when God *p* me
Ps 37:28 they are *p* for ever
Is 49:6 and to restore the *p* of Israel
Hos 12:13 Egypt, and by a prophet was he *p*
Mt 9:17 into new bottles, and both are *p*
Lk 5:38 and both are *p*
1Th 5:23 body be *p* blameless unto the
Jude 1 *p* in Jesus Christ, and called

## PRESERVETH

Job 36:6 He *p* not the life of the wicked
Ps 31:23 for the LORD *p* the faithful
Ps 97:10 he *p* the souls of his saints
Ps 116:6 The LORD *p* the simple
Ps 145:20 The LORD *p* all them that love him
Ps 146:9 The LORD *p* the strangers
Prov 2:8 and *p* the way of his saints
Prov 16:17 that keepeth his way *p* his soul

## PRESIDENTS

Dan 6:2 And over these three *p*
Dan 6:3 Daniel was preferred above the *p*
Dan 6:4 Then the *p* and princes sought to
Dan 6:6 Then these *p* and princes assembled
Dan 6:7 All the *p* of the kingdom, the

## PRESS

Joel 3:13 for the *p* is full, the fats
Hag 2:16 out fifty vessels out of the *p*
Mk 2:4 not come nigh unto him for the *p*
Mk 5:27 of Jesus, came in the *p* behind
Mk 5:30 of him, turned him about in the *p*
Lk 8:19 could not come at him for the *p*
Lk 8:45 *p* thee, and sayest thou, Who
Lk 19:3 and could not for the *p*, because
Phil 3:14 I *p* toward the mark for the prize

## PRESSED

Gen 19:3 And he *p* upon them greatly
Gen 19:9 they *p* sore upon the man, even
Gen 40:11 *p* them into Pharaoh's cup, and I
Judg 16:16 when she *p* him daily with her
2Sa 13:25 And he *p* him
2Sa 13:27 But Absalom *p* him, that he let
Est 8:14 *p* on by the king's commandment
Eze 23:3 there were their breasts *p*
Amos 2:13 I am *p* under you, as a cart is
Amos 2:13 as a cart is *p* that is full of
Mk 3:10 insomuch that they *p* upon him for
Lk 5:1 as the people *p* upon him to hear
Lk 6:38 *p* down, and shaken together, and
Acts 18:5 Paul was *p* in the spirit, and
2Cor 1:8 that we were *p* out of measure,

## PRESUMPTUOUSLY

Ex 21:14 But if a man come *p* upon his
Num 15:30 But the soul that doeth ought *p*
Deut 1:43 LORD, and went *p* up into the hill
Deut 17:12 And the man that will do *p*
Deut 17:13 hear, and fear, and do no more *p*
Deut 18:22 but the prophet hath spoken it *p*

## PREVAIL

Gen 7:20 cubits upward did the waters *p*
Num 22:6 peradventure I shall *p*, that we
Judg 16:5 what means we may *p* against him
1Sa 2:9 for by strength shall no man *p*
1Sa 17:9 but if I *p* against him, and kill
1Sa 26:25 things, and also shalt still *p*
1Kin 22:22 shalt persuade him, and *p* also
2Chr 14:11 let not man *p* against thee
2Chr 18:21 entice him, and thou shalt also *p*
Est 6:13 thou shalt not *p* against him
Job 15:24 they shall *p* against him, as a
Job 18:9 and the robber shall *p* against him
Ps 9:19 let not man *p*
Ps 12:4 said, With our tongue will we *p*
Ps 65:3 Iniquities *p* against me
Eccl 4:12 if one *p* against him, two shall
Is 7:1 it, but could not *p* against it
Is 16:12 but he shall not *p*
Is 42:13 he shall *p* against his enemies
Is 47:12 to profit, if so be thou mayest *p*
Jer 1:19 but they shall not *p* against thee
Jer 5:22 themselves, yet can they not *p*
Jer 15:20 but they shall not *p* against thee
Jer 20:10 we shall *p* against him, and we
Jer 20:11 stumble, and they shall not *p*
Dan 11:7 deal against them, and shall *p*
Mt 16:18 of hell shall not *p* against it
Mt 27:24 saw that he could *p* nothing
Jn 12:19 Perceive ye how ye *p* nothing

## PREVAILED

Gen 7:18 And the waters *p*, and were
Gen 7:19 the waters *p* exceedingly upon the
Gen 7:24 the waters *p* upon the earth an
Gen 30:8 with my sister, and I have *p*
Gen 32:25 he saw that he *p* not against him
Gen 32:28 with God and with men, and hast *p*
Gen 47:20 because the famine *p* over them
Gen 49:26 have *p* above the blessings of my
Ex 17:11 held up his hand, that Israel *p*
Ex 17:11 he let down his hand, Amalek *p*
Judg 1:35 the hand of the house of Joseph *p*
Judg 3:10 and his hand *p* against
Judg 4:24 *p* against Jabin the king of
Judg 6:2 hand of Midian *p* against Israel
1Sa 17:50 So David *p* over the Philistine
2Sa 11:23 Surely the men *p* against us
2Sa 24:4 the king's word *p* against Joab
1Kin 16:22 Omri *p* against the people that
2Kin 25:3 month the famine *p* in the city
1Chr 5:2 For Judah *p* above his brethren,
1Chr 21:4 the king's word *p* against Joab
2Chr 8:3 to Hamath-zobah, and *p* against it
2Chr 13:18 time, and the children of Judah *p*
2Chr 27:5 the Ammonites, and *p* against them
Ps 13:4 enemy say, I have *p* against him
Ps 129:2 yet they have not *p* against me
Jer 20:7 art stronger than I, and hast *p*
Jer 38:22 thee on, and have *p* against thee
Lam 1:16 are desolate, because the enemy *p*
Dan 7:21 the saints, and *p* against them
Hos 12:4 he had power over the angel, and *p*
Obad 7 deceived thee, and *p* against thee
Lk 23:23 of them and of the chief priests *p*
Acts 19:16 *p* against them, so that they fled
Acts 19:20 grew the word of God and *p*
Rev 5:5 hath *p* to open the book, and to
Rev 12:8 And *p* not

## PREVENT

Job 3:12 Why did the knees *p* me
Ps 59:10 The God of my mercy shall *p* me
Ps 79:8 thy tender mercies speedily *p* us
Ps 88:13 morning shall my prayer *p* thee
Ps 119:148 Mine eyes *p* the night watches,
Amos 9:10 evil shall not overtake nor *p* us
1Th 4:15 shall not *p* them which are asleep

## PREVENTED

2Sa 22:6 the snares of death *p* me
2Sa 22:19 They *p* me in the day of my
Job 30:27 the days of affliction *p* me
Job 41:11 Who hath *p* me, that I should
Ps 18:5 the snares of death *p* me
Ps 18:18 They *p* me in the day of my
Ps 119:147 I *p* the dawning of the morning,
Is 21:14 they *p* with their bread him that
Mt 17:25 come into the house, Jesus *p* him

## PREY

Gen 49:9 from the *p*, my son, thou art gone
Gen 49:27 the morning he shall devour the *p*
Num 14:3 and our children should be a *p*
Num 14:31 ones, which ye said should be a *p*
Num 23:24 lie down until he eat of the *p*
Num 31:11 took all the spoil, and all the *p*
Num 31:12 brought the captives, and the *p*
Num 31:26 the sum of the *p* that was taken
Num 31:27 divide the *p* into two parts
Num 31:32 being the rest of the *p* which the
Deut 1:39 ones, which ye said should be a *p*
Deut 2:35 we took for a *p* unto ourselves

Deut 3:7 we took for a *p* to ourselves
Josh 8:2 ye take for a *p* unto yourselves
Josh 8:27 took for a *p* unto themselves
Josh 11:14 took for a *p* unto themselves
Judg 5:30 have they not divided the *p*
Judg 5:30 to Sisera a *p* of divers colours,
Judg 5:30 a *p* of divers colours of
Judg 8:24 every man the earrings of his *p*
Judg 8:25 every man the earrings of his *p*
2Kin 21:14 and they shall become a *p* and a
Neh 4:4 give them for a *p* in the land of
Est 3:13 to take the spoil of them for a *p*
Est 8:11 to take the spoil of them for a *p*
Est 9:15 but on the *p* they laid not their
Est 9:16 laid not their hands on the *p*
Job 4:11 old lion perisheth for lack of *p*
Job 9:26 the eagle that hasteth to the *p*
Job 24:5 rising betimes for a *p*
Job 38:39 Wilt thou hunt the *p* for the lion
Job 39:29 From thence she seeketh the *p*
Ps 17:12 as a lion that is greedy of his *p*
Ps 76:4 excellent than the mountains of *p*
Ps 104:21 young lions roar after their *p*
Ps 124:6 given us as a *p* to their teeth
Prov 23:28 She also lieth in wait as for a *p*
Is 5:29 shall roar, and lay hold of the *p*
Is 10:2 that widows may be their *p*
Is 10:6 take the spoil, and to take the *p*
Is 31:4 the young lion roaring on his *p*
Is 33:23 then is the *p* of a great spoil
Is 33:23 the lame take the *p*
Is 42:22 they are for a *p*, and none
Is 49:24 Shall the *p* be taken from the
Is 49:25 the *p* of the terrible shall be
Is 59:15 from evil maketh himself a *p*
Jer 21:9 life shall be unto him for a *p*
Jer 30:16 all that *p* upon thee will I give
Jer 30:16 upon thee will I give for a *p*
Jer 38:2 he shall have his life for a *p*
Jer 39:18 life shall be for a *p* unto thee
Jer 45:5 a *p* in all places whither thou
Eze 7:21 hands of the strangers for a *p*
Eze 19:3 and it learned to catch the *p*
Eze 19:6 lion, and learned to catch the *p*
Eze 22:25 a roaring lion ravening the *p*
Eze 22:27 are like wolves ravening the *p*
Eze 26:12 make a *p* of thy merchandise
Eze 29:19 and take her spoil, and take her *p*
Eze 34:8 because my flock became a *p*
Eze 34:22 and they shall no more be a *p*
Eze 34:28 no more be a *p* to the heathen
Eze 36:4 are forsaken, which became a *p*
Eze 36:5 minds, to cast it out for a *p*
Eze 38:12 To take a spoil, and to take a *p*
Eze 38:13 gathered thy company to take a *p*
Dan 11:24 he shall scatter among them the *p*
Amos 3:4 in the forest, when he hath no *p*
Nah 2:12 and filled his holes with *p*
Nah 2:13 will cut off thy *p* from the earth
Nah 3:1 the *p* departeth not
Zeph 3:8 the day that I rise up to the *p*

### PRICE

Lev 25:16 thou shalt increase the *p* thereof
Lev 25:16 thou shalt diminish the *p* of it
Lev 25:50 the *p* of his sale shall be
Lev 25:51 *p* of his redemption out of the
Lev 25:52 him again the *p* of his redemption
Deut 23:18 or the *p* of a dog, into the house
2Sa 24:24 will surely buy it of thee at a *p*
1Kin 10:28 received the linen yarn at a *p*
1Chr 21:22 shalt grant it me for the full *p*
1Chr 21:24 will verily buy it for the full *p*
2Chr 1:16 received the linen yarn at a *p*
Job 28:13 Man knoweth not the *p* thereof
Job 28:15 be weighed for the *p* thereof
Job 28:18 for the *p* of wisdom is above
Ps 44:12 increase thy wealth by their *p*
Prov 17:16 Wherefore is there a *p* in the
Prov 27:26 the goats are the *p* of the field
Prov 31:10 for her *p* is far above rubies
Is 45:13 not for *p* nor reward, saith the
Is 55:1 milk without money and without *p*
Jer 15:13 I give to the spoil without *p*
Zec 11:12 If ye think good, give me my *p*
Zec 11:12 So they weighed for my *p* thirty
Zec 11:13 a goodly *p* that I was prised at
Mt 13:46 he had found one pearl of great *p*
Mt 27:6 because it is the *p* of blood
Mt 27:9 the *p* of him that was valued,
Acts 5:2 And kept back part of the *p*
Acts 5:3 back part of the *p* of the land
Acts 19:19 and they counted the *p* of them
1Cor 6:20 For ye are bought with a *p*
1Cor 7:23 Ye are bought with a *p*
1Pet 3:4 is in the sight of God of great *p*

### PRIDE

Lev 26:19 I will break the *p* of your power
1Sa 17:28 I know thy *p*, and the naughtiness
2Chr 32:26 himself for the *p* of his heart
Job 33:17 his purpose, and hide *p* from man
Job 35:12 because of the *p* of evil men
Job 41:15 His scales are his *p*, shut up
Job 41:34 a king over all the children of *p*
Ps 10:2 The wicked in his *p* doth
Ps 10:4 through the *p* of his countenance,
Ps 31:20 of thy presence from the *p* of man
Ps 36:11 not the foot of *p* come against me
Ps 59:12 let them even be taken in their *p*
Ps 73:6 Therefore *p* compasseth them about
Prov 8:13 *p*, and arrogancy, and the evil way,
Prov 11:2 When *p* cometh, then cometh shame
Prov 13:10 Only by *p* cometh contention
Prov 14:3 of the foolish is a rod of *p*
Prov 16:18 *P* goeth before destruction, and an
Prov 29:23 A man's *p* shall bring him low
Is 9:9 of Samaria, that say in the *p*
Is 16:6 We have heard of the *p* of Moab
Is 16:6 even of his haughtiness, and his *p*
Is 23:9 it, to stain the *p* of all glory
Is 25:11 he shall bring down their *p*
Is 28:1 Woe to the crown of *p*, to the
Is 28:3 The crown of *p*, the drunkards of
Jer 13:9 manner will I mar the *p* of Judah
Jer 13:9 and the great *p* of Jerusalem
Jer 13:17 weep in secret places for your *p*
Jer 48:29 We have heard the *p* of Moab
Jer 48:29 and his arrogancy, and his *p*
Jer 49:16 the *p* of thine heart, O thou that
Eze 7:10 rod hath blossomed, *p* hath budded
Eze 16:49 iniquity of thy sister Sodom, *p*
Eze 16:56 by thy mouth in the day of thy *p*
Eze 30:6 the *p* of her power shall come
Dan 4:37 those that walk in *p* he is able
Dan 5:20 up, and his mind hardened in *p*
Hos 5:5 the *p* of Israel doth testify to
Hos 7:10 the *p* of Israel testifieth to his
Obad 3 The *p* of thine heart hath
Zeph 2:10 This shall they have for their *p*
Zeph 3:11 thee them that rejoice in thy *p*
Zec 9:6 cut off the *p* of the Philistines
Zec 10:11 the *p* of Assyria shall be brought
Zec 11:3 for the *p* of Jordan is spoiled
Mk 7:22 an evil eye, blasphemy, *p*
1Ti 3:6 lest being lifted up with *p* he
1Jn 2:16 the *p* of life, is not of the

### PRIESTHOOD

Ex 40:15 *p* throughout their generations
Num 16:10 and seek ye the *p* also
Num 18:1 shall bear the iniquity of your *p*
Num 25:13 the covenant of an everlasting *p*
Josh 18:7 for the *p* of the LORD is their
Ezr 2:62 they, as polluted, put from the *p*
Neh 7:64 they, as polluted, put from the *p*
Neh 13:29 because they have defiled the *p*
Neh 13:29 and the covenant of the *p*
Heb 7:5 who receive the office of the *p*
Heb 7:11 were by the Levitical *p*, (for
Heb 7:12 For the *p* being changed, there is
Heb 7:14 Moses spake nothing concerning *p*
Heb 7:24 ever, hath an unchangeable *p*
1Pet 2:5 up a spiritual house, an holy *p*
1Pet 2:9 a chosen generation, a royal *p*

### PRIESTS'

Josh 4:3 place where the *p* feet stood firm
Josh 4:18 the soles of the *p* feet were
1Sa 2:36 thee, into one of the *p* offices
2Kin 12:16 it was the *p*
Ezr 2:69 silver, and one hundred *p* garments
Neh 7:70 five hundred and thirty *p* garments
Neh 7:72 and threescore and seven *p* garments
Neh 12:35 certain of the *p* sons with

### PRINCE

Gen 23:6 thou art a mighty *p* among us
Gen 32:28 for as a *p* hast thou power with
Gen 34:2 *p* of the country, saw her, he
Ex 2:14 And he said, Who made thee a *p*
Num 7:11 each *p* on his day, for the
Num 7:18 of Zuar, *p* of Issachar, did offer
Num 7:24 *p* of the children of Zebulun, did
Num 7:30 *p* of the children of Reuben, did
Num 7:36 *p* of the children of Simeon, did
Num 7:42 *p* of the children of Gad, offered
Num 7:48 *p* of the children of Ephraim,
Num 7:54 *p* of the children of Manasseh
Num 7:60 *p* of the children of Benjamin,
Num 7:66 *p* of the children of Dan, offered
Num 7:72 *p* of the children of Asher,
Num 7:78 *p* of the children of Naphtali,
Num 16:13 thyself altogether a *p* over us
Num 17:6 him a rod apiece, for each *p* one
Num 25:14 a *p* of a chief house among the
Num 25:18 the daughter of a *p* of Midian
Num 34:18 shall take one *p* of every tribe
Num 34:22 the *p* of the tribe of the
Num 34:23 The *p* of the children of Joseph,
Num 34:24 the *p* of the tribe of the
Num 34:25 the *p* of the tribe of the
Num 34:26 the *p* of the tribe of the
Num 34:27 the *p* of the tribe of the
Num 34:28 the *p* of the tribe of the
Josh 22:14 princes, of each chief house a *p*
2Sa 3:38 Know ye not that there is a *p*
1Kin 11:34 but I will make him *p* all the
1Kin 14:7 made thee *p* over my people Israel
1Kin 16:2 made thee *p* over my people Israel
1Chr 2:10 *p* of the children of Judah
1Chr 5:6 he was *p* of the Reubenites
Ezr 1:8 unto Sheshbazzar, the *p* of Judah
Job 21:28 say, Where is the house of the *p*
Job 31:37 as a *p* would I go near unto him
Prov 14:28 is the destruction of the *p*
Prov 17:7 much less do lying lips a *p*
Prov 19:6 will intreat the favour of the *p*
Prov 25:7 the *p* whom thine eyes have seen
Prov 25:15 long forbearing is a *p* persuaded
Prov 28:16 The *p* that wanteth understanding
Is 9:6 Father, The *P* of Peace
Jer 51:59 And this Seraiah was a quiet *p*
Eze 7:27 the *p* shall be clothed with
Eze 12:10 concerneth the *p* in Jerusalem
Eze 12:12 the *p* that is among them shall
Eze 21:25 thou, profane wicked *p* of Israel
Eze 28:2 of man, say unto the *p* of Tyrus
Eze 30:13 no more a *p* of the land of Egypt
Eze 34:24 my servant David a *p* among them
Eze 37:25 David shall be their *p* for ever
Eze 38:2 the chief *p* of Meshech and Tubal,
Eze 38:3 the chief *p* of Meshech and Tubal
Eze 39:1 the chief *p* of Meshech and Tubal
Eze 44:3 It is for the *p*
Eze 44:3 the *p*, he shall sit in it to eat
Eze 45:7 be for the *p* on the one side
Eze 45:16 this oblation for the *p* in Israel
Eze 45:22 shall the *p* prepare for himself
Eze 46:2 the *p* shall enter by the way of
Eze 46:4 the burnt offering that the *p*
Eze 46:8 when the *p* shall enter, he shall
Eze 46:10 the *p* in the midst of them, when
Eze 46:12 Now when the *p* shall prepare a
Eze 46:16 If the *p* give a gift unto any of
Eze 46:17 after, it shall return to the *p*
Eze 46:18 Moreover the *p* shall not take of
Eze 48:21 And the residue shall be for the *p*
Eze 48:21 against the portions for the *p*
Eze 48:22 of Benjamin, shall be for the *p*
Dan 1:7 Unto whom the *p* of the eunuchs
Dan 1:8 *p* of the eunuchs that he might
Dan 1:9 love with the *p* of the eunuchs
Dan 1:10 the *p* of the eunuchs said unto
Dan 1:11 whom the *p* of the eunuchs had set
Dan 1:18 then the *p* of the eunuchs brought
Dan 8:11 himself even to the *p* of the host
Dan 8:25 stand up against the *P* of princes
Dan 9:25 the *P* shall be seven weeks
Dan 9:26 the people of the *p* that shall
Dan 10:13 But the *p* of the kingdom of
Dan 10:20 to fight with the *p* of Persia
Dan 10:20 the *p* of Grecia shall come
Dan 10:21 these things, but Michael your *p*
Dan 11:18 but a *p* for his own behalf shall
Dan 11:22 also the *p* of the covenant
Dan 12:1 the great *p* which standeth for
Hos 3:4 without a king, and without a *p*
Mic 7:3 the *p* asketh, and the judge asketh
Mt 9:34 through the *p* of the devils
Mt 12:24 by Beelzebub the *p* of the devils
Mk 3:22 by the *p* of the devils casteth he

Jn 12:31 now shall the *p* of this world be
Jn 14:30 for the *p* of this world cometh,
Jn 16:11 because the *p* of this world is
Acts 3:15 And killed the *P* of life, whom God
Acts 5:31 with his right hand to be a *P*
Eph 2:2 according to the *p* of the power
Rev 1:5 the *p* of the kings of the earth

**PRINCIPAL**
Ex 30:23 Take thou also unto thee *p* spices
Lev 6:5 he shall even restore it in the *p*
Num 5:7 his trespass with the *p* thereof
1Kin 4:5 the son of Nathan was *p* officer
2Kin 25:19 the *p* scribe of the host, which
1Chr 24:6 one *p* household being taken for
1Chr 24:31 even the *p* fathers over against
Neh 11:17 of Asaph, was the *p* to begin the
Prov 4:7 Wisdom is the *p* thing
Is 16:8 broken down the *p* plants thereof
Is 28:25 cummin, and cast in the *p* wheat
Jer 25:34 in the ashes, ye *p* of the flock
Jer 25:35 nor the *p* of the flock to escape
Jer 25:36 an howling of the *p* of the flock
Jer 52:25 the *p* scribe of the host, who
Mic 5:5 seven shepherds, and eight *p* men
*p* men of the city, at Acts 25:23

**PRINCIPALITIES**
Jer 13:18 for your *p* shall come down, even
Rom 8:38 nor life, nor angels, nor *p*
Eph 3:10 To the intent that now unto the *p*
Eph 6:12 flesh and blood, but against *p*
Col 1:16 be thrones, or dominions, or *p*
Col 2:15 And having spoiled *p* and powers, he
Titus 3:1 them in mind to be subject to *p*

**PRISCA** *(pris'-cah)* See PRISCILLA. *Same as Priscilla.*
2Ti 4:19 Salute *P* and Aquila, and the

**PRISCILLA** *(pris-sil'-lah)* See PRISCA. *Wife of Aquila and co-worker of Paul.*
Acts 18:2 come from Italy, with his wife *P*
Acts 18:18 thence into Syria, and with him *P*
Acts 18:26 *P* had heard, they took him unto
Rom 16:3 Greet *P* and Aquila my helpers in
1Cor 16:19 *P* salute you much in the Lord,

**PRISON**
Gen 39:20 took him, and put him into the *p*
Gen 39:20 and he was there in the *p*
Gen 39:21 the sight of the keeper of the *p*
Gen 39:22 the keeper of the *p* committed to
Gen 39:22 the prisoners that were in the *p*
Gen 39:23 The keeper of the *p* looked not to
Gen 40:3 captain of the guard, into the *p*
Gen 40:5 Egypt, which were bound in the *p*
Gen 42:16 brother, and ye shall be kept in *p*
Gen 42:19 be bound in the house of your *p*
Judg 16:21 and he did grind in the *p* house
Judg 16:25 for Samson out of the *p* house
1Kin 22:27 king, Put this fellow in the *p*
2Kin 17:4 shut him up, and bound him in *p*
2Kin 25:27 Jehoiachin king of Judah out of *p*
2Kin 25:29 And changed his *p* garments
2Chr 16:10 the seer, and put him in a *p* house
2Chr 18:26 king, Put this fellow in the *p*
Neh 3:25 that was by the court of the *p*
Neh 12:39 and they stood still in the *p* gate
Ps 142:7 Bring my soul out of *p*, that I
Eccl 4:14 For out of *p* he cometh to reign
Is 24:22 pit, and shall be shut up in the *p*
Is 42:7 out the prisoners from the *p*
Is 42:7 in darkness out of the *p* house
Is 42:22 and they are hid in *p* houses
Is 53:8 He was taken from *p* and from
Is 61:1 the opening of the *p* to them that
Jer 29:26 that thou shouldest put him in *p*
Jer 32:2 was shut up in the court of the *p*
Jer 32:8 *p* according to the word of the
Jer 32:12 that sat in the court of the *p*
Jer 33:1 yet shut up in the court of the *p*
Jer 37:4 for they had not put him into *p*
Jer 37:15 put him in *p* in the house of
Jer 37:15 for they had made that the *p*
Jer 37:18 people, that ye have put me in *p*
Jer 37:21 Jeremiah into the court of the *p*
Jer 37:21 remained in the court of the *p*
Jer 38:6 that was in the court of the *p*
Jer 38:13 remained in the court of the *p*
Jer 38:28 abode in the court of the *p* until
Jer 39:14 out of the court of the *p*
Jer 39:15 was shut up in the court of the *p*
Jer 52:11 put him in *p* till the day of his
Jer 52:31 and brought him forth out of *p*
Jer 52:33 And changed his *p* garments
Mt 4:12 heard that John was cast into *p*
Mt 5:25 officer, and thou be cast into *p*
Mt 11:2 in the *p* the works of Christ
Mt 14:3 put him in *p* for Herodias' sake,
Mt 14:10 sent, and beheaded John in the *p*
Mt 18:30 but went and cast him into *p*
Mt 25:36 I was in *p*, and ye came unto me
Mt 25:39 Or when saw we thee sick, or in *p*
Mt 25:43 sick, and in *p*, and ye visited me
Mt 25:44 or naked, or sick, or in *p*
Mk 1:14 Now after that John was put in *p*
Mk 6:17 bound him in *p* for Herodias' sake
Mk 6:27 he went and beheaded him in the *p*
Lk 3:20 all, that he shut up John in *p*
Lk 12:58 and the officer cast thee into *p*
Lk 22:33 to go with thee, both into *p*
Lk 23:19 and for murder, was cast into *p*
Lk 23:25 and murder was cast into *p*
Jn 3:24 For John was not yet cast into *p*
Acts 5:18 and put them in the common *p*
Acts 5:19 Lord by night opened the *p* doors
Acts 5:21 sent to the *p* to have them
Acts 5:22 came, and found them not in the *p*
Acts 5:23 The *p* truly found we shut with
Acts 5:25 the men whom ye put in *p* are
Acts 8:3 men and women committed them to *p*
Acts 12:4 apprehended him, he put him in *p*
Acts 12:5 Peter therefore was kept in *p*
Acts 12:6 before the door kept the *p*
Acts 12:7 him, and a light shined in the *p*
Acts 12:17 Lord had brought him out of the *p*
Acts 16:23 upon them, they cast them into *p*
Acts 16:24 thrust them into the inner *p*
Acts 16:26 foundations of the *p* were shaken
Acts 16:27 the keeper of the *p* awaking out
Acts 16:27 sleep, and seeing the *p* doors open
Acts 16:36 the keeper of the *p* told this
Acts 16:37 Romans, and have cast us into *p*
Acts 16:40 And they went out of the *p*
Acts 26:10 of the saints did I shut up in *p*
1Pet 3:19 and preached unto the spirits in *p*
Rev 2:10 shall cast some of you into *p*
Rev 20:7 shall be loosed out of his *p*

**PRISONER**
Ps 79:11 sighing of the *p* come before thee
Ps 102:20 To hear the groaning of the *p*
Mt 27:15 to release unto the people a *p*
Mt 27:16 And they had then a notable *p*
Mk 15:6 feast he released unto them one *p*
Acts 23:18 Paul the *p* called me unto him, and
Acts 25:27 to me unreasonable to send a *p*
Acts 28:17 yet was I delivered *p* from
Eph 3:1 the *p* of Jesus Christ for you
Eph 4:1 the *p* of the Lord, beseech you
2Ti 1:8 of our Lord, nor of me his *p*
Philem 1 a *p* of Jesus Christ, and Timothy
Philem 9 now also a *p* of Jesus Christ

**PRISONERS**
Gen 39:20 where the king's *p* were bound
Gen 39:22 all the *p* that were in the prison
Num 21:1 Israel, and took some of them *p*
Job 3:18 There the *p* rest together
Ps 69:33 the poor, and despiseth not his *p*
Ps 146:7 The LORD looseth the *p*
Is 10:4 they shall bow down under the *p*
Is 14:17 opened not the house of his *p*
Is 20:4 Assyria lead away the Egyptians *p*
Is 24:22 as *p* are gathered in the pit, and
Is 42:7 bring out the *p* from the prison
Is 49:9 That thou mayest say to the *p*
Lam 3:34 his feet all the *p* of the earth
Zec 9:11 *p* out of the pit wherein is no
Zec 9:12 to the strong hold, ye *p* of hope
Acts 16:25 and the *p* heard them
Acts 16:27 that the *p* had been fled
Acts 27:1 certain other *p* unto one named
Acts 27:42 counsel was to kill the *p*
Acts 28:16 the *p* to the captain of the guard

**PRIVATELY**
Mt 24:3 the disciples came unto him *p*
Mk 6:32 into a desert place by ship *p*
Mk 9:28 house, his disciples asked him *p*
Mk 13:3 John and Andrew asked him *p*
Lk 9:10 went aside *p* into a desert place
Lk 10:23 him unto his disciples, and said *p*
Acts 23:19 hand, and went with him aside *p*
Gal 2:2 but *p* to them which were of

**PRIVILY**
Judg 9:31 sent messengers unto Abimelech *p*
1Sa 24:4 off the skirt of Saul's robe *p*
Ps 10:8 his eyes are *p* set against the
Ps 11:2 that they may *p* shoot at the
Ps 31:4 net that they have laid *p* for me
Ps 64:5 they commune of laying snares *p*
Ps 101:5 Whoso *p* slandereth his neighbour,
Ps 142:3 have they *p* laid a snare for me
Prov 1:11 let us lurk *p* for the innocent
Prov 1:18 they lurk *p* for their own lives
Mt 1:19 was minded to put her away *p*
Mt 2:7 when he had *p* called the wise men
Acts 16:37 and now do they thrust us out *p*
Gal 2:4 who came in *p* to spy out our
2Pet 2:1 who *p* shall bring in damnable

**PRIVY**
Deut 23:1 or hath his *p* member cut off,
1Kin 2:44 which thine heart is *p* to
Eze 21:14 entereth into their *p* chambers
Acts 5:2 his wife also being *p* to it

**PROCEED**
Ex 25:35 that *p* out of the candlestick
Josh 6:10 any word *p* out of your mouth
2Sa 7:12 which shall *p* out of thy bowels,
Job 40:5 but I will *p* no further
Is 29:14 I will *p* to do a marvellous work
Is 51:4 for a law shall *p* from me
Jer 9:3 for they *p* from evil to evil, and
Jer 30:19 out of them shall *p* thanksgiving
Jer 30:21 their governor shall *p* from the
Hab 1:7 dignity shall *p* of themselves
Mt 15:18 But those things which *p* out of
Mt 15:19 out of the heart *p* evil thoughts
Mk 7:21 *p* evil thoughts, adulteries,
Eph 4:29 communication *p* out of your mouth
2Ti 3:9 But they shall *p* no further

**PROCEEDED**
Num 30:12 then whatsoever *p* out of her lips
Num 32:24 which hath *p* out of your mouth
Judg 11:36 which hath *p* out of thy mouth
Job 36:1 Elihu also *p*, and said,
Lk 4:22 words which *p* out of his mouth
Jn 8:42 for I *p* forth and came from God
Acts 12:3 he *p* further to take Peter also
Rev 4:5 And out of the throne *p* lightnings
Rev 19:21 which sword *p* out of his mouth

**PROCEEDETH**
Gen 24:50 The thing *p* from the LORD
Num 30:2 to all that *p* out of his mouth
Deut 8:3 but by every word that *p* out of
1Sa 24:13 Wickedness *p* from the wicked
Eccl 10:5 an error which *p* from the ruler
Lam 3:38 mouth of the most High *p* not evil
Hab 1:4 therefore wrong judgment *p*
Mt 4:4 but by every word that *p* out of
Jn 15:26 which *p* from the Father, he shall
Jas 3:10 Out of the same mouth *p* blessing
Rev 11:5 fire *p* out of their mouth, and

**PROCESS**
Gen 4:3 in *p* of time it came to pass,
Gen 38:12 in *p* of time the daughter of
Ex 2:23 And it came to pass in *p* of time
Judg 11:4 And it came to pass in *p* of time
2Chr 21:19 came to pass, that in *p* of time

**PROCHORUS** *(prok'-o-rus) A leader in the Jerusalem church.*
Acts 6:5 the Holy Ghost, and Philip, and *P*

**PROCLAIM**
Ex 33:19 I will *p* the name of the LORD
Lev 23:2 which ye shall *p* to be holy
Lev 23:4 which ye shall *p* in their seasons
Lev 23:21 ye shall *p* on the selfsame day,
Lev 23:37 which ye shall *p* to be holy
Lev 25:10 *p* liberty throughout all the land
Deut 20:10 against it, then *p* peace unto it
Judg 7:3 *p* in the ears of the people,
1Kin 21:9 *P* a fast, and set Naboth on high
2Kin 10:20 *P* a solemn assembly for Baal
Neh 8:15 *p* in all their cities, and in
Est 6:9 *p* before him, Thus shall it be
Prov 20:6 Most men will *p* every one his own
Is 61:1 to *p* liberty to the captives, and
Is 61:2 To *p* the acceptable year of the
Jer 3:12 *p* these words toward the north,

Jer 7:2 p there this word, and say, Hear
Jer 11:6 P all these words in the cities
Jer 19:2 p there the words that I shall
Jer 34:8 Jerusalem, to p liberty unto them
Jer 34:17 I p a liberty for you, saith the
Joel 3:9 P ye this among the Gentiles
Amos 4:5 of thanksgiving with leaven, and p

## PROCLAIMED
Ex 34:5 there, and p the name of the LORD
Ex 34:6 LORD passed by before him, and p
Ex 36:6 it to be p throughout the camp
1Kin 21:12 They p a fast, and set Naboth on
2Kin 10:20 And they p it
2Kin 23:16 God p, who p these words
2Kin 23:17 p these things that thou hast
2Chr 20:3 p a fast throughout all Judah
Ezr 8:21 Then I p a fast there, at the
Est 6:11 p before him, Thus shall it be
Is 62:11 the LORD hath p unto the end of
Jer 36:9 that they p a fast before the
Jonah 3:5 p a fast, and put on sackcloth,
Jonah 3:7 And he caused it to be p and
Lk 12:3 shall be p upon the housetops

## PROCLAMATION
Ex 32:5 and Aaron made p, and said, To
1Kin 15:22 Asa made a p throughout all Judah
1Kin 22:36 there went a p throughout the
2Chr 24:9 they made a p through Judah and
2Chr 30:5 to make p throughout all Israel
2Chr 36:22 that he made a p throughout all
Ezr 1:1 that he made a p throughout all
Ezr 10:7 they made p throughout Judah
Dan 5:29 made a p concerning him, that he

## PROFANE
Lev 18:21 neither shalt thou p the name of
Lev 19:12 neither shalt thou p the name of
Lev 20:3 sanctuary, and to p my holy name
Lev 21:4 among his people, to p himself
Lev 21:6 not p the name of their God
Lev 21:7 take a wife that is a whore, or p
Lev 21:9 if she p herself by playing the
Lev 21:12 nor p the sanctuary of his God
Lev 21:14 widow, or a divorced woman, or p
Lev 21:15 Neither shall he p his seed among
Lev 21:23 that he p not my sanctuaries
Lev 22:2 that they p not my holy name in
Lev 22:9 and die therefore, if they p it
Lev 22:15 they shall not p the holy things
Lev 22:32 Neither shall ye p my holy name
Neh 13:17 that ye do, and p the sabbath day
Jer 23:11 For both prophet and priest are p
Eze 21:25 p wicked prince of Israel, whose
Eze 22:26 difference between the holy and p
Eze 23:39 day into my sanctuary to p it
Eze 24:21 I will p my sanctuary, the
Eze 28:16 as p out of the mountain of God
Eze 42:20 the sanctuary and the p place
Eze 44:23 difference between the holy and p
Eze 48:15 shall be a p place for the city,
Amos 2:7 the same maid, to p my holy name
Mt 12:5 in the temple p the sabbath
Acts 24:6 hath gone about to p the temple
1Ti 1:9 and for sinners, for unholy and p
1Ti 4:7 But refuse p and old wives' fables
1Ti 6:20 to thy trust, avoiding p and vain
2Ti 2:16 But shun p and vain babblings
Heb 12:16 or p person, as Esau, who for one

## PROFANED
Lev 19:8 because he hath p the hallowed
Ps 89:39 thou hast p his crown by casting
Is 43:28 Therefore I have p the princes of
Eze 22:8 things, and hast p my sabbaths
Eze 22:26 law, and have p mine holy things
Eze 22:26 my sabbaths, and I am p among them
Eze 23:38 same day, and have p my sabbaths
Eze 25:3 my sanctuary, when it was p
Eze 36:20 they p my holy name, when they
Eze 36:21 of Israel had p among the heathen
Eze 36:22 which ye have p among the heathen
Eze 36:23 which was p among the heathen,
Eze 36:23 which ye have p in the midst of
Mal 1:12 But ye have p it, in that ye say,
Mal 2:11 for Judah hath p the holiness of

## PROFESSION
1Ti 6:12 a good p before many witnesses
Heb 3:1 Apostle and High Priest of our p
Heb 4:14 of God, let us hold fast our p
Heb 10:23 Let us hold fast the p of our

## PROFIT
Gen 25:32 what p shall this birthright do
Gen 37:26 What p is it if we slay our
1Sa 12:21 which cannot p nor deliver
Est 3:8 for the king's p to suffer them
Job 21:15 what p should we have, if we pray
Job 30:2 the strength of their hands p me
Job 35:3 What p shall I have, if I be
Job 35:8 may p the son of man
Ps 30:9 What p is there in my blood, when
Prov 10:2 Treasures of wickedness p nothing
Prov 11:4 Riches p not in the day of wrath
Prov 14:23 In all labour there is p
Eccl 1:3 What p hath a man of all his
Eccl 2:11 there was no p under the sun
Eccl 3:9 What p hath he that worketh in
Eccl 5:9 Moreover the p of the earth is
Eccl 5:16 what p hath he that hath laboured
Eccl 7:11 by it there is p to them that see
Is 30:5 of a people that could not p them
Is 30:5 nor be an help nor p
Is 30:6 to a people that shall not p them
Is 44:9 delectable things shall not p
Is 47:12 if so be thou shalt be able to p
Is 48:17 thy God which teacheth thee to p
Is 57:12 for they shall not p thee
Jer 2:8 walked after things that do not p
Jer 2:11 glory for that which doth not p
Jer 7:8 in lying words, that cannot p
Jer 12:13 to pain, but shall not p
Jer 16:19 and things wherein there is no p
Jer 23:32 shall not p this people at all
Mal 3:14 what p is it that we have kept
Mk 8:36 For what shall it p a man
Rom 3:1 or what p is there of
1Cor 7:35 And this I speak for your own p
1Cor 10:33 own p, but the p of many
1Cor 12:7 is given to every man to p withal
1Cor 14:6 with tongues, what shall I p you
Gal 5:2 Christ shall p you nothing
2Ti 2:14 strive not about words to no p
Heb 4:2 the word preached did not p them
Heb 12:10 but he for our p, that we might
Jas 2:14 What doth it p, my brethren,
Jas 2:16 what doth it p

## PROFITABLE
Job 22:2 Can a man be p unto God, as he
Job 22:2 is wise may be p unto himself
Eccl 10:10 but wisdom is p to direct
Is 44:10 image that is p for nothing
Jer 13:7 was marred, it was p for nothing
Mt 5:29 for it is p for thee that one of
Mt 5:30 for it is p for thee that one of
Acts 20:20 back nothing that was p unto you
1Ti 4:8 godliness is p unto all things
2Ti 3:16 is p for doctrine, for reproof,
2Ti 4:11 for he is p to me for the
Titus 3:8 things are good and p unto men
Philem 11 unprofitable, but now p to thee

## PROFITED
Job 33:27 which was right, and it p me not
Mt 15:5 thou mightest be p by me
Mt 16:26 For what is a man p, if he shall
Mk 7:11 thou mightest be p by me
Gal 1:14 p in the Jews' religion above
Heb 13:9 which have not p them that have

## PROFITETH
Job 34:9 It p a man nothing that he should
Hab 2:18 What p the graven image that the
Jn 6:63 the flesh p nothing
Rom 2:25 For circumcision verily p
1Cor 13:3 have not charity, it p me nothing
1Ti 4:8 For bodily exercise p little

## PROLONG
Deut 4:26 ye shall not p your days upon it,
Deut 4:40 that thou mayest p thy days upon
Deut 5:33 that ye may p your days in the
Deut 11:9 that ye may p your days in the
Deut 17:20 to the end that he may p his days
Deut 22:7 and that thou mayest p thy days
Deut 30:18 that ye shall not p your days
Deut 32:47 ye shall p your days in the land
Job 6:11 mine end, that I should p my life
Job 15:29 neither shall he p the perfection
Ps 61:6 Thou wilt p the king's life
Prov 28:16 covetousness shall p his days
Eccl 8:13 neither shall he p his days
Is 53:10 see his seed, he shall p his days

## PROLONGED
Deut 5:16 that thy days may be p, and that
Deut 6:2 and that thy days may be p
Prov 28:2 the state thereof shall be p
Eccl 8:12 hundred times, and his days be p
Is 13:22 come, and her days shall not be p
Eze 12:22 of Israel, saying, The days are p
Eze 12:25 it shall be no more p
Eze 12:28 none of my words be p any more
Dan 7:12 their lives were p for a season

## PROMISE
Num 14:34 and ye shall know my breach of p
1Kin 8:56 failed one word of all his good p
2Chr 1:9 let thy p unto David my father be
Neh 5:12 should do according to this p
Neh 5:13 that performeth not this p
Neh 5:13 people did according to this p
Ps 77:8 doth his p fail for evermore
Ps 105:42 For he remembered his holy p
Lk 24:49 I send the p of my Father upon
Acts 1:4 but wait for the p of the Father
Acts 2:33 Father the p of the Holy Ghost
Acts 2:39 For the p is unto you, and to your
Acts 7:17 when the time of the p drew nigh
Acts 13:23 p raised unto Israel a Saviour
Acts 13:32 how that the p which was made
Acts 23:21 ready, looking for a p from thee
Acts 26:6 p made of God unto our fathers
Acts 26:7 Unto which p our twelve tribes,
Rom 4:13 For the p, that he should be the
Rom 4:14 the p made of none effect
Rom 4:16 to the end the p might be sure to
Rom 4:20 at the p of God through unbelief
Rom 9:8 but the children of the p are
Rom 9:9 For this is the word of p
Gal 3:14 that we might receive the p of
Gal 3:17 should make the p of none effect
Gal 3:18 be of the law, it is no more of p
Gal 3:18 but God gave it to Abraham by p
Gal 3:19 come to whom the p was made
Gal 3:22 that the p by faith of Jesus
Gal 3:29 seed, and heirs according to the p
Gal 4:23 but he of the freewoman was by p
Gal 4:28 Isaac was, are the children of p
Eph 1:13 sealed with that holy Spirit of p
Eph 2:12 strangers from the covenants of p
Eph 3:6 partakers of his p in Christ by
Eph 6:2 is the first commandment with p
1Ti 4:8 having p of the life that now is,
2Ti 1:1 according to the p of life which
Heb 4:1 a p being left us of entering
Heb 6:13 For when God made p to Abraham
Heb 6:15 endured, he obtained the p
Heb 6:17 to shew unto the heirs of p the
Heb 9:15 the p of eternal inheritance
Heb 10:36 of God, ye might receive the p
Heb 11:9 he sojourned in the land of p
Heb 11:9 the heirs with him of the same p
Heb 11:39 through faith, received not the p
2Pet 2:19 While they p them liberty, they
2Pet 3:4 Where is the p of his coming
2Pet 3:9 is not slack concerning his p
2Pet 3:13 we, according to his p, look for
1Jn 2:25 this is the p that he hath

## PROMISED
Ex 12:25 give you, according as he hath p
Num 14:40 the place which the LORD hath p
Deut 1:11 and bless you, as he hath p you
Deut 6:3 God of thy fathers hath p thee
Deut 9:28 into the land which he p them
Deut 10:9 as the LORD thy God p him
Deut 12:20 thy border, as he hath p thee
Deut 15:6 God blesseth thee, as he p thee
Deut 19:8 he p to give unto thy fathers
Deut 23:23 which thou hast p with thy mouth
Deut 26:18 people, as he hath p thee
Deut 27:3 God of thy fathers hath p thee
Josh 9:21 as the princes had p them
Josh 22:4 unto your brethren, as he p them
Josh 23:5 the LORD your God hath p unto you
Josh 23:10 for you, as he hath p you
Josh 23:15 which the LORD your God p you
2Sa 7:28 thou hast p this goodness unto
1Kin 2:24 hath made me an house, as he p
1Kin 5:12 gave Solomon wisdom, as he p him
1Kin 8:20 throne of Israel, as the LORD p
1Kin 8:56 according to all that he p
1Kin 8:56 which he p by the hand of Moses
1Kin 9:5 as I p to David thy father,

2Kin 8:19 as he *p* him to give him alway a
1Chr 17:26 hast *p* this goodness unto thy
2Chr 6:10 throne of Israel, as the LORD *p*
2Chr 6:15 father that which thou hast *p* him
2Chr 6:16 father that which thou hast *p* him
2Chr 21:7 as he *p* to give a light to him and
Neh 9:23 thou hadst *p* to their fathers
Est 4:7 *p* to pay to the king's treasuries
Jer 32:42 all the good that I have *p* them
Jer 33:14 I have *p* unto the house of Israel
Mt 14:7 Whereupon he *p* with an oath to
Mk 14:11 were glad, and *p* to give him money
Lk 1:72 the mercy *p* to our fathers
Lk 22:6 And he *p*, and sought opportunity to
Acts 7:5 yet he *p* that he would give it to
Rom 1:2 (Which he had *p* afore by his
Rom 4:21 persuaded that, what he had *p*
Titus 1:2 lie, *p* before the world began
Heb 10:23 (for he is faithful that *p*
Heb 11:11 she judged him faithful who had *p*
Heb 12:26 but now he hath *p*, saying, Yet
Jas 1:12 which the Lord hath *p* to them
Jas 2:5 he hath *p* to them that love him
1Jn 2:25 is the promise that he hath *p* us

## PROMISES
Rom 9:4 and the service of God, and the *p*
Rom 15:8 to confirm the *p* made unto the
2Cor 1:20 For all the *p* of God in him are
2Cor 7:1 therefore these *p* dearly beloved
Gal 3:16 and his seed were the *p* made
Gal 3:21 the law then against the *p* of God
Heb 6:12 faith and patience inherit the *p*
Heb 7:6 and blessed him that had the *p*
Heb 8:6 was established upon better *p*
Heb 11:13 faith, not having received the *p*
Heb 11:17 he that had received the *p*
Heb 11:33 wrought righteousness, obtained *p*
2Pet 1:4 us exceeding great and precious *p*

## PROMOTE
Num 22:17 For I will *p* thee unto very great
Num 22:37 able indeed to *p* thee to honour
Num 24:11 I thought to *p* thee unto great
Est 3:1 *p* Haman the son of Hammedatha the
Prov 4:8 Exalt her, and she shall *p* thee

## PROMOTED
Judg 9:9 go to be *p* over the trees
Judg 9:11 go to be *p* over the trees
Judg 9:13 go to be *p* over the trees
Est 5:11 things wherein the king had *p* him
Dan 3:30 Then the king *p* Shadrach, Meshach

## PRONOUNCE
Lev 5:4 that a man shall *p* with an oath
Lev 13:3 look on him, and *p* him unclean
Lev 13:6 the priest shall *p* him clean
Lev 13:8 the priest shall *p* him unclean
Lev 13:11 and the priest shall *p* him unclean
Lev 13:13 he shall *p* him clean that hath
Lev 13:15 raw flesh, and *p* him to be unclean
Lev 13:17 then the priest shall *p* him clean
Lev 13:20 the priest shall *p* him unclean
Lev 13:22 the priest shall *p* him unclean
Lev 13:23 and the priest shall *p* him clean
Lev 13:25 the priest shall *p* him unclean
Lev 13:27 the priest shall *p* him unclean
Lev 13:28 and the priest shall *p* him clean
Lev 13:30 the priest shall *p* him unclean
Lev 13:34 then the priest shall *p* him clean
Lev 13:37 and the priest shall *p* him clean
Lev 13:44 the priest shall *p* him utterly
Lev 13:59 to *p* it clean, or to *p* it
Lev 14:7 shall *p* him clean, and shall let
Lev 14:48 priest shall *p* the house clean
Judg 12:6 he could not frame to *p* it right

## PRONOUNCED
Neh 6:12 but that he *p* this prophecy
Jer 11:17 hath *p* evil against thee, for the
Jer 16:10 Wherefore hath the LORD *p* all
Jer 18:8 nation, against whom I have *p*
Jer 19:15 the evil that I have *p* against it
Jer 25:13 words which I have *p* against it
Jer 26:13 evil that he hath *p* against you
Jer 26:19 evil which he had *p* against them
Jer 34:5 for I have *p* the word, saith the
Jer 35:17 evil that I have *p* against them
Jer 36:7 LORD hath *p* against this people
Jer 36:18 He *p* all these words unto me with
Jer 36:31 evil that I have *p* against them
Jer 40:2 The LORD thy God hath *p* this evil

## PROOF
2Cor 2:9 that I might know the *p* of you
2Cor 8:24 the *p* of your love, and of our
2Cor 13:3 Since ye seek a *p* of Christ
Phil 2:22 But ye know the *p* of him, that,
2Ti 4:5 make full *p* of thy ministry

## PROPER
1Chr 29:3 my God, I have of mine own *p* good
Acts 1:19 field is called in their *p* tongue
1Cor 7:7 every man hath his *p* gift of God
Heb 11:23 because they saw he was a *p* child

## PROPHECY
2Chr 9:29 in the *p* of Ahijah the Shilonite,
2Chr 15:8 the *p* of Oded the prophet, he
Neh 6:12 he pronounced this *p* against me
Prov 30:1 Agur the son of Jakeh, even the *p*
Prov 31:1 the *p* that his mother taught him
Dan 9:24 and to seal up the vision and *p*
Mt 13:14 them is fulfilled the *p* of Esaias
Rom 12:6 that is given to us, whether *p*
1Cor 12:10 to another *p*
1Cor 13:2 And though I have the gift of *p*
1Ti 4:14 thee, which was given thee by *p*
2Pet 1:19 have also a more sure word of *p*
2Pet 1:20 that no *p* of the scripture is of
2Pet 1:21 For the *p* came not in old time by
Rev 1:3 that hear the words of this *p*
Rev 11:6 rain not in the days of their *p*
Rev 19:10 of Jesus is the spirit of *p*
Rev 22:7 the sayings of the *p* of this book
Rev 22:10 the sayings of the *p* of this book
Rev 22:18 the words of the *p* of this book
Rev 22:19 the words of the book of this *p*

## PROPHESIED
Num 11:25 spirit rested upon them, they *p*
Num 11:26 and they *p* in the camp
1Sa 10:10 came upon him, and he *p* among them
1Sa 10:11 he *p* among the prophets, then the
1Sa 18:10 he *p* in the midst of the house
1Sa 19:20 of Saul, and they also *p*
1Sa 19:21 messengers, and they *p* likewise
1Sa 19:21 the third time, and they *p* also
1Sa 19:23 him also, and he went on, and *p*
1Sa 19:24 *p* before Samuel in like manner,
1Kin 18:29 they *p* until the time of the
1Kin 22:10 and all the prophets *p* before them
1Kin 22:12 And all the prophets *p* so, saying,
1Chr 25:2 which *p* according to the order of
1Chr 25:3 who *p* with a harp, to give thanks
2Chr 18:7 for he never *p* good unto me
2Chr 18:9 and all the prophets *p* before them
2Chr 18:11 And all the prophets *p* so, saying,
2Chr 20:37 of Mareshah *p* against Jehoshaphat
Ezr 5:1 *p* unto the Jews that were in
Jer 2:8 me, and the prophets *p* by Baal
Jer 20:1 that Jeremiah *p* these things
Jer 20:6 friends, to whom thou hast *p* lies
Jer 23:13 they *p* in Baal, and caused my
Jer 23:21 not spoken to them, yet they *p*
Jer 25:13 which Jeremiah hath *p* against all
Jer 26:9 Why hast thou *p* in the name of
Jer 26:11 for he hath *p* against this city,
Jer 26:18 Micah the Morasthite *p* in the
Jer 26:20 that *p* in the name of the LORD
Jer 26:20 who *p* against this city and
Jer 28:6 thy words which thou hast *p*
Jer 28:8 before thee of old *p* both against
Jer 29:31 that Shemaiah hath *p* unto you
Jer 37:19 your prophets which *p* unto you
Eze 11:13 And it came to pass, when I *p*
Eze 37:7 So I *p* as I was commanded
Eze 37:7 and as I *p*, there was a noise, and
Eze 37:10 So I *p* as he commanded me, and the
Eze 38:17 which *p* in those days many years
Zec 13:4 one of his vision, when he hath *p*
Mt 7:22 Lord, have we not *p* in thy name
Mt 11:13 prophets and the law *p* until John
Mk 7:6 Well hath Esaias *p* of you
Lk 1:67 filled with the Holy Ghost, and *p*
Jn 11:51 he *p* that Jesus should die for
Acts 19:6 and they spake with tongues, and *p*
1Cor 14:5 tongues, but rather that ye *p*
1Pet 1:10 who *p* of the grace that should
Jude 14 *p* of these, saying, Behold, the

## PROPHESIETH
Jer 28:9 The prophet which *p* of peace
Eze 12:27 he *p* of the times that are far
Zec 13:3 thrust him through when he *p*
1Cor 11:5 or *p* with her head uncovered
1Cor 14:3 But he that *p* speaketh unto men
1Cor 14:4 but he that *p* edifieth the church
1Cor 14:5 for greater is he that *p* than he

## PROPHESY
Num 11:27 Eldad and Medad do *p* in the camp
1Sa 10:5 and they shall *p*
1Sa 10:6 thee, and thou shalt *p* with them
1Kin 22:8 for he doth not *p* good concerning
1Kin 22:18 he would *p* no good concerning me
1Chr 25:1 Jeduthun, who should *p* with harps
2Chr 18:17 that he would not *p* good unto me
Is 30:10 *P* not unto us right things, speak
Is 30:10 unto us smooth things, *p* deceits
Jer 5:31 The prophets *p* falsely, and the
Jer 11:21 *P* not in the name of the LORD,
Jer 14:14 The prophets *p* lies in my name
Jer 14:14 they *p* unto you a false vision and
Jer 14:15 the prophets that *p* in my name
Jer 14:16 the people to whom they *p* shall
Jer 19:14 the LORD had sent him to *p*
Jer 23:16 of the prophets that *p* unto you
Jer 23:25 that *p* lies in my name, saying, I
Jer 23:26 heart of the prophets that *p* lies
Jer 23:32 against them that *p* false dreams
Jer 25:30 Therefore *p* thou against them all
Jer 26:12 sent me to *p* against this house
Jer 27:10 For they *p* a lie unto you, to
Jer 27:14 for they *p* a lie unto you
Jer 27:15 yet they *p* a lie in my name
Jer 27:15 and the prophets that *p* unto you
Jer 27:16 of your prophets that *p* unto you
Jer 27:16 for they *p* a lie unto you
Jer 29:9 For they *p* falsely unto you in my
Jer 29:21 which *p* a lie unto you in my name
Jer 32:3 up, saying, Wherefore dost thou *p*
Eze 4:7 and thou shalt *p* against it
Eze 6:2 of Israel, and *p* against them,
Eze 11:4 *p* against them, *p*, O son
Eze 13:2 *p* against the prophets of Israel
Eze 13:2 the prophets of Israel that *p*
Eze 13:2 that *p* out of their own hearts
Eze 13:16 which *p* concerning Jerusalem
Eze 13:17 which *p* out of their own heart
Eze 13:17 and *p* thou against them,
Eze 20:46 *p* against the forest of the south
Eze 21:2 *p* against the land of Israel,
Eze 21:9 Son of man, *p*, and say, Thus saith
Eze 21:14 Thou therefore, son of man, *p*
Eze 21:28 And thou, son of man, *p* and say,
Eze 25:2 the Ammonites, and *p* against them
Eze 28:21 against Zidon, and *p* against it,
Eze 29:2 *p* against him, and against all
Eze 30:2 Son of man, *p* and say, Thus saith
Eze 34:2 *p* against the shepherds of Israel
Eze 34:2 the shepherds of Israel, *p*
Eze 35:2 mount Seir, and *p* against it,
Eze 36:1 *p* unto the mountains of Israel,
Eze 36:3 Therefore *p* and say, Thus saith
Eze 36:6 *P* therefore concerning the land
Eze 37:4 *P* upon these bones, and say unto
Eze 37:9 *P* unto the wind, *p*, son of
Eze 37:12 Therefore *p* and say unto them,
Eze 38:2 and Tubal, and *p* against him,
Eze 38:14 Therefore, son of man, *p* and say
Eze 39:1 *p* against Gog, and say, Thus saith
Joel 2:28 sons and your daughters shall *p*
Amos 2:12 the prophets, saying, *P* not
Amos 3:8 GOD hath spoken, who can but *p*
Amos 7:12 and there eat bread, and *p* there
Amos 7:13 But *p* not again any more at
Amos 7:15 me, Go, *p* unto my people Israel
Amos 7:16 *P* not against Israel, and drop not
Mic 2:6 *P* ye not, say they to them that
Mic 2:6 ye not, say they to them that *p*
Mic 2:6 they shall not *p* to them, that
Mic 2:11 I will *p* unto thee of wine and of
Zec 13:3 pass, that when any shall yet *p*
Mt 15:7 well did Esaias *p* of you
Mt 26:68 *P* unto us, thou Christ, Who is he
Mk 14:65 buffet him, and to say unto him, *P*
Lk 22:64 the face, and asked him, saying, *P*
Acts 2:17 sons and your daughters shall *p*
Acts 2:18 and they shall *p*
Acts 21:9 daughters, virgins, which did *p*
Rom 12:6 let us *p* according to the
1Cor 13:9 we know in part, and we *p* in part
1Cor 14:1 gifts, but rather that ye may *p*
1Cor 14:24 But if all *p*, and there come in

1Cor 14:31 For ye may all *p* one by one
1Cor 14:39 Wherefore, brethren, covet to *p*
Rev 10:11 Thou must *p* again before many
Rev 11:3 they shall *p* a thousand two

## PROPHESYING

1Sa 10:13 And when he had made an end of *p*
1Sa 19:20 saw the company of the prophets *p*
Ezr 6:14 the *p* of Haggai the prophet
1Cor 11:4 Every man praying or *p*, having
1Cor 14:6 or by knowledge, or by *p*
1Cor 14:22 but *p* serveth not for them that

## PROPHET

Gen 20:7 for he is a *p*, and he shall pray
Ex 7:1 Aaron thy brother shall be thy *p*
Num 12:6 If there be a *p* among you
Deut 13:1 If there arise among you a *p*
Deut 13:3 hearken unto the words of that *p*
Deut 13:5 And that *p*, or that dreamer of
Deut 18:15 thee a *P* from the midst of thee
Deut 18:18 I will raise them up a *P* from
Deut 18:20 But the *p*, which shall presume to
Deut 18:20 other gods, even that *p* shall die
Deut 18:22 When a *p* speaketh in the name of
Deut 18:22 spoken, but the *p* hath spoken it
Deut 34:10 there arose not a *p* since in
Judg 6:8 That the LORD sent a *p* unto the
1Sa 3:20 established to be a *p* of the LORD
1Sa 9:9 for he that is now called a *P* was
1Sa 22:5 the *p* Gad said unto David, Abide
2Sa 7:2 the king said unto Nathan the *p*
2Sa 12:25 sent by the hand of Nathan the *p*
2Sa 24:11 of the LORD came unto the *p* Gad
1Kin 1:8 son of Jehoiada, and Nathan the *p*
1Kin 1:10 But Nathan the *p*, and Benaiah, and
1Kin 1:22 Nathan the *p* also came in
1Kin 1:23 king, saying, Behold Nathan the *p*
1Kin 1:32 Zadok the priest, and Nathan the *p*
1Kin 1:34 Nathan the *p* anoint him there
1Kin 1:38 Zadok the priest, and Nathan the *p*
1Kin 1:44 Zadok the priest, and Nathan the *p*
1Kin 1:45 Nathan the *p* have anointed him
1Kin 11:29 that the *p* Ahijah the Shilonite
1Kin 13:11 there dwelt an old *p* in Beth-el
1Kin 13:18 I am a *p* also as thou art
1Kin 13:20 unto the *p* that brought him back
1Kin 13:23 for the *p* whom he had brought
1Kin 13:25 in the city where the old *p* dwelt
1Kin 13:26 when the *p* that brought him back
1Kin 13:29 the *p* took up the carcase of the
1Kin 13:29 the old *p* came to the city, to
1Kin 14:2 behold, there is Ahijah the *p*
1Kin 14:18 hand of his servant Ahijah the *p*
1Kin 16:7 also by the hand of the *p* Jehu
1Kin 16:12 against Baasha by Jehu the *p*
1Kin 18:22 I only, remain a *p* of the LORD
1Kin 18:36 that Elijah the *p* came near
1Kin 19:16 thou anoint to be *p* in thy room
1Kin 20:13 there came a *p* unto Ahab king of
1Kin 20:22 the *p* came to the king of Israel,
1Kin 20:38 So the *p* departed, and waited for
1Kin 22:7 not here a *p* of the LORD besides
2Kin 3:11 Is there not here a *p* of the LORD
2Kin 5:3 with the *p* that is in Samaria
2Kin 5:8 know that there is a *p* in Israel
2Kin 5:13 if the *p* had bid thee do some
2Kin 6:12 the *p* that is in Israel, telleth
2Kin 9:1 Elisha the *p* called one of the
2Kin 9:4 man, even the young man the *p*
2Kin 14:25 Jonah, the son of Amittai, the *p*
2Kin 19:2 to Isaiah the *p* the son of Amoz
2Kin 20:1 the *p* Isaiah the son of Amoz came
2Kin 20:11 Isaiah the *p* cried unto the LORD
2Kin 20:14 Isaiah the *p* unto king Hezekiah
2Kin 23:18 with the bones of the *p* that came
1Chr 17:1 that David said to Nathan the *p*
1Chr 29:29 and in the book of Nathan the *p*
2Chr 9:29 in the book of Nathan the *p*
2Chr 12:5 came Shemaiah the *p* to Rehoboam
2Chr 12:15 in the book of Shemaiah the *p*
2Chr 13:22 in the story of the *p* Iddo
2Chr 15:8 and the prophecy of Oded the *p*
2Chr 18:6 not here a *p* of the LORD besides
2Chr 21:12 writing to him from Elijah the *p*
2Chr 25:15 Amaziah, and he sent unto him a *p*
2Chr 25:16 Then the *p* forbare, and said, I
2Chr 26:22 first and last, did Isaiah the *p*
2Chr 28:9 But a *p* of the LORD was there,
2Chr 29:25 the king's seer, and Nathan the *p*
2Chr 32:20 the *p* Isaiah the son of Amoz,
2Chr 32:32 in the vision of Isaiah the *p*
2Chr 35:18 from the days of Samuel the *p*
2Chr 36:12 *p* speaking from the mouth of the
Ezr 5:1 Then the prophets, Haggai the *p*
Ezr 6:14 the prophesying of Haggai the *p*
Ps 51:*t* when Nathan the *p* came unto him
Ps 74:9 there is no more any *p*
Is 3:2 man of war, the judge, and the *p*
Is 9:15 the *p* that teacheth lies, he is
Is 28:7 the *p* have erred through strong
Is 37:2 unto Isaiah the *p* the son of Amoz
Is 38:1 Isaiah the *p* the son of Amoz came
Is 39:3 Isaiah the *p* unto king Hezekiah
Jer 1:5 thee a *p* unto the nations
Jer 6:13 from the *p* even unto the priest
Jer 8:10 from the *p* even unto the priest
Jer 14:18 yea, both the *p* and the priest go
Jer 18:18 the wise, nor the word from the *p*
Jer 20:2 Then Pashur smote Jeremiah the *p*
Jer 23:11 For both *p* and priest are profane
Jer 23:28 The *p* that hath a dream, let him
Jer 23:33 And when this people, or the *p*
Jer 23:34 And as for the *p*, and the priest,
Jer 23:37 Thus shalt thou say to the *p*
Jer 25:2 The which Jeremiah the *p* spake
Jer 28:1 Hananiah the son of Azur the *p*
Jer 28:5 *p* Jeremiah said unto the *p*
Jer 28:6 Even the *p* Jeremiah said, Amen
Jer 28:9 The *p* which prophesieth of peace,
Jer 28:9 word of the *p* shall come to pass
Jer 28:9 then shall the *p* be known
Jer 28:10 Then Hananiah the *p* took the yoke
Jer 28:10 from off the *p* Jeremiah's neck
Jer 28:11 the *p* Jeremiah went his way
Jer 28:12 the LORD came unto Jeremiah the *p*
Jer 28:12 after that Hananiah the *p* had
Jer 28:12 off the neck of the *p* Jeremiah
Jer 28:15 Then said the *p* Jeremiah unto
Jer 28:15 Jeremiah unto Hananiah the *p*
Jer 28:17 So Hananiah the *p* died the same
Jer 29:1 *p* sent from Jerusalem unto the
Jer 29:26 is mad, and maketh himself a *p*
Jer 29:27 which maketh himself a *p* to you
Jer 29:29 in the ears of Jeremiah the *p*
Jer 32:2 Jeremiah the *p* was shut up in the
Jer 34:6 Then Jeremiah the *p* spake all
Jer 36:8 that Jeremiah the *p* commanded him
Jer 36:26 the scribe and Jeremiah the *p*
Jer 37:2 which he spake by the *p* Jeremiah
Jer 37:3 the priest to the *p* Jeremiah
Jer 37:6 of the LORD unto the *p* Jeremiah
Jer 37:13 and he took Jeremiah the *p*
Jer 38:9 they have done to Jeremiah the *p*
Jer 38:10 Jeremiah the *p* out of the dungeon
Jer 38:14 took Jeremiah the *p* unto him into
Jer 42:2 And said unto Jeremiah the *p*
Jer 42:4 Jeremiah the *p* said unto them
Jer 43:6 son of Shaphan, and Jeremiah the *p*
Jer 45:1 The word that Jeremiah the *p*
Jer 46:1 the *p* against the Gentiles
Jer 46:13 the LORD spake to Jeremiah the *p*
Jer 47:1 the *p* against the Philistines
Jer 49:34 *p* against Elam in the beginning
Jer 50:1 the Chaldeans by Jeremiah the *p*
Jer 51:59 The word which Jeremiah the *p*
Lam 2:20 the *p* be slain in the sanctuary
Eze 2:5 there hath been a *p* among them
Eze 7:26 shall they seek a vision of the *p*
Eze 14:4 his face, and cometh to the *p*
Eze 14:7 cometh to a *p* to enquire of him
Eze 14:9 if the *p* be deceived when he hath
Eze 14:9 I the LORD have deceived that *p*
Eze 14:10 the punishment of the *p* shall be
Eze 33:33 that a *p* hath been among them
Dan 9:2 the LORD came to Jeremiah the *p*
Hos 4:5 the *p* also shall fall with thee
Hos 9:7 the *p* is a fool, the spiritual
Hos 9:8 but the *p* is a snare of a fowler
Hos 12:13 by a *p* the LORD brought Israel
Hos 12:13 Egypt, and by a *p* was he preserved
Amos 7:14 and said to Amaziah, I was no *p*
Mic 2:11 even be the *p* of this people
Hab 1:1 which Habakkuk the *p* did see
Hab 3:1 of Habakkuk the *p* upon Shigionoth
Hag 1:1 the *p* unto Zerubbabel the son of
Hag 1:3 word of the LORD by Haggai the *p*
Hag 1:12 God, and the words of Haggai the *p*
Hag 2:1 word of the LORD by the *p* Haggai
Hag 2:10 word of the LORD by Haggai the *p*
Zec 1:1 Berechiah, the son of Iddo the *p*
Zec 1:7 Berechiah, the son of Iddo the *p*
Zec 13:5 But he shall say, I am no *p*
Mal 4:5 I will send you Elijah the *p*
Mt 1:22 was spoken of the Lord by the *p*
Mt 2:5 for thus it is written by the *p*
Mt 2:15 was spoken of the Lord by the *p*
Mt 2:17 which was spoken by Jeremy the *p*
Mt 3:3 was spoken of by the *p* Esaias
Mt 4:14 which was spoken by Esaias the *p*
Mt 8:17 which was spoken by Esaias the *p*
Mt 10:41 He that receiveth a *p* in the name
Mt 10:41 of a *p* shall receive a prophet's
Mt 11:9 for to see? A *p*?
Mt 11:9 I say unto you, and more than a *p*
Mt 12:17 which was spoken by Esaias the *p*
Mt 12:39 it, but the sign of the *p* Jonas
Mt 13:35 which was spoken by the *p*
Mt 13:57 A *p* is not without honour, save
Mt 14:5 because they counted him as a *p*
Mt 16:4 it, but the sign of the *p* Jonas
Mt 21:4 which was spoken by the *p*
Mt 21:11 This is Jesus the *p* of Nazareth
Mt 21:26 for all hold John as a *p*
Mt 21:46 because they took him for a *p*
Mt 24:15 spoken of by Daniel the *p*
Mt 27:9 which was spoken by Jeremy the *p*
Mt 27:35 which was spoken by the *p*
Mk 6:4 A *p* is not without honour, but in
Mk 6:15 And others said, That it is a *p*
Mk 11:32 John, that he was a *p* indeed
Mk 13:14 spoken of by Daniel the *p*
Lk 1:76 be called the *p* of the Highest
Lk 3:4 book of the words of Esaias the *p*
Lk 4:17 unto him the book of the *p* Esaias
Lk 4:24 No *p* is accepted in his own
Lk 4:27 in the time of Eliseus the *p*
Lk 7:16 That a great *p* is risen up among
Lk 7:26 for to see? A *p*?
Lk 7:26 unto you, and much more than a *p*
Lk 7:28 a greater *p* than John the Baptist
Lk 7:39 saying, This man, if he were a *p*
Lk 11:29 it, but the sign of Jonas the *p*
Lk 13:33 that a *p* perish out of Jerusalem
Lk 20:6 be persuaded that John was a *p*
Lk 24:19 which was a *p* mighty in deed and
Jn 1:21 Art thou that *p*
Jn 1:23 of the Lord, as said the *p* Esaias
Jn 1:25 Christ, nor Elias, neither that *p*
Jn 4:19 Sir, I perceive that thou art a *p*
Jn 4:44 that a *p* hath no honour in his
Jn 6:14 This is of a truth that *p* that
Jn 7:40 said, Of a truth this is the *P*
Jn 7:52 for out of Galilee ariseth no *p*
Jn 9:17 He said, He is a *p*
Jn 12:38 Esaias the *p* might be fulfilled
Acts 2:16 which was spoken by the *p* Joel
Acts 2:30 Therefore being a *p*, and knowing
Acts 3:22 A *p* shall the Lord your God raise
Acts 3:23 soul, which will not hear that *p*
Acts 7:37 A *p* shall the Lord your God raise
Acts 7:48 as saith the *p*,
Acts 8:28 in his chariot read Esaias the *p*
Acts 8:30 and heard him read the *p* Esaias
Acts 8:34 thee, of whom speaketh the *p* this
Acts 13:6 a certain sorcerer, a false *p*
Acts 13:20 fifty years, until Samuel the *p*
Acts 21:10 came down from Judaea a certain *p*
Acts 28:25 by Esaias the *p* unto our fathers
1Cor 14:37 any man think himself to be a *p*
Titus 1:12 even a *p* of their own, said, The
2Pet 2:16 voice forbad the madness of the *p*
Rev 16:13 out of the mouth of the false *p*
Rev 19:20 with him the false *p* that wrought
Rev 20:10 the beast and the false *p* are

## PROPHETESS

Ex 15:20 And Miriam the *p*, the sister of
Judg 4:4 And Deborah, a *p*, the wife of
2Kin 22:14 Asahiah, went unto Huldah the *p*
2Chr 34:22 appointed, went to Huldah the *p*
Neh 6:14 on the *p* Noadiah, and the rest of
Is 8:3 And I went unto the *p*
Lk 2:36 And there was one Anna, a *p*
Rev 2:20 which calleth herself a *p*

## PROPHETS

Num 11:29 that all the LORD's people were *p*
1Sa 10:5 thou shalt meet a company of *p*
1Sa 10:10 behold, a company of *p* met him
1Sa 10:11 behold, he prophesied among the *p*
1Sa 10:11 Is Saul also among the *p*

1Sa 10:12 proverb, Is Saul also among the *p*
1Sa 19:20 the company of the *p* prophesying
1Sa 19:24 say, Is Saul also among the *p*
1Sa 28:6 by dreams, nor by Urim, nor by *p*
1Sa 28:15 me no more, neither by *p*, nor by
1Kin 18:4 Jezebel cut off the *p* of the LORD
1Kin 18:4 that Obadiah took an hundred *p*
1Kin 18:13 Jezebel slew the *p* of the LORD
1Kin 18:13 the LORD's *p* by fifty in a cave
1Kin 18:19 the *p* of Baal four hundred and
1Kin 18:19 the *p* of the groves four hundred,
1Kin 18:20 gathered the *p* together unto
1Kin 18:22 but Baal's *p* are four hundred and
1Kin 18:25 And Elijah said unto the *p* of Baal
1Kin 18:40 unto them, Take the *p* of Baal
1Kin 19:1 slain all the *p* with the sword
1Kin 19:10 slain thy *p* with the sword
1Kin 19:14 slain thy *p* with the sword
1Kin 20:35 *p* said unto his neighbour in the
1Kin 20:41 him that he was of the *p*
1Kin 22:6 of Israel gathered the *p* together
1Kin 22:10 all the *p* prophesied before them
1Kin 22:12 all the *p* prophesied so, saying,
1Kin 22:13 the words of the *p* declare good
1Kin 22:22 spirit in the mouth of all his *p*
1Kin 22:23 in the mouth of all these thy *p*
2Kin 2:3 the sons of the *p* that were at
2Kin 2:5 the sons of the *p* that were at
2Kin 2:7 men of the sons of the *p* went
2Kin 2:15 when the sons of the *p* which were
2Kin 3:13 get thee to the *p* of thy father
2Kin 3:13 and to the *p* of thy mother
2Kin 4:1 of the sons of the *p* unto Elisha
2Kin 4:38 the sons of the *p* were sitting
2Kin 4:38 pottage for the sons of the *p*
2Kin 5:22 young men of the sons of the *p*
2Kin 6:1 the sons of the *p* said unto
2Kin 9:1 one of the children of the *p*
2Kin 9:7 the blood of my servants the *p*
2Kin 10:19 call unto me all the *p* of Baal
2Kin 17:13 and against Judah, by all the *p*
2Kin 17:13 sent to you by my servants the *p*
2Kin 17:23 said by all his servants the *p*
2Kin 21:10 LORD spake by his servants the *p*
2Kin 23:2 him, and the priests, and the *p*
2Kin 24:2 he spake by his servants the *p*
1Chr 16:22 mine anointed, and do my *p* no harm
2Chr 18:5 together of *p* four hundred men
2Chr 18:9 all the *p* prophesied before them
2Chr 18:11 all the *p* prophesied so, saying,
2Chr 18:12 the words of the *p* declare good
2Chr 18:21 spirit in the mouth of all his *p*
2Chr 18:22 in the mouth of these thy *p*
2Chr 20:20 believe his *p*, so shall ye
2Chr 24:19 Yet he sent *p* to them, to bring
2Chr 29:25 commandment of the LORD by his *p*
2Chr 36:16 his words, and misused his *p*
Ezr 5:1 Then the *p*, Haggai the prophet,
Ezr 5:2 with them were the *p* of God
Ezr 9:11 commanded by thy servants the *p*
Neh 6:7 thou hast also appointed *p* to
Neh 6:14 Noadiah, and the rest of the *p*
Neh 9:26 slew thy *p* which testified
Neh 9:30 them by thy spirit in thy *p*
Neh 9:32 and on our priests, and on our *p*
Ps 105:15 mine anointed, and do my *p* no harm
Is 29:10 the *p* and your rulers, the seers
Is 30:10 and to the *p*, Prophesy not unto us
Jer 2:8 the *p* prophesied by Baal, and
Jer 2:26 and their priests, and their *p*
Jer 2:30 own sword hath devoured your *p*
Jer 4:9 astonished, and the *p* shall wonder
Jer 5:13 the *p* shall become wind, and the
Jer 5:31 The *p* prophesy falsely, and the
Jer 7:25 unto you all my servants the *p*
Jer 8:1 priests, and the bones of the *p*
Jer 13:13 throne, and the priests, and the *p*
Jer 14:13 the *p* say unto them, Ye shall not
Jer 14:14 The *p* prophesy lies in my name
Jer 14:15 the *p* that prophesy in my name
Jer 14:15 famine shall those *p* be consumed
Jer 23:9 me is broken because of the *p*
Jer 23:13 seen folly in the *p* of Samaria
Jer 23:14 I have seen also in the *p* of
Jer 23:15 LORD of hosts concerning the *p*
Jer 23:15 for from the *p* of Jerusalem is
Jer 23:16 of the *p* that prophesy unto you
Jer 23:21 I have not sent these *p*, yet they
Jer 23:25 I have heard what the *p* said
Jer 23:26 heart of the *p* that prophesy lies
Jer 23:26 they are *p* of the deceit of their
Jer 23:30 behold, I am against the *p*
Jer 23:31 Behold, I am against the *p*
Jer 25:4 unto you all his servants the *p*
Jer 26:5 to the words of my servants the *p*
Jer 26:7 So the priests and the *p* and all
Jer 26:8 people, that the priests and the *p*
Jer 26:11 the *p* unto the princes and to all
Jer 26:16 unto the priests and to the *p*
Jer 27:9 hearken not ye to your *p*, nor to
Jer 27:14 of the *p* that speak unto you
Jer 27:15 the *p* that prophesy unto you
Jer 27:16 of your *p* that prophesy unto you
Jer 27:18 But if they be *p*, and if the word
Jer 28:8 The *p* that have been before me and
Jer 29:1 and to the priests, and to the *p*
Jer 29:8 Let not your *p* and your diviners,
Jer 29:15 hath raised us up *p* in Babylon
Jer 29:19 unto them by my servants the *p*
Jer 32:32 their priests, and their *p*
Jer 35:15 unto you all my servants the *p*
Jer 37:19 Where are now your *p* which
Jer 44:4 unto you all my servants the *p*
Lam 2:9 her *p* also find no vision from
Lam 2:14 Thy *p* have seen vain and foolish
Lam 4:13 For the sins of her *p*, and the
Eze 13:2 prophesy against the *p* of Israel
Eze 13:3 Woe unto the foolish *p*, that
Eze 13:4 thy *p* are like the foxes in the
Eze 13:9 be upon the *p* that see vanity
Eze 13:16 the *p* of Israel which prophesy
Eze 22:25 of her *p* in the midst thereof
Eze 22:28 her *p* have daubed them with
Eze 38:17 by my servants the *p* of Israel
Dan 9:6 hearkened unto thy servants the *p*
Dan 9:10 before us by his servants the *p*
Hos 6:5 have I hewed them by the *p*
Hos 12:10 I have also spoken by the *p*
Hos 12:10 by the ministry of the *p*
Amos 2:11 And I raised up of your sons for *p*
Amos 2:12 and commanded the *p*, saying,
Amos 3:7 secret unto his servants the *p*
Mic 3:5 the *p* that make my people err
Mic 3:6 the sun shall go down over the *p*
Mic 3:11 the *p* thereof divine for money
Zeph 3:4 Her *p* are light and treacherous
Zec 1:4 unto whom the former *p* have cried
Zec 1:5 and the *p*, do they live for ever
Zec 1:6 I commanded my servants the *p*
Zec 7:3 of the LORD of hosts, and to the *p*
Zec 7:7 LORD hath cried by the former *p*
Zec 7:12 in his spirit by the former *p*
Zec 8:9 these words by the mouth of the *p*
Zec 13:2 and also I will cause the *p*
Zec 13:4 that the *p* shall be ashamed every
Mt 2:23 which was spoken by the *p*
Mt 5:12 they the *p* which were before you
Mt 5:17 come to destroy the law, or the *p*
Mt 7:12 for this is the law and the *p*
Mt 7:15 Beware of false *p*, which come to
Mt 11:13 For all the *p* and the law
Mt 13:17 I say unto you, That many *p*
Mt 16:14 others, Jeremias, or one of the *p*
Mt 22:40 hang all the law and the *p*
Mt 23:29 ye build the tombs of the *p*
Mt 23:30 with them in the blood of the *p*
Mt 23:31 of them which killed the *p*
Mt 23:34 behold, I send unto you *p*
Mt 23:37 thou that killest the *p*, and
Mt 24:11 And many false *p* shall rise
Mt 24:24 arise false Christs, and false *p*
Mt 26:56 of the *p* might be fulfilled
Mk 1:2 As it is written in the *p*
Mk 6:15 is a prophet, or as one of the *p*
Mk 8:28 and others, One of the *p*
Mk 13:22 false *p* shall rise, and shall shew
Lk 1:70 spake by the mouth of his holy *p*
Lk 6:23 did their fathers unto the *p*
Lk 6:26 did their fathers to the false *p*
Lk 9:8 one of the old *p* was risen again
Lk 9:19 one of the old *p* is risen again
Lk 10:24 For I tell you, that many *p*
Lk 11:47 ye build the sepulchres of the *p*
Lk 11:49 wisdom of God, I will send them *p*
Lk 11:50 That the blood of all the *p*
Lk 13:28 and Isaac, and Jacob, and all the *p*
Lk 13:34 Jerusalem, which killest the *p*
Lk 16:16 The law and the *p* were until John
Lk 16:29 him, They have Moses and the *p*
Lk 16:31 If they hear not Moses and the *p*
Lk 18:31 things that are written by the *p*
Lk 24:25 all that the *p* have spoken
Lk 24:27 beginning at Moses and all the *p*
Lk 24:44 in the law of Moses, and in the *p*
Jn 1:45 whom Moses in the law, and the *p*
Jn 6:45 It is written in the *p*, And they
Jn 8:52 Abraham is dead, and the *p*
Jn 8:53 and the *p* are dead
Acts 3:18 shewed by the mouth of all his *p*
Acts 3:21 his holy *p* since the world began
Acts 3:24 all the *p* from Samuel and those
Acts 3:25 Ye are the children of the *p*
Acts 7:42 is written in the book of the *p*
Acts 7:52 Which of the *p* have not your
Acts 10:43 To him give all the *p* witness
Acts 11:27 in these days came *p* from
Acts 13:1 that was at Antioch certain *p*
Acts 13:15 the *p* the rulers of the synagogue
Acts 13:27 nor yet the voices of the *p* which
Acts 13:40 you, which is spoken of in the *p*
Acts 15:15 to this agree the words of the *p*
Acts 15:32 being *p* also themselves, exhorted
Acts 24:14 written in the law and in the *p*
Acts 26:22 things than those which the *p*
Acts 26:27 Agrippa, believest thou the *p*
Acts 28:23 the law of Moses, and out of the *p*
Rom 1:2 by his *p* in the holy scriptures
Rom 3:21 witnessed by the law and the *p*
Rom 11:3 Lord, they have killed thy *p*
Rom 16:26 and by the scriptures of the *p*
1Cor 12:28 first apostles, secondarily *p*
1Cor 12:29 are all *p*?
1Cor 14:29 Let the *p* speak two or three, and
1Cor 14:32 the *p* are subject to the *p*
Eph 2:20 foundation of the apostles and *p*
Eph 3:5 holy apostles and *p* by the Spirit
Eph 4:11 and some, *p*
1Th 2:15 the Lord Jesus, and their own *p*
Heb 1:1 past unto the fathers by the *p*
Heb 11:32 also, and Samuel, and of the *p*
Jas 5:10 Take, my brethren, the *p*, who
1Pet 1:10 salvation the *p* have enquired
2Pet 2:1 But there were false *p* also among
2Pet 3:2 were spoken before by the holy *p*
1Jn 4:1 because many false *p* are gone out
Rev 10:7 declared to his servants the *p*
Rev 11:10 because these two *p* tormented
Rev 11:18 reward unto thy servants the *p*
Rev 16:6 shed the blood of saints and *p*
Rev 18:20 heaven, and ye holy apostles and *p*
Rev 18:24 in her was found the blood of *p*
Rev 22:6 the Lord God of the holy *p* sent
Rev 22:9 and of thy brethren the *p*

**PROSPECT**

Eze 40:44 their *p* was toward the south
Eze 40:44 having the *p* toward the north
Eze 40:45 whose *p* is toward the south, is
Eze 40:46 the chamber whose *p* is toward the
Eze 42:15 gate whose *p* is toward the east
Eze 43:4 gate whose *p* is toward the east

**PROSPER**

Gen 24:40 his angel with thee, and *p* thy way
Gen 24:42 if now thou do *p* my way which I
Gen 39:3 all that he did to *p* in his hand
Gen 39:23 he did, the LORD made it to *p*
Num 14:41 but it shall not *p*
Deut 28:29 and thou shalt not *p* in thy ways
Deut 29:9 that ye may *p* in all that ye do
Josh 1:7 that thou mayest *p* whithersoever
1Kin 2:3 that thou mayest *p* in all that
1Kin 22:12 Go up to Ramoth-gilead, and *p*
1Kin 22:15 And he answered him, Go, and *p*
1Chr 22:11 *p* thou, and build the house of the
1Chr 22:13 Then shalt thou *p*, if thou takest
2Chr 13:12 for ye shall not *p*
2Chr 18:11 Go up to Ramoth-gilead, and *p*
2Chr 18:14 And he said, Go ye up, and *p*
2Chr 20:20 his prophets, so shall ye *p*
2Chr 24:20 of the LORD, that ye cannot *p*
2Chr 26:5 the LORD, God made him to *p*
Neh 1:11 and *p*, I pray thee, thy servant
Neh 2:20 The God of heaven, he will *p* us
Job 12:6 The tabernacles of robbers *p*
Ps 1:3 and whatsoever he doeth shall *p*
Ps 73:12 the ungodly, who *p* in the world
Ps 122:6 they shall *p* that love thee
Prov 28:13 covereth his sins shall not *p*
Eccl 11:6 thou knowest not whether shall *p*
Is 53:10 of the LORD shall *p* in his hand

Is 54:17 is formed against thee shall *p*
Is 55:11 it shall *p* in the thing whereto I
Jer 2:37 and thou shalt not *p* in them
Jer 5:28 of the fatherless, yet they *p*
Jer 10:21 therefore they shall not *p*
Jer 12:1 doth the way of the wicked *p*
Jer 20:11 for they shall not *p*
Jer 22:30 man that shall not *p* in his days
Jer 22:30 for no man of his seed shall *p*
Jer 23:5 and a King shall reign and *p*
Jer 32:5 the Chaldeans, ye shall not *p*
Lam 1:5 are the chief, her enemies *p*
Eze 16:13 thou didst *p* into a kingdom
Eze 17:9 Shall it *p*?
Eze 17:10 behold, being planted, shall it *p*
Eze 17:15 Shall he *p*?
Dan 8:24 destroy wonderfully, and shall *p*
Dan 8:25 cause craft to *p* in his hand
Dan 11:27 but it shall not *p*
Dan 11:36 shall *p* till the indignation be
3Jn 2 all things that thou mayest *p*

## PROSPERED
Gen 24:56 seeing the LORD hath *p* my way
Judg 4:24 hand of the children of Israel *p*
2Sa 11:7 the people did, and how the war *p*
2Kin 18:7 he *p* whithersoever he went forth
1Chr 29:23 instead of David his father, and *p*
2Chr 14:7 So they built and *p*
2Chr 31:21 did it with all his heart, and *p*
2Chr 32:30 Hezekiah *p* in all his works
Ezr 6:14 they *p* through the prophesying of
Job 9:4 himself against him, and hath *p*
Dan 6:28 So this Daniel *p* in the reign of
Dan 8:12 and it practised, and *p*
1Cor 16:2 him in store, as God hath *p* him

## PROSPERETH
Ezr 5:8 fast on, and *p* in their hands
Ps 37:7 because of him who *p* in his way
Prov 17:8 whithersoever it turneth, it *p*
3Jn 2 be in health, even as thy soul *p*

## PROSPERITY
Deut 23:6 nor their *p* all thy days for ever
1Sa 25:6 ye say to him that liveth in *p*
1Kin 10:7 *p* exceedeth the fame which I
Job 15:21 in *p* the destroyer shall come
Job 36:11 they shall spend their days in *p*
Ps 30:6 in my *p* I said, I shall never be
Ps 35:27 pleasure in the *p* of his servant
Ps 73:3 when I saw the *p* of the wicked
Ps 118:25 LORD, I beseech thee, send now *p*
Ps 122:7 walls, and *p* within thy palaces
Prov 1:32 the *p* of fools shall destroy them
Eccl 7:14 In the day of *p* be joyful
Jer 22:21 I spake unto thee in thy *p*
Jer 33:9 for all the *p* that I procure unto
Lam 3:17 I forgat *p*
Zec 1:17 My cities through *p* shall yet be
Zec 7:7 Jerusalem was inhabited and in *p*

## PROSPEROUS
Gen 24:21 had made his journey *p* or not
Gen 39:2 with Joseph, and he was a *p* man
Josh 1:8 then thou shalt make thy way *p*
Judg 18:5 our way which we go shall be *p*
Job 8:6 habitation of thy righteousness *p*
Is 48:15 him, and he shall make his way *p*
Zec 8:12 For the seed shall be *p*
Rom 1:10 now at length I might have a *p*

## PROUD
Job 9:13 the *p* helpers do stoop under him
Job 26:12 he smiteth through the *p*
Job 38:11 here shall thy *p* waves be stayed
Job 40:11 and behold every one that is *p*
Job 40:12 Look on every one that is *p*
Ps 12:3 the tongue that speaketh *p* things
Ps 31:23 plentifully rewardeth the *p* doer
Ps 40:4 trust, and respecteth not the *p*
Ps 86:14 the *p* are risen against me, and
Ps 94:2 render a reward to the *p*
Ps 101:5 a *p* heart will not I suffer
Ps 119:21 rebuked the *p* that are cursed
Ps 119:51 The *p* have had me greatly in
Ps 119:69 The *p* have forged a lie against
Ps 119:78 Let the *p* be ashamed
Ps 119:85 The *p* have digged pits for me,
Ps 119:122 let not the *p* oppress me
Ps 123:4 and with the contempt of the *p*
Ps 124:5 Then the *p* waters had gone over
Ps 138:6 but the *p* he knoweth afar off
Ps 140:5 The *p* have hid a snare for me, and
Prov 6:17 A *p* look, a lying tongue, and
Prov 15:25 will destroy the house of the *p*
Prov 16:5 Every one that is *p* in heart is
Prov 16:19 to divide the spoil with the *p*
Prov 21:4 a *p* heart, and the plowing of the
Prov 21:24 *P* and haughty scorner is his name,
Prov 21:24 who dealeth in *p* wrath
Prov 28:25 He that is of a *p* heart stirreth
Eccl 7:8 is better than the *p* in spirit
Is 2:12 shall be upon every one that is *p*
Is 13:11 the arrogancy of the *p* to cease
Is 16:6 he is very *p*
Jer 13:15 be not *p*
Jer 43:2 son of Kareah, and all the *p* men
Jer 48:29 (he is exceeding *p*) his loftiness
Jer 50:29 she hath been *p* against the LORD
Jer 50:31 I am against thee, O thou most *p*
Jer 50:32 the most *p* shall stumble and fall,
Hab 2:5 by wine, he is a *p* man, neither
Mal 3:15 And now we call the *p* happy
Mal 4:1 and all the *p*, yea, and all that do
Lk 1:51 he hath scattered the *p* in the
Rom 1:30 haters of God, despiteful, *p*
1Ti 6:4 He is *p*, knowing nothing, but
2Ti 3:2 own selves, covetous, boasters, *p*
Jas 4:6 he saith, God resisteth the *p*
1Pet 5:5 for God resisteth the *p*, and

## PROUDLY
Ex 18:11 they dealt *p* he was above them
1Sa 2:3 Talk no more so exceeding *p*
Neh 9:10 that they dealt *p* against them
Neh 9:16 But they and our fathers dealt *p*
Neh 9:29 yet they dealt *p*, and hearkened
Ps 17:10 with their mouth they speak *p*
Ps 31:18 which speak grievous things *p*
Is 3:5 himself *p* against the ancient
Obad 12 spoken *p* in the day of distress

## PROVE
Ex 16:4 rate every day, that I may *p* them
Ex 20:20 for God is come to *p* you, and that
Deut 8:2 to *p* thee, to know what was in
Deut 8:16 thee, and that he might *p* thee
Deut 33:8 one, whom thou didst *p* at Massah
Judg 2:22 That through them I may *p* Israel
Judg 3:1 to *p* Israel by them, even as many
Judg 3:4 they were to *p* Israel by them, to
Judg 6:39 let me *p*, I pray thee, but this
1Kin 10:1 she came to *p* him with hard
2Chr 9:1 she came to *p* Solomon with hard
Job 9:20 it shall also *p* me perverse
Ps 26:2 Examine me, O LORD, and *p* me
Eccl 2:1 I will *p* thee with mirth,
Dan 1:12 *P* thy servants, I beseech thee,
Mal 3:10 *p* me now herewith, saith the LORD
Lk 14:19 yoke of oxen, and I go to *p* them
Jn 6:6 And this he said to *p* him
Acts 24:13 Neither can they *p* the things
Acts 25:7 Paul, which they could not *p*
Rom 12:2 that ye may *p* what is that good,
2Cor 8:8 to *p* the sincerity of your love
2Cor 13:5 *p* your own selves
Gal 6:4 But let every man *p* his own work
1Th 5:21 *P* all things

## PROVED
Gen 42:15 Hereby ye shall be *p*
Gen 42:16 prison, that your words may be *p*
Ex 15:25 an ordinance, and there he *p* them
1Sa 17:39 for he had not *p* it
1Sa 17:39 for I have not *p* them
Ps 17:3 Thou hast *p* mine heart
Ps 66:10 For thou, O God, hast *p* us
Ps 81:7 I *p* thee at the waters of Meribah
Ps 95:9 tempted me, *p* me, and saw my work
Eccl 7:23 All this have I *p* by wisdom
Dan 1:14 this matter, and *p* them ten days
Rom 3:9 for we have before *p* both Jews
2Cor 8:22 *p* diligent in many things
1Ti 3:10 And let these also first be *p*
Heb 3:9 *p* me, and saw my works forty years

## PROVENDER
Gen 24:25 *p* enough, and room to lodge in
Gen 24:32 *p* for the camels, and water to
Gen 42:27 sack to give his ass *p* in the inn
Gen 43:24 and he gave their asses *p*
Judg 19:19 is both straw and *p* for our asses
Judg 19:21 house, and gave *p* unto the asses
Is 30:24 ear the ground shall eat clean *p*

## PROVERB
Deut 28:37 shalt become an astonishment, a *p*
1Sa 10:12 Therefore it became a *p*, Is Saul
1Sa 24:13 As saith the *p* of the ancients,
1Kin 9:7 and Israel shall be a *p* and a
2Chr 7:20 sight, and will make it to be a *p*
Ps 69:11 and I became a *p* to them
Prov 1:6 To understand a *p*, and the
Is 14:4 *p* against the king of Babylon
Jer 24:9 hurt, to be a reproach and a *p*
Eze 12:22 what is that *p* that ye have in
Eze 12:23 I will make this *p* to cease
Eze 12:23 no more use it as a *p* in Israel
Eze 14:8 and will make him a sign and a *p*
Eze 16:44 shall use this *p* against thee
Eze 18:2 that ye use this *p* concerning the
Eze 18:3 any more to use this *p* in Israel
Hab 2:6 a taunting *p* against him, and say,
Lk 4:23 Ye will surely say unto me this *p*
Jn 16:29 thou plainly, and speakest no *p*
2Pet 2:22 unto them according to the true *p*

## PROVERBS
Num 21:27 they that speak in *p* say, Come
1Kin 4:32 And he spake three thousand *p*
Prov 1:1 The *P* of Solomon the son of David
Prov 10:1 The *p* of Solomon
Prov 25:1 These are also *p* of Solomon
Eccl 12:9 out, and set in order many *p*
Eze 16:44 every one that useth *p* shall use
Jn 16:25 have I spoken unto you in *p*
Jn 16:25 shall no more speak unto you in *p*

## PROVIDE
Gen 22:8 God will *p* himself a lamb for a
Gen 30:30 now when shall I *p* for mine own
Ex 18:21 Moreover thou shalt *p* out of all
1Sa 16:17 *P* me now a man that can play well
2Chr 2:7 whom David my father did *p*
Ps 78:20 can he *p* flesh for his people
Mt 10:9 *P* neither gold, nor silver, nor
Lk 12:33 *p* yourselves bags which wax not
Acts 23:24 *p* them beasts, that they may set
Rom 12:17 *P* things honest in the sight of
1Ti 5:8 But if any *p* not for his own, and

## PROVIDED
Deut 33:21 he *p* the first part for himself,
1Sa 16:1 for I have *p* me a king among his
2Sa 19:32 he had *p* the king of sustenance
1Kin 4:7 which *p* victuals for the king and
1Kin 4:27 those officers *p* victual for king
2Chr 32:29 Moreover he *p* him cities, and
Ps 65:9 corn, when thou hast so *p* for it
Lk 12:20 things be, which thou hast *p*
Heb 11:40 God having *p* some better thing

## PROVINCE
Ezr 2:1 of the *p* that went up out of the
Ezr 5:8 that we went into the *p* of Judea
Ezr 6:2 that is in the *p* of the Medes
Ezr 7:16 find in all the *p* of Babylon
Neh 1:3 in the *p* are in great affliction
Neh 7:6 These are the children of the *p*
Neh 11:3 of the *p* that dwelt in Jerusalem
Est 1:22 into every *p* according to the
Est 3:12 governors that were over every *p*
Est 3:12 every *p* according to the writing
Est 3:14 to be given in every *p* was
Est 4:3 And in every *p*, whithersoever the
Est 8:9 unto every *p* according to the
Est 8:11 *p* that would assault them, both
Est 8:13 to be given in every *p* was
Est 8:17 And in every *p*, and in every city,
Est 9:28 generation, every family, every *p*
Eccl 5:8 of judgment and justice in a *p*
Dan 2:48 ruler over the whole *p* of Babylon
Dan 2:49 the affairs of the *p* of Babylon
Dan 3:1 of Dura, in the *p* of Babylon
Dan 3:12 the affairs of the *p* of Babylon
Dan 3:30 and Abed-nego, in the *p* of Babylon
Dan 8:2 palace, which is in the *p* of Elam
Dan 11:24 upon the fattest places of the *p*
Acts 23:34 letter, he asked of what *p* he was
Acts 25:1 when Festus was come into the *p*

## PROVINCES
1Kin 20:14 young men of the princes of the *p*
1Kin 20:15 young men of the princes of the *p*
1Kin 20:17 princes of the *p* went out first
1Kin 20:19 of the *p* came out of the city
Ezr 4:15 city, and hurtful unto kings and *p*
Est 1:1 an hundred and seven and twenty *p*

Est 1:3 the nobles and princes of the *p*
Est 1:16 all the *p* of the king Ahasuerus
Est 1:22 letters into all the king's *p*
Est 2:3 in all the *p* of his kingdom
Est 2:18 and he made a release to the *p*
Est 3:8 in all the *p* of thy kingdom
Est 3:13 by posts into all the king's *p*
Est 4:11 and the people of the king's *p*
Est 8:5 which are in all the king's *p*
Est 8:9 rulers of the *p* which are from
Est 8:9 an hundred twenty and seven *p*
Est 8:12 in all the *p* of king Ahasuerus
Est 9:2 all the *p* of the king Ahasuerus
Est 9:3 And all the rulers of the *p*
Est 9:4 went out throughout all the *p*
Est 9:12 done in the rest of the king's *p*
Est 9:16 *p* gathered themselves together
Est 9:20 all the *p* of the king Ahasuerus
Est 9:30 seven *p* of the kingdom of
Eccl 2:8 treasure of kings and of the *p*
Lam 1:1 nations, and princess among the *p*
Eze 19:8 him on every side from the *p*
Dan 3:2 and all the rulers of the *p*
Dan 3:3 and all the rulers of the *p*

## PROVISION

Gen 42:25 and to give them *p* for the way
Gen 45:21 and gave them *p* for the way
Josh 9:5 all the bread of their *p* was dry
Josh 9:12 our bread we took hot for our *p*
1Kin 4:7 man his month in a year made *p*
1Kin 4:22 Solomon's *p* for one day was
2Kin 6:23 And he prepared great *p* for them
1Chr 29:19 for the which I have made *p*
Ps 132:15 I will abundantly bless her *p*
Dan 1:5 them a daily *p* of the king's meat
Rom 13:14 make not *p* for the flesh, to

## PROVOCATION

1Kin 15:30 by his *p* wherewith he provoked
1Kin 21:22 for the *p* wherewith thou hast
Job 17:2 not mine eye continue in their *p*
Ps 95:8 not your heart, as in the *p*
Jer 32:31 been to me as a *p* of mine anger
Eze 20:28 presented the *p* of their offering
Heb 3:8 not your hearts, as in the *p*
Heb 3:15 not your hearts, as in the *p*

## PROVOKE

Ex 23:21 him, and obey his voice, *p* him not
Num 14:11 How long will this people *p* me
Deut 4:25 LORD thy God, to *p* him to anger
Deut 9:18 of the LORD, to *p* him to anger
Deut 31:20 *p* me, and break my covenant
Deut 31:29 to *p* him to anger through the
Deut 32:21 I will *p* them to anger with a
1Kin 14:9 to *p* me to anger, and hast cast me
1Kin 16:2 to *p* me to anger with their sins
1Kin 16:26 to *p* the LORD God of Israel to
1Kin 16:33 Ahab did more to *p* the LORD God
2Kin 17:11 things to *p* the LORD to anger
2Kin 17:17 of the LORD, to *p* him to anger
2Kin 21:6 of the LORD, to *p* him to anger
2Kin 22:17 that they might *p* me to anger
2Kin 23:19 had made to *p* the LORD to anger
2Chr 33:6 of the LORD, to *p* him to anger
2Chr 34:25 that they might *p* me to anger
Job 12:6 they that *p* God are secure
Ps 78:40 How oft did they *p* him in the
Is 3:8 to *p* the eyes of his glory
Jer 7:18 gods, that they may *p* me to anger
Jer 7:19 Do they *p* me to anger
Jer 7:19 do they not *p* themselves to the
Jer 11:17 *p* me to anger in offering incense
Jer 25:6 *p* me not to anger with the works
Jer 25:7 that ye might *p* me to anger with
Jer 32:29 unto other gods, to *p* me to anger
Jer 32:32 they have done to *p* me to anger
Jer 44:3 have committed to *p* me to anger
Jer 44:8 In that ye *p* me unto wrath with
Eze 8:17 and have returned to *p* me to anger
Eze 16:26 thy whoredoms, to *p* me to anger
Lk 11:53 to *p* him to speak of many things
Rom 10:19 I will *p* you to jealousy by them
Rom 11:11 for to *p* them to jealousy
Rom 11:14 If by any means I may *p* to
1Cor 10:22 Do we *p* the Lord to jealousy
Eph 6:4 *p* not your children to wrath
Col 3:21 *p* not your children to anger,
Heb 3:16 some, when they had heard, did *p*
Heb 10:24 one another to *p* unto love

## PROVOKED

Num 14:23 any of them that *p* me see it
Num 16:30 that these men have *p* the LORD
Deut 9:8 Also in Horeb ye *p* the LORD to
Deut 9:22 ye *p* the LORD to wrath
Deut 32:16 They *p* him to jealousy with
Deut 32:16 abominations *p* they him to anger
Deut 32:21 they have *p* me to anger with
Judg 2:12 unto them, and *p* the LORD to anger
1Sa 1:6 And her adversary also *p* her sore
1Sa 1:7 house of the LORD, so she *p* her
1Kin 14:22 they *p* him to jealousy with their
1Kin 15:30 *p* the LORD God of Israel to anger
1Kin 21:22 wherewith thou hast *p* me to anger
1Kin 22:53 *p* to anger the LORD God of Israel
2Kin 21:15 have *p* me to anger, since the day
2Kin 23:26 that Manasseh had *p* him withal
1Chr 21:1 and *p* David to number Israel
2Chr 28:25 *p* to anger the LORD God of his
Ezr 5:12 *p* the God of heaven unto wrath
Neh 4:5 for they have *p* thee to anger
Ps 78:56 *p* the most high God, and kept not
Ps 78:58 For they *p* him to anger with
Ps 106:7 but *p* him at the sea, even at the
Ps 106:29 Thus they *p* him to anger with
Ps 106:33 Because they *p* his spirit
Ps 106:43 but they *p* him with their counsel
Is 1:4 they have *p* the Holy One of
Jer 8:19 Why have they *p* me to anger with
Jer 32:30 *p* me to anger with the work of
Hos 12:14 Ephraim *p* him to anger most
Zec 8:14 when your fathers *p* me to wrath
1Cor 13:5 not her own, is not easily *p*
2Cor 9:2 and your zeal hath *p* very many

## PROVOKING

Deut 32:19 because of the *p* of his sons
1Kin 14:15 their groves, *p* the LORD to anger
1Kin 16:7 in *p* him to anger with the work
1Kin 16:13 in *p* the LORD God of Israel to
Ps 78:17 sinned yet more against him by *p*
Gal 5:26 *p* one another, envying one

## PRUDENT

1Sa 16:18 *p* in matters, and a comely person,
Prov 12:16 but a *p* man covereth shame
Prov 12:23 A *p* man concealeth knowledge
Prov 13:16 Every *p* man dealeth with
Prov 14:8 The wisdom of the *p* is to
Prov 14:15 but the *p* man looketh well to his
Prov 14:18 but the *p* are crowned with
Prov 15:5 he that regardeth reproof is *p*
Prov 16:21 wise in heart shall be called *p*
Prov 18:15 The heart of the *p* getteth
Prov 19:14 a *p* wife is from the LORD
Prov 22:3 A *p* man foreseeth the evil, and
Prov 27:12 A *p* man foreseeth the evil, and
Is 3:2 judge, and the prophet, and the *p*
Is 5:21 own eyes, and *p* in their own sight
Is 10:13 for I am *p*
Is 29:14 of their *p* men shall be hid
Jer 49:7 is counsel perished from the *p*
Hos 14:9 *p*, and he shall know them
Amos 5:13 Therefore the *p* shall keep
Mt 11:25 these things from the wise and *p*
Lk 10:21 these things from the wise and *p*
Acts 13:7 country, Sergius Paulus, a *p* man
1Cor 1:19 the understanding of the *p*

## PRUNINGHOOKS

Is 2:4 and their spears into *p*
Is 18:5 both cut off the sprigs with *p*
Joel 3:10 swords, and your *p* into spears
Mic 4:3 and their spears into *p*

## PSALMS

1Chr 16:9 sing *p* unto him, talk ye of all
Ps 95:2 a joyful noise unto him with *p*
Ps 105:2 Sing unto him, sing *p* unto him
Lk 20:42 himself saith in the book of *P*
Lk 24:44 and in the prophets, and in the *p*
Acts 1:20 it is written in the book of *P*
Eph 5:19 Speaking to yourselves in *p*
Col 3:16 and admonishing one another in *p*
Jas 5:13 let him sing *p*

## PSALTERIES

2Sa 6:5 fir wood, even on harps, and on *p*
1Kin 10:12 harps also and *p* for singers
1Chr 13:8 singing, and with harps, and with *p*
1Chr 15:16 with instruments of musick, *p*
1Chr 15:20 and Benaiah, with *p* on Alamoth
1Chr 15:28 cymbals, making a noise with *p*
1Chr 16:5 and Jeiel with *p* and with harps
1Chr 25:1 prophesy with harps, with *p*
1Chr 25:6 of the LORD, with cymbals, *p*
2Chr 5:12 white linen, having cymbals and *p*
2Chr 9:11 palace, and harps and *p* for singers
2Chr 20:28 And they came to Jerusalem with *p*
2Chr 29:25 of the LORD with cymbals, with *p*
Neh 12:27 and with singing, with cymbals, *p*

## PSALTERY

1Sa 10:5 down from the high place with a *p*
Ps 33:2 sing unto him with the *p* and an
Ps 57:8 awake, *p* and harp
Ps 71:22 will also praise thee with the *p*
Ps 81:2 the pleasant harp with the *p*
Ps 92:3 of ten strings, and upon the *p*
Ps 108:2 Awake, *p* and harp
Ps 144:9 upon a *p* and an instrument of ten
Ps 150:3 praise him with the *p* and harp
Dan 3:5 cornet, flute, harp, sackbut, *p*
Dan 3:7 cornet, flute, harp, sackbut, *p*
Dan 3:10 cornet, flute, harp, sackbut, *p*
Dan 3:15 cornet, flute, harp, sackbut, *p*

**PTOLEMAIS** *(tol-e-ma'-is)* See ACCHO. *A seaport between Carmel and Tyre.*
Acts 21:7 course from Tyre, we came to *P*

**PUA** *(pu'ah)* See PUAH. *A son of Issachar.*
Num 26:23 of *P*, the family of the Punites

**PUAH** *(pu'-ah)* See PHUVAH, PUA, PUNITES.
*1. Same as Pua.*
1Chr 7:1 sons of Issachar were, Tola, and *P*
*2. Father of Tola.*
Judg 10:1 defend Israel Tola the son of *P*
*3. A Hebrew midwife in Egypt.*
Ex 1:15 and the name of the other *P*

## PUBLICAN

Mt 10:3 Thomas, and Matthew the *p*
Mt 18:17 thee as an heathen man and a *p*
Lk 5:27 things he went forth, and saw a *p*
Lk 18:10 one a Pharisee, and the other a *p*
Lk 18:11 adulterers, or even as this *p*
Lk 18:13 And the *p*, standing afar off,

## PUBLICANS

Mt 5:46 do not even the *p* the same
Mt 5:47 do not even the *p* so
Mt 9:10 meat in the house, behold, many *p*
Mt 9:11 Why eateth your Master with *p*
Mt 11:19 and a winebibber, a friend of *p*
Mt 21:31 Verily I say unto you, That the *p*
Mt 21:32 but the *p* and the harlots believed
Mk 2:15 sat at meat in his house, many *p*
Mk 2:16 and Pharisees saw him eat with *p*
Mk 2:16 that he eateth and drinketh with *p*
Lk 3:12 Then came also *p* to be baptized
Lk 5:29 and there was a great company of *p*
Lk 5:30 Why do ye eat and drink with *p*
Lk 7:29 people that heard him, and the *p*
Lk 7:34 and a winebibber, a friend of *p*
Lk 15:1 Then drew near unto him all the *p*
Lk 19:2 which was the chief among the *p*

## PUBLISH

Deut 32:3 Because I will *p* the name of the
1Sa 31:9 to *p* it in the house of their
2Sa 1:20 *p* it not in the streets of
Neh 8:15 And that they should *p* and proclaim
Ps 26:7 That I may *p* with the voice of
Jer 4:5 ye in Judah, and *p* in Jerusalem
Jer 4:16 *p* against Jerusalem, that
Jer 5:20 Jacob, and *p* it in Judah, saying,
Jer 31:7 *p* ye, praise ye, and say, O LORD,
Jer 46:14 *p* in Migdol, and *p* in Noph
Jer 50:2 ye among the nations, and *p*
Jer 50:2 *p*, and conceal not
Amos 3:9 *P* in the palaces at Ashdod, and in
Amos 4:5 proclaim and *p* the free offerings
Mk 1:45 went out, and began to *p* it much
Mk 5:20 began to *p* in Decapolis how great

## PUBLISHED

Est 1:20 be *p* throughout all his empire
Est 1:22 that it should be *p* according to
Est 3:14 province was *p* unto all people
Est 8:13 province was *p* unto all people
Ps 68:11 the company of those that *p* it
Jonah 3:7 *p* through Nineveh by the decree
Mk 7:36 the more a great deal they *p* it
Mk 13:10 must first be *p* among all nations
Lk 8:39 *p* throughout the whole city how

Acts 10:37 which was *p* throughout all Judaea
Acts 13:49 the word of the Lord was *p*

**PUBLIUS** *(pub'-le-us) A chief man on Melita.*
Acts 28:7 of the island, whose name was *P*
Acts 28:8 that the father of *P* lay sick of

**PUDENS** *(pu'-denz) A Christian in Rome.*
2Ti 4:21 Eubulus greeteth thee, and *P*

**PUFFED**
1Cor 4:6 that no one of you be *p* up for
1Cor 4:18 Now some are *p* up, as though I
1Cor 4:19 the speech of them which are *p* up
1Cor 5:2 And ye are *p* up, and have not
1Cor 13:4 vaunteth not itself, is not *p* up
Col 2:18 vainly *p* up by his fleshly mind,

**PUHITES** *(pu'-hites) A family descended from Caleb.*
1Chr 2:53 the Ithrites, and the *P*, and the

**PUL** *(pul)*
*1. Same as Tiglath-pileser.*
2Kin 15:19 *P* the king of Assyria came
2Kin 15:19 Menahem gave *P* a thousand talents
1Chr 5:26 the spirit of *P* king of Assyria
*2. A place near Libya.*
Is 66:19 unto the nations, to Tarshish, *P*

**PULL**
1Kin 13:4 he could not *p* it in again to him
Ps 31:4 *P* me out of the net that they
Is 22:19 thy state shall he *p* thee down
Jer 1:10 to *p* down, and to destroy, and to
Jer 12:3 *p* them out like sheep for the
Jer 18:7 to *p* down, and to destroy it
Jer 24:6 build them, and not *p* them down
Jer 42:10 not *p* you down, and I will plant
Eze 17:9 shall he not *p* up the roots
Mic 2:8 ye *p* off the robe with the
Mt 7:4 Let me *p* out the mote out of
Lk 6:42 let me *p* out the mote that is in
Lk 6:42 to *p* out the mote that is in thy
Lk 12:18 I will *p* down my barns, and build
Lk 14:5 will not straightway *p* him out on

**PULLED**
Gen 8:9 *p* her in unto him into the ark
Gen 19:10 *p* Lot into the house to them, and
Ezr 6:11 let timber be *p* down from his
Lam 3:11 aside my ways, and *p* me in pieces
Amos 9:15 they shall no more be *p* up out of
Zec 7:11 *p* away the shoulder, and stopped
Acts 23:10 have been *p* in pieces of them

**PUNISH**
Lev 26:18 then I will *p* you seven times
Lev 26:24 will *p* you yet seven times for
Prov 17:26 Also to *p* the just is not good,
Is 10:12 I will *p* the fruit of the stout
Is 13:11 I will *p* the world for their evil
Is 24:21 that the LORD shall *p* the host of
Is 26:21 to *p* the inhabitants of the earth
Is 27:1 strong sword shall *p* leviathan
Jer 9:25 that I will *p* all them which are
Jer 11:22 of hosts, Behold, I will *p* them
Jer 13:21 thou say when he shall *p* thee
Jer 21:14 But I will *p* you according to the
Jer 23:34 the LORD, I will even *p* that man
Jer 25:12 that I will *p* the king of Babylon
Jer 27:8 of Babylon, that nation will I *p*
Jer 29:32 I will *p* Shemaiah the Nehelamite,
Jer 30:20 I will *p* all that oppress them
Jer 36:31 And I will *p* him and his seed and
Jer 44:13 For I will *p* them that dwell in
Jer 44:29 that I will *p* you in this place,
Jer 46:25 I will *p* the multitude of No, and
Jer 50:18 I will *p* the king of Babylon and
Jer 51:44 I will *p* Bel in Babylon, and I
Hos 4:9 I will *p* them for their ways, and
Hos 4:14 I will not *p* your daughters when
Hos 12:2 will *p* Jacob according to his
Amos 3:2 therefore I will *p* you for all
Zeph 1:8 that I will *p* the princes
Zeph 1:9 I *p* all those that leap on the
Zeph 1:12 *p* the men that are settled on
Zec 8:14 As I thought to *p* you, when your
Acts 4:21 nothing how they might *p* them

**PUNISHED**
Ex 21:20 he shall be surely *p*
Ex 21:21 a day or two, he shall not be *p*
Ex 21:22 he shall be surely *p*, according
Ezr 9:13 *p* us less than our iniquities
Job 31:11 an iniquity to be *p* by the judges
Job 31:28 an iniquity to be *p* by the judge
Prov 21:11 When the scorner is *p*, the simple
Prov 22:3 but the simple pass on, and are *p*
Prov 27:12 but the simple pass on, and are *p*
Jer 44:13 of Egypt, as I have *p* Jerusalem
Jer 50:18 as I have *p* the king of Assyria
Zeph 3:7 be cut off, howsoever I *p* them
Zec 10:3 the shepherds, and I *p* the goats
Acts 22:5 bound unto Jerusalem, for to be *p*
Acts 26:11 I *p* them oft in every synagogue,
2Th 1:9 Who shall be *p* with everlasting
2Pet 2:9 unto the day of judgment to be *p*

**PUNISHMENT**
Gen 4:13 My *p* is greater than I can bear
Lev 26:41 accept of the *p* of their iniquity
Lev 26:43 accept of the *p* of their iniquity
1Sa 28:10 there shall no *p* happen to thee
Job 31:3 a strange *p* to the workers of
Prov 19:19 man of great wrath shall suffer *p*
Lam 3:39 a man for the *p* of his sins
Lam 4:6 For the *p* of the iniquity of the
Lam 4:6 than the *p* of the sin of Sodom
Lam 4:22 The *p* of thine iniquity is
Eze 14:10 bear the *p* of their iniquity
Eze 14:10 the *p* of the prophet shall be
Eze 14:10 *p* of him that seeketh unto him
Amos 1:3 will not turn away the *p* thereof
Amos 1:6 will not turn away the *p* thereof
Amos 1:9 will not turn away the *p* thereof
Amos 1:11 will not turn away the *p* thereof
Amos 1:13 will not turn away the *p* thereof
Amos 2:1 will not turn away the *p* thereof
Amos 2:4 will not turn away the *p* thereof
Amos 2:6 will not turn away the *p* thereof
Zec 14:19 This shall be the *p* of Egypt
Zec 14:19 the *p* of all nations that come
Mt 25:46 shall go away into everlasting *p*
2Cor 2:6 to such a man is this *p*, which
Heb 10:29 Of how much sorer *p*, suppose ye,
1Pet 2:14 by him for the *p* of evildoers

**PUNITES** *(pu'-nites) Descendents of Pua.*
Num 26:23 of Pua, the family of the *P*

**PUNON** *(pu'-non) An Edomite city.*
Num 33:42 from Zalmonah, and pitched in *P*
Num 33:43 And they departed from *P*, and

**PUR** *(pur)* See PURIM. *Same as Purim.*
Est 3:7 of king Ahasuerus, they cast *P*
Est 9:24 to destroy them, and had cast *P*
Est 9:26 days Purim after the name of *P*

**PURCHASE**
Gen 49:32 The *p* of the field and of the cave
Lev 25:33 if a man *p* of the Levites, then
Jer 32:11 So I took the evidence of the *p*
Jer 32:12 I gave the evidence of the *p* unto
Jer 32:12 that subscribed the book of the *p*
Jer 32:14 evidences, this evidence of the *p*
Jer 32:16 *p* unto Baruch the son of Neriah
1Ti 3:13 *p* to themselves a good degree

**PURCHASED**
Gen 25:10 Abraham *p* of the sons of Heth
Ex 15:16 pass over, which thou hast *p*
Ruth 4:10 have I *p* to be my wife, to raise
Ps 74:2 which thou hast *p* of old
Ps 78:54 which his right hand had *p*
Acts 1:18 Now this man *p* a field with the
Acts 8:20 gift of God may be *p* with money
Acts 20:28 which he hath *p* with his own
Eph 1:14 redemption of the *p* possession

**PURE**
Ex 25:11 thou shalt overlay it with *p* gold
Ex 25:17 shalt make a mercy seat of *p* gold
Ex 25:24 thou shalt overlay it with *p* gold
Ex 25:29 of *p* gold shalt thou make them
Ex 25:31 make a candlestick of *p* gold
Ex 25:36 be one beaten work of *p* gold
Ex 25:38 thereof, shall be of *p* gold
Ex 25:39 Of a talent of *p* gold shall he
Ex 27:20 that they bring thee *p* oil olive
Ex 28:14 two chains of *p* gold at the ends
Ex 28:22 ends of wreathen work of *p* gold
Ex 28:36 thou shalt make a plate of *p* gold
Ex 30:3 thou shalt overlay it with *p* gold
Ex 30:23 of *p* myrrh five hundred shekels
Ex 30:34 sweet spices with *p* frankincense
Ex 30:35 apothecary, tempered together, *p*
Ex 31:8 the *p* candlestick with all his
Ex 37:2 he overlaid it with *p* gold within
Ex 37:6 he made the mercy seat of *p* gold
Ex 37:11 And he overlaid it with *p* gold
Ex 37:16 covers to cover withal, of *p* gold
Ex 37:17 he made the candlestick of *p* gold
Ex 37:22 it was one beaten work of *p* gold
Ex 37:23 and his snuffdishes, of *p* gold
Ex 37:24 Of a talent of *p* gold made he it,
Ex 37:26 And he overlaid it with *p* gold
Ex 37:29 the *p* incense of sweet spices,
Ex 39:15 ends, of wreathen work of *p* gold
Ex 39:25 And they made bells of *p* gold
Ex 39:30 plate of the holy crown of *p* gold
Ex 39:37 The *p* candlestick, with the lamps
Lev 24:2 that they bring unto thee *p* oil
Lev 24:4 the *p* candlestick before the LORD
Lev 24:6 upon the *p* table before the LORD
Lev 24:7 thou shalt put *p* frankincense
Deut 32:14 drink the *p* blood of the grape
2Sa 22:27 With the *p* thou wilt shew thyself
2Sa 22:27 thou wilt shew thyself *p*
1Kin 5:11 and twenty measures of *p* oil
1Kin 6:20 and he overlaid it with *p* gold
1Kin 6:21 the house within with *p* gold
1Kin 7:49 And the candlesticks of *p* gold
1Kin 7:50 spoons, and the censers of *p* gold
1Kin 10:21 forest of Lebanon were of *p* gold
1Chr 28:17 Also *p* gold for the fleshhooks,
2Chr 3:4 he overlaid it within with *p* gold
2Chr 4:20 before the oracle, of *p* gold
2Chr 4:22 spoons, and the censers, of *p* gold
2Chr 9:17 ivory, and overlaid it with *p* gold
2Chr 9:20 forest of Lebanon were of *p* gold
2Chr 13:11 they in order upon the *p* table
Ezr 6:20 together, all of them were *p*
Job 4:17 a man be more *p* than his maker
Job 8:6 If thou wert *p* and upright
Job 11:4 thou hast said, My doctrine is *p*
Job 16:17 also my prayer is *p*
Job 25:5 the stars are not *p* in his sight
Job 28:19 shall it be valued with *p* gold
Ps 12:6 The words of the LORD are *p* words
Ps 18:26 With the *p* thou wilt shew thyself
Ps 18:26 thou wilt shew thyself *p*
Ps 19:8 the commandment of the LORD is *p*
Ps 21:3 a crown of *p* gold on his head
Ps 24:4 hath clean hands, and a *p* heart
Ps 119:140 Thy word is very *p*
Prov 15:26 words of the *p* are pleasant words
Prov 20:9 heart clean, I am *p* from my sin
Prov 20:11 his doings, whether his work be *p*
Prov 21:8 but as for the *p*, his work is
Prov 30:5 Every word of God is *p*
Prov 30:12 that are *p* in their own eyes
Dan 7:9 hair of his head like the *p* wool
Mic 6:11 Shall I count them *p* with the
Zeph 3:9 I turn to the people a *p* language
Mal 1:11 unto my name, and a *p* offering
Mt 5:8 Blessed are the *p* in heart
Acts 20:26 that I am *p* from the blood of all
Rom 14:20 All things indeed are *p*
Phil 4:8 are just, whatsoever things are *p*
1Ti 1:5 is charity out of a *p* heart
1Ti 3:9 of the faith in a *p* conscience
1Ti 5:22 keep thyself *p*
2Ti 1:3 my forefathers with *p* conscience
2Ti 2:22 call on the Lord out of a *p* heart
Titus 1:15 Unto the *p* all things are *p*
Titus 1:15 and unbelieving is nothing *p*
Heb 10:22 and our bodies washed with *p* water
Jas 1:27 *P* religion and undefiled before
Jas 3:17 that is from above is first *p*
1Pet 1:22 another with a *p* heart fervently
2Pet 3:1 *p* minds by way of remembrance
1Jn 3:3 himself, even as he is *p*
Rev 15:6 the seven plagues, clothed in *p*
Rev 21:18 and the city was *p* gold, like unto
Rev 21:21 the street of the city was *p* gold
Rev 22:1 he shewed me a *p* river of water

**PURGE**
2Chr 34:3 twelfth year he began to *p* Judah
Ps 51:7 *P* me with hyssop, and I shall be
Ps 65:3 thou shalt *p* them away
Ps 79:9 *p* away our sins, for thy name's
Is 1:25 purely *p* away thy dross, and take
Eze 20:38 I will *p* out from among you the
Eze 43:20 thus shalt thou cleanse and *p* it
Eze 43:26 Seven days shall they *p* the altar
Dan 11:35 shall fall, to try them, and to *p*

Jer 52:8 of the Chaldeans *p* after the king
Lam 4:19 they *p* us upon the mountains,

**PURSUETH**
Lev 26:17 and ye shall flee when none *p* you
Lev 26:36 and they shall fall when none *p*
Lev 26:37 were before a sword, when none *p*
Prov 11:19 so he that *p* evil *p* it to
Prov 11:19 evil *p* it to his own death
Prov 13:21 Evil *p* sinners
Prov 19:7 he *p* them with words, yet they
Prov 28:1 The wicked flee when no man *p*

**PURSUING**
Judg 8:4 were with him, faint, yet *p* them
Judg 8:5 I am *p* after Zebah and Zalmunna,
1Sa 23:28 Saul returned from *p* after David
2Sa 3:22 David and Joab came from *p* a troop
2Sa 18:16 returned from *p* after Israel
1Kin 18:27 either he is talking, or he is *p*
1Kin 22:33 that they turned back from *p* him
2Chr 18:32 they turned back again from *p* him

**PUSH**
Ex 21:29 to *p* with his horn in time past
Ex 21:32 If the ox shall *p* a manservant or
Ex 21:36 ox hath used to *p* in time past
Deut 33:17 with them he shall *p* the people
1Kin 22:11 these shalt thou *p* the Syrians
2Chr 18:10 With these thou shalt *p* Syria
Job 30:12 they *p* away my feet, and they
Ps 44:5 thee will we *p* down our enemies
Dan 11:40 the king of the south *p* at him

**PUT** *(put)* See also PHUT.
*2. Descendant of Put 3.*
Nah 3:9 *P* and Lubim were thy helpers
*3. Son of Ham.*
1Chr 1:8 Cush, and Mizraim, P, and Canaan

**PUTEOLI** *(pu-te'-o-li) A seaport in Italy.*
Acts 28:13 and we came the next day to P

**PUTIEL** *(pu'-te-el) Father-in-law of Eleazar.*
Ex 6:25 one of the daughters of *P* to wife

# Q

**QUAILS**
Ex 16:13 pass, that at even the *q* came up
Num 11:31 brought *q* from the sea, and let
Num 11:32 next day, and they gathered the *q*
Ps 105:40 The people asked, and he brought *q*

**QUAKE**
Joel 2:10 The earth shall *q* before them
Nah 1:5 The mountains *q* at him, and the
Mt 27:51 and the earth did *q*, and the rocks
Heb 12:21 said, I exceedingly fear and *q*

**QUARREL**
Lev 26:25 shall avenge the *q* of my covenant
2Kin 5:7 see how he seeketh a *q* against me
Mk 6:19 Herodias had a *q* against him
Col 3:13 if any man have a *q* against any

**QUARTER**
Gen 19:4 all the people from every *q*
Num 34:3 Then your south *q* shall be from
Josh 15:5 their border in the north *q* was
Josh 18:14 this was the west *q*
Josh 18:15 the south *q* was from the end of
Is 47:15 shall wander every one to his *q*
Is 56:11 one for his gain, from his *q*
Mk 1:45 and they came to him from every *q*

**QUARTERS**
Ex 13:7 seen with thee in all thy *q*
Deut 22:12 upon the four *q* of thy vesture
1Chr 9:24 In four *q* were the porters,
Jer 49:36 winds from the four *q* of heaven
Eze 38:6 house of Togarmah of the north *q*
Acts 9:32 as Peter passed throughout all *q*
Acts 16:3 of the Jews which were in those *q*
Acts 28:7 In the same *q* were possessions of
Rev 20:8 are in the four *q* of the earth

**QUARTUS** *(quar'-tus) A Christian in Rome.*
Rom 16:23 city saluteth you, and *Q* a brother

**QUEEN**
1Kin 10:1 when the *q* of Sheba heard of the
1Kin 10:4 when the *q* of Sheba had seen all
1Kin 10:10 of spices as these which the *q* of
1Kin 10:13 the *q* of Sheba all her desire
1Kin 11:19 the sister of Tahpenes the *q*
1Kin 15:13 even her he removed from being *q*
2Kin 10:13 the king and the children of the *q*
2Chr 9:1 when the *q* of Sheba heard of the
2Chr 9:3 when the *q* of Sheba had seen the
2Chr 9:9 the *q* of Sheba gave king Solomon
2Chr 9:12 to the *q* of Sheba all her desire
2Chr 15:16 king, he removed her from being *q*
Neh 2:6 (the *q* also sitting by him,) For
Est 1:9 Also Vashti the *q* made a feast
Est 1:11 To bring Vashti the *q* before the
Est 1:12 But the *q* Vashti refused to come
Est 1:15 the *q* Vashti according to law
Est 1:16 Vashti the *q* hath not done wrong
Est 1:17 For this deed of the *q* shall come
Est 1:17 the *q* to be brought in before him
Est 1:18 have heard of the deed of the *q*
Est 2:4 the king be *q* instead of Vashti
Est 2:17 made her *q* instead of Vashti
Est 2:22 who told it unto Esther the *q*
Est 4:4 Then was the *q* exceedingly
Est 5:2 the *q* standing in the court
Est 5:3 her, What wilt thou, *q* Esther
Est 5:12 Esther the *q* did let no man come
Est 7:1 came to banquet with Esther the *q*
Est 7:2 What is thy petition, *q* Esther
Est 7:3 Then Esther the *q* answered
Est 7:5 and said unto Esther the *q*
Est 7:6 afraid before the king and the *q*
Est 7:7 for his life to Esther the *q*
Est 7:8 Will he force the *q* also before
Est 8:1 the Jews' enemy unto Esther the *q*
Est 8:7 Ahasuerus said unto Esther the *q*
Est 9:12 the king said unto Esther the *q*
Est 9:29 Then Esther the *q*, the daughter
Est 9:31 Esther the *q* had enjoined them,
Ps 45:9 did stand the *q* in gold of Ophir
Jer 7:18 to make cakes to the *q* of heaven
Jer 13:18 Say unto the king and to the *q*
Jer 29:2 that Jeconiah the king, and the *q*
Jer 44:17 burn incense unto the *q* of heaven
Jer 44:18 burn incense to the *q* of heaven
Jer 44:19 burned incense to the *q* of heaven
Jer 44:25 burn incense to the *q* of heaven
Dan 5:10 Now the *q*, by reason of the words
Dan 5:10 the *q* spake and said, O king, live
Mt 12:42 The *q* of the south shall rise up
Lk 11:31 The *q* of the south shall rise up
Acts 8:27 under Candace *q* of the Ethiopians
Rev 18:7 she saith in her heart, I sit a *q*

**QUENCH**
2Sa 14:7 so they shall *q* my coal which is
2Sa 21:17 that thou *q* not the light of
Ps 104:11 the wild asses *q* their thirst
Song 8:7 Many waters cannot *q* love
Is 1:31 together, and none shall *q* them
Is 42:3 the smoking flax shall he not *q*
Jer 4:4 burn that none can *q* it because
Jer 21:12 fire, and burn that none can *q* it
Amos 5:6 there be none to *q* it in Beth-el
Mt 12:20 and smoking flax shall he not *q*
Eph 6:16 to *q* all the fiery darts of the
1Th 5:19 *Q* not the Spirit

**QUENCHED**
Num 11:2 unto the LORD, the fire was *q*
2Kin 22:17 this place, and shall not be *q*
2Chr 34:25 this place, and shall not be *q*
Ps 118:12 they are *q* as the fire of thorns
Is 34:10 It shall not be *q* night nor day
Is 43:17 are extinct, they are *q* as tow
Is 66:24 neither shall their fire be *q*
Jer 7:20 it shall burn, and shall not be *q*
Jer 17:27 Jerusalem, and it shall not be *q*
Eze 20:47 the flaming flame shall not be *q*
Eze 20:48 it shall not be *q*
Mk 9:43 the fire that never shall be *q*
Mk 9:44 dieth not, and the fire is not *q*
Mk 9:45 the fire that never shall be *q*
Mk 9:46 dieth not, and the fire is not *q*
Mk 9:48 dieth not, and the fire is not *q*
Heb 11:34 *Q* the violence of fire, escaped

**QUESTION**
Mt 22:35 which was a lawyer, asked him a *q*
Mk 8:11 forth, and began to *q* with him
Mk 9:16 the scribes, What *q* ye with them
Mk 11:29 I will also ask of you one *q*
Mk 12:34 after that durst ask him any *q*
Lk 20:40 durst not ask him any *q* at all
Jn 3:25 Then there arose a *q* between some
Acts 15:2 apostles and elders about this *q*
Acts 18:15 But if it be a *q* of words
Acts 19:40 called in *q* for this day's uproar
Acts 23:6 of the dead I am called in *q*
Acts 24:21 I am called in *q* by you this day
1Cor 10:25 asking no *q* for conscience sake
1Cor 10:27 asking no *q* for conscience sake

**QUESTIONS**
1Kin 10:1 she came to prove him with hard *q*
1Kin 10:3 And Solomon told her all her *q*
2Chr 9:1 Solomon with hard *q* at Jerusalem
2Chr 9:2 And Solomon told her all her *q*
Mt 22:46 that day forth ask him any more *q*
Lk 2:46 hearing them, and asking them *q*
Acts 23:29 to be accused of *q* of their law
Acts 25:19 But had certain *q* against him of
Acts 25:20 I doubted of such manner of *q*
Acts 26:3 *q* which are among the Jews
1Ti 1:4 genealogies, which minister *q*
1Ti 6:4 nothing, but doting about *q*
2Ti 2:23 But foolish and unlearned *q* avoid
Titus 3:9 But avoid foolish *q*, and

**QUICK**
Lev 13:10 there be *q* raw flesh in the
Lev 13:24 the *q* flesh that burneth have a
Num 16:30 and they go down *q* into the pit
Ps 55:15 and let them go down *q* into hell
Ps 124:3 Then they had swallowed us up *q*
Is 11:3 shall make him of *q* understanding
Acts 10:42 of God to be the Judge of *q*
2Ti 4:1 Christ, who shall judge the *q*
Heb 4:12 For the word of God is *q*, and
1Pet 4:5 him that is ready to judge the *q*

**QUICKEN**
Ps 71:20 shalt *q* me again, and shalt bring
Ps 80:18 *q* us, and we will call upon thy
Ps 119:25 *q* thou me according to thy word
Ps 119:37 and *q* thou me in thy way
Ps 119:40 *q* me in thy righteousness
Ps 119:88 *Q* me after thy lovingkindness
Ps 119:107 *q* me, O LORD, according unto thy
Ps 119:149 *q* me according to thy judgment
Ps 119:154 *q* me according to thy word
Ps 119:156 *q* me according to thy judgments
Ps 119:159 *q* me, O LORD, according to thy
Ps 143:11 *Q* me, O LORD, for thy name's sake
Rom 8:11 also *q* your mortal bodies by his

**QUICKENED**
Ps 119:50 for thy word hath *q* me
Ps 119:93 for with them thou hast *q* me
1Cor 15:36 that which thou sowest is not *q*
Eph 2:1 And you hath he *q*, who were dead
Eph 2:5 hath *q* us together with Christ,
Col 2:13 hath he *q* together with him,
1Pet 3:18 in the flesh, but *q* by the Spirit

**QUICKENETH**
Jn 5:21 raiseth up the dead, and *q* them
Jn 5:21 even so the Son *q* whom he will
Jn 6:63 It is the spirit that *q*
Rom 4:17 who *q* the dead, and calleth those
1Ti 6:13 who *q* all things, and before

**QUICKLY**
Gen 18:6 Make ready *q* three measures of
Gen 27:20 it that thou hast found it so *q*
Ex 32:8 aside *q* out of the way which I

Num 16:46 go *q* unto the congregation, and
Deut 9:3 drive them out, and destroy them *q*
Deut 9:12 Arise, get thee down *q* from hence
Deut 9:12 they are *q* turned aside out of
Deut 9:16 ye had turned aside *q* out of the
Deut 11:17 lest ye perish *q* from off the
Deut 28:20 destroyed, and until thou perish *q*
Josh 2:5 pursue after them *q*
Josh 8:19 the ambush arose *q* out of their
Josh 10:6 come up to us *q*, and save us, and
Josh 23:16 ye shall perish *q* from off the
Judg 2:17 they turned *q* out of the way
1Sa 20:19 days, then thou shalt go down *q*
2Sa 17:16 Now therefore send *q*, and tell
2Sa 17:18 but they went both of them away *q*
2Sa 17:21 Arise, and pass *q* over the water
2Kin 1:11 Come down *q*
2Chr 18:8 Fetch *q* Micaiah the son of Imla
Eccl 4:12 a threefold cord is not *q* broken
Mt 5:25 Agree with thine adversary *q*
Mt 28:7 And go *q*, and tell his disciples
Mt 28:8 And they departed *q* from the
Mk 16:8 And they went out *q*, and fled from
Lk 14:21 Go out *q* into the streets and
Lk 16:6 him, Take thy bill, and sit down *q*
Jn 11:29 as she heard that, she arose *q*
Jn 13:27 unto him, That thou doest, do *q*
Acts 12:7 raised him up, saying, Arise up *q*
Acts 22:18 get thee *q* out of Jerusalem
Rev 2:5 or else I will come unto thee *q*
Rev 2:16 or else I will come unto thee *q*
Rev 3:11 Behold, I come *q*
Rev 11:14 behold, the third woe cometh *q*
Rev 22:7 Behold, I come *q*
Rev 22:12 And, behold, I come *q*
Rev 22:20 things saith, Surely I come *q*

**QUIET**
Judg 16:2 were *q* all the night, saying, In
Judg 18:7 the manner of the Zidonians, *q*
Judg 18:27 unto a people that were at *q*
2Kin 11:20 rejoiced, and the city was in *q*
1Chr 4:40 good, and the land was wide, and *q*
2Chr 14:1 his days the land was *q* ten years
2Chr 14:5 and the kingdom was *q* before him
2Chr 20:30 So the realm of Jehoshaphat was *q*
2Chr 23:21 and the city was *q*, after that
Job 3:13 I have lain still and been *q*
Job 3:26 had I rest, neither was I *q*
Job 21:23 being wholly at ease and *q*
Ps 35:20 them that are *q* in the land
Ps 107:30 are they glad because they be *q*
Prov 1:33 shall be *q* from fear of evil
Eccl 9:17 *q* more than the cry of him that
Is 7:4 say unto him, Take heed, and be *q*
Is 14:7 whole earth is at rest, and is *q*
Is 32:18 dwellings, and in *q* resting places
Is 33:20 see Jerusalem a *q* habitation
Jer 30:10 and shall be in rest, and be *q*
Jer 47:6 how long will it be ere thou be *q*
Jer 47:7 How can it be *q*, seeing the LORD
Jer 49:23 it cannot be *q*
Jer 51:59 And this Seraiah was a *q* prince
Eze 16:42 depart from thee, and I will be *q*
Nah 1:12 Though they be *q*, and likewise
Acts 19:36 spoken against, ye ought to be *q*
1Th 4:11 And that ye study to be *q*, and to
1Ti 2:2 that we may lead a *q* and peaceable
1Pet 3:4 *q* spirit, which is in the sight

**QUIETNESS**
Judg 8:28 the country was in *q* forty years
1Chr 22:9 *q* unto Israel in his days
Job 20:20 he shall not feel *q* in his belly
Job 34:29 When he giveth *q*, who then can
Prov 17:1 *q* therewith, than an house full
Eccl 4:6 Better is an handful with *q*
Is 30:15 in *q* and in confidence shall be
Is 32:17 and the effect of righteousness *q*
Acts 24:2 that by thee we enjoy great *q*
2Th 3:12 Christ, that with *q* they work

**QUIT**
Ex 21:19 then shall he that smote him be *q*
Ex 21:28 the owner of the ox shall be *q*
Josh 2:20 then we will be *q* of thine oath
1Sa 4:9 *q* yourselves like men, O ye
1Sa 4:9 *q* yourselves like men, and fight
1Cor 16:13 *q* you like men, be strong

**QUITE**
Gen 31:15 hath *q* devoured also our money
Ex 23:24 *q* break down their images
Num 17:10 thou shalt *q* take away their
Num 33:52 *q* pluck down all their high
2Sa 3:24 sent him away, and he is *q* gone
Job 6:13 and is wisdom driven *q* from me
Hab 3:9 Thy bow was made *q* naked,

**QUIVER**
Gen 27:3 I pray thee, thy weapons, thy *q*
Job 39:23 The *q* rattleth against him, the
Ps 127:5 man that hath his *q* full of them
Is 22:6 Elam bare the *q* with chariots of
Is 49:2 in his *q* hath he hid me
Jer 5:16 Their *q* is as an open sepulchre,
Lam 3:13 of his *q* to enter into my reins

# R

**RAAMAH** *(ra'-a-mah)*
*1. A son of Cush.*
Gen 10:7 Seba, and Havilah, and Sabtah, and *R*
Gen 10:7 and the sons of *R*
1Chr 1:9 Seba, and Havilah, and Sabta, and *R*
1Chr 1:9 And the sons of *R*
*2. A place in Arabia.*
Eze 27:22 The merchants of Sheba and *R*

**RAAMIAH** *(ra-a-mi'-ah) A clan leader in exile.*
Neh 7:7 Jeshua, Nehemiah, Azariah, *R*

**RAAMSES** *(ra-am'-seze)* See RAMESES. *An Egyptian city.*
Ex 1:11 treasure cities, Pithom and *R*

**RABBAH** *(rab'-bah)* See RABBATH.
*1. An Ammonite city.*
Josh 13:25 unto Aroer that is before *R*
2Sa 11:1 children of Ammon, and besieged *R*
2Sa 12:26 Joab fought against *R* of the
2Sa 12:27 and said, I have fought against *R*
2Sa 12:29 the people together, and went to *R*
2Sa 17:27 of *R* of the children of Ammon
1Chr 20:1 of Ammon, and came and besieged *R*
1Chr 20:1 And Joab smote *R*, and destroyed it
Jer 49:2 to be heard in *R* of the Ammonites
Jer 49:3 cry, ye daughters of *R*, gird you
Eze 25:5 I will make *R* a stable for camels
Amos 1:14 kindle a fire in the wall of *R*
*2. A city in Judah.*
Josh 15:60 which is Kirjath-jearim, and *R*

**RABBATH** *(rab'-bath)* See RABBAH. *Same as Rabbah 1.*
Deut 3:11 is it not in *R* of the children of
Eze 21:20 may come to *R* of the Ammonites

**RABBI** *(rab'-bi)* See RABBONI. *A Jewish title meaning "teacher."*
Mt 23:7 and to be called of men, *R*, *R*
Mt 23:8 But be not ye called *R*
Jn 1:38 They said unto him, *R*, (which is
Jn 1:49 answered and saith unto him, *R*
Jn 3:2 by night, and said unto him, *R*
Jn 3:26 unto John, and said unto him, *R*
Jn 6:25 of the sea, they said unto him, *R*

**RABBITH** *(rab'-bith) A city in Issachar.*
Josh 19:20 And *R*, and Kishion, and Abez,

**RABBONI** *(rab-bo'-ni)* See RABBI. *A Jewish title of respect.*
Jn 20:16 herself, and saith unto him, *R*

**RAB-MAG** *A Babylonian prince.*
Jer 39:3 Rab-saris, Nergal-sharezer, *R*
Jer 39:13 Rab-saris, and Nergal-sharezer, *R*

**RAB-SARIS**
*1. A Babylonian prince.*
Jer 39:3 Samgar-nebo, Sarsechim, *R*
Jer 39:13 the guard sent, and Nebushasban, *R*
*2. An Assyrian officer.*
2Kin 18:17 king of Assyria sent Tartan and *R*

**RAB-SHAKEH** *(rab'-sha-keh)* See RABSHAKEH. *An Assyrian officer.*
2Kin 18:17 *R* from Lachish to king Hezekiah
2Kin 18:19 *R* said unto them, Speak ye now to
2Kin 18:26 and Shebna, and Joah, unto *R*
2Kin 18:27 But *R* said unto them, Hath my
2Kin 18:28 Then *R* stood and cried with a loud
2Kin 18:37 rent, and told him the words of *R*
2Kin 19:4 God will hear all the words of *R*
2Kin 19:8 So *R* returned, and found the king

**RABSHAKEH** *(rab'-sha-keh)* See RAB-SHAKEH. *Same as Rab-shakeh.*
Is 36:2 the king of Assyria sent *R* from
Is 36:4 *R* said unto them, Say ye now to
Is 36:11 Eliakim and Shebna and Joah unto *R*
Is 36:12 But *R* said, Hath my master sent
Is 36:13 Then *R* stood, and cried with a
Is 36:22 rent, and told him the words of *R*
Is 37:4 thy God will hear the words of *R*
Is 37:8 So *R* returned, and found the king

**RACA** *(ra'-cah) A Jewish term of disrespect.*
Mt 5:22 shall say to his brother, *R*

**RACE**
Ps 19:5 as a strong man to run a *r*
Eccl 9:11 that the *r* is not to the swift,
1Cor 9:24 they which run in a *r* run all
Heb 12:1 the *r* that is set before us

**RACHAB** *(ra'kab)* See RAHAB. *Same as Rahab; ancestor of Jesus.*
Mt 1:5 And Salmon begat Booz of *R*

**RACHAL** *(ra'-kal) A city in Judah.*
1Sa 30:29 And to them which were in *R*

**RACHEL** *(ra'-chel)* See RACHEL'S, RAHEL. *Wife of Jacob.*
Gen 29:6 *R* his daughter cometh with the
Gen 29:9 *R* came with her father's sheep
Gen 29:10 when Jacob saw *R* the daughter of
Gen 29:11 And Jacob kissed *R*, and lifted up
Gen 29:12 Jacob told *R* that he was her
Gen 29:16 and the name of the younger was *R*
Gen 29:17 but *R* was beautiful and well
Gen 29:18 And Jacob loved *R*
Gen 29:18 years for *R* thy younger daughter
Gen 29:20 And Jacob served seven years for *R*
Gen 29:25 did not I serve with thee for *R*
Gen 29:28 he gave him *R* his daughter to
Gen 29:29 Laban gave to *R* his daughter
Gen 29:30 And he went in also unto *R*
Gen 29:30 he loved also *R* more than Leah,
Gen 29:31 but *R* was barren
Gen 30:1 when *R* saw that she bare Jacob no
Gen 30:1 no children, *R* envied her sister
Gen 30:2 anger was kindled against *R*
Gen 30:6 *R* said, God hath judged me, and
Gen 30:8 *R* said, With great wrestlings
Gen 30:14 Then *R* said to Leah, Give me, I
Gen 30:15 *R* said, Therefore he shall lie
Gen 30:22 And God remembered *R*, and God
Gen 30:25 when *R* had born Joseph, that
Gen 31:4 And Jacob sent and called *R*
Gen 31:14 And *R* and Leah answered and said
Gen 31:19 *R* had stolen the images that were
Gen 31:32 knew not that *R* had stolen them
Gen 31:34 Now *R* had taken the images, and
Gen 33:1 the children unto Leah, and unto *R*
Gen 33:2 Leah and her children after, and *R*
Gen 33:7 and after came Joseph near and *R*
Gen 35:16 *R* travailed, and she had hard
Gen 35:19 *R* died, and was buried in the way
Gen 35:24 The sons of *R*
Gen 46:19 The sons of *R* Jacob's wife
Gen 46:22 These are the sons of *R*, which

Gen 46:25 Laban gave unto *R* his daughter
Gen 48:7 *R* died by me in the land of
Ruth 4:11 is come into thine house like *R*
Mt 2:18 *R* weeping for her children, and

**RACHEL'S** *(ra'-chelz)*
Gen 30:7 Bilhah *R* maid conceived again, and
Gen 31:33 tent, and entered into *R* tent
Gen 35:20 pillar of *R* grave unto this day
Gen 35:25 And the sons of Bilhah, *R* handmaid
1Sa 10:2 by *R* sepulchre in the border of

**RADDAI** *(rad'-dahee) Son of Jesse.*
1Chr 2:14 the fourth, *R* the fifth,

**RAGAU** *(ra'-gaw)* See Reu. *Father of Saruch; ancestor of Jesus.*
Lk 3:35 of Saruch, which was the son of *R*

**RAGE**
2Kin 5:12 So he turned and went away in a *r*
2Kin 19:27 coming in, and thy *r* against me
2Kin 19:28 Because thy *r* against me and thy
2Chr 16:10 for he was in a *r* with him
2Chr 28:9 ye have slain them in a *r* that
Job 39:24 the ground with fierceness and *r*
Job 40:11 Cast abroad the *r* of thy wrath
Ps 2:1 Why do the heathen *r*, and the
Ps 7:6 because of the *r* of mine enemies
Prov 6:34 For jealousy is the *r* of a man
Prov 29:9 man, whether he *r* or laugh
Is 37:28 coming in, and thy *r* against me
Is 37:29 Because thy *r* against me, and thy
Jer 46:9 and *r*, ye chariots
Dan 3:13 Then Nebuchadnezzar in his *r*
Hos 7:16 sword for the *r* of their tongue
Nah 2:4 chariots shall *r* in the streets
Acts 4:25 hast said, Why did the heathen *r*

**RAGING**
Ps 89:9 Thou rulest the *r* of the sea
Prov 20:1 is a mocker, strong drink is *r*
Jonah 1:15 and the sea ceased from her *r*
Lk 8:24 the wind and the *r* of the water
Jude 13 *R* waves of the sea, foaming out

**RAGS**
Prov 23:21 shall clothe a man with *r*
Is 64:6 righteousnesses are as filthy *r*
Jer 38:11 old cast clouts and old rotten *r*
Jer 38:12 rotten *r* under thine armholes

**RAGUEL** *(ra-gu'-el) Father-in-law of Moses.*
Num 10:29 the son of *R* the Midianite,

**RAHAB** *(ra'-hab)* See Rachab.
*1. A Jericho woman who befriended the spies.*
Josh 2:1 into an harlot's house, named *R*
Josh 2:3 the king of Jericho sent unto *R*
Josh 6:17 only *R* the harlot shall live, she
Josh 6:23 spies went in, and brought out *R*
Josh 6:25 Joshua saved *R* the harlot alive,
Heb 11:31 By faith the harlot *R* perished
Jas 2:25 Likewise also was not *R* the
*2. A symbolic name for Egypt.*
Ps 87:4 I will make mention of *R* and
Ps 89:10 Thou hast broken *R* in pieces
Is 51:9 Art thou not it that hath cut *R*

**RAHAM** *(ra'-ham) Son of Shema.*
1Chr 2:44 And Shema begat *R*, the father of

**RAHEL** *(ra'-hel)* See Rachel. *Same as Rachel.*
Jer 31:15 *R* weeping for her children

**RAIMENT**
Gen 24:53 silver, and jewels of gold, and *r*
Gen 27:15 Rebekah took goodly *r* of her
Gen 27:27 and he smelled the smell of his *r*
Gen 28:20 me bread to eat, and *r* to put on,
Gen 41:14 shaved himself, and changed his *r*
Gen 45:22 he gave each man changes of *r*
Gen 45:22 of silver, and five changes of *r*
Ex 3:22 silver, and jewels of gold, and *r*
Ex 12:35 silver, and jewels of gold, and *r*
Ex 21:10 her food, her *r*, and her duty of
Ex 22:9 for ox, for ass, for sheep, for *r*
Ex 22:26 take thy neighbour's *r* to pledge
Ex 22:27 only, it is his *r* for his skin
Lev 11:32 it be any vessel of wood, or *r*
Num 31:20 And purify all your *r*, and all that
Deut 8:4 Thy *r* waxed not old upon thee,
Deut 10:18 stranger, in giving him food and *r*
Deut 21:13 she shall put the *r* of her
Deut 22:3 and so shalt thou do with his *r*
Deut 24:13 that he may sleep in his own *r*
Deut 24:17 nor take a widow's *r* to pledge
Josh 22:8 and with iron, and with very much *r*
Judg 3:16 under his *r* upon his right thigh
Judg 8:26 purple *r* that was on the kings of
Ruth 3:3 put thy *r* upon thee, and get thee
1Sa 28:8 himself, and put on other *r*
2Kin 5:5 of gold, and ten changes of *r*
2Kin 7:8 thence silver, and gold, and *r*
2Chr 9:24 silver, and vessels of gold, and *r*
Est 4:4 she sent *r* to clothe Mordecai, and
Job 27:16 dust, and prepare *r* as the clay
Ps 45:14 unto the king in *r* of needlework
Is 14:19 as the *r* of those that are slain,
Is 63:3 and I will stain all my *r*
Eze 16:13 thy *r* was of fine linen, and silk,
Zec 3:4 will clothe thee with change of *r*
Mt 3:4 John had his *r* of camel's hair
Mt 6:25 than meat, and the body than *r*
Mt 6:28 And why take ye thought for *r*
Mt 11:8 A man clothed in soft *r*
Mt 17:2 his *r* was white as the light
Mt 27:31 from him, and put his own *r* on him
Mt 28:3 lightning, and his *r* white as snow
Mk 9:3 his *r* became shining, exceeding
Lk 7:25 A man clothed in soft *r*
Lk 9:29 his *r* was white and glistering
Lk 10:30 which stripped him of his *r*
Lk 12:23 meat, and the body is more than *r*
Lk 23:34 And they parted his *r*, and cast
Jn 19:24 They parted my *r* among them
Acts 18:6 and blasphemed, he shook his *r*
Acts 22:20 kept the *r* of them that slew him
1Ti 6:8 *r* let us be therewith content
Jas 2:2 come in also a poor man in vile *r*
Rev 3:5 same shall be clothed in white *r*
Rev 3:18 and white *r*, that thou mayest be
Rev 4:4 sitting, clothed in white *r*

**RAIN**
Gen 2:5 not caused it to *r* upon the earth
Gen 7:4 I will cause it to *r* upon the
Gen 7:12 the *r* was upon the earth forty
Gen 8:2 the *r* from heaven was restrained
Ex 9:18 it to *r* a very grievous hail
Ex 9:33 the *r* was not poured upon the
Ex 9:34 And when Pharaoh saw that the *r*
Ex 16:4 I will *r* bread from heaven for
Lev 26:4 I will give you *r* in due season
Deut 11:11 drinketh water of the *r* of heaven
Deut 11:14 That I will give you the *r* of
Deut 11:14 in his due season, the first *r*
Deut 11:14 and the latter *r*
Deut 11:17 up the heaven, that there be no *r*
Deut 28:12 the heaven to give the *r* unto thy
Deut 28:24 make the *r* of thy land powder
Deut 32:2 My doctrine shall drop as the *r*
Deut 32:2 as the small *r* upon the tender
1Sa 12:17 and he shall send thunder and *r*
1Sa 12:18 LORD sent thunder and *r* that day
2Sa 1:21 be no dew, neither let there be *r*
2Sa 23:4 earth by clear shining after *r*
1Kin 8:35 is shut up, and there is no *r*
1Kin 8:36 give *r* upon thy land, which thou
1Kin 17:1 not be dew nor *r* these years
1Kin 17:7 there had been no *r* in the land
1Kin 17:14 the LORD sendeth *r* upon the earth
1Kin 18:1 I will send *r* upon the earth
1Kin 18:41 is a sound of abundance of *r*
1Kin 18:44 down, that the *r* stop thee not
1Kin 18:45 and wind, and there was a great *r*
2Kin 3:17 see wind, neither shall ye see *r*
2Chr 6:26 is shut up, and there is no *r*
2Chr 6:27 send *r* upon thy land, which thou
2Chr 7:13 shut up heaven that there be no *r*
Ezr 10:9 this matter, and for the great *r*
Ezr 10:13 many, and it is a time of much *r*
Job 5:10 Who giveth *r* upon the earth, and
Job 20:23 shall *r* it upon him while he is
Job 28:26 When he made a decree for the *r*
Job 29:23 they waited for me as for the *r*
Job 29:23 mouth wide as for the latter *r*
Job 36:27 they pour down *r* according to the
Job 37:6 likewise to the small *r*, and to
Job 37:6 to the great *r* of his strength
Job 38:26 To cause it to *r* on the earth
Job 38:28 Hath the *r* a father
Ps 11:6 Upon the wicked he shall *r* snares
Ps 68:9 O God, didst send a plentiful *r*
Ps 72:6 down like *r* upon the mown grass
Ps 84:6 the *r* also filleth the pools
Ps 105:32 He gave them hail for *r*, and
Ps 135:7 he maketh lightnings for the *r*
Ps 147:8 who prepareth *r* for the earth
Prov 16:15 is as a cloud of the latter *r*
Prov 25:14 is like clouds and wind without *r*
Prov 25:23 The north wind driveth away *r*
Prov 26:1 as *r* in harvest, so honour is not
Prov 28:3 sweeping *r* which leaveth no food
Eccl 11:3 If the clouds be full of *r*
Eccl 12:2 nor the clouds return after the *r*
Song 2:11 is past, the *r* is over and gone
Is 4:6 for a covert from storm and from *r*
Is 5:6 that they *r* no *r* upon it
Is 5:6 that they *r* no *r* upon it
Is 30:23 shall he give the *r* of thy seed
Is 44:14 an ash, and the *r* doth nourish it
Is 55:10 For as the *r* cometh down, and the
Jer 3:3 and there hath been no latter *r*
Jer 5:24 the LORD our God, that giveth *r*
Jer 10:13 he maketh lightnings with *r*
Jer 14:4 for there was no *r* in the earth
Jer 14:22 of the Gentiles that can cause *r*
Jer 51:16 he maketh lightnings with *r*
Eze 1:28 is in the cloud in the day of *r*
Eze 38:22 I will *r* upon him, and upon his
Eze 38:22 are with him, and overflowing *r*
Hos 6:3 and he shall come unto us as the *r*
Hos 6:3 latter and former *r* unto the earth
Hos 10:12 come and *r* righteousness upon you
Joel 2:23 given you the former *r* moderately
Joel 2:23 cause to come down for you the *r*
Joel 2:23 the former *r*, and the latter
Joel 2:23 the latter *r* in the first month
Amos 4:7 I have withholden the *r* from you
Amos 4:7 and I caused it to *r* upon one city
Amos 4:7 caused it not to *r* upon another
Zec 10:1 Ask ye of the LORD *r* in the time
Zec 10:1 in the time of the latter *r*
Zec 10:1 clouds, and give them showers of *r*
Zec 14:17 even upon them shall be no *r*
Zec 14:18 up, and come not, that have no *r*
Mt 5:45 sendeth *r* on the just and on the
Mt 7:25 the *r* descended, and the floods
Mt 7:27 the *r* descended, and the floods
Acts 14:17 gave us *r* from heaven, and
Acts 28:2 one, because of the present *r*
Heb 6:7 in the *r* that cometh oft upon it
Jas 5:7 he receive the early and latter *r*
Jas 5:17 earnestly that it might not *r*
Jas 5:18 again, and the heaven gave *r*
Rev 11:6 that it *r* not in the days of

**RAINED**
Gen 19:24 Then the LORD *r* upon Sodom
Ex 9:23 the LORD *r* hail upon the land of
Ps 78:24 had *r* down manna upon them to eat
Ps 78:27 He *r* flesh also upon them as dust
Eze 22:24 nor *r* upon in the day of
Amos 4:7 one piece was *r* upon, and the
Amos 4:7 piece whereupon it *r* not withered
Lk 17:29 Lot went out of Sodom it *r* fire
Jas 5:17 it *r* not on the earth by the

**RAISE**
Gen 38:8 her, and *r* up seed to thy brother
Ex 23:1 Thou shalt not *r* a false report
Deut 18:15 The LORD thy God will *r* up unto
Deut 18:18 I will *r* them up a Prophet from
Deut 25:7 *r* up unto his brother a name in
Josh 8:29 *r* thereon a great heap of stones,
Ruth 4:5 to *r* up the name of the dead upon
Ruth 4:10 to *r* up the name of the dead upon
1Sa 2:35 I will *r* me up a faithful priest,
2Sa 12:11 I will *r* up evil against thee out
2Sa 12:17 to *r* him up from the earth
1Kin 14:14 Moreover the LORD shall *r* him up
1Chr 17:11 that I will *r* up thy seed after
Job 3:8 who are ready to *r* up their
Job 19:12 *r* up their way against me, and
Job 30:12 they *r* up against me the ways of
Ps 41:10 *r* me up, that I may requite them
Is 15:5 shall *r* up a cry of destruction
Is 29:3 I will *r* forts against thee
Is 44:26 I will *r* up the decayed places
Is 49:6 to *r* up the tribes of Jacob
Is 58:12 thou shalt *r* up the foundations
Is 61:4 they shall *r* up the former
Jer 23:5 that I will *r* unto David a
Jer 30:9 whom I will *r* up unto them
Jer 50:9 For, lo, I will *r* and cause to

Jer 50:32 and fall, and none shall *r* him up
Jer 51:1 I will *r* up against Babylon, and
Eze 23:22 I will *r* up thy lovers against
Eze 34:29 I will *r* up for them a plant of
Hos 6:2 in the third day he will *r* us up
Joel 3:7 I will *r* them out of the place
Amos 5:2 there is none to *r* her up
Amos 6:14 I will *r* up against you a nation,
Amos 9:11 In that day will I *r* up the
Amos 9:11 I will *r* up his ruins, and I will
Mic 5:5 then shall we *r* against him seven
Hab 1:3 and there are that *r* up strife
Hab 1:6 I *r* up the Chaldeans, that bitter
Zec 11:16 I will *r* up a shepherd in the
Mt 3:9 to *r* up children unto Abraham
Mt 10:8 *r* the dead, cast out devils
Mt 22:24 *r* up seed unto his brother
Mk 12:19 *r* up seed unto his brother
Lk 3:8 to *r* up children unto Abraham
Lk 20:28 *r* up seed unto his brother
Jn 2:19 and in three days I will *r* it up
Jn 6:39 but should *r* it up again at the
Jn 6:40 I will *r* him up at the last day
Jn 6:44 I will *r* him up at the last day
Jn 6:54 I will *r* him up at the last day
Acts 2:30 he would *r* up Christ to sit on
Acts 3:22 *r* up unto you of your brethren
Acts 7:37 *r* up unto you of your brethren
Acts 26:8 you, that God should *r* the dead
1Cor 6:14 will also *r* up us by his own
2Cor 4:14 Jesus shall *r* up us also by Jesus
Heb 11:19 that God was able to *r* him up
Jas 5:15 sick, and the Lord shall *r* him up

**RAISED**
Ex 9:16 for this cause have I *r* thee up
Josh 5:7 whom he *r* up in their stead, them
Josh 7:26 they *r* over him a great heap of
Judg 2:16 Nevertheless the LORD *r* up judges
Judg 2:18 when the LORD *r* them up judges,
Judg 3:9 the LORD *r* up a deliverer to the
Judg 3:15 the LORD *r* them up a deliverer,
2Sa 23:1 and the man who was *r* up on high
1Kin 5:13 king Solomon *r* a levy out of all
1Kin 9:15 of the levy which king Solomon *r*
2Chr 32:5 *r* it up to the towers, and another
2Chr 33:14 *r* it up a very great height, and
Ezr 1:5 all them whose spirit God had *r*
Job 14:12 nor be *r* out of their sleep
Song 8:5 I *r* thee up under the apple tree
Is 14:9 it hath *r* up from their thrones
Is 23:13 they *r* up the palaces thereof
Is 41:2 Who *r* up the righteous man from
Is 41:25 I have *r* up one from the north,
Is 45:13 I have *r* him up in righteousness,
Jer 6:22 a great nation shall be *r* from
Jer 25:32 a great whirlwind shall be *r* up
Jer 29:15 The LORD hath *r* us up prophets in
Jer 50:41 many kings shall be *r* up from the
Jer 51:11 the LORD hath *r* up the spirit of
Dan 7:5 it *r* up itself on one side, and it
Amos 2:11 I *r* up of your sons for prophets,
Zec 2:13 for he is *r* up out of his holy
Zec 9:13 *r* up thy sons, O Zion, against
Mt 1:24 Then Joseph being *r* from sleep
Mt 11:5 the deaf hear, the dead are *r* up
Mt 16:21 and be *r* again the third day
Mt 17:23 the third day he shall be *r* again
Lk 1:69 hath *r* up an horn of salvation
Lk 7:22 the deaf hear, the dead are *r*
Lk 9:22 be slain, and be *r* the third day
Lk 20:37 Now that the dead are *r*, even
Jn 12:1 dead, whom he *r* from the dead
Jn 12:9 whom he had *r* from the dead
Jn 12:17 *r* him from the dead, bare record
Acts 2:24 Whom God hath *r* up, having loosed
Acts 2:32 This Jesus hath God *r* up, whereof
Acts 3:15 whom God hath *r* from the dead
Acts 3:26 having *r* up his Son Jesus, sent
Acts 4:10 whom God *r* from the dead, even by
Acts 5:30 The God of our fathers *r* up Jesus
Acts 10:40 Him God *r* up the third day, and
Acts 12:7 *r* him up, saying, Arise up
Acts 13:22 he *r* up unto them David to be
Acts 13:23 promise *r* unto Israel a Saviour
Acts 13:30 But God *r* him from the dead
Acts 13:33 in that he hath *r* up Jesus again
Acts 13:34 that he *r* him up from the dead
Acts 13:37 But he, whom God *r* again, saw no
Acts 13:50 *r* persecution against Paul and
Acts 17:31 in that he hath *r* him from the
Rom 4:24 if we believe on him that *r* up
Rom 4:25 was *r* again for our justification
Rom 6:4 that like as Christ was *r* up from
Rom 6:9 Knowing that Christ being *r* from
Rom 7:4 to him who is *r* from the dead
Rom 8:11 But if the Spirit of him that *r*
Rom 8:11 he that *r* up Christ from the dead
Rom 9:17 same purpose have I *r* thee up
Rom 10:9 that God hath *r* him from the dead
1Cor 6:14 And God hath both *r* up the Lord
1Cor 15:15 of God that he *r* up Christ
1Cor 15:15 whom he *r* not up, if so be that
1Cor 15:16 rise not, then is not Christ *r*
1Cor 15:17 And if Christ be not *r*, your faith
1Cor 15:35 will say, How are the dead *r* up
1Cor 15:42 it is *r* in incorruption
1Cor 15:43 it is *r* in glory
1Cor 15:43 it is *r* in power
1Cor 15:44 it is *r* a spiritual body
1Cor 15:52 the dead shall be *r* incorruptible
2Cor 4:14 Knowing that he which *r* up the
Gal 1:1 Father, who *r* him from the dead
Eph 1:20 when he *r* him from the dead, and
Eph 2:6 hath *r* us up together, and made us
Col 2:12 who hath *r* him from the dead
1Th 1:10 whom he *r* from the dead, even
2Ti 2:8 *r* from the dead according to my
Heb 11:35 their dead *r* to life again
1Pet 1:21 that *r* him up from the dead, and

**RAISETH**
1Sa 2:8 He *r* up the poor out of the dust,
Job 41:25 When he *r* up himself, the mighty
Ps 107:25 *r* the stormy wind, which lifteth
Ps 113:7 He *r* up the poor out of the dust,
Ps 145:14 *r* up all those that be bowed down
Ps 146:8 the LORD *r* them that are bowed
Jn 5:21 For as the Father *r* up the dead
2Cor 1:9 but in God which *r* the dead

**RAISINS**
1Sa 25:18 corn, and an hundred clusters of *r*
1Sa 30:12 of figs, and two clusters of *r*
2Sa 16:1 bread, and an hundred bunches of *r*
1Chr 12:40 cakes of figs, and bunches of *r*

**RAKEM** *(ra'-kem) Son of Sheresh.*
1Chr 7:16 and his sons were Ulam and *R*

**RAKKATH** *(rah'-kath) A city in Naphtali.*
Josh 19:35 are Ziddim, Zer, and Hammath, *R*

**RAKKON** *(rak'-kon) A city in Dan.*
Josh 19:46 And Me-jarkon, and *R*, with the

**RAM** *(ram)*
*1. Father of Aminadab.*
Ruth 4:19 And Hezron begat *R*
Ruth 4:19 and *R* begat Amminadab
1Chr 2:9 Jerahmeel, and *R*, and Chelubai
1Chr 2:10 And *R* begat Amminadab
*2. Son of Jerahmeel.*
1Chr 2:25 *R* the firstborn, and Bunah, and
1Chr 2:27 the sons of *R* the firstborn of
*3. Head of Elihu's family.*
Job 32:2 the Buzite, of the kindred of *R*
*4. Male sheep.*
Gen 15:9 a *r* of three years old, and a
Gen 22:13 behold behind him a *r* caught in a
Gen 22:13 and Abraham went and took the *r*
Ex 29:15 Thou shalt also take one *r*
Ex 29:15 hands upon the head of the *r*
Ex 29:16 And thou shalt slay the *r*, and thou
Ex 29:17 And thou shalt cut the *r* in pieces
Ex 29:18 burn the whole *r* upon the altar
Ex 29:19 And thou shalt take the other *r*
Ex 29:19 hands upon the head of the *r*
Ex 29:20 Then shalt thou kill the *r*
Ex 29:22 thou shalt take of the *r* the fat
Ex 29:22 for it is a *r* of consecration
Ex 29:26 of the *r* of Aaron's consecration
Ex 29:27 of the *r* of the consecration,
Ex 29:31 take the *r* of the consecration
Ex 29:32 sons shall eat the flesh of the *r*
Lev 5:15 a *r* without blemish out of the
Lev 5:16 the *r* of the trespass offering
Lev 5:18 he shall bring a *r* without
Lev 6:6 a *r* without blemish out of the
Lev 8:18 he brought the *r* for the burnt
Lev 8:18 hands upon the head of the *r*
Lev 8:20 And he cut the *r* into pieces
Lev 8:21 burnt the whole *r* upon the altar
Lev 8:22 other ram, the *r* of consecration
Lev 8:22 hands upon the head of the *r*
Lev 8:29 for of the *r* of consecration it
Lev 9:2 a *r* for a burnt offering, without
Lev 9:4 a *r* for peace offerings, to
Lev 9:18 the *r* for a sacrifice of peace
Lev 9:19 fat of the bullock and of the *r*
Lev 16:3 and a *r* for a burnt offering
Lev 16:5 one *r* for a burnt offering
Lev 19:21 even a *r* for a trespass offering
Lev 19:22 an atonement for him with the *r*
Num 5:8 beside the *r* of the atonement,
Num 6:14 one *r* without blemish for peace
Num 6:17 he shall offer the *r* for a
Num 6:19 take the sodden shoulder of the *r*
Num 7:15 One young bullock, one *r*, one
Num 7:21 One young bullock, one *r*, one
Num 7:27 One young bullock, one *r*, one
Num 7:33 One young bullock, one *r*, one
Num 7:39 One young bullock, one *r*, one
Num 7:45 One young bullock, one *r*, one
Num 7:51 One young bullock, one *r*, one
Num 7:57 One young bullock, one *r*, one
Num 7:63 One young bullock, one *r*, one
Num 7:69 One young bullock, one *r*, one
Num 7:75 One young bullock, one *r*, one
Num 7:81 One young bullock, one *r*, one
Num 15:6 Or for a *r*, thou shalt prepare
Num 15:11 for one bullock, or for one *r*
Num 23:2 on every altar a bullock and a *r*
Num 23:4 upon every altar a bullock and a *r*
Num 23:14 a bullock and a *r* on every altar
Num 23:30 a bullock and a *r* on every altar
Num 28:11 two young bullocks, and one *r*
Num 28:12 mingled with oil, for one *r*
Num 28:14 the third part of an hin unto a *r*
Num 28:19 two young bullocks, and one *r*
Num 28:20 and two tenth deals for a *r*
Num 28:27 two young bullocks, one *r*
Num 28:28 two tenth deals unto one *r*
Num 29:2 one young bullock, one *r*, and
Num 29:3 and two tenth deals for a *r*
Num 29:8 one young bullock, one *r*, and
Num 29:9 and two tenth deals to one *r*
Num 29:14 deals to each *r* of the two rams
Num 29:36 one bullock, one *r*, seven lambs
Num 29:37 for the bullock, for the *r*
Ezr 10:19 they offered a *r* of the flock for
Eze 43:23 a *r* out of the flock without
Eze 43:25 a *r* out of the flock, without
Eze 45:24 a bullock, and an ephah for a *r*
Eze 46:4 blemish, and a *r* without blemish
Eze 46:5 shall be an ephah for a *r*
Eze 46:6 blemish, and six lambs, and a *r*
Eze 46:7 a bullock, and an ephah for a *r*
Eze 46:11 to a bullock, and an ephah to a *r*
Dan 8:3 the river a *r* which had two horns
Dan 8:4 I saw the *r* pushing westward, and
Dan 8:6 he came to the *r* that had two
Dan 8:7 I saw him come close unto the *r*
Dan 8:7 against him, and smote the *r*
Dan 8:7 in the *r* to stand before him
Dan 8:7 deliver the *r* out of his hand
Dan 8:20 The *r* which thou sawest having

**RAMA** *(ra-mah)* See RAMAH. *Same as Ramah 1.*
Mt 2:18 In *R* was there a voice heard,

**RAMAH** *(ra'-mah)* See RAMA, RAMATH.
*1. A city in Benjamin.*
Josh 18:25 Gibeon, and *R*, and Beeroth,
Judg 4:5 palm tree of Deborah between *R*
Judg 19:13 all night, in Gibeah, or in *R*
1Kin 15:17 went up against Judah, and built *R*
1Kin 15:21 that he left off building of *R*
1Kin 15:22 and they took away the stones of *R*
2Chr 16:1 came up against Judah, and built *R*
2Chr 16:5 that he left off building of *R*
2Chr 16:6 they carried away the stones of *R*
Ezr 2:26 The children of *R* and Gaba, six
Neh 7:30 The men of *R* and Gaba, six hundred
Neh 11:33 Hazor, *R*, Gittaim,
Is 10:29 *R* is afraid
Jer 40:1 the guard had let him go from *R*
Hos 5:8 in Gibeah, and the trumpet in *R*
*2. A city in Naphtali.*
Josh 19:29 And then the coast turneth to *R*
Josh 19:36 And Adamah, and *R*, and Hazor,
*3. A city in Ephraim.*
1Sa 1:19 and came to their house to *R*
1Sa 2:11 And Elkanah went to *R* to his house

1Sa 7:17 And his return was to R
1Sa 8:4 and came to Samuel unto R
1Sa 15:34 Then Samuel went to R
1Sa 16:13 So Samuel rose up, and went to R
1Sa 19:18 escaped, and came to Samuel to R
1Sa 19:19 Behold, David is at Naioth in R
1Sa 19:22 Then went he also to R, and came
1Sa 19:22 Behold, they be at Naioth in R
1Sa 19:23 And he went thither to Naioth in R
1Sa 19:23 until he came to Naioth in R
1Sa 20:1 And David fled from Naioth in R
1Sa 22:6 abode in Gibeah under a tree in R
1Sa 25:1 and buried him in his house at R
1Sa 28:3 lamented him, and buried him in R
Jer 31:15 A voice was heard in R,
*4. A short form of Ramoth-Gilead.*
2Kin 8:29 the Syrians had given him at R
2Chr 22:6 wounds which were given him at R

**RAMATH** *(ra-math) A city in Simeon.*
Josh 19:8 to Baalath-beer, R of the south

**RAMATHAIM-ZOPHIM** *(ram-a-tha'-im-zo'-fim) A city on Mt. Ephraim.*
1Sa 1:1 Now there was a certain man of R

**RAMATHITE** *(ra'-math-ite) An inhabitant of Ramah 1.*
1Chr 27:27 the vineyards was Shimei the R

**RAMATH-LEHI** *(ra'-math-le'-hi) A place in Judah.*
Judg 15:17 his hand, and called that place R

**RAMATH-MIZPEH** *(ra'-math-miz'-peh) A city in Gad.*
Josh 13:26 And from Heshbon unto R, and

**RAMESES** *(ram'-e-seze)* See RAAMSES. *A city in Goshen.*
Gen 47:11 of the land, in the land of R
Ex 12:37 journeyed from R to Succoth
Num 33:3 from R in the first month
Num 33:5 children of Israel removed from R

**RAMIAH** *(ra'-mi-ah) Married a foreigner while in exile.*
Ezr 10:25 R, and Jeziah, and Malchiah, and

**RAMOTH** *(ra'-moth)* See JARMUTH, RAMAH, RAMOTH-GILEAD, REMETH.
*1. A Levitical city in Gad.*
Deut 4:43 R in Gilead, of the Gadites
Josh 20:8 R in Gilead out of the tribe of
Josh 21:38 R in Gilead with her suburbs, to
1Chr 6:80 R in Gilead with her suburbs, and
*2. A Levitical city in Issachar.*
1Chr 6:73 R with her suburbs, and Anem with
*3. Married a foreigner in exile.*
Ezr 10:29 and Adaiah, Jashub, and Sheal, and R
*4. A city in Simeon.*
1Sa 30:27 and to them which were in south R
*5. Same as Ramoth-gilead.*
1Kin 22:3 Know ye that R in Gilead is ours,

**RAMOTH-GILEAD** *(ra'-moth-ghil'-e-ad) A city in Gad.*
1Kin 4:13 The son of Geber, in R
1Kin 22:4 thou go with me to battle to R
1Kin 22:6 Shall I go against R to battle
1Kin 22:12 prophesied so, saying, Go up to R
1Kin 22:15 shall we go against R to battle
1Kin 22:20 that he may go up and fall at R
1Kin 22:29 the king of Judah went up to R
2Kin 8:28 against Hazael king of Syria in R
2Kin 9:1 of oil in thine hand, and go to R
2Kin 9:4 young man the prophet, went to R
2Kin 9:14 (Now Joram had kept R, he and all
2Chr 18:2 him to go up with him to R
2Chr 18:3 Judah, Wilt thou go with me to R
2Chr 18:5 them, Shall we go to R to battle
2Chr 18:11 prophesied so, saying, Go up to R
2Chr 18:14 shall we go to R to battle
2Chr 18:19 that he may go up and fall at R
2Chr 18:28 the king of Judah went up to R
2Chr 22:5 against Hazael king of Syria at R

**RAMS**
Gen 31:10 the r which leaped upon the
Gen 31:12 all the r which leap upon the
Gen 31:38 the r of thy flock have I not
Gen 32:14 two hundred ewes, and twenty r
Ex 29:1 and two r without blemish,
Ex 29:3 with the bullock and the two r
Ex 35:23 and goats' hair, and red skins of r
Lev 8:2 for the sin offering, and two r
Lev 23:18 and one young bullock, and two r
Num 7:17 peace offerings, two oxen, five r
Num 7:23 peace offerings, two oxen, five r
Num 7:29 peace offerings, two oxen, five r
Num 7:35 peace offerings, two oxen, five r
Num 7:41 peace offerings, two oxen, five r
Num 7:47 peace offerings, two oxen, five r
Num 7:53 peace offerings, two oxen, five r
Num 7:59 peace offerings, two oxen, five r
Num 7:65 peace offerings, two oxen, five r
Num 7:71 peace offerings, two oxen, five r
Num 7:77 peace offerings, two oxen, five r
Num 7:83 peace offerings, two oxen, five r
Num 7:87 the r twelve, the lambs of the
Num 7:88 the r sixty, the he goats sixty,
Num 23:1 me here seven oxen and seven r
Num 23:29 me here seven bullocks and seven r
Num 29:13 thirteen young bullocks, two r
Num 29:14 deals to each ram of the two r
Num 29:17 twelve young bullocks, two r
Num 29:18 for the bullocks, for the r
Num 29:20 third day eleven bullocks, two r
Num 29:21 for the bullocks, for the r
Num 29:23 fourth day ten bullocks, two r
Num 29:24 for the bullocks, for the r
Num 29:26 fifth day nine bullocks, two r
Num 29:27 for the bullocks, for the r
Num 29:29 sixth day eight bullocks, two r
Num 29:30 for the bullocks, for the r
Num 29:32 seventh day seven bullocks, two r
Num 29:33 for the bullocks, for the r
Deut 32:14 r of the breed of Bashan, and
1Sa 15:22 and to hearken than the fat of r
2Kin 3:4 lambs, and an hundred thousand r
1Chr 15:26 offered seven bullocks and seven r
1Chr 29:21 a thousand bullocks, a thousand r
2Chr 13:9 with a young bullock and seven r
2Chr 17:11 seven thousand and seven hundred r
2Chr 29:21 seven bullocks, and seven r
2Chr 29:22 when they had killed the r
2Chr 29:32 and ten bullocks, an hundred r
Ezr 6:9 of, both young bullocks, and r
Ezr 6:17 hundred bullocks, two hundred r
Ezr 7:17 with this money bullocks, r
Ezr 8:35 for all Israel, ninety and six r
Job 42:8 you now seven bullocks and seven r
Ps 66:15 fatlings, with the incense of r
Ps 114:4 The mountains skipped like r
Ps 114:6 mountains, that ye skipped like r
Is 1:11 full of the burnt offerings of r
Is 34:6 with the fat of the kidneys of r
Is 60:7 the r of Nebaioth shall minister
Jer 51:40 slaughter, like r with he goats
Eze 4:2 set battering r against it round
Eze 21:22 battering r against the gates
Eze 27:21 occupied with thee in lambs, and r
Eze 34:17 cattle and cattle, between the r
Eze 39:18 of the princes of the earth, of r
Eze 45:23 seven r without blemish daily the
Mic 6:7 be pleased with thousands of r

**RAMS'**
Ex 25:5 r skins dyed red, and badgers'
Ex 26:14 for the tent of r skins dyed red
Ex 35:7 r skins dyed red, and badgers'
Ex 36:19 for the tent of r skins dyed red
Ex 39:34 the covering of r skins dyed red
Josh 6:4 the ark seven trumpets of r horns
Josh 6:6 of r horns before the ark of the
Josh 6:8 bearing the seven trumpets of r
Josh 6:13 bearing seven trumpets of r horns

**RAN**
Gen 18:2 he r to meet them from the tent
Gen 18:7 Abraham r unto the herd, and
Gen 24:17 And the servant r to meet her
Gen 24:20 r again unto the well to draw
Gen 24:28 And the damsel r, and told them of
Gen 24:29 Laban r out unto the man, unto
Gen 29:12 and she r and told her father
Gen 29:13 that he r to meet him, and
Gen 33:4 Esau r to meet him, and embraced
Ex 9:23 the fire r along upon the ground
Num 11:27 there r a young man, and told
Num 16:47 and r into the midst of the
Josh 7:22 and they r unto the tent
Josh 8:19 and they r as soon as he had
Judg 7:21 and all the host r, and cried, and
Judg 9:21 And Jotham r away, and fled, and
Judg 9:44 the two other companies r upon
Judg 13:10 And the woman made haste, and r
1Sa 3:5 he r unto Eli, and said, Here am I
1Sa 4:12 there r a man of Benjamin out of
1Sa 10:23 And they r and fetched him thence
1Sa 17:22 r into the army, and came and
1Sa 17:48 r toward the army to meet the
1Sa 17:51 Therefore David r, and stood upon
1Sa 20:36 And as the lad r, he shot an arrow
2Sa 18:21 bowed himself unto Joab, and r
2Sa 18:23 Then Ahimaaz r by the way of the
1Kin 2:39 two of the servants of Shimei r
1Kin 18:35 the water r round about the altar
1Kin 18:46 r before Ahab to the entrance of
1Kin 19:20 r after Elijah, and said, Let me,
1Kin 22:35 the blood r out of the wound into
2Chr 32:4 the brook that r through the
Ps 77:2 my sore r in the night, and ceased
Ps 105:41 they r in the dry places like a
Ps 133:2 that r down upon the beard, even
Jer 23:21 sent these prophets, yet they r
Eze 1:14 And the living creatures r
Eze 47:2 there r out waters on the right
Dan 8:6 r unto him in the fury of his
Mt 8:32 the whole herd of swine r
Mt 27:48 And straightway one of them r
Mk 5:6 when he saw Jesus afar off, he r
Mk 5:13 the herd r violently down a steep
Mk 6:33 r afoot thither out of all cities
Mk 6:55 r through that whole region round
Mk 15:36 And one r and filled a spunge full
Lk 8:33 the herd r violently down a steep
Lk 15:20 saw him, and had compassion, and r
Lk 19:4 he r before, and climbed up into a
Lk 24:12 Peter, and r unto the sepulchre
Jn 20:4 So they r both together
Acts 3:11 all the people r together unto
Acts 7:57 r upon him with one accord,
Acts 8:30 Philip r thither to him, and heard
Acts 12:14 the gate for gladness, but r in
Acts 14:14 r in among the people, crying out
Acts 21:30 moved, and the people r together
Acts 21:32 centurions, and r down unto them
Acts 27:41 seas met, they r the ship aground
Jude 11 r greedily after the error of

**RANGES**
Lev 11:35 or r for pots, they shall be
2Kin 11:8 and he that cometh within the r
2Kin 11:15 Have her forth without the r
2Chr 23:14 them, Have her forth of the r

**RANK**
Gen 41:5 of corn came up upon one stalk, r
Gen 41:7 thin ears devoured the seven r
Num 2:16 shall set forth in the second r
Num 2:24 shall go forward in the third r
1Chr 12:33 thousand, which could keep r
1Chr 12:38 men of war, that could keep r

**RANKS**
1Kin 7:4 was against light in three r
1Kin 7:5 was against light in three r
Joel 2:7 and they shall not break their r
Mk 6:40 And they sat down in r, by

**RANSOM**
Ex 21:30 then he shall give for the r of
Ex 30:12 a r for his soul unto the LORD
Job 33:24 I have found a r
Job 36:18 then a great r cannot deliver
Ps 49:7 nor give to God a r for him
Prov 6:35 He will not regard any r
Prov 13:8 The r of a man's life are his
Prov 21:18 shall be a r for the righteous
Is 43:3 I gave Egypt for thy r, Ethiopia
Hos 13:14 I will r them from the power of
Mt 20:28 and to give his life a r for many
Mk 10:45 and to give his life a r for many
1Ti 2:6 Who gave himself a r for all

**RANSOMED**
Is 35:10 the r of the LORD shall return,
Is 51:10 sea a way for the r to pass over
Jer 31:11 r him from the hand of him that

**RAPHA** *(ra'-fah)* See BETH-RAPHA, REPHAIAH.
*1. Son of Benjamin.*
1Chr 8:2 Nohah the fourth, and R the fifth
*2. A member of Saul's family.*
1Chr 8:37 R was his son, Eleasah his son,

**RAPHU** *(ra'-fu) A Benjamite spy sent to the Promised Land.*
Num 13:9 of Benjamin, Palti the son of R

**RATE**
Ex 16:4 and gather a certain *r* every day
1Kin 10:25 and mules, a *r* year by year
2Kin 25:30 a daily *r* for every day, all the
2Chr 8:13 Even after a certain *r* every day
2Chr 9:24 and mules, a *r* year by year

**RAVEN**
Gen 8:7 And he sent forth a *r*, which went
Lev 11:15 Every *r* after his kind
Deut 14:14 And every *r* after his kind,
Job 38:41 Who provideth for the *r* his food
Song 5:11 locks are bushy, and black as a *r*
Is 34:11 also and the *r* shall dwell in it

**RAVENING**
Ps 22:13 upon me with their mouths, as a *r*
Eze 22:25 like a roaring lion *r* the prey
Eze 22:27 are like wolves *r* the prey
Mt 7:15 but inwardly they are *r* wolves
Lk 11:39 but your inward part is full of *r*

**RAVENOUS**
Is 35:9 nor any *r* beast shall go up
Is 46:11 Calling a *r* bird from the east,
Eze 39:4 unto the *r* birds of every sort

**RAVENS**
1Kin 17:4 the *r* to feed thee there
1Kin 17:6 the *r* brought him bread and flesh
Ps 147:9 food, and to the young *r* which cry
Prov 30:17 the *r* of the valley shall pick it
Lk 12:24 Consider the *r*

**RAVISHED**
Prov 5:19 be thou *r* always with her love
Prov 5:20 be *r* with a strange woman, and
Song 4:9 Thou hast *r* my heart, my sister,
Song 4:9 thou hast *r* my heart with one of
Is 13:16 be spoiled, and their wives *r*
Lam 5:11 They *r* the women in Zion, and the
Zec 14:2 the houses rifled, and the women *r*

**RAZOR**
Num 6:5 shall no *r* come upon his head
Judg 13:5 no *r* shall come on his head
Judg 16:17 hath not come a *r* upon mine head
1Sa 1:11 there shall no *r* come upon his
Is 7:20 Lord shave with a *r* that is hired
Eze 5:1 knife, take thee a barber's *r*

**READ**
Ex 24:7 *r* in the audience of the people
Deut 17:19 he shall *r* therein all the days
Deut 31:11 thou shalt *r* this law before all
Josh 8:34 afterward he *r* all the words of
Josh 8:35 which Joshua *r* not before all the
2Kin 5:7 king of Israel had *r* the letter
2Kin 19:14 hand of the messengers, and *r* it
2Kin 22:8 the book to Shaphan, and he *r* it
2Kin 22:10 Shaphan *r* it before the king
2Kin 22:16 which the king of Judah hath *r*
2Kin 23:2 he *r* in their ears all the words
2Chr 34:18 Shaphan *r* it before the king
2Chr 34:24 have *r* before the king of Judah
2Chr 34:30 he *r* in their ears all the words
Ezr 4:18 us hath been plainly *r* before me
Ezr 4:23 letter was *r* before Rehum
Neh 8:3 he *r* therein before the street
Neh 8:8 So they *r* in the book in the law
Neh 8:18 he *r* in the book of the law of
Neh 9:3 *r* in the book of the law of the
Neh 13:1 On that day they *r* in the book of
Est 6:1 they were *r* before the king
Is 29:11 saying, *R* this, I pray thee
Is 29:12 saying, *R* this, I pray thee
Is 34:16 out of the book of the LORD, and *r*
Is 37:14 hand of the messengers, and *r* it
Jer 29:29 Zephaniah the priest *r* this
Jer 36:6 *r* in the roll, which thou hast
Jer 36:6 also thou shalt *r* them in the
Jer 36:10 Then *r* Baruch in the book the
Jer 36:13 when Baruch *r* the book in the
Jer 36:14 hast *r* in the ears of the people
Jer 36:15 Sit down now, and *r* it in our ears
Jer 36:15 So Baruch *r* it in their ears
Jer 36:21 Jehudi *r* it in the ears of the
Jer 36:23 Jehudi had *r* three or four leaves
Jer 51:61 see, and shalt *r* all these words
Dan 5:7 Whosoever shall *r* this writing
Dan 5:8 but they could not *r* the writing
Dan 5:15 that they should *r* this writing
Dan 5:16 now if thou canst *r* the writing
Dan 5:17 yet I will *r* the writing unto the
Mt 12:3 Have ye not *r* what David did,
Mt 12:5 Or have ye not *r* in the law
Mt 19:4 and said unto them, Have ye not *r*
Mt 21:16 have ye never *r*, Out of the mouth
Mt 21:42 Did ye never *r* in the scriptures,
Mt 22:31 have ye not *r* that which was
Mk 2:25 Have ye never *r* what David did,
Mk 12:10 have ye not *r* this scripture
Mk 12:26 have ye not *r* in the book of
Lk 4:16 sabbath day, and stood up for to *r*
Lk 6:3 Have ye not *r* so much as this,
Jn 19:20 This title then *r* many of the
Acts 8:28 his chariot *r* Esaias the prophet
Acts 8:30 heard him *r* the prophet Esaias,
Acts 8:32 the scripture which he *r* was this
Acts 13:27 which are *r* every sabbath day
Acts 15:21 being *r* in the synagogues every
Acts 15:31 Which when they had *r*, they
Acts 23:34 the governor had *r* the letter
2Cor 1:13 than what ye *r* or acknowledge
2Cor 3:2 our hearts, known and *r* of all men
2Cor 3:15 unto this day, when Moses is *r*
Eph 3:4 Whereby, when ye *r*, ye may
Col 4:16 when this epistle is *r* among you
Col 4:16 cause that it be *r* also in the
Col 4:16 that ye likewise *r* the epistle
1Th 5:27 be *r* unto all the holy brethren
Rev 5:4 to *r* the book, neither to look

**READETH**
Hab 2:2 tables, that he may run that *r* it
Mt 24:15 stand in the holy place, (whoso *r*
Mk 13:14 not, (let him that *r* understand
Rev 1:3 Blessed is he that *r*, and they

**READING**
Neh 8:8 caused them to understand the *r*
Jer 36:8 *r* in the book the words of the
Jer 51:63 hast made an end of *r* this book
Acts 13:15 after the *r* of the law and the
2Cor 3:14 in the *r* of the old testament
1Ti 4:13 Till I come, give attendance to *r*

**READY**
Gen 18:6 Make *r* quickly three measures of
Gen 43:16 men home, and slay, and make *r*
Gen 43:25 they made *r* the present against
Gen 46:29 And Joseph made *r* his chariot
Ex 14:6 he made *r* his chariot, and took
Ex 17:4 they be almost *r* to stone me
Ex 19:11 be *r* against the third day
Ex 19:15 Be *r* against the third day
Ex 34:2 be *r* in the morning, and come up
Num 32:17 But we ourselves will go *r* armed
Deut 1:41 ye were *r* to go up into the hill
Deut 26:5 A Syrian *r* to perish was my
Josh 8:4 from the city, but be ye all *r*
Judg 6:19 made *r* a kid, and unleavened cakes
Judg 13:15 shall have made *r* a kid for thee
1Sa 25:18 of wine, and five sheep *r* dressed
2Sa 15:15 Behold, thy servants are *r* to do
2Sa 18:22 that thou hast no tidings *r*
1Kin 6:7 was built of stone made *r* before
2Kin 9:21 And Joram said, Make *r*
2Kin 9:21 And his chariot was made *r*
1Chr 12:23 that were *r* armed to the war
1Chr 12:24 eight hundred, *r* armed to the war
1Chr 28:2 had made *r* for the building
2Chr 17:18 fourscore thousand *r* prepared for
2Chr 35:14 they made *r* for themselves
Ezr 7:6 he was a *r* scribe in the law of
Neh 9:17 but thou art a God *r* to pardon
Est 3:14 they should be *r* against that day
Est 8:13 that the Jews should be *r* against
Job 3:8 who are *r* to raise up their
Job 12:5 He that is *r* to slip with his
Job 15:23 day of darkness is *r* at his hand
Job 15:24 as a king *r* to the battle
Job 15:28 which are *r* to become heaps
Job 17:1 extinct, the graves are *r* for me
Job 18:12 shall be *r* at his side
Job 29:13 that was *r* to perish came upon me
Job 32:19 it is *r* to burst like new bottles
Ps 7:12 hath bent his bow, and made it *r*
Ps 11:2 they make *r* their arrow upon the
Ps 21:12 when thou shalt make *r* thine
Ps 38:17 For I am *r* to halt, and my sorrow
Ps 45:1 tongue is the pen of a *r* writer
Ps 86:5 Lord, art good, and *r* to forgive
Ps 88:15 *r* to die from my youth up
Prov 24:11 and those that are *r* to be slain
Prov 31:6 unto him that is *r* to perish
Eccl 5:1 of God, and be more *r* to hear
Is 27:13 were *r* to perish in the land of
Is 30:13 be to you as a breach *r* to fall
Is 32:4 shall be *r* to speak plainly
Is 38:20 The LORD was *r* to save me
Is 41:7 saying, It is *r* for the sodering
Is 51:13 as if he were *r* to destroy
Eze 7:14 the trumpet, even to make all *r*
Dan 3:15 Now if ye be *r* that at what time
Hos 7:6 For they have made *r* their heart
Mt 22:4 are killed, and all things are *r*
Mt 22:8 to his servants, The wedding is *r*
Mt 24:44 Therefore be ye also *r*
Mt 25:10 they that were *r* went in with him
Mt 26:19 and they made *r* the passover
Mk 14:15 there make *r* for us
Mk 14:16 and they made *r* the passover
Mk 14:38 The spirit truly is *r*, but the
Lk 1:17 to make *r* a people prepared for
Lk 7:2 unto him, was sick, and *r* to die
Lk 9:52 the Samaritans, to make *r* for him
Lk 12:40 Be ye therefore *r* also
Lk 14:17 for all things are now *r*
Lk 17:8 Make *r* wherewith I may sup, and
Lk 22:12 there make *r*
Lk 22:13 and they made *r* the passover
Lk 22:33 I am *r* to go with thee, both into
Jn 7:6 but your time is alway *r*
Acts 10:10 but while they made *r*, he fell
Acts 20:7 *r* to depart on the morrow
Acts 21:13 for I am *r* not to be bound only,
Acts 23:15 he come near, are *r* to kill him
Acts 23:21 and now are they *r*, looking for a
Acts 23:23 Make *r* two hundred soldiers to go
Rom 1:15 I am *r* to preach the gospel to
2Cor 8:19 and declaration of your *r* mind
2Cor 9:2 that Achaia was *r* a year ago
2Cor 9:3 that, as I said, ye may be *r*
2Cor 9:5 before, that the same might be *r*
2Cor 10:16 line of things made *r* to our hand
2Cor 12:14 third time I am *r* to come to you
1Ti 6:18 *r* to distribute, willing to
2Ti 4:6 For I am now *r* to be offered, and
Titus 3:1 to be *r* to every good work,
Heb 8:13 waxeth old is *r* to vanish away
1Pet 1:5 through faith unto salvation *r* to
1Pet 3:15 be *r* always to give an answer to
1Pet 4:5 him that is *r* to judge the quick
1Pet 5:2 for filthy lucre, but of a *r* mind
Rev 3:2 which remain, that are *r* to die
Rev 12:4 woman which was *r* to be delivered
Rev 19:7 and his wife hath made herself *r*

**REAIA** *(re-ah'-yah) Grandfather of Beerah.*
1Chr 5:5 his son, *R* his son, Baal his son,

**REAIAH** *(re-ah'-yah)* See REAIA.
*1. Son of Shobal.*
1Chr 4:2 *R* the son of Shobal begat Jahath
*2. A family of exiles.*
Ezr 2:47 of Gahar, the children of *R*
Neh 7:50 The children of *R*, the children

**REALM**
2Chr 20:30 So the *r* of Jehoshaphat was quiet
Ezr 7:13 his priests and Levites, in my *r*
Ezr 7:23 wrath against the *r* of the king
Dan 1:20 that were in all his *r*
Dan 6:3 to set him over the whole *r*
Dan 9:1 king over the *r* of the Chaldeans
Dan 11:2 up all against the *r* of Grecia

**REAP**
Lev 19:9 when ye *r* the harvest of your
Lev 19:9 thou shalt not wholly *r* the
Lev 23:10 shall *r* the harvest thereof, then
Lev 23:22 when ye *r* the harvest of your
Lev 25:5 of thy harvest thou shalt not *r*
Lev 25:11 neither *r* that which groweth of
Ruth 2:9 be on the field that they do *r*
1Sa 8:12 to *r* his harvest, and to make his
2Kin 19:29 and in the third year sow ye, and *r*
Job 4:8 and sow wickedness, *r* the same
Job 24:6 They *r* every one his corn in the
Ps 126:5 that sow in tears shall *r* in joy
Prov 22:8 soweth iniquity shall *r* vanity
Eccl 11:4 regardeth the clouds shall not *r*
Is 37:30 and in the third year sow ye, and *r*
Jer 12:13 sown wheat, but shall *r* thorns
Hos 8:7 they shall *r* the whirlwind
Hos 10:12 in righteousness, *r* in mercy
Mic 6:15 shalt sow, but thou shalt not *r*

Mt 6:26 they sow not, neither do they *r*
Mt 25:26 that I *r* where I sowed not
Lk 12:24 for they neither sow nor *r*
Jn 4:38 I sent you to *r* that whereon ye
1Cor 9:11 if we shall *r* your carnal things
2Cor 9:6 sparingly shall *r* also sparingly
2Cor 9:6 shall *r* also bountifully
Gal 6:7 man soweth, that shall he also *r*
Gal 6:8 shall of the flesh *r* corruption
Gal 6:8 of the Spirit *r* life everlasting
Gal 6:9 for in due season we shall *r*
Rev 14:15 cloud, Thrust in thy sickle, and *r*
Rev 14:15 the time is come for thee to *r*

**REAPERS**
Ruth 2:3 gleaned in the field after the *r*
Ruth 2:4 Beth-lehem, and said unto the *r*
Ruth 2:5 servant that was set over the *r*
Ruth 2:6 that was set over the *r* answered
Ruth 2:7 gather after the *r* among the
Ruth 2:14 And she sat beside the *r*
2Kin 4:18 went out to his father to the *r*
Mt 13:30 of harvest I will say to the *r*
Mt 13:39 and the *r* are the angels

**REAR**
Ex 26:30 thou shalt *r* up the tabernacle
Lev 26:1 neither *r* you up a standing image
2Sa 24:18 *r* an altar unto the LORD in the
Jn 2:20 wilt thou *r* it up in three days

**REARED**
Ex 40:17 that the tabernacle was *r* up
Ex 40:18 Moses *r* up the tabernacle, and
Ex 40:18 bars thereof, and *r* up his pillars
Ex 40:33 he *r* up the court round about the
Num 9:15 was *r* up the cloud covered the
2Sa 18:18 *r* up for himself a pillar, which
1Kin 16:32 he *r* up an altar for Baal in the
2Kin 21:3 he *r* up altars for Baal, and made
2Chr 3:17 he *r* up the pillars before the
2Chr 33:3 he *r* up altars for Baalim, and

**REASON**
Gen 41:31 by *r* of that famine following
Gen 47:13 Canaan fainted by *r* of the famine
Ex 2:23 Israel sighed by *r* of the bondage
Ex 2:23 up unto God by *r* of the bondage
Ex 3:7 cry by *r* of their taskmasters
Ex 8:24 by *r* of the swarm of flies
Num 9:10 be unclean by *r* of a dead body
Num 18:8 given them by *r* of the anointing
Num 18:32 ye shall bear no sin by *r* of it
Deut 5:5 ye were afraid by *r* of the fire
Deut 23:10 that is not clean by *r* of
Josh 9:13 old by *r* of the very long journey
Judg 2:18 by *r* of them that oppressed them
1Sa 12:7 that I may *r* with you before the
1Kin 9:15 this is the *r* of the levy which
1Kin 14:4 his eyes were set by *r* of his age
2Chr 5:14 to minister by *r* of the cloud
2Chr 20:15 by *r* of this great multitude
2Chr 21:15 by *r* of the sickness day by day
2Chr 21:19 fell out by *r* of his sickness
Job 6:16 are blackish by *r* of the ice
Job 9:14 choose out my words to *r* with him
Job 13:3 and I desire to *r* with God
Job 15:3 Should he *r* with unprofitable
Job 17:7 eye also is dim by *r* of sorrow
Job 31:23 by *r* of his highness I could not
Job 35:9 By *r* of the multitude of
Job 35:9 they cry out by *r* of the arm of
Job 37:19 order our speech by *r* of darkness
Job 41:25 by *r* of breakings they purify
Ps 38:8 I have roared by *r* of the
Ps 44:16 by *r* of the enemy and avenger
Ps 78:65 man that shouteth by *r* of wine
Ps 88:9 eye mourneth by *r* of affliction
Ps 90:10 if by *r* of strength they be
Ps 102:5 By *r* of the voice of my groaning
Prov 20:4 will not plow by *r* of the cold
Prov 26:16 seven men that can render a *r*
Eccl 7:25 the *r* of things, and to know the
Is 1:18 let us *r* together, saith the LORD
Is 49:19 narrow by *r* of the inhabitants
Eze 19:10 of branches by *r* of many waters
Eze 21:12 terrors by *r* of the sword shall
Eze 26:10 By *r* of the abundance of his
Eze 27:12 Tarshish was thy merchant by *r* of
Eze 27:16 Syria was thy merchant by *r* of
Eze 28:17 thy wisdom by *r* of thy brightness
Dan 4:36 same time my *r* returned unto me
Dan 5:10 by *r* of the words of the king and
Dan 8:12 sacrifice by *r* of transgression
Jonah 2:2 I cried by *r* of mine affliction
Mic 2:12 by *r* of the multitude of men
Mt 16:8 why *r* ye among yourselves,
Mk 2:8 Why *r* ye these things in your
Mk 8:17 it, he saith unto them, Why *r* ye
Lk 5:21 and the Pharisees began to *r*
Lk 5:22 them, What *r* ye in your hearts
Jn 6:18 the sea arose by *r* of a great
Jn 12:11 Because that by *r* of him many of
Acts 6:2 It is not *r* that we should leave
Acts 18:14 *r* would that I should bear with
Rom 8:20 but by *r* of him who hath
2Cor 3:10 by *r* of the glory that excelleth
Heb 5:3 by *r* hereof he ought, as for the
Heb 5:14 even those who by *r* of use have
Heb 7:23 to continue by *r* of death
1Pet 3:15 to every man that asketh you a *r*
2Pet 2:2 by *r* of whom the way of truth
Rev 8:13 by *r* of the other voices of the
Rev 9:2 by *r* of the smoke of the pit
Rev 18:19 in the sea by *r* of her costliness

**REASONED**
Mt 16:7 they *r* among themselves, saying,
Mt 21:25 they *r* with themselves, saying,
Mk 2:8 that they so *r* within themselves
Mk 8:16 they *r* among themselves, saying,
Mk 11:31 they *r* with themselves, saying,
Lk 20:5 they *r* with themselves, saying,
Lk 20:14 they *r* among themselves, saying,
Lk 24:15 while they communed together and *r*
Acts 17:2 three sabbath days *r* with them
Acts 18:4 he *r* in the synagogue every
Acts 18:19 the synagogue, and *r* with the Jews
Acts 24:25 as he *r* of righteousness,

**REASONING**
Job 13:6 Hear now my *r*, and hearken to the
Mk 2:6 there, and *r* in their hearts,
Mk 12:28 and having heard them *r* together
Lk 9:46 Then there arose a *r* among them
Acts 28:29 had great *r* among themselves

**REBA** *(re'-bah) A king of Midian.*
Num 31:8 and Rekem, and Zur, and Hur, and *R*
Josh 13:21 and Rekem, and Zur, and Hur, and *R*

**REBECCA** *(re-bek'-kah)* See REBEKAH. *Greek form of Rebekah.*
Rom 9:10 but when *R* also had conceived by

**REBEKAH** *(re-bek'-kah)* See REBECCA, REBEKAH'S. *Wife of Isaac.*
Gen 22:23 And Bethuel begat *R*
Gen 24:15 *R* came out, who was born to
Gen 24:29 *R* had a brother, and his name was
Gen 24:30 heard the words of *R* his sister
Gen 24:45 *R* came forth with her pitcher on
Gen 24:51 *R* is before thee, take her, and go
Gen 24:53 and raiment, and gave them to *R*
Gen 24:58 And they called *R*, and said unto
Gen 24:59 And they sent away *R* their sister
Gen 24:60 And they blessed *R*, and said unto
Gen 24:61 *R* arose, and her damsels, and they
Gen 24:61 and the servant took *R*, and went
Gen 24:64 *R* lifted up her eyes, and when she
Gen 24:67 mother Sarah's tent, and took *R*
Gen 25:20 years old when he took *R* to wife
Gen 25:21 of him, and *R* his wife conceived
Gen 25:28 but *R* loved Jacob
Gen 26:7 of the place should kill me for *R*
Gen 26:8 was sporting with *R* his wife
Gen 26:35 grief of mind unto Isaac and to *R*
Gen 27:5 *R* heard when Isaac spake to Esau
Gen 27:6 *R* spake unto Jacob her son,
Gen 27:11 And Jacob said to *R* his mother
Gen 27:15 *R* took goodly raiment of her
Gen 27:42 Esau her elder son were told to *R*
Gen 27:46 *R* said to Isaac, I am weary of my
Gen 28:5 the Syrian, the brother of *R*
Gen 49:31 they buried Isaac and *R* his wife

**REBEKAH'S** *(re-bek'-kahz)*
Gen 29:12 brother, and that he was *R* son
Gen 35:8 But Deborah *R* nurse died, and she

**REBEL**
Num 14:9 Only *r* not ye against the LORD,
Josh 1:18 doth *r* against thy commandment
Josh 22:16 that ye might *r* this day against
Josh 22:18 seeing ye *r* to day against the
Josh 22:19 but *r* not against the LORD
Josh 22:19 nor *r* against us, in building you
Josh 22:29 that we should *r* against the LORD
1Sa 12:14 not *r* against the commandment of
1Sa 12:15 but *r* against the commandment of
Neh 2:19 will ye *r* against the king
Neh 6:6 that thou and the Jews think to *r*
Job 24:13 of those that *r* against the light
Is 1:20 But if ye refuse and *r*, ye shall
Hos 7:14 and wine, and they *r* against me

**REBELLED**
Gen 14:4 and in the thirteenth year they *r*
Num 20:24 because ye *r* against my word at
Num 27:14 For ye *r* against my commandment
Deut 1:26 but *r* against the commandment of
Deut 1:43 but *r* against the commandment of
Deut 9:23 then ye *r* against the commandment
1Kin 12:19 So Israel *r* against the house of
2Kin 1:1 Then Moab *r* against Israel after
2Kin 3:5 that the king of Moab *r* against
2Kin 3:7 king of Moab hath *r* against me
2Kin 18:7 he *r* against the king of Assyria,
2Kin 24:1 then he turned and *r* against him
2Kin 24:20 that Zedekiah *r* against the king
2Chr 10:19 Israel *r* against the house of
2Chr 13:6 up, and hath *r* against his lord
2Chr 36:13 And he also *r* against king
Neh 9:26 *r* against thee, and cast thy law
Ps 5:10 for they have *r* against thee
Ps 105:28 they *r* not against his word
Ps 107:11 Because they *r* against the words
Is 1:2 and they have *r* against me
Is 63:10 But they *r*, and vexed his holy
Jer 52:3 that Zedekiah *r* against the king
Lam 1:18 for I have *r* against his
Lam 1:20 for I have grievously *r*
Lam 3:42 We have transgressed and have *r*
Eze 2:3 nation that hath *r* against me
Eze 17:15 But he *r* against him in sending
Eze 20:8 But they *r* against me, and would
Eze 20:13 But the house of Israel *r* against
Eze 20:21 the children *r* against me
Dan 9:5 and have done wickedly, and have *r*
Dan 9:9 though we have *r* against him
Hos 13:16 for she hath *r* against her God

**REBELLION**
Deut 31:27 For I know thy *r*, and thy stiff
Josh 22:22 if it be in *r*, or if in
1Sa 15:23 For *r* is as the sin of witchcraft
Ezr 4:19 against kings, and that *r* and
Neh 9:17 in their *r* appointed a captain to
Job 34:37 For he addeth *r* unto his sin
Prov 17:11 An evil man seeketh only *r*
Jer 28:16 hast taught *r* against the LORD
Jer 29:32 he hath taught *r* against the LORD

**REBELLIOUS**
Deut 9:7 ye have been *r* against the LORD
Deut 9:24 Ye have been *r* against the LORD
Deut 21:18 *r* son, which will not obey the
Deut 21:20 This our son is stubborn and *r*
Deut 31:27 ye have been *r* against the LORD
1Sa 20:30 Thou son of the perverse *r* woman
Ezr 4:12 unto Jerusalem, building the *r*
Ezr 4:15 know that this city is a *r* city
Ps 66:7 let not the *r* exalt themselves
Ps 68:6 but the *r* dwell in a dry land
Ps 68:18 yea, for the *r* also, that the
Ps 78:8 a stubborn and *r* generation
Is 1:23 Thy princes are *r*, and companions
Is 30:1 Woe to the *r* children, saith the
Is 30:9 That this is a *r* people, lying
Is 50:5 opened mine ear, and I was not *r*
Is 65:2 hands all the day unto a *r* people
Jer 4:17 she hath been *r* against me
Jer 5:23 hath a revolting and a *r* heart
Eze 2:3 to a *r* nation that hath rebelled
Eze 2:5 forbear, (for they are a *r* house
Eze 2:6 looks, though they be a *r* house
Eze 2:7 for they are most *r*
Eze 2:8 Be not thou *r* like that
Eze 2:8 like that *r* house
Eze 3:9 looks, though they be a *r* house
Eze 3:26 for they are a *r* house
Eze 3:27 for they are a *r* house
Eze 12:2 in the midst of a *r* house
Eze 12:2 for they are a *r* house
Eze 12:3 though they be a *r* house
Eze 12:9 the *r* house, said unto thee, What
Eze 12:25 O *r* house, will I say the word,
Eze 17:12 Say now to the *r* house, Know ye

Eze 24:3 utter a parable unto the r house
Eze 44:6 And thou shalt say to the r

### REBUKE

Lev 19:17 shalt in any wise r thy neighbour
Deut 28:20 upon thee cursing, vexation, and r
Ruth 2:16 she may glean them, and r her not
2Kin 19:3 day is a day of trouble, and of r
1Chr 12:17 our fathers look thereon, and r it
Ps 6:1 r me not in thine anger, neither
Ps 18:15 world were discovered at thy r
Ps 38:1 O LORD, r me not in thy wrath
Ps 68:30 R the company of spearmen, the
Ps 76:6 At thy r, O God of Jacob, both
Ps 80:16 at the r of thy countenance
Ps 104:7 At thy r they fled
Prov 9:8 r a wise man, and he will love
Prov 13:1 but a scorner heareth not r
Prov 13:8 but the poor heareth not r
Prov 24:25 But to them that r him shall be
Prov 27:5 Open r is better than secret love
Eccl 7:5 better to hear the r of the wise
Is 2:4 nations, and shall r many people
Is 17:13 but God shall r them, and they
Is 25:8 the r of his people shall he take
Is 30:17 shall flee at the r of one
Is 30:17 at the r of five shall ye flee
Is 37:3 day is a day of trouble, and of r
Is 50:2 at my r I dry up the sea, I make
Is 51:20 of the LORD, the r of thy God
Is 54:9 be wroth with thee, nor r thee
Is 66:15 his r with flames of fire
Jer 15:15 for thy sake I have suffered r
Hos 5:9 shall be desolate in the day of r
Mic 4:3 r strong nations afar off
Zec 3:2 said unto Satan, The LORD r thee
Zec 3:2 that hath chosen Jerusalem r thee
Mal 3:11 I will r the devourer for your
Mt 16:22 Peter took him, and began to r him
Mk 8:32 Peter took him, and began to r him
Lk 17:3 trespass against thee, r him
Lk 19:39 unto him, Master, r thy disciples
Phil 2:15 the sons of God, without r
1Ti 5:1 R not an elder, but intreat him
1Ti 5:20 Them that sin r before all
2Ti 4:2 reprove, r, exhort with all
Titus 1:13 Wherefore r them sharply, that
Titus 2:15 exhort, and r with all authority
Jude 9 but said, The Lord r thee
Rev 3:19 As many as I love, I r and chasten

### REBUKED

Gen 31:42 my hands, and r thee yesternight
Gen 37:10 and his father r him, and said unto
Neh 5:7 I r the nobles, and the rulers, and
Ps 9:5 Thou hast r the heathen, thou
Ps 106:9 He r the Red sea also, and it was
Ps 119:21 Thou hast r the proud that are
Mt 8:26 arose, and r the winds and the sea
Mt 17:18 And Jesus r the devil
Mt 19:13 and the disciples r them
Mt 20:31 And the multitude r them, because
Mk 1:25 And Jesus r him, saying, Hold thy
Mk 4:39 r the wind, and said unto the sea,
Mk 8:33 he r Peter, saying, Get thee
Mk 9:25 he r the foul spirit, saying unto
Mk 10:13 his disciples r those that
Lk 4:35 And Jesus r him, saying, Hold thy
Lk 4:39 he stood over her, and r the fever
Lk 8:24 r the wind and the raging of the
Lk 9:42 Jesus r the unclean spirit, and
Lk 9:55 r them, and said, Ye know not what
Lk 18:15 his disciples saw it, they r them
Lk 18:39 And they which went before r him
Lk 23:40 But the other answering r him
Heb 12:5 nor faint when thou art r of him
2Pet 2:16 But was r for his iniquity

### REBUKETH

Prov 9:7 he that r a wicked man getteth
Prov 28:23 He that r a man afterwards shall
Amos 5:10 They hate him that r in the gate
Nah 1:4 He r the sea, and maketh it dry,

### RECEIVE

Gen 4:11 to r thy brother's blood from thy
Gen 33:10 then r my present at my hand
Gen 38:20 to r his pledge from the woman's
Ex 27:3 make his pans to r his ashes
Ex 29:25 thou shalt r them of their hands,
Num 18:28 which ye r of the children of
Deut 9:9 mount to r the tables of stone
Deut 33:3 every one shall r of thy words
1Sa 10:4 which thou shalt r of their hands
2Sa 18:12 Though I should r a thousand
1Kin 5:9 there, and thou shalt r them
1Kin 8:64 little to r the burnt offerings
2Kin 5:16 whom I stand, I will r none
2Kin 5:26 Is it a time to r money
2Kin 5:26 to r garments, and oliveyards, and
2Kin 12:7 now therefore r no more money of
2Kin 12:8 the priests consented to r no
2Chr 7:7 not able to r the burnt offerings
Job 2:10 shall we r good at the hand of
Job 2:10 of God, and shall we not r evil
Job 22:22 R, I pray thee, the law from his
Job 27:13 they shall r of the Almighty
Ps 6:9 the LORD will r my prayer
Ps 24:5 He shall r the blessing from the
Ps 49:15 for he shall r me
Ps 73:24 and afterward r me to glory
Ps 75:2 When I shall r the congregation I
Prov 1:3 To r the instruction of wisdom,
Prov 2:1 My son, if thou wilt r my words
Prov 4:10 Hear, O my son, and r my sayings
Prov 8:10 R my instruction, and not silver
Prov 10:8 wise in heart will r commandments
Prov 19:20 r instruction, that thou mayest
Is 57:6 Should I r comfort in these
Jer 5:3 they have refused to r correction
Jer 9:20 let your ear r the word of his
Jer 17:23 might not hear, nor r instruction
Jer 32:33 not hearkened to r instruction
Jer 35:13 Will ye not r instruction to
Eze 3:10 speak unto thee r in thine heart
Eze 16:61 when thou shalt r thy sisters
Eze 36:30 that ye shall r no more reproach
Dan 2:6 ye shall r of me gifts and rewards
Hos 10:6 Ephraim shall r shame, and Israel
Hos 14:2 all iniquity, and r us graciously
Mic 1:11 he shall r of you his standing
Zeph 3:7 fear me, thou wilt r instruction
Mal 3:10 shall not be room enough to r it
Mt 10:14 And whosoever shall not r you
Mt 10:41 shall r a prophet's reward
Mt 10:41 shall r a righteous man's reward
Mt 11:5 The blind r their sight, and the
Mt 11:14 And if ye will r it, this is Elias
Mt 18:5 whoso shall r one such little
Mt 19:11 All men cannot r this saying
Mt 19:12 He that is able to r it
Mt 19:12 let him r it
Mt 19:29 shall r an hundredfold, and shall
Mt 20:7 is right, that shall ye r
Mt 21:22 in prayer, believing, ye shall r
Mt 21:34 that they might r the fruits of
Mt 23:14 therefore ye shall r the greater
Mk 2:2 that there was no room to r them
Mk 4:16 immediately r it with gladness
Mk 4:20 r it, and bring forth fruit, some
Mk 6:11 And whosoever shall not r you
Mk 9:37 Whosoever shall r one of such
Mk 9:37 and whosoever shall r me,
Mk 10:15 Whosoever shall not r the kingdom
Mk 10:30 But he shall r an hundredfold now
Mk 10:51 Lord, that I might r my sight
Mk 11:24 ye pray, believe that ye r them
Mk 12:2 servant, that he might r from the
Mk 12:40 these shall r greater damnation
Lk 6:34 lend to them of whom ye hope to r
Lk 6:34 to sinners, to r as much again
Lk 8:13 they hear, r the word with joy
Lk 9:5 And whosoever will not r you
Lk 9:48 Whosoever shall r this child in
Lk 9:48 whosoever shall r me receiveth
Lk 9:53 And they did not r him, because
Lk 10:8 city ye enter, and they r you
Lk 10:10 they r you not, go your ways out
Lk 16:4 they may r me into their houses
Lk 16:9 they may r you into everlasting
Lk 18:17 Whosoever shall not r the kingdom
Lk 18:30 Who shall not r manifold more in
Lk 18:41 said, Lord, that I may r my sight
Lk 18:42 Jesus said unto him, R thy sight
Lk 19:12 to r for himself a kingdom
Lk 20:47 the same shall r greater
Lk 23:41 for we r the due reward of our
Jn 3:11 and ye r not our witness
Jn 3:27 and said, A man can r nothing
Jn 5:34 But I r not testimony from man
Jn 5:41 I r not honour from men
Jn 5:43 my Father's name, and ye r me not
Jn 5:43 in his own name, him ye will r
Jn 5:44 which r honour one of another, and
Jn 7:23 on the sabbath day r circumcision
Jn 7:39 they that believe on him should r
Jn 14:3 come again, and r you unto myself
Jn 14:17 whom the world cannot r, because
Jn 16:14 for he shall r of mine, and shall
Jn 16:24 ask, and ye shall r, that your joy
Jn 20:22 unto them, R ye the Holy Ghost
Acts 1:8 But ye shall r power, after that
Acts 2:38 ye shall r the gift of the Holy
Acts 3:5 expecting to r something of them
Acts 3:21 Whom the heaven must r until the
Acts 7:59 saying, Lord Jesus, r my spirit
Acts 8:15 that they might r the Holy Ghost
Acts 8:19 hands, he may r the Holy Ghost
Acts 9:12 on him, that he might r his sight
Acts 9:17 that thou mightest r thy sight
Acts 10:43 in him shall r remission of sins
Acts 16:21 which are not lawful for us to r
Acts 18:27 exhorting the disciples to r him
Acts 20:35 is more blessed to give than to r
Acts 22:13 me, Brother Saul, r thy sight
Acts 22:18 for they will not r thy testimony
Acts 26:18 that they may r forgiveness of
Rom 5:17 they which r abundance of grace
Rom 13:2 they that resist shall r to
Rom 14:1 that is weak in the faith r ye
Rom 15:7 Wherefore r ye one another, as
Rom 16:2 That ye r her in the Lord, as
1Cor 3:8 every man shall r his own reward
1Cor 3:14 thereupon, he shall r a reward
1Cor 4:7 hast thou that thou didst not r
1Cor 4:7 now if thou didst r it, why dost
1Cor 14:5 that the church may r edifying
2Cor 5:10 that every one may r the things
2Cor 6:1 beseech you also that ye r not
2Cor 6:17 and I will r you,
2Cor 7:2 R us; we have wronged
2Cor 7:9 that ye might r damage by us in
2Cor 8:4 intreaty that we would r the gift
2Cor 11:4 or if ye r another spirit, which
2Cor 11:16 if otherwise, yet as a fool r me
Gal 3:14 that we might r the promise of
Gal 4:5 that we might r the adoption of
Eph 6:8 the same shall he r of the Lord
Phil 2:29 R him therefore in the Lord with
Col 3:24 that of the Lord ye shall r the
Col 3:25 r for the wrong which he hath
Col 4:10 if he come unto you, r him
1Ti 5:19 Against an elder r not an
Philem 12 thou therefore r him, that is,
Philem 15 thou shouldest r him for ever
Philem 17 a partner, r him as myself
Heb 7:5 of Levi, who r the office of the
Heb 7:8 And here men that die r tithes
Heb 9:15 might r the promise of eternal
Heb 10:36 of God, ye might r the promise
Heb 11:8 should after r for an inheritance
Jas 1:7 he shall r any thing of the Lord
Jas 1:12 he shall r the crown of life,
Jas 1:21 r with meekness the engrafted
Jas 3:1 knowing that we shall r the
Jas 4:3 r not, because ye ask amiss, that
Jas 5:7 until he r the early and latter
1Pet 5:4 ye shall r a crown of glory that
2Pet 2:13 And shall r the reward of
1Jn 3:22 we r of him, because we keep his
1Jn 5:9 If we r the witness of men, the
2Jn 8 but that we r a full reward
2Jn 10 r him not into your house,
3Jn 8 We therefore ought to r such
3Jn 10 doth he himself r the brethren
Rev 4:11 to r glory and honour and power
Rev 5:12 Lamb that was slain to r power
Rev 13:16 to r a mark in their right hand,
Rev 14:9 r his mark in his forehead, or in
Rev 17:12 but r power as kings one hour
Rev 18:4 that ye r not of her plagues

### RECEIVED

Gen 26:12 r in the same year an hundredfold
Ex 32:4 he r them at their hand, and
Ex 36:3 they r of Moses all the offering,
Num 12:14 after that let her be r in again
Num 23:20 I have r commandment to bless
Num 34:14 fathers, have r their inheritance
Num 34:14 Manasseh have r their inheritance
Num 34:15 the half tribe have r their
Num 36:3 of the tribe whereunto they are r

Num 36:4 of the tribe whereunto they are *r*
Josh 13:8 and the Gadites have *r* their
Josh 18:2 had not yet *r* their inheritance
Josh 18:7 have *r* their inheritance beyond
Judg 13:23 would not have *r* a burnt offering
1Sa 12:3 or of whose hand have I *r* any
1Sa 25:35 So David *r* of her hand that which
1Kin 10:28 the king's merchants *r* the linen
2Kin 19:14 Hezekiah *r* the letter of the hand
1Chr 12:18 Then David *r* them, and made them
2Chr 1:16 the king's merchants *r* the linen
2Chr 4:5 and it *r* and held three thousand
2Chr 29:22 and the priests *r* the blood
2Chr 30:16 which they *r* of the hand of the
Est 4:4 but he *r* it not
Job 4:12 mine ear *r* a little thereof
Ps 68:18 thou hast *r* gifts for men
Prov 24:32 looked upon it, and *r* instruction
Is 37:14 Hezekiah *r* the letter from the
Is 40:2 for she hath *r* of the LORD's hand
Jer 2:30 they *r* no correction
Eze 18:17 that hath not *r* usury nor
Zeph 3:2 she *r* not correction
Mt 10:8 freely ye have *r*, freely give
Mt 13:19 This is he which *r* seed by the
Mt 13:20 But he that *r* the seed into stony
Mt 13:22 He also that *r* seed among the
Mt 13:23 But he that *r* seed into the good
Mt 17:24 they that *r* tribute money came to
Mt 20:9 hour, they *r* every man a penny
Mt 20:10 that they should have *r* more
Mt 20:10 they likewise *r* every man a penny
Mt 20:11 And when they had *r* it, they
Mt 20:34 and immediately their eyes *r* sight
Mt 25:16 Then he that had *r* the five
Mt 25:17 And likewise he that had *r* two
Mt 25:18 But he that had *r* one went
Mt 25:20 so he that had *r* five talents
Mt 25:22 also that had *r* two talents came
Mt 25:24 Then he which had *r* the one
Mt 25:27 should have *r* mine own with usury
Mk 7:4 be, which they have *r* to hold
Mk 10:52 And immediately he *r* his sight
Mk 15:23 but he *r* it not
Mk 16:19 he was *r* up into heaven, and sat
Lk 6:24 for ye have *r* your consolation
Lk 8:40 returned, the people gladly *r* him
Lk 9:11 he *r* them, and spake unto them of
Lk 9:51 was come that he should be *r* up
Lk 10:38 named Martha *r* him into her house
Lk 15:27 calf, because he hath *r* him safe
Lk 18:43 And immediately he *r* his sight
Lk 19:6 and came down, and *r* him joyfully
Lk 19:15 having *r* the kingdom, then he
Jn 1:11 his own, and his own *r* him not
Jn 1:12 But as many as *r* him, to them
Jn 1:16 And of his fulness have all we *r*
Jn 3:33 He that hath *r* his testimony hath
Jn 4:45 Galilee, the Galilaeans *r* him
Jn 6:21 willingly *r* him into the ship
Jn 9:11 and I went and washed, and I *r* sight
Jn 9:15 asked him how he had *r* his sight
Jn 9:18 *r* his sight, until they called
Jn 9:18 of him that had *r* his sight
Jn 10:18 commandment have I *r* of my Father
Jn 13:30 He then having *r* the sop went
Jn 17:8 and they have *r* them, and have
Jn 18:3 having *r* a band of men and
Jn 19:30 Jesus therefore had *r* the vinegar
Acts 1:9 a cloud *r* him out of their sight
Acts 2:33 having *r* of the Father the
Acts 2:41 Then they that gladly *r* his word
Acts 3:7 feet and ancle bones *r* strength
Acts 7:38 who *r* the lively oracles to give
Acts 7:53 Who have *r* the law by the
Acts 8:14 Samaria had *r* the word of God
Acts 8:17 on them, and they *r* the Holy Ghost
Acts 9:18 he *r* sight forthwith, and arose,
Acts 9:19 And when he had *r* meat, he was
Acts 10:16 the vessel was *r* up again into
Acts 10:47 which have *r* the Holy Ghost as
Acts 11:1 had also *r* the word of God
Acts 15:4 they were *r* of the church, and of
Acts 16:24 having *r* such a charge, thrust
Acts 17:7 Whom Jason hath *r*
Acts 17:11 in that they *r* the word with all
Acts 19:2 Have ye *r* the Holy Ghost since ye
Acts 20:24 which I have *r* of the Lord Jesus,
Acts 21:17 the brethren *r* us gladly
Acts 22:5 from whom also I *r* letters unto
Acts 26:10 having *r* authority from the chief
Acts 28:2 *r* us every one, because of the
Acts 28:7 who *r* us, and lodged us three days
Acts 28:21 We neither *r* letters out of
Acts 28:30 *r* all that came in unto him,
Rom 1:5 By whom we have *r* grace and
Rom 4:11 he *r* the sign of circumcision, a
Rom 5:11 whom we have now *r* the atonement
Rom 8:15 For ye have not *r* the spirit of
Rom 8:15 but ye have *r* the Spirit of
Rom 14:3 for God hath *r* him
Rom 15:7 as Christ also *r* us to the glory
1Cor 2:12 Now we have *r*, not the spirit of
1Cor 4:7 glory, as if thou hadst not *r* it
1Cor 11:23 For I have *r* of the Lord that
1Cor 15:1 unto you, which also ye have *r*
1Cor 15:3 first of all that which I also *r*
2Cor 4:1 this ministry, as we have *r* mercy
2Cor 7:15 with fear and trembling ye *r* him
2Cor 11:4 spirit, which ye have not *r*
2Cor 11:24 Of the Jews five times *r* I forty
Gal 1:9 unto you than that ye have *r*
Gal 1:12 For I neither *r* it of man
Gal 3:2 *R* ye the Spirit by the works of
Gal 4:14 but *r* me as an angel of God, even
Phil 4:9 which ye have both learned, and *r*
Phil 4:18 having *r* of Epaphroditus the
Col 2:6 As ye have therefore *r* Christ
Col 4:10 (touching whom ye *r* commandments
Col 4:17 which thou hast *r* in the Lord
1Th 1:6 having *r* the word in much
1Th 2:13 when ye *r* the word of God which
1Th 2:13 ye *r* it not as the word of men,
1Th 4:1 that as ye have *r* of us how ye
2Th 2:10 because they *r* not the love of
2Th 3:6 the tradition which he *r* of us
1Ti 3:16 on in the world, *r* up into glory
1Ti 4:3 which God hath created to be *r*
1Ti 4:4 if it be *r* with thanksgiving
Heb 2:2 disobedience *r* a just recompence
Heb 7:6 from them *r* tithes of Abraham
Heb 7:11 for under it the people *r* the law
Heb 10:26 have *r* the knowledge of the truth
Heb 11:11 *r* strength to conceive seed
Heb 11:13 not having *r* the promises, but
Heb 11:17 he that had *r* the promises
Heb 11:19 whence also he *r* him in a figure
Heb 11:31 when she had *r* the spies with
Heb 11:35 Women *r* their dead raised to life
Heb 11:39 through faith, *r* not the promise
Jas 2:25 when she had *r* the messengers, and
1Pet 1:18 from your vain conversation *r* by
1Pet 4:10 As every man hath *r* the gift
2Pet 1:17 For he *r* from God the Father
1Jn 2:27 ye have *r* of him abideth in you
2Jn 4 as we have *r* a commandment from
Rev 2:27 even as I *r* of my Father
Rev 3:3 therefore how thou hast *r*
Rev 17:12 which have *r* no kingdom as yet
Rev 19:20 that had *r* the mark of the beast
Rev 20:4 neither had *r* his mark upon their

**RECEIVETH**

Judg 19:18 is no man that *r* me to house
Job 35:7 or what *r* he of thine hand
Prov 21:11 is instructed, he *r* knowledge
Prov 29:4 but he that *r* gifts overthroweth
Jer 7:28 LORD their God, nor *r* correction
Mal 2:13 or *r* it with good will at your
Mt 7:8 For every one that asketh *r*
Mt 10:40 He that *r* you *r* me, and he
Mt 10:40 *r* me *r* him that sent me
Mt 10:41 He that *r* a prophet in the name
Mt 10:41 he that *r* a righteous man in the
Mt 13:20 the word, and anon with joy *r* it
Mt 18:5 such little child in my name *r* me
Mk 9:37 of such children in my name, *r* me
Mk 9:37 *r* not me, but him that sent me
Lk 9:48 this child in my name *r* me
Lk 9:48 receive me *r* him that sent me
Lk 11:10 For every one that asketh *r*
Lk 15:2 saying, This man *r* sinners
Jn 3:32 and no man *r* his testimony
Jn 4:36 And he that reapeth *r* wages
Jn 12:48 *r* not my words, hath one that
Jn 13:20 *r* whomsoever I send *r* me
Jn 13:20 *r* me *r* him that sent me
1Cor 2:14 But the natural man *r* not the
1Cor 9:24 race run all, but one *r* the prize
Heb 6:7 is dressed, *r* blessing from God
Heb 7:8 but there he *r* them, of whom it
Heb 7:9 who *r* tithes, payed tithes in
Heb 12:6 and scourgeth every son whom he *r*
3Jn 9 preeminence among them, *r* us not
Rev 2:17 man knoweth saving he that *r* it
Rev 14:11 whosoever *r* the mark of his name

**RECEIVING**

2Kin 5:20 in not *r* at his hands that which
Acts 17:15 *r* a commandment unto Silas and
Rom 1:27 *r* in themselves that recompence
Rom 11:15 what shall the *r* of them be
Phil 4:15 with me as concerning giving and *r*
Heb 12:28 Wherefore we *r* a kingdom which
1Pet 1:9 *R* the end of your faith, even the

**RECHAB** *(re'-kab)* See RECHABITES.

*1. A son of Rimmon.*

2Sa 4:2 and the name of the other *R*
2Sa 4:5 sons of Rimmon the Beerothite, *R*
2Sa 4:6 and *R* and Baanah his brother
2Sa 4:9 And David answered *R* and Baanah

*2. Founder of the Rechabites.*

2Kin 10:15 the son of *R* coming to meet him
2Kin 10:23 went, and Jehonadab the son of *R*
Jer 35:6 for Jonadab the son of *R* our
Jer 35:8 *R* our father in all that he hath
Jer 35:14 The words of Jonadab the son of *R*
Jer 35:16 *R* have performed the commandment
Jer 35:19 Jonadab the son of *R* shall not

*3. A descendant of Hemath.*

1Chr 2:55 the father of the house of *R*

*4. Father of Malchiah.*

Neh 3:14 repaired Malchiah the son of *R*

**RECHABITES** *(rek'-ab-ites) Descendants of Rechab 2.*

Jer 35:2 Go unto the house of the *R*
Jer 35:3 sons, and the whole house of the *R*
Jer 35:5 house of the *R* pots full of wine
Jer 35:18 said unto the house of the *R*

**RECHAH** *A family of Judah.*

1Chr 4:12 These are the men of *R*

**RECKON**

Lev 25:50 he shall *r* with him that bought
Lev 27:18 then the priest shall *r* unto him
Lev 27:23 Then the priest shall *r* unto him
Num 4:32 and by name ye shall *r* the
Eze 44:26 they shall *r* unto him seven days
Mt 18:24 And when he had begun to *r*
Rom 6:11 Likewise *r* ye also yourselves to
Rom 8:18 For I *r* that the sufferings of

**RECKONED**

Num 18:27 offering shall be *r* unto you
Num 23:9 shall not be *r* among the nations
2Sa 4:2 Beeroth also was *r* to Benjamin
2Kin 12:15 Moreover they *r* not with the men,
1Chr 5:1 not to be *r* after the birthright
1Chr 5:7 of their generations was *r*
1Chr 5:17 All these were *r* by genealogies
1Chr 7:5 *r* in all by their genealogies
1Chr 7:7 were *r* by their genealogies
1Chr 9:1 all Israel were *r* by genealogies
1Chr 9:22 These were *r* by their genealogy
2Chr 31:19 to all that were *r* by genealogies
Ezr 2:62 those that were *r* by genealogy
Ezr 8:3 with him were *r* by genealogy of
Neh 7:5 that they might be *r* by genealogy
Neh 7:64 those that were *r* by genealogy
Ps 40:5 they cannot be *r* up in order unto
Is 38:13 I *r* till morning, that, as a lion
Lk 22:37 he was *r* among the transgressors
Rom 4:4 is the reward not *r* of grace
Rom 4:9 for we say that faith was *r* to
Rom 4:10 How was it then *r*

**RECOMPENCE**

Deut 32:35 To me belongeth vengeance, and *r*
Job 15:31 for vanity shall be his *r*
Is 35:4 with vengeance, even God with a *r*
Is 59:18 his adversaries, *r* to his enemies
Is 59:18 to the islands he will repay *r*
Is 66:6 that rendereth *r* to his enemies
Jer 51:6 he will render unto her a *r*
Lam 3:64 Render unto them a *r*, O LORD,
Hos 9:7 are come, the days of *r* are come
Joel 3:4 will ye render me a *r*
Joel 3:4 return your *r* upon your own head
Joel 3:7 will return your *r* upon your own
Lk 14:12 thee again, and a *r* be made thee
Rom 1:27 receiving in themselves that *r* of

Rom 11:9 stumblingblock, and a *r* unto them
2Cor 6:13 Now for a *r* in the same, (I speak
Heb 2:2 received a just *r* of reward
Heb 10:35 which hath great *r* of reward
Heb 11:26 respect unto the *r* of the reward

**RECOMPENSE**

Num 5:7 he shall *r* his trespass with the
Num 5:8 no kinsman to *r* the trespass unto
Ruth 2:12 The LORD *r* thy work, and a full
2Sa 19:36 why should the king *r* it me with
Job 34:33 he will *r* it, whether thou refuse
Prov 12:14 the *r* of a man's hands shall be
Prov 20:22 Say not thou, I will *r* evil
Is 65:6 will not keep silence, but will *r*
Is 65:6 even *r* into their bosom,
Jer 16:18 first I will *r* their iniquity and
Jer 25:14 I will *r* them according to their
Jer 50:29 *r* her according to her work
Eze 7:3 will *r* upon thee all thine
Eze 7:4 but I will *r* thy ways upon thee,
Eze 7:8 will *r* thee for all thine
Eze 7:9 I will *r* thee according to thy
Eze 9:10 but I will *r* their way upon their
Eze 11:21 I will *r* their way upon their own
Eze 16:43 therefore I also will *r* thy way
Eze 17:19 even it will I *r* upon his own
Eze 23:49 they shall *r* your lewdness upon
Hos 12:2 to his doings will he *r* him
Joel 3:4 and if ye *r* me, swiftly and
Lk 14:14 for they cannot *r* thee
Rom 12:17 *R* to no man evil for evil
2Th 1:6 God to *r* tribulation to them that
Heb 10:30 belongeth unto me, I will *r*

**RECOMPENSED**

Num 5:8 the trespass be *r* unto the LORD
2Sa 22:21 of my hands hath he *r* me
2Sa 22:25 LORD hath *r* me according to my
Ps 18:20 of my hands hath he *r* me
Ps 18:24 the LORD *r* me according to my
Prov 11:31 righteous shall be *r* in the earth
Jer 18:20 Shall evil be *r* for good
Eze 22:31 own way have I *r* upon their heads
Lk 14:14 for thou shalt be *r* at the
Rom 11:35 it shall be *r* unto him again

**RECONCILE**

Lev 6:30 of the congregation to *r* withal
1Sa 29:4 he *r* himself unto his master
Eze 45:20 so shall ye *r* the house
Eph 2:16 that he might *r* both unto God in
Col 1:20 by him to *r* all things unto

**RECONCILED**

Mt 5:24 first be *r* to thy brother, and
Rom 5:10 we were *r* to God by the death of
Rom 5:10 of his Son, much more, being *r*
1Cor 7:11 unmarried, or be *r* to her husband
2Cor 5:18 who hath *r* us to himself by Jesus
2Cor 5:20 in Christ's stead, be ye *r* to God
Col 1:21 wicked works, yet now hath he *r*

**RECONCILIATION**

Lev 8:15 sanctified it, to make *r* upon it
2Chr 29:24 they made *r* with their blood upon
Eze 45:15 to make *r* for them, saith the
Eze 45:17 to make *r* for the house of Israel
Dan 9:24 to make *r* for iniquity, and to
2Cor 5:18 given to us the ministry of *r*
2Cor 5:19 committed unto us the word of *r*
Heb 2:17 to make *r* for the sins of the

**RECONCILING**

Lev 16:20 made an end of *r* the holy place
Rom 11:15 of them be the *r* of the world
2Cor 5:19 *r* the world unto himself, not

**RECORD**

Ex 20:24 in all places where I *r* my name I
Deut 30:19 earth to *r* this day against you,
Deut 31:28 heaven and earth to *r* against them
1Chr 16:4 the ark of the LORD, and to *r*
Ezr 6:2 and therein was a *r* thus written
Job 16:19 is in heaven, and my *r* is on high
Is 8:2 unto me faithful witnesses to *r*
Jn 1:19 And this is the *r* of John, when
Jn 1:32 And John bare *r*, saying, I saw the
Jn 1:34 bare *r* that this is the Son of
Jn 8:13 him, Thou bearest *r* of thyself
Jn 8:13 thy *r* is not true
Jn 8:14 them, Though I bear *r* of myself
Jn 8:14 yet my *r* is true
Jn 12:17 raised him from the dead, bare *r*
Jn 19:35 And he that saw it bare *r*, and his
Jn 19:35 and his *r* is true
Acts 20:26 I take you to *r* this day, that I
Rom 10:2 For I bear them *r* that they have
2Cor 1:23 I call God for a *r* upon my soul
2Cor 8:3 For to their power, I bear *r*
Gal 4:15 for I bear you *r*, that, if it had
Phil 1:8 For God is my *r*, how greatly I
Col 4:13 For I bear him *r*, that he hath a
1Jn 5:7 are three that bear *r* in heaven
1Jn 5:10 the *r* that God gave of his Son
1Jn 5:11 And this is the *r*, that God hath
3Jn 12 yea, and we also bear *r*
3Jn 12 and ye know that our *r* is true
Rev 1:2 Who bare *r* of the word of God, and

**RECORDER**

2Sa 8:16 the son of Ahilud was *r*
2Sa 20:24 the son of Ahilud was *r*
1Kin 4:3 the son of Ahilud, the *r*
2Kin 18:18 and Joah the son of Asaph the *r*
2Kin 18:37 and Joah the son of Asaph the *r*
1Chr 18:15 Jehoshaphat the son of Ahilud, *r*
2Chr 34:8 and Joah the son of Joahaz the *r*
Is 36:3 and Joah, Asaph's son, the *r*
Is 36:22 and Joah, the son of Asaph, the *r*

**RECOVER**

Judg 11:26 ye not *r* them within that time
1Sa 30:8 them, and without fail *r* all
2Sa 8:3 as he went to *r* his border at the
2Kin 1:2 whether I shall *r* of this disease
2Kin 5:3 for he would *r* him of his leprosy
2Kin 5:6 that thou mayest *r* him of his
2Kin 5:7 unto me to *r* a man of his leprosy
2Kin 5:11 over the place, and *r* the leper
2Kin 8:8 Shall I *r* of this disease
2Kin 8:9 Shall I *r* of this disease
2Kin 8:10 unto him, Thou mayest certainly *r*
2Kin 8:14 me that thou shouldest surely *r*
2Chr 13:20 Neither did Jeroboam *r* strength
2Chr 14:13 that they could not *r* themselves
Ps 39:13 O spare me, that I may *r* strength
Is 11:11 to *r* the remnant of his people
Is 38:16 so wilt thou *r* me, and make me to
Is 38:21 upon the boil, and he shall *r*
Hos 2:9 will *r* my wool and my flax given
Mk 16:18 on the sick, and they shall *r*
2Ti 2:26 that they may *r* themselves out of

**RECOVERED**

1Sa 30:18 David *r* all that the Amalekites
1Sa 30:19 David *r* all
1Sa 30:22 ought of the spoil that we have *r*
2Kin 13:25 him, and *r* the cities of Israel
2Kin 14:28 how he *r* Damascus, and Hamath,
2Kin 16:6 king of Syria *r* Elath to Syria
2Kin 20:7 and laid it on the boil, and he *r*
Is 38:9 sick, and was *r* of his sickness
Is 39:1 that he had been sick, and was *r*
Jer 8:22 of the daughter of my people *r*
Jer 41:16 he had *r* from Ishmael the son of

**RED** *The sea dividing Egypt and Arabia.*

Gen 25:25 And the first came out *r*, all over
Gen 25:30 thee, with that same *r* pottage
Gen 49:12 His eyes shall be *r* with wine
Ex 10:19 and cast them into the *R* sea
Ex 13:18 of the wilderness of the *R* sea
Ex 15:4 also are drowned in the *R* sea
Ex 15:22 brought Israel from the *R* sea
Ex 23:31 *R* sea even unto the sea of the
Ex 25:5 And rams' skins dyed *r*, and
Ex 26:14 the tent of rams' skins dyed *r*
Ex 35:7 And rams' skins dyed *r*, and
Ex 35:23 *r* skins of rams, and badgers'
Ex 36:19 the tent of rams' skins dyed *r*
Ex 39:34 covering of rams' skins dyed *r*
Num 14:25 by the way of the *R* sea
Num 19:2 thee a *r* heifer without spot
Num 21:4 mount Hor by the way of the *R* sea
Num 21:14 LORD, What he did in the *R* sea
Num 33:10 Elim, and encamped by the *R* sea
Num 33:11 And they removed from the *R* sea
Deut 1:1 the plain over against the *R* sea
Deut 1:40 by the way of the *R* sea
Deut 2:1 by the way of the *R* sea, as the
Deut 11:4 *R* sea to overflow them as they
Josh 2:10 up the water of the *R* sea for you
Josh 4:23 LORD your God did to the *R* sea
Josh 24:6 and horsemen unto the *R* sea
Judg 11:16 the wilderness unto the *R* sea
1Kin 9:26 Eloth, on the shore of the *R* sea
2Kin 3:22 on the other side as *r* as blood
Neh 9:9 heardest their cry by the *R* sea
Est 1:6 and silver, upon a pavement of *r*
Ps 75:8 there is a cup, and the wine is *r*
Ps 106:7 him at the sea, even at the *R* sea
Ps 106:9 He rebuked the *R* sea also
Ps 106:22 and terrible things by the *R* sea
Ps 136:13 divided the *R* sea into parts
Ps 136:15 Pharaoh and his host in the *R* sea
Prov 23:31 thou upon the wine when it is *r*
Is 1:18 though they be *r* like crimson
Is 27:2 ye unto her, A vineyard of *r* wine
Is 63:2 art thou *r* in thine apparel
Jer 49:21 thereof was heard in the *R* sea
Nah 2:3 of his mighty men is made *r*
Zec 1:8 a man riding upon a *r* horse
Zec 1:8 and behind him were there *r* horses
Zec 6:2 the first chariot were *r* horses
Mt 16:2 for the sky is *r*
Mt 16:3 for the sky is *r* and lowring
Acts 7:36 land of Egypt, and in the *R* sea
Heb 11:29 through the *R* sea as by dry land
Rev 6:4 went out another horse that was *r*
Rev 12:3 and behold a great *r* dragon

**REDEEM**

Ex 6:6 I will *r* you with a stretched out
Ex 13:13 an ass thou shalt *r* with a lamb
Ex 13:13 and if thou wilt not *r* it, then
Ex 13:13 among thy children shalt thou *r*
Ex 13:15 the firstborn of my children I *r*
Ex 34:20 an ass thou shalt *r* with a lamb
Ex 34:20 and if thou *r* him not, then shalt
Ex 34:20 of thy sons thou shalt *r*
Lev 25:25 and if any of his kin come to *r* it
Lev 25:25 then shall he *r* that which his
Lev 25:26 And if the man have none to *r* it
Lev 25:26 and himself be able to *r* it
Lev 25:29 then he may *r* it within a whole
Lev 25:29 within a full year may he *r* it
Lev 25:32 may the Levites *r* at any time
Lev 25:48 one of his brethren may *r* him
Lev 25:49 or his uncle's son, may *r* him
Lev 25:49 unto him of his family may *r* him
Lev 25:49 if he be able, he may *r* himself
Lev 27:13 But if he will at all *r* it
Lev 27:15 sanctified it will *r* his house
Lev 27:19 the field will in any wise *r* it
Lev 27:20 And if he will not *r* the field
Lev 27:27 then he shall *r* it according to
Lev 27:31 will at all *r* ought of his tithes
Num 18:15 of man shalt thou surely *r*
Num 18:15 of unclean beasts shalt thou *r*
Num 18:16 from a month old shalt thou *r*
Num 18:17 of a goat, thou shalt not *r*
Ruth 4:4 If thou wilt *r* it
Ruth 4:4 *r* it: but if thou wilt
Ruth 4:4 but if thou wilt not *r* it
Ruth 4:4 there is none to *r* it beside thee
Ruth 4:4 And he said, I will *r* it
Ruth 4:6 I cannot *r* it for myself, lest I
Ruth 4:6 *r* thou my right to thyself
Ruth 4:6 for I cannot *r* it
2Sa 7:23 whom God went to *r* for a people
1Chr 17:21 whom God went to *r* to be his own
Neh 5:5 is it in our power to *r* them
Job 5:20 famine he shall *r* thee from death
Job 6:23 *R* me from the hand of the mighty
Ps 25:22 *R* Israel, O God, out of all his
Ps 26:11 *r* me, and be merciful unto me
Ps 44:26 *r* us for thy mercies' sake
Ps 49:7 can by any means *r* his brother
Ps 49:15 But God will *r* my soul from the
Ps 69:18 Draw nigh unto my soul, and *r* it
Ps 72:14 He shall *r* their soul from deceit
Ps 130:8 he shall *r* Israel from all his
Is 50:2 at all, that it cannot *r*
Jer 15:21 I will *r* thee out of the hand of
Hos 13:14 I will *r* them from death
Mic 4:10 there the LORD shall *r* thee from
Gal 4:5 To *r* them that were under the law
Titus 2:14 that he might *r* us from all

**REDEEMED**

Gen 48:16 The angel which *r* me from all
Ex 15:13 the people which thou hast *r*
Ex 21:8 then shall he let her be *r*
Lev 19:20 to an husband, and not at all *r*
Lev 25:30 if it be not *r* within the space
Lev 25:31 they may be *r*, and they shall go

Lev 25:48 that he is sold he may be *r* again
Lev 25:54 if he be not *r* in these years,
Lev 27:20 man, it shall not be *r* any more
Lev 27:27 or if it be not *r*, then it shall
Lev 27:28 possession, shall be sold or *r*
Lev 27:29 be devoted of men, shall be *r*
Lev 27:33 it shall not be *r*
Num 3:46 are to be *r* of the two hundred
Num 3:48 the odd number of them is to be *r*
Num 3:49 them that were *r* by the Levites
Num 3:51 of them that were *r* unto Aaron
Num 18:16 those that are to be *r* from a
Deut 7:8 *r* you out of the house of bondmen
Deut 9:26 which thou hast *r* through thy
Deut 13:5 *r* you out of the house of bondage
Deut 15:15 Egypt, and the LORD thy God *r* thee
Deut 21:8 people Israel, whom thou hast *r*
Deut 24:18 and the LORD thy God *r* thee thence
2Sa 4:9 who hath *r* my soul out of all
1Kin 1:29 that hath *r* my soul out of all
1Chr 17:21 whom thou hast *r* out of Egypt
Neh 1:10 whom thou hast *r* by thy great
Neh 5:8 have *r* our brethren the Jews
Ps 31:5 thou hast *r* me, O LORD God of
Ps 71:23 and my soul, which thou hast *r*
Ps 74:2 inheritance, which thou hast *r*
Ps 77:15 hast with thine arm *r* thy people
Ps 106:10 *r* them from the hand of the enemy
Ps 107:2 Let the *r* of the LORD say so,
Ps 107:2 whom he hath *r* from the hand of
Ps 136:24 hath *r* us from our enemies
Is 1:27 Zion shall be *r* with judgment
Is 29:22 who *r* Abraham, concerning the
Is 35:9 but the *r* shall walk there
Is 43:1 for I have *r* thee, I have called
Is 44:22 for I have *r* thee
Is 44:23 for the LORD hath *r* Jacob
Is 48:20 The LORD hath *r* his servant Jacob
Is 51:11 Therefore the *r* of the LORD shall
Is 52:3 ye shall be *r* without money
Is 52:9 his people, he hath *r* Jerusalem
Is 62:12 holy people, The *r* of the LORD
Is 63:4 and the year of my *r* is come
Is 63:9 his love and in his pity he *r* them
Jer 31:11 For the LORD hath *r* Jacob
Lam 3:58 thou hast *r* my life
Hos 7:13 though I have *r* them, yet they
Mic 6:4 *r* thee out of the house of
Zec 10:8 for I have *r* them
Lk 1:68 he hath visited and *r* his people,
Lk 24:21 he which should have *r* Israel
Gal 3:13 Christ hath *r* us from the curse
1Pet 1:18 not *r* with corruptible things
Rev 5:9 hast *r* us to God by thy blood out
Rev 14:3 which were *r* from the earth
Rev 14:4 These were *r* from among men,

### REDEEMER
Job 19:25 For I know that my *r* liveth
Ps 19:14 O LORD, my strength, and my *r*
Ps 78:35 rock, and the high God their *r*
Prov 23:11 For their *r* is mighty
Is 41:14 thee, saith the LORD, and thy *r*
Is 43:14 Thus saith the LORD, your *r*
Is 44:6 and his *r* the LORD of hosts
Is 44:24 Thus saith the LORD, thy *r*
Is 47:4 As for our *r*, the LORD of hosts
Is 48:17 Thus saith the LORD, thy *R*
Is 49:7 the *R* of Israel, and his Holy One,
Is 49:26 the LORD am thy Saviour and thy *R*
Is 54:5 thy *R* the Holy One of Israel
Is 54:8 on thee, saith the LORD thy *R*
Is 59:20 the *R* shall come to Zion, and unto
Is 60:16 the LORD am thy Saviour and thy *R*
Is 63:16 O LORD, art our father, our *r*
Jer 50:34 Their *R* is strong

### REDEMPTION
Lev 25:24 ye shall grant a *r* for the land
Lev 25:51 give again the price of his *r* out
Lev 25:52 give him again the price of his *r*
Num 3:49 Moses took the *r* money of them
Ps 49:8 (For the *r* of their soul is
Ps 111:9 He sent *r* unto his people
Ps 130:7 mercy, and with him is plenteous *r*
Jer 32:7 for the right of *r* is thine to
Jer 32:8 is thine, and the *r* is thine
Lk 2:38 that looked for *r* in Jerusalem
Lk 21:28 for your *r* draweth nigh
Rom 3:24 the *r* that is in Christ Jesus
Rom 8:23 to wit, the *r* of our body
1Cor 1:30 and sanctification, and *r*
Eph 1:7 In whom we have *r* through his
Eph 1:14 the *r* of the purchased possession
Eph 4:30 ye are sealed unto the day of *r*
Col 1:14 In whom we have *r* through his
Heb 9:12 having obtained eternal *r* for us
Heb 9:15 for the *r* of the transgressions

### REED
1Kin 14:15 as a *r* is shaken in the water, and
2Kin 18:21 upon the staff of this bruised *r*
Job 40:21 trees, in the covert of the *r*
Is 36:6 in the staff of this broken *r*
Is 42:3 A bruised *r* shall he not break,
Eze 29:6 staff of *r* to the house of Israel
Eze 40:3 in his hand, and a measuring *r*
Eze 40:5 in the man's hand a measuring *r*
Eze 40:5 breadth of the building, one *r*
Eze 40:5 and the height, one *r*
Eze 40:6 the gate, which was one *r* broad
Eze 40:6 the gate, which was one *r* broad
Eze 40:7 was one *r* long, and one *r* broad
Eze 40:7 of the gate within was one *r*
Eze 40:8 porch of the gate within, one *r*
Eze 41:8 were a full *r* of six great cubits
Eze 42:16 east side with the measuring *r*
Eze 42:16 with the measuring *r* round about
Eze 42:17 with the measuring *r* round about
Eze 42:18 reeds, with the measuring *r*
Eze 42:19 reeds with the measuring *r*
Mt 11:7 A *r* shaken with the wind
Mt 12:20 A bruised *r* shall he not break,
Mt 27:29 head, and a *r* in his right hand
Mt 27:30 they spit upon him, and took the *r*
Mt 27:48 it with vinegar, and put it on a *r*
Mk 15:19 smote him on the head with a *r*
Mk 15:36 full of vinegar, and put it on a *r*
Lk 7:24 A *r* shaken with the wind
Rev 11:1 was given me a *r* like unto a rod
Rev 21:15 a golden *r* to measure the city
Rev 21:16 he measured the city with the *r*

### REEDS
Is 19:6 the *r* and flags shall wither
Is 19:7 The paper *r* by the brooks, by the
Is 35:7 each lay, shall be grass with *r*
Jer 51:32 the *r* they have burned with fire,
Eze 42:16 measuring reed, five hundred *r*
Eze 42:17 the north side, five hundred *r*
Eze 42:18 the south side, five hundred *r*
Eze 42:19 measured five hundred *r* with the
Eze 42:20 round about, five hundred *r* long
Eze 45:1 of five and twenty thousand *r*
Eze 48:8 and twenty thousand *r* in breadth

### REELAIAH *(re-el-ah'-yah) A clan leader with Zerubbabel.*
Ezr 2:2 Jeshua, Nehemiah, Seraiah, *R*

### REFINED
1Chr 28:18 altar of incense *r* gold by weight
1Chr 29:4 thousand talents of *r* silver
Is 25:6 of wines on the lees well *r*
Is 48:10 Behold, I have *r* thee, but not
Zec 13:9 will refine them as silver is *r*

### REFRAIN
Gen 45:1 Then Joseph could not *r* himself
Job 7:11 Therefore I will not *r* my mouth
Prov 1:15 *r* thy foot from their path
Eccl 3:5 a time to *r* from embracing
Is 48:9 for my praise will I *r* for thee
Is 64:12 Wilt thou *r* thyself for these
Jer 31:16 *R* thy voice from weeping, and
Acts 5:38 *R* from these men, and let them
1Pet 3:10 let him *r* his tongue from evil,

### REFRAINED
Gen 43:31 *r* himself, and said, Set on bread
Est 5:10 Nevertheless Haman *r* himself
Job 29:9 The princes *r* talking, and laid
Ps 40:9 lo, I have not *r* my lips, O LORD,
Ps 119:101 I have *r* my feet from every evil
Is 42:14 I have been still, and *r* myself
Jer 14:10 they have not *r* their feet

### REFRESHED
Ex 23:12 and the stranger, may be *r*
Ex 31:17 seventh day he rested, and was *r*
1Sa 16:23 so Saul was *r*, and was well, and
2Sa 16:14 came weary, and *r* themselves there
Job 32:20 I will speak, that I may be *r*
Rom 15:32 will of God, and may with you be *r*
1Cor 16:18 For they have *r* my spirit
2Cor 7:13 his spirit was *r* by you all
2Ti 1:16 for he oft *r* me, and was not
Philem 7 of the saints are *r* by thee

### REFUGE
Num 35:6 there shall be six cities for *r*
Num 35:11 cities to be cities of *r* for you
Num 35:12 you cities for *r* from the avenger
Num 35:13 six cities shall ye have for *r*
Num 35:14 which shall be cities of *r*
Num 35:15 These six cities shall be a *r*
Num 35:25 restore him to the city of his *r*
Num 35:26 the border of the city of his *r*
Num 35:27 the borders of the city of his *r*
Num 35:28 his *r* until the death of the high
Num 35:32 that is fled to the city of his *r*
Deut 33:27 The eternal God is thy *r*, and
Josh 20:2 Appoint out for you cities of *r*
Josh 20:3 they shall be your *r* from the
Josh 21:13 to be a city of *r* for the slayer
Josh 21:21 to be a city of *r* for the slayer
Josh 21:27 to be a city of *r* for the slayer
Josh 21:32 to be a city of *r* for the slayer
Josh 21:38 to be a city of *r* for the slayer
2Sa 22:3 salvation, my high tower, and my *r*
1Chr 6:57 namely, Hebron, the city of *r*
1Chr 6:67 unto them, of the cities of *r*
Ps 9:9 will be a *r* for the oppressed
Ps 9:9 a *r* in times of trouble
Ps 14:6 poor, because the LORD is his *r*
Ps 46:1 God is our *r* and strength, a very
Ps 46:7 the God of Jacob is our *r*
Ps 46:11 the God of Jacob is our *r*
Ps 48:3 is known in her palaces for a *r*
Ps 57:1 of thy wings will I make my *r*
Ps 59:16 *r* in the day of my trouble
Ps 62:7 the rock of my strength, and my *r*
Ps 62:8 God is a *r* for us
Ps 71:7 but thou art my strong *r*
Ps 91:2 will say of the LORD, He is my *r*
Ps 91:9 hast made the LORD, which is my *r*
Ps 94:22 and my God is the rock of my *r*
Ps 104:18 hills are a *r* for the wild goats
Ps 142:4 *r* failed me
Ps 142:5 I said, Thou art my *r* and my
Prov 14:26 children shall have a place of *r*
Is 4:6 the heat, and for a place of *r*
Is 25:4 a *r* from the storm, a shadow from
Is 28:15 for we have made lies our *r*
Is 28:17 shall sweep away the *r* of lies
Jer 16:19 my *r* in the day of affliction,
Heb 6:18 who have fled for *r* to lay hold

### REFUSE
Ex 4:23 if thou *r* to let him go, behold,
Ex 8:2 if thou *r* to let them go, behold,
Ex 9:2 For if thou *r* to let them go, and
Ex 10:3 How long wilt thou *r* to humble
Ex 10:4 if thou *r* to let my people go,
Ex 16:28 Moses, How long *r* ye to keep my
Ex 22:17 utterly *r* to give her unto him
1Sa 15:9 every thing that was vile and *r*
Job 34:33 recompense it, whether thou *r*
Prov 8:33 and be wise, and *r* it not
Prov 21:7 because they *r* to do judgment
Prov 21:25 for his hands *r* to labour
Is 1:20 But if ye *r* and rebel, ye shall be
Is 7:15 that he may know to *r* the evil
Is 7:16 child shall know to *r* the evil
Jer 8:5 fast deceit, they *r* to return
Jer 9:6 through deceit they *r* to know me
Jer 13:10 which *r* to hear my words, which
Jer 25:28 if they *r* to take the cup at
Jer 38:21 But if thou *r* to go forth
Lam 3:45 *r* in the midst of the people
Amos 8:6 yea, and sell the *r* of the wheat
Acts 25:11 worthy of death, I *r* not to die
1Ti 4:7 But *r* profane and old wives'
1Ti 5:11 But the younger widows *r*
Heb 12:25 See that ye *r* not him that

### REFUSED
Gen 37:35 but he *r* to be comforted
Gen 39:8 But he *r*, and said unto his
Gen 48:19 And his father *r*, and said, I know
Num 20:21 Thus Edom *r* to give Israel
1Sa 8:19 Nevertheless the people *r* to obey
1Sa 16:7 because I have *r* him
1Sa 28:23 But he *r*, and said, I will not eat
2Sa 2:23 Howbeit he *r* to turn aside
2Sa 13:9 but he *r* to eat
1Kin 20:35 And the man *r* to smite him

1Kin 21:15 which he r to give thee for money
2Kin 5:16 to take it; but he r
Neh 9:17 r to obey, neither were mindful
Est 1:12 But the queen Vashti r to come at
Job 6:7 The things that my soul r to
Ps 77:2 my soul r to be comforted
Ps 78:10 of God, and r to walk in his law
Ps 78:67 Moreover he r the tabernacle of
Ps 118:22 The stone which the builders r is
Prov 1:24 Because I have called, and ye r
Is 54:6 a wife of youth, when thou wast r
Jer 5:3 but they have r to receive
Jer 5:3 they have r to return
Jer 11:10 which r to hear my words
Jer 31:15 r to be comforted for her
Jer 50:33 they r to let them go
Eze 5:6 for they have r my judgments
Hos 11:5 king, because they r to return
Zec 7:11 But they r to hearken, and pulled
Acts 7:35 This Moses whom they r, saying,
1Ti 4:4 God is good, and nothing to be r
Heb 11:24 r to be called the son of
Heb 12:25 not who r him that spake on earth

**REFUSETH**

Ex 7:14 he r to let the people go
Num 22:13 for the LORD r to give me leave
Num 22:14 and said, Balaam r to come with us
Deut 25:7 My husband's brother r to raise
Prov 10:17 but he that r reproof erreth
Prov 13:18 be to him that r instruction
Prov 15:32 He that r instruction despiseth
Is 8:6 Forasmuch as this people r the
Jer 15:18 incurable, which r to be healed

**REGARD**

Gen 45:20 Also r not your stuff
Ex 5:9 and let them not r vain words
Lev 19:31 R not them that have familiar
Deut 28:50 which shall not r the person of
1Sa 4:20 not, neither did she r it
1Sa 25:25 r this man of Belial, even Nabal
2Sa 13:20 r not this thing
2Kin 3:14 were it not that I r the presence
Job 3:4 let not God r it from above,
Job 35:13 neither will the Almighty r it
Job 36:21 Take heed, r not iniquity
Ps 28:5 Because they r not the works of
Ps 31:6 hated them that r lying vanities
Ps 66:18 If I r iniquity in my heart, the
Ps 94:7 shall the God of Jacob r it
Ps 102:17 He will r the prayer of the
Prov 5:2 That thou mayest r discretion
Prov 6:35 He will not r any ransom
Eccl 8:2 that in r of the oath of God
Is 5:12 but they r not the work of the
Is 13:17 them, which shall not r silver
Lam 4:16 he will no more r them
Dan 11:37 Neither shall he r the God of his
Dan 11:37 desire of women, nor r any god
Amos 5:22 neither will I r the peace
Hab 1:5 Behold ye among the heathen, and r
Mal 1:9 will he r your persons
Lk 18:4 Though I fear not God, nor r man
Acts 8:11 And to him they had r, because
Rom 14:6 day, to the Lord he doth not r it

**REGARDED**

Ex 9:21 he that r not the word of the
1Kin 18:29 nor any to answer, nor any that r
1Chr 17:17 hast r me according to the estate
Ps 106:44 Nevertheless he r their
Prov 1:24 out my hand, and no man r
Dan 3:12 men, O king, have not r thee
Lk 1:48 For he hath r the low estate of
Lk 18:2 feared not God, neither r man
Heb 8:9 I r them not, saith the Lord

**REGARDEST**

2Sa 19:6 that thou r neither princes nor
Job 30:20 I stand up, and thou r me not
Mt 22:16 for thou r not the person of men
Mk 12:14 for thou r not the person of men,

**REGARDETH**

Deut 10:17 which r not persons, nor taketh
Job 34:19 nor r the rich more than the poor
Job 39:7 neither r he the crying of the
Prov 12:10 A righteous man r the life of his
Prov 13:18 but he that r reproof shall be
Prov 15:5 but he that r reproof is prudent
Prov 29:7 but the wicked r not to know it
Eccl 5:8 that is higher than the highest r
Eccl 11:4 he that r the clouds shall not
Is 33:8 despised the cities, he r no man
Dan 6:13 r not thee, O king, nor the
Mal 2:13 insomuch that he r not the
Rom 14:6 He that r the day, r it
Rom 14:6 he that r not the day, to the

**REGEM** *(re'-ghem) A son of Jahdai.*

1Chr 2:47 R, and Jotham, and Gesham, and

**REGEM-MELECH** *(re'-ghem-me'-lek) A messenger for Zechariah.*

Zec 7:2 the house of God Sherezer and R

**REGION**

Deut 3:4 all the r of Argob, the kingdom
Deut 3:13 all the r of Argob, with all
1Kin 4:11 of Abinadab, in all the r of Dor
1Kin 4:13 him also pertained the r of Argob
1Kin 4:24 all the r on this side the river
Mt 3:5 all the r round about Jordan,
Mt 4:16 and to them which sat in the r
Mk 1:28 all the r round about Galilee
Mk 6:55 through that whole r round about
Lk 3:1 of the r of Trachonitis, and
Lk 4:14 him through all the r round about
Lk 7:17 throughout all the r round about
Acts 13:49 published throughout all the r
Acts 14:6 unto the r that lieth round about
Acts 16:6 the r of Galatia, and were

**REGIONS**

Acts 8:1 abroad throughout the r of Judaea
2Cor 10:16 the gospel in the r beyond you
2Cor 11:10 this boasting in the r of Achaia
Gal 1:21 I came into the r of Syria

**REHABIAH** *(re-hab-i'-ah) A son of Eliezer.*

1Chr 23:17 sons of Eliezer were, R the chief
1Chr 23:17 but the sons of R were very many
1Chr 24:21 Concerning R
1Chr 24:21 of the sons of R, the first was
1Chr 26:25 R his son, and Jeshaiah his son,

**REHEARSED**

1Sa 8:21 he r them in the ears of the LORD
1Sa 17:31 spake, they r them before Saul
Acts 11:4 But Peter r the matter from the
Acts 14:27 they r all that God had done with

**REHOB** *(re'-hob)*

*1. A Levitical city in Asher.*
Num 13:21 from the wilderness of Zin unto R
Josh 19:28 and R, and Hammon, and
Josh 19:30 Ummah also, and Aphek, and R
Josh 21:31 suburbs, and R with her suburbs
Judg 1:31 of Helbah, nor of Aphik, nor of R
2Sa 10:8 and the Syrians of Zoba, and of R
1Chr 6:75 suburbs, and R with her suburbs
*2. Father of Hadadezer.*
2Sa 8:3 also Hadadezer, the son of R
2Sa 8:12 the spoil of Hadadezer, son of R
*3. A Levite.*
Neh 10:11 Micha, R, Hashabiah,

**REHOBOAM** *(re-ho-bo'-am)* See ROBOAM. *A son of Solomon and king of Judah.*

1Kin 11:43 R his son reigned in his stead
1Kin 12:1 And R went to Shechem
1Kin 12:3 of Israel came, and spake unto R
1Kin 12:6 king R consulted with the old men
1Kin 12:12 people came to R the third day
1Kin 12:17 of Judah, R reigned over them
1Kin 12:18 Then king R sent Adoram, who was
1Kin 12:18 Therefore king R made speed to
1Kin 12:21 when R was come to Jerusalem, he
1Kin 12:21 again to R the son of Solomon
1Kin 12:23 Speak unto R, the son of Solomon,
1Kin 12:27 even unto R king of Judah, and
1Kin 12:27 go again to R king of Judah
1Kin 14:21 R the son of Solomon reigned in
1Kin 14:21 R was forty and one years old when
1Kin 14:25 pass in the fifth year of king R
1Kin 14:27 king R made in their stead brasen
1Kin 14:29 Now the rest of the acts of R
1Kin 14:30 And there was war between R
1Kin 14:31 R slept with his fathers, and was
1Kin 15:6 And there was war between R
1Chr 3:10 And Solomon's son was R, Abia his
2Chr 9:31 R his son reigned in his stead
2Chr 10:1 And R went to Shechem
2Chr 10:3 and all Israel came and spake to R
2Chr 10:6 king R took counsel with the old
2Chr 10:12 people came to R on the third day
2Chr 10:13 king R forsook the counsel of the
2Chr 10:17 of Judah, R reigned over them
2Chr 10:18 Then king R sent Hadoram that was
2Chr 10:18 But king R made speed to get him
2Chr 11:1 when R was come to Jerusalem, he
2Chr 11:1 bring the kingdom again to R
2Chr 11:3 Speak unto R the son of Solomon,
2Chr 11:5 R dwelt in Jerusalem, and built
2Chr 11:17 made R the son of Solomon strong,
2Chr 11:18 R took him Mahalath the daughter
2Chr 11:21 R loved Maachah the daughter of
2Chr 11:22 R made Abijah the son of Maachah
2Chr 12:1 when R had established the
2Chr 12:2 R Shishak king of Egypt came up
2Chr 12:5 came Shemaiah the prophet to R
2Chr 12:10 king R made shields of brass
2Chr 12:13 So king R strengthened himself in
2Chr 12:13 for R was one and forty years old
2Chr 12:15 Now the acts of R, first and last,
2Chr 12:15 And there were wars between R
2Chr 12:16 R slept with his fathers, and was
2Chr 13:7 against R the son of Solomon
2Chr 13:7 when R was young and tenderhearted

**REHOBOTH** *(re'-ho-both)*

*1. A city in Assyria.*
Gen 10:11 and builded Nineveh, and the city R
Gen 36:37 Saul of R by the river reigned in
1Chr 1:48 Shaul of R by the river reigned
*2. A well Isaac dug.*
Gen 26:22 and he called the name of it R

**REHUM** *(re'-hum)* See NEHUM.

*1. A clan leader with Zerubbabel.*
Ezr 2:2 Bilshan, Mizpar, Bigvai, R
Neh 12:3 Shechaniah, R, Meremoth,
*2. An officer of King Artaxerxes.*
Ezr 4:8 R the chancellor and Shimshai the
Ezr 4:9 Then wrote R the chancellor, and
Ezr 4:17 an answer unto R the chancellor
Ezr 4:23 letter was read before R, and
*3. A Levite rebuilder of Jerusalem's wall.*
Neh 3:17 the Levites, R the son of Bani
*4. A renewer of the covenant.*
Neh 10:25 R, Hashabnah, Maaseiah,

**REI** *(re'-i) A friend of David.*

1Kin 1:8 the prophet, and Shimei, and R

**REINS**

Job 16:13 about, he cleaveth my r asunder
Job 19:27 though my r be consumed within me
Ps 7:9 God trieth the hearts and r
Ps 16:7 my r also instruct me in the
Ps 26:2 try my r and my heart
Ps 73:21 grieved, and I was pricked in my r
Ps 139:13 For thou hast possessed my r
Prov 23:16 my r shall rejoice, when thy lips
Is 11:5 faithfulness the girdle of his r
Jer 11:20 righteously, that triest the r
Jer 12:2 their mouth, and far from their r
Jer 17:10 search the heart, I try the r
Jer 20:12 the righteous, and seest the r
Lam 3:13 of his quiver to enter into my r
Rev 2:23 I am he which searcheth the r

**REJECT**

Hos 4:6 knowledge, I will also r thee
Mk 6:26 sat with him, he would not r her
Mk 7:9 Full well ye r the commandment of
Titus 3:10 the first and second admonition r

**REJECTED**

1Sa 8:7 r thee, but they have r me
1Sa 10:19 And ye have this day r your God
1Sa 15:23 Because thou hast r the word of
1Sa 15:23 he hath also r thee from being
1Sa 15:26 for thou hast r the word of the
1Sa 15:26 the LORD hath r thee from being
1Sa 16:1 seeing I have r him from reigning
2Kin 17:15 they r his statutes, and his
2Kin 17:20 the LORD r all the seed of Israel
Is 53:3 He is despised and r of men
Jer 2:37 the LORD hath r thy confidences
Jer 6:19 my words, nor to my law, but r it
Jer 6:30 because the LORD hath r them
Jer 7:29 for the LORD hath r and forsaken
Jer 8:9 they have r the word of the LORD
Jer 14:19 Hast thou utterly r Judah
Lam 5:22 But thou hast utterly r us
Hos 4:6 because thou hast r knowledge
Mt 21:42 The stone which the builders r
Mk 8:31 be r of the elders, and of the

Mk 12:10 *r* is become the head of the
Lk 7:30 lawyers *r* the counsel of God
Lk 9:22 be *r* of the elders and chief
Lk 17:25 and be *r* of this generation
Lk 20:17 The stone which the builders *r*
Gal 4:14 my flesh ye despised not, nor *r*
Heb 6:8 beareth thorns and briers is *r*
Heb 12:17 inherited the blessing, he was *r*

### REJOICE

Lev 23:40 ye shall *r* before the LORD your
Deut 12:7 ye shall *r* in all that ye put
Deut 12:12 ye shall *r* before the LORD your
Deut 12:18 thou shalt *r* before the LORD thy
Deut 14:26 the LORD thy God, and thou shalt *r*
Deut 16:11 thou shalt *r* before the LORD thy
Deut 16:14 thou shalt *r* in thy feast, thou,
Deut 16:15 therefore thou shalt surely *r*
Deut 26:11 thou shalt *r* in every good thing
Deut 27:7 *r* before the LORD thy God
Deut 28:63 so the LORD will *r* over you to
Deut 30:9 will again *r* over thee for good
Deut 32:43 *R*, O ye nations, with his people
Deut 33:18 And of Zebulun he said, *R*, Zebulun
Judg 9:19 then *r* ye in Abimelech
Judg 9:19 and let him also *r* in you
Judg 16:23 unto Dagon their god, and to *r*
1Sa 2:1 because I *r* in thy salvation
1Sa 19:5 thou sawest it, and didst *r*
2Sa 1:20 daughters of the Philistines *r*
1Chr 16:10 of them *r* that seek the LORD
1Chr 16:31 be glad, and let the earth *r*
1Chr 16:32 let the fields *r*, and all that is
2Chr 6:41 and let thy saints *r* in goodness
2Chr 20:27 made them to *r* over their enemies
Neh 12:43 had made them *r* with great joy
Job 3:22 Which *r* exceedingly, and are glad,
Job 20:18 be, and he shall not *r* therein
Job 21:12 *r* at the sound of the organ
Ps 2:11 with fear, and *r* with trembling
Ps 5:11 that put their trust in thee *r*
Ps 9:2 I will be glad and *r* in thee
Ps 9:14 I will *r* in thy salvation
Ps 13:4 that trouble me *r* when I am moved
Ps 13:5 my heart shall *r* in thy salvation
Ps 14:7 of his people, Jacob shall *r*
Ps 20:5 We will *r* in thy salvation, and in
Ps 21:1 salvation how greatly shall he *r*
Ps 30:1 not made my foes to *r* over me
Ps 31:7 I will be glad and *r* in thy mercy
Ps 32:11 Be glad in the LORD, and *r*
Ps 33:1 *R* in the LORD, O ye righteous
Ps 33:21 For our heart shall *r* in him
Ps 35:9 it shall *r* in his salvation
Ps 35:19 mine enemies wrongfully *r* over me
Ps 35:24 and let them not *r* over me
Ps 35:26 together that *r* at mine hurt
Ps 38:16 otherwise they should *r* over me
Ps 40:16 Let all those that seek thee *r*
Ps 48:11 Let mount Zion *r*, let the
Ps 51:8 which thou hast broken may *r*
Ps 53:6 of his people, Jacob shall *r*
Ps 58:10 The righteous shall *r* when he
Ps 60:6 I will *r*, I will divide Shechem,
Ps 63:7 the shadow of thy wings will I *r*
Ps 63:11 But the king shall *r* in God
Ps 65:8 of the morning and evening to *r*
Ps 65:12 the little hills *r* on every side
Ps 66:6 there did we *r* in him
Ps 68:3 let them *r* before God
Ps 68:3 yea, let them exceedingly *r*
Ps 68:4 by his name JAH, and *r* before him
Ps 70:4 Let all those that seek thee *r*
Ps 71:23 greatly *r* when I sing unto thee
Ps 85:6 that thy people may *r* in thee
Ps 86:4 *R* the soul of thy servant
Ps 89:12 and Hermon shall *r* in thy name
Ps 89:16 thy name shall they *r* all the day
Ps 89:42 hast made all his enemies to *r*
Ps 90:14 that we may *r* and be glad all our
Ps 96:11 Let the heavens *r*, and let the
Ps 96:12 shall all the trees of the wood *r*
Ps 97:1 let the earth *r*
Ps 97:12 *R* in the LORD, ye righteous
Ps 98:4 make a loud noise, and *r*, and sing
Ps 104:31 the LORD shall *r* in his works
Ps 105:3 of them *r* that seek the LORD
Ps 106:5 that I may *r* in the gladness of
Ps 107:42 The righteous shall see it, and *r*
Ps 108:7 I will *r*, I will divide Shechem,
Ps 109:28 but let thy servant *r*
Ps 118:24 we will *r* and be glad in it
Ps 119:162 I *r* at thy word, as one that
Ps 149:2 Let Israel *r* in him that made him
Prov 2:14 Who *r* to do evil, and delight in
Prov 5:18 *r* with the wife of thy youth
Prov 23:15 heart be wise, my heart shall *r*
Prov 23:16 Yea, my reins shall *r*, when thy
Prov 23:24 of the righteous shall greatly *r*
Prov 23:25 and she that bare thee shall *r*
Prov 24:17 *R* not when thine enemy falleth,
Prov 27:9 Ointment and perfume *r* the heart
Prov 28:12 When righteous men do *r*, there is
Prov 29:2 are in authority, the people *r*
Prov 29:6 but the righteous doth sing and *r*
Prov 31:25 she shall *r* in time to come
Eccl 3:12 good in them, but for a man to *r*
Eccl 3:22 a man should *r* in his own works
Eccl 4:16 come after shall not *r* in him
Eccl 5:19 portion, and to *r* in his labour
Eccl 11:8 live many years, and *r* in them all
Eccl 11:9 *R*, O young man, in thy youth
Song 1:4 *r* in thee, we will remember thy
Is 8:6 *r* in Rezin and Remaliah's son
Is 9:3 as men *r* when they divide the
Is 13:3 even them that *r* in my highness
Is 14:8 Yea, the fir trees *r* at thee
Is 14:29 *R* not thou, whole Palestina,
Is 23:12 And he said, Thou shalt no more *r*
Is 24:8 the noise of them that *r* endeth
Is 25:9 be glad and *r* in his salvation
Is 29:19 the poor among men shall *r* in the
Is 35:1 and the desert shall *r*, and blossom
Is 35:2 *r* even with joy and singing
Is 41:16 thou shalt *r* in the LORD, and
Is 61:7 they shall *r* in their portion
Is 61:10 I will greatly *r* in the LORD
Is 62:5 so shall thy God *r* over thee
Is 65:13 behold, my servants shall *r*
Is 65:18 *r* for ever in that which I create
Is 65:19 I will *r* in Jerusalem, and joy in
Is 66:10 *R* ye with Jerusalem, and be glad
Is 66:10 *r* for joy with her, all ye that
Is 66:14 ye see this, your heart shall *r*
Jer 31:13 shall the virgin *r* in the dance
Jer 31:13 make them *r* from their sorrow
Jer 32:41 I will *r* over them to do them
Jer 51:39 them drunken, that they may *r*
Lam 2:17 caused thine enemy to *r* over thee
Lam 4:21 *R* and be glad, O daughter of Edom,
Eze 7:12 let not the buyer *r*, nor the
Eze 35:15 As thou didst *r* at the
Hos 9:1 *R* not, O Israel, for joy, as
Joel 2:21 be glad and *r*
Joel 2:23 Zion, and *r* in the LORD your God
Amos 6:13 Ye which *r* in a thing of nought,
Mic 7:8 *R* not against me, O mine enemy
Hab 1:15 therefore they *r* and are glad
Hab 3:18 Yet I will *r* in the LORD, I will
Zeph 3:11 of thee them that *r* in thy pride
Zeph 3:14 *r* with all the heart, O daughter
Zeph 3:17 he will *r* over thee with joy
Zec 2:10 Sing and *r*, O daughter of Zion
Zec 4:10 for they shall *r*, and shall see
Zec 9:9 *R* greatly, O daughter of Zion
Zec 10:7 heart shall *r* as through wine
Zec 10:7 their heart shall *r* in the LORD
Mt 5:12 *R*, and be exceeding glad
Lk 1:14 many shall *r* at his birth
Lk 6:23 *R* ye in that day, and leap for joy
Lk 10:20 Notwithstanding in this *r* not
Lk 10:20 but rather *r*, because your names
Lk 15:6 saying unto them, *R* with me
Lk 15:9 together, saying, *R* with me
Lk 19:37 of the disciples began to *r*
Jn 4:36 and he that reapeth may *r* together
Jn 5:35 for a season to *r* in his light
Jn 14:28 If ye loved me, ye would *r*
Jn 16:20 and lament, but the world shall *r*
Jn 16:22 you again, and your heart shall *r*
Acts 2:26 Therefore did my heart *r*, and my
Rom 5:2 *r* in hope of the glory of God
Rom 12:15 *R* with them that do *r*
Rom 15:10 And again he saith, *R*, ye Gentiles
1Cor 7:30 and they that *r*, as though they
1Cor 12:26 all the members *r* with it
2Cor 2:3 from them of whom I ought to *r*
2Cor 7:9 Now I *r*, not that ye were made
2Cor 7:16 I *r* therefore that I have
Gal 4:27 For it is written, *R*, thou barren
Phil 1:18 do *r*, yea, and will *r*
Phil 2:16 that I may *r* in the day of Christ
Phil 2:17 faith, I joy, and *r* with you all
Phil 2:18 also do ye joy, and *r* with me
Phil 2:28 when ye see him again, ye may *r*
Phil 3:1 my brethren, *r* in the Lord
Phil 3:3 *r* in Christ Jesus, and have no
Phil 4:4 *R* in the Lord alway
Phil 4:4 and again I say, *R*
Col 1:24 Who now *r* in my sufferings for
1Th 5:16 *R* evermore
Jas 1:9 degree *r* in that he is exalted
Jas 4:16 But now ye *r* in your boastings
1Pet 1:6 Wherein ye greatly *r*, though now
1Pet 1:8 ye *r* with joy unspeakable and full
1Pet 4:13 But *r*, inasmuch as ye are
Rev 11:10 upon the earth shall *r* over them
Rev 12:12 Therefore *r*, ye heavens, and ye
Rev 18:20 *R* over her, thou heaven, and ye
Rev 19:7 Let us be glad and *r*, and give

### REJOICED

Ex 18:9 Jethro *r* for all the goodness
Deut 28:63 that as the LORD *r* over you to do
Deut 30:9 good, as he *r* over thy fathers
Judg 19:3 damsel saw him, he *r* to meet him
1Sa 6:13 and saw the ark, and *r* to see it
1Sa 11:15 all the men of Israel *r* greatly
1Kin 1:40 *r* with great joy, so that the
1Kin 5:7 of Solomon, that he *r* greatly
2Kin 11:14 and all the people of the land *r*
2Kin 11:20 And all the people of the land *r*
1Chr 29:9 Then the people *r*, for that they
1Chr 29:9 the king also *r* with great joy
2Chr 15:15 And all Judah *r* at the oath
2Chr 23:13 and all the people of the land *r*
2Chr 23:21 And all the people of the land *r*
2Chr 24:10 the princes and all the people *r*
2Chr 29:36 And Hezekiah *r*, and all the people,
2Chr 30:25 Israel, and that dwelt in Judah, *r*
Neh 12:43 offered great sacrifices, and *r*
Neh 12:43 the wives also and the children *r*
Neh 12:44 for Judah *r* for the priests and
Est 8:15 and the city of Shushan *r* and was
Job 31:25 If I *r* because my wealth was
Job 31:29 If I *r* at the destruction of him
Ps 35:15 But in mine adversity they *r*
Ps 97:8 the daughters of Judah *r* because
Ps 119:14 I have *r* in the way of thy
Eccl 2:10 for my heart *r* in all my labour
Jer 15:17 assembly of the mockers, nor *r*
Jer 50:11 ye were glad, because ye *r*
Eze 25:6 *r* in heart with all thy despite
Hos 10:5 the priests thereof that *r* on it
Obad 12 neither shouldest thou have *r*
Mt 2:10 they *r* with exceeding great joy
Lk 1:47 my spirit hath *r* in God my
Lk 1:58 and they *r* with her
Lk 10:21 In that hour Jesus *r* in spirit
Lk 13:17 all the people *r* for all the
Jn 8:56 father Abraham *r* to see my day
Acts 7:41 *r* in the works of their own hands
Acts 15:31 they *r* for the consolation
Acts 16:34 he set meat before them, and *r*
1Cor 7:30 rejoice, as though they *r* not
2Cor 7:7 so that I *r* the more
Phil 4:10 But I *r* in the Lord greatly, that
2Jn 4 I *r* greatly that I found of thy
3Jn 3 For I *r* greatly, when the

### REJOICETH

1Sa 2:1 My heart *r* in the LORD, mine horn
Job 39:21 the valley, and *r* in his strength
Ps 16:9 my heart is glad, and my glory *r*
Ps 19:5 *r* as a strong man to run a race
Ps 28:7 therefore my heart greatly *r*
Prov 11:10 with the righteous, the city *r*
Prov 13:9 The light of the righteous *r*
Prov 15:30 The light of the eyes *r* the heart
Prov 29:3 Whoso loveth wisdom *r* his father
Is 5:14 and their pomp, and he that *r*
Is 62:5 the bridegroom *r* over the bride
Is 64:5 Thou meetest him that *r* and
Eze 35:14 When the whole earth *r*, I will
Mt 18:13 he *r* more of that sheep, than of
Jn 3:29 him, *r* greatly because of the
1Cor 13:6 *R* not in iniquity
1Cor 13:6 but *r* in the truth
Jas 2:13 and mercy *r* against judgment

### REJOICING
1Kin 1:45 and they are come up from thence *r*
2Chr 23:18 in the law of Moses, with *r*
Job 8:21 with laughing, and thy lips with *r*
Ps 19:8 the LORD are right, *r* the heart
Ps 45:15 and *r* shall they be brought
Ps 107:22 and declare his works with *r*
Ps 118:15 The voice of *r* and salvation is in
Ps 119:111 for they are the *r* of my heart
Ps 126:6 shall doubtless come again with *r*
Prov 8:30 his delight, *r* always before him
Prov 8:31 *R* in the habitable part of his
Is 65:18 behold, I create Jerusalem a *r*
Jer 15:16 me the joy and *r* of mine heart
Hab 3:14 their *r* was as to devour the poor
Zeph 2:15 This is the *r* city that dwelt
Lk 15:5 he layeth it on his shoulders, *r*
Acts 5:41 *r* that they were counted worthy
Acts 8:39 and he went on his way *r*
Rom 12:12 *R* in hope
1Cor 15:31 I protest by your *r* which I have
2Cor 1:12 For our *r* is this, the testimony
2Cor 1:14 us in part, that we are your *r*
2Cor 6:10 As sorrowful, yet alway *r*
Gal 6:4 shall he have *r* in himself alone
Phil 1:26 That your *r* may be more abundant
1Th 2:19 our hope, or joy, or crown of *r*
Heb 3:6 the *r* of the hope firm unto the
Jas 4:16 all such *r* is evil

### REKEM *(re'-kem)*
*1. A prince of Midian.*
Num 31:8 namely, Evi, and *R*, and Zur, and Hur
Josh 13:21 the princes of Midian, Evi, and *R*
*2. A son of Hebron.*
1Chr 2:43 Korah, and Tappuah, and *R*,
1Chr 2:44 and *R* begat Shammai
*3. A city in Benjamin.*
Josh 18:27 And *R*, and Irpeel, and Taralah,

### RELEASE
Deut 15:1 seven years thou shalt make a *r*
Deut 15:2 And this is the manner of the *r*
Deut 15:2 unto his neighbour shall *r* it
Deut 15:2 because it is called the LORD's *r*
Deut 15:3 thy brother thine hand shall *r*
Deut 15:9 The seventh year, the year of *r*
Deut 31:10 in the solemnity of the year of *r*
Est 2:18 he made a *r* to the provinces, and
Mt 27:15 to *r* unto the people a prisoner
Mt 27:17 Whom will ye that I *r* unto you
Mt 27:21 twain will ye that I *r* unto you
Mk 15:9 Will ye that I *r* unto you the
Mk 15:11 rather *r* Barabbas unto them
Lk 23:16 therefore chastise him, and *r* him
Lk 23:17 (For of necessity he must *r* one
Lk 23:18 this man, and *r* unto us Barabbas
Lk 23:20 therefore, willing to *r* Jesus
Jn 18:39 that I should *r* unto you one at
Jn 18:39 will ye therefore that I *r* unto
Jn 19:10 thee, and have power to *r* thee
Jn 19:12 Pilate sought to *r* him

### RELEASED
Mt 27:26 Then *r* he Barabbas unto them
Mk 15:6 Now at that feast he *r* unto them
Mk 15:15 people, *r* Barabbas unto them, and
Lk 23:25 he *r* unto them him that for

### RELIED
2Chr 13:18 because they *r* upon the LORD God
2Chr 16:7 Because thou hast *r* on the king
2Chr 16:7 not *r* on the LORD thy God,

### RELIEVE
Lev 25:35 then thou shalt *r* him
Is 1:17 *r* the oppressed, judge the
Lam 1:11 things for meat to *r* the soul
Lam 1:16 should *r* my soul is far from me
Lam 1:19 their meat to *r* their souls
1Ti 5:16 have widows, let them *r* them
1Ti 5:16 that it may *r* them that are

### RELIGION
Acts 26:5 sect of our *r* I lived a Pharisee
Gal 1:13 in time past in the Jews' *r*
Gal 1:14 profited in the Jews' *r* above
Jas 1:26 own heart, this man's *r* is vain
Jas 1:27 Pure *r* and undefiled before God and

### REMAIN
Gen 38:11 *R* a widow at thy father's house,
Ex 8:9 that they may *r* in the river only
Ex 8:11 they shall *r* in the river only
Ex 12:10 nothing of it *r* until the morning
Ex 23:18 my sacrifice *r* until the morning
Ex 29:34 *r* unto the morning, then thou
Lev 19:6 if ought *r* until the third day,
Lev 25:28 *r* in the hand of him that hath
Lev 25:52 if there *r* but few years unto the
Lev 27:18 according to the years that *r*
Num 33:55 that those which ye let *r* of them
Deut 2:34 of every city, we left none to *r*
Deut 16:4 *r* all night until the morning
Deut 19:20 And those which *r* shall hear
Deut 21:13 shall *r* in thine house, and bewail
Deut 21:23 His body shall not *r* all night
Josh 1:14 shall *r* in the land which Moses
Josh 2:11 neither did there *r* any more
Josh 8:22 they let none of them *r* or escape
Josh 10:27 which *r* until this very day
Josh 10:28 he let none *r*
Josh 10:30 he let none *r* in it
Josh 23:4 you by lot these nations that *r*
Josh 23:7 nations, these that *r* among you
Josh 23:12 even these that *r* among you
Judg 5:17 and why did Dan *r* in ships
Judg 21:7 we do for wives for them that *r*
Judg 21:16 we do for wives for them that *r*
1Sa 20:19 shalt *r* by the stone Ezel
1Kin 11:16 did Joab *r* there with all Israel
1Kin 18:22 I only, *r* a prophet of the LORD
2Kin 7:13 thee, five of the horses that *r*
Ezr 9:15 for we *r* yet escaped, as it is
Job 21:32 the grave, and shall *r* in the tomb
Job 27:15 Those that *r* of him shall be
Job 37:8 into dens, and *r* in their places
Ps 55:7 far off, and *r* in the wilderness
Prov 2:21 and the perfect shall *r* in it
Prov 21:16 the way of understanding shall *r*
Is 10:32 As yet shall he *r* at Nob that day
Is 32:16 righteousness *r* in the fruitful
Is 44:13 that it may *r* in the house
Is 65:4 Which *r* among the graves, and
Is 66:22 shall *r* before me, saith the LORD
Is 66:22 so shall your seed and your name *r*
Jer 8:3 them that *r* of this evil family
Jer 8:3 which *r* in all the places whither
Jer 17:25 and this city shall *r* for ever
Jer 24:8 that *r* in this land, and them that
Jer 27:11 those will I let *r* still in their
Jer 27:19 the vessels that *r* in this city
Jer 27:21 that *r* in the house of the LORD
Jer 30:18 the palace shall *r* after the
Jer 38:4 men of war that *r* in this city
Jer 42:17 none of them shall *r* or escape
Jer 44:7 of Judah, to leave you none to *r*
Jer 44:14 sojourn there, shall escape or *r*
Jer 51:62 it off, that none shall *r* in it
Eze 7:11 none of them shall *r*, nor of
Eze 17:21 they that *r* shall be scattered
Eze 31:13 all the fowls of the heaven *r*
Eze 32:4 of the heaven to *r* upon thee
Eze 39:14 that *r* upon the face of the earth
Amos 6:9 if there *r* ten men in one house,
Obad 14 that did *r* in the day of distress
Zec 5:4 it shall *r* in the midst of his
Zec 12:14 All the families that *r*, every
Lk 10:7 And in the same house *r*, eating and
Jn 6:12 Gather up the fragments that *r*
Jn 15:11 you, that my joy might *r* in you
Jn 15:16 and that your fruit should *r*
Jn 19:31 that the bodies should not *r* upon
1Cor 7:11 let her *r* unmarried, or be
1Cor 15:6 greater part *r* unto this present
1Th 4:15 *r* unto the coming of the Lord
1Th 4:17 *r* shall be caught up together
Heb 12:27 which cannot be shaken may *r*
1Jn 2:24 from the beginning shall *r* in you
Rev 3:2 and strengthen the things which *r*

### REMAINDER
Ex 29:34 thou shalt burn the *r* with fire
Lev 6:16 the *r* thereof shall Aaron and his
Lev 7:16 also the *r* of it shall be eaten
Lev 7:17 But the *r* of the flesh of the
2Sa 14:7 neither name nor *r* upon the earth
Ps 76:10 the *r* of wrath shalt thou

### REMAINED
Gen 7:23 and Noah only *r* alive, and they
Gen 14:10 they that *r* fled to the mountain
Ex 8:31 there *r* not one
Ex 10:15 there *r* not any green thing in
Ex 10:19 there *r* not one locust in all the
Ex 14:28 there *r* not so much as one of
Num 11:26 But there *r* two of the men in the
Num 35:28 Because he should have *r* in the
Num 36:12 their inheritance *r* in the tribe
Deut 3:11 Bashan *r* of the remnant of giants
Deut 4:25 ye shall have *r* long in the land,
Josh 10:20 that the rest which *r* of them
Josh 11:22 in Gath, and in Ashdod, there *r*
Josh 13:12 who *r* of the remnant of the
Josh 18:2 there *r* among the children of
Josh 21:20 the Levites which *r* of the
Josh 21:26 of the children of Kohath that *r*
Judg 7:3 and there *r* ten thousand
1Sa 11:11 that they which *r* were scattered
1Sa 23:14 *r* in a mountain in the wilderness
1Sa 24:3 his men *r* in the sides of the
2Sa 13:20 So Tamar *r* desolate in her
1Kin 22:46 which *r* in the days of his father
2Kin 10:11 So Jehu slew all that *r* of the
2Kin 10:17 he slew all that *r* unto Ahab in
2Kin 13:6 there *r* the grove also in Samaria
2Kin 24:14 none *r*, save the poorest sort of
2Kin 25:22 that *r* in the land of Judah
1Chr 13:14 the ark of God *r* with the family
Eccl 2:9 also my wisdom *r* with me
Jer 34:7 cities *r* of the cities of Judah
Jer 37:10 there *r* but wounded men among
Jer 37:16 Jeremiah had *r* there many days
Jer 37:21 Thus Jeremiah *r* in the court of
Jer 38:13 Jeremiah *r* in the court of the
Jer 39:9 of the people that *r* in the city
Jer 39:9 the rest of the people that *r*
Jer 41:10 all the people that *r* in Mizpah
Jer 48:11 therefore his taste *r* in him
Jer 51:30 they have *r* in their holds
Jer 52:15 of the people that *r* in the city
Lam 2:22 LORD's anger none escaped nor *r*
Eze 3:15 *r* there astonished among them
Dan 10:8 there *r* no strength in me
Dan 10:13 I *r* there with the kings of
Dan 10:17 there *r* no strength in me
Mt 11:23 it would have *r* until this day
Mt 14:20 that *r* twelve baskets full
Lk 1:22 unto them, and *r* speechless
Lk 9:17 that *r* to them twelve baskets
Jn 6:13 five barley loaves, which *r* over
Acts 5:4 Whiles it *r*, was it not thine own
Acts 27:41 *r* unmoveable, but the hinder part

### REMAINETH
Gen 8:22 While the earth *r*, seedtime and
Ex 10:5 which *r* unto you from the hail,
Ex 12:10 that which *r* of it until the
Ex 16:23 that which *r* over lay up for you
Ex 26:12 the remnant that *r* of the
Ex 26:12 the tent, the half curtain that *r*
Ex 26:13 *r* in the length of the curtains
Lev 8:32 that which *r* of the flesh and of
Lev 10:12 Take the meat offering that *r* of
Lev 16:16 that *r* among them in the midst of
Num 24:19 destroy him that *r* of the city
Josh 8:29 of stones, that *r* unto this day
Josh 13:1 there *r* yet very much land to be
Josh 13:2 This is the land that yet *r*
Judg 5:13 Then he made him that *r* have
1Sa 6:18 which stone *r* unto this day in
1Sa 16:11 There *r* yet the youngest, and,
1Chr 17:1 of the LORD *r* under curtains
Ezr 1:4 whosoever *r* in any place where he
Job 19:4 erred, mine error *r* with myself
Job 21:34 in your answers there *r* falsehood
Job 41:22 In his neck *r* strength, and sorrow
Is 4:3 he that *r* in Jerusalem, shall be
Jer 38:2 He that *r* in this city shall die
Jer 47:4 and Zidon every helper that *r*
Eze 6:12 and he that *r* and is besieged shall
Hag 2:5 Egypt, so my spirit *r* among you
Zec 9:7 but he that *r*, even he, shall be
Jn 9:41 therefore your sin *r*
1Cor 7:29 it *r*, that both they that have
2Cor 3:11 more that which *r* is glorious
2Cor 3:14 for until this day *r* the same
2Cor 9:9 his righteousness *r* for ever
Heb 4:6 Seeing therefore it *r* that some
Heb 4:9 There *r* therefore a rest to the
Heb 10:26 there *r* no more sacrifice for
1Jn 3:9 for his seed *r* in him

### REMAINING
Num 9:22 *r* thereon, the children of Israel
Deut 3:3 him until none was left to him *r*

Josh 10:33 until he had left him none r
Josh 10:37 he left none r, according to all
Josh 10:39 he left none r
Josh 10:40 he left none r, but utterly
Josh 11:8 them, until they left them none r
Josh 21:40 which were r of the families of
2Sa 21:5 we should be destroyed from r in
2Kin 10:11 priests, until he left him none r
1Chr 9:33 who r in the chambers were free
Job 18:19 nor any r in his dwellings
Obad 18 not be any r of the house of Esau
Jn 1:33 r on him, the same is he which

**REMALIAH** *(rem-a-li'-ah)* See REMALIAH'S. *Father of Pekah.*
2Kin 15:25 But Pekah the son of R, a captain
2Kin 15:27 R began to reign over Israel in
2Kin 15:30 against Pekah the son of R
2Kin 15:32 R king of Israel began Jotham the
2Kin 15:37 of Syria, and Pekah the son of R
2Kin 16:1 year of Pekah the son of R Ahaz
2Kin 16:5 Pekah son of R king of Israel
2Chr 28:6 For Pekah the son of R slew in
Is 7:1 of Syria, and Pekah the son of R
Is 7:4 with Syria, and of the son of R
Is 7:5 Syria, Ephraim, and the son of R

**REMALIAH'S** *(rem-a-li'-ahs)*
Is 7:9 and the head of Samaria is R son
Is 8:6 and rejoice in Rezin and R son

**REMEMBER**
Gen 9:15 I will r my covenant, which is
Gen 9:16 that I may r the everlasting
Gen 40:23 did not the chief butler r Joseph
Gen 41:9 I do r my faults this day
Ex 13:3 R this day, in which ye came out
Ex 20:8 R the sabbath day, to keep it
Ex 32:13 R Abraham, Isaac, and Israel, thy
Lev 26:42 Then will I r my covenant with
Lev 26:42 my covenant with Abraham will I r
Lev 26:42 and I will r the land
Lev 26:45 But I will for their sakes r the
Num 11:5 We r the fish, which we did eat
Num 15:39 r all the commandments of the
Num 15:40 That ye may r, and do all my
Deut 5:15 r that thou wast a servant in the
Deut 7:18 but shalt well r what the LORD
Deut 8:2 thou shalt r all the way which
Deut 8:18 But thou shalt r the LORD thy God
Deut 9:7 R, and forget not, how thou
Deut 9:27 R thy servants, Abraham, Isaac,
Deut 15:15 thou shalt r that thou wast a
Deut 16:3 that thou mayest r the day when
Deut 16:12 thou shalt r that thou wast a
Deut 24:9 R what the LORD thy God did unto
Deut 24:18 But thou shalt r that thou wast a
Deut 24:22 thou shalt r that thou wast a
Deut 25:17 R what Amalek did unto thee by
Deut 32:7 R the days of old, consider the
Josh 1:13 R the word which Moses the
Judg 9:2 r also that I am your bone and
Judg 16:28 r me, I pray thee, and strengthen
1Sa 1:11 r me, and not forget thine
1Sa 15:2 I r that which Amalek did to
1Sa 25:31 my lord, then r thine handmaid
2Sa 14:11 let the king r the LORD thy God,
2Sa 19:19 neither do thou r that which thy
2Kin 9:25 for r how that, when I and thou
2Kin 20:3 r now how I have walked before
1Chr 16:12 R his marvellous works that he
2Chr 6:42 r the mercies of David thy
Neh 1:8 R, I beseech thee, the word that
Neh 4:14 r the LORD, which is great and
Neh 13:14 R me, O my God, concerning this,
Neh 13:22 R me, O my God, concerning this
Neh 13:29 R them, O my God, because they
Neh 13:31 R me, O my God, for good
Job 4:7 R, I pray thee, who ever perished
Job 7:7 O r that my life is wind
Job 10:9 R, I beseech thee, that thou hast
Job 11:16 r it as waters that pass away
Job 14:13 appoint me a set time, and r me
Job 21:6 Even when I r I am afraid
Job 36:24 R that thou magnify his work,
Job 41:8 him, r the battle, do no more
Ps 20:3 R all thy offerings, and accept
Ps 20:7 but we will r the name of the
Ps 22:27 All the ends of the world shall r
Ps 25:6 R, O LORD, thy tender mercies and
Ps 25:7 R not the sins of my youth, nor
Ps 25:7 according to thy mercy r thou me
Ps 42:4 When I r these things, I pour out
Ps 42:6 therefore will I r thee from the
Ps 63:6 When I r thee upon my bed, and
Ps 74:2 R thy congregation, which thou
Ps 74:18 R this, that the enemy hath
Ps 74:22 r how the foolish man reproacheth
Ps 77:10 but I will r the years of the
Ps 77:11 I will r the works of the LORD
Ps 77:11 surely I will r thy wonders of
Ps 79:8 O r not against us former
Ps 89:47 R how short my time is
Ps 89:50 R, Lord, the reproach of thy
Ps 103:18 to those that r his commandments
Ps 105:5 R his marvellous works that he
Ps 106:4 R me, O LORD, with the favour
Ps 119:49 R the word unto thy servant, upon
Ps 132:1 r David, and all his afflictions
Ps 137:6 If I do not r thee, let my tongue
Ps 137:7 R, O LORD, the children of Edom
Ps 143:5 I r the days of old
Prov 31:7 poverty, and r his misery no more
Eccl 5:20 not much r the days of his life
Eccl 11:8 yet let him r the days of
Eccl 12:1 R now thy Creator in the days of
Song 1:4 we will r thy love more than wine
Is 38:3 R now, O LORD, I beseech thee,
Is 43:18 R ye not the former things,
Is 43:25 own sake, and will not r thy sins
Is 44:21 R these, O Jacob and Israel
Is 46:8 R this, and shew yourselves men
Is 46:9 R the former things of old
Is 47:7 neither didst r the latter end of
Is 54:4 shalt not r the reproach of thy
Is 64:5 those that r thee in thy ways
Is 64:9 neither r iniquity for ever
Jer 2:2 I r thee, the kindness of thy
Jer 3:16 neither shall they r it
Jer 14:10 he will now r their iniquity, and
Jer 14:21 r, break not thy covenant with us
Jer 15:15 r me, and visit me, and revenge me
Jer 17:2 their children r their altars
Jer 18:20 R that I stood before thee to
Jer 31:20 him, I do earnestly r him still
Jer 31:34 I will r their sin no more
Jer 44:21 the land, did not the LORD r them
Jer 51:50 r the LORD afar off, and let
Lam 5:1 R, O LORD, what is come upon us
Eze 6:9 r me among the nations whither
Eze 16:60 Nevertheless I will r my covenant
Eze 16:61 Then thou shalt r thy ways
Eze 16:63 That thou mayest r, and be
Eze 20:43 And there shall ye r your ways
Eze 23:27 unto them, nor r Egypt any more
Eze 36:31 Then shall ye r your own evil
Hos 7:2 that I r all their wickedness
Hos 8:13 now will he r their iniquity, and
Hos 9:9 he will r their iniquity, he will
Mic 6:5 r now what Balak king of Moab
Hab 3:2 in wrath r mercy
Zec 10:9 they shall r me in far countries
Mal 4:4 R ye the law of Moses my servant,
Mt 16:9 neither r the five loaves of the
Mt 27:63 we r that that deceiver said,
Mk 8:18 and do ye not r
Lk 1:72 and to r his holy covenant
Lk 16:25 r that thou in thy lifetime
Lk 17:32 R Lot's wife
Lk 23:42 r me when thou comest into thy
Lk 24:6 r how he spake unto you when he
Jn 15:20 R the word that I said unto you,
Jn 16:4 ye may r that I told you of them
Acts 20:31 Therefore watch, and r, that by
Acts 20:35 to r the words of the Lord Jesus,
1Cor 11:2 that ye r me in all things, and
Gal 2:10 would that we should r the poor
Eph 2:11 Wherefore r, that ye being in
Col 4:18 R my bonds
1Th 2:9 For ye r, brethren, our labour and
2Th 2:5 R ye not, that, when I was yet
2Ti 2:8 R that Jesus Christ of the seed
Heb 8:12 their iniquities will I r no more
Heb 10:17 and iniquities will I r no more
Heb 13:3 R them that are in bonds, as
Heb 13:7 R them which have the rule over
3Jn 10 I will r his deeds which he doeth
Jude 17 r ye the words which were spoken
Rev 2:5 R therefore from whence thou art
Rev 3:3 R therefore how thou hast

**REMEMBERED**
Gen 8:1 God r Noah, and every living thing
Gen 19:29 of the plain, that God r Abraham
Gen 30:22 God r Rachel, and God hearkened to
Gen 42:9 Joseph r the dreams which he
Ex 2:24 God r his covenant with Abraham,
Ex 6:5 and I have r my covenant
Num 10:9 ye shall be r before the LORD
Judg 8:34 Israel r not the LORD their God
1Sa 1:19 and the LORD r her
2Chr 24:22 Thus Joash the king r not the
Est 2:1 he r Vashti, and what she had done
Est 9:28 And that these days should be r
Job 24:20 he shall be no more r
Ps 45:17 name to be r in all generations
Ps 77:3 I r God, and was troubled
Ps 78:35 they r that God was their rock,
Ps 78:39 For he r that they were but flesh
Ps 78:42 They r not his hand, nor the day
Ps 98:3 He hath r his mercy and his truth
Ps 105:8 He hath r his covenant for ever,
Ps 105:42 For he r his holy promise, and
Ps 106:7 they r not the multitude of thy
Ps 106:45 he r for them his covenant, and
Ps 109:14 of his fathers be r with the LORD
Ps 109:16 Because that he r not to shew
Ps 111:4 made his wonderful works to be r
Ps 119:52 I r thy judgments of old, O LORD
Ps 119:55 I have r thy name, O LORD, in the
Ps 136:23 Who r us in our low estate
Ps 137:1 yea, we wept, when we r Zion
Eccl 9:15 yet no man r that same poor man
Is 23:16 many songs, that thou mayest be r
Is 57:11 thou hast lied, and hast not r me
Is 63:11 Then he r the days of old, Moses,
Is 65:17 and the former shall not be r
Jer 11:19 that his name may be no more r
Lam 1:7 Jerusalem r in the days of her
Lam 2:1 r not his footstool in the day of
Eze 3:20 which he hath done shall not be r
Eze 16:22 hast not r the days of thy youth
Eze 16:43 hast not r the days of thy youth
Eze 21:24 have made your iniquity to be r
Eze 21:32 thou shalt be no more r
Eze 25:10 may not be r among the nations
Eze 33:13 righteousnesses shall not be r
Hos 2:17 shall no more be r by their name
Amos 1:9 r not the brotherly covenant
Jonah 2:7 fainted within me I r the LORD
Zec 13:2 land, and they shall no more be r
Mt 26:75 Peter r the word of Jesus, which
Lk 22:61 Peter r the word of the Lord, how
Lk 24:8 And they r his words,
Jn 2:17 his disciples r that it was
Jn 2:22 his disciples r that he had said
Jn 12:16 then r they that these things
Acts 11:16 Then r I the word of the Lord,
Rev 18:5 God hath r her iniquities

**REMEMBERETH**
Ps 9:12 inquisition for blood, he r them
Ps 103:14 he r that we are dust
Lam 1:9 she r not her last end
Jn 16:21 she r no more the anguish, for
2Cor 7:15 whilst he r the obedience of you

**REMEMBRANCE**
Ex 17:14 the r of Amalek from under heaven
Num 5:15 memorial, bringing iniquity to r
Deut 25:19 the r of Amalek from under heaven
Deut 32:26 I would make the r of them to
2Sa 18:18 have no son to keep my name in r
1Kin 17:18 come unto me to call my sin to r
Job 18:17 His r shall perish from the earth
Ps 6:5 in death there is no r of thee
Ps 30:4 thanks at the r of his holiness
Ps 34:16 to cut off the r of them from the
Ps 38:t A Psalm of David, to bring to r
Ps 70:t A Psalm of David, to bring to r
Ps 77:6 I call to r my song in the night
Ps 83:4 of Israel may be no more in r
Ps 97:12 thanks at the r of his holiness
Ps 102:12 thy r unto all generations
Ps 112:6 shall be in everlasting r
Eccl 1:11 There is no r of former things
Eccl 1:11 neither shall there be any r of
Eccl 2:16 For there is no r of the wise
Is 26:8 to thy name, and to the r of thee
Is 43:26 Put me in r
Is 57:8 the posts hast thou set up thy r
Lam 3:20 My soul hath them still in r

Eze 21:23 he will call to *r* the iniquity
Eze 21:24 I say, that ye are come to *r*
Eze 23:19 in calling to *r* the days of her
Eze 23:21 Thus thou calledst to *r* the
Eze 29:16 bringeth their iniquity to *r*
Mal 3:16 a book of *r* was written before
Mk 11:21 Peter calling to *r* saith unto him
Lk 1:54 servant Israel, in *r* of his mercy
Lk 22:19 this do in *r* of me
Jn 14:26 and bring all things to your *r*
Acts 10:31 are had in *r* in the sight of God
1Cor 4:17 who shall bring you into *r* of my
1Cor 11:24 this do in *r* of me
1Cor 11:25 as oft as ye drink it, in *r* of me
Phil 1:3 thank my God upon every *r* of you
1Th 3:6 that ye have good *r* of us always
1Ti 4:6 the brethren in *r* of these things
2Ti 1:3 *r* of thee in my prayers night
2Ti 1:5 When I call to *r* the unfeigned
2Ti 1:6 Wherefore I put thee in *r* that
2Ti 2:14 Of these things put them in *r*
Heb 10:3 a *r* again made of sins every year
Heb 10:32 But call to *r* the former days, in
2Pet 1:12 you always in *r* of these things
2Pet 1:13 stir you up by putting you in *r*
2Pet 1:15 to have these things always in *r*
2Pet 3:1 up your pure minds by way of *r*
Jude 5 I will therefore put you in *r*
Rev 16:19 Babylon came in *r* before God

**REMETH** *(re'-meth)* See RAMOTH, JARMUTH. *A Levitical city in Issachar.*
Josh 19:21 And *R*, and En-gannim,

**REMISSION**
Mt 26:28 shed for many for the *r* of sins
Mk 1:4 of repentance for the *r* of sins
Lk 1:77 his people by the *r* of their sins
Lk 3:3 of repentance for the *r* of sins
Lk 24:47 *r* of sins should be preached in
Acts 2:38 of Jesus Christ for the *r* of sins
Acts 10:43 in him shall receive *r* of sins
Rom 3:25 for the *r* of sins that are past
Heb 9:22 without shedding of blood is no *r*
Heb 10:18 Now where *r* of these is, there is

**REMMON** *(rem'-mon)* See RIMMON. *A city in Judah.*
Josh 19:7 Ain, *R*, and Ether, and Ashan

**REMMON-METHOAR** *(rem'-mon-meth'-o-ar) A city in Zebulun.*
Josh 19:13 and goeth out to *R* to Neah

**REMNANT**
Ex 26:12 the *r* that remaineth of the
Lev 2:3 the *r* of the meat offerings shall
Lev 5:13 the *r* shall be the priest's, as a
Lev 14:18 the *r* of the oil that is in the
Deut 3:11 remained of the *r* of giants
Deut 28:54 toward the *r* of his children
Josh 12:4 which was of the *r* of the giants
Josh 13:12 remained of the *r* of the giants
Josh 23:12 cleave unto the *r* of these
2Sa 21:2 but of the *r* of the Amorites
1Kin 12:23 to the *r* of the people, saying,
1Kin 14:10 will take away the *r* of the house
1Kin 22:46 the *r* of the sodomites, which
2Kin 19:4 prayer for the *r* that are left
2Kin 19:30 the *r* that is escaped of the
2Kin 19:31 of Jerusalem shall go forth a *r*
2Kin 21:14 I will forsake the *r* of mine
2Kin 25:11 with the *r* of the multitude, did
1Chr 6:70 of the *r* of the sons of Kohath
2Chr 30:6 and he will return to the *r* of you
2Chr 34:9 and of all the *r* of Israel
Ezr 3:8 the *r* of their brethren the
Ezr 9:8 God, to leave us a *r* to escape
Ezr 9:14 there should be no *r* nor escaping
Neh 1:3 The *r* that are left of the
Job 22:20 but the *r* of them the fire
Is 1:9 had left unto us a very small *r*
Is 10:20 that the *r* of Israel, and such as
Is 10:21 The *r* shall return, even the
Is 10:21 shall return, even the *r* of Jacob
Is 10:22 yet a *r* of them shall return
Is 11:11 to recover the *r* of his people
Is 11:16 highway for the *r* of his people
Is 14:22 off from Babylon the name, and *r*
Is 14:30 famine, and he shall slay thy *r*
Is 15:9 Moab, and upon the *r* of the land
Is 16:14 the *r* shall be very small and
Is 17:3 from Damascus, and the *r* of Syria
Is 37:4 thy prayer for the *r* that is left
Is 37:31 the *r* that is escaped of the
Is 37:32 of Jerusalem shall go forth a *r*
Is 46:3 all the *r* of the house of Israel,
Jer 6:9 glean the *r* of Israel as a vine
Jer 11:23 And there shall be no *r* of them
Jer 15:11 it shall be well with thy *r*
Jer 23:3 I will gather the *r* of my flock
Jer 25:20 and Ekron, and the *r* of Ashdod,
Jer 31:7 save thy people, the *r* of Israel
Jer 39:9 away captive into Babylon the *r*
Jer 40:11 of Babylon had left a *r* of Judah
Jer 40:15 and the *r* in Judah perish
Jer 41:16 all the *r* of the people whom he
Jer 42:2 LORD thy God, even for all this *r*
Jer 42:15 word of the LORD, ye *r* of Judah
Jer 42:19 concerning you, O ye *r* of Judah
Jer 43:5 forces, took all the *r* of Judah
Jer 44:12 And I will take the *r* of Judah
Jer 44:14 So that none of the *r* of Judah
Jer 44:28 all the *r* of Judah, that are gone
Jer 47:4 the *r* of the country of Caphtor
Jer 47:5 off with the *r* of their valley
Eze 5:10 the whole *r* of thee will I
Eze 6:8 Yet will I leave a *r*, that ye may
Eze 11:13 a full end of the *r* of Israel
Eze 14:22 therein shall be left a *r* that
Eze 23:25 thy *r* shall fall by the sword
Eze 25:16 destroy the *r* of the sea coast
Joel 2:32 in the *r* whom the LORD shall call
Amos 1:8 the *r* of the Philistines shall
Amos 5:15 be gracious unto the *r* of Joseph
Amos 9:12 they may possess the *r* of Edom
Mic 2:12 surely gather the *r* of Israel
Mic 4:7 I will make her that halted a *r*
Mic 5:3 then the *r* of his brethren shall
Mic 5:7 the *r* of Jacob shall be in the
Mic 5:8 the *r* of Jacob shall be among the
Mic 7:18 of the *r* of his heritage
Hab 2:8 all the *r* of the people shall
Zeph 1:4 I will cut off the *r* of Baal from
Zeph 2:7 for the *r* of the house of Judah
Zeph 2:9 the *r* of my people shall possess
Zeph 3:13 The *r* of Israel shall not do
Hag 1:12 with all the *r* of the people,
Hag 1:14 spirit of all the *r* of the people
Zec 8:6 *r* of this people in these days
Zec 8:12 I will cause the *r* of this people
Mt 22:6 the *r* took his servants, and
Rom 9:27 of the sea, a *r* shall be saved
Rom 11:5 a *r* according to the election of
Rev 11:13 the *r* were affrighted, and gave
Rev 12:17 make war with the *r* of her seed
Rev 19:21 the *r* were slain with the sword

**REMOVE**
Gen 48:17 to *r* it from Ephraim's head unto
Num 36:7 of Israel *r* from tribe to tribe
Num 36:9 Neither shall the inheritance *r*
Deut 19:14 Thou shalt not *r* thy neighbour's
Josh 3:3 then ye shall *r* from your place,
Judg 9:29 then would I *r* Abimelech
2Sa 6:10 So David would not *r* the ark of
2Kin 23:27 I will *r* Judah also out of my
2Kin 24:3 to *r* them out of his sight, for
2Chr 33:8 Neither will I any more *r* the
Job 24:2 Some *r* the landmarks
Job 27:5 till I die I will not *r* mine
Ps 36:11 not the hand of the wicked *r* me
Ps 39:10 *R* thy stroke away from me
Ps 119:22 *R* from me reproach and contempt
Ps 119:29 *R* from me the way of lying
Prov 4:27 *r* thy foot from evil
Prov 5:8 *R* thy way far from her, and come
Prov 22:28 *R* not the ancient landmark, which
Prov 23:10 *R* not the old landmark
Prov 30:8 *R* far from me vanity and lies
Eccl 11:10 Therefore *r* sorrow from thy heart
Is 13:13 the earth shall *r* out of her
Is 46:7 from his place shall he not *r*
Jer 4:1 my sight, then shalt thou not *r*
Jer 27:10 to *r* you far from your land
Jer 32:31 that I should *r* it from before my
Jer 50:3 they shall *r*, they shall depart,
Jer 50:8 *R* out of the midst of Babylon, and
Eze 12:3 and *r* by day in their sight
Eze 12:3 thou shalt *r* from thy place to
Eze 12:11 they shall *r* and go into captivity
Eze 21:26 *R* the diadem, and take off the
Eze 45:9 *r* violence and spoil, and execute
Hos 5:10 were like them that *r* the bound
Joel 2:20 But I will *r* far off from you the
Joel 3:6 that ye might *r* them far from
Mic 2:3 which ye shall not *r* your necks
Zec 3:9 I will *r* the iniquity of that
Zec 14:4 mountain shall *r* toward the north
Mt 17:20 mountain, *R* hence to yonder place
Mt 17:20 and it shall *r*
Lk 22:42 be willing, *r* this cup from me
1Cor 13:2 so that I could *r* mountains
Rev 2:5 will *r* thy candlestick out of his

**REMOVED**
Gen 8:13 Noah *r* the covering of the ark,
Gen 12:8 he *r* from thence unto a mountain
Gen 13:18 Then Abram *r* his tent, and came and
Gen 26:22 he *r* from thence, and digged
Gen 30:35 he *r* that day the he goats that
Gen 47:21 he *r* them to cities from one end
Ex 8:31 he *r* the swarms of flies from
Ex 14:19 went before the camp of Israel, *r*
Ex 20:18 and when the people saw it, they *r*
Num 12:16 the people *r* from Hazeroth
Num 21:12 From thence they *r*, and pitched in
Num 21:13 From thence they *r*, and pitched on
Num 33:5 children of Israel *r* from Rameses
Num 33:7 they *r* from Etham, and turned
Num 33:9 they *r* from Marah, and came unto
Num 33:10 they *r* from Elim, and encamped by
Num 33:11 they *r* from the Red sea, and
Num 33:14 they *r* from Alush, and encamped at
Num 33:16 they *r* from the desert of Sinai,
Num 33:21 they *r* from Libnah, and pitched at
Num 33:24 they *r* from mount Shapher, and
Num 33:25 they *r* from Haradah, and pitched
Num 33:26 they *r* from Makheloth, and
Num 33:28 they *r* from Tarah, and pitched in
Num 33:32 they *r* from Bene-jaakan, and
Num 33:34 they *r* from Jotbathah, and
Num 33:36 they *r* from Ezion-gaber, and
Num 33:37 they *r* from Kadesh, and pitched in
Num 33:46 they *r* from Dibon-gad, and
Num 33:47 they *r* from Almon-diblathaim, and
Deut 28:25 shalt be *r* into all the kingdoms
Josh 3:1 they *r* from Shittim, and came to
Josh 3:14 when the people *r* from their
1Sa 6:3 why his hand is not *r* from you
1Sa 18:13 Therefore Saul *r* him from him
2Sa 20:12 he *r* Amasa out of the highway
2Sa 20:13 When he was *r* out of the highway,
1Kin 15:12 *r* all the idols that his fathers
1Kin 15:13 even her he *r* from being queen,
1Kin 15:14 But the high places were not *r*
2Kin 15:4 that the high places were not *r*
2Kin 15:35 the high places were not *r*
2Kin 16:17 *r* the laver from off them
2Kin 17:18 and *r* them out of his sight
2Kin 17:23 Until the LORD *r* Israel out of
2Kin 17:26 The nations which thou hast *r*
2Kin 18:4 He *r* the high places, and brake
2Kin 23:27 of my sight, as I have *r* Israel
1Chr 8:6 Geba, and they *r* them to Manahath
1Chr 8:7 he *r* them, and begat Uzza, and
2Chr 15:16 he *r* her from being queen,
2Chr 35:12 they *r* the burnt offerings, that
Job 14:18 the rock is *r* out of his place
Job 18:4 the rock be *r* out of his place
Job 19:10 mine hope hath he *r* like a tree
Job 36:16 Even so would he have *r* thee out
Ps 46:2 we fear, though the earth be *r*
Ps 81:6 I *r* his shoulder from the burden
Ps 103:12 the west, so far hath he *r* our
Ps 104:5 that it should not be *r* for ever
Ps 125:1 as mount Zion, which cannot be *r*
Prov 10:30 The righteous shall never be *r*
Is 6:12 And the LORD have *r* men far away
Is 10:13 I have *r* the bounds of the people
Is 10:31 Madmenah is *r*
Is 22:25 fastened in the sure place be *r*
Is 24:20 shall be *r* like a cottage
Is 26:15 thou hadst *r* it far unto all the
Is 29:13 but have *r* their heart far from
Is 30:20 be *r* into a corner any more
Is 33:20 stakes thereof shall ever be *r*
Is 38:12 is *r* from me as a shepherd's tent
Is 54:10 shall depart, and the hills be *r*
Is 54:10 the covenant of my peace be *r*
Jer 15:4 I will cause them to be *r* into
Jer 24:9 I will deliver them to be *r* into
Jer 29:18 will deliver them to be *r* to all

Jer 34:17 I will make you to be *r* into all
Lam 1:8 therefore she is *r*
Lam 3:17 thou hast *r* my soul far off from
Eze 7:19 streets, and their gold shall be *r*
Eze 23:46 them, and will give them to be *r*
Eze 36:17 as the uncleanness of a *r* woman
Amos 6:7 stretched themselves shall be *r*
Mic 2:4 how hath he *r* it from me
Mic 7:11 day shall the decree be far *r*
Mt 21:21 say unto this mountain, Be thou *r*
Mk 11:23 say unto this mountain, Be thou *r*
Acts 7:4 he *r* him into this land, wherein
Acts 13:22 And when he had *r* him, he raised
Gal 1:6 I marvel that ye are so soon *r*

**REMPHAN** *(rem'-fan) An idol worshipped by Israel.*
Acts 7:43 Moloch, and the star of your god *R*

**REND**
Ex 39:23 the hole, that it should not *r*
Lev 10:6 heads, neither *r* your clothes
Lev 13:56 then he shall *r* it out of the
Lev 21:10 his head, nor *r* his clothes
2Sa 3:31 *R* your clothes, and gird you with
1Kin 11:11 I will surely *r* the kingdom from
1Kin 11:12 but I will *r* it out of the hand
1Kin 11:13 Howbeit I will not *r* away all the
1Kin 11:31 I will *r* the kingdom out of the
2Chr 34:27 didst *r* thy clothes, and weep
Eccl 3:7 A time to *r*, and a time to sew
Is 64:1 that thou wouldest *r* the heavens
Eze 13:11 and a stormy wind shall *r* it
Eze 13:13 I will even *r* it with a stormy
Eze 29:7 break, and *r* all their shoulder
Hos 13:8 will *r* the caul of their heart,
Joel 2:13 *r* your heart, and not your
Mt 7:6 feet, and turn again and *r* you
Jn 19:24 among themselves, Let us not *r* it

**RENDER**
Num 18:9 which they shall *r* unto me
Deut 32:41 I will *r* vengeance to mine
Deut 32:43 and will *r* vengeance to his
Judg 9:57 did God *r* upon their heads
1Sa 26:23 The LORD *r* to every man his
2Chr 6:30 *r* unto every man according unto
Job 33:26 for he will *r* unto man his
Job 34:11 work of a man shall he *r* unto him
Ps 28:4 *r* to them their desert
Ps 38:20 They also that *r* evil for good
Ps 56:12 I will *r* praises unto thee
Ps 79:12 *r* unto our neighbours sevenfold
Ps 94:2 *r* a reward to the proud
Ps 116:12 What shall I *r* unto the LORD for
Prov 24:12 shall not he *r* to every man
Prov 24:29 I will *r* to the man according to
Prov 26:16 seven men that can *r* a reason
Is 66:15 to *r* his anger with fury, and his
Jer 51:6 he will *r* unto her a recompence
Jer 51:24 I will *r* unto Babylon and to all
Lam 3:64 *R* unto them a recompence, O LORD,
Hos 14:2 so will we *r* the calves of our
Joel 3:4 will ye *r* me a recompence
Zec 9:12 that I will *r* double unto thee
Mt 21:41 which shall *r* him the fruits in
Mt 22:21 *R* therefore unto Caesar the
Mk 12:17 *R* to Caesar the things that are
Lk 20:25 *R* therefore unto Caesar the
Rom 2:6 Who will *r* to every man according
Rom 13:7 *R* therefore to all their dues
1Cor 7:3 Let the husband *r* unto the wife
1Th 3:9 can we *r* to God again for you
1Th 5:15 See that none *r* evil for evil

**RENDERED**
Judg 9:56 Thus God *r* the wickedness of
2Kin 3:4 *r* unto the king of Israel an
2Chr 32:25 But Hezekiah *r* not again
Prov 12:14 a man's hands shall be *r* unto him

**RENEW**
1Sa 11:14 to Gilgal, and *r* the kingdom there
Ps 51:10 *r* a right spirit within me
Is 40:31 the LORD shall *r* their strength
Is 41:1 let the people *r* their strength
Lam 5:21 *r* our days as of old
Heb 6:6 to *r* them again unto repentance

**RENEWED**
2Chr 15:8 *r* the altar of the LORD, that was
Job 29:20 in me, and my bow was *r* in my hand
Ps 103:5 thy youth is *r* like the eagle's
2Cor 4:16 the inward man is *r* day by day
Eph 4:23 be *r* in the spirit of your mind
Col 3:10 which is *r* in knowledge after the

**RENOWN**
Gen 6:4 men which were of old, men of *r*
Num 16:2 in the congregation, men of *r*
Eze 16:14 thy *r* went forth among the
Eze 16:15 the harlot because of thy *r*
Eze 34:29 raise up for them a plant of *r*
Eze 39:13 it shall be to them a *r* the day
Dan 9:15 hand, and hast gotten thee *r*

**RENOWNED**
Num 1:16 These were the *r* of the
Is 14:20 of evildoers shall never be *r*
Eze 23:23 and rulers, great lords and *r*
Eze 26:17 the *r* city, which wast strong in

**RENT**
Gen 37:29 and he *r* his clothes
Gen 37:33 is without doubt *r* in pieces
Gen 37:34 Jacob *r* his clothes, and put
Gen 44:13 Then they *r* their clothes, and
Ex 28:32 of an habergeon, that it be not *r*
Lev 13:45 plague is, his clothes shall be *r*
Num 14:6 the land, *r* their clothes
Josh 7:6 Joshua *r* his clothes, and fell to
Josh 9:4 asses, and wine bottles, old, and *r*
Josh 9:13 and, behold, they be *r*
Judg 11:35 that he *r* his clothes, and said,
Judg 14:6 he *r* him as he would have *r* a
Judg 14:6 *r* him as he would have *r* a kid
1Sa 4:12 the same day with his clothes *r*
1Sa 15:27 the skirt of his mantle, and it *r*
1Sa 15:28 The LORD hath *r* the kingdom of
1Sa 28:17 for the LORD hath *r* the kingdom
2Sa 1:2 camp from Saul with his clothes *r*
2Sa 1:11 hold on his clothes, and *r* them
2Sa 13:19 *r* her garment of divers colours
2Sa 13:31 stood by with their clothes *r*
2Sa 15:32 came to meet him with his coat *r*
1Kin 1:40 so that the earth *r* with the
1Kin 11:30 on him, and *r* it in twelve pieces
1Kin 13:3 Behold, the altar shall be *r*
1Kin 13:5 The altar also was *r*, and the
1Kin 14:8 *r* the kingdom away from the house
1Kin 19:11 strong wind *r* the mountains, and
1Kin 21:27 that he *r* his clothes, and put
2Kin 2:12 clothes, and *r* them in two pieces
2Kin 5:7 that he *r* his clothes, and said,
2Kin 5:8 king of Israel had *r* his clothes
2Kin 5:8 Wherefore hast thou *r* thy clothes
2Kin 6:30 the woman, that he *r* his clothes
2Kin 11:14 Athaliah *r* her clothes, and cried,
2Kin 17:21 For he *r* Israel from the house of
2Kin 18:37 to Hezekiah with their clothes *r*
2Kin 19:1 that he *r* his clothes, and covered
2Kin 22:11 of the law, that he *r* his clothes
2Kin 22:19 hast *r* thy clothes, and wept
2Chr 23:13 Then Athaliah *r* her clothes
2Chr 34:19 of the law, that he *r* his clothes
Ezr 9:3 I *r* my garment and my mantle, and
Ezr 9:5 having *r* my garment and my mantle,
Est 4:1 Mordecai *r* his clothes, and put on
Job 1:20 *r* his mantle, and shaved his head,
Job 2:12 they *r* every one his mantle, and
Job 26:8 and the cloud is not *r* under them
Is 3:24 and instead of a girdle a *r*
Is 36:22 to Hezekiah with their clothes *r*
Is 37:1 that he *r* his clothes, and covered
Jer 36:24 nor *r* their garments, neither the
Jer 41:5 beards shaven, and their clothes *r*
Eze 30:16 pain, and No shall be *r* asunder
Mt 9:16 garment, and the *r* is made worse
Mt 26:65 the high priest *r* his clothes
Mt 27:51 the veil of the temple was *r* in
Mt 27:51 earth did quake, and the rocks *r*
Mk 2:21 the old, and the *r* is made worse
Mk 9:26 *r* him sore, and came out of him
Mk 14:63 the high priest *r* his clothes
Mk 15:38 the veil of the temple was *r* in
Lk 5:36 then both the new maketh a *r*
Lk 23:45 of the temple was *r* in the midst
Acts 14:14 they *r* their clothes, and ran in
Acts 16:22 the magistrates *r* off their

**REPAIR**
2Kin 12:5 let them *r* the breaches of the
2Kin 12:7 Why *r* ye not the breaches of the
2Kin 12:8 neither to *r* the breaches of the
2Kin 12:12 hewed stone to *r* the breaches of
2Kin 12:12 laid out for the house to *r* it
2Kin 22:5 to *r* the breaches of the house,
2Kin 22:6 and hewn stone to *r* the house
2Chr 24:4 minded to *r* the house of the LORD
2Chr 24:5 gather of all Israel money to *r*
2Chr 24:12 carpenters to *r* the house of the
2Chr 34:8 to *r* the house of the LORD his
2Chr 34:10 in the house of the LORD, to *r*
Ezr 9:9 to *r* the desolations thereof, and
Is 61:4 they shall *r* the waste cities,

**REPAIRED**
Judg 21:23 *r* the cities, and dwelt in them
1Kin 11:27 *r* the breaches of the city of
1Kin 18:30 he *r* the altar of the LORD that
2Kin 12:6 not *r* the breaches of the house
2Kin 12:14 *r* therewith the house of the LORD
1Chr 11:8 Joab *r* the rest of the city
2Chr 29:3 the house of the LORD, and *r* them
2Chr 32:5 *r* Millo in the city of David, and
2Chr 33:16 he *r* the altar of the LORD, and
Neh 3:4 next unto them *r* Meremoth the son
Neh 3:4 next unto them *r* Meshullam the
Neh 3:4 next unto them *r* Zadok the son of
Neh 3:5 And next unto them the Tekoites *r*
Neh 3:6 Moreover the old gate *r* Jehoiada
Neh 3:7 next unto them *r* Melatiah the
Neh 3:8 Next unto him *r* Uzziel the son of
Neh 3:8 Next unto him also *r* Hananiah the
Neh 3:9 next unto them *r* Rephaiah the son
Neh 3:10 next unto them *r* Jedaiah the son
Neh 3:10 next unto him *r* Hattush the son
Neh 3:11 *r* the other piece, and the tower
Neh 3:12 next unto him *r* Shallum the son
Neh 3:13 The valley gate *r* Hanun, and the
Neh 3:14 But the dung gate *r* Malchiah the
Neh 3:15 *r* Shallun the son of Colhozeh
Neh 3:16 After him *r* Nehemiah the son of
Neh 3:17 After him *r* the Levites, Rehum
Neh 3:17 Next unto him *r* Hashabiah
Neh 3:18 After him *r* their brethren, Bavai
Neh 3:19 next to him *r* Ezer the son of
Neh 3:20 earnestly *r* the other piece
Neh 3:21 After him *r* Meremoth the son of
Neh 3:22 after him *r* the priests, the men
Neh 3:23 After him *r* Benjamin and Hashub
Neh 3:23 After him *r* Azariah the son of
Neh 3:24 After him *r* Binnui the son of
Neh 3:27 them the Tekoites *r* another piece
Neh 3:28 the horse gate *r* the priests
Neh 3:29 After them *r* Zadok the son of
Neh 3:29 After him *r* also Shemaiah the son
Neh 3:30 After him *r* Hananiah the son of
Neh 3:30 After him *r* Meshullam the son of
Neh 3:31 After him *r* Malchiah the
Neh 3:32 the sheep gate *r* the goldsmiths

**REPAY**
Deut 7:10 he will *r* him to his face
Job 21:31 who shall *r* him what he hath done
Job 41:11 prevented me, that I should *r* him
Is 59:18 deeds, accordingly he will *r*
Is 59:18 the islands he will *r* recompence
Lk 10:35 when I come again, I will *r* thee
Rom 12:19 I will *r*, saith the Lord
Philem 19 with mine own hand, I will *r* it

**REPENT**
Ex 13:17 the people *r* when they see war
Ex 32:12 *r* of this evil against thy people
Num 23:19 the son of man, that he should *r*
Deut 32:36 *r* himself for his servants, when
1Sa 15:29 of Israel will not lie nor *r*
1Sa 15:29 he is not a man, that he should *r*
1Kin 8:47 they were carried captives, and *r*
Job 42:6 myself, and *r* in dust and ashes
Ps 90:13 let it *r* thee concerning thy
Ps 110:4 LORD hath sworn, and will not *r*
Ps 135:14 he will *r* himself concerning his
Jer 4:28 I have purposed it, and will not *r*
Jer 18:8 I will *r* of the evil that I
Jer 18:10 voice, then I will *r* of the good
Jer 26:3 that I may *r* me of the evil,
Jer 26:13 the LORD will *r* him of the evil
Jer 42:10 for I *r* me of the evil that I
Eze 14:6 *R*, and turn yourselves from your
Eze 18:30 *R*, and turn yourselves from all
Eze 24:14 will I spare, neither will I *r*
Joel 2:14 knoweth if he will return and *r*
Jonah 3:9 can tell if God will turn and *r*
Mt 3:2 And saying, *R* ye
Mt 4:17 began to preach, and to say, *R*
Mk 1:15 *r* ye, and believe the gospel

Mk 6:12 and preached that men should r
Lk 13:3 but, except ye r, ye shall all
Lk 13:5 but, except ye r, ye shall all
Lk 16:30 them from the dead, they will r
Lk 17:3 and if he r, forgive him
Lk 17:4 turn again to thee, saying, I r
Acts 2:38 Then Peter said unto them, R
Acts 3:19 R ye therefore, and be converted,
Acts 8:22 R therefore of this thy
Acts 17:30 all men every where to r
Acts 26:20 the Gentiles, that they should r
2Cor 7:8 I do not r, though I did r
Heb 7:21 him, The Lord sware and will not r
Rev 2:5 from whence thou art fallen, and r
Rev 2:5 out of his place, except thou r
Rev 2:16 R; or else I will
Rev 2:21 her space to r of her fornication
Rev 2:22 except they r of their deeds
Rev 3:3 and heard, and hold fast, and r
Rev 3:19 be zealous therefore, and r

**REPENTANCE**
Hos 13:14 r shall be hid from mine eyes
Mt 3:8 forth therefore fruits meet for r
Mt 3:11 baptize you with water unto r
Mt 9:13 the righteous, but sinners to r
Mk 1:4 preach the baptism of r for the
Mk 2:17 the righteous, but sinners to r
Lk 3:3 preaching the baptism of r for
Lk 3:8 therefore fruits worthy of r
Lk 5:32 the righteous, but sinners to r
Lk 15:7 just persons, which need no r
Lk 24:47 And that r and remission of sins
Acts 5:31 Saviour, for to give r to Israel
Acts 11:18 the Gentiles granted r unto life
Acts 13:24 his coming the baptism of r to
Acts 19:4 baptized with the baptism of r
Acts 20:21 r toward God, and faith toward our
Acts 26:20 to God, and do works meet for r
Rom 2:4 goodness of God leadeth thee to r
Rom 11:29 and calling of God are without r
2Cor 7:9 sorry, but that ye sorrowed to r
2Cor 7:10 For godly sorrow worketh r to
2Ti 2:25 r to the acknowledging of the
Heb 6:1 foundation of r from dead works
Heb 6:6 away, to renew them again unto r
Heb 12:17 for he found no place of r
2Pet 3:9 but that all should come to r

**REPENTED**
Gen 6:6 it r the LORD that he had made
Ex 32:14 the LORD r of the evil which he
Judg 2:18 for it r the LORD because of
Judg 21:6 the children of Israel r them for
Judg 21:15 the people r them for Benjamin,
1Sa 15:35 the LORD r that he had made Saul
2Sa 24:16 the LORD r him of the evil, and
1Chr 21:15 he r him of the evil, and said to
Ps 106:45 r according to the multitude of
Jer 8:6 no man r him of his wickedness,
Jer 20:16 the LORD overthrew, and r not
Jer 26:19 the LORD r him of the evil which
Jer 31:19 after that I was turned, I r
Amos 7:3 The LORD r for this
Amos 7:6 The LORD r for this
Jonah 3:10 God r of the evil, that he had
Zec 8:14 the LORD of hosts, and I r not
Mt 11:20 were done, because they r not
Mt 11:21 they would have r long ago in
Mt 12:41 because they r at the preaching
Mt 21:29 but afterward he r, and went
Mt 21:32 r not afterward, that ye might
Mt 27:3 r himself, and brought again the
Lk 10:13 you, they had a great while ago r
Lk 11:32 for they r at the preaching of
2Cor 7:10 to salvation not to be r of
2Cor 12:21 have not r of the uncleanness and
Rev 2:21 and she r not
Rev 9:20 r not of the works of their hands
Rev 9:21 Neither r they of their murders,
Rev 16:9 they r not to give him glory
Rev 16:11 sores, and r not of their deeds

**REPENTETH**
Gen 6:7 for it r me that I have made them
1Sa 15:11 It r me that I have set up Saul
Joel 2:13 kindness, and r him of the evil
Lk 15:7 in heaven over one sinner that r
Lk 15:10 of God over one sinner that r

**REPHAEL** *(re'-fa-el) A sanctuary servant.*
1Chr 26:7 Othni, and R, and Obed, Elzabad,

**REPHAH** *(re'-fah) A grandson of Ephraim.*
1Chr 7:25 R was his son, also Resheph, and

**REPHAIAH** *(ref-a-i'-ah)* See RAPHA, RHESA.
*1. Head of a family.*
1Chr 3:21 the sons of R, the sons of Arnan,
*2. A captain of Simeon.*
1Chr 4:42 Pelatiah, and Neariah, and R
*3. A son of Tola.*
1Chr 7:2 Uzzi, and R, and Jeriel, and Jahmai,
*4. Son of Binea.*
1Chr 9:43 R his son, Eleasah his son, Azel
*5. A repairer of Jerusalem's wall.*
Neh 3:9 them repaired R the son of Hur

**REPHAIM** *(re-fa'-im)* See REPHAIMS. *A valley near Jerusalem.*
2Sa 5:18 themselves in the valley of R
2Sa 5:22 themselves in the valley of R
2Sa 23:13 pitched in the valley of R
1Chr 11:15 encamped in the valley of R
1Chr 14:9 themselves in the valley of R
Is 17:5 gathereth ears in the valley of R

**REPHAIMS** *(re-fa'-ims)* See REPHAIM. *A tribe of Canaanites.*
Gen 14:5 smote the R in Ashteroth Karnaim,
Gen 15:20 and the Perizzites, and the R

**REPHIDIM** *(ref'-i-dim) An Israelite encampment in the wilderness.*
Ex 17:1 of the LORD, and pitched in R
Ex 17:8 and fought with Israel in R
Ex 19:2 For they were departed from R
Num 33:14 from Alush, and encamped at R
Num 33:15 And they departed from R, and

**REPLENISHED**
Is 2:6 because they be r from the east
Is 23:2 that pass over the sea, have r
Jer 31:25 I have r every sorrowful soul
Eze 26:2 I shall be r, now she is laid
Eze 27:25 and thou wast r, and made very

**REPORT**
Gen 37:2 unto his father their evil r
Ex 23:1 Thou shalt not raise a false r
Num 13:32 they brought up an evil r of the
Num 14:37 bring up the evil r upon the land
Deut 2:25 heaven, who shall hear r of thee
1Sa 2:24 for it is no good r that I hear
1Kin 10:6 It was a true r that I heard in
2Chr 9:5 It was a true r which I heard in
Neh 6:13 might have matter for an evil r
Prov 15:30 a good r maketh the bones fat
Is 23:5 As at the r concerning Egypt, so
Is 23:5 be sorely pained at the r of Tyre
Is 28:19 vexation only to understand the r
Is 53:1 Who hath believed our r
Jer 20:10 R, say they, and we will r it
Jer 50:43 Babylon hath heard the r of them
Jn 12:38 Lord, who hath believed our r
Acts 6:3 among you seven men of honest r
Acts 10:22 of good r among all the nation of
Acts 22:12 having a good r of all the Jews
Rom 10:16 Lord, who hath believed our r
1Cor 14:25 r that God is in you of a truth
2Cor 6:8 By honour and dishonour, by evil r
2Cor 6:8 and good r: as deceivers
Phil 4:8 whatsoever things are of good r
1Ti 3:7 good r of them which are without
Heb 11:2 it the elders obtained a good r
Heb 11:39 obtained a good r through faith
3Jn 12 Demetrius hath good r of all men

**REPORTED**
Neh 6:6 It is r among the heathen, and
Neh 6:7 now shall it be r to the king
Neh 6:19 Also they r his good deeds before
Est 1:17 in their eyes, when it shall be r
Eze 9:11 r the matter, saying, I have done
Mt 28:15 this saying is commonly r among
Acts 4:23 r all that the chief priests and
Acts 16:2 Which was well r of by the
Rom 3:8 rather, (as we be slanderously r
1Cor 5:1 It is r commonly that there is
1Ti 5:10 Well r of for good works
1Pet 1:12 which are now r unto you by them

**REPROACH**
Gen 30:23 and said, God hath taken away my r
Gen 34:14 for that were a r unto us
Josh 5:9 away the r of Egypt from off you
Ruth 2:15 among the sheaves, and r her not
1Sa 11:2 lay it for a r upon all Israel
1Sa 17:26 and taketh away the r from Israel
1Sa 25:39 of my r from the hand of Nabal
2Kin 19:4 hath sent to r the living God
2Kin 19:16 hath sent him to r the living God
Neh 1:3 are in great affliction and r
Neh 2:17 Jerusalem, that we be no more a r
Neh 4:4 turn their r upon their own head,
Neh 5:9 the r of the heathen our enemies
Neh 6:13 evil report, that they might r me
Job 19:5 me, and plead against me my r
Job 20:3 I have heard the check of my r
Job 27:6 my heart shall not r me so long
Ps 15:3 nor taketh up a r against his
Ps 22:6 a r of men, and despised of the
Ps 31:11 I was a r among all mine enemies,
Ps 39:8 make me not the r of the foolish
Ps 42:10 in my bones, mine enemies r me
Ps 44:13 Thou makest us a r to our
Ps 57:3 save me from the r of him that
Ps 69:7 for thy sake I have borne r
Ps 69:10 with fasting, that was to my r
Ps 69:19 Thou hast known my r, and my shame
Ps 69:20 R hath broken my heart
Ps 71:13 let them be covered with r
Ps 74:10 how long shall the adversary r
Ps 78:66 he put them to a perpetual r
Ps 79:4 We are become a r to our
Ps 79:12 into their bosom their r,
Ps 89:41 he is a r to his neighbours
Ps 89:50 Lord, the r of thy servants
Ps 89:50 the r of all the mighty people
Ps 102:8 Mine enemies r me all the day
Ps 109:25 I became also a r unto them
Ps 119:22 Remove from me r and contempt
Ps 119:39 Turn away my r which I fear
Prov 6:33 his r shall not be wiped away
Prov 14:34 but sin is a r to any people
Prov 18:3 also contempt, and with ignominy r
Prov 19:26 that causeth shame, and bringeth r
Prov 22:10 yea, strife and r shall cease
Is 4:1 by thy name, to take away our r
Is 30:5 profit, but a shame, and also a r
Is 37:4 hath sent to r the living God
Is 37:17 hath sent to r the living God
Is 51:7 fear ye not the r of men, neither
Is 54:4 shalt not remember the r of thy
Jer 6:10 word of the LORD is unto them a r
Jer 20:8 of the LORD was made a r unto me
Jer 23:40 bring an everlasting r upon you
Jer 24:9 earth for their hurt, to be a r
Jer 29:18 and an hissing, and a r, among all
Jer 31:19 I did bear the r of my youth
Jer 42:18 astonishment, and a curse, and a r
Jer 44:8 a r among all the nations of the
Jer 44:12 astonishment, and a curse, and a r
Jer 49:13 shall become a desolation, a r
Jer 51:51 because we have heard r
Lam 3:30 he is filled full with r
Lam 3:61 Thou hast heard their r, O LORD,
Lam 5:1 consider, and behold our r
Eze 5:14 a r among the nations that are
Eze 5:15 So it shall be a r and a taunt, an
Eze 16:57 as at the time of thy r of the
Eze 21:28 Ammonites, and concerning their r
Eze 22:4 I made thee a r unto the heathen
Eze 36:15 bear the r of the people any more
Eze 36:30 r of famine among the heathen
Dan 9:16 thy people are become a r to all
Dan 11:18 the r offered by him to cease
Dan 11:18 without his own r he shall cause
Hos 12:14 his r shall his Lord return unto
Joel 2:17 and give not thine heritage to r
Joel 2:19 make you a r among the heathen
Mic 6:16 ye shall bear the r of my people
Zeph 2:8 I have heard the r of Moab
Zeph 3:18 to whom the r of it was a burden
Lk 1:25 me, to take away my r among men
Lk 6:22 their company, and shall r you
2Cor 11:21 I speak as concerning r, as
1Ti 3:7 lest he fall into r and the snare
1Ti 4:10 we both labour and suffer r
Heb 11:26 Esteeming the r of Christ greater
Heb 13:13 without the camp, bearing his r

**REPROACHED**
2Kin 19:22 Whom hast thou r and blasphemed
2Kin 19:23 messengers thou hast r the Lord
Job 19:3 These ten times have ye r me
Ps 55:12 For it was not an enemy that r me

**RESORTED**
2Chr 11:13 *r* to him out of all their coasts
Mk 2:13 and all the multitude *r* unto him
Jn 10:41 many *r* unto him, and said, John
Jn 18:2 for Jesus ofttimes *r* thither with
Acts 16:13 unto the women which *r* thither

**RESPECT**
Gen 4:4 And the LORD had *r* unto Abel
Gen 4:5 and to his offering he had not *r*
Ex 2:25 of Israel, and God had *r* unto them
Lev 19:15 thou shalt not *r* the person of
Lev 26:9 For I will have *r* unto you
Num 16:15 *R* not thou their offering
Deut 1:17 Ye shall not *r* persons in
Deut 16:19 thou shalt not *r* persons, neither
2Sa 14:14 neither doth God *r* any person
1Kin 8:28 Yet have thou *r* unto the prayer
2Kin 13:23 had *r* unto them, because of his
2Chr 6:19 Have *r* therefore to the prayer of
2Chr 19:7 nor *r* of persons, nor taking of
Ps 74:20 Have *r* unto the covenant
Ps 119:6 when I have *r* unto all thy
Ps 119:15 precepts, and have *r* unto thy ways
Ps 119:117 I will have *r* unto thy statutes
Ps 138:6 yet hath he *r* unto the lowly
Prov 24:23 to have *r* of persons in judgment
Prov 28:21 To have *r* of persons is not good
Is 17:7 his eyes shall have *r* to the Holy
Is 17:8 neither shall *r* that which his
Is 22:11 neither had *r* unto him that
Rom 2:11 For there is no *r* of persons with
2Cor 3:10 glorious had no glory in this *r*
Eph 6:9 neither is there *r* of persons
Phil 4:11 Not that I speak in *r* of want
Col 2:16 or in *r* of an holyday, or of the
Col 3:25 and there is no *r* of persons
Heb 11:26 for he had *r* unto the recompence
Jas 2:1 Lord of glory, with *r* of persons
Jas 2:3 ye have *r* to him that weareth the
Jas 2:9 But if ye have *r* to persons
1Pet 1:17 who without *r* of persons judgeth

**RESTED**
Gen 2:2 he *r* on the seventh day from all
Gen 2:3 because that in it he had *r* from
Gen 8:4 the ark *r* in the seventh month,
Ex 10:14 *r* in all the coasts of Egypt
Ex 16:30 So the people *r* on the seventh
Ex 20:11 in them is, and *r* the seventh day
Ex 31:17 earth, and on the seventh day he *r*
Num 9:18 tabernacle they *r* in their tents
Num 9:23 of the LORD they *r* in the tents
Num 10:12 the cloud *r* in the wilderness of
Num 10:36 And when it *r*, he said, Return, O
Num 11:25 that, when the spirit *r* upon them
Num 11:26 and the spirit *r* upon them
Josh 11:23 And the land *r* from war
1Kin 6:10 they *r* on the house with timber
2Chr 32:8 the people *r* themselves upon the
Est 9:17 fourteenth day of the same *r* they
Est 9:18 fifteenth day of the same they *r*
Est 9:22 the Jews *r* from their enemies
Job 30:27 My bowels boiled, and *r* not
Lk 23:56 *r* the sabbath day according to

**RESTETH**
Job 24:23 him to be in safety, whereon he *r*
Prov 14:33 Wisdom *r* in the heart of him that
Eccl 7:9 for anger *r* in the bosom of fools
1Pet 4:14 of glory and of God *r* upon you

**RESTING**
Num 10:33 to search out a *r* place for them
2Chr 6:41 O LORD God, into thy *r* place
Prov 24:15 spoil not his *r* place
Is 32:18 dwellings, and in quiet *r* places

**RESTITUTION**
Ex 22:3 for he should make full *r*
Ex 22:5 his own vineyard, shall he make *r*
Ex 22:6 the fire shall surely make *r*
Ex 22:12 he shall make *r* unto the owner
Job 20:18 to his substance shall the *r* be
Acts 3:21 the times of *r* of all things

**RESTORE**
Gen 20:7 Now therefore *r* the man his wife
Gen 20:7 and if thou *r* her not, know thou
Gen 40:13 head, and *r* thee unto thy place
Gen 42:25 to *r* every man's money into his
Ex 22:1 he shall *r* five oxen for an ox,
Ex 22:4 he shall *r* double
Lev 6:4 that he shall *r* that which he
Lev 6:5 he shall even *r* it in the
Lev 24:21 killeth a beast, he shall *r* it
Lev 25:27 *r* the overplus unto the man to
Lev 25:28 if he be not able to *r* it to him
Num 35:25 the congregation shall *r* him to
Deut 22:2 thou shalt *r* it to him again
Judg 11:13 now therefore *r* those lands again
Judg 17:3 therefore I will *r* it unto thee
1Sa 12:3 and I will *r* it you
2Sa 9:7 will *r* thee all the land of Saul
2Sa 12:6 he shall *r* the lamb fourfold,
2Sa 16:3 *r* me the kingdom of my father
1Kin 20:34 took from thy father, I will *r*
2Kin 8:6 *R* all that was hers, and all the
Neh 5:11 *R*, I pray you, to them, even this
Neh 5:12 Then said they, We will *r* them
Job 20:10 and his hands shall *r* their goods
Job 20:18 which he laboured for shall he *r*
Ps 51:12 *R* unto me the joy of thy
Prov 6:31 he be found, he shall *r* sevenfold
Is 1:26 I will *r* thy judges as at the
Is 42:22 for a spoil, and none saith, *R*
Is 49:6 to *r* the preserved of Israel
Is 57:18 *r* comforts unto him and to his
Jer 27:22 them up, and *r* them to this place
Jer 30:17 For I will *r* health unto thee, and
Eze 33:15 If the wicked *r* the pledge
Dan 9:25 forth of the commandment to *r*
Joel 2:25 I will *r* to you the years that
Mt 17:11 shall first come, and *r* all things
Lk 19:8 accusation, I *r* him fourfold
Acts 1:6 wilt thou at this time *r* again
Gal 6:1 *r* such an one in the spirit of

**RESTORED**
Gen 20:14 Abraham, and *r* him Sarah his wife
Gen 40:21 he *r* the chief butler unto his
Gen 41:13 me he *r* unto mine office, and him
Gen 42:28 unto his brethren, My money is *r*
Deut 28:31 face, and shall not be *r* to thee
Judg 17:3 when he had *r* the eleven hundred
Judg 17:4 Yet he *r* the money unto his
1Sa 7:14 from Israel were *r* to Israel
1Kin 13:6 that my hand may be *r* me again
1Kin 13:6 the king's hand was *r* him again
2Kin 8:1 woman, whose son he had *r* to life
2Kin 8:5 how he had *r* a dead body to life
2Kin 8:5 woman, whose son he had *r* to life
2Kin 8:5 is her son, whom Elisha *r* to life
2Kin 14:22 *r* it to Judah, after that the
2Kin 14:25 He *r* the coast of Israel from the
2Chr 8:2 which Huram had *r* to Solomon
2Chr 26:2 *r* it to Judah, after that the
Ezr 6:5 and brought unto Babylon, be *r*
Ps 69:4 then I *r* that which I took not
Eze 18:7 but hath *r* to the debtor his
Eze 18:12 hath not *r* the pledge, and hath
Mt 12:13 and it was *r* whole, like as the
Mk 3:5 his hand was *r* whole as the other
Mk 8:25 and he was *r*, and saw every man
Lk 6:10 his hand was *r* whole as the other
Heb 13:19 that I may be *r* to you the sooner

**RESTORER**
Ruth 4:15 be unto thee a *r* of thy life
Is 58:12 The *r* of paths to dwell in

**RESTORETH**
Ps 23:3 He *r* my soul
Mk 9:12 cometh first, and *r* all things

**RESTRAIN**
Job 15:8 dost thou *r* wisdom to thyself
Ps 76:10 remainder of wrath shalt thou *r*

**RESTRAINED**
Gen 8:2 and the rain from heaven was *r*
Gen 11:6 now nothing will be *r* from them
Gen 16:2 the LORD hath *r* me from bearing
Ex 36:6 the people were *r* from bringing
1Sa 3:13 themselves vile, and he *r* them not
Is 63:15 are they *r*
Eze 31:15 I *r* the floods thereof, and the
Acts 14:18 sayings scarce *r* they the people

**RESURRECTION**
Mt 22:23 which say that there is no *r*
Mt 22:28 Therefore in the *r* whose wife
Mt 22:30 For in the *r* they neither marry,
Mt 22:31 But as touching the *r* of the dead
Mt 27:53 out of the graves after his *r*
Mk 12:18 which say there is no *r*
Mk 12:23 In the *r* therefore, when they
Lk 14:14 recompensed at the *r* of the just
Lk 20:27 which deny that there is any *r*
Lk 20:33 Therefore in the *r* whose wife of
Lk 20:35 the *r* from the dead, neither
Lk 20:36 God, being the children of the *r*
Jn 5:29 done good, unto the *r* of life
Jn 5:29 evil, unto the *r* of damnation
Jn 11:24 again in the *r* at the last day
Jn 11:25 Jesus said unto her, I am the *r*
Acts 1:22 to be a witness with us of his *r*
Acts 2:31 before spake of the *r* of Christ
Acts 4:2 through Jesus the *r* from the dead
Acts 4:33 of the *r* of the Lord Jesus
Acts 17:18 unto them Jesus, and the *r*
Acts 17:32 they heard of the *r* of the dead
Acts 23:6 *r* of the dead I am called in
Acts 23:8 Sadducees say that there is no *r*
Acts 24:15 there shall be a *r* of the dead
Acts 24:21 Touching the *r* of the dead I am
Rom 1:4 holiness, by the *r* from the dead
Rom 6:5 be also in the likeness of his *r*
1Cor 15:12 that there is no *r* of the dead
1Cor 15:13 But if there be no *r* of the dead
1Cor 15:21 man came also the *r* of the dead
1Cor 15:42 So also is the *r* of the dead
Phil 3:10 know him, and the power of his *r*
Phil 3:11 attain unto the *r* of the dead
2Ti 2:18 saying that the *r* is past already
Heb 6:2 of *r* of the dead, and of eternal
Heb 11:35 that they might obtain a better *r*
1Pet 1:3 *r* of Jesus Christ from the dead
1Pet 3:21 by the *r* of Jesus Christ
Rev 20:5 This is the first *r*
Rev 20:6 he that hath part in the first *r*

**RETAIN**
Job 2:9 Dost thou still *r* thine integrity
Prov 4:4 me, Let thine heart *r* my words
Prov 11:16 and strong men *r* riches
Eccl 8:8 over the spirit to *r* the spirit
Dan 11:6 but she shall not *r* the power of
Jn 20:23 and whose soever sins ye *r*
Rom 1:28 like to *r* God in their knowledge

**RETAINED**
Judg 7:8 *r* those three hundred men
Judg 19:4 law, the damsel's father, *r* him
Dan 10:8 corruption, and I *r* no strength
Dan 10:16 upon me, and I have *r* no strength
Jn 20:23 soever sins ye retain, they are *r*
Philem 13 Whom I would have *r* with me

**REU** *(re'-u)* See RAGAU. *Son of Peleg.*
Gen 11:18 lived thirty years, and begat *R*
Gen 11:19 after he begat *R* two hundred
Gen 11:20 *R* lived two and thirty years, and
Gen 11:21 *R* lived after he begat Serug two
1Chr 1:25 Eber, Peleg, *R*,

**REUBEN** *(ru'-ben)* See REUBENITE.
*1. A son of Jacob and Leah.*
Gen 29:32 a son, and she called his name *R*
Gen 30:14 *R* went in the days of wheat
Gen 35:22 dwelt in that land, that *R* went
Gen 35:23 *R*, Jacob's firstborn, and Simeon,
Gen 37:21 *R* heard it, and he delivered him
Gen 37:22 *R* said unto them, Shed no blood,
Gen 37:29 And *R* returned unto the pit
Gen 42:22 *R* answered them, saying, Spake I
Gen 42:37 *R* spake unto his father, saying,
Gen 46:8 *R*, Jacob's firstborn
Gen 46:9 And the sons of *R*
Gen 48:5 as *R* and Simeon, they shall be
Gen 49:3 *R*, thou art my firstborn, my
Ex 1:2 *R*, Simeon, Levi, and Judah,
Ex 6:14 The sons of *R* the firstborn of
Ex 6:14 these be the families of *R*
Num 1:20 And the children of *R*, Israel's
Num 16:1 On, the son of Peleth, sons of *R*
Num 26:5 *R*, the eldest son of Israel
Num 26:5 the children of *R*
Deut 11:6 the sons of Eliab, the son of *R*
Josh 15:6 the stone of Bohan the son of *R*
Josh 18:17 the stone of Bohan the son of *R*
1Chr 2:1 *R*, Simeon, Levi, and Judah,
1Chr 5:1 Now the sons of *R* the firstborn
1Chr 5:3 of *R* the firstborn of Israel were
*2. Descendants of Reuben 1.*
Num 1:5 of the tribe of *R*
Num 1:21 of them, even of the tribe of *R*
Num 2:10 of *R* according to their armies
Num 2:10 of *R* shall be Elizur the son of
Num 2:16 of *R* were an hundred thousand

Num 7:30 prince of the children of *R*
Num 10:18 the standard of the camp of *R* set
Num 13:4 of the tribe of *R*, Shammua the
Num 32:1 Now the children of *R* and the
Num 32:2 of Gad and the children of *R* came
Num 32:6 of Gad and to the children of *R*
Num 32:25 the children of *R* spake unto
Num 32:29 the children of *R* will pass with
Num 32:31 Gad and the children of *R* answered
Num 32:33 of Gad, and to the children of *R*
Num 32:37 the children of *R* built Heshbon
Num 34:14 the tribe of the children of *R*
Deut 27:13 *R*, Gad, and Asher, and Zebulun, Dan
Deut 33:6 Let *R* live, and not die
Josh 4:12 And the children of *R*, and the
Josh 13:15 the tribe of the children of *R*
Josh 13:23 of the children of *R* was Jordan
Josh 13:23 of *R* after their families
Josh 18:7 and Gad, and *R*, and half the tribe
Josh 20:8 the plain out of the tribe of *R*
Josh 21:7 had out of the tribe of *R*
Josh 21:36 And out of the tribe of *R*, Bezer
Josh 22:9 And the children of *R* and the
Josh 22:10 land of Canaan, the children of *R*
Josh 22:11 say, Behold, the children of *R*
Josh 22:13 sent unto the children of *R*
Josh 22:15 they came unto the children of *R*
Josh 22:21 Then the children of *R* and the
Josh 22:25 us and you, ye children of *R*
Josh 22:30 the words that the children of *R*
Josh 22:31 said unto the children of *R*
Josh 22:32 returned from the children of *R*
Josh 22:33 land wherein the children of *R*
Josh 22:34 And the children of *R* and the
Judg 5:15 For the divisions of *R* there were
Judg 5:16 For the divisions of *R* there were
1Chr 5:18 The sons of *R*, and the Gadites, and
1Chr 6:63 families, out of the tribe of *R*
1Chr 6:78 given them out of the tribe of *R*
Eze 48:6 the west side, a portion for *R*
Eze 48:7 And by the border of *R*, from the
Eze 48:31 one gate of *R*, one gate of Judah,
Rev 7:5 Of the tribe of *R* were sealed

**REUBENITE** *(ru'-ben-ite)* See REUBENITES. *A descendant of Reuben.*
1Chr 11:42 Adina the son of Shiza the *R*

**REUBENITES** *(ru'-ben-ites)*
Num 26:7 These are the families of the *R*
Deut 3:12 cities thereof, gave I unto the *R*
Deut 3:16 And unto the *R* and unto the Gadites
Deut 4:43 in the plain country, of the *R*
Deut 29:8 it for an inheritance unto the *R*
Josh 1:12 And to the *R*, and to the Gadites,
Josh 12:6 it for a possession unto the *R*
Josh 13:8 With whom the *R* and the Gadites
Josh 22:1 Then Joshua called the *R*, and the
2Kin 10:33 of Gilead, the Gadites, and the *R*
1Chr 5:6 he was prince of the *R*
1Chr 5:26 he carried them away, even the *R*
1Chr 11:42 the Reubenite, a captain of the *R*
1Chr 12:37 other side of Jordan, of the *R*
1Chr 26:32 king David made rulers over the *R*
1Chr 27:16 the ruler of the *R* was Eliezer

**REUEL** *(re-u'-el)* See DEUEL, JETHRO, RAGUEL.
*1. A son of Esau.*
Gen 36:4 and Bashemath bare *R*
Gen 36:10 *R* the son of Bashemath the wife
Gen 36:13 And these are the sons of *R*
Gen 36:17 are the sons of *R* Esau's son
Gen 36:17 came of *R* in the land of Edom
1Chr 1:35 Eliphaz, *R*, and Jeush, and Jaalam,
1Chr 1:37 The sons of *R*
*2. Same as Jethro.*
Ex 2:18 when they came to *R* their father
*3. Father of Eliasaph.*
Num 2:14 shall be Eliasaph the son of *R*
*4. A Benjamite.*
1Chr 9:8 son of Shephatiah, the son of *R*

**REUMAH** *(re-u'-mah) Concubine of Nahor.*
Gen 22:24 his concubine, whose name was *R*

**REVEAL**
Job 20:27 The heaven shall *r* his iniquity
Jer 33:6 will *r* unto them the abundance of
Dan 2:47 seeing thou couldst *r* this secret
Mt 11:27 to whomsoever the Son will *r* him
Lk 10:22 and he to whom the Son will *r* him
Gal 1:16 To *r* his Son in me, that I might
Phil 3:15 God shall *r* even this unto you

**REVEALED**
Deut 29:29 things which are *r* belong unto us
1Sa 3:7 word of the LORD yet *r* unto him
1Sa 3:21 for the LORD *r* himself to Samuel
2Sa 7:27 hast *r* to thy servant, saying, I
Is 22:14 it was *r* in mine ears by the LORD
Is 23:1 land of Chittim it is *r* to them
Is 40:5 the glory of the LORD shall be *r*
Is 53:1 to whom is the arm of the LORD *r*
Is 56:1 come, and my righteousness to be *r*
Jer 11:20 for unto thee have I *r* my cause
Dan 2:19 Then was the secret *r* unto Daniel
Dan 2:30 this secret is not *r* to me for
Dan 10:1 Persia a thing was *r* unto Daniel
Mt 10:26 covered, that shall not be *r*
Mt 11:25 and hast *r* them unto babes
Mt 16:17 and blood hath not *r* it unto thee
Lk 2:26 it was *r* unto him by the Holy
Lk 2:35 thoughts of many hearts may be *r*
Lk 10:21 and hast *r* them unto babes
Lk 12:2 covered, that shall not be *r*
Lk 17:30 the day when the Son of man is *r*
Jn 12:38 hath the arm of the Lord been *r*
Rom 1:17 of God *r* from faith to faith
Rom 1:18 God is *r* from heaven against all
Rom 8:18 the glory which shall be *r* in us
1Cor 2:10 But God hath *r* them unto us by
1Cor 3:13 it, because it shall be *r* by fire
1Cor 14:30 If any thing be *r* to another that
Gal 3:23 which should afterwards be *r*
Eph 3:5 as it is now *r* unto his holy
2Th 1:7 be *r* from heaven with his mighty
2Th 2:3 first, and that man of sin be *r*
2Th 2:6 that he might be *r* in his time
2Th 2:8 And then shall that Wicked be *r*
1Pet 1:5 ready to be *r* in the last time
1Pet 1:12 Unto whom it was *r*, that not unto
1Pet 4:13 that, when his glory shall be *r*
1Pet 5:1 of the glory that shall be *r*

**REVEALETH**
Prov 11:13 A talebearer *r* secrets
Prov 20:19 about as a talebearer *r* secrets
Dan 2:22 He *r* the deep and secret things
Dan 2:28 is a God in heaven that *r* secrets
Dan 2:29 he that *r* secrets maketh known to
Amos 3:7 but he *r* his secret unto his

**REVELATION**
Rom 2:5 *r* of the righteous judgment of
Rom 16:25 according to the *r* of the mystery
1Cor 14:6 I shall speak to you either by *r*
1Cor 14:26 doctrine, hath a tongue, hath a *r*
Gal 1:12 but by the *r* of Jesus Christ
Gal 2:2 And I went up by *r*, and
Eph 1:17 *r* in the knowledge of him
Eph 3:3 How that by *r* he made known unto
1Pet 1:13 unto you at the *r* of Jesus Christ
Rev 1:1 The *R* of Jesus Christ, which God

**REVENGE**
Jer 15:15 me, and *r* me of my persecutors
Jer 20:10 and we shall take our *r* on him
Eze 25:15 the Philistines have dealt by *r*
2Cor 7:11 yea, what zeal, yea, what *r*
2Cor 10:6 a readiness to *r* all disobedience

**REVENGER**
Num 35:19 The *r* of blood himself shall slay
Num 35:21 the *r* of blood shall slay the
Num 35:24 the *r* of blood according to these
Num 35:25 out of the hand of the *r* of blood
Num 35:27 the *r* of blood find him without
Num 35:27 the *r* of blood kill the slayer
Rom 13:4 a *r* to execute wrath upon him

**REVENUE**
Ezr 4:13 shalt endamage the *r* of the kings
Prov 8:19 and my *r* than choice silver
Is 23:3 harvest of the river, is her *r*

**REVERENCE**
Lev 19:30 my sabbaths, and *r* my sanctuary
Lev 26:2 my sabbaths, and *r* my sanctuary
2Sa 9:6 he fell on his face, and did *r*
1Kin 1:31 did *r* to the king, and said, Let
Est 3:2 Mordecai bowed not, nor did him *r*
Est 3:5 Mordecai bowed not, nor did him *r*
Ps 89:7 to be had in *r* of all them that
Mt 21:37 son, saying, They will *r* my son
Mk 12:6 them, saying, They will *r* my son
Lk 20:13 it may be they will *r* him when
Eph 5:33 wife see that she *r* her husband
Heb 12:9 corrected us, and we gave them *r*
Heb 12:28 may serve God acceptably with *r*

**REVILED**
Mt 27:39 And they that passed by *r* him
Mk 15:32 were crucified with him *r* him
Jn 9:28 Then they *r* him, and said, Thou
1Cor 4:12 being *r*, we bless
1Pet 2:23 when he was *r*, *r* not again

**REVIVE**
Neh 4:2 will they *r* the stones out of the
Ps 85:6 Wilt thou not *r* us again
Ps 138:7 midst of trouble, thou wilt *r* me
Is 57:15 to *r* the spirit of the humble, and
Is 57:15 to *r* the heart of the contrite
Hos 6:2 After two days will he *r* us
Hos 14:7 they shall *r* as the corn, and grow
Hab 3:2 *r* thy work in the midst of the

**REVIVED**
Gen 45:27 spirit of Jacob their father *r*
Judg 15:19 his spirit came again, and he *r*
1Kin 17:22 came into him again, and he *r*
2Kin 13:21 touched the bones of Elisha, he *r*
Rom 7:9 when the commandment came, sin *r*
Rom 14:9 Christ both died, and rose, and *r*

**REVOLTED**
2Kin 8:20 In his days Edom *r* from under the
2Kin 8:22 Yet Edom *r* from under the hand of
2Kin 8:22 Then Libnah *r* at the same time
2Chr 21:8 In his days the Edomites *r* from
2Chr 21:10 So the Edomites *r* from under the
Is 31:6 children of Israel have deeply *r*
Jer 5:23 they are *r* and gone

**REWARD**
Gen 15:1 shield, and thy exceeding great *r*
Num 18:31 for it is your *r* for your service
Deut 10:17 not persons, nor taketh *r*
Deut 27:25 Cursed be he that taketh *r* to
Deut 32:41 and will *r* them that hate me
Ruth 2:12 a full *r* be given thee of the
1Sa 24:19 wherefore the LORD *r* thee good
2Sa 3:39 the LORD shall *r* the doer of evil
2Sa 4:10 given him a *r* for his tidings
2Sa 19:36 recompense it me with such a *r*
1Kin 13:7 thyself, and I will give thee a *r*
2Chr 20:11 Behold, I say, how they *r* us
Job 6:22 Give a *r* for me of your substance
Job 7:2 looketh for the *r* of his work
Ps 15:5 nor taketh *r* against the innocent
Ps 19:11 keeping of them there is great *r*
Ps 40:15 Let them be desolate for a *r* of
Ps 54:5 He shall *r* evil unto mine enemies
Ps 58:11 there is a *r* for the righteous
Ps 70:3 for a *r* of their shame that say
Ps 91:8 behold and see the *r* of the wicked
Ps 94:2 render a *r* to the proud
Ps 109:20 Let this be the *r* of mine
Ps 127:3 and the fruit of the womb is his *r*
Prov 11:18 righteousness shall be a sure *r*
Prov 21:14 a *r* in the bosom strong wrath
Prov 24:14 found it, then there shall be a *r*
Prov 24:20 shall be no *r* to the evil man
Prov 25:22 head, and the LORD shall *r* thee
Eccl 4:9 have a good *r* for their labour
Eccl 9:5 neither have they any more a *r*
Is 3:11 for the *r* of his hands shall be
Is 5:23 Which justify the wicked for *r*
Is 40:10 his *r* is with him, and his work
Is 45:13 my captives, not for price nor *r*
Is 62:11 his *r* is with him, and his work
Jer 40:5 guard gave him victuals and a *r*
Eze 16:34 and in that thou givest a *r*
Eze 16:34 and no *r* is given unto thee,
Hos 4:9 ways, and *r* them their doings
Hos 9:1 thou hast loved a *r* upon every
Obad 15 thy *r* shall return upon thine own
Mic 3:11 The heads thereof judge for *r*
Mic 7:3 and the judge asketh for a *r*
Mt 5:12 for great is your *r* in heaven
Mt 5:46 which love you, what *r* have ye
Mt 6:1 otherwise ye have no *r* of your
Mt 6:2 I say unto you, They have their *r*
Mt 6:4 himself shall *r* thee openly
Mt 6:5 I say unto you, They have their *r*
Mt 6:6 in secret shall *r* thee openly
Mt 6:16 I say unto you, They have their *r*
Mt 6:18 in secret, shall *r* thee openly

Mt 10:41 shall receive a prophet's *r*
Mt 10:41 shall receive a righteous man's *r*
Mt 10:42 he shall in no wise lose his *r*
Mt 16:27 then he shall *r* every man
Mk 9:41 unto you, he shall not lose his *r*
Lk 6:23 your *r* is great in heaven
Lk 6:35 your *r* shall be great, and ye
Lk 23:41 we receive the due *r* of our deeds
Acts 1:18 a field with the *r* of iniquity
Rom 4:4 is the *r* not reckoned of grace
1Cor 3:8 own *r* according to his own labour
1Cor 3:14 thereupon, he shall receive a *r*
1Cor 9:17 this thing willingly, I have a *r*
1Cor 9:18 What is my *r* then
Col 2:18 of your *r* in a voluntary humility
Col 3:24 receive the *r* of the inheritance
1Ti 5:18 The labourer is worthy of his *r*
2Ti 4:14 the Lord *r* him according to his
Heb 2:2 received a just recompence of *r*
Heb 10:35 which hath great recompence of *r*
Heb 11:26 unto the recompence of the *r*
2Pet 2:13 And shall receive the *r* of
2Jn 8 but that we receive a full *r*
Jude 11 after the error of Balaam for *r*
Rev 11:18 that thou shouldest give *r* unto
Rev 18:6 *R* her even as she rewarded you,
Rev 22:12 my *r* is with me, to give every

### REWARDED
Gen 44:4 Wherefore have ye *r* evil for good
1Sa 24:17 for thou hast *r* me good, whereas
1Sa 24:17 good, whereas I have *r* thee evil
2Sa 22:21 The LORD *r* me according to my
2Chr 15:7 for your work shall be *r*
Ps 7:4 If I have *r* evil unto him that
Ps 18:20 The LORD *r* me according to my
Ps 35:12 They *r* me evil for good to the
Ps 103:10 nor *r* us according to our
Ps 109:5 they have *r* me evil for good, and
Prov 13:13 the commandment shall be *r*
Is 3:9 for they have *r* evil unto
Jer 31:16 for thy work shall be *r*, saith
Rev 18:6 Reward her even as she *r* you

### REWARDETH
Job 21:19 he *r* him, and he shall know it
Ps 31:23 plentifully *r* the proud doer
Ps 137:8 that *r* thee as thou hast served
Prov 17:13 Whoso *r* evil for good, evil shall
Prov 26:10 formed all things both *r* the fool
Prov 26:10 and *r* transgressors

### REWARDS
Num 22:7 the *r* of divination in their hand
Is 1:23 gifts, and followeth after *r*
Dan 2:6 ye shall receive of me gifts and *r*
Dan 5:17 thyself, and give thy *r* to another
Hos 2:12 These are my *r* that my lovers

### REZEPH *(re'-zef) A fortress near Haran.*
2Kin 19:12 as Gozan, and Haran, and *R*, and the
Is 37:12 as Gozan, and Haran, and *R*

### REZIA *(re-zi'-ah) Son of Ulla.*
1Chr 7:39 Arah, and Haniel, and *R*

### REZIN *(re'-zin)*
*1. A king of Syria.*
2Kin 15:37 against Judah *R* the king of Syria
2Kin 16:5 Then *R* king of Syria and Pekah son
2Kin 16:6 At that time *R* king of Syria
2Kin 16:9 of it captive to Kir, and slew *R*
Is 7:4 the fierce anger of *R* with Syria
Is 7:8 and the head of Damascus is *R*
Is 8:6 that go softly, and rejoice in *R*
Is 9:11 the adversaries of *R* against him
*2. A family of exiles.*
Ezr 2:48 The children of *R*, the children
Neh 7:50 of Reaiah, the children of *R*

### REZON *(re'-zon) An enemy of Solomon.*
1Kin 11:23 *R* the son of Eliadah, which fled

### RHEGIUM *(re'-je-um) A port of southern Italy.*
Acts 28:13 fetched a compass, and came to *R*

### RHESA *(re'-sah) Son of Zorobabel; an ancestor of Jesus.*
Lk 3:27 of Joanna, which was the son of *R*

### RHODA *(ro'-dah) A maiden in Mary's house.*
Acts 12:13 a damsel came to hearken, named *R*

### RHODES *(rodes) A Mediterranean island.*
Acts 21:1 Coos, and the day following unto *R*

### RIB
Gen 2:22 And the *r*, which the LORD God had
2Sa 2:23 spear smote him under the fifth *r*
2Sa 3:27 smote him there under the fifth *r*
2Sa 4:6 they smote him under the fifth *r*
2Sa 20:10 him therewith in the fifth *r*

### RIBAI *(rib'-ahee) Father of Ittai.*
2Sa 23:29 Ittai the son of *R* out of Gibeah
1Chr 11:31 Ithai the son of *R* of Gibeah

### RIBLAH *(rib'-lah) A city on the Orontes River.*
Num 34:11 shall go down from Shepham to *R*
2Kin 23:33 put him in bands at *R* in the land
2Kin 25:6 up to the king of Babylon to *R*
2Kin 25:20 them to the king of Babylon to *R*
2Kin 25:21 slew them at *R* in the land of
Jer 39:5 king of Babylon to *R* in the land
Jer 39:6 of Zedekiah in *R* before his eyes
Jer 52:9 to *R* in the land of Hamath
Jer 52:10 all the princes of Judah in *R*
Jer 52:26 them to the king of Babylon to *R*
Jer 52:27 put them to death in *R* in the

### RICH
Gen 13:2 And Abram was very *r* in cattle
Gen 14:23 say, I have made Abram *r*
Ex 30:15 The *r* shall not give more, and the
Lev 25:47 or stranger wax *r* by thee
Ruth 3:10 not young men, whether poor or *r*
1Sa 2:7 The LORD maketh poor, and maketh *r*
2Sa 12:1 the one *r*, and the other poor
2Sa 12:2 The *r* man had exceeding many
2Sa 12:4 came a traveller unto the *r* man
Job 15:29 He shall not be *r*, neither shall
Job 27:19 The *r* man shall lie down, but he
Job 34:19 nor regardeth the *r* more than the
Ps 45:12 even the *r* among the people shall
Ps 49:2 Both low and high, *r* and poor,
Ps 49:16 thou afraid when one is made *r*
Prov 10:4 the hand of the diligent maketh *r*
Prov 10:15 The *r* man's wealth is his strong
Prov 10:22 blessing of the LORD, it maketh *r*
Prov 13:7 There is that maketh himself *r*
Prov 14:20 but the *r* hath many friends
Prov 18:11 The *r* man's wealth is his strong
Prov 18:23 but the *r* answereth roughly
Prov 21:17 loveth wine and oil shall not be *r*
Prov 22:2 The *r* and poor meet together
Prov 22:7 The *r* ruleth over the poor, and
Prov 22:16 and he that giveth to the *r*
Prov 23:4 Labour not to be *r*
Prov 28:6 in his ways, though he be *r*
Prov 28:11 The *r* man is wise in his own
Prov 28:20 to be *r* shall not be innocent
Prov 28:22 hasteth to be *r* hath an evil eye
Eccl 5:12 but the abundance of the *r* will
Eccl 10:6 and the *r* sit in low place
Eccl 10:20 curse not the *r* in thy bedchamber
Is 53:9 and with the *r* in his death
Jer 5:27 they are become great, and waxen *r*
Jer 9:23 let not the *r* man glory in his
Eze 27:24 work, and in chests of *r* apparel
Hos 12:8 Ephraim said, Yet I am become *r*
Mic 6:12 For the *r* men thereof are full of
Zec 11:5 for I am *r*
Mt 19:23 That a *r* man shall hardly enter
Mt 19:24 than for a *r* man to enter into
Mt 27:57 there came a *r* man of Arimathaea,
Mk 10:25 than for a *r* man to enter into
Mk 12:41 and many that were *r* cast in much
Lk 1:53 the *r* he hath sent empty away
Lk 6:24 But woe unto you that are *r*
Lk 12:16 The ground of a certain *r* man
Lk 12:21 himself, and is not *r* toward God
Lk 14:12 thy kinsmen, nor thy *r* neighbours
Lk 16:1 There was a certain *r* man
Lk 16:19 There was a certain *r* man
Lk 16:21 which fell from the *r* man's table
Lk 16:22 the *r* man also died, and was
Lk 18:23 for he was very *r*
Lk 18:25 than for a *r* man to enter into
Lk 19:2 among the publicans, and he was *r*
Lk 21:1 saw the *r* men casting their gifts
Rom 10:12 is *r* unto all that call upon him
1Cor 4:8 Now ye are full, now ye are *r*
2Cor 6:10 as poor, yet making many *r*
2Cor 8:9 Christ, that, though he was *r*
2Cor 8:9 ye through his poverty might be *r*
Eph 2:4 who is *r* in mercy, for his great
1Ti 6:9 will be *r* fall into temptation
1Ti 6:17 them that are *r* in this world
1Ti 6:18 that they be *r* in good works,
Jas 1:10 But the *r*, in that he is made low
Jas 1:11 so also shall the *r* man fade away
Jas 2:5 the poor of this world *r* in faith
Jas 2:6 Do not *r* men oppress you, and draw
Jas 5:1 ye *r* men, weep and howl for your
Rev 2:9 and poverty, (but thou art *r*)
Rev 3:17 Because thou sayest, I am *r*
Rev 3:18 the fire, that thou mayest be *r*
Rev 6:15 and the great men, and the *r* men
Rev 13:16 all, both small and great, *r*
Rev 18:3 of the earth are waxed *r* through
Rev 18:15 things, which were made *r* by her
Rev 18:19 wherein were made *r* all that had

### RICHES
Gen 31:16 For all the *r* which God hath
Gen 36:7 For their *r* were more than that
Josh 22:8 with much *r* unto your tents
1Sa 17:25 king will enrich him with great *r*
1Kin 3:11 neither hast asked *r* for thyself
1Kin 3:13 which thou hast not asked, both *r*
1Kin 10:23 all the kings of the earth for *r*
1Chr 29:12 Both *r* and honour come of thee, and
1Chr 29:28 a good old age, full of days, *r*
2Chr 1:11 heart, and thou hast not asked *r*
2Chr 1:12 and I will give thee *r*, and wealth,
2Chr 9:22 all the kings of the earth in *r*
2Chr 17:5 and he had *r* and honour in
2Chr 18:1 Now Jehoshaphat had *r* and honour
2Chr 20:25 both *r* with the dead bodies
2Chr 32:27 And Hezekiah had exceeding much *r*
Est 1:4 When he shewed the *r* of his
Est 5:11 told them of the glory of his *r*
Job 20:15 He hath swallowed down *r*, and he
Job 36:19 Will he esteem thy *r*
Ps 37:16 better than the *r* of many wicked
Ps 39:6 he heapeth up *r*, and knoweth not
Ps 49:6 in the multitude of their *r*
Ps 52:7 trusted in the abundance of his *r*
Ps 62:10 if *r* increase, set not your heart
Ps 73:12 they increase in *r*
Ps 104:24 the earth is full of thy *r*
Ps 112:3 Wealth and *r* shall be in his house
Ps 119:14 testimonies, as much as in all *r*
Prov 3:16 and in her left hand *r* and honour
Prov 8:18 *R* and honour are with me
Prov 8:18 yea, durable *r* and righteousness
Prov 11:4 *R* profit not in the day of wrath
Prov 11:16 and strong men retain *r*
Prov 11:28 that trusteth in his *r* shall fall
Prov 13:7 himself poor, yet hath great *r*
Prov 13:8 ransom of a man's life are his *r*
Prov 14:24 The crown of the wise is their *r*
Prov 19:14 *r* are the inheritance of fathers
Prov 22:1 rather to be chosen than great *r*
Prov 22:4 and the fear of the LORD are *r*
Prov 22:16 the poor to increase his *r*
Prov 23:5 for *r* certainly make themselves
Prov 24:4 with all precious and pleasant *r*
Prov 27:24 For *r* are not for ever
Prov 30:8 give me neither poverty nor *r*
Eccl 4:8 is his eye satisfied with *r*
Eccl 5:13 *r* kept for the owners thereof to
Eccl 5:14 But those *r* perish by evil
Eccl 5:19 man also to whom God hath given *r*
Eccl 6:2 A man to whom God hath given *r*
Eccl 9:11 nor yet *r* to men of understanding
Is 8:4 the *r* of Damascus and the spoil of
Is 10:14 as a nest the *r* of the people
Is 30:6 they will carry their *r* upon the
Is 45:3 hidden *r* of secret places, that
Is 61:6 shall eat the *r* of the Gentiles
Jer 9:23 not the rich man glory in his *r*
Jer 17:11 so he that getteth *r*, and not by
Jer 48:36 because the *r* that he hath gotten
Eze 26:12 they shall make a spoil of thy *r*
Eze 27:12 of the multitude of all kind of *r*
Eze 27:18 for the multitude of all *r*
Eze 27:27 Thy *r*, and thy fairs, thy
Eze 27:33 earth with the multitude of thy *r*
Eze 28:4 thou hast gotten thee *r*, and hast
Eze 28:5 hast thou increased thy *r*
Eze 28:5 is lifted up because of thy *r*
Dan 11:2 by his strength through his *r* he
Dan 11:13 with a great army and with much *r*
Dan 11:24 them the prey, and spoil, and *r*
Dan 11:28 return into his land with great *r*
Mt 13:22 world, and the deceitfulness of *r*

Mk 4:19 world, and the deceitfulness of *r*
Mk 10:23 *r* enter into the kingdom of God
Mk 10:24 in *r* to enter into the kingdom of
Lk 8:14 and are choked with cares and *r*
Lk 16:11 commit to your trust the true *r*
Lk 18:24 *r* enter into the kingdom of God
Rom 2:4 thou the *r* of his goodness
Rom 9:23 that he might make known the *r* of
Rom 11:12 of them be the *r* of the world
Rom 11:12 of them the *r* of the Gentiles
Rom 11:33 depth of the *r* both of the wisdom
2Cor 8:2 unto the *r* of their liberality
Eph 1:7 according to the *r* of his grace
Eph 1:18 what the *r* of the glory of his
Eph 2:7 he might shew the exceeding *r* of
Eph 3:8 the unsearchable *r* of Christ
Eph 3:16 according to the *r* of his glory
Phil 4:19 to his *r* in glory by Christ Jesus
Col 1:27 *r* of the glory of this mystery
Col 2:2 unto all *r* of the full assurance
1Ti 6:17 nor trust in uncertain *r*
Heb 11:26 *r* than the treasures in Egypt
Jas 5:2 Your *r* are corrupted, and your
Rev 5:12 was slain to receive power, and *r*
Rev 18:17 hour so great *r* is come to nought

## RID

Gen 37:22 that he might *r* him out of their
Ex 6:6 I will *r* you out of their bondage
Lev 26:6 I will *r* evil beasts out of the
Ps 82:4 *r* them out of the hand of the
Ps 144:7 *r* me, and deliver me out of great
Ps 144:11 *R* me, and deliver me from the hand

## RIDE

Gen 41:43 he made him to *r* in the second
Deut 32:13 He made him *r* on the high places
Judg 5:10 ye that *r* on white asses, ye that
2Sa 16:2 for the king's household to *r* on
2Sa 19:26 me an ass, that I may *r* thereon
1Kin 1:33 my son to *r* upon mine own mule
1Kin 1:38 caused Solomon to *r* upon king
1Kin 1:44 him to *r* upon the king's mule
2Kin 10:16 So they made him *r* in his chariot
Job 30:22 thou causest me to *r* upon it
Ps 45:4 in thy majesty *r* prosperously
Ps 66:12 caused men to *r* over our heads
Is 30:16 and, We will *r* upon the swift
Is 58:14 I will cause thee to *r* upon the
Jer 6:23 they *r* upon horses, set in array
Jer 50:42 they shall *r* upon horses, every
Hos 10:11 I will make Ephraim to *r*
Hos 14:3 we will not *r* upon horses
Hab 3:8 that thou didst *r* upon thine
Hag 2:22 chariots, and those that *r* in them

## RIDER

Gen 49:17 so that his *r* shall fall backward
Ex 15:1 his *r* hath he thrown into the sea
Ex 15:21 his *r* hath he thrown into the sea
Job 39:18 she scorneth the horse and his *r*
Jer 51:21 in pieces the horse and his *r*
Jer 51:21 in pieces the chariot and his *r*
Zec 12:4 and his *r* with madness

## RIDERS

2Kin 18:23 on thy part to set *r* upon them
Est 8:10 *r* on mules, camels, and young
Is 36:8 on thy part to set *r* upon them
Hag 2:22 their *r* shall come down, every
Zec 10:5 them, and the *r* on horses shall be

## RIDETH

Lev 15:9 what saddle soever he *r* upon that
Deut 33:26 who *r* upon the heaven in thy help
Est 6:8 and the horse that the king *r* upon
Ps 68:4 extol him that *r* upon the heavens
Ps 68:33 To him that *r* upon the heavens of
Is 19:1 the LORD *r* upon a swift cloud, and
Amos 2:15 neither shall he that *r* the horse

## RIDING

Num 22:22 Now he was *r* upon his ass, and his
2Kin 4:24 slack not thy *r* for me, except I
Jer 17:25 *r* in chariots and on horses, they,
Jer 22:4 *r* in chariots and on horses, he,
Eze 23:6 young men, horsemen *r* upon horses
Eze 23:12 horsemen *r* upon horses, all of
Eze 23:23 all of them *r* upon horses
Eze 38:15 thee, all of them *r* upon horses
Zec 1:8 behold a man *r* upon a red horse,
Zec 9:9 *r* upon an ass, and upon a colt the

## RIGHTEOUS

Gen 7:1 for thee have I seen *r* before me
Gen 18:23 destroy the *r* with the wicked
Gen 18:24 there be fifty *r* within the city
Gen 18:24 for the fifty *r* that are therein
Gen 18:25 to slay the *r* with the wicked
Gen 18:25 that the *r* should be as the
Gen 18:26 in Sodom fifty *r* within the city
Gen 18:28 shall lack five of the fifty *r*
Gen 20:4 wilt thou slay also a *r* nation
Gen 38:26 said, She hath been more *r* than I
Ex 9:27 the LORD is *r*, and I and my people
Ex 23:7 the innocent and *r* slay thou not
Ex 23:8 and perverteth the words of the *r*
Num 23:10 Let me die the death of the *r*
Deut 4:8 judgments so *r* as all this law,
Deut 16:19 and pervert the words of the *r*
Deut 25:1 then they shall justify the *r*
Judg 5:11 rehearse the *r* acts of the LORD
Judg 5:11 even the *r* acts toward the
1Sa 12:7 of all the *r* acts of the LORD
1Sa 24:17 to David, Thou art more *r* than I
2Sa 4:11 a *r* person in his own house upon
1Kin 2:32 who fell upon two men more *r*
1Kin 8:32 and justifying the *r*, to give him
2Kin 10:9 said to all the people, Ye be *r*
2Chr 6:23 and by justifying the *r*, by giving
2Chr 12:6 and they said, The LORD is *r*
Ezr 9:15 O LORD God of Israel, thou art *r*
Neh 9:8 for thou art *r*
Job 4:7 or where were the *r* cut off
Job 9:15 Whom, though I were *r*, yet would
Job 10:15 and if I be *r*, yet will I not lift
Job 15:14 of a woman, that he should be *r*
Job 17:9 The *r* also shall hold on his way,
Job 22:3 to the Almighty, that thou art *r*
Job 22:19 The *r* see it, and are glad
Job 23:7 There the *r* might dispute with
Job 32:1 because he was *r* in his own eyes
Job 34:5 For Job hath said, I am *r*
Job 35:7 If thou be *r*, what givest thou
Job 36:7 not his eyes from the *r*
Job 40:8 condemn me, that thou mayest be *r*
Ps 1:5 in the congregation of the *r*
Ps 1:6 the LORD knoweth the way of the *r*
Ps 5:12 For thou, LORD, wilt bless the *r*
Ps 7:9 for the *r* God trieth the hearts
Ps 7:11 God judgeth the *r*, and God is
Ps 11:3 be destroyed, what can the *r* do
Ps 11:5 The LORD trieth the *r*
Ps 11:7 For the *r* LORD loveth
Ps 14:5 God is in the generation of the *r*
Ps 19:9 the LORD are true and *r* altogether
Ps 31:18 and contemptuously against the *r*
Ps 32:11 in the LORD, and rejoice, ye *r*
Ps 33:1 Rejoice in the LORD, O ye *r*
Ps 34:15 eyes of the LORD are upon the *r*
Ps 34:17 The *r* cry, and the LORD heareth,
Ps 34:19 Many are the afflictions of the *r*
Ps 34:21 that hate the *r* shall be desolate
Ps 35:27 be glad, that favour my *r* cause
Ps 37:16 A little that a *r* man hath is
Ps 37:17 but the LORD upholdeth the *r*
Ps 37:21 but the *r* sheweth mercy, and
Ps 37:25 have I not seen the *r* forsaken
Ps 37:29 The *r* shall inherit the land, and
Ps 37:30 mouth of the *r* speaketh wisdom
Ps 37:32 The wicked watcheth the *r*
Ps 37:39 salvation of the *r* is of the LORD
Ps 52:6 The *r* also shall see, and fear, and
Ps 55:22 never suffer the *r* to be moved
Ps 58:10 The *r* shall rejoice when he seeth
Ps 58:11 there is a reward for the *r*
Ps 64:10 The *r* shall be glad in the LORD,
Ps 68:3 But let the *r* be glad
Ps 69:28 and not be written with the *r*
Ps 72:7 In his days shall the *r* flourish
Ps 75:10 horns of the *r* shall be exalted
Ps 92:12 The *r* shall flourish like the
Ps 94:21 against the soul of the *r*
Ps 97:11 Light is sown for the *r*, and
Ps 97:12 Rejoice in the LORD, ye *r*
Ps 107:42 The *r* shall see it, and rejoice
Ps 112:4 and full of compassion, and *r*
Ps 112:6 the *r* shall be in everlasting
Ps 116:5 Gracious is the LORD, and *r*
Ps 118:15 is in the tabernacles of the *r*
Ps 118:20 into which the *r* shall enter
Ps 119:7 have learned thy *r* judgments
Ps 119:62 thee because of thy *r* judgments
Ps 119:106 that I will keep thy *r* judgments
Ps 119:137 *R* art thou, O LORD, and upright
Ps 119:138 that thou hast commanded are *r*
Ps 119:160 every one of thy *r* judgments
Ps 119:164 thee because of thy *r* judgments
Ps 125:3 not rest upon the lot of the *r*
Ps 125:3 lest the *r* put forth their hands
Ps 129:4 The LORD is *r*
Ps 140:13 Surely the *r* shall give thanks
Ps 141:5 Let the *r* smite me
Ps 142:7 the *r* shall compass me about
Ps 145:17 The LORD is *r* in all his ways, and
Ps 146:8 the LORD loveth the *r*
Prov 2:7 layeth up sound wisdom for the *r*
Prov 2:20 men, and keep the paths of the *r*
Prov 3:32 but his secret is with the *r*
Prov 10:3 the soul of the *r* to famish
Prov 10:11 The mouth of a *r* man is a well of
Prov 10:16 labour of the *r* tendeth to life
Prov 10:21 The lips of the *r* feed many
Prov 10:24 desire of the *r* shall be granted
Prov 10:25 but the *r* is an everlasting
Prov 10:28 The hope of the *r* shall be
Prov 10:30 The *r* shall never be removed
Prov 10:32 The lips of the *r* know what is
Prov 11:8 The *r* is delivered out of trouble
Prov 11:10 When it goeth well with the *r*
Prov 11:21 seed of the *r* shall be delivered
Prov 11:23 The desire of the *r* is only good
Prov 11:28 but the *r* shall flourish as a
Prov 11:30 The fruit of the *r* is a tree of
Prov 11:31 the *r* shall be recompensed in the
Prov 12:3 root of the *r* shall not be moved
Prov 12:5 The thoughts of the *r* are right
Prov 12:7 the house of the *r* shall stand
Prov 12:10 A *r* man regardeth the life of his
Prov 12:12 the root of the *r* yieldeth fruit
Prov 12:26 The *r* is more excellent than his
Prov 13:5 A *r* man hateth lying
Prov 13:9 The light of the *r* rejoiceth
Prov 13:21 but to the *r* good shall be repaid
Prov 13:25 The *r* eateth to the satisfying of
Prov 14:9 but among the *r* there is favour
Prov 14:19 the wicked at the gates of the *r*
Prov 14:32 but the *r* hath hope in his death
Prov 15:6 house of the *r* is much treasure
Prov 15:19 the way of the *r* is made plain
Prov 15:28 The heart of the *r* studieth to
Prov 15:29 he heareth the prayer of the *r*
Prov 16:13 *R* lips are the delight of kings
Prov 18:5 to overthrow the *r* in judgment
Prov 18:10 the *r* runneth into it, and is safe
Prov 21:12 The *r* man wisely considereth the
Prov 21:18 shall be a ransom for the *r*
Prov 21:26 but the *r* giveth and spareth not
Prov 23:24 The father of the *r* shall greatly
Prov 24:15 against the dwelling of the *r*
Prov 24:24 saith unto the wicked, Thou art *r*
Prov 25:26 A *r* man falling down before the
Prov 28:1 but the *r* are bold as a lion
Prov 28:10 Whoso causeth the *r* to go astray
Prov 28:12 When *r* men do rejoice, there is
Prov 28:28 when they perish, the *r* increase
Prov 29:2 When the *r* are in authority, the
Prov 29:6 but the *r* doth sing and rejoice
Prov 29:7 The *r* considereth the cause of
Prov 29:16 but the *r* shall see their fall
Eccl 3:17 mine heart, God shall judge the *r*
Eccl 7:16 Be not *r* over much
Eccl 8:14 according to the work of the *r*
Eccl 9:1 to declare all this, that the *r*
Eccl 9:2 there is one event to the *r*
Is 3:10 Say ye to the *r*, that it shall be
Is 5:23 righteousness of the *r* from him
Is 24:16 heard songs, even glory to the *r*
Is 26:2 that the *r* nation which keepeth
Is 41:2 raised up the *r* man from the east
Is 41:26 that we may say, He is *r*
Is 53:11 shall my *r* servant justify many
Is 57:1 The *r* perisheth, and no man layeth
Is 57:1 none considering that the *r* is
Is 60:21 Thy people also shall be all *r*
Jer 12:1 *R* art thou, O LORD, when I plead
Jer 20:12 LORD of hosts, that triest the *r*
Jer 23:5 will raise unto David a *r* Branch
Lam 1:18 The LORD is *r*
Eze 3:20 When a *r* man doth turn from his
Eze 3:21 if thou warn the *r* man
Eze 3:21 that the *r* sin not
Eze 13:22 have made the heart of the *r* sad

Eze 16:52 they are more *r* than thou
Eze 18:20 of the *r* shall be upon him
Eze 18:24 But when the *r* turneth away from
Eze 18:26 When a *r* man turneth away from
Eze 21:3 and will cut off from thee the *r*
Eze 21:4 I will cut off from thee the *r*
Eze 23:45 And the *r* men, they shall judge
Eze 33:12 The righteousness of the *r* shall
Eze 33:12 neither shall the *r* be able to
Eze 33:13 When I shall say to the *r*
Eze 33:18 When the *r* turneth from his
Dan 9:14 for the LORD our God is *r* in all
Amos 2:6 they sold the *r* for silver
Hab 1:4 wicked doth compass about the *r*
Hab 1:13 the man that is more *r* than he
Mal 3:18 return, and discern between the *r*
Mt 9:13 for I am not come to call the *r*
Mt 10:41 he that receiveth a *r* man in the
Mt 10:41 a *r* man shall receive a *r*
Mt 13:17 *r* men have desired to see those
Mt 13:43 Then shall the *r* shine forth as
Mt 23:28 also outwardly appear *r* unto men
Mt 23:29 garnish the sepulchres of the *r*
Mt 23:35 the *r* blood shed upon the earth
Mt 23:35 from the blood of *r* Abel unto the
Mt 25:37 Then shall the *r* answer him
Mt 25:46 but the *r* into life eternal
Mk 2:17 I came not to call the *r*, but
Lk 1:6 And they were both *r* before God
Lk 5:32 I came not to call the *r*, but
Lk 18:9 in themselves that they were *r*
Lk 23:47 Certainly this was a *r* man
Jn 7:24 appearance, but judge *r* judgment
Jn 17:25 O *r* Father, the world hath not
Rom 2:5 of the *r* judgment of God
Rom 3:10 As it is written, There is none *r*
Rom 5:7 scarcely for a *r* man will one die
Rom 5:19 of one shall many be made *r*
2Th 1:5 token of the *r* judgment of God
2Th 1:6 Seeing it is a *r* thing with God
1Ti 1:9 the law is not made for a *r* man
2Ti 4:8 the *r* judge, shall give me at
Heb 11:4 he obtained witness that he was *r*
Jas 5:16 prayer of a *r* man availeth much
1Pet 3:12 eyes of the Lord are over the *r*
1Pet 4:18 if the *r* scarcely be saved, where
2Pet 2:8 (For that *r* man dwelling among
2Pet 2:8 vexed his *r* soul from day to day
1Jn 2:1 the Father, Jesus Christ the *r*
1Jn 2:29 If ye know that he is *r*, ye know
1Jn 3:7 he that doeth righteousness is *r*
1Jn 3:7 even as he is *r*
1Jn 3:12 were evil, and his brother's *r*
Rev 16:5 of the waters say, Thou art *r*
Rev 16:7 true and *r* are thy judgments
Rev 19:2 For true and *r* are his judgments
Rev 22:11 is *r*, let him be *r* still

## RIGHTEOUSLY

Deut 1:16 judge *r* between every man and his
Ps 67:4 for thou shalt judge the people *r*
Ps 96:10 he shall judge the people *r*
Prov 31:9 Open thy mouth, judge *r*, and plead
Is 33:15 He that walketh *r*, and speaketh
Jer 11:20 O LORD of hosts, that judgest *r*
Titus 2:12 lusts, we should live soberly, *r*
1Pet 2:23 himself to him that judgeth *r*

## RIGHTEOUSNESS

Gen 15:6 and he counted it to him for *r*
Gen 30:33 So shall my *r* answer for me in
Lev 19:15 but in *r* shalt thou judge thy
Deut 6:25 And it shall be our *r*, if we
Deut 9:4 For my *r* the LORD hath brought me
Deut 9:5 Not for thy *r*, or for the
Deut 9:6 good land to possess it for thy *r*
Deut 24:13 it shall be *r* unto thee before
Deut 33:19 they shall offer sacrifices of *r*
1Sa 26:23 LORD render to every man his *r*
2Sa 22:21 rewarded me according to my *r*
2Sa 22:25 recompensed me according to my *r*
1Kin 3:6 before thee in truth, and in *r*
1Kin 8:32 to give him according to his *r*
2Chr 6:23 by giving him according to his *r*
Job 6:29 yea, return again, my *r* is in it
Job 8:6 habitation of thy *r* prosperous
Job 27:6 My *r* I hold fast, and will not let
Job 29:14 I put on *r*, and it clothed me
Job 33:26 for he will render unto man his *r*
Job 35:2 saidst, My *r* is more than God's
Job 35:8 thy *r* may profit the son of man
Job 36:3 and will ascribe *r* to my Maker
Ps 4:1 me when I call, O God of my *r*
Ps 4:5 Offer the sacrifices of *r*
Ps 5:8 in thy *r* because of mine enemies
Ps 7:8 me, O LORD, according to my *r*
Ps 7:17 the LORD according to his *r*
Ps 9:8 And he shall judge the world in *r*
Ps 11:7 For the righteous LORD loveth *r*
Ps 15:2 walketh uprightly, and worketh *r*
Ps 17:15 me, I will behold thy face in *r*
Ps 18:20 rewarded me according to my *r*
Ps 18:24 recompensed me according to my *r*
Ps 22:31 shall declare his *r* unto a people
Ps 23:3 paths of *r* for his name's sake
Ps 24:5 *r* from the God of his salvation
Ps 31:1 deliver me in thy *r*
Ps 33:5 He loveth *r* and judgment
Ps 35:24 O LORD my God, according to thy *r*
Ps 35:28 And my tongue shall speak of thy *r*
Ps 36:6 Thy *r* is like the great mountains
Ps 36:10 thy *r* to the upright in heart
Ps 37:6 bring forth thy *r* as the light
Ps 40:9 I have preached *r* in the great
Ps 40:10 not hid thy *r* within my heart
Ps 45:4 because of truth and meekness and *r*
Ps 45:7 Thou lovest *r*, and hatest
Ps 48:10 thy right hand is full of *r*
Ps 50:6 the heavens shall declare his *r*
Ps 51:14 tongue shall sing aloud of thy *r*
Ps 51:19 pleased with the sacrifices of *r*
Ps 52:3 and lying rather than to speak *r*
Ps 58:1 Do ye indeed speak *r*, O
Ps 65:5 things in *r* wilt thou answer us
Ps 69:27 and let them not come into thy *r*
Ps 71:2 Deliver me in thy *r*, and cause me
Ps 71:15 My mouth shall shew forth thy *r*
Ps 71:16 I will make mention of thy *r*
Ps 71:19 Thy *r* also, O God, is very high,
Ps 71:24 talk of thy *r* all the day long
Ps 72:1 thy *r* unto the king's son
Ps 72:2 He shall judge thy people with *r*
Ps 72:3 people, and the little hills, by *r*
Ps 85:10 *r* and peace have kissed each other
Ps 85:11 *r* shall look down from heaven
Ps 85:13 *R* shall go before him
Ps 88:12 and thy *r* in the land of
Ps 89:16 in thy *r* shall they be exalted
Ps 94:15 But judgment shall return unto *r*
Ps 96:13 he shall judge the world with *r*
Ps 97:2 *r* and judgment are the habitation
Ps 97:6 The heavens declare his *r*
Ps 98:2 his *r* hath he openly shewed in
Ps 98:9 with *r* shall he judge the world,
Ps 99:4 executest judgment and *r* in Jacob
Ps 103:6 The LORD executeth *r* and judgment
Ps 103:17 his *r* unto children's children
Ps 106:3 and he that doeth *r* at all times
Ps 106:31 for *r* unto all generations for
Ps 111:3 and his *r* endureth for ever
Ps 112:3 and his *r* endureth for ever
Ps 112:9 his *r* endureth for ever
Ps 118:19 Open to me the gates of *r*
Ps 119:40 quicken me in thy *r*
Ps 119:123 and for the word of thy *r*
Ps 119:142 Thy *r* is an everlasting
Ps 119:142 *r* is an everlasting *r*
Ps 119:144 The *r* of thy testimonies is
Ps 119:172 for all thy commandments are *r*
Ps 132:9 Let thy priests be clothed with *r*
Ps 143:1 answer me, and in thy *r*
Ps 145:7 goodness, and shall sing of thy *r*
Prov 2:9 Then shalt thou understand *r*
Prov 8:8 the words of my mouth are in *r*
Prov 8:18 yea, durable riches and *r*
Prov 8:20 I lead in the way of *r*, in the
Prov 10:2 but *r* delivereth from death
Prov 11:4 but *r* delivereth from death
Prov 11:5 The *r* of the perfect shall direct
Prov 11:6 The *r* of the upright shall
Prov 11:18 soweth *r* shall be a sure reward
Prov 11:19 As *r* tendeth to life
Prov 12:17 speaketh truth sheweth forth *r*
Prov 12:28 In the way of *r* is life
Prov 13:6 *R* keepeth him that is upright in
Prov 14:34 *R* exalteth a nation
Prov 15:9 loveth him that followeth after *r*
Prov 16:8 Better is a little with *r* than
Prov 16:12 the throne is established by *r*
Prov 16:31 if it be found in the way of *r*
Prov 21:21 He that followeth after *r*
Prov 21:21 and mercy findeth life, *r*, and
Prov 25:5 throne shall be established in *r*
Eccl 3:16 and the place of *r*, that iniquity
Eccl 7:15 just man that perisheth in his *r*
Is 1:21 *r* lodged in it
Is 1:26 shalt be called, The city of *r*
Is 1:27 judgment, and her converts with *r*
Is 5:7 for *r*, but behold a cry
Is 5:16 is holy shall be sanctified in *r*
Is 5:23 take away the *r* of the righteous
Is 10:22 decreed shall overflow with *r*
Is 11:4 But with *r* shall he judge the
Is 11:5 *r* shall be the girdle of his
Is 16:5 and seeking judgment, and hasting *r*
Is 26:9 of the world will learn *r*
Is 26:10 wicked, yet will he not learn *r*
Is 28:17 to the line, and *r* to the plummet
Is 32:1 Behold, a king shall reign in *r*
Is 32:16 *r* remain in the fruitful field
Is 32:17 the work of *r* shall be peace
Is 32:17 and the effect of *r* quietness
Is 33:5 filled Zion with judgment and *r*
Is 41:10 thee with the right hand of my *r*
Is 42:6 I the LORD have called thee in *r*
Is 45:8 and let the skies pour down *r*
Is 45:8 and let *r* spring up together
Is 45:13 I have raised him up in *r*
Is 45:19 I the LORD speak *r*, I declare
Is 45:23 word is gone out of my mouth in *r*
Is 45:24 one say, in the LORD have I *r*
Is 46:12 stouthearted, that are far from *r*
Is 46:13 I bring near my *r*
Is 48:1 but not in truth, nor in *r*
Is 48:18 thy *r* as the waves of the sea
Is 51:1 to me, ye that follow after *r*
Is 51:5 My *r* is near
Is 51:6 my *r* shall not be abolished
Is 51:7 Hearken unto me, ye that know *r*
Is 51:8 but my *r* shall be for ever, and my
Is 54:14 In *r* shalt thou be established
Is 54:17 their *r* is of me, saith the LORD
Is 56:1 to come, and my *r* to be revealed
Is 57:12 I will declare thy *r*, and thy
Is 58:2 my ways, as a nation that did *r*
Is 58:8 thy *r* shall go before thee
Is 59:16 and his *r*, it sustained him
Is 59:17 For he put on *r* as a breastplate,
Is 60:17 peace, and thine exactors *r*
Is 61:3 they might be called trees of *r*
Is 61:10 covered me with the robe of *r*
Is 61:11 so the Lord GOD will cause *r*
Is 62:1 until the *r* thereof go forth as
Is 62:2 And the Gentiles shall see thy *r*
Is 63:1 I that speak in *r*, mighty to save
Is 64:5 him that rejoiceth and worketh *r*
Jer 4:2 in truth, in judgment, and in *r*
Jer 9:24 lovingkindness, judgment, and *r*
Jer 22:3 Execute ye judgment and *r*, and
Jer 23:6 shall be called, THE LORD OUR *R*
Jer 33:15 Branch of *r* to grow up unto David
Jer 33:15 execute judgment and *r* in the land
Jer 33:16 shall be called, The LORD our *r*
Jer 51:10 The LORD hath brought forth our *r*
Eze 3:20 man doth turn from his *r*, and
Eze 3:20 his *r* which he hath done shall
Eze 14:14 but their own souls by their *r*
Eze 14:20 their own souls by their *r*
Eze 18:20 the *r* of the righteous shall be
Eze 18:22 in his *r* that he hath done he
Eze 18:24 righteous turneth away from his *r*
Eze 18:24 All his *r* that he hath done shall
Eze 18:26 man turneth away from his *r*
Eze 33:12 The *r* of the righteous shall not
Eze 33:12 be able to live for his *r* in the
Eze 33:13 if he trust to his own *r*, and
Eze 33:18 the righteous turneth from his *r*
Dan 4:27 thee, and break off thy sins by *r*
Dan 9:7 *r* belongeth unto thee, but unto
Dan 9:16 O Lord, according to all thy *r*
Dan 9:24 and to bring in everlasting *r*
Dan 12:3 many to *r* as the stars for ever
Hos 2:19 I will betroth thee unto me in *r*
Hos 10:12 Sow to yourselves in *r*, reap in
Hos 10:12 till he come and rain *r* upon you
Amos 5:7 leave off *r* in the earth,
Amos 5:24 waters, and *r* as a mighty stream
Amos 6:12 and the fruit of *r* into hemlock
Mic 6:5 ye may know the *r* of the LORD
Mic 7:9 light, and I shall behold his *r*
Zeph 2:3 seek *r*, seek meekness

Zec 8:8 be their God, in truth and in *r*
Mal 3:3 unto the LORD an offering in *r*
Mal 4:2 fear my name shall the Sun of *r*
Mt 3:15 it becometh us to fulfil all *r*
Mt 5:6 which do hunger and thirst after *r*
Mt 5:20 That except your *r* shall exceed
Mt 5:20 shall exceed the *r* of the scribes
Mt 6:33 the kingdom of God, and his *r*
Mt 21:32 came unto you in the way of *r*
Lk 1:75 *r* before him, all the days of our
Jn 16:8 reprove the world of sin, and of *r*
Jn 16:10 Of *r*, because I go to my Father,
Acts 10:35 he that feareth him, and worketh *r*
Acts 13:10 of the devil, thou enemy of all *r*
Acts 17:31 in *r* by that man whom he hath
Acts 24:25 And as he reasoned of *r*,
Rom 1:17 For therein is the *r* of God
Rom 2:26 keep the *r* of the law, shall not
Rom 3:5 commend the *r* of God, what shall
Rom 3:21 But now the *r* of God without the
Rom 3:22 Even the *r* of God which is by
Rom 3:25 blood, to declare his *r* for the
Rom 3:26 I say, at this time his *r*
Rom 4:3 and it was counted unto him for *r*
Rom 4:5 his faith is counted for *r*
Rom 4:6 whom God imputeth *r* without works
Rom 4:9 was reckoned to Abraham for *r*
Rom 4:11 a seal of the *r* of the faith
Rom 4:11 that *r* might be imputed unto them
Rom 4:13 law, but through the *r* of faith
Rom 4:22 it was imputed to him for *r*
Rom 5:17 of the gift of *r* shall reign in
Rom 5:18 even so by the *r* of one the free
Rom 5:21 *r* unto eternal life by Jesus
Rom 6:13 as instruments of *r* unto God
Rom 6:16 death, or of obedience unto *r*
Rom 6:18 sin, ye became the servants of *r*
Rom 6:19 servants to *r* unto holiness
Rom 6:20 of sin, ye were free from *r*
Rom 8:4 That the *r* of the law might be
Rom 8:10 the Spirit is life because of *r*
Rom 9:28 the work, and cut it short in *r*
Rom 9:30 which followed not after *r*
Rom 9:30 have attained to *r*
Rom 9:30 even the *r* which is of faith
Rom 9:31 which followed after the law of *r*
Rom 9:31 hath not attained to the law of *r*
Rom 10:3 they being ignorant of God's *r*
Rom 10:3 about to establish their own *r*
Rom 10:3 themselves unto the *r* of God
Rom 10:4 is the end of the law for *r* to
Rom 10:5 the *r* which is of the law
Rom 10:6 But the *r* which is of faith
Rom 10:10 the heart man believeth unto *r*
Rom 14:17 but *r*, and peace, and joy in the
1Cor 1:30 God is made unto us wisdom, and *r*
1Cor 15:34 Awake to *r*, and sin not
2Cor 3:9 ministration of *r* exceed in glory
2Cor 5:21 might be made the *r* of God in him
2Cor 6:7 by the armour of *r* on the right
2Cor 6:14 hath *r* with unrighteousness
2Cor 9:9 his *r* remaineth for ever
2Cor 9:10 and increase the fruits of your *r*
2Cor 11:15 transformed as the ministers of *r*
Gal 2:21 for if *r* come by the law, then
Gal 3:6 and it was accounted to him for *r*
Gal 3:21 verily *r* should have been by the
Gal 5:5 wait for the hope of *r* by faith
Eph 4:24 which after God is created in *r*
Eph 5:9 Spirit is in all goodness and *r*
Eph 6:14 and having on the breastplate of *r*
Phil 1:11 Being filled with the fruits of *r*
Phil 3:6 touching the *r* which is in the
Phil 3:9 in him, not having mine own *r*
Phil 3:9 the *r* which is of God by faith
1Ti 6:11 and follow after *r*, godliness,
2Ti 2:22 but follow *r*, faith, charity,
2Ti 3:16 correction, for instruction in *r*
2Ti 4:8 is laid up for me a crown of *r*
Titus 3:5 Not by works of *r* which we have
Heb 1:8 a sceptre of *r* is the sceptre of
Heb 1:9 Thou hast loved *r*, and hated
Heb 5:13 is unskilful in the word of *r*
Heb 7:2 being by interpretation King of *r*
Heb 11:7 heir of the *r* which is by faith
Heb 11:33 faith subdued kingdoms, wrought *r*
Heb 12:11 *r* unto them which are exercised
Jas 1:20 of man worketh not the *r* of God
Jas 2:23 and it was imputed unto him for *r*
Jas 3:18 the fruit of *r* is sown in peace
1Pet 2:24 dead to sins, should live unto *r*
2Pet 1:1 with us through the *r* of God
2Pet 2:5 eighth person, a preacher of *r*
2Pet 2:21 not to have known the way of *r*
2Pet 3:13 a new earth, wherein dwelleth *r*
1Jn 2:29 one that doeth *r* is born of him
1Jn 3:7 he that doeth *r* is righteous
1Jn 3:10 doeth not *r* is not of God
Rev 19:8 the fine linen is the *r* of saints
Rev 19:11 in *r* he doth judge and make war

**RIGHTEOUSNESS'**
Ps 143:11 for thy *r* sake bring my soul out
Is 42:21 is well pleased for his *r* sake
Mt 5:10 which are persecuted for *r* sake
1Pet 3:14 But and if ye suffer for *r* sake

**RIGHTLY**
Gen 27:36 he said, Is not he *r* named Jacob
Lk 7:43 said unto him, Thou hast *r* judged
Lk 20:21 that thou sayest and teachest *r*
2Ti 2:15 *r* dividing the word of truth

**RIGOUR**
Ex 1:13 of Israel to serve with *r*
Ex 1:14 they made them serve, was with *r*
Lev 25:43 shalt not rule over him with *r*
Lev 25:46 not rule one over another with *r*
Lev 25:53 rule with *r* over him in thy sight

**RIMMON** *(rim'-mon)*
*1. A city in Zebulun.*
Josh 15:32 Lebaoth, and Shilhim, and Ain, and *R*
1Chr 6:77 *R* with her suburbs, Tabor with
Zec 14:10 from Geba to *R* south of Jerusalem
*2. A rock near Gibeah.*
Judg 20:45 the wilderness unto the rock of *R*
Judg 20:47 to the wilderness unto the rock *R*
Judg 20:47 abode in the rock *R* four months
Judg 21:13 Benjamin that were in the rock *R*
*3. Father of Baanah and Rechab.*
2Sa 4:2 the sons of *R* a Beerothite, of
2Sa 4:5 the sons of *R* the Beerothite,
2Sa 4:9 the sons of *R* the Beerothite, and
*4. A Syrian god.*
2Kin 5:18 the house of *R* to worship there
2Kin 5:18 and I bow myself in the house of *R*
2Kin 5:18 bow down myself in the house of *R*
*5. A city in Simeon.*
1Chr 4:32 villages were, Etam, and Ain, *R*

**RIMMON-PAREZ** *(rim'-mon-pa'-rez) An Israelite encampment in the wilderness.*
Num 33:19 from Rithmah, and pitched at *R*
Num 33:20 And they departed from *R*, and

**RING**
Gen 41:42 took off his *r* from his hand
Ex 26:24 above the head of it unto one *r*
Ex 36:29 at the head thereof, to one *r*
Est 3:10 the king took his *r* from his hand
Est 3:12 and sealed with the king's *r*
Est 8:2 And the king took off his *r*
Est 8:8 and seal it with the king's *r*
Est 8:8 name, and sealed with the king's *r*
Est 8:10 and sealed it with the king's *r*
Lk 15:22 put a *r* on his hand, and shoes on
Jas 2:2 your assembly a man with a gold *r*

**RINGS**
Ex 25:12 shalt cast four *r* of gold for it
Ex 25:12 two *r* shall be in the one side of
Ex 25:12 two *r* in the other side of it
Ex 25:14 the *r* by the sides of the ark
Ex 25:15 shall be in the *r* of the ark
Ex 25:26 shalt make for it four *r* of gold
Ex 25:26 put the *r* in the four corners
Ex 25:27 against the border shall the *r* be
Ex 26:29 make their *r* of gold for places
Ex 27:4 *r* in the four corners thereof
Ex 27:7 staves shall be put into the *r*
Ex 28:23 the breastplate two *r* of gold
Ex 28:23 shalt put the two *r* on the two
Ex 28:24 chains of gold in the two *r* which
Ex 28:26 And thou shalt make two *r* of gold
Ex 28:27 two other *r* of gold thou shalt
Ex 28:28 bind the breastplate by the *r*
Ex 28:28 the *r* of the ephod with a lace of
Ex 30:4 two golden *r* shalt thou make to
Ex 35:22 bracelets, and earrings, and *r*
Ex 36:34 made their *r* of gold to be places
Ex 37:3 And he cast for it four *r* of gold
Ex 37:3 even two *r* upon the one side of
Ex 37:3 two *r* upon the other side of it
Ex 37:5 the *r* by the sides of the ark
Ex 37:13 And he cast for it four *r* of gold
Ex 37:13 put the *r* upon the four corners
Ex 37:14 against the border were the *r*
Ex 37:27 he made two *r* of gold for it
Ex 38:5 he cast four *r* for the four ends
Ex 38:7 the *r* on the sides of the altar
Ex 39:16 two ouches of gold, and two gold *r*
Ex 39:16 put the two *r* in the two ends of
Ex 39:17 chains of gold in the two *r* on
Ex 39:19 And they made two *r* of gold
Ex 39:20 And they made two other golden *r*
Ex 39:21 his *r* unto the *r* of the ephod
Num 31:50 of gold, chains, and bracelets, *r*
Est 1:6 fine linen and purple to silver *r*
Song 5:14 are as gold *r* set with the beryl
Is 3:21 The *r*, and nose jewels,
Eze 1:18 As for their *r*, they were so high
Eze 1:18 their *r* were full of eyes round

**RINGSTRAKED**
Gen 30:35 that day the he goats that were *r*
Gen 30:39 rods, and brought forth cattle *r*
Gen 30:40 faces of the flocks toward the *r*
Gen 31:8 thus, The *r* shall be thy hire
Gen 31:8 then bare all the cattle *r*
Gen 31:10 leaped upon the cattle were *r*
Gen 31:12 which leap upon the cattle are *r*

**RINNAH** *(rin'-nah) A descendant of Caleb.*
1Chr 4:20 sons of Shimon were, Amnon, and *R*

**RIPE**
Gen 40:10 thereof brought forth *r* grapes
Ex 22:29 offer the first of thy *r* fruits
Num 18:13 whatsoever is first *r* in the land
Jer 24:2 like the figs that are first *r*
Joel 3:13 the sickle, for the harvest is *r*
Rev 14:15 for the harvest of the earth is *r*
Rev 14:18 for her grapes are fully *r*

**RIPHATH** *(ri'-fath) A son of Gomer.*
Gen 10:3 Ashkenaz, and *R*, and Togarmah
1Chr 1:6 Ashchenaz, and *R*, and Togarmah

**RISE**
Gen 19:2 your feet, and ye shall *r* up early
Gen 31:35 that I cannot *r* up before thee
Ex 8:20 *R* up early in the morning, and
Ex 9:13 *R* up early in the morning, and
Ex 12:31 *R* up, and get you forth from among
Ex 21:19 If he *r* again, and walk abroad
Lev 19:32 Thou shalt *r* up before the hoary
Num 10:35 *R* up, LORD, and let thine enemies
Num 22:20 call thee, *r* up, and go with them
Num 23:18 and said, *R* up, Balak, and hear
Num 23:24 the people shall *r* up as a great
Num 24:17 a Sceptre shall *r* out of Israel
Deut 2:13 Now *r* up, said I, and get you over
Deut 2:24 *R* ye up, take your journey, and
Deut 19:11 *r* up against him, and smite him
Deut 19:15 One witness shall not *r* up
Deut 19:16 If a false witness *r* up against
Deut 28:7 *r* up against thee to be smitten
Deut 29:22 that shall *r* up after you
Deut 31:16 and this people will *r* up, and go a
Deut 32:38 Let them *r* up and help you, and be
Deut 33:11 loins of them that *r* against him
Deut 33:11 hate him, that they *r* not again
Josh 8:7 Then ye shall *r* up from the
Josh 18:4 I will send them, and they shall *r*
Judg 8:21 said, *R* thou, and fall upon us
Judg 9:33 the sun is up, thou shalt *r* early
Judg 20:38 with smoke *r* up out of the city
1Sa 22:13 him, that he should *r* against me
1Sa 24:7 them not to *r* against Saul
1Sa 29:10 Wherefore now *r* up early in the
2Sa 12:21 the child was dead, thou didst *r*
2Sa 18:32 all that *r* against thee to do
2Kin 16:7 of Israel, which *r* up against me
Neh 2:18 And they said, Let us *r* up
Job 20:27 the earth shall *r* up against him
Job 30:12 Upon my right hand *r* the youth
Ps 3:1 are they that *r* up against me
Ps 17:7 from those that *r* up against them
Ps 18:38 them that they were not able to *r*
Ps 18:48 above those that *r* up against me
Ps 27:3 though war should *r* against me
Ps 35:11 False witnesses did *r* up
Ps 36:12 down, and shall not be able to *r*
Ps 41:8 he lieth he shall *r* up no more
Ps 44:5 them under that *r* up against us
Ps 59:1 me from them that *r* up against me

Ps 74:23 the tumult of those that *r* up
Ps 92:11 the wicked that *r* up against me
Ps 94:16 Who will *r* up for me against the
Ps 119:62 At midnight I will *r* to give
Ps 127:2 It is vain for you to *r* up early
Ps 139:21 with those that *r* up against thee
Ps 140:10 pits, that they *r* not up again
Prov 24:22 their calamity shall *r* suddenly
Prov 28:12 but when the wicked *r*, a man is
Prov 28:28 When the wicked *r*, men hide
Eccl 10:4 of the ruler *r* up against thee
Eccl 12:4 he shall *r* up at the voice of the
Song 2:10 *R* up, my love, my fair one, and
Song 3:2 I will *r* now, and go about the
Is 5:11 Woe unto them that *r* up early in
Is 14:21 that they do not *r*, nor possess
Is 14:22 For I will *r* up against them,
Is 24:20 and it shall fall, and not *r* again
Is 26:14 are deceased, they shall not *r*
Is 28:21 For the LORD shall *r* up as in
Is 32:9 *R* up, ye women that are at ease
Is 33:10 Now will I *r*, saith the LORD
Is 43:17 down together, they shall not *r*
Is 54:17 every tongue that shall *r* against
Is 58:10 shall thy light *r* in obscurity
Jer 25:27 *r* no more, because of the sword
Jer 37:10 yet should they *r* up every man in
Jer 47:2 waters *r* up out of the north, and
Jer 49:14 her, and *r* up to the battle
Jer 51:1 of them that *r* up against me
Jer 51:64 shall not *r* from the evil that I
Lam 1:14 from whom I am not able to *r* up
Dan 7:24 and another shall *r* after them
Amos 5:2 she shall no more *r*
Amos 7:9 I will *r* against the house of
Amos 8:8 it shall *r* up wholly as a flood
Amos 8:14 shall fall, and never *r* up again
Amos 9:5 it shall *r* up wholly like a flood
Obad 1 let us *r* up against her in battle
Nah 1:9 shall not *r* up the second time
Hab 2:7 Shall they not *r* up suddenly that
Zeph 3:8 the day that I *r* up to the prey
Zec 14:13 his hand shall *r* up against the
Mt 5:45 maketh his sun to *r* on the evil
Mt 10:21 the children shall *r* up against
Mt 12:41 shall *r* in judgment with this
Mt 12:42 *r* up in the judgment with this
Mt 20:19 and the third day he shall *r* again
Mt 24:7 For nation shall *r* against nation
Mt 24:11 And many false prophets shall *r*
Mt 26:46 *R*, let us be going
Mt 27:63 After three days I will *r* again
Mk 3:26 if Satan *r* up against himself, and
Mk 4:27 *r* night and day, and the seed
Mk 8:31 and after three days *r* again
Mk 9:31 killed, he shall *r* the third day
Mk 10:34 and the third day he shall *r* again
Mk 10:49 unto him, Be of good comfort, *r*
Mk 12:23 therefore, when they shall *r*
Mk 12:25 when they shall *r* from the dead
Mk 12:26 as touching the dead, that they *r*
Mk 13:8 For nation shall *r* against nation
Mk 13:12 children shall *r* up against their
Mk 13:22 Christs and false prophets shall *r*
Mk 14:42 *R* up, let us go
Lk 5:23 or to say, *R* up and walk
Lk 6:8 *R* up, and stand forth in the midst
Lk 11:7 I cannot *r* and give thee
Lk 11:8 unto you, Though he will not *r*
Lk 11:8 of his importunity he will *r*
Lk 11:31 The queen of the south shall *r* up
Lk 11:32 The men of Nineve shall *r* up in
Lk 12:54 ye see a cloud *r* out of the west
Lk 18:33 and the third day he shall *r* again
Lk 21:10 Nation shall *r* against nation, and
Lk 22:46 *r* and pray, lest ye enter into
Lk 24:7 and the third day *r* again
Lk 24:46 to *r* from the dead the third day
Jn 5:8 Jesus saith unto him, *R*, take up
Jn 11:23 her, Thy brother shall *r* again
Jn 11:24 I know that he shall *r* again in
Jn 20:9 that he must *r* again from the
Acts 3:6 of Jesus Christ of Nazareth *r* up
Acts 10:13 And there came a voice to him, *R*
Acts 26:16 But *r*, and stand upon thy feet
Acts 26:23 first that should *r* from the dead
Rom 15:12 he that shall *r* to reign over the
1Cor 15:15 up, if so be that the dead *r* not
1Cor 15:16 For if the dead *r* not, then is
1Cor 15:29 dead, if the dead *r* not at all
1Cor 15:32 it me, if the dead *r* not
1Th 4:16 the dead in Christ shall *r* first
Heb 7:11 that another priest should *r*
Rev 11:1 and the angel stood, saying, *R*
Rev 13:1 saw a beast *r* up out of the sea,

## RISEN

Gen 19:23 The sun was *r* upon the earth when
Ex 22:3 If the sun be *r* upon him, there
Num 32:14 ye are *r* up in your fathers'
Judg 9:18 ye are *r* up against my father's
Ruth 2:15 And when she was *r* up to glean
1Sa 25:29 Yet a man is *r* to pursue thee, and
2Sa 14:7 the whole family is *r* against
1Kin 8:20 I am *r* up in the room of David my
2Kin 6:15 of the man of God was *r* early
2Chr 6:10 for I am *r* up in the room of
2Chr 13:6 Solomon the son of David, is *r* up
2Chr 21:4 Now when Jehoram was *r* up to the
Ps 20:8 but we are *r*, and stand upright
Ps 27:12 witnesses are *r* up against me
Ps 54:3 For strangers are *r* up against me
Ps 86:14 O God, the proud are *r* against me
Is 60:1 glory of the LORD is *r* upon thee
Eze 7:11 Violence is *r* up into a rod of
Eze 47:5 for the waters were *r*, waters to
Mic 2:8 my people is *r* up as an enemy
Mt 11:11 born of women there hath not *r* a
Mt 14:2 he is *r* from the dead
Mt 17:9 of man be *r* again from the dead
Mt 26:32 But after I am *r* again, I will go
Mt 27:64 the people, He is *r* from the dead
Mt 28:6 for he is *r*, as he said
Mt 28:7 that he is *r* from the dead
Mk 6:14 the Baptist was *r* from the dead
Mk 6:16 he is *r* from the dead
Mk 9:9 Son of man were *r* from the dead
Mk 14:28 But after that I am *r*, I will go
Mk 16:6 he is *r*
Mk 16:9 Now when Jesus was *r* early the
Mk 16:14 which had seen him after he was *r*
Lk 7:16 a great prophet is *r* up among us
Lk 9:7 that John was *r* from the dead
Lk 9:8 of the old prophets was *r* again
Lk 9:19 of the old prophets is *r* again
Lk 13:25 the master of the house is *r* up
Lk 24:6 He is not here, but is *r*
Lk 24:34 Saying, The Lord is *r* indeed
Jn 2:22 therefore he was *r* from the dead
Jn 21:14 after that he was *r* from the dead
Acts 17:3 and *r* again from the dead
Rom 8:34 died, yea rather, that is *r* again
1Cor 15:13 of the dead, then is Christ not *r*
1Cor 15:14 And if Christ be not *r*, then is
1Cor 15:20 But now is Christ *r* from the dead
Col 2:12 wherein also ye are *r* with him
Col 3:1 If ye then be *r* with Christ
Jas 1:11 no sooner *r* with a burning heat

## RISETH

Deut 22:26 for as when a man *r* against his
Josh 6:26 man before the LORD, that *r* up
2Sa 23:4 of the morning, when the sun *r*
Job 9:7 commandeth the sun, and it *r* not
Job 14:12 So man lieth down, and *r* not
Job 24:22 he *r* up, and no man is sure of
Job 27:7 he that *r* up against me as the
Job 31:14 then shall I do when God *r* up
Prov 24:16 seven times, and *r* up again
Prov 31:15 She *r* also while it is yet night,
Is 47:11 shalt not know from whence it *r*
Jer 46:8 Egypt *r* up like a flood, and his
Mic 7:6 the daughter *r* up against her
Jn 13:4 He *r* from supper, and laid aside

## RISING

Lev 13:2 have in the skin of his flesh a *r*
Lev 13:10 if the *r* be white in the skin, and
Lev 13:10 there be quick raw flesh in the *r*
Lev 13:19 of the boil there be a white *r*
Lev 13:28 it is a *r* of the burning, and the
Lev 13:43 if the *r* of the sore be white
Lev 14:56 And for a *r*, and for a scab, and for
Num 2:3 on the east side toward the *r* of
Josh 12:1 Jordan toward the *r* of the sun
2Chr 36:15 *r* up betimes, and sending
Neh 4:21 *r* of the morning till the stars
Job 16:8 my leanness *r* up in me beareth
Job 24:5 *r* betimes for a prey
Job 24:14 The murderer *r* with the light
Ps 50:1 called the earth from the *r* of
Ps 113:3 From the *r* of the sun unto the
Prov 27:14 *r* early in the morning, it shall
Prov 30:31 against whom there is no *r* up
Is 41:25 from the *r* of the sun shall he
Is 45:6 may know from the *r* of the sun
Is 59:19 his glory from the *r* of the sun
Is 60:3 kings to the brightness of thy *r*
Jer 7:13 *r* up early and speaking, but ye
Jer 7:25 daily *r* up early and sending them
Jer 11:7 *r* early and protesting, saying,
Jer 25:3 unto you, *r* early and speaking
Jer 25:4 prophets, *r* early and sending them
Jer 26:5 both *r* up early, and sending them,
Jer 29:19 *r* up early and sending them
Jer 32:33 *r* up early and teaching them, yet
Jer 35:14 unto you, *r* early and speaking
Jer 35:15 *r* up early and sending them,
Jer 44:4 *r* early and sending them, saying,
Lam 3:63 their sitting down, and their *r* up
Mal 1:11 For from the *r* of the sun even
Mk 1:35 *r* up a great while before day, he
Mk 9:10 the *r* from the dead should mean
Mk 16:2 the sepulchre at the *r* of the sun
Lk 2:34 *r* again of many in Israel

## RISSAH *(ris'-sah) An Israelite encampment in the wilderness.*

Num 33:21 from Libnah, and pitched at *R*
Num 33:22 And they journeyed from *R*, and

## RITHMAH *(rith'-mah) An Israelite encampment in the wilderness.*

Num 33:18 from Hazeroth, and pitched in *R*
Num 33:19 And they departed from *R*, and

## RIZPAH *(riz'-pah) A concubine of Saul.*

2Sa 3:7 had a concubine, whose name was *R*
2Sa 21:8 sons of *R* the daughter of Aiah
2Sa 21:10 *R* the daughter of Aiah took
2Sa 21:11 David what *R* the daughter of Aiah

## ROAR

1Chr 16:32 Let the sea *r*, and the fulness
Ps 46:3 Though the waters thereof *r*
Ps 74:4 Thine enemies *r* in the midst of
Ps 96:11 let the sea *r*, and the fulness
Ps 98:7 Let the sea *r*, and the fulness
Ps 104:21 The young lions *r* after their
Is 5:29 they shall *r* like young lions
Is 5:29 yea, they shall *r*, and lay hold of
Is 5:30 in that day they shall *r* against
Is 42:13 he shall cry, yea, *r*
Is 59:11 We *r* all like bears, and mourn
Jer 5:22 though they *r*, yet can they not
Jer 25:30 The LORD shall *r* from on high
Jer 25:30 he shall mightily *r* upon his
Jer 31:35 the sea when the waves thereof *r*
Jer 50:42 their voice shall *r* like the sea
Jer 51:38 They shall *r* together like lions
Jer 51:55 her waves do *r* like great waters
Hos 11:10 he shall *r* like a lion
Hos 11:10 when he shall *r*, then the
Joel 3:16 The LORD also shall *r* out of Zion
Amos 1:2 said, The LORD will *r* from Zion
Amos 3:4 Will a lion *r* in the forest, when

## ROARED

Judg 14:5 a young lion *r* against him
Ps 38:8 I have *r* by reason of the
Is 51:15 divided the sea, whose waves *r*
Jer 2:15 The young lions *r* upon him
Amos 3:8 The lion hath *r*, who will not

## ROARING

Job 4:10 The *r* of the lion, and the voice
Ps 22:1 me, and from the words of my *r*
Ps 22:13 mouths, as a ravening and a *r* lion
Ps 32:3 old through my *r* all the day long
Prov 19:12 wrath is as the *r* of a lion
Prov 20:2 of a king is as the *r* of a lion
Prov 28:15 As a *r* lion, and a ranging bear
Is 5:29 Their *r* shall be like a lion,
Is 5:30 them like the *r* of the sea
Is 31:4 and the young lion *r* on his prey
Eze 19:7 thereof, by the noise of his *r*
Eze 22:25 like a *r* lion ravening the prey
Zeph 3:3 princes within her are *r* lions
Zec 11:3 a voice of the *r* of young lions
Lk 21:25 the sea and the waves *r*
1Pet 5:8 adversary the devil, as a *r* lion

## ROAST

Ex 12:8 *r* with fire, and unleavened bread
Ex 12:9 all with water, but *r* with fire
Deut 16:7 And thou shalt *r* and eat it in the

1Sa 2:15 Give flesh to *r* for the priest
Is 44:16 he roasteth *r*, and is satisfied

**ROB**
Lev 19:13 thy neighbour, neither *r* him
Lev 26:22 which shall *r* you of your
1Sa 23:1 they *r* the threshingfloors
Prov 22:22 *R* not the poor, because he is
Is 10:2 that they may *r* the fatherless
Is 17:14 us, and the lot of them that *r* us
Eze 39:10 *r* those that robbed them, saith
Mal 3:8 Will a man *r* God

**ROBBED**
Judg 9:25 they *r* all that came along that
2Sa 17:8 as a bear *r* of her whelps in the
Ps 119:61 The bands of the wicked have *r* me
Prov 17:12 Let a bear *r* of her whelps meet a
Is 10:13 have *r* their treasures, and I have
Is 42:22 But this is a people *r* and spoiled
Jer 50:37 and they shall be *r*
Eze 33:15 pledge, give again that he had *r*
Eze 39:10 them, and rob those that *r* them
Mal 3:8 Yet ye have *r* me
Mal 3:8 ye say, Wherein have we *r* thee
Mal 3:9 for ye have *r* me, even this whole
2Cor 11:8 I *r* other churches, taking wages

**ROBBER**
Job 5:5 the *r* swalloweth up their
Job 18:9 the *r* shall prevail against him
Eze 18:10 If he beget a son that is a *r*
Jn 10:1 way, the same is a thief and a *r*
Jn 18:40 Now Barabbas was a *r*

**ROBBERS**
Job 12:6 The tabernacles of *r* prosper
Is 42:24 for a spoil, and Israel to the *r*
Jer 7:11 become a den of *r* in your eyes
Eze 7:22 for the *r* shall enter into it, and
Dan 11:14 also the *r* of thy people shall
Hos 6:9 as troops of *r* wait for a man, so
Hos 7:1 the troop of *r* spoileth without
Obad 5 if *r* by night, (how art thou cut
Jn 10:8 came before me are thieves and *r*
Acts 19:37 which are neither *r* of churches
2Cor 11:26 perils of waters, in perils of *r*

**ROBBERY**
Ps 62:10 and become not vain in *r*
Prov 21:7 The *r* of the wicked shall destroy
Is 61:8 I hate *r* for burnt offering
Eze 22:29 used oppression, and exercised *r*
Amos 3:10 up violence and *r* in their palaces
Nah 3:1 it is all full of lies and *r*
Phil 2:6 thought it not *r* to be equal with

**ROBE**
Ex 28:4 breastplate, and an ephod, and a *r*
Ex 28:31 thou shalt make the *r* of the
Ex 28:34 upon the hem of the *r* round about
Ex 29:5 the *r* of the ephod, and the ephod,
Ex 39:22 he made the *r* of the ephod of
Ex 39:23 was an hole in the midst of the *r*
Ex 39:24 of the *r* pomegranates of blue
Ex 39:25 upon the hem of the *r*, round
Ex 39:26 the hem of the *r* to minister in
Lev 8:7 girdle, and clothed him with the *r*
1Sa 18:4 of the *r* that was upon him
1Sa 24:4 off the skirt of Saul's *r* privily
1Sa 24:11 see the skirt of thy *r* in my hand
1Sa 24:11 that I cut off the skirt of thy *r*
1Chr 15:27 clothed with a *r* of fine linen
Job 29:14 my judgment was as a *r* and a
Is 22:21 And I will clothe him with thy *r*
Is 61:10 me with the *r* of righteousness
Jonah 3:6 throne, and he laid his *r* from him
Mic 2:8 ye pull off the *r* with the
Mt 27:28 him, and put on him a scarlet *r*
Mt 27:31 him, they took the *r* off from him
Lk 15:22 servants, Bring forth the best *r*
Lk 23:11 and arrayed him in a gorgeous *r*
Jn 19:2 and they put on him a purple *r*
Jn 19:5 crown of thorns, and the purple *r*

**ROBES**
2Sa 13:18 for with such *r* were the king's
1Kin 22:10 his throne, having put on their *r*
1Kin 22:30 but put thou on thy *r*
2Chr 18:9 on his throne, clothed in their *r*
2Chr 18:29 but put thou on thy *r*
Eze 26:16 thrones, and lay away their *r*
Lk 20:46 which desire to walk in long *r*
Rev 6:11 white *r* were given unto every one
Rev 7:9 the Lamb, clothed with white *r*
Rev 7:13 which are arrayed in white *r*
Rev 7:14 and have washed their *r*, and made

**ROBOAM** *(ro-bo'-am)* See REHOBOAM. *Same as Rehoboam; an ancestor of Jesus.*
Mt 1:7 And Solomon begat *R*
Mt 1:7 and *R* begat Abia

**ROCK**
Ex 17:6 thee there upon the *r* in Horeb
Ex 17:6 and thou shalt smite the *r*
Ex 33:21 me, and thou shalt stand upon a *r*
Ex 33:22 will put thee in a clift of the *r*
Num 20:8 ye unto the *r* before their eyes
Num 20:8 forth to them water out of the *r*
Num 20:10 together before the *r*, and he said
Num 20:10 we fetch you water out of this *r*
Num 20:11 with his rod he smote the *r* twice
Num 24:21 and thou puttest thy nest in a *r*
Deut 8:15 forth water out of the *r* of flint
Deut 32:4 He is the *R*, his work is perfect
Deut 32:13 him to suck honey out of the *r*
Deut 32:13 and oil out of the flinty *r*
Deut 32:15 esteemed the *R* of his salvation
Deut 32:18 Of the *R* that begat thee thou art
Deut 32:30 except their *R* had sold them, and
Deut 32:31 For their *r* is not as our *R*,
Deut 32:37 their *r* in whom they trusted,
Judg 1:36 going up to Akrabbim, from the *r*
Judg 6:20 cakes, and lay them upon this *r*
Judg 6:21 there rose up fire out of the *r*
Judg 6:26 thy God upon the top of this *r*
Judg 7:25 and they slew Oreb upon the *r* Oreb
Judg 13:19 offered it upon a *r* unto the LORD
Judg 15:8 and dwelt in the top of the *r* Etam
Judg 15:11 went to the top of the *r* Etam
Judg 15:13 and brought him up from the *r*
Judg 20:45 wilderness unto the *r* of Rimmon
Judg 20:47 the wilderness unto the *r* Rimmon
Judg 20:47 abode in the *r* Rimmon four months
Judg 21:13 that were in the *r* Rimmon
1Sa 2:2 is there any *r* like our God
1Sa 14:4 was a sharp *r* on the one side
1Sa 14:4 a sharp *r* on the other side
1Sa 23:25 wherefore he came down into a *r*
2Sa 21:10 and spread it for her upon the *r*
2Sa 22:2 And he said, The LORD is my *r*
2Sa 22:3 The God of my *r*
2Sa 22:32 and who is a *r*, save our God
2Sa 22:47 and blessed be my *r*
2Sa 22:47 the God of the *r* of my salvation
2Sa 23:3 the *R* of Israel spake to me, He
1Chr 11:15 went down to the *r* to David
2Chr 25:12 them unto the top of the *r*
2Chr 25:12 them down from the top of the *r*
Neh 9:15 out of the *r* for their thirst
Job 14:18 the *r* is removed out of his place
Job 18:4 shall the *r* be removed out of his
Job 19:24 pen and lead in the *r* for ever
Job 24:8 embrace the *r* for want of a
Job 28:9 putteth forth his hand upon the *r*
Job 29:6 the *r* poured me out rivers of oil
Job 39:1 wild goats of the *r* bring forth
Job 39:28 She dwelleth and abideth on the *r*
Job 39:28 upon the crag of the *r*
Ps 18:2 The LORD is my *r*, and my fortress,
Ps 18:31 or who is a *r* save our God
Ps 18:46 and blessed be my *r*
Ps 27:5 he shall set me up upon a *r*
Ps 28:1 Unto thee will I cry, O LORD my *r*
Ps 31:2 be thou my strong *r*, for an house
Ps 31:3 For thou art my *r* and my fortress
Ps 40:2 clay, and set my feet upon a *r*
Ps 42:9 I will say unto God my *r*, Why
Ps 61:2 lead me to the *r* that is higher
Ps 62:2 He only is my *r* and my salvation
Ps 62:6 He only is my *r* and my salvation
Ps 62:7 the *r* of my strength, and my
Ps 71:3 to save me, for thou art my *r*
Ps 78:16 brought streams also out of the *r*
Ps 78:20 Behold, he smote the *r*, that the
Ps 78:35 remembered that God was their *r*
Ps 81:16 with honey out of the *r* should I
Ps 89:26 my God, and the *r* of my salvation
Ps 92:15 he is my *r*, and there is no
Ps 94:22 and my God is the *r* of my refuge
Ps 95:1 noise to the *r* of our salvation
Ps 105:41 He opened the *r*, and the waters
Ps 114:8 Which turned the *r* into a
Prov 30:19 the way of a serpent upon a *r*
Song 2:14 that art in the clefts of the *r*
Is 2:10 Enter into the *r*, and hide thee in
Is 8:14 for a *r* of offence to both the
Is 10:26 of Midian at the *r* of Oreb
Is 17:10 mindful of the *r* of thy strength
Is 22:16 an habitation for himself in a *r*
Is 32:2 of a great *r* in a weary land
Is 42:11 let the inhabitants of the *r* sing
Is 48:21 to flow out of the *r* for them
Is 48:21 he clave the *r* also, and the
Is 51:1 look unto the *r* whence ye are
Jer 5:3 made their faces harder than a *r*
Jer 13:4 hide it there in a hole of the *r*
Jer 18:14 cometh from the *r* of the field
Jer 21:13 *r* of the plain, saith the LORD
Jer 23:29 that breaketh the *r* in pieces
Jer 48:28 the cities, and dwell in the *r*
Jer 49:16 dwellest in the clefts of the *r*
Eze 24:7 she set it upon the top of a *r*
Eze 24:8 set her blood upon the top of a *r*
Eze 26:4 and make her like the top of a *r*
Eze 26:14 make thee like the top of a *r*
Amos 6:12 Shall horses run upon the *r*
Obad 3 dwellest in the clefts of the *r*
Mt 7:24 which built his house upon a *r*
Mt 7:25 for it was founded upon a *r*
Mt 16:18 upon this *r* I will build my
Mt 27:60 which he had hewn out in the *r*
Mk 15:46 which was hewn out of a *r*
Lk 6:48 and laid the foundation on a *r*
Lk 6:48 for it was founded upon a *r*
Lk 8:6 And some fell upon a *r*
Lk 8:13 They on the *r* are they, which,
Rom 9:33 a stumblingstone and *r* of offence
1Cor 10:4 spiritual *R* that followed them
1Cor 10:4 and that *R* was Christ
1Pet 2:8 a *r* of offence, even to them

**ROCKS**
Num 23:9 from the top of the *r* I see him
1Sa 13:6 in caves, and in thickets, and in *r*
1Sa 24:2 his men upon the *r* of the wild
1Kin 19:11 in pieces the *r* before the LORD
Job 28:10 He cutteth out rivers among the *r*
Job 30:6 caves of the earth, and in the *r*
Ps 78:15 He clave the *r* in the wilderness,
Ps 104:18 and the *r* for the conies
Prov 30:26 make they their houses in the *r*
Is 2:19 shall go into the holes of the *r*
Is 2:21 To go into the clefts of the *r*
Is 2:21 and into the tops of the ragged *r*
Is 7:19 valleys, and in the holes of the *r*
Is 33:16 shall be the munitions of *r*
Is 57:5 valleys under the clifts of the *r*
Jer 4:29 thickets, and climb up upon the *r*
Jer 16:16 and out of the holes of the *r*
Jer 51:25 and roll thee down from the *r*
Nah 1:6 the *r* are thrown down by him
Mt 27:51 earth did quake, and the *r* rent
Acts 27:29 lest we should have fallen upon *r*
Rev 6:15 in the *r* of the mountains
Rev 6:16 And said to the mountains and *r*

**ROD**
Ex 4:2 And he said, A *r*
Ex 4:4 it, and it became a *r* in his hand
Ex 4:17 shalt take this *r* in thine hand
Ex 4:20 Moses took the *r* of God in his
Ex 7:9 shalt say unto Aaron, Take thy *r*
Ex 7:10 cast down his *r* before Pharaoh
Ex 7:12 they cast down every man his *r*
Ex 7:12 but Aaron's *r* swallowed up their
Ex 7:15 the *r* which was turned to a
Ex 7:17 I will smite with the *r* that is
Ex 7:19 Moses, Say unto Aaron, Take thy *r*
Ex 7:20 and he lifted up the *r*, and smote
Ex 8:5 hand with thy *r* over the streams
Ex 8:16 Say unto Aaron, Stretch out thy *r*
Ex 8:17 stretched out his hand with his *r*
Ex 9:23 forth his *r* toward heaven
Ex 10:13 his *r* over the land of Egypt
Ex 14:16 But lift thou up thy *r*, and
Ex 17:5 and thy *r*, wherewith thou smotest
Ex 17:9 with the *r* of God in mine hand
Ex 21:20 servant, or his maid, with a *r*
Lev 27:32 of whatsoever passeth under the *r*
Num 17:2 take of every one of them a *r*
Num 17:2 thou every man's name upon his *r*
Num 17:3 Aaron's name upon the *r* of Levi
Num 17:3 for one *r* shall be for the head

Num 17:5 come to pass, that the man's *r*
Num 17:6 their princes gave him a *r* apiece
Num 17:6 the *r* of Aaron was among their
Num 17:8 the *r* of Aaron for the house of
Num 17:9 looked, and took every man his *r*
Num 17:10 Bring Aaron's *r* again before the
Num 20:8 Take the *r*, and gather thou the
Num 20:9 Moses took the *r* from before the
Num 20:11 with his *r* he smote the rock
1Sa 14:27 end of the *r* that was in his hand
1Sa 14:43 of the *r* that was in mine hand
2Sa 7:14 chasten him with the *r* of men
Job 9:34 Let him take his *r* away from me
Job 21:9 neither is the *r* of God upon them
Ps 2:9 shalt break them with a *r* of iron
Ps 23:4 thy *r* and thy staff they comfort
Ps 74:2 the *r* of thine inheritance, which
Ps 89:32 their transgression with the *r*
Ps 110:2 The LORD shall send the *r* of thy
Ps 125:3 For the *r* of the wicked shall not
Prov 10:13 but a *r* is for the back of him
Prov 13:24 that spareth his *r* hateth his son
Prov 14:3 of the foolish is a *r* of pride
Prov 22:8 the *r* of his anger shall fail
Prov 22:15 but the *r* of correction shall
Prov 23:13 if thou beatest him with the *r*
Prov 23:14 Thou shalt beat him with the *r*
Prov 26:3 ass, and a *r* for the fool's back
Prov 29:15 The *r* and reproof give wisdom
Is 9:4 the *r* of his oppressor, as in the
Is 10:5 the *r* of mine anger, and the staff
Is 10:15 as if the *r* should shake itself
Is 10:24 he shall smite thee with a *r*
Is 10:26 as his *r* was upon the sea, so
Is 11:1 a *r* out of the stem of Jesse
Is 11:4 the earth with the *r* of his mouth
Is 14:29 because the *r* of him that smote
Is 28:27 a staff, and the cummin with a *r*
Is 30:31 beaten down, which smote with a *r*
Jer 1:11 I see a *r* of an almond tree
Jer 10:16 and Israel is the *r* of his
Jer 48:17 staff broken, and the beautiful *r*
Jer 51:19 and Israel is the *r* of his
Lam 3:1 affliction by the *r* of his wrath
Eze 7:10 the *r* hath blossomed, pride hath
Eze 7:11 risen up into a *r* of wickedness
Eze 19:14 gone out of a *r* of her branches
Eze 19:14 strong *r* to be a sceptre to rule
Eze 20:37 cause you to pass under the *r*
Eze 21:10 it contemneth the *r* of my son
Eze 21:13 if the sword contemn even the *r*
Mic 5:1 of Israel with a *r* upon the cheek
Mic 6:9 hear ye the *r*, and who hath
Mic 7:14 Feed thy people with thy *r*
1Cor 4:21 shall I come unto you with a *r*
Heb 9:4 Aaron's *r* that budded, and the
Rev 2:27 shall rule them with a *r* of iron
Rev 11:1 was given me a reed like unto a *r*
Rev 12:5 rule all nations with a *r* of iron
Rev 19:15 shall rule them with a *r* of iron

**RODE**
Gen 24:61 they *r* upon the camels, and
Judg 10:4 sons that *r* on thirty ass colts
Judg 12:14 that *r* on threescore and ten ass
1Sa 25:20 as she *r* on the ass, that she
1Sa 25:42 *r* upon an ass, with five damsels
1Sa 30:17 which *r* upon camels, and fled
2Sa 18:9 Absalom *r* upon a mule, and the
2Sa 22:11 he *r* upon a cherub, and did fly
1Kin 13:13 and he *r* thereon,
1Kin 18:45 And Ahab *r*, and went to Jezreel
2Kin 9:16 So Jehu *r* in a chariot, and went
2Kin 9:25 thou *r* together after Ahab his
Neh 2:12 me, save the beast that I *r* upon
Est 8:14 So the posts that *r* upon mules
Ps 18:10 he *r* upon a cherub, and did fly

**RODS**
Gen 30:37 Jacob took him *r* of green poplar,
Gen 30:37 white appear which was in the *r*
Gen 30:38 he set the *r* which he had pilled
Gen 30:39 the flocks conceived before the *r*
Gen 30:41 that Jacob laid the *r* before the
Gen 30:41 they might conceive among the *r*
Ex 7:12 Aaron's rod swallowed up their *r*
Num 17:2 house of their fathers twelve *r*
Num 17:6 fathers' houses, even twelve *r*
Num 17:6 rod of Aaron was among their *r*
Num 17:7 Moses laid up the *r* before the
Num 17:9 Moses brought out all the *r* from
Eze 19:11 she had strong *r* for the sceptres
Eze 19:12 her strong *r* were broken and
2Cor 11:25 Thrice was I beaten with *r*

**ROE**
2Sa 2:18 was as light of foot as a wild *r*
Prov 5:19 as the loving hind and pleasant *r*
Prov 6:5 Deliver thyself as a *r* from the
Song 2:9 is like a *r* or a young hart
Song 2:17 be thou like a *r* or a young hart
Song 8:14 be thou like to a *r* or to a young
Is 13:14 And it shall be as the chased *r*

**ROEBUCK**
Deut 12:15 may eat thereof, as of the *r*
Deut 12:22 Even as the *r* and the hart is
Deut 14:5 The hart, and the *r*, and the fallow
Deut 15:22 shall eat it alike, as the *r*

**ROES**
1Chr 12:8 swift as the *r* upon the mountains
Song 2:7 daughters of Jerusalem, by the *r*
Song 3:5 daughters of Jerusalem, by the *r*
Song 4:5 like two young *r* that are twins
Song 7:3 like two young *r* that are twins

**ROGELIM** *(ro'-ghel-im) A city in Gilead.*
2Sa 17:27 and Barzillai the Gileadite of *R*
2Sa 19:31 the Gileadite came down from *R*

**ROHGAH** *(ro'-gah) A son of Shamer.*
1Chr 7:34 Ahi, and *R*, Jehubbah, and Aram

**ROLL**
Gen 29:8 till they *r* the stone from the
Josh 10:18 *R* great stones upon the mouth of
1Sa 14:33 *r* a great stone unto me this day
Ezr 6:2 in the province of the Medes, a *r*
Is 8:1 said unto me, Take thee a great *r*
Jer 36:2 Take thee a *r* of a book, and write
Jer 36:4 unto him, upon a *r* of a book
Jer 36:6 go thou, and read in the *r*
Jer 36:14 Take in thine hand the *r* wherein
Jer 36:14 of Neriah took the *r* in his hand
Jer 36:20 but they laid up the *r* in the
Jer 36:21 king sent Jehudi to fetch the *r*
Jer 36:23 until all the *r* was consumed in
Jer 36:25 king that he would not burn the *r*
Jer 36:27 that the king had burned the *r*
Jer 36:28 Take thee again another *r*
Jer 36:28 words that were in the first *r*
Jer 36:29 Thou hast burned this *r*, saying,
Jer 36:32 Then took Jeremiah another *r*
Jer 51:25 *r* thee down from the rocks, and
Eze 2:9 a *r* of a book was therein
Eze 3:1 eat this *r*, and go speak unto the
Eze 3:2 and he caused me to eat that *r*
Eze 3:3 with this *r* that I give thee
Mic 1:10 of Aphrah *r* thyself in the dust
Zec 5:1 and looked, and behold a flying *r*
Zec 5:2 And I answered, I see a flying *r*
Mk 16:3 Who shall *r* us away the stone

**ROLLED**
Gen 29:3 they *r* the stone from the well's
Gen 29:10 *r* the stone from the well's mouth
Josh 5:9 This day have I *r* away the
Job 30:14 they *r* themselves upon me
Is 9:5 noise, and garments *r* in blood
Is 34:4 shall be *r* together as a scroll
Mt 27:60 he *r* a great stone to the door of
Mt 28:2 *r* back the stone from the door,
Mk 15:46 *r* a stone unto the door of the
Mk 16:4 saw that the stone was *r* away
Lk 24:2 they found the stone *r* away from
Rev 6:14 as a scroll when it is *r* together

**ROMAMTI-EZER** *(romam'-ti-e'-zur) A sanctuary servant.*
1Chr 25:4 Hanani, Eliathah, Giddalti, and *R*
1Chr 25:31 The four and twentieth to *R*

**ROMAN** *(ro'-mun)* See ROMANS. *A citizen of Rome.*
Acts 22:25 you to scourge a man that is a *R*
Acts 22:26 for this man is a *R*
Acts 22:27 unto him, Tell me, art thou a *R*
Acts 22:29 after he knew that he was a *R*
Acts 23:27 having understood that he was a *R*

**ROMANS** *(ro'-muns)*
Jn 11:48 the *R* shall come and take away
Acts 16:21 neither to observe, being *R*
Acts 16:37 us openly uncondemned, being *R*
Acts 16:38 when they heard that they were *R*
Acts 25:16 the *R* to deliver any man to die
Acts 28:17 Jerusalem into the hands of the *R*
Rom *s* Written to the *R* from Corinthus

**ROME** *(rome)* See ROMAN. *Administrative center of the Roman Empire.*
Acts 2:10 about Cyrene, and strangers of *R*
Acts 18:2 all Jews to depart from *R*
Acts 19:21 been there, I must also see *R*
Acts 23:11 must thou bear witness also at *R*
Acts 28:14 and so we went toward *R*
Acts 28:16 And when we came to *R*, the
Rom 1:7 To all that be in *R*, beloved of
Rom 1:15 gospel to you that are at *R* also
Gal *s* Unto the Galatians written from *R*
Eph *s* Written from *R* unto the Ephesians
Phil *s* from *R* by Epaphroditus
Col *s* Written from *R* to the Colossians
2Ti 1:17 But, when he was in *R*, he sought
2Ti *s* the Ephesians, was written from *R*
Philem *s* Written from *R* to Philemon

**ROOF**
Gen 19:8 they under the shadow of my *r*
Deut 22:8 shalt make a battlement for thy *r*
Josh 2:6 them up to the *r* of the house
Josh 2:6 she had laid in order upon the *r*
Josh 2:8 she came up unto them upon the *r*
Judg 16:27 there were upon the *r* about three
2Sa 11:2 walked upon the *r* of the king's
2Sa 11:2 from the *r* he saw a woman washing
2Sa 18:24 the *r* over the gate unto the wall
Neh 8:16 every one upon the *r* of his house
Job 29:10 cleaved to the *r* of their mouth
Ps 137:6 cleave to the *r* of my mouth
Song 7:9 the *r* of thy mouth like the best
Lam 4:4 to the *r* of his mouth for thirst
Eze 3:26 cleave to the *r* of thy mouth
Eze 40:13 *r* of one little chamber to the
Eze 40:13 chamber to the *r* of another
Mt 8:8 thou shouldest come under my *r*
Mk 2:4 they uncovered the *r* where he was
Lk 7:6 thou shouldest enter under my *r*

**ROOM**
Gen 24:23 is there *r* in thy father's house
Gen 24:25 enough, and *r* to lodge in
Gen 24:31 the house, and *r* for the camels
Gen 26:22 now the LORD hath made *r* for us
2Sa 19:13 me continually in the *r* of Joab
1Kin 2:35 Jehoiada in his *r* over the host
1Kin 2:35 the king put in the *r* of Abiathar
1Kin 5:1 him king in the *r* of his father
1Kin 5:5 will set upon thy throne in thy *r*
1Kin 8:20 up in the *r* of David my father
1Kin 19:16 anoint to be prophet in thy *r*
2Kin 15:25 killed him, and reigned in his *r*
2Kin 23:34 in the *r* of Josiah his father
2Chr 6:10 up in the *r* of David my father
2Chr 26:1 made him king in the *r* of his
Ps 31:8 hast set my feet in a large *r*
Ps 80:9 Thou preparedst *r* before it
Prov 18:16 A man's gift maketh *r* for him
Mal 3:10 not be *r* enough to receive it
Mt 2:22 in the *r* of his father Herod
Mk 2:2 there was no *r* to receive them
Mk 14:15 you a large upper *r* furnished
Lk 2:7 was no *r* for them in the inn
Lk 12:17 because I have no *r* where to
Lk 14:8 sit not down in the highest *r*
Lk 14:9 with shame to take the lowest *r*
Lk 14:10 go and sit down in the lowest *r*
Lk 14:22 hast commanded, and yet there is *r*
Lk 22:12 you a large upper *r* furnished
Acts 1:13 in, they went up into an upper *r*
Acts 24:27 Porcius Festus came into Felix' *r*
1Cor 14:16 *r* of the unlearned say Amen at

**ROOMS**
Gen 6:14 *r* shalt thou make in the ark, and
1Kin 20:24 place, and put captains in their *r*
1Chr 4:41 this day, and dwelt in their *r*
Mt 23:6 And love the uppermost *r* at feasts
Mk 12:39 and the uppermost *r* at feasts
Lk 14:7 how they chose out the chief *r*
Lk 20:46 and the chief *r* at feasts

**ROOT**
Deut 29:18 among you a *r* that beareth gall
Judg 5:14 there a *r* of them against Amalek
1Kin 14:15 he shall *r* up Israel out of this
2Kin 19:30 shall yet again take *r* downward
Job 5:3 I have seen the foolish taking *r*
Job 14:8 Though the *r* thereof wax old in

Job 19:28 seeing the *r* of the matter is
Job 29:19 My *r* was spread out by the waters
Job 31:12 would *r* out all mine increase
Ps 52:5 *r* thee out of the land of the
Ps 80:9 and didst cause it to take deep *r*
Prov 12:3 but the *r* of the righteous shall
Prov 12:12 but the *r* of the righteous
Is 5:24 so their *r* shall be as rottenness
Is 11:10 day there shall be a *r* of Jesse
Is 14:29 for out of the serpent's *r* shall
Is 14:30 and I will kill thy *r* with famine
Is 27:6 them that come of Jacob to take *r*
Is 37:31 Judah shall again take *r* downward
Is 40:24 shall not take *r* in the earth
Is 53:2 as a *r* out of a dry ground
Jer 1:10 to *r* out, and to pull down, and to
Jer 12:2 them, yea, they have taken *r*
Eze 31:7 for his *r* was by great waters
Hos 9:16 their *r* is dried up, they shall
Mal 4:1 leave them neither *r* nor branch
Mt 3:10 is laid unto the *r* of the trees
Mt 13:6 and because they had no *r*, they
Mt 13:21 Yet hath he not *r* in himself
Mt 13:29 ye *r* up also the wheat with them
Mk 4:6 and because it had no *r*, it
Mk 4:17 have no *r* in themselves, and so
Lk 3:9 is laid unto the *r* of the trees
Lk 8:13 and these have no *r*, which for a
Lk 17:6 tree, Be thou plucked up by the *r*
Rom 11:16 if the *r* be holy, so are the
Rom 11:17 and with them partakest of the *r*
Rom 11:18 not the *r*, but the *r* thee
Rom 15:12 There shall be a *r* of Jesse
1Ti 6:10 of money is the *r* of all evil
Heb 12:15 lest any *r* of bitterness
Rev 5:5 the *R* of David, hath prevailed to
Rev 22:16 I am the *r* and the offspring of

**ROOTED**
Deut 29:28 the LORD *r* them out of their land
Job 18:14 shall be *r* out of his tabernacle
Job 31:8 yea, let my offspring be *r* out
Prov 2:22 shall be *r* out of it
Zeph 2:4 noonday, and Ekron shall be *r* up
Mt 15:13 hath not planted, shall be *r* up
Eph 3:17 that ye, being *r* and grounded in
Col 2:7 *R* and built up in him, and

**ROOTS**
2Chr 7:20 the *r* out of my land which I have
Job 8:17 His *r* are wrapped about the heap,
Job 18:16 His *r* shall be dried up beneath,
Job 28:9 the mountains by the *r*
Job 30:4 and juniper *r* for their meat
Is 11:1 a Branch shall grow out of his *r*
Jer 17:8 spreadeth out her *r* by the river
Eze 17:6 the *r* thereof were under him
Eze 17:7 vine did bend her *r* toward him
Eze 17:9 he not pull up the *r* thereof
Eze 17:9 to pluck it up by the *r* thereof
Dan 4:15 the stump of his *r* in the earth
Dan 4:23 of the *r* thereof in the earth
Dan 4:26 to leave the stump of the tree *r*
Dan 7:8 first horns plucked up by the *r*
Dan 11:7 her *r* shall one stand up in his
Hos 14:5 and cast forth his *r* as Lebanon
Amos 2:9 from above, and his *r* from beneath
Mk 11:20 the fig tree dried up from the *r*
Jude 12 twice dead, plucked up by the *r*

**ROPES**
Judg 16:11 new *r* that never were occupied
Judg 16:12 Delilah therefore took new *r*
2Sa 17:13 all Israel bring *r* to that city
1Kin 20:31 *r* upon our heads, and go out to
1Kin 20:32 put *r* on their heads, and came to
Acts 27:32 cut off the *r* of the boat

**ROSE**
Gen 4:8 that Cain *r* up against Abel his
Gen 18:16 the men *r* up from thence, and
Gen 19:1 Lot seeing them *r* up to meet them
Gen 20:8 Therefore Abimelech *r* early in
Gen 21:14 Abraham *r* up early in the morning
Gen 21:32 then Abimelech *r* up, and Phichol
Gen 22:3 Abraham *r* up early in the morning
Gen 22:3 *r* up, and went unto the place of
Gen 22:19 unto his young men, and they *r* up
Gen 24:54 they *r* up in the morning, and he
Gen 25:34 drink, and *r* up, and went his way
Gen 26:31 they *r* up betimes in the morning,
Gen 28:18 Jacob *r* up early in the morning,
Gen 31:17 Then Jacob *r* up, and set his sons
Gen 31:21 and he *r* up, and passed over the
Gen 31:55 early in the morning Laban *r* up
Gen 32:22 he *r* up that night, and took his
Gen 32:31 over Penuel the sun *r* upon him
Gen 37:35 his daughters *r* up to comfort him
Gen 43:15 *r* up, and went down to Egypt, and
Gen 46:5 Jacob *r* up from Beer-sheba
Ex 10:23 neither *r* any from his place for
Ex 12:30 Pharaoh *r* up in the night, he, and
Ex 15:7 them that *r* up against thee
Ex 24:4 *r* up early in the morning, and
Ex 24:13 And Moses *r* up, and his minister
Ex 32:6 they *r* up early on the morrow, and
Ex 32:6 eat and to drink, and *r* up to play
Ex 33:8 that all the people *r* up
Ex 33:10 and all the people *r* up and
Ex 34:4 Moses *r* up early in the morning,
Num 14:40 they *r* up early in the morning,
Num 16:2 they *r* up before Moses, with
Num 16:25 And Moses *r* up and went unto
Num 22:13 Balaam *r* up in the morning, and
Num 22:14 And the princes of Moab *r* up
Num 22:21 Balaam *r* up in the morning, and
Num 24:25 And Balaam *r* up, and went and
Num 25:7 saw it, he *r* up from among the
Deut 33:2 and *r* up from Seir unto them
Josh 3:1 Joshua *r* early in the morning
Josh 3:16 *r* up upon an heap very far from
Josh 6:12 Joshua *r* early in the morning, and
Josh 6:15 that they *r* early about the
Josh 7:16 So Joshua *r* up early in the
Josh 8:10 Joshua *r* up early in the morning,
Josh 8:14 *r* up early, and the men of the
Judg 6:21 there *r* up fire out of the rock,
Judg 6:38 for he *r* up early on the morrow,
Judg 7:1 *r* up early, and pitched beside the
Judg 9:34 And Abimelech *r* up, and all the
Judg 9:35 and Abimelech *r* up, and the people
Judg 9:43 he *r* up against them, and smote
Judg 19:5 morning, that he *r* up to depart
Judg 19:7 And when the man *r* up to depart
Judg 19:9 And when the man *r* up to depart
Judg 19:10 not tarry that night, but he *r* up
Judg 19:27 her lord *r* up in the morning, and
Judg 19:28 up upon an ass, and the man *r* up
Judg 20:5 And the men of Gibeah *r* against me
Judg 20:19 of Israel *r* up in the morning
Judg 20:33 of Israel *r* up out of their place
Judg 21:4 morrow, that the people *r* early
Ruth 3:14 she *r* up before one could know
1Sa 1:9 So Hannah *r* up after they had
1Sa 1:19 they *r* up in the morning early,
1Sa 15:12 when Samuel *r* early to meet Saul
1Sa 16:13 So Samuel *r* up, and went to Ramah
1Sa 17:20 David *r* up early in the morning,
1Sa 24:7 But Saul *r* up out of the cave, and
1Sa 28:25 Then they *r* up, and went away that
1Sa 29:11 his men *r* up early to depart in
2Sa 15:2 Absalom *r* up early, and stood
2Sa 18:31 all them that *r* up against thee
2Sa 22:40 them that *r* up against me hast
2Sa 22:49 above them that *r* up against me
1Kin 1:49 *r* up, and went every man his way
1Kin 2:19 the king *r* up to meet her, and
1Kin 3:21 when I *r* in the morning to give
1Kin 21:16 that Ahab *r* up to go down to the
2Kin 3:22 they *r* up early in the morning,
2Kin 3:24 of Israel, the Israelites *r* up
2Kin 7:5 they *r* up in the twilight, to go
2Kin 8:21 he *r* by night, and smote the
2Chr 20:20 they *r* early in the morning, and
2Chr 21:9 he *r* up by night, and smote the
2Chr 26:19 the leprosy even *r* up in his
2Chr 28:15 which were expressed by name *r* up
2Chr 29:20 Then Hezekiah the king *r* early
Ezr 1:5 Then *r* up the chief of the
Ezr 5:2 Then *r* up Zerubbabel the son of
Ezr 10:6 Then Ezra *r* up from before the
Neh 3:1 priest *r* up with his brethren the
Neh 4:14 *r* up, and said unto the nobles, and
Job 1:5 *r* up early in the morning, and
Ps 18:39 me those that *r* up against me
Ps 124:2 side, when men *r* up against us
Song 2:1 I am the *r* of Sharon, and the lily
Song 5:5 I *r* up to open to my beloved
Is 35:1 rejoice, and blossom as the *r*
Jer 26:17 Then *r* up certain of the elders
Lam 3:62 of those that *r* up against me
Dan 3:24 *r* up in haste, and spake, and said
Dan 8:27 afterward I *r* up, and did the
Jonah 1:3 But Jonah *r* up to flee unto
Jonah 4:7 when the morning *r* the next day
Zeph 3:7 but they *r* early, and corrupted
Mk 10:50 he, casting away his garment, *r*
Lk 4:29 *r* up, and thrust him out of the
Lk 5:25 immediately he *r* up before them
Lk 5:28 left all, *r* up, and followed him
Lk 16:31 though one *r* from the dead
Lk 22:45 when he *r* up from prayer, and was
Lk 24:33 they *r* up the same hour, and
Jn 11:31 that she *r* up hastily and went out
Acts 5:17 Then the high priest *r* up
Acts 5:36 before these days *r* up Theudas
Acts 5:37 After this man *r* up Judas of
Acts 10:41 with him after he *r* from the dead
Acts 14:20 stood round about him, he *r* up
Acts 15:5 But there *r* up certain of the
Acts 15:7 been much disputing, Peter *r* up
Acts 16:22 the multitude *r* up together
Acts 26:30 he had thus spoken, the king *r* up
Rom 14:9 this end Christ both died, and *r*
1Cor 10:7 to eat and drink, and *r* up to play
1Cor 15:4 that he *r* again the third day
1Cor 15:12 preached that he *r* from the dead
2Cor 5:15 which died for them, and *r* again
1Th 4:14 *r* again, even so them also which
Rev 19:3 her smoke *r* up for ever and ever

**ROT**
Num 5:21 the LORD doth make thy thigh to *r*
Num 5:22 belly to swell, and thy thigh to *r*
Num 5:27 shall swell, and her thigh shall *r*
Prov 10:7 the name of the wicked shall *r*
Is 40:20 chooseth a tree that will not *r*

**ROTTEN**
Job 13:28 as a *r* thing, consumeth, as a
Job 41:27 iron as straw, and brass as *r* wood
Jer 38:11 old *r* rags, and let them down by
Jer 38:12 *r* rags under thine armholes under
Joel 1:17 The seed is *r* under their clods,

**ROTTENNESS**
Prov 12:4 ashamed is as *r* in his bones
Prov 14:30 but envy the *r* of the bones
Is 5:24 so their root shall be as *r*
Hos 5:12 and to the house of Judah as *r*
Hab 3:16 *r* entered into my bones, and I

**ROUGH**
Deut 21:4 down the heifer unto a *r* valley
Is 27:8 he stayeth his *r* wind in the day
Is 40:4 straight, and the *r* places plain
Jer 51:27 to come up as the *r* caterpillers
Dan 8:21 the *r* goat is the king of Grecia
Zec 13:4 they wear a *r* garment to deceive
Lk 3:5 the *r* ways shall be made smooth

**ROUGHLY**
Gen 42:7 unto them, and spake *r* unto them
Gen 42:30 lord of the land, spake *r* to us
1Sa 20:10 what if thy father answer thee *r*
1Kin 12:13 And the king answered the people *r*
2Chr 10:13 And the king answered them *r*
Prov 18:23 but the rich answereth *r*

**ROW**
Ex 28:17 the first *r* shall be a sardius, a
Ex 28:17 this shall be the first *r*
Ex 28:18 the second *r* shall be an emerald,
Ex 28:19 And the third *r* a ligure, an agate
Ex 28:20 And the fourth *r* a beryl, and an
Ex 39:10 the first *r* was a sardius, a
Ex 39:10 this was the first *r*
Ex 39:11 And the second *r*, an emerald, a
Ex 39:12 And the third *r*, a ligure, an
Ex 39:13 And the fourth *r*, a beryl, an onyx
Lev 24:6 set them in two rows, six on a *r*
Lev 24:7 put pure frankincense upon each *r*
1Kin 6:36 stone, and a *r* of cedar beams
1Kin 7:3 five pillars, fifteen in a *r*
1Kin 7:12 a *r* of cedar beams, both for the
Ezr 6:4 stones, and a *r* of new timber
Eze 46:23 there was a *r* of building round

**ROWS**
Ex 28:17 of stones, even four *r* of stones
Ex 39:10 they set in it four *r* of stones
Lev 24:6 And thou shalt set them in two *r*
1Kin 6:36 court with three *r* of hewed stone
1Kin 7:2 upon four *r* of cedar pillars,
1Kin 7:4 And there were windows in three *r*
1Kin 7:12 was with three *r* of hewed stones

1Kin 7:18 two *r* round about upon the one
1Kin 7:20 were two hundred in *r* round about
1Kin 7:24 the knops were cast in two *r*
1Kin 7:42 even two *r* of pomegranates for
2Chr 4:3 Two *r* of oxen were cast, when it
2Chr 4:13 two *r* of pomegranates on each
Ezr 6:4 With three *r* of great stones, and
Song 1:10 are comely with *r* of jewels
Eze 46:23 places under the *r* round about

**ROYAL**
Gen 49:20 fat, and he shall yield *r* dainties
Josh 10:2 city, as one of the *r* cities
1Sa 27:5 dwell in the *r* city with thee
2Sa 12:26 of Ammon, and took the *r* city
1Kin 10:13 Solomon gave her of his *r* bounty
2Kin 11:1 arose and destroyed all the seed *r*
2Kin 25:25 son of Elishama, of the seed *r*
1Chr 29:25 bestowed upon him such *r* majesty
2Chr 22:10 the seed *r* of the house of Judah
Est 1:7 *r* wine in abundance, according to
Est 1:9 *r* house which belonged to king
Est 1:11 before the king with the crown *r*
Est 1:19 let there go a *r* commandment from
Est 1:19 let the king give her *r* estate
Est 2:16 his house *r* in the tenth month
Est 2:17 so that he set the *r* crown upon
Est 5:1 that Esther put on her *r* apparel
Est 5:1 his *r* throne in the *r* house
Est 6:8 Let the *r* apparel be brought
Est 6:8 the crown *r* which is set upon his
Est 8:15 of the king in *r* apparel of blue
Is 62:3 a *r* diadem in the hand of thy God
Jer 41:1 son of Elishama, of the seed *r*
Jer 43:10 spread his *r* pavilion over them
Dan 6:7 together to establish a *r* statute
Acts 12:21 day Herod, arrayed in *r* apparel
Jas 2:8 If ye fulfil the *r* law according
1Pet 2:9 a *r* priesthood, an holy nation, a

**RUBIES**
Job 28:18 the price of wisdom is above *r*
Prov 3:15 She is more precious than *r*
Prov 8:11 For wisdom is better than *r*
Prov 20:15 is gold, and a multitude of *r*
Prov 31:10 for her price is far above *r*
Lam 4:7 were more ruddy in body than *r*

**RUDDY**
1Sa 16:12 Now he was *r*, and withal of a
1Sa 17:42 for he was but a youth, and *r*
Song 5:10 My beloved is white and *r*, the
Lam 4:7 they were more *r* in body than

**RUFUS** *(ru'-fus)*
*1. Son of Simon the Cyrenian.*
Mk 15:21 the father of Alexander and *R*
*2. A Christian in Rome.*
Rom 16:13 Salute *R* chosen in the Lord, and

**RUHAMAH** *(ru-ha'-mah) A symbolic name of Israel.*
Hos 2:1 and to your sisters, *R*

**RUIN**
2Chr 28:23 But they were the *r* of him
Ps 89:40 brought his strong holds to *r*
Prov 24:22 and who knoweth the *r* of them both
Prov 26:28 and a flattering mouth worketh *r*
Is 3:6 let this *r* be under thy hand
Is 23:13 and he brought it to *r*
Is 25:2 of a defenced city a *r*
Eze 18:30 so iniquity shall not be your *r*
Eze 27:27 of the seas in the day of thy *r*
Eze 31:13 Upon his *r* shall all the fowls of
Lk 6:49 the *r* of that house was great

**RULE**
Gen 1:16 the greater light to *r* the day
Gen 1:16 the lesser light to *r* the night
Gen 1:18 to *r* over the day and over the
Gen 3:16 husband, and he shall *r* over thee
Gen 4:7 desire, and thou shalt *r* over him
Lev 25:43 Thou shalt not *r* over him with
Lev 25:46 ye shall not *r* one over another
Lev 25:53 the other shall not *r* with rigour
Judg 8:22 *R* thou over us, both thou, and thy
Judg 8:23 unto them, I will not *r* over you
Judg 8:23 neither shall my son *r* over you
Judg 8:23 the LORD shall *r* over you
1Kin 9:23 which bare *r* over the people that
1Kin 22:31 that had *r* over his chariots
2Chr 8:10 that bare *r* over the people
Neh 5:15 servants bare *r* over the people
Est 1:22 should bear *r* in his own house
Est 9:1 that the Jews had *r* over them
Ps 110:2 *r* thou in the midst of thine
Ps 136:8 The sun to *r* by day
Ps 136:9 The moon and stars to *r* by night
Prov 8:16 By me princes *r*, and nobles, even
Prov 12:24 hand of the diligent shall bear *r*
Prov 17:2 A wise servant shall have *r* over
Prov 19:10 a servant to have *r* over princes
Prov 25:28 He that hath no *r* over his own
Prov 29:2 but when the wicked beareth *r*
Eccl 2:19 yet shall he have *r* over all my
Is 3:4 and babes shall *r* over them
Is 3:12 oppressors, and women *r* over them
Is 14:2 and they shall *r* over their
Is 19:4 a fierce king shall *r* over them
Is 28:14 that *r* this people which is in
Is 32:1 and princes shall *r* in judgment
Is 40:10 hand, and his arm shall *r* for him
Is 41:2 him, and made him *r* over kings
Is 44:13 carpenter stretcheth out his *r*
Is 52:5 they that *r* over them make them
Is 63:19 thou never barest *r* over them
Jer 5:31 the priests bear *r* by their means
Eze 19:11 the sceptres of them that bare *r*
Eze 19:14 strong rod to be a sceptre to *r*
Eze 20:33 poured out, will I *r* over you
Eze 29:15 shall no more *r* over the nations
Dan 2:39 which shall bear *r* over all the
Dan 4:26 have known that the heavens do *r*
Dan 11:3 that shall *r* with great dominion,
Dan 11:39 shall cause them to *r* over many
Joel 2:17 the heathen should *r* over them
Zec 6:13 and shall sit and *r* upon his throne
Mt 2:6 that shall *r* my people Israel
Mk 10:42 to *r* over the Gentiles exercise
1Cor 15:24 when he shall have put down all *r*
2Cor 10:13 *r* which God hath distributed to
2Cor 10:15 you according to our *r* abundantly
Gal 6:16 many as walk according to this *r*
Phil 3:16 let us walk by the same *r*
Col 3:15 the peace of God *r* in your hearts
1Ti 3:5 know not how to *r* his own house
1Ti 5:17 Let the elders that *r* well be
Heb 13:7 them which have the *r* over you
Heb 13:17 them that have the *r* over you
Heb 13:24 all them that have the *r* over you
Rev 2:27 he shall *r* them with a rod of
Rev 12:5 who was to *r* all nations with a
Rev 19:15 he shall *r* them with a rod of

**RULED**
Gen 24:2 that *r* over all that he had, Put,
Gen 41:40 thy word shall all my people be *r*
Josh 12:2 *r* from Aroer, which is upon the
Ruth 1:1 in the days when the judges *r*
1Kin 5:16 which *r* over the people that
1Chr 26:6 that *r* throughout the house of
Ezr 4:20 which have *r* over all countries
Ps 106:41 they that hated them *r* over them
Is 14:6 he that *r* the nations in anger,
Lam 5:8 Servants have *r* over us
Eze 34:4 and with cruelty have ye *r* them
Dan 5:21 high God *r* in the kingdom of men
Dan 11:4 to his dominion which he *r*

**RULER**
Gen 41:43 he made him *r* over all the land
Gen 43:16 he said to the *r* of his house
Gen 45:8 a *r* throughout all the land of
Ex 22:28 nor curse the *r* of thy people
Lev 4:22 When a *r* hath sinned, and done
Num 13:2 a man, every one a *r* among them
Judg 9:30 when Zebul the *r* of the city
1Sa 25:30 have appointed thee *r* over Israel
2Sa 6:21 to appoint me *r* over the people
2Sa 7:8 to be *r* over my people, over
2Sa 20:26 Jairite was a chief *r* about David
1Kin 1:35 appointed him to be *r* over Israel
1Kin 11:28 he made him *r* over all the charge
2Kin 25:22 of Ahikam, the son of Shaphan, *r*
1Chr 5:2 and of him came the chief *r*
1Chr 9:11 the *r* of the house of God
1Chr 9:20 was the *r* over them in time past
1Chr 11:2 thou shalt be *r* over my people
1Chr 17:7 be *r* over my people Israel
1Chr 26:24 of Moses, was *r* of the treasures
1Chr 27:4 his course was Mikloth also the *r*
1Chr 27:16 the *r* of the Reubenites was
1Chr 28:4 he hath chosen Judah to be the *r*
2Chr 6:5 to be a *r* over my people Israel
2Chr 7:18 fail thee a man to be *r* in Israel
2Chr 11:22 to be *r* among his brethren
2Chr 19:11 the *r* of the house of Judah, for
2Chr 26:11 the scribe and Maaseiah the *r*
2Chr 31:12 which Cononiah the Levite was *r*
2Chr 31:13 Azariah the *r* of the house of God
Neh 3:9 the *r* of the half part of
Neh 3:12 the *r* of the half part of
Neh 3:14 the *r* of part of Beth-haccerem
Neh 3:15 Colhozeh, the *r* of part of Mizpah
Neh 3:16 the *r* of the half part of
Neh 3:17 the *r* of the half part of Keilah,
Neh 3:18 the *r* of the half part of Keilah
Neh 3:19 the *r* of Mizpah, another piece
Neh 7:2 Hananiah the *r* of the palace,
Neh 11:11 was the *r* of the house of God
Ps 68:27 is little Benjamin with their *r*
Ps 105:20 even the *r* of the people, and let
Ps 105:21 house, and *r* of all his substance
Prov 6:7 having no guide, overseer, or *r*
Prov 23:1 When thou sittest to eat with a *r*
Prov 28:15 so is a wicked *r* over the poor
Prov 29:12 If a *r* hearken to lies, all his
Eccl 10:4 of the *r* rise up against thee
Eccl 10:5 error which proceedeth from the *r*
Is 3:6 Thou hast clothing, be thou our *r*
Is 3:7 make me not a *r* of the people
Is 16:1 Send ye the lamb to the *r* of the
Jer 51:46 in the land, *r* against *r*
Dan 2:10 there is no king, lord, nor *r*
Dan 2:38 and hath made thee *r* over them all
Dan 2:48 made him *r* over the whole
Dan 5:7 be the third *r* in the kingdom
Dan 5:16 be the third *r* in the kingdom
Dan 5:29 be the third *r* in the kingdom
Mic 5:2 unto me that is to be *r* in Israel
Hab 1:14 things, that have no *r* over them
Mt 9:18 behold, there came a certain *r*
Mt 24:45 hath made *r* over his household
Mt 24:47 make him *r* over all his goods
Mt 25:21 will make thee *r* over many things
Mt 25:23 will make thee *r* over many things
Mk 5:35 there came from the *r* of the
Mk 5:36 saith unto the *r* of the synagogue
Mk 5:38 house of the *r* of the synagogue
Lk 8:41 he was a *r* of the synagogue
Lk 8:49 the *r* of the synagogue's house
Lk 12:42 shall make *r* over his household
Lk 12:44 make him *r* over all that he hath
Lk 13:14 the *r* of the synagogue answered
Lk 18:18 And a certain *r* asked him, saying,
Jn 2:9 When the *r* of the feast had
Jn 3:1 named Nicodemus, a *r* of the Jews
Acts 7:27 away, saying, Who made thee a *r*
Acts 7:35 saying, Who made thee a *r*
Acts 7:35 the same did God send to be a *r*
Acts 18:8 the chief *r* of the synagogue,
Acts 18:17 the chief *r* of the synagogue, and
Acts 23:5 speak evil of the *r* of thy people

**RULERS**
Gen 47:6 then make them *r* over my cattle
Ex 16:22 all the *r* of the congregation
Ex 18:21 to be *r* of thousands
Ex 18:21 *r* of hundreds, *r* of fifties,
Ex 18:21 *r* of fifties, and *r* of tens
Ex 18:25 *r* of thousands
Ex 18:25 *r* of hundreds, *r* of fifties,
Ex 18:25 *r* of fifties, and *r* of tens
Ex 34:31 all the *r* of the congregation
Ex 35:27 the *r* brought onyx stones, and
Deut 1:13 and I will make them *r* over you
Judg 15:11 the Philistines are *r* over us
2Sa 8:18 and David's sons were chief *r*
1Kin 9:22 *r* of his chariots, and his
2Kin 10:1 unto the *r* of Jezreel, to the
2Kin 11:4 fetched the *r* over hundreds, with
2Kin 11:19 he took the *r* over hundreds, and
1Chr 21:2 to the *r* of the people, Go,
1Chr 26:32 David made *r* over the Reubenites
1Chr 27:31 All these were the *r* of the
1Chr 29:6 with the *r* of the king's work,
2Chr 29:20 and gathered the *r* of the city
2Chr 35:8 *r* of the house of God, gave unto
Ezr 9:2 *r* hath been chief in this
Ezr 10:14 Let now our *r* of all the
Neh 2:16 the *r* knew not whither I went, or
Neh 2:16 nor to the nobles, nor to the *r*
Neh 4:14 said unto the nobles, and to the *r*
Neh 4:16 the *r* were behind all the house

# S

Lev 16:31 It shall be a s of rest unto you,
Lev 23:3 the seventh day is the s of rest
Lev 23:3 it is the s of the LORD in all
Lev 23:11 on the morrow after the s the
Lev 23:15 you from the morrow after the s
Lev 23:16 s shall ye number fifty days
Lev 23:24 of the month, shall ye have a s
Lev 23:32 It shall be unto you a s of rest
Lev 23:32 even, shall ye celebrate your s
Lev 23:39 on the first day shall be a s
Lev 23:39 and on the eighth day shall be a s
Lev 24:8 Every s he shall set it in order
Lev 25:2 the land keep a s unto the LORD
Lev 25:4 be a s of rest unto the land
Lev 25:4 unto the land, a s for the LORD
Lev 25:6 the s of the land shall be meat
Num 15:32 gathered sticks upon the s day
Num 28:9 on the s day two lambs of the
Num 28:10 is the burnt offering of every s
Deut 5:12 Keep the s day to sanctify it, as
Deut 5:14 day is the s of the LORD thy God
Deut 5:15 commanded thee to keep the s day
2Kin 4:23 it is neither new moon, nor s
2Kin 11:5 of you that enter in on the s
2Kin 11:7 of all you that go forth on the s
2Kin 11:9 men that were to come in on the s
2Kin 11:9 them that should go out on the s
2Kin 16:18 the covert for the s that they
1Chr 9:32 shewbread, to prepare it every s
2Chr 23:4 part of you entering on the s
2Chr 23:8 men that were to come in on the s
2Chr 23:8 them that were to go out on the s
2Chr 36:21 as she lay desolate she kept s
Neh 9:14 madest known unto them thy holy s
Neh 10:31 any victuals on the s day to sell
Neh 10:31 would not buy it of them on the s
Neh 13:15 treading winepresses on the s
Neh 13:15 into Jerusalem on the s day
Neh 13:16 sold on the s unto the children
Neh 13:17 that ye do, and profane the s day
Neh 13:18 upon Israel by profaning the s
Neh 13:19 began to be dark before the s
Neh 13:19 not be opened till after the s
Neh 13:19 burden be brought in on the s day
Neh 13:21 forth came they no more on the s
Neh 13:22 the gates, to sanctify the s day
Ps 92:t A Psalm or Song for the s day
Is 56:2 that keepeth the s from polluting
Is 56:6 keepeth the s from polluting it
Is 58:13 turn away thy foot from the s
Is 58:13 call the s a delight, the holy of
Is 66:23 from one s to another, shall all
Jer 17:21 and bear no burden on the s day
Jer 17:22 out of your houses on the s day
Jer 17:22 any work, but hallow ye the s day
Jer 17:24 gates of this city on the s day
Jer 17:24 but hallow the s day
Jer 17:27 unto me to hallow the s day
Jer 17:27 gates of Jerusalem on the s day
Eze 46:1 but on the s it shall be opened,
Eze 46:4 offer unto the LORD in the s day
Eze 46:12 offerings, as he did on the s day
Amos 8:5 and the s, that we may set forth
Mt 12:1 on the s day through the corn
Mt 12:2 not lawful to do upon the s day
Mt 12:5 how that on the s days the
Mt 12:5 in the temple profane the s
Mt 12:8 of man is Lord even of the s day
Mt 12:10 it lawful to heal on the s days
Mt 12:11 it fall into a pit on the s day
Mt 12:12 lawful to do well on the s days
Mt 24:20 the winter, neither on the s day
Mt 28:1 In the end of the s, as it began
Mk 1:21 straightway on the s day he
Mk 2:23 the corn fields on the s day
Mk 2:24 why do they on the s day that
Mk 2:27 The s was made for man
Mk 2:27 and not man for the s
Mk 2:28 Son of man is Lord also of the s
Mk 3:2 he would heal him on the s day
Mk 3:4 lawful to do good on the s days
Mk 6:2 when the s day was come, he began
Mk 15:42 that is, the day before the s
Mk 16:1 And when the s was past, Mary
Lk 4:16 into the synagogue on the s day
Lk 4:31 and taught them on the s days
Lk 6:1 on the second s after the first
Lk 6:2 is not lawful to do on the s days
Lk 6:5 Son of man is Lord also of the s
Lk 6:6 it came to pass also on another s
Lk 6:7 he would heal on the s day
Lk 6:9 lawful on the s days to do good
Lk 13:10 in one of the synagogues on the s
Lk 13:14 Jesus had healed on the s day
Lk 13:14 and be healed, and not on the s day
Lk 13:15 s loose his ox or his ass from
Lk 13:16 from this bond on the s day
Lk 14:1 to eat bread on the s day
Lk 14:3 Is it lawful to heal on the s day
Lk 14:5 pull him out on the s day
Lk 23:54 the preparation, and the s drew on
Lk 23:56 rested the s day according to the
Jn 5:9 and on the same day was the s
Jn 5:10 that was cured, It is the s day
Jn 5:16 done these things on the s day
Jn 5:18 he not only had broken the s
Jn 7:22 ye on the s day circumcise a man
Jn 7:23 If a man on the s day receive
Jn 7:23 man every whit whole on the s day
Jn 9:14 it was the s day when Jesus made
Jn 9:16 because he keepeth not the s day
Jn 19:31 upon the cross on the s day
Jn 19:31 (for that s day was an high day,)
Acts 1:12 from Jerusalem a s day's journey
Acts 13:14 into the synagogue on the s day
Acts 13:27 which are read every s day
Acts 13:42 be preached to them the next s
Acts 13:44 the next s day came almost the
Acts 15:21 in the synagogues every s day
Acts 16:13 on the s we went out of the city
Acts 17:2 three s days reasoned with them
Acts 18:4 reasoned in the synagogue every s
Col 2:16 of the new moon, or of the s days

**SABBATHS**
Ex 31:13 Verily my s ye shall keep
Lev 19:3 and his father, and keep my s
Lev 19:30 Ye shall keep my s, and reverence
Lev 23:15 seven s shall be complete
Lev 23:38 Beside the s of the LORD, and
Lev 25:8 number seven s of years unto thee
Lev 25:8 the space of the seven s of years
Lev 26:2 Ye shall keep my s, and reverence
Lev 26:34 Then shall the land enjoy her s
Lev 26:34 the land rest, and enjoy her s
Lev 26:35 because it did not rest in your s
Lev 26:43 of them, and shall enjoy her s
1Chr 23:31 sacrifices unto the LORD in the s
2Chr 2:4 morning and evening, on the s
2Chr 8:13 commandment of Moses, on the s
2Chr 31:3 and the burnt offerings for the s
2Chr 36:21 until the land had enjoyed her s
Neh 10:33 burnt offering, of the s, of the
Is 1:13 the new moons and s, the calling
Is 56:4 unto the eunuchs that keep my s
Lam 1:7 saw her, and did mock at her s
Lam 2:6 s to be forgotten in Zion, and
Eze 20:12 Moreover also I gave them my s
Eze 20:13 my s they greatly polluted
Eze 20:16 in my statutes, but polluted my s
Eze 20:20 And hallow my s
Eze 20:21 they polluted my s
Eze 20:24 my statutes, and had polluted my s
Eze 22:8 things, and hast profaned my s
Eze 22:26 and have hid their eyes from my s
Eze 23:38 same day, and have profaned my s
Eze 44:24 and they shall hallow my s
Eze 45:17 and in the new moons, and in the s
Eze 46:3 gate before the LORD in the s
Hos 2:11 days, her new moons, and her s

**SABEANS** *(sab-e'-uns)*
*1. Descendants of Sheba.*
Job 1:15 the S fell upon them, and took
Joel 3:8 and they shall sell them to the S
*2. Descendants of Seba.*
Is 45:14 of Ethiopia and of the S, men of
Eze 23:42 brought S from the wilderness

**SABTA** *(sab'-tah)* See SABTAH. *A son of Cush.*
1Chr 1:9 Seba, and Havilah, and S, and Raamah

**SABTAH** *(sab'-tah)* See SABTA. *Same as Sabta.*
Gen 10:7 Seba, and Havilah, and S, and Raamah

**SABTECHA** *(sab'-te-kah)* See SABTECHAH. *A son of Cush.*
1Chr 1:9 and Sabta, and Raamah, and S

**SABTECHAH** *(sab'-te-kah)* See SABTECHA. *Same as Sabtecha.*
Gen 10:7 and Sabtah, and Raamah, and S

**SACAR** *(sa'-kar)* See SHARAR.
*1. Father of Ahiham.*
1Chr 11:35 Ahiam the son of S the Hararite
*2. A sanctuary servant.*
1Chr 26:4 S the fourth, and Nethaneel the

**SACK**
Gen 42:25 every man's money into his s
Gen 42:27 as one of them opened his s to
Gen 42:28 and, lo, it is even in my s
Gen 42:35 bundle of money was in his s
Gen 43:21 money was in the mouth of his s
Gen 44:11 every man his s to the ground
Gen 44:11 and opened every man his s
Gen 44:12 the cup was found in Benjamin's s
Lev 11:32 wood, or raiment, or skin, or s

**SACKCLOTH**
Gen 37:34 put s upon his loins, and mourned
2Sa 3:31 your clothes, and gird you with s
2Sa 21:10 the daughter of Aiah took s
1Kin 20:31 put s on our loins, and ropes upon
1Kin 20:32 So they girded s on their loins
1Kin 21:27 put s upon his flesh, and fasted,
1Kin 21:27 his flesh, and fasted, and lay in s
2Kin 6:30 he had s within upon his flesh
2Kin 19:1 and covered himself with s
2Kin 19:2 of the priests, covered with s
1Chr 21:16 of Israel, who were clothed in s
Est 4:1 put on s with ashes, and went out
Est 4:2 the king's gate clothed with s
Est 4:3 and many lay in s and ashes
Est 4:4 and to take away his s from him
Job 16:15 I have sewed s upon my skin
Ps 30:11 thou hast put off my s, and girded
Ps 35:13 they were sick, my clothing was s
Ps 69:11 I made s also my garment
Is 3:24 of a stomacher a girding of s
Is 15:3 they shall gird themselves with s
Is 20:2 loose the s from off thy loins,
Is 22:12 to baldness, and to girding with s
Is 32:11 bare, and gird s upon your loins
Is 37:1 and covered himself with s
Is 37:2 of the priests covered with s
Is 50:3 and I make s their covering
Is 58:5 head as a bulrush, and to spread s
Jer 4:8 For this gird you with s, lament
Jer 6:26 of my people, gird thee with s
Jer 48:37 be cuttings, and upon the loins s
Jer 49:3 of Rabbah, gird you with s
Lam 2:10 have girded themselves with s
Eze 7:18 shall also gird themselves with s
Eze 27:31 for thee, and gird them with s
Dan 9:3 supplications, with fasting, and s
Joel 1:8 like a virgin girded with s for
Joel 1:13 come, lie all night in s, ye
Amos 8:10 I will bring up s upon all loins
Jonah 3:5 and proclaimed a fast, and put on s
Jonah 3:6 from him, and covered him with s
Jonah 3:8 man and beast be covered with s
Mt 11:21 would have repented long ago in s
Lk 10:13 while ago repented, sitting in s
Rev 6:12 the sun became black as s of hair
Rev 11:3 and threescore days, clothed in s

**SACKS**
Gen 42:25 to fill their s with corn
Gen 42:35 to pass as they emptied their s
Gen 43:12 again in the mouth of your s
Gen 43:18 in our s at the first time are we
Gen 43:21 to the inn, that we opened our s
Gen 43:22 tell who put our money in our s
Gen 43:23 hath given you treasure in your s
Gen 44:1 Fill the men's s with food
Josh 9:4 took old s upon their asses, and

**SACRIFICE**
Gen 31:54 Jacob offered s upon the mount
Ex 3:18 that we may s to the LORD our God
Ex 5:3 and s unto the LORD our God
Ex 5:8 saying, Let us go and s to our God
Ex 5:17 Let us go and do s to the LORD
Ex 8:8 that they may do s unto the LORD
Ex 8:25 s to your God in the land
Ex 8:26 for we shall s the abomination of
Ex 8:26 shall we s the abomination of the
Ex 8:27 s to the LORD our God, as he
Ex 8:28 that ye may s to the LORD your
Ex 8:29 the people go to s to the LORD
Ex 10:25 that we may s unto the LORD our
Ex 12:27 It is the s of the LORD's
Ex 13:15 therefore I s to the LORD all

Ex 20:24 shalt s thereon thy burnt
Ex 23:18 blood of my s with leavened bread
Ex 23:18 of my s remain until the morning
Ex 29:28 of the s of their peace offerings
Ex 30:9 incense thereon, nor burnt s
Ex 34:15 do s unto their gods, and one call
Ex 34:15 call thee, and thou eat of his s
Ex 34:25 the blood of my s with leaven
Ex 34:25 neither shall the s of the feast
Lev 1:3 offering be a burnt s of the herd
Lev 1:9 all on the altar, to be a burnt s
Lev 1:10 or of the goats, for a burnt s
Lev 1:13 it is a burnt s, an offering made
Lev 1:14 if the burnt s for his offering
Lev 1:17 it is a burnt s, an offering made
Lev 3:1 oblation be a s of peace offering
Lev 3:3 he shall offer of the s of the
Lev 3:5 it on the altar upon the burnt s
Lev 3:6 if his offering for a s of peace
Lev 3:9 he shall offer of the s of the
Lev 4:10 of the s of peace offerings
Lev 4:26 as the fat of the s of peace
Lev 4:31 from off the s of peace offerings
Lev 4:35 from the s of the peace offerings
Lev 7:11 law of the s of peace offerings
Lev 7:12 the s of thanksgiving unleavened
Lev 7:13 leavened bread with the s of
Lev 7:15 the flesh of the s of his peace
Lev 7:16 But if the s of his offering be a
Lev 7:16 same day that he offereth his s
Lev 7:17 remainder of the flesh of the s
Lev 7:18 if any of the flesh of the s of
Lev 7:20 flesh of the s of peace offerings
Lev 7:21 flesh of the s of peace offerings
Lev 7:29 He that offereth the s of his
Lev 7:29 of the s of his peace offerings
Lev 7:37 of the s of the peace offerings
Lev 8:21 it was a burnt s for a sweet
Lev 9:4 offerings, to s before the LORD
Lev 9:17 beside the burnt s of the morning
Lev 9:18 and the ram for a s of peace
Lev 17:8 offereth a burnt offering or s
Lev 19:5 And if ye offer a s of peace
Lev 22:21 whosoever offereth a s of peace
Lev 22:29 when ye will offer a s of
Lev 23:19 Then ye shall s one kid of the
Lev 23:19 year for a s of peace offerings
Lev 23:37 offering, and a meat offering, a s
Lev 27:11 do not offer a s unto the LORD
Num 6:17 a s of peace offerings unto the
Num 6:18 the s of the peace offerings
Num 7:17 for a s of peace offerings, two
Num 7:23 for a s of peace offerings, two
Num 7:29 for a s of peace offerings, two
Num 7:35 for a s of peace offerings, two
Num 7:41 for a s of peace offerings, two
Num 7:47 for a s of peace offerings, two
Num 7:53 for a s of peace offerings, two
Num 7:59 for a s of peace offerings, two
Num 7:65 for a s of peace offerings, two
Num 7:71 for a s of peace offerings, two
Num 7:77 for a s of peace offerings, two
Num 7:83 for a s of peace offerings, two
Num 7:88 all the oxen for the s of the
Num 15:3 or a s in performing a vow, or in
Num 15:5 with the burnt offering or s
Num 15:8 or for a s in performing a vow,
Num 15:25 a s made by fire unto the LORD,
Num 23:6 and, lo, he stood by his burnt s
Num 28:6 a s made by fire unto the LORD
Num 28:8 a s made by fire, of a sweet
Num 28:13 a s made by fire unto the LORD
Num 28:19 But ye shall offer a s made by
Num 28:24 the meat of the s made by fire
Num 29:6 a s made by fire unto the LORD
Num 29:13 a s made by fire, of a sweet
Num 29:36 a s made by fire, of a sweet
Deut 15:21 thou shalt not s it unto the LORD
Deut 16:2 Thou shalt therefore s the
Deut 16:5 Thou mayest not s the passover
Deut 16:6 there thou shalt s the passover
Deut 17:1 Thou shalt not s unto the LORD
Deut 18:3 people, from them that offer a s
Deut 33:10 whole burnt s upon thine altar
Josh 22:26 not for burnt offering, nor for s
Judg 6:26 offer a burnt s with the wood of
Judg 16:23 a great s unto Dagon their god
1Sa 1:3 to s unto the LORD of hosts in
1Sa 1:21 offer unto the LORD the yearly s
1Sa 2:13 was, that, when any man offered s
1Sa 2:19 her husband to offer the yearly s
1Sa 2:29 Wherefore kick ye at my s
1Sa 3:14 with s nor offering for ever
1Sa 9:12 for there is a s of the people to
1Sa 9:13 come, because he doth bless the s
1Sa 10:8 and to s sacrifices of peace
1Sa 15:15 to s unto the LORD thy God
1Sa 15:21 to s unto the LORD thy God in
1Sa 15:22 Behold, to obey is better than s
1Sa 16:2 say, I am come to s to the LORD
1Sa 16:3 And call Jesse to the s, and I will
1Sa 16:5 I am come to s unto the LORD
1Sa 16:5 and come with me to the s
1Sa 16:5 his sons, and called them to the s
1Sa 20:6 for there is a yearly s there for
1Sa 20:29 our family hath a s in the city
2Sa 24:22 behold, here be oxen for burnt s
1Kin 3:4 king went to Gibeon to s there
1Kin 8:62 offered s before the LORD
1Kin 8:63 Solomon offered a s of peace
1Kin 12:27 If this people go up to do s in
1Kin 18:29 of the offering of the evening s
1Kin 18:33 water, and pour it on the burnt s
1Kin 18:36 of the offering of the evening s
1Kin 18:38 fell, and consumed the burnt s
2Kin 5:17 offering nor s unto other gods
2Kin 10:19 I have a great s to do to Baal
2Kin 14:4 as yet the people did s and burnt
2Kin 16:15 offering, and the king's burnt s
2Kin 16:15 and all the blood of the s
2Kin 17:35 nor serve them, nor s to them
2Kin 17:36 worship, and to him shall ye do s
2Chr 2:6 save only to burn s before him
2Chr 7:5 Solomon offered a s of twenty
2Chr 7:12 place to myself for an house of s
2Chr 11:16 to s unto the LORD God of their
2Chr 28:23 them, therefore will I s to them
2Chr 33:17 did s still in the high places
Ezr 4:2 we do s unto him since the days
Ezr 9:4 sat astonied until the evening s
Ezr 9:5 at the evening s I arose up from
Neh 4:2 will they s
Ps 20:3 offerings, and accept thy burnt s
Ps 40:6 S and offering thou didst not
Ps 50:5 have made a covenant with me by s
Ps 51:16 For thou desirest not s
Ps 54:6 I will freely s unto thee
Ps 107:22 let them s the sacrifices of
Ps 116:17 to thee the s of thanksgiving
Ps 118:27 bind the s with cords, even unto
Ps 141:2 up of my hands as the evening s
Prov 15:8 The s of the wicked is an
Prov 21:3 acceptable to the LORD than s
Prov 21:27 The s of the wicked is
Eccl 5:1 hear, than to give the s of fools
Is 19:21 LORD in that day, and shall do s
Is 34:6 for the LORD hath a s in Bozrah
Is 57:7 wentest thou up to offer s
Jer 33:11 of them that shall bring the s of
Jer 33:18 offerings, and to do s continually
Jer 46:10 a s in the north country by the
Eze 39:17 every side to my s
Eze 39:17 that I do s for you
Eze 39:17 even a great s upon the mountains
Eze 39:19 of my s which I have sacrificed
Eze 40:42 slew the burnt offering and the s
Eze 44:11 the s for the people, and they
Eze 46:24 shall boil the s of the people
Dan 8:11 by him the daily s was taken away
Dan 8:12 s by reason of transgression
Dan 8:13 the vision concerning the daily s
Dan 9:27 of the week he shall cause the s
Dan 11:31 and shall take away the daily s
Dan 12:11 the daily s shall be taken away
Hos 3:4 without a prince, and without a s
Hos 4:13 They s upon the tops of the
Hos 4:14 whores, and they s with harlots
Hos 6:6 For I desired mercy, and not s
Hos 8:13 They s flesh for the sacrifices
Hos 12:11 they s bullocks in Gilgal
Hos 13:2 the men that s kiss the calves
Amos 4:5 offer a s of thanksgiving with
Jonah 1:16 offered a s unto the LORD, and
Jonah 2:9 But I will s unto thee with the
Hab 1:16 Therefore they s unto their net
Zeph 1:7 for the LORD hath prepared a s
Zeph 1:8 pass in the day of the LORD's s
Zec 14:21 and all they that s shall come
Mal 1:8 And if ye offer the blind for s
Mt 9:13 I will have mercy, and not s
Mt 12:7 I will have mercy, and not s
Mk 9:49 every s shall be salted with salt
Lk 2:24 to offer a s according to that
Acts 7:41 offered s unto the idol, and
Acts 14:13 would have done s with the people
Acts 14:18 they had not done s unto them
Rom 12:1 ye present your bodies a living s
1Cor 8:4 that are offered in s unto idols
1Cor 10:19 in s to idols is any thing
1Cor 10:20 the things which the Gentiles s
1Cor 10:20 they s to devils, and not to God
1Cor 10:28 This is offered in s unto idols
Eph 5:2 a s to God for a sweetsmelling
Phil 2:17 and if I be offered upon the s
Phil 4:18 a s acceptable, wellpleasing to
Heb 7:27 those high priests, to offer up s
Heb 9:26 put away sin by the s of himself
Heb 10:5 into the world, he saith, S
Heb 10:8 Above when he said, S and offering
Heb 10:12 offered one s for sins for ever
Heb 10:26 remaineth no more s for sins
Heb 11:4 God a more excellent s than Cain
Heb 13:15 s of praise to God continually

## SACRIFICED

Ex 24:5 s peace offerings of oxen unto
Ex 32:8 have s thereunto, and said, These
Deut 32:17 They s unto devils, not to God
Josh 8:31 the LORD, and s peace offerings
Judg 2:5 they s there unto the LORD
1Sa 2:15 came, and said to the man that s
1Sa 6:15 s sacrifices the same day unto
1Sa 11:15 there they s sacrifices of peace
2Sa 6:13 six paces, he s oxen and fatlings
1Kin 3:2 Only the people s in high places
1Kin 3:3 only he s and burnt incense in
1Kin 11:8 incense and s unto their gods
2Kin 12:3 the people still s and burnt
2Kin 15:4 the people s and burnt incense
2Kin 15:35 the people s and burned incense
2Kin 16:4 And he s and burnt incense in the
2Kin 17:32 which s for them in the houses of
1Chr 21:28 the Jebusite, then he s there
1Chr 29:21 they s sacrifices unto the LORD,
2Chr 5:6 s sheep and oxen, which could not
2Chr 28:4 He s also and burnt incense in the
2Chr 28:23 For he s unto the gods of
2Chr 33:16 s thereon peace offerings and
2Chr 33:22 for Amon s unto all the carved
2Chr 34:4 of them that had s unto them
Ps 106:37 they s their sons and their
Ps 106:38 whom they s unto the idols of
Eze 16:20 these hast thou s unto them to be
Eze 39:19 sacrifice which I have s for you
Hos 11:2 they s unto Baalim, and burned
1Cor 5:7 Christ our passover is s for us
Rev 2:14 to eat things s unto idols
Rev 2:20 and to eat things s unto idols

## SACRIFICES

Gen 46:1 offered s unto the God of his
Ex 10:25 said, Thou must give us also s
Ex 18:12 a burnt offering and s for God
Lev 7:32 of the s of your peace offerings
Lev 7:34 the s of their peace offerings
Lev 10:13 of the s of the LORD made by fire
Lev 10:14 the s of peace offerings of the
Lev 17:5 of Israel may bring their s
Lev 17:7 no more offer their s unto devils
Num 10:10 and over the s of your peace
Num 25:2 people unto the s of their gods
Num 28:2 and my bread for my s made by fire
Deut 12:6 your burnt offerings, and your s
Deut 12:11 your burnt offerings, and your s
Deut 12:27 the blood of thy s shall be
Deut 32:38 Which did eat the fat of their s
Deut 33:19 shall offer s of righteousness
Josh 13:14 the s of the LORD God of Israel
Josh 22:27 burnt offerings, and with our s
Josh 22:28 for burnt offerings, nor for s
Josh 22:29 for meat offerings, or for s
1Sa 6:15 sacrificed s the same day unto
1Sa 10:8 to sacrifice s of peace offerings
1Sa 11:15 there they sacrificed s of peace
1Sa 15:22 delight in burnt offerings and s
2Sa 15:12 from Giloh, while he offered s
2Kin 10:24 And when they went in to offer s
1Chr 16:1 and they offered burnt s and peace
1Chr 23:31 to offer all burnt s unto the
1Chr 29:21 they sacrificed s unto the LORD
1Chr 29:21 s in abundance for all Israel

2Chr 7:1 the burnt offering and the s
2Chr 7:4 people offered s before the LORD
2Chr 13:11 morning and every evening burnt s
2Chr 29:31 the LORD, come near and bring s
2Chr 29:31 And the congregation brought in s
Ezr 6:3 the place where they offered s
Ezr 6:10 That they may offer s of sweet
Neh 12:43 that day they offered great s
Ps 4:5 Offer the s of righteousness, and
Ps 27:6 offer in his tabernacle s of joy
Ps 50:8 for thy s or thy burnt offerings
Ps 51:17 The s of God are a broken spirit
Ps 51:19 with the s of righteousness
Ps 66:15 unto thee burnt s of fatlings
Ps 106:28 and ate the s of the dead
Ps 107:22 sacrifice the s of thanksgiving
Prov 17:1 an house full of s with strife
Is 1:11 the multitude of your s unto me
Is 29:1 let them kill s
Is 43:23 hast thou honoured me with thy s
Is 43:24 filled me with the fat of thy s
Is 56:7 their s shall be accepted upon
Jer 6:20 nor your s sweet unto me
Jer 7:21 your burnt offerings unto your s
Jer 7:22 concerning burnt offerings or s
Jer 17:26 bringing burnt offerings, and s
Jer 17:26 bringing s of praise, unto the
Eze 20:28 and they offered there their s
Eze 40:41 whereupon they slew their s
Hos 4:19 be ashamed because of their s
Hos 8:13 flesh for the s of mine offerings
Hos 9:4 their s shall be unto them as the
Amos 4:4 bring your s every morning, and
Amos 5:25 Have ye offered unto me s
Mk 12:33 all whole burnt offerings and s
Lk 13:1 Pilate had mingled with their s
Acts 7:42 s by the space of forty years in
1Cor 10:18 of the s partakers of the altar
Heb 5:1 offer both gifts and s for sins
Heb 8:3 is ordained to offer gifts and s
Heb 9:9 were offered both gifts and s
Heb 9:23 with better s than these
Heb 10:1 can never with those s which they
Heb 10:3 But in those s there is a
Heb 10:6 s for sin thou hast had no
Heb 10:11 and offering oftentimes the same s
Heb 13:16 for with such s God is well
1Pet 2:5 to offer up spiritual s,

**SACRIFICETH**

Ex 22:20 He that s unto any god, save unto
Eccl 9:2 to him that s, and to him that
Eccl 9:2 s, and to him that s not
Is 65:3 that s in gardens, and burneth
Is 66:3 he that s a lamb, as if he cut
Mal 1:14 s unto the Lord a corrupt thing

**SAD**

Gen 40:6 them, and, behold, they were s
1Sa 1:18 and her countenance was no more s
1Kin 21:5 unto him, Why is thy spirit so s
Neh 2:1 been beforetime s in his presence
Neh 2:2 unto me, Why is thy countenance s
Neh 2:3 should not my countenance be s
Eze 13:22 made the heart of the righteous s
Eze 13:22 s, whom I have not made s
Mt 6:16 hypocrites, of a s countenance
Mk 10:22 he was s at that saying, and went
Lk 24:17 to another, as ye walk, and are s

**SADDLE**

Lev 15:9 what s soever he rideth upon that
2Sa 19:26 I will s me an ass, that I may
1Kin 13:13 said unto his sons, S me the ass
1Kin 13:27 to his sons, saying, S me the ass

**SADDLED**

Gen 22:3 s his ass, and took two of his
Num 22:21 s his ass, and went with the
Judg 19:10 there were with him two asses s
2Sa 16:1 met him, with a couple of asses s
2Sa 17:23 he s his ass, and arose, and gat
1Kin 2:40 s his ass, and went to Gath to
1Kin 13:13 So they s him the ass
1Kin 13:23 that he s for him the ass, to wit
1Kin 13:27 And they s him
2Kin 4:24 Then she s an ass, and said to her

**SADDUCEES** *(sad'-du-sees) Members of a Jewish sect.*

Mt 3:7 S come to his baptism, he said
Mt 16:1 Pharisees also with the S came
Mt 16:6 of the Pharisees and of the S
Mt 16:11 of the Pharisees and of the S
Mt 16:12 of the Pharisees and of the S
Mt 22:23 The same day came to him the S
Mt 22:34 that he had put the S to silence
Mk 12:18 Then come unto him the S, which
Lk 20:27 Then came to him certain of the S
Acts 4:1 captain of the temple, and the S
Acts 5:17 him, (which is the sect of the S
Acts 23:6 that the one part were S, and the
Acts 23:7 between the Pharisees and the S
Acts 23:8 For the S say that there is no

**SADOC** *(sa'-dok) Father of Achim; an ancestor of Jesus.*

Mt 1:14 And Azor begat S
Mt 1:14 and S begat Achim

**SAFE**

1Sa 12:11 on every side, and ye dwelled s
2Sa 18:29 said, Is the young man Absalom s
2Sa 18:32 Cushi, Is the young man Absalom s
Job 21:9 Their houses are s from fear
Ps 119:117 Hold thou me up, and I shall be s
Prov 18:10 runneth into it, and is s
Prov 29:25 his trust in the LORD shall be s
Is 5:29 prey, and shall carry it away s
Eze 34:27 and they shall be s in their land
Lk 15:27 because he hath received him s
Acts 23:24 bring him s unto Felix the
Acts 27:44 that they escaped all s to land
Phil 3:1 not grievous, but for you it is s

**SAFELY**

Lev 26:5 the full, and dwell in your land s
1Kin 4:25 And Judah and Israel dwelt s
Ps 78:53 And he led them on s, so that they
Prov 1:33 hearkeneth unto me shall dwell s
Prov 3:23 Then shalt thou walk in thy way s
Prov 31:11 her husband doth s trust in her
Is 41:3 He pursued them, and passed s
Jer 23:6 be saved, and Israel shall dwell s
Jer 32:37 and I will cause them to dwell s
Jer 33:16 saved, and Jerusalem shall dwell s
Eze 28:26 And they shall dwell s therein
Eze 34:25 they shall dwell s in the
Eze 34:28 but they shall dwell s, and none
Eze 38:8 and they shall dwell s all of them
Eze 38:11 that are at rest, that dwell s
Eze 38:14 my people of Israel dwelleth s
Eze 39:26 when they dwelt s in their land
Hos 2:18 and will make them to lie down s
Zec 14:11 Jerusalem shall be s inhabited
Mk 14:44 take him, and lead him away s
Acts 16:23 the jailer to keep them s

**SAFETY**

Lev 25:18 ye shall dwell in the land in s
Lev 25:19 your fill, and dwell therein in s
Deut 12:10 about, so that ye dwell in s
Deut 33:12 the LORD shall dwell in s by him
Deut 33:28 then shall dwell in s alone
Job 3:26 I was not in s, neither had I
Job 5:4 His children are far from s
Job 5:11 which mourn may be exalted to s
Job 11:18 and thou shalt take thy rest in s
Job 24:23 Though it be given him to be in s
Ps 4:8 LORD, only makest me dwell in s
Ps 12:5 I will set him in s from him that
Ps 33:17 An horse is a vain thing for s
Prov 11:14 of counsellors there is s
Prov 21:31 but s is of the LORD
Prov 24:6 of counsellors there is s
Is 14:30 and the needy shall lie down in s
Acts 5:23 truly found we shut with all s
1Th 5:3 when they shall say, Peace and s

**SAIL**

Is 33:23 mast, they could not spread the s
Eze 27:7 thou spreadest forth to be thy s
Acts 20:3 as he was about to s into Syria
Acts 20:16 had determined to s by Ephesus
Acts 27:1 that we should s into Italy
Acts 27:2 meaning to s by the coasts of
Acts 27:17 into the quicksands, strake s
Acts 27:24 thee all them that s with thee

**SAILED**

Lk 8:23 But as they s he fell asleep
Acts 13:4 and from thence they s to Cyprus
Acts 14:26 thence s to Antioch, from whence
Acts 15:39 took Mark, and s unto Cyprus
Acts 18:18 s thence into Syria, and with him
Acts 18:21 And he s from Ephesus
Acts 20:6 we s away from Philippi after the
Acts 20:13 s unto Assos, there intending to
Acts 20:15 we s thence, and came the next day
Acts 21:3 s into Syria, and landed at Tyre
Acts 27:4 we s under Cyprus, because the
Acts 27:5 when we had s over the sea of
Acts 27:7 when we had s slowly many days,
Acts 27:7 we s under Crete, over against
Acts 27:13 thence, they s close by Crete

**SAINTS**

Deut 33:2 he came with ten thousands of s
Deut 33:3 all his s are in thy hand
1Sa 2:9 He will keep the feet of his s
2Chr 6:41 let thy s rejoice in goodness
Job 5:1 to which of the s wilt thou turn
Job 15:15 he putteth no trust in his s
Ps 16:3 But to the s that are in the
Ps 30:4 O ye s of his, and give thanks at
Ps 31:23 O love the LORD, all ye his s
Ps 34:9 O fear the LORD, ye his s
Ps 37:28 judgment, and forsaketh not his s
Ps 50:5 Gather my s together unto me
Ps 52:9 for it is good before thy s
Ps 79:2 the flesh of thy s unto the
Ps 85:8 unto his people, and to his s
Ps 89:5 also in the congregation of the s
Ps 89:7 feared in the assembly of the s
Ps 97:10 he preserveth the souls of his s
Ps 116:15 of the LORD is the death of his s
Ps 132:9 and let thy s shout for joy
Ps 132:16 her s shall shout aloud for joy
Ps 145:10 and thy s shall bless thee
Ps 148:14 people, the praise of all his s
Ps 149:1 praise in the congregation of s
Ps 149:5 Let the s be joyful in glory
Ps 149:9 this honour have all his s
Prov 2:8 and preserveth the way of his s
Dan 7:18 But the s of the most High shall
Dan 7:21 the same horn made war with the s
Dan 7:22 given to the s of the most High
Dan 7:22 that the s possessed the kingdom
Dan 7:25 wear out the s of the most High
Dan 7:27 people of the s of the most High
Hos 11:12 God, and is faithful with the s
Zec 14:5 come, and all the s with thee
Mt 27:52 bodies of the s which slept arose
Acts 9:13 hath done to thy s at Jerusalem
Acts 9:32 to the s which dwelt at Lydda
Acts 9:41 up, and when he had called the s
Acts 26:10 many of the s did I shut up in
Rom 1:7 beloved of God, called to be s
Rom 8:27 s according to the will of God
Rom 12:13 to the necessity of s
Rom 15:25 Jerusalem to minister unto the s
Rom 15:26 the poor s which are at Jerusalem
Rom 15:31 may be accepted of the s
Rom 16:2 her in the Lord, as becometh s
Rom 16:15 all the s which are with them
1Cor 1:2 in Christ Jesus, called to be s
1Cor 6:1 the unjust, and not before the s
1Cor 6:2 that the s shall judge the world
1Cor 14:33 as in all churches of the s
1Cor 16:1 the collection for the s, as I
1Cor 16:15 to the ministry of the s,)
2Cor 1:1 with all the s which are in all
2Cor 8:4 of the ministering to the s
2Cor 9:1 touching the ministering to the s
2Cor 9:12 only supplieth the want of the s
2Cor 13:13 All the s salute you
Eph 1:1 to the s which are at Ephesus, and
Eph 1:15 Jesus, and love unto all the s
Eph 1:18 glory of his inheritance in the s
Eph 2:19 but fellowcitizens with the s
Eph 3:8 am less than the least of all s
Eph 3:18 with all s what is the breadth
Eph 4:12 For the perfecting of the s
Eph 5:3 named among you, as becometh s
Eph 6:18 and supplication for all s
Phil 1:1 to all the s in Christ Jesus
Phil 4:22 All the s salute you, chiefly
Col 1:2 To the s and faithful brethren in
Col 1:4 love which ye have to all the s
Col 1:12 the inheritance of the s in light
Col 1:26 but now is made manifest to his s
1Th 3:13 Lord Jesus Christ with all his s
2Th 1:10 come to be glorified in his s
Philem 5 the Lord Jesus, and toward all s
Philem 7 of the s are refreshed by thee
Heb 6:10 that ye have ministered to the s
Heb 13:24 the rule over you, and all the s

Jude 3 was once delivered unto the s
Jude 14 with ten thousands of his s
Rev 5:8 which are the prayers of s
Rev 8:3 it with the prayers of all s upon
Rev 8:4 came with the prayers of the s
Rev 11:18 the prophets, and to the s
Rev 13:7 unto him to make war with the s
Rev 13:10 patience and the faith of the s
Rev 14:12 Here is the patience of the s
Rev 15:3 true are thy ways, thou King of s
Rev 16:6 For they have shed the blood of s
Rev 17:6 drunken with the blood of the s
Rev 18:24 the blood of prophets, and of s
Rev 19:8 linen is the righteousness of s
Rev 20:9 compassed the camp of the s about

**SAKE**

Gen 3:17 cursed is the ground for thy s
Gen 8:21 the ground any more for man's s
Gen 12:13 it may be well with me for thy s
Gen 12:16 he entreated Abram well for her s
Gen 18:29 I will not do it for forty's s
Gen 18:31 not destroy it for twenty's s
Gen 18:32 I will not destroy it for ten's s
Gen 20:11 they will slay me for my wife's s
Gen 26:24 seed for my servant Abraham's s
Gen 30:27 LORD hath blessed me for thy s
Gen 39:5 Egyptian's house for Joseph's s
Ex 18:8 to the Egyptians for Israel's s
Ex 21:26 let him go free for his eye's s
Ex 21:27 let him go free for his tooth's s
Num 11:29 unto him, Enviest thou for my s
Num 25:11 was zealous for my s among them
Num 25:18 day of the plague for Peor's s
1Sa 12:22 his people for his great name's s
1Sa 23:10 to destroy the city for my s
2Sa 5:12 kingdom for his people Israel's s
2Sa 7:21 For thy word's s, and according to
2Sa 9:1 him kindness for Jonathan's s
2Sa 9:7 for Jonathan thy father's s
2Sa 18:5 for my s with the young man
1Kin 8:41 of a far country for thy name's s
1Kin 11:12 do it for David thy father's s
1Kin 11:13 thy son for David my servant's s
1Kin 11:13 for Jerusalem's s which I have
1Kin 11:32 tribe for my servant David's s
1Kin 11:32 and for Jerusalem's s
1Kin 11:34 his life for David my servant's s
1Kin 15:4 Nevertheless for David's s did
2Kin 8:19 Judah for David his servant's s
2Kin 19:34 city, to save it, for mine own s
2Kin 19:34 s, and for my servant David's s
2Kin 20:6 defend this city for mine own s
2Kin 20:6 and for my servant David's s
1Chr 17:19 O LORD, for thy servant's s
2Chr 6:32 country for thy great name's s
Neh 9:31 for thy great mercies' s thou
Job 19:17 the children's s of mine own body
Ps 6:4 oh save me for thy mercies' s
Ps 23:3 of righteousness for his name's s
Ps 25:7 thou me for thy goodness' s
Ps 25:11 For thy name's s, O LORD, pardon
Ps 31:3 for thy name's s lead me, and
Ps 31:16 save me for thy mercies' s
Ps 44:22 for thy s are we killed all the
Ps 44:26 and redeem us for thy mercies' s
Ps 69:6 GOD of hosts, be ashamed for my s
Ps 69:6 seek thee be confounded for my s
Ps 69:7 Because for thy s I have borne
Ps 79:9 away our sins, for thy name's s
Ps 106:8 he saved them for his name's s
Ps 109:21 O GOD the Lord, for thy name's s
Ps 115:1 thy mercy, and for thy truth's s
Ps 132:10 For thy servant David's s turn
Ps 143:11 me, O LORD, for thy name's s
Ps 143:11 for thy righteousness' s bring my
Is 37:35 city to save it for mine own s
Is 37:35 and for my servant David's s
Is 42:21 pleased for his righteousness' s
Is 43:14 For your s I have sent to Babylon
Is 43:25 thy transgressions for mine own s
Is 45:4 For Jacob my servant's s, and
Is 48:9 For my name's s will I defer mine
Is 48:11 own s, even for mine own s
Is 54:15 against thee shall fall for thy s
Is 62:1 For Zion's s will I not hold my
Is 62:1 for Jerusalem's s I will not rest
Is 63:17 Return for thy servants' s
Is 66:5 that cast you out for my name's s
Jer 14:7 us, do thou it for thy name's s
Jer 14:21 Do not abhor us, for thy name's s
Jer 15:15 know that for thy s I have
Eze 20:9 But I wrought for my name's s
Eze 20:14 But I wrought for my name's s
Eze 20:22 hand, and wrought for my name's s
Eze 20:44 wrought with you for my name's s
Eze 36:22 but for mine holy name's s
Dan 9:17 is desolate, for the Lord's s
Dan 9:19 defer not, for thine own s
Jonah 1:12 for I know that for my s this
Mic 3:12 for your s be plowed as a field
Mt 5:10 persecuted for righteousness' s
Mt 5:11 against you falsely, for my s
Mt 10:18 governors and kings for my s
Mt 10:22 hated of all men for my name's s
Mt 10:39 his life for my s shall find it
Mt 14:3 put him in prison for Herodias' s
Mt 14:9 nevertheless for the oath's s
Mt 16:25 his life for my s shall find it
Mt 19:12 for the kingdom of heaven's s
Mt 19:29 or lands, for my name's s
Mt 24:9 of all nations for my name's s
Mt 24:22 but for the elect's s those days
Mk 4:17 ariseth for the word's s,
Mk 6:17 him in prison for Herodias' s
Mk 6:26 yet for his oath's s, and for
Mk 8:35 shall lose his life for my s
Mk 10:29 or children, or lands, for my s
Mk 13:9 before rulers and kings for my s
Mk 13:13 hated of all men for my name's s
Mk 13:20 but for the elect's s, whom he
Lk 6:22 as evil, for the Son of man's s
Lk 9:24 will lose his life for my s
Lk 18:29 for the kingdom of God's s
Lk 21:12 kings and rulers for my name's s
Lk 21:17 hated of all men for my name's s
Jn 12:9 they came not for Jesus' s only
Jn 13:37 I will lay down my life for thy s
Jn 13:38 thou lay down thy life for my s
Jn 14:11 believe me for the very works' s
Jn 15:21 they do unto you for my name's s
Acts 9:16 he must suffer for my name's s
Acts 26:7 For which hope's s, king Agrippa,
Rom 4:23 was not written for his s alone
Rom 8:36 For thy s we are killed all the
Rom 13:5 wrath, but also for conscience s
Rom 15:30 for the Lord Jesus Christ's s
1Cor 4:10 We are fools for Christ's s
1Cor 9:23 And this I do for the gospel's s
1Cor 10:25 no question for conscience s
1Cor 10:27 no question for conscience s
1Cor 10:28 eat not for his s that shewed it
1Cor 10:28 shewed it, and for conscience s
2Cor 4:5 your servants for Jesus' s
2Cor 4:11 delivered unto death for Jesus' s
2Cor 12:10 in distresses for Christ's s
Eph 4:32 for Christ's s hath forgiven you
Phil 1:29 him, but also to suffer for his s
Col 1:24 in my flesh for his body's s
Col 3:6 For which things' s the wrath of
1Th 1:5 men we were among you for your s
1Th 5:13 highly in love for their work's s
1Ti 5:23 a little wine for thy stomach's s
Titus 1:11 ought not, for filthy lucre's s
Philem 9 Yet for love's s I rather beseech
1Pet 2:13 ordinance of man for the Lord's s
1Pet 3:14 if ye suffer for righteousness' s
1Jn 2:12 are forgiven you for his name's s
2Jn 2 For the truth's s, which dwelleth
3Jn 7 for his name's s they went forth
Rev 2:3 and for my name's s hast laboured

**SAKES**

Gen 18:26 spare all the place for their s
Lev 26:45 But I will for their s remember
Deut 1:37 LORD was angry with me for your s
Deut 3:26 LORD was wroth with me for your s
Deut 4:21 LORD was angry with me for your s
Judg 21:22 Be favourable unto them for our s
Ruth 1:13 s that the hand of the LORD is
1Chr 16:21 he reproved kings for their s
Ps 7:7 for their s therefore return thou
Ps 105:14 he reproved kings for their s
Ps 106:32 went ill with Moses for their s
Ps 122:8 For my brethren and companions' s
Is 65:8 so will I do for my servants' s
Eze 36:22 I do not this for your s, O house
Eze 36:32 Not for your s do I this, saith
Dan 2:30 but for their s that shall make
Mal 3:11 rebuke the devourer for your s
Mk 6:26 for their s which sat with him,
Jn 11:15 I am glad for your s that I was
Jn 12:30 not because of me, but for your s
Jn 17:19 for their s I sanctify myself,
Rom 11:28 they are enemies for your s
Rom 11:28 are beloved for the fathers' s
1Cor 4:6 myself and to Apollos for your s
1Cor 9:10 saith he it altogether for our s
1Cor 9:10 For our s, no doubt, this is
2Cor 2:10 for your s forgave I it in the
2Cor 4:15 For all things are for your s
2Cor 8:9 yet for your s he became poor,
1Th 3:9 we joy for your s before our God
2Ti 2:10 all things for the elect's s

**SALA** *(sa'-lah)* See SALAH. *Father of Heber; an ancestor of Jesus.*
Lk 3:35 of Heber, which was the son of S

**SALAH** *(sa'-lah)* See SALA. *Son of Arphaxad.*
Gen 10:24 And Arphaxad begat S
Gen 10:24 and S begat Eber
Gen 11:12 five and thirty years, and begat S
Gen 11:13 after he begat S four hundred
Gen 11:14 S lived thirty years, and begat
Gen 11:15 S lived after he begat Eber four

**SALAMIS** *(sal'-a-mis) A city on Cyprus.*
Acts 13:5 And when they were at S, they

**SALATHIEL** *(sa-la'-the-el)* See SHEALTIEL. *Descendant of Jehoiakim; an ancestor of Jesus.*
1Chr 3:17 Assir, S his son,
Mt 1:12 to Babylon, Jechonias begat S
Mt 1:12 and S begat Zorobabel
Lk 3:27 Zorobabel, which was the son of S

**SALCAH** *(sal'-kah)* See SALCHAH. *A city in Gad.*
Josh 12:5 reigned in mount Hermon, and in S
Josh 13:11 Hermon, and all Bashan unto S

**SALCHAH** *(sal'-kah)* See SALCAH. *Same as Salcah.*
Deut 3:10 all Gilead, and all Bashan, unto S
1Chr 5:11 in the land of Bashan unto S

**SALEM** *(sa'-lem)* See JERUSALEM. *The city of Melchizedek.*
Gen 14:18 king of S brought forth bread
Ps 76:2 In S also is his tabernacle, and
Heb 7:1 For this Melchisedec, king of S
Heb 7:2 and after that also King of S

**SALIM** *(sa'-lim) A city near Aenon.*
Jn 3:23 was baptizing in Aenon near to S

**SALLAI** *(sal'-lahee)* See SALLU.
*1. An exile.*
Neh 11:8 And after him Gabbai, S, nine
*2. A priest with Zerubbabel.*
Neh 12:20 Of S, Kallai

**SALLU** *(sal'-lu)* See SALLAI. *A priest with Zerubbabel.*
Neh 12:7 S, Amok, Hilkiah, Jedaiah
1Chr 9:7 S the son of Meshullam, the son
Neh 11:7 S the son of Meshullam, the son

**SALMA** *(sal'-mah)* See SALMON, ZALMA.
*1. Father of Boaz.*
1Chr 2:11 And Nahshon begat S, and S
*2. A son of Caleb.*
1Chr 2:11 begat Salma, and S begat Boaz,
1Chr 2:51 S the father of Beth-lehem,
1Chr 2:54 The sons of S

**SALMON** *(sal'-mon)* See SALMA.
*1. Father of Boaz.*
Ruth 4:20 begat Nahshon, and Nahshon begat S
Ruth 4:21 S begat Boaz, and Boaz begat Obed,
Mt 1:4 and Naasson begat S
Mt 1:5 And S begat Booz of Rachab
Lk 3:32 of Booz, which was the son of S
*2. A mountain near Shechem.*
Ps 68:14 in it, it was white as snow in S

**SALMONE** *(sal-mo'-ne) A promontory on Crete.*
Acts 27:7 under Crete, over against S

**SALOME** *(sa-lo'-me) A female follower of Jesus.*
Mk 15:40 James the less and of Joses, and S
Mk 16:1 and Mary the mother of James, and S

**SALT**
Gen 14:3 of Siddim, which is the S Sea
Gen 19:26 him, and she became a pillar of s
Lev 2:13 offering shalt thou season with s
Lev 2:13 s of the covenant of thy God to
Lev 2:13 offerings thou shalt offer s
Num 18:19 it is a covenant of s for ever
Num 34:3 coast of the s sea eastward
Num 34:12 out of it shall be at the s sea
Deut 3:17 sea of the plain, even the s sea
Deut 29:23 land thereof is brimstone, and s
Josh 3:16 sea of the plain, even the s sea
Josh 12:3 even the s sea on the east, the
Josh 15:2 was from the shore of the s sea
Josh 15:5 And the east border was the s sea
Josh 15:62 And Nibshan, and the city of S
Josh 18:19 were at the north bay of the s
Judg 9:45 down the city, and sowed it with s
2Sa 8:13 of the Syrians in the valley of s
2Kin 2:20 me a new cruse, and put s therein
2Kin 2:21 waters, and cast the s in there
2Kin 14:7 in the valley of s ten thousand
1Chr 18:12 the valley of s eighteen thousand
2Chr 13:5 and to his sons by a covenant of s
2Chr 25:11 and went to the valley of s
Ezr 6:9 of the God of heaven, wheat, s
Ezr 7:22 s without prescribing how much
Job 6:6 is unsavoury be eaten without s
Ps 60:t the valley of s twelve thousand
Jer 17:6 in the wilderness, in a s land
Eze 43:24 priests shall cast s upon them
Eze 47:11 they shall be given to s
Mt 5:13 Ye are the s of the earth
Mt 5:13 but if the s have lost his savour
Mk 9:49 sacrifice shall be salted with s
Mk 9:50 S is good
Mk 9:50 but if the s have lost his
Mk 9:50 Have s in yourselves, and have
Lk 14:34 S is good
Lk 14:34 but if the s have lost his savour
Col 4:6 alway with grace, seasoned with s
Jas 3:12 no fountain both yield s water

**SALTED**
Eze 16:4 thou wast not s at all, nor
Mt 5:13 savour, wherewith shall it be s
Mk 9:49 every one shall be s with fire
Mk 9:49 sacrifice shall be s with salt

**SALU** *(sa'-lu) Father of Zimri.*
Num 25:14 woman, was Zimri, the son of S

**SALUTATION**
Lk 1:29 what manner of s this should be
Lk 1:41 Elisabeth heard the s of Mary
Lk 1:44 of thy s sounded in mine ears
1Cor 16:21 The s of me Paul with mine own
Col 4:18 The s by the hand of me Paul
2Th 3:17 The s of Paul with mine own hand,

**SALUTE**
1Sa 10:4 And they will s thee, and give thee
1Sa 13:10 to meet him, that he might s him
1Sa 25:14 of the wilderness to s our master
2Sa 8:10 to s him, and to bless him,
2Kin 4:29 if thou meet any man, s him not
2Kin 4:29 and if any s thee, answer him not
2Kin 10:13 we go down to s the children of
Mt 5:47 if ye s your brethren only, what
Mt 10:12 when ye come into an house, s it
Mk 15:18 And began to s him, Hail, King of
Lk 10:4 and s no man by the way
Acts 25:13 came unto Caesarea to s Festus
Rom 16:5 S my wellbeloved Epaenetus, who
Rom 16:7 S Andronicus and Junia, my kinsmen
Rom 16:9 S Urbane, our helper in Christ,
Rom 16:10 S Apelles approved in Christ
Rom 16:10 S them which are of Aristobulus'
Rom 16:11 S Herodion my kinsman
Rom 16:12 S Tryphena and Tryphosa, who
Rom 16:12 S the beloved Persis, which
Rom 16:13 S Rufus chosen in the Lord, and
Rom 16:14 S Asyncritus, Phlegon, Hermas,
Rom 16:15 S Philologus, and Julia, Nereus,
Rom 16:16 S one another with an holy kiss
Rom 16:16 The churches of Christ s you
Rom 16:21 and Sosipater, my kinsmen, s you
Rom 16:22 this epistle, s you in the Lord
1Cor 16:19 The churches of Asia s you
1Cor 16:19 Priscilla s you much in the Lord,
2Cor 13:13 All the saints s you
Phil 4:21 S every saint in Christ Jesus
Phil 4:22 All the saints s you, chiefly
Col 4:15 S the brethren which are in
2Ti 4:19 S Prisca and Aquila, and the
Titus 3:15 All that are with me s thee
Philem 23 There s thee Epaphras, my
Heb 13:24 S all them that have the rule
Heb 13:24 They of Italy s you
3Jn 14 Our friends s thee

**SALUTED**
Judg 18:15 the house of Micah, and s him
1Sa 17:22 and came and s his brethren
1Sa 30:21 near to the people, he s them
2Kin 10:15 he s him, and said to him, Is
Mk 9:15 amazed, and running to him s him
Lk 1:40 of Zacharias, and s Elisabeth
Acts 18:22 s the church, he went down to
Acts 21:7 s the brethren, and abode with
Acts 21:19 And when he had s them, he

**SALUTETH**
Rom 16:23 and of the whole church, s you
Rom 16:23 the chamberlain of the city s you
Col 4:10 my fellowprisoner s you, and
Col 4:12 s you, always labouring fervently
1Pet 5:13 elected together with you, s you

**SALVATION**
Gen 49:18 I have waited for thy s, O LORD
Ex 14:13 see the s of the LORD, which he
Ex 15:2 and song, and he is become my s
Deut 32:15 esteemed the Rock of his s
1Sa 2:1 because I rejoice in thy s
1Sa 11:13 the LORD hath wrought s in Israel
1Sa 14:45 wrought this great s in Israel
1Sa 19:5 wrought a great s for all Israel
2Sa 22:3 is my shield, and the horn of my s
2Sa 22:36 also given me the shield of thy s
2Sa 22:47 be the God of the rock of my s
2Sa 22:51 He is the tower of s for his king
2Sa 23:5 for this is all my s, and all my
1Chr 16:23 shew forth from day to day his s
1Chr 16:35 say ye, Save us, O God of our s
2Chr 6:41 O LORD God, be clothed with s
2Chr 20:17 see the s of the LORD with you, O
Job 13:16 He also shall be my s
Ps 3:8 S belongeth unto the LORD
Ps 9:14 I will rejoice in thy s
Ps 13:5 my heart shall rejoice in thy s
Ps 14:7 Oh that the s of Israel were come
Ps 18:2 my buckler, and the horn of my s
Ps 18:35 also given me the shield of thy s
Ps 18:46 and let the God of my s be exalted
Ps 20:5 We will rejoice in thy s, and in
Ps 21:1 in thy s how greatly shall he
Ps 21:5 His glory is great in thy s
Ps 24:5 from the God of his s
Ps 25:5 for thou art the God of my s
Ps 27:1 The LORD is my light and my s
Ps 27:9 neither forsake me, O God of my s
Ps 35:3 say unto my soul, I am thy s
Ps 35:9 it shall rejoice in his s
Ps 37:39 But the s of the righteous is of
Ps 38:22 haste to help me, O Lord my s
Ps 40:10 thy faithfulness and thy s
Ps 40:16 as love thy s say continually
Ps 50:23 aright will I shew the s of God
Ps 51:12 Restore unto me the joy of thy s
Ps 51:14 O God, thou God of my s
Ps 53:6 Oh that the s of Israel were come
Ps 62:1 from him cometh my s
Ps 62:2 He only is my rock and my s
Ps 62:6 He only is my rock and my s
Ps 62:7 In God is my s and my glory
Ps 65:5 thou answer us, O God of our s
Ps 68:19 benefits, even the God of our s
Ps 68:20 that is our God is the God of s
Ps 69:13 hear me, in the truth of thy s
Ps 69:29 let thy s, O God, set me up on
Ps 70:4 as love thy s say continually
Ps 71:15 and thy s all the day
Ps 74:12 working s in the midst of the
Ps 78:22 in God, and trusted not in his s
Ps 79:9 Help us, O God of our s, for the
Ps 85:4 Turn us, O God of our s, and cause
Ps 85:7 mercy, O LORD, and grant us thy s
Ps 85:9 Surely his s is nigh them that
Ps 88:1 O lord God of my s, I have cried
Ps 89:26 my God, and the rock of my s
Ps 91:16 I satisfy him, and shew him my s
Ps 95:1 joyful noise to the rock of our s
Ps 96:2 shew forth his s from day to day
Ps 98:2 The LORD hath made known his s
Ps 98:3 earth have seen the s of our God
Ps 106:4 O visit me with thy s
Ps 116:13 I will take the cup of s, and call
Ps 118:14 and song, and is become my s
Ps 118:15 s is in the tabernacles of the
Ps 118:21 hast heard me, and art become my s
Ps 119:41 also unto me, O LORD, even thy s
Ps 119:81 My soul fainteth for thy s
Ps 119:123 Mine eyes fail for thy s, and for
Ps 119:155 S is far from the wicked
Ps 119:166 LORD, I have hoped for thy s
Ps 119:174 I have longed for thy s, O LORD
Ps 132:16 also clothe her priests with s
Ps 140:7 the Lord, the strength of my s
Ps 144:10 It is he that giveth s unto kings
Ps 149:4 he will beautify the meek with s
Is 12:2 Behold, God is my s
Is 12:2 he also is become my s
Is 12:3 draw water out of the wells of s
Is 17:10 hast forgotten the God of thy s
Is 25:9 will be glad and rejoice in his s
Is 26:1 s will God appoint for walls and
Is 33:2 our s also in the time of trouble
Is 33:6 of thy times, and strength of s
Is 45:8 open, and let them bring forth s
Is 45:17 in the LORD with an everlasting s
Is 46:13 far off, and my s shall not tarry
Is 46:13 I will place s in Zion for Israel
Is 49:6 that thou mayest be my s unto the
Is 49:8 in a day of s have I helped thee
Is 51:5 my s is gone forth, and mine arms
Is 51:6 but my s shall be for ever, and my
Is 51:8 ever, and my s from generation to
Is 52:7 of good, that publisheth s
Is 52:10 earth shall see the s of our God
Is 56:1 for my s is near to come, and my
Is 59:11 for s, but it is far off from us
Is 59:16 his arm brought s unto him
Is 59:17 an helmet of s upon his head
Is 60:18 but thou shalt call thy walls S
Is 61:10 clothed me with the garments of s
Is 62:1 the s thereof as a lamp that
Is 62:11 of Zion, Behold, thy s cometh
Is 63:5 mine own arm brought s unto me
Jer 3:23 Truly in vain is s hoped for from
Jer 3:23 LORD our God is the s of Israel
Lam 3:26 wait for the s of the LORD
Jonah 2:9 S is of the LORD
Mic 7:7 I will wait for the God of my s
Hab 3:8 thine horses and thy chariots of s
Hab 3:13 forth for the s of thy people
Hab 3:13 even for s with thine anointed
Hab 3:18 I will joy in the God of my s
Zec 9:9 he is just, and having s
Lk 1:69 hath raised up an horn of s for
Lk 1:77 To give knowledge of s unto his
Lk 2:30 For mine eyes have seen thy s
Lk 3:6 all flesh shall see the s of God
Lk 19:9 This day is s come to this house,
Jn 4:22 for s is of the Jews
Acts 4:12 Neither is there s in any other
Acts 13:26 to you is the word of this s sent
Acts 13:47 for s unto the ends of the earth
Acts 16:17 which shew unto us the way of s
Acts 28:28 that the s of God is sent unto
Rom 1:16 s to every one that believeth
Rom 10:10 mouth confession is made unto s
Rom 11:11 fall s is come unto the Gentiles
Rom 13:11 for now is our s nearer than when
2Cor 1:6 it is for your consolation and s
2Cor 1:6 it is for your consolation and s
2Cor 6:2 in the day of s have I succoured
2Cor 6:2 behold, now is the day of s
2Cor 7:10 to s not to be repented of
Eph 1:13 of truth, the gospel of your s
Eph 6:17 And take the helmet of s, and the
Phil 1:19 turn to my s through your prayer
Phil 1:28 of perdition, but to you of s
Phil 2:12 work out your own s with fear
1Th 5:8 and for an helmet, the hope of s
1Th 5:9 but to obtain s by our Lord Jesus
2Th 2:13 the beginning chosen you to s
2Ti 2:10 s which is in Christ Jesus with
2Ti 3:15 unto s through faith which is in
Titus 2:11 s hath appeared to all men
Heb 1:14 for them who shall be heirs of s
Heb 2:3 escape, if we neglect so great s
Heb 2:10 s perfect through sufferings
Heb 5:9 s unto all them that obey him

Heb 6:9 you, and things that accompany s
Heb 9:28 second time without sin unto s
1Pet 1:5 s ready to be revealed in the
1Pet 1:9 faith, even the s of your souls
1Pet 1:10 Of which s the prophets have
2Pet 3:15 longsuffering of our Lord is s
Jude 3 to write unto you of the common s
Rev 7:10 S to our God which sitteth upon
Rev 12:10 saying in heaven, Now is come s
Rev 19:1 S, and glory, and honour, and power,

**SAMARIA** *(sa-ma'-re-ah)* See SAMARITAN.

*1. A city in Ephraim.*
1Kin 16:24 he bought the hill S of Shemer
1Kin 16:24 of Shemer, owner of the hill, S
1Kin 16:28 his fathers, and was buried in S
1Kin 16:29 reigned over Israel in S twenty
1Kin 16:32 of Baal, which he had built in S
1Kin 18:2 And there was a sore famine in S
1Kin 20:1 and he went up and besieged S
1Kin 20:10 if the dust of S shall suffice
1Kin 20:17 There are men come out of S
1Kin 20:34 Damascus, as my father made in S
1Kin 20:43 heavy and displeased, and came to S
1Kin 21:18 king of Israel, which is in S
1Kin 22:10 in the entrance of the gate of S
1Kin 22:37 king died, and was brought to S
1Kin 22:37 and they buried the king in S
1Kin 22:38 the chariot in the pool of S
1Kin 22:51 in S the seventeenth year of
2Kin 1:2 his upper chamber that was in S
2Kin 2:25 and from thence he returned to S
2Kin 3:1 in S the eighteenth year of
2Kin 3:6 went out of S the same time
2Kin 5:3 with the prophet that is in S
2Kin 6:19 But he led them to S
2Kin 6:20 pass, when they were come into S
2Kin 6:20 they were in the midst of S
2Kin 6:24 host, and went up, and besieged S
2Kin 6:25 And there was a great famine in S
2Kin 7:1 for a shekel, in the gate of S
2Kin 7:18 about this time in the gate of S
2Kin 10:1 And Ahab had seventy sons in S
2Kin 10:1 Jehu wrote letters, and sent to S
2Kin 10:12 arose and departed, and came to S
2Kin 10:17 And when he came to S, he slew all
2Kin 10:17 all that remained unto Ahab in S
2Kin 10:35 and they buried him in S
2Kin 10:36 over Israel in S was twenty
2Kin 13:1 began to reign over Israel in S
2Kin 13:6 remained the grove also in S
2Kin 13:9 and they buried him in S
2Kin 13:10 to reign over Israel in S
2Kin 13:13 Joash was buried in S with the
2Kin 14:14 and hostages, and returned to S
2Kin 14:16 was buried in S with the kings of
2Kin 14:23 of Israel began to reign in S
2Kin 15:8 reign over Israel in S six months
2Kin 15:13 and he reigned a full month in S
2Kin 15:14 went up from Tirzah, and came to S
2Kin 15:14 Shallum the son of Jabesh in S
2Kin 15:17 Israel, and reigned ten years in S
2Kin 15:23 began to reign over Israel in S
2Kin 15:25 against him, and smote him in S
2Kin 15:27 began to reign over Israel in S
2Kin 17:1 reign in S over Israel nine years
2Kin 17:5 all the land, and went up to S
2Kin 17:6 Hoshea the king of Assyria took S
2Kin 18:9 king of Assyria came up against S
2Kin 18:10 king of Israel, S was taken
2Kin 18:34 they delivered S out of mine hand
2Kin 21:13 over Jerusalem the line of S
2Chr 18:9 the entering in of the gate of S
2Chr 22:9 caught him, (for he was hid in S
2Chr 25:13 from S even unto Beth-horon, and
2Chr 25:24 hostages also, and returned to S
2Chr 28:8 them, and brought the spoil to S
2Chr 28:9 before the host that came to S
2Chr 28:15 then they returned to S
Is 7:9 And the head of Ephraim is S
Is 7:9 the head of S is Remaliah's son
Is 8:4 the spoil of S shall be taken
Is 9:9 Ephraim and the inhabitant of S
Is 10:9 is not S as Damascus
Is 10:10 excel them of Jerusalem and of S
Is 10:11 I not, as I have done unto S
Eze 16:46 And thine elder sister is S
Eze 16:51 Neither hath S committed half of
Eze 16:53 daughters, and the captivity of S
Eze 16:55 to their former estate, and S
Eze 23:4 S is Aholah, and Jerusalem
Eze 23:33 with the cup of thy sister S
Hos 13:16 S shall become desolate
Amos 3:12 dwell in S in the corner of a bed
Mic 1:1 Judah, which he saw concerning S
Mic 1:5 is it not S
Mic 1:6 Therefore I will make S as an
Acts 8:5 Philip went down to the city of S
Acts 8:9 and bewitched the people of S
Acts 8:14 S had received the word of God

*2. Territory of the northern tribes.*
1Kin 13:32 which are in the cities of S
1Kin 21:1 by the palace of Ahab king of S
2Kin 1:3 the messengers of the king of S
2Kin 17:24 of S instead of the children of
2Kin 17:24 and they possessed S, and dwelt in
2Kin 17:26 and placed in the cities of S
2Kin 17:28 they had carried away from S came
2Kin 23:18 of the prophet that came out of S
2Kin 23:19 that were in the cities of S
2Chr 18:2 years he went down to Ahab to S
Ezr 4:10 over, and set in the cities of S
Ezr 4:17 their companions that dwell in S
Neh 4:2 his brethren and the army of S
Is 36:19 they delivered S out of my hand
Jer 23:13 seen folly in the prophets of S
Jer 31:5 vines upon the mountains of S
Jer 41:5 Shechem, from Shiloh, and from S
Hos 7:1 and the wickedness of S
Hos 8:5 Thy calf, O S, hath cast thee off
Hos 8:6 but the calf of S shall be broken
Hos 10:5 The inhabitants of S shall fear
Hos 10:7 As for S, her king is cut off as
Amos 3:9 upon the mountains of S, and
Amos 4:1 that are in the mountain of S
Amos 6:1 and trust in the mountain of S
Amos 8:14 They that swear by the sin of S
Obad 19 of Ephraim, and the fields of S

*3. District north of Judah.*
Lk 17:11 he passed through the midst of S
Jn 4:4 And he must needs go through S
Jn 4:5 Then cometh he to a city of S
Jn 4:7 cometh a woman of S to draw water
Jn 4:9 saith the woman of S unto him
Jn 4:9 of me, which am a woman of S
Acts 1:8 and in all Judaea, and in S
Acts 8:1 the regions of Judaea and S
Acts 9:31 all Judaea and Galilee and S
Acts 15:3 they passed through Phenice and S

**SAMARITAN** *(sa-mar'-i-tun)* See SAMARITANS. *An inhabitant of Samaria.*
Lk 10:33 But a certain S, as he journeyed,
Lk 17:16 and he was a S
Jn 8:48 Say we not well that thou art a S

**SAMARITANS** *(sa-mar'-i-tuns)*
2Kin 17:29 high places which the S had made
Mt 10:5 any city of the S enter ye not
Lk 9:52 entered into a village of the S
Jn 4:9 Jews have no dealings with the S
Jn 4:39 many of the S of that city
Jn 4:40 So when the S were come unto him,
Acts 8:25 gospel in many villages of the S

**SAMGAR-NEBO** *(sam'-gar-ne'-bo) A prince of Babylon.*
Jer 39:3 gate, even Nergal-sharezer, S

**SAMLAH** *(sam'-lah) A king of Edom.*
Gen 36:36 S of Masrekah reigned in his
Gen 36:37 S died, and Saul of Rehoboth by
1Chr 1:47 S of Masrekah reigned in his
1Chr 1:48 when S was dead, Shaul of

**SAMOS** *(sa'-mos) An island in the Aegean Sea.*
Acts 20:15 and the next day we arrived at S

**SAMOTHRACIA** *(sam-o-thra'-she-ah) An island in the Aegean Sea.*
Acts 16:11 came with a straight course to S

**SAMSON** *(sam'-sun)* See SAMSON'S. *A judge of Israel.*
Judg 13:24 bare a son, and called his name S
Judg 14:1 S went down to Timnath, and saw a
Judg 14:3 S said unto his father, Get her
Judg 14:5 Then went S down, and his father
Judg 14:7 and she pleased S well
Judg 14:10 and S made there a feast
Judg 14:12 S said unto them, I will now put
Judg 15:1 that S visited his wife with a
Judg 15:3 S said concerning them, Now shall
Judg 15:4 S went and caught three hundred
Judg 15:6 And they answered, S, the son in
Judg 15:7 S said unto them, Though ye have
Judg 15:10 To bind S are we come up, to do
Judg 15:11 of the rock Etam, and said to S
Judg 15:12 S said unto them, Swear unto me,
Judg 15:16 S said, With the jawbone of an
Judg 16:1 Then went S to Gaza, and saw there
Judg 16:2 Gazites, saying, S is come hither
Judg 16:3 S lay till midnight, and arose at
Judg 16:6 And Delilah said to S, Tell me, I
Judg 16:7 S said unto her, If they bind me
Judg 16:9 The Philistines be upon thee, S
Judg 16:10 And Delilah said unto S, Behold,
Judg 16:12 The Philistines be upon thee, S
Judg 16:13 And Delilah said unto S, Hitherto
Judg 16:14 The Philistines be upon thee, S
Judg 16:20 The Philistines be upon thee, S
Judg 16:23 Our god hath delivered S our
Judg 16:25 merry, that they said, Call for S
Judg 16:25 they called for S out of the
Judg 16:26 S said unto the lad that held him
Judg 16:27 that beheld while S made sport
Judg 16:28 S called unto the LORD, and said,
Judg 16:29 S took hold of the two middle
Judg 16:30 S said, Let me die with the
Heb 11:32 of Gedeon, and of Barak, and of S

**SAMSON'S** *(sam'-suns)*
Judg 14:15 day, that they said unto S wife
Judg 14:16 S wife wept before him, and said,
Judg 14:20 But S wife was given to his

**SAMUEL** *(sam'-u-el)* See SHEMUEL. *A priest and judge of Israel.*
1Sa 1:20 bare a son, and called his name S
1Sa 2:18 But S ministered before the LORD,
1Sa 2:21 the child S grew before the LORD
1Sa 2:26 And the child S grew on, and was in
1Sa 3:1 the child S ministered unto the
1Sa 3:3 was, and S was laid down to sleep
1Sa 3:4 That the LORD called S
1Sa 3:6 And the LORD called yet again, S
1Sa 3:6 S arose and went to Eli, and said,
1Sa 3:7 Now S did not yet know the LORD,
1Sa 3:8 the LORD called S again the third
1Sa 3:9 Therefore Eli said unto S
1Sa 3:9 So S went and lay down in his
1Sa 3:10 as at other times, S, S
1Sa 3:10 Then S answered, Speak
1Sa 3:11 And the LORD said to S, Behold, I
1Sa 3:15 S lay until the morning, and
1Sa 3:15 S feared to shew Eli the vision
1Sa 3:16 Eli called S, and said, S
1Sa 3:18 S told him every whit, and hid
1Sa 3:19 S grew, and the LORD was with him,
1Sa 3:20 even to Beer-sheba knew that S
1Sa 3:21 to S in Shiloh by the word of the
1Sa 4:1 the word of S came to all Israel
1Sa 7:3 S spake unto all the house of
1Sa 7:5 S said, Gather all Israel to
1Sa 7:6 S judged the children of Israel
1Sa 7:8 the children of Israel said to S
1Sa 7:9 S took a sucking lamb, and offered
1Sa 7:9 S cried unto the LORD for Israel
1Sa 7:10 as S was offering up the burnt
1Sa 7:12 Then S took a stone, and set it
1Sa 7:13 the Philistines all the days of S
1Sa 7:15 S judged Israel all the days of
1Sa 8:1 when S was old, that he made his
1Sa 8:4 and came to S unto Ramah,
1Sa 8:6 But the thing displeased S
1Sa 8:6 And S prayed unto the LORD
1Sa 8:7 And the LORD said unto S, Hearken
1Sa 8:10 S told all the words of the LORD
1Sa 8:19 refused to obey the voice of S
1Sa 8:21 S heard all the words of the
1Sa 8:22 And the LORD said to S, Hearken
1Sa 8:22 S said unto the men of Israel, Go
1Sa 9:14 S came out against them, for to
1Sa 9:15 Now the LORD had told S in his
1Sa 9:17 when S saw Saul, the LORD said
1Sa 9:18 Saul drew near to S in the gate
1Sa 9:19 S answered Saul, and said, I am
1Sa 9:22 S took Saul and his servant, and
1Sa 9:23 S said unto the cook, Bring the
1Sa 9:24 S said, Behold that which is left
1Sa 9:24 So Saul did eat with S that day
1Sa 9:25 S communed with Saul upon the top
1Sa 9:26 that S called Saul to the top of

1Sa 9:26 went out both of them, he and *S*
1Sa 9:27 *S* said to Saul, Bid the servant
1Sa 10:1 Then *S* took a vial of oil, and
1Sa 10:9 had turned his back to go from *S*
1Sa 10:14 they were no where, we came to *S*
1Sa 10:15 I pray thee, what *S* said unto you
1Sa 10:16 of the kingdom, whereof *S* spake
1Sa 10:17 *S* called the people together unto
1Sa 10:20 when *S* had caused all the tribes
1Sa 10:24 *S* said to all the people, See ye
1Sa 10:25 Then *S* told the people the manner
1Sa 10:25 *S* sent all the people away, every
1Sa 11:7 not forth after Saul and after *S*
1Sa 11:12 And the people said unto *S*
1Sa 11:14 Then said *S* to the people, Come,
1Sa 12:1 *S* said unto all Israel, Behold, I
1Sa 12:6 *S* said unto the people, It is the
1Sa 12:11 and Bedan, and Jephthah, and *S*
1Sa 12:18 So *S* called unto the LORD
1Sa 12:18 greatly feared the LORD and *S*
1Sa 12:19 And all the people said unto *S*
1Sa 12:20 *S* said unto the people, Fear not
1Sa 13:8 the set time that *S* had appointed
1Sa 13:8 but *S* came not to Gilgal
1Sa 13:10 burnt offering, behold, *S* came
1Sa 13:11 *S* said, What hast thou done
1Sa 13:13 *S* said to Saul, Thou hast done
1Sa 13:15 *S* arose, and gat him up from
1Sa 15:1 *S* also said unto Saul, The LORD
1Sa 15:10 came the word of the LORD unto *S*
1Sa 15:11 And it grieved *S*
1Sa 15:12 when *S* rose early to meet Saul in
1Sa 15:12 in the morning, it was told *S*
1Sa 15:13 And *S* came to Saul
1Sa 15:14 *S* said, What meaneth then this
1Sa 15:16 Then *S* said unto Saul, Stay, and I
1Sa 15:17 *S* said, When thou wast little in
1Sa 15:20 And Saul said unto *S*, Yea, I have
1Sa 15:22 *S* said, Hath the LORD as great
1Sa 15:24 And Saul said unto *S*, I have
1Sa 15:26 *S* said unto Saul, I will not
1Sa 15:27 as *S* turned about to go away, he
1Sa 15:28 *S* said unto him, The LORD hath
1Sa 15:31 So *S* turned again after Saul
1Sa 15:32 Then said *S*, Bring ye hither to
1Sa 15:33 *S* said, As thy sword hath made
1Sa 15:33 *S* hewed Agag in pieces before the
1Sa 15:34 Then *S* went to Ramah
1Sa 15:35 *S* came no more to see Saul until
1Sa 15:35 nevertheless *S* mourned for Saul
1Sa 16:1 And the LORD said unto *S*, How long
1Sa 16:2 And *S* said, How can I go
1Sa 16:4 *S* did that which the LORD spake,
1Sa 16:7 But the LORD said unto *S*, Look
1Sa 16:8 and made him pass before *S*
1Sa 16:10 of his sons to pass before *S*
1Sa 16:10 *S* said unto Jesse, The LORD hath
1Sa 16:11 *S* said unto Jesse, Are here all
1Sa 16:11 *S* said unto Jesse, Send and fetch
1Sa 16:13 Then *S* took the horn of oil, and
1Sa 16:13 So *S* rose up, and went to Ramah
1Sa 19:18 came to *S* to Ramah, and told him
1Sa 19:18 *S* went and dwelt in Naioth
1Sa 19:20 *S* standing as appointed over them
1Sa 19:22 and he asked and said, Where are *S*
1Sa 19:24 before *S* in like manner, and lay
1Sa 25:1 And *S* died
1Sa 28:3 Now *S* was dead, and all Israel had
1Sa 28:11 And he said, Bring me up *S*
1Sa 28:12 And when the woman saw *S*, she
1Sa 28:14 And Saul perceived that it was *S*
1Sa 28:15 *S* said to Saul, Why hast thou
1Sa 28:16 Then said *S*, Wherefore then dost
1Sa 28:20 afraid, because of the words of *S*
1Chr 6:28 And the sons of *S*
1Chr 9:22 *S* the seer did ordain in their
1Chr 11:3 to the word of the LORD by *S*
1Chr 26:28 And all that *S* the seer, and Saul
1Chr 29:29 written in the book of *S* the seer
2Chr 35:18 from the days of *S* the prophet
Ps 99:6 *S* among them that call upon his
Jer 15:1 *S* stood before me, yet my mind
Acts 3:24 Yea, and all the prophets from *S*
Acts 13:20 fifty years, until *S* the prophet
Heb 11:32 of David also, and *S*, and of the

**SANBALLAT** *(san-bal'-lat) An opponent of Nehemiah.*
Neh 2:10 When *S* the Horonite, and Tobiah
Neh 2:19 But when *S* the Horonite, and
Neh 4:1 that when *S* heard that we builded
Neh 4:7 But it came to pass, that when *S*
Neh 6:1 Now it came to pass, when *S*
Neh 6:2 That *S* and Geshem sent unto me,
Neh 6:5 Then sent *S* his servant unto me
Neh 6:12 for Tobiah and *S* had hired him
Neh 6:14 *S* according to these their works,
Neh 13:28 was son in law to *S* the Horonite

**SANCTIFICATION**
1Cor 1:30 us wisdom, and righteousness, and *s*
1Th 4:3 is the will of God, even your *s*
1Th 4:4 how to possess his vessel in *s*
2Th 2:13 salvation through *s* of the Spirit
1Pet 1:2 through *s* of the Spirit, unto

**SANCTIFIED**
Gen 2:3 blessed the seventh day, and *s* it
Ex 19:14 unto the people, and *s* the people
Ex 29:43 tabernacle shall be *s* by my glory
Lev 8:10 all that was therein, and *s* them
Lev 8:15 *s* it, to make reconciliation upon
Lev 8:30 *s* Aaron, and his garments, and his
Lev 10:3 I will be *s* in them that come
Lev 27:15 if he that *s* it will redeem his
Lev 27:19 if he that *s* the field will in
Num 7:1 *s* it, and all the instruments
Num 7:1 and had anointed them, and *s* them
Num 8:17 land of Egypt I *s* them for myself
Num 20:13 the LORD, and he was *s* in them
Deut 32:51 because ye *s* me not in the midst
1Sa 7:1 *s* Eleazar his son to keep the ark
1Sa 16:5 he *s* Jesse and his sons, and called
1Sa 21:5 though it were *s* this day in the
1Chr 15:14 the Levites *s* themselves to bring
2Chr 5:11 priests that were present were *s*
2Chr 7:16 *s* this house, that my name may be
2Chr 7:20 house, which I have *s* for my name
2Chr 29:15 *s* themselves, and came, according
2Chr 29:17 so they *s* the house of the LORD
2Chr 29:19 have we prepared and *s*, and,
2Chr 29:34 other priests had *s* themselves
2Chr 30:3 had not *s* themselves sufficiently
2Chr 30:8 which he hath *s* for ever
2Chr 30:15 *s* themselves, and brought in the
2Chr 30:17 the congregation that were not *s*
2Chr 30:24 number of priests *s* themselves
2Chr 31:18 they *s* themselves in holiness
Neh 3:1 they *s* it, and set up the doors of
Neh 3:1 unto the tower of Meah they *s* it
Neh 12:47 they *s* holy things unto the
Neh 12:47 the Levites *s* them unto the
Job 1:5 *s* them, and rose up early in the
Is 5:16 holy shall be *s* in righteousness
Is 13:3 I have commanded my *s* ones
Jer 1:5 forth out of the womb I *s* thee
Eze 20:41 I will be *s* in you before the
Eze 28:22 in her, and shall be *s* in her
Eze 28:25 shall be *s* in them in the sight
Eze 36:23 when I shall be *s* in you before
Eze 38:16 me, when I shall be *s* in thee
Eze 39:27 am *s* in them in the sight of many
Eze 48:11 that are *s* of the sons of Zadok
Jn 10:36 ye of him, whom the Father hath *s*
Jn 17:19 also might be *s* through the truth
Acts 20:32 among all them which are *s*
Acts 26:18 among them which are *s* by faith
Rom 15:16 being *s* by the Holy Ghost
1Cor 1:2 them that are *s* in Christ Jesus
1Cor 6:11 but ye are washed, but ye are *s*
1Cor 7:14 husband is *s* by the wife, and the
1Cor 7:14 wife is *s* by the husband
1Ti 4:5 For it is *s* by the word of God and
2Ti 2:21 shall be a vessel unto honour, *s*
Heb 2:11 they who are *s* are all of one
Heb 10:10 By the which will we are *s*
Heb 10:14 for ever them that are *s*
Heb 10:29 the covenant, wherewith he was *s*
Jude 1 to them that are *s* by God the

**SANCTIFIETH**
Mt 23:17 or the temple that *s* the gold
Mt 23:19 or the altar that *s* the gift
Heb 2:11 For both he that *s* and they who
Heb 9:13 *s* to the purifying of the flesh

**SANCTIFY**
Ex 13:2 *S* unto me all the firstborn,
Ex 19:10 *s* them to day and to morrow, and
Ex 19:22 *s* themselves, lest the LORD break
Ex 19:23 bounds about the mount, and *s* it
Ex 28:41 *s* them, that they may minister
Ex 29:27 thou shalt *s* the breast of the
Ex 29:33 made, to consecrate and to *s* them
Ex 29:36 and thou shalt anoint it, to *s* it
Ex 29:37 atonement for the altar, and *s* it
Ex 29:44 I will *s* the tabernacle of the
Ex 29:44 I will *s* also both Aaron and his
Ex 30:29 And thou shalt *s* them, that they
Ex 31:13 I am the LORD that doth *s* you
Ex 40:10 all his vessels, and *s* the altar
Ex 40:11 the laver and his foot, and *s* it
Ex 40:13 garments, and anoint him, and *s* him
Lev 8:11 the laver and his foot, to *s* them
Lev 8:12 head, and anointed him, to *s* him
Lev 11:44 ye shall therefore *s* yourselves
Lev 20:7 *S* yourselves therefore, and be ye
Lev 20:8 I am the LORD which *s* you
Lev 21:8 Thou shalt *s* him therefore
Lev 21:8 for I the LORD, which *s* you
Lev 21:15 for I the LORD do *s* him
Lev 21:23 for I the LORD do *s* them
Lev 22:9 I the LORD do *s* them
Lev 22:16 for I the LORD do *s* them
Lev 27:14 when a man shall *s* his house to
Lev 27:16 if a man shall *s* unto the LORD
Lev 27:17 If he *s* his field from the year
Lev 27:18 But if he *s* his field after the
Lev 27:22 if a man *s* unto the LORD a field
Lev 27:26 firstling, no man shall *s* it
Num 11:18 *S* yourselves against to morrow,
Num 20:12 to *s* me in the eyes of the
Num 27:14 to *s* me at the water before their
Deut 5:12 Keep the sabbath day to *s* it
Deut 15:19 shalt *s* unto the LORD thy God
Josh 3:5 unto the people, *S* yourselves
Josh 7:13 *s* the people, and say, *S*
1Sa 16:5 *s* yourselves, and come with me to
1Chr 15:12 *s* yourselves, both ye and your
1Chr 23:13 that he should *s* the most holy
2Chr 29:5 *s* now yourselves
2Chr 29:5 *s* the house of the LORD God of
2Chr 29:17 first day of the first month to *s*
2Chr 29:34 to *s* themselves than the priests
2Chr 30:17 clean, to *s* them unto the LORD
2Chr 35:6 *s* yourselves, and prepare your
Neh 13:22 the gates, to *s* the sabbath day
Is 8:13 *S* the LORD of hosts himself
Is 29:23 of him, they shall *s* my name
Is 29:23 *s* the Holy One of Jacob, and shall
Is 66:17 They that *s* themselves, and purify
Eze 20:12 that I am the LORD that *s* them
Eze 36:23 I will *s* my great name, which was
Eze 37:28 know that I the LORD do *s* Israel
Eze 38:23 I magnify myself, and *s* myself
Eze 44:19 they shall not *s* the people with
Eze 46:20 the utter court, to *s* the people
Joel 1:14 *S* ye a fast, call a solemn
Joel 2:15 *s* a fast, call a solemn assembly
Joel 2:16 *s* the congregation, assemble the
Jn 17:17 *S* them through thy truth
Jn 17:19 And for their sakes I *s* myself
Eph 5:26 That he might *s* and cleanse it
1Th 5:23 very God of peace *s* you wholly
Heb 13:12 that he might *s* the people with
1Pet 3:15 But *s* the Lord God in your hearts

**SANCTUARIES**
Lev 21:23 that he profane not my *s*
Lev 26:31 bring your *s* unto desolation, and
Jer 51:51 into the *s* of the LORD's house
Eze 28:18 Thou hast defiled thy *s* by the
Amos 7:9 the *s* of Israel shall be laid

**SANCTUARY**
Ex 15:17 for thee to dwell in, in the *S*
Ex 25:8 And let them make me a *s*
Ex 30:13 shekel after the shekel of the *s*
Ex 30:24 after the shekel of the *s*
Ex 36:1 of work for the service of the *s*
Ex 36:3 the work of the service of the *s*
Ex 36:4 wrought all the work of the *s*
Ex 36:6 work for the offering of the *s*
Ex 38:24 after the shekel of the *s*
Ex 38:25 after the shekel of the *s*
Ex 38:26 shekel, after the shekel of the *s*
Ex 38:27 were cast the sockets of the *s*
Lev 4:6 LORD, before the vail of the *s*
Lev 5:15 silver, after the shekel of the *s*
Lev 10:4 from before the *s* out of the camp
Lev 12:4 thing, nor come into the *s*
Lev 16:33 make an atonement for the holy *s*
Lev 19:30 my sabbaths, and reverence my *s*

Lev 20:3 seed unto Molech, to defile my *s*
Lev 21:12 Neither shall he go out of the *s*
Lev 21:12 nor profane the *s* of his God
Lev 26:2 my sabbaths, and reverence my *s*
Lev 27:3 silver, after the shekel of the *s*
Lev 27:25 according to the shekel of the *s*
Num 3:28 keeping the charge of the *s*
Num 3:31 the vessels of the *s* wherewith
Num 3:32 that keep the charge of the *s*
Num 3:38 keeping the charge of the *s* for
Num 3:47 of the *s* shalt thou take them
Num 3:50 after the shekel of the *s*
Num 4:12 wherewith they minister in the *s*
Num 4:15 made an end of covering the *s*
Num 4:15 and all the vessels of the *s*
Num 4:16 of all that therein is, in the *s*
Num 7:9 because the service of the *s*
Num 7:13 after the shekel of the *s*
Num 7:19 after the shekel of the *s*
Num 7:25 after the shekel of the *s*
Num 7:31 after the shekel of the *s*
Num 7:37 after the shekel of the *s*
Num 7:43 after the shekel of the *s*
Num 7:49 after the shekel of the *s*
Num 7:55 after the shekel of the *s*
Num 7:61 after the shekel of the *s*
Num 7:67 after the shekel of the *s*
Num 7:73 after the shekel of the *s*
Num 7:79 after the shekel of the *s*
Num 7:85 after the shekel of the *s*
Num 7:86 apiece, after the shekel of the *s*
Num 8:19 of Israel come nigh unto the *s*
Num 10:21 set forward, bearing the *s*
Num 18:1 shall bear the iniquity of the *s*
Num 18:3 come nigh the vessels of the *s*
Num 18:5 ye shall keep the charge of the *s*
Num 18:16 after the shekel of the *s*
Num 19:20 he hath defiled the *s* of the LORD
Josh 24:26 that was by the *s* of the LORD
1Chr 9:29 and all the instruments of the *s*
1Chr 22:19 build ye the *s* of the LORD God,
1Chr 24:5 for the governors of the *s*
1Chr 28:10 thee to build an house for the *s*
2Chr 20:8 have built thee a *s* therein for
2Chr 26:18 go out of the *s*
2Chr 29:21 for the kingdom, and for the *s*
2Chr 30:8 the LORD, and enter into his *s*
2Chr 30:19 to the purification of the *s*
2Chr 36:17 the sword in the house of their *s*
Neh 10:39 where are the vessels of the *s*
Ps 20:2 Send thee help from the *s*
Ps 63:2 so as I have seen thee in the *s*
Ps 68:24 of my God, my King, in the *s*
Ps 73:17 Until I went into the *s* of God
Ps 74:3 enemy hath done wickedly in the *s*
Ps 74:7 They have cast fire into thy *s*
Ps 77:13 Thy way, O God, is in the *s*
Ps 78:54 them to the border of his *s*
Ps 78:69 he built his *s* like high palaces,
Ps 96:6 strength and beauty are in his *s*
Ps 102:19 down from the height of his *s*
Ps 114:2 Judah was his *s*, and Israel his
Ps 134:2 Lift up your hands in the *s*
Ps 150:1 Praise God in his *s*
Is 8:14 And he shall be for a *s*
Is 16:12 he shall come to his *s* to pray
Is 43:28 profaned the princes of the *s*
Is 60:13 to beautify the place of my *s*
Is 63:18 have trodden down thy *s*
Jer 17:12 beginning is the place of our *s*
Lam 1:10 the heathen entered into her *s*
Lam 2:7 his altar, he hath abhorred his *s*
Lam 2:20 be slain in the *s* of the Lord
Lam 4:1 the stones of the *s* are poured
Eze 5:11 because thou hast defiled my *s*
Eze 8:6 I should go far off from my *s*
Eze 9:6 and begin at my *s*
Eze 11:16 *s* in the countries where they
Eze 23:38 have defiled my *s* in the same day
Eze 23:39 same day into my *s* to profane it
Eze 24:21 Behold, I will profane my *s*
Eze 25:3 thou saidst, Aha, against my *s*
Eze 37:26 will set my *s* in the midst of
Eze 37:28 when my *s* shall be in the midst
Eze 41:21 squared, and the face of the *s*
Eze 41:23 the temple and the *s* had two doors
Eze 42:20 make a separation between the *s*
Eze 43:21 place of the house, without the *s*
Eze 44:1 *s* which looketh toward the east
Eze 44:5 with every going forth of the *s*
Eze 44:7 have brought into my *s* strangers
Eze 44:7 in flesh, to be in my *s*, to
Eze 44:8 my charge in my *s* for yourselves
Eze 44:9 in flesh, shall enter into my *s*
Eze 44:11 they shall be ministers in my *s*
Eze 44:15 that kept the charge of my *s* when
Eze 44:16 They shall enter into my *s*
Eze 44:27 the day that he goeth into the *s*
Eze 44:27 inner court, to minister in the *s*
Eze 45:2 for the *s* five hundred in length
Eze 45:3 and in it shall be the *s* and the
Eze 45:4 priests the ministers of the *s*
Eze 45:4 and an holy place for the *s*
Eze 45:18 without blemish, and cleanse the *s*
Eze 47:12 they they issued out of the *s*
Eze 48:8 the *s* shall be in the midst of it
Eze 48:10 the *s* of the LORD shall be in the
Eze 48:21 the *s* of the house shall be in
Dan 8:11 the place of his *s* was cast down
Dan 8:13 of desolation, to give both the *s*
Dan 8:14 then shall the *s* be cleansed
Dan 9:17 shine upon thy *s* that is desolate
Dan 9:26 shall destroy the city and the *s*
Dan 11:31 shall pollute the *s* of strength
Zeph 3:4 her priests have polluted the *s*
Heb 8:2 A minister of the *s*, and of the
Heb 9:1 of divine service, and a worldly *s*
Heb 9:2 which is called the *s*
Heb 13:11 the *s* by the high priest for sin

**SAND**
Gen 22:17 as the *s* which is upon the sea
Gen 32:12 make thy seed as the *s* of the sea
Gen 41:49 gathered corn as the *s* of the sea
Ex 2:12 the Egyptian, and hid him in the *s*
Deut 33:19 and of treasures hid in the *s*
Josh 11:4 even as the *s* that is upon the
Judg 7:12 as the *s* by the sea side for
1Sa 13:5 people as the *s* which is on the
2Sa 17:11 as the *s* that is by the sea for
1Kin 4:20 as the *s* which is by the sea in
1Kin 4:29 even as the *s* that is on the sea
Job 6:3 be heavier than the *s* of the sea
Job 29:18 I shall multiply my days as the *s*
Ps 78:27 fowls like as the *s* of the sea
Ps 139:18 are more in number than the *s*
Prov 27:3 stone is heavy, and the *s* weighty
Is 10:22 Israel be as the *s* of the sea
Is 48:19 Thy seed also had been as the *s*
Jer 5:22 which have placed the *s* for the
Jer 15:8 to me above the *s* of the seas
Jer 33:22 neither the *s* of the sea measured
Hos 1:10 shall be as the *s* of the sea
Hab 1:9 gather the captivity as the *s*
Mt 7:26 which built his house upon the *s*
Rom 9:27 of Israel be as the *s* of the sea
Heb 11:12 as the *s* which is by the sea
Rev 13:1 And I stood upon the *s* of the sea
Rev 20:8 of whom is as the *s* of the sea

**SANG**
Ex 15:1 Then *s* Moses and the children of
Num 21:17 Then Israel *s* this song, Spring
Judg 5:1 Then *s* Deborah and Barak the son
1Sa 29:5 of whom they *s* one to another in
2Chr 29:28 worshipped, and the singers *s*
2Chr 29:30 they *s* praises with gladness, and
Ezr 3:11 they *s* together by course in
Neh 12:42 And the singers *s* loud, with
Job 38:7 When the morning stars *s* together
Ps 7:*t* which he *s* unto the LORD,
Ps 106:12 they *s* his praise
Acts 16:25 prayed, and *s* praises unto God

**SANSANNAH** *(san-san'-nah) A city in Judah.*
Josh 15:31 And Ziklag, and Madmannah, and *S*

**SAPH** *(saf)* See SIPHAI. *A descendant of Rapha.*
2Sa 21:18 Sibbechai the Hushathite slew *S*

**SAPHIR** *(sa'-fur) A city in Ephraim.*
Mic 1:11 ye away, thou inhabitant of *S*

**SAPPHIRA** *(saf-fi'-rah) Wife of Ananias.*
Acts 5:1 Ananias, with *S* his wife, sold a

**SAPPHIRE**
Ex 24:10 it were a paved work of a *s* stone
Ex 28:18 row shall be an emerald, a *s*
Ex 39:11 the second row, an emerald, a *s*
Job 28:16 with the precious onyx, or the *s*
Lam 4:7 rubies, their polishing was of *s*
Eze 1:26 as the appearance of a *s* stone
Eze 10:1 over them as it were a *s* stone
Eze 28:13 the onyx, and the jasper, the *s*
Rev 21:19 the second, *s*

**SARA** *(sa'-rah)* See SARAH. *Greek form of Sarah 1.*
Heb 11:11 Through faith also *S* herself

**SARAH** *(sa'-rah)* See SARA, SARAH'S, SARAI, SERAH.
*1. Wife of Abraham.*
Gen 17:15 Sarai, but *S* shall her name be
Gen 17:17 and shall *S*, that is ninety years
Gen 17:19 *S* thy wife shall bear thee a son
Gen 17:21 which *S* shall bear unto thee at
Gen 18:6 hastened into the tent unto *S*
Gen 18:9 unto him, Where is *S* thy wife
Gen 18:10 *S* thy wife shall have a son
Gen 18:10 *S* heard it in the tent door,
Gen 18:11 *S* were old and well stricken in
Gen 18:11 it ceased to be with *S* after the
Gen 18:12 Therefore *S* laughed within
Gen 18:13 Abraham, Wherefore did *S* laugh
Gen 18:14 of life, and *S* shall have a son
Gen 18:15 Then *S* denied, saying, I laughed
Gen 20:2 And Abraham said of *S* his wife
Gen 20:2 king of Gerar sent, and took *S*
Gen 20:14 and restored him *S* his wife
Gen 20:16 unto *S* he said, Behold, I have
Gen 20:18 because of *S* Abraham's wife
Gen 21:1 the LORD visited *S* as he had said
Gen 21:1 LORD did unto *S* as he had spoken
Gen 21:2 For *S* conceived, and bare Abraham
Gen 21:3 whom *S* bare to him, Isaac
Gen 21:6 *S* said, God hath made me to laugh
Gen 21:7 that *S* should have given children
Gen 21:9 *S* saw the son of Hagar the
Gen 21:12 in all that *S* hath said unto thee
Gen 23:1 *S* was an hundred and seven and
Gen 23:1 were the years of the life of *S*
Gen 23:2 And *S* died in Kirjath-arba
Gen 23:2 and Abraham came to mourn for *S*
Gen 23:19 Abraham buried *S* his wife in the
Gen 24:36 *S* my master's wife bare a son to
Gen 25:10 was Abraham buried, and *S* his wife
Gen 49:31 they buried Abraham and *S* his wife
Is 51:2 father, and unto *S* that bare you
Rom 9:9 I come, and *S* shall have a son
1Pet 3:6 Even as *S* obeyed Abraham, calling
*2. A daughter of Asher.*
Num 26:46 of the daughter of Asher was *S*

**SARAI** *(sa'-rahee)* See SARAH, SARAI'S. *The original name of Sarah.*
Gen 11:29 the name of Abram's wife was *S*
Gen 11:30 But *S* was barren
Gen 11:31 *S* his daughter in law, his son
Gen 12:5 And Abram took *S* his wife, and Lot
Gen 12:11 that he said unto *S* his wife
Gen 12:17 plagues because of *S* Abram's wife
Gen 16:1 Now *S* Abram's wife bare him no
Gen 16:2 *S* said unto Abram, Behold now,
Gen 16:2 Abram hearkened to the voice of *S*
Gen 16:3 *S* Abram's wife took Hagar her
Gen 16:5 *S* said unto Abram, My wrong be
Gen 16:6 But Abram said unto *S*, Behold,
Gen 16:6 when *S* dealt hardly with her, she
Gen 16:8 from the face of my mistress *S*
Gen 17:15 As for *S* thy wife, thou shalt not
Gen 17:15 thou shalt not call her name *S*

**SARAI'S** *(sa'-rahees)*
Gen 16:8 *S* maid, whence camest thou

**SARAPH** *(sa'-raf) A descendant of Shelah.*
1Chr 4:22 men of Chozeba, and Joash, and *S*

**SARDIS** *(sar'-dis) A city in Lydia in Asia Minor.*
Rev 1:11 and unto Thyatira, and unto *S*
Rev 3:1 angel of the church in *S* write
Rev 3:4 in *S* which have not defiled their

**SARDITES** *(sar'-dites) Descendants of Sered.*
Num 26:26 of Sered, the family of the *S*

**SARDIUS**
Ex 28:17 the first row shall be a *s*
Ex 39:10 the first row was a *s*, a topaz,
Eze 28:13 stone was thy covering, the *s*
Rev 21:20 the sixth, *s*

**SAREPTA** *(sa-rep'-tah)* See ZAREPHATH. *A city near Sidon.*
Lk 4:26 them was Elias sent, save unto *S*

**SARGON** *(sar'-gon) An Assyrian king.*
Is 20:1 (when *S* the king of Assyria sent

**SARID** *(sa'-rid) A city in Zebulun.*
Josh 19:10 of their inheritance was unto *S*
Josh 19:12 turned from *S* eastward toward the

**SARON** *(sa'-ron)* See SHARON. *The area between Joppa and Caesarea.*
Acts 9:35 *S* saw him, and turned to the Lord

**SARSECHIM** *(sar'-se-kim) A prince of Babylon.*
Jer 39:3 Nergal-sharezer, Samgar-nebo, *S*

**SARUCH** *(sa'-ruk)* See SERUG. *Father of Nahor; an ancestor of Jesus.*
Lk 3:35 Which was the son of *S*, which was

**SAT**
Gen 18:1 he *s* in the tent door in the heat
Gen 19:1 Lot *s* in the gate of Sodom
Gen 21:16 *s* her down over against him a
Gen 21:16 she *s* over against him, and lift
Gen 31:34 camel's furniture, and *s* upon them
Gen 37:25 And they *s* down to eat bread
Gen 38:14 *s* in an open place, which is by
Gen 43:33 they *s* before him, the firstborn
Gen 48:2 himself, and *s* upon the bed
Ex 2:15 and he *s* down by a well
Ex 12:29 that *s* on his throne unto the
Ex 16:3 when we *s* by the flesh pots, and
Ex 17:12 put it under him, and he *s* thereon
Ex 18:13 that Moses *s* to judge the people
Ex 32:6 the people *s* down to eat and to
Lev 15:6 *s* that hath the issue shall wash
Lev 15:22 she *s* upon shall wash his clothes
Deut 33:3 and they *s* down at thy feet
Judg 6:11 *s* under an oak which was in
Judg 13:9 the woman as she *s* in the field
Judg 19:6 And they *s* down, and did eat and
Judg 19:15 he *s* him down in a street of the
Judg 20:26 *s* there before the LORD, and
Ruth 2:14 And she *s* beside the reapers
Ruth 4:1 to the gate, and *s* him down there
Ruth 4:1 And he turned aside, and *s* down
Ruth 4:2 And they *s* down
1Sa 1:9 Now Eli the priest *s* upon a seat
1Sa 4:13 Eli *s* upon a seat by the wayside
1Sa 19:9 as he *s* in his house with his
1Sa 20:24 the king *s* him down to eat meat
1Sa 20:25 the king *s* upon his seat, as at
1Sa 20:25 Abner *s* by Saul's side, and
1Sa 28:23 from the earth, and *s* upon the bed
2Sa 2:13 and they *s* down, the one on the
2Sa 7:1 when the king *s* in his house
2Sa 7:18 *s* before the LORD, and he said,
2Sa 18:24 David *s* between the two gates
2Sa 19:8 the king arose, and *s* in the gate
2Sa 23:8 The Tachmonite that *s* in the seat
1Kin 2:12 Then *s* Solomon upon the throne of
1Kin 2:19 *s* down on his throne, and caused a
1Kin 2:19 and she *s* on his right hand
1Kin 13:20 as they *s* at the table, that the
1Kin 16:11 as soon as he *s* on his throne
1Kin 19:4 *s* down under a juniper tree
1Kin 21:13 of Belial, and *s* before him
1Kin 22:10 of Judah *s* each on his throne
2Kin 1:9 he *s* on the top of an hill
2Kin 4:20 he *s* on her knees till noon, and
2Kin 6:32 But Elisha *s* in his house, and the
2Kin 6:32 house, and the elders *s* with him
2Kin 11:19 he *s* on the throne of the kings
2Kin 13:13 Jeroboam *s* upon his throne
1Chr 17:1 as David *s* in his house, that
1Chr 17:16 *s* before the LORD, and said, Who
1Chr 29:23 Then Solomon *s* on the throne of
2Chr 18:9 Jehoshaphat king of Judah *s*
2Chr 18:9 they *s* in a void place at the
Ezr 9:3 of my beard, and *s* down astonied
Ezr 9:4 I *s* astonied until the evening
Ezr 10:9 all the people *s* in the street of
Ezr 10:16 *s* down in the first day of the
Neh 1:4 heard these words, that I *s* down
Neh 8:17 booths, and *s* under the booths
Est 1:2 when the king Ahasuerus *s* on the
Est 1:14 which *s* the first in the kingdom
Est 2:19 then Mordecai *s* in the king's
Est 2:21 while Mordecai *s* in the king's
Est 3:15 the king and Haman *s* down to drink
Est 5:1 the king *s* upon his royal throne
Job 2:8 he *s* down among the ashes
Job 2:13 So they *s* down with him upon the
Job 29:25 *s* chief, and dwelt as a king in
Ps 26:4 I have not *s* with vain persons,
Ps 137:1 of Babylon, there we *s* down
Song 2:3 I *s* down under his shadow with
Jer 3:2 In the ways hast thou *s* for them
Jer 15:17 I *s* not in the assembly of the
Jer 15:17 I *s* alone because of thy hand
Jer 26:10 *s* down in the entry of the new
Jer 32:12 before all the Jews that *s* in the
Jer 36:12 and, lo, all the princes *s* there
Jer 36:22 Now the king *s* in the winterhouse
Jer 39:3 *s* in the middle gate, even
Eze 3:15 I *s* where they *s*, and remained
Eze 3:15 of Chebar, and I *s* where they *s*
Eze 8:1 as I *s* in mine house, and the
Eze 8:1 the elders of Judah *s* before me
Eze 8:14 there *s* women weeping for Tammuz
Eze 14:1 of Israel unto me, and *s* before me
Eze 20:1 of the LORD, and *s* before me
Dan 2:49 but Daniel *s* in the gate of the
Jonah 3:6 him with sackcloth, and *s* in ashes
Jonah 4:5 *s* on the east side of the city,
Jonah 4:5 *s* under it in the shadow, till he
Mt 4:16 The people which *s* in darkness
Mt 4:16 and to them which *s* in the region
Mt 9:10 as Jesus *s* at meat in the house,
Mt 9:10 *s* down with him and his disciples
Mt 13:1 the house, and *s* by the sea side
Mt 13:2 so that he went into a ship, and *s*
Mt 13:48 *s* down, and gathered the good into
Mt 14:9 them which *s* with him at meat, he
Mt 15:29 into a mountain, and *s* down there
Mt 24:3 as he *s* upon the mount of Olives,
Mt 26:7 it on his head, as he *s* at meat
Mt 26:20 he *s* down with the twelve
Mt 26:55 I *s* daily with you teaching in
Mt 26:58 *s* with the servants, to see the
Mt 26:69 Now Peter *s* without in the palace
Mt 28:2 stone from the door, and *s* upon it
Mk 2:15 as Jesus *s* at meat in his house,
Mk 2:15 sinners *s* also together with
Mk 3:32 And the multitude *s* about him
Mk 3:34 about on them which *s* about him
Mk 4:1 into a ship, and *s* in the sea
Mk 6:22 Herod and them that *s* with him
Mk 6:26 for their sakes which *s* with him
Mk 6:40 they *s* down in ranks, by hundreds
Mk 9:35 he *s* down, and called the twelve,
Mk 10:46 *s* by the highway side begging
Mk 11:2 a colt tied, whereon never man *s*
Mk 11:7 and he *s* upon him
Mk 12:41 Jesus *s* over against the treasury
Mk 13:3 as he *s* upon the mount of Olives
Mk 14:3 as he *s* at meat, there came a
Mk 14:18 And as they *s* and did eat, Jesus
Mk 14:54 he *s* with the servants, and warmed
Mk 16:14 unto the eleven as they *s* at meat
Mk 16:19 *s* on the right hand of God
Lk 4:20 again to the minister, and *s* down
Lk 5:3 he *s* down, and taught the people
Lk 5:29 of others that *s* down with them
Lk 7:15 And he that was dead *s* up, and
Lk 7:36 house, and *s* down to meat
Lk 7:37 when she knew that Jesus *s* at
Lk 7:49 they that *s* at meat with him
Lk 10:39 which also *s* at Jesus' feet, and
Lk 11:37 and he went in, and *s* down to meat
Lk 14:15 when one of them that *s* at meat
Lk 18:35 a certain blind man *s* by the way
Lk 19:30 tied, whereon yet never man *s*
Lk 22:14 he *s* down, and the twelve apostles
Lk 22:55 together, Peter *s* down among them
Lk 22:56 beheld him as he *s* by the fire
Lk 24:30 as he *s* at meat with them, he
Jn 4:6 his journey, *s* thus on the well
Jn 6:3 there he *s* with his disciples
Jn 6:10 So the men *s* down, in number
Jn 8:2 he *s* down, and taught them
Jn 9:8 said, Is not this he that *s*
Jn 11:20 but Mary *s* still in the house
Jn 12:2 them that *s* at the table with him
Jn 12:14 had found a young ass, *s* thereon
Jn 19:13 *s* down in the judgment seat in a
Acts 2:3 fire, and it *s* upon each of them
Acts 3:10 *s* for alms at the Beautiful gate
Acts 6:15 all that *s* in the council,
Acts 9:40 and when she saw Peter, she *s* up
Acts 12:21 *s* upon his throne, and made an
Acts 13:14 on the sabbath day, and *s* down
Acts 14:8 there *s* a certain man at Lystra,
Acts 16:13 we *s* down, and spake unto the
Acts 20:9 there *s* in a window a certain
Acts 25:17 morrow I *s* on the judgment seat
Acts 26:30 Bernice, and they that *s* with them
1Cor 10:7 The people *s* down to eat and drink
Heb 1:3 *s* down on the right hand of the
Heb 10:12 *s* down on the right hand of God
Rev 4:2 in heaven, and one *s* on the throne
Rev 4:3 he that *s* was to look upon like a
Rev 4:9 to him that *s* on the throne
Rev 4:10 before him that *s* on the throne
Rev 5:1 *s* on the throne a book written
Rev 5:7 of him that *s* upon the throne
Rev 6:2 he that *s* on him had a bow
Rev 6:4 power was given to him that *s*
Rev 6:5 he that *s* on him had a pair of
Rev 6:8 his name that *s* on him was Death,
Rev 9:17 vision, and them that *s* on them
Rev 11:16 which *s* before God on their seats
Rev 14:14 upon the cloud one *s* like unto
Rev 14:15 voice to him that *s* on the cloud
Rev 14:16 he that *s* on the cloud thrust in
Rev 19:4 God that *s* on the throne, saying,
Rev 19:11 he that *s* upon him was called
Rev 19:19 against him that *s* on the horse
Rev 19:21 of him that *s* upon the horse
Rev 20:4 they *s* upon them, and judgment was
Rev 20:11 white throne, and him that *s* on it
Rev 21:5 he that *s* upon the throne said,

**SATAN** *(sa'-tun) The adversary.*
1Chr 21:1 *S* stood up against Israel, and
Job 1:6 LORD, and *S* came also among them
Job 1:7 And the LORD said unto *S*, Whence
Job 1:7 Then *S* answered the LORD, and said
Job 1:8 And the LORD said unto *S*, Hast
Job 1:9 Then *S* answered the LORD, and said
Job 1:12 And the LORD said unto *S*, Behold,
Job 1:12 So *S* went forth from the presence
Job 2:1 *S* came also among them to present
Job 2:2 And the LORD said unto *S*, From
Job 2:2 *S* answered the LORD, and said,
Job 2:3 And the LORD said unto *S*, Hast
Job 2:4 *S* answered the LORD, and said,
Job 2:6 And the LORD said unto *S*, Behold,
Job 2:7 So went *S* forth from the presence
Ps 109:6 let *S* stand at his right hand
Zec 3:1 *S* standing at his right hand to
Zec 3:2 *S*, The LORD rebuke thee, O *S*
Mt 4:10 Jesus unto him, Get thee hence, *S*
Mt 12:26 And if *S* cast out *S*, he is
Mt 16:23 unto Peter, Get thee behind me, *S*
Mk 1:13 forty days, tempted of *S*
Mk 3:23 How can *S* cast out *S*
Mk 3:26 if *S* rise up against himself, and
Mk 4:15 *S* cometh immediately, and taketh
Mk 8:33 saying, Get thee behind me, *S*
Lk 4:8 unto him, Get thee behind me, *S*
Lk 10:18 I beheld *S* as lightning fall from
Lk 11:18 If *S* also be divided against
Lk 13:16 whom *S* hath bound, lo, these
Lk 22:3 Then entered *S* into Judas
Lk 22:31 *S* hath desired to have you, that
Jn 13:27 after the sop *S* entered into him
Acts 5:3 why hath *S* filled thine heart to
Acts 26:18 and from the power of *S* unto God
Rom 16:20 bruise *S* under your feet shortly
1Cor 5:5 unto *S* for the destruction of the
1Cor 7:5 that *S* tempt you not for your
2Cor 2:11 Lest *S* should get an advantage of
2Cor 11:14 for *S* himself is transformed into
2Cor 12:7 the messenger of *S* to buffet me
1Th 2:18 but *S* hindered us
2Th 2:9 the working of *S* with all power
1Ti 1:20 whom I have delivered unto *S*
1Ti 5:15 are already turned aside after *S*
Rev 2:9 not, but are the synagogue of *S*
Rev 2:13 slain among you, where *S* dwelleth
Rev 2:24 have not known the depths of *S*
Rev 3:9 make them of the synagogue of *S*
Rev 12:9 serpent, called the Devil, and *S*
Rev 20:2 serpent, which is the Devil, and *S*
Rev 20:7 *S* shall be loosed out of his

**SATISFIED**
Ex 15:9 my lust shall be *s* upon them
Lev 26:26 and ye shall eat, and not be *s*
Deut 14:29 shall come, and shall eat and be *s*

Deut 33:23 s with favour, and full with the
Job 19:22 God, and are not s with my flesh
Job 27:14 shall not be s with bread
Job 31:31 we cannot be s
Ps 17:15 I shall be s, when I awake, with
Ps 22:26 The meek shall eat and be s
Ps 36:8 They shall be abundantly s with
Ps 37:19 days of famine they shall be s
Ps 59:15 meat, and grudge if they be not s
Ps 63:5 My soul shall be s as with marrow
Ps 65:4 we shall be s with the goodness
Ps 81:16 of the rock should I have s thee
Ps 104:13 the earth is s with the fruit of
Prov 12:11 his land shall be s with bread
Prov 12:14 A man shall be s with good by the
Prov 14:14 good man shall be s from himself
Prov 18:20 A man's belly shall be s with the
Prov 19:23 and he that hath it shall abide s
Prov 20:13 and thou shalt be s with bread
Prov 27:20 so the eyes of man are never s
Prov 30:15 are three things that are never s
Eccl 1:8 the eye is not s with seeing
Eccl 4:8 neither is his eye s with riches
Eccl 5:10 silver shall not be s with silver
Is 9:20 left hand, and they shall not be s
Is 44:16 he roasteth roast, and is s
Is 53:11 of his soul, and shall be s
Is 66:11 be s with the breasts of her
Jer 31:14 shall be s with my goodness
Jer 50:10 all that spoil her shall be s
Jer 50:19 his soul shall be s upon mount
Lam 5:6 the Assyrians, to be s with bread
Eze 16:28 them, and yet couldest not be s
Eze 16:29 and yet thou wast not s herewith
Joel 2:19 oil, and ye shall be s therewith
Joel 2:26 ye shall eat in plenty, and be s
Amos 4:8 but they were not s
Mic 6:14 Thou shalt eat, but not be s
Hab 2:5 and is as death, and cannot be s

**SATISFY**

Job 38:27 To s the desolate and waste ground
Ps 90:14 O s us early with thy mercy
Ps 91:16 With long life will I s him
Ps 132:15 I will s her poor with bread
Prov 5:19 let her breasts s thee at all
Prov 6:30 if he steal to s his soul when he
Is 58:10 hungry, and s the afflicted soul
Is 58:11 s thy soul in drought, and make
Eze 7:19 they shall not s their souls
Mk 8:4 From whence can a man s these men

**SAUL** *(sawl)* See PAUL, SAUL'S, SHAUL.

*1. The first king of Israel.*

1Sa 9:2 And he had a son, whose name was S
1Sa 9:3 And Kish said to S his son
1Sa 9:5 S said to his servant that was
1Sa 9:7 Then said S to his servant, But,
1Sa 9:8 And the servant answered S again
1Sa 9:10 Then said S to his servant, Well
1Sa 9:15 in his ear a day before S came
1Sa 9:17 And when Samuel saw S, the LORD
1Sa 9:18 Then S drew near to Samuel in the
1Sa 9:19 And Samuel answered S, and said, I
1Sa 9:21 S answered and said, Am not I a
1Sa 9:22 And Samuel took S and his servant,
1Sa 9:24 was upon it, and set it before S
1Sa 9:24 So S did eat with Samuel that day
1Sa 9:25 Samuel communed with S upon the
1Sa 9:26 that Samuel called S to the top
1Sa 9:26 S arose, and they went out both of
1Sa 9:27 end of the city, Samuel said to S
1Sa 10:11 Is S also among the prophets
1Sa 10:12 Is S also among the prophets
1Sa 10:16 S said unto his uncle, He told us
1Sa 10:21 S the son of Kish was taken
1Sa 10:26 S also went home to Gibeah
1Sa 11:4 the messengers to Gibeah of S
1Sa 11:5 S came after the herd out of the
1Sa 11:5 S said, What aileth the people
1Sa 11:6 S when he heard those tidings
1Sa 11:7 cometh not forth after S and after
1Sa 11:11 that S put the people in three
1Sa 11:12 that said, Shall S reign over us
1Sa 11:13 S said, There shall not a man be
1Sa 11:15 there they made S king before the
1Sa 11:15 and there S and all the men of
1Sa 13:1 S reigned one year
1Sa 13:2 S chose him three thousand men of
1Sa 13:2 thousand were with S in Michmash
1Sa 13:3 S blew the trumpet throughout all
1Sa 13:4 all Israel heard say that S had
1Sa 13:4 called together after S to Gilgal
1Sa 13:7 As for S, he was yet in Gilgal,
1Sa 13:9 S said, Bring hither a burnt
1Sa 13:10 S went out to meet him, that he
1Sa 13:11 S said, Because I saw that the
1Sa 13:13 And Samuel said to S, Thou hast
1Sa 13:15 S numbered the people that were
1Sa 13:16 And S, and Jonathan his son, and the
1Sa 13:22 of the people that were with S
1Sa 13:22 but with S and with Jonathan his
1Sa 14:1 that Jonathan the son of S said
1Sa 14:2 S tarried in the uttermost part
1Sa 14:16 the watchmen of S in Gibeah of
1Sa 14:17 Then said S unto the people that
1Sa 14:18 S said unto Ahiah, Bring hither
1Sa 14:19 while S talked unto the priest,
1Sa 14:19 S said unto the priest, Withdraw
1Sa 14:20 And S and all the people that were
1Sa 14:21 the Israelites that were with S
1Sa 14:24 for S had adjured the people,
1Sa 14:33 Then they told S, saying, Behold,
1Sa 14:34 S said, Disperse yourselves among
1Sa 14:35 S built an altar unto the LORD
1Sa 14:36 S said, Let us go down after the
1Sa 14:37 S asked counsel of God, Shall I
1Sa 14:38 S said, Draw ye near hither, all
1Sa 14:40 And the people said unto S
1Sa 14:41 Therefore S said unto the LORD
1Sa 14:41 And S and Jonathan were taken
1Sa 14:42 S said, Cast lots between me and
1Sa 14:43 Then S said to Jonathan, Tell me
1Sa 14:44 S answered, God do so and more
1Sa 14:45 And the people said unto S
1Sa 14:46 Then S went up from following the
1Sa 14:47 So S took the kingdom over Israel
1Sa 14:49 Now the sons of S were Jonathan
1Sa 14:51 And Kish was the father of S
1Sa 14:52 the Philistines all the days of S
1Sa 14:52 when S saw any strong man, or any
1Sa 15:1 Samuel also said unto S, The LORD
1Sa 15:4 S gathered the people together,
1Sa 15:5 S came to a city of Amalek, and
1Sa 15:6 S said unto the Kenites, Go,
1Sa 15:7 S smote the Amalekites from
1Sa 15:9 But S and the people spared Agag,
1Sa 15:11 that I have set up S to be king
1Sa 15:12 early to meet S in the morning
1Sa 15:12 S came to Carmel, and, behold, he
1Sa 15:13 And Samuel came to S
1Sa 15:13 S said unto him, Blessed be thou
1Sa 15:15 S said, They have brought them
1Sa 15:16 Then Samuel said unto S, Stay, and
1Sa 15:20 S said unto Samuel, Yea, I have
1Sa 15:24 S said unto Samuel, I have sinned
1Sa 15:26 And Samuel said unto S, I will not
1Sa 15:31 So Samuel turned again after S
1Sa 15:31 and S worshipped the LORD
1Sa 15:34 S went up to his house to Gibeah
1Sa 15:34 up to his house to Gibeah of S
1Sa 15:35 see S until the day of his death
1Sa 15:35 nevertheless Samuel mourned for S
1Sa 15:35 he had made S king over Israel
1Sa 16:1 How long wilt thou mourn for S
1Sa 16:2 if S hear it, he will kill me
1Sa 16:14 of the LORD departed from S
1Sa 16:17 S said unto his servants, Provide
1Sa 16:19 Wherefore S sent messengers unto
1Sa 16:20 sent them by David his son unto S
1Sa 16:21 And David came to S, and stood
1Sa 16:22 S sent to Jesse, saying, Let
1Sa 16:23 evil spirit from God was upon S
1Sa 16:23 so S was refreshed, and was well,
1Sa 17:2 And S and the men of Israel were
1Sa 17:8 a Philistine, and ye servants to S
1Sa 17:11 When S and all Israel heard those
1Sa 17:12 for an old man in the days of S
1Sa 17:13 went and followed S to the battle
1Sa 17:14 and the three eldest followed S
1Sa 17:15 returned from S to feed his
1Sa 17:19 Now S, and they, and all the men of
1Sa 17:31 they rehearsed them before S
1Sa 17:32 And David said to S, Let no man's
1Sa 17:33 S said to David, Thou art not
1Sa 17:34 And David said unto S, Thy servant
1Sa 17:37 S said unto David, Go, and the
1Sa 17:38 S armed David with his armour, and
1Sa 17:39 And David said unto S, I cannot go
1Sa 17:55 when S saw David go forth against
1Sa 17:57 brought him before S with the
1Sa 17:58 S said to him, Whose son art thou
1Sa 18:1 made an end of speaking unto S
1Sa 18:2 S took him that day, and would let
1Sa 18:5 went out whithersoever S sent him
1Sa 18:5 S set him over the men of war, and
1Sa 18:6 and dancing, to meet king S
1Sa 18:7 S hath slain his thousands, and
1Sa 18:8 S was very wroth, and the saying
1Sa 18:9 S eyed David from that day and
1Sa 18:10 evil spirit from God came upon S
1Sa 18:11 And S cast the javelin
1Sa 18:12 S was afraid of David, because
1Sa 18:12 with him, and was departed from S
1Sa 18:13 Therefore S removed him from him,
1Sa 18:15 Wherefore when S saw that he
1Sa 18:17 S said to David, Behold my elder
1Sa 18:17 For S said, Let not mine hand be
1Sa 18:18 And David said unto S, Who am I
1Sa 18:20 and they told S, and the thing
1Sa 18:21 S said, I will give him her, that
1Sa 18:21 Wherefore S said to David, Thou
1Sa 18:22 S commanded his servants, saying,
1Sa 18:24 And the servants of S told him
1Sa 18:25 S said, Thus shall ye say to
1Sa 18:25 But S thought to make David fall
1Sa 18:27 S gave him Michal his daughter to
1Sa 18:28 S saw and knew that the LORD was
1Sa 18:29 S was yet the more afraid of
1Sa 18:29 and S became David's enemy
1Sa 18:30 wisely than all the servants of S
1Sa 19:1 S spake to Jonathan his son, and
1Sa 19:2 S my father seeketh to kill thee
1Sa 19:4 good of David unto S his father
1Sa 19:6 S hearkened unto the voice of
1Sa 19:6 S sware, As the LORD liveth, he
1Sa 19:7 And Jonathan brought David to S
1Sa 19:9 spirit from the LORD was upon S
1Sa 19:10 S sought to smite David even to
1Sa 19:11 S also sent messengers unto
1Sa 19:14 when S sent messengers to take
1Sa 19:15 S sent the messengers again to
1Sa 19:17 S said unto Michal, Why hast thou
1Sa 19:17 And Michal answered S, He said
1Sa 19:18 him all that S had done to him
1Sa 19:19 And it was told S, saying, Behold,
1Sa 19:20 S sent messengers to take David
1Sa 19:20 God was upon the messengers of S
1Sa 19:21 And when it was told S, he sent
1Sa 19:21 S sent messengers again the third
1Sa 19:24 Is S also among the prophets
1Sa 20:26 Nevertheless S spake not any
1Sa 20:27 S said unto Jonathan his son,
1Sa 20:28 And Jonathan answered S, David
1Sa 20:32 And Jonathan answered S his father
1Sa 20:33 S cast a javelin at him to smite
1Sa 21:7 servants of S was there that day
1Sa 21:7 of the herdmen that belonged to S
1Sa 21:10 and fled that day for fear of S
1Sa 21:11 S hath slain his thousands, and
1Sa 22:6 When S heard that David was
1Sa 22:6 (now S abode in Gibeah under a
1Sa 22:7 Then S said unto his servants
1Sa 22:9 was set over the servants of S
1Sa 22:12 S said, Hear now, thou son of
1Sa 22:13 S said unto him, Why have ye
1Sa 22:21 Abiathar shewed David that S had
1Sa 22:22 that he would surely tell S
1Sa 23:7 it was told S that David was come
1Sa 23:7 S said, God hath delivered him
1Sa 23:8 S called all the people together
1Sa 23:9 David knew that S secretly
1Sa 23:10 that S seeketh to come to Keilah
1Sa 23:11 will S come down, as thy servant
1Sa 23:12 me and my men into the hand of S
1Sa 23:13 it was told S that David was
1Sa 23:14 S sought him every day, but God
1Sa 23:15 David saw that S was come out to
1Sa 23:17 for the hand of S my father shall
1Sa 23:17 that also S my father knoweth
1Sa 23:19 up the Ziphites to S to Gibeah
1Sa 23:21 S said, Blessed be ye of the LORD
1Sa 23:24 arose, and went to Ziph before S
1Sa 23:25 S also and his men went to seek
1Sa 23:25 when S heard that, he pursued
1Sa 23:26 S went on this side of the
1Sa 23:26 haste to get away for fear of S
1Sa 23:26 for S and his men compassed David
1Sa 23:27 But there came a messenger unto S
1Sa 23:28 Wherefore S returned from
1Sa 24:1 to pass, when S was returned from

1Sa 24:2 Then *S* took three thousand chosen
1Sa 24:3 *S* went in to cover his feet
1Sa 24:7 them not to rise against *S*
1Sa 24:7 But *S* rose up out of the cave, and
1Sa 24:8 out of the cave, and cried after *S*
1Sa 24:8 when *S* looked behind him, David
1Sa 24:9 And David said to *S*, Wherefore
1Sa 24:16 words unto *S*, that *S* said
1Sa 24:16 *S* lifted up his voice, and wept
1Sa 24:22 And David sware unto *S*
1Sa 24:22 And *S* went home
1Sa 25:44 But *S* had given Michal his
1Sa 26:1 Ziphites came unto *S* to Gibeah
1Sa 26:2 Then *S* arose, and went down to the
1Sa 26:3 *S* pitched in the hill of Hachilah
1Sa 26:3 he saw that *S* came after him into
1Sa 26:4 understood that *S* was come in
1Sa 26:5 to the place where *S* had pitched
1Sa 26:5 beheld the place where *S* lay
1Sa 26:5 *S* lay in the trench, and the
1Sa 26:6 go down with me to *S* to the camp
1Sa 26:7 *S* lay sleeping within the trench,
1Sa 26:17 *S* knew David's voice, and said, Is
1Sa 26:21 Then said *S*, I have sinned
1Sa 26:25 Then *S* said to David, Blessed be
1Sa 26:25 way, and *S* returned to his place
1Sa 27:1 perish one day by the hand of *S*
1Sa 27:1 *S* shall despair of me, to seek me
1Sa 27:4 it was told *S* that David was fled
1Sa 28:3 *S* had put away those that had
1Sa 28:4 *S* gathered all Israel together,
1Sa 28:5 when *S* saw the host of the
1Sa 28:6 when *S* enquired of the LORD, the
1Sa 28:7 Then said *S* unto his servants,
1Sa 28:8 *S* disguised himself, and put on
1Sa 28:9 thou knowest what *S* hath done
1Sa 28:10 *S* sware to her by the LORD,
1Sa 28:12 and the woman spake to *S*, saying,
1Sa 28:12 for thou art *S*
1Sa 28:13 And the woman said unto *S*, I saw
1Sa 28:14 *S* perceived that it was Samuel,
1Sa 28:15 And Samuel said to *S*, Why hast
1Sa 28:15 *S* answered, I am sore distressed
1Sa 28:20 Then *S* fell straightway all along
1Sa 28:21 And the woman came unto *S*, and saw
1Sa 28:25 And she brought it before *S*
1Sa 29:3 the servant of *S* the king of
1Sa 29:5 *S* slew his thousands, and David
1Sa 31:2 Philistines followed hard upon *S*
1Sa 31:3 And the battle went sore against *S*
1Sa 31:4 Then said *S* unto his armourbearer
1Sa 31:4 Therefore *S* took a sword, and fell
1Sa 31:5 armourbearer saw that *S* was dead
1Sa 31:6 So *S* died, and his three sons, and
1Sa 31:7 the men of Israel fled, and that *S*
1Sa 31:8 the slain, that they found *S*
1Sa 31:11 the Philistines had done to *S*
1Sa 31:12 all night, and took the body of *S*
2Sa 1:1 came to pass after the death of *S*
2Sa 1:2 camp from *S* with his clothes rent
2Sa 1:4 and *S* and Jonathan his son are dead
2Sa 1:5 told him, How knowest thou that *S*
2Sa 1:6 behold, *S* leaned upon his spear
2Sa 1:12 wept, and fasted until even, for *S*
2Sa 1:17 with this lamentation over *S*
2Sa 1:21 vilely cast away, the shield of *S*
2Sa 1:22 the sword of *S* returned not empty
2Sa 1:23 *S* and Jonathan were lovely and
2Sa 1:24 daughters of Israel, weep over *S*
2Sa 2:4 were they that buried *S*
2Sa 2:5 unto your lord, even unto *S*
2Sa 2:7 for your master *S* is dead
2Sa 2:8 took Ish-bosheth the son of *S*
2Sa 2:12 of Ish-bosheth the son of *S*
2Sa 2:15 to Ish-bosheth the son of *S*
2Sa 3:1 long war between the house of *S*
2Sa 3:1 and the house of *S* waxed weaker
2Sa 3:6 was war between the house of *S*
2Sa 3:6 himself strong for the house of *S*
2Sa 3:7 *S* had a concubine, whose name was
2Sa 3:8 unto the house of *S* thy father
2Sa 3:10 the kingdom from the house of *S*
2Sa 4:4 old when the tidings came of *S*
2Sa 4:8 the son of *S* thine enemy, which
2Sa 4:8 my lord the king this day of *S*
2Sa 4:10 *S* is dead, thinking to have
2Sa 5:2 when *S* was king over us, thou
2Sa 6:20 of *S* came out to meet David
2Sa 6:23 Michal the daughter of *S* had no
2Sa 7:15 from him, as I took it from *S*
2Sa 9:1 that is left of the house of *S*
2Sa 9:2 there was of the house of *S* a
2Sa 9:3 not yet any of the house of *S*
2Sa 9:6 the son of Jonathan, the son of *S*
2Sa 9:7 thee all the land of *S* thy father
2Sa 9:9 son all that pertained to *S*
2Sa 12:7 thee out of the hand of *S*
2Sa 16:5 of the family of the house of *S*
2Sa 16:8 all the blood of the house of *S*
2Sa 19:17 the servant of the house of *S*
2Sa 19:24 Mephibosheth the son of *S* came
2Sa 21:1 And the LORD answered, It is for *S*
2Sa 21:2 *S* sought to slay them in his zeal
2Sa 21:4 will have no silver nor gold of *S*
2Sa 21:6 up unto the LORD in Gibeah of *S*
2Sa 21:7 the son of Jonathan the son of *S*
2Sa 21:7 David and Jonathan the son of *S*
2Sa 21:8 of Aiah, whom she bare unto *S*
2Sa 21:8 sons of Michal the daughter of *S*
2Sa 21:11 of Aiah, the concubine of *S*
2Sa 21:12 David went and took the bones of *S*
2Sa 21:12 Philistines had slain *S* in Gilboa
2Sa 21:13 up from thence the bones of *S*
2Sa 21:14 And the bones of *S* and Jonathan his
2Sa 22:1 enemies, and out of the hand of *S*
1Chr 5:10 in the days of *S* they made war
1Chr 8:33 Ner begat Kish, and Kish begat *S*
1Chr 8:33 *S* begat Jonathan, and Malchi-shua,
1Chr 9:39 and Kish begat *S*
1Chr 9:39 *S* begat Jonathan, and Malchi-shua,
1Chr 10:2 Philistines followed hard after *S*
1Chr 10:2 and Malchi-shua, the sons of *S*
1Chr 10:3 And the battle went sore against *S*
1Chr 10:4 Then said *S* to his armourbearer,
1Chr 10:4 So *S* took a sword, and fell upon
1Chr 10:5 armourbearer saw that *S* was dead
1Chr 10:6 So *S* died, and his three sons, and
1Chr 10:7 saw that they fled, and that *S*
1Chr 10:8 the slain, that they found *S*
1Chr 10:11 the Philistines had done to *S*
1Chr 10:12 men, and took away the body of *S*
1Chr 10:13 So *S* died for his transgression
1Chr 11:2 time past, even when *S* was king
1Chr 12:1 because of *S* the son of Kish
1Chr 12:19 Philistines against *S* to battle
1Chr 12:19 He will fall to his master *S* to
1Chr 12:23 to turn the kingdom of *S* to him
1Chr 12:29 of Benjamin, the kindred of *S*
1Chr 12:29 kept the ward of the house of *S*
1Chr 13:3 not at it in the days of *S*
1Chr 15:29 of *S* looking out at a window saw
1Chr 26:28 *S* the son of Kish, and Abner the
Ps 18:*t* enemies, and from the hand of *S*
Ps 52:*t* Doeg the Edomite came and told *S*
Ps 54:*t* the Ziphims came and said to *S*
Ps 57:*t* when he fled from *S* in the cave
Ps 59:*t* when *S* sent, and they watched the
Is 10:29 Gibeah of *S* is fled
Acts 13:21 gave unto them *S* the son of Cis

*2. An Edomite king.*
Gen 36:37 *S* of Rehoboth by the river
Gen 36:38 *S* died, and Baal-hanan the son of

*3. Original name of Paul.*
Acts 7:58 man's feet, whose name was *S*
Acts 8:1 *S* was consenting unto his death
Acts 8:3 As for *S*, he made havock of the
Acts 9:1 And *S*, yet breathing out
Acts 9:4 a voice saying unto him, Saul, *S*
Acts 9:8 And *S* arose from the earth
Acts 9:11 house of Judas for one called *S*
Acts 9:17 his hands on him said, Brother *S*
Acts 9:19 Then was *S* certain days with the
Acts 9:22 But *S* increased the more in
Acts 9:24 their laying await was known of *S*
Acts 9:26 when *S* was come to Jerusalem, he
Acts 11:25 Barnabas to Tarsus, for to seek *S*
Acts 11:30 by the hands of Barnabas and *S*
Acts 12:25 *S* returned from Jerusalem, when
Acts 13:1 up with Herod the tetrarch, and *S*
Acts 13:2 *S* for the work whereunto I have
Acts 13:7 who called for Barnabas and *S*
Acts 13:9 Then *S*, (who also is called Paul,
Acts 22:7 a voice saying unto me, Saul, *S*
Acts 22:13 stood, and said unto me, Brother *S*
Acts 26:14 in the Hebrew tongue, Saul, *S*

**SAUL'S** *Refers to Saul 1.*
1Sa 9:3 asses of Kish *S* father were lost
1Sa 10:14 *S* uncle said unto him and to his
1Sa 10:15 *S* uncle said, Tell me, I pray
1Sa 14:50 the name of *S* wife was Ahinoam,
1Sa 14:50 Abner, the son of Ner, *S* uncle
1Sa 16:15 *S* servants said unto him, Behold
1Sa 18:5 also in the sight of *S* servants
1Sa 18:10 and there was a javelin in *S* hand
1Sa 18:19 to pass at the time when Merab *S*
1Sa 18:20 Michal *S* daughter loved David
1Sa 18:23 *S* servants spake those words in
1Sa 18:28 that Michal *S* daughter loved him
1Sa 19:2 But Jonathan *S* son delighted much
1Sa 19:10 he slipped away out of *S* presence
1Sa 20:25 arose, and Abner sat by *S* side
1Sa 20:30 Then *S* anger was kindled against
1Sa 23:16 Jonathan *S* son arose, and went to
1Sa 24:4 off the skirt of *S* robe privily
1Sa 24:5 because he had cut off *S* skirt
1Sa 26:12 the cruse of water from *S* bolster
1Sa 31:2 Abinadab, and Melchi-shua, *S* sons
2Sa 2:8 the son of Ner, captain of *S* host
2Sa 2:10 Ish-bosheth *S* son was forty years
2Sa 3:13 first bring Michal *S* daughter
2Sa 3:14 messengers to Ish-bosheth *S* son
2Sa 4:1 when *S* son heard that Abner was
2Sa 4:2 *S* son had two men that were
2Sa 4:4 *S* son, had a son that was lame of
2Sa 6:16 Michal *S* daughter looked through
2Sa 9:9 *S* servant, and said unto him, I
1Chr 12:2 even of *S* brethren of Benjamin

**SAVE**
Gen 12:12 me, but they will *s* thee alive
Gen 14:24 *S* only that which the young men
Gen 39:6 *s* the bread which he did eat
Gen 45:7 to *s* your lives by a great
Gen 50:20 this day, to *s* much people alive
Ex 1:22 every daughter ye shall *s* alive
Ex 12:16 *s* that which every man must eat,
Ex 22:20 *s* unto the LORD only, he shall be
Num 14:30 *s* Caleb the son of Jephunneh, and
Num 26:65 *s* Caleb the son of Jephunneh, and
Num 32:12 *S* Caleb the son of Jephunneh the
Deut 1:36 *S* Caleb the son of Jephunneh
Deut 15:4 *S* when there shall be no poor
Deut 20:4 against your enemies, to *s* you
Deut 20:16 thou shalt *s* alive nothing that
Deut 22:27 cried, and there was none to *s* her
Deut 28:29 evermore, and no man shall *s* thee
Josh 2:13 that ye will *s* alive my father,
Josh 10:6 us quickly, and *s* us, and help us
Josh 11:13 burned none of them, *s* Hazor only
Josh 11:19 *s* the Hivites the inhabitants of
Josh 14:4 *s* cities to dwell in, with their
Josh 22:22 the LORD, (*s* us not this day,)
Judg 6:14 thou shalt *s* Israel from the hand
Judg 6:15 Lord, wherewith shall I *s* Israel
Judg 6:31 will ye *s* him
Judg 6:36 If thou wilt *s* Israel by mine
Judg 6:37 thou wilt *s* Israel by mine hand
Judg 7:7 men that lapped will I *s* you
Judg 7:14 This is nothing else *s* the sword
1Sa 4:3 it may *s* us out of the hand of
1Sa 7:8 that he will *s* us out of the hand
1Sa 9:16 that he may *s* my people out of
1Sa 10:24 shouted, and said, God *s* the king
1Sa 10:27 said, How shall this man *s* us
1Sa 11:3 then, if there be no man to *s* us
1Sa 14:6 the LORD to *s* by many or by few
1Sa 19:11 If thou *s* not thy to night, to
1Sa 21:9 for there is no other *s* that here
1Sa 23:2 the Philistines, and *s* Keilah
1Sa 30:17 *s* four hundred young men, which
1Sa 30:22 *s* to every man his wife and his
2Sa 3:18 *s* my people Israel out of the
2Sa 12:3 *s* one little ewe lamb, which he
2Sa 16:16 God *s* the king, God *s* the king
2Sa 16:16 God *s* the king, God *s* the king
2Sa 22:28 the afflicted people thou wilt *s*
2Sa 22:32 For who is God, *s* the LORD
2Sa 22:32 and who is a rock, *s* our God
2Sa 22:42 looked, but there was none to *s*
1Kin 1:12 that thou mayest *s* thine own life
1Kin 1:25 him, and say, God *s* king Adonijah
1Kin 1:34 and say, God *s* king Solomon
1Kin 1:39 people said, God *s* king Solomon
1Kin 3:18 the house, *s* we two in the house
1Kin 8:9 the ark *s* the two tables of stone
1Kin 15:5 *s* only in the matter of Uriah the
1Kin 18:5 we may find grass to *s* the horses
1Kin 20:31 peradventure he will *s* thy life
1Kin 22:31 *s* only with the king of Israel

2Kin 4:2 in the house, *s* a pot of oil
2Kin 7:4 if they *s* us alive, we shall live
2Kin 11:12 hands, and said, God *s* the king
2Kin 15:4 *S* that the high places were not
2Kin 16:7 *s* me out of the hand of the king
2Kin 19:19 *s* thou us out of his hand, that
2Kin 19:34 I will defend this city, to *s* it
2Kin 24:14 *s* the poorest sort of the people
1Chr 16:35 *S* us, O God of our salvation, and
2Chr 2:6 *s* only to burn sacrifice before
2Chr 5:10 There was nothing in the ark *s*
2Chr 18:30 *s* only with the king of Israel
2Chr 21:17 *s* Jehoahaz, the youngest of his
2Chr 23:6 *s* the priests, and they that
2Chr 23:11 him, and said, God *s* the king
Neh 2:12 *s* the beast that I rode upon
Neh 6:11 go into the temple to *s* his life
Job 2:6 but *s* his life
Job 20:20 he shall not *s* of that which he
Job 22:29 he shall *s* the humble person
Job 40:14 thine own right hand can *s* thee
Ps 3:7 *s* me, O my God
Ps 6:4 oh *s* me for thy mercies' sake
Ps 7:1 *s* me from all them that persecute
Ps 18:27 For thou wilt *s* the afflicted
Ps 18:31 For who is God *s* the LORD
Ps 18:31 or who is a rock *s* our God
Ps 18:41 but there was none to *s* them
Ps 20:9 *S*, LORD
Ps 22:21 *S* me from the lion's mouth
Ps 28:9 *S* thy people, and bless thine
Ps 31:2 for an house of defence to *s* me
Ps 31:16 *s* me for thy mercies' sake
Ps 37:40 *s* them, because they trust in him
Ps 44:3 neither did their own arm *s* them
Ps 44:6 bow, neither shall my sword *s* me
Ps 54:1 *S* me, O God, by thy name, and
Ps 55:16 and the LORD shall *s* me
Ps 57:3 *s* me from the reproach of him
Ps 59:2 iniquity, and *s* me from bloody men
Ps 60:5 *s* with thy right hand, and hear me
Ps 69:1 *S* me, O God
Ps 69:35 For God will *s* Zion, and will
Ps 71:2 thine ear unto me, and *s* me
Ps 71:3 hast given commandment to *s* me
Ps 72:4 he shall *s* the children of the
Ps 72:13 shall *s* the souls of the needy
Ps 76:9 to *s* all the meek of the earth
Ps 80:2 up thy strength, and come and *s* us
Ps 86:2 *s* thy servant that trusteth in
Ps 86:16 *s* the son of thine handmaid
Ps 106:47 *S* us, O LORD our God, and gather
Ps 108:6 *s* with thy right hand, and answer
Ps 109:26 O *s* me according to thy mercy
Ps 109:31 to *s* him from those that condemn
Ps 118:25 *S* now, I beseech thee, O LORD
Ps 119:94 I am thine, *s* me
Ps 119:146 *s* me, and I shall keep thy
Ps 138:7 and thy right hand shall *s* me
Ps 145:19 hear their cry, and will *s* them
Prov 20:22 on the LORD, and he shall *s* thee
Is 25:9 waited for him, and he will *s* us
Is 33:22 he will *s* us
Is 35:4 he will come and *s* you
Is 37:20 *s* us from his hand, that all the
Is 37:35 city to *s* it for mine own sake
Is 38:20 The LORD was ready to *s* me
Is 45:20 and pray unto a god that cannot *s*
Is 46:7 nor *s* him out of his trouble
Is 47:13 *s* thee from these things that
Is 47:15 none shall *s* thee
Is 49:25 thee, and I will *s* thy children
Is 59:1 not shortened, that it cannot *s*
Is 63:1 in righteousness, mighty to *s*
Jer 2:27 they will say, Arise, and *s* us
Jer 2:28 if they can *s* thee in the time of
Jer 11:12 but they shall not *s* them at all
Jer 14:9 as a mighty man that cannot *s*
Jer 15:20 for I am with thee to *s* thee
Jer 17:14 *s* me, and I shall be saved
Jer 30:10 I will *s* thee from afar, and thy
Jer 30:11 thee, saith the LORD, to *s* thee
Jer 31:7 *s* thy people, the remnant of
Jer 42:11 for I am with you to *s* you
Jer 46:27 I will *s* thee from afar off, and
Jer 48:6 *s* your lives, and be like the
Lam 4:17 for a nation that could not *s* us
Eze 3:18 his wicked way, to *s* his life
Eze 13:18 will ye *s* the souls alive that
Eze 13:19 to *s* the souls alive that should
Eze 18:27 he shall *s* his soul alive
Eze 34:22 Therefore will I *s* my flock
Eze 36:29 I will also *s* you from all your
Eze 37:23 but I will *s* them out of all
Dan 6:7 *s* of thee, O king, he shall be
Dan 6:12 *s* of thee, O king, shall be cast
Hos 1:7 will *s* them by the LORD their God
Hos 1:7 will not *s* them by bow, nor by
Hos 13:10 that may *s* thee in all thy cities
Hos 14:3 Asshur shall not *s* us
Hab 1:2 of violence, and thou wilt not *s*
Zeph 3:17 he will *s*, he will rejoice over
Zeph 3:19 I will *s* her that halteth, and
Zec 8:7 I will *s* my people from the east
Zec 8:13 so will I *s* you, and ye shall be a
Zec 9:16 the LORD their God shall *s* them
Zec 10:6 I will *s* the house of Joseph, and
Zec 12:7 The LORD also shall *s* the tents
Mt 1:21 for he shall *s* his people from
Mt 8:25 and awoke him, saying, Lord, *s* us
Mt 11:27 *s* the Son, and he to whomsoever
Mt 13:57 *s* in his own country, and in his
Mt 14:30 he cried, saying, Lord, *s* me
Mt 16:25 For whosoever will *s* his life
Mt 17:8 they saw no man, *s* Jesus only
Mt 18:11 is come to *s* that which was lost
Mt 19:11 *s* they to whom it is given
Mt 27:40 it in three days, *s* thyself
Mt 27:42 himself he cannot *s*
Mt 27:49 whether Elias will come to *s* him
Mk 3:4 to *s* life, or to kill
Mk 5:37 *s* Peter, and James, and John the
Mk 6:5 *s* that he laid his hands upon a
Mk 6:8 for their journey, *s* a staff only
Mk 8:35 For whosoever will *s* his life
Mk 8:35 the gospel's, the same shall *s* it
Mk 9:8 *s* Jesus only with themselves
Mk 15:30 *S* thyself, and come down from the
Mk 15:31 himself he cannot *s*
Lk 4:26 *s* unto Sarepta, a city of Sidon,
Lk 6:9 to *s* life, or to destroy it
Lk 8:51 *s* Peter, and James, and John, and
Lk 9:24 For whosoever will *s* his life
Lk 9:24 for my sake, the same shall *s* it
Lk 9:56 men's lives, but to *s* them
Lk 17:18 glory to God, *s* this stranger
Lk 17:33 seek to *s* his life shall lose it
Lk 18:19 none is good, *s* one, that is, God
Lk 19:10 seek and to *s* that which was lost
Lk 23:35 let him *s* himself, if he be
Lk 23:37 the king of the Jews, *s* thyself
Lk 23:39 thou be Christ, *s* thyself and us
Jn 6:22 there, *s* that one whereinto his
Jn 6:46 *s* he which is of God, he hath
Jn 12:27 Father, *s* me from this hour
Jn 12:47 the world, but to *s* the world
Jn 13:10 needeth not *s* to wash his feet
Acts 2:40 *S* yourselves from this untoward
Acts 20:23 *S* that the Holy Ghost witnesseth
Acts 21:25 *s* only that they keep themselves
Acts 27:43 the centurion, willing to *s* Paul
Rom 11:14 my flesh, and might *s* some of them
1Cor 1:21 preaching to *s* them that believe
1Cor 2:2 *s* Jesus Christ, and him crucified
1Cor 2:11 *s* the spirit of man which is in
1Cor 7:16 whether thou shalt *s* thy husband
1Cor 7:16 whether thou shalt *s* thy wife
1Cor 9:22 that I might by all means *s* some
2Cor 11:24 received I forty stripes *s* one
Gal 1:19 *s* James the Lord's brother
Gal 6:14 *s* in the cross of our Lord Jesus
1Ti 1:15 came into the world to *s* sinners
1Ti 4:16 this thou shalt both *s* thyself
Heb 5:7 that was able to *s* him from death
Heb 7:25 Wherefore he is able also to *s*
Jas 1:21 which is able to *s* your souls
Jas 2:14 can faith *s* him
Jas 4:12 is one lawgiver, who is able to *s*
Jas 5:15 prayer of faith shall *s* the sick
Jas 5:20 his way shall *s* a soul from death
1Pet 3:21 even baptism doth also now *s* us
Jude 23 others *s* with fear, pulling them
Rev 13:17 *s* he that had the mark, or the

**SAVED**

Gen 47:25 they said, Thou hast *s* our lives
Ex 1:17 but *s* the men children alive
Ex 1:18 have *s* the men children alive
Ex 14:30 Thus the LORD *s* Israel that day
Num 10:9 ye shall be *s* from your enemies
Num 22:33 I had slain thee, and *s* her alive
Num 31:15 Have ye *s* all the women alive
Deut 33:29 O people *s* by the LORD, the
Josh 6:25 Joshua *s* Rahab the harlot alive,
Judg 7:2 saying, Mine own hand hath *s* me
Judg 8:19 if ye had *s* them alive, I would
Judg 21:14 they had *s* alive of the women of
1Sa 10:19 who himself *s* you out of all your
1Sa 14:23 So the LORD *s* Israel that day
1Sa 23:5 So David *s* the inhabitants of
1Sa 27:11 David *s* neither man nor woman
2Sa 19:5 which this day have *s* thy life
2Sa 19:9 The king *s* us out of the hand of
2Sa 22:4 so shall I be *s* from mine enemies
2Kin 6:10 *s* himself there, not once nor
2Kin 14:27 but he *s* them by the hand of
1Chr 11:14 the LORD *s* them by a great
2Chr 32:22 Thus the LORD *s* Hezekiah and the
Neh 9:27 who *s* them out of the hand of
Ps 18:3 so shall I be *s* from mine enemies
Ps 33:16 There is no king *s* by the
Ps 34:6 *s* him out of all his troubles
Ps 44:7 But thou hast *s* us from our
Ps 80:3 and we shall be *s*
Ps 80:7 and we shall be *s*
Ps 80:19 and we shall be *s*
Ps 106:8 Nevertheless he *s* them for his
Ps 106:10 he *s* them from the hand of him
Ps 107:13 he *s* them out of their distresses
Prov 28:18 walketh uprightly shall be *s*
Is 30:15 returning and rest shall ye be *s*
Is 43:12 I have declared, and have *s*
Is 45:17 But Israel shall be *s* in the LORD
Is 45:22 Look unto me, and be ye *s*, all the
Is 63:9 the angel of his presence *s* them
Is 64:5 is continuance, and we shall be *s*
Jer 4:14 wickedness, that thou mayest be *s*
Jer 8:20 summer is ended, and we are not *s*
Jer 17:14 save me, and I shall be *s*
Jer 23:6 In his days Judah shall be *s*
Jer 30:7 but he shall be *s* out of it
Jer 33:16 In those days shall Judah be *s*
Mt 10:22 endureth to the end shall be *s*
Mt 19:25 amazed, saying, Who then can be *s*
Mt 24:13 unto the end, the same shall be *s*
Mt 24:22 there should no flesh be *s*
Mt 27:42 He *s* others; himself he
Mk 10:26 themselves, Who then can be *s*
Mk 13:13 unto the end, the same shall be *s*
Mk 13:20 those days, no flesh should be *s*
Mk 15:31 with the scribes, He *s* others
Mk 16:16 and is baptized shall be *s*
Lk 1:71 we should be *s* from our enemies
Lk 7:50 the woman, Thy faith hath *s* thee
Lk 8:12 lest they should believe and be *s*
Lk 13:23 Lord, are there few that be *s*
Lk 18:26 heard it said, Who then can be *s*
Lk 18:42 thy faith hath *s* thee
Lk 23:35 derided him, saying, He *s* others
Jn 3:17 the world through him might be *s*
Jn 5:34 things I say, that ye might be *s*
Jn 10:9 any man enter in, he shall be *s*
Acts 2:21 the name of the Lord shall be *s*
Acts 2:47 church daily such as should be *s*
Acts 4:12 among men, whereby we must be *s*
Acts 11:14 thou and all thy house shall be *s*
Acts 15:1 manner of Moses, ye cannot be *s*
Acts 15:11 Lord Jesus Christ we shall be *s*
Acts 16:30 Sirs, what must I do to be *s*
Acts 16:31 Jesus Christ, and thou shalt be *s*
Acts 27:20 should be *s* was then taken away
Acts 27:31 abide in the ship, ye cannot be *s*
Rom 5:9 we shall be *s* from wrath through
Rom 5:10 we shall be *s* by his life
Rom 8:24 For we are *s* by hope
Rom 9:27 of the sea, a remnant shall be *s*
Rom 10:1 Israel is, that they might be *s*
Rom 10:9 from the dead, thou shalt be *s*
Rom 10:13 the name of the Lord shall be *s*
Rom 11:26 And so all Israel shall be *s*
1Cor 1:18 but unto us which are *s* it is the
1Cor 3:15 but he himself shall be *s*
1Cor 5:5 that the spirit may be *s* in the
1Cor 10:33 of many, that they may be *s*
1Cor 15:2 By which also ye are *s*, if ye
2Cor 2:15 of Christ, in them that are *s*
Eph 2:5 with Christ, (by grace ye are *s*
Eph 2:8 by grace are ye *s* through faith
1Th 2:16 the Gentiles that they might be *s*
2Th 2:10 the truth, that they might be *s*

1Ti 2:4 Who will have all men to be *s*
1Ti 2:15 she shall be *s* in childbearing
2Ti 1:9 Who hath *s* us, and called us with
Titus 3:5 according to his mercy he *s* us
1Pet 3:20 is, eight souls were *s* by water
1Pet 4:18 And if the righteous scarcely be *s*
2Pet 2:5 but *s* Noah the eighth person, a
Jude 5 having *s* the people out of the
Rev 21:24 *s* shall walk in the light of it

## SAVETH

1Sa 14:39 which *s* Israel, though it be in
1Sa 17:47 that the LORD *s* not with sword
Job 5:15 But he *s* the poor from the sword,
Ps 7:10 which *s* the upright in heart
Ps 20:6 I that the LORD *s* his anointed
Ps 34:18 *s* such as be of a contrite spirit
Ps 107:19 he *s* them out of their distresses

## SAVING

Gen 19:19 hast shewed unto me in *s* my life
Neh 4:23 *s* that every one put them off for
Ps 20:6 the *s* strength of his right hand
Ps 28:8 he is the *s* strength of his
Ps 67:2 thy *s* health among all nations
Eccl 5:11 *s* the beholding of them with
Amos 9:8 *s* that I will not utterly destroy
Mt 5:32 *s* for the cause of fornication,
Lk 4:27 was cleansed, *s* Naaman the Syrian
Heb 10:39 that believe to the *s* of the soul
Heb 11:7 an ark to the *s* of his house
Rev 2:17 knoweth *s* he that receiveth it

## SAVIOUR

2Sa 22:3 my high tower, and my refuge, my *s*
2Kin 13:5 (And the LORD gave Israel a *s*
Ps 106:21 They forgat God their *s*, which
Is 19:20 and he shall send them a *s*
Is 43:3 the Holy One of Israel, thy *S*
Is 43:11 and beside me there is no *s*
Is 45:15 thyself, O God of Israel, the *S*
Is 45:21 a just God and a *S*
Is 49:26 know that I the LORD am thy *S*
Is 60:16 know that I the LORD am thy *S*
Is 63:8 so he was their *S*
Jer 14:8 the *s* thereof in time of trouble,
Hos 13:4 for there is no *s* beside me
Lk 1:47 spirit hath rejoiced in God my *S*
Lk 2:11 this day in the city of David a *S*
Jn 4:42 the Christ, the *S* of the world
Acts 5:31 right hand to be a Prince and a *S*
Acts 13:23 promise raised unto Israel a *S*
Eph 5:23 and he is the *s* of the body
Phil 3:20 whence also we look for the *S*
1Ti 1:1 by the commandment of God our *S*
1Ti 2:3 in the sight of God our *S*
1Ti 4:10 God, who is the *S* of all men
2Ti 1:10 appearing of our *S* Jesus Christ
Titus 1:3 to the commandment of God our *S*
Titus 1:4 and the Lord Jesus Christ our *S*
Titus 2:10 of God our *S* in all things
Titus 2:13 great God and our *S* Jesus Christ
Titus 3:4 love of God our *S* toward man
Titus 3:6 through Jesus Christ our *S*
2Pet 1:1 of God and our *S* Jesus Christ
2Pet 1:11 of our Lord and *S* Jesus Christ
2Pet 2:20 *S* Jesus Christ, they are again
2Pet 3:2 us the apostles of the Lord and *S*
2Pet 3:18 of our Lord and *S* Jesus Christ
1Jn 4:14 the Son to be the *S* of the world
Jude 25 To the only wise God our *S*

## SAVOUR

Gen 8:21 And the LORD smelled a sweet *s*
Ex 5:21 because ye have made our *s* to be
Ex 29:18 it is a sweet *s*, an offering made
Ex 29:25 for a sweet *s* before the LORD
Ex 29:41 offering thereof, for a sweet *s*
Lev 1:9 of a sweet *s* unto the LORD
Lev 1:13 of a sweet *s* unto the LORD
Lev 1:17 of a sweet *s* unto the LORD
Lev 2:2 of a sweet *s* unto the LORD
Lev 2:9 of a sweet *s* unto the LORD
Lev 2:12 burnt on the altar for a sweet *s*
Lev 3:5 of a sweet *s* unto the LORD
Lev 3:16 made by fire for a sweet *s*
Lev 4:31 altar for a sweet *s* unto the LORD
Lev 6:15 it upon the altar for a sweet *s*
Lev 6:21 offer for a sweet *s* unto the LORD
Lev 8:21 a burnt sacrifice for a sweet *s*
Lev 8:28 were consecrations for a sweet *s*
Lev 17:6 fat for a sweet *s* unto the LORD
Lev 23:13 fire unto the LORD for a sweet *s*
Lev 23:18 by fire, of sweet *s* unto the LORD
Lev 26:31 smell the *s* of your sweet odours
Num 15:3 to make a sweet *s* unto the LORD
Num 15:7 for a sweet *s* unto the LORD
Num 15:10 of a sweet *s* unto the LORD
Num 15:13 of a sweet *s* unto the LORD
Num 15:14 of a sweet *s* unto the LORD
Num 15:24 for a sweet *s* unto the LORD, with
Num 18:17 for a sweet *s* unto the LORD
Num 28:2 by fire, for a sweet *s* unto me
Num 28:6 in mount Sinai for a sweet *s*
Num 28:8 of a sweet *s* unto the LORD
Num 28:13 for a burnt offering of a sweet *s*
Num 28:24 of a sweet *s* unto the LORD
Num 28:27 for a sweet *s* unto the LORD
Num 29:2 for a sweet *s* unto the LORD
Num 29:6 unto their manner, for a sweet *s*
Num 29:8 unto the LORD for a sweet *s*
Num 29:13 of a sweet *s* unto the LORD
Num 29:36 of a sweet *s* unto the LORD
Eccl 10:1 to send forth a stinking *s*
Song 1:3 Because of the *s* of thy good
Eze 6:13 offer sweet *s* to all their idols
Eze 16:19 set it before them for a sweet *s*
Eze 20:28 also they made their sweet *s*
Eze 20:41 will accept you with your sweet *s*
Joel 2:20 his ill *s* shall come up, because
Mt 5:13 but if the salt have lost his *s*
Lk 14:34 but if the salt have lost his *s*
2Cor 2:14 maketh manifest the *s* of his
2Cor 2:15 are unto God a sweet *s* of Christ
2Cor 2:16 we are the *s* of death unto death
2Cor 2:16 to the other the *s* of life unto
Eph 5:2 to God for a sweetsmelling *s*

## SCAB

Lev 13:2 skin of his flesh a rising, a *s*
Lev 13:6 it is but a *s*
Lev 13:7 But if the *s* spread much abroad
Lev 13:8 the *s* spreadeth in the skin, then
Lev 14:56 And for a rising, and for a *s*
Deut 28:27 with the emerods, and with the *s*
Is 3:17 the Lord will smite with a *s* the

## SCALES

Lev 11:9 *s* in the waters, in the seas, and
Lev 11:10 *s* in the seas, and in the rivers,
Lev 11:12 hath no fins nor *s* in the waters
Deut 14:9 that have fins and *s* shall ye eat
Deut 14:10 hath not fins and *s* ye may not eat
Job 41:15 His *s* are his pride, shut up
Is 40:12 and weighed the mountains in *s*
Eze 29:4 of thy rivers to stick unto thy *s*
Eze 29:4 thy rivers shall stick unto thy *s*
Acts 9:18 from his eyes as it had been *s*

## SCALL

Lev 13:30 it is a dry *s*, even a leprosy
Lev 13:31 look on the plague of the *s*
Lev 13:31 the plague of the *s* seven days
Lev 13:32 if the *s* spread not, and there be
Lev 13:32 the *s* be not in sight deeper than
Lev 13:33 but the *s* shall he not shave
Lev 13:33 that hath the *s* seven days more
Lev 13:34 the priest shall look on the *s*
Lev 13:34 if the *s* be not spread in the
Lev 13:35 But if the *s* spread much in the
Lev 13:36 if the *s* be spread in the skin,
Lev 13:37 But if the *s* be in his sight at a
Lev 13:37 the *s* is healed, he is clean
Lev 14:54 manner of plague of leprosy, and *s*

## SCARLET

Gen 38:28 and bound upon his hand a *s* thread
Gen 38:30 that had the *s* thread upon his
Ex 25:4 blue, and purple, and *s*, and fine
Ex 26:1 linen, and blue, and purple, and *s*
Ex 26:31 a vail of blue, and purple, and *s*
Ex 26:36 tent, of blue, and purple, and *s*
Ex 27:16 cubits, of blue, and purple, and *s*
Ex 28:5 gold, and blue, and purple, and *s*
Ex 28:6 gold, of blue, and of purple, of *s*
Ex 28:8 of gold, of blue, and purple, and *s*
Ex 28:15 of blue, and of purple, and of *s*
Ex 28:33 of blue, and of purple, and of *s*
Ex 35:6 blue, and purple, and *s*, and fine
Ex 35:23 was found blue, and purple, and *s*
Ex 35:25 of blue, and of purple, and of *s*
Ex 35:35 in blue, and in purple, in *s*
Ex 36:8 linen, and blue, and purple, and *s*
Ex 36:35 a vail of blue, and purple, and *s*
Ex 36:37 door of blue, and purple, and *s*
Ex 38:18 of blue, and purple, and *s*
Ex 38:23 in blue, and in purple, and in *s*
Ex 39:1 And of the blue, and purple, and *s*
Ex 39:2 of gold, blue, and purple, and *s*
Ex 39:3 and in the purple, and in the *s*
Ex 39:5 of gold, blue, and purple, and *s*
Ex 39:8 of gold, blue, and purple, and *s*
Ex 39:24 of blue, and purple, and *s*, and
Ex 39:29 linen, and blue, and purple, and *s*
Lev 14:4 and clean, and cedar wood, and *s*
Lev 14:6 it, and the cedar wood, and the *s*
Lev 14:49 two birds, and cedar wood, and *s*
Lev 14:51 wood, and the hyssop, and the *s*
Lev 14:52 with the hyssop, and with the *s*
Num 4:8 spread upon them a cloth of *s*
Num 19:6 cedar wood, and hyssop, and *s*
Josh 2:18 thou shalt bind this line of *s*
Josh 2:21 she bound the *s* line in the
2Sa 1:24 over Saul, who clothed you in *s*
Prov 31:21 her household are clothed with *s*
Song 4:3 Thy lips are like a thread of *s*
Is 1:18 though your sins be as *s*, they
Lam 4:5 brought up in *s* embrace dunghills
Dan 5:7 thereof, shall be clothed with *s*
Dan 5:16 thou shalt be clothed with *s*
Dan 5:29 and they clothed Daniel with *s*
Nah 2:3 red, the valiant men are in *s*
Mt 27:28 him, and put on him a *s* robe
Heb 9:19 *s* wool, and hyssop, and sprinkled
Rev 17:3 woman sit upon a *s* coloured beast
Rev 17:4 *s* colour, and decked with gold and
Rev 18:12 linen, and purple, and silk, and *s*
Rev 18:16 in fine linen, and purple, and *s*

## SCATTER

Gen 11:9 from thence did the LORD *s* them
Gen 49:7 in Jacob, and *s* them in Israel
Lev 26:33 I will *s* you among the heathen,
Num 16:37 and *s* thou the fire yonder
Deut 4:27 the LORD shall *s* you among the
Deut 28:64 the LORD shall *s* thee among all
Deut 32:26 I would *s* them into corners, I
1Kin 14:15 shall *s* them beyond the river,
Neh 1:8 I will *s* you abroad among the
Ps 59:11 *s* them by thy power
Ps 68:30 *s* thou the people that delight in
Ps 106:27 and to *s* them in the lands
Ps 144:6 Cast forth lightning, and *s* them
Is 28:25 *s* the cummin, and cast in the
Is 41:16 and the whirlwind shall *s* them
Jer 9:16 I will *s* them also among the
Jer 13:24 Therefore will I *s* them as the
Jer 18:17 I will *s* them as with an east
Jer 23:1 *s* the sheep of my pasture
Jer 49:32 I will *s* into all winds them that
Jer 49:36 will *s* them toward all those
Eze 5:2 part thou shalt *s* in the wind
Eze 5:10 thee will I *s* into all the winds
Eze 5:12 I will *s* a third part into all
Eze 6:5 I will *s* your bones round about
Eze 10:2 and *s* them over the city
Eze 12:14 I will *s* toward every wind all
Eze 12:15 when I shall *s* them among the
Eze 20:23 that I would *s* them among the
Eze 22:15 I will *s* thee among the heathen,
Eze 29:12 I will *s* the Egyptians among the
Eze 30:23 I will *s* the Egyptians among the
Eze 30:26 I will *s* the Egyptians among the
Dan 4:14 off his leaves, and *s* his fruit
Dan 11:24 he shall *s* among them the prey,
Dan 12:7 to *s* the power of the holy people
Hab 3:14 came out as a whirlwind to *s* me
Zec 1:21 over the land of Judah to *s* it

## SCATTERED

Gen 11:4 lest we be *s* abroad upon the face
Gen 11:8 So the LORD *s* them abroad from
Ex 5:12 So the people were *s* abroad
Num 10:35 LORD, and let thine enemies be *s*
Deut 30:3 the LORD thy God hath *s* thee
1Sa 11:11 that they which remained were *s*
1Sa 13:8 and the people were *s* from him
1Sa 13:11 that the people were *s* from me
2Sa 18:8 there *s* over the face of all the
2Sa 22:15 And he sent out arrows, and *s* them
1Kin 22:17 I saw all Israel *s* upon the hills
2Kin 25:5 and all his army were *s* from him
2Chr 18:16 all Israel *s* upon the mountains
Est 3:8 is a certain people *s* abroad
Job 4:11 stout lion's whelps are *s* abroad

Job 18:15 brimstone shall be *s* upon his
Ps 18:14 he sent out his arrows, and *s* them
Ps 44:11 hast *s* us among the heathen
Ps 53:5 for God hath *s* the bones of him
Ps 60:1 hast cast us off, thou hast *s* us
Ps 68:1 God arise, let his enemies be *s*
Ps 68:14 When the Almighty *s* kings in it
Ps 89:10 thou hast *s* thine enemies with
Ps 92:9 workers of iniquity shall be *s*
Ps 141:7 Our bones are *s* at the grave's
Is 18:2 swift messengers, to a nation *s*
Is 18:7 the LORD of hosts of a people *s*
Is 33:3 up of thyself the nations were *s*
Jer 3:13 hast *s* thy ways to the strangers
Jer 10:21 and all their flocks shall be *s*
Jer 23:2 Ye have *s* my flock, and driven
Jer 30:11 all nations whither I have *s* thee
Jer 31:10 He that *s* Israel will gather him,
Jer 40:15 gathered unto thee should be *s*
Jer 50:17 Israel is a *s* sheep
Jer 52:8 and all his army was *s* from him
Eze 6:8 when ye shall be *s* through the
Eze 11:16 although I have *s* them among the
Eze 11:17 countries where ye have been *s*
Eze 17:21 shall be *s* toward all winds
Eze 20:34 of the countries wherein ye are *s*
Eze 20:41 countries wherein ye have been *s*
Eze 28:25 the people among whom they are *s*
Eze 29:13 the people whither they were *s*
Eze 34:5 And they were *s*, because there is
Eze 34:5 of the field, when they were *s*
Eze 34:6 my flock was *s* upon all the face
Eze 34:12 he is among his sheep that are *s*
Eze 34:12 they have been *s* in the cloudy
Eze 34:21 horns, till ye have *s* them abroad
Eze 36:19 I *s* them among the heathen, and
Eze 46:18 that my people be not *s* every man
Joel 3:2 whom they have *s* among the
Nah 3:18 thy people is *s* upon the
Hab 3:6 the everlasting mountains were *s*
Zec 1:19 are the horns which have *s* Judah
Zec 1:21 are the horns which have *s* Judah
Zec 7:14 But I *s* them with a whirlwind
Zec 13:7 shepherd, and the sheep shall be *s*
Mt 9:36 were *s* abroad, as sheep having no
Mt 26:31 of the flock shall be *s* abroad
Mk 14:27 shepherd, and the sheep shall be *s*
Lk 1:51 he hath *s* the proud in the
Jn 11:52 of God that were *s* abroad
Jn 16:32 is now come, that ye shall be *s*
Acts 5:36 as many as obeyed him, were *s*
Acts 8:1 they were all *s* abroad throughout
Acts 8:4 were *s* abroad went every where
Acts 11:19 Now they which were *s* abroad upon
Jas 1:1 twelve tribes which are *s* abroad
1Pet 1:1 to the strangers *s* throughout

## SCATTERETH

Job 37:11 he *s* his bright cloud
Job 38:24 which *s* the east wind upon the
Ps 147:16 he *s* the hoar frost like ashes
Prov 11:24 There is that *s*, and yet
Prov 20:8 in the throne of judgment *s* away
Prov 20:26 A wise king *s* the wicked, and
Is 24:1 *s* abroad the inhabitants thereof
Mt 12:30 gathereth not with me *s* abroad
Lk 11:23 he that gathereth not with me *s*
Jn 10:12 catcheth them, and *s* the sheep

## SCEPTRE

Gen 49:10 The *s* shall not depart from Judah
Num 24:17 a *S* shall rise out of Israel, and
Est 4:11 king shall hold out the golden *s*
Est 5:2 the golden *s* that was in his hand
Est 5:2 near, and touched the top of the *s*
Est 8:4 out the golden *s* toward Esther
Ps 45:6 the *s* of thy kingdom is a right
Ps 45:6 of thy kingdom is a right *s*
Is 14:5 wicked, and the *s* of the rulers
Eze 19:14 no strong rod to be a *s* to rule
Amos 1:5 him that holdeth the *s* from the
Amos 1:8 that holdeth the *s* from Ashkelon
Zec 10:11 the *s* of Egypt shall depart away
Heb 1:8 a *s* of righteousness is the
Heb 1:8 is the *s* of thy kingdom

**SCEVA** *(see'-vah) A Jewish priest at Ephesus.*

Acts 19:14 And there were seven sons of one *S*

## SCORN

2Kin 19:21 thee, and laughed thee to *s*
2Chr 30:10 but they laughed them to *s*
Neh 2:19 heard it, they laughed us to *s*
Est 3:6 he thought *s* to lay hands on
Job 12:4 just upright man is laughed to *s*
Job 16:20 My friends *s* me
Job 22:19 and the innocent laugh them to *s*
Ps 22:7 they that see me laugh me to *s*
Ps 44:13 a reproach to our neighbours, a *s*
Ps 79:4 a reproach to our neighbours, a *s*
Is 37:22 thee, and laughed thee to *s*
Eze 23:32 thou shalt be laughed to *s*
Hab 1:10 princes shall be a *s* unto them
Mt 9:24 And they laughed him to *s*
Mk 5:40 And they laughed him to *s*
Lk 8:53 And they laughed him to *s*, knowing

## SCORNER

Prov 9:7 He that reproveth a *s* getteth to
Prov 9:8 Reprove not a *s*, lest he hate
Prov 13:1 but a *s* heareth not rebuke
Prov 14:6 A *s* seeketh wisdom, and findeth it
Prov 15:12 A *s* loveth not one that reproveth
Prov 19:25 Smite a *s*, and the simple will
Prov 21:11 When the *s* is punished, the
Prov 21:24 haughty *s* is his name, who
Prov 22:10 Cast out the *s*, and contention
Prov 24:9 the *s* is an abomination to men
Is 29:20 the *s* is consumed, and all that

## SCORNERS

Prov 1:22 the *s* delight in their scorning,
Prov 3:34 Surely he scorneth the *s*
Prov 19:29 Judgments are prepared for *s*
Hos 7:5 he stretched out his hand with *s*

## SCORNETH

Job 39:7 He *s* the multitude of the city,
Job 39:18 she *s* the horse and his rider
Prov 3:34 Surely he *s* the scorners
Prov 19:28 An ungodly witness *s* judgment

## SCORPIONS

Deut 8:15 wherein were fiery serpents, and *s*
1Kin 12:11 but I will chastise you with *s*
1Kin 12:14 but I will chastise you with *s*
2Chr 10:11 but I will chastise you with *s*
2Chr 10:14 but I will chastise you with *s*
Eze 2:6 thee, and thou dost dwell among *s*
Lk 10:19 power to tread on serpents and *s*
Rev 9:3 as the *s* of the earth have power
Rev 9:10 And they had tails like unto *s*

## SCOURGE

Job 5:21 be hid from the *s* of the tongue
Job 9:23 If the *s* slay suddenly, he will
Is 10:26 up a *s* for him according to the
Is 28:15 overflowing *s* shall pass through
Is 28:18 overflowing *s* shall pass through
Mt 10:17 and they will *s* you in their
Mt 20:19 to the Gentiles to mock, and to *s*
Mt 23:34 shall ye *s* in your synagogues
Mk 10:34 shall mock him, and shall *s* him
Lk 18:33 And they shall *s* him, and put him
Jn 2:15 he had made a *s* of small cords
Acts 22:25 you to *s* a man that is a Roman

## SCOURGED

Lev 19:20 she shall be *s*
Mt 27:26 and when he had *s* Jesus, he
Mk 15:15 Jesus, when he had *s* him, to be
Jn 19:1 therefore took Jesus, and *s* him

## SCRIBE

2Sa 8:17 and Seraiah was the *s*
2Sa 20:25 And Sheva was *s*
2Kin 12:10 in the chest, that the king's *s*
2Kin 18:18 the household, and Shebna the *s*
2Kin 18:37 the household, and Shebna the *s*
2Kin 19:2 the household, and Shebna the *s*
2Kin 22:3 the son of Meshullam, the *s*
2Kin 22:8 priest said unto Shaphan the *s*
2Kin 22:9 Shaphan the *s* came to the king,
2Kin 22:10 Shaphan the *s* shewed the king,
2Kin 22:12 son of Michaiah, and Shaphan the *s*
2Kin 25:19 and the principal *s* of the host
1Chr 18:16 and Shavsha was *s*
1Chr 24:6 the son of Nethaneel the *s*
1Chr 27:32 a counsellor, a wise man, and a *s*
2Chr 24:11 was much money, the king's *s*
2Chr 26:11 by the hand of Jeiel the *s*
2Chr 34:15 answered and said to Shaphan the *s*
2Chr 34:18 Then Shaphan the *s* told the king
2Chr 34:20 son of Micah, and Shaphan the *s*
Ezr 4:8 Shimshai the *s* wrote a letter
Ezr 4:9 the chancellor, and Shimshai the *s*
Ezr 4:17 chancellor, and to Shimshai the *s*
Ezr 4:23 before Rehum, and Shimshai the *s*
Ezr 7:6 he was a ready *s* in the law of
Ezr 7:11 gave unto Ezra the priest, the *s*
Ezr 7:11 even a *s* of the words of the
Ezr 7:12 a *s* of the law of the God of
Ezr 7:21 the *s* of the law of the God of
Neh 8:1 they spake unto Ezra the *s* to
Neh 8:4 Ezra the *s* stood upon a pulpit of
Neh 8:9 and Ezra the priest the *s*
Neh 8:13 and the Levites, unto Ezra the *s*
Neh 12:26 and of Ezra the priest, the *s*
Neh 12:36 of God, and Ezra the *s* before them
Neh 13:13 the priest, and Zadok the *s*
Is 33:18 Where is the *s*
Is 36:3 over the house, and Shebna the *s*
Is 36:22 the household, and Shebna the *s*
Is 37:2 the household, and Shebna the *s*
Jer 36:10 Gemariah the son of Shaphan the *s*
Jer 36:12 sat there, even Elishama the *s*
Jer 36:20 in the chamber of Elishama the *s*
Jer 36:26 of Abdeel, to take Baruch the *s*
Jer 36:32 roll, and gave it to Baruch the *s*
Jer 37:15 in the house of Jonathan the *s*
Jer 37:20 to the house of Jonathan the *s*
Jer 52:25 and the principal *s* of the host
Mt 8:19 And a certain *s* came, and said unto
Mt 13:52 Therefore every *s* which is
Mk 12:32 the *s* said unto him, Well, Master
1Cor 1:20 where is the *s*

## SCRIBES

1Kin 4:3 and Ahiah, the sons of Shisha, *s*
1Chr 2:55 the families of the *s* which dwelt
2Chr 34:13 and of the Levites there were *s*
Est 3:12 Then were the king's *s* called on
Est 8:9 Then were the king's *s* called at
Jer 8:8 the pen of the *s* is in vain
Mt 2:4 *s* of the people together, he
Mt 5:20 exceed the righteousness of the *s*
Mt 7:29 having authority, and not as the *s*
Mt 9:3 certain of the *s* said within
Mt 12:38 Then certain of the *s* and of the
Mt 15:1 Then came to Jesus *s* and Pharisees
Mt 16:21 the elders and chief priests and *s*
Mt 17:10 Why then say the *s* that Elias
Mt 20:18 the chief priests and unto the *s*
Mt 21:15 *s* saw the wonderful things that
Mt 23:2 Saying, The *s* and the Pharisees
Mt 23:13 But woe unto you, *s* and Pharisees,
Mt 23:14 Woe unto you, *s* and Pharisees,
Mt 23:15 Woe unto you, *s* and Pharisees,
Mt 23:23 Woe unto you, *s* and Pharisees,
Mt 23:25 Woe unto you, *s* and Pharisees,
Mt 23:27 Woe unto you, *s* and Pharisees,
Mt 23:29 Woe unto you, *s* and Pharisees,
Mt 23:34 you prophets, and wise men, and *s*
Mt 26:3 the chief priests, and the *s*
Mt 26:57 the high priest, where the *s*
Mt 27:41 priests mocking him, with the *s*
Mk 1:22 had authority, and not as the *s*
Mk 2:6 certain of the *s* sitting there
Mk 2:16 And when the *s* and Pharisees saw
Mk 3:22 the *s* which came down from
Mk 7:1 Pharisees, and certain of the *s*
Mk 7:5 *s* asked him, Why walk not thy
Mk 8:31 and of the chief priests, and *s*
Mk 9:11 Why say the *s* that Elias must
Mk 9:14 the *s* questioning with them
Mk 9:16 And he asked the *s*, What question
Mk 10:33 the chief priests, and unto the *s*
Mk 11:18 And the *s* and chief priests heard
Mk 11:27 him the chief priests, and the *s*
Mk 12:28 And one of the *s* came, and having
Mk 12:35 How say the *s* that Christ is the
Mk 12:38 in his doctrine, Beware of the *s*
Mk 14:1 the *s* sought how they might take
Mk 14:43 from the chief priest and the *s*
Mk 14:53 priests and the elders and the *s*
Mk 15:1 consultation with the elders and *s*
Mk 15:31 said among themselves with the *s*
Lk 5:21 And the *s* and the Pharisees began
Lk 5:30 But their *s* and Pharisees murmured
Lk 6:7 And the *s* and Pharisees watched him
Lk 9:22 the elders and chief priests and *s*
Lk 11:44 Woe unto you, *s* and Pharisees,
Lk 11:53 these things unto them, the *s*

Lk 15:2 *s* murmured, saying, This man
Lk 19:47 But the chief priests and the *s*
Lk 20:1 the *s* came upon him with the
Lk 20:19 the *s* the same hour sought to lay
Lk 20:39 certain of the *s* answering said
Lk 20:46 Beware of the *s*, which desire to
Lk 22:2 *s* sought how they might kill him
Lk 22:66 the *s* came together, and led him
Lk 23:10 *s* stood and vehemently accused him
Jn 8:3 And the *s* and Pharisees brought
Acts 4:5 their rulers, and elders, and *s*
Acts 6:12 people, and the elders, and the *s*
Acts 23:9 the *s* that were of the Pharisees'

## SCRIP
1Sa 17:40 bag which he had, even in a *s*
Mt 10:10 Nor *s* for your journey, neither
Mk 6:8 no *s*, no bread, no money in their
Lk 9:3 journey, neither staves, nor *s*
Lk 10:4 Carry neither purse, nor *s*
Lk 22:35 I sent you without purse, and *s*
Lk 22:36 him take it, and likewise his *s*

## SCRIPTURE
Dan 10:21 which is noted in the *s* of truth
Mk 12:10 And have ye not read this *s*
Mk 15:28 the *s* was fulfilled, which saith,
Lk 4:21 This day is this *s* fulfilled in
Jn 2:22 and they believed the *s*, and the
Jn 7:38 as the *s* hath said, out of his
Jn 7:42 Hath not the *s* said, That Christ
Jn 10:35 came, and the *s* cannot be broken
Jn 13:18 but that the *s* may be fulfilled,
Jn 17:12 that the *s* might be fulfilled
Jn 19:24 that the *s* might be fulfilled,
Jn 19:28 that the *s* might be fulfilled,
Jn 19:36 that the *s* should be fulfilled, A
Jn 19:37 And again another *s* saith, They
Jn 20:9 For as yet they knew not the *s*
Acts 1:16 this *s* must needs have been
Acts 8:32 The place of the *s* which he read
Acts 8:35 his mouth, and began at the same *s*
Rom 4:3 For what saith the *s*
Rom 9:17 For the *s* saith unto Pharaoh,
Rom 10:11 For the *s* saith, Whosoever
Rom 11:2 ye not what the *s* saith of Elias
Gal 3:8 And the *s*, foreseeing that God
Gal 3:22 But the *s* hath concluded all
Gal 4:30 Nevertheless what saith the *s*
1Ti 5:18 For the *s* saith, Thou shalt not
2Ti 3:16 All *s* is given by inspiration of
Jas 2:8 the royal law according to the *s*
Jas 2:23 the *s* was fulfilled which saith,
Jas 4:5 ye think that the *s* saith in vain
1Pet 2:6 also it is contained in the *s*
2Pet 1:20 of the *s* is of any private

## SCRIPTURES
Mt 21:42 them, Did ye never read in the *s*
Mt 22:29 Ye do err, not knowing the *s*
Mt 26:54 how then shall the *s* be fulfilled
Mt 26:56 that the *s* of the prophets might
Mk 12:24 err, because ye know not the *s*
Mk 14:49 but the *s* must be fulfilled
Lk 24:27 *s* the things concerning himself
Lk 24:32 and while he opened to us the *s*
Lk 24:45 that they might understand the *s*
Jn 5:39 Search the *s*
Acts 17:2 reasoned with them out of the *s*
Acts 17:11 of mind, and searched the *s* daily
Acts 18:24 eloquent man, and mighty in the *s*
Acts 18:28 shewing by the *s* that Jesus was
Rom 1:2 by his prophets in the holy *s*
Rom 15:4 comfort of the *s* might have hope
Rom 16:26 by the *s* of the prophets,
1Cor 15:3 for our sins according to the *s*
1Cor 15:4 the third day according to the *s*
2Ti 3:15 child thou hast known the holy *s*
2Pet 3:16 as they do also the other *s*

## SCYTHIAN *(sith'-e-un) A barbarous people north of the Black Sea.*
Col 3:11 nor uncircumcision, Barbarian, *S*

## SEAL
1Kin 21:8 name, and sealed them with his *s*
Neh 9:38 Levites, and priests, *s* unto it
Est 8:8 *s* it with the king's ring
Job 38:14 It is turned as clay to the *s*
Job 41:15 up together as with a close *s*
Song 8:6 Set me as a *s* upon thine heart,
Song 8:6 heart, as a *s* upon thine arm
Is 8:16 *s* the law among my disciples
Jer 32:44 *s* them, and take witnesses in the
Dan 9:24 to *s* up the vision and prophecy,
Dan 12:4 *s* the book, even to the time of
Jn 3:33 set to his *s* that God is true
Rom 4:11 a *s* of the righteousness of the
1Cor 9:2 for the *s* of mine apostleship are
2Ti 2:19 God standeth sure, having this *s*
Rev 6:3 when he had opened the second *s*
Rev 6:5 And when he had opened the third *s*
Rev 6:7 when he had opened the fourth *s*
Rev 6:9 And when he had opened the fifth *s*
Rev 6:12 when he had opened the sixth *s*
Rev 7:2 having the *s* of the living God
Rev 8:1 when he had opened the seventh *s*
Rev 9:4 the *s* of God in their foreheads
Rev 10:4 *S* up those things which the seven
Rev 20:3 set a *s* upon him, that he should
Rev 22:10 *S* not the sayings of the prophecy

## SEALED
Deut 32:34 me, and *s* up among my treasures
1Kin 21:8 *s* them with his seal, and sent the
Neh 10:1 Now those that *s* were, Nehemiah,
Est 3:12 and *s* with the king's ring
Est 8:8 *s* with the king's ring, may no
Est 8:10 *s* it with the king's ring, and
Job 14:17 My transgression is *s* up in a bag
Song 4:12 a spring shut up, a fountain *s*
Is 29:11 as the words of a book that is *s*
Is 29:11 for it is *s*
Jer 32:10 *s* it, and took witnesses, and
Jer 32:11 both that which was *s* according
Jer 32:14 of the purchase, both which is *s*
Dan 6:17 the king *s* it with his own signet
Dan 12:9 *s* till the time of the end
Jn 6:27 for him hath God the Father *s*
Rom 15:28 have *s* to them this fruit, I will
2Cor 1:22 Who hath also *s* us, and given the
Eph 1:13 ye were *s* with that holy Spirit
Eph 4:30 whereby ye are *s* unto the day of
Rev 5:1 the backside, *s* with seven seals
Rev 7:3 till we have *s* the servants of
Rev 7:4 the number of them which were *s*
Rev 7:4 and there were *s* an hundred
Rev 7:5 of Juda were *s* twelve thousand
Rev 7:5 of Reuben were *s* twelve thousand
Rev 7:5 of Gad were *s* twelve thousand
Rev 7:6 of Aser were *s* twelve thousand
Rev 7:6 Nepthalim were *s* twelve thousand
Rev 7:6 Manasses were *s* twelve thousand
Rev 7:7 of Simeon were *s* twelve thousand
Rev 7:7 of Levi were *s* twelve thousand
Rev 7:7 Issachar were *s* twelve thousand
Rev 7:8 of Zabulon were *s* twelve thousand
Rev 7:8 of Joseph were *s* twelve thousand
Rev 7:8 Benjamin were *s* twelve thousand

## SEALS
Rev 5:1 the backside, sealed with seven *s*
Rev 5:2 book, and to loose the *s* thereof
Rev 5:5 and to loose the seven *s* thereof
Rev 5:9 book, and to open the *s* thereof
Rev 6:1 when the Lamb opened one of the *s*

## SEARCH
Lev 27:33 He shall not *s* whether it be good
Num 10:33 to *s* out a resting place for them
Num 13:2 that they may *s* the land of
Num 13:32 which we have gone to *s* it
Num 14:7 which we passed through to *s* it
Num 14:36 which Moses sent to *s* the land
Num 14:38 the men that went to *s* the land
Deut 1:22 they shall *s* us out the land, and
Deut 1:33 to *s* you out a place to pitch
Deut 13:14 shalt thou enquire, and make *s*
Josh 2:2 of Israel to *s* out the country
Josh 2:3 be come to *s* out all the country
Judg 18:2 to spy out the land, and to *s* it
Judg 18:2 said unto them, Go, *s* the land
1Sa 23:23 that I will *s* him out throughout
2Sa 10:3 to *s* the city, and to spy it out,
1Kin 20:6 they shall *s* thine house, and the
2Kin 10:23 unto the worshippers of Baal, *S*
1Chr 19:3 servants come unto thee for to *s*
Ezr 4:15 That *s* may be made in the book of
Ezr 4:19 *s* hath been made, and it is found
Ezr 5:17 let there be *s* made in the king's
Ezr 6:1 *s* was made in the house of the
Job 8:8 thyself to the *s* of their fathers
Job 13:9 it good that he should *s* you out
Job 38:16 thou walked in the *s* of the depth
Ps 44:21 Shall not God *s* this out
Ps 64:6 They *s* out iniquities
Ps 64:6 they accomplish a diligent *s*
Ps 77:6 and my spirit made diligent *s*
Ps 139:23 *S* me, O God, and know my heart
Prov 25:2 of kings is to *s* out a matter
Prov 25:27 so for men to *s* their own glory
Eccl 1:13 *s* out by wisdom concerning all
Eccl 7:25 mine heart to know, and to *s*
Jer 2:34 I have not found it by secret *s*
Jer 17:10 I the LORD *s* the heart, I try the
Jer 29:13 when ye shall *s* for me with all
Lam 3:40 Let us *s* and try our ways, and turn
Eze 34:6 none did *s* or seek after them
Eze 34:8 did my shepherds *s* for my flock
Eze 34:11 I, even I, will both *s* my sheep
Eze 39:14 end of seven months shall they *s*
Amos 9:3 in the top of Carmel, I will *s*
Zeph 1:12 that I will *s* Jerusalem with
Mt 2:8 *s* diligently for the young child
Jn 5:39 *S* the scriptures
Jn 7:52 *S*, and look

## SEARCHED
Gen 31:34 Laban *s* all the tent, but found
Gen 31:35 And he *s*, but found not the images
Gen 31:37 Whereas thou hast *s* all my stuff
Gen 44:12 And he *s*, and began at the eldest,
Num 13:21 *s* the land from the wilderness of
Num 13:32 of the land which they had *s* unto
Num 14:6 were of them that *s* the land
Num 14:34 the days in which ye *s* the land
Deut 1:24 the valley of Eshcol, and *s* it out
Job 5:27 Lo this, we have *s* it, so it is
Job 28:27 he prepared it, yea, and *s* it out
Job 29:16 cause which I knew not I *s* out
Job 32:11 whilst ye *s* out what to say
Job 36:26 the number of his years be *s* out
Ps 139:1 O lord, thou hast *s* me, and known
Jer 31:37 of the earth *s* out beneath
Jer 46:23 the LORD, though it cannot be *s*
Obad 6 How are the things of Esau *s* out
Acts 17:11 *s* the scriptures daily, whether
1Pet 1:10 *s* diligently, who prophesied of

## SEARCHETH
1Chr 28:9 for the LORD *s* all hearts
Job 28:3 darkness, and *s* out all perfection
Job 39:8 he *s* after every green thing
Prov 18:17 but his neighbour cometh and *s* him
Prov 28:11 that hath understanding *s* him out
Rom 8:27 he that *s* the hearts knoweth what
1Cor 2:10 for the Spirit *s* all things
Rev 2:23 that I am he which *s* the reins

## SEARCHING
Num 13:25 they returned from *s* of the land
Job 11:7 Canst thou by *s* find out God
Prov 20:27 *s* all the inward parts of the
Is 40:28 there is no *s* of his
1Pet 1:11 *S* what, or what manner of time

## SEASON
Gen 40:4 and they continued a *s* in ward
Ex 13:10 in his *s* from year to year
Lev 2:13 offering shalt thou *s* with salt
Lev 26:4 I will give you rain in due *s*
Num 9:2 the passover at his appointed *s*
Num 9:3 shall keep it in his appointed *s*
Num 9:7 *s* among the children of Israel
Num 9:13 of the LORD in his appointed *s*
Num 28:2 to offer unto me in their due *s*
Deut 11:14 rain of your land in his due *s*
Deut 16:6 at the *s* that thou camest forth
Deut 28:12 the rain unto thy land in his *s*
Josh 24:7 dwelt in the wilderness a long *s*
2Kin 4:16 And he said, About this *s*,
2Kin 4:17 bare a son at that *s* that Elisha
1Chr 21:29 were at that *s* in the high place
2Chr 15:3 Now for a long *s* Israel hath been
Job 5:26 shock of corn cometh in in his *s*
Job 30:17 are pierced in me in the night *s*
Job 38:32 bring forth Mazzaroth in his *s*
Ps 1:3 bringeth forth his fruit in his *s*
Ps 22:2 and in the night *s*, and am not
Ps 104:27 give them their meat in due *s*
Ps 145:15 givest them their meat in due *s*
Prov 15:23 and a word spoken in due *s*
Eccl 3:1 To every thing there is a *s*
Eccl 10:17 and thy princes eat in due *s*
Is 50:4 a word in *s* to him that is weary
Jer 5:24 former and the latter, in his *s*
Jer 33:20 not be day and night in their *s*

Eze 34:26 the shower to come down in his *s*
Dan 7:12 lives were prolonged for a *s*
Hos 2:9 and my wine in the *s* thereof
Mt 24:45 to give them meat in due *s*
Mk 9:50 saltness, wherewith will ye *s* it
Mk 12:2 And at the *s* he sent to the
Lk 1:20 shall be fulfilled in their *s*
Lk 4:13 he departed from him for a *s*
Lk 12:42 their portion of meat in due *s*
Lk 13:1 that *s* some that told him of the
Lk 20:10 at the *s* he sent a servant to the
Lk 23:8 desirous to see him of a long *s*
Jn 5:4 down at a certain *s* into the pool
Jn 5:35 ye were willing for a *s* to
Acts 13:11 blind, not seeing the sun for a *s*
Acts 19:22 he himself stayed in Asia for a *s*
Acts 24:25 when I have a convenient *s*
2Cor 7:8 sorry, though it were but for a *s*
Gal 6:9 for in due *s* we shall reap, if we
2Ti 4:2 be instant in *s*
2Ti 4:2 out of *s*; reprove
Philem 15 he therefore departed for a *s*
Heb 11:25 the pleasures of sin for a *s*
1Pet 1:6 rejoice, though now for a *s*
Rev 6:11 should rest yet for a little *s*
Rev 20:3 that he must be loosed a little *s*

## SEASONS

Gen 1:14 let them be for signs, and for *s*
Ex 18:22 them judge the people at all *s*
Ex 18:26 they judged the people at all *s*
Lev 23:4 ye shall proclaim in their *s*
Ps 16:7 also instruct me in the night *s*
Ps 104:19 He appointed the moon for *s*
Dan 2:21 And he changeth the times and the *s*
Mt 21:41 render him the fruits in their *s*
Acts 1:7 you to know the times or the *s*
Acts 14:17 rain from heaven, and fruitful *s*
Acts 20:18 I have been with you at all *s*
1Th 5:1 But of the times and the *s*

## SEAT

Ex 25:17 shalt make a mercy *s* of pure gold
Ex 25:18 in the two ends of the mercy *s*
Ex 25:19 even of the mercy *s* shall ye make
Ex 25:20 the mercy *s* with their wings
Ex 25:20 toward the mercy *s* shall the
Ex 25:21 the mercy *s* above upon the ark
Ex 25:22 with thee from above the mercy *s*
Ex 26:34 thou shalt put the mercy *s* upon
Ex 30:6 before the mercy *s* that is over
Ex 31:7 the mercy *s* that is thereupon, and
Ex 35:12 staves thereof, with the mercy *s*
Ex 37:6 he made the mercy *s* of pure gold
Ex 37:7 on the two ends of the mercy *s*
Ex 37:8 out of the mercy *s* made he the
Ex 37:9 with their wings over the mercy *s*
Ex 39:35 staves thereof, and the mercy *s*
Ex 40:20 put the mercy *s* above upon the
Lev 16:2 the vail before the mercy *s*
Lev 16:2 in the cloud upon the mercy *s*
Lev 16:13 *s* that is upon the testimony
Lev 16:14 finger upon the mercy *s* eastward
Lev 16:14 before the mercy *s* shall he
Lev 16:15 and sprinkle it upon the mercy *s*
Lev 16:15 and before the mercy *s*
Num 7:89 mercy *s* that was upon the ark of
Judg 3:20 And he arose out of his *s*
1Sa 1:9 Now Eli the priest sat upon a *s*
1Sa 4:13 Eli sat upon a *s* by the wayside
1Sa 4:18 that he fell from off the *s*
1Sa 20:18 because thy *s* will be empty
1Sa 20:25 And the king sat upon his *s*
1Sa 20:25 times, even upon a *s* by the wall
2Sa 23:8 The Tachmonite that sat in the *s*
1Kin 2:19 caused a *s* to be set for the
1Kin 10:19 either side on the place of the *s*
1Chr 28:11 and of the place of the mercy *s*
Est 3:1 set his *s* above all the princes
Job 23:3 that I might come even to his *s*
Job 29:7 I prepared my *s* in the street
Ps 1:1 sitteth in the *s* of the scornful
Prov 9:14 on a *s* in the high places of the
Eze 8:3 where was the *s* of the image of
Eze 28:2 I am a God, I sit in the *s* of God
Amos 6:3 cause the *s* of violence to come
Mt 23:2 and the Pharisees sit in Moses' *s*
Mt 27:19 he was set down on the judgment *s*
Jn 19:13 sat down in the judgment *s* in a
Acts 18:12 and brought him to the judgment *s*
Acts 18:16 he drave them from the judgment *s*
Acts 18:17 and beat him before the judgment *s*
Acts 25:6 day sitting on the judgment *s*
Acts 25:10 I stand at Caesar's judgment *s*
Acts 25:17 morrow I sat on the judgment *s*
Rom 14:10 before the judgment *s* of Christ
2Cor 5:10 before the judgment *s* of Christ
Rev 2:13 dwellest, even where Satan's *s* is
Rev 13:2 gave him his power, and his *s*
Rev 16:10 his vial upon the *s* of the beast

## SEATS

Mt 21:12 the *s* of them that sold doves,
Mt 23:6 the chief *s* in the synagogues,
Mk 11:15 the *s* of them that sold doves
Mk 12:39 the chief *s* in the synagogues, and
Lk 1:52 put down the mighty from their *s*
Lk 11:43 the uppermost *s* in the synagogues
Lk 20:46 the highest *s* in the synagogues,
Jas 2:6 and draw you before the judgment *s*
Rev 4:4 the throne were four and twenty *s*
Rev 4:4 upon the *s* I saw four and twenty
Rev 11:16 which sat before God on their *s*

## SEBA *(se'-bah)* See SABEANS, SHEBA.

*1. A son of Cush.*
Gen 10:7 *S*, and Havilah, and Sabtah, and
1Chr 1:9 *S*, and Havilah, and Sabta, and
*2. The land.*
Ps 72:10 of Sheba and *S* shall offer gifts
Is 43:3 ransom, Ethiopia and *S* for thee

## SEBAT *(se'-bat) The eleventh month of the Hebrew year.*

Zec 1:7 month, which is the month *S*

## SECACAH *(se-ca'-cah) A village in Judah.*

Josh 15:61 Beth-arabah, Middin, and *S*

## SECHU *(se'-ku) A city in Benjamin.*

1Sa 19:22 came to a great well that is in *S*

## SECOND

Gen 1:8 and the morning were the *s* day
Gen 2:13 the name of the *s* river is Gihon
Gen 6:16 with lower, *s*, and third stories
Gen 7:11 of Noah's life, in the *s* month
Gen 8:14 And in the *s* month, on the seven
Gen 22:15 Abraham out of heaven the *s* time
Gen 30:7 again, and bare Jacob a *s* son
Gen 30:12 Leah's maid bare Jacob a *s* son
Gen 32:19 And so commanded he the *s*, and the
Gen 41:5 And he slept and dreamed the *s* time
Gen 41:43 in the *s* chariot which he had
Gen 41:52 the name of the *s* called he
Gen 43:10 now we had returned this *s* time
Gen 47:18 they came unto him the *s* year
Ex 2:13 And when he went out the *s* day
Ex 16:1 on the fifteenth day of the *s*
Ex 26:4 curtain, in the coupling of the *s*
Ex 26:5 that is in the coupling of the *s*
Ex 26:10 the curtain which coupleth the *s*
Ex 26:20 for the *s* side of the tabernacle
Ex 28:18 the *s* row shall be an emerald, a
Ex 36:11 curtain, in the coupling of the *s*
Ex 36:12 was in the coupling of the *s*
Ex 36:17 the curtain which coupleth the *s*
Ex 39:11 And the *s* row, an emerald, a
Ex 40:17 in the first month in the *s* year
Lev 5:10 he shall offer the *s* for a burnt
Lev 13:58 it shall be washed the *s* time
Num 1:1 on the first day of the *s* month
Num 1:1 in the *s* year after they were
Num 1:18 on the first day of the *s* month
Num 2:16 shall set forth in the *s* rank
Num 7:18 On the *s* day Nethaneel the son of
Num 9:1 in the first month of the *s* year
Num 9:11 The fourteenth day of the *s* month
Num 10:6 When ye blow an alarm the *s* time
Num 10:11 the *s* month, in the *s* year
Num 29:17 on the *s* day ye shall offer
Josh 5:2 the children of Israel the *s* time
Josh 6:14 the *s* day they compassed the city
Josh 10:32 which took it on the *s* day
Josh 19:1 the *s* lot came forth to Simeon,
Judg 6:25 even the *s* bullock of seven years
Judg 6:26 place, and take the *s* bullock
Judg 6:28 the *s* bullock was offered upon
Judg 20:24 children of Benjamin the *s* day
Judg 20:25 them out of Gibeah the *s* day
1Sa 8:2 and the name of his *s*, Abiah
1Sa 20:27 which was the *s* day of the month,
1Sa 20:34 no meat the *s* day of the month
1Sa 26:8 I will not smite him the *s* time
2Sa 3:3 And his *s*, Chileab, of Abigail the
2Sa 14:29 and when he sent again the *s* time
1Kin 6:1 month Zif, which is the *s* month
1Kin 9:2 appeared to Solomon the *s* time
1Kin 15:25 the *s* year of Asa king of Judah
1Kin 18:34 And he said, Do it the *s* time
1Kin 18:34 And they did it the *s* time
1Kin 19:7 of the LORD came again the *s* time
2Kin 1:17 the *s* year of Jehoram the son of
2Kin 9:19 Then he sent out a *s* on horseback
2Kin 10:6 wrote a letter the *s* time to them
2Kin 14:1 In the *s* year of Joash son of
2Kin 15:32 In the *s* year of Pekah the son of
2Kin 19:29 and in the *s* year that which
2Kin 23:4 and the priests of the *s* order
2Kin 25:17 like unto these had the *s* pillar
2Kin 25:18 priest, and Zephaniah the *s* priest
1Chr 2:13 Eliab, and Abinadab the *s*, and
1Chr 3:1 the *s* Daniel, of Abigail the
1Chr 3:15 the *s* Jehoiakim, the third
1Chr 7:15 the name of the *s* was Zelophehad
1Chr 8:1 Bela his firstborn, Ashbel the *s*
1Chr 8:39 Ulam his firstborn, Jehush the *s*
1Chr 12:9 Ezer the first, Obadiah the *s*
1Chr 15:18 their brethren of the *s* degree
1Chr 23:11 was the chief, and Zizah the *s*
1Chr 23:19 Jeriah the first, Amariah the *s*
1Chr 23:20 Micah the first, and Jesiah the *s*
1Chr 24:7 to Jehoiarib, the *s* to Jedaiah,
1Chr 24:23 Jeriah the first, Amariah the *s*
1Chr 25:9 the *s* to Gedaliah, who with his
1Chr 26:2 the firstborn, Jediael the *s*
1Chr 26:4 the firstborn, Jehozabad the *s*
1Chr 26:11 Hilkiah the *s*, Tebaliah the third
1Chr 27:4 over the course of the *s* month
1Chr 29:22 the son of David king the *s* time
2Chr 3:2 in the *s* day of the *s* month
2Chr 27:5 pay unto him, both the *s* year
2Chr 30:2 keep the passover in the *s* month
2Chr 30:13 unleavened bread in the *s* month
2Chr 30:15 the fourteenth day of the *s* month
2Chr 35:24 put him in the *s* chariot that he
Ezr 1:10 basons of a *s* sort four hundred
Ezr 3:8 Now in the *s* year of their coming
Ezr 3:8 God at Jerusalem, in the *s* month
Ezr 4:24 So it ceased unto the *s* year of
Neh 8:13 on the *s* day were gathered
Neh 11:9 son of Senuah was *s* over the city
Neh 11:17 Bakbukiah the *s* among his
Est 2:14 into the *s* house of the women
Est 2:19 were gathered together the *s* time
Est 7:2 the *s* day at the banquet of wine
Est 9:29 to confirm this *s* letter of Purim
Job 42:14 and the name of the *s*, Kezia
Eccl 4:8 is one alone, and there is not a *s*
Eccl 4:15 with the *s* child that shall stand
Is 11:11 shall set his hand again the *s*
Is 37:30 the *s* year that which springeth
Jer 1:13 the LORD came unto me the *s* time
Jer 13:3 the LORD came unto me the *s* time
Jer 33:1 came unto Jeremiah the *s* time
Jer 41:4 it came to pass the *s* day after
Jer 52:22 The *s* pillar also and the
Jer 52:24 priest, and Zephaniah the *s* priest
Eze 10:14 the *s* face was the face of a man,
Eze 43:22 on the *s* day thou shalt offer a
Dan 2:1 in the *s* year of the reign of
Dan 7:5 And behold another beast, a *s*
Jonah 3:1 LORD came unto Jonah the *s* time
Nah 1:9 shall not rise up the *s* time
Zeph 1:10 gate, and an howling from the *s*
Hag 1:1 In the *s* year of Darius the king,
Hag 1:15 in the *s* year of Darius the king
Hag 2:10 in the *s* year of Darius, came the
Zec 1:1 in the *s* year of Darius, came the
Zec 1:7 in the *s* year of Darius, came the
Zec 6:2 in the *s* chariot black horses
Mt 21:30 And he came to the *s*, and said
Mt 22:26 Likewise the *s* also, and the third
Mt 22:39 the *s* is like unto it, Thou shalt
Mt 26:42 He went away again the *s* time
Mk 12:21 the *s* took her, and died, neither
Mk 12:31 the *s* is like, namely this, Thou
Mk 14:72 And the *s* time the cock crew
Lk 6:1 it came to pass on the *s* sabbath
Lk 12:38 if he shall come in the *s* watch
Lk 19:18 the *s* came, saying, Lord, thy
Lk 20:30 the *s* took her to wife, and he
Jn 3:4 can he enter the *s* time into his
Jn 4:54 This is again the *s* miracle that
Jn 21:16 He saith to him again the *s* time

Acts 7:13 at the *s* time Joseph was made
Acts 10:15 spake unto him again the *s* time
Acts 12:10 the *s* ward, they came unto the
Acts 13:33 it is also written in the *s* psalm
1Cor 15:47 the *s* man is the Lord from heaven
2Cor 1:15 that ye might have a *s* benefit
2Cor 13:2 as if I were present, the *s* time
2Cor *s* The *s* epistle to the Corinthians
2Th *s* The *s* epistle to the
2Ti *s* The *s* epistle unto Timotheus,
2Ti *s* brought before Nero the *s* time
Titus 3:10 the first and *s* admonition reject
Heb 8:7 place have been sought for the *s*
Heb 9:3 And after the *s* veil, the
Heb 9:7 But into the *s* went the high
Heb 9:28 for him shall he appear the *s*
Heb 10:9 that he may establish the *s*
2Pet 3:1 This *s* epistle, beloved, I now
Rev 2:11 shall not be hurt of the *s* death
Rev 4:7 the *s* beast like a calf, and the
Rev 6:3 And when he had opened the *s* seal
Rev 6:3 I heard the *s* beast say
Rev 8:8 the *s* angel sounded, and as it
Rev 11:14 The *s* woe is past
Rev 16:3 the *s* angel poured out his vial
Rev 20:6 on such the *s* death hath no power
Rev 20:14 This is the *s* death
Rev 21:8 which is the *s* death
Rev 21:19 the *s*, sapphire

## SECRET

Gen 49:6 soul, come not thou into their *s*
Deut 27:15 and putteth it in a *s* place
Deut 29:29 The *s* things belong unto the LORD
Judg 3:19 I have a *s* errand unto thee, O
Judg 13:18 after my name, seeing it is *s*
1Sa 5:9 they had emerods in their *s* parts
1Sa 19:2 morning, and abide in a *s* place
Job 14:13 that thou wouldest keep me *s*
Job 15:8 Hast thou heard the *s* of God
Job 15:11 is there any *s* thing with thee
Job 20:26 shall be hid in his *s* places
Job 29:4 when the *s* of God was upon my
Job 40:13 and bind their faces in *s*
Ps 10:8 in the *s* places doth he murder
Ps 17:12 a young lion lurking in *s* places
Ps 18:11 He made darkness his *s* place
Ps 19:12 cleanse thou me from *s* faults
Ps 25:14 The *s* of the LORD is with them
Ps 27:5 in the *s* of his tabernacle shall
Ps 31:20 Thou shalt hide them in the *s* of
Ps 64:2 Hide me from the *s* counsel of the
Ps 64:4 may shoot in *s* at the perfect
Ps 81:7 thee in the *s* place of thunder
Ps 90:8 our *s* sins in the light of thy
Ps 91:1 He that dwelleth in the *s* place
Ps 139:15 from thee, when I was made in *s*
Prov 3:32 but his *s* is with the righteous
Prov 9:17 and bread eaten in *s* is pleasant
Prov 21:14 A gift in *s* pacifieth anger
Prov 25:9 and discover not a *s* to another
Prov 27:5 Open rebuke is better than *s* love
Eccl 12:14 into judgment, with every *s* thing
Song 2:14 in the *s* places of the stairs,
Is 3:17 LORD will discover their *s* parts
Is 45:3 and hidden riches of *s* places
Is 45:19 I have not spoken in *s*, in a dark
Is 48:16 spoken in *s* from the beginning
Jer 2:34 I have not found it by *s* search
Jer 13:17 weep in *s* places for your pride
Jer 23:24 Can any hide himself in *s* places
Jer 49:10 I have uncovered his *s* places
Lam 3:10 in wait, and as a lion in *s* places
Eze 7:22 and they shall pollute my *s* place
Eze 28:3 there is no *s* that they can hide
Dan 2:18 God of heaven concerning this *s*
Dan 2:19 Then was the *s* revealed unto
Dan 2:22 He revealeth the deep and *s* things
Dan 2:27 The *s* which the king hath
Dan 2:30 this *s* is not revealed to me for
Dan 2:47 seeing thou couldst reveal this *s*
Dan 4:9 no *s* troubleth thee, tell me the
Amos 3:7 but he revealeth his *s* unto his
Mt 6:4 That thine alms may be in *s*
Mt 6:4 in *s* himself shall reward thee
Mt 6:6 pray to thy Father which is in *s*
Mt 6:6 in *s* shall reward thee openly
Mt 6:18 but unto thy Father which is in *s*
Mt 6:18 and thy Father, which seeth in *s*
Mt 13:35 kept *s* from the foundation of the
Mt 24:26 behold, he is in the *s* chambers
Mk 4:22 neither was any thing kept *s*
Lk 8:17 For nothing is *s*, that shall not
Lk 11:33 a candle, putteth it in a *s* place
Jn 7:4 no man that doeth any thing in *s*
Jn 7:10 not openly, but as it were in *s*
Jn 18:20 and in *s* have I said nothing
Rom 16:25 which was kept *s* since the world
Eph 5:12 which are done of them in *s*

## SECRETLY

Gen 31:27 Wherefore didst thou flee away *s*
Deut 13:6 as thine own soul, entice thee *s*
Deut 27:24 he that smiteth his neighbour *s*
Deut 28:57 want of all things *s* in the siege
Josh 2:1 out of Shittim two men to spy *s*
1Sa 18:22 saying, Commune with David *s*
1Sa 23:9 David knew that Saul *s* practised
2Sa 12:12 For thou didst it *s*
2Kin 17:9 did *s* those things that were not
Job 4:12 Now a thing was *s* brought to me
Job 13:10 if ye do *s* accept persons
Job 31:27 And my heart hath been *s* enticed
Ps 10:9 He lieth in wait *s* as a lion in
Ps 31:20 thou shalt keep them *s* in a
Jer 37:17 the king asked him *s* in his house
Jer 38:16 the king sware *s* unto Jeremiah
Jer 40:15 spake to Gedaliah in Mizpah *s*
Hab 3:14 was as to devour the poor *s*
Jn 11:28 way, and called Mary her sister *s*
Jn 19:38 but *s* for fear of the Jews,

## SECRETS

Deut 25:11 her hand, and taketh him by the *s*
Job 11:6 would shew thee the *s* of wisdom
Ps 44:21 for he knoweth the *s* of the heart
Prov 11:13 A talebearer revealeth *s*
Prov 20:19 about as a talebearer revealeth *s*
Dan 2:28 a God in heaven that revealeth *s*
Dan 2:29 he that revealeth *s* maketh known
Dan 2:47 LORD of kings, and a revealer of *s*
Rom 2:16 the *s* of men by Jesus Christ
1Cor 14:25 thus are the *s* of his heart made

## SECT

Acts 5:17 (which is the *s* of the Sadducees,
Acts 15:5 there rose up certain of the *s* of
Acts 24:5 of the *s* of the Nazarenes
Acts 26:5 *s* of our religion I lived a
Acts 28:22 for as concerning this *s*, we know

## SECUNDUS *(se-cun'-dus) A Christian in Thessalonica.*

Acts 20:4 Thessalonians, Aristarchus and *S*

## SECURE

Judg 8:11 for the host was *s*
Judg 18:7 of the Zidonians, quiet and *s*
Judg 18:10 go, ye shall come unto a people *s*
Judg 18:27 a people that were at quiet and *s*
Job 11:18 And thou shalt be *s*, because there
Job 12:6 and they that provoke God are *s*
Mt 28:14 we will persuade him, and *s* you

## SEDITION

Ezr 4:15 that they have moved *s* within the
Ezr 4:19 and *s* have been made therein
Lk 23:19 for a certain *s* made in the city
Lk 23:25 released unto them him that for *s*
Acts 24:5 a mover of *s* among all the Jews

## SEED

Gen 1:11 forth grass, the herb yielding *s*
Gen 1:11 whose *s* is in itself, upon the
Gen 1:12 herb yielding *s* after his kind,
Gen 1:12 whose *s* was in itself, after his
Gen 1:29 given you every herb bearing *s*
Gen 1:29 is the fruit of a tree yielding *s*
Gen 3:15 and between thy *s* and her *s*
Gen 4:25 me another *s* instead of Abel
Gen 7:3 to keep *s* alive upon the face of
Gen 9:9 you, and with your *s* after you
Gen 12:7 Unto thy *s* will I give this land
Gen 13:15 I give it, and to thy *s* for ever
Gen 13:16 I will make thy *s* as the dust of
Gen 13:16 then shall thy *s* also be numbered
Gen 15:3 to me thou hast given no *s*
Gen 15:5 said unto him, So shall thy *s* be
Gen 15:13 Know of a surety that thy *s* shall
Gen 15:18 Unto thy *s* have I given this land
Gen 16:10 I will multiply thy *s* exceedingly
Gen 17:7 thy *s* after thee in their
Gen 17:7 unto thee, and to thy *s* after thee
Gen 17:8 to thy *s* after thee, the land
Gen 17:9 thy *s* after thee in their
Gen 17:10 me and you and thy *s* after thee
Gen 17:12 stranger, which is not of thy *s*
Gen 17:19 covenant, and with his *s* after him
Gen 19:32 we may preserve *s* of our father
Gen 19:34 we may preserve *s* of our father
Gen 21:12 in Isaac shall thy *s* be called
Gen 21:13 a nation, because he is thy *s*
Gen 22:17 thy *s* as the stars of the heaven
Gen 22:17 thy *s* shall possess the gate of
Gen 22:18 in thy *s* shall all the nations of
Gen 24:7 Unto thy *s* will I give this land
Gen 24:60 let thy *s* possess the gate of
Gen 26:3 for unto thee, and unto thy *s*
Gen 26:4 I will make thy *s* to multiply as
Gen 26:4 will give unto thy *s* all these
Gen 26:4 in thy *s* shall all the nations of
Gen 26:24 multiply thy *s* for my servant
Gen 28:4 to thee, and to thy *s* with thee
Gen 28:13 thee will I give it, and to thy *s*
Gen 28:14 thy *s* shall be as the dust of the
Gen 28:14 in thy *s* shall all the families
Gen 32:12 make thy *s* as the sand of the sea
Gen 35:12 to thy *s* after thee will I give
Gen 38:8 raise up *s* to thy brother
Gen 38:9 knew that the *s* should not be his
Gen 38:9 he should give *s* to his brother
Gen 46:6 Jacob, and all his *s* with him
Gen 46:7 all his *s* brought he with him
Gen 47:19 and give us *s*, that we may live,
Gen 47:23 lo, here is *s* for you, and ye
Gen 47:24 for *s* of the field, and for your
Gen 48:4 will give this land to thy *s*
Gen 48:11 lo, God hath shewed me also thy *s*
Gen 48:19 his *s* shall become a multitude of
Ex 16:31 and it was like coriander *s*
Ex 28:43 ever unto him and his *s* after him
Ex 30:21 to his *s* throughout their
Ex 32:13 I will multiply your *s* as the
Ex 32:13 spoken of will I give unto your *s*
Ex 33:1 Unto thy *s* will I give it
Lev 11:37 any sowing *s* which is to be sown
Lev 11:38 if any water be put upon the *s*
Lev 12:2 If a woman have conceived *s*
Lev 15:16 if any man's *s* of copulation go
Lev 15:17 whereon is the *s* of copulation
Lev 15:18 shall lie with *s* of copulation
Lev 15:32 of him whose *s* goeth from him, and
Lev 18:21 thou shalt not let any of thy *s*
Lev 19:19 not sow thy field with mingled *s*
Lev 20:2 giveth any of his *s* unto Molech
Lev 20:3 hath given of his *s* unto Molech
Lev 20:4 he giveth of his *s* unto Molech
Lev 21:15 he profane his *s* among his people
Lev 21:17 Whosoever he be of thy *s* in their
Lev 21:21 *s* of Aaron the priest shall come
Lev 22:3 all your *s* among your generations
Lev 22:4 of the *s* of Aaron is a leper
Lev 22:4 or a man whose *s* goeth from him
Lev 26:16 and ye shall sow your *s* in vain
Lev 27:16 be according to the *s* thereof
Lev 27:16 a homer of barley *s* shall be
Lev 27:30 whether of the *s* of the land
Num 5:28 be free, and shall conceive *s*
Num 11:7 And the manna was as coriander *s*
Num 14:24 and his *s* shall possess it
Num 16:40 which is not of the *s* of Aaron
Num 18:19 unto thee and to thy *s* with thee
Num 20:5 it is no place of *s*, or of figs,
Num 24:7 his *s* shall be in many waters, and
Num 25:13 his *s* after him, even the
Deut 1:8 them and to their *s* after them
Deut 4:37 he chose their *s* after them
Deut 10:15 and he chose their *s* after them
Deut 11:9 to give unto them and to their *s*
Deut 11:10 out, where thou sowedst thy *s*
Deut 14:22 tithe all the increase of thy *s*
Deut 22:9 of thy *s* which thou hast sown
Deut 28:38 carry much *s* out into the field
Deut 28:46 a wonder, and upon thy *s* for ever
Deut 28:59 and the plagues of thy *s*, even
Deut 30:6 heart, and the heart of thy *s*
Deut 30:19 that both thou and thy *s* may live
Deut 31:21 out of the mouths of their *s*
Deut 34:4 saying, I will give it unto thy *s*
Josh 24:3 of Canaan, and multiplied his *s*
Ruth 4:12 of the *s* which the LORD shall
1Sa 2:20 The LORD give thee *s* of this
1Sa 8:15 he will take the tenth of your *s*
1Sa 20:42 between my *s* and thy *s* for ever

1Sa 24:21 wilt not cut off my *s* after me
2Sa 4:8 this day of Saul, and of his *s*
2Sa 7:12 I will set up thy *s* after thee
2Sa 22:51 David, and to his *s* for evermore
1Kin 2:33 upon the head of his *s* for ever
1Kin 2:33 but upon David, and upon his *s*
1Kin 11:14 he was of the king's *s* in Edom
1Kin 11:39 for this afflict the *s* of David
1Kin 18:32 would contain two measures of *s*
2Kin 5:27 unto thee, and unto thy *s* for ever
2Kin 11:1 and destroyed all the *s* royal
2Kin 17:20 LORD rejected all the *s* of Israel
2Kin 25:25 son of Elishama, of the *s* royal
1Chr 16:13 O ye *s* of Israel his servant, ye
1Chr 17:11 I will raise up thy *s* after thee
2Chr 20:7 gavest it to the *s* of Abraham thy
2Chr 22:10 destroyed all the *s* royal of the
Ezr 2:59 their father's house, and their *s*
Ezr 9:2 so that the holy *s* have mingled
Neh 7:61 their father's house, nor their *s*
Neh 9:2 the *s* of Israel separated
Neh 9:8 to give it, I say, to his *s*
Est 6:13 Mordecai be of the *s* of the Jews
Est 9:27 took upon them, and upon their *s*
Est 9:28 of them perish from their *s*
Est 9:31 for themselves and for their *s*
Est 10:3 and speaking peace to all his *s*
Job 5:25 also that thy *s* shall be great
Job 21:8 Their *s* is established in their
Job 39:12 that he will bring home thy *s*
Ps 18:50 David, and to his *s* for evermore
Ps 21:10 their *s* from among the children
Ps 22:23 all ye the *s* of Jacob, glorify
Ps 22:23 fear him, all ye the *s* of Israel
Ps 22:30 A *s* shall serve him
Ps 25:13 his *s* shall inherit the earth
Ps 37:25 forsaken, nor his *s* begging bread
Ps 37:26 and his *s* is blessed
Ps 37:28 but the *s* of the wicked shall be
Ps 69:36 The *s* also of his servants shall
Ps 89:4 Thy *s* will I establish for ever,
Ps 89:29 His *s* also will I make to endure
Ps 89:36 His *s* shall endure for ever, and
Ps 102:28 their *s* shall be established
Ps 105:6 O ye *s* of Abraham his servant, ye
Ps 106:27 To overthrow their *s* also among
Ps 112:2 His *s* shall be mighty upon earth
Ps 126:6 and weepeth, bearing precious *s*
Prov 11:21 but the *s* of the righteous shall
Eccl 11:6 In the morning sow thy *s*, and in
Is 1:4 a *s* of evildoers, children that
Is 5:10 the *s* of an homer shall yield an
Is 6:13 so the holy *s* shall be the
Is 14:20 the *s* of evildoers shall never be
Is 17:11 shalt thou make thy *s* to flourish
Is 23:3 And by great waters the *s* of Sihor
Is 30:23 shall he give the rain of thy *s*
Is 41:8 the *s* of Abraham my friend
Is 43:5 I will bring thy *s* from the east
Is 44:3 I will pour my spirit upon thy *s*
Is 45:19 I said not unto the *s* of Jacob
Is 45:25 all the *s* of Israel be justified
Is 48:19 Thy *s* also had been as the sand,
Is 53:10 for sin, he shall see his *s*
Is 54:3 thy *s* shall inherit the Gentiles,
Is 55:10 that it may give *s* to the sower
Is 57:3 the *s* of the adulterer and the
Is 57:4 transgression, a *s* of falsehood,
Is 59:21 nor out of the mouth of thy *s*
Is 59:21 out of the mouth of thy seed's *s*
Is 61:9 their *s* shall be known among the
Is 61:9 that they are the *s* which the
Is 65:9 will bring forth a *s* out of Jacob
Is 65:23 for they are the *s* of the blessed
Is 66:22 saith the LORD, so shall your *s*
Jer 2:21 a noble vine, wholly a right *s*
Jer 7:15 even the whole *s* of Ephraim
Jer 22:28 are they cast out, he and his *s*
Jer 22:30 for no man of his *s* shall prosper
Jer 23:8 which led the *s* of the house of
Jer 29:32 Shemaiah the Nehelamite, and his *s*
Jer 30:10 thy *s* from the land of their
Jer 31:27 house of Judah with the *s* of man
Jer 31:27 of man, and with the *s* of beast
Jer 31:36 then the *s* of Israel also shall
Jer 31:37 the *s* of Israel for all that they
Jer 33:22 the *s* of David my servant
Jer 33:26 will I cast away the *s* of Jacob
Jer 33:26 *s* to be rulers over the *s* of
Jer 33:26 be rulers over the *s* of Abraham
Jer 35:7 shall ye build house, nor sow *s*
Jer 35:9 we vineyard, nor field, nor *s*
Jer 36:31 And I will punish him and his *s*
Jer 41:1 son of Elishama, of the *s* royal
Jer 46:27 thy *s* from the land of their
Jer 49:10 his *s* is spoiled, and his brethren
Eze 17:5 He took also of the *s* of the land
Eze 17:13 And hath taken of the king's *s*
Eze 20:5 unto the *s* of the house of Jacob
Eze 43:19 Levites that be of the *s* of Zadok
Eze 44:22 of the *s* of the house of Israel
Dan 1:3 of Israel, and of the king's *s*
Dan 2:43 themselves with the *s* of men
Dan 9:1 of the *s* of the Medes, which was
Joel 1:17 The *s* is rotten under their clods
Amos 9:13 of grapes him that soweth *s*
Hag 2:19 Is the *s* yet in the barn
Zec 8:12 For the *s* shall be prosperous
Mal 2:3 Behold, I will corrupt your *s*
Mal 2:15 That he might seek a godly *s*
Mt 13:19 which received *s* by the way side
Mt 13:20 received the *s* into stony places
Mt 13:22 He also that received *s* among the
Mt 13:23 But he that received *s* into the
Mt 13:24 which sowed good *s* in his field
Mt 13:27 not thou sow good *s* in thy field
Mt 13:31 is like to a grain of mustard *s*
Mt 13:37 the good *s* is the Son of man
Mt 13:38 the good *s* are the children of
Mt 17:20 faith as a grain of mustard *s*
Mt 22:24 raise up *s* unto his brother
Mk 4:26 man should cast *s* into the ground
Mk 4:27 the *s* should spring and grow up,
Mk 4:31 It is like a grain of mustard *s*
Mk 12:19 raise up *s* unto his brother
Mk 12:20 took a wife, and dying left no *s*
Mk 12:21 and died, neither left he any *s*
Mk 12:22 the seven had her, and left no *s*
Lk 1:55 to Abraham, and to his *s* for ever
Lk 8:5 A sower went out to sow his *s*
Lk 8:11 The *s* is the word of God
Lk 13:19 It is like a grain of mustard *s*
Lk 17:6 had faith as a grain of mustard *s*
Lk 20:28 raise up *s* unto his brother
Jn 7:42 Christ cometh of the *s* of David
Jn 8:33 answered him, We be Abraham's *s*
Jn 8:37 I know that ye are Abraham's *s*
Acts 3:25 in thy *s* shall all the kindreds
Acts 7:5 to his *s* after him, when as yet
Acts 7:6 That his *s* should sojourn in a
Acts 13:23 Of this man's *s* hath God
Rom 1:3 which was made of the *s* of David
Rom 4:13 was not to Abraham, or to his *s*
Rom 4:16 might be sure to all the *s*
Rom 4:18 was spoken, So shall thy *s* be
Rom 9:7 because they are the *s* of Abraham
Rom 9:7 In Isaac shall thy *s* be called
Rom 9:8 the promise are counted for the *s*
Rom 9:29 Lord of Sabaoth had left us a *s*
Rom 11:1 of the *s* of Abraham, of the tribe
1Cor 15:38 him, and to every *s* his own body
2Cor 9:10 Now he that ministereth *s* to the
2Cor 9:10 food, and multiply your *s* sown
2Cor 11:22 Are they the *s* of Abraham
Gal 3:16 his *s* were the promises made
Gal 3:16 but as of one, And to thy *s*
Gal 3:19 till the *s* should come to whom
Gal 3:29 Christ's, then are ye Abraham's *s*
2Ti 2:8 that Jesus Christ of the *s* of
Heb 2:16 he took on him the *s* of Abraham
Heb 11:11 received strength to conceive *s*
Heb 11:18 in Isaac shall thy *s* be called
1Pet 1:23 born again, not of corruptible *s*
1Jn 3:9 for his *s* remaineth in him
Rev 12:17 war with the remnant of her *s*

## SEEDS

Deut 22:9 sow thy vineyard with divers *s*
Mt 13:4 some *s* fell by the way side, and
Mt 13:32 indeed is the least of all *s*
Mk 4:31 all the *s* that be in the earth
Gal 3:16 He saith not, And to *s*, as of many

## SEEK

Gen 37:16 And he said, I *s* my brethren
Gen 43:18 that he may *s* occasion against us
Lev 13:36 shall not *s* for yellow hair
Lev 19:31 neither *s* after wizards, to be
Num 15:39 that ye *s* not after your own
Num 16:10 and *s* ye the priesthood also
Num 24:1 to *s* for enchantments, but he set
Deut 4:29 thou shalt *s* the LORD thy God
Deut 4:29 if thou *s* him with all thy heart
Deut 12:5 unto his habitation shall ye *s*
Deut 22:2 thee until thy brother *s* after it
Deut 23:6 Thou shalt not *s* their peace nor
Ruth 3:1 shall I not *s* rest for thee, that
1Sa 9:3 thee, and arise, go *s* the asses
1Sa 10:2 which thou wentest to *s* are found
1Sa 10:14 And he said, To *s* the asses
1Sa 16:16 to *s* out a man, who is a cunning
1Sa 23:15 Saul was come out to *s* his life
1Sa 23:25 also and his men went to *s* him
1Sa 24:2 of all Israel, and went to *s* David
1Sa 25:26 they that *s* evil to my lord, be
1Sa 25:29 to pursue thee, and to *s* thy soul
1Sa 26:2 to *s* David in the wilderness of
1Sa 26:20 of Israel is come out to *s* a flea
1Sa 27:1 to *s* me any more in any coast of
1Sa 28:7 *S* me a woman that hath a familiar
2Sa 5:17 Philistines came up to *s* David
1Kin 2:40 Gath to Achish to *s* his servants
1Kin 18:10 my lord hath not sent to *s* thee
1Kin 19:10 they *s* my life, to take it away
1Kin 19:14 they *s* my life, to take it away
2Kin 2:16 go, we pray thee, and *s* thy master
2Kin 6:19 bring you to the man whom ye *s*
1Chr 4:39 to *s* pasture for their flocks
1Chr 14:8 Philistines went up to *s* David
1Chr 16:10 of them rejoice that *s* the LORD
1Chr 16:11 *S* the LORD and his strength
1Chr 16:11 *s* his face continually
1Chr 22:19 your soul to *s* the LORD your God
1Chr 28:8 *s* for all the commandments of the
1Chr 28:9 if thou *s* him, he will be found
2Chr 7:14 *s* my face, and turn from their
2Chr 11:16 such as set their hearts to *s* the
2Chr 12:14 not his heart to *s* the LORD
2Chr 14:4 commanded Judah to *s* the LORD God
2Chr 15:2 and if ye *s* him, he will be found
2Chr 15:12 *s* the LORD God of their fathers
2Chr 15:13 That whosoever would not *s* the
2Chr 19:3 prepared thine heart to *s* God
2Chr 20:3 and set himself to *s* the LORD
2Chr 20:4 of Judah they came to *s* the LORD
2Chr 30:19 That prepareth his heart to *s* God
2Chr 31:21 to *s* his God, he did it with all
2Chr 34:3 he began to *s* after the God of
Ezr 4:2 for we *s* your God, as ye do
Ezr 6:21 to *s* the LORD God of Israel, did
Ezr 7:10 heart to *s* the law of the LORD
Ezr 8:21 to *s* of him a right way for us,
Ezr 8:22 upon all them for good that *s* him
Ezr 9:12 nor *s* their peace or their wealth
Neh 2:10 that there was come a man to *s*
Job 5:8 I would *s* unto God, and unto God
Job 7:21 thou shalt *s* me in the morning,
Job 8:5 thou wouldest *s* unto God betimes
Job 20:10 shall *s* to please the poor
Ps 4:2 love vanity, and *s* after leasing
Ps 9:10 not forsaken them that *s* thee
Ps 10:4 countenance, will not *s* after God
Ps 10:15 *s* out his wickedness till thou
Ps 14:2 any that did understand, and *s* God
Ps 22:26 shall praise the LORD that *s* him
Ps 24:6 the generation of them that *s* him
Ps 24:6 him, that *s* thy face, O Jacob
Ps 27:4 of the LORD, that will I *s* after
Ps 27:8 When thou saidst, *S* ye my face
Ps 27:8 thee, Thy face, LORD, will I *s*
Ps 34:10 but they that *s* the LORD shall
Ps 34:14 *s* peace, and pursue it
Ps 35:4 put to shame that *s* after my soul
Ps 38:12 They also that *s* after my life
Ps 38:12 they that *s* my hurt speak
Ps 40:14 confounded together that *s* after
Ps 40:16 Let all those that *s* thee rejoice
Ps 53:2 did understand, that did *s* God
Ps 54:3 oppressors *s* after my soul
Ps 63:1 early will I *s* thee
Ps 63:9 But those that *s* my soul, to
Ps 69:6 let not those that *s* thee be
Ps 69:32 your heart shall live that *s* God
Ps 70:2 confounded that *s* after my soul
Ps 70:4 Let all those that *s* thee rejoice
Ps 71:13 and dishonour that *s* my hurt
Ps 71:24 unto shame, that *s* my hurt
Ps 83:16 that they may *s* thy name, O LORD
Ps 104:21 prey, and *s* their meat from God
Ps 105:3 of them rejoice that *s* the LORD
Ps 105:4 *S* the LORD, and his strength

Ps 105:4 *s* his face evermore
Ps 109:10 let them *s* their bread also out
Ps 119:2 that *s* him with the whole heart
Ps 119:45 for I *s* thy precepts
Ps 119:155 for they *s* not thy statutes
Ps 119:176 *s* thy servant
Ps 122:9 LORD our God I will *s* thy good
Prov 1:28 they shall *s* me early, but they
Prov 7:15 thee, diligently to *s* thy face
Prov 8:17 those that *s* me early shall find
Prov 21:6 to and fro of them that *s* death
Prov 23:30 they that go to *s* mixed wine
Prov 23:35 I will *s* it yet again
Prov 28:5 but they that *s* the LORD
Prov 29:10 but the just *s* his soul
Prov 29:26 Many *s* the ruler's favour
Eccl 1:13 And I gave my heart to *s* and search
Eccl 7:25 to *s* out wisdom, and the reason of
Eccl 8:17 though a man labour to *s* it out
Song 3:2 I will *s* him whom my soul loveth
Song 6:1 that we may *s* him with thee
Is 1:17 *s* judgment, relieve the oppressed
Is 8:19 *S* unto them that have familiar
Is 8:19 not a people *s* unto their God
Is 9:13 neither do they *s* the LORD of
Is 11:10 to it shall the Gentiles *s*
Is 19:3 they shall *s* to the idols, and to
Is 26:9 within me will I *s* thee early
Is 29:15 Woe unto them that *s* deep to hide
Is 31:1 One of Israel, neither *s* the LORD
Is 34:16 *S* ye out of the book of the LORD,
Is 41:12 Thou shalt *s* them, and shalt not
Is 41:17 When the poor and needy *s* water
Is 45:19 seed of Jacob, *S* ye me in vain
Is 51:1 righteousness, ye that *s* the LORD
Is 55:6 *S* ye the LORD while he may be
Is 58:2 Yet they *s* me daily, and delight
Jer 2:24 all they that *s* her will not
Jer 2:33 trimmest thou thy way to *s* love
Jer 4:30 thee, they will *s* thy life
Jer 5:1 *s* in the broad places thereof, if
Jer 11:21 that *s* thy life, saying, Prophesy
Jer 19:7 hands of them that *s* their lives
Jer 19:9 they that *s* their lives, shall
Jer 21:7 hand of those that *s* their life
Jer 22:25 the hand of them that *s* thy life
Jer 29:7 *s* the peace of the city whither I
Jer 29:13 And ye shall *s* me, and find me,
Jer 30:14 they *s* thee not
Jer 34:20 hand of them that *s* their life
Jer 34:21 hand of them that *s* their life
Jer 38:16 hand of these men that *s* thy life
Jer 44:30 the hand of them that *s* his life
Jer 45:5 *s* them not
Jer 46:26 hand of those that *s* their lives
Jer 49:37 and before them that *s* their life
Jer 50:4 shall go, and *s* the LORD their God
Lam 1:11 All her people sigh, they *s* bread
Eze 7:25 and they shall *s* peace, and there
Eze 7:26 then shall they *s* a vision of the
Eze 34:6 none did search or *s* after them
Eze 34:11 search my sheep, and *s* them out
Eze 34:12 so will I *s* out my sheep, and will
Eze 34:16 I will *s* that which was lost, and
Dan 9:3 to *s* by prayer and supplications,
Hos 2:7 and she shall *s* them, but shall
Hos 3:5 *s* the LORD their God, and David
Hos 5:6 and with their herds to *s* the LORD
Hos 5:15 their offence, and *s* my face
Hos 5:15 affliction they will *s* me early
Hos 7:10 their God, nor *s* him for all this
Hos 10:12 for it is time to *s* the LORD
Amos 5:4 *S* ye me, and ye shall live
Amos 5:5 But *s* not Beth-el, nor enter into
Amos 5:6 *S* the LORD, and ye shall live
Amos 5:8 *S* him that maketh the seven stars
Amos 5:14 *S* good, and not evil, that ye may
Amos 8:12 fro to *s* the word of the LORD, and
Nah 3:7 whence shall I *s* comforters for
Nah 3:11 thou also shalt *s* strength
Zeph 2:3 *S* ye the LORD, all ye meek of the
Zeph 2:3 *s* righteousness, *s* meekness
Zec 8:21 LORD, and to *s* the LORD of hosts
Zec 8:22 strong nations shall come to *s*
Zec 11:16 neither shall *s* the young one
Zec 12:9 that I will *s* to destroy all the
Mal 2:7 they should *s* the law at his
Mal 2:15 That he might *s* a godly seed
Mal 3:1 and the Lord, whom ye *s*, shall
Mt 2:13 for Herod will *s* the young child
Mt 6:32 these things do the Gentiles *s*
Mt 6:33 But *s* ye first the kingdom of God
Mt 7:7 *s*, and ye shall find
Mt 28:5 for I know that ye *s* Jesus
Mk 1:37 said unto him, All men *s* for thee
Mk 3:32 thy brethren without *s* for thee
Mk 8:12 this generation *s* after a sign
Mk 16:6 Ye *s* Jesus of Nazareth, which was
Lk 11:9 *s*, and ye shall find
Lk 11:29 they *s* a sign
Lk 12:29 *s* not ye what ye shall eat, or
Lk 12:30 the nations of the world *s* after
Lk 12:31 But rather *s* ye the kingdom of
Lk 13:24 will *s* to enter in, and shall not
Lk 15:8 *s* diligently till she find it
Lk 17:33 Whosoever shall *s* to save his
Lk 19:10 For the Son of man is come to *s*
Lk 24:5 Why *s* ye the living among the
Jn 1:38 and saith unto them, What *s* ye
Jn 5:30 because I *s* not mine own will,
Jn 5:44 *s* not the honour that cometh from
Jn 6:26 verily, I say unto you, Ye *s* me
Jn 7:25 not this he, whom they *s* to kill
Jn 7:34 Ye shall *s* me, and shall not find
Jn 7:36 this that he said, Ye shall *s* me
Jn 8:21 I go my way, and ye shall *s* me
Jn 8:37 but ye *s* to kill me, because my
Jn 8:40 But now ye *s* to kill me, a man
Jn 8:50 And I *s* not mine own glory
Jn 13:33 Ye shall *s* me
Jn 18:4 and said unto them, Whom *s* ye
Jn 18:7 asked he them again, Whom *s* ye
Jn 18:8 if therefore ye *s* me, let these
Acts 10:19 him, Behold, three men *s* thee
Acts 10:21 said, Behold, I am he whom ye *s*
Acts 11:25 Barnabas to Tarsus, for to *s* Saul
Acts 15:17 of men might *s* after the Lord
Acts 17:27 That they should *s* the Lord
Rom 2:7 in well doing *s* for glory
Rom 11:3 am left alone, and they *s* my life
1Cor 1:22 the Greeks *s* after wisdom
1Cor 7:27 *s* not to be loosed
1Cor 7:27 *s* not a wife
1Cor 10:24 Let no man *s* his own, but every
1Cor 14:12 *s* that ye may excel to the
2Cor 12:14 for I *s* not yours, but you
2Cor 13:3 Since ye *s* a proof of Christ
Gal 1:10 or do I *s* to please men
Gal 2:17 while we *s* to be justified by
Phil 2:21 For all *s* their own, not the
Col 3:1 *s* those things which are above,
Heb 11:6 of them that diligently *s* him
Heb 11:14 plainly that they *s* a country
Heb 13:14 city, but we *s* one to come
1Pet 3:11 let him *s* peace, and ensue it
Rev 9:6 in those days shall men *s* death

## SEEKEST

Gen 37:15 asked him, saying, What *s* thou
Judg 4:22 shew thee the man whom thou *s*
2Sa 17:3 the man whom thou *s* is as if all
2Sa 20:19 thou *s* to destroy a city and a
1Kin 11:22 thou *s* to go to thine own country
Prov 2:4 If thou *s* her as silver, and
Jer 45:5 *s* thou great things for thyself
Jn 4:27 yet no man said, What *s* thou
Jn 20:15 whom *s* thou

## SEEKETH

1Sa 19:2 Saul my father *s* to kill thee
1Sa 20:1 thy father, that he *s* my life
1Sa 22:23 for he that *s* my life *s* thy
1Sa 22:23 that *s* my life *s* thy life
1Sa 23:10 that Saul *s* to come to Keilah
1Sa 24:9 saying, Behold, David *s* thy hurt
2Sa 16:11 forth of my bowels, *s* my life
1Kin 20:7 and see how this man *s* mischief
2Kin 5:7 see how he *s* a quarrel against me
Job 39:29 From thence she *s* the prey
Ps 37:32 the righteous, and *s* to slay him
Prov 11:27 He that diligently *s* good
Prov 11:27 but he that *s* mischief, it shall
Prov 14:6 A scorner *s* wisdom, and findeth it
Prov 15:14 hath understanding *s* knowledge
Prov 17:9 covereth a transgression *s* love
Prov 17:11 An evil man *s* only rebellion
Prov 17:19 exalteth his gate *s* destruction
Prov 18:1 man, having separated himself, *s*
Prov 18:15 the ear of the wise *s* knowledge
Prov 31:13 She *s* wool, and flax, and worketh
Eccl 7:28 Which yet my soul *s*, but I find
Is 40:20 he *s* unto him a cunning workman
Jer 5:1 judgment, that *s* the truth
Jer 30:17 This is Zion, whom no man *s* after
Jer 38:4 for this man *s* not the welfare of
Lam 3:25 for him, to the soul that *s* him
Eze 14:10 punishment of him that *s* unto him
Eze 34:12 As a shepherd *s* out his flock in
Mt 7:8 and he that *s* findeth
Mt 12:39 generation *s* after a sign
Mt 16:4 generation *s* after a sign
Mt 18:12 *s* that which is gone astray
Lk 11:10 and he that *s* findeth
Jn 4:23 for the Father *s* such to worship
Jn 7:4 he himself *s* to be known openly
Jn 7:18 of himself *s* his own glory
Jn 7:18 but he that *s* his glory that sent
Jn 8:50 there is one that *s* and judgeth
Rom 3:11 there is none that *s* after God
Rom 11:7 not obtained that which he *s* for
1Cor 13:5 *s* not her own, is not easily

## SEEKING

Est 10:3 *s* the wealth of his people, and
Is 16:5 and *s* judgment, and hasting
Mt 12:43 places, *s* rest, and findeth none
Mt 13:45 a merchant man, *s* goodly pearls
Mk 8:11 *s* of him a sign from heaven,
Lk 2:45 back again to Jerusalem, *s* him
Lk 11:24 through dry places, *s* rest
Lk 11:54 *s* to catch something out of his
Lk 13:7 I come *s* fruit on this fig tree
Jn 6:24 and came to Capernaum, *s* for Jesus
Acts 13:8 *s* to turn away the deputy from
Acts 13:11 he went about *s* some to lead him
1Cor 10:33 not *s* mine own profit, but the
1Pet 5:8 about, *s* whom he may devour

## SEEN

Gen 7:1 for thee have I *s* righteous
Gen 8:5 were the tops of the mountains *s*
Gen 9:14 the bow shall be *s* in the cloud
Gen 22:14 mount of the LORD it shall be *s*
Gen 31:12 for I have *s* all that Laban doeth
Gen 31:42 God hath *s* mine affliction and the
Gen 32:30 for I have *s* God face to face, and
Gen 33:10 for therefore I have *s* thy face
Gen 33:10 as though I had *s* the face of God
Gen 45:13 Egypt, and of all that ye have *s*
Gen 46:30 me die, since I have *s* thy face
Ex 3:7 I have surely *s* the affliction of
Ex 3:9 I have also *s* the oppression
Ex 3:16 *s* that which is done to you in
Ex 10:6 nor thy fathers' fathers have *s*
Ex 13:7 no leavened bread be *s* with thee
Ex 13:7 *s* with thee in all thy quarters
Ex 14:13 Egyptians whom ye have *s* to day
Ex 19:4 Ye have *s* what I did unto the
Ex 20:22 Ye have *s* that I have talked with
Ex 32:9 I have *s* this people, and, behold,
Ex 33:23 but my face shall not be *s*
Ex 34:3 thee, neither let any man be *s*
Lev 5:1 whether he hath *s* or known of it
Lev 13:7 after that he hath been *s* of the
Lev 13:7 he shall be *s* of the priest again
Num 14:14 that thou LORD art *s* face to face
Num 14:22 those men which have *s* my glory
Num 23:21 neither hath he *s* perverseness in
Num 27:13 And when thou hast *s* it, thou also
Deut 1:28 moreover we have *s* the sons of
Deut 1:31 where thou hast *s* how that the
Deut 3:21 Thine eyes have *s* all that the
Deut 4:3 Your eyes have *s* what the LORD
Deut 4:9 things which thine eyes have *s*
Deut 5:24 we have *s* this day that God doth
Deut 9:13 I have *s* this people, and, behold,
Deut 10:21 things, which thine eyes have *s*
Deut 11:2 which have not *s* the chastisement
Deut 11:7 But your eyes have *s* all the
Deut 16:4 *s* with thee in all thy coast
Deut 21:7 blood, neither have our eyes *s* it
Deut 29:2 Ye have *s* all that the LORD did
Deut 29:3 which thine eyes have *s*, the
Deut 29:17 ye have *s* their abominations, and
Deut 33:9 to his mother, I have not *s* him
Josh 23:3 ye have *s* all that the LORD your
Josh 24:7 your eyes have *s* what I have done
Judg 2:7 who had *s* all the great works of
Judg 5:8 was there a shield or spear *s*
Judg 6:22 for because I have *s* an angel of
Judg 9:48 with him, What ye have *s* me do
Judg 13:22 surely die, because we have *s* God

Judg 14:2 I have s a woman in Timnath of
Judg 18:9 for we have s the land, and,
Judg 19:30 s from the day that the children
1Sa 6:16 lords of the Philistines had s it
1Sa 16:18 I have s a son of Jesse the
1Sa 17:25 Have ye s this man that is come
1Sa 23:22 haunt is, and who hath s him there
1Sa 24:10 this day thine eyes have s how
2Sa 17:17 not be s to come into the city
2Sa 18:21 Go tell the king what thou hast s
2Sa 22:11 he was s upon the wings of the
1Kin 6:18 there was no stone s
1Kin 8:8 the ends of the staves were s out
1Kin 8:8 and they were not s without
1Kin 10:4 Sheba had s all Solomon's wisdom
1Kin 10:7 I came, and mine eyes had s it
1Kin 10:12 trees, nor were s unto this day
1Kin 13:12 For his sons had s what way the
1Kin 20:13 Hast thou s all this great
2Kin 9:26 Surely I have s yesterday the
2Kin 20:5 thy prayer, I have s thy tears
2Kin 20:15 What have they s in thine house
2Kin 20:15 are in mine house have they s
2Kin 23:29 him at Megiddo, when he had s him
1Chr 29:17 now have I s with joy thy people,
2Chr 5:9 the ends of the staves were s
2Chr 5:9 but they were not s without
2Chr 9:3 Sheba had s the wisdom of Solomon
2Chr 9:6 I came, and mine eyes had s it
2Chr 9:11 there were none such s before in
Ezr 3:12 that had s the first house, when
Est 9:26 they had s concerning this matter
Job 4:8 Even as I have s, they that plow
Job 5:3 I have s the foolish taking root
Job 7:8 hath s me shall see me no more
Job 8:18 him, saying, I have not s thee
Job 10:18 up the ghost, and no eye had s me
Job 13:1 Lo, mine eye hath s all this
Job 15:17 which I have s I will declare
Job 20:7 they which have s him shall say
Job 27:12 all ye yourselves have s it
Job 28:7 the vulture's eye hath not s
Job 31:19 If I have s any perish for want
Job 33:21 away, that it cannot be s
Job 33:21 bones that were not s stick out
Job 38:17 or hast thou s the doors of the
Job 38:22 or hast thou s the treasures of
Ps 10:14 Thou hast s it
Ps 18:15 the channels of waters were s
Ps 35:21 said, Aha, aha, our eye hath s it
Ps 35:22 This thou hast s, O LORD
Ps 37:25 yet have I not s the righteous
Ps 37:35 I have s the wicked in great
Ps 48:8 so have we s in the city of the
Ps 54:7 mine eye hath s his desire upon
Ps 55:9 for I have s violence and strife
Ps 63:2 so as I have s thee in the
Ps 68:24 They have s thy goings, O God
Ps 90:15 the years wherein we have s evil
Ps 98:3 have s the salvation of our God
Ps 119:96 I have s an end of all perfection
Prov 25:7 the prince whom thine eyes have s
Eccl 1:14 I have s all the works that are
Eccl 3:10 I have s the travail, which God
Eccl 4:3 who hath not s the evil work that
Eccl 5:13 evil which I have s under the sun
Eccl 5:18 Behold that which I have s
Eccl 6:1 evil which I have s under the sun
Eccl 6:5 Moreover he hath not s the sun
Eccl 6:6 twice told, yet hath he s no good
Eccl 7:15 All things have I s in the days
Eccl 8:9 All this have I s, and applied my
Eccl 9:13 have I s also under the sun
Eccl 10:5 evil which I have s under the sun
Eccl 10:7 I have s servants upon horses, and
Is 6:5 for mine eyes have s the King
Is 9:2 in darkness have s a great light
Is 16:12 when it is s that Moab is weary
Is 22:9 Ye have s also the breaches of
Is 38:5 thy prayer, I have s thy tears
Is 39:4 What have they s in thine house
Is 39:4 that is in mine house have they s
Is 44:16 Aha, I am warm, I have s the fire
Is 47:3 yea, thy shame shall be s
Is 57:18 I have s his ways, and will heal
Is 60:2 and his glory shall be s upon thee
Is 64:4 the ear, neither hath the eye s
Is 66:8 who hath s such things
Is 66:19 my fame, neither have s my glory
Jer 1:12 LORD unto me, Thou hast well s
Jer 3:6 the king, Hast thou s that which
Jer 7:11 Behold, even I have s it, saith
Jer 12:3 thou hast s me, and tried mine
Jer 13:27 I have s thine adulteries, and thy
Jer 23:13 I have s folly in the prophets of
Jer 23:14 I have s also in the prophets of
Jer 44:2 Ye have s all the evil that I
Jer 46:5 Wherefore have I s them dismayed
Lam 1:8 because they have s her nakedness
Lam 1:10 for she hath s that the heathen
Lam 2:14 Thy prophets have s vain and
Lam 2:14 but have s for thee false burdens
Lam 2:16 we have found, we have s it
Lam 3:1 I am the man that hath s
Lam 3:59 O LORD, thou hast s my wrong
Lam 3:60 Thou hast s all their vengeance
Eze 8:12 hast thou s what the ancients of
Eze 8:15 said he unto me, Hast thou s this
Eze 8:17 he said unto me, Hast thou s this
Eze 11:24 that I had s went up from me
Eze 13:3 own spirit, and have s nothing
Eze 13:6 They have s vanity and lying
Eze 13:7 Have ye not s a vain vision, and
Eze 13:8 s lies, therefore, behold, I am
Eze 47:6 me, Son of man, hast thou s this
Dan 2:26 unto me the dream which I have s
Dan 4:9 visions of my dream that I have s
Dan 4:18 I king Nebuchadnezzar have s
Dan 8:6 which I had s standing before the
Dan 8:15 had s the vision, and sought for
Dan 9:21 whom I had s in the vision at the
Hos 6:10 I have s an horrible thing in the
Zec 9:8 for now have I s with mine eyes
Zec 9:14 And the LORD shall be s over them
Zec 10:2 and the diviners have s a lie
Mt 2:2 for we have s his star in the
Mt 6:1 alms before men, to be s of them
Mt 6:5 that they may be s of men
Mt 9:33 It was never so s in Israel
Mt 13:17 which ye see, and have not s them
Mt 21:32 and ye, when ye had s it, repented
Mt 23:5 works they do for to be s of men
Mk 9:1 till they have s the kingdom of
Mk 9:9 no man what things they had s
Mk 16:11 was alive, and had been s of her
Mk 16:14 had s him after he was risen
Lk 1:22 he had s a vision in the temple
Lk 2:17 And when they had s it, they made
Lk 2:20 things that they had heard and s
Lk 2:26 before he had s the Lord's Christ
Lk 2:30 mine eyes have s thy salvation
Lk 5:26 We have s strange things to day
Lk 7:22 tell John what things ye have s
Lk 9:36 of those things which they had s
Lk 10:24 which ye see, and have not s them
Lk 19:37 the mighty works that they had s
Lk 23:8 he hoped to have s some miracle
Lk 24:23 had also s a vision of angels
Lk 24:37 supposed that they had s a spirit
Jn 1:18 No man hath s God at any time
Jn 3:11 know, and testify that we have s
Jn 3:32 And what he hath s and heard, that
Jn 4:45 having s all the things that he
Jn 5:37 at any time, nor s his shape
Jn 6:14 when they had s the miracle that
Jn 6:36 unto you, That ye also have s me
Jn 6:46 that any man hath s the Father
Jn 6:46 is of God, he hath s the Father
Jn 8:38 which I have s with my Father
Jn 8:38 which ye have s with your father
Jn 8:57 years old, and hast thou s Abraham
Jn 9:8 had s him that he was blind
Jn 9:37 unto him, Thou hast both s him
Jn 11:45 had s the things which Jesus did,
Jn 14:7 ye know him, and have s him
Jn 14:9 hath s me hath s the Father
Jn 15:24 but now have they both s and hated
Jn 20:18 disciples that she had s the Lord
Jn 20:25 said unto him, We have s the Lord
Jn 20:29 Thomas, because thou hast s me
Jn 20:29 blessed are they that have not s
Acts 1:3 being s of them forty days, and
Acts 1:11 as ye have s him go into heaven
Acts 4:20 speak the things which we have s
Acts 7:34 I have s, I have s the
Acts 7:44 to the fashion that he had s
Acts 9:12 hath s in a vision a man named
Acts 9:27 how he had s the Lord in the way
Acts 10:17 vision which he had s should mean
Acts 11:13 he had s an angel in his house
Acts 11:23 had s the grace of God, was glad,
Acts 13:31 he was s many days of them which
Acts 16:10 And after he had s the vision
Acts 16:40 and when they had s the brethren
Acts 21:29 (For they had s before with him
Acts 22:15 unto all men of what thou hast s
Acts 26:16 of these things which thou hast s
Rom 1:20 of the world are clearly s
Rom 8:24 but hope that is s is not hope
1Cor 2:9 as it is written, Eye hath not s
1Cor 9:1 have I not s Jesus Christ our
1Cor 15:5 And that he was s of Cephas
1Cor 15:6 he was s of above five hundred
1Cor 15:7 After that, he was s of James
1Cor 15:8 last of all he was s of me also
2Cor 4:18 not at the things which are s
2Cor 4:18 but at the things which are not s
2Cor 4:18 things which are s are temporal
2Cor 4:18 which are not s are eternal
Phil 4:9 and heard, and s in me, do
Col 2:1 have not s my face in the flesh
Col 2:18 those things which he hath not s
1Ti 3:16 s of angels, preached unto the
1Ti 6:16 whom no man hath s, nor can see
Heb 11:1 for, the evidence of things not s
Heb 11:3 so that things which are s were
Heb 11:7 of God of things not s as yet
Heb 11:13 but having s them afar off, and
Jas 5:11 have s the end of the Lord
1Pet 1:8 Whom having not s, ye love
1Jn 1:1 which we have s with our eyes
1Jn 1:2 was manifested, and we have s it
1Jn 1:3 That which we have s and heard
1Jn 3:6 whosoever sinneth hath not s him
1Jn 4:12 No man hath s God at any time
1Jn 4:14 And we have s and do testify that
1Jn 4:20 not his brother whom he hath s
1Jn 4:20 he love God whom he hath not s
3Jn 11 he that doeth evil hath not s God
Rev 1:19 the things which thou hast s
Rev 11:19 there was s in his temple the ark
Rev 22:8 And when I had heard and s, I fell

**SEER**
1Sa 9:9 Come, and let us go to the s
1Sa 9:9 Prophet was beforetime called a S
1Sa 9:11 and said unto them, Is the s here
1Sa 9:19 Saul, and said, I am the s
2Sa 15:27 the priest, Art not thou a s
2Sa 24:11 unto the prophet Gad, David's s
1Chr 9:22 Samuel the s did ordain in their
1Chr 21:9 LORD spake unto Gad, David's s
1Chr 25:5 the king's s in the words of God
1Chr 26:28 And all that Samuel the s, and Saul
1Chr 29:29 in the book of Samuel the s
1Chr 29:29 and in the book of Gad the s
2Chr 9:29 in the visions of Iddo the s
2Chr 12:15 and of Iddo the s concerning
2Chr 16:7 at that time Hanani the s came to
2Chr 16:10 Then Asa was wroth with the s
2Chr 19:2 Hanani the s went out to meet him
2Chr 29:25 of David, and of Gad the king's s
2Chr 29:30 words of David, and of Asaph the s
2Chr 35:15 Heman, and Jeduthun the king's s
Amos 7:12 Amaziah said unto Amos, O thou s

**SEERS**
2Kin 17:13 all the prophets, and by all the s
2Chr 33:18 the words of the s that spake to
2Chr 33:19 among the sayings of the s
Is 29:10 rulers, the s hath he covered
Is 30:10 Which say to the s, See not
Mic 3:7 Then shall the s be ashamed

**SEGUB** *(se'-gub)*
*1. A son of Hiel.*
1Kin 16:34 thereof in his youngest son S
*2. A son of Hezron.*
1Chr 2:21 and she bare him S
1Chr 2:22 S begat Jair, who had three and

**SEIR** *(se'-ur)*
*1. A region south of the Dead Sea.*
Gen 14:6 And the Horites in their mount S
Gen 32:3 his brother unto the land of S
Gen 33:14 until I come unto my lord unto S
Gen 33:16 that day on his way unto S
Gen 36:8 Thus dwelt Esau in mount S
Gen 36:9 father of the Edomites in mount S
Gen 36:21 the children of S in the land of
Gen 36:30 their dukes in the land of S
Num 24:18 S also shall be a possession for

Deut 1:2 way of mount *S* unto Kadesh-barnea
Deut 1:44 as bees do, and destroyed you in *S*
Deut 2:1 we compassed mount *S* many days
Deut 2:4 of Esau, which dwell in *S*
Deut 2:5 *S* unto Esau for a possession
Deut 2:8 of Esau, which dwelt in *S*
Deut 2:12 Horims also dwelt in *S* beforetime
Deut 2:22 of Esau, which dwelt in *S*
Deut 2:29 children of Esau which dwell in *S*
Deut 33:2 and rose up from *S* unto them
Josh 11:17 mount Halak, that goeth up to *S*
Josh 12:7 mount Halak, that goeth up to *S*
Josh 15:10 from Baalah westward unto mount *S*
Josh 24:4 and I gave unto Esau mount *S*
Judg 5:4 LORD, when thou wentest out of *S*
1Chr 4:42 five hundred men, went to mount *S*
2Chr 20:10 of Ammon and Moab and mount *S*
2Chr 20:22 of Ammon, Moab, and mount *S*
2Chr 20:23 the inhabitants of mount *S*
2Chr 20:23 an end of the inhabitants of *S*
2Chr 25:11 of the children of *S* ten thousand
2Chr 25:14 the gods of the children of *S*
Is 21:11 He calleth to me out of *S*
Eze 25:8 *S* do say, Behold, the house of
Eze 35:2 man, set thy face against mount *S*
Eze 35:3 Behold, O mount *S*, I am against
Eze 35:7 will I make mount *S* most desolate
Eze 35:15 thou shalt be desolate, O mount *S*

*2. Grandfather of Hori.*
Gen 36:20 are the sons of *S* the Horite
1Chr 1:38 And the sons of *S*

**SEIRATH** *(se'-ur-ath) A city in Ephraim.*
Judg 3:26 the quarries, and escaped unto *S*

**SEIZE**
Josh 8:7 the ambush, and *s* upon the city
Job 3:6 night, let darkness *s* upon it
Ps 55:15 Let death *s* upon them, and let
Mt 21:38 let us *s* on his inheritance

**SELA** *(se'-lah)* See SELAH. *Same as Selah 1.*
Is 16:1 the land from *S* to the wilderness

**SELAH** *(se'-lah)* See JOKTHEEL, SELA.

*1. Capital of Edom.*
2Kin 14:7 took *S* by war, and called the name

*2. A musical notation.*
Ps 3:2 no help for him in God. *S*
Ps 3:4 me out of his holy hill. *S*
Ps 3:8 blessing is upon thy people. *S*
Ps 4:2 vanity, and seek after leasing? *S*
Ps 4:4 your bed, and be still. *S*
Ps 7:5 mine honour in the dust. *S*
Ps 9:16 his own hands. Higgaion. *S*
Ps 9:20 themselves to be but men. *S*
Ps 20:3 accept thy burnt sacrifice; *S*
Ps 21:2 the request of his lips. *S*
Ps 24:6 thy face, O Jacob. *S*
Ps 24:10 he is the King of glory. *S*
Ps 32:4 the drought of summer. *S*
Ps 32:5 the iniquity of my sin. *S*
Ps 32:7 songs of deliverance. *S*
Ps 39:5 state is altogether vanity. *S*
Ps 39:11 every man is vanity. *S*
Ps 44:8 thy name for ever. *S*
Ps 46:3 with the swelling thereof. *S*
Ps 46:7 Jacob is our refuge. *S*
Ps 46:11 Jacob is our refuge. *S*
Ps 47:4 Jacob whom he loved. *S*
Ps 48:8 establish it for ever. *S*
Ps 49:13 approve their sayings. *S*
Ps 49:15 he shall receive me. *S*
Ps 50:6 God is judge himself. *S*
Ps 52:3 to speak righteousness. *S*
Ps 52:5 land of the living. *S*
Ps 54:3 set God before them. *S*
Ps 55:7 remain in the wilderness. *S*
Ps 55:19 that abideth of old. *S*
Ps 57:3 swallow me up. *S*
Ps 57:6 are fallen themselves. *S*
Ps 59:5 wicked transgressors. *S*
Ps 59:13 ends of the earth. *S*
Ps 60:4 because of the truth. *S*
Ps 61:4 the covert of thy wings. *S*
Ps 62:4 but they curse inwardly. *S*
Ps 62:8 is a refuge for us. *S*
Ps 66:4 sing to thy name. *S*
Ps 66:7 exalt themselves. *S*
Ps 66:15 offer bullocks with goats. *S*
Ps 67:1 face to shine upon us; *S*
Ps 67:4 the nations upon earth. *S*
Ps 68:7 through the wilderness; *S*
Ps 68:19 the God of our salvation. *S*
Ps 68:32 praises unto the Lord. *S*
Ps 75:3 up the pillars of it. *S*
Ps 76:3 sword, and the battle. *S*
Ps 76:9 the meek of the earth. *S*
Ps 77:3 was overwhelmed. *S*
Ps 77:9 up his tender mercies? *S*
Ps 77:15 of Jacob and Joseph. *S*
Ps 81:7 the waters of Meribah. *S*
Ps 82:2 persons of the wicked? *S*
Ps 83:8 the children of Lot. *S*
Ps 84:4 be still praising thee. *S*
Ps 84:8 O God of Jacob. *S*
Ps 85:2 covered all their sin. *S*
Ps 87:3 O city of God. *S*
Ps 87:6 man was born there. *S*
Ps 88:7 me with all thy waves. *S*
Ps 88:10 dead arise and praise thee? *S*
Ps 89:4 throne to all generations. *S*
Ps 89:37 witness in heaven. *S*
Ps 89:45 him with shame. *S*
Ps 89:48 hand of the grave? *S*
Ps 140:3 is under their lips. *S*
Ps 140:5 have set gins for me. *S*
Ps 140:8 they exalt themselves. *S*
Ps 143:6 as a thirsty land. *S*
Hab 3:3 from mount Paran. *S*
Hab 3:9 even thy word. *S*
Hab 3:13 foundation unto the neck. *S*

**SELA-HAMMAHLEKOTH** *(se'-lah-ham-mah'-le-koth) A hill in the wilderness of Maon.*
1Sa 23:28 they called that place *S*

**SELED** *(se'-led) A descendant of Jerahmeel.*
1Chr 2:30 *S*, and Appaim: but *S* died

**SELEUCIA** *(sel-u-si'-ah) A city in Syria.*
Acts 13:4 the Holy Ghost, departed unto *S*

**SELL**
Gen 25:31 *S* me this day thy birthright
Gen 37:27 let us *s* him to the Ishmeelites,
Ex 21:7 if a man *s* his daughter to be a
Ex 21:8 to *s* her unto a strange nation he
Ex 21:35 then they shall *s* the live ox
Ex 22:1 or a sheep, and kill it, or *s* it
Lev 25:14 And if thou *s* ought unto thy
Lev 25:15 the fruits he shall *s* unto thee
Lev 25:16 of the fruits doth he *s* unto thee
Lev 25:29 if a man *s* a dwelling house in a
Lev 25:47 *s* himself unto the stranger or
Deut 2:28 Thou shalt *s* me meat for money,
Deut 14:21 or thou mayest *s* it unto an alien
Deut 21:14 but thou shalt not *s* her at all
Judg 4:9 for the LORD shall *s* Sisera into
1Kin 21:25 which did *s* himself to work
2Kin 4:7 *s* the oil, and pay thy debt, and
Neh 5:8 will ye even *s* your brethren
Neh 10:31 victuals on the sabbath day to *s*
Prov 23:23 Buy the truth, and *s* it not
Eze 30:12 *s* the land into the hand of the
Eze 48:14 And they shall not *s* of it
Joel 3:8 I will *s* your sons and your
Joel 3:8 they shall *s* them to the Sabeans,
Amos 8:5 moon be gone, that we may *s* corn
Amos 8:6 *s* the refuse of the wheat
Zec 11:5 and they that *s* them say, Blessed
Mt 19:21 *s* that thou hast, and give to the
Mt 25:9 but go ye rather to them that *s*
Mk 10:21 *s* whatsoever thou hast, and give
Lk 12:33 *S* that ye have, and give alms
Lk 18:22 *s* all that thou hast, and
Lk 22:36 let him *s* his garment, and buy one
Jas 4:13 there a year, and buy and *s*
Rev 13:17 And that no man might buy or *s*

**SELLETH**
Ex 21:16 *s* him, or if he be found in his
Deut 24:7 merchandise of him, or *s* him
Ruth 4:3 *s* a parcel of land, which was our
Prov 11:26 be upon the head of him that *s* it
Prov 31:24 She maketh fine linen, and *s* it
Nah 3:4 that *s* nations through her
Mt 13:44 *s* all that he hath, and buyeth

**SELVES**
Lk 21:30 know of your own *s* that summer is
Acts 20:30 of your own *s* shall men arise
2Cor 8:5 gave their own *s* to the Lord
2Cor 13:5 prove your own *s*
2Cor 13:5 Know ye not your own *s*, how that
2Ti 3:2 shall be lovers of their own *s*
Jas 1:22 only, deceiving your own *s*

**SEM** *(sem)* See SHEM. *Greek form of Shem.*
Lk 3:36 Arphaxad, which was the son of *S*

**SEMACHIAH** *(sem-a-ki'-ah) A sanctuary servant.*
1Chr 26:7 were strong men, Elihu, and *S*

**SEMEI** *(sem'-e-i)* See SHEMAIAH. *A son of Joseph; an ancestor of Jesus.*
Lk 3:26 which was the son of *S*, which

**SENAAH** *(sen'-a-ah)* See HASSENAAH. *A city in Judah.*
Ezr 2:35 The children of *S*, three thousand
Neh 7:38 The children of *S*, three thousand

**SEND**
Gen 24:7 he shall *s* his angel before thee,
Gen 24:12 *s* me good speed this day, and shew
Gen 24:40 will *s* his angel with thee, and
Gen 24:54 he said, *S* me away unto my master
Gen 24:56 *s* me away that I may go to my
Gen 27:45 then I will *s*, and fetch thee from
Gen 30:25 *S* me away, that I may go unto
Gen 37:13 come, and I will *s* thee unto them
Gen 38:17 I will *s* thee a kid from the
Gen 38:17 give me a pledge, till thou *s* it
Gen 42:16 *S* one of you, and let him fetch
Gen 43:4 If thou wilt *s* our brother with
Gen 43:5 But if thou wilt not *s* him
Gen 43:8 *S* the lad with me, and we will
Gen 43:14 that he may *s* away your other
Gen 45:5 for God did *s* me before you to
Ex 3:10 I will *s* thee unto Pharaoh, that
Ex 4:13 And he said, O my Lord, *s*, I pray
Ex 4:13 the hand of him whom thou wilt *s*
Ex 7:2 that he *s* the children of Israel
Ex 8:21 I will *s* swarms of flies upon
Ex 9:14 For I will at this time *s* all my
Ex 9:19 *S* therefore now, and gather thy
Ex 12:33 that they might *s* them out of the
Ex 23:20 I *s* an Angel before thee, to keep
Ex 23:27 I will *s* my fear before thee, and
Ex 23:28 I will *s* hornets before thee,
Ex 33:2 I will *s* an angel before thee
Ex 33:12 me know whom thou wilt *s* with me
Lev 16:21 shall *s* him away by the hand of a
Lev 26:22 I will also *s* wild beasts among
Lev 26:25 I will *s* the pestilence among you
Lev 26:36 are left alive of you I will *s* a
Num 13:2 *S* thou men, that they may search
Num 13:2 of their fathers shall ye *s* a man
Num 22:37 Did I not earnestly *s* unto thee
Num 31:4 of Israel, shall ye *s* to the war
Deut 1:22 We will *s* men before us, and they
Deut 7:20 God will *s* the hornet among them
Deut 11:15 I will *s* grass in thy fields for
Deut 19:12 the elders of his city shall *s*
Deut 24:1 hand, and *s* her out of his house
Deut 28:20 The LORD shall *s* upon thee
Deut 28:48 the LORD shall *s* against thee
Deut 32:24 I will also *s* the teeth of beasts
Josh 18:4 and I will *s* them, and they shall
Judg 13:8 thou didst *s* come again unto us
1Sa 5:11 *S* away the ark of the God of
1Sa 6:2 we shall *s* it to his place
1Sa 6:3 If ye *s* away the ark of the God
1Sa 6:3 the God of Israel, *s* it not empty
1Sa 6:8 *s* it away, that it may go
1Sa 9:16 *s* thee a man out of the land of
1Sa 9:26 Up, that I may *s* thee away
1Sa 11:3 that we may *s* messengers unto all
1Sa 12:17 the LORD, and he shall *s* thunder
1Sa 16:1 I will *s* thee to Jesse the
1Sa 16:11 And Samuel said unto Jesse, *S*
1Sa 16:19 *S* me David thy son, which is with
1Sa 20:12 I then *s* not unto thee, and shew
1Sa 20:13 *s* thee away, that thou mayest go
1Sa 20:21 And, behold, I will *s* a lad
1Sa 20:31 Wherefore now *s* and fetch him unto
1Sa 21:2 the business whereabout I *s* thee
1Sa 25:25 men of my lord, whom thou didst *s*
2Sa 11:6 saying, *S* me Uriah the Hittite
2Sa 14:32 that I may *s* thee to the king, to
2Sa 15:36 by them ye shall *s* unto me every
2Sa 17:16 Now therefore *s* quickly, and tell
1Kin 8:44 whithersoever thou shalt *s* them

1Kin 18:1 I will *s* rain upon the earth
1Kin 18:19 Now therefore *s*, and gather to me
1Kin 20:6 Yet I will *s* my servants unto
1Kin 20:9 All that thou didst *s* for to thy
1Kin 20:34 I will *s* thee away with this
2Kin 2:16 And he said, Ye shall not *s*
2Kin 2:17 till he was ashamed, he said, *S*
2Kin 4:22 *S* me, I pray thee, one of the
2Kin 5:5 I will *s* a letter unto the king
2Kin 5:7 that this man doth *s* unto me to
2Kin 6:13 and spy where he is, that I may *s*
2Kin 7:13 and let us *s* and see
2Kin 9:17 *s* to meet them, and let him say,
2Kin 15:37 *s* against Judah Rezin the king of
2Kin 19:7 I will *s* a blast upon him, and he
1Chr 13:2 let us *s* abroad unto our brethren
2Chr 2:3 didst *s* him cedars to build him
2Chr 2:7 *S* me now therefore a man cunning
2Chr 2:8 *S* me also cedar trees, fir trees,
2Chr 2:15 let him *s* unto his servants
2Chr 6:27 *s* rain upon thy land, which thou
2Chr 6:34 by the way that thou shalt *s* them
2Chr 7:13 or if I *s* pestilence among my
2Chr 28:16 At that time did king Ahaz *s* unto
2Chr 32:9 *s* his servants to Jerusalem
Ezr 5:17 let the king *s* his pleasure to us
Neh 2:5 thou wouldest *s* me unto Judah
Neh 2:6 So it pleased the king to *s* me
Neh 8:10 *s* portions unto them for whom
Neh 8:12 to *s* portions, and to make great
Job 21:11 They *s* forth their little ones
Job 38:35 Canst thou *s* lightnings, that
Ps 20:2 *S* thee help from the sanctuary,
Ps 43:3 O *s* out thy light and thy truth
Ps 57:3 He shall *s* from heaven, and save
Ps 57:3 God shall *s* forth his mercy and
Ps 68:9 didst *s* a plentiful rain, whereby
Ps 68:33 he doth *s* out his voice, and that
Ps 110:2 The LORD shall *s* the rod of thy
Ps 118:25 I beseech thee, *s* now prosperity
Ps 144:7 *S* thine hand from above
Prov 10:26 the sluggard to them that *s* him
Prov 22:21 of truth to them that *s* unto thee
Prov 25:13 messenger to them that *s* him
Eccl 10:1 to *s* forth a stinking savour
Is 6:8 the Lord, saying, Whom shall I *s*
Is 6:8 Here am I; *s* me
Is 10:6 I will *s* him against an
Is 10:16 *s* among his fat ones leanness
Is 16:1 *S* ye the lamb to the ruler of the
Is 19:20 he shall *s* them a saviour, and a
Is 32:20 that *s* forth thither the feet of
Is 37:7 I will *s* a blast upon him, and he
Is 57:9 didst *s* thy messengers far off,
Is 66:19 I will *s* those that escape of
Jer 1:7 go to all that I shall *s* thee
Jer 2:10 *s* unto Kedar, and consider
Jer 8:17 I will *s* serpents, cockatrices,
Jer 9:16 I will *s* a sword after them, till
Jer 9:17 *s* for cunning women, that they
Jer 16:16 I will *s* for many fishers, saith
Jer 16:16 after will I *s* for many hunters,
Jer 24:10 I will *s* the sword, the famine,
Jer 25:9 Behold, I will *s* and take all the
Jer 25:15 all the nations, to whom I *s* thee
Jer 25:16 sword that I will *s* among them
Jer 25:27 sword which I will *s* among you
Jer 27:3 *s* them to the king of Edom, and to
Jer 29:17 I will *s* upon them the sword, the
Jer 29:31 *S* to all them of the captivity,
Jer 42:5 LORD thy God shall *s* thee to us
Jer 42:6 LORD our God, to whom we *s* thee
Jer 43:10 Behold, I will *s* and take
Jer 48:12 that I will *s* unto him wanderers,
Jer 49:37 I will *s* the sword after them,
Jer 51:2 will *s* unto Babylon fanners, that
Eze 2:3 I *s* thee to the children of
Eze 2:4 I do *s* thee unto them
Eze 5:16 When I shall *s* upon them the evil
Eze 5:16 which I will *s* to destroy you
Eze 5:17 So will I *s* upon you famine and
Eze 7:3 I will *s* mine anger upon thee, and
Eze 14:13 will *s* famine upon it, and will
Eze 14:19 Or if I *s* a pestilence into that
Eze 14:21 How much more when I *s* my four
Eze 28:23 For I will *s* into her pestilence,
Eze 39:6 I will *s* a fire on Magog, and
Hos 8:14 but I will *s* a fire upon his
Joel 2:19 I will *s* you corn, and wine, and
Amos 1:4 But I will *s* a fire into the
Amos 1:7 But I will *s* a fire on the wall
Amos 1:10 But I will *s* a fire on the wall
Amos 1:12 But I will *s* a fire upon Teman,
Amos 2:2 But I will *s* a fire upon Moab, and
Amos 2:5 But I will *s* a fire upon Judah,
Amos 8:11 that I will *s* a famine in the
Mal 2:2 I will even *s* a curse upon you,
Mal 3:1 I will *s* my messenger, and he
Mal 4:5 I will *s* you Elijah the prophet
Mt 9:38 that he will *s* forth labourers
Mt 10:16 I *s* you forth as sheep in the
Mt 10:34 I am come to *s* peace on earth
Mt 10:34 I came not to *s* peace, but a
Mt 11:10 I *s* my messenger before thy face,
Mt 12:20 till he *s* forth judgment unto
Mt 13:41 of man shall *s* forth his angels
Mt 14:15 *s* the multitude away, that they
Mt 15:23 besought him, saying, *S* her away
Mt 15:32 I will not *s* them away fasting,
Mt 21:3 and straightway he will *s* them
Mt 23:34 I *s* unto you prophets, and wise
Mt 24:31 he shall *s* his angels with a
Mk 1:2 I *s* my messenger before thy face,
Mk 3:14 that he might *s* them forth to
Mk 5:10 him much that he would not *s* them
Mk 5:12 *S* us into the swine, that we may
Mk 6:7 began to *s* them forth by two and
Mk 6:36 *S* them away, that they may go
Mk 8:3 if I *s* them away fasting to their
Mk 11:3 straightway he will *s* him hither
Mk 12:13 they *s* unto him certain of the
Mk 13:27 And then shall he *s* his angels
Lk 7:27 I *s* my messenger before thy face,
Lk 9:12 *S* the multitude away, that they
Lk 10:2 that he would *s* forth labourers
Lk 10:3 I *s* you forth as lambs among
Lk 11:49 I will *s* them prophets and
Lk 12:49 I am come to *s* fire on the earth
Lk 16:24 *s* Lazarus, that he may dip the
Lk 16:27 that thou wouldest *s* him to my
Lk 20:13 I will *s* my beloved son
Lk 24:49 I *s* the promise of my Father upon
Jn 13:20 whomsoever I *s* receiveth me
Jn 14:26 whom the Father will *s* in my name
Jn 15:26 whom I will *s* unto you from the
Jn 16:7 I depart, I will *s* him unto you
Jn 17:8 believed that thou didst *s* me
Jn 20:21 hath sent me, even so *s* I you
Acts 3:20 he shall *s* Jesus Christ, which
Acts 7:34 come, I will *s* thee into Egypt
Acts 7:35 the same did God *s* to be a ruler
Acts 10:5 now *s* men to Joppa, and call for
Acts 10:22 to *s* for thee into his house
Acts 10:32 *S* therefore to Joppa, and call
Acts 11:13 *S* men to Joppa, and call for Simon
Acts 11:29 determined to *s* relief unto the
Acts 15:22 to *s* chosen men of their own
Acts 15:23 brethren *s* greeting unto the
Acts 15:25 to *s* chosen men unto you with our
Acts 22:21 for I will *s* thee far hence unto
Acts 25:3 that he would *s* for him to
Acts 25:21 kept till I might *s* him to Caesar
Acts 25:25 I have determined to *s* him
Acts 25:27 me unreasonable to *s* a prisoner
Acts 26:17 Gentiles, unto whom now I *s* thee
1Cor 16:3 them will I *s* to bring your
Phil 2:19 to *s* Timotheus shortly unto you
Phil 2:23 therefore I hope to *s* presently
Phil 2:25 to *s* to you Epaphroditus, my
2Th 2:11 God shall *s* them strong delusion
Titus 3:12 When I shall *s* Artemas unto thee,
Jas 3:11 Doth a fountain *s* forth at the
Rev 1:11 *s* it unto the seven churches
Rev 11:10 shall *s* gifts one to another

**SENDEST**
Deut 15:13 when thou *s* him out free from
Deut 15:18 when thou *s* him away free from
Josh 1:16 do, and whithersoever thou *s* us
2Kin 1:6 that thou *s* to enquire of
Job 14:20 his countenance, and *s* him away
Ps 104:30 Thou *s* forth thy spirit, they are

**SENDETH**
Deut 24:3 hand, and *s* her out of his house
1Kin 17:14 the LORD *s* rain upon the earth
Job 5:10 and *s* waters upon the fields
Job 12:15 also he *s* them out, and they
Ps 104:10 He *s* the springs into the valleys
Ps 147:15 He *s* forth his commandment upon
Ps 147:18 He *s* out his word, and melteth
Prov 26:6 He that *s* a message by the hand
Song 1:12 my spikenard *s* forth the smell
Is 18:2 That *s* ambassadors by the sea,
Mt 5:45 *s* rain on the just and on the
Mk 11:1 he *s* forth two of his disciples,
Mk 14:13 he *s* forth two of his disciples,
Lk 14:32 he *s* an ambassage, and desireth
Acts 23:26 governor Felix *s* greeting

**SENDING**
2Sa 13:16 this evil in *s* me away is greater
2Chr 36:15 rising up betimes, and *s*
Est 9:19 of *s* portions one to another
Est 9:22 of *s* portions one to another, and
Ps 78:49 by *s* evil angels among them
Is 7:25 shall be for the *s* forth of oxen
Jer 7:25 daily rising up early and *s* them
Jer 25:4 prophets, rising early and *s* them
Jer 26:5 *s* them, but ye have not hearkened
Jer 29:19 rising up early and *s* them
Jer 35:15 *s* them, saying, Return ye now
Jer 44:4 *s* them, saying, Oh, do not this
Eze 17:15 in *s* his ambassadors into Egypt
Rom 8:3 God *s* his own Son in the likeness

**SENEH** *(se'-neh) A rock in Benjamin.*
1Sa 14:4 Bozez, and the name of the other *S*

**SENIR** *(se'-nur)* See SHENIR. *A mountain between Amana and Hermon.*
1Chr 5:23 from Bashan unto Baal-hermon and *S*
Eze 27:5 thy ship boards of fir trees of *S*

**SENNACHERIB** *(sen-nak'-er-ib) An Assyrian king.*
2Kin 18:13 year of king Hezekiah did *S* king
2Kin 19:16 and hear the words of *S*, which
2Kin 19:20 *S* king of Assyria I have heard
2Kin 19:36 So *S* king of Assyria departed, and
2Chr 32:1 *S* king of Assyria came, and
2Chr 32:2 when Hezekiah saw that *S* was come
2Chr 32:9 After this did *S* king of Assyria
2Chr 32:10 Thus saith *S* king of Assyria,
2Chr 32:22 the hand of *S* the king of Assyria
Is 36:1 that *S* king of Assyria came up
Is 37:17 and hear all the words of *S*
Is 37:21 to me against *S* king of Assyria
Is 37:37 So *S* king of Assyria departed, and

**SENTENCE**
Deut 17:9 shall shew thee the *s* of judgment
Deut 17:10 thou shalt do according to the *s*
Deut 17:11 According to the *s* of the law
Deut 17:11 the *s* which they shall shew thee
Ps 17:2 Let my *s* come forth from thy
Prov 16:10 A divine *s* is in the lips of the
Eccl 8:11 Because *s* against an evil work is
Jer 4:12 also will I give *s* against them
Lk 23:24 Pilate gave *s* that it should be
Acts 15:19 Wherefore my *s* is, that we
2Cor 1:9 But we had the *s* of death in

**SENUAH** *(sen'-u-ah)* See HASSENUAH. *Father of Judah.*
Neh 11:9 Judah the son of *S* was second

**SEORIM** *(se-o'-rim) A sanctuary servant.*
1Chr 24:8 third to Harim, the fourth to *S*

**SEPARATE**
Gen 13:9 *s* thyself, I pray thee, from me
Gen 30:40 And Jacob did *s* the lambs, and set
Gen 49:26 him that was *s* from his brethren
Lev 15:31 Thus shall ye *s* the children of
Lev 22:2 that they *s* themselves from the
Num 6:2 *s* themselves to vow a vow of a
Num 6:2 to *s* themselves unto the LORD
Num 6:3 He shall *s* himself from wine and
Num 8:14 Thus shalt thou *s* the Levites
Num 16:21 *S* yourselves from among this
Deut 19:2 Thou shalt *s* three cities for
Deut 19:7 Thou shalt *s* three cities for
Deut 29:21 the LORD shall *s* him unto evil
Josh 16:9 the *s* cities for the children of
1Kin 8:53 For thou didst *s* them from among
Ezr 10:11 *s* yourselves from the people of
Jer 37:12 to *s* himself thence in the midst
Eze 41:12 the *s* place at the end toward the
Eze 41:13 the *s* place, and the building,
Eze 41:14 of the *s* place toward the east,
Eze 41:15 the *s* place which was behind it
Eze 42:1 that was over against the *s* place
Eze 42:10 east, over against the *s* place
Eze 42:13 which are before the *s* place
Mt 25:32 he shall *s* them one from another,

| | |
|---|---|
| Lk 6:22 | when they shall *s* you from their |
| Acts 13:2 | *S* me Barnabas and Saul for the |
| Rom 8:35 | Who shall *s* us from the love of |
| Rom 8:39 | shall be able to *s* us from the |
| 2Cor 6:17 | out from among them, and be ye *s* |
| Heb 7:26 | *s* from sinners, and made higher |
| Jude 19 | These be they who *s* themselves |

**SEPARATED**

| | |
|---|---|
| Gen 13:11 | they *s* themselves the one from |
| Gen 13:14 | after that Lot was *s* from him |
| Gen 25:23 | people shall be *s* from thy bowels |
| Ex 33:16 | so shall we be *s*, I and thy people |
| Lev 20:24 | which have *s* you from other |
| Lev 20:25 | which I have *s* from you as |
| Num 16:9 | that the God of Israel hath *s* you |
| Deut 10:8 | time the LORD *s* the tribe of Levi |
| Deut 32:8 | when he *s* the sons of Adam, he |
| Deut 33:16 | him that was *s* from his brethren |
| 1Chr 12:8 | of the Gadites there *s* themselves |
| 1Chr 23:13 | and Aaron was *s*, that he should |
| 1Chr 25:1 | the captains of the host *s* to the |
| 2Chr 25:10 | Then Amaziah *s* them, to wit, the |
| Ezr 6:21 | all such as had *s* themselves unto |
| Ezr 8:24 | Then I *s* twelve of the chief of |
| Ezr 9:1 | have not *s* themselves from the |
| Ezr 10:8 | himself *s* from the congregation |
| Ezr 10:16 | of them by their names, were *s* |
| Neh 4:19 | we are *s* upon the wall, one far |
| Neh 9:2 | the seed of Israel *s* themselves |
| Neh 10:28 | all they that had *s* themselves |
| Neh 13:3 | that they *s* from Israel all the |
| Prov 18:1 | having *s* himself, seeketh and |
| Prov 19:4 | but the poor is *s* from his |
| Is 56:3 | hath utterly *s* me from his people |
| Is 59:2 | iniquities have *s* between you |
| Hos 4:14 | for themselves are *s* with whores |
| Hos 9:10 | *s* themselves unto that shame |
| Acts 19:9 | *s* the disciples, disputing daily |
| Rom 1:1 | *s* unto the gospel of God, |
| Gal 1:15 | who *s* me from my mother's womb, |
| Gal 2:12 | *s* himself, fearing them which |

**SEPARATETH**

| | |
|---|---|
| Num 6:5 | in the which he *s* himself unto |
| Num 6:6 | All the days that he *s* himself |
| Prov 16:28 | a whisperer *s* chief friends |
| Prov 17:9 | repeateth a matter *s* very friends |
| Eze 14:7 | which *s* himself from me, and |

**SEPARATION**

| | |
|---|---|
| Lev 12:2 | according to the days of the *s* |
| Lev 12:5 | be unclean two weeks, as in her *s* |
| Lev 15:20 | upon in her *s* shall be unclean |
| Lev 15:25 | days out of the time of her *s* |
| Lev 15:25 | it run beyond the time of her *s* |
| Lev 15:25 | shall be as the days of her *s* |
| Lev 15:26 | be unto her as the bed of her *s* |
| Lev 15:26 | as the uncleanness of her *s* |
| Num 6:4 | All the days of his *s* shall he |
| Num 6:5 | *s* there shall no razor come upon |
| Num 6:8 | All the days of his *s* he is holy |
| Num 6:12 | unto the LORD the days of his *s* |
| Num 6:12 | lost, because his *s* was defiled |
| Num 6:13 | the days of his *s* are fulfilled |
| Num 6:18 | shall shave the head of his *s* at |
| Num 6:18 | the hair of the head of his *s* |
| Num 6:19 | after the hair of his *s* is shaven |
| Num 6:21 | offering unto the LORD for his *s* |
| Num 6:21 | he must do after the law of his *s* |
| Num 19:9 | of Israel for a water of *s* |
| Num 19:13 | because the water of *s* was not |
| Num 19:20 | the water of *s* hath not been |
| Num 19:21 | water of *s* shall wash his clothes |
| Num 19:21 | of *s* shall be unclean until even |
| Num 31:23 | be purified with the water of *s* |
| Eze 42:20 | to make a *s* between the sanctuary |

**SEPHAR** *(se'-far) A mountain in Arabia.*

| | |
|---|---|
| Gen 10:30 | as thou goest unto *S* a mount of |

**SEPHARAD** *(sef'-a-rad) A city in Media.*

| | |
|---|---|
| Obad 20 | of Jerusalem, which is in *S* |

**SEPHARVAIM** *(sef-ar-va'-im)* See SEPHARVITES. *A city in Mesopotamia.*

| | |
|---|---|
| 2Kin 17:24 | Ava, and from Hamath, and from *S* |
| 2Kin 17:31 | and Anammelech, the gods of *S* |
| 2Kin 18:34 | where are the gods of *S*, Hena, and |
| 2Kin 19:13 | and the king of the city of *S* |
| Is 36:19 | where are the gods of *S* |
| Is 37:13 | and the king of the city of *S* |

**SEPHARVITES** *(sef'-ar-vites) Inhabitants of Sepharvaim.*

| | |
|---|---|
| 2Kin 17:31 | the *S* burnt their children in |

**SEPULCHRE**

| | |
|---|---|
| Gen 23:6 | us shall withhold from thee his *s* |
| Deut 34:6 | knoweth of his *s* unto this day |
| Judg 8:32 | was buried in the *s* of Joash his |
| 1Sa 10:2 | *s* in the border of Benjamin at |
| 2Sa 2:32 | buried him in the *s* of his father |
| 2Sa 4:12 | buried it in the *s* of Abner in |
| 2Sa 17:23 | was buried in the *s* of his father |
| 2Sa 21:14 | in the *s* of Kish his father |
| 1Kin 13:22 | come unto the *s* of thy fathers |
| 1Kin 13:31 | then bury me in the *s* wherein the |
| 2Kin 9:28 | buried him in his *s* with his |
| 2Kin 13:21 | cast the man into the *s* of Elisha |
| 2Kin 21:26 | he was buried in his *s* in the |
| 2Kin 23:17 | It is the *s* of the man of God, |
| 2Kin 23:30 | and buried him in his own *s* |
| Ps 5:9 | their throat is an open *s* |
| Is 22:16 | thou hast hewed thee out a *s* here |
| Is 22:16 | that heweth him out an *s* on high |
| Jer 5:16 | Their quiver is as an open *s* |
| Mt 27:60 | great stone to the door of the *s* |
| Mt 27:61 | Mary, sitting over against the *s* |
| Mt 27:64 | Command therefore that the *s* be |
| Mt 27:66 | So they went, and made the *s* sure |
| Mt 28:1 | and the other Mary to see the *s* |
| Mt 28:8 | quickly from the *s* with fear |
| Mk 15:46 | laid him in a *s* which was hewn |
| Mk 15:46 | a stone unto the door of the *s* |
| Mk 16:2 | they came unto the *s* at the |
| Mk 16:3 | the stone from the door of the *s* |
| Mk 16:5 | And entering into the *s*, they saw |
| Mk 16:8 | out quickly, and fled from the *s* |
| Lk 23:53 | laid it in a *s* that was hewn in |
| Lk 23:55 | followed after, and beheld the *s* |
| Lk 24:1 | the morning, they came unto the *s* |
| Lk 24:2 | the stone rolled away from the *s* |
| Lk 24:9 | And returned from the *s*, and told |
| Lk 24:12 | arose Peter, and ran unto the *s* |
| Lk 24:22 | which were early at the *s* |
| Lk 24:24 | which were with us went to the *s* |
| Jn 19:41 | and in the garden a new *s*, wherein |
| Jn 19:42 | for the *s* was nigh at hand |
| Jn 20:1 | when it was yet dark, unto the *s* |
| Jn 20:1 | the stone taken away from the *s* |
| Jn 20:2 | taken away the Lord out of the *s* |
| Jn 20:3 | other disciple, and came to the *s* |
| Jn 20:4 | Peter, and came first to the *s* |
| Jn 20:6 | following him, and went into the *s* |
| Jn 20:8 | which came first to the *s* |
| Jn 20:11 | stood without at the *s* weeping |
| Jn 20:11 | down, and looked into the *s* |
| Acts 2:29 | his *s* is with us unto this day |
| Acts 7:16 | laid in the *s* that Abraham bought |
| Acts 13:29 | from the tree, and laid him in a *s* |
| Rom 3:13 | Their throat is an open *s* |

**SEPULCHRES**

| | |
|---|---|
| Gen 23:6 | the choice of our *s* bury thy dead |
| 2Kin 23:16 | he spied the *s* that were there in |
| 2Kin 23:16 | and took the bones out of the *s* |
| 2Chr 16:14 | And they buried him in his own *s* |
| 2Chr 21:20 | but not in the *s* of the kings |
| 2Chr 24:25 | him not in the *s* of the kings |
| 2Chr 28:27 | into the *s* of the kings of Israel |
| 2Chr 32:33 | of the *s* of the sons of David |
| 2Chr 35:24 | in one of the *s* of his fathers |
| Neh 2:3 | city, the place of my fathers' *s* |
| Neh 2:5 | unto the city of my fathers' *s* |
| Neh 3:16 | place over against the *s* of David |
| Mt 23:27 | for ye are like unto whited *s* |
| Mt 23:29 | garnish the *s* of the righteous, |
| Lk 11:47 | ye build the *s* of the prophets |
| Lk 11:48 | killed them, and ye build their *s* |

**SERAH** *(se'-rah)* See SARAH. *A daughter of Asher.*

| | |
|---|---|
| Gen 46:17 | and Beriah, and *S* their sister |
| 1Chr 7:30 | and Beriah, and *S* their sister |

**SERAIAH** *(se-ra-i'-ah)* See SHAVSHA.

*1. David's scribe.*

| | |
|---|---|
| 2Sa 8:17 | and *S* was the scribe |

*2. High priest in Zedekiah's time.*

| | |
|---|---|
| 2Kin 25:18 | the guard took *S* the chief priest |
| 1Chr 6:14 | And Azariah begat *S*, and Seraiah |
| 1Chr 6:14 | Seraiah, and *S* begat Jehozadak, |
| Ezr 7:1 | king of Persia, Ezra the son of *S* |
| Jer 52:24 | the guard took *S* the chief priest |

*3. Son of Tanhumeth.*

| | |
|---|---|
| 2Kin 25:23 | *S* the son of Tanhumeth the |
| Jer 40:8 | *S* the son of Tanhumeth, and the |

*4. A son of Kenaz.*

| | |
|---|---|
| 1Chr 4:13 | Othniel, and *S* |
| 1Chr 4:14 | *S* begat Joab, the father of the |

*5. Son of Asiel.*

| | |
|---|---|
| 1Chr 4:35 | the son of Josibiah, the son of *S* |

*6. A priest with Zerubbabel.*

| | |
|---|---|
| Ezr 2:2 | Jeshua, Nehemiah, *S*, Reelaiah, |
| Neh 10:2 | *S*, Azariah, Jeremiah, |
| Neh 12:1 | *S*, Jeremiah, Ezra, |
| Neh 12:12 | of *S*, Meraiah |

*7. An exile.*

| | |
|---|---|
| Neh 11:11 | *S* the son of Hilkiah, the son of |

*8. Son of Azriel.*

| | |
|---|---|
| Jer 36:26 | *S* the son of Azriel, and Shelemiah |

*9. Son of Neriah.*

| | |
|---|---|
| Jer 51:59 | commanded *S* the son of Neriah |
| Jer 51:59 | this *S* was a quiet prince |
| Jer 51:61 | And Jeremiah said to *S*, When thou |

**SERAPHIMS**

| | |
|---|---|
| Is 6:2 | Above it stood the *s* |
| Is 6:6 | Then flew one of the *s* unto me |

**SERED** *(se'-red)* See SARDITES. *A son of Zebulun.*

| | |
|---|---|
| Gen 46:14 | *S*, and Elon, and Jahleel |
| Num 26:26 | of *S*, the family of the Sardites |

**SERGIUS** *(sur'-je-us) Roman governor of Cyprus.*

| | |
|---|---|
| Acts 13:7 | country, *S* Paulus, a prudent man |

**SERPENT**

| | |
|---|---|
| Gen 3:1 | Now the *s* was more subtil than |
| Gen 3:2 | And the woman said unto the *s* |
| Gen 3:4 | the *s* said unto the woman, Ye |
| Gen 3:13 | The *s* beguiled me, and I did eat |
| Gen 3:14 | And the LORD God said unto the *s* |
| Gen 49:17 | Dan shall be a *s* by the way |
| Ex 4:3 | on the ground, and it became a *s* |
| Ex 7:9 | Pharaoh, and it shall become a *s* |
| Ex 7:10 | his servants, and it became a *s* |
| Ex 7:15 | a *s* shalt thou take in thine hand |
| Num 21:8 | unto Moses, Make thee a fiery *s* |
| Num 21:9 | And Moses made a *s* of brass |
| Num 21:9 | that if a *s* had bitten any man, |
| Num 21:9 | when he beheld the *s* of brass |
| 2Kin 18:4 | the brasen *s* that Moses had made |
| Job 26:13 | hand hath formed the crooked *s* |
| Ps 58:4 | poison is like the poison of a *s* |
| Ps 140:3 | sharpened their tongues like a *s* |
| Prov 23:32 | At the last it biteth like a *s* |
| Prov 30:19 | the way of a *s* upon a rock |
| Eccl 10:8 | an hedge, a *s* shall bite him |
| Eccl 10:11 | Surely the *s* will bite without |
| Is 14:29 | fruit shall be a fiery flying *s* |
| Is 27:1 | punish leviathan the piercing *s* |
| Is 27:1 | even leviathan that crooked *s* |
| Is 30:6 | lion, the viper and fiery flying *s* |
| Jer 46:22 | voice thereof shall go like a *s* |
| Amos 5:19 | hand on the wall, and a *s* bit him |
| Amos 9:3 | sea, thence will I command the *s* |
| Mic 7:17 | They shall lick the dust like a *s* |
| Mt 7:10 | ask a fish, will he give him a *s* |
| Lk 11:11 | will he for a fish give him a *s* |
| Jn 3:14 | lifted up the *s* in the wilderness |
| 2Cor 11:3 | as the *s* beguiled Eve through his |
| Rev 12:9 | dragon was cast out, that old *s* |
| Rev 12:14 | a time, from the face of the *s* |
| Rev 12:15 | the *s* cast out of his mouth water |
| Rev 20:2 | hold on the dragon, that old *s* |

**SERPENTS**

| | |
|---|---|
| Ex 7:12 | man his rod, and they became *s* |
| Num 21:6 | sent fiery *s* among the people |
| Num 21:7 | that he take away the *s* from us |
| Deut 8:15 | wilderness, wherein were fiery *s* |
| Deut 32:24 | with the poison of *s* of the dust |
| Jer 8:17 | For, behold, I will send *s* |
| Mt 10:16 | be ye therefore wise as *s* |
| Mt 23:33 | Ye *s*, ye generation of vipers, |
| Mk 16:18 | They shall take up *s* |
| Lk 10:19 | give unto you power to tread on *s* |
| 1Cor 10:9 | tempted, and were destroyed of *s* |
| Jas 3:7 | of beasts, and of birds, and of *s* |
| Rev 9:19 | for their tails were like unto *s* |

**SERUG** *(se'-rug)* See SARUCH. *Father of Nahor.*

| | |
|---|---|
| Gen 11:20 | two and thirty years, and begat *S* |
| Gen 11:21 | after he begat *S* two hundred |

Gen 11:22 S lived thirty years, and begat
Gen 11:23 S lived after he begat Nahor two
1Chr 1:26 S, Nahor, Terah,

## SERVE

Gen 15:13 is not theirs, and shall s them
Gen 15:14 that nation, whom they shall s
Gen 25:23 and the elder shall s the younger
Gen 27:29 Let people s thee, and nations bow
Gen 27:40 thou live, and shalt s thy brother
Gen 29:15 thou therefore s me for nought
Gen 29:18 I will s thee seven years for
Gen 29:25 did not I s with thee for Rachel
Gen 29:27 the service which thou shalt s
Ex 1:13 of Israel to s with rigour
Ex 1:14 service, wherein they made them s
Ex 3:12 ye shall s God upon this mountain
Ex 4:23 Let my son go, that he may s me
Ex 7:16 that they may s me in the
Ex 8:1 my people go, that they may s me
Ex 8:20 my people go, that they may s me
Ex 9:1 my people go, that they may s me
Ex 9:13 my people go, that they may s me
Ex 10:3 my people go, that they may s me
Ex 10:7 that they may s the LORD their
Ex 10:8 them, Go, s the LORD your God
Ex 10:11 ye that are men, and s the LORD
Ex 10:24 Moses, and said, Go ye, s the LORD
Ex 10:26 we take to s the LORD our God
Ex 10:26 not with what we must s the LORD
Ex 12:31 s the LORD, as ye have said
Ex 14:12 that we may s the Egyptians
Ex 14:12 better for us to s the Egyptians
Ex 20:5 down thyself to them, nor s them
Ex 21:2 servant, six years he shall s
Ex 21:6 and he shall s him for ever
Ex 23:24 nor s them, nor do after their
Ex 23:25 ye shall s the LORD your God, and
Ex 23:33 for if thou s their gods, it will
Lev 25:39 compel him to s as a bondservant
Lev 25:40 shall s thee unto the year of
Num 4:24 families of the Gershonites, to s
Num 4:26 so shall they s
Num 8:25 thereof, and shall s no more
Num 18:7 and ye shall s
Num 18:21 for their service which they s
Deut 4:19 s them, which the LORD thy God
Deut 4:28 And there ye shall s gods, the
Deut 5:9 thyself unto them, nor s them
Deut 6:13 s him, and shalt swear by his name
Deut 7:4 me, that they may s other gods
Deut 7:16 neither shalt thou s their gods
Deut 8:19 s them, and worship them, I
Deut 10:12 to s the LORD thy God with all
Deut 10:20 him shalt thou s, and to him shalt
Deut 11:13 to s him with all your heart and
Deut 11:16 s other gods, and worship them
Deut 12:30 did these nations s their gods
Deut 13:2 hast not known, and let us s them
Deut 13:4 obey his voice, and ye shall s him
Deut 13:6 s other gods, which thou hast not
Deut 13:13 s other gods, which ye have not
Deut 15:12 unto thee, and s thee six years
Deut 20:11 unto thee, and they shall s thee
Deut 28:14 to go after other gods to s them
Deut 28:36 and there shalt thou s other gods
Deut 28:48 Therefore shalt thou s thine
Deut 28:64 and there thou shalt s other gods
Deut 29:18 s the gods of these nations
Deut 30:17 and worship other gods, and s them
Deut 31:20 s them, and provoke me, and break
Josh 16:10 unto this day, and s under tribute
Josh 22:5 to s him with all your heart and
Josh 23:7 to swear by them, neither s them
Josh 24:14 s him in sincerity and in truth
Josh 24:14 and s ye the LORD
Josh 24:15 seem evil unto you to s the LORD
Josh 24:15 you this day whom ye will s
Josh 24:15 and my house, we will s the LORD
Josh 24:16 forsake the LORD, to s other gods
Josh 24:18 therefore will we also s the LORD
Josh 24:19 the people, Ye cannot s the LORD
Josh 24:20 s strange gods, then he will turn
Josh 24:21 but we will s the LORD
Josh 24:22 chosen you the LORD, to s him
Josh 24:24 The LORD our God will we s
Judg 2:19 in following other gods to s them
Judg 9:28 is Shechem, that we should s him
Judg 9:28 s the men of Hamor the father of
Judg 9:28 for why should we s him
Judg 9:38 Abimelech, that we should s him
1Sa 7:3 unto the LORD, and s him only
1Sa 10:7 that thou do as occasion s thee
1Sa 11:1 with us, and we will s thee
1Sa 12:10 of our enemies, and we will s thee
1Sa 12:14 s him, and obey his voice, and not
1Sa 12:20 but s the LORD with all your
1Sa 12:24 s him in truth with all your
1Sa 17:9 shall ye be our servants, and s us
1Sa 26:19 LORD, saying, Go, s other gods
2Sa 15:8 Jerusalem, then I will s the LORD
2Sa 16:19 And again, whom should I s
2Sa 16:19 should I not s in the presence of
2Sa 22:44 which I knew not shall s me
1Kin 9:6 s other gods, and worship them
1Kin 12:4 us, lighter, and we will s thee
1Kin 12:7 people this day, and wilt s them
2Kin 10:18 but Jehu shall s him much
2Kin 17:35 nor s them, nor sacrifice to them
2Kin 25:24 land, and s the king of Babylon
1Chr 28:9 s him with a perfect heart and
2Chr 7:19 s other gods, and worship them
2Chr 10:4 he put upon us, and we will s thee
2Chr 29:11 to s him, and that ye should
2Chr 30:8 s the LORD your God, that the
2Chr 33:16 commanded Judah to s the LORD God
2Chr 34:33 that were present in Israel to s
2Chr 34:33 even to s the LORD their God
2Chr 35:3 s now the LORD your God, and his
Job 21:15 Almighty, that we should s him
Job 36:11 s him, they shall spend their
Job 39:9 the unicorn be willing to s thee
Ps 2:11 S the LORD with fear, and rejoice
Ps 18:43 whom I have not known shall s me
Ps 22:30 A seed shall s him
Ps 72:11 all nations shall s him
Ps 97:7 be all they that s graven images
Ps 100:2 S the LORD with gladness
Ps 101:6 in a perfect way, he shall s me
Ps 102:22 and the kingdoms, to s the LORD
Is 14:3 wherein thou wast made to s
Is 19:23 shall s with the Assyrians
Is 43:23 caused thee to s with an offering
Is 43:24 hast made me to s with thy sins
Is 56:6 to s him, and to love the name of
Is 60:12 that will not s thee shall perish
Jer 5:19 so shall ye s strangers in a land
Jer 11:10 went after other gods to s them
Jer 13:10 to s them, and to worship them,
Jer 16:13 there shall ye s other gods day
Jer 17:4 I will cause thee to s thine
Jer 25:6 go not after other gods to s them
Jer 25:11 these nations shall s the king of
Jer 25:14 great kings shall s themselves of
Jer 27:6 field have I given also to s him
Jer 27:7 And all nations shall s him
Jer 27:7 kings shall s themselves of him
Jer 27:8 kingdom which will not s the same
Jer 27:9 Ye shall not s the king of
Jer 27:11 s him, those will I let remain
Jer 27:12 s him and his people, and live
Jer 27:13 will not s the king of Babylon
Jer 27:14 Ye shall not s the king of
Jer 27:17 s the king of Babylon, and live
Jer 28:14 that they may s Nebuchadnezzar
Jer 28:14 and they shall s him
Jer 30:8 shall no more s themselves of him
Jer 30:9 But they shall s the LORD their
Jer 34:9 none should s himself of them
Jer 34:10 that none should s themselves of
Jer 35:15 go not after other gods to s them
Jer 40:9 Fear not to s the Chaldeans
Jer 40:9 s the king of Babylon, and it
Jer 40:10 at Mizpah to s the Chaldeans
Jer 44:3 to s other gods, whom they knew
Eze 20:32 the countries, to s wood and stone
Eze 20:39 s ye every one his idols, and
Eze 20:40 all of them in the land, s me
Eze 29:18 s a great service against Tyrus
Eze 48:18 food unto them that s the city
Eze 48:19 they that s the city shall s
Dan 3:12 they s not thy gods, nor worship
Dan 3:14 and Abed-nego, do not ye s my gods
Dan 3:17 our God whom we s is able to
Dan 3:18 king, that we will not s thy gods
Dan 3:28 might not s nor worship any god
Dan 7:14 and languages, should s him
Dan 7:27 kingdom, and all dominions shall s
Zeph 3:9 to s him with one consent
Mal 3:14 Ye have said, It is vain to s God
Mt 4:10 thy God, and him only shalt thou s
Mt 6:24 No man can s two masters
Mt 6:24 Ye cannot s God and mammon
Lk 1:74 enemies might s him without fear
Lk 4:8 thy God, and him only shalt thou s
Lk 10:40 my sister hath left me to s alone
Lk 12:37 and will come forth and s them
Lk 15:29 Lo, these many years do I s thee
Lk 16:13 No servant can s two masters
Lk 16:13 Ye cannot s God and mammon
Lk 17:8 s me, till I have eaten and
Lk 22:26 that is chief, as he that doth s
Jn 12:26 If any man s me, let him follow
Jn 12:26 if any man s me, him will my
Acts 6:2 the word of God, and s tables
Acts 7:7 come forth, and s me in this place
Acts 27:23 of God, whose I am, and whom I s
Rom 1:9 whom I s with my spirit in the
Rom 6:6 henceforth we should not s sin
Rom 7:6 that we should s in newness of
Rom 7:25 mind I myself s the law of God
Rom 9:12 The elder shall s the younger
Rom 16:18 For they that are such s not our
Gal 5:13 flesh, but by love s one another
Col 3:24 for ye s the Lord Christ
1Th 1:9 to God from idols to s the living
2Ti 1:3 whom I s from my forefathers with
Heb 8:5 Who s unto the example and shadow
Heb 9:14 dead works to s the living God
Heb 12:28 whereby we may s God acceptably
Heb 13:10 to eat which s the tabernacle
Rev 7:15 s him day and night in his temple
Rev 22:3 and his servants shall s him

## SERVED

Gen 14:4 Twelve years they s Chedorlaomer
Gen 29:20 Jacob s seven years for Rachel
Gen 29:30 s with him yet seven other years
Gen 30:26 children, for whom I have s thee
Gen 30:29 Thou knowest how I have s thee
Gen 31:6 all my power I have s your father
Gen 31:41 I s thee fourteen years for thy
Gen 39:4 grace in his sight, and he s him
Gen 40:4 Joseph with them, and he s them
Deut 12:2 ye shall possess s their gods
Deut 17:3 s other gods, and worshipped them,
Deut 29:26 s other gods, and worshipped them,
Josh 23:16 s other gods, and bowed yourselves
Josh 24:2 and they s other gods
Josh 24:14 the gods which your fathers s on
Josh 24:15 the gods which your fathers s
Josh 24:31 Israel s the LORD all the days of
Judg 2:7 the people s the LORD all the
Judg 2:11 sight of the LORD, and s Baalim
Judg 2:13 the LORD, and s Baal and Ashtaroth
Judg 3:6 to their sons, and s their gods
Judg 3:7 God, and s Baalim and the groves
Judg 3:8 and the children of Israel s
Judg 3:14 So the children of Israel s Eglon
Judg 8:1 unto him, Why hast thou s us thus
Judg 10:6 s Baalim, and Ashtaroth, and the
Judg 10:6 and forsook the LORD, and s not him
Judg 10:10 our God, and also s Baalim
Judg 10:13 have forsaken me, and s other gods
Judg 10:16 from among them, and s the LORD
1Sa 7:4 and Ashtaroth, and s the LORD only
1Sa 8:8 s other gods, so do they also
1Sa 12:10 have s Baalim and Ashtaroth
2Sa 10:19 made peace with Israel, and s them
2Sa 16:19 as I have s in thy father's
1Kin 4:21 s Solomon all the days of his
1Kin 9:9 have worshipped them, and s them
1Kin 16:31 s Baal, and worshipped him
1Kin 22:53 For he s Baal, and worshipped him,
2Kin 10:18 unto them, Ahab s Baal a little
2Kin 17:12 For they s idols, whereof the
2Kin 17:16 all the host of heaven, and s Baal
2Kin 17:33 s their own gods, after the
2Kin 17:41 s their graven images, both their
2Kin 18:7 the king of Assyria, and s him not
2Kin 21:3 all the host of heaven, and s them
2Kin 21:21 s the idols that his father
2Kin 21:21 the idols that his father s
1Chr 19:5 and told David how the men were s
1Chr 27:1 their officers that s the king in
2Chr 7:22 and worshipped them, and s them
2Chr 24:18 fathers, and s groves and idols
2Chr 33:3 all the host of heaven, and s them
2Chr 33:22 his father had made, and s them
Neh 9:35 For they have not s thee in their

Est 1:10 the seven chamberlains that *s* in
Ps 106:36 And they *s* their idols
Ps 137:8 rewardeth thee as thou hast *s* us
Eccl 5:9 king himself is *s* by the field
Jer 5:19 *s* strange gods in your land, so
Jer 8:2 have loved, and whom they have *s*
Jer 16:11 after other gods, and have *s* them
Jer 22:9 worshipped other gods, and *s* them
Jer 34:14 when he hath *s* thee six years,
Jer 52:12 which *s* the king of Babylon, into
Eze 29:18 service that he had *s* against it
Eze 29:20 labour wherewith he *s* against it
Eze 34:27 those that *s* themselves of them
Hos 12:12 Israel *s* for a wife, and for a
Lk 2:37 but *s* God with fastings and
Jn 12:2 and Martha *s*
Acts 13:36 after he had *s* his own generation
Rom 1:25 *s* the creature more than the
Phil 2:22 he hath *s* with me in the gospel

### SERVETH
Num 3:36 thereof, and all that *s* thereto
Mal 3:17 spareth his own son that *s* him
Mal 3:18 *s* God and him that *s* him not
Lk 22:27 sitteth at meat, or he that *s*
Lk 22:27 but I am among you as he that *s*
Rom 14:18 *s* Christ is acceptable to God
1Cor 14:22 but prophesying *s* not for them
Gal 3:19 Wherefore then *s* the law

### SERVICE
Gen 29:27 give thee this also for the *s*
Gen 30:26 for thou knowest my *s* which I
Ex 1:14 in all manner of *s* in the field
Ex 1:14 all their *s*, wherein they made
Ex 12:25 that ye shall keep this *s*
Ex 12:26 unto you, What mean ye by this *s*
Ex 13:5 shalt keep this *s* in this month
Ex 27:19 tabernacle in all the *s* thereof
Ex 30:16 the *s* of the tabernacle of the
Ex 31:10 And the cloths of *s*, and the holy
Ex 35:19 The cloths of *s*, to do *s* in
Ex 35:19 to do *s* in the holy place, the
Ex 35:21 congregation, and for all his *s*
Ex 35:24 wood for any work of the *s*
Ex 36:1 work for the *s* of the sanctuary
Ex 36:3 work of the *s* of the sanctuary
Ex 36:5 than enough for the *s* of the work
Ex 38:21 for the *s* of the Levites, by the
Ex 39:1 and scarlet, they made cloths of *s*
Ex 39:1 to do *s* in the holy place, and
Ex 39:40 of the *s* of the tabernacle
Ex 39:41 The cloths of *s* to do
Ex 39:41 to do *s* in the holy place
Num 3:7 to do the *s* of the tabernacle
Num 3:8 to do the *s* of the tabernacle
Num 3:26 cords of it for all the *s* thereof
Num 3:31 the hanging, and all the *s* thereof
Num 4:4 This shall be the *s* of the sons
Num 4:19 appoint them every one to his *s*
Num 4:23 that enter in to perform the *s*
Num 4:24 This is the *s* of the families of
Num 4:26 and all the instruments of their *s*
Num 4:27 his sons shall be all the *s* of
Num 4:27 their burdens, and in all their *s*
Num 4:28 This is the *s* of the families of
Num 4:30 one that entereth into the *s*
Num 4:31 according to all their *s* in the
Num 4:32 instruments, and with all their *s*
Num 4:33 This is the *s* of the families of
Num 4:33 Merari, according to all their *s*
Num 4:35 one that entereth into the *s*
Num 4:37 all that might do *s* in the
Num 4:39 one that entereth into the *s*
Num 4:41 of all that might do *s* in the
Num 4:43 one that entereth into the *s*
Num 4:47 came to do the *s* of the ministry
Num 4:47 the *s* of the burden in the
Num 4:49 every one according to his *s*
Num 7:5 do the *s* of the tabernacle of the
Num 7:5 to every man according to his *s*
Num 7:7 of Gershon, according to their *s*
Num 7:8 of Merari, according unto their *s*
Num 7:9 because the *s* of the sanctuary
Num 8:11 may execute the *s* of the LORD
Num 8:15 do the *s* of the tabernacle of the
Num 8:19 to do the *s* of the children of
Num 8:22 their *s* in the tabernacle of the
Num 8:24 the *s* of the tabernacle of the
Num 8:25 cease waiting upon the *s* thereof
Num 8:26 keep the charge, and shall do no *s*
Num 16:9 *s* of the tabernacle of the LORD
Num 18:4 for all the *s* of the tabernacle
Num 18:6 to do the *s* of the tabernacle of
Num 18:7 office unto you as a *s* of gift
Num 18:21 for their *s* which they serve,
Num 18:21 even the *s* of the tabernacle of
Num 18:23 do the *s* of the tabernacle of the
Num 18:31 your *s* in the tabernacle of the
Josh 22:27 that we might do the *s* of the
1Kin 12:4 thou the grievous *s* of thy father
1Chr 6:31 the *s* of song in the house of the
1Chr 6:48 appointed unto all manner of *s* of
1Chr 9:13 work of the *s* of the house of God
1Chr 9:19 were over the work of the *s*
1Chr 23:24 the *s* of the house of the LORD
1Chr 23:26 vessels of it for the *s* thereof
1Chr 23:28 the *s* of the house of the LORD
1Chr 23:28 the work of the *s* of the house of
1Chr 23:32 in the *s* of the house of the LORD
1Chr 24:3 to their offices in their *s*
1Chr 24:19 *s* to come into the house of the
1Chr 25:1 to the *s* of the sons of Asaph
1Chr 25:1 workmen according to their *s* was
1Chr 25:6 for the *s* of the house of God,
1Chr 26:8 able men for strength for the *s*
1Chr 26:30 the LORD, and in the *s* of the king
1Chr 28:13 for all the work of the *s* of the
1Chr 28:13 for all the vessels of *s* in the
1Chr 28:14 instruments of all manner of *s*
1Chr 28:14 instruments of every kind of *s*
1Chr 28:20 the *s* of the house of the LORD
1Chr 28:21 for all the *s* of the house of God
1Chr 28:21 skilful man, for any manner of *s*
1Chr 29:5 his *s* this day unto the LORD
1Chr 29:7 gave for the *s* of the house of
2Chr 8:14 courses of the priests to their *s*
2Chr 12:8 that they may know my *s*, and the
2Chr 12:8 the *s* of the kingdoms of the
2Chr 24:12 of the *s* of the house of the LORD
2Chr 29:35 So the *s* of the house of the LORD
2Chr 31:2 every man according to his *s*
2Chr 31:16 his daily portion for their *s* in
2Chr 31:21 in the *s* of the house of God
2Chr 34:13 the work in any manner of *s*
2Chr 35:2 encouraged them to the *s* of the
2Chr 35:10 So the *s* was prepared, and the
2Chr 35:15 might not depart from their *s*
2Chr 35:16 So all the *s* of the LORD was
Ezr 6:18 their courses, for the *s* of God
Ezr 7:19 for the *s* of the house of thy God
Ezr 8:20 for the *s* of the Levites, two
Neh 10:32 for the *s* of the house of our God
Ps 104:14 cattle, and herb for the *s* of man
Jer 22:13 his neighbour's *s* without wages
Eze 29:18 to serve a great *s* against Tyrus
Eze 29:18 for the *s* that he had served
Eze 44:14 the house, for all the *s* thereof
Jn 16:2 will think that he doeth God *s*
Rom 9:4 the *s* of God, and the promises
Rom 12:1 God, which is your reasonable *s*
Rom 15:31 that my *s* which I have for
2Cor 9:12 *s* not only supplieth the want of
2Cor 11:8 taking wages of them, to do you *s*
Gal 4:8 ye did *s* unto them which by
Eph 6:7 With good will doing *s*, as to the
Phil 2:17 *s* of your faith, I joy, and
Phil 2:30 supply your lack of *s* toward me
1Ti 6:2 but rather do them *s*, because
Heb 9:1 had also ordinances of divine *s*
Heb 9:6 accomplishing the *s* of God
Heb 9:9 make him that did the *s* perfect
Rev 2:19 know thy works, and charity, and *s*

### SERVING
Ex 14:5 we have let Israel go from *s* us
Deut 15:18 to thee, in *s* thee six years
Lk 10:40 Martha was cumbered about much *s*
Acts 20:19 *S* the Lord with all humility of
Acts 26:7 tribes, instantly *s* God day
Rom 12:11 fervent in spirit; *s* the Lord
Titus 3:3 *s* divers lusts and pleasures,

### SETH *(seth)* See SHETH. *A son of Adam and Eve.*
Gen 4:25 bare a son, and called his name *S*
Gen 4:26 And to *S*, to him also there was
Gen 5:3 and called his name *S*
Gen 5:4 *S* were eight hundred years
Gen 5:6 *S* lived an hundred and five years,
Gen 5:7 *S* lived after he begat Enos eight
Gen 5:8 all the days of *S* were nine
Lk 3:38 of Enos, which was the son of *S*

### SETHUR *(se'-thur) A spy sent to the Promised Land.*
Num 13:13 of Asher, *S* the son of Michael

### SETTLE
1Chr 17:14 But I will *s* him in mine house and
Eze 36:11 I will *s* you after your old
Eze 43:14 the lower *s* shall be two cubits
Eze 43:14 from the lesser *s* even to the
Eze 43:14 greater *s* shall be four cubits
Eze 43:17 the *s* shall be fourteen cubits
Eze 43:20 and on the four corners of the *s*
Eze 45:19 corners of the *s* of the altar
Lk 21:14 *S* it therefore in your hearts,
1Pet 5:10 stablish, strengthen, *s* you

### SETTLED
1Kin 8:13 a *s* place for thee to abide in
2Kin 8:11 he *s* his countenance stedfastly,
Ps 119:89 O LORD, thy word is *s* in heaven
Prov 8:25 Before the mountains were *s*
Jer 48:11 he hath *s* on his lees, and hath
Zeph 1:12 the men that are *s* on their lees
Col 1:23 in the faith grounded and *s*

### SEVEN
Gen 5:7 *s* years, and begat sons and
Gen 5:25 and *s* years, and begat Lamech
Gen 5:26 he begat Lamech *s* hundred eighty
Gen 5:31 *s* hundred seventy and *s* years
Gen 7:4 For yet *s* days, and I will cause
Gen 7:10 And it came to pass after *s* days
Gen 8:10 And he stayed yet other *s* days
Gen 8:12 And he stayed yet other *s* days
Gen 8:14 And in the second month, on the *s*
Gen 11:21 *s* years, and begat sons and
Gen 21:28 Abraham set *s* ewe lambs of the
Gen 21:29 What mean these *s* ewe lambs which
Gen 21:30 For these *s* ewe lambs shalt thou
Gen 23:1 And Sarah was an hundred and *s*
Gen 25:17 an hundred and thirty and *s* years
Gen 29:18 I will serve thee *s* years for
Gen 29:20 Jacob served *s* years for Rachel
Gen 29:27 serve with me yet *s* other years
Gen 29:30 served with him yet *s* other years
Gen 31:23 pursued after him *s* days' journey
Gen 33:3 himself to the ground *s* times
Gen 41:2 of the river *s* well favoured kine
Gen 41:3 *s* other kine came up after them
Gen 41:4 did eat up the *s* well favoured
Gen 41:5 *s* ears of corn came up upon one
Gen 41:6 *s* thin ears and blasted with the
Gen 41:7 the *s* thin ears devoured the
Gen 41:7 thin ears devoured the *s* rank
Gen 41:18 came up out of the river *s* kine
Gen 41:19 *s* other kine came up after them,
Gen 41:20 did eat up the first *s* fat kine
Gen 41:22 *s* ears came up in one stalk, full
Gen 41:23 *s* ears, withered, thin, and
Gen 41:24 ears devoured the *s* good ears
Gen 41:26 The *s* good kine are *s* years
Gen 41:26 the *s* good ears are *s* years
Gen 41:27 the *s* thin and ill favoured kine
Gen 41:27 came up after them are *s* years
Gen 41:27 the *s* empty ears blasted with the
Gen 41:27 wind shall be *s* years of famine
Gen 41:29 there come *s* years of great
Gen 41:30 after them *s* years of famine
Gen 41:34 of Egypt in the *s* plenteous years
Gen 41:36 against the *s* years of famine
Gen 41:47 in the *s* plenteous years the
Gen 41:48 up all the food of the *s* years
Gen 41:53 the *s* years of plenteousness,
Gen 41:54 the *s* years of dearth began to
Gen 46:25 all the souls were *s*
Gen 47:28 was an hundred forty and *s* years
Gen 50:10 a mourning for his father *s* days
Ex 2:16 priest of Midian had *s* daughters
Ex 6:16 were an hundred thirty and *s* years
Ex 6:20 an hundred and thirty and *s* years
Ex 7:25 *s* days were fulfilled, after that
Ex 12:15 *S* days shall ye eat unleavened
Ex 12:19 *S* days shall there be no leaven
Ex 13:6 *S* days thou shalt eat unleavened
Ex 13:7 bread shall be eaten *s* days
Ex 22:30 *s* days it shall be with his dam
Ex 23:15 shalt eat unleavened bread *s* days
Ex 25:37 shalt make the *s* lamps thereof
Ex 29:30 stead shall put them on *s* days

Ex 29:35 *s* days shalt thou consecrate them
Ex 29:37 *S* days thou shalt make an
Ex 34:18 *S* days thou shalt eat unleavened
Ex 37:23 And he made his *s* lamps, and his
Ex 38:24 *s* hundred and thirty shekels,
Ex 38:25 talents, and a thousand *s* hundred
Ex 38:28 of the thousand *s* hundred seventy
Lev 4:6 the blood *s* times before the LORD
Lev 4:17 sprinkle it *s* times before the
Lev 8:11 thereof upon the altar *s* times
Lev 8:33 of the congregation in *s* days
Lev 8:33 for *s* days shall he consecrate
Lev 8:35 congregation day and night *s* days
Lev 12:2 then she shall be unclean *s* days
Lev 13:4 him that hath the plague *s* days
Lev 13:5 shall shut him up *s* days more
Lev 13:21 priest shall shut him up *s* days
Lev 13:26 priest shall shut him up *s* days
Lev 13:31 the plague of the scall *s* days
Lev 13:33 that hath the scall *s* days more
Lev 13:50 up it that hath the plague *s* days
Lev 13:54 he shall shut it up *s* days more
Lev 14:7 cleansed from the leprosy *s* times
Lev 14:8 abroad out of his tent *s* days
Lev 14:16 finger *s* times before the LORD
Lev 14:27 left hand *s* times before the LORD
Lev 14:38 and shut up the house *s* days
Lev 14:51 and sprinkle the house *s* times
Lev 15:13 himself *s* days for his cleansing
Lev 15:19 she shall be put apart *s* days
Lev 15:24 him, he shall be unclean *s* days
Lev 15:28 shall number to herself *s* days
Lev 16:14 the blood with his finger *s* times
Lev 16:19 upon it with his finger *s* times
Lev 22:27 then it shall be *s* days under the
Lev 23:6 *s* days ye must eat unleavened
Lev 23:8 made by fire unto the LORD *s* days
Lev 23:15 *s* sabbaths shall be complete
Lev 23:18 *s* lambs without blemish of the
Lev 23:34 for *s* days unto the LORD
Lev 23:36 *S* days ye shall offer an offering
Lev 23:39 keep a feast unto the LORD *s* days
Lev 23:40 before the LORD your God *s* days
Lev 23:41 unto the LORD *s* days in the year
Lev 23:42 Ye shall dwell in booths *s* days
Lev 25:8 thou shalt number *s* sabbaths of
Lev 25:8 unto thee, *s* times *s* years
Lev 25:8 the space of the *s* sabbaths of
Lev 26:18 then I will punish you *s* times
Lev 26:21 I will bring *s* times more plagues
Lev 26:24 you yet *s* times for your sins
Lev 26:28 will chastise you *s* times for
Num 1:31 *s* thousand and four hundred
Num 1:39 and two thousand and *s* hundred
Num 2:8 *s* thousand and four hundred
Num 2:26 and two thousand and *s* hundred
Num 2:31 *s* thousand and six hundred
Num 3:22 numbered of them were *s* thousand
Num 4:36 were two thousand *s* hundred
Num 8:2 the *s* lamps shall give light over
Num 12:14 should she not be ashamed *s* days
Num 12:14 be shut out from the camp *s* days
Num 12:15 was shut out from the camp *s* days
Num 13:22 (Now Hebron was built *s* years
Num 16:49 *s* hundred, beside them that died
Num 19:4 of the congregation *s* times
Num 19:11 any man shall be unclean *s* days
Num 19:14 the tent, shall be unclean *s* days
Num 19:16 a grave, shall be unclean *s* days
Num 23:1 Balak, Build me here *s* altars
Num 23:1 me here *s* oxen and *s* rams
Num 23:4 him, I have prepared *s* altars
Num 23:14 built *s* altars, and offered a
Num 23:29 Balak, Build me here *s* altars
Num 23:29 me here *s* bullocks and *s* rams
Num 26:7 thousand and *s* hundred and thirty
Num 26:34 and two thousand and *s* hundred
Num 26:51 thousand and a thousand *s* hundred
Num 28:11 *s* lambs of the first year without
Num 28:17 *s* days shall unleavened bread be
Num 28:19 *s* lambs of the first year
Num 28:21 lamb, throughout the *s* lambs
Num 28:24 daily, throughout the *s* days
Num 28:27 *s* lambs of the first year
Num 28:29 one lamb, throughout the *s* lambs
Num 29:2 *s* lambs of the first year without
Num 29:4 one lamb, throughout the *s* lambs
Num 29:8 *s* lambs of the first year
Num 29:10 one lamb, throughout the *s* lambs
Num 29:12 keep a feast unto the LORD *s* days
Num 29:32 And on the seventh day *s* bullocks
Num 29:36 *s* lambs of the first year without
Num 31:19 ye abide without the camp *s* days
Num 31:36 three hundred thousand and *s*
Num 31:43 *s* thousand and five hundred sheep,
Num 31:52 was sixteen thousand *s* hundred
Deut 7:1 *s* nations greater and mightier
Deut 15:1 At the end of every *s* years thou
Deut 16:3 *s* days shalt thou eat unleavened
Deut 16:4 with thee in all thy coast *s* days
Deut 16:9 *S* weeks shalt thou number unto
Deut 16:9 begin to number the *s* weeks from
Deut 16:13 the feast of tabernacles *s* days
Deut 16:15 *S* days shalt thou keep a solemn
Deut 28:7 way, and flee before thee *s* ways
Deut 28:25 them, and flee *s* ways before them
Deut 31:10 At the end of every *s* years
Josh 6:4 *s* priests shall bear before the
Josh 6:4 the ark *s* trumpets of rams' horns
Josh 6:4 ye shall compass the city *s* times
Josh 6:6 let *s* priests bear *s* trumpets
Josh 6:8 the *s* priests bearing the *s*
Josh 6:13 *s* priests bearing *s* trumpets
Josh 6:15 after the same manner *s* times
Josh 6:15 they compassed the city *s* times
Josh 18:2 the children of Israel *s* tribes
Josh 18:5 they shall divide it into *s* parts
Josh 18:6 describe the land into *s* parts
Josh 18:9 by cities into *s* parts in a book
Judg 6:1 into the hand of Midian *s* years
Judg 6:25 the second bullock of *s* years old
Judg 8:26 *s* hundred shekels of gold
Judg 12:9 And he judged Israel *s* years
Judg 14:12 me within the *s* days of the feast
Judg 14:17 And she wept before him the *s* days
Judg 16:7 If they bind me with *s* green
Judg 16:8 Philistines brought up to her *s*
Judg 16:13 If thou weavest the *s* locks of my
Judg 16:19 shave off the *s* locks of his head
Judg 20:15 numbered *s* hundred chosen men
Judg 20:16 all this people there were *s*
Ruth 4:15 is better to thee than *s* sons
1Sa 2:5 so that the barren hath born *s*
1Sa 6:1 of the Philistines *s* months
1Sa 10:8 *s* days shalt thou tarry, till I
1Sa 11:3 Give us *s* days' respite, that we
1Sa 13:8 And he tarried *s* days, according
1Sa 16:10 Jesse made *s* of his sons to pass
1Sa 31:13 tree at Jabesh, and fasted *s* days
2Sa 2:11 the house of Judah was *s* years
2Sa 5:5 he reigned over Judah *s* years
2Sa 8:4 *s* hundred horsemen, and twenty
2Sa 10:18 David slew the men of *s* hundred
2Sa 21:6 Let *s* men of his sons be
2Sa 21:9 and they fell all *s* together
2Sa 23:39 thirty and *s* in all
2Sa 24:13 Shall *s* years of famine come unto
1Kin 2:11 *s* years reigned he in Hebron, and
1Kin 6:6 and the third was *s* cubits broad
1Kin 6:38 So was he *s* years in building it
1Kin 7:17 *s* for the one chapiter
1Kin 7:17 and *s* for the other chapiter
1Kin 8:65 *s* days and *s* days, even
1Kin 11:3 And he had *s* hundred wives,
1Kin 16:15 did Zimri reign *s* days in Tirzah
1Kin 18:43 And he said, Go again *s* times
1Kin 19:18 have left me *s* thousand in Israel
1Kin 20:15 of Israel, being *s* thousand
1Kin 20:29 one over against the other *s* days
1Kin 20:30 *s* thousand of the men that were
2Kin 3:9 a compass of *s* days' journey
2Kin 3:26 he took with him *s* hundred men
2Kin 4:35 and the child sneezed *s* times
2Kin 5:10 Go and wash in Jordan *s* times
2Kin 5:14 dipped himself *s* times in Jordan,
2Kin 8:1 also come upon the land *s* years
2Kin 8:2 land of the Philistines *s* years
2Kin 8:3 came to pass at the *s* years' end
2Kin 11:21 *S* years old was Jehoash when he
2Kin 24:16 even *s* thousand, and craftsmen and
2Kin 25:27 And it came to pass in the *s*
2Kin 25:27 in the twelfth month, on the *s*
1Chr 3:4 and there he reigned *s* years
1Chr 3:24 Johanan, and Dalaiah, and Anani, *s*
1Chr 5:13 and Jachan, and Zia, and Heber, *s*
1Chr 5:18 four and forty thousand *s* hundred
1Chr 7:5 fourscore and *s* thousand
1Chr 9:13 and *s* hundred and threescore
1Chr 9:25 were to come after *s* days from
1Chr 10:12 oak in Jabesh, and fasted *s* days
1Chr 12:25 *s* thousand and one hundred
1Chr 12:27 were three thousand and *s* hundred
1Chr 12:34 and spear thirty and *s* thousand
1Chr 15:26 offered *s* bullocks and *s* rams
1Chr 18:4 *s* thousand horsemen, and twenty
1Chr 19:18 David slew of the Syrians *s*
1Chr 26:30 *s* hundred, were officers among
1Chr 26:32 *s* hundred chief fathers, whom
1Chr 29:4 *s* thousand talents of refined
1Chr 29:27 *s* years reigned he in Hebron, and
2Chr 7:8 Solomon kept the feast *s* days
2Chr 7:9 dedication of the altar *s* days
2Chr 7:9 *s* days, and the feast *s* days
2Chr 13:9 *s* rams, the same may be a priest
2Chr 15:11 *s* hundred oxen and *s* thousand
2Chr 17:11 *s* thousand and *s* hundred rams,
2Chr 17:11 *s* thousand and *s* hundred he
2Chr 24:1 Joash was *s* years old when he
2Chr 26:13 *s* thousand and five hundred, that
2Chr 29:21 And they brought *s* bullocks
2Chr 29:21 *s* rams, and *s* lambs
2Chr 29:21 *s* he goats, for a sin offering
2Chr 30:21 bread *s* days with great gladness
2Chr 30:22 eat throughout the feast *s* days
2Chr 30:23 took counsel to keep other *s* days
2Chr 30:23 they kept other *s* days with
2Chr 30:24 bullocks and *s* thousand sheep
2Chr 35:17 feast of unleavened bread *s* days
Ezr 2:5 *s* hundred seventy and five
Ezr 2:9 Zaccai, *s* hundred and threescore
Ezr 2:25 *s* hundred and forty and three
Ezr 2:33 and Ono, *s* hundred twenty and five
Ezr 2:38 a thousand two hundred forty and *s*
Ezr 2:65 of whom there were *s* thousand
Ezr 2:65 three hundred thirty and *s*
Ezr 2:66 horses were *s* hundred thirty
Ezr 2:67 asses, six thousand *s* hundred
Ezr 6:22 unleavened bread *s* days with joy
Ezr 7:14 of his *s* counsellors, to enquire
Ezr 8:35 *s* lambs, twelve he goats for a
Neh 7:14 Zaccai, *s* hundred and threescore
Neh 7:18 six hundred threescore and *s*
Neh 7:19 two thousand threescore and *s*
Neh 7:29 Beeroth, *s* hundred forty and three
Neh 7:37 and Ono, *s* hundred twenty and one
Neh 7:41 a thousand two hundred forty and *s*
Neh 7:67 of whom there were *s* thousand
Neh 7:67 three hundred thirty and *s*
Neh 7:68 horses, *s* hundred thirty and six
Neh 7:69 six thousand *s* hundred and twenty
Neh 7:72 threescore and *s* priests' garments
Neh 8:18 And they kept the feast *s* days
Est 1:1 Ethiopia, over an hundred and *s*
Est 1:5 *s* days, in the court of the
Est 1:10 the *s* chamberlains that served in
Est 1:14 the *s* princes of Persia and Media,
Est 2:9 *s* maidens, which were meet to be
Est 8:9 *s* provinces, unto every province
Est 9:30 *s* provinces of the kingdom of
Job 1:2 there were born unto him *s* sons
Job 1:3 also was *s* thousand sheep
Job 2:13 with him upon the ground *s* days
Job 2:13 *s* nights, and none spake a word
Job 5:19 in *s* there shall no evil touch
Job 42:8 take unto you now *s* bullocks
Job 42:8 *s* rams, and go to my servant Job,
Job 42:13 He had also *s* sons and three
Ps 12:6 of earth, purified *s* times
Ps 119:164 *S* times a day do I praise thee
Prov 6:16 *s* are an abomination unto him
Prov 9:1 she hath hewn out her *s* pillars
Prov 24:16 For a just man falleth *s* times
Prov 26:16 *s* men that can render a reason
Prov 26:25 for there are *s* abominations in
Eccl 11:2 Give a portion to *s*, and also to
Is 4:1 in that day *s* women shall take
Is 11:15 shall smite it in the *s* streams
Is 30:26 sevenfold, as the light of *s* days
Jer 15:9 She that hath borne *s* languisheth
Jer 34:14 At the end of *s* years let ye go
Jer 52:25 *s* men of them that were near the
Jer 52:30 of the Jews *s* hundred forty
Jer 52:31 And it came to pass in the *s*
Eze 3:15 astonished among them *s* days
Eze 3:16 came to pass at the end of *s* days
Eze 29:17 And it came to pass in the *s*
Eze 39:9 shall burn them with fire *s* years
Eze 39:12 *s* months shall the house of
Eze 39:14 after the end of *s* months shall
Eze 40:22 they went up unto it by *s* steps

Eze 40:26 there were *s* steps to go up to it
Eze 41:3 the breadth of the door, *s* cubits
Eze 43:25 *S* days shalt thou prepare every
Eze 43:26 *S* days shall they purge the altar
Eze 44:26 they shall reckon unto him *s* days
Eze 45:21 the passover, a feast of *s* days
Eze 45:23 *s* days of the feast he shall
Eze 45:23 *s* bullocks and *s* rams without
Eze 45:23 *s* rams without blemish daily the
Eze 45:23 without blemish daily the *s* days
Eze 45:25 like in the feast of the *s* days
Dan 3:19 should heat the furnace one *s*
Dan 4:16 let *s* times pass over him
Dan 4:23 till *s* times pass over him
Dan 4:25 *s* times shall pass over thee,
Dan 4:32 *s* times shall pass over thee,
Dan 9:25 the Prince shall be *s* weeks
Amos 5:8 Seek him that maketh the *s* stars
Mic 5:5 we raise against him *s* shepherds
Zec 3:9 upon one stone shall be *s* eyes
Zec 4:2 his *s* lamps thereon
Zec 4:2 and *s* pipes to the *s* lamps
Zec 4:10 hand of Zerubbabel with those *s*
Mt 12:45 taketh with himself *s* other
Mt 15:34 And they said, *S*, and a few little
Mt 15:36 And he took the *s* loaves and the
Mt 15:37 meat that was left *s* baskets full
Mt 16:10 Neither the *s* loaves of the four
Mt 18:21 till *s* times
Mt 18:22 say not unto thee, Until *s* times
Mt 18:22 but, Until seventy times *s*
Mt 22:25 Now there were with us *s* brethren
Mt 22:28 whose wife shall she be of the *s*
Mk 8:5 And they said, *S*
Mk 8:6 and he took the *s* loaves, and gave
Mk 8:8 meat that was left *s* baskets
Mk 8:20 when the *s* among four thousand,
Mk 8:20 And they said, *S*
Mk 12:20 Now there were *s* brethren
Mk 12:22 the *s* had her, and left no seed
Mk 12:23 for the *s* had her to wife
Mk 16:9 out of whom he had cast *s* devils
Lk 2:36 *s* years from her virginity
Lk 8:2 out of whom went *s* devils
Lk 11:26 taketh to him *s* other spirits
Lk 17:4 against thee *s* times in a day
Lk 17:4 *s* times in a day turn again to
Lk 20:29 There were therefore *s* brethren
Lk 20:31 and in like manner the *s* also
Lk 20:33 for *s* had her to wife
Acts 6:3 among you *s* men of honest report
Acts 13:19 when he had destroyed *s* nations
Acts 19:14 there were *s* sons of one Sceva, a
Acts 20:6 where we abode *s* days
Acts 21:4 we tarried there *s* days
Acts 21:8 which was one of the *s*
Acts 21:27 when the *s* days were almost ended
Acts 28:14 desired to tarry with them *s* days
Rom 11:4 reserved to myself *s* thousand men
Heb 11:30 they were compassed about *s* days
Rev 1:4 John to the *s* churches which are
Rev 1:4 from the *s* Spirits which are
Rev 1:11 send it unto the *s* churches which
Rev 1:12 I saw *s* golden candlesticks
Rev 1:13 And in the midst of the *s*
Rev 1:16 he had in his right hand *s* stars
Rev 1:20 The mystery of the *s* stars which
Rev 1:20 the *s* golden candlesticks
Rev 1:20 The *s* stars are the angels of the
Rev 1:20 are the angels of the *s* churches
Rev 1:20 the *s* candlesticks which thou
Rev 1:20 thou sawest are the *s* churches
Rev 2:1 the *s* stars in his right hand
Rev 2:1 of the *s* golden candlesticks
Rev 3:1 he that hath the *s* Spirits of God
Rev 3:1 Spirits of God, and the *s* stars
Rev 4:5 there were *s* lamps of fire
Rev 4:5 which are the *s* Spirits of God
Rev 5:1 the backside, sealed with *s* seals
Rev 5:5 to loose the *s* seals thereof
Rev 5:6 it had been slain, having *s* horns
Rev 5:6 horns and *s* eyes, which are
Rev 5:6 which are the *s* Spirits of God
Rev 8:2 I saw the *s* angels which stood
Rev 8:2 and to them were given *s* trumpets
Rev 8:6 the *s* angels which had the *s*
Rev 10:3 *s* thunders uttered their voices
Rev 10:4 when the *s* thunders had uttered
Rev 10:4 which the *s* thunders uttered
Rev 11:13 were slain of men *s* thousand
Rev 12:3 great red dragon, having *s* heads
Rev 12:3 horns, and *s* crowns upon his heads
Rev 13:1 up out of the sea, having *s* heads
Rev 15:1 *s* angels having the *s* last
Rev 15:6 the *s* angels came out of the
Rev 15:6 the temple, having the *s* plagues
Rev 15:7 gave unto the *s* angels *s*
Rev 15:8 till the *s* plagues of the *s*
Rev 16:1 the temple saying to the *s* angels
Rev 17:1 there came one of the *s* angels
Rev 17:1 angels which had the *s* vials
Rev 17:3 of blasphemy, having *s* heads
Rev 17:7 her, which hath the *s* heads
Rev 17:9 The *s* heads are *s* mountains,
Rev 17:10 And there are *s* kings
Rev 17:11 he is the eighth, and is of the *s*
Rev 21:9 the *s* angels which had the
Rev 21:9 *s* vials full of the *s* last

## SEVENFOLD

Gen 4:15 vengeance shall be taken on him *s*
Gen 4:24 If Cain shall be avenged *s*
Gen 4:24 truly Lamech seventy and *s*
Ps 79:12 render unto our neighbours *s* into
Prov 6:31 he be found, he shall restore *s*
Is 30:26 the light of the sun shall be *s*

## SEVENTEEN

Gen 37:2 being *s* years old, was feeding
Gen 47:28 in the land of Egypt *s* years
Judg 8:14 thereof, even threescore and *s* men
1Kin 14:21 he reigned *s* years in Jerusalem,
2Kin 13:1 in Samaria, and reigned *s* years
1Chr 7:11 were *s* thousand and two hundred
2Chr 12:13 he reigned *s* years in Jerusalem,
Ezr 2:39 of Harim, a thousand and *s*
Neh 7:42 of Harim, a thousand and *s*
Jer 32:9 money, even *s* shekels of silver

## SEVENTEENTH

Gen 7:11 the *s* day of the month, the same
Gen 8:4 on the *s* day of the month, upon
1Kin 22:51 over Israel in Samaria the *s* year
2Kin 16:1 In the *s* year of Pekah the son of
1Chr 24:15 The *s* to Hezir, the eighteenth to
1Chr 25:24 The *s* to Joshbekashah, he, his

## SEVENTH

Gen 2:2 on the *s* day God ended his work
Gen 2:2 he rested on the *s* day from all
Gen 2:3 And God blessed the *s* day, and
Gen 8:4 And the ark rested in the *s* month
Ex 12:15 the first day until the *s* day
Ex 12:16 in the *s* day there shall be an
Ex 13:6 in the *s* day shall be a feast to
Ex 16:26 but on the *s* day, which is the
Ex 16:27 people on the *s* day for to gather
Ex 16:29 go out of his place on the *s* day
Ex 16:30 So the people rested on the *s* day
Ex 20:10 But the *s* day is the sabbath of
Ex 20:11 in them is, and rested the *s* day
Ex 21:2 in the *s* he shall go out free for
Ex 23:11 But the *s* year thou shalt let it
Ex 23:12 on the *s* day thou shalt rest
Ex 24:16 the *s* day he called unto Moses
Ex 31:15 but in the *s* is the sabbath of
Ex 31:17 on the *s* day he rested, and was
Ex 34:21 but on the *s* day thou shalt rest
Ex 35:2 but on the *s* day there shall be
Lev 13:5 shall look on him the *s* day
Lev 13:6 shall look on him again the *s* day
Lev 13:27 shall look upon him the *s* day
Lev 13:32 in the *s* day the priest shall
Lev 13:34 in the *s* day the priest shall
Lev 13:51 look on the plague on the *s* day
Lev 14:9 But it shall be on the *s* day
Lev 14:39 priest shall come again the *s* day
Lev 16:29 that in the *s* month, on the tenth
Lev 23:3 but the *s* day is the sabbath of
Lev 23:8 in the *s* day is an holy
Lev 23:16 *s* sabbath shall ye number fifty
Lev 23:24 of Israel, saying, In the *s* month
Lev 23:27 *s* month there shall be a day of
Lev 23:34 The fifteenth day of this *s* month
Lev 23:39 the fifteenth day of the *s* month
Lev 23:41 shall celebrate it in the *s* month
Lev 25:4 But in the *s* year shall be a
Lev 25:9 on the tenth day of the *s* month
Lev 25:20 say, What shall we eat the *s* year
Num 6:9 on the *s* day shall he shave it
Num 7:48 On the *s* day Elishama the son of
Num 19:12 on the *s* day he shall be clean
Num 19:12 then the *s* day he shall not be
Num 19:19 on the third day, and on the *s* day
Num 19:19 on the *s* day he shall purify
Num 28:25 on the *s* day ye shall have an
Num 29:1 And in the *s* month, on the first
Num 29:7 this *s* month an holy convocation
Num 29:12 the *s* month ye shall have an holy
Num 29:32 on the *s* day seven bullocks, two
Num 31:19 on the third day, and on the *s* day
Num 31:24 wash your clothes on the *s* day
Deut 5:14 But the *s* day is the sabbath of
Deut 15:9 The *s* year, the year of release,
Deut 15:12 then in the *s* year thou shalt let
Deut 16:8 on the *s* day shall be a solemn
Josh 6:4 the *s* day ye shall compass the
Josh 6:15 And it came to pass on the *s* day
Josh 6:16 And it came to pass at the *s* time
Josh 19:40 the *s* lot came out for the tribe
Judg 14:15 And it came to pass on the *s* day
Judg 14:17 and it came to pass on the *s* day
Judg 14:18 *s* day before the sun went down
2Sa 12:18 And it came to pass on the *s* day
1Kin 8:2 Ethanim, which is the *s* month
1Kin 16:10 *s* year of Asa king of Judah, and
1Kin 16:15 *s* year of Asa king of Judah did
1Kin 18:44 And it came to pass at the *s* time
1Kin 20:29 that in the *s* day the battle was
2Kin 11:4 the *s* year Jehoiada sent and
2Kin 12:1 In the *s* year of Jehu Jehoash
2Kin 13:10 *s* year of Joash king of Judah
2Kin 15:1 *s* year of Jeroboam king of Israel
2Kin 18:9 which was the *s* year of Hoshea
2Kin 25:8 on the *s* day of the month, which
2Kin 25:25 it came to pass in the *s* month
1Chr 2:15 Ozem the sixth, David the *s*
1Chr 12:11 Attai the sixth, Eliel the *s*
1Chr 24:10 The *s* to Hakkoz, the eighth to
1Chr 25:14 The *s* to Jesharelah, he, his sons
1Chr 26:3 the sixth, Elioenai the *s*
1Chr 26:5 Ammiel the sixth, Issachar the *s*
1Chr 27:10 The *s* captain for the *s*
2Chr 5:3 feast which was in the *s* month
2Chr 7:10 twentieth day of the *s* month he
2Chr 23:1 And in the *s* year Jehoiada
2Chr 31:7 and finished them in the *s* month
Ezr 3:1 when the *s* month was come, and the
Ezr 3:6 From the first day of the *s* month
Ezr 7:7 in the *s* year of Artaxerxes the
Ezr 7:8 was in the *s* year of the king
Neh 7:73 when the *s* month came, the
Neh 8:2 upon the first day of the *s* month
Neh 8:14 in the feast of the *s* month
Neh 10:31 and that we would leave the *s* year
Est 1:10 On the *s* day, when the heart of
Est 2:16 in the *s* year of his reign
Jer 28:17 died the same year in the *s* month
Jer 41:1 it came to pass in the *s* month
Jer 52:28 in the *s* year three thousand Jews
Eze 20:1 And it came to pass in the *s* year
Eze 30:20 in the *s* day of the month, that
Eze 45:20 so thou shalt do the *s* day of the
Eze 45:25 In the *s* month, in the fifteenth
Hag 2:1 In the *s* month, in the one and
Zec 7:5 *s* month, even those seventy years
Zec 8:19 the fifth, and the fast of the *s*
Mt 22:26 also, and the third, unto the *s*
Jn 4:52 Yesterday at the *s* hour the fever
Heb 4:4 place of the *s* day on this wise
Heb 4:4 God did rest the *s* day from all
Jude 14 the *s* from Adam, prophesied of
Rev 8:1 And when he had opened the *s* seal
Rev 10:7 days of the voice of the *s* angel
Rev 11:15 And the *s* angel sounded
Rev 16:17 the *s* angel poured out his vial
Rev 21:20 the *s*, chrysolite

## SEVENTY

Gen 4:24 avenged sevenfold, truly Lamech *s*
Gen 5:12 And Cainan lived *s* years, and begat
Gen 5:31 of Lamech were seven hundred *s*
Gen 11:26 And Terah lived *s* years, and begat
Gen 12:4 and Abram was *s* and five years old
Ex 1:5 the loins of Jacob were *s* souls
Ex 24:1 *s* of the elders of Israel
Ex 24:9 *s* of the elders of Israel
Ex 38:28 of the thousand seven hundred *s*
Ex 38:29 of the offering was *s* talents
Num 7:13 one silver bowl of *s* shekels
Num 7:19 one silver bowl of *s* shekels
Num 7:25 one silver bowl of *s* shekels

Num 7:31 one silver bowl of *s* shekels
Num 7:37 one silver bowl of *s* shekels
Num 7:43 a silver bowl of *s* shekels
Num 7:49 one silver bowl of *s* shekels
Num 7:55 one silver bowl of *s* shekels
Num 7:61 one silver bowl of *s* shekels
Num 7:67 one silver bowl of *s* shekels
Num 7:73 one silver bowl of *s* shekels
Num 7:79 one silver bowl of *s* shekels
Num 7:85 and thirty shekels, each bowl *s*
Num 11:16 Gather unto me *s* men of the
Num 11:24 gathered the *s* men of the elders
Num 11:25 him, and gave it unto the *s* elders
Num 31:32 *s* thousand and five thousand sheep
Judg 9:56 father, in slaying his *s* brethren
2Sa 24:15 even to Beer-sheba *s* thousand men
2Kin 10:1 Ahab had *s* sons in Samaria
2Kin 10:6 being *s* persons, were with the
2Kin 10:7 slew *s* persons, and put their
1Chr 21:14 fell of Israel *s* thousand men
Ezr 2:3 Parosh, two thousand an hundred *s*
Ezr 2:4 of Shephatiah, three hundred *s*
Ezr 2:5 children of Arah, seven hundred *s*
Ezr 2:36 house of Jeshua, nine hundred *s*
Ezr 2:40 of the children of Hodaviah, *s*
Ezr 8:7 of Athaliah, and with him *s* males
Ezr 8:14 and Zabbud, and with them *s* males
Ezr 8:35 all Israel, ninety and six rams, *s*
Neh 7:8 Parosh, two thousand an hundred *s*
Neh 7:9 of Shephatiah, three hundred *s*
Neh 7:39 house of Jeshua, nine hundred *s*
Neh 7:43 and of the children of Hodevah, *s*
Neh 11:19 kept the gates, were an hundred *s*
Est 9:16 enemies, and slew of their foes *s*
Is 23:15 Tyre shall be forgotten *s* years
Is 23:15 after the end of *s* years shall
Is 23:17 to pass after the end of *s* years
Jer 25:11 serve the king of Babylon *s* years
Jer 25:12 when *s* years are accomplished,
Jer 29:10 the LORD, That after *s* years be
Eze 8:11 there stood before them *s* men of
Eze 41:12 the west was *s* cubits broad
Dan 9:2 that he would accomplish *s* years
Dan 9:24 *S* weeks are determined upon thy
Zec 7:5 seventh month, even those *s* years
Mt 18:22 but, Until *s* times seven
Lk 10:1 the Lord appointed other *s* also
Lk 10:17 the *s* returned again with joy,

**SEVER**
Ex 8:22 I will *s* in that day the land of
Ex 9:4 the LORD shall *s* between the
Eze 39:14 they shall *s* out men of continual
Mt 13:49 *s* the wicked from among the just,

**SHAALABBIN** *(sha-al-ab'-bin)* See SHAALBIM. *A city in Dan.*
Josh 19:42 And *S*, and Ajalon, and Jethlah,

**SHAALBIM** *(sha-al'-bim)* See SHAALABBIN, SHAALBONITE. *Same as Shaalabbin.*
Judg 1:35 mount Heres in Aijalon, and in *S*
1Kin 4:9 son of Dekar, in Makaz, and in *S*

**SHAALBONITE** *(sha-al'-bo-nite) A native of Shaalabbin.*
2Sa 23:32 Eliahba the *S*, of the sons of
1Chr 11:33 the Baharumite, Eliahba the *S*

**SHAAPH** *(sha'-af) A son of Jahdai.*
1Chr 2:47 Gesham, and Pelet, and Ephah, and *S*
1Chr 2:49 She bare also *S* the father of

**SHAARAIM** *(sha-a-ra'-im)* See SHARAIM, SHARUHEN. *A city in Judah.*
1Sa 17:52 fell down by the way to *S*
1Chr 4:31 and at Beth-birei, and at *S*

**SHAASHGAZ** *(sha-ash'-gaz) A servant of King Ahasuerus.*
Est 2:14 of the women, to the custody of *S*

**SHABBETHAI** *(shab'-be-thahee)*
*1. A Levite who dealt with the foreign wife problem.*
Ezr 10:15 and *S* the Levite helped them
*2. A Levite who aided Ezra.*
Neh 8:7 and Sherebiah, Jamin, Akkub, *S*
*3. A family of exiles.*
Neh 11:16 And *S* and Jozabad, of the chief of

**SHACHIA** *(sha-ki'-ah) A son of Shaharaim.*
1Chr 8:10 And Jeuz, and *S*, and Mirma

**SHADOW**
Gen 19:8 came they under the *s* of my roof
Judg 9:15 come and put your trust in my *s*
Judg 9:36 Thou seest the *s* of the mountains
2Kin 20:9 shall the *s* go forward ten
2Kin 20:10 for the *s* to go down ten degrees
2Kin 20:10 but let the *s* return backward ten
2Kin 20:11 he brought the *s* ten degrees
1Chr 29:15 our days on the earth are as a *s*
Job 3:5 and the *s* of death stain it
Job 7:2 servant earnestly desireth the *s*
Job 8:9 our days upon earth are a *s*
Job 10:21 of darkness and the *s* of death
Job 10:22 of the *s* of death, without any
Job 12:22 out to light the *s* of death
Job 14:2 he fleeth also as a *s*, and
Job 16:16 on my eyelids is the *s* of death
Job 17:7 and all my members are as a *s*
Job 24:17 is to them even as the *s* of death
Job 24:17 in the terrors of the *s* of death
Job 28:3 of darkness, and the *s* of death
Job 34:22 nor *s* of death, where the workers
Job 38:17 seen the doors of the *s* of death
Job 40:22 trees cover him with their *s*
Ps 17:8 hide me under the *s* of thy wings
Ps 23:4 the valley of the *s* of death
Ps 36:7 trust under the *s* of thy wings
Ps 44:19 and covered us with the *s* of death
Ps 57:1 in the *s* of thy wings will I make
Ps 63:7 therefore in the *s* of thy wings
Ps 80:10 were covered with the *s* of it
Ps 91:1 abide under the *s* of the Almighty
Ps 102:11 days are like a *s* that declineth
Ps 107:10 in the *s* of death, being bound in
Ps 107:14 the *s* of death, and brake their
Ps 109:23 gone like the *s* when it declineth
Ps 144:4 days are as a *s* that passeth away
Eccl 6:12 life which he spendeth as a *s*
Eccl 8:13 his days, which are as a *s*
Song 2:3 under his *s* with great delight
Is 4:6 shall be a tabernacle for a *s* in
Is 9:2 in the land of the *s* of death
Is 16:3 make thy *s* as the night in the
Is 25:4 a *s* from the heat, when the blast
Is 25:5 the heat with the *s* of a cloud
Is 30:2 and to trust in the *s* of Egypt
Is 30:3 the trust in the *s* of Egypt your
Is 32:2 as the *s* of a great rock in a
Is 34:15 and hatch, and gather under her *s*
Is 38:8 bring again the *s* of the degrees
Is 49:2 in the *s* of his hand hath he hid
Is 51:16 thee in the *s* of mine hand
Jer 2:6 of the *s* of death, through a land
Jer 13:16 he turn it into the *s* of death
Jer 48:45 They that fled stood under the *s*
Lam 4:20 Under his *s* we shall live among
Eze 17:23 in the *s* of the branches thereof
Eze 31:6 under his *s* dwelt all great
Eze 31:12 earth are gone down from his *s*
Eze 31:17 that dwelt under his *s* in the
Dan 4:12 of the field had *s* under it
Hos 4:13 because the *s* thereof is good
Hos 14:7 dwell under his *s* shall return
Amos 5:8 turneth the *s* of death into the
Jonah 4:5 a booth, and sat under it in the *s*
Jonah 4:6 it might be a *s* over his head
Mt 4:16 *s* of death light is sprung up
Mk 4:32 air may lodge under the *s* of it
Lk 1:79 in the *s* of death, to guide our
Acts 5:15 that at the least the *s* of Peter
Col 2:17 Which are a *s* of things to come
Heb 8:5 *s* of heavenly things, as Moses
Heb 10:1 For the law having a *s* of good
Jas 1:17 neither *s* of turning

**SHADRACH** *(sha'-drak)* See HANANIAH. *A companion of Daniel.*
Dan 1:7 and to Hananiah, of *S*
Dan 2:49 of the king, and he set *S*, Meshach
Dan 3:12 of the province of Babylon, *S*
Dan 3:13 rage and fury commanded to bring *S*
Dan 3:14 said unto them, Is it true, O *S*
Dan 3:16 *S*, Meshach, and Abed-nego,
Dan 3:19 his visage was changed against *S*
Dan 3:20 that were in his army to bind *S*
Dan 3:22 slew those men that took up *S*
Dan 3:23 And these three men, *S*, Meshach,
Dan 3:26 furnace, and spake, and said, *S*
Dan 3:26 Then *S*, Meshach, and Abed-nego,
Dan 3:28 and said, Blessed be the God of *S*
Dan 3:29 thing amiss against the God of *S*
Dan 3:30 Then the king promoted *S*, Meshach

**SHAFT**
Ex 25:31 his *s*, and his branches, his bowls
Ex 37:17 his *s*, and his branch, his bowls,
Num 8:4 beaten gold, unto the *s* thereof
Is 49:2 hid me, and made me a polished *s*

**SHAGE** *(sha'-ghe) A "mighty man" of David.*
1Chr 11:34 the son of *S* the Hararite

**SHAHAR** *(sha'-har) A musical notation.*
Ps 22:t chief Musician upon Aijeleth *S*

**SHAHARAIM** *(sha-ha-ra'-im) A Benjamite from Moab.*
1Chr 8:8 *S* begat children in the country

**SHAHAZIMAH** *(sha-haz'-i-mah) A city in Issachar.*
Josh 19:22 the coast reacheth to Tabor, and *S*

**SHAKE**
Judg 16:20 other times before, and *s* myself
Neh 5:13 So God *s* out every man from his
Job 4:14 which made all my bones to *s*
Job 15:33 He shall *s* off his unripe grape
Job 16:4 you, and *s* mine head at you
Ps 22:7 the lip, they *s* the head, saying,
Ps 46:3 though the mountains *s* with the
Ps 69:23 make their loins continually to *s*
Ps 72:16 thereof shall *s* like Lebanon
Is 2:19 ariseth to *s* terribly the earth
Is 2:21 ariseth to *s* terribly the earth
Is 10:15 as if the rod should *s* itself
Is 10:32 he shall *s* his hand against the
Is 11:15 he *s* his hand over the river
Is 13:2 *s* the hand, that they may go into
Is 13:13 Therefore I will *s* the heavens
Is 14:16 to tremble, that did *s* kingdoms
Is 24:18 the foundations of the earth do *s*
Is 33:9 Carmel *s* off their fruits
Is 52:2 *S* thyself from the dust
Jer 23:9 all my bones *s*
Eze 26:10 thy walls shall *s* at the noise of
Eze 26:15 Shall not the isles *s* at the
Eze 27:28 The suburbs shall *s* at the sound
Eze 31:16 I made the nations to *s* at the
Eze 38:20 shall *s* at my presence, and the
Dan 4:14 *s* off his leaves, and scatter his
Joel 3:16 the heavens and the earth shall *s*
Amos 9:1 of the door, that the posts may *s*
Hag 2:6 I will *s* the heavens, and the
Hag 2:7 I will *s* all nations, and the
Hag 2:21 I will *s* the heavens and the earth
Zec 2:9 I will *s* mine hand upon them, and
Mt 10:14 *s* off the dust of your feet
Mt 28:4 for fear of him the keepers did *s*
Mk 6:11 *s* off the dust under your feet
Lk 6:48 that house, and could not *s* it
Lk 9:5 *s* off the very dust from your
Heb 12:26 Yet once more I *s* not the earth

**SHAKEN**
Lev 26:36 the sound of a *s* leaf shall chase
1Kin 14:15 as a reed is *s* in the water
2Kin 19:21 Jerusalem hath *s* her head at thee
Neh 5:13 promise, even thus be he *s* out
Job 16:12 *s* me to pieces, and set me up for
Job 38:13 the wicked might be *s* out of it
Ps 18:7 also of the hills moved and were *s*
Is 37:22 Jerusalem hath *s* her head at thee
Nah 2:3 the fir trees shall be terribly *s*
Nah 3:12 if they be *s*, they shall even
Mt 11:7 A reed *s* with the wind
Mt 24:29 powers of the heavens shall be *s*
Mk 13:25 that are in heaven shall be *s*
Lk 6:38 *s* together, and running over,
Lk 7:24 A reed *s* with the wind
Lk 21:26 the powers of heaven shall be *s*
Acts 4:31 the place was *s* where they were
Acts 16:26 foundations of the prison were *s*
2Th 2:2 That ye be not soon *s* in mind
Heb 12:27 of those things that are *s*
Heb 12:27 which cannot be *s* may remain
Rev 6:13 when she is *s* of a mighty wind

**SHAKETH**
Job 9:6 Which *s* the earth out of her
Ps 29:8 of the LORD *s* the wilderness
Ps 29:8 the LORD *s* the wilderness of
Ps 60:2 thereof; for it *s*
Is 10:15 itself against him that *s* it

Is 19:16 LORD of hosts, which he s over it
Is 33:15 that s his hands from holding of

**SHAKING**
Job 41:29 he laugheth at the s of a spear
Ps 44:14 a s of the head among the people
Is 17:6 as the s of an olive tree, two or
Is 19:16 fear because of the s of the hand
Is 24:13 be as the s of an olive tree
Is 30:32 in battles of s will he fight
Eze 37:7 there was a noise, and behold a s
Eze 38:19 a great s in the land of Israel

**SHALEM** *(sha'-lem) A city in Ephraim.*
Gen 33:18 And Jacob came to S, a city of

**SHALIM** *(sha'-lim) A district in Dan.*
1Sa 9:4 they passed through the land of S

**SHALISHA** *(shal'-i-shah) A district in Ephraim.*
1Sa 9:4 and passed through the land of S

**SHALLECHETH** *(shal'-le-keth) A gate of the First Temple.*
1Chr 26:16 forth westward, with the gate S

**SHALLUM** *(shal'-lum)* See JEHOAHAZ, MESHELEMIAH, SHILLEM.
*1. A king of Israel.*
2Kin 15:10 S the son of Jabesh conspired
2Kin 15:13 S the son of Jabesh began to
2Kin 15:14 smote S the son of Jabesh in
2Kin 15:15 And the rest of the acts of S
*2. Husband of Huldah.*
2Kin 22:14 the wife of S the son of Tikvah,
2Chr 34:22 the wife of S the son of Tikvath,
*3. A descendant of Jerahmeel.*
1Chr 2:40 begat Sisamai, and Sisamai begat S
1Chr 2:41 S begat Jekamiah, and Jekamiah
*4. A son of King Josiah.*
1Chr 3:15 the third Zedekiah, the fourth S
Jer 22:11 thus saith the LORD touching S
*5. Grandson of Simeon.*
1Chr 4:25 S his son, Mibsam his son, Mishma
*6. Father of Hilkiah.*
1Chr 6:12 begat Zadok, and Zadok begat S
1Chr 6:13 S begat Hilkiah, and Hilkiah begat
Ezr 7:2 The son of S, the son of Zadok,
*7. Son of Naphtali.*
1Chr 7:13 Jahziel, and Guni, and Jezer, and S
*8. A family of exiles.*
1Chr 9:17 And the porters were, S, and Akkub,
1Chr 9:17 S was the chief
1Chr 9:19 S the son of Kore, the son of
1Chr 9:31 the firstborn of S the Korahite
Ezr 2:42 the children of S, the children
Neh 7:45 the children of S, the children
*9. Father of Jehizkiah.*
2Chr 28:12 and Jehizkiah the son of S
*10. A gatekeeper who married a foreigner.*
Ezr 10:24 S, and Telem, and Uri
*11. A son of Bani who married a foreigner.*
Ezr 10:42 S, Amariah, and Joseph
*12. A rebuilder of Jerusalem's wall.*
Neh 3:12 repaired S the son of Halohesh
*13. Father of Hanameel.*
Jer 32:7 Hanameel the son of S thine uncle
*14. Father of Maaseiah.*
Jer 35:4 chamber of Maaseiah the son of S

**SHALLUN** *(shal'-lun) A rebuilder of Jerusalem's wall.*
Neh 3:15 repaired S the son of Colhozeh

**SHALMAI** *(shal'-mahee) A family of exiles.*
Ezr 2:46 of Hagab, the children of S
Neh 7:48 of Hagaba, the children of S

**SHALMAN** *(shal'-man)* See SHALMANESER. *A king of Assyria.*
Hos 10:14 as S spoiled Beth-arbel in the

**SHALMANESER** *(shal-man-e'-zer)* See SHALMAN. *A king of Assyria.*
2Kin 17:3 him came up S king of Assyria
2Kin 18:9 that S king of Assyria came up

**SHAMA** *(sha'-mah) A "mighty man" of David.*
1Chr 11:44 Uzzia the Ashterathite, S

**SHAMARIAH** *Son of Rehoboam.*
2Chr 11:19 Jeush, and S, and Zaham

**SHAME**
Ex 32:25 unto their s among their enemies
Judg 18:7 might put them to s in any thing
1Sa 20:34 because his father had done him s
2Sa 13:13 whither shall I cause my s to go
2Chr 32:21 So he returned with s of face to
Job 8:22 hate thee shall be clothed with s
Ps 4:2 long will ye turn my glory into s
Ps 35:4 put to s that seek after my soul
Ps 35:26 let them be clothed with s
Ps 40:14 put to s that wish me evil
Ps 40:15 of their s that say unto me
Ps 44:7 hast put them to s that hated us
Ps 44:9 hast cast off, and put us to s
Ps 44:15 the s of my face hath covered me,
Ps 53:5 thou hast put them to s, because
Ps 69:7 s hath covered my face
Ps 69:19 hast known my reproach, and my s
Ps 70:3 for a reward of their s that say
Ps 71:24 for they are brought unto s
Ps 83:16 Fill their faces with s
Ps 83:17 yea, let them be put to s
Ps 89:45 thou hast covered him with s
Ps 109:29 adversaries be clothed with s
Ps 119:31 O LORD, put me not to s
Ps 132:18 His enemies will I clothe with s
Prov 3:35 but s shall be the promotion of
Prov 9:7 a scorner getteth to himself s
Prov 10:5 harvest is a son that causeth s
Prov 11:2 When pride cometh, then cometh s
Prov 12:16 but a prudent man covereth s
Prov 13:5 man is loathsome, and cometh to s
Prov 13:18 s shall be to him that refuseth
Prov 14:35 is against him that causeth s
Prov 17:2 rule over a son that causeth s
Prov 18:13 it, it is folly and s unto him
Prov 19:26 mother, is a son that causeth s
Prov 25:8 thy neighbour hath put thee to s
Prov 25:10 he that heareth it put thee to s
Prov 29:15 himself bringeth his mother to s
Is 20:4 uncovered, to the s of Egypt
Is 22:18 be the s of thy lord's house
Is 30:3 the strength of Pharaoh be your s
Is 30:5 be an help nor profit, but a s
Is 47:3 yea, thy s shall be seen
Is 50:6 I hid not my face from s and
Is 54:4 for thou shalt not be put to s
Is 54:4 shalt forget the s of thy youth
Is 61:7 For your s ye shall have double
Jer 3:24 For s hath devoured the labour of
Jer 3:25 We lie down in our s, and our
Jer 13:26 thy face, that thy s may appear
Jer 20:18 my days should be consumed with s
Jer 23:40 upon you, and a perpetual s
Jer 46:12 The nations have heard of thy s
Jer 48:39 hath Moab turned the back with s
Jer 51:51 s hath covered our faces
Eze 7:18 s shall be upon all faces, and
Eze 16:52 bear thine own s for thy sins
Eze 16:52 confounded also, and bear thy s
Eze 16:54 That thou mayest bear thine own s
Eze 16:63 mouth any more because of thy s
Eze 32:24 yet have they borne their s with
Eze 32:25 yet have they borne their s with
Eze 32:30 bear their s with them that go
Eze 34:29 neither bear the s of the heathen
Eze 36:6 have borne the s of the heathen
Eze 36:7 you, they shall bear their s
Eze 36:15 the s of the heathen any more
Eze 39:26 that they have borne their s
Eze 44:13 but they shall bear their s
Dan 12:2 to everlasting life, and some to s
Hos 4:7 will I change their glory into s
Hos 4:18 her rulers with s do love
Hos 9:10 separated themselves unto that s
Hos 10:6 Ephraim shall receive s, and
Obad 10 brother Jacob s shall cover thee
Mic 1:11 of Saphir, having thy s naked
Mic 2:6 them, that they shall not take s
Mic 7:10 s shall cover her which said unto
Nah 3:5 nakedness, and the kingdoms thy s
Hab 2:10 Thou hast consulted s to thy
Hab 2:16 Thou art filled with s for glory
Zeph 3:5 but the unjust knoweth no s
Zeph 3:19 where they have been put to s
Lk 14:9 thou begin with s to take the
Acts 5:41 worthy to suffer s for his name
1Cor 4:14 I write not these things to s you
1Cor 6:5 I speak to your s
1Cor 11:6 but if it be a s for a woman to
1Cor 11:14 long hair, it is a s unto him
1Cor 11:22 of God, and s them that have not
1Cor 14:35 for it is a s for women to speak
1Cor 15:34 I speak this to your s
Eph 5:12 For it is a s even to speak of
Phil 3:19 and whose glory is in their s
Heb 6:6 afresh, and put him to an open s
Heb 12:2 the cross, despising the s
Jude 13 the sea, foaming out their own s
Rev 3:18 that the s of thy nakedness do
Rev 16:15 he walk naked, and they see his s

**SHAMED** *(sha'-med) A son of Elpaal.*
Gen 38:23 her take it to her, lest we be s
2Sa 19:5 said Thou hast s this day the
1Chr 8:12 Eber, and Misham, and S, who built
Ps 14:6 Ye have s the counsel of the poor

**SHAMEFULLY**
Hos 2:5 that conceived them hath done s
Mk 12:4 head, and sent him away s handled
Lk 20:11 beat him also, and entreated him s
1Th 2:2 were s entreated, as ye know, at

**SHAMER** *(sha'-mur)* See SHOMER.
*1. Son of Mahli.*
1Chr 6:46 the son of Bani, the son of S
*2. Son of Heber.*
1Chr 7:34 And the sons of S

**SHAMGAR** *(sham'-gar) A judge of Israel.*
Judg 3:31 after him was S the son of Anath,
Judg 5:6 In the days of S the son of Anath

**SHAMHUTH** *(sham'-huth)* See SHAMMOTH. *A captain in David's army.*
1Chr 27:8 fifth month was S the Izrahite

**SHAMIR** *(sha'-mur)*
*1. A city in Judah.*
Josh 15:48 And in the mountains, S, and Jattir
*2. A city near Mt. Ephraim.*
Judg 10:1 he dwelt in S in mount Ephraim
Judg 10:2 and died, and was buried in S
*3. Son of Micah the Levite.*
1Chr 24:24 the sons of Michah; S

**SHAMMA** *(sham'-mah)* See SHAMMAH. *A son of Zophah.*
1Chr 7:37 Bezer, and Hod, and S, and Shilshah,

**SHAMMAH** *(sham'-mah)* See SHAMMA, SHAMMOTH, SHIMEA, SHIMMA.
*1. A son of Reuel.*
Gen 36:13 Nahath, and Zerah, S, and Mizzah
Gen 36:17 duke Nahath, duke Zerah, duke S
1Chr 1:37 Nahath, Zerah, S, and Mizzah
*2. A son of Jesse.*
1Sa 16:9 Then Jesse made S to pass by
1Sa 17:13 unto him Abinadab, and the third S
*3. A "mighty man" of David.*
2Sa 23:11 after him was S the son of Agee
*4. A Hararite "mighty man" of David.*
2Sa 23:33 S the Hararite, Ahiam the son of
*5. A Harodite "mighty man" of David.*
2Sa 23:25 S the Harodite, Elika the

**SHAMMAI** *(sham'-mahee)*
*1. A son of Onan.*
1Chr 2:28 And the sons of Onam were, S
1Chr 2:28 And the sons of S
1Chr 2:32 the sons of Jada the brother of S
*2. Father of Maon.*
1Chr 2:44 and Rekem begat S
1Chr 2:45 And the son of S was Maon
*3. A descendant of Caleb.*
1Chr 4:17 and she bare Miriam, and S, and

**SHAMMOTH** *(sham'-moth)* See SHAMMAH, SHAMHUTH. *A "mighty man" of David.*
1Chr 11:27 S the Harorite, Helez the

**SHAMMUA** *(sham-mu'-ah)* See SHAMMUAH, SHEMAIH, SHIMEA.
*1. A spy sent to the Promised Land.*
Num 13:4 of Reuben, S the son of Zaccur
*2. A son of David.*
1Chr 14:4 S, and Shobab, Nathan, and Solomon,
*3. A family of exiles.*
Neh 11:17 brethren, and Abda the son of S
*4. A priest with Zerubbabel.*
Neh 12:18 Of Bilgah, S

**SHAMMUAH** *(sham-mu'-ah)* See SHAMMUA. *Same as Shammua 2.*
2Sa 5:14 S, and Shobab, and Nathan, and

**SHAMSHERAI** *(sham'-she-rahee) A son of Jeroham.*
1Chr 8:26 And S, and Shehariah, and Athaliah,

**SHAPHAM** *(sha'-fam) A Gadite chief.*
1Chr 5:12 S the next, and Jaanai, and Shaphat

**SHAPHAN** *(sha'-fan)*
*1. A scribe in Josiah's time.*
2Kin 22:3 king sent S the son of Azaliah
2Kin 22:8 priest said unto S the scribe
2Kin 22:8 And Hilkiah gave the book to S
2Kin 22:9 S the scribe came to the king, and
2Kin 22:10 S the scribe shewed the king,
2Kin 22:10 S read it before the king
2Kin 22:12 S the scribe, and Asahiah a
2Kin 22:14 and Ahikam, and Achbor, and S
2Chr 34:8 he sent S the son of Azaliah, and
2Chr 34:15 said to S the scribe, I have
2Chr 34:15 Hilkiah delivered the book to S
2Chr 34:16 S carried the book to the king,
2Chr 34:18 Then S the scribe told the king,
2Chr 34:18 S read it before the king
2Chr 34:20 S the scribe, and Asaiah a servant
Jer 36:10 Gemariah the son of S the scribe
Jer 36:11 the son of Gemariah, the son of S
Jer 36:12 Achbor, and Gemariah the son of S
*2. Father of Ahikam.*
2Kin 22:12 priest, and Ahikam the son of S
2Kin 25:22 the son of Ahikam, the son of S
2Chr 34:20 Hilkiah, and Ahikam the son of S
Jer 26:24 the son of S was with Jeremiah
Jer 39:14 the son of Ahikam the son of S
Jer 40:5 the son of Ahikam the son of S
Jer 40:9 the son of S sware unto them
Jer 40:11 the son of Ahikam the son of S
Jer 41:2 the son of S with the sword
Jer 43:6 the son of Ahikam the son of S
*3. Messenger for Jeremiah.*
Jer 29:3 the hand of Elasah the son of S
*4. Father of Jaazaniah.*
Eze 8:11 them stood Jaazaniah the son of S

**SHAPHAT** *(sha'-fat)*
*1. A spy sent to the Promised Land.*
Num 13:5 of Simeon, S the son of Hori
*2. Father of Elisha the prophet.*
1Kin 19:16 and Elisha the son of S of
1Kin 19:19 and found Elisha the son of S
2Kin 3:11 said, Here is Elisha the son of S
2Kin 6:31 of S shall stand on him this day
*3. A grandson of Shechaniah.*
1Chr 3:22 and Bariah, and Neariah, and S
*4. A chief Gadite.*
1Chr 5:12 next, and Jaanai, and S in Bashan
*5. A shepherd of David's herds.*
1Chr 27:29 valleys was S the son of Adlai

**SHAPHER** *(sha'-fur) An Israelite encampment in the wilderness.*
Num 33:23 Kehelathah, and pitched in mount S
Num 33:24 And they removed from mount S

**SHARAI** *(sha'-rahee) Married a foreigner in exile.*
Ezr 10:40 Machnadebai, Shashai, S,

**SHARAIM** *(sha-ra'-im)* See SHAARAIM. *Same as Shaaraim.*
Josh 15:36 And S, and Adithaim, and Gederah, and

**SHARAR** *(sha'-rar)* See SARAR. *A "mighty man" of David.*
2Sa 23:33 Ahiam the son of S the Hararite

**SHAREZER** *(sha-re'-zur)* See SHEREZER. *Son of Sennacherib.*
2Kin 19:37 S his sons smote him with the
Is 37:38 S his sons smote him with the

**SHARON** *(sha'-run)* See SARON, SHARONITE.
*1. A plain of Ephraim.*
1Chr 27:29 in S was Shitrai the Sharonite
Song 2:1 I am the rose of S, and the lily
Is 33:9 S is like a wilderness
Is 35:2 it, the excellency of Carmel and S
Is 65:10 S shall be a fold of flocks, and
*2. A plain or city in Gad.*
1Chr 5:16 towns, and in all the suburbs of S

**SHARONITE** *(sha'-run-ite) An inhabitant of Sharon 1.*
1Chr 27:29 fed in Sharon was Shitrai the S

**SHARP**
Ex 4:25 Then Zipporah took a s stone
Josh 5:2 unto Joshua, Make thee s knives
Josh 5:3 And Joshua made him s knives
1Sa 14:4 there was a s rock on the one
1Sa 14:4 a s rock on the other side
Job 41:30 S stones are under him
Job 41:30 he spreadeth s pointed things
Ps 45:5 Thine arrows are s in the heart
Ps 52:2 like a s rasor, working
Ps 57:4 arrows, and their tongue a s sword
Ps 120:4 S arrows of the mighty, with
Prov 5:4 wormwood, s as a twoedged sword
Prov 25:18 a maul, and a sword, and a s arrow
Is 5:28 Whose arrows are s, and all their
Is 41:15 Behold, I will make thee a new s
Is 49:2 hath made my mouth like a s sword
Eze 5:1 son of man, take thee a s knife
Acts 15:39 contention was so s between them
Rev 1:16 his mouth went a s twoedged sword
Rev 2:12 hath the s sword with two edges
Rev 14:14 crown, and in his hand a s sickle
Rev 14:17 heaven, he also having a s sickle
Rev 14:18 cry to him that had the s sickle
Rev 14:18 saying, Thrust in thy s sickle
Rev 19:15 out of his mouth goeth a s sword

**SHARPENED**
Ps 140:3 They have s their tongues like a
Eze 21:9 Say, A sword, a sword is s
Eze 21:10 It is s to make a sore slaughter
Eze 21:11 this sword is s, and it is

**SHARUHEN** *(sha-ru'-hen)* See SHAARAIM, SHILHIM. *A city in Simeon.*
Josh 19:6 And Beth-lebaoth, and S

**SHASHAI** *(sha'-shahee) Married a foreigner in exile.*
Ezr 10:40 Machnadebai, S, Sharai,

**SHASHAK** *(sha'-shak) A son of Elpaal.*
1Chr 8:14 And Ahio, S, and Jeremoth,
1Chr 8:25 and Penuel, the sons of S

**SHAUL** *(sha'-ul)* See SAUL, SHAULITES.
*1. A son of Simeon.*
Gen 46:10 S the son of a Canaanitish woman
Ex 6:15 S the son of a Canaanitish woman
Num 26:13 of S, the family of the Shaulites
1Chr 4:24 and Jamin, Jarib, Zerah, and S
*2. A king of Edom.*
1Chr 1:48 S of Rehoboth by the river
1Chr 1:49 when S was dead, Baal-hanan the
*3. Son of Kohath.*
1Chr 6:24 son, Uzziah his son, and S his son

**SHAULITES** *(sha'-ul-ites) Decendants of Shaul 1.*
Num 26:13 of Shaul, the family of the S

**SHAVE**
Lev 13:33 but the scall shall he not s
Lev 14:8 s off all his hair, and wash
Lev 14:9 that he shall s all his hair off
Lev 14:9 even all his hair he shall s off
Lev 21:5 neither shall they s off the
Num 6:9 then he shall s his head in the
Num 6:9 on the seventh day shall he s it
Num 6:18 the Nazarite shall s the head of
Num 8:7 let them s all their flesh, and
Deut 21:12 and she shall s her head, and pare
Judg 16:19 she caused him to s off the seven
Is 7:20 Lord s with a razor that is hired
Eze 44:20 Neither shall they s their heads
Acts 21:24 them, that they may s their heads

**SHAVED**
Gen 41:14 he s himself, and changed his
2Sa 10:4 s off the one half of their
1Chr 19:4 s them, and cut off their garments
Job 1:20 s his head, and fell down upon the

**SHAVEH** *(sha'-veh) A valley near Aenon.*
Gen 14:5 Ham, and the Emims in S Kiriathaim
Gen 14:17 were with him, at the valley of S

**SHAVEN**
Lev 13:33 He shall be s, but the scall
Num 6:19 the hair of his separation is s
Judg 16:17 if I be s, then my strength will
Judg 16:22 to grow again after he was s
Jer 41:5 men, having their beards s
1Cor 11:5 is even all one as if she were s
1Cor 11:6 for a woman to be shorn or s

**SHAVSHA** *(shav'-shah)* See SERAIAH, SHEVA, SHISHA. *David's scribe.*
1Chr 18:16 and S was scribe

**SHEAF**
Gen 37:7 my s arose, and also stood upright
Gen 37:7 about, and made obeisance to my s
Lev 23:10 then ye shall bring a s of the
Lev 23:11 shall wave the s before the LORD
Lev 23:12 s an he lamb without blemish of
Lev 23:15 the s of the wave offering
Deut 24:19 and hast forgot a s in the field
Job 24:10 take away the s from the hungry
Zec 12:6 and like a torch of fire in a s

**SHEAL** *(she'-al) Married a foreigner in exile.*
Ezr 10:29 Malluch, and Adaiah, Jashub, and S

**SHEALTIEL** *(she-al'-te-el)* See SALATHIEL. *Father of Zerubbabel.*
Ezr 3:2 and Zerubbabel the son of S
Ezr 3:8 began Zerubbabel the son of S
Ezr 5:2 rose up Zerubbabel the son of S
Neh 12:1 up with Zerubbabel the son of S
Hag 1:1 unto Zerubbabel the son of S
Hag 1:12 Then Zerubbabel the son of S
Hag 1:14 spirit of Zerubbabel the son of S
Hag 2:2 now to Zerubbabel the son of S
Hag 2:23 my servant, the son of S

**SHEAR**
Gen 31:19 And Laban went to s his sheep
Gen 38:13 up to Timnath to s his sheep
Deut 15:19 nor s the firstling of thy sheep
1Sa 25:4 that Nabal did s his sheep

**SHEARIAH** *(she-a-ri'-ah) Son of Azel.*
1Chr 8:38 Bocheru, and Ishmael, and S
1Chr 9:44 Bocheru, and Ishmael, and S

**SHEAR-JASHUB** *(she'-ar-ja'-shub) Symbolic name of a son of Isaiah.*
Is 7:3 S thy son, at the end of the

**SHEATH**
1Sa 17:51 and drew it out of the s thereof
2Sa 20:8 upon his loins in the s thereof
1Chr 21:27 sword again into the s thereof
Eze 21:3 draw forth my sword out of his s
Eze 21:4 his s against all flesh from the
Eze 21:5 drawn forth my sword out of his s
Eze 21:30 I cause it to return into his s
Jn 18:11 Put up thy sword into the s

**SHEAVES**
Gen 37:7 we were binding s in the field
Gen 37:7 your s stood round about, and made
Ruth 2:7 after the reapers among the s
Ruth 2:15 Let her glean even among the s
Neh 13:15 on the sabbath, and bringing in s
Ps 126:6 bringing his s with him
Ps 129:7 nor he that bindeth s his bosom
Amos 2:13 cart is pressed that is full of s
Mic 4:12 them as the s into the floor

**SHEBA** *(she'-bah)* See BATH-SHEBA, BEER-SHEBA, SHEBAH.
*1. Son of Raamah.*
Gen 10:7 Raamah; S, and Dedan
1Chr 1:9 Raamah; S, and Dedan
*2. Son of Yoktan.*
Gen 10:28 And Obal, and Abimael, and S
1Chr 1:22 And Ebal, and Abimael, and S
*3. Son of Yokshan.*
Gen 25:3 And Jokshan begat S, and Dedan
1Chr 1:32 Jokshan; S, and Dedan
*4. A region in southwestern Arabia.*
1Kin 10:1 when the queen of S heard of the
1Kin 10:4 when the queen of S had seen all
1Kin 10:10 queen of S gave to king Solomon
1Kin 10:13 the queen of S all her desire
2Chr 9:1 when the queen of S heard of the
2Chr 9:3 when the queen of S had seen the
2Chr 9:9 the queen of S gave king Solomon
2Chr 9:12 to the queen of S all her desire
Job 6:19 companies of S waited for them
Ps 72:10 the kings of S and Seba shall
Ps 72:15 shall be given of the gold of S
Is 60:6 all they from S shall come
Jer 6:20 cometh there to me incense from S
Eze 27:22 The merchants of S and Raamah,
Eze 27:23 and Eden, the merchants of S
Eze 38:13 S, and Dedan, and the merchants of
*5. A city in Simeon.*
Josh 19:2 inheritance Beer-sheba, or S
*6. A son of Bichri.*
2Sa 20:1 a man of Belial, whose name was S
2Sa 20:2 followed S the son of Bichri

2Sa 20:6 Now shall *S* the son of Bichri do
2Sa 20:7 to pursue after *S* the son of
2Sa 20:10 pursued after *S* the son of Bichri
2Sa 20:13 to pursue after *S* the son of
2Sa 20:21 *S* the son of Bichri by name, hath
2Sa 20:22 the head of *S* the son of Bichri
*7. A chief Gadite.*
1Chr 5:13 were, Michael, and Meshullam, and *S*

**SHEBAH** *(she'-bah)* See SHEBA. *A well at Beersheba.*
Gen 26:33 And he called it *S*

**SHEBAM** *(she'-bam)* See SHIBMAH. *A city in Reuben.*
Num 32:3 and Heshbon, and Elealeh, and *S*

**SHEBANIAH** *(sheb-a-ni'-ah)* See SHECHANIAH.
*1. A priest who moved the Ark.*
1Chr 15:24 And *S*, and Jehoshaphat, and
*2. A Levite who aided Ezra.*
Neh 9:4 Jeshua, and Bani, Kadmiel, *S*
Neh 9:5 Hashabniah, Sherebiah, Hodijah, *S*
Neh 10:10 And their brethren, *S*, Hodijah,
*3. A priest who renewed the covenant.*
Neh 10:4 Hattush, *S*, Malluch,
Neh 12:14 of *S*, Joseph
*4. A Levite who renewed the covenant.*
Neh 10:12 Zaccur, Sherebiah, *S*,

**SHEBARIM** *(sheb'-a-rim) A place near Jericho.*
Josh 7:5 from before the gate even unto *S*

**SHEBER** *(she'-bur) A son of Caleb.*
1Chr 2:48 Caleb's concubine, bare *S*

**SHEBNA** *(sheb'-nah)*
*1. King Hezekiah's scribe.*
2Kin 18:18 *S* the scribe, and Joah the son of
2Kin 18:26 Eliakim the son of Hilkiah, and *S*
2Kin 18:37 *S* the scribe, and Joah the son of
2Kin 19:2 *S* the scribe, and the elders of
Is 36:3 *S* the scribe, and Joah, Asaph's
Is 36:11 Then said Eliakim and *S* and Joah
Is 36:22 *S* the scribe, and Joah, the son of
Is 37:2 *S* the scribe, and the elders of
*2. An unspecified treasurer.*
Is 22:15 unto this treasurer, even unto *S*

**SHEBUEL** *(she-bu'-el)* See SHUBAEL.
*1. A son of Gershom.*
1Chr 23:16 sons of Gershom, *S* was the chief
1Chr 26:24 *S* the son of Gershom, the son of
*2. A son of Haman.*
1Chr 25:4 Bukkiah, Mattaniah, Uzziel, *S*

**SHECANIAH** *(shek-a-ni'-ah)* See SHEBANIAH, SHECHANIAH.
*1. A priest in David's time.*
1Chr 24:11 ninth to Jeshua, the tenth to *S*
*2. A priest in Hezekiah's time.*
2Chr 31:15 and Shemaiah, Amariah, and *S*

**SHECHANIAH** *(shek-a-ni'-ah)* See SHEBANIAH, SHECANIAH.
*1. Head of a Davidic family.*
1Chr 3:21 sons of Obadiah, the sons of *S*
1Chr 3:22 And the sons of *S*
*2. A family of exiles.*
Ezr 8:3 Of the sons of *S*, of the sons of
*3. Another family of exiles.*
Ezr 8:5 Of the sons of *S*
*4. Married a foreigner in exile.*
Ezr 10:2 *S* the son of Jehiel, one of the
*5. Father of Shemaiah.*
Neh 3:29 also Shemaiah the son of *S*
*6. Son of Arah.*
Neh 6:18 son in law of *S* the son of Arah
*7. A priest with Zerubbabel.*
Neh 12:3 *S*, Rehum, Meremoth,

**SHECHEM** *(she'-kem)* See SHECHEMITES, SHECHEM'S, SICHEM, SYCHEM.
*1. A Levitical city near Mt. Ephraim.*
Gen 33:18 Jacob came to Shalem, a city of *S*
Gen 35:4 them under the oak which was by *S*
Gen 37:12 to feed their father's flock in *S*
Gen 37:13 thy brethren feed the flock in *S*
Gen 37:14 vale of Hebron, and he came to *S*
Josh 17:7 Michmethah, that lieth before *S*
Josh 20:7 and *S* in mount Ephraim, and
Josh 21:21 For they gave them *S* with her
Josh 24:1 all the tribes of Israel to *S*
Josh 24:25 a statute and an ordinance in *S*
Judg 8:31 And his concubine that was in *S*
Judg 9:1 to *S* unto his mother's brethren
Judg 9:2 in the ears of all the men of *S*
Judg 9:3 all the men of *S* all these words
Judg 9:6 all the men of *S* gathered
Judg 9:6 plain of the pillar that was in *S*
Judg 9:7 Hearken unto me, ye men of *S*
Judg 9:18 king over the men of *S*, because
Judg 9:20 Abimelech, and devour the men of *S*
Judg 9:20 fire come out from the men of *S*
Judg 9:23 between Abimelech and the men of *S*
Judg 9:23 the men of *S* dealt treacherously
Judg 9:24 and upon the men of *S*, which aided
Judg 9:25 the men of *S* set liers in wait
Judg 9:26 his brethren, and went over to *S*
Judg 9:26 the men of *S* put their confidence
Judg 9:31 Ebed and his brethren be come to *S*
Judg 9:34 wait against *S* in four companies
Judg 9:39 Gaal went out before the men of *S*
Judg 9:41 that they should not dwell in *S*
Judg 9:46 men of the tower of *S* heard that
Judg 9:47 tower of *S* were gathered together
Judg 9:49 men of the tower of *S* died also
Judg 9:57 all the evil of the men of *S* did
Judg 21:19 that goeth up from Beth-el to *S*
1Kin 12:1 And Rehoboam went to *S*
1Kin 12:1 were come to *S* to make him king
1Kin 12:25 Jeroboam built *S* in mount Ephraim
1Chr 6:67 *S* in mount Ephraim with her
1Chr 7:28 *S* also and the towns thereof, unto
2Chr 10:1 And Rehoboam went to *S*
2Chr 10:1 for to *S* were all Israel come to
Ps 60:6 I will rejoice, I will divide *S*
Ps 108:7 I will rejoice, I will divide *S*
Jer 41:5 That there came certain from *S*
*2. Son of Hamor.*
Gen 34:2 when *S* the son of Hamor the
Gen 34:4 *S* spake unto his father Hamor,
Gen 34:6 Hamor the father of *S* went out
Gen 34:8 The soul of my son *S* longeth for
Gen 34:11 *S* said unto her father and unto
Gen 34:13 And the sons of Jacob answered *S*
Gen 34:18 pleased Hamor, and *S* Hamor's son
Gen 34:20 *S* his son came unto the gate of
Gen 34:24 unto *S* his son hearkened all that
Gen 34:26 *S* his son with the edge of the
Josh 24:32 up out of Egypt, buried they in *S*
Josh 24:32 *S* for an hundred pieces of silver
Judg 9:28 Who is Abimelech, and who is *S*
Judg 9:28 the men of Hamor the father of *S*
*3. Son of Gilead.*
Num 26:31 and of *S*, the family of the
Josh 17:2 Asriel, and for the children of *S*
*4. A son of Shemidah.*
1Chr 7:19 of Shemidah were, Ahian, and *S*

**SHECHEMITES** *(she'-kem-ites) Descendants of Shechem.*
Num 26:31 of Shechem, the family of the *S*

**SHECHEM'S** *(she'-kems) Refers to Shechem 2.*
Gen 33:19 *S* father, for an hundred pieces
Gen 34:26 and took Dinah out of *S* house

**SHED**
Gen 9:6 by man shall his blood be *s*
Gen 37:22 *S* no blood, but cast him into
Ex 22:2 there shall no blood be *s* for him
Ex 22:3 there shall be blood *s* for him
Lev 17:4 he hath *s* blood
Num 35:33 of the blood that is *s* therein
Num 35:33 but by the blood of him that *s* it
Deut 19:10 blood be not *s* in thy land
Deut 21:7 Our hands have not *s* this blood
1Sa 25:26 thee from coming to *s* blood
1Sa 25:31 that thou hast *s* blood causeless
1Sa 25:33 this day from coming to *s* blood
2Sa 20:10 *s* out his bowels to the ground,
1Kin 2:5 *s* the blood of war in peace, and
1Kin 2:31 the innocent blood, which Joab *s*
2Kin 21:16 Moreover Manasseh *s* innocent
2Kin 24:4 for the innocent blood that he *s*
1Chr 22:8 Thou hast *s* blood abundantly, and
1Chr 22:8 because thou hast *s* much blood
1Chr 28:3 a man of war, and hast *s* blood
Ps 79:3 Their blood have they *s* like
Ps 79:10 blood of thy servants which is *s*
Ps 106:38 *s* innocent blood, even the blood
Prov 1:16 to evil, and make haste to *s* blood
Prov 6:17 hands that *s* innocent blood,
Is 59:7 make haste to *s* innocent blood
Jer 7:6 *s* not innocent blood in this
Jer 22:3 neither *s* innocent blood in this
Jer 22:17 for to *s* innocent blood, and for
Lam 4:13 that have *s* the blood of the just
Eze 16:38 wedlock and *s* blood are judged
Eze 22:4 in thy blood that thou hast *s*
Eze 22:6 in thee to their power to *s* blood
Eze 22:9 men that carry tales to *s* blood
Eze 22:12 have they taken gifts to *s* blood
Eze 22:27 to *s* blood, and to destroy souls,
Eze 23:45 the manner of women that *s* blood
Eze 33:25 toward your idols, and *s* blood
Eze 35:5 hast *s* the blood of the children
Eze 36:18 that they had *s* upon the land
Joel 3:19 because they have *s* innocent
Mt 23:35 righteous blood *s* upon the earth
Mt 26:28 which is *s* for many for the
Mk 14:24 testament, which is *s* for many
Lk 11:50 which was *s* from the foundation
Lk 22:20 in my blood, which is *s* for you
Acts 2:33 he hath *s* forth this, which ye
Acts 22:20 blood of thy martyr Stephen was *s*
Rom 3:15 Their feet are swift to *s* blood
Rom 5:5 because the love of God is *s*
Titus 3:6 Which he *s* on us abundantly
Rev 16:6 For they have *s* the blood of

**SHEDEUR** *(shed'-e-ur) A Reubenite who counted the people.*
Num 1:5 Elizur the son of *S*
Num 2:10 shall be Elizur the son of *S*
Num 7:30 fourth day Elizur the son of *S*
Num 7:35 offering of Elizur the son of *S*
Num 10:18 his host was Elizur the son of *S*

**SHEEP**
Gen 4:2 And Abel was a keeper of *s*
Gen 12:16 and he had *s*, and oxen, and he asses
Gen 20:14 And Abimelech took *s*, and oxen, and
Gen 21:27 And Abraham took *s* and oxen, and
Gen 29:2 three flocks of *s* lying by it
Gen 29:3 well's mouth, and watered the *s*
Gen 29:6 his daughter cometh with the *s*
Gen 29:7 water ye the *s*, and go and feed
Gen 29:8 then we water the *s*
Gen 29:9 Rachel came with her father's *s*
Gen 29:10 the *s* of Laban his mother's
Gen 30:32 all the brown cattle among the *s*
Gen 30:33 the goats, and brown among the *s*
Gen 30:35 it, and all the brown among the *s*
Gen 31:19 And Laban went to shear his *s*
Gen 34:28 They took their *s*, and their oxen,
Gen 38:13 up to Timnath to shear his *s*
Ex 9:3 upon the oxen, and upon the *s*
Ex 12:5 ye shall take it out from the *s*
Ex 20:24 and thy peace offerings, thy *s*
Ex 22:1 a man shall steal an ox, or a *s*
Ex 22:1 for an ox, and four *s* for a *s*
Ex 22:4 whether it be ox, or ass, or *s*
Ex 22:9 it be for ox, for ass, for *s*
Ex 22:10 an ass, or an ox, or a *s*, or any
Ex 22:30 do with thine oxen, and with thy *s*
Ex 34:19 among thy cattle, whether ox or *s*
Lev 1:10 of the flocks, namely, of the *s*
Lev 7:23 no manner of fat, of ox, or of *s*
Lev 22:19 blemish, of the beeves, of the *s*
Lev 22:21 freewill offering in beeves or *s*
Lev 22:27 When a bullock, or a *s*, or a goat
Lev 27:26 whether it be ox, or *s*
Num 18:17 of a cow, or the firstling of a *s*
Num 22:40 And Balak offered oxen and *s*
Num 27:17 of the LORD be not as *s* which
Num 31:28 and of the asses, and of the *s*
Num 31:32 thousand and five thousand *s*
Num 31:36 thirty thousand and five hundred *s*
Num 31:37 tribute of the *s* was six hundred
Num 31:43 seven thousand and five hundred *s*
Num 32:24 little ones, and folds for your *s*
Num 32:36 and folds of *s*
Deut 7:13 thy kine, and the flocks of thy *s*
Deut 14:4 the ox, the *s*, and the goat,
Deut 14:26 lusteth after, for oxen, or for *s*
Deut 15:19 nor shear the firstling of thy *s*
Deut 17:1 LORD thy God any bullock, or *s*
Deut 18:3 sacrifice, whether it be ox or *s*
Deut 18:4 the first of the fleece of thy *s*
Deut 22:1 brother's ox or his *s* go astray
Deut 28:4 thy kine, and the flocks of thy *s*
Deut 28:18 thy kine, and the flocks of thy *s*
Deut 28:31 thy *s* shall be given unto thine
Deut 28:51 of thy kine, or flocks of thy *s*

Deut 32:14 Butter of kine, and milk of *s*
Josh 6:21 woman, young and old, and ox, and *s*
Josh 7:24 his oxen, and his asses, and his *s*
Judg 6:4 sustenance for Israel, neither *s*
1Sa 8:17 He will take the tenth of your *s*
1Sa 14:32 flew upon the spoil, and took *s*
1Sa 14:34 man his ox, and every man his *s*
1Sa 15:3 infant and suckling, ox and *s*
1Sa 15:9 spared Agag, and the best of the *s*
1Sa 15:14 bleating of the *s* in mine ears
1Sa 15:15 people spared the best of the *s*
1Sa 15:21 the people took of the spoil, *s*
1Sa 16:11 and, behold, he keepeth the *s*
1Sa 16:19 thy son, which is with the *s*
1Sa 17:15 feed his father's *s* at Beth-lehem
1Sa 17:20 left the *s* with a keeper, and took
1Sa 17:28 those few *s* in the wilderness
1Sa 17:34 Thy servant kept his father's *s*
1Sa 22:19 and oxen, and asses, and *s*, with
1Sa 25:2 great, and he had three thousand *s*
1Sa 25:2 he was shearing his *s* in Carmel
1Sa 25:4 that Nabal did shear his *s*
1Sa 25:16 we were with them keeping the *s*
1Sa 25:18 five *s* ready dressed, and five
1Sa 27:9 woman alive, and took away the *s*
2Sa 7:8 sheepcote, from following the *s*
2Sa 17:29 And honey, and butter, and *s*
2Sa 24:17 but these *s*, what have they done
1Kin 1:9 And Adonijah slew *s* and oxen and fat
1Kin 1:19 *s* in abundance, and hath called
1Kin 1:25 *s* in abundance, and hath called
1Kin 4:23 of the pastures, and an hundred *s*
1Kin 8:5 him before the ark, sacrificing *s*
1Kin 8:63 an hundred and twenty thousand *s*
1Kin 22:17 as *s* that have not a shepherd
2Kin 5:26 and oliveyards, and vineyards, and *s*
1Chr 5:21 of *s* two hundred and fifty
1Chr 12:40 and oil, and oxen, and *s* abundantly
1Chr 17:7 even from following the *s*
1Chr 21:17 but as for these *s*, what have
2Chr 5:6 him before the ark, sacrificed *s*
2Chr 7:5 an hundred and twenty thousand *s*
2Chr 14:15 of cattle, and carried away *s*
2Chr 15:11 hundred oxen and seven thousand *s*
2Chr 18:2 And Ahab killed *s* and oxen for him
2Chr 18:16 as *s* that have no shepherd
2Chr 29:33 hundred oxen and three thousand *s*
2Chr 30:24 bullocks and seven thousand *s*
2Chr 30:24 bullocks and ten thousand *s*
2Chr 31:6 brought in the tithe of oxen and *s*
Neh 3:1 and they builded the *s* gate
Neh 3:32 *s* gate repaired the goldsmiths
Neh 5:18 daily was one ox and six choice *s*
Neh 12:39 of Meah, even unto the *s* gate
Job 1:3 also was seven thousand *s*
Job 1:16 heaven, and hath burned up the *s*
Job 31:20 warmed with the fleece of my *s*
Job 42:12 for he had fourteen thousand *s*
Ps 8:7 All *s* and oxen, yea, and the beasts
Ps 44:11 us like *s* appointed for meat
Ps 44:22 counted as *s* for the slaughter
Ps 49:14 Like *s* they are laid in the grave
Ps 74:1 against the *s* of thy pasture
Ps 78:52 his own people to go forth like *s*
Ps 79:13 *s* of thy pasture will give thee
Ps 95:7 his pasture, and the *s* of his hand
Ps 100:3 people, and the *s* of his pasture
Ps 119:176 I have gone astray like a lost *s*
Ps 144:13 that our *s* may bring forth
Song 4:2 a flock of *s* that are even shorn
Song 6:6 Thy teeth are as a flock of *s*
Is 7:21 nourish a young cow, and two *s*
Is 13:14 as a *s* that no man taketh up
Is 22:13 slaying oxen, and killing *s*
Is 53:6 All we like *s* have gone astray
Is 53:7 as a *s* before her shearers is
Jer 12:3 them out like *s* for the slaughter
Jer 23:1 scatter the *s* of my pasture
Jer 50:6 My people hath been lost *s*
Jer 50:17 Israel is a scattered *s*
Eze 34:6 My *s* wandered through all the
Eze 34:11 I, even I, will both search my *s*
Eze 34:12 is among his *s* that are scattered
Eze 34:12 so will I seek out my *s*, and will
Hos 12:12 a wife, and for a wife he kept *s*
Joel 1:18 the flocks of *s* are made desolate
Mic 2:12 them together as the *s* of Bozrah
Mic 5:8 young lion among the flocks of *s*
Zec 13:7 and the *s* shall be scattered
Mt 9:36 abroad, as *s* having no shepherd
Mt 10:6 the lost *s* of the house of Israel
Mt 10:16 I send you forth as *s* in the
Mt 12:11 among you, that shall have one *s*
Mt 12:12 then is a man better than a *s*
Mt 15:24 the lost *s* of the house of Israel
Mt 18:12 if a man have an hundred *s*
Mt 18:13 you, he rejoiceth more of that *s*
Mt 25:32 divideth his *s* from the goats
Mt 25:33 he shall set the *s* on his right
Mt 26:31 the *s* of the flock shall be
Mk 6:34 because they were as *s* not having
Mk 14:27 and the *s* shall be scattered
Lk 15:4 man of you, having an hundred *s*
Lk 15:6 I have found my *s* which was lost
Jn 2:14 temple those that sold oxen and *s*
Jn 2:15 all out of the temple, and the *s*
Jn 5:2 Jerusalem by the *s* market a pool
Jn 10:2 the door is the shepherd of the *s*
Jn 10:3 and the *s* hear his voice
Jn 10:3 and he calleth his own *s* by name
Jn 10:4 when he putteth forth his own *s*
Jn 10:4 before them, and the *s* follow him
Jn 10:7 unto you, I am the door of the *s*
Jn 10:8 but the *s* did not hear them
Jn 10:11 giveth his life for the *s*
Jn 10:12 shepherd, whose own the *s* are not
Jn 10:12 the wolf coming, and leaveth the *s*
Jn 10:12 them, and scattereth the *s*
Jn 10:13 hireling, and careth not for the *s*
Jn 10:14 the good shepherd, and know my *s*
Jn 10:15 and I lay down my life for the *s*
Jn 10:16 other *s* I have, which are not of
Jn 10:26 not, because ye are not of my *s*
Jn 10:27 My *s* hear my voice, and I know
Jn 21:16 He saith unto him, Feed my *s*
Jn 21:17 Jesus saith unto him, Feed my *s*
Acts 8:32 this, He was led as a *s* to the
Rom 8:36 accounted as *s* for the slaughter
Heb 13:20 that great shepherd of the *s*
1Pet 2:25 For ye were as *s* going astray
Rev 18:13 flour, and wheat, and beasts, and *s*

**SHEHARIAH** *(she-ha-ri'-ah) A son of Jeroham.*

1Chr 8:26 And Shamsherai, and *S*, and Athaliah,

**SHEKEL**

Gen 24:22 golden earring of half a *s* weight
Ex 30:13 half a *s* after the *s* of the
Ex 30:13 (a *s* is twenty gerahs
Ex 30:13 an half *s* shall be the offering
Ex 30:15 shall not give less than half a *s*
Ex 30:24 after the *s* of the sanctuary, and
Ex 38:24 after the *s* of the sanctuary
Ex 38:25 after the *s* of the sanctuary
Ex 38:26 for every man, that is, half a *s*
Ex 38:26 after the *s* of the sanctuary, for
Lev 5:15 after the *s* of the sanctuary, for
Lev 27:3 after the *s* of the sanctuary
Lev 27:25 to the *s* of the sanctuary
Lev 27:25 twenty gerahs shall be the *s*
Num 3:47 after the *s* of the sanctuary
Num 3:47 (the *s* is twenty gerahs
Num 3:50 after the *s* of the sanctuary
Num 7:13 after the *s* of the sanctuary
Num 7:19 after the *s* of the sanctuary
Num 7:25 after the *s* of the sanctuary
Num 7:31 after the *s* of the sanctuary
Num 7:37 after the *s* of the sanctuary
Num 7:43 after the *s* of the sanctuary
Num 7:49 after the *s* of the sanctuary
Num 7:55 after the *s* of the sanctuary
Num 7:61 after the *s* of the sanctuary
Num 7:67 after the *s* of the sanctuary
Num 7:73 after the *s* of the sanctuary
Num 7:79 after the *s* of the sanctuary
Num 7:85 after the *s* of the sanctuary
Num 7:86 after the *s* of the sanctuary
Num 18:16 after the *s* of the sanctuary,
1Sa 9:8 the fourth part of a *s* of silver
2Kin 7:1 of fine flour be sold for a *s*
2Kin 7:1 and two measures of barley for a *s*
2Kin 7:16 of fine flour was sold for a *s*
2Kin 7:16 and two measures of barley for a *s*
2Kin 7:18 Two measures of barley for a *s*
2Kin 7:18 a measure of fine flour for a *s*
Neh 10:32 *s* for the service of the house of
Eze 45:12 the *s* shall be twenty gerahs
Amos 8:5 the *s* great, and falsifying the

**SHEKELS**

Gen 23:15 is worth four hundred *s* of silver
Gen 23:16 of Heth, four hundred *s* of silver
Gen 24:22 her hands of ten *s* weight of gold
Ex 21:32 their master thirty *s* of silver
Ex 30:23 of pure myrrh five hundred *s*
Ex 30:23 much, even two hundred and fifty *s*
Ex 30:23 calamus two hundred and fifty *s*
Ex 30:24 And of cassia five hundred *s*
Ex 38:24 and seven hundred and thirty *s*
Ex 38:25 and threescore and fifteen *s*
Ex 38:28 five *s* he made hooks for the
Ex 38:29 and two thousand and four hundred *s*
Lev 5:15 thy estimation by *s* of silver
Lev 27:3 shall be fifty *s* of silver
Lev 27:4 thy estimation shall be thirty *s*
Lev 27:5 shall be of the male twenty *s*
Lev 27:5 and for the female ten *s*
Lev 27:6 be of the male five *s* of silver
Lev 27:6 shall be three *s* of silver
Lev 27:7 thy estimation shall be fifteen *s*
Lev 27:7 and for the female ten *s*
Lev 27:16 be valued at fifty *s* of silver
Num 3:47 take five *s* apiece by the poll
Num 3:50 hundred and threescore and five *s*
Num 7:13 was an hundred and thirty *s*
Num 7:13 one silver bowl of seventy *s*
Num 7:14 One spoon of ten *s* of gold
Num 7:19 was an hundred and thirty *s*
Num 7:19 one silver bowl of seventy *s*
Num 7:20 One spoon of gold of ten *s*
Num 7:25 was an hundred and thirty *s*
Num 7:25 one silver bowl of seventy *s*
Num 7:26 One golden spoon of ten *s*
Num 7:31 weight of an hundred and thirty *s*
Num 7:31 one silver bowl of seventy *s*
Num 7:32 One golden spoon of ten *s*
Num 7:37 was an hundred and thirty *s*
Num 7:37 one silver bowl of seventy *s*
Num 7:38 One golden spoon of ten *s*
Num 7:43 weight of an hundred and thirty *s*
Num 7:43 a silver bowl of seventy *s*
Num 7:44 One golden spoon of ten *s*
Num 7:49 was an hundred and thirty *s*
Num 7:49 one silver bowl of seventy *s*
Num 7:50 One golden spoon of ten *s*
Num 7:55 weight of an hundred and thirty *s*
Num 7:55 one silver bowl of seventy *s*
Num 7:56 One golden spoon of ten *s*
Num 7:61 was an hundred and thirty *s*
Num 7:61 one silver bowl of seventy *s*
Num 7:62 One golden spoon of ten *s*
Num 7:67 was an hundred and thirty *s*
Num 7:67 one silver bowl of seventy *s*
Num 7:68 One golden spoon of ten *s*
Num 7:73 was an hundred and thirty *s*
Num 7:73 one silver bowl of seventy *s*
Num 7:74 One golden spoon of ten *s*
Num 7:79 was an hundred and thirty *s*
Num 7:79 one silver bowl of seventy *s*
Num 7:80 One golden spoon of ten *s*
Num 7:85 weighing an hundred and thirty *s*
Num 7:85 two thousand and four hundred *s*
Num 7:86 of incense, weighing ten *s* apiece
Num 7:86 spoons was an hundred and twenty *s*
Num 18:16 for the money of five *s*, after
Num 31:52 thousand seven hundred and fifty *s*
Deut 22:19 him in an hundred *s* of silver
Deut 22:29 damsel's father fifty *s* of silver
Josh 7:21 and two hundred *s* of silver
Josh 7:21 a wedge of gold of fifty *s* weight
Judg 8:26 and seven hundred *s* of gold
Judg 17:2 The eleven hundred *s* of silver
Judg 17:3 hundred *s* of silver to his mother
Judg 17:4 took two hundred *s* of silver
Judg 17:10 I will give thee ten *s* of silver
1Sa 17:5 coat was five thousand *s* of brass
1Sa 17:7 weighed six hundred *s* of iron
2Sa 14:26 hundred *s* after the king's weight
2Sa 18:11 have given thee ten *s* of silver
2Sa 18:12 thousand *s* of silver in mine hand
2Sa 21:16 hundred *s* of brass in weight
2Sa 24:24 and the oxen for fifty *s* of silver
1Kin 10:16 six hundred *s* of gold went to one
1Kin 10:29 Egypt for six hundred *s* of silver
2Kin 15:20 of each man fifty *s* of silver
1Chr 21:25 six hundred *s* of gold by weight
2Chr 1:17 for six hundred *s* of silver
2Chr 3:9 of the nails was fifty *s* of gold
2Chr 9:15 six hundred *s* of beaten gold went

2Chr 9:16 three hundred *s* of gold went to
Neh 5:15 and wine, beside forty *s* of silver
Jer 32:9 money, even seventeen *s* of silver
Eze 4:10 be by weight, twenty *s* a day
Eze 45:12 twenty *s*, five and twenty
Eze 45:12 five and twenty *s*, fifteen *s*

**SHELAH** *(she'-lah)* See SALAH, SHELANITES.
*1. Son of Judah.*
Gen 38:5 and called his name *S*
Gen 38:11 house, till *S* my son be grown
Gen 38:14 for she saw that *S* was grown
Gen 38:26 that I gave her not to *S* my son
Gen 46:12 Er, and Onan, and *S*, and Pharez, and
Num 26:20 of *S*, the family of the
1Chr 2:3 Er, and Onan, and *S*
1Chr 4:21 The sons of *S* the son of Judah
*2. Son of Arphaxad.*
1Chr 1:18 And Arphaxad begat *S*, and Shelah
1Chr 1:18 begat Shelah, and *S* begat Eber
1Chr 1:24 Shem, Arphaxad, *S*,

**SHELANITES** *(she'-lan-ites) Descendants of Shelah.*
Num 26:20 of Shelah, the family of the *S*

**SHELEMIAH** *(shel-e-mi'-ah)* See MESHELEMIAH, SHALLUM.
*1. A sanctuary servant.*
1Chr 26:14 And the lot eastward fell to *S*
*2. A son of Bani who married a foreigner.*
Ezr 10:39 And *S*, and Nathan, and Adaiah,
*3. Another son of Bani.*
Ezr 10:41 Azareel, and *S*, Shemariah,
*4. Father of Hananiah.*
Neh 3:30 repaired Hananiah the son of *S*
*5. A treasury sevant.*
Neh 13:13 *S* the priest, and Zadok the scribe
*6. Son of Cushi.*
Jer 36:14 son of Nethaniah, the son of *S*
*7. Son of Abdeel.*
Jer 36:26 *S* the son of Abdeel, to take
*8. Father of Jehucal.*
Jer 37:3 king sent Jehucal the son of *S*
Jer 38:1 of Pashur, and Jucal the son of *S*
*9. Father of Irijah.*
Jer 37:13 name was Irijah, the son of *S*

**SHELEPH** *(she'-lef) A son of Joktan.*
Gen 10:26 And Joktan begat Almodad, and *S*
1Chr 1:20 And Joktan begat Almodad, and *S*

**SHELESH** *(she'-lesh) A son of Helem.*
1Chr 7:35 Zophah, and Imna, and *S*, and Amal

**SHELOMI** *(shel'-o-mi) Father of Ahihud.*
Num 34:27 of Asher, Ahihud the son of *S*

**SHELOMITH** *(shel'-o-mith)*
*1. Daughter of Debri.*
Lev 24:11 (and his mother's name was *S*
*2. Daughter of Zerubbabel.*
1Chr 3:19 and Hananiah, and *S* their sister
*3. A son of Shimei.*
1Chr 23:9 *S*, and Haziel, and Haran, three
*4. A son of Izhar.*
1Chr 23:18 *S* the chief
*5. A descendant of Eliezer.*
1Chr 26:25 and Zichri his son, and *S* his son
1Chr 26:26 Which *S* and his brethren were over
1Chr 26:28 thing, it was under the hand of *S*
*6. A child of King Rehoboam.*
2Chr 11:20 Abijah, and Attai, and Ziza, and *S*
*7. A family of exiles.*
Ezr 8:10 And of the sons of *S*

**SHELOMOTH** *(shel'-o-moth)* See SHELOMITH. *A descendant of Izhar.*
1Chr 24:22 *S*: of the sons of *S*

**SHELUMIEL**
Num 1:6 *S* the son of Zurishaddai
Num 2:12 shall be *S* the son of Zurishaddai
Num 7:36 On the fifth day *S* the son of
Num 7:41 of *S* the son of Zurishaddai
Num 10:19 was *S* the son of Zurishaddai

**SHEM** *(shem)* See SEM. *A son of Noah.*
Gen 5:32 and Noah begat *S*, Ham, and Japheth
Gen 6:10 And Noah begat three sons, *S*
Gen 7:13 selfsame day entered Noah, and *S*
Gen 9:18 went forth of the ark, were *S*
Gen 9:23 And *S* and Japheth took a garment,
Gen 9:26 Blessed be the LORD God of *S*
Gen 9:27 he shall dwell in the tents of *S*
Gen 10:1 of the sons of Noah, *S*, Ham, and
Gen 10:21 Unto *S* also, the father of all
Gen 10:22 The children of *S*
Gen 10:31 These are the sons of *S*, after
Gen 11:10 These are the generations of *S*
Gen 11:10 *S* was an hundred years old, and
Gen 11:11 *S* lived after he begat Arphaxad
1Chr 1:4 Noah, *S*, Ham, and Japheth
1Chr 1:17 The sons of *S*
1Chr 1:24 *S*, Arphaxad, Shelah,

**SHEMA** *(she'-mah)* See SHEMAIAH, SHIMHI.
*1. A city in Judah.*
Josh 15:26 Amam, and *S*, and Moladah,
*2. A son of Hebron.*
1Chr 2:43 Korah, and Tappuah, and Rekem, and *S*
1Chr 2:44 *S* begat Raham, the father of
*3. Father of Azaz.*
1Chr 5:8 the son of Azaz, the son of *S*
*4. A Benjamite Chief.*
1Chr 8:13 Beriah aldo, and *S*, who were heads
*5. A priest who aided Ezra.*
Neh 8:4 beside him stood Mattithiah, and *S*

**SHEMAAH** *(shem'-a-ah) Father of two warriors in David's army.*
1Chr 12:3 the sons of *S* the Gibeathite

**SHEMAIAH** *(shem-a-i'-ah)* See SHAMMUA, SHEMA, SHIMEI, SIMEI.
*1. A prophet in King Rehoboam's time.*
1Kin 12:22 of God came unto *S* the man of God
2Chr 11:2 the LORD came to *S* the man of God
2Chr 12:5 Then came *S* the prophet to
2Chr 12:7 the word of the LORD came to *S*
2Chr 12:15 in the book of *S* the prophet
*2. Son of Shechaniah.*
1Chr 3:22 *S*: and the sons of Shemaiah
*3. Father of Shimri.*
1Chr 4:37 the son of Shimri, the son of *S*
*4. Son of Joel.*
1Chr 5:4 *S* his son, Gog his son, Shimei
*5. Son of Hasshub.*
1Chr 9:14 *S* the son of Hasshub, the son of
Neh 11:15 *S* the son of Hashub, the son of
*6. Father of Obadiah.*
1Chr 9:16 And Obadiah the son of *S*, the son
*7. A priest who moved the Ark.*
1Chr 15:8 *S* the chief, and his brethren two
1Chr 15:11 for Uriel, Asaiah, and Joel, *S*
*8. Son of Nathaneel.*
1Chr 24:6 *S* the son of Nethaneel the scribe
*9. A sanctuary servant.*
1Chr 26:4 *S* the firstborn, Jehozabad the
1Chr 26:6 Also unto *S* his son were sons
1Chr 26:7 The sons of *S*
*10. A Levite teacher of the people.*
2Chr 17:8 with them he sent Levites, even *S*
*11. A Levite who cleansed the temple.*
2Chr 29:14 *S*, and Uzziel
*12. A Levite in Hezekiah's time.*
2Chr 31:15 and Miniamin, and Jeshua, and *S*
*13. A Levite in Josiah's time.*
2Chr 35:9 Conaniah also, and *S* and Nethaneel,
*14. A family of exiles.*
Ezr 8:13 are these, Eliphelet, Jeiel, and *S*
*15. A messenger of Ezra.*
Ezr 8:16 I for Eliezer, for Ariel, for *S*
*16. A priest who married a foreigner.*
Ezr 10:21 Maaseiah, and Elijah, and *S*
*17. A son of Harim.*
Ezr 10:31 Eliezer, Ishijah, Malchiah, *S*
*18. A rebuilder of Jerusalem's wall.*
Neh 3:29 also *S* the son of Shechaniah
*19. Son of Delaiah.*
Neh 6:10 I came unto the house of *S* the
*20. A priest who renewed the covenant.*
Neh 10:8 Maaziah, Bilgai, *S*
Neh 12:6 *S*, and Joiarib, Jedaiah,
Neh 12:18 of *S*, Jehonathan
Neh 12:34 Judah, and Benjamin, and *S*, and
Neh 12:35 the son of Jonathan, the son of *S*
*21. A priest who dedicated the wall.*
Neh 12:36 And his brethren, *S*, and Azarael,
*22. A priest who gave thanks at the wall.*
Neh 12:42 And Maaseiah, and *S*, and Eleazar, and
*23. Father of Urijah.*
Jer 26:20 the son of *S* of Kirjath-jearim
*24. A false prophet.*
Jer 29:24 also speak to *S* the Nehelamite
Jer 29:31 LORD concerning *S* the Nehelamite
Jer 29:31 Because that *S* hath prophesied
Jer 29:32 I will punish *S* the Nehelamite,
*25. Father of Delaiah.*
Jer 36:12 scribe, and Delaiah the son of *S*

**SHEMARIAH** *(shem-a-ri'-ah)*
*1. A warrior in David's army.*
1Chr 12:5 and Jerimoth, and Bealiah, and *S*
*2. Married a foreigner in exile.*
Ezr 10:32 Benjamin, Malluch, and *S*
*3. Married a foreigner in exile.*
Ezr 10:41 Azareel, and Shelemiah, *S*,

**SHEMEBER** *(shem-e'-ber) King of Zeboim.*
Gen 14:2 *S* king of Zeboiim, and the king of

**SHEMER** *(she'-mur) Owner of a hill, later the site of Samaria.*
1Kin 16:24 of *S* for two talents of silver
1Kin 16:24 he built, after the name of *S*

**SHEMIDA** *(shem-i'-dah)* See SHEMIDAH. *Son of Gilead.*
Num 26:32 And of *S*, the family of the
Josh 17:2 Hepher, and for the children of *S*

**SHEMIDAH** *(shem-i'-dah)* See SHEMIDA, SHEMIDAITES. *Same as Shemida.*
1Chr 7:19 And the sons of *S* were, Ahian, and

**SHEMIDAITES** *(shem'-i-dah-ites) Descendants of Shemida.*
Num 26:32 of Shemida, the family of the *S*

**SHEMINITH** *(shem'-i-nith) A musical notation.*
1Chr 15:21 with harps on the *S* to excel
Ps 6:*t* chief Musician on Neginoth upon *S*
Ps 12:*t* To the chief Musician upon *S*

**SHEMIRAMOTH** *(she-mir'-a-moth)*
*1. A priest who moved the Ark.*
1Chr 15:18 Zechariah, Ben, and Jaaziel, and *S*
1Chr 15:20 And Zechariah, and Aziel, and *S*
1Chr 16:5 to him Zechariah, Jeiel, and *S*
*2. A Levite in Jehoshaphat's time.*
2Chr 17:8 and Zebadiah, and Asahel, and *S*

**SHEMUEL** *(shem-u'-el)* See SAMUEL.
*1. A Simeonite prince.*
Num 34:20 of Simeon, *S* the son of Ammihud
*2. Another name for Samuel the prophet.*
1Chr 6:33 the son of Joel, the son of *S*
*3. Head of a family in Issachar.*
1Chr 7:2 and Jahmai, and Jibsam, and *S*

**SHEN** *(shen) A place in Benjamin.*
1Sa 7:12 and set it between Mizpeh and *S*

**SHENAZAR** *(she-na'-zar) Descendant of King Jehoiakim.*
1Chr 3:18 Malchiram also, and Pedaiah, and *S*

**SHENIR** *(she'-nur)* See SENIR, SION. *A mountain between Amana and Hermon.*
Deut 3:9 and the Amorites call it *S*
Song 4:8 top of Amana, from the top of *S*

**SHEPHAM** *(she'-fam)* See SHIPMITE. *A place east of the Sea of Cinneroth.*
Num 34:10 east border from Hazar-enan to *S*
Num 34:11 shall go down from *S* to Riblah

**SHEPHATIAH** *(shef-a-ti'-ah)*
*1. A son of David.*
2Sa 3:4 and the fifth, *S* the son of Abital
1Chr 3:3 The fifth, *S* of Abital
1Chr 9:8 Michri, and Meshullam the son of *S*
*2. A warrior in David's army.*
1Chr 12:5 and Shemariah, and *S* the Haruphite,
*3. A Simeonite prince.*
1Chr 27:16 Simeonites, *S* the son of Maachah
*4. A son of King Jehoshaphat.*
2Chr 21:2 and Azariah, and Michael, and *S*
*5. A family of exiles with Zerubbabel.*
Ezr 2:4 The children of *S*, three hundred
Neh 7:9 The children of *S*, three hundred
*6. Descendants of a servant of Solomon.*
Ezr 2:57 The children of *S*, the children
Neh 7:59 The children of *S*, the children
*7. A family of exiles with Ezra.*
Ezr 8:8 And of the sons of *S*
*8. A family of exiles who resettled in Jerusalem.*
Neh 11:4 the son of Amariah, the son of *S*

*9. A prince of Judah.*
Jer 38:1 Then S the son of Mattan, and

**SHEPHERD**
Gen 46:34 for every s is an abomination
Gen 49:24 (from thence is the s, the stone
Num 27:17 be not as sheep which have no s
1Kin 22:17 hills, as sheep that have not a s
2Chr 18:16 as sheep that have no s
Ps 23:1 The LORD is my s
Ps 80:1 O S of Israel, thou that leadest
Eccl 12:11 which are given from one s
Is 40:11 He shall feed his flock like a s
Is 44:28 That saith of Cyrus, He is my s
Is 63:11 the sea with the s of his flock
Jer 31:10 keep him, as a s doth his flock
Jer 43:12 as a s putteth on his garment
Jer 49:19 who is that s that will stand
Jer 50:44 who is that s that will stand
Jer 51:23 break in pieces with thee the s
Eze 34:5 scattered, because there is no s
Eze 34:8 the field, because there was no s
Eze 34:12 As a s seeketh out his flock in
Eze 34:23 And I will set up one s over them
Eze 34:23 feed them, and he shall be their s
Eze 37:24 and they all shall have one s
Amos 3:12 As the s taketh out of the mouth
Zec 10:2 troubled, because there was no s
Zec 11:15 the instruments of a foolish s
Zec 11:16 I will raise up a s in the land
Zec 11:17 Woe to the idol s that leaveth
Zec 13:7 Awake, O sword, against my s
Zec 13:7 smite the s, and the sheep shall
Mt 9:36 abroad, as sheep having no s
Mt 25:32 as a s divideth his sheep from
Mt 26:31 it is written, I will smite the s
Mk 6:34 they were as sheep not having a s
Mk 14:27 it is written, I will smite the s
Jn 10:2 by the door is the s of the sheep
Jn 10:11 I am the good s
Jn 10:11 the good s giveth his life for
Jn 10:12 that is an hireling, and not the s
Jn 10:14 I am the good s, and know my sheep
Jn 10:16 there shall be one fold, and one s
Heb 13:20 that great s of the sheep,
1Pet 2:25 but are now returned unto the S
1Pet 5:4 And when the chief S shall appear

**SHEPHERDS**
Gen 46:32 And the men are s, for their trade
Gen 47:3 unto Pharaoh, Thy servants are s
Ex 2:17 the s came and drove them away
Ex 2:19 us out of the hand of the s
1Sa 25:7 now thy s which were with us, we
Is 13:20 neither shall the s make their
Is 31:4 when a multitude of s is called
Is 56:11 they are s that cannot understand
Jer 6:3 The s with their flocks shall
Jer 23:4 I will set up s over them which
Jer 25:34 Howl, ye s, and cry
Jer 25:35 the s shall have no way to flee,
Jer 25:36 A voice of the cry of the s
Jer 33:12 shall be an habitation of s
Jer 50:6 their s have caused them to go
Eze 34:2 prophesy against the s of Israel
Eze 34:2 saith the Lord GOD unto the s
Eze 34:2 Woe be to the s of Israel that do
Eze 34:2 should not the s feed the flocks
Eze 34:7 Therefore, ye s, hear the word of
Eze 34:8 neither did my s search for my
Eze 34:8 but the s fed themselves, and fed
Eze 34:9 Therefore, O ye s, hear the word
Eze 34:10 Behold, I am against the s
Eze 34:10 neither shall the s feed
Amos 1:2 habitations of the s shall mourn
Mic 5:5 we raise against him seven s
Nah 3:18 Thy s slumber, O king of Assyria
Zeph 2:6 be dwellings and cottages for s
Zec 10:3 anger was kindled against the s
Zec 11:3 a voice of the howling of the s
Zec 11:5 their own s pity them not
Zec 11:8 Three s also I cut off in one
Lk 2:8 country s abiding in the field
Lk 2:15 the s said one to another, Let us
Lk 2:18 which were told them by the s
Lk 2:20 the s returned, glorifying and

**SHEPHI** *(she'-fi)* See SHEPHO. *A son of Shobal.*
1Chr 1:40 Alian, and Manahath, and Ebal, S

**SHEPHO** *(she'-fo)* See SHEPHI. *Same as Shephi.*
Gen 36:23 Alvan, and Manahath, and Ebal, S

**SHEPHUPHAN** *(shef'-u-fan)* See SHUPHAM, SHUPPIM. *A son of Bela.*
1Chr 8:5 And Gera, and S, and Huram

**SHERAH** *(she'-rah) Daughter of Beriah.*
1Chr 7:24 (And his daughter was S, who built

**SHEREBIAH** *(sher-e-bi'-ah)*
*1. A family of exiles.*
Ezr 8:18 and S, with his sons and his
Ezr 8:24 of the chief of the priests, S
Neh 8:7 Also Jeshua, and Bani, and S
Neh 9:4 Kadmiel, Shebaniah, Bunni, S
Neh 9:5 and Kadmiel, Bani, Hashabniah, S
*2. A Levite who renewed the covenant.*
Neh 10:12 Zaccur, S, Shebaniah,
Neh 12:8 Jeshua, Binnui, Kadmiel, S
Neh 12:24 Hashabiah, S, and Jeshua the son

**SHERESH** *(she'-resh) Son of Machir.*
1Chr 7:16 and the name of his brother was S

**SHEREZER** *(she-re'-zur)* See SHAREZER. *A messenger in Zechariah's time.*
Zec 7:2 had sent unto the house of God S

**SHESHACH** *(she'-shak)* See BABYLON. *Another name for Babylon.*
Jer 25:26 the king of S shall drink after
Jer 51:41 How is S taken

**SHESHAI** *(she'-shahee) A son of Anak.*
Num 13:22 where Ahiman, S, and Talmai, the
Josh 15:14 thence the three sons of Anak, S
Judg 1:10 and they slew S, and Ahiman, and

**SHESHAN** *(she'-shan) A descendant of Jerahmeel.*
1Chr 2:31 S. And the children of S
1Chr 2:34 Now S had no sons, but daughters
1Chr 2:34 S had a servant, an Egyptian,
1Chr 2:35 S gave his daughter to Jarha his

**SHESHBAZZAR** *(shesh-baz'-zur)* See ZERUBBABEL. *Same as Zerubbabel.*
Ezr 1:8 and numbered them unto S, the
Ezr 1:11 All these did S bring up with
Ezr 5:14 unto one, whose name was S
Ezr 5:16 Then came the same S, and laid the

**SHETH** *(sheth)* See SETH.
*1. A Moabite chief.*
Num 24:17 and destroy all the children of S
*2. Same as Seth.*
1Chr 1:1 Adam, S, Enosh,

**SHETHAR** *(she'-thar) A prince of Media and Persia.*
Est 1:14 the next unto him was Carshena, S

**SHETHAR-BOZNAI** *(she'-thar-boz'-nahee) A Persian official.*
Ezr 5:3 on this side the river, and S
Ezr 5:6 on this side the river, and S
Ezr 6:6 governor beyond the river, S
Ezr 6:13 on this side the river, S

**SHETHER BAZNAI** See SHETHAR BOZNAI.

**SHEVA** *(she'-vah)* See SHAVSHA.
*1. David's scribe.*
2Sa 20:25 And S was scribe
*2. Son of Maachah.*
1Chr 2:49 S the father of Machbenah, and the

**SHEW**
Gen 12:1 unto a land that I will s thee
Gen 20:13 which thou shalt s unto me
Gen 24:12 s kindness unto my master Abraham
Gen 40:14 s kindness, I pray thee, unto me,
Gen 46:31 s Pharaoh, and say unto him, My
Ex 7:9 you, saying, S a miracle for you
Ex 9:16 for to s in thee my power
Ex 10:1 that I might s these my signs
Ex 13:8 thou shalt s thy son in that day,
Ex 14:13 which he will s to you to day
Ex 18:20 shalt s them the way wherein they
Ex 25:9 According to all that I s thee
Ex 33:13 s me now thy way, that I may know
Ex 33:18 I beseech thee, s me thy glory
Ex 33:19 s mercy on whom I will s mercy
Num 16:5 the LORD will s who are his
Deut 1:33 to s you by what way ye should go
Deut 3:24 thou hast begun to s thy servant
Deut 5:5 to s you the word of the LORD
Deut 7:2 with them, nor s mercy unto them
Deut 13:17 s thee mercy, and have compassion
Deut 17:9 they shall s thee the sentence of
Deut 17:10 LORD shall choose shall s thee
Deut 17:11 sentence which they shall s thee
Deut 28:50 nor s favour to the young
Deut 32:7 ask thy father, and he will s thee
Josh 2:12 that ye will also s kindness unto
Josh 5:6 that he would not s them the land
Judg 1:24 S us, we pray thee, the entrance
Judg 1:24 the city, and we will s thee mercy
Judg 4:22 I will s thee the man whom thou
Judg 6:17 then s me a sign that thou
1Sa 3:15 Samuel feared to s Eli the vision
1Sa 8:9 s them the manner of the king
1Sa 9:6 peradventure he can s us our way
1Sa 9:27 that I may s thee the word of God
1Sa 10:8 s thee what thou shalt do
1Sa 14:12 to us, and we will s you a thing
1Sa 16:3 I will s thee what thou shalt do
1Sa 20:2 small, but that he will s it me
1Sa 20:12 send not unto thee, and s it thee
1Sa 20:13 thee evil, then I will s it thee
1Sa 20:14 s me the kindness of the LORD
1Sa 22:17 he fled, and did not s it to me
1Sa 25:8 young men, and they will s thee
2Sa 2:6 And now the LORD s kindness
2Sa 3:8 which against Judah do s kindness
2Sa 9:1 that I may s him kindness for
2Sa 9:3 that I may s the kindness of God
2Sa 9:7 for I will surely s thee kindness
2Sa 10:2 I will s kindness unto Hanun the
2Sa 15:25 s me both it, and his habitation
2Sa 22:26 thou wilt s thyself merciful
2Sa 22:26 man thou wilt s thyself upright
2Sa 22:27 the pure thou wilt s thyself pure
2Sa 22:27 thou wilt s thyself unsavoury
1Kin 1:52 If he will s himself a worthy man
1Kin 2:2 therefore, and s thyself a man
1Kin 2:7 But s kindness unto the sons of
1Kin 18:1 saying, Go, s thyself unto Ahab
1Kin 18:2 Elijah went to s himself unto
1Kin 18:15 I will surely s myself unto him
2Kin 6:11 Will ye not s me which of us is
2Kin 7:12 I will now s you what the Syrians
1Chr 16:23 s forth from day to day his
1Chr 19:2 I will s kindness unto Hanun the
2Chr 16:9 to s himself strong in the behalf
Ezr 2:59 but they could not s their
Neh 7:61 but they could not s their
Neh 9:19 to s them light, and the way
Est 1:11 to s the people and the princes
Est 2:10 her that she should not s it
Est 4:8 to s it unto Esther, and to
Job 10:2 s me wherefore thou contendest
Job 11:6 that he would s thee the secrets
Job 15:17 I will s thee, hear me
Job 32:6 durst not s you mine opinion
Job 32:10 I also will s mine opinion
Job 32:17 I also will s mine opinion
Job 33:23 to s unto man his uprightness
Job 36:2 I will s thee that I have yet to
Ps 4:6 that say, Who will s us any good
Ps 9:1 I will s forth all thy marvellous
Ps 9:14 That I may s forth all thy praise
Ps 16:11 Thou wilt s me the path of life
Ps 17:7 S thy marvellous lovingkindness,
Ps 18:25 thou wilt s thyself merciful
Ps 18:25 man thou wilt s thyself upright
Ps 18:26 the pure thou wilt s thyself pure
Ps 18:26 thou wilt s thyself froward
Ps 25:4 S me thy ways, O LORD
Ps 25:14 he will s them his covenant
Ps 39:6 every man walketh in a vain s
Ps 50:23 will I s the salvation of God
Ps 51:15 my mouth shall s forth thy praise
Ps 71:15 My mouth shall s forth thy
Ps 79:13 we will s forth thy praise to all
Ps 85:7 S us thy mercy, O LORD, and grant
Ps 86:17 S me a token for good
Ps 88:10 Wilt thou s wonders to the dead
Ps 91:16 him, and s him my salvation
Ps 92:2 To s forth thy lovingkindness in
Ps 92:15 To s that the LORD is upright
Ps 94:1 vengeance belongeth, s thyself
Ps 96:2 s forth his salvation from day to
Ps 106:2 who can s forth all his praise
Ps 109:16 that he remembered not to s mercy
Prov 18:24 friends must s himself friendly
Is 3:9 The s of their countenance doth

Is 27:11 formed them will *s* them no favour
Is 30:30 shall *s* the lighting down of his
Is 41:22 forth, and *s* us what shall happen
Is 41:22 let them *s* the former things,
Is 41:23 *S* the things that are to come
Is 43:9 this, and *s* us former things
Is 43:21 they shall *s* forth my praise
Is 44:7 shall come, let them *s* unto them
Is 46:8 this, and *s* yourselves men
Is 47:6 thou didst *s* them no mercy
Is 49:9 are in darkness, *S* yourselves
Is 58:1 *s* my people their transgression,
Is 60:6 they shall *s* forth the praises of
Jer 16:10 when thou shalt *s* this people all
Jer 16:13 where I will not *s* you favour
Jer 18:17 I will *s* them the back, and not
Jer 33:3 *s* thee great and mighty things,
Jer 42:3 That the LORD thy God may *s* us
Jer 42:12 I will *s* mercies unto you, that
Jer 50:42 are cruel, and will not *s* mercy
Jer 51:31 to *s* the king of Babylon that his
Eze 22:2 yea, thou shalt *s* her all her
Eze 33:31 with their mouth they *s* much love
Eze 37:18 Wilt thou not *s* us what thou
Eze 40:4 upon all that I shall *s* thee
Eze 40:4 for to the intent that I might *s*
Eze 43:10 *s* the house to the house of
Eze 43:11 *s* them the form of the house, and
Dan 2:2 for to *s* the king his dreams
Dan 2:4 we will *s* the interpretation
Dan 2:6 But if ye *s* the dream, and the
Dan 2:6 therefore *s* me the dream, and the
Dan 2:7 we will *s* the interpretation of
Dan 2:9 I shall know that ye can *s* me the
Dan 2:10 that can *s* the king's matter
Dan 2:11 that can *s* it before the king
Dan 2:16 that he would *s* the king the
Dan 2:24 I will *s* unto the king the
Dan 2:27 the soothsayers, *s* unto the king
Dan 4:2 I thought it good to *s* the signs
Dan 5:7 *s* me the interpretation thereof,
Dan 5:12 he will *s* the interpretation
Dan 5:15 but they could not *s* the
Dan 9:23 forth, and I am come to *s* thee
Dan 10:21 But I will *s* thee that which is
Dan 11:2 now will I *s* thee the truth
Joel 2:30 I will *s* wonders in the heavens
Mic 7:15 I *s* unto him marvellous things
Nah 3:5 face, and I will *s* the nations thy
Hab 1:3 Why dost thou *s* me iniquity
Zec 1:9 I will *s* thee what these be
Zec 7:9 *s* mercy and compassions every man
Mt 8:4 *s* thyself to the priest, and offer
Mt 11:4 *s* John again those things which
Mt 12:18 he shall *s* judgment to the
Mt 14:2 do *s* forth themselves in him
Mt 16:1 would *s* them a sign from heaven
Mt 16:21 Jesus to *s* unto his disciples
Mt 22:19 *S* me the tribute money
Mt 24:1 disciples came to him for to *s*
Mt 24:24 shall *s* great signs and wonders
Mk 1:44 *s* thyself to the priest, and offer
Mk 6:14 do *s* forth themselves in him
Mk 13:22 shall rise, and shall *s* signs
Mk 14:15 he will *s* you a large upper room
Lk 1:19 to *s* thee these glad tidings
Lk 5:14 *s* thyself to the priest, and offer
Lk 6:47 I will *s* you to whom he is like
Lk 8:39 *s* how great things God hath done
Lk 17:14 Go *s* yourselves unto the priests
Lk 20:24 *S* me a penny
Lk 20:47 for a *s* make long prayers
Lk 22:12 he shall *s* you a large upper room
Jn 5:20 he will *s* him greater works than
Jn 7:4 things, *s* thyself to the world
Jn 11:57 where he were, he should *s* it
Jn 14:8 *s* us the Father, and it sufficeth
Jn 14:9 sayest thou then, *S* us the Father
Jn 16:13 he will *s* you things to come
Jn 16:14 of mine, and shall *s* it unto you
Jn 16:15 of mine, and shall *s* it unto you
Jn 16:25 but I shall *s* you plainly of the
Acts 1:24 *s* whether of these two thou hast
Acts 2:19 I will *s* wonders in heaven above,
Acts 7:3 the land which I shall *s* thee
Acts 9:16 For I will *s* him how great things
Acts 12:17 Go *s* these things unto James, and
Acts 16:17 which *s* unto us the way of
Acts 24:27 willing to *s* the Jews a pleasure,
Acts 26:23 should *s* light unto the people,
Rom 2:15 Which *s* the work of the law
Rom 9:17 that I might *s* my power in thee,
Rom 9:22 if God, willing to *s* his wrath
1Cor 11:26 ye do *s* the Lord's death till he
1Cor 12:31 yet *s* I unto you a more excellent
1Cor 15:51 Behold, I *s* you a mystery
2Cor 8:24 Wherefore *s* ye to them, and before
Gal 6:12 to make a fair *s* in the flesh
Eph 2:7 *s* the exceeding riches of his
Col 2:15 he made a *s* of them openly,
Col 2:23 a *s* of wisdom in will worship
1Th 1:9 For they themselves *s* of us what
1Ti 1:16 might *s* forth all longsuffering
1Ti 5:4 learn first to *s* piety at home
1Ti 6:15 Which in his times he shall *s*
2Ti 2:15 Study to *s* thyself approved unto
Heb 6:11 *s* the same diligence to the full
Heb 6:17 willing more abundantly to *s* unto
Jas 2:18 *s* me thy faith without thy works,
Jas 2:18 I will *s* thee my faith by my
Jas 3:13 let him *s* out of a good
1Pet 2:9 that ye should *s* forth the
1Jn 1:2 *s* unto you that eternal life,
Rev 1:1 to *s* unto his servants things
Rev 4:1 I will *s* thee things which must
Rev 17:1 I will *s* unto thee the judgment
Rev 21:9 I will *s* thee the bride, the
Rev 22:6 to *s* unto his servants the things

## SHEWBREAD

Ex 25:30 upon the table *s* before me alway
Ex 35:13 and all his vessels, and the *s*
Ex 39:36 all the vessels thereof, and the *s*
Num 4:7 upon the table of *s* they shall
1Sa 21:6 was no bread there but the *s*
1Kin 7:48 of gold, whereupon the *s* was
1Chr 9:32 the Kohathites, were over the *s*
1Chr 23:29 Both for the *s*, and for the fine
1Chr 28:16 he gave gold for the tables of *s*
2Chr 2:4 incense, and for the continual *s*
2Chr 4:19 the tables whereon the *s* was set
2Chr 13:11 the *s* also set they in order upon
2Chr 29:18 the *s* table, with all the vessels
Neh 10:33 For the *s*, and for the continual
Mt 12:4 house of God, and did eat the *s*
Mk 2:26 the high priest, and did eat the *s*
Lk 6:4 of God, and did take and eat the *s*
Heb 9:2 and the table, and the *s*

## SHEWED

Gen 19:19 which thou hast *s* unto me in
Gen 24:14 hast *s* kindness unto my master
Gen 32:10 which thou hast *s* unto thy
Gen 39:21 *s* him mercy, and gave him favour
Gen 41:25 God hath *s* Pharaoh what he is
Gen 41:39 as God hath *s* thee all this
Gen 48:11 God hath *s* me also thy seed
Ex 15:25 the LORD *s* him a tree, which when
Ex 25:40 which was *s* thee in the mount
Ex 26:30 which was *s* thee in the mount
Ex 27:8 as it was *s* thee in the mount, so
Lev 13:19 reddish, and it be *s* to the priest
Lev 13:49 shall be *s* unto the priest
Lev 24:12 mind of the LORD might be *s* them
Num 8:4 which the LORD had *s* Moses
Num 13:26 *s* them the fruit of the land
Num 14:11 signs which I have *s* among them
Deut 4:35 Unto thee it was *s*, that thou
Deut 4:36 upon earth he *s* thee his great
Deut 5:24 LORD our God hath *s* us his glory
Deut 6:22 And the LORD *s* signs and wonders,
Deut 34:1 the LORD *s* him all the land of
Deut 34:12 *s* in the sight of all Israel
Josh 2:12 LORD, since I have *s* you kindness
Judg 1:25 when he *s* them the entrance into
Judg 4:12 they *s* Sisera that Barak the son
Judg 8:35 Neither *s* they kindness to the
Judg 8:35 which he had *s* unto Israel
Judg 13:10 *s* her husband, and said unto him,
Judg 13:23 he have *s* us all these things
Judg 16:18 for he hath *s* me all his heart
Ruth 2:11 unto her, It hath fully been *s* me
Ruth 2:19 she *s* her mother in law with whom
Ruth 3:10 for thou hast *s* more kindness in
1Sa 11:9 *s* it to the men of Jabesh
1Sa 15:6 for ye *s* kindness to all the
1Sa 19:7 Jonathan *s* him all those things
1Sa 22:21 Abiathar *s* David that Saul had
1Sa 24:18 thou hast *s* this day how that
2Sa 2:5 that ye have *s* this kindness unto
2Sa 10:2 as his father *s* kindness unto me
2Sa 11:22 *s* David all that Joab had sent
1Kin 1:27 thou hast not *s* it unto thy
1Kin 3:6 Thou hast *s* unto thy servant
1Kin 16:27 he did, and his might that he *s*
1Kin 22:45 and his might that he *s*, and how
2Kin 6:6 And he *s* him the place
2Kin 8:10 howbeit the LORD hath *s* me that
2Kin 8:13 The LORD hath *s* me that thou
2Kin 11:4 LORD, and *s* them the king's son
2Kin 20:13 *s* them all the house of his
2Kin 20:13 that Hezekiah *s* them not
2Kin 20:15 treasures that I have not *s* them
2Kin 22:10 And Shaphan the scribe *s* the king
1Chr 19:2 his father *s* kindness to me
2Chr 1:8 Thou hast *s* great mercy unto
2Chr 7:10 that the LORD had *s* unto David
Ezr 9:8 hath been *s* from the LORD our God
Est 1:4 When he *s* the riches of his
Est 2:10 Esther had not *s* her people nor
Est 2:20 Esther had not yet *s* her kindred
Est 3:6 for they had *s* him the people of
Job 6:14 pity should be *s* from his friend
Ps 31:21 for he hath *s* me his marvellous
Ps 60:3 Thou hast *s* thy people hard
Ps 71:18 until I have *s* thy strength unto
Ps 71:20 Thou, which hast *s* me great
Ps 78:11 and his wonders that he had *s* them
Ps 98:2 *s* in the sight of the heathen
Ps 105:27 They *s* his signs among them, and
Ps 111:6 He hath *s* his people the power of
Ps 118:27 the LORD, which hath *s* us light
Ps 142:2 I *s* before him my trouble
Prov 26:26 his wickedness shall be *s* before
Eccl 2:19 wherein I have *s* myself wise
Is 26:10 Let favour be *s* to the wicked
Is 39:2 *s* them the house of his precious
Is 39:2 that Hezekiah *s* them not
Is 39:4 treasures that I have not *s* them
Is 40:14 *s* to him the way of understanding
Is 43:12 and have saved, and I have *s*
Is 48:3 out of my mouth, and I *s* them
Is 48:5 it came to pass I *s* it thee
Is 48:6 I have *s* thee new things from
Jer 24:1 The LORD *s* me, and, behold, two
Jer 38:21 the word that the LORD hath *s* me
Eze 11:25 the things that the LORD had *s* me
Eze 20:11 *s* them my judgments, which if a
Eze 22:26 neither have they *s* difference
Amos 7:1 Thus hath the Lord GOD *s* unto me
Amos 7:4 Thus hath the Lord GOD *s* unto me
Amos 7:7 Thus he *s* me
Amos 8:1 Thus hath the Lord GOD *s* unto me
Mic 6:8 He hath *s* thee, O man, what is
Zec 1:20 the LORD *s* me four carpenters
Zec 3:1 he *s* me Joshua the high priest
Mt 28:11 *s* unto the chief priests all the
Lk 1:51 He hath *s* strength with his arm
Lk 1:58 Lord had *s* great mercy upon her
Lk 4:5 *s* unto him all the kingdoms of
Lk 7:18 the disciples of John *s* him of
Lk 10:37 he said, He that *s* mercy on him
Lk 14:21 came, and *s* his lord these things
Lk 20:37 even Moses *s* at the bush, when he
Lk 24:40 he *s* them his hands and his feet
Jn 10:32 works have I *s* you from my Father
Jn 20:20 he *s* unto them his hands and his
Jn 21:1 After these things Jesus *s*
Jn 21:1 and on this wise *s* he himself
Jn 21:14 Jesus *s* himself to his disciples
Acts 1:3 To whom also he *s* himself alive
Acts 3:18 which God before had *s* by the
Acts 4:22 this miracle of healing was *s*
Acts 7:26 the next day he *s* himself unto
Acts 7:36 out, after that he had *s* wonders
Acts 7:52 they have slain them which *s*
Acts 10:28 but God hath *s* me that I should
Acts 10:40 up the third day, and *s* him
Acts 11:13 he *s* us how he had seen an angel
Acts 19:18 and confessed, and *s* their deeds
Acts 20:20 unto you, but have *s* you, and have
Acts 20:35 I have *s* you all things, how that
Acts 23:22 thou hast *s* these things to me
Acts 26:20 But *s* first unto them of Damascus
Acts 28:2 the barbarous people *s* us no
Acts 28:21 came *s* or spake any harm of thee
Rom 1:19 for God hath *s* it unto them
1Cor 10:28 eat not for his sake that *s* it
Heb 6:10 which ye have *s* toward his name,
Heb 8:5 pattern *s* to thee in the mount
Jas 2:13 mercy, that hath *s* no mercy

2Pet 1:14 our Lord Jesus Christ hath *s* me
Rev 21:10 *s* me that great city, the holy
Rev 22:1 he *s* me a pure river of water of
Rev 22:8 the angel which *s* me these things

**SHEWEST**
2Chr 6:14 *s* mercy unto thy servants, that
Job 10:16 again thou *s* thyself marvellous
Jer 32:18 Thou *s* lovingkindness unto
Jn 2:18 What sign *s* thou unto us, seeing
Jn 6:30 unto him, What sign *s* thou then

**SHEWETH**
Gen 41:28 is about to do he *s* unto Pharaoh
Num 23:3 whatsoever he *s* me I will tell
1Sa 22:8 there is none that *s* me that my
1Sa 22:8 or *s* unto me that my son hath
2Sa 22:51 *s* mercy to his anointed, unto
Job 36:9 Then he *s* them their work, and
Job 36:33 The noise thereof *s* concerning it
Ps 18:50 *s* mercy to his anointed, to David
Ps 19:1 and the firmament *s* his handywork
Ps 19:2 and night unto night *s* knowledge
Ps 37:21 but the righteous *s* mercy
Ps 112:5 A good man *s* favour, and lendeth
Ps 147:19 He *s* his word unto Jacob, his
Prov 12:17 truth *s* forth righteousness
Prov 27:25 and the tender grass *s* itself
Is 41:26 yea, there is none that *s*
Mt 4:8 *s* him all the kingdoms of the
Jn 5:20 *s* him all things that himself
Rom 9:16 runneth, but of God that *s* mercy
Rom 12:8 he that *s* mercy, with

**SHEWING**
Ex 20:6 *s* mercy unto thousands of them
Deut 5:10 *s* mercy unto thousands of them
Ps 78:4 *s* to the generation to come the
Song 2:9 *s* himself through the lattice
Dan 4:27 iniquities by *s* mercy to the poor
Dan 5:12 and *s* of hard sentences, and
Lk 1:80 till the day of his *s* unto Israel
Lk 8:1 *s* the glad tidings of the kingdom
Acts 9:39 *s* the coats and garments which
Acts 18:28 *s* by the scriptures that Jesus
2Th 2:4 of God, *s* himself that he is God
Titus 2:7 In all things *s* thyself a pattern
Titus 2:7 in doctrine *s* uncorruptness,
Titus 2:10 but *s* all good fidelity
Titus 3:2 *s* all meekness unto all men

**SHIBBOLETH** *(shib'-bo-leth)* See SIBBOLETH. *Password that distinguished Gileadites from Ephraimites.*
Judg 12:6 said they unto him, Say now *S*

**SHIBMAH** *(shib'-mah)* See SHEBAM, SIBMAH. *A city in Reuben.*
Num 32:38 (their names being changed,) and *S*

**SHICRON** *(shi'-cron) A city in Judah.*
Josh 15:11 and the border was drawn to *S*

**SHIELD**
Gen 15:1 I am thy *s*, and thy exceeding
Deut 33:29 the *s* of thy help, and who is the
Judg 5:8 was there a *s* or spear seen among
1Sa 17:7 one bearing a *s* went before him
1Sa 17:41 that bare the *s* went before him
1Sa 17:45 and with a spear, and with a *s*
2Sa 1:21 for there the *s* of the mighty is
2Sa 1:21 the *s* of Saul, as though he had
2Sa 22:3 he is my *s*, and the horn of my
2Sa 22:36 given me the *s* of thy salvation
1Kin 10:17 three pound of gold went to one *s*
2Kin 19:32 there, nor come before it with *s*
1Chr 12:8 the battle, that could handle *s*
1Chr 12:24 The children of Judah that bare *s*
1Chr 12:34 captains, and with them with *s*
2Chr 9:16 shekels of gold went to one *s*
2Chr 17:17 bow and *s* two hundred thousand
2Chr 25:5 war, that could handle spear and *s*
Job 39:23 the glittering spear and the *s*
Ps 3:3 But thou, O LORD, art a *s* for me
Ps 5:12 wilt thou compass him as with a *s*
Ps 18:35 given me the *s* of thy salvation
Ps 28:7 The LORD is my strength and my *s*
Ps 33:20 he is our help and our *s*
Ps 35:2 Take hold of *s* and buckler, and
Ps 59:11 and bring them down, O Lord our *s*
Ps 76:3 he the arrows of the bow, the *s*
Ps 84:9 Behold, O God our *s*, and look upon
Ps 84:11 For the LORD God is a sun and *s*
Ps 91:4 his truth shall be thy *s* and
Ps 115:9 he is their help and their *s*
Ps 115:10 he is their help and their *s*
Ps 115:11 he is their help and their *s*
Ps 119:114 Thou art my hiding place and my *s*
Ps 144:2 my *s*, and he in whom I trust
Prov 30:5 he is a *s* unto them that put
Is 21:5 ye princes, and anoint the *s*
Is 22:6 horsemen, and Kir uncovered the *s*
Jer 46:3 Order ye the buckler and *s*
Jer 46:9 and the Libyans, that handle the *s*
Eze 23:24 set against thee buckler and *s*
Eze 27:10 they hanged the *s* and helmet in
Eze 38:5 all of them with *s* and helmet
Nah 2:3 The *s* of his mighty men is made
Eph 6:16 Above all, taking the *s* of faith

**SHIELDS**
2Sa 8:7 David took the *s* of gold that
1Kin 10:17 three hundred *s* of beaten gold
1Kin 14:26 he took away all the *s* of gold
1Kin 14:27 made in their stead brasen *s*
2Kin 11:10 give king David's spears and *s*
1Chr 18:7 David took the *s* of gold that
2Chr 9:16 three hundred *s* made he of beaten
2Chr 11:12 And in every several city he put *s*
2Chr 12:9 he carried away also the *s* of
2Chr 12:10 king Rehoboam made *s* of brass
2Chr 14:8 and out of Benjamin, that bare *s*
2Chr 23:9 spears, and bucklers, and *s*
2Chr 26:14 them throughout all the host *s*
2Chr 32:5 and made darts and *s* in abundance
2Chr 32:27 stones, and for spices, and for *s*
Neh 4:16 them held both the spears, the *s*
Ps 47:9 for the *s* of the earth belong
Song 4:4 bucklers, all *s* of mighty men
Is 37:33 there, nor come before it with *s*
Jer 51:11 gather the *s*
Eze 27:11 they hanged their *s* upon thy
Eze 38:4 great company with bucklers and *s*
Eze 39:9 and burn the weapons, both the *s*

**SHIGGAION** *(shig-gah'-yon)* See SHIGIONOTH. *A musical notation.*
Ps 7:*t* *S* of David, which he sang unto

**SHIGIONOTH** *(shig-i'-o-noth)* See SHIGGAION. *A musical notation.*
Hab 3:1 of Habakkuk the prophet upon *S*

**SHIHON** *(shi'-hon) A city in Issachar.*
Josh 19:19 Haphraim, and *S*, and Anaharath,

**SHIHOR** *(shi'-hor)* See SHIHOR-LIBNATH. *Same as Sihor.*
1Chr 13:5 from *S* of Egypt even unto the

**SHIHOR-LIBNATH** *(shi'-hor-lib'-nath) A small river in Asher.*
Josh 19:26 to Carmel westward, and to *S*

**SHILHI** *(shil'-hi) Father of Azubah.*
1Kin 22:42 name was Azubah the daughter of *S*
2Chr 20:31 name was Azubah the daughter of *S*

**SHILHIM** *(shil'-him)* See SHAARAIM, SHARUHEN. *A city in Judah.*
Josh 15:32 And Lebaoth, and *S*, and Ain, and

**SHILLEM** *(shil'-lem)* See SHALLUM, SHILLEMITES. *A son of Naphtali.*
Gen 46:24 Jahzeel, and Guni, and Jezer, and *S*
Num 26:49 of *S*, the family of the

**SHILLEMITES** *(shil'-lem-ites) Descendants of Shillem.*
Num 26:49 of Shillem, the family of the *S*

**SHILOAH** *(shi-lo'-ah)* See SILOAH, SILOAM. *A fountain in Jerusalem.*
Is 8:6 the waters of *S* that go softly

**SHILOH** *(shi'-loh)* See SHILONITE.
*1. Symbolic name for the Ruler from Judah.*
Gen 49:10 between his feet, until *S* come
*2. A city in Ephraim.*
Josh 18:1 of Israel assembled together at *S*
Josh 18:8 lots for you before the LORD in *S*
Josh 18:9 again to Joshua to the host at *S*
Josh 18:10 for them in *S* before the LORD
Josh 19:51 by lot in *S* before the LORD
Josh 21:2 them at *S* in the land of Canaan
Josh 22:9 the children of Israel out of *S*
Josh 22:12 gathered themselves together at *S*
Judg 18:31 that the house of God was in *S*
Judg 21:12 brought them unto the camp to *S*
Judg 21:19 *S* yearly in a place which is on
Judg 21:21 if the daughters of *S* come out to
Judg 21:21 his wife of the daughters of *S*
1Sa 1:3 unto the LORD of hosts in *S*
1Sa 1:9 rose up after they had eaten in *S*
1Sa 1:24 unto the house of the LORD in *S*
1Sa 2:14 So they did in *S* unto all the
1Sa 3:21 And the LORD appeared again in *S*
1Sa 3:21 in *S* by the word of the LORD
1Sa 4:3 of the LORD out of *S* unto us
1Sa 4:4 So the people sent to *S*, that
1Sa 4:12 came to *S* the same day with his
1Sa 14:3 of Eli, the LORD's priest in *S*
1Kin 2:27 concerning the house of Eli in *S*
1Kin 14:2 and get thee to *S*
1Kin 14:4 did so, and arose, and went to *S*
Ps 78:60 he forsook the tabernacle of *S*
Jer 7:12 now unto my place which was in *S*
Jer 7:14 your fathers, as I have done to *S*
Jer 26:6 will I make this house like *S*
Jer 26:9 This house shall be like *S*
Jer 41:5 came certain from Shechem, from *S*

**SHILONI** *(shi-lo'-ni)* See SHILONITE. *Father of Zechariah.*
Neh 11:5 son of Zechariah, the son of *S*

**SHILONITE** *(shi'-lon-ite)* See SHILONI, SHILONITES. *An inhabitant of Shiloh.*
1Kin 11:29 Ahijah the *S* found him in the way
1Kin 12:15 the LORD spake by Ahijah the *S*
1Kin 15:29 spake by his servant Ahijah the *S*
2Chr 9:29 in the prophecy of Ahijah the *S*
2Chr 10:15 *S* to Jeroboam the son of Nebat

**SHILONITES** *(shi'-lon-ites)*
1Chr 9:5 And of the *S*

**SHILSHAH** *(shil'-shah) Son of Zophah.*
1Chr 7:37 Bezer, and Hod, and Shamma, and *S*

**SHIMEA** *(shim'-e-ah)* See SHAMMAH, SHAMMUA, SHAMMUAH, SHIMEAH, SHIMEATHITES, SHIMMA.
*1. David's brother.*
1Chr 20:7 Jonathan the son of *S* David's
*2. A son of David.*
1Chr 3:5 *S*, and Shobab, and Nathan, and
*3. Father of Haggiah.*
1Chr 6:30 *S* his son, Haggiah his son,
*4. Father of Berachiah.*
1Chr 6:39 son of Berachiah, the son of *S*

**SHIMEAH** *(shim'-e-ah)* See SHIMEA, SHIMEAM.
*1. Same as Shimea 1.*
2Sa 13:3 the son of *S* David's brother
2Sa 13:32 the son of *S* David's brother,
2Sa 21:21 Jonathan the son of *S* the brother
*2. A relative of King Saul.*
1Chr 8:32 And Mikloth begat *S*

**SHIMEAM** *(shim'-e-am)* See SHIMEA. *Son of Mikloth.*
1Chr 9:38 And Mikloth begat *S*

**SHIMEATH** *(shim'-e-ath) Mother of Jozachar.*
2Kin 12:21 For Jozachar the son of *S*
2Chr 24:26 Zabad the son of *S* an Ammonitess

**SHIMEATHITES** *(shim'-e-ath-ites) A family of scribes.*
1Chr 2:55 the Tirathites, the *S*, and

**SHIMEI** *(shim'-e-i)* See SHEMAIAH, SHIMHI, SHIMI, SHIMITES.
*1. A son of Gershon.*
Num 3:18 families; Libni, and *S*
1Chr 6:17 Gershom; Libni, and *S*
1Chr 6:42 the son of Zimmah, the son of *S*
1Chr 23:7 Gershonites were, Laadan, and *S*
1Chr 23:10 And the sons of *S* were, Jahath,
1Chr 23:10 These four were the sons of *S*
*2. A son of Gera.*
2Sa 16:5 house of Saul, whose name was *S*
2Sa 16:7 thus said *S* when he cursed, Come
2Sa 16:13 *S* went along on the hill's side
2Sa 19:16 *S* the son of Gera, a Benjamite,
2Sa 19:18 *S* the son of Gera fell down
2Sa 19:21 Shall not *S* be put to death for
2Sa 19:23 Therefore the king said unto *S*
1Kin 2:8 hast with thee *S* the son of Gera
1Kin 2:36 And the king sent and called for *S*
1Kin 2:38 *S* said unto the king, The saying
1Kin 2:38 *S* dwelt in Jerusalem many days
1Kin 2:39 of *S* ran away unto Achish son of
1Kin 2:39 And they told *S*, saying, Behold,
1Kin 2:40 *S* arose, and saddled his ass, and

1Kin 2:40 *S* went, and brought his servants
1Kin 2:41 it was told Solomon that *S* had
1Kin 2:42 And the king sent and called for *S*
1Kin 2:44 The king said moreover to *S*
*3. An officer of David.*
1Kin 1:8 and Nathan the prophet, and *S*
*4. An officer of Solomon.*
1Kin 4:18 *S* the son of Elah, in Benjamin
*5. A descendant of King Jehoiakim.*
1Chr 3:19 of Pedaiah were, Zerubbabel, and *S*
*6. Son of Zacchur.*
1Chr 4:26 son, Zacchur his son, *S* his son
1Chr 4:27 *S* had sixteen sons and six
*7. Son of Gog.*
1Chr 5:4 his son, Gog his son, *S* his son,
*8. Son of Libni.*
1Chr 6:29 his son, *S* his son, Uzza his son,
*9. A Levite of the Laadan family.*
1Chr 23:9 The sons of *S*
*10. A sanctuary servant.*
1Chr 25:17 The tenth to *S*, he, his sons, and
*11. A vineyard keeper.*
1Chr 27:27 the vineyards was *S* the Ramathite
*12. A Levite who cleansed the Temple.*
2Chr 29:14 Jehiel, and *S*
*13. A Temple servant in Hezekiah's time.*
2Chr 31:12 *S* his brother was the next
2Chr 31:13 *S* his brother, at the commandment
*14. A Levite who married a foreigner.*
Ezr 10:23 Jozabad, and *S*, and Kelaiah, (the
*15. A Hashumite who married a foreigner.*
Ezr 10:33 Jeremai, Manasseh, and *S*
*16. A Banite who married a foreigner.*
Ezr 10:38 And Bani, and Binnui, *S*,
*17. Grandfather of Mordecai.*
Est 2:5 the son of Jair, the son of *S*
*18. A representative of the Gershonites.*
Zec 12:13 the family of *S* apart, and their

**SHIMEON** *(shim'-e-on)* See SIMEON. *A member of the Harim family.*
Ezr 10:31 Ishijah, Malchiah, Shemaiah, *S*

**SHIMHI** *(shim'-hi)* See SHEMA, SHIMEI. *Father of a chief family in Judah.*
1Chr 8:21 and Shimrath, the sons of *S*

**SHIMI** *(shi'-mi)* See SHIMEI, SHIMITES. *Same as Shimei 1.*
Ex 6:17 Libni, and *S*, according to their

**SHIMITES** *(shi'-mites) Descendants of Shimei 1.*
Num 3:21 Libnites, and the family of the *S*

**SHIMMA** *(shim'-mah)* See SHAMMAH. *Same as Shamma.*
1Chr 2:13 the second, and *S* the third,

**SHIMON** *(shi'-mon) A descendant of Caleb.*
1Chr 4:20 And the sons of *S* were, Amnon, and

**SHIMRATH** *(shim'-rath) A son of Shimri.*
1Chr 8:21 And Adaiah, and Beraiah, and *S*

**SHIMRI** *(shim'-ri)* See SIMRI.
*1. Head of a family in Simeon.*
1Chr 4:37 the son of Jedaiah, the son of *S*
*2. Father of Jedaiah.*
1Chr 11:45 Jediael the son of *S*, and Joha his
*3. A Levite who cleansed the Temple.*
2Chr 29:13 *S*, and Jeiel

**SHIMRITH** *(shim'-rith)* See SHOMER. *Mother of Jehozabad.*
2Chr 24:26 the son of *S* a Moabitess

**SHIMROM** *(shim'-rom)* See SHIMRON. *A son of Issachar.*
1Chr 7:1 were, Tola, and Puah, Jashub, and *S*

**SHIMRON** *(shim'-ron)* See SHIMROM, SHIMRONITES. *Same as Shimron.*
Gen 46:13 Tola, and Phuvah, and Job, and *S*
Num 26:24 of *S*, the family of the
Josh 11:1 of Madon, and to the king of *S*
Josh 19:15 And Kattath, and Nahallal, and *S*

**SHIMRONITES** *(shim'-ron-ites) Descendants of Shimrom.*
Num 26:24 of Shimron, the family of the *S*

**SHIMRON-MERON** *(shim'-ron-me'-ron) A city in Galilee.*
Josh 12:20 The king of *S*, one

**SHIMSHAI** *(shim'-shahee) An opponent of Nehemiah.*
Ezr 4:8 *S* the scribe wrote a letter
Ezr 4:9 *S* the scribe, and the rest of
Ezr 4:17 to *S* the scribe, and to the rest
Ezr 4:23 *S* the scribe, and their companions

**SHINAB** *(shi'-nab) King of Admah.*
Gen 14:2 *S* king of Admah, and Shemeber king

**SHINAR** *(shi'-nar) A nation in Babylonia.*
Gen 10:10 and Calneh, in the land of *S*
Gen 11:2 found a plain in the land of *S*
Gen 14:1 in the days of Amraphel king of *S*
Gen 14:9 of nations, and Amraphel king of *S*
Is 11:11 Cush, and from Elam, and from *S*
Dan 1:2 land of *S* to the house of his god
Zec 5:11 it an house in the land of *S*

**SHINE**
Num 6:25 LORD make his face *s* upon thee
Job 3:4 neither let the light *s* upon it
Job 10:3 *s* upon the counsel of the wicked
Job 11:17 thou shalt *s* forth, thou shalt be
Job 18:5 the spark of his fire shall not *s*
Job 22:28 the light shall *s* upon thy ways
Job 36:32 commandeth it not to *s* by the
Job 37:15 the light of his cloud to *s*
Job 41:18 By his neesings a light doth *s*
Job 41:32 He maketh a path to *s* after him
Ps 31:16 thy face to *s* upon thy servant
Ps 67:1 and cause his face to *s* upon us
Ps 80:1 between the cherubims, *s* forth
Ps 80:3 O God, and cause thy face to *s*
Ps 80:7 of hosts, and cause thy face to *s*
Ps 80:19 God of hosts, cause thy face to *s*
Ps 104:15 man, and oil to make his face to *s*
Ps 119:135 thy face to *s* upon thy servant
Eccl 8:1 man's wisdom maketh his face to *s*
Is 13:10 shall not cause her light to *s*
Is 60:1 Arise, *s*; for thy light
Jer 5:28 They are waxen fat, they *s*
Dan 9:17 cause thy face to *s* upon thy
Dan 12:3 they that be wise shall *s* as the
Mt 5:16 Let your light so *s* before men
Mt 13:43 Then shall the righteous *s* forth
Mt 17:2 and his face did *s* as the sun
2Cor 4:4 image of God, should *s* unto them
2Cor 4:6 the light to *s* out of darkness
Phil 2:15 among whom ye *s* as lights in the
Rev 18:23 shall *s* no more at all in thee
Rev 21:23 neither of the moon, to *s* in it

**SHINED**
Deut 33:2 he *s* forth from mount Paran, and
Job 29:3 When his candle *s* upon my head
Job 31:26 If I beheld the sun when it *s*
Ps 50:2 perfection of beauty, God hath *s*
Is 9:2 death, upon them hath the light *s*
Eze 43:2 the earth *s* with his glory
Acts 9:3 suddenly there *s* round about him
Acts 12:7 him, and a light *s* in the prison
2Cor 4:6 hath *s* in our hearts, to give the

**SHINETH**
Job 25:5 even to the moon, and it *s* not
Ps 139:12 but the night *s* as the day
Prov 4:18 as the shining light, that *s* more
Mt 24:27 the east, and *s* even unto the west
Lk 17:24 *s* unto the other part under
Jn 1:5 And the light *s* in darkness
2Pet 1:19 a light that *s* in a dark place
1Jn 2:8 is past, and the true light now *s*
Rev 1:16 was as the sun *s* in his strength

**SHINING**
2Sa 23:4 the earth by clear *s* after rain
Prov 4:18 of the just is as the *s* light
Is 4:5 the *s* of a flaming fire by night
Joel 2:10 the stars shall withdraw their *s*
Joel 3:15 the stars shall withdraw their *s*
Hab 3:11 at the *s* of thy glittering spear
Mk 9:3 And his raiment became *s*,
Lk 11:36 as when the bright *s* of a candle
Lk 24:4 men stood by them in *s* garments
Jn 5:35 He was a burning and a *s* light
Acts 26:13 *s* round about me and them which

**SHIP**
Prov 30:19 the way of a *s* in the midst of
Is 33:21 shall gallant *s* pass thereby
Eze 27:5 They have made all thy *s* boards
Jonah 1:3 he found a *s* going to Tarshish
Jonah 1:4 so that the *s* was like to be
Jonah 1:5 that were in the *s* into the sea
Jonah 1:5 gone down into the sides of the *s*
Mt 4:21 in a *s* with Zebedee their father,
Mt 4:22 And they immediately left the *s*
Mt 8:23 And when he was entered into a *s*
Mt 8:24 insomuch that the *s* was covered
Mt 9:1 And he entered into a *s*, and passed
Mt 13:2 him, so that he went into a *s*
Mt 14:13 he departed thence by *s* into a
Mt 14:22 his disciples to get into a *s*
Mt 14:24 But the *s* was now in the midst of
Mt 14:29 Peter was come down out of the *s*
Mt 14:32 And when they were come into the *s*
Mt 14:33 Then they that were in the *s* came
Mt 15:39 away the multitude, and took *s*
Mk 1:19 were in the *s* mending their nets
Mk 1:20 in the *s* with the hired servants
Mk 3:9 that a small *s* should wait on him
Mk 4:1 so that he entered into a *s*
Mk 4:36 took him even as he was in the *s*
Mk 4:37 and the waves beat into the *s*
Mk 4:38 was in the hinder part of the *s*
Mk 5:2 And when he was come out of the *s*
Mk 5:18 And when he was come into the *s*
Mk 5:21 again by *s* unto the other side
Mk 6:32 a desert place by *s* privately
Mk 6:45 his disciples to get into the *s*
Mk 6:47 the *s* was in the midst of the sea
Mk 6:51 he went up unto them into the *s*
Mk 6:54 when they were come out of the *s*
Mk 8:10 into a *s* with his disciples
Mk 8:13 entering into the *s* again
Mk 8:14 neither had they in the *s* with
Lk 5:3 and taught the people out of the *s*
Lk 5:7 which were in the other *s*
Lk 8:22 went into a *s* with his disciples
Lk 8:37 and he went up into the *s*, and
Jn 6:17 And entered into a *s*, and went over
Jn 6:19 sea, and drawing nigh unto the *s*
Jn 6:21 willingly received him into the *s*
Jn 6:21 immediately the *s* was at the land
Jn 21:3 and entered into a *s* immediately
Jn 21:6 net on the right side of the *s*
Jn 21:8 disciples came in a little *s*
Acts 20:13 And we went before to *s*, and sailed
Acts 20:38 they accompanied him unto the *s*
Acts 21:2 finding a *s* sailing over unto
Acts 21:3 for there the *s* was to unlade her
Acts 21:6 leave one of another, we took *s*
Acts 27:2 entering into a *s* of Adramyttium
Acts 27:6 a *s* of Alexandria sailing into
Acts 27:10 not only of the lading and *s*
Acts 27:11 the master and the owner of the *s*
Acts 27:15 when the *s* was caught, and could
Acts 27:17 used helps, undergirding the *s*
Acts 27:18 the next day they lightened the *s*
Acts 27:19 own hands the tackling of the *s*
Acts 27:22 life among you, but of the *s*
Acts 27:30 were about to flee out of the *s*
Acts 27:31 Except these abide in the *s*
Acts 27:37 we were in all in the *s* two
Acts 27:38 enough, they lightened the *s*
Acts 27:39 were possible, to thrust in the *s*
Acts 27:41 seas met, they ran the *s* aground
Acts 27:44 and some on broken pieces of the *s*
Acts 28:11 we departed in a *s* of Alexandria

**SHIPHI** *(shi'-fi) Father of Ziza.*
1Chr 4:37 And Ziza the son of *S*, the son of

**SHIPHMITE** *(shif'-mite) Family name of Zabdi.*
1Chr 27:27 the wine cellars was Zabdi the *S*

**SHIPHRAH** *(shif'-rah) A Hebrew midwife in Egypt.*
Ex 1:15 which the name of the one was *S*

**SHIPHTAN** *(shif'-tan) Father of Kemuel.*
Num 34:24 of Ephraim, Kemuel the son of *S*

**SHIPS**
Gen 49:13 and he shall be for an haven of *s*
Num 24:24 *s* shall come come from the coast
Deut 28:68 thee into Egypt again with *s*
Judg 5:17 and why did Dan remain in *s*
1Kin 9:26 made a navy of *s* in Ezion-geber
1Kin 22:48 Jehoshaphat made *s* of Tharshish
1Kin 22:48 for the *s* were broken at
1Kin 22:49 go with thy servants in the *s*
2Chr 8:18 by the hands of his servants *s*
2Chr 9:21 For the king's *s* went to Tarshish
2Chr 9:21 the *s* of Tarshish bringing gold

2Chr 20:36 him to make *s* to go to Tarshish
2Chr 20:36 they made the *s* in Ezion-gaber
2Chr 20:37 the *s* were broken, that they were
Job 9:26 are passed away as the swift *s*
Ps 48:7 Thou breakest the *s* of Tarshish
Ps 104:26 There go the *s*
Ps 107:23 They that go down to the sea in *s*
Prov 31:14 She is like the merchants' *s*
Is 2:16 And upon all the *s* of Tarshish
Is 23:1 Howl, ye *s* of Tarshish
Is 23:14 Howl, ye *s* of Tarshish
Is 43:14 Chaldeans, whose cry is in the *s*
Is 60:9 the *s* of Tarshish first, to bring
Eze 27:9 all the *s* of the sea with their
Eze 27:25 The *s* of Tarshish did sing of
Eze 27:29 sea, shall come down from their *s*
Eze 30:9 messengers go forth from me in *s*
Dan 11:30 For the *s* of Chittim shall come
Dan 11:40 and with horsemen, and with many *s*
Mk 4:36 were also with him other little *s*
Lk 5:2 saw two *s* standing by the lake
Lk 5:3 And he entered into one of the *s*
Lk 5:7 they came, and filled both the *s*
Lk 5:11 they had brought their *s* to land
Jas 3:4 Behold also the *s*, which though
Rev 8:9 part of the *s* were destroyed
Rev 18:17 and all the company in *s*, and
Rev 18:19 had *s* in the sea by reason of her

**SHISHA** *(shi'-shah)* See SHAVSHA. *Father of Elihoreph and Ahiah.*
1Kin 4:3 Elihoreph and Ahiah, the sons of *S*

**SHISHAK** *(shi'-shak) A king of Egypt.*
1Kin 11:40 unto *S* king of Egypt, and was in
1Kin 14:25 that *S* king of Egypt came up
2Chr 12:2 *S* king of Egypt came up against
2Chr 12:5 to Jerusalem because of *S*
2Chr 12:5 I also left you in the hand of *S*
2Chr 12:7 upon Jerusalem by the hand of *S*
2Chr 12:9 So *S* king of Egypt came up

**SHITRAI** *(shit'-ra-i) A herdsman in David's court.*
1Chr 27:29 fed in Sharon was *S* the Sharonite

**SHITTIM** *(shit'-tim) A place in Moab.*
Ex 25:5 and badgers' skins, and *s* wood,
Ex 25:10 they shall make an ark of *s* wood
Ex 25:13 thou shalt make staves of *s* wood
Ex 25:23 shalt also make a table of *s* wood
Ex 25:28 shalt make the staves of *s* wood
Ex 26:15 tabernacle of *s* wood standing up
Ex 26:26 And thou shalt make bars of *s* wood
Ex 26:32 of *s* wood overlaid with gold
Ex 26:37 hanging five pillars of *s* wood
Ex 27:1 shalt make an altar of *s* wood
Ex 27:6 for the altar, staves of *s* wood
Ex 30:1 of *s* wood shalt thou make it
Ex 30:5 shalt make the staves of *s* wood
Ex 35:7 and badgers' skins, and *s* wood,
Ex 35:24 with whom was found *s* wood for
Ex 36:20 for the tabernacle of *s* wood
Ex 36:31 And he made bars of *s* wood
Ex 36:36 thereunto four pillars of *s* wood
Ex 37:1 Bezaleel made the ark of *s* wood
Ex 37:4 And he made staves of *s* wood
Ex 37:10 And he made the table of *s* wood
Ex 37:15 And he made the staves of *s* wood
Ex 37:25 made the incense altar of *s* wood
Ex 37:28 And he made the staves of *s* wood
Ex 38:1 altar of burnt offering of *s* wood
Ex 38:6 And he made the staves of *s* wood
Num 25:1 And Israel abode in *S*, and the
Deut 10:3 And I made an ark of *s* wood
Josh 2:1 out of *S* two men to spy secretly
Josh 3:1 and they removed from *S*, and came
Joel 3:18 and shall water the valley of *S*
Mic 6:5 answered him from *S* unto Gilgal

**SHIZA** *(shi'-zah) A "mighty man" of David.*
1Chr 11:42 Adina the son of *S* the Reubenite

**SHOA** *(sho'-ah) A tribal enemy of Israel.*
Eze 23:23 and all the Chaldeans, Pekod, and *S*

**SHOBAB** *(sho'-bab)*
*1. A son of David.*
2Sa 5:14 Shammuah, and *S*, and Nathan, and
1Chr 3:5 Shimea, and *S*, and Nathan, and
1Chr 14:4 and *S*, Nathan, and Solomon
*2. A son of Caleb.*
1Chr 2:18 Jesher, and *S*, and Ardon

**SHOBACH** *(sho'-bak)* See SHOPHACH. *A Syrian defeated by David.*
2Sa 10:16 *S* the captain of the host of
2Sa 10:18 smote *S* the captain of their host

**SHOBAI** *(sho'-bahee) A family of exiles.*
Ezr 2:42 of Hatita, the children of *S*
Neh 7:45 of Hatita, the children of *S*

**SHOBAL** *(sho'-bal)*
*1. A son of Seir.*
Gen 36:20 Lotan, and *S*, and Zibeon, and Anah,
Gen 36:23 And the children of *S* were these
Gen 36:29 duke Lotan, duke *S*, duke Zibeon,
1Chr 1:38 Lotan, and *S*, and Zibeon, and Anah,
1Chr 1:40 The sons of *S*
*2. A son of Caleb.*
1Chr 2:50 *S* the father of Kirjath-jearim,
1Chr 2:52 *S* the father of Kirjath-jearim
*3. A son of Judah.*
1Chr 4:1 Hezron, and Carmi, and Hur, and *S*
1Chr 4:2 Reaiah the son of *S* begat Jahath

**SHOBEK** *(sho'-bek) A clan leader who renewed the covenant.*
Neh 10:24 Hallohesh, Pileha, *S*,

**SHOBI** *(sho'-bi) A son of Nahash.*
2Sa 17:27 that *S* the son of Nahash of

**SHOCHO** *(sho'-ko)* See CHOCHO. *A city in Judah.*
2Chr 28:18 *S* with the villages thereof, and

**SHOCHOH** *(sho'-ko)* See SHOCHO, SHOCO, SOCHOH, SOCO, SOCOH. *Same as Shocho.*
1Sa 17:1 and were gathered together at *S*
1Sa 17:1 to Judah, and pitched between *S*

**SHOCO** *(sho'-ko)* See SHOCHOH. *Same as Shocho.*
2Chr 11:7 And Beth-zur, and *S*, and Adullam,

**SHOD**
2Chr 28:15 *s* them, and gave them to eat and to
Eze 16:10 *s* thee with badgers' skin, and I
Mk 6:9 But be *s* with sandals
Eph 6:15 your feet *s* with the preparation

**SHOE**
Deut 25:9 loose his *s* from off his foot, and
Deut 25:10 of him that hath his *s* loosed
Deut 29:5 thy *s* is not waxen old upon thy
Josh 5:15 Loose thy *s* from off thy foot
Ruth 4:7 a man plucked off his *s*, and gave
Ruth 4:8 So he drew off his *s*
Ps 60:8 over Edom will I cast out my *s*
Ps 108:9 over Edom will I cast out my *s*
Is 20:2 put off thy *s* from thy foot

**SHOES**
Ex 3:5 put off thy *s* from off thy feet,
Ex 12:11 your *s* on your feet, and your
Deut 33:25 Thy *s* shall be iron and brass
Josh 9:5 And old *s* and clouted upon their
Josh 9:13 our *s* are become old by reason of
1Kin 2:5 in his *s* that were on his feet
Song 7:1 How beautiful are thy feet with *s*
Is 5:27 the latchet of their *s* be broken
Eze 24:17 put on thy *s* upon thy feet, and
Eze 24:23 heads, and your *s* upon your feet
Amos 2:6 and the poor for a pair of *s*
Amos 8:6 and the needy for a pair of *s*
Mt 3:11 whose *s* I am not worthy to bear
Mt 10:10 neither two coats, neither *s*
Mk 1:7 the latchet of whose *s* I am not
Lk 3:16 the latchet of whose *s* I am not
Lk 10:4 neither purse, nor scrip, nor *s*
Lk 15:22 on his hand, and *s* on his feet
Lk 22:35 you without purse, and scrip, and *s*
Acts 7:33 Put off thy *s* from thy feet
Acts 13:25 whose *s* of his feet I am not

**SHOHAM** *(sho'-ham) A Merarite.*
1Chr 24:27 Beno, and *S*, and Zaccur, and Ibri

**SHOMER** *(sho'-mur)* See SHAMER, SHIMRITH.
*1. Same as Shimrith.*
2Kin 12:21 and Jehozabad the son of *S*
*2. Son of Heber.*
1Chr 7:32 And Heber begat Japhlet, and *S*

**SHONE**
Ex 34:29 face *s* while he talked with him
Ex 34:30 behold, the skin of his face *s*
Ex 34:35 that the skin of Moses' face *s*
2Kin 3:22 the sun *s* upon the water, and the
Lk 2:9 of the Lord *s* round about them
Acts 22:6 suddenly there *s* from heaven a
Rev 8:12 the day *s* not for a third part of

**SHOOK**
2Sa 6:6 for the oxen *s* it
2Sa 22:8 Then the earth *s* and trembled
2Sa 22:8 foundations of heaven moved and *s*
Neh 5:13 Also I *s* my lap, and said, So God
Ps 18:7 Then the earth *s* and trembled
Ps 68:8 The earth *s*, the heavens also
Ps 77:18 the earth trembled and *s*
Is 23:11 over the sea, he *s* the kingdoms
Acts 13:51 But they *s* off the dust of their
Acts 18:6 he *s* his raiment, and said unto
Acts 28:5 he *s* off the beast into the fire,
Heb 12:26 Whose voice then *s* the earth

**SHOOT**
Ex 36:33 he made the middle bar to *s*
1Sa 20:20 I will *s* three arrows on the side
1Sa 20:36 find out now the arrows which I *s*
2Sa 11:20 that they would *s* from the wall
2Kin 13:17 Then Elisha said, *S*
2Kin 19:32 nor *s* an arrow there, nor come
1Chr 5:18 to *s* with bow, and skilful in war,
2Chr 26:15 to *s* arrows and great stones
Ps 11:2 that they may privily *s* at the
Ps 22:7 they *s* out the lip, they shake
Ps 58:7 bendeth his bow to *s* his arrows
Ps 64:3 bend their bows to *s* their arrows
Ps 64:4 That they may *s* in secret at the
Ps 64:4 suddenly do they *s* at him
Ps 64:7 But God shall *s* at them with an
Ps 144:6 *s* out thine arrows, and destroy
Is 37:33 nor *s* an arrow there, nor come
Jer 50:14 *s* at her, spare no arrows
Eze 31:14 neither *s* up their top among the
Eze 36:8 ye shall *s* forth your branches,
Lk 21:30 When they now *s* forth, ye see and

**SHOPHACH** *(sho'-fak)* See SHOBACH. *Same as Shoback.*
1Chr 19:16 *S* the captain of the host of
1Chr 19:18 killed *S* the captain of the host

**SHOPHAN** *(sho'-fan)* See ZAPHON. *A city in Gad.*
Num 32:35 And Atroth, *S*, and Jaazer, and

**SHORE**
Gen 22:17 the sand which is upon the sea *s*
Ex 14:30 the Egyptians dead upon the sea *s*
Josh 11:4 is upon the sea *s* in multitude
Josh 15:2 was from the *s* of the salt sea
Judg 5:17 Asher continued on the sea *s*
1Sa 13:5 is on the sea *s* in multitude
1Kin 4:29 as the sand that is on the sea *s*
1Kin 9:26 on the *s* of the Red sea, in the
Jer 47:7 Ashkelon, and against the sea *s*
Mt 13:2 whole multitude stood on the *s*
Mt 13:48 when it was full, they drew to *s*
Mk 6:53 of Gennesaret, and drew to the *s*
Jn 21:4 now come, Jesus stood on the *s*
Acts 21:5 and we kneeled down on the *s*
Acts 27:39 a certain creek with a *s*, into
Acts 27:40 to the wind, and made toward *s*
Heb 11:12 which is by the sea *s* innumerable

**SHORT**
Num 11:23 Moses, Is the LORD's hand waxed *s*
2Kin 10:32 the LORD began to cut Israel *s*
Job 17:12 the light is *s* because of
Job 20:5 the triumphing of the wicked is *s*
Ps 89:47 Remember how *s* my time is
Rom 3:23 come *s* of the glory of God
Rom 9:28 cut it *s* in righteousness
Rom 9:28 because a *s* work will the Lord
1Cor 7:29 I say, brethren, the time is *s*
1Th 2:17 from you for a *s* time in presence
Heb 4:1 you should seem to come *s* of it
Rev 12:12 knoweth that he hath but a *s* time
Rev 17:10 he must continue a *s* space

**SHORTENED**
Ps 89:45 The days of his youth hast thou *s*
Ps 102:23 he *s* my days
Prov 10:27 years of the wicked shall be *s*
Is 50:2 Is my hand *s* at all, that it
Is 59:1 Behold, the LORD's hand is not *s*
Mt 24:22 And except those days should be *s*
Mt 24:22 sake those days shall be *s*
Mk 13:20 that the Lord had *s* those days
Mk 13:20 hath chosen, he hath *s* the days

**SHORTLY**
Gen 41:32 God will *s* bring it to pass
Jer 27:16 *s* be brought again from Babylon
Eze 7:8 Now will I *s* pour out my fury
Acts 25:4 he himself would depart *s* thither
Rom 16:20 bruise Satan under your feet *s*
1Cor 4:19 But I will come to you *s*, if the
Phil 2:19 to send Timotheus *s* unto you
Phil 2:24 that I also myself shall come *s*
1Ti 3:14 thee, hoping to come unto thee *s*
2Ti 4:9 thy diligence to come *s* unto me
Heb 13:23 with whom, if he come *s*, I will
2Pet 1:14 Knowing that *s* I must put off
3Jn 14 But I trust I shall *s* see thee
Rev 1:1 things which must *s* come to pass
Rev 22:6 the things which must *s* be done

**SHOSHANNIM** *(sho-shan'-nim) A musical notation.*
Ps 45:*t* To the chief Musician upon *S*
Ps 69:*t* To the chief Musician upon *S*

**SHOSHANNIM-EDUTH** *(sho-shan'-nim-e'-duth) A musical notation.*
Ps 80:*t* To the chief Musician upon *S*

**SHOT**
Gen 40:10 budded, and her blossoms *s* forth
Gen 49:23 him, and *s* at him, and hated him
Ex 19:13 surely be stoned, or *s* through
Num 21:30 We have *s* at them
1Sa 20:20 thereof, as though I *s* at a mark
1Sa 20:36 lad ran, he *s* an arrow beyond him
1Sa 20:37 of the arrow which Jonathan had *s*
2Sa 11:24 the shooters *s* from off the wall
2Kin 13:17 said, Shoot. And he *s*.
2Chr 35:23 the archers *s* at king Josiah
Ps 18:14 and he *s* out lightnings, and
Jer 9:8 Their tongue is as an arrow *s* out
Eze 17:6 forth branches, and *s* forth sprigs
Eze 17:7 *s* forth her branches toward him,
Eze 31:5 of waters, when he *s* forth
Eze 31:10 he hath *s* up his top among the

**SHOULDER**
Gen 21:14 unto Hagar, putting it on her *s*
Gen 24:15 with her pitcher upon her *s*
Gen 24:45 forth with her pitcher on her *s*
Gen 24:46 let down her pitcher from her *s*
Gen 49:15 and bowed his *s* to bear, and became
Ex 29:22 that is upon them, and the right *s*
Ex 29:27 the *s* of the heave offering,
Lev 7:32 the right *s* shall ye give unto
Lev 7:33 have the right *s* for his part
Lev 7:34 the heave *s* have I taken of the
Lev 8:25 and their fat, and the right *s*
Lev 8:26 on the fat, and upon the right *s*
Lev 9:21 the right *s* Aaron waved for a
Lev 10:14 heave *s* shall ye eat in a clean
Lev 10:15 The heave *s* and the wave breast
Num 6:19 take the sodden *s* of the ram
Num 6:20 with the wave breast and heave *s*
Num 18:18 and as the right *s* are thine
Deut 18:3 shall give unto the priest the *s*
Josh 4:5 man of you a stone upon his *s*
Judg 9:48 and took it, and laid it on his *s*
1Sa 9:24 And the cook took up the *s*
Neh 9:29 and withdrew the *s*, and hardened
Job 31:22 let mine arm fall from my *s* blade
Job 31:36 Surely I would take it upon my *s*
Ps 81:6 I removed his *s* from the burden
Is 9:4 his burden, and the staff of his *s*
Is 9:6 government shall be upon his *s*
Is 10:27 be taken away from off thy *s*
Is 22:22 of David will I lay upon his *s*
Is 46:7 They bear him upon the *s*, they
Eze 12:7 bare it upon my *s* in their sight
Eze 12:12 bear upon his *s* in the twilight
Eze 24:4 good piece, the thigh, and the *s*
Eze 29:7 didst break, and rend all their *s*
Eze 29:18 made bald, and every *s* was peeled
Eze 34:21 have thrust with side and with *s*
Zec 7:11 to hearken, and pulled away the *s*

**SHOULDERPIECES**
Ex 28:7 It shall have the two *s* thereof
Ex 28:25 put them on the *s* of the ephod
Ex 39:4 They made *s* for it, to couple it
Ex 39:18 and put them on the *s* of the ephod

**SHOULDERS**
Gen 9:23 and laid it upon both their *s*
Ex 12:34 up in their clothes upon their *s*
Ex 28:12 the *s* of the ephod for stones of
Ex 28:12 upon his two *s* for a memorial
Ex 39:7 he put them on the *s* of the ephod
Num 7:9 they should bear upon their *s*
Deut 33:12 and he shall dwell between his *s*
Judg 16:3 and all, and put them upon his *s*
1Sa 9:2 from his *s* and upward he was
1Sa 10:23 than any of the people from his *s*
1Sa 17:6 a target of brass between his *s*
1Chr 15:15 their *s* with the staves thereon
2Chr 35:3 shall not be a burden upon your *s*
Is 11:14 But they shall fly upon the *s* of
Is 14:25 burden depart from off their *s*
Is 30:6 riches upon the *s* of young asses
Is 49:22 shall be carried upon their *s*
Eze 12:6 shalt thou bear it upon thy *s*
Mt 23:4 be borne, and lay them on men's *s*
Lk 15:5 found it, he layeth it on his *s*

**SHOUT**
Ex 32:18 voice of them that *s* for mastery
Num 23:21 the *s* of a king is among them
Josh 6:5 people shall *s* with a great *s*
Josh 6:5 people shall *s* with a great *s*
Josh 6:10 people, saying, Ye shall not *s*
Josh 6:10 mouth, until the day I bid you *s*
Josh 6:10 then shall ye *s*
Josh 6:16 Joshua said unto the people, *S*
Josh 6:20 the people shouted with a great *s*
1Sa 4:5 all Israel shouted with a great *s*
1Sa 4:6 heard the noise of the *s*, they
1Sa 4:6 *s* in the camp of the Hebrews
2Chr 13:15 Then the men of Judah gave a *s*
Ezr 3:11 the people shouted with a great *s*
Ezr 3:13 *s* of joy from the noise of the
Ezr 3:13 the people shouted with a loud *s*
Ps 5:11 let them ever *s* for joy, because
Ps 32:11 *s* for joy, all ye that are
Ps 35:27 Let them *s* for joy, and be glad,
Ps 47:1 *s* unto God with the voice of
Ps 47:5 God is gone up with a *s*, the LORD
Ps 65:13 they *s* for joy, they also sing
Ps 132:9 and let thy saints *s* for joy
Ps 132:16 her saints shall *s* aloud for joy
Is 12:6 Cry out and *s*, thou inhabitant of
Is 42:11 let them *s* from the top of the
Is 44:23 *s*, ye lower parts of the earth
Jer 25:30 he shall give a *s*, as they that
Jer 31:7 *s* among the chief of the nations
Jer 50:15 *S* against her round about
Jer 51:14 shall lift up a *s* against thee
Lam 3:8 Also when I cry and *s*, he shutteth
Zeph 3:14 *s*, O Israel
Zec 9:9 *s*, O daughter of Jerusalem
Acts 12:22 And the people gave a *s*, saying,
1Th 4:16 descend from heaven with a *s*

**SHOUTED**
Ex 32:17 the noise of the people as they *s*
Lev 9:24 when all the people saw, they *s*
Josh 6:20 So the people *s* when the priests
Josh 6:20 the people *s* with a great shout,
Judg 15:14 the Philistines *s* against him
1Sa 4:5 all Israel *s* with a great shout,
1Sa 10:24 And all the people *s*, and said, God
1Sa 17:20 to the fight, and *s* for the battle
1Sa 17:52 of Israel and of Judah arose, and *s*
2Chr 13:15 and as the men of Judah *s*, it came
Ezr 3:11 all the people *s* with a great
Ezr 3:12 and many *s* aloud for joy
Ezr 3:13 for the people *s* with a loud
Job 38:7 and all the sons of God *s* for joy

**SHOUTING**
2Sa 6:15 up the ark of the LORD with *s*
1Chr 15:28 the covenant of the LORD with *s*
2Chr 15:14 LORD with a loud voice, and with *s*
Job 39:25 thunder of the captains, and the *s*
Prov 11:10 the wicked perish, there is *s*
Is 16:9 for the *s* for thy summer fruits
Is 16:10 singing, neither shall there be *s*
Is 16:10 made their vintage *s* to cease
Jer 20:16 the morning, and the *s* at noontide
Jer 48:33 none shall tread with *s*
Jer 48:33 their *s* shall be no *s*
Eze 21:22 to lift up the voice with *s*
Amos 1:14 with *s* in the day of battle, with
Amos 2:2 shall die with tumult, with *s*

**SHOVELS**
Ex 27:3 to receive his ashes, and his *s*
Ex 38:3 of the altar, the pots, and the *s*
Num 4:14 censers, the fleshhooks, and the *s*
1Kin 7:40 Hiram made the lavers, and the *s*
1Kin 7:45 And the pots, and the *s*, and the
2Kin 25:14 And the pots, and the *s*, and the
2Chr 4:11 And Huram made the pots, and the *s*
2Chr 4:16 The pots also, and the *s*, and the
Jer 52:18 The caldrons also, and the *s*

**SHOWER**
Eze 13:11 there shall be an overflowing *s*
Eze 13:13 be an overflowing *s* in mine anger
Eze 34:26 I will cause the *s* to come down
Lk 12:54 ye say, There cometh a *s*

**SHOWERS**
Deut 32:2 herb, and as the *s* upon the grass
Job 24:8 wet with the *s* of the mountains
Ps 65:10 thou makest it soft with *s*
Ps 72:6 as *s* that water the earth
Jer 3:3 Therefore the *s* have been
Jer 14:22 or can the heavens give *s*
Eze 34:26 there shall be *s* of blessing
Mic 5:7 as the *s* upon the grass, that
Zec 10:1 clouds, and give them *s* of rain

**SHUA** *(shu'-ah)* See SHUAH.
*1. Daughter of Judah.*
1Chr 2:3 the daughter of *S* the Canaanitess
*2. Daughter of Heber.*
1Chr 7:32 and Hotham, and *S* their sister

**SHUAH** *(shu'-ah)*
*1. A son of Abraham.*
Gen 25:2 and Midian, and Ishbak, and *S*
1Chr 1:32 and Midian, and Ishbak, and *S*
*2. Same as Shua 1.*
Gen 38:2 Canaanite, whose name was *S*
Gen 38:12 daughter of *S* Judah's wife died
*3. A descendant of Caleb.*
1Chr 4:11 the brother of *S* begat Mehir

**SHUAL** *(shu'-al)*
*1. A district in Benjamin.*
1Sa 13:17 to Ophrah, unto the land of *S*
*2. Son of Zophah.*
1Chr 7:36 Suah, and Harnepher, and *S*, and Beri

**SHUBAEL** *(shu'-ba-el)* See SHEBUEL.
*1. Son of Amram.*
1Chr 24:20 sons of Amram; *S*
1Chr 24:20 of the sons of *S*
*2. A sanctuary servant.*
1Chr 25:20 The thirteenth to *S*, he, his sons

**SHUHAM** *(shu'-ham)* See HUSHIM, SHUHAMITES. *A son of Dan.*
Num 26:42 of *S*, the family of the

**SHUHAMITES** *(shu'-ham-ites) Descendants of Shuham.*
Num 26:42 of Shuham, the family of the *S*
Num 26:43 All the families of the *S*

**SHUHITE** *(shu'-hite) A descendant of Shuah.*
Job 2:11 the Temanite, and Bildad the *S*
Job 8:1 Then answered Bildad the *S*
Job 18:1 Then answered Bildad the *S*
Job 25:1 Then answered Bildad the *S*
Job 42:9 the Temanite and Bildad the *S*

**SHULAMITE** *(shu'-lam-ite) An inhabitant of Shulam.*
Song 6:13 Return, return, O *S*
Song 6:13 What will ye see in the *S*

**SHUMATHITES** *(shu'-math-ites) Descendants of Shobal.*
1Chr 2:53 and the Puhites, and the *S*

**SHUNAMMITE** *(shu'-nam-mite) An inhabitant of Shunem.*
1Kin 1:3 of Israel, and found Abishag a *S*
1Kin 1:15 Abishag the *S* ministered unto the
1Kin 2:17 he give me Abishag the *S* to wife
1Kin 2:21 Let Abishag the *S* be given to
1Kin 2:22 ask Abishag the *S* for Adonijah
2Kin 4:12 Gehazi his servant, Call this *S*
2Kin 4:25 servant, Behold, yonder is that *S*
2Kin 4:36 Gehazi, and said, Call this *S*

**SHUNEM** *(shu'-nem)* See SHUNAMMITE. *A city in Issachar.*
Josh 19:18 Jezreel, and Chesulloth, and *S*
1Sa 28:4 together, and came and pitched in *S*
2Kin 4:8 on a day, that Elisha passed to *S*

**SHUNI** *(shu'-ni)* See SHUNITES. *A son of Gad.*
Gen 46:16 Ziphion, and Haggi, *S*, and Ezbon,
Num 26:15 of *S*, the family of the Shunites

**SHUNITES** *(shu'-nites) Descendants of Shuni.*
Num 26:15 of Shuni, the family of the *S*

**SHUPHAM** *(shu'-fam)* See SHEPHUPHAN, SHUPHAMITES. *A son of Benjamin.*
Num 26:39 Of *S*, the family of the

**SHUPHAMITES** *(shu'-fam-ites) Descendants of Shupham.*
Num 26:39 Of Shupham, the family of the *S*

**SHUPPIM** *(shup'-pim)* See MUPPIM, SHEPHUPHAN.
*1. A Benjamite.*
1Chr 7:12 *S* also, and Huppim, the children
1Chr 7:15 to wife the sister of Huppim and *S*
*2. A Levite gatekeeper.*
1Chr 26:16 To *S* and Hosah the lot came forth

**SHUR** *(shur) A wilderness east of Egypt.*
Gen 16:7 by the fountain in the way to *S*
Gen 20:1 and dwelled between Kadesh and *S*
Gen 25:18 And they dwelt from Havilah unto *S*
Ex 15:22 went out into the wilderness of *S*
1Sa 15:7 Havilah until thou comest to *S*
1Sa 27:8 of the land, as thou goest to *S*

**SHUSHAN** *(shu'-shan)* See SHOSHANNIM. *Capital of Persia.*
Neh 1:1 year, as I was in *S* the palace
Est 1:2 which was in *S* the palace
Est 1:5 that were present in *S* the palace
Est 2:3 young virgins unto *S* the palace
Est 2:5 Now in *S* the palace there was a
Est 2:8 together unto *S* the palace
Est 3:15 decree was given in *S* the palace
Est 3:15 but the city *S* was perplexed
Est 4:8 was given at *S* to destroy them
Est 4:16 the Jews that are present in *S*
Est 8:14 decree was given at *S* the palace
Est 8:15 and the city of *S* rejoiced
Est 9:6 in *S* the palace the Jews slew and
Est 9:11 of those that were slain in *S* the
Est 9:12 five hundred men in *S* the palace
Est 9:13 to the Jews which are in *S* to do
Est 9:14 and the decree was given at *S*
Est 9:15 For the Jews that were in *S*
Est 9:15 and slew three hundred men at *S*
Est 9:18 at *S* assembled together on the
Dan 8:2 that I was at *S* in the palace

**SHUSHAN-EDUTH** *(shu'-shan-e'-duth)*
Ps 60:*t* To the chief Musician upon *S*

**SHUT**
Gen 7:16 and the LORD *s* him in
Gen 19:6 them, and *s* the door after him,
Gen 19:10 house to them, and *s* to the door
Ex 14:3 the wilderness hath *s* them in
Lev 13:4 then the priest shall *s* up him
Lev 13:5 then the priest shall *s* him up
Lev 13:11 unclean, and shall not *s* him up
Lev 13:21 priest shall *s* him up seven days
Lev 13:26 priest shall *s* him up seven days
Lev 13:31 then the priest shall *s* up him
Lev 13:33 the priest shall *s* up him that
Lev 13:50 *s* up it that hath the plague
Lev 13:54 he shall *s* it up seven days more
Lev 14:38 *s* up the house seven days
Lev 14:46 *s* up shall be unclean until the
Num 12:14 let her be *s* out from the camp
Num 12:15 Miriam was *s* out from the camp
Deut 11:17 he *s* up the heaven, that there be
Deut 15:7 nor *s* thine hand from thy poor
Deut 32:30 them, and the LORD had *s* them up
Deut 32:36 is gone, and there is none *s* up
Josh 2:7 were gone out, they *s* the gate
Josh 6:1 Now Jericho was straitly *s* up
Judg 3:23 *s* the doors of the parlour upon
Judg 9:51 *s* it to them, and gat them up to
1Sa 1:5 but the LORD had *s* up her womb
1Sa 1:6 the LORD had *s* up her womb
1Sa 6:10 *s* up their calves at home
1Sa 23:7 for he is *s* in, by entering into
2Sa 20:3 So they were *s* up unto the day of
1Kin 8:35 When heaven is *s* up, and there is
1Kin 14:10 the wall, and him that is *s* up
1Kin 21:21 the wall, and him that is *s* up
2Kin 4:4 thou shalt *s* the door upon thee
2Kin 4:5 *s* the door upon her and upon her
2Kin 4:21 *s* the door upon him, and went out
2Kin 4:33 *s* the door upon them twain, and
2Kin 6:32 *s* the door, and hold him fast at
2Kin 9:8 the wall, and him that is *s* up
2Kin 14:26 for there was not any *s* up
2Kin 17:4 the king of Assyria *s* him up
2Chr 6:26 When the heaven is *s* up, and there
2Chr 7:13 If I *s* up heaven that there be no
2Chr 28:24 *s* up the doors of the house of
2Chr 29:7 Also they have *s* up the doors of
Neh 6:10 son of Mehetabeel, who was *s* up
Neh 6:10 let us *s* the doors of the temple
Neh 7:3 let them *s* the doors, and bar them
Neh 13:19 that the gates should be *s*
Job 3:10 Because it *s* not up the doors of
Job 11:10 *s* up, or gather together, then
Job 38:8 Or who *s* up the sea with doors,
Job 41:15 *s* up together as with a close
Ps 31:8 hast not *s* me up into the hand of
Ps 69:15 let not the pit *s* her mouth upon
Ps 77:9 hath he in anger *s* up his tender
Ps 88:8 I am *s* up, and I cannot come forth
Eccl 12:4 doors shall be *s* in the streets
Song 4:12 a spring *s* up, a fountain sealed
Is 6:10 their ears heavy, and *s* their eyes
Is 22:22 so he shall open, and none shall *s*
Is 22:22 and he shall *s*, and none shall open
Is 24:10 every house is *s* up, that no man
Is 24:22 shall be *s* up in the prison, and
Is 26:20 and *s* thy doors about thee
Is 44:18 for he hath *s* their eyes, that
Is 45:1 and the gates shall not be *s*
Is 52:15 the kings shall *s* their mouths at
Is 60:11 they shall not be *s* day nor night
Is 66:9 to bring forth, and *s* the womb
Jer 13:19 cities of the south shall be *s* up
Jer 20:9 a burning fire *s* up in my bones
Jer 32:2 Jeremiah the prophet was *s* up in
Jer 32:3 king of Judah had *s* him up
Jer 33:1 while he was yet *s* up in the
Jer 36:5 Baruch, saying, I am *s* up
Jer 39:15 while he was *s* up in the court of
Eze 3:24 *s* thyself within thine house
Eze 44:1 and it was *s*
Eze 44:2 This gate shall be *s*, it shall
Eze 44:2 in by it, therefore it shall be *s*
Eze 46:1 shall be *s* the six working days
Eze 46:2 shall not be *s* until the evening
Eze 46:12 going forth one shall *s* the gate
Dan 6:22 hath *s* the lions' mouths, that
Dan 8:26 wherefore *s* thou up the vision
Dan 12:4 *s* up the words, and seal the book,
Mal 1:10 that would *s* the doors for nought
Mt 6:6 and when thou hast *s* thy door
Mt 23:13 for ye *s* up the kingdom of heaven
Mt 25:10 and the door was *s*
Lk 3:20 that he *s* up John in prison
Lk 4:25 the heaven was *s* up three years
Lk 11:7 the door is now *s*, and my children
Lk 13:25 hath *s* to the door, and ye begin
Jn 20:19 when the doors were *s* where the
Jn 20:26 came Jesus, the doors being *s*
Acts 5:23 truly found we *s* with all safety
Acts 21:30 and forthwith the doors were *s*
Acts 26:10 the saints did I *s* up in prison
Gal 3:23 *s* up unto the faith which should
Rev 3:8 an open door, and no man can *s* it
Rev 11:6 These have power to *s* heaven
Rev 20:3 *s* him up, and set a seal upon him,
Rev 21:25 it shall not be *s* at all by day

**SHUTHALHITES** *(shu'-thal-hites) Descendants of Shuthelah.*
Num 26:35 of Shuthelah, the family of the *S*

**SHUTHELAH** *(shu'-the-lah)* See SHUTHALHITES.
*1. A son of Ephraim.*
Num 26:35 of *S*, the family of the
Num 26:36 And these are the sons of *S*
1Chr 7:20 *S*, and Bered his son, and Tahath
*2. Son of Zabad.*
1Chr 7:21 *S* his son, and Ezer, and Elead,

**SHUTTETH**
Job 12:14 he *s* up a man, and there can be no
Prov 16:30 He *s* his eyes to devise froward
Prov 17:28 he that *s* his lips is esteemed a
Is 33:15 *s* his eyes from seeing evil
Lam 3:8 cry and shout, he *s* out my prayer
1Jn 3:17 *s* up his bowels of compassion
Rev 3:7 he that openeth, and no man *s*
Rev 3:7 and *s*, and no man openeth

**SIA** *(si'-ah)* See SIAHA. *A family of exiles.*
Neh 7:47 of Keros, the children of *S*

**SIAHA** *(si'-a-hah)* See SIA. *Same as Sia.*
Ezr 2:44 of Keros, the children of *S*

**SIBBECAI** *(sib'-be-cahee)* See SIBBECHAI. *A "mighty man" of David.*
1Chr 11:29 *S* the Hushathite, Ilai the
1Chr 27:11 eighth month was *S* the Hushathite

**SIBBECHAI** *(sib'-be-kahee)* See SIBBECAI. *Same as Sibbecai.*
2Sa 21:18 then *S* the Hushathite slew Saph,
1Chr 20:4 at which time *S* the Hushathite

**SIBBOLETH** *(sib'-bo-leth)* See SHIBBOLETH. *The Ephraimite pronunciation of Shibboleth.*
Judg 12:6 and he said *S*

**SIBMAH** *(sib'-mah) A city in Reuben.*
Josh 13:19 And Kirjathaim, and *S*, and
Is 16:8 languish, and the vine of *S*
Is 16:9 weeping of Jazer the vine of *S*
Jer 48:32 O vine of *S*, I will weep for thee

**SIBRAIM** *(sib'-ra-im) A city in Syria between Damascus and Hamath.*
Eze 47:16 Hamath, Berothah, *S*, which is

**SICHEM** *(si'-kem)* See SHECHEM, SYCHEM. *A place on the plain of Moreh.*
Gen 12:6 the land unto the place of *S*

**SICK**
Gen 48:1 Joseph, Behold, thy father is *s*
Lev 15:33 of her that is *s* of her flowers
1Sa 19:14 to take David, she said, He is *s*
1Sa 30:13 because three days agone I fell *s*
2Sa 12:15 bare unto David, and it was very *s*
2Sa 13:2 that he fell *s* for his sister
2Sa 13:5 on thy bed, and make thyself *s*
2Sa 13:6 Amnon lay down, and made himself *s*
1Kin 14:1 Abijah the son of Jeroboam fell *s*
1Kin 14:5 for he is *s*
1Kin 17:17 the mistress of the house, fell *s*
2Kin 1:2 that was in Samaria, and was *s*
2Kin 8:7 Ben-hadad the king of Syria was *s*
2Kin 8:29 Ahab in Jezreel, because he was *s*
2Kin 13:14 Now Elisha was fallen *s* of his
2Kin 20:1 days was Hezekiah *s* unto death
2Kin 20:12 heard that Hezekiah had been *s*
2Chr 22:6 Ahab at Jezreel, because he was *s*
2Chr 32:24 days Hezekiah was *s* to the death
Neh 2:2 sad, seeing thou art not *s*
Ps 35:13 But as for me, when they were *s*
Prov 13:12 Hope deferred maketh the heart *s*
Prov 23:35 shalt thou say, and I was not *s*
Song 2:5 for I am *s* of love
Song 5:8 ye tell him, that I am *s* of love
Is 1:5 the whole head is *s*, and the whole
Is 33:24 inhabitant shall not say, I am *s*
Is 38:1 days was Hezekiah *s* unto death
Is 38:9 king of Judah, when he had been *s*
Is 39:1 he had heard that he had been *s*
Jer 14:18 them that are *s* with famine
Eze 34:4 have ye healed that which was *s*
Eze 34:16 will strengthen that which was *s*
Dan 8:27 fainted, and was *s* certain days
Hos 7:5 made him *s* with bottles of wine
Mic 6:13 I make thee *s* in smiting thee
Mal 1:8 and if ye offer the lame and *s*
Mal 1:13 was torn, and the lame, and the *s*
Mt 4:24 they brought unto him all *s*
Mt 8:6 lieth at home *s* of the palsy
Mt 8:14 mother laid, and *s* of a fever
Mt 8:16 word, and healed all that were *s*
Mt 9:2 to him a man *s* of the palsy
Mt 9:2 said unto the *s* of the palsy
Mt 9:6 saith he to the *s* of the palsy
Mt 9:12 a physician, but they that are *s*
Mt 10:8 Heal the *s*, cleanse the lepers,
Mt 14:14 toward them, and he healed their *s*
Mt 25:36 I was *s*, and ye visited me
Mt 25:39 Or when saw we thee *s*, or in
Mt 25:43 *s*, and in prison, and ye visited me
Mt 25:44 or a stranger, or naked, or *s*
Mk 1:30 wife's mother lay *s* of a fever
Mk 1:34 that were *s* of divers diseases
Mk 2:3 him, bringing one *s* of the palsy
Mk 2:4 wherein the *s* of the palsy lay
Mk 2:5 he said unto the *s* of the palsy

Mk 2:9 to say to the *s* of the palsy
Mk 2:10 (he saith to the *s* of the palsy
Mk 2:17 physician, but they that are *s*
Mk 6:5 laid his hands upon a few *s* folk
Mk 6:13 with oil many that were *s*
Mk 6:55 about in beds those that were *s*
Mk 6:56 they laid the *s* in the streets,
Mk 16:18 they shall lay hands on the *s*
Lk 4:40 all they that had any *s* with
Lk 5:24 (he said unto the *s* of the palsy
Lk 5:31 but they that are *s*
Lk 7:2 who was dear unto him, was *s*
Lk 7:10 the servant whole that had been *s*
Lk 9:2 kingdom of God, and to heal the *s*
Lk 10:9 heal the *s* that are therein, and
Jn 4:46 whose son was *s* at Capernaum
Jn 11:1 Now a certain man was *s*, named
Jn 11:2 hair, whose brother Lazarus was *s*
Jn 11:3 behold, he whom thou lovest is *s*
Jn 11:6 had heard therefore that he was *s*
Acts 5:15 forth the *s* into the streets
Acts 5:16 unto Jerusalem, bringing *s* folks
Acts 9:33 years, and was *s* of the palsy
Acts 9:37 in those days, that she was *s*
Acts 19:12 the *s* handkerchiefs or aprons
Acts 28:8 of Publius lay *s* of a fever
Phil 2:26 ye had heard that he had been *s*
Phil 2:27 indeed he was *s* nigh unto death
2Ti 4:20 have I left at Miletum *s*
Jas 5:14 Is any *s* among you
Jas 5:15 prayer of faith shall save the *s*

**SICKLE**
Deut 16:9 to put the *s* to the corn
Deut 23:25 but thou shalt not move a *s* unto
Jer 50:16 him that handleth the *s* in the
Joel 3:13 Put ye in the *s*, for the harvest
Mk 4:29 immediately he putteth in the *s*
Rev 14:14 crown, and in his hand a sharp *s*
Rev 14:15 sat on the cloud, Thrust in thy *s*
Rev 14:16 thrust in his *s* on the earth
Rev 14:17 heaven, he also having a sharp *s*
Rev 14:18 cry to him that had the sharp *s*
Rev 14:18 saying, Thrust in thy sharp *s*
Rev 14:19 thrust in his *s* into the earth

**SICKNESS**
Ex 23:25 I will take *s* away from the midst
Lev 20:18 lie with a woman having her *s*
Deut 7:15 will take away from thee all *s*
Deut 28:61 Also every *s*, and every plague,
1Kin 8:37 plague, whatsoever *s* there be
1Kin 17:17 his *s* was so sore, that there was
2Kin 13:14 sick of his *s* whereof he died
2Chr 6:28 sore or whatsoever *s* there be
2Chr 21:15 thou shalt have great *s* by
2Chr 21:15 out by reason of the *s* day by day
2Chr 21:19 fell out by reason of his *s*
Ps 41:3 wilt make all his bed in his *s*
Eccl 5:17 much sorrow and wrath with his *s*
Is 38:9 sick, and was recovered of his *s*
Is 38:12 he will cut me off with pining *s*
Hos 5:13 When Ephraim saw his *s*, and Judah
Mt 4:23 and healing all manner of *s*
Mt 9:35 the kingdom, and healing every *s*
Mt 10:1 out, and to heal all manner of *s*
Jn 11:4 This *s* is not unto death, but for

**SICKNESSES**
Deut 28:59 and of long continuance, and sore *s*
Deut 29:22 the *s* which the LORD hath laid
Mt 8:17 our infirmities, and bare our *s*
Mk 3:15 And to have power to heal *s*

**SIDDIM** *(sid'-dim) Area of Sodom and Gomorrah.*
Gen 14:3 joined together in the vale of *S*
Gen 14:8 battle with them in the vale of *S*
Gen 14:10 the vale of *S* was full of

**SIDES**
Ex 25:14 the rings by the *s* of the ark
Ex 25:32 shall come out of the *s* of it
Ex 26:13 it shall hang over the *s* of the
Ex 26:22 for the *s* of the tabernacle
Ex 26:23 of the tabernacle in the two *s*
Ex 26:27 for the two *s* westward
Ex 27:7 be upon the two *s* of the altar
Ex 28:27 the two *s* of the ephod underneath
Ex 30:3 the *s* thereof round about, and the
Ex 30:4 upon the two *s* of it shalt thou
Ex 32:15 were written on both their *s*
Ex 36:27 for the *s* of the tabernacle
Ex 36:28 of the tabernacle in the two *s*
Ex 36:32 the tabernacle for the *s* westward
Ex 37:5 the rings by the *s* of the ark
Ex 37:18 going out of the *s* thereof
Ex 37:26 the *s* thereof round about, and the
Ex 37:27 of it, upon the two *s* thereof
Ex 38:7 the rings on the *s* of the altar
Ex 39:20 put them on the two *s* of the
Num 33:55 in your eyes, and thorns in your *s*
Josh 23:13 unto you, and scourges in your *s*
Judg 2:3 they shall be as thorns in your *s*
Judg 5:30 colours of needlework on both *s*
1Sa 24:3 men remained in the *s* of the cave
1Kin 4:24 peace on all *s* round about him
1Kin 6:16 cubits on the *s* of the house
2Kin 19:23 to the *s* of Lebanon, and will cut
Ps 48:2 on the *s* of the north, the city
Ps 128:3 vine by the *s* of thine house
Is 14:13 in the *s* of the north
Is 14:15 down to hell, to the *s* of the pit
Is 37:24 mountains, to the *s* of Lebanon
Is 66:12 ye shall be borne upon her *s*
Jer 6:22 be raised from the *s* of the earth
Jer 48:28 nest in the *s* of the hole's mouth
Jer 49:32 their calamity from all *s* thereof
Eze 1:8 under their wings on their four *s*
Eze 1:17 went, they went upon their four *s*
Eze 10:11 went, they went upon their four *s*
Eze 32:23 are set in the *s* of the pit
Eze 41:2 the *s* of the door were five
Eze 41:26 on the *s* of the porch, and upon
Eze 42:20 He measured it by the four *s*
Eze 46:19 was a place on the two *s* westward
Eze 48:1 for these are his *s* east and west
Amos 6:10 him that is by the *s* of the house
Jonah 1:5 gone down into the *s* of the ship

**SIDON** *(si'-don)* See SIDONIANS, ZIDON.
*1. Son of Canaan.*
Gen 10:15 Canaan begat *S* his firstborn, and
*2. Phoenician city north of Tyre.*
Gen 10:19 of the Canaanites was from *S*
Mt 11:21 you, had been done in Tyre and *S*
Mt 11:22 *S* at the day of judgment, than
Mt 15:21 into the coasts of Tyre and *S*
Mk 3:8 and they about Tyre and *S*, a great
Mk 7:24 into the borders of Tyre and *S*
Mk 7:31 from the coasts of Tyre and *S*
Lk 4:26 save unto Sarepta, a city of *S*
Lk 6:17 from the sea coast of Tyre and *S*
Lk 10:13 works had been done in Tyre and *S*
Lk 10:14 *S* at the judgment, than for you
Acts 12:20 displeased with them of Tyre and *S*
Acts 27:3 And the next day we touched at *S*

**SIDONIANS** *(si-do'-ne-uns)* See ZIDONIANS. *Inhabitants of Sidon.*
Deut 3:9 (Which Hermon the *S* call Sirion
Josh 13:4 and Mearah that is beside the *S*
Josh 13:6 Misrephoth-maim, and all the *S*
Judg 3:3 and all the Canaanites, and the *S*
1Kin 5:6 to hew timber like unto the *S*

**SIEGE**
Deut 20:19 life) to employ them in the *s*
Deut 28:53 thy God hath given thee, in the *s*
Deut 28:55 he hath nothing left him in the *s*
Deut 28:57 of all things secretly in the *s*
1Kin 15:27 and all Israel laid *s* to Gibbethon
2Chr 32:9 he himself laid *s* against Lachish
2Chr 32:10 ye abide in the *s* in Jerusalem
Is 29:3 will lay *s* against thee with a
Jer 19:9 the flesh of his friend in the *s*
Eze 4:2 lay *s* against it, and build a fort
Eze 4:3 and thou shalt lay *s* against it
Eze 4:7 face toward the *s* of Jerusalem
Eze 4:8 thou hast ended the days of thy *s*
Eze 5:2 the days of the *s* are fulfilled
Mic 5:1 he hath laid *s* against us
Nah 3:14 Draw thee waters for the *s*
Zec 12:2 be in the *s* both against Judah

**SIGH**
Is 24:7 all the merryhearted do *s*
Lam 1:4 her priests *s*, her virgins are
Lam 1:11 All her people *s*, they seek bread
Lam 1:21 They have heard that I *s*
Eze 9:4 the foreheads of the men that *s*
Eze 21:6 *S* therefore, thou son of man,
Eze 21:6 with bitterness *s* before their

**SIGHING**
Job 3:24 For my *s* cometh before I eat, and
Ps 12:5 for the *s* of the needy, now will
Ps 31:10 with grief, and my years with *s*
Ps 79:11 Let the *s* of the prisoner come
Is 21:2 all the *s* thereof have I made to
Is 35:10 and sorrow and *s* shall flee away
Jer 45:3 I fainted in my *s*, and I find no

**SIGHTS**
Lk 21:11 and fearful *s* and great signs shall

**SIGN**
Ex 4:8 to the voice of the first *s*
Ex 4:8 believe the voice of the latter *s*
Ex 8:23 to morrow shall this *s* be
Ex 13:9 it shall be for a *s* unto thee
Ex 31:13 for it is a *s* between me and you
Ex 31:17 It is a *s* between me and the
Num 16:38 they shall be a *s* unto the
Num 26:10 and they became a *s*
Deut 6:8 bind them for a *s* upon thine hand
Deut 11:18 bind them for a *s* upon your hand
Deut 13:1 and giveth thee a *s* or a wonder
Deut 13:2 the *s* or the wonder come to pass,
Deut 28:46 they shall be upon thee for a *s*
Josh 4:6 That this may be a *s* among you
Judg 6:17 then shew me a *s* that thou
Judg 20:38 *s* between the men of Israel
1Sa 2:34 And this shall be a *s* unto thee
1Sa 14:10 and this shall be a *s* unto us
1Kin 13:3 he gave a *s* the same day, saying,
1Kin 13:3 This is the *s* which the LORD hath
1Kin 13:5 according to the *s* which the man
2Kin 19:29 And this shall be a *s* unto thee
2Kin 20:8 What shall be the *s* that the LORD
2Kin 20:9 This *s* shalt thou have of the
2Chr 32:24 unto him, and he gave him a *s*
Is 7:11 Ask thee a *s* of the LORD thy God
Is 7:14 Lord himself shall give you a *s*
Is 19:20 And it shall be for a *s* and for a
Is 20:3 and barefoot three years for a *s*
Is 37:30 And this shall be a *s* unto thee
Is 38:7 this shall be a *s* unto thee from
Is 38:22 What is the *s* that I shall go up
Is 55:13 for an everlasting *s* that shall
Is 66:19 And I will set a *s* among them
Jer 6:1 Tekoa, and set up a *s* of fire in
Jer 44:29 And this shall be a *s* unto you
Eze 4:3 This shall be a *s* to the house of
Eze 12:6 for a *s* unto the house of Israel
Eze 12:11 Say, I am your *s*
Eze 14:8 that man, and will make him a *s*
Eze 20:12 to be a *s* between me and them,
Eze 20:20 and they shall be a *s* between me
Eze 24:24 Thus Ezekiel is unto you a *s*
Eze 24:27 and thou shalt be a *s* unto them
Eze 39:15 then shall he set up a *s* by it
Dan 6:8 *s* the writing, that it be not
Mt 12:38 we would see a *s* from thee
Mt 12:39 generation seeketh after a *s*
Mt 12:39 there shall no *s* be given to it
Mt 12:39 but the *s* of the prophet Jonas
Mt 16:1 would shew them a *s* from heaven
Mt 16:4 generation seeketh after a *s*
Mt 16:4 there shall no *s* be given unto it
Mt 16:4 but the *s* of the prophet Jonas
Mt 24:3 what shall be the *s* of thy coming
Mt 24:30 then shall appear the *s* of the
Mt 26:48 that betrayed him gave them a *s*
Mk 8:11 seeking of him a *s* from heaven
Mk 8:12 this generation seek after a *s*
Mk 8:12 There shall no *s* be given unto
Mk 13:4 what shall be the *s* when all
Lk 2:12 And this shall be a *s* unto you
Lk 2:34 for a *s* which shall be spoken
Lk 11:16 sought of him a *s* from heaven
Lk 11:29 they seek a *s*
Lk 11:29 and there shall no *s* be given it
Lk 11:29 but the *s* of Jonas the prophet
Lk 11:30 Jonas was a *s* unto the Ninevites
Lk 21:7 what *s* will there be when these
Jn 2:18 What *s* shewest thou unto us,
Jn 6:30 What *s* shewest thou then, that we
Acts 28:11 whose *s* was Castor and Pollux
Rom 4:11 he received the *s* of circumcision
1Cor 1:22 For the Jews require a *s*, and the
1Cor 14:22 Wherefore tongues are for a *s*
Rev 15:1 And I saw another *s* in heaven

**SIGNED**
Dan 6:9 king Darius s the writing
Dan 6:10 knew that the writing was s
Dan 6:12 Hast thou not s a decree, that
Dan 6:13 nor the decree that thou hast s

**SIGNET**
Gen 38:18 And she said, Thy s, and thy
Gen 38:25 pray thee, whose are these, the s
Ex 28:11 stone, like the engravings of a s
Ex 28:21 names, like the engravings of a s
Ex 28:36 it, like the engravings of a s
Ex 39:14 names, like the engravings of a s
Ex 39:30 like to the engravings of a s
Jer 22:24 were the s upon my right hand
Dan 6:17 the king sealed it with his own s
Dan 6:17 and with the s of his lords
Hag 2:23 LORD, and will make thee as a s

**SIGNIFY**
Acts 21:26 to s the accomplishment of the
Acts 23:15 s to the chief captain that he
Acts 25:27 not withal to s the crimes laid
1Pet 1:11 of Christ which was in them did s

**SIGNIFYING**
Jn 12:33 s what death he should die
Jn 18:32 s what death he should die
Jn 21:19 s by what death he should glorify
Heb 9:8 The Holy Ghost this s, that the

**SIGNS**
Gen 1:14 and let them be for s, and for
Ex 4:9 will not believe also these two s
Ex 4:17 hand, wherewith thou shalt do s
Ex 4:28 all the s which he had commanded
Ex 4:30 did the s in the sight of the
Ex 7:3 Pharaoh's heart, and multiply my s
Ex 10:1 might shew these my s before him
Ex 10:2 my s which I have done among them
Num 14:11 for all the s which I have shewed
Deut 4:34 nation, by temptations, by s
Deut 6:22 And the LORD shewed s and wonders,
Deut 7:19 which thine eyes saw, and the s
Deut 26:8 great terribleness, and with s
Deut 29:3 which thine eyes have seen, the s
Deut 34:11 In all the s and the wonders,
Josh 24:17 did those great s in our sight
1Sa 10:7 when these s are come unto thee,
1Sa 10:9 all those s came to pass that day
Neh 9:10 And shewedst s and wonders upon
Ps 74:4 they set up their ensigns for s
Ps 74:9 We see not our s
Ps 78:43 How he had wrought his s in Egypt
Ps 105:27 They shewed his s among them
Is 8:18 the LORD hath given me are for s
Jer 10:2 not dismayed at the s of heaven
Jer 32:20 Which hast set s and wonders in
Jer 32:21 out of the land of Egypt with s
Dan 4:2 I thought it good to shew the s
Dan 4:3 How great are his s
Dan 6:27 and rescueth, and he worketh s
Mt 16:3 ye not discern the s of the times
Mt 24:24 prophets, and shall shew great s
Mk 13:22 shall rise, and shall shew s
Mk 16:17 these s shall follow them that
Mk 16:20 the word with s following
Lk 1:62 they made s to his father, how he
Lk 21:11 great s shall there be from
Lk 21:25 And there shall be s in the sun
Jn 4:48 Jesus unto him, Except ye see s
Jn 20:30 many other s truly did Jesus in
Acts 2:19 above, and s in the earth beneath
Acts 2:22 you by miracles and wonders and s
Acts 2:43 s were done by the apostles
Acts 4:30 and that s and wonders may be done
Acts 5:12 hands of the apostles were many s
Acts 7:36 s in the land of Egypt, and in the
Acts 8:13 the miracles and s which were done
Acts 14:3 word of his grace, and granted s
Rom 15:19 Through mighty s and wonders, by
2Cor 12:12 Truly the s of an apostle were
2Cor 12:12 among you in all patience, in s
2Th 2:9 of Satan with all power and s
Heb 2:4 bearing them witness, both with s

**SIHON** *(si'-hon) An Amorite king.*
Num 21:21 unto S king of the Amorites
Num 21:23 S would not suffer Israel to pass
Num 21:23 but S gathered all his people
Num 21:26 of S the king of the Amorites
Num 21:27 let the city of S be built
Num 21:28 a flame from the city of S
Num 21:29 into captivity unto S king of the
Num 21:34 didst unto S king of the Amorites
Num 32:33 the kingdom of S king of the
Deut 1:4 After he had slain S the king of
Deut 2:24 into thine hand S the Amorite
Deut 2:26 S king of Heshbon with words of
Deut 2:30 But S king of Heshbon would not
Deut 2:31 Behold, I have begun to give S
Deut 2:32 Then S came out against us, he and
Deut 3:2 didst unto S king of the Amorites
Deut 3:6 as we did unto S king of Heshbon,
Deut 4:46 in the land of S king of the
Deut 29:7 S the king of Heshbon, and Og the
Deut 31:4 shall do unto them as he did to S
Josh 2:10 were on the other side Jordan, S
Josh 9:10 to S king of Heshbon, and to Og
Josh 12:2 S king of the Amorites, who dwelt
Josh 12:5 the border of S king of Heshbon
Josh 13:10 all the cities of S king of the
Josh 13:21 all the kingdom of S king of the
Josh 13:21 and Reba, which were dukes of S
Josh 13:27 the kingdom of S king of Heshbon
Judg 11:19 unto S king of the Amorites
Judg 11:20 But S trusted not Israel to pass
Judg 11:20 but S gathered all his people
Judg 11:21 LORD God of Israel delivered S
1Kin 4:19 in the country of S king of the
Neh 9:22 so they possessed the land of S
Ps 135:11 S king of the Amorites, and Og
Ps 136:19 S king of the Amorites
Jer 48:45 and a flame from the midst of S

**SIHOR** *(si'-hor)* See SHIHOR. *A river in southern Canaan.*
Josh 13:3 From S, which is before Egypt,
Is 23:3 And by great waters the seed of S
Jer 2:18 Egypt, to drink the waters of S

**SILAS** *(si'-las)* See SILVANUS. *A co-worker with Paul.*
Acts 15:22 Judas surnamed Barsabas, and S
Acts 15:27 We have sent therefore Judas and S
Acts 15:32 And Judas and S, being prophets
Acts 15:34 it pleased S to abide there still
Acts 15:40 And Paul chose S, and departed,
Acts 16:19 was gone, they caught Paul and S
Acts 16:25 S prayed, and sang praises unto
Acts 16:29 and fell down before Paul and S
Acts 17:4 and consorted with Paul and S
Acts 17:10 Paul and S by night unto Berea
Acts 17:14 but S and Timotheus abode there
Acts 17:15 and receiving a commandment unto S
Acts 18:5 And when S and Timotheus were come

**SILENCE**
Judg 3:19 who said, Keep s
Job 4:16 was before mine eyes, there was s
Job 29:21 waited, and kept s at my counsel
Job 31:34 terrify me, that I kept s
Ps 31:18 Let the lying lips be put to s
Ps 32:3 When I kept s, my bones waxed old
Ps 35:22 keep not s
Ps 39:2 I was dumb with s, I held my
Ps 50:3 shall come, and shall not keep s
Ps 50:21 hast thou done, and I kept s
Ps 83:1 Keep not thou s, O God
Ps 94:17 my soul had almost dwelt in s
Ps 115:17 neither any that go down into s
Eccl 3:7 a time to keep s, and a time to
Is 15:1 is laid waste, and brought to s
Is 15:1 is laid waste, and brought to s
Is 41:1 Keep s before me, O islands
Is 62:6 mention of the LORD, keep not s
Is 65:6 I will not keep s, but will
Jer 8:14 the LORD our God hath put us to s
Lam 2:10 sit upon the ground, and keep s
Lam 3:28 He sitteth alone and keepeth s
Amos 5:13 prudent shall keep s in that time
Amos 8:3 they shall cast them forth with s
Hab 2:20 all the earth keep s before him
Mt 22:34 he had put the Sadducees to s
Acts 15:12 Then all the multitude kept s
Acts 21:40 And when there was made a great s
Acts 22:2 to them, they kept the more s
1Cor 14:28 let him keep s in the church
1Cor 14:34 your women keep s in the churches
1Ti 2:11 learn in s with all subjection
1Ti 2:12 over the man, but to be in s
1Pet 2:15 to s the ignorance of foolish men
Rev 8:1 there was s in heaven about the

**SILENT**
1Sa 2:9 the wicked shall be s in darkness
Ps 22:2 in the night season, and am not s
Ps 28:1 be not s to me
Ps 28:1 lest, if thou be s to me, I
Ps 30:12 sing praise to thee, and not be s
Ps 31:17 let them be s in the grave
Is 47:5 Sit thou s, and get thee into
Jer 8:14 cities, and let us be s there
Zec 2:13 Be s, O all flesh, before the

**SILK**
Prov 31:22 her clothing is s and purple
Eze 16:10 linen, and I covered thee with s
Eze 16:13 raiment was of fine linen, and s
Rev 18:12 and fine linen, and purple, and s

**SILLA** *(sil'-lah) A place near Jerusalem.*
2Kin 12:20 of Millo, which goeth down to S

**SILLY**
Job 5:2 man, and envy slayeth the s one
Hos 7:11 is like a s dove without heart
2Ti 3:6 lead captive s women laden with

**SILOAH** *(si-lo'-ah)* See SHILOAH, SILOAM. *Same as Siloam.*
Neh 3:15 pool of S by the king's garden

**SILOAM** *(si'-lo-am)* See SILOAH. *A pool south of Jerusalem.*
Lk 13:4 upon whom the tower in S fell
Jn 9:7 him, Go, wash in the pool of S
Jn 9:11 said unto me, Go to the pool of S

**SILVANUS** *(sil-va'-nus)* See SILAS.
*1. A co-worker with Paul.*
2Cor 1:19 among you by us, even by me and S
1Th 1:1 Paul, and S, and Timotheus, unto
2Th 1:1 Paul, and S, and Timotheus, unto
*2. A messenger for Peter.*
1Pet 5:12 By S, a faithful brother unto you

**SIMEON** *(sim'-e-un)* See SHIMEON, SIMEONITES, SIMON.
*1. A son of Jacob.*
Gen 29:33 and she called his name S
Gen 34:25 that two of the sons of Jacob, S
Gen 34:30 And Jacob said to S and Levi, Ye
Gen 35:23 Reuben, Jacob's firstborn, and S
Gen 42:24 with them, and took from them S
Gen 42:36 S is not, and ye will take
Gen 43:23 he brought S out unto them
Gen 46:10 And the sons of S
Gen 48:5 as Reuben and S, they shall be
Gen 49:5 S and Levi are brethren
Ex 1:2 Reuben, S, Levi, and Judah,
Ex 6:15 And the sons of S
Ex 6:15 these are the families of S
*2. Descendants of Simeon 1 and their land.*
Num 1:6 Of S
Num 1:22 Of the children of S, by their
Num 1:23 of them, even of the tribe of S
Num 2:12 by him shall be the tribe of S
Num 2:12 S shall be Shelumiel the son of
Num 7:36 prince of the children of S
Num 10:19 of S was Shelumiel the son of
Num 13:5 Of the tribe of S, Shaphat the
Num 26:12 The sons of S after their
Num 34:20 of the tribe of the children of S
Deut 27:12 S, and Levi, and Judah, and Issachar
Josh 19:1 And the second lot came forth to S
Josh 19:1 of S according to their families
Josh 19:8 of S according to their families
Josh 19:9 inheritance of the children of S
Josh 19:9 therefore the children of S had
Josh 21:4 Judah, and out of the tribe of S
Josh 21:9 of the tribe of the children of S
Judg 1:3 And Judah said unto S his brother
Judg 1:3 So S went with him
Judg 1:17 And Judah went with S his brother
1Chr 2:1 Reuben, S, Levi, and Judah,
1Chr 4:24 The sons of S were, Nemuel, and
1Chr 4:42 of them, even of the sons of S
1Chr 6:65 of the tribe of the children of S
1Chr 12:25 Of the children of S, mighty men
2Chr 15:9 Ephraim and Manasseh, and out of S
2Chr 34:6 of Manasseh, and Ephraim, and S
Eze 48:24 west side, S shall have a portion
Eze 48:25 And by the border of S, from the
Eze 48:33 one gate of S, one gate of
Rev 7:7 Of the tribe of S were sealed

*3. A devout man who blessed Jesus.*
Lk 2:25 in Jerusalem, whose name was *S*
Lk 2:34 *S* blessed them, and said unto Mary
*4. Father of Levi; an ancestor of Jesus.*
Lk 3:30 Which was the son of *S*, which was
*5. A prophet of Antioch.*
Acts 13:1 *S* that was called Niger, and
*6. Same as Simon Peter.*
Acts 15:14 *S* hath declared how God at the

**SIMEONITES** *(sim'-e-un-ites) Descendants of Simeon 1.*
Num 25:14 of a chief house among the *S*
Num 26:14 These are the families of the *S*
1Chr 27:16 of the *S*, Shephatiah the son of

**SIMILITUDE**
Num 12:8 the *s* of the LORD shall he behold
Deut 4:12 voice of the words, but saw no *s*
Deut 4:15 for ye saw no manner of *s* on the
Deut 4:16 the *s* of any figure, the likeness
2Chr 4:3 And under it was the *s* of oxen
Ps 106:20 the *s* of an ox that eateth grass
Ps 144:12 polished after the *s* of a palace
Dan 10:16 one like the *s* of the sons of men
Rom 5:14 the *s* of Adam's transgression
Heb 7:15 for that after the *s* of
Jas 3:9 which are made after the *s* of God

**SIMON** *(si'mun)* See BAR-JONA, NIGER, PETER, SIMEON, SIMON'S, ZELOTES.
*1. Same as Peter.*
Mt 4:18 *S* called Peter, and Andrew his
Mt 10:2 The first, *S*, who is called Peter
Mt 16:16 *S* Peter answered and said, Thou
Mt 16:17 him, Blessed art thou, *S* Bar-jona
Mt 17:25 saying, What thinkest thou, *S*
Mk 1:16 by the sea of Galilee, he saw *S*
Mk 1:29 they entered into the house of *S*
Mk 1:36 And *S* and they that were with him
Mk 3:16 And *S* he surnamed Peter
Mk 14:37 sleeping, and saith unto Peter, *S*
Lk 5:4 had left speaking, he said unto *S*
Lk 5:5 *S* answering said unto him, Master
Lk 5:8 When *S* Peter saw it, he fell down
Lk 5:10 which were partners with *S*
Lk 5:10 And Jesus said unto *S*, Fear not
Lk 6:14 *S*, (whom he also named Peter,) and
Lk 22:31 And the Lord said, *S*, *S*,
Lk 24:34 indeed, and hath appeared to *S*
Jn 1:40 was Andrew, *S* Peter's brother
Jn 1:41 first findeth his own brother *S*
Jn 1:42 Thou art *S* the son of Jona
Jn 6:8 *S* Peter's brother, saith unto him
Jn 6:68 Then *S* Peter answered him, Lord,
Jn 13:6 Then cometh he to *S* Peter
Jn 13:9 *S* Peter saith unto him, Lord, not
Jn 13:24 *S* Peter therefore beckoned to him
Jn 13:36 *S* Peter said unto him, Lord,
Jn 18:10 Then *S* Peter having a sword drew
Jn 18:15 *S* Peter followed Jesus, and so did
Jn 18:25 *S* Peter stood and warmed himself
Jn 20:2 she runneth, and cometh to *S* Peter
Jn 20:6 Then cometh *S* Peter following him
Jn 21:2 There were together *S* Peter
Jn 21:3 *S* Peter saith unto them, I go a
Jn 21:7 Now when *S* Peter heard that it
Jn 21:11 *S* Peter went up, and drew the net
Jn 21:15 Jesus saith to *S* Peter, *S*
Jn 21:16 to him again the second time, *S*
Jn 21:17 saith unto him the third time, *S*
Acts 10:5 men to Joppa, and call for one *S*
Acts 10:18 And called, and asked whether *S*
Acts 10:32 to Joppa, and call hither *S*
Acts 11:13 Send men to Joppa, and call for *S*
2Pet 1:1 *S* Peter, a servant and an apostle
*2. A Canaanite disciple of Jesus.*
Mt 10:4 *S* the Canaanite, and Judas
Mk 3:18 and Thaddaeus, and *S* the Canaanite,
Lk 6:15 of Alphaeus, and *S* called Zelotes,
Acts 1:13 *S* Zelotes, and Judas the brother
*3. A brother of Jesus.*
Mt 13:55 brethren, James, and Joses, and *S*
Mk 6:3 James, and Joses, and of Juda, and *S*
*4. A leper in Bethany.*
Mt 26:6 in the house of *S* the leper
Mk 14:3 in the house of *S* the leper
*5. A Cyrenian who bore Jesus' cross.*
Mt 27:32 found a man of Cyrene, *S* by name
Mk 15:21 And they compel one *S* a Cyrenian
Lk 23:26 away, they laid hold upon one *S*
*6. A Pharisee.*
Lk 7:40 Jesus answering said unto him, *S*
Lk 7:43 *S* answered and said, I suppose
Lk 7:44 to the woman, and said unto *S*
*7. Father of Judas Iscariot.*
Jn 6:71 of Judas Iscariot the son of *S*
Jn 13:26 to Judas Iscariot, the son of *S*
*8. A Samaritan sorcerer.*
Acts 8:9 there was a certain man, called *S*
Acts 8:13 Then *S* himself believed also
Acts 8:18 when *S* saw that through laying on
Acts 8:24 Then answered *S*, and said, Pray ye
*9. A tanner at Joppa.*
Acts 9:43 days in Joppa with one *S* a tanner
Acts 10:6 He lodgeth with one *S* a tanner
Acts 10:32 of one *S* a tanner by the sea side

**SIMON'S** *(si'-muns)*
*1. Refers to Simon 1.*
Mk 1:30 But *S* wife's mother lay sick of a
Lk 4:38 and entered into *S* house
Lk 4:38 *S* wife's mother was taken with a
Lk 5:3 one of the ships, which was *S*
*2. Refers to Simon 7.*
Jn 12:4 *S* son, which should betray him,
Jn 13:2 Iscariot, *S* son, to betray him
*3. Refers to Simon 9.*
Acts 10:17 had made enquiry for *S* house

**SIMPLE**
Ps 19:7 LORD is sure, making wise the *s*
Ps 116:6 The LORD preserveth the *s*
Ps 119:130 giveth understanding unto the *s*
Prov 1:4 To give subtilty to the *s*
Prov 1:22 How long, ye *s* ones, will ye love
Prov 1:32 away of the *s* shall slay them
Prov 7:7 And beheld among the *s* ones
Prov 8:5 O ye *s*, understand wisdom
Prov 9:4 Whoso is *s*, let him turn in
Prov 9:13 she is *s*, and knoweth nothing
Prov 9:16 Whoso is *s*, let him turn in
Prov 14:15 The *s* believeth every word
Prov 14:18 The *s* inherit folly
Prov 19:25 a scorner, and the *s* will beware
Prov 21:11 is punished, the *s* is made wise
Prov 22:3 but the *s* pass on, and are
Prov 27:12 but the *s* pass on, and are
Eze 45:20 that erreth, and for him that is *s*
Rom 16:18 deceive the hearts of the *s*
Rom 16:19 is good, and *s* concerning evil

**SIMPLICITY**
2Sa 15:11 and they went in their *s*, and they
Prov 1:22 ye simple ones, will ye love *s*
Rom 12:8 that giveth, let him do it with *s*
2Cor 1:12 of our conscience, that in *s*
2Cor 11:3 from the *s* that is in Christ

**SIMRI** *(sim'-ri)* See SHIMRI. *A sanctuary servant.*
1Chr 26:10 *S* the chief, (for though he was

**SIN** *(sin)*
*1. A transgression.*
Gen 4:7 not well, *s* lieth at the door
Gen 18:20 because their *s* is very grievous
Gen 20:9 on me and on my kingdom a great *s*
Gen 31:36 what is my *s*, that thou hast so
Gen 39:9 wickedness, and *s* against God
Gen 42:22 Do not *s* against the child
Gen 50:17 of thy brethren, and their *s*
Ex 10:17 my *s* only this once, and intreat
Ex 20:20 before your faces, that ye *s* not
Ex 23:33 lest they make thee *s* against me
Ex 29:14 it is a *s* offering
Ex 29:36 for a *s* offering for atonement
Ex 30:10 of the *s* offering of atonements
Ex 32:21 brought so great a *s* upon them
Ex 32:30 people, Ye have sinned a great *s*
Ex 32:30 make an atonement for your *s*
Ex 32:31 this people have sinned a great *s*
Ex 32:32 now, if thou wilt forgive their *s*
Ex 32:34 I will visit their *s* upon them
Ex 34:7 iniquity and transgression and *s*
Ex 34:9 and pardon our iniquity and our *s*
Lev 4:2 If a soul shall *s* through
Lev 4:3 do *s* according to the
Lev 4:3 according to the *s* of the people
Lev 4:3 then let him bring for his *s*
Lev 4:3 unto the LORD for a *s* offering
Lev 4:8 of the bullock for the *s* offering
Lev 4:13 of Israel *s* through ignorance
Lev 4:14 When the *s*, which they have
Lev 4:14 offer a young bullock for the *s*
Lev 4:20 with the bullock for a *s* offering
Lev 4:21 it is a *s* offering for the
Lev 4:23 Or if his *s*, wherein he hath
Lev 4:24 it is a *s* offering
Lev 4:25 of the *s* offering with his finger
Lev 4:26 for him as concerning his *s*
Lev 4:27 common people *s* through ignorance
Lev 4:28 Or if his *s*, which he hath sinned
Lev 4:28 for his *s* which he hath sinned
Lev 4:29 upon the head of the *s* offering
Lev 4:29 slay the *s* offering in the place
Lev 4:32 he bring a lamb for a *s* offering
Lev 4:33 upon the head of the *s* offering
Lev 4:33 slay it for a *s* offering in the
Lev 4:34 of the *s* offering with his finger
Lev 4:35 for his *s* that he hath committed
Lev 5:1 And if a soul *s*, and hear the voice
Lev 5:6 for his *s* which he hath sinned
Lev 5:6 of the goats, for a *s* offering
Lev 5:6 for him concerning his *s*
Lev 5:7 one for a *s* offering, and the
Lev 5:8 which is for the *s* offering first
Lev 5:9 sprinkle of the blood of the *s*
Lev 5:9 it is a *s* offering
Lev 5:10 for his *s* which he hath sinned
Lev 5:11 of fine flour for a *s* offering
Lev 5:11 for it is a *s* offering
Lev 5:12 it is a *s* offering
Lev 5:13 for him as touching his *s* that he
Lev 5:15 *s* through ignorance, in the holy
Lev 5:17 And if a soul *s*, and commit any of
Lev 6:2 If a soul *s*, and commit a trespass
Lev 6:17 most holy, as is the *s* offering
Lev 6:25 This is the law of the *s* offering
Lev 6:25 offering is killed shall the *s*
Lev 6:26 offereth it for *s* shall eat it
Lev 6:30 no *s* offering, whereof any of the
Lev 7:7 As the *s* offering is, so is the
Lev 7:37 of the *s* offering, and of the
Lev 8:2 and a bullock for the *s* offering
Lev 8:14 the bullock for the *s* offering
Lev 8:14 of the bullock for the *s* offering
Lev 9:2 a young calf for a *s* offering
Lev 9:3 kid of the goats for a *s* offering
Lev 9:7 altar, and offer thy *s* offering
Lev 9:8 slew the calf of the *s* offering
Lev 9:10 above the liver of the *s* offering
Lev 9:15 which was the *s* offering for the
Lev 9:15 and slew it, and offered it for *s*
Lev 9:22 from offering of the *s* offering
Lev 10:16 sought the goat of the *s* offering
Lev 10:17 the *s* offering in the holy place
Lev 10:19 they offered their *s* offering
Lev 10:19 I had eaten the *s* offering to day
Lev 12:6 for a *s* offering, unto the door
Lev 12:8 and the other for a *s* offering
Lev 14:13 he shall kill the *s* offering
Lev 14:13 for as the *s* offering is the
Lev 14:19 priest shall offer the *s* offering
Lev 14:22 and the one shall be a *s* offering
Lev 14:31 to get, the one for a *s* offering
Lev 15:15 them, the one for a *s* offering
Lev 15:30 offer the one for a *s* offering
Lev 16:3 a young bullock for a *s* offering
Lev 16:5 of the goats for a *s* offering
Lev 16:6 his bullock of the *s* offering
Lev 16:9 and offer him for a *s* offering
Lev 16:11 the bullock of the *s* offering
Lev 16:11 *s* offering which is for himself
Lev 16:15 kill the goat of the *s* offering
Lev 16:25 the fat of the *s* offering shall
Lev 16:27 And the bullock for the *s* offering
Lev 16:27 and the goat for the *s* offering
Lev 19:17 and not suffer *s* upon him
Lev 19:22 LORD for his *s* which he hath done
Lev 19:22 the *s* which he hath done shall be
Lev 20:20 they shall bear their *s*
Lev 22:9 lest they bear *s* for it, and die
Lev 23:19 kid of the goats for a *s* offering
Lev 24:15 curseth his God shall bear his *s*
Num 5:6 commit any *s* that men commit
Num 5:7 their *s* which they have done
Num 6:11 offer the one for a *s* offering
Num 6:14 without blemish for a *s* offering
Num 6:16 and shall offer his *s* offering
Num 7:16 kid of the goats for a *s* offering
Num 7:22 kid of the goats for a *s* offering
Num 7:28 kid of the goats for a *s* offering
Num 7:34 kid of the goats for a *s* offering

Num 7:40 kid of the goats for a s offering
Num 7:46 kid of the goats for a s offering
Num 7:52 kid of the goats for a s offering
Num 7:58 kid of the goats for a s offering
Num 7:64 kid of the goats for a s offering
Num 7:70 kid of the goats for a s offering
Num 7:76 kid of the goats for a s offering
Num 7:82 kid of the goats for a s offering
Num 7:87 the goats for s offering twelve
Num 8:8 shalt thou take for a s offering
Num 8:12 offer the one for a s offering
Num 9:13 season, that man shall bear his s
Num 12:11 thee, lay not the s upon us
Num 15:24 kid of the goats for a s offering
Num 15:25 their s offering before the LORD,
Num 15:27 if any soul s through ignorance,
Num 15:27 the first year for a s offering
Num 16:22 of all flesh, shall one man s
Num 18:9 every s offering of theirs, and
Num 18:22 congregation, lest they bear s
Num 18:32 shall bear no s by reason of it
Num 19:9 it is a purification for s
Num 19:17 heifer of purification for s
Num 27:3 but died in his own s, and had no
Num 28:15 one kid of the goats for a s
Num 28:22 And one goat for a s offering
Num 29:5 kid of the goats for a s offering
Num 29:11 kid of the goats for a s offering
Num 29:11 beside the s offering of
Num 29:16 kid of the goats for a s offering
Num 29:19 kid of the goats for a s offering
Num 29:22 And one goat for a s offering
Num 29:25 kid of the goats for a s offering
Num 29:28 And one goat for a s offering
Num 29:31 And one goat for a s offering
Num 29:34 And one goat for a s offering
Num 29:38 And one goat for a s offering
Num 32:23 be sure your s will find you out
Deut 9:21 And I took your s, the calf which
Deut 9:27 their wickedness, nor to their s
Deut 15:9 thee, and it be s unto thee
Deut 19:15 for any iniquity, or for any s
Deut 19:15 in any s that he sinneth
Deut 20:18 so should ye s against the LORD
Deut 21:22 committed a s worthy of death
Deut 22:26 the damsel no s worthy of death
Deut 23:21 and it would be s in thee
Deut 23:22 to vow, it shall be no s in thee
Deut 24:4 shalt not cause the land to s
Deut 24:15 the LORD, and it be s unto thee
Deut 24:16 be put to death for his own s
1Sa 2:17 Wherefore the s of the young men
1Sa 2:25 If one man s against another, the
1Sa 2:25 but if a man s against the LORD,
1Sa 12:23 God forbid that I should s
1Sa 14:33 the people s against the LORD, in
1Sa 14:34 s not against the LORD in eating
1Sa 14:38 see wherein this s hath been this
1Sa 15:23 is as the s of witchcraft
1Sa 15:25 I pray thee, pardon my s
1Sa 19:4 Let not the king s against his
1Sa 19:5 thou s against innocent blood
1Sa 20:1 what is my s before thy father,
2Sa 12:13 The LORD also hath put away thy s
1Kin 8:34 forgive the s of thy people
1Kin 8:35 thy name, and turn from their s
1Kin 8:36 forgive the s of thy servants, and
1Kin 8:46 If they s against thee, (for
1Kin 12:30 And this thing became a s
1Kin 13:34 this thing became s unto the
1Kin 14:16 the sins of Jeroboam, who did s
1Kin 14:16 and who made Israel to s
1Kin 15:26 in his s wherewith he made Israel
1Kin 15:26 wherewith he made Israel to s
1Kin 15:30 sinned, and which he made Israel s
1Kin 15:34 in his s wherewith he made Israel
1Kin 15:34 wherewith he made Israel to s
1Kin 16:2 hast made my people Israel to s
1Kin 16:13 and by which they made Israel to s
1Kin 16:19 in his s which he did, to make
1Kin 16:19 which he did, to make Israel to s
1Kin 16:26 in his s wherewith he made Israel
1Kin 16:26 wherewith he made Israel to s
1Kin 17:18 me to call my s to remembrance
1Kin 21:22 me to anger, and made Israel to s
1Kin 22:52 of Nebat, who made Israel to s
2Kin 3:3 of Nebat, which made Israel to s
2Kin 10:29 of Nebat, who made Israel to s
2Kin 10:31 Jeroboam, which made Israel to s
2Kin 12:16 s money was not brought into the
2Kin 13:2 of Nebat, which made Israel to s
2Kin 13:6 of Jeroboam, who made Israel s
2Kin 13:11 son of Nebat, who made Israel s
2Kin 14:6 be put to death for his own s
2Kin 14:24 of Nebat, who made Israel to s
2Kin 15:9 of Nebat, who made Israel to s
2Kin 15:18 of Nebat, who made Israel to s
2Kin 15:24 of Nebat, who made Israel to s
2Kin 15:28 of Nebat, who made Israel to s
2Kin 17:21 LORD, and made them s
2Kin 17:21 a great s
2Kin 21:11 Judah also to s with his idols
2Kin 21:16 beside his s wherewith he made
2Kin 21:16 wherewith he made Judah to s
2Kin 21:17 his s that he sinned, are they
2Kin 23:15 of Nebat, who made Israel to s
2Chr 6:22 If a man s against his neighbour,
2Chr 6:25 forgive the s of thy people
2Chr 6:26 thy name, and turn from their s
2Chr 6:27 forgive the s of thy servants, and
2Chr 6:36 If they s against thee, (for
2Chr 7:14 heaven, and will forgive their s
2Chr 25:4 every man shall die for his own s
2Chr 29:21 for a s offering for the kingdom,
2Chr 29:23 the s offering before the king
2Chr 29:24 the s offering should be made for
2Chr 33:19 intreated of him, and all his s
Ezr 6:17 for a s offering for all Israel,
Ezr 8:35 twelve he goats for a s offering
Neh 4:5 let not their s be blotted out
Neh 6:13 should be afraid, and do so, and s
Neh 10:33 for the s offerings to make an
Neh 13:26 king of Israel s by these things
Neh 13:26 did outlandish women cause to s
Job 2:10 this did not Job s with his lips
Job 5:24 thy habitation, and shalt not s
Job 10:6 iniquity, and searchest after my s
Job 10:14 If I s, then thou markest me, and
Job 13:23 to know my transgression and my s
Job 14:16 dost thou not watch over my s
Job 20:11 are full of the s of his youth
Job 31:30 have I suffered my mouth to s by
Job 34:37 he addeth rebellion unto his s
Job 35:3 have, if I be cleansed from my s
Ps 4:4 Stand in awe, and s not
Ps 32:1 is forgiven, whose s is covered
Ps 32:5 I acknowledged my s unto thee
Ps 32:5 forgavest the iniquity of my s
Ps 38:3 rest in my bones because of my s
Ps 38:18 I will be sorry for my s
Ps 39:1 that I s not with my tongue
Ps 40:6 s offering hast thou not required
Ps 51:2 iniquity, and cleanse me from my s
Ps 51:3 and my s is ever before me
Ps 51:5 in s did my mother conceive me
Ps 59:3 my transgression, nor for my s
Ps 59:12 For the s of their mouth and the
Ps 85:2 thou hast covered all their s
Ps 109:7 and let his prayer become s
Ps 109:14 let not the s of his mother be
Ps 119:11 that I might not s against thee
Prov 10:16 the fruit of the wicked to s
Prov 10:19 of words there wanteth not s
Prov 14:9 Fools make a mock at s
Prov 14:34 but s is a reproach to any people
Prov 20:9 heart clean, I am pure from my s
Prov 21:4 the plowing of the wicked, is s
Prov 24:9 The thought of foolishness is s
Eccl 5:6 thy mouth to cause thy flesh to s
Is 3:9 and they declare their s as Sodom
Is 5:18 s as it were with a cart rope
Is 6:7 is taken away, and thy s purged
Is 27:9 all the fruit to take away his s
Is 30:1 that they may add s to s
Is 31:7 hands have made unto you for a s
Is 53:10 make his soul an offering for s
Is 53:12 and he bare the s of many, and made
Jer 16:10 or what is our s that we have
Jer 16:18 their iniquity and their s double
Jer 17:1 The s of Judah is written with a
Jer 17:3 spoil, and thy high places for s
Jer 18:23 blot out their s from thy sight
Jer 31:34 I will remember their s no more
Jer 32:35 abomination, to cause Judah to s
Jer 36:3 forgive their iniquity and their s
Jer 51:5 their land was filled with s
Lam 4:6 the punishment of the s of Sodom
Eze 3:20 warning, he shall die in his s
Eze 3:21 s not, and he doth not s
Eze 18:24 in his s that he hath sinned, in
Eze 33:14 if he turn from his s, and do that
Eze 40:39 the s offering and the trespass
Eze 42:13 the s offering, and the trespass
Eze 43:19 a young bullock for a s offering
Eze 43:21 bullock also of the s offering
Eze 43:22 without blemish for a s offering
Eze 43:25 every day a goat for a s offering
Eze 44:27 he shall offer his s offering
Eze 44:29 the s offering, and the trespass
Eze 45:17 he shall prepare the s offering
Eze 45:19 of the blood of the s offering
Eze 45:22 land a bullock for a s offering
Eze 45:23 the goats daily for a s offering
Eze 45:25 days, according to the s offering
Eze 46:20 the s offering, where they shall
Dan 9:20 and praying, and confessing my s
Dan 9:20 the s of my people Israel, and
Hos 4:8 They eat up the s of my people
Hos 8:11 hath made many altars to s
Hos 8:11 altars shall be unto him to s
Hos 10:8 the s of Israel, shall be
Hos 12:8 none iniquity in me that were s
Hos 13:2 And now they s more and more, and
Hos 13:12 his s is hid
Amos 8:14 that swear by the s of Samaria
Mic 1:13 of the s to the daughter of Zion
Mic 3:8 transgression, and to Israel his s
Mic 6:7 of my body for the s of my soul
Zec 13:1 inhabitants of Jerusalem for s
Mt 12:31 I say unto you, All manner of s
Mt 18:21 oft shall my brother s against me
Jn 1:29 taketh away the s of the world
Jn 5:14 s no more, lest a worse thing
Jn 8:7 He that is without s among you
Jn 8:11 go, and s no more
Jn 8:34 Whosoever committeth s is the
Jn 8:34 is the servant of s
Jn 8:46 Which of you convinceth me of s
Jn 9:2 him, saying, Master, who did s
Jn 9:41 were blind, ye should have no s
Jn 9:41 therefore your s remaineth
Jn 15:22 unto them, they had not had s
Jn 15:22 they have no cloke for their s
Jn 15:24 other man did, they had not had s
Jn 16:8 he will reprove the world of s
Jn 16:9 Of s, because they believe not on
Jn 19:11 me unto thee hath the greater s
Acts 7:60 lay not this s to their charge
Rom 3:9 that they are all under s
Rom 3:20 by the law is the knowledge of s
Rom 4:8 whom the Lord will not impute s
Rom 5:12 as by one man s entered into the
Rom 5:12 into the world, and death by s
Rom 5:13 until the law s was in the world
Rom 5:13 but s is not imputed when there
Rom 5:20 But where s abounded, grace did
Rom 5:21 That as s hath reigned unto death
Rom 6:1 Shall we continue in s, that
Rom 6:2 How shall we, that are dead to s
Rom 6:6 that the body of s might be
Rom 6:6 henceforth we should not serve s
Rom 6:7 he that is dead is freed from s
Rom 6:10 that he died, he died unto s once
Rom 6:11 to be dead indeed unto s, but
Rom 6:12 Let not s therefore reign in your
Rom 6:13 of unrighteousness unto s
Rom 6:14 For s shall not have dominion
Rom 6:15 shall we s, because we are not
Rom 6:16 whether of s unto death, or of
Rom 6:17 that ye were the servants of s
Rom 6:18 Being then made free from s
Rom 6:20 when ye were the servants of s
Rom 6:22 But now being made free from s
Rom 6:23 For the wages of s is death
Rom 7:7 Is the law s
Rom 7:7 Nay, I had not known s, but by
Rom 7:8 But s, taking occasion by the
Rom 7:8 For without the law s was dead
Rom 7:9 came, s revived, and I died
Rom 7:11 For s, taking occasion by the
Rom 7:13 But s, that it might appear s,
Rom 7:13 that s by the commandment might
Rom 7:14 but I am carnal, sold under s
Rom 7:17 but s that dwelleth in me
Rom 7:20 but s that dwelleth in me
Rom 7:23 law of s which is in my members
Rom 7:25 but with the flesh the law of s
Rom 8:2 made me free from the law of s
Rom 8:3 for s, condemned s in the flesh
Rom 8:10 the body is dead because of s

Rom 14:23 whatsoever is not of faith is *s*
1Cor 6:18 Every *s* that a man doeth is
1Cor 8:12 But when ye *s* so against the
1Cor 8:12 conscience, ye *s* against Christ
1Cor 15:34 Awake to righteousness, and *s* not
1Cor 15:56 The sting of death is *s*
1Cor 15:56 and the strength of *s* is the law
2Cor 5:21 to be *s* for us, who knew no *s*
Gal 2:17 Christ the minister of *s*
Gal 3:22 hath concluded all under *s*
Eph 4:26 Be ye angry, and *s* not
2Th 2:3 and that man of *s* be revealed
1Ti 5:20 Them that *s* rebuke before all,
Heb 3:13 through the deceitfulness of *s*
Heb 4:15 like as we are, yet without *s*
Heb 9:26 *s* by the sacrifice of himself
Heb 9:28 time without *s* unto salvation
Heb 10:6 sacrifices for *s* thou hast had no
Heb 10:8 offering for *s* thou wouldest not,
Heb 10:18 there is no more offering for *s*
Heb 10:26 For if we *s* wilfully after that
Heb 11:25 the pleasures of *s* for a season
Heb 12:1 the *s* which doth so easily beset
Heb 12:4 unto blood, striving against *s*
Heb 13:11 by the high priest for *s*, are
Jas 1:15 conceived, it bringeth forth *s*
Jas 1:15 and *s*, when it is finished,
Jas 2:9 respect to persons, ye commit *s*
Jas 4:17 and doeth it not, to him it is *s*
1Pet 2:22 Who did no *s*, neither was guile
1Pet 4:1 in the flesh hath ceased from *s*
2Pet 2:14 and that cannot cease from *s*
1Jn 1:7 his Son cleanseth us from all *s*
1Jn 1:8 If we say that we have no *s*
1Jn 2:1 write I unto you, that ye *s* not
1Jn 2:1 And if any man *s*, we have an
1Jn 3:4 Whosoever committeth *s*
1Jn 3:4 for *s* is the transgression of the
1Jn 3:5 and in him is no *s*
1Jn 3:8 that committeth *s* is of the devil
1Jn 3:9 is born of God doth not commit *s*
1Jn 3:9 and he cannot *s*, because he is
1Jn 5:16 *s* a *s* which is not unto death
1Jn 5:16 for them that *s* not unto death
1Jn 5:16 There is a *s* unto death
1Jn 5:17 All unrighteousness is *s*
1Jn 5:17 there is a *s* not unto death

*2. Eastern border of Egypt.*

Eze 30:15 And I will pour my fury upon *S*
Eze 30:16 *S* shall have great pain, and No

*3. Desert between Elim and Sinai.*

Ex 16:1 came unto the wilderness of *S*
Ex 17:1 from the wilderness of *S*, after
Num 33:11 encamped in the wilderness of *S*
Num 33:12 out of the wilderness of *S*

**SINA** *(si'-nah)* See SINAI. *Greek form of Sinai.*

Acts 7:30 him in the wilderness of mount *S*
Acts 7:38 which spake to him in the mount *S*

**SINAI** *(si'-nahee)* See HOREB, SINA. *Mountainous district in the southern Sinai peninsula.*

Ex 16:1 Sin, which is between Elim and *S*
Ex 19:1 they into the wilderness of *S*
Ex 19:2 and were come to the desert of *S*
Ex 19:11 of all the people upon mount *S*
Ex 19:18 mount *S* was altogether on a smoke
Ex 19:20 the LORD came down upon mount *S*
Ex 19:23 people cannot come up to mount *S*
Ex 24:16 of the LORD abode upon mount *S*
Ex 31:18 communing with him upon mount *S*
Ex 34:2 up in the morning unto mount *S*
Ex 34:4 morning, and went up unto mount *S*
Ex 34:29 mount *S* with the two tables of
Ex 34:32 had spoken with him in mount *S*
Lev 7:38 LORD commanded Moses in mount *S*
Lev 7:38 the LORD, in the wilderness of *S*
Lev 25:1 LORD spake unto Moses in mount *S*
Lev 26:46 in mount *S* by the hand of Moses
Lev 27:34 the children of Israel in mount *S*
Num 1:1 unto Moses in the wilderness of *S*
Num 1:19 them in the wilderness of *S*
Num 3:1 LORD spake with Moses in mount *S*
Num 3:4 the LORD, in the wilderness of *S*
Num 3:14 unto Moses in the wilderness of *S*
Num 9:1 unto Moses in the wilderness of *S*
Num 9:5 at even in the wilderness of *S*
Num 10:12 out of the wilderness of *S*
Num 26:64 of Israel in the wilderness of *S*
Num 28:6 in mount *S* for a sweet savour
Num 33:15 and pitched in the wilderness of *S*
Num 33:16 they removed from the desert of *S*
Deut 33:2 And he said, The LORD came from *S*
Judg 5:5 even that *S* from before the LORD
Neh 9:13 camest down also upon mount *S*
Ps 68:8 even *S* itself was moved at the
Ps 68:17 the Lord is among them, as in *S*
Gal 4:24 the one from the mount *S*, which
Gal 4:25 this Agar is mount *S* in Arabia

**SINCERITY**

Josh 24:14 fear the LORD, and serve him in *s*
1Cor 5:8 with the unleavened bread of *s*
2Cor 1:12 that in simplicity and godly *s*
2Cor 2:17 but as of *s*, but as of God, in
2Cor 8:8 and to prove the *s* of your love
Eph 6:24 love our Lord Jesus Christ in *s*
Titus 2:7 shewing uncorruptness, gravity, *s*

**SINEWS**

Job 10:11 and hast fenced me with bones and *s*
Job 30:17 and my *s* take no rest
Job 40:17 the *s* of his stones are wrapped
Eze 37:6 And I will lay *s* upon you, and will
Eze 37:8 And when I beheld, lo, the *s*

**SINFUL**

Num 32:14 stead, an increase of *s* men
Is 1:4 Ah *s* nation, a people laden with
Amos 9:8 Lord GOD are upon the *s* kingdom
Mk 8:38 this adulterous and *s* generation
Lk 5:8 for I am a *s* man, O Lord
Lk 24:7 delivered into the hands of *s* men
Rom 7:13 might become exceeding *s*
Rom 8:3 Son in the likeness of *s* flesh

**SING**

Ex 15:1 I will *s* unto the LORD, for he
Ex 15:21 *S* ye to the LORD, for he hath
Ex 32:18 noise of them that *s* do I hear
Num 21:17 *s* ye unto it
Judg 5:3 I, even I, will *s* unto the LORD
Judg 5:3 I will *s* praise to the LORD God
1Sa 21:11 did they not *s* one to another of
1Chr 16:9 *S* unto him, *s* psalms unto him,
1Chr 16:23 *S* unto the LORD, all the earth
1Chr 16:33 shall the trees of the wood *s* out
2Chr 20:22 And when they began to *s* and to
2Chr 23:13 and such as taught to *s* praise
2Chr 29:30 commanded the Levites to *s* praise
Job 29:13 the widow's heart to *s* for joy
Ps 7:17 will *s* praise to the name of the
Ps 9:2 I will *s* praise to thy name, O
Ps 9:11 *S* praises to the LORD, which
Ps 13:6 I will *s* unto the LORD, because
Ps 18:49 and *s* praises unto thy name
Ps 21:13 so will we *s* and praise thy power
Ps 27:6 I will *s*, yea
Ps 27:6 I will *s* praises unto the LORD
Ps 30:4 *S* unto the LORD, O ye saints of
Ps 30:12 my glory may *s* praise to thee
Ps 33:2 *s* unto him with the psaltery and
Ps 33:3 *S* unto him a new song
Ps 47:6 *S* praises to God, *s* praises
Ps 47:6 *s* praises unto our King, *s*
Ps 47:7 *s* ye praises with understanding
Ps 51:14 my tongue shall *s* aloud of thy
Ps 57:7 I will *s* and give praise
Ps 57:9 I will *s* unto thee among the
Ps 59:16 But I will *s* of thy power
Ps 59:16 I will *s* aloud of thy mercy in
Ps 59:17 thee, O my strength, will I *s*
Ps 61:8 So will I *s* praise unto thy name
Ps 65:13 they shout for joy, they also *s*
Ps 66:2 *S* forth the honour of his name
Ps 66:4 thee, and shall *s* unto thee
Ps 66:4 they shall *s* to thy name
Ps 67:4 the nations be glad and *s* for joy
Ps 68:4 *S* unto God
Ps 68:4 *s* praises to his name
Ps 68:32 *S* unto God, ye kingdoms of the
Ps 68:32 O *s* praises unto the Lord
Ps 71:22 unto thee will I *s* with the harp
Ps 71:23 rejoice when I *s* unto thee
Ps 75:9 I will *s* praises to the God of
Ps 81:1 *S* aloud unto God our strength
Ps 89:1 I will *s* of the mercies of the
Ps 92:1 to *s* praises unto thy name, O
Ps 95:1 O come, let us *s* unto the LORD
Ps 96:1 O *s* unto the LORD a new song
Ps 96:1 *s* unto the LORD, all the earth
Ps 96:2 *S* unto the LORD, bless his name
Ps 98:1 O *s* unto the LORD a new song
Ps 98:4 noise, and rejoice, and *s* praise
Ps 98:5 *S* unto the LORD with the harp
Ps 101:1 I will *s* of mercy and judgment
Ps 101:1 unto thee, O LORD, will I *s*
Ps 104:12 which *s* among the branches
Ps 104:33 I will *s* unto the LORD as long as
Ps 104:33 I will *s* praise to my God while I
Ps 105:2 *S* unto him
Ps 105:2 *s* psalms unto him
Ps 108:1 I will *s* and give praise, even
Ps 108:3 I will *s* praises unto thee among
Ps 135:3 *s* praises unto his name
Ps 137:3 *S* us one of the songs of Zion
Ps 137:4 How shall we *s* the LORD's song in
Ps 138:1 gods will I *s* praise unto thee
Ps 138:5 they shall *s* in the ways of the
Ps 144:9 I will *s* a new song unto thee, O
Ps 144:9 will I *s* praises unto thee
Ps 145:7 shall *s* of thy righteousness
Ps 146:2 I will *s* praises unto my God
Ps 147:1 for it is good to *s* praises unto
Ps 147:7 *S* unto the LORD with thanksgiving
Ps 147:7 *s* praise upon the harp unto our
Ps 149:1 *S* unto the LORD a new song, and
Ps 149:3 let them *s* praises unto him with
Ps 149:5 let them *s* aloud upon their beds
Prov 29:6 but the righteous doth *s* and
Is 5:1 Now will I *s* to my wellbeloved a
Is 12:5 *S* unto the LORD
Is 23:15 years shall Tyre *s* as an harlot
Is 23:16 *s* many songs, that thou mayest be
Is 24:14 they shall *s* for the majesty of
Is 26:19 Awake and *s*, ye that dwell in dust
Is 27:2 In that day *s* ye unto her
Is 35:6 hart, and the tongue of the dumb *s*
Is 38:20 therefore we will *s* my songs to
Is 42:10 *S* unto the LORD a new song, and
Is 42:11 let the inhabitants of the rock *s*
Is 44:23 *S*, O ye heavens
Is 49:13 *S*, O heavens
Is 52:8 the voice together shall they *s*
Is 52:9 *s* together, ye waste places of
Is 54:1 *S*, O barren, thou that didst not
Is 65:14 servants shall *s* for joy of heart
Jer 20:13 *S* unto the LORD, praise ye the
Jer 31:7 *S* with gladness for Jacob, and
Jer 31:12 *s* in the height of Zion, and shall
Jer 51:48 is therein, shall *s* for Babylon
Eze 27:25 did *s* of thee in thy market
Hos 2:15 and she shall *s* there, as in the
Zeph 2:14 voice shall *s* in the windows
Zeph 3:14 *S*, O daughter of Zion
Zec 2:10 *S* and rejoice, O daughter of Zion
Rom 15:9 the Gentiles, and *s* unto thy name
1Cor 14:15 I will *s* with the spirit
1Cor 14:15 I will *s* with the understanding
Heb 2:12 church will I *s* praise unto thee
Jas 5:13 let him *s* psalms
Rev 15:3 they *s* the song of Moses the

**SINGERS**

1Kin 10:12 harps also and psalteries for *s*
1Chr 9:33 And these are the *s*, chief of the
1Chr 15:16 their brethren to be the *s* with
1Chr 15:19 So the *s*, Heman, Asaph, and Ethan,
1Chr 15:27 that bare the ark, and the *s*
1Chr 15:27 the master of the song with the *s*
2Chr 5:12 Also the Levites which were the *s*
2Chr 5:13 *s* were as one, to make one sound
2Chr 9:11 and harps and psalteries for *s*
2Chr 20:21 he appointed *s* unto the LORD, and
2Chr 23:13 also the *s* with instruments of
2Chr 29:28 the *s* sang, and the trumpeters
2Chr 35:15 the *s* the sons of Asaph were in
Ezr 2:41 The *s*: the children of Asaph
Ezr 2:70 and some of the people, and the *s*
Ezr 7:7 priests, and the Levites, and the *s*
Ezr 7:24 any of the priests and Levites, *s*
Ezr 10:24 Of the *s* also
Neh 7:1 doors, and the porters and the *s*
Neh 7:44 The *s*: the children of Asaph
Neh 7:73 Levites, and the porters, and the *s*
Neh 10:28 the Levites, the porters, the *s*
Neh 10:39 and the porters, and the *s*
Neh 11:22 the *s* were over the business of
Neh 11:23 portion should be for the *s*
Neh 12:28 the sons of the *s* gathered
Neh 12:29 for the *s* had builded them

Neh 12:42 the *s* sang loud, with Jezrahiah
Neh 12:45 And both the *s* and the porters kept
Neh 12:46 of old there were chief of the *s*
Neh 12:47 gave the portions of the *s*
Neh 13:5 be given to the Levites, and the *s*
Neh 13:10 for the Levites and the *s*, that
Ps 68:25 The *s* went before, the players on
Ps 87:7 As well the *s* as the players on
Eccl 2:8 I gat me men *s* and women *s*
Eze 40:44 of the *s* in the inner court

**SINGING**
1Sa 18:6 out of all cities of Israel, *s*
2Sa 19:35 voice of *s* men and *s* women
1Chr 6:32 of the congregation with *s*
1Chr 13:8 with all their might, and with *s*
2Chr 23:18 Moses, with rejoicing and with *s*
2Chr 30:21 *s* with loud instruments unto the
2Chr 35:25 and all the *s* men and the *s*
Ezr 2:65 hundred *s* men and *s* women
Neh 7:67 and five *s* men and *s* women
Neh 12:27 with thanksgivings, and with *s*
Ps 100:2 come before his presence with *s*
Ps 126:2 laughter, and our tongue with *s*
Song 2:12 the time of the *s* of birds is
Is 14:7 they break forth into *s*
Is 16:10 the vineyards there shall be no *s*
Is 35:2 and rejoice even with joy and *s*
Is 44:23 break forth into *s*, ye mountains,
Is 48:20 with a voice of *s* declare ye
Is 49:13 and break forth into *s*, O
Is 51:11 return, and come with *s* unto Zion
Is 54:1 break forth into *s*, and cry aloud,
Is 55:12 break forth before you into *s*
Zeph 3:17 he will joy over thee with *s*
Eph 5:19 and hymns and spiritual songs, *s*
Col 3:16 *s* with grace in your hearts to

**SINIM** *(si'-nim) An unspecified people.*
Is 49:12 and these from the land of *S*

**SINITE** *(si'-nite) A tribe of Canaanites.*
Gen 10:17 Hivite, and the Arkite, and the *S*
1Chr 1:15 Hivite, and the Arkite, and the *S*

**SINK**
Ps 69:2 I *s* in deep mire, where there is
Ps 69:14 out of the mire, and let me not *s*
Jer 51:64 shalt say, Thus shall Babylon *s*
Mt 14:30 and beginning to *s*, he cried,
Lk 5:7 ships, so that they began to *s*
Lk 9:44 Let these sayings *s* down into

**SINNED**
Ex 9:27 unto them, I have *s* this time
Ex 9:34 he *s* yet more, and hardened his
Ex 10:16 I have *s* against the LORD your
Ex 32:30 the people, Ye have *s* a great sin
Ex 32:31 this people have *s* a great sin
Ex 32:33 Whosoever hath *s* against me
Lev 4:3 for his sin, which he hath *s*
Lev 4:14 sin, which they have *s* against it
Lev 4:22 When a ruler hath *s*, and done
Lev 4:23 Or if his sin, wherein he hath *s*
Lev 4:28 Or if his sin, which he hath *s*
Lev 4:28 for his sin which he hath *s*
Lev 5:5 that he hath *s* in that thing
Lev 5:6 LORD for his sin which he hath *s*
Lev 5:10 him for his sin which he hath *s*
Lev 5:11 then he that *s* shall bring for
Lev 5:13 that he hath *s* in one of these
Lev 6:4 it shall be, because he hath *s*
Num 6:11 him, for that he *s* by the dead
Num 12:11 foolishly, and wherein we have *s*
Num 14:40 for we have *s*
Num 21:7 came to Moses, and said, We have *s*
Num 22:34 the angel of the LORD, I have *s*
Num 32:23 ye have *s* against the LORD
Deut 1:41 We have *s* against the LORD, we
Deut 9:16 ye had *s* against the LORD your
Deut 9:18 of all your sins which ye *s*
Josh 7:11 Israel hath *s*, and they have also
Josh 7:20 Indeed I have *s* against the LORD
Judg 10:10 We have *s* against thee, both
Judg 10:15 said unto the LORD, We have *s*
Judg 11:27 I have not *s* against thee
1Sa 7:6 We have *s* against the LORD
1Sa 12:10 unto the LORD, and said, We have *s*
1Sa 15:24 Saul said unto Samuel, I have *s*
1Sa 15:30 Then he said, I have *s*
1Sa 19:4 he hath not *s* against thee
1Sa 24:11 I have not *s* against thee
1Sa 26:21 Then said Saul, I have *s*
2Sa 12:13 I have *s* against the LORD
2Sa 19:20 servant doth know that I have *s*
2Sa 24:10 I have *s* greatly in that I have
2Sa 24:17 the people, and said, Lo, I have *s*
1Kin 8:33 because they have *s* against thee
1Kin 8:35 because they have *s* against thee
1Kin 8:47 them captives, saying, We have *s*
1Kin 8:50 people that have *s* against thee
1Kin 15:30 the sins of Jeroboam which he *s*
1Kin 16:13 of Elah his son, by which they *s*
1Kin 16:19 For his sins which he *s* in doing
1Kin 18:9 And he said, What have I *s*
2Kin 17:7 had *s* against the LORD their God
2Kin 21:17 that he did, and his sin that he *s*
1Chr 21:8 I have *s* greatly, because I have
1Chr 21:17 even I it is that have *s* and done
2Chr 6:24 because they have *s* against thee
2Chr 6:26 because they have *s* against thee
2Chr 6:37 captivity, saying, We have *s*
2Chr 6:39 people which have *s* against thee
Neh 1:6 which we have *s* against thee
Neh 1:6 I and my father's house have *s*
Neh 9:29 but *s* against thy judgments,
Job 1:5 It may be that my sons have *s*
Job 1:22 In all this Job *s* not, nor
Job 7:20 I have *s*
Job 8:4 thy children have *s* against him
Job 24:19 doth the grave those which have *s*
Job 33:27 upon men, and if any say, I have *s*
Ps 41:4 for I have *s* against thee
Ps 51:4 Against thee, thee only, have I *s*
Ps 78:17 they *s* yet more against him by
Ps 78:32 For all this they *s* still
Ps 106:6 We have *s* with our fathers, we
Is 42:24 LORD, he against whom we have *s*
Is 43:27 Thy first father hath *s*, and thy
Is 64:5 for we have *s*
Jer 2:35 because thou sayest, I have not *s*
Jer 3:25 for we have *s* against the LORD
Jer 8:14 because we have *s* against the
Jer 14:7 we have *s* against thee
Jer 14:20 for we have *s* against thee
Jer 33:8 whereby they have *s* against me
Jer 33:8 iniquities, whereby they have *s*
Jer 40:3 because ye have *s* against the
Jer 44:23 because ye have *s* against the
Jer 50:7 they have *s* against the LORD
Jer 50:14 for she hath *s* against the LORD
Lam 1:8 Jerusalem hath grievously *s*
Lam 5:7 Our fathers have *s*, and are not
Lam 5:16 woe unto us, that we have *s*
Eze 18:24 and in his sin that he hath *s*
Eze 28:16 with violence, and thou hast *s*
Eze 37:23 wherein they have *s*, and will
Dan 9:5 We have *s*, and have committed
Dan 9:8 because we have *s* against thee
Dan 9:11 because we have *s* against him
Dan 9:15 we have *s*, we have done wickedly
Hos 4:7 increased, so they *s* against me
Hos 10:9 thou hast *s* from the days of
Mic 7:9 because I have *s* against him
Hab 2:10 and hast *s* against thy soul
Zeph 1:17 they have *s* against the LORD
Mt 27:4 I have *s* in that I have betrayed
Lk 15:18 I have *s* against heaven, and
Lk 15:21 I have *s* against heaven, and in
Jn 9:3 answered, Neither hath this man *s*
Rom 2:12 For as many as have *s* without law
Rom 2:12 as many as have *s* in the law
Rom 3:23 For all have *s*, and come short of
Rom 5:12 upon all men, for that all have *s*
Rom 5:14 even over them that had not *s*
Rom 5:16 And not as it was by one that *s*
1Cor 7:28 and if thou marry, thou hast not *s*
1Cor 7:28 if a virgin marry, she hath not *s*
2Cor 12:21 bewail many which have *s* already
2Cor 13:2 to them which heretofore have *s*
Heb 3:17 was it not with them that had *s*
2Pet 2:4 God spared not the angels that *s*
1Jn 1:10 If we say that we have not *s*

**SINNER**
Prov 11:31 much more the wicked and the *s*
Prov 13:6 but wickedness overthroweth the *s*
Prov 13:22 the wealth of the *s* is laid up
Eccl 2:26 but to the *s* he giveth travail,
Eccl 7:26 but the *s* shall be taken by her
Eccl 8:12 Though a *s* do evil an hundred
Eccl 9:2 as is the good, so is the *s*
Eccl 9:18 but one *s* destroyeth much good
Is 65:20 but the *s* being an hundred years
Lk 7:37 woman in the city, which was a *s*
Lk 7:39 for she is a *s*
Lk 15:7 heaven over one *s* that repenteth
Lk 15:10 of God over one *s* that repenteth
Lk 18:13 saying, God be merciful to me a *s*
Lk 19:7 be guest with a man that is a *s*
Jn 9:16 man that is a *s* do such miracles
Jn 9:24 we know that this man is a *s*
Jn 9:25 and said, Whether he be a *s* or no
Rom 3:7 why yet am I also judged as a *s*
Jas 5:20 that he which converteth the *s*
1Pet 4:18 shall the ungodly and the *s* appear

**SINNERS**
Gen 13:13 *s* before the LORD exceedingly
Num 16:38 The censers of these *s* against
1Sa 15:18 destroy the *s* the Amalekites
Ps 1:1 nor standeth in the way of *s*
Ps 1:5 nor *s* in the congregation of the
Ps 25:8 will he teach *s* in the way
Ps 26:9 Gather not my soul with *s*
Ps 51:13 *s* shall be converted unto thee
Ps 104:35 Let the *s* be consumed out of the
Prov 1:10 if *s* entice thee, consent thou
Prov 13:21 Evil pursueth *s*
Prov 23:17 Let not thine heart envy *s*
Is 1:28 of the *s* shall be together, and
Is 13:9 destroy the *s* thereof out of it
Is 33:14 The *s* in Zion are afraid
Amos 9:10 All the *s* of my people shall die
Mt 9:10 *s* came and sat down with him and
Mt 9:11 your Master with publicans and *s*
Mt 9:13 righteous, but *s* to repentance
Mt 11:19 a friend of publicans and *s*
Mt 26:45 is betrayed into the hands of *s*
Mk 2:15 *s* sat also together with Jesus and
Mk 2:16 saw him eat with publicans and *s*
Mk 2:16 and drinketh with publicans and *s*
Mk 2:17 righteous, but *s* to repentance
Mk 14:41 is betrayed into the hands of *s*
Lk 5:30 eat and drink with publicans and *s*
Lk 5:32 righteous, but *s* to repentance
Lk 6:32 for *s* also love those that love
Lk 6:33 for *s* also do even the same
Lk 6:34 for *s* also lend to *s*
Lk 7:34 a friend of publicans and *s*
Lk 13:2 were *s* above all the Galilaeans
Lk 13:4 think ye that they were *s* above
Lk 15:1 publicans and *s* for to hear him
Lk 15:2 saying, This man receiveth *s*
Jn 9:31 we know that God heareth not *s*
Rom 5:8 us, in that, while we were yet *s*
Rom 5:19 disobedience many were made *s*
Gal 2:15 nature, and not *s* of the Gentiles,
Gal 2:17 we ourselves also are found *s*
1Ti 1:9 for the ungodly and for *s*
1Ti 1:15 came into the world to save *s*
Heb 7:26 undefiled, separate from *s*
Heb 12:3 of *s* against himself, lest ye be
Jas 4:8 Cleanse your hands, ye *s*
Jude 15 ungodly *s* have spoken against him

**SINNETH**
Num 15:28 for the soul that *s* ignorantly
Num 15:28 when he *s* by ignorance before the
Num 15:29 for him that *s* through ignorance
Deut 19:15 for any sin, in any sin that he *s*
1Kin 8:46 (for there is no man that *s* not
2Chr 6:36 (for there is no man which *s* not
Prov 8:36 But he that *s* against me wrongeth
Prov 14:21 He that despiseth his neighbour *s*
Prov 19:2 he that hasteth with his feet *s*
Prov 20:2 to anger *s* against his own soul
Eccl 7:20 earth, that doeth good, and *s* not
Eze 14:13 when the land *s* against me by
Eze 18:4 the soul that *s*, it shall die
Eze 18:20 The soul that *s*, it shall die
Eze 33:12 in the day that he *s*
1Cor 6:18 *s* against his own body
1Cor 7:36 let him do what he will, he *s* not
Titus 3:11 that is such is subverted, and *s*
1Jn 3:6 Whosoever abideth in him *s* not
1Jn 3:6 whosoever *s* hath not seen him,
1Jn 3:8 for the devil *s* from the
1Jn 5:18 whosoever is born of God *s* not

**SINS**
Lev 16:16 transgressions in all their *s*
Lev 16:21 transgressions in all their *s*
Lev 16:30 from all your *s* before the LORD
Lev 16:34 for all their *s* once a year

Lev 26:18 you seven times more for your *s*
Lev 26:21 upon you according to your *s*
Lev 26:24 you yet seven times for your *s*
Lev 26:28 you seven times for your *s*
Num 16:26 ye be consumed in all their *s*
Deut 9:18 of all your *s* which ye sinned
Josh 24:19 your transgressions nor your *s*
1Sa 12:19 added unto all our *s* this evil
1Kin 14:16 up because of the *s* of Jeroboam
1Kin 14:22 their *s* which they had committed
1Kin 15:3 walked in all the *s* of his father
1Kin 15:30 Because of the *s* of Jeroboam
1Kin 16:2 provoke me to anger with their *s*
1Kin 16:13 For all the *s* of Baasha, and the
1Kin 16:13 the *s* of Elah his son, by which
1Kin 16:19 For his *s* which he sinned in
1Kin 16:31 *s* of Jeroboam the son of Nebat
2Kin 3:3 he cleaved unto the *s* of Jeroboam
2Kin 10:29 Howbeit from the *s* of Jeroboam
2Kin 10:31 not from the *s* of Jeroboam
2Kin 13:2 followed the *s* of Jeroboam the
2Kin 13:6 the *s* of the house of Jeroboam
2Kin 13:11 *s* of Jeroboam the son of Nebat
2Kin 14:24 *s* of Jeroboam the son of Nebat
2Kin 15:9 he departed not from the *s* of
2Kin 15:18 not all his days from the *s* of
2Kin 15:24 he departed not from the *s* of
2Kin 15:28 he departed not from the *s* of
2Kin 17:22 the *s* of Jeroboam which he did
2Kin 24:3 for the *s* of Manasseh, according
2Chr 28:10 *s* against the LORD your God
2Chr 28:13 ye intend to add more to our *s*
Neh 1:6 confess the *s* of the children of
Neh 9:2 and stood and confessed their *s*
Neh 9:37 hast set over us because of our *s*
Job 13:23 How many are mine iniquities and *s*
Ps 19:13 servant also from presumptuous *s*
Ps 25:7 Remember not the *s* of my youth
Ps 25:18 and forgive all my *s*
Ps 51:9 Hide thy face from my *s*, and blot
Ps 69:5 my *s* are not hid from thee
Ps 79:9 deliver us, and purge away our *s*
Ps 90:8 our secret *s* in the light of thy
Ps 103:10 not dealt with us after our *s*
Prov 5:22 be holden with the cords of his *s*
Prov 10:12 but love covereth all *s*
Prov 28:13 covereth his *s* shall not prosper
Is 1:18 though your *s* be as scarlet, they
Is 38:17 cast all my *s* behind thy back
Is 40:2 LORD's hand double for all her *s*
Is 43:24 hast made me to serve with thy *s*
Is 43:25 sake, and will not remember thy *s*
Is 44:22 and, as a cloud, thy *s*
Is 58:1 and the house of Jacob their *s*
Is 59:2 your *s* have hid his face from you
Is 59:12 thee, and our *s* testify against us
Jer 5:25 your *s* have withholden good
Jer 14:10 their iniquity, and visit their *s*
Jer 15:13 price, and that for all thy *s*
Jer 30:14 because thy *s* were increased
Jer 30:15 because thy *s* were increased, I
Jer 50:20 the *s* of Judah, and they shall not
Lam 3:39 a man for the punishment of his *s*
Lam 4:13 For the *s* of her prophets, and the
Lam 4:22 he will discover thy *s*
Eze 16:51 Samaria committed half of thy *s*
Eze 16:52 bear thine own shame for thy *s*
Eze 18:14 his father's *s* which he hath done
Eze 18:21 all his *s* that he hath committed
Eze 21:24 all your doings your *s* do appear
Eze 23:49 ye shall bear the *s* of your idols
Eze 33:10 our *s* be upon us, and we pine away
Eze 33:16 None of his *s* that he hath
Dan 4:27 break off thy *s* by righteousness,
Dan 9:16 because for our *s*, and for the
Dan 9:24 and to make an end of *s*, and to
Hos 8:13 their iniquity, and visit their *s*
Hos 9:9 iniquity, he will visit their *s*
Amos 5:12 transgressions and your mighty *s*
Mic 1:5 for the *s* of the house of Israel
Mic 6:13 thee desolate because of thy *s*
Mic 7:19 thou wilt cast all their *s* into
Mt 1:21 save his people from their *s*
Mt 3:6 him in Jordan, confessing their *s*
Mt 9:2 thy *s* be forgiven thee
Mt 9:5 to say, Thy *s* be forgiven thee
Mt 9:6 hath power on earth to forgive *s*
Mt 26:28 for many for the remission of *s*
Mk 1:4 repentance for the remission of *s*
Mk 1:5 of Jordan, confessing their *s*
Mk 2:5 Son, thy *s* be forgiven thee
Mk 2:7 who can forgive *s* but God only
Mk 2:9 the palsy, Thy *s* be forgiven thee
Mk 2:10 hath power on earth to forgive *s*
Mk 3:28 All *s* shall be forgiven unto the
Mk 4:12 their *s* should be forgiven them
Lk 1:77 by the remission of their *s*
Lk 3:3 repentance for the remission of *s*
Lk 5:20 him, Man, thy *s* are forgiven thee
Lk 5:21 Who can forgive *s*, but God alone
Lk 5:23 to say, Thy *s* be forgiven thee
Lk 5:24 power upon earth to forgive *s*
Lk 7:47 Wherefore I say unto thee, Her *s*
Lk 7:48 said unto her, Thy *s* are forgiven
Lk 7:49 Who is this that forgiveth *s* also
Lk 11:4 And forgive us our *s*
Lk 24:47 remission of *s* should be preached
Jn 8:21 seek me, and shall die in your *s*
Jn 8:24 you, that ye shall die in your *s*
Jn 8:24 I am he, ye shall die in your *s*
Jn 9:34 Thou wast altogether born in *s*
Jn 20:23 Whose soever *s* ye remit, they are
Jn 20:23 and whose soever *s* ye retain
Acts 2:38 Christ for the remission of *s*
Acts 3:19 that your *s* may be blotted out,
Acts 5:31 to Israel, and forgiveness of *s*
Acts 10:43 him shall receive remission of *s*
Acts 13:38 unto you the forgiveness of *s*
Acts 22:16 be baptized, and wash away thy *s*
Acts 26:18 they may receive forgiveness of *s*
Rom 3:25 the remission of *s* that are past
Rom 4:7 forgiven, and whose *s* are covered
Rom 7:5 in the flesh, the motions of *s*
Rom 11:27 when I shall take away their *s*
1Cor 15:3 our *s* according to the scriptures
1Cor 15:17 ye are yet in your *s*
Gal 1:4 Who gave himself for our *s*
Eph 1:7 his blood, the forgiveness of *s*
Eph 2:1 who were dead in trespasses and *s*
Eph 2:5 Even when we were dead in *s*
Col 1:14 blood, even the forgiveness of *s*
Col 2:11 body of the *s* of the flesh by the
Col 2:13 And you, being dead in your *s*
1Th 2:16 saved, to fill up their *s* alway
1Ti 5:22 be partaker of other men's *s*
1Ti 5:24 Some men's *s* are open beforehand,
2Ti 3:6 captive silly women laden with *s*
Heb 1:3 he had by himself purged our *s*
Heb 2:17 for the *s* of the people
Heb 5:1 both gifts and sacrifices for *s*
Heb 5:3 also for himself, to offer for *s*
Heb 7:27 up sacrifice, first for his own *s*
Heb 8:12 their unrighteousness, and their *s*
Heb 9:28 offered to bear the *s* of many
Heb 10:2 have had no more conscience of *s*
Heb 10:3 again made of *s* every year
Heb 10:4 and of goats should take away *s*
Heb 10:11 which can never take away *s*
Heb 10:12 one sacrifice for *s* for ever
Heb 10:17 And their *s* and iniquities will I
Heb 10:26 remaineth no more sacrifice for *s*
Jas 5:15 and if he have committed *s*
Jas 5:20 and shall hide a multitude of *s*
1Pet 2:24 Who his own self bare our *s* in
1Pet 2:24 tree, that we, being dead to *s*
1Pet 3:18 also hath once suffered for *s*
1Pet 4:8 shall cover the multitude of *s*
2Pet 1:9 that he was purged from his old *s*
1Jn 1:9 If we confess our *s*, he is
1Jn 1:9 and just to forgive us our *s*
1Jn 2:2 he is the propitiation for our *s*
1Jn 2:2 but also for the *s* of the whole
1Jn 2:12 because your *s* are forgiven you
1Jn 3:5 was manifested to take away our *s*
1Jn 4:10 to be the propitiation for our *s*
Rev 1:5 us from our *s* in his own blood
Rev 18:4 that ye be not partakers of her *s*
Rev 18:5 For her *s* have reached unto

**SION** *(si'-on)* See SHENIR, SIRION, ZION.
*1. The peak of Mount Hermon.*
Deut 4:48 even unto mount *S* which is Hermon
*2. A district of Jerusalem.*
Ps 65:1 waiteth for thee, O God in *S*
Mt 21:5 Tell ye the daughter of *S*
Jn 12:15 Fear not, daughter of *S*
Rom 9:33 I lay in *S* a stumblingstone and
Rom 11:26 shall come out of *S* the Deliverer
Heb 12:22 But ye are come unto mount *S*
1Pet 2:6 I lay in *S* a chief corner stone,
Rev 14:1 lo, a Lamb stood on the mount *S*

**SIPHMOTH** *(sif'-moth) A city in Judah.*
1Sa 30:28 Aroer, and to them which were in *S*

**SIPPAI** *(sip'-pahee)* See SAPH. *Son of Rapha.*
1Chr 20:4 Sibbechai the Hushathite slew *S*

**SIR**
Gen 43:20 And said, O *s*, we came indeed down
Mt 13:27 came and said unto him, *S*, didst
Mt 21:30 And he answered and said, I go *s*
Mt 27:63 Saying, *S*, we remember that that
Jn 4:11 The woman saith unto him, *S*
Jn 4:15 The woman saith unto him, *S*
Jn 4:19 The woman saith unto him, *S*
Jn 4:49 The nobleman saith unto him, *S*
Jn 5:7 The impotent man answered him, *S*
Jn 12:21 and desired him, saying, *S*
Jn 20:15 the gardener, saith unto him, *S*
Rev 7:14 And I said unto him, *S*, thou

**SIRAH** *(si'-rah) A well near Hebron.*
2Sa 3:26 him again from the well of *S*

**SIRION** *(sir'-e-on)* See HERMON. *A Sidonian name for Mount Hermon.*
Deut 3:9 Which Hermon the Sidonians call *S*
Ps 29:6 Lebanon and *S* like a young unicorn

**SIRS**
Acts 7:26 set them at one again, saying, *S*
Acts 14:15 And saying, *S*, why do ye these
Acts 16:30 And brought them out, and said, *S*
Acts 19:25 of like occupation, and said, *S*
Acts 27:10 And said unto them, *S*, I perceive
Acts 27:21 in the midst of them, and said, *S*
Acts 27:25 Wherefore, *s*, be of good cheer

**SISAMAI** *(sis'-a-mahee) Son of Eleasah.*
1Chr 2:40 And Eleasah begat *S*
1Chr 2:40 and *S* begat Shallum

**SISERA** *(sis'-e-rah)*
*1. A captain in the Canaanite army.*
Judg 4:2 the captain of whose host was *S*
Judg 4:7 unto thee to the river Kishon, *S*
Judg 4:9 for the LORD shall sell *S* into
Judg 4:12 they shewed *S* that Barak the son
Judg 4:13 *S* gathered together all his
Judg 4:14 hath delivered *S* into thine hand
Judg 4:15 And the LORD discomfited *S*
Judg 4:15 so that *S* lighted down off his
Judg 4:16 all the host of *S* fell upon the
Judg 4:17 Howbeit *S* fled away on his feet
Judg 4:18 And Jael went out to meet *S*
Judg 4:22 And, behold, as Barak pursued *S*
Judg 4:22 *S* lay dead, and the nail was in
Judg 5:20 in their courses fought against *S*
Judg 5:26 and with the hammer she smote *S*
Judg 5:28 The mother of *S* looked out at a
Judg 5:30 to *S* a prey of divers colours, a
1Sa 12:9 he sold them into the hand of *S*
Ps 83:9 as to *S*, as to Jabin, at the
*2. A family of exiles.*
Ezr 2:53 of Barkos, the children of *S*
Neh 7:55 of Barkos, the children of *S*

**SISTER**
Gen 4:22 the *s* of Tubal-cain was Naamah
Gen 12:13 Say, I pray thee, thou art my *s*
Gen 12:19 Why saidst thou, She is my *s*
Gen 20:2 of Sarah his wife, She is my *s*
Gen 20:5 Said he not unto me, She is my *s*
Gen 20:12 And yet indeed she is my *s*
Gen 24:30 heard the words of Rebekah his *s*
Gen 24:59 And they sent away Rebekah their *s*
Gen 24:60 and said unto her, Thou art our *s*
Gen 25:20 the *s* to Laban the Syrian
Gen 26:7 and he said, She is my *s*
Gen 26:9 and how saidst thou, She is my *s*
Gen 28:9 the *s* of Nebajoth, to be his wife
Gen 30:1 no children, Rachel envied her *s*
Gen 30:8 have I wrestled with my *s*
Gen 34:13 he had defiled Dinah their *s*
Gen 34:14 to give our *s* to one that is
Gen 34:27 because they had defiled their *s*
Gen 34:31 deal with our *s* as with an harlot
Gen 36:3 Ishmael's daughter, *s* of Nebajoth
Gen 36:22 and Lotan's *s* was Timna
Gen 46:17 Isui, and Beriah, and Serah their *s*
Ex 2:4 his *s* stood afar off, to wit what
Ex 2:7 Then said his *s* to Pharaoh's
Ex 6:20 Jochebed his father's *s* to wife

Ex 6:23 Amminadab, s of Naashon, to wife
Ex 15:20 the s of Aaron, took a timbrel in
Lev 18:9 The nakedness of thy s, the
Lev 18:11 of thy father, she is thy s
Lev 18:12 the nakedness of thy father's s
Lev 18:13 the nakedness of thy mother's s
Lev 18:18 shalt thou take a wife to her s
Lev 20:17 And if a man shall take his s
Lev 20:19 the nakedness of thy mother's s
Lev 20:19 nor of thy father's s
Lev 21:3 for his s a virgin, that is nigh
Num 6:7 for his brother, or for his s
Num 25:18 of a prince of Midian, their s
Num 26:59 Aaron and Moses, and Miriam their s
Deut 27:22 be he that lieth with his s
Judg 15:2 not her younger s fairer than she
Ruth 1:15 thy s in law is gone back unto
Ruth 1:15 return thou after thy s in law
2Sa 13:1 the son of David had a fair s
2Sa 13:2 that he fell sick for his s Tamar
2Sa 13:4 Tamar, my brother Absalom's s
2Sa 13:5 let my s Tamar come, and give me
2Sa 13:6 I pray thee, let Tamar my s come
2Sa 13:11 unto her, Come lie with me, my s
2Sa 13:20 but hold now thy peace, my s
2Sa 13:22 because he had forced his s Tamar
2Sa 13:32 day that he forced his s Tamar
2Sa 17:25 s to Zeruiah Joab's mother
1Kin 11:19 him to wife the s of his own wife
1Kin 11:19 the s of Tahpenes the queen
1Kin 11:20 the s of Tahpenes bare him
2Kin 11:2 s of Ahaziah, took Joash the son
1Chr 1:39 and Timna was Lotan's s
1Chr 3:9 the concubines, and Tamar their s
1Chr 3:19 and Hananiah, and Shelomith their s
1Chr 4:3 name of their s was Hazelelponi
1Chr 4:19 of his wife Hodiah the s of Naham
1Chr 7:15 took to wife the s of Huppim
1Chr 7:18 his s Hammoleketh bare Ishod, and
1Chr 7:30 and Beriah, and Serah their s
1Chr 7:32 and Hotham, and Shua their s
2Chr 22:11 (for she was the s of Ahaziah
Job 17:14 worm, Thou art my mother, and my s
Prov 7:4 Say unto wisdom, Thou art my s
Song 4:9 Thou hast ravished my heart, my s
Song 4:10 How fair is thy love, my s
Song 4:12 A garden inclosed is my s
Song 5:1 I am come into my garden, my s
Song 5:2 saying, Open to me, my s
Song 8:8 We have a little s, and she hath
Song 8:8 what shall we do for our s in the
Jer 3:7 And her treacherous s Judah saw it
Jer 3:8 treacherous s Judah feared not
Jer 3:10 for all this her treacherous s
Jer 22:18 my brother! or, Ah s!
Eze 16:45 thou art the s of thy sisters,
Eze 16:46 And thine elder s is Samaria
Eze 16:46 and thy younger s, that dwelleth
Eze 16:48 Sodom thy s hath not done, she
Eze 16:49 was the iniquity of thy s Sodom
Eze 16:56 For thy s Sodom was not mentioned
Eze 22:11 in thee hath humbled his s
Eze 23:4 the elder, and Aholibah her s
Eze 23:11 when her s Aholibah saw this, she
Eze 23:11 more than her s in her whoredoms
Eze 23:18 my mind was alienated from her s
Eze 23:31 hast walked in the way of thy s
Eze 23:33 with the cup of thy s Samaria
Eze 44:25 or for s that hath had no husband
Mt 12:50 the same is my brother, and s
Mk 3:35 the same is my brother, and my s
Lk 10:39 she had a s called Mary, which
Lk 10:40 dost thou not care that my s hath
Jn 11:1 the town of Mary and her s Martha
Jn 11:5 Now Jesus loved Martha, and her s
Jn 11:28 and called Mary her s secretly
Jn 11:39 the s of him that was dead, saith
Jn 19:25 his mother, and his mother's s
Rom 16:1 I commend unto you Phebe our s
Rom 16:15 and Julia, Nereus, and his s
1Cor 7:15 A brother or a s is not under
1Cor 9:5 we not power to lead about a s
Jas 2:15 If a brother or s be naked
2Jn 13 of thy elect s greet thee

## SISTER'S

Gen 24:30 and bracelets upon his s hands
Gen 29:13 the tidings of Jacob his s son
Lev 20:17 he hath uncovered his s nakedness
1Chr 7:15 Shuppim, whose s name was Maachah
Eze 23:32 shalt drink of thy s cup deep
Acts 23:16 when Paul's s son heard of their
Col 4:10 s son to Barnabas, (touching whom

## SISTERS

Josh 2:13 mother, and my brethren, and my s
1Chr 2:16 Whose s were Zeruiah, and Abigail
Job 1:4 called for their three s to eat
Job 42:11 all his brethren, and all his s
Eze 16:45 and thou art the sister of thy s
Eze 16:51 hast justified thy s in all thine
Eze 16:52 also, which hast judged thy s
Eze 16:52 in that thou hast justified thy s
Eze 16:55 When thy s, Sodom and her
Eze 16:61 when thou shalt receive thy s
Hos 2:1 and to your s, Ruhamah
Mt 13:56 And his s, are they not all with
Mt 19:29 houses, or brethren, or s
Mk 6:3 are not his s here with us
Mk 10:29 left house, or brethren, or s
Mk 10:30 time, houses, and brethren, and s
Lk 14:26 and children, and brethren, and s
Jn 11:3 Therefore his s sent unto him
1Ti 5:2 the younger as s, with all purity

## SIT

Gen 27:19 arise, I pray thee, s and eat of
Num 32:6 go to war, and shall ye s here
Judg 5:10 ye that s in judgment, and walk by
Ruth 3:18 S still, my daughter, until thou
Ruth 4:1 turn aside, s down here
Ruth 4:2 the city, and said, S ye down here
1Sa 9:22 made them s in the chiefest place
1Sa 16:11 for we will not s down till he
1Sa 20:5 I should not fail to s with the
2Sa 19:8 the king doth s in the gate
1Kin 1:13 he shall s upon my throne
1Kin 1:17 he shall s upon my throne
1Kin 1:20 s on the throne of my lord the
1Kin 1:24 he shall s upon my throne
1Kin 1:27 who should s on the throne of my
1Kin 1:30 he shall s upon my throne in my
1Kin 1:35 he may come and s upon my throne
1Kin 1:48 one to s on my throne this day
1Kin 3:6 him a son to s on his throne
1Kin 8:20 s on the throne of Israel, as the
1Kin 8:25 to s on the throne of Israel
2Kin 7:3 Why s we here until we die
2Kin 7:4 if we s still here, we die also
2Kin 10:30 shall s on the throne of Israel
2Kin 15:12 Thy sons shall s on the throne of
2Kin 18:27 me to the men which s on the wall
1Chr 28:5 hath chosen Solomon my son to s
2Chr 6:16 to s upon the throne of Israel
Ps 26:5 will not s with the wicked
Ps 69:12 They that s in the gate speak
Ps 107:10 Such as s in darkness and in the
Ps 110:1 S thou at my right hand, until I
Ps 119:23 Princes also did s and speak
Ps 127:2 to s up late, to eat the bread of
Ps 132:12 their children shall also s upon
Eccl 10:6 and the rich s in low place
Is 3:26 desolate shall s upon the ground
Is 14:13 I will s also upon the mount of
Is 16:5 he shall s upon it in truth in
Is 30:7 Their strength is to s still
Is 36:12 to the men that s upon the wall
Is 42:7 them that s in darkness out of
Is 47:1 s in the dust, O virgin daughter
Is 47:1 of Babylon, s on the ground
Is 47:5 S thou silent, and get thee into
Is 47:8 I shall not s as a widow, neither
Is 47:14 warm at, nor fire to s before it
Is 52:2 arise, and s down, O Jerusalem
Jer 8:14 Why do we s still
Jer 13:13 kings that s upon David's throne
Jer 13:18 queen, Humble yourselves, s down
Jer 16:8 to s with them to eat and to drink
Jer 33:17 s upon the throne of the house of
Jer 36:15 S down now, and read it in our
Jer 36:30 He shall have none to s upon the
Jer 48:18 from thy glory, and s in thirst
Lam 1:1 How doth the city s solitary
Lam 2:10 of Zion s upon the ground
Eze 26:16 they shall s upon the ground, and
Eze 28:2 I s in the seat of God, in the
Eze 33:31 they s before thee as my people,
Eze 44:3 he shall s in it to eat bread
Dan 7:9 and the Ancient of days did s
Dan 7:26 But the judgment shall s, and they
Joel 3:12 for there will I s to judge all
Mic 4:4 But they shall s every man under
Mic 7:8 when I s in darkness, the LORD
Zec 3:8 and thy fellows that s before thee
Zec 6:13 shall bear the glory, and shall s
Mal 3:3 he shall s as a refiner and
Mt 8:11 shall s down with Abraham, and
Mt 14:19 multitude to s down on the grass
Mt 15:35 multitude to s down on the ground
Mt 19:28 when the Son of man shall s in
Mt 19:28 ye also shall s upon twelve
Mt 20:21 that these my two sons may s
Mt 20:23 but to s on my right hand, and on
Mt 22:44 S thou on my right hand, till I
Mt 23:2 the Pharisees s in Moses' seat
Mt 25:31 then shall he s upon the throne
Mt 26:36 S ye here, while I go and pray
Mk 6:39 all s down by companies upon the
Mk 8:6 people to s down on the ground
Mk 10:37 him, Grant unto us that we may s
Mk 10:40 But to s on my right hand and on
Mk 12:36 S thou on my right hand, till I
Mk 14:32 S ye here, while I shall pray
Lk 1:79 light to them that s in darkness
Lk 9:14 Make them s down by fifties in a
Lk 9:15 did so, and made them all s down
Lk 12:37 and make them to s down to meat
Lk 13:29 shall s down in the kingdom of
Lk 14:8 s not down in the highest room
Lk 14:10 s down in the lowest room
Lk 14:10 of them that s at meat with thee
Lk 16:6 s down quickly, and write fifty
Lk 17:7 the field, Go and s down to meat
Lk 20:42 my Lord, S thou on my right hand,
Lk 22:30 s on thrones judging the twelve
Lk 22:69 s on the right hand of the power
Jn 6:10 Jesus said, Make the men s down
Acts 2:30 up Christ to s on his throne
Acts 2:34 my Lord, S thou on my right hand,
Acts 8:31 he would come up and s with him
1Cor 8:10 s at meat in the idol's temple
Eph 2:6 made us s together in heavenly
Heb 1:13 S on my right hand, until I make
Jas 2:3 S thou here in a good place
Jas 2:3 or s here under my footstool
Rev 3:21 I grant to s with me in my throne
Rev 17:3 I saw a woman s upon a scarlet
Rev 18:7 I s a queen, and am no widow, and
Rev 19:18 horses, and of them that s on them

## SITNAH *(sit'-nah) A well near Gerar.*

Gen 26:21 and he called the name of it S

## SITTEST

Ex 18:14 why s thou thyself alone, and all
Deut 6:7 them when thou s in thine house
Deut 11:19 them when thou s in thine house
Ps 50:20 Thou s and speakest against thy
Prov 23:1 When thou s to eat with a ruler,
Jer 22:2 that s upon the throne of David,
Acts 23:3 for s thou to judge me after the

## SITTETH

Ex 11:5 of Pharaoh that s upon his throne
Lev 15:4 and every thing, whereon he s
Lev 15:6 he that s on any thing whereon he
Lev 15:20 that she s upon shall be unclean
Lev 15:23 or on any thing whereon she s
Lev 15:26 whatsoever she s upon shall be
Deut 17:18 when he s upon the throne of his
1Kin 1:46 also Solomon s on the throne of
Est 6:10 that s at the king's gate
Ps 1:1 nor s in the seat of the scornful
Ps 2:4 He that s in the heavens shall
Ps 10:8 He s in the lurking places of the
Ps 29:10 The LORD s upon the flood
Ps 29:10 yea, the LORD s King for ever
Ps 47:8 God s upon the throne of his
Ps 99:1 he s between the cherubims
Prov 9:14 For she s at the door of her
Prov 20:8 A king that s in the throne of
Prov 31:23 when he s among the elders of the
Song 1:12 While the king s at his table
Is 28:6 to him that s in judgment
Is 40:22 It is he that s upon the circle
Jer 17:11 As the partridge s on eggs
Jer 29:16 that s upon the throne of David
Lam 3:28 He s alone and keepeth silence,
Zec 1:11 and, behold, all the earth s still
Zec 5:7 this is a woman that s in the
Mt 23:22 of God, and by him that s thereon
Lk 14:28 s not down first, and counteth the
Lk 14:31 s not down first, and consulteth

Lk 22:27 is greater, he that *s* at meat
Lk 22:27 is not he that *s* at meat
1Cor 14:30 be revealed to another that *s* by
Col 3:1 where Christ *s* on the right hand
2Th 2:4 so that he as God *s* in the temple
Rev 5:13 unto him that *s* upon the throne
Rev 6:16 face of him that *s* on the throne
Rev 7:10 our God which *s* upon the throne
Rev 7:15 he that *s* on the throne shall
Rev 17:1 whore that *s* upon many waters
Rev 17:9 mountains, on which the woman *s*
Rev 17:15 thou sawest, where the whore *s*

**SITTING**
Deut 22:6 the dam *s* upon the young, or upon
Judg 3:20 he was *s* in a summer parlour,
1Kin 10:5 the *s* of his servants, and the
1Kin 13:14 God, and found him *s* under an oak
1Kin 22:19 I saw the LORD *s* on his throne
2Kin 4:38 of the prophets were *s* before him
2Kin 9:5 the captains of the host were *s*
2Chr 9:4 the *s* of his servants, and the
2Chr 9:18 stays on each side of the *s* place
2Chr 18:18 I saw the LORD *s* upon his throne,
Neh 2:6 unto me, (the queen also *s* by him
Est 5:13 the Jew *s* at the king's gate
Is 6:1 saw also the Lord *s* upon a throne
Jer 17:25 princes *s* upon the throne of
Jer 22:4 kings *s* upon the throne of David
Jer 22:30 *s* upon the throne of David, and
Jer 38:7 the king then *s* in the gate of
Lam 3:63 Behold their *s* down, and their
Mt 9:9 *s* at the receipt of custom
Mt 11:16 unto children *s* in the markets
Mt 20:30 two blind men *s* by the way side,
Mt 21:5 *s* upon an ass, and a colt the foal
Mt 26:64 man *s* on the right hand of power
Mt 27:36 *s* down they watched him there
Mt 27:61 *s* over against the sepulchre
Mk 2:6 certain of the scribes *s* there
Mk 2:14 *s* at the receipt of custom
Mk 5:15 the devil, and had the legion, *s*
Mk 14:62 man *s* on the right hand of power
Mk 16:5 a young man *s* on the right side
Lk 2:46 *s* in the midst of the doctors,
Lk 5:17 and doctors of the law *s* by
Lk 5:27 *s* at the receipt of custom
Lk 7:32 children *s* in the marketplace
Lk 8:35 *s* at the feet of Jesus, clothed,
Lk 10:13 repented, *s* in sackcloth and ashes
Jn 2:14 doves, and the changers of money *s*
Jn 12:15 King cometh, *s* on an ass's colt
Jn 20:12 And seeth two angels in white *s*
Acts 2:2 all the house where they were *s*
Acts 8:28 *s* in his chariot read Esaias the
Acts 25:6 the next day *s* on the judgment
Rev 4:4 I saw four and twenty elders *s*

**SIVAN** *(si'-van) Third month of the Hebrew year.*
Est 8:9 third month, that is, the month *S*

**SIX**
Gen 7:6 Noah was *s* hundred years old when
Gen 7:11 In the *s* hundredth year of Noah's
Gen 8:13 came to pass in the *s* hundredth
Gen 16:16 *s* years old, when Hagar bare
Gen 30:20 because I have born him *s* sons
Gen 31:41 and *s* years for thy cattle
Gen 46:26 the souls were threescore and *s*
Ex 12:37 about *s* hundred thousand on foot
Ex 14:7 he took *s* hundred chosen chariots
Ex 16:26 *S* days ye shall gather it
Ex 20:9 *S* days shalt thou labour, and do
Ex 20:11 For in *s* days the LORD made
Ex 21:2 servant, *s* years he shall serve
Ex 23:10 *s* years thou shalt sow thy land,
Ex 23:12 *S* days thou shalt do thy work, and
Ex 24:16 and the cloud covered it *s* days
Ex 25:32 *s* branches shall come out of the
Ex 25:33 so in the *s* branches that come
Ex 25:35 according to the *s* branches that
Ex 26:9 *s* curtains by themselves, and
Ex 26:22 westward thou shalt make *s* boards
Ex 28:10 *S* of their names on one stone, and
Ex 28:10 the other *s* names of the rest on
Ex 31:15 *S* days may work be done
Ex 31:17 for in *s* days the LORD made
Ex 34:21 *S* days thou shalt work, but on
Ex 35:2 *S* days shall work be done, but on
Ex 36:16 and *s* curtains by themselves
Ex 36:27 westward he made *s* boards
Ex 37:18 *s* branches going out of the sides
Ex 37:19 so throughout the *s* branches
Ex 37:21 according to the *s* branches going
Ex 38:26 for *s* hundred thousand and three
Lev 12:5 purifying threescore and *s* days
Lev 23:3 *S* days shall work be done
Lev 24:6 *s* on a row, upon the pure table
Lev 25:3 *S* years thou shalt sow thy field,
Lev 25:3 *s* years thou shalt prune thy
Num 1:21 *s* thousand and five hundred
Num 1:25 forty and five thousand *s* hundred
Num 1:27 and fourteen thousand and *s* hundred
Num 1:46 numbered were *s* hundred thousand
Num 2:4 and fourteen thousand and *s* hundred
Num 2:9 *s* thousand and four hundred,
Num 2:11 *s* thousand and five hundred
Num 2:15 thousand and *s* hundred and fifty
Num 2:31 and seven thousand and *s* hundred
Num 2:32 hosts were *s* hundred thousand
Num 3:28 *s* hundred, keeping the charge of
Num 3:34 were *s* thousand and two hundred
Num 4:40 thousand and *s* hundred and thirty
Num 7:3 *s* covered wagons, and twelve oxen
Num 11:21 are *s* hundred thousand footmen
Num 26:41 and five thousand and *s* hundred
Num 26:51 *s* hundred thousand and a thousand
Num 31:32 was *s* hundred thousand and seventy
Num 31:37 of the sheep was *s* hundred
Num 31:38 beeves were thirty and *s* thousand
Num 31:44 And thirty and *s* thousand beeves,
Num 35:6 shall be *s* cities for refuge
Num 35:13 cities which ye shall give *s*
Num 35:15 These *s* cities shall be a refuge,
Deut 5:13 *S* days thou shalt labour, and do
Deut 15:12 unto thee, and serve thee *s* years
Deut 15:18 to thee, in serving thee *s* years
Deut 16:8 *S* days thou shalt eat unleavened
Josh 6:3 Thus shalt thou do *s* days
Josh 6:14 so they did *s* days
Josh 7:5 of them about thirty and *s* men
Josh 15:59 *s* cities with their villages
Josh 15:62 *s* cities with their villages
Judg 3:31 *s* hundred men with an ox goad
Judg 12:7 And Jephthah judged Israel *s* years
Judg 18:11 *s* hundred men appointed with
Judg 18:16 the *s* hundred men appointed with
Judg 18:17 entering of the gate with the *s*
Judg 20:15 *s* thousand men that drew sword,
Judg 20:47 But *s* hundred men turned and fled
Ruth 3:15 he measured *s* measures of barley,
Ruth 3:17 These *s* measures of barley gave
1Sa 13:5 *s* thousand horsemen, and people as
1Sa 13:15 with him, about *s* hundred men
1Sa 14:2 with him were about *s* hundred men
1Sa 17:4 Gath, whose height was *s* cubits
1Sa 17:7 weighed *s* hundred shekels of iron
1Sa 23:13 men, which were about *s* hundred
1Sa 27:2 he passed over with the *s* hundred
1Sa 30:9 the *s* hundred men that were with
2Sa 2:11 Judah was seven years and *s* months
2Sa 5:5 Judah seven years and *s* months
2Sa 6:13 ark of the LORD had gone *s* paces
2Sa 15:18 *s* hundred men which came after
2Sa 21:20 that had on every hand *s* fingers
2Sa 21:20 fingers, and on every foot *s* toes
1Kin 6:6 and the middle was *s* cubits broad
1Kin 10:14 one year was *s* hundred threescore
1Kin 10:14 threescore and *s* talents of gold,
1Kin 10:16 *s* hundred shekels of gold went to
1Kin 10:19 The throne had *s* steps, and the
1Kin 10:20 and on the other upon the *s* steps
1Kin 10:29 went out of Egypt for *s* hundred
1Kin 11:16 (For *s* months did Joab remain
1Kin 16:23 *s* years reigned he in Tirzah
2Kin 5:5 *s* thousand pieces of gold, and ten
2Kin 11:3 in the house of the LORD *s* years
2Kin 13:19 have smitten five or *s* times
2Kin 15:8 over Israel in Samaria *s* months
1Chr 3:4 These *s* were born unto him in
1Chr 3:4 reigned seven years and *s* months
1Chr 3:22 Bariah, and Neariah, and Shaphat, *s*
1Chr 4:27 had sixteen sons and *s* daughters
1Chr 7:2 and twenty thousand and *s* hundred
1Chr 7:4 were bands of soldiers for war, *s*
1Chr 7:40 was twenty and *s* thousand men
1Chr 8:38 And Azel had *s* sons, whose names
1Chr 9:6 brethren, *s* hundred and ninety
1Chr 9:9 nine hundred and fifty and *s*
1Chr 9:44 And Azel had *s* sons, whose names
1Chr 12:24 shield and spear were *s* thousand
1Chr 12:26 Levi four thousand and *s* hundred
1Chr 12:35 and eight thousand and *s* hundred
1Chr 20:6 *s* on each hand, and *s* on each
1Chr 21:25 *s* hundred shekels of gold by
1Chr 23:4 *s* thousand were officers and
1Chr 25:3 Hashabiah, and Mattithiah, *s*
1Chr 26:17 Eastward were *s* Levites,
2Chr 1:17 for *s* hundred shekels of silver
2Chr 2:2 *s* hundred to oversee them
2Chr 2:17 and three thousand and *s* hundred
2Chr 2:18 *s* hundred overseers to set the
2Chr 3:8 amounting to *s* hundred talents
2Chr 9:13 Solomon in one year was *s* hundred
2Chr 9:13 threescore and *s* talents of gold
2Chr 9:15 *s* hundred shekels of beaten gold
2Chr 9:18 there were *s* steps to the throne,
2Chr 9:19 and on the other upon the *s* steps
2Chr 16:1 In the *s* and thirtieth year of the
2Chr 22:12 hid in the house of God *s* years
2Chr 26:12 were two thousand and *s* hundred
2Chr 29:33 things were *s* hundred oxen
2Chr 35:8 *s* hundred small cattle, and three
Ezr 2:10 of Bani, *s* hundred forty and two
Ezr 2:11 *s* hundred twenty and three
Ezr 2:13 Adonikam, *s* hundred sixty and *s*
Ezr 2:14 Bigvai, two thousand fifty and *s*
Ezr 2:22 The men of Netophah, fifty and *s*
Ezr 2:26 and Gaba, *s* hundred twenty and one
Ezr 2:30 of Magbish, an hundred fifty and *s*
Ezr 2:35 thousand and *s* hundred and thirty
Ezr 2:60 of Nekoda, *s* hundred fifty and two
Ezr 2:66 were seven hundred thirty and *s*
Ezr 2:67 *s* thousand seven hundred and
Ezr 8:26 weighed unto their hand *s* hundred
Ezr 8:35 *s* rams, seventy and seven lambs,
Neh 5:18 was one ox and *s* choice sheep
Neh 7:10 of Arah, *s* hundred fifty and two
Neh 7:15 Binnui, *s* hundred forty and eight
Neh 7:16 *s* hundred twenty and eight
Neh 7:18 *s* hundred threescore and seven
Neh 7:20 of Adin, *s* hundred fifty and five
Neh 7:30 and Gaba, *s* hundred twenty and one
Neh 7:62 of Nekoda, *s* hundred forty and two
Neh 7:68 horses, seven hundred thirty and *s*
Neh 7:69 *s* thousand seven hundred and
Est 2:12 *s* months with oil of myrrh, and
Est 2:12 *s* months with sweet odours, and
Job 5:19 shall deliver thee in *s* troubles
Job 42:12 *s* thousand camels, and a thousand
Prov 6:16 These *s* things doth the LORD hate
Is 6:2 each one had *s* wings
Jer 34:14 when he hath served thee *s* years
Jer 52:23 and *s* pomegranates on a side
Jer 52:30 were four thousand and *s* hundred
Eze 9:2 *s* men came from the way of the
Eze 40:5 of *s* cubits long by the cubit
Eze 40:12 were *s* cubits on this side
Eze 40:12 and *s* cubits on that side
Eze 41:1 *s* cubits broad on the one side,
Eze 41:1 *s* cubits broad on the other side,
Eze 41:3 and the door, *s* cubits
Eze 41:5 the wall of the house, *s* cubits
Eze 41:8 a full reed of *s* great cubits
Eze 46:1 shall be shut the *s* working days
Eze 46:4 shall be *s* lambs without blemish
Eze 46:6 blemish, and *s* lambs, and a ram
Dan 3:1 and the breadth thereof *s* cubits
Mt 17:1 after *s* days Jesus taketh Peter,
Mk 9:2 after *s* days Jesus taketh with
Lk 4:25 *s* months, when great famine was
Lk 13:14 There are *s* days in which men
Jn 2:6 set there *s* waterpots of stone
Jn 2:20 *s* years was this temple in
Jn 12:1 Then Jesus *s* days before the
Acts 11:12 Moreover these *s* brethren
Acts 18:11 *s* months, teaching the word of
Jas 5:17 space of three years and *s* months
Rev 4:8 each of them *s* wings about him
Rev 13:18 is *s* hundred threescore and *s*
Rev 14:20 a thousand and *s* hundred furlongs

**SIXTEEN**
Gen 46:18 she bare unto Jacob, even *s* souls
Ex 26:25 sockets of silver, *s* sockets
Ex 36:30 sockets were *s* sockets of silver
Num 26:22 *s* thousand and five hundred
Num 31:40 And the persons were *s* thousand
Num 31:46 And *s* thousand persons
Num 31:52 was *s* thousand seven hundred
Josh 15:41 *s* cities with their villages

Josh 19:22 s cities with their villages
2Kin 13:10 in Samaria, and reigned s years
2Kin 14:21 Azariah, which was s years old
2Kin 15:2 S years old was he when he began
2Kin 15:33 he reigned s years in Jerusalem
2Kin 16:2 reigned s years in Jerusalem, and
1Chr 4:27 And Shimei had s sons and six
1Chr 24:4 the sons of Eleazar there were s
2Chr 13:21 and two sons, and s daughters
2Chr 26:1 was s years old, and made him
2Chr 26:3 S years old was Uzziah when he
2Chr 27:1 he reigned s years in Jerusalem
2Chr 27:8 reigned s years in Jerusalem
2Chr 28:1 he reigned s years in Jerusalem
Acts 27:37 two hundred threescore and s

## SIXTH

Gen 1:31 and the morning were the s day
Gen 30:19 again, and bare Jacob the s son
Ex 16:5 that on the s day they shall
Ex 16:22 that on the s day they gathered
Ex 16:29 the s day the bread of two days
Ex 26:9 shalt double the s curtain in the
Lev 25:21 blessing upon you in the s year
Num 7:42 On the s day Eliasaph the son of
Num 29:29 on the s day eight bullocks, two
Josh 19:32 The s lot came out to the
2Sa 3:5 And the s, Ithream, by Eglah
1Kin 16:8 s year of Asa king of Judah began
2Kin 18:10 even in the s year of Hezekiah,
1Chr 2:15 Ozem the s, David the seventh
1Chr 3:3 the s, Ithream by Eglah his wife
1Chr 12:11 Attai the s, Eliel the seventh,
1Chr 24:9 to Malchijah, the s to Mijamin,
1Chr 25:13 The s to Bukkiah, he, his sons,
1Chr 26:3 Elam the fifth, Jehohanan the s
1Chr 26:5 Ammiel the s, Issachar the
1Chr 27:9 The s captain for the s month
Ezr 6:15 which was in the s year of the
Neh 3:30 Hanun the s son of Zalaph,
Eze 4:11 by measure, the s part of an hin
Eze 8:1 in the s year, in the s month
Eze 39:2 and leave but the s part of thee
Eze 45:13 the s part of an ephah of an
Eze 45:13 ye shall give the s part of an
Eze 46:14 the s part of an ephah, and the
Hag 1:1 Darius the king, in the s month
Hag 1:15 and twentieth day of the s month
Mt 20:5 Again he went out about the s
Mt 27:45 Now from the s hour there was
Mk 15:33 when the s hour was come, there
Lk 1:26 in the s month the angel Gabriel
Lk 1:36 this is the s month with her, who
Lk 23:44 And it was about the s hour
Jn 4:6 and it was about the s hour
Jn 19:14 the passover, and about the s hour
Acts 10:9 housetop to pray about the s hour
Rev 6:12 when he had opened the s seal
Rev 9:13 the s angel sounded, and I heard a
Rev 9:14 Saying to the s angel which had
Rev 16:12 the s angel poured out his vial
Rev 21:20 the s, sardius

## SIXTY

Gen 5:15 And Mahalaleel lived s and five
Gen 5:18 And Jared lived an hundred s
Gen 5:20 days of Jared were nine hundred s
Gen 5:21 And Enoch lived s and five years,
Gen 5:23 of Enoch were three hundred s
Gen 5:27 of Methuselah were nine hundred s
Lev 27:3 years old even unto s years old
Lev 27:7 And if it be from s years old
Num 7:88 the rams s, the he goats s
Num 7:88 the lambs of the first year s
Ezr 2:13 of Adonikam, six hundred s
Mt 13:23 some an hundredfold, some s
Mk 4:8 forth, some thirty, and some s
Mk 4:20 fruit, some thirtyfold, some s

## SIZE

Ex 36:9 the curtains were all of one s
Ex 36:15 the eleven curtains were of one s
1Kin 6:25 were of one measure and one s
1Kin 7:37 casting, one measure, and one s
1Chr 23:29 and for all manner of measure and s

## SKIES

2Sa 22:12 waters, and thick clouds of the s
Ps 18:11 waters and thick clouds of the s
Ps 77:17 the s sent out a sound
Is 45:8 let the s pour down righteousness
Jer 51:9 and is lifted up even to the s

## SKILFUL

1Chr 5:18 s in war, were four and forty
1Chr 15:22 about the song, because he was s
1Chr 28:21 workmanship every willing s man
2Chr 2:14 s to work in gold, and in silver,
Eze 21:31 of brutish men, and s to destroy
Dan 1:4 s in all wisdom, and cunning in
Amos 5:16 such as are s of lamentation to

## SKILL

1Kin 5:6 can s to hew timber like unto the
2Chr 2:7 that can s to grave with the
2Chr 2:8 can s to cut timber in Lebanon
2Chr 34:12 all that could s of instruments
Eccl 9:11 nor yet favour to men of s
Dan 1:17 s in all learning and wisdom
Dan 9:22 am now come forth to give thee s

## SKIN

Ex 22:27 only, it is his raiment for his s
Ex 29:14 flesh of the bullock, and his s
Ex 34:29 the s of his face shone while he
Ex 34:30 behold, the s of his face shone
Ex 34:35 that the s of Moses' face shone
Lev 4:11 the s of the bullock, and all his
Lev 7:8 shall have to himself the s of
Lev 11:32 vessel of wood, or raiment, or s
Lev 13:2 in the s of his flesh a rising
Lev 13:2 it be in the s of his flesh like
Lev 13:3 the plague in the s of the flesh
Lev 13:3 be deeper than the s of his flesh
Lev 13:4 be white in the s of his flesh
Lev 13:4 in sight be not deeper than the s
Lev 13:5 and the plague spread not in the s
Lev 13:6 and the plague spread not in the s
Lev 13:7 scab spread much abroad in the s
Lev 13:8 the scab spreadeth in the s
Lev 13:10 if the rising be white in the s
Lev 13:11 old leprosy in the s of his flesh
Lev 13:12 leprosy break out abroad in the s
Lev 13:12 the leprosy cover all the s of
Lev 13:18 in which, even in the s thereof
Lev 13:20 it be in sight lower than the s
Lev 13:21 and if it be not lower than the s
Lev 13:22 if it spread much abroad in the s
Lev 13:24 in the s whereof there is a hot
Lev 13:25 it be in sight deeper than the s
Lev 13:26 it be no lower than the other s
Lev 13:27 it be spread much abroad in the s
Lev 13:28 his place, and spread not in the s
Lev 13:30 it be in sight deeper than the s
Lev 13:31 be not in sight deeper than the s
Lev 13:32 be not in sight deeper than the s
Lev 13:34 the scall be not spread in the s
Lev 13:34 nor be in sight deeper than the s
Lev 13:35 much in the s after his cleansing
Lev 13:36 if the scall be spread in the s
Lev 13:38 the s of their flesh bright spots
Lev 13:39 if the bright spots in the s of
Lev 13:39 spot that groweth in the s
Lev 13:43 appeareth in the s of the flesh
Lev 13:48 a s, or in any thing made of s
Lev 13:49 in the garment, or in the s
Lev 13:49 in the woof, or in any thing of s
Lev 13:51 warp, or in the woof, or in a s
Lev 13:51 or in any work that is made of s
Lev 13:52 or in linen, or any thing of s
Lev 13:53 in the woof, or in any thing of s
Lev 13:56 of the garment, or out of the s
Lev 13:57 in the woof, or in any thing of s
Lev 13:58 or whatsoever thing of s it be
Lev 15:17 And every garment, and every s
Num 19:5 her s, and her flesh, and her blood
Job 2:4 S for s, yea, all that a man
Job 7:5 my s is broken, and become
Job 10:11 Thou hast clothed me with s
Job 16:15 I have sewed sackcloth upon my s
Job 18:13 devour the strength of his s
Job 19:20 My bone cleaveth to my s and to my
Job 19:20 am escaped with the s of my teeth
Job 19:26 though after my s worms destroy
Job 30:30 My s is black upon me, and my
Job 41:7 thou fill his s with barbed irons
Ps 102:5 groaning my bones cleave to my s
Jer 13:23 Can the Ethiopian change his s
Lam 3:4 My flesh and my s hath he made old
Lam 4:8 their s cleaveth to their bones
Lam 5:10 Our s was black like an oven
Eze 16:10 and shod thee with badgers' s
Eze 37:6 upon you, and cover you with s
Eze 37:8 them, and the s covered them above
Mic 3:2 pluck off their s from off them
Mic 3:3 flay their s from off them
Mk 1:6 a girdle of a s about his loins

## SKINS

Gen 3:21 did the LORD God make coats of s
Gen 27:16 she put the s of the kids of the
Ex 25:5 s dyed red, and badgers' s
Ex 26:14 for the tent of rams' s dyed red
Ex 26:14 and a covering above of badgers' s
Ex 35:7 s dyed red, and badgers' s
Ex 35:23 red s of rams, and badgers' s
Ex 36:19 for the tent of rams' s dyed red
Ex 36:19 covering of badgers' s above that
Ex 39:34 the covering of rams' s dyed red
Ex 39:34 and the covering of badgers' s
Lev 13:59 warp, or woof, or any thing of s
Lev 16:27 shall burn in the fire their s
Num 4:6 the covering of badgers' s
Num 4:8 with a covering of badgers' s
Num 4:10 within a covering of badgers' s
Num 4:11 it with a covering of badgers' s
Num 4:12 with a covering of badgers' s
Num 4:14 upon it a covering of badgers' s
Num 4:25 badgers' s that is above upon it
Num 31:20 raiment, and all that is made of s

## SKIRT

Deut 22:30 wife, nor discover his father's s
Deut 27:20 he uncovereth his father's s
Ruth 3:9 thy s over thine handmaid
1Sa 15:27 hold upon the s of his mantle
1Sa 24:4 cut off the s of Saul's robe
1Sa 24:5 because he had cut off Saul's s
1Sa 24:11 see the s of thy robe in my hand
1Sa 24:11 that I cut off the s of thy robe
Eze 16:8 and I spread my s over thee
Hag 2:12 flesh in the s of his garment
Hag 2:12 with his s do touch bread, or
Zec 8:23 of the s of him that is a Jew

## SKIRTS

Ps 133:2 down to the s of his garments
Jer 2:34 Also in thy s is found the blood
Jer 13:22 iniquity are thy s discovered
Jer 13:26 I discover thy s upon thy face
Lam 1:9 Her filthiness is in her s
Eze 5:3 in number, and bind them in thy s
Nah 3:5 will discover thy s upon thy face

## SKULL

Judg 9:53 head, and all to brake his s
2Kin 9:35 found no more of her than the s
Mt 27:33 that is to say, a place of a s
Mk 15:22 interpreted, The place of a s
Jn 19:17 a place called the place of a s

## SKY

Deut 33:26 and in his excellency on the s
Job 37:18 thou with him spread out the s
Mt 16:2 for the s is red
Mt 16:3 for the s is red and lowring
Mt 16:3 ye can discern the face of the s
Lk 12:56 ye can discern the face of the s
Heb 11:12 the stars of the s in multitude

## SLACK

Deut 7:10 he will not be s to him that
Deut 23:21 God, thou shalt not s to pay it
Josh 10:6 S not thy hand from thy servants
Josh 18:3 How long are ye s to go to
2Kin 4:24 s not thy riding for me, except I
Prov 10:4 poor that dealeth with a s hand
Zeph 3:16 to Zion, Let not thine hands be s
2Pet 3:9 The Lord is not s concerning his

## SLAIN

Gen 4:23 for I have s a man to my wounding
Gen 34:27 The sons of Jacob came upon the s
Lev 14:51 them in the blood of the s bird
Lev 26:17 ye shall be s before your enemies
Num 11:22 flocks and the herds be s for them
Num 14:16 therefore he hath s them in the
Num 19:16 whosoever toucheth one that is s
Num 19:18 him that touched a bone, or one s
Num 22:33 me, surely now also I had s thee
Num 23:24 prey, and drink the blood of the s
Num 25:14 name of the Israelite that was s
Num 25:14 even that was s with the
Num 25:15 woman that was s was Cozbi
Num 25:18 which was s in the day of the
Num 31:8 the rest of them that were s
Num 31:19 and whosoever hath touched any s
Deut 1:4 After he had s Sihon the king of

Deut 21:1 If one be found s in the land
Deut 21:1 and it be not known who hath s him
Deut 21:2 are round about him that is s
Deut 21:3 city which is next unto the s man
Deut 21:6 that are next unto the s man
Deut 28:31 ox shall be s before thine eyes
Deut 32:42 and that with the blood of the s
Josh 11:6 them up all s before Israel
Josh 13:22 among them that were s by them
Judg 9:18 have s his sons, threescore and
Judg 15:16 of an ass have I s a thousand men
Judg 20:4 husband of the woman that was s
Judg 20:5 by night, and thought to have s me
1Sa 4:11 Eli, Hophni and Phinehas, were s
1Sa 18:7 Saul hath s his thousands, and
1Sa 19:6 LORD liveth, he shall not be s
1Sa 19:11 night, to morrow thou shalt be s
1Sa 20:32 unto him, Wherefore shall he be s
1Sa 21:11 Saul hath s his thousands, and
1Sa 22:21 Saul had s the LORD's priests
1Sa 31:1 fell down s in mount Gilboa
1Sa 31:8 Philistines came to strip the s
2Sa 1:16 I have s the LORD's anointed
2Sa 1:19 Israel is s upon thy high places
2Sa 1:22 From the blood of the s, from the
2Sa 1:25 thou wast s in thine high places
2Sa 3:30 because he had s their brother
2Sa 4:11 more, when wicked men have s a
2Sa 12:9 hast s him with the sword of the
2Sa 13:30 Absalom hath s all the king's
2Sa 13:32 s all the young men the king's
2Sa 18:7 s before the servants of David
2Sa 21:12 Philistines had s Saul in Gilboa
2Sa 21:16 sword, thought to have s David
1Kin 1:19 And he hath s oxen and fat cattle
1Kin 1:25 down this day, and hath s oxen
1Kin 9:16 s the Canaanites that dwelt in
1Kin 11:15 host was gone up to bury the s
1Kin 13:26 s him, according to the word of
1Kin 16:16 and hath also s the king
1Kin 19:1 withal how he had s all the
1Kin 19:10 s thy prophets with the sword
1Kin 19:14 s thy prophets with the sword
2Kin 3:23 the kings are surely s, and they
2Kin 11:2 the king's sons which were s
2Kin 11:2 Athaliah, so that he was not s
2Kin 11:8 within the ranges, let him be s
2Kin 11:15 Let her not be s in the house of
2Kin 11:16 and there was she s
2Kin 14:5 which had s the king his father
1Chr 5:22 For there fell down many s
1Chr 10:1 fell down s in mount Gilboa
1Chr 10:8 Philistines came to strip the s
1Chr 11:11 hundred s by him at one time
2Chr 13:17 so there fell down s of Israel
2Chr 21:13 also hast s thy brethren of thy
2Chr 22:1 to the camp had s all the eldest
2Chr 22:9 and when they had s him, they
2Chr 22:11 among the king's sons that were s
2Chr 23:14 let him be s with the sword
2Chr 23:21 after that they had s Athaliah
2Chr 28:9 ye have s them in a rage that
Est 7:4 people, to be destroyed, to be s
Est 9:11 were s in Shushan the palace was
Est 9:12 Esther the queen, The Jews have s
Job 1:15 they have s the servants with the
Job 1:17 s the servants with the edge of
Job 39:30 and where the s are, there is she
Ps 62:3 ye shall be s all of you
Ps 88:5 like the s that lie in the grave,
Ps 89:10 Rahab in pieces, as one that is s
Prov 7:26 strong men have been s by her
Prov 22:13 I shall be s in the streets
Prov 24:11 and those that are ready to be s
Is 10:4 and they shall fall under the s
Is 14:19 the raiment of those that are s
Is 14:20 thy land, and s thy people
Is 22:2 thy s men are not s with the
Is 26:21 and shall no more cover her s
Is 27:7 or is he s according to the
Is 27:7 of them that are s by him
Is 34:3 Their s also shall be cast out,
Is 66:16 the s of the LORD shall be many
Jer 9:1 night for the s of the daughter
Jer 14:18 then behold the s with the sword
Jer 18:21 men be s by the sword in battle
Jer 25:33 the s of the LORD shall be at
Jer 33:5 whom I have s in mine anger and in
Jer 41:4 day after he had s Gedaliah
Jer 41:9 whom he had s because of Gedaliah
Jer 41:9 filled it with them that were s
Jer 41:16 after that he had s Gedaliah the
Jer 41:18 the son of Nethaniah had s
Jer 51:4 Thus the s shall fall in the land
Jer 51:47 all her s shall fall in the midst
Jer 51:49 caused the s of Israel to fall
Jer 51:49 shall fall the s of all the earth
Lam 2:20 the prophet be s in the sanctuary
Lam 2:21 thou hast s them in the day of
Lam 3:43 thou hast s, thou hast not pitied
Lam 4:9 They that be s with the sword are
Lam 4:9 than they that be s with hunger
Eze 6:4 down your s men before your idols
Eze 6:7 the s shall fall in the midst of
Eze 6:13 when their s men shall be among
Eze 9:7 and fill the courts with the s
Eze 11:6 multiplied your s in this city
Eze 11:6 the streets thereof with the s
Eze 11:7 Your s whom ye have laid in the
Eze 16:21 That thou hast s my children
Eze 21:14 third time, the sword of the s
Eze 21:14 sword of the great men that are s
Eze 21:29 upon the necks of them that are s
Eze 23:39 For when they had s their
Eze 26:6 the field shall be s by the sword
Eze 28:8 are s in the midst of the seas
Eze 30:4 when the s shall fall in Egypt,
Eze 30:11 and fill the land with the s
Eze 31:17 them that be s with the sword
Eze 31:18 with them that be s by the sword
Eze 32:20 of them that are s by the sword
Eze 32:21 lie uncircumcised, s by the sword
Eze 32:22 all of them s, fallen by the
Eze 32:23 all of them s, fallen by the
Eze 32:24 about her grave, all of them s
Eze 32:25 of the s with all her multitude
Eze 32:25 uncircumcised, s by the sword
Eze 32:25 in the midst of them that be s
Eze 32:26 s by the sword, though they
Eze 32:28 them that are s with the sword
Eze 32:29 by them that were s by the sword
Eze 32:30 which are gone down with the s
Eze 32:30 with them that be s by the sword
Eze 32:31 and all his army s by the sword
Eze 32:32 them that are s with the sword
Eze 35:8 fill his mountains with his s men
Eze 35:8 fall that are s with the sword
Eze 37:9 O breath, and breathe upon these s
Dan 2:13 that the wise men should be s
Dan 2:13 Daniel and his fellows to be s
Dan 5:30 the king of the Chaldeans s
Dan 7:11 beheld even till the beast was s
Dan 11:26 and many shall fall down s
Hos 6:5 I have s them by the words of my
Amos 4:10 young men have I s with the sword
Nah 3:3 and there is a multitude of s
Zeph 2:12 also, ye shall be s by my sword
Lk 9:22 chief priests and scribes, and be s
Acts 2:23 wicked hands have crucified and s
Acts 5:36 who was s; and all
Acts 7:42 have ye offered to me s beasts
Acts 7:52 they have s them which shewed
Acts 13:28 they Pilate that he should be s
Acts 23:14 eat nothing until we have s Paul
Eph 2:16 having s the enmity thereby
Heb 11:37 were s with the sword
Rev 2:13 who was s among you, where Satan
Rev 5:6 stood a Lamb as it had been s
Rev 5:9 for thou wast s, and hast redeemed
Rev 5:12 Lamb that was s to receive power
Rev 6:9 that were s for the word of God
Rev 11:13 were s of men seven thousand
Rev 13:8 Lamb s from the foundation of the
Rev 18:24 of all that were s upon the earth
Rev 19:21 the remnant were s with the sword

## SLAUGHTER

Gen 14:17 return from the s of Chedorlaomer
Josh 10:10 them with a great s at Gibeon
Josh 10:20 slaying them with a very great s
Judg 11:33 vineyards, with a very great s
Judg 15:8 them hip and thigh with a great s
1Sa 4:10 and there was a very great s
1Sa 4:17 also a great s among the people
1Sa 6:19 many of the people with a great s
1Sa 14:14 And that first s, which Jonathan
1Sa 14:30 greater s among the Philistines
1Sa 17:57 from the s of the Philistine
1Sa 18:6 from the s of the Philistine
1Sa 19:8 and slew them with a great s
1Sa 23:5 and smote them with a great s
2Sa 1:1 from the s of the Amalekites
2Sa 17:9 There is a s among the people
2Sa 18:7 there was there a great s that
1Kin 20:21 slew the Syrians with a great s
2Chr 13:17 people slew them with a great s
2Chr 25:14 come from the s of the Edomites
2Chr 28:5 who smote him with a great s
Est 9:5 the stroke of the sword, and s
Ps 44:22 we are counted as sheep for the s
Prov 7:22 as an ox goeth to the s, or as a
Is 10:26 for him according to the s of
Is 14:21 Prepare s for his children for
Is 27:7 s of them that are slain by him
Is 30:25 waters in the day of the great s
Is 34:2 he hath delivered them to the s
Is 34:6 a great s in the land of Idumea
Is 53:7 he is brought as a lamb to the s
Is 65:12 and ye shall all bow down to the s
Jer 7:32 of Hinnom, but the valley of s
Jer 11:19 or an ox that is brought to the s
Jer 12:3 them out like sheep for the s
Jer 12:3 and prepare them for the day of s
Jer 19:6 of Hinnom, but The valley of s
Jer 25:34 for the days of your s and of your
Jer 48:15 young men are gone down to the s
Jer 50:27 let them go down to the s
Jer 51:40 them down like lambs to the s
Eze 9:2 every man a s weapon in his hand
Eze 21:10 It is sharpened to make a sore s
Eze 21:15 it is wrapped up for the s
Eze 21:22 to open the mouth in the s
Eze 21:28 for the s it is furbished, to
Eze 26:15 when the s is made in the midst
Hos 5:2 revolters are profound to make s
Obad 9 mount of Esau may be cut off by s
Zec 11:4 Feed the flock of the s
Zec 11:7 And I will feed the flock of s
Acts 8:32 He was led as a sheep to the s
Acts 9:1 s against the disciples of the
Rom 8:36 are accounted as sheep for the s
Heb 7:1 returning from the s of the kings
Jas 5:5 your hearts, as in a day of s

## SLAY

Gen 4:14 one that findeth me shall s me
Gen 18:25 to s the righteous with the
Gen 20:4 wilt thou s also a righteous
Gen 20:11 they will s me for my wife's sake
Gen 22:10 and took the knife to s his son
Gen 27:41 then will I s my brother Jacob
Gen 34:30 together against me, and s me
Gen 37:18 conspired against him to s him
Gen 37:20 now therefore, and let us s him
Gen 37:26 profit is it if we s our brother
Gen 42:37 S my two sons, if I bring him not
Gen 43:16 house, Bring these men home, and s
Ex 2:15 this thing, he sought to s Moses
Ex 4:23 I will s thy son, even thy
Ex 5:21 put a sword in their hand to s us
Ex 21:14 neighbour, to s him with guile
Ex 23:7 innocent and righteous s thou not
Ex 29:16 And thou shalt s the ram, and thou
Ex 32:12 to s them in the mountains, and to
Ex 32:27 s every man his brother, and every
Lev 4:29 s the sin offering in the place
Lev 4:33 s it for a sin offering in the
Lev 14:13 he shall s the lamb in the place
Lev 20:15 and ye shall s the beast
Num 19:3 one shall s her before his face
Num 25:5 S ye every one his men that were
Num 35:19 himself shall s the murderer
Num 35:19 he meeteth him, he shall s him
Num 35:21 of blood shall s the murderer
Deut 9:28 out to s them in the wilderness
Deut 19:6 because the way is long, and s him
Deut 27:25 reward to s an innocent person
Josh 13:22 did the children of Israel s with
Judg 8:19 them alive, I would not s you
Judg 8:20 his firstborn, Up, and s them
Judg 9:54 s me, that men say not of me, A
1Sa 2:25 because the LORD would s them
1Sa 5:10 the God of Israel to us, to s us
1Sa 5:11 his own place, that it s us not
1Sa 14:34 his sheep, and s them here, and eat
1Sa 15:3 but s both man and woman, infant
1Sa 19:5 to s David without a cause
1Sa 19:11 him, and to s him in the morning
1Sa 19:15 me in the bed, that I may s him
1Sa 20:8 be in me iniquity, s me thyself

1Sa 20:33 of his father to s David
1Sa 22:17 s the priests of the LORD
2Sa 1:9 I pray thee, upon me, and s me
2Sa 3:37 king to s Abner the son of Ner
2Sa 21:2 Saul sought to s them in his zeal
1Kin 1:51 not s his servant with the sword
1Kin 3:26 living child, and in no wise s it
1Kin 3:27 living child, and in no wise s it
1Kin 15:28 king of Judah did Baasha s him
1Kin 17:18 to remembrance, and to s my son
1Kin 18:9 into the hand of Ahab, to s me
1Kin 18:12 cannot find thee, he shall s me
1Kin 18:14 and he shall s me
1Kin 19:17 the sword of Hazael shall Jehu s
1Kin 19:17 the sword of Jehu shall Elisha s
1Kin 20:36 from me, a lion shall s thee
2Kin 8:12 men wilt thou s with the sword
2Kin 10:25 to the captains, Go in, and s them
2Kin 17:26 them, and, behold, they s them
2Chr 20:23 of mount Seir, utterly to s
2Chr 23:14 S her not in the house of the
Neh 4:11 s them, and cause the work to
Neh 6:10 for they will come to s thee
Neh 6:10 night will they come to s thee
Est 8:11 for their life, to destroy, to s
Job 9:23 If the scourge s suddenly
Job 13:15 Though he s me, yet will I trust
Job 20:16 the viper's tongue shall s him
Ps 34:21 Evil shall s the wicked
Ps 37:14 to s such as be of upright
Ps 37:32 righteous, and seeketh to s him
Ps 59:11 S them not, lest my people forget
Ps 94:6 They s the widow and the stranger,
Ps 109:16 that he might even s the broken
Ps 139:19 Surely thou wilt s the wicked
Prov 1:32 away of the simple shall s them
Is 11:4 of his lips shall he s the wicked
Is 14:30 famine, and he shall s thy remnant
Is 27:1 he shall s the dragon that is in
Is 65:15 for the Lord GOD shall s thee
Jer 5:6 out of the forest shall s them
Jer 15:3 the sword to s, and the dogs to
Jer 18:23 their counsel against me to s me
Jer 20:4 shall s them with the sword
Jer 29:21 he shall s them before your eyes
Jer 40:14 the son of Nethaniah to s thee
Jer 40:15 I will s Ishmael the son of
Jer 40:15 wherefore should he s thee
Jer 41:8 that said unto Ishmael, S us not
Jer 50:27 S all her bullocks
Eze 9:6 S utterly old and young, both
Eze 13:19 to s the souls that should not
Eze 23:47 they shall s their sons and their
Eze 26:8 He shall s with the sword thy
Eze 26:11 he shall s thy people by the
Eze 40:39 to s thereon the burnt offering
Eze 44:11 they shall s the burnt offering
Dan 2:14 to s the wise men of Babylon
Hos 2:3 a dry land, and s her with thirst
Hos 9:16 yet will I s even the beloved
Amos 2:3 will s all the princes thereof
Amos 9:1 I will s the last of them with
Amos 9:4 the sword, and it shall s them
Hab 1:17 continually to s the nations
Zec 11:5 Whose possessors s them, and hold
Lk 11:49 and some of them they shall s
Lk 19:27 bring hither, and s them before me
Jn 5:16 Jesus, and sought to s him
Acts 5:33 heart, and took counsel to s them
Acts 9:29 but they went about to s him
Acts 11:7 s and eat
Rev 9:15 for to s the third part of men

## SLAYER
Num 35:11 that the s may flee thither,
Num 35:24 shall judge between the s
Num 35:25 congregation shall deliver the s
Num 35:26 But if the s shall at any time
Num 35:27 the revenger of blood kill the s
Num 35:28 death of the high priest the s
Deut 4:42 That the s might flee thither,
Deut 19:3 that every s may flee thither
Deut 19:4 And this is the case of the s
Deut 19:6 avenger of the blood pursue the s
Josh 20:3 That the s that killeth any
Josh 20:5 deliver the s up into his hand
Josh 20:6 then shall the s return, and come
Josh 21:13 to be a city of refuge for the s
Josh 21:21 to be a city of refuge for the s
Josh 21:27 to be a city of refuge for the s
Josh 21:32 to be a city of refuge for the s
Josh 21:38 to be a city of refuge for the s
Eze 21:11 to give it into the hand of the s

## SLAYETH
Gen 4:15 him, Therefore whosoever s Cain
Deut 22:26 s him, even so is this matter
Job 5:2 man, and envy s the silly one
Eze 28:9 yet say before him that s thee
Eze 28:9 in the hand of him that s thee

## SLAYING
Josh 8:24 of s all the inhabitants of Ai in
Josh 10:20 end of s them with a very great
Judg 9:56 in s his seventy brethren
1Kin 17:20 with whom I sojourn, by s her son
Is 22:13 s oxen, and killing sheep, eating
Is 57:5 s the children in the valleys
Eze 9:8 to pass, while they were s them

## SLEEP
Gen 2:21 caused a deep s to fall upon Adam
Gen 15:12 down, a deep s fell upon Abram
Gen 28:11 and lay down in that place to s
Gen 28:16 And Jacob awaked out of his s
Gen 31:40 my s departed from mine eyes
Ex 22:27 wherein shall he s
Deut 24:12 thou shalt not s with his pledge
Deut 24:13 that he may s in his own raiment,
Deut 31:16 thou shalt s with thy fathers
Judg 16:14 And he awaked out of his s
Judg 16:19 she made him s upon her knees
Judg 16:20 And he awoke out of his s, and said
1Sa 3:3 was, and Samuel was laid down to s
1Sa 26:12 because a deep s from the LORD
2Sa 7:12 thou shalt s with thy fathers, I
1Kin 1:21 the king shall s with his fathers
Est 6:1 that night could not the king s
Job 4:13 when deep s falleth on men,
Job 7:21 for now shall I s in the dust
Job 14:12 nor be raised out of their s
Job 33:15 when deep s falleth upon men, in
Ps 4:8 both lay me down in peace, and s
Ps 13:3 lest I s the s of death
Ps 76:5 spoiled, they have slept their s
Ps 76:6 and horse are cast into a dead s
Ps 78:65 the Lord awaked as one out of s
Ps 90:5 they are as a s
Ps 121:4 shall neither slumber nor s
Ps 127:2 for so he giveth his beloved s
Ps 132:4 I will not give s to mine eyes
Prov 3:24 lie down, and thy s shall be sweet
Prov 4:16 For they s not, except they have
Prov 4:16 their s is taken away, unless
Prov 6:4 Give not s to thine eyes, nor
Prov 6:9 How long wilt thou s, O sluggard
Prov 6:9 when wilt thou arise out of thy s
Prov 6:10 Yet a little s, a little slumber,
Prov 6:10 little folding of the hands to s
Prov 19:15 casteth into a deep s
Prov 20:13 Love not s, lest thou come to
Prov 24:33 Yet a little s, a little slumber,
Prov 24:33 little folding of the hands to s
Eccl 5:12 The s of a labouring man is sweet
Eccl 5:12 the rich will not suffer him to s
Eccl 8:16 nor night seeth s with his eyes
Song 5:2 I s, but my heart waketh
Is 5:27 none shall slumber nor s
Is 29:10 out upon you the spirit of deep s
Jer 31:26 and my s was sweet unto me
Jer 51:39 they may rejoice, and s
Jer 51:39 a perpetual s, and not wake
Jer 51:57 they shall s a perpetual s,
Jer 51:57 and they shall s a perpetual s
Eze 34:25 the wilderness, and s in the woods
Dan 2:1 troubled, and his s brake from him
Dan 6:18 and his s went from him
Dan 8:18 I was in a deep s on my face
Dan 10:9 then was I in a deep s on my face
Dan 12:2 many of them that s in the dust
Zec 4:1 man that is wakened out of his s
Mt 1:24 s did as the angel of the Lord
Mt 26:45 S on now, and take your rest
Mk 4:27 And should s, and rise night and day
Mk 14:41 S on now, and take your rest
Lk 9:32 were with him were heavy with s
Lk 22:46 And said unto them, Why s ye
Jn 11:11 go, that I may awake him out of s
Jn 11:12 said his disciples, Lord, if he s
Jn 11:13 had spoken of taking of rest in s
Acts 13:36 by the will of God, fell on s
Acts 16:27 the prison awaking out of his s
Acts 20:9 being fallen into a deep s
Acts 20:9 preaching, he sunk down with s
Rom 13:11 it is high time to awake out of s
1Cor 11:30 and sickly among you, and many s
1Cor 15:51 We shall not all s, but we shall
1Th 4:14 even so them also which s in
1Th 5:6 Therefore let us not s, as do
1Th 5:7 they that s s in the night
1Th 5:10 us, that, whether we wake or s

## SLEEPETH
1Kin 18:27 a journey, or peradventure he s
Prov 10:5 but he that s in harvest is a son
Hos 7:6 their baker s all the night
Mt 9:24 for the maid is not dead, but s
Mk 5:39 the damsel is not dead, but s
Lk 8:52 she is not dead, but s
Jn 11:11 unto them, Our friend Lazarus s

## SLEEPING
1Sa 26:7 Saul lay s within the trench, and
Is 56:10 s, lying down, loving to slumber
Mk 13:36 coming suddenly he find you s
Mk 14:37 And he cometh, and findeth them s
Lk 22:45 he found them s for sorrow
Acts 12:6 Peter was s between two soldiers

## SLEPT
Gen 2:21 sleep to fall upon Adam, and he s
Gen 41:5 And he s and dreamed the second
2Sa 11:9 But Uriah s at the door of the
1Kin 2:10 So David s with his fathers, and
1Kin 3:20 beside me, while thine handmaid s
1Kin 11:21 that David s with his fathers
1Kin 11:43 Solomon s with his fathers, and
1Kin 14:20 he s with his fathers, and Nadab
1Kin 14:31 Rehoboam s with his fathers, and
1Kin 15:8 Abijam s with his fathers
1Kin 15:24 Asa s with his fathers, and was
1Kin 16:6 So Baasha s with his fathers, and
1Kin 16:28 So Omri s with his fathers, and
1Kin 19:5 s under a juniper tree, behold,
1Kin 22:40 So Ahab s with his fathers
1Kin 22:50 Jehoshaphat s with his fathers,
2Kin 8:24 Joram s with his fathers, and was
2Kin 10:35 And Jehu s with his fathers
2Kin 13:9 Jehoahaz s with his fathers
2Kin 13:13 And Joash s with his fathers
2Kin 14:16 Jehoash s with his fathers, and
2Kin 14:22 that the king s with his fathers
2Kin 14:29 Jeroboam s with his fathers, even
2Kin 15:7 So Azariah s with his fathers
2Kin 15:22 Menahem s with his fathers
2Kin 15:38 Jotham s with his fathers, and was
2Kin 16:20 Ahaz s with his fathers, and was
2Kin 20:21 Hezekiah s with his fathers
2Kin 21:18 Manasseh s with his fathers, and
2Kin 24:6 So Jehoiakim s with his fathers
2Chr 9:31 Solomon s with his fathers, and he
2Chr 12:16 Rehoboam s with his fathers, and
2Chr 14:1 So Abijah s with his fathers, and
2Chr 16:13 Asa s with his fathers, and died
2Chr 21:1 Now Jehoshaphat s with his
2Chr 26:2 that the king s with his fathers
2Chr 26:23 So Uzziah s with his fathers, and
2Chr 27:9 Jotham s with his fathers, and
2Chr 28:27 Ahaz s with his fathers, and they
2Chr 32:33 Hezekiah s with his fathers, and
2Chr 33:20 So Manasseh s with his fathers,
Job 3:13 and been quiet, I should have s
Ps 3:5 I laid me down and s
Ps 76:5 spoiled, they have s their sleep
Mt 13:25 But while men s, his enemy came
Mt 25:5 tarried, they all slumbered and s
Mt 27:52 of the saints which s arose
Mt 28:13 and stole him away while we s
1Cor 15:20 the firstfruits of them that s

## SLEW
Gen 4:8 Abel his brother, and s him
Gen 4:25 seed instead of Abel, whom Cain s
Gen 34:25 city boldly, and s all the males
Gen 34:26 they s Hamor and Shechem his son
Gen 38:7 and the LORD s him
Gen 38:10 wherefore he s him also
Gen 49:6 for in their anger they s a man
Ex 2:12 he s the Egyptian, and hid him in
Ex 13:15 that the LORD s all the firstborn
Lev 8:15 And he s it
Lev 8:23 And he s it
Lev 9:8 s the calf of the sin offering,
Lev 9:12 And he s the burnt offering

Lev 9:15 s it, and offered it for sin, as
Lev 9:18 He s also the bullock and the ram
Num 31:7 and they s all the males
Num 31:8 they s the kings of Midian,
Num 31:8 son of Beor they s with the sword
Josh 8:21 turned again, and s the men of Ai
Josh 9:26 of Israel, that they s them not
Josh 10:10 s them with a great slaughter at
Josh 10:11 of Israel s with the sword
Josh 10:26 s them, and hanged them on five
Josh 11:17 he took, and smote them, and s them
Judg 1:4 they s of them in Bezek ten
Judg 1:5 they s the Canaanites and the
Judg 1:10 they s Sheshai, and Ahiman, and
Judg 1:17 they s the Canaanites that
Judg 3:29 they s of Moab at that time about
Judg 3:31 which s of the Philistines six
Judg 7:25 they s Oreb upon the rock Oreb,
Judg 7:25 Zeeb they s at the winepress of
Judg 8:17 Penuel, and s the men of the city
Judg 8:18 men were they whom ye s at Tabor
Judg 8:21 s Zebah and Zalmunna,
Judg 9:5 s his brethren the sons of
Judg 9:24 their brother, which s them
Judg 9:44 were in the fields, and s them
Judg 9:45 s the people that was therein, and
Judg 9:54 men say not of me, A woman s him
Judg 12:6 s him at the passages of Jordan
Judg 14:19 s thirty men of them, and took
Judg 15:15 s a thousand men therewith
Judg 16:24 our country, which s many of us
Judg 16:30 So the dead which he s at his
Judg 16:30 than they which he s in his life
Judg 20:45 s two thousand men of them
1Sa 1:25 they s a bullock, and brought the
1Sa 4:2 they s of the army in the field
1Sa 11:11 s the Ammonites until the heat of
1Sa 14:13 and his armourbearer s after him
1Sa 14:32 calves, and s them on the ground
1Sa 14:34 him that night, and s them there
1Sa 17:35 his beard, and smote him, and s him
1Sa 17:36 Thy servant s both the lion and
1Sa 17:50 and smote the Philistine, and s him
1Sa 17:51 s him, and cut off his head
1Sa 18:27 s of the Philistines two hundred
1Sa 19:5 s the Philistine, and the LORD
1Sa 19:8 s them with a great slaughter
1Sa 22:18 s on that day fourscore and five
1Sa 29:5 Saul s his thousands, and David
1Sa 30:2 they s not any, either great or
1Sa 31:2 and the Philistines s Jonathan
2Sa 1:10 s him, because I was sure that he
2Sa 3:30 and Abishai his brother s Abner
2Sa 4:7 s him, and beheaded him, and took
2Sa 4:10 s him in Ziklag, who thought that
2Sa 4:12 his young men, and they s them
2Sa 8:5 David s of the Syrians two and
2Sa 10:18 David s the men of seven hundred
2Sa 14:6 the one smote the other, and s him
2Sa 14:7 the life of his brother whom he s
2Sa 18:15 about and smote Absalom, and s him
2Sa 21:1 because he s the Gibeonites
2Sa 21:18 Sibbechai the Hushathite s Saph
2Sa 21:19 s the brother of Goliath the
2Sa 21:21 the brother of David s him
2Sa 23:8 hundred, whom he s at one time
2Sa 23:12 defended it, and s the Philistines
2Sa 23:18 s them, and had the name among
2Sa 23:20 he s two lionlike men of Moab
2Sa 23:20 s a lion in the midst of a pit in
2Sa 23:21 he s an Egyptian, a goodly man
2Sa 23:21 hand, and s him with his own spear
1Kin 1:9 And Adonijah s sheep and oxen and
1Kin 2:5 the son of Jether, whom he s
1Kin 2:32 s them with the sword, my father
1Kin 2:34 up, and fell upon him, and s him
1Kin 11:24 when David s them of Zobah
1Kin 13:24 lion met him by the way, and s him
1Kin 16:11 that he s all the house of Baasha
1Kin 18:13 s the prophets of the LORD
1Kin 18:40 the brook Kishon, and s them there
1Kin 19:21 s them, and boiled their flesh
1Kin 20:20 And they s every one his man
1Kin 20:21 s the Syrians with a great
1Kin 20:29 the children of Israel s of the
1Kin 20:36 him, a lion found him, and s him
2Kin 9:31 Had Zimri peace, who s his master
2Kin 10:7 s seventy persons, and put their
2Kin 10:9 against my master, and s him
2Kin 10:9 but who s all these
2Kin 10:11 So Jehu s all that remained of
2Kin 10:14 s them at the pit of the shearing
2Kin 10:17 he s all that remained unto Ahab
2Kin 11:18 s Mattan the priest of Baal
2Kin 11:20 they s Athaliah with the sword
2Kin 12:20 s Joash in the house of Millo,
2Kin 14:5 that he s his servants which had
2Kin 14:6 of the murderers he s not
2Kin 14:7 He s of Edom in the valley of
2Kin 14:19 him to Lachish, and s him there
2Kin 15:10 s him, and reigned in his stead
2Kin 15:14 s him, and reigned in his stead
2Kin 15:30 s him, and reigned in his stead,
2Kin 16:9 of it captive to Kir, and s Rezin
2Kin 17:25 among them, which s some of them
2Kin 21:23 s the king in his own house
2Kin 21:24 the people of the land s all them
2Kin 23:20 he s all the priests of the high
2Kin 23:29 he s him at Megiddo, when he had
2Kin 25:7 they s the sons of Zedekiah
2Kin 25:21 s them at Riblah in the land of
1Chr 2:3 and he s him
1Chr 7:21 that were born in that land s
1Chr 10:2 and the Philistines s Jonathan
1Chr 10:14 therefore he s him, and turned the
1Chr 11:14 it, and s the Philistines
1Chr 11:20 he s them, and had a name among
1Chr 11:22 he s two lionlike men of Moab
1Chr 11:22 s a lion in a pit in a snowy day
1Chr 11:23 he s an Egyptian, a man of great
1Chr 11:23 hand, and s him with his own spear
1Chr 18:5 David s of the Syrians two and
1Chr 18:12 Abishai the son Zeruiah s of the
1Chr 19:18 David s of the Syrians seven
1Chr 20:4 Sibbechai the Hushathite s Sippai
1Chr 20:5 Elhanan the son of Jair s Lahmi
1Chr 20:7 of Shimea David's brother s him
2Chr 13:17 his people s them with a great
2Chr 21:4 s all his brethren with the sword
2Chr 22:8 ministered to Ahaziah, he s them
2Chr 22:11 Athaliah, so that she s him not
2Chr 23:15 king's house, they s her there
2Chr 23:17 s Mattan the priest of Baal
2Chr 24:22 had done to him, but s his son
2Chr 24:25 s him on his bed, and he died
2Chr 25:3 that he s his servants that had
2Chr 25:4 But he s not their children, but
2Chr 25:27 Lachish after him, and s him there
2Chr 28:6 of Remaliah s in Judah an hundred
2Chr 28:7 s Maaseiah the king's son, and
2Chr 32:21 bowels s him there with the sword
2Chr 33:24 him, and s him in his own house
2Chr 33:25 But the people of the land s all
2Chr 36:17 who s their young men with the
Neh 9:26 s thy prophets which testified
Est 9:6 in Shushan the palace the Jews s
Est 9:10 the enemy of the Jews, s they
Est 9:15 s three hundred men at Shushan
Est 9:16 s of their foes seventy and five
Ps 78:31 s the fattest of them, and smote
Ps 78:34 When he s them, then they sought
Ps 105:29 into blood, and s their fish
Ps 135:10 great nations, and s mighty kings
Ps 136:18 And s famous kings
Is 66:3 killeth an ox is as if he s a man
Jer 20:17 Because he s me not from the womb
Jer 26:23 who s him with the sword, and cast
Jer 39:6 Then the king of Babylon s the
Jer 39:6 Babylon s all the nobles of Judah
Jer 41:2 s him, whom the king of Babylon
Jer 41:3 Ishmael also s all the Jews that
Jer 41:7 the son of Nethaniah s them
Jer 41:8 s them not among their brethren
Jer 52:10 the king of Babylon s the sons of
Jer 52:10 he s also all the princes of
Lam 2:4 s all that were pleasant to the
Eze 9:7 they went forth, and s in the city
Eze 23:10 and s her with the sword
Eze 40:41 whereupon they s their sacrifices
Eze 40:42 they s the burnt offering
Dan 3:22 the flame of the fire s those men
Dan 5:19 whom he would he s
Mt 2:16 s all the children that were in
Mt 21:39 him out of the vineyard, and s him
Mt 22:6 them spitefully, and s them
Mt 23:35 whom ye s between the temple and
Lk 13:4 s them, think ye that they were
Acts 5:30 raised up Jesus, whom ye s
Acts 10:39 whom they s and hanged on a tree
Acts 22:20 the raiment of them that s him
Rom 7:11 deceived me, and by it s me
1Jn 3:12 that wicked one, and s his brother
1Jn 3:12 And wherefore s he him

## SLING
Judg 20:16 every one could s stones at an
1Sa 17:40 and his s was in his hand
1Sa 17:50 over the Philistine with a s
1Sa 25:29 enemies, them shall he s out
1Sa 25:29 as out of the middle of a s
Prov 26:8 As he that bindeth a stone in a s
Jer 10:18 I will s out the inhabitants of
Zec 9:15 devour, and subdue with s stones

## SLIP
2Sa 22:37 so that my feet did not s
Job 12:5 He that is ready to s with his
Ps 17:5 paths, that my footsteps s not
Ps 18:36 under me, that my feet did not s
Heb 2:1 at any time we should let them s

## SLOTHFUL
Judg 18:9 be not s to go, and to enter to
Prov 12:24 but the s shall be under tribute
Prov 12:27 The s man roasteth not that which
Prov 15:19 The way of the s man is as an
Prov 18:9 He also that is s in his work is
Prov 19:24 A s man hideth his hand in his
Prov 21:25 The desire of the s killeth him
Prov 22:13 The s man saith, There is a lion
Prov 24:30 I went by the field of the s
Prov 26:13 The s man saith, There is a lion
Prov 26:14 so doth the s upon his bed
Prov 26:15 The s hideth his hand in his
Mt 25:26 s servant, thou knewest that I
Rom 12:11 Not s in business
Heb 6:12 That ye be not s, but followers

## SLOW
Ex 4:10 but I am s of speech
Ex 4:10 and of a s tongue
Neh 9:17 s to anger, and of great kindness,
Ps 103:8 s to anger, and plenteous in mercy
Ps 145:8 s to anger, and of great mercy
Prov 14:29 He that is s to wrath is of great
Prov 15:18 but he that is s to anger
Prov 16:32 He that is s to anger is better
Joel 2:13 s to anger, and of great kindness,
Jonah 4:2 s to anger, and of great kindness,
Nah 1:3 The LORD is s to anger, and great
Lk 24:25 s of heart to believe all that
Titus 1:12 liars, evil beasts, s bellies
Jas 1:19 s to speak, s to wrath

## SLUGGARD
Prov 6:6 Go to the ant, thou s
Prov 6:9 How long wilt thou sleep, O s
Prov 10:26 so is the s to them that send him
Prov 13:4 The soul of the s desireth
Prov 20:4 The s will not plow by reason of
Prov 26:16 The s is wiser in his own conceit

## SLUICES
Is 19:10 purposes thereof, all that make s

## SLUMBER
Ps 121:3 he that keepeth thee will not s
Ps 121:4 Israel shall neither s nor sleep
Ps 132:4 mine eyes, or s to mine eyelids,
Prov 6:4 eyes, nor s to thine eyelids
Prov 6:10 Yet a little sleep, a little s
Prov 24:33 Yet a little sleep, a little s
Is 5:27 none shall s nor sleep
Is 56:10 sleeping, lying down, loving to s
Nah 3:18 Thy shepherds s, O king of
Rom 11:8 hath given them the spirit of s

## SMALL
Gen 19:11 the house with blindness, both s
Gen 30:15 Is it a s matter that thou hast
Ex 9:9 it shall become s dust in all the
Ex 16:14 there lay a s round thing
Ex 16:14 as s as the hoar frost on the
Ex 18:22 but every s matter they shall
Ex 18:26 but every s matter they judged
Ex 30:36 thou shalt beat some of it very s
Lev 16:12 full of sweet incense beaten s
Num 16:9 Seemeth it but a s thing unto you
Num 16:13 Is it a s thing that thou hast
Num 32:41 took the s towns thereof, and
Deut 1:17 hear the s as well as the great
Deut 9:21 stamped it, and ground it very s
Deut 9:21 even until it was as s as dust
Deut 25:13 divers weights, a great and a s
Deut 25:14 divers measures, a great and a s

Deut 32:2 as the *s* rain upon the tender
1Sa 5:9 smote the men of the city, both *s*
1Sa 20:2 will do nothing either great or *s*
1Sa 30:2 slew not any, either great or *s*
1Sa 30:19 neither *s* nor great, neither sons
2Sa 7:19 this was yet a *s* thing in thy
2Sa 17:13 be not one *s* stone found there
2Sa 22:43 Then did I beat them as *s* as the
1Kin 2:20 I desire one *s* petition of thee
1Kin 19:12 and after the fire a still *s* voice
1Kin 22:31 Fight neither with *s* nor great
2Kin 19:26 their inhabitants were of *s* power
2Kin 23:2 and all the people, both *s*
2Kin 23:6 Kidron, and stamped it *s* to powder
2Kin 23:15 place, and stamped it *s* to powder
2Kin 25:26 And all the people, both *s*
1Chr 17:17 yet this was a *s* thing in thine
1Chr 25:8 as well the *s* as the great, the
1Chr 26:13 as well the *s* as the great,
2Chr 15:13 whether *s* or great, whether man
2Chr 18:30 Fight ye not with *s* or great
2Chr 24:24 came with a *s* company of men
2Chr 31:15 as well to the great as to the *s*
2Chr 34:30 and all the people, great and *s*
2Chr 35:8 thousand and six hundred *s* cattle
2Chr 35:9 offerings five thousand *s* cattle
2Chr 36:18 of the house of God, great and *s*
Est 1:5 the palace, both unto great and *s*
Est 1:20 honour, both to great and *s*
Job 3:19 The *s* and great are there
Job 8:7 Though thy beginning was *s*
Job 15:11 consolations of God *s* with thee
Job 36:27 For he maketh *s* the drops of
Job 37:6 likewise to the *s* rain, and to the
Ps 18:42 Then did I beat them *s* as the
Ps 104:25 creeping innumerable, both *s*
Ps 115:13 them that fear the LORD, both *s*
Ps 119:141 I am *s* and despised
Prov 24:10 of adversity, thy strength is *s*
Eccl 2:7 *s* cattle above all that were in
Is 1:9 had left unto us a very *s* remnant
Is 7:13 Is it a *s* thing for you to weary
Is 16:14 and the remnant shall be very *s*
Is 22:24 issue, all vessels of *s* quantity
Is 29:5 strangers shall be like *s* dust
Is 37:27 their inhabitants were of *s* power
Is 40:15 are counted as the *s* dust of the
Is 41:15 the mountains, and beat them *s*
Is 43:23 Thou hast not brought me the *s*
Is 54:7 For a *s* moment have I forsaken
Is 60:22 and a *s* one a strong nation
Jer 16:6 the *s* shall die in this land
Jer 30:19 them, and they shall not be *s*
Jer 44:28 Yet a *s* number that escape the
Jer 49:15 I will make thee *s* among the
Eze 16:20 this of thy whoredoms a *s* matter
Eze 34:18 Seemeth it a *s* thing unto you to
Dan 11:23 become strong with a *s* people
Amos 7:2 for he is *s*
Amos 7:5 for he is *s*
Amos 8:5 forth wheat, making the ephah *s*
Obad 2 I have made thee *s* among the
Zec 4:10 hath despised the day of *s* things
Mk 3:9 that a *s* ship should wait on him
Mk 8:7 And they had a few *s* fishes
Jn 2:15 he had made a scourge of *s* cords
Jn 6:9 barley loaves, and two *s* fishes
Acts 12:18 there was no *s* stir among the
Acts 15:2 and Barnabas had no *s* dissension
Acts 19:23 arose no *s* stir about that way
Acts 19:24 brought no *s* gain unto the
Acts 26:22 this day, witnessing both to *s*
Acts 27:20 no *s* tempest lay on us, all hope
1Cor 4:3 But with me it is a very *s* thing
Jas 3:4 turned about with a very *s* helm
Rev 11:18 and them that fear thy name, *s*
Rev 13:16 And he causeth all, both *s*
Rev 19:5 and ye that fear him, both *s*
Rev 19:18 men, both free and bond, both *s*
Rev 20:12 And I saw the dead, *s* and great,

**SMELL**

Gen 27:27 he smelled the *s* of his raiment
Gen 27:27 the *s* of my son is as the *s*
Ex 30:38 to *s* thereto, shall even be cut
Lev 26:31 I will not *s* the savour of your
Deut 4:28 see, nor hear, nor eat, nor *s*
Ps 45:8 All thy garments *s* of myrrh
Ps 115:6 noses have they, but they *s* not
Song 1:12 sendeth forth the *s* thereof
Song 2:13 the tender grape give a good *s*
Song 4:10 the *s* of thine ointments than all
Song 4:11 the *s* of thy garments is like the
Song 4:11 garments is like the *s* of Lebanon
Song 7:8 the *s* of thy nose like apples
Song 7:13 The mandrakes give a *s*, and at our
Is 3:24 of sweet *s* there shall be stink
Dan 3:27 nor the *s* of fire had passed on
Hos 14:6 olive tree, and his *s* as Lebanon
Amos 5:21 I will not *s* in your solemn
Phil 4:18 from you, an odour of a sweet *s*

**SMITE**

Gen 8:21 neither will I again *s* any more
Gen 32:8 *s* it, then the other company
Gen 32:11 *s* me, and the mother with the
Ex 3:20 *s* Egypt with all my wonders which
Ex 7:17 I will *s* with the rod that is in
Ex 8:2 I will *s* all thy borders with
Ex 8:16 *s* the dust of the land, that it
Ex 9:15 out my hand, that I may *s* thee
Ex 12:12 will *s* all the firstborn in the
Ex 12:13 when I *s* the land of Egypt
Ex 12:23 pass through to *s* the Egyptians
Ex 12:23 come in unto your houses to *s* you
Ex 17:6 and thou shalt *s* the rock, and
Ex 21:18 one *s* another with a stone, or
Ex 21:20 if a man *s* his servant, or his
Ex 21:26 if a man *s* the eye of his servant
Ex 21:27 if he *s* out his manservant's
Num 14:12 I will *s* them with the pestilence
Num 22:6 shall prevail, that we may *s* them
Num 24:17 shall *s* the corners of Moab, and
Num 25:17 Vex the Midianites, and *s* them
Num 35:16 if he *s* him with an instrument of
Num 35:17 if he *s* him with throwing a stone
Num 35:18 Or if he *s* him with an hand
Num 35:21 Or in enmity *s* him with his hand,
Deut 7:2 thou shalt *s* them, and utterly
Deut 13:15 Thou shalt surely *s* the
Deut 19:11 *s* him mortally that he die, and
Deut 20:13 thou shalt *s* every male thereof
Deut 28:22 The LORD shall *s* thee with a
Deut 28:27 The LORD will *s* thee with the
Deut 28:28 The LORD shall *s* thee with
Deut 28:35 The LORD shall *s* thee in the
Deut 33:11 *s* through the loins of them that
Josh 7:3 three thousand men go up and *s* Ai
Josh 10:4 and help me, that we may *s* Gibeon
Josh 10:19 and *s* the hindmost of them
Josh 12:6 LORD and the children of Israel *s*
Josh 13:12 for these did Moses *s*, and cast
Judg 6:16 thou shalt *s* the Midianites as
Judg 20:31 and they began to *s* of the people
Judg 20:39 the battle, Benjamin began to *s*
Judg 21:10 Go and *s* the inhabitants of
1Sa 15:3 *s* Amalek, and utterly destroy all
1Sa 17:46 and I will *s* thee, and take thine
1Sa 18:11 I will *s* David even to the wall
1Sa 19:10 Saul sought to *s* David even to
1Sa 20:33 cast a javelin at him to *s* him
1Sa 23:2 Shall I go and *s* these Philistines
1Sa 23:2 *s* the Philistines, and save Keilah
1Sa 26:8 now therefore let me *s* him
1Sa 26:8 I will not *s* him the second time
1Sa 26:10 LORD liveth, the LORD shall *s* him
2Sa 2:22 should I *s* thee to the ground
2Sa 5:24 to *s* the host of the Philistines
2Sa 13:28 and when I say unto you, *S* Amnon
2Sa 15:14 *s* the city with the edge of the
2Sa 17:2 and I will *s* the king only
2Sa 18:11 why didst thou not *s* him there to
1Kin 14:15 For the LORD shall *s* Israel
1Kin 20:35 of the LORD, *S* me, I pray thee
1Kin 20:35 And the man refused to *s* him
1Kin 20:37 man, and said, *S* me, I pray thee
2Kin 3:19 ye shall *s* every fenced city, and
2Kin 6:18 *S* this people, I pray thee, with
2Kin 6:21 them, My father, shall I *s* them
2Kin 6:21 shall I *s* them
2Kin 6:22 answered, Thou shalt not *s* them
2Kin 6:22 wouldest thou *s* those whom thou
2Kin 9:7 thou shalt *s* the house of Ahab
2Kin 9:27 *S* him also in the chariot
2Kin 13:17 for thou shalt *s* the Syrians in
2Kin 13:18 king of Israel, *S* upon the ground
2Kin 13:19 now thou shalt *s* Syria but thrice
1Chr 14:15 to *s* the host of the Philistines
2Chr 21:14 plague will the LORD *s* thy people
Ps 121:6 The sun shall not *s* thee by day
Ps 141:5 Let the righteous *s* me
Prov 19:25 *S* a scorner, and the simple will
Is 3:17 Therefore the Lord will *s* with a
Is 10:24 he shall *s* thee with a rod, and
Is 11:4 he shall *s* the earth with the rod
Is 11:15 shall *s* it in the seven streams,
Is 19:22 And the LORD shall *s* Egypt
Is 19:22 he shall *s* and heal it
Is 49:10 shall the heat nor sun *s* them
Is 58:4 to *s* with the fist of wickedness
Jer 18:18 let us *s* him with the tongue, and
Jer 21:6 I will *s* the inhabitants of this
Jer 21:7 he shall *s* them with the edge of
Jer 43:11 he shall *s* the land of Egypt, and
Jer 46:13 come and *s* the land of Egypt
Jer 49:28 king of Babylon shall *s*, thus
Eze 5:2 part, and *s* about it with a knife
Eze 6:11 *S* with thine hand, and stamp with
Eze 9:5 after him through the city, and *s*
Eze 21:12 *s* therefore upon thy thigh
Eze 21:14 *s* thine hands together, and let
Eze 21:17 I will also *s* mine hands together
Eze 32:15 when I shall *s* all them that
Eze 39:3 I will *s* thy bow out of thy left
Amos 3:15 I will *s* the winter house with
Amos 6:11 he will *s* the great house with
Amos 9:1 *S* the lintel of the door, that
Mic 5:1 they shall *s* the judge of Israel
Nah 2:10 melteth, and the knees *s* together
Zec 9:4 he will *s* her power in the sea
Zec 10:11 shall *s* the waves in the sea, and
Zec 11:6 and they shall *s* the land, and out
Zec 12:4 I will *s* every horse with
Zec 12:4 will *s* every horse of the people
Zec 13:7 *s* the shepherd, and the sheep
Zec 14:12 plague wherewith the LORD will *s*
Zec 14:18 wherewith the LORD will *s* the
Mal 4:6 come and *s* the earth with a curse
Mt 5:39 but whosoever shall *s* thee on thy
Mt 24:49 And shall begin to *s* his
Mt 26:31 I will *s* the shepherd, and the
Mk 14:27 I will *s* the shepherd, and the
Lk 22:49 shall we *s* with the sword
Acts 23:2 by him to *s* him on the mouth
Acts 23:3 Paul unto him, God shall *s* thee
2Cor 11:20 if a man *s* you on the face
Rev 11:6 to *s* the earth with all plagues,
Rev 19:15 with it he should *s* the nations

**SMITETH**

Ex 21:12 He that *s* a man, so that he die,
Ex 21:15 he that *s* his father, or his
Deut 25:11 out of the hand of him that *s* him
Deut 27:24 Cursed be he that *s* his neighbour
Josh 15:16 He that *s* Kirjath-sepher, and
Judg 1:12 He that *s* Kirjath-sepher, and
2Sa 5:8 *s* the Jebusites, and the lame and
1Chr 11:6 Whosoever *s* the Jebusites first
Job 26:12 he *s* through the proud
Is 9:13 turneth not unto him that *s* them
Lam 3:30 his cheek to him that *s* him
Eze 7:9 know that I am the LORD that *s*
Lk 6:29 unto him that *s* thee on the one

**SMITHS**

2Kin 24:14 and all the craftsmen and *s*
2Kin 24:16 *s* a thousand, all that were
Jer 24:1 Judah, with the carpenters and *s*
Jer 29:2 and the carpenters, and the *s*

**SMITING**

Ex 2:11 he spied an Egyptian *s* an Hebrew
2Sa 8:13 a name when he returned from *s* of
1Kin 20:37 so that in *s* he wounded him
2Kin 3:24 they went forward *s* the Moabites
Mic 6:13 will I make thee sick in *s* thee

**SMITTEN**

Ex 7:25 that the LORD had *s* the river
Ex 9:31 And the flax and the barley was *s*
Ex 9:32 the wheat and the rie were not *s*
Ex 22:2 be *s* that he die, there shall no
Num 14:42 that ye be not *s* before your
Num 22:28 that thou hast *s* me these three
Num 22:32 Wherefore hast thou *s* thine ass
Num 33:4 which the LORD had *s* among them
Deut 1:42 lest ye be *s* before your enemies
Deut 28:7 thee to be *s* before thy face
Deut 28:25 thee to be *s* before thine enemies
Judg 1:8 *s* it with the edge of the sword,
Judg 20:32 They are *s* down before us, as at
Judg 20:36 of Benjamin saw that they were *s*

Judg 20:39 Surely they are *s* down before us
1Sa 4:2 battle, Israel was *s* before the
1Sa 4:3 the LORD *s* us to day before the
1Sa 4:10 fought, and Israel was *s*, and they
1Sa 5:12 died not were *s* with the emerods
1Sa 6:19 because the LORD had *s* many of
1Sa 7:10 they were *s* before Israel
1Sa 13:4 *s* a garrison of the Philistines
1Sa 30:1 *s* Ziklag, and burned it with fire
2Sa 2:31 of David had *s* of Benjamin
2Sa 8:9 had *s* all the host of Hadadezer
2Sa 8:10 against Hadadezer, and *s* him
2Sa 10:15 that they were *s* before Israel
2Sa 10:19 that they were *s* before Israel
2Sa 11:15 ye from him, that he may be *s*
1Kin 8:33 Israel be *s* down before the enemy
1Kin 11:15 after he had *s* every male in Edom
2Kin 2:14 and when he also had *s* the waters
2Kin 3:23 slain, and they have *s* one another
2Kin 13:19 have *s* five or six times
2Kin 13:19 then hadst thou *s* Syria till thou
2Kin 14:10 Thou hast indeed *s* Edom, and thine
1Chr 18:9 of Hamath heard how David had *s*
1Chr 18:10 against Hadarezer, and *s* him
2Chr 20:22 and they were *s*
2Chr 25:16 why shouldest thou be *s*
2Chr 25:19 Lo, thou hast *s* the Edomites
2Chr 26:20 out, because the LORD had *s* him
2Chr 28:17 *s* Judah, and carried away captives
Job 16:10 they have *s* me upon the cheek
Ps 3:7 for thou hast *s* all mine enemies
Ps 69:26 persecute him whom thou hast *s*
Ps 102:4 My heart is *s*, and withered like
Ps 143:3 he hath *s* my life down to the
Is 5:25 hand against them, and hath *s* them
Is 24:12 the gate is *s* with destruction
Is 27:7 Hath he *s* him, as he smote those
Is 53:4 stricken, *s* of God, and afflicted
Jer 2:30 In vain have I *s* your children
Jer 14:19 why hast thou *s* us, and there is
Jer 37:10 For though ye had *s* the whole
Eze 22:13 therefore I have *s* mine hand at
Eze 33:21 unto me, saying, The city is *s*
Eze 40:1 year after that the city was *s*
Hos 6:1 he hath *s*, and he will bind us up
Hos 9:16 Ephraim is *s*, their root is dried
Amos 4:9 I have *s* you with blasting and
Acts 23:3 me to be *s* contrary to the law
Rev 8:12 the third part of the sun was *s*

## SMOKE

Gen 19:28 the *s* of the country went up as
Gen 19:28 went up as the *s* of a furnace
Ex 19:18 mount Sinai was altogether on a *s*
Ex 19:18 the *s* thereof ascended as the
Ex 19:18 ascended as the *s* of a furnace
Deut 29:20 jealousy shall *s* against that man
Josh 8:20 the *s* of the city ascended up to
Josh 8:21 that the *s* of the city ascended,
Judg 20:38 with *s* rise up out of the city
Judg 20:40 of the city with a pillar of *s*
2Sa 22:9 There went up a *s* out of his
Job 41:20 Out of his nostrils goeth *s*
Ps 18:8 There went up a *s* out of his
Ps 37:20 into *s* shall they consume away
Ps 68:2 As *s* is driven away, so drive
Ps 74:1 why doth thine anger *s* against
Ps 102:3 For my days are consumed like *s*
Ps 104:32 he toucheth the hills, and they *s*
Ps 119:83 am become like a bottle in the *s*
Ps 144:5 the mountains, and they shall *s*
Prov 10:26 as *s* to the eyes, so is the
Song 3:6 the wilderness like pillars of *s*
Is 4:5 *s* by day, and the shining of a
Is 6:4 and the house was filled with *s*
Is 9:18 mount up like the lifting up of *s*
Is 14:31 shall come from the north a *s*
Is 34:10 the *s* thereof shall go up for
Is 51:6 heavens shall vanish away like *s*
Is 65:5 These are a *s* in my nose, a fire
Hos 13:3 as the *s* out of the chimney
Joel 2:30 blood, and fire, and pillars of *s*
Nah 2:13 I will burn her chariots in the *s*
Acts 2:19 blood, and fire, and vapour of *s*
Rev 8:4 the *s* of the incense, which came
Rev 9:2 there arose a *s* out of the pit,
Rev 9:2 as the *s* of a great furnace
Rev 9:2 by reason of the *s* of the pit
Rev 9:3 there came out of the *s* locusts
Rev 9:17 of their mouths issued fire and *s*
Rev 9:18 killed, by the fire, and by the *s*
Rev 14:11 the *s* of their torment ascendeth
Rev 15:8 with *s* from the glory of God
Rev 18:9 shall see the *s* of her burning
Rev 18:18 they saw the *s* of her burning
Rev 19:3 her *s* rose up for ever and ever

## SMOKING

Gen 15:17 it was dark, behold a *s* furnace
Ex 20:18 of the trumpet, and the mountain *s*
Is 7:4 two tails of these *s* firebrands
Is 42:3 the *s* flax shall he not quench
Mt 12:20 *s* flax shall he not quench, till

## SMOOTH

Gen 27:11 is a hairy man, and I am a *s* man
Gen 27:16 hands, and upon the *s* of his neck
1Sa 17:40 chose him five *s* stones out of
Is 30:10 things, speak unto us *s* things
Is 57:6 Among the *s* stones of the stream
Lk 3:5 and the rough ways shall be made *s*

## SMOTE

Gen 14:5 *s* the Rephaims in Ashteroth
Gen 14:7 and *s* all the country of the
Gen 14:15 *s* them, and pursued them unto
Gen 19:11 they *s* the men that were at the
Gen 36:35 who *s* Midian in the field of Moab
Ex 7:20 *s* the waters that were in the
Ex 8:17 *s* the dust of the earth, and it
Ex 9:25 the hail *s* throughout all the
Ex 9:25 the hail *s* every herb of the
Ex 12:27 when he *s* the Egyptians, and
Ex 12:29 that at midnight the LORD *s* all
Ex 21:19 then shall he that *s* him be quit
Num 3:13 for on the day that I *s* all the
Num 8:17 on the day that I *s* every
Num 11:33 the LORD *s* the people with a very
Num 14:45 *s* them, and discomfited them, even
Num 20:11 with his rod he *s* the rock twice
Num 21:24 Israel *s* him with the edge of the
Num 21:35 So they *s* him, and his sons, and
Num 22:23 Balaam *s* the ass, to turn her
Num 22:25 and he *s* her again
Num 22:27 he *s* the ass with a staff
Num 24:10 and he *s* his hands together
Num 32:4 LORD *s* before the congregation of
Num 35:21 he that *s* him shall surely be put
Deut 2:33 we *s* him, and his sons, and all his
Deut 3:3 we *s* him until none was left to
Deut 4:46 Moses and the children of Israel *s*
Deut 25:18 *s* the hindmost of thee, even all
Deut 29:7 us unto battle, and we *s* them
Josh 7:5 the men of Ai *s* of them about
Josh 7:5 and *s* them in the going down
Josh 8:22 and they *s* them, so that they let
Josh 8:24 *s* it with the edge of the sword
Josh 9:18 the children of Israel *s* them not
Josh 10:10 *s* them to Azekah, and unto
Josh 10:26 And afterward Joshua *s* them
Josh 10:28 *s* it with the edge of the sword,
Josh 10:30 he *s* it with the edge of the
Josh 10:32 *s* it with the edge of the sword,
Josh 10:33 and Joshua *s* him and his people,
Josh 10:35 *s* it with the edge of the sword,
Josh 10:37 *s* it with the edge of the sword,
Josh 10:39 they *s* them with the edge of the
Josh 10:40 So Joshua *s* all the country of
Josh 10:41 Joshua *s* them from Kadesh-barnea
Josh 11:8 who *s* them, and chased them unto
Josh 11:8 and they *s* them, until they left
Josh 11:10 *s* the king thereof with the sword
Josh 11:11 they *s* all the souls that were
Josh 11:12 *s* them with the edge of the sword
Josh 11:14 but every man they *s* with the
Josh 11:17 he took, and *s* them, and slew them
Josh 12:1 which the children of Israel *s*
Josh 12:7 the children of Israel *s* on this
Josh 13:21 whom Moses *s* with the princes of
Josh 19:47 *s* it with the edge of the sword,
Josh 20:5 because he *s* his neighbour
Judg 1:25 they *s* the city with the edge of
Judg 3:13 *s* Israel, and possessed the city
Judg 4:21 *s* the nail into his temples, and
Judg 5:26 and with the hammer she *s* Sisera
Judg 5:26 she *s* off his head, when she had
Judg 7:13 *s* it that it fell, and overturned
Judg 8:11 Nobah and Jogbehah, and *s* the host
Judg 9:43 rose up against them, and *s* them
Judg 11:21 hand of Israel, and they *s* them
Judg 11:33 he *s* them from Aroer, even till
Judg 12:4 and the men of Gilead *s* Ephraim
Judg 15:8 he *s* them hip and thigh with a
Judg 18:27 they *s* them with the edge of the
Judg 20:35 the LORD *s* Benjamin before Israel
Judg 20:37 *s* all the city with the edge of
Judg 20:48 *s* them with the edge of the sword
1Sa 4:8 these are the Gods that *s* the
1Sa 5:6 *s* them with emerods, even Ashdod
1Sa 5:9 he *s* the men of the city, both
1Sa 6:9 that it is not his hand that *s* us
1Sa 6:19 he *s* the men of Beth-shemesh,
1Sa 6:19 even he *s* of the people fifty
1Sa 7:11 *s* them, until they came under
1Sa 13:3 Jonathan *s* the garrison of the
1Sa 14:31 they *s* the Philistines that day
1Sa 14:48 *s* the Amalekites, and delivered
1Sa 15:7 Saul *s* the Amalekites from
1Sa 17:35 *s* him, and delivered it out of his
1Sa 17:35 his beard, and *s* him, and slew him
1Sa 17:49 *s* the Philistine in his forehead,
1Sa 17:50 *s* the Philistine, and slew him
1Sa 19:10 he *s* the javelin into the wall
1Sa 22:19 *s* he with the edge of the sword,
1Sa 23:5 *s* them with a great slaughter
1Sa 24:5 that David's heart *s* him
1Sa 25:38 days after, that the LORD *s* Nabal
1Sa 27:9 David *s* the land, and left neither
1Sa 30:17 David *s* them from the twilight
2Sa 1:15 And he *s* him that he died
2Sa 2:23 spear *s* him under the fifth rib
2Sa 3:27 *s* him there under the fifth rib,
2Sa 4:6 they *s* him under the fifth rib
2Sa 4:7 in his bedchamber, and they *s* him
2Sa 5:20 David *s* them there, and said, The
2Sa 5:25 *s* the Philistines from Geba until
2Sa 6:7 God *s* him there for his error
2Sa 8:1 that David *s* the Philistines, and
2Sa 8:2 he *s* Moab, and measured them with
2Sa 8:3 David *s* also Hadadezer, the son
2Sa 10:18 *s* Shobach the captain of their
2Sa 11:21 Who *s* Abimelech the son of
2Sa 14:6 them, but the one *s* the other
2Sa 14:7 Deliver him that *s* his brother
2Sa 18:15 about and *s* Absalom, and slew him
2Sa 20:10 so he *s* him therewith in the
2Sa 21:17 *s* the Philistine, and killed him
2Sa 23:10 *s* the Philistines until his hand
2Sa 24:10 David's heart *s* him after that he
2Sa 24:17 saw the angel that *s* the people
1Kin 15:20 of Israel, and *s* Ijon, and Dan, and
1Kin 15:27 Baasha *s* him at Gibbethon, which
1Kin 15:29 that he *s* all the house of
1Kin 16:10 *s* him, and killed him, in the
1Kin 20:21 *s* the horses and chariots, and slew
1Kin 20:37 And the man *s* him, so that in
1Kin 22:24 *s* Micaiah on the cheek, and said,
1Kin 22:34 *s* the king of Israel between the
2Kin 2:8 *s* the waters, and they were
2Kin 2:14 *s* the waters, and said, Where is
2Kin 3:24 *s* the Moabites, so that they fled
2Kin 3:25 slingers went about it, and *s* it
2Kin 6:18 And he *s* them with blindness
2Kin 8:21 *s* the Edomites which compassed
2Kin 9:24 *s* Jehoram between his arms, and
2Kin 10:25 they *s* them with the edge of the
2Kin 10:32 Hazael *s* them in all the coasts
2Kin 12:21 his servants, *s* him, and he died
2Kin 13:18 And he *s* thrice, and stayed
2Kin 15:5 And the LORD *s* the king, so that
2Kin 15:10 *s* him before the people, and slew
2Kin 15:14 *s* Shallum the son of Jabesh in
2Kin 15:16 Then Menahem *s* Tiphsah, and all
2Kin 15:16 not to him, therefore he *s* it
2Kin 15:25 *s* him in Samaria, in the palace
2Kin 15:30 *s* him, and slew him, and reigned in
2Kin 18:8 He *s* the Philistines, even unto
2Kin 19:35 *s* in the camp of the Assyrians an
2Kin 19:37 Sharezer his sons *s* him with the
2Kin 25:21 And the king of Babylon *s* them
2Kin 25:25 *s* Gedaliah, that he died, and the
1Chr 1:46 which *s* Midian in the field of
1Chr 4:41 *s* their tents, and the habitations
1Chr 4:43 they *s* the rest of the Amalekites
1Chr 13:10 he *s* him, because he put his hand
1Chr 14:11 and David *s* them there
1Chr 14:16 and they *s* the host of the
1Chr 18:1 that David *s* the Philistines, and
1Chr 18:2 And he *s* Moab
1Chr 18:3 David *s* Hadarezer king of Zobah
1Chr 20:1 Joab *s* Rabbah, and destroyed it
1Chr 21:7 therefore he *s* Israel

2Chr 13:15 came to pass, that God *s* Jeroboam
2Chr 14:12 So the LORD *s* the Ethiopians
2Chr 14:14 they *s* all the cities round about
2Chr 14:15 They *s* also the tents of cattle,
2Chr 16:4 and they *s* Ijon, and Dan, and
2Chr 18:23 *s* Micaiah upon the cheek, and said
2Chr 18:33 *s* the king of Israel between the
2Chr 21:9 *s* the Edomites which compassed
2Chr 21:18 after all this the LORD *s* him in
2Chr 22:5 and the Syrians *s* Joram
2Chr 25:11 *s* of the children of Seir ten
2Chr 25:13 *s* three thousand of them, and took
2Chr 28:5 and they *s* him, and carried away a
2Chr 28:5 who *s* him with a great slaughter
2Chr 28:23 the gods of Damascus, which *s* him
Neh 13:25 *s* certain of them, and plucked off
Est 9:5 Thus the Jews *s* all their enemies
Job 1:19 *s* the four corners of the house,
Job 2:7 *s* Job with sore boils from the
Ps 60:*t* *s* of Edom in the valley of salt
Ps 78:20 he *s* the rock, that the waters
Ps 78:31 *s* down the chosen men of Israel
Ps 78:51 *s* all the firstborn in Egypt
Ps 78:66 he *s* his enemies in the hinder
Ps 105:33 He *s* their vines also and their
Ps 105:36 He *s* also all the firstborn in
Ps 135:8 Who *s* the firstborn of Egypt,
Ps 135:10 Who *s* great nations, and slew
Ps 136:10 To him that *s* Egypt in their
Ps 136:17 To him which *s* great kings
Song 5:7 the city found me, they *s* me
Is 10:20 again stay upon him that *s* them
Is 14:6 He who *s* the people in wrath with
Is 14:29 rod of him that *s* thee is broken
Is 27:7 as he *s* those that
Is 27:7 those that *s* him
Is 30:31 beaten down, which *s* with a rod
Is 37:36 *s* in the camp of the Assyrians an
Is 37:38 Sharezer his sons *s* him with the
Is 41:7 the hammer him that *s* the anvil
Is 57:17 was I wroth, and *s* him
Is 60:10 for in my wrath I *s* thee, but in
Jer 20:2 Then Pashur *s* Jeremiah the
Jer 31:19 was instructed, I *s* upon my thigh
Jer 37:15 *s* him, and put him in prison in
Jer 41:2 *s* Gedaliah the son of Ahikam the
Jer 46:2 Nebuchadrezzar king of Babylon *s*
Jer 47:1 before that Pharaoh *s* Gaza
Jer 52:27 And the king of Babylon *s* them
Dan 2:34 which *s* the image upon his feet
Dan 2:35 the stone that *s* the image became
Dan 5:6 his knees *s* one against another
Dan 8:7 *s* the ram, and brake his two horns
Jonah 4:7 it *s* the gourd that it withered
Hag 2:17 I *s* you with blasting and with
Mt 26:51 high priest's, and *s* off his ear
Mt 26:67 others *s* him with the palms of
Mt 26:68 Christ, Who is he that *s* thee
Mt 27:30 the reed, and *s* him on the head
Mk 14:47 *s* a servant of the high priest,
Mk 15:19 they *s* him on the head with a
Lk 18:13 but *s* upon his breast, saying,
Lk 22:50 one of them *s* the servant of the
Lk 22:63 held Jesus mocked him, and *s* him
Lk 22:64 Prophesy, who is it that *s* thee
Lk 23:48 *s* their breasts, and returned
Jn 18:10 *s* the high priest's servant, and
Jn 19:3 they *s* him with their hands
Acts 7:24 was oppressed, and *s* the Egyptian
Acts 12:7 he *s* Peter on the side, and raised
Acts 12:23 the angel of the Lord *s* him

**SMYRNA** *(smir'-na) A city of Ionia in Asia Minor.*
Rev 1:11 unto Ephesus, and unto *S*, and unto
Rev 2:8 angel of the church in *S* write

**SNARE**
Ex 10:7 shall this man be a *s* unto us
Ex 23:33 it will surely be a *s* unto thee
Ex 34:12 lest it be for a *s* in the midst
Deut 7:16 for that will be a *s* unto thee
Judg 2:3 their gods shall be a *s* unto you
Judg 8:27 thing became a *s* unto Gideon
1Sa 18:21 her, that she may be a *s* to him
1Sa 28:9 then layest thou a *s* for my life
Job 18:8 own feet, and he walketh upon a *s*
Job 18:10 The *s* is laid for him in the
Ps 69:22 table become a *s* before them
Ps 91:3 thee from the *s* of the fowler
Ps 106:36 which were a *s* unto them
Ps 119:110 The wicked have laid a *s* for me
Ps 124:7 bird out of the *s* of the fowlers
Ps 124:7 the *s* is broken, and we are
Ps 140:5 The proud have hid a *s* for me
Ps 142:3 have they privily laid a *s* for me
Prov 7:23 as a bird hasteth to the *s*
Prov 18:7 and his lips are the *s* of his soul
Prov 20:25 It is a *s* to the man who
Prov 22:25 his ways, and get a *s* to thy soul
Prov 29:6 of an evil man there is a *s*
Prov 29:8 men bring a city into a *s*
Prov 29:25 The fear of man bringeth a *s*
Eccl 9:12 birds that are caught in the *s*
Is 8:14 for a *s* to the inhabitants of
Is 24:17 Fear, and the pit, and the *s*
Is 24:18 the pit shall be taken in the *s*
Is 29:21 lay a *s* for him that reproveth in
Jer 48:43 Fear, and the pit, and the *s*
Jer 48:44 the pit shall be taken in the *s*
Jer 50:24 I have laid a *s* for thee, and thou
Lam 3:47 a *s* is come upon us, desolation
Eze 12:13 him, and he shall be taken in my *s*
Eze 17:20 him, and he shall be taken in my *s*
Hos 5:1 ye have been a *s* on Mizpah
Hos 9:8 but the prophet is a *s* of a
Amos 3:5 a bird fall in a *s* upon the earth
Amos 3:5 one take up a *s* from the earth
Lk 21:35 For as a *s* shall it come on all
Rom 11:9 Let their table be made a *s*
1Cor 7:35 not that I may cast a *s* upon you
1Ti 3:7 reproach and the *s* of the devil
1Ti 6:9 rich fall into temptation and a *s*
2Ti 2:26 out of the *s* of the devil

**SNARED**
Deut 7:25 unto thee, lest thou be *s* therein
Deut 12:30 thou be not *s* by following them
Ps 9:16 the wicked is *s* in the work of
Prov 6:2 Thou art *s* with the words of thy
Prov 12:13 The wicked is *s* by the
Eccl 9:12 the sons of men *s* in an evil time
Is 8:15 and fall, and be broken, and be *s*
Is 28:13 fall backward, and be broken, and *s*
Is 42:22 they are all of them *s* in holes

**SNARES**
Josh 23:13 but they shall be *s* and traps unto
2Sa 22:6 the *s* of death prevented me
Job 22:10 Therefore *s* are round about thee,
Job 40:24 his nose pierceth through *s*
Ps 11:6 Upon the wicked he shall rain *s*
Ps 18:5 the *s* of death prevented me
Ps 38:12 seek after my life lay *s* for me
Ps 64:5 they commune of laying *s* privily
Ps 141:9 Keep me from the *s* which they
Prov 13:14 to depart from the *s* of death
Prov 14:27 to depart from the *s* of death
Prov 22:5 *s* are in the way of the froward
Eccl 7:26 death the woman, whose heart is *s*
Jer 5:26 lay wait, as he that setteth *s*
Jer 18:22 to take me, and hid *s* for my feet

**SNOW**
Ex 4:6 behold, his hand was leprous as *s*
Num 12:10 Miriam became leprous, white as *s*
2Sa 23:20 the midst of a pit in time of *s*
2Kin 5:27 presence a leper as white as *s*
Job 6:16 the ice, and wherein the *s* is hid
Job 9:30 If I wash myself with *s* water
Job 24:19 and heat consume the *s* waters
Job 37:6 For he saith to the *s*, Be thou on
Job 38:22 into the treasures of the *s*
Ps 51:7 me, and I shall be whiter than *s*
Ps 68:14 it, it was white as *s* in Salmon
Ps 147:16 He giveth *s* like wool
Ps 148:8 Fire, and hail; *s*, and vapours
Prov 25:13 As the cold of *s* in the time of
Prov 26:1 As *s* in summer, and as rain in
Prov 31:21 afraid of the *s* for her household
Is 1:18 they shall be as white as *s*
Is 55:10 the *s* from heaven, and returneth
Jer 18:14 Will a man leave the *s* of Lebanon
Lam 4:7 Her Nazarites were purer than *s*
Dan 7:9 sit, whose garment was white as *s*
Mt 28:3 and his raiment white as *s*
Mk 9:3 shining, exceeding white as *s*
Rev 1:14 white like wool, as white as *s*

**SNUFFERS**
Ex 37:23 he made his seven lamps, and his *s*
1Kin 7:50 And the bowls, and the *s*, and the
2Kin 12:13 of the LORD bowls of silver, *s*
2Kin 25:14 pots, and the shovels, and the *s*
2Chr 4:22 And the *s*, and the basons, and the
Jer 52:18 also, and the shovels, and the *s*

**SOBER**
2Cor 5:13 or whether we be *s*, it is for
1Th 5:6 but let us watch and be *s*
1Th 5:8 let us, who are of the day, be *s*
1Ti 3:2 husband of one wife, vigilant, *s*
1Ti 3:11 wives be grave, not slanderers, *s*
Titus 1:8 a lover of good men, *s*, just,
Titus 2:2 That the aged men be *s*, grave,
Titus 2:4 may teach the young women to be *s*
Titus 2:6 likewise exhort to be *s* minded
1Pet 1:13 up the loins of your mind, be *s*
1Pet 4:7 be ye therefore *s*, and watch unto
1Pet 5:8 Be *s*, be vigilant

**SOCHO** *(so'-ko)* See SOCHOH. *A son of Heber.*
1Chr 4:18 Gedor, and Heber the father of *S*

**SOCHOH** *(so'-ko)* See SHOCHOH, SOCHO, SOCOH. *A city in Judah near Adullam.*
1Kin 4:10 to him pertained *S*, and all the

**SOCKETS**
Ex 26:19 thou shalt make forty *s* of silver
Ex 26:19 two *s* under one board for his two
Ex 26:19 two *s* under another board for his
Ex 26:21 And their forty *s* of silver
Ex 26:21 two *s* under one board
Ex 26:21 two *s* under another board
Ex 26:25 *s* of silver, sixteen *s*
Ex 26:25 two *s* under one board
Ex 26:25 two *s* under another board
Ex 26:32 gold, upon the four *s* of silver
Ex 26:37 cast five *s* of brass for them
Ex 27:10 their twenty *s* shall be of brass
Ex 27:11 and their twenty *s* of brass
Ex 27:12 their pillars ten, and their *s* ten
Ex 27:14 pillars three, and their *s* three
Ex 27:15 pillars three, and their *s* three
Ex 27:16 shall be four, and their *s* four
Ex 27:17 be of silver, and their *s* of brass
Ex 27:18 twined linen, and their *s* of brass
Ex 35:11 his bars, his pillars, and his *s*
Ex 35:17 court, his pillars, and their *s*
Ex 36:24 forty *s* of silver he made under
Ex 36:24 two *s* under one board for his two
Ex 36:24 two *s* under another board for his
Ex 36:26 And their forty *s* of silver
Ex 36:26 two *s* under one board
Ex 36:26 two *s* under another board
Ex 36:30 *s* were sixteen *s* of silver
Ex 36:30 under every board two *s*
Ex 36:36 he cast for them four *s* of silver
Ex 36:38 but their five *s* were of brass
Ex 38:10 twenty, and their brasen *s* twenty
Ex 38:11 and their *s* of brass twenty
Ex 38:12 their pillars ten, and their *s* ten
Ex 38:14 pillars three, and their *s* three
Ex 38:15 pillars three, and their *s* three
Ex 38:17 the *s* for the pillars were of
Ex 38:19 four, and their *s* of brass four
Ex 38:27 were cast the *s* of the sanctuary
Ex 38:27 and the *s* of the vail
Ex 38:27 an hundred *s* of the hundred
Ex 38:30 therewith he made the *s* to the
Ex 38:31 the *s* of the court round about,
Ex 38:31 the *s* of the court gate, and all
Ex 39:33 bars, and his pillars, and his *s*
Ex 39:40 the court, his pillars, and his *s*
Ex 40:18 the tabernacle, and fastened his *s*
Num 3:36 the *s* thereof, and all the vessels
Num 3:37 the court round about, and their *s*
Num 4:31 pillars thereof, and *s* thereof,
Num 4:32 the court round about, and their *s*
Song 5:15 marble, set upon *s* of fine gold

**SOCOH** *(so'-ko)* See SOCHOH.
*1. Same as Sochoh.*
Josh 15:35 Jarmuth, and Adullam, *S*, and Azekah
*2. A city in the hill country of Judah.*
Josh 15:48 Shamir, and Jattir, and *S*,

**SODDEN**
Ex 12:9 nor *s* at all with water, but
Lev 6:28 wherein it is *s* shall be broken
Lev 6:28 if it be *s* in a brasen pot, it
Num 6:19 take the *s* shoulder of the ram
1Sa 2:15 he will not have *s* flesh of thee
Lam 4:10 women have *s* their own children

**SODI** *(so'-di) A spy sent to the Promised Land.*
Num 13:10 of Zebulun, Gaddiel the son of *S*

**SODOM** *(sod'-om)* See SODOMA, SODOMITE. *A city on the Salt Sea.*
Gen 10:19 as thou goest, unto *S*, and
Gen 13:10 before the LORD destroyed *S*
Gen 13:12 and pitched his tent toward *S*
Gen 13:13 But the men of *S* were wicked
Gen 14:2 made war with Bera king of *S*
Gen 14:8 And there went out the king of *S*
Gen 14:10 and the kings of *S* and Gomorrah
Gen 14:11 And they took all the goods of *S*
Gen 14:12 brother's son, who dwelt in *S*
Gen 14:17 the king of *S* went out to meet
Gen 14:21 the king of *S* said unto Abram,
Gen 14:22 And Abram said to the king of *S*
Gen 18:16 from thence, and looked toward *S*
Gen 18:20 LORD said, Because the cry of *S*
Gen 18:22 from thence, and went toward *S*
Gen 18:26 If I find in *S* fifty righteous
Gen 19:1 came two angels to *S* at even
Gen 19:1 and Lot sat in the gate of *S*
Gen 19:4 of the city, even the men of *S*
Gen 19:24 Then the LORD rained upon *S*
Gen 19:28 he looked toward *S* and Gomorrah
Deut 29:23 therein, like the overthrow of *S*
Deut 32:32 their vine is of the vine of *S*
Is 1:9 remnant, we should have been as *S*
Is 1:10 word of the LORD, ye rulers of *S*
Is 3:9 and they declare their sin as *S*
Is 13:19 shall be as when God overthrew *S*
Jer 23:14 they are all of them unto me as *S*
Jer 49:18 As in the overthrow of *S* and
Jer 50:40 As God overthrew *S* and Gomorrah
Lam 4:6 the punishment of the sin of *S*
Eze 16:46 dwelleth at thy right hand, is *S*
Eze 16:48 *S* thy sister hath not done, she
Eze 16:49 was the iniquity of thy sister *S*
Eze 16:53 captivity, the captivity of *S*
Eze 16:55 When thy sisters, *S* and her
Eze 16:56 For thy sister *S* was not
Amos 4:11 some of you, as God overthrew *S*
Zeph 2:9 Israel, Surely Moab shall be as *S*
Mt 10:15 more tolerable for the land of *S*
Mt 11:23 done in thee, had been done in *S*
Mt 11:24 land of *S* in the day of judgment
Mk 6:11 It shall be more tolerable for *S*
Lk 10:12 more tolerable in that day for *S*
Lk 17:29 Lot went out of *S* it rained fire
2Pet 2:6 And turning the cities of *S*
Jude 7 Even as *S* and Gomorrha, and the
Rev 11:8 which spiritually is called *S*

**SODOMA** *(sod'-o-mah)* See SODOM. *Greek form of Sodom.*
Rom 9:29 left us a seed, we had been as *S*

**SOEVER**
Lev 15:9 what saddle *s* he rideth upon that
Lev 17:3 What man *s* there be of the house
Lev 22:4 What man *s* of the seed of Aaron
Deut 12:32 What thing *s* I command you,
2Sa 15:35 that what thing *s* thou shalt hear
2Sa 24:3 the people, how many *s* they be
1Kin 8:38 supplication *s* be made by any man
2Chr 6:29 *s* shall be made of any man
2Chr 19:10 what cause *s* shall come to you of
Mk 3:28 wherewith *s* they shall blaspheme
Mk 6:10 In what place *s* ye enter into a
Mk 11:24 unto you, What things *s* ye desire
Jn 5:19 for what things *s* he doeth
Jn 20:23 Whose *s* sins ye remit, they are
Jn 20:23 whose *s* sins ye retain, they are
Rom 3:19 that what things *s* the law saith

**SOFT**
Job 23:16 For God maketh my heart *s*
Job 41:3 will he speak *s* words unto thee
Ps 65:10 thou makest it *s* with showers
Prov 15:1 A *s* answer turneth away wrath
Prov 25:15 a *s* tongue breaketh the bone
Mt 11:8 A man clothed in *s* raiment
Mt 11:8 they that wear *s* clothing are in
Lk 7:25 A man clothed in *s* raiment

**SOFTLY**
Gen 33:14 and I will lead on *s*, according as
Judg 4:21 went *s* unto him, and smote the
Ruth 3:7 and she came *s*, and uncovered his
1Kin 21:27 and lay in sackcloth, and went *s*
Is 8:6 the waters of Shiloah that go *s*
Is 38:15 I shall go *s* all my years in the
Acts 27:13 And when the south wind blew *s*

**SOJOURN**
Gen 12:10 went down into Egypt to *s* there
Gen 19:9 This one fellow came in to *s*
Gen 26:3 *S* in this land, and I will be with
Gen 47:4 For to *s* in the land are we come
Ex 12:48 when a stranger shall *s* with thee
Lev 17:8 the strangers which *s* among you
Lev 17:10 of the strangers that *s* among you
Lev 17:13 of the strangers that *s* among you
Lev 19:33 if a stranger *s* with thee in your
Lev 20:2 of the strangers that *s* in Israel
Lev 25:45 the strangers that do *s* among you
Num 9:14 if a stranger shall *s* among you
Num 15:14 And if a stranger *s* with you
Judg 17:8 to *s* where he could find a place
Judg 17:9 I go to *s* where I may find a
Ruth 1:1 went to *s* in the country of Moab
1Kin 17:20 evil upon the widow with whom I *s*
2Kin 8:1 *s* wheresoever thou canst *s*
Ps 120:5 that I *s* in Mesech, that I dwell
Is 23:7 shall carry her afar off to *s*
Is 52:4 aforetime into Egypt to *s* there
Jer 42:15 into Egypt, and go to *s* there
Jer 42:17 faces to go into Egypt to *s* there
Jer 42:22 whither ye desire to go and to *s*
Jer 43:2 say, Go not into Egypt to *s* there
Jer 44:12 into the land of Egypt to *s* there
Jer 44:14 into the land of Egypt to *s* there
Jer 44:28 into the land of Egypt to *s* there
Lam 4:15 They shall no more *s* there
Eze 20:38 out of the country where they *s*
Eze 47:22 to the strangers that *s* among you
Acts 7:6 seed should *s* in a strange land

**SOJOURNED**
Gen 20:1 Kadesh and Shur, and *s* in Gerar
Gen 21:23 to the land wherein thou hast *s*
Gen 21:34 Abraham *s* in the Philistines'
Gen 32:4 I have *s* with Laban, and stayed
Gen 35:27 Hebron, where Abraham and Isaac *s*
Deut 18:6 out of all Israel, where he *s*
Deut 26:5 *s* there with a few, and became
Judg 17:7 who was a Levite, and he *s* there
Judg 19:16 and he *s* in Gibeah
2Kin 8:2 *s* in the land of the Philistines
Ps 105:23 Jacob *s* in the land of Ham
Heb 11:9 By faith he *s* in the land of

**SOJOURNER**
Gen 23:4 I am a stranger and a *s* with you
Lev 22:10 a *s* of the priest, or an hired
Lev 25:35 though he be a stranger, or a *s*
Lev 25:40 as an hired servant, and as a *s*
Lev 25:47 if a *s* or stranger wax rich by
Lev 25:47 unto the stranger or *s* by thee
Num 35:15 stranger, and for the *s* among them
Ps 39:12 I am a stranger with thee, and a *s*

**SOJOURNETH**
Ex 3:22 of her that *s* in her house,
Ex 12:49 the stranger that *s* among you
Lev 16:29 or a stranger that *s* among you
Lev 17:12 that *s* among you eat blood
Lev 18:26 nor any stranger that *s* among you
Lev 25:6 for thy stranger that *s* with thee
Num 15:15 for the stranger that *s* with you
Num 15:16 for the stranger that *s* with you
Num 15:26 and the stranger that *s* among them
Num 15:29 the stranger that *s* among them
Num 19:10 the stranger that *s* among them
Josh 20:9 the stranger that *s* among them
Ezr 1:4 remaineth in any place where he *s*
Eze 14:7 of the stranger that *s* in Israel
Eze 47:23 that in what tribe the stranger *s*

**SOLD**
Gen 25:33 he *s* his birthright unto Jacob
Gen 31:15 for he hath *s* us, and hath quite
Gen 37:28 *s* Joseph to the Ishmeelites for
Gen 37:36 the Midianites *s* him into Egypt
Gen 41:56 and *s* unto the Egyptians
Gen 42:6 he it was that *s* to all the
Gen 45:4 brother, whom ye *s* into Egypt
Gen 45:5 yourselves, that ye *s* me hither
Gen 47:20 for the Egyptians *s* every man his
Gen 47:22 wherefore they *s* not their lands
Ex 22:3 then he shall be *s* for his theft
Lev 25:23 The land shall not be *s* for ever
Lev 25:25 poor, and hath *s* away some of his
Lev 25:25 redeem that which his brother *s*
Lev 25:27 unto the man to whom he *s* it
Lev 25:28 then that which is *s* shall remain
Lev 25:29 within a whole year after it is *s*
Lev 25:33 then the house that was *s*
Lev 25:34 of their cities may not be *s*
Lev 25:39 be waxen poor, and be *s* unto thee
Lev 25:42 they shall not be *s* as bondmen
Lev 25:48 After that he is *s* he may be
Lev 25:50 him from the year that he was *s*
Lev 27:20 or if he have *s* the field to
Lev 27:27 then it shall be *s* according to
Lev 27:28 shall be *s* or redeemed
Deut 15:12 be *s* unto thee, and serve thee six
Deut 28:68 there ye shall be *s* unto your
Deut 32:30 except their Rock had *s* them
Judg 2:14 he *s* them into the hands of their
Judg 3:8 he *s* them into the hand of
Judg 4:2 the LORD *s* them into the hand of
Judg 10:7 he *s* them into the hands of the
1Sa 12:9 he *s* them into the hand of Sisera
1Kin 21:20 because thou hast *s* thyself to
2Kin 6:25 until an ass's head was *s* for
2Kin 7:1 of fine flour be *s* for a shekel
2Kin 7:16 of fine flour was *s* for a shekel
2Kin 17:17 *s* themselves to do evil in the
Neh 5:8 which were *s* unto the heathen
Neh 5:8 or shall they be *s* unto us
Neh 13:15 the day wherein they *s* victuals
Neh 13:16 *s* on the sabbath unto the
Est 7:4 For we are *s*, I and my people, to
Est 7:4 But if we had been *s* for bondmen
Ps 105:17 Joseph, who was *s* for a servant
Is 50:1 is it to whom I have *s* you
Is 50:1 iniquities have ye *s* yourselves
Is 52:3 Ye have *s* yourselves for nought
Jer 34:14 which hath been *s* unto thee
Lam 5:4 our wood is *s* unto us
Eze 7:13 not return to that which is *s*
Joel 3:3 *s* a girl for wine, that they
Joel 3:6 have ye *s* unto the Grecians
Joel 3:7 the place whither ye have *s* them
Amos 2:6 because they *s* the righteous for
Mt 10:29 not two sparrows *s* for a farthing
Mt 13:46 *s* all that he had, and bought it
Mt 18:25 his lord commanded him to be *s*
Mt 21:12 God, and cast out all them that *s*
Mt 21:12 and the seats of them that *s* doves
Mt 26:9 might have been *s* for much
Mk 11:15 and began to cast out them that *s*
Mk 11:15 and the seats of them that *s* doves
Mk 14:5 For it might have been *s* for more
Lk 12:6 five sparrows *s* for two farthings
Lk 17:28 they drank, they bought, they *s*
Lk 19:45 to cast out them that *s* therein
Jn 2:14 in the temple those that *s* oxen
Jn 2:16 And said unto them that *s* doves
Jn 12:5 *s* for three hundred pence
Acts 2:45 *s* their possessions and goods, and
Acts 4:34 of lands or houses *s* them
Acts 4:34 prices of the things that were *s*
Acts 4:37 *s* it, and brought the money, and
Acts 5:1 his wife, *s* a possession,
Acts 5:4 and after it was *s*, was it not in
Acts 5:8 Tell me whether ye *s* the land for
Acts 7:9 with envy, *s* Joseph into Egypt
Rom 7:14 but I am carnal, *s* under sin
1Cor 10:25 Whatsoever is *s* in the shambles,
Heb 12:16 morsel of meat *s* his birthright

**SOLDIER**
Jn 19:23 four parts, to every *s* a part
Acts 10:7 a devout *s* of them that waited on
Acts 28:16 by himself with a *s* that kept him
Phil 2:25 companion in labour, and fellow *s*
2Ti 2:3 as a good *s* of Jesus Christ
2Ti 2:4 him who hath chosen him to be a *s*

**SOLDIERS**
1Chr 7:4 fathers, were bands of *s* for war
1Chr 7:11 thousand and two hundred *s*
2Chr 25:13 But the *s* of the army which
Ezr 8:22 require of the king a band of *s*
Is 15:4 therefore the armed *s* of Moab
Mt 8:9 authority, having *s* under me
Mt 27:27 Then the *s* of the governor took
Mt 27:27 unto him the whole band of *s*
Mt 28:12 they gave large money unto the *s*
Mk 15:16 the *s* led him away into the hall,
Lk 3:14 the *s* likewise demanded of him,
Lk 7:8 authority, having under me *s*
Lk 23:36 the *s* also mocked him, coming to

Jn 19:2 the s platted a crown of thorns,
Jn 19:23 Then the s, when they had
Jn 19:24 These things therefore the s did
Jn 19:32 Then came the s, and brake the
Jn 19:34 But one of the s with a spear
Acts 12:4 four quaternions of s to keep him
Acts 12:6 Peter was sleeping between two s
Acts 12:18 was no small stir among the s
Acts 21:32 Who immediately took s and
Acts 21:32 saw the chief captain and the s
Acts 21:35 that he was borne of the s for
Acts 23:10 them, commanded the s to go down
Acts 23:23 two hundred s to go to Caesarea
Acts 23:31 Then the s, as it was commanded
Acts 27:31 said to the centurion and to the s
Acts 27:32 Then the s cut off the ropes of

**SOLE**
Gen 8:9 no rest for the s of her foot
Deut 28:35 from the s of thy foot unto the
Deut 28:56 would not adventure to set the s
Deut 28:65 neither shall the s of thy foot
Josh 1:3 Every place that the s of your
2Sa 14:25 from the s of his foot even to
2Kin 19:24 with the s of my feet have I
Job 2:7 the s of his foot unto his crown
Is 1:6 From the s of the foot even unto
Is 37:25 with the s of my feet have I
Eze 1:7 the s of their feet was like the
Eze 1:7 was like the s of a calf's foot

**SOLEMN**
Lev 23:36 it is a s assembly
Num 10:10 your gladness, and in your s days
Num 15:3 offering, or in your s feasts
Num 29:35 day ye shall have a s assembly
Deut 16:8 a s assembly to the LORD thy God
Deut 16:15 Seven days shalt thou keep a s
2Kin 10:20 Proclaim a s assembly for Baal
2Chr 2:4 on the s feasts of the LORD our
2Chr 7:9 eighth day they made a s assembly
2Chr 8:13 the new moons, and on the s feasts
Neh 8:18 the eighth day was a s assembly
Ps 81:3 appointed, on our s feast day
Ps 92:3 upon the harp with a s sound
Is 1:13 is iniquity, even the s meeting
Lam 1:4 because none come to the s feasts
Lam 2:6 the LORD hath caused the s feasts
Lam 2:7 LORD, as in the day of a s feast
Lam 2:22 Thou hast called as in a s day my
Eze 36:38 of Jerusalem in her s feasts
Eze 46:9 before the LORD in the s feasts
Hos 2:11 her sabbaths, and all her s feasts
Hos 9:5 What will ye do in the s day
Hos 12:9 as in the days of the s feast
Joel 1:14 call a s assembly, gather the
Joel 2:15 a fast, call a s assembly
Amos 5:21 not smell in your s assemblies
Nah 1:15 O Judah, keep thy s feasts
Zeph 3:18 are sorrowful for the s assembly
Mal 2:3 even the dung of your s feasts

**SOLES**
Deut 11:24 Every place whereon the s of your
Josh 3:13 as soon as the s of the feet of
Josh 4:18 the s of the priests' feet were
1Kin 5:3 put them under the s of his feet
Is 60:14 down at the s of thy feet
Eze 43:7 and the place of the s of my feet
Mal 4:3 they shall be ashes under the s

**SOLITARY**
Job 3:7 Lo, let that night be s
Job 30:3 For want and famine they were s
Ps 68:6 God setteth the s in families
Ps 107:4 in the wilderness in a s way
Is 35:1 the s place shall be glad for
Lam 1:1 How doth the city sit s, that was
Mk 1:35 out, and departed into a s place

**SOLOMON** *(sol'-o-mun)* See JEDIDIAH, SOLOMON'S. *Son of David; king of Israel.*
2Sa 5:14 and Shobab, and Nathan, and S
2Sa 12:24 a son, and he called his name S
1Kin 1:10 S his brother, he called not
1Kin 1:11 unto Bath-sheba the mother of S
1Kin 1:12 life, and the life of thy son S
1Kin 1:13 Assuredly S thy son shall reign
1Kin 1:17 Assuredly S thy son shall reign
1Kin 1:19 but S thy servant hath he not
1Kin 1:21 my son S shall be counted
1Kin 1:26 son of Jehoiada, and thy servant S
1Kin 1:30 Assuredly S thy son shall reign
1Kin 1:33 cause S my son to ride upon mine
1Kin 1:34 trumpet, and say, God save king S
1Kin 1:37 the king, even so be he with S
1Kin 1:38 caused S to ride upon king
1Kin 1:39 of the tabernacle, and anointed S
1Kin 1:39 the people said, God save king S
1Kin 1:43 lord king David hath made S king
1Kin 1:46 also S sitteth on the throne of
1Kin 1:47 name of S better than thy name
1Kin 1:50 And Adonijah feared because of S
1Kin 1:51 And it was told S, saying, Behold,
1Kin 1:51 Behold, Adonijah feareth king S
1Kin 1:51 Let king S swear unto me to day
1Kin 1:52 S said, If he will shew himself a
1Kin 1:53 So king S sent, and they brought
1Kin 1:53 came and bowed himself to king S
1Kin 1:53 S said unto him, Go to thine
1Kin 2:1 and he charged S his son, saying,
1Kin 2:12 Then sat S upon the throne of
1Kin 2:13 to Bath-sheba the mother of S
1Kin 2:17 unto S the king, (for he will not
1Kin 2:19 therefore went unto king S
1Kin 2:22 king S answered and said unto his
1Kin 2:23 Then king S sware by the LORD,
1Kin 2:25 king S sent by the hand of
1Kin 2:27 So S thrust out Abiathar from
1Kin 2:29 it was told king S that Joab was
1Kin 2:29 Then S sent Benaiah the son of
1Kin 2:41 it was told S that Shimei had
1Kin 2:45 king S shall be blessed, and the
1Kin 2:46 was established in the hand of S
1Kin 3:1 S made affinity with Pharaoh king
1Kin 3:3 S loved the LORD, walking in the
1Kin 3:4 did S offer upon that altar
1Kin 3:5 appeared to S in a dream by night
1Kin 3:6 S said, Thou hast shewed unto thy
1Kin 3:10 that S had asked this thing
1Kin 3:15 And S awoke
1Kin 4:1 So king S was king over all
1Kin 4:7 S had twelve officers over all
1Kin 4:11 Taphath the daughter of S to wife
1Kin 4:15 Basmath the daughter of S to wife
1Kin 4:21 S reigned over all kingdoms from
1Kin 4:21 served S all the days of his life
1Kin 4:25 to Beer-sheba, all the days of S
1Kin 4:26 S had forty thousand stalls of
1Kin 4:27 provided victual for king S
1Kin 4:29 And God gave S wisdom and
1Kin 4:34 people to hear the wisdom of S
1Kin 5:1 of Tyre sent his servants unto S
1Kin 5:2 And S sent to Hiram, saying,
1Kin 5:7 when Hiram heard the words of S
1Kin 5:8 And Hiram sent to S, saying, I
1Kin 5:10 So Hiram gave S cedar trees
1Kin 5:11 S gave Hiram twenty thousand
1Kin 5:11 thus gave S to Hiram year by year
1Kin 5:12 And the LORD gave S wisdom
1Kin 5:12 was peace between Hiram and S
1Kin 5:13 king S raised a levy out of all
1Kin 5:15 S had threescore and ten thousand
1Kin 6:2 which king S built for the LORD
1Kin 6:11 And the word of the LORD came to S
1Kin 6:14 So S built the house, and finished
1Kin 6:21 So S overlaid the house within
1Kin 7:1 But S was building his own house
1Kin 7:8 S made also an house for
1Kin 7:13 And king S sent and fetched Hiram
1Kin 7:14 And he came to king S, and wrought
1Kin 7:40 king S for the house of the LORD
1Kin 7:45 which Hiram made to king S for
1Kin 7:47 S left all the vessels unweighed,
1Kin 7:48 S made all the vessels that
1Kin 7:51 ended all the work that king S
1Kin 7:51 S brought in the things which
1Kin 8:1 Then S assembled the elders of
1Kin 8:1 unto king S in Jerusalem, that
1Kin 8:2 king S at the feast in the month
1Kin 8:5 And king S, and all the
1Kin 8:12 Then spake S, The LORD said that
1Kin 8:22 S stood before the altar of the
1Kin 8:54 that when S had made an end of
1Kin 8:63 S offered a sacrifice of peace
1Kin 8:65 And at that time S held a feast
1Kin 9:1 when S had finished the building
1Kin 9:2 appeared to S the second time
1Kin 9:10 when S had built the two houses,
1Kin 9:11 had furnished S with cedar trees
1Kin 9:11 that then king S gave Hiram
1Kin 9:12 the cities which S had given him
1Kin 9:15 of the levy which king S raised
1Kin 9:17 S built Gezer, and Beth-horon the
1Kin 9:19 the cities of store that S had
1Kin 9:19 that which S desired to build in
1Kin 9:21 upon those did S levy a tribute
1Kin 9:22 of Israel did S make no bondmen
1Kin 9:24 house which S had built for her
1Kin 9:25 year did S offer burnt offerings
1Kin 9:26 king S made a navy of ships in
1Kin 9:27 the sea, with the servants of S
1Kin 9:28 talents, and brought it to king S
1Kin 10:1 of Sheba heard of the fame of S
1Kin 10:2 and when she was come to S
1Kin 10:3 S told her all her questions
1Kin 10:10 the queen of Sheba gave to king S
1Kin 10:13 king S gave unto the queen of
1Kin 10:13 beside that which S gave her of
1Kin 10:14 to S in one year was six hundred
1Kin 10:16 king S made two hundred targets
1Kin 10:21 accounted of in the days of S
1Kin 10:23 So king S exceeded all the kings
1Kin 10:24 And all the earth sought to S
1Kin 10:26 S gathered together chariots and
1Kin 10:28 S had horses brought out of Egypt
1Kin 11:1 But king S loved many strange
1Kin 11:2 S clave unto these in love
1Kin 11:4 when S was old, that his wives
1Kin 11:5 For S went after Ashtoreth the
1Kin 11:6 S did evil in the sight of the
1Kin 11:7 Then did S build an high place
1Kin 11:9 And the LORD was angry with S
1Kin 11:11 Wherefore the LORD said unto S
1Kin 11:14 stirred up an adversary unto S
1Kin 11:25 to Israel all the days of S
1Kin 11:27 S built Millo, and repaired the
1Kin 11:28 S seeing the young man that he
1Kin 11:31 the kingdom out of the hand of S
1Kin 11:40 S sought therefore to kill
1Kin 11:40 was in Egypt until the death of S
1Kin 11:41 And the rest of the acts of S
1Kin 11:41 in the book of the acts of S
1Kin 11:42 the time that S reigned in
1Kin 11:43 S slept with his fathers, and was
1Kin 12:2 fled from the presence of king S
1Kin 12:6 that stood before S his father
1Kin 12:21 again to Rehoboam the son of S
1Kin 12:23 Speak unto Rehoboam, the son of S
1Kin 14:21 the son of S reigned in Judah
1Kin 14:26 shields of gold which S had made
2Kin 21:7 to S his son, In this house, and
2Kin 23:13 which S the king of Israel had
2Kin 24:13 all the vessels of gold which S
2Kin 25:16 the bases which S had made for
1Chr 3:5 and Shobab, and Nathan, and S
1Chr 6:10 temple that S built in Jerusalem
1Chr 6:32 until S had built the house of
1Chr 14:4 and Shobab, Nathan, and S
1Chr 18:8 wherewith S made the brasen sea,
1Chr 22:5 S my son is young and tender, and
1Chr 22:6 Then he called for S his son
1Chr 22:7 And David said to S, My son, as
1Chr 22:9 for his name shall be S, and I
1Chr 22:17 of Israel to help S his son
1Chr 23:1 he made S his son king over
1Chr 28:5 he hath chosen S my son to sit
1Chr 28:6 S thy son, he shall build my
1Chr 28:9 S my son, know thou the God of
1Chr 28:11 Then David gave to S his son the
1Chr 28:20 And David said to S his son
1Chr 29:1 S my son, whom alone God hath
1Chr 29:19 give unto S my son a perfect
1Chr 29:22 they made S the son of David king
1Chr 29:23 Then S sat on the throne of the
1Chr 29:24 themselves unto S the king
1Chr 29:25 the LORD magnified S exceedingly
1Chr 29:28 S his son reigned in his stead
2Chr 1:1 And S the son of David was
2Chr 1:2 Then S spake unto all Israel, to
2Chr 1:3 So S, and all the congregation
2Chr 1:5 and S and the congregation sought
2Chr 1:6 S went up thither to the brasen
2Chr 1:7 that night did God appear unto S
2Chr 1:8 S said unto God, Thou hast shewed
2Chr 1:11 And God said to S, Because this
2Chr 1:13 Then S came from his journey to
2Chr 1:14 S gathered chariots and horsemen
2Chr 1:16 S had horses brought out of Egypt
2Chr 2:1 S determined to build an house
2Chr 2:2 S told out threescore and ten
2Chr 2:3 S sent to Huram the king of Tyre,

2Chr 2:11 in writing, which he sent to *S*
2Chr 2:17 *S* numbered all the strangers that
2Chr 3:1 Then *S* began to build the house
2Chr 3:3 these are the things wherein *S*
2Chr 4:11 for king *S* for the house of God
2Chr 4:16 *S* for the house of the LORD of
2Chr 4:18 Thus *S* made all these vessels in
2Chr 4:19 *S* made all the vessels that were
2Chr 5:1 Thus all the work that *S* made for
2Chr 5:1 *S* brought in all the things that
2Chr 5:2 Then *S* assembled the elders of
2Chr 5:6 Also king *S*, and all the
2Chr 6:1 Then said *S*, The LORD hath said
2Chr 6:13 For *S* had made a brasen scaffold,
2Chr 7:1 Now when *S* had made an end of
2Chr 7:5 king *S* offered a sacrifice of
2Chr 7:7 Moreover *S* hallowed the middle of
2Chr 7:7 which *S* had made was not able to
2Chr 7:8 Also at the same time *S* kept the
2Chr 7:10 had shewed unto David, and to *S*
2Chr 7:11 Thus *S* finished the house of the
2Chr 7:12 the LORD appeared to *S* by night
2Chr 8:1 wherein *S* had built the house of
2Chr 8:2 which Huram had restored to *S*
2Chr 8:2 *S* built them, and caused the
2Chr 8:3 *S* went to Hamath-zobah, and
2Chr 8:6 all the store cities that *S* had
2Chr 8:6 all that *S* desired to build in
2Chr 8:8 them did *S* make to pay tribute
2Chr 8:9 *S* make no servants for his work
2Chr 8:11 *S* brought up the daughter of
2Chr 8:12 Then *S* offered burnt offerings
2Chr 8:16 Now all the work of *S* was
2Chr 8:17 Then went *S* to Ezion-geber, and to
2Chr 8:18 with the servants of *S* to Ophir
2Chr 8:18 gold, and brought them to king *S*
2Chr 9:1 of Sheba heard of the fame of *S*
2Chr 9:1 she came to prove *S* with hard
2Chr 9:1 and when she was come to *S*
2Chr 9:2 *S* told her all her questions
2Chr 9:2 hid from *S* which he told her not
2Chr 9:3 of Sheba had seen the wisdom of *S*
2Chr 9:9 as the queen of Sheba gave king *S*
2Chr 9:10 of Huram, and the servants of *S*
2Chr 9:12 king *S* gave to the queen of Sheba
2Chr 9:13 to *S* in one year was six hundred
2Chr 9:14 brought gold and silver to *S*
2Chr 9:15 king *S* made two hundred targets
2Chr 9:20 vessels of king *S* were of gold
2Chr 9:20 accounted of in the days of *S*
2Chr 9:22 king *S* passed all the kings of
2Chr 9:23 earth sought the presence of *S*
2Chr 9:25 *S* had four thousand stalls for
2Chr 9:28 they brought unto *S* horses out of
2Chr 9:29 Now the rest of the acts of *S*
2Chr 9:30 *S* reigned in Jerusalem over all
2Chr 9:31 *S* slept with his fathers, and he
2Chr 10:2 from the presence of *S* the king
2Chr 10:6 *S* his father while he yet lived
2Chr 11:3 Speak unto Rehoboam the son of *S*
2Chr 11:17 made Rehoboam the son of *S* strong
2Chr 11:17 walked in the way of David and *S*
2Chr 12:9 shields of gold which *S* had made
2Chr 13:6 the servant of *S* the son of David
2Chr 13:7 against Rehoboam the son of *S*
2Chr 30:26 for since the time of *S* the son
2Chr 33:7 to *S* his son, In this house, and
2Chr 35:3 *S* the son of David king of Israel
2Chr 35:4 to the writing of *S* his son
Neh 12:45 of David, and of *S* his son
Neh 13:26 Did not *S* king of Israel sin by
Ps 72:*t* A Psalm for *S*
Ps 127:*t* A Song of degrees for *S*
Prov 1:1 The Proverbs of *S* the son of
Prov 10:1 The proverbs of *S*
Prov 25:1 These are also proverbs of *S*
Song 1:5 of Kedar, as the curtains of *S*
Song 3:9 King *S* made himself a chariot of
Song 3:11 behold king *S* with the crown
Song 8:11 *S* had a vineyard at Baal-hamon
Song 8:12 thou, O *S*, must have a thousand,
Jer 52:20 which king *S* had made in the
Mt 1:6 David the king begat *S* of her
Mt 1:7 And *S* begat Roboam
Mt 6:29 That even *S* in all his glory was
Mt 12:42 the earth to hear the wisdom of *S*
Mt 12:42 behold, a greater than *S* is here
Lk 11:31 the earth to hear the wisdom of *S*
Lk 11:31 behold, a greater than *S* is here
Lk 12:27 that *S* in all his glory was not
Acts 7:47 But *S* built him an house

## SOLOMON'S *(sol'-o-muns)*

1Kin 4:22 *S* provision for one day was
1Kin 4:27 all that came unto king *S* table
1Kin 4:30 *S* wisdom excelled the wisdom of
1Kin 5:16 Beside the chief of *S* officers
1Kin 5:18 *S* builders and Hiram's builders
1Kin 6:1 year of *S* reign over Israel
1Kin 9:1 all *S* desire which he was pleased
1Kin 9:16 present unto his daughter, *S* wife
1Kin 9:23 officers that were over *S* work
1Kin 10:4 of Sheba had seen all *S* wisdom
1Kin 10:21 all king *S* drinking vessels were
1Kin 11:26 *S* servant, whose mother's name
1Chr 3:10 *S* son was Rehoboam, Abia his son,
2Chr 7:11 all that came into *S* heart to
2Chr 8:10 were the chief of king *S* officers
Ezr 2:55 The children of *S* servants
Ezr 2:58 and the children of *S* servants
Neh 7:57 The children of *S* servants
Neh 7:60 and the children of *S* servants
Neh 11:3 and the children of *S* servants
Song 1:1 The song of songs, which is *S*
Song 3:7 Behold his bed, which is *S*
Jn 10:23 walked in the temple in *S* porch
Acts 3:11 in the porch that is called *S*
Acts 5:12 all with one accord in *S* porch

## SONG

Ex 15:1 of Israel this *s* unto the LORD
Ex 15:2 The LORD is my strength and *s*
Num 21:17 Then Israel sang this *s*, Spring
Deut 31:19 therefore write ye this *s* for you
Deut 31:19 that this *s* may be a witness for
Deut 31:21 that this *s* shall testify against
Deut 31:22 wrote this *s* the same day
Deut 31:30 of Israel the words of this *s*
Deut 32:44 this *s* in the ears of the people
Judg 5:12 awake, awake, utter a *s*
2Sa 22:1 unto the LORD the words of this *s*
1Chr 6:31 of *s* in the house of the LORD
1Chr 15:22 chief of the Levites, was for *s*
1Chr 15:22 he instructed about the *s*
1Chr 15:27 master of the *s* with the singers
1Chr 25:6 for *s* in the house of the LORD
2Chr 29:27 the *s* of the LORD began also with
Job 30:9 And now am I their *s*, yea, I am
Ps 18:*t* this *s* in the day that the LORD
Ps 28:7 with my *s* will I praise him
Ps 30:*t* *S* at the dedication of the house
Ps 33:3 Sing unto him a new *s*
Ps 40:3 he hath put a new *s* in my mouth
Ps 42:8 the night his *s* shall be with me
Ps 45:*t* of Korah, A Maschil, A *S* of loves
Ps 46:*t* sons of Korah, A *S* upon Alamoth
Ps 48:*t* A *S* and Psalm for the sons of
Ps 65:*t* Musician, A Psalm and *S* of David
Ps 66:*t* the chief Musician, A *S* or Psalm
Ps 67:*t* on Neginoth, A Psalm or *S*
Ps 68:*t* Musician, A Psalm or *S* of David
Ps 69:12 I was the *s* of the drunkards
Ps 69:30 praise the name of God with a *s*
Ps 75:*t* Altaschith, A Psalm or *S* of Asaph
Ps 76:*t* Neginoth, A Psalm or *S* of Asaph
Ps 77:6 to remembrance my *s* in the night
Ps 83:*t* A *S* or Psalm of Asaph
Ps 87:*t* A Psalm or *S* for the sons of
Ps 88:*t* A *S* or Psalm for the sons of
Ps 92:*t* A Psalm or *S* for the sabbath day
Ps 96:1 O sing unto the LORD a new *s*
Ps 98:1 O sing unto the LORD a new *s*
Ps 108:*t* A *S* or Psalm of David
Ps 118:14 The LORD is my strength and *s*
Ps 120:*t* A *S* of degrees
Ps 121:*t* A *S* of degrees
Ps 122:*t* A *S* of degrees of David
Ps 123:*t* A *S* of degrees
Ps 124:*t* A *S* of degrees of David
Ps 125:*t* A *S* of degrees
Ps 126:*t* A *S* of degrees
Ps 127:*t* A *S* of degrees for Solomon
Ps 128:*t* A *S* of degrees
Ps 129:*t* A *S* of degrees
Ps 130:*t* A *S* of degrees
Ps 131:*t* A *S* of degrees of David
Ps 132:*t* A *S* of degrees
Ps 133:*t* A *S* of degrees of David
Ps 134:*t* A *S* of degrees
Ps 137:3 away captive required of us a *s*
Ps 137:4 the LORD's *s* in a strange land
Ps 144:9 I will sing a new *s* unto thee
Ps 149:1 Sing unto the LORD a new *s*
Eccl 7:5 for a man to hear the *s* of fools
Song 1:1 The *s* of songs, which is
Is 5:1 a *s* of my beloved touching his
Is 12:2 JEHOVAH is my strength and my *s*
Is 24:9 shall not drink wine with a *s*
Is 26:1 In that day shall this *s* be sung
Is 30:29 Ye shall have a *s*, as in the
Is 42:10 Sing unto the LORD a new *s*
Lam 3:14 and their *s* all the day
Eze 33:32 *s* of one that hath a pleasant
Rev 5:9 And they sung a new *s*, saying,
Rev 14:3 it were a new *s* before the throne
Rev 14:3 learn that *s* but the hundred
Rev 15:3 they sing the *s* of Moses the
Rev 15:3 the *s* of the Lamb, saying, Great

## SONGS

Gen 31:27 thee away with mirth, and with *s*
1Kin 4:32 his *s* were a thousand and five
1Chr 25:7 instructed in the *s* of the LORD
Neh 12:46 *s* of praise and thanksgiving unto
Job 35:10 who giveth *s* in the night
Ps 32:7 me about with *s* of deliverance
Ps 119:54 Thy statutes have been my *s* in
Ps 137:3 Sing us one of the *s* of Zion
Prov 25:20 that singeth *s* to an heavy heart
Song 1:1 The song of *s*, which is Solomon's
Is 23:16 make sweet melody, sing many *s*
Is 24:16 part of the earth have we heard *s*
Is 35:10 return, and come to Zion with *s*
Is 38:20 therefore we will sing my *s* to
Eze 26:13 cause the noise of thy *s* to cease
Amos 5:23 away from me the noise of thy *s*
Amos 8:3 the *s* of the temple shall be
Amos 8:10 all your *s* into lamentation
Eph 5:19 in psalms and hymns and spiritual *s*
Col 3:16 in psalms and hymns and spiritual *s*

## SON'S

Gen 11:31 and Lot the son of Haran his *s* son
Gen 16:15 and Abram called his *s* name
Gen 21:23 with my son, nor with my *s* son
Gen 24:51 and let her be thy master's *s* wife
Gen 27:25 me, and I will eat of my *s* venison
Gen 27:31 arise, and eat of his *s* venison
Gen 30:14 I pray thee, of thy *s* mandrakes
Gen 30:15 take away my *s* mandrakes also
Gen 30:15 thee to night for thy *s* mandrakes
Gen 30:16 hired thee with my *s* mandrakes
Gen 37:32 whether it be thy *s* coat or no
Gen 37:33 knew it, and said, It is my *s* coat
Ex 10:2 ears of thy son, and of thy *s* son
Lev 18:10 The nakedness of thy *s* daughter
Lev 18:15 she is thy *s* wife
Lev 18:17 shalt thou take her *s* daughter
Deut 6:2 thou, and thy son, and thy *s* son
Judg 8:22 and thy son, and thy *s* son also
1Kin 11:35 the kingdom out of his *s* hand
1Kin 21:29 but in his *s* days will I bring
Prov 30:4 his name, and what is his *s* name
Jer 27:7 him, and his son, and his *s* son

## SONS'

Gen 6:18 wife, and thy *s* wives with thee
Gen 7:7 his *s* wives with him, into the
Gen 8:16 sons, and thy *s* wives with thee
Gen 8:18 his wife, and his *s* wives with him
Gen 46:7 sons, and his *s* sons with him, his
Gen 46:7 his *s* daughters, and all his seed
Gen 46:26 loins, besides Jacob's *s* wives
Ex 29:21 sons, and his *s* garments with him
Ex 29:28 his *s* by a statute for ever from
Ex 29:29 of Aaron shall be his *s* after him
Ex 39:41 his *s* garments, to minister in
Lev 2:3 shall be Aaron's and his *s*
Lev 2:10 shall be Aaron's and his *s*
Lev 7:31 breast shall be Aaron's and his *s*
Lev 8:27 hands, and upon his *s* hands
Lev 8:30 upon his *s* garments with him
Lev 8:30 sons, and his *s* garments with him
Lev 10:13 it is thy due, and thy *s* due
Lev 10:14 for they be thy due, and thy *s* due
Lev 10:15 thy *s* with thee, by a statute for
Lev 24:9 And it shall be Aaron's and his *s*
Deut 4:9 them thy sons, and thy *s* sons
1Chr 8:40 *s* sons, an hundred and fifty
Job 42:16 his *s* sons, even four generations
Eze 46:16 thereof shall be his *s*
Eze 46:17 shall be his *s* for them

## SOON
Gen 18:33 as s as he had left communing
Gen 27:30 as s as Isaac had made an end of
Gen 44:3 As s as the morning was light,
Ex 2:18 it that ye are come so s to day
Ex 9:29 As s as I am gone out of the city
Ex 32:19 as s as he came nigh unto the
Deut 4:26 that ye shall s utterly perish
Josh 2:7 as s as they which pursued after
Josh 2:11 as s as we had heard these things
Josh 3:13 as s as the soles of the feet of
Josh 8:19 they ran as s as he had stretched
Josh 8:29 as s as the sun was down, Joshua
Judg 8:33 as s as Gideon was dead, that the
Judg 9:33 as s as the sun is up, thou shalt
1Sa 9:13 As s as ye be come into the city,
1Sa 13:10 that as s as he had made an end
1Sa 20:41 as s as the lad was gone, David
1Sa 29:10 as s as ye be up early in the
2Sa 6:18 as s as David had made an end of
2Sa 13:36 as s as he had made an end of
2Sa 15:10 As s as ye hear the sound of the
2Sa 22:45 as s as they hear, they shall be
1Kin 16:11 as s as he sat on his throne,
1Kin 18:12 as s as I am gone from thee, that
1Kin 20:36 as s as thou art departed from me
1Kin 20:36 as s as he was departed from him,
2Kin 10:2 Now as s as this letter cometh to
2Kin 10:25 as s as he had made an end of
2Kin 14:5 as s as the kingdom was confirmed
2Chr 31:5 as s as the commandment came
Job 32:22 my maker would s take me away
Ps 18:44 As s as they hear of me, they
Ps 37:2 For they shall s be cut down like
Ps 58:3 go astray as s as they be born
Ps 68:31 Ethiopia shall s stretch out her
Ps 81:14 I should s have subdued their
Ps 90:10 for it is s cut off, and we fly
Ps 106:13 They s forgat his works
Prov 14:17 He that is s angry dealeth
Is 66:8 for as s as Zion travailed, she
Eze 23:16 as s as she saw them with her
Mt 21:20 How s is the fig tree withered
Mk 1:42 And as s as he had spoken,
Mk 5:36 As s as Jesus heard the word that
Mk 11:2 as s as ye be entered into it, ye
Mk 14:45 as s as he was come, he goeth
Lk 1:23 that, as s as the days of his
Lk 1:44 For, lo, as s as the voice of thy
Lk 8:6 as s as it was sprung up, it
Lk 15:30 But as s as this thy son was come
Lk 22:66 as s as it was day, the elders of
Lk 23:7 as s as he knew that he belonged
Jn 11:20 as s as she heard that Jesus was
Jn 11:29 As s as she heard that, she arose
Jn 16:21 but as s as she is delivered of
Jn 18:6 As s then as he had said unto
Jn 21:9 As s then as they were come to
Acts 10:29 as s as I was sent for
Acts 12:18 Now as s as it was day, there was
Gal 1:6 I marvel that ye are so s removed
Phil 2:23 so s as I shall see how it will
2Th 2:2 That ye be not s shaken in mind
Titus 1:7 not s angry, not given to wine,
Rev 10:10 as s as I had eaten it, my belly
Rev 12:4 her child as s as it was born

## SOOTHSAYERS
Is 2:6 are s like the Philistines, and
Dan 2:27 astrologers, the magicians, the s
Dan 4:7 the Chaldeans, and the s
Dan 5:7 the Chaldeans, and the s
Dan 5:11 astrologers, Chaldeans, and s
Mic 5:12 and thou shalt have no more s

**SOPATER** *(so'-pa-ter)* See SOSIPATER. *A Christian from Berea.*
Acts 20:4 him into Asia *S* of Berea

**SOPHERETH** *(so-fe'-reth) A family of exiles.*
Ezr 2:55 of Sotai, the children of *S*
Neh 7:57 of Sotai, the children of *S*

## SORCERERS
Ex 7:11 also called the wise men and the s
Jer 27:9 to your enchanters, nor to your s
Dan 2:2 and the astrologers, and the s
Mal 3:5 be a swift witness against the s
Rev 21:8 murderers, and whoremongers, and s
Rev 22:15 For without are dogs, and s

## SORCERIES
Is 47:9 for the multitude of thy s
Is 47:12 and with the multitude of thy s
Acts 8:11 time he had bewitched them with s
Rev 9:21 of their murders, nor of their s
Rev 18:23 for by thy s were all nations

## SORE
Gen 19:9 And they pressed s upon the man
Gen 20:8 and the men were s afraid
Gen 31:30 because thou s longedst after thy
Gen 34:25 the third day, when they were s
Gen 41:56 the famine waxed s in the land of
Gen 41:57 the famine was so s in all lands
Gen 43:1 And the famine was s in the land
Gen 47:4 for the famine is s in the land
Gen 47:13 for the famine was very s
Gen 50:10 a great and very s lamentation
Ex 14:10 and they were s afraid
Lev 13:42 bald forehead, a white reddish s
Lev 13:43 if the rising of the s be white
Num 22:3 Moab was s afraid of the people,
Deut 6:22 signs and wonders, great and s
Deut 28:35 with a s botch that cannot be
Deut 28:59 and s sicknesses, and of long
Josh 9:24 therefore we were s afraid of our
Judg 10:9 so that Israel was s distressed
Judg 14:17 her, because she lay s upon him
Judg 15:18 he was s athirst, and called on
Judg 20:34 all Israel, and the battle was s
Judg 21:2 lifted up their voices, and wept s
1Sa 1:6 her adversary also provoked her s
1Sa 1:10 prayed unto the LORD, and wept s
1Sa 5:7 for his hand is s upon us
1Sa 14:52 there was s war against the
1Sa 17:24 fled from him, and were s afraid
1Sa 21:12 was s afraid of Achish the king
1Sa 28:15 Saul answered, I am s distressed
1Sa 28:20 was s afraid, because of the
1Sa 28:21 and saw that he was s troubled
1Sa 31:3 And the battle went s against Saul
1Sa 31:3 he was s wounded of the archers
1Sa 31:4 for he was s afraid
2Sa 2:17 was a very s battle that day
2Sa 13:36 and all his servants wept very s
1Kin 17:17 and his sickness was so s, that
1Kin 18:2 there was a s famine in Samaria
2Kin 3:26 that the battle was too s for him
2Kin 6:11 was s troubled for this thing
2Kin 20:3 And Hezekiah wept s
1Chr 10:3 And the battle went s against Saul
1Chr 10:4 for he was s afraid
2Chr 6:28 whatsoever s or whatsoever
2Chr 6:29 every one shall know his own s
2Chr 21:19 so he died of s diseases
2Chr 28:19 transgressed s against the LORD
2Chr 35:23 for I am s wounded
Ezr 10:1 for the people wept very s
Neh 2:2 Then I was very s afraid,
Neh 13:8 And it grieved me s
Job 2:7 smote Job with s boils from the
Job 5:18 For he maketh s, and bindeth up
Ps 2:5 and vex them in his s displeasure
Ps 6:3 My soul is also s vexed
Ps 6:10 enemies be ashamed and s vexed
Ps 38:2 in me, and thy hand presseth me s
Ps 38:8 I am feeble and s broken
Ps 38:11 my friends stand aloof from my s
Ps 44:19 Though thou hast s broken us in
Ps 55:4 My heart is s pained within me
Ps 71:20 s troubles, shalt quicken me
Ps 77:2 my s ran in the night, and ceased
Ps 118:13 Thou hast thrust s at me that I
Ps 118:18 The LORD hath chastened me s
Eccl 1:13 this s travail hath God given to
Eccl 4:8 vanity, yea, it is a s travail
Eccl 5:13 There is a s evil which I have
Eccl 5:16 And this also is a s evil, that in
Is 27:1 In that day the LORD with his s
Is 38:3 And Hezekiah wept s
Is 59:11 like bears, and mourn s like doves
Is 64:9 Be not wroth very s, O LORD,
Is 64:12 thy peace, and afflict us very s
Jer 13:17 and mine eye shall weep s, and run
Jer 22:10 but weep s for him that goeth
Jer 50:12 Your mother shall be s confounded
Jer 52:6 the famine was s in the city
Lam 1:2 She weepeth s in the night, and
Lam 3:52 Mine enemies chased me s, like a
Eze 14:21 four s judgments upon Jerusalem
Eze 21:10 sharpened to make a s slaughter
Eze 27:35 and their kings shall be s afraid
Dan 6:14 was s displeased with himself, and
Mic 2:10 you, even with a s destruction
Zec 1:2 The LORD hath been s displeased
Zec 1:15 I am very s displeased with the
Mt 17:6 on their face, and were s afraid
Mt 17:15 for he is lunatick, and s vexed
Mt 21:15 they were s displeased,
Mk 6:51 they were s amazed in themselves
Mk 9:6 for they were s afraid
Mk 9:26 the spirit cried, and rent him s
Mk 14:33 and John, and began to be s amazed
Lk 2:9 and they were s afraid
Acts 20:37 And they all wept s, and fell on
Rev 16:2 grievous s upon the men which had

**SOREK** *(so'-rek) A valley between Ashkelon and Gaza.*
Judg 16:4 loved a woman in the valley of *S*

## SORES
Is 1:6 and bruises, and putrifying s
Lk 16:20 was laid at his gate, full of s
Lk 16:21 the dogs came and licked his s
Rev 16:11 because of their pains and their s

## SORROW
Gen 3:16 I will greatly multiply thy s
Gen 3:16 in s thou shalt bring forth
Gen 3:17 in s shalt thou eat of it all the
Gen 42:38 my gray hairs with s to the grave
Gen 44:29 my gray hairs with s to the grave
Gen 44:31 our father with s to the grave
Ex 15:14 s shall take hold on the
Lev 26:16 the eyes, and cause s of heart
Deut 28:65 and failing of eyes, and s of mind
1Chr 4:9 saying, Because I bare him with s
Neh 2:2 is nothing else but s of heart
Est 9:22 turned unto them from s to joy
Job 3:10 womb, nor hid s from mine eyes
Job 6:10 yea, I would harden myself in s
Job 17:7 eye also is dim by reason of s
Job 41:22 s is turned into joy before him
Ps 13:2 having s in my heart daily
Ps 38:17 my s is continually before me
Ps 39:2 and my s was stirred
Ps 55:10 also and s are in the midst of it
Ps 90:10 yet is their strength labour and s
Ps 107:39 oppression, affliction, and s
Ps 116:3 I found trouble and s
Prov 10:10 winketh with the eye causeth s
Prov 10:22 rich, and he addeth no s with it
Prov 15:13 but by s of the heart the spirit
Prov 17:21 a fool doeth it to his s
Prov 23:29 who hath s
Eccl 1:18 increaseth knowledge increaseth s
Eccl 5:17 in darkness, and he hath much s
Eccl 7:3 *S* is better than laughter
Eccl 11:10 Therefore remove s from thy heart
Is 5:30 the land, behold darkness and s
Is 14:3 shall give thee rest from thy s
Is 17:11 day of grief and of desperate s
Is 29:2 and there shall be heaviness and s
Is 35:10 obtain joy and gladness, and s
Is 50:11 ye shall lie down in s
Is 51:11 and s and mourning shall flee away
Is 65:14 but ye shall cry for s of heart
Jer 8:18 I would comfort myself against s
Jer 20:18 of the womb to see labour and s
Jer 30:15 thy s is incurable for the
Jer 31:12 they shall not s any more at all
Jer 31:13 and make them rejoice from their s
Jer 45:3 the LORD hath added grief to my s
Jer 49:23 there is s on the sea
Jer 51:29 And the land shall tremble and s
Lam 1:12 be any s like unto my s
Lam 1:18 you, all people, and behold my s
Lam 3:65 Give them s of heart, thy curse
Eze 23:33 be filled with drunkenness and s
Hos 8:10 they shall s a little for the
Lk 22:45 he found them sleeping for s
Jn 16:6 you, s hath filled your heart
Jn 16:20 but your s shall be turned into
Jn 16:21 when she is in travail hath s
Jn 16:22 And ye now therefore have s
Rom 9:2 and continual s in my heart
2Cor 2:3 I should have s from them of whom
2Cor 2:7 be swallowed up with overmuch s
2Cor 7:10 For godly s worketh repentance to
2Cor 7:10 but the s of the world worketh
Phil 2:27 lest I should have s upon s

1Th 4:13 which are asleep, that ye s not
Rev 18:7 so much torment and s give her
Rev 18:7 and am no widow, and shall see no s
Rev 21:4 shall be no more death, neither s

**SORROWFUL**
1Sa 1:15 lord, I am a woman of a s spirit
Job 6:7 refused to touch are as my s meat
Ps 69:29 But I am poor and s
Prov 14:13 Even in laughter the heart is s
Jer 31:25 I have replenished every s soul
Zeph 3:18 are s for the solemn assembly
Zec 9:5 also shall see it, and be very s
Mt 19:22 heard that saying, he went away s
Mt 26:22 And they were exceeding s, and
Mt 26:37 sons of Zebedee, and began to be s
Mt 26:38 unto them, My soul is exceeding s
Mk 14:19 And they began to be s, and to say
Mk 14:34 My soul is exceeding s unto death
Lk 18:23 when he heard this, he was very s
Lk 18:24 when Jesus saw that he was very s
Jn 16:20 and ye shall be s, but your sorrow
2Cor 6:10 As s, yet alway rejoicing
Phil 2:28 and that I may be the less s

**SORROWS**
Ex 3:7 for I know their s
2Sa 22:6 The s of hell compassed me about
Job 9:28 I am afraid of all my s, I know
Job 21:17 God distributeth s in his anger
Job 39:3 young ones, they cast out their s
Ps 16:4 Their s shall be multiplied that
Ps 18:4 The s of death compassed me, and
Ps 18:5 The s of hell compassed me about
Ps 32:10 Many s shall be to the wicked
Ps 116:3 The s of death compassed me, and
Ps 127:2 up late, to eat the bread of s
Eccl 2:23 For all his days are s, and his
Is 13:8 s shall take hold of them
Is 53:3 a man of s, and acquainted with
Is 53:4 our griefs, and carried our s
Jer 13:21 shall not s take thee, as a woman
Jer 49:24 s have taken her, as a woman in
Dan 10:16 by the vision my s are turned
Hos 13:13 The s of a travailing woman shall
Mt 24:8 All these are the beginning of s
Mk 13:8 these are the beginnings of s
1Ti 6:10 themselves through with many s

**SORRY**
1Sa 22:8 is none of you that is s for me
Neh 8:10 neither be ye s
Ps 38:18 I will be s for my sin
Is 51:19 who shall be s for thee
Mt 14:9 And the king was s
Mt 17:23 And they were exceeding s
Mt 18:31 what was done, they were very s
Mk 6:26 And the king was exceeding s
2Cor 2:2 For if I make you s, who is he
2Cor 2:2 the same which is made s by me
2Cor 7:8 though I made you s with a letter
2Cor 7:8 the same epistle hath made you s
2Cor 7:9 rejoice, not that ye were made s
2Cor 7:9 for ye were made s after a godly

**SORT**
Gen 6:19 two of every s shalt thou bring
Gen 6:20 two of every s shall come unto
Gen 7:14 his kind, every bird of every s
2Kin 24:14 save the poorest s of the people
1Chr 24:5 by lot, one s with another
1Chr 29:14 offer so willingly after this s
2Chr 30:5 time in such s as it was written
Ezr 1:10 basons of a second s four hundred
Ezr 4:8 to Artaxerxes the king in this s
Neh 6:4 unto me four times after this s
Eze 23:42 with the men of the common s were
Eze 39:4 the ravenous birds of every s
Eze 44:30 of every s of your oblations,
Dan 1:10 the children which are of your s
Dan 3:29 God that can deliver after this s
Acts 17:5 lewd fellows of the baser s
Rom 15:15 more boldly unto you in some s
1Cor 3:13 every man's work of what s it is
2Cor 7:11 that ye sorrowed after a godly s
2Ti 3:6 For of this s are they which
3Jn 6 on their journey after a godly s

**SORTS**
Deut 22:11 not wear a garment of divers s
Neh 5:18 ten days store of all s of wine
Ps 78:45 He sent divers s of flies among
Ps 105:31 and there came divers s of flies
Eccl 2:8 instruments, and that of all s
Eze 27:24 thy merchants in all s of things
Eze 38:4 them clothed with all s of armour

**SOSIPATER** *(so-sip'-a-tur)* See SOPATER. *A relative of Paul.*
Rom 16:21 and Lucius, and Jason, and S

**SOSTHENES** *(sos'-the-neze)*
*1. Chief ruler of a synagogue in Corinth.*
Acts 18:17 Then all the Greeks took S
*2. A co-worker with Paul.*
1Cor 1:1 will of God, and S our brother,

**SOTAI** *(so'-tahee) A family of Temple servants.*
Ezr 2:55 the children of S, the children
Neh 7:57 the children of S, the children

**SOUGHT**
Gen 43:30 and he s where to weep
Ex 2:15 this thing, he s to slay Moses
Ex 4:19 the men are dead which s thy life
Ex 4:24 LORD met him, and s to kill him
Ex 33:7 that every one which s the LORD
Lev 10:16 Moses diligently s the goat of
Num 35:23 not his enemy, neither s his harm
Deut 13:10 because he hath s to thrust thee
Josh 2:22 the pursuers s them throughout
Judg 14:4 that he s an occasion against the
Judg 18:1 days the tribe of the Danites s
1Sa 10:21 and when they s him, he could not
1Sa 13:14 the LORD hath s him a man after
1Sa 14:4 by which Jonathan s to go over
1Sa 19:10 Saul s to smite David even to the
1Sa 23:14 Saul s him every day, but God
1Sa 27:4 he s no more again for him
2Sa 3:17 Ye s for David in times past to
2Sa 4:8 thine enemy, which s thy life
2Sa 17:20 And when they had s and could not
2Sa 21:2 Saul s to slay them in his zeal
1Kin 1:2 Let there be s for my lord the
1Kin 1:3 So they s for a fair damsel
1Kin 10:24 And all the earth s to Solomon
1Kin 11:40 Solomon s therefore to kill
2Kin 2:17 they s three days, but found him
1Chr 15:13 for that we s him not after the
1Chr 26:31 reign of David they were s for
2Chr 1:5 and the congregation s unto it
2Chr 9:23 earth s the presence of Solomon
2Chr 14:7 because we have s the LORD our
2Chr 14:7 the LORD our God, we have s him
2Chr 15:4 s him, he was found of them
2Chr 15:15 s him with their whole desire
2Chr 16:12 his disease he s not to the LORD
2Chr 17:3 David, and s not unto Baalim
2Chr 17:4 But s to the LORD God of his
Jer 4:22 they are s children, and they have
2Chr 22:9 And he s Ahaziah
2Chr 22:9 who s the LORD with all his heart
2Chr 25:15 Why hast thou s after the gods of
2Chr 25:20 because they s after the gods of
2Chr 26:5 he s God in the days of Zechariah
2Chr 26:5 and as long as he s the LORD
Ezr 2:62 These s their register among
Neh 7:64 These s their register among
Neh 12:27 s the Levites out of all their
Est 2:2 fair young virgins s for the king
Est 2:21 s to lay hand on the king
Est 3:6 wherefore Haman s to destroy all
Est 6:2 who s to lay hand on the king
Est 9:2 lay hand on such as s their hurt
Ps 34:4 I s the LORD, and he heard me, and
Ps 37:36 I s him, but he could not be
Ps 77:2 day of my trouble I s the Lord
Ps 78:34 he slew them, then they s him
Ps 86:14 violent men have s after my soul
Ps 111:2 s out of all them that have
Ps 119:10 With my whole heart have I s thee
Ps 119:94 for I have s thy precepts
Eccl 2:3 I s in mine heart to give myself
Eccl 7:29 but they have s out many
Eccl 12:9 s out, and set in order many
Eccl 12:10 The preacher s to find out
Song 3:1 By night on my bed I s him whom
Song 3:1 I s him, but I found him not
Song 3:2 I s him, but I found him not
Song 5:6 I s him, but I could not find him
Is 62:12 S out, A city not forsaken
Is 65:1 I am s of them that asked not for
Is 65:1 I am found of them that s me not
Is 65:10 in, for my people that have s me
Jer 8:2 have walked, and whom they have s
Jer 10:21 brutish, and have not s the LORD
Jer 26:21 the king s to put him to death
Jer 44:30 his enemy, and that s his life
Jer 50:20 iniquity of Israel shall be s for
Lam 1:19 while they s their meat to
Eze 22:30 I s for a man among them, that
Eze 26:21 though thou be s for, yet shalt
Eze 34:4 neither have ye s that which was
Dan 2:13 they s Daniel and his fellows to
Dan 4:36 counsellors and my lords s unto me
Dan 6:4 princes s to find occasion
Dan 8:15 s for the meaning, then, behold,
Obad 6 how are his hidden things s up
Zeph 1:6 and those that have not s the LORD
Zec 6:7 s to go that they might walk to
Mt 2:20 which s the young child's life
Mt 21:46 But when they s to lay hands on
Mt 26:16 from that time he s opportunity
Mt 26:59 s false witness against Jesus, to
Mk 11:18 s how they might destroy him
Mk 12:12 they s to lay hold on him, but
Mk 14:1 the scribes s how they might take
Mk 14:11 he s how he might conveniently
Mk 14:55 all the council s for witness
Lk 2:44 they s him among their kinsfolk
Lk 2:48 father and I have s thee sorrowing
Lk 2:49 unto them, How is it that ye s me
Lk 4:42 and the people s him, and came unto
Lk 5:18 they s means to bring him in, and
Lk 6:19 whole multitude s to touch him
Lk 11:16 s of him a sign from heaven
Lk 13:6 s fruit thereon, and found none
Lk 19:3 he s to see Jesus who he was
Lk 19:47 of the people s to destroy him
Lk 20:19 same hour s to lay hands on him
Lk 22:2 scribes s how they might kill him
Lk 22:6 s opportunity to betray him unto
Jn 5:16 s to slay him, because he had
Jn 5:18 Therefore the Jews s the more to
Jn 7:1 because the Jews s to kill him
Jn 7:11 Then the Jews s him at the feast,
Jn 7:30 Then they s to take him
Jn 10:39 Therefore they s again to take
Jn 11:8 the Jews of late s to stone thee
Jn 11:56 Then s they for Jesus, and spake
Jn 19:12 Pilate s to release him
Acts 12:19 And when Herod had s for him
Acts 17:5 s to bring them out to the people
Rom 9:32 Because they s it not by faith,
Rom 10:20 I was found of them that s me not
1Th 2:6 Nor of men s we glory, neither of
2Ti 1:17 he s me out very diligently, and
Heb 8:7 place have been s for the second
Heb 12:17 though he s it carefully with

**SOUND**
Ex 28:35 his s shall be heard when he
Lev 25:9 the trumpet of the jubile to s on
Lev 25:9 s throughout all your land
Lev 26:36 the s of a shaken leaf shall
Num 10:7 blow, but ye shall not s an alarm
Josh 6:5 when ye hear the s of the trumpet
Josh 6:20 people heard the s of the trumpet
2Sa 5:24 when thou hearest the s of a
2Sa 6:15 with the s of the trumpet
2Sa 15:10 as ye hear the s of the trumpet
1Kin 1:40 the earth rent with the s of them
1Kin 1:41 Joab heard the s of the trumpet
1Kin 14:6 Ahijah heard the s of her feet
1Kin 18:41 for there is a s of abundance of
2Kin 6:32 is not the s of his master's feet
1Chr 14:15 when thou shalt hear a s of going
1Chr 15:19 were appointed to s with cymbals
1Chr 15:28 with s of the cornet, and with
1Chr 16:5 but Asaph made a s with cymbals
1Chr 16:42 for those that should make a s
2Chr 5:13 to make one s to be heard in
Neh 4:20 ye hear the s of the trumpet
Job 15:21 A dreadful s is in his ears
Job 21:12 and rejoice at the s of the organ
Job 37:2 the s that goeth out of his mouth
Job 39:24 that it is the s of the trumpet
Ps 47:5 the LORD with the s of a trumpet
Ps 77:17 the skies sent out a s
Ps 89:15 the people that know the joyful s
Ps 92:3 upon the harp with a solemn s
Ps 98:6 s of cornet make a joyful noise
Ps 119:80 Let my heart be s in thy statutes
Ps 150:3 him with the s of the trumpet

Prov 2:7 He layeth up *s* wisdom for the
Prov 3:21 keep *s* wisdom and discretion
Prov 8:14 Counsel is mine, and *s* wisdom
Prov 14:30 A *s* heart is the life of the
Eccl 12:4 when the *s* of the grinding is low
Is 16:11 shall *s* like an harp for Moab
Jer 4:19 the *s* of the trumpet, the alarm
Jer 4:21 hear the *s* of the trumpet
Jer 6:17 Hearken to the *s* of the trumpet
Jer 8:16 *s* of the neighing of his strong
Jer 25:10 the *s* of the millstones, and the
Jer 42:14 nor hear the *s* of the trumpet,
Jer 48:36 heart shall *s* for Moab like pipes
Jer 48:36 mine heart shall *s* like pipes for
Jer 50:22 A *s* of battle is in the land, and
Jer 51:54 A *s* of a cry cometh from Babylon,
Eze 10:5 the *s* of the cherubims' wings was
Eze 26:13 the *s* of thy harps shall be no
Eze 26:15 isles shake at the *s* of thy fall
Eze 27:28 at the *s* of the cry of thy pilots
Eze 31:16 to shake at the *s* of his fall
Eze 33:4 heareth the *s* of the trumpet
Eze 33:5 He heard the *s* of the trumpet, and
Dan 3:5 time ye hear the *s* of the cornet
Dan 3:7 people heard the *s* of the cornet
Dan 3:10 shall hear the *s* of the cornet
Dan 3:15 time ye hear the *s* of the cornet
Joel 2:1 *s* an alarm in my holy mountain
Amos 2:2 with the *s* of the trumpet
Amos 6:5 That chant to the *s* of the viol
Mt 6:2 do not *s* a trumpet before thee,
Mt 24:31 with a great *s* of a trumpet
Lk 15:27 he hath received him safe and *s*
Jn 3:8 and thou hearest the *s* thereof
Acts 2:2 suddenly there came a *s* from
Rom 10:18 their *s* went into all the earth,
1Cor 14:7 even things without life giving *s*
1Cor 14:8 the trumpet give an uncertain *s*
1Cor 15:52 for the trumpet shall *s*, and the
1Ti 1:10 that is contrary to *s* doctrine
2Ti 1:7 power, and of love, and of a *s* mind
2Ti 1:13 Hold fast the form of *s* words
2Ti 4:3 they will not endure *s* doctrine
Titus 1:9 that he may be able by *s* doctrine
Titus 1:13 that they may be *s* in the faith
Titus 2:1 things which become *s* doctrine
Titus 2:2 *s* in faith, in charity, in
Titus 2:8 *S* speech, that cannot be
Heb 12:19 the *s* of a trumpet, and the voice
Rev 1:15 his voice as the *s* of many waters
Rev 8:6 trumpets prepared themselves to *s*
Rev 8:13 three angels, which are yet to *s*
Rev 9:9 the *s* of their wings was as the
Rev 9:9 the *s* of chariots of many horses
Rev 10:7 angel, when he shall begin to *s*
Rev 18:22 the *s* of a millstone shall be

## SOUNDED

Ex 19:19 the voice of the trumpet *s* long
1Sa 20:12 when I have *s* my father about to
2Chr 7:6 the priests *s* trumpets before
2Chr 13:14 the priests *s* with the trumpets
2Chr 23:13 *s* with trumpets, also the singers
2Chr 29:28 singers sang, and the trumpeters *s*
Neh 4:18 he that *s* the trumpet was by me
Lk 1:44 of thy salutation *s* in mine ears
Acts 27:28 And *s*, and found it twenty fathoms
Acts 27:28 they *s* again, and found it fifteen
1Th 1:8 For from you *s* out the word of
Rev 8:7 The first angel *s*, and there
Rev 8:8 And the second angel *s*, and as it
Rev 8:10 And the third angel *s*, and there
Rev 8:12 And the fourth angel *s*, and the
Rev 9:1 And the fifth angel *s*, and I saw a
Rev 9:13 And the sixth angel *s*, and I heard
Rev 11:15 And the seventh angel *s*

## SOUNDING

1Chr 15:16 psalteries and harps and cymbals, *s*
2Chr 5:12 and twenty priests *s* with trumpets
2Chr 13:12 his priests with *s* trumpets to
Ps 150:5 him upon the high *s* cymbals
Is 63:15 the *s* of thy bowels and of thy
Eze 7:7 not the *s* again of the mountains
1Cor 13:1 charity, I am become as *s* brass

## SOUNDNESS

Ps 38:3 There is no *s* in my flesh because
Ps 38:7 and there is no *s* in my flesh
Is 1:6 unto the head there is no *s* in it
Acts 3:16 *s* in the presence of you all

## SOUR

Is 18:5 the *s* grape is ripening in the
Jer 31:29 The fathers have eaten a *s* grape
Jer 31:30 every man that eateth the *s* grape
Eze 18:2 The fathers have eaten *s* grapes
Hos 4:18 Their drink is *s*

## SOUTH

Gen 12:9 going on still toward the *s*
Gen 13:1 had, and Lot with him, into the *s*
Gen 13:3 from the *s* even to Beth-el
Gen 20:1 from thence toward the *s* country
Gen 24:62 for he dwelt in the *s* country
Gen 28:14 and to the north, and to the *s*
Ex 26:18 boards on the *s* side southward
Ex 26:35 of the tabernacle toward the *s*
Ex 27:9 for the *s* side southward there
Ex 36:23 boards for the *s* side southward
Ex 38:9 on the *s* side southward the
Num 2:10 On the *s* side shall be the
Num 10:6 *s* side shall take their journey
Num 13:22 And they ascended by the *s*
Num 13:29 dwell in the land of the *s*
Num 21:1 Canaanite, which dwelt in the *s*
Num 33:40 which dwelt in the *s* in the land
Num 34:3 Then your *s* quarter shall be from
Num 34:3 your *s* border shall be the
Num 34:4 the *s* to the ascent of Akrabbim
Num 34:4 be from the *s* to Kadesh-barnea
Num 35:5 on the *s* side two thousand cubits
Deut 1:7 and in the vale, and in the *s*
Deut 33:23 possess thou the west and the *s*
Deut 34:3 And the *s*, and the plain of the
Josh 10:40 country of the hills, and of the *s*
Josh 11:2 and of the plains *s* of Chinneroth
Josh 11:16 the hills, and all the *s* country
Josh 12:3 and from the *s*, under
Josh 12:8 wilderness, and in the *s* country
Josh 13:4 From the *s*, all the land of the
Josh 15:1 the uttermost part of the *s* coast
Josh 15:2 their *s* border was from the shore
Josh 15:3 it went out to the *s* side to
Josh 15:3 ascended up on the *s* side unto
Josh 15:4 this shall be your *s* coast
Josh 15:7 which is on the *s* side of the
Josh 15:8 unto the *s* side of the Jebusite
Josh 15:19 for thou hast given me a *s* land
Josh 18:5 abide in their coast on the *s*
Josh 18:13 *s* side of the nether Beth-horon
Josh 18:15 the *s* quarter was from the end of
Josh 18:16 to the side of Jebusi on the *s*
Josh 18:19 salt sea at the *s* end of Jordan
Josh 18:19 this was the *s* coast
Josh 19:8 to Baalath-beer, Ramath of the *s*
Josh 19:34 reacheth to Zebulun on the *s* side
Judg 1:9 in the mountain, and in the *s*
Judg 1:15 for thou hast given me a *s* land
Judg 1:16 which lieth in the *s* of Arad
Judg 21:19 Shechem, and on the *s* of Lebonah
1Sa 20:41 arose out of a place toward the *s*
1Sa 23:19 which is on the *s* of Jeshimon
1Sa 23:24 in the plain on the *s* of Jeshimon
1Sa 27:10 said, Against the *s* of Judah
1Sa 27:10 of Judah, and against the *s* of the
1Sa 27:10 against the *s* of the Kenites
1Sa 30:1 the Amalekites had invaded the *s*
1Sa 30:14 upon the *s* of the Cherethites
1Sa 30:14 to Judah, and upon the *s* of Caleb
1Sa 30:27 and to them which were in *s* Ramoth
2Sa 24:7 they went out to the *s* of Judah
1Kin 7:25 and three looking toward the *s*
1Kin 7:39 house eastward over against the *s*
1Chr 9:24 the east, west, north, and *s*
2Chr 4:4 and three looking toward the *s*
2Chr 4:10 the east end, over against the *s*
2Chr 28:18 of the *s* of Judah, and had taken
Job 9:9 and the chambers of the *s*
Job 37:9 Out of the *s* cometh the whirlwind
Job 37:17 quieteth the earth by the *s* wind
Job 39:26 and stretch her wings toward the *s*
Ps 75:6 nor from the west, nor from the *s*
Ps 78:26 power he brought in the *s* wind
Ps 89:12 the *s* thou hast created them
Ps 107:3 from the north, and from the *s*
Ps 126:4 O LORD, as the streams in the *s*
Eccl 1:6 The wind goeth toward the *s*
Eccl 11:3 and if the tree fall toward the *s*
Song 4:16 and come, thou *s*
Is 21:1 whirlwinds in the *s* pass through
Is 30:6 The burden of the beasts of the *s*
Is 43:6 and to the *s*, Keep not back
Jer 13:19 cities of the *s* shall be shut up
Jer 17:26 from the mountains, and from the *s*
Jer 32:44 valley, and in the cities of the *s*
Jer 33:13 vale, and in the cities of the *s*
Eze 20:46 of man, set thy face toward the *s*
Eze 20:46 and drop thy word toward the *s*
Eze 20:46 against the forest of the *s* field
Eze 20:47 And say to the forest of the *s*
Eze 20:47 all faces from the *s* to the north
Eze 21:4 all flesh from the *s* to the north
Eze 40:2 as the frame of a city on the *s*
Eze 40:24 that he brought me toward the *s*
Eze 40:24 and behold a gate toward the *s*
Eze 40:27 in the inner court toward the *s*
Eze 40:27 toward the *s* an hundred cubits
Eze 40:28 to the inner court by the *s* gate
Eze 40:28 he measured the *s* gate according
Eze 40:44 their prospect was toward the *s*
Eze 40:45 whose prospect is toward the *s*
Eze 41:11 and another door toward the *s*
Eze 42:12 *s* was a door in the head of the
Eze 42:13 the *s* chambers, which are before
Eze 42:18 He measured the *s* side, five
Eze 46:9 go out by the way of the *s* gate
Eze 46:9 *s* gate shall go forth by the way
Eze 47:1 at the *s* side of the altar
Eze 47:19 the *s* side southward, from Tamar
Eze 47:19 this is the *s* side southward
Eze 48:10 in breadth, and toward the *s* five
Eze 48:16 the *s* side four thousand and five
Eze 48:17 toward the *s* two hundred and fifty
Eze 48:28 at the *s* side southward, the
Eze 48:33 at the *s* side four thousand and
Dan 8:9 exceeding great, toward the *s*
Dan 11:5 the king of the *s* shall be strong
Dan 11:6 *s* shall come to the king of the
Dan 11:9 So the king of the *s* shall come
Dan 11:11 the king of the *s* shall be moved
Dan 11:14 up against the king of the *s*
Dan 11:15 the arms of the *s* shall not
Dan 11:25 king of the *s* with a great army
Dan 11:25 the king of the *s* shall be
Dan 11:29 return, and come toward the *s*
Dan 11:40 the king of the *s* push at him
Obad 19 they of the *s* shall possess the
Obad 20 shall possess the cities of the *s*
Zec 6:6 go forth toward the *s* country
Zec 7:7 her, when men inhabited the *s*
Zec 9:14 shall go with whirlwinds of the *s*
Zec 14:4 north, and half of it toward the *s*
Zec 14:10 Geba to Rimmon *s* of Jerusalem
Mt 12:42 The queen of the *s* shall rise up
Lk 11:31 The queen of the *s* shall rise up
Lk 12:55 And when ye see the *s* wind blow
Lk 13:29 and from the north, and from the *s*
Acts 8:26 go toward the *s* unto the way that
Acts 27:12 Crete, and lieth toward the *s* west
Acts 27:13 when the *s* wind blew softly,
Acts 28:13 and after one day the *s* wind blew
Rev 21:13 on the *s* three gates

## SOUTHWARD

Gen 13:14 where thou art northward, and *s*
Ex 26:18 twenty boards on the south side *s*
Ex 27:9 for the south side *s* there shall
Ex 36:23 boards for the south side *s*
Ex 38:9 on the south side *s* the hangings
Ex 40:24 on the side of the tabernacle *s*
Num 3:29 on the side of the tabernacle *s*
Num 13:17 unto them, Get you up this way *s*
Deut 3:27 eyes westward, and northward, and *s*
Josh 15:1 *s* was the uttermost part of the
Josh 15:2 sea, from the bay that looketh *s*
Josh 15:21 the coast of Edom *s* were Kabzeel
Josh 17:9 the river Kanah, *s* of the river
Josh 17:10 *S* it was Ephraim's, and northward
Josh 18:13 side of Luz, which is Beth-el, *s*
Josh 18:14 compassed the corner of the sea *s*
Josh 18:14 that lieth before Beth-horon *s*
1Sa 14:5 the other *s* over against Gibeah
1Chr 26:15 To Obed-edom *s*
1Chr 26:17 *s* four a day, and toward Asuppim
Eze 47:19 And the south side *s*, from Tamar
Eze 47:19 And this is the south side *s*
Eze 48:28 of Gad, at the south side *s*
Dan 8:4 westward, and northward, and *s*

## SOW

Gen 47:23 for you, and ye shall *s* the land
Ex 23:10 six years thou shalt *s* thy land

Lev 19:19 thou shalt not *s* thy field with
Lev 25:3 Six years thou shalt *s* thy field
Lev 25:4 thou shalt neither *s* thy field
Lev 25:11 ye shall not *s*, neither reap that
Lev 25:20 behold, we shall not *s*, nor
Lev 25:22 ye shall *s* the eighth year, and
Lev 26:16 ye shall *s* your seed in vain, for
Deut 22:9 Thou shalt not *s* thy vineyard
2Kin 19:29 and in the third year *s* ye
Job 4:8 *s* wickedness, reap the same
Job 31:8 Then let me *s*, and let another eat
Ps 107:37 *s* the fields, and plant vineyards,
Ps 126:5 They that *s* in tears shall reap
Eccl 11:4 observeth the wind shall not *s*
Eccl 11:6 In the morning *s* thy seed
Is 28:24 the plowman plow all day to *s*
Is 30:23 that thou shalt *s* the ground
Is 32:20 are ye that *s* beside all waters
Is 37:30 and in the third year *s* ye
Jer 4:3 ground, and *s* not among thorns
Jer 31:27 that I will *s* the house of Israel
Jer 35:7 nor *s* seed, nor plant vineyard,
Hos 2:23 I will *s* her unto me in the earth
Hos 10:12 *S* to yourselves in righteousness,
Mic 6:15 Thou shalt *s*, but thou shalt not
Zec 10:9 I will *s* them among the people
Mt 6:26 for they *s* not, neither do they
Mt 13:3 Behold, a sower went forth to *s*
Mt 13:27 didst not thou *s* good seed in thy
Mk 4:3 there went out a sower to *s*
Lk 8:5 A sower went out to *s* his seed
Lk 12:24 for they neither *s* nor reap
Lk 19:21 and reapest that thou didst not *s*
Lk 19:22 down, and reaping that I did not *s*
2Pet 2:22 the *s* that was washed to her

### SOWED
Gen 26:12 Then Isaac *s* in that land, and
Judg 9:45 down the city, and *s* it with salt
Mt 13:4 And when he *s*, some seeds fell by
Mt 13:24 which *s* good seed in his field
Mt 13:25 *s* tares among the wheat, and went
Mt 13:31 a man took, and *s* in his field
Mt 13:39 The enemy that *s* them is the
Mt 25:26 knewest that I reap where I *s* not
Mk 4:4 And it came to pass, as he *s*
Lk 8:5 and as he *s*, some fell by the way

### SOWER
Is 55:10 that it may give seed to the *s*
Jer 50:16 Cut off the *s* from Babylon, and
Mt 13:3 Behold, a *s* went forth to sow
Mt 13:18 ye therefore the parable of the *s*
Mk 4:3 Behold, there went out a *s* to sow
Mk 4:14 The *s* soweth the word
Lk 8:5 A *s* went out to sow his seed
2Cor 9:10 *s* both minister bread for your

### SOWETH
Prov 6:14 he *s* discord
Prov 6:19 he that *s* discord among brethren
Prov 11:18 but to him that *s* righteousness
Prov 16:28 A froward man *s* strife
Prov 22:8 He that *s* iniquity shall reap
Amos 9:13 treader of grapes him that *s* seed
Mt 13:37 He that *s* the good seed is the
Mk 4:14 The sower *s* the word
Jn 4:36 that both he that *s* and he that
Jn 4:37 herein is that saying true, One *s*
2Cor 9:6 He which *s* sparingly shall reap
2Cor 9:6 he which *s* bountifully shall reap
Gal 6:7 for whatsoever a man *s*, that
Gal 6:8 For he that *s* to his flesh shall
Gal 6:8 but he that *s* to the Spirit shall

### SOWN
Ex 23:16 which thou hast *s* in the field
Lev 11:37 any sowing seed which is to be *s*
Deut 21:4 which is neither eared nor *s*
Deut 22:9 of thy seed which thou hast *s*
Deut 29:23 and burning, that it is not *s*
Judg 6:3 And so it was, when Israel had *s*
Ps 97:11 Light is *s* for the righteous, and
Is 19:7 every thing *s* by the brooks,
Is 40:24 yea, they shall not be *s*
Is 61:11 that are *s* in it to spring forth
Jer 2:2 in a land that was not *s*
Jer 12:13 They have *s* wheat, but shall reap
Eze 36:9 you, and ye shall be tilled and *s*
Hos 8:7 For they have *s* the wind, and they
Nah 1:14 that no more of thy name be *s*
Hag 1:6 Ye have *s* much, and bring in
Mt 13:19 that which was *s* in his heart
Mt 25:24 reaping where thou hast not *s*
Mk 4:15 the way side, where the word is *s*
Mk 4:15 word that was *s* in their hearts
Mk 4:16 which are *s* on stony ground
Mk 4:18 are they which are *s* among thorns
Mk 4:20 they which are *s* on good ground
Mk 4:31 when it is *s* in the earth, is
Mk 4:32 But when it is *s*, it groweth up,
1Cor 9:11 If we have *s* unto you spiritual
1Cor 15:42 It is *s* in corruption
1Cor 15:43 It is *s* in dishonour
1Cor 15:43 it is *s* in weakness
1Cor 15:44 It is *s* a natural body
2Cor 9:10 food, and multiply your seed *s*
Jas 3:18 is *s* in peace of them that make

### SPACE
Gen 29:14 abode with him the *s* of a month
Gen 32:16 put a *s* betwixt drove and drove
Lev 25:8 the *s* of the seven sabbaths of
Lev 25:30 within the *s* of a full year
Deut 2:14 the *s* in which we came from
Josh 3:4 there shall be a *s* between you
1Sa 26:13 a great *s* being between them
Ezr 9:8 now for a little *s* grace hath
Jer 28:11 within the *s* of two full years
Eze 40:12 The *s* also before the little
Eze 40:12 the *s* was one cubit on that side
Lk 22:59 about the *s* of one hour after
Acts 5:7 it was about the *s* of three hours
Acts 5:34 put the apostles forth a little *s*
Acts 7:42 sacrifices by the *s* of forty
Acts 13:20 about the *s* of four hundred
Acts 13:21 Benjamin, by the *s* of forty years
Acts 15:33 after they had tarried there a *s*
Acts 19:8 boldly for the *s* of three months
Acts 19:10 continued by the *s* of two years
Acts 19:34 the *s* of two hours cried out
Acts 20:31 that by the *s* of three years I
Jas 5:17 the earth by the *s* of three years
Rev 2:21 I gave her *s* to repent of her
Rev 8:1 about the *s* of half an hour
Rev 14:20 by the *s* of a thousand and six
Rev 17:10 he must continue a short *s*

### SPAIN *(spane) Land at the western extremity of the Mediterranean Sea.*
Rom 15:24 I take my journey into *S*, I will
Rom 15:28 fruit, I will come by you into *S*

### SPAN
Ex 28:16 a *s* shall be the length thereof,
Ex 28:16 a *s* shall be the breadth thereof
Ex 39:9 a *s* was the length thereof, and a
Ex 39:9 a *s* the breadth thereof, being
1Sa 17:4 height was six cubits and a *s*
Is 40:12 and meted out heaven with the *s*
Lam 2:20 fruit, and children of a *s* long
Eze 43:13 thereof round about shall be a *s*

### SPARE
Gen 18:24 not *s* the place for the fifty
Gen 18:26 then I will *s* all the place for
Deut 13:8 pity him, neither shalt thou *s*
Deut 29:20 The LORD will not *s* him, but then
1Sa 15:3 all that they have, and *s* them not
Neh 13:22 *s* me according to the greatness
Job 6:10 let him not *s*
Job 16:13 my reins asunder, and doth not *s*
Job 20:13 Though he *s* it, and forsake it not
Job 27:22 God shall cast upon him, and not *s*
Job 30:10 me, and *s* not to spit in my face
Ps 39:13 O *s* me, that I may recover
Ps 72:13 He shall *s* the poor and needy, and
Prov 6:34 therefore he will not *s* in the
Prov 19:18 let not thy soul *s* for his crying
Is 9:19 no man shall *s* his brother
Is 13:18 their eye shall not *s* children
Is 30:14 he shall not *s*
Is 54:2 *s* not, lengthen thy cords, and
Is 58:1 *s* not, lift up thy voice like a
Jer 13:14 I will not pity, nor *s*, nor have
Jer 21:7 he shall not *s* them, neither have
Jer 50:14 bow, shoot at her, *s* no arrows
Jer 51:3 and *s* ye not her young men
Eze 5:11 neither shall mine eye *s*, neither
Eze 7:4 And mine eye shall not *s* thee
Eze 7:9 And mine eye shall not *s*, neither
Eze 8:18 mine eye shall not *s*, neither
Eze 9:5 let not your eye *s*, neither have
Eze 9:10 for me also, mine eye shall not *s*
Eze 24:14 not go back, neither will I *s*
Joel 2:17 *S* thy people, O LORD, and give not
Jonah 4:11 And should not I *s* Nineveh
Hab 1:17 not *s* continually to slay the
Mal 3:17 and I will *s* them, as a man
Lk 15:17 have bread enough and to *s*
Rom 11:21 take heed lest he also *s* not thee
1Cor 7:28 but I *s* you
2Cor 1:23 that to *s* you I came not as yet
2Cor 13:2 if I come again, I will not *s*

### SPARED
1Sa 15:9 But Saul and the people *s* Agag
1Sa 15:15 for the people *s* the best of the
1Sa 24:10 but mine eye *s* thee
2Sa 12:4 he *s* to take of his own flock and
2Sa 21:7 But the king *s* Mephibosheth
2Kin 5:20 my master hath *s* Naaman this
Ps 78:50 he *s* not their soul from death,
Eze 20:17 Nevertheless mine eye *s* them from
Rom 8:32 He that *s* not his own Son, but
Rom 11:21 For if God *s* not the natural
2Pet 2:4 For if God *s* not the angels that
2Pet 2:5 *s* not the old world, but saved

### SPARETH
Prov 13:24 He that *s* his rod hateth his son
Prov 17:27 that hath knowledge *s* his words
Prov 21:26 but the righteous giveth and *s* not
Mal 3:17 as a man *s* his own son that

### SPARROWS
Mt 10:29 Are not two *s* sold for a farthing
Mt 10:31 ye are of more value than many *s*
Lk 12:6 Are not five *s* sold for two
Lk 12:7 ye are of more value than many *s*

### SPEAKEST
1Sa 9:21 wherefore then *s* thou so to me
2Sa 19:29 Why *s* thou any more of thy
2Kin 6:12 that thou *s* in thy bedchamber
Job 2:10 Thou *s* as one of the foolish
Ps 50:20 sittest and *s* against thy brother
Ps 51:4 mightest be justified when thou *s*
Is 40:27 Why sayest thou, O Jacob, and *s*
Jer 40:16 for thou *s* falsely of Ishmael
Jer 43:2 unto Jeremiah, Thou *s* falsely
Eze 3:18 nor *s* to warn the wicked from his
Zec 13:3 for thou *s* lies in the name of
Mt 13:10 Why *s* thou unto them in parables
Lk 12:41 *s* thou this parable unto us, or
Jn 16:29 now *s* thou plainly
Jn 16:29 thou plainly, and *s* no proverb
Jn 19:10 unto him, *S* thou not unto me
Acts 17:19 this new doctrine, whereof thou *s*

### SPEAKETH
Gen 45:12 it is my mouth that *s* unto you
Ex 33:11 as a man *s* unto his friend
Num 23:26 thee, saying, All that the LORD *s*
Deut 18:22 When a prophet *s* in the name of
1Kin 20:5 Thus *s* Ben-hadad, saying,
Job 2:10 as one of the foolish women *s*
Job 17:5 He that *s* flattery to his friends
Job 33:14 For God *s* once, yea twice, yet
Ps 12:3 and the tongue that *s* proud things
Ps 15:2 and *s* the truth in his heart
Ps 37:30 mouth of the righteous *s* wisdom
Ps 41:6 if he come to see me, he *s* vanity
Ps 144:8 Whose mouth *s* vanity, and their
Ps 144:11 children, whose mouth *s* vanity
Prov 2:12 the man that *s* froward things
Prov 6:13 he *s* with his feet, he teacheth
Prov 6:19 A false witness that *s* lies
Prov 10:32 mouth of the wicked *s* frowardness
Prov 12:17 He that *s* truth sheweth forth
Prov 12:18 There is that *s* like the
Prov 14:25 but a deceitful witness *s* lies
Prov 16:13 and they love him that *s* right
Prov 19:5 he that *s* lies shall not escape
Prov 19:9 he that *s* lies shall perish
Prov 21:28 the man that heareth *s* constantly
Prov 26:25 When he *s* fair, believe him not
Is 9:17 evildoer, and every mouth *s* folly
Is 32:7 even when the needy *s* right
Is 33:15 righteously, and *s* uprightly
Jer 9:8 it *s* deceit
Jer 9:8 one *s* peaceably to his neighbour
Jer 10:1 word which the LORD *s* unto you
Jer 28:2 Thus *s* the LORD of hosts, the God
Jer 29:25 Thus *s* the LORD of hosts, the God
Jer 30:2 Thus *s* the LORD God of Israel,
Eze 10:5 of the Almighty God when he *s*

Amos 5:10 they abhor him that *s* uprightly
Hag 1:2 Thus *s* the LORD of hosts, saying,
Zec 6:12 Thus *s* the LORD of hosts, saying,
Zec 7:9 Thus *s* the LORD of hosts, saying,
Mt 10:20 of your Father which *s* in you
Mt 12:32 but whosoever *s* against the Holy
Mt 12:34 of the heart the mouth *s*
Lk 5:21 Who is this which *s* blasphemies
Lk 6:45 of the heart his mouth *s*
Jn 3:31 is earthly, and *s* of the earth
Jn 3:34 God hath sent *s* the words of God
Jn 7:18 He that *s* of himself seeketh his
Jn 7:26 he *s* boldly, and they say nothing
Jn 8:44 *s* a lie, he *s* of his own
Jn 19:12 himself a king *s* against Caesar
Acts 2:25 For David *s* concerning him, I
Acts 8:34 of whom *s* the prophet this
Rom 10:6 which is of faith *s* on this wise
1Cor 14:2 For he that *s* in an unknown
1Cor 14:2 an unknown tongue *s* not unto men
1Cor 14:2 in the spirit he *s* mysteries
1Cor 14:3 *s* unto men to edification
1Cor 14:4 He that *s* in an unknown tongue
1Cor 14:5 than he that *s* with tongues
1Cor 14:11 be unto him that *s* a barbarian
1Cor 14:11 he that *s* shall be a barbarian
1Cor 14:13 Wherefore let him that *s* in an
1Ti 4:1 Now the Spirit *s* expressly
Heb 11:4 and by it he being dead yet *s*
Heb 12:5 which *s* unto you as unto children
Heb 12:24 that *s* better things than that of
Heb 12:25 See that ye refuse not him that *s*
Heb 12:25 away from him that *s* from heaven
Jas 4:11 He that *s* evil of his brother, and
Jas 4:11 *s* evil of the law, and judgeth the
Jude 16 their mouth *s* great swelling

**SPEAKING**

Gen 24:15 to pass, before he had done *s*
Gen 24:45 before I had done *s* in mine heart
Ex 34:33 till Moses had done *s* with them
Num 7:89 one *s* unto him from off the mercy
Num 16:31 made an end of *s* all these words
Deut 4:33 *s* out of the midst of the fire
Deut 5:26 the voice of the living God *s* out
Deut 11:19 *s* of them when thou sittest in
Deut 20:9 made an end of *s* unto the people
Deut 32:45 Moses made an end of *s* all these
Judg 15:17 when he had made an end of *s*
Ruth 1:18 her, then she left *s* unto her
1Sa 18:1 he had made an end of *s* unto Saul
1Sa 24:16 an end of *s* these words unto Saul
2Sa 13:36 soon as he had made an end of *s*
2Chr 36:12 *s* from the mouth of the LORD
Est 10:3 and *s* peace to all his seed
Job 1:16 While he was yet *s*, there came
Job 1:17 While he was yet *s*, there came
Job 1:18 While he was yet *s*, there came
Job 4:2 who can withhold himself from *s*
Job 32:15 they left off *s*
Ps 34:13 evil, and thy lips from *s* guile
Ps 58:3 as soon as they be born, *s* lies
Is 58:9 forth of the finger, and *s* vanity
Is 58:13 pleasure, nor *s* thine own words
Is 59:13 our God, *s* oppression and revolt,
Is 65:24 and while they are yet *s*, I will
Jer 7:13 unto you, rising up early and *s*
Jer 25:3 unto you, rising early and *s*
Jer 26:7 all the people heard Jeremiah *s*
Jer 26:8 Jeremiah had made an end of *s* all
Jer 35:14 unto you, rising early and *s*
Jer 38:4 in *s* such words unto them
Jer 38:27 So they left off *s* with him
Jer 43:1 of *s* unto all the people all the
Eze 43:6 I heard him *s* unto me out of the
Dan 7:8 of man, and a mouth *s* great things
Dan 8:13 Then I heard one saint *s*, and
Dan 8:18 Now as he was *s* with me, I was in
Dan 9:20 And whiles I was *s*, and praying, and
Dan 9:21 Yea, whiles I was *s* in prayer
Mt 6:7 shall be heard for their much *s*
Lk 5:4 Now when he had left *s*, he said
Acts 1:3 *s* of the things pertaining to the
Acts 7:44 *s* unto Moses, that he should make
Acts 13:43 *s* to them, persuaded them to
Acts 14:3 abode they *s* boldly in the Lord
Acts 20:30 *s* perverse things, to draw away
Acts 26:14 earth, I heard a voice *s* unto me
1Cor 12:3 that no man *s* by the Spirit of
1Cor 14:6 if I come unto you *s* with tongues
2Cor 13:3 ye seek a proof of Christ *s* in me
Eph 4:15 But *s* the truth in love, may grow
Eph 4:31 and anger, and clamour, and evil *s*
Eph 5:19 *S* to yourselves in psalms and
1Ti 4:2 *S* lies in hypocrisy
1Ti 5:13 *s* things which they ought not
1Pet 4:4 excess of riot, *s* evil of you
2Pet 2:16 the dumb ass *s* with man's voice
2Pet 3:16 *s* in them of these things
Rev 13:5 unto him a mouth *s* great things

**SPEAR**

Josh 8:18 Stretch out the *s* that is in thy
Josh 8:18 Joshua stretched out the *s* that
Josh 8:26 wherewith he stretched out the *s*
Judg 5:8 was there a shield or *s* seen
1Sa 13:22 there was neither sword nor *s*
1Sa 17:7 the staff of his *s* was like a
1Sa 17:45 to me with a sword, and with a *s*
1Sa 17:47 LORD saveth not with sword and *s*
1Sa 21:8 here under thine hand *s* or sword
1Sa 22:6 having his *s* in his hand, and all
1Sa 26:7 his *s* stuck in the ground at his
1Sa 26:8 with the *s* even to the earth at
1Sa 26:11 take thou now the *s* that is at
1Sa 26:12 So David took the *s* and the cruse
1Sa 26:16 And now see where the king's *s* is
1Sa 26:22 and said, Behold the king's *s*
2Sa 1:6 behold, Saul leaned upon his *s*
2Sa 2:23 with the hinder end of the *s*
2Sa 2:23 that the *s* came out behind him
2Sa 21:16 the weight of whose *s* weighed
2Sa 21:19 the staff of whose *s* was like a
2Sa 23:7 with iron and the staff of a *s*
2Sa 23:8 he lift up his *s* against eight
2Sa 23:18 he lifted up his *s* against three
2Sa 23:21 the Egyptian had a *s* in his hand
2Sa 23:21 and plucked the *s* out of the
2Sa 23:21 hand, and slew him with his own *s*
1Chr 11:11 he lifted up his *s* against three
1Chr 11:20 for lifting up his *s* against
1Chr 11:23 hand was a *s* like a weaver's beam
1Chr 11:23 and plucked the *s* out of the
1Chr 11:23 hand, and slew him with his own *s*
1Chr 12:24 *s* were six thousand and eight
1Chr 12:34 *s* thirty and seven thousand
1Chr 20:5 whose *s* staff was like a weaver's
2Chr 25:5 forth to war, that could handle *s*
Job 39:23 against him, the glittering *s*
Job 41:26 the *s*, the dart, nor the
Job 41:29 he laugheth at the shaking of a *s*
Ps 35:3 Draw out also the *s*, and stop the
Ps 46:9 bow, and cutteth the *s* in sunder
Jer 6:23 They shall lay hold on bow and *s*
Nah 3:3 bright sword and the glittering *s*
Hab 3:11 the shining of thy glittering *s*
Jn 19:34 with a *s* pierced his side

**SPEARS**

1Sa 13:19 the Hebrews make them swords or *s*
2Kin 11:10 the priest give king David's *s*
2Chr 11:12 several city he put shields and *s*
2Chr 14:8 of men that bare targets and *s*
2Chr 23:9 to the captains of hundreds *s*
2Chr 26:14 all the host shields, and *s*
Neh 4:13 with their swords, their *s*
Neh 4:16 half of them held both the *s*
Neh 4:21 half of them held the *s* from the
Job 41:7 or his head with fish *s*
Ps 57:4 sons of men, whose teeth are *s*
Is 2:4 their *s* into pruninghooks
Jer 46:4 furbish the *s*, and put on the
Eze 39:9 and the handstaves, and the *s*
Joel 3:10 and your pruninghooks into *s*
Mic 4:3 their *s* into pruninghooks

**SPECIALLY**

Deut 4:10 *S* the day that thou stoodest
Acts 25:26 *s* before thee, O king Agrippa,
1Ti 4:10 all men, *s* of those that believe
1Ti 5:8 *s* for those of his own house, he
Titus 1:10 *s* they of the circumcision
Philem 16 *s* to me, but how much more unto

**SPECKLED**

Gen 30:32 removing from thence all the *s*
Gen 30:32 the spotted and *s* among the goats
Gen 30:33 every one that is not *s* and
Gen 30:35 and all the she goats that were *s*
Gen 30:39 forth cattle ringstraked, *s*
Gen 31:8 thus, The *s* shall be thy wages
Gen 31:8 then all the cattle bare *s*
Gen 31:10 the cattle were ringstraked, *s*
Gen 31:12 the cattle are ringstraked, *s*
Jer 12:9 heritage is unto me as a *s* bird
Zec 1:8 him were there red horses, *s*

**SPEECH**

Gen 4:23 of Lamech, hearken unto my *s*
Gen 11:1 was of one language, and of one *s*
Gen 11:7 not understand one another's *s*
Ex 4:10 but I am slow of *s*, and of a slow
Deut 22:14 give occasions of *s* against her
Deut 22:17 given occasions of *s* against her
Deut 32:2 my *s* shall distil as the dew, as
2Sa 14:20 To fetch about this form of *s*
2Sa 19:11 seeing the *s* of all Israel is
1Kin 3:10 the *s* pleased the Lord, that
2Chr 32:18 *s* unto the people of Jerusalem
Neh 13:24 spake half in the *s* of Ashdod
Job 12:20 removeth away the *s* of the trusty
Job 13:17 Hear diligently my *s*, and my
Job 21:2 Hear diligently my *s*, and let this
Job 24:25 liar, and make my *s* nothing worth
Job 29:22 and my *s* dropped upon them
Job 37:19 order our *s* by reason of darkness
Ps 17:6 thine ear unto me, and hear my *s*
Ps 19:2 Day unto day uttereth *s*, and night
Ps 19:3 There is no *s* nor language, where
Prov 7:21 With her much fair *s* she caused
Prov 17:7 Excellent *s* becometh not a fool
Song 4:3 of scarlet, and thy *s* is comely
Is 28:23 hearken, and hear my *s*
Is 29:4 thy *s* shall be low out of the
Is 29:4 thy *s* shall whisper out of the
Is 32:9 give ear unto my *s*
Is 33:19 a people of a deeper *s* than thou
Jer 31:23 use this *s* in the land of Judah
Eze 1:24 of the Almighty, the voice of *s*
Eze 3:5 sent to a people of a strange *s*
Eze 3:6 Not to many people of a strange *s*
Hab 3:2 O LORD, I have heard thy *s*
Mt 26:73 for thy *s* bewrayeth thee
Mk 7:32 and had an impediment in his *s*
Mk 14:70 and thy *s* agreeth thereto
Jn 8:43 Why do ye not understand my *s*
Acts 14:11 saying in the *s* of Lycaonia
Acts 20:7 continued his *s* until midnight
1Cor 2:1 with excellency of *s* or of wisdom
1Cor 2:4 And my *s* and my preaching was not
1Cor 4:19 not the *s* of them which are
2Cor 3:12 hope, we use great plainness of *s*
2Cor 7:4 is my boldness of *s* toward you
2Cor 10:10 is weak, and his *s* contemptible
2Cor 11:6 But though I be rude in *s*
Col 4:6 Let your *s* be alway with grace,
Titus 2:8 Sound *s*, that cannot be condemned

**SPEECHES**

Num 12:8 even apparently, and not in dark *s*
Job 6:26 the *s* of one that is desperate,
Job 15:3 or with *s* wherewith he can do no
Job 32:14 will I answer him with your *s*
Job 33:1 Job, I pray thee, hear my *s*
Rom 16:18 fair *s* deceive the hearts of the
Jude 15 of all their hard *s* which ungodly

**SPEED**

Gen 24:12 thee, send me good *s* this day
1Sa 20:38 cried after the lad, Make *s*
2Sa 15:14 make *s* to depart, lest he
1Kin 12:18 *s* to get him up to his chariot
2Chr 10:18 But king Rehoboam made *s* to get
Ezr 6:12 let it be done with *s*
Is 5:19 That say, Let him make *s*, and
Is 5:26 they shall come with *s* swiftly
Acts 17:15 for to come to him with all *s*
2Jn 10 your house, neither bid him God *s*
2Jn 11 For he that biddeth him God *s* is

**SPEEDILY**

Gen 44:11 Then they *s* took down every man
1Sa 27:1 for me than that I should *s*
2Sa 17:16 the wilderness, but *s* pass over
2Chr 35:13 divided them *s* among all the
Ezr 6:13 the king had sent, so they did *s*
Ezr 7:17 That thou mayest buy *s* with this
Ezr 7:21 require of you, it be done *s*
Ezr 7:26 judgment be executed *s* upon him
Est 2:9 he *s* gave her her things for
Ps 31:2 deliver me *s*
Ps 69:17 hear me *s*
Ps 79:8 thy tender mercies *s* prevent us
Ps 102:2 the day when I call answer me *s*

Ps 143:7 Hear me s, O LORD
Eccl 8:11 an evil work is not executed s
Is 58:8 thine health shall spring forth s
Joel 3:4 s will I return your recompence
Zec 8:21 Let us go s to pray before the
Lk 18:8 you that he will avenge them s

## SPEND

Deut 32:23 I will s mine arrows upon them
Job 21:13 They s their days in wealth, and
Job 36:11 they shall s their days in
Ps 90:9 we s our years as a tale that is
Is 55:2 Wherefore do ye s money for that
Acts 20:16 he would not s the time in Asia
2Cor 12:15 And I will very gladly s and be

## SPENT

Gen 21:15 And the water was s in the bottle
Gen 47:18 my lord, how that our money is s
Lev 26:20 your strength shall be s in vain
Judg 19:11 were by Jebus, the day was far s
1Sa 9:7 for the bread is s in our vessels
Job 7:6 shuttle, and are s without hope
Ps 31:10 For my life is s with grief
Is 49:4 I have s my strength for nought,
Jer 37:21 all the bread in the city were s
Mk 5:26 had s all that she had, and was
Mk 6:35 And when the day was now far s
Lk 8:43 which had s all her living upon
Lk 15:14 And when he had s all, there arose
Lk 24:29 evening, and the day is far s
Acts 17:21 s their time in nothing else
Acts 18:23 after he had s some time there,
Acts 27:9 Now when much time was s, and when
Rom 13:12 The night is far s, the day is at
2Cor 12:15 very gladly spend and be s for you

## SPICE

Ex 35:28 And s, and oil for the light, and
1Kin 10:15 the traffick of the s merchants
2Chr 9:9 neither was there any such s as
Song 5:1 have gathered my myrrh with my s
Eze 24:10 s it well, and let the bones be

## SPICES

Gen 43:11 little balm, and a little honey, s
Ex 25:6 s for anointing oil, and for sweet
Ex 30:23 s of pure myrrh five hundred
Ex 30:34 Moses, Take unto thee sweet s
Ex 30:34 these sweet s with pure
Ex 35:8 s for anointing oil, and for the
Ex 37:29 and the pure incense of sweet s
1Kin 10:2 train, with camels that bare s
1Kin 10:10 of s very great store, and
1Kin 10:10 of s as these which the queen of
1Kin 10:25 and garments, and armour, and s
2Kin 20:13 the silver, and the gold, and the s
1Chr 9:29 and the frankincense, and the s
1Chr 9:30 made the ointment of the s
2Chr 9:1 company, and camels that bare s
2Chr 9:9 of s great abundance, and precious
2Chr 9:24 gold, and raiment, harness, and s
2Chr 16:14 divers kinds of s prepared by the
2Chr 32:27 and for precious stones, and for s
Song 4:10 of thine ointments than all s
Song 4:14 and aloes, with all the chief s
Song 4:16 that the s thereof may flow out
Song 5:13 His cheeks are as a bed of s
Song 6:2 into his garden, to the beds of s
Song 8:14 hart upon the mountains of s
Is 39:2 the silver, and the gold, and the s
Eze 27:22 in thy fairs with chief of all s
Mk 16:1 and Salome, had bought sweet s
Lk 23:56 And they returned, and prepared s
Lk 24:1 bringing the s which they had
Jn 19:40 it in linen clothes with the s

## SPIED

Ex 2:11 he s an Egyptian smiting an
Josh 6:22 men that had s out the country
2Kin 9:17 he s the company of Jehu as he
2Kin 13:21 behold, they s a band of men
2Kin 23:16 he s the sepulchres that were
2Kin 23:24 that were s in the land of Judah

## SPIES

Gen 42:9 them, and said unto them, Ye are s
Gen 42:11 true men, thy servants are no s
Gen 42:14 spake unto you, saying, Ye are s
Gen 42:16 life of Pharaoh surely ye are s
Gen 42:30 took us for s of the country
Gen 42:31 we are no s
Gen 42:34 shall I know that ye are no s
Num 21:1 Israel came by the way of the s
Josh 6:23 the young men that were s went in
Judg 1:24 the s saw a man come forth out of
1Sa 26:4 David therefore sent out s
2Sa 15:10 But Absalom sent s throughout all
Lk 20:20 they watched him, and sent forth s
Heb 11:31 she had received the s with peace

## SPIKENARD

Song 1:12 my s sendeth forth the smell
Song 4:13 camphire, with s,
Song 4:14 S and saffron
Mk 14:3 of ointment of s very precious
Jn 12:3 Mary a pound of ointment of s

## SPIRIT

Gen 1:2 the S of God moved upon the face
Gen 6:3 My s shall not always strive with
Gen 41:8 morning that his s was troubled
Gen 41:38 is, a man in whom the S of God is
Gen 45:27 the s of Jacob their father
Ex 6:9 not unto Moses for anguish of s
Ex 28:3 have filled with the s of wisdom
Ex 31:3 have filled him with the s of God
Ex 35:21 every one whom his s made willing
Ex 35:31 hath filled him with the s of God
Lev 20:27 or woman that hath a familiar s
Num 5:14 the s of jealousy come upon him,
Num 5:14 or if the s of jealousy come upon
Num 5:30 Or when the s of jealousy cometh
Num 11:17 take of the s which is upon thee
Num 11:25 took of the s that was upon him,
Num 11:25 when the s rested upon them, they
Num 11:26 and the s rested upon them
Num 11:29 LORD would put his s upon them
Num 14:24 because he had another s with him
Num 24:2 the s of God came upon him
Num 27:18 of Nun, a man in whom is the s
Deut 2:30 the LORD thy God hardened his s
Deut 34:9 Nun was full of the s of wisdom
Josh 5:1 was there s in them any more
Judg 3:10 the s of the LORD came upon him,
Judg 6:34 But the S of the LORD came upon
Judg 9:23 sent an evil s between Abimelech
Judg 11:29 Then the S of the LORD came upon
Judg 13:25 the S of the LORD began to move
Judg 14:6 the S of the LORD came mightily
Judg 14:19 the S of the LORD came upon him,
Judg 15:14 the S of the LORD came mightily
Judg 15:19 his s came again, and he revived
1Sa 1:15 I am a woman of a sorrowful s
1Sa 10:6 the S of the LORD will come upon
1Sa 10:10 the S of God came upon him, and he
1Sa 11:6 the S of God came upon Saul when
1Sa 16:13 the S of the LORD came upon David
1Sa 16:14 But the S of the LORD departed
1Sa 16:14 an evil s from the LORD troubled
1Sa 16:15 an evil s from God troubleth thee
1Sa 16:16 when the evil s from God is upon
1Sa 16:23 when the evil s from God was upon
1Sa 16:23 the evil s departed from him
1Sa 18:10 that the evil s from God came
1Sa 19:9 the evil s from the LORD was upon
1Sa 19:20 the S of God was upon the
1Sa 19:23 the S of God was upon him also,
1Sa 28:7 me a woman that hath a familiar s
1Sa 28:7 that hath a familiar s at En-dor
1Sa 28:8 divine unto me by the familiar s
1Sa 30:12 eaten, his s came again to him
2Sa 23:2 The S of the LORD spake by me, and
1Kin 10:5 there was no more s in her
1Kin 18:12 that the S of the LORD shall
1Kin 21:5 unto him, Why is thy s so sad
1Kin 22:21 And there came forth a s, and stood
1Kin 22:22 I will be a lying s in the mouth
1Kin 22:23 the LORD hath put a lying s in
1Kin 22:24 Which way went the S of the LORD
2Kin 2:9 portion of thy s be upon me
2Kin 2:15 The s of Elijah doth rest on
2Kin 2:16 lest peradventure the S of the
1Chr 5:26 up the s of Pul king of Assyria
1Chr 5:26 the s of Tilgath-pilneser king of
1Chr 10:13 of one that had a familiar s
1Chr 12:18 Then the s came upon Amasai, who
1Chr 28:12 of all that he had by the s
2Chr 9:4 there was no more s in her
2Chr 15:1 the S of God came upon Azariah
2Chr 18:20 Then there came out a s, and stood
2Chr 18:21 be a lying s in the mouth of all
2Chr 18:22 lying s in the mouth of these thy
2Chr 18:23 Which way went the S of the LORD
2Chr 20:14 came the S of the LORD in the
2Chr 21:16 Jehoram the s of the Philistines
2Chr 24:20 the S of God came upon Zechariah
2Chr 33:6 and dealt with a familiar s
2Chr 36:22 up the s of Cyrus king of Persia
Ezr 1:1 up the s of Cyrus king of Persia
Ezr 1:5 all them whose s God had raised
Neh 9:20 also thy good s to instruct them
Neh 9:30 them by thy s in thy prophets
Job 4:15 Then a s passed before my face
Job 6:4 poison whereof drinketh up my s
Job 7:11 will speak in the anguish of my s
Job 10:12 visitation hath preserved my s
Job 15:13 thou turnest thy s against God
Job 20:3 the s of my understanding causeth
Job 21:4 why should not my s be troubled
Job 26:4 and whose s came from thee
Job 26:13 By his s he hath garnished the
Job 27:3 the s of God is in my nostrils
Job 32:8 But there is a s in man
Job 32:18 the s within me constraineth me
Job 33:4 The s of God hath made me, and the
Job 34:14 if he gather unto himself his s
Ps 31:5 Into thine hand I commit my s
Ps 32:2 in whose s there is no guile
Ps 34:18 saveth such as be of a contrite s
Ps 51:10 and renew a right s within me
Ps 51:11 and take not thy holy s from me
Ps 51:12 and uphold me with thy free s
Ps 51:17 sacrifices of God are a broken s
Ps 76:12 He shall cut off the s of princes
Ps 77:3 and my s was overwhelmed
Ps 77:6 my s made diligent search
Ps 78:8 whose s was not stedfast with God
Ps 104:30 Thou sendest forth thy s, they
Ps 106:33 Because they provoked his s
Ps 139:7 Whither shall I go from thy s
Ps 142:3 When my s was overwhelmed within
Ps 143:4 Therefore is my s overwhelmed
Ps 143:7 my s faileth
Ps 143:10 thy s is good
Prov 1:23 I will pour out my s unto you
Prov 11:13 faithful s concealeth the matter
Prov 14:29 that is hasty of s exalteth folly
Prov 15:4 therein is a breach in the s
Prov 15:13 of the heart the s is broken
Prov 16:18 an haughty s before a fall
Prov 16:19 be of an humble s with the lowly
Prov 16:32 he that ruleth his s than he that
Prov 17:22 but a broken s drieth the bones
Prov 17:27 is of an excellent s
Prov 18:14 The s of a man will sustain his
Prov 18:14 but a wounded s who can bear
Prov 20:27 The s of man is the candle of the
Prov 25:28 s is like a city that is broken
Prov 29:23 shall uphold the humble in s
Eccl 1:14 all is vanity and vexation of s
Eccl 1:17 that this also is vexation of s
Eccl 2:11 all was vanity and vexation of s
Eccl 2:17 all is vanity and vexation of s
Eccl 2:26 also is vanity and vexation of s
Eccl 3:21 Who knoweth the s of man that
Eccl 3:21 the s of the beast that goeth
Eccl 4:4 is also vanity and vexation of s
Eccl 4:6 with travail and vexation of s
Eccl 4:16 also is vanity and vexation of s
Eccl 6:9 is also vanity and vexation of s
Eccl 7:8 the patient in s is better than
Eccl 7:8 is better than the proud in s
Eccl 7:9 Be not hasty in thy s to be angry
Eccl 8:8 over the s to retain the s
Eccl 10:4 If the s of the ruler rise up
Eccl 11:5 not what is the way of the s
Eccl 12:7 the s shall return unto God who
Is 4:4 thereof by the s of judgment
Is 4:4 and by the s of burning
Is 11:2 the s of the LORD shall rest upon
Is 11:2 the s of wisdom and understanding,
Is 11:2 the s of counsel and might
Is 11:2 the s of knowledge and of the fear
Is 19:3 the s of Egypt shall fail in the
Is 19:14 a perverse s in the midst thereof
Is 26:9 with my s within me will I seek
Is 28:6 for a s of judgment to him that
Is 29:4 as of one that hath a familiar s
Is 29:10 out upon you the s of deep sleep
Is 29:24 They also that erred in s shall
Is 30:1 with a covering, but not of my s
Is 31:3 and their horses flesh, and not s
Is 32:15 Until the s be poured upon us
Is 34:16 his s it hath gathered them

Is 38:16 these things is the life of my *s*
Is 40:7 because the *s* of the LORD bloweth
Is 40:13 hath directed the *S* of the LORD
Is 42:1 I have put my *s* upon him
Is 42:5 *s* to them that walk therein
Is 44:3 I will pour my *s* upon thy seed
Is 48:16 and now the Lord GOD, and his *S*
Is 54:6 a woman forsaken and grieved in *s*
Is 57:15 that is of a contrite and humble *s*
Is 57:15 to revive the *s* of the humble
Is 57:16 for the *s* should fail before me,
Is 59:19 the *S* of the LORD shall lift up a
Is 59:21 My *s* that is upon thee, and my
Is 61:1 The *S* of the Lord GOD is upon me
Is 61:3 of praise for the *s* of heaviness
Is 63:10 rebelled, and vexed his holy *S*
Is 63:11 he that put his holy *S* within him
Is 63:14 the *S* of the LORD caused him to
Is 65:14 and shall howl for vexation of *s*
Is 66:2 that is poor and of a contrite *s*
Jer 51:11 the *s* of the kings of the Medes
Eze 1:12 whither the *s* was to go, they
Eze 1:20 Whithersoever the *s* was to go
Eze 1:20 went, thither was their *s* to go
Eze 1:20 for the *s* of the living creature
Eze 1:21 for the *s* of the living creature
Eze 2:2 the *s* entered into me when he
Eze 3:12 Then the *s* took me up, and I heard
Eze 3:14 So the *s* lifted me up, and took me
Eze 3:14 bitterness, in the heat of my *s*
Eze 3:24 Then the *s* entered into me, and
Eze 8:3 the *s* lifted me up between the
Eze 10:17 for the *s* of the living creature
Eze 11:1 Moreover the *s* lifted me up
Eze 11:5 the *S* of the LORD fell upon me,
Eze 11:19 and I will put a new *s* within you
Eze 11:24 Afterwards the *s* took me up
Eze 11:24 by the *S* of God into Chaldea
Eze 13:3 prophets, that follow their own *s*
Eze 18:31 make you a new heart and a new *s*
Eze 21:7 every *s* shall faint, and all knees
Eze 36:26 a new *s* will I put within you
Eze 36:27 And I will put my *s* within you
Eze 37:1 me out in the *s* of the LORD
Eze 37:14 And shall put my *s* in you, and ye
Eze 39:29 out my *s* upon the house of Israel
Eze 43:5 So the *s* took me up, and brought
Dan 2:1 wherewith his *s* was troubled
Dan 2:3 my *s* was troubled to know the
Dan 4:8 in whom is the *s* of the holy gods
Dan 4:9 because I know that the *s* of the
Dan 4:18 for the *s* of the holy gods is in
Dan 5:11 in whom is the *s* of the holy gods
Dan 5:12 Forasmuch as an excellent *s*
Dan 5:14 that the *s* of the gods is in thee
Dan 6:3 because an excellent *s* was in him
Dan 7:15 in my *s* in the midst of my body
Hos 4:12 for the *s* of whoredoms hath
Hos 5:4 for the *s* of whoredoms is in the
Joel 2:28 will pour out my *s* upon all flesh
Joel 2:29 those days will I pour out my *s*
Mic 2:7 is the *s* of the LORD straitened
Mic 2:11 If a man walking in the *s*
Mic 3:8 of power by the *s* of the LORD
Hag 1:14 the LORD stirred up the *s* of
Hag 1:14 the *s* of Joshua the son of
Hag 1:14 the *s* of all the remnant of the
Hag 2:5 so my *s* remaineth among you
Zec 4:6 might, nor by power, but by my *s*
Zec 6:8 quieted my *s* in the north country
Zec 7:12 in his *s* by the former prophets
Zec 12:1 formeth the *s* of man within him
Zec 12:10 Jerusalem, the *s* of grace and of
Zec 13:2 the unclean *s* to pass out of the
Mal 2:15 Yet had he the residue of the *s*
Mal 2:15 Therefore take heed to your *s*
Mal 2:16 therefore take heed to your *s*
Mt 3:16 he saw the *S* of God descending
Mt 4:1 the *s* into the wilderness to be
Mt 5:3 Blessed are the poor in *s*
Mt 10:20 but the *S* of your Father which
Mt 12:18 I will put my *S* upon him, and he
Mt 12:28 I cast out devils by the *S* of God
Mt 12:43 When the unclean *s* is gone out of
Mt 14:26 were troubled, saying, It is a *s*
Mt 22:43 doth David in *s* call him Lord
Mt 26:41 the *s* indeed is willing, but the
Mk 1:10 the *S* like a dove descending upon
Mk 1:12 immediately the *s* driveth him
Mk 1:23 synagogue a man with an unclean *s*
Mk 1:26 when the unclean *s* had torn him
Mk 2:8 when Jesus perceived in his *s*
Mk 3:30 they said, He hath an unclean *s*
Mk 5:2 the tombs a man with an unclean *s*
Mk 5:8 out of the man, thou unclean *s*
Mk 6:49 they supposed it had been a *s*
Mk 7:25 young daughter had an unclean *s*
Mk 8:12 And he sighed deeply in his *s*
Mk 9:17 thee my son, which hath a dumb *s*
Mk 9:20 him, straightway the *s* tare him
Mk 9:25 together, he rebuked the foul *s*
Mk 9:25 unto him, Thou dumb and deaf *s*
Mk 9:26 the *s* cried, and rent him sore, and
Mk 14:38 The *s* truly is ready, but the
Lk 1:17 he shall go before him in the *s*
Lk 1:47 my *s* hath rejoiced in God my
Lk 1:80 child grew, and waxed strong in *s*
Lk 2:27 he came by the *S* into the temple
Lk 2:40 child grew, and waxed strong in *s*
Lk 4:1 was led by the *S* into the
Lk 4:14 the power of the *S* into Galilee
Lk 4:18 The *S* of the Lord is upon me,
Lk 4:33 which had a *s* of an unclean devil
Lk 8:29 unclean *s* to come out of the man
Lk 8:55 her *s* came again, and she arose
Lk 9:39 a *s* taketh him, and he suddenly
Lk 9:42 And Jesus rebuked the unclean *s*
Lk 9:55 not what manner of *s* ye are of
Lk 10:21 In that hour Jesus rejoiced in *s*
Lk 11:13 the Holy *S* to them that ask him
Lk 11:24 When the unclean *s* is gone out of
Lk 13:11 a *s* of infirmity eighteen years
Lk 23:46 into thy hands I commend my *s*
Lk 24:37 supposed that they had seen a *s*
Lk 24:39 for a *s* hath not flesh and bones,
Jn 1:32 I saw the *S* descending from
Jn 1:33 thou shalt see the *S* descending
Jn 3:5 man be born of water and of the *S*
Jn 3:6 which is born of the *S* is *s*
Jn 3:8 every one that is born of the *S*
Jn 3:34 not the *S* by measure unto him
Jn 4:23 shall worship the Father in *s*
Jn 4:24 God is a *S*
Jn 4:24 worship him must worship him in *s*
Jn 6:63 It is the *s* that quickeneth
Jn 6:63 that I speak unto you, they are *s*
Jn 7:39 (But this spake he of the *S*
Jn 11:33 with her, he groaned in the *s*
Jn 13:21 thus said, he was troubled in *s*
Jn 14:17 Even the *S* of truth
Jn 15:26 the Father, even the *S* of truth
Jn 16:13 the *S* of truth, is come, he will
Acts 2:4 as the *S* gave them utterance
Acts 2:17 pour out of my *S* upon all flesh
Acts 2:18 pour out in those days of my *S*
Acts 5:9 to tempt the *S* of the Lord
Acts 6:10 wisdom and the *s* by which he spake
Acts 7:59 saying, Lord Jesus, receive my *s*
Acts 8:29 Then the *S* said unto Philip, Go
Acts 8:39 the *S* of the Lord caught away
Acts 10:19 the *S* said unto him, Behold,
Acts 11:12 the *S* bade me go with them,
Acts 11:28 signified by the *S* that there
Acts 16:7 but the *S* suffered them not
Acts 16:16 with a *s* of divination met us
Acts 16:18 grieved, turned and said to the *s*
Acts 17:16 his *s* was stirred in him, when he
Acts 18:5 Paul was pressed in the *s*
Acts 18:25 and being fervent in the *s*
Acts 19:15 And the evil *s* answered and said,
Acts 19:16 the evil *s* was leaped on them
Acts 19:21 ended, Paul purposed in the *s*
Acts 20:22 go bound in the *s* unto Jerusalem
Acts 21:4 who said to Paul through the *S*
Acts 23:8 neither angel, nor *s*
Acts 23:9 but if a *s* or an angel hath
Rom 1:4 according to the *s* of holiness
Rom 1:9 whom I serve with my *s* in the
Rom 2:29 is that of the heart, in the *s*
Rom 7:6 we should serve in newness of *s*
Rom 8:1 after the flesh, but after the *S*
Rom 8:2 For the law of the the *S* of life
Rom 8:4 after the flesh, but after the *S*
Rom 8:5 the *S* the things of the *S*
Rom 8:9 not in the flesh, but in the *S*
Rom 8:9 if so be that the *S* of God dwell
Rom 8:9 any man have not the *S* of Christ
Rom 8:10 but the *S* is life because of
Rom 8:11 But if the *S* of him that raised
Rom 8:11 by his *S* that dwelleth in you
Rom 8:13 but if ye through the *S* do
Rom 8:14 many as are led by the *S* of God
Rom 8:15 the *s* of bondage again to fear
Rom 8:15 have received the *S* of adoption
Rom 8:16 The *S* itself beareth witness with
Rom 8:16 itself beareth witness with our *s*
Rom 8:23 have the firstfruits of the *S*
Rom 8:26 Likewise the *S* also helpeth our
Rom 8:26 but the *S* itself maketh
Rom 8:27 knoweth what is the mind of the *S*
Rom 11:8 hath given them the *s* of slumber
Rom 12:11 fervent in *s*
Rom 15:19 by the power of the *S* of God
Rom 15:30 sake, and for the love of the *S*
1Cor 2:4 but in demonstration of the *S*
1Cor 2:10 revealed them unto us by his *S*
1Cor 2:10 for the *S* searcheth all things,
1Cor 2:11 save the *s* of man which is in him
1Cor 2:11 knoweth no man, but the *S* of God
1Cor 2:12 not the *s* of the world
1Cor 2:12 but the *s* which is of God
1Cor 2:14 not the things of the *S* of God
1Cor 3:16 that the *S* of God dwelleth in you
1Cor 4:21 in love, and in the *s* of meekness
1Cor 5:3 absent in body, but present in *s*
1Cor 5:4 ye are gathered together, and my *s*
1Cor 5:5 that the *s* may be saved in the
1Cor 6:11 Jesus, and by the *S* of our God
1Cor 6:17 is joined unto the Lord is one *s*
1Cor 6:20 God in your body, and in your *s*
1Cor 7:34 may be holy both in body and in *s*
1Cor 7:40 also that I have the *S* of God
1Cor 12:3 that no man speaking by the *S* of
1Cor 12:4 of gifts, but the same *S*
1Cor 12:7 But the manifestation of the *S* is
1Cor 12:8 given by the *S* the word of wisdom
1Cor 12:8 word of knowledge by the same *S*
1Cor 12:9 To another faith by the same *S*
1Cor 12:9 gifts of healing by the same *S*
1Cor 12:11 that one and the selfsame *S*
1Cor 12:13 For by one *S* are we all baptized
1Cor 12:13 been all made to drink into one *S*
1Cor 14:2 howbeit in the *s* he speaketh
1Cor 14:14 tongue, my *s* prayeth, but my
1Cor 14:15 I will pray with the *s*, and I will
1Cor 14:15 I will sing with the *s*, and I will
1Cor 14:16 when thou shalt bless with the *s*
1Cor 15:45 last Adam was made a quickening *s*
1Cor 16:18 For they have refreshed my *s*
2Cor 1:22 earnest of the *S* in our hearts
2Cor 2:13 I had no rest in my *s*, because I
2Cor 3:3 but with the *S* of the living God
2Cor 3:6 not of the letter, but of the *s*
2Cor 3:6 killeth, but the *s* giveth life
2Cor 3:8 of the *s* be rather glorious
2Cor 3:17 Now the Lord is that *S*
2Cor 3:17 where the *S* of the Lord is, there
2Cor 3:18 even as by the *S* of the Lord
2Cor 4:13 We having the same *s* of faith
2Cor 5:5 unto us the earnest of the *S*
2Cor 7:1 all filthiness of the flesh and *s*
2Cor 7:13 because his *s* was refreshed by
2Cor 11:4 or if ye receive another *s*
2Cor 12:18 walked we not in the same *s*
Gal 3:2 Received ye the *S* by the works of
Gal 3:3 having begun in the *S*, are ye now
Gal 3:5 that ministereth to you the *S*
Gal 3:14 promise of the *S* through faith
Gal 4:6 God hath sent forth the *S* of his
Gal 4:29 him that was born after the *S*
Gal 5:5 For we through the *S* wait for the
Gal 5:16 This I say then, Walk in the *S*
Gal 5:17 the flesh lusteth against the *S*
Gal 5:17 and the *S* against the flesh
Gal 5:18 But if ye be led of the *S*
Gal 5:22 But the fruit of the *S* is love
Gal 5:25 If we live in the *S*, let us also
Gal 5:25 let us also walk in the *S*
Gal 6:1 such an one in the *s* of meekness
Gal 6:8 but he that soweth to the *S* shall
Gal 6:8 of the *S* reap life everlasting
Gal 6:18 Lord Jesus Christ be with your *s*
Eph 1:13 with that holy *S* of promise
Eph 1:17 may give unto you the *s* of wisdom
Eph 2:2 the *s* that now worketh in the
Eph 2:18 access by one *S* unto the Father
Eph 2:22 habitation of God through the *S*
Eph 3:5 apostles and prophets by the *S*
Eph 3:16 might by his *S* in the inner man
Eph 4:3 of the *S* in the bond of peace

Eph 4:4 There is one body, and one S
Eph 4:23 be renewed in the s of your mind
Eph 4:30 And grieve not the holy S of God
Eph 5:9 fruit of the S is in all goodness
Eph 5:18 but be filled with the S
Eph 6:17 salvation, and the sword of the S
Eph 6:18 prayer and supplication in the S
Phil 1:19 supply of the S of Jesus Christ
Phil 1:27 that ye stand fast in one s
Phil 2:1 love, if any fellowship of the S
Phil 3:3 which worship God in the s
Col 1:8 unto us your love in the S
Col 2:5 flesh, yet am I with you in the s
1Th 4:8 also given unto us his holy S
1Th 5:19 Quench not the S
1Th 5:23 and I pray God your whole s
2Th 2:2 or be troubled, neither by s
2Th 2:8 consume with the s of his mouth
2Th 2:13 through sanctification of the S
1Ti 3:16 in the flesh, justified in the S
1Ti 4:1 Now the S speaketh expressly,
1Ti 4:12 in conversation, in charity, in s
2Ti 1:7 hath not given us the s of fear
2Ti 4:22 Lord Jesus Christ be with thy s
Philem 25 Lord Jesus Christ be with your s
Heb 4:12 the dividing asunder of soul and s
Heb 9:14 who through the eternal S offered
Heb 10:29 done despite unto the S of grace
Jas 2:26 as the body without the s is dead
Jas 4:5 The s that dwelleth in us lusteth
1Pet 1:2 through sanctification of the S
1Pet 1:11 or what manner of time the S of
1Pet 1:22 the S unto unfeigned love of the
1Pet 3:4 the ornament of a meek and quiet s
1Pet 3:18 the flesh, but quickened by the S
1Pet 4:6 live according to God in the s
1Pet 4:14 for the s of glory and of God
1Jn 3:24 by the S which he hath given us
1Jn 4:1 Beloved, believe not every s
1Jn 4:2 Hereby know ye the S of God
1Jn 4:2 Every s that confesseth that
1Jn 4:3 every s that confesseth not that
1Jn 4:3 this is that s of antichrist,
1Jn 4:6 Hereby know we the s of truth
1Jn 4:6 of truth, and the s of error
1Jn 4:13 because he hath given us of his S
1Jn 5:6 it is the S that beareth witness,
1Jn 5:6 witness, because the S is truth
1Jn 5:8 that bear witness in earth, the s
Jude 19 sensual, having not the S
Rev 1:10 I was in the S on the Lord's day,
Rev 2:7 let him hear what the S saith
Rev 2:11 let him hear what the S saith
Rev 2:17 let him hear what the S saith
Rev 2:29 let him hear what the S saith
Rev 3:6 let him hear what the S saith
Rev 3:13 let him hear what the S saith
Rev 3:22 let him hear what the S saith
Rev 4:2 And immediately I was in the s
Rev 11:11 an half the S of life from God
Rev 14:13 Yea, saith the S, that they may
Rev 17:3 away in the s into the wilderness
Rev 18:2 and the hold of every foul s
Rev 19:10 of Jesus is the s of prophecy
Rev 21:10 me away in the s to a great
Rev 22:17 And the S and the bride say, Come

## SPIRITS

Lev 19:31 not them that have familiar s
Lev 20:6 after such as have familiar s
Num 16:22 the God of the s of all flesh
Num 27:16 the God of the s of all flesh
Deut 18:11 or a consulter with familiar s
1Sa 28:3 away those that had familiar s
1Sa 28:9 off those that have familiar s
2Kin 21:6 and dealt with familiar s
2Kin 23:24 the workers with familiar s
Ps 104:4 Who maketh his angels s
Prov 16:2 but the LORD weigheth the s
Is 8:19 unto them that have familiar s
Is 19:3 and to them that have familiar s
Zec 6:5 are the four s of the heavens
Mt 8:16 he cast out the s with his word
Mt 10:1 gave them power against unclean s
Mt 12:45 other s more wicked than himself
Mk 1:27 commandeth he even the unclean s
Mk 3:11 And unclean s, when they saw him,
Mk 5:13 And the unclean s went out
Mk 6:7 and gave them power over unclean s
Lk 4:36 power he commandeth the unclean s
Lk 6:18 that were vexed with unclean s
Lk 7:21 and plagues, and of evil s
Lk 8:2 which had been healed of evil s
Lk 10:20 that the s are subject unto you
Lk 11:26 other s more wicked than himself
Acts 5:16 which were vexed with unclean s
Acts 8:7 For unclean s, crying with loud
Acts 19:12 the evil s went out of them
Acts 19:13 evil s the name of the Lord Jesus
1Cor 12:10 to another discerning of s
1Cor 14:32 the s of the prophets are subject
1Ti 4:1 faith, giving heed to seducing s
Heb 1:7 he saith, Who maketh his angels s
Heb 1:14 Are they not all ministering s
Heb 12:9 subjection unto the Father of s
Heb 12:23 to the s of just men made perfect
1Pet 3:19 and preached unto the s in prison
1Jn 4:1 but try the s whether they are of
Rev 1:4 from the seven S which are before
Rev 3:1 he that hath the seven S of God
Rev 4:5 which are the seven S of God
Rev 5:6 which are the seven S of God sent
Rev 16:13 I saw three unclean s like frogs
Rev 16:14 For they are the s of devils

## SPIRITUAL

Hos 9:7 the s man is mad, for the
Rom 1:11 I may impart unto you some s gift
Rom 7:14 For we know that the law is s
Rom 15:27 made partakers of their s things
1Cor 2:13 comparing s things with s
1Cor 2:15 But he that is s judgeth all
1Cor 3:1 not speak unto you as unto s
1Cor 9:11 If we have sown unto you s things
1Cor 10:3 And did all eat the same s meat
1Cor 10:4 And did all drink the same s drink
1Cor 10:4 for they drank of that s Rock
1Cor 12:1 Now concerning s gifts, brethren,
1Cor 14:1 after charity, and desire s gifts
1Cor 14:12 as ye are zealous of s gifts
1Cor 14:37 himself to be a prophet, or s
1Cor 15:44 it is raised a s body
1Cor 15:44 body, and there is a s body
1Cor 15:46 that was not first which is s
1Cor 15:46 and afterward that which is s
Gal 6:1 in a fault, ye which are s
Eph 1:3 who hath blessed us with all s
Eph 5:19 s songs, singing and making melody
Eph 6:12 against s wickedness in high
Col 1:9 in all wisdom and s understanding
Col 3:16 s songs, singing with grace in
1Pet 2:5 stones, are built up a s house
1Pet 2:5 to offer up s sacrifices

## SPIT

Lev 15:8 issue s upon him that is clean
Num 12:14 her father had but s in her face
Deut 25:9 s in his face, and shall answer and
Job 30:10 me, and spare not to s in my face
Mt 26:67 Then did they s in his face
Mt 27:30 they s upon him, and took the reed
Mk 7:33 fingers into his ears, and he s
Mk 8:23 and when he had s on his eyes
Mk 10:34 shall s upon him, and shall kill
Mk 14:65 And some began to s on him
Mk 15:19 did s upon him, and bowing their

## SPOIL

Gen 49:27 and at night he shall divide the s
Ex 3:22 and ye shall s the Egyptians
Ex 15:9 overtake, I will divide the s
Num 31:9 took the s of all their cattle,
Num 31:11 And they took all the s, and all
Num 31:12 captives, and the prey, and the s
Num 31:53 (For the men of war had taken s
Deut 2:35 the s of the cities which we took
Deut 3:7 the s of the cities, we took for
Deut 13:16 thou shalt gather all the s of it
Deut 13:16 all the s thereof every whit, for
Deut 20:14 the city, even all the s thereof
Deut 20:14 shalt eat the s of thine enemies
Josh 8:2 only the s thereof, and the cattle
Josh 8:27 the s of that city Israel took
Josh 11:14 all the s of these cities, and the
Josh 22:8 divide the s of your enemies with
Judg 5:30 the necks of them that take the s
Judg 14:19 men of them, and took their s
1Sa 14:30 the s of their enemies which they
1Sa 14:32 And the people flew upon the s
1Sa 14:36 s them until the morning light,
1Sa 15:19 LORD, but didst fly upon the s
1Sa 15:21 But the people took of the s
1Sa 30:16 because of all the great s that
1Sa 30:19 sons nor daughters, neither s
1Sa 30:20 and said, This is David's s
1Sa 30:22 of the s that we have recovered
1Sa 30:26 he sent of the s unto the elders
1Sa 30:26 the s of the enemies of the LORD
2Sa 3:22 and brought in a great s with them
2Sa 8:12 of the s of Hadadezer, son of
2Sa 12:30 he brought forth the s of the
2Sa 23:10 returned after him only to s
2Kin 3:23 now therefore, Moab, to the s
2Kin 21:14 prey and a s to all their enemies
1Chr 20:2 exceeding much s out of the city
2Chr 14:13 and they carried away very much s
2Chr 14:14 was exceeding much s in them
2Chr 15:11 of the s which they had brought,
2Chr 20:25 came to take away the s of them
2Chr 20:25 three days in gathering of the s
2Chr 24:23 sent all the s of them unto the
2Chr 25:13 thousand of them, and took much s
2Chr 28:8 took also away much s from them
2Chr 28:8 and brought the s to Samaria
2Chr 28:14 the s before the princes and all
2Chr 28:15 with the s clothed all that were
Ezr 9:7 sword, to captivity, and to a s
Est 3:13 to take the s of them for a prey
Est 8:11 to take the s of them for a prey,
Est 9:10 but on the s laid they not their
Job 29:17 plucked the s out of his teeth
Ps 44:10 which hate us s for themselves
Ps 68:12 tarried at home divided the s
Ps 89:41 All that pass by the way s him
Ps 109:11 and let the strangers s his labour
Ps 119:162 word, as one that findeth great s
Prov 1:13 we shall fill our houses with s
Prov 16:19 to divide the s with the proud
Prov 22:23 s the soul of those that spoiled
Prov 24:15 s not his resting place
Prov 31:11 that he shall have no need of s
Song 2:15 little foxes, that s the vines
Is 3:14 the s of the poor is in your
Is 8:4 the s of Samaria shall be taken
Is 9:3 rejoice when they divide the s
Is 10:6 give him a charge, to take the s
Is 11:14 they shall s them of the east
Is 17:14 is the portion of them that s us
Is 33:1 when thou shalt cease to s
Is 33:4 your s shall be gathered like the
Is 33:23 is the prey of a great s divided
Is 42:22 for a s, and none saith, Restore
Is 42:24 Who gave Jacob for a s, and Israel
Is 53:12 divide the s with the strong
Jer 5:6 wolf of the evenings shall s them
Jer 6:7 violence and s is heard in her
Jer 15:13 I give to the s without price
Jer 17:3 and all thy treasures to the s
Jer 20:5 their enemies, which shall s them
Jer 20:8 cried out, I cried violence and s
Jer 30:16 they that s thee shall be a
Jer 30:16 thee shall be a s
Jer 47:4 cometh to s all the Philistines
Jer 47:4 the LORD will s the Philistines
Jer 49:28 Kedar, and s the men of the east
Jer 49:32 the multitude of their cattle a s
Jer 50:10 And Chaldea shall be a s
Jer 50:10 all that s her shall be satisfied
Eze 7:21 the wicked of the earth for a s
Eze 14:15 through the land, and they s it
Eze 25:7 thee for a s to the heathen
Eze 26:5 shall become a s to the nations
Eze 26:12 they shall make a s of thy riches
Eze 29:19 take her multitude, and take her s
Eze 32:12 they shall s the pomp of Egypt,
Eze 38:12 To take a s, and to take a prey
Eze 38:13 thee, Art thou come to take a s
Eze 38:13 and goods, to take a great s
Eze 39:10 they shall s those that spoiled
Eze 45:9 remove violence and s, and execute
Dan 11:24 scatter among them the prey, and s
Dan 11:33 by flame, by captivity, and by s
Hos 10:2 altars, he shall s their images
Hos 13:15 he shall s the treasure of all
Nah 2:9 Take ye the s of silver, take the
Nah 2:9 of silver, take the s of gold
Hab 2:8 of the people shall s thee
Hab 2:17 the s of beasts, which made them
Zeph 2:9 residue of my people shall s them
Zec 2:9 they shall be a s to their
Zec 14:1 thy s shall be divided in the
Mt 12:29 s his goods, except he first bind

Mt 12:29 and then he will *s* his house
Mk 3:27 *s* his goods, except he will first
Mk 3:27 and then he will *s* his house
Col 2:8 Beware lest any man *s* you through

## SPOILED

Gen 34:27 *s* the city, because they had
Gen 34:29 *s* even all that was in the house
Ex 12:36 And they *s* the Egyptians
Deut 28:29 *s* evermore, and no man shall save
Judg 2:14 the hands of spoilers that *s* them
Judg 2:16 of the hand of those that *s* them
1Sa 14:48 of the hands of them that *s* them
1Sa 17:53 and they *s* their tents
2Kin 7:16 *s* the tents of the Syrians
2Chr 14:14 and they *s* all the cities
Job 12:17 He leadeth counsellors away *s*
Job 12:19 He leadeth princes away *s*
Ps 76:5 The stouthearted are *s*, they have
Prov 22:23 the soul of those that *s* them
Is 13:16 their houses shall be *s*, and their
Is 18:2 whose land the rivers have *s*
Is 18:7 whose land the rivers have *s*
Is 24:3 be utterly emptied, and utterly *s*
Is 33:1 that spoilest, and thou wast not *s*
Is 33:1 cease to spoil, thou shalt be *s*
Is 42:22 But this is a people robbed and *s*
Jer 2:14 why is he *s*
Jer 4:13 for we are *s*
Jer 4:20 for the whole land is *s*
Jer 4:20 suddenly are my tents *s*, and my
Jer 4:30 And when thou art *s*, what wilt
Jer 9:19 heard out of Zion, How are we *s*
Jer 10:20 My tabernacle is *s*, and all my
Jer 21:12 deliver him that is *s* out of the
Jer 22:3 deliver the *s* out of the hand of
Jer 25:36 for the LORD hath *s* their pasture
Jer 48:1 for it is *s*
Jer 48:15 Moab is *s*, and gone up out of her
Jer 48:20 ye it in Arnon, that Moab is *s*
Jer 49:3 Howl, O Heshbon, for Ai is *s*
Jer 49:10 his seed is *s*, and his brethren,
Jer 51:55 Because the LORD hath *s* Babylon
Eze 18:7 hath *s* none by violence, hath
Eze 18:12 hath *s* by violence, hath not
Eze 18:16 neither hath *s* by violence
Eze 18:18 *s* his brother by violence, and did
Eze 23:46 will give them to be removed and *s*
Eze 39:10 shall spoil those that *s* them
Hos 10:14 and all thy fortresses shall be *s*
Hos 10:14 as Shalman *s* Beth-arbel in the
Amos 3:11 thee, and thy palaces shall be *s*
Amos 5:9 the *s* against the strong, so that
Amos 5:9 so that the *s* shall come against
Mic 2:4 and say, We be utterly *s*
Hab 2:8 Because thou hast *s* many nations
Zec 2:8 me unto the nations which *s* you
Zec 11:2 because the mighty are *s*
Zec 11:3 for their glory is *s*
Zec 11:3 for the pride of Jordan is *s*
Col 2:15 having *s* principalities and powers

## SPOILER

Is 16:4 to them from the face of the *s*
Is 16:4 the *s* ceaseth, the oppressors are
Is 21:2 treacherously, and the *s* spoileth
Jer 6:26 for the *s* shall suddenly come
Jer 15:8 of the young men a *s* at noonday
Jer 48:8 the *s* shall come upon every city,
Jer 48:18 for the *s* of Moab shall come upon
Jer 48:32 the *s* is fallen upon thy summer
Jer 51:56 Because the *s* is come upon her,

## SPOILERS

Judg 2:14 the hands of *s* that spoiled them
1Sa 13:17 the *s* came out of the camp of the
1Sa 14:15 the garrison, and the *s*, they also
2Kin 17:20 delivered them into the hand of *s*
Jer 12:12 The *s* are come upon all high
Jer 51:48 for the *s* shall come unto her
Jer 51:53 yet from me shall *s* come unto her

## SPOILETH

Ps 35:10 and the needy from him that *s* him
Is 21:2 treacherously, and the spoiler *s*
Hos 7:1 and the troop of robbers *s* without
Nah 3:16 the cankerworm *s*, and fleeth away

## SPOILING

Ps 35:12 evil for good to the *s* of my soul
Is 22:4 because of the *s* of the daughter
Jer 48:3 crying shall be from Horonaim, *s*
Hab 1:3 for *s* and violence are before me
Heb 10:34 took joyfully the *s* of your goods

## SPOILS

Josh 7:21 When I saw among the *s* a goodly
1Chr 26:27 Out of the *s* won in battles did
Is 25:11 with the *s* of their hands
Lk 11:22 he trusted, and divideth his *s*
Heb 7:4 Abraham gave the tenth of the *s*

## SPOONS

Ex 25:29 *s* thereof, and covers thereof, and
Ex 37:16 the table, his dishes, and his *s*
Num 4:7 put thereon the dishes, and the *s*
Num 7:84 silver bowls, twelve *s* of gold
Num 7:86 The golden *s* were twelve, full of
Num 7:86 the gold of the *s* was an hundred
1Kin 7:50 snuffers, and the basons, and the *s*
2Kin 25:14 and the snuffers, and the *s*
2Chr 4:22 snuffers, and the basons, and the *s*
2Chr 24:14 and to offer withal, and *s*
Jer 52:18 snuffers, and the bowls, and the *s*
Jer 52:19 and the candlesticks, and the *s*

## SPORT

Judg 16:25 for Samson, that he may make us *s*
Judg 16:25 and he made them *s*
Judg 16:27 that beheld while Samson made *s*
Prov 10:23 It is as *s* to a fool to do
Prov 26:19 and saith, Am not I in *s*
Is 57:4 Against whom do ye *s* yourselves

## SPOT

Lev 13:2 a rising, a scab, or bright *s*
Lev 13:4 If the bright *s* be white in the
Lev 13:19 be a white rising, or a bright *s*
Lev 13:23 if the bright *s* stay in his place
Lev 13:24 burneth have a white bright *s*
Lev 13:25 in the bright *s* be turned white
Lev 13:26 be no white hair in the bright *s*
Lev 13:28 if the bright *s* stay in his place
Lev 13:39 it is a freckled *s* that groweth
Lev 14:56 and for a scab, and for a bright *s*
Num 19:2 bring thee a red heifer without *s*
Num 28:3 first year without *s* day by day
Num 28:9 lambs of the first year without *s*
Num 28:11 lambs of the first year without *s*
Num 29:17 lambs of the first year without *s*
Num 29:26 lambs of the first year without *s*
Deut 32:5 their *s* is not the *s* of his
Deut 32:5 is not the *s* of his children
Job 11:15 thou lift up thy face without *s*
Song 4:7 there is no *s* in thee
Eph 5:27 a glorious church, not having *s*
1Ti 6:14 keep this commandment without *s*
Heb 9:14 offered himself without *s* to God
1Pet 1:19 lamb without blemish and without *s*
2Pet 3:14 found of him in peace, without *s*

## SPOTS

Lev 13:38 bright *s*, even white bright *s*
Lev 13:39 if the bright *s* in the skin of
Jer 13:23 his skin, or the leopard his *s*
2Pet 2:13 *S* they are and blemishes, sporting
Jude 12 These are *s* in your feasts of

## SPOTTED

Gen 30:32 *s* cattle, and all the brown cattle
Gen 30:32 cattle among the sheep, and the *s*
Gen 30:33 *s* among the goats, and brown among
Gen 30:35 goats that were ringstraked and *s*
Gen 30:35 she goats that were speckled and *s*
Gen 30:39 ringstraked, speckled, and *s*
Jude 23 even the garment *s* by the flesh

## SPOUSE

Song 4:8 Come with me from Lebanon, my *s*
Song 4:9 my heart, my sister, my *s*
Song 4:10 fair is thy love, my sister, my *s*
Song 4:11 Thy lips, O my *s*, drop as the
Song 4:12 inclosed is my sister, my *s*
Song 5:1 into my garden, my sister, my *s*

## SPRANG

Mk 4:5 and immediately it *s* up, because
Mk 4:8 and did yield fruit that *s* up
Lk 8:7 and the thorns *s* up with it
Lk 8:8 ground, and *s* up, and bare fruit an
Acts 16:29 *s* in, and came trembling, and fell
Heb 7:14 that our Lord *s* out of Juda
Heb 11:12 Therefore *s* there even of one, and

## SPREAD

Gen 10:18 of the Canaanites *s* abroad
Gen 28:14 thou shalt *s* abroad to the west,
Gen 33:19 a field, where he had *s* his tent
Gen 35:21 *s* his tent beyond the tower of
Ex 9:29 I will *s* abroad my hands unto the
Ex 9:33 *s* abroad his hands unto the LORD
Ex 37:9 the cherubims *s* out their wings
Ex 40:19 he *s* abroad the tent over the
Lev 13:5 the plague *s* not in the skin
Lev 13:6 the plague *s* not in the skin, the
Lev 13:7 But if the scab *s* much abroad in
Lev 13:22 if it *s* much abroad in the skin,
Lev 13:23 *s* not, it is a burning boil
Lev 13:27 if it be *s* much abroad in the
Lev 13:28 *s* not in the skin, but it be
Lev 13:32 and, behold, if the scall *s* not
Lev 13:34 if the scall be not *s* in the skin
Lev 13:35 But if the scall *s* much in the
Lev 13:36 if the scall be *s* in the skin
Lev 13:51 if the plague be *s* in the garment
Lev 13:53 plague be not *s* in the garment
Lev 13:55 colour, and the plague be not *s*
Lev 14:39 if the plague be *s* in the walls
Lev 14:44 if the plague be *s* in the house
Lev 14:48 plague hath not *s* in the house
Num 4:6 shall *s* over it a cloth wholly of
Num 4:7 they shall *s* a cloth of blue
Num 4:8 they shall *s* upon them a cloth of
Num 4:11 they shall *s* a cloth of blue
Num 4:13 and *s* a purple cloth thereon
Num 4:14 they shall *s* upon it a covering
Num 11:32 they *s* them all abroad for
Num 24:6 As the valleys are they *s* forth
Deut 22:17 they shall *s* the cloth before the
Judg 8:25 they *s* a garment, and did cast
Judg 15:9 in Judah, and *s* themselves in Lehi
Ruth 3:9 *s* therefore thy skirt over thine
1Sa 30:16 they were *s* abroad upon all the
2Sa 5:18 *s* themselves in the valley of
2Sa 5:22 *s* themselves in the valley of
2Sa 16:22 So they *s* Absalom a tent upon the
2Sa 17:19 *s* a covering over the well's
2Sa 17:19 mouth, and *s* ground corn thereon
2Sa 21:10 *s* it for her upon the rock, from
2Sa 22:43 the street, and did *s* them abroad
1Kin 6:32 *s* gold upon the cherubims, and
1Kin 8:7 For the cherubims *s* forth their
1Kin 8:22 *s* forth his hands toward heaven
1Kin 8:38 *s* forth his hands toward this
1Kin 8:54 with his hands *s* up to heaven
2Kin 8:15 *s* it on his face, so that he died
2Kin 19:14 the LORD, and *s* it before the LORD
1Chr 14:9 *s* themselves in the valley of
1Chr 14:13 the Philistines yet again *s*
1Chr 28:18 that *s* out their wings, and
2Chr 3:13 The wings of these cherubims *s*
2Chr 5:8 For the cherubims *s* forth their
2Chr 6:12 of Israel, and *s* forth his hands
2Chr 6:13 *s* forth his hands toward heaven,
2Chr 6:29 shall *s* forth his hands in this
2Chr 26:8 his name *s* abroad even to the
2Chr 26:15 And his name *s* far abroad
Ezr 9:5 *s* out my hands unto the LORD my
Job 29:19 My root was *s* out by the waters,
Job 37:18 Hast thou with him *s* out the sky
Ps 105:39 He *s* a cloud for a covering
Ps 140:5 they have *s* a net by the wayside
Prov 1:17 net is *s* in the sight of any bird
Is 1:15 when ye *s* forth your hands, I
Is 14:11 the worm is *s* under thee, and the
Is 19:8 they that *s* nets upon the waters
Is 25:7 vail that is *s* over all nations
Is 25:11 he shall *s* forth his hands in the
Is 33:23 mast, they could not *s* the sail
Is 37:14 the LORD, and *s* it before the LORD
Is 42:5 he that *s* forth the earth, and
Is 58:5 to *s* sackcloth and ashes under him
Is 65:2 I have *s* out my hands all the day
Jer 8:2 they shall *s* them before the sun,
Jer 10:9 Silver *s* into plates is brought
Jer 43:10 he shall *s* his royal pavilion
Jer 48:40 shall *s* his wings over Moab
Jer 49:22 eagle, and *s* his wings over Bozrah
Lam 1:10 The adversary hath *s* out his hand
Lam 1:13 he hath *s* a net for my feet, he
Eze 2:10 And he *s* it before me
Eze 12:13 My net also will I *s* upon him
Eze 16:8 I *s* my skirt over thee, and
Eze 17:20 I will *s* my net upon him, and he
Eze 19:8 and *s* their net over him
Eze 26:14 shalt be a place to *s* nets upon
Eze 32:3 I will therefore *s* out my net
Eze 47:10 shall be a place to *s* forth nets

Hos 5:1 on Mizpah, and a net *s* upon Tabor
Hos 7:12 I will *s* my net upon them
Hos 14:6 His branches shall *s*, and his
Joel 2:2 as the morning *s* upon the
Hab 1:8 their horsemen shall *s* themselves
Zec 1:17 prosperity shall yet be *s* abroad
Zec 2:6 for I have *s* you abroad as the
Mal 2:3 *s* dung upon your faces, even the
Mt 9:31 *s* abroad his fame in all that
Mt 21:8 a very great multitude *s* their
Mk 1:28 immediately his fame *s* abroad
Mk 6:14 (for his name was *s* abroad
Mk 11:8 many *s* their garments in the way
Lk 19:36 they *s* their clothes in the way
Acts 4:17 But that it *s* no further among
1Th 1:8 faith to God-ward is *s* abroad

## SPREADETH
Lev 13:8 the scab *s* in the skin, then the
Deut 32:11 *s* abroad her wings, taketh them,
Job 9:8 Which alone *s* out the heavens, and
Job 26:9 throne, and *s* his cloud upon it
Job 36:30 he *s* his light upon it, and
Job 41:30 he *s* sharp pointed things upon
Prov 29:5 neighbour *s* a net for his feet
Is 25:11 as he that swimmeth *s* forth his
Is 40:19 the goldsmith *s* it over with gold
Is 40:22 *s* them out as a tent to dwell in
Is 44:24 that *s* abroad the earth by myself
Jer 4:31 that *s* her hands, saying, Woe is
Jer 17:8 that *s* out her roots by the river
Lam 1:17 Zion *s* forth her hands, and there

## SPREADING
Lev 13:57 it is a *s* plague
Ps 37:35 *s* himself like a green bay tree
Eze 17:6 became a *s* vine of low stature,
Eze 26:5 It shall be a place for the *s* of

## SPRING
Num 21:17 sang this song, *S* up, O well
Deut 8:7 depths that *s* out of valleys and
Judg 19:25 and when the day began to *s*
1Sa 9:26 to pass about the *s* of the day
2Kin 2:21 forth unto the *s* of the waters
Job 5:6 doth trouble *s* out of the ground
Job 38:27 bud of the tender herb to *s* forth
Ps 85:11 Truth shall *s* out of the earth
Ps 92:7 When the wicked *s* as the grass
Prov 25:26 troubled fountain, and a corrupt *s*
Song 4:12 a *s* shut up, a fountain sealed
Is 42:9 before they *s* forth I tell you of
Is 43:19 now it shall *s* forth
Is 44:4 they shall *s* up as among the
Is 45:8 let righteousness *s* up together
Is 58:8 health shall *s* forth speedily
Is 58:11 like a *s* of water, whose waters
Is 61:11 that are sown in it to *s* forth
Is 61:11 praise to *s* forth before all the
Eze 17:9 wither in all the leaves of her *s*
Hos 13:15 his *s* shall become dry, and his
Joel 2:22 pastures of the wilderness do *s*
Mk 4:27 and day, and the seed should *s*

## SPRINGETH
1Kin 4:33 the hyssop that *s* out of the wall
2Kin 19:29 year that which *s* of the same
Is 37:30 year that which *s* of the same
Hos 10:4 thus judgment *s* up as hemlock in

## SPRINGING
Gen 26:19 and found there a well of *s* water
2Sa 23:4 as the tender grass *s* out of the
Ps 65:10 thou blessest the *s* thereof
Jn 4:14 water *s* up into everlasting life
Heb 12:15 of bitterness *s* up trouble you

## SPRINGS
Deut 4:49 the plain, under the *s* of Pisgah
Josh 10:40 and of the vale, and of the *s*
Josh 12:8 and in the plains, and in the *s*
Josh 15:19 give me also *s* of water
Josh 15:19 upper *s*, and the nether *s*
Judg 1:15 give me also *s* of water
Judg 1:15 the upper *s* and the nether *s*
Job 38:16 entered into the *s* of the sea
Ps 87:7 all my *s* are in thee
Ps 104:10 He sendeth the *s* into the valleys
Is 35:7 and the thirsty land *s* of water
Is 41:18 water, and the dry land *s* of water
Is 49:10 even by the *s* of water shall he
Jer 51:36 dry up her sea, and make her *s* dry

## SPRINKLE
Ex 9:8 let Moses *s* it toward the heaven
Ex 29:16 *s* it round about upon the altar
Ex 29:20 *s* the blood upon the altar round
Ex 29:21 *s* it upon Aaron, and upon his
Lev 1:5 *s* the blood round about upon the
Lev 1:11 shall *s* his blood round about
Lev 3:2 *s* the blood upon the altar round
Lev 3:8 Aaron's sons shall *s* the blood
Lev 3:13 the sons of Aaron shall *s* the
Lev 4:6 *s* of the blood seven times before
Lev 4:17 *s* it seven times before the LORD,
Lev 5:9 he shall *s* of the blood of the
Lev 7:2 he *s* round about upon the altar
Lev 14:7 he shall *s* upon him that is to be
Lev 14:16 shall *s* of the oil with his
Lev 14:27 the priest shall *s* with his right
Lev 14:51 water, and *s* the house seven times
Lev 16:14 *s* it with his finger upon the
Lev 16:14 he *s* of the blood with his finger
Lev 16:15 *s* it upon the mercy seat, and
Lev 16:19 he shall *s* of the blood upon it
Lev 17:6 the priest shall *s* the blood upon
Num 8:7 *S* water of purifying upon them,
Num 18:17 thou shalt *s* their blood upon the
Num 19:4 *s* of her blood directly before
Num 19:18 *s* it upon the tent, and upon all
Num 19:19 the clean person shall *s* upon the
2Kin 16:15 *s* upon it all the blood of the
Is 52:15 So shall he *s* many nations
Eze 36:25 Then will I *s* clean water upon
Eze 43:18 thereon, and to *s* blood thereon

## SPRINKLED
Ex 9:10 Moses *s* it up toward heaven
Ex 24:6 of the blood he *s* on the altar
Ex 24:8 *s* it on the people, and said,
Lev 6:27 when there is *s* of the blood
Lev 6:27 it was *s* in the holy place
Lev 8:11 he *s* thereof upon the altar seven
Lev 8:19 Moses *s* the blood upon the altar
Lev 8:24 Moses *s* the blood upon the altar
Lev 8:30 *s* it upon Aaron, and upon his
Lev 9:12 which he *s* round about upon the
Lev 9:18 which he *s* upon the altar round
Num 19:13 of separation was not *s* upon him
Num 19:20 hath not been *s* upon him
2Kin 9:33 of her blood was *s* on the wall
2Kin 16:13 and *s* the blood of his peace
2Chr 29:22 the blood, and *s* it on the altar
2Chr 29:22 they *s* the blood upon the altar
2Chr 29:22 they *s* the blood upon the altar
2Chr 30:16 the priests *s* the blood, which
2Chr 35:11 the priests *s* the blood from
Job 2:12 *s* dust upon their heads toward
Is 63:3 blood shall be *s* upon my garments
Heb 9:19 *s* both the book, and all the
Heb 9:21 Moreover he *s* with blood both the
Heb 10:22 having our hearts *s* from an evil

## SPRINKLING
Heb 9:13 ashes of an heifer *s* the unclean
Heb 11:28 the *s* of blood, lest he that
Heb 12:24 covenant, and to the blood of *s*
1Pet 1:2 *s* of the blood of Jesus Christ

## SPRUNG
Gen 41:6 the east wind *s* up after them
Gen 41:23 the east wind, *s* up after them
Lev 13:42 it is a leprosy *s* up in his bald
Mt 4:16 and shadow of death light is *s* up
Mt 13:5 and forthwith they *s* up, because
Mt 13:7 and the thorns *s* up, and choked
Mt 13:26 But when the blade was *s* up
Lk 8:6 and as soon as it was *s* up

## SPUE
Lev 18:28 That the land *s* not you out also,
Lev 20:22 to dwell therein, *s* you not out
Jer 25:27 Drink ye, and be drunken, and *s*
Rev 3:16 I will *s* thee out of my mouth

## SPY
Num 13:16 Moses sent to *s* out the land
Num 13:17 Moses sent them to *s* out the land
Num 21:32 And Moses sent to *s* out Jaazer
Josh 2:1 of Shittim two men to *s* secretly
Josh 6:25 Joshua sent to *s* out Jericho
Judg 18:2 to *s* out the land, and to search
Judg 18:14 to *s* out the country of Laish
Judg 18:17 went to *s* out the land went up
2Sa 10:3 to *s* it out, and to overthrow it
2Kin 6:13 *s* where he is, that I may send and
1Chr 19:3 overthrow, and to *s* out the land
Gal 2:4 who came in privily to *s* out our

## STABLISH
2Sa 7:13 I will *s* the throne of his
1Chr 17:12 I will *s* his throne for ever
1Chr 18:3 as he went to *s* his dominion by
2Chr 7:18 Then will I *s* the throne of thy
Est 9:21 To *s* this among them, that they
Ps 119:38 *S* thy word unto thy servant, who
Rom 16:25 to *s* you according to my gospel
1Th 3:13 To the end he may *s* your hearts
2Th 2:17 *s* you in every good word and work
2Th 3:3 Lord is faithful, who shall *s* you
Jas 5:8 *s* your hearts
1Pet 5:10 a while, make you perfect, *s*

## STABLISHED
2Chr 17:5 Therefore the LORD *s* the kingdom
Ps 93:1 the world also is *s*, that it
Ps 148:6 He hath also *s* them for ever and
Col 2:7 *s* in the faith, as ye have been

## STACHYS *(sta'-kis) A Christian in Rome.*
Rom 16:9 helper in Christ, and *S* my beloved

## STAFF
Gen 32:10 for with my *s* I passed over this
Gen 38:18 thy *s* that is in thine hand
Gen 38:25 the signet, and bracelets, and *s*
Ex 12:11 your feet, and your *s* in your hand
Ex 21:19 again, and walk abroad upon his *s*
Lev 26:26 I have broken the *s* of your bread
Num 13:23 they bare it between two upon a *s*
Num 22:27 and he smote the ass with a *s*
Judg 6:21 end of the *s* that was in his hand
1Sa 17:7 the *s* of his spear was like a
1Sa 17:40 And he took his *s* in his hand
2Sa 3:29 a leper, or that leaneth on a *s*
2Sa 21:19 the *s* of whose spear was like a
2Sa 23:7 with iron and the *s* of a spear
2Sa 23:21 but he went down to him with a *s*
2Kin 4:29 take my *s* in thine hand, and go
2Kin 4:29 lay my *s* upon the face of the
2Kin 4:31 laid the *s* upon the face of the
2Kin 18:21 upon the *s* of this bruised reed
1Chr 11:23 and he went down to him with a *s*
1Chr 20:5 whose spear *s* was like a weaver's
Ps 23:4 thy rod and thy *s* they comfort me
Ps 105:16 he brake the whole *s* of bread
Is 3:1 and from Judah the stay and the *s*
Is 9:4 the *s* of his shoulder, the rod of
Is 10:5 the *s* in their hand is mine
Is 10:15 or as if the *s* should lift up
Is 10:24 shall lift up his *s* against thee
Is 14:5 hath broken the *s* of the wicked
Is 28:27 fitches are beaten out with a *s*
Is 30:32 where the grounded *s* shall pass
Is 36:6 in the *s* of this broken reed
Jer 48:17 say, How is the strong *s* broken
Eze 4:16 I will break the *s* of bread in
Eze 5:16 and will break your *s* of bread
Eze 14:13 will break the *s* of the bread
Eze 29:6 because they have been a *s* of
Hos 4:12 their *s* declareth unto them
Zec 8:4 every man with his *s* in his hand
Zec 11:10 And I took my *s*, even Beauty, and
Zec 11:14 Then I cut asunder mine other *s*
Mk 6:8 for their journey, save a *s* only
Heb 11:21 leaning upon the top of his *s*

## STAIRS
1Kin 6:8 winding *s* into the middle chamber
2Kin 9:13 it under him on the top of the *s*
Neh 3:15 unto the *s* that go down from the
Neh 9:4 Then stood up upon the *s*, of the
Neh 12:37 they went up by the *s* of the city
Song 2:14 in the secret places of the *s*
Eze 40:6 east, and went up the *s* thereof
Eze 43:17 his *s* shall look toward the east
Acts 21:35 And when he came upon the *s*
Acts 21:40 him licence, Paul stood on the *s*

## STALLS
1Kin 4:26 *s* of horses for his chariots
2Chr 9:25 had four thousand *s* for horses
2Chr 32:28 *s* for all manner of beasts, and
Hab 3:17 there shall be no herd in the *s*

## STAMPED
Deut 9:21 *s* it, and ground it very small,
2Kin 23:6 *s* it small to powder, and cast the
2Kin 23:15 *s* it small to powder, and burned
2Chr 15:16 *s* it, and burnt it at the brook

Eze 25:6 s with the feet, and rejoiced in
Dan 7:7 s the residue with the feet of it
Dan 7:19 s the residue with his feet
Dan 8:7 down to the ground, and s upon him
Dan 8:10 to the ground, and s upon them

**STANDARD**
Num 1:52 camp, and every man by his own s
Num 2:2 Israel shall pitch by his own s
Num 2:3 the s of the camp of Judah pitch
Num 2:10 On the south side shall be the s
Num 2:18 be the s of the camp of Ephraim
Num 2:25 The s of the camp of Dan shall be
Num 10:14 In the first place went the s of
Num 10:18 the s of the camp of Reuben set
Num 10:22 the s of the camp of the children
Num 10:25 the s of the camp of the children
Is 49:22 set up my s to the people
Is 59:19 shall lift up a s against him
Is 62:10 lift up a s for the people
Jer 4:6 Set up the s toward Zion
Jer 4:21 How long shall I see the s
Jer 50:2 and publish, and set up a s
Jer 51:12 Set up the s upon the walls of
Jer 51:27 Set ye up a s in the land

**STANDEST**
Gen 24:31 wherefore s thou without
Ex 3:5 whereon thou s is holy ground
Josh 5:15 the place whereon thou s is holy
Ps 10:1 Why s thou afar off, O LORD
Acts 7:33 place where thou s is holy ground
Rom 11:20 broken off, and thou s by faith

**STANDETH**
Num 14:14 and that thy cloud s over them
Deut 1:38 which s before thee, he shall go
Deut 17:12 s to minister there before the
Deut 29:15 But with him that s here with us
Judg 16:26 the pillars whereupon the house s
Est 6:5 him, Behold, Haman s in the court
Est 7:9 the king, s in the house of Haman
Ps 1:1 nor s in the way of sinners, nor
Ps 26:12 My foot s in an even place
Ps 33:11 counsel of the LORD s for ever
Ps 82:1 God s in the congregation of the
Ps 119:161 but my heart s in awe of thy word
Prov 8:2 She s in the top of high places,
Song 2:9 he s behind our wall, he looketh
Is 3:13 The LORD s up to plead
Is 3:13 and s to judge the people
Is 46:7 and set him in his place, and he s
Is 59:14 backward, and justice s afar off
Dan 12:1 the great prince which s for the
Zec 11:16 nor feed that that s still
Jn 1:26 but there s one among you, whom
Jn 3:29 friend of the bridegroom, which s
Rom 14:4 to his own master he s or falleth
1Cor 7:37 Nevertheless he that s stedfast
1Cor 8:13 eat no flesh while the world s
1Cor 10:12 he s take heed lest he fall
2Ti 2:19 the foundation of God s sure
Heb 10:11 every priest s daily ministering
Jas 5:9 the judge s before the door
Rev 10:8 of the angel which s upon the sea

**STANDING**
Ex 22:6 the stacks of corn, or the s corn
Ex 26:15 tabernacle of shittim wood s up
Ex 36:20 tabernacle of shittim wood, s up
Lev 26:1 neither rear you up a s image
Num 22:23 angel of the LORD s in the way
Num 22:31 angel of the LORD s in the way
Deut 23:25 into the s corn of thy neighbour
Deut 23:25 unto thy neighbour's s corn
Judg 15:5 the s corn of the Philistines
Judg 15:5 the shocks, and also the s corn
1Sa 19:20 Samuel s as appointed over them,
1Sa 22:6 all his servants were s about him
1Kin 13:25 the lion s by the carcase
1Kin 13:28 the lion s by the carcase
1Kin 22:19 all the host of heaven s by him
2Chr 9:18 and two lions s by the stays
2Chr 18:18 of heaven s on his right hand
Est 5:2 Esther the queen s in the court
Ps 69:2 in deep mire, where there is no s
Ps 107:35 the wilderness into a s water
Ps 114:8 turned the rock into a s water
Dan 8:6 I had seen s before the river
Amos 9:1 I saw the Lord s upon the altar
Mic 1:11 he shall receive of you his s
Mic 5:13 thy s images out of the midst of
Zec 3:1 me Joshua the high priest s
Zec 3:1 Satan s at his right hand to
Zec 6:5 which go forth from s before the
Mt 6:5 love to pray s in the synagogues
Mt 16:28 unto you, There be some s here
Mt 20:3 hour, and saw others s idle in the
Mt 20:6 went out, and found others s idle
Mk 3:31 s without, sent unto him, calling
Mk 13:14 s where it ought not, (let him
Lk 1:11 unto him an angel of the Lord s
Lk 5:2 And saw two ships s by the lake
Lk 9:27 of a truth, there be some s here
Lk 18:13 s afar off, would not lift up so
Jn 8:9 and the woman s in the midst
Jn 19:26 his mother, and the disciple s by
Jn 20:14 herself back, and saw Jesus s
Acts 2:14 s up with the eleven, lifted up
Acts 4:14 man which was healed s with them
Acts 5:23 the keepers s without before the
Acts 5:25 put in prison are s in the temple
Acts 7:55 Jesus s on the right hand of God,
Acts 7:56 the Son of man s on the right
Acts 22:20 Stephen was shed, I also was s by
Acts 24:21 voice, that I cried s among them
Heb 9:8 as the first tabernacle was yet s
2Pet 3:5 the earth s out of the water and
Rev 7:1 s on the four corners of the
Rev 11:4 the two candlesticks s before the
Rev 18:10 S afar off for the fear of her
Rev 19:17 And I saw an angel s in the sun

**STANK**
Ex 7:21 and the river s, and the Egyptians
Ex 8:14 and the land s
Ex 16:20 morning, and it bred worms, and s
2Sa 10:6 saw that they s before David

**STAR**
Num 24:17 there shall come a S out of Jacob
Amos 5:26 the s of your god, which ye made
Mt 2:2 we have seen his s in the east
Mt 2:7 what time the s appeared
Mt 2:9 and, lo, the s, which they saw in
Mt 2:10 When they saw the s, they
Acts 7:43 the s of your god Remphan,
1Cor 15:41 for one s differeth from another
1Cor 15:41 differeth from another s in glory
2Pet 1:19 the day s arise in your hearts
Rev 2:28 And I will give him the morning s
Rev 8:10 there fell a great s from heaven
Rev 8:11 the name of the s is called
Rev 9:1 I saw a s fall from heaven unto
Rev 22:16 David, and the bright and morning s

**STARS**
Gen 1:16 he made the s also
Gen 15:5 now toward heaven, and tell the s
Gen 22:17 thy seed as the s of the heaven
Gen 26:4 to multiply as the s of heaven
Gen 37:9 the eleven s made obeisance to me
Ex 32:13 your seed as the s of heaven
Deut 1:10 ye are this day as the s of
Deut 4:19 the sun, and the moon, and the s
Deut 10:22 as the s of heaven for multitude
Deut 28:62 whereas ye were as the s of
Judg 5:20 the s in their courses fought
1Chr 27:23 like to the s of the heavens
Neh 4:21 the morning till the s appeared
Neh 9:23 thou as the s of heaven, and
Job 3:9 Let the s of the twilight thereof
Job 9:7 and sealeth up the s
Job 22:12 and behold the height of the s
Job 25:5 the s are not pure in his sight
Job 38:7 When the morning s sang together
Ps 8:3 of thy fingers, the moon and the s
Ps 136:9 The moon and s to rule by night
Ps 147:4 He telleth the number of the s
Ps 148:3 praise him, all ye s of light
Eccl 12:2 the light, or the moon, or the s
Is 13:10 For the s of heaven and the
Is 14:13 my throne above the s of God
Jer 31:35 of the s for a light by night,
Eze 32:7 and make the s thereof dark
Dan 8:10 of the s to the ground, and
Dan 12:3 righteousness as the s for ever
Joel 2:10 the s shall withdraw their
Joel 3:15 the s shall withdraw their
Amos 5:8 Seek him that maketh the seven s
Obad 4 thou set thy nest among the s
Nah 3:16 merchants above the s of heaven
Mt 24:29 the s shall fall from heaven, and
Mk 13:25 the s of heaven shall fall, and
Lk 21:25 sun, and in the moon, and in the s
Acts 27:20 when neither sun nor s in many
1Cor 15:41 moon, and another glory of the s
Heb 11:12 so many as the s of the sky in
Jude 13 wandering s, to whom is reserved
Rev 1:16 he had in his right hand seven s
Rev 1:20 The mystery of the seven s which
Rev 1:20 The seven s are the angels of the
Rev 2:1 the seven s in his right hand
Rev 3:1 Spirits of God, and the seven s
Rev 6:13 the s of heaven fell unto the
Rev 8:12 moon, and the third part of the s
Rev 12:1 upon her head a crown of twelve s
Rev 12:4 the third part of the s of heaven

**STATE**
Gen 43:7 man asked us straitly of our s
2Chr 24:13 set the house of God in his s
Est 1:7 according to the s of the king
Est 2:18 according to the s of the king
Ps 39:5 his best s is altogether vanity
Prov 27:23 to know the s of thy flocks
Prov 28:2 knowledge the s thereof shall be
Is 22:19 from thy s shall he pull thee
Mt 12:45 the last s of that man is worse
Lk 11:26 the last s of that man is worse
Phil 2:19 good comfort, when I know your s
Phil 2:20 will naturally care for your s
Phil 4:11 learned, in whatsoever s I am
Col 4:7 All my s shall Tychicus declare

**STATURE**
Num 13:32 we saw in it are men of a great s
1Sa 16:7 or on the height of his s
2Sa 21:20 Gath, where was a man of great s
1Chr 11:23 an Egyptian, a man of great s
1Chr 20:6 Gath, where was a man of great s
Song 7:7 This thy s is like to a palm tree
Is 10:33 the high ones of s shall be hewn
Is 45:14 and of the Sabeans, men of s
Eze 13:18 the head of every s to hunt souls
Eze 17:6 became a spreading vine of low s
Eze 19:11 her s was exalted among the thick
Eze 31:3 shadowing shroud, and of an high s
Mt 6:27 can add one cubit unto his s
Lk 2:52 And Jesus increased in wisdom and s
Lk 12:25 can add to his s one cubit
Lk 19:3 press, because he was little of s
Eph 4:13 unto the measure of the s of the

**STATUTE**
Ex 15:25 there he made for them a s
Ex 27:21 it shall be a s for ever unto
Ex 28:43 it shall be a s for ever unto him
Ex 29:9 shall be theirs for a perpetual s
Ex 29:28 his sons' by a s for ever from
Ex 30:21 it shall be a s for ever to them,
Lev 3:17 It shall be a perpetual s for
Lev 6:18 It shall be a s for ever in your
Lev 6:22 it is a s for ever unto the LORD
Lev 7:34 unto his sons by a s for ever
Lev 7:36 by a s for ever throughout their
Lev 10:9 it shall be a s for ever
Lev 10:15 sons' with thee, by a s for ever
Lev 16:29 this shall be a s for ever unto
Lev 16:31 your souls, by a s for ever
Lev 16:34 be an everlasting s unto you
Lev 17:7 This shall be a s for ever unto
Lev 23:14 it shall be a s for ever
Lev 23:21 it shall be a s for ever in all
Lev 23:31 it shall be a s for ever
Lev 23:41 It shall be a s for ever in your
Lev 24:3 it shall be a s for ever in your
Lev 24:9 made by fire by a perpetual s
Num 18:11 with thee, by a s for ever
Num 18:19 with thee, by a s for ever
Num 18:23 it shall be a s for ever
Num 19:10 among them, for a s for ever
Num 19:21 shall be a perpetual s unto them
Num 27:11 of Israel a s of judgment
Num 35:29 So these things shall be for a s
Josh 24:25 people that day, and set them a s
1Sa 30:25 day forward, that he made it a s
Ps 81:4 For this was a s for Israel
Dan 6:7 together to establish a royal s
Dan 6:15 That no decree nor s which the

**STATUTES**
Gen 26:5 my charge, my commandments, my s
Ex 15:26 commandments, and keep all his s
Ex 18:16 I do make them know the s of God
Lev 10:11 the children of Israel all the s

Lev 18:5 Ye shall therefore keep my s
Lev 18:26 Ye shall therefore keep my s
Lev 19:19 Ye shall keep my s
Lev 19:37 shall ye observe all my s
Lev 20:8 And ye shall keep my s, and do them
Lev 20:22 Ye shall therefore keep all my s
Lev 25:18 Wherefore ye shall do my s
Lev 26:3 If ye walk in my s, and keep my
Lev 26:15 And if ye shall despise my s
Lev 26:43 because their soul abhorred my s
Lev 26:46 These are the s and judgments and
Num 30:16 These are the s, which the LORD
Deut 4:1 hearken, O Israel, unto the s
Deut 4:5 Behold, I have taught you s
Deut 4:6 which shall hear all these s
Deut 4:8 is there so great, that hath s
Deut 4:14 me at that time to teach you s
Deut 4:40 Thou shalt keep therefore his s
Deut 4:45 are the testimonies, and the s
Deut 5:1 unto them, Hear, O Israel, the s
Deut 5:31 all the commandments, and the s
Deut 6:1 these are the commandments, the s
Deut 6:2 LORD thy God, to keep all his s
Deut 6:17 God, and his testimonies, and his s
Deut 6:20 mean the testimonies, and the s
Deut 6:24 commanded us to do all these s
Deut 7:11 keep the commandments, and the s
Deut 8:11 and his judgments, and his s
Deut 10:13 of the LORD, and his s, which I
Deut 11:1 God, and keep his charge, and his s
Deut 11:32 ye shall observe to do all the s
Deut 12:1 These are the s and judgments,
Deut 16:12 thou shalt observe and do these s
Deut 17:19 the words of this law and these s
Deut 26:16 hath commanded thee to do these s
Deut 26:17 in his ways, and to keep his s
Deut 27:10 and do his commandments and his s
Deut 28:15 his s which I command thee this
Deut 28:45 his s which he commanded thee
Deut 30:10 his s which are written in this
Deut 30:16 to keep his commandments and his s
2Sa 22:23 and as for his s, I did not depart
1Kin 2:3 walk in his ways, to keep his s
1Kin 3:3 walking in the s of David his
1Kin 3:14 walk in my ways, to keep my s
1Kin 6:12 if thou wilt walk in my s
1Kin 8:58 keep his commandments, and his s
1Kin 8:61 LORD our God, to walk in his s
1Kin 9:4 commanded thee, and wilt keep my s
1Kin 9:6 my s which I have set before you,
1Kin 11:11 hast not kept my covenant and my s
1Kin 11:33 in mine eyes, and to keep my s
1Kin 11:34 he kept my commandments and my s
1Kin 11:38 right in my sight, to keep my s
2Kin 17:8 walked in the s of the heathen,
2Kin 17:13 keep my commandments and my s
2Kin 17:15 And they rejected his s, and his
2Kin 17:19 but walked in the s of Israel
2Kin 17:34 neither do they after their s
2Kin 17:37 And the s, and the ordinances, and
2Kin 23:3 his s with all their heart and all
1Chr 22:13 thou takest heed to fulfil the s
1Chr 29:19 thy testimonies, and thy s
2Chr 7:17 thee, and shalt observe my s
2Chr 7:19 if ye turn away, and forsake my s
2Chr 19:10 between law and commandment, s
2Chr 33:8 to the whole law and the s
2Chr 34:31 and his testimonies, and his s
Ezr 7:10 to do it, and to teach in Israel s
Ezr 7:11 the LORD, and of his s to Israel
Neh 1:7 kept the commandments, nor the s
Neh 9:13 judgments, and true laws, good s
Neh 9:14 and commandedst them precepts, s
Neh 10:29 Lord, and his judgments and his s
Ps 18:22 I did not put away his s from me
Ps 19:8 The s of the LORD are right,
Ps 50:16 hast thou to do to declare my s
Ps 89:31 If they break my s, and keep not
Ps 105:45 That they might observe his s
Ps 119:5 ways were directed to keep thy s
Ps 119:8 I will keep thy s
Ps 119:12 teach me thy s
Ps 119:16 I will delight myself in thy s
Ps 119:23 thy servant did meditate in thy s
Ps 119:26 teach me thy s
Ps 119:33 me, O LORD, the way of thy s
Ps 119:48 and I will meditate in thy s
Ps 119:54 Thy s have been my songs in the
Ps 119:64 teach me thy s
Ps 119:68 teach me thy s
Ps 119:71 that I might learn thy s
Ps 119:80 Let my heart be sound in thy s
Ps 119:83 yet do I not forget thy s
Ps 119:112 mine heart to perform thy s alway
Ps 119:117 respect unto thy s continually
Ps 119:118 down all them that err from thy s
Ps 119:124 unto thy mercy, and teach me thy s
Ps 119:135 and teach me thy s
Ps 119:145 I will keep thy s
Ps 119:155 for they seek not thy s
Ps 119:171 when thou hast taught me thy s
Ps 147:19 his word unto Jacob, his s
Jer 44:10 nor walked in my law, nor in my s
Jer 44:23 walked in his law, nor in his s
Eze 5:6 my s more than the countries that
Eze 5:6 have refused my judgments and my s
Eze 5:7 you, and have not walked in my s
Eze 11:12 for ye have not walked in my s
Eze 11:20 That they may walk in my s
Eze 18:9 Hath walked in my s, and hath kept
Eze 18:17 my judgments, hath walked in my s
Eze 18:19 and right, and hath kept all my s
Eze 18:21 hath committed, and keep all my s
Eze 20:11 And I gave them my s, and shewed
Eze 20:13 they walked not in my s, and they
Eze 20:16 judgments, and walked not in my s
Eze 20:18 ye not in the s of your fathers
Eze 20:19 walk in my s, and keep my
Eze 20:21 they walked not in my s, neither
Eze 20:24 judgments, but had despised my s
Eze 20:25 them also s that were not good
Eze 33:15 had robbed, walk in the s of life
Eze 36:27 you, and cause you to walk in my s
Eze 37:24 in my judgments, and observe my s
Eze 44:24 my s in all mine assemblies
Mic 6:16 For the s of Omri are kept, and
Zec 1:6 But my words and my s, which I
Mal 4:4 Horeb for all Israel, with the s

**STAVES**
Ex 25:13 thou shalt make s of shittim wood
Ex 25:14 thou shalt put the s into the
Ex 25:15 The s shall be in the rings of
Ex 25:27 places of the s to bear the table
Ex 25:28 shalt make the s of shittim wood
Ex 27:6 thou shalt make s for the altar
Ex 27:6 s of shittim wood, and overlay
Ex 27:7 the s shall be put into the rings
Ex 27:7 the s shall be upon the two sides
Ex 30:4 for the s to bear it withal
Ex 30:5 shalt make the s of shittim wood
Ex 35:12 the s thereof, with the mercy
Ex 35:13 The table, and his s, and all his
Ex 35:15 And the incense altar, and his s
Ex 35:16 with his brasen grate, his s
Ex 37:4 he made s of shittim wood, and
Ex 37:5 he put the s into the rings by
Ex 37:14 for the s to bear the table
Ex 37:15 he made the s of shittim wood, and
Ex 37:27 for the s to bear it withal
Ex 37:28 he made the s of shittim wood, and
Ex 38:5 of brass, to be places for the s
Ex 38:6 he made the s of shittim wood, and
Ex 38:7 he put the s into the rings on
Ex 39:35 the s thereof, and the mercy seat,
Ex 39:39 and his grate of brass, his s
Ex 40:20 set the s on the ark, and put the
Num 4:6 and shall put in the s thereof
Num 4:8 and shall put in the s thereof
Num 4:11 and shall put to the s thereof
Num 4:14 skins, and put to the s of it
Num 21:18 of the lawgiver, with their s
1Sa 17:43 that thou comest to me with s
1Kin 8:7 the ark and the s thereof above
1Kin 8:8 And they drew out the s, that the
1Kin 8:8 that the ends of the s were seen
1Chr 15:15 shoulders with the s thereon
2Chr 5:8 the ark and the s thereof above
2Chr 5:9 And they drew out the s of the ark
2Chr 5:9 that the ends of the s were seen
Hab 3:14 his s the head of his villages
Zec 11:7 And I took unto me two s
Mt 10:10 coats, neither shoes, nor yet s
Mt 26:47 great multitude with swords and s
Mt 26:55 with swords and s for to take me
Mk 14:43 great multitude with swords and s
Mk 14:48 with swords and with s to take me
Lk 9:3 for your journey, neither s
Lk 22:52 against a thief, with swords and s

**STEAL**
Gen 31:27 away secretly, and s away from me
Gen 44:8 how then should we s out of thy
Ex 20:15 Thou shalt not s
Ex 22:1 If a man shall s an ox, or a
Lev 19:11 Ye shall not s, neither deal
Deut 5:19 Neither shalt thou s
2Sa 19:3 as people being ashamed s away
Prov 6:30 if he s to satisfy his soul when
Prov 30:9 or lest I be poor, and s, and take
Jer 7:9 Will ye s, murder, and commit
Jer 23:30 that s my words every one from
Mt 6:19 where thieves break through and s
Mt 6:20 do not break through nor s
Mt 19:18 commit adultery, Thou shalt not s
Mt 27:64 s him away, and say unto the
Mk 10:19 adultery, Do not kill, Do not s
Lk 18:20 adultery, Do not kill, Do not s
Jn 10:10 thief cometh not, but for to s
Rom 2:21 man should not s, dost thou s
Rom 13:9 shalt not kill, Thou shalt not s
Eph 4:28 Let him that stole s no more

**STEDFAST**
Job 11:15 yea, thou shalt be s, and shalt
Ps 78:8 whose spirit was not s with God
Ps 78:37 were they s in his covenant
Dan 6:26 s for ever, and his kingdom that
1Cor 7:37 he that standeth s in his heart
1Cor 15:58 my beloved brethren, be ye s
2Cor 1:7 And our hope of you is s, knowing,
Heb 2:2 the word spoken by angels was s
Heb 3:14 of our confidence s unto the end
Heb 6:19 of the soul, both sure and s
1Pet 5:9 Whom resist s in the faith,

**STEDFASTLY**
Ruth 1:18 she was s minded to go with her
2Kin 8:11 And he settled his countenance s
Lk 9:51 he s set his face to go to
Acts 1:10 while they looked s toward heaven
Acts 2:42 they continued s in the apostles'
Acts 6:15 in the council, looking s on him
Acts 7:55 looked up s into heaven, and saw
Acts 14:9 who s beholding him, and
2Cor 3:7 s behold the face of Moses for
2Cor 3:13 children of Israel could not s

**STEEL**
2Sa 22:35 so that a bow of s is broken by
Job 20:24 the bow of s shall strike him
Ps 18:34 so that a bow of s is broken by
Jer 15:12 break the northern iron and the s

**STEEP**
Eze 38:20 the s places shall fall, and every
Mic 1:4 that are poured down a s place
Mt 8:32 down a s place into the sea
Mk 5:13 down a s place into the sea
Lk 8:33 down a s place into the lake

**STEPHANAS** *(stef'-a-nas) A convert of Paul from Achaia.*
1Cor 1:16 baptized also the household of S
1Cor 16:15 brethren, (ye know the house of S
1Cor 16:17 I am glad of the coming of S

**STEPHANUS**
1Cor s was written from Philippi by S

**STEPHEN** *(ste'-ven) A leader of the Jerusalem church.*
Acts 6:5 and they chose S, a man full of
Acts 6:8 And S, full of faith and power, did
Acts 6:9 and of Asia, disputing with S
Acts 7:59 And they stoned S, calling upon
Acts 8:2 men carried S to his burial
Acts 11:19 S travelled as far as Phenice
Acts 22:20 blood of thy martyr S was shed

**STEPS**
Ex 20:26 thou go up by s unto mine altar
2Sa 22:37 Thou hast enlarged my s under me
1Kin 10:19 The throne had six s, and the top
1Kin 10:20 and on the other upon the six s
2Chr 9:18 And there were six s to the throne
2Chr 9:19 and on the other upon the six s
Job 14:16 For now thou numberest my s
Job 18:7 The s of his strength shall be
Job 23:11 My foot hath held his s, his way
Job 29:6 When I washed my s with butter
Job 31:4 he see my ways, and count all my s
Job 31:37 unto him the number of my s
Ps 17:11 have now compassed us in our s
Ps 18:36 Thou hast enlarged my s under me

Ps 37:23 The *s* of a good man are ordered
Ps 37:31 none of his *s* shall slide
Ps 44:18 neither have our *s* declined from
Ps 56:6 hide themselves, they mark my *s*
Ps 57:6 They have prepared a net for my *s*
Ps 73:2 my *s* had well nigh slipped
Ps 85:13 shall set us in the way of his *s*
Ps 119:133 Order my *s* in thy word
Prov 4:12 thy *s* shall not be straitened
Prov 5:5 her *s* take hold on hell
Prov 16:9 but the LORD directeth his *s*
Is 26:6 the poor, and the *s* of the needy
Jer 10:23 man that walketh to direct his *s*
Lam 4:18 They hunt our *s*, that we cannot
Eze 40:22 they went up unto it by seven *s*
Eze 40:26 there were seven *s* to go up to it
Eze 40:31 and the going up to it had eight *s*
Eze 40:34 and the going up to it had eight *s*
Eze 40:37 and the going up to it had eight *s*
Eze 40:49 he brought me by the *s* whereby
Dan 11:43 the Ethiopians shall be at his *s*
Rom 4:12 but who also walk in the *s* of
2Cor 12:18 walked we not in the same *s*
1Pet 2:21 that ye should follow his *s*

### STEWARD
Gen 15:2 the *s* of my house is this Eliezer
Gen 43:19 near to the *s* of Joseph's house
Gen 44:1 he commanded the *s* of his house
Gen 44:4 far off, Joseph said unto his *s*
1Kin 16:9 of Arza *s* of his house in Tirzah
Mt 20:8 of the vineyard saith unto his *s*
Lk 8:3 the wife of Chuza Herod's *s*
Lk 12:42 then is that faithful and wise *s*
Lk 16:1 a certain rich man, which had a *s*
Lk 16:2 for thou mayest be no longer *s*
Lk 16:3 Then the *s* said within himself,
Lk 16:8 the lord commended the unjust *s*
Titus 1:7 be blameless, as the *s* of God

### STEWARDS
1Chr 28:1 the *s* over all the substance and
1Cor 4:1 *s* of the mysteries of God
1Cor 4:2 Moreover it is required in *s*
1Pet 4:10 as good *s* of the manifold grace

### STICK
2Kin 6:6 And he cut down a *s*, and cast it in
Job 33:21 bones that were not seen *s* out
Job 41:17 they *s* together, that they cannot
Ps 38:2 For thine arrows *s* fast in me
Lam 4:8 withered, it is become like a *s*
Eze 29:4 thy rivers to *s* unto thy scales
Eze 29:4 rivers shall *s* unto thy scales
Eze 37:16 thou son of man, take thee one *s*
Eze 37:16 then take another *s*, and write
Eze 37:16 the *s* of Ephraim, and for all the
Eze 37:17 them one to another into one *s*
Eze 37:19 I will take the *s* of Joseph
Eze 37:19 him, even with the *s* of Judah
Eze 37:19 of Judah, and make them one *s*

### STICKS
Num 15:32 gathered *s* upon the sabbath day
Num 15:33 *s* brought him unto Moses and Aaron
1Kin 17:10 woman was there gathering of *s*
1Kin 17:12 and, behold, I am gathering two *s*
Eze 37:20 the *s* whereon thou writest shall
Acts 28:3 Paul had gathered a bundle of *s*

### STIFF
Deut 31:27 know thy rebellion, and thy *s* neck
Ps 75:5 speak not with a *s* neck
Jer 17:23 their ear, but made their neck *s*

### STIFFNECKED
Ex 32:9 and, behold, it is a *s* people
Ex 33:3 for thou art a *s* people
Ex 33:5 of Israel, Ye are a *s* people
Ex 34:9 for it is a *s* people
Deut 9:6 for thou art a *s* people
Deut 9:13 and, behold, it is a *s* people
Deut 10:16 of your heart, and be no more *s*
2Chr 30:8 Now be ye not *s*, as your fathers
Acts 7:51 Ye *s* and uncircumcised in heart and

### STILL
Gen 12:9 going on *s* toward the south
Gen 41:21 but they were *s* ill favoured
Ex 9:2 let them go, and wilt hold them *s*
Ex 14:13 the people, Fear ye not, stand *s*
Ex 15:16 arm they shall be as *s* as a stone
Ex 23:11 thou shalt let it rest and lie *s*
Lev 13:57 if it appear *s* in the garment,
Num 9:8 And Moses said unto them, Stand *s*
Num 14:38 went to search the land, lived *s*
Josh 3:8 ye shall stand *s* in Jordan
Josh 10:12 Sun, stand thou *s* upon Gibeon
Josh 10:13 And the sun stood *s*, and the moon
Josh 10:13 So the sun stood *s* in the midst
Josh 11:13 that stood *s* in their strength
Josh 24:10 therefore he blessed you *s*
Judg 18:9 and are ye *s*
Ruth 3:18 Then said she, Sit *s*, my daughter
1Sa 9:27 on,) but stand thou *s* a while
1Sa 12:7 Now therefore stand *s*, that I may
1Sa 12:25 But if ye shall *s* do wickedly
1Sa 14:9 then we will stand *s* in our place
1Sa 26:25 things, and also shalt *s* prevail
2Sa 2:23 Asahel fell down and died stood *s*
2Sa 2:28 and all the people stood *s*
2Sa 11:1 But David tarried *s* at Jerusalem
2Sa 14:32 good for me to have been there *s*
2Sa 16:5 forth, and cursed *s* as he came
2Sa 18:30 And he turned aside, and stood *s*
2Sa 20:12 saw that all the people stood *s*
2Sa 20:12 one that came by him stood *s*
1Kin 19:12 and after the fire a *s* small voice
1Kin 22:3 in Gilead is ours, and we be *s*
2Kin 2:11 came to pass, as they *s* went on
2Kin 7:4 and if we sit *s* here, we die also
2Kin 12:3 the people *s* sacrificed and burnt
2Kin 15:4 burnt incense *s* on the high
2Kin 15:35 burned incense *s* in the high
2Chr 20:17 set yourselves, stand ye *s*
2Chr 22:9 no power to keep *s* the kingdom
2Chr 33:17 sacrifice *s* in the high places
Neh 12:39 they stood *s* in the prison gate
Job 2:3 *s* he holdeth fast his integrity,
Job 2:9 him, Dost thou *s* retain thine
Job 3:13 For now should I have lain *s*
Job 4:16 It stood *s*, but I could not
Job 20:13 but keep it *s* within his mouth
Job 32:16 (for they spake not, but stood *s*
Job 37:14 stand *s*, and consider the wondrous
Ps 4:4 own heart upon your bed, and be *s*
Ps 8:2 that thou mightest *s* the enemy
Ps 23:2 he leadeth me beside the *s* waters
Ps 46:10 Be *s*, and know that I am God
Ps 49:9 That he should *s* live for ever
Ps 68:21 as goeth on *s* in his trespasses
Ps 76:8 the earth feared, and was *s*
Ps 78:32 For all this they sinned *s*
Ps 83:1 hold not thy peace, and be not *s*
Ps 84:4 they will be *s* praising thee
Ps 92:14 They shall *s* bring forth fruit in
Ps 107:29 so that the waves thereof are *s*
Ps 139:18 when I awake, I am *s* with thee
Eccl 12:9 he *s* taught the people knowledge
Is 5:25 but his hand is stretched out *s*
Is 9:12 but his hand is stretched out *s*
Is 9:17 but his hand is stretched out *s*
Is 9:21 but his hand is stretched out *s*
Is 10:4 but his hand is stretched out *s*
Is 23:2 Be *s*, ye inhabitants of the isle
Is 30:7 this, Their strength is to sit *s*
Is 42:14 I have been *s*, and refrained
Jer 8:14 Why do we sit *s*
Jer 23:17 They say *s* unto them that despise
Jer 27:11 I let remain *s* in their own land
Jer 31:20 I do earnestly remember him *s*
Jer 42:10 If ye will *s* abide in this land,
Jer 47:6 into thy scabbard, rest, and be *s*
Jer 51:50 the sword, go away, stand not *s*
Lam 3:20 soul hath them *s* in remembrance
Eze 33:30 the children of thy people *s* are
Eze 41:7 a winding about *s* upward to the
Eze 41:7 *s* upward round about the house
Eze 41:7 breadth of the house was *s* upward
Hab 3:11 moon stood *s* in their habitation
Zec 1:11 behold, all the earth sitteth *s*
Zec 11:16 nor feed that that standeth *s*
Mt 20:32 And Jesus stood *s*, and called them,
Mk 4:39 and said unto the sea, Peace, be *s*
Mk 10:49 And Jesus stood *s*, and commanded
Lk 7:14 and they that bare him stood *s*
Jn 7:9 unto them, he abode *s* in Galilee
Jn 11:6 he abode two days *s* in the same
Jn 11:20 but Mary sat *s* in the house
Acts 8:38 commanded the chariot to stand *s*
Acts 15:34 it pleased Silas to abide there *s*
Acts 17:14 Silas and Timotheus abode there *s*
Rom 11:23 if they abide not *s* in unbelief
1Ti 1:3 thee to abide *s* at Ephesus
Rev 22:11 is unjust, let him be unjust *s*
Rev 22:11 is filthy, let him be filthy *s*
Rev 22:11 righteous, let him be righteous *s*
Rev 22:11 that is holy, let him be holy *s*

### STINK
Gen 34:30 to *s* among the inhabitants of the
Ex 7:18 shall die, and the river shall *s*
Ex 16:24 and it did not *s*, neither was
Ps 38:5 My wounds *s* and are corrupt
Is 3:24 of sweet smell there shall be *s*
Is 34:3 their *s* shall come up out of
Joel 2:20 his *s* shall come up, and his ill
Amos 4:10 I have made the *s* of your camps

### STIR
Num 24:9 who shall *s* him up
Job 17:8 the innocent shall *s* up himself
Job 41:10 is so fierce that dare *s* him up
Ps 35:23 *S* up thyself, and awake to my
Ps 78:38 did not *s* up all his wrath
Ps 80:2 Manasseh *s* up thy strength, and
Prov 15:1 but grievous words *s* up anger
Song 2:7 of the field, that ye *s* not up
Song 3:5 of the field, that ye *s* not up
Song 8:4 of Jerusalem, that ye *s* not up
Is 10:26 the LORD of hosts shall *s* up a
Is 13:17 I will *s* up the Medes against
Is 42:13 he shall *s* up jealousy like a man
Dan 11:2 *s* up all against the realm of
Dan 11:25 he shall *s* up his power and his
Acts 12:18 was no small *s* among the soldiers
Acts 19:23 arose no small *s* about that way
2Ti 1:6 that thou *s* up the gift of God
2Pet 1:13 to *s* you up by putting you in
2Pet 3:1 in both which I *s* up your pure

### STIRRED
Ex 35:21 every one whose heart *s* him up
Ex 35:26 all the women whose heart *s* them
Ex 36:2 even every one whose heart *s* him
1Sa 22:8 hath *s* up my servant against me
1Sa 26:19 If the LORD have *s* thee up
1Kin 11:14 the LORD *s* up an adversary unto
1Kin 11:23 God *s* him up another adversary,
1Kin 21:25 LORD, whom Jezebel his wife *s* up
1Chr 5:26 the God of Israel *s* up the spirit
2Chr 21:16 Moreover the LORD *s* up against
2Chr 36:22 the LORD *s* up the spirit of Cyrus
Ezr 1:1 the LORD *s* up the spirit of Cyrus
Ps 39:2 and my sorrow was *s*
Dan 11:10 But his sons shall be *s* up
Dan 11:10 then shall he return, and be *s* up
Dan 11:25 *s* up to battle with a very great
Hag 1:14 the LORD *s* up the spirit of
Acts 6:12 they *s* up the people, and the
Acts 13:50 But the Jews *s* up the devout and
Acts 14:2 Jews *s* up the Gentiles, and made
Acts 17:13 thither also, and *s* up the people
Acts 17:16 Athens, his spirit was *s* in him
Acts 21:27 *s* up all the people, and laid

### STIRRETH
Deut 32:11 As an eagle *s* up her nest
Prov 10:12 Hatred *s* up strifes
Prov 15:18 A wrathful man *s* up strife
Prov 28:25 is of a proud heart *s* up strife
Prov 29:22 An angry man *s* up strife, and a
Is 14:9 it *s* up the dead for thee, even
Is 64:7 that *s* up himself to take hold of
Lk 23:5 He *s* up the people, teaching

### STIRS
Is 22:2 Thou that art full of *s*, a

### STOCK
Lev 25:47 or to the *s* of the stranger's
Job 14:8 the *s* thereof die in the ground
Is 40:24 their *s* shall not take root in
Is 44:19 I fall down to the *s* of a tree
Jer 2:27 Saying to a *s*, Thou art my father
Jer 10:8 the *s* is a doctrine of vanities
Acts 13:26 children of the *s* of Abraham
Phil 3:5 of the *s* of Israel, of the tribe

### STOCKS
Job 13:27 puttest my feet also in the *s*
Job 33:11 He putteth my feet in the *s*
Prov 7:22 a fool to the correction of the *s*
Jer 3:9 adultery with stones and with *s*
Jer 20:2 put him in the *s* that were in the
Jer 20:3 forth Jeremiah out of the *s*
Jer 29:26 put him in prison, and in the *s*

Hos 4:12 My people ask counsel at their *s*
Acts 16:24 and made their feet fast in the *s*

**STOICKS** *(sto'-ics) A sect of Greek philosophers.*
Acts 17:18 of the Epicureans, and of the *S*

**STOLE**
Gen 31:20 Jacob *s* away unawares to Laban
2Sa 15:6 so Absalom *s* the hearts of the
2Kin 11:2 *s* him from among the king's sons
2Chr 22:11 *s* him from among the king's sons
Mt 28:13 *s* him away while we slept
Eph 4:28 Let him that *s* steal no more

**STOLEN**
Gen 30:33 that shall be counted *s* with me
Gen 31:19 Rachel had *s* the images that were
Gen 31:26 that thou hast *s* away unawares to
Gen 31:30 yet wherefore hast thou *s* my gods
Gen 31:32 knew not that Rachel had *s* them
Gen 31:39 *s* by day, or *s* by night
Gen 40:15 For indeed I was *s* away out of
Ex 22:7 it be *s* out of the man's house
Ex 22:12 And if it be *s* from him, he shall
Josh 7:11 accursed thing, and have also *s*
2Sa 19:41 the men of Judah *s* thee away
2Sa 21:12 which had *s* them from the street
Prov 9:17 *S* waters are sweet, and bread
Obad 5 not have *s* till they had enough

**STOMACHER**
Is 3:24 instead of a *s* a girding of

**STOMACH'S**
1Ti 5:23 use a little wine for thy *s* sake

**STONE**
Gen 2:12 there is bdellium and the onyx *s*
Gen 11:3 And they had brick for *s*, and slime
Gen 28:18 took the *s* that he had put for
Gen 28:22 And this *s*, which I have set for a
Gen 29:2 a great *s* was upon the well's
Gen 29:3 they rolled the *s* from the well's
Gen 29:3 put the *s* again upon the well's
Gen 29:8 till they roll the *s* from the
Gen 29:10 rolled the *s* from the well's
Gen 31:45 And Jacob took a *s*, and set it up
Gen 35:14 with him, even a pillar of *s*
Gen 49:24 is the shepherd, the *s* of Israel
Ex 4:25 Then Zipporah took a sharp *s*
Ex 7:19 of wood, and in vessels of *s*
Ex 8:26 their eyes, and will they not *s* us
Ex 15:5 they sank into the bottom as a *s*
Ex 15:16 arm they shall be as still as a *s*
Ex 17:4 they be almost ready to *s* me
Ex 17:12 and they took a *s*, and put it under
Ex 20:25 thou wilt make me an altar of *s*
Ex 20:25 thou shalt not build it of hewn *s*
Ex 21:18 and one smite another with a *s*
Ex 24:10 were a paved work of a sapphire *s*
Ex 24:12 and I will give thee tables of *s*
Ex 28:10 Six of their names on one *s*
Ex 28:10 names of the rest on the other *s*
Ex 28:11 With the work of an engraver in *s*
Ex 31:18 tables of testimony, tables of *s*
Ex 34:1 tables of *s* like unto the first
Ex 34:4 tables of *s* like unto the first
Ex 34:4 in his hand the two tables of *s*
Lev 20:2 the land shall *s* him with stones
Lev 20:27 they shall *s* them with stones
Lev 24:14 and let all the congregation *s* him
Lev 24:16 shall certainly *s* him
Lev 24:23 of the camp, and *s* him with stones
Lev 26:1 up any image of *s* in your land
Num 14:10 bade *s* them with stones
Num 15:35 all the congregation shall *s* him
Num 35:17 if he smite him with throwing a *s*
Num 35:23 Or with any *s*, wherewith a man
Deut 4:13 wrote them upon two tables of *s*
Deut 4:28 work of men's hands, wood and *s*
Deut 5:22 he wrote them in two tables of *s*
Deut 9:9 mount to receive the tables of *s*
Deut 9:10 *s* written with the finger of God
Deut 9:11 LORD gave me the two tables of *s*
Deut 10:1 tables of *s* like unto the first
Deut 10:3 tables of *s* like unto the first
Deut 13:10 thou shalt *s* him with stones,
Deut 17:5 shalt *s* them with stones, till
Deut 21:21 his city shall *s* him with stones
Deut 22:21 the men of her city shall *s* her
Deut 22:24 ye shall *s* them with stones that
Deut 28:36 thou serve other gods, wood and *s*
Deut 28:64 have known, even wood and *s*
Deut 29:17 and their idols, wood and *s*
Josh 4:5 man of you a *s* upon his shoulder
Josh 15:6 the border went up to the *s* of
Josh 18:17 descended to the *s* of Bohan the
Josh 24:26 the law of God, and took a great *s*
Josh 24:27 this *s* shall be a witness unto us
Judg 9:5 and ten persons, upon one *s*
Judg 9:18 and ten persons, upon one *s*
1Sa 6:14 there, where there was a great *s*
1Sa 6:15 were, and put them on the great *s*
1Sa 6:18 even unto the great *s* of Abel
1Sa 6:18 which *s* remaineth unto this day
1Sa 7:12 Then Samuel took a *s*, and set it
1Sa 14:33 roll a great *s* unto me this day
1Sa 17:49 in his bag, and took thence a *s*
1Sa 17:49 that the *s* sunk into his forehead
1Sa 17:50 with a sling and with a *s*, and
1Sa 20:19 and shalt remain by the *s* Ezel
1Sa 25:37 within him, and he became as a *s*
2Sa 17:13 be not one small *s* found there
2Sa 20:8 at the great *s* which is in Gibeon
1Kin 1:9 fat cattle by the *s* of Zoheleth
1Kin 6:7 was built of *s* made ready before
1Kin 6:18 there was no *s* seen
1Kin 6:36 court with three rows of hewed *s*
1Kin 8:9 the ark save the two tables of *s*
1Kin 21:10 out, and *s* him, that he may die
2Kin 3:25 of land cast every man his *s*
2Kin 12:12 And to masons, and hewers of *s*
2Kin 12:12 hewed *s* to repair the breaches of
2Kin 19:18 work of men's hands, wood and *s*
2Kin 22:6 hewn *s* to repair the house
1Chr 22:14 timber also and *s* have I prepared
1Chr 22:15 abundance, hewers and workers of *s*
2Chr 2:14 silver, in brass, in iron, in *s*
2Chr 34:11 gave they it, to buy hewn *s*
Neh 4:3 even break down their *s* wall
Neh 9:11 as a *s* into the mighty waters
Job 28:2 and brass is molten out of the *s*
Job 38:6 or who laid the corner *s* thereof
Job 38:30 The waters are hid as with a *s*
Job 41:24 His heart is as firm as a *s*
Ps 91:12 thou dash thy foot against a *s*
Ps 118:22 The *s* which the builders refused
Ps 118:22 become the head *s* of the corner
Prov 17:8 A gift is as a precious *s* in the
Prov 24:31 the *s* wall thereof was broken
Prov 26:8 As he that bindeth a *s* in a sling
Prov 26:27 and he that rolleth a *s*, it will
Prov 27:3 A *s* is heavy, and the sand weighty
Is 8:14 but for a *s* of stumbling and for a
Is 28:16 a foundation a *s*, a tried *s*
Is 28:16 a precious corner *s*
Is 37:19 work of men's hands, wood and *s*
Jer 2:27 and to a *s*, Thou hast brought me
Jer 51:26 not take of thee a *s* for a corner
Jer 51:26 a corner, nor a *s* for foundations
Jer 51:63 that thou shalt bind a *s* to it
Lam 3:9 hath inclosed my ways with hewn *s*
Lam 3:53 the dungeon, and cast a *s* upon me
Eze 1:26 as the appearance of a sapphire *s*
Eze 10:1 over them as it were a sapphire *s*
Eze 10:9 was as the colour of a beryl *s*
Eze 16:40 they shall *s* thee with stones, and
Eze 20:32 the countries, to serve wood and *s*
Eze 23:47 company shall *s* them with stones
Eze 28:13 every precious *s* was thy covering
Eze 40:42 of hewn *s* for the burnt offering
Dan 2:34 Thou sawest till that a *s* was cut
Dan 2:35 the *s* that smote the image became
Dan 2:45 as thou sawest that the *s* was cut
Dan 5:4 brass, of iron, of wood, and of *s*
Dan 5:23 gold, of brass, iron, wood, and *s*
Dan 6:17 a *s* was brought, and laid upon the
Amos 5:11 ye have built houses of hewn *s*
Hab 2:11 For the *s* shall cry out of the
Hab 2:19 to the dumb *s*, Arise, it shall
Hag 2:15 from before a *s* was laid upon a
Hag 2:15 a *s* in the temple of the LORD
Zec 3:9 For behold the *s* that I have laid
Zec 3:9 upon one *s* shall be seven eyes
Zec 7:12 made their hearts as an adamant *s*
Zec 12:3 a burdensome *s* for all people
Mt 4:6 thou dash thy foot against a *s*
Mt 7:9 ask bread, will he give him a *s*
Mt 21:42 The *s* which the builders rejected
Mt 21:44 fall on this *s* shall be broken
Mt 24:2 be left here one *s* upon another
Mt 27:60 he rolled a great *s* to the door
Mt 27:66 the sepulchre sure, sealing the *s*
Mt 28:2 rolled back the *s* from the door
Mk 12:10 The *s* which the builders rejected
Mk 13:2 not be left one *s* upon another
Mk 15:46 rolled a *s* unto the door of the
Mk 16:3 Who shall roll us away the *s* from
Mk 16:4 saw that the *s* was rolled away
Lk 4:3 command this *s* that it be made
Lk 4:11 thou dash thy foot against a *s*
Lk 11:11 is a father, will he give him a *s*
Lk 19:44 leave in thee one *s* upon another
Lk 20:6 all the people will *s* us
Lk 20:17 The *s* which the builders rejected
Lk 20:18 fall upon that *s* shall be broken
Lk 21:6 not be left one *s* upon another
Lk 23:53 in a sepulchre that was hewn in *s*
Lk 24:2 they found the *s* rolled away from
Jn 1:42 which is by interpretation, A *s*
Jn 2:6 were set there six waterpots of *s*
Jn 8:7 let him first cast a *s* at her
Jn 10:31 took up stones again to *s* him
Jn 10:32 which of those works do ye *s* me
Jn 10:33 For a good work we *s* thee not
Jn 11:8 the Jews of late sought to *s* thee
Jn 11:38 It was a cave, and a *s* lay upon it
Jn 11:39 Jesus said, Take ye away the *s*
Jn 11:41 Then they took away the *s* from
Jn 20:1 seeth the *s* taken away from the
Acts 4:11 This is the *s* which was set at
Acts 14:5 them despitefully, and to *s* them,
Acts 17:29 like unto gold, or silver, or *s*
2Cor 3:3 not in tables of *s*, but in
Eph 2:20 himself being the chief corner *s*
1Pet 2:4 whom coming, as unto a living *s*
1Pet 2:6 I lay in Sion a chief corner *s*
1Pet 2:7 the *s* which the builders
1Pet 2:8 a *s* of stumbling, and a rock of
Rev 2:17 manna, and will give him a white *s*
Rev 2:17 in the *s* a new name written,
Rev 4:3 upon like a jasper and a sardine *s*
Rev 9:20 gold, and silver, and brass, and *s*
Rev 16:21 every *s* about the weight of a
Rev 18:21 up a *s* like a great millstone
Rev 21:11 was like unto a *s* most precious
Rev 21:11 precious, even like a jasper *s*

**STONED**
Ex 19:13 it, but he shall surely be *s*
Ex 21:28 then the ox shall be surely *s*
Ex 21:29 the ox shall be *s*, and his owner
Ex 21:32 of silver, and the ox shall be *s*
Num 15:36 *s* him with stones, and he died
Josh 7:25 all Israel *s* him with stones, and
Josh 7:25 after they had *s* them with stones
1Kin 12:18 all Israel *s* him with stones,
1Kin 21:13 *s* him with stones, that he died
1Kin 21:14 to Jezebel, saying, Naboth is *s*
1Kin 21:15 Jezebel heard that Naboth was *s*
2Chr 10:18 of Israel *s* him with stones
2Chr 24:21 him, and *s* him with stones at the
Mt 21:35 and killed another, and *s* another
Jn 8:5 us, that such should be *s*
Acts 5:26 lest they should have been *s*
Acts 7:58 him out of the city, and *s* him
Acts 7:59 they *s* Stephen, calling upon God,
Acts 14:19 the people, and, having *s* Paul
2Cor 11:25 I beaten with rods, once was I *s*
Heb 11:37 They were *s*, they were sawn
Heb 12:20 touch the mountain, it shall be *s*

**STONE'S**
Lk 22:41 from them about a *s* cast, and

**STONES**
Gen 28:11 and he took of the *s* of that place
Gen 31:46 said unto his brethren, Gather *s*
Gen 31:46 and they took *s*, and made an heap
Ex 25:7 Onyx *s*, and *s* to be set in
Ex 28:9 And thou shalt take two onyx *s*
Ex 28:11 shalt thou engrave the two *s* with
Ex 28:12 thou shalt put the two *s* upon the
Ex 28:12 *s* of memorial unto the children
Ex 28:17 shalt set in it settings of *s*
Ex 28:17 even four rows of *s*
Ex 28:21 the *s* shall be with the names of
Ex 31:5 And in cutting of *s*, to set them,
Ex 35:9 And onyx *s*, and *s* to be set
Ex 35:27 And the rulers brought onyx *s*
Ex 35:27 *s* to be set, for the ephod, and
Ex 35:33 And in the cutting of *s*, to set
Ex 39:6 they wrought onyx *s* inclosed in
Ex 39:7 that they should be *s* for a
Ex 39:10 And they set in it four rows of *s*

Ex 39:14 the s were according to the names
Lev 14:40 away the s in which the plague is
Lev 14:42 And they shall take other s
Lev 14:42 put them in the place of those s
Lev 14:43 that he hath taken away the s
Lev 14:45 the s of it, and the timber
Lev 20:2 the land shall stone him with s
Lev 20:27 they shall stone them with s
Lev 21:20 or scabbed, or hath his s broken
Lev 24:23 of the camp, and stone him with s
Num 14:10 bade stone them with s
Num 15:35 stone him with s without the camp
Num 15:36 the camp, and stoned him with s
Deut 8:9 a land whose s are iron, and out
Deut 13:10 And thou shalt stone him with s
Deut 17:5 woman, and shalt stone them with s
Deut 21:21 his city shall stone him with s
Deut 22:21 stone her with s that she die
Deut 22:24 stone them with s that they die
Deut 23:1 He that is wounded in the s
Deut 27:2 thou shalt set thee up great s
Deut 27:4 that ye shall set up these s
Deut 27:5 the LORD thy God, an altar of s
Deut 27:6 of the LORD thy God of whole s
Deut 27:8 thou shalt write upon the s all
Josh 4:3 feet stood firm, twelve s
Josh 4:6 saying, What mean ye by these s
Josh 4:7 these s shall be for a memorial
Josh 4:8 took up twelve s out of the midst
Josh 4:9 Joshua set up twelve s in the
Josh 4:20 And those twelve s, which they
Josh 4:21 come, saying, What mean these s
Josh 7:25 And all Israel stoned him with s
Josh 7:25 after they had stoned them with s
Josh 7:26 a great heap of s unto this day
Josh 8:29 raise thereon a great heap of s
Josh 8:31 law of Moses, an altar of whole s
Josh 8:32 he wrote there upon the s a copy
Josh 10:11 s from heaven upon them unto
Josh 10:18 Roll great s upon the mouth of
Josh 10:27 laid great s in the cave's mouth,
Judg 20:16 could sling s at an hair breadth
1Sa 17:40 five smooth s out of the brook
2Sa 12:30 of gold with the precious s
2Sa 16:6 he cast s at David, and at all the
2Sa 16:13 threw s at him, and cast dust
2Sa 18:17 a very great heap of s upon him
1Kin 5:17 s, costly s, and hewed s
1Kin 5:18 timber and s to build the house
1Kin 7:9 All these were of costly s
1Kin 7:9 to the measures of hewed s
1Kin 7:10 of costly s, even great s
1Kin 7:10 s of ten cubits, and s of
1Kin 7:11 And above were costly s, after the
1Kin 7:11 after the measures of hewed s
1Kin 7:12 was with three rows of hewed s
1Kin 10:2 and very much gold, and precious s
1Kin 10:10 very great store, and precious s
1Kin 10:11 of almug trees, and precious s
1Kin 10:27 silver to be in Jerusalem as s
1Kin 12:18 and all Israel stoned him with s
1Kin 15:22 and they took away the s of Ramah
1Kin 18:31 And Elijah took twelve s,
1Kin 18:32 with the s he built an altar in
1Kin 18:38 sacrifice, and the wood, and the s
1Kin 21:13 of the city, and stoned him with s
2Kin 3:19 every good piece of land with s
2Kin 3:25 left they the s thereof
2Kin 16:17 and put it upon a pavement of s
1Chr 12:2 hand and the left in hurling s
1Chr 20:2 and there were precious s in it
1Chr 22:2 s to build the house of God
1Chr 29:2 onyx s, and s to be set,
1Chr 29:2 to be set, glistering s
1Chr 29:2 and all manner of precious s
1Chr 29:2 s, and marble s in abundance
1Chr 29:8 they with whom precious s were
2Chr 1:15 at Jerusalem as plenteous as s
2Chr 3:6 house with precious s for beauty
2Chr 9:1 gold in abundance, and precious s
2Chr 9:9 great abundance, and precious s
2Chr 9:10 brought algum trees and precious s
2Chr 9:27 made silver in Jerusalem as s
2Chr 10:18 of Israel stoned him with s
2Chr 16:6 they carried away the s of Ramah
2Chr 24:21 him, and stoned him with s at the
2Chr 26:14 and bows, and slings to cast s
2Chr 26:15 to shoot arrows and great s withal
2Chr 32:27 and for gold, and for precious s
Ezr 5:8 which is builded with great s
Ezr 6:4 With three rows of great s
Neh 4:2 will they revive the s out of the
Job 5:23 in league with the s of the field
Job 6:12 Is my strength the strength of s
Job 8:17 the heap, and seeth the place of s
Job 14:19 The waters wear the s
Job 22:24 of Ophir as the s of the brooks
Job 28:3 the s of darkness, and the shadow
Job 28:6 The s of it are the place of
Job 40:17 the sinews of his s are wrapped
Job 41:30 Sharp s are under him
Ps 18:12 his thick clouds passed, hail s
Ps 18:13 hail s and coals of fire
Ps 102:14 servants take pleasure in her s
Ps 137:9 thy little ones against the s
Ps 144:12 our daughters may be as corner s
Eccl 3:5 A time to cast away s, and a time
Eccl 3:5 and a time to gather s together
Eccl 10:9 Whoso removeth s shall be hurt
Is 5:2 it, and gathered out the s thereof
Is 9:10 but we will build with hewn s
Is 14:19 that go down to the s of the pit
Is 27:9 when he maketh all the s of the
Is 34:11 confusion, and the s of emptiness
Is 54:11 I will lay thy s with fair colors
Is 54:12 and all thy borders of pleasant s
Is 57:6 Among the smooth s of the stream
Is 60:17 and for wood brass, and for s iron
Is 62:10 gather out the s
Jer 3:9 and committed adultery with s
Jer 43:9 Take great s in thine hand, and
Jer 43:10 upon these s that I have hid
Lam 3:16 broken my teeth with gravel s
Lam 4:1 the s of the sanctuary are poured
Eze 16:40 and they shall stone thee with s
Eze 23:47 company shall stone them with s
Eze 26:12 and they shall lay thy s and thy
Eze 27:22 spices, and with all precious s
Eze 28:14 in the midst of the s of fire
Eze 28:16 from the midst of the s of fire
Dan 11:38 and silver, and with precious s
Mic 1:6 I will pour down the s thereof
Zec 5:4 timber thereof and the s thereof
Zec 9:15 devour, and subdue with sling s
Zec 9:16 they shall be as the s of a crown
Mt 3:9 these s to raise up children unto
Mt 4:3 that these s be made bread
Mk 5:5 crying, and cutting himself with s
Mk 12:4 and at him they cast s, and wounded
Mk 13:1 him, Master, see what manner of s
Lk 3:8 these s to raise up children unto
Lk 19:40 the s would immediately cry out
Lk 21:5 how it was adorned with goodly s
Jn 8:59 took they up s to cast at him
Jn 10:31 Jews took up s again to stone him
1Cor 3:12 gold, silver, precious s, wood,
2Cor 3:7 death, written and engraven in s
1Pet 2:5 Ye also, as lively s, are built
Rev 17:4 and decked with gold and precious s
Rev 18:12 of gold, and silver, and precious s
Rev 18:16 decked with gold, and precious s
Rev 21:19 with all manner of precious s

## STONESQUARERS

1Kin 5:18 builders did hew them, and the s

## STONEST

Mt 23:37 s them which are sent unto thee,
Lk 13:34 s them that are sent unto thee

## STONING

1Sa 30:6 for the people spake of s him

## STONY

Ps 141:6 judges are overthrown in s places
Eze 11:19 I will take the s heart out of
Eze 36:26 I will take away the s heart out
Mt 13:5 Some fell upon s places, where
Mt 13:20 received the seed into s places
Mk 4:5 And some fell on s ground, where
Mk 4:16 which are sown on s ground

## STOOD

Gen 18:2 and, lo, three men s by him
Gen 18:8 he s by them under the tree, and
Gen 18:22 but Abraham s yet before the LORD
Gen 19:27 place where he s before the LORD
Gen 23:3 Abraham s up from before his dead
Gen 23:7 Abraham s up, and bowed himself
Gen 24:30 he s by the camels at the well
Gen 28:13 And, behold, the LORD s above it
Gen 37:7 my sheaf arose, and also s upright
Gen 37:7 your sheaves s round about
Gen 41:1 and, behold, he s by the river
Gen 41:3 s by the other kine upon the
Gen 41:17 I s upon the bank of the river
Gen 41:46 he s before Pharaoh king of Egypt
Gen 43:15 down to Egypt, and s before Joseph
Gen 45:1 before all them that s by him
Gen 45:1 there s no man with him, while
Ex 2:4 And his sister s afar off, to wit
Ex 2:17 but Moses s up and helped them, and
Ex 5:20 who s in the way, as they came
Ex 9:10 the furnace, and s before Pharaoh
Ex 14:19 their face, and s behind them
Ex 15:8 the floods s upright as an heap,
Ex 18:13 the people s by Moses from the
Ex 19:17 they s at the nether part of the
Ex 20:18 it, they removed, and s afar off
Ex 20:21 And the people s afar off, and
Ex 32:26 Then Moses s in the gate of the
Ex 33:8 s every man at his tent door, and
Ex 33:9 s at the door of the tabernacle,
Ex 34:5 s with him there, and proclaimed
Lev 9:5 drew near and s before the LORD
Num 11:32 the people s up all that day, and
Num 12:5 s in the door of the tabernacle,
Num 16:18 s in the door of the tabernacle
Num 16:27 s in the door of their tents, and
Num 16:48 he s between the dead and the
Num 22:22 the angel of the LORD s in the
Num 22:24 But the angel of the LORD s in a
Num 22:26 s in a narrow place, where was no
Num 23:6 he s by his burnt sacrifice, he,
Num 23:17 he s by his burnt offering, and
Num 27:2 they s before Moses, and before
Deut 4:11 came near and s under the mountain
Deut 5:5 (I s between the LORD and you at
Deut 31:15 the pillar of the cloud s over
Josh 3:16 which came down from above s
Josh 3:17 s firm on dry ground in the midst
Josh 4:3 where the priests' feet s firm
Josh 4:9 bare the ark of the covenant s
Josh 4:10 the ark s in the midst of Jordan
Josh 5:13 there s a man over against him
Josh 8:33 s on this side the ark and on that
Josh 10:13 And the sun s still, and the moon
Josh 10:13 So the sun s still in the midst
Josh 11:13 that s still in their strength
Josh 20:9 of blood, until he s before the
Josh 21:44 there s not a man of all their
Judg 3:19 all that s by him went out from
Judg 6:31 said unto all that s against him
Judg 7:21 they s every man in his place
Judg 9:7 s in the top of mount Gerizim, and
Judg 9:35 s in the entering of the gate of
Judg 9:44 s in the entering of the gate of
Judg 16:29 pillars upon which the house s
Judg 18:16 s by the entering of the gate
Judg 18:17 the priest s in the entering of
Judg 20:28 s before it in those days,)
1Sa 1:26 am the woman that s by thee here
1Sa 3:10 And the LORD came, and s, and called
1Sa 4:20 women that s by her said unto her
1Sa 6:14 s there, where there was a great
1Sa 10:23 when he s among the people, he
1Sa 16:21 came to Saul, and s before him
1Sa 17:3 the Philistines s on a mountain
1Sa 17:3 Israel s on a mountain on the
1Sa 17:8 And he s and cried unto the armies
1Sa 17:26 spake to the men that s by him
1Sa 17:51 s upon the Philistine, and took
1Sa 22:7 his servants that s about him
1Sa 22:17 unto the footmen that s about him
1Sa 26:13 s on the top of an hill afar off
2Sa 1:10 So I s upon him, and slew him,
2Sa 2:23 Asahel fell down and died s still
2Sa 2:25 troop, and s on the top of an hill
2Sa 2:28 and all the people s still
2Sa 13:31 all his servants s by with their
2Sa 15:2 s beside the way of the gate
2Sa 18:4 the king s by the gate side, and
2Sa 18:30 And he turned aside, and s still
2Sa 20:11 And one of Joab's men s by him
2Sa 20:12 saw that all the people s still
2Sa 20:12 one that came by him s still
2Sa 20:15 the city, and it s in the trench
2Sa 23:12 But he s in the midst of the
1Kin 1:28 presence, and s before the king
1Kin 3:15 s before the ark of the covenant
1Kin 3:16 unto the king, and s before him
1Kin 7:25 It s upon twelve oxen, three
1Kin 8:14 all the congregation of Israel s

1Kin 8:22 Solomon *s* before the altar of the
1Kin 8:55 And he *s*, and blessed all the
1Kin 10:19 two lions *s* beside the stays
1Kin 10:20 twelve lions *s* there on the one
1Kin 12:6 that *s* before Solomon his father
1Kin 12:8 with him, and which *s* before him
1Kin 13:1 Jeroboam *s* by the altar to burn
1Kin 13:24 in the way, and the ass *s* by it
1Kin 13:24 the lion also *s* by the carcase
1Kin 19:13 *s* in the entering in of the cave
1Kin 22:21 *s* before the LORD, and said, I
2Kin 2:7 went, and *s* to view afar off
2Kin 2:7 and they two *s* by Jordan
2Kin 2:13 back, and *s* by the bank of Jordan
2Kin 3:21 and upward, and *s* in the border
2Kin 4:12 had called her, she *s* before him
2Kin 4:15 had called her, she *s* in the door
2Kin 5:9 *s* at the door of the house of
2Kin 5:15 company, and came, and *s* before him
2Kin 5:25 went in, and *s* before his master
2Kin 8:9 *s* before him, and said, Thy son
2Kin 9:17 there *s* a watchman on the tower
2Kin 10:4 two kings *s* not before him
2Kin 10:9 morning, that he went out, and *s*
2Kin 11:11 And the guard *s*, every man with
2Kin 11:14 the king *s* by a pillar, as the
2Kin 13:21 he revived, and *s* up on his feet
2Kin 18:17 *s* by the conduit of the upper
2Kin 18:28 Then Rab-shakeh *s* and cried with a
2Kin 23:3 the king *s* by a pillar, and made a
2Kin 23:3 all the people *s* to the covenant
1Chr 6:39 who *s* on his right hand, even
1Chr 6:44 sons of Merari *s* on the left hand
1Chr 21:1 Satan *s* up against Israel, and
1Chr 21:15 the angel of the LORD *s* by the
1Chr 28:2 David the king *s* up upon his feet
2Chr 3:13 they *s* on their feet, and their
2Chr 4:4 It *s* upon twelve oxen, three
2Chr 5:12 *s* at the east end of the altar,
2Chr 6:3 all the congregation of Israel *s*
2Chr 6:12 he *s* before the altar of the LORD
2Chr 6:13 and upon it he *s*, and kneeled down
2Chr 7:6 before them, and all Israel *s*
2Chr 9:19 twelve lions *s* there on the one
2Chr 10:6 with the old men that had *s*
2Chr 10:8 up with him, that *s* before him
2Chr 13:4 Abijah *s* up upon mount Zemaraim,
2Chr 18:20 *s* before the LORD, and said, I
2Chr 20:5 Jehoshaphat *s* in the congregation
2Chr 20:13 all Judah *s* before the LORD, with
2Chr 20:19 *s* up to praise the LORD God of
2Chr 20:20 as they went forth, Jehoshaphat *s*
2Chr 20:23 Moab *s* up against the inhabitants
2Chr 23:13 the king *s* at his pillar at the
2Chr 24:20 which *s* above the people, and said
2Chr 28:12 *s* up against them that came from
2Chr 29:26 And the Levites *s* with the
2Chr 30:16 they *s* in their place after their
2Chr 34:31 the king *s* in his place, and made
2Chr 35:10 the priests *s* in their place, and
Ezr 2:63 till there *s* up a priest with
Ezr 3:2 Then *s* up Jeshua the son of
Ezr 3:9 Then *s* Jeshua with his sons and
Ezr 10:10 And Ezra the priest *s* up, and said
Neh 7:65 till there *s* up a priest with
Neh 8:4 Ezra the scribe *s* upon a pulpit
Neh 8:4 and beside him *s* Mattithiah
Neh 8:5 he opened it, all the people *s* up
Neh 8:7 the people *s* in their place
Neh 9:2 from all strangers, and *s* and
Neh 9:3 they *s* up in their place, and read
Neh 9:4 Then *s* up upon the stairs, of the
Neh 12:39 they *s* still in the prison gate
Neh 12:40 So *s* the two companies of them
Est 5:1 *s* in the inner court of the
Est 5:9 the king's gate, that he *s* not up
Est 7:7 Haman *s* up to make request for
Est 8:4 arose, and *s* before the king,
Est 9:16 *s* for their lives, and had rest
Job 4:15 the hair of my flesh *s* up
Job 4:16 It *s* still, but I could not
Job 29:8 and the aged arose, and *s* up
Job 30:28 I *s* up, and I cried in the
Job 32:16 but *s* still, and answered no more
Ps 33:9 he commanded, and it *s* fast
Ps 104:6 the waters *s* above the mountains
Ps 106:23 chosen *s* before him in the breach
Ps 106:30 Then *s* up Phinehas, and executed
Is 6:2 Above it *s* the seraphims
Is 36:2 he *s* by the conduit of the upper
Is 36:13 Then Rabshakeh *s*, and cried with a
Jer 15:1 Samuel *s* before me, yet my mind
Jer 18:20 Remember that I *s* before thee to
Jer 19:14 he *s* in the court of the LORD's
Jer 23:18 For who hath *s* in the counsel of
Jer 23:22 But if they had *s* in my counsel
Jer 28:5 that *s* in the house of the LORD
Jer 36:21 princes which *s* beside the king
Jer 44:15 gods, and all the women that *s* by
Jer 46:15 they *s* not, because the LORD did
Jer 48:45 They that fled *s* under the shadow
Lam 2:4 he *s* with his right hand as an
Eze 1:21 and when those *s*, these *s*
Eze 1:24 when they *s*, they let down their
Eze 1:25 was over their heads, when they *s*
Eze 3:23 the glory of the LORD *s* there
Eze 8:11 there *s* before them seventy men
Eze 8:11 in the midst of them *s* Jaazaniah
Eze 9:2 *s* beside the brasen altar
Eze 10:3 Now the cherubims *s* on the right
Eze 10:4 *s* over the threshold of the house
Eze 10:6 went in, and *s* beside the wheels
Eze 10:17 When they *s*, these *s*
Eze 10:18 house, and *s* over the cherubims
Eze 10:19 every one *s* at the door of the
Eze 11:23 *s* upon the mountain which is on
Eze 21:21 For the king of Babylon *s* at the
Eze 37:10 and *s* up upon their feet, an
Eze 40:3 and he *s* in the gate
Eze 43:6 and the man *s* by me
Eze 47:1 of the house *s* toward the east
Dan 1:19 therefore *s* they before the king
Dan 2:2 So they came and *s* before the king
Dan 2:31 was excellent, *s* before thee
Dan 3:3 they *s* before the image that
Dan 7:10 times ten thousand *s* before him
Dan 7:16 near unto one of them that *s* by
Dan 8:3 there *s* before the river a ram
Dan 8:15 behold, there *s* before me as the
Dan 8:17 So he came near where I *s*
Dan 8:22 broken, whereas four *s* up for it
Dan 10:11 this word unto me, I *s* trembling
Dan 10:16 and said unto him that *s* before me
Dan 11:1 *s* to confirm and to strengthen him
Dan 12:5 there *s* other two, the one on
Hos 10:9 there they *s*
Amos 7:7 the Lord *s* upon a wall made by a
Obad 14 thou have *s* in the crossway
Hab 3:6 He *s*, and measured the earth
Hab 3:11 moon *s* still in their habitation
Zec 1:8 he *s* among the myrtle trees that
Zec 1:10 the man that *s* among the myrtle
Zec 1:11 that *s* among the myrtle trees
Zec 3:3 garments, and *s* before the angel
Zec 3:4 unto those that *s* before him
Zec 3:5 And the angel of the LORD *s* by
Mt 2:9 *s* over where the young child was
Mt 12:46 mother and his brethren *s* without
Mt 13:2 whole multitude *s* on the shore
Mt 20:32 And Jesus *s* still, and called them,
Mt 26:73 came unto him they that *s* by
Mt 27:11 Jesus *s* before the governor
Mt 27:47 Some of them that *s* there
Mk 10:49 And Jesus *s* still, and commanded
Mk 11:5 them that *s* there said unto them
Mk 14:47 of them that *s* by drew a sword
Mk 14:60 the high priest *s* up in the midst
Mk 14:69 and began to say to them that *s* by
Mk 14:70 they that *s* by said again to
Mk 15:35 And some of them that *s* by
Mk 15:39 which *s* over against him, saw
Lk 4:16 sabbath day, and *s* up for to read
Lk 4:39 he *s* over her, and rebuked the
Lk 5:1 he *s* by the lake of Gennesaret,
Lk 6:8 And he arose and *s* forth
Lk 6:17 *s* in the plain, and the company of
Lk 7:14 and they that bare him *s* still
Lk 7:38 *s* at his feet behind him weeping,
Lk 9:32 and the two men that *s* with him
Lk 10:25 And, behold, a certain lawyer *s* up
Lk 17:12 were lepers, which *s* afar off
Lk 18:11 The Pharisee *s* and prayed thus
Lk 18:40 And Jesus *s*, and commanded him to
Lk 19:8 And Zacchaeus *s*, and said unto the
Lk 19:24 And he said unto them that *s* by
Lk 23:10 And the chief priests and scribes *s*
Lk 23:35 And the people *s* beholding
Lk 23:49 *s* afar off, beholding these
Lk 24:4 two men *s* by them in shining
Lk 24:36 Jesus himself *s* in the midst of
Jn 1:35 Again the next day after John *s*
Jn 6:22 when the people which *s* on the
Jn 7:37 great day of the feast, Jesus *s*
Jn 11:56 as they *s* in the temple, What
Jn 12:29 The people therefore, that *s* by
Jn 18:5 which betrayed him, *s* with them
Jn 18:16 But Peter *s* at the door without
Jn 18:18 the servants and officers *s* there
Jn 18:18 Peter *s* with them, and warmed
Jn 18:22 one of the officers which *s* by
Jn 18:25 And Simon Peter *s* and warmed
Jn 19:25 Now there *s* by the cross of Jesus
Jn 20:11 But Mary *s* without at the
Jn 20:19 *s* in the midst, and saith unto
Jn 20:26 *s* in the midst, and said, Peace be
Jn 21:4 now come, Jesus *s* on the shore
Acts 1:10 two men *s* by them in white
Acts 1:15 in those days Peter *s* up in the
Acts 3:8 And he leaping up *s*, and walked, and
Acts 4:26 The kings of the earth *s* up
Acts 5:34 Then *s* there up one in the
Acts 9:7 journeyed with him *s* speechless
Acts 9:39 all the widows *s* by him weeping
Acts 10:17 house, and *s* before the gate,
Acts 10:30 a man *s* before me in bright
Acts 11:13 an angel in his house, which *s*
Acts 11:28 there *s* up one of them named
Acts 12:14 told how Peter *s* before the gate
Acts 13:16 Then Paul *s* up, and beckoning with
Acts 14:20 the disciples *s* round about him
Acts 16:9 There *s* a man of Macedonia, and
Acts 17:22 Then Paul *s* in the midst of Mars'
Acts 21:40 Paul *s* on the stairs, and beckoned
Acts 22:13 Came unto me, and *s*, and said unto
Acts 22:25 said unto the centurion that *s* by
Acts 23:2 that *s* by him to smite him on the
Acts 23:4 And they that *s* by said, Revilest
Acts 23:11 night following the Lord *s* by him
Acts 24:20 while I *s* before the council,
Acts 25:7 down from Jerusalem *s* round about
Acts 25:18 whom when the accusers *s* up
Acts 27:21 Paul *s* forth in the midst of them
Acts 27:23 For there *s* by me this night the
2Ti 4:16 my first answer no man *s* with me
2Ti 4:17 the Lord *s* with me, and
Heb 9:10 Which *s* only in meats and drinks,
Rev 5:6 *s* a Lamb as it had been slain,
Rev 7:9 *s* before the throne, and before
Rev 7:11 all the angels *s* round about the
Rev 8:2 seven angels which *s* before God
Rev 8:3 *s* at the altar, having a golden
Rev 11:1 and the angel *s*, saying, Rise, and
Rev 11:11 them, and they *s* upon their feet
Rev 12:4 the dragon *s* before the woman
Rev 13:1 I *s* upon the sand of the sea, and
Rev 14:1 a Lamb *s* on the mount Sion, and
Rev 18:17 many as trade by sea, *s* afar off,

## STOODEST
Num 22:34 that thou *s* in the way against me
Deut 4:10 thou *s* before the LORD thy God in
Obad 11 day that thou *s* on the other side

## STOOL
2Kin 4:10 there a bed, and a table, and a *s*

## STOOLS
Ex 1:16 women, and see them upon the *s*

## STOOP
Job 9:13 the proud helpers do *s* under him
Prov 12:25 in the heart of man maketh it *s*
Is 46:2 They *s*, they bow down together
Mk 1:7 shoes I am not worthy to *s* down

## STOOPED
Gen 49:9 he *s* down, he couched as a lion,
1Sa 24:8 David *s* with his face to the
1Sa 28:14 he *s* with his face to the ground,
2Chr 36:17 old man, or him that *s* for age
Jn 8:6 But Jesus *s* down, and with his
Jn 8:8 And again he *s* down, and wrote on
Jn 20:11 she *s* down, and looked into the

## STOOPETH
Is 46:1 Bel boweth down, Nebo *s*, their

## STOOPING
Lk 24:12 *s* down, he beheld the linen
Jn 20:5 he *s* down, and looking in, saw the

## STOP
1Kin 18:44 down, that the rain *s* thee not
2Kin 3:19 *s* all wells of water, and mar
2Chr 32:3 his mighty men to *s* the waters of

Ps 35:3 *s* the way against them that
Ps 107:42 and all iniquity shall *s* her mouth
Eze 39:11 it shall *s* the noses of the
2Cor 11:10 no man shall *s* me of this

### STOPPED

Gen 8:2 and the windows of heaven were *s*
Gen 26:15 the Philistines had *s* them
Gen 26:18 for the Philistines had *s* them
Lev 15:3 or his flesh be *s* from his issue
2Kin 3:25 they *s* all the wells of water, and
2Chr 32:4 who *s* all the fountains, and the
2Chr 32:30 This same Hezekiah also *s* the
Neh 4:7 that the breaches began to be *s*
Ps 63:11 them that speak lies shall be *s*
Jer 51:32 And that the passages are *s*
Zec 7:11 *s* their ears, that they should
Acts 7:57 *s* their ears, and ran upon him
Rom 3:19 that every mouth may be *s*
Titus 1:11 Whose mouths must be *s*, who
Heb 11:33 promises, *s* the mouths of lions,

### STOPPETH

Job 5:16 hope, and iniquity *s* her mouth
Ps 58:4 the deaf adder that *s* her ear
Prov 21:13 Whoso *s* his ears at the cry of
Is 33:15 that *s* his ears from hearing of

### STORE

Gen 26:14 of herds, and great *s* of servants
Gen 41:36 that food shall be for *s* to the
Lev 25:22 come in ye shall eat of the old *s*
Lev 26:10 And ye shall eat old *s*, and bring
Deut 28:5 shall be thy basket and thy *s*
Deut 28:17 shall be thy basket and thy *s*
Deut 32:34 Is not this laid up in *s* with me
1Kin 9:19 the cities of *s* that Solomon had
1Kin 10:10 gold, and of spices very great *s*
2Kin 20:17 have laid up in *s* unto this day
1Chr 29:16 all this *s* that we have prepared
2Chr 8:4 wilderness, and all the *s* cities
2Chr 8:6 all the *s* cities that Solomon had
2Chr 11:11 *s* of victual, and of oil and wine
2Chr 16:4 all the *s* cities of Naphtali
2Chr 17:12 in Judah castles, and cities of *s*
2Chr 31:10 which is left is this great *s*
Neh 5:18 once in ten days *s* of all sorts
Ps 144:13 full, affording all manner of *s*
Is 39:6 have laid up in *s* until this day
Amos 3:10 who *s* up violence and robbery in
Nah 2:9 for there is none end of the *s*
1Cor 16:2 every one of you lay by him in *s*
1Ti 6:19 Laying up in *s* for themselves a
2Pet 3:7 by the same word are kept in *s*

### STOREHOUSE

Mal 3:10 ye all the tithes into the *s*
Lk 12:24 which neither have *s* nor barn

### STOREHOUSES

Gen 41:56 And Joseph opened all the *s*
Deut 28:8 the blessing upon thee in thy *s*
1Chr 27:25 over the *s* in the fields, in the
2Chr 32:28 *S* also for the increase of corn,
Ps 33:7 he layeth up the depth in *s*
Jer 50:26 the utmost border, open her *s*

### STORIES

Gen 6:16 third *s* shalt thou make it
Eze 41:16 round about on their three *s*
Eze 42:3 against gallery in three *s*
Eze 42:6 For they were in three *s*, but had
Amos 9:6 that buildeth his *s* in the heaven

### STORK

Lev 11:19 And the *s*, the heron after her
Deut 14:18 And the *s*, and the heron after her
Ps 104:17 as for the *s*, the fir trees are
Jer 8:7 the *s* in the heaven knoweth her
Zec 5:9 had wings like the wings of a *s*

### STORM

Job 21:18 as chaff that the *s* carrieth away
Job 27:21 as a *s* hurleth him out of his
Ps 55:8 hasten my escape from the windy *s*
Ps 83:15 and make them afraid with thy *s*
Ps 107:29 He maketh the *s* a calm, so that
Is 4:6 of refuge, and for a covert from *s*
Is 25:4 his distress, a refuge from the *s*
Is 25:4 ones is as a *s* against the wall
Is 28:2 tempest of hail and a destroying *s*
Is 29:6 and great noise, with *s* and
Eze 38:9 shalt ascend and come like a *s*
Nah 1:3 way in the whirlwind and in the *s*
Mk 4:37 And there arose a great *s* of wind
Lk 8:23 there came down a *s* of wind on

### STORMY

Ps 107:25 commandeth, and raiseth the *s* wind
Ps 148:8 *s* wind fulfilling his word
Eze 13:11 and a *s* wind shall rend it
Eze 13:13 rend it with a *s* wind in my fury

### STORY

2Chr 13:22 are written in the *s* of the
2Chr 24:27 they are written in the *s* of the

### STOUT

Job 4:11 the *s* lion's whelps are scattered
Is 10:12 *s* heart of the king of Assyria
Dan 7:20 look was more *s* than his fellows
Mal 3:13 Your words have been *s* against me

### STOUTHEARTED

Ps 76:5 The *s* are spoiled, they have
Is 46:12 Hearken unto me, ye *s*, that are

### STOUTNESS

Is 9:9 say in the pride and *s* of heart,

### STRAIGHT

Josh 6:5 ascend up every man *s* before him
Josh 6:20 every man *s* before him, and they
1Sa 6:12 the kine took the *s* way to the
2Chr 32:30 brought it *s* down to the west
Ps 5:8 make thy way *s* before my face
Prov 4:25 thine eyelids look *s* before thee
Eccl 1:15 which is crooked cannot be made *s*
Eccl 7:13 for who can make that *s*, which he
Is 40:3 make *s* in the desert a highway
Is 40:4 and the crooked shall be made *s*
Is 42:16 before them, and crooked things *s*
Is 45:2 and make the crooked places *s*
Jer 31:9 the rivers of waters in a *s* way
Eze 1:7 And their feet were *s* feet
Eze 1:9 they went every one *s* forward
Eze 1:12 And they went every one *s* forward
Eze 1:23 the firmament were their wings *s*
Eze 10:22 they went every one *s* forward
Mt 3:3 way of the Lord, make his paths *s*
Mk 1:3 way of the Lord, make his paths *s*
Lk 3:4 way of the Lord, make his paths *s*
Lk 3:5 and the crooked shall be made *s*
Lk 13:13 and immediately she was made *s*
Jn 1:23 Make *s* the way of the Lord, as
Acts 9:11 into the street which is called *S*
Acts 16:11 we came with a *s* course to
Acts 21:1 we came with a *s* course unto Coos
Heb 12:13 make *s* paths for your feet, lest

### STRAIGHTWAY

1Sa 9:13 the city, ye shall *s* find him
1Sa 28:20 Then Saul fell *s* all along on the
Prov 7:22 He goeth after her *s*, as an ox
Dan 10:17 *s* there remained no strength in
Mt 3:16 went up *s* out of the water
Mt 4:20 they *s* left their nets, and
Mt 14:22 And *s* Jesus constrained his
Mt 14:27 But *s* Jesus spake unto them,
Mt 21:2 *s* ye shall find an ass tied, and a
Mt 21:3 and *s* he will send them
Mt 25:15 and *s* took his journey
Mt 27:48 *s* one of them ran, and took a
Mk 1:10 *s* coming up out of the water, he
Mk 1:18 *s* they forsook their nets, and
Mk 1:20 And *s* he called them
Mk 1:21 *s* on the sabbath day he entered
Mk 2:2 *s* many were gathered together,
Mk 3:6 *s* took counsel with the Herodians
Mk 5:29 *s* the fountain of her blood was
Mk 5:42 *s* the damsel arose, and walked
Mk 6:25 she came in *s* with haste unto the
Mk 6:45 *s* he constrained his disciples to
Mk 6:54 out of the ship, *s* they knew him,
Mk 7:35 *s* his ears were opened, and the
Mk 8:10 *s* he entered into a ship with his
Mk 9:15 *s* all the people, when they
Mk 9:20 he saw him, *s* the spirit tare him
Mk 9:24 *s* the father of the child cried
Mk 11:3 *s* he will send him hither
Mk 14:45 as he was come, he goeth *s* to him
Mk 15:1 *s* in the morning the chief
Lk 5:39 drunk old wine *s* desireth new
Lk 8:55 spirit came again, and she arose *s*
Lk 12:54 *s* ye say, There cometh a shower
Lk 14:5 will not *s* pull him out on the
Jn 13:32 himself, and shall *s* glorify him
Acts 5:10 Then fell she down *s* at his feet
Acts 9:20 *s* he preached Christ in the
Acts 16:33 and was baptized, he and all his, *s*
Acts 22:29 Then *s* they departed from him
Acts 23:30 I sent *s* to thee, and gave
Jas 1:24 *s* forgetteth what manner of man

### STRAIN

Mt 23:24 which *s* at a gnat, and swallow a

### STRAIT

1Sa 13:6 Israel saw that they were in a *s*
2Sa 24:14 said unto Gad, I am in a great *s*
2Kin 6:1 dwell with thee is too *s* for us
1Chr 21:13 said unto Gad, I am in a great *s*
Job 36:16 out of the *s* into a broad place
Is 49:20 ears, The place is too *s* for me
Mt 7:13 Enter ye in at the *s* gate
Mt 7:14 Because *s* is the gate, and narrow
Lk 13:24 Strive to enter in at the *s* gate
Phil 1:23 For I am in a *s* betwixt two

### STRAITEN

Jer 19:9 seek their lives, shall *s* them

### STRAITENED

Job 18:7 steps of his strength shall be *s*
Job 37:10 and the breadth of the waters is *s*
Prov 4:12 goest, thy steps shall not be *s*
Eze 42:6 was *s* more than the lowest
Mic 2:7 is the spirit of the LORD *s*
Lk 12:50 and how am I *s* till it be
2Cor 6:12 Ye are not *s* in us, but ye are
2Cor 6:12 but ye are *s* in your own bowels

### STRAITENETH

Job 12:23 the nations, and *s* them again

### STRAITEST

Acts 26:5 that after the most *s* sect of our

### STRAITLY

Gen 43:7 The man asked us *s* of our state
Ex 13:19 for he had *s* sworn the children
Josh 6:1 Now Jericho was *s* shut up because
1Sa 14:28 Thy father *s* charged the people
Mt 9:30 Jesus *s* charged them, saying, See
Mk 1:43 he *s* charged him, and forthwith
Mk 3:12 he *s* charged them that they
Mk 5:43 he charged them *s* that no man
Lk 9:21 he *s* charged them, and commanded
Acts 4:17 let us *s* threaten them, that they
Acts 5:28 Did not we *s* command you that ye

### STRAITNESS

Deut 28:53 thee, in the siege, and in the *s*
Deut 28:55 him in the siege, and in the *s*
Deut 28:57 things secretly in the siege and *s*
Job 36:16 broad place, where there is no *s*
Jer 19:9 of his friend in the siege and *s*

### STRAITS

Job 20:22 his sufficiency he shall be in *s*
Lam 1:3 overtook her between the *s*

### STRAKE

Acts 27:17 *s* sail, and so were driven

### STRAKES

Gen 30:37 and pilled white *s* in them
Lev 14:37 walls of the house with hollow *s*

### STRANGE

Gen 35:2 Put away the *s* gods that are
Gen 35:4 they gave unto Jacob all the *s*
Gen 42:7 but made himself *s* unto them
Ex 2:22 have been a stranger in a *s* land
Ex 18:3 I have been an alien in a *s* land
Ex 21:8 to sell her unto a *s* nation he
Ex 30:9 shall offer no *s* incense thereon
Lev 10:1 offered *s* fire before the LORD,
Num 3:4 when they offered *s* fire before
Num 26:61 when they offered *s* fire before
Deut 32:12 and there was no *s* god with him
Deut 32:16 him to jealousy with *s* gods
Josh 24:20 forsake the LORD, and serve *s* gods
Josh 24:23 the *s* gods which are among you,
Judg 10:16 they put away the *s* gods from
Judg 11:2 for thou art the son of a *s* woman
1Sa 7:3 hearts, then put away the *s* gods
1Kin 11:1 king Solomon loved many *s* women
1Kin 11:8 did he for all his *s* wives
2Kin 19:24 drunk *s* waters, and with the sole
2Chr 14:3 away the altars of the *s* gods
2Chr 33:15 And he took away the *s* gods
Ezr 10:2 have taken *s* wives of the people
Ezr 10:10 and have taken *s* wives, to
Ezr 10:11 of the land, and from the *s* wives
Ezr 10:14 *s* wives in our cities come at

Ezr 10:17 *s* wives by the first day of the
Ezr 10:18 were found that had taken *s* wives
Ezr 10:44 All these had taken *s* wives
Neh 13:27 our God in marrying *s* wives
Job 19:3 that ye make yourselves *s* to me
Job 19:17 My breath is *s* to my wife
Job 31:3 a *s* punishment to the workers of
Ps 44:20 out our hands to a *s* god
Ps 81:9 There shall no *s* god be in thee
Ps 81:9 shalt thou worship any *s* god
Ps 114:1 Jacob from a people of *s* language
Ps 137:4 sing the LORD's song in a *s* land
Ps 144:7 from the hand of *s* children
Ps 144:11 me from the hand of *s* children
Prov 2:16 To deliver thee from the *s* woman
Prov 5:3 For the lips of a *s* woman drop as
Prov 5:20 son, be ravished with a *s* woman
Prov 6:24 of the tongue of a *s* woman
Prov 7:5 may keep thee from the *s* woman
Prov 20:16 a pledge of him for a *s* woman
Prov 21:8 The way of man is froward and *s*
Prov 22:14 The mouth of *s* women is a deep
Prov 23:27 a *s* woman is a narrow pit
Prov 23:33 Thine eyes shall behold *s* women
Prov 27:13 a pledge of him for a *s* woman
Is 17:10 and shalt set it with *s* slips
Is 28:21 he may do his work, his *s* work
Is 28:21 bring to pass his act, his *s* act
Is 43:12 when there was no *s* god among you
Jer 2:21 plant of a *s* vine unto me
Jer 5:19 served *s* gods in your land, so
Jer 8:19 graven images, and with *s* vanities
Eze 3:5 sent to a people of a *s* speech
Eze 3:6 Not to many people of a *s* speech
Dan 11:39 most strong holds with a *s* god
Hos 5:7 for they have begotten *s* children
Hos 8:12 they were counted as a *s* thing
Zeph 1:8 as are clothed with *s* apparel
Mal 2:11 married the daughter of a *s* god
Lk 5:26 We have seen *s* things to day
Acts 7:6 seed should sojourn in a *s* land
Acts 17:18 to be a setter forth of *s* gods
Acts 17:20 certain *s* things to our ears
Acts 26:11 them even unto *s* cities
Heb 11:9 of promise, as in a *s* country
Heb 13:9 about with divers and *s* doctrines
1Pet 4:4 Wherein they think it *s* that ye
1Pet 4:12 think it not *s* concerning the
1Pet 4:12 as though some *s* thing happened
Jude 7 and going after *s* flesh, are set

## STRANGELY

Deut 32:27 should behave themselves *s*

## STRANGER

Gen 15:13 a *s* in a land that is not theirs
Gen 17:8 the land wherein thou art a *s*
Gen 17:12 or bought with money of any *s*
Gen 17:27 and bought with money of the *s*
Gen 23:4 I am a *s* and a sojourner with you
Gen 28:4 the land wherein thou art a *s*
Gen 37:1 land wherein his father was a *s*
Ex 2:22 I have been a *s* in a strange land
Ex 12:19 of Israel, whether he be a *s*
Ex 12:43 There shall no *s* eat thereof
Ex 12:48 when a *s* shall sojourn with thee,
Ex 12:49 unto the *s* that sojourneth among
Ex 20:10 nor thy *s* that is within thy
Ex 22:21 Thou shalt neither vex a *s*
Ex 23:9 Also thou shalt not oppress a *s*
Ex 23:9 for ye know the heart of a *s*
Ex 23:12 the son of thy handmaid, and the *s*
Ex 29:33 but a *s* shall not eat thereof,
Ex 30:33 putteth any of it upon a *s*
Lev 16:29 or a *s* that sojourneth among you
Lev 17:12 blood, neither shall any *s* that
Lev 17:15 one of your own country, or a *s*
Lev 18:26 nor any *s* that sojourneth among
Lev 19:10 leave them for the poor and *s*
Lev 19:33 if a *s* sojourn with thee in your
Lev 19:34 But the *s* that dwelleth with you
Lev 22:10 There shall no *s* eat of the holy
Lev 22:12 daughter also be married unto a *s*
Lev 22:13 but there shall no *s* eat thereof
Lev 23:22 them unto the poor, and to the *s*
Lev 24:16 as well the *s*, as he that is born
Lev 24:22 manner of law, as well for the *s*
Lev 25:6 for thy *s* that sojourneth with
Lev 25:35 yea, though he be a *s*, or a
Lev 25:47 a sojourner or *s* wax rich by thee
Lev 25:47 unto the *s* or sojourner by thee
Num 1:51 the *s* that cometh nigh shall be
Num 3:10 the *s* that cometh nigh shall be
Num 3:38 the *s* that cometh nigh shall be
Num 9:14 if a *s* shall sojourn among you,
Num 9:14 one ordinance, both for the *s*
Num 15:14 if a *s* sojourn with you, or
Num 15:15 also for the *s* that sojourneth
Num 15:15 so shall the *s* be before the LORD
Num 15:16 for the *s* that sojourneth with
Num 15:26 the *s* that sojourneth among them
Num 15:29 for the *s* that sojourneth among
Num 15:30 he be born in the land, or a *s*
Num 16:40 the children of Israel, that no *s*
Num 18:4 a *s* shall not come nigh unto you
Num 18:7 the *s* that cometh nigh shall be
Num 19:10 unto the *s* that sojourneth among
Num 35:15 children of Israel, and for the *s*
Deut 1:16 and the *s* that is with him
Deut 5:14 nor thy *s* that is within thy
Deut 10:18 and widow, and loveth the *s*
Deut 10:19 Love ye therefore the *s*
Deut 14:21 unto the *s* that is in thy gates
Deut 14:29 inheritance with thee,) and the *s*
Deut 16:11 is within thy gates, and the *s*
Deut 16:14 maidservant, and the Levite, the *s*
Deut 17:15 thou mayest not set a *s* over thee
Deut 23:7 because thou wast a *s* in his land
Deut 23:20 Unto a *s* thou mayest lend upon
Deut 24:17 not pervert the judgment of the *s*
Deut 24:19 it shall be for the *s*, for the
Deut 24:20 it shall be for the *s*, for the
Deut 24:21 it shall be for the *s*, for the
Deut 25:5 shall not marry without unto a *s*
Deut 26:11 and the *s* that is among you
Deut 26:12 given it unto the Levite, the *s*
Deut 26:13 unto the Levite, and unto the *s*
Deut 27:19 perverteth the judgment of the *s*
Deut 28:43 The *s* that is within thee shall
Deut 29:11 thy *s* that is in thy camp, from
Deut 29:22 the *s* that shall come from a far
Deut 31:12 thy *s* that is within thy gates,
Josh 8:33 of the LORD, as well the *s*
Josh 20:9 for the *s* that sojourneth among
Judg 19:12 aside hither into the city of a *s*
Ruth 2:10 knowledge of me, seeing I am a *s*
2Sa 1:13 he answered, I am the son of a *s*
2Sa 15:19 for thou art a *s*, and also an
1Kin 3:18 there was no *s* with us in the
1Kin 8:41 Moreover concerning a *s*, that is
1Kin 8:43 that the *s* calleth to thee for
2Chr 6:32 Moreover concerning the *s*
2Chr 6:33 that the *s* calleth to thee for
Job 15:19 given, and no *s* passed among them
Job 19:15 and my maids, count me for a *s*
Job 31:32 The *s* did not lodge in the street
Ps 39:12 for I am a *s* with thee, and a
Ps 69:8 I am become a *s* unto my brethren,
Ps 94:6 They slay the widow and the *s*
Ps 119:19 I am a *s* in the earth
Prov 2:16 even from the *s* which flattereth
Prov 5:10 labours be in the house of a *s*
Prov 5:20 and embrace the bosom of a *s*
Prov 6:1 hast stricken thy hand with a *s*
Prov 7:5 from the *s* which flattereth with
Prov 11:15 surety for a *s* shall smart for it
Prov 14:10 a *s* doth not intermeddle with his
Prov 20:16 garment that is surety for a *s*
Prov 27:2 a *s*, and not thine own lips
Prov 27:13 garment that is surety for a *s*
Eccl 6:2 to eat thereof, but a *s* eateth it
Is 56:3 Neither let the son of the *s*
Is 56:6 Also the sons of the *s*, that join
Is 62:8 the sons of the *s* shall not drink
Jer 7:6 If ye oppress not the *s*, the
Jer 14:8 thou be as a *s* in the land
Jer 22:3 no wrong, do no violence to the *s*
Eze 14:7 or of the *s* that sojourneth in
Eze 22:7 dealt by oppression with the *s*
Eze 22:29 have oppressed the *s* wrongfully
Eze 44:9 No *s*, uncircumcised in heart, nor
Eze 44:9 of any *s* that is among the
Eze 47:23 in what tribe the *s* sojourneth
Obad 12 in the day that he became a *s*
Zec 7:10 widow, nor the fatherless, the *s*
Mal 3:5 turn aside the *s* from his right
Mt 25:35 I was a *s*, and ye took me in
Mt 25:38 When saw we thee a *s*, and took
Mt 25:43 I was a *s*, and ye took me not in
Mt 25:44 an hungred, or athirst, or a *s*
Lk 17:18 to give glory to God, save this *s*
Lk 24:18 Art thou only a *s* in Jerusalem
Jn 10:5 a *s* will they not follow, but
Acts 7:29 was a *s* in the land of Madian,

## STRANGER'S

Lev 22:25 Neither from a *s* hand shall ye
Lev 25:47 or to the stock of the *s* family

## STRANGERS

Gen 31:15 Are we not counted of him *s*
Gen 36:7 the land wherein they were *s*
Ex 6:4 pilgrimage, wherein they were *s*
Ex 22:21 for ye were *s* in the land of
Ex 23:9 seeing ye were *s* in the land of
Lev 17:8 or of the *s* which sojourn among
Lev 17:10 or of the *s* that sojourn among
Lev 17:13 or of the *s* that sojourn among
Lev 19:34 for ye were *s* in the land of
Lev 20:2 or of the *s* that sojourn in
Lev 22:18 of Israel, or of the *s* in Israel
Lev 25:23 for ye are *s* and sojourners with
Lev 25:45 the *s* that do sojourn among you
Deut 10:19 for ye were *s* in the land of
Deut 24:14 or of thy *s* that are in thy land
Deut 31:16 the gods of the *s* of the land
Josh 8:35 the *s* that were conversant among
2Sa 22:45 *S* shall submit themselves unto me
2Sa 22:46 *S* shall fade away, and they shall
1Chr 16:19 but few, even a few, and *s* in it
1Chr 22:2 to gather together the *s* that
1Chr 29:15 For we are *s* before thee, and
2Chr 2:17 Solomon numbered all the *s* that
2Chr 15:9 the *s* with them out of Ephraim and
2Chr 30:25 the *s* that came out of the land
Neh 9:2 separated themselves from all *s*
Neh 13:30 Thus cleansed I them from all *s*
Ps 18:44 the *s* shall submit themselves
Ps 18:45 The *s* shall fade away, and be
Ps 54:3 For *s* are risen up against me, and
Ps 105:12 yea, very few, and *s* in it
Ps 109:11 let the *s* spoil his labour
Ps 146:9 The LORD preserveth the *s*
Prov 5:10 Lest *s* be filled with thy wealth
Is 1:7 *s* devour it in your presence, and
Is 1:7 is desolate, as overthrown by *s*
Is 2:6 themselves in the children of *s*
Is 5:17 of the fat ones shall *s* eat
Is 14:1 the *s* shall be joined with them,
Is 25:2 a palace of *s* to be no city
Is 25:5 shalt bring down the noise of *s*
Is 29:5 of thy *s* shall be like small dust
Is 60:10 the sons of *s* shall build up thy
Is 61:5 *s* shall stand and feed your flocks
Jer 2:25 for I have loved *s*, and after them
Jer 3:13 to the *s* under every green tree
Jer 5:19 so shall ye serve *s* in a land
Jer 30:8 *s* shall no more serve themselves
Jer 35:7 days in the land where ye be *s*
Jer 51:51 for *s* are come into the
Lam 5:2 Our inheritance is turned to *s*
Eze 7:21 the hands of the *s* for a prey
Eze 11:9 deliver you into the hands of *s*
Eze 16:32 which taketh *s* instead of her
Eze 28:7 I will bring *s* upon thee, the
Eze 28:10 uncircumcised by the hand of *s*
Eze 30:12 that is therein, by the hand of *s*
Eze 31:12 And *s*, the terrible of the nations
Eze 44:7 have brought into my sanctuary *s*
Eze 47:22 to the *s* that sojourn among you,
Hos 7:9 *S* have devoured his strength, and
Hos 8:7 the *s* shall swallow it up
Joel 3:17 there shall no *s* pass through her
Obad 11 in the day that the *s* carried
Mt 17:25 of their own children, or of *s*
Mt 17:26 Peter saith unto him, Of *s*
Mt 27:7 the potter's field, to bury *s* in
Jn 10:5 for they know not the voice of *s*
Acts 2:10 *s* of Rome, Jews and proselytes,
Acts 13:17 dwelt as *s* in the land of Egypt
Acts 17:21 *s* which were there spent their
Eph 2:12 *s* from the covenants of promise,
Eph 2:19 Now therefore ye are no more *s*
1Ti 5:10 up children, if she have lodged *s*
Heb 11:13 and confessed that they were *s*
Heb 13:2 Be not forgetful to entertain *s*
1Pet 1:1 to the *s* scattered throughout
1Pet 2:11 beloved, I beseech you as *s*
3Jn 5 doest to the brethren, and to *s*

## STRANGERS'

Prov 5:17 thine own, and not *s* with thee

### STRANGLED
Nah 2:12 *s* for his lionesses, and filled
Acts 15:20 fornication, and from things *s*
Acts 15:29 and from blood, and from things *s*
Acts 21:25 idols, and from blood, and from *s*

### STRANGLING
Job 7:15 So that my soul chooseth *s*

### STRAW
Gen 24:25 moreover unto him, We have both *s*
Gen 24:32 he ungirded his camels, and gave *s*
Ex 5:7 give the people *s* to make brick
Ex 5:7 go and gather *s* for themselves
Ex 5:10 Pharaoh, I will not give you *s*
Ex 5:11 get you *s* where ye can find it
Ex 5:12 to gather stubble instead of *s*
Ex 5:13 daily tasks, as when there was *s*
Ex 5:16 There is no *s* given unto thy
Ex 5:18 for there shall no *s* be given you
Judg 19:19 Yet there is both *s* and provender
1Kin 4:28 *s* for the horses and dromedaries
Job 41:27 He esteemeth iron as *s*, and brass
Is 11:7 the lion shall eat *s* like the ox
Is 25:10 even as *s* is trodden down for the
Is 65:25 lion shall eat *s* like the bullock

### STRAWED
Ex 32:20 *s* it upon the water, and made the
Mt 21:8 the trees, and *s* them in the way
Mt 25:24 gathering where thou hast not *s*
Mt 25:26 not, and gather where I have not *s*
Mk 11:8 the trees, and *s* them in the way

### STREAM
Num 21:15 at the *s* of the brooks that goeth
Job 6:15 as the *s* of brooks they pass away
Ps 124:4 the *s* had gone over our soul
Is 27:12 of the river unto the *s* of Egypt
Is 30:28 his breath, as an overflowing *s*
Is 30:33 like a *s* of brimstone, doth
Is 57:6 stones of the *s* is thy portion
Is 66:12 of the Gentiles like a flowing *s*
Dan 7:10 A fiery *s* issued and came forth
Amos 5:24 and righteousness as a mighty *s*
Lk 6:48 the *s* beat vehemently upon that
Lk 6:49 against which the *s* did beat

### STREAMS
Ex 7:19 the waters of Egypt, upon their *s*
Ex 8:5 hand with thy rod over the *s*
Ps 46:4 the *s* whereof shall make glad the
Ps 78:16 He brought *s* also out of the rock
Ps 78:20 gushed out, and the *s* overflowed
Ps 126:4 O LORD, as the *s* in the south
Song 4:15 living waters, and *s* from Lebanon
Is 11:15 and shall smite it in the seven *s*
Is 30:25 *s* of waters in the day of the
Is 33:21 us a place of broad rivers and *s*
Is 34:9 the *s* thereof shall be turned
Is 35:6 break out, and *s* in the desert

### STREET
Gen 19:2 we will abide in the *s* all night
Deut 13:16 into the midst of the *s* thereof
Josh 2:19 the doors of thy house into the *s*
Judg 19:15 sat him down in a *s* of the city
Judg 19:17 man in the *s* of the city
Judg 19:20 only lodge not in the *s*
2Sa 21:12 them from the *s* of Beth-shan
2Sa 22:43 stamp them as the mire of the *s*
2Chr 29:4 them together into the east *s*
2Chr 32:6 in the *s* of the gate of the city
Ezr 10:9 sat in the *s* of the house of God
Neh 8:1 together as one man into the *s*
Neh 8:3 he read therein before the *s* that
Neh 8:16 in the *s* of the water gate, and in
Neh 8:16 in the *s* of the gate of Ephraim
Est 4:6 Mordecai unto the *s* of the city
Est 6:9 through the *s* of the city
Est 6:11 through the *s* of the city
Job 18:17 and he shall have no name in the *s*
Job 29:7 when I prepared my seat in the *s*
Job 31:32 stranger did not lodge in the *s*
Prov 7:8 through the *s* near her corner
Is 42:2 his voice to be heard in the *s*
Is 51:23 body as the ground, and as the *s*
Is 59:14 for truth is fallen in the *s*
Jer 37:21 of bread out of the bakers' *s*
Lam 2:19 for hunger in the top of every *s*
Lam 4:1 poured out in the top of every *s*
Eze 16:24 thee an high place in every *s*
Eze 16:31 thine high place in every *s*
Eze 28:23 pestilence, and blood into her *s*
Dan 9:25 the *s* shall be built again, and
Acts 9:11 go into the *s* which is called
Acts 12:10 out, and passed on through one *s*
Rev 11:8 lie in the *s* of the great city
Rev 21:21 the *s* of the city was pure gold,
Rev 22:2 In the midst of the *s* of it

### STREETS
2Sa 1:20 it not in the *s* of Askelon
1Kin 20:34 thou shalt make *s* for thee in
Ps 18:42 them out as the dirt in the *s*
Ps 55:11 and guile depart not from her *s*
Ps 144:13 and ten thousands in our *s*
Ps 144:14 there be no complaining in our *s*
Prov 1:20 she uttereth her voice in the *s*
Prov 5:16 and rivers of waters in the *s*
Prov 7:12 Now is she without, now in the *s*
Prov 22:13 I shall be slain in the *s*
Prov 26:13 a lion is in the *s*
Eccl 12:4 the doors shall be shut in the *s*
Eccl 12:5 and the mourners go about the *s*
Song 3:2 and go about the city in the *s*
Is 5:25 were torn in the midst of the *s*
Is 10:6 them down like the mire of the *s*
Is 15:3 In their *s* they shall gird
Is 15:3 of their houses, and in their *s*
Is 24:11 is a crying for wine in the *s*
Is 51:20 they lie at the head of all the *s*
Jer 5:1 and fro through the *s* of Jerusalem
Jer 7:17 of Judah and in the *s* of Jerusalem
Jer 7:34 from the *s* of Jerusalem, the
Jer 9:21 and the young men from the *s*
Jer 11:6 in the *s* of Jerusalem, saying,
Jer 11:13 the *s* of Jerusalem have ye set up
Jer 14:16 shall be cast out in the *s* of
Jer 33:10 in the *s* of Jerusalem, that are
Jer 44:6 of Judah and in the *s* of Jerusalem
Jer 44:9 Judah, and in the *s* of Jerusalem
Jer 44:17 Judah, and in the *s* of Jerusalem
Jer 44:21 in the *s* of Jerusalem, ye, and
Jer 48:38 of Moab, and in the *s* thereof
Jer 49:26 her young men shall fall in her *s*
Jer 50:30 shall her young men fall in the *s*
Jer 51:4 that are thrust through in her *s*
Lam 2:11 swoon in the *s* of the city
Lam 2:12 the wounded in the *s* of the city
Lam 2:21 old lie on the ground in the *s*
Lam 4:5 delicately are desolate in the *s*
Lam 4:8 they are not known in the *s*
Lam 4:14 wandered as blind men in the *s*
Lam 4:18 steps, that we cannot go in our *s*
Eze 7:19 shall cast their silver in the *s*
Eze 11:6 ye have filled the *s* thereof with
Eze 26:11 shall he tread down all thy *s*
Amos 5:16 Wailing shall be in all *s*
Mic 7:10 trodden down as the mire of the *s*
Nah 2:4 The chariots shall rage in the *s*
Nah 3:10 in pieces at the top of all the *s*
Zeph 3:6 I made their *s* waste, that none
Zec 8:4 women dwell in the *s* of Jerusalem
Zec 8:5 the *s* of the city shall be full
Zec 8:5 and girls playing in the *s* thereof
Zec 9:3 and fine gold as the mire of the *s*
Zec 10:5 the mire of the *s* in the battle
Mt 6:2 do in the synagogues and in the *s*
Mt 6:5 and in the corners of the *s*
Mt 12:19 any man hear his voice in the *s*
Mk 6:56 they laid the sick in the *s*
Lk 10:10 ways out into the *s* of the same
Lk 13:26 and thou hast taught in our *s*
Lk 14:21 Go out quickly into the *s*
Acts 5:15 brought forth the sick into the *s*

### STRENGTH
Gen 4:12 henceforth yield unto thee her *s*
Gen 49:3 might, and the beginning of my *s*
Gen 49:24 But his bow abode in *s*, and the
Ex 13:3 for by *s* of hand the LORD brought
Ex 13:14 By *s* of hand the LORD brought us
Ex 13:16 for by *s* of hand the LORD brought
Ex 14:27 the sea returned to his *s* when
Ex 15:2 The LORD is my *s* and song, and he
Ex 15:13 in thy *s* unto thy holy habitation
Lev 26:20 your *s* shall be spent in vain
Num 23:22 as it were the *s* of a unicorn
Num 24:8 as it were the *s* of a unicorn
Deut 21:17 for he is the beginning of his *s*
Deut 33:25 and as thy days, so shall thy *s* be
Josh 11:13 that stood still in their *s*
Josh 14:11 as my *s* was then, even so is my
Josh 14:11 was then, even so is my *s* now
Judg 5:21 my soul, thou hast trodden down *s*
Judg 8:21 for as the man is, so is his *s*
Judg 16:5 and see wherein his great *s* lieth
Judg 16:6 thee, wherein thy great *s* lieth
Judg 16:9 So his *s* was not known
Judg 16:15 told me wherein thy great *s* lieth
Judg 16:17 then my *s* will go from me, and I
Judg 16:19 him, and his *s* went from him
1Sa 2:4 that stumbled are girded with *s*
1Sa 2:9 for by *s* shall no man prevail
1Sa 2:10 and he shall give *s* unto his king
1Sa 15:29 also the *S* of Israel will not lie
1Sa 28:20 and there was no *s* in him
1Sa 28:22 and eat, that thou mayest have *s*
2Sa 22:33 God is my *s* and power
2Sa 22:40 hast girded me with *s* to battle
1Kin 19:8 went in the *s* of that meat forty
2Kin 9:24 Jehu drew a bow with his full *s*
2Kin 18:20 I have counsel and *s* for the war
2Kin 19:3 there is not *s* to bring forth
1Chr 16:11 Seek the LORD and his *s*, seek his
1Chr 16:27 *s* and gladness are in his place
1Chr 16:28 give unto the LORD glory and *s*
1Chr 26:8 able men for *s* for the service,
1Chr 29:12 make great, and to give *s* unto all
2Chr 6:41 place, thou, and the ark of thy *s*
2Chr 13:20 *s* again in the days of Abijah
Neh 4:10 The *s* of the bearers of burdens
Neh 8:10 for the joy of the LORD is your *s*
Job 6:11 What is my *s*, that I should hope
Job 6:12 Is my *s* the *s* of stones
Job 9:4 is wise in heart, and mighty in *s*
Job 9:19 If I speak of *s*, lo, he is strong
Job 12:13 With him is wisdom and *s*, he hath
Job 12:16 With him is *s* and wisdom
Job 12:21 and weakeneth the *s* of the mighty
Job 18:7 The steps of his *s* shall be
Job 18:12 His *s* shall be hungerbitten, and
Job 18:13 It shall devour the *s* of his skin
Job 18:13 of death shall devour his *s*
Job 21:23 One dieth in his full *s*, being
Job 23:6 but he would put *s* in me
Job 26:2 thou the arm that hath no *s*
Job 30:2 whereto might the *s* of their
Job 36:5 he is mighty in *s* and wisdom
Job 36:19 not gold, nor all the forces of *s*
Job 37:6 and to the great rain of his *s*
Job 39:11 trust him, because his *s* is great
Job 39:19 Hath thou given the horse *s*
Job 39:21 the valley, and rejoiceth in his *s*
Job 40:16 his *s* is in his loins, and his
Job 41:22 In his neck remaineth *s*, and
Ps 8:2 *s* because of thine enemies
Ps 18:1 I will love thee, O LORD, my *s*
Ps 18:2 my God, my *s*, in whom I will
Ps 18:32 It is God that girdeth me with *s*
Ps 18:39 girded me with *s* unto the battle
Ps 19:14 in thy sight, O LORD, my *s*
Ps 20:6 the saving *s* of his right hand
Ps 21:1 The king shall joy in thy *s*
Ps 21:13 exalted, LORD, in thine own *s*
Ps 22:15 My *s* is dried up like a potsherd
Ps 22:19 O my *s*, haste thee to help me
Ps 27:1 the LORD is the *s* of my life
Ps 28:7 The LORD is my *s* and my shield
Ps 28:8 The LORD is their *s*, and he is the
Ps 28:8 is the saving *s* of his anointed
Ps 29:1 give unto the LORD glory and *s*
Ps 29:11 LORD will give *s* unto his people
Ps 31:4 for thou art my *s*
Ps 31:10 my *s* faileth because of mine
Ps 33:16 man is not delivered by much *s*
Ps 33:17 he deliver any by his great *s*
Ps 37:39 he is their *s* in the time of
Ps 38:10 My heart panteth, my *s* faileth me
Ps 39:13 O spare me, that I may recover *s*
Ps 43:2 For thou art the God of my *s*
Ps 46:1 God is our refuge and *s*, a very
Ps 52:7 the man that made not God his *s*
Ps 54:1 by thy name, and judge me by thy *s*
Ps 59:9 Because of his *s* will I wait upon
Ps 59:17 Unto thee, O my *s*, will I sing
Ps 60:7 also is the *s* of mine head
Ps 62:7 the rock of my *s*, and my refuge,
Ps 65:6 Which by his *s* setteth fast the
Ps 68:28 Thy God hath commanded thy *s*
Ps 68:34 Ascribe ye *s* unto God
Ps 68:34 Israel, and his *s* is in the clouds
Ps 68:35 God of Israel is he that giveth *s*
Ps 71:9 forsake me not when my *s* faileth

Ps 71:16 will go in the *s* of the Lord GOD
Ps 71:18 shewed thy *s* unto this generation
Ps 73:4 but their *s* is firm
Ps 73:26 but God is the *s* of my heart
Ps 74:13 didst divide the sea by thy *s*
Ps 77:14 declared thy *s* among the people
Ps 78:4 the praises of the LORD, and his *s*
Ps 78:51 the chief of their *s* in the
Ps 78:61 delivered his *s* into captivity,
Ps 80:2 and Manasseh stir up thy *s*
Ps 81:1 Sing aloud unto God our *s*
Ps 84:5 is the man whose *s* is in thee
Ps 84:7 They go from *s* to *s*
Ps 86:16 give thy *s* unto thy servant, and
Ps 88:4 I am as a man that hath no *s*
Ps 89:17 For thou art the glory of their *s*
Ps 90:10 if by reason of *s* they be
Ps 90:10 years, yet is their *s* labour
Ps 93:1 the LORD is clothed with *s*
Ps 95:4 the *s* of the hills is his also
Ps 96:6 *s* and beauty are in his sanctuary
Ps 96:7 give unto the LORD glory and *s*
Ps 99:4 The king's *s* also loveth judgment
Ps 102:23 He weakened my *s* in the way
Ps 103:20 ye his angels, that excel in *s*
Ps 105:4 Seek the LORD, and his *s*
Ps 105:36 land, the chief of all their *s*
Ps 108:8 also is the *s* of mine head
Ps 110:2 send the rod of thy *s* out of Zion
Ps 118:14 The LORD is my *s* and song, and is
Ps 132:8 thou, and the ark of thy *s*
Ps 138:3 me with *s* in my soul
Ps 140:7 the *s* of my salvation, thou hast
Ps 144:1 Blessed be the LORD my *s*, which
Ps 147:10 not in the *s* of the horse
Prov 8:14 I have *s*
Prov 10:29 of the LORD is *s* to the upright
Prov 14:4 increase is by the *s* of the ox
Prov 20:29 The glory of young men is their *s*
Prov 21:22 casteth down the *s* of the
Prov 24:5 a man of knowledge increaseth *s*
Prov 24:10 day of adversity, thy *s* is small
Prov 31:3 Give not thy *s* unto women
Prov 31:17 She girdeth her loins with *s*
Prov 31:25 *S* and honour are her clothing
Eccl 9:16 said I, Wisdom is better than *s*
Eccl 10:10 edge, then must he put to more *s*
Eccl 10:17 princes eat in due season, for *s*
Is 5:22 men of *s* to mingle strong drink
Is 10:13 By the *s* of my hand I have done
Is 12:2 for the LORD JEHOVAH is my *s*
Is 17:10 been mindful of the rock of thy *s*
Is 23:4 even the *s* of the sea, saying, I
Is 23:10 there is no more *s*
Is 23:14 for your *s* is laid waste
Is 25:4 thou hast been a *s* to the poor
Is 25:4 a *s* to the needy in his distress,
Is 26:4 the LORD JEHOVAH is everlasting *s*
Is 27:5 Or let him take hold of my *s*
Is 28:6 for *s* to them that turn the
Is 30:2 themselves in the *s* of Pharaoh
Is 30:3 Therefore shall the *s* of Pharaoh
Is 30:7 this, Their *s* is to sit still
Is 30:15 and in confidence shall be your *s*
Is 33:6 of thy times, and *s* of salvation
Is 36:5 I have counsel and *s* for war
Is 37:3 there is not *s* to bring forth
Is 40:9 tidings, lift up thy voice with *s*
Is 40:29 have no might he increaseth *s*
Is 40:31 upon the LORD shall renew their *s*
Is 41:1 and let the people renew their *s*
Is 42:25 of his anger, and the *s* of battle
Is 44:12 worketh it with the *s* of his arms
Is 44:12 he is hungry, and his *s* faileth
Is 45:24 LORD have I righteousness and *s*
Is 49:4 I have spent my *s* for nought
Is 49:5 the LORD, and my God shall be my *s*
Is 51:9 Awake, awake, put on *s*, O arm of
Is 52:1 put on thy *s*, O Zion
Is 62:8 hand, and by the arm of his *s*
Is 63:1 in the greatness of his *s*
Is 63:6 bring down their *s* to the earth
Is 63:15 where is thy zeal and thy *s*
Jer 16:19 O LORD, my *s*, and my fortress, and
Jer 20:5 deliver all the *s* of this city
Jer 51:53 fortify the height of her *s*
Lam 1:6 gone without *s* before the pursuer
Lam 1:14 he hath made my *s* to fall
Lam 3:18 And I said, My *s* and my hope is
Eze 24:21 the excellency of your *s*
Eze 24:25 day when I take from them their *s*
Eze 30:15 my fury upon Sin, the *s* of Egypt
Eze 30:18 the pomp of her *s* shall cease in
Eze 33:28 and the pomp of her *s* shall cease
Dan 2:37 given thee a kingdom, power, and *s*
Dan 2:41 be in it of the *s* of the iron
Dan 10:8 and there remained no *s* in me
Dan 10:8 corruption, and I retained no *s*
Dan 10:16 upon me, and I have retained no *s*
Dan 10:17 there remained no *s* in me
Dan 11:2 by his *s* through his riches he
Dan 11:15 shall there be any *s* to withstand
Dan 11:17 with the *s* of his whole kingdom
Dan 11:31 shall pollute the sanctuary of *s*
Hos 7:9 Strangers have devoured his *s*
Hos 12:3 by his *s* he had power with God
Joel 2:22 tree and the vine do yield their *s*
Joel 3:16 the *s* of the children of Israel
Amos 3:11 shall bring down thy *s* from thee
Amos 6:13 taken to us horns by our own *s*
Mic 5:4 and feed in the *s* of the LORD
Nah 3:9 Ethiopia and Egypt were her *s*
Nah 3:11 shalt seek *s* because of the enemy
Hab 3:19 The LORD God is my *s*, and he will
Hag 2:22 I will destroy the *s* of the
Zec 12:5 of Jerusalem shall be my *s* in the
Mk 12:30 all thy mind, and with all thy *s*
Mk 12:33 all the soul, and with all the *s*
Lk 1:51 He hath shewed *s* with his arm
Lk 10:27 all thy soul, and with all thy *s*
Acts 3:7 feet and ancle bones received *s*
Acts 9:22 But Saul increased the more in *s*
Rom 5:6 For when we were yet without *s*
1Cor 15:56 and the *s* of sin is the law
2Cor 1:8 pressed out of measure, above *s*
2Cor 12:9 for my *s* is made perfect in
Heb 9:17 otherwise it is of no *s* at all
Heb 11:11 received *s* to conceive seed
Rev 1:16 was as the sun shineth in his *s*
Rev 3:8 for thou hast a little *s*, and hast
Rev 5:12 power, and riches, and wisdom, and *s*
Rev 12:10 Now is come salvation, and *s*
Rev 17:13 their power and *s* unto the beast

## STRENGTHEN

Deut 3:28 and encourage him, and *s* him
Judg 16:28 *s* me, I pray thee, only this once
1Kin 20:22 *s* thyself, and mark, and see what
Ezr 6:22 to *s* their hands in the work of
Neh 6:9 Now therefore, O God, *s* my hands
Job 16:5 But I would *s* you with my mouth,
Ps 20:2 sanctuary, and *s* thee out of Zion
Ps 27:14 and he shall *s* thine heart
Ps 31:24 he shall *s* your heart, all ye
Ps 41:3 The LORD will *s* him upon the bed
Ps 68:28 *s*, O God, that which thou hast
Ps 89:21 mine arm also shall *s* him
Ps 119:28 *s* thou me according unto thy word
Is 22:21 *s* him with thy girdle, and I will
Is 30:2 to *s* themselves in the strength
Is 33:23 they could not well *s* their mast
Is 35:3 *S* ye the weak hands, and confirm
Is 41:10 I will *s* thee
Is 54:2 thy cords, and *s* thy stakes
Jer 23:14 they *s* also the hands of
Eze 7:13 neither shall any *s* himself in
Eze 16:49 neither did she *s* the hand of the
Eze 30:24 I will *s* the arms of the king of
Eze 30:25 But I will *s* the arms of the king
Eze 34:16 will *s* that which was sick
Dan 11:1 I, stood to confirm and to *s* him
Amos 2:14 the strong shall not *s* his force
Zec 10:6 I will *s* the house of Judah, and I
Zec 10:12 I will *s* them in the LORD
Lk 22:32 art converted, *s* thy brethren
1Pet 5:10 make you perfect, stablish, *s*
Rev 3:2 *s* the things which remain, that

## STRENGTHENED

Gen 48:2 Israel *s* himself, and sat upon the
Judg 3:12 the LORD *s* Eglon the king of Moab
Judg 7:11 be *s* to go down unto the host
1Sa 23:16 the wood, and *s* his hand in God
2Sa 2:7 Therefore now let your hands be *s*
1Chr 11:10 who *s* themselves with him in his
2Chr 1:1 son of David was *s* in his kingdom
2Chr 11:17 So they *s* the kingdom of Judah,
2Chr 12:1 had *s* himself, he forsook the law
2Chr 12:13 So king Rehoboam *s* himself in
2Chr 13:7 have *s* themselves against
2Chr 17:1 and *s* himself against Israel
2Chr 21:4 he *s* himself, and slew all his
2Chr 23:1 seventh year Jehoiada *s* himself
2Chr 24:13 of God in his state, and *s* it
2Chr 25:11 And Amaziah *s* himself, and led
2Chr 26:8 for he *s* himself exceedingly
2Chr 28:20 and distressed him, but *s* him not
2Chr 32:5 Also he *s* himself, and built up
Ezr 1:6 *s* their hands with vessels of
Ezr 7:28 I was *s* as the hand of the LORD
Neh 2:18 So they *s* their hands for this
Job 4:3 thou hast *s* the weak hands
Job 4:4 thou hast *s* the feeble knees
Ps 52:7 *s* himself in his wickedness
Ps 147:13 For he hath *s* the bars of thy
Prov 8:28 when he *s* the fountains of the
Eze 13:22 *s* the hands of the wicked, that
Eze 34:4 The diseased have ye not *s*
Dan 10:18 appearance of a man, and he *s* me
Dan 10:19 he had spoken unto me, I was *s*
Dan 10:19 for thou hast *s* me
Dan 11:6 he that *s* her in these times
Dan 11:12 but he shall not be *s* by it
Hos 7:15 *s* their arms, yet do they imagine
Acts 9:19 he had received meat, he was *s*
Eph 3:16 to be *s* with might by his Spirit
Col 1:11 *S* with all might, according to
2Ti 4:17 the Lord stood with me, and *s* me

## STRENGTHENEDST

Ps 138:3 *s* me with strength in my soul

## STRENGTHENETH

Job 15:25 *s* himself against the Almighty
Ps 104:15 and bread which *s* man's heart
Prov 31:17 with strength, and *s* her arms
Eccl 7:19 Wisdom *s* the wise more than ten
Is 44:14 which he *s* for himself among the
Amos 5:9 That *s* the spoiled against the
Phil 4:13 things through Christ which *s* me

## STRENGTHENING

Lk 22:43 angel unto him from heaven, *s* him
Acts 18:23 in order, *s* all the disciples

## STRETCH

Ex 3:20 I will *s* out my hand, and smite
Ex 7:5 when I *s* forth mine hand upon
Ex 7:19 *s* out thine hand upon the waters
Ex 8:5 *S* forth thine hand with thy rod
Ex 8:16 *S* out thy rod, and smite the dust
Ex 9:15 For now I will *s* out my hand
Ex 9:22 *S* forth thine hand toward heaven,
Ex 10:12 *S* out thine hand over the land of
Ex 10:21 *S* out thine hand toward heaven,
Ex 14:16 *s* out thine hand over the sea, and
Ex 14:26 *S* out thine hand over the sea,
Ex 25:20 the cherubim shall *s* forth their
Josh 8:18 *S* out the spear that is in thy
1Sa 24:6 to *s* forth mine hand against him,
1Sa 26:9 for who can *s* forth his hand
1Sa 26:11 *s* forth mine hand against the
1Sa 26:23 but I would not *s* forth mine hand
2Sa 1:14 How wast thou not afraid to *s*
2Kin 21:13 I will *s* over Jerusalem the line
Job 11:13 *s* out thine hands toward him
Job 30:24 Howbeit he will not *s* out his
Job 39:26 *s* her wings toward the south
Ps 68:31 Ethiopia shall soon *s* out her
Ps 138:7 thou shalt *s* forth thine hand
Ps 143:6 I *s* forth my hands unto thee
Is 28:20 that a man can *s* himself on it
Is 31:3 the LORD shall *s* out his hand
Is 34:11 he shall *s* out upon it the line
Is 54:2 let them *s* forth the curtains of
Jer 6:12 for I will *s* out my hand upon the
Jer 10:20 there is none to *s* forth my tent
Jer 15:6 therefore will I *s* out my hand
Jer 51:25 I will *s* out mine hand upon thee,
Eze 6:14 So will I *s* out my hand upon them
Eze 14:9 I will *s* out my hand upon him, and
Eze 14:13 then will I *s* out mine hand upon
Eze 25:7 therefore I will *s* out mine hand
Eze 25:13 I will also *s* out mine hand upon
Eze 25:16 I will *s* out mine hand upon the
Eze 30:25 he shall *s* it out upon the land
Eze 35:3 I will *s* out mine hand against
Dan 11:42 He shall *s* forth his hand also
Amos 6:4 *s* themselves upon their couches,
Zeph 1:4 I will also *s* out mine hand upon
Zeph 2:13 he will *s* out his hand against
Mt 12:13 he to the man, *S* forth thine hand
Mk 3:5 unto the man, *S* forth thine hand

Lk 6:10 unto the man, S forth thy hand
Jn 21:18 thou shalt s forth thy hands, and
2Cor 10:14 For we s not ourselves beyond our

## STRETCHED

Gen 22:10 Abraham s forth his hand, and took
Gen 48:14 Israel s out his right hand, and
Ex 6:6 will redeem you with a s out arm
Ex 8:6 Aaron s out his hand over the
Ex 8:17 for Aaron s out his hand with his
Ex 9:23 Moses s forth his rod toward
Ex 10:13 Moses s forth his rod over the
Ex 10:22 Moses s forth his hand toward
Ex 14:21 Moses s out his hand over the sea
Ex 14:27 Moses s forth his hand over the
Deut 4:34 by a s out arm, and by great
Deut 5:15 a mighty hand and by a s out arm
Deut 7:19 the s out arm, whereby the LORD
Deut 9:29 mighty power and by thy s out arm
Deut 11:2 mighty hand, and his s out arm,
Josh 8:18 Joshua s out the spear that he
Josh 8:19 as soon as he had s out his hand
Josh 8:26 wherewith he s out the spear,
2Sa 24:16 when the angel s out his hand
1Kin 6:27 they s forth the wings of the
1Kin 8:42 strong hand, and of thy s out arm
1Kin 17:21 he s himself upon the child three
2Kin 4:34 he s himself upon the child
2Kin 4:35 and went up, and s himself upon him
2Kin 17:36 a s out arm, him shall ye fear,
1Chr 21:16 in his hand s out over Jerusalem
2Chr 6:32 thy mighty hand, and thy s out arm
Job 38:5 or who hath s the line upon it
Ps 44:20 or s out our hands to a strange
Ps 88:9 I have s out my hands unto thee
Ps 136:6 To him that s out the earth above
Ps 136:12 strong hand, and with a s out arm
Prov 1:24 I have s out my hand, and no man
Is 3:16 walk with s forth necks and wanton
Is 5:25 he hath s forth his hand against
Is 5:25 away, but his hand is s out still
Is 9:12 away, but his hand is s out still
Is 9:17 away, but his hand is s out still
Is 9:21 away, but his hand is s out still
Is 10:4 away, but his hand is s out still
Is 14:26 is s out upon all the nations
Is 14:27 and his hand is s out, and who
Is 16:8 her branches are s out, they are
Is 23:11 He s out his hand over the sea,
Is 42:5 the heavens, and s them out
Is 45:12 have s out the heavens, and all
Is 51:13 that hath s forth the heavens, and
Jer 6:4 shadows of the evening are s out
Jer 10:12 hath s out the heavens by his
Jer 32:17 s out arm, and there is nothing
Jer 32:21 with a s out arm, and with great
Jer 51:15 hath s out the heaven by his
Lam 2:8 he hath s out a line, he hath not
Eze 1:11 and their wings were s upward
Eze 1:22 s forth over their heads above
Eze 10:7 one cherub s forth his hand from
Eze 16:27 therefore I have s out my hand
Eze 20:33 with a s out arm, and with fury
Eze 20:34 with a s out arm, and with fury
Hos 7:5 he s out his hand with scorners
Amos 6:7 the banquet of them that s
Zec 1:16 a line shall be s forth upon
Mt 12:13 And he s it forth
Mt 12:49 he s forth his hand toward his
Mt 14:31 Jesus s forth his hand, and caught
Mt 26:51 were with Jesus s out his hand
Mk 3:5 And he s it out
Lk 22:53 ye s forth no hands against me
Acts 12:1 s forth his hands to vex certain
Acts 26:1 Then Paul s forth the hand, and
Rom 10:21 All day long I have s forth my

## STRETCHEDST

Ex 15:12 Thou s out thy right hand, the

## STRETCHEST

Ps 104:2 who s out the heavens like a

## STRETCHETH

Job 15:25 For he s out his hand against God
Job 26:7 He s out the north over the empty
Prov 31:20 She s out her hand to the poor
Is 40:22 that s out the heavens as a
Is 44:13 The carpenter s out his rule
Is 44:24 that s forth the heavens alone
Zec 12:1 which s forth the heavens, and

## STRETCHING

Is 8:8 the s out of his wings shall fill
Acts 4:30 By s forth thine hand to heal

## STRICKEN

Gen 18:11 Sarah were old and well s in age
Gen 24:1 Abraham was old, and well s in age
Josh 13:1 Now Joshua was old and s in years
Josh 13:1 s in years, and there remaineth
Josh 23:1 that Joshua waxed old and s in age
Josh 23:2 unto them, I am old and s in age
Judg 5:26 pierced and s through his temples
1Kin 1:1 king David was old and s in years
Prov 6:1 if thou hast s thy hand with a
Prov 23:35 They have s me, shalt thou say,
Is 1:5 Why should ye be s any more
Is 16:7 surely they are s
Is 53:4 yet we did esteem him s, smitten
Is 53:8 of my people was he s
Jer 5:3 thou hast s them, but they have
Lam 4:9 s through for want of the fruits
Lk 1:7 both were now well s in years
Lk 1:18 man, and my wife well s in years

## STRIFE

Gen 13:7 there was a s between the herdmen
Gen 13:8 said unto Lot, Let there be no s
Num 27:14 in the s of the congregation, to
Deut 1:12 and your burden, and your s
Judg 12:2 my people were at great s with
2Sa 19:9 And all the people were at s
Ps 31:20 a pavilion from the s of tongues
Ps 55:9 seen violence and s in the city
Ps 80:6 Thou makest us a s unto our
Ps 106:32 him also at the waters of s
Prov 15:18 A wrathful man stirreth up s
Prov 15:18 that is slow to anger appeaseth s
Prov 16:28 A froward man soweth s
Prov 17:1 house full of sacrifices with s
Prov 17:14 The beginning of s is as when one
Prov 17:19 transgression that loveth s
Prov 20:3 honour for a man to cease from s
Prov 22:10 yea, s and reproach shall cease
Prov 26:17 meddleth with s belonging not to
Prov 26:20 is no talebearer, the s ceaseth
Prov 26:21 is a contentious man to kindle s
Prov 28:25 is of a proud heart stirreth up s
Prov 29:22 An angry man stirreth up s
Prov 30:33 forcing of wrath bringeth forth s
Is 58:4 Behold, ye fast for s and debate,
Jer 15:10 thou hast borne me a man of s
Eze 47:19 even to the waters of s in Kadesh
Eze 48:28 unto the waters of s in Kadesh
Hab 1:3 and there are that raise up s
Lk 22:24 And there was also a s among them
Rom 13:13 and wantonness, not in s and
1Cor 3:3 there is among you envying, and s
Gal 5:20 variance, emulations, wrath, s
Phil 1:15 preach Christ even of envy and s
Phil 2:3 be done through s or vainglory
1Ti 6:4 of words, whereof cometh envy, s
Heb 6:16 is to them an end of all s
Jas 3:14 s in your hearts, glory not, and
Jas 3:16 s is, there is confusion and every

## STRIFES

Prov 10:12 Hatred stirreth up s
2Cor 12:20 be debates, envyings, wraths, s
1Ti 6:4 s of words, whereof cometh envy,
2Ti 2:23 knowing that they do gender s

## STRIKE

Ex 12:7 s it on the two side posts and on
Ex 12:22 s the lintel and the two side
Deut 21:4 shall s off the heifer's neck
2Kin 5:11 s his hand over the place, and
Job 17:3 is he that will s hands with me
Job 20:24 bow of steel shall s him through
Ps 110:5 LORD at thy right hand shall s
Prov 7:23 Till a dart s through his liver
Prov 17:26 nor to s princes for equity
Prov 22:26 not thou one of them that s hands
Hab 3:14 Thou didst s through with his
Mk 14:65 the servants did s him with the

## STRIKER

1Ti 3:3 Not given to wine, no s, not
Titus 1:7 angry, not given to wine, no s

## STRIKETH

Job 34:26 He s them as wicked men in the
Prov 17:18 man void of understanding s hands
Rev 9:5 of a scorpion, when he s a man

## STRING

Ps 11:2 make ready their arrow upon the s
Mk 7:35 the s of his tongue was loosed,

## STRINGED

Ps 150:4 praise him with s instruments
Is 38:20 we will sing my songs to the s
Hab 3:19 chief singer on my s instruments

## STRINGS

Ps 21:12 thy s against the face of them
Ps 33:2 and an instrument of ten s
Ps 92:3 Upon an instrument of ten s
Ps 144:9 an instrument of ten s will I

## STRIP

Num 20:26 s Aaron of his garments, and put
1Sa 31:8 Philistines came to s the slain
1Chr 10:8 Philistines came to s the slain
Is 32:11 s you, and make you bare, and gird
Eze 16:39 they shall s thee also of thy
Eze 23:26 They shall also s thee out of thy
Hos 2:3 Lest I s her naked, and set her as

## STRIPE

Ex 21:25 wound for wound, s for s

## STRIPES

Deut 25:3 Forty s he may give him, and not
Deut 25:3 beat him above these with many s
2Sa 7:14 with the s of the children of men
Ps 89:32 the rod, and their iniquity with s
Prov 17:10 man than an hundred s into a fool
Prov 19:29 and s for the back of fools
Prov 20:30 so do s the inward parts of the
Is 53:5 and with his s we are healed
Lk 12:47 will, shall be beaten with many s
Lk 12:48 and did commit things worthy of s
Lk 12:48 shall be beaten with few s
Acts 16:23 they had laid many s upon them
Acts 16:33 of the night, and washed their s
2Cor 6:5 In s, in imprisonments, in
2Cor 11:23 in s above measure, in prisons
2Cor 11:24 times received I forty s save one
1Pet 2:24 by whose s ye were healed

## STRIPLING

1Sa 17:56 Enquire thou whose son the s is

## STRIPPED

Ex 33:6 And the children of Israel s
Num 20:28 Moses s Aaron of his garments, and
1Sa 18:4 Jonathan s himself of the robe
1Sa 31:9 s off his armour, and sent into
1Chr 10:9 And when they had s him, they took
2Chr 20:25 which they s off for themselves,
Job 19:9 He hath s me of my glory, and
Job 22:6 s the naked of their clothing
Mic 1:8 I will wail and howl, I will go s
Mt 27:28 And they s him, and put on him a
Lk 10:30 which s him of his raiment, and

## STRIPT

Gen 37:23 that they s Joseph out of his
1Sa 19:24 he s off his clothes also, and

## STRIVE

Gen 6:3 shall not always s with man
Gen 26:20 Gerar did s with Isaac's herdmen
Ex 21:18 if men s together, and one smite
Ex 21:22 If men s, and hurt a woman with
Deut 25:11 When men s together one with
Deut 33:8 with whom thou didst s at the
Judg 11:25 did he ever s against Israel, or
Job 33:13 Why dost thou s against him
Ps 35:1 O LORD, with them that s with me
Prov 3:30 S not with a man without cause,
Prov 25:8 Go not forth hastily to s
Is 41:11 they that s with thee shall
Is 45:9 Let the potsherd s with the
Hos 4:4 Yet let no man s, nor reprove
Hos 4:4 as they that s with the priest
Mt 12:19 He shall not s, nor cry
Lk 13:24 S to enter in at the strait gate
Rom 15:30 that ye s together with me in
2Ti 2:5 And if a man also s for masteries
2Ti 2:5 not crowned, except he s lawfully
2Ti 2:14 s not about words to no profit
2Ti 2:24 servant of the Lord must not s

## STRIVED

Rom 15:20 so have I s to preach the gospel,

## STRIVEN

Jer 50:24 thou hast s against the LORD

## STRIVETH

Is 45:9 unto him that s with his Maker
1Cor 9:25 every man that s for the mastery

## STRIVING

Phil 1:27 with one mind s together for the
Col 1:29 s according to his working, which
Heb 12:4 unto blood, s against sin

## STRIVINGS

2Sa 22:44 me from the s of my people
Ps 18:43 me from the s of the people
Titus 3:9 contentions, and s about the law

## STROKE

Deut 17:8 and plea, and between s and s
Deut 19:5 his hand fetcheth a s with the
Deut 21:5 controversy and every s be tried
Est 9:5 enemies with the s of the sword
Job 23:2 my s is heavier than my groaning
Job 36:18 lest he take thee away with his s
Ps 39:10 Remove thy s away from me
Is 14:6 in wrath with a continual s
Is 30:26 healeth the s of their wound
Eze 24:16 the desire of thine eyes with a s

## STROKES

Prov 18:6 and his mouth calleth for s

## STRONG

Gen 49:14 Issachar is a s ass couching down
Gen 49:24 s by the hands of the mighty God
Ex 6:1 for with a s hand shall he let
Ex 6:1 with a s hand shall he drive them
Ex 10:19 LORD turned a mighty s west wind
Ex 13:9 for with a s hand hath the LORD
Ex 14:21 by a s east wind all that night
Lev 10:9 Do not drink wine nor s drink
Num 6:3 s drink, and shall drink no
Num 6:3 of wine, or vinegar of s drink
Num 13:18 whether they be s or weak
Num 13:19 whether in tents, or in s holds
Num 13:28 be s that dwell in the land
Num 20:20 much people, and with a s hand
Num 21:24 of the children of Ammon was s
Num 24:21 S is thy dwellingplace, and thou
Num 28:7 s wine to be poured unto the LORD
Deut 2:36 was not one city too s for us
Deut 11:8 you this day, that ye may be s
Deut 14:26 or for wine, or for s drink
Deut 29:6 have ye drunk wine or s drink
Deut 31:6 Be s and of a good courage, fear
Deut 31:7 in the sight of all Israel, Be s
Deut 31:23 of Nun a charge, and said, Be s
Josh 1:6 Be s and of a good courage
Josh 1:7 Only be thou s and very courageous
Josh 1:9 Be s and of a good courage
Josh 1:18 only be s and of a good courage
Josh 10:25 Fear not, nor be dismayed, be s
Josh 14:11 As yet I am as s this day as I
Josh 17:13 children of Israel were waxen s
Josh 17:18 chariots, and though they be s
Josh 19:29 to Ramah, and to the s city Tyre
Josh 23:9 before you great nations and s
Judg 1:28 came to pass, when Israel was s
Judg 6:2 mountains, and caves, and s holds
Judg 9:51 But there was a s tower within
Judg 13:4 and drink not wine nor s drink
Judg 13:7 and now drink no wine nor s drink
Judg 13:14 let her drink wine or s drink
Judg 14:14 out of the s came forth sweetness
Judg 18:26 saw that they were too s for him
1Sa 1:15 drunken neither wine nor s drink
1Sa 4:9 Be s, and quit yourselves like men
1Sa 14:52 and when Saul saw any s man
1Sa 23:14 in the wilderness in s holds
1Sa 23:19 with us in s holds in the wood
1Sa 23:29 dwelt in s holds at En-gedi
2Sa 3:6 himself s for the house of Saul
2Sa 5:7 David took the s hold of Zion
2Sa 10:11 If the Syrians be too s for me
2Sa 10:11 of Ammon be too s for thee
2Sa 11:25 battle more s against the city
2Sa 15:12 And the conspiracy was s
2Sa 16:21 of all that are with thee be s
2Sa 22:18 He delivered me from my s enemy
2Sa 22:18 for they were too s for me
2Sa 24:7 came to the s hold of Tyre, and to
1Kin 2:2 be thou s therefore, and shew
1Kin 8:42 thy great name, and of thy s hand
1Kin 19:11 s wind rent the mountains, and
2Kin 2:16 be with thy servants fifty s men
2Kin 8:12 their s holds wilt thou set on
2Kin 24:16 a thousand, all that were s
1Chr 19:12 If the Syrians be too s for me
1Chr 19:12 of Ammon be too s for thee
1Chr 22:13 be s, and of good courage
1Chr 26:7 whose brethren were s men
1Chr 26:9 sons and brethren, s men, eighteen
1Chr 28:10 be s, and do it
1Chr 28:20 said to Solomon his son, Be s
2Chr 11:11 And he fortified the s holds
2Chr 11:12 spears, and made them exceeding s
2Chr 11:17 Rehoboam the son of Solomon s
2Chr 15:7 Be ye s therefore, and let not
2Chr 16:9 to shew himself s in the behalf
2Chr 25:8 go, do it, be s for the battle
2Chr 26:15 helped, till he was s
2Chr 26:16 But when he was s, his heart was
2Chr 32:7 Be s and courageous, be not afraid
Ezr 9:12 that ye may be s, and eat the good
Neh 1:10 thy great power, and by thy s hand
Neh 9:25 And they took s cities, and a fat
Job 8:2 of thy mouth be like a s wind
Job 9:19 I speak of strength, lo, he is s
Job 30:21 with thy s hand thou opposest
Job 33:19 of his bones with s pain
Job 37:18 spread out the sky, which is s
Job 39:28 crag of the rock, and the s place
Job 40:18 bones are as s pieces of brass
Ps 10:10 the poor may fall by his s ones
Ps 18:17 He delivered me from my s enemy
Ps 18:17 for they were too s for me
Ps 19:5 rejoiceth as a s man to run a
Ps 22:12 s bulls of Bashan have beset me
Ps 24:8 The LORD s and mighty, the LORD
Ps 30:7 hast made my mountain to stand s
Ps 31:2 be thou my s rock, for an house
Ps 31:21 marvellous kindness in a s city
Ps 35:10 from him that is too s for him
Ps 38:19 enemies are lively, and they are s
Ps 60:9 Who will bring me into the s city
Ps 61:3 me, and a s tower from the enemy
Ps 71:3 Be thou my s habitation,
Ps 71:7 but thou art my s refuge
Ps 80:15 that thou madest s for thyself
Ps 80:17 whom thou madest s for thyself
Ps 89:8 who is a s LORD like unto thee
Ps 89:10 thine enemies with thy s arm
Ps 89:13 s is thy hand, and high is thy
Ps 89:40 hast brought his s holds to ruin
Ps 108:10 Who will bring me into the s city
Ps 136:12 With a s hand, and with a
Ps 144:14 That our oxen may be s to labour
Prov 7:26 many s men have been slain by her
Prov 10:15 rich man's wealth is his s city
Prov 11:16 and s men retain riches
Prov 14:26 fear of the LORD is s confidence
Prov 18:10 The name of the LORD is a s tower
Prov 18:11 rich man's wealth is his s city
Prov 18:19 is harder to be won than a s city
Prov 20:1 is a mocker, s drink is raging
Prov 21:14 and a reward in the bosom s wrath
Prov 24:5 A wise man is s
Prov 30:25 The ants are a people not s
Prov 31:4 nor for princes s drink
Prov 31:6 Give s drink unto him that is
Eccl 9:11 swift, nor the battle to the s
Eccl 12:3 the s men shall bow themselves,
Song 8:6 for love is s as death
Is 1:31 the s shall be as tow, and the
Is 5:11 that they may follow s drink
Is 5:22 men of strength to mingle s drink
Is 8:7 them the waters of the river, s
Is 8:11 spake thus to me with a s hand
Is 17:9 In that day shall his s cities be
Is 23:11 to destroy the s holds thereof
Is 24:9 s drink shall be bitter to them
Is 25:3 shall the s people glorify thee
Is 26:1 We have a s city
Is 27:1 s sword shall punish leviathan
Is 28:2 s one, which as a tempest of hail
Is 28:7 through s drink are out of the
Is 28:7 have erred through s drink
Is 28:7 out of the way through s drink
Is 28:22 lest your bands be made s
Is 29:9 stagger, but not with s drink
Is 31:1 horsemen, because they are very s
Is 31:9 pass over to his s hold for fear
Is 35:4 that are of a fearful heart, Be s
Is 40:10 Lord GOD will come with s hand
Is 40:26 might, for that he is s in power
Is 41:21 bring forth your s reasons
Is 53:12 shall divide the spoil with the s
Is 56:12 will fill ourselves with s drink
Is 60:22 and a small one a s nation
Jer 8:16 of the neighing of his s ones
Jer 21:5 outstretched hand and with a s arm
Jer 32:21 and with wonders, and with a s hand
Jer 47:3 of the hoofs of his s horses
Jer 48:14 are mighty and s men for the war
Jer 48:17 How is the s staff broken, and the
Jer 48:18 and he shall destroy thy s holds
Jer 48:41 the s holds are surprised, and the
Jer 49:19 against the habitation of the s
Jer 50:34 Their Redeemer is s
Jer 50:44 unto the habitation of the s
Jer 51:12 of Babylon, make the watch s
Lam 2:2 thrown down in his wrath the s
Lam 2:5 he hath destroyed his s holds
Eze 3:8 thy face s against their faces
Eze 3:8 thy forehead s against their
Eze 3:14 hand of the LORD was s upon me
Eze 7:24 make the pomp of the s to cease
Eze 19:11 she had s rods for the sceptres
Eze 19:12 her s rods were broken and
Eze 19:14 so that she hath no s rod to be a
Eze 22:14 endure, or can thine hands be s
Eze 26:11 thy s garrisons shall go down to
Eze 26:17 city, which wast s in the sea
Eze 30:21 to make it s to hold the sword
Eze 30:22 and will break his arms, the s
Eze 32:21 The s among the mighty shall
Eze 34:16 I will destroy the fat and the s
Dan 2:40 fourth kingdom shall be s as iron
Dan 2:42 so the kingdom shall be partly s
Dan 4:11 The tree grew, and was s, and the
Dan 4:20 thou sawest, which grew, and was s
Dan 4:22 king, that art grown and become s
Dan 7:7 and terrible, and s exceedingly
Dan 8:8 and when he was s, the great horn
Dan 10:19 unto thee, be s, yea, be s
Dan 11:5 the king of the south shall be s
Dan 11:5 and he shall be s above him
Dan 11:23 shall become s with a small
Dan 11:24 his devices against the s holds
Dan 11:32 that do know their God shall be s
Dan 11:39 most s holds with a strange god
Joel 1:6 nation is come up upon my land, s
Joel 2:2 a great people and a s
Joel 2:5 as a s people set in battle array
Joel 2:11 for he is s that executeth his
Joel 3:10 let the weak say, I am s
Amos 2:9 cedars, and he was s as the oaks
Amos 2:14 the s shall not strengthen his
Amos 5:9 the spoiled against the s
Mic 2:11 unto thee of wine and of s drink
Mic 4:3 rebuke s nations afar off
Mic 4:7 that was cast far off a s nation
Mic 4:8 the s hold of the daughter of
Mic 5:11 and throw down all thy s holds
Mic 6:2 ye s foundations of the earth
Nah 1:7 a s hold in the day of trouble
Nah 2:1 watch the way, make thy loins s
Nah 3:12 All thy s holds shall be like fig
Nah 3:14 the siege, fortify thy s holds
Nah 3:14 the morter, make s the brickkiln
Hab 1:10 they shall deride every s hold
Hag 2:4 Yet now be s, O Zerubbabel, saith
Hag 2:4 and be s, O Joshua, son of
Hag 2:4 and be s, all ye people of the
Zec 8:9 Let your hands be s, ye that hear
Zec 8:13 fear not, but let your hands be s
Zec 8:22 s nations shall come to seek the
Zec 9:3 Tyrus did build herself a s hold
Zec 9:12 Turn you to the s hold, ye
Mt 12:29 one enter into a s man's house
Mt 12:29 except he first bind the s man
Mk 3:27 can enter into a s man's house
Mk 3:27 he will first bind the s man
Lk 1:15 drink neither wine nor s drink
Lk 1:80 waxed s in spirit, and was in the
Lk 2:40 waxed s in spirit, filled with
Lk 11:21 When a s man armed keepeth his
Acts 3:16 in his name hath made this man s
Rom 4:20 but was s in faith, giving glory
Rom 15:1 We then that are s ought to bear
1Cor 4:10 we are weak, but ye are s
1Cor 16:13 faith, quit you like men, be s
2Cor 10:4 to the pulling down of s holds
2Cor 12:10 for when I am weak, then am I s
2Cor 13:9 when we are weak, and ye are s
Eph 6:10 be s in the Lord, and in the power

2Th 2:11 God shall send them *s* delusion
2Ti 2:1 be *s* in the grace that is in
Heb 5:7 and supplications with *s* crying
Heb 5:12 need of milk, and not of *s* meat
Heb 5:14 But *s* meat belongeth to them that
Heb 6:18 we might have a *s* consolation
Heb 11:34 out of weakness were made *s*
1Jn 2:14 you, young men, because ye are *s*
Rev 5:2 I saw a *s* angel proclaiming with
Rev 18:2 he cried mightily with a *s* voice
Rev 18:8 for *s* is the Lord God who judgeth

### STRONGER
Gen 25:23 shall be *s* than the other people
Gen 30:41 whensoever the *s* cattle did
Gen 30:42 were Laban's, and the *s* Jacob's
Num 13:31 for they are *s* than we
Judg 14:18 And what is *s* than a lion
2Sa 1:23 eagles, they were *s* than lions
2Sa 3:1 but David waxed *s* and *s*, and
2Sa 13:14 being *s* than she, forced her, and
1Kin 20:23 therefore they were *s* than we
1Kin 20:23 and surely we shall be *s* than they
1Kin 20:25 and surely we shall be *s* than they
Job 17:9 hands shall be *s* and *s*
Ps 105:24 made them *s* than their enemies
Ps 142:6 for they are *s* than I
Jer 20:7 thou art *s* than I, and hast
Jer 31:11 hand of him that was *s* than he
Lk 11:22 But when a *s* than he shall come
1Cor 1:25 the weakness of God is *s* than men
1Cor 10:22 are we *s* than he

### STRONGEST
Prov 30:30 A lion which is *s* among beasts

### STRONGLY
Ezr 6:3 the foundations thereof be *s* laid

### STROVE
Gen 26:20 because they *s* with him
Gen 26:21 another well, and *s* for that also
Gen 26:22 and for that they *s* not
Ex 2:13 two men of the Hebrews *s* together
Lev 24:10 a man of Israel *s* together in the
Num 20:13 of Israel *s* with the LORD
Num 26:9 who *s* against Moses and against
Num 26:9 when they *s* against the LORD
2Sa 14:6 they two *s* together in the field,
Ps 60:*t* when he *s* with Aram-naharaim and
Dan 7:2 the heaven *s* upon the great sea
Jn 6:52 Jews therefore *s* among themselves
Acts 7:26 himself unto them as they *s*
Acts 23:9 the Pharisees' part arose, and *s*

### STROWED
2Chr 34:4 *s* it upon the graves of them that

### STRUCK
1Sa 2:14 he *s* it into the pan, or kettle,
2Sa 12:15 the LORD *s* the child that Uriah's
2Sa 20:10 to the ground, and *s* him not again
2Chr 13:20 and the LORD *s* him, and he died
Mt 26:51 *s* a servant of the high priest's,
Lk 22:64 they *s* him on the face, and asked
Jn 18:22 of the officers which stood by *s*

### STRUGGLED
Gen 25:22 the children *s* together within

### STUBBLE
Ex 5:12 to gather *s* instead of straw
Ex 15:7 wrath, which consumed them as *s*
Job 13:25 and wilt thou pursue the dry *s*
Job 21:18 They are as *s* before the wind, and
Job 41:28 are turned with him into *s*
Job 41:29 Darts are counted as *s*
Ps 83:13 as the *s* before the wind
Is 5:24 as the fire devoureth the *s*
Is 33:11 chaff, ye shall bring forth *s*
Is 40:24 shall take them away as *s*
Is 41:2 sword, and as driven *s* to his bow
Is 47:14 Behold, they shall be as *s*
Jer 13:24 will I scatter them as the *s* that
Joel 2:5 of fire that devoureth the *s*
Obad 18 flame, and the house of Esau for *s*
Nah 1:10 shall be devoured as *s* fully dry
Mal 4:1 all that do wickedly, shall be *s*
1Cor 3:12 precious stones, wood, hay, *s*

### STUBBORN
Deut 21:18 If a man have a *s* and rebellious
Deut 21:20 of his city, This our son is *s*
Judg 2:19 own doings, nor from their *s* way
Ps 78:8 not be as their fathers, a *s*
Prov 7:11 (She is loud and *s*

### STUBBORNNESS
Deut 9:27 not unto the *s* of this people
1Sa 15:23 *s* is as iniquity and idolatry

### STUCK
1Sa 26:7 his spear *s* in the ground at his
Ps 119:31 I have *s* unto thy testimonies
Acts 27:41 and the forepart *s* fast, and

### STUDIETH
Prov 15:28 of the righteous *s* to answer
Prov 24:2 For their heart *s* destruction

### STUDS
Song 1:11 borders of gold with *s* of silver

### STUDY
Eccl 12:12 much *s* is a weariness of the
1Th 4:11 that ye *s* to be quiet, and to do
2Ti 2:15 *S* to shew thyself approved unto

### STUFF
Gen 31:37 thou hast searched all my *s*
Gen 31:37 thou found of all thy household *s*
Gen 45:20 Also regard not your *s*
Ex 22:7 his neighbour money or *s* to keep
Ex 36:7 For the *s* they had was sufficient
Josh 7:11 put it even among their own *s*
1Sa 10:22 he hath hid himself among the *s*
1Sa 25:13 and two hundred abode by the *s*
1Sa 30:24 part be that tarrieth by the *s*
Neh 13:8 *s* of Tobiah out of the chamber
Eze 12:3 man, prepare thee *s* for removing
Eze 12:4 forth thy *s* by day in their sight
Eze 12:4 in their sight, as *s* for removing
Eze 12:7 I brought forth my *s* by day
Eze 12:7 as *s* for captivity, and in the
Lk 17:31 his *s* in the house, let him not

### STUMBLE
Prov 3:23 safely, and thy foot shall not *s*
Prov 4:12 thou runnest, thou shalt not *s*
Prov 4:19 they know not at what they *s*
Is 5:27 shall be weary nor *s* among them
Is 8:15 And many among them shall *s*
Is 28:7 err in vision, they *s* in judgment
Is 59:10 we *s* at noonday as in the night
Is 63:13 that they should not *s*
Jer 13:16 before your feet *s* upon the dark
Jer 18:15 they have caused them to *s* in
Jer 20:11 therefore my persecutors shall *s*
Jer 31:9 way, wherein they shall not *s*
Jer 46:6 they shall *s*, and fall toward the
Jer 50:32 And the most proud shall *s*
Dan 11:19 but he shall *s* and fall, and not be
Nah 2:5 they shall *s* in their walk
Nah 3:3 they *s* upon their corpses
Mal 2:8 have caused many to *s* at the law
1Pet 2:8 even to them which *s* at the word

### STUMBLED
1Sa 2:4 they that *s* are girded with
1Chr 13:9 for the oxen *s*
Ps 27:2 me to eat up my flesh, they *s*
Jer 46:12 man hath *s* against the mighty
Rom 9:32 For they *s* at that stumblingstone
Rom 11:11 Have they *s* that they should fall

### STUMBLETH
Prov 24:17 not thine heart be glad when he *s*
Jn 11:9 he *s* not, because he seeth the
Jn 11:10 if a man walk in the night, he *s*
Rom 14:21 any thing whereby thy brother *s*

### STUMBLING
Is 8:14 but for a stone of *s* and for a
1Pet 2:8 And a stone of *s*, and a rock of
1Jn 2:10 is none occasion of *s* in him

### STUMBLINGBLOCK
Lev 19:14 nor put a *s* before the blind, but
Is 57:14 take up the *s* out of the way of
Eze 3:20 I lay a *s* before him, he shall
Eze 7:19 it is the *s* of their iniquity
Eze 14:3 put the *s* of their iniquity
Eze 14:4 putteth the *s* of his iniquity
Eze 14:7 putteth the *s* of his iniquity
Rom 11:9 made a snare, and a trap, and a *s*
Rom 14:13 that no man put a *s* or an
1Cor 1:23 crucified, unto the Jews a *s*
1Cor 8:9 become a *s* to them that are weak
Rev 2:14 who taught Balac to cast a *s*

### STUMBLINGBLOCKS
Jer 6:21 I will lay *s* before this people,
Zeph 1:3 the sea, and the *s* with the wicked

### STUMBLINGSTONE
Rom 9:32 For they stumbled at that *s*
Rom 9:33 Behold, I lay in Sion a *s*

### STUMP
1Sa 5:4 only the *s* of Dagon was left to
Dan 4:15 Nevertheless leave the *s* of his
Dan 4:23 yet leave the *s* of the roots
Dan 4:26 to leave the *s* of the tree roots

### SUAH *(su'-ah) Son of Zophah.*
1Chr 7:36 *S*, and Harnepher, and Shual, and

### SUBDUE
Gen 1:28 and replenish the earth, and *s* it
1Chr 17:10 Moreover I will *s* all thine
Ps 47:3 He shall *s* the people under us,
Is 45:1 holden, to *s* nations before him
Dan 7:24 first, and he shall *s* three kings
Mic 7:19 he will *s* our iniquities
Zec 9:15 devour, and *s* with sling stones
Phil 3:21 even to *s* all things unto himself

### SUBDUED
Num 32:22 the land be *s* before the LORD
Num 32:29 and the land shall be *s* before you
Deut 20:20 war with thee, until it be *s*
Josh 18:1 And the land was *s* before them
Judg 3:30 So Moab was *s* that day under the
Judg 4:23 So God *s* on that day Jabin the
Judg 8:28 Thus was Midian *s* before the
Judg 11:33 *s* before the children of Israel
1Sa 7:13 So the Philistines were *s*
2Sa 8:1 smote the Philistines, and *s* them
2Sa 8:11 of all nations which he *s*
2Sa 22:40 against me hast thou *s* under me
1Chr 18:1 *s* them, and took Gath and her towns
1Chr 20:4 and they were *s*
1Chr 22:18 the land is *s* before the LORD, and
Ps 18:39 thou hast *s* under me those that
Ps 81:14 should soon have *s* their enemies
1Cor 15:28 all things shall be *s* unto him
Heb 11:33 Who through faith *s* kingdoms

### SUBDUEDST
Neh 9:24 land, and thou *s* before them the

### SUBDUETH
Ps 18:47 me, and *s* the people under me
Ps 144:2 who *s* my people under me
Dan 2:40 in pieces and *s* all things

### SUBJECT
Lk 2:51 to Nazareth, and was *s* unto them
Lk 10:17 even the devils are *s* unto us
Lk 10:20 that the spirits are *s* unto you
Rom 8:7 for it is not *s* to the law of God
Rom 8:20 the creature was made *s* to vanity
Rom 13:1 Let every soul be *s* unto the
Rom 13:5 Wherefore ye must needs be *s*
1Cor 14:32 prophets are *s* to the prophets
1Cor 15:28 be *s* unto him that put all things
Eph 5:24 as the church is *s* unto Christ
Col 2:20 world, are ye *s* to ordinances,
Titus 3:1 in mind to be *s* to principalities
Heb 2:15 all their lifetime *s* to bondage
Jas 5:17 Elias was a man *s* to like
1Pet 2:18 be *s* to your masters with all
1Pet 3:22 and powers being made *s* unto him
1Pet 5:5 all of you be *s* one to another,

### SUBJECTED
Rom 8:20 him who hath *s* the same in hope

### SUBJECTION
Ps 106:42 brought into *s* under their hand
Jer 34:11 brought them into *s* for servants
Jer 34:16 to return, and brought them into *s*
1Cor 9:27 under my body, and bring it into *s*
2Cor 9:13 *s* into the gospel of Christ
Gal 2:5 To whom we gave place by *s*
1Ti 2:11 woman learn in silence with all *s*
1Ti 3:4 children in *s* with all gravity
Heb 2:5 he not put in *s* the world to come
Heb 2:8 all things in *s* under his feet
Heb 2:8 in that he put all in *s* under him
Heb 12:9 in *s* unto the Father of spirits
1Pet 3:1 be in *s* to your own husbands
1Pet 3:5 being in *s* unto their own

### SUBMIT
Gen 16:9 *s* thyself under her hands
2Sa 22:45 Strangers shall *s* themselves unto
Ps 18:44 shall *s* themselves unto me
Ps 66:3 enemies *s* themselves unto thee
Ps 68:30 till every one *s* himself with

1Cor 16:16 That ye *s* yourselves unto such,
Eph 5:22 *s* yourselves unto your own
Col 3:18 *s* yourselves unto your own
Heb 13:17 rule over you, and *s* yourselves
Jas 4:7 *S* yourselves therefore to God
1Pet 2:13 *S* yourselves to every ordinance
1Pet 5:5 *s* yourselves unto the elder

### SUBMITTED
1Chr 29:24 *s* themselves unto Solomon the
Ps 81:15 should have *s* themselves unto him
Rom 10:3 have not *s* themselves unto the

### SUBMITTING
Eph 5:21 *S* yourselves one to another in

### SUBORNED
Acts 6:11 Then they *s* men, which said, We

### SUBSCRIBE
Is 44:5 another shall *s* with his hand
Jer 32:44 *s* evidences, and seal them, and

### SUBSCRIBED
Jer 32:10 I *s* the evidence, and sealed it,
Jer 32:12 that *s* the book of the purchase

### SUBSTANCE
Gen 7:4 every living *s* that I have made
Gen 7:23 every living *s* was destroyed
Gen 12:5 all their *s* that they had
Gen 13:6 for their *s* was great, so that
Gen 15:14 shall they come out with great *s*
Gen 34:23 Shall not their cattle and their *s*
Gen 36:6 and all his beasts, and all his *s*
Deut 11:6 all the *s* that was in their
Deut 33:11 Bless, LORD, his *s*, and accept the
Josh 14:4 for their cattle and for their *s*
1Chr 27:31 of the *s* which was king David's
1Chr 28:1 and the stewards over all the *s*
2Chr 21:17 carried away all the *s* that was
2Chr 31:3 of his *s* for the burnt offerings
2Chr 32:29 for God had given him *s* very much
2Chr 35:7 these were of the king's *s*
Ezr 8:21 our little ones, and for all our *s*
Ezr 10:8 all his *s* should be forfeited, and
Job 1:3 His *s* also was seven thousand
Job 1:10 his *s* is increased in the land
Job 5:5 the robber swalloweth up their *s*
Job 6:22 Give a reward for me of your *s*
Job 15:29 neither shall his *s* continue
Job 20:18 according to his *s* shall the
Job 22:20 Whereas our *s* is not cut down,
Job 30:22 ride upon it, and dissolvest my *s*
Ps 17:14 rest of their *s* to their babes
Ps 105:21 his house, and ruler of all his *s*
Ps 139:15 My *s* was not hid from thee, when
Ps 139:16 Thine eyes did see my *s*, yet
Prov 1:13 We shall find all precious *s*
Prov 3:9 Honour the LORD with thy *s*
Prov 6:31 shall give all the *s* of his house
Prov 8:21 those that love me to inherit *s*
Prov 10:3 casteth away the *s* of the wicked
Prov 12:27 but the *s* of a diligent man is
Prov 28:8 and unjust gain increaseth his *s*
Prov 29:3 with harlots spendeth his *s*
Song 8:7 all the *s* of his house for love
Is 6:13 whose *s* is in them, when they
Is 6:13 holy seed shall be the *s* thereof
Jer 15:13 Thy *s* and thy treasures will I
Jer 17:3 in the field, I will give thy *s*
Hos 12:8 rich, I have found me out *s*
Obad 13 *s* in the day of their calamity
Mic 4:13 their *s* unto the Lord of the
Lk 8:3 ministered unto him of their *s*
Lk 15:13 there wasted his *s* with riotous
Heb 10:34 heaven a better and an enduring *s*
Heb 11:1 Now faith is the *s* of things

### SUBTIL
Gen 3:1 Now the serpent was more *s* than
2Sa 13:3 and Jonadab was a very *s* man
Prov 7:10 of an harlot, and *s* of heart

### SUBTILLY
1Sa 23:22 is told me that he dealeth very *s*
Ps 105:25 to deal *s* with his servants
Acts 7:19 The same dealt *s* with our kindred

### SUBTILTY
Gen 27:35 he said, Thy brother came with *s*
2Kin 10:19 But Jehu did it in *s*, to the
Prov 1:4 To give *s* to the simple, to the
Mt 26:4 that they might take Jesus by *s*
Acts 13:10 And said, O full of all *s* and all
2Cor 11:3 beguiled Eve through his *s*

### SUBURBS
Lev 25:34 But the field of the *s* of their
Num 35:2 give also unto the Levites *s* for
Num 35:3 the *s* of them shall be for their
Num 35:4 the *s* of the cities, which ye
Num 35:5 be to them the *s* of the cities
Num 35:7 them shall ye give with their *s*
Josh 14:4 with their *s* for their cattle and
Josh 21:2 with the *s* thereof for our cattle
Josh 21:3 the LORD, these cities and their *s*
Josh 21:8 Levites these cities with their *s*
Josh 21:11 with the *s* thereof round about it
Josh 21:13 the priest Hebron with her *s*
Josh 21:13 and Libnah with her *s*,
Josh 21:14 And Jattir with her *s*, and Eshtemoa
Josh 21:14 and Eshtemoa with her *s*
Josh 21:15 And Holon with her *s*, and Debir
Josh 21:15 and Debir with her *s*
Josh 21:16 And Ain with her *s*, and Juttah with
Josh 21:16 and Juttah with her *s*
Josh 21:16 and Beth-shemesh with her *s*
Josh 21:17 of Benjamin, Gibeon with her *s*
Josh 21:17 Geba with her *s*
Josh 21:18 Anathoth with her *s*, and Almon
Josh 21:18 and Almon with her *s*
Josh 21:19 were thirteen cities with their *s*
Josh 21:21 with her *s* in mount Ephraim
Josh 21:21 and Gezer with her *s*,
Josh 21:22 And Kibzaim with her *s*, and
Josh 21:22 and Beth-horon with her *s*
Josh 21:23 tribe of Dan, Eltekeh with her *s*
Josh 21:23 Gibbethon with her *s*
Josh 21:24 Aijalon with her *s*, Gath-rimmon
Josh 21:24 Gath-rimmon with her *s*
Josh 21:25 of Manasseh, Tanach with her *s*
Josh 21:25 and Gath-rimmon with her *s*
Josh 21:26 their *s* for the families of the
Josh 21:27 gave Golan in Bashan with her *s*
Josh 21:27 and Beesh-terah with her *s*
Josh 21:28 of Issachar, Kishon with her *s*
Josh 21:28 Dabareh with her *s*
Josh 21:29 Jarmuth with her *s*, En-gannim
Josh 21:29 En-gannim with her *s*
Josh 21:30 tribe of Asher, Mishal with her *s*
Josh 21:30 Abdon with her *s*
Josh 21:31 Helkath with her *s*, and Rehob with
Josh 21:31 Rehob with her *s*
Josh 21:32 Kedesh in Galilee with her *s*
Josh 21:32 and Hammoth-dor with her *s*
Josh 21:32 and Kartan with her *s*
Josh 21:33 were thirteen cities with their *s*
Josh 21:34 of Zebulun, Jokneam with her *s*
Josh 21:34 and Kartah with her *s*
Josh 21:35 Dimnah with her *s*, Nahalal with
Josh 21:35 her *s*, Nahalal with her *s*
Josh 21:36 tribe of Reuben, Bezer with her *s*
Josh 21:36 and Jahazah with her *s*
Josh 21:37 Kedemoth with her *s*, and Mephaath
Josh 21:37 and Mephaath with her *s*
Josh 21:38 Gad, Ramoth in Gilead with her *s*
Josh 21:38 and Mahanaim with her *s*,
Josh 21:39 Heshbon with her *s*, Jazer with
Josh 21:39 Jazer with her *s*
Josh 21:41 and eight cities with their *s*
Josh 21:42 one with their *s* round about them
2Kin 23:11 chamberlain, which was in the *s*
1Chr 5:16 towns, and in all the *s* of Sharon
1Chr 6:55 the *s* thereof round about it
1Chr 6:57 of refuge, and Libnah with her *s*
1Chr 6:57 Jattir, and Eshtemoa, with their *s*
1Chr 6:58 And Hilen with her *s*, Debir with
1Chr 6:58 Debir with her *s*
1Chr 6:59 And Ashan with her *s*, and
1Chr 6:59 and Beth-shemesh with her *s*
1Chr 6:60 Geba with her *s*
1Chr 6:60 and Alemeth with her *s*
1Chr 6:60 and Anathoth with her *s*
1Chr 6:64 Levites these cities with their *s*
1Chr 6:67 in mount Ephraim with her *s*
1Chr 6:67 they gave also Gezer with her *s*
1Chr 6:68 And Jokmeam with her *s*, and
1Chr 6:68 and Beth-horon with her *s*
1Chr 6:69 And Aijalon with her *s*, and
1Chr 6:69 and Gath-rimmon with her *s*
1Chr 6:70 Aner with her *s*, and Bileam with
1Chr 6:70 and Bileam with her *s*
1Chr 6:71 Golan in Bashan with her *s*
1Chr 6:71 and Ashtaroth with her *s*
1Chr 6:72 Kedesh with her *s*
1Chr 6:72 Daberath with her *s*
1Chr 6:73 And Ramoth with her *s*
1Chr 6:73 and Anem with her *s*
1Chr 6:74 Mashal with her *s*
1Chr 6:74 and Abdon with her *s*
1Chr 6:75 And Hukok with her *s*
1Chr 6:75 and Rehob with her *s*
1Chr 6:76 Kedesh in Galilee with her *s*
1Chr 6:76 and Hammon with her *s*
1Chr 6:76 and Kirjathaim with her *s*
1Chr 6:77 of Zebulun, Rimmon with her *s*
1Chr 6:77 Tabor with her *s*
1Chr 6:78 in the wilderness with her *s*
1Chr 6:78 and Jahzah with her *s*
1Chr 6:79 Kedemoth also with her *s*, and
1Chr 6:79 and Mephaath with her *s*
1Chr 6:80 Ramoth in Gilead with her *s*
1Chr 6:80 and Mahanaim with her *s*
1Chr 6:81 And Heshbon with her *s*, and Jazer
1Chr 6:81 and Jazer with her *s*
1Chr 13:2 which are in their cities and *s*
2Chr 11:14 For the Levites left their *s*
2Chr 31:19 fields of the *s* of their cities
Eze 27:28 The *s* shall shake at the sound of
Eze 45:2 round about for the *s* thereof
Eze 48:15 the city, for dwelling, and for *s*
Eze 48:17 the *s* of the city shall be toward

### SUBVERT
Lam 3:36 To *s* a man in his cause, the Lord
Titus 1:11 who *s* whole houses, teaching

### SUBVERTED
Titus 3:11 Knowing that he that is such is *s*

### SUBVERTING
Acts 15:24 *s* your souls, saying, Ye must be
2Ti 2:14 but to the *s* of the hearers

### SUCCEED
Deut 25:6 which she beareth shall *s* in the

### SUCCEEDED
Deut 2:12 but the children of Esau *s* them
Deut 2:21 and they *s* them, and dwelt in their
Deut 2:22 and they *s* them, and dwelt in their

### SUCCEEDEST
Deut 12:29 to possess them, and thou *s* them
Deut 19:1 God giveth thee, and thou *s* them

### SUCCESS
Josh 1:8 and then thou shalt have good *s*

### SUCCOTH *(suc'-coth)*
*1. A place east of the Jordan.*
Gen 33:17 And Jacob journeyed to *S*, and built
Gen 33:17 the name of the place is called *S*
*2. An Israelite encampment in the wilderness.*
Ex 12:37 journeyed from Rameses to *S*
Ex 13:20 And they took their journey from *S*
Num 33:5 from Rameses, and pitched in *S*
Num 33:6 And they departed from *S*, and
*3. A place in Gad.*
Josh 13:27 Beth-aram, and Beth-nimrah, and *S*
Judg 8:5 And he said unto the men of *S*
Judg 8:6 And the princes of *S* said, Are the
Judg 8:8 as the men of *S* had answered him
Judg 8:14 a young man of the men of *S*
Judg 8:14 unto him the princes of *S*
Judg 8:15 And he came unto the men of *S*
Judg 8:16 with them he taught the men of *S*
*4. A city in Ephraim.*
1Kin 7:46 in the clay ground between *S*
2Chr 4:17 in the clay ground between *S*
Ps 60:6 and mete out the valley of *S*
Ps 108:7 and mete out the valley of *S*

### SUCCOTH-BENOTH *(suc'-coth-be'-noth) A Babylonian god.*
2Kin 17:30 And the men of Babylon made *S*

### SUCCOUR
2Sa 8:5 came to *s* Hadadezer king of Zobah
2Sa 18:3 that thou *s* us out of the city
Heb 2:18 he is able to *s* them that are

### SUCCOURED
2Sa 21:17 Abishai the son of Zeruiah *s* him
2Cor 6:2 day of salvation have I *s* thee

### SUCCOURER
Rom 16:2 for she hath been a *s* of many

### SUCHATHITES *(soo'-kath-ites) A family of scribes.*
1Chr 2:55 the Shimeathites, and *S*

### SUCK
Gen 21:7 should have given children *s*
Deut 32:13 he made him to *s* honey out of the
Deut 33:19 for they shall *s* of the abundance
1Sa 1:23 gave her son *s* until she weaned
1Kin 3:21 in the morning to give my child *s*
Job 3:12 why the breasts that I should *s*
Job 20:16 He shall *s* the poison of asps
Job 39:30 Her young ones also *s* up blood
Is 60:16 Thou shalt also *s* the milk of the
Is 60:16 shalt *s* the breast of kings
Is 66:11 That ye may *s*, and be satisfied
Is 66:12 then shall ye *s*, ye shall be
Lam 4:3 they give *s* to their young ones
Eze 23:34 *s* it out, and thou shalt break the
Joel 2:16 and those that *s* the breasts
Mt 24:19 to them that give *s* in those days
Mk 13:17 to them that give *s* in those days
Lk 21:23 child, and to them that give *s*
Lk 23:29 and the paps which never gave *s*

### SUCKED
Song 8:1 that *s* the breasts of my mother
Lk 11:27 and the paps which thou hast *s*

### SUCKING
Num 11:12 father beareth the *s* child
1Sa 7:9 And Samuel took a *s* lamb, and
Is 11:8 the *s* child shall play on the
Is 49:15 Can a woman forget her *s* child
Lam 4:4 The tongue of the *s* child

### SUCKLING
Deut 32:25 the *s* also with the man of gray
1Sa 15:3 both man and woman, infant and *s*
Jer 44:7 man and woman, child and *s*

### SUCKLINGS
1Sa 22:19 both men and women, children and *s*
Ps 8:2 *s* hast thou ordained strength
Lam 2:11 the *s* swoon in the streets of the
Mt 21:16 *s* thou hast perfected praise

### SUDDEN
Job 22:10 thee, and *s* fear troubleth thee
Prov 3:25 Be not afraid of *s* fear, neither
1Th 5:3 then *s* destruction cometh upon

### SUDDENLY
Num 6:9 And if any man die very *s* by him
Num 12:4 And the LORD spake *s* unto Moses
Num 35:22 if he thrust him *s* without enmity
Deut 7:4 against you, and destroy thee *s*
Josh 10:9 Joshua therefore came unto them *s*
Josh 11:7 them by the waters of Merom *s*
2Sa 15:14 to depart, lest he overtake us *s*
2Chr 29:36 for the thing was done *s*
Job 5:3 but *s* I cursed his habitation
Job 9:23 If the scourge slay *s*, he will
Ps 6:10 let them return and be ashamed *s*
Ps 64:4 *s* do they shoot at him, and fear
Ps 64:7 *s* shall they be wounded
Prov 6:15 shall his calamity come *s*
Prov 6:15 *s* shall he be broken without
Prov 24:22 For their calamity shall rise *s*
Prov 29:1 shall *s* be destroyed, and that
Eccl 9:12 time, when it falleth *s* upon them
Is 29:5 yea, it shall be at an instant *s*
Is 30:13 breaking cometh *s* at an instant
Is 47:11 desolation shall come upon thee *s*
Is 48:3 I did them *s*, and they came to
Jer 4:20 *s* are my tents spoiled, and my
Jer 6:26 the spoiler shall *s* come upon us
Jer 15:8 have caused him to fall upon it *s*
Jer 18:22 shalt bring a troop *s* upon them
Jer 49:19 but I will *s* make him run away
Jer 50:44 make them *s* run away from her
Jer 51:8 Babylon is *s* fallen and destroyed
Hab 2:7 rise up *s* that shall bite thee
Mal 3:1 shall *s* come to his temple, even
Mk 9:8 And *s*, when they had looked round
Mk 13:36 Lest coming *s* he find you
Lk 2:13 *s* there was with the angel a
Lk 9:39 taketh him, and he *s* crieth out
Acts 2:2 *s* there came a sound from heaven
Acts 9:3 *s* there shined round about him a
Acts 16:26 *s* there was a great earthquake,
Acts 22:6 *s* there shone from heaven a great
Acts 28:6 swollen, or fallen down dead *s*
1Ti 5:22 Lay hands *s* on no man, neither be

### SUE
Mt 5:40 if any man will *s* thee at the law

### SUFFER
Ex 12:23 will not *s* the destroyer to come
Ex 22:18 Thou shalt not *s* a witch to live
Lev 2:13 neither shalt thou *s* the salt of
Lev 19:17 neighbour, and not *s* sin upon him
Lev 22:16 Or *s* them to bear the iniquity of
Num 21:23 Sihon would not *s* Israel to pass
Josh 10:19 *s* them not to enter into their
Judg 1:34 for they would not *s* them to come
Judg 15:1 father would not *s* him to go in
Judg 16:26 *S* me that I may feel the pillars
2Sa 14:11 that thou wouldest not *s* the
1Kin 15:17 that he might not *s* any to go out
Est 3:8 for the king's profit to *s* them
Job 9:18 He will not *s* me to take my
Job 21:3 *S* me that I may speak
Job 24:11 their winepresses, and *s* thirst
Job 36:2 *S* me a little, and I will shew
Ps 9:13 which I *s* of them that hate me
Ps 16:10 neither wilt thou *s* thine Holy
Ps 34:10 young lions do lack, and *s* hunger
Ps 55:22 he shall never *s* the righteous to
Ps 88:15 while I *s* thy terrors I am
Ps 89:33 nor *s* my faithfulness to fail
Ps 101:5 and a proud heart will not I *s*
Ps 121:3 He will not *s* thy foot to be
Prov 10:3 The LORD will not *s* the soul of
Prov 19:15 and an idle soul shall *s* hunger
Prov 19:19 of great wrath shall *s* punishment
Eccl 5:6 *S* not thy mouth to cause thy
Eccl 5:12 the rich will not *s* him to sleep
Eze 44:20 nor *s* their locks to grow long
Mt 3:15 said unto him, *S* it to be so now
Mt 8:21 *s* me first to go and bury my
Mt 8:31 *s* us to go away into the herd of
Mt 16:21 *s* many things of the elders and
Mt 17:12 also the Son of man *s* of them
Mt 17:17 how long shall I *s* you
Mt 19:14 *S* little children, and forbid them
Mt 23:13 neither *s* ye them that are
Mk 7:12 ye *s* him no more to do ought for
Mk 8:31 the Son of man must *s* many things
Mk 9:12 man, that he must *s* many things
Mk 9:19 how long shall I *s* you
Mk 10:14 *S* the little children to come
Mk 11:16 would not *s* that any man should
Lk 8:32 would *s* them to enter into them
Lk 9:22 The Son of man must *s* many things
Lk 9:41 shall I be with you, and *s* you
Lk 9:59 *s* me first to go and bury my
Lk 17:25 But first must he *s* many things
Lk 18:16 *S* little children to come unto me
Lk 22:15 this passover with you before I *s*
Lk 22:51 answered and said, *S* ye thus far
Lk 24:46 and thus it behoved Christ to *s*
Acts 2:27 neither wilt thou *s* thine Holy
Acts 3:18 prophets, that Christ should *s*
Acts 5:41 worthy to *s* shame for his name
Acts 7:24 And seeing one of them *s* wrong
Acts 9:16 he must *s* for my name's sake
Acts 13:35 Thou shalt not *s* thine Holy One
Acts 21:39 *s* me to speak unto the people
Acts 26:23 That Christ should *s*, and that he
Rom 8:17 if so be that we *s* with him
1Cor 3:15 shall be burned, he shall *s* loss
1Cor 4:12 being persecuted, we *s* it
1Cor 6:7 why do ye not rather *s* yourselves
1Cor 9:12 but *s* all things, lest we should
1Cor 10:13 who will not *s* you to be tempted
1Cor 12:26 And whether one member *s*, all the
1Cor 12:26 *s*, all the members *s* with it
2Cor 1:6 same sufferings which we also *s*
2Cor 11:19 For ye *s* fools gladly, seeing ye
2Cor 11:20 For ye *s*, if a man bring you into
Gal 5:11 why do I yet *s* persecution
Gal 6:12 only lest they should *s*
Phil 1:29 but also to *s* for his sake
Phil 4:12 both to abound and to *s* need
1Th 3:4 that we should *s* tribulation
2Th 1:5 of God, for which ye also *s*
1Ti 2:12 But I *s* not a woman to teach, nor
1Ti 4:10 *s* reproach, because we trust in
2Ti 1:12 which cause I also *s* these things
2Ti 2:9 Wherein I *s* trouble, as an evil
2Ti 2:12 If we *s*, we shall also reign with
2Ti 3:12 Christ Jesus shall *s* persecution
Heb 11:25 Choosing rather to *s* affliction
Heb 13:3 and them which *s* adversity
Heb 13:22 *s* the word of exhortation
1Pet 2:20 *s* for it, ye take it patiently,
1Pet 3:14 if ye *s* for righteousness' sake,
1Pet 3:17 that ye *s* for well doing, than
1Pet 4:15 let none of you *s* as a murderer
1Pet 4:16 Yet if any man *s* as a Christian
1Pet 4:19 Wherefore let them that *s*
Rev 2:10 those things which thou shalt *s*
Rev 11:9 shall not *s* their dead bodies to

### SUFFERED
Gen 20:6 therefore *s* I thee not to touch
Gen 31:7 but God *s* him not to hurt me
Gen 31:28 hast not *s* me to kiss my sons and
Deut 8:3 *s* thee to hunger, and fed thee
Deut 18:14 thy God hath not *s* thee so to do
Judg 3:28 Moab, and *s* not a man to pass over
1Sa 24:7 *s* them not to rise against Saul
2Sa 21:10 *s* neither the birds of the air to
1Chr 16:21 He *s* no man to do them wrong
Job 31:30 (Neither have I *s* my mouth to sin
Ps 105:14 He *s* no man to do them wrong
Jer 15:15 that for thy sake I have *s* rebuke
Mt 3:15 Then he *s* him
Mt 19:8 *s* you to put away your wives
Mt 24:43 would not have *s* his house to be
Mt 27:19 for I have *s* many things this day
Mk 1:34 *s* not the devils to speak,
Mk 5:19 Howbeit Jesus *s* him not, but
Mk 5:26 had *s* many things of many
Mk 5:37 he *s* no man to follow him, save
Mk 10:4 Moses *s* to write a bill of
Lk 4:41 he rebuking them *s* them not to
Lk 8:32 And he *s* them
Lk 8:51 he *s* no man to go in, save Peter,
Lk 12:39 not have *s* his house to be broken
Lk 13:2 because they *s* such things
Lk 24:26 not Christ to have *s* these things
Acts 13:18 years *s* he their manners in the
Acts 14:16 Who in times past *s* all nations
Acts 16:7 but the Spirit *s* them not
Acts 17:3 that Christ must needs have *s*
Acts 19:30 people, the disciples *s* him not
Acts 28:16 but Paul was *s* to dwell by
2Cor 7:12 nor for his cause that *s* wrong
2Cor 11:25 thrice I *s* shipwreck, a night and
Gal 3:4 Have ye *s* so many things in vain
Phil 3:8 for whom I have *s* the loss of all
1Th 2:2 even after that we had *s* before
1Th 2:14 for ye also have *s* like things of
Heb 2:18 he himself hath *s* being tempted
Heb 5:8 by the things which he *s*
Heb 7:23 because they were not *s* to
Heb 9:26 *s* since the foundation of the
Heb 13:12 his own blood, *s* without the gate
1Pet 2:21 because Christ also *s* for us
1Pet 2:23 when he *s*, he threatened not
1Pet 3:18 Christ also hath once *s* for sins
1Pet 4:1 Christ hath *s* for us in the flesh
1Pet 4:1 for he that hath *s* in the flesh
1Pet 5:10 after that ye have *s* a while

### SUFFEREST
Rev 2:20 because thou *s* that woman Jezebel

### SUFFERETH
Ps 66:9 *s* not our feet to be moved
Ps 107:38 *s* not their cattle to decrease
Mt 11:12 the kingdom of heaven *s* violence
Acts 28:4 sea, yet vengeance *s* not to live
1Cor 13:4 Charity *s* long, and is kind

### SUFFERING
Acts 27:7 against Cnidus, the wind not *s* us
Heb 2:9 the angels for the *s* of death
Jas 5:10 for an example of *s* affliction
1Pet 2:19 God endure grief, *s* wrongfully
Jude 7 *s* the vengeance of eternal fire

### SUFFERINGS
Rom 8:18 For I reckon that the *s* of this
2Cor 1:5 For as the *s* of Christ abound in
2Cor 1:6 the same *s* which we also suffer
2Cor 1:7 that as ye are partakers of the *s*
Phil 3:10 and the fellowship of his *s*
Col 1:24 Who now rejoice in my *s* for you
Heb 2:10 their salvation perfect through *s*
1Pet 1:11 beforehand the *s* of Christ
1Pet 4:13 as ye are partakers of Christ's *s*
1Pet 5:1 and a witness of the *s* of Christ

### SUFFICE
Num 11:22 be slain for them, to *s* them
Num 11:22 together for them, to *s* them
Deut 3:26 LORD said unto me, Let it *s* thee
1Kin 20:10 if the dust of Samaria shall *s*

Eze 44:6 Israel, let it *s* you of all your
Eze 45:9 Let it *s* you, O princes of Israel
1Pet 4:3 the time past of our life may *s*

**SUFFICED**
Judg 21:14 and yet so they *s* them not
Ruth 2:14 corn, and she did eat, and was *s*
Ruth 2:18 she had reserved after she was *s*

**SUFFICETH**
Jn 14:8 shew us the Father, and it *s* us

**SUFFICIENCY**
Job 20:22 In the fulness of his *s* he shall
2Cor 3:5 but our *s* is of God
2Cor 9:8 always having all *s* in all things

**SUFFICIENT**
Ex 36:7 For the stuff they had was *s* for
Deut 15:8 surely lend him *s* for his need
Deut 33:7 let his hands be *s* for him
Prov 25:16 eat so much as is *s* for thee
Is 40:16 And Lebanon is not *s* to burn
Is 40:16 thereof *s* for a burnt offering
Mt 6:34 *S* unto the day is the evil
Lk 14:28 whether he have *s* to finish it
Jn 6:7 of bread is not *s* for them
2Cor 2:6 *S* to such a man is this
2Cor 2:16 who is *s* for these things
2Cor 3:5 Not that we are *s* of ourselves to
2Cor 12:9 unto me, My grace is *s* for thee

**SUFFICIENTLY**
2Chr 30:3 had not sanctified themselves *s*
Is 23:18 dwell before the LORD, to eat *s*

**SUIT**
Judg 17:10 a *s* of apparel, and thy victuals
2Sa 15:4 any *s* or cause might come unto me
Job 11:19 yea, many shall make *s* unto thee

**SUITS**
Is 3:22 The changeable *s* of apparel

**SUKKIIMS** *(suk'-ke-ims) An Egyptian tribe.*
2Chr 12:3 the Lubim, the *S*, and the

**SUM**
Ex 21:30 there be laid on him a *s* of money
Ex 30:12 When thou takest the *s* of the
Ex 38:21 This is the *s* of the tabernacle,
Num 1:2 Take ye the *s* of all the
Num 1:49 neither take the *s* of them among
Num 4:2 Take the *s* of the sons of Kohath
Num 4:22 Take also the *s* of the sons of
Num 26:2 Take the *s* of all the
Num 26:4 Take the *s* of the people, from
Num 31:26 Take the *s* of the prey that was
Num 31:49 the *s* of the men of war which are
2Sa 24:9 Joab gave up the *s* of the number
2Kin 22:4 that he may *s* the silver which is
1Chr 21:5 Joab gave the *s* of the number of
Est 4:7 of the *s* of the money that Haman
Ps 139:17 How great is the *s* of them
Eze 28:12 Thou sealest up the *s*, full of
Dan 7:1 told the *s* of the matters
Acts 7:16 that Abraham bought for a *s* of
Acts 22:28 With a great *s* obtained I this
Heb 8:1 we have spoken this is the *s*

**SUMMER**
Gen 8:22 and harvest, and cold and heat, and *s*
Judg 3:20 and he was sitting in a *s* parlour
Judg 3:24 his feet in his *s* chamber
2Sa 16:1 and an hundred of *s* fruits
2Sa 16:2 *s* fruit for the young men to eat
Ps 32:4 is turned into the drought of *s*
Ps 74:17 thou hast made *s* and winter
Prov 6:8 Provideth her meat in the *s*
Prov 10:5 that gathereth in *s* is a wise son
Prov 26:1 As snow in *s*, and as rain in
Prov 30:25 they prepare their meat in the *s*
Is 16:9 for the shouting for thy *s* fruits
Is 18:6 and the fowls shall *s* upon them
Is 28:4 as the hasty fruit before the *s*
Jer 8:20 the *s* is ended, and we are not
Jer 40:10 *s* fruits, and oil, and put them in
Jer 40:12 wine and *s* fruits very much
Jer 48:32 is fallen upon thy *s* fruits
Dan 2:35 chaff of the *s* threshingfloors
Amos 3:15 the winter house with the *s* house
Amos 8:1 and behold a basket of *s* fruit
Amos 8:2 And I said, A basket of *s* fruit
Mic 7:1 they have gathered the *s* fruits
Zec 14:8 in *s* and in winter shall it be

Mt 24:32 leaves, ye know that *s* is nigh
Mk 13:28 leaves, ye know that *s* is near
Lk 21:30 selves that *s* is now nigh at hand

**SUMPTUOUSLY**
Lk 16:19 fine linen, and fared *s* every day

**SUN**
Gen 15:12 when the *s* was going down, a deep
Gen 15:17 when the *s* went down, and it was
Gen 19:23 The *s* was risen upon the earth
Gen 28:11 all night, because the *s* was set
Gen 32:31 over Penuel the *s* rose upon him
Gen 37:9 and, behold, the *s* and the moon and
Ex 16:21 when the *s* waxed hot, it melted
Ex 17:12 until the going down of the *s*
Ex 22:3 If the *s* be risen upon him, there
Ex 22:26 unto him by that the *s* goeth down
Lev 22:7 And when the *s* is down, he shall
Num 2:3 *s* shall they of the standard of
Num 25:4 up before the LORD against the *s*
Deut 4:19 heaven, and when thou seest the *s*
Deut 11:30 by the way where the *s* goeth down
Deut 16:6 even, at the going down of the *s*
Deut 17:3 and worshipped them, either the *s*
Deut 23:11 and when the *s* is down, he shall
Deut 24:13 again when the *s* goeth down
Deut 24:15 shall the *s* go down upon it
Deut 33:14 fruits brought forth by the *s*
Josh 1:4 toward the going down of the *s*
Josh 8:29 and as soon as the *s* was down
Josh 10:12 he said in the sight of Israel, *S*
Josh 10:13 the *s* stood still, and the moon
Josh 10:13 So the *s* stood still in the midst
Josh 10:27 time of the going down of the *s*
Josh 12:1 Jordan toward the rising of the *s*
Judg 5:31 the *s* when he goeth forth in his
Judg 8:13 from battle before the *s* was up
Judg 9:33 morning, as soon as the *s* is up
Judg 14:18 day before the *s* went down
Judg 19:14 the *s* went down upon them when
1Sa 11:9 morrow, by that time the *s* be hot
2Sa 2:24 the *s* went down when they were
2Sa 3:35 or ought else, till the *s* be down
2Sa 12:11 thy wives in the sight of this *s*
2Sa 12:12 all Israel, and before the *s*
2Sa 23:4 of the morning, when the *s* riseth
1Kin 22:36 about the going down of the *s*
2Kin 3:22 the *s* shone upon the water, and
2Kin 23:5 incense unto Baal, to the *s*
2Kin 23:11 kings of Judah had given to the *s*
2Kin 23:11 the chariots of the *s* with fire
2Chr 18:34 time of the *s* going down he died
Neh 7:3 be opened until the *s* be hot
Job 8:16 He is green before the *s*, and his
Job 9:7 Which commandeth the *s*, and it
Job 30:28 I went mourning without the *s*
Job 31:26 If I beheld the *s* when it shined
Ps 19:4 he set a tabernacle for the *s*
Ps 50:1 the *s* unto the going down thereof
Ps 58:8 that they may not see the *s*
Ps 72:5 shall fear thee as long as the *s*
Ps 72:17 be continued as long as the *s*
Ps 74:16 hast prepared the light and the *s*
Ps 84:11 For the LORD God is a *s* and shield
Ps 89:36 and his throne as the *s* before me
Ps 104:19 the *s* knoweth his going down
Ps 104:22 The *s* ariseth, they gather
Ps 113:3 From the rising of the *s* unto the
Ps 121:6 The *s* shall not smite thee by day
Ps 136:8 The *s* to rule by day
Ps 148:3 Praise ye him, *s* and moon
Eccl 1:3 which he taketh under the *s*
Eccl 1:5 The *s* also ariseth
Eccl 1:5 the *s* goeth down, and hasteth to
Eccl 1:9 there is no new thing under the *s*
Eccl 1:14 works that are done under the *s*
Eccl 2:11 there was no profit under the *s*
Eccl 2:17 under the *s* is grievous unto me
Eccl 2:18 which I had taken under the *s*
Eccl 2:19 shewed myself wise under the *s*
Eccl 2:20 labour which I took under the *s*
Eccl 2:22 he hath laboured under the *s*
Eccl 3:16 under the *s* the place of judgment
Eccl 4:1 that are done under the *s*
Eccl 4:3 work that is done under the *s*
Eccl 4:7 and I saw vanity under the *s*
Eccl 4:15 the living which walk under the *s*
Eccl 5:13 which I have seen under the *s*
Eccl 5:18 the *s* all the days of his life
Eccl 6:1 which I have seen under the *s*

Eccl 6:5 Moreover he hath not seen the *s*
Eccl 6:12 shall be after him under the *s*
Eccl 7:11 is profit to them that see the *s*
Eccl 8:9 work that is done under the *s*
Eccl 8:15 hath no better thing under the *s*
Eccl 8:15 which God giveth him under the *s*
Eccl 8:17 the work that is done under the *s*
Eccl 9:3 things that are done under the *s*
Eccl 9:6 thing that is done under the *s*
Eccl 9:9 he hath given thee under the *s*
Eccl 9:9 which thou takest under the *s*
Eccl 9:11 I returned, and saw under the *s*
Eccl 9:13 have I seen also under the *s*
Eccl 10:5 which I have seen under the *s*
Eccl 11:7 is for the eyes to behold the *s*
Eccl 12:2 While the *s*, or the light, or the
Song 1:6 because the *s* hath looked upon me
Song 6:10 fair as the moon, clear as the *s*
Is 13:10 the *s* shall be darkened in his
Is 24:23 the *s* ashamed, when the LORD of
Is 30:26 shall be as the light of the *s*
Is 30:26 the light of the *s* shall be
Is 38:8 gone down in the *s* dial of Ahaz
Is 38:8 So the *s* returned ten degrees, by
Is 41:25 from the rising of the *s* shall he
Is 45:6 may know from the rising of the *s*
Is 49:10 shall the heat nor *s* smite them
Is 59:19 glory from the rising of the *s*
Is 60:19 The *s* shall be no more thy light
Is 60:20 Thy *s* shall no more go down
Jer 8:2 shall spread them before the *s*
Jer 15:9 her *s* is gone down while it was
Jer 31:35 which giveth the *s* for a light by
Eze 8:16 worshipped the *s* toward the east
Eze 32:7 I will cover the *s* with a cloud
Dan 6:14 down of the *s* to deliver him
Joel 2:10 the *s* and the moon shall be dark,
Joel 2:31 The *s* shall be turned into
Joel 3:15 The *s* and the moon shall be
Amos 8:9 cause the *s* to go down at noon
Jonah 4:8 when the *s* did arise, that God
Jonah 4:8 the *s* beat upon the head of Jonah
Mic 3:6 the *s* shall go down over the
Nah 3:17 but when the *s* ariseth they flee
Hab 3:11 The *s* and moon stood still in
Mal 1:11 For from the rising of the *s* even
Mal 4:2 the *S* of righteousness arise with
Mt 5:45 for he maketh his *s* to rise on
Mt 13:6 And when the *s* was up, they were
Mt 13:43 righteous shine forth as the *s* in
Mt 17:2 and his face did shine as the *s*
Mt 24:29 days shall the *s* be darkened
Mk 1:32 And at even, when the *s* did set
Mk 4:6 But when the *s* was up, it was
Mk 13:24 the *s* shall be darkened, and the
Mk 16:2 sepulchre at the rising of the *s*
Lk 4:40 Now when the *s* was setting
Lk 21:25 And there shall be signs in the *s*
Lk 23:45 the *s* was darkened, and the veil
Acts 2:20 The *s* shall be turned into
Acts 13:11 not seeing the *s* for a season
Acts 26:13 above the brightness of the *s*
Acts 27:20 when neither *s* nor stars in many
1Cor 15:41 There is one glory of the *s*
Eph 4:26 let not the *s* go down upon your
Jas 1:11 For the *s* is no sooner risen with
Rev 1:16 as the *s* shineth in his strength
Rev 6:12 the *s* became black as sackcloth
Rev 7:16 neither shall the *s* light on them
Rev 8:12 third part of the *s* was smitten
Rev 9:2 and the *s* and the air were darkened
Rev 10:1 and his face was as it were the *s*
Rev 12:1 a woman clothed with the *s*
Rev 16:8 poured out his vial upon the *s*
Rev 19:17 I saw an angel standing in the *s*
Rev 21:23 And the city had no need of the *s*
Rev 22:5 no candle, neither light of the *s*

**SUNDER**
Ps 46:9 bow, and cutteth the spear in *s*
Ps 107:14 death, and brake their bands in *s*
Ps 107:16 and cut the bars of iron in *s*
Is 27:9 chalkstones that are beaten in *s*
Is 45:2 cut in *s* the bars of iron
Nah 1:13 and will burst thy bonds in *s*
Lk 12:46 not aware, and will cut him in *s*

**SUNDERED**
Job 41:17 together, that they cannot be *s*

**SUNDRY**
Heb 1:1 God, who at *s* times and in divers

**SUNG**
Is 26:1 song be s in the land of Judah
Mt 26:30 And when they had s an hymn
Mk 14:26 And when they had s an hymn
Rev 5:9 they s a new song, saying, Thou
Rev 14:3 they s as it were a new song

**SUNK**
1Sa 17:49 that the stone s into his
2Kin 9:24 and he s down in his chariot
Ps 9:15 The heathen are s down in the pit
Jer 38:6 so Jeremiah s in the mire
Jer 38:22 thy feet are s in the mire
Lam 2:9 Her gates are s into the ground
Acts 20:9 he s down with sleep, and fell

**SUNRISING**
Num 21:11 is before Moab, toward the s
Num 34:15 Jericho eastward, toward the s
Deut 4:41 on this side Jordan toward the s
Deut 4:47 on this side Jordan toward the s
Josh 1:15 on this side Jordan toward the s
Josh 13:5 and all Lebanon, toward the s
Josh 19:12 toward the s unto the border of
Josh 19:27 toward the s to Beth-dagon
Josh 19:34 to Judah upon Jordan toward the s
Judg 20:43 over against Gibeah toward the s

**SUP**
Hab 1:9 their faces shall s up as the
Lk 17:8 him, Make ready wherewith I may s
Rev 3:20 will s with him, and he with me

**SUPERFLUITY**
Jas 1:21 s of naughtiness, and receive with

**SUPERFLUOUS**
Lev 21:18 hath a flat nose, or any thing s
Lev 22:23 thing s or lacking in his parts
2Cor 9:1 it is s for me to write to you

**SUPERSCRIPTION**
Mt 22:20 them, Whose is this image and s
Mk 12:16 them, Whose is this image and s
Mk 15:26 the s of his accusation was
Lk 20:24 Whose image and s hath it
Lk 23:38 a s also was written over him in

**SUPERSTITION**
Acts 25:19 against him of their own s

**SUPERSTITIOUS**
Acts 17:22 that in all things ye are too s

**SUPPED**
1Cor 11:25 he took the cup, when he had s

**SUPPER**
Mk 6:21 birthday made a s to his lords
Lk 14:12 When thou makest a dinner or a s
Lk 14:16 him, A certain man made a great s
Lk 14:17 sent his servant at s time to say
Lk 14:24 were bidden shall taste of my s
Lk 22:20 Likewise also the cup after s
Jn 12:2 There they made him a s
Jn 13:2 s being ended, the devil having
Jn 13:4 He riseth from s, and laid aside
Jn 21:20 also leaned on his breast at s
1Cor 11:20 this is not to eat the Lord's s
1Cor 11:21 one taketh before other his own s
Rev 19:9 unto the marriage s of the Lamb
Rev 19:17 unto the s of the great God

**SUPPLANT**
Jer 9:4 for every brother will utterly s

**SUPPLANTED**
Gen 27:36 for he hath s me these two times

**SUPPLE**
Eze 16:4 thou washed in water to s thee

**SUPPLIANTS**
Zeph 3:10 the rivers of Ethiopia my s

**SUPPLICATION**
1Sa 13:12 I have not made s unto the LORD
1Kin 8:28 of thy servant, and to his s
1Kin 8:30 thou to the s of thy servant
1Kin 8:33 make s unto thee in this house
1Kin 8:38 s soever be made by any man, or
1Kin 8:45 in heaven their prayer and their s
1Kin 8:47 make s unto thee in the land of
1Kin 8:49 their s in heaven thy dwelling
1Kin 8:52 be open unto the s of thy servant
1Kin 8:52 unto the s of thy people Israel,
1Kin 8:54 s unto the LORD, he arose from
1Kin 8:59 I have made s before the LORD
1Kin 9:3 I have heard thy prayer and thy s
2Chr 6:19 of thy servant, and to his s
2Chr 6:24 make s before thee in this house
2Chr 6:29 Then what prayer or what s soever
2Chr 6:35 heavens their prayer and their s
2Chr 33:13 intreated of him, and heard his s
Est 4:8 to make s unto him, and to make
Job 8:5 make thy s to the Almighty
Job 9:15 but I would make s to my judge
Ps 6:9 The LORD hath heard my s
Ps 30:8 and unto the LORD I made s
Ps 55:1 and hide not thyself from my s
Ps 119:170 Let my s come before thee
Ps 142:1 unto the LORD did I make my s
Is 45:14 thee, they shall make s unto thee
Jer 36:7 present their s before the LORD
Jer 37:20 let my s, I pray thee, be
Jer 38:26 I presented my s before the king,
Jer 42:2 our s be accepted before thee, and
Jer 42:9 me to present your s before him
Dan 6:11 and making s before his God
Dan 9:20 presenting my s before the LORD
Hos 12:4 he wept, and made s unto him
Acts 1:14 with one accord in prayer and s
Eph 6:18 s in the Spirit, and watching
Eph 6:18 perseverance and s for all saints
Phil 4:6 s with thanksgiving let your

**SUPPLICATIONS**
2Chr 6:21 unto the s of thy servant
2Chr 6:39 place, their prayer and their s
Job 41:3 Will he make many s unto thee
Ps 28:2 Hear the voice of my s, when I
Ps 28:6 he hath heard the voice of my s
Ps 31:22 of my s when I cried unto thee
Ps 86:6 and attend to the voice of my s
Ps 116:1 he hath heard my voice and my s
Ps 130:2 be attentive to the voice of my s
Ps 140:6 hear the voice of my s, O LORD
Ps 143:1 prayer, O LORD, give ear to my s
Jer 3:21 s of the children of Israel
Jer 31:9 and with s will I lead them
Dan 9:3 Lord God, to seek by prayer and s
Dan 9:17 prayer of thy servant, and his s
Dan 9:18 present our s before thee for our
Dan 9:23 At the beginning of thy s the
Zec 12:10 the spirit of grace and of s
1Ti 2:1 therefore, that, first of all, s
1Ti 5:5 in God, and continueth in s
Heb 5:7 s with strong crying and tears

**SUPPLIED**
1Cor 16:17 lacking on your part they have s
2Cor 11:9 which came from Macedonia s

**SUPPLIETH**
2Cor 9:12 not only s the want of the saints
Eph 4:16 by that which every joint s

**SUPPLY**
2Cor 8:14 may be a s for their want
2Cor 8:14 also may be a s for your want
Phil 1:19 the s of the Spirit of Jesus
Phil 2:30 to s your lack of service toward
Phil 4:19 But my God shall s all your need

**SUPPORT**
Acts 20:35 labouring ye ought to s the weak
1Th 5:14 s the weak, be patient toward all

**SUPPOSE**
2Sa 13:32 Let not my lord s that they have
Lk 7:43 I s that he, to whom he forgave
Lk 12:51 S ye that I am come to give peace
Lk 13:2 S ye that these Galilaeans were
Jn 21:25 I s that even the world itself
Acts 2:15 these are not drunken, as ye s
1Cor 7:26 I s therefore that this is good
2Cor 11:5 For I s I was not a whit behind
Heb 10:29 s ye, shall he be thought worthy,
1Pet 5:12 faithful brother unto you, as I s

**SUPPOSED**
Mt 20:10 they s that they should have
Mk 6:49 they s it had been a spirit, and
Lk 3:23 being (as was s) the son of
Lk 24:37 s that they had seen a spirit
Acts 7:25 For he s his brethren would have
Acts 21:29 whom they s that Paul had brought
Acts 25:18 accusation of such things as I s
Phil 2:25 Yet I s it necessary to send to

**SUPPOSING**
Lk 2:44 s him to have been in the company
Jn 20:15 s him to be the gardener, saith
Acts 14:19 of the city, s he had been dead
Acts 16:27 s that the prisoners had been
Acts 27:13 s that they had obtained their
Phil 1:16 s to add affliction to my bonds
1Ti 6:5 truth, s that gain is godliness

**SUPREME**
1Pet 2:13 whether it be to the king, as s

**SUR** *(sur) A gate of the Temple.*
2Kin 11:6 part shall be at the gate of S

**SURE**
Gen 23:17 borders round about, were made s
Gen 23:20 were made s unto Abraham for a
Ex 3:19 I am s that the king of Egypt
Num 32:23 be s your sin will find you out
Deut 12:23 Only be s that thou eat not the
1Sa 2:35 and I will build him a s house
1Sa 20:7 then be s that evil is determined
1Sa 25:28 certainly make my lord a s house
2Sa 1:10 because I was s that he could not
2Sa 23:5 ordered in all things, and s
1Kin 11:38 thee, and build thee a s house
Neh 9:38 of all this we make a s covenant
Job 24:22 riseth up, and no man is s of life
Ps 19:7 the testimony of the LORD is s
Ps 93:5 Thy testimonies are very s
Ps 111:7 all his commandments are s
Prov 6:3 thyself, and make s thy friend
Prov 11:15 and he that hateth suretiship is s
Prov 11:18 righteousness shall be a s reward
Is 22:23 fasten him as a nail in a s place
Is 22:25 in the s place be removed
Is 28:16 corner stone, a s foundation
Is 32:18 in s dwellings, and in quiet
Is 33:16 his waters shall be s
Is 55:3 even the s mercies of David
Dan 2:45 and the interpretation thereof s
Dan 4:26 thy kingdom shall be s unto thee
Mt 27:64 be made s until the third day
Mt 27:65 your way, make it as s as ye can
Mt 27:66 went, and made the sepulchre s
Lk 10:11 notwithstanding be ye s of this
Jn 6:69 are s that thou art that Christ,
Jn 16:30 Now are we s that thou knowest
Acts 13:34 give you the s mercies of David
Rom 2:2 But we are s that the judgment of
Rom 4:16 might be s to all the seed
Rom 15:29 And I am s that, when I come unto
2Ti 2:19 the foundation of God standeth s
Heb 6:19 as an anchor of the soul, both s
2Pet 1:10 make your calling and election s
2Pet 1:19 also a more s word of prophecy

**SURETIES**
Prov 22:26 or of them that are s for debts

**SURETISHIP**
Prov 11:15 and he that hateth s is sure

**SURETY**
Gen 15:13 Know of a s that thy seed shall
Gen 18:13 Shall I of a s bear a child
Gen 26:9 Behold, of a s she is thy wife
Gen 43:9 I will be s for him
Gen 44:32 For thy servant became s for the
Job 17:3 down now, put me in a s with thee
Ps 119:122 Be s for thy servant for good
Prov 6:1 if thou be s for thy friend, if
Prov 11:15 He that is s for a stranger shall
Prov 17:18 becometh s in the presence of his
Prov 20:16 garment that is s for a stranger
Prov 27:13 garment that is s for a stranger
Acts 12:11 he said, Now I know of a s
Heb 7:22 made a s of a better testament

**SURFEITING**
Lk 21:34 your hearts be overcharged with s

**SURMISINGS**
1Ti 6:4 envy, strife, railings, evil s

**SURNAME**
Is 44:5 s himself by the name of Israel
Mt 10:3 Lebbaeus, whose s was Thaddaeus
Acts 10:5 for one Simon, whose s is Peter
Acts 10:32 hither Simon, whose s is Peter
Acts 11:13 call for Simon, whose s is Peter
Acts 12:12 mother of John, whose s was Mark
Acts 12:25 with them John, whose s was Mark
Acts 15:37 with them John, whose s was Mark

**SURNAMED**
Is 45:4 I have s thee, though thou hast
Mk 3:16 And Simon he s Peter
Mk 3:17 he s them Boanerges, which is,
Lk 22:3 Satan into Judas s Iscariot

Acts 1:23 called Barsabas, who was *s* Justus
Acts 4:36 by the apostles was *s* Barnabas
Acts 10:18 whether Simon, which was *s* Peter
Acts 15:22 Judas *s* Barsabas, and Silas, chief

**SURPRISED**
Is 33:14 fearfulness hath *s* the hypocrites
Jer 48:41 taken, and the strong holds are *s*
Jer 51:41 the praise of the whole earth *s*

**SUSANCHITES** *(su'-san-kites) Resettled foreigners in Israel.*
Ezr 4:9 the Babylonians, the *S*, the

**SUSANNA** *(su'-zan'-nah) A woman follower of Jesus.*
Lk 8:3 of Chuza Herod's steward, and *S*

**SUSI** *(su'-si) Father of Gaddi.*
Num 13:11 of Manasseh, Gaddi the son of *S*

**SUSTAIN**
1Kin 17:9 a widow woman there to *s* thee
Neh 9:21 thou *s* them in the wilderness
Ps 55:22 upon the LORD, and he shall *s* thee
Prov 18:14 of a man will *s* his infirmity

**SUSTAINED**
Gen 27:37 and with corn and wine have I *s* him
Ps 3:5 for the LORD *s* me
Is 59:16 and his righteousness, it *s* him

**SUSTENANCE**
Judg 6:4 left no *s* for Israel, neither
2Sa 19:32 of *s* while he lay at Mahanaim
Acts 7:11 and our fathers found no *s*

**SWADDLED**
Lam 2:22 those that I have *s* and brought up
Eze 16:4 not salted at all, nor *s* at all

**SWADDLING**
Lk 2:7 son, and wrapped him in *s* clothes
Lk 2:12 the babe wrapped in *s* clothes

**SWADDLINGBAND**
Job 38:9 and thick darkness a *s* for it

**SWALLOW**
Num 16:30 and *s* them up, with all that
Num 16:34 said, Lest the earth *s* us up also
2Sa 20:19 why wilt thou *s* up the
2Sa 20:20 me, that I should *s* up or destroy
Job 7:19 me alone till I *s* down my spittle
Job 20:18 restore, and shall not *s* it down
Ps 21:9 the LORD shall *s* them up in his
Ps 56:1 for man would *s* me up
Ps 56:2 Mine enemies would daily *s* me up
Ps 57:3 of him that would *s* me up
Ps 69:15 me, neither let the deep *s* me up
Ps 84:3 the *s* a nest for herself, where
Prov 1:12 Let us *s* them up alive as the
Prov 26:2 as the *s* by flying, so the curse
Eccl 10:12 lips of a fool will *s* up himself
Is 25:8 He will *s* up death in victory
Is 38:14 Like a crane or a *s*, so did I
Jer 8:7 the *s* observe the time of their
Hos 8:7 the strangers shall *s* it up
Amos 8:4 O ye that *s* up the needy, even to
Obad 16 shall drink, and they shall *s* down
Jonah 1:17 a great fish to *s* up Jonah
Mt 23:24 strain at a gnat, and *s* a camel

**SWALLOWED**
Ex 7:12 but Aaron's rod *s* up their rods
Ex 15:12 thy right hand, the earth *s* them
Num 16:32 *s* them up, and their houses, and
Num 26:10 *s* them up together with Korah,
Deut 11:6 *s* them up, and their households,
2Sa 17:16 lest the king be *s* up, and all the
Job 6:3 therefore my words are *s* up
Job 20:15 He hath *s* down riches, and he
Job 37:20 speak, surely he shall be *s* up
Ps 35:25 them not say, We have *s* him up
Ps 106:17 *s* up Dathan, and covered the
Ps 124:3 Then they had *s* us up quick
Is 28:7 they are *s* up of wine, they are
Is 49:19 they that *s* thee up shall be far
Jer 51:34 he hath *s* me up like a dragon, he
Jer 51:44 his mouth that which he hath *s* up
Lam 2:2 The Lord hath *s* up all the
Lam 2:5 he hath *s* up Israel, he hath
Lam 2:5 he hath *s* up all her palaces
Lam 2:16 they say, We have *s* her up
Eze 36:3 *s* you up on every side, that ye
Hos 8:8 Israel is *s* up
1Cor 15:54 written, Death is *s* up in victory
2Cor 2:7 be *s* up with overmuch sorrow
2Cor 5:4 mortality might be *s* up of life
Rev 12:16 *s* up the flood which the dragon

**SWALLOWETH**
Job 5:5 the robber *s* up their substance
Job 39:24 He *s* the ground with fierceness

**SWAN**
Lev 11:18 And the *s*, and the pelican, and the
Deut 14:16 owl, and the great owl, and the *s*

**SWARE**
Gen 21:31 because there they *s* both of them
Gen 24:7 that *s* unto me, saying, Unto thy
Gen 24:9 *s* to him concerning that matter
Gen 25:33 and he *s* unto him
Gen 26:3 which I *s* unto Abraham thy father
Gen 26:31 the morning, and *s* one to another
Gen 31:53 Jacob *s* by the fear of his father
Gen 47:31 And he *s* unto him
Gen 50:24 the land which he *s* to Abraham
Ex 13:5 which he *s* unto thy fathers to
Ex 13:11 as he *s* unto thee and to thy
Ex 33:1 the land which I *s* unto Abraham
Num 14:16 the land which he *s* unto them
Num 14:23 land which I *s* unto their fathers
Num 14:30 concerning which I *s* to make you
Num 32:10 kindled the same time, and he *s*
Num 32:11 the land which I *s* unto Abraham
Deut 1:8 the LORD *s* unto your fathers
Deut 1:34 of your words, and was wroth, and *s*
Deut 1:35 which I *s* to give unto your
Deut 2:14 the host, as the LORD *s* unto them
Deut 4:21 *s* that I should not go over
Deut 4:31 thy fathers which he *s* unto them
Deut 6:10 land which he *s* unto thy fathers
Deut 6:18 which the LORD *s* unto thy fathers
Deut 6:23 land which he *s* unto our fathers
Deut 7:12 mercy which he *s* unto thy fathers
Deut 7:13 in the land which he *s* unto thy
Deut 8:1 the LORD *s* unto your fathers
Deut 8:18 which he *s* unto thy fathers
Deut 9:5 which the LORD *s* unto thy fathers
Deut 10:11 which I *s* unto their fathers to
Deut 11:9 which the LORD *s* unto your
Deut 11:21 in the land which the LORD *s* unto
Deut 26:3 *s* unto our fathers for to give us
Deut 28:11 in the land which the LORD *s* unto
Deut 30:20 which the LORD *s* unto thy fathers
Deut 31:20 land which I *s* unto their fathers
Deut 31:21 them into the land which I *s*
Deut 31:23 into the land which I *s* unto them
Deut 34:4 the land which I *s* unto Abraham
Josh 1:6 which I *s* unto their fathers to
Josh 5:6 unto whom the LORD *s* that he
Josh 5:6 which the LORD *s* unto their
Josh 6:22 that she hath, as ye *s* unto her
Josh 9:15 of the congregation *s* unto them
Josh 9:20 of the oath which we *s* unto them
Josh 14:9 Moses *s* on that day, saying,
Josh 21:43 he *s* to give unto their fathers
Josh 21:44 all that he *s* unto their fathers
Judg 2:1 land which I *s* unto your fathers
1Sa 19:6 and Saul *s*, As the LORD liveth, he
1Sa 20:3 David *s* moreover, and said, Thy
1Sa 24:22 And David *s* unto Saul
1Sa 28:10 Saul *s* to her by the LORD, saying
2Sa 3:35 while it was yet day, David *s*
2Sa 19:23 And the king *s* unto him
2Sa 21:17 Then the men of David *s* unto him
1Kin 1:29 And the king *s*, and said, As the
1Kin 1:30 Even as I *s* unto thee by the LORD
1Kin 2:8 I *s* to him by the LORD, saying, I
1Kin 2:23 Then king Solomon *s* by the LORD
2Kin 25:24 And Gedaliah *s* to them, and to
2Chr 15:14 they *s* unto the LORD with a loud
Ezr 10:5 And they *s*
Ps 95:11 Unto whom I *s* in my wrath that
Ps 132:2 How he *s* unto the LORD, and vowed
Jer 38:16 So Zedekiah the king *s* secretly
Jer 40:9 the son of Shaphan *s* unto them
Eze 16:8 I *s* unto thee, and entered into a
Dan 12:7 *s* by him that liveth for ever
Mk 6:23 he *s* unto her, Whatsoever thou
Lk 1:73 The oath which he *s* to our father
Heb 3:11 So I *s* in my wrath, They shall
Heb 3:18 to whom *s* he that they should not
Heb 6:13 by no greater, he *s* by himself,
Heb 7:21 that said unto him, The Lord *s*
Rev 10:6 *s* by him that liveth for ever and

**SWAREST**
Ex 32:13 to whom thou *s* by thine own self,
Num 11:12 which thou *s* unto their fathers
Deut 26:15 as thou *s* unto our fathers, a
1Kin 1:17 thou *s* by the LORD thy God unto
Ps 89:49 which thou *s* unto David in thy

**SWARM**
Ex 8:24 there came a grievous *s* of flies
Ex 8:24 by reason of the *s* of flies
Judg 14:8 and, behold, there was a *s* of bees

**SWARMS**
Ex 8:21 I will send *s* of flies upon thee,
Ex 8:21 shall be full of *s* of flies
Ex 8:22 that no *s* of flies shall be there
Ex 8:29 the *s* of flies may depart from
Ex 8:31 he removed the *s* of flies from

**SWEAR**
Gen 21:23 Now therefore *s* unto me here by
Gen 21:24 And Abraham said, I will *s*
Gen 24:3 And I will make thee *s* by the LORD
Gen 24:37 And my master made me *s*, saying,
Gen 25:33 And Jacob said, *S* to me this day
Gen 47:31 And he said, *S* unto me
Gen 50:5 My father made me *s*, saying, Lo,
Gen 50:6 according as he made thee *s*
Ex 6:8 I did *s* to give it to Abraham
Lev 5:4 Or if a soul *s*, pronouncing with
Lev 19:12 ye shall not *s* by my name falsely
Num 30:2 or *s* an oath to bind his soul
Deut 6:13 serve him, and shalt *s* by his name
Deut 10:20 thou cleave, and *s* by his name
Josh 2:12 *s* unto me by the LORD, since I
Josh 2:17 oath which thou hast made us *s*
Josh 2:20 oath which thou hast made us to *s*
Josh 23:7 gods, nor cause to *s* by them
Judg 15:12 *S* unto me, that ye will not fall
1Sa 20:17 Jonathan caused David to *s* again
1Sa 24:21 *S* now therefore unto me by the
1Sa 30:15 *S* unto me by God, that thou wilt
2Sa 19:7 for I *s* by the LORD, if thou go
1Kin 1:13 *s* unto thine handmaid, saying,
1Kin 1:51 Let king Solomon *s* unto me to day
1Kin 2:42 I not make thee to *s* by the LORD
1Kin 8:31 laid upon him to cause him to *s*
2Chr 6:22 be laid upon him to make him *s*
2Chr 36:13 who had made him *s* by God
Ezr 10:5 Israel, to *s* that they should do
Neh 13:25 their hair, and made them *s* by God
Is 3:7 In that day shall he *s*, saying, I
Is 19:18 Canaan, and *s* to the LORD of hosts
Is 45:23 shall bow, every tongue shall *s*
Is 48:1 which *s* by the name of the LORD,
Is 65:16 earth shall *s* by the God of truth
Jer 4:2 And thou shalt *s*, The LORD liveth,
Jer 5:2 surely they *s* falsely
Jer 7:9 *s* falsely, and burn incense unto
Jer 12:16 to *s* by my name, The LORD liveth
Jer 12:16 taught my people to *s* by Baal
Jer 22:5 I *s* by myself, saith the LORD,
Jer 32:22 which thou didst *s* to their
Hos 4:15 go ye up to Beth-aven, nor *s*
Amos 8:14 They that *s* by the sin of Samaria
Zeph 1:5 that *s* by the LORD
Zeph 1:5 and that *s* by Malcham
Mt 5:34 But I say unto you, *S* not at all
Mt 5:36 Neither shalt thou *s* by thy head
Mt 23:16 Whosoever shall *s* by the temple
Mt 23:16 but whosoever shall *s* by the gold
Mt 23:18 Whosoever shall *s* by the altar
Mt 23:20 therefore shall *s* by the altar
Mt 23:21 whoso shall *s* by the temple,
Mt 23:22 And he that shall *s* by heaven
Mt 26:74 Then began he to curse and to *s*
Mk 14:71 But he began to curse and to *s*
Heb 6:13 because he could *s* by no greater
Heb 6:16 For men verily *s* by the greater
Jas 5:12 *s* not, neither by heaven, neither

**SWEARERS**
Mal 3:5 adulterers, and against false *s*

**SWEARETH**
Lev 6:3 lieth concerning it, and *s* falsely
Ps 15:4 He that *s* to his own hurt, and
Ps 63:11 every one that *s* by him shall
Eccl 9:2 and he that *s*, as he that feareth
Is 65:16 he that *s* in the earth shall
Zec 5:3 every one that *s* shall be cut off
Zec 5:4 of him that *s* falsely by my name
Mt 23:18 but whosoever *s* by the gift that

Mt 23:20 s by it, and by all things thereon
Mt 23:21 s by it, and by him that dwelleth
Mt 23:22 s by the throne of God, and by him

### SWEARING
Lev 5:1 soul sin, and hear the voice of s
Jer 23:10 for because of s the land
Hos 4:2 By s, and lying, and killing, and
Hos 10:4 s falsely in making a covenant

### SWEAT
Gen 3:19 In the s of thy face shalt thou
Eze 44:18 with any thing that causeth s
Lk 22:44 his s was as it were great drops

### SWEEP
Is 14:23 I will s it with the besom of
Is 28:17 the hail shall s away the refuge
Lk 15:8 s the house, and seek diligently

### SWEEPING
Prov 28:3 a s rain which leaveth no food

### SWEET
Gen 8:21 And the LORD smelled a s savour
Ex 15:25 waters, the waters were made s
Ex 25:6 anointing oil, and for s incense,
Ex 29:18 it is a s savour, an offering
Ex 29:25 for a s savour before the LORD
Ex 29:41 for a s savour, an offering made
Ex 30:7 thereon s incense every morning
Ex 30:23 of s cinnamon half so much, even
Ex 30:23 of s calamus two hundred and fifty
Ex 30:34 Moses, Take unto thee s spices
Ex 30:34 these s spices with pure
Ex 31:11 s incense for the holy place
Ex 35:8 oil, and for the s incense
Ex 35:15 the s incense, and the hanging for
Ex 35:28 oil, and for the s incense
Ex 37:29 and the pure incense of s spices
Ex 39:38 the s incense, and the hanging for
Ex 40:27 he burnt s incense thereon
Lev 1:9 of a s savour unto the LORD
Lev 1:13 of a s savour unto the LORD
Lev 1:17 of a s savour unto the LORD
Lev 2:2 of a s savour unto the LORD
Lev 2:9 of a s savour unto the LORD
Lev 2:12 burnt on the altar for a s savour
Lev 3:5 of a s savour unto the LORD
Lev 3:16 made by fire for a s savour
Lev 4:7 of s incense before the LORD
Lev 4:31 for a s savour unto the LORD
Lev 6:15 it upon the altar for a s savour
Lev 6:21 for a s savour unto the LORD
Lev 8:21 a burnt sacrifice for a s savour
Lev 8:28 were consecrations for a s savour
Lev 16:12 his hands full of s incense
Lev 17:6 burn the fat for a s savour unto
Lev 23:13 fire unto the LORD for a s savour
Lev 23:18 of s savour unto the LORD
Lev 26:31 smell the savour of your s odours
Num 4:16 the s incense, and the daily meat
Num 15:3 to make a s savour unto the LORD,
Num 15:7 for a s savour unto the LORD
Num 15:10 of a s savour unto the LORD
Num 15:13 of a s savour unto the LORD
Num 15:14 of a s savour unto the LORD
Num 15:24 for a s savour unto the LORD,
Num 18:17 for a s savour unto the LORD
Num 28:2 for a s savour unto me, shall ye
Num 28:6 in mount Sinai for a s savour
Num 28:8 of a s savour unto the LORD
Num 28:13 a burnt offering of a s savour
Num 28:24 of a s savour unto the LORD
Num 28:27 for a s savour unto the LORD
Num 29:2 for a s savour unto the LORD
Num 29:6 for a s savour, a sacrifice made
Num 29:8 unto the LORD for a s savour
Num 29:13 of a s savour unto the LORD
Num 29:36 of a s savour unto the LORD
2Sa 23:1 the s psalmist of Israel, said,
2Chr 2:4 and to burn before him s incense
2Chr 13:11 burnt sacrifices and s incense
2Chr 16:14 which was filled with s odours
Ezr 6:10 they may offer sacrifices of s
Neh 8:10 way, eat the fat, and drink the s
Est 2:12 and six months with s odours
Job 20:12 wickedness be s in his mouth
Job 21:33 of the valley shall be s unto him
Job 38:31 Canst thou bind the s influences
Ps 55:14 We took s counsel together, and
Ps 104:34 My meditation of him shall be s
Ps 119:103 How s are thy words unto my taste
Ps 141:6 for they are s
Prov 3:24 lie down, and thy sleep shall be s
Prov 9:17 Stolen waters are s, and bread
Prov 13:19 accomplished is s to the soul
Prov 16:24 s to the soul, and health to the
Prov 20:17 Bread of deceit is s to a man
Prov 23:8 vomit up, and lose thy s words
Prov 24:13 which is s to thy taste
Prov 27:7 soul every bitter thing is s
Eccl 5:12 The sleep of a labouring man is s
Eccl 11:7 Truly the light is s, and a
Song 2:3 and his fruit was s to my taste
Song 2:14 for s is thy voice, and thy
Song 5:5 my fingers with s smelling myrrh
Song 5:13 as a bed of spices, as s flowers
Song 5:13 dropping s smelling myrrh
Song 5:16 His mouth is most s
Is 3:24 that instead of s smell there
Is 5:20 bitter for s, and s for bitter
Is 23:16 make s melody, sing many songs,
Is 43:24 bought me no s cane with money
Is 49:26 their own blood, as with s wine
Jer 6:20 the s cane from a far country
Jer 6:20 nor your sacrifices s unto me
Jer 31:26 and my sleep was s unto me
Eze 6:13 offer s savour to all their idols
Eze 16:19 set it before them for a s savour
Eze 20:28 also they made their s savour
Eze 20:41 accept you with your s savour
Dan 2:46 an oblation and s odours unto him
Amos 9:13 the mountains shall drop s wine
Mic 6:15 s wine, but shalt not drink wine
Mk 16:1 and Salome, had bought s spices
2Cor 2:15 are unto God a s savour of Christ
Phil 4:18 from you, an odour of a s smell
Jas 3:11 forth at the same place s water
Rev 10:9 shall be in thy mouth s as honey
Rev 10:10 and it was in my mouth s as honey

### SWEETER
Judg 14:18 went down, What is s than honey
Ps 19:10 s also than honey and the
Ps 119:103 yea, s than honey to my mouth

### SWEETLY
Job 24:20 the worm shall feed s on him
Song 7:9 for my beloved, that goeth down s

### SWEETNESS
Judg 9:11 unto them, Should I forsake my s
Judg 14:14 and out of the strong came forth s
Prov 16:21 the s of the lips increaseth
Prov 27:9 so doth the s of a man's friend
Eze 3:3 it was in my mouth as honey for s

### SWEETSMELLING
Eph 5:2 a sacrifice to God for a s savour

### SWELL
Num 5:21 thigh to rot, and thy belly to s
Num 5:22 bowels, to make thy belly to s
Num 5:27 bitter, and her belly shall s
Deut 8:4 upon thee, neither did thy foot s

### SWELLED
Neh 9:21 not old, and their feet s not

### SWELLING
Ps 46:3 shake with the s thereof
Is 30:13 s out in a high wall, whose
Jer 12:5 wilt thou do in the s of Jordan
Jer 49:19 from the s of Jordan against the
Jer 50:44 come up like a lion from the s of
2Pet 2:18 speak great s words of vanity
Jude 16 mouth speaketh great s words

### SWELLINGS
2Cor 12:20 backbitings, whisperings, s

### SWEPT
Judg 5:21 The river of Kishon s them away
Jer 46:15 Why are thy valiant men s away
Mt 12:44 is come, he findeth it empty, s
Lk 11:25 when he cometh, he findeth it s

### SWERVED
1Ti 1:6 From which some having s have

### SWIFT
Deut 28:49 earth, as s as the eagle flieth
1Chr 12:8 were as s as the roes upon the
Job 9:26 are passed away as the s ships
Job 24:18 He is s as the waters
Prov 6:18 feet that be s in running to
Eccl 9:11 that the race is not to the s
Is 18:2 ye s messengers, to a nation
Is 19:1 the LORD rideth upon a s cloud
Is 30:16 and, We will ride upon the s
Is 30:16 shall they that pursue you be s
Is 66:20 upon s beasts, to my holy
Jer 2:23 thou art a s dromedary traversing
Jer 46:6 Let not the s flee away, nor the
Amos 2:14 flight shall perish from the s
Amos 2:15 he that is s of foot shall not
Mic 1:13 bind the chariot to the s beast
Mal 3:5 I will be a s witness against the
Rom 3:15 Their feet are s to shed blood
Jas 1:19 let every man be s to hear
2Pet 2:1 upon themselves s destruction

### SWIFTER
2Sa 1:23 they were s than eagles, they
Job 7:6 My days are s than a weaver's
Job 9:25 Now my days are s than a post
Jer 4:13 his horses are s than eagles
Lam 4:19 Our persecutors are s than the
Hab 1:8 also are s than the leopards

### SWIFTLY
Ps 147:15 his word runneth very s
Is 5:26 they shall come with speed s
Dan 9:21 beginning, being caused to fly s
Joel 3:4 and if ye recompense me, s

### SWIM
2Kin 6:6 and the iron did s
Ps 6:6 all the night make I my bed to s
Is 25:11 spreadeth forth his hands to s
Eze 47:5 waters were risen, waters to s in
Acts 27:42 lest any of them should s out
Acts 27:43 s should cast themselves first

### SWIMMEST
Eze 32:6 thy blood the land wherein thou s

### SWIMMETH
Is 25:11 as he that s spreadeth forth his

### SWINE
Lev 11:7 And the s, though he divide the
Deut 14:8 And the s, because it divideth the
Mt 7:6 cast ye your pearls before s
Mt 8:30 them an herd of many s feeding
Mt 8:31 us to go away into the herd of s
Mt 8:32 out, they went into the herd of s
Mt 8:32 the whole herd of s ran violently
Mk 5:11 a great herd of s feeding
Mk 5:12 him, saying, Send us into the s
Mk 5:13 went out, and entered into the s
Mk 5:14 And they that fed the s fled
Mk 5:16 devil, and also concerning the s
Lk 8:32 of many s feeding on the mountain
Lk 8:33 of the man, and entered into the s
Lk 15:15 him into his fields to feed s
Lk 15:16 with the husks that the s did eat

### SWINE'S
Prov 11:22 As a jewel of gold in a s snout
Is 65:4 the monuments, which eat s flesh
Is 66:3 as if he offered s blood
Is 66:17 tree in the midst, eating s flesh

### SWOLLEN
Acts 28:6 they looked when he should have s

### SWOON
Lam 2:11 the sucklings s in the streets of

### SWOONED
Lam 2:12 when they s as the wounded in the

### SWORD
Gen 3:24 a flaming s which turned every
Gen 27:40 by thy s shalt thou live, and
Gen 31:26 as captives taken with the s
Gen 34:25 brethren, took each man his s
Gen 34:26 his son with the edge of the s
Gen 48:22 the hand of the Amorite with my s
Ex 5:3 us with pestilence, or with the s
Ex 5:21 to put a s in their hand to slay
Ex 15:9 I will draw my s, my hand shall
Ex 17:13 his people with the edge of the s
Ex 18:4 me from the s of Pharaoh
Ex 22:24 and I will kill you with the s
Ex 32:27 Put every man his s by his side
Lev 26:6 neither shall the s go through
Lev 26:7 shall fall before you by the s
Lev 26:8 shall fall before you by the s
Lev 26:25 And I will bring a s upon you
Lev 26:33 and will draw out a s after you
Lev 26:36 shall flee, as fleeing from a s
Lev 26:37 another, as it were before a s
Num 14:3 unto this land, to fall by the s
Num 14:43 you, and ye shall fall by the s

| | |
|---|---|
| Num 19:16 | slain with a *s* in the open fields |
| Num 20:18 | come out against thee with the *s* |
| Num 21:24 | smote him with the edge of the *s* |
| Num 22:23 | way, and his *s* drawn in his hand |
| Num 22:29 | would there were a *s* in mine hand |
| Num 22:31 | way, and his *s* drawn in his hand |
| Num 31:8 | son of Beor they slew with the *s* |
| Deut 13:15 | that city with the edge of the *s* |
| Deut 13:15 | thereof, with the edge of the *s* |
| Deut 20:13 | thereof with the edge of the *s* |
| Deut 28:22 | an extreme burning, and with the *s* |
| Deut 32:25 | The *s* without, and terror within, |
| Deut 32:41 | If I whet my glittering *s* |
| Deut 32:42 | blood, and my *s* shall devour flesh |
| Deut 33:29 | who is the *s* of thy excellency |
| Josh 5:13 | him with his *s* drawn in his hand |
| Josh 6:21 | and ass, with the edge of the *s* |
| Josh 8:24 | all fallen on the edge of the *s* |
| Josh 8:24 | smote it with the edge of the *s* |
| Josh 10:11 | of Israel slew with the *s* |
| Josh 10:28 | smote it with the edge of the *s* |
| Josh 10:30 | smote it with the edge of the *s* |
| Josh 10:32 | smote it with the edge of the *s* |
| Josh 10:35 | smote it with the edge of the *s* |
| Josh 10:37 | smote it with the edge of the *s* |
| Josh 10:39 | smote them with the edge of the *s* |
| Josh 11:10 | smote the king thereof with the *s* |
| Josh 11:11 | therein with the edge of the *s* |
| Josh 11:12 | smote them with the edge of the *s* |
| Josh 11:14 | they smote with the edge of the *s* |
| Josh 13:22 | of Israel slay with the *s* among |
| Josh 19:47 | smote it with the edge of the *s* |
| Josh 24:12 | but not with thy *s*, nor with thy |
| Judg 1:8 | smitten it with the edge of the *s* |
| Judg 1:25 | the city with the edge of the *s* |
| Judg 4:15 | the edge of the *s* before Barak |
| Judg 4:16 | fell upon the edge of the *s* |
| Judg 7:14 | the *s* of Gideon the son of Joash |
| Judg 7:18 | The *s* of the LORD, and of Gideon |
| Judg 7:20 | The *s* of the LORD, and of Gideon |
| Judg 7:22 | every man's *s* against his fellow |
| Judg 8:10 | twenty thousand men that drew *s* |
| Judg 8:20 | But the youth drew not his *s* |
| Judg 9:54 | and said unto him, Draw thy *s* |
| Judg 18:27 | smote them with the edge of the *s* |
| Judg 20:2 | thousand footmen that drew *s* |
| Judg 20:15 | and six thousand men that drew *s* |
| Judg 20:17 | hundred thousand men that drew *s* |
| Judg 20:25 | all these drew the *s* |
| Judg 20:35 | all these drew the *s* |
| Judg 20:37 | the city with the edge of the *s* |
| Judg 20:46 | five thousand men that drew the *s* |
| Judg 20:48 | smote them with the edge of the *s* |
| Judg 21:10 | with the edge of the *s*, with the |
| 1Sa 13:22 | that there was neither *s* nor |
| 1Sa 14:20 | every man's *s* was against his |
| 1Sa 15:8 | the people with the edge of the *s* |
| 1Sa 15:33 | said, As thy *s* hath made women |
| 1Sa 17:39 | girded his *s* upon his armour |
| 1Sa 17:45 | Thou comest to me with a *s* |
| 1Sa 17:47 | that the LORD saveth not with *s* |
| 1Sa 17:50 | but there was no *s* in the hand of |
| 1Sa 17:51 | the Philistine, and took his *s* |
| 1Sa 18:4 | and his garments, even to his *s* |
| 1Sa 21:8 | here under thine hand spear or *s* |
| 1Sa 21:8 | my *s* nor my weapons with me |
| 1Sa 21:9 | The *s* of Goliath the Philistine, |
| 1Sa 22:10 | gave him the *s* of Goliath the |
| 1Sa 22:13 | thou hast given him bread, and a *s* |
| 1Sa 22:19 | smote he with the edge of the *s* |
| 1Sa 22:19 | and sheep, with the edge of the *s* |
| 1Sa 25:13 | men, Gird ye on every man his *s* |
| 1Sa 25:13 | And they girded on every man his *s* |
| 1Sa 25:13 | and David also girded on his *s* |
| 1Sa 31:4 | unto his armourbearer, Draw thy *s* |
| 1Sa 31:4 | Therefore Saul took a *s*, and fell |
| 1Sa 31:5 | dead, he fell likewise upon his *s* |
| 2Sa 1:12 | because they were fallen by the *s* |
| 2Sa 1:22 | the *s* of Saul returned not empty |
| 2Sa 2:16 | thrust his *s* in his fellow's side |
| 2Sa 2:26 | Shall the *s* devour for ever |
| 2Sa 3:29 | a staff, or that falleth on the *s* |
| 2Sa 11:25 | for the *s* devoureth one as well |
| 2Sa 12:9 | Uriah the Hittite with the *s* |
| 2Sa 12:9 | hast slain him with the *s* of the |
| 2Sa 12:10 | Now therefore the *s* shall never |
| 2Sa 15:14 | the city with the edge of the *s* |
| 2Sa 18:8 | that day than the *s* devoured |
| 2Sa 20:8 | upon it a girdle with a *s* |
| 2Sa 20:10 | to the *s* that was in Joab's hand |
| 2Sa 21:16 | he being girded with a new *s* |
| 2Sa 23:10 | and his hand clave unto the *s* |
| 2Sa 24:9 | valiant men that drew the *s* |
| 1Kin 1:51 | not slay his servant with the *s* |
| 1Kin 2:8 | not put thee to death with the *s* |
| 1Kin 2:32 | than he, and slew them with the *s* |
| 1Kin 3:24 | And the king said, Bring me a *s* |
| 1Kin 3:24 | they brought a *s* before the king |
| 1Kin 19:1 | slain all the prophets with the *s* |
| 1Kin 19:10 | and slain thy prophets with the *s* |
| 1Kin 19:14 | and slain thy prophets with the *s* |
| 1Kin 19:17 | the *s* of Hazael shall Jehu slay |
| 1Kin 19:17 | the *s* of Jehu shall Elisha slay |
| 2Kin 6:22 | hast taken captive with thy *s* |
| 2Kin 8:12 | men wilt thou slay with the *s* |
| 2Kin 10:25 | smote them with the edge of the *s* |
| 2Kin 11:15 | followeth her kill with the *s* |
| 2Kin 11:20 | the *s* beside the king's house |
| 2Kin 19:7 | to fall by the *s* in his own land |
| 2Kin 19:37 | his sons smote him with the *s* |
| 1Chr 5:18 | men able to bear buckler and *s* |
| 1Chr 10:4 | to his armourbearer, Draw thy *s* |
| 1Chr 10:4 | So Saul took a *s*, and fell upon it |
| 1Chr 10:5 | dead, he fell likewise on the *s* |
| 1Chr 21:5 | hundred thousand men that drew *s* |
| 1Chr 21:5 | and ten thousand men that drew *s* |
| 1Chr 21:12 | while that the *s* of thine enemies |
| 1Chr 21:12 | else three days the *s* of the LORD |
| 1Chr 21:16 | having a drawn *s* in his hand |
| 1Chr 21:27 | he put up his *s* again into the |
| 1Chr 21:30 | of the *s* of the angel of the LORD |
| 2Chr 20:9 | evil cometh upon us, as the *s* |
| 2Chr 21:4 | slew all his brethren with the *s* |
| 2Chr 23:14 | her, let him be slain with the *s* |
| 2Chr 23:21 | had slain Athaliah with the *s* |
| 2Chr 29:9 | our fathers have fallen by the *s* |
| 2Chr 32:21 | bowels slew him there with the *s* |
| 2Chr 36:17 | slew their young men with the *s* |
| 2Chr 36:20 | the *s* carried he away to Babylon |
| Ezr 9:7 | the kings of the lands, to the *s* |
| Neh 4:18 | every one had his *s* girded by his |
| Est 9:5 | enemies with the stroke of the *s* |
| Job 1:15 | servants with the edge of the *s* |
| Job 1:17 | servants with the edge of the *s* |
| Job 5:15 | But he saveth the poor from the *s* |
| Job 5:20 | and in war from the power of the *s* |
| Job 15:22 | and he is waited for of the *s* |
| Job 19:29 | Be ye afraid of the *s* |
| Job 19:29 | bringeth the punishments of the *s* |
| Job 20:25 | the glittering *s* cometh out of |
| Job 27:14 | be multiplied, it is for the *s* |
| Job 33:18 | his life from perishing by the *s* |
| Job 36:12 | not, they shall perish by the *s* |
| Job 39:22 | turneth he back from the *s* |
| Job 40:19 | make his *s* to approach unto him |
| Job 41:26 | The *s* of him that layeth at him |
| Ps 7:12 | he turn not, he will whet his *s* |
| Ps 17:13 | from the wicked, which is thy *s* |
| Ps 22:20 | Deliver my soul from the *s* |
| Ps 37:14 | The wicked have drawn out the *s* |
| Ps 37:15 | Their *s* shall enter into their |
| Ps 42:10 | As with a *s* in my bones, mine |
| Ps 44:3 | land in possession by their own *s* |
| Ps 44:6 | bow, neither shall my *s* save me |
| Ps 45:3 | Gird thy *s* upon thy thigh, O most |
| Ps 57:4 | arrows, and their tongue a sharp *s* |
| Ps 63:10 | They shall fall by the *s* |
| Ps 64:3 | Who whet their tongue like a *s* |
| Ps 76:3 | of the bow, the shield, and the *s* |
| Ps 78:62 | his people over also unto the *s* |
| Ps 78:64 | Their priests fell by the *s* |
| Ps 89:43 | also turned the edge of his *s* |
| Ps 144:10 | his servant from the hurtful *s* |
| Ps 149:6 | a twoedged *s* in their hand |
| Prov 5:4 | wormwood, sharp as a twoedged *s* |
| Prov 12:18 | like the piercings of a *s* |
| Prov 25:18 | his neighbour is a maul, and a *s* |
| Song 3:8 | every man hath his *s* upon his |
| Is 1:20 | ye shall be devoured with the *s* |
| Is 2:4 | not lift up *s* against nation |
| Is 3:25 | Thy men shall fall by the *s* |
| Is 13:15 | unto them shall fall by the *s* |
| Is 14:19 | slain, thrust through with a *s* |
| Is 21:15 | from the swords, from the drawn *s* |
| Is 22:2 | men are not slain with the *s* |
| Is 27:1 | strong *s* shall punish leviathan |
| Is 31:8 | the Assyrian fall with the *s* |
| Is 31:8 | and the *s*, not of a mean man, |
| Is 31:8 | but he shall flee from the *s* |
| Is 34:5 | For my *s* shall be bathed in |
| Is 34:6 | The *s* of the LORD is filled with |
| Is 37:7 | to fall by the *s* in his own land |
| Is 37:38 | his sons smote him with the *s* |
| Is 41:2 | he gave them as the dust to his *s* |
| Is 49:2 | hath made my mouth like a sharp *s* |
| Is 51:19 | and the famine, and the *s* |
| Is 65:12 | will I number you to the *s* |
| Is 66:16 | by his *s* will the LORD plead with |
| Jer 2:30 | your own *s* hath devoured your |
| Jer 4:10 | whereas the *s* reacheth unto the |
| Jer 5:12 | neither shall we see *s* nor famine |
| Jer 5:17 | thou trustedst, with the *s* |
| Jer 6:25 | for the *s* of the enemy and fear is |
| Jer 9:16 | and I will send a *s* after them |
| Jer 11:22 | the young men shall die by the *s* |
| Jer 12:12 | for the *s* of the LORD shall |
| Jer 14:12 | but I will consume them by the *s* |
| Jer 14:13 | unto them, Ye shall not see the *s* |
| Jer 14:15 | I sent them not, yet they say, *S* |
| Jer 14:15 | By *s* and famine shall those |
| Jer 14:16 | because of the famine and the *s* |
| Jer 14:18 | then behold the slain with the *s* |
| Jer 15:2 | as are for the *s*, to the *s* |
| Jer 15:3 | the *s* to slay, and the dogs to |
| Jer 15:9 | to the *s* before their enemies |
| Jer 16:4 | they shall be consumed by the *s* |
| Jer 18:21 | their blood by the force of the *s* |
| Jer 18:21 | men be slain by the *s* in battle |
| Jer 19:7 | by the *s* before their enemies |
| Jer 20:4 | fall by the *s* of their enemies |
| Jer 20:4 | and shall slay them with the *s* |
| Jer 21:7 | from the pestilence, from the *s* |
| Jer 21:7 | smite them with the edge of the *s* |
| Jer 21:9 | in this city shall die by the *s* |
| Jer 24:10 | And I will send the *s*, the famine, |
| Jer 25:16 | because of the *s* that I will send |
| Jer 25:27 | because of the *s* which I will |
| Jer 25:29 | for I will call for a *s* upon all |
| Jer 25:31 | them that are wicked to the *s* |
| Jer 26:23 | who slew him with the *s*, and cast |
| Jer 27:8 | saith the LORD, with the *s* |
| Jer 27:13 | die, thou and thy people, by the *s* |
| Jer 29:17 | I will send upon them the *s* |
| Jer 29:18 | I will persecute them with the *s* |
| Jer 31:2 | *s* found grace in the wilderness |
| Jer 32:24 | against it, because of the *s* |
| Jer 32:36 | of the king of Babylon by the *s* |
| Jer 33:4 | down by the mounts, and by the *s* |
| Jer 34:4 | thee, Thou shalt not die by the *s* |
| Jer 34:17 | for you, saith the LORD, to the *s* |
| Jer 38:2 | in this city shall die by the *s* |
| Jer 39:18 | and thou shalt not fall by the *s* |
| Jer 41:2 | the son of Shaphan with the *s* |
| Jer 42:16 | it shall come to pass, that the *s* |
| Jer 42:17 | they shall die by the *s*, by the |
| Jer 42:22 | that ye shall die by the *s* |
| Jer 43:11 | as are for the *s* to the *s* |
| Jer 44:12 | shall even be consumed by the *s* |
| Jer 44:12 | even unto the greatest, by the *s* |
| Jer 44:13 | have punished Jerusalem, by the *s* |
| Jer 44:18 | and have been consumed by the *s* |
| Jer 44:27 | Egypt shall be consumed by the *s* |
| Jer 44:28 | a small number that escape the *s* |
| Jer 46:10 | the *s* shall devour, and it shall |
| Jer 46:14 | for the *s* shall devour round |
| Jer 46:16 | nativity, from the oppressing *s* |
| Jer 47:6 | O thou *s* of the LORD, how long |
| Jer 48:2 | the *s* shall pursue thee |
| Jer 48:10 | keepeth back his *s* from blood |
| Jer 49:37 | and I will send the *s* after them |
| Jer 50:16 | for fear of the oppressing *s* they |
| Jer 50:35 | A *s* is upon the Chaldeans, saith |
| Jer 50:36 | A *s* is upon the liars |
| Jer 50:36 | a *s* is upon her mighty men |
| Jer 50:37 | A *s* is upon their horses, and upon |
| Jer 50:37 | a *s* is upon her treasures |
| Jer 51:50 | Ye that have escaped the *s* |
| Lam 1:20 | abroad the *s* bereaveth, at home |
| Lam 2:21 | my young men are fallen by the *s* |
| Lam 4:9 | They that be slain with the *s* are |
| Lam 5:9 | of the *s* of the wilderness |
| Eze 5:2 | and I will draw out a *s* after them |
| Eze 5:12 | fall by the *s* round about thee |
| Eze 5:12 | and I will draw out a *s* after them |
| Eze 5:17 | and I will bring the *s* upon thee |
| Eze 6:3 | even I, will bring a *s* upon you |
| Eze 6:8 | escape the *s* among the nations |
| Eze 6:11 | for they shall fall by the *s* |
| Eze 6:12 | that is near shall fall by the *s* |
| Eze 7:15 | The *s* is without, and the |

Eze 7:15 in the field shall die with the s
Eze 11:8 Ye have feared the s
Eze 11:8 and I will bring a s upon you
Eze 11:10 Ye shall fall by the s
Eze 12:14 I will draw out the s after them
Eze 12:16 a few men of them from the s
Eze 14:17 a s upon that land, and say, S
Eze 14:21 judgments upon Jerusalem, the s
Eze 17:21 all his bands shall fall by the s
Eze 21:3 draw forth my s out of his sheath
Eze 21:4 therefore shall my s go forth out
Eze 21:5 forth my s out of his sheath
Eze 21:9 Say, A s, a s is sharpened,
Eze 21:11 this s is sharpened, and it is
Eze 21:12 of the s shall be upon my people
Eze 21:13 what if the s contemn even the
Eze 21:14 let the s be doubled the third
Eze 21:14 third time, the s of the slain
Eze 21:14 it is the s of the great men that
Eze 21:15 of the s against all their gates
Eze 21:19 that the s of the king of Babylon
Eze 21:20 that the s may come to Rabbath of
Eze 21:28 thou, The s, the s is drawn
Eze 23:10 daughters, and slew her with the s
Eze 23:25 thy remnant shall fall by the s
Eze 24:21 ye have left shall fall by the s
Eze 25:13 they of Dedan shall fall by the s
Eze 26:6 the field shall be slain by the s
Eze 26:8 He shall slay with the s thy
Eze 26:11 he shall slay thy people by the s
Eze 28:23 by the s upon her on every side
Eze 29:8 I will bring a s upon thee
Eze 30:4 the s shall come upon Egypt, and
Eze 30:5 shall fall with them by the s
Eze 30:6 shall they fall in it by the s
Eze 30:17 of Pi-beseth shall fall by the s
Eze 30:21 to make it strong to hold the s
Eze 30:22 I will cause the s to fall out of
Eze 30:24 Babylon, and put my s in his hand
Eze 30:25 when I shall put my s into the
Eze 31:17 them that be slain with the s
Eze 31:18 with them that be slain by the s
Eze 32:10 I shall brandish my s before them
Eze 32:11 The s of the king of Babylon
Eze 32:20 of them that are slain by the s
Eze 32:20 she is delivered to the s
Eze 32:21 lie uncircumcised, slain by the s
Eze 32:22 of them slain, fallen by the s
Eze 32:23 of them slain, fallen by the s
Eze 32:24 of them slain, fallen by the s
Eze 32:25 uncircumcised, slain by the s
Eze 32:26 uncircumcised, slain by the s
Eze 32:28 them that are slain with the s
Eze 32:29 by them that were slain by the s
Eze 32:30 with them that be slain by the s
Eze 32:31 and all his army slain by the s
Eze 32:32 them that are slain with the s
Eze 33:2 When I bring the s upon a land
Eze 33:3 he seeth the s come upon the land
Eze 33:4 if the s come, and take him away,
Eze 33:6 if the watchman see the s come
Eze 33:6 if the s come, and take any person
Eze 33:26 Ye stand upon your s, ye work
Eze 33:27 in the wastes shall fall by the s
Eze 35:5 s in the time of their calamity
Eze 35:8 fall that are slain with the s
Eze 38:8 that is brought back from the s
Eze 38:21 I will call for a s against him
Eze 38:21 every man's s shall be against
Eze 39:23 so fell they all by the s
Dan 11:33 yet they shall fall by the s
Hos 1:7 not save them by bow, nor by s
Hos 2:18 and I will break the bow and the s
Hos 7:16 s for the rage of their tongue
Hos 11:6 the s shall abide on his cities,
Hos 13:16 they shall fall by the s
Joel 2:8 and when they fall upon the s
Amos 1:11 did pursue his brother with the s
Amos 4:10 young men have I slain with the s
Amos 7:9 the house of Jeroboam with the s
Amos 7:11 Jeroboam shall die by the s
Amos 7:17 thy daughters shall fall by the s
Amos 9:1 slay the last of them with the s
Amos 9:4 thence will I command the s
Amos 9:10 of my people shall die by the s
Mic 4:3 not lift up a s against nation
Mic 5:6 the land of Assyria with the s
Mic 6:14 will I give up to the s
Nah 2:13 the s shall devour thy young
Nah 3:3 lifteth up both the bright s
Nah 3:15 the s shall cut thee off, it
Zeph 2:12 also, ye shall be slain by my s
Hag 2:22 every one by the s of his brother
Zec 9:13 thee as the s of a mighty man
Zec 11:17 the s shall be upon his arm, and
Zec 13:7 Awake, O s, against my shepherd,
Mt 10:34 I came not to send peace, but a s
Mt 26:51 out his hand, and drew his s
Mt 26:52 Put up again thy s into his place
Mt 26:52 the s shall perish with the s
Mk 14:47 of them that stood by drew a s
Lk 2:35 a s shall pierce through thy own
Lk 21:24 shall fall by the edge of the s
Lk 22:36 and he that hath no s, let him
Lk 22:49 Lord, shall we smite with the s
Jn 18:10 Simon Peter having a s drew it
Jn 18:11 Put up thy s into the sheath
Acts 12:2 the brother of John with the s
Acts 16:27 doors open, he drew out his s
Rom 8:35 or nakedness, or peril, or s
Rom 13:4 for he beareth not the s in vain
Eph 6:17 the s of the Spirit, which is the
Heb 4:12 and sharper than any twoedged s
Heb 11:34 fire, escaped the edge of the s
Heb 11:37 tempted, were slain with the s
Rev 1:16 his mouth went a sharp twoedged s
Rev 2:12 hath the sharp s with two edges
Rev 2:16 them with the s of my mouth
Rev 6:4 was given unto him a great s
Rev 6:8 part of the earth, to kill with s
Rev 13:10 he that killeth with the s must
Rev 13:10 must be killed with the s
Rev 13:14 beast, which had the wound by a s
Rev 19:15 out of his mouth goeth a sharp s
Rev 19:21 s of him that sat upon the horse
Rev 19:21 which s proceeded out of his

**SWORDS**
1Sa 13:19 the Hebrews make them s or spears
2Kin 3:26 him seven hundred men that drew s
Neh 4:13 after their families with their s
Ps 55:21 than oil, yet were they drawn s
Ps 59:7 s are in their lips
Prov 30:14 generation, whose teeth are as s
Song 3:8 They all hold s, being expert in
Is 2:4 beat their s into plowshares
Is 21:15 For they fled from the s, from
Eze 16:40 thrust thee through with their s
Eze 23:47 and dispatch them with their s
Eze 28:7 they shall draw their s against
Eze 30:11 shall draw their s against Egypt
Eze 32:12 By the s of the mighty will I
Eze 32:27 laid their s under their heads
Eze 38:4 shields, all of them handling s
Joel 3:10 Beat your plowshares into s
Mic 4:3 beat their s into plowshares
Mt 26:47 with him a great multitude with s
Mt 26:55 out as against a thief with s
Mk 14:43 with him a great multitude with s
Mk 14:48 out, as against a thief, with s
Lk 22:38 Lord, behold, here are two s
Lk 22:52 out, as against a thief, with s

**SWORN**
Gen 22:16 And said, By myself have I s
Ex 13:19 for he had straitly s the
Ex 17:16 Because the LORD hath s
Lev 6:5 about which he hath s falsely
Deut 7:8 which he had s unto your fathers
Deut 13:17 as he hath s unto thy fathers
Deut 19:8 as he hath s unto thy fathers, and
Deut 28:9 himself, as he hath s unto thee
Deut 29:13 as he hath s unto thy fathers, to
Deut 31:7 the land which the LORD hath s
Josh 9:18 s unto them by the LORD God of
Josh 9:19 We have s unto them by the LORD
Judg 2:15 and as the LORD had s unto them
Judg 21:1 the men of Israel had s in Mizpeh
Judg 21:7 seeing we have s by the LORD that
Judg 21:18 for the children of Israel have s
1Sa 3:14 therefore I have s unto the house
1Sa 20:42 forasmuch as we have s both of us
2Sa 3:9 as the LORD hath s to David
2Sa 21:2 of Israel had s unto them
2Chr 15:15 for they had s with all their
Neh 6:18 were many in Judah s unto him
Neh 9:15 which thou hadst s to give them
Ps 24:4 unto vanity, nor s deceitfully
Ps 89:3 I have s unto David my servant,
Ps 89:35 Once have I s by my holiness that
Ps 102:8 mad against me are s against me
Ps 110:4 The LORD hath s, and will not
Ps 119:106 I have s, and I will perform it,
Ps 132:11 The LORD hath s in truth unto
Is 14:24 The LORD of hosts hath s, saying,
Is 45:23 I have s by myself, the word is
Is 54:9 for as I have s that the waters
Is 54:9 so have I s that I would not be
Is 62:8 The LORD hath s by his right hand
Jer 5:7 s by them that are no gods
Jer 11:5 which I have s unto your fathers
Jer 44:26 I have s by my great name, saith
Jer 49:13 For I have s by myself, saith the
Jer 51:14 LORD of hosts hath s by himself
Eze 21:23 sight, to them that have s oaths
Amos 4:2 Lord GOD hath s by his holiness
Amos 6:8 The Lord GOD hath s by himself
Amos 8:7 The LORD hath s by the excellency
Mic 7:20 which thou hast s unto our
Acts 2:30 God had s with an oath to him
Acts 7:17 nigh, which God had s to Abraham
Heb 4:3 As I have s in my wrath, if they

**SYCAMINE**
Lk 17:6 ye might say unto this s tree

**SYCHAR** *(si'-kar)* See SHECHEM. *A city in Samaria.*
Jn 4:5 of Samaria, which is called S

**SYCHEM** *(si'-kem)* See SHECHEM. *Same as Shechem.*
Acts 7:16 And were carried over into S
Acts 7:16 the sons of Emmor the father of S

**SYCOMORE**
1Kin 10:27 the s trees that are in the vale
1Chr 27:28 the s trees that were in the low
2Chr 1:15 cedar trees made he as the s
2Chr 9:27 the s trees that are in the low
Ps 78:47 hail, and their s trees with frost
Amos 7:14 herdman, and a gatherer of s fruit
Lk 19:4 up into a s tree to see him

**SYCOMORES**
Is 9:10 the s are cut down, but we will

**SYENE** *(si-e'-ne) An Egyptian city.*
Eze 29:10 from the tower of S even unto the
Eze 30:6 from the tower of S shall they

**SYNAGOGUE**
Mt 12:9 thence, he went into their s
Mt 13:54 he taught them in their s
Mk 1:21 sabbath day he entered into the s
Mk 1:23 there was in their s a man with
Mk 1:29 when they were come out of the s
Mk 3:1 And he entered again into the s
Mk 5:22 cometh one of the rulers of the s
Mk 5:36 he saith unto the ruler of the s
Mk 5:38 the house of the ruler of the s
Mk 6:2 come, he began to teach in the s
Lk 4:16 he went into the s on the sabbath
Lk 4:20 in the s were fastened on him
Lk 4:28 And all they in the s, when they
Lk 4:33 in the s there was a man, which
Lk 4:38 And he arose out of the s, and
Lk 6:6 that he entered into the s
Lk 7:5 nation, and he hath built us a s
Lk 8:41 and he was a ruler of the s
Lk 13:14 the ruler of the s answered with
Jn 6:59 These things said he in the s
Jn 9:22 he should be put out of the s
Jn 12:42 they should be put out of the s
Jn 18:20 I ever taught in the s, and in the
Acts 6:9 Then there arose certain of the s
Acts 6:9 is called the s of the Libertines
Acts 13:14 went into the s on the sabbath
Acts 13:15 rulers of the s sent unto them
Acts 13:42 the Jews were gone out of the s
Acts 14:1 together into the s of the Jews
Acts 17:1 where was a s of the Jews
Acts 17:10 went into the s of the Jews
Acts 17:17 he in the s with the Jews
Acts 18:4 reasoned in the s every sabbath
Acts 18:7 whose house joined hard to the s
Acts 18:8 Crispus, the chief ruler of the s
Acts 18:17 the chief ruler of the s
Acts 18:19 but he himself entered into the s
Acts 18:26 he began to speak boldly in the s
Acts 19:8 And he went into the s, and spake
Acts 22:19 beat in every s them that
Acts 26:11 And I punished them oft in every s
Rev 2:9 are not, but are the s of Satan
Rev 3:9 will make them of the s of Satan

**SYNAGOGUE'S**
Mk 5:35 of the *s* house certain which said
Lk 8:49 one from the ruler of the *s* house

**SYNAGOGUES**
Ps 74:8 up all the *s* of God in the land
Mt 4:23 all Galilee, teaching in their *s*
Mt 6:2 as the hypocrites do in the *s*
Mt 6:5 love to pray standing in the *s*
Mt 9:35 and villages, teaching in their *s*
Mt 10:17 they will scourge you in their *s*
Mt 23:6 and the chief seats in the *s*
Mt 23:34 them shall ye scourge in your *s*
Mk 1:39 he preached in their *s* throughout
Mk 12:39 And the chief seats in the *s*
Mk 13:9 in the *s* ye shall be beaten
Lk 4:15 And he taught in their *s*, being
Lk 4:44 he preached in the *s* of Galilee
Lk 11:43 love the uppermost seats in the *s*
Lk 12:11 And when they bring you unto the *s*
Lk 13:10 in one of the *s* on the sabbath
Lk 20:46 and the highest seats in the *s*
Lk 21:12 you, delivering you up to the *s*
Jn 16:2 They shall put you out of the *s*
Acts 9:2 him letters to Damascus to the *s*
Acts 9:20 he preached Christ in the *s*
Acts 13:5 word of God in the *s* of the Jews
Acts 15:21 read in the *s* every sabbath day
Acts 24:12 up the people, neither in the *s*

**SYNTYCHE** *(sin'-ti-ke) A Christian at Philippi.*
Phil 4:2 I beseech Euodias, and beseech *S*

**SYRACUSE** *(sir'-a-cuse) A city on Sicily.*
Acts 28:12 And landing at *S*, we tarried there

**SYRIA** *(sir'-e-ah)* See ARAM, SYRIA-DAMASCUS, SYRIA-MAACHAH, SYRIAN. *Nation north of Israel.*
Judg 10:6 and Ashtaroth, and the gods of *S*
2Sa 8:6 put garrisons in *S* of Damascus
2Sa 8:12 Of *S*, and of Moab, and of the
2Sa 15:8 vow while I abode at Geshur in *S*
1Kin 10:29 Hittites, and for the kings of *S*
1Kin 11:25 Israel, and reigned over *S*
1Kin 15:18 the son of Hezion, king of *S*
1Kin 19:15 anoint Hazael to be king over *S*
1Kin 20:1 Ben-hadad the king of *S* gathered
1Kin 20:20 Ben-hadad the king of *S* escaped
1Kin 20:22 of *S* will come up against thee
1Kin 20:23 of the king of *S* said unto him
1Kin 22:1 three years without war between *S*
1Kin 22:3 out of the hand of the king of *S*
1Kin 22:31 But the king of *S* commanded his
2Kin 5:1 of the host of the king of *S*
2Kin 5:1 LORD had given deliverance unto *S*
2Kin 5:5 And the king of *S* said, Go to, go,
2Kin 6:8 Then the king of *S* warred against
2Kin 6:11 the heart of the king of *S* was
2Kin 6:23 So the bands of *S* came no more
2Kin 6:24 king of *S* gathered all his host
2Kin 7:5 uttermost part of the camp of *S*
2Kin 8:7 Ben-hadad the king of *S* was sick
2Kin 8:9 king of *S* hath sent me to thee
2Kin 8:13 me that thou shalt be king over *S*
2Kin 8:28 Hazael king of *S* in Ramoth-gilead
2Kin 8:29 fought against Hazael king of *S*
2Kin 9:14 because of Hazael king of *S*
2Kin 9:15 he fought with Hazael king of *S*
2Kin 12:17 Then Hazael king of *S* went up
2Kin 12:18 and sent it to Hazael king of *S*
2Kin 13:3 into the hand of Hazael king of *S*
2Kin 13:4 the king of *S* oppressed them
2Kin 13:7 for the king of *S* had destroyed
2Kin 13:17 the arrow of deliverance from *S*
2Kin 13:19 then hadst thou smitten *S* till
2Kin 13:19 now thou shalt smite *S* but thrice
2Kin 13:22 But Hazael king of *S* oppressed
2Kin 13:24 So Hazael king of *S* died
2Kin 15:37 against Judah Rezin the king of *S*
2Kin 16:5 Then Rezin king of *S* and Pekah son
2Kin 16:6 of *S* recovered Elath to *S*
2Kin 16:7 out of the hand of the king of *S*
2Chr 1:17 Hittites, and for the kings of *S*
2Chr 16:2 and sent to Ben-hadad king of *S*
2Chr 16:7 thou hast relied on the king of *S*
2Chr 16:7 of *S* escaped out of thine hand
2Chr 18:10 push *S* until they be consumed
2Chr 18:30 Now the king of *S* had commanded
2Chr 20:2 beyond the sea on this side *S*
2Chr 22:5 Hazael king of *S* at Ramoth-gilead
2Chr 22:6 he fought with Hazael king of *S*
2Chr 24:23 that the host of *S* came up
2Chr 28:5 into the hand of the king of *S*
2Chr 28:23 gods of the kings of *S* help them
Is 7:1 Judah, that Rezin the king of *S*
Is 7:2 *S* is confederate with Ephraim
Is 7:4 the fierce anger of Rezin with *S*
Is 7:5 Because *S*, Ephraim, and the son of
Is 7:8 For the head of *S* is Damascus
Is 17:3 Damascus, and the remnant of *S*
Eze 16:57 reproach of the daughters of *S*
Eze 27:16 *S* was thy merchant by reason of
Hos 12:12 Jacob fled into the country of *S*
Amos 1:5 the people of *S* shall go into
Mt 4:24 And his fame went throughout all *S*
Lk 2:2 when Cyrenius was governor of *S*
Acts 15:23 of the Gentiles in Antioch and *S*
Acts 15:41 And he went through *S* and Cilicia,
Acts 18:18 brethren, and sailed thence into *S*
Acts 20:3 as he was about to sail into *S*
Acts 21:3 the left hand, and sailed into *S*
Gal 1:21 I came into the regions of *S*

**SYRIACK** *(sir'-e-ak)* See SYRIAN. *Language of the Syrians.*
Dan 2:4 the Chaldeans to the king in *S*

**SYRIA-DAMASCUS** *(sir'-e-ah-da-mas'-cus)* See SYRIA, DAMASCUS. *Same as Damascus.*
1Chr 18:6 Then David put garrisons in *S*

**SYRIA-MAACHAH** *(sir'-e-ah-ma-a-kah) A Syrian city-state.*
1Chr 19:6 out of Mesopotamia, and out of *S*

**SYRIAN** *(sir'-e-un)* See ARAMITES, SYRIANS, SYROPHENICIAN.
*1. An inhabitant of Syria.*
Gen 25:20 of Bethuel the *S* of Padan-aram
Gen 25:20 the sister to Laban the *S*
Gen 28:5 unto Laban, son of Bethuel the *S*
Gen 31:20 away unawares to Laban the *S*
Gen 31:24 Laban the *S* in a dream by night
Deut 26:5 A *S* ready to perish was my father
2Kin 5:20 master hath spared Naaman this *S*
Lk 4:27 was cleansed, saving Naaman the *S*
*2. The language of Syria.*
2Kin 18:26 to thy servants in the *S* language
Ezr 4:7 was written in the *S* tongue
Ezr 4:7 and interpreted in the *S* tongue
Is 36:11 thy servants in the *S* language

**SYRIANS**
2Sa 8:5 when the *S* of Damascus came to
2Sa 8:5 of Zobah, David slew of the *S* two
2Sa 8:6 the *S* became servants to David,
2Sa 8:13 of the *S* in the valley of salt
2Sa 10:6 hired the *S* of Beth-rehob, and the
2Sa 10:6 the *S* of Zoba, twenty thousand
2Sa 10:8 the *S* of Zoba, and of Rehob, and
2Sa 10:9 put them in array against the *S*
2Sa 10:11 If the *S* be too strong for me,
2Sa 10:13 unto the battle against the *S*
2Sa 10:14 of Ammon saw that the *S* were fled
2Sa 10:15 when the *S* saw that they were
2Sa 10:16 brought out the *S* that were
2Sa 10:17 the *S* set themselves in array
2Sa 10:18 And the *S* fled before Israel
2Sa 10:18 seven hundred chariots of the *S*
2Sa 10:19 So the *S* feared to help the
1Kin 20:20 and the *S* fled
1Kin 20:21 slew the *S* with a great slaughter
1Kin 20:26 that Ben-hadad numbered the *S*
1Kin 20:27 but the *S* filled the country
1Kin 20:28 the LORD, Because the *S* have said
1Kin 20:29 *S* an hundred thousand footmen in
1Kin 22:11 With these shalt thou push the *S*
1Kin 22:35 up in his chariot against the *S*
2Kin 5:2 the *S* had gone out by companies,
2Kin 6:9 for thither the *S* are come down
2Kin 7:4 us fall unto the host of the *S*
2Kin 7:5 to go unto the camp of the *S*
2Kin 7:6 the *S* to hear a noise of chariots
2Kin 7:10 We came to the camp of the *S*
2Kin 7:12 you what the *S* have done to us
2Kin 7:14 king sent after the host of the *S*
2Kin 7:15 which the *S* had cast away in
2Kin 7:16 and spoiled the tents of the *S*
2Kin 8:28 and the *S* wounded Joram
2Kin 8:29 the *S* had given him at Ramah
2Kin 9:15 wounds which the *S* had given him
2Kin 13:5 out from under the hand of the *S*
2Kin 13:17 thou shalt smite the *S* in Aphek
2Kin 16:6 the *S* came to Elath, and dwelt
2Kin 24:2 the Chaldees, and bands of the *S*
1Chr 18:5 when the *S* of Damascus came to
1Chr 18:5 of Zobah, David slew of the *S* two
1Chr 18:6 the *S* became David's servants, and
1Chr 19:10 put them in array against the *S*
1Chr 19:12 If the *S* be too strong for me,
1Chr 19:14 nigh before the *S* unto the battle
1Chr 19:15 of Ammon saw that the *S* were fled
1Chr 19:16 when the *S* saw that they were put
1Chr 19:16 drew forth the *S* that were beyond
1Chr 19:17 the battle in array against the *S*
1Chr 19:18 But the *S* fled before Israel
1Chr 19:18 David slew of the *S* seven
1Chr 19:19 neither would the *S* help the
2Chr 18:34 against the *S* until the even
2Chr 22:5 and the *S* smote Joram
2Chr 24:24 For the army of the *S* came with a
Is 9:12 The *S* before, and the Philistines
Jer 35:11 and for fear of the army of the *S*
Amos 9:7 from Caphtor, and the *S* from Kir

**SYROPHENICIAN** *(sy'-ro-fe-ne'-she-un) A citizen of Phenicia in Syria.*
Mk 7:26 woman was a Greek, a *S* by nation

# T

**TAANACH** *(ta'-a-nak)* See TANACH. *A Levitical city in Manasseh.*
Josh 12:21 The king of *T*, one
Josh 17:11 towns, and the inhabitants of *T*
Judg 1:27 of Beth-shean and her towns, nor *T*
Judg 5:19 in *T* by the waters of Megiddo
1Kin 4:12 to him pertained *T* and Megiddo, and
1Chr 7:29 Beth-shean and her towns, *T*

**TAANATH-SHILOH** *(ta'-a-nath-shi'-lo) A city on the border of Benjamin.*
Josh 16:6 border went about eastward unto *T*

**TABBAOTH** *(tab'-ba-oth) A family of exiles.*
Ezr 2:43 of Hasupha, the children of *T*
Neh 7:46 of Hashupha, the children of *T*

**TABBATH** *(tab'-bath) A city in Issachar.*
Judg 7:22 border of Abel-meholah, unto *T*

**TABEAL** *(tab'-e-al)* See TABEEL. *Father of a would-be king of Israel.*
Is 7:6 midst of it, even the son of *T*

**TABEEL** *(tab'-e-el)* See TABEAL. *A Persian official in Samaria.*
Ezr 4:7 wrote Bishlam, Mithredath, *T*

**TABERAH** *(tab'-e-rah) A place in the wilderness of Paran.*
Num 11:3 he called the name of the place *T*
Deut 9:22 And at *T*, and at Massah, and at

**TABERING**
Nah 2:7 of doves, *t* upon their breasts

**TABERNACLE**
Ex 25:9 thee, after the pattern of the *t*
Ex 26:1 the *t* with ten curtains of fine
Ex 26:6 and it shall be one *t*
Ex 26:7 hair to be a covering upon the *t*
Ex 26:9 curtain in the forefront of the *t*

Ex 26:12 hang over the backside of the *t*
Ex 26:13 the sides of the *t* on this side
Ex 26:15 the *t* of shittim wood standing up
Ex 26:17 make for all the boards of the *t*
Ex 26:18 shalt make the boards for the *t*
Ex 26:20 for the second side of the *t* on
Ex 26:22 for the sides of the *t* westward
Ex 26:23 corners of the *t* in the two sides
Ex 26:26 boards of the one side of the *t*
Ex 26:27 boards of the other side of the *t*
Ex 26:27 the boards of the side of the *t*
Ex 26:30 And thou shalt rear up the *t*
Ex 26:35 side of the *t* toward the south
Ex 27:9 shalt make the court of the *t*
Ex 27:19 All the vessels of the *t* in all
Ex 27:21 In the *t* of the congregation
Ex 28:43 in unto the *t* of the congregation
Ex 29:4 door of the *t* of the congregation
Ex 29:10 before the *t* of the congregation
Ex 29:11 by the door of the *t* of the
Ex 29:30 when he cometh into the *t* of the
Ex 29:32 by the door of the *t* of the
Ex 29:42 *t* of the congregation before the
Ex 29:43 the *t* shall be sanctified by my
Ex 29:44 the *t* of the congregation
Ex 30:16 of the *t* of the congregation
Ex 30:18 between the *t* of the congregation
Ex 30:20 go into the *t* of the congregation
Ex 30:26 thou shalt anoint the *t* of the
Ex 30:36 in the *t* of the congregation
Ex 31:7 The *t* of the congregation, and the
Ex 31:7 and all the furniture of the *t*
Ex 33:7 And Moses took the *t*, and pitched
Ex 33:7 camp, and called it the *T* of the
Ex 33:7 unto the *t* of the congregation
Ex 33:8 when Moses went out unto the *t*
Ex 33:8 until he was gone into the *t*
Ex 33:9 pass, as Moses entered into the *t*
Ex 33:9 and stood at the door of the *t*
Ex 33:10 cloudy pillar stand at the *t* door
Ex 33:11 man, departed not out of the *t*
Ex 35:11 The *t*, his tent, and his covering,
Ex 35:15 door at the entering in of the *t*
Ex 35:18 The pins of the *t*, and the pins of
Ex 35:21 work of the *t* of the congregation
Ex 36:8 the *t* made ten curtains of fine
Ex 36:13 so it became one *t*
Ex 36:14 hair for the tent over the *t*
Ex 36:20 boards for the *t* of shittim wood
Ex 36:22 make for all the boards of the *t*
Ex 36:23 And he made boards for the *t*
Ex 36:25 And for the other side of the *t*
Ex 36:27 for the sides of the *t* westward
Ex 36:28 corners of the *t* in the two sides
Ex 36:31 boards of the one side of the *t*
Ex 36:32 boards of the other side of the *t*
Ex 36:32 of the *t* for the sides westward
Ex 36:37 an hanging for the *t* door of blue
Ex 38:8 door of the *t* of the congregation
Ex 38:20 And all the pins of the *t*, and of
Ex 38:21 This is the sum of the *t*, even of
Ex 38:21 even of the *t* of testimony, as it
Ex 38:30 door of the *t* of the congregation
Ex 38:31 gate, and all the pins of the *t*
Ex 39:32 Thus was all the work of the *t* of
Ex 39:33 And they brought the *t* unto Moses
Ex 39:38 and the hanging for the *t* door
Ex 39:40 vessels of the service of the *t*
Ex 40:2 month shalt thou set up the *t* of
Ex 40:5 the hanging of the door to the *t*
Ex 40:6 *t* of the tent of the congregation
Ex 40:9 anointing oil, and anoint the *t*
Ex 40:12 door of the *t* of the congregation
Ex 40:17 month, that the *t* was reared up
Ex 40:18 And Moses reared up the *t*, and
Ex 40:19 spread abroad the tent over the *t*
Ex 40:21 And he brought the ark into the *t*
Ex 40:22 upon the side of the *t* northward
Ex 40:24 on the side of the *t* southward
Ex 40:28 the hanging at the door of the *t*
Ex 40:29 offering by the door of the *t* of
Ex 40:33 up the court round about the *t*
Ex 40:34 glory of the LORD filled the *t*
Ex 40:35 glory of the LORD filled the *t*
Ex 40:36 was taken up from over the *t*
Ex 40:38 of the LORD was upon the *t* by day
Lev 1:1 out of the *t* of the congregation
Lev 1:3 will at the door of the *t* of the
Lev 1:5 door of the *t* of the congregation
Lev 3:2 door of the *t* of the congregation
Lev 3:8 kill it before the *t* of the
Lev 3:13 kill it before the *t* of the
Lev 4:4 bullock unto the door of the *t* of
Lev 4:5 and bring it to the *t* of the
Lev 4:7 LORD, which is in the *t* of the
Lev 4:7 door of the *t* of the congregation
Lev 4:14 before the *t* of the congregation
Lev 4:16 to the *t* of the congregation
Lev 4:18 the LORD, that is in the *t* of the
Lev 4:18 door of the *t* of the congregation
Lev 6:16 in the court of the *t* of the
Lev 6:26 of the *t* of the congregation
Lev 6:30 into the *t* of the congregation to
Lev 8:3 door of the *t* of the congregation
Lev 8:4 door of the *t* of the congregation
Lev 8:10 anointing oil, and anointed the *t*
Lev 8:31 door of the *t* of the congregation
Lev 8:33 *t* of the congregation in seven
Lev 8:35 of the *t* of the congregation day
Lev 9:5 before the *t* of the congregation
Lev 9:23 into the *t* of the congregation
Lev 10:7 door of the *t* of the congregation
Lev 10:9 go into the *t* of the congregation
Lev 12:6 door of the *t* of the congregation
Lev 14:11 at the door of the *t* of the
Lev 14:23 door of the *t* of the congregation
Lev 15:14 door of the *t* of the congregation
Lev 15:29 to the door of the *t* of the
Lev 15:31 defile my *t* that is among them
Lev 16:7 door of the *t* of the congregation
Lev 16:16 do for the *t* of the congregation
Lev 16:17 the *t* of the congregation when he
Lev 16:20 the *t* of the congregation, and the
Lev 16:23 into the *t* of the congregation
Lev 16:33 for the *t* of the congregation
Lev 17:4 door of the *t* of the congregation
Lev 17:4 the LORD before the *t* of the LORD
Lev 17:5 door of the *t* of the congregation
Lev 17:6 door of the *t* of the congregation
Lev 17:9 door of the *t* of the congregation
Lev 19:21 door of the *t* of the congregation
Lev 24:3 in the *t* of the congregation,
Lev 26:11 And I will set my *t* among you
Num 1:1 in the *t* of the congregation, on
Num 1:50 Levites over the *t* of testimony
Num 1:50 they shall bear the *t*, and all the
Num 1:50 and shall encamp round about the *t*
Num 1:51 when the *t* setteth forward, the
Num 1:51 when the *t* is to be pitched, the
Num 1:53 round about the *t* of testimony
Num 1:53 the charge of the *t* of testimony
Num 2:2 far off about the *t* of the
Num 2:17 Then the *t* of the congregation
Num 3:7 before the *t* of the congregation
Num 3:7 to do the service of the *t*
Num 3:8 of the *t* of the congregation
Num 3:8 to do the service of the *t*
Num 3:23 shall pitch behind the *t* westward
Num 3:25 *t* of the congregation shall be
Num 3:25 the congregation shall be the *t*
Num 3:25 door of the *t* of the congregation
Num 3:26 of the court, which is by the *t*
Num 3:29 on the side of the *t* southward
Num 3:35 on the side of the *t* northward
Num 3:36 shall be the boards of the *t*
Num 3:38 before the *t* toward the east
Num 3:38 even before the *t* of the
Num 4:3 work in the *t* of the congregation
Num 4:4 in the *t* of the congregation
Num 4:15 in the *t* of the congregation
Num 4:16 and the oversight of all the *t*
Num 4:23 work in the *t* of the congregation
Num 4:25 shall bear the curtains of the *t*
Num 4:25 the *t* of the congregation, his
Num 4:25 door of the *t* of the congregation
Num 4:26 of the court, which is by the *t*
Num 4:28 in the *t* of the congregation
Num 4:30 work of the *t* of the congregation
Num 4:31 in the *t* of the congregation
Num 4:31 the boards of the *t*, and the bars
Num 4:33 in the *t* of the congregation,
Num 4:35 work in the *t* of the congregation
Num 4:37 in the *t* of the congregation
Num 4:39 work in the *t* of the congregation
Num 4:41 in the *t* of the congregation
Num 4:43 work in the *t* of the congregation
Num 4:47 in the *t* of the congregation
Num 5:17 of the *t* the priest shall take
Num 6:10 to the door of the *t* of the
Num 6:13 door of the *t* of the congregation
Num 6:18 door of the *t* of the congregation
Num 7:1 that Moses had fully set up the *t*
Num 7:3 and they brought them before the *t*
Num 7:5 of the *t* of the congregation
Num 7:89 *t* of the congregation to speak
Num 8:9 before the *t* of the congregation
Num 8:15 of the *t* of the congregation
Num 8:19 in the *t* of the congregation
Num 8:22 the *t* of the congregation before
Num 8:24 of the *t* of the congregation
Num 8:26 in the *t* of the congregation
Num 9:15 on the day that the *t* was reared
Num 9:15 reared up the cloud covered the *t*
Num 9:15 at even there was upon the *t* as
Num 9:17 the cloud was taken up from the *t*
Num 9:18 the *t* they rested in their tents
Num 9:19 tarried long upon the *t* many days
Num 9:20 cloud was a few days upon the *t*
Num 9:22 that the cloud tarried upon the *t*
Num 10:3 door of the *t* of the congregation
Num 10:11 from off the *t* of the testimony
Num 10:17 And the *t* was taken down
Num 10:17 Merari set forward, bearing the *t*
Num 10:21 set up the *t* against they came
Num 11:16 unto the *t* of the congregation
Num 11:24 and set them round about the *t*
Num 11:26 but went not out unto the *t*
Num 12:4 unto the *t* of the congregation
Num 12:5 and stood in the door of the *t*
Num 12:10 the cloud departed from off the *t*
Num 14:10 of the LORD appeared in the *t* of
Num 16:9 the service of the *t* of the LORD
Num 16:18 stood in the door of the *t* of the
Num 16:19 door of the *t* of the congregation
Num 16:24 you up from about the *t* of Korah
Num 16:27 they gat up from the *t* of Korah
Num 16:42 toward the *t* of the congregation
Num 16:43 before the *t* of the congregation
Num 16:50 door of the *t* of the congregation
Num 17:4 thou shalt lay them up in the *t*
Num 17:7 the LORD in the *t* of witness
Num 17:8 Moses went into the *t* of witness
Num 17:13 unto the *t* of the LORD shall die
Num 18:2 minister before the *t* of witness
Num 18:3 and the charge of all the *t*
Num 18:4 of the *t* of the congregation
Num 18:4 for all the service of the *t*
Num 18:6 of the *t* of the congregation
Num 18:21 of the *t* of the congregation
Num 18:22 nigh the *t* of the congregation
Num 18:23 of the *t* of the congregation
Num 18:31 in the *t* of the congregation
Num 19:4 her blood directly before the *t*
Num 19:13 defileth the *t* of the LORD
Num 20:6 door of the *t* of the congregation
Num 25:6 door of the *t* of the congregation
Num 27:2 by the door of the *t* of the
Num 31:30 the charge of the *t* of the LORD
Num 31:47 the charge of the *t* of the LORD
Num 31:54 it into the *t* of the congregation
Deut 31:14 in the *t* of the congregation
Deut 31:14 in the *t* of the congregation
Deut 31:15 in the *t* in a pillar of a cloud
Deut 31:15 stood over the door of the *t*
Josh 18:1 set up the *t* of the congregation
Josh 19:51 at the door of the *t* of the
Josh 22:19 wherein the LORD's *t* dwelleth
Josh 22:29 LORD our God that is before his *t*
1Sa 2:22 door of the *t* of the congregation
2Sa 6:17 in the midst of the *t* that David
2Sa 7:6 have walked in a tent and in a *t*
1Kin 1:39 took an horn of oil out of the *t*
1Kin 2:28 Joab fled unto the *t* of the LORD
1Kin 2:29 was fled unto the *t* of the LORD
1Kin 2:30 Benaiah came to the *t* of the LORD
1Kin 8:4 the *t* of the congregation, and all
1Kin 8:4 holy vessels that were in the *t*
1Chr 6:32 of the *t* of the congregation with
1Chr 6:48 of the *t* of the house of God
1Chr 9:19 keepers of the gates of the *t*
1Chr 9:21 door of the *t* of the congregation
1Chr 9:23 LORD, namely, the house of the *t*
1Chr 16:39 before the *t* of the LORD in the
1Chr 17:5 to tent, and from one *t* to another
1Chr 21:29 For the *t* of the LORD, which
1Chr 23:26 they shall no more carry the *t*
1Chr 23:32 of the *t* of the congregation
2Chr 1:3 for there was the *t* of the
2Chr 1:5 he put before the *t* of the LORD
2Chr 1:6 which was at the *t* of the

2Chr 1:13 from before the *t* of the
2Chr 5:5 the *t* of the congregation, and all
2Chr 5:5 holy vessels that were in the *t*
2Chr 24:6 of Israel, for the *t* of witness
Job 5:24 know that thy *t* shall be in peace
Job 18:6 The light shall be dark in his *t*
Job 18:14 shall be rooted out of his *t*
Job 18:15 It shall dwell in his *t*, because
Job 19:12 me, and encamp round about my *t*
Job 20:26 with him that is left in his *t*
Job 29:4 the secret of God was upon my *t*
Job 31:31 If the men of my *t* said not
Job 36:29 the clouds, or the noise of his *t*
Ps 15:1 Lord, who shall abide in thy *t*
Ps 19:4 them hath he set a *t* for the sun
Ps 27:5 secret of his *t* shall he hide me
Ps 27:6 offer in his *t* sacrifices of joy
Ps 61:4 I will abide in thy *t* for ever
Ps 76:2 In Salem also is his *t*, and his
Ps 78:60 that he forsook the *t* of Shiloh
Ps 78:67 he refused the *t* of Joseph
Ps 132:3 not come into the *t* of my house
Prov 14:11 but the *t* of the upright shall
Is 4:6 there shall be a *t* for a shadow
Is 16:5 it in truth in the *t* of David
Is 33:20 a *t* that shall not be taken down
Jer 10:20 My *t* is spoiled, and all my cords
Lam 2:4 in the *t* of the daughter of Zion
Lam 2:6 hath violently taken away his *t*
Eze 37:27 My *t* also shall be with them
Eze 41:1 which was the breadth of the *t*
Amos 5:26 have borne the *t* of your Moloch
Amos 9:11 up the *t* of David that is fallen
Acts 7:43 Yea, ye took up the *t* of Moloch
Acts 7:44 Our fathers had the *t* of witness
Acts 7:46 desired to find a *t* for the God
Acts 15:16 will build again the *t* of David
2Cor 5:1 house of this *t* were dissolved
2Cor 5:4 we that are in this *t* do groan
Heb 8:2 the sanctuary, and of the true *t*
Heb 8:5 when he was about to make the *t*
Heb 9:2 For there was a *t* made
Heb 9:3 the *t* which is called the Holiest
Heb 9:6 went always into the first *t*
Heb 9:8 as the first *t* was yet standing
Heb 9:11 by a greater and more perfect *t*
Heb 9:21 sprinkled with blood both the *t*
Heb 13:10 no right to eat which serve the *t*
2Pet 1:13 meet, as long as I am in this *t*
2Pet 1:14 shortly I must put off this my *t*
Rev 13:6 to blaspheme his name, and his *t*
Rev 15:5 the temple of the *t* of the
Rev 21:3 the *t* of God is with men, and he

## TABERNACLES

Lev 23:34 month shall be the feast of *t* for
Num 24:5 are thy tents, O Jacob, and thy *t*
Deut 16:13 observe the feast of *t* seven days
Deut 16:16 of weeks, and in the feast of *t*
Deut 31:10 of release, in the feast of *t*
2Chr 8:13 of weeks, and in the feast of *t*
Ezr 3:4 They kept also the feast of *t*
Job 11:14 let not wickedness dwell in thy *t*
Job 12:6 The *t* of robbers prosper, and they
Job 15:34 shall consume the *t* of bribery
Job 22:23 put away iniquity far from thy *t*
Ps 43:3 unto thy holy hill, and to thy *t*
Ps 46:4 place of the *t* of the most High
Ps 78:51 of their strength in the *t* of Ham
Ps 83:6 The *t* of Edom, and the Ishmaelites
Ps 84:1 How amiable are thy *t*, O LORD of
Ps 118:15 is in the *t* of the righteous
Ps 132:7 We will go into his *t*
Dan 11:45 he shall plant the *t* of his
Hos 9:6 thorns shall be in their *t*
Hos 12:9 will yet make thee to dwell in *t*
Zec 14:16 hosts, and to keep the feast of *t*
Zec 14:18 not up to keep the feast of *t*
Zec 14:19 not up to keep the feast of *t*
Mal 2:12 scholar, out of the *t* of Jacob
Mt 17:4 wilt, let us make here three *t*
Mk 9:5 and let us make three *t*
Lk 9:33 and let us make three *t*
Jn 7:2 the Jews' feast of *t* was at hand
Heb 11:9 country, dwelling in *t* with Isaac

## TABITHA *(tab'-ith-ah) Woman raised from the dead by Peter.*

Acts 9:36 Joppa a certain disciple named *T*
Acts 9:40 turning him to the body said, *T*

## TABLE

Ex 25:23 also make a *t* of shittim wood
Ex 25:27 of the staves to bear the *t*
Ex 25:28 that the *t* may be borne with them
Ex 25:30 thou shalt set upon the *t*
Ex 26:35 shalt set the *t* without the vail
Ex 26:35 candlestick over against the *t* on
Ex 26:35 shalt put the *t* on the north side
Ex 30:27 And the *t* and all his vessels, and
Ex 31:8 And the *t* and his furniture, and the
Ex 35:13 The *t*, and his staves, and all his
Ex 37:10 he made the *t* of shittim wood
Ex 37:14 for the staves to bear the *t*
Ex 37:15 them with gold, to bear the *t*
Ex 37:16 the vessels which were upon the *t*
Ex 39:36 The *t*, and all the vessels thereof
Ex 40:4 And thou shalt bring in the *t*
Ex 40:22 he put the *t* in the tent of the
Ex 40:24 congregation, over against the *t*
Lev 24:6 upon the pure *t* before the LORD
Num 3:31 charge shall be the ark, and the *t*
Num 4:7 upon the *t* of shewbread they
Judg 1:7 gathered their meat under my *t*
1Sa 20:29 he cometh not unto the king's *t*
1Sa 20:34 arose from the *t* in fierce anger
2Sa 9:7 eat bread at my *t* continually
2Sa 9:10 son shall eat bread alway at my *t*
2Sa 9:11 the king, he shall eat at my *t*
2Sa 9:13 eat continually at the king's *t*
2Sa 19:28 them that did eat at thine own *t*
1Kin 2:7 be of those that eat at thy *t*
1Kin 4:27 that came unto king Solomon's *t*
1Kin 7:48 the *t* of gold, whereupon the
1Kin 10:5 And the meat of his *t*, and the
1Kin 13:20 to pass, as they sat at the *t*
1Kin 18:19 hundred, which eat at Jezebel's *t*
2Kin 4:10 set for him there a bed, and a *t*
1Chr 28:16 tables of shewbread, for every *t*
2Chr 9:4 And the meat of his *t*, and the
2Chr 13:11 set they in order upon the pure *t*
2Chr 29:18 thereof, and the shewbread *t*
Neh 5:17 there were at my *t* an hundred
Job 36:16 thy *t* should be full of fatness
Ps 23:5 Thou preparest a *t* before me in
Ps 69:22 Let their *t* become a snare before
Ps 78:19 God furnish a *t* in the wilderness
Ps 128:3 olive plants round about thy *t*
Prov 3:3 them upon the *t* of thine heart
Prov 7:3 them upon the *t* of thine heart
Prov 9:2 she hath also furnished her *t*
Song 1:12 While the king sitteth at his *t*
Is 21:5 Prepare the *t*, watch in the
Is 30:8 go, write it before them in a *t*
Is 65:11 that prepare a *t* for that troop
Jer 17:1 graven upon the *t* of their heart
Eze 23:41 a *t* prepared before it, whereupon
Eze 39:20 be filled at my *t* with horses
Eze 41:22 This is the *t* that is before the
Eze 44:16 and they shall come near to my *t*
Dan 11:27 and they shall speak lies at one *t*
Mal 1:7 The *t* of the LORD is contemptible
Mal 1:12 The *t* of the LORD is polluted
Mt 15:27 which fall from their masters' *t*
Mk 7:28 yet the dogs under the *t* eat of
Lk 1:63 And he asked for a writing *t*
Lk 16:21 which fell from the rich man's *t*
Lk 22:21 betrayeth me is with me on the *t*
Lk 22:30 drink at my *t* in my kingdom, and
Jn 12:2 them that sat at the *t* with him
Jn 13:28 Now no man at the *t* knew for what
Rom 11:9 Let their *t* be made a snare, and a
1Cor 10:21 be partakers of the Lord's *t*
1Cor 10:21 and of the *t* of devils
Heb 9:2 was the candlestick, and the *t*

## TABLES

Ex 24:12 and I will give thee *t* of stone
Ex 31:18 two *t* of testimony, *t* of
Ex 31:18 *t* of stone, written with the
Ex 32:15 the two *t* of the testimony were
Ex 32:15 the *t* were written on both their
Ex 32:16 the *t* were the work of God, and
Ex 32:16 writing of God, graven upon the *t*
Ex 32:19 he cast the *t* out of his hands,
Ex 34:1 Hew thee two *t* of stone like unto
Ex 34:1 I will write upon these *t* the
Ex 34:1 words that were in the first *t*
Ex 34:4 he hewed two *t* of stone like unto
Ex 34:4 in his hand the two *t* of stone
Ex 34:28 he wrote upon the *t* the words of
Ex 34:29 two *t* of testimony in Moses' hand
Deut 4:13 he wrote them upon two *t* of stone
Deut 5:22 he wrote them in two *t* of stone
Deut 9:9 mount to receive the *t* of stone
Deut 9:9 even the *t* of the covenant which
Deut 9:10 two *t* of stone written with the
Deut 9:11 LORD gave me the two *t* of stone
Deut 9:11 even the *t* of the covenant
Deut 9:15 the two *t* of the covenant were in
Deut 9:17 And I took the two *t*, and cast them
Deut 10:1 Hew thee two *t* of stone like unto
Deut 10:2 I will write on the *t* the words
Deut 10:2 in the first *t* which thou brakest
Deut 10:3 hewed two *t* of stone like unto
Deut 10:3 having the two *t* in mine hand
Deut 10:4 And he wrote on the *t*, according
Deut 10:5 put the *t* in the ark which I had
1Kin 8:9 the ark save the two *t* of stone
1Chr 28:16 gave gold for the *t* of shewbread
1Chr 28:16 silver for the *t* of silver
2Chr 4:8 He made also ten *t*, and placed
2Chr 4:19 the *t* whereon the shewbread was
2Chr 5:10 two *t* which Moses put therein at
Is 28:8 For all *t* are full of vomit and
Eze 40:39 the gate were two *t* on this side
Eze 40:39 two *t* on that side, to slay
Eze 40:40 of the north gate, were two *t*
Eze 40:40 the porch of the gate, were two *t*
Eze 40:41 Four *t* were on this side, and four
Eze 40:41 four *t* on that side, by the side
Eze 40:41 eight *t*, whereupon they slew
Eze 40:42 the four *t* were of hewn stone for
Eze 40:43 upon the *t* was the flesh of the
Hab 2:2 vision, and make it plain upon *t*
Mt 21:12 temple, and overthrew the *t* of the
Mk 7:4 and pots, brasen vessels, and of *t*
Mk 11:15 temple, and overthrew the *t* of the
Jn 2:15 money, and overthrew the *t*
Acts 6:2 leave the word of God, and serve *t*
2Cor 3:3 not in *t* of stone, but in fleshly
2Cor 3:3 but in fleshly *t* of the heart
Heb 9:4 budded, and the *t* of the covenant

## TABLETS

Ex 35:22 and earrings, and rings, and *t*
Num 31:50 bracelets, rings, earrings, and *t*
Is 3:20 legs, and the headbands, and the *t*

## TABOR *(ta'-bor)*

*1. A mountain in Issachar and Zebulun.*
Josh 19:22 And the coast reacheth to *T*
Judg 4:6 saying, Go and draw toward mount *T*
Judg 4:12 of Abinoam was gone up to mount *T*
Judg 4:14 So Barak went down from mount *T*
Judg 8:18 men were they whom ye slew at *T*
Ps 89:12 *T* and Hermon shall rejoice in thy
Jer 46:18 hosts, Surely as *T* is among the
Hos 5:1 on Mizpah, and a net spread upon *T*
*2. A plain in Benjamin.*
1Sa 10:3 thou shalt come to the plain of *T*
*3. A Levitical city in Zebulun.*
1Chr 6:77 her suburbs, *T* with her suburbs

## TABRET

Gen 31:27 with mirth, and with songs, with *t*
1Sa 10:5 place with a psaltery, and a *t*
Job 17:6 and aforetime I was as a *t*
Is 5:12 And the harp, and the viol, the *t*

## TABRETS

1Sa 18:6 to meet king Saul, with *t*
Is 24:8 The mirth of *t* ceaseth, the noise
Is 30:32 lay upon him, it shall be with *t*
Jer 31:4 shalt again be adorned with thy *t*
Eze 28:13 the workmanship of thy *t* and of

## TABRIMON *(tab'-rim-on) Father of Ben-hadad, king of Syria.*

1Kin 15:18 them to Ben-hadad, the son of *T*

## TACHES

Ex 26:6 thou shalt make fifty *t* of gold
Ex 26:6 the curtains together with the *t*
Ex 26:11 thou shalt make fifty *t* of brass
Ex 26:11 put the *t* into the loops, and
Ex 26:33 hang up the vail under the *t*
Ex 35:11 his tent, and his covering, his *t*
Ex 36:13 And he made fifty *t* of gold
Ex 36:13 one unto another with the *t*
Ex 36:18 he made fifty *t* of brass to
Ex 39:33 tent, and all his furniture, his *t*

**TACHMONITE** *(tak'-mun-ite)* See HACHMONITE. *Family name of a "mighty man" of David.*
2Sa 23:8 The *T* that sat in the seat, chief

**TACKLING**
Acts 27:19 our own hands the *t* of the ship

**TACKLINGS**
Is 33:23 Thy *t* are loosed

**TADMOR** *(tad'-mor) A city rebuilt by Solomon.*
1Kin 9:18 *T* in the wilderness, in the land,
2Chr 8:4 he built *T* in the wilderness, and

**TAHAN** *(ta'-han)* See TAHANITES.
*1. A son of Ephraim.*
Num 26:35 of *T*, the family of the Tahanites
*2. A descendant of Ephraim.*
1Chr 7:25 and Telah his son, and *T* his son,

**TAHANITES** *(ta'-han-ites) Descendants of Tahan 1.*
Num 26:35 of Tahan, the family of the *T*

**TAHAPANES** *(ta-hap'-a-neze)* See TAHAPANHES. *A city in Egypt.*
Jer 2:16 *T* have broken the crown of thy

**TAHATH** *(ta'-hath)*
*1. An Israelite encampment in the wilderness.*
Num 33:26 from Makheloth, and encamped at *T*
Num 33:27 And they departed from *T*, and
*2. Father of Uriel.*
1Chr 6:24 *T* his son, Uriel his son, Uzziah
1Chr 6:37 The son of *T*, the son of Assir,
*3. Father of Eladah.*
1Chr 7:20 *T* his son, and Eladah his son, and
*4. Son of Eladah.*
1Chr 7:20 and Eladah his son, and *T* his son,

**TAHPANHES** *(tah'-pan-heze)* See TAHAPANES, TAHPENES, TEHAPHNEHES. *Same as Tahapanes.*
Jer 43:7 thus came they even to *T*
Jer 43:8 of the LORD unto Jeremiah in *T*
Jer 43:9 the entry of Pharaoh's house in *T*
Jer 44:1 which dwell at Migdol, and at *T*
Jer 46:14 and publish in Noph and in *T*

**TAHPENES** *(tah'-pe-neze)* See TAHPANHES. *Queen of a pharaoh.*
1Kin 11:19 wife, the sister of *T* the queen
1Kin 11:20 the sister of *T* bare him Genubath
1Kin 11:20 whom *T* weaned in Pharaoh's house

**TAHREA** *(tah'-re-ah)* See TAREA. *Son of Micah.*
1Chr 9:41 were, Pithon, and Melech, and *T*

**TAHTIM-HODSHI** *(tah'-tim-hod'-shi) A district north of Gilead in Bashan.*
2Sa 24:6 to Gilead, and to the land of *T*

**TAIL**
Ex 4:4 thine hand, and take it by the *t*
Deut 28:13 make thee the head, and not the *t*
Deut 28:44 the head, and thou shalt be the *t*
Judg 15:4 firebrands, and turned *t* to *t*
Job 40:17 He moveth his *t* like a cedar
Is 9:14 cut off from Israel head and *t*
Is 9:15 that teacheth lies, he is the *t*
Is 19:15 for Egypt, which the head or *t*
Rev 12:4 his *t* drew the third part of the

**TAILS**
Judg 15:4 in the midst between two *t*
Is 7:4 two *t* of these smoking firebrands
Rev 9:10 they had *t* like unto scorpions,
Rev 9:10 and there were stings in their *t*
Rev 9:19 is in their mouth, and in their *t*
Rev 9:19 for their *t* were like unto

**TAKE**
Gen 3:22 *t* also of the tree of life, and
Gen 6:21 *t* thou unto thee of all food that
Gen 7:2 thou shalt *t* to thee by sevens
Gen 12:19 thy wife, *t* her, and go thy way
Gen 13:9 if thou wilt *t* the left hand,
Gen 14:21 and *t* the goods to thyself
Gen 14:23 That I will not *t* from a thread
Gen 14:23 that I will not *t* any thing that
Gen 14:24 let them *t* their portion
Gen 15:9 *T* me an heifer of three years old
Gen 19:15 *t* thy wife, and thy two daughters,
Gen 19:19 the mountain, lest some evil *t* me
Gen 21:30 ewe lambs shalt thou *t* of my hand
Gen 22:2 *T* now thy son, thine only son
Gen 23:13 *t* it of me, and I will bury my
Gen 24:3 that thou shalt not *t* a wife unto
Gen 24:4 *t* a wife unto my son Isaac
Gen 24:7 thou shalt *t* a wife unto my son
Gen 24:37 Thou shalt not *t* a wife to my son
Gen 24:38 kindred, and *t* a wife unto my son
Gen 24:40 thou shalt *t* a wife for my son of
Gen 24:48 *t* my master's brother's daughter
Gen 24:51 *t* her, and go, and let her be thy
Gen 27:3 Now therefore *t*, I pray thee, thy
Gen 27:3 the field, and *t* me some venison
Gen 27:46 if Jacob *t* a wife of the
Gen 28:1 Thou shalt not *t* a wife of the
Gen 28:2 *t* thee a wife from thence of the
Gen 28:6 to *t* him a wife from thence
Gen 28:6 Thou shalt not *t* a wife of the
Gen 30:15 wouldest thou *t* away my son's
Gen 31:24 *T* heed that thou speak not to
Gen 31:29 *T* thou heed that thou speak not
Gen 31:31 Peradventure thou wouldest *t* by
Gen 31:32 is thine with me, and *t* it to thee
Gen 31:50 or if thou shalt *t* other wives
Gen 33:11 *T*, I pray thee, my blessing that
Gen 33:12 Let us *t* our journey, and let us
Gen 34:9 us, and *t* our daughters unto you
Gen 34:16 we will *t* your daughters to us,
Gen 34:17 then will we *t* our daughter
Gen 34:21 let us *t* their daughters to us
Gen 38:23 Let her *t* it to her, lest we be
Gen 41:34 *t* up the fifth part of the land
Gen 42:33 *t* food for the famine of your
Gen 42:36 not, and ye will *t* Benjamin away
Gen 43:11 *t* of the best fruits in the land
Gen 43:12 *t* double money in your hand
Gen 43:13 *T* also your brother, and arise, go
Gen 43:18 *t* us for bondmen, and our asses
Gen 44:29 if ye *t* this also from me, and
Gen 45:18 *t* your father and your households,
Gen 45:19 *t* you wagons out of the land of
Ex 2:9 *T* this child away, and nurse it
Ex 4:4 thine hand, and *t* it by the tail
Ex 4:9 that thou shalt *t* of the water of
Ex 4:17 thou shalt *t* this rod in thine
Ex 6:7 I will *t* you to me for a people,
Ex 7:9 *T* thy rod, and cast it before
Ex 7:15 shalt thou *t* in thine hand
Ex 7:19 *T* thy rod, and stretch out thine
Ex 8:8 that he may *t* away the frogs from
Ex 9:8 *T* to you handfuls of ashes of the
Ex 10:17 that he may *t* away from me this
Ex 10:26 for thereof must we *t* to serve
Ex 10:28 *t* heed to thyself, see my face no
Ex 12:3 shall *t* to them every man a lamb
Ex 12:4 *t* it according to the number of
Ex 12:5 ye shall *t* it out from the sheep,
Ex 12:7 they shall *t* of the blood, and
Ex 12:21 *t* you a lamb according to your
Ex 12:22 ye shall *t* a bunch of hyssop, and
Ex 12:32 Also *t* your flocks and your herds,
Ex 15:14 sorrow shall *t* hold on the
Ex 15:15 trembling shall *t* hold upon them
Ex 16:16 *t* ye every man for them which are
Ex 16:33 *T* a pot, and put an omer full of
Ex 17:5 *t* with thee of the elders of
Ex 17:5 the river, *t* in thine hand, and go
Ex 19:12 *T* heed to yourselves, that ye go
Ex 20:7 Thou shalt not *t* the name of the
Ex 21:10 If he *t* him another wife
Ex 21:14 thou shalt *t* him from mine altar,
Ex 22:26 If thou at all *t* thy neighbour's
Ex 23:8 And thou shalt *t* no gift
Ex 23:25 I will *t* sickness away from the
Ex 25:2 his heart ye shall *t* my offering
Ex 25:3 offering which ye shall *t* of them
Ex 26:5 that the loops may *t* hold one of
Ex 28:1 *t* thou unto thee Aaron thy
Ex 28:5 And they shall *t* gold, and blue, and
Ex 28:9 thou shalt *t* two onyx stones, and
Ex 29:1 *T* one young bullock, and two rams
Ex 29:5 thou shalt *t* the garments, and put
Ex 29:7 Then shalt thou *t* the anointing
Ex 29:12 thou shalt *t* of the blood of the
Ex 29:13 thou shalt *t* all the fat that
Ex 29:15 Thou shalt also *t* one ram
Ex 29:16 ram, and thou shalt *t* his blood
Ex 29:19 thou shalt *t* the other ram
Ex 29:20 *t* of his blood, and put it upon
Ex 29:21 thou shalt *t* of the blood that is
Ex 29:22 Also thou shalt *t* of the ram the
Ex 29:26 thou shalt *t* the breast of the
Ex 29:31 thou shalt *t* the ram of the
Ex 30:16 thou shalt *t* the atonement money
Ex 30:23 *T* thou also unto thee principal
Ex 30:34 *T* unto thee sweet spices, stacte,
Ex 33:23 I will *t* away mine hand, and thou
Ex 34:9 *t* us for thine inheritance
Ex 34:12 *T* heed to thyself, lest thou make
Ex 34:16 thou *t* of their daughters unto
Ex 35:5 *T* ye from among you an offering
Ex 40:9 thou shalt *t* the anointing oil,
Lev 2:2 he shall *t* thereout his handful
Lev 2:9 the priest shall *t* from the meat
Lev 3:4 the kidneys, it shall he *t* away
Lev 3:9 it shall he *t* off hard by the
Lev 3:10 the kidneys, it shall he *t* away
Lev 3:15 the kidneys, it shall he *t* away
Lev 4:5 shall *t* of the bullock's blood
Lev 4:8 he shall *t* off from it all the
Lev 4:9 the kidneys, it shall he *t* away
Lev 4:19 he shall *t* all his fat from him,
Lev 4:25 the priest shall *t* of the blood
Lev 4:30 the priest shall *t* of the blood
Lev 4:31 he shall *t* away all the fat
Lev 4:34 the priest shall *t* of the blood
Lev 4:35 he shall *t* away all the fat
Lev 5:12 the priest shall *t* his handful of
Lev 6:10 *t* up the ashes which the fire
Lev 6:15 he shall *t* of it his handful, of
Lev 7:4 the kidneys, it shall he *t* away
Lev 8:2 *T* Aaron and his sons with him, and
Lev 9:2 *T* thee a young calf for a sin
Lev 9:3 *T* ye a kid of the goats for a sin
Lev 10:12 left, *T* the meat offering that
Lev 14:4 shall the priest command to *t* for
Lev 14:6 the living bird, he shall *t* it
Lev 14:10 on the eighth day he shall *t* two
Lev 14:12 And the priest shall *t* one he lamb
Lev 14:14 the priest shall *t* some of the
Lev 14:15 the priest shall *t* some of the
Lev 14:21 then he shall *t* one lamb for a
Lev 14:24 the priest shall *t* the lamb of
Lev 14:25 the priest shall *t* some of the
Lev 14:40 *t* away the stones in which the
Lev 14:42 they shall *t* other stones, and put
Lev 14:42 he shall *t* other morter, and shall
Lev 14:49 he shall *t* to cleanse the house
Lev 14:51 he shall *t* the cedar wood, and the
Lev 15:14 he shall *t* to him two turtledoves
Lev 15:29 she shall *t* unto her two turtles
Lev 16:5 he shall *t* of the congregation of
Lev 16:7 he shall *t* the two goats, and
Lev 16:12 he shall *t* a censer full of
Lev 16:14 he shall *t* of the blood of the
Lev 16:18 shall *t* of the blood of the
Lev 18:17 shalt thou *t* her son's daughter
Lev 18:18 Neither shalt thou *t* a wife to
Lev 20:14 And if a man *t* a wife and her
Lev 20:17 And if a man shall *t* his sister
Lev 20:21 if a man shall *t* his brother's
Lev 21:7 They shall not *t* a wife that is a
Lev 21:7 neither shall they *t* a woman put
Lev 21:13 And he shall *t* a wife in her
Lev 21:14 an harlot, these shall he not *t*
Lev 21:14 but he shall *t* a virgin of his
Lev 22:5 man of whom he may *t* uncleanness
Lev 23:40 ye shall *t* you on the first day
Lev 24:5 And thou shalt *t* fine flour
Lev 25:36 *T* thou no usury of him, or
Lev 25:46 ye shall *t* them as an inheritance
Num 1:2 *T* ye the sum of all the
Num 1:49 neither *t* the sum of them among
Num 1:51 the Levites shall *t* it down
Num 3:40 *t* the number of their names
Num 3:41 thou shalt *t* the Levites for me
Num 3:45 *T* the Levites instead of all the
Num 3:47 Thou shalt even *t* five shekels
Num 3:47 the sanctuary shalt thou *t* them
Num 4:2 *T* the sum of the sons of Kohath
Num 4:5 they shall *t* down the covering
Num 4:9 they shall *t* a cloth of blue, and
Num 4:12 they shall *t* all the instruments
Num 4:13 they shall *t* away the ashes from
Num 4:22 *T* also the sum of the sons of
Num 5:17 the priest shall *t* holy water in
Num 5:17 the tabernacle the priest shall *t*
Num 5:25 Then the priest shall *t* the
Num 5:26 the priest shall *t* an handful of
Num 6:18 shall *t* the hair of the head of
Num 6:19 the priest shall *t* the sodden
Num 7:5 *T* it of them, that they may be to

| | |
|---|---|
| Num 8:6 | *T* the Levites from among the |
| Num 8:8 | Then let them *t* a young bullock |
| Num 8:8 | shalt thou *t* for a sin offering |
| Num 10:6 | south side shall *t* their journey |
| Num 11:17 | I will *t* of the spirit which is |
| Num 16:3 | Ye *t* too much upon you, seeing |
| Num 16:6 | *T* you censers, Korah, and all his |
| Num 16:7 | ye *t* too much upon you, ye sons |
| Num 16:17 | *t* every man his censer, and put |
| Num 16:37 | that he *t* up the censers out of |
| Num 16:46 | *T* a censer, and put fire therein |
| Num 17:2 | *t* of every one of them a rod |
| Num 17:10 | thou shalt quite *t* away their |
| Num 18:26 | When ye *t* of the children of |
| Num 19:4 | Eleazar the priest shall *t* of her |
| Num 19:6 | And the priest shall *t* cedar wood |
| Num 19:17 | shall *t* of the ashes of the burnt |
| Num 19:18 | And a clean person shall *t* hyssop |
| Num 20:8 | *T* the rod, and gather thou the |
| Num 20:25 | *T* Aaron and Eleazar his son, and |
| Num 21:7 | that he *t* away the serpents from |
| Num 23:12 | Must I not *t* heed to speak that |
| Num 25:4 | *T* all the heads of the people, and |
| Num 26:2 | *T* the sum of all the congregation |
| Num 26:4 | *T* the sum of the people, from |
| Num 27:18 | *T* thee Joshua the son of Nun, a |
| Num 31:26 | *T* the sum of the prey that was |
| Num 31:29 | *T* it of their half, and give it |
| Num 31:30 | thou shalt *t* one portion of fifty |
| Num 34:18 | ye shall *t* one prince of every |
| Num 35:31 | Moreover ye shall *t* no |
| Num 35:32 | ye shall *t* no satisfaction for |
| Deut 1:7 | *t* your journey, and go to the |
| Deut 1:13 | *T* you wise men, and understanding, |
| Deut 1:40 | you, and *t* your journey into the |
| Deut 2:4 | *t* ye good heed unto yourselves |
| Deut 2:24 | *t* your journey, and pass over the |
| Deut 4:9 | Only *t* heed to thyself, and keep |
| Deut 4:15 | *T* ye therefore good heed unto |
| Deut 4:23 | *T* heed unto yourselves, lest ye |
| Deut 4:34 | *t* him a nation from the midst of |
| Deut 5:11 | Thou shalt not *t* the name of the |
| Deut 7:3 | shalt thou *t* unto thy son |
| Deut 7:15 | the LORD will *t* away from thee |
| Deut 7:25 | nor *t* it unto thee, lest thou be |
| Deut 10:11 | *t* thy journey before the people, |
| Deut 11:16 | *T* heed to yourselves, that your |
| Deut 12:13 | *T* heed to thyself that thou offer |
| Deut 12:19 | *T* heed to thyself that thou |
| Deut 12:26 | hast, and thy vows, thou shalt *t* |
| Deut 12:30 | *T* heed to thyself that thou be |
| Deut 15:17 | Then thou shalt *t* an aul, and |
| Deut 16:19 | respect persons, neither *t* a gift |
| Deut 20:7 | the battle, and another man *t* her |
| Deut 20:14 | shalt thou *t* unto thyself |
| Deut 20:19 | in making war against it to *t* it |
| Deut 21:3 | of that city shall *t* an heifer |
| Deut 22:6 | thou shalt not *t* the dam with the |
| Deut 22:7 | dam go, and *t* the young to thee |
| Deut 22:13 | If any man *t* a wife, and go in |
| Deut 22:15 | of the damsel, and her mother, *t* |
| Deut 22:18 | of that city shall *t* that man |
| Deut 22:30 | A man shall not *t* his father's |
| Deut 24:4 | may not *t* her again to be his |
| Deut 24:6 | No man shall *t* the nether or the |
| Deut 24:8 | *T* heed in the plague of leprosy, |
| Deut 24:17 | nor *t* a widow's raiment to pledge |
| Deut 25:5 | *t* her to him to wife, and perform |
| Deut 25:7 | like not to *t* his brother's wife |
| Deut 25:8 | it, and say, I like not to *t* her |
| Deut 26:2 | That thou shalt *t* of the first of |
| Deut 26:4 | the priest shall *t* the basket out |
| Deut 27:9 | *T* heed, and hearken, O Israel |
| Deut 31:26 | *T* this book of the law, and put it |
| Deut 32:41 | mine hand *t* hold on judgment |
| Josh 3:6 | *T* up the ark of the covenant, and |
| Josh 3:12 | Now therefore *t* you twelve men |
| Josh 4:2 | *T* you twelve men out of the |
| Josh 4:3 | *T* you hence out of the midst of |
| Josh 4:5 | *t* you up every man of you a stone |
| Josh 6:6 | *T* up the ark of the covenant, and |
| Josh 6:18 | when ye *t* of the accursed thing, |
| Josh 7:13 | until ye *t* away the accursed |
| Josh 7:14 | shall *t* shall come by households |
| Josh 7:14 | shall *t* shall come man by man |
| Josh 8:1 | *t* all the people of war with thee |
| Josh 8:2 | shall ye *t* for a prey unto |
| Josh 8:29 | commanded that they should *t* his |
| Josh 9:11 | *T* victuals with you for the |
| Josh 10:42 | land did Joshua *t* at one time |
| Josh 11:12 | the kings of them, did Joshua *t* |
| Josh 20:4 | they shall *t* him into the city |
| Josh 22:5 | But *t* diligent heed to do the |
| Josh 22:19 | and *t* possession among us |
| Josh 23:11 | *T* good heed therefore unto |
| Judg 4:6 | *t* with thee ten thousand men of |
| Judg 5:30 | necks of them that *t* the spoil |
| Judg 6:20 | *T* the flesh and the unleavened |
| Judg 6:25 | *T* thy father's young bullock, |
| Judg 6:26 | *t* the second bullock, and offer a |
| Judg 7:24 | *t* before them the waters unto |
| Judg 14:3 | that thou goest to *t* a wife of |
| Judg 14:8 | after a time he returned to *t* her |
| Judg 14:15 | ye called us to *t* that we have |
| Judg 15:2 | *t* her, I pray thee, instead of |
| Judg 19:30 | *t* advice, and speak your minds |
| Judg 20:10 | we will *t* ten men of an hundred |
| Ruth 2:10 | thou shouldest *t* knowledge of me |
| Ruth 2:19 | he that did *t* knowledge of thee |
| 1Sa 2:16 | then *t* as much as thy soul |
| 1Sa 2:16 | and if not, I will *t* it by force |
| 1Sa 6:7 | *t* two milch kine, on which there |
| 1Sa 6:8 | *t* the ark of the LORD, and lay it |
| 1Sa 8:11 | He will *t* your sons, and appoint |
| 1Sa 8:13 | he will *t* your daughters to be |
| 1Sa 8:14 | he will *t* your fields, and your |
| 1Sa 8:15 | he will *t* the tenth of your seed, |
| 1Sa 8:16 | he will *t* your menservants, and |
| 1Sa 8:17 | He will *t* the tenth of your sheep |
| 1Sa 9:3 | *T* now one of the servants with |
| 1Sa 9:5 | the asses, and *t* thought for us |
| 1Sa 16:2 | *T* an heifer with thee, and say, I |
| 1Sa 17:17 | *T* now for thy brethren an ephah |
| 1Sa 17:18 | brethren fare, and *t* their pledge |
| 1Sa 17:46 | thee, and *t* thine head from thee |
| 1Sa 19:2 | *t* heed to thyself until the |
| 1Sa 19:14 | Saul sent messengers to *t* David |
| 1Sa 19:20 | Saul sent messengers to *t* David |
| 1Sa 20:21 | are on this side of thee, *t* them |
| 1Sa 21:9 | if thou wilt *t* that, *t* it |
| 1Sa 23:23 | *t* knowledge of all the lurking |
| 1Sa 23:26 | and his men round about to *t* them |
| 1Sa 24:11 | yet thou huntest my soul to *t* it |
| 1Sa 25:11 | Shall I then *t* my bread, and my |
| 1Sa 25:39 | Abigail, to *t* her to him to wife |
| 1Sa 25:40 | thee, to *t* thee to him to wife |
| 1Sa 26:11 | *t* thou now the spear that is at |
| 2Sa 2:21 | young men, and *t* thee his armour |
| 2Sa 4:11 | *t* you away from the earth |
| 2Sa 5:6 | Except thou *t* away the blind and |
| 2Sa 12:4 | he spared to *t* of his own flock |
| 2Sa 12:11 | I will *t* thy wives before thine |
| 2Sa 12:28 | encamp against the city, and *t* it |
| 2Sa 12:28 | lest I *t* the city, and it be |
| 2Sa 13:33 | the king *t* the thing to his heart |
| 2Sa 15:20 | thou, and *t* back thy brethren |
| 2Sa 16:9 | I pray thee, and *t* off his head |
| 2Sa 19:19 | the king should *t* it to his heart |
| 2Sa 19:30 | unto the king, Yea, let him *t* all |
| 2Sa 20:6 | *t* thou thy lord's servants, and |
| 2Sa 24:10 | *t* away the iniquity of thy |
| 2Sa 24:22 | David, Let my lord the king *t* |
| 1Kin 1:33 | *T* with you the servants of your |
| 1Kin 2:4 | If thy children *t* heed to their |
| 1Kin 2:31 | that thou mayest *t* away the |
| 1Kin 8:25 | thy children *t* heed to their way |
| 1Kin 11:31 | to Jeroboam, *T* thee ten pieces |
| 1Kin 11:34 | Howbeit I will not *t* the whole |
| 1Kin 11:35 | But I will *t* the kingdom out of |
| 1Kin 11:37 | And I will *t* thee, and thou shalt |
| 1Kin 14:3 | *t* with thee ten loaves, and |
| 1Kin 14:10 | will *t* away the remnant of the |
| 1Kin 16:3 | I will *t* away the posterity of |
| 1Kin 18:40 | unto them, *T* the prophets of Baal |
| 1Kin 19:4 | now, O LORD, *t* away my life |
| 1Kin 19:10 | they seek my life, to *t* it away |
| 1Kin 19:14 | they seek my life, to *t* it away |
| 1Kin 20:6 | it in their hand, and *t* it away |
| 1Kin 20:18 | come out for peace, *t* them alive |
| 1Kin 20:18 | be come out for war, *t* them alive |
| 1Kin 20:24 | *T* the kings away, every man out |
| 1Kin 21:15 | *t* possession of the vineyard of |
| 1Kin 21:16 | Jezreelite, to *t* possession of it |
| 1Kin 21:21 | will *t* away thy posterity, and |
| 1Kin 22:3 | *t* it not out of the hand of the |
| 1Kin 22:26 | *T* Micaiah, and carry him back unto |
| 2Kin 2:1 | when the LORD would *t* up Elijah |
| 2Kin 2:3 | *t* away thy master from thy head |
| 2Kin 2:5 | *t* away thy master from thy head |
| 2Kin 4:1 | the creditor is come to *t* unto |
| 2Kin 4:29 | *t* my staff in thine hand, and go |
| 2Kin 4:36 | unto him, he said, *T* up thy son |
| 2Kin 5:15 | *t* a blessing of thy servant |
| 2Kin 5:16 | And he urged him to *t* it |
| 2Kin 5:20 | after him, and *t* somewhat of him |
| 2Kin 5:23 | said, Be content, *t* two talents |
| 2Kin 6:2 | *t* thence every man a beam, and let |
| 2Kin 6:7 | said he, *T* it up to thee |
| 2Kin 6:32 | hath sent to *t* away mine head |
| 2Kin 7:13 | answered and said, Let some *t* |
| 2Kin 8:8 | *T* a present in thine hand, and go, |
| 2Kin 9:1 | *t* this box of oil in thine hand, |
| 2Kin 9:3 | Then *t* the box of oil, and pour it |
| 2Kin 9:17 | *T* an horseman, and send to meet |
| 2Kin 9:25 | *T* up, and cast him in the portion |
| 2Kin 9:26 | Now therefore *t* and cast him into |
| 2Kin 10:6 | *t* ye the heads of the men your |
| 2Kin 10:14 | And he said, *T* them alive |
| 2Kin 12:5 | Let the priests *t* it to them |
| 2Kin 13:15 | said unto him, *T* bow and arrows |
| 2Kin 13:18 | And he said, *T* the arrows |
| 2Kin 18:32 | *t* you away to a land like your |
| 2Kin 19:30 | shall yet again *t* root downward |
| 2Kin 20:7 | And Isaiah said, *T* a lump of figs |
| 2Kin 20:18 | shalt beget, shall they *t* away |
| 1Chr 7:21 | came down to *t* away their cattle |
| 1Chr 17:13 | I will not *t* my mercy away from |
| 1Chr 21:23 | *T* it to thee, and let my lord the |
| 1Chr 21:24 | for I will not *t* that which is |
| 1Chr 28:10 | *T* heed now |
| 2Chr 6:16 | yet so that thy children *t* heed |
| 2Chr 18:25 | *T* ye Micaiah, and carry him back |
| 2Chr 19:6 | to the judges, *T* heed what ye do |
| 2Chr 19:7 | *t* heed and do it |
| 2Chr 20:25 | his people came to *t* away the |
| 2Chr 32:18 | that they might *t* the city |
| 2Chr 33:8 | so that they will *t* heed to do |
| Ezr 4:22 | *T* heed now that ye fail not to do |
| Ezr 5:14 | those did Cyrus the king *t* out of |
| Ezr 5:15 | *T* these vessels, go, carry them |
| Ezr 9:12 | neither *t* their daughters unto |
| Neh 5:2 | therefore we *t* up corn for them, |
| Neh 6:7 | let us *t* counsel together |
| Neh 10:30 | nor *t* their daughters for our |
| Neh 10:38 | when the Levites *t* tithes |
| Neh 13:25 | nor *t* their daughters unto your |
| Est 3:13 | to *t* the spoil of them for a prey |
| Est 4:4 | to *t* away his sackcloth from him |
| Est 6:10 | *t* the apparel and the horse, as |
| Est 8:11 | to *t* the spoil of them for a prey |
| Job 7:21 | and *t* away mine iniquity |
| Job 9:18 | will not suffer me to *t* my breath |
| Job 9:34 | Let him *t* his rod away from me, |
| Job 10:20 | that I may *t* comfort a little, |
| Job 11:18 | thou shalt *t* thy rest in safety |
| Job 13:14 | Wherefore do I *t* my flesh in my |
| Job 18:9 | The gin shall *t* him by the heel, |
| Job 21:12 | They *t* the timbrel and harp, and |
| Job 23:10 | But he knoweth the way that I *t* |
| Job 24:2 | they violently *t* away flocks |
| Job 24:3 | they *t* the widow's ox for a |
| Job 24:9 | breast, and *t* a pledge of the poor |
| Job 24:10 | they *t* away the sheaf from the |
| Job 27:20 | Terrors *t* hold on him as waters, |
| Job 30:17 | and my sinews *t* no rest |
| Job 31:36 | Surely I would *t* it upon my |
| Job 32:22 | my maker would soon *t* me away |
| Job 36:17 | and justice *t* hold on thee |
| Job 36:18 | beware lest he *t* thee away with |
| Job 36:21 | *T* heed, regard not iniquity |
| Job 38:13 | That it might *t* hold of the ends |
| Job 38:20 | That thou shouldest *t* it to the |
| Job 41:4 | wilt thou *t* him for a servant for |
| Job 42:8 | Therefore *t* unto you now seven |
| Ps 2:2 | the rulers *t* counsel together, |
| Ps 7:5 | enemy persecute my soul, and *t* it |
| Ps 13:2 | How long shall I *t* counsel in my |
| Ps 16:4 | nor *t* up their names into my lips |
| Ps 27:10 | me, then the LORD will *t* me up |
| Ps 31:13 | they devised to *t* away my life |
| Ps 35:2 | *T* hold of shield and buckler, and |
| Ps 39:1 | I will *t* heed to my ways, that I |
| Ps 50:9 | I will *t* no bullock out of thy |
| Ps 50:16 | or that thou shouldest *t* my |
| Ps 51:11 | *t* not thy holy spirit from me |
| Ps 52:5 | he shall *t* thee away, and pluck |
| Ps 58:9 | he shall *t* them away as with a |
| Ps 69:20 | and I looked for some to *t* pity |
| Ps 69:24 | thy wrathful anger *t* hold of them |
| Ps 71:10 | for my soul *t* counsel together |

Ps 71:11 persecute and *t* him
Ps 80:9 and didst cause it to *t* deep root
Ps 81:2 *T* a psalm, and bring hither the
Ps 83:12 Let us *t* to ourselves the houses
Ps 89:33 will I not utterly *t* from him
Ps 102:14 For thy servants *t* pleasure in
Ps 102:24 *t* me not away in the midst of my
Ps 109:8 and let another *t* his office
Ps 116:13 I will *t* the cup of salvation, and
Ps 119:43 *t* not the word of truth utterly
Ps 139:9 If I *t* the wings of the morning,
Ps 139:20 thine enemies *t* thy name in vain
Prov 2:19 neither *t* they hold of the paths
Prov 4:13 *T* fast hold of instruction
Prov 5:5 her steps *t* hold on hell
Prov 5:22 shall *t* the wicked himself
Prov 6:25 neither let her *t* thee with her
Prov 6:27 Can a man *t* fire in his bosom, and
Prov 7:18 let us *t* our fill of love until
Prov 20:16 *T* his garment that is surety for
Prov 20:16 *t* a pledge of him for a strange
Prov 22:27 why should he *t* away thy bed from
Prov 25:4 *T* away the dross from the silver,
Prov 25:5 *T* away the wicked from before the
Prov 27:13 *T* his garment that is surety for
Prov 27:13 *t* a pledge of him for a strange
Prov 30:9 *t* the name of my God in vain
Eccl 5:15 shall *t* nothing of his labour,
Eccl 5:19 to *t* his portion, and to rejoice
Eccl 7:18 thou shouldest *t* hold of this
Eccl 7:21 Also *t* no heed unto all words
Song 2:15 *T* us the foxes, the little foxes,
Song 7:8 I will *t* hold of the boughs
Is 1:25 thy dross, and *t* away all thy tin
Is 3:1 doth *t* away from Jerusalem and
Is 3:6 When a man shall *t* hold of his
Is 3:18 will *t* away the bravery of their
Is 4:1 women shall *t* hold of one man
Is 4:1 thy name, to *t* away our reproach
Is 5:5 I will *t* away the hedge thereof,
Is 5:23 *t* away the righteousness of the
Is 7:4 say unto him, *T* heed, and be quiet
Is 8:1 *T* thee a great roll, and write in
Is 8:10 *T* counsel together, and it shall
Is 10:2 to *t* away the right from the poor
Is 10:6 to *t* the spoil, and to
Is 10:6 to *t* the prey, and to tread them
Is 13:8 and sorrows shall *t* hold of them
Is 14:2 And the people shall *t* them
Is 14:2 they shall *t* them captives, whose
Is 14:4 That thou shalt *t* up this proverb
Is 16:3 *T* counsel, execute judgment
Is 18:4 I will *t* my rest, and I will
Is 18:5 *t* away and cut down the branches
Is 23:16 *T* an harp, go about the city,
Is 25:8 he *t* away from off all the earth
Is 27:5 Or let him *t* hold of my strength,
Is 27:6 them that come of Jacob to *t* root
Is 27:9 all the fruit to *t* away his sin
Is 28:19 it goeth forth it shall *t* you
Is 30:1 that *t* counsel, but not of me
Is 30:14 a sherd to *t* fire from the hearth
Is 30:14 or to *t* water withal out of the
Is 33:23 the lame *t* the prey
Is 36:17 *t* you away to a land like your
Is 37:31 Judah shall again *t* root downward
Is 38:21 Let them *t* a lump of figs, and lay
Is 39:7 shall beget, shall they *t* away
Is 40:24 shall not *t* root in the earth
Is 40:24 the whirlwind shall *t* them away
Is 44:15 for he will *t* thereof, and warm
Is 45:21 let them *t* counsel together
Is 47:2 *T* the millstones, and grind meal
Is 47:3 I will *t* vengeance, and I will not
Is 56:4 me, and *t* hold of my covenant
Is 57:13 vanity shall *t* them
Is 57:14 *t* up the stumblingblock out of
Is 58:2 they *t* delight in approaching to
Is 58:9 If thou *t* away from the midst of
Is 64:7 up himself to *t* hold of thee
Is 66:21 I will also *t* of them for priests
Jer 2:22 *t* thee much sope, yet thine
Jer 3:14 I will *t* you one of a city, and
Jer 4:4 *t* away the foreskins of your
Jer 5:10 *t* away her battlements
Jer 7:29 *t* up a lamentation on high places
Jer 9:4 *T* ye heed every one of his
Jer 9:10 mountains will I *t* up a weeping
Jer 9:18 *t* up a wailing for us, that our
Jer 13:4 *T* the girdle that thou hast got,
Jer 13:6 *t* the girdle from thence, which I
Jer 13:21 shall not sorrows *t* thee, as a
Jer 15:15 *t* me not away in thy
Jer 15:19 if thou *t* forth the precious from
Jer 16:2 Thou shalt not *t* thee a wife
Jer 17:21 *T* heed to yourselves, and bear no
Jer 18:22 they have digged a pit to *t* me
Jer 19:1 *t* of the ancients of the people,
Jer 20:5 *t* them, and carry them to Babylon
Jer 20:10 we shall *t* our revenge on him
Jer 25:9 *t* all the families of the north,
Jer 25:10 Moreover I will *t* from them the
Jer 25:15 *T* the wine cup of this fury at my
Jer 25:28 if they refuse to *t* the cup at
Jer 29:6 *T* ye wives, and beget sons and
Jer 29:6 *t* wives for your sons, and give
Jer 32:3 king of Babylon, and he shall *t* it
Jer 32:14 *T* these evidences, this evidence
Jer 32:24 are come unto the city to *t* it
Jer 32:25 field for money, and *t* witnesses
Jer 32:28 king of Babylon, and he shall *t* it
Jer 32:44 *t* witnesses in the land of
Jer 33:26 so that I will not *t* any of his
Jer 34:22 *t* it, and burn it with fire
Jer 36:2 *T* thee a roll of a book, and write
Jer 36:14 *T* in thine hand the roll wherein
Jer 36:26 to *t* Baruch the scribe and
Jer 36:28 *T* thee again another roll, and
Jer 37:8 *t* it, and burn it with fire
Jer 38:3 Babylon's army, which shall *t* it
Jer 38:10 *T* from hence thirty men with thee
Jer 38:10 *t* up Jeremiah the prophet out of
Jer 39:12 *T* him, and look well to him, and do
Jer 43:9 *T* great stones in thine hand, and
Jer 43:10 *t* Nebuchadrezzar the king of
Jer 44:12 I will *t* the remnant of Judah,
Jer 46:11 *t* balm, O virgin, the daughter of
Jer 49:29 and their flocks shall they *t* away
Jer 49:29 they shall *t* to themselves their
Jer 50:15 *t* vengeance upon her
Jer 51:8 *t* balm for her pain, if so be she
Jer 51:26 they shall not *t* of thee a stone
Jer 51:36 cause, and *t* vengeance for thee
Lam 2:13 What thing shall I *t* to witness
Eze 4:1 *t* thee a tile, and lay it before
Eze 4:3 Moreover *t* thou unto thee an iron
Eze 4:9 *T* thou also unto thee wheat, and
Eze 5:1 *t* thee a sharp knife
Eze 5:1 *t* thee a barber's razor, and cause
Eze 5:1 then *t* thee balances to weigh, and
Eze 5:2 thou shalt *t* a third part, and
Eze 5:3 Thou shalt also *t* thereof a few
Eze 5:4 Then *t* of them again, and cast
Eze 10:6 *T* fire from between the wheels,
Eze 11:18 they shall *t* away all the
Eze 11:19 I will *t* the stony heart out of
Eze 14:5 That I may *t* the house of Israel
Eze 15:3 or will men *t* a pin of it to hang
Eze 16:16 And of thy garments thou didst *t*
Eze 16:39 shall *t* thy fair jewels, and leave
Eze 17:22 I will also *t* of the highest
Eze 19:1 Moreover *t* thou up a lamentation
Eze 21:26 the diadem, and *t* off the crown
Eze 22:16 thou shalt *t* thine inheritance in
Eze 23:25 they shall *t* away thy nose and
Eze 23:25 they shall *t* thy sons and thy
Eze 23:26 and *t* away thy fair jewels
Eze 23:29 shall *t* away all thy labour, and
Eze 24:5 *T* the choice of the flock, and
Eze 24:8 fury to come up to *t* vengeance
Eze 24:16 I *t* away from thee the desire of
Eze 24:25 when I *t* from them their strength
Eze 26:17 they shall *t* up a lamentation for
Eze 27:2 *t* up a lamentation for Tyrus
Eze 27:32 shall *t* up a lamentation for thee
Eze 28:12 *t* up a lamentation upon the king
Eze 29:19 he shall *t* her multitude
Eze 29:19 multitude, and *t* her spoil
Eze 29:19 her spoil, and *t* her prey
Eze 30:4 they shall *t* away her multitude,
Eze 32:2 *t* up a lamentation for Pharaoh
Eze 33:2 the land *t* a man of their coasts
Eze 33:4 *t* him away, his blood shall be
Eze 33:6 *t* any person from among them, he
Eze 36:24 For I will *t* you from among the
Eze 36:26 I will *t* away the stony heart out
Eze 37:16 *t* thee one stick, and write upon
Eze 37:16 then *t* another stick, and write
Eze 37:19 I will *t* the stick of Joseph,
Eze 37:21 I will *t* the children of Israel
Eze 38:12 To *t* a spoil, and to
Eze 38:12 a spoil, and to *t* a prey
Eze 38:13 thee, Art thou come to *t* a spoil
Eze 38:13 gathered thy company to *t* a prey
Eze 38:13 to *t* away cattle and goods, to
Eze 38:13 and goods, to *t* a great spoil
Eze 39:10 So that they shall *t* no wood out
Eze 43:20 thou shalt *t* of the blood thereof
Eze 43:21 Thou shalt *t* the bullock also of
Eze 44:22 Neither shall they *t* for their
Eze 44:22 but they shall *t* maidens of the
Eze 45:9 *t* away your exactions from my
Eze 45:18 thou shalt *t* a young bullock
Eze 45:19 the priest shall *t* of the blood
Eze 46:18 Moreover the prince shall not *t*
Dan 6:23 should *t* Daniel up out of the den
Dan 7:18 the most High shall *t* the kingdom
Dan 7:26 they shall *t* away his dominion,
Dan 11:15 and *t* the most fenced cities
Dan 11:18 unto the isles, and shall *t* many
Dan 11:31 shall *t* away the daily sacrifice,
Hos 1:2 *t* unto thee a wife of whoredoms
Hos 1:6 but I will utterly *t* them away
Hos 2:9 *t* away my corn in the time
Hos 2:17 For I will *t* away the names of
Hos 4:10 left off to *t* heed to the LORD
Hos 4:11 new wine *t* away the heart
Hos 5:14 I will *t* away, and none shall
Hos 11:4 that *t* off the yoke on their jaws
Hos 14:2 *T* with you words, and turn to the
Hos 14:2 *T* away all iniquity, and receive
Amos 3:5 shall one *t* up a snare from the
Amos 4:2 that he will *t* you away with
Amos 5:1 word which I *t* up against you
Amos 5:11 ye *t* from him burdens of wheat
Amos 5:12 they *t* a bribe, and they turn
Amos 5:23 *T* thou away from me the noise of
Amos 6:10 And a man's uncle shall *t* him up
Amos 9:2 thence shall mine hand *t* them
Amos 9:3 will search and *t* them out thence
Jonah 1:12 *T* me up, and cast me forth into
Jonah 4:3 Therefore now, O LORD, *t*, I
Mic 2:2 fields, and *t* them by violence
Mic 2:2 and houses, and *t* them away
Mic 2:4 In that day shall one *t* up a
Mic 2:6 them, that they shall not *t* shame
Mic 6:14 and thou shalt *t* hold, but shalt
Nah 1:2 the LORD will *t* vengeance on his
Nah 2:9 *T* ye the spoil of silver
Nah 2:9 *t* the spoil of gold
Hab 1:10 for they shall heap dust, and *t* it
Hab 1:15 They *t* up all of them with the
Hab 2:6 Shall not all these *t* up a
Zeph 3:11 for then I will *t* away out of the
Hag 1:8 I will *t* pleasure in it, and I
Hag 2:23 the LORD of hosts, will I *t* thee
Zec 1:6 did they not *t* hold of your
Zec 3:4 *T* away the filthy garments from
Zec 6:10 *T* of them of the captivity, even
Zec 6:11 Then *t* silver and gold, and make
Zec 8:23 that ten men shall *t* hold out of
Zec 8:23 even shall *t* hold of the skirt of
Zec 9:7 I will *t* away his blood out of
Zec 11:15 *T* unto thee yet the instruments
Zec 14:21 *t* of them, and seethe therein
Mal 2:3 one shall *t* you away with it
Mal 2:15 Therefore *t* heed to your spirit,
Mal 2:16 therefore *t* heed to your spirit,
Mt 1:20 fear not to *t* unto thee Mary thy
Mt 2:13 *t* the young child and his mother,
Mt 2:20 *t* the young child and his mother,
Mt 5:40 *t* away thy coat, let him have thy
Mt 6:1 *T* heed that ye do not your alms
Mt 6:25 *T* no thought for your life, what
Mt 6:28 why *t* ye thought for raiment
Mt 6:31 Therefore *t* no thought, saying,
Mt 6:34 *T* therefore no thought for the
Mt 6:34 for the morrow shall *t* thought
Mt 9:6 *t* up thy bed, and go unto thine
Mt 10:19 *t* no thought how or what ye shall
Mt 11:12 and the violent *t* it by force
Mt 11:29 *T* my yoke upon you, and learn of
Mt 15:26 and said, It is not meet to *t* the
Mt 16:5 they had forgotten to *t* bread
Mt 16:6 *T* heed and beware of the leaven of
Mt 16:24 *t* up his cross, and follow me
Mt 17:25 of the earth *t* custom or tribute
Mt 17:27 *t* up the fish that first cometh
Mt 17:27 that *t*, and give unto them for me
Mt 18:10 *T* heed that ye despise not one of

Mt 18:16 then *t* with thee one or two more,
Mt 18:23 which would *t* account of his
Mt 20:14 *T* that thine is, and go thy way
Mt 22:13 *t* him away, and cast him into
Mt 24:4 *T* heed that no man deceive you
Mt 24:17 to *t* any thing out of his house
Mt 24:18 return back to *t* his clothes
Mt 25:28 *T* therefore the talent from him,
Mt 26:4 they might *t* Jesus by subtilty
Mt 26:26 it to the disciples, and said, *T*
Mt 26:45 Sleep on now, and *t* your rest
Mt 26:52 for all they that *t* the sword
Mt 26:55 with swords and staves for to *t* me
Mk 2:9 Arise, and *t* up thy bed, and walk
Mk 2:11 *t* up thy bed, and go thy way into
Mk 4:24 unto them, *T* heed what ye hear
Mk 6:8 *t* nothing for their journey
Mk 7:27 meet to *t* the children's bread
Mk 8:14 had forgotten to *t* bread, neither
Mk 8:15 *T* heed, beware of the leaven of
Mk 8:34 *t* up his cross, and follow me
Mk 10:21 *t* up the cross, and follow me
Mk 12:19 his brother should *t* his wife
Mk 13:5 *T* heed lest any man deceive you
Mk 13:9 But *t* heed to yourselves
Mk 13:11 *t* no thought beforehand what ye
Mk 13:15 to *t* any thing out of his house
Mk 13:16 again for to *t* up his garment
Mk 13:23 But *t* ye heed
Mk 13:33 *T* ye heed, watch and pray
Mk 14:1 how they might *t* him by craft
Mk 14:22 it and gave to them, and said, *T*
Mk 14:36 *t* away this cup from me
Mk 14:41 Sleep on now, and *t* your rest
Mk 14:44 *t* him, and lead him away safely
Mk 14:48 swords and with staves to *t* me
Mk 15:24 them, what every man should *t*
Mk 15:36 Elias will come to *t* him down
Mk 16:18 They shall *t* up serpents
Lk 1:25 to *t* away my reproach among men
Lk 5:24 *t* up thy couch, and go into thine
Lk 6:4 into the house of God, and did *t*
Lk 6:29 forbid not to *t* thy coat also
Lk 8:18 *T* heed therefore how ye hear
Lk 9:3 *T* nothing for your journey,
Lk 9:23 *t* up his cross daily, and follow
Lk 10:35 and said unto him, *T* care of him
Lk 11:35 *T* heed therefore that the light
Lk 12:11 *t* ye no thought how or what thing
Lk 12:15 *T* heed, and beware of covetousness
Lk 12:19 *t* thine ease, eat, drink, and be
Lk 12:22 *T* no thought for your life, what
Lk 12:26 why *t* ye thought for the rest
Lk 14:9 with shame to *t* the lowest room
Lk 16:6 *T* thy bill, and sit down quickly,
Lk 16:7 *T* thy bill, and write fourscore
Lk 17:3 *T* heed to yourselves
Lk 17:31 him not come down to *t* it away
Lk 19:24 *T* from him the pound, and give it
Lk 20:20 that they might *t* hold of his
Lk 20:26 they could not *t* hold of his
Lk 20:28 his brother should *t* his wife
Lk 21:8 *T* heed that ye be not deceived
Lk 21:34 *t* heed to yourselves, lest at any
Lk 22:17 *T* this, and divide it among
Lk 22:36 that hath a purse, let him *t* it
Jn 2:16 sold doves, *T* these things hence
Jn 5:8 him, Rise, *t* up thy bed, and walk
Jn 5:11 unto me, *T* up thy bed, and walk
Jn 5:12 unto thee, *T* up thy bed, and walk
Jn 6:7 every one of them may *t* a little
Jn 6:15 *t* him by force, to make him a
Jn 7:30 Then they sought to *t* him
Jn 7:32 priests sent officers to *t* him
Jn 10:17 my life, that I might *t* it again
Jn 10:18 and I have power to *t* it again
Jn 10:39 they sought again to *t* him
Jn 11:39 Jesus said, *T* ye away the stone
Jn 11:48 *t* away both our place and nation
Jn 11:57 shew it, that they might *t* him
Jn 16:15 said I, that he shall *t* of mine
Jn 17:15 shouldest *t* them out of the world
Jn 18:31 *T* ye him, and judge him according
Jn 19:6 them, *T* ye him, and crucify him
Jn 19:38 he might *t* away the body of Jesus
Jn 20:15 laid him, and I will *t* him away
Acts 1:20 and his bishoprick let another *t*
Acts 1:25 That he may *t* part of this
Acts 5:35 *t* heed to yourselves what ye
Acts 12:3 proceeded further to *t* Peter also
Acts 15:14 to *t* out of them a people for his
Acts 15:37 determined to *t* with them John
Acts 15:38 not good to *t* him with them
Acts 20:13 there intending to *t* in Paul
Acts 20:26 Wherefore I *t* you to record this
Acts 20:28 *T* heed therefore unto yourselves,
Acts 21:24 Them *t*, and purify thyself with
Acts 22:26 saying, *T* heed what thou doest
Acts 23:10 to *t* him by force from among them
Acts 24:8 of whom thyself mayest *t*
Acts 27:33 Paul besought them all to *t* meat
Acts 27:34 I pray you to *t* some meat
Rom 11:21 *t* heed lest he also spare not
Rom 11:27 when I shall *t* away their sins
Rom 15:24 Whensoever I *t* my journey into
1Cor 3:10 But let every man *t* heed how he
1Cor 6:7 Why do ye not rather *t* wrong
1Cor 6:15 shall I then *t* the members of
1Cor 8:9 But *t* heed lest by any means this
1Cor 9:9 Doth God *t* care for oxen
1Cor 10:12 he standeth *t* heed lest he fall
1Cor 11:24 thanks, he brake it, and said, *T*
2Cor 8:4 *t* upon us the fellowship of the
2Cor 11:20 man devour you, if a man *t* of you
2Cor 12:10 Therefore I *t* pleasure in
Gal 5:15 *t* heed that ye be not consumed
Eph 6:13 Wherefore *t* unto you the whole
Eph 6:17 *t* the helmet of salvation, and the
Col 4:17 *T* heed to the ministry which thou
1Ti 3:5 how shall he *t* care of the church
1Ti 4:16 *T* heed unto thyself, and unto the
2Ti 4:11 *T* Mark, and bring him with thee
Heb 3:12 *T* heed, brethren, lest there be
Heb 7:5 have a commandment to *t* tithes of
Heb 10:4 and of goats should *t* away sins
Heb 10:11 which can never *t* away sins
Jas 5:10 *T*, my brethren, the prophets, who
1Pet 2:20 faults, ye shall *t* it patiently
1Pet 2:20 ye *t* it patiently, this is
2Pet 1:19 ye do well that ye *t* heed
1Jn 3:5 was manifested to *t* away our sins
Rev 3:11 hast, that no man *t* thy crown
Rev 5:9 Thou art worthy to *t* the book
Rev 6:4 thereon to *t* peace from the earth
Rev 10:8 *t* the little book which is open
Rev 10:9 said unto me, *T* it, and eat it up
Rev 22:17 let him *t* the water of life
Rev 22:19 if any man shall *t* away from the
Rev 22:19 God shall *t* away his part out of

**TAKEN**

Gen 2:22 which the LORD God had *t* from man
Gen 2:23 because she was *t* out of Man
Gen 3:19 for out of it wast thou *t*
Gen 3:23 the ground from whence he was *t*
Gen 4:15 shall be *t* on him sevenfold
Gen 12:15 the woman was *t* into Pharaoh's
Gen 12:19 so I might have *t* her to me to
Gen 14:14 that his brother was *t* captive
Gen 18:27 I have *t* upon me to speak unto
Gen 18:31 I have *t* upon me to speak unto
Gen 20:3 for the woman which thou hast *t*
Gen 21:25 servants had violently *t* away
Gen 27:33 where is he that hath *t* venison
Gen 27:35 and hath *t* away thy blessing
Gen 27:36 now he hath *t* away my blessing
Gen 30:15 that thou hast *t* my husband
Gen 30:23 God hath *t* away my reproach
Gen 31:1 Jacob hath *t* away all that was
Gen 31:9 Thus God hath *t* away the cattle
Gen 31:16 which God hath *t* from our father
Gen 31:26 as captives *t* with the sword
Gen 31:34 Now Rachel had *t* the images
Ex 14:11 hast thou *t* us away to die in the
Ex 25:15 they shall not be *t* from it
Ex 40:36 when the cloud was *t* up from over
Ex 40:37 But if the cloud were not *t* up
Ex 40:37 not till the day that it was *t* up
Lev 4:10 As it was *t* off from the bullock
Lev 4:31 as the fat is *t* away from off the
Lev 4:35 as the fat of the lamb is *t* away
Lev 6:2 or in a thing *t* away by violence,
Lev 7:34 the heave shoulder have I *t* of
Lev 14:43 that he hath *t* away the stones
Lev 24:8 being *t* from the children of
Num 3:12 I have *t* the Levites from among
Num 5:13 neither she be *t* with the manner
Num 8:16 of Israel, have I *t* them unto me
Num 8:18 I have *t* the Levites for all the
Num 9:17 when the cloud was *t* up from the
Num 9:21 the cloud was *t* up in the morning
Num 9:21 by night that the cloud was *t* up
Num 9:22 but when it was *t* up, they
Num 10:11 that the cloud was *t* up from off
Num 10:17 And the tabernacle was *t* down
Num 16:15 I have not *t* one ass from them,
Num 18:6 I have *t* your brethren the
Num 21:26 *t* all his land out of his hand,
Num 31:26 the sum of the prey that was *t*
Num 31:49 Thy servants have *t* the sum of
Num 31:53 (For the men of war had *t* spoil
Num 36:3 be *t* from the inheritance of our
Num 36:3 so shall it be *t* from the lot of
Num 36:4 be *t* away from the inheritance of
Deut 4:20 But the LORD hath *t* you, and
Deut 20:7 a wife, and hath not *t* her
Deut 21:10 thou hast *t* them captive,
Deut 24:1 When a man hath *t* a wife, and
Deut 24:5 When a man hath *t* a new wife
Deut 24:5 cheer up his wife which he hath *t*
Deut 26:14 neither have I *t* away ought
Deut 28:31 *t* away from before thy face
Josh 7:11 for they have even *t* of the
Josh 7:15 that he that is *t* with the
Josh 7:16 and the tribe of Judah was *t*
Josh 7:17 and Zabdi was *t*
Josh 7:18 of the tribe of Judah, was *t*
Josh 8:8 shall be, when ye have *t* the city
Josh 8:21 that the ambush had *t* the city
Josh 10:1 had heard how Joshua had *t* Ai
Judg 1:8 against Jerusalem, and had *t* it
Judg 11:36 forasmuch as the LORD hath *t*
Judg 14:9 he told not them that he had *t*
Judg 15:6 because he had *t* his wife
Judg 17:2 of silver that were *t* from thee
Judg 18:24 Ye have *t* away my gods which I
1Sa 4:11 And the ark of God was *t*
1Sa 4:17 are dead, and the ark of God is *t*
1Sa 4:19 tidings that the ark of God was *t*
1Sa 4:21 because the ark of God was *t*
1Sa 4:22 for the ark of God is *t*
1Sa 7:14 which the Philistines had *t* from
1Sa 10:20 near, the tribe of Benjamin was *t*
1Sa 10:21 the family of Matri was *t*
1Sa 10:21 and Saul the son of Kish was *t*
1Sa 12:3 whose ox have I *t*
1Sa 12:3 or whose ass have I *t*
1Sa 12:4 neither hast thou *t* ought of any
1Sa 14:41 And Saul and Jonathan were *t*
1Sa 14:42 And Jonathan was *t*
1Sa 21:6 that was *t* from before the LORD,
1Sa 21:6 in the day when it was *t* away
1Sa 30:2 had *t* the women captives, that
1Sa 30:3 their daughters, were *t* captives
1Sa 30:5 David's two wives were *t* captives
1Sa 30:16 they had *t* out of the land of the
1Sa 30:19 any thing that they had *t* to them
2Sa 12:9 hast *t* his wife to be thy wife,
2Sa 12:10 hast *t* the wife of Uriah the
2Sa 12:27 have *t* the city of waters
2Sa 16:8 thou art *t* in thy mischief,
2Sa 18:9 he was *t* up between the heaven and
2Sa 18:18 Now Absalom in his lifetime had *t*
2Sa 23:6 they cannot be *t* with hands
1Kin 7:8 daughter, whom he had *t* to wife
1Kin 9:9 have *t* hold upon other gods, and
1Kin 9:16 *t* Gezer, and burnt it with fire,
1Kin 16:18 Zimri saw that the city was *t*
1Kin 21:19 thou killed, and also *t* possession
1Kin 22:43 the high places were not *t* away
2Kin 2:9 before I be *t* away from thee
2Kin 2:10 thou see me when I am *t* from thee
2Kin 2:16 Spirit of the LORD hath *t* him up
2Kin 4:20 And when he had *t* him, and brought
2Kin 6:22 hast *t* captive with thy sword
2Kin 12:3 the high places were not *t* away
2Kin 13:25 which he had *t* out of the hand of
2Kin 14:4 the high places were not *t* away
2Kin 18:10 king of Israel, Samaria was *t*
2Kin 18:22 whose altars Hezekiah hath *t* away
2Kin 24:7 for the king of Babylon had *t*
1Chr 24:6 household being *t* for Eleazar
1Chr 24:6 for Eleazar, and one *t* for Ithamar
2Chr 15:8 which he had *t* from mount Ephraim
2Chr 15:17 were not *t* away out of Israel
2Chr 17:2 which Asa his father had *t*
2Chr 19:3 in that thou hast *t* away the
2Chr 20:33 the high places were not *t* away
2Chr 28:11 which ye have *t* captive of your
2Chr 28:18 had *t* Beth-shemesh, and Ajalon, and

2Chr 30:2 For the king had *t* counsel
2Chr 32:12 Hezekiah *t* away his high places
Ezr 9:2 For they have *t* of their
Ezr 10:2 have *t* strange wives of the
Ezr 10:10 have *t* strange wives, to increase
Ezr 10:14 let all them which have *t* strange
Ezr 10:17 end with all the men that had *t*
Ezr 10:18 found that had *t* strange wives
Ezr 10:44 All these had *t* strange wives
Neh 5:15 had *t* of them bread and wine,
Neh 6:18 his son Johanan had *t* the
Est 2:15 who had *t* her for his daughter,
Est 2:16 So Esther was *t* unto king
Est 8:2 ring, which he had *t* from Haman
Job 1:21 gave, and the LORD hath *t* away
Job 16:12 he hath also *t* me by my neck, and
Job 19:9 and *t* the crown from my head
Job 20:19 because he hath violently *t* away
Job 22:6 For thou hast *t* a pledge from thy
Job 24:24 they are *t* out of the way as all
Job 27:2 who hath *t* away my judgment
Job 28:2 Iron is *t* out of the earth, and
Job 30:16 of affliction have *t* hold upon me
Job 34:5 God hath *t* away my judgment
Job 34:20 shall be *t* away without hand
Ps 9:15 they hid is their own foot *t*
Ps 10:2 let them be *t* in the devices that
Ps 40:12 iniquities have *t* hold upon me
Ps 59:12 let them even be *t* in their pride
Ps 83:3 They have *t* crafty counsel
Ps 85:3 Thou hast *t* away all thy wrath
Ps 119:53 Horror hath *t* hold upon me
Ps 119:111 Thy testimonies have I *t* as an
Ps 119:143 and anguish have *t* hold on me
Prov 3:26 shall keep thy foot from being *t*
Prov 4:16 and their sleep is *t* away, unless
Prov 6:2 thou art *t* with the words of thy
Prov 7:20 He hath *t* a bag of money with him
Prov 11:6 be *t* in their own naughtiness
Eccl 2:18 which I had *t* under the sun
Eccl 3:14 to it, nor any thing *t* from it
Eccl 7:26 but the sinner shall be *t* by her
Eccl 9:12 fishes that are *t* in an evil net
Is 6:6 which he had *t* with the tongs
Is 6:7 and thine iniquity is *t* away
Is 7:5 have *t* evil counsel against thee,
Is 8:4 the spoil of Samaria shall be *t*
Is 8:15 be broken, and be snared, and be *t*
Is 10:27 that his burden shall be *t* away
Is 10:29 they have *t* up their lodging at
Is 16:10 And gladness is *t* away, and joy out
Is 17:1 Damascus is *t* away from being a
Is 21:3 pangs have *t* hold upon me, as the
Is 23:8 Who hath *t* this counsel against
Is 24:18 the pit shall be *t* in the snare
Is 28:13 and be broken, and snared, and *t*
Is 33:20 that shall not be *t* down
Is 36:7 whose altars Hezekiah hath *t* away
Is 41:9 Thou whom I have *t* from the ends
Is 49:24 the prey be *t* from the mighty
Is 49:25 of the mighty shall be *t* away
Is 51:22 I have *t* out of thine hand the
Is 52:5 my people is *t* away for nought
Is 53:8 He was *t* from prison and from
Is 57:1 and merciful men are *t* away
Is 57:1 that the righteous is *t* away from
Is 64:6 like the wind, have *t* us away
Jer 6:11 husband with the wife shall be *t*
Jer 6:24 anguish hath *t* hold of us
Jer 8:9 ashamed, they are dismayed and *t*
Jer 8:21 astonishment hath *t* hold on me
Jer 12:2 them, yea, they have *t* root
Jer 16:5 for I have *t* away my peace from
Jer 29:22 of them shall be *t* up a curse by
Jer 34:3 his hand, but shalt surely be *t*
Jer 38:23 but shalt be *t* by the hand of the
Jer 38:28 the day that Jerusalem was *t*
Jer 38:28 he was there when Jerusalem was *t*
Jer 39:5 and when they had *t* him, they
Jer 40:1 when he had *t* him being bound in
Jer 40:10 in your cities that ye have *t*
Jer 48:1 Kiriathaim is confounded and *t*
Jer 48:7 treasures, thou shalt also be *t*
Jer 48:33 gladness is *t* from the plentiful
Jer 48:41 Kerioth is *t*, and the strong holds
Jer 48:44 the pit shall be *t* in the snare
Jer 48:46 for thy sons are *t* captives
Jer 49:20 LORD, that he hath *t* against Edom
Jer 49:24 anguish and sorrows have *t* her
Jer 49:30 hath *t* counsel against you
Jer 50:2 say, Babylon is *t*, Bel is
Jer 50:9 from thence she shall be *t*
Jer 50:24 for thee, and thou art also *t*
Jer 50:45 that he hath *t* against Babylon
Jer 51:31 that his city is *t* at one end
Jer 51:41 How is Sheshach *t*
Jer 51:56 Babylon, and her mighty men are *t*
Lam 2:6 he hath violently *t* away his
Lam 4:20 was *t* in their pits, of whom we
Eze 12:13 him, and he shall be *t* in my snare
Eze 15:3 Shall wood be *t* thereof to do any
Eze 16:17 Thou hast also *t* thy fair jewels
Eze 16:20 Moreover thou hast *t* thy sons
Eze 16:37 with whom thou hast *t* pleasure
Eze 17:12 hath *t* the king thereof, and the
Eze 17:13 hath *t* of the king's seed, and
Eze 17:13 him, and hath *t* an oath of him
Eze 17:13 he hath also *t* the mighty of the
Eze 17:20 him, and he shall be *t* in my snare
Eze 18:8 neither hath *t* any increase
Eze 18:13 upon usury, and hath *t* increase
Eze 18:17 That hath *t* off his hand from the
Eze 19:4 he was *t* in their pit, and they
Eze 19:8 he was *t* in their pit
Eze 21:23 the iniquity, that they may be *t*
Eze 21:24 ye shall be *t* with the hand
Eze 22:12 In thee have they *t* gifts to shed
Eze 22:12 thou hast *t* usury and increase, and
Eze 22:25 they have *t* the treasure and
Eze 25:15 and have *t* vengeance with a
Eze 27:5 they have *t* cedars from Lebanon
Eze 33:6 he is *t* away in his iniquity
Eze 36:3 ye are *t* up in the lips of
Dan 5:2 his father Nebuchadnezzar had *t*
Dan 5:3 the golden vessels that were *t*
Dan 6:23 So Daniel was *t* up out of the den
Dan 7:12 they had their dominion *t* away
Dan 8:11 the daily sacrifice was *t* away
Dan 11:12 when he hath *t* away the multitude
Dan 12:11 daily sacrifice shall be *t* away
Hos 4:3 of the sea also shall be *t* away
Joel 3:5 Because ye have *t* my silver
Amos 3:4 of his den, if he have *t* nothing
Amos 3:5 earth, and have *t* nothing at all
Amos 3:12 be *t* out that dwell in Samaria in
Amos 4:10 sword, and have *t* away your horses
Amos 6:13 Have we not *t* to us horns by our
Mic 2:9 have ye *t* away my glory for ever
Mic 4:9 for pangs have *t* thee as a woman
Zeph 3:15 The LORD hath *t* away thy
Zec 14:2 and the city shall be *t*, and the
Mt 4:24 that were *t* with divers diseases
Mt 9:15 bridegroom shall be *t* from them
Mt 13:12 from him shall be *t* away even
Mt 16:7 It is because we have *t* no bread
Mt 21:43 of God shall be *t* from you
Mt 24:40 the one shall be *t*, and the other
Mt 24:41 the one shall be *t*, and the other
Mt 25:29 be *t* away even that which he hath
Mt 27:59 And when Joseph had *t* the body
Mt 28:12 had *t* counsel, they gave large
Mk 2:20 shall be *t* away from them
Mk 4:25 from him shall be *t* even that
Mk 6:41 when he had *t* the five loaves and
Mk 9:36 when he had *t* him in his arms, he
Lk 1:1 Forasmuch as many have *t* in hand
Lk 4:38 mother was *t* with a great fever
Lk 5:5 all the night, and have *t* nothing
Lk 5:9 of the fishes which they had *t*
Lk 5:18 a man which was *t* with a palsy
Lk 5:35 shall be *t* away from them
Lk 5:36 the piece that was *t* out of the
Lk 8:18 from him shall be *t* even that
Lk 8:37 for they were *t* with great fear
Lk 9:17 there was *t* up of fragments that
Lk 10:42 shall not be *t* away from her
Lk 11:52 for ye have *t* away the key of
Lk 17:34 the one shall be *t*, and the other
Lk 17:35 the one shall be *t*, and the other
Lk 17:36 the one shall be *t*, and the other
Lk 19:8 if I have *t* any thing from any
Lk 19:26 he hath shall be *t* away from him
Jn 7:44 And some of them would have *t* him
Jn 8:3 unto him a woman *t* in adultery
Jn 8:4 this woman was *t* in adultery
Jn 13:12 had *t* his garments, and was set
Jn 19:31 and that they might be *t* away
Jn 20:1 seeth the stone *t* away from the
Jn 20:2 They have *t* away the Lord out of
Jn 20:13 Because they have *t* away my Lord
Acts 1:2 the day in which he was *t* up
Acts 1:9 while they beheld, he was *t* up
Acts 1:11 which is *t* up from you into
Acts 1:22 same day that he was *t* up from us
Acts 2:23 foreknowledge of God, ye have *t*
Acts 8:7 many *t* with palsies, and that were
Acts 8:33 his judgment was *t* away
Acts 8:33 for his life is *t* from the earth
Acts 17:9 when they had *t* security of Jason
Acts 20:9 the third loft, and was *t* up dead
Acts 21:6 when we had *t* our leave one of
Acts 23:27 This man was *t* of the Jews
Acts 27:17 Which when they had *t* up, they
Acts 27:20 should be saved was then *t* away
Acts 27:33 fasting, having *t* nothing
Acts 27:40 when they had *t* up the anchors,
Rom 9:6 word of God hath *t* none effect
1Cor 5:2 might be *t* away from among you
1Cor 10:13 There hath no temptation *t* you
2Cor 3:16 Lord, the vail shall be *t* away
1Th 2:17 being *t* from you for a short time
2Th 2:7 until he be *t* out of the way
1Ti 5:9 Let not a widow be *t* into the
2Ti 2:26 who are *t* captive by him at his
Heb 5:1 For every high priest *t* from
2Pet 2:12 brute beasts, made to be *t*
Rev 5:8 And when he had *t* the book
Rev 11:17 because thou hast *t* to thee thy
Rev 19:20 And the beast was *t*, and with him

## TAKER

Is 24:2 as with the *t* of usury, so with

## TAKEST

Ex 4:9 the water which thou *t* out of the
Ex 30:12 When thou *t* the sum of the
Judg 4:9 the journey that thou *t* shall not
1Chr 22:13 if thou *t* heed to fulfil the
Ps 104:29 thou *t* away their breath, they
Ps 144:3 that thou *t* knowledge of him
Eccl 9:9 labour which thou *t* under the sun
Is 58:3 our soul, and thou *t* no knowledge
Lk 19:21 thou *t* up that thou layedst not

## TAKETH

Ex 20:7 guiltless that *t* his name in vain
Deut 5:11 guiltless that *t* his name in vain
Deut 10:17 not persons, nor *t* reward
Deut 24:6 for he *t* a man's life to pledge
Deut 25:11 her hand, and *t* him by the secrets
Deut 27:25 Cursed be he that *t* reward to
Deut 32:11 *t* them, beareth them on her wings
Josh 7:14 *t* shall come according to the
Josh 15:16 *t* it, to him will I give Achsah
Judg 1:12 *t* it, to him will I give Achsah
1Sa 17:26 *t* away the reproach from Israel
1Kin 14:10 as a man *t* away dung, till it be
Job 5:5 *t* it even out of the thorns, and
Job 5:13 He *t* the wise in their own
Job 9:12 he *t* away, who can hinder him
Job 12:20 *t* away the understanding of the
Job 12:24 He *t* away the heart of the chief
Job 21:6 trembling *t* hold on my flesh
Job 27:8 gained, when God *t* away his soul
Job 40:24 He *t* it with his eyes
Ps 15:3 nor *t* up a reproach against his
Ps 15:5 nor *t* reward against the innocent
Ps 118:7 The LORD *t* my part with them that
Ps 137:9 Happy shall he be, that *t*
Ps 147:10 he *t* not pleasure in the legs of
Ps 147:11 The LORD *t* pleasure in them that
Ps 149:4 For the LORD *t* pleasure in his
Prov 1:19 which *t* away the life of the
Prov 16:32 his spirit than he that *t* a city
Prov 17:23 A wicked man *t* a gift out of the
Prov 25:20 As he that *t* away a garment in
Prov 26:17 is like one that *t* a dog by the
Prov 30:28 The spider *t* hold with her hands,
Eccl 1:3 labour which he *t* under the sun
Eccl 2:23 his heart *t* not rest in the night
Eccl 5:18 *t* under the sun all the days of
Is 13:14 and as a sheep that no man *t* up
Is 40:15 he *t* up the isles as a very
Is 44:14 *t* the cypress and the oak, which
Is 51:18 neither is there any that *t* her
Is 56:6 it, and *t* hold of my covenant
Eze 16:32 which *t* strangers instead of her
Eze 33:4 of the trumpet, and *t* not warning
Eze 33:5 But he that *t* warning shall
Amos 3:12 As the shepherd *t* out of the
Mt 4:5 Then the devil *t* him up into the
Mt 4:8 the devil *t* him up into an

Mt 9:16 to fill it up *t* from the garment
Mt 10:38 he that *t* not his cross, and
Mt 12:45 *t* with himself seven other
Mt 17:1 And after six days Jesus *t* Peter
Mk 2:21 filled it up *t* away from the old
Mk 4:15 *t* away the word that was sown in
Mk 5:40 he *t* the father and the mother of
Mk 9:2 six days Jesus *t* with him Peter
Mk 9:18 And wheresoever he *t* him, he
Mk 14:33 he *t* with him Peter and James and
Lk 6:29 him that *t* away thy cloke forbid
Lk 6:30 of him that *t* away thy goods ask
Lk 8:12 *t* away the word out of their
Lk 9:39 And, lo, a spirit *t* him, and he
Lk 11:22 he *t* from him all his armour
Lk 11:26 *t* to him seven other spirits more
Lk 16:3 for my lord *t* away from me the
Jn 1:29 which *t* away the sin of the world
Jn 10:18 No man *t* it from me, but I lay it
Jn 15:2 that beareth not fruit he *t* away
Jn 16:22 and your joy no man *t* from you
Jn 21:13 *t* bread, and giveth them, and fish
Rom 3:5 God unrighteous who *t* vengeance
1Cor 3:19 He *t* the wise in their own
1Cor 11:21 For in eating every one *t* before
Heb 5:4 no man *t* this honour unto himself
Heb 10:9 He *t* away the first, that he may

**TAKING**
2Chr 19:7 of persons, nor *t* of gifts
Job 5:3 I have seen the foolish *t* root
Ps 119:9 by *t* heed thereto according to
Jer 50:46 At the noise of the *t* of Babylon
Eze 25:12 the house of Judah by *t* vengeance
Hos 11:3 also to go, *t* them by their arms
Mt 6:27 Which of you by *t* thought can add
Mk 13:34 man is as a man *t* a far journey
Lk 4:5 *t* him up into an high mountain,
Lk 12:25 which of you with *t* thought can
Lk 19:22 *t* up that I laid not down, and
Jn 11:13 had spoken of *t* of rest in sleep
Rom 7:8 *t* occasion by the commandment,
Rom 7:11 *t* occasion by the commandment,
2Cor 2:13 but *t* my leave of them, I went
2Cor 11:8 *t* wages of them, to do you
Eph 6:16 *t* the shield of faith, wherewith
2Th 1:8 In flaming fire *t* vengeance on
1Pet 5:2 *t* the oversight thereof, not by
3Jn 7 *t* nothing of the Gentiles

**TALE**
Ex 5:8 the *t* of the bricks, which they
Ex 5:18 shall ye deliver the *t* of bricks
1Sa 18:27 gave them in full *t* to the king
1Chr 9:28 should bring them in and out by *t*
Ps 90:9 our years as a *t* that is told

**TALEBEARER**
Lev 19:16 down as a *t* among thy people
Prov 11:13 A *t* revealeth secrets
Prov 18:8 The words of a *t* are as wounds
Prov 20:19 about as a *t* revealeth secrets
Prov 26:20 so where there is no *t*, the
Prov 26:22 The words of a *t* are as wounds

**TALENT**
Ex 25:39 Of a *t* of pure gold shall he make
Ex 37:24 Of a *t* of pure gold made he it,
Ex 38:27 hundred talents, a *t* for a socket
2Sa 12:30 the weight whereof was a *t* of
1Kin 20:39 else thou shalt pay a *t* of silver
2Kin 5:22 a *t* of silver, and two changes of
2Kin 23:33 talents of silver, and a *t* of gold
1Chr 20:2 and found it to weigh a *t* of gold
2Chr 36:3 talents of silver and a *t* of gold
Zec 5:7 there was lifted up a *t* of lead
Mt 25:24 which had received the one *t* came
Mt 25:25 and went and hid thy *t* in the earth
Mt 25:28 Take therefore the *t* from him
Rev 16:21 stone about the weight of a *t*

**TALENTS**
Ex 38:24 offering, was twenty and nine *t*
Ex 38:25 the congregation was an hundred *t*
Ex 38:27 of the hundred *t* of silver were
Ex 38:27 hundred sockets of the hundred *t*
Ex 38:29 of the offering was seventy *t*
1Kin 9:14 to the king sixscore *t* of gold
1Kin 9:28 gold, four hundred and twenty *t*
1Kin 10:10 twenty *t* of gold, and of spices
1Kin 10:14 threescore and six *t* of gold,
1Kin 16:24 of Shemer for two *t* of silver
2Kin 5:5 and took with him ten *t* of silver
2Kin 5:23 said, Be content, take two *t*
2Kin 5:23 bound two *t* of silver in two bags
2Kin 15:19 gave Pul a thousand *t* of silver
2Kin 18:14 Judah three hundred *t* of silver
2Kin 18:14 of silver and thirty *t* of gold
2Kin 23:33 tribute of an hundred *t* of silver
1Chr 19:6 of Ammon sent a thousand *t* of
1Chr 22:14 an hundred thousand *t* of gold
1Chr 22:14 a thousand thousand *t* of silver
1Chr 29:4 Even three thousand *t* of gold
1Chr 29:4 seven thousand *t* of refined
1Chr 29:7 of God of gold five thousand *t*
1Chr 29:7 and of silver ten thousand *t*
1Chr 29:7 and of brass eighteen thousand *t*
1Chr 29:7 and one hundred thousand *t* of iron
2Chr 3:8 gold, amounting to six hundred *t*
2Chr 8:18 fifty *t* of gold, and brought them
2Chr 9:9 twenty *t* of gold, and of spices
2Chr 9:13 and threescore and six *t* of gold
2Chr 25:6 Israel for an hundred *t* of silver
2Chr 25:9 shall we do for the hundred *t*
2Chr 27:5 same year an hundred *t* of silver
2Chr 36:3 land in an hundred *t* of silver
Ezr 7:22 Unto an hundred *t* of silver
Ezr 8:26 fifty *t* of silver, and silver
Ezr 8:26 and silver vessels an hundred *t*
Ezr 8:26 and of gold an hundred *t*
Est 3:9 I will pay ten thousand *t* of
Mt 18:24 which owed him ten thousand *t*
Mt 25:15 And unto one he gave five *t*
Mt 25:16 that had received the five *t* went
Mt 25:16 same, and made them other five *t*
Mt 25:20 he that had received five *t* came
Mt 25:20 came and brought other five *t*
Mt 25:20 thou deliveredst unto me five *t*
Mt 25:20 gained beside them five *t* more
Mt 25:22 also that had received two *t* came
Mt 25:22 thou deliveredst unto me two *t*
Mt 25:22 gained two other *t* beside them
Mt 25:28 give it unto him which hath ten *t*

**TALES**
Eze 22:9 men that carry *t* to shed blood
Lk 24:11 words seemed to them as idle *t*

**TALITHA** *(tal'-ith-ah) Aramaic for damsel.*
Mk 5:41 hand, and said unto her, *T* cumi

**TALKERS**
Eze 36:3 ye are taken up in the lips of *t*
Titus 1:10 there are many unruly and vain *t*

**TALL**
Deut 2:10 a people great, and many, and *t*
Deut 2:21 A people great, and many, and *t*
Deut 9:2 A people great and *t*, the children
2Kin 19:23 will cut down the *t* cedar trees
Is 37:24 cut down the *t* cedars thereof

**TALLER**
Deut 1:28 people is greater and *t* than we

**TALMAI** *(tal'-mahee)*
*1. A son of Anak.*
Num 13:22 where Ahiman, Sheshai, and *T*
Josh 15:14 of Anak, Sheshai, and Ahiman, and *T*
Judg 1:10 slew Sheshai, and Ahiman, and *T*
*2. A king of Geshur.*
2Sa 3:3 the daughter of *T* king of Geshur
2Sa 13:37 But Absalom fled, and went to *T*
1Chr 3:2 the daughter of *T* king of Geshur

**TALMON** *(tal'-mon) A Levite in Jerusalem.*
1Chr 9:17 were, Shallum, and Akkub, and *T*
Ezr 2:42 of Ater, the children of *T*
Neh 7:45 of Ater, the children of *T*
Neh 11:19 Moreover the porters, Akkub, *T*
Neh 12:25 Bakbukiah, Obadiah, Meshullam, *T*

**TAMAH** *(ta'-mah)* See THAMAH. *A family of exiles.*
Neh 7:55 of Sisera, the children of *T*

**TAMAR** *(ta'-mar)* See THAMAR.
*1. Wife of Er.*
Gen 38:6 his firstborn, whose name was *T*
Gen 38:11 Then said Judah to *T* his daughter
Gen 38:11 *T* went and dwelt in her father's
Gen 38:13 And it was told *T*, saying, Behold
Gen 38:24 *T* thy daughter in law hath played
Ruth 4:12 whom *T* bare unto Judah, of the
1Chr 2:4 *T* his daughter in law bare him
*2. A daughter of David.*
2Sa 13:1 a fair sister, whose name was *T*
2Sa 13:2 he fell sick for his sister *T*
2Sa 13:4 And Amnon said unto him, I love *T*
2Sa 13:5 I pray thee, let my sister *T* come
2Sa 13:6 let *T* my sister come, and make me
2Sa 13:7 Then David sent home to *T*
2Sa 13:8 So *T* went to her brother Amnon's
2Sa 13:10 And Amnon said unto *T*, Bring the
2Sa 13:10 *T* took the cakes which she had
2Sa 13:19 *T* put ashes on her head, and rent
2Sa 13:20 So *T* remained desolate in her
2Sa 13:22 he had forced his sister *T*
2Sa 13:32 day that he forced his sister *T*
1Chr 3:9 the concubines, and *T* their sister
*3. A daughter of Absalom.*
2Sa 14:27 and one daughter, whose name was *T*
*4. A city in Judah.*
Eze 47:19 from *T* even to the waters of
Eze 48:28 *T* unto the waters of strife in

**TAME**
Mk 5:4 neither could any man *t* him
Jas 3:8 But the tongue can no man *t*

**TAMED**
Jas 3:7 and of things in the sea, is *t*
Jas 3:7 and hath been *t* of mankind

**TAMMUZ** *(tam'-muz) A Syrian god.*
Eze 8:14 there sat women weeping for *T*

**TANACH** *(ta'-nak)* See TAANACH. *Same as Taanach.*
Josh 21:25 Manasseh, *T* with her suburbs, and

**TANHUMETH** *(tan'-hu-meth) Father of Seraiah.*
2Kin 25:23 the son of *T* the Netophathite
Jer 40:8 Kareah, and Seraiah the son of *T*

**TANNER**
Acts 9:43 days in Joppa with one Simon a *t*
Acts 10:6 He lodgeth with one Simon a *t*
Acts 10:32 of one Simon a *t* by the sea side

**TAPESTRY**
Prov 7:16 decked my bed with coverings of *t*
Prov 31:22 She maketh herself coverings of *t*

**TAPHATH** *(ta'-fath) A daughter of Solomon.*
1Kin 4:11 which had *T* the daughter of

**TAPPUAH** *(tap'-pu-ah)*
*1. A city in Judah.*
Josh 12:17 The king of *T*, one
Josh 15:34 And Zanoah, and En-gannim, *T*
*2. A city in Ephraim.*
Josh 16:8 The border went out from *T*
Josh 17:8 Now Manasseh had the land of *T*
Josh 17:8 but *T* on the border of Manasseh
*3. A son of Hebron.*
1Chr 2:43 Korah, and *T*, and Rekem, and Shema

**TARAH** *(ta'-rah) An Israelite encampment in the wilderness.*
Num 33:27 from Tahath, and pitched at *T*
Num 33:28 And they removed from *T*, and

**TARALAH** *(tar'-a-lah) A city in Benjamin.*
Josh 18:27 And Rekem, and Irpeel, and *T*

**TARE**
2Sa 13:31 *t* his garments, and lay on the
2Kin 2:24 *t* forty and two children of them
Mk 9:20 him, straightway the spirit *t* him
Lk 9:42 devil threw him down, and *t* him

**TAREA** *(ta'-re-ah)* See TAHREA. *A son of Micah.*
1Chr 8:35 were, Pithon, and Melech, and *T*

**TARES**
Mt 13:25 sowed *t* among the wheat, and went
Mt 13:26 fruit, then appeared the *t* also
Mt 13:27 from whence then hath it *t*
Mt 13:29 lest while ye gather up the *t*
Mt 13:30 Gather ye together first the *t*
Mt 13:36 the parable of the *t* of the field
Mt 13:38 but the *t* are the children of the
Mt 13:40 As therefore the *t* are gathered

**TARGET**
1Sa 17:6 legs, and a *t* of brass between his
1Kin 10:16 shekels of gold went to one *t*
2Chr 9:15 of beaten gold went to one *t*

**TARGETS**
1Kin 10:16 made two hundred *t* of beaten gold
2Chr 9:15 made two hundred *t* of beaten gold
2Chr 14:8 had an army of men that bare *t*

**TARPELITES** *(tar'-pel-ites) Foreigners resettled in Israel.*
Ezr 4:9 the Apharsathchites, the *T*

**TARRIED**
Gen 24:54 were with him, and *t* all night
Gen 28:11 *t* there all night, because the
Gen 31:54 and *t* all night in the mount
Num 9:19 when the cloud *t* long upon the
Num 9:22 that the cloud *t* upon the
Judg 3:25 they *t* till they were ashamed
Judg 3:26 And Ehud escaped while they *t*
Judg 19:8 they *t* until afternoon, and they
Ruth 2:7 that she *t* a little in the house
1Sa 13:8 he *t* seven days, according to the
1Sa 14:2 Saul *t* in the uttermost part of
2Sa 11:1 But David *t* still at Jerusalem
2Sa 15:17 *t* in a place that was far off
2Sa 15:29 and they *t* there
2Sa 20:5 but he *t* longer than the set time
2Kin 2:18 (for he *t* at Jericho,) he said
1Chr 20:1 But David *t* at Jerusalem
Ps 68:12 she that *t* at home divided the
Mt 25:5 While the bridegroom *t*, they all
Lk 1:21 marvelled that he *t* so long in
Lk 2:43 the child Jesus *t* behind in
Jn 3:22 there he *t* with them, and baptized
Acts 9:43 that he *t* many days in Joppa with
Acts 15:33 And after they had *t* there a space
Acts 18:18 Paul after this *t* there yet a
Acts 20:5 going before *t* for us at Troas
Acts 20:15 at Samos, and *t* at Trogyllium
Acts 21:4 disciples, we *t* there seven days
Acts 21:10 as we *t* there many days, there
Acts 25:6 when he had *t* among them more
Acts 27:33 the fourteenth day that ye have *t*
Acts 28:12 Syracuse, we *t* there three days

**TARRIEST**
Acts 22:16 And now why *t* thou

**TARRIETH**
1Sa 30:24 his part be that *t* by the stuff
Mic 5:7 that *t* not for man, nor waiteth

**TARRY**
Gen 19:2 *t* all night, and wash your feet,
Gen 27:44 *t* with him a few days, until thy
Gen 30:27 found favour in thine eyes, *t*
Gen 45:9 come down unto me, *t* not
Ex 12:39 out of Egypt, and could not *t*
Ex 24:14 *T* ye here for us, until we come
Lev 14:8 shall *t* abroad out of his tent
Num 22:19 *t* ye also here this night, that I
Judg 5:28 Why *t* the wheels of his chariots
Judg 6:18 I will *t* until thou come again
Judg 19:6 *t* all night, and let thine heart
Judg 19:9 evening, I pray you *t* all night
Judg 19:10 the man would not *t* that night
Ruth 1:13 Would ye *t* for them till they
Ruth 3:13 *T* this night, and it shall be in
1Sa 1:23 *t* until thou have weaned him
1Sa 10:8 seven days shalt thou *t*, till I
1Sa 14:9 unto us, *T* until we come to you
2Sa 10:5 *T* at Jericho until your beards be
2Sa 11:12 *T* here to day also, and to morrow
2Sa 15:28 I will *t* in the plain of the
2Sa 18:14 I may not *t* thus with thee
2Sa 19:7 there will not *t* one with thee
2Kin 2:2 unto Elisha, *T* here, I pray thee
2Kin 2:4 him, Elisha, *t* here, I pray thee
2Kin 2:6 And Elijah said unto him, *T*
2Kin 7:9 if we *t* till the morning light,
2Kin 9:3 open the door, and flee, and *t* not
2Kin 14:10 glory of this, and *t* at home
1Chr 19:5 *T* at Jericho until your beards be
Ps 101:7 lies shall not *t* in my sight
Prov 23:30 They that *t* long at the wine
Is 46:13 off, and my salvation shall not *t*
Jer 14:8 turneth aside to *t* for a night
Hab 2:3 though it *t*, wait for it
Hab 2:3 will surely come, it will not *t*
Mt 26:38 *t* ye here, and watch with me
Mk 14:34 *t* ye here, and watch
Lk 24:29 And he went in to *t* with them
Lk 24:49 but *t* ye in the city of Jerusalem
Jn 4:40 him that he would *t* with them
Jn 21:22 If I will that he *t* till I come
Jn 21:23 If I will that he *t* till I come
Acts 10:48 prayed they him to *t* certain days
Acts 18:20 him to *t* longer time with them
Acts 28:14 were desired to *t* with them seven
1Cor 11:33 to eat, *t* one for another
1Cor 16:7 but I trust to *t* a while with you
1Cor 16:8 But I will *t* at Ephesus until
1Ti 3:15 But if I *t* long, that thou mayest
Heb 10:37 come will come, and will not *t*

**TARRYING**
Ps 40:17 make no *t*, O my God
Ps 70:5 O LORD, make no *t*

**TARSHISH** *(tar'-shish)* See THARSHISH.
*1. A son of Javan.*
Gen 10:4 Elishah, and *T*, Kittim, and Dodanim
1Chr 1:7 Elishah, and *T*, Kittim, and Dodanim
*2. Spain.*
2Chr 9:21 to *T* with the servants of Huram
2Chr 9:21 came the ships of *T* bringing gold
2Chr 20:36 with him to make ships to go to *T*
2Chr 20:37 they were not able to go to *T*
Ps 48:7 the ships of *T* with an east wind
Ps 72:10 The kings of *T* and of the isles
Is 2:16 And upon all the ships of *T*
Is 23:1 Howl, ye ships of *T*
Is 23:6 Pass ye over to *T*
Is 23:10 land as a river, O daughter of *T*
Is 23:14 Howl, ye ships of *T*
Is 60:9 for me, and the ships of *T* first
Is 66:19 of them unto the nations, to *T*
Jer 10:9 into plates is brought from *T*
Eze 27:12 *T* was thy merchant by reason of
Eze 27:25 The ships of *T* did sing of thee
Eze 38:13 and Dedan, and the merchants of *T*
Jonah 1:3 *T* from the presence of the LORD
Jonah 1:3 and he found a ship going to *T*
Jonah 1:3 to go with them unto *T* from the
Jonah 4:2 Therefore I fled before unto *T*
*3. A prince of Persia.*
Est 1:14 was Carshena, Shethar, Admatha, *T*

**TARSUS** *(tar'-sus) Capital of Roman province of Cilicia.*
Acts 9:11 Judas for one called Saul, of *T*
Acts 9:30 Caesarea, and sent him forth to *T*
Acts 11:25 Then departed Barnabas to *T*
Acts 21:39 I am a man which am a Jew of *T*
Acts 22:3 a man which am a Jew, born in *T*

**TARTAK** *(tar'-tak) A god of the Avites.*
2Kin 17:31 And the Avites made Nibhaz and *T*

**TARTAN** *(tar'-tan) The commander of the Assyrian army.*
2Kin 18:17 And the king of Assyria sent *T*
Is 20:1 the year that *T* came unto Ashdod

**TASK**
Ex 5:14 have ye not fulfilled your *t* in
Ex 5:19 from your bricks of your daily *t*

**TASKMASTERS**
Ex 1:11 they did set over them *t* to
Ex 3:7 their cry by reason of their *t*
Ex 5:6 the same day the *t* of the people
Ex 5:10 the *t* of the people went out, and
Ex 5:13 the *t* hasted them, saying, Fulfil
Ex 5:14 which Pharaoh's *t* had set over

**TASKS**
Ex 5:13 Fulfil your works, your daily *t*

**TASTE**
Ex 16:31 the *t* of it was like wafers made
Num 11:8 the *t* of it was as the
Num 11:8 of it was as the *t* of fresh oil
1Sa 14:43 I did but *t* a little honey with
2Sa 3:35 if I *t* bread, or ought else, till
2Sa 19:35 can thy servant *t* what I eat or
Job 6:6 or is there any *t* in the white of
Job 6:30 cannot my *t* discern perverse
Job 12:11 and the mouth *t* his meat
Ps 34:8 O *t* and see that the LORD is good
Ps 119:103 How sweet are thy words unto my *t*
Prov 24:13 which is sweet to thy *t*
Song 2:3 and his fruit was sweet to my *t*
Jer 48:11 therefore his *t* remained in him,
Jonah 3:7 herd nor flock, *t* any thing
Mt 16:28 here, which shall not *t* of death
Mk 9:1 here, which shall not *t* of death
Lk 9:27 here, which shall not *t* of death
Lk 14:24 were bidden shall *t* of my supper
Jn 8:52 saying, he shall never *t* of death
Col 2:21 *t* not
Heb 2:9 God should *t* death for every man

**TASTED**
1Sa 14:24 So none of the people *t* any food
1Sa 14:29 because I *t* a little of this
Dan 5:2 Belshazzar, whiles he *t* the wine
Mt 27:34 and when he had *t* thereof, he
Jn 2:9 *t* the water that was made wine
Heb 6:4 have *t* of the heavenly gift, and
Heb 6:5 have *t* the good word of God, and
1Pet 2:3 If so be ye have *t* that the Lord

**TASTETH**
Job 34:3 trieth words, as the mouth *t* meat

**TATNAI** *(tat'-nahee) Persian governor of Samaria.*
Ezr 5:3 At the same time came to them *T*
Ezr 5:6 The copy of the letter that *T*
Ezr 6:6 Now therefore, *T*, governor beyond
Ezr 6:13 Then *T*, governor on this side the

**TATTLERS**
1Ti 5:13 but *t* also and busybodies,

**TAUGHT**
Deut 4:5 Behold, I have *t* you statutes and
Deut 31:22 *t* it the children of Israel
Judg 8:16 with them he *t* the men of Succoth
2Kin 17:28 *t* them how they should fear the
2Chr 6:27 when thou hast *t* them the good
2Chr 17:9 they *t* in Judah, and had the book
2Chr 17:9 cities of Judah, and *t* the people
2Chr 23:13 and such as *t* to sing praise
2Chr 30:22 unto all the Levites that *t* the
2Chr 35:3 the Levites that *t* all Israel
Neh 8:9 and the Levites that *t* the people
Ps 71:17 thou hast *t* me from my youth
Ps 119:102 for thou hast *t* me
Ps 119:171 when thou hast *t* me thy statutes
Prov 4:4 He *t* me also, and said unto me,
Prov 4:11 I have *t* thee in the way of
Prov 31:1 prophecy that his mother *t* him
Eccl 12:9 he still *t* the people knowledge
Is 29:13 me is *t* by the precept of men
Is 40:13 being his counsellor hath *t* him
Is 40:14 *t* him in the path of judgment, and
Is 40:14 *t* him knowledge, and shewed to him
Is 54:13 children shall be *t* of the LORD
Jer 2:33 also *t* the wicked ones thy ways
Jer 9:5 they have *t* their tongue to speak
Jer 9:14 which their fathers *t* them
Jer 12:16 as they *t* my people to swear by
Jer 13:21 for thou hast *t* them to be
Jer 28:16 because thou hast *t* rebellion
Jer 29:32 because he hath *t* rebellion
Jer 32:33 though I *t* them, rising up early
Eze 23:48 that all women may be *t* not to do
Hos 10:11 Ephraim is as an heifer that is *t*
Hos 11:3 I *t* Ephraim also to go, taking
Zec 13:5 for man *t* me to keep cattle from
Mt 5:2 his mouth, and *t* them, saying,
Mt 7:29 For he *t* them as one having
Mt 13:54 he *t* them in their synagogue,
Mt 28:15 the money, and did as they were *t*
Mk 1:21 entered into the synagogue, and *t*
Mk 1:22 for he *t* them as one that had
Mk 2:13 resorted unto him, and he *t* them
Mk 4:2 he *t* them many things by parables
Mk 6:30 they had done, and what they had *t*
Mk 9:31 For he *t* his disciples, and said
Mk 10:1 as he was wont, he *t* them again
Mk 11:17 And he *t*, saying unto them, Is it
Mk 12:35 while he *t* in the temple, How say
Lk 4:15 he *t* in their synagogues, being
Lk 4:31 *t* them on the sabbath days
Lk 5:3 *t* the people out of the ship
Lk 6:6 entered into the synagogue and *t*
Lk 11:1 as John also *t* his disciples
Lk 13:26 thou hast *t* in our streets
Lk 19:47 And he *t* daily in the temple
Lk 20:1 as he *t* the people in the temple,
Jn 6:45 And they shall be all *t* of God
Jn 6:59 synagogue, as he *t* in Capernaum
Jn 7:14 went up into the temple, and *t*
Jn 7:28 cried Jesus in the temple as he *t*
Jn 8:2 and he sat down, and *t* them
Jn 8:20 treasury, as he *t* in the temple
Jn 8:28 but as my Father hath *t* me
Jn 18:20 I ever *t* in the synagogue, and in
Acts 4:2 grieved that they *t* the people

Acts 5:21 temple early in the morning, and *t*
Acts 11:26 with the church, and *t* much people
Acts 14:21 had *t* many, they returned again
Acts 15:1 down from Judaea *t* the brethren
Acts 18:25 *t* diligently the things of the
Acts 20:20 have *t* you publickly, and from
Acts 22:3 *t* according to the perfect manner
Gal 1:12 it of man, neither was I *t* it
Gal 6:6 Let him that is *t* in the word
Eph 4:21 heard him, and have been *t* by him
Col 2:7 in the faith, as ye have been *t*
1Th 4:9 for ye yourselves are *t* of God to
2Th 2:15 traditions which ye have been *t*
Titus 1:9 faithful word as he hath been *t*
1Jn 2:27 no lie, and even as it hath *t* you
Rev 2:14 of Balaam, who *t* Balac to cast a

### TAUNT
Jer 24:9 be a reproach and a proverb, a *t*
Eze 5:15 So it shall be a reproach and a *t*

### TAUNTING
Hab 2:6 a *t* proverb against him, and say,

### TAVERNS
Acts 28:15 as Appii forum, and The three *t*

### TAXATION
2Kin 23:35 of every one according to his *t*

### TAXED
2Kin 23:35 but he *t* the land to give the
Lk 2:1 that all the world should be *t*
Lk 2:3 And all went to be *t*, every one
Lk 2:5 To be *t* with Mary his espoused

### TAXES
Dan 11:20 of *t* in the glory of the kingdom

### TAXING
Lk 2:2 this *t* was first made when
Acts 5:37 of Galilee in the days of the *t*

### TEACH
Ex 4:12 *t* thee what thou shalt say
Ex 4:15 will *t* you what ye shall do
Ex 18:20 thou shalt *t* them ordinances and
Ex 24:12 that thou mayest *t* them
Ex 35:34 put in his heart that he may *t*
Lev 10:11 that ye may *t* the children of
Lev 14:57 To *t* when it is unclean, and when
Deut 4:1 unto the judgments, which I *t* you
Deut 4:9 but *t* them thy sons, and thy sons'
Deut 4:10 that they may *t* their children
Deut 4:14 me at that time to *t* you statutes
Deut 5:31 which thou shalt *t* them, that
Deut 6:1 LORD your God commanded to *t* you
Deut 6:7 thou shalt *t* them diligently unto
Deut 11:19 ye shall *t* them your children,
Deut 17:11 the law which they shall *t* thee
Deut 20:18 That they *t* you not to do after
Deut 24:8 priests the Levites shall *t* you
Deut 31:19 *t* it the children of Israel
Deut 33:10 They shall *t* Jacob thy judgments,
Judg 3:2 to *t* them war, at the least such
Judg 13:8 *t* us what we shall do unto the
1Sa 12:23 but I will *t* you the good and the
2Sa 1:18 (Also he bade them *t* the children
1Kin 8:36 that thou *t* them the good way
2Kin 17:27 let him *t* them the manner of the
2Chr 17:7 to *t* in the cities of Judah
Ezr 7:10 to *t* in Israel statutes and
Ezr 7:25 *t* ye them that know them not
Job 6:24 *T* me, and I will hold my tongue
Job 8:10 Shall not they *t* thee, and tell
Job 12:7 the beasts, and they shall *t* thee
Job 12:8 to the earth, and it shall *t* thee
Job 21:22 Shall any *t* God knowledge
Job 27:11 I will *t* you by the hand of God
Job 32:7 of years should *t* wisdom
Job 33:33 peace, and I shall *t* thee wisdom
Job 34:32 That which I see not *t* thou me
Job 37:19 *T* us what we shall say unto him
Ps 25:4 *t* me thy paths
Ps 25:5 Lead me in thy truth, and *t* me
Ps 25:8 therefore will he *t* sinners in
Ps 25:9 and the meek will he *t* his way
Ps 25:12 him shall he *t* in the way that he
Ps 27:11 *T* me thy way, O LORD, and lead me
Ps 32:8 *t* thee in the way which thou
Ps 34:11 I will *t* you the fear of the LORD
Ps 45:4 hand shall *t* thee terrible things
Ps 51:13 Then will I *t* transgressors thy
Ps 60:*t* Michtam of David, to *t*
Ps 86:11 *T* me thy way, O LORD
Ps 90:12 So *t* us to number our days, that
Ps 105:22 and *t* his senators wisdom
Ps 119:12 *t* me thy statutes
Ps 119:26 *t* me thy statutes
Ps 119:33 *T* me, O LORD, the way of thy
Ps 119:64 *t* me thy statutes
Ps 119:66 *T* me good judgment and knowledge
Ps 119:68 *t* me thy statutes
Ps 119:108 O LORD, and *t* me thy judgments
Ps 119:124 thy mercy, and *t* me thy statutes
Ps 119:135 and *t* me thy statutes
Ps 132:12 my testimony that I shall *t* them
Ps 143:10 *T* me to do thy will
Prov 9:9 *t* a just man, and he will increase
Is 2:3 he will *t* us of his ways, and we
Is 28:9 Whom shall he *t* knowledge
Is 28:26 him to discretion, and doth *t* him
Jer 9:20 *t* your daughters wailing, and
Jer 31:34 they shall *t* no more every man
Eze 44:23 they shall *t* my people the
Dan 1:4 and whom they might *t* the learning
Mic 3:11 and the priests thereof *t* for hire
Mic 4:2 he will *t* us of his ways, and we
Hab 2:19 the dumb stone, Arise, it shall *t*
Mt 5:19 shall *t* men so, he shall be
Mt 5:19 *t* them, the same shall be called
Mt 11:1 he departed thence to *t* and to
Mt 28:19 *t* all nations, baptizing them in
Mk 4:1 began again to *t* by the sea side
Mk 6:2 he began to *t* in the synagogue
Mk 6:34 he began to *t* them many things
Mk 8:31 And he began to *t* them, that the
Lk 11:1 *t* us to pray, as John also taught
Lk 12:12 For the Holy Ghost shall *t* you in
Jn 7:35 the Gentiles, and *t* the Gentiles
Jn 9:34 born in sins, and dost thou *t* us
Jn 14:26 he shall *t* you all things, and
Acts 1:1 that Jesus began both to do and *t*
Acts 4:18 at all nor *t* in the name of Jesus
Acts 5:28 that ye should not *t* in this name
Acts 5:42 every house, they ceased not to *t*
Acts 16:21 *t* customs, which are not lawful
1Cor 4:17 as I *t* every where in every
1Cor 11:14 Doth not even nature itself *t* you
1Cor 14:19 by my voice I might *t* others also
1Ti 1:3 that they *t* no other doctrine
1Ti 2:12 But I suffer not a woman to *t*
1Ti 3:2 given to hospitality, apt to *t*
1Ti 4:11 These things command and *t*
1Ti 6:2 These things *t* and exhort
1Ti 6:3 If any man *t* otherwise, and
2Ti 2:2 shall be able to *t* others also
2Ti 2:24 be gentle unto all men, apt to *t*
Titus 2:4 That they may *t* the young women
Heb 5:12 ye have need that one *t* you again
Heb 8:11 they shall not *t* every man his
1Jn 2:27 and ye need not that any man *t* you
Rev 2:20 herself a prophetess, to *t*

### TEACHER
1Chr 25:8 the great, the *t* as the scholar
Hab 2:18 a *t* of lies, that the maker of
Jn 3:2 that thou art a *t* come from God
Rom 2:20 a *t* of babes, which hast the form
1Ti 2:7 a *t* of the Gentiles in faith and
2Ti 1:11 apostle, and a *t* of the Gentiles

### TEACHERS
Ps 119:99 more understanding than all my *t*
Prov 5:13 have not obeyed the voice of my *t*
Is 30:20 yet shall not thy *t* be removed
Is 30:20 but thine eyes shall see thy *t*
Is 43:27 thy *t* have transgressed against
Acts 13:1 at Antioch certain prophets and *t*
1Cor 12:28 secondarily prophets, thirdly *t*
1Cor 12:29 are all *t*?
Eph 4:11 and some, pastors and *t*
1Ti 1:7 Desiring to be *t* of the law
2Ti 4:3 shall they heap to themselves *t*
Titus 2:3 to much wine, *t* of good things
Heb 5:12 for the time ye ought to be *t*
2Pet 2:1 there shall be false *t* among you

### TEACHEST
Ps 94:12 O LORD, and *t* him out of thy law
Mt 22:16 *t* the way of God in truth,
Mk 12:14 but *t* the way of God in truth
Lk 20:21 *t* rightly, neither acceptest thou
Lk 20:21 but *t* the way of God truly
Acts 21:21 that thou *t* all the Jews which
Rom 2:21 Thou therefore which *t* another
Rom 2:21 *t* thou not thyself?

### TEACHETH
2Sa 22:35 He *t* my hands to war
Job 35:11 Who *t* us more than the beasts of
Job 36:22 who *t* like him
Ps 18:34 He *t* my hands to war, so that a
Ps 94:10 he that *t* man knowledge, shall
Ps 144:1 which *t* my hands to war, and my
Prov 6:13 his feet, he *t* with his fingers
Prov 16:23 The heart of the wise *t* his mouth
Is 9:15 and the prophet that *t* lies
Is 48:17 thy God which *t* thee to profit
Acts 21:28 that *t* all men every where
Rom 12:7 or he that *t*, on teaching
1Cor 2:13 in the words which man's wisdom *t*
1Cor 2:13 but which the Holy Ghost *t*
Gal 6:6 him that *t* in all good things
1Jn 2:27 anointing *t* you of all things

### TEACHING
2Chr 15:3 true God, and without a *t* priest
Jer 32:33 *t* them, yet they have not
Mt 4:23 *t* in their synagogues, and
Mt 9:35 *t* in their synagogues, and
Mt 15:9 *t* for doctrines the commandments
Mt 21:23 people came unto him as he was *t*
Mt 26:55 daily with you *t* in the temple
Mt 28:20 *T* them to observe all things
Mk 6:6 went round about the villages, *t*
Mk 7:7 *t* for doctrines the commandments
Mk 14:49 daily with you in the temple *t*
Lk 5:17 on a certain day, as he was *t*
Lk 13:10 he was *t* in one of the synagogues
Lk 13:22 through the cities and villages, *t*
Lk 21:37 day time he was *t* in the temple
Lk 23:5 *t* throughout all Jewry, beginning
Acts 5:25 in the temple, and *t* the people
Acts 15:35 Barnabas continued in Antioch, *t*
Acts 18:11 *t* the word of God among them
Acts 28:31 *t* those things which concern the
Rom 12:7 or he that teacheth, on *t*
Col 1:28 *t* every man in all wisdom
Col 3:16 *t* and admonishing one another in
Titus 1:11 *t* things which they ought not,
Titus 2:12 *T* us that, denying ungodliness and

### TEAR
Judg 8:7 then I will *t* your flesh with the
Ps 7:2 Lest he *t* my soul like a lion,
Ps 35:15 they did *t* me, and ceased not
Ps 50:22 lest I *t* you in pieces, and there
Jer 15:3 sword to slay, and the dogs to *t*
Jer 16:7 Neither shall men *t* themselves
Eze 13:20 I will *t* them from your arms, and
Eze 13:21 Your kerchiefs also will I *t*
Hos 5:14 I, even I, will *t* and go away
Hos 13:8 the wild beast shall *t* them
Amos 1:11 and his anger did *t* perpetually
Nah 2:12 The lion did *t* in pieces enough
Zec 11:16 fat, and *t* their claws in pieces

### TEARETH
Deut 33:20 *t* the arm with the crown of the
Job 16:9 He *t* me in his wrath, who hateth
Job 18:4 He *t* himself in his anger
Mic 5:8 *t* in pieces, and none can deliver
Mk 9:18 he taketh him, he *t* him
Lk 9:39 it *t* him that he foameth again,

### TEARS
2Kin 20:5 thy prayer, I have seen thy *t*
Est 8:3 besought him with *t* to put away
Job 16:20 mine eye poureth out *t* unto God
Ps 6:6 I water my couch with my *t*
Ps 39:12 hold not thy peace at my *t*
Ps 42:3 My *t* have been my meat day and
Ps 56:8 put thou my *t* into thy bottle
Ps 80:5 feedest them with the bread of *t*
Ps 80:5 givest them *t* to drink in great
Ps 116:8 soul from death, mine eyes from *t*
Ps 126:5 They that sow in *t* shall reap in
Eccl 4:1 behold the *t* of such as were
Is 16:9 I will water thee with my *t*
Is 25:8 wipe away *t* from off all faces
Is 38:5 thy prayer, I have seen thy *t*
Jer 9:1 and mine eyes a fountain of *t*
Jer 9:18 that our eyes may run down with *t*
Jer 13:17 weep sore, and run down with *t*
Jer 14:17 mine eyes run down with *t* night
Jer 31:16 weeping, and thine eyes from *t*
Lam 1:2 night, and her *t* are on her cheeks
Lam 2:11 Mine eyes do fail with *t*, my
Lam 2:18 let *t* run down like a river day

Eze 24:16 neither shall thy *t* run down
Mal 2:13 the altar of the LORD with *t*
Mk 9:24 child cried out, and said with *t*
Lk 7:38 and began to wash his feet with *t*
Lk 7:44 she hath washed my feet with *t*
Acts 20:19 humility of mind, and with many *t*
Acts 20:31 every one night and day with *t*
2Cor 2:4 I wrote unto you with many *t*
2Ti 1:4 see thee, being mindful of thy *t*
Heb 5:7 *t* unto him that was able to save
Heb 12:17 he sought it carefully with *t*
Rev 7:17 wipe away all *t* from their eyes
Rev 21:4 wipe away all *t* from their eyes

**TEATS**
Is 32:12 They shall lament for the *t*
Eze 23:3 bruised the *t* of their virginity
Eze 23:21 youth, in bruising thy *t* by the

**TEBAH** *(te'-bah) A son of Nahor.*
Gen 22:24 name was Reumah, she bare also *T*

**TEBALIAH** *(teb-a-li'-ah) A sanctuary servant.*
1Chr 26:11 *T* the third, Zechariah the fourth

**TEBETH** *(te'-beth) Tenth month of the Hebrew year.*
Est 2:16 tenth month, which is the month *T*

**TEDIOUS**
Acts 24:4 that I be not further *t* unto thee

**TEETH**
Gen 49:12 wine, and his *t* white with milk
Num 11:33 the flesh was yet between their *t*
Deut 32:24 send the *t* of beasts upon them
1Sa 2:13 fleshhook of three *t* in his hand
Job 4:10 the *t* of the young lions, are
Job 13:14 do I take my flesh in my *t*
Job 16:9 he gnasheth upon me with his *t*
Job 19:20 am escaped with the skin of my *t*
Job 29:17 and plucked the spoil out of his *t*
Job 41:14 his *t* are terrible round about
Ps 3:7 hast broken the *t* of the ungodly
Ps 35:16 they gnashed upon me with their *t*
Ps 37:12 and gnasheth upon him with his *t*
Ps 57:4 whose *t* are spears and arrows, and
Ps 58:6 Break their *t*, O God, in their
Ps 58:6 the great *t* of the young lions
Ps 112:10 he shall gnash with his *t*
Ps 124:6 not given us as a prey to their *t*
Prov 10:26 As vinegar to the *t*, and as smoke
Prov 30:14 whose *t* are as swords, and their
Prov 30:14 swords, and their jaw *t* as knives
Song 4:2 Thy *t* are like a flock of sheep
Song 6:6 Thy *t* are as a flock of sheep
Is 41:15 threshing instrument having *t*
Jer 31:29 the children's *t* are set on edge
Jer 31:30 his *t* shall be set on edge
Lam 2:16 they hiss and gnash the *t*
Lam 3:16 broken my *t* with gravel stones
Eze 18:2 the children's *t* are set on edge
Dan 7:5 mouth of it between the *t* of it
Dan 7:7 and it had great iron *t*
Dan 7:19 whose *t* were of iron, and his
Joel 1:6 whose *t* are the
Joel 1:6 are the *t* of a lion
Joel 1:6 hath the cheek *t* of a great lion
Amos 4:6 cleanness of *t* in all your cities
Mic 3:5 err, that bite with their *t*
Zec 9:7 abominations from between his *t*
Mt 8:12 shall be weeping and gnashing of *t*
Mt 13:42 shall be wailing and gnashing of *t*
Mt 13:50 shall be wailing and gnashing of *t*
Mt 22:13 shall be weeping and gnashing of *t*
Mt 24:51 shall be weeping and gnashing of *t*
Mt 25:30 shall be weeping and gnashing of *t*
Mt 27:44 with him, cast the same in his *t*
Mk 9:18 foameth, and gnasheth with his *t*
Lk 13:28 shall be weeping and gnashing of *t*
Acts 7:54 they gnashed on him with their *t*
Rev 9:8 their *t* were as the
Rev 9:8 were as the *t* of lions

**TEHAPHNEHES** *(te-haf'-ne-heze) Same as Tahpanhes.*
Eze 30:18 At *T* also the day shall be

**TEHINNAH** *(te-hin'-nah) A descendant of Judah.*
1Chr 4:12 *T* the father of Ir-nahash

**TEIL**
Is 6:13 as a *t* tree, and as an oak, whose

**TEKEL** *(te'-kel) Part of the "handwriting of the wall."*
Dan 5:25 that was written, MENE, MENE, *T*
Dan 5:27 *T*; Thou art weighed

**TEKOA** *(te'-ko-ah)* See TEKOAH, TEKOITE.
*1. Son of Ashur.*
1Chr 2:24 bare him Ashur the father of *T*
1Chr 4:5 the father of *T* had two wives
*2. A city in Judah.*
2Chr 11:6 even Beth-lehem, and Etam, and *T*
2Chr 20:20 forth into the wilderness of *T*
Jer 6:1 and blow the trumpet in *T*
Amos 1:1 who was among the herdmen of *T*

**TEKOAH** *(te'-ko-ah)* See TEKOA. *Same as Tekoa 2.*
2Sa 14:2 And Joab sent to *T*, and fetched
2Sa 14:4 the woman of *T* spake to the king
2Sa 14:9 the woman of *T* said unto the king

**TEKOITE** *(te'-ko-ite)* See TEKOITES. *An inhabitant of Tekoa.*
2Sa 23:26 Ira the son of Ikkesh the *T*
1Chr 11:28 Ira the son of Ikkesh the *T*
1Chr 27:9 was Ira the son of Ikkesh the *T*

**TEKOITES** *(te'-ko-ites)*
Neh 3:5 And next unto them the *T* repaired
Neh 3:27 After them the *T* repaired another

**TEL-ABIB** *(tel-a'-bib) Town on the River Chebar.*
Eze 3:15 to them of the captivity at *T*

**TELAH** *(te'-lah) Father of Tahan.*
1Chr 7:25 *T* his son, and Tahan his son,

**TELAIM** *(tel'-a-im)* See TELEM. *A place in Judah.*
1Sa 15:4 together, and numbered them in *T*

**TELASSAR** *(te-las'-sar)* See THELASAR. *A city in Mesopotamia.*
Is 37:12 children of Eden which were in *T*

**TELEM** *(te'-lem)* See TELAIM.
*1. A city in Judah.*
Josh 15:24 Ziph, and *T*, and Bealoth,
*2. Married a foreigner in exile.*
Ezr 10:24 Shallum, and *T*, and Uri

**TEL-HARESHA** *(tel-ha-re'-sha)* See TEL-HARSA. *A Babylonian settlement of exiles.*
Neh 7:61 went up also from Tel-melah, *T*

**TEL-HARSA** *(tel'-har-sah)* See TEL-HARESHA. *Same as Tel-haresha.*
Ezr 2:59 which went up from Tel-melah, *T*

**TEL-MELAH** *(tel-me'-lah) A place where the exiles lived.*
Ezr 2:59 were they which went up from *T*
Neh 7:61 they which went up also from *T*

**TEMA** *(te'-mah)*
*1. A son of Ishmael.*
Gen 25:15 Hadar, and *T*, Jetur, Naphish, and
1Chr 1:30 and Dumah, Massa, Hadad, and *T*
Is 21:14 *T* brought water to him that was
Jer 25:23 Dedan, and *T*, and Buz, and all that
*2. A city in northern Arabia.*
Job 6:19 The troops of *T* looked, the

**TEMAN** *(te'-man)* See TEMANITE.
*1. A son of Eliphaz.*
Gen 36:11 And the sons of Eliphaz were *T*
Gen 36:15 duke *T*, duke Omar, duke Zepho,
Gen 36:42 Duke Kenaz, duke *T*, duke Mibzar,
1Chr 1:36 *T*, and Omar, Zephi, and Gatam,
1Chr 1:53 Duke Kenaz, duke *T*, duke Mibzar,
*2. A race and district of Edom.*
Jer 49:7 Is wisdom no more in *T*
Jer 49:20 against the inhabitants of *T*
Eze 25:13 and I will make it desolate from *T*
Amos 1:12 But I will send a fire upon *T*
Obad 9 And thy mighty men, O *T*, shall be
Hab 3:3 God came from *T*, and the Holy One

**TEMANI** *(te'-ma-ni)* See TEMANITE. *A son of Ashur.*
Gen 36:34 land of *T* reigned in his stead

**TEMANITE** *(te'-man-ite)* See TEMANI, TEMANITES. *An inhabitant of Teman 2.*
Job 2:11 Eliphaz the *T*, and Bildad the
Job 4:1 Then Eliphaz the *T* answered
Job 15:1 Then answered Eliphaz the *T*
Job 22:1 Then Eliphaz the *T* answered
Job 42:7 the LORD said to Eliphaz the *T*
Job 42:9 So Eliphaz the *T* and Bildad the

**TEMANITES** *(te'-man-ites)*
1Chr 1:45 of the *T* reigned in his stead

**TEMENI** *(tem'-e-ni) A descendant of Caleb.*
1Chr 4:6 bare him Ahuzam, and Hepher, and *T*

**TEMPER**
Eze 46:14 of oil, to *t* with the fine flour

**TEMPERANCE**
Acts 24:25 he reasoned of righteousness, *t*
Gal 5:23 Meekness, *t*
2Pet 1:6 And to knowledge *t*
2Pet 1:6 and to *t* patience

**TEMPERATE**
1Cor 9:25 the mastery is *t* in all things
Titus 1:8 of good men, sober, just, holy, *t*
Titus 2:2 the aged men be sober, grave, *t*

**TEMPERED**
Ex 29:2 and cakes unleavened *t* with oil
Ex 30:35 *t* together, pure and holy
1Cor 12:24 but God hath *t* the body together,

**TEMPEST**
Job 9:17 For he breaketh me with a *t*
Job 27:20 a *t* stealeth him away in the
Ps 11:6 and brimstone, and an horrible *t*
Ps 55:8 escape from the windy storm and *t*
Ps 83:15 So persecute them with thy *t*
Is 28:2 strong one, which as a *t* of hail
Is 29:6 and great noise, with storm and *t*
Is 30:30 fire, with scattering, and *t*
Is 32:2 the wind, and a covert from the *t*
Is 54:11 O thou afflicted, tossed with *t*
Amos 1:14 with a *t* in the day of the
Jonah 1:4 there was a mighty *t* in the sea
Jonah 1:12 my sake this great *t* is upon you
Mt 8:24 there arose a great *t* in the sea
Acts 27:18 being exceedingly tossed with a *t*
Acts 27:20 no small *t* lay on us, all hope
Heb 12:18 unto blackness, and darkness, and *t*
2Pet 2:17 clouds that are carried with a *t*

**TEMPESTUOUS**
Ps 50:3 shall be very *t* round about him
Jonah 1:11 for the sea wrought, and was *t*
Jonah 1:13 wrought, and was *t* against them
Acts 27:14 there arose against it a *t* wind

**TEMPLE**
1Sa 1:9 by a post of the *t* of the LORD
1Sa 3:3 God went out in the *t* of the LORD
2Sa 22:7 he did hear my voice out of his *t*
1Kin 6:3 porch before the *t* of the house
1Kin 6:5 house round about, both of the *t*
1Kin 6:17 the *t* before it, was forty cubits
1Kin 6:33 door of the *t* posts of olive tree
1Kin 7:21 the pillars in the porch of the *t*
1Kin 7:50 of the house, to wit, of the *t*
2Kin 11:10 that were in the *t* of the LORD
2Kin 11:11 the *t* to the left corner of the
2Kin 11:11 to the left corner of the *t*
2Kin 11:11 along by the altar and the *t*
2Kin 11:13 the people into the *t* of the LORD
2Kin 18:16 the doors of the *t* of the LORD
2Kin 23:4 to bring forth out of the *t* of
2Kin 24:13 had made in the *t* of the LORD
1Chr 6:10 the priest's office in the *t* that
1Chr 10:10 his head in the *t* of Dagon
2Chr 3:17 up the pillars before the *t*
2Chr 4:7 their form, and set them in the *t*
2Chr 4:8 tables, and placed them in the *t*
2Chr 4:22 the doors of the house of the *t*
2Chr 23:10 from the right side of the *t* to
2Chr 23:10 to the left side of the *t*
2Chr 23:10 along by the altar and the *t*
2Chr 26:16 went into the *t* of the LORD to
2Chr 27:2 not into the *t* of the LORD
2Chr 29:16 that they found in the *t* of the
2Chr 35:20 when Josiah had prepared the *t*
2Chr 36:7 and put them in his *t* at Babylon
Ezr 3:6 But the foundation of the *t* of
Ezr 3:10 foundation of the *t* of the LORD
Ezr 4:1 the *t* unto the LORD God of Israel
Ezr 5:14 of the *t* that was in Jerusalem
Ezr 5:14 them into the *t* of Babylon
Ezr 5:14 king take out of the *t* of Babylon
Ezr 5:15 carry them into the *t* that is in
Ezr 6:5 of the *t* which is at Jerusalem
Ezr 6:5 unto the *t* which is at Jerusalem

Neh 6:10 in the house of God, within the *t*
Neh 6:10 and let us shut the doors of the *t*
Neh 6:11 go into the *t* to save his life
Ps 5:7 will I worship toward thy holy *t*
Ps 11:4 The LORD is in his holy *t*
Ps 18:6 he heard my voice out of his *t*
Ps 27:4 the LORD, and to enquire in his *t*
Ps 29:9 in his *t* doth every one speak of
Ps 48:9 O God, in the midst of thy *t*
Ps 65:4 of thy house, even of thy holy *t*
Ps 68:29 Because of thy *t* at Jerusalem
Ps 79:1 thy holy *t* have they defiled
Ps 138:2 I will worship toward thy holy *t*
Is 6:1 up, and his train filled the *t*
Is 44:28 and to the *t*, Thy foundation shall
Is 66:6 from the city, a voice from the *t*
Jer 7:4 The *t* of the LORD
Jer 7:4 The *t* of the LORD
Jer 7:4 The *t* of the LORD, are these
Jer 24:1 were set before the *t* of the LORD
Jer 50:28 our God, the vengeance of his *t*
Jer 51:11 the LORD, the vengeance of his *t*
Eze 8:16 at the door of the *t* of the LORD
Eze 8:16 backs toward the *t* of the LORD
Eze 41:1 Afterward he brought me to the *t*
Eze 41:4 twenty cubits, before the *t*
Eze 41:15 hundred cubits, with the inner *t*
Eze 41:20 made, and on the wall of the *t*
Eze 41:21 The posts of the *t* were squared
Eze 41:23 And the *t* and the sanctuary had two
Eze 41:25 on them, on the doors of the *t*
Eze 42:8 before the *t* were an hundred
Dan 5:2 had taken out of the *t* which was
Dan 5:3 that were taken out of the *t* of
Amos 8:3 the songs of the *t* shall be
Jonah 2:4 will look again toward thy holy *t*
Jonah 2:7 in unto thee, into thine holy *t*
Mic 1:2 you, the Lord from his holy *t*
Hab 2:20 But the LORD is in his holy *t*
Hag 2:15 upon a stone in the *t* of the LORD
Hag 2:18 of the LORD's *t* was laid,
Zec 6:12 he shall build the *t* of the LORD
Zec 6:13 he shall build the *t* of the LORD
Zec 6:14 a memorial in the *t* of the LORD
Zec 6:15 and build in the *t* of the LORD
Zec 8:9 that the *t* might be built
Mal 3:1 shall suddenly come to his *t*
Mt 4:5 him on a pinnacle of the *t*
Mt 12:5 in the *t* profane the sabbath
Mt 12:6 place is one greater than the *t*
Mt 21:12 And Jesus went into the *t* of God
Mt 21:12 them that sold and bought in the *t*
Mt 21:14 and the lame came to him in the *t*
Mt 21:15 and the children crying in the *t*
Mt 21:23 And when he was come into the *t*
Mt 23:16 Whosoever shall swear by the *t*
Mt 23:16 shall swear by the gold of the *t*
Mt 23:17 or the *t* that sanctifieth the
Mt 23:21 And whoso shall swear by the *t*
Mt 23:35 whom ye slew between the *t*
Mt 24:1 went out, and departed from the *t*
Mt 24:1 shew him the buildings of the *t*
Mt 26:55 daily with you teaching in the *t*
Mt 26:61 I am able to destroy the *t* of God
Mt 27:5 the pieces of silver in the *t*
Mt 27:40 Thou that destroyest the *t*
Mt 27:51 the veil of the *t* was rent in
Mk 11:11 into Jerusalem, and into the *t*
Mk 11:15 and Jesus went into the *t*, and
Mk 11:15 them that sold and bought in the *t*
Mk 11:16 carry any vessel through the *t*
Mk 11:27 and as he was walking in the *t*
Mk 12:35 and said, while he taught in the *t*
Mk 13:1 And as he went out of the *t*
Mk 13:3 of Olives over against the *t*
Mk 14:49 daily with you in the *t* teaching
Mk 14:58 I will destroy this *t* that is
Mk 15:29 Ah, thou that destroyest the *t*
Mk 15:38 the veil of the *t* was rent in
Lk 1:9 he went into the *t* of the Lord
Lk 1:21 that he tarried so long in the *t*
Lk 1:22 he had seen a vision in the *t*
Lk 2:27 he came by the Spirit into the *t*
Lk 2:37 which departed not from the *t*
Lk 2:46 days they found him in the *t*
Lk 4:9 and set him on a pinnacle of the *t*
Lk 11:51 between the altar and the *t*
Lk 18:10 men went up into the *t* to pray
Lk 19:45 And he went into the *t*, and began
Lk 19:47 And he taught daily in the *t*
Lk 20:1 as he taught the people in the *t*
Lk 21:5 And as some spake of the *t*
Lk 21:37 day time he was teaching in the *t*
Lk 21:38 in the morning to him in the *t*
Lk 22:52 priests, and captains of the *t*
Lk 22:53 I was daily with you in the *t*
Lk 23:45 the veil of the *t* was rent in the
Lk 24:53 And were continually in the *t*
Jn 2:14 found in the *t* those that sold
Jn 2:15 he drove them all out of the *t*
Jn 2:19 and said unto them, Destroy this *t*
Jn 2:20 six years was this *t* in building
Jn 2:21 But he spake of the *t* of his body
Jn 5:14 Jesus findeth him in the *t*
Jn 7:14 feast Jesus went up into the *t*
Jn 7:28 cried Jesus in the *t* as he taught
Jn 8:2 morning he came again into the *t*
Jn 8:20 treasury, as he taught in the *t*
Jn 8:59 hid himself, and went out of the *t*
Jn 10:23 in the *t* in Solomon's porch
Jn 11:56 as they stood in the *t*, What
Jn 18:20 in the synagogue, and in the *t*
Acts 2:46 daily with one accord in the *t*
Acts 3:1 into the *t* at the hour of prayer
Acts 3:2 the *t* which is called Beautiful
Acts 3:2 of them that entered into the *t*
Acts 3:3 to go into the *t* asked an alms
Acts 3:8 and entered with them into the *t*
Acts 3:10 at the Beautiful gate of the *t*
Acts 4:1 priests, and the captain of the *t*
Acts 5:20 speak in the *t* to the people all
Acts 5:21 into the *t* early in the morning
Acts 5:24 priest and the captain of the *t*
Acts 5:25 in prison are standing in the *t*
Acts 5:42 And daily in the *t*, and in every
Acts 19:27 but also that the *t* of the great
Acts 21:26 with them entered into the *t*
Acts 21:27 Asia, when they saw him in the *t*
Acts 21:28 brought Greeks also into the *t*
Acts 21:29 that Paul had brought into the *t*
Acts 21:30 Paul, and drew him out of the *t*
Acts 22:17 even while I prayed in the *t*
Acts 24:6 hath gone about to profane the *t*
Acts 24:12 in the *t* disputing with any man
Acts 24:18 Asia found me purified in the *t*
Acts 25:8 the Jews, neither against the *t*
Acts 26:21 the Jews caught me in the *t*
1Cor 3:16 ye not that ye are the *t* of God
1Cor 3:17 If any man defile the *t* of God
1Cor 3:17 for the *t* of God is holy, which
1Cor 3:17 of God is holy, which *t* ye are
1Cor 6:19 ye not that your body is the *t* of
1Cor 8:10 sit at meat in the idol's *t*
1Cor 9:13 live of the things of the *t*
2Cor 6:16 hath the *t* of God with idols
2Cor 6:16 for ye are the *t* of the living
Eph 2:21 unto an holy *t* in the Lord
2Th 2:4 he as God sitteth in the *t* of God
Rev 3:12 make a pillar in the *t* of my God
Rev 7:15 serve him day and night in his *t*
Rev 11:1 Rise, and measure the *t* of God
Rev 11:2 which is without the *t* leave out
Rev 11:19 the *t* of God was opened in heaven
Rev 11:19 there was seen in his *t* the ark
Rev 14:15 another angel came out of the *t*
Rev 14:17 out of the *t* which is in heaven
Rev 15:5 the *t* of the tabernacle of the
Rev 15:6 seven angels came out of the *t*
Rev 15:8 the *t* was filled with smoke from
Rev 15:8 man was able to enter into the *t*
Rev 16:1 the *t* saying to the seven angels
Rev 16:17 voice out of the *t* of heaven
Rev 21:22 And I saw no *t* therein
Rev 21:22 and the Lamb are the *t* of it

## TEMPLES

Judg 4:21 him, and smote the nail into his *t*
Judg 4:22 dead, and the nail was in his *t*
Judg 5:26 pierced and stricken through his *t*
Song 4:3 thy *t* are like a piece of a
Song 6:7 are thy *t* within thy locks
Hos 8:14 his Maker, and buildeth *t*
Joel 3:5 have carried into your *t* my
Acts 7:48 dwelleth not in *t* made with hands
Acts 17:24 dwelleth not in *t* made with hands

## TEMPORAL

2Cor 4:18 the things which are seen are *t*

## TEMPT

Gen 22:1 things, that God did *t* Abraham
Ex 17:2 wherefore do ye *t* the LORD
Deut 6:16 Ye shall not *t* the LORD your God,
Is 7:12 ask, neither will I *t* the LORD
Mal 3:15 yea, they that *t* God are even
Mt 4:7 Thou shalt not *t* the Lord thy God
Mt 22:18 Why *t* ye me, ye hypocrites
Mk 12:15 said unto them, Why *t* ye me
Lk 4:12 Thou shalt not *t* the Lord thy God
Lk 20:23 and said unto them, Why *t* ye me
Acts 5:9 to *t* the Spirit of the Lord
Acts 15:10 Now therefore why *t* ye God
1Cor 7:5 that Satan *t* you not for your
1Cor 10:9 Neither let us *t* Christ, as some

## TEMPTATION

Ps 95:8 as in the day of *t* in the
Mt 6:13 And lead us not into *t*, but
Mt 26:41 and pray, that ye enter not into *t*
Mk 14:38 ye and pray, lest ye enter into *t*
Lk 4:13 the devil had ended all the *t*
Lk 8:13 and in time of *t* fall away
Lk 11:4 And lead us not into *t*
Lk 22:40 Pray that ye enter not into *t*
Lk 22:46 and pray, lest ye enter into *t*
1Cor 10:13 There hath no *t* taken you but
1Cor 10:13 but will with the *t* also make a
Gal 4:14 my *t* which was in my flesh ye
1Ti 6:9 that will be rich fall into *t*
Heb 3:8 in the day of *t* in the wilderness
Jas 1:12 is the man that endureth *t*
Rev 3:10 will keep thee from the hour of *t*

## TEMPTATIONS

Deut 4:34 the midst of another nation, by *t*
Deut 7:19 The great *t* which thine eyes saw,
Deut 29:3 The great *t* which thine eyes have
Lk 22:28 have continued with me in my *t*
Acts 20:19 of mind, and with many tears, and *t*
Jas 1:2 joy when ye fall into divers *t*
1Pet 1:6 in heaviness through manifold *t*
2Pet 2:9 how to deliver the godly out of *t*

## TEMPTED

Ex 17:7 and because they *t* the LORD
Num 14:22 have *t* me now these ten times, and
Deut 6:16 your God, as ye *t* him in Massah
Ps 78:18 they *t* God in their heart by
Ps 78:41 *t* God, and limited the Holy One of
Ps 78:56 Yet they *t* and provoked the most
Ps 95:9 When your fathers *t* me, proved me
Ps 106:14 and *t* God in the desert
Mt 4:1 wilderness to be *t* of the devil
Mk 1:13 wilderness forty days, *t* of Satan
Lk 4:2 Being forty days *t* of the devil
Lk 10:25 *t* him, saying, Master, what shall
1Cor 10:9 Christ, as some of them also *t*
1Cor 10:13 to be *t* above that ye are able
Gal 6:1 thyself, lest thou also be *t*
1Th 3:5 some means the tempter have *t* you
Heb 2:18 he himself hath suffered being *t*
Heb 2:18 able to succour them that are *t*
Heb 3:9 When your fathers *t* me, proved me
Heb 4:15 in all points *t* like as we are
Heb 11:37 they were sawn asunder, were *t*
Jas 1:13 when he is *t*, I am *t* of God
Jas 1:13 for God cannot be *t* with evil
Jas 1:14 But every man is *t*, when he is

## TEMPTER

Mt 4:3 when the *t* came to him, he said,
1Th 3:5 some means the *t* have tempted you

## TEMPTETH

Jas 1:13 with evil, neither *t* he any man

## TEMPTING

Mt 16:1 *t* desired him that he would shew
Mt 19:3 *t* him, and saying unto him, Is it
Mt 22:35 him a question, *t* him, and saying,
Mk 8:11 of him a sign from heaven, *t* him
Mk 10:2 put away his wife? *t* him
Lk 11:16 *t* him, sought of him a sign from
Jn 8:6 *t* him, that they might have to

## TEN

Gen 5:14 were nine hundred and *t* years
Gen 16:3 after Abram had dwelt *t* years in
Gen 18:32 Peradventure *t* shall be found
Gen 24:10 the servant took *t* camels of the
Gen 24:22 hands of *t* shekels weight of gold
Gen 24:55 us a few days, at the least *t*
Gen 31:7 me, and changed my wages *t* times
Gen 31:41 hast changed my wages *t* times
Gen 32:15 *t* bulls, twenty she asses
Gen 32:15 twenty she asses, and *t* foals

Gen 42:3 Joseph's *t* brethren went down to
Gen 45:23 *t* asses laden with the good
Gen 45:23 *t* she asses laden with corn and
Gen 46:27 into Egypt, were threescore and *t*
Gen 50:3 for him threescore and *t* days
Gen 50:22 lived an hundred and *t* years
Gen 50:26 being an hundred and *t* years old
Ex 15:27 and threescore and *t* palm trees
Ex 26:1 *t* curtains of fine twined linen
Ex 26:16 *T* cubits shall be the length of a
Ex 27:12 pillars *t*, and their sockets *t*
Ex 34:28 the covenant, the *t* commandments
Ex 36:8 *t* curtains of fine twined linen
Ex 36:21 length of a board was *t* cubits
Ex 38:12 pillars *t*, and their sockets *t*
Lev 26:8 shall put *t* thousand to flight
Lev 26:26 *t* women shall bake your bread in
Lev 27:5 and for the female *t* shekels
Lev 27:7 and for the female *t* shekels
Num 7:14 One spoon of *t* shekels of gold,
Num 7:20 One spoon of gold of *t* shekels
Num 7:26 One golden spoon of *t* shekels
Num 7:32 One golden spoon of *t* shekels
Num 7:38 One golden spoon of *t* shekels
Num 7:44 One golden spoon of *t* shekels
Num 7:50 One golden spoon of *t* shekels
Num 7:56 One golden spoon of *t* shekels
Num 7:62 One golden spoon of *t* shekels
Num 7:68 One golden spoon of *t* shekels
Num 7:74 One golden spoon of *t* shekels
Num 7:80 One golden spoon of *t* shekels
Num 7:86 weighing *t* shekels apiece, after
Num 11:19 nor five days, neither *t* days
Num 11:32 gathered least gathered *t* homers
Num 14:22 have tempted me now these *t* times
Num 29:23 And on the fourth day *t* bullocks
Num 33:9 and threescore and *t* palm trees
Deut 4:13 to perform, even *t* commandments
Deut 10:4 the *t* commandments, which the
Deut 10:22 with threescore and *t* persons
Deut 32:30 two put *t* thousand to flight,
Deut 33:2 he came with *t* thousands of
Deut 33:17 they are the *t* thousands of
Josh 15:57 *t* cities with their villages
Josh 17:5 there fell *t* portions to Manasseh
Josh 21:5 half tribe of Manasseh, *t* cities
Josh 21:26 All the cities were *t* with their
Josh 22:14 And with him *t* princes, of each
Josh 24:29 being an hundred and *t* years old
Judg 1:4 of them in Bezek *t* thousand men
Judg 1:7 *t* kings, having their thumbs and
Judg 2:8 being an hundred and *t* years old
Judg 3:29 at that time about *t* thousand men
Judg 4:6 take with thee *t* thousand men of
Judg 4:10 he went up with *t* thousand men at
Judg 4:14 and *t* thousand men after him
Judg 6:27 Then Gideon took *t* men of his
Judg 7:3 and there remained *t* thousand
Judg 8:30 *t* sons of his body begotten
Judg 9:2 *t* persons, reign over you, or
Judg 9:4 *t* pieces of silver out of the
Judg 9:5 *t* persons, upon one stone
Judg 9:18 *t* persons, upon one stone, and
Judg 9:24 *t* sons of Jerubbaal might come,
Judg 12:11 and he judged Israel *t* years
Judg 12:14 rode on threescore and *t* ass colts
Judg 17:10 I will give thee *t* shekels of
Judg 20:10 we will take *t* men of an hundred
Judg 20:10 and a thousand out of *t* thousand
Judg 20:34 there came against Gibeah *t*
Ruth 1:4 they dwelled there about *t* years
Ruth 4:2 he took *t* men of the elders of
1Sa 1:8 not I better to thee than *t* sons
1Sa 6:19 thousand and threescore and *t* men
1Sa 15:4 and *t* thousand men of Judah
1Sa 17:17 these *t* loaves, and run to the
1Sa 17:18 carry these *t* cheeses unto the
1Sa 18:7 and David his *t* thousands
1Sa 18:8 ascribed unto David *t* thousands
1Sa 21:11 and David his *t* thousands
1Sa 25:5 And David sent out *t* young men
1Sa 25:38 came to pass about *t* days after
1Sa 29:5 and David his *t* thousands
2Sa 15:16 And the king left *t* women, which
2Sa 18:3 thou art worth *t* thousand of us
2Sa 18:11 given thee *t* shekels of silver
2Sa 18:15 *t* young men that bare Joab's
2Sa 19:43 We have *t* parts in the king, and
2Sa 20:3 the king took the *t* women his
1Kin 4:23 *T* fat oxen, and twenty oxen out of
1Kin 5:14 *t* thousand a month by courses
1Kin 5:15 *t* thousand that bare burdens, and
1Kin 6:3 *t* cubits was the breadth thereof
1Kin 6:23 of olive tree, each *t* cubits high
1Kin 6:24 part of the other were *t* cubits
1Kin 6:25 And the other cherub was *t* cubits
1Kin 6:26 of the one cherub was *t* cubits
1Kin 7:10 great stones, stones of *t* cubits
1Kin 7:23 *t* cubits from the one brim to the
1Kin 7:24 *t* in a cubit, compassing the sea
1Kin 7:27 And he made *t* bases of brass
1Kin 7:37 this manner he made the *t* bases
1Kin 7:38 Then made he *t* lavers of brass
1Kin 7:38 one of the *t* bases one laver
1Kin 7:43 bases, and *t* lavers on the bases
1Kin 11:31 to Jeroboam, Take thee *t* pieces
1Kin 11:31 will give *t* tribes to thee
1Kin 11:35 give it unto thee, even *t* tribes
1Kin 14:3 And take with thee *t* loaves
2Kin 5:5 took with him *t* talents of silver
2Kin 5:5 of gold, and *t* changes of raiment
2Kin 13:7 *t* chariots, and *t* thousand
2Kin 14:7 in the valley of salt *t* thousand
2Kin 15:17 reigned *t* years in Samaria
2Kin 20:9 *t* degrees, or go back *t* degrees
2Kin 20:10 the shadow to go down *t* degrees
2Kin 20:10 shadow return backward *t* degrees
2Kin 20:11 the shadow *t* degrees backward
2Kin 24:14 even *t* thousand captives, and all
2Kin 25:25 *t* men with him, and smote Gedaliah
1Chr 6:61 of Manasseh, by lot, *t* cities
1Chr 21:5 *t* thousand men that drew sword
1Chr 29:7 *t* thousand drams, and of silver
1Chr 29:7 of silver *t* thousand talents, and
2Chr 2:2 *t* thousand men to bear burdens,
2Chr 2:18 *t* thousand of them to be bearers
2Chr 4:1 *t* cubits the height thereof
2Chr 4:2 sea of *t* cubits from brim to brim
2Chr 4:3 *t* in a cubit, compassing the sea
2Chr 4:6 He made also *t* lavers, and put
2Chr 4:7 he made *t* candlesticks of gold
2Chr 4:8 He made also *t* tables, and placed
2Chr 14:1 days the land was quiet *t* years
2Chr 25:11 the children of Seir *t* thousand
2Chr 25:12 other *t* thousand left alive did
2Chr 27:5 *t* thousand measures of wheat
2Chr 27:5 and *t* thousand of barley
2Chr 29:32 *t* bullocks, an hundred rams, and
2Chr 30:24 bullocks and *t* thousand sheep
2Chr 36:9 months and *t* days in Jerusalem
2Chr 36:21 to fulfil threescore and *t* years
Ezr 1:10 a second sort four hundred and *t*
Ezr 8:12 and with him an hundred and *t* males
Ezr 8:24 *t* of their brethren with them,
Neh 4:12 came, they said unto us *t* times
Neh 5:18 once in *t* days store of all sorts
Neh 11:1 to bring one of *t* to dwell in
Est 3:9 I will pay *t* thousand talents of
Est 9:10 The *t* sons of Haman the son of
Est 9:12 palace, and the *t* sons of Haman
Est 9:13 let Haman's *t* sons be hanged upon
Est 9:14 and they hanged Haman's *t* sons
Job 19:3 These *t* times have ye reproached
Ps 3:6 afraid of *t* thousands of people
Ps 33:2 and an instrument of *t* strings
Ps 90:10 years are threescore years and *t*
Ps 91:7 *t* thousand at thy right hand
Ps 92:3 Upon an instrument of *t* strings
Ps 144:9 an instrument of *t* strings will I
Ps 144:13 *t* thousands in our streets
Eccl 7:19 the wise more than *t* mighty men
Song 5:10 the chiefest among *t* thousand
Is 5:10 *t* acres of vineyard shall yield
Is 38:8 dial of Ahaz, *t* degrees backward
Is 38:8 So the sun returned *t* degrees
Jer 41:1 even *t* men with him, came unto
Jer 41:2 the *t* men that were with him, and
Jer 41:8 But *t* men were found among them
Jer 42:7 And it came to pass after *t* days
Eze 40:11 the entry of the gate, *t* cubits
Eze 41:2 breadth of the door was *t* cubits
Eze 42:4 a walk of *t* cubits breadth inward
Eze 45:1 the breadth shall be *t* thousand
Eze 45:3 and the breadth of *t* thousand
Eze 45:5 the *t* thousand of breadth, shall
Eze 45:14 cor, which is an homer of *t* baths
Eze 45:14 for *t* baths are an homer
Eze 48:9 and of *t* thousand in breadth
Eze 48:10 toward the west *t* thousand in
Eze 48:10 toward the east *t* thousand in
Eze 48:13 length, and *t* thousand in breadth
Eze 48:13 and the breadth *t* thousand
Eze 48:18 shall be *t* thousand eastward
Eze 48:18 and *t* thousand westward
Dan 1:12 servants, I beseech thee, *t* days
Dan 1:14 matter, and proved them *t* days
Dan 1:15 at the end of *t* days their
Dan 1:20 he found them *t* times better than
Dan 7:7 and it had *t* horns
Dan 7:10 unto him, and *t* thousand times
Dan 7:10 *t* thousand stood before him
Dan 7:20 of the *t* horns that were in his
Dan 7:24 the *t* horns out of this kingdom
Dan 7:24 are *t* kings that shall arise
Dan 11:12 shall cast down many *t* thousands
Amos 5:3 forth by an hundred shall leave *t*
Amos 6:9 if there remain *t* men in one
Mic 6:7 or with *t* thousands of rivers of
Hag 2:16 twenty measures, there were but *t*
Zec 1:12 these threescore and *t* years
Zec 5:2 and the breadth thereof *t* cubits
Zec 8:23 that *t* men shall take hold out of
Mt 18:24 which owed him *t* thousand talents
Mt 20:24 And when the *t* heard it, they were
Mt 25:1 heaven be likened unto *t* virgins
Mt 25:28 it unto him which hath *t* talents
Mk 10:41 And when the *t* heard it, they
Lk 14:31 whether he be able with *t*
Lk 15:8 woman having *t* pieces of silver
Lk 17:12 there met him *t* men that were
Lk 17:17 said, Were there not *t* cleansed
Lk 19:13 And he called his *t* servants
Lk 19:13 and delivered them *t* pounds
Lk 19:16 thy pound hath gained *t* pounds
Lk 19:17 have thou authority over *t* cities
Lk 19:24 give it to him that hath *t* pounds
Lk 19:25 unto him, Lord, he hath *t* pounds
Acts 23:23 and horsemen threescore and *t*
Acts 25:6 among them more than *t* days
1Cor 4:15 For though ye have *t* thousand
1Cor 14:19 than *t* thousand words in an
Jude 14 the Lord cometh with *t* thousands
Rev 2:10 ye shall have tribulation *t* days
Rev 5:11 the number of them was *t* thousand
Rev 5:11 thousand times *t* thousand
Rev 12:3 *t* horns, and seven crowns upon his
Rev 13:1 *t* horns, and upon his horns
Rev 13:1 and upon his horns *t* crowns
Rev 17:3 having seven heads and *t* horns
Rev 17:7 hath the seven heads and *t* horns
Rev 17:12 the *t* horns which thou sawest are
Rev 17:12 which thou sawest are *t* kings
Rev 17:16 the *t* horns which thou sawest

## TEND

Prov 21:5 diligent *t* only to plenteousness

## TENDER

Gen 18:7 unto the herd, and fetcht a calf *t*
Gen 29:17 Leah was *t* eyed
Gen 33:13 knoweth that the children are *t*
Deut 28:54 that the man that is *t* among you
Deut 28:56 The *t* and delicate woman among you
Deut 32:2 as the small rain upon the *t* herb
2Sa 23:4 as the *t* grass springing out of
2Kin 22:19 Because thine heart was *t*
1Chr 22:5 Solomon my son is young and *t*
1Chr 29:1 hath chosen, is yet young and *t*
2Chr 34:27 Because thine heart was *t*
Job 14:7 that the *t* branch thereof will
Job 38:27 bud of the *t* herb to spring forth
Ps 25:6 O LORD, thy *t* mercies and thy
Ps 40:11 not thou thy *t* mercies from me
Ps 51:1 of thy *t* mercies blot out my
Ps 69:16 to the multitude of thy *t* mercies
Ps 77:9 he in anger shut up his *t* mercies
Ps 79:8 let thy *t* mercies speedily
Ps 103:4 with lovingkindness and *t* mercies
Ps 119:77 Let thy *t* mercies come unto me,
Ps 119:156 Great are thy *t* mercies, O LORD
Ps 145:9 his *t* mercies are over all his
Prov 4:3 For I was my father's son, *t*
Prov 12:10 but the *t* mercies of the wicked
Prov 27:25 the *t* grass sheweth itself, and
Song 2:13 the vines with the *t* grape give a
Song 2:15 for our vines have *t* grapes
Song 7:12 whether the *t* grape appear, and
Is 47:1 thou shalt no more be called *t*
Is 53:2 grow up before him as a *t* plant
Eze 17:22 top of his young twigs a *t* one
Dan 1:9 *t* love with the prince of the

Dan 4:15 in the *t* grass of the field
Dan 4:23 in the *t* grass of the field
Mt 24:32 When his branch is yet *t*, and
Mk 13:28 When her branch is yet *t*, and
Lk 1:78 Through the *t* mercy of our God
Jas 5:11 is very pitiful, and of *t* mercy

**TENDERHEARTED**

2Chr 13:7 when Rehoboam was young and *t*
Eph 4:32 And be ye kind one to another, *t*

**TENDERNESS**

Deut 28:56 the ground for delicateness and *t*

**TENDETH**

Prov 10:16 labour of the righteous *t* to life
Prov 11:19 As righteousness *t* to life
Prov 11:24 than is meet, but it *t* to poverty
Prov 14:23 talk of the lips *t* only to penury
Prov 19:23 The fear of the LORD *t* to life

**TENONS**

Ex 26:17 Two *t* shall there be in one board
Ex 26:19 under one board for his two *t*
Ex 26:19 under another board for his two *t*
Ex 36:22 One board had two *t*, equally
Ex 36:24 under one board for his two *t*
Ex 36:24 under another board for his two *t*

**TENOR**

Gen 43:7 according to the *t* of these words
Ex 34:27 for after the *t* of these words I

**TEN'S**

Gen 18:32 I will not destroy it for *t* sake

**TENS**

Ex 18:21 rulers of fifties, and rulers of *t*
Ex 18:25 rulers of fifties, and rulers of *t*
Deut 1:15 over fifties, and captains over *t*

**TENT**

Gen 9:21 and he was uncovered within his *t*
Gen 12:8 east of Beth-el, and pitched his *t*
Gen 13:3 unto the place where his *t* had
Gen 13:12 pitched his *t* toward Sodom
Gen 13:18 Then Abram removed his *t*, and came
Gen 18:1 he sat in the *t* door in the heat
Gen 18:2 ran to meet them from the *t* door
Gen 18:6 hastened into the *t* unto Sarah
Gen 18:9 And he said, Behold, in the *t*
Gen 18:10 And Sarah heard it in the *t* door
Gen 24:67 her into his mother Sarah's *t*
Gen 26:17 pitched his *t* in the valley of
Gen 26:25 the LORD, and pitched his *t* there
Gen 31:25 had pitched his *t* in the mount
Gen 31:33 Jacob's *t*, and into Leah's *t*
Gen 31:33 Then went he out of Leah's *t*
Gen 31:33 and entered into Rachel's *t*
Gen 31:34 And Laban searched all the *t*
Gen 33:18 pitched his *t* before the city
Gen 33:19 field, where he had spread his *t*
Gen 35:21 spread his *t* beyond the tower of
Ex 18:7 and they came into the *t*
Ex 26:11 loops, and couple the *t* together
Ex 26:12 of the curtains of the *t*, the
Ex 26:13 length of the curtains of the *t*
Ex 26:14 for the *t* of rams' skins dyed red
Ex 26:36 an hanging for the door of the *t*
Ex 33:8 and stood every man at his *t* door
Ex 33:10 every man in his *t* door
Ex 35:11 The tabernacle, his *t*, and his
Ex 36:14 for the *t* over the tabernacle
Ex 36:18 of brass to couple the *t* together
Ex 36:19 for the *t* of rams' skins dyed red
Ex 39:32 *t* of the congregation finished
Ex 39:33 the tabernacle unto Moses, the *t*
Ex 39:40 for the *t* of the congregation,
Ex 40:2 of the *t* of the congregation
Ex 40:6 of the *t* of the congregation
Ex 40:7 between the *t* of the congregation
Ex 40:19 abroad the *t* over the tabernacle
Ex 40:19 covering of the *t* above upon it
Ex 40:22 in the *t* of the congregation
Ex 40:24 in the *t* of the congregation
Ex 40:26 *t* of the congregation before the
Ex 40:29 of the *t* of the congregation
Ex 40:30 between the *t* of the congregation
Ex 40:32 into the *t* of the congregation
Ex 40:34 covered the *t* of the congregation
Ex 40:35 into the *t* of the congregation
Lev 14:8 abroad out of his *t* seven days
Num 3:25 shall be the tabernacle, and the *t*
Num 9:15 namely, the *t* of the testimony
Num 11:10 every man in the door of his *t*
Num 19:14 the law, when a man dieth in a *t*
Num 19:14 all that come into the *t*, and all
Num 19:14 and all that is in the *t*
Num 19:18 water, and sprinkle it upon the *t*
Num 25:8 the man of Israel into the *t*
Josh 7:21 in the earth in the midst of my *t*
Josh 7:22 and they ran unto the *t*
Josh 7:22 and, behold, it was hid in his *t*
Josh 7:23 them out of the midst of the *t*
Josh 7:24 his asses, and his sheep, and his *t*
Judg 4:11 pitched his *t* unto the plain of
Judg 4:17 fled away on his feet to the *t* of
Judg 4:18 had turned in unto her into the *t*
Judg 4:20 her, Stand in the door of the *t*
Judg 4:21 Heber's wife took a nail of the *t*
Judg 4:22 And when he came into her *t*
Judg 5:24 shall she be above women in the *t*
Judg 7:8 of Israel every man unto his *t*
Judg 7:13 host of Midian, and came unto a *t*
Judg 7:13 it, that the *t* lay along
Judg 20:8 We will not any of us go to his *t*
1Sa 4:10 and they fled every man into his *t*
1Sa 13:2 people he sent every man to his *t*
1Sa 17:54 but he put his armour in his *t*
2Sa 7:6 this day, but have walked in a *t*
2Sa 16:22 So they spread Absalom a *t* upon
2Sa 18:17 Israel fled every one to his *t*
2Sa 19:8 had fled every man to his *t*
2Sa 20:22 from the city, every man to his *t*
2Kin 7:8 of the camp, they went into one *t*
2Kin 7:8 again, and entered into another *t*
1Chr 15:1 ark of God, and pitched for it a *t*
1Chr 16:1 set it in the midst of the *t* that
1Chr 17:5 but have gone from *t* to *t*
2Chr 1:4 pitched a *t* for it at Jerusalem
2Chr 25:22 and they fled every man to his *t*
Ps 78:60 the *t* which he placed among men
Is 13:20 shall the Arabian pitch *t* there
Is 38:12 removed from me as a shepherd's *t*
Is 40:22 them out as a *t* to dwell in
Is 54:2 Enlarge the place of thy *t*
Jer 10:20 to stretch forth my *t* any more
Jer 37:10 they rise up every man in his *t*

**TENTH**

Gen 8:5 continually until the *t* month
Gen 8:5 in the *t* month, on the first day
Gen 28:22 will surely give the *t* unto thee
Ex 12:3 In the *t* day of this month they
Ex 16:36 an omer is the *t* part of an ephah
Ex 29:40 with the one lamb a *t* deal of
Lev 5:11 bring for his offering the *t* part
Lev 6:20 the *t* part of an ephah of fine
Lev 14:10 three *t* deals of fine flour for a
Lev 14:21 one *t* deal of fine flour mingled
Lev 16:29 on the *t* day of the month, ye
Lev 23:13 two *t* deals of fine flour mingled
Lev 23:17 two wave loaves of two *t* deals
Lev 23:27 Also on the *t* day of this seventh
Lev 24:5 two *t* deals shall be in one cake
Lev 25:9 on the *t* day of the seventh month
Lev 27:32 the *t* shall be holy unto the LORD
Num 5:15 the *t* part of an ephah of barley
Num 7:66 On the *t* day Ahiezer the son of
Num 15:4 *t* deal of flour mingled with the
Num 15:6 *t* deals of flour mingled with the
Num 15:9 a meat offering of three *t* deals
Num 18:21 *t* in Israel for an inheritance
Num 18:26 even a *t* part of the tithe
Num 28:5 a *t* part of an ephah of flour for
Num 28:9 two *t* deals of flour for a meat
Num 28:12 three *t* deals of flour for a meat
Num 28:12 two *t* deals of flour for a meat
Num 28:13 a several *t* deal of flour mingled
Num 28:20 three *t* deals shall ye offer for
Num 28:20 bullock, and two *t* deals for a ram
Num 28:21 A several *t* deal shalt thou offer
Num 28:28 three *t* deals unto one bullock,
Num 28:28 two *t* deals unto one ram,
Num 28:29 A several *t* deal unto one lamb,
Num 29:3 three *t* deals for a bullock
Num 29:3 and two *t* deals for a ram,
Num 29:4 And one *t* deal for one lamb,
Num 29:7 ye shall have on the *t* day of
Num 29:9 three *t* deals to a bullock
Num 29:9 and two *t* deals to one ram,
Num 29:10 A several *t* deal for one lamb,
Num 29:14 three *t* deals unto every bullock
Num 29:14 two *t* deals to each ram of the
Num 29:15 a several *t* deal to each lamb of
Deut 23:2 even to his *t* generation shall he
Deut 23:3 even to their *t* generation shall
Josh 4:19 on the *t* day of the first month
1Sa 8:15 he will take the *t* of your seed
1Sa 8:17 He will take the *t* of your sheep
2Kin 25:1 year of his reign, in the *t* month
2Kin 25:1 in the *t* day of the month, that
1Chr 12:13 Jeremiah the *t*, Machbanai the
1Chr 24:11 to Jeshua, the *t* to Shecaniah,
1Chr 25:17 The *t* to Shimei, he, his sons, and
1Chr 27:13 The *t* captain for the *t* month
Ezr 10:16 the *t* month to examine the matter
Est 2:16 his house royal in the *t* month
Is 6:13 But yet in it shall be a *t*
Jer 32:1 Jeremiah from the LORD in the *t*
Jer 39:1 king of Judah, in the *t* month
Jer 52:4 year of his reign, in the *t* month
Jer 52:4 in the *t* day of the month, that
Jer 52:12 in the *t* day of the month, which
Eze 20:1 the *t* day of the month, that
Eze 24:1 in the ninth year, in the *t* month
Eze 24:1 in the *t* day of the month, the
Eze 29:1 In the *t* year, in the *t* month
Eze 33:21 of our captivity, in the *t* month
Eze 40:1 in the *t* day of the month, in the
Eze 45:11 contain the *t* part of an homer
Eze 45:11 the ephah the *t* part of an homer
Eze 45:14 ye shall offer the *t* part of a
Zec 8:19 the seventh, and the fast of the *t*
Jn 1:39 for it was about the *t* hour
Heb 7:2 also Abraham gave a *t* part of all
Heb 7:4 Abraham gave the *t* of the spoils
Rev 11:13 the *t* part of the city fell, and
Rev 21:20 the *t*, a chrysoprasus

**TENTMAKERS**

Acts 18:3 by their occupation they were *t*

**TENTS**

Gen 4:20 the father of such as dwell in *t*
Gen 9:27 he shall dwell in the *t* of Shem
Gen 13:5 Abram, had flocks, and herds, and *t*
Gen 25:27 was a plain man, dwelling in *t*
Gen 31:33 and into the two maidservants' *t*
Ex 16:16 man for them which are in his *t*
Num 1:52 of Israel shall pitch their *t*
Num 9:17 of Israel pitched their *t*
Num 9:18 tabernacle they rested in their *t*
Num 9:20 of the LORD they abode in their *t*
Num 9:22 of Israel abode in their *t*
Num 9:23 of the LORD they rested in the *t*
Num 13:19 that they dwell in, whether in *t*
Num 16:26 from the *t* of these wicked men,
Num 16:27 and stood in the door of their *t*
Num 24:2 his *t* according to their tribes
Num 24:5 How goodly are thy *t*, O Jacob, and
Deut 1:27 And ye murmured in your *t*, and said
Deut 1:33 out a place to pitch your *t* in
Deut 5:30 them, Get you into your *t* again
Deut 11:6 and their households, and their *t*
Deut 16:7 in the morning, and go unto thy *t*
Deut 33:18 and, Issachar, in thy *t*
Josh 3:14 the people removed from their *t*
Josh 22:4 return ye, and get you unto your *t*
Josh 22:6 and they went unto their *t*
Josh 22:7 sent them away also unto their *t*
Josh 22:8 with much riches unto your *t*
Judg 6:5 up with their cattle and their *t*
Judg 8:11 dwelt in *t* on the east of Nobah
1Sa 17:53 and they spoiled their *t*
2Sa 11:11 and Israel, and Judah, abide in *t*
2Sa 20:1 every man to his *t*, O Israel
1Kin 8:66 king, and went unto their *t* joyful
1Kin 12:16 to your *t*, O Israel
1Kin 12:16 So Israel departed unto their *t*
2Kin 7:7 in the twilight, and left their *t*
2Kin 7:10 asses tied, and the *t* as they were
2Kin 7:16 spoiled the *t* of the Syrians
2Kin 8:21 and the people fled into their *t*
2Kin 13:5 of Israel dwelt in their *t*
2Kin 14:12 and they fled every man to their *t*
1Chr 4:41 king of Judah, and smote their *t*
1Chr 5:10 they dwelt in their *t* throughout
2Chr 7:10 sent the people away into their *t*
2Chr 10:16 every man to your *t*, O Israel, and
2Chr 10:16 So all Israel went to their *t*
2Chr 14:15 They smote also the *t* of cattle
2Chr 31:2 in the gates of the *t* of the LORD
Ezr 8:15 and there abode we in *t* three days
Ps 69:25 and let none dwell in their *t*
Ps 78:55 of Israel to dwell in their *t*

Ps 84:10 to dwell in the *t* of wickedness
Ps 106:25 But murmured in their *t*, and
Ps 120:5 that I dwell in the *t* of Kedar
Song 1:5 as the *t* of Kedar, as the
Song 1:8 thy kids beside the shepherds' *t*
Jer 4:20 suddenly are my *t* spoiled
Jer 6:3 they shall pitch their *t* against
Jer 30:18 again the captivity of Jacob's *t*
Jer 35:7 all your days ye shall dwell in *t*
Jer 35:10 But we have dwelt in *t*, and have
Jer 49:29 Their *t* and their flocks shall
Hab 3:7 I saw the *t* of Cushan in
Zec 12:7 shall save the *t* of Judah first
Zec 14:15 beasts that shall be in these *t*

**TERAH** *(te'-rah)* See THARA. *Father of Abraham.*
Gen 11:24 nine and twenty years, and begat *T*
Gen 11:25 lived after he begat *T* an hundred
Gen 11:26 *T* lived seventy years, and begat
Gen 11:27 these are the generations of *T*
Gen 11:27 *T* begat Abram, Nahor, and Haran
Gen 11:28 *T* in the land of his nativity
Gen 11:31 *T* took Abram his son, and Lot the
Gen 11:32 the days of *T* were two hundred and
Gen 11:32 and *T* died in Haran
Josh 24:2 of the flood in old time, even *T*
1Chr 1:26 Serug, Nahor, *T*,

**TERAPHIM**
Judg 17:5 of gods, and made an ephod, and *t*
Judg 18:14 is in these houses an ephod, and *t*
Judg 18:17 image, and the ephod, and the *t*
Judg 18:18 carved image, the ephod, and the *t*
Judg 18:20 and he took the ephod, and the *t*
Hos 3:4 and without an ephod, and without *t*

**TERESH** *(te'-resh) A servant of King Ahasuerus.*
Est 2:21 king's chamberlains, Bigthan and *T*
Est 6:2 had told of Bigthana and *T*

**TERMED**
Is 62:4 Thou shalt no more be *t* Forsaken
Is 62:4 thy land any more be *t* Desolate

**TERRACES**
2Chr 9:11 trees *t* to the house of the LORD

**TERRESTRIAL**
1Cor 15:40 celestial bodies, and bodies *t*
1Cor 15:40 and the glory of the *t* is another

**TERRIBLE**
Ex 34:10 for it is a *t* thing that I will
Deut 1:19 *t* wilderness, which ye saw by the
Deut 7:21 is among you, a mighty God and *t*
Deut 8:15 *t* wilderness, wherein were fiery
Deut 10:17 a great God, a mighty, and a *t*
Deut 10:21 *t* things, which thine eyes have
Judg 13:6 of an angel of God, very *t*
2Sa 7:23 to do for you great things and *t*
Neh 1:5 *t* God, that keepeth covenant and
Neh 4:14 the LORD, which is great and *t*
Neh 9:32 great, the mighty, and the *t* God
Job 37:22 with God is *t* majesty
Job 39:20 the glory of his nostrils is *t*
Job 41:14 his teeth are *t* round about
Ps 45:4 hand shall teach thee *t* things
Ps 47:2 For the LORD most high is *t*
Ps 65:5 By *t* things in righteousness wilt
Ps 66:3 How *t* art thou in thy works
Ps 66:5 he is *t* in his doing toward the
Ps 68:35 thou art *t* out of thy holy places
Ps 76:12 he is *t* to the kings of the earth
Ps 99:3 them praise thy great and *t* name
Ps 106:22 Ham, and *t* things by the Red sea
Ps 145:6 speak of the might of thy *t* acts
Song 6:4 *t* as an army with banners
Song 6:10 *t* as an army with banners
Is 13:11 lay low the haughtiness of the *t*
Is 18:2 peeled, to a people *t* from their
Is 18:7 from a people *t* from their
Is 21:1 from the desert, from a *t* land
Is 25:3 the city of the *t* nations shall
Is 25:4 when the blast of the *t* ones is
Is 25:5 the branch of the *t* ones shall be
Is 29:5 the multitude of the *t* ones shall
Is 29:20 For the *t* one is brought to
Is 49:25 the prey of the *t* shall be
Is 64:3 When thou didst *t* things which we
Jer 15:21 thee out of the hand of the *t*
Jer 20:11 LORD is with me as a mighty *t* one
Lam 5:10 an oven because of the *t* famine
Eze 1:22 as the colour of the *t* crystal
Eze 28:7 upon thee, the *t* of the nations
Eze 30:11 the *t* of the nations, shall be
Eze 31:12 the *t* of the nations, have cut
Eze 32:12 the *t* of the nations, all of them
Dan 2:31 and the form thereof was *t*
Dan 7:7 a fourth beast, dreadful and *t*
Joel 2:11 of the LORD is great and very *t*
Joel 2:31 the *t* day of the LORD come
Hab 1:7 They are *t* and dreadful
Zeph 2:11 The LORD will be *t* unto them
Heb 12:21 so *t* was the sight, that Moses

**TERRIBLENESS**
Deut 26:8 outstretched arm, and with great *t*
1Chr 17:21 thee a name of greatness and *t*
Jer 49:16 Thy *t* hath deceived thee, and the

**TERRIBLY**
Is 2:19 he ariseth to shake *t* the earth
Is 2:21 he ariseth to shake *t* the earth
Nah 2:3 the fir trees shall be *t* shaken

**TERRIFIED**
Deut 20:3 neither be ye *t* because of them
Lk 21:9 of wars and commotions, be not *t*
Lk 24:37 But they were *t* and affrighted, and
Phil 1:28 in nothing *t* by your adversaries

**TERRIFIEST**
Job 7:14 dreams, and *t* me through visions

**TERRIFY**
Job 3:5 let the blackness of the day *t* it
Job 9:34 from me, and let not his fear *t* me
Job 31:34 did the contempt of families *t* me
2Cor 10:9 as if I would *t* you by letters

**TERROR**
Gen 35:5 the *t* of God was upon the cities
Lev 26:16 I will even appoint over you *t*
Deut 32:25 *t* within, shall destroy both the
Deut 34:12 in all the great *t* which Moses
Josh 2:9 that your *t* is fallen upon us, and
Job 31:23 from God was a *t* to me, and by
Job 33:7 my *t* shall not make thee afraid,
Ps 91:5 not be afraid for the *t* by night
Is 10:33 hosts, shall lop the bough with *t*
Is 19:17 of Judah shall be a *t* unto Egypt
Is 33:18 Thine heart shall meditate *t*
Is 54:14 and from *t*
Jer 17:17 Be not a *t* unto me
Jer 20:4 I will make thee a *t* to thyself
Jer 32:21 out arm, and with great *t*
Eze 26:17 which cause their *t* to be on all
Eze 26:21 I will make thee a *t*, and thou
Eze 27:36 thou shalt be a *t*, and never shalt
Eze 28:19 thou shalt be a *t*, and never shalt
Eze 32:23 which caused *t* in the land of the
Eze 32:24 which caused their *t* in the land
Eze 32:25 though their *t* was caused in the
Eze 32:26 though they caused their *t* in the
Eze 32:27 though they were the *t* of the
Eze 32:30 with their *t* they are ashamed of
Eze 32:32 For I have caused my *t* in the
Rom 13:3 rulers are not a *t* to good works
2Cor 5:11 therefore the *t* of the Lord
1Pet 3:14 and be not afraid of their *t*

**TERRORS**
Deut 4:34 stretched out arm, and by great *t*
Job 6:4 the *t* of God do set themselves in
Job 18:11 *T* shall make him afraid on every
Job 18:14 shall bring him to the king of *t*
Job 20:25 *t* are upon him
Job 24:17 they are in the *t* of the shadow
Job 27:20 *T* take hold on him as waters, a
Job 30:15 *T* are turned upon me
Ps 55:4 the *t* of death are fallen upon me
Ps 73:19 they are utterly consumed with *t*
Ps 88:15 I suffer thy *t* I am distracted
Ps 88:16 thy *t* have cut me off
Jer 15:8 it suddenly, and *t* upon the city
Lam 2:22 in a solemn day my *t* round about
Eze 21:12 *t* by reason of the sword shall be

**TERTIUS** *(tur'-she-us) An assistant of Paul.*
Rom 16:22 I *T*, who wrote this epistle,

**TERTULLUS** *(tur-tul'-lus) An orator who opposed Paul.*
Acts 24:1 and with a certain orator named *T*
Acts 24:2 *T* began to accuse him, saying,

**TESTAMENT**
Mt 26:28 For this is my blood of the new *t*
Mk 14:24 This is my blood of the new *t*
Lk 22:20 This cup is the new *t* in my blood
1Cor 11:25 This cup is the new *t* in my blood
2Cor 3:6 us able ministers of the new *t*
2Cor 3:14 away in the reading of the old *t*
Heb 7:22 Jesus made a surety of a better *t*
Heb 9:15 he is the mediator of the new *t*
Heb 9:15 that were under the first *t*
Heb 9:16 For where a *t* is, there must also
Heb 9:17 For a *t* is of force after men are
Heb 9:18 *t* was dedicated without blood
Heb 9:20 This is the blood of the *t* which
Rev 11:19 in his temple the ark of his *t*

**TESTATOR**
Heb 9:16 necessity be the death of the *t*
Heb 9:17 at all while the *t* liveth

**TESTIFIED**
Ex 21:29 and it hath been *t* to his owner
Deut 19:18 hath *t* falsely against his
Ruth 1:21 seeing the LORD hath *t* against me
2Sa 1:16 for thy mouth hath *t* against thee
2Kin 17:13 Yet the LORD *t* against Israel, and
2Kin 17:15 which he *t* against them
2Chr 24:19 and they *t* against them
Neh 9:26 slew thy prophets which *t* against
Neh 13:15 I *t* against them in the day
Neh 13:21 Then I *t* against them, and said
Jn 4:39 the saying of the woman, which *t*
Jn 4:44 For Jesus himself *t*, that a
Jn 13:21 he was troubled in spirit, and *t*
Acts 8:25 And they, when they had *t* and
Acts 18:5 *t* to the Jews that Jesus was
Acts 23:11 for as thou hast *t* of me in
Acts 28:23 *t* the kingdom of God, persuading
1Cor 15:15 because we have *t* of God that he
1Th 4:6 we also have forewarned you and *t*
1Ti 2:6 for all, to be *t* in due time
Heb 2:6 But one in a certain place *t*
1Pet 1:11 signify, when it *t* beforehand the
1Jn 5:9 of God which he hath *t* of his Son
3Jn 3 *t* of the truth that is in thee,

**TESTIFIEDST**
Neh 9:29 *t* against them, that thou
Neh 9:30 *t* against them by thy spirit in

**TESTIFIETH**
Hos 7:10 the pride of Israel *t* to his face
Jn 3:32 he hath seen and heard, that he *t*
Jn 21:24 disciple which *t* of these things
Heb 7:17 For he *t*, Thou art a priest for
Rev 22:20 He which *t* these things saith,

**TESTIFY**
Num 35:30 but one witness shall not *t*
Deut 8:19 I *t* against you this day that ye
Deut 19:16 rise up against any man to *t*
Deut 31:21 that this song shall *t* against
Deut 32:46 which I *t* among you this day
Neh 9:34 thou didst *t* against them
Job 15:6 thine own lips *t* against thee
Ps 50:7 Israel, and I will *t* against thee
Ps 81:8 my people, and I will *t* unto thee
Is 59:12 thee, and our sins *t* against us
Jer 14:7 our iniquities *t* against us
Hos 5:5 of Israel doth *t* to his face
Amos 3:13 *t* in the house of Jacob, saith
Mic 6:3 *t* against me
Lk 16:28 that he may *t* unto them, lest
Jn 2:25 not that any should *t* of man
Jn 3:11 do know, and *t* that we have seen
Jn 5:39 and they are they which *t* of me
Jn 7:7 me it hateth, because I *t* of it
Jn 15:26 from the Father, he shall *t* of me
Acts 2:40 And with many other words did he *t*
Acts 10:42 to *t* that it is he which was
Acts 20:24 to *t* the gospel of the grace of
Acts 26:5 the beginning, if they would *t*
Gal 5:3 For I *t* again to every man that
Eph 4:17 *t* in the Lord, that ye henceforth
1Jn 4:14 do *t* that the Father sent the Son
Rev 22:16 to *t* unto you these things in the
Rev 22:18 For I *t* unto every man that

**TESTIFYING**
Acts 20:21 *T* both to the Jews, and also to
Heb 11:4 was righteous, God *t* of his gifts
1Pet 5:12 *t* that this is the true grace of

**TESTIMONIES**
Deut 4:45 These are the *t*, and the statutes,
Deut 6:17 of the LORD your God, and his *t*
Deut 6:20 to come, saying, What mean the *t*
1Kin 2:3 and his judgments, and his *t*
2Kin 17:15 his *t* which he testified against
2Kin 23:3 to keep his commandments and his *t*
1Chr 29:19 to keep thy commandments, thy *t*
2Chr 34:31 keep his commandments, and his *t*
Neh 9:34 unto thy commandments and thy *t*
Ps 25:10 as keep his covenant and his *t*
Ps 78:56 most high God, and kept not his *t*
Ps 93:5 Thy *t* are very sure
Ps 99:7 they kept his *t*, and the ordinance
Ps 119:2 Blessed are they that keep his *t*
Ps 119:14 have rejoiced in the way of thy *t*
Ps 119:22 for I have kept thy *t*
Ps 119:24 Thy *t* also are my delight, and my
Ps 119:31 I have stuck unto thy *t*
Ps 119:36 Incline my heart unto thy *t*
Ps 119:46 speak of thy *t* also before kings
Ps 119:59 and turned my feet unto thy *t*
Ps 119:79 and those that have known thy *t*
Ps 119:95 but I will consider thy *t*
Ps 119:99 for thy *t* are my meditation
Ps 119:111 Thy *t* have I taken as an heritage
Ps 119:119 therefore I love thy *t*
Ps 119:125 that I may know thy *t*
Ps 119:129 Thy *t* are wonderful
Ps 119:138 Thy *t* that thou hast commanded
Ps 119:144 of thy *t* is everlasting
Ps 119:146 save me, and I shall keep thy *t*
Ps 119:152 Concerning thy *t*, I have known of
Ps 119:157 yet do I not decline from thy *t*
Ps 119:167 My soul hath kept thy *t*
Ps 119:168 I have kept thy precepts and thy *t*
Jer 44:23 nor in his statutes, nor in his *t*

**TESTIMONY**
Ex 16:34 so Aaron laid it up before the *T*
Ex 25:16 ark the *t* which I shall give thee
Ex 25:21 put the *t* that I shall give thee
Ex 25:22 which are upon the ark of the *t*
Ex 26:33 within the vail the ark of the *t*
Ex 26:34 of the *t* in the most holy place
Ex 27:21 the vail, which is before the *t*
Ex 30:6 vail that is by the ark of the *t*
Ex 30:6 the mercy seat that is over the *t*
Ex 30:26 therewith, and the ark of the *t*
Ex 30:36 put of it before the *t* in the
Ex 31:7 congregation, and the ark of the *t*
Ex 31:18 upon mount Sinai, two tables of *t*
Ex 32:15 tables of the *t* were in his hand
Ex 34:29 two tables of *t* in Moses' hand
Ex 38:21 even of the tabernacle of *t*
Ex 39:35 The ark of the *t*, and the staves
Ex 40:3 put therein the ark of the *t*
Ex 40:5 incense before the ark of the *t*
Ex 40:20 put the *t* into the ark, and set
Ex 40:21 and covered the ark of the *t*
Lev 16:13 the mercy seat that is upon the *t*
Lev 24:3 Without the vail of the *t*
Num 1:50 Levites over the tabernacle of *t*
Num 1:53 round about the tabernacle of *t*
Num 1:53 the charge of the tabernacle of *t*
Num 4:5 and cover the ark of *t* with it
Num 7:89 seat that was upon the ark of *t*
Num 9:15 namely, the tent of the *t*
Num 10:11 from off the tabernacle of the *t*
Num 17:4 of the congregation before the *t*
Num 17:10 Aaron's rod again before the *t*
Josh 4:16 that bear the ark of the *t*
Ruth 4:7 and this was a *t* in Israel
2Kin 11:12 crown upon him, and gave him the *t*
2Chr 23:11 him the crown, and gave him the *t*
Ps 19:7 the *t* of the LORD is sure, making
Ps 78:5 For he established a *t* in Jacob
Ps 81:5 he ordained in Joseph for a *t*
Ps 119:88 shall I keep the *t* of thy mouth
Ps 122:4 unto the *t* of Israel, to give
Ps 132:12 my *t* that I shall teach them,
Is 8:16 Bind up the *t*, seal the law among
Is 8:20 To the law and to the *t*
Mt 8:4 commanded, for a *t* unto them
Mt 10:18 for a *t* against them and the
Mk 1:44 commanded, for a *t* unto them
Mk 6:11 your feet for a *t* against them
Mk 13:9 for my sake, for a *t* against them
Lk 5:14 commanded, for a *t* unto them
Lk 9:5 your feet for a *t* against them
Lk 21:13 And it shall turn to you for a *t*
Jn 3:32 and no man receiveth his *t*
Jn 3:33 He that hath received his *t* hath
Jn 5:34 But I receive not *t* from man
Jn 8:17 that the *t* of two men is true
Jn 21:24 and we know that his *t* is true
Acts 13:22 to whom also he gave *t*, and said,
Acts 14:3 which gave *t* unto the word of his
Acts 22:18 not receive thy *t* concerning me
1Cor 1:6 Even as the *t* of Christ was
1Cor 2:1 declaring unto you the *t* of God
2Cor 1:12 the *t* of our conscience, that in
2Th 1:10 them that believe (because our *t*
2Ti 1:8 ashamed of the *t* of our Lord
Heb 3:5 for a *t* of those things which
Heb 11:5 his translation he had this *t*
Rev 1:2 of the *t* of Jesus Christ, and of
Rev 1:9 for the *t* of Jesus Christ
Rev 6:9 for the *t* which they held
Rev 11:7 they shall have finished their *t*
Rev 12:11 Lamb, and by the word of their *t*
Rev 12:17 have the *t* of Jesus Christ
Rev 15:5 of the *t* in heaven was opened
Rev 19:10 brethren that have the *t* of Jesus
Rev 19:10 for the *t* of Jesus is the spirit

**TETRARCH**
Mt 14:1 At that time Herod the *t* heard of
Lk 3:1 and Herod being *t* of Galilee
Lk 3:1 his brother Philip *t* of Ituraea
Lk 3:1 and Lysanias the *t* of Abilene
Lk 3:19 But Herod the *t*, being reproved
Lk 9:7 Now Herod the *t* heard of all that
Acts 13:1 been brought up with Herod the *t*

**THADDAEUS** *(thad-de'-us)* See JUDE, LEBBAEUS. *A disciple of Jesus.*
Mt 10:3 and Lebbaeus, whose surname was *T*
Mk 3:18 James the son of Alphaeus, and *T*

**THAHASH** *(tha'-hash) A son of Reumah.*
Gen 22:24 bare also Tebah, and Gaham, and *T*

**THAMAH** *(tha'-mah)* See TAMAH. *A family of exiles.*
Ezr 2:53 of Sisera, the children of *T*

**THAMAR** *(tha'-mar)* See TAMAR. *Mother of Phares and Zara; ancestor of Jesus.*
Mt 1:3 Judas begat Phares and Zara of *T*

**THANK**
1Chr 16:4 the LORD, and to record, and to *t*
1Chr 16:7 delivered first this psalm to *t*
1Chr 23:30 And to stand every morning to *t*
1Chr 29:13 we *t* thee, and praise thy glorious
2Chr 29:31 *t* offerings into the house of the
2Chr 29:31 in sacrifices and *t* offerings
2Chr 33:16 *t* offerings, and commanded Judah
Dan 2:23 I *t* thee, and praise thee, O thou
Mt 11:25 I *t* thee, O Father, Lord of
Lk 6:32 which love you, what *t* have ye
Lk 6:33 do good to you, what *t* have ye
Lk 6:34 hope to receive, what *t* have ye
Lk 10:21 I *t* thee, O Father, Lord of
Lk 17:9 Doth he *t* that servant because he
Lk 18:11 I *t* thee, that I am not as other
Jn 11:41 I *t* thee that thou hast heard me
Rom 1:8 I *t* my God through Jesus Christ
Rom 7:25 I *t* God through Jesus Christ our
1Cor 1:4 I *t* my God always on your behalf,
1Cor 1:14 I *t* God that I baptized none of
1Cor 14:18 I *t* my God, I speak with tongues
Phil 1:3 I *t* my God upon every remembrance
1Th 2:13 For this cause also *t* we God
2Th 1:3 We are bound to *t* God always for
1Ti 1:12 I *t* Christ Jesus our Lord, who
2Ti 1:3 I *t* God, whom I serve from my
Philem 4 I *t* my God, making mention of

**THANKED**
2Sa 14:22 and bowed himself, and *t* the king
Acts 28:15 he *t* God, and took courage
Rom 6:17 But God be *t*, that ye were the

**THANKFUL**
Ps 100:4 be *t* unto him, and bless his name
Rom 1:21 him not as God, neither were *t*
Col 3:15 and be ye *t*

**THANKFULNESS**
Acts 24:3 most noble Felix, with all *t*

**THANKING**
2Chr 5:13 heard in praising and *t* the LORD

**THANKS**
2Sa 22:50 Therefore I will give *t* unto thee
1Chr 16:8 Give *t* unto the LORD, call upon
1Chr 16:34 O give *t* unto the LORD
1Chr 16:35 we may give *t* to thy holy name
1Chr 16:41 to give *t* to the LORD, because
1Chr 25:3 prophesied with a harp, to give *t*
2Chr 31:2 to minister, and to give *t*
Ezr 3:11 and giving *t* unto the LORD
Neh 12:24 them, to praise and to give *t*
Neh 12:31 companies of them that gave *t*
Neh 12:38 gave *t* went over against them
Neh 12:40 that gave *t* in the house of God
Ps 6:5 the grave who shall give thee *t*
Ps 18:49 Therefore will I give *t* unto thee
Ps 30:4 give *t* at the remembrance of his
Ps 30:12 I will give *t* unto thee for ever
Ps 35:18 I will give thee *t* in the great
Ps 75:1 Unto thee, O God, do we give *t*
Ps 75:1 unto thee do we give *t*
Ps 79:13 pasture will give thee *t* for ever
Ps 92:1 thing to give *t* unto the LORD
Ps 97:12 give *t* at the remembrance of his
Ps 105:1 O give *t* unto the LORD
Ps 106:1 O give *t* unto the LORD
Ps 106:47 to give *t* unto thy holy name, and
Ps 107:1 O give *t* unto the LORD, for he is
Ps 118:1 O give *t* unto the LORD
Ps 118:29 O give *t* unto the LORD
Ps 119:62 give *t* unto thee because of thy
Ps 122:4 to give *t* unto the name of the
Ps 136:1 O Give *t* unto the LORD
Ps 136:2 O give *t* unto the God of gods
Ps 136:3 O give *t* to the Lord of lords
Ps 136:26 O give *t* unto the God of heaven
Ps 140:13 shall give *t* unto thy name
Dan 6:10 gave *t* before his God, as he did
Mt 15:36 loaves and the fishes, and gave *t*
Mt 26:27 And he took the cup, and gave *t*
Mk 8:6 took the seven loaves, and gave *t*
Mk 14:23 the cup, and when he had given *t*
Lk 2:38 gave *t* likewise unto the Lord
Lk 17:16 face at his feet, giving him *t*
Lk 22:17 And he took the cup, and gave *t*
Lk 22:19 And he took bread, and gave *t*
Jn 6:11 and when he had given *t*, he
Jn 6:23 after that the Lord had given *t*
Acts 27:35 gave *t* to God in presence of them
Rom 14:6 to the Lord, for he giveth God *t*
Rom 14:6 he eateth not, and giveth God *t*
Rom 16:4 unto whom not only I give *t*
1Cor 10:30 of for that for which I give *t*
1Cor 11:24 And when he had given *t*, he brake
1Cor 14:16 say Amen at thy giving of *t*
1Cor 14:17 For thou verily givest *t* well
1Cor 15:57 But *t* be to God, which giveth us
2Cor 1:11 *t* may be given by many on our
2Cor 2:14 Now *t* be unto God, which always
2Cor 8:16 But *t* be to God, which put the
2Cor 9:15 *T* be unto God for his unspeakable
Eph 1:16 Cease not to give *t* for you
Eph 5:4 but rather giving of *t*
Eph 5:20 Giving *t* always for all things
Col 1:3 We give *t* to God and the Father of
Col 1:12 Giving *t* unto the Father, which
Col 3:17 the Lord Jesus, giving *t* to God
1Th 1:2 We give *t* to God always for you
1Th 3:9 For what *t* can we render to God
1Th 5:18 In every thing give *t*
2Th 2:13 to give *t* alway to God for you
1Ti 2:1 intercessions, and giving of *t*
Heb 13:15 of our lips giving *t* to his name
Rev 4:9 *t* to him that sat on the throne,
Rev 11:17 Saying, We give thee *t*, O Lord

**THANKSGIVING**
Lev 7:12 If he offer it for a *t*, then he
Lev 7:12 offer with the sacrifice of *t*
Lev 7:13 of *t* of his peace offerings
Lev 7:15 of his peace offerings for *t*
Lev 22:29 a sacrifice of *t* unto the LORD
Neh 11:17 to begin the *t* in prayer
Neh 12:8 Mattaniah, which was over the *t*
Neh 12:46 and songs of praise and *t* unto God
Ps 26:7 I may publish with the voice of *t*
Ps 50:14 Offer unto God *t*
Ps 69:30 song, and will magnify him with *t*
Ps 95:2 come before his presence with *t*
Ps 100:4 Enter into his gates with *t*
Ps 107:22 sacrifice the sacrifices of *t*

Ps 116:17 offer to thee the sacrifice of *t*
Ps 147:7 Sing unto the LORD with *t*
Is 51:3 shall be found therein, *t*
Jer 30:19 And out of them shall proceed *t*
Amos 4:5 a sacrifice of *t* with leaven
Jonah 2:9 unto thee with the voice of *t*
2Cor 4:15 grace might through the *t* of many
2Cor 9:11 which causeth through us *t* to God
Phil 4:6 supplication with *t* let your
Col 2:7 taught, abounding therein with *t*
Col 4:2 and watch in the same with *t*
1Ti 4:3 with *t* of them which believe
1Ti 4:4 refused, if it be received with *t*
Rev 7:12 and glory, and wisdom, and *t*

**THANKSGIVINGS**
Neh 12:27 with gladness, both with *t*
2Cor 9:12 abundant also by many *t* unto God

**THANKWORTHY**
1Pet 2:19 For this is *t*, if a man for

**THARA** *(tha'-rah)* See TERAH. *Greek form of Terah.*
Lk 3:34 Abraham, which was the son of *T*

**THARSHISH** *(thar'-shish)* See TARSHISH.
*1. Ships fitted for long voyages.*
1Kin 10:22 navy of *T* with the navy of Hiram
1Kin 10:22 in three years came the navy of *T*
1Kin 22:48 of *T* to go to Ophir for gold
*2. Son of Bilhan.*
1Chr 7:10 and Chenaanah, and Zethan, and *T*

**THEATRE**
Acts 19:29 rushed with one accord into the *t*
Acts 19:31 not adventure himself into the *t*

**THEBEZ** *(the'-bez) A city in Ephraim.*
Judg 9:50 Then went Abimelech to *T*, and
Judg 9:50 to *T*, and encamped against *T*
2Sa 11:21 from the wall, that he died in *T*

**THEE-WARD**
1Sa 19:4 works have been to *t* very good

**THEFT**
Ex 22:3 then he shall be sold for his *t*
Ex 22:4 If the *t* be certainly found in

**THEFTS**
Mt 15:19 adulteries, fornications, *t*
Mk 7:22 *T*, covetousness, wickedness,
Rev 9:21 their fornication, nor of their *t*

**THELASAR** *(the-la'-sar)* See TELASSAR. *Same as Telassar.*
2Kin 19:12 children of Eden which were in *T*

**THEOPHILUS** *(the-of'-il-us) To whom the gospel of Luke and the Acts of the Apostles are addressed.*
Lk 1:3 thee in order, most excellent *T*
Acts 1:1 former treatise have I made, O *T*

**THESSALONIANS** *(thes-sa-lo'-ne-uns) The inhabitants of Thessalonica.*
Acts 20:4 and of the *T*, Aristarchus and
1Th 1:1 unto the church of the *T* which is
1Th *s* the *T* was written from Athens
2Th 1:1 church of the *T* in God our Father
2Th *s* to the *T* was written from Athens

**THESSALONICA** *(thes-sa-lo-ni'-cah) A city in Macedonia.*
Acts 17:1 and Apollonia, they came to *T*
Acts 17:11 were more noble than those in *T*
Acts 17:13 But when the Jews of *T* had
Acts 27:2 Aristarchus, a Macedonian of *T*
Phil 4:16 For even in *T* ye sent once and
2Ti 4:10 world, and is departed unto *T*

**THEUDAS** *(thew'-das) A false Jewish Messiah.*
Acts 5:36 For before these days rose up *T*

**THICK**
Ex 10:22 there was a *t* darkness in all the
Ex 19:9 Lo, I come unto thee in a *t* cloud
Ex 19:16 a *t* cloud upon the mount, and the
Ex 20:21 unto the *t* darkness where God was
Lev 23:40 trees, and the boughs of *t* trees
Deut 4:11 darkness, clouds, and *t* darkness
Deut 5:22 of the *t* darkness, with a great
Deut 32:15 art waxen fat, thou art grown *t*
2Sa 18:9 under the *t* boughs of a great oak
2Sa 22:12 waters, and *t* clouds of the skies
1Kin 7:6 the *t* beam were before them
1Kin 7:26 And it was an hand breadth *t*
1Kin 8:12 he would dwell in the *t* darkness
2Kin 8:15 morrow, that he took a *t* cloth
2Chr 6:1 he would dwell in the *t* darkness
Neh 8:15 branches, and branches of *t* trees
Job 15:26 upon the *t* bosses of his bucklers
Job 22:14 *T* clouds are a covering to him,
Job 26:8 up the waters in his *t* clouds
Job 37:11 watering he wearieth the *t* cloud
Job 38:9 *t* darkness a swaddlingband for it
Ps 18:11 waters and *t* clouds of the skies
Ps 18:12 before him his *t* clouds passed
Ps 74:5 lifted up axes upon the *t* trees
Is 44:22 as a *t* cloud, thy transgressions,
Eze 6:13 green tree, and under every *t* oak
Eze 8:11 a *t* cloud of incense went up
Eze 19:11 was exalted among the *t* branches
Eze 20:28 high hill, and all the *t* trees
Eze 31:3 and his top was among the *t* boughs
Eze 31:10 up his top among the *t* boughs
Eze 31:14 up their top among the *t* boughs
Eze 41:12 was five cubits *t* round about
Eze 41:25 there were *t* planks upon the face
Eze 41:26 of the house, and *t* planks
Joel 2:2 of *t* darkness, as the morning
Hab 2:6 that ladeth himself with *t* clay
Zeph 1:15 a day of clouds and *t* darkness,
Lk 11:29 people were gathered *t* together

**THICKER**
1Kin 12:10 shall be *t* than my father's loins
2Chr 10:10 shall be *t* than my father's loins

**THICKET**
Gen 22:13 a ram caught in a *t* by his horns
Jer 4:7 The lion is come up from his *t*

**THICKETS**
1Sa 13:6 hide themselves in caves, and in *t*
Is 9:18 kindle in the *t* of the forest
Is 10:34 he shall cut down the *t* of the
Jer 4:29 they shall go into *t*, and climb up

**THICKNESS**
2Chr 4:5 the *t* of it was an handbreadth,
Jer 52:21 the *t* thereof was four fingers
Eze 41:9 The *t* of the wall, which was for
Eze 42:10 The chambers were in the *t* of the

**THIEF**
Ex 22:2 If a *t* be found breaking up, and
Ex 22:7 if the *t* be found, let him pay
Ex 22:8 If the *t* be not found, then the
Deut 24:7 then that *t* shall die
Job 24:14 needy, and in the night is as a *t*
Job 30:5 cried after them as after a *t*
Ps 50:18 When thou sawest a *t*, then thou
Prov 6:30 Men do not despise a *t*, if he
Prov 29:24 with a *t* hateth his own soul
Jer 2:26 As the *t* is ashamed when he is
Hos 7:1 the *t* cometh in, and the troop of
Joel 2:9 enter in at the windows like a *t*
Zec 5:4 enter into the house of the *t*
Mt 24:43 in what watch the *t* would come
Mt 26:55 out as against a *t* with swords
Mk 14:48 Are ye come out, as against a *t*
Lk 12:33 where no *t* approacheth, neither
Lk 12:39 known what hour the *t* would come
Lk 22:52 Be ye come out, as against a *t*
Jn 10:1 some other way, the same is a *t*
Jn 10:10 The *t* cometh not, but for to
Jn 12:6 but because he was a *t*, and had
1Th 5:2 so cometh as a *t* in the night
1Th 5:4 day should overtake you as a *t*
1Pet 4:15 suffer as a murderer, or as a *t*
2Pet 3:10 will come as a *t* in the night
Rev 3:3 watch, I will come on thee as a *t*
Rev 16:15 Behold, I come as a *t*

**THIEVES**
Is 1:23 rebellious, and companions of *t*
Jer 48:27 was he found among *t*
Jer 49:9 if *t* by night, they will destroy
Obad 5 If *t* came to thee, if robbers by
Mt 6:19 where *t* break through and steal
Mt 6:20 where *t* do not break through nor
Mt 21:13 but ye have made it a den of *t*
Mt 27:38 there two *t* crucified with him
Mt 27:44 The *t* also, which were crucified
Mk 11:17 but ye have made it a den of *t*
Mk 15:27 And with him they crucify two *t*
Lk 10:30 to Jericho, and fell among *t*
Lk 10:36 unto him that fell among the *t*
Lk 19:46 but ye have made it a den of *t*
Jn 10:8 that ever came before me are *t*
1Cor 6:10 Nor *t*, nor covetous, nor

**THIGH**
Gen 24:2 I pray thee, thy hand under my *t*
Gen 24:9 under the *t* of Abraham his master
Gen 32:25 he touched the hollow of his *t*
Gen 32:25 of Jacob's *t* was out of joint
Gen 32:31 upon him, and he halted upon his *t*
Gen 32:32 which is upon the hollow of the *t*
Gen 32:32 *t* in the sinew that shrank
Gen 47:29 I pray thee, thy hand under my *t*
Num 5:21 the LORD doth make thy *t* to rot
Num 5:22 belly to swell, and thy *t* to rot
Num 5:27 shall swell, and her *t* shall rot
Judg 3:16 his raiment upon his right *t*
Judg 3:21 took the dagger from his right *t*
Judg 15:8 hip and *t* with a great slaughter
Ps 45:3 Gird thy sword upon thy *t*
Song 3:8 man hath his sword upon his *t*
Is 47:2 make bare the leg, uncover the *t*
Jer 31:19 was instructed, I smote upon my *t*
Eze 21:12 smite therefore upon thy *t*
Eze 24:4 it, even every good piece, the *t*
Rev 19:16 on his *t* a name written, KING OF

**THIGHS**
Ex 28:42 even unto the *t* they shall reach
Song 7:1 joints of thy *t* are like jewels
Dan 2:32 his belly and his *t* of brass,

**THIMNATHAH** *(thim'-nath-ah)* See TIMNAH. *A city in Dan.*
Josh 19:43 And Elon, and *T*, and Ekron,

**THIN**
Gen 41:6 And, behold, seven *t* ears and
Gen 41:7 the seven *t* ears devoured the
Gen 41:23 behold, seven ears, withered, *t*
Gen 41:24 the *t* ears devoured the seven
Gen 41:27 And the seven *t* and ill favoured
Ex 39:3 did beat the gold into *t* plates
Lev 13:30 and there be in it a yellow *t* hair
1Kin 7:29 certain additions made of *t* work
Is 17:4 glory of Jacob shall be made *t*

**THINK**
Gen 40:14 But *t* on me when it shall be well
Num 36:6 them marry to whom they *t* best
2Sa 13:33 to *t* that all the king's sons are
2Chr 13:8 now ye *t* to withstand the kingdom
Neh 5:19 *T* upon me, my God, for good,
Neh 6:6 that thou and the Jews *t* to rebel
Neh 6:14 *t* thou upon Tobiah and Sanballat
Est 4:13 *T* not with thyself that thou
Job 31:1 why then should I *t* upon a maid
Job 41:32 one would *t* the deep to be hoary
Eccl 8:17 though a wise man *t* to know it
Is 10:7 so, neither doth his heart *t* so
Jer 23:27 Which *t* to cause my people to
Jer 29:11 the thoughts that I *t* toward you
Eze 38:10 thou shalt *t* an evil thought
Dan 7:25 *t* to change times and laws
Jonah 1:6 if so be that God will *t* upon us
Zec 11:12 And I said unto them, If ye *t* good
Mt 3:9 *t* not to say within yourselves,
Mt 5:17 *T* not that I am come to destroy
Mt 6:7 for they *t* that they shall be
Mt 9:4 Wherefore *t* ye evil in your
Mt 10:34 *T* not that I am come to send
Mt 18:12 How *t* ye?
Mt 21:28 But what *t* ye
Mt 22:42 Saying, What *t* ye of Christ
Mt 24:44 as ye *t* not the Son of man cometh
Mt 26:66 What *t* ye?
Mk 14:64 what *t* ye?
Lk 12:40 cometh at an hour when ye *t* not
Lk 13:4 *t* ye that they were sinners above
Jn 5:39 for in them ye *t* ye have eternal
Jn 5:45 Do not *t* that I will accuse you
Jn 11:56 stood in the temple, What *t* ye
Jn 16:2 will *t* that he doeth God service
Acts 13:25 he said, Whom *t* ye that I am
Acts 17:29 we ought not to *t* that the
Acts 26:2 I *t* myself happy, king Agrippa,
Rom 12:3 not to *t* of himself more highly
Rom 12:3 more highly than he ought to *t*
Rom 12:3 but to *t* soberly, according as
1Cor 4:6 to *t* of men above that which is
1Cor 4:9 For I *t* that God hath set forth
1Cor 7:36 But if any man *t* that he behaveth
1Cor 7:40 I *t* also that I have the Spirit
1Cor 8:2 if any man *t* that he knoweth any
1Cor 12:23 which we *t* to be less honourable,
1Cor 14:37 If any man *t* himself to be a

2Cor 3:5 to *t* any thing as of ourselves
2Cor 10:2 wherewith I *t* to be bold against
2Cor 10:2 which *t* of us as if we walked
2Cor 10:7 let him of himself *t* this again
2Cor 10:11 Let such an one *t* this, that,
2Cor 11:16 say again, Let no man *t* me a fool
2Cor 12:6 lest any man should *t* of me above
2Cor 12:19 *t* ye that we excuse ourselves
Gal 6:3 For if a man *t* himself to be
Eph 3:20 above all that we ask or *t*
Phil 1:7 meet for me to *t* this of you all
Phil 4:8 be any praise, *t* on these things
Jas 1:7 For let not that man *t* that he
Jas 4:5 Do ye *t* that the scripture saith
1Pet 4:4 Wherein they *t* it strange that ye
1Pet 4:12 *t* it not strange concerning the
2Pet 1:13 I *t* it meet, as long as I am in

**THINKEST**
2Sa 10:3 *T* thou that David doth honour thy
1Chr 19:3 *T* thou that David doth honour thy
Job 35:2 *T* thou this to be right, that
Mt 17:25 him, saying, What *t* thou, Simon
Mt 22:17 Tell us therefore, What *t* thou
Mt 26:53 *T* thou that I cannot now pray to
Lk 10:36 *t* thou, was neighbour unto him
Acts 28:22 to hear of thee what thou *t*
Rom 2:3 *t* thou this, O man, that judgest

**THINKETH**
2Sa 18:27 Me *t* the running of the foremost
Ps 40:17 yet the Lord *t* upon me
Prov 23:7 For as he *t* in his heart, so is
1Cor 10:12 Wherefore let him that *t* he
1Cor 13:5 is not easily provoked, *t* no evil
Phil 3:4 If any other man *t* that he hath

**THINKING**
2Sa 4:10 *t* to have brought good tidings, I
2Sa 5:6 *t*, David cannot come in

**THIRD**
Gen 1:13 and the morning were the *t* day
Gen 2:14 the name of the *t* river is
Gen 6:16 *t* stories shalt thou make it
Gen 22:4 Then on the *t* day Abraham lifted
Gen 31:22 on the *t* day that Jacob was fled
Gen 32:19 commanded he the second, and the *t*
Gen 34:25 And it came to pass on the *t* day
Gen 40:20 And it came to pass the *t* day
Gen 42:18 Joseph said unto them the *t* day
Gen 50:23 children of the *t* generation
Ex 19:1 In the *t* month, when the children
Ex 19:11 And be ready against the *t* day
Ex 19:11 for the *t* day the LORD will come
Ex 19:15 Be ready against the *t* day
Ex 19:16 pass on the *t* day in the morning
Ex 20:5 upon the children unto the *t*
Ex 28:19 the *t* row a ligure, an agate, and
Ex 34:7 children's children, unto the *t*
Ex 39:12 And the *t* row, a ligure, an agate,
Lev 7:17 *t* day shall be burnt with fire
Lev 7:18 be eaten at all on the *t* day
Lev 19:6 if ought remain until the *t* day
Lev 19:7 it be eaten at all on the *t* day
Num 2:24 shall go forward in the *t* rank
Num 7:24 On the *t* day Eliab the son of
Num 14:18 upon the children unto the *t*
Num 15:6 with the *t* part of an hin of oil
Num 15:7 the *t* part of an hin of wine
Num 19:12 himself with it on the *t* day
Num 19:12 he purify not himself the *t* day
Num 19:19 upon the unclean on the *t* day
Num 28:14 the *t* part of an hin unto a ram,
Num 29:20 on the *t* day eleven bullocks, two
Num 31:19 and your captives on the *t* day
Deut 5:9 upon the children unto the *t*
Deut 23:8 of the LORD in their *t* generation
Deut 26:12 of thine increase the *t* year
Josh 9:17 unto their cities on the *t* day
Josh 19:10 the *t* lot came up for the
Judg 20:30 children of Benjamin on the *t* day
1Sa 3:8 called Samuel again the *t* time
1Sa 17:13 him Abinadab, and the *t* Shammah
1Sa 19:21 sent messengers again the *t* time
1Sa 20:5 the field unto the *t* day at even
1Sa 20:12 to morrow any time, or the *t* day
1Sa 30:1 were come to Ziklag on the *t* day
2Sa 1:2 It came even to pass on the *t* day
2Sa 3:3 and the *t*, Absalom the son of
2Sa 18:2 David sent forth a *t* part of the
2Sa 18:2 a *t* part under the hand of
2Sa 18:2 a *t* part under the hand of Ittai
1Kin 3:18 it came to pass the *t* day after
1Kin 6:6 the *t* was seven cubits broad
1Kin 6:8 and out of the middle into the *t*
1Kin 12:12 people came to Rehoboam the *t* day
1Kin 12:12 Come to me again the *t* day
1Kin 15:28 Even in the *t* year of Asa king of
1Kin 15:33 In the *t* year of Asa king of
1Kin 18:1 LORD came to Elijah in the *t* year
1Kin 18:34 And he said, Do it the *t* time
1Kin 18:34 And they did it the *t* time
1Kin 22:2 And it came to pass in the *t* year
2Kin 1:13 of the *t* fifty with his fifty
2Kin 1:13 the *t* captain of fifty went up,
2Kin 11:5 A *t* part of you that enter in on
2Kin 11:6 a *t* part shall be at the gate of
2Kin 11:6 a *t* part at the gate behind the
2Kin 18:1 Now it came to pass in the *t* year
2Kin 19:29 in the *t* year sow ye, and reap, and
2Kin 20:5 on the *t* day thou shalt go up
2Kin 20:8 the house of the LORD the *t* day
1Chr 2:13 the second, and Shimma the *t*
1Chr 3:2 The *t*, Absalom the son of Maachah
1Chr 3:15 the *t* Zedekiah, the fourth
1Chr 8:1 the second, and Aharah the *t*
1Chr 8:39 the second, and Eliphelet the *t*
1Chr 12:9 Obadiah the second, Eliab the *t*
1Chr 23:19 the second, Jahaziel the *t*
1Chr 24:8 The *t* to Harim, the fourth to
1Chr 24:23 the second, Jahaziel the *t*
1Chr 25:10 The *t* to Zaccur, he, his sons, and
1Chr 26:2 the second, Zebadiah the *t*
1Chr 26:4 Jehozabad the second, Joah the *t*
1Chr 26:11 the second, Tebaliah the *t*
1Chr 27:5 The *t* captain of the host for the
1Chr 27:5 captain of the host for the *t*
2Chr 10:12 came to Rehoboam on the *t* day
2Chr 10:12 Come again to me on the *t* day
2Chr 15:10 at Jerusalem in the *t* month
2Chr 17:7 Also in the *t* year of his reign
2Chr 23:4 A *t* part of you entering on the
2Chr 23:5 a *t* part shall be at the king's
2Chr 23:5 a *t* part at the gate of the
2Chr 27:5 both the second year, and the *t*
2Chr 31:7 In the *t* month they began to lay
Ezr 6:15 on the *t* day of the month Adar
Neh 10:32 the *t* part of a shekel for the
Est 1:3 In the *t* year of his reign, he
Est 5:1 Now it came to pass on the *t* day
Est 8:9 at that time in the *t* month
Job 42:14 and the name of the *t*,
Is 19:24 shall Israel be the *t* with Egypt
Is 37:30 in the *t* year sow ye, and reap, and
Jer 38:14 *t* entry that is in the house of
Eze 5:2 Thou shalt burn with fire a *t*
Eze 5:2 and thou shalt take a *t* part
Eze 5:2 a *t* part thou shalt scatter in
Eze 5:12 A *t* part of thee shall die with
Eze 5:12 a *t* part shall fall by the sword
Eze 5:12 I will scatter a *t* part into all
Eze 10:14 the *t* the face of a lion, and the
Eze 21:14 the sword be doubled the *t* time
Eze 31:1 the eleventh year, in the *t* month
Eze 46:14 the *t* part of an hin of oil, to
Dan 1:1 In the *t* year of the reign of
Dan 2:39 another *t* kingdom of brass, which
Dan 5:7 shall be the *t* ruler in the
Dan 5:16 shalt be the *t* ruler in the
Dan 5:29 be the *t* ruler in the kingdom
Dan 8:1 In the *t* year of the reign of
Dan 10:1 In the *t* year of Cyrus king of
Hos 6:2 in the *t* day he will raise us up,
Zec 6:3 in the *t* chariot white horses
Zec 13:8 but the *t* shall be left therein
Zec 13:9 I will bring the *t* part through
Mt 16:21 and be raised again the *t* day
Mt 17:23 the *t* day he shall be raised
Mt 20:3 And he went out about the *t* hour
Mt 20:19 the *t* day he shall rise again
Mt 22:26 the second also, and the *t*
Mt 26:44 away again, and prayed the *t* time
Mt 27:64 be made sure until the *t* day
Mk 9:31 killed, he shall rise the *t* day
Mk 10:34 the *t* day he shall rise again
Mk 12:21 and the *t* likewise
Mk 14:41 And he cometh the *t* time, and saith
Mk 15:25 And it was the *t* hour, and they
Lk 9:22 be slain, and be raised the *t* day
Lk 12:38 watch, or come in the *t* watch
Lk 13:32 the *t* day I shall be perfected
Lk 18:33 the *t* day he shall rise again
Lk 20:12 And again he sent a *t*
Lk 20:31 And the *t* took her
Lk 23:22 And he said unto them the *t* time
Lk 24:7 and the *t* day rise again
Lk 24:21 to day is the *t* day since these
Lk 24:46 to rise from the dead the *t* day
Jn 2:1 the *t* day there was a marriage in
Jn 21:14 This is now the *t* time that Jesus
Jn 21:17 He saith unto him the *t* time
Jn 21:17 he said unto him the *t* time
Acts 2:15 it is but the *t* hour of the day
Acts 10:40 Him God raised up the *t* day
Acts 20:9 and fell down from the *t* loft
Acts 23:23 at the *t* hour of the night
Acts 27:19 the *t* day we cast out with our
1Cor 15:4 that he rose again the *t* day
2Cor 12:2 an one caught up to the *t* heaven
2Cor 12:14 the *t* time I am ready to come to
2Cor 13:1 This is the *t* time I am coming to
Rev 4:7 the *t* beast had a face as a man,
Rev 6:5 And when he had opened the *t* seal
Rev 6:5 I heard the *t* beast say
Rev 8:7 the *t* part of trees was burnt up,
Rev 8:8 the *t* part of the sea became
Rev 8:9 the *t* part of the creatures which
Rev 8:9 the *t* part of the ships were
Rev 8:10 the *t* angel sounded, and there
Rev 8:10 it fell upon the *t* part of the
Rev 8:11 the *t* part of the waters became
Rev 8:12 the *t* part of the sun was smitten
Rev 8:12 the *t* part of the moon, and the
Rev 8:12 moon, and the *t* part of the stars
Rev 8:12 so as the *t* part of them was
Rev 8:12 day shone not for a *t* part of it
Rev 9:15 for to slay the *t* part of men
Rev 9:18 was the *t* part of men killed
Rev 11:14 behold, the *t* woe cometh quickly
Rev 12:4 his tail drew the *t* part of the
Rev 14:9 the *t* angel followed them, saying
Rev 16:4 the *t* angel poured out his vial
Rev 21:19 the *t*, a chalcedony

**THIRDLY**
1Cor 12:28 *t* teachers, after that miracles,

**THIRST**
Ex 17:3 our children and our cattle with *t*
Deut 28:48 against thee, in hunger, and in *t*
Deut 29:19 heart, to add drunkenness to *t*
Judg 15:18 and now shall I die for *t*, and fall
2Chr 32:11 to die by famine and by *t*, saying,
Neh 9:15 them out of the rock for their *t*
Neh 9:20 and gavest them water for their *t*
Job 24:11 their winepresses, and suffer *t*
Ps 69:21 in my *t* they gave me vinegar to
Ps 104:11 the wild asses quench their *t*
Is 5:13 their multitude dried up with *t*
Is 41:17 and their tongue faileth for *t*
Is 49:10 They shall not hunger nor *t*
Is 50:2 there is no water, and dieth for *t*
Jer 2:25 unshod, and thy throat from *t*
Jer 48:18 down from thy glory, and sit in *t*
Lam 4:4 to the roof of his mouth for *t*
Hos 2:3 a dry land, and slay her with *t*
Amos 8:11 nor a *t* for water, but of hearing
Amos 8:13 virgins and young men faint for *t*
Mt 5:6 hunger and *t* after righteousness
Jn 4:13 of this water shall *t* again
Jn 4:14 I shall give him shall never *t*
Jn 4:15 give me this water, that I *t* not
Jn 6:35 believeth on me shall never *t*
Jn 7:37 and cried, saying, If any man *t*
Jn 19:28 might be fulfilled, saith, I *t*
Rom 12:20 if he *t*, give him drink
1Cor 4:11 present hour we both hunger, and *t*
2Cor 11:27 watchings often, in hunger and *t*
Rev 7:16 no more, neither *t* any more

**THIRSTED**
Ex 17:3 the people *t* there for water
Is 48:21 they *t* not when he led them

**THIRSTETH**
Ps 42:2 My soul *t* for God, for the living
Ps 63:1 my soul *t* for thee, my flesh
Ps 143:6 my soul *t* after thee, as a
Is 55:1 Ho, every one that *t*, come ye to

**THIRSTY**
Judg 4:19 for I am *t*
2Sa 17:29 people is hungry, and weary, and *t*
Ps 63:1 *t* land, where no water is

Ps 107:5 Hungry and *t*, their soul fainted
Ps 143:6 thirsteth after thee, as a *t* land
Prov 25:21 and if he be *t*, give him water to
Prov 25:25 As cold waters to a *t* soul
Is 21:14 brought water to him that was *t*
Is 29:8 or as when a *t* man dreameth
Is 32:6 cause the drink of the *t* to fail
Is 35:7 the *t* land springs of water
Is 44:3 pour water upon him that is *t*
Is 65:13 shall drink, but ye shall be *t*
Eze 19:13 wilderness, in a dry and *t* ground
Mt 25:35 I was *t*, and ye gave me drink
Mt 25:37 or *t*, and gave thee drink
Mt 25:42 I was *t*, and ye gave me no drink

**THIRTEEN**
Gen 17:25 Ishmael his son was *t* years old
Num 3:43 two hundred and threescore and *t*
Num 3:46 *t* of the firstborn of the
Num 29:13 *t* young bullocks, two rams, and
Num 29:14 every bullock of the *t* bullocks
Josh 19:6 *t* cities and their villages
Josh 21:4 the tribe of Benjamin, *t* cities
Josh 21:6 of Manasseh in Bashan, *t* cities
Josh 21:19 were *t* cities with their suburbs
Josh 21:33 to their families were *t* cities
1Kin 7:1 building his own house *t* years
1Chr 6:60 their families were *t* cities
1Chr 6:62 of Manasseh in Bashan, *t* cities
1Chr 26:11 sons and brethren of Hosah were *t*
Eze 40:11 the length of the gate, *t* cubits

**THIRTEENTH**
Gen 14:4 in the *t* year they rebelled
1Chr 24:13 The *t* to Huppah, the fourteenth
1Chr 25:20 The *t* to Shubael, he, his sons,
Est 3:12 on the *t* day of the first month
Est 3:13 even upon the *t* day of the
Est 8:12 upon the *t* day of the twelfth
Est 9:1 on the *t* day of the same, when
Est 9:17 On the *t* day of the month Adar
Est 9:18 together on the *t* day thereof
Jer 1:2 in the *t* year of his reign
Jer 25:3 From the *t* year of Josiah the son

**THIRTIETH**
2Kin 15:13 *t* year of Uzziah king of Judah
2Kin 15:17 *t* year of Azariah king of Judah
2Kin 25:27 *t* year of the captivity of
2Chr 15:19 *t* year of the reign of Asa
2Chr 16:1 *t* year of the reign of Asa Baasha
Neh 5:14 *t* year of Artaxerxes the king,
Neh 13:6 *t* year of Artaxerxes king of
Jer 52:31 *t* year of the captivity of
Eze 1:1 Now it came to pass in the *t* year

**THIRTY**
Gen 5:3 *t* years, and begat a son in his
Gen 5:5 were nine hundred and *t* years
Gen 5:16 *t* years, and begat sons and
Gen 6:15 and the height of it *t* cubits
Gen 11:12 five and *t* years, and begat Salah
Gen 11:14 And Salah lived *t* years, and begat
Gen 11:16 four and *t* years, and begat Peleg
Gen 11:17 *t* years, and begat sons and
Gen 11:18 And Peleg lived *t* years, and begat
Gen 11:20 two and *t* years, and begat Serug
Gen 11:22 And Serug lived *t* years, and begat
Gen 18:30 there shall *t* be found there
Gen 18:30 will not do it, if I find *t* there
Gen 25:17 life of Ishmael, an hundred and *t*
Gen 32:15 *T* milch camels with their colts,
Gen 41:46 Joseph was *t* years old when he
Gen 46:15 his sons and his daughters were *t*
Gen 47:9 are an hundred and *t* years
Ex 6:16 life of Levi were an hundred *t*
Ex 6:18 life of Kohath were an hundred *t*
Ex 6:20 of Amram were an hundred and *t*
Ex 12:40 was four hundred and *t* years
Ex 12:41 *t* years, even the selfsame day it
Ex 21:32 their master *t* shekels of silver
Ex 26:8 of one curtain shall be *t* cubits
Ex 36:15 of one curtain was *t* cubits
Ex 38:24 *t* shekels, after the shekel of
Lev 12:4 of her purifying three and *t* days
Lev 27:4 thy estimation shall be *t* shekels
Num 1:35 of the tribe of Manasseh, were *t*
Num 1:37 of the tribe of Benjamin, were *t*
Num 2:21 were numbered of them, were *t*
Num 2:23 were numbered of them, were *t*
Num 4:3 From *t* years old and upward even
Num 4:23 From *t* years old and upward until
Num 4:30 From *t* years old and upward even
Num 4:35 From *t* years old and upward even
Num 4:39 From *t* years old and upward even
Num 4:40 two thousand and six hundred and *t*
Num 4:43 From *t* years old and upward even
Num 4:47 From *t* years old and upward even
Num 7:13 *t* shekels, one silver bowl of
Num 7:19 *t* shekels, one silver bowl of
Num 7:25 *t* shekels, one silver bowl of
Num 7:31 *t* shekels, one silver bowl of
Num 7:37 *t* shekels, one silver bowl of
Num 7:43 *t* shekels, a silver bowl of
Num 7:49 *t* shekels, one silver bowl of
Num 7:55 *t* shekels, one silver bowl of
Num 7:61 *t* shekels, one silver bowl of
Num 7:67 *t* shekels, one silver bowl of
Num 7:73 *t* shekels, one silver bowl of
Num 7:79 *t* shekels, one silver bowl of
Num 7:85 *t* shekels, each bowl seventy
Num 20:29 they mourned for Aaron *t* days
Num 26:7 thousand and seven hundred and *t*
Num 26:37 that were numbered of them, *t*
Num 26:51 and a thousand seven hundred and *t*
Num 31:35 And *t* and two thousand persons in
Num 31:36 *t* thousand and five hundred sheep
Num 31:38 And the beeves were *t* and six
Num 31:39 And the asses were *t* thousand
Num 31:40 of which the LORD's tribute was *t*
Num 31:43 *t* thousand and seven thousand and
Num 31:44 And *t* and six thousand beeves,
Num 31:45 *t* thousand asses and five hundred,
Deut 2:14 come over the brook Zered, was *t*
Deut 34:8 in the plains of Moab *t* days
Josh 7:5 men of Ai smote of them about *t*
Josh 8:3 Joshua chose out *t* thousand
Josh 12:24 all the kings *t* and one
Judg 10:4 he had *t* sons that rode
Judg 10:4 sons that rode on *t* ass colts
Judg 10:4 ass colts, and they had *t* cities
Judg 12:9 And he had *t* sons
Judg 12:9 *t* daughters, whom he sent abroad,
Judg 12:9 took in *t* daughters from abroad
Judg 12:14 sons and *t* nephews, that rode on
Judg 14:11 that they brought *t* companions to
Judg 14:12 then I will give you *t* sheets
Judg 14:12 sheets and *t* change of garments
Judg 14:13 then shall ye give me *t* sheets
Judg 14:13 sheets and *t* change of garments
Judg 14:19 slew *t* men of them, and took their
Judg 20:31 the field, about *t* men of Israel
Judg 20:39 the men of Israel about *t* persons
1Sa 4:10 fell of Israel *t* thousand footmen
1Sa 9:22 which were about *t* persons
1Sa 11:8 and the men of Judah *t* thousand
1Sa 13:5 *t* thousand chariots, and six
2Sa 5:4 David was *t* years old when he
2Sa 5:5 and in Jerusalem he reigned *t*
2Sa 6:1 chosen men of Israel, *t* thousand
2Sa 23:13 three of the *t* chief went down,
2Sa 23:23 He was more honourable than the *t*
2Sa 23:24 brother of Joab was one of the *t*
2Sa 23:39 *t* and seven in all
1Kin 2:11 years reigned he in Hebron, and *t*
1Kin 4:22 day was *t* measures of fine flour
1Kin 5:13 and the levy was *t* thousand men
1Kin 6:2 and the height thereof *t* cubits
1Kin 7:2 and the height thereof *t* cubits
1Kin 7:6 and the breadth thereof *t* cubits
1Kin 7:23 a line of *t* cubits did compass it
1Kin 16:23 In the *t* and first year of Asa
1Kin 16:29 And in the *t* and eighth year of Asa
1Kin 20:1 and there were *t* and two kings with
1Kin 20:15 and they were two hundred and *t* two
1Kin 20:16 pavilions, he and the kings, the *t*
1Kin 22:31 the king of Syria commanded his *t*
1Kin 22:42 Jehoshaphat was *t* and five years
2Kin 8:17 *T* and two years old was he when he
2Kin 13:10 In the *t* and seventh year of Joash
2Kin 15:8 In the *t* and eighth year of
2Kin 18:14 of silver and *t* talents of gold
2Kin 22:1 began to reign, and he reigned *t*
1Chr 3:4 and in Jerusalem he reigned *t*
1Chr 7:4 for war, six and *t* thousand men
1Chr 7:7 twenty and two thousand and *t*
1Chr 11:15 Now three of the *t* captains went
1Chr 11:25 he was honourable among the *t*
1Chr 11:42 of the Reubenites, and *t* with him,
1Chr 12:4 among the *t*, and over the *t*
1Chr 12:34 with them with shield and spear *t*
1Chr 15:7 and his brethren an hundred and *t*
1Chr 19:7 So they hired *t* and two thousand
1Chr 23:3 numbered from the age of *t* years
1Chr 23:3 by their polls, man by man, was *t*
1Chr 27:6 among the *t*, and above the *t*
1Chr 29:27 years reigned he in Hebron, and *t*
2Chr 3:15 before the house two pillars of *t*
2Chr 4:2 a line of *t* cubits did compass it
2Chr 16:12 And Asa in the *t* and ninth year of
2Chr 20:31 he was *t* and five years old when
2Chr 21:5 Jehoram was *t* and two years old
2Chr 21:20 *T* and two years old was he when he
2Chr 24:15 *t* years old was he when he died
2Chr 34:1 in Jerusalem one and *t* years
2Chr 35:7 to the number of *t* thousand
Ezr 1:9 *t* chargers of gold, a thousand
Ezr 1:10 *T* basons of gold, silver basons
Ezr 2:35 thousand and six hundred and *t*
Ezr 2:42 of Shobai, in all an hundred *t*
Ezr 2:65 seven thousand three hundred *t*
Ezr 2:66 Their horses were seven hundred *t*
Ezr 2:67 Their camels, four hundred *t*
Neh 7:38 three thousand nine hundred and *t*
Neh 7:45 children of Shobai, an hundred *t*
Neh 7:67 seven thousand three hundred *t*
Neh 7:68 Their horses, seven hundred *t*
Neh 7:69 Their camels, four hundred *t*
Neh 7:70 hundred and *t* priests' garments
Est 4:11 in unto the king these *t* days
Jer 38:10 Take from hence *t* men with thee
Jer 52:29 from Jerusalem eight hundred *t*
Eze 40:17 *t* chambers were upon the pavement
Eze 41:6 one over another, and *t* in order
Eze 46:22 of forty cubits long and *t* broad
Dan 6:7 of any God or man for *t* days
Dan 6:12 of any God or man within *t* days
Dan 12:12 three hundred and five and *t* days
Zec 11:12 for my price *t* pieces of silver
Zec 11:13 I took the *t* pieces of silver, and
Mt 13:23 hundredfold, some sixty, some *t*
Mt 26:15 with him for *t* pieces of silver
Mt 27:3 brought again the *t* pieces of
Mt 27:9 they took the *t* pieces of silver,
Mk 4:8 and brought forth, some *t*, and some
Lk 3:23 began to be about *t* years of age
Jn 5:5 there, which had an infirmity *t*
Jn 6:19 five and twenty or *t* furlongs
Gal 3:17 *t* years after, cannot disannul,

**THIRTYFOLD**
Mt 13:8 some sixtyfold, some *t*
Mk 4:20 it, and bring forth fruit, some *t*

**THISTLE**
2Kin 14:9 The *t* that was in Lebanon sent to
2Kin 14:9 in Lebanon, and trode down the *t*
2Chr 25:18 The *t* that was in Lebanon sent to
2Chr 25:18 in Lebanon, and trode down the *t*
Hos 10:8 the *t* shall come up on their

**THISTLES**
Gen 3:18 *t* shall it bring forth to thee
Job 31:40 Let *t* grow instead of wheat, and
Mt 7:16 grapes of thorns, or figs of *t*

**THOMAS** *(tom'-us)* See DIDYMUS. *One of the twelve apostles.*
Mt 10:3 *T*, and Matthew the publican
Mk 3:18 and Bartholomew, and Matthew, and *T*
Lk 6:15 Matthew and *T*, James the son of
Jn 11:16 Then said *T*, which is called
Jn 14:5 *T* saith unto him, Lord, we know
Jn 20:24 But *T*, one of the twelve, called
Jn 20:26 were within, and *T* with them
Jn 20:27 Then saith he to *T*, Reach hither
Jn 20:28 *T* answered and said unto him, My
Jn 20:29 Jesus saith unto him, *T*, because
Jn 21:2 *T* called Didymus, and Nathanael of
Acts 1:13 and John, and Andrew, Philip, and *T*

**THONGS**
Acts 22:25 And as they bound him with *t*

**THORN**
Job 41:2 or bore his jaw through with a *t*
Prov 26:9 As a *t* goeth up into the hand of
Is 55:13 Instead of the *t* shall come
Eze 28:24 nor any grieving *t* of all that
Hos 10:8 the *t* and the thistle shall come
Mic 7:4 upright is sharper than a *t* hedge
2Cor 12:7 was given to me a *t* in the flesh

**THORNS**
Gen 3:18 *T* also and thistles shall it bring
Ex 22:6 If fire break out, and catch in *t*

Num 33:55 *t* in your sides, and shall vex you
Josh 23:13 *t* in your eyes, until ye perish
Judg 2:3 they shall be as *t* in your sides
Judg 8:7 with the *t* of the wilderness
Judg 8:16 *t* of the wilderness and briers, and
2Sa 23:6 be all of them as *t* thrust away
2Chr 33:11 which took Manasseh among the *t*
Job 5:5 and taketh it even out of the *t*
Ps 58:9 Before your pots can feel the *t*
Ps 118:12 are quenched as the fire of *t*
Prov 15:19 slothful man is as an hedge of *t*
Prov 22:5 *T* and snares are in the way of the
Prov 24:31 lo, it was all grown over with *t*
Eccl 7:6 as the crackling of *t* under a pot
Song 2:2 As the lily among *t*, so is my
Is 5:6 there shall come up briers and *t*
Is 7:19 holes of the rocks, and upon all *t*
Is 7:23 it shall even be for briers and *t*
Is 7:24 the land shall become briers and *t*
Is 7:25 thither the fear of briers and *t*
Is 9:18 it shall devour the briers and *t*
Is 10:17 and it shall burn and devour his *t*
Is 27:4 briers and *t* against me in battle
Is 32:13 land of my people shall come up *t*
Is 33:12 as *t* cut up shall they be burned
Is 34:13 *t* shall come up in her palaces,
Jer 4:3 fallow ground, and sow not among *t*
Jer 12:13 have sown wheat, but shall reap *t*
Eze 2:6 *t* be with thee, and thou dost
Hos 2:6 I will hedge up thy way with *t*
Hos 9:6 *t* shall be in their tabernacles
Nah 1:10 they be folden together as *t*
Mt 7:16 Do men gather grapes of *t*
Mt 13:7 And some fell among *t*
Mt 13:7 the *t* sprung up, and choked them
Mt 13:22 the *t* is he that heareth the word
Mt 27:29 they had platted a crown of *t*
Mk 4:7 And some fell among *t*, and the
Mk 4:7 the *t* grew up, and choked it, and
Mk 4:18 are they which are sown among *t*
Mk 15:17 purple, and platted a crown of *t*
Lk 6:44 For of *t* men do not gather figs,
Lk 8:7 And some fell among *t*
Lk 8:7 the *t* sprang up with it, and
Lk 8:14 that which fell among *t* are they
Jn 19:2 the soldiers platted a crown of *t*
Jn 19:5 forth, wearing the crown of *t*
Heb 6:8 But that which beareth *t* and

## THOUGHT

Gen 20:11 And Abraham said, Because I *t*
Gen 38:15 saw her, he *t* her to be an harlot
Gen 48:11 I had not *t* to see thy face
Gen 50:20 as for you, ye *t* evil against me
Ex 32:14 which he *t* to do unto his people
Num 24:11 I *t* to promote thee unto great
Num 33:56 unto you, as I *t* to do unto them
Deut 15:9 be not a *t* in thy wicked heart
Deut 19:19 as he had *t* to have done unto his
Judg 15:2 I verily *t* that thou hadst
Judg 20:5 by night, and *t* to have slain me
Ruth 4:4 I *t* to advertise thee, saying,
1Sa 1:13 therefore Eli *t* she had been
1Sa 9:5 for the asses, and take *t* for us
1Sa 18:25 But Saul *t* to make David fall by
1Sa 20:26 for he *t*, Something hath befallen
2Sa 4:10 who *t* that I would have given him
2Sa 13:2 Amnon *t* it hard for him to do any
2Sa 14:13 Wherefore then hast thou *t* such a
2Sa 19:18 and to do what he *t* good
2Sa 21:16 new sword, *t* to have slain David
2Kin 5:11 went away, and said, Behold, I *t*
2Chr 11:22 for he *t* to make him king
2Chr 32:1 *t* to win them for himself
Neh 6:2 But they *t* to do me mischief
Est 3:6 he *t* scorn to lay hands on
Est 6:6 Now Haman *t* in his heart, To whom
Job 12:5 in the *t* of him that is at ease
Job 42:2 that no *t* can be withholden from
Ps 48:9 We have *t* of thy lovingkindness,
Ps 49:11 Their inward *t* is, that their
Ps 64:6 both the inward *t* of every one of
Ps 73:16 When I *t* to know this, it was too
Ps 119:59 I *t* on my ways, and turned my feet
Ps 139:2 thou understandest my *t* afar off
Prov 24:9 The *t* of foolishness is sin
Prov 30:32 thyself, or if thou hast *t* evil
Eccl 10:20 not the king, no not in thy *t*
Is 14:24 sworn, saying, Surely as I have *t*
Jer 18:8 the evil that I *t* to do unto them
Eze 38:10 and thou shalt think an evil *t*
Dan 4:2 I *t* it good to shew the signs and
Dan 6:3 the king *t* to set him over the
Amos 4:13 declareth unto man what is his *t*
Zec 1:6 the LORD of hosts *t* to do unto us
Zec 8:14 As I *t* to punish you, when your
Zec 8:15 So again have I *t* in these days
Mal 3:16 the LORD, and that *t* upon his name
Mt 1:20 But while he *t* on these things,
Mt 6:25 Take no *t* for your life, what ye
Mt 6:27 Which of you by taking *t* can add
Mt 6:28 And why take ye *t* for raiment
Mt 6:31 Therefore take no *t*, saying, What
Mt 6:34 therefore no *t* for the morrow
Mt 6:34 take *t* for the things of itself
Mt 10:19 take no *t* how or what ye shall
Mk 13:11 take no *t* beforehand what ye
Mk 14:72 And when he *t* thereon, he wept
Lk 7:7 Wherefore neither *t* I myself
Lk 9:47 perceiving the *t* of their heart
Lk 12:11 take ye no *t* how or what thing ye
Lk 12:17 he *t* within himself, saying, What
Lk 12:22 Take no *t* for your life, what ye
Lk 12:25 which of you with taking *t* can
Lk 12:26 why take ye *t* for the rest
Lk 19:11 because they *t* that the kingdom
Jn 11:13 but they *t* that he had spoken of
Jn 13:29 For some of them *t*, because Judas
Acts 8:20 because thou hast *t* that the gift
Acts 8:22 if perhaps the *t* of thine heart
Acts 10:19 While Peter *t* on the vision, the
Acts 12:9 but *t* he saw a vision
Acts 15:38 But Paul *t* not good to take him
Acts 26:8 Why should it be *t* a thing
Acts 26:9 I verily *t* with myself, that I
1Cor 13:11 as a child, I *t* as a child
2Cor 9:5 Therefore I *t* it necessary to
2Cor 10:5 *t* to the obedience of Christ
Phil 2:6 *t* it not robbery to be equal with
1Th 3:1 we *t* it good to be left at Athens
Heb 10:29 suppose ye, shall he be *t* worthy

## THOUGHTS

Gen 6:5 the *t* of his heart was only evil
Judg 5:15 there were great *t* of heart
1Chr 28:9 all the imaginations of the *t*
1Chr 29:18 the *t* of the heart of thy people
Job 4:13 In *t* from the visions of the
Job 17:11 off, even the *t* of my heart
Job 20:2 Therefore do my *t* cause me to
Job 21:27 Behold, I know your *t*, and the
Ps 10:4 God is not in all his *t*
Ps 33:11 the *t* of his heart to all
Ps 40:5 thy *t* which are to us-ward
Ps 56:5 all their *t* are against me for
Ps 92:5 and thy *t* are very deep
Ps 94:11 The LORD knoweth the *t* of man
Ps 94:19 In the multitude of my *t* within
Ps 119:113 I hate vain *t*
Ps 139:17 precious also are thy *t* unto me
Ps 139:23 try me, and know my *t*
Ps 146:4 in that very day his *t* perish
Prov 12:5 The *t* of the righteous are right
Prov 15:26 The *t* of the wicked are an
Prov 16:3 thy *t* shall be established
Prov 21:5 The *t* of the diligent tend only
Is 55:7 way, and the unrighteous man his *t*
Is 55:8 For my *t* are not your *t*,
Is 55:9 ways, and my *t* than your *t*
Is 59:7 their *t* are *t* of iniquity
Is 65:2 was not good, after their own *t*
Is 66:18 For I know their works and their *t*
Jer 4:14 thy vain *t* lodge within thee
Jer 6:19 people, even the fruit of their *t*
Jer 23:20 have performed the *t* of his heart
Jer 29:11 For I know the *t* that I think
Jer 29:11 *t* of peace, and not of evil, to
Dan 2:29 thy *t* came into thy mind upon thy
Dan 2:30 mightest know the *t* of thy heart
Dan 4:5 the *t* upon my bed and the visions
Dan 4:19 one hour, and his *t* troubled him
Dan 5:6 his *t* troubled him, so that the
Dan 5:10 let not thy *t* trouble thee, nor
Mic 4:12 they know not the *t* of the LORD
Mt 9:4 And Jesus knowing their *t* said
Mt 12:25 And Jesus knew their *t*, and said
Mt 15:19 out of the heart proceed evil *t*
Mk 7:21 the heart of men, proceed evil *t*
Lk 2:35 that the *t* of many hearts may be
Lk 5:22 But when Jesus perceived their *t*
Lk 6:8 But he knew their *t*, and said to
Lk 11:17 But he, knowing their *t*, said
Lk 24:38 why do *t* arise in your hearts
Rom 2:15 their *t* the mean while accusing
1Cor 3:20 Lord knoweth the *t* of the wise
Heb 4:12 and is a discerner of the *t*
Jas 2:4 and are become judges of evil *t*

## THOUSAND

Gen 20:16 thy brother a *t* pieces of silver
Ex 12:37 about six hundred *t* on foot that
Ex 32:28 people that day about three *t* men
Ex 38:25 a *t* seven hundred and threescore
Ex 38:26 six hundred *t* and three *t*
Ex 38:28 of the *t* seven hundred seventy and
Ex 38:29 was seventy talents, and two *t*
Lev 26:8 of you shall put ten *t* to flight
Num 1:21 of Reuben, were forty and six *t*
Num 1:23 of Simeon, were fifty and nine *t*
Num 1:25 five *t* six hundred and fifty
Num 1:27 were threescore and fourteen *t*
Num 1:29 of Issachar, were fifty and four *t*
Num 1:31 of Zebulun, were fifty and seven *t*
Num 1:33 tribe of Ephraim, were forty *t*
Num 1:35 of Manasseh, were thirty and two *t*
Num 1:37 Benjamin, were thirty and five *t*
Num 1:39 of Dan, were threescore and two *t*
Num 1:41 of Asher, were forty and one *t*
Num 1:43 Naphtali, were fifty and three *t*
Num 1:46 were numbered were six hundred *t*
Num 1:46 six hundred *t* and three *t*
Num 2:4 were threescore and fourteen *t*
Num 2:6 thereof, were fifty and four *t*
Num 2:8 thereof, were fifty and seven *t*
Num 2:9 camp of Judah were an hundred *t*
Num 2:9 and fourscore *t* and six *t*
Num 2:11 thereof, were forty and six *t*
Num 2:13 of them, were fifty and nine *t*
Num 2:15 of them, were forty and five *t*
Num 2:16 camp of Reuben were an hundred *t*
Num 2:16 *t* and fifty and one *t*
Num 2:19 numbered of them, were forty *t*
Num 2:21 of them, were thirty and two *t*
Num 2:23 of them, were thirty and five *t*
Num 2:24 an hundred *t* and eight *t*
Num 2:26 of them, were threescore and two *t*
Num 2:28 of them, were forty and one *t*
Num 2:30 of them, were fifty and three *t*
Num 2:31 the camp of Dan were an hundred *t*
Num 2:31 and fifty and seven *t*
Num 2:32 six hundred *t* and three *t*
Num 3:22 numbered of them were seven *t*
Num 3:28 month old and upward, were eight *t*
Num 3:34 a month old and upward, were six *t*
Num 3:39 and upward, were twenty and two *t*
Num 3:43 two *t* two hundred and threescore
Num 3:50 a *t* three hundred and threescore
Num 4:36 families were two *t* seven hundred
Num 4:40 of their fathers, were two *t*
Num 4:44 their families, were three *t*
Num 4:48 numbered of them, were eight *t*
Num 7:85 the silver vessels weighed two *t*
Num 11:21 I am, are six hundred *t* footmen
Num 16:49 in the plague were fourteen *t*
Num 25:9 the plague were twenty and four *t*
Num 26:7 of them were forty and three *t*
Num 26:14 the Simeonites, twenty and two *t*
Num 26:18 were numbered of them, forty *t*
Num 26:22 of them, threescore and sixteen *t*
Num 26:25 of them, threescore and four *t*
Num 26:27 numbered of them, threescore *t*
Num 26:34 numbered of them, fifty and two *t*
Num 26:37 numbered of them, thirty and two *t*
Num 26:41 of them were forty and five *t*
Num 26:43 them, were threescore and four *t*
Num 26:47 who were fifty and three *t*
Num 26:50 of them were forty and five *t*
Num 26:51 children of Israel, six hundred *t*
Num 26:51 a *t* seven hundred and thirty
Num 26:62 of them were twenty and three *t*
Num 31:4 Of every tribe a *t*, throughout
Num 31:5 a *t* of every tribe, twelve
Num 31:5 tribe, twelve *t* armed for war
Num 31:6 a *t* of every tribe, them and
Num 31:32 war had caught, was six hundred *t*
Num 31:32 seventy *t* and five *t* sheep,
Num 31:33 And threescore and twelve *t* beeves
Num 31:34 And threescore and one *t* asses,
Num 31:35 two *t* persons in all, of women
Num 31:36 was in number three hundred *t*

Num 31:36 and seven and thirty *t*
Num 31:38 the beeves were thirty and six *t*
Num 31:39 And the asses were thirty *t*
Num 31:40 And the persons were sixteen *t*
Num 31:43 congregation was three hundred *t*
Num 31:43 and thirty *t* and seven *t*
Num 31:44 And thirty and six *t* beeves,
Num 31:45 And thirty *t* asses and five hundred
Num 31:46 And sixteen *t* persons
Num 31:52 was sixteen *t* seven hundred and
Num 35:4 outward a *t* cubits round about
Num 35:5 on the east side two *t* cubits
Num 35:5 and on the south side two *t* cubits
Num 35:5 and on the west side two *t* cubits
Num 35:5 and on the north side two *t* cubits
Deut 1:11 a *t* times so many more as ye are
Deut 7:9 commandments to a *t* generations
Deut 32:30 How should one chase a *t*, and two
Deut 32:30 and two put ten *t* to flight
Josh 3:4 about two *t* cubits by measure
Josh 4:13 About forty *t* prepared for war
Josh 7:3 about two or three *t* men go up
Josh 7:4 of the people about three *t* men
Josh 8:3 out thirty *t* mighty men of valour
Josh 8:12 And he took about five *t* men
Josh 8:25 of men and women, were twelve *t*
Josh 23:10 One man of you shall chase a *t*
Judg 1:4 slew of them in Bezek ten *t* men
Judg 3:29 Moab at that time about ten *t* men
Judg 4:6 take with thee ten *t* men of the
Judg 4:10 up with ten *t* men at his feet
Judg 4:14 Tabor, and ten *t* men after him
Judg 5:8 seen among forty *t* in Israel
Judg 7:3 of the people twenty and two *t*
Judg 7:3 and there remained ten *t*
Judg 8:10 with them, about fifteen *t* men
Judg 8:10 twenty *t* men that drew sword
Judg 8:26 that he requested was a *t*
Judg 9:49 Shechem died also, about a *t* men
Judg 12:6 of the Ephraimites forty and two *t*
Judg 15:11 Then three *t* men of Judah went to
Judg 15:15 it, and slew a *t* men therewith
Judg 15:16 of an ass have I slain a *t* men
Judg 16:27 upon the roof about three *t* men
Judg 20:2 four hundred *t* footmen that drew
Judg 20:10 of Israel, and an hundred of a *t*
Judg 20:10 and a *t* out of ten *t*
Judg 20:15 six *t* men that drew sword, beside
Judg 20:17 hundred *t* men that drew sword
Judg 20:21 that day twenty and two *t* men
Judg 20:25 of Israel again eighteen *t* men
Judg 20:34 *t* chosen men out of all Israel
Judg 20:35 that day twenty and five *t*
Judg 20:44 fell of Benjamin eighteen *t* men
Judg 20:45 them in the highways five *t* men
Judg 20:45 Gidom, and slew two *t* men of them
Judg 20:46 five *t* men that drew the sword
Judg 21:10 sent thither twelve *t* men of the
1Sa 4:2 in the field about four *t* men
1Sa 4:10 fell of Israel thirty *t* footmen
1Sa 6:19 he smote of the people fifty *t*
1Sa 11:8 of Israel were three hundred *t*
1Sa 11:8 and the men of Judah thirty *t*
1Sa 13:2 chose him three *t* men of Israel
1Sa 13:2 whereof two *t* were with Saul in
1Sa 13:2 a *t* were with Jonathan in Gibeah
1Sa 13:5 thirty *t* chariots, and six
1Sa 13:5 six *t* horsemen, and people as the
1Sa 15:4 in Telaim, two hundred *t* footmen
1Sa 15:4 footmen, and ten *t* men of Judah
1Sa 17:5 coat was five *t* shekels of brass
1Sa 17:18 unto the captain of their *t*
1Sa 18:13 and made him his captain over a *t*
1Sa 24:2 Then Saul took three *t* chosen men
1Sa 25:2 great, and he had three *t* sheep
1Sa 25:2 sheep, and a *t* goats
1Sa 26:2 having three *t* chosen men of
2Sa 6:1 chosen men of Israel, thirty *t*
2Sa 8:4 David took from him a *t* chariots
2Sa 8:4 horsemen, and twenty *t* footmen
2Sa 8:5 the Syrians two and twenty *t* men
2Sa 8:13 of salt, being eighteen *t* men
2Sa 10:6 twenty *t* footmen, and of king
2Sa 10:6 and of king Maacah a *t* men
2Sa 10:6 and of Ish-tob twelve *t* men
2Sa 10:18 forty *t* horsemen, and smote
2Sa 17:1 me now choose out twelve *t* men
2Sa 18:3 now thou art worth ten *t* of us
2Sa 18:7 that day of twenty *t* men
2Sa 18:12 Though I should receive a *t*
2Sa 19:17 there were a *t* men of Benjamin
2Sa 24:9 were in Israel eight hundred *t*
2Sa 24:9 of Judah were five hundred *t* men
2Sa 24:15 even to Beer-sheba seventy *t* men
1Kin 3:4 a *t* burnt offerings did Solomon
1Kin 4:26 Solomon had forty *t* stalls of
1Kin 4:26 chariots, and twelve *t* horsemen
1Kin 4:32 And he spake three *t* proverbs
1Kin 4:32 and his songs were a *t* and five
1Kin 5:11 Solomon gave Hiram twenty *t*
1Kin 5:13 and the levy was thirty *t* men
1Kin 5:14 Lebanon, ten *t* a month by courses
1Kin 5:15 ten *t* that bare burdens, and
1Kin 5:15 fourscore *t* hewers in the
1Kin 5:16 which were over the work, three *t*
1Kin 7:26 it contained two *t* baths
1Kin 8:63 the LORD, two and twenty *t* oxen
1Kin 8:63 and an hundred and twenty *t* sheep
1Kin 10:26 and he had a *t* and four hundred
1Kin 10:26 twelve *t* horsemen, whom he
1Kin 12:21 fourscore *t* chosen men, which
1Kin 19:18 I have left me seven *t* in Israel
1Kin 20:15 children of Israel, being seven *t*
1Kin 20:29 an hundred *t* footmen in one day
1Kin 20:30 seven *t* of the men that were left
2Kin 3:4 king of Israel an hundred *t* lambs
2Kin 3:4 lambs, and an hundred *t* rams
2Kin 5:5 six *t* pieces of gold, and ten
2Kin 13:7 and ten chariots, and ten *t* footmen
2Kin 14:7 Edom in the valley of salt ten *t*
2Kin 15:19 gave Pul a *t* talents of silver
2Kin 18:23 I will deliver thee two *t* horses
2Kin 19:35 an hundred fourscore and five *t*
2Kin 24:14 of valour, even ten *t* captives
2Kin 24:16 the men of might, even seven *t*
2Kin 24:16 and craftsmen and smiths a *t*
1Chr 5:18 four and forty *t* seven hundred and
1Chr 5:21 of their camels fifty *t*, and of
1Chr 5:21 fifty *t*, and of asses two *t*
1Chr 5:21 and of men an hundred *t*
1Chr 7:2 the days of David two and twenty *t*
1Chr 7:4 for war, six and thirty *t* men
1Chr 7:5 genealogies fourscore and seven *t*
1Chr 7:7 their genealogies twenty and two *t*
1Chr 7:9 men of valour, was twenty *t*
1Chr 7:11 men of valour, were seventeen *t*
1Chr 7:40 to battle was twenty and six *t* men
1Chr 9:13 the house of their fathers, a *t*
1Chr 12:14 hundred, and the greatest over a *t*
1Chr 12:24 bare shield and spear were six *t*
1Chr 12:25 of valour for the war, seven *t*
1Chr 12:26 Of the children of Levi four *t*
1Chr 12:27 and with him were three *t*
1Chr 12:29 the kindred of Saul, three *t*
1Chr 12:30 the children of Ephraim twenty *t*
1Chr 12:31 half tribe of Manasseh eighteen *t*
1Chr 12:33 all instruments of war, fifty *t*
1Chr 12:34 And of Naphtali a *t* captains
1Chr 12:34 shield and spear thirty and seven *t*
1Chr 12:35 expert in war twenty and eight *t*
1Chr 12:36 to battle, expert in war, forty *t*
1Chr 12:37 battle, an hundred and twenty *t*
1Chr 16:15 he commanded to a *t* generations
1Chr 18:4 David took from him a *t* chariots
1Chr 18:4 seven *t* horsemen, and twenty
1Chr 18:4 horsemen, and twenty *t* footmen
1Chr 18:5 the Syrians two and twenty *t* men
1Chr 18:12 in the valley of salt eighteen *t*
1Chr 19:6 the children of Ammon sent a *t*
1Chr 19:7 two *t* chariots, and the king of
1Chr 19:18 *t* men which fought in chariots
1Chr 19:18 forty *t* footmen, and killed
1Chr 21:5 they of Israel were a *t* *t*
1Chr 21:5 an hundred *t* men that drew sword
1Chr 21:5 ten *t* men that drew sword
1Chr 21:14 fell of Israel seventy *t* men
1Chr 22:14 LORD an hundred *t* talents of gold
1Chr 22:14 a *t* *t* talents of silver
1Chr 23:3 man by man, was thirty and eight *t*
1Chr 23:4 four *t* were to set forward the
1Chr 23:4 six *t* were officers and judges
1Chr 23:5 Moreover four *t* were porters
1Chr 23:5 four *t* praised the LORD with the
1Chr 26:30 his brethren, men of valour, a *t*
1Chr 26:32 men of valour, were two *t*
1Chr 27:1 course were twenty and four *t*
1Chr 27:2 his course were twenty and four *t*
1Chr 27:4 likewise were twenty and four *t*
1Chr 27:5 his course were twenty and four *t*
1Chr 27:7 his course were twenty and four *t*
1Chr 27:8 his course were twenty and four *t*
1Chr 27:9 his course were twenty and four *t*
1Chr 27:10 his course were twenty and four *t*
1Chr 27:11 his course were twenty and four *t*
1Chr 27:12 his course were twenty and four *t*
1Chr 27:13 his course were twenty and four *t*
1Chr 27:14 his course were twenty and four *t*
1Chr 27:15 his course were twenty and four *t*
1Chr 29:4 Even three *t* talents of gold, of
1Chr 29:4 seven *t* talents of refined silver
1Chr 29:7 of God of gold five *t* talents
1Chr 29:7 ten *t* drams, and of silver ten
1Chr 29:7 drams, and of silver ten *t* talents
1Chr 29:7 and of brass eighteen *t* talents
1Chr 29:7 one hundred *t* talents of iron
1Chr 29:21 even a *t* bullocks, a *t*
1Chr 29:21 a *t* rams, and a *t* lambs,
2Chr 1:6 offered a *t* burnt offerings upon
2Chr 1:14 and he had a *t* and four hundred
2Chr 1:14 twelve *t* horsemen, which he
2Chr 2:2 ten *t* men to bear burdens, and
2Chr 2:2 fourscore *t* to hew in the
2Chr 2:2 hew in the mountain, and three *t*
2Chr 2:10 twenty *t* measures of beaten wheat
2Chr 2:10 twenty *t* measures of barley, and
2Chr 2:10 twenty *t* baths of wine, and twenty
2Chr 2:10 of wine, and twenty *t* baths of oil
2Chr 2:17 and fifty *t* and three *t*
2Chr 2:18 ten *t* of them to be bearers of
2Chr 2:18 fourscore *t* to be hewers in the
2Chr 2:18 in the mountain, and three *t*
2Chr 4:5 it received and held three *t* baths
2Chr 7:5 two *t* oxen, and an hundred and
2Chr 7:5 and an hundred and twenty *t* sheep
2Chr 9:25 Solomon had four *t* stalls for
2Chr 9:25 and chariots, and twelve *t* horsemen
2Chr 11:1 fourscore *t* chosen men, which
2Chr 12:3 and threescore *t* horsemen
2Chr 13:3 even four hundred *t* chosen men
2Chr 13:3 with eight hundred *t* chosen men
2Chr 13:17 Israel five hundred *t* chosen men
2Chr 14:8 out of Judah three hundred *t*
2Chr 14:8 bows, two hundred and fourscore *t*
2Chr 14:9 with an host of a *t* *t*
2Chr 15:11 hundred oxen and seven *t* sheep
2Chr 17:11 brought him flocks, seven *t*
2Chr 17:11 and seven hundred rams, and seven *t*
2Chr 17:14 men of valour three hundred *t*
2Chr 17:15 him two hundred and fourscore *t*
2Chr 17:16 hundred *t* mighty men of valour
2Chr 17:17 with bow and shield two hundred *t*
2Chr 17:18 fourscore *t* ready prepared for
2Chr 25:5 them three hundred *t* choice men
2Chr 25:6 He hired also an hundred *t* mighty
2Chr 25:11 of the children of Seir ten *t*
2Chr 25:12 other ten *t* left alive did the
2Chr 25:13 and smote three *t* of them
2Chr 26:12 mighty men of valour were two *t*
2Chr 26:13 three hundred *t* and seven *t*
2Chr 27:5 ten *t* measures of wheat, and ten
2Chr 27:5 of wheat, and ten *t* of barley
2Chr 28:6 twenty *t* in one day, which were
2Chr 28:8 of their brethren two hundred *t*
2Chr 29:33 six hundred oxen and three *t* sheep
2Chr 30:24 to the congregation a *t* bullocks
2Chr 30:24 bullocks and seven *t* sheep
2Chr 30:24 to the congregation a *t* bullocks
2Chr 30:24 *t* bullocks and ten *t* sheep
2Chr 35:7 to the number of thirty *t*
2Chr 35:7 and three *t* bullocks
2Chr 35:8 for the passover offerings two *t*
2Chr 35:9 offerings five *t* small cattle
Ezr 1:9 a *t* chargers of silver, nine and
Ezr 1:10 and ten, and other vessels a *t*
Ezr 1:11 of gold and of silver were five *t*
Ezr 2:3 two *t* an hundred seventy and two
Ezr 2:6 two *t* eight hundred and twelve
Ezr 2:7 a *t* two hundred fifty and four
Ezr 2:12 a *t* two hundred twenty and two
Ezr 2:14 of Bigvai, two *t* fifty and six
Ezr 2:31 a *t* two hundred fifty and four
Ezr 2:35 The children of Senaah, three *t*
Ezr 2:37 of Immer, a *t* fifty and two
Ezr 2:38 a *t* two hundred forty and seven
Ezr 2:39 The children of Harim, a *t*
Ezr 2:64 two *t* three hundred and threescore
Ezr 2:65 were seven *t* three hundred thirty
Ezr 2:67 six *t* seven hundred and twenty
Ezr 2:69 one *t* drams of gold, and five
Ezr 2:69 five *t* pound of silver, and one

Ezr 8:27 basons of gold, of a *t* drams
Neh 3:13 a *t* cubits on the wall unto the
Neh 7:8 two *t* an hundred seventy and two
Neh 7:11 children of Jeshua and Joab, two *t*
Neh 7:12 a *t* two hundred fifty and four
Neh 7:17 two *t* three hundred twenty and two
Neh 7:19 two *t* threescore and seven
Neh 7:34 a *t* two hundred fifty and four
Neh 7:38 three *t* nine hundred and thirty
Neh 7:40 of Immer, a *t* fifty and two
Neh 7:41 a *t* two hundred forty and seven
Neh 7:42 The children of Harim, a *t*
Neh 7:66 two *t* three hundred and threescore
Neh 7:67 were seven *t* three hundred thirty
Neh 7:69 six *t* seven hundred and twenty
Neh 7:70 to the treasure a *t* drams of gold
Neh 7:71 the work twenty *t* drams of gold
Neh 7:71 of gold, and two *t*
Neh 7:72 gave was twenty *t* drams of gold
Neh 7:72 two *t* pounds of silver, and
Est 3:9 I will pay ten *t* talents of
Est 9:16 of their foes seventy and five *t*
Job 1:3 substance also was seven *t* sheep
Job 1:3 three *t* camels, and five hundred
Job 9:3 he cannot answer him one of a *t*
Job 33:23 an interpreter, one among a *t*
Job 42:12 for he had fourteen *t* sheep
Job 42:12 six *t* camels, and a *t* yoke
Job 42:12 yoke of oxen, and a *t* she asses
Ps 50:10 and the cattle upon a *t* hills
Ps 60:*t* in the valley of salt twelve *t*
Ps 68:17 The chariots of God are twenty *t*
Ps 84:10 in thy courts is better than a *t*
Ps 90:4 For a *t* years in thy sight are
Ps 91:7 A *t* shall fall at thy side, and
Ps 91:7 side, and ten *t* at thy right hand
Ps 105:8 he commanded to a *t* generations
Eccl 6:6 he live a *t* years twice told
Eccl 7:28 one man among a *t* have I found
Song 4:4 whereon there hang a *t* bucklers
Song 5:10 ruddy, the chiefest among ten *t*
Song 8:11 was to bring a *t* pieces of silver
Song 8:12 thou, O Solomon, must have a *t*
Is 7:23 *t* vines at a *t* silverlings
Is 30:17 One *t* shall flee at the rebuke of
Is 36:8 and I will give thee two *t* horses
Is 37:36 an hundred and fourscore and five *t*
Is 60:22 A little one shall become a *t*
Jer 52:28 in the seventh year three *t* Jews
Jer 52:30 all the persons were four *t*
Eze 45:1 length of five and twenty *t* reeds
Eze 45:1 and the breadth shall be ten *t*
Eze 45:3 the length of five and twenty *t*
Eze 45:3 and the breadth of ten *t*
Eze 45:5 twenty *t* of length, and the ten
Eze 45:5 the ten *t* of breadth, shall also
Eze 45:6 of the city five *t* broad, and five
Eze 45:6 broad, and five and twenty *t* long
Eze 47:3 eastward, he measured a *t* cubits
Eze 47:4 Again he measured a *t*, and brought
Eze 47:4 Again he measured a *t*, and brought
Eze 47:5 Afterward he measured a *t*
Eze 48:8 twenty *t* reeds in breadth, and in
Eze 48:9 twenty *t* in length, and of ten
Eze 48:9 in length, and of ten *t* in breadth
Eze 48:10 twenty *t* in length, and toward the
Eze 48:10 toward the west ten *t* in breadth
Eze 48:10 toward the east ten *t* in breadth
Eze 48:10 south five and twenty *t* in length
Eze 48:13 twenty *t* in length, and ten
Eze 48:13 in length, and ten *t* in breadth
Eze 48:13 length shall be five and twenty *t*
Eze 48:13 and the breadth ten *t*
Eze 48:15 And the five *t*, that are left in
Eze 48:15 over against the five and twenty *t*
Eze 48:16 the north side four *t* and five
Eze 48:16 hundred, and the south side four *t*
Eze 48:16 and on the east side four *t*
Eze 48:16 hundred, and the west side four *t*
Eze 48:18 portion shall be ten *t* eastward
Eze 48:18 eastward, and ten *t* westward
Eze 48:20 twenty *t* by five and twenty
Eze 48:20 by five and twenty *t*
Eze 48:21 twenty *t* of the oblation toward
Eze 48:21 twenty *t* toward the west border,
Eze 48:30 city on the north side, four *t*
Eze 48:32 And at the east side four *t*
Eze 48:33 And at the south side four *t*
Eze 48:34 At the west side four *t* and five
Eze 48:35 round about eighteen *t* measures
Dan 5:1 a great feast to a *t* of his lords
Dan 5:1 lords, and drank wine before the *t*
Dan 7:10 *t* thousands ministered unto him,
Dan 7:10 ten *t* times ten *t* stood
Dan 8:14 And he said unto me, Unto two *t*
Dan 12:11 there shall be a *t* two hundred
Dan 12:12 and cometh to the *t* three hundred
Amos 5:3 out by a *t* shall leave an hundred
Jonah 4:11 *t* persons that cannot discern
Mt 14:21 had eaten were about five *t* men
Mt 15:38 they that did eat were four *t* men
Mt 16:9 the five loaves of the five *t*
Mt 16:10 the seven loaves of the four *t*
Mt 18:24 him, which owed him ten *t* talents
Mk 5:13 the sea, (they were about two *t*
Mk 6:44 the loaves were about five *t* men
Mk 8:9 that had eaten were about four *t*
Mk 8:19 the five loaves among five *t*
Mk 8:20 And when the seven among four *t*
Lk 9:14 For they were about five *t* men
Lk 14:31 whether he be able with ten *t* to
Lk 14:31 cometh against him with twenty *t*
Jn 6:10 sat down, in number about five *t*
Acts 2:41 unto them about three *t* souls
Acts 4:4 of the men was about five *t*
Acts 19:19 found it fifty *t* pieces of silver
Acts 21:38 four *t* men that were murderers
Rom 11:4 reserved to myself seven *t* men
1Cor 4:15 have ten *t* instructers in Christ
1Cor 10:8 fell in one day three and twenty *t*
1Cor 14:19 than ten *t* words in an unknown
2Pet 3:8 day is with the Lord as a *t* years
2Pet 3:8 years, and a *t* years as one day
Rev 5:11 them was ten *t* times ten *t*
Rev 7:4 four *t* of all the tribes of the
Rev 7:5 of Juda were sealed twelve *t*
Rev 7:5 of Reuben were sealed twelve *t*
Rev 7:5 tribe of Gad were sealed twelve *t*
Rev 7:6 of Aser were sealed twelve *t*
Rev 7:6 of Nepthalim were sealed twelve *t*
Rev 7:6 of Manasses were sealed twelve *t*
Rev 7:7 of Simeon were sealed twelve *t*
Rev 7:7 of Levi were sealed twelve *t*
Rev 7:7 of Issachar were sealed twelve *t*
Rev 7:8 of Zabulon were sealed twelve *t*
Rev 7:8 of Joseph were sealed twelve *t*
Rev 7:8 of Benjamin were sealed twelve *t*
Rev 9:16 were two hundred *t t*
Rev 11:3 shall prophesy a *t* two hundred
Rev 11:13 were slain of men seven *t*
Rev 12:6 feed her there a *t* two hundred
Rev 14:1 him an hundred forty and four *t*
Rev 14:3 the hundred and forty and four *t*
Rev 14:20 bridles, by the space of a *t*
Rev 20:2 and Satan, and bound him a *t* years
Rev 20:3 till the *t* years should be
Rev 20:4 and reigned with Christ a *t* years
Rev 20:5 until the *t* years were finished
Rev 20:6 and shall reign with him a *t* years
Rev 20:7 when the *t* years are expired,
Rev 21:16 with the reed, twelve *t* furlongs

## THOUSANDS

Gen 24:60 thou the mother of *t* of millions
Ex 18:21 such over them, to be rulers of *t*
Ex 18:25 over the people, rulers of *t*
Ex 20:6 shewing mercy unto *t* of them that
Ex 34:7 Keeping mercy for *t*, forgiving
Num 1:16 fathers, heads of *t* in Israel
Num 10:4 are heads of the *t* of Israel
Num 10:36 O LORD, unto the many *t* of Israel
Num 31:5 delivered out of the *t* of Israel
Num 31:14 host, with the captains over *t*
Num 31:48 which were over *t* of the host
Num 31:48 of the host, the captains of *t*
Num 31:52 to the LORD, of the captains of *t*
Num 31:54 the gold of the captains of *t*
Deut 1:15 heads over you, captains over *t*
Deut 5:10 shewing mercy unto *t* of them that
Deut 33:2 and he came with ten *t* of saints
Deut 33:17 and they are the ten *t* of Ephraim
Deut 33:17 and they are the *t* of Manasseh
Josh 22:14 fathers among the *t* of Israel
Josh 22:21 unto the heads of the *t* of Israel
Josh 22:30 heads of the *t* of Israel which
1Sa 8:12 will appoint him captains over *t*
1Sa 10:19 LORD by your tribes, and by your *t*
1Sa 18:7 his *t*, and David his ten *t*
1Sa 18:8 have ascribed unto David ten *t*
1Sa 18:8 and to me they have ascribed but *t*
1Sa 21:11 saying, Saul hath slain his *t*
1Sa 21:11 and David his ten *t*
1Sa 22:7 and make you all captains of *t*
1Sa 23:23 out throughout all the *t* of Judah
1Sa 29:2 passed on by hundreds, and by *t*
1Sa 29:5 dances, saying, Saul slew his *t*
1Sa 29:5 and David his ten *t*
2Sa 18:1 with him, and set captains of *t*
2Sa 18:4 came out by hundreds and by *t*
1Chr 12:20 captains of the *t* that were of
1Chr 13:1 consulted with the captains of *t*
1Chr 15:25 of Israel, and the captains over *t*
1Chr 26:26 fathers, the captains over *t*
1Chr 27:1 chief fathers and captains of *t*
1Chr 28:1 and the captains over the *t*
1Chr 29:6 of Israel, and the captains of *t*
2Chr 1:2 all Israel, to the captains of *t*
2Chr 17:14 Of Judah, the captains of *t*
2Chr 25:5 and made them captains over *t*
Ps 3:6 not be afraid of ten *t* of people
Ps 68:17 twenty thousand, even *t* of angels
Ps 119:72 is better unto me than *t* of gold
Ps 144:13 that our sheep may bring forth *t*
Ps 144:13 and ten *t* in our streets
Jer 32:18 shewest lovingkindness unto *t*
Dan 7:10 thousand *t* ministered unto him,
Dan 11:12 and he shall cast down many ten *t*
Mic 5:2 be little among the *t* of Judah
Mic 6:7 LORD be pleased with *t* of rams
Mic 6:7 or with ten *t* of rivers of oil
Acts 21:20 how many *t* of Jews there are
Jude 14 cometh with ten *t* of his saints
Rev 5:11 ten thousand, and *t* of *t*

## THREAD

Gen 14:23 from a *t* even to a shoelatchet
Gen 38:28 bound upon his hand a scarlet *t*
Gen 38:30 had the scarlet *t* upon his hand
Josh 2:18 *t* in the window which thou didst
Judg 16:9 as a *t* of tow is broken when it
Judg 16:12 them from off his arms like a *t*
Song 4:3 Thy lips are like a *t* of scarlet

## THREATEN

Acts 4:17 people, let us straitly *t* them

## THREATENED

Acts 4:21 So when they had further *t* them
1Pet 2:23 when he suffered, he *t* not

## THREATENING

Eph 6:9 things unto them, forbearing *t*

## THREATENINGS

Acts 4:29 And now, Lord, behold their *t*
Acts 9:1 And Saul, yet breathing out *t*

## THREE

Gen 5:22 begat Methuselah *t* hundred years
Gen 5:23 of Enoch were *t* hundred sixty
Gen 6:10 And Noah begat *t* sons, Shem, Ham,
Gen 6:15 the ark shall be *t* hundred cubits
Gen 7:13 the *t* wives of his sons with them
Gen 9:19 These are the *t* sons of Noah
Gen 9:28 lived after the flood *t* hundred
Gen 11:13 *t* years, and begat sons and
Gen 11:15 *t* years, and begat sons and
Gen 14:14 *t* hundred and eighteen, and pursued
Gen 15:9 Take me an heifer of *t* years old
Gen 15:9 old, and a she goat of *t* years old
Gen 15:9 a ram of *t* years old, and a
Gen 18:2 and, lo, *t* men stood by him
Gen 18:6 Make ready quickly *t* measures of
Gen 29:2 there were *t* flocks of sheep
Gen 29:34 because I have born him *t* sons
Gen 30:36 he set *t* days' journey betwixt
Gen 38:24 came to pass about *t* months after
Gen 40:10 And in the vine were *t* branches
Gen 40:12 The *t* branches are *t* days
Gen 40:13 Yet within *t* days shall Pharaoh
Gen 40:16 I had *t* white baskets on my head
Gen 40:18 The *t* baskets are *t* days
Gen 40:19 Yet within *t* days shall Pharaoh
Gen 42:17 all together into ward *t* days
Gen 45:22 but to Benjamin he gave *t* hundred
Gen 46:15 and his daughters were thirty and *t*
Ex 2:2 child, she hid him *t* months
Ex 3:18 thee, *t* days' journey into the
Ex 5:3 *t* days' journey into the desert,
Ex 6:18 were an hundred thirty and *t* years
Ex 7:7 *t* years old, when they spake unto
Ex 8:27 We will go *t* days' journey into
Ex 10:22 in all the land of Egypt *t* days
Ex 10:23 any from his place for *t* days

Ex 15:22 and they went *t* days in the
Ex 21:11 And if he do not these *t* unto her
Ex 23:14 *T* times thou shalt keep a feast
Ex 23:17 *T* times in the year all thy males
Ex 25:32 *t* branches of the candlestick out
Ex 25:32 *t* branches of the candlestick out
Ex 25:33 *T* bowls made like unto almonds,
Ex 25:33 *t* bowls made like almonds in the
Ex 27:1 height thereof shall be *t* cubits
Ex 27:14 pillars *t*, and their sockets *t*
Ex 27:15 pillars *t*, and their sockets *t*
Ex 32:28 that day about *t* thousand men
Ex 37:18 *t* branches of the candlestick out
Ex 37:18 *t* branches of the candlestick out
Ex 37:19 *T* bowls made after the fashion of
Ex 37:19 *t* bowls made like almonds in
Ex 38:1 *t* cubits the height thereof
Ex 38:14 pillars *t*, and their sockets *t*
Ex 38:15 pillars *t*, and their sockets *t*
Ex 38:26 *t* thousand and five hundred and
Lev 12:4 in the blood of her purifying *t*
Lev 14:10 *t* tenth deals of fine flour for a
Lev 19:23 *t* years shall it be as
Lev 25:21 bring forth fruit for *t* years
Lev 27:6 shall be *t* shekels of silver
Num 1:23 and nine thousand and *t* hundred
Num 1:43 *t* thousand and four hundred
Num 1:46 *t* thousand and five hundred and
Num 2:13 and nine thousand and *t* hundred
Num 2:30 *t* thousand and four hundred
Num 2:32 *t* thousand and five hundred and
Num 3:50 a thousand *t* hundred and
Num 4:44 were *t* thousand and two hundred
Num 10:33 mount of the LORD *t* days' journey
Num 10:33 them in the *t* days' journey
Num 12:4 Come out ye *t* unto the tabernacle
Num 12:4 And they *t* came out
Num 15:9 of *t* tenth deals of flour mingled
Num 22:28 hast smitten me these *t* times
Num 22:32 smitten thine ass these *t* times
Num 22:33 and turned from me these *t* times
Num 24:10 blessed them these *t* times
Num 26:7 *t* thousand and seven hundred and
Num 26:25 and four thousand and *t* hundred
Num 26:47 *t* thousand and four hundred
Num 26:62 *t* thousand, all males from a
Num 28:12 *t* tenth deals of flour for a meat
Num 28:20 *t* tenth deals shall ye offer for
Num 28:28 *t* tenth deals unto one bullock,
Num 29:3 *t* tenth deals for a bullock, and
Num 29:9 *t* tenth deals to a bullock, and
Num 29:14 *t* tenth deals unto every bullock
Num 31:36 was in number *t* hundred thousand
Num 31:43 was *t* hundred thousand and thirty
Num 33:8 went *t* days' journey in the
Num 33:39 *t* years old when he died in mount
Num 35:14 Ye shall give *t* cities on this
Num 35:14 *t* cities shall ye give in the
Deut 4:41 Then Moses severed *t* cities on
Deut 14:28 At the end of *t* years thou shalt
Deut 16:16 *T* times in a year shall all thy
Deut 17:6 or *t* witnesses, shall he that is
Deut 19:2 Thou shalt separate *t* cities for
Deut 19:3 into *t* parts, that every slayer
Deut 19:7 shalt separate *t* cities for thee
Deut 19:9 then shalt thou add *t* cities more
Deut 19:9 more for thee, beside these *t*
Deut 19:15 or at the mouth of *t* witnesses
Josh 1:11 for within *t* days ye shall pass
Josh 2:16 and hide yourselves there *t* days
Josh 2:22 mountain, and abode there *t* days
Josh 3:2 And it came to pass after *t* days
Josh 7:3 about two or *t* thousand men go up
Josh 7:4 the people about *t* thousand men
Josh 9:16 of *t* days after they had made a
Josh 15:14 drove thence the *t* sons of Anak
Josh 17:11 and her towns, even *t* countries
Josh 18:4 among you *t* men for each tribe
Josh 21:32 with her suburbs; *t* cities
Judg 1:20 thence the *t* sons of Anak
Judg 7:6 their mouth, were *t* hundred men
Judg 7:7 By the *t* hundred men that lapped
Judg 7:8 and retained those *t* hundred men
Judg 7:16 he divided the *t* hundred men into
Judg 7:16 hundred men into *t* companies
Judg 7:20 the *t* companies blew the trumpets
Judg 7:22 the *t* hundred blew the trumpets,
Judg 8:4 the *t* hundred men that were with
Judg 9:22 had reigned *t* years over Israel
Judg 9:43 and divided them into *t* companies
Judg 10:2 *t* years, and died, and was buried
Judg 11:26 coasts of Arnon, *t* hundred years
Judg 14:14 they could not in *t* days expound
Judg 15:4 caught *t* hundred foxes, and took
Judg 15:11 Then *t* thousand men of Judah went
Judg 16:15 thou hast mocked me these *t* times
Judg 16:27 the roof about *t* thousand men
Judg 19:4 and he abode with him *t* days
1Sa 1:24 with *t* bullocks, and one ephah of
1Sa 2:13 fleshhook of *t* teeth in his hand
1Sa 2:21 she conceived, and bare *t* sons
1Sa 9:20 asses that were lost *t* days ago
1Sa 10:3 there shall meet thee *t* men going
1Sa 10:3 to Beth-el, one carrying *t* kids
1Sa 10:3 carrying *t* loaves of bread
1Sa 11:8 of Israel were *t* hundred thousand
1Sa 11:11 put the people in *t* companies
1Sa 13:2 Saul chose him *t* thousand men of
1Sa 13:17 of the Philistines in *t* companies
1Sa 17:13 the *t* eldest sons of Jesse went
1Sa 17:13 the names of his *t* sons that went
1Sa 17:14 the *t* eldest followed Saul
1Sa 20:19 And when thou hast stayed *t* days
1Sa 20:20 I will shoot *t* arrows on the side
1Sa 20:41 ground, and bowed himself *t* times
1Sa 21:5 kept from us about these *t* days
1Sa 24:2 Then Saul took *t* thousand chosen
1Sa 25:2 he had *t* thousand sheep, and a
1Sa 26:2 having *t* thousand chosen men of
1Sa 30:12 any water, *t* days and *t* nights
1Sa 30:13 because *t* days agone I fell sick
1Sa 31:6 his *t* sons, and his armourbearer,
1Sa 31:8 his *t* sons fallen in mount Gilboa
2Sa 2:18 there were *t* sons of Zeruiah
2Sa 2:31 of Abner's men, so that *t* hundred
2Sa 5:5 *t* years over all Israel and Judah
2Sa 6:11 of Obed-edom the Gittite *t* months
2Sa 13:38 to Geshur, and was there *t* years
2Sa 14:27 Absalom there were born *t* sons
2Sa 18:14 he took *t* darts in his hand, and
2Sa 20:4 me the men of Judah within *t* days
2Sa 21:1 in the days of David *t* years
2Sa 21:16 *t* hundred shekels of brass in
2Sa 23:9 one of the *t* mighty men with
2Sa 23:13 *t* of the thirty chief went down,
2Sa 23:16 the *t* mighty men brake through
2Sa 23:17 things did these *t* mighty men
2Sa 23:18 son of Zeruiah, was chief among *t*
2Sa 23:18 up his spear against *t* hundred
2Sa 23:18 them, and had the name among *t*
2Sa 23:19 Was he not most honourable of *t*
2Sa 23:19 he attained not unto the first *t*
2Sa 23:22 had the name among *t* mighty men
2Sa 23:23 he attained not to the first *t*
2Sa 24:12 the LORD, I offer thee *t* things
2Sa 24:13 or wilt thou flee *t* months before
2Sa 24:13 or that there be *t* days'
1Kin 2:11 *t* years reigned he in Jerusalem
1Kin 2:39 to pass at the end of *t* years
1Kin 4:32 he spake *t* thousand proverbs
1Kin 5:16 *t* thousand and *t* hundred,
1Kin 6:36 court with *t* rows of hewed stone
1Kin 7:4 And there were windows in *t* rows
1Kin 7:4 was against light in *t* ranks
1Kin 7:5 was against light in *t* ranks
1Kin 7:12 was with *t* rows of hewed stones
1Kin 7:25 *t* looking toward the north, and
1Kin 7:25 *t* looking toward the west, and
1Kin 7:25 *t* looking toward the south, and
1Kin 7:25 *t* looking toward the east
1Kin 7:27 *t* cubits the height of it
1Kin 9:25 *t* times in a year did Solomon
1Kin 10:17 he made *t* hundred shields of
1Kin 10:17 *t* pound of gold went to one
1Kin 10:22 once in *t* years came the navy of
1Kin 11:3 and *t* hundred concubines
1Kin 12:5 unto them, Depart yet for *t* days
1Kin 15:2 *T* years reigned he in Jerusalem
1Kin 17:21 himself upon the child *t* times
1Kin 22:1 they continued *t* years without
2Kin 2:17 and they sought *t* days, but found
2Kin 3:10 called these *t* kings together
2Kin 3:13 called these *t* kings together
2Kin 9:32 out to him two or *t* eunuchs
2Kin 12:6 But it was so, that in the *t*
2Kin 13:1 In the *t* and twentieth year of
2Kin 13:25 *T* times did Joash beat him, and
2Kin 17:5 Samaria, and besieged it *t* years
2Kin 18:10 at the end of *t* years they took
2Kin 18:14 Judah *t* hundred talents of silver
2Kin 23:31 *t* years old when he began to
2Kin 23:31 he reigned *t* months in Jerusalem
2Kin 24:1 became his servant *t* years
2Kin 24:8 he reigned in Jerusalem *t* months
2Kin 25:17 height of the chapiter *t* cubits
2Kin 25:18 the *t* keepers of the door
1Chr 2:3 which *t* were born unto him of the
1Chr 2:16 Abishai, and Joab, and Asahel, *t*
1Chr 2:22 And Segub begat Jair, who had *t*
1Chr 3:4 he reigned thirty and *t* years
1Chr 3:23 and Hezekiah, and Azrikam, *t*
1Chr 7:6 Bela, and Becher, and Jediael, *t*
1Chr 10:6 his *t* sons, and all his house died
1Chr 11:11 *t* hundred slain by him at one
1Chr 11:12 who was one of the *t* mighties
1Chr 11:15 Now *t* of the thirty captains went
1Chr 11:18 the *t* brake through the host of
1Chr 11:19 things did these *t* mightiest
1Chr 11:20 of Joab, he was chief of the *t*
1Chr 11:20 up his spear against *t* hundred
1Chr 11:20 them, and had a name among the *t*
1Chr 11:21 Of the *t*, he was more honourable
1Chr 11:21 he attained not to the first *t*
1Chr 11:24 had the name among the *t* mighties
1Chr 11:25 but attained not to the first *t*
1Chr 12:27 and with him were *t* thousand
1Chr 12:29 the kindred of Saul, *t* thousand
1Chr 12:39 there they were with David *t* days
1Chr 13:14 Obed-edom in his house *t* months
1Chr 21:10 the LORD, I offer thee *t* things
1Chr 21:12 Either *t* years' famine
1Chr 21:12 or *t* months to be destroyed
1Chr 21:12 or else *t* days the sword of the
1Chr 23:8 was Jehiel, and Zetham, and Joel, *t*
1Chr 23:9 Shelomith, and Haziel, and Haran, *t*
1Chr 23:23 Mahli, and Eder, and Jeremoth, *t*
1Chr 24:18 The *t* and twentieth to Delaiah,
1Chr 25:5 fourteen sons and *t* daughters
1Chr 25:30 The *t* and twentieth to Mahazioth,
1Chr 29:4 Even *t* thousand talents of gold,
1Chr 29:27 *t* years reigned he in Jerusalem
2Chr 2:2 *t* thousand and six hundred to
2Chr 2:17 *t* thousand and six hundred
2Chr 2:18 *t* thousand and six hundred
2Chr 4:4 *t* looking toward the north, and
2Chr 4:4 *t* looking toward the west, and
2Chr 4:4 *t* looking toward the south, and
2Chr 4:4 *t* looking toward the east
2Chr 4:5 received and held *t* thousand baths
2Chr 6:13 *t* cubits high, and had set it in
2Chr 7:10 And on the *t* and twentieth day of
2Chr 8:13 *t* times in the year, even in the
2Chr 9:16 *t* hundred shields made he of
2Chr 9:16 *t* hundred shekels of gold went to
2Chr 9:21 every *t* years once came the ships
2Chr 10:5 Come again unto me after *t* days
2Chr 11:17 son of Solomon strong, *t* years
2Chr 11:17 for *t* years they walked in the
2Chr 13:2 He reigned *t* years in Jerusalem
2Chr 14:8 out of Judah *t* hundred thousand
2Chr 14:9 thousand, and *t* hundred chariots
2Chr 17:14 men of valour *t* hundred thousand
2Chr 20:25 they were *t* days in gathering of
2Chr 25:5 found them *t* hundred thousand
2Chr 25:13 smote *t* thousand of them, and took
2Chr 26:13 *t* hundred thousand and seven
2Chr 29:33 hundred oxen and *t* thousand sheep
2Chr 31:16 from *t* years old and upward, even
2Chr 35:7 thousand, and *t* thousand bullocks
2Chr 35:8 small cattle, and *t* hundred oxen
2Chr 36:2 *t* years old when he began to
2Chr 36:2 he reigned *t* months in Jerusalem
2Chr 36:9 to reign, and he reigned *t* months
Ezr 2:4 *t* hundred seventy and two
Ezr 2:11 of Bebai, six hundred twenty and *t*
Ezr 2:17 Bezai, *t* hundred twenty and *t*
Ezr 2:19 Hashum, two hundred twenty and *t*
Ezr 2:21 an hundred twenty and *t*
Ezr 2:25 seven hundred and forty and *t*
Ezr 2:28 and Ai, two hundred twenty and *t*
Ezr 2:32 of Harim, *t* hundred and twenty
Ezr 2:34 Jericho, *t* hundred forty and five
Ezr 2:35 *t* thousand and six hundred and
Ezr 2:36 Jeshua, nine hundred seventy and *t*
Ezr 2:58 were *t* hundred ninety and two
Ezr 2:64 forty and two thousand *t* hundred
Ezr 2:65 seven thousand *t* hundred thirty
Ezr 6:4 With *t* rows of great stones, and a
Ezr 8:5 and with him *t* hundred males
Ezr 8:15 and there abode we in tents *t* days

Ezr 8:32 Jerusalem, and abode there *t* days
Ezr 10:8 would not come within *t* days
Ezr 10:9 unto Jerusalem within *t* days
Neh 2:11 to Jerusalem, and was there *t* days
Neh 7:9 *t* hundred seventy and two
Neh 7:17 two thousand *t* hundred twenty and
Neh 7:22 *t* hundred twenty and eight
Neh 7:23 Bezai, *t* hundred twenty and four
Neh 7:29 Beeroth, seven hundred forty and *t*
Neh 7:32 and Ai, an hundred twenty and *t*
Neh 7:35 of Harim, *t* hundred and twenty
Neh 7:36 Jericho, *t* hundred forty and five
Neh 7:38 *t* thousand nine hundred and thirty
Neh 7:39 Jeshua, nine hundred seventy and *t*
Neh 7:60 were *t* hundred ninety and two
Neh 7:66 forty and two thousand *t* hundred
Neh 7:67 seven thousand *t* hundred thirty
Est 4:16 and neither eat nor drink *t* days
Est 8:9 is, the month Sivan, on the *t*
Est 9:15 slew *t* hundred men at Shushan
Job 1:2 him seven sons and *t* daughters
Job 1:3 *t* thousand camels, and five
Job 1:4 called for their *t* sisters to eat
Job 1:17 The Chaldeans made out *t* bands
Job 2:11 Now when Job's *t* friends heard of
Job 32:1 So these *t* men ceased to answer
Job 32:3 Also against his *t* friends was
Job 32:5 in the mouth of these *t* men
Job 42:13 also seven sons and *t* daughters
Prov 30:15 There are *t* things that are never
Prov 30:18 There be *t* things which are too
Prov 30:21 For *t* things the earth is
Prov 30:29 There be *t* things which go well,
Is 15:5 Zoar, an heifer of *t* years old
Is 16:14 spoken, saying, Within *t* years
Is 17:6 two or *t* berries in the top of
Is 20:3 barefoot *t* years for a sign and
Jer 25:3 even unto this day, that is the *t*
Jer 36:23 Jehudi had read *t* or four leaves
Jer 48:34 as an heifer of *t* years old
Jer 52:24 the *t* keepers of the door
Jer 52:28 year *t* thousand Jews and *t*
Jer 52:30 In the *t* and twentieth year of
Eze 4:5 days, *t* hundred and ninety days
Eze 4:9 *t* hundred and ninety days shalt
Eze 14:14 Though these *t* men, Noah, Daniel,
Eze 14:16 Though these *t* men were in it, as
Eze 14:18 Though these *t* men were in it, as
Eze 40:10 gate eastward were *t* on this side
Eze 40:10 on this side, and *t* on that side
Eze 40:10 they *t* were of one measure
Eze 40:21 thereof were *t* on this side
Eze 40:21 on this side and *t* on that side
Eze 40:48 gate was *t* cubits on this side
Eze 40:48 side, and *t* cubits on that side
Eze 41:6 And the side chambers were *t*
Eze 41:16 round about on their *t* stories
Eze 41:22 altar of wood was *t* cubits high
Eze 42:3 against gallery in *t* stories
Eze 42:6 For they were in *t* stories
Eze 48:31 *t* gates northward
Eze 48:32 five hundred: and *t* gates
Eze 48:33 hundred measures: and *t* gates
Eze 48:34 five hundred, with their *t* gates
Dan 1:5 so nourishing them *t* years
Dan 3:23 And these *t* men, Shadrach, Meshach
Dan 3:24 Did not we cast *t* men bound into
Dan 6:2 And over these *t* presidents
Dan 6:10 upon his knees *t* times a day
Dan 6:13 maketh his petition *t* times a day
Dan 7:5 it had *t* ribs in the mouth of it
Dan 7:8 before whom there were *t* of the
Dan 7:20 came up, and before whom *t* fell
Dan 7:24 first, and he shall subdue *t* kings
Dan 8:14 two thousand and *t* hundred days
Dan 10:2 Daniel was mourning *t* full weeks
Dan 10:3 till *t* whole weeks were fulfilled
Dan 11:2 stand up yet *t* kings in Persia
Dan 12:12 cometh to the thousand *t* hundred
Amos 1:3 For *t* transgressions of Damascus,
Amos 1:6 For *t* transgressions of Gaza, and
Amos 1:9 For *t* transgressions of Tyrus, and
Amos 1:11 For *t* transgressions of Edom, and
Amos 1:13 For *t* transgressions of the
Amos 2:1 For *t* transgressions of Moab, and
Amos 2:4 For *t* transgressions of Judah, and
Amos 2:6 For *t* transgressions of Israel,
Amos 4:4 and your tithes after *t* years
Amos 4:7 when there were yet *t* months to
Amos 4:8 So two or *t* cities wandered unto
Jonah 1:17 the fish *t* days and *t* nights
Jonah 3:3 great city of *t* days' journey
Zec 11:8 *T* shepherds also I cut off in one
Mt 12:40 For as Jonas was *t* days
Mt 12:40 *t* nights in the whale's belly
Mt 12:40 so shall the Son of man be *t* days
Mt 12:40 *t* nights in the heart of the
Mt 13:33 hid in *t* measures of meal, till
Mt 15:32 they continue with me now *t* days
Mt 17:4 let us make here *t* tabernacles
Mt 18:16 or *t* witnesses every word may be
Mt 18:20 For where two or *t* are gathered
Mt 26:61 of God, and to build it in *t* days
Mt 27:40 temple, and buildest it in *t* days
Mt 27:63 After *t* days I will rise again
Mk 8:2 they have now been with me *t* days
Mk 8:31 and after *t* days rise again
Mk 9:5 and let us make *t* tabernacles
Mk 14:5 for more than *t* hundred pence
Mk 14:58 within *t* days I will build
Mk 15:29 temple, and buildest it in *t* days
Lk 1:56 abode with her about *t* months
Lk 2:46 that after *t* days they found him
Lk 4:25 the heaven was shut up *t* years
Lk 9:33 and let us make *t* tabernacles
Lk 10:36 Which now of these *t*, thinkest
Lk 11:5 him, Friend, lend me *t* loaves
Lk 12:52 *t* against two, and two against
Lk 12:52 against two, and two against *t*
Lk 13:7 these *t* years I come seeking
Lk 13:21 hid in *t* measures of meal, till
Jn 2:6 two or *t* firkins apiece
Jn 2:19 in *t* days I will raise it up
Jn 2:20 and wilt thou rear it up in *t* days
Jn 12:5 ointment sold for *t* hundred pence
Jn 21:11 fishes, an hundred and fifty and *t*
Acts 2:41 unto them about *t* thousand souls
Acts 5:7 about the space of *t* hours after
Acts 7:20 up in his father's house *t* months
Acts 9:9 he was *t* days without sight, and
Acts 10:19 unto him, Behold, *t* men seek thee
Acts 11:10 And this was done *t* times
Acts 11:11 immediately there were *t* men
Acts 17:2 *t* sabbath days reasoned with them
Acts 19:8 boldly for the space of *t* months
Acts 20:3 And there abode *t* months
Acts 20:31 that by the space of *t* years I
Acts 25:1 after *t* days he ascended from
Acts 28:7 lodged us *t* days courteously
Acts 28:11 after *t* months we departed in a
Acts 28:12 Syracuse, we tarried there *t* days
Acts 28:15 as Appii forum, and The *t* taverns
Acts 28:17 that after *t* days Paul called the
1Cor 10:8 committed, and fell in one day *t*
1Cor 13:13 faith, hope, charity, these *t*
1Cor 14:27 it be by two, or at the most by *t*
1Cor 14:29 Let the prophets speak two or *t*
2Cor 13:1 In the mouth of two or *t*
Gal 1:18 Then after *t* years I went up to
1Ti 5:19 but before two or *t* witnesses
Heb 10:28 mercy under two or *t* witnesses
Heb 11:23 was hid *t* months of his parents,
Jas 5:17 the earth by the space of *t* years
1Jn 5:7 For there are *t* that bear record
1Jn 5:7 and these *t* are one
1Jn 5:8 there are *t* that bear witness in
1Jn 5:8 and these *t* agree in one
Rev 6:6 *t* measures of barley for a penny
Rev 8:13 of the trumpet of the *t* angels
Rev 9:18 By these *t* was the third part of
Rev 11:9 see their dead bodies *t* days
Rev 11:11 And after *t* days and an half the
Rev 16:13 I saw *t* unclean spirits like
Rev 16:19 city was divided into *t* parts
Rev 21:13 On the east *t* gates
Rev 21:13 on the north *t* gates
Rev 21:13 on the south *t* gates
Rev 21:13 and on the west *t* gates

## THREEFOLD

Eccl 4:12 a *t* cord is not quickly broken

## THREESCORE

Gen 25:7 life which he lived, an hundred *t*
Gen 25:26 Isaac was *t* years old when she
Gen 46:26 sons' wives, all the souls were *t*
Gen 46:27 which came into Egypt, were *t*
Gen 50:3 the Egyptians mourned for him *t*
Ex 15:27 were twelve wells of water, and *t*
Ex 38:25 and a thousand seven hundred and *t*
Lev 12:5 in the blood of her purifying *t*
Num 1:27 of the tribe of Judah, were *t*
Num 1:39 even of the tribe of Dan, were *t*
Num 2:4 were numbered of them, were *t*
Num 2:26 were numbered of them, were *t*
Num 3:43 and two thousand two hundred and *t*
Num 3:46 redeemed of the two hundred and *t*
Num 3:50 a thousand three hundred and *t*
Num 26:22 that were numbered of them, *t*
Num 26:25 that were numbered of them, *t*
Num 26:27 *t* thousand and five hundred
Num 26:43 were numbered of them, were *t*
Num 31:33 And *t* and twelve thousand beeves,
Num 31:34 And *t* and one thousand asses,
Num 31:37 of the sheep was six hundred and *t*
Num 31:38 of which the LORD's tribute was *t*
Num 31:39 of which the LORD's tribute was *t*
Num 33:9 twelve fountains of water, and *t*
Deut 3:4 *t* cities, all the region of Argob
Deut 10:22 went down into Egypt with *t*
Josh 13:30 which are in Bashan, *t* cities
Judg 1:7 And Adoni-bezek said, *T* and ten
Judg 8:14 and the elders thereof, even *t*
Judg 8:30 And Gideon had *t* and ten sons of
Judg 9:2 sons of Jerubbaal, which are *t*
Judg 9:4 And they gave him *t* and ten pieces
Judg 9:5 the sons of Jerubbaal, being *t*
Judg 9:18 day, and have slain his sons, *t*
Judg 9:24 That the cruelty done to the *t*
Judg 12:14 and thirty nephews, that rode on *t*
1Sa 6:19 of the people fifty thousand and *t*
2Sa 2:31 that three hundred and *t* men died
1Kin 4:13 *t* great cities with walls and
1Kin 4:22 flour, and *t* measures of meal,
1Kin 5:15 And Solomon had *t* and ten thousand
1Kin 6:2 the length thereof was *t* cubits
1Kin 10:14 in one year was six hundred *t*
2Kin 25:19 *t* men of the people of the land
1Chr 2:21 married when he was *t* years old
1Chr 2:23 the towns thereof, even *t* cities
1Chr 5:18 forty thousand seven hundred and *t*
1Chr 9:13 a thousand and seven hundred and *t*
1Chr 16:38 Obed-edom with their brethren, *t*
1Chr 21:5 and Judah was four hundred *t*
1Chr 26:8 strength for the service, were *t*
2Chr 2:2 And Solomon told out *t* and ten
2Chr 2:18 And he set *t* and ten thousand of
2Chr 3:3 the first measure was *t* cubits
2Chr 9:13 in one year was six hundred and *t*
2Chr 11:21 eighteen wives, and *t* concubines
2Chr 11:21 and eight sons, and *t* daughters
2Chr 12:3 chariots, and *t* thousand horsemen
2Chr 29:32 the congregation brought, was *t*
2Chr 36:21 she kept sabbath, to fulfil *t*
Ezr 2:9 of Zaccai, seven hundred and *t*
Ezr 2:64 two thousand three hundred and *t*
Ezr 2:69 unto the treasure of the work *t*
Ezr 6:3 the height thereof *t* cubits
Ezr 6:3 and the breadth thereof *t* cubits
Ezr 8:10 and with him an hundred and *t* males
Ezr 8:13 and Shemaiah, and with them *t* males
Neh 7:14 of Zaccai, seven hundred and *t*
Neh 7:18 of Adonikam, six hundred *t*
Neh 7:19 of Bigvai, two thousand *t*
Neh 7:66 two thousand three hundred and *t*
Neh 7:72 thousand pounds of silver, and *t*
Neh 11:6 at Jerusalem were four hundred *t*
Ps 90:10 The days of our years are *t* years
Song 3:7 *t* valiant men are about it, of
Song 6:8 There are *t* queens, and fourscore
Is 7:8 and within *t* and five years shall
Jer 52:25 *t* men of the people of the land,
Eze 40:14 He made also posts of *t* cubits
Dan 3:1 gold, whose height was *t* cubits
Dan 5:31 took the kingdom, being about *t*
Dan 9:25 Prince shall be seven weeks, and *t*
Dan 9:26 And after *t* and two weeks shall
Zec 1:12 thou hast had indignation these *t*
Lk 24:13 from Jerusalem about *t* furlongs
Acts 7:14 to him, and all his kindred, *t*
Acts 23:23 to go to Caesarea, and horsemen *t*
Acts 27:37 in all the ship two hundred *t*
1Ti 5:9 into the number under *t* years old
Rev 11:3 *t* days, clothed in sackcloth
Rev 12:6 a thousand two hundred and *t* days
Rev 13:18 and his number is six hundred *t*

## THRESH

Is 41:15 thou shalt *t* the mountains, and
Jer 51:33 it is time to *t* her

Mic 4:13 Arise and *t*, O daughter of Zion
Hab 3:12 thou didst *t* the heathen in anger

### THRESHED
Judg 6:11 his son Gideon *t* wheat by the
Is 28:27 For the fitches are not *t* with a
Amos 1:3 because they have *t* Gilead with

### THRESHETH
1Cor 9:10 that he that *t* in hope should be

### THRESHING
Lev 26:5 your *t* shall reach unto the
2Sa 24:22 and *t* instruments and other
2Kin 13:7 had made them like the dust by *t*
1Chr 21:20 Now Ornan was *t* wheat
1Chr 21:23 the *t* instruments for wood, and
Is 21:10 O my *t*, and the corn of my floor
Is 28:27 not threshed with a *t* instrument
Is 28:28 because he will not ever be *t* it
Is 41:15 sharp *t* instrument having teeth
Amos 1:3 Gilead with *t* instruments of iron

### THRESHINGFLOOR
Gen 50:10 And they came to the *t* of Atad
Num 15:20 ye do the heave offering of the *t*
Num 18:27 though it were the corn of the *t*
Num 18:30 Levites as the increase of the *t*
Ruth 3:2 barley to night in the *t*
2Sa 6:6 And when they came to Nachon's *t*
2Sa 24:18 in the *t* of Araunah the Jebusite
2Sa 24:21 David said, To buy the *t* of thee
2Sa 24:24 So David bought the *t* and the oxen
1Chr 13:9 they came unto the *t* of Chidon
1Chr 21:15 by the *t* of Ornan the Jebusite
1Chr 21:18 in the *t* of Ornan the Jebusite
1Chr 21:21 saw David, and went out of the *t*
1Chr 21:22 Grant me the place of this *t*
1Chr 21:28 in the *t* of Ornan the Jebusite
2Chr 3:1 in the *t* of Ornan the Jebusite
Jer 51:33 daughter of Babylon is like a *t*

### THRESHINGFLOORS
1Sa 23:1 against Keilah, and they rob the *t*
Dan 2:35 like the chaff of the summer *t*

### THRESHINGPLACE
2Sa 24:16 by the *t* of Araunah the Jebusite

### THRESHOLD
Judg 19:27 and her hands were upon the *t*
1Sa 5:4 his hands were cut off upon the *t*
1Sa 5:5 tread on the *t* of Dagon in Ashdod
1Kin 14:17 she came to the *t* of the door
Eze 9:3 he was, to the *t* of the house
Eze 10:4 and stood over the *t* of the house
Eze 10:18 from off the *t* of the house
Eze 40:6 and measured the *t* of the gate
Eze 40:6 the other *t* of the gate, which
Eze 40:7 the *t* of the gate by the porch of
Eze 43:8 of their *t* by my thresholds
Eze 46:2 worship at the *t* of the gate
Eze 47:1 under the *t* of the house eastward
Zeph 1:9 all those that leap on the *t*

### THRESHOLDS
Neh 12:25 the ward at the *t* of the gates
Eze 43:8 of their threshold by my *t*
Zeph 2:14 desolation shall be in the *t*

### THREW
2Sa 16:13 *t* stones at him, and cast dust
2Kin 9:33 So they *t* her down
2Chr 31:1 *t* down the high places and the
Mk 12:42 she *t* in two mites, which make a
Lk 9:42 a coming, the devil *t* him down
Acts 22:23 clothes, and *t* dust into the air,

### THREWEST
Neh 9:11 persecutors thou *t* into the deeps

### THRICE
Ex 34:23 *T* in the year shall all your men
Ex 34:24 the LORD thy God *t* in the year
2Kin 13:18 And he smote *t*, and stayed
2Kin 13:19 now thou shalt smite Syria but *t*
Mt 26:34 cock crow, thou shalt deny me *t*
Mt 26:75 cock crow, thou shalt deny me *t*
Mk 14:30 crow twice, thou shalt deny me *t*
Mk 14:72 crow twice, thou shalt deny me *t*
Lk 22:34 before that thou shalt *t* deny
Lk 22:61 cock crow, thou shalt deny me *t*
Jn 13:38 crow, till thou hast denied me *t*
Acts 10:16 This was done *t*
2Cor 11:25 *T* was I beaten with rods, once
2Cor 11:25 *t* I suffered shipwreck, a night
2Cor 12:8 this thing I besought the Lord *t*

### THROAT
Ps 5:9 their *t* is an open sepulchre
Ps 69:3 my *t* is dried
Ps 115:7 speak they through their *t*
Prov 23:2 And put a knife to thy *t*, if thou
Jer 2:25 unshod, and thy *t* from thirst
Mt 18:28 on him, and took him by the *t*
Rom 3:13 Their *t* is an open sepulchre

### THRONE
Gen 41:40 only in the *t* will I be greater
Ex 11:5 Pharaoh that sitteth upon his *t*
Ex 12:29 his *t* unto the firstborn of the
Deut 17:18 sitteth upon the *t* of his kingdom
1Sa 2:8 make them inherit the *t* of glory
2Sa 3:10 to set up the *t* of David over
2Sa 7:13 I will stablish the *t* of his
2Sa 7:16 thy *t* shall be established for
2Sa 14:9 and the king and his *t* be guiltless
1Kin 1:13 me, and he shall sit upon my *t*
1Kin 1:17 me, and he shall sit upon my *t*
1Kin 1:20 *t* of my lord the king after him
1Kin 1:24 me, and he shall sit upon my *t*
1Kin 1:27 who should sit on the *t* of my
1Kin 1:30 shall sit upon my *t* in my stead
1Kin 1:35 that he may come and sit upon my *t*
1Kin 1:37 make his *t* greater than the
1Kin 1:37 than the *t* of my lord king David
1Kin 1:46 sitteth on the *t* of the kingdom
1Kin 1:47 his *t* greater than thy *t*
1Kin 1:48 given one to sit on my *t* this day
1Kin 2:4 said he) a man on the *t* of Israel
1Kin 2:12 upon the *t* of David his father
1Kin 2:19 unto her, and sat down on his *t*
1Kin 2:24 set me on the *t* of David my
1Kin 2:33 and upon his house, and upon his *t*
1Kin 2:45 and the *t* of David shall be
1Kin 3:6 given him a son to sit on his *t*
1Kin 5:5 I will set upon thy *t* in thy room
1Kin 7:7 for the *t* where he might judge
1Kin 8:20 father, and sit on the *t* of Israel
1Kin 8:25 sight to sit on the *t* of Israel
1Kin 9:5 Then I will establish the *t* of
1Kin 9:5 thee a man upon the *t* of Israel
1Kin 10:9 to set thee on the *t* of Israel
1Kin 10:18 the king made a great *t* of ivory
1Kin 10:19 The *t* had six steps, and the top
1Kin 10:19 the top of the *t* was round behind
1Kin 16:11 reign, as soon as he sat on his *t*
1Kin 22:10 king of Judah sat each on his *t*
1Kin 22:19 I saw the LORD sitting on his *t*
2Kin 10:3 and set him on his father's *t*
2Kin 10:30 shall sit on the *t* of Israel
2Kin 11:19 And he sat on the *t* of the kings
2Kin 13:13 and Jeroboam sat upon his *t*
2Kin 15:12 the *t* of Israel unto the fourth
2Kin 25:28 set his *t* above the *t* of the
1Chr 17:12 and I will stablish his *t* for ever
1Chr 17:14 his *t* shall be established for
1Chr 22:10 I will establish the *t* of his
1Chr 28:5 Solomon my son to sit upon the *t*
1Chr 29:23 Then Solomon sat on the *t* of the
2Chr 6:10 and am set on the *t* of Israel
2Chr 6:16 sight to sit upon the *t* of Israel
2Chr 7:18 I stablish the *t* of thy kingdom
2Chr 9:8 in thee to set thee on his *t*
2Chr 9:17 the king made a great *t* of ivory
2Chr 9:18 And there were six steps to the *t*
2Chr 9:18 which were fastened to the *t*
2Chr 18:9 Judah sat either of them on his *t*
2Chr 18:18 I saw the LORD sitting upon his *t*
2Chr 23:20 king upon the *t* of the kingdom
Neh 3:7 unto the *t* of the governor on
Est 1:2 sat on the *t* of his kingdom
Est 5:1 his royal *t* in the royal house
Job 26:9 He holdeth back the face of his *t*
Job 36:7 but with kings are they on the *t*
Ps 9:4 satest in the *t* judging right
Ps 9:7 hath prepared his *t* for judgment
Ps 11:4 the LORD's *t* is in heaven
Ps 45:6 Thy *t*, O God, is for ever and ever
Ps 47:8 upon the *t* of his holiness
Ps 89:4 build up thy *t* to all generations
Ps 89:14 are the habitation of thy *t*
Ps 89:29 his *t* as the days of heaven
Ps 89:36 his *t* as the sun before me
Ps 89:44 cast his *t* down to the ground
Ps 93:2 Thy *t* is established of old
Ps 94:20 Shall the *t* of iniquity have
Ps 97:2 are the habitation of his *t*
Ps 103:19 prepared his *t* in the heavens
Ps 132:11 of thy body will I set upon thy *t*
Ps 132:12 also sit upon thy *t* for evermore
Prov 16:12 for the *t* is established by
Prov 20:8 A king that sitteth in the *t* of
Prov 20:28 his *t* is upholden by mercy
Prov 25:5 his *t* shall be established in
Prov 29:14 his *t* shall be established for
Is 6:1 also the Lord sitting upon a *t*
Is 9:7 be no end, upon the *t* of David
Is 14:13 I will exalt my *t* above the stars
Is 16:5 mercy shall the *t* be established
Is 22:23 glorious *t* to his father's house
Is 47:1 there is no *t*, O daughter of the
Is 66:1 the LORD, The heaven is my *t*
Jer 1:15 they shall set every one his *t* at
Jer 3:17 call Jerusalem the *t* of the LORD
Jer 13:13 the kings that sit upon David's *t*
Jer 14:21 not disgrace the *t* of thy glory
Jer 17:12 A glorious high *t* from the
Jer 17:25 sitting upon the *t* of David
Jer 22:2 that sittest upon the *t* of David
Jer 22:4 kings sitting upon the *t* of David
Jer 22:30 sitting upon the *t* of David
Jer 29:16 that sitteth upon the *t* of David
Jer 33:17 upon the *t* of the house of Israel
Jer 33:21 have a son to reign upon his *t*
Jer 36:30 none to sit upon the *t* of David
Jer 43:10 will set his *t* upon these stones
Jer 49:38 And I will set my *t* in Elam
Jer 52:32 set his *t* above the *t* of the
Lam 5:19 thy *t* from generation to
Eze 1:26 heads was the likeness of a *t*
Eze 1:26 of the *t* was the likeness as the
Eze 10:1 appearance of the likeness of a *t*
Eze 43:7 me, Son of man, the place of my *t*
Dan 5:20 he was deposed from his kingly *t*
Dan 7:9 his *t* was like the fiery flame,
Jonah 3:6 Nineveh, and he arose from his *t*
Hag 2:22 will overthrow the *t* of kingdoms
Zec 6:13 and shall sit and rule upon his *t*
Zec 6:13 he shall be a priest upon his *t*
Mt 5:34 for it is God's *t*
Mt 19:28 shall sit in the *t* of his glory
Mt 23:22 heaven, sweareth by the *t* of God
Mt 25:31 he sit upon the *t* of his glory
Lk 1:32 him the *t* of his father David
Acts 2:30 raise up Christ to sit on his *t*
Acts 7:49 Heaven is my *t*, and earth is my
Acts 12:21 in royal apparel, sat upon his *t*
Heb 1:8 But unto the Son he saith, Thy *t*
Heb 4:16 come boldly unto the *t* of grace
Heb 8:1 *t* of the Majesty in the heavens
Heb 12:2 at the right hand of the *t* of God
Rev 1:4 Spirits which are before his *t*
Rev 3:21 I grant to sit with me in my *t*
Rev 3:21 set down with my Father in his *t*
Rev 4:2 a *t* was set in heaven, and one sat
Rev 4:2 in heaven, and one sat on the *t*
Rev 4:3 was a rainbow round about the *t*
Rev 4:4 And round about the *t* were four
Rev 4:5 out of the *t* proceeded lightnings
Rev 4:5 of fire burning before the *t*
Rev 4:6 before the *t* there was a sea of
Rev 4:6 and in the midst of the *t*, and
Rev 4:6 and round about the *t*
Rev 4:9 thanks to him that sat on the *t*
Rev 4:10 down before him that sat on the *t*
Rev 4:10 and cast their crowns before the *t*
Rev 5:1 on the *t* a book written within
Rev 5:6 and, lo, in the midst of the *t*
Rev 5:7 hand of him that sat upon the *t*
Rev 5:11 of many angels round about the *t*
Rev 5:13 unto him that sitteth upon the *t*
Rev 6:16 face of him that sitteth on the *t*
Rev 7:9 and tongues, stood before the *t*
Rev 7:10 our God which sitteth upon the *t*
Rev 7:11 angels stood round about the *t*
Rev 7:11 fell before the *t* on their faces
Rev 7:15 are they before the *t* of God
Rev 7:15 on the *t* shall dwell among them
Rev 7:17 midst of the *t* shall feed them
Rev 8:3 altar which was before the *t*
Rev 12:5 caught up unto God, and to his *t*
Rev 14:3 it were a new song before the *t*
Rev 14:5 without fault before the *t* of God
Rev 16:17 the temple of heaven, from the *t*
Rev 19:4 worshipped God that sat on the *t*
Rev 19:5 And a voice came out of the *t*
Rev 20:11 And I saw a great white *t*, and him

Rev 21:5 And he that sat upon the *t* said
Rev 22:1 proceeding out of the *t* of God
Rev 22:3 but the *t* of God and of the Lamb

**THRONES**
Ps 122:5 For there are set *t* of judgment
Ps 122:5 the *t* of the house of David
Is 14:9 *t* all the kings of the nations
Eze 26:16 sea shall come down from their *t*
Dan 7:9 beheld till the *t* were cast down
Mt 19:28 ye also shall sit upon twelve *t*
Lk 22:30 sit on *t* judging the twelve
Col 1:16 and invisible, whether they be *t*
Rev 20:4 And I saw *t*, and they sat upon them

**THRONG**
Mk 3:9 multitude, lest they should *t* him
Lk 8:45 Master, the multitude *t* thee

**THRONGED**
Mk 5:24 people followed him, and *t* him
Lk 8:42 But as he went the people *t* him

**THRONGING**
Mk 5:31 Thou seest the multitude *t* thee

**THROW**
Judg 2:2 ye shall *t* down their altars
Judg 6:25 *t* down the altar of Baal that thy
2Sa 20:15 battered the wall, to *t* it down
2Kin 9:33 And he said, *T* her down
Jer 1:10 to *t* down, to build, and to plant
Jer 31:28 to *t* down, and to destroy, and to
Eze 16:39 they shall *t* down thine eminent
Mic 5:11 *t* down all thy strong holds
Mal 1:4 shall build, but I will *t* down

**THROWING**
Num 35:17 And if he smite him with *t* a stone

**THROWN**
Ex 15:1 his rider hath he *t* into the sea
Ex 15:21 his rider hath he *t* into the sea
Judg 6:32 because he hath *t* down his altar
2Sa 20:21 his head shall be *t* to thee over
1Kin 19:10 *t* down thine altars, and slain thy
1Kin 19:14 *t* down thine altars, and slain thy
Jer 31:40 nor *t* down any more for ever
Jer 33:4 which are *t* down by the mounts,
Jer 50:15 are fallen, her walls are *t* down
Lam 2:2 he hath *t* down in his wrath the
Lam 2:17 he hath *t* down, and hath not
Eze 29:5 I will leave thee *t* into the
Eze 38:20 and the mountains shall be *t* down
Nah 1:6 and the rocks are *t* down by him
Mt 24:2 another, that shall not be *t* down
Mk 13:2 another, that shall not be *t* down
Lk 4:35 the devil had *t* him in the midst
Lk 21:6 another, that shall not be *t* down
Rev 18:21 that great city Babylon be *t* down

**THRUST**
Ex 11:1 he shall surely *t* you out hence
Ex 12:39 because they were *t* out of Egypt
Num 22:25 she *t* herself unto the wall, and
Num 25:8 *t* both of them through, the man
Num 35:20 But if he *t* him of hatred, or
Num 35:22 But if he *t* him suddenly without
Deut 13:5 to *t* thee out of the way which
Deut 13:10 because he hath sought to *t* thee
Deut 15:17 *t* it through his ear unto the
Deut 33:27 he shall *t* out the enemy from
Judg 3:21 thigh, and *t* it into his belly
Judg 6:38 *t* the fleece together, and wringed
Judg 9:41 Zebul *t* out Gaal and his brethren,
Judg 9:54 And his young man *t* him through
Judg 11:2 they *t* out Jephthah, and said unto
1Sa 11:2 that I may *t* out all your right
1Sa 31:4 sword, and *t* me through therewith
1Sa 31:4 *t* me through, and abuse me
2Sa 2:16 *t* his sword in his fellow's side
2Sa 18:14 *t* them through the heart of
2Sa 23:6 be all of them as thorns *t* away
1Kin 2:27 So Solomon *t* out Abiathar from
2Kin 4:27 Gehazi came near to *t* her away
1Chr 10:4 sword, and *t* me through therewith
2Chr 26:20 they *t* him out from thence
Ps 118:13 Thou hast *t* sore at me that I
Is 13:15 that is found shall be *t* through
Is 14:19 *t* through with a sword, that go
Jer 51:4 they that are *t* through in her
Eze 16:40 *t* thee through with their swords
Eze 34:21 Because ye have *t* with side
Eze 46:18 to *t* them out of their possession
Joel 2:8 Neither shall one *t* another
Zec 13:3 *t* him through when he prophesieth
Lk 4:29 *t* him out of the city, and led him
Lk 5:3 prayed him that he would *t* out a
Lk 10:15 heaven, shalt be *t* down to hell
Lk 13:28 of God, and you yourselves *t* out
Jn 20:25 *t* my hand into his side, I will
Jn 20:27 thy hand, and *t* it into my side
Acts 7:27 his neighbour wrong *t* him away
Acts 7:39 but *t* him from them, and in their
Acts 16:24 *t* them into the inner prison, and
Acts 16:37 now do they *t* us out privily
Acts 27:39 were possible, to *t* in the ship
Heb 12:20 stoned, or *t* through with a dart
Rev 14:15 cloud, *T* in thy sickle, and reap
Rev 14:16 he that sat on the cloud *t* in his
Rev 14:18 *T* in thy sharp sickle, and gather
Rev 14:19 the angel *t* in his sickle into

**THRUSTETH**
Job 32:13 God *t* him down, not man

**THUMB**
Ex 29:20 upon the *t* of their right hand,
Lev 8:23 upon the *t* of his right hand, and
Lev 14:14 upon the *t* of his right hand, and
Lev 14:17 upon the *t* of his right hand, and
Lev 14:25 upon the *t* of his right hand, and
Lev 14:28 upon the *t* of his right hand, and

**THUMBS**
Lev 8:24 upon the *t* of their right hands,
Judg 1:6 and caught him, and cut off his *t*
Judg 1:7 and ten kings, having their *t*

**THUMMIM** *(thum'-mim) A symbolic object in the High Priest's breastplate.*
Ex 28:30 of judgment the Urim and the *T*
Lev 8:8 the breastplate the Urim and the *T*
Deut 33:8 And of Levi he said, Let thy *T*
Ezr 2:63 up a priest with Urim and with *T*
Neh 7:65 stood up a priest with Urim and *T*

**THUNDER**
Ex 9:23 and the LORD sent *t* and hail, and
Ex 9:29 the *t* shall cease, neither shall
1Sa 2:10 of heaven shall he *t* upon them
1Sa 7:10 a great *t* on that day upon the
1Sa 12:17 unto the LORD, and he shall send *t*
1Sa 12:18 and the LORD sent *t* and rain that
Job 26:14 but the *t* of his power who can
Job 28:26 a way for the lightning of the *t*
Job 38:25 or a way for the lightning of *t*
Job 39:19 hast thou clothed his neck with *t*
Job 39:25 the *t* of the captains, and the
Job 40:9 or canst thou *t* with a voice like
Ps 77:18 The voice of thy *t* was in the
Ps 81:7 thee in the secret place of *t*
Ps 104:7 voice of thy *t* they hasted away
Is 29:6 of the LORD of hosts with *t*
Mk 3:17 which is, The sons of *t*
Rev 6:1 heard, as it were the noise of *t*
Rev 14:2 and as the voice of a great *t*

**THUNDERBOLTS**
Ps 78:48 hail, and their flocks to hot *t*

**THUNDERED**
1Sa 7:10 but the LORD *t* with a great
2Sa 22:14 The LORD *t* from heaven, and the
Ps 18:13 The LORD also *t* in the heavens,
Jn 12:29 by, and heard it, said that it *t*

**THUNDERETH**
Job 37:4 he *t* with the voice of his
Job 37:5 God *t* marvellously with his voice
Ps 29:3 the God of glory *t*

**THUNDERINGS**
Ex 9:28 that there be no more mighty *t*
Ex 20:18 And all the people saw the *t*
Rev 4:5 throne proceeded lightnings and *t*
Rev 8:5 and there were voices, and *t*
Rev 11:19 were lightnings, and voices, and *t*
Rev 19:6 and as the voice of mighty *t*

**THUNDERS**
Ex 9:33 and the *t* and hail ceased, and the
Ex 9:34 the *t* were ceased, he sinned yet
Ex 19:16 in the morning, that there were *t*
Rev 10:3 seven *t* uttered their voices
Rev 10:4 when the seven *t* had uttered
Rev 10:4 things which the seven *t* uttered
Rev 16:18 And there were voices, and *t*

**THYATIRA** *(thi-a-ti'-rah) A city in Lydia in Asia Minor.*
Acts 16:14 of purple, of the city of *T*
Rev 1:11 and unto Pergamos, and unto *T*
Rev 2:18 angel of the church in *T* write
Rev 2:24 you I say, and unto the rest in *T*

**THYINE**
Rev 18:12 all *t* wood, and all manner vessels

**TIBERIAS** *(ti-be'-re-as) A city on the Sea of Galilee.*
Jn 6:1 of Galilee, which is the sea of *T*
Jn 6:23 there came other boats from *T*
Jn 21:1 to the disciples at the sea of *T*

**TIBERIUS** *(ti-be'-re-us)* See CAESAR. *A Roman emperor.*
Lk 3:1 year of the reign of *T* Caesar

**TIBHATH** *(tib'-hath) A city in Aram Zobah.*
1Chr 18:8 Likewise from *T*, and from Chun,

**TIBNI** *(tib'-ni) Son of Ginath.*
1Kin 16:21 followed *T* the son of Ginath
1Kin 16:22 that followed *T* the son of Ginath
1Kin 16:22 so *T* died, and Omri reigned

**TIDAL** *(ti'-dal) A king of Goyim.*
Gen 14:1 of Elam, and *T* king of nations
Gen 14:9 with *T* king of nations, and

**TIDINGS**
Gen 29:13 when Laban heard the *t* of Jacob
Ex 33:4 the people heard these evil *t*
1Sa 4:19 when she heard the *t* that the ark
1Sa 11:4 told the *t* in the ears of the
1Sa 11:5 they told him the *t* of the men of
1Sa 11:6 upon Saul when he heard those *t*
1Sa 27:11 woman alive, to bring *t* to Gath
2Sa 4:4 years old when the *t* came of Saul
2Sa 4:10 thinking to have brought good *t*
2Sa 4:10 have given him a reward for his *t*
2Sa 13:30 that *t* came to David, saying,
2Sa 18:19 me now run, and bear the king *t*
2Sa 18:20 Thou shalt not bear *t* this day
2Sa 18:20 but thou shalt bear *t* another day
2Sa 18:20 but this day thou shalt bear no *t*
2Sa 18:22 seeing that thou hast no *t* ready
2Sa 18:25 be alone, there is *t* in his mouth
2Sa 18:26 the king said, He also bringeth *t*
2Sa 18:27 a good man, and cometh with good *t*
2Sa 18:31 and Cushi said, *T*, my lord the
1Kin 1:42 a valiant man, and bringest good *t*
1Kin 2:28 Then *t* came to Joab
1Kin 14:6 I am sent to thee with heavy *t*
2Kin 7:9 this day is a day of good *t*
1Chr 10:9 to carry *t* unto their idols, and
Ps 112:7 He shall not be afraid of evil *t*
Is 40:9 O Zion, that bringest good *t*
Is 40:9 O Jerusalem, that bringest good *t*
Is 41:27 one that bringeth good *t*
Is 52:7 feet of him that bringeth good *t*
Is 52:7 that bringeth good *t* of good
Is 61:1 me to preach good *t* unto the meek
Jer 20:15 man who brought *t* to my father
Jer 37:5 Jerusalem heard *t* of them
Jer 49:23 for they have heard evil *t*
Eze 21:7 that thou shalt answer, For the *t*
Dan 11:44 But *t* out of the east and out of
Nah 1:15 feet of him that bringeth good *t*
Lk 1:19 and to shew thee these glad *t*
Lk 2:10 I bring you good *t* of great joy
Lk 8:1 shewing the glad *t* of the kingdom
Acts 11:22 Then *t* of these things came unto
Acts 13:32 And we declare unto you glad *t*
Acts 21:31 *t* came unto the chief captain of
Rom 10:15 bring glad *t* of good things
1Th 3:6 brought us good *t* of your faith

**TIE**
1Sa 6:7 *t* the kine to the cart, and bring
Prov 6:21 heart, and *t* them about thy neck

**TIED**
Ex 39:31 they *t* unto it a lace of blue, to
1Sa 6:10 *t* them to the cart, and shut up
2Kin 7:10 voice of man, but horses *t*
2Kin 7:10 man, but horses *t*, and asses *t*
Mt 21:2 ye shall find an ass *t*, and a colt
Mk 11:2 into it, ye shall find a colt *t*
Mk 11:4 found the colt *t* by the door
Lk 19:30 entering ye shall find a colt *t*

**TIGLATH-PILESER** *(tig'-lath-pi-le'-zur)* See TIGLATH-PILNESER. *An Assyrian king.*
2Kin 15:29 of Israel came *T* king of Assyria
2Kin 16:7 messengers to *T* king of Assyria
2Kin 16:10 to meet *T* king of Assyria

**TIKVAH** *(tik'-vah)* See TIKVATH.
*1. Father-in-law of Huldah.*
2Kin 22:14 the wife of Shallum the son of *T*
*2. Father of Jahaziah.*
Ezr 10:15 Jahaziah the son of *T* were

**TIKVATH** *(tik'-vath)* See TIKVAH. *Same as Tikvah 1.*
2Chr 34:22 the wife of Shallum the son of *T*

**TIL**
Is 23:13 *t* the Assyrian founded it for

**TILE**
Eze 4:1 also, son of man, take thee a *t*

**TILGATH-PILNESER** *(til'-gath-pil-ne'-zur)* See TIGLATH-PILESER. *Same as Tiglath-pileser.*
1Chr 5:6 whom *T* king of Assyria carried
1Chr 5:26 the spirit of *T* king of Assyria,
2Chr 28:20 *T* king of Assyria came unto him,

**TILING**
Lk 5:19 let him down through the *t* with

**TILLAGE**
1Chr 27:26 did the work of the field for *t*
Neh 10:37 tithes in all the cities of our *t*
Prov 13:23 Much food is in the *t* of the poor

**TILLED**
Eze 36:9 turn unto you, and ye shall be *t*
Eze 36:34 And the desolate land shall be *t*

**TILLER**
Gen 4:2 but Cain was a *t* of the ground

**TILLEST**
Gen 4:12 When thou *t* the ground, it shall

**TILLETH**
Prov 12:11 He that *t* his land shall be
Prov 28:19 He that *t* his land shall have

**TILON** *(ti'-lon) A descendant of Judah.*
1Chr 4:20 and Rinnah, Ben-hanan, and *T*

**TIMAEUS** *(ti-me'-us)* See BARTIMAEUS. *Father of Bartimaeus.*
Mk 10:46 blind Bartimaeus, the son of *T*

**TIMBER**
Ex 31:5 to set them, and in carving of *t*
Lev 14:45 the *t* thereof, and all the morter
1Kin 5:6 to hew *t* like unto the Sidonians
1Kin 5:8 thy desire concerning *t* of cedar
1Kin 5:8 of cedar, and concerning *t* of fir
1Kin 5:18 so they prepared *t* and stones to
1Kin 6:10 on the house with *t* of cedar
1Kin 15:22 the *t* thereof, wherewith Baasha
2Kin 12:12 and hewers of stone, and to buy *t*
2Kin 22:6 builders, and masons, and to buy *t*
1Chr 14:1 *t* of cedars, with masons and
1Chr 22:14 *t* also and stone have I prepared
1Chr 22:15 hewers and workers of stone and *t*
2Chr 2:8 can skill to cut *t* in Lebanon
2Chr 2:9 Even to prepare me *t* in abundance
2Chr 2:10 servants, the hewers that cut *t*
2Chr 2:14 brass, in iron, in stone, and in *t*
2Chr 16:6 the *t* thereof, wherewith Baasha
2Chr 34:11 *t* for couplings, and to floor the
Ezr 5:8 *t* is laid in the walls, and this
Ezr 6:4 great stones, and a row of new *t*
Ezr 6:11 let *t* be pulled down from his
Neh 2:8 that he may give me *t* to make
Eze 26:12 shall lay thy stones and thy *t*
Hab 2:11 beam out of the *t* shall answer it
Zec 5:4 consume it with the *t* thereof

**TIMBREL**
Ex 15:20 of Aaron, took a *t* in her hand
Job 21:12 They take the *t* and harp, and
Ps 81:2 a psalm, and bring hither the *t*
Ps 149:3 sing praises unto him with the *t*
Ps 150:4 Praise him with the *t* and dance

**TIMBRELS**
Ex 15:20 women went out after her with *t*
Judg 11:34 came out to meet him with *t*
2Sa 6:5 harps, and on psalteries, and on *t*
1Chr 13:8 and with psalteries, and with *t*
Ps 68:25 were the damsels playing with *t*

**TIME**
Gen 4:3 in process of *t* it came to pass,
Gen 17:21 at this set *t* in the next year
Gen 18:10 thee according to the *t* of life
Gen 18:14 At the *t* appointed I will return
Gen 18:14 thee, according to the *t* of life
Gen 21:2 at the set *t* of which God had
Gen 21:22 And it came to pass at that *t*
Gen 22:15 out of heaven the second *t*
Gen 24:11 of water at the *t* of the evening
Gen 24:11 even the *t* that women go out to
Gen 26:8 when he had been there a long *t*
Gen 29:7 neither is it *t* that the cattle
Gen 29:34 Now this *t* will my husband be
Gen 30:33 answer for me in *t* to come
Gen 31:10 it came to pass at the *t* that the
Gen 38:1 And it came to pass at that *t*
Gen 38:12 in process of *t* the daughter of
Gen 38:27 to pass in the *t* of her travail
Gen 39:5 it came to pass from the *t* that
Gen 39:11 And it came to pass about this *t*
Gen 41:5 he slept and dreamed the second *t*
Gen 43:10 now we had returned this second *t*
Gen 43:18 at the first *t* are we brought in
Gen 43:20 down at the first *t* to buy food
Gen 47:29 the *t* drew nigh that Israel must
Ex 2:23 it came to pass in process of *t*
Ex 8:32 hardened his heart at this *t* also
Ex 9:5 And the LORD appointed a set *t*
Ex 9:14 For I will at this *t* send all my
Ex 9:18 to morrow about this *t* I will
Ex 9:27 unto them, I have sinned this *t*
Ex 13:14 thy son asketh thee in *t* to come
Ex 21:19 shall pay for the loss of his *t*
Ex 21:29 to push with his horn in *t* past
Ex 21:36 ox hath used to push in *t* past
Ex 23:15 in the *t* appointed of the month
Ex 34:18 in the *t* of the month Abib
Ex 34:21 in earing *t* and in harvest thou
Lev 13:58 it shall be washed the second *t*
Lev 15:25 out of the *t* of her separation
Lev 15:25 beyond the *t* of her separation
Lev 18:18 beside the other in her life *t*
Lev 25:32 may the Levites redeem at any *t*
Lev 25:50 according to the *t* of an hired
Lev 26:5 shall reach unto the sowing *t*
Num 10:6 ye blow an alarm the second *t*
Num 13:20 Now the *t* was the *t* of the
Num 20:15 we have dwelt in Egypt a long *t*
Num 22:4 king of the Moabites at that *t*
Num 23:23 according to this *t* it shall be
Num 26:10 what *t* the fire devoured two
Num 32:10 anger was kindled the same *t*
Num 35:26 *t* come without the border of the
Deut 1:9 And I spake unto you at that *t*
Deut 1:16 I charged your judges at that *t*
Deut 1:18 I commanded you at that *t* all the
Deut 2:20 giants dwelt therein in old *t*
Deut 2:34 we took all his cities at that *t*
Deut 3:4 we took all his cities at that *t*
Deut 3:8 we took at that *t* out of the hand
Deut 3:12 which we possessed at that *t*
Deut 3:18 And I commanded you at that *t*
Deut 3:21 And I commanded Joshua at that *t*
Deut 3:23 And I besought the LORD at that *t*
Deut 4:14 at that *t* to teach you statutes
Deut 5:5 between the LORD and you at that *t*
Deut 6:20 thy son asketh thee in *t* to come
Deut 9:19 hearkened unto me at that *t* also
Deut 9:20 prayed for Aaron also the same *t*
Deut 10:1 At that *t* the LORD said unto me,
Deut 10:8 At that *t* the LORD separated the
Deut 10:10 mount, according to the first *t*
Deut 10:10 hearkened unto me at that *t* also
Deut 16:9 the seven weeks from such *t* as
Deut 19:4 whom he hated not in *t* past
Deut 19:6 as he hated him not in *t* past
Deut 19:14 which they of old *t* have set in
Deut 20:19 shalt besiege a city a long *t*
Deut 32:35 their foot shall slide in due *t*
Josh 2:5 the *t* of shutting of the gate
Josh 3:15 his banks all the *t* of harvest
Josh 4:6 ask their fathers in *t* to come
Josh 4:21 ask their fathers in *t* to come
Josh 5:2 At that *t* the LORD said unto
Josh 5:2 children of Israel the second *t*
Josh 6:16 it came to pass at the seventh *t*
Josh 6:26 And Joshua adjured them at that *t*
Josh 8:14 at a *t* appointed, before the
Josh 10:27 it came to pass at the *t* of the
Josh 10:42 land did Joshua take at one *t*
Josh 11:6 for to morrow about this *t* will I
Josh 11:10 And Joshua at that *t* turned back
Josh 11:18 war a long *t* with all those kings
Josh 11:21 at that *t* came Joshua, and cut off
Josh 22:24 In *t* to come your children might
Josh 22:27 say to our children in *t* to come
Josh 22:28 to our generations in *t* to come
Josh 23:1 it came to pass a long *t* after
Josh 24:2 other side of the flood in old *t*
Judg 3:29 at that *t* about ten thousand men
Judg 4:4 she judged Israel at that *t*
Judg 9:8 The trees went forth on a *t* to
Judg 10:14 you in the *t* of your tribulation
Judg 11:4 it came to pass in process of *t*
Judg 11:26 ye not recover them within that *t*
Judg 12:6 there fell at that *t* of the
Judg 13:23 nor would as at this *t* have told
Judg 14:4 for at that *t* the Philistines had
Judg 14:8 after a *t* he returned to take her
Judg 15:1 in the *t* of wheat harvest, that
Judg 18:31 all the *t* that the house of God
Judg 20:15 that *t* out of the cities twenty
Judg 21:14 And Benjamin came again at that *t*
Judg 21:22 did not give unto them at this *t*
Judg 21:24 Israel departed thence at that *t*
Ruth 4:7 this was the manner in former *t*
1Sa 1:4 when the *t* was that Elkanah
1Sa 1:20 when the *t* was come about after
1Sa 3:2 And it came to pass at that *t*
1Sa 3:8 called Samuel again the third *t*
1Sa 4:20 about the *t* of her death the
1Sa 7:2 that the *t* was long
1Sa 9:13 for about this *t* ye shall find
1Sa 9:16 To morrow about this *t* I will
1Sa 9:24 for unto this *t* hath it been kept
1Sa 11:9 by that *t* the sun be hot, ye
1Sa 13:8 according to the set *t* that
1Sa 14:18 *t* with the children of Israel
1Sa 14:21 the Philistines before that *t*
1Sa 18:19 the *t* when Merab Saul's daughter
1Sa 19:21 sent messengers again the third *t*
1Sa 20:12 my father about to morrow any *t*
1Sa 20:35 at the *t* appointed with David
1Sa 26:8 I will not smite him the second *t*
1Sa 27:7 the *t* that David dwelt in the
2Sa 2:11 the *t* that David was king in
2Sa 5:2 Also in *t* past, when Saul was
2Sa 7:6 dwelt in any house since the *t*
2Sa 7:11 as since the *t* that I commanded
2Sa 11:1 at the *t* when kings go forth to
2Sa 14:2 had a long *t* mourned for the dead
2Sa 14:29 when he sent again the second *t*
2Sa 17:7 hath given is not good at this *t*
2Sa 20:5 set *t* which he had appointed him
2Sa 20:18 They were wont to speak in old *t*
2Sa 23:8 hundred, whom he slew at one *t*
2Sa 23:13 *t* unto the cave of Adullam
2Sa 23:20 the midst of a pit in *t* of snow
2Sa 24:15 morning even to the *t* appointed
1Kin 1:6 displeased him at any *t* in saying
1Kin 2:26 not at this *t* put thee to death
1Kin 8:65 at that *t* Solomon held a feast,
1Kin 9:2 appeared to Solomon the second *t*
1Kin 11:29 it came to pass at that *t* when
1Kin 11:42 the *t* that Solomon reigned in
1Kin 14:1 At that *t* Abijah the son of
1Kin 15:23 Nevertheless in the *t* of his old
1Kin 18:29 they prophesied until the *t* of
1Kin 18:34 And he said, Do it the second *t*
1Kin 18:34 And they did it the second *t*
1Kin 18:34 And he said, Do it the third *t*
1Kin 18:34 And they did it the third *t*
1Kin 18:36 it came to pass at the *t* of the
1Kin 18:44 it came to pass at the seventh *t*
1Kin 19:2 of them by to morrow about this *t*
1Kin 19:7 the LORD came again the second *t*
1Kin 20:6 unto thee to morrow about this *t*
2Kin 3:6 went out of Samaria the same *t*
2Kin 4:16 according to the *t* of life
2Kin 4:17 her, according to the *t* of life
2Kin 5:26 Is it a *t* to receive money, and to
2Kin 7:1 To morrow about this *t* shall a
2Kin 7:18 this *t* in the gate of Samaria
2Kin 8:22 Libnah revolted at the same *t*
2Kin 10:6 a letter the second *t* to them
2Kin 10:6 me to Jezreel by to morrow this *t*
2Kin 10:36 the *t* that Jehu reigned over
2Kin 16:6 At that *t* Rezin king of Syria
2Kin 18:16 At that *t* did Hezekiah cut off

2Kin 20:12 At that *t* Berodach-baladan, the
2Kin 24:10 At that *t* the servants of
1Chr 9:20 was the ruler over them in *t* past
1Chr 9:25 days from *t* to *t* with them
1Chr 11:2 And moreover in *t* past, even when
1Chr 11:11 hundred slain by him at one *t*
1Chr 12:22 For at that *t* day by day there
1Chr 17:10 since the *t* that I commanded
1Chr 20:1 at the *t* that kings go out to
1Chr 20:4 at which *t* Sibbechai the
1Chr 21:28 At that *t* when David saw that the
1Chr 29:22 son of David king the second *t*
1Chr 29:27 the *t* that he reigned over Israel
2Chr 7:8 Also at the same *t* Solomon kept
2Chr 13:18 were brought under at that *t*
2Chr 15:11 offered unto the LORD the same *t*
2Chr 16:7 at that *t* Hanani the seer came to
2Chr 16:10 some of the people the same *t*
2Chr 18:34 about the *t* of the sun going down
2Chr 21:10 The same *t* also did Libnah revolt
2Chr 21:19 to pass, that in process of *t*
2Chr 24:11 that at what *t* the chest was
2Chr 25:27 Now after the *t* that Amaziah did
2Chr 28:16 At that *t* did king Ahaz send unto
2Chr 28:22 in the *t* of his distress did he
2Chr 30:3 they could not keep it at that *t*
2Chr 30:5 *t* in such sort as it was written
2Chr 30:26 for since the *t* of Solomon the
2Chr 35:17 kept the passover at that *t*
Ezr 4:10 side the river, and at such a *t*
Ezr 4:11 side the river, and at such a *t*
Ezr 4:15 sedition within the same of old *t*
Ezr 4:17 the river, Peace, and at such a *t*
Ezr 4:19 *t* hath made insurrection against
Ezr 5:3 At the same *t* came to them Tatnai
Ezr 5:16 since that *t* even until now hath
Ezr 7:12 perfect peace, and at such a *t*
Ezr 8:34 the weight was written at that *t*
Ezr 10:13 it is a *t* of much rain, and we are
Neh 2:6 and I set him a *t*
Neh 4:16 it came to pass from that *t* forth
Neh 4:22 Likewise at the same *t* said I
Neh 5:14 Moreover from the *t* that I was
Neh 6:1 (though at that *t* I had not set
Neh 6:5 me in like manner the fifth *t*
Neh 9:27 in the *t* of their trouble, when
Neh 9:32 since the *t* of the kings of
Neh 12:44 at that *t* were some appointed
Neh 13:6 But in all this *t* was not I at
Neh 13:21 From that *t* forth came they no
Est 2:19 gathered together the second *t*
Est 4:14 holdest thy peace at this *t*
Est 4:14 the kingdom for such a *t* as this
Est 8:9 at that *t* in the third month
Est 9:27 to their appointed *t* every year
Job 6:17 What *t* they wax warm, they vanish
Job 7:1 an appointed *t* to man upon earth
Job 9:19 who shall set me a *t* to plead
Job 14:13 thou wouldest appoint me a set *t*
Job 14:14 of my appointed *t* will I wait
Job 15:32 be accomplished before his *t*
Job 22:16 Which were cut down out of *t*
Job 30:3 wilderness in former *t* desolate
Job 38:23 reserved against the *t* of trouble
Job 39:1 Knowest thou the *t* when the wild
Job 39:2 or knowest thou the *t* when they
Job 39:18 What *t* she lifteth up herself on
Ps 4:7 than in the *t* that their corn
Ps 21:9 oven in the *t* of thine anger
Ps 27:5 For in the *t* of trouble he shall
Ps 32:6 in a *t* when thou mayest be found
Ps 37:19 not be ashamed in the evil *t*
Ps 37:39 strength in the *t* of trouble
Ps 41:1 will deliver him in *t* of trouble
Ps 56:3 What *t* I am afraid, I will trust
Ps 69:13 thee, O LORD, in an acceptable *t*
Ps 71:9 me not off in the *t* of old age
Ps 78:38 many a *t* turned he his anger away
Ps 81:3 in the *t* appointed, on our solemn
Ps 81:15 but their *t* should have endured
Ps 89:47 Remember how short my *t* is
Ps 102:13 for the *t* to favour her, yea, the
Ps 102:13 to favour her, yea, the set *t*
Ps 105:19 Until the *t* that his word came
Ps 113:2 of the LORD from this *t* forth
Ps 115:18 bless the LORD from this *t* forth
Ps 119:126 It is *t* for thee, LORD, to work
Ps 121:8 thy coming in from this *t* forth
Ps 129:1 Many a *t* have they afflicted me
Ps 129:2 Many a *t* have they afflicted me

Prov 25:13 cold of snow in the *t* of harvest
Prov 25:19 in an unfaithful man in *t* of
Prov 31:25 and she shall rejoice in *t* to come
Eccl 1:10 it hath been already of old *t*
Eccl 3:1 a *t* to every purpose under the
Eccl 3:2 A *t* to be born, and a *t* to die
Eccl 3:2 a *t* to plant, and a *t* to pluck
Eccl 3:3 A *t* to kill, and a *t* to heal
Eccl 3:3 a *t* to break down
Eccl 3:3 and a *t* to build up
Eccl 3:4 A *t* to weep, and a *t* to laugh
Eccl 3:4 a *t* to mourn, and a *t* to dance
Eccl 3:5 A *t* to cast away stones, and a
Eccl 3:5 a *t* to gather stones together
Eccl 3:5 a *t* to embrace
Eccl 3:5 a *t* to refrain from embracing
Eccl 3:6 A *t* to get, and a *t* to lose
Eccl 3:6 *t* to keep, and a *t* to cast away
Eccl 3:7 A *t* to rend, and a *t* to sew
Eccl 3:7 a *t* to keep silence
Eccl 3:7 and a *t* to speak
Eccl 3:8 A *t* to love, and a *t* to hate
Eccl 3:8 a *t* of war, and a *t* of peace
Eccl 3:11 every thing beautiful in his *t*
Eccl 3:17 for there is a *t* there for every
Eccl 7:17 shouldest thou die before thy *t*
Eccl 8:5 man's heart discerneth both *t*
Eccl 8:6 to every purpose there is *t*
Eccl 8:9 there is a *t* wherein one man
Eccl 9:11 but *t* and chance happeneth to them
Eccl 9:12 For man also knoweth not his *t*
Eccl 9:12 sons of men snared in an evil *t*
Song 2:12 the *t* of the singing of birds is
Is 11:11 *t* to recover the remnant of his
Is 13:22 her *t* is near to come, and her
Is 16:13 concerning Moab since that *t*
Is 18:7 In that *t* shall the present be
Is 20:2 At the same *t* spake the LORD by
Is 26:17 near the *t* of her delivery
Is 28:19 From the *t* that it goeth forth it
Is 30:8 may be for the *t* to come for ever
Is 33:2 also in the *t* of trouble
Is 39:1 At that *t* Merodach-baladan, the
Is 42:14 I have long *t* holden my peace
Is 42:23 hearken and hear for the *t* to come
Is 44:8 have not I told thee from that *t*
Is 45:21 hath declared this from ancient *t*
Is 45:21 who hath told it from that *t*
Is 48:6 thee new things from this *t*
Is 48:8 from that *t* that thine ear was
Is 48:16 from the *t* that it was, there am
Is 49:8 In an acceptable *t* have I heard
Is 60:22 the LORD will hasten it in his *t*
Jer 1:13 LORD came unto me the second *t*
Jer 2:20 For of old *t* I have broken thy
Jer 2:27 but in the *t* of their trouble
Jer 2:28 save thee in the *t* of thy trouble
Jer 3:4 thou not from this *t* cry unto me
Jer 3:17 At that *t* they shall call
Jer 4:11 At that *t* shall it be said to
Jer 6:15 at the *t* that I visit them they
Jer 8:1 At that *t*, saith the LORD, they
Jer 8:7 observe the *t* of their coming
Jer 8:12 in the *t* of their visitation they
Jer 8:15 for a *t* of health, and behold
Jer 10:15 in the *t* of their visitation they
Jer 11:12 at all in the *t* of their trouble
Jer 11:14 *t* that they cry unto me for their
Jer 13:3 LORD came unto me the second *t*
Jer 14:8 saviour thereof in *t* of trouble
Jer 14:19 for the *t* of healing, and behold
Jer 15:11 thee well in the *t* of evil
Jer 15:11 of evil and in the *t* of affliction
Jer 18:23 with them in the *t* of thine anger
Jer 27:7 until the very *t* of his land come
Jer 30:7 it is even the *t* of Jacob's
Jer 31:1 At the same *t*, saith the LORD,
Jer 33:1 came unto Jeremiah the second *t*
Jer 33:15 In those days, and at that *t*
Jer 39:10 vineyards and fields at the same *t*
Jer 46:17 he hath passed the *t* appointed
Jer 46:21 the *t* of their visitation
Jer 49:8 the *t* that I will visit him
Jer 49:19 and who will appoint me the *t*
Jer 50:4 In those days, and in that *t*
Jer 50:16 the sickle in the *t* of harvest
Jer 50:20 In those days, and in that *t*
Jer 50:27 the *t* of their visitation
Jer 50:31 the *t* that I will visit thee
Jer 50:44 and who will appoint me the *t*

Jer 51:6 for this is the *t* of the LORD's
Jer 51:18 in the *t* of their visitation they
Jer 51:33 it is *t* to thresh her
Jer 51:33 the *t* of her harvest shall come
Lam 5:20 for ever, and forsake us so long *t*
Eze 4:10 from *t* to *t* shalt thou eat it
Eze 4:11 from *t* to *t* shalt thou drink
Eze 7:7 the *t* is come, the day of trouble
Eze 7:12 The *t* is come, the day draweth
Eze 16:8 thy *t* was the *t* of love
Eze 16:57 as at the *t* of thy reproach of
Eze 21:14 the sword be doubled the third *t*
Eze 22:3 midst of it, that her *t* may come
Eze 26:20 the pit, with the people of old *t*
Eze 27:34 In the *t* when thou shalt be
Eze 30:3 it shall be the *t* of the heathen
Eze 35:5 sword in the *t* of their calamity
Eze 35:5 in the *t* that their iniquity had
Eze 38:10 that at the same *t* shall things
Eze 38:17 *t* by my servants the prophets of
Eze 38:18 shall come to pass at the same *t*
Dan 2:8 that ye would gain the *t*, because
Dan 2:9 before me, till the *t* be changed
Dan 2:16 the king that he would give him *t*
Dan 3:5 That at what *t* ye hear the sound
Dan 3:7 Therefore at that *t*, when all the
Dan 3:8 Wherefore at that *t* certain
Dan 3:15 *t* ye hear the sound of the cornet
Dan 4:36 At the same *t* my reason returned
Dan 7:12 were prolonged for a season and *t*
Dan 7:22 the *t* came that the saints
Dan 7:25 be given into his hand until a *t*
Dan 7:25 and times and the dividing of *t*
Dan 8:17 for at the *t* of the end shall be
Dan 8:19 for at the *t* appointed the end
Dan 8:23 in the latter *t* of their kingdom,
Dan 9:21 touched me about the *t* of the
Dan 10:1 but the *t* appointed was long
Dan 11:24 the strong holds, even for a *t*
Dan 11:27 end shall be at the *t* appointed
Dan 11:29 At the *t* appointed he shall
Dan 11:35 white, even to the *t* of the end
Dan 11:35 it is yet for a *t* appointed
Dan 11:40 at the *t* of the end shall the
Dan 12:1 at that *t* shall Michael stand up,
Dan 12:1 and there shall be a *t* of trouble
Dan 12:1 was a nation even to that same *t*
Dan 12:1 at that *t* thy people shall be
Dan 12:4 book, even to the *t* of the end
Dan 12:7 for ever that it shall be for a *t*
Dan 12:9 and sealed till the *t* of the end
Dan 12:11 from the *t* that the daily
Hos 2:9 away my corn in the *t* thereof
Hos 9:10 in the fig tree at her first *t*
Hos 10:12 for it is *t* to seek the LORD,
Joel 3:1 in those days, and in that *t*
Amos 5:13 shall keep silence in that *t*
Amos 5:13 for it is an evil *t*
Jonah 3:1 LORD came unto Jonah the second *t*
Mic 2:3 for this *t* is evil
Mic 3:4 hide his face from them at that *t*
Mic 5:3 until the *t* that she which
Nah 1:9 shall not rise up the second *t*
Hab 2:3 vision is yet for an appointed *t*
Zeph 1:12 it shall come to pass at that *t*
Zeph 3:19 at that *t* I will undo all that
Zeph 3:20 At that *t* will I bring you again,
Zeph 3:20 even in the *t* that I gather you
Hag 1:2 The *t* is not come
Hag 1:2 the *t* that the LORD's house
Hag 1:4 Is it *t* for you, O ye, to dwell
Zec 10:1 rain in the *t* of the latter rain
Zec 14:7 that at evening *t* it shall be
Mal 3:11 fruit before the *t* in the field
Mt 1:11 about the *t* they were carried
Mt 2:7 what *t* the star appeared
Mt 2:16 according to the *t* which he had
Mt 4:6 lest at any *t* thou dash thy foot
Mt 4:17 From that *t* Jesus began to preach
Mt 5:21 that it was said by them of old *t*
Mt 5:25 lest at any *t* the adversary
Mt 5:27 that it was said by them of old *t*
Mt 5:33 hath been said by them of old *t*
Mt 8:29 hither to torment us before the *t*
Mt 11:25 At that *t* Jesus answered and said,
Mt 12:1 At that *t* Jesus went on the
Mt 13:15 lest at any *t* they should see
Mt 13:30 in the *t* of harvest I will say to
Mt 14:1 At that *t* Herod the tetrarch
Mt 14:15 place, and the *t* is now past

Mt 16:21 From that *t* forth began Jesus to
Mt 18:1 At the same *t* came the disciples
Mt 21:34 when the *t* of the fruit drew near
Mt 24:21 beginning of the world to this *t*
Mt 25:19 After a long *t* the lord of those
Mt 26:16 from that *t* he sought opportunity
Mt 26:18 The Master saith, My *t* is at hand
Mt 26:42 He went away again the second *t*
Mt 26:44 away again, and prayed the third *t*
Mk 1:15 The *t* is fulfilled, and the
Mk 4:12 lest at any *t* they should be
Mk 4:17 and so endure but for a *t*
Mk 6:35 place, and now the *t* is far passed
Mk 10:30 an hundredfold now in this *t*
Mk 11:13 for the *t* of figs was not yet
Mk 13:19 which God created unto this *t*
Mk 13:33 for ye know not when the *t* is
Mk 14:41 And he cometh the third *t*, and
Mk 14:72 the second *t* the cock crew
Lk 1:10 without at the *t* of incense
Lk 1:57 Now Elisabeth's full *t* came that
Lk 4:5 of the world in a moment of *t*
Lk 4:11 lest at any *t* thou dash thy foot
Lk 4:27 in the *t* of Eliseus the prophet
Lk 7:45 but this woman since the *t* I came
Lk 8:13 in *t* of temptation fall away
Lk 8:27 man, which had devils long *t*
Lk 9:51 when the *t* was come that he
Lk 12:1 In the mean *t*, when there were
Lk 12:56 it that ye do not discern this *t*
Lk 13:35 until the *t* come when ye shall
Lk 14:17 sent his servant at supper *t* to
Lk 15:29 I at any *t* thy commandment
Lk 16:16 since that *t* the kingdom of God
Lk 18:30 manifold more in this present *t*
Lk 19:44 not the *t* of thy visitation
Lk 20:9 into a far country for a long *t*
Lk 21:8 and the *t* draweth near
Lk 21:34 lest at any *t* your hearts be
Lk 21:37 in the day *t* he was teaching in
Lk 23:7 also was at Jerusalem at that *t*
Lk 23:22 And he said unto them the third *t*
Jn 1:18 No man hath seen God at any *t*
Jn 3:4 second *t* into his mother's womb
Jn 5:6 been now a long *t* in that case
Jn 5:37 neither heard his voice at any *t*
Jn 6:66 From that *t* many of his disciples
Jn 7:6 unto them, My *t* is not yet come
Jn 7:6 but your *t* is alway ready
Jn 7:8 for my *t* is not yet full come
Jn 11:39 him, Lord, by this *t* he stinketh
Jn 14:9 Have I been so long *t* with you
Jn 16:2 the *t* cometh, that whosoever
Jn 16:4 you, that when the *t* shall come
Jn 16:25 but the *t* cometh, when I shall no
Jn 21:14 This is now the third *t* that
Jn 21:16 saith to him again the second *t*
Jn 21:17 He saith unto him the third *t*
Jn 21:17 he said unto him the third *t*
Acts 1:6 wilt thou at this *t* restore again
Acts 1:21 the *t* that the Lord Jesus went in
Acts 7:13 at the second *t* Joseph was made
Acts 7:17 But when the *t* of the promise
Acts 7:20 In which *t* Moses was born, and was
Acts 8:1 at that *t* there was a great
Acts 8:11 because that of long *t* he had
Acts 10:15 spake unto him again the second *t*
Acts 11:8 at any *t* entered into my mouth
Acts 12:1 Now about that *t* Herod the king
Acts 13:18 about the *t* of forty years
Acts 14:3 Long *t* therefore abode they
Acts 14:28 abode long *t* with the disciples
Acts 15:21 For Moses of old *t* hath in every
Acts 17:21 spent their *t* in nothing else
Acts 18:20 him to tarry longer *t* with them
Acts 18:23 after he had spent some *t* there
Acts 19:23 the same *t* there arose no small
Acts 20:16 he would not spend the *t* in Asia
Acts 24:25 answered, Go thy way for this *t*
Acts 27:9 Now when much *t* was spent
Rom 3:26 at this *t* his righteousness
Rom 5:6 in due *t* Christ died for the
Rom 8:18 *t* are not worthy to be compared
Rom 9:9 At this *t* will I come, and Sarah
Rom 11:5 present *t* also there is a remnant
Rom 13:11 And that, knowing the *t*, that now
Rom 13:11 that now it is high *t* to awake
1Cor 4:5 judge nothing before the *t*
1Cor 7:5 except it be with consent for a *t*
1Cor 7:29 I say, brethren, the *t* is short
1Cor 9:7 warfare any *t* at his own charges
1Cor 15:8 also, as of one born out of due *t*
1Cor 16:12 was not at all to come at this *t*
1Cor 16:12 when he shall have convenient *t*
2Cor 6:2 I have heard thee in a *t* accepted
2Cor 6:2 behold, now is the accepted *t*
2Cor 8:14 that now at this *t* your abundance
2Cor 12:14 the third *t* I am ready to come to
2Cor 13:1 This is the third *t* I am coming
2Cor 13:2 if I were present, the second *t*
Gal 1:13 in *t* past in the Jews' religion
Gal 4:2 governors until the *t* appointed
Gal 4:4 the fulness of the *t* was come
Gal 5:21 as I have also told you in *t* past
Eph 2:2 Wherein in *t* past ye walked
Eph 2:11 that ye being in *t* past Gentiles
Eph 2:12 That at that *t* ye were without
Eph 5:16 Redeeming the *t*, because the days
Col 3:7 the which ye also walked some *t*
Col 4:5 that are without, redeeming the *t*
1Th 2:5 For neither at any *t* used we
1Th 2:17 you for a short *t* in presence
2Th 2:6 he might be revealed in his *t*
1Ti 2:6 for all, to be testified in due *t*
1Ti 6:19 foundation against the *t* to come
2Ti 4:3 For the *t* will come when they
2Ti 4:6 the *t* of my departure is at hand
2Ti *s* brought before Nero the second *t*
Philem 11 Which in *t* past was to thee
Heb 1:1 in divers manners spake in *t* past
Heb 1:5 of the angels said he at any *t*
Heb 2:1 lest at any *t* we should let them
Heb 4:7 David, To day, after so long a *t*
Heb 4:16 find grace to help in *t* of need
Heb 5:12 For when for the *t* ye ought to be
Heb 9:9 a figure for the *t* then present
Heb 9:10 them until the *t* of reformation
Heb 9:28 *t* without sin unto salvation
Heb 11:32 for the *t* would fail me to tell
Jas 4:14 that appeareth for a little *t*
1Pet 1:5 to be revealed in the last *t*
1Pet 1:11 or what manner of *t* the Spirit of
1Pet 1:17 pass the *t* of your sojourning
1Pet 2:10 Which in *t* past were not a people
1Pet 3:5 in the old *t* the holy women also
1Pet 4:2 should live the rest of his *t* in
1Pet 4:3 For the *t* past of our life may
1Pet 4:17 For the *t* is come that judgment
1Pet 5:6 that he may exalt you in due *t*
2Pet 1:21 not in old *t* by the will of man
2Pet 2:3 now of a long *t* lingereth not
1Jn 2:18 Little children, it is the last *t*
1Jn 2:18 we know that it is the last *t*
1Jn 4:12 No man hath seen God at any *t*
Jude 18 should be mockers in the last *t*
Rev 1:3 for the *t* is at hand
Rev 10:6 that there should be *t* no longer
Rev 11:18 the *t* of the dead, that they
Rev 12:12 that he hath but a short *t*
Rev 12:14 for a *t*, and times, and half a *t*
Rev 14:15 for the *t* is come for thee to
Rev 22:10 for the *t* is at hand

## TIMES

Gen 27:36 he hath supplanted me these two *t*
Gen 31:7 me, and changed my wages ten *t*
Gen 31:41 thou hast changed my wages ten *t*
Gen 33:3 himself to the ground seven *t*
Gen 43:34 five *t* so much as any of theirs
Ex 23:14 Three *t* thou shalt keep a feast
Ex 23:17 Three *t* in the year all thy males
Lev 4:6 the blood seven *t* before the LORD
Lev 4:17 it seven *t* before the LORD
Lev 8:11 thereof upon the altar seven *t*
Lev 14:7 cleansed from the leprosy seven *t*
Lev 14:16 finger seven *t* before the LORD
Lev 14:27 left hand seven *t* before the LORD
Lev 14:51 and sprinkle the house seven *t*
Lev 16:2 that he come not at all *t* into
Lev 16:14 the blood with his finger seven *t*
Lev 16:19 upon it with his finger seven *t*
Lev 19:26 ye use enchantment, nor observe *t*
Lev 25:8 unto thee, seven *t* seven years
Lev 26:18 you seven *t* more for your sins
Lev 26:21 I will bring seven *t* more plagues
Lev 26:24 you yet seven *t* for your sins
Lev 26:28 you seven *t* for your sins
Num 14:22 have tempted me now these ten *t*
Num 19:4 of the congregation seven *t*
Num 22:28 hast smitten me these three *t*
Num 22:32 smitten thine ass these three *t*
Num 22:33 and turned from me these three *t*
Num 24:1 he went not, as at other *t*
Num 24:10 blessed them these three *t*
Deut 1:11 thousand *t* so many more as ye are
Deut 2:10 The Emims dwelt therein in *t* past
Deut 4:42 and hated him not in *t* past
Deut 16:16 Three *t* in a year shall all thy
Deut 18:10 divination, or an observer of *t*
Deut 18:14 hearkened unto observers of *t*
Josh 6:4 ye shall compass the city seven *t*
Josh 6:15 after the same manner seven *t*
Josh 6:15 they compassed the city seven *t*
Judg 13:25 at *t* in the camp of Dan between
Judg 16:15 thou hast mocked me these three *t*
Judg 16:20 will go out as at other *t* before
Judg 20:30 against Gibeah, as at other *t*
Judg 20:31 people, and kill, as at other *t*
1Sa 3:10 and stood, and called as at other *t*
1Sa 18:10 with his hand, as at other *t*
1Sa 19:7 was in his presence, as in *t* past
1Sa 20:25 sat upon his seat, as at other *t*
1Sa 20:41 ground, and bowed himself three *t*
2Sa 3:17 Ye sought for David in *t* past to
1Kin 8:59 of his people Israel at all *t*
1Kin 9:25 three *t* in a year did Solomon
1Kin 17:21 himself upon the child three *t*
1Kin 18:43 And he said, Go again seven *t*
1Kin 22:16 How many *t* shall I adjure thee
2Kin 4:35 and the child sneezed seven *t*
2Kin 5:10 Go and wash in Jordan seven *t*
2Kin 5:14 dipped himself seven *t* in Jordan
2Kin 13:19 have smitten five or six *t*
2Kin 13:25 Three *t* did Joash beat him, and
2Kin 19:25 of ancient *t* that I have formed
2Kin 21:6 through the fire, and observed *t*
1Chr 12:32 that had understanding of the *t*
1Chr 21:3 hundred *t* so many more as they be
1Chr 29:30 the *t* that went over him, and over
2Chr 8:13 three *t* in the year, even in the
2Chr 15:5 in those *t* there was no peace to
2Chr 18:15 How many *t* shall I adjure thee
2Chr 33:6 also he observed *t*, and used
Ezr 10:14 in our cities come at appointed *t*
Neh 4:12 came, they said unto us ten *t*
Neh 6:4 unto me four *t* after this sort
Neh 9:28 many *t* didst thou deliver them
Neh 10:34 at *t* appointed year by year, to
Neh 13:31 at *t* appointed, and for the
Est 1:13 to the wise men, which knew the *t*
Est 9:31 of Purim in their *t* appointed
Job 19:3 These ten *t* have ye reproached me
Job 24:1 seeing *t* are not hidden from the
Ps 9:9 a refuge in *t* of trouble
Ps 10:1 thou thyself in *t* of trouble
Ps 12:6 of earth, purified seven *t*
Ps 31:15 My *t* are in thy hand
Ps 34:1 I will bless the LORD at all *t*
Ps 44:1 in their days, in the *t* of old
Ps 62:8 Trust in him at all *t*
Ps 77:5 of old, the years of ancient *t*
Ps 106:3 that doeth righteousness at all *t*
Ps 106:43 Many *t* did he deliver them
Ps 119:20 hath unto thy judgments at all *t*
Ps 119:164 Seven *t* a day do I praise thee
Prov 5:19 her breasts satisfy thee at all *t*
Prov 17:17 A friend loveth at all *t*, and a
Prov 24:16 For a just man falleth seven *t*
Eccl 8:12 a sinner do evil an hundred *t*
Is 14:31 shall be alone in his appointed *t*
Is 33:6 shall be the stability of thy *t*
Is 37:26 and of ancient *t*, that I have
Is 46:10 from ancient *t* the things that
Jer 8:7 heaven knoweth her appointed *t*
Eze 12:27 of the *t* that are far off
Dan 1:20 he found them ten *t* better than
Dan 2:21 And he changeth the *t* and the
Dan 3:19 heat the furnace one seven *t* more
Dan 4:16 let seven *t* pass over him
Dan 4:23 till seven *t* pass over him
Dan 4:25 seven *t* shall pass over thee,
Dan 4:32 seven *t* shall pass over thee,
Dan 6:10 upon his knees three *t* a day
Dan 6:13 maketh his petition three *t* a day
Dan 7:10 ten thousand *t* ten thousand stood
Dan 7:25 most High, and think to change *t*
Dan 7:25 into his hand until a time and *t*
Dan 9:25 and the wall, even in troublous *t*
Dan 11:6 that strengthened her in these *t*
Dan 11:14 in those *t* there shall many stand

Dan 12:7 that it shall be for a time, *t*
Mt 16:3 ye not discern the signs of the *t*
Mt 18:21 till seven *t*
Mt 18:22 say not unto thee, Until seven *t*
Mt 18:22 but, Until seventy *t* seven
Lk 17:4 against thee seven *t* in a day
Lk 17:4 seven *t* in a day turn again to
Lk 21:24 until the *t* of the Gentiles be
Acts 1:7 you to know the *t* or the seasons
Acts 3:19 when the *t* of refreshing shall
Acts 3:21 *t* of restitution of all things
Acts 11:10 And this was done three *t*
Acts 14:16 Who in *t* past suffered all
Acts 17:26 determined the *t* before appointed
Acts 17:30 the *t* of this ignorance God
Rom 11:30 For as ye in *t* past have not
2Cor 11:24 Of the Jews five *t* received I
Gal 1:23 in *t* past now preacheth the faith
Gal 4:10 Ye observe days, and months, and *t*
Eph 1:10 dispensation of the fulness of *t*
Eph 2:3 *t* past in the lusts of our flesh
1Th 5:1 But of the *t* and the seasons,
1Ti 4:1 that in the latter *t* some shall
1Ti 6:15 Which in his *t* he shall shew, who
2Ti 3:1 last days perilous *t* shall come
Titus 1:3 But hath in due *t* manifested his
Heb 1:1 God, who at sundry *t* and in divers
Heb 1:13 of the angels said he at any *t*
1Pet 1:20 manifest in these last *t* for you
Rev 5:11 was ten thousand *t* ten thousand
Rev 12:14 she is nourished for a time, and *t*

**TIMNA** *(tim'-nah)* See TIMNATH.
*1. Concubine of Eliphaz.*
Gen 36:12 *T* was concubine to Eliphaz Esau's
*2. Daughter of Seir.*
Gen 36:22 and Lotan's sister was *T*
1Chr 1:39 and *T* was Lotan's sister
*3. A son of Eliphaz.*
1Chr 1:36 Zephi, and Gatam, Kenaz, and *T*

**TIMNAH** *(tim'-nah)* See TIMNA, TIMNATH.
*1. A chief of Edom.*
Gen 36:40 duke *T*, duke Alvah, duke Jetheth,
1Chr 1:51 duke *T*, duke Aliah, duke Jetheth,
*2. A city in Judah.*
Josh 15:57 Cain, Gibeah, and *T*
*3. A city in Dan.*
Josh 15:10 Beth-shemesh, and passed on to *T*
2Chr 28:18 *T* with the villages thereof,

**TIMNATH** *(tim'-nath)* See THIMNATHAH, TIMNAH.
*1. Same as Timnah 2.*
Gen 38:12 up unto his sheepshearers to *T*
Gen 38:13 goeth up to *T* to shear his sheep
Gen 38:14 place, which is by the way to *T*
*2. Same as Timnah 3.*
Judg 14:1 And Samson went down to *T*, and saw
Judg 14:1 saw a woman in *T* of the daughters
Judg 14:2 I have seen a woman in *T* of the
Judg 14:5 and his father and his mother, to *T*
Judg 14:5 and came to the vineyards of *T*

**TIMNATH-HERES** *(tim'-nath-he'-rez)* See TIMNATH-SERAH. *Land near Mount Ephraim.*
Judg 2:9 border of his inheritance in *T*

**TIMNATH-SERAH** *(tim'-nath-se'-rah)* See TIMNATH-HERES. *Same as Timnath-heres.*
Josh 19:50 he asked, even *T* in mount Ephraim
Josh 24:30 border of his inheritance in *T*

**TIMNITE** *(tim'-nite) An inhabitant of Timnath.*
Judg 15:6 Samson, the son in law of the *T*

**TIMON** *(ti'-mon) A leader in the Jerusalem church.*
Acts 6:5 and Prochorus, and Nicanor, and *T*

**TIMOTHEOUS**
1Cor *s* and Fortunatus, and Achaicus, and *T*

**TIMOTHEUS** *(tim-o'-the-us)* See TIMOTHY. *Same as Timothy.*
Acts 16:1 disciple was there, named *T*
Acts 17:14 but Silas and *T* abode there still
Acts 17:15 *T* for to come to him with all
Acts 18:5 *T* were come from Macedonia, Paul
Acts 19:22 them that ministered unto him, *T*
Acts 20:4 and Gaius of Derbe, and *T*
Rom 16:21 *T* my workfellow, and Lucius, and
1Cor 4:17 this cause have I sent unto you *T*
1Cor 16:10 Now if *T* come, see that he may be
2Cor 1:19 us, even by me and Silvanus and *T*
Phil 1:1 Paul and *T*, the servants of Jesus
Phil 2:19 Jesus to send *T* shortly unto you
Col 1:1 will of God, and *T* our brother,
1Th 1:1 Paul, and Silvanus, and *T*, unto the
1Th 3:2 And sent *T*, our brother, and
1Th 3:6 But now when *T* came from you unto
2Th 1:1 Paul, and Silvanus, and *T*, unto the
2Ti *s* The second epistle unto *T*

**TIMOTHY** *(tim'-o-thy)* See TIMOTHEUS. *A co-worker with Paul.*
2Cor 1:1 *T* our brother, unto the church of
1Ti 1:2 Unto *T*, my own son in the faith
1Ti 1:18 charge I commit unto thee, son *T*
1Ti 6:20 O *T*, keep that which is committed
1Ti *s* The first to *T* was written from
2Ti 1:2 To *T*, my dearly beloved son
Philem 1 *T* our brother, unto Philemon our
Heb 13:23 our brother *T* is set at liberty
Heb *s* to the Hebrews from Italy by *T*

**TIN**
Num 31:22 the brass, the iron, the *t*
Is 1:25 thy dross, and take away all thy *t*
Eze 22:18 all they are brass, and *t*, and iron
Eze 22:20 and brass, and iron, and lead, and *t*
Eze 27:12 with silver, iron, *t*, and lead,

**TINGLE**
1Sa 3:11 every one that heareth it shall *t*
2Kin 21:12 of it, both his ears shall *t*
Jer 19:3 heareth, his ears shall *t*

**TINKLING**
Is 3:16 making a *t* with their feet
Is 3:18 *t* ornaments about their feet
1Cor 13:1 as sounding brass, or a *t* cymbal

**TIP**
Ex 29:20 put it upon the *t* of the right
Ex 29:20 upon the *t* of the right ear of
Lev 8:23 put it upon the *t* of Aaron's
Lev 8:24 upon the *t* of their right ear
Lev 14:14 priest shall put it upon the *t* of
Lev 14:17 shall the priest put upon the *t*
Lev 14:25 put it upon the *t* of the right
Lev 14:28 that is in his hand upon the *t* of
Lk 16:24 that he may dip the *t* of his

**TIPHSAH** *(tif'-sah)*
*1. A city on the Euphrates River.*
1Kin 4:24 from *T* even to Azzah, over all
*2. A city in Judah.*
2Kin 15:16 Then Menahem smote *T*, and all that

**TIRAS** *(Ti'-ras) A son of Japheth.*
Gen 10:2 Javan, and Tubal, and Meshech, and *T*
1Chr 1:5 Javan, and Tubal, and Meshech, and *T*

**TIRATHITES** *(ti'-rath-ites) A family of scribes.*
1Chr 2:55 the *T*, the Shimeathites, and

**TIRE**
Eze 24:17 bind the *t* of thine head upon

**TIRED**
2Kin 9:30 *t* her head, and looked out at a

**TIRES**
Is 3:18 their round *t* like the moon,
Eze 24:23 your *t* shall be upon your heads,

**TIRHAKAH** *(tur-ha'-kah) A king of Ethiopia.*
2Kin 19:9 heard say of *T* king of Ethiopia
Is 37:9 say concerning *T* king of Ethiopia

**TIRHANAH** *(tur-ha'-nah) A son of Caleb.*
1Chr 2:48 concubine, bare Sheber, and *T*

**TIRIA** *(tir'-e-ah) A descendant of Judah.*
1Chr 4:16 Ziph, and Ziphah, *T*, and Asareel

**TIRSHATHA** *(tur'-sha-thah) Persian governors of Judah.*
Ezr 2:63 the *T* said unto them, that they
Neh 7:65 the *T* said unto them, that they
Neh 7:70 The *T* gave to the treasure a
Neh 8:9 And Nehemiah, which is the *T*
Neh 10:1 that sealed were, Nehemiah, the *T*

**TIRZAH** *(tur'-zah)*
*1. A daughter of Zelophehad.*
Num 26:33 and Noah, Hoglah, Milcah, and *T*
Num 27:1 Noah, and Hoglah, and Milcah, and *T*
Num 36:11 For Mahlah, *T*, and Hoglah, and
Josh 17:3 and Noah, Hoglah, Milcah, and *T*
*2. A city in Ephraim.*
Josh 12:24 The king of *T*, one
1Kin 14:17 arose, and departed, and came to *T*
1Kin 15:21 building of Ramah, and dwelt in *T*
1Kin 15:33 to reign over all Israel in *T*
1Kin 16:6 his fathers, and was buried in *T*
1Kin 16:8 Baasha to reign over Israel in *T*
1Kin 16:9 against him, as he was in *T*
1Kin 16:9 of Arza steward of his house in *T*
1Kin 16:15 did Zimri reign seven days in *T*
1Kin 16:17 with him, and they besieged *T*
1Kin 16:23 six years reigned he in *T*
2Kin 15:14 the son of Gadi went up from *T*
2Kin 15:16 and the coasts thereof from *T*
Song 6:4 art beautiful, O my love, as *T*

**TISHBITE** *(tish'-bite) An inhabitant of Tishbeh.*
1Kin 17:1 And Elijah the *T*, who was of the
1Kin 21:17 of the LORD came to Elijah the *T*
1Kin 21:28 of the LORD came to Elijah the *T*
2Kin 1:3 of the LORD said to Elijah the *T*
2Kin 1:8 And he said, It is Elijah the *T*
2Kin 9:36 spake by his servant Elijah the *T*

**TITHE**
Lev 27:30 all the *t* of the land, whether of
Lev 27:32 And concerning the *t* of the herd
Num 18:26 LORD, even a tenth part of the *t*
Deut 12:17 thy gates the *t* of thy corn
Deut 14:22 Thou shalt truly *t* all the
Deut 14:23 the *t* of thy corn, of thy wine,
Deut 14:28 thou shalt bring forth all the *t*
2Chr 31:5 the *t* of all things brought they
2Chr 31:6 also brought in the *t* of oxen
2Chr 31:6 the *t* of holy things which were
Neh 10:38 the Levites shall bring up the *t*
Neh 13:12 all Judah the *t* of the corn
Mt 23:23 for ye pay *t* of mint and anise and
Lk 11:42 for ye *t* mint and rue and all

**TITHES**
Gen 14:20 And he gave him *t* of all
Lev 27:31 will at all redeem ought of his *t*
Num 18:24 But the *t* of the children of
Num 18:26 the *t* which I have given you from
Num 18:28 unto the LORD of all your *t*
Deut 12:6 and your sacrifices, and your *t*
Deut 12:11 and your sacrifices, your *t*
Deut 26:12 the *t* of thine increase the third
2Chr 31:12 brought in the offerings and the *t*
Neh 10:37 the *t* of our ground unto the
Neh 10:37 the *t* in all the cities of our
Neh 10:38 Levites, when the Levites take *t*
Neh 10:38 the *t* unto the house of our God
Neh 12:44 for the firstfruits, and for the *t*
Neh 13:5 the *t* of the corn, the new wine,
Amos 4:4 and your *t* after three years
Mal 3:8 In *t* and offerings
Mal 3:10 Bring ye all the *t* into the
Lk 18:12 I give *t* of all that I possess
Heb 7:5 have a commandment to take *t* of
Heb 7:6 from them received *t* of Abraham
Heb 7:8 And here men that die receive *t*
Heb 7:9 say, Levi also, who receiveth *t*
Heb 7:9 payed *t* in Abraham

**TITHING**
Deut 26:12 end of *t* all the tithes of thine
Deut 26:12 year, which is the year of *t*

**TITLE**
2Kin 23:17 What *t* is that that I see
Jn 19:19 And Pilate wrote a *t*, and put it on
Jn 19:20 This *t* then read many of the Jews

**TITLES**
Job 32:21 let me give flattering *t* unto man
Job 32:22 I know not to give flattering *t*

**TITTLE**
Mt 5:18 one jot or one *t* shall in no wise
Lk 16:17 than one *t* of the law to fail

**TITUS** *(ti'-tus) A co-worker with Paul.*
2Cor 2:13 because I found not *T* my brother
2Cor 7:6 comforted us by the coming of *T*
2Cor 7:13 more joyed we for the joy of *T*
2Cor 7:14 boasting, which I made before *T*
2Cor 8:6 Insomuch that we desired *T*
2Cor 8:16 care into the heart of *T* for you
2Cor 8:23 Whether any do enquire of *T*
2Cor 12:18 I desired *T*, and with him I sent a
2Cor 12:18 Did *T* make a gain of you
2Cor *s* a city of Macedonia, by *T*

Gal 2:1 Barnabas, and took *T* with me also
Gal 2:3 But neither *T*, who was with me,
2Ti 4:10 to Galatia, *T* unto Dalmatia
Titus 1:4 To *T*, mine own son after the
Titus *s* It was written to *T*, ordained the

**TIZITE** *(ti'-zite) Family name of Joha.*
1Chr 11:45 and Joha his brother, the *T*

**TOAH** *(to'-ah)* See NAHATH, TOHU. *An ancestor of Samuel.*
1Chr 6:34 the son of Eliel, the son of *T*

**TOB** *(tob) A district in Syria.*
Judg 11:3 and dwelt in the land of *T*
Judg 11:5 Jephthah out of the land of *T*

**TOB-ADONIJAH** *(tob'-ad-o-ni-jah) A Levite messenger of King Jehoshaphat.*
2Chr 17:8 and Adonijah, and Tobijah, and *T*

**TOBIAH** *(to-bi'-ah)* See TOBIJAH.
*1. A family of exiles.*
Ezr 2:60 of Delaiah, the children of *T*
Neh 7:62 of Delaiah, the children of *T*
*2. An Ammonite who opposed Nehemiah.*
Neh 2:10 *T* the servant, the Ammonite,
Neh 2:19 *T* the servant, the Ammonite, and
Neh 4:3 Now *T* the Ammonite was by him, and
Neh 4:7 pass, that when Sanballat, and *T*
Neh 6:1 to pass, when Sanballat, and *T*
Neh 6:12 for *T* and Sanballat had hired him
Neh 6:14 My God, think thou upon *T*
Neh 6:17 of Judah sent many letters unto *T*
Neh 6:17 the letters of *T* came unto them
Neh 6:19 *T* sent letters to put me in fear
Neh 13:4 of our God, was allied unto *T*
Neh 13:7 the evil that Eliashib did for *T*
Neh 13:8 stuff of *T* out of the chamber

**TOBIJAH** *(to-bi'-jah)* See TOBIAH.
*1. A Levite messenger of King Jehoshaphat.*
2Chr 17:8 and Jehonathan, and Adonijah, and *T*
*2. A clan leader of exiles.*
Zec 6:10 captivity, even of Heldai, of *T*
Zec 6:14 crowns shall be to Helem, and to *T*

**TOCHEN** *(to'-ken) A city in Simeon.*
1Chr 4:32 were, Etam, and Ain, Rimmon, and *T*

**TODAY**
2Sa 6:20 glorious was the king of Israel *t*
2Sa 14:22 *T* thy servant knoweth that I have
2Sa 16:3 *T* shall the house of Israel

**TOE**
Ex 29:20 upon the great *t* of their right
Lev 8:23 upon the great *t* of his right
Lev 14:14 upon the great *t* of his right
Lev 14:17 upon the great *t* of his right
Lev 14:25 upon the great *t* of his right
Lev 14:28 upon the great *t* of his right

**TOES**
Lev 8:24 upon the great *t* of their right
Judg 1:6 cut off his thumbs and his great *t*
Judg 1:7 thumbs and their great *t* cut off
2Sa 21:20 fingers, and on every foot six *t*
1Chr 20:6 *t* were four and twenty, six on
Dan 2:41 whereas thou sawest the feet and *t*
Dan 2:42 as the *t* of the feet were part of

**TOGARMAH** *(to-gar'-mah) A son of Gomer.*
Gen 10:3 Ashkenaz, and Riphath, and *T*
1Chr 1:6 Ashchenaz, and Riphath, and *T*
Eze 27:14 They of the house of *T* traded in
Eze 38:6 the house of *T* of the north

**TOHU** *(to'-hu)* See NAHATH, TOAH. *An ancestor of Samuel.*
1Sa 1:1 the son of Elihu, the son of *T*

**TOI** *(to'-i)* See TOU. *King of Hamath.*
2Sa 8:9 When *T* king of Hamath heard that
2Sa 8:10 Then *T* sent Joram his son unto
2Sa 8:10 for Hadadezer had wars with *T*

**TOIL**
Gen 5:29 *t* of our hands, because of the
Gen 41:51 he, hath made me forget all my *t*
Mt 6:28 they *t* not, neither do they spin
Lk 12:27 they *t* not, they spin not

**TOILED**
Lk 5:5 we have *t* all the night, and have

**TOILING**
Mk 6:48 And he saw them *t* in rowing

**TOKEN**
Gen 9:12 This is the *t* of the covenant
Gen 9:13 it shall be for a *t* of a covenant
Gen 9:17 This is the *t* of the covenant,
Gen 17:11 it shall be a *t* of the covenant
Ex 3:12 and this shall be a *t* unto thee
Ex 12:13 a *t* upon the houses where ye are
Ex 13:16 shall be for a *t* upon thine hand
Num 17:10 to be kept for a *t* against the
Josh 2:12 house, and give me a true *t*
Ps 86:17 Shew me a *t* for good
Mk 14:44 betrayed him had given them a *t*
Phil 1:28 to them an evident *t* of perdition
2Th 1:5 Which is a manifest *t* of the
2Th 3:17 which is the *t* in every epistle

**TOKENS**
Deut 22:15 bring forth the *t* of the damsel's
Deut 22:17 yet these are the *t* of my
Deut 22:20 the *t* of virginity be not found
Job 21:29 and do ye not know their *t*
Ps 65:8 parts are afraid at thy *t*
Ps 135:9 Who sent *t* and wonders into the
Is 44:25 frustrateth the *t* of the liars

**TOLA** *(to'-lah)* See TOLAITES.
*1. A son of Issachar.*
Gen 46:13 *T*, and Phuvah, and Job, and Shimron
Num 26:23 of *T*, the family of the Tolaites
1Chr 7:1 Now the sons of Issachar were, *T*
1Chr 7:2 And the sons of *T*
1Chr 7:2 father's house, to wit, of *T*
*2. A judge of Israel.*
Judg 10:1 defend Israel *T* the son of Puah

**TOLAD** *(to'-lad)* See EL-TOLAD. *A city in Simeon.*
1Chr 4:29 And at Bilhah, and at Ezem, and at *T*

**TOLAITES** *(to'-lah-ites) Descendants of Tola.*
Num 26:23 of Tola, the family of the *T*

**TOLERABLE**
Mt 10:15 It shall be more *t* for the land
Mt 11:22 you, It shall be more *t* for Tyre
Mt 11:24 That it shall be more *t* for the
Mk 6:11 you, It shall be more *t* for Sodom
Lk 10:12 be more *t* in that day for Sodom
Lk 10:14 But it shall be more *t* for Tyre

**TOLL**
Ezr 4:13 again, then will they not pay *t*
Ezr 4:20 and *t*, tribute, and custom, was
Ezr 7:24 shall not be lawful to impose *t*

**TOMB**
Job 21:32 grave, and shall remain in the *t*
Mt 27:60 And laid it in his own new *t*
Mk 6:29 up his corpse, and laid it in a *t*

**TOMBS**
Mt 8:28 with devils, coming out of the *t*
Mt 23:29 ye build the *t* of the prophets
Mk 5:2 there met him out of the *t* a man
Mk 5:3 Who had his dwelling among the *t*
Mk 5:5 was in the mountains, and in the *t*
Lk 8:27 abode in any house, but in the *t*

**TONGS**
Ex 25:38 the *t* thereof, and the snuffdishes
Num 4:9 the light, and his lamps, and his *t*
1Kin 7:49 and the lamps, and the *t* of gold,
2Chr 4:21 flowers, and the lamps, and the *t*
Is 6:6 with the *t* from off the altar
Is 44:12 The smith with the *t* both worketh

**TONGUE**
Gen 10:5 every one after his *t*, after
Ex 4:10 am slow of speech, and of a slow *t*
Ex 11:7 Israel shall not a dog move his *t*
Deut 28:49 a nation whose *t* thou shalt not
Josh 10:21 none moved his *t* against any of
Judg 7:5 lappeth of the water with his *t*
2Sa 23:2 by me, and his word was in my *t*
Ezr 4:7 was written in the Syrian *t*
Ezr 4:7 and interpreted in the Syrian *t*
Est 7:4 and bondwomen, I had held my *t*
Job 5:21 be hid from the scourge of the *t*
Job 6:24 Teach me, and I will hold my *t*
Job 6:30 Is there iniquity in my *t*
Job 13:19 for now, if I hold my *t*, I shall
Job 15:5 thou choosest the *t* of the crafty
Job 20:12 though he hide it under his *t*
Job 20:16 the viper's *t* shall slay him
Job 27:4 wickedness, nor my *t* utter deceit
Job 29:10 their *t* cleaved to the roof of
Job 33:2 my *t* hath spoken in my mouth
Job 41:1 or his *t* with a cord which thou
Ps 5:9 they flatter with their *t*
Ps 10:7 under his *t* is mischief and vanity
Ps 12:3 the *t* that speaketh proud things
Ps 12:4 With our *t* will we prevail
Ps 15:3 He that backbiteth not with his *t*
Ps 22:15 and my *t* cleaveth to my jaws
Ps 34:13 Keep thy *t* from evil, and thy lips
Ps 35:28 And my *t* shall speak of thy
Ps 37:30 his *t* talketh of judgment
Ps 39:1 my ways, that I sin not with my *t*
Ps 39:3 then spake I with my *t*,
Ps 45:1 my *t* is the pen of a ready writer
Ps 50:19 to evil, and thy *t* frameth deceit
Ps 51:14 my *t* shall sing aloud of thy
Ps 52:2 Thy *t* deviseth mischiefs
Ps 52:4 words, O thou deceitful *t*
Ps 57:4 arrows, and their *t* a sharp sword
Ps 64:3 Who whet their *t* like a sword
Ps 64:8 own *t* to fall upon themselves
Ps 66:17 and he was extolled with my *t*
Ps 68:23 the *t* of thy dogs in the same
Ps 71:24 My *t* also shall talk of thy
Ps 73:9 their *t* walketh through the earth
Ps 109:2 spoken against me with a lying *t*
Ps 119:172 My *t* shall speak of thy word
Ps 120:2 lying lips, and from a deceitful *t*
Ps 120:3 be done unto thee, thou false *t*
Ps 126:2 laughter, and our *t* with singing
Ps 137:6 let my *t* cleave to the roof of my
Ps 139:4 For there is not a word in my *t*
Prov 6:17 A proud look, a lying *t*, and hands
Prov 6:24 of the *t* of a strange woman
Prov 10:20 The *t* of the just is as choice
Prov 10:31 but the froward *t* shall be cut
Prov 12:18 but the *t* of the wise is health
Prov 12:19 but a lying *t* is but for a moment
Prov 15:2 The *t* of the wise useth knowledge
Prov 15:4 A wholesome *t* is a tree of life
Prov 16:1 in man, and the answer of the *t*
Prov 17:4 a liar giveth ear to a naughty *t*
Prov 17:20 perverse *t* falleth into mischief
Prov 18:21 and life are in the power of the *t*
Prov 21:6 a lying *t* is a vanity tossed to
Prov 21:23 his *t* keepeth his soul from
Prov 25:15 a soft *t* breaketh the bone
Prov 25:23 angry countenance a backbiting *t*
Prov 26:28 A lying *t* hateth those that are
Prov 28:23 he that flattereth with the *t*
Prov 31:26 in her *t* is the law of kindness
Song 4:11 honey and milk are under thy *t*
Is 3:8 because their *t* and their doings
Is 11:15 destroy the *t* of the Egyptian sea
Is 28:11 another *t* will he speak to this
Is 30:27 his *t* as a devouring fire
Is 32:4 the *t* of the stammerers shall be
Is 33:19 of a stammering *t*, that thou
Is 35:6 hart, and the *t* of the dumb sing
Is 41:17 their *t* faileth for thirst, I the
Is 45:23 shall bow, every *t* shall swear
Is 50:4 given me the *t* of the learned
Is 54:17 every *t* that shall rise against
Is 57:4 a wide mouth, and draw out the *t*
Is 59:3 your *t* hath muttered perverseness
Jer 9:5 have taught their *t* to speak lies
Jer 9:8 Their *t* is as an arrow shot out
Jer 18:18 and let us smite him with the *t*
Lam 4:4 The *t* of the sucking child
Eze 3:26 I will make thy *t* cleave to the
Dan 1:4 and the *t* of the Chaldeans
Hos 7:16 the sword for the rage of their *t*
Amos 6:10 Then shall he say, Hold thy *t*
Mic 6:12 their *t* is deceitful in their
Hab 1:13 holdest thy *t* when the wicked
Zeph 3:13 *t* be found in their mouth
Zec 14:12 their *t* shall consume away in
Mk 7:33 and he spit, and touched his *t*
Mk 7:35 and the string of his *t* was loosed
Lk 1:64 his *t* loosed, and he spake, and
Lk 16:24 his finger in water, and cool my *t*
Jn 5:2 called in the Hebrew *t* Bethesda
Acts 1:19 field is called in their proper *t*
Acts 2:8 hear we every man in our own *t*
Acts 2:26 heart rejoice, and my *t* was glad
Acts 21:40 spake unto them in the Hebrew *t*
Acts 22:2 he spake in the Hebrew *t* to them
Acts 26:14 me, and saying in the Hebrew *t*
Rom 14:11 every *t* shall confess to God

1Cor 14:2 unknown *t* speaketh not unto men
1Cor 14:4 in an unknown *t* edifieth himself
1Cor 14:9 except ye utter by the *t* words
1Cor 14:13 *t* pray that he may interpret
1Cor 14:14 For if I pray in an unknown *t*
1Cor 14:19 thousand words in an unknown *t*
1Cor 14:26 psalm, hath a doctrine, hath a *t*
1Cor 14:27 If any man speak in an unknown *t*
Phil 2:11 that every *t* should confess that
Jas 1:26 religious, and bridleth not his *t*
Jas 3:5 Even so the *t* is a little member,
Jas 3:6 the *t* is a fire, a world of
Jas 3:6 so is the *t* among our members,
Jas 3:8 But the *t* can no man tame
1Pet 3:10 let him refrain his *t* from evil
1Jn 3:18 us not love in word, neither in *t*
Rev 5:9 blood out of every kindred, and *t*
Rev 9:11 name in the Hebrew *t* is Abaddon
Rev 9:11 but in the Greek *t* hath his name
Rev 14:6 to every nation, and kindred, and *t*
Rev 16:16 called in the Hebrew *t* Armageddon

**TONGUES**
Gen 10:20 their families, after their *t*
Gen 10:31 their families, after their *t*
Ps 31:20 a pavilion from the strife of *t*
Ps 55:9 O Lord, and divide their *t*
Ps 78:36 they lied unto him with their *t*
Ps 140:3 sharpened their *t* like a serpent
Is 66:18 I will gather all nations and *t*
Jer 9:3 they bend their *t* like their bow
Jer 23:31 saith the LORD, that use their *t*
Mk 16:17 they shall speak with new *t*
Acts 2:3 them cloven *t* like as of fire
Acts 2:4 and began to speak with other *t*
Acts 2:11 our *t* the wonderful works of God
Acts 10:46 For they heard them speak with *t*
Acts 19:6 and they spake with *t*, and
Rom 3:13 with their *t* they have used
1Cor 12:10 to another divers kinds of *t*
1Cor 12:10 another the interpretation of *t*
1Cor 12:28 governments, diversities of *t*
1Cor 12:30 do all speak with *t*
1Cor 13:1 Though I speak with the *t* of men
1Cor 13:8 whether there be *t*, they shall
1Cor 14:5 I would that ye all spake with *t*
1Cor 14:5 than he that speaketh with *t*
1Cor 14:6 I come unto you speaking with *t*
1Cor 14:18 I speak with *t* more than ye all
1Cor 14:21 is written, With men of other *t*
1Cor 14:22 Wherefore *t* are for a sign, not
1Cor 14:23 one place, and all speak with *t*
1Cor 14:39 and forbid not to speak with *t*
Rev 7:9 and kindreds, and people, and *t*
Rev 10:11 many peoples, and nations, and *t*
Rev 11:9 of the people and kindreds and *t*
Rev 13:7 given him over all kindreds, and *t*
Rev 16:10 and they gnawed their *t* for pain
Rev 17:15 and multitudes, and nations, and *t*

**TOOK**
Gen 2:15 And the LORD God *t* the man
Gen 2:21 he *t* one of his ribs, and closed
Gen 3:6 she *t* of the fruit thereof, and
Gen 4:19 Lamech *t* unto him two wives
Gen 5:24 for God *t* him
Gen 6:2 they *t* them wives of all which
Gen 8:9 *t* her, and pulled her in unto him
Gen 8:20 *t* of every clean beast, and of
Gen 9:23 Japheth *t* a garment, and laid it
Gen 11:29 And Abram and Nahor *t* them wives
Gen 11:31 Terah *t* Abram his son, and Lot the
Gen 12:5 Abram *t* Sarai his wife, and Lot
Gen 14:11 they *t* all the goods of Sodom and
Gen 14:12 And they *t* Lot, Abram's brother's
Gen 15:10 he *t* unto him all these, and
Gen 16:3 Sarai Abram's wife *t* Hagar her
Gen 17:23 Abraham *t* Ishmael his son, and all
Gen 18:8 he *t* butter, and milk, and the calf
Gen 20:2 king of Gerar sent, and *t* Sarah
Gen 20:14 And Abimelech *t* sheep, and oxen, and
Gen 21:14 *t* bread, and a bottle of water, and
Gen 21:21 his mother *t* him a wife out of
Gen 21:27 And Abraham *t* sheep and oxen, and
Gen 22:3 *t* two of his young men with him,
Gen 22:6 Abraham *t* the wood of the burnt
Gen 22:6 he *t* the fire in his hand, and a
Gen 22:10 *t* the knife to slay his son
Gen 22:13 *t* the ram, and offered him up for
Gen 24:7 which *t* me from my father's house
Gen 24:10 the servant *t* ten camels of the
Gen 24:22 that the man *t* a golden earring
Gen 24:61 and the servant *t* Rebekah, and went
Gen 24:65 therefore she *t* a vail, and
Gen 24:67 *t* Rebekah, and she became his wife
Gen 25:1 Then again Abraham *t* a wife
Gen 25:20 old when he *t* Rebekah to wife
Gen 25:26 his hand *t* hold on Esau's heel
Gen 26:34 was forty years old when he *t* to
Gen 27:15 Rebekah *t* goodly raiment of her
Gen 27:36 he *t* away my birthright
Gen 28:9 *t* unto the wives which he had
Gen 28:11 he *t* of the stones of that place,
Gen 28:18 *t* the stone that he had put for
Gen 29:23 that he *t* Leah his daughter, and
Gen 30:9 she *t* Zilpah her maid, and gave
Gen 30:37 Jacob *t* him rods of green poplar,
Gen 31:23 he *t* his brethren with him, and
Gen 31:45 Jacob *t* a stone, and set it up for
Gen 31:46 they *t* stones, and made an heap
Gen 32:13 *t* of that which came to his hand
Gen 32:22 *t* his two wives, and his two
Gen 32:23 he *t* them, and sent them over the
Gen 33:11 And he urged him, and he *t* it
Gen 34:2 he *t* her, and lay with her, and
Gen 34:25 *t* each man his sword, and came
Gen 34:26 *t* Dinah out of Shechem's house,
Gen 34:28 They *t* their sheep, and their oxen
Gen 34:29 their wives *t* they captive, and
Gen 36:2 Esau *t* his wives of the daughters
Gen 36:6 Esau *t* his wives, and his sons, and
Gen 37:24 And they *t* him, and cast him into a
Gen 37:31 they *t* Joseph's coat, and killed a
Gen 38:2 he *t* her, and went in unto her
Gen 38:6 Judah *t* a wife for Er his
Gen 38:28 and the midwife *t* and bound upon
Gen 39:20 And Joseph's master *t* him, and put
Gen 40:11 I *t* the grapes, and pressed them
Gen 41:42 Pharaoh *t* off his ring from his
Gen 42:24 *t* from them Simeon, and bound him
Gen 42:30 *t* us for spies of the country
Gen 43:15 the men *t* that present, and they
Gen 43:15 they *t* double money in their hand
Gen 43:34 And he *t* and sent messes unto them
Gen 44:11 Then they speedily *t* down every
Gen 46:1 Israel *t* his journey with all
Gen 46:6 they *t* their cattle, and their
Gen 47:2 he *t* some of his brethren, even
Gen 48:1 he *t* with him his two sons,
Gen 48:13 Joseph *t* them both, Ephraim in
Gen 48:22 which I *t* out of the hand of the
Gen 50:25 Joseph *t* an oath of the children
Ex 2:1 *t* to wife a daughter of Levi
Ex 2:3 she *t* for him an ark of bulrushes
Ex 2:9 And the woman *t* the child, and
Ex 4:6 and when he *t* it out, behold, his
Ex 4:20 Moses *t* his wife and his sons, and
Ex 4:20 Moses *t* the rod of God in his
Ex 4:25 Then Zipporah *t* a sharp stone
Ex 6:20 Amram *t* him Jochebed his father's
Ex 6:23 Aaron *t* him Elisheba, daughter of
Ex 6:25 Eleazar Aaron's son *t* him one of
Ex 9:10 they *t* ashes of the furnace, and
Ex 10:19 which *t* away the locusts, and cast
Ex 12:34 the people *t* their dough before
Ex 13:19 Moses *t* the bones of Joseph with
Ex 13:20 they *t* their journey from Succoth
Ex 13:22 He *t* not away the pillar of the
Ex 14:6 chariot, and *t* his people with him
Ex 14:7 he *t* six hundred chosen chariots,
Ex 14:25 *t* off their chariot wheels, that
Ex 15:20 of Aaron, *t* a timbrel in her hand
Ex 16:1 they *t* their journey from Elim,
Ex 17:12 they *t* a stone, and put it under
Ex 18:2 *t* Zipporah, Moses' wife, after he
Ex 18:12 *t* a burnt offering and sacrifices
Ex 24:6 Moses *t* half of the blood, and put
Ex 24:7 he *t* the book of the covenant, and
Ex 24:8 Moses *t* the blood, and sprinkled
Ex 32:20 he *t* the calf which they had made
Ex 33:7 Moses *t* the tabernacle, and
Ex 34:4 *t* in his hand the two tables of
Ex 34:34 he *t* the vail off, until he came
Ex 40:20 And he *t* and put the testimony into
Lev 6:4 that which he *t* violently away
Lev 8:10 Moses *t* the anointing oil, and
Lev 8:15 Moses *t* the blood, and put it upon
Lev 8:16 he *t* all the fat that was upon
Lev 8:23 Moses *t* of the blood of it, and
Lev 8:25 he *t* the fat, and the rump, and all
Lev 8:26 he *t* one unleavened cake, and a
Lev 8:28 Moses *t* them from off their hands
Lev 8:29 Moses *t* the breast, and waved it
Lev 8:30 Moses *t* of the anointing oil, and
Lev 9:15 *t* the goat, which was the sin
Lev 9:17 *t* an handful thereof, and burnt it
Lev 10:1 *t* either of them his censer, and
Num 1:17 Aaron *t* these men which are
Num 3:49 Moses *t* the redemption money of
Num 3:50 children of Israel *t* he the money
Num 7:6 Moses *t* the wagons and the oxen,
Num 10:12 the children of Israel *t* their
Num 10:13 they first *t* their journey
Num 11:25 *t* of the spirit that was upon him
Num 16:1 of Peleth, sons of Reuben, *t* men
Num 16:18 they *t* every man his censer, and
Num 16:39 the priest *t* the brasen censers
Num 16:47 Aaron *t* as Moses commanded, and
Num 17:9 looked, and *t* every man his rod
Num 20:9 Moses *t* the rod from before the
Num 21:1 and *t* some of them prisoners
Num 21:25 Israel *t* all these cities
Num 21:32 they *t* the villages thereof, and
Num 22:41 the morrow, that Balak *t* Balaam
Num 23:7 he *t* up his parable, and said,
Num 23:11 I *t* thee to curse mine enemies,
Num 23:18 he *t* up his parable, and said,
Num 24:3 he *t* up his parable, and said,
Num 24:15 he *t* up his parable, and said,
Num 24:20 he *t* up his parable, and said,
Num 24:21 *t* up his parable, and said, Strong
Num 24:23 he *t* up his parable, and said,
Num 25:7 and *t* a javelin in his hand
Num 27:22 he *t* Joshua, and set him before
Num 31:9 the children of Israel *t* all the
Num 31:9 *t* the spoil of all their cattle,
Num 31:11 they *t* all the spoil, and all the
Num 31:27 them that *t* the war upon them
Num 31:47 Moses *t* one portion of fifty,
Num 31:51 the priest *t* the gold of them
Num 31:54 Eleazar the priest *t* the gold of
Num 32:39 *t* it, and dispossessed the Amorite
Num 32:41 *t* the small towns thereof, and
Num 32:42 *t* Kenath, and the villages thereof
Num 33:12 they *t* their journey out of the
Deut 1:15 So I *t* the chief of your tribes,
Deut 1:23 I *t* twelve men of you, one of a
Deut 1:25 they *t* of the fruit of the land
Deut 2:1 *t* our journey into the wilderness
Deut 2:34 we *t* all his cities at that time,
Deut 2:35 Only the cattle we *t* for a prey
Deut 2:35 spoil of the cities which we *t*
Deut 3:4 we *t* all his cities at that time,
Deut 3:4 a city which we *t* not from them
Deut 3:7 we *t* for a prey to ourselves
Deut 3:8 we *t* at that time out of the hand
Deut 3:14 Jair the son of Manasseh *t* all
Deut 9:17 I *t* the two tables, and cast them
Deut 9:21 I *t* your sin, the calf which ye
Deut 10:6 the children of Israel *t* their
Deut 22:14 I *t* this woman, and when I came to
Deut 24:3 which *t* her to be his wife
Deut 29:8 we *t* their land, and gave it for
Josh 2:4 the woman *t* the two men, and hid
Josh 3:6 they *t* up the ark of the covenant
Josh 4:8 *t* up twelve stones out of the
Josh 4:20 which they *t* out of Jordan, did
Josh 6:12 the priests *t* up the ark of the
Josh 6:20 before him, and they *t* the city
Josh 7:1 of Judah, *t* of the accursed thing
Josh 7:17 he *t* the family of the Zarhites
Josh 7:21 then I coveted them, and *t* them
Josh 7:23 they *t* them out of the midst of
Josh 7:24 *t* Achan the son of Zerah, and the
Josh 8:12 he *t* about five thousand men, and
Josh 8:19 *t* it, and hasted and set the city
Josh 8:23 And the king of Ai they *t* alive
Josh 8:27 *t* for a prey unto themselves
Josh 9:4 *t* old sacks upon their asses, and
Josh 9:12 This our bread we *t* hot for our
Josh 9:14 the men *t* of their victuals, and
Josh 10:27 they *t* them down off the trees,
Josh 10:28 And that day Joshua *t* Makkedah
Josh 10:32 which *t* it on the second day, and
Josh 10:35 they *t* it on that day, and smote
Josh 10:37 And they *t* it, and smote it with
Josh 10:39 And he *t* it, and the king thereof,
Josh 11:10 *t* Hazor, and smote the king
Josh 11:14 the children of Israel *t* for a
Josh 11:16 So Joshua *t* all that land, the
Josh 11:17 and all their kings he *t*, and smote

Josh 11:19 all other they *t* in battle
Josh 11:23 So Joshua *t* the whole land,
Josh 15:17 Kenaz, the brother of Caleb, *t* it
Josh 16:4 and Ephraim, *t* their inheritance
Josh 19:47 *t* it, and smote it with the edge
Josh 24:3 I *t* your father Abraham from the
Josh 24:26 *t* a great stone, and set it up
Judg 1:13 Caleb's younger brother, *t* it
Judg 1:18 Also Judah *t* Gaza with the coast
Judg 3:6 they *t* their daughters to be
Judg 3:21 *t* the dagger from his right thigh
Judg 3:25 therefore they *t* a key, and opened
Judg 3:28 *t* the fords of Jordan toward Moab
Judg 4:21 Heber's wife *t* a nail of the tent
Judg 4:21 *t* an hammer in her hand, and went
Judg 5:19 they *t* no gain of money
Judg 6:27 Then Gideon *t* ten men of his
Judg 7:8 So the people *t* victuals in their
Judg 7:24 *t* the waters unto Beth-barah and
Judg 7:25 they *t* two princes of the
Judg 8:12 *t* the two kings of Midian, Zebah
Judg 8:16 he *t* the elders of the city, and
Judg 8:21 *t* away the ornaments that were on
Judg 9:43 he *t* the people, and divided them
Judg 9:45 he *t* the city, and slew the people
Judg 9:48 Abimelech *t* an axe in his hand,
Judg 9:48 *t* it, and laid it on his shoulder,
Judg 9:50 encamped against Thebez, and *t* it
Judg 11:13 Because Israel *t* away my land
Judg 11:15 Israel *t* not away the land of
Judg 12:5 the Gileadites *t* the passages of
Judg 12:6 Then they *t* him, and slew him at
Judg 12:9 *t* in thirty daughters from abroad
Judg 13:19 So Manoah *t* a kid with a meat
Judg 14:9 he *t* thereof in his hands, and
Judg 14:19 *t* their spoil, and gave change of
Judg 15:4 *t* firebrands, and turned tail to
Judg 15:15 *t* it, and slew a thousand men
Judg 16:3 *t* the doors of the gate of the
Judg 16:12 Delilah therefore *t* new ropes
Judg 16:21 But the Philistines *t* him
Judg 16:29 Samson *t* hold of the two middle
Judg 16:31 *t* him, and brought him up, and
Judg 17:2 I *t* it
Judg 17:4 his mother *t* two hundred shekels
Judg 18:17 *t* the graven image, and the ephod,
Judg 18:20 he *t* the ephod, and the teraphim,
Judg 18:27 they *t* the things which Micah had
Judg 19:1 who *t* to him a concubine out of
Judg 19:15 for there was no man that *t* them
Judg 19:25 so the man *t* his concubine, and
Judg 19:28 Then the man *t* her up upon an ass
Judg 19:29 he *t* a knife, and laid hold on his
Judg 20:6 I *t* my concubine, and cut her in
Judg 21:23 *t* them wives, according to their
Ruth 1:4 they *t* them wives of the women of
Ruth 2:18 she *t* it up, and went into the
Ruth 4:2 he *t* ten men of the elders of the
Ruth 4:13 So Boaz *t* Ruth, and she was his
Ruth 4:16 Naomi *t* the child, and laid it in
1Sa 1:24 she *t* him up with her, with three
1Sa 2:14 up the priest *t* for himself
1Sa 5:1 the Philistines *t* the ark of God
1Sa 5:2 the Philistines *t* the ark of God
1Sa 5:3 they *t* Dagon, and set him in his
1Sa 6:10 *t* two milch kine, and tied them to
1Sa 6:12 the kine *t* the straight way to
1Sa 6:15 the Levites *t* down the ark of the
1Sa 7:9 Samuel *t* a sucking lamb, and
1Sa 7:12 Then Samuel *t* a stone, and set it
1Sa 8:3 *t* bribes, and perverted judgment
1Sa 9:22 And Samuel *t* Saul and his servant,
1Sa 9:24 the cook *t* up the shoulder, and
1Sa 10:1 Then Samuel *t* a vial of oil, and
1Sa 11:7 he *t* a yoke of oxen, and hewed
1Sa 14:32 *t* sheep, and oxen, and calves, and
1Sa 14:47 So Saul *t* the kingdom over Israel
1Sa 14:52 valiant man, he *t* him unto him
1Sa 15:8 he *t* Agag the king of the
1Sa 15:21 But the people *t* of the spoil
1Sa 16:13 Then Samuel *t* the horn of oil, and
1Sa 16:20 Jesse *t* an ass laden with bread,
1Sa 16:23 upon Saul, that David *t* an harp
1Sa 17:20 the sheep with a keeper, and *t*
1Sa 17:34 *t* a lamb out of the flock
1Sa 17:40 he *t* his staff in his hand, and
1Sa 17:49 *t* thence a stone, and slang it, and
1Sa 17:51 *t* his sword, and drew it out of
1Sa 17:54 And David *t* the head of the
1Sa 17:57 of the Philistine, Abner *t* him
1Sa 18:2 Saul *t* him that day, and would let
1Sa 19:13 Michal *t* an image, and laid it in
1Sa 24:2 Then Saul *t* three thousand chosen
1Sa 25:18 *t* two hundred loaves, and two
1Sa 25:43 David also *t* Ahinoam of Jezreel
1Sa 26:12 So David *t* the spear and the cruse
1Sa 27:9 *t* away the sheep, and the oxen, and
1Sa 28:24 *t* flour, and kneaded it, and did
1Sa 30:20 David *t* all the flocks and the
1Sa 31:4 Therefore Saul *t* a sword, and fell
1Sa 31:12 *t* the body of Saul and the bodies
1Sa 31:13 they *t* their bones, and buried
2Sa 1:10 I *t* the crown that was upon his
2Sa 1:11 Then David *t* hold on his clothes,
2Sa 2:8 *t* Ish-bosheth the son of Saul, and
2Sa 2:32 they *t* up Asahel, and buried him
2Sa 3:15 *t* her from her husband, even from
2Sa 3:27 Joab *t* him aside in the gate to
2Sa 3:36 And all the people *t* notice of it
2Sa 4:4 of Jezreel, and his nurse *t* him up
2Sa 4:7 *t* his head, and gat them away
2Sa 4:10 I *t* hold of him, and slew him in
2Sa 4:12 But they *t* the head of
2Sa 5:7 Nevertheless David *t* the strong
2Sa 5:13 David *t* him more concubines and
2Sa 6:6 the ark of God, and *t* hold of it
2Sa 7:8 I *t* thee from the sheepcote, from
2Sa 7:15 as I *t* it from Saul, whom I put
2Sa 8:1 David *t* Metheg-ammah out of the
2Sa 8:4 David *t* from him a thousand
2Sa 8:7 David *t* the shields of gold that
2Sa 8:8 king David *t* exceeding much brass
2Sa 10:4 Wherefore Hanun *t* David's
2Sa 11:4 David sent messengers, and *t* her
2Sa 12:4 but *t* the poor man's lamb, and
2Sa 12:26 of Ammon, and *t* the royal city
2Sa 12:29 and fought against it, and *t* it
2Sa 12:30 he *t* their king's crown from off
2Sa 13:8 she *t* flour, and kneaded it, and
2Sa 13:9 she *t* a pan, and poured them out
2Sa 13:10 Tamar *t* the cakes which she had
2Sa 13:11 he *t* hold of her, and said unto
2Sa 15:5 his hand, and *t* him, and kissed him
2Sa 17:19 And the woman *t* and spread a
2Sa 18:14 he *t* three darts in his hand, and
2Sa 18:17 they *t* Absalom, and cast him into
2Sa 20:3 the king *t* the ten women his
2Sa 20:9 Joab *t* Amasa, by the beard with
2Sa 20:10 But Amasa *t* no heed to the sword
2Sa 21:8 But the king *t* the two sons of
2Sa 21:10 the daughter of Aiah *t* sackcloth
2Sa 21:12 *t* the bones of Saul and the bones
2Sa 22:17 He sent from above, he *t* me
2Sa 23:16 *t* it, and brought it to David
1Kin 1:39 Zadok the priest *t* an horn of oil
1Kin 3:1 *t* Pharaoh's daughter, and brought
1Kin 3:20 *t* my son from beside me, while
1Kin 4:15 he also *t* Basmath the daughter of
1Kin 8:3 came, and the priests *t* up the ark
1Kin 11:18 they *t* men with them out of Paran
1Kin 12:28 Whereupon the king *t* counsel
1Kin 13:29 the prophet *t* up the carcase of
1Kin 14:26 he *t* away the treasures of the
1Kin 14:26 he even *t* away all
1Kin 14:26 he *t* away all the shields of gold
1Kin 15:12 he *t* away the sodomites out of
1Kin 15:18 Then Asa *t* all the silver and the
1Kin 15:22 they *t* away the stones of Ramah,
1Kin 16:31 that he *t* to wife Jezebel the
1Kin 17:19 he *t* him out of her bosom, and
1Kin 17:23 Elijah *t* the child, and brought
1Kin 18:4 that Obadiah *t* an hundred
1Kin 18:10 he *t* an oath of the kingdom and
1Kin 18:26 they *t* the bullock which was
1Kin 18:31 Elijah *t* twelve stones, according
1Kin 18:40 And they *t* them
1Kin 19:21 *t* a yoke of oxen, and slew them,
1Kin 20:34 which my father *t* from thy father
1Kin 20:41 *t* the ashes away from his face
1Kin 22:46 father Asa, he *t* out of the land
2Kin 2:8 Elijah *t* his mantle, and wrapped
2Kin 2:12 he *t* hold of his own clothes, and
2Kin 2:13 He *t* up also the mantle of Elijah
2Kin 2:14 he *t* the mantle of Elijah that
2Kin 3:26 he *t* with him seven hundred men
2Kin 3:27 Then he *t* his eldest son that
2Kin 4:37 *t* up her son, and went out
2Kin 5:5 *t* with him ten talents of silver,
2Kin 5:24 he *t* them from their hand, and
2Kin 6:7 And he put out his hand, and *t* it
2Kin 6:8 *t* counsel with his servants,
2Kin 7:14 They *t* therefore two chariot
2Kin 8:9 *t* a present with him, even of
2Kin 8:15 that he *t* a thick cloth, and
2Kin 9:13 *t* every man his garment, and put
2Kin 10:7 that they *t* the king's sons, and
2Kin 10:14 they *t* them alive, and slew them
2Kin 10:15 he *t* him up to him into the
2Kin 10:31 But Jehu *t* no heed to walk in the
2Kin 11:2 *t* Joash the son of Ahaziah, and
2Kin 11:4 *t* an oath of them in the house of
2Kin 11:9 they *t* every man his men that
2Kin 11:19 he *t* the rulers over hundreds, and
2Kin 12:9 But Jehoiada the priest *t* a chest
2Kin 12:17 and fought against Gath, and *t* it
2Kin 12:18 Jehoash king of Judah *t* all the
2Kin 13:15 he *t* unto him bow and arrows
2Kin 13:18 And he *t* them
2Kin 13:25 *t* again out of the hand of
2Kin 14:7 *t* Selah by war, and called the
2Kin 14:13 of Israel *t* Amaziah king of Judah
2Kin 14:14 he *t* all the gold and silver, and
2Kin 14:21 all the people of Judah *t* Azariah
2Kin 15:29 *t* Ijon, and Abel-beth-maachah, and
2Kin 16:8 Ahaz *t* the silver and gold that
2Kin 16:9 *t* it, and carried the people of it
2Kin 16:17 *t* down the sea from off the
2Kin 17:6 the king of Assyria *t* Samaria
2Kin 18:10 the end of three years they *t* it
2Kin 18:13 fenced cities of Judah, and *t* them
2Kin 20:7 And they *t* and laid it on the boil,
2Kin 23:11 he *t* away the horses that the
2Kin 23:16 *t* the bones out of the sepulchres
2Kin 23:19 the LORD to anger, Josiah *t* away
2Kin 23:30 the people of the land *t* Jehoahaz
2Kin 23:34 to Jehoiakim, and *t* Jehoahaz away
2Kin 24:12 the king of Babylon *t* him in the
2Kin 25:6 So they *t* the king, and brought
2Kin 25:14 they ministered, *t* they away
2Kin 25:15 the captain of the guard *t* away
2Kin 25:18 guard *t* Seraiah the chief priest
2Kin 25:19 out of the city he *t* an officer
2Kin 25:20 captain of the guard *t* these
1Chr 2:19 Caleb *t* unto him Ephrath, which
1Chr 2:23 he *t* Geshur, and Aram, with the
1Chr 4:18 of Pharaoh, which Mered *t*
1Chr 5:21 And they *t* away their cattle
1Chr 7:15 Machir *t* to wife the sister of
1Chr 10:4 So Saul *t* a sword, and fell upon
1Chr 10:9 they *t* his head, and his armour,
1Chr 10:12 *t* away the body of Saul, and the
1Chr 11:5 David *t* the castle of Zion
1Chr 11:18 *t* it, and brought it to David
1Chr 14:3 David *t* more wives at Jerusalem
1Chr 17:7 I *t* thee from the sheepcote, even
1Chr 17:13 as I *t* it from him that was
1Chr 18:1 *t* Gath and her towns out of the
1Chr 18:4 David *t* from him a thousand
1Chr 18:7 David *t* the shields of gold that
1Chr 19:4 Wherefore Hanun *t* David's
1Chr 20:2 David *t* the crown of their king
1Chr 23:22 brethren the sons of Kish *t* them
1Chr 27:23 But David *t* not the number of
2Chr 5:4 and the Levites *t* up the ark
2Chr 8:18 *t* thence four hundred and fifty
2Chr 10:6 king Rehoboam *t* counsel with the
2Chr 10:8 *t* counsel with the young men that
2Chr 11:18 Rehoboam *t* him Mahalath the
2Chr 11:20 after her he *t* Maachah the
2Chr 11:21 (for he *t* eighteen wives, and
2Chr 12:4 he *t* the fenced cities which
2Chr 12:9 *t* away the treasures of the house
2Chr 12:9 he *t* all
2Chr 13:19 *t* cities from him, Beth-el with
2Chr 14:3 For he *t* away the altars of the
2Chr 14:5 Also he *t* away out of all the
2Chr 15:8 he *t* courage, and put away the
2Chr 16:6 Then Asa the king *t* all Judah
2Chr 17:6 moreover he *t* away the high
2Chr 22:11 *t* Joash the son of Ahaziah, and
2Chr 23:1 *t* the captains of hundreds,
2Chr 23:8 *t* every man his men that were to
2Chr 23:20 he *t* the captains of hundreds, and
2Chr 24:3 Jehoiada *t* for him two wives
2Chr 24:11 *t* it, and carried it to his place
2Chr 25:13 thousand of them, and *t* much spoil
2Chr 25:17 Amaziah king of Judah *t* advice
2Chr 25:23 of Israel *t* Amaziah king of Judah
2Chr 25:24 he *t* all the gold and the sliver,
2Chr 26:1 all the people of Judah *t* Uzziah

Rev 10:10 I *t* the little book out of the
Rev 18:21 a mighty angel *t* up a stone like

**TOOKEST**
Ps 99:8 though thou *t* vengeance of their
Eze 16:18 *t* thy broidered garments, and

**TOOL**
Ex 20:25 for if thou lift up thy *t* upon it
Ex 32:4 and fashioned it with a graving *t*
Deut 27:5 not lift up any iron *t* upon them
1Kin 6:7 any *t* of iron heard in the house

**TOOTH**
Ex 21:24 Eye for eye, *t* for *t*, hand
Ex 21:27 he smite out his manservant's *t*
Ex 21:27 or his maidservant's *t*
Lev 24:20 breach, eye for eye, *t* for *t*
Deut 19:21 life, eye for eye, *t* for *t*
Prov 25:19 of trouble is like a broken *t*
Mt 5:38 for an eye, and a *t* for a *t*

**TOOTH'S**
Ex 21:27 let him go free for his *t* sake

**TOP**
Gen 11:4 whose *t* may reach unto heaven
Gen 28:12 the *t* of it reached to heaven
Gen 28:18 and poured oil upon the *t* of it
Ex 17:9 to morrow I will stand on the *t*
Ex 17:10 Hur went up to the *t* of the hill
Ex 19:20 Sinai, on the *t* of the mount
Ex 19:20 Moses up to the *t* of the mount
Ex 24:17 was like devouring fire on the *t*
Ex 28:32 shall be an hole in the *t* of it
Ex 30:3 the *t* thereof, and the sides
Ex 34:2 there to me in the *t* of the mount
Ex 37:26 with pure gold, both the *t* of it
Num 14:40 up into the *t* of the mountain
Num 14:44 presumed to go up unto the hill *t*
Num 20:28 died there in the *t* of the mount
Num 21:20 to the *t* of Pisgah, which looketh
Num 23:9 For from the *t* of the rocks I see
Num 23:14 to the *t* of Pisgah, and built
Num 23:28 brought Balaam unto the *t* of Peor
Deut 3:27 Get thee up into the *t* of Pisgah
Deut 28:35 thy foot unto the *t* of thy head
Deut 33:16 upon the *t* of the head of him
Deut 34:1 to the *t* of Pisgah, that is over
Josh 15:8 the border went up to the *t* of
Josh 15:9 *t* of the hill unto the fountain
Judg 6:26 thy God upon the *t* of this rock
Judg 9:7 stood in the *t* of mount Gerizim,
Judg 9:25 for him in the *t* of the mountains
Judg 9:36 down from the *t* of the mountains
Judg 9:51 gat them up to the *t* of the tower
Judg 15:8 dwelt in the *t* of the rock Etam
Judg 15:11 went to the *t* of the rock Etam
Judg 16:3 carried them up to the *t* of an
1Sa 9:25 with Saul upon the *t* of the house
1Sa 9:26 called Saul to the *t* of the house
1Sa 26:13 stood on the *t* of an hill afar
2Sa 2:25 and stood on the *t* of an hill
2Sa 15:32 was come to the *t* of the mount
2Sa 16:1 a little past the *t* of the hill
2Sa 16:22 a tent upon the *t* of the house
1Kin 7:17 were upon the *t* of the pillars
1Kin 7:18 chapiters that were upon the *t*
1Kin 7:19 the *t* of the pillars were of lily
1Kin 7:22 upon the *t* of the pillars was
1Kin 7:35 in the *t* of the base was there a
1Kin 7:35 on the *t* of the base the ledges
1Kin 7:41 were on the *t* of the two pillars
1Kin 7:41 were upon the *t* of the pillars
1Kin 10:19 the *t* of the throne was round
1Kin 18:42 Elijah went up to the *t* of Carmel
2Kin 1:9 he sat on the *t* of an hill
2Kin 9:13 under him on the *t* of the stairs
2Kin 23:12 the altars that were on the *t* of
2Chr 3:15 the chapiter that was on the *t* of
2Chr 4:12 were on the *t* of the two pillars
2Chr 4:12 were on the *t* of the pillars
2Chr 25:12 them unto the *t* of the rock
2Chr 25:12 them down from the *t* of the rock
Est 5:2 touched the *t* of the sceptre
Ps 72:16 earth upon the *t* of the mountains
Ps 102:7 a sparrow alone upon the house *t*
Prov 8:2 standeth in the *t* of high places
Prov 23:34 that lieth upon the *t* of a mast
Song 4:8 look from the *t* of Amana, from
Song 4:8 from the *t* of Shenir and Hermon,
Is 2:2 in the *t* of the mountains
Is 17:6 in the *t* of the uppermost bough
Is 30:17 a beacon upon the *t* of a mountain
Is 42:11 shout from the *t* of the mountains
Lam 2:19 hunger in the *t* of every street
Lam 4:1 out in the *t* of every street
Eze 17:4 off the *t* of his young twigs
Eze 17:22 I will crop off from the *t* of his
Eze 24:7 she set it upon the *t* of a rock
Eze 24:8 her blood upon the *t* of a rock
Eze 26:4 and make her like the *t* of a rock
Eze 26:14 make thee like the *t* of a rock
Eze 31:3 his *t* was among the thick boughs
Eze 31:10 he hath shot up his *t* among the
Eze 31:14 up their *t* among the thick boughs
Eze 43:12 Upon the *t* of the mountain the
Amos 1:2 the *t* of Carmel shall wither
Amos 9:3 themselves in the *t* of Carmel
Mic 4:1 in the *t* of the mountains
Nah 3:10 at the *t* of all the streets
Zec 4:2 with a bowl upon the *t* of it
Zec 4:2 which are upon the *t* thereof
Mt 27:51 in twain from the *t* to the bottom
Mk 15:38 in twain from the *t* to the bottom
Jn 19:23 seam, woven from the *t* throughout
Heb 11:21 leaning upon the *t* of his staff

**TOPAZ**
Ex 28:17 first row shall be a sardius, a *t*
Ex 39:10 the first row was a sardius, a *t*
Job 28:19 The *t* of Ethiopia shall not equal
Eze 28:13 was thy covering, the sardius, *t*
Rev 21:20 the ninth, a *t*

**TOPHEL** *(to'-fel) A place in the Sinai wilderness.*
Deut 1:1 the Red sea, between Paran, and *T*

**TOPHET** *(to'-fet)* See TOPHETH. *A place in the valley of Hinnom.*
Is 30:33 For *T* is ordained of old
Jer 7:31 have built the high places of *T*
Jer 7:32 that it shall no more be called *T*
Jer 7:32 for they shall bury in *T*, till
Jer 19:6 place shall no more be called *T*
Jer 19:11 and they shall bury them in *T*
Jer 19:12 and even make this city as *T*
Jer 19:13 be defiled as the place of *T*
Jer 19:14 Then came Jeremiah from *T*

**TOPHETH** *(to'-feth)* See TOPHET. *Same as Tophet.*
2Kin 23:10 And he defiled *T*, which is in the

**TOPS**
Gen 8:5 were the *t* of the mountains seen
2Sa 5:24 in the *t* of the mulberry trees
1Kin 7:16 to set upon the *t* of the pillars
2Kin 19:26 herb, as the grass on the house *t*
1Chr 14:15 in the *t* of the mulberry trees
Job 24:24 cut off as the *t* of the ears of
Is 2:21 into the *t* of the ragged rocks,
Is 15:3 on the *t* of their houses, and in
Eze 6:13 in all the *t* of the mountains, and
Hos 4:13 upon the *t* of the mountains
Joel 2:5 *t* of mountains shall they leap

**TORCH**
Zec 12:6 like a *t* of fire in a sheaf

**TORCHES**
Nah 2:3 *t* in the day of his preparation
Nah 2:4 they shall seem like *t*, they
Jn 18:3 cometh thither with lanterns and *t*

**TORMENT**
Mt 8:29 hither to *t* us before the time
Mk 5:7 thee by God, that thou *t* me not
Lk 8:28 I beseech thee, *t* me not
Lk 16:28 also come into this place of *t*
1Jn 4:18 because fear hath *t*
Rev 9:5 their *t* was as the *t* of a
Rev 9:5 was as the *t* of a scorpion
Rev 14:11 the smoke of their *t* ascendeth up
Rev 18:7 and lived deliciously, so much *t*
Rev 18:10 afar off for the fear of her *t*
Rev 18:15 afar off for the fear of her *t*

**TORMENTED**
Mt 8:6 sick of the palsy, grievously *t*
Lk 16:24 for I am *t* in this flame
Lk 16:25 he is comforted, and thou art *t*
Heb 11:37 being destitute, afflicted, *t*
Rev 9:5 that they should be *t* five months
Rev 11:10 because these two prophets *t* them
Rev 14:10 and he shall be *t* with fire
Rev 20:10 prophet are, and shall be *t* day

**TORMENTORS**
Mt 18:34 wroth, and delivered him to the *t*

**TORMENTS**
Mt 4:24 taken with divers diseases and *t*
Lk 16:23 he lift up his eyes, being in *t*

**TORN**
Gen 31:39 That which was *t* of beasts I
Gen 44:28 I said, Surely he is *t* in pieces
Ex 22:13 If it be *t* in pieces, then let
Ex 22:13 not make good that which was *t*
Ex 22:31 that is *t* of beasts in the field
Lev 7:24 of that which is *t* with beasts
Lev 17:15 or that which was *t* with beasts
Lev 22:8 or is *t* with beasts, he shall not
1Kin 13:26 unto the lion, which hath *t* him
1Kin 13:28 eaten the carcase, nor *t* the ass
Is 5:25 their carcases were *t* in the
Jer 5:6 out thence shall be *t* in pieces
Eze 4:14 of itself, or is *t* in pieces
Eze 44:31 that is dead of itself, or *t*
Hos 6:1 for he hath *t*, and he will heal us
Mal 1:13 and ye brought that which was *t*
Mk 1:26 when the unclean spirit had *t* him

**TORTOISE**
Lev 11:29 mouse, and the *t* after his kind,

**TORTURED**
Heb 11:35 and others were *t*, not accepting

**TOSS**
Is 22:18 *t* thee like a ball into a large
Jer 5:22 the waves thereof *t* themselves

**TOSSED**
Ps 109:23 I am *t* up and down as the locust
Prov 21:6 a lying tongue is a vanity *t* to
Is 54:11 *t* with tempest, and not comforted,
Mt 14:24 midst of the sea, *t* with waves
Acts 27:18 exceedingly *t* with a tempest
Eph 4:14 *t* to and fro, and carried about
Jas 1:6 the sea driven with the wind and *t*

**TOSSINGS**
Job 7:4 and I am full of *t* to and fro unto

**TOTTERING**
Ps 62:3 wall shall ye be, and as a *t* fence

**TOU** *(to'-u)* See TOI. *Same as Toi.*
1Chr 18:9 Now when *T* king of Hamath heard
1Chr 18:10 (for Hadarezer had war with *T*

**TOUCH**
Gen 3:3 eat of it, neither shall ye *t* it
Gen 20:6 suffered I thee not to *t* her
Ex 19:12 the mount, or *t* the border of it
Ex 19:13 There shall not an hand *t* it
Lev 5:2 Or if a soul *t* any unclean thing,
Lev 5:3 Or if he *t* the uncleanness of man
Lev 6:27 Whatsoever shall *t* the flesh
Lev 7:21 that shall *t* any unclean thing
Lev 11:8 and their carcase shall ye not *t*
Lev 11:31 whosoever doth *t* them, when they
Lev 12:4 she shall *t* no hallowed thing,
Num 4:15 they shall not *t* any holy thing
Num 16:26 *t* nothing of theirs, lest ye be
Deut 14:8 flesh, nor *t* their dead carcase
Josh 9:19 now therefore we may not *t* them
Ruth 2:9 men that they shall not *t* thee
2Sa 14:10 he shall not *t* thee any more
2Sa 18:12 Beware that none *t* the young man
2Sa 23:7 But the man that shall *t* them
1Chr 16:22 *T* not mine anointed, and do my
Job 1:11 *t* all that he hath, and he will
Job 2:5 *t* his bone and his flesh, and he
Job 5:19 seven there shall no evil *t* thee
Job 6:7 to *t* are as my sorrowful meat
Ps 105:15 *T* not mine anointed, and do my
Ps 144:5 *t* the mountains, and they shall
Is 52:11 from thence, *t* no unclean thing
Jer 12:14 that *t* the inheritance which I
Lam 4:14 men could not *t* their garments
Lam 4:15 depart, depart, *t* not
Hag 2:12 and with his skirt do *t* bread
Hag 2:13 by a dead body *t* any of these
Mt 9:21 If I may but *t* his garment
Mt 14:36 only *t* the hem of his garment
Mk 3:10 pressed upon him for to *t* him
Mk 5:28 If I may *t* but his clothes, I
Mk 6:56 *t* if it were but the border of
Mk 8:22 him, and besought him to *t* him
Mk 10:13 to him, that he should *t* them
Lk 6:19 whole multitude sought to *t* him

Lk 11:46 ye yourselves *t* not the burdens
Lk 18:15 infants, that he would *t* them
Jn 20:17 Jesus saith unto her, *T* me not
1Cor 7:1 good for a man not to *t* a woman
2Cor 6:17 Lord, and *t* not the unclean thing
Col 2:21 *T* not; taste not
Heb 11:28 the firstborn should *t* them
Heb 12:20 so much as a beast *t* the mountain

## TOUCHED

Gen 26:29 us no hurt, as we have not *t* thee
Gen 32:25 he *t* the hollow of his thigh
Gen 32:32 because he *t* the hollow of
Lev 22:6 The soul which hath *t* any such
Num 19:18 there, and upon him that *t* a bone
Num 31:19 and whosoever hath *t* any slain
Judg 6:21 *t* the flesh and the unleavened
1Sa 10:26 of men, whose hearts God had *t*
1Kin 6:27 wing of the one *t* the one wall
1Kin 6:27 the other cherub *t* the other wall
1Kin 6:27 their wings *t* one another in the
1Kin 19:5 tree, behold, then an angel *t* him
1Kin 19:7 *t* him, and said, Arise and eat
2Kin 13:21 *t* the bones of Elisha, he revived
Est 5:2 near, and *t* the top of the sceptre
Job 19:21 for the hand of God hath *t* me
Is 6:7 and said, Lo, this hath *t* thy lips
Jer 1:9 put forth his hand, and *t* my mouth
Eze 3:13 creatures that *t* one another
Dan 8:5 whole earth, and *t* not the ground
Dan 8:18 but he *t* me, and set me upright
Dan 9:21 *t* me about the time of the
Dan 10:10 And, behold, an hand *t* me, which
Dan 10:16 of the sons of men *t* my lips
Dan 10:18 *t* me one like the appearance of a
Mt 8:3 hand, and *t* him, saying, I will
Mt 8:15 he *t* her hand, and the fever left
Mt 9:20 him, and *t* the hem of his garment
Mt 9:29 Then *t* he their eyes, saying,
Mt 14:36 as many as *t* were made perfectly
Mt 17:7 *t* them, and said, Arise, and be not
Mt 20:34 on them, and *t* their eyes
Mk 1:41 *t* him, and saith unto him, I will
Mk 5:27 press behind, and *t* his garment
Mk 5:30 press, and said, Who *t* my clothes
Mk 5:31 thee, and sayest thou, Who *t* me
Mk 6:56 as many as *t* him were made whole
Mk 7:33 ears, and he spit, and *t* his tongue
Lk 5:13 hand, and *t* him, saying, I will
Lk 7:14 And he came and *t* the bier
Lk 8:44 *t* the border of his garment
Lk 8:45 And Jesus said, Who *t* me
Lk 8:45 thee, and sayest thou, Who *t* me
Lk 8:46 And Jesus said, Somebody hath *t* me
Lk 8:47 for what cause she had *t* him
Lk 22:51 he *t* his ear, and healed him
Acts 27:3 And the next day we *t* at Sidon
Heb 4:15 be *t* with the feeling of our
Heb 12:18 unto the mount that might be *t*

## TOUCHETH

Gen 26:11 He that *t* this man or his wife
Ex 19:12 whosoever *t* the mount shall be
Ex 29:37 whatsoever *t* the altar shall be
Ex 30:29 whatsoever *t* them shall be holy
Lev 6:18 every one that *t* them shall be
Lev 7:19 the flesh that *t* any unclean
Lev 11:24 whosoever *t* the carcase of them
Lev 11:26 every one that *t* them shall be
Lev 11:27 whoso *t* their carcase shall be
Lev 11:36 but that which *t* their carcase
Lev 11:39 he that *t* the carcase thereof
Lev 15:5 whosoever *t* his bed shall wash
Lev 15:7 he that *t* the flesh of him that
Lev 15:10 whosoever *t* any thing that was
Lev 15:11 whomsoever he *t* that hath the
Lev 15:12 that he *t* which hath the issue,
Lev 15:19 whosoever *t* her shall be unclean
Lev 15:21 whosoever *t* her bed shall wash
Lev 15:22 whosoever *t* any thing that she
Lev 15:23 whereon she sitteth, when he *t* it
Lev 15:27 whosoever *t* those things shall be
Lev 22:4 whoso *t* any thing that is unclean
Lev 22:5 Or whosoever *t* any creeping thing
Num 19:11 He that *t* the dead body of any
Num 19:13 Whosoever *t* the dead body of any
Num 19:16 whosoever *t* one that is slain
Num 19:21 he that *t* the water of separation
Num 19:22 unclean person *t* shall be unclean
Num 19:22 the soul that *t* it shall be
Judg 16:9 tow is broken when it *t* the fire
Job 4:5 it *t* thee, and thou art troubled
Ps 104:32 he *t* the hills, and they smoke
Prov 6:29 whosoever *t* her shall not be
Eze 17:10 wither, when the east wind *t* it
Hos 4:2 they break out, and blood *t* blood
Amos 9:5 of hosts is he that *t* the land
Zec 2:8 for he that *t* you
Zec 2:8 you *t* the apple of his eye
Lk 7:39 of woman this is that *t* him
1Jn 5:18 and that wicked one *t* him not

## TOUCHING

Gen 27:42 as *t* thee, doth comfort himself,
Lev 5:13 make an atonement for him as *t*
Num 8:26 unto the Levites *t* their charge
1Sa 20:23 as *t* the matter which thou and I
2Kin 22:18 As *t* the words which thou hast
Ezr 7:24 that *t* any of the priests and
Job 37:23 *T* the Almighty, we cannot find
Ps 45:1 which I have made *t* the king
Is 5:1 song of my beloved *t* his vineyard
Jer 1:16 them *t* all their wickedness
Jer 21:11 *t* the house of the king of Judah,
Jer 22:11 For thus saith the LORD *t* Shallum
Eze 7:13 for the vision is *t* the whole
Mt 18:19 *t* any thing that they shall ask
Mt 22:31 But as *t* the resurrection of the
Mk 12:26 as *t* the dead, that they rise
Lk 23:14 *t* those things whereof ye accuse
Acts 5:35 ye intend to do as *t* these men
Acts 21:25 As *t* the Gentiles which believe,
Acts 24:21 *T* the resurrection of the dead I
Acts 26:2 *t* all the things whereof I am
Rom 11:28 but as *t* the election, they are
1Cor 8:1 Now as *t* things offered unto
1Cor 16:12 As *t* our brother Apollos, I
2Cor 9:1 For as *t* the ministering to the
Phil 3:5 as *t* the law, a Pharisee
Phil 3:6 *t* the righteousness which is in
Col 4:10 (*t* whom ye received commandments
1Th 4:9 But as *t* brotherly love ye need
2Th 3:4 have confidence in the Lord *t* you

## TOW

Judg 16:9 as a thread of *t* is broken when
Is 1:31 And the strong shall be as *t*
Is 43:17 extinct, they are quenched as *t*

## TOWEL

Jn 13:4 and took a *t*, and girded himself
Jn 13:5 to wipe them with the *t* wherewith

## TOWER

Gen 11:4 to, let us build us a city and a *t*
Gen 11:5 down to see the city and the *t*
Gen 35:21 his tent beyond the *t* of Edar
Judg 8:9 peace, I will break down this *t*
Judg 8:17 And he beat down the *t* of Penuel
Judg 9:46 of the *t* of Shechem heard that
Judg 9:47 that all the men of the *t* of
Judg 9:49 men of the *t* of Shechem died also
Judg 9:51 was a strong *t* within the city
Judg 9:51 gat them up to the top of the *t*
Judg 9:52 And Abimelech came unto the *t*
Judg 9:52 of the *t* to burn it with fire
2Sa 22:3 horn of my salvation, my high *t*
2Sa 22:51 He is the *t* of salvation for his
2Kin 5:24 And when he came to the *t*, he took
2Kin 9:17 a watchman on the *t* in Jezreel
2Kin 17:9 from the *t* of the watchmen to the
2Kin 18:8 from the *t* of the watchmen to the
2Chr 20:24 the watch *t* in the wilderness
Neh 3:1 even unto the *t* of Meah they
Neh 3:1 it, unto the *t* of Hananeel
Neh 3:11 piece, and the *t* of the furnaces
Neh 3:25 the *t* which lieth out from the
Neh 3:26 the east, and the *t* that lieth out
Neh 3:27 the great *t* that lieth out
Neh 12:38 from beyond the *t* of the furnaces
Neh 12:39 the *t* of Hananeel
Neh 12:39 the *t* of Meah, even unto the
Ps 18:2 of my salvation, and my high *t*
Ps 61:3 a strong *t* from the enemy
Ps 144:2 my high *t*, and my deliverer
Prov 18:10 name of the LORD is a strong *t*
Song 4:4 Thy neck is like the *t* of David
Song 7:4 Thy neck is as a *t* of ivory
Song 7:4 thy nose is as the *t* of Lebanon
Is 2:15 And upon every high *t*, and upon
Is 5:2 built a *t* in the midst of it, and
Jer 6:27 I have set thee for a *t* and a
Jer 31:38 *t* of Hananeel unto the gate of
Eze 29:10 from the *t* of Syene even unto the
Eze 30:6 from the *t* of Syene shall they
Mic 4:8 O *t* of the flock, the strong hold
Hab 2:1 my watch, and set me upon the *t*
Zec 14:10 from the *t* of Hananeel unto the
Mt 21:33 a winepress in it, and built a *t*
Mk 12:1 for the winefat, and built a *t*
Lk 13:4 upon whom the *t* in Siloam fell,
Lk 14:28 of you, intending to build a *t*

## TOWERS

2Chr 14:7 and make about them walls, and *t*
2Chr 26:9 Moreover Uzziah built *t* in
2Chr 26:10 Also he built *t* in the desert
2Chr 26:15 by cunning men, to be on the *t*
2Chr 27:4 the forests he built castles and *t*
2Chr 32:5 broken, and raised it up to the *t*
Ps 48:12 tell the *t* thereof
Song 8:10 I am a wall, and my breasts like *t*
Is 23:13 they set up the *t* thereof
Is 30:25 great slaughter, when the *t* fall
Is 32:14 *t* shall be for dens for ever, a
Is 33:18 where is he that counted the *t*
Eze 26:4 of Tyrus, and break down her *t*
Eze 26:9 axes he shall break down thy *t*
Eze 27:11 and the Gammadims were in thy *t*
Zeph 1:16 cities, and against the high *t*
Zeph 3:6 their *t* are desolate

## TOWN

Josh 2:15 for her house was upon the *t* wall
1Sa 16:4 the elders of the *t* trembled at
1Sa 23:7 entering into a *t* that hath gates
1Sa 27:5 a place in some *t* in the country
Hab 2:12 him that buildeth a *t* with blood
Mt 10:11 city or *t* ye shall enter, enquire
Mk 8:23 the hand, and led him out of the *t*
Mk 8:26 saying, Neither go into the *t*
Mk 8:26 nor tell it to any in the *t*
Lk 5:17 come out of every *t* of Galilee
Jn 7:42 out of the *t* of Bethlehem, where
Jn 11:1 the *t* of Mary and her sister
Jn 11:30 Jesus was not yet come into the *t*

## TOWNCLERK

Acts 19:35 when the *t* had appeased the

## TOWNS

Gen 25:16 these are their names, by their *t*
Num 32:41 went and took the small *t* thereof
Deut 3:5 beside unwalled *t* a great many
Josh 13:30 of Bashan, and all the *t* of Jair
Josh 15:45 Ekron, with her *t* and her villages
Josh 15:47 Ashdod with her *t* and her villages
Josh 15:47 and her villages, Gaza with her *t*
Josh 17:11 and in Asher Beth-shean and her *t*
Josh 17:11 and Ibleam and her *t*
Josh 17:11 the inhabitants of Dor and her *t*
Josh 17:11 inhabitants of En-dor and her *t*
Josh 17:11 inhabitants of Taanach and her *t*
Josh 17:11 inhabitants of Megiddo and her *t*
Josh 17:16 who are of Beth-shean and her *t*
Judg 1:27 of Beth-shean and her *t*, nor
Judg 1:27 nor Taanach and her *t*
Judg 1:27 the inhabitants of Dor and her *t*
Judg 1:27 inhabitants of Ibleam and her *t*
Judg 1:27 inhabitants of Megiddo and her *t*
Judg 11:26 Israel dwelt in Heshbon and her *t*
Judg 11:26 and in Aroer and her *t*
1Kin 4:13 to him pertained the *t* of Jair
1Chr 2:23 and Aram, with the *t* of Jair
1Chr 2:23 the *t* thereof, even threescore
1Chr 5:16 in Gilead in Bashan, and in her *t*
1Chr 7:28 the *t* thereof, and eastward Naaran
1Chr 7:28 Gezer, with the *t* thereof
1Chr 7:28 unto Gaza and the *t* thereof
1Chr 7:29 of Manasseh, Beth-shean and her *t*
1Chr 7:29 Taanach and her *t*
1Chr 7:29 Megiddo and her *t*
1Chr 7:29 Dor and her *t*
1Chr 8:12 Ono, and Lod, with the *t* thereof
1Chr 18:1 her *t* out of the hand of the
2Chr 13:19 him, Beth-el with the *t* thereof
2Chr 13:19 and Jeshanah with the *t* thereof
2Chr 13:19 and Ephrain with the *t* thereof
Est 9:19 that dwelt in the unwalled *t*
Jer 19:15 upon all her *t* all the evil that
Zec 2:4 *t* without walls for the multitude
Mk 1:38 them, Let us go into the next *t*
Mk 8:27 into the *t* of Caesarea Philippi
Lk 9:6 departed, and went through the *t*
Lk 9:12 away, that they may go into the *t*

**TRACHONITIS** *(trak-o-nï'-tis) A rocky district east of the Jordan.*
Lk 3:1 of Ituraea and of the region of *T*

**TRADE**
Gen 34:10 dwell and *t* ye therein, and get you
Gen 34:21 dwell in the land, and *t* therein
Gen 46:32 for their *t* hath been to feed
Gen 46:34 Thy servants' *t* hath been about
Rev 18:17 sailors, and as many as *t* by sea

**TRADED**
Eze 27:12 tin, and lead, they *t* in thy fairs
Eze 27:13 they *t* the persons of men and
Eze 27:14 *t* in thy fairs with horses
Eze 27:17 they *t* in thy market wheat of
Mt 25:16 *t* with the same, and made them

**TRADING**
Lk 19:15 much every man had gained by *t*

**TRADITION**
Mt 15:2 transgress the *t* of the elders
Mt 15:3 the commandment of God by your *t*
Mt 15:6 of God of none effect by your *t*
Mk 7:3 holding the *t* of the elders
Mk 7:5 according to the *t* of the elders
Mk 7:8 of God, ye hold the *t* of men
Mk 7:9 God, that ye may keep your own *t*
Mk 7:13 God of none effect through your *t*
Col 2:8 vain deceit, after the *t* of men
2Th 3:6 not after the *t* which he received
1Pet 1:18 received by *t* from your fathers

**TRADITIONS**
Gal 1:14 zealous of the *t* of my fathers
2Th 2:15 hold the *t* which ye have been

**TRAFFICK**
Gen 42:34 and ye shall *t* in the land
1Kin 10:15 of the *t* of the spice merchants,
Eze 17:4 and carried it into a land of *t*
Eze 28:5 by thy *t* hast thou increased thy
Eze 28:18 by the iniquity of thy *t*

**TRAFFICKERS**
Is 23:8 whose *t* are the honourable of the

**TRAIN**
1Kin 10:2 to Jerusalem with a very great *t*
Prov 22:6 *T* up a child in the way he should
Is 6:1 up, and his *t* filled the temple

**TRAINED**
Gen 14:14 captive, he armed his *t* servants

**TRAITOR**
Lk 6:16 Iscariot, which also was the *t*

**TRAITORS**
2Ti 3:4 *T*, heady, highminded, lovers of

**TRAMPLE**
Ps 91:13 dragon shalt thou *t* under feet
Is 63:3 mine anger, and *t* them in my fury
Mt 7:6 lest they *t* them under their feet

**TRANCE**
Num 24:4 of the Almighty, falling into a *t*
Num 24:16 of the Almighty, falling into a *t*
Acts 10:10 they made ready, he fell into a *t*
Acts 11:5 in a *t* I saw a vision, A certain
Acts 22:17 in the temple, I was in a *t*

**TRANQUILITY**
Dan 4:27 it may be a lengthening of thy *t*

**TRANSFERRED**
1Cor 4:6 I have in a figure *t* to myself

**TRANSFIGURED**
Mt 17:2 And was *t* before them
Mk 9:2 and he was *t* before them

**TRANSFORMED**
Rom 12:2 but be ye *t* by the renewing of
2Cor 11:14 for Satan himself is *t* into an
2Cor 11:15 also be *t* as the ministers of

**TRANSFORMING**
2Cor 11:13 *t* themselves into the apostles of

**TRANSGRESS**
Num 14:41 Wherefore now do ye *t* the
1Sa 2:24 ye make the LORD's people to *t*
2Chr 24:20 Why *t* ye the commandments of the
Neh 1:8 servant Moses, saying, If ye *t*
Neh 13:27 to *t* against our God in marrying
Ps 17:3 that my mouth shall not *t*
Ps 25:3 be ashamed which *t* without cause
Prov 28:21 a piece of bread that man will *t*
Jer 2:20 and thou saidst, I will not *t*
Eze 20:38 rebels, and them that *t* against me
Amos 4:4 Come to Beth-el, and *t*
Mt 15:2 Why do thy disciples *t* the
Mt 15:3 Why do ye also *t* the commandment
Rom 2:27 and circumcision dost *t* the law

**TRANSGRESSED**
Deut 26:13 I have not *t* thy commandments,
Josh 7:11 they have also *t* my covenant
Josh 7:15 because he hath *t* the covenant of
Josh 23:16 When ye have *t* the covenant of
Judg 2:20 *t* my covenant which I commanded
1Sa 14:33 And he said, Ye have *t*
1Sa 15:24 for I have *t* the commandment of
1Kin 8:50 wherein they have *t* against thee
2Kin 18:12 but *t* his covenant, and all that
1Chr 2:7 who *t* in the thing accursed
1Chr 5:25 they *t* against the God of their
2Chr 12:2 they had *t* against the LORD
2Chr 26:16 for he *t* against the LORD his God
2Chr 28:19 naked, and *t* sore against the LORD
2Chr 36:14 *t* very much after all the
Ezr 10:10 up, and said unto them, Ye have *t*
Ezr 10:13 many that have *t* in this thing
Is 24:5 because they have *t* the laws
Is 43:27 and thy teachers have *t* against me
Is 66:24 of the men that have *t* against me
Jer 2:8 the pastors also *t* against me
Jer 2:29 ye all have *t* against me, saith
Jer 3:13 that thou hast *t* against the LORD
Jer 33:8 and whereby they have *t* against me
Jer 34:18 the men that have *t* my covenant
Lam 3:42 We have *t* and have rebelled
Eze 2:3 their fathers have *t* against me
Eze 18:31 transgressions, whereby ye have *t*
Dan 9:11 Yea, all Israel have *t* thy law
Hos 6:7 they like men have *t* the covenant
Hos 7:13 because they have *t* against me
Hos 8:1 because they have *t* my covenant
Zeph 3:11 wherein thou hast *t* against me
Lk 15:29 neither *t* I at any time thy

**TRANSGRESSEST**
Est 3:3 Why *t* thou the king's commandment

**TRANSGRESSETH**
Prov 16:10 his mouth *t* not in judgment
Hab 2:5 Yea also, because he *t* by wine
1Jn 3:4 committeth sin *t* also the law
2Jn 9 Whosoever *t*, and abideth not in

**TRANSGRESSING**
Deut 17:2 LORD thy God, in *t* his covenant,
Is 59:13 In *t* and lying against the LORD,

**TRANSGRESSION**
Ex 34:7 forgiving iniquity and *t* and sin,
Num 14:18 mercy, forgiving iniquity and *t*
Josh 22:22 or if in *t* against the LORD,
1Sa 24:11 neither evil nor *t* in mine hand
1Chr 9:1 away to Babylon for their *t*
1Chr 10:13 So Saul died for his *t* which he
2Chr 29:19 his reign did cast away in his *t*
Ezr 9:4 because of the *t* of those that
Ezr 10:6 *t* of them that had been carried
Job 7:21 And why dost thou not pardon my *t*
Job 8:4 have cast them away for their *t*
Job 13:23 make me to know my *t* and my sin
Job 14:17 My *t* is sealed up in a bag, and
Job 33:9 I am clean without *t*, I am
Job 34:6 my wound is incurable without *t*
Ps 19:13 be innocent from the great *t*
Ps 32:1 Blessed is he whose *t* is forgiven
Ps 36:1 The *t* of the wicked saith within
Ps 59:3 not for my *t*, nor for my sin, O
Ps 89:32 will I visit their *t* with the rod
Ps 107:17 Fools, because of their *t*
Prov 12:13 is snared by the *t* of his lips
Prov 17:9 He that covereth a *t* seeketh love
Prov 17:19 He loveth *t* that loveth strife
Prov 19:11 it is his glory to pass over a *t*
Prov 28:2 For the *t* of a land many are the
Prov 28:24 his mother, and saith, It is no *t*
Prov 29:6 In the *t* of an evil man there is
Prov 29:16 are multiplied, *t* increaseth
Prov 29:22 and a furious man aboundeth in *t*
Is 24:20 the *t* thereof shall be heavy upon
Is 53:8 for the *t* of my people was he
Is 57:4 are ye not children of *t*, a seed
Is 58:1 and shew my people their *t*
Is 59:20 them that turn from *t* in Jacob
Eze 33:12 deliver him in the day of his *t*
Dan 8:12 daily sacrifice by reason of *t*
Dan 8:13 the *t* of desolation, to give both
Dan 9:24 thy holy city, to finish the *t*
Amos 4:4 at Gilgal multiply *t*
Mic 1:5 For the *t* of Jacob is all this,
Mic 1:5 What is the *t* of Jacob
Mic 3:8 to declare unto Jacob his *t*
Mic 6:7 I give my firstborn for my *t*
Mic 7:18 passeth by the *t* of the remnant
Acts 1:25 from which Judas by *t* fell
Rom 4:15 where no law is, there is no *t*
Rom 5:14 after the similitude of Adam's *t*
1Ti 2:14 woman being deceived was in the *t*
Heb 2:2 angels was stedfast, and every *t*
1Jn 3:4 for sin is the *t* of the law

**TRANSGRESSIONS**
Ex 23:21 for he will not pardon your *t*
Lev 16:16 because of their *t* in all their
Lev 16:21 all their *t* in all their sins,
Josh 24:19 not forgive your *t* nor your sins
1Kin 8:50 all their *t* wherein they have
Job 31:33 If I covered my *t* as Adam
Job 35:6 or if thy *t* be multiplied, what
Job 36:9 their *t* that they have exceeded
Ps 5:10 out in the multitude of their *t*
Ps 25:7 the sins of my youth, nor my *t*
Ps 32:5 I will confess my *t* unto the LORD
Ps 39:8 Deliver me from all my *t*
Ps 51:1 thy tender mercies blot out my *t*
Ps 51:3 For I acknowledge my *t*
Ps 65:3 as for our *t*, thou shalt purge
Ps 103:12 far hath he removed our *t* from us
Is 43:25 out thy *t* for mine own sake
Is 44:22 out, as a thick cloud, thy *t*
Is 50:1 for your *t* is your mother put
Is 53:5 But he was wounded for our *t*
Is 59:12 For our *t* are multiplied before
Is 59:12 for our *t* are with us
Jer 5:6 because their *t* are many, and
Lam 1:5 her for the multitude of her *t*
Lam 1:14 The yoke of my *t* is bound by his
Lam 1:22 hast done unto me for all my *t*
Eze 14:11 any more with all their *t*
Eze 18:22 All his *t* that he hath committed,
Eze 18:28 all his *t* that he hath committed
Eze 18:30 turn yourselves from all your *t*
Eze 18:31 Cast away from you all your *t*
Eze 21:24 in that your *t* are discovered, so
Eze 33:10 Thus ye speak, saying, If our *t*
Eze 37:23 things, nor with any of their *t*
Eze 39:24 according to their *t* have I done
Amos 1:3 For three *t* of Damascus, and for
Amos 1:6 For three *t* of Gaza, and for four,
Amos 1:9 For three *t* of Tyrus, and for four
Amos 1:11 For three *t* of Edom, and for four,
Amos 1:13 For three *t* of the children of
Amos 2:1 For three *t* of Moab, and for four,
Amos 2:4 For three *t* of Judah, and for four
Amos 2:6 For three *t* of Israel, and for
Amos 3:14 *t* of Israel upon him I will also
Amos 5:12 For I know your manifold *t*
Mic 1:13 for the *t* of Israel were found in
Gal 3:19 It was added because of *t*
Heb 9:15 the *t* that were under the first

**TRANSGRESSOR**
Prov 21:18 and the *t* for the upright
Prov 22:12 overthroweth the words of the *t*
Is 48:8 and wast called a *t* from the womb
Gal 2:18 I destroyed, I make myself a *t*
Jas 2:11 thou art become a *t* of the law

**TRANSGRESSORS**
Ps 37:38 But the *t* shall be destroyed
Ps 51:13 Then will I teach *t* thy ways
Ps 59:5 be not merciful to any wicked *t*
Ps 119:158 I beheld the *t*, and was grieved
Prov 2:22 the *t* shall be rooted out of it
Prov 11:3 of *t* shall destroy them
Prov 11:6 but *t* shall be taken in their own
Prov 13:2 soul of the *t* shall eat violence
Prov 13:15 but the way of *t* is hard
Prov 23:28 and increaseth the *t* among men
Prov 26:10 the fool, and rewardeth *t*
Is 1:28 And the destruction of the *t*
Is 46:8 bring it again to mind, O ye *t*
Is 53:12 and he was numbered with the *t*
Is 53:12 and made intercession for the *t*
Dan 8:23 when the *t* are come to the full,
Hos 14:9 but the *t* shall fall therein
Mk 15:28 And he was numbered with the *t*
Lk 22:37 And he was reckoned among the *t*
Jas 2:9 and are convinced of the law as *t*

### TRANSLATE
2Sa 3:10 To *t* the kingdom from the house

### TRANSLATED
Col 1:13 hath *t* us into the kingdom of his
Heb 11:5 By faith Enoch was *t* that he
Heb 11:5 not found, because God had *t* him

### TRANSLATION
Heb 11:5 for before his *t* he had this

### TRANSPARENT
Rev 21:21 was pure gold, as it were *t* glass

### TRAP
Job 18:10 ground, and a *t* for him in the way
Ps 69:22 their welfare, let it become a *t*
Jer 5:26 they set a *t*, they catch men
Rom 11:9 table be made a snare, and a *t*

### TRAPS
Josh 23:13 *t* unto you, and scourges in your

### TRAVAIL
Gen 38:27 came to pass in the time of her *t*
Ex 18:8 all the *t* that had come upon them
Ps 48:6 and pain, as of a woman in *t*
Eccl 1:13 this sore *t* hath God given to the
Eccl 2:23 days are sorrows, and his *t* grief
Eccl 2:26 but to the sinner he giveth *t*
Eccl 3:10 I have seen the *t*, which God hath
Eccl 4:4 Again, I considered all *t*
Eccl 4:6 than both the hands full with *t*
Eccl 4:8 also vanity, yea, it is a sore *t*
Eccl 5:14 But those riches perish by evil *t*
Is 23:4 I *t* not, nor bring forth children
Is 53:11 He shall see of the *t* of his soul
Is 54:1 thou that didst not *t* with child
Jer 4:31 heard a voice as of a woman in *t*
Jer 6:24 us, and pain, as of a woman in *t*
Jer 13:21 take thee, as a woman in *t*
Jer 22:23 thee, the pain as of a woman in *t*
Jer 30:6 whether a man doth *t* with child
Jer 30:6 on his loins, as a woman in *t*
Jer 49:24 have taken her, as a woman in *t*
Jer 50:43 him, and pangs as of a woman in *t*
Mic 4:9 have taken thee as a woman in *t*
Mic 4:10 of Zion, like a woman in *t*
Jn 16:21 when she is in *t* hath sorrow
Gal 4:19 of whom I *t* in birth again until
1Th 2:9 brethren, our labour and *t*
1Th 5:3 as *t* upon a woman with child
2Th 3:8 *t* night and day, that we might not

### TRAVAILED
Gen 35:16 and Rachel *t*, and she had hard
Gen 38:28 And it came to pass, when she *t*
1Sa 4:19 were dead, she bowed herself and *t*
Is 66:7 Before she *t*, she brought forth
Is 66:8 for as soon as Zion *t*, she

### TRAVAILEST
Gal 4:27 forth and cry, thou that *t* not

### TRAVAILETH
Job 15:20 The wicked man *t* with pain all
Ps 7:14 he *t* with iniquity, and hath
Is 13:8 be in pain as a woman that *t*
Is 21:3 as the pangs of a woman that *t*
Jer 31:8 her that *t* with child together
Mic 5:3 she which *t* hath brought forth
Rom 8:22 *t* in pain together until now

### TRAVAILING
Is 42:14 now will I cry like a *t* woman
Hos 13:13 The sorrows of a *t* woman shall
Rev 12:2 *t* in birth, and pained to be

### TRAVEL
Num 20:14 Thou knowest all the *t* that hath
Lam 3:5 and compassed me with gall and *t*
Acts 19:29 Macedonia, Paul's companions in *t*
2Cor 8:19 to *t* with us with this grace

### TRAVELERS
Judg 5:6 the *t* walked through byways

### TRAVELLED
Acts 11:19 about Stephen *t* as far as Phenice

### TRAVELLER
2Sa 12:4 there came a *t* unto the rich man,
Job 31:32 but I opened my doors to the *t*

### TRAVELLETH
Prov 6:11 thy poverty come as one that *t*
Prov 24:34 thy poverty come as one that *t*

### TRAVELLING
Is 21:13 O ye *t* companies of Dedanim
Is 63:1 *t* in the greatness of his
Mt 25:14 is as a man *t* into a far country

### TRAVERSING
Jer 2:23 art a swift dromedary *t* her ways

### TREACHEROUS
Is 21:2 the *t* dealer dealeth
Is 24:16 the *t* dealers have dealt
Is 24:16 the *t* dealers have dealt very
Jer 3:7 her *t* sister Judah saw it
Jer 3:8 yet her *t* sister Judah feared not
Jer 3:10 yet for all this her *t* sister
Jer 3:11 herself more than *t* Judah
Jer 9:2 adulterers, an assembly of *t* men
Zeph 3:4 prophets are light and *t* persons

### TREACHEROUSLY
Judg 9:23 of Shechem dealt *t* with Abimelech
Is 21:2 the treacherous dealer dealeth *t*
Is 24:16 treacherous dealers have dealt *t*
Is 24:16 dealers have dealt very *t*
Is 33:1 and dealest *t*, and they dealt not
Is 33:1 and they dealt not *t* with thee
Is 33:1 thou shalt make an end to deal *t*
Is 33:1 they shall deal *t* with thee
Is 48:8 that thou wouldest deal very *t*
Jer 3:20 Surely as a wife *t* departeth from
Jer 3:20 so have ye dealt *t* with me
Jer 5:11 have dealt very *t* against me
Jer 12:1 all they happy that deal very *t*
Jer 12:6 even they have dealt *t* with thee
Lam 1:2 her friends have dealt *t* with her
Hos 5:7 They have dealt *t* against the
Hos 6:7 have they dealt *t* against me
Hab 1:13 thou upon them that deal *t*
Mal 2:10 why do we deal *t* every man
Mal 2:11 Judah hath dealt *t*, and an
Mal 2:14 against whom thou hast dealt *t*
Mal 2:15 let none deal *t* against the wife
Mal 2:16 your spirit, that ye deal not *t*

### TREACHERY
2Kin 9:23 and said to Ahaziah, There is *t*

### TREAD
Deut 11:24 your feet shall *t* shall be yours
Deut 11:25 all the land that ye shall *t* upon
Deut 33:29 thou shalt *t* upon their high
Josh 1:3 sole of your foot shall *t* upon
1Sa 5:5 *t* on the threshold of Dagon in
Job 24:11 *t* their winepresses, and suffer
Job 40:12 *t* down the wicked in their place
Ps 7:5 let him *t* down my life upon the
Ps 44:5 through thy name will we *t* them
Ps 60:12 is that shall *t* down our enemies
Ps 91:13 Thou shalt *t* upon the lion and
Ps 108:13 is that shall *t* down our enemies
Is 1:12 this at your hand, to *t* my courts
Is 10:6 to *t* them down like the mire of
Is 14:25 my mountains *t* him under foot
Is 16:10 the treaders shall *t* out no wine
Is 26:6 The foot shall *t* it down, even
Is 63:3 for I will *t* them in mine anger,
Is 63:6 I will *t* down the people in mine
Jer 25:30 shout, as they that *t* the grapes
Jer 48:33 none shall *t* with shouting
Eze 26:11 shall he *t* down all thy streets
Eze 34:18 but ye must *t* down with your feet
Dan 7:23 shall *t* it down, and break it in
Hos 10:11 and loveth to *t* out the corn
Mic 1:3 *t* upon the high places of the
Mic 5:5 when he shall *t* in our palaces,
Mic 6:15 thou shalt *t* the olives, but thou
Nah 3:14 *t* the morter, make strong the
Zec 10:5 which *t* down their enemies in the
Mal 4:3 ye shall *t* down the wicked
Lk 10:19 unto you power to *t* on serpents
Rev 11:2 shall they *t* under foot forty

### TREADER
Amos 9:13 the *t* of grapes him that soweth

### TREADERS
Is 16:10 the *t* shall tread out no wine in

### TREADETH
Deut 25:4 the ox when he *t* out the corn
Job 9:8 *t* upon the waves of the sea
Is 41:25 morter, and as the potter *t* clay
Is 63:2 like him that *t* in the winefat
Amos 4:13 *t* upon the high places of the
Mic 5:6 when he *t* within our borders
Mic 5:8 if he go through, both *t* down
1Cor 9:9 of the ox that *t* out the corn
1Ti 5:18 muzzle the ox that *t* out the corn
Rev 19:15 he *t* the winepress of the

### TREADING
Neh 13:15 some *t* winepresses on the sabbath
Is 7:25 for the *t* of lesser cattle
Is 22:5 of *t* down, and of perplexity by
Amos 5:11 as your *t* is upon the poor

### TREASON
1Kin 16:20 his *t* that he wrought, are they
2Kin 11:14 rent her clothes, and cried, *T*
2Kin 11:14 her clothes, and cried, *T*, *T*
2Chr 23:13 rent her clothes, and said, *T*
2Chr 23:13 her clothes, and said, *T*, *T*

### TREASURE
Gen 43:23 hath given you *t* in your sacks
Ex 1:11 they built for Pharaoh *t* cities
Ex 19:5 *t* unto me above all people
Deut 28:12 shall open unto thee his good *t*
1Chr 29:8 to the *t* of the house of the LORD
Ezr 2:69 unto the *t* of the work threescore
Ezr 5:17 search made in the king's *t* house
Ezr 7:20 it out of the king's *t* house
Neh 7:70 to the *t* a thousand drams of gold
Neh 7:71 of the fathers gave to the *t* of
Neh 10:38 to the chambers, into the *t* house
Ps 17:14 belly thou fillest with thy hid *t*
Ps 135:4 and Israel for his peculiar *t*
Prov 15:6 house of the righteous is much *t*
Prov 15:16 the fear of the LORD than great *t*
Prov 21:20 There is *t* to be desired and oil
Eccl 2:8 gold, and the peculiar *t* of kings
Is 33:6 the fear of the LORD is his *t*
Eze 22:25 they have taken the *t* and precious
Dan 1:2 into the *t* house of his god
Hos 13:15 he shall spoil the *t* of all
Mt 6:21 For where your *t* is, there will
Mt 12:35 A good man out of the good *t* of
Mt 12:35 evil *t* bringeth forth evil things
Mt 13:44 is like unto *t* hid in a field
Mt 13:52 forth out of his *t* things new
Mt 19:21 and thou shalt have *t* in heaven
Mk 10:21 and thou shalt have *t* in heaven
Lk 6:45 A good man out of the good *t* of
Lk 6:45 *t* of his heart bringeth forth
Lk 12:21 he that layeth up *t* for himself
Lk 12:33 a *t* in the heavens that faileth
Lk 12:34 For where your *t* is, there will
Lk 18:22 and thou shalt have *t* in heaven
Acts 8:27 who had the charge of all her *t*
2Cor 4:7 But we have this *t* in earthen
Jas 5:3 Ye have heaped *t* together for the

### TREASURED
Is 23:18 it shall not be *t* nor laid up

### TREASURER
Ezr 1:8 by the hand of Mithredath the *t*
Is 22:15 hosts, Go, get thee unto this *t*

### TREASURERS
Ezr 7:21 the *t* which are beyond the river
Neh 13:13 I made *t* over the treasuries,
Dan 3:2 the captains, the judges, the *t*
Dan 3:3 and captains, the judges, the *t*

### TREASURES
Deut 32:34 with me, and sealed up among my *t*
Deut 33:19 the seas, and of *t* hid in the sand
1Kin 7:51 did he put among the *t* of the
1Kin 14:26 he took away the *t* of the house
1Kin 14:26 the *t* of the king's house
1Kin 15:18 in the *t* of the house of the LORD
1Kin 15:18 the *t* of the king's house, and
2Kin 12:18 in the *t* of the house of the LORD
2Kin 14:14 in the *t* of the king's house, and
2Kin 16:8 in the *t* of the king's house, and
2Kin 18:15 in the *t* of the king's house
2Kin 20:13 and all that was found in his *t*
2Kin 20:15 there is nothing among my *t* that
2Kin 24:13 the *t* of the house of the LORD
2Kin 24:13 the *t* of the king's house, and cut
1Chr 26:20 over the *t* of the house of God
1Chr 26:20 over the *t* of the dedicated
1Chr 26:22 which were over the *t* of the
1Chr 26:24 son of Moses, was ruler of the *t*
1Chr 26:26 all the *t* of the dedicated things
1Chr 27:25 over the king's *t* was Azmaveth
2Chr 5:1 put he among the *t* of the house
2Chr 8:15 any matter, or concerning the *t*

2Chr 12:9 took away the *t* of the house of
2Chr 12:9 the *t* of the king's house
2Chr 16:2 gold out of the *t* of the house of
2Chr 25:24 the *t* of the king's house, the
2Chr 36:18 the *t* of the house of the LORD,
2Chr 36:18 the *t* of the king, and of his
Ezr 6:1 where the *t* were laid up in
Neh 12:44 over the chambers for the *t*
Job 3:21 and dig for it more than for hid *t*
Job 38:22 entered into the *t* of the snow
Job 38:22 hast thou seen the *t* of the hail
Prov 2:4 and searchest for her as for hid *t*
Prov 8:21 and I will fill their *t*
Prov 10:2 *T* of wickedness profit nothing
Prov 21:6 The getting of *t* by a lying
Is 2:7 is there any end of their *t*
Is 10:13 people, and have robbed their *t*
Is 30:6 their *t* upon the bunches of
Is 39:2 and all that was found in his *t*
Is 39:4 there is nothing among my *t* that
Is 45:3 will give thee the *t* of darkness
Jer 10:13 forth the wind out of his *t*
Jer 15:13 thy *t* will I give to the spoil
Jer 17:3 all thy *t* to the spoil, and thy
Jer 20:5 all the *t* of the kings of Judah
Jer 41:8 for we have *t* in the field, of
Jer 48:7 trusted in thy works and in thy *t*
Jer 49:4 that trusted in her *t*, saying,
Jer 50:37 a sword is upon her *t*
Jer 51:13 upon many waters, abundant in *t*
Jer 51:16 forth the wind out of his *t*
Eze 28:4 gotten gold and silver into thy *t*
Dan 11:43 have power over the *t* of gold
Mic 6:10 Are there yet the *t* of wickedness
Mt 2:11 and when they had opened their *t*
Mt 6:19 up for yourselves *t* upon earth
Mt 6:20 lay up for yourselves *t* in heaven
Col 2:3 whom are hid all the *t* of wisdom
Heb 11:26 riches than the *t* in Egypt

### TREASUREST
Rom 2:5 impenitent heart *t* up unto

### TREASURIES
1Chr 9:26 chambers and *t* of the house of God
1Chr 28:11 of the *t* thereof, and of the upper
1Chr 28:12 of the *t* of the house of God, and
1Chr 28:12 of the *t* of the dedicated things
2Chr 32:27 and he made himself *t* for silver
Neh 13:12 new wine and the oil unto the *t*
Neh 13:13 And I made treasurers over the *t*
Est 3:9 to bring it into the king's *t*
Est 4:7 pay to the king's *t* for the Jews
Ps 135:7 he bringeth the wind out of his *t*

### TREASURY
Josh 6:19 shall come into the *t* of the LORD
Josh 6:24 they put into the *t* of the house
Jer 38:11 the house of the king under the *t*
Mt 27:6 lawful for to put them into the *t*
Mk 12:41 And Jesus sat over against the *t*
Mk 12:41 the people cast money into the *t*
Mk 12:43 they which have cast into the *t*
Lk 21:1 casting their gifts into the *t*
Jn 8:20 These words spake Jesus in the *t*

### TREATISE
Acts 1:1 The former *t* have I made, O

### TREE
Gen 1:11 the fruit *t* yielding fruit after
Gen 1:12 the *t* yielding fruit, whose seed
Gen 1:29 face of all the earth, and every *t*
Gen 1:29 is the fruit of a *t* yielding seed
Gen 2:9 *t* that is pleasant to the sight
Gen 2:9 the *t* of life also in the midst
Gen 2:9 the *t* of knowledge of good and
Gen 2:16 Of every *t* of the garden thou
Gen 2:17 But of the *t* of the knowledge of
Gen 3:1 not eat of every *t* of the garden
Gen 3:3 But of the fruit of the *t* which
Gen 3:6 saw that the *t* was good for food
Gen 3:6 a *t* to be desired to make one
Gen 3:11 Hast thou eaten of the *t*, whereof
Gen 3:12 be with me, she gave me of the *t*
Gen 3:17 thy wife, and hast eaten of the *t*
Gen 3:22 and take also of the *t* of life
Gen 3:24 to keep the way of the *t* of life
Gen 18:4 and rest yourselves under the *t*
Gen 18:8 and he stood by them under the *t*
Gen 30:37 and of the hazel and chesnut *t*
Gen 40:19 thee, and shall hang thee on a *t*
Ex 9:25 brake every *t* of the field
Ex 10:5 shall eat every *t* which groweth
Ex 15:25 and the LORD shewed him a *t*
Lev 27:30 land, or of the fruit of the *t*
Num 6:4 that is made of the vine *t*
Deut 12:2 the hills, and under every green *t*
Deut 19:5 with the axe to cut down the *t*
Deut 20:19 not cut them down (for the *t* of
Deut 21:22 to death, and thou hang him on a *t*
Deut 21:23 not remain all night upon the *t*
Deut 22:6 before thee in the way in any *t*
Deut 24:20 When thou beatest thine olive *t*
Josh 8:29 he hanged on a *t* until eventide
Josh 8:29 take his carcase down from the *t*
Judg 4:5 palm *t* of Deborah between Ramah
Judg 9:8 and they said unto the olive *t*
Judg 9:9 But the olive *t* said unto them,
Judg 9:10 And the trees said to the fig *t*
Judg 9:11 But the fig *t* said unto them,
1Sa 14:2 pomegranate *t* which is in Migron
1Sa 22:6 in Gibeah under a *t* in Ramah
1Sa 31:13 buried them under a *t* at Jabesh
1Kin 4:25 under his vine and under his fig *t*
1Kin 4:33 from the cedar *t* that is in
1Kin 6:23 he made two cherubims of olive *t*
1Kin 6:31 oracle he made doors of olive *t*
1Kin 6:32 two doors also were of olive *t*
1Kin 6:33 of the temple posts of olive *t*
1Kin 6:34 And the two doors were of fir *t*
1Kin 14:23 high hill, and under every green *t*
1Kin 19:4 and sat down under a juniper *t*
1Kin 19:5 he lay and slept under a juniper *t*
2Kin 3:19 city, and shall fell every good *t*
2Kin 16:4 the hills, and under every green *t*
2Kin 17:10 high hill, and under every green *t*
2Kin 18:31 vine, and every one of his fig *t*
2Chr 3:5 house he cieled with fir *t*
2Chr 28:4 the hills, and under every green *t*
Est 2:23 they were both hanged on a *t*
Job 14:7 For there is hope of a *t*, if it
Job 19:10 hope hath he removed like a *t*
Job 24:20 wickedness shall be broken as a *t*
Ps 1:3 he shall be like a *t* planted by
Ps 37:35 himself like a green bay *t*
Ps 52:8 green olive *t* in the house of God
Ps 92:12 shall flourish like the palm *t*
Prov 3:18 She is a *t* of life to them that
Prov 11:30 of the righteous is a *t* of life
Prov 13:12 desire cometh, it is a *t* of life
Prov 15:4 A wholesome tongue is a *t* of life
Prov 27:18 Whoso keepeth the fig *t* shall eat
Eccl 11:3 if the *t* fall toward the south,
Eccl 11:3 in the place where the *t* falleth
Eccl 12:5 the almond *t* shall flourish, and
Song 2:3 As the apple *t* among the trees of
Song 2:13 The fig *t* putteth forth her green
Song 7:7 thy stature is like to a palm *t*
Song 7:8 said, I will go up to the palm *t*
Song 8:5 raised thee up under the apple *t*
Is 6:13 as a teil *t*, and as an oak, whose
Is 17:6 it, as the shaking of an olive *t*
Is 24:13 be as the shaking of an olive *t*
Is 34:4 as a falling fig from the fig *t*
Is 36:16 vine, and every one of his fig *t*
Is 40:20 chooseth a *t* that will not rot
Is 41:19 the cedar, the shittah *t*, and the
Is 41:19 *t*, and the myrtle, and the oil *t*
Is 41:19 will set in the desert the fir *t*
Is 41:19 the pine, and the box *t* together
Is 44:19 I fall down to the stock of a *t*
Is 44:23 O forest, and every *t* therein
Is 55:13 the thorn shall come up the fir *t*
Is 55:13 brier shall come up the myrtle *t*
Is 56:3 eunuch say, Behold, I am a dry *t*
Is 57:5 with idols under every green *t*
Is 60:13 shall come unto thee, the fir *t*
Is 60:13 thee, the fir *t*, the pine *t*
Is 65:22 for as the days of a *t* are the
Is 66:17 gardens behind one *t* in the midst
Jer 1:11 said, I see a rod of an almond *t*
Jer 2:20 every green *t* thou wanderest
Jer 3:6 mountain and under every green *t*
Jer 3:13 the strangers under every green *t*
Jer 8:13 the vine, nor figs on the fig *t*
Jer 10:3 one cutteth a *t* out of the forest
Jer 10:5 They are upright as the palm *t*
Jer 11:16 called thy name, A green olive *t*
Jer 11:19 Let us destroy the *t* with the
Jer 17:8 For he shall be as a *t* planted by
Eze 6:13 mountains, and under every green *t*
Eze 15:2 is the vine *t* more than any *t*
Eze 15:6 As the vine *t* among the trees of
Eze 17:5 waters, and set it as a willow *t*
Eze 17:24 LORD have brought down the high *t*
Eze 17:24 have exalted the low *t*
Eze 17:24 *t*, have dried up the green *t*
Eze 17:24 have made the dry *t* to flourish
Eze 20:47 devour every green *t* in thee
Eze 20:47 and every dry *t*
Eze 21:10 the rod of my son, as every *t*
Eze 31:8 nor any *t* in the garden of God
Eze 34:27 the *t* of the field shall yield
Eze 36:30 will multiply the fruit of the *t*
Eze 41:18 so that a palm *t* was between a
Eze 41:19 toward the palm *t* on the one side
Eze 41:19 the palm *t* on the other side
Dan 4:10 behold a *t* in the midst of the
Dan 4:11 The *t* grew, and was strong, and the
Dan 4:14 and said thus, Hew down the *t*
Dan 4:20 The *t* that thou sawest, which
Dan 4:23 heaven, and saying, Hew the *t* down
Dan 4:26 to leave the stump of the *t* roots
Hos 9:10 in the fig *t* at her first time
Hos 14:6 beauty shall be as the olive *t*
Hos 14:8 I am like a green fir *t*
Joel 1:7 my vine waste, and barked my fig *t*
Joel 1:12 up, and the fig *t* languisheth
Joel 1:12 pomegranate *t*, the palm *t* also
Joel 1:12 also, and the apple *t*
Joel 2:22 for the *t* beareth her fruit, the
Joel 2:22 beareth her fruit, the fig *t*
Mic 4:4 under his vine and under his fig *t*
Hab 3:17 Although the fig *t* shall not
Hag 2:19 as yet the vine, and the fig *t*
Hag 2:19 the pomegranate, and the olive *t*
Zec 3:10 under the vine and under the fig *t*
Zec 11:2 Howl, fir *t*
Mt 3:10 therefore every *t* which bringeth
Mt 7:17 Even so every good *t* bringeth
Mt 7:17 but a corrupt *t* bringeth forth
Mt 7:18 A good *t* cannot bring forth evil
Mt 7:18 neither can a corrupt *t* bring
Mt 7:19 Every *t* that bringeth not forth
Mt 12:33 Either make the *t* good, and his
Mt 12:33 or else make the *t* corrupt
Mt 12:33 for the *t* is known by his fruit
Mt 13:32 among herbs, and becometh a *t*
Mt 21:19 And when he saw a fig *t* in the way
Mt 21:19 presently the fig *t* withered away
Mt 21:20 soon is the fig *t* withered away
Mt 21:21 this which is done to the fig *t*
Mt 24:32 Now learn a parable of the fig *t*
Mk 11:13 seeing a fig *t* afar off having
Mk 11:20 they saw the fig *t* dried up from
Mk 11:21 the fig *t* which thou cursedst is
Mk 13:28 Now learn a parable of the fig *t*
Lk 3:9 every *t* therefore which bringeth
Lk 6:43 For a good *t* bringeth not forth
Lk 6:43 corrupt *t* bring forth good fruit
Lk 6:44 For every *t* is known by his own
Lk 13:6 a fig *t* planted in his vineyard
Lk 13:7 come seeking fruit on this fig *t*
Lk 13:19 and it grew, and waxed a great *t*
Lk 17:6 ye might say unto this sycamine *t*
Lk 19:4 up into a sycomore *t* to see him
Lk 21:29 Behold the fig *t*, and all the
Lk 23:31 they do these things in a green *t*
Jn 1:48 when thou wast under the fig *t*
Jn 1:50 thee, I saw thee under the fig *t*
Acts 5:30 whom ye slew and hanged on a *t*
Acts 10:39 whom they slew and hanged on a *t*
Acts 13:29 they took him down from the *t*
Rom 11:17 and thou, being a wild olive *t*
Rom 11:17 root and fatness of the olive *t*
Rom 11:24 olive *t* which is wild by nature
Rom 11:24 to nature into a good olive *t*
Rom 11:24 be graffed into their own olive *t*
Gal 3:13 is every one that hangeth on a *t*
Jas 3:12 Can the fig *t*, my brethren, bear
1Pet 2:24 our sins in his own body on the *t*
Rev 2:7 I give to eat of the *t* of life
Rev 6:13 even as a fig *t* casteth her
Rev 7:1 nor on the sea, nor on any *t*
Rev 9:4 any green thing, neither any *t*
Rev 22:2 river, was there the *t* of life
Rev 22:2 the leaves of the *t* were for the
Rev 22:14 may have right to the *t* of life

### TREES
Gen 3:2 the fruit of the *t* of the garden
Gen 3:8 God amongst the *t* of the garden

Gen 23:17 all the *t* that were in the field,
Ex 10:15 all the fruit of the *t* which the
Ex 10:15 not any green thing in the *t*
Ex 15:27 and threescore and ten palm *t*
Lev 19:23 planted all manner of *t* for food
Lev 23:40 first day the boughs of goodly *t*
Lev 23:40 branches of palm *t*
Lev 23:40 and the boughs of thick *t*
Lev 26:4 the *t* of the field shall yield
Lev 26:20 neither shall the *t* of the land
Num 24:6 as the *t* of lign aloes which the
Num 24:6 as cedar *t* beside the waters
Num 33:9 and threescore and ten palm *t*
Deut 6:11 not, vineyards and olive *t*
Deut 8:8 and barley, and vines, and fig *t*
Deut 16:21 not plant thee a grove of any *t*
Deut 20:19 the *t* thereof by forcing an ax
Deut 20:20 Only the *t* which thou knowest
Deut 20:20 that they be not *t* for meat
Deut 28:40 Thou shalt have olive *t*
Deut 28:42 All thy *t* and fruit of thy land
Deut 34:3 of Jericho, the city of palm *t*
Josh 10:26 them, and hanged them on five *t*
Josh 10:26 upon the *t* until the evening
Josh 10:27 and they took them down off the *t*
Judg 1:16 *t* with the children of Judah into
Judg 3:13 and possessed the city of palm *t*
Judg 9:8 The *t* went forth on a time to
Judg 9:9 and go to be promoted over the *t*
Judg 9:10 the *t* said to the fig tree, Come
Judg 9:11 and go to be promoted over the *t*
Judg 9:12 Then said the *t* unto the vine
Judg 9:13 and go to be promoted over the *t*
Judg 9:14 said all the *t* unto the bramble
Judg 9:15 And the bramble said unto the *t*
Judg 9:48 and cut down a bough from the *t*
2Sa 5:11 messengers to David, and cedar *t*
2Sa 5:23 them over against the mulberry *t*
2Sa 5:24 in the tops of the mulberry *t*
1Kin 4:33 And he spake of *t*, from the cedar
1Kin 5:6 hew me cedar *t* out of Lebanon
1Kin 5:10 So Hiram gave Solomon cedar *t*
1Kin 5:10 fir *t* according to all his desire
1Kin 6:29 figures of cherubims and palm *t*
1Kin 6:32 carvings of cherubims and palm *t*
1Kin 6:32 the cherubims, and upon the palm *t*
1Kin 6:35 thereon cherubims and palm *t*
1Kin 7:36 cherubims, lions, and palm *t*
1Kin 9:11 Solomon with cedar *t* and fir *t*
1Kin 10:11 Ophir great plenty of almug *t*
1Kin 10:12 the king made of the almug *t*
1Kin 10:12 there came no such almug *t*
1Kin 10:27 sycomore *t* that are in the vale
2Kin 3:25 water, and felled all the good *t*
2Kin 19:23 cut down the tall cedar *t* thereof
2Kin 19:23 and the choice fir *t* thereof
1Chr 14:14 them over against the mulberry *t*
1Chr 14:15 in the tops of the mulberry *t*
1Chr 16:33 Then shall the *t* of the wood sing
1Chr 22:4 Also cedar *t* in abundance
1Chr 27:28 And over the olive *t* and the
1Chr 27:28 the sycomore *t* that were in the
2Chr 1:15 cedar *t* made he as the sycomore
2Chr 1:15 *t* that are in the vale for
2Chr 2:8 Send me also cedar *t*
2Chr 2:8 fir *t*, and algum *t*
2Chr 3:5 fine gold, and set thereon palm *t*
2Chr 9:10 gold from Ophir, brought algum *t*
2Chr 9:11 the king made of the algum *t*
2Chr 9:27 cedar *t* made he as the sycomore
2Chr 9:27 *t* that are in the low plains in
2Chr 28:15 to Jericho, the city of palm *t*
Ezr 3:7 to bring cedar *t* from Lebanon to
Neh 8:15 branches, and branches of thick *t*
Neh 9:25 and fruit *t* in abundance
Neh 10:35 firstfruits of all fruit of all *t*
Neh 10:37 and the fruit of all manner of *t*
Job 40:21 He lieth under the shady *t*
Job 40:22 The shady *t* cover him with their
Ps 74:5 lifted up axes upon the thick *t*
Ps 78:47 and their sycomore *t* with frost
Ps 96:12 then shall all the *t* of the wood
Ps 104:16 The *t* of the LORD are full of sap
Ps 104:17 stork, the fir *t* are her house
Ps 105:33 their vines also and their fig *t*
Ps 105:33 brake the *t* of their coasts
Ps 148:9 fruitful *t*, and all cedars
Eccl 2:5 I planted *t* in them of all kind
Eccl 2:6 the wood that bringeth forth *t*
Song 2:3 tree among the *t* of the wood
Song 4:14 with all *t* of frankincense
Is 7:2 as the *t* of the wood are moved
Is 10:19 the rest of the *t* of his forest
Is 14:8 the fir *t* rejoice at thee, and the
Is 37:24 and the choice fir *t* thereof
Is 44:14 himself among the *t* of the forest
Is 55:12 all the *t* of the field shall clap
Is 61:3 be called *t* of righteousness
Jer 5:17 eat up thy vines and thy fig *t*
Jer 6:6 LORD of hosts said, Hew ye down *t*
Jer 7:20 upon the *t* of the field, and upon
Jer 17:2 the green *t* upon the high hills
Eze 15:2 is among the *t* of the forest
Eze 15:6 tree among the *t* of the forest
Eze 17:24 all the *t* of the field shall know
Eze 20:28 high hill, and all the thick *t*
Eze 27:5 thy ship boards of fir *t* of Senir
Eze 31:4 unto all the *t* of the field
Eze 31:5 above all the *t* of the field
Eze 31:8 the fir *t* were not like his
Eze 31:8 the chesnut *t* were not like his
Eze 31:9 so that all the *t* of Eden
Eze 31:14 *t* by the waters exalt themselves
Eze 31:14 neither their *t* stand up in their
Eze 31:15 all the *t* of the field fainted
Eze 31:16 and all the *t* of Eden, the choice
Eze 31:18 in greatness among the *t* of Eden
Eze 31:18 *t* of Eden unto the nether parts
Eze 40:16 and upon each post were palm *t*
Eze 40:22 and their arches, and their palm *t*
Eze 40:26 and it had palm *t*, one on this
Eze 40:31 palm *t* were upon the posts
Eze 40:34 palm *t* were upon the posts
Eze 40:37 palm *t* were upon the posts
Eze 41:18 was made with cherubims and palm *t*
Eze 41:20 were cherubims and palm *t* made
Eze 41:25 the temple, cherubims and palm *t*
Eze 41:26 palm *t* on the one side and on the
Eze 47:7 were very many *t* on the one side
Eze 47:12 side, shall grow all *t* for meat
Hos 2:12 destroy her vines and her fig *t*
Joel 1:12 tree, even all the *t* of the field
Joel 1:19 burned all the *t* of the field
Amos 4:9 and your vineyards and your fig *t*
Amos 4:9 and your olive *t* increased
Nah 2:3 the fir *t* shall be terribly
Nah 3:12 fig *t* with the firstripe figs
Zec 1:8 myrtle *t* that were in the bottom
Zec 1:10 stood among the myrtle *t* answered
Zec 1:11 that stood among the myrtle *t*
Zec 4:3 And two olive *t* by it, one upon
Zec 4:11 What are these two olive *t* upon
Mt 3:10 ax is laid unto the root of the *t*
Mt 21:8 cut down branches from the *t*
Mk 8:24 up, and said, I see men as *t*
Mk 11:8 cut down branches off the *t*
Lk 3:9 is laid unto the root of the *t*
Lk 21:29 Behold the fig tree, and all the *t*
Jn 12:13 Took branches of palm *t*, and went
Jude 12 *t* whose fruit withereth, without
Rev 7:3 earth, neither the sea, nor the *t*
Rev 8:7 the third part of *t* was burnt up
Rev 11:4 These are the two olive *t*

## TREMBLE
Deut 2:25 hear report of thee, and shall *t*
Deut 20:3 faint, fear not, and do not *t*
Ezr 10:3 lord, and of those that *t* at the
Job 9:6 place, and the pillars thereof *t*
Job 26:11 The pillars of heaven *t*, and are
Ps 60:2 Thou hast made the earth to *t*
Ps 99:1 let the people *t*
Ps 114:7 *T*, thou earth, at the presence of
Eccl 12:3 the keepers of the house shall *t*
Is 5:25 and the hills did *t*, and their
Is 14:16 the man that made the earth to *t*
Is 32:11 *T*, ye women that are at ease
Is 64:2 the nations may *t* at thy presence
Is 66:5 the LORD, ye that *t* at his word
Jer 5:22 will ye not *t* at my presence,
Jer 10:10 at his wrath the earth shall *t*
Jer 33:9 *t* for all the goodness and for all
Jer 51:29 And the land shall *t* and sorrow
Eze 26:16 shall *t* at every moment, and be
Eze 26:18 Now shall the isles *t* in the day
Eze 32:10 they shall *t* at every moment,
Dan 6:26 dominion of my kingdom men *t*
Hos 11:10 children shall *t* from the west
Hos 11:11 They shall *t* as a bird out of
Joel 2:1 all the inhabitants of the land *t*
Joel 2:10 the heavens shall *t*
Amos 8:8 Shall not the land *t* for this
Hab 3:7 of the land of Midian did *t*
Jas 2:19 the devils also believe, and *t*

## TREMBLED
Gen 27:33 Isaac *t* very exceedingly, and said
Ex 19:16 the people that was in the camp *t*
Judg 5:4 of the field of Edom, the earth *t*
1Sa 4:13 for his heart *t* for the ark of
1Sa 14:15 and the spoilers, they also *t*
1Sa 16:4 of the town *t* at his coming
1Sa 28:5 afraid, and his heart greatly *t*
2Sa 22:8 Then the earth shook and *t*
Ezr 9:4 unto me every one that *t* at the
Ps 18:7 Then the earth shook and *t*
Ps 77:18 the earth *t* and shook
Ps 97:4 the earth saw, and *t*
Jer 4:24 the mountains, and, lo, they *t*
Jer 8:16 the whole land *t* at the sound of
Dan 5:19 people, nations, and languages, *t*
Hab 3:10 The mountains saw thee, and they *t*
Hab 3:16 When I heard, my belly *t*
Hab 3:16 I *t* in myself, that I might rest
Mk 16:8 for they *t* and were amazed
Acts 7:32 Then Moses *t*, and durst not
Acts 24:25 and judgment to come, Felix *t*

## TREMBLETH
Job 37:1 At this also my heart *t*, and is
Ps 104:32 He looketh on the earth, and it *t*
Ps 119:120 My flesh *t* for fear of thee
Is 66:2 contrite spirit, and *t* at my word

## TREMBLING
Ex 15:15 *t* shall take hold upon them
Deut 28:65 shall give thee there a *t* heart
1Sa 13:7 and all the people followed him *t*
1Sa 14:15 there was *t* in the host, in the
1Sa 14:15 so it was a very great *t*
Ezr 10:9 *t* because of this matter, and for
Job 4:14 Fear came upon me, and *t*, which
Job 21:6 *t* taketh hold on my flesh
Ps 2:11 LORD with fear, and rejoice with *t*
Ps 55:5 *t* are come upon me, and horror
Is 51:17 drunken the dregs of the cup of *t*
Is 51:22 out of thine hand the cup of *t*
Jer 30:5 We have heard a voice of *t*
Eze 12:18 and drink thy water with *t*
Eze 26:16 shall clothe themselves with *t*
Dan 10:11 this word unto me, I stood *t*
Hos 13:1 When Ephraim spake *t*, he exalted
Zec 12:2 I will make Jerusalem a cup of *t*
Mk 5:33 But the woman fearing and *t*
Lk 8:47 that she was not hid, she came *t*
Acts 9:6 And he *t* and astonished said, Lord,
Acts 16:29 a light, and sprang in, and came *t*
1Cor 2:3 and in fear, and in much *t*
2Cor 7:15 with fear and *t* ye received him
Eph 6:5 to the flesh, with fear and *t*
Phil 2:12 your own salvation with fear and *t*

## TRENCH
1Sa 17:20 and he came to the *t*, as the host
1Sa 26:5 and Saul lay in the *t*, and the
1Sa 26:7 Saul lay sleeping within the *t*
2Sa 20:15 the city, and it stood in the *t*
1Kin 18:32 he made a *t* about the altar, as
1Kin 18:35 he filled the *t* also with water
1Kin 18:38 up the water that was in the *t*
Lk 19:43 enemies shall cast a *t* about thee

## TRESPASS
Gen 31:36 and said to Laban, What is my *t*
Gen 50:17 the *t* of thy brethren, and their
Gen 50:17 forgive the *t* of the servants of
Ex 22:9 For all manner of *t*, whether it
Lev 5:6 he shall bring his *t* offering
Lev 5:7 then he shall bring for his *t*
Lev 5:15 If a soul commit a *t*, and sin
Lev 5:15 his *t* unto the LORD a ram without
Lev 5:15 the sanctuary, for a *t* offering
Lev 5:16 with the ram of the *t* offering
Lev 5:18 for a *t* offering, unto the priest
Lev 5:19 It is a *t* offering
Lev 6:2 commit a *t* against the LORD, and
Lev 6:5 in the day of his *t* offering
Lev 6:6 he shall bring his *t* offering
Lev 6:6 for a *t* offering, unto the priest
Lev 6:17 offering, and as the *t* offering
Lev 7:1 this is the law of the *t* offering
Lev 7:2 shall they kill the *t* offering
Lev 7:5 it is a *t* offering

Lev 7:7 offering is, so is the *t* offering
Lev 7:37 of the *t* offering, and of the
Lev 14:12 and offer him for a *t* offering
Lev 14:13 priest's, so is the *t* offering
Lev 14:14 of the blood of the *t* offering
Lev 14:17 upon the blood of the *t* offering
Lev 14:21 lamb for a *t* offering to be waved
Lev 14:24 take the lamb of the *t* offering
Lev 14:25 kill the lamb of the *t* offering
Lev 14:25 of the blood of the *t* offering
Lev 14:28 of the blood of the *t* offering
Lev 19:21 he shall bring his *t* offering
Lev 19:21 even a ram for a *t* offering
Lev 19:22 for him with the ram of the *t*
Lev 22:16 them to bear the iniquity of *t*
Lev 26:40 fathers, with their *t* which they
Num 5:6 to do a *t* against the LORD, and
Num 5:7 he shall recompense his *t* with
Num 5:8 kinsman to recompense the *t* unto
Num 5:8 let the *t* be recompensed unto the
Num 5:12 aside, and commit a *t* against him,
Num 5:27 have done *t* against her husband,
Num 6:12 the first year for a *t* offering
Num 18:9 every *t* offering of theirs, which
Num 31:16 to commit *t* against the LORD in
Josh 7:1 a *t* in the accursed thing
Josh 22:16 What *t* is this that ye have
Josh 22:20 commit a *t* in the accursed thing
Josh 22:31 committed this *t* against the LORD
1Sa 6:3 any wise return him a *t* offering
1Sa 6:4 What shall be the *t* offering
1Sa 6:8 ye return him for a *t* offering
1Sa 6:17 for a *t* offering unto the LORD
1Sa 25:28 forgive the *t* of thine handmaid
1Kin 8:31 If any man *t* against his
2Kin 12:16 The *t* money and sin money was not
1Chr 21:3 will he be a cause of *t* to Israel
2Chr 19:10 that they *t* not against the LORD
2Chr 19:10 this do, and ye shall not *t*
2Chr 24:18 and Jerusalem for this their *t*
2Chr 28:13 add more to our sins and to our *t*
2Chr 28:13 for our *t* is great, and there is
2Chr 28:22 he *t* yet more against the LORD
2Chr 33:19 of him, and all his sin, and his *t*
Ezr 9:2 rulers hath been chief in this *t*
Ezr 9:6 our *t* is grown up unto the
Ezr 9:7 been in a great *t* unto this day
Ezr 9:13 evil deeds, and for our great *t*
Ezr 10:10 to increase the *t* of Israel
Ezr 10:19 a ram of the flock for their *t*
Eze 15:8 because they have committed a *t*
Eze 17:20 plead with him there for his *t*
Eze 18:24 in his *t* that he hath trespassed,
Eze 20:27 have committed a *t* against me
Eze 40:39 sin offering and the *t* offering
Eze 42:13 sin offering, and the *t* offering
Eze 44:29 sin offering, and the *t* offering
Eze 46:20 priests shall boil the *t* offering
Dan 9:7 because of their *t* that they have
Mt 18:15 thy brother shall *t* against thee
Lk 17:3 If thy brother *t* against thee
Lk 17:4 if he *t* against thee seven times

## TRESPASSED

Lev 5:19 hath certainly *t* against the LORD
Lev 26:40 trespass which they *t* against me
Num 5:7 unto him against whom he hath *t*
Deut 32:51 Because ye *t* against me among the
2Chr 26:18 for thou hast *t*
2Chr 29:6 For our fathers have *t*, and done
2Chr 30:7 which *t* against the LORD God of
2Chr 33:23 but Amon *t* more and more
Ezr 10:2 We have *t* against our God, and
Eze 17:20 that he hath *t* against me
Eze 18:24 in his trespass that he hath *t*
Eze 39:23 because they *t* against me
Eze 39:26 whereby they have *t* against me
Dan 9:7 that they have *t* against thee
Hos 8:1 my covenant, and *t* against my law

## TRESPASSES

Ezr 9:15 we are before thee in our *t*
Ps 68:21 an one as goeth on still in his *t*
Eze 39:26 all their *t* whereby they have
Mt 6:14 For if ye forgive men their *t*
Mt 6:15 But if ye forgive not men their *t*
Mt 6:15 will your Father forgive your *t*
Mt 18:35 not every one his brother their *t*
Mk 11:25 in heaven may forgive you your *t*
Mk 11:26 which is in heaven forgive your *t*
2Cor 5:19 not imputing their *t* unto them
Eph 2:1 he quickened, who were dead in *t*
Col 2:13 him, having forgiven you all *t*

## TRESPASSING

Lev 6:7 that he hath done in *t* therein
Eze 14:13 against me by *t* grievously

## TRIAL

Job 9:23 laugh at the *t* of the innocent
Eze 21:13 Because it is a *t*, and what if the
2Cor 8:2 How that in a great *t* of
Heb 11:36 others had *t* of cruel mockings and
1Pet 1:7 That the *t* of your faith, being
1Pet 4:12 the fiery *t* which is to try you

## TRIBE

Ex 31:2 the son of Hur, of the *t* of Judah
Ex 31:6 son of Ahisamach, of the *t* of Dan
Ex 35:30 the son of Hur, of the *t* of Judah
Ex 35:34 son of Ahisamach, of the *t* of Dan
Ex 38:22 of the *t* of Judah, made all that
Ex 38:23 son of Ahisamach, of the *t* of Dan
Lev 24:11 of Dibri, of the *t* of Dan
Num 1:4 there shall be a man of every *t*
Num 1:5 of the *t* of Reuben
Num 1:21 of them, even of the *t* of Reuben
Num 1:23 of them, even of the *t* of Simeon
Num 1:25 of them, even of the *t* of Gad
Num 1:27 of them, even of the *t* of Judah
Num 1:29 them, even of the *t* of Issachar
Num 1:31 of them, even of the *t* of Zebulun
Num 1:33 of them, even of the *t* of Ephraim
Num 1:35 them, even of the *t* of Manasseh
Num 1:37 them, even of the *t* of Benjamin
Num 1:39 of them, even of the *t* of Dan
Num 1:41 of them, even of the *t* of Asher
Num 1:43 them, even of the *t* of Naphtali
Num 1:47 the *t* of their fathers were not
Num 1:49 shalt not number the *t* of Levi
Num 2:5 him shall be the *t* of Issachar
Num 2:7 Then the *t* of Zebulun
Num 2:12 by him shall be the *t* of Simeon
Num 2:14 Then the *t* of Gad
Num 2:20 by him shall be the *t* of Manasseh
Num 2:22 Then the *t* of Benjamin
Num 2:27 by him shall be the *t* of Asher
Num 2:29 Then the *t* of Naphtali
Num 3:6 Bring the *t* of Levi near, and
Num 4:18 Cut ye not off the *t* of the
Num 7:12 of Amminadab, of the *t* of Judah
Num 10:15 over the host of the *t* of the
Num 10:16 over the host of the *t* of the
Num 10:19 over the host of the *t* of the
Num 10:20 over the host of the *t* of the
Num 10:23 over the host of the *t* of the
Num 10:24 over the host of the *t* of the
Num 10:26 over the host of the *t* of the
Num 10:27 over the host of the *t* of the
Num 13:2 of every *t* of their fathers shall
Num 13:4 of the *t* of Reuben, Shammua the
Num 13:5 Of the *t* of Simeon, Shaphat the
Num 13:6 Of the *t* of Judah, Caleb the son
Num 13:7 Of the *t* of Issachar, Igal the
Num 13:8 Of the *t* of Ephraim, Oshea the
Num 13:9 Of the *t* of Benjamin, Palti the
Num 13:10 Of the *t* of Zebulun, Gaddiel the
Num 13:11 Of the *t* of Joseph, namely, of
Num 13:11 of the *t* of Manasseh, Gaddi the
Num 13:12 Of the *t* of Dan, Ammiel the son
Num 13:13 Of the *t* of Asher, Sethur the son
Num 13:14 Of the *t* of Naphtali, Nahbi the
Num 13:15 Of the *t* of Gad, Geuel the son of
Num 18:2 brethren also of the *t* of Levi
Num 18:2 the *t* of thy father, bring thou
Num 31:4 Of every *t* a thousand, throughout
Num 31:5 of Israel, a thousand of every *t*
Num 31:6 to the war, a thousand of every *t*
Num 32:33 unto half the *t* of Manasseh the
Num 34:13 the nine tribes, and to the half *t*
Num 34:14 For the *t* of the children of
Num 34:14 the *t* of the children of Gad
Num 34:14 half the *t* of Manasseh have
Num 34:15 the half *t* have received their
Num 34:18 shall take one prince of every *t*
Num 34:19 Of the *t* of Judah, Caleb the son
Num 34:20 of the *t* of the children of
Num 34:21 Of the *t* of Benjamin, Elidad the
Num 34:22 the prince of the *t* of the
Num 34:23 for the *t* of the children of
Num 34:24 the prince of the *t* of the
Num 34:25 the prince of the *t* of the
Num 34:26 the prince of the *t* of the
Num 34:27 the prince of the *t* of the
Num 34:28 the prince of the *t* of the
Num 36:3 the *t* whereunto they are received
Num 36:4 the *t* whereunto they are received
Num 36:4 of the *t* of our fathers
Num 36:5 The *t* of the sons of Joseph hath
Num 36:6 only to the family of the *t* of
Num 36:7 of Israel remove from *t* to *t*
Num 36:7 of the *t* of his fathers
Num 36:8 an inheritance in any *t* of the
Num 36:8 the family of the *t* of her father
Num 36:9 from one *t* to another *t*
Num 36:12 inheritance remained in the *t* of
Deut 1:23 twelve men of you, one of a *t*
Deut 3:13 I unto the half *t* of Manasseh
Deut 10:8 the LORD separated the *t* of Levi
Deut 18:1 the Levites, and all the *t* of Levi
Deut 29:8 and to the half *t* of Manasseh
Deut 29:18 man, or woman, or family, or *t*
Josh 1:12 and to half the *t* of Manasseh
Josh 3:12 of Israel, out of every *t* a man
Josh 4:2 the people, out of every *t* a man
Josh 4:4 of Israel, out of every *t* a man
Josh 4:12 half the *t* of Manasseh, passed
Josh 7:1 of the *t* of Judah, took of the
Josh 7:14 that the *t* which the LORD taketh
Josh 7:16 and the *t* of Judah was taken
Josh 7:18 of the *t* of Judah, was taken
Josh 12:6 and the half *t* of Manasseh
Josh 13:7 and the half *t* of Manasseh,
Josh 13:14 Only unto the *t* of Levi he gave
Josh 13:15 Moses gave unto the *t* of the
Josh 13:24 inheritance unto the *t* of Gad
Josh 13:29 unto the half *t* of Manasseh
Josh 13:29 *t* of the children of Manasseh by
Josh 13:33 But unto the *t* of Levi Moses gave
Josh 14:2 nine tribes, and for the half *t*
Josh 14:3 an half *t* on the other side
Josh 15:1 the *t* of the children of Judah by
Josh 15:20 of the *t* of the children of Judah
Josh 15:21 the uttermost cities of the *t* of
Josh 16:8 *t* of the children of Ephraim by
Josh 17:1 also a lot for the *t* of Manasseh
Josh 18:4 among you three men for each *t*
Josh 18:7 half the *t* of Manasseh, have
Josh 18:11 the lot of the *t* of the children
Josh 18:21 Now the cities of the *t* of the
Josh 19:1 even for the *t* of the children of
Josh 19:8 the *t* of the children of Simeon
Josh 19:23 the *t* of the children of Issachar
Josh 19:24 the *t* of the children of Asher
Josh 19:31 of the *t* of the children of Asher
Josh 19:39 the *t* of the children of Naphtali
Josh 19:40 for the *t* of the children of Dan
Josh 19:48 of the *t* of the children of Dan
Josh 20:8 the plain out of the *t* of Reuben
Josh 20:8 in Gilead out of the *t* of Gad
Josh 20:8 Bashan out of the *t* of Manasseh
Josh 21:4 had by lot out of the *t* of Judah
Josh 21:4 Judah, and out of the *t* of Simeon
Josh 21:4 out of the *t* of Benjamin,
Josh 21:5 the families of the *t* of Ephraim
Josh 21:5 Ephraim, and out of the *t* of Dan
Josh 21:5 and out of the half *t* of Manasseh
Josh 21:6 the families of the *t* of Issachar
Josh 21:6 and out of the *t* of Asher
Josh 21:6 out of the *t* of Naphtali, and out
Josh 21:6 out of the half *t* of Manasseh in
Josh 21:7 had out of the *t* of Reuben
Josh 21:7 of Reuben, and out of the *t* of Gad
Josh 21:7 Gad, and out of the *t* of Zebulun
Josh 21:9 they gave out of the *t* of the
Josh 21:9 out of the *t* of the children of
Josh 21:17 out of the *t* of Benjamin, Gibeon
Josh 21:20 their lot out of the *t* of Ephraim
Josh 21:23 And out of the *t* of Dan, Eltekeh
Josh 21:25 And out of the half *t* of Manasseh
Josh 21:27 out of the other half *t* of
Josh 21:28 out of the *t* of Issachar, Kishon
Josh 21:30 And out of the *t* of Asher, Mishal
Josh 21:32 out of the *t* of Naphtali, Kedesh
Josh 21:34 Levites, out of the *t* of Zebulun
Josh 21:36 And out of the *t* of Reuben
Josh 21:38 And out of the *t* of Gad, Ramoth in
Josh 22:1 and the half *t* of Manasseh,
Josh 22:7 Now to the one half of the *t* of
Josh 22:9 the half *t* of Manasseh returned,
Josh 22:10 the half *t* of Manasseh built
Josh 22:11 the half *t* of Manasseh have built
Josh 22:13 Gad, and to the half *t* of Manasseh

Josh 22:15 Gad, and to the half *t* of Manasseh
Josh 22:21 the half *t* of Manasseh answered,
Judg 18:1 in those days the *t* of the
Judg 18:19 or that thou be a priest unto a *t*
Judg 18:30 the *t* of Dan until the day of the
Judg 20:12 men through all the *t* of Benjamin
Judg 21:3 be to day one *t* lacking in Israel
Judg 21:6 There is one *t* cut off from
Judg 21:17 that a *t* be not destroyed out of
Judg 21:24 at that time, every man to his *t*
1Sa 9:21 the families of the *t* of Benjamin
1Sa 10:20 the *t* of Benjamin was taken
1Sa 10:21 When he had caused the *t* of
1Kin 7:14 widow's son of the *t* of Naphtali
1Kin 11:13 but will give one *t* to thy son
1Kin 11:32 (But he shall have one *t* for my
1Kin 11:36 And unto his son will I give one *t*
1Kin 12:20 of David, but the *t* of Judah only
1Kin 12:21 with the *t* of Benjamin, an
2Kin 17:18 none left but the *t* of Judah only
1Chr 5:18 half the *t* of Manasseh, of
1Chr 5:23 the children of the half *t* of
1Chr 5:26 the half *t* of Manasseh, and
1Chr 6:60 And out of the *t* of Benjamin
1Chr 6:61 were left of the family of that *t*
1Chr 6:61 cities given out of the half *t*
1Chr 6:61 out of the half *t* of Manasseh
1Chr 6:62 families out of the *t* of Issachar
1Chr 6:62 and out of the *t* of Asher
1Chr 6:62 out of the *t* of Naphtali, and out
1Chr 6:62 out of the *t* of Manasseh in
1Chr 6:63 families, out of the *t* of Reuben
1Chr 6:63 of Reuben, and out of the *t* of Gad
1Chr 6:63 Gad, and out of the *t* of Zebulun
1Chr 6:65 of the *t* of the children of Judah
1Chr 6:65 out of the *t* of the children of
1Chr 6:65 out of the *t* of the children of
1Chr 6:66 coasts out of the *t* of Ephraim
1Chr 6:70 And out of the half *t* of Manasseh
1Chr 6:71 family of the half *t* of Manasseh
1Chr 6:72 And out of the *t* of Issachar
1Chr 6:74 And out of the *t* of Asher
1Chr 6:76 And out of the *t* of Naphtali
1Chr 6:77 given out of the *t* of Zebulun
1Chr 6:78 given them out of the *t* of Reuben
1Chr 6:80 And out of the *t* of Gad
1Chr 12:31 of the half *t* of Manasseh
1Chr 12:37 and of the half *t* of Manasseh
1Chr 23:14 sons were named of the *t* of Levi
1Chr 26:32 the half *t* of Manasseh, for every
1Chr 27:20 of the half *t* of Manasseh
1Chr 27:21 Of the half *t* of Manasseh in
Ps 78:67 and chose not the *t* of Ephraim
Ps 78:68 But chose the *t* of Judah, the
Eze 47:23 that in what *t* the stranger
Lk 2:36 of Phanuel, of the *t* of Aser
Acts 13:21 Cis, a man of the *t* of Benjamin
Rom 11:1 of Abraham, of the *t* of Benjamin
Phil 3:5 of the *t* of Benjamin, an Hebrew
Heb 7:13 spoken pertaineth to another *t*
Heb 7:14 of which *t* Moses spake nothing
Rev 5:5 behold, the Lion of the *t* of Juda
Rev 7:5 Of the *t* of Juda were sealed
Rev 7:5 Of the *t* of Reuben were sealed
Rev 7:5 Of the *t* of Gad were sealed
Rev 7:6 Of the *t* of Aser were sealed
Rev 7:6 Of the *t* of Nepthalim were sealed
Rev 7:6 Of the *t* of Manasses were sealed
Rev 7:7 Of the *t* of Simeon were sealed
Rev 7:7 Of the *t* of Levi were sealed
Rev 7:7 Of the *t* of Issachar were sealed
Rev 7:8 Of the *t* of Zabulon were sealed
Rev 7:8 Of the *t* of Joseph were sealed
Rev 7:8 Of the *t* of Benjamin were sealed

**TRIBES**

Gen 49:16 people, as one of the *t* of Israel
Gen 49:28 these are the twelve *t* of Israel
Ex 24:4 to the twelve *t* of Israel
Ex 28:21 they be according to the twelve *t*
Ex 39:14 name, according to the twelve *t*
Num 1:16 princes of the *t* of their fathers
Num 7:2 who were the princes of the *t*
Num 24:2 in his tents according to their *t*
Num 26:55 the *t* of their fathers they shall
Num 30:1 the *t* concerning the children of
Num 31:4 throughout all the *t* of Israel
Num 32:28 the chief fathers of the *t* of the
Num 33:54 according to the *t* of your
Num 34:13 commanded to give unto the nine *t*
Num 34:15 The two *t* and the half tribe have
Num 36:3 other *t* of the children of Israel
Num 36:9 but every one of the *t* of the
Deut 1:13 and known among your *t*, and I will
Deut 1:15 So I took the chief of your *t*
Deut 1:15 tens, and officers among your *t*
Deut 5:23 me, even all the heads of your *t*
Deut 12:5 all your *t* to put his name there
Deut 12:14 LORD shall choose in one of thy *t*
Deut 16:18 God giveth thee, throughout thy *t*
Deut 18:5 hath chosen him out of all thy *t*
Deut 29:10 your captains of your *t*, your
Deut 29:21 evil out of all the *t* of Israel
Deut 31:28 unto me all the elders of your *t*
Deut 33:5 the *t* of Israel were gathered
Josh 3:12 twelve men out of the *t* of Israel
Josh 4:5 unto the number of the *t* of the
Josh 4:8 the *t* of the children of Israel
Josh 7:14 be brought according to your *t*
Josh 7:16 and brought Israel by their *t*
Josh 11:23 to their divisions by their *t*
Josh 12:7 the *t* of Israel for a possession
Josh 13:7 an inheritance unto the nine *t*
Josh 14:1 the *t* of the children of Israel
Josh 14:2 the hand of Moses, for the nine *t*
Josh 14:3 given the inheritance of two *t*
Josh 14:4 the children of Joseph were two *t*
Josh 18:2 the children of Israel seven *t*
Josh 19:51 the *t* of the children of Israel
Josh 21:1 the *t* of the children of Israel
Josh 21:16 nine cities out of those two *t*
Josh 22:14 throughout all the *t* of Israel
Josh 23:4 to be an inheritance for your *t*
Josh 24:1 all the *t* of Israel to Shechem
Judg 18:1 unto them among the *t* of Israel
Judg 20:2 even of all the *t* of Israel
Judg 20:10 throughout all the *t* of Israel
Judg 20:12 the *t* of Israel sent men through
Judg 21:5 Who is there among all the *t* of
Judg 21:8 What one is there of the *t* of
Judg 21:15 made a breach in the *t* of Israel
1Sa 2:28 the *t* of Israel to be my priest
1Sa 9:21 the smallest of the *t* of Israel
1Sa 10:19 before the LORD by your *t*
1Sa 10:20 all the *t* of Israel to come near
1Sa 15:17 made the head of the *t* of Israel
2Sa 5:1 Then came all the *t* of Israel to
2Sa 7:7 word with any of the *t* of Israel
2Sa 15:2 is of one of the *t* of Israel
2Sa 15:10 throughout all the *t* of Israel
2Sa 19:9 throughout all the *t* of Israel
2Sa 20:14 all the *t* of Israel unto Abel
2Sa 24:2 now through all the *t* of Israel
1Kin 8:1 Israel, and all the heads of the *t*
1Kin 8:16 the *t* of Israel to build an house
1Kin 11:31 and will give ten *t* to thee
1Kin 11:32 chosen out of all the *t* of Israel
1Kin 11:35 give it unto thee, even ten *t*
1Kin 14:21 choose out of all the *t* of Israel
1Kin 18:31 of the *t* of the sons of Jacob
2Kin 21:7 chosen out of all *t* of Israel
1Chr 27:16 Furthermore over the *t* of Israel
1Chr 27:22 the princes of the *t* of Israel
1Chr 28:1 of Israel, the princes of the *t*
1Chr 29:6 and princes of the *t* of Israel
2Chr 5:2 Israel, and all the heads of the *t*
2Chr 6:5 I chose no city among all the *t*
2Chr 11:16 after them out of all the *t* of
2Chr 12:13 chosen out of all the *t* of Israel
2Chr 33:7 chosen before all the *t* of Israel
Ezr 6:17 to the number of the *t* of Israel
Ps 78:55 made the *t* of Israel to dwell in
Ps 105:37 one feeble person among their *t*
Ps 122:4 Whither the *t* go up, the *t*
Ps 122:4 the *t* of the LORD, unto the
Is 19:13 are the stay of the *t* thereof
Is 49:6 to raise up the *t* of Jacob
Is 63:17 the *t* of thine inheritance
Eze 37:19 the *t* of Israel his fellows, and
Eze 45:8 of Israel according to their *t*
Eze 47:13 to the twelve *t* of Israel
Eze 47:21 you according to the *t* of Israel
Eze 47:22 with you among the *t* of Israel
Eze 48:1 Now these are the names of the *t*
Eze 48:19 it out of all the *t* of Israel
Eze 48:23 As for the rest of the *t*, from
Eze 48:29 the *t* of Israel for inheritance
Eze 48:31 the names of the *t* of Israel
Hos 5:9 among the *t* of Israel have I made
Hab 3:9 according to the oaths of the *t*
Zec 9:1 of man, as of all the *t* of Israel
Mt 19:28 judging the twelve *t* of Israel
Mt 24:30 all the *t* of the earth mourn
Lk 22:30 judging the twelve *t* of Israel
Acts 26:7 Unto which promise our twelve *t*
Jas 1:1 to the twelve *t* which are
Rev 7:4 four thousand of all the *t* of the
Rev 21:12 *t* of the children of Israel

**TRIBULATION**

Deut 4:30 When thou art in *t*, and all these
Judg 10:14 deliver you in the time of your *t*
1Sa 26:24 let him deliver me out of all *t*
Mt 13:21 for when *t* or persecution ariseth
Mt 24:21 For then shall be great *t*
Mt 24:29 Immediately after the *t* of those
Mk 13:24 But in those days, after that *t*
Jn 16:33 In the world ye shall have *t*
Acts 14:22 that we must through much *t* enter
Rom 2:9 *T* and anguish, upon every soul of
Rom 5:3 knowing that *t* worketh patience
Rom 8:35 shall *t*, or distress, or
Rom 12:12 patient in *t*
2Cor 1:4 Who comforteth us in all our *t*
2Cor 7:4 am exceeding joyful in all our *t*
1Th 3:4 before that we should suffer *t*
2Th 1:6 *t* to them that trouble you
Rev 1:9 your brother, and companion in *t*
Rev 2:9 I know thy works, and *t*, and
Rev 2:10 and ye shall have *t* ten days
Rev 2:22 adultery with her into great *t*
Rev 7:14 they which came out of great *t*

**TRIBULATIONS**

1Sa 10:19 of all your adversities and your *t*
Rom 5:3 only so, but we glory in *t* also
Eph 3:13 that ye faint not at my *t* for you
2Th 1:4 persecutions and *t* that ye endure

**TRIBUTARIES**

Deut 20:11 therein shall be *t* unto thee
Judg 1:30 dwelt among them, and became *t*
Judg 1:33 of Beth-anath became *t* unto them
Judg 1:35 prevailed, so that they became *t*

**TRIBUTARY**

Lam 1:1 provinces, how is she become *t*

**TRIBUTE**

Gen 49:15 bear, and became a servant unto *t*
Num 31:28 levy a *t* unto the LORD of the men
Num 31:37 the LORD's *t* of the sheep was six
Num 31:38 which the LORD's *t* was threescore
Num 31:39 which the LORD's *t* was threescore
Num 31:40 of which the LORD's *t* was thirty
Num 31:41 And Moses gave the *t*, which was
Deut 16:10 unto the LORD thy God with a *t* of
Josh 16:10 unto this day, and serve under *t*
Josh 17:13 that they put the Canaanites to *t*
Judg 1:28 that they put the Canaanites to *t*
2Sa 20:24 And Adoram was over the *t*
1Kin 4:6 the son of Abda was over the *t*
1Kin 9:21 a *t* of bondservice unto this day
1Kin 12:18 sent Adoram, who was over the *t*
2Kin 23:33 put the land to a *t* of an hundred
2Chr 8:8 make to pay *t* until this day
2Chr 10:18 sent Hadoram that was over the *t*
2Chr 17:11 Jehoshaphat presents, and *t* silver
Ezr 4:13 then will they not pay toll, *t*
Ezr 4:20 and toll, *t*, and custom, was paid
Ezr 6:8 even of the *t* beyond the river,
Ezr 7:24 not be lawful to impose toll, *t*
Neh 5:4 borrowed money for the king's *t*
Est 10:1 Ahasuerus laid a *t* upon the land
Prov 12:24 but the slothful shall be under *t*
Mt 17:24 they that received *t* money came
Mt 17:24 said, Doth not your master pay *t*
Mt 17:25 of the earth take custom or *t*
Mt 22:17 it lawful to give *t* unto Caesar
Mt 22:19 Shew me the *t* money
Mk 12:14 Is it lawful to give *t* to Caesar
Lk 20:22 for us to give *t* unto Caesar
Lk 23:2 and forbidding to give *t* to Caesar
Rom 13:6 For for this cause pay ye *t* also
Rom 13:7 *t* to whom *t* is due

**TRICKLETH**

Lam 3:49 Mine eye *t* down, and ceaseth not,

**TRIED**

Deut 21:5 controversy and every stroke be *t*
2Sa 22:31 the word of the LORD is *t*
Job 23:10 when he hath *t* me, I shall come
Job 34:36 is that Job may be *t* unto the end

Ps 12:6 as silver *t* in a furnace of earth
Ps 17:3 thou hast *t* me, and shalt find
Ps 18:30 the word of the LORD is *t*
Ps 66:10 hast *t* us, as silver is *t*
Ps 105:19 the word of the LORD *t* him
Is 28:16 a *t* stone, a precious corner
Jer 12:3 me, and *t* mine heart toward thee
Dan 12:10 be purified, and made white, and *t*
Zec 13:9 and will try them as gold is *t*
Heb 11:17 By faith Abraham, when he was *t*
Jas 1:12 for when he is *t*, he shall
1Pet 1:7 though it be *t* with fire
Rev 2:2 thou hast *t* them which say they
Rev 2:10 you into prison, that ye may be *t*
Rev 3:18 to buy of me gold *t* in the fire

**TRIEST**
1Chr 29:17 my God, that thou *t* the heart
Jer 11:20 that *t* the reins and the heart,
Jer 20:12 that *t* the righteous, and seest

**TRIETH**
Job 34:3 For the ear *t* words, as the mouth
Ps 7:9 the righteous God *t* the hearts
Ps 11:5 The LORD *t* the righteous
Prov 17:3 but the LORD *t* the hearts
1Th 2:4 men, but God, which *t* our hearts

**TRIMMED**
2Sa 19:24 nor *t* his beard, nor washed his
Mt 25:7 virgins arose, and *t* their lamps

**TRIMMEST**
Jer 2:33 Why *t* thou thy way to seek love

**TRIUMPH**
2Sa 1:20 daughters of the uncircumcised *t*
Ps 25:2 let not mine enemies *t* over me
Ps 41:11 mine enemy doth not *t* over me
Ps 47:1 unto God with the voice of *t*
Ps 60:8 Philistia, *t* thou because of me
Ps 92:4 I will *t* in the works of thy
Ps 94:3 how long shall the wicked *t*
Ps 106:47 holy name, and to *t* in thy praise
Ps 108:9 over Philistia will I *t*
2Cor 2:14 always causeth us to *t* in Christ

**TRIUMPHED**
Ex 15:1 LORD, for he hath *t* gloriously
Ex 15:21 LORD, for he hath *t* gloriously

**TRIUMPHING**
Job 20:5 That the *t* of the wicked is short
Col 2:15 of them openly, *t* over them in it

**TROAS** *(tro'-as) A seaport of Phrygia in Asia Minor.*
Acts 16:8 passing by Mysia came down to *T*
Acts 16:11 Therefore loosing from *T*, we came
Acts 20:5 going before tarried for us at *T*
Acts 20:6 came unto them to *T* in five days
2Cor 2:12 when I came to *T* to preach
2Ti 4:13 that I left at *T* with Carpus

**TRODDEN**
Deut 1:36 give the land that he hath *t* upon
Josh 14:9 have *t* shall be thine inheritance
Judg 5:21 thou hast *t* down strength
Job 22:15 old way which wicked men have *t*
Job 28:8 The lion's whelps have not *t* it
Ps 119:118 Thou hast *t* down all them that
Is 5:5 thereof, and it shall be *t* down
Is 14:19 as a carcase *t* under feet
Is 18:2 *t* down, whose land the rivers
Is 18:7 *t* under foot, whose land the
Is 25:10 Moab shall be *t* down under him,
Is 25:10 even as straw is *t* down for the
Is 28:3 of Ephraim, shall be *t* under feet
Is 28:18 then ye shall be *t* down by it
Is 63:3 I have *t* the winepress alone
Is 63:18 have *t* down thy sanctuary
Jer 12:10 they have *t* my portion under foot
Lam 1:15 The Lord hath *t* under foot all my
Lam 1:15 the Lord hath *t* the virgin
Eze 34:19 which ye have *t* with your feet
Dan 8:13 and the host to be *t* under foot
Mic 7:10 now shall she be *t* down as the
Mt 5:13 to be *t* under foot of men
Lk 8:5 and it was *t* down, and the fowls of
Lk 21:24 Jerusalem shall be *t* down of the
Heb 10:29 who hath *t* under foot the Son of
Rev 14:20 winepress was *t* without the city

**TRODE**
Judg 9:27 *t* the grapes, and made merry, and
Judg 20:43 *t* them down with ease over
2Kin 7:17 the people *t* upon him in the gate
2Kin 7:20 for the people *t* upon him in the
2Kin 9:33 and he *t* her under foot
2Kin 14:9 in Lebanon, and *t* down the thistle
2Chr 25:18 in Lebanon, and *t* down the thistle
Lk 12:1 that they *t* one upon another

**TROGYLLIUM** *(tro-jil'-le-um) A coastal town in Ionia in Asia Minor.*
Acts 20:15 arrived at Samos, and tarried at *T*

**TROOP**
Gen 30:11 And Leah said, A *t* cometh
Gen 49:19 Gad, a *t* shall overcome him
1Sa 30:8 Shall I pursue after this *t*
2Sa 2:25 after Abner, and became one *t*
2Sa 3:22 and Joab came from pursuing a *t*
2Sa 22:30 by thee I have run through a *t*
2Sa 23:11 were gathered together into a *t*
2Sa 23:13 the *t* of the Philistines pitched
Ps 18:29 by thee I have run through a *t*
Is 65:11 that prepare a table for that *t*
Jer 18:22 bring a *t* suddenly upon them
Hos 7:1 the *t* of robbers spoileth without
Amos 9:6 hath founded his *t* in the earth

**TROOPS**
Job 6:19 The *t* of Tema looked, the
Job 19:12 His *t* come together, and raise up
Jer 5:7 by *t* in the harlots' houses
Hos 6:9 as *t* of robbers wait for a man,
Mic 5:1 in *t*, O daughter of *t*
Hab 3:16 he will invade them with his *t*

**TROPHIMUS** *(trof'-im-us) A companion of Paul.*
Acts 20:4 and of Asia, Tychicus and *T*
Acts 21:29 him in the city *T* an Ephesian
2Ti 4:20 but *T* have I left at Miletum sick

**TROUBLE**
Josh 6:18 camp of Israel a curse, and *t* it
Josh 7:25 the LORD shall *t* thee this day
Judg 11:35 and thou art one of them that *t* me
2Kin 19:3 Hezekiah, This day is a day of *t*
1Chr 22:14 in my *t* I have prepared for the
2Chr 15:4 But when they in their *t* did turn
2Chr 29:8 and he hath delivered them to *t*
2Chr 32:18 to affright them, and to *t* them
Neh 9:27 and in the time of their *t*
Neh 9:32 let not all the *t* seem little
Job 3:26 yet *t* came
Job 5:6 neither doth *t* spring out of the
Job 5:7 Yet man is born unto *t*, as the
Job 14:1 is of few days, and full of *t*
Job 15:24 *T* and anguish shall make him
Job 27:9 his cry when *t* cometh upon him
Job 30:25 not I weep for him that was in *t*
Job 34:29 quietness, who then can make *t*
Job 38:23 reserved against the time of *t*
Ps 3:1 how are they increased that *t* me
Ps 9:9 oppressed, a refuge in times of *t*
Ps 9:13 consider my *t* which I suffer of
Ps 10:1 hidest thou thyself in times of *t*
Ps 13:4 those that *t* me rejoice when I am
Ps 20:1 LORD hear thee in the day of *t*
Ps 22:11 for *t* is near
Ps 27:5 For in the time of *t* he shall
Ps 31:7 for thou hast considered my *t*
Ps 31:9 upon me, O LORD, for I am in *t*
Ps 32:7 thou shalt preserve me from *t*
Ps 37:39 their strength in the time of *t*
Ps 41:1 will deliver him in time of *t*
Ps 46:1 a very present help in *t*
Ps 50:15 And call upon me in the day of *t*
Ps 54:7 he hath delivered me out of all *t*
Ps 59:16 and refuge in the day of my *t*
Ps 60:11 Give us help from *t*
Ps 66:14 hath spoken, when I was in *t*
Ps 69:17 for I am in *t*
Ps 73:5 They are not in *t* as other men
Ps 77:2 In the day of my *t* I sought the
Ps 78:33 in vanity, and their years in *t*
Ps 78:49 wrath, and indignation, and *t*
Ps 81:7 Thou calledst in *t*, and I
Ps 86:7 In the day of my *t* I will call
Ps 91:15 I will be with him in *t*
Ps 102:2 from me in the day when I am in *t*
Ps 107:6 cried unto the LORD in their *t*
Ps 107:13 cried unto the LORD in their *t*
Ps 107:19 they cry unto the LORD in their *t*
Ps 107:26 their soul is melted because of *t*
Ps 107:28 they cry unto the LORD in their *t*
Ps 108:12 Give us help from *t*
Ps 116:3 I found *t* and sorrow
Ps 119:143 *T* and anguish have taken hold on
Ps 138:7 Though I walk in the midst of *t*
Ps 142:2 I shewed before him my *t*
Ps 143:11 sake bring my soul out of *t*
Prov 11:8 righteous is delivered out of *t*
Prov 12:13 but the just shall come out of *t*
Prov 15:6 the revenues of the wicked is *t*
Prov 15:16 great treasure and *t* therewith
Prov 25:19 time of *t* is like a broken tooth
Is 1:14 they are a *t* unto me
Is 8:22 and behold *t* and darkness, dimness
Is 17:14 And behold at eveningtide *t*
Is 22:5 For it is a day of *t*, and of
Is 26:16 in *t* have they visited thee
Is 30:6 into the land of *t* and anguish,
Is 33:2 salvation also in the time of *t*
Is 37:3 Hezekiah, This day is a day of *t*
Is 46:7 answer, nor save him out of his *t*
Is 65:23 in vain, nor bring forth for *t*
Jer 2:27 the time of their *t* they will say
Jer 2:28 save thee in the time of thy *t*
Jer 8:15 for a time of health, and behold *t*
Jer 11:12 at all in the time of their *t*
Jer 11:14 that they cry unto me for their *t*
Jer 14:8 the saviour thereof in time of *t*
Jer 14:19 the time of healing, and behold *t*
Jer 30:7 it is even the time of Jacob's *t*
Jer 51:2 for in the day of *t* they shall be
Lam 1:21 mine enemies have heard of my *t*
Eze 7:7 is come, the day of *t* is near
Eze 32:13 the foot of man *t* them any more
Eze 32:13 nor the hoofs of beasts *t* them
Dan 4:19 interpretation thereof, *t* thee
Dan 5:10 let not thy thoughts *t* thee
Dan 11:44 and out of the north shall *t* him
Dan 12:1 and there shall be a time of *t*
Nah 1:7 a strong hold in the day of *t*
Hab 3:16 that I might rest in the day of *t*
Zeph 1:15 day is a day of wrath, a day of *t*
Mt 26:10 unto them, Why *t* ye the woman
Mk 14:6 why *t* ye her
Lk 7:6 unto him, Lord, *t* not thyself
Lk 8:49 *t* not the Master
Lk 11:7 shall answer and say, *T* me not
Acts 15:19 that we *t* not them, which from
Acts 16:20 Jews, do exceedingly *t* our city
Acts 20:10 him said, *T* not yourselves
1Cor 7:28 such shall have *t* in the flesh
2Cor 1:4 comfort them which are in any *t*
2Cor 1:8 of our *t* which came to us in Asia
Gal 1:7 but there be some that *t* you
Gal 5:12 were even cut off which *t* you
Gal 6:17 From henceforth let no man *t* me
2Th 1:6 tribulation to them that *t* you
2Ti 2:9 Wherein I suffer *t*, as an evil
Heb 12:15 of bitterness springing up *t* you

**TROUBLED**
Gen 34:30 Ye have *t* me to make me to stink
Gen 41:8 the morning that his spirit was *t*
Gen 45:3 for they were *t* at his presence
Ex 14:24 *t* the host of the Egyptians,
Josh 7:25 Joshua said, Why hast thou *t* us
1Sa 14:29 My father hath *t* the land
1Sa 16:14 evil spirit from the LORD *t* him
1Sa 28:21 Saul, and saw that he was sore *t*
2Sa 4:1 and all the Israelites were *t*
1Kin 18:18 he answered, I have not *t* Israel
2Kin 6:11 Syria was sore *t* for this thing
Ezr 4:4 of Judah, and *t* them in building,
Job 4:5 it toucheth thee, and thou art *t*
Job 21:4 so, why should not my spirit be *t*
Job 23:15 Therefore am I *t* at his presence
Job 34:20 the people shall be *t* at midnight
Ps 30:7 didst hide thy face, and I was *t*
Ps 38:6 I am *t*
Ps 46:3 the waters thereof roar and be *t*
Ps 48:5 they were *t*, and hasted away
Ps 77:3 I remembered God, and was *t*
Ps 77:4 I am so *t* that I cannot speak
Ps 77:16 the depths also were *t*
Ps 83:17 them be confounded and *t* for ever
Ps 90:7 anger, and by thy wrath are we *t*
Ps 104:29 Thou hidest thy face, they are *t*
Prov 25:26 the wicked is as a *t* fountain
Is 32:10 Many days and years shall ye be *t*
Is 32:11 be *t*, ye careless ones
Is 57:20 But the wicked are like the *t* sea

Jer 31:20 therefore my bowels are *t* for him
Lam 1:20 my bowels are *t*
Lam 2:11 fail with tears, my bowels are *t*
Eze 7:27 the people of the land shall be *t*
Eze 26:18 sea shall be *t* at thy departure
Eze 27:35 afraid, they shall be *t* in their
Dan 2:1 wherewith his spirit was *t*
Dan 2:3 my spirit was *t* to know the dream
Dan 4:5 and the visions of my head *t* me
Dan 4:19 one hour, and his thoughts *t* him
Dan 5:6 changed, and his thoughts *t* him
Dan 5:9 was king Belshazzar greatly *t*
Dan 7:15 and the visions of my head *t* me
Dan 7:28 Daniel, my cogitations much *t* me
Zec 10:2 their way as a flock, they were *t*
Mt 2:3 had heard these things, he was *t*
Mt 14:26 walking on the sea, they were *t*
Mt 24:6 see that ye be not *t*
Mk 6:50 For they all saw him, and were *t*
Mk 13:7 and rumours of wars, be ye not *t*
Lk 1:12 when Zacharias saw him, he was *t*
Lk 1:29 she was *t* at his saying, and cast
Lk 10:41 careful and *t* about many things
Lk 24:38 he said unto them, Why are ye *t*
Jn 5:4 into the pool, and *t* the water
Jn 5:7 have no man, when the water is *t*
Jn 11:33 groaned in the spirit, and was *t*
Jn 12:27 Now is my soul *t*
Jn 13:21 he was *t* in spirit, and testified,
Jn 14:1 Let not your heart be *t*
Jn 14:27 Let not your heart be *t*, neither
Acts 15:24 out from us have *t* you with words
Acts 17:8 they *t* the people and the rulers
2Cor 4:8 We are *t* on every side, yet not
2Cor 7:5 but we were *t* on every side
2Th 1:7 And to you who are *t* rest with us
2Th 2:2 not soon shaken in mind, or be *t*
1Pet 3:14 of their terror, neither be *t*

**TROUBLEDST**
Eze 32:2 *t* the waters with thy feet, and

**TROUBLER**
1Chr 2:7 the *t* of Israel, who transgressed

**TROUBLES**
Deut 31:17 many evils and *t* shall befall them
Deut 31:21 *t* are befallen them, that this
Job 5:19 He shall deliver thee in six *t*
Ps 25:17 The *t* of my heart are enlarged
Ps 25:22 Israel, O God, out of all his *t*
Ps 34:6 and saved him out of all his *t*
Ps 34:17 them out of all their *t*
Ps 71:20 hast shewed me great and sore *t*
Ps 88:3 For my soul is full of *t*
Prov 21:23 tongue keepeth his soul from *t*
Is 65:16 the former *t* are forgotten
Mk 13:8 and there shall be famines and *t*

**TROUBLEST**
Mk 5:35 why *t* thou the Master any further

**TROUBLETH**
1Sa 16:15 an evil spirit from God *t* thee
1Kin 18:17 him, Art thou he that *t* Israel
Job 22:10 about thee, and sudden fear *t* thee
Job 23:16 heart soft, and the Almighty *t* me
Prov 11:17 he that is cruel *t* his own flesh
Prov 11:29 He that *t* his own house shall
Prov 15:27 is greedy of gain *t* his own house
Dan 4:9 is in thee, and no secret *t* thee
Lk 18:5 Yet because this widow *t* me
Gal 5:10 but he that *t* you shall bear his

**TROUBLING**
Job 3:17 There the wicked cease from *t*
Jn 5:4 the *t* of the water stepped in was

**TROUBLOUS**
Dan 9:25 and the wall, even in *t* times

**TROUGH**
Gen 24:20 and emptied her pitcher into the *t*

**TROUGHS**
Gen 30:38 *t* when the flocks came to drink
Ex 2:16 filled the *t* to water their

**TROW**
Lk 17:9 I *t* not

**TRUCEBREAKERS**
2Ti 3:3 Without natural affection, *t*

**TRUE**
Gen 42:11 we are *t* men, thy servants are no
Gen 42:19 If ye be *t* men, let one of your
Gen 42:31 And we said unto him, We are *t* men
Gen 42:33 shall I know that ye are *t* men
Gen 42:34 no spies, but that ye are *t* men
Deut 17:4 diligently, and, behold, it be *t*
Deut 22:20 But if this thing be *t*, and the
Josh 2:12 house, and give me a *t* token
Ruth 3:12 now it is *t* that I am thy near
2Sa 7:28 art that God, and thy words be *t*
1Kin 10:6 It was a *t* report that I heard in
1Kin 22:16 is *t* in the name of the LORD
2Chr 9:5 It was a *t* report which I heard
2Chr 15:3 hath been without the *t* God
Neh 9:13 and *t* laws, good statutes and
Ps 19:9 the judgments of the LORD are *t*
Ps 119:160 Thy word is *t* from the beginning
Prov 14:25 A *t* witness delivereth souls
Jer 10:10 But the LORD is the *t* God
Jer 42:5 said to Jeremiah, The LORD be a *t*
Eze 18:8 hath executed *t* judgment between
Dan 3:14 spake and said unto them, Is it *t*
Dan 3:24 answered and said unto the king, *T*
Dan 6:12 answered and said, The thing is *t*
Dan 8:26 the morning which was told is *t*
Dan 10:1 and the thing was *t*, but the time
Zec 7:9 Execute *t* judgment, and shew mercy
Mt 22:16 Master, we know that thou art *t*
Mk 12:14 Master, we know that thou art *t*
Lk 16:11 commit to your trust the *t* riches
Jn 1:9 That was the *t* Light, which
Jn 3:33 set to his seal that God is *t*
Jn 4:23 when the *t* worshippers shall
Jn 4:37 And herein is that saying *t*
Jn 5:31 of myself, my witness is not *t*
Jn 5:32 which he witnesseth of me is *t*
Jn 6:32 you the *t* bread from heaven
Jn 7:18 that sent him, the same is *t*
Jn 7:28 myself, but he that sent me is *t*
Jn 8:13 thy record is not *t*
Jn 8:14 of myself, yet my record is *t*
Jn 8:16 yet if I judge, my judgment is *t*
Jn 8:17 the testimony of two men is *t*
Jn 8:26 but he that sent me is *t*
Jn 10:41 John spake of this man were *t*
Jn 15:1 I am the *t* vine, and my Father is
Jn 17:3 might know thee the only *t* God
Jn 19:35 bare record, and his record is *t*
Jn 19:35 and he knoweth that he saith *t*
Jn 21:24 we know that his testimony is *t*
Acts 12:9 wist not that it was *t* which was
Rom 3:4 yea, let God be *t*, but every man
2Cor 1:18 But as God is *t*, our word toward
2Cor 6:8 as deceivers, and yet *t*
Eph 4:24 in righteousness and *t* holiness
Phil 4:3 *t* yokefellow, help those women
Phil 4:8 brethren, whatsoever things are *t*
1Th 1:9 to serve the living and *t* God
1Ti 3:1 This is a *t* saying, If a man
Titus 1:13 This witness is *t*
Heb 8:2 of the *t* tabernacle, which the
Heb 9:24 which are the figures of the *t*
Heb 10:22 Let us draw near with a *t* heart
1Pet 5:12 testifying that this is the *t*
2Pet 2:22 them according to the *t* proverb
1Jn 2:8 unto you, which thing is *t* in him
1Jn 2:8 past, and the *t* light now shineth
1Jn 5:20 that we may know him that is *t*
1Jn 5:20 and we are in him that is *t*
1Jn 5:20 This is the *t* God, and eternal
3Jn 12 and ye know that our record is *t*
Rev 3:7 he that is holy, he that is *t*
Rev 3:14 *t* witness, the beginning of the
Rev 6:10 How long, O Lord, holy and *t*
Rev 15:3 *t* are thy ways, thou King of
Rev 16:7 Even so, Lord God Almighty, *t*
Rev 19:2 For *t* and righteous are his
Rev 19:9 These are the *t* sayings of God
Rev 19:11 upon him was called Faithful and *T*
Rev 21:5 for these words are *t* and faithful
Rev 22:6 These sayings are faithful and *t*

**TRULY**
Gen 4:24 *t* Lamech seventy and sevenfold
Gen 24:49 *t* with my master, tell me
Gen 47:29 and deal kindly and *t* with me
Gen 48:19 but *t* his younger brother shall
Num 14:21 But as *t* as I live, all the earth
Num 14:28 As *t* as I live, saith the LORD,
Deut 14:22 Thou shalt *t* tithe all the
Josh 2:14 will deal kindly and *t* with thee
Josh 2:24 *T* the LORD hath delivered into
Judg 9:16 Now therefore, if ye have done *t*
Judg 9:19 If ye then have dealt *t* and
1Sa 20:3 but *t* as the LORD liveth, and as
Job 36:4 For *t* my words shall not be false
Ps 62:1 *T* my soul waiteth upon God
Ps 73:1 *T* God is good to Israel, even to
Ps 116:16 O LORD, *t* I am thy servant
Prov 12:22 they that deal *t* are his delight
Eccl 11:7 *T* the light is sweet, and a
Jer 3:23 *T* in vain is salvation hoped for
Jer 3:23 *t* in the LORD our God is the
Jer 10:19 *T* this is a grief, and I must bear
Jer 28:9 that the LORD hath *t* sent him
Eze 18:9 hath kept my judgments, to deal *t*
Mic 3:8 But *t* I am full of power by the
Mt 9:37 The harvest *t* is plenteous, but
Mt 17:11 Elias *t* shall first come, and
Mt 27:54 *T* this was the Son of God
Mk 14:38 The spirit *t* is ready, but the
Mk 15:39 *T* this man was the Son of God
Lk 10:2 unto them, The harvest *t* is great
Lk 11:48 *T* ye bear witness that ye allow
Lk 20:21 but teachest the way of God *t*
Lk 22:22 *t* the Son of man goeth, as it was
Jn 4:18 in that saidst thou *t*
Jn 20:30 many other signs *t* did Jesus in
Acts 1:5 For John *t* baptized with water
Acts 3:22 For Moses *t* said unto the fathers
Acts 5:23 The prison *t* found we shut with
2Cor 12:12 *T* the signs of an apostle were
Heb 7:23 they *t* were many priests, because
Heb 11:15 And *t*, if they had been mindful of
1Jn 1:3 *t* our fellowship is with the

**TRUMP**
Jer 4:19 O my soul, the sound of the *t*
Hos 5:8 in Gibeah, and the *t* in Ramah
1Cor 15:52 of an eye, at the last *t*
1Th 4:16 archangel, and with the *t* of God

**TRUMPET**
Ex 19:13 when the *t* soundeth long, they
Ex 19:16 the voice of the *t* exceeding loud
Ex 19:19 the voice of the *t* sounded long
Ex 20:18 lightnings, and the noise of the *t*
Lev 25:9 Then shalt thou cause the *t* of
Lev 25:9 *t* sound throughout all your land
Num 10:4 And if they blow but with one *t*
Josh 6:5 when ye hear the sound of the *t*
Josh 6:20 people heard the sound of the *t*
Judg 3:27 that he blew a *t* in the mountain
Judg 6:34 came upon Gideon, and he blew a *t*
Judg 7:16 he put a *t* in every man's hand,
Judg 7:18 When I blow with a *t*, I and all
1Sa 13:3 Saul blew the *t* throughout all
2Sa 2:28 So Joab blew a *t*, and all the
2Sa 6:15 and with the sound of the *t*
2Sa 15:10 as ye hear the sound of the *t*
2Sa 18:16 And Joab blew the *t*, and the people
2Sa 20:1 and he blew a *t*, and said, We have
2Sa 20:22 And he blew a *t*, and they retired
1Kin 1:34 and blow ye with the *t*, and say,
1Kin 1:39 And they blew the *t*
1Kin 1:41 Joab heard the sound of the *t*
Neh 4:18 he that sounded the *t* was by me
Neh 4:20 ye hear the sound of the *t*
Job 39:24 he that it is the sound of the *t*
Ps 47:5 the LORD with the sound of a *t*
Ps 81:3 Blow up the *t* in the new moon, in
Ps 150:3 him with the sound of the *t*
Is 18:3 and when he bloweth a *t*, hear ye
Is 27:13 that the great *t* shall be blown
Is 58:1 not, lift up thy voice like a *t*
Jer 4:5 and say, Blow ye the *t* in the land
Jer 4:21 and hear the sound of the *t*
Jer 6:1 Jerusalem, and blow the *t* in Tekoa
Jer 6:17 Hearken to the sound of the *t*
Jer 42:14 war, nor hear the sound of the *t*
Jer 51:27 blow the *t* among the nations,
Eze 7:14 They have blown the *t*, even to
Eze 33:3 come upon the land, he blow the *t*
Eze 33:4 heareth the sound of the *t*
Eze 33:5 He heard the sound of the *t*
Eze 33:6 the sword come, and blow not the *t*
Hos 8:1 Set the *t* to thy mouth
Joel 2:1 Blow ye the *t* in Zion, and sound
Joel 2:15 Blow the *t* in Zion, sanctify a
Amos 2:2 and with the sound of the *t*
Amos 3:6 Shall a *t* be blown in the city,
Zeph 1:16 A day of the *t* and alarm against
Zec 9:14 and the Lord GOD shall blow the *t*
Mt 6:2 do not sound a *t* before thee

Mt 24:31 angels with a great sound of a *t*
1Cor 14:8 For if the *t* give an uncertain
1Cor 15:52 for the *t* shall sound, and the
Heb 12:19 And the sound of a *t*, and the voice
Rev 1:10 me a great voice, as of a *t*
Rev 4:1 as it were of a *t* talking with me
Rev 8:13 of the *t* of the three angels
Rev 9:14 the sixth angel which had the *t*

## TRUMPETERS

2Kin 11:14 the *t* by the king, and all the
2Chr 5:13 It came even to pass, as the *t*
2Chr 29:28 singers sang, and the *t* sounded
Rev 18:22 and musicians, and of pipers, and *t*

## TRUMPETS

Lev 23:24 a memorial of blowing of *t*
Num 10:2 Make thee two *t* of silver
Num 10:8 priests, shall blow with the *t*
Num 10:9 ye shall blow an alarm with the *t*
Num 10:10 ye shall blow with the *t* over
Num 29:1 a day of blowing the *t* unto you
Num 31:6 the *t* to blow in his hand
Josh 6:4 the ark seven *t* of rams' horns
Josh 6:4 the priests shall blow with the *t*
Josh 6:6 let seven priests bear seven *t* of
Josh 6:8 *t* of rams' horns passed on before
Josh 6:8 the LORD, and blew with the *t*
Josh 6:9 the priests that blew with the *t*
Josh 6:9 going on, and blowing with the *t*
Josh 6:13 seven priests bearing seven *t* of
Josh 6:13 continually, and blew with the *t*
Josh 6:13 going on, and blowing with the *t*
Josh 6:16 when the priests blew with the *t*
Josh 6:20 when the priests blew with the *t*
Judg 7:8 in their hand, and their *t*
Judg 7:18 then blow ye the *t* also on every
Judg 7:19 and they blew the *t*, and brake the
Judg 7:20 And the three companies blew the *t*
Judg 7:20 the *t* in their right hands to
Judg 7:22 And the three hundred blew the *t*
2Kin 9:13 top of the stairs, and blew with *t*
2Kin 11:14 the land rejoiced, and blew with *t*
2Kin 12:13 of silver, snuffers, basons, *t*
1Chr 13:8 and with cymbals, and with *t*
1Chr 15:24 did blow with the *t* before the
1Chr 15:28 sound of the cornet, and with *t*
1Chr 16:6 Jahaziel the priests with *t*
1Chr 16:42 them Heman and Jeduthun with *t*
2Chr 5:12 and twenty priests sounding with *t*
2Chr 5:13 lifted up their voice with the *t*
2Chr 7:6 the priests sounded *t* before them
2Chr 13:12 *t* to cry alarm against you
2Chr 13:14 and the priests sounded with the *t*
2Chr 15:14 and with shouting, and with *t*
2Chr 20:28 *t* unto the house of the LORD
2Chr 23:13 the princes and the *t* by the king
2Chr 23:13 land rejoiced, and sounded with *t*
2Chr 29:26 David, and the priests with the *t*
2Chr 29:27 of the LORD began also with the *t*
Ezr 3:10 priests in their apparel with *t*
Neh 12:35 of the priests' sons with *t*
Neh 12:41 Zechariah, and Hananiah, with *t*
Job 39:25 He saith among the *t*, Ha, ha
Ps 98:6 With *t* and sound of cornet make a
Rev 8:2 and to them were given seven *t*
Rev 8:6 angels which had the seven *t*

## TRUST

Judg 9:15 come and put your *t* in my shadow
Ruth 2:12 whose wings thou art come to *t*
2Sa 22:3 in him will I *t*
2Sa 22:31 buckler to all them that *t* in him
2Kin 18:20 Now on whom dost thou *t*, that
2Kin 18:21 of Egypt unto all that *t* on him
2Kin 18:22 unto me, We *t* in the LORD our God
2Kin 18:24 put thy *t* on Egypt for chariots
2Kin 18:30 Hezekiah make you *t* in the LORD
1Chr 5:20 because they put their *t* in him
2Chr 32:10 king of Assyria, Whereon do ye *t*
Job 4:18 he put no *t* in his servants
Job 8:14 whose *t* shall be a spider's web
Job 13:15 he slay me, yet will I *t* in him
Job 15:15 he putteth no *t* in his saints
Job 15:31 him that is deceived *t* in vanity
Job 35:14 therefore *t* thou in him
Job 39:11 Wilt thou *t* him, because his
Ps 2:12 all they that put their *t* in him
Ps 4:5 and put your *t* in the LORD
Ps 5:11 that put their *t* in thee rejoice
Ps 7:1 my God, in thee do I put my *t*
Ps 9:10 thy name will put their *t* in thee
Ps 11:1 In the LORD put I my *t*
Ps 16:1 for in thee do I put my *t*
Ps 17:7 *t* in thee from those that rise up
Ps 18:2 my strength, in whom I will *t*
Ps 18:30 to all those that *t* in him
Ps 20:7 Some *t* in chariots, and some in
Ps 25:2 O my God, I *t* in thee
Ps 25:20 for I put my *t* in thee
Ps 31:1 In thee, O LORD, do I put my *t*
Ps 31:6 but I *t* in the LORD
Ps 31:19 *t* in thee before the sons of men
Ps 34:22 none of them that *t* in him shall
Ps 36:7 *t* under the shadow of thy wings
Ps 37:3 *T* in the LORD, and do good
Ps 37:5 *t* also in him
Ps 37:40 save them, because they *t* in him
Ps 40:3 and fear, and shall *t* in the LORD
Ps 40:4 man that maketh the LORD his *t*
Ps 44:6 For I will not *t* in my bow
Ps 49:6 They that *t* in their wealth, and
Ps 52:8 I *t* in the mercy of God for ever
Ps 55:23 but I will *t* in thee
Ps 56:3 I am afraid, I will *t* in thee
Ps 56:4 his word, in God I have put my *t*
Ps 56:11 In God have I put my *t*
Ps 61:4 I will *t* in the covert of thy
Ps 62:8 *T* in him at all times
Ps 62:10 *T* not in oppression, and become
Ps 64:10 in the LORD, and shall *t* in him
Ps 71:1 In thee, O LORD, do I put my *t*
Ps 71:5 thou art my *t* from my youth
Ps 73:28 I have put my *t* in the Lord GOD,
Ps 91:2 in him will I *t*
Ps 91:4 and under his wings shalt thou *t*
Ps 115:9 O Israel, *t* thou in the LORD
Ps 115:10 O house of Aaron, *t* in the LORD
Ps 115:11 that fear the LORD, *t* in the LORD
Ps 118:8 It is better to *t* in the LORD
Ps 118:9 It is better to *t* in the LORD
Ps 119:42 for I *t* in thy word
Ps 125:1 They that *t* in the LORD shall be
Ps 141:8 in thee is my *t*
Ps 143:8 for in thee do I *t*
Ps 144:2 my shield, and he in whom I *t*
Ps 146:3 Put not your *t* in princes
Prov 3:5 *T* in the LORD with all thine
Prov 22:19 That thy *t* may be in the LORD, I
Prov 28:25 but he that putteth his *t* in the
Prov 29:25 but whoso putteth his *t* in the
Prov 30:5 unto them that put their *t* in him
Prov 31:11 her husband doth safely *t* in her
Is 12:2 I will *t*, and not be afraid
Is 14:32 poor of his people shall *t* in it
Is 26:4 *T* ye in the LORD for ever
Is 30:2 to *t* in the shadow of Egypt
Is 30:3 the *t* in the shadow of Egypt your
Is 30:12 *t* in oppression and perverseness,
Is 31:1 *t* in chariots, because they are
Is 36:5 now on whom dost thou *t*, that
Is 36:6 of Egypt to all that *t* in him
Is 36:7 to me, We *t* in the LORD our God
Is 36:9 put thy *t* on Egypt for chariots
Is 36:15 Hezekiah make you *t* in the LORD
Is 42:17 that *t* in graven images, that say
Is 50:10 let him *t* in the name of the LORD
Is 51:5 me, and on mine arm shall they *t*
Is 57:13 but he that putteth his *t* in me
Is 59:4 they *t* in vanity, and speak lies
Jer 7:4 *T* ye not in lying words, saying,
Jer 7:8 ye *t* in lying words, that cannot
Jer 7:14 called by my name, wherein ye *t*
Jer 9:4 and *t* ye not in any brother
Jer 28:15 makest this people to *t* in a lie
Jer 29:31 and he caused you to *t* in a lie
Jer 39:18 because thou hast put thy *t* in me
Jer 46:25 and all them that *t* in him
Jer 49:11 and let thy widows *t* in me
Eze 16:15 But thou didst *t* in thine own
Eze 33:13 if he *t* to his own righteousness,
Hos 10:13 because thou didst *t* in thy way
Amos 6:1 *t* in the mountain of Samaria,
Mic 7:5 *T* ye not in a friend, put ye not
Nah 1:7 and he knoweth them that *t* in him
Zeph 3:12 they shall *t* in the name of the
Mt 12:21 in his name shall the Gentiles *t*
Mk 10:24 *t* in riches to enter into the
Lk 16:11 commit to your *t* the true riches
Jn 5:45 you, even Moses, in whom ye *t*
Rom 15:12 in him shall the Gentiles *t*
Rom 15:24 for I *t* to see you in my journey,
1Cor 16:7 but I *t* to tarry a while with you
2Cor 1:9 that we should not *t* in ourselves
2Cor 1:10 in whom we *t* that he will yet
2Cor 1:13 I *t* ye shall acknowledge even to
2Cor 3:4 such *t* have we through Christ to
2Cor 5:11 I *t* also are made manifest in
2Cor 10:7 If any man *t* to himself that he
2Cor 13:6 But I *t* that ye shall know that
Phil 2:19 But I *t* in the Lord Jesus to send
Phil 2:24 But I *t* in the Lord that I also
Phil 3:4 whereof he might *t* in the flesh
1Th 2:4 to be put in *t* with the gospel
1Ti 1:11 God, which was committed to my *t*
1Ti 4:10 because we *t* in the living God,
1Ti 6:17 nor *t* in uncertain riches, but in
1Ti 6:20 that which is committed to thy *t*
Philem 22 for I *t* that through your prayers
Heb 2:13 And again, I will put my *t* in him
Heb 13:18 for we *t* we have a good
2Jn 12 but I *t* to come unto you, and
3Jn 14 But I *t* I shall shortly see thee,

## TRUSTED

Deut 32:37 gods, their rock in whom they *t*
Judg 11:20 But Sihon *t* not Israel to pass
Judg 20:36 because they *t* unto the liers in
2Kin 18:5 He *t* in the LORD God of Israel
Ps 13:5 But I have *t* in thy mercy
Ps 22:4 Our fathers *t* in thee
Ps 22:4 they *t*, and thou didst deliver
Ps 22:5 they *t* in thee, and were not
Ps 22:8 He *t* on the LORD that he would
Ps 26:1 I have *t* also in the LORD
Ps 28:7 my heart *t* in him, and I am helped
Ps 31:14 But I *t* in thee, O LORD
Ps 33:21 because we have *t* in his holy
Ps 41:9 own familiar friend, in whom I *t*
Ps 52:7 but *t* in the abundance of his
Ps 78:22 in God, and *t* not in his salvation
Is 47:10 For thou hast *t* in thy wickedness
Jer 13:25 forgotten me, and *t* in falsehood
Jer 48:7 because thou hast *t* in thy works
Jer 49:4 that *t* in her treasures, saying,
Dan 3:28 his servants that *t* in him
Zeph 3:2 she *t* not in the LORD
Mt 27:43 He *t* in God
Lk 11:22 him all his armour wherein he *t*
Lk 18:9 *t* in themselves that they were
Lk 24:21 But we *t* that it had been he
Eph 1:12 his glory, who first *t* in Christ
Eph 1:13 In whom ye also *t*, after that ye
1Pet 3:5 who *t* in God, adorned themselves,

## TRUSTEDST

Deut 28:52 walls come down, wherein thou *t*
Jer 5:17 thy fenced cities, wherein thou *t*
Jer 12:5 the land of peace, wherein thou *t*

## TRUSTEST

2Kin 18:19 confidence is this wherein thou *t*
2Kin 18:21 thou *t* upon the staff of this
2Kin 19:10 God in whom thou *t* deceive thee
Is 36:4 confidence is this wherein thou *t*
Is 36:6 thou *t* in the staff of this
Is 37:10 Let not thy God, in whom thou *t*

## TRUSTETH

Job 40:23 he *t* that he can draw up Jordan
Ps 21:7 For the king *t* in the LORD
Ps 32:10 but he that *t* in the LORD
Ps 34:8 blessed is the man that *t* in him
Ps 57:1 for my soul *t* in thee
Ps 84:12 blessed is the man that *t* in thee
Ps 86:2 save thy servant that *t* in thee
Ps 115:8 so is every one that *t* in them
Ps 135:18 so is every one that *t* in them
Prov 11:28 He that *t* in his riches shall
Prov 16:20 whoso *t* in the LORD, happy is he
Prov 28:26 He that *t* in his own heart is a
Is 26:3 because he *t* in thee
Jer 17:5 Cursed be the man that *t* in man
Jer 17:7 is the man that *t* in the LORD
Hab 2:18 the maker of his work *t* therein
1Ti 5:5 *t* in God, and continueth in

## TRUSTING

Ps 112:7 his heart is fixed, *t* in the LORD

## TRUSTY

Job 12:20 removeth away the speech of the *t*

## TRUTH

Gen 24:27 my master of his mercy and his *t*
Gen 32:10 all the mercies, and of all the *t*

Gen 42:16 whether there be any *t* in you
Ex 18:21 men, such as fear God, men of *t*
Ex 34:6 and abundant in goodness and *t*
Deut 13:14 and, behold, if it be *t*, and the
Deut 32:4 a God of *t* and without iniquity,
Josh 24:14 and serve him in sincerity and in *t*
Judg 9:15 If in *t* ye anoint me king over
1Sa 12:24 serve him in *t* with all your
1Sa 21:5 Of a *t* women have been kept from
2Sa 2:6 LORD shew kindness and *t* unto you
2Sa 15:20 mercy and *t* be with thee
1Kin 2:4 me in *t* with all their heart
1Kin 3:6 as he walked before thee in *t*
1Kin 17:24 of the LORD in thy mouth is *t*
2Kin 19:17 Of a *t*, LORD, the kings of
2Kin 20:3 I have walked before thee in *t*
2Kin 20:19 good, if peace and *t* be in my days
2Chr 18:15 *t* to me in the name of the LORD
2Chr 31:20 *t* before the LORD his God
Est 9:30 with words of peace and *t*
Job 9:2 I know it is so of a *t*
Ps 15:2 and speaketh the *t* in his heart
Ps 25:5 Lead me in thy *t*, and teach me
Ps 25:10 *t* unto such as keep his covenant
Ps 26:3 and I have walked in thy *t*
Ps 30:9 shall it declare thy *t*
Ps 31:5 hast redeemed me, O LORD God of *t*
Ps 33:4 and all his works are done in *t*
Ps 40:10 thy *t* from the great congregation
Ps 40:11 thy *t* continually preserve me
Ps 43:3 O send out thy light and thy *t*
Ps 45:4 ride prosperously because of *t*
Ps 51:6 thou desirest *t* in the inward
Ps 54:5 cut them off in thy *t*
Ps 57:3 send forth his mercy and his *t*
Ps 57:10 heavens, and thy *t* unto the clouds
Ps 60:4 may be displayed because of the *t*
Ps 61:7 O prepare mercy and *t*, which may
Ps 69:13 in the *t* of thy salvation
Ps 71:22 with the psaltery, even thy *t*
Ps 85:10 Mercy and *t* are met together
Ps 85:11 *T* shall spring out of the earth
Ps 86:11 I will walk in thy *t*
Ps 86:15 and plenteous in mercy and *t*
Ps 89:14 *t* shall go before thy face
Ps 89:49 thou swarest unto David in thy *t*
Ps 91:4 his *t* shall be thy shield and
Ps 96:13 and the people with his *t*
Ps 98:3 his *t* toward the house of Israel
Ps 100:5 his *t* endureth to all generations
Ps 108:4 thy *t* reacheth unto the clouds
Ps 111:8 ever and ever, and are done in *t*
Ps 117:2 the *t* of the LORD endureth for
Ps 119:30 I have chosen the way of *t*
Ps 119:43 take not the word of *t* utterly
Ps 119:142 and thy law is the *t*
Ps 119:151 and all thy commandments are *t*
Ps 132:11 LORD hath sworn in *t* unto David
Ps 138:2 thy lovingkindness and for thy *t*
Ps 145:18 to all that call upon him in *t*
Ps 146:6 which keepeth *t* for ever
Prov 3:3 Let not mercy and *t* forsake thee
Prov 8:7 For my mouth shall speak *t*
Prov 12:17 He that speaketh *t* sheweth forth
Prov 12:19 The lip of *t* shall be established
Prov 14:22 *t* shall be to them that devise
Prov 16:6 By mercy and *t* iniquity is purged
Prov 20:28 Mercy and *t* preserve the king
Prov 22:21 the certainty of the words of *t*
Prov 22:21 of *t* to them that send unto thee
Prov 23:23 Buy the *t*, and sell it not
Eccl 12:10 was upright, even words of *t*
Is 5:9 Of a *t* many houses shall be
Is 10:20 the Holy One of Israel, in *t*
Is 16:5 he shall sit upon it in *t* in the
Is 25:1 of old are faithfulness and *t*
Is 26:2 which keepeth the *t* may enter in
Is 37:18 Of a *t*, LORD, the kings of
Is 38:3 I have walked before thee in *t*
Is 38:18 the pit cannot hope for thy *t*
Is 38:19 children shall make known thy *t*
Is 39:8 shall be peace and *t* in my days
Is 42:3 shall bring forth judgment unto *t*
Is 43:9 or let them hear, and say, It is *t*
Is 48:1 the God of Israel, but not in *t*
Is 59:4 justice, nor any pleadeth for *t*
Is 59:14 for *t* is fallen in the street, and
Is 59:15 Yea, *t* faileth
Is 61:8 and I will direct their work in *t*
Is 65:16 bless himself in the God of *t*
Is 65:16 earth shall swear by the God of *t*
Jer 4:2 swear, The LORD liveth, in *t*
Jer 5:1 judgment, that seeketh the *t*
Jer 5:3 are not thine eyes upon the *t*
Jer 7:28 *t* is perished, and is cut off from
Jer 9:3 valiant for the *t* upon the earth
Jer 9:5 and will not speak the *t*
Jer 26:15 for of a *t* the LORD hath sent me
Jer 33:6 them the abundance of peace and *t*
Dan 2:47 Of a *t* it is, that your God is a
Dan 4:37 of heaven, all whose works are *t*
Dan 7:16 and asked him the *t* of all this
Dan 7:19 know the *t* of the fourth beast
Dan 8:12 it cast down the *t* to the ground
Dan 9:13 iniquities, and understand thy *t*
Dan 10:21 is noted in the scripture of *t*
Dan 11:2 And now will I shew thee the *t*
Hos 4:1 the land, because there is no *t*
Mic 7:20 Thou wilt perform the *t* to Jacob
Zec 8:3 shall be called a city of *t*
Zec 8:8 and I will be their God, in *t*
Zec 8:16 every man the *t* to his neighbour
Zec 8:16 execute the judgment of *t*
Zec 8:19 therefore love the *t* and peace
Mal 2:6 The law of *t* was in his mouth, and
Mt 14:33 Of a *t* thou art the Son of God
Mt 15:27 And she said, *T*, Lord
Mt 22:16 and teachest the way of God in *t*
Mk 5:33 before him, and told him all the *t*
Mk 12:14 but teachest the way of God in *t*
Mk 12:32 Master, thou hast said the *t*
Lk 4:25 But I tell you of a *t*, many
Lk 9:27 But I tell you of a *t*, there be
Lk 12:44 Of a *t* I say unto you, that he
Lk 21:3 Of a *t* I say unto you, that this
Lk 22:59 Of a *t* this fellow also was with
Jn 1:14 the Father,) full of grace and *t*
Jn 1:17 grace and *t* came by Jesus Christ
Jn 3:21 But he that doeth *t* cometh to the
Jn 4:23 the Father in spirit and in *t*
Jn 4:24 worship him in spirit and in *t*
Jn 5:33 and he bare witness unto the *t*
Jn 6:14 This is of a *t* that prophet that
Jn 7:40 Of a *t* this is the Prophet
Jn 8:32 And ye shall know the *t*, and the
Jn 8:32 the *t* shall make you free
Jn 8:40 a man that hath told you the *t*
Jn 8:44 beginning, and abode not in the *t*
Jn 8:44 because there is no *t* in him
Jn 8:45 And because I tell you the *t*
Jn 8:46 And if I say the *t*, why do ye not
Jn 14:6 unto him, I am the way, the *t*
Jn 14:17 Even the Spirit of *t*
Jn 15:26 the Father, even the Spirit of *t*
Jn 16:7 Nevertheless I tell you the *t*
Jn 16:13 Howbeit when he, the Spirit of *t*
Jn 16:13 he will guide you into all *t*
Jn 17:17 Sanctify them through thy *t*
Jn 17:17 thy word is *t*
Jn 17:19 might be sanctified through the *t*
Jn 18:37 I should bear witness unto the *t*
Jn 18:37 that is of the *t* heareth my voice
Jn 18:38 Pilate saith unto him, What is *t*
Acts 4:27 For of a *t* against thy holy child
Acts 10:34 Of a *t* I perceive that God is no
Acts 26:25 but speak forth the words of *t*
Rom 1:18 who hold the *t* in unrighteousness
Rom 1:25 Who changed the *t* of God into a
Rom 2:2 *t* against them which commit such
Rom 2:8 contentious, and do not obey the *t*
Rom 2:20 knowledge and of the *t* in the law
Rom 3:7 For if the *t* of God hath more
Rom 9:1 I say the *t* in Christ, I lie not,
Rom 15:8 the circumcision for the *t* of God
1Cor 5:8 bread of sincerity and *t*
1Cor 13:6 iniquity, but rejoiceth in the *t*
1Cor 14:25 report that God is in you of a *t*
2Cor 4:2 but by manifestation of the *t*
2Cor 6:7 By the word of *t*, by the power of
2Cor 7:14 we spake all things to you in *t*
2Cor 7:14 I made before Titus, is found a *t*
2Cor 11:10 As the *t* of Christ is in me, no
2Cor 12:6 for I will say the *t*
2Cor 13:8 against the *t*, but for the *t*
Gal 2:5 that the *t* of the gospel might
Gal 2:14 according to the *t* of the gospel
Gal 3:1 that ye should not obey the *t*
Gal 4:16 enemy, because I tell you the *t*
Gal 5:7 you that ye should not obey the *t*
Eph 1:13 after that ye heard the word of *t*
Eph 4:15 But speaking the *t* in love
Eph 4:21 by him, as the *t* is in Jesus
Eph 4:25 speak every man *t* with his
Eph 5:9 goodness and righteousness and *t*
Eph 6:14 your loins girt about with *t*
Phil 1:18 way, whether in pretence, or in *t*
Col 1:5 the word of the *t* of the gospel
Col 1:6 it, and knew the grace of God in *t*
1Th 2:13 word of men, but as it is in *t*
2Th 2:10 received not the love of the *t*
2Th 2:12 be damned who believed not the *t*
2Th 2:13 of the Spirit and belief of the *t*
1Ti 2:4 come unto the knowledge of the *t*
1Ti 2:7 apostle, (I speak the *t* in Christ
1Ti 3:15 the pillar and ground of the *t*
1Ti 4:3 them which believe and know the *t*
1Ti 6:5 minds, and destitute of the *t*
2Ti 2:15 rightly dividing the word of *t*
2Ti 2:18 Who concerning the *t* have erred
2Ti 2:25 to the acknowledging of the *t*
2Ti 3:7 to come to the knowledge of the *t*
2Ti 3:8 so do these also resist the *t*
2Ti 4:4 turn away their ears from the *t*
Titus 1:1 of the *t* which is after godliness
Titus 1:14 of men, that turn from the *t*
Heb 10:26 received the knowledge of the *t*
Jas 1:18 begat he us with the word of *t*
Jas 3:14 not, and lie not against the *t*
Jas 5:19 if any of you do err from the *t*
1Pet 1:22 the *t* through the Spirit unto
2Pet 1:12 be established in the present *t*
2Pet 2:2 way of *t* shall be evil spoken of
1Jn 1:6 darkness, we lie, and do not the *t*
1Jn 1:8 ourselves, and the *t* is not in us
1Jn 2:4 is a liar, and the *t* is not in him
1Jn 2:21 you because ye know not the *t*
1Jn 2:21 it, and that no lie is of the *t*
1Jn 2:27 you of all things, and is *t*
1Jn 3:18 but in deed and in *t*
1Jn 3:19 we know that we are of the *t*
1Jn 4:6 Hereby know we the spirit of *t*
1Jn 5:6 witness, because the Spirit is *t*
2Jn 1 children, whom I love in the *t*
2Jn 1 all they that have known the *t*
2Jn 3 the Son of the Father, in *t*
2Jn 4 of thy children walking in *t*
3Jn 1 Gaius, whom I love in the *t*
3Jn 3 of the *t* that is in thee, even as
3Jn 3 even as thou walkest in the *t*
3Jn 4 hear that my children walk in *t*
3Jn 8 might be fellowhelpers to the *t*
3Jn 12 of all men, and of the *t* itself

**TRUTH'S**
Ps 115:1 for thy mercy, and for thy *t* sake
2Jn 2 For the *t* sake, which dwelleth in

**TRY**
Judg 7:4 I will *t* them for thee there
2Chr 32:31 to *t* him, that he might know all
Job 7:18 morning, and *t* him every moment
Job 12:11 Doth not the ear *t* words
Ps 11:4 his eyes behold, his eyelids *t*
Ps 26:2 *t* my reins and my heart
Ps 139:23 *t* me, and know my thoughts
Jer 6:27 thou mayest know and *t* their way
Jer 9:7 I will melt them, and *t* them
Jer 17:10 I *t* the reins, even to give every
Lam 3:40 *t* our ways, and turn again to the
Dan 11:35 to *t* them, and to purge, and to
Zec 13:9 will *t* them as gold is tried
1Cor 3:13 the fire shall *t* every man's work
1Pet 4:12 the fiery trial which is to *t* you
1Jn 4:1 but *t* the spirits whether they
Rev 3:10 to *t* them that dwell upon the

**TRYING**
Jas 1:3 that the *t* of your faith worketh

**TRYPHENA** *(tri-fe'-nah) A Christian in Rome.*
Rom 16:12 Salute *T* and Tryphosa, who labour

**TRYPHOSA** *(tri-fo'-sah) A Christian in Rome.*
Rom 16:12 Salute Tryphena and *T*, who labour

**TUBAL** *(tu'-bal)*
*1. A son of Japeth.*
Gen 10:2 Magog, and Madai, and Javan, and *T*
1Chr 1:5 Magog, and Madai, and Javan, and *T*
*2. Migrants to Sicily and Spain.*
Is 66:19 and Lud, that draw the bow, to *T*
Eze 27:13 Javan, *T*, and Meshech, they were

Eze 32:26 There is Meshech, *T*, and all her
Eze 38:2 the chief prince of Meshech and *T*
Eze 38:3 the chief prince of Meshech and *T*
Eze 39:1 the chief prince of Meshech and *T*

**TUBAL-CAIN** *(tu'-bal-cain) Son of Lamech.*
Gen 4:22 And Zillah, she also bare *T*
Gen 4:22 and the sister of *T* was Naamah

**TUMBLED**
Judg 7:13 a cake of barley bread *t* into the

**TUMULT**
1Sa 4:14 What meaneth the noise of this *t*
2Sa 18:29 me thy servant, I saw a great *t*
2Kin 19:28 thy *t* is come up into mine ears,
Ps 65:7 waves, and the *t* of the people
Ps 74:23 the *t* of those that rise up
Ps 83:2 For, lo, thine enemies make a *t*
Is 33:3 noise of the *t* the people fled
Is 37:29 thy rage against me, and thy *t*
Jer 11:16 with the noise of a great *t* he
Hos 10:14 Therefore shall a *t* arise among
Amos 2:2 and Moab shall die with *t*, with
Zec 14:13 that a great *t* from the LORD
Mt 27:24 but that rather a *t* was made
Mk 5:38 of the synagogue, and seeth the *t*
Acts 21:34 not know the certainty for the *t*
Acts 24:18 with multitude, nor with *t*

**TUMULTS**
Amos 3:9 behold the great *t* in the midst
2Cor 6:5 stripes, in imprisonments, in *t*
2Cor 12:20 whisperings, swellings, *t*

**TUMULTUOUS**
Is 13:4 a *t* noise of the kingdoms of
Is 22:2 of stirs, a *t* city, a joyous city
Jer 48:45 crown of the head of the *t* ones

**TURN**
Gen 19:2 *t* in, I pray you, into your
Gen 24:49 that I may *t* to the right hand,
Gen 27:44 until thy brother's fury *t* away
Gen 27:45 brother's anger *t* away from thee
Ex 3:3 And Moses said, I will now *t* aside
Ex 14:2 children of Israel, that they *t*
Ex 23:27 enemies *t* their backs unto thee
Ex 32:12 *T* from thy fierce wrath, and
Lev 13:16 Or if the raw flesh *t* again
Lev 19:4 *T* ye not unto idols, nor make to
Num 14:25 To morrow *t* you, and get you into
Num 20:17 we will not *t* to the right hand
Num 21:22 we will not *t* into the fields, or
Num 22:23 the ass, to *t* her into the way
Num 22:26 where was no way to *t* either to
Num 32:15 For if ye *t* away from after him,
Num 34:4 your border shall *t* from the
Deut 1:7 *T* you, and take your journey, and
Deut 1:40 *t* you, and take your journey into
Deut 2:3 *t* you northward
Deut 2:27 I will neither *t* unto the right
Deut 4:30 if thou *t* to the LORD thy God, and
Deut 5:32 ye shall not *t* aside to the right
Deut 7:4 For they will *t* away thy son from
Deut 11:16 ye *t* aside, and serve other gods,
Deut 11:28 but *t* aside out of the way which
Deut 13:5 because he hath spoken to *t* you
Deut 13:17 that the LORD may *t* from the
Deut 14:25 Then shalt thou *t* it into money
Deut 16:7 thou shalt *t* in the morning, and
Deut 17:17 that his heart *t* not away
Deut 17:20 that he *t* not aside from the
Deut 23:13 dig therewith, and shalt *t* back
Deut 23:14 in thee, and *t* away from thee
Deut 30:3 LORD thy God will *t* thy captivity
Deut 30:10 if thou *t* unto the LORD thy God
Deut 30:17 But if thine heart *t* away
Deut 31:20 then will they *t* unto other gods,
Deut 31:29 *t* aside from the way which I have
Josh 1:7 *t* not from it to the right hand
Josh 22:16 to *t* away this day from following
Josh 22:18 But that ye must *t* away this day
Josh 22:23 to *t* from following the LORD
Josh 22:29 *t* this day from following the
Josh 23:6 that ye *t* not aside therefrom to
Josh 24:20 strange gods, then he will *t*
Judg 4:18 *T* in, my lord, *t* in to me
Judg 11:8 Therefore we *t* again to thee now,
Judg 19:11 let us *t* in into this city of the
Judg 19:12 We will not *t* aside hither into
Judg 20:8 we any of us *t* into his house
Ruth 1:11 Naomi said, *T* again, my daughters
Ruth 1:12 *T* again, my daughters, go your
Ruth 4:1 *t* aside, sit down here
1Sa 12:20 yet *t* not aside from following
1Sa 12:21 And *t* ye not aside
1Sa 14:7 *t* thee; behold, I am
1Sa 15:25 *t* again with me, that I may
1Sa 15:30 *t* again with me, that I may
1Sa 22:17 footmen that stood about him, *T*
1Sa 22:18 *T* thou, and fall upon the priests
2Sa 2:21 *T* thee aside to thy right hand or
2Sa 2:21 But Asahel would not *t* aside from
2Sa 2:22 *T* thee aside from following me
2Sa 2:23 Howbeit he refused to *t* aside
2Sa 14:19 none can *t* to the right hand or
2Sa 14:24 Let him *t* to his own house, and
2Sa 15:31 *t* the counsel of Ahithophel into
2Sa 18:30 unto him, *T* aside, and stand here
2Sa 19:37 *t* back again, that I may die in
1Kin 8:33 shall *t* again to thee, and confess
1Kin 8:35 *t* from their sin, when thou
1Kin 9:6 shall at all *t* from following me
1Kin 11:2 for surely they will *t* away your
1Kin 12:27 people *t* again unto their lord
1Kin 13:9 nor *t* again by the same way that
1Kin 13:17 nor *t* again to go by the way that
1Kin 17:3 *t* thee eastward, and hide thyself
1Kin 22:34 *T* thine hand, and carry me out of
2Kin 1:6 *t* again unto the king that sent
2Kin 4:10 to us, that he shall *t* in thither
2Kin 9:18 *t* thee behind me
2Kin 9:19 *t* thee behind me
2Kin 17:13 *T* ye from your evil ways, and keep
2Kin 18:24 How then wilt thou *t* away the
2Kin 19:28 I will *t* thee back by the way by
2Kin 20:5 *T* again, and tell Hezekiah the
1Chr 12:23 to *t* the kingdom of Saul to him,
1Chr 14:14 *t* away from them, and come upon
2Chr 6:26 *t* from their sin, when thou dost
2Chr 6:37 they are carried captive, and *t*
2Chr 6:42 *t* not away the face of thine
2Chr 7:14 face, and *t* from their wicked ways
2Chr 7:19 But if ye *t* away, and forsake my
2Chr 15:4 did *t* unto the LORD God of Israel
2Chr 18:33 *T* thine hand, that thou mayest
2Chr 25:27 *t* away from following the LORD
2Chr 29:10 fierce wrath may *t* away from us
2Chr 30:6 *t* again unto the LORD God of
2Chr 30:8 of his wrath may *t* away from you
2Chr 30:9 For if ye *t* again unto the LORD,
2Chr 30:9 will not *t* away his face from you
2Chr 35:22 would not *t* his face from him
Neh 1:9 But if ye *t* unto me, and keep my
Neh 4:4 *t* their reproach upon their own
Neh 9:26 against them to *t* them to thee
Est 2:12 Now when every maid's *t* was come
Est 2:15 Now when the *t* of Esther, the
Job 5:1 which of the saints wilt thou *t*
Job 14:6 *T* from him, that he may rest,
Job 23:13 is in one mind, and who can *t* him
Job 24:4 They *t* the needy out of the way
Job 34:15 man shall *t* again unto dust
Ps 4:2 how long will ye *t* my glory into
Ps 7:12 If he *t* not, he will whet his
Ps 18:37 neither did I *t* again till they
Ps 21:12 shalt thou make them *t* their back
Ps 22:27 shall remember and *t* unto the LORD
Ps 25:16 *T* thee unto me, and have mercy
Ps 40:4 nor such as *t* aside to lies
Ps 44:10 Thou makest us to *t* back from the
Ps 56:9 then shall mine enemies *t* back
Ps 60:1 O *t* thyself to us again
Ps 69:16 *t* unto me according to the
Ps 80:3 *T* us again, O God, and cause thy
Ps 80:7 *T* us again, O God of hosts, and
Ps 80:19 *T* us again, O LORD God of hosts,
Ps 85:4 *T* us, O God of our salvation, and
Ps 85:8 but let them not *t* again to folly
Ps 86:16 O *t* unto me, and have mercy upon
Ps 101:3 the work of them that *t* aside
Ps 104:9 that they *t* not again to cover
Ps 106:23 to *t* away his wrath, lest he
Ps 119:37 *T* away mine eyes from beholding
Ps 119:39 *T* away my reproach which I fear
Ps 119:79 those that fear thee *t* unto me
Ps 125:5 As for such as *t* aside unto their
Ps 126:4 *T* again our captivity, O LORD, as
Ps 132:10 sake *t* not away the face of thine
Ps 132:11 he will not *t* from it
Prov 1:23 *T* you at my reproof
Prov 4:15 by it, *t* from it, and pass away
Prov 4:27 *T* not to the right hand nor to
Prov 9:4 is simple, let him *t* in hither
Prov 9:16 is simple, let him *t* in hither
Prov 24:18 he *t* away his wrath from him
Prov 25:10 shame, and thine infamy *t* not away
Prov 29:8 but wise men *t* away wrath
Eccl 3:20 the dust, and all *t* to dust again
Song 2:17 and the shadows flee away, *t*
Song 6:5 *T* away thine eyes from me, for
Is 1:25 I will *t* my hand upon thee, and
Is 10:2 To *t* aside the needy from
Is 13:14 every man *t* to his own people
Is 14:27 out, and who shall *t* it back
Is 19:6 they shall *t* the rivers far away
Is 22:18 He will surely violently *t*
Is 23:17 she shall *t* to her hire, and shall
Is 28:6 that *t* the battle to the gate
Is 29:21 *t* aside the just for a thing of
Is 30:11 *t* aside out of the path, cause
Is 30:21 when ye *t* to the right hand, and
Is 30:21 hand, and when ye *t* to the left
Is 31:6 *T* ye unto him from whom the
Is 36:9 How then wilt thou *t* away the
Is 37:29 I will *t* thee back by the way by
Is 58:13 If thou *t* away thy foot from the
Is 59:20 to Zion, and unto them that *t* from
Jer 2:24 her occasion who can *t* her away
Jer 2:35 surely his anger shall *t* from me
Jer 3:7 all these things, *T* thou unto me
Jer 3:14 *T*, O backsliding children, saith
Jer 3:19 and shalt not *t* away from me
Jer 4:28 neither will I *t* back from it
Jer 6:9 *t* back thine hand as a
Jer 8:4 shall he *t* away, and not return
Jer 13:16 he *t* it into the shadow of death,
Jer 18:8 *t* from their evil, I will repent
Jer 18:20 to *t* away thy wrath from them
Jer 21:4 I will *t* back the weapons of war
Jer 25:5 *T* ye again now every one from his
Jer 26:3 *t* every man from his evil way,
Jer 29:14 I will *t* away your captivity, and
Jer 31:13 for I will *t* their mourning into
Jer 31:18 *t* thou me, and I shall be turned
Jer 31:21 *t* again, O virgin of Israel
Jer 31:21 *t* again to these thy cities
Jer 32:40 that I will not *t* away from them
Jer 44:5 ear to *t* from their wickedness
Jer 49:8 *t* back, dwell deep, O inhabitants
Jer 50:16 shall *t* every one to his people
Lam 2:14 iniquity, to *t* away thy captivity
Lam 3:35 To *t* aside the right of a man
Lam 3:40 our ways, and *t* again to the LORD
Lam 5:21 *T* thou us unto thee, O LORD, and
Eze 3:19 he *t* not from his wickedness, nor
Eze 3:20 man doth *t* from his righteousness
Eze 4:8 thou shalt not *t* thee from one
Eze 7:22 My face will I *t* also from them
Eze 8:6 but *t* thee yet again, and thou
Eze 8:13 *T* thee yet again, and thou shalt
Eze 8:15 *t* thee yet again, and thou shalt
Eze 14:6 *t* yourselves from your idols
Eze 14:6 *t* away your faces from all your
Eze 18:21 But if the wicked will *t* from all
Eze 18:30 *t* yourselves from all your
Eze 18:32 wherefore *t* yourselves, and live
Eze 33:9 wicked of his way to *t* from it
Eze 33:9 if he do not *t* from his way
Eze 33:11 that the wicked *t* from his way
Eze 33:11 *t* ye, *t* ye from your evil ways
Eze 33:14 if he *t* from his sin, and do that
Eze 33:19 But if the wicked *t* from his
Eze 36:9 I will *t* unto you, and ye shall be
Eze 38:4 I will *t* thee back, and put hooks
Eze 38:12 to *t* thine hand upon the desolate
Eze 39:2 I will *t* thee back, and leave but
Dan 9:13 our God, that we might *t* from our
Dan 11:18 After this shall he *t* his face
Dan 11:18 he shall cause it to *t* upon him
Dan 11:19 Then he shall *t* his face toward
Dan 12:3 they that *t* many to righteousness
Hos 5:4 their doings to *t* unto their God
Hos 12:6 Therefore *t* thou to thy God
Hos 14:2 with you words, and *t* to the LORD
Joel 2:12 *t* ye even to me with all your
Joel 2:13 and *t* unto the LORD your God
Amos 1:3 I will not *t* away the punishment
Amos 1:6 I will not *t* away the punishment
Amos 1:8 I will *t* mine hand against Ekron
Amos 1:9 I will not *t* away the punishment
Amos 1:11 I will not *t* away the punishment

Amos 1:13 I will not *t* away the punishment
Amos 2:1 I will not *t* away the punishment
Amos 2:4 I will not *t* away the punishment
Amos 2:6 I will not *t* away the punishment
Amos 2:7 *t* aside the way of the meek
Amos 5:7 Ye who *t* judgment to wormwood, and
Amos 5:12 they *t* aside the poor in the gate
Amos 8:10 I will *t* your feasts into
Jonah 3:8 let them *t* every one from his
Jonah 3:9 Who can tell if God will *t*
Jonah 3:9 *t* away from his fierce anger,
Mic 7:19 He will *t* again, he will have
Zeph 2:7 them, and *t* away their captivity
Zeph 3:9 For then will I *t* to the people a
Zeph 3:20 when I *t* back your captivity
Zec 1:3 *T* ye unto me, saith the LORD of
Zec 1:3 I will *t* unto you, saith the LORD
Zec 1:4 *T* ye now from your evil ways, and
Zec 9:12 *T* you to the strong hold, ye
Zec 10:9 with their children, and *t* again
Zec 13:7 I will *t* mine hand upon the
Mal 2:6 did *t* many away from iniquity
Mal 3:5 that *t* aside the stranger from
Mal 4:6 he shall *t* the heart of the
Mt 5:39 cheek, *t* to him the other also
Mt 5:42 borrow of thee *t* not thou away
Mt 7:6 feet, and *t* again and rend you
Mk 13:16 him that is in the field not *t*
Lk 1:16 shall he *t* to the Lord their God
Lk 1:17 to *t* the hearts of the fathers to
Lk 10:6 if not, it shall *t* to you again
Lk 17:4 times in a day *t* again to thee
Lk 21:13 it shall *t* to you for a testimony
Acts 13:8 seeking to *t* away the deputy from
Acts 13:46 life, lo, we *t* to the Gentiles
Acts 14:15 *t* from these vanities unto the
Acts 26:18 to *t* them from darkness to light,
Acts 26:20 *t* to God, and do works meet for
Rom 11:26 shall *t* away ungodliness from
2Cor 3:16 when it shall *t* to the Lord
Gal 4:9 how *t* ye again to the weak and
Phil 1:19 For I know that this shall *t* to
2Ti 3:5 from such *t* away
2Ti 4:4 they shall *t* away their ears from
Titus 1:14 of men, that *t* from the truth
Heb 12:25 if we *t* away from him that
Jas 3:3 we *t* about their whole body
2Pet 2:21 to *t* from the holy commandment
Rev 11:6 over waters to *t* them to blood

**TURNED**

Gen 3:24 a flaming sword which *t* every way
Gen 18:22 the men *t* their faces from thence
Gen 19:3 they *t* in unto him, and entered
Gen 38:1 *t* in to a certain Adullamite,
Gen 38:16 he *t* unto her by the way, and said
Gen 42:24 he *t* himself about from them, and
Ex 3:4 LORD saw that he *t* aside to see
Ex 4:7 it was *t* again as his other flesh
Ex 7:15 the rod which was *t* to a serpent
Ex 7:17 and they shall be *t* to blood
Ex 7:20 were in the river were *t* to blood
Ex 7:23 And Pharaoh *t* and went into his
Ex 10:6 he *t* himself, and went out from
Ex 10:19 the LORD *t* a mighty strong west
Ex 14:5 servants was *t* against the people
Ex 32:8 They have *t* aside quickly out of
Ex 32:15 And Moses *t*, and went down from the
Ex 33:11 And he *t* again into the camp
Lev 13:3 the hair in the plague is *t* white
Lev 13:4 the hair thereof be not *t* white
Lev 13:10 it have *t* the hair white, and
Lev 13:13 it is all *t* white
Lev 13:17 if the plague be *t* into white
Lev 13:20 and the hair thereof be *t* white
Lev 13:25 in the bright spot be *t* white
Num 14:43 because ye are *t* away from the
Num 20:21 wherefore Israel *t* away from him
Num 21:33 And they *t* and went up by the way
Num 22:23 the ass *t* aside out of the way,
Num 22:33 *t* from me these three times
Num 22:33 unless she had *t* from me, surely
Num 25:4 LORD may be *t* away from Israel
Num 25:11 hath *t* my wrath away from the
Num 33:7 *t* again unto Pi-hahiroth, which
Deut 1:24 And they *t* and went up into the
Deut 2:1 Then we *t*, and took our journey
Deut 2:8 Elath, and from Ezion-gaber, we *t*
Deut 3:1 Then we *t*, and went up the way to
Deut 9:12 they are quickly *t* aside out of
Deut 9:15 So I *t* and came down from the
Deut 9:16 ye had *t* aside quickly out of the
Deut 10:5 I *t* myself and came down from the
Deut 23:5 but the LORD thy God *t* the curse
Deut 31:18 that they are *t* unto other gods
Josh 7:12 but *t* their backs before their
Josh 7:26 So the LORD *t* from the fierceness
Josh 8:20 *t* back upon the pursuers
Josh 8:21 city ascended, then they *t* again
Josh 11:10 And Joshua at that time *t* back
Josh 19:12 *t* from Sarid eastward toward the
Judg 2:17 they *t* quickly out of the way
Judg 3:19 But he himself *t* again from the
Judg 4:18 when he had *t* in unto her into
Judg 8:33 the children of Israel *t* again
Judg 14:8 he *t* aside to see the carcase of
Judg 15:4 and *t* tail to tail, and put a
Judg 18:3 they *t* in thither, and said unto
Judg 18:15 they *t* thitherward, and came to
Judg 18:21 So they *t* and departed, and put the
Judg 18:23 they *t* their faces, and said unto
Judg 18:26 were too strong for him, he *t*
Judg 19:15 they *t* aside thither, to go in and
Judg 20:41 And when the men of Israel *t* again
Judg 20:42 Therefore they *t* their backs
Judg 20:45 And they *t* and fled toward the
Judg 20:47 But six hundred men *t* and fled to
Judg 20:48 the men of Israel *t* again upon
Ruth 3:8 the man was afraid, and *t* himself
Ruth 4:1 And he *t* aside, and sat down
1Sa 6:12 *t* not aside to the right hand or
1Sa 8:3 but *t* aside after lucre, and took
1Sa 10:6 shalt be *t* into another man
1Sa 10:9 that when he had *t* his back to go
1Sa 13:17 one company *t* unto the way that
1Sa 13:18 another company *t* the way to
1Sa 13:18 another company *t* to the way of
1Sa 14:21 even they also *t* to be with the
1Sa 14:47 and whithersoever he *t* himself
1Sa 15:11 for he is *t* back from following
1Sa 15:27 as Samuel *t* about to go away, he
1Sa 15:31 So Samuel *t* again after Saul
1Sa 17:30 he *t* from him toward another, and
1Sa 22:18 And Doeg the Edomite *t*, and he fell
1Sa 25:12 So David's young men *t* their way
2Sa 1:22 the bow of Jonathan *t* not back
2Sa 2:19 in going he *t* not to the right
2Sa 18:30 he *t* aside, and stood still
2Sa 19:2 the victory that day was *t* into
2Sa 22:38 *t* not again until I had consumed
1Kin 2:15 howbeit the kingdom is *t* about
1Kin 2:28 for Joab had *t* after Adonijah,
1Kin 2:28 though he *t* not after Absalom
1Kin 8:14 the king *t* his face about, and
1Kin 10:13 So she *t* and went to her own
1Kin 11:3 his wives *t* away his heart
1Kin 11:4 that his wives *t* away his heart
1Kin 11:9 because his heart was *t* from the
1Kin 15:5 *t* not aside from any thing that
1Kin 18:37 that thou hast *t* their heart back
1Kin 20:39 and, behold, a man *t* aside
1Kin 21:4 *t* away his face, and would eat no
1Kin 22:32 they *t* aside to fight against him
1Kin 22:33 that they *t* back from pursuing
1Kin 22:43 he *t* not aside from it, doing
2Kin 1:5 the messengers *t* back unto him
2Kin 1:5 unto them, Why are ye now *t* back
2Kin 2:24 he *t* back, and looked on them, and
2Kin 4:8 he *t* in thither to eat bread
2Kin 4:11 he *t* into the chamber, and lay
2Kin 5:12 So he *t* and went away in a rage
2Kin 5:26 when the man *t* again from his
2Kin 9:23 Joram *t* his hands, and fled, and
2Kin 15:20 So the king of Assyria *t* back
2Kin 16:18 *t* he from the house of the LORD
2Kin 20:2 Then he *t* his face to the wall,
2Kin 22:2 *t* not aside to the right hand or
2Kin 23:16 And as Josiah *t* himself, he spied
2Kin 23:25 that *t* to the LORD with all his
2Kin 23:26 Notwithstanding the LORD *t* not
2Kin 23:34 *t* his name to Jehoiakim, and took
2Kin 24:1 then he *t* and rebelled against him
1Chr 10:14 *t* the kingdom unto David the son
1Chr 21:20 And Ornan *t* back, and saw the angel
2Chr 6:3 And the king *t* his face, and
2Chr 9:12 So she *t*, and went away to her own
2Chr 12:12 the wrath of the LORD *t* from him
2Chr 18:32 they *t* back again from pursuing
2Chr 20:10 Egypt, but they *t* from them, and
2Chr 29:6 have *t* away their faces from the
2Chr 29:6 of the LORD, and *t* their backs
2Chr 36:4 and *t* his name to Jehoiakim
Ezr 6:22 *t* the heart of the king of
Ezr 10:14 God for this matter be *t* from us
Neh 2:15 *t* back, and entered by the gate of
Neh 9:35 neither *t* they from their wicked
Neh 13:2 howbeit our God *t* the curse into
Est 9:1 (though it was *t* to the contrary,
Est 9:22 the month which was *t* unto them
Job 6:18 paths of their way are *t* aside
Job 16:11 *t* me over into the hands of the
Job 19:19 whom I loved are *t* against me
Job 20:14 Yet his meat in his bowels is *t*
Job 28:5 under it is *t* up as it were fire
Job 30:15 Terrors are *t* upon me
Job 30:31 My harp also is *t* to mourning
Job 31:7 If my step hath *t* out of the way
Job 34:27 Because they *t* back from him, and
Job 37:12 it is *t* round about by his
Job 38:14 It is *t* as clay to the seal
Job 41:22 sorrow is *t* into joy before him
Job 41:28 slingstones are *t* with him into
Job 42:10 the LORD *t* the captivity of Job,
Ps 9:3 When mine enemies are *t* back
Ps 9:17 The wicked shall be *t* into hell
Ps 30:11 Thou hast *t* for me my mourning
Ps 32:4 my moisture is *t* into the drought
Ps 35:4 let them be *t* back and brought to
Ps 44:18 Our heart is not *t* back, neither
Ps 66:6 He *t* the sea into dry land
Ps 66:20 which hath not *t* away my prayer
Ps 70:2 let them be *t* backward, and put to
Ps 70:3 Let them be *t* back for a reward
Ps 78:9 *t* back in the day of battle
Ps 78:38 many a time *t* he his anger away,
Ps 78:41 Yea, they *t* back and tempted God,
Ps 78:44 had *t* their rivers into blood
Ps 78:57 But *t* back, and dealt unfaithfully
Ps 78:57 they were *t* aside like a
Ps 81:14 and *t* my hand against their
Ps 85:3 thou hast *t* thyself from the
Ps 89:43 Thou hast also *t* the edge of his
Ps 105:25 He *t* their heart to hate his
Ps 105:29 He *t* their waters into blood, and
Ps 114:8 Which *t* the rock into a standing
Ps 119:59 *t* my feet unto thy testimonies
Ps 126:1 When the LORD *t* again the
Ps 129:5 and *t* back that hate Zion
Eccl 2:12 I *t* myself to behold wisdom, and
Song 6:1 whither is thy beloved *t* aside
Is 5:25 all this his anger is not *t* away
Is 9:12 all this his anger is not *t* away
Is 9:17 all this his anger is not *t* away
Is 9:21 all this his anger is not *t* away
Is 10:4 all this his anger is not *t* away
Is 12:1 with me, thine anger is *t* away
Is 21:4 hath he *t* into fear unto me
Is 28:27 wheel *t* about upon the cummin
Is 29:17 Lebanon shall be *t* into a
Is 34:9 thereof shall be *t* into pitch
Is 38:2 Then Hezekiah *t* his face toward
Is 42:17 They shall be *t* back, they shall
Is 44:20 a deceived heart hath *t* him aside
Is 50:5 rebellious, neither *t* away back
Is 53:6 we have *t* every one to his own
Is 59:14 judgment is *t* away backward, and
Is 63:10 therefore he was *t* to be their
Jer 2:21 how then art thou *t* into the
Jer 2:27 for they have *t* their back unto
Jer 3:10 sister Judah hath not *t* unto me
Jer 4:8 of the LORD is not *t* back from us
Jer 5:25 have *t* away these things, and your
Jer 6:12 houses shall be *t* unto others
Jer 8:6 every one *t* to his course, as the
Jer 11:10 They are *t* back to the iniquities
Jer 23:22 then they should have *t* them from
Jer 30:6 and all faces are *t* into paleness
Jer 31:18 turn thou me, and I shall be *t*
Jer 31:19 Surely after that I was *t*
Jer 32:33 they have *t* unto me the back, and
Jer 34:11 But afterward they *t*, and caused
Jer 34:15 And ye were now *t*, and had done
Jer 34:16 But ye *t* and polluted my name, and
Jer 38:22 the mire, and they are *t* away back
Jer 46:5 seen them dismayed and *t* away back
Jer 46:21 for they also are *t* back, and are
Jer 48:39 how hath Moab *t* the back with
Jer 50:6 they have *t* them away on the
Lam 1:13 for my feet, he hath *t* me back
Lam 1:20 mine heart is *t* within me

Lam 3:3 Surely against me is he *t*
Lam 3:11 He hath *t* aside my ways, and
Lam 5:2 Our inheritance is *t* to strangers
Lam 5:15 our dance is *t* into mourning
Lam 5:21 thee, O LORD, and we shall be *t*
Eze 1:9 they *t* not when they went
Eze 1:12 they *t* not when they went
Eze 1:17 they *t* not when they went
Eze 10:11 they *t* not as they went, but to
Eze 10:11 they *t* not as they went
Eze 10:16 also *t* not from beside them
Eze 17:6 whose branches *t* toward him
Eze 26:2 she is *t* unto me
Eze 42:19 He *t* about to the west side, and
Dan 9:16 thy fury be *t* away from thy city
Dan 10:8 was *t* in me into corruption
Dan 10:16 vision my sorrows are *t* upon me
Hos 7:8 Ephraim is a cake not *t*
Hos 11:8 mine heart is *t* within me
Hos 14:4 for mine anger is *t* away from him
Joel 2:31 The sun shall be *t* into darkness
Amos 6:12 for ye have *t* judgment into gall,
Jonah 3:10 that they *t* from their evil way
Nah 2:2 For the LORD hath *t* away the
Hab 2:16 right hand shall be *t* unto thee
Zeph 1:6 them that are *t* back from the
Hag 2:17 yet ye *t* not to me, saith the
Zec 5:1 Then I *t*, and lifted up mine eyes,
Zec 6:1 And I *t*, and lifted up mine eyes,
Zec 14:10 All the land shall be *t* as a
Mt 2:22 he *t* aside into the parts of
Mt 9:22 But Jesus *t* him about, and when he
Mt 16:23 But he *t*, and said unto Peter, Get
Mk 5:30 *t* him about in the press, and said
Mk 8:33 But when he had *t* about and looked
Lk 2:45 they *t* back again to Jerusalem,
Lk 7:9 *t* him about, and said unto the
Lk 7:44 he *t* to the woman, and said unto
Lk 9:55 But he *t*, and rebuked them, and
Lk 10:23 he *t* him unto his disciples, and
Lk 14:25 and he *t*, and said unto them,
Lk 17:15 *t* back, and with a loud voice
Lk 22:61 And the Lord *t*, and looked upon
Jn 1:38 Then Jesus *t*, and saw them
Jn 16:20 your sorrow shall be *t* into joy
Jn 20:14 she *t* herself back, and saw Jesus
Jn 20:16 She *t* herself, and saith unto him,
Acts 2:20 The sun shall be *t* into darkness
Acts 7:39 in their hearts *t* back again into
Acts 7:42 Then God *t*, and gave them up to
Acts 9:35 Saron saw him, and *t* to the Lord
Acts 11:21 believed, and *t* unto the Lord
Acts 15:19 among the Gentiles are *t* to God
Acts 16:18 But Paul, being grieved, *t*
Acts 17:6 These that have *t* the world
Acts 19:26 *t* away much people, saying that
1Th 1:9 how ye *t* to God from idols to
1Ti 1:6 have *t* aside unto vain jangling
1Ti 5:15 are already *t* aside after Satan
2Ti 1:15 are in Asia be *t* away from me
2Ti 4:4 truth, and shall be *t* unto fables
Heb 11:34 *t* to flight the armies of the
Heb 12:13 which is lame be *t* out of the way
Jas 3:4 yet are they *t* about with a very
Jas 4:9 your laughter be *t* to mourning
2Pet 2:22 The dog is *t* to his own vomit
Rev 1:12 I *t* to see the voice that spake
Rev 1:12 And being *t*, I saw seven golden

## TURNEST

1Kin 2:3 and whithersoever thou *t* thyself
Job 15:13 That thou *t* thy spirit against
Ps 90:3 Thou *t* man to destruction

## TURNETH

Lev 20:6 the soul that *t* after such as
Deut 29:18 whose heart *t* away this day from
Josh 7:8 when Israel *t* their backs before
Josh 19:27 *t* toward the sunrising to
Josh 19:29 And then the coast *t* to Ramah
Josh 19:29 and the coast *t* to Hosah
Josh 19:34 then the coast *t* westward to
Job 39:22 neither *t* he back from the sword
Ps 107:33 He *t* rivers into a wilderness, and
Ps 107:35 He *t* the wilderness into a
Ps 146:9 of the wicked he *t* upside down
Prov 15:1 A soft answer *t* away wrath
Prov 17:8 whithersoever it *t*, it prospereth
Prov 21:1 he *t* it whithersoever he will
Prov 26:14 As the door *t* upon his hinges, so
Prov 28:9 He that *t* away his ear from
Prov 30:30 beasts, and *t* not away for any
Eccl 1:6 south, and *t* about unto the north
Song 1:7 that *t* aside by the flocks of thy
Is 9:13 For the people *t* not unto him
Is 24:1 *t* it upside down, and scattereth
Is 44:25 that *t* wise men backward, and
Jer 14:8 as a wayfaring man that *t* aside
Jer 49:24 *t* herself to flee, and fear hath
Lam 1:8 yea, she sigheth, and *t* backward
Lam 3:3 he *t* his hand against me all the
Eze 18:24 But when the righteous *t* away
Eze 18:26 When a righteous man *t* away from
Eze 18:27 when the wicked man *t* away from
Eze 18:28 and *t* away from all his
Eze 33:12 day that he *t* from his wickedness
Eze 33:18 When the righteous *t* from his
Amos 5:8 *t* the shadow of death into the

## TURNING

2Kin 21:13 wiping it, and *t* it upside down
2Chr 26:9 gate, and at the *t* of the wall, and
2Chr 36:13 hardened his heart from *t* unto
Neh 3:19 the armoury at the *t* of the wall
Neh 3:20 from the *t* of the wall unto the
Neh 3:24 of Azariah unto the *t* of the wall
Neh 3:25 over against the *t* of the wall
Prov 1:32 For the *t* away of the simple
Is 29:16 Surely your *t* of things upside
Eze 41:24 two leaves apiece, two *t* leaves
Mic 2:4 *t* away he hath divided our fields
Lk 23:28 But Jesus *t* unto them said,
Jn 21:20 *t* about, seeth the disciple whom
Acts 3:26 in *t* away every one of you from
Acts 9:40 *t* him to the body said, Tabitha,
Jas 1:17 variableness, neither shadow of *t*
2Pet 2:6 *t* the cities of Sodom and Gomorrah
Jude 4 *t* the grace of our God into

## TURTLE

Song 2:12 the voice of the *t* is heard in
Jer 8:7 and the *t* and the crane and the

## TURTLEDOVE

Gen 15:9 a ram of three years old, and a *t*
Lev 12:6 and a young pigeon, or a *t*
Ps 74:19 thy *t* unto the multitude of the

## TURTLEDOVES

Lev 1:14 he shall bring his offering of *t*
Lev 5:7 which he hath committed, two *t*
Lev 5:11 if he be not able to bring two *t*
Lev 14:22 And two *t*, or two young pigeons,
Lev 14:30 he shall offer the one of the *t*
Lev 15:14 day he shall take to him two *t*
Lk 2:24 the law of the Lord, A pair of *t*

## TURTLES

Lev 12:8 lamb, then she shall bring two *t*
Lev 15:29 day she shall take unto her two *t*
Num 6:10 eighth day he shall bring two *t*

## TUTORS

Gal 4:2 But is under *t* and governors until

## TWAIN

1Sa 18:21 my son in law in the one of the *t*
2Kin 4:33 and shut the door upon them *t*
Is 6:2 with *t* he covered his face, and
Is 6:2 with *t* he covered his feet, and
Is 6:2 his feet, and with *t* he did fly
Jer 34:18 me, when they cut the calf in *t*
Eze 21:19 both *t* shall come forth out of
Mt 5:41 thee to go a mile, go with him *t*
Mt 19:5 they *t* shall be one flesh
Mt 19:6 Wherefore they are no more *t*
Mt 21:31 Whether of them *t* did the will of
Mt 27:21 Whether of the *t* will ye that I
Mt 27:51 in *t* from the top to the bottom
Mk 10:8 they *t* shall be one flesh
Mk 10:8 so then they are no more *t*
Mk 15:38 in *t* from the top to the bottom
Eph 2:15 make in himself of *t* one new man

## TWELFTH

Num 7:78 On the *t* day Ahira the son of
1Kin 19:19 oxen before him, and he with the *t*
2Kin 8:25 In the *t* year of Joram the son of
2Kin 17:1 In the *t* year of Ahaz king of
2Kin 25:27 king of Judah, in the *t* month
1Chr 24:12 to Eliashib, the *t* to Jakim,
1Chr 25:19 The *t* to Hashabiah, he, his sons,
1Chr 27:15 The *t* captain for the *t*
2Chr 34:3 in the *t* year he began to purge
Ezr 8:31 on the *t* day of the first month
Est 3:7 in the *t* year of king Ahasuerus,
Est 3:7 month to month, to the *t* month
Est 3:13 the thirteenth day of the *t* month
Est 8:12 the thirteenth day of the *t* month
Est 9:1 Now in the *t* month, that is, the
Jer 52:31 king of Judah, in the *t* month
Eze 29:1 in the *t* day of the month, the
Eze 32:1 the *t* year, in the *t* month
Eze 32:17 came to pass also in the *t* year
Eze 33:21 in the *t* year of our captivity
Rev 21:20 the *t*, an amethyst

## TWELVE

Gen 5:8 Seth were nine hundred and *t*
Gen 14:4 *T* years they served Chedorlaomer,
Gen 17:20 *t* princes shall he beget, and I
Gen 25:16 *t* princes according to their
Gen 35:22 Now the sons of Jacob were *t*
Gen 42:13 said, Thy servants are *t* brethren
Gen 42:32 We be *t* brethren, sons of our
Gen 49:28 these are the *t* tribes of Israel
Ex 15:27 where were *t* wells of water, and
Ex 24:4 *t* pillars, according to the
Ex 24:4 to the *t* tribes of Israel
Ex 28:21 of the children of Israel, *t*
Ex 28:21 they be according to the *t* tribes
Ex 39:14 of the children of Israel, *t*
Ex 39:14 name, according to the *t* tribes
Lev 24:5 flour, and bake *t* cakes thereof
Num 1:44 princes of Israel, being *t* men
Num 7:3 six covered wagons, and *t* oxen
Num 7:84 *t* chargers of silver
Num 7:84 *t* silver bowls, *t* spoons of
Num 7:86 The golden spoons were *t*, full of
Num 7:87 were *t* bullocks, the rams *t*
Num 7:87 the lambs of the first year *t*
Num 7:87 of the goats for sin offering *t*
Num 17:2 the house of their fathers *t* rods
Num 17:6 fathers' houses, even *t* rods
Num 29:17 ye shall offer *t* young bullocks
Num 31:5 tribe, *t* thousand armed for war
Num 31:33 threescore and *t* thousand beeves,
Num 31:38 tribute was threescore and *t*
Num 33:9 in Elim were *t* fountains of water
Deut 1:23 I took *t* men of you, one of a
Josh 3:12 Now therefore take you *t* men out
Josh 4:2 Take you *t* men out of the people,
Josh 4:3 *t* stones, and ye shall carry them
Josh 4:4 Then Joshua called the *t* men
Josh 4:8 took up *t* stones out of the midst
Josh 4:9 Joshua set up *t* stones in the
Josh 4:20 those *t* stones, which they took
Josh 8:25 were *t* thousand, even all the men
Josh 18:24 *t* cities with their villages
Josh 19:15 *t* cities with their villages
Josh 21:7 of the tribe of Zebulun, *t* cities
Josh 21:40 were by their lot *t* cities
Judg 19:29 into *t* pieces, and sent her into
Judg 21:10 the congregation sent thither *t*
2Sa 2:15 over by number *t* of Benjamin
2Sa 2:15 *t* of the servants of David
2Sa 10:6 of Ish-tob *t* thousand men
2Sa 17:1 me now choose out *t* thousand
1Kin 4:7 Solomon had *t* officers over all
1Kin 4:26 chariots, and *t* thousand horsemen
1Kin 7:15 a line of *t* cubits did compass
1Kin 7:25 It stood upon *t* oxen, three
1Kin 7:44 one sea, and *t* oxen under the sea
1Kin 10:20 *t* lions stood there on the one
1Kin 10:26 *t* thousand horsemen, whom he
1Kin 11:30 on him, and rent it in *t* pieces
1Kin 16:23 to reign over Israel, *t* years
1Kin 18:31 And Elijah took *t* stones,
1Kin 19:19 who was plowing with *t* yoke of
2Kin 3:1 king of Judah, and reigned *t* years
2Kin 21:1 Manasseh was *t* years old when
1Chr 6:63 of the tribe of Zebulun, *t* cities
1Chr 9:22 the gates were two hundred and *t*
1Chr 15:10 and his brethren an hundred and *t*
1Chr 25:9 with his brethren and sons were *t*
1Chr 25:10 his sons, and his brethren, were *t*
1Chr 25:11 his sons, and his brethren, were *t*
1Chr 25:12 his sons, and his brethren, were *t*
1Chr 25:13 his sons, and his brethren, were *t*
1Chr 25:14 his sons, and his brethren, were *t*
1Chr 25:15 his sons, and his brethren, were *t*
1Chr 25:16 his sons, and his brethren, were *t*
1Chr 25:17 his sons, and his brethren, were *t*
1Chr 25:18 his sons, and his brethren, were *t*
1Chr 25:19 his sons, and his brethren, were *t*
1Chr 25:20 his sons, and his brethren, were *t*

1Chr 25:21 his sons, and his brethren, were *t*
1Chr 25:22 his sons, and his brethren, were *t*
1Chr 25:23 his sons, and his brethren, were *t*
1Chr 25:24 his sons, and his brethren, were *t*
1Chr 25:25 his sons, and his brethren, were *t*
1Chr 25:26 his sons, and his brethren, were *t*
1Chr 25:27 his sons, and his brethren, were *t*
1Chr 25:28 his sons, and his brethren, were *t*
1Chr 25:29 his sons, and his brethren, were *t*
1Chr 25:30 his sons, and his brethren, were *t*
1Chr 25:31 his sons, and his brethren, were *t*
2Chr 1:14 *t* thousand horsemen, which he
2Chr 4:4 It stood upon *t* oxen, three
2Chr 4:15 One sea, and *t* oxen under it
2Chr 9:19 *t* lions stood there on the one
2Chr 9:25 chariots, and *t* thousand horsemen
2Chr 12:3 With *t* hundred chariots, and
2Chr 33:1 Manasseh was *t* years old when
Ezr 2:6 two thousand eight hundred and *t*
Ezr 2:18 of Jorah, an hundred and *t*
Ezr 6:17 *t* he goats, according to the
Ezr 8:24 Then I separated *t* of the chief
Ezr 8:35 *t* bullocks for all Israel, ninety
Ezr 8:35 *t* he goats for a sin offering
Neh 5:14 *t* years, I and my brethren have
Neh 7:24 of Hariph, an hundred and *t*
Est 2:12 after that she had been *t* months
Ps 60:*t* in the valley of salt *t* thousand
Jer 52:20 *t* brasen bulls that were under
Jer 52:21 a fillet of *t* cubits did compass
Eze 43:16 the altar shall be *t* cubits long
Eze 43:16 *t* broad, square in the four
Eze 47:13 to the *t* tribes of Israel
Dan 4:29 At the end of *t* months he walked
Mt 9:20 with an issue of blood *t* years
Mt 10:1 called unto him his *t* disciples
Mt 10:2 names of the *t* apostles are these
Mt 10:5 These *t* Jesus sent forth, and
Mt 11:1 end of commanding his *t* disciples
Mt 14:20 that remained *t* baskets full
Mt 19:28 ye also shall sit upon *t* thrones
Mt 19:28 judging the *t* tribes of Israel
Mt 20:17 the *t* disciples apart in the way
Mt 26:14 Then one of the *t*, called Judas
Mt 26:20 was come, he sat down with the *t*
Mt 26:47 spake, lo, Judas, one of the *t*
Mt 26:53 me more than *t* legions of angels
Mk 3:14 And he ordained *t*, that they
Mk 4:10 the *t* asked of him the parable
Mk 5:25 had an issue of blood *t* years
Mk 5:42 for she was of the age of *t* years
Mk 6:7 And he called unto him the *t*
Mk 6:43 they took up *t* baskets full of
Mk 8:19 They say unto him, *T*
Mk 9:35 And he sat down, and called the *t*
Mk 10:32 And he took again the *t*, and began
Mk 11:11 went out unto Bethany with the *t*
Mk 14:10 And Judas Iscariot, one of the *t*
Mk 14:17 the evening he cometh with the *t*
Mk 14:20 unto them, It is one of the *t*
Mk 14:43 spake, cometh Judas, one of the *t*
Lk 2:42 And when he was *t* years old
Lk 6:13 and of them he chose *t*, whom also
Lk 8:1 and the *t* were with him,
Lk 8:42 about *t* years of age, and she lay
Lk 8:43 having an issue of blood *t* years
Lk 9:1 called his *t* disciples together
Lk 9:12 to wear away, then came the *t*
Lk 9:17 that remained to them *t* baskets
Lk 18:31 Then he took unto him the *t*
Lk 22:3 being of the number of the *t*
Lk 22:14 down, and the *t* apostles with him
Lk 22:30 judging the *t* tribes of Israel
Lk 22:47 was called Judas, one of the *t*
Jn 6:13 filled *t* baskets with the
Jn 6:67 Then said Jesus unto the *t*
Jn 6:70 them, Have not I chosen you *t*
Jn 6:71 betray him, being one of the *t*
Jn 11:9 Are there not *t* hours in the day
Jn 20:24 But Thomas, one of the *t*, called
Acts 6:2 Then the *t* called the multitude
Acts 7:8 and Jacob begat the *t* patriarchs
Acts 19:7 And all the men were about *t*
Acts 24:11 that there are yet but *t* days
Acts 26:7 Unto which promise our *t* tribes
1Cor 15:5 was seen of Cephas, then of the *t*
Jas 1:1 to the *t* tribes which are
Rev 7:5 of Juda were sealed *t* thousand
Rev 7:5 of Reuben were sealed *t* thousand
Rev 7:5 of Gad were sealed *t* thousand
Rev 7:6 of Aser were sealed *t* thousand
Rev 7:6 Nepthalim were sealed *t* thousand
Rev 7:6 Manasses were sealed *t* thousand
Rev 7:7 of Simeon were sealed *t* thousand
Rev 7:7 of Levi were sealed *t* thousand
Rev 7:7 Issachar were sealed *t* thousand
Rev 7:8 of Zabulon were sealed *t* thousand
Rev 7:8 of Joseph were sealed *t* thousand
Rev 7:8 Benjamin were sealed *t* thousand
Rev 12:1 upon her head a crown of *t* stars
Rev 21:12 had *t* gates, and at the gates
Rev 21:12 gates, and at the gates *t* angels
Rev 21:12 the *t* tribes of the children of
Rev 21:14 of the city had *t* foundations
Rev 21:14 of the *t* apostles of the Lamb
Rev 21:16 the reed, *t* thousand furlongs
Rev 21:21 the *t* gates were *t* pearls
Rev 22:2 which bare *t* manner of fruits, and

## TWENTIETH

Gen 8:14 *t* day of the month, was the earth
Ex 12:18 *t* day of the month at even
Num 10:11 it came to pass on the *t* day of
1Kin 15:9 in the *t* year of Jeroboam king of
2Kin 12:6 *t* year of king Jehoash the
2Kin 13:1 *t* year of Joash the son of
2Kin 15:30 in the *t* year of Jotham the son
2Kin 25:27 seven and *t* day of the month, that
1Chr 24:16 to Pethahiah, the *t* to Jehezekel,
1Chr 24:17 *t* to Jachin, the two and
1Chr 24:17 to Jachin, the two and *t* to Gamul,
1Chr 24:18 *t* to Delaiah, the four and
1Chr 24:18 Delaiah, the four and *t* to Maaziah
1Chr 25:27 The *t* to Eliathah, he, his sons,
1Chr 25:28 *t* to Hothir, he, his sons, and his
1Chr 25:29 *t* to Giddalti, he, his sons, and
1Chr 25:30 *t* to Mahazioth, he, his sons, and
1Chr 25:31 *t* to Romamti-ezer, he, his sons,
2Chr 7:10 *t* day of the seventh month he
Ezr 10:9 on the *t* day of the month
Neh 1:1 the month Chisleu, in the *t* year
Neh 2:1 in the *t* year of Artaxerxes the
Neh 5:14 from the *t* year even unto the two
Est 8:9 on the three and *t* day thereof
Jer 25:3 *t* year, the word of the LORD hath
Jer 52:30 three and *t* year of Nebuchadrezzar
Jer 52:31 five and *t* day of the month, that
Eze 29:17 *t* year, in the first month, in
Eze 40:1 *t* year of our captivity, in the
Dan 10:4 *t* day of the first month, as I
Hag 1:15 *t* day of the sixth month, in the
Hag 2:1 *t* day of the month, came the word
Hag 2:10 *t* day of the ninth month, in the
Hag 2:18 *t* day of the ninth month, even
Hag 2:20 *t* day of the month, saying,
Zec 1:7 *t* day of the eleventh month,

## TWENTY

Gen 6:3 shall be an hundred and *t* years
Gen 11:24 nine and *t* years, and begat Terah
Gen 18:31 there shall be *t* found there
Gen 23:1 hundred and seven and *t* years old
Gen 31:38 This *t* years have I been with
Gen 31:41 Thus have I been *t* years in thy
Gen 32:14 *t* he goats, two hundred ewes, and
Gen 32:14 two hundred ewes, and *t* rams,
Gen 32:15 *t* she asses, and ten foals
Gen 37:28 for *t* pieces of silver
Ex 26:2 *t* cubits, and the breadth of one
Ex 26:18 *t* boards on the south side
Ex 26:19 of silver under the *t* boards
Ex 26:20 side there shall be *t* boards
Ex 27:10 the *t* pillars thereof and their
Ex 27:10 their *t* sockets shall be of brass
Ex 27:11 his *t* pillars and their *t*
Ex 27:16 shall be an hanging of *t* cubits
Ex 30:13 (a shekel is *t* gerahs
Ex 30:14 from *t* years old and above, shall
Ex 36:9 The length of one curtain was *t*
Ex 36:23 *t* boards for the south side
Ex 36:24 silver he made under the *t* boards
Ex 36:25 north corner, he made *t* boards
Ex 38:10 Their pillars were *t*, and their
Ex 38:10 and their brasen sockets *t*
Ex 38:11 cubits, their pillars were *t*
Ex 38:11 and their sockets of brass *t*
Ex 38:18 *t* cubits was the length, and the
Ex 38:24 the gold of the offering, was *t*
Ex 38:26 from *t* years old and upward, for
Lev 27:3 shall be of the male from *t* years
Lev 27:5 years old even unto *t* years old
Lev 27:5 shall be of the male *t* shekels
Lev 27:25 *t* gerahs shall be the shekel
Num 1:3 From *t* years old and upward, all
Num 1:18 from *t* years old and upward, by
Num 1:20 every male from *t* years old
Num 1:22 every male from *t* years old
Num 1:24 from *t* years old and upward, all
Num 1:26 from *t* years old and upward, all
Num 1:28 from *t* years old and upward, all
Num 1:30 from *t* years old and upward, all
Num 1:32 from *t* years old and upward, all
Num 1:34 from *t* years old and upward, all
Num 1:36 from *t* years old and upward, all
Num 1:38 from *t* years old and upward, all
Num 1:40 from *t* years old and upward, all
Num 1:42 from *t* years old and upward, all
Num 1:45 from *t* years old and upward, all
Num 3:39 a month old and upward, were *t*
Num 3:43 were numbered of them, were *t*
Num 3:47 (the shekel is *t* gerahs
Num 7:86 was an hundred and *t* shekels
Num 7:88 of the peace offerings were *t*
Num 8:24 from *t* and five years old and
Num 11:19 neither ten days, nor *t* days
Num 14:29 from *t* years old and upward, which
Num 18:16 the sanctuary, which is *t* gerahs
Num 25:9 that died in the plague were *t*
Num 26:2 from *t* years old and upward,
Num 26:4 from *t* years old and upward
Num 26:14 the families of the Simeonites, *t*
Num 26:62 that were numbered of them were *t*
Num 32:11 from *t* years old and upward, shall
Num 33:39 And Aaron was an hundred and *t*
Deut 31:2 hundred and *t* years old this day
Deut 34:7 and *t* years old when he died
Josh 15:32 all the cities are *t* and nine,
Josh 19:30 *t* and two cities with their
Judg 4:3 *t* years he mightily oppressed the
Judg 7:3 And there returned of the people *t*
Judg 8:10 *t* thousand men that drew sword
Judg 10:2 And he judged Israel *t* and three
Judg 10:3 a Gileadite, and judged Israel *t*
Judg 11:33 even *t* cities, and unto the plain
Judg 15:20 days of the Philistines *t* years
Judg 16:31 And he judged Israel *t* years
Judg 20:15 at that time out of the cities *t*
Judg 20:21 of the Israelites that day *t*
Judg 20:35 of the Benjamites that day *t*
Judg 20:46 fell that day of Benjamin were *t*
1Sa 7:2 for it was *t* years
1Sa 14:14 made, was about *t* men, within as
2Sa 3:20 to Hebron, and *t* men with him
2Sa 8:4 horsemen, and *t* thousand footmen
2Sa 8:5 the Syrians two and *t* thousand men
2Sa 9:10 had fifteen sons and *t* servants
2Sa 10:6 *t* thousand footmen, and of king
2Sa 18:7 that day of *t* thousand men
2Sa 19:17 sons and his *t* servants with him
2Sa 21:20 six toes, four and *t* in number
2Sa 24:8 the end of nine months and *t* days
1Kin 4:23 *t* oxen out of the pastures, and an
1Kin 5:11 Solomon gave Hiram *t* thousand
1Kin 5:11 and *t* measures of pure oil
1Kin 6:2 and the breadth thereof *t* cubits
1Kin 6:3 *t* cubits was the length thereof,
1Kin 6:16 he built *t* cubits on the sides of
1Kin 6:20 forepart was *t* cubits in length
1Kin 6:20 *t* cubits in breadth
1Kin 6:20 *t* cubits in the height thereof
1Kin 8:63 *t* thousand oxen, and an hundred and
1Kin 8:63 and an hundred and *t* thousand sheep
1Kin 9:10 to pass at the end of *t* years
1Kin 9:11 then king Solomon gave Hiram *t*
1Kin 9:28 *t* talents, and brought it to king
1Kin 10:10 *t* talents of gold, and of spices
1Kin 14:20 reigned were two and *t* years
1Kin 15:33 over all Israel in Tirzah, *t*
1Kin 16:8 In the *t* and sixth year of Asa
1Kin 16:10 him, and killed him, in the *t*
1Kin 16:15 In the *t* and seventh year of Asa
1Kin 16:29 reigned over Israel in Samaria *t*
1Kin 20:30 and there a wall fell upon *t*
1Kin 22:42 and he reigned *t* and five years in
2Kin 4:42 *t* loaves of barley, and full ears
2Kin 8:26 *t* years old was Ahaziah when he
2Kin 10:36 over Israel in Samaria was *t*
2Kin 14:2 He was *t* and five years old when
2Kin 14:2 he began to reign, and reigned *t*
2Kin 15:1 In the *t* and seventh year of
2Kin 15:27 in Samaria, and reigned *t* years

2Kin 15:33 *t* years old was he when he began
2Kin 16:2 *T* years old was Ahaz when he
2Kin 18:2 *T* and five years old was he when
2Kin 18:2 and he reigned *t* and nine years in
2Kin 21:19 Amon was *t* and two years old when
2Kin 23:31 Jehoahaz was *t* and three years old
2Kin 23:36 Jehoiakim was *t* and five years old
2Kin 24:18 Zedekiah was *t* and one years old
1Chr 2:22 *t* cities in the land of Gilead
1Chr 7:2 *t* thousand and six hundred
1Chr 7:7 reckoned by their genealogies *t*
1Chr 7:9 was *t* thousand and two hundred
1Chr 7:40 apt to the war and to battle was *t*
1Chr 12:28 and of his father's house *t*
1Chr 12:30 children of Ephraim *t* thousand
1Chr 12:35 And of the Danites expert in war *t*
1Chr 12:37 battle, an hundred and *t* thousand
1Chr 15:5 and his brethren an hundred and *t*
1Chr 15:6 and his brethren two hundred and *t*
1Chr 18:4 horsemen, and *t* thousand footmen
1Chr 18:5 the Syrians two and *t* thousand men
1Chr 20:6 fingers and toes were four and *t*
1Chr 23:4 Of which, *t* and four thousand were
1Chr 23:24 the LORD, from the age of *t* years
1Chr 23:27 were numbered from *t* years old
1Chr 27:1 the year, of every course were *t*
1Chr 27:2 and in his course were *t* and four
1Chr 27:4 in his course likewise were *t*
1Chr 27:5 and in his course were *t* and four
1Chr 27:7 and in his course were *t* and four
1Chr 27:8 and in his course were *t* and four
1Chr 27:9 and in his course were *t* and four
1Chr 27:10 and in his course were *t* and four
1Chr 27:11 and in his course were *t* and four
1Chr 27:12 and in his course were *t* and four
1Chr 27:13 and in his course were *t* and four
1Chr 27:14 and in his course were *t* and four
1Chr 27:15 and in his course were *t* and four
1Chr 27:23 number of them from *t* years old
2Chr 2:10 *t* thousand measures of beaten
2Chr 2:10 *t* thousand measures of barley, and
2Chr 2:10 *t* thousand baths of wine, and
2Chr 2:10 wine, and *t* thousand baths of oil
2Chr 3:3 cubits, and the breadth *t* cubits
2Chr 3:4 *t* cubits, and the height was an
2Chr 3:4 and the height was an hundred and *t*
2Chr 3:8 *t* cubits, and the breadth thereof
2Chr 3:8 and the breadth thereof *t* cubits
2Chr 3:11 the cherubims were *t* cubits long
2Chr 3:13 spread themselves forth *t* cubits
2Chr 4:1 *t* cubits the length thereof, and
2Chr 4:1 *t* cubits the breadth thereof, and
2Chr 5:12 *t* priests sounding with trumpets
2Chr 7:5 Solomon offered a sacrifice of *t*
2Chr 7:5 and an hundred and *t* thousand sheep
2Chr 8:1 to pass at the end of *t* years
2Chr 9:9 *t* talents of gold, and of spices
2Chr 11:21 and begat *t* and eight sons, and
2Chr 13:21 fourteen wives, and begat *t*
2Chr 20:31 began to reign, and he reigned *t*
2Chr 25:1 Amaziah was *t* and five years old
2Chr 25:1 began to reign, and he reigned *t*
2Chr 25:5 he numbered them from *t* years old
2Chr 27:1 Jotham was *t* and five years old
2Chr 27:8 *t* years old when he began to
2Chr 28:1 Ahaz was *t* years old when he
2Chr 28:6 *t* thousand in one day, which were
2Chr 29:1 *t* years old, and he reigned nine
2Chr 29:1 nine and *t* years in Jerusalem
2Chr 31:17 and the Levites from *t* years old
2Chr 33:21 *t* years old when he began to
2Chr 36:2 Jehoahaz was *t* and three years old
2Chr 36:5 Jehoiakim was *t* and five years old
2Chr 36:11 *t* years old when he began to
Ezr 1:9 of silver, nine and *t* knives,
Ezr 2:11 children of Bebai, six hundred *t*
Ezr 2:12 Azgad, a thousand two hundred *t*
Ezr 2:17 of Bezai, three hundred *t*
Ezr 2:19 children of Hashum, two hundred *t*
Ezr 2:21 of Beth-lehem, an hundred *t*
Ezr 2:23 The men of Anathoth, an hundred *t*
Ezr 2:26 of Ramah and Gaba, six hundred *t*
Ezr 2:27 The men of Michmas, an hundred *t*
Ezr 2:28 of Beth-el and Ai, two hundred *t*
Ezr 2:32 of Harim, three hundred and *t*
Ezr 2:33 Hadid, and Ono, seven hundred *t*
Ezr 2:41 children of Asaph, an hundred *t*
Ezr 2:67 six thousand seven hundred and *t*
Ezr 3:8 from *t* years old and upward, to
Ezr 8:11 the son of Bebai, and with him *t*
Ezr 8:19 his brethren and their sons, *t*
Ezr 8:20 two hundred and *t* Nethinims
Ezr 8:27 Also *t* basons of gold, of a
Neh 6:15 So the wall was finished in the *t*
Neh 7:16 children of Bebai, six hundred *t*
Neh 7:17 two thousand three hundred *t*
Neh 7:22 of Hashum, three hundred *t*
Neh 7:23 of Bezai, three hundred *t*
Neh 7:27 The men of Anathoth, an hundred *t*
Neh 7:30 of Ramah and Gaba, six hundred *t*
Neh 7:31 men of Michmas, an hundred and *t*
Neh 7:32 of Beth-el and Ai, an hundred *t*
Neh 7:35 of Harim, three hundred and *t*
Neh 7:37 Hadid, and Ono, seven hundred *t*
Neh 7:69 thousand seven hundred and *t* asses
Neh 7:71 the work *t* thousand drams of gold
Neh 7:72 gave was *t* thousand drams of gold
Neh 9:1 Now in the *t* and fourth day of
Neh 11:8 Gabbai, Sallai, nine hundred *t*
Neh 11:12 of the house were eight hundred *t*
Neh 11:14 men of valour, an hundred *t*
Est 1:1 hundred and seven and *t* provinces
Est 8:9 India unto Ethiopia, an hundred *t*
Est 9:30 all the Jews, to the hundred *t*
Ps 68:17 chariots of God are *t* thousand
Jer 52:1 *t* years old when he began to
Jer 52:28 three thousand Jews and three and *t*
Eze 4:10 be by weight, *t* shekels a day
Eze 8:16 *t* men, with their backs toward
Eze 11:1 door of the gate five and *t* men
Eze 40:13 *t* cubits, door against door
Eze 40:21 and the breadth five and *t* cubits
Eze 40:25 and the breadth five and *t* cubits
Eze 40:29 long, and five and *t* cubits broad
Eze 40:30 *t* cubits long, and five cubits
Eze 40:33 long, and five and *t* cubits broad
Eze 40:36 and the breadth five and *t* cubits
Eze 40:49 length of the porch was *t* cubits
Eze 41:2 and the breadth, *t* cubits
Eze 41:4 the length thereof, *t* cubits
Eze 41:4 *t* cubits, before the temple
Eze 41:10 chambers was the wideness of *t*
Eze 42:3 Over against the *t* cubits which
Eze 45:1 *t* thousand reeds, and the breadth
Eze 45:3 *t* thousand, and the breadth of ten
Eze 45:5 *t* thousand of length, and the ten
Eze 45:5 for a possession for *t* chambers
Eze 45:6 *t* thousand long, over against the
Eze 45:12 And the shekel shall be *t* gerahs
Eze 45:12 *t* shekels, five and *t* shekels
Eze 48:8 *t* thousand reeds in breadth, and
Eze 48:9 *t* thousand in length, and of ten
Eze 48:10 *t* thousand in length, and toward
Eze 48:10 five and *t* thousand in length
Eze 48:13 *t* thousand in length, and ten
Eze 48:13 *t* thousand, and the breadth ten
Eze 48:15 *t* thousand, shall be a profane
Eze 48:20 *t* thousand by five and
Eze 48:20 thousand by five and *t* thousand
Eze 48:21 *t* thousand of the oblation toward
Eze 48:21 *t* thousand toward the west border
Dan 6:1 *t* princes, which should be over
Dan 10:13 Persia withstood me one and *t* days
Hag 2:16 one came to an heap of *t* measures
Hag 2:16 of the press, there were but *t*
Zec 5:2 the length thereof is *t* cubits
Lk 14:31 against him with *t* thousand
Jn 6:19 *t* or thirty furlongs, they see
Acts 1:15 were about an hundred and *t*
Acts 27:28 And sounded, and found it *t* fathoms
1Cor 10:8 in one day three and *t* thousand
Rev 4:4 the throne were four and *t* seats
Rev 4:4 *t* elders sitting, clothed in
Rev 4:10 *t* elders fall down before him
Rev 5:8 *t* elders fell down before the
Rev 5:14 *t* elders fell down and worshipped
Rev 11:16 *t* elders, which sat before God on
Rev 19:4 *t* elders and the four beasts fell

## TWENTY'S

Gen 18:31 I will not destroy it for *t* sake

## TWICE

Gen 41:32 dream was doubled unto Pharaoh *t*
Ex 16:5 it shall be *t* as much as they
Ex 16:22 day they gathered *t* as much bread
Num 20:11 with his rod he smote the rock *t*
1Sa 18:11 avoided out of his presence *t*
1Kin 11:9 which had appeared unto him *t*
2Kin 6:10 himself there, not once nor *t*
Neh 13:20 without Jerusalem once or *t*
Job 33:14 For God speaketh once, yea *t*
Job 40:5 will not answer: yea, *t*
Job 42:10 also the LORD gave Job *t* as much
Ps 62:11 *t* have I heard this
Eccl 6:6 he live a thousand years *t* told
Mk 14:30 night, before the cock crow *t*
Mk 14:72 unto him, Before the cock crow *t*
Lk 18:12 I fast *t* in the week, I give
Jude 12 *t* dead, plucked up by the roots

## TWIGS

Eze 17:4 off the top of his young *t*
Eze 17:22 top of his young *t* a tender one

## TWILIGHT

1Sa 30:17 David smote them from the *t* even
2Kin 7:5 And they rose up in the *t*, to go
2Kin 7:7 they arose and fled in the *t*
Job 3:9 stars of the *t* thereof be dark
Job 24:15 the adulterer waiteth for the *t*
Prov 7:9 In the *t*, in the evening, in the
Eze 12:6 and carry it forth in the *t*
Eze 12:7 I brought it forth in the *t*
Eze 12:12 bear upon his shoulder in the *t*

## TWINED

Ex 26:1 with ten curtains of fine *t* linen
Ex 26:31 fine *t* linen of cunning work
Ex 26:36 fine *t* linen, wrought with
Ex 27:9 hangings for the court of fine *t*
Ex 27:16 fine *t* linen, wrought with
Ex 27:18 five cubits of fine *t* linen
Ex 28:6 fine *t* linen, with cunning work
Ex 28:8 and scarlet, and fine *t* linen
Ex 28:15 and of scarlet, and of fine *t* linen
Ex 36:8 made ten curtains of fine *t* linen
Ex 36:35 and scarlet, and fine *t* linen
Ex 36:37 fine *t* linen, of needlework
Ex 38:9 of the court were of fine *t* linen
Ex 38:16 round about were of fine *t* linen
Ex 38:18 and scarlet, and fine *t* linen
Ex 39:2 and scarlet, and fine *t* linen
Ex 39:5 and scarlet, and fine *t* linen
Ex 39:8 and scarlet, and fine *t* linen
Ex 39:24 and purple, and scarlet, and *t* linen
Ex 39:28 and linen breeches of fine *t* linen
Ex 39:29 And a girdle of fine *t* linen

## TWINKLING

1Cor 15:52 in the *t* of an eye, at the last

## TWINS

Gen 25:24 behold, there were *t* in her womb
Gen 38:27 that, behold, *t* were in her womb
Song 4:2 whereof every one bear *t*, and none
Song 4:5 like two young roes that are *t*
Song 6:6 whereof every one beareth *t*
Song 7:3 like two young roes that are *t*

## TWOEDGED

Ps 149:6 mouth, and a *t* sword in their hand
Prov 5:4 as wormwood, sharp as a *t* sword
Heb 4:12 and sharper than any *t* sword
Rev 1:16 of his mouth went a sharp *t* sword

## TWOFOLD

Mt 23:15 ye make him *t* more the child of

## TYCHICUS *(tik'-ik-us) A co-worker with Paul.*

Acts 20:4 and of Asia, *T* and Trophimus
Eph 6:21 know my affairs, and how I do, *T*
Eph *s* from Rome unto the Ephesians by *T*
Col 4:7 my state shall *T* declare unto you
Col *s* from Rome to the Colossians by *T*
2Ti 4:12 And *T* have I sent to Ephesus
Titus 3:12 send Artemas unto thee, or *T*

## TYRANNUS *(ti-ran'-nus) An Ephesian schoolmaster.*

Acts 19:9 daily in the school of one *T*

## TYRE *(tire)* See TYRUS. *A coastal city of Phoenicia.*

Josh 19:29 to Ramah, and to the strong city *T*
2Sa 5:11 Hiram king of *T* sent messengers
2Sa 24:7 And came to the strong hold of *T*
1Kin 5:1 Hiram king of *T* sent his servants
1Kin 7:13 sent and fetched Hiram out of *T*
1Kin 7:14 and his father was a man of *T*
1Kin 9:11 (Now Hiram the king of *T* had
1Kin 9:12 Hiram came out from *T* to see the
1Chr 14:1 Now Hiram king of *T* sent
1Chr 22:4 they of *T* brought much cedar wood
2Chr 2:3 sent to Huram the king of *T*
2Chr 2:11 the king of *T* answered in writing

# U

Lev 11:43 ye make yourselves *u* with them
Lev 11:47 make a difference between the *u*
Lev 12:2 then she shall be *u* seven days
Lev 12:2 for her infirmity shall she be *u*
Lev 12:5 then she shall be *u* two weeks
Lev 13:3 look on him, and pronounce him *u*
Lev 13:8 the priest shall pronounce him *u*
Lev 13:11 the priest shall pronounce him *u*
Lev 13:11 for he is *u*
Lev 13:14 appeareth in him, he shall be *u*
Lev 13:15 flesh, and pronounce him to be *u*
Lev 13:15 for the raw flesh is *u*
Lev 13:20 the priest shall pronounce him *u*
Lev 13:22 the priest shall pronounce him *u*
Lev 13:25 the priest shall pronounce him *u*
Lev 13:27 the priest shall pronounce him *u*
Lev 13:30 the priest shall pronounce him *u*
Lev 13:36 he is *u*
Lev 13:44 He is a leprous man, he is *u*
Lev 13:44 shall pronounce him utterly *u*
Lev 13:45 lip, and shall cry, *U*, *u*
Lev 13:46 he is *u*
Lev 13:51 it is *u*
Lev 13:55 it is *u*
Lev 13:59 it clean, or to pronounce it *u*
Lev 14:36 is in the house be not made *u*
Lev 14:40 into an *u* place without the city
Lev 14:41 without the city into an *u* place
Lev 14:44 it is *u*
Lev 14:45 out of the city into an *u* place
Lev 14:46 shut up shall be *u* until the even
Lev 14:57 To teach when it is *u*, and when it
Lev 15:2 because of his issue he is *u*
Lev 15:4 lieth that hath the issue, is *u*
Lev 15:4 whereon he sitteth, shall be *u*
Lev 15:5 in water, and be *u* until the even
Lev 15:6 in water, and be *u* until the even
Lev 15:7 in water, and be *u* until the even
Lev 15:8 in water, and be *u* until the even
Lev 15:9 that hath the issue shall be *u*
Lev 15:10 him shall be *u* until the even
Lev 15:10 in water, and be *u* until the even
Lev 15:11 in water, and be *u* until the even
Lev 15:16 in water, and be *u* until the even
Lev 15:17 water, and be *u* until the even
Lev 15:18 in water, and be *u* until the even
Lev 15:19 her shall be *u* until the even
Lev 15:20 upon in her separation shall be *u*
Lev 15:20 that she sitteth upon shall be *u*
Lev 15:21 in water, and be *u* until the even
Lev 15:22 in water, and be *u* until the even
Lev 15:23 he shall be *u* until the even
Lev 15:24 him, he shall be *u* seven days
Lev 15:24 bed whereon he lieth shall be *u*
Lev 15:25 she shall be *u*
Lev 15:26 she sitteth upon shall be *u*
Lev 15:27 toucheth those things shall be *u*
Lev 15:27 in water, and be *u* until the even
Lev 15:33 him that lieth with her that is *u*
Lev 17:15 in water, and be *u* until the even
Lev 20:21 brother's wife, it is an *u* thing
Lev 20:25 between clean beasts and *u*
Lev 20:25 and between *u* fowls
Lev 20:25 I have separated from you as *u*
Lev 22:4 any thing that is *u* by the dead
Lev 22:5 thing, whereby he may be made *u*
Lev 22:6 any such shall be *u* until even
Lev 27:11 And if it be any *u* beast, of which
Lev 27:27 And if it be of an *u* beast
Num 6:7 not make himself *u* for his father
Num 9:10 be *u* by reason of a dead body
Num 18:15 the firstling of *u* beasts shalt
Num 19:7 priest shall be *u* until the even
Num 19:8 shall be *u* until the even
Num 19:10 clothes, and be *u* until the even
Num 19:11 of any man shall be *u* seven days
Num 19:13 sprinkled upon him, he shall be *u*
Num 19:14 the tent, shall be *u* seven days
Num 19:15 no covering bound upon it, is *u*
Num 19:16 or a grave, shall be *u* seven days
Num 19:17 for an *u* person they shall take
Num 19:19 upon the *u* on the third day
Num 19:20 But the man that shall be *u*
Num 19:20 he is *u*
Num 19:21 separation shall be *u* until even
Num 19:22 whatsoever the *u* person toucheth
Num 19:22 person toucheth shall be *u*
Num 19:22 toucheth it shall be *u* until even
Deut 12:15 the *u* and the clean may eat
Deut 12:22 the *u* and the clean shall eat of
Deut 14:7 therefore they are *u* unto you
Deut 14:8 not the cud, it is *u* unto you
Deut 14:10 it is *u* unto you
Deut 14:19 thing that flieth is *u* unto you
Deut 15:22 the *u* and the clean person shall
Deut 23:14 that he see no *u* thing in thee
Deut 26:14 away ought thereof for any *u* use
Josh 22:19 the land of your possession be *u*
Judg 13:4 drink, and eat not any *u* thing
Judg 13:7 drink, neither eat any *u* thing
Judg 13:14 strong drink, nor eat any *u* thing
2Chr 23:19 that none which was *u* in any
Ezr 9:11 is an *u* land with the filthiness
Job 14:4 bring a clean thing out of an *u*
Job 36:14 and their life is among the *u*
Eccl 9:2 good and to the clean, and to the *u*
Is 6:5 because I am a man of *u* lips
Is 6:5 the midst of a people of *u* lips
Is 35:8 the *u* shall not pass over it
Is 52:1 thee the uncircumcised and the *u*
Is 52:11 out from thence, touch no *u* thing
Is 64:6 But we are all as an *u* thing
Lam 4:15 it is *u*
Eze 22:26 shewed difference between the *u*
Eze 44:23 them to discern between the *u*
Hos 9:3 they shall eat *u* things in
Hag 2:13 If one that is *u* by a dead body
Hag 2:13 touch any of these, shall it be *u*
Hag 2:13 answered and said, It shall be *u*
Hag 2:14 that which they offer there is *u*
Zec 13:2 the *u* spirit to pass out of the
Mt 10:1 gave them power against *u* spirits
Mt 12:43 When the *u* spirit is gone out of
Mk 1:23 synagogue a man with an *u* spirit
Mk 1:26 when the *u* spirit had torn him,
Mk 1:27 commandeth he even the *u* spirits
Mk 3:11 *u* spirits, when they saw him,
Mk 3:30 they said, He hath an *u* spirit
Mk 5:2 the tombs a man with an *u* spirit
Mk 5:8 out of the man, thou *u* spirit
Mk 5:13 the *u* spirits went out, and
Mk 6:7 and gave them power over *u* spirits
Mk 7:25 young daughter had an *u* spirit
Lk 4:33 which had a spirit of an *u* devil
Lk 4:36 power he commandeth the *u* spirits
Lk 6:18 that were vexed with *u* spirits
Lk 8:29 (For he had commanded the *u*
Lk 9:42 And Jesus rebuked the *u* spirit
Lk 11:24 When the *u* spirit is gone out of
Acts 5:16 which were vexed with *u* spirits
Acts 8:7 For *u* spirits, crying with loud
Acts 10:14 any thing that is common or *u*
Acts 10:28 not call any man common or *u*
Acts 11:8 for nothing common or *u* hath at
Rom 14:14 that there is nothing *u* of itself
Rom 14:14 that esteemeth any thing to be *u*
Rom 14:14 to him it is *u*
1Cor 7:14 else were your children *u*
2Cor 6:17 Lord, and touch not the *u* thing
Eph 5:5 nor *u* person, nor covetous man,
Heb 9:13 of an heifer sprinkling the *u*
Rev 16:13 I saw three *u* spirits like frogs
Rev 18:2 foul spirit, and a cage of every *u*

## UNCLEANNESS

Lev 5:3 Or if he touch the *u* of man
Lev 5:3 whatsoever *u* it be that a man
Lev 7:20 the LORD, having his *u* upon him
Lev 7:21 unclean thing, as the *u* of man
Lev 14:19 that is to be cleansed from his *u*
Lev 15:3 this shall be his *u* in his issue
Lev 15:3 from his issue, it is his *u*
Lev 15:25 her *u* shall be as the days of her
Lev 15:26 as the *u* of her separation
Lev 15:30 the LORD for the issue of her *u*
Lev 15:31 children of Israel from their *u*
Lev 15:31 that they die not in their *u*
Lev 16:16 because of the *u* of the children
Lev 16:16 them in the midst of their *u*
Lev 16:19 hallow it from the *u* of the
Lev 18:19 as she is put apart for her *u*
Lev 22:3 the LORD, having his *u* upon him
Lev 22:5 or a man of whom he may take *u*
Lev 22:5 whatsoever *u* he hath
Num 5:19 to *u* with another instead of thy
Num 19:13 his *u* is yet upon him
Deut 23:10 of *u* that chanceth him by night
Deut 24:1 he hath found some *u* in her
2Sa 11:4 for she was purified from her *u*
2Chr 29:16 brought out all the *u* that they
Ezr 9:11 one end to another with their *u*
Eze 36:17 me as the *u* of a removed woman
Eze 39:24 According to their *u* and according
Zec 13:1 of Jerusalem for sin and for *u*
Mt 23:27 of dead men's bones, and of all *u*
Rom 1:24 God also gave them up to *u*
Rom 6:19 your members servants to *u*
2Cor 12:21 and have not repented of the *u*
Gal 5:19 Adultery, fornication, *u*,
Eph 4:19 to work all *u* with greediness
Eph 5:3 But fornication, and all *u*
Col 3:5 fornication, *u*, inordinate
1Th 2:3 was not of deceit, nor of *u*
1Th 4:7 For God hath not called us unto *u*
2Pet 2:10 after the flesh in the lust of *u*

## UNCLEANNESSES

Eze 36:29 also save you from all your *u*

## UNCLE'S

Lev 20:20 a man shall lie with his *u* wife
Lev 20:20 he hath uncovered his *u* nakedness
Lev 25:49 Either his uncle, or his *u* son
Est 2:7 that is, Esther, his *u* daughter
Jer 32:8 So Hanameel mine *u* son came to me
Jer 32:9 the field of Hanameel my *u* son
Jer 32:12 the sight of Hanameel mine *u* son

## UNCLOTHED

2Cor 5:4 not for that we would be *u*

## UNCOMELY

1Cor 7:36 himself *u* toward his virgin
1Cor 12:23 our *u* parts have more abundant

## UNCONDEMNED

Acts 16:37 They have beaten us openly *u*
Acts 22:25 a man that is a Roman, and *u*

## UNCORRUPTIBLE

Rom 1:23 changed the glory of the *u* God

## UNCORRUPTNESS

Titus 2:7 in doctrine shewing *u*, gravity,

## UNCOVER

Lev 10:6 *U* not your heads, neither rend
Lev 18:6 kin to him, to *u* their nakedness
Lev 18:7 of thy mother, shalt thou not *u*
Lev 18:7 thou shalt not *u* her nakedness
Lev 18:8 father's wife shalt thou not *u*
Lev 18:9 their nakedness thou shalt not *u*
Lev 18:10 their nakedness thou shalt not *u*
Lev 18:11 thou shalt not *u* her nakedness
Lev 18:12 Thou shalt not *u* the nakedness of
Lev 18:13 Thou shalt not *u* the nakedness of
Lev 18:14 Thou shalt not *u* the nakedness of
Lev 18:15 Thou shalt not *u* the nakedness of
Lev 18:15 thou shalt not *u* her nakedness
Lev 18:16 Thou shalt not *u* the nakedness of
Lev 18:17 Thou shalt not *u* the nakedness of
Lev 18:17 daughter, to *u* her nakedness
Lev 18:18 to *u* her nakedness, beside the
Lev 18:19 unto a woman to *u* her nakedness
Lev 20:18 and shall *u* her nakedness
Lev 20:19 thou shalt not *u* the nakedness of
Lev 21:10 garments, shall not *u* his head
Num 5:18 *u* the woman's head, and put the
Ruth 3:4 *u* his feet, and lay thee down
Is 47:2 *u* thy locks, make bare the leg,
Is 47:2 *u* the thigh, pass over the rivers
Zeph 2:14 for he shall *u* the cedar work

## UNCOVERED

Gen 9:21 and he was *u* within his tent
Lev 20:11 hath *u* his father's nakedness
Lev 20:17 he hath *u* his sister's nakedness
Lev 20:18 she hath *u* the fountain of her
Lev 20:20 he hath *u* his uncle's nakedness
Lev 20:21 he hath *u* his brother's nakedness
Ruth 3:7 *u* his feet, and laid her down
2Sa 6:20 of Israel today, who *u* himself
Is 20:4 even with their buttocks *u*
Is 22:6 and horsemen, and Kir *u* the shield
Is 47:3 Thy nakedness shall be *u*, yea,
Jer 49:10 I have *u* his secret places, and he
Eze 4:7 and thine arm shall be *u*, and thou
Hab 2:16 also, and let thy foreskin be *u*
Mk 2:4 they *u* the roof where he was
1Cor 11:5 her head *u* dishonoureth her head
1Cor 11:13 that a woman pray unto God *u*

## UNCOVERETH

Lev 20:19 for he *u* his near kin
Deut 27:20 because he *u* his father's skirt
2Sa 6:20 fellows shamelessly *u* himself

## UNCTION
1Jn 2:20 But ye have an *u* from the Holy

## UNDEFILED
Ps 119:1 Blessed are the *u* in the way
Song 5:2 my sister, my love, my dove, my *u*
Song 6:9 My dove, my *u* is but one
Heb 7:26 us, who is holy, harmless, *u*
Heb 13:4 honourable in all, and the bed *u*
Jas 1:27 *u* before God and the Father is
1Pet 1:4 inheritance incorruptible, and *u*

## UNDERGIRDING
Acts 27:17 up, they used helps, *u* the ship

## UNDERSETTERS
1Kin 7:30 and the four corners thereof had *u*
1Kin 7:30 under the laver were *u* molten
1Kin 7:34 there were four *u* to the four
1Kin 7:34 the *u* were of the very base

## UNDERSTAND
Gen 11:7 that they may not *u* one another's
Gen 41:15 that thou canst *u* a dream to
Num 16:30 then ye shall *u* that these men
Deut 9:3 *U* therefore this day, that the
Deut 9:6 *U* therefore, that the LORD thy
Deut 28:49 whose tongue thou shalt not *u*
2Kin 18:26 for we *u* it
1Chr 28:19 the LORD made me *u* in writing by
Neh 8:3 the women, and those that could *u*
Neh 8:7 caused the people to *u* the law
Neh 8:8 and caused them to *u* the reading
Neh 8:13 even to *u* the words of the law
Job 6:24 cause me to *u* wherein I have
Job 23:5 *u* what he would say unto me
Job 26:14 thunder of his power who can *u*
Job 32:9 neither do the aged *u* judgment
Job 36:29 Also can any *u* the spreadings of
Ps 14:2 see if there were any that did *u*
Ps 19:12 Who can *u* his errors
Ps 53:2 see if there were any that did *u*
Ps 82:5 know not, neither will they *u*
Ps 92:6 neither doth a fool *u* this
Ps 94:8 *U*, ye brutish among the people
Ps 107:43 things, even they shall *u* the
Ps 119:27 Make me to *u* the way of thy
Ps 119:100 I *u* more than the ancients,
Prov 1:6 To *u* a proverb, and the
Prov 2:5 Then shalt thou *u* the fear of the
Prov 2:9 Then shalt thou *u* righteousness
Prov 8:5 O ye simple, *u* wisdom
Prov 14:8 of the prudent is to *u* his way
Prov 19:25 and he will *u* knowledge
Prov 20:24 how can a man then *u* his own way
Prov 28:5 Evil men *u* not judgment
Prov 28:5 that seek the LORD *u* all things
Prov 29:19 for though he *u* he will not
Is 6:9 people, Hear ye indeed, but *u* not
Is 6:10 *u* with their heart, and convert,
Is 28:9 whom shall he make to *u* doctrine
Is 28:19 a vexation only to *u* the report
Is 32:4 of the rash shall *u* knowledge
Is 33:19 tongue, that thou canst not *u*
Is 36:11 for we *u* it
Is 41:20 *u* together, that the hand of the
Is 43:10 and believe me, and *u* that I am he
Is 44:18 their hearts, that they cannot *u*
Is 56:11 they are shepherds that cannot *u*
Jer 9:12 is the wise man, that may *u* this
Eze 3:6 whose words thou canst not *u*
Dan 8:16 make this man to *u* the vision
Dan 8:17 but he said unto me, *U*, O son of
Dan 9:13 our iniquities, and *u* thy truth
Dan 9:23 therefore *u* the matter, and
Dan 9:25 Know therefore and *u*, that from
Dan 10:11 *u* the words that I speak unto
Dan 10:12 thou didst set thine heart to *u*
Dan 10:14 Now I am come to make thee *u* what
Dan 11:33 they that *u* among the people
Dan 12:10 and none of the wicked shall *u*
Dan 12:10 but the wise shall *u*
Hos 4:14 people that doth not *u* shall fall
Hos 14:9 wise, and he shall *u* these things
Mic 4:12 neither *u* they his counsel
Mt 13:13 they hear not, neither do they *u*
Mt 13:14 ye shall hear, and shall not *u*
Mt 13:15 should *u* with their heart, and
Mt 15:10 and said unto them, Hear, and *u*
Mt 15:17 Do not ye yet *u*, that whatsoever
Mt 16:9 Do ye not yet *u*, neither remember
Mt 16:11 How is it that ye do not *u* that I
Mt 24:15 place, (whoso readeth, let him *u*
Mk 4:12 hearing they may hear, and not *u*
Mk 7:14 unto me every one of you, and *u*
Mk 8:17 perceive ye not yet, neither *u*
Mk 8:21 them, How is it that ye do not *u*
Mk 13:14 not, (let him that readeth *u*
Mk 14:68 neither *u* I what thou sayest
Lk 8:10 see, and hearing they might not *u*
Lk 24:45 that they might *u* the scriptures
Jn 8:43 Why do ye not *u* my speech
Jn 12:40 nor *u* with their heart, and be
Acts 24:11 Because that thou mayest *u*
Acts 28:26 ye shall hear, and shall not *u*
Acts 28:27 *u* with their heart, and should be
Rom 15:21 they that have not heard shall *u*
1Cor 12:3 Wherefore I give you to *u*
1Cor 13:2 *u* all mysteries, and all knowledge
Eph 3:4 ye may *u* my knowledge in the
Phil 1:12 But I would ye should *u*, brethren
Heb 11:3 Through faith we *u* that the
2Pet 2:12 of the things that they *u* not

## UNDERSTANDEST
Job 15:9 what *u* thou, which is not in us
Ps 139:2 thou *u* my thought afar off
Jer 5:15 not, neither *u* what they say
Acts 8:30 and said, *U* thou what thou readest

## UNDERSTANDETH
1Chr 28:9 *u* all the imaginations of the
Job 28:23 God *u* the way thereof, and he
Ps 49:20 *u* not, is like the beasts that
Prov 8:9 They are all plain to him that *u*
Prov 14:6 knowledge is easy unto him that *u*
Jer 9:24 glorieth glory in this, that he *u*
Mt 13:19 *u* it not, then cometh the wicked
Mt 13:23 he that heareth the word, and *u* it
Rom 3:11 There is none that *u*, there is
1Cor 14:2 for no man *u* him
1Cor 14:16 seeing he *u* not what thou sayest

## UNDERSTANDING
Ex 31:3 spirit of God, in wisdom, and in *u*
Ex 35:31 spirit of God, in wisdom, in *u*
Ex 36:1 *u* to know how to work all manner
Deut 1:13 Take you wise men, and *u*, and known
Deut 4:6 your *u* in the sight of the
Deut 4:6 nation is a wise and *u* people
Deut 32:28 neither is there any *u* in them
1Sa 25:3 and she was a woman of good *u*
1Kin 3:9 an *u* heart to judge thy people
1Kin 3:11 for thyself *u* to discern judgment
1Kin 3:12 given thee a wise and an *u* heart
1Kin 4:29 *u* exceeding much, and largeness of
1Kin 7:14 he was filled with wisdom, and *u*
1Chr 12:32 were men that had *u* of the times
1Chr 22:12 the LORD give thee wisdom and *u*
2Chr 2:12 son, endued with prudence and *u*
2Chr 2:13 sent a cunning man, endued with *u*
2Chr 26:5 who had *u* in the visions of God
Ezr 8:16 and for Elnathan, men of *u*
Ezr 8:18 us they brought us a man of *u*
Neh 8:2 and all that could hear with *u*
Neh 10:28 one having knowledge, and having *u*
Job 12:3 But I have *u* as well as you
Job 12:12 and in length of days *u*
Job 12:13 and strength, he hath counsel and *u*
Job 12:20 and taketh away the *u* of the aged
Job 17:4 thou hast hid their heart from *u*
Job 20:3 the spirit of my *u* causeth me to
Job 26:12 by his *u* he smiteth through the
Job 28:12 and where is the place of *u*
Job 28:20 and where is the place of *u*
Job 28:28 and to depart from evil is *u*
Job 32:8 of the Almighty giveth them *u*
Job 34:10 hearken unto me, ye men of *u*
Job 34:16 If now thou hast *u*, hear this
Job 34:34 Let men of *u* tell me, and let a
Job 38:4 declare, if thou hast *u*
Job 38:36 or who hath given *u* to the heart
Job 39:17 neither hath he imparted to her *u*
Ps 32:9 or as the mule, which have no *u*
Ps 47:7 sing ye praises with *u*
Ps 49:3 of my heart shall be of *u*
Ps 111:10 a good *u* have all they that do
Ps 119:34 Give me *u*, and I shall keep thy
Ps 119:73 give me *u*, that I may learn thy
Ps 119:99 I have more *u* than all my
Ps 119:104 Through thy precepts I get *u*
Ps 119:125 give me *u*, that I may know thy
Ps 119:130 it giveth *u* unto the simple
Ps 119:144 give me *u*, and I shall live
Ps 119:169 give me *u* according to thy word
Ps 147:5 his *u* is infinite
Prov 1:2 to perceive the words of *u*
Prov 1:5 a man of *u* shall attain unto wise
Prov 2:2 wisdom, and apply thine heart to *u*
Prov 2:3 and liftest up thy voice for *u*
Prov 2:6 his mouth cometh knowledge and *u*
Prov 2:11 preserve thee, *u* shall keep thee
Prov 3:4 good *u* in the sight of God and man
Prov 3:5 and lean not unto thine own *u*
Prov 3:13 wisdom, and the man that getteth *u*
Prov 3:19 by *u* hath he established the
Prov 4:1 of a father, and attend to know *u*
Prov 4:5 Get wisdom, get *u*
Prov 4:7 and with all thy getting get *u*
Prov 5:1 wisdom, and bow thine ear to my *u*
Prov 6:32 adultery with a woman lacketh *u*
Prov 7:4 and call *u* thy kinswoman
Prov 7:7 the youths, a young man void of *u*
Prov 8:1 and *u* put forth her voice
Prov 8:5 and, ye fools, be ye of an *u* heart
Prov 8:14 I am *u*
Prov 9:4 as for him that wanteth *u*
Prov 9:6 and go in the way of *u*
Prov 9:10 and the knowledge of the holy is *u*
Prov 9:16 and as for him that wanteth *u*
Prov 10:13 him that hath *u* wisdom is found
Prov 10:13 the back of him that is void of *u*
Prov 10:23 but a man of *u* hath wisdom
Prov 11:12 but a man of *u* holdeth his peace
Prov 12:11 vain persons is void of *u*
Prov 13:15 Good *u* giveth favour
Prov 14:29 is slow to wrath is of great *u*
Prov 14:33 in the heart of him that hath *u*
Prov 15:14 him that hath *u* seeketh knowledge
Prov 15:21 but a man of *u* walketh uprightly
Prov 15:32 he that heareth reproof getteth *u*
Prov 16:16 to get *u* rather to be chosen than
Prov 16:22 *U* is a wellspring of life unto
Prov 17:18 A man void of *u* striketh hands,
Prov 17:24 Wisdom is before him that hath *u*
Prov 17:27 a man of *u* is of an excellent
Prov 17:28 his lips is esteemed a man of *u*
Prov 18:2 A fool hath no delight in *u*
Prov 19:8 he that keepeth *u* shall find good
Prov 19:25 and reprove one that hath *u*
Prov 20:5 but a man of *u* will draw it out
Prov 21:16 the way of *u* shall remain in the
Prov 21:30 There is no wisdom nor *u* nor
Prov 23:23 also wisdom, and instruction, and *u*
Prov 24:3 and by *u* it is established
Prov 24:30 the vineyard of the man void of *u*
Prov 28:2 but by a man of *u* and knowledge
Prov 28:11 that hath *u* searcheth him out
Prov 28:16 The prince that wanteth *u* is also
Prov 30:2 man, and have not the *u* of a man
Eccl 9:11 wise, nor yet riches to men of *u*
Is 11:2 him, the spirit of wisdom and *u*
Is 11:3 quick *u* in the fear of the LORD
Is 27:11 for it is a people of no *u*
Is 29:14 the *u* of their prudent men shall
Is 29:16 him that framed it, He had no *u*
Is 29:24 erred in spirit shall come to *u*
Is 40:14 and shewed to him the way of *u*
Is 40:28 there is no searching of his *u*
Is 44:19 is there knowledge nor *u* to say
Jer 3:15 feed you with knowledge and *u*
Jer 4:22 children, and they have none *u*
Jer 5:21 O foolish people, and without *u*
Jer 51:15 stretched out the heaven by his *u*
Eze 28:4 with thine *u* thou hast gotten
Dan 1:4 *u* science, and such as had ability
Dan 1:17 Daniel had *u* in all visions and
Dan 1:20 And in all matters of wisdom and *u*
Dan 2:21 and knowledge to them that know *u*
Dan 4:34 mine *u* returned unto me, and I
Dan 5:11 the days of thy father light and *u*
Dan 5:12 spirit, and knowledge, and *u*
Dan 5:14 is in thee, and that light and *u*
Dan 8:23 *u* dark sentences, shall stand up
Dan 9:22 forth to give thee skill and *u*
Dan 10:1 the thing, and had *u* of the vision
Dan 11:35 And some of them of *u* shall fall
Hos 13:2 and idols according to their own *u*
Obad 7 there is none *u* in him
Obad 8 *u* out of the mount of Esau
Mt 15:16 said, Are ye also yet without *u*
Mk 7:18 them, Are ye so without *u* also
Mk 12:33 all the heart, and with all the *u*
Lk 1:3 having had perfect *u* of all

Lk 2:47 him were astonished at his *u*
Lk 24:45 Then opened he their *u*, that they
Rom 1:31 Without *u*, covenantbreakers,
1Cor 1:19 to nothing the *u* of the prudent
1Cor 14:14 prayeth, but my *u* is unfruitful
1Cor 14:15 and I will pray with the *u* also
1Cor 14:15 and I will sing with the *u* also
1Cor 14:19 rather speak five words with my *u*
1Cor 14:20 Brethren, be not children in *u*
1Cor 14:20 be ye children, but in *u* be men
Eph 1:18 The eyes of your *u* being
Eph 4:18 Having the *u* darkened, being
Eph 5:17 but *u* what the will of the Lord
Phil 4:7 peace of God, which passeth all *u*
Col 1:9 will in all wisdom and spiritual *u*
Col 2:2 riches of the full assurance of *u*
1Ti 1:7 *u* neither what they say, nor
2Ti 2:7 Lord give thee *u* in all things
1Jn 5:20 is come, and hath given us an *u*
Rev 13:18 Let him that hath *u* count the

### UNDERSTOOD

Gen 42:23 they knew not that Joseph *u* them
Deut 32:29 they were wise, that they *u* this
1Sa 4:6 they *u* that the ark of the LORD
1Sa 26:4 *u* that Saul was come in very deed
2Sa 3:37 all Israel *u* that day that it was
Neh 8:12 because they had *u* the words that
Neh 13:7 *u* of the evil that Eliashib did
Job 13:1 this, mine ear hath heard and *u* it
Job 42:3 have I uttered that I *u* not
Ps 73:17 then *u* I their end
Ps 81:5 I heard a language that I *u* not
Ps 106:7 Our fathers *u* not thy wonders in
Is 40:21 have ye not *u* from the
Is 44:18 They have not known nor *u*
Dan 8:27 at the vision, but none *u* it
Dan 9:2 *u* by books the number of the
Dan 10:1 and he *u* the thing, and had
Dan 12:8 And I heard, but I *u* not
Mt 13:51 Have ye *u* all these things
Mt 16:12 Then *u* they how that he bade them
Mt 17:13 Then the disciples *u* that he
Mt 26:10 When Jesus *u* it, he said unto
Mk 9:32 But they *u* not that saying, and
Lk 2:50 they *u* not the saying which he
Lk 9:45 But they *u* not this saying, and it
Lk 18:34 they *u* none of these things
Jn 8:27 They *u* not that he spake to them
Jn 10:6 but they *u* not what things they
Jn 12:16 These things *u* not his disciples
Acts 7:25 his brethren would have *u* how
Acts 7:25 but they *u* not
Acts 23:27 having *u* that he was a Roman
Acts 23:34 when he *u* that he was of Cilicia
Rom 1:20 being *u* by the things that are
1Cor 13:11 I *u* as a child, I thought as a
1Cor 14:9 by the tongue words easy to be *u*
2Pet 3:16 are some things hard to be *u*

### UNDERTAKE

Is 38:14 oppressed; *u* for me

### UNDERTOOK

Est 9:23 the Jews *u* to do as they had

### UNDO

Is 58:6 to *u* the heavy burdens, and to let
Zeph 3:19 at that time I will *u* all that

### UNDONE

Num 21:29 thou art *u*, O people of Chemosh
Josh 11:15 he left nothing *u* of all that the
Is 6:5 for I am *u*
Mt 23:23 done, and not to leave the other *u*
Lk 11:42 done, and not to leave the other *u*

### UNDRESSED

Lev 25:5 gather the grapes of thy vine *u*
Lev 25:11 the grapes in it of thy vine *u*

### UNEQUAL

Eze 18:25 are not your ways *u*
Eze 18:29 are not your ways *u*

### UNEQUALLY

2Cor 6:14 Be ye not *u* yoked together with

### UNFAITHFUL

Prov 25:19 Confidence in an *u* man in time of

### UNFAITHFULLY

Ps 78:57 dealt *u* like their fathers

### UNFEIGNED

2Cor 6:6 by the Holy Ghost, by love *u*
1Ti 1:5 a good conscience, and of faith *u*
2Ti 1:5 the *u* faith that is in thee
1Pet 1:22 unto *u* love of the brethren

### UNFRUITFUL

Mt 13:22 choke the word, and he becometh *u*
Mk 4:19 choke the word, and it becometh *u*
1Cor 14:14 but my understanding is *u*
Eph 5:11 with the *u* works of darkness
Titus 3:14 uses, that they be not *u*
2Pet 1:8 *u* in the knowledge of our Lord

### UNGIRDED

Gen 24:32 he *u* his camels, and gave straw and

### UNGODLINESS

Rom 1:18 from heaven against all *u*
Rom 11:26 and shall turn away *u* from Jacob
2Ti 2:16 they will increase unto more *u*
Titus 2:12 Teaching us that, denying *u*

### UNGODLY

2Sa 22:5 the floods of *u* men made me
2Chr 19:2 Shouldest thou help the *u*
Job 16:11 God hath delivered me to the *u*
Job 34:18 and to princes, Ye are *u*
Ps 1:1 not in the counsel of the *u*
Ps 1:4 The *u* are not so
Ps 1:5 Therefore the *u* shall not stand
Ps 1:6 but the way of the *u* shall perish
Ps 3:7 hast broken the teeth of the *u*
Ps 18:4 the floods of *u* men made me
Ps 43:1 my cause against an *u* nation
Ps 73:12 Behold, these are the *u*, who
Prov 16:27 An *u* man diggeth up evil
Prov 19:28 An *u* witness scorneth judgment
Rom 4:5 on him that justifieth the *u*
Rom 5:6 in due time Christ died for the *u*
1Ti 1:9 lawless and disobedient, for the *u*
1Pet 4:18 be saved, where shall the *u*
2Pet 2:5 the flood upon the world of the *u*
2Pet 2:6 those that after should live *u*
2Pet 3:7 of judgment and perdition of *u* men
Jude 4 *u* men, turning the grace of our
Jude 15 to convince all that are *u* among
Jude 15 *u* deeds which they have
Jude 15 deeds which they have *u* committed
Jude 15 all their hard speeches which *u*
Jude 18 walk after their own *u* lusts

### UNHOLY

Lev 10:10 put difference between holy and *u*
1Ti 1:9 the ungodly and for sinners, for *u*
2Ti 3:2 to parents, unthankful, *u*
Heb 10:29 an *u* thing, and hath done despite

### UNICORN

Num 23:22 as it were the strength of a *u*
Num 24:8 as it were the strength of a *u*
Job 39:9 Will the *u* be willing to serve
Job 39:10 Canst thou bind the *u* with his
Ps 29:6 Lebanon and Sirion like a young *u*
Ps 92:10 thou exalt like the horn of an *u*

### UNICORNS

Deut 33:17 his horns are like the horns of *u*
Ps 22:21 heard me from the horns of the *u*
Is 34:7 the *u* shall come down with them,

### UNITE

Ps 86:11 *u* my heart to fear thy name

### UNITED

Gen 49:6 mine honour, be not thou *u*

### UNITY

Ps 133:1 brethren to dwell together in *u*
Eph 4:3 Endeavouring to keep the *u* of the
Eph 4:13 we all come in the *u* of the faith

### UNJUST

Ps 43:1 me from the deceitful and *u* man
Prov 11:7 the hope of *u* men perisheth
Prov 28:8 *u* gain increaseth his substance,
Prov 29:27 An *u* man is an abomination to the
Zeph 3:5 but the *u* knoweth no shame
Mt 5:45 rain on the just and on the *u*
Lk 16:8 the lord commended the *u* steward
Lk 16:10 he that is *u* in the least is
Lk 16:10 in the least is *u* also in much
Lk 18:6 said, Hear what the *u* judge saith
Lk 18:11 as other men are, extortioners, *u*
Acts 24:15 the dead, both of the just and *u*
1Cor 6:1 another, go to law before the *u*
1Pet 3:18 for sins, the just for the *u*
2Pet 2:9 to reserve the *u* unto the day of
Rev 22:11 He that is *u*, let him be *u*

### UNJUSTLY

Ps 82:2 How long will ye judge *u*, and
Is 26:10 of uprightness will he deal *u*

### UNKNOWN

Acts 17:23 this inscription, TO THE *U* GOD
1Cor 14:2 For he that speaketh in an *u*
1Cor 14:4 He that speaketh in an *u* tongue
1Cor 14:13 in an *u* tongue pray that he may
1Cor 14:14 For if I pray in an *u* tongue
1Cor 14:19 ten thousand words in an *u* tongue
1Cor 14:27 If any man speak in an *u* tongue
2Cor 6:9 As *u*, and yet well known
Gal 1:22 was *u* by face unto the churches

### UNLADE

Acts 21:3 the ship was to *u* her burden

### UNLAWFUL

Acts 10:28 Ye know how that it is an *u* thing
2Pet 2:8 day to day with their *u* deeds

### UNLEARNED

Acts 4:13 and perceived that they were *u*
1Cor 14:16 the *u* say Amen at thy giving of
1Cor 14:23 and there come in those that are *u*
1Cor 14:24 one that believeth not, or one *u*
2Ti 2:23 *u* questions avoid, knowing that
2Pet 3:16 understood, which they that are *u*

### UNLEAVENED

Gen 19:3 them a feast, and did bake *u* bread
Ex 12:8 roast with fire, and *u* bread
Ex 12:15 Seven days shall ye eat *u* bread
Ex 12:17 observe the feast of *u* bread
Ex 12:18 at even, ye shall eat *u* bread
Ex 12:20 habitations shall ye eat *u* bread
Ex 12:39 they baked *u* cakes of the dough
Ex 13:6 Seven days thou shalt eat *u* bread
Ex 13:7 *U* bread shall be eaten seven days
Ex 23:15 shalt keep the feast of *u* bread
Ex 23:15 (thou shalt eat *u* bread seven
Ex 29:2 *u* bread, and cakes *u*
Ex 29:2 wafers *u* anointed with oil
Ex 29:23 *u* bread that is before the LORD
Ex 34:18 The feast of *u* bread shalt thou
Ex 34:18 Seven days thou shalt eat *u* bread
Lev 2:4 it shall be *u* cakes of fine flour
Lev 2:4 or *u* wafers anointed with oil
Lev 2:5 pan, it shall be of fine flour *u*
Lev 6:16 with *u* bread shall it be eaten in
Lev 7:12 *u* cakes mingled with oil, and
Lev 7:12 *u* wafers anointed with oil, and
Lev 8:2 two rams, and a basket of *u* bread
Lev 8:26 And out of the basket of *u* bread
Lev 8:26 the LORD, he took one *u* cake
Lev 23:6 feast of *u* bread unto the LORD
Lev 23:6 seven days ye must eat *u* bread
Num 6:15 And a basket of *u* bread, cakes of
Num 6:15 wafers of *u* bread anointed with
Num 6:17 LORD, with the basket of *u* bread
Num 6:19 one *u* cake out of the basket, and
Num 6:19 one *u* wafer, and shall put them
Num 9:11 keep it, and eat it with *u* bread
Num 28:17 seven days shall *u* bread be eaten
Deut 16:3 shalt thou eat *u* bread therewith
Deut 16:8 Six days thou shalt eat *u* bread
Deut 16:16 in the feast of *u* bread, and in
Josh 5:11 *u* cakes, and parched corn in the
Judg 6:19 *u* cakes of an ephah of flour
Judg 6:20 the *u* cakes, and lay them upon
Judg 6:21 touched the flesh and the *u* cakes
Judg 6:21 consumed the flesh and the *u* cakes
1Sa 28:24 it, and did bake *u* bread thereof
2Kin 23:9 but they did eat of the *u* bread
1Chr 23:29 meat offering, and for the *u* cakes
2Chr 8:13 even in the feast of *u* bread
2Chr 30:13 of *u* bread in the second month
2Chr 30:21 of *u* bread seven days with great
2Chr 35:17 the feast of *u* bread seven days
Ezr 6:22 kept the feast of *u* bread seven
Eze 45:21 *u* bread shall be eaten
Mt 26:17 of *u* bread the disciples came to
Mk 14:1 of the passover, and of *u* bread
Mk 14:12 And the first day of *u* bread
Lk 22:1 the feast of *u* bread drew nigh
Lk 22:7 Then came the day of *u* bread
Acts 12:3 (Then were the days of *u* bread
Acts 20:6 after the days of *u* bread
1Cor 5:7 ye may be a new lump, as ye are *u*
1Cor 5:8 but with the *u* bread of sincerity

**UNLOOSE**
Mk 1:7 am not worthy to stoop down and *u*
Lk 3:16 whose shoes I am not worthy to *u*
Jn 1:27 latchet I am not worthy to *u*

**UNMARRIED**
1Cor 7:8 I say therefore to the *u* and
1Cor 7:11 if she depart, let her remain *u*
1Cor 7:32 He that is *u* careth for the
1Cor 7:34 The *u* woman careth for the things

**UNMERCIFUL**
Rom 1:31 natural affection, implacable, *u*

**UNMINDFUL**
Deut 32:18 Rock that begat thee thou art *u*

**UNMOVABLE**
1Cor 15:58 brethren, be ye stedfast, *u*

**UNMOVEABLE**
Acts 27:41 stuck fast, and remained *u*

**UNNI** *(un'-nee) A Levite.*
1Chr 15:18 and Shemiramoth, and Jehiel, and *U*
1Chr 15:20 and Shemiramoth, and Jehiel, and *U*
Neh 12:9 Also Bakbukiah and *U*, their

**UNOCCUPIED**
Judg 5:6 days of Jael, the highways were *u*

**UNPERFECT**
Ps 139:16 did see my substance, yet being *u*

**UNPREPARED**
2Cor 9:4 come with me, and find you *u*

**UNPROFITABLE**
Job 15:3 Should he reason with *u* talk
Mt 25:30 cast ye the *u* servant into outer
Lk 17:10 you, say, We are *u* servants
Rom 3:12 way, they are together become *u*
Titus 3:9 for they are *u* and vain
Philem 11 Which in time past was to thee *u*
Heb 13:17 for that is *u* for you

**UNPROFITABLENESS**
Heb 7:18 for the weakness and *u* thereof

**UNPUNISHED**
Prov 11:21 hand, the wicked shall not be *u*
Prov 16:5 join in hand, he shall not be *u*
Prov 17:5 glad at calamities shall not be *u*
Prov 19:5 A false witness shall not be *u*
Prov 19:9 A false witness shall not be *u*
Jer 25:29 name, and should ye be utterly *u*
Jer 25:29 Ye shall not be *u*
Jer 30:11 will not leave thee altogether *u*
Jer 46:28 will I not leave thee wholly *u*
Jer 49:12 he that shall altogether go *u*
Jer 49:12 thou shalt not go *u*, but thou

**UNQUENCHABLE**
Mt 3:12 burn up the chaff with *u* fire
Lk 3:17 chaff he will burn with fire *u*

**UNREASONABLE**
Acts 25:27 to me *u* to send a prisoner
2Th 3:2 that we may be delivered from *u*

**UNREBUKEABLE**
1Ti 6:14 this commandment without spot, *u*

**UNREPROVEABLE**
Col 1:22 and unblameable and *u* in his sight

**UNRIGHTEOUS**
Ex 23:1 the wicked to be an *u* witness
Job 27:7 riseth up against me as the *u*
Ps 71:4 wicked, out of the hand of the *u*
Is 10:1 unto them that decree *u* decrees
Is 55:7 way, and the *u* man his thoughts
Lk 16:11 not been faithful in the *u* mammon
Rom 3:5 Is God *u* who taketh vengeance
1Cor 6:9 Know ye not that the *u* shall not
Heb 6:10 For God is not *u* to forget your

**UNRIGHTEOUSLY**
Deut 25:16 do such things, and all that do *u*

**UNRIGHTEOUSNESS**
Lev 19:15 Ye shall do no *u* in judgment
Lev 19:35 Ye shall do no *u* in judgment
Ps 92:15 my rock, and there is no *u* in him
Jer 22:13 him that buildeth his house by *u*
Lk 16:9 friends of the mammon of *u*
Jn 7:18 same is true, and no *u* is in him
Rom 1:18 *u* of men, who hold the truth in
Rom 1:18 of men, who hold the truth in *u*
Rom 1:29 Being filled with all *u*,
Rom 2:8 do not obey the truth, but obey *u*
Rom 3:5 But if our *u* commend the
Rom 6:13 as instruments of *u* unto sin
Rom 9:14 Is there *u* with God
2Cor 6:14 hath righteousness with *u*
2Th 2:10 of *u* in them that perish
2Th 2:12 the truth, but had pleasure in *u*
Heb 8:12 For I will be merciful to their *u*
2Pet 2:13 And shall receive the reward of *u*
2Pet 2:15 Bosor, who loved the wages of *u*
1Jn 1:9 sins, and to cleanse us from all *u*
1Jn 5:17 All *u* is sin

**UNRIPE**
Job 15:33 shake off his *u* grape as the vine

**UNRULY**
1Th 5:14 brethren, warn them that are *u*
Titus 1:6 children not accused of riot or *u*
Titus 1:10 For there are many *u* and vain
Jas 3:8 it is an *u* evil, full of deadly

**UNSATIABLE**
Eze 16:28 Assyrians, because thou wast *u*

**UNSAVOURY**
2Sa 22:27 froward thou wilt shew thyself *u*
Job 6:6 Can that which is *u* be eaten

**UNSEARCHABLE**
Job 5:9 Which doeth great things and *u*
Ps 145:3 and his greatness is *u*
Prov 25:3 depth, and the heart of kings is *u*
Rom 11:33 how *u* are his judgments, and his
Eph 3:8 Gentiles the *u* riches of Christ

**UNSEEMLY**
Rom 1:27 with men working that which is *u*
1Cor 13:5 Doth not behave itself *u*, seeketh

**UNSHOD**
Jer 2:25 Withhold thy foot from being *u*

**UNSKILFUL**
Heb 5:13 is *u* in the word of righteousness

**UNSPEAKABLE**
2Cor 9:15 Thanks be unto God for his *u* gift
2Cor 12:4 into paradise, and heard *u* words
1Pet 1:8 believing, ye rejoice with joy *u*

**UNSPOTTED**
Jas 1:27 to keep himself *u* from the world

**UNSTABLE**
Gen 49:4 *U* as water, thou shalt not excel
Jas 1:8 minded man is *u* in all his ways
2Pet 2:14 beguiling *u* souls
2Pet 3:16 *u* wrest, as they do also the

**UNSTOPPED**
Is 35:5 the ears of the deaf shall be *u*

**UNTAKEN**
2Cor 3:14 day remaineth the same vail *u*

**UNTEMPERED**
Eze 13:10 others daubed it with *u* morter
Eze 13:11 them which daub it with *u* morter
Eze 13:14 that ye have daubed with *u* morter
Eze 13:15 that have daubed it with *u* morter
Eze 22:28 have daubed them with *u* morter

**UNTHANKFUL**
Lk 6:35 for he is kind unto the *u*
2Ti 3:2 disobedient to parents, *u*

**UNTIMELY**
Job 3:16 Or as an hidden *u* birth I had not
Ps 58:8 like the *u* birth of a woman, that
Eccl 6:3 that an *u* birth is better than he
Rev 6:13 as a fig tree casteth her *u* figs

**UNTOWARD**
Acts 2:40 yourselves from this *u* generation

**UNWALLED**
Deut 3:5 beside *u* towns a great many
Est 9:19 that dwelt in the *u* towns
Eze 38:11 go up to the land of *u* villages

**UNWASHEN**
Mt 15:20 but to eat with *u* hands defileth
Mk 7:2 defiled, that is to say, with *u*
Mk 7:5 but eat bread with *u* hands

**UNWEIGHED**
1Kin 7:47 And Solomon left all the vessels *u*

**UNWISE**
Deut 32:6 the LORD, O foolish people and *u*
Hos 13:13 he is an *u* son
Rom 1:14 both to the wise, and to the *u*
Eph 5:17 Wherefore be ye not *u*, but

**UNWITTINGLY**
Lev 22:14 if a man eat of the holy thing *u*
Josh 20:3 unawares and *u* may flee thither
Josh 20:5 because he smote his neighbour *u*

**UNWORTHILY**
1Cor 11:27 and drink this cup of the Lord, *u*
1Cor 11:29 For he that eateth and drinketh *u*

**UNWORTHY**
Acts 13:46 judge yourselves *u* of everlasting
1Cor 6:2 are ye *u* to judge the smallest

**UPBRAID**
Judg 8:15 Zalmunna, with whom ye did *u* me
Mt 11:20 Then began he to *u* the cities

**UPBRAIDED**
Mk 16:14 *u* them with their unbelief and

**UPBRAIDETH**
Jas 1:5 to all men liberally, and *u* not

**UPHARSIN** *(u-far'-sin) See* PERES. *Part of the "handwriting on the wall."*
Dan 5:25 written, MENE, MENE, TEKEL, *U*

**UPHAZ** *(u'-faz) A place in southern Arabia.*
Jer 10:9 from Tarshish, and gold from *U*
Dan 10:5 were girded with fine gold of *U*

**UPHELD**
Is 63:5 and my fury, it *u* me

**UPHOLD**
Ps 51:12 *u* me with thy free spirit
Ps 54:4 Lord is with them that *u* my soul
Ps 119:116 *U* me according unto thy word,
Prov 29:23 but honour shall *u* the humble in
Is 41:10 I will *u* thee with the right hand
Is 42:1 Behold my servant, whom I *u*
Is 63:5 wondered that there was none to *u*
Eze 30:6 They also that *u* Egypt shall fall

**UPHOLDEN**
Job 4:4 Thy words have *u* him that was
Prov 20:28 and his throne is *u* by mercy

**UPHOLDEST**
Ps 41:12 thou *u* me in mine integrity, and

**UPHOLDETH**
Ps 37:17 but the LORD *u* the righteous
Ps 37:24 for the LORD *u* him with his hand
Ps 63:8 thy right hand *u* me
Ps 145:14 The LORD *u* all that fall, and

**UPHOLDING**
Heb 1:3 *u* all things by the word of his

**UPPER**
Ex 12:7 on the *u* door post of the houses,
Lev 13:45 put a covering upon his *u* lip
Deut 24:6 or the *u* millstone to pledge
Josh 15:19 And he gave her the *u* springs
Josh 16:5 unto Beth-horon the *u*
Judg 1:15 And Caleb gave her the *u* springs
2Kin 1:2 his *u* chamber that was in Samaria
2Kin 18:17 by the conduit of the *u* pool
2Kin 23:12 the top of the *u* chamber of Ahaz
1Chr 7:24 Beth-horon the nether, and the *u*
1Chr 28:11 of the *u* chambers thereof, and of
2Chr 3:9 he overlaid the *u* chambers with
2Chr 8:5 Also he built Beth-horon the *u*
2Chr 32:30 the *u* watercourse of Gihon
Is 7:3 the *u* pool in the highway of the
Is 36:2 the *u* pool in the highway of the
Eze 42:5 Now the *u* chambers were shorter
Zeph 2:14 lodge in the *u* lintels of it
Mk 14:15 shew you a large *u* room furnished
Lk 22:12 shew you a large *u* room furnished
Acts 1:13 in, they went up into an *u* room
Acts 9:37 they laid her in an *u* chamber
Acts 9:39 brought him into the *u* chamber
Acts 19:1 the *u* coasts came to Ephesus
Acts 20:8 were many lights in the *u* chamber

**UPPERMOST**
Gen 40:17 in the *u* basket there was of all
Is 17:6 berries in the top of the *u* bough
Is 17:9 an *u* branch, which they left
Mt 23:6 love the *u* rooms at feasts, and
Mk 12:39 and the *u* rooms at feasts
Lk 11:43 for ye love the *u* seats in the

**UPRIGHT**
Gen 37:7 my sheaf arose, and also stood *u*
Ex 15:8 the floods stood *u* as an heap
Lev 26:13 of your yoke, and made you go *u*
1Sa 29:6 the LORD liveth, thou hast been *u*

2Sa 22:24 I was also *u* before him, and have
2Sa 22:26 with the *u* man thou wilt shew
2Sa 22:26 man thou wilt shew thyself *u*
2Chr 29:34 for the Levites were more *u* in
Job 1:1 and that man was perfect and *u*
Job 1:8 an *u* man, one that feareth God,
Job 2:3 an *u* man, one that feareth God,
Job 8:6 If thou wert pure and *u*
Job 12:4 the just *u* man is laughed to
Job 17:8 *U* men shall be astonied at this,
Ps 7:10 God, which saveth the *u* in heart
Ps 11:2 privily shoot at the *u* in heart
Ps 11:7 his countenance doth behold the *u*
Ps 18:23 I was also *u* before him, and I
Ps 18:25 with an *u* man thou wilt shew
Ps 18:25 man thou wilt shew thyself *u*
Ps 19:13 then shall I be *u*, and I shall be
Ps 20:8 but we are risen, and stand *u*
Ps 25:8 Good and *u* is the LORD
Ps 32:11 joy, all ye that are *u* in heart
Ps 33:1 for praise is comely for the *u*
Ps 36:10 righteousness to the *u* in heart
Ps 37:14 slay such as be of *u* conversation
Ps 37:18 LORD knoweth the days of the *u*
Ps 37:37 the perfect man, and behold the *u*
Ps 49:14 the *u* shall have dominion over
Ps 64:10 all the *u* in heart shall glory
Ps 92:15 To shew that the LORD is *u*
Ps 94:15 all the *u* in heart shall follow
Ps 97:11 and gladness for the *u* in heart
Ps 111:1 heart, in the assembly of the *u*
Ps 112:2 of the *u* shall be blessed
Ps 112:4 Unto the *u* there ariseth light in
Ps 119:137 O LORD, and *u* are thy judgments
Ps 125:4 them that are *u* in their hearts
Ps 140:13 the *u* shall dwell in thy presence
Prov 2:21 For the *u* shall dwell in the land
Prov 10:29 of the LORD is strength to the *u*
Prov 11:3 of the *u* shall guide them
Prov 11:6 of the *u* shall deliver them
Prov 11:11 of the *u* the city is exalted
Prov 11:20 but such as are *u* in their way
Prov 12:6 mouth of the *u* shall deliver them
Prov 13:6 keepeth him that is *u* in the way
Prov 14:11 of the *u* shall flourish
Prov 15:8 prayer of the *u* is his delight
Prov 16:17 The highway of the *u* is to depart
Prov 21:18 and the transgressor for the *u*
Prov 21:29 but as for the *u*, he directeth
Prov 28:10 but the *u* shall have good things
Prov 29:10 The bloodthirsty hate the *u*
Prov 29:27 he that is *u* in the way is
Eccl 7:29 I found, that God hath made man *u*
Eccl 12:10 and that which was written was *u*
Song 1:4 the *u* love thee
Is 26:7 thou, most *u*, dost weigh the path
Jer 10:5 They are *u* as the palm tree, but
Dan 8:18 but he touched me, and set me *u*
Dan 10:11 I speak unto thee, and stand *u*
Dan 11:17 whole kingdom, and *u* ones with him
Mic 7:2 and there is none *u* among men
Mic 7:4 the most *u* is sharper than a
Hab 2:4 is lifted up is not *u* in him
Acts 14:10 a loud voice, Stand *u* on thy feet

**UPRIGHTLY**
Ps 15:2 He that walketh *u*, and worketh
Ps 58:1 do ye judge *u*, O ye sons of men
Ps 75:2 the congregation I will judge *u*
Ps 84:11 he withhold from them that walk *u*
Prov 2:7 is a buckler to them that walk *u*
Prov 10:9 He that walketh *u* walketh surely
Prov 15:21 a man of understanding walketh *u*
Prov 28:18 Whoso walketh *u* shall be saved
Is 33:15 righteously, and speaketh *u*
Amos 5:10 and they abhor him that speaketh *u*
Mic 2:7 do good to him that walketh *u*
Gal 2:14 *u* according to the truth of the

**UPRIGHTNESS**
Deut 9:5 or for the *u* of thine heart, dost
1Kin 3:6 and in *u* of heart with thee
1Kin 9:4 in integrity of heart, and in *u*
1Chr 29:17 the heart, and hast pleasure in *u*
1Chr 29:17 in the *u* of mine heart I have
Job 4:6 thy hope, and the *u* of thy ways
Job 33:3 shall be of the *u* of my heart
Job 33:23 thousand, to shew unto man his *u*
Ps 9:8 judgment to the people in *u*
Ps 25:21 Let integrity and *u* preserve me
Ps 111:8 ever, and are done in truth and *u*
Ps 119:7 will praise thee with *u* of heart
Ps 143:10 lead me into the land of *u*
Prov 2:13 Who leave the paths of *u*, to walk
Prov 14:2 walketh in his *u* feareth the LORD
Prov 28:6 is the poor that walketh in his *u*
Is 26:7 The way of the just is *u*
Is 26:10 in the land of *u* will he deal
Is 57:2 beds, each one walking in his *u*

**UPRISING**
Ps 139:2 knowest my downsitting and mine *u*

**UPROAR**
1Kin 1:41 noise of the city being in an *u*
Mt 26:5 there be an *u* among the people
Mk 14:2 lest there be an *u* of the people
Acts 17:5 and set all the city on an *u*
Acts 19:40 in question for this day's *u*
Acts 20:1 after the *u* was ceased, Paul
Acts 21:31 that all Jerusalem was in an *u*
Acts 21:38 before these days madest an *u*

**UPSIDE**
2Kin 21:13 wiping it, and turning it *u* down
Ps 146:9 of the wicked he turneth *u* down
Is 24:1 it waste, and turneth it *u* down
Is 29:16 *u* down shall be esteemed as the
Acts 17:6 world *u* down are come hither also

**UPWARD**
Gen 7:20 Fifteen cubits *u* did the waters
Ex 38:26 from twenty years old and *u*
Num 1:3 From twenty years old and *u*
Num 1:18 names, from twenty years old and *u*
Num 1:20 male from twenty years old and *u*
Num 1:22 male from twenty years old and *u*
Num 1:24 names, from twenty years old and *u*
Num 1:26 names, from twenty years old and *u*
Num 1:28 names, from twenty years old and *u*
Num 1:30 names, from twenty years old and *u*
Num 1:32 names, from twenty years old and *u*
Num 1:34 names, from twenty years old and *u*
Num 1:36 names, from twenty years old and *u*
Num 1:38 names, from twenty years old and *u*
Num 1:40 names, from twenty years old and *u*
Num 1:42 names, from twenty years old and *u*
Num 1:45 from twenty years old and *u*
Num 3:15 old and *u* shalt thou number them
Num 3:22 the males, from a month old and *u*
Num 3:28 the males, from a month old and *u*
Num 3:34 the males, from a month old and *u*
Num 3:39 the males from a month old and *u*
Num 3:40 of Israel from a month old and *u*
Num 3:43 of names, from a month old and *u*
Num 4:3 *u* even until fifty years old, all
Num 4:23 *u* until fifty years old shalt
Num 4:30 *u* even unto fifty years old shalt
Num 4:35 *u* even unto fifty years old,
Num 4:39 *u* even unto fifty years old,
Num 4:43 *u* even unto fifty years old,
Num 4:47 *u* even unto fifty years old,
Num 8:24 *u* they shall go in to wait upon
Num 14:29 from twenty years old and *u*
Num 26:2 from twenty years old and *u*
Num 26:4 from twenty years old and *u*
Num 26:62 all males from a month old and *u*
Num 32:11 Egypt, from twenty years old and *u*
Judg 1:36 to Akrabbim, from the rock, and *u*
1Sa 9:2 *u* he was higher than any of the
1Sa 10:23 people from his shoulders and *u*
2Kin 3:21 were able to put on armour, and *u*
2Kin 19:30 root downward, and bear fruit *u*
1Chr 23:3 from the age of thirty years and *u*
1Chr 23:24 from the age of twenty years and *u*
2Chr 31:16 males, from three years old and *u*
2Chr 31:17 from twenty years old and *u*
Ezr 3:8 from twenty years old and *u*
Job 5:7 unto trouble, as the sparks fly *u*
Eccl 3:21 the spirit of man that goeth *u*
Is 8:21 king and their God, and look *u*
Is 37:31 root downward, and bear fruit *u*
Is 38:14 mine eyes fail with looking *u*
Eze 1:11 and their wings were stretched *u*
Eze 1:27 appearance of his loins even *u*
Eze 8:2 and from his loins even *u*, as the
Eze 41:7 still *u* to the side chambers
Eze 41:7 still *u* round about the house
Eze 41:7 breadth of the house was still *u*
Eze 43:15 altar and *u* shall be four horns
Hag 2:15 you, consider from this day and *u*
Hag 2:18 Consider now from this day and *u*

**UR** *(ur)*
*1. A district in Mesopotamia.*
Gen 11:28 nativity, in *U* of the Chaldees
Gen 11:31 with them from *U* of the Chaldees
Gen 15:7 thee out of *U* of the Chaldees
Neh 9:7 forth out of *U* of the Chaldees
*2. Father of Eliphal.*
1Chr 11:35 Hararite, Eliphal the son of *U*

**URBANE** *(ur'-bane) A Christian in Rome.*
Rom 16:9 Salute *U*, our helper in Christ,

**URGE**
Lk 11:53 began to *u* him vehemently

**URGED**
Gen 33:11 And he *u* him, and he took it
Judg 16:16 *u* him, so that his soul was vexed
Judg 19:7 depart, his father in law *u* him
2Kin 2:17 when they *u* him till he was
2Kin 5:16 And he *u* him to take it
2Kin 5:23 he *u* him, and bound two talents of

**URGENT**
Ex 12:33 Egyptians were *u* upon the people
Dan 3:22 the king's commandment was *u*

**URI** *(u'-ri)*
*1. Father of Bezaleel.*
Ex 31:2 by name Bezaleel the son of *U*
Ex 35:30 by name Bezaleel the son of *U*
Ex 38:22 And Bezaleel the son of *U*, the son
1Chr 2:20 And Hur begat *U*
1Chr 2:20 and *U* begat Bezaleel
2Chr 1:5 altar, that Bezaleel the son of *U*
*2. Father of Geber.*
1Kin 4:19 Geber the son of *U* was in the
Ezr 10:24 Shallum, and Telem, and *U*

**URIAH** *(u-ri'-ah)* See URIAH'S, URIAS, URIJAH.
*1. Husband of Bathsheba.*
2Sa 11:3 Eliam, the wife of *U* the Hittite
2Sa 11:6 saying, Send me *U* the Hittite
2Sa 11:6 And Joab sent *U* to David
2Sa 11:7 when *U* was come unto him, David
2Sa 11:8 And David said to *U*, Go down to
2Sa 11:8 *U* departed out of the king's
2Sa 11:9 But *U* slept at the door of the
2Sa 11:10 *U* went not down unto his house,
2Sa 11:10 unto his house, David said unto *U*
2Sa 11:11 *U* said unto David, The ark, and
2Sa 11:12 And David said to *U*, Tarry here to
2Sa 11:12 So *U* abode in Jerusalem that day,
2Sa 11:14 Joab, and sent it by the hand of *U*
2Sa 11:15 Set ye *U* in the forefront of the
2Sa 11:16 that he assigned *U* unto a place
2Sa 11:17 and *U* the Hittite died also
2Sa 11:21 Thy servant *U* the Hittite is dead
2Sa 11:24 thy servant *U* the Hittite is dead
2Sa 11:26 when the wife of *U* heard that
2Sa 11:26 heard that *U* her husband was dead
2Sa 12:9 thou hast killed *U* the Hittite
2Sa 12:10 hast taken the wife of *U* the
2Sa 23:39 *U* the Hittite
1Kin 15:5 in the matter of *U* the Hittite
1Chr 11:41 *U* the Hittite, Zabad the son of
*2. A rebuilder of Jerusalem's wall.*
Ezr 8:33 Meremoth the son of *U* the priest
*3. A priest who aided Isaiah.*
Is 8:2 *U* the priest, and Zechariah the

**URIAH'S** *(u-ri'-ahz) Refers to Uriah 1.*
2Sa 12:15 child that *U* wife bare unto David

**URIAS** *(u-ri'-as) Greek form of Uriah 1.*
Mt 1:6 her that had been the wife of *U*

**URIEL** *(u'-re-el)*
*1. Son of Tahath.*
1Chr 6:24 *U* his son, Uzziah his son, and
1Chr 15:5 *U* the chief, and his brethren an
1Chr 15:11 and for the Levites, for *U*
*2. Father of Micaiah.*
2Chr 13:2 the daughter of *U* of Gibeah

**URIJAH** *(u-ri'-jah)* See URIAH.
*1. A priest in Jerusalem.*
2Kin 16:10 king Ahaz sent to *U* the priest
2Kin 16:11 *U* the priest built an altar
2Kin 16:11 so *U* the priest made it against
2Kin 16:15 king Ahaz commanded *U* the priest
2Kin 16:16 Thus did *U* the priest, according
*2. A priest who rebuilt the wall.*
Neh 3:4 repaired Meremoth the son of *U*
Neh 3:21 of *U* the son of Koz another piece

*3. A priest who aided Ezra.*
Neh 8:4 and Shema, and Anaiah, and *U*
*4. A prophet killed by Jehoiakim.*
Jer 26:20 LORD, *U* the son of Shemaiah of
Jer 26:21 but when *U* heard it, he was
Jer 26:23 they fetched forth *U* out of Egypt

**URIM** *(u'-rim) A symbolic object in the High Priest's breastplate.*
Ex 28:30 the breastplate of judgment the *U*
Lev 8:8 he put in the breastplate the *U*
Num 27:21 the judgment of *U* before the LORD
Deut 33:8 thy *U* be with thy holy one, whom
1Sa 28:6 not, neither by dreams, nor by *U*
Ezr 2:63 there stood up a priest with *U*
Neh 7:65 there stood up a priest with *U*

**USURER**
Ex 22:25 thou shalt not be to him as a *u*

**USURP**
1Ti 2:12 nor to *u* authority over the man,

**USURY**
Ex 22:25 neither shalt thou lay upon him *u*
Lev 25:36 Take thou no *u* of him, or
Lev 25:37 not give him thy money upon *u*
Deut 23:19 not lend upon *u* to thy brother
Deut 23:19 *u* of money, *u* of victuals,
Deut 23:19 *u* of any thing that is lent upon
Deut 23:19 of any thing that is lent upon *u*
Deut 23:20 stranger thou mayest lend upon *u*
Deut 23:20 thou shalt not lend upon *u*
Neh 5:7 and said unto them, Ye exact *u*
Neh 5:10 pray you, let us leave off this *u*
Ps 15:5 putteth not out his money to *u*
Prov 28:8 He that by *u* and unjust gain
Is 24:2 as with the taker of *u*
Is 24:2 so with the giver of *u* to him
Jer 15:10 I have neither lent on *u*
Jer 15:10 nor men have lent to me on *u*
Eze 18:8 that hath not given forth upon *u*
Eze 18:13 Hath given forth upon *u*, and hath
Eze 18:17 hath not received *u* nor increase
Eze 22:12 thou hast taken *u* and increase, and
Mt 25:27 have received mine own with *u*
Lk 19:23 have required mine own with *u*

**US-WARD**
Ps 40:5 and thy thoughts which are to *u*
Eph 1:19 of his power to *u* who believe
2Pet 3:9 but is longsuffering to *u*

**UTHAI** *(u'-thahee)*
*1. Son of Ammihud.*
1Chr 9:4 *U* the son of Ammihud, the son of
*2. A clan leader with Ezra.*
Ezr 8:14 *U*, and Zabbud, and with them

**UTMOST**
Gen 49:26 of my progenitors unto the *u*
Num 22:36 of Arnon, which is in the *u* coast
Num 22:41 see the *u* part of the people
Num 23:13 shalt see but the *u* part of them
Deut 34:2 the land of Judah, unto the *u* sea
Jer 9:26 and all that are in the *u* corners
Jer 25:23 and all that are in the *u* corners
Jer 49:32 them that are in the *u* corners
Jer 50:26 against her from the *u* border
Joel 2:20 his hinder part toward the *u* sea
Lk 11:31 for she came from the *u* parts of

**UTTER**
Lev 5:1 if he do not *u* it, then he shall
Josh 2:14 if ye *u* not this our business
Josh 2:20 if thou *u* this our business, then
Judg 5:12 awake, awake, *u* a song
1Kin 20:42 whom I appointed to *u* destruction
Job 8:10 *u* words out of their heart
Job 15:2 a wise man *u* vain knowledge
Job 27:4 nor my tongue *u* deceit
Job 33:3 my lips shall *u* knowledge clearly
Ps 78:2 I will *u* dark sayings of old
Ps 94:4 How long shall they *u* and speak
Ps 106:2 Who can *u* the mighty acts of the
Ps 119:171 My lips shall *u* praise, when thou
Ps 145:7 They shall abundantly *u* the
Prov 14:5 but a false witness will *u* lies
Prov 23:33 heart shall *u* perverse things
Eccl 1:8 man cannot *u* it
Eccl 5:2 hasty to *u* any thing before God
Is 32:6 to *u* error against the LORD, to
Is 48:20 *u* it even to the end of the earth
Jer 1:16 I will *u* my judgments against
Jer 25:30 *u* his voice from his holy
Eze 24:3 *u* a parable unto the rebellious
Eze 40:31 thereof were toward the *u* court
Eze 40:37 thereof were toward the *u* court
Eze 42:1 brought me forth into the *u* court
Eze 42:3 which was for the *u* court
Eze 42:7 toward the *u* court on the
Eze 42:8 in the *u* court was fifty cubits
Eze 42:9 goeth into them from the *u* court
Eze 42:14 the holy place into the *u* court
Eze 44:19 they go forth into the *u* court
Eze 44:19 even into the *u* court to the
Eze 46:20 them not out into the *u* court
Eze 46:21 brought me forth into the *u* court
Eze 47:2 *u* gate by the way that looketh
Joel 2:11 the LORD shall *u* his voice before
Joel 3:16 *u* his voice from Jerusalem
Amos 1:2 *u* his voice from Jerusalem
Nah 1:8 flood he will make an *u* end of
Nah 1:9 he will make an *u* end
Zec 14:11 shall be no more *u* destruction
Mt 13:35 I will *u* things which have been
1Cor 14:9 except ye *u* by the tongue words
2Cor 12:4 it is not lawful for a man to *u*

**UTTERANCE**
Acts 2:4 as the Spirit gave them *u*
1Cor 1:5 ye are enriched by him, in all *u*
2Cor 8:7 in every thing, in faith, and *u*
Eph 6:19 that *u* may be given unto me, that
Col 4:3 would open unto us a door of *u*

**UTTERED**
Num 30:6 or *u* ought out of her lips,
Num 30:8 and that which she *u* with her lips
Judg 11:11 Jephthah *u* all his words before
2Sa 22:14 and the most High *u* his voice
Neh 6:19 before me, and *u* my words to him
Job 26:4 To whom hast thou *u* words
Job 42:3 therefore have I *u* that I
Ps 46:6 he *u* his voice, the earth melted
Ps 66:14 Which my lips have *u*, and my mouth
Jer 48:34 have they *u* their voice, from
Jer 51:55 a noise of their voice is *u*
Hab 3:10 the deep *u* his voice, and lifted
Rom 8:26 with groanings which cannot be *u*
Heb 5:11 things to say, and hard to be *u*
Rev 10:3 seven thunders *u* their voices
Rev 10:4 seven thunders had *u* their voices
Rev 10:4 things which the seven thunders *u*

**UTTERETH**
Job 15:5 For thy mouth *u* thine iniquity,
Ps 19:2 Day unto day *u* speech, and night
Prov 1:20 she *u* her voice in the streets
Prov 1:21 in the city she *u* her words
Prov 10:18 he that *u* a slander, is a fool
Prov 29:11 A fool *u* all his mind
Jer 10:13 When he *u* his voice, there is a
Jer 51:16 When he *u* his voice, there is a
Mic 7:3 he *u* his mischievous desire

**UTTERING**
Is 59:13 *u* from the heart words of

**UTTERLY**
Ex 17:14 for I will *u* put out the
Ex 22:17 If her father *u* refuse to give
Ex 22:20 only, he shall be *u* destroyed
Ex 23:24 but thou shalt *u* overthrow them
Lev 13:44 shall pronounce him *u* unclean
Lev 26:44 I abhor them, to destroy them *u*
Num 15:31 that soul shall *u* be cut off
Num 21:2 then I will *u* destroy their
Num 21:3 they *u* destroyed them and their
Num 30:12 But if her husband hath *u* made
Deut 2:34 *u* destroyed the men, and the women
Deut 3:6 we *u* destroyed them, as we did
Deut 3:6 *u* destroying the men, women, and
Deut 4:26 that ye shall soon *u* perish from
Deut 4:26 upon it, but shall *u* be destroyed
Deut 7:2 smite them, and *u* destroy them
Deut 7:26 but thou shalt *u* detest it
Deut 7:26 and thou shalt *u* abhor it
Deut 12:2 Ye shall *u* destroy all the places
Deut 13:15 of the sword, destroying it *u*
Deut 20:17 But thou shalt *u* destroy them
Deut 31:29 ye will *u* corrupt yourselves
Josh 2:10 Sihon and Og, whom ye *u* destroyed
Josh 6:21 they *u* destroyed all that was in
Josh 8:26 until he had *u* destroyed all the
Josh 10:1 taken Ai, and had *u* destroyed it
Josh 10:28 the king thereof he *u* destroyed
Josh 10:35 therein he *u* destroyed that day
Josh 10:37 but destroyed it *u*, and all the
Josh 10:39 *u* destroyed all the souls that
Josh 10:40 but *u* destroyed all that breathed
Josh 11:11 of the sword, *u* destroying them
Josh 11:12 he *u* destroyed them, as Moses the
Josh 11:20 that he might destroy them *u*
Josh 11:21 them *u* with their cities
Josh 17:13 but did not *u* drive them out
Judg 1:17 Zephath, and *u* destroyed it
Judg 1:28 and did not *u* drive them out
Judg 15:2 that thou hadst *u* hated her
Judg 21:11 Ye shall *u* destroy every male, and
1Sa 15:3 *u* destroy all that they have, and
1Sa 15:8 *u* destroyed all the people with
1Sa 15:9 good, and would not *u* destroy them
1Sa 15:9 and refuse, that they destroyed *u*
1Sa 15:15 and the rest we have *u* destroyed
1Sa 15:18 *u* destroy the sinners the
1Sa 15:20 have *u* destroyed the Amalekites
1Sa 15:21 should have been *u* destroyed
1Sa 27:12 his people Israel *u* to abhor him
2Sa 17:10 the heart of a lion, shall *u* melt
2Sa 23:7 they shall be *u* burned with fire
1Kin 9:21 also were not able *u* to destroy
2Kin 19:11 all lands, by destroying them *u*
1Chr 4:41 and destroyed them *u* unto this day
2Chr 20:23 *u* to slay and destroy them
2Chr 31:1 until they had *u* destroyed them
2Chr 32:14 that my fathers *u* destroyed
Neh 9:31 thou didst not *u* consume them
Ps 37:24 fall, he shall not be *u* cast down
Ps 73:19 they are *u* consumed with terrors
Ps 89:33 will I not *u* take from him
Ps 119:8 O forsake me not *u*
Ps 119:43 word of truth *u* out of my mouth
Song 8:7 for love, it would *u* be contemned
Is 2:18 And the idols he shall *u* abolish
Is 6:11 man, and the land be *u* desolate
Is 11:15 the LORD shall *u* destroy the
Is 24:3 be *u* emptied, and *u* spoiled
Is 24:19 The earth is *u* broken down
Is 34:2 he hath *u* destroyed them, he hath
Is 37:11 to all lands by destroying them *u*
Is 40:30 and the young men shall *u* fall
Is 56:3 The LORD hath *u* separated me from
Is 60:12 those nations shall be *u* wasted
Jer 9:4 for every brother will *u* supplant
Jer 12:17 I will *u* pluck up and destroy that
Jer 14:19 Hast thou *u* rejected Judah
Jer 23:39 will *u* forget you, and I will
Jer 25:9 will *u* destroy them, and make them
Jer 25:29 and should ye be *u* unpunished
Jer 50:21 *u* destroy after them, saith the
Jer 50:26 her up as heaps, and destroy her *u*
Jer 51:3 destroy ye *u* all her host
Jer 51:58 of Babylon shall be *u* broken
Lam 5:22 But thou hast *u* rejected us
Eze 9:6 Slay *u* old and young, both maids,
Eze 17:10 shall it not *u* wither, when the
Eze 27:31 make themselves *u* bald for thee
Eze 29:10 make the land of Egypt *u* waste
Dan 11:44 destroy, and *u* to make away many
Hos 1:6 but I will *u* take them away
Hos 10:15 the king of Israel *u* be cut off
Amos 9:8 saving that I will not *u* destroy
Mic 2:4 and say, We be *u* spoiled
Nah 1:15 he is *u* cut off
Zeph 1:2 I will *u* consume all things from
Zec 11:17 his right eye shall be *u* darkened
1Cor 6:7 there is *u* a fault among you
2Pet 2:12 shall *u* perish in their own
Rev 18:8 she shall be *u* burned with fire

**UTTERMOST**
Ex 26:4 in the *u* edge of another curtain
Ex 36:11 in the *u* side of another curtain
Ex 36:17 the *u* edge of the curtain in the
Num 11:1 were in the *u* parts of the camp
Num 20:16 a city in the *u* of thy border
Deut 11:24 even unto the *u* sea shall your
Josh 15:1 was the *u* part of the south coast
Josh 15:5 the sea at the *u* part of Jordan
Josh 15:21 the *u* cities of the tribe of the
1Sa 14:2 Saul tarried in the *u* part of
1Kin 6:24 from the *u* part of the one wing
1Kin 6:24 the *u* part of the other were ten
2Kin 7:5 the *u* part of the camp of Syria
2Kin 7:8 came to the *u* part of the camp
Neh 1:9 out unto the *u* part of the heaven
Ps 2:8 the *u* parts of the earth for thy

Ps 65:8 They also that dwell in the *u*
Ps 139:9 dwell in the *u* parts of the sea
Is 7:18 the *u* part of the rivers of Egypt
Is 24:16 From the *u* part of the earth have
Mt 5:26 thou hast paid the *u* farthing
Mt 12:42 for she came from the *u* parts of
Mk 13:27 from the *u* part of the earth to
Mk 13:27 the earth to the *u* part of heaven
Acts 1:8 unto the *u* part of the earth
Acts 24:22 I will know the *u* of your matter
1Th 2:16 wrath is come upon them to the *u*
Heb 7:25 the *u* that come unto God by him

**UZ** *(uz) A son of Aram.*
Gen 10:23 *U*, and Hul, and Gether, and Mash
Gen 36:28 are these; *U*, and Aran
1Chr 1:17 Arphaxad, and Lud, and Aram, and *U*
1Chr 1:42 of Dishan; *U*, and Aran
Job 1:1 There was a man in the land of *U*
Jer 25:20 and all the kings of the land of *U*
Lam 4:21 that dwellest in the land of *U*

**UZAI** *(u'-zahee) Father of Palal.*
Neh 3:25 Palal the son of *U*, over against

**UZAL** *(u'-zal) A son of Joktan.*
Gen 10:27 And Hadoram, and *U*, and Diklah,
1Chr 1:21 Hadoram also, and *U*, and Diklah,

**UZZA** *(uz'-zah)* See UZZAH.
*1. Name of the burial ground of Manasseh and Amon.*
2Kin 21:18 his own house, in the garden of *U*
2Kin 21:26 his sepulchre in the garden of *U*
*2. Son of Shimei.*
1Chr 6:29 son, Shimei his son, *U* his son,
*3. A brother of Ahihud.*
1Chr 8:7 Gera, he removed them, and begat *U*
*4. Touched the Ark and died.*
1Chr 13:7 and *U* and Ahio drave the cart
1Chr 13:9 *U* put forth his hand to hold the
1Chr 13:10 of the LORD was kindled against *U*
1Chr 13:11 the LORD had made a breach upon *U*
*5. A family of Nethinims.*
Ezr 2:49 The children of *U*, the children
Neh 7:51 of Gazzam, the children of *U*

**UZZAH** *(uz'-zah)* See UZZA. *Same as Uzza 4.*
2Sa 6:3 and *U* and Ahio, the sons of
2Sa 6:6 *U* put forth his hand to the ark
2Sa 6:7 of the LORD was kindled against *U*
2Sa 6:8 the LORD had made a breach upon *U*

**UZZEN-SHERAH** *(uz'-zen-she'-rah) A city in Ephraim.*
1Chr 7:24 the nether, and the upper, and *U*

**UZZI** *(uz'-zi)*
*1. A son of Bukki.*
1Chr 6:5 begat Bukki, and Bukki begat *U*
1Chr 6:6 *U* begat Zerahiah, and Zerahiah
1Chr 6:51 *U* his son, Zerahiah his son,
Ezr 7:4 The son of Zerahiah, the son of *U*
*2. Father of Izrahiah.*
1Chr 7:2 *U*, and Rephaiah, and Jeriel, and
1Chr 7:3 And the sons of *U*
*3. Son of Bela.*
1Chr 7:7 Ezbon, and *U*, and Uzziel, and
*4. A family of exiles.*
1Chr 9:8 of Jeroham, and Elah the son of *U*
*5. An overseer of Levites.*
Neh 11:22 Jerusalem was *U* the son of Bani
*6. A priest descended from Jedaiah.*
Neh 12:19 of Jedaiah, *U*
Neh 12:42 and Shemaiah, and Eleazar, and *U*

**UZZIA** *(uz-zi'-ah) A "mighty man" of David.*
1Chr 11:44 *U* the Ashterathite, Shama and

**UZZIAH** *(uz-zi'-ah)*
*1. A king of Judah.*
2Kin 15:13 thirtieth year of *U* king of Judah
2Kin 15:30 year of Jotham the son of *U*
2Kin 15:32 son of *U* king of Judah to reign
2Kin 15:34 to all that his father *U* had done
2Chr 26:1 all the people of Judah took *U*
2Chr 26:3 Sixteen years old was *U* when he
2Chr 26:8 And the Ammonites gave gifts to *U*
2Chr 26:9 Moreover *U* built towers in
2Chr 26:11 Moreover *U* had an host of
2Chr 26:14 *U* prepared for them throughout
2Chr 26:18 And they withstood *U* the king
2Chr 26:18 It appertaineth not unto thee, *U*
2Chr 26:19 Then *U* was wroth, and had a censer
2Chr 26:21 *U* the king was a leper unto the
2Chr 26:22 Now the rest of the acts of *U*
2Chr 26:23 So *U* slept with his fathers, and
2Chr 27:2 to all that his father *U* did
Is 1:1 and Jerusalem in the days of *U*
Is 6:1 In the year that king *U* died I
Is 7:1 the son of Jotham, the son of *U*
Hos 1:1 son of Beeri, in the days of *U*
Amos 1:1 in the days of *U* king of Judah
Zec 14:5 in the days of *U* king of Judah
*2. Son of Uriel.*
1Chr 6:24 *U* his son, and Shaul his son
*3. Father of Jehonathan.*
1Chr 27:25 was Jehonathan the son of *U*
*4. Married a foreigner in exile.*
Ezr 10:21 and Shemaiah, and Jehiel, and *U*
*5. A family of exiles.*
Neh 11:4 Athaiah the son of *U*, the son of

**UZZIEL** *(uz-zi'-el)*
*1. A son of Kohath.*
Ex 6:18 Amram, and Izhar, and Hebron, and *U*
Ex 6:22 And the sons of *U*
Lev 10:4 the sons of *U* the uncle of Aaron,
Num 3:19 Amram, and Izehar, Hebron, and *U*
Num 3:30 shall be Elizaphan the son of *U*
1Chr 6:2 Amram, Izhar, and Hebron, and *U*
1Chr 6:18 Amram, and Izhar, and Hebron, and *U*
1Chr 15:10 Of the sons of *U*
1Chr 23:12 Amram, Izhar, Hebron, and *U*
1Chr 23:20 Of the sons of *U*
1Chr 24:24 Of the sons of *U*
*2. A son of Ishi.*
1Chr 4:42 and Neariah, and Rephaiah, and *U*
*3. A son of Bela.*
1Chr 7:7 Ezbon, and Uzzi, and *U*, and Jerimoth
*4. A sanctuary servant.*
1Chr 25:4 Bukkiah, Mattaniah, *U*, Shebuel,
*5. A Levite who cleansed the Temple.*
2Chr 29:14 Shemaiah, and *U*
*6. A repairer of Jerusalem's wall.*
Neh 3:8 repaired *U* the son of Harhaiah

**UZZIELITES** *(uz-zi'-el-ites) Descendants of Uzziel 1.*
Num 3:27 and the family of the *U*
1Chr 26:23 the Hebronites, and the *U*

# V

**VAGABOND**
Gen 4:12 a *v* shalt thou be in the earth
Gen 4:14 be a fugitive and a *v* in the earth
Acts 19:13 Then certain of the *v* Jews

**VAGABONDS**
Ps 109:10 Let his children be continually *v*

**VAIL**
Gen 24:65 therefore she took a *v*, and
Gen 38:14 from her, and covered her with a *v*
Gen 38:19 away, and laid by her *v* from her
Ex 26:31 And thou shalt make a *v* of blue
Ex 26:33 hang up the *v* under the taches
Ex 26:33 the *v* the ark of the testimony
Ex 26:33 the *v* shall divide unto you
Ex 26:35 shalt set the table without the *v*
Ex 27:21 of the congregation without the *v*
Ex 30:6 the *v* that is by the ark of the
Ex 34:33 with them, he put a *v* on his face
Ex 34:34 speak with him, he took the *v* off
Ex 34:35 Moses put the *v* upon his face
Ex 35:12 seat, and the *v* of the covering,
Ex 36:35 And he made a *v* of blue, and purple
Ex 38:27 and the sockets of the *v*
Ex 39:34 skins, and the *v* of the covering,
Ex 40:3 and cover the ark with the *v*
Ex 40:21 set up the *v* of the covering, and
Ex 40:22 northward, without the *v*
Ex 40:26 of the congregation before the *v*
Lev 4:6 before the *v* of the sanctuary
Lev 4:17 the LORD, even before the *v*
Lev 16:2 the *v* before the mercy seat
Lev 16:12 small, and bring it within the *v*
Lev 16:15 and bring his blood within the *v*
Lev 21:23 he shall not go in unto the *v*
Lev 24:3 Without the *v* of the testimony,
Num 4:5 shall take down the covering *v*
Num 18:7 of the altar, and within the *v*
Ruth 3:15 Bring the *v* that thou hast upon
2Chr 3:14 And he made the *v* of blue, and
Is 25:7 the *v* that is spread over all
2Cor 3:13 which put a *v* over his face, that
2Cor 3:14 this day remaineth the same *v*
2Cor 3:14 which *v* is done away in Christ
2Cor 3:15 the *v* is upon their heart
2Cor 3:16 the *v* shall be taken away

**VAILS**
Is 3:23 linen, and the hoods, and the *v*

**VAIN**
Ex 5:9 and let them not regard *v* words
Ex 20:7 the name of the LORD thy God in *v*
Ex 20:7 that taketh his name in *v*
Lev 26:16 and ye shall sow your seed in *v*
Lev 26:20 your strength shall be spent in *v*
Deut 5:11 the name of the LORD thy God in *v*
Deut 5:11 that taketh his name in *v*
Deut 32:47 For it is not a *v* thing for you
Judg 9:4 wherewith Abimelech hired *v*
Judg 11:3 were gathered *v* men to Jephthah
1Sa 12:21 then should ye go after *v* things
1Sa 12:21 for they are *v*
1Sa 25:21 Surely in *v* have I kept all that
2Sa 6:20 servants, as one of the *v* fellows
2Kin 17:15 they followed vanity, and became *v*
2Kin 18:20 sayest, (but they are but *v* words
2Chr 13:7 there are gathered unto him *v* men
Job 9:29 be wicked, why then labour I in *v*
Job 11:11 For he knoweth *v* men
Job 11:12 For *v* man would be wise, though
Job 15:2 a wise man utter *v* knowledge
Job 16:3 Shall *v* words have an end
Job 21:34 How then comfort ye me in *v*
Job 27:12 why then are ye thus altogether *v*
Job 35:16 doth Job open his mouth in *v*
Job 39:16 her labour is in *v* without fear
Job 41:9 Behold, the hope of him is in *v*
Ps 2:1 and the people imagine a *v* thing
Ps 26:4 I have not sat with *v* persons
Ps 33:17 An horse is a *v* thing for safety
Ps 39:6 every man walketh in a *v* shew
Ps 39:6 surely they are disquieted in *v*
Ps 60:11 for *v* is the help of man
Ps 62:10 and become not *v* in robbery
Ps 73:13 I have cleansed my heart in *v*
Ps 89:47 hast thou made all men in *v*
Ps 108:12 for *v* is the help of man
Ps 119:113 I hate *v* thoughts
Ps 127:1 they labour in *v* that build it
Ps 127:1 the watchman waketh but in *v*
Ps 127:2 It is *v* for you to rise up early,
Ps 139:20 thine enemies take thy name in *v*
Prov 1:17 Surely in *v* the net is spread in
Prov 12:11 followeth *v* persons is void of
Prov 28:19 *v* persons shall have poverty
Prov 30:9 and take the name of my God in *v*
Prov 31:30 is deceitful, and beauty is *v*
Eccl 6:12 all the days of his *v* life which
Is 1:13 Bring no more *v* oblations
Is 30:7 For the Egyptians shall help in *v*
Is 36:5 (but they are but *v* words) I have

Is 45:18 it, he created it not in v
Is 45:19 seed of Jacob, Seek ye me in v
Is 49:4 Then I said, I have laboured in v
Is 49:4 my strength for nought, and in v
Is 65:23 They shall not labour in v
Jer 2:5 after vanity, and are become v
Jer 2:30 In v have I smitten your children
Jer 3:23 Truly in v is salvation hoped for
Jer 4:14 How long shall thy v thoughts
Jer 4:30 in v shalt thou make thyself fair
Jer 6:29 the founder melteth in v
Jer 8:8 Lo, certainly in v made he it
Jer 8:8 the pen of the scribes is in v
Jer 10:3 the customs of the people are v
Jer 23:16 they make you v
Jer 46:11 in v shalt thou use many
Jer 50:9 none shall return in v
Jer 51:58 and the people shall labour in v
Lam 2:14 Thy prophets have seen v and
Lam 4:17 eyes as yet failed for our v help
Eze 6:10 that I have not said in v that I
Eze 12:24 more any v vision nor flattering
Eze 13:7 Have ye not seen a v vision
Zec 10:2 they comfort in v
Mal 3:14 have said, It is v to serve God
Mt 6:7 use not v repetitions, as the
Mt 15:9 But in v they do worship me,
Mk 7:7 Howbeit in v do they worship me,
Acts 4:25 and the people imagine v things
Rom 1:21 but became v in their
Rom 13:4 for he beareth not the sword in v
1Cor 3:20 of the wise, that they are v
1Cor 15:2 you, unless ye have believed in v
1Cor 15:10 was bestowed upon me was not in v
1Cor 15:14 risen, then is our preaching v
1Cor 15:14 and your faith is also v
1Cor 15:17 be not raised, your faith is v
1Cor 15:58 labour is not in v in the Lord
2Cor 6:1 receive not the grace of God in v
2Cor 9:3 you should be in v in this behalf
Gal 2:2 I should run, or had run, in v
Gal 2:21 the law, then Christ is dead in v
Gal 3:4 ye suffered so many things in v
Gal 3:4 if it be yet in v
Gal 4:11 bestowed upon you labour in v
Gal 5:26 Let us not be desirous of v glory
Eph 5:6 no man deceive you with v words
Phil 2:16 Christ, that I have not run in v
Phil 2:16 neither laboured in v
Col 2:8 v deceit, after the tradition of
1Th 2:1 in unto you, that it was not in v
1Th 3:5 you, and our labour be in v
1Ti 1:6 have turned aside unto v jangling
1Ti 6:20 v babblings, and oppositions of
2Ti 2:16 But shun profane and v babblings
Titus 1:10 v talkers and deceivers, specially
Titus 3:9 for they are unprofitable and v
Jas 1:26 heart, this man's religion is v
Jas 2:20 O v man, that faith without works
Jas 4:5 that the scripture saith in v
1Pet 1:18 from your v conversation received

**VAINGLORY**
Phil 2:3 be done through strife or v

**VAINLY**
Col 2:18 v puffed up by his fleshly mind,

**VAJEZATHA** *(va-jez'-a-thah) A son of Haman.*
Est 9:9 and Arisai, and Aridai, and V

**VALE**
Gen 14:3 together in the v of Siddim
Gen 14:8 with them in the v of Siddim
Gen 14:10 the v of Siddim was full of
Gen 37:14 sent him out of the v of Hebron
Deut 1:7 plain, in the hills, and in the v
Josh 10:40 and of the south, and of the v
1Kin 10:27 sycomore trees that are in the v
2Chr 1:15 that are in the v for abundance
Jer 33:13 mountains, in the cities of the v

**VALIANT**
1Sa 14:52 saw any strong man, or any v man
1Sa 16:18 in playing, and a mighty v man
1Sa 18:17 only be thou v for me, and fight
1Sa 26:15 to Abner, Art not thou a v man
1Sa 31:12 All the v men arose, and went all
2Sa 2:7 be strengthened, and be ye v
2Sa 11:16 where he knew that v men were
2Sa 13:28 be courageous, and be v
2Sa 17:10 And he also that is v, whose heart
2Sa 17:10 they which be with him are v men
2Sa 23:20 of Jehoiada, the son of a v man
2Sa 24:9 v men that drew the sword
1Kin 1:42 for thou art a v man, and bringest
1Chr 5:18 of v men, men able to bear
1Chr 7:2 they were v men of might in their
1Chr 7:5 of Issachar were v men of might
1Chr 10:12 They arose, all the v men
1Chr 11:22 the son of a v man of Kabzeel,
1Chr 11:26 Also the v men of the armies were
1Chr 28:1 mighty men, and with all the v men
2Chr 13:3 with an army of v men of war
2Chr 26:17 of the LORD, that were v men
2Chr 28:6 in one day, which were all v men
Neh 11:6 hundred threescore and eight v men
Song 3:7 threescore v men are about it, of
Song 3:7 are about it, of the v of Israel
Is 10:13 down the inhabitants like a v man
Is 33:7 their v ones shall cry without
Jer 9:3 but they are not v for the truth
Jer 46:15 Why are thy v men swept away
Nah 2:3 red, the v men are in scarlet
Heb 11:34 waxed v in fight, turned to

**VALIANTEST**
Judg 21:10 twelve thousand men of the v

**VALIANTLY**
Num 24:18 and Israel shall do v
1Chr 19:13 behave ourselves v for our people
Ps 60:12 Through God we shall do v
Ps 108:13 Through God we shall do v
Ps 118:15 right hand of the LORD doeth v
Ps 118:16 right hand of the LORD doeth v

**VALLEY**
Gen 14:17 at the v of Shaveh, which is the
Gen 26:17 his tent in the v of Gerar
Gen 26:19 Isaac's servants digged in the v
Num 14:25 and the Canaanites dwelt in the v
Num 21:12 and pitched in the v of Zared
Num 21:20 And from Bamoth in the v, that is
Num 32:9 they went up unto the v of Eshcol
Deut 1:24 and came unto the v of Eshcol
Deut 3:16 unto the river Arnon half the v
Deut 3:29 So we abode in the v over against
Deut 4:46 in the v over against Beth-peor,
Deut 21:4 down the heifer unto a rough v
Deut 21:4 the heifer's neck there in the v
Deut 21:6 heifer that is beheaded in the v
Deut 34:3 and the plain of the v of Jericho
Deut 34:6 he buried him in a v in the land
Josh 7:24 brought them unto the v of Achor
Josh 7:26 The v of Achor, unto this day
Josh 8:11 now there was a v between them
Josh 8:13 night into the midst of the v
Josh 10:12 and thou, Moon, in the v of Ajalon
Josh 11:2 south of Chinneroth, and in the v
Josh 11:8 unto the v of Mizpeh eastward
Josh 11:16 all the land of Goshen, and the v
Josh 11:16 of Israel, and the v of the same
Josh 11:17 even unto Baal-gad in the v of
Josh 12:7 from Baal-gad in the v of Lebanon
Josh 13:19 in the mount of the v,
Josh 13:27 And in the v, Beth-aram, and
Josh 15:7 toward Debir from the v of Achor
Josh 15:8 the border went up by the v of
Josh 15:8 before the v of Hinnom westward
Josh 15:8 of the v of the giants northward
Josh 15:33 And in the v, Eshtaol, and Zoreah,
Josh 17:16 of the v have chariots of iron
Josh 17:16 they who are of the v of Jezreel
Josh 18:16 before the v of the son of Hinnom
Josh 18:16 which is in the v of the giants
Josh 18:16 and descended to the v of Hinnom
Josh 18:21 Beth-hoglah, and the v of Keziz,
Josh 19:14 are in the v of Jiphthah-el
Josh 19:27 to the v of Jiphthah-el toward
Judg 1:9 and in the south, and in the v
Judg 1:19 out the inhabitants of the v
Judg 1:34 suffer them to come down to the v
Judg 5:15 he was sent on foot into the v
Judg 6:33 and pitched in the v of Jezreel
Judg 7:1 by the hill of Moreh, in the v
Judg 7:8 Midian was beneath him in the v
Judg 7:12 of the east lay along in the v
Judg 16:4 loved a woman in the v of Sorek
Judg 18:28 it was in the v that lieth by
1Sa 6:13 their wheat harvest in the v
1Sa 13:18 the border that looketh to the v
1Sa 15:5 of Amalek, and laid wait in the v
1Sa 17:2 and pitched by the v of Elah
1Sa 17:3 there was a v between them
1Sa 17:19 of Israel, were in the v of Elah
1Sa 17:52 until thou come to the v
1Sa 21:9 thou slewest in the v of Elah
1Sa 31:7 were on the other side of the v
2Sa 5:18 themselves in the v of Rephaim
2Sa 5:22 themselves in the v of Rephaim
2Sa 8:13 of the Syrians in the v of salt
2Sa 23:13 pitched in the v of Rephaim
2Kin 2:16 some mountain, or into some v
2Kin 3:16 Make this v full of ditches
2Kin 3:17 yet that v shall be filled with
2Kin 14:7 in the v of salt ten thousand
2Kin 23:10 which is in the v of the children
1Chr 4:14 the father of the v of Charashim
1Chr 4:39 even unto the east side of the v
1Chr 10:7 were in the v saw that they fled
1Chr 11:15 encamped in the v of Rephaim
1Chr 14:9 themselves in the v of Rephaim
1Chr 14:13 spread themselves abroad in the v
1Chr 18:12 the v of salt eighteen thousand
2Chr 14:10 in the v of Zephathah at Mareshah
2Chr 20:26 themselves in the v of Berachah
2Chr 20:26 The v of Berachah, unto this day
2Chr 25:11 people, and went to the v of salt
2Chr 26:9 the corner gate, and at the v gate
2Chr 28:3 in the v of the son of Hinnom
2Chr 33:6 in the v of the son of Hinnom
2Chr 33:14 the west side of Gihon, in the v
2Chr 35:22 came to fight in the v of Megiddo
Neh 2:13 out by night by the gate of the v
Neh 2:15 and entered by the gate of the v
Neh 3:13 The v gate repaired Hanun, and the
Neh 11:30 Beer-sheba unto the v of Hinnom
Neh 11:35 Lod, and Ono, the v of craftsmen
Job 21:33 The clods of the v shall be sweet
Job 39:21 He paweth in the v, and rejoiceth
Ps 23:4 the v of the shadow of death
Ps 60:*t* smote of Edom in the v of salt
Ps 60:6 and mete out the v of Succoth
Ps 84:6 the v of Baca make it a well
Ps 108:7 and mete out the v of Succoth
Prov 30:17 ravens of the v shall pick it out
Song 6:11 nuts to see the fruits of the v
Is 17:5 ears in the v of Rephaim
Is 22:1 The burden of the v of vision
Is 22:5 GOD of hosts in the v of vision
Is 28:4 which is on the head of the fat v
Is 28:21 be wroth as in the v of Gibeon
Is 40:4 Every v shall be exalted, and
Is 63:14 As a beast goeth down into the v
Is 65:10 the v of Achor a place for the
Jer 2:23 see thy way in the v, know what
Jer 7:31 which is in the v of the son of
Jer 7:32 nor the v of the son of Hinnom,
Jer 7:32 of Hinnom, but the v of slaughter
Jer 19:2 go forth unto the v of the son of
Jer 19:6 nor The v of the son of Hinnom,
Jer 19:6 of Hinnom, but The v of slaughter
Jer 21:13 thee, O inhabitant of the v
Jer 31:40 the whole v of the dead bodies,
Jer 32:35 which are in the v of the son of
Jer 32:44 and in the cities of the v
Jer 47:5 off with the remnant of their v
Jer 48:8 the v also shall perish, and the
Jer 49:4 in the valleys, thy flowing v
Eze 37:1 of the v which was full of bones
Eze 37:2 were very many in the open v
Eze 39:11 the v of the passengers on the
Eze 39:11 shall call it The v of Hamon-gog
Eze 39:15 buried it in the v of Hamon-gog
Hos 1:5 bow of Israel in the v of Jezreel
Hos 2:15 the v of Achor for a door of hope
Joel 3:2 down into the v of Jehoshaphat
Joel 3:12 come up to the v of Jehoshaphat
Joel 3:14 multitudes in the v of decision
Joel 3:14 LORD is near in the v of decision
Joel 3:18 and shall water the v of Shittim
Mic 1:6 the stones thereof into the v
Zec 12:11 Hadadrimmon in the v of Megiddon
Zec 14:4 and there shall be a very great v
Zec 14:5 flee to the v of the mountains
Zec 14:5 for the v of the mountains shall
Lk 3:5 Every v shall be filled, and every

**VALLEYS**
Num 24:6 As the v are they spread forth,
Deut 8:7 and depths that spring out of v
Deut 11:11 it, is a land of hills and v
Josh 9:1 Jordan, in the hills, and in the v

Josh 12:8 In the mountains, and in the v
1Kin 20:28 hills, but he is not God of the v
1Chr 12:15 put to flight all them of the v
1Chr 27:29 v was Shaphat the son of Adlai
Job 30:6 To dwell in the cliffs of the v
Job 39:10 will he harrow the v after thee
Ps 65:13 the v also are covered over with
Ps 104:8 they go down by the v unto the
Ps 104:10 He sendeth the springs into the v
Song 2:1 of Sharon, and the lily of the v
Is 7:19 all of them in the desolate v
Is 22:7 that thy choicest v shall be full
Is 28:1 are on the head of the fat v of
Is 41:18 fountains in the midst of the v
Is 57:5 slaying the children in the v
Jer 49:4 Wherefore gloriest thou in the v
Eze 6:3 hills, to the rivers, and to the v
Eze 7:16 the mountains like doves of the v
Eze 31:12 in all the v his branches are
Eze 32:5 fill the v with thy height
Eze 35:8 in thy hills, and in thy v
Eze 36:4 hills, to the rivers, and to the v
Eze 36:6 hills, to the rivers, and to the v
Mic 1:4 the v shall be cleft, as wax

**VALOUR**
Josh 1:14 armed, all the mighty men of v
Josh 6:2 thereof, and the mighty men of v
Josh 8:3 thirty thousand mighty men of v
Josh 10:7 him, and all the mighty men of v
Judg 3:29 men, all lusty, and all men of v
Judg 6:12 with thee, thou mighty man of v
Judg 11:1 Gileadite was a mighty man of v
Judg 18:2 men from their coasts, men of v
Judg 20:44 all these were men of v
Judg 20:46 all these were men of v
1Kin 11:28 Jeroboam was a mighty man of v
2Kin 5:1 he was also a mighty man in v
2Kin 24:14 and all the mighty men of v
1Chr 5:24 and Jahdiel, mighty men of v
1Chr 7:7 of their fathers, mighty men of v
1Chr 7:9 of their fathers, mighty men of v
1Chr 7:11 of their fathers, mighty men of v
1Chr 7:40 house, choice and mighty men of v
1Chr 8:40 sons of Ulam were mighty men of v
1Chr 12:21 for they were all mighty men of v
1Chr 12:25 mighty men of v for the war
1Chr 12:28 And Zadok, a young man mighty of v
1Chr 12:30 and eight hundred, mighty men of v
1Chr 26:6 for they were mighty men of v
1Chr 26:30 and his brethren, men of v
1Chr 26:31 men of v at Jazer of Gilead
1Chr 26:32 And his brethren, men of v
2Chr 13:3 chosen men, being mighty men of v
2Chr 14:8 all these were mighty men of v
2Chr 17:13 the men of war, mighty men of v
2Chr 17:14 men of v three hundred thousand
2Chr 17:16 hundred thousand mighty men of v
2Chr 17:17 Eliada a mighty man of v, and with
2Chr 25:6 of v out of Israel for an hundred
2Chr 26:12 mighty men of v were two thousand
2Chr 32:21 cut off all the mighty men of v
Neh 11:14 their brethren, mighty men of v

**VALUE**
Lev 27:8 priest, and the priest shall v him
Lev 27:8 that vowed shall the priest v him
Lev 27:12 And the priest shall v it, whether
Job 13:4 ye are all physicians of no v
Mt 10:31 ye are of more v than many
Mt 27:9 of the children of Israel did v
Lk 12:7 ye are of more v than many

**VALUED**
Lev 27:16 be v at fifty shekels of silver
Job 28:16 It cannot be v with the gold of
Job 28:19 shall it be v with pure gold
Mt 27:9 the price of him that was v

**VALUEST**
Lev 27:12 as thou v it, who art the priest,

**VANIAH** *(va-ni'-ah) Married a foreigner in exile.*
Ezr 10:36 V, Meremoth, Eliashib,

**VANISH**
Job 6:17 What time they wax warm, they v
Is 51:6 heavens shall v away like smoke
1Cor 13:8 be knowledge, it shall v away
Heb 8:13 and waxeth old is ready to v away

**VANISHED**
Jer 49:7 is their wisdom v
Lk 24:31 and he v out of their sight

**VANISHETH**
Job 7:9 the cloud is consumed and v away
Jas 4:14 for a little time, and then v away

**VANITIES**
Deut 32:21 provoked me to anger with their v
1Kin 16:13 of Israel to anger with their v
1Kin 16:26 of Israel to anger with their v
Ps 31:6 hated them that regard lying v
Eccl 1:2 Vanity of v, saith the Preacher,
Eccl 1:2 saith the Preacher, vanity of v
Eccl 5:7 words there are also divers v
Eccl 12:8 Vanity of v, saith the preacher
Jer 8:19 graven images, and with strange v
Jer 10:8 the stock is a doctrine of v
Jer 14:22 Are there any among the v of the
Jonah 2:8 lying v forsake their own mercy
Acts 14:15 from these v unto the living God

**VANITY**
2Kin 17:15 and they followed v, and became
Job 7:3 am I made to possess months of v
Job 7:16 for my days are v
Job 15:31 him that is deceived trust in v
Job 15:31 for v shall be his recompence
Job 15:35 mischief, and bring forth v
Job 31:5 If I have walked with v, or if my
Job 35:13 Surely God will not hear v
Ps 4:2 how long will ye love v, and seek
Ps 10:7 under his tongue is mischief and v
Ps 12:2 They speak v every one with his
Ps 24:4 not lifted up his soul unto v
Ps 39:5 at his best state is altogether v
Ps 39:11 surely every man is v
Ps 41:6 he come to see me, he speaketh v
Ps 62:9 Surely men of low degree are v
Ps 62:9 are altogether lighter than v
Ps 78:33 their days did he consume in v
Ps 94:11 thoughts of man, that they are v
Ps 119:37 away mine eyes from beholding v
Ps 144:4 Man is like to v
Ps 144:8 Whose mouth speaketh v, and their
Ps 144:11 children, whose mouth speaketh v
Prov 13:11 Wealth gotten by v shall be
Prov 21:6 a lying tongue is a v tossed to
Prov 22:8 that soweth iniquity shall reap v
Prov 30:8 Remove far from me v and lies
Eccl 1:2 V of vanities, saith the Preacher
Eccl 1:2 saith the Preacher, v of vanities
Eccl 1:2 all is v
Eccl 1:14 and, behold, all is v and vexation
Eccl 2:1 and, behold, this also is v
Eccl 2:11 and, behold, all was v and vexation
Eccl 2:15 in my heart, that this also is v
Eccl 2:17 for all is v and vexation of
Eccl 2:19 This is also v
Eccl 2:21 This also is v and a great evil
Eccl 2:23 This is also v
Eccl 2:26 This also is v and vexation of
Eccl 3:19 for all is v
Eccl 4:4 This is also v and vexation of
Eccl 4:7 and I saw v under the sun
Eccl 4:8 This is also v, yea, it is a sore
Eccl 4:16 Surely this also is v and vexation
Eccl 5:10 this is also v
Eccl 6:2 this is v, and it is an evil
Eccl 6:4 For he cometh in with v, and
Eccl 6:9 this is also v and vexation of
Eccl 6:11 be many things that increase v
Eccl 7:6 this also is v
Eccl 7:15 have I seen in the days of my v
Eccl 8:10 this is also v
Eccl 8:14 There is a v which is done upon
Eccl 8:14 I said that this also is v
Eccl 9:9 all the days of the life of thy v
Eccl 9:9 the sun, all the days of thy v
Eccl 11:8 All that cometh is v
Eccl 11:10 for childhood and youth are v
Eccl 12:8 V of vanities, saith the preacher
Eccl 12:8 all is v
Is 5:18 draw iniquity with cords of v
Is 30:28 the nations with the sieve of v
Is 40:17 to him less than nothing, and v
Is 40:23 the judges of the earth as v
Is 41:29 Behold, they are all v
Is 44:9 a graven image are all of them v
Is 57:13 v shall take them
Is 58:9 of the finger, and speaking v
Is 59:4 they trust in v, and speak lies
Jer 2:5 from me, and have walked after v
Jer 10:15 They are v, and the work of errors
Jer 16:19 fathers have inherited lies, v
Jer 18:15 me, they have burned incense to v
Jer 51:18 They are v, the work of errors
Eze 13:6 They have seen v and lying
Eze 13:8 Because ye have spoken v, and seen
Eze 13:9 be upon the prophets that see v
Eze 13:23 Therefore ye shall see no more v
Eze 21:29 Whiles they see v unto thee
Eze 22:28 with untempered morter, seeing v
Hos 12:11 surely they are v
Hab 2:13 shall weary themselves for very v
Zec 10:2 For the idols have spoken v
Rom 8:20 creature was made subject to v
Eph 4:17 walk, in the v of their mind,
2Pet 2:18 speak great swelling words of v

**VAPORS**
Jer 10:13 he causeth the v to ascend from
Jer 51:16 he causeth the v to ascend from

**VAPOUR**
Job 36:27 rain according to the v thereof
Job 36:33 the cattle also concerning the v
Acts 2:19 blood, and fire, and v of smoke
Jas 4:14 It is even a v, that appeareth

**VAPOURS**
Ps 135:7 He causeth the v to ascend from
Ps 148:8 and hail; snow, and v

**VARIABLENESS**
Jas 1:17 of lights, with whom is no v

**VARIANCE**
Mt 10:35 set a man at v against his father
Gal 5:20 Idolatry, witchcraft, hatred, v

**VASHNI** *(vash'-ni) A son of Samuel.*
1Chr 6:28 the firstborn V, and Abiah

**VASHTI** *(vash'-ti) A Persian queen, succeeded by Esther.*
Est 1:9 Also V the queen made a feast for
Est 1:11 To bring V the queen before the
Est 1:12 But the queen V refused to come
Est 1:15 unto the queen V according to law
Est 1:16 V the queen hath not done wrong
Est 1:17 V the queen to be brought in
Est 1:19 That V come no more before king
Est 2:1 was appeased, he remembered V
Est 2:4 the king be queen instead of V
Est 2:17 and made her queen instead of V

**VAUNT**
Judg 7:2 lest Israel v themselves against

**VAUNTETH**
1Cor 13:4 charity v not itself, is not

**VEHEMENT**
Song 8:6 fire, which hath a most v flame
Jonah 4:8 that God prepared a v east wind
2Cor 7:11 what v desire, yea, what zeal,

**VEHEMENTLY**
Mk 14:31 But he spake the more v, If I
Lk 6:48 the stream beat v upon that house
Lk 6:49 which the stream did beat v
Lk 11:53 the Pharisees began to urge him v
Lk 23:10 and scribes stood and v accused him

**VEIL**
Song 5:7 the walls took away my v from me
Mt 27:51 the v of the temple was rent in
Mk 15:38 the v of the temple was rent in
Lk 23:45 the v of the temple was rent in
Heb 6:19 entereth into that within the v
Heb 9:3 And after the second v, the
Heb 10:20 consecrated for us, through the v

**VEIN**
Job 28:1 there is a v for the silver

**VENGEANCE**
Gen 4:15 v shall be taken on him sevenfold
Deut 32:35 To me belongeth v, and recompence
Deut 32:41 I will render v to mine enemies,
Deut 32:43 will render v to his adversaries,
Judg 11:36 as the LORD hath taken v for thee
Ps 58:10 shall rejoice when he seeth the v
Ps 94:1 O LORD God, to whom v belongeth
Ps 94:1 to whom v belongeth, shew thyself
Ps 99:8 tookest v of their inventions
Ps 149:7 To execute v upon the heathen, and
Prov 6:34 he will not spare in the day of v
Is 34:8 For it is the day of the LORD's v

Is 35:4 behold, your God will come with *v*
Is 47:3 I will take *v*, and I will not meet
Is 59:17 on the garments of *v* for clothing
Is 61:2 LORD, and the day of *v* of our God
Is 63:4 For the day of *v* is in mine heart
Jer 11:20 heart, let me see thy *v* on them
Jer 20:12 heart, let me see thy *v* on them
Jer 46:10 the Lord GOD of hosts, a day of *v*
Jer 50:15 for it is the *v* of the LORD
Jer 50:15 take *v* upon her
Jer 50:28 in Zion the *v* of the LORD our God
Jer 50:28 LORD our God, the *v* of his temple
Jer 51:6 this is the time of the LORD's *v*
Jer 51:11 because it is the *v* of the LORD
Jer 51:11 of the LORD, the *v* of his temple
Jer 51:36 thy cause, and take *v* for thee
Lam 3:60 Thou hast seen all their *v*
Eze 24:8 cause fury to come up to take *v*
Eze 25:12 the house of Judah by taking *v*
Eze 25:14 I will lay my *v* upon Edom by the
Eze 25:14 and they shall know my *v*, saith
Eze 25:15 have taken *v* with a despiteful
Eze 25:17 I will execute great *v* upon them
Eze 25:17 when I shall lay my *v* upon them
Mic 5:15 And I will execute *v* in anger
Nah 1:2 will take *v* on his adversaries
Lk 21:22 For these be the days of *v*
Acts 28:4 yet *v* suffereth not to live
Rom 3:5 Is God unrighteous who taketh *v*
Rom 12:19 for it is written, *V* is mine
2Th 1:8 In flaming fire taking *v* on them
Heb 10:30 *V* belongeth unto me, I will
Jude 7 suffering the *v* of eternal fire

## VENISON
Gen 25:28 Esau, because he did eat of his *v*
Gen 27:3 to the field, and take me some *v*
Gen 27:5 went to the field to hunt for *v*
Gen 27:7 Bring me *v*, and make me savoury
Gen 27:19 I pray thee, sit and eat of my *v*
Gen 27:25 me, and I will eat of my son's *v*
Gen 27:31 arise, and eat of his son's *v*
Gen 27:33 where is he that hath taken *v*

## VENOM
Deut 32:33 dragons, and the cruel *v* of asps

## VENOMOUS
Acts 28:4 saw the *v* beast hang on his hand

## VENT
Job 32:19 belly is as wine which hath no *v*

## VENTURE
1Kin 22:34 a certain man drew a bow at a *v*
2Chr 18:33 a certain man drew a bow at a *v*

## VERIFIED
Gen 42:20 so shall your words be *v*, and ye
1Kin 8:26 let thy word, I pray thee, be *v*
2Chr 6:17 God of Israel, let thy word be *v*

## VERILY
Gen 42:21 We are *v* guilty concerning our
Ex 31:13 *V* my sabbaths ye shall keep
Judg 15:2 I *v* thought that thou hadst
1Kin 1:43 *V* our lord king David hath made
2Kin 4:14 *V* she hath no child, and her
1Chr 21:24 but I will *v* buy it for the full
Job 19:13 are *v* estranged from me
Ps 37:3 the land, and *v* thou shalt be fed
Ps 39:5 *v* every man at his best state is
Ps 58:11 *V* there is a reward for the
Ps 58:11 *v* he is a God that judgeth in the
Ps 66:19 But *v* God hath heard me
Ps 73:13 *V* I have cleansed my heart in
Is 45:15 *V* thou art a God that hidest
Jer 15:11 *V* it shall be well with thy
Jer 15:11 *v* I will cause the enemy to
Mt 5:18 For *v* I say unto you, Till heaven
Mt 5:26 *V* I say unto thee, Thou shalt by
Mt 6:2 *V* I say unto you, They have their
Mt 6:5 *V* I say unto you, They have their
Mt 6:16 *V* I say unto you, They have their
Mt 8:10 *V* I say unto you, I have not
Mt 10:15 *V* I say unto you, It shall be
Mt 10:23 for *v* I say unto you, Ye shall
Mt 10:42 *v* I say unto you, he shall in no
Mt 11:11 *V* I say unto you, Among them that
Mt 13:17 For *v* I say unto you, That many
Mt 16:28 *V* I say unto you, There be some
Mt 17:20 for *v* I say unto you, If ye have
Mt 18:3 *V* I say unto you, Except ye be
Mt 18:13 *v* I say unto you, he rejoiceth
Mt 18:18 *V* I say unto you, Whatsoever ye
Mt 19:23 *V* I say unto you, That a rich man
Mt 19:28 *V* I say unto you, That ye which
Mt 21:21 *V* I say unto you, If ye have
Mt 21:31 *V* I say unto you, That the
Mt 23:36 *V* I say unto you, All these
Mt 24:2 *v* I say unto you, There shall not
Mt 24:34 *V* I say unto you, This generation
Mt 24:47 *V* I say unto you, That he shall
Mt 25:12 *V* I say unto you, I know you not
Mt 25:40 *V* I say unto you, Inasmuch as ye
Mt 25:45 *V* I say unto you, Inasmuch as ye
Mt 26:13 *V* I say unto you, Wheresoever
Mt 26:21 *V* I say unto you, that one of you
Mt 26:34 *V* I say unto thee, That this
Mk 3:28 *V* I say unto you, All sins shall
Mk 6:11 *V* I say unto you, It shall be
Mk 8:12 *v* I say unto you, There shall no
Mk 9:1 *V* I say unto you, That there be
Mk 9:12 them, Elias *v* cometh first, and
Mk 9:41 *v* I say unto you, he shall not
Mk 10:15 *V* I say unto you, Whosoever shall
Mk 10:29 *V* I say unto you, There is no man
Mk 11:23 For *v* I say unto you, That
Mk 12:43 *V* I say unto you, That this poor
Mk 13:30 *V* I say unto you, that this
Mk 14:9 *V* I say unto you, Wheresoever
Mk 14:18 *V* I say unto you, One of you
Mk 14:25 *V* I say unto you, I will drink no
Mk 14:30 *V* I say unto thee, That this day,
Lk 4:24 *V* I say unto you, No prophet is
Lk 11:51 *v* I say unto you, It shall be
Lk 12:37 *v* I say unto you, that he shall
Lk 13:35 *v* I say unto you, Ye shall not
Lk 18:17 *V* I say unto you, Whosoever shall
Lk 18:29 *V* I say unto you, There is no man
Lk 21:32 *V* I say unto you, This generation
Lk 23:43 *V* I say unto thee, To day shalt
Jn 1:51 And he saith unto him, *V*, *v*,
Jn 3:3 and said unto him, *V*, *v*
Jn 3:5 Jesus answered, *V*, *v*
Jn 3:11 *V*, *v*, I say unto thee, We
Jn 5:19 and said unto them, *V*, *v*
Jn 5:24 *V*, *v*, I say unto you, He
Jn 5:25 *V*, *v*, I say unto you, The
Jn 6:26 answered them and said, *V*, *v*
Jn 6:32 Jesus said unto them, *V*, *v*
Jn 6:47 *V*, *v*, I say unto you, He
Jn 6:53 Jesus said unto them, *V*, *v*
Jn 8:34 Jesus answered them, *V*, *v*
Jn 8:51 *V*, *v*, I say unto you, If a
Jn 8:58 Jesus said unto them, *V*, *v*
Jn 10:1 *V*, *v*, I say unto you, He
Jn 10:7 Jesus unto them again, *V*, *v*
Jn 12:24 *V*, *v*, I say unto you, Except
Jn 13:16 *V*, *v*, I say unto you, The
Jn 13:20 *V*, *v*, I say unto you, He
Jn 13:21 and testified, and said, *V*, *v*
Jn 13:38 *V*, *v*, I say unto thee, The
Jn 14:12 *V*, *v*, I say unto you, He
Jn 16:20 *V*, *v*, I say unto you, That
Jn 16:23 *V*, *v*, I say unto you,
Jn 21:18 *V*, *v*, I say unto thee, When
Acts 16:37 nay *v*; but let them
Acts 19:4 John *v* baptized with the baptism
Acts 22:3 I am *v* a man which am a Jew, born
Acts 26:9 I *v* thought with myself, that I
Rom 2:25 For circumcision *v* profiteth
Rom 10:18 Yes *v*, their sound went into all
Rom 15:27 It hath pleased them *v*
1Cor 5:3 For I *v*, as absent in body, but
1Cor 9:18 *V* that, when I preach the gospel,
1Cor 14:17 For thou *v* givest thanks well,
Gal 3:21 *v* righteousness should have been
1Th 3:4 For *v*, when we were with you, we
Heb 2:16 For *v* he took not on him the
Heb 3:5 Moses *v* was faithful in all his
Heb 6:16 For men *v* swear by the greater
Heb 7:5 *v* they that are of the sons of
Heb 7:18 For there is *v* a disannulling of
Heb 9:1 Then *v* the first covenant had
Heb 12:10 For they *v* for a few days
1Pet 1:20 Who *v* was foreordained before the
1Jn 2:5 in him *v* is the love of God

## VERITY
Ps 111:7 The works of his hands are *v*
1Ti 2:7 of the Gentiles in faith and *v*

## VERMILION
Jer 22:14 with cedar, and painted with *v*
Eze 23:14 the Chaldeans pourtrayed with *v*

## VESSEL
Lev 6:28 But the earthen *v* wherein it is
Lev 11:32 whether it be any *v* of wood
Lev 11:32 skin, or sack, whatsoever *v* it be
Lev 11:33 And every earthen *v*, whereinto any
Lev 11:34 in every such *v* shall be unclean
Lev 14:5 an earthen *v* over running water
Lev 14:50 an earthen *v* over running water
Lev 15:12 the *v* of earth, that he toucheth
Lev 15:12 every *v* of wood shall be rinsed
Num 5:17 take holy water in an earthen *v*
Num 19:15 And every open *v*, which hath no
Num 19:17 water shall be put thereto in a *v*
Deut 23:24 thou shalt not put any in thy *v*
1Sa 21:5 were sanctified this day in the *v*
1Kin 17:10 pray thee, a little water in a *v*
2Kin 4:6 unto her son, Bring me yet a *v*
2Kin 4:6 unto her, There is not a *v* more
Ps 2:9 them in pieces like a potter's *v*
Ps 31:12 I am like a broken *v*
Prov 25:4 come forth a *v* for the finer
Is 30:14 *v* that is broken in pieces
Is 66:20 *v* into the house of the LORD
Jer 18:4 the *v* that he made of clay was
Jer 18:4 so he made it again another *v*
Jer 19:11 as one breaketh a potter's *v*
Jer 22:28 is he a *v* wherein is no pleasure
Jer 25:34 ye shall fall like a pleasant *v*
Jer 32:14 and put them in an earthen *v*
Jer 48:11 not been emptied from *v* to *v*
Jer 48:38 like a *v* wherein is no pleasure
Jer 51:34 me, he hath made me an empty *v*
Eze 4:9 and fitches, and put them in one *v*
Eze 15:3 a pin of it to hang any *v* thereon
Hos 8:8 as a *v* wherein is no pleasure
Mk 11:16 carry any *v* through the temple
Lk 8:16 a candle, covereth it with a *v*
Jn 19:29 there was set a *v* full of vinegar
Acts 9:15 for he is a chosen *v* unto me
Acts 10:11 a certain *v* descending unto him,
Acts 10:16 the *v* was received up again into
Acts 11:5 saw a vision, A certain *v* descend
Rom 9:21 lump to make one *v* unto honour
1Th 4:4 possess his *v* in sanctification
2Ti 2:21 he shall be a *v* unto honour
1Pet 3:7 the wife, as unto the weaker *v*

## VESSELS
Gen 43:11 best fruits in the land in your *v*
Ex 7:19 *v* of wood, and in *v* of stone
Ex 25:39 he make it, with all these *v*
Ex 27:3 all the *v* thereof thou shalt make
Ex 27:19 All the *v* of the tabernacle in
Ex 30:27 And the table and all his *v*
Ex 30:27 and the candlestick and his *v*
Ex 30:28 of burnt offering with all his *v*
Ex 35:13 and his staves, and all his *v*
Ex 35:16 grate, his staves, and all his *v*
Ex 37:16 he made the *v* which were upon the
Ex 37:24 made he it, and all the *v* thereof
Ex 38:3 And he made all the *v* of the altar
Ex 38:3 all the *v* thereof made he of
Ex 38:30 it, and all the *v* of the altar,
Ex 39:36 The table, and all the *v* thereof
Ex 39:37 in order, and all the *v* thereof
Ex 39:39 brass, his staves, and all his *v*
Ex 39:40 all the *v* of the service of the
Ex 40:9 hallow it, and all the *v* thereof
Ex 40:10 the burnt offering, and all his *v*
Lev 8:11 anointed the altar and all his *v*
Num 1:50 and over all the *v* thereof
Num 1:50 tabernacle, and all the *v* thereof
Num 3:31 the *v* of the sanctuary wherewith
Num 3:36 thereof, and all the *v* thereof
Num 4:9 and all the oil *v* thereof
Num 4:10 all the *v* thereof within a
Num 4:14 put upon it all the *v* thereof
Num 4:14 basons, all the *v* of the altar
Num 4:15 all the *v* of the sanctuary, as
Num 4:16 sanctuary, and in the *v* thereof
Num 7:1 the altar and all the *v* thereof
Num 7:85 all the silver *v* weighed two
Num 18:3 come nigh the *v* of the sanctuary
Num 19:18 upon the tent, and upon all the *v*
Josh 6:19 gold, and *v* of brass and iron, are
Josh 6:24 the *v* of brass and of iron, they
Ruth 2:9 thou art athirst, go unto the *v*

1Sa 9:7 for the bread is spent in our *v*
1Sa 21:5 the *v* of the young men are holy,
2Sa 8:10 brought with him *v* of silver
2Sa 8:10 and *v* of gold, and *v* of brass
2Sa 17:28 beds, and basons, and earthen *v*
1Kin 7:45 and all these *v*, which Hiram made
1Kin 7:47 Solomon left all the *v* unweighed
1Kin 7:48 Solomon made all the *v* that
1Kin 7:51 the silver, and the gold, and the *v*
1Kin 8:4 all the holy *v* that were in the
1Kin 10:21 Solomon's drinking *v* were of gold
1Kin 10:21 all the *v* of the house of the
1Kin 10:25 *v* of silver, and *v* of gold,
1Kin 15:15 the LORD, silver, and gold, and *v*
2Kin 4:3 borrow thee *v* abroad of all thy
2Kin 4:3 all thy neighbours, even empty *v*
2Kin 4:4 shalt pour out into all those *v*
2Kin 4:5 sons, who brought the *v* to her
2Kin 4:6 when the *v* were full, that she
2Kin 7:15 the way was full of garments and *v*
2Kin 12:13 any *v* of gold
2Kin 12:13 or *v* of silver, of the money that
2Kin 14:14 all the *v* that were found in the
2Kin 23:4 all the *v* that were made for Baal
2Kin 24:13 cut in pieces all the *v* of gold
2Kin 25:14 all the *v* of brass wherewith they
2Kin 25:16 of all these *v* was without weight
1Chr 9:28 the charge of the ministering *v*
1Chr 9:29 were appointed to oversee the *v*
1Chr 18:8 and the pillars, and the *v* of brass
1Chr 18:10 with him all manner of *v* of gold
1Chr 22:19 of the LORD, and the holy *v* of God
1Chr 23:26 nor any *v* of it for the service
1Chr 28:13 for all the *v* of service in the
2Chr 4:18 all these *v* in great abundance
2Chr 4:19 Solomon made all the *v* that were
2Chr 5:5 all the holy *v* that were in the
2Chr 9:20 all the drinking *v* of king
2Chr 9:20 all the *v* of the house of the
2Chr 9:24 *v* of silver, and *v* of gold,
2Chr 15:18 dedicated, silver, and gold, and *v*
2Chr 24:14 whereof were made *v* for the house
2Chr 24:14 even *v* to minister, and to offer
2Chr 24:14 and spoons, and *v* of gold and silver
2Chr 25:24 all the *v* that were found in the
2Chr 28:24 the *v* of the house of God
2Chr 28:24 cut in pieces the *v* of the house
2Chr 29:18 offering, with all the *v* thereof
2Chr 29:18 table, with all the *v* thereof
2Chr 29:19 Moreover all the *v*, which king
2Chr 36:7 also carried of the *v* of the
2Chr 36:10 with the goodly *v* of the house of
2Chr 36:18 all the *v* of the house of God,
2Chr 36:19 all the goodly *v* thereof
Ezr 1:6 their hands with *v* of silver
Ezr 1:7 the *v* of the house of the LORD
Ezr 1:10 and ten, and other *v* a thousand
Ezr 1:11 All the *v* of gold and of silver
Ezr 5:14 the *v* also of gold and silver of
Ezr 5:15 And said unto him, Take these *v*
Ezr 6:5 silver *v* of the house of God,
Ezr 7:19 The *v* also that are given thee
Ezr 8:25 the silver, and the gold, and the *v*
Ezr 8:26 silver *v* an hundred talents, and
Ezr 8:27 two *v* of fine copper, precious as
Ezr 8:28 the *v* are holy also
Ezr 8:30 the silver, and the gold, and the *v*
Ezr 8:33 the *v* weighed in the house of our
Neh 10:39 where are the *v* of the sanctuary,
Neh 13:5 the frankincense, and the *v*
Neh 13:9 I again the *v* of the house of God
Est 1:7 they gave them drink in *v* of gold
Est 1:7 (the *v* being diverse one from
Is 18:2 even in *v* of bulrushes upon the
Is 22:24 all *v* of small quantity, from the
Is 22:24 quantity, from the *v* of cups
Is 22:24 even to all the *v* of flagons
Is 52:11 that bear the *v* of the LORD
Is 65:4 abominable things is in their *v*
Jer 14:3 they returned with their *v* empty
Jer 27:16 the *v* of the LORD's house shall
Jer 27:18 that the *v* which are left in the
Jer 27:19 of the *v* that remain in this city
Jer 27:21 concerning the *v* that remain in
Jer 28:3 all the *v* of the LORD's house
Jer 28:6 to bring again the *v* of the
Jer 40:10 and oil, and put them in your *v*
Jer 48:12 to wander, and shall empty his *v*
Jer 49:29 their curtains, and all their *v*
Jer 52:18 all the *v* of brass wherewith they
Jer 52:20 of all these *v* was without weight
Eze 27:13 men and *v* of brass in thy market
Dan 1:2 with part of the *v* of the house
Dan 1:2 he brought the *v* into the
Dan 5:2 silver *v* which his father
Dan 5:3 *v* that were taken out of the
Dan 5:23 they have brought the *v* of his
Dan 11:8 with their precious *v* of silver
Hos 13:15 the treasure of all pleasant *v*
Hag 2:16 draw out fifty *v* out of the press
Mt 13:48 down, and gathered the good into *v*
Mt 25:4 oil in their *v* with their lamps
Mk 7:4 of cups, and pots, brasen *v*
Rom 9:22 with much longsuffering the *v* of
Rom 9:23 of his glory on the *v* of mercy
2Cor 4:7 have this treasure in earthen *v*
2Ti 2:20 there are not only *v* of gold
Heb 9:21 all the *v* of the ministry
Rev 2:27 as the *v* of a potter shall they
Rev 18:12 wood, and all manner *v* of ivory
Rev 18:12 all manner *v* of most precious

## VESTMENTS
2Kin 10:22 Bring forth *v* for all the
2Kin 10:22 And he brought them forth *v*

## VESTRY
2Kin 10:22 said unto him that was over the *v*

## VESTURE
Deut 22:12 upon the four quarters of thy *v*
Ps 22:18 them, and cast lots upon my *v*
Ps 102:26 as a *v* shalt thou change them, and
Mt 27:35 upon my *v* did they cast lots
Jn 19:24 for my *v* they did cast lots
Heb 1:12 as a *v* shalt thou fold them up,
Rev 19:13 clothed with a *v* dipped in blood
Rev 19:16 And he hath on his *v* and on his

## VESTURES
Gen 41:42 and arrayed him in *v* of fine linen

## VEX
Ex 22:21 Thou shalt neither *v* a stranger
Lev 18:18 sister, to *v* her, to uncover her
Lev 19:33 in your land, ye shall not *v* him
Num 25:17 *V* the Midianites, and smite them
Num 25:18 For they *v* you with their wiles
Num 33:55 shall *v* you in the land wherein
2Sa 12:18 how will he then *v* himself
2Chr 15:6 for God did *v* them with all
Job 19:2 How long will ye *v* my soul
Ps 2:5 *v* them in his sore displeasure
Is 7:6 *v* it, and let us make a breach
Is 11:13 and Judah shall not *v* Ephraim
Eze 32:9 I will also *v* the hearts of many
Hab 2:7 thee, and awake that shall *v* thee
Acts 12:1 hands to *v* certain of the church

## VEXATION
Deut 28:20 shall send upon thee cursing, *v*
Eccl 1:14 all is vanity and *v* of spirit
Eccl 1:17 that this also is *v* of spirit
Eccl 2:11 *v* of spirit, and there was no
Eccl 2:17 for all is vanity and *v* of spirit
Eccl 2:22 of the *v* of his heart, wherein he
Eccl 2:26 also is vanity and *v* of spirit
Eccl 4:4 is also vanity and *v* of spirit
Eccl 4:6 full with travail and *v* of spirit
Eccl 4:16 also is vanity and *v* of spirit
Eccl 6:9 is also vanity and *v* of spirit
Is 9:1 shall not be such as was in her *v*
Is 28:19 and it shall be a *v* only to
Is 65:14 and shall howl for *v* of spirit

## VEXATIONS
2Chr 15:5 but great *v* were upon all the

## VEXED
Num 20:15 and the Egyptians *v* us, and our
Judg 2:18 that oppressed them and *v* them
Judg 10:8 And that year they *v* and oppressed
Judg 16:16 so that his soul was *v* unto death
1Sa 14:47 he turned himself, he *v* them
2Sa 13:2 And Amnon was so *v*, that he fell
2Kin 4:27 for her soul is *v* within her
Neh 9:27 hand of their enemies, who *v* them
Job 27:2 the Almighty, who hath *v* my soul
Ps 6:2 for my bones are *v*
Ps 6:3 My soul is also sore *v*
Ps 6:10 mine enemies be ashamed and sore *v*
Is 63:10 rebelled, and *v* his holy Spirit
Eze 22:5 which art infamous and much *v*
Eze 22:7 thee have they *v* the fatherless
Eze 22:29 and have *v* the poor and needy
Mt 15:22 is grievously *v* with a devil
Mt 17:15 for he is lunatick, and sore *v*
Lk 6:18 they that were *v* with unclean
Acts 5:16 them which were *v* with unclean
2Pet 2:7 *v* with the filthy conversation of
2Pet 2:8 *v* his righteous soul from day to

## VIAL
1Sa 10:1 Then Samuel took a *v* of oil
Rev 16:2 poured out his *v* upon the earth
Rev 16:3 poured out his *v* upon the sea
Rev 16:4 poured out his *v* upon the rivers
Rev 16:8 poured out his *v* upon the sun
Rev 16:10 his *v* upon the seat of the beast
Rev 16:12 *v* upon the great river Euphrates
Rev 16:17 poured out his *v* into the air

## VIALS
Rev 5:8 golden *v* full of odours, which
Rev 15:7 golden *v* full of the wrath of God
Rev 16:1 pour out the *v* of the wrath of
Rev 17:1 angels which had the seven *v*
Rev 21:9 angels which had the seven *v* full

## VICTORY
2Sa 19:2 the *v* that day was turned into
2Sa 23:10 LORD wrought a great *v* that day
2Sa 23:12 and the LORD wrought a great *v*
1Chr 29:11 the power, and the glory, and the *v*
Ps 98:1 holy arm, hath gotten him the *v*
Is 25:8 He will swallow up death in *v*
Mt 12:20 he send forth judgment unto *v*
1Cor 15:54 Death is swallowed up in *v*
1Cor 15:55 O grave, where is thy *v*
1Cor 15:57 which giveth us the *v* through our
1Jn 5:4 this is the *v* that overcometh the
Rev 15:2 had gotten the *v* over the beast

## VICTUAL
Ex 12:39 prepared for themselves any *v*
Judg 20:10 to fetch *v* for the people, that
1Kin 4:27 provided *v* for king Solomon
2Chr 11:11 captains in them, and store of *v*
2Chr 11:23 and he gave them *v* in abundance

## VICTUALS
Gen 14:11 Sodom and Gomorrah, and all their *v*
Lev 25:37 nor lend him thy *v* for increase
Deut 23:19 usury of money, usury of *v*
Josh 1:11 the people, saying, Prepare you *v*
Josh 9:11 Take *v* with you for the journey,
Josh 9:14 And the men took of their *v*
Judg 7:8 the people took *v* in their hand
Judg 17:10 and a suit of apparel, and thy *v*
1Sa 22:10 the LORD for him, and gave him *v*
1Kin 4:7 which provided *v* for the king
1Kin 11:18 him an house, and appointed him *v*
Neh 10:31 any *v* on the sabbath day to sell
Neh 13:15 in the day wherein they sold *v*
Jer 40:5 captain of the guard gave him *v*
Jer 44:17 for then had we plenty of *v*
Mt 14:15 the villages, and buy themselves *v*
Lk 9:12 round about, and lodge, and get *v*

## VIEW
Josh 2:1 Go *v* the land, even Jericho
Josh 7:2 saying, Go up and *v* the country
2Kin 2:7 went, and stood to *v* afar off
2Kin 2:15 were to *v* at Jericho saw him

## VIEWED
Josh 7:2 And the men went up and *v* Ai
Ezr 8:15 I *v* the people, and the priests,
Neh 2:13 *v* the walls of Jerusalem, which
Neh 2:15 *v* the wall, and turned back, and

## VIGILANT
1Ti 3:2 the husband of one wife, *v*
1Pet 5:8 Be sober, be *v*

## VILE
Deut 25:3 brother should seem *v* unto thee
Judg 19:24 unto this man do not so *v* a thing
1Sa 3:13 his sons made themselves *v*
1Sa 15:9 but every thing that was *v*
2Sa 6:22 And I will yet be more *v* than thus
Job 18:3 and reputed *v* in your sight
Job 40:4 Behold, I am *v*
Ps 15:4 In whose eyes a *v* person is
Is 32:5 The *v* person shall be no more
Is 32:6 For the *v* person will speak
Jer 15:19 forth the precious from the *v*
Jer 29:17 and will make them like *v* figs
Lam 1:11 for I am become *v*
Dan 11:21 estate shall stand up a *v* person
Nah 1:14 for thou art *v*

Nah 3:6 filth upon thee, and make thee v
Rom 1:26 gave them up unto v affections
Phil 3:21 Who shall change our v body
Jas 2:2 in also a poor man in v raiment

## VILELY
2Sa 1:21 of the mighty is v cast away

## VILER
Job 30:8 they were v than the earth

## VILEST
Ps 12:8 when the v men are exalted

## VILLAGE
Mt 21:2 Go into the v over against you,
Mk 11:2 way into the v over against you
Lk 8:1 went throughout every city and v
Lk 9:52 went, and entered into a v of the
Lk 9:56 And they went to another v
Lk 10:38 that he entered into a certain v
Lk 17:12 And as he entered into a certain v
Lk 19:30 Go ye into the v over against you
Lk 24:13 same day to a v called Emmaus
Lk 24:28 And they drew nigh unto the v

## VILLAGES
Ex 8:13 out of the houses, out of the v
Lev 25:31 But the houses of the v which
Num 21:25 Heshbon, and in all the v thereof
Num 21:32 and they took the v thereof
Num 32:42 the v thereof, and called it Nobah
Josh 13:23 the cities and the v thereof
Josh 13:28 families, the cities, and their v
Josh 15:32 are twenty and nine, with their v
Josh 15:36 fourteen cities with their v
Josh 15:41 sixteen cities with their v
Josh 15:44 nine cities with their v
Josh 15:45 Ekron, with her towns and her v
Josh 15:46 lay near Ashdod, with their v
Josh 15:47 Ashdod with her towns and her v
Josh 15:47 Gaza with her towns and her v
Josh 15:51 eleven cities with their v
Josh 15:54 nine cities with their v
Josh 15:57 ten cities with their v
Josh 15:59 six cities with their v
Josh 15:60 two cities with their v
Josh 15:62 six cities with their v
Josh 16:9 all the cities with their v
Josh 18:24 twelve cities with their v
Josh 18:28 fourteen cities with their v
Josh 19:6 thirteen cities and their v
Josh 19:7 four cities and their v
Josh 19:8 all the v that were round about
Josh 19:15 twelve cities with their v
Josh 19:16 these cities with their v
Josh 19:22 sixteen cities with their v
Josh 19:23 families, the cities and their v
Josh 19:30 twenty and two cities with their v
Josh 19:31 these cities with their v
Josh 19:38 nineteen cities with their v
Josh 19:39 families, the cities and their v
Josh 19:48 these cities with their v
Josh 21:12 the v thereof, gave they to Caleb
Judg 5:7 The inhabitants of the v ceased
Judg 5:11 inhabitants of his v in Israel
1Sa 6:18 of fenced cities, and of country v
1Chr 4:32 And their v were, Etam, and Ain,
1Chr 4:33 all their v that were round about
1Chr 6:56 the v thereof, they gave to Caleb
1Chr 9:16 that dwelt in the v of the
1Chr 9:22 by their genealogy in their v
1Chr 9:25 brethren, which were in their v
1Chr 27:25 in the cities, and in the v
2Chr 28:18 and Shocho with the v thereof
2Chr 28:18 and Timnah with the v thereof
2Chr 28:18 Gimzo also and the v thereof
Neh 6:2 one of the v in the plain of Ono
Neh 11:25 And for the v, with their fields,
Neh 11:25 in the v thereof, and at Dibon, and
Neh 11:25 in the v thereof, and at Jekabzeel
Neh 11:25 Jekabzeel, and in the v thereof,
Neh 11:27 Beer-sheba, and in the v thereof,
Neh 11:28 at Mekonah, and in the v thereof,
Neh 11:30 Zanoah, Adullam, and in their v
Neh 11:30 at Azekah, and in the v thereof
Neh 11:31 Aija, and Beth-el, and in their v
Neh 12:28 and from the v of Netophathi
Neh 12:29 them v round about Jerusalem
Est 9:19 Therefore the Jews of the v
Ps 10:8 in the lurking places of the v
Song 7:11 let us lodge in the v
Is 42:11 the v that Kedar doth inhabit
Eze 38:11 go up to the land of unwalled v
Hab 3:14 with his staves the head of his v
Mt 9:35 went about all the cities and v
Mt 14:15 away, that they may go into the v
Mk 6:6 And he went round about the v
Mk 6:36 round about, and into the v
Mk 6:56 whithersoever he entered, into v
Lk 13:22 he went through the cities and v
Acts 8:25 in many v of the Samaritans

## VILLANY
Is 32:6 For the vile person will speak v
Jer 29:23 they have committed v in Israel

## VINE
Gen 40:9 dream, behold, a v was before me
Gen 40:10 in the v were three branches
Gen 49:11 Binding his foal unto the v
Gen 49:11 his ass's colt unto the choice v
Lev 25:5 the grapes of thy v undressed
Lev 25:11 grapes in it of thy v undressed
Num 6:4 that is made of the v tree
Deut 32:32 their v is of the v of Sodom
Judg 9:12 Then said the trees unto the v
Judg 9:13 the v said unto them, Should I
Judg 13:14 of any thing that cometh of the v
1Kin 4:25 safely, every man under his v
2Kin 4:39 gather herbs, and found a wild v
2Kin 18:31 eat ye every man of his own v
2Chr 26:10 v dressers in the mountains, and
Job 15:33 off his unripe grape as the v
Ps 80:8 hast brought a v out of Egypt
Ps 80:14 and behold, and visit this v
Ps 128:3 v by the sides of thine house
Song 6:11 to see whether the v flourished
Song 7:8 shall be as clusters of the v
Song 7:12 let us see if the v flourish
Is 5:2 and planted it with the choicest v
Is 16:8 languish, and the v of Sibmah
Is 16:9 weeping of Jazer the v of Sibmah
Is 24:7 the v languisheth, all the
Is 32:12 fields, for the fruitful v
Is 34:4 the leaf falleth off from the v
Is 36:16 and eat ye every one of his v
Jer 2:21 Yet I had planted thee a noble v
Jer 2:21 plant of a strange v unto me
Jer 6:9 the remnant of Israel as a v
Jer 8:13 there shall be no grapes on the v
Jer 48:32 O v of Sibmah, I will weep for
Eze 15:2 What is the v tree more than any
Eze 15:6 As the v tree among the trees of
Eze 17:6 a spreading v of low stature
Eze 17:6 so it became a v, and brought
Eze 17:7 this v did bend her roots toward
Eze 17:8 that it might be a goodly v
Eze 19:10 mother is like a v in thy blood
Hos 10:1 Israel is an empty v, he bringeth
Hos 14:7 as the corn, and grow as the v
Joel 1:7 He hath laid my v waste, and
Joel 1:12 The v is dried up, and the fig
Joel 2:22 the v do yield their strength
Mic 4:4 shall sit every man under his v
Nah 2:2 out, and marred their v branches
Hag 2:19 yea, as yet the v, and the fig
Zec 3:10 man his neighbour under the v
Zec 8:12 the v shall give her fruit, and
Mal 3:11 neither shall your v cast her
Mt 26:29 henceforth of this fruit of the v
Mk 14:25 no more of the fruit of the v
Lk 22:18 not drink of the fruit of the v
Jn 15:1 I am the true v, and my Father is
Jn 15:4 itself, except it abide in the v
Jn 15:5 I am the v, ye are the branches
Jas 3:12 either a v, figs?
Rev 14:18 clusters of the v of the earth
Rev 14:19 and gathered the v of the earth

## VINEDRESSERS
2Kin 25:12 of the poor of the land to be v
Is 61:5 shall be your plowmen and your v
Jer 52:16 of the poor of the land for v
Joel 1:11 howl, O ye v, for the wheat and

## VINEGAR
Num 6:3 and shall drink no v of wine
Num 6:3 or v of strong drink, neither
Ruth 2:14 bread, and dip thy morsel in the v
Ps 69:21 my thirst they gave me v to drink
Prov 10:26 As v to the teeth, and as smoke to
Prov 25:20 as v upon nitre, so is he that
Mt 27:34 They gave him v to drink mingled
Mt 27:48 a spunge, and filled it with v
Mk 15:36 ran and filled a spunge full of v
Lk 23:36 coming to him, and offering him v
Jn 19:29 there was set a vessel full of v
Jn 19:29 and they filled a spunge with v
Jn 19:30 therefore had received the v

## VINES
Num 20:5 of seed, or of figs, or of v
Deut 8:8 A land of wheat, and barley, and v
Ps 78:47 He destroyed their v with hail
Ps 105:33 He smote their v also and their
Song 2:13 the v with the tender grape give
Song 2:15 little foxes, that spoil the v
Song 2:15 for our v have tender grapes
Is 7:23 v at a thousand silverlings
Jer 5:17 they shall eat up thy v and thy
Jer 31:5 Thou shalt yet plant v upon the
Hos 2:12 And I will destroy her v and her
Hab 3:17 neither shall fruit be in the v

## VINEYARD
Gen 9:20 an husbandman, and he planted a v
Ex 22:5 cause a field or v to be eaten
Ex 22:5 and of the best of his own v
Ex 23:11 manner thou shalt deal with thy v
Lev 19:10 And thou shalt not glean thy v
Lev 19:10 thou gather every grape of thy v
Lev 25:3 six years thou shalt prune thy v
Lev 25:4 sow thy field, nor prune thy v
Deut 20:6 man is he that hath planted a v
Deut 22:9 not sow thy v with divers seeds
Deut 22:9 hast sown, and the fruit of thy v
Deut 23:24 comest into thy neighbour's v
Deut 24:21 gatherest the grapes of thy v
Deut 28:30 thou shalt plant a v, and shalt
1Kin 21:1 Naboth the Jezreelite had a v
1Kin 21:2 Naboth, saying, Give me thy v
1Kin 21:2 thee for it a better v than it
1Kin 21:6 unto him, Give me thy v for money
1Kin 21:6 I will give thee another v for it
1Kin 21:6 I will not give thee my v
1Kin 21:7 I will give thee the v of Naboth
1Kin 21:15 take possession of the v of
1Kin 21:16 to the v of Naboth the Jezreelite
1Kin 21:18 behold, he is in the v of Naboth
Ps 80:15 the v which thy right hand hath
Prov 24:30 by the v of the man void of
Prov 31:16 of her hands she planteth a v
Song 1:6 but mine own v have I not kept
Song 8:11 Solomon had a v at Baal-hamon
Song 8:11 he let out the v unto keepers
Song 8:12 My v, which is mine, is before me
Is 1:8 Zion is left as a cottage in a v
Is 3:14 for ye have eaten up the v
Is 5:1 song of my beloved touching his v
Is 5:1 My wellbeloved hath a v in a very
Is 5:3 I pray you, betwixt me and my v
Is 5:4 could have been done more to my v
Is 5:5 tell you what I will do to my v
Is 5:7 For the v of the LORD of hosts is
Is 5:10 ten acres of v shall yield one
Is 27:2 sing ye unto her, A v of red wine
Jer 12:10 Many pastors have destroyed my v
Jer 35:7 house, nor sow seed, nor plant v
Jer 35:9 neither have we v, nor field, nor
Mic 1:6 the field, and as plantings of a v
Mt 20:1 to hire labourers into his v
Mt 20:2 a day, he sent them into his v
Mt 20:4 Go ye also into the v, and
Mt 20:7 unto them, Go ye also into the v
Mt 20:8 the lord of the v saith unto his
Mt 21:28 said, Son, go work to day in my v
Mt 21:33 householder, which planted a v
Mt 21:39 him, and cast him out of the v
Mt 21:40 lord therefore of the v cometh
Mt 21:41 will let out his v unto other
Mk 12:1 A certain man planted a v
Mk 12:2 husbandmen of the fruit of the v
Mk 12:8 him, and cast him out of the v
Mk 12:9 therefore the lord of the v do
Mk 12:9 and will give the v unto others
Lk 13:6 had a fig tree planted in his v
Lk 13:7 said he unto the dresser of his v
Lk 20:9 A certain man planted a v
Lk 20:10 give him of the fruit of the v
Lk 20:13 Then said the lord of the v
Lk 20:15 So they cast him out of the v
Lk 20:15 the lord of the v do unto them
Lk 20:16 and shall give the v to others
1Cor 9:7 who planteth a v, and eateth not

**VINEYARDS**
Num 16:14 us inheritance of fields and *v*
Num 20:17 the fields, or through the *v*
Num 21:22 into the fields, or into the *v*
Num 22:24 the LORD stood in a path of the *v*
Deut 6:11 which thou diggedst not, *v*
Deut 28:39 Thou shalt plant *v*, and dress them
Josh 24:13 of the *v* and oliveyards which ye
Judg 9:27 the fields, and gathered their *v*
Judg 11:33 and unto the plain of the *v*
Judg 14:5 and came to the *v* of Timnath
Judg 15:5 the standing corn, with the *v*
Judg 21:20 Go and lie in wait in the *v*
Judg 21:21 dances, then come ye out of the *v*
1Sa 8:14 will take your fields, and your *v*
1Sa 8:15 tenth of your seed, and of your *v*
1Sa 22:7 give every one of you fields and *v*
2Kin 5:26 garments, and oliveyards, and *v*
2Kin 18:32 and wine, a land of bread and *v*
2Kin 19:29 year sow ye, and reap, and plant *v*
1Chr 27:27 over the *v* was Shimei the
1Chr 27:27 over the increase of the *v* for
Neh 5:3 We have mortgaged our lands, *v*
Neh 5:4 and that upon our lands and *v*
Neh 5:5 for other men have our lands and *v*
Neh 5:11 this day, their lands, their *v*
Neh 9:25 of all goods, wells digged, *v*
Job 24:18 he beholdeth not the way of the *v*
Ps 107:37 And sow the fields, and plant *v*
Eccl 2:4 I planted me *v*
Song 1:6 they made me the keeper of the *v*
Song 1:14 of camphire in the *v* of En-gedi
Song 7:12 Let us get up early to the *v*
Is 16:10 in the *v* there shall be no
Is 36:17 and wine, a land of bread and *v*
Is 37:30 year sow ye, and reap, and plant *v*
Is 65:21 and they shall plant *v*, and eat the
Jer 32:15 *v* shall be possessed again in
Jer 39:10 the land of Judah, and gave them *v*
Eze 28:26 and shall build houses, and plant *v*
Hos 2:15 I will give her her *v* from thence
Amos 4:9 when your gardens and your *v*
Amos 5:11 ye have planted pleasant *v*
Amos 5:17 in all *v* shall be wailing
Amos 9:14 and they shall plant *v*, and drink
Zeph 1:13 and they shall plant *v*, but not

**VINTAGE**
Lev 26:5 threshing shall reach unto the *v*
Lev 26:5 the *v* shall reach unto the sowing
Judg 8:2 better than the *v* of Abi-ezer
Job 24:6 they gather the *v* of the wicked
Is 16:10 made their *v* shouting to cease
Is 24:13 grapes when the *v* is done
Is 32:10 for the *v* shall fail, the
Jer 48:32 thy summer fruits and upon thy *v*
Mic 7:1 as the grapegleanings of the *v*
Zec 11:2 the forest of the *v* is come down

**VIOL**
Is 5:12 And the harp, and the *v*, the tabret
Amos 6:5 That chant to the sound of the *v*

**VIOLATED**
Eze 22:26 Her priests have *v* my law

**VIOLENCE**
Gen 6:11 and the earth was filled with *v*
Gen 6:13 is filled with *v* through them
Lev 6:2 or in a thing taken away by *v*
2Sa 22:3 thou savest me from *v*
Ps 11:5 him that loveth *v* his soul hateth
Ps 55:9 for I have seen *v* and strife in
Ps 58:2 ye weigh the *v* of your hands in
Ps 72:14 their soul from deceit and *v*
Ps 73:6 *v* covereth them as a garment
Prov 4:17 and drink the wine of *v*
Prov 10:6 but *v* covereth the mouth of the
Prov 10:11 but *v* covereth the mouth of the
Prov 13:2 of the transgressors shall eat *v*
Prov 28:17 A man that doeth *v* to the blood
Is 53:9 because he had done no *v*, neither
Is 59:6 the act of *v* is in their hands
Is 60:18 *V* shall no more be heard in thy
Jer 6:7 *v* and spoil is heard in her
Jer 20:8 I spake, I cried out, I cried *v*
Jer 22:3 do no *v* to the stranger, the
Jer 22:17 and for oppression, and for *v*
Jer 51:35 The *v* done to me and to my flesh
Jer 51:46 *v* in the land, ruler against
Eze 7:11 *V* is risen up into a rod of
Eze 7:23 crimes, and the city is full of *v*
Eze 8:17 they have filled the land with *v*
Eze 12:19 because of the *v* of all them that
Eze 18:7 pledge, hath spoiled none by *v*
Eze 18:12 poor and needy, hath spoiled by *v*
Eze 18:16 pledge, neither hath spoiled by *v*
Eze 18:18 spoiled his brother by *v*
Eze 28:16 filled the midst of thee with *v*
Eze 45:9 remove *v* and spoil, and execute
Joel 3:19 for the *v* against the children of
Amos 3:10 saith the LORD, who store up *v*
Amos 6:3 cause the seat of *v* to come near
Obad 10 For thy *v* against thy brother
Jonah 3:8 from the *v* that is in their hands
Mic 2:2 covet fields, and take them by *v*
Mic 6:12 rich men thereof are full of *v*
Hab 1:2 even cry out unto thee of *v*
Hab 1:3 for spoiling and *v* are before me
Hab 1:9 They shall come all for *v*
Hab 2:8 for the *v* of the land, of the
Hab 2:17 For the *v* of Lebanon shall cover
Hab 2:17 for the *v* of the land, of the
Zeph 1:9 fill their masters' houses with *v*
Zeph 3:4 they have done *v* to the law
Mal 2:16 one covereth *v* with his garment
Mt 11:12 the kingdom of heaven suffereth *v*
Lk 3:14 Do *v* to no man, neither accuse
Acts 5:26 and brought them without *v*
Acts 21:35 soldiers for the *v* of the people
Acts 24:7 with great *v* took him away out of
Acts 27:41 broken with the *v* of the waves
Heb 11:34 Quenched the *v* of fire, escaped
Rev 18:21 Thus with *v* shall that great city

**VIOLENT**
2Sa 22:49 hast delivered me from the *v* man
Ps 7:16 his *v* dealing shall come down
Ps 18:48 hast delivered me from the *v* man
Ps 86:14 the assemblies of *v* men have
Ps 140:1 preserve me from the *v* man
Ps 140:4 preserve me from the *v* man
Ps 140:11 evil shall hunt the *v* man to
Prov 16:29 A *v* man enticeth his neighbour,
Eccl 5:8 *v* perverting of judgment and
Mt 11:12 and the *v* take it by force

**VIOLENTLY**
Gen 21:25 servants had *v* taken away
Lev 6:4 restore that which he took *v* away
Deut 28:31 thine ass shall be *v* taken away
Job 20:19 because he hath *v* taken away an
Job 24:2 they *v* take away flocks, and feed
Is 22:18 He will surely *v* turn and toss
Lam 2:6 And he hath *v* taken away his
Mt 8:32 the whole herd of swine ran *v*
Mk 5:13 the herd ran *v* down a steep place
Lk 8:33 the herd ran *v* down a steep place

**VIOLS**
Is 14:11 the grave, and the noise of thy *v*
Amos 5:23 will not hear the melody of thy *v*

**VIPER**
Is 30:6 come the young and old lion, the *v*
Is 59:5 is crushed breaketh out into a *v*
Acts 28:3 there came a *v* out of the heat,

**VIPER'S**
Job 20:16 the *v* tongue shall slay him

**VIPERS**
Mt 3:7 said unto them, O generation of *v*
Mt 12:34 O generation of *v*, how can ye,
Mt 23:33 Ye serpents, ye generation of *v*
Lk 3:7 of him, O generation of *v*

**VIRGIN**
Gen 24:16 was very fair to look upon, a *v*
Gen 24:43 that when the *v* cometh forth to
Lev 21:3 And for his sister a *v*, that is
Lev 21:14 but he shall take a *v* of his own
Deut 22:19 an evil name upon a *v* of Israel
Deut 22:23 If a damsel that is a *v* be
Deut 22:28 a man find a damsel that is a *v*
Deut 32:25 both the young man and the *v*
2Sa 13:2 for she was a *v*
1Kin 1:2 for my lord the king a young *v*
2Kin 19:21 The *v* the daughter of Zion hath
Is 7:14 a *v* shall conceive, and bear a son
Is 23:12 more rejoice, O thou oppressed *v*
Is 37:22 The *v*, the daughter of Zion, hath
Is 47:1 O *v* daughter of Babylon, sit on
Is 62:5 For as a young man marrieth a *v*
Jer 14:17 for the *v* daughter of my people
Jer 18:13 the *v* of Israel hath done a very
Jer 31:4 shalt be built, O *v* of Israel
Jer 31:13 Then shall the *v* rejoice in the
Jer 31:21 O *v* of Israel, turn again to
Jer 46:11 up into Gilead, and take balm, O *v*
Lam 1:15 the Lord hath trodden the *v*
Lam 2:13 thee, O *v* daughter of Zion
Joel 1:8 Lament like a *v* girded with
Amos 5:2 The *v* of Israel is fallen
Mt 1:23 a *v* shall be with child, and shall
Lk 1:27 To a *v* espoused to a man whose
1Cor 7:28 if a *v* marry, she hath not sinned
1Cor 7:34 also between a wife and a *v*
1Cor 7:36 himself uncomely toward his *v*
1Cor 7:37 his heart that he will keep his *v*
2Cor 11:2 you as a chaste *v* to Christ

**VIRGINITY**
Lev 21:13 And he shall take a wife in her *v*
Deut 22:15 the tokens of the damsel's *v* unto
Deut 22:17 are the tokens of my daughter's *v*
Deut 22:20 the tokens of *v* be not found for
Judg 11:37 the mountains, and bewail my *v*
Judg 11:38 bewailed her *v* upon the mountains
Eze 23:3 they bruised the teats of their *v*
Eze 23:8 they bruised the breasts of her *v*
Lk 2:36 an husband seven years from her *v*

**VIRGIN'S**
Lk 1:27 and the *v* name was Mary

**VIRGINS**
Ex 22:17 money according to the dowry of *v*
Judg 21:12 four hundred young *v*, that had
2Sa 13:18 daughters that were *v* apparelled
Est 2:2 fair young *v* sought for the king
Est 2:3 young *v* unto Shushan the palace
Est 2:17 in his sight more than all the *v*
Est 2:19 when the *v* were gathered together
Ps 45:14 the *v* her companions that follow
Song 1:3 therefore do the *v* love thee
Song 6:8 concubines, and *v* without number
Is 23:4 up young men, nor bring up *v*
Lam 1:4 her *v* are afflicted, and she is in
Lam 1:18 my *v* and my young men are gone
Lam 2:10 the *v* of Jerusalem hang down
Lam 2:21 my *v* and my young men are fallen
Amos 8:13 In that day shall the fair *v*
Mt 25:1 of heaven be likened unto ten *v*
Mt 25:7 Then all those *v* arose, and
Mt 25:11 Afterward came also the other *v*
Acts 21:9 same man had four daughters, *v*
1Cor 7:25 Now concerning *v* I have no
Rev 14:4 for they are *v*

**VIRTUE**
Mk 5:30 that *v* had gone out of him
Lk 6:19 for there went *v* out of him
Lk 8:46 perceive that *v* is gone out of me
Phil 4:8 if there be any *v*, and if there be
2Pet 1:3 that hath called us to glory and *v*
2Pet 1:5 diligence, add to your faith *v*
2Pet 1:5 and to *v* knowledge

**VIRTUOUS**
Ruth 3:11 doth know that thou art a *v* woman
Prov 12:4 A *v* woman is a crown to her
Prov 31:10 Who can find a *v* woman

**VIRTUOUSLY**
Prov 31:29 Many daughters have done *v*

**VISAGE**
Is 52:14 his *v* was so marred more than any
Lam 4:8 Their *v* is blacker than a coal
Dan 3:19 the form of his *v* was changed

**VISIBLE**
Col 1:16 heaven, and that are in earth, *v*

**VISION**
Gen 15:1 the LORD came unto Abram in a *v*
Num 12:6 make myself known unto him in a *v*
Num 24:4 which saw the *v* of the Almighty,
Num 24:16 which saw the *v* of the Almighty,
1Sa 3:1 there was no open *v*
1Sa 3:15 Samuel feared to shew Eli the *v*
2Sa 7:17 words, and according to all this *v*
1Chr 17:15 words, and according to all this *v*
2Chr 32:32 in the *v* of Isaiah the prophet
Job 20:8 chased away as a *v* of the night
Job 33:15 in a *v* of the night, when deep
Ps 89:19 thou spakest in *v* to thy holy one
Prov 29:18 Where there is no *v*, the people
Is 1:1 The *v* of Isaiah the son of Amoz,
Is 21:2 A grievous *v* is declared unto me
Is 22:1 The burden of the valley of *v*

Is 22:5 GOD of hosts in the valley of v
Is 28:7 they err in v, they stumble in
Is 29:7 shall be as a dream of a night v
Is 29:11 the v of all is become unto you
Jer 14:14 they prophesy unto you a false v
Jer 23:16 they speak a v of their own heart
Lam 2:9 also find no v from the LORD
Eze 7:13 for the v is touching the whole
Eze 7:26 they seek a v of the prophet
Eze 8:4 according to the v that I saw in
Eze 11:24 brought me in a v by the Spirit
Eze 11:24 So the v that I had seen went up
Eze 12:22 are prolonged, and every v faileth
Eze 12:23 at hand, and the effect of every v
Eze 12:24 vain v nor flattering divination
Eze 12:27 The v that he seeth is for many
Eze 13:7 Have ye not seen a vain v
Eze 43:3 appearance of the v which I saw
Eze 43:3 even according to the v that I
Eze 43:3 the visions were like the v that
Dan 2:19 revealed unto Daniel in a night v
Dan 7:2 and said, I saw in my v by night
Dan 8:1 Belshazzar a v appeared unto me
Dan 8:2 And I saw in a v
Dan 8:2 and I saw in a v, and I was by the
Dan 8:13 spake, How long shall be the v
Dan 8:15 I, even I Daniel, had seen the v
Dan 8:16 make this man to understand the v
Dan 8:17 time of the end shall be the v
Dan 8:26 the v of the evening and the
Dan 8:26 wherefore shut thou up the v
Dan 8:27 and I was astonished at the v
Dan 9:21 seen in the v at the beginning
Dan 9:23 the matter, and consider the v
Dan 9:24 and to seal up the v and prophecy,
Dan 10:1 and had understanding of the v
Dan 10:7 And I Daniel alone saw the v
Dan 10:7 that were with me saw not the v
Dan 10:8 left alone, and saw this great v
Dan 10:14 for yet the v is for many days
Dan 10:16 by the v my sorrows are turned
Dan 11:14 themselves to establish the v
Obad 1 The v of Obadiah
Mic 3:6 you, that ye shall not have a v
Nah 1:1 The book of the v of Nahum the
Hab 2:2 answered me, and said, Write the v
Hab 2:3 For the v is yet for an appointed
Zec 13:4 be ashamed every one of his v
Mt 17:9 Tell the v to no man, until the
Lk 1:22 he had seen a v in the temple
Lk 24:23 they had also seen a v of angels
Acts 9:10 and to him said the Lord in a v
Acts 9:12 hath seen in a v a man named
Acts 10:3 He saw in a v evidently about the
Acts 10:17 doubted in himself what this v
Acts 10:19 While Peter thought on the v
Acts 11:5 and in a trance I saw a v, A
Acts 12:9 but thought he saw a v
Acts 16:9 a v appeared to Paul in the night
Acts 16:10 And after he had seen the v
Acts 18:9 Lord to Paul in the night by a v
Acts 26:19 disobedient unto the heavenly v
Rev 9:17 And thus I saw the horses in the v

## VISIONS

Gen 46:2 unto Israel in the v of the night
2Chr 9:29 in the v of Iddo the seer against
2Chr 26:5 had understanding in the v of God
Job 4:13 thoughts from the v of the night
Job 7:14 and terrifiest me through v
Eze 1:1 were opened, and I saw v of God
Eze 8:3 brought me in the v of God to
Eze 13:16 which see v of peace for her, and
Eze 40:2 In the v of God brought he me
Eze 43:3 the v were like the vision that I
Dan 1:17 Daniel had understanding in all v
Dan 2:28 the v of thy head upon thy bed,
Dan 4:5 the v of my head troubled me
Dan 4:9 tell me the v of my dream that I
Dan 4:10 Thus were the v of mine head in
Dan 4:13 I saw in the v of my head upon my
Dan 7:1 v of his head upon his bed
Dan 7:7 After this I saw in the night v
Dan 7:13 I saw in the night v, and, behold,
Dan 7:15 the v of my head troubled me
Hos 12:10 prophets, and I have multiplied v
Joel 2:28 your young men shall see v
Acts 2:17 and your young men shall see v
2Cor 12:1 I will come to v and revelations

## VISIT

Gen 50:24 and God will surely v you, and
Gen 50:25 saying, God will surely v you
Ex 13:19 saying, God will surely v you
Ex 32:34 I v I will v their sin upon
Lev 18:25 therefore I do v the iniquity
Job 5:24 thou shalt v thy habitation, and
Job 7:18 shouldest v him every morning
Ps 59:5 awake to v all the heathen
Ps 80:14 heaven, and behold, and v this vine
Ps 89:32 Then will I v their transgression
Ps 106:4 O v me with thy salvation
Is 23:17 years, that the LORD will v Tyre
Jer 3:16 neither shall they v it
Jer 5:9 Shall I not v for these things
Jer 5:29 Shall I not v for these things
Jer 6:15 at the time that I v them they
Jer 9:9 Shall I not v them for these
Jer 14:10 their iniquity, and v their sins
Jer 15:15 v me, and revenge me of my
Jer 23:2 I will v upon you the evil of
Jer 27:22 be until the day that I v them
Jer 29:10 at Babylon I will v you, and
Jer 32:5 there shall he be until I v him
Jer 49:8 him, the time that I will v him
Jer 50:31 come, the time that I will v thee
Lam 4:22 he will v thine iniquity, O
Hos 2:13 I will v upon her the days of
Hos 8:13 their iniquity, and v their sins
Hos 9:9 iniquity, he will v their sins
Amos 3:14 v the transgressions of Israel
Amos 3:14 will also v the altars of Beth-el
Zeph 2:7 the LORD their God shall v them
Zec 11:16 which shall not v those that be
Acts 7:23 it came into his heart to v his
Acts 15:14 at the first did v the Gentiles
Acts 15:36 v our brethren in every city
Jas 1:27 To v the fatherless and widows in

## VISITATION

Num 16:29 be visited after the v of all men
Job 10:12 thy v hath preserved my spirit
Is 10:3 what will ye do in the day of v
Jer 8:12 in the time of their v they shall
Jer 10:15 time of their v they shall perish
Jer 11:23 even the year of their v
Jer 23:12 them, even the year of their v
Jer 46:21 upon them, and the time of their v
Jer 48:44 upon Moab, the year of their v
Jer 50:27 day is come, the time of their v
Jer 51:18 time of their v they shall perish
Hos 9:7 The days of v are come, the days
Mic 7:4 of thy watchmen and thy v cometh
Lk 19:44 knewest not the time of thy v
1Pet 2:12 glorify God in the day of v

## VISITED

Gen 21:1 the LORD v Sarah as he had said,
Ex 3:16 me, saying, I have surely v you
Ex 4:31 LORD had v the children of Israel
Num 16:29 or if they be v after the
Judg 15:1 that Samson v his wife with a kid
Ruth 1:6 of Moab how that the LORD had v
1Sa 2:21 And the LORD v Hannah, so that she
Job 35:15 is not so, he hath v in his anger
Ps 17:3 thou hast v me in the night
Prov 19:23 he shall not be v with evil
Is 24:22 after many days shall they be v
Is 26:14 therefore hast thou v and
Is 26:16 LORD, in trouble have they v thee
Is 29:6 Thou shalt be v of the LORD of
Jer 6:6 this is the city to be v
Jer 23:2 them away, and have not v them
Eze 38:8 After many days thou shalt be v
Zec 10:3 for the LORD of hosts hath v his
Mt 25:36 I was sick, and ye v me
Mt 25:43 and in prison, and ye v me not
Lk 1:68 for he hath v and redeemed his
Lk 1:78 dayspring from on high hath v us
Lk 7:16 and, That God hath v his people

## VISITEST

Ps 8:4 the son of man, that thou v him
Ps 65:9 Thou v the earth, and waterest it
Heb 2:6 the son of man, that thou v him

## VISITETH

Job 31:14 and when he v, what shall I answer

## VISITING

Ex 20:5 v the iniquity of the fathers
Ex 34:7 v the iniquity of the fathers
Num 14:18 v the iniquity of the fathers
Deut 5:9 v the iniquity of the fathers

## VOCATION

Eph 4:1 of the v wherewith ye are called

## VOICE

Gen 3:8 they heard the v of the LORD God
Gen 3:10 I heard thy v in the garden, and I
Gen 3:17 hearkened unto the v of thy wife
Gen 4:10 the v of thy brother's blood
Gen 4:23 wives, Adah and Zillah, Hear my v
Gen 16:2 Abram hearkened to the v of Sarai
Gen 21:12 unto thee, hearken unto her v
Gen 21:16 against him, and lift up her v
Gen 21:17 And God heard the v of the lad
Gen 21:17 the v of the lad where he is
Gen 22:18 because thou hast obeyed my v
Gen 26:5 Because that Abraham obeyed my v
Gen 27:8 obey my v according to that which
Gen 27:13 only obey my v, and go fetch me
Gen 27:22 and said, The v is Jacob's v
Gen 27:38 And Esau lifted up his v, and wept
Gen 27:43 Now therefore, my son, obey my v
Gen 29:11 kissed Rachel, and lifted up his v
Gen 30:6 me, and hath also heard my v
Gen 39:14 with me, and I cried with a loud v
Gen 39:15 he heard that I lifted up my v
Gen 39:18 came to pass, as I lifted up my v
Ex 3:18 And they shall hearken to thy v
Ex 4:1 believe me, nor hearken unto my v
Ex 4:8 to the v of the first sign
Ex 4:8 believe the v of the latter sign
Ex 4:9 signs, neither hearken unto thy v
Ex 5:2 obey his v to let Israel go
Ex 15:26 to the v of the LORD thy God
Ex 18:19 Hearken now unto my v, I will
Ex 18:24 to the v of his father in law
Ex 19:5 if ye will obey my v indeed
Ex 19:16 the v of the trumpet exceeding
Ex 19:19 when the v of the trumpet sounded
Ex 19:19 spake, and God answered him by a v
Ex 23:21 Beware of him, and obey his v
Ex 23:22 if thou shalt indeed obey his v
Ex 24:3 the people answered with one v
Ex 32:18 It is not the v of them that
Ex 32:18 neither is it the v of them that
Lev 5:1 hear the v of swearing, and is a
Num 7:89 then he heard the v of one
Num 14:1 congregation lifted up their v
Num 14:22 and have not hearkened to my v
Num 20:16 unto the LORD, he heard our v
Num 21:3 LORD hearkened to the v of Israel
Deut 1:34 LORD heard the v of your words
Deut 1:45 LORD would not hearken to your v
Deut 4:12 ye heard the v of the words
Deut 4:12 only ye heard a v
Deut 4:30 and shalt be obedient unto his v
Deut 4:33 Did ever people hear the v of God
Deut 4:36 heaven he made thee to hear his v
Deut 5:22 thick darkness, with a great v
Deut 5:23 when ye heard the v out of the
Deut 5:24 we have heard his v out of the
Deut 5:25 if we hear the v of the LORD our
Deut 5:26 that hath heard the v of the
Deut 5:28 LORD heard the v of your words
Deut 5:28 I have heard the v of the words
Deut 8:20 unto the v of the LORD your God
Deut 9:23 him not, nor hearkened to his v
Deut 13:4 his commandments, and obey his v
Deut 13:18 to the v of the LORD thy God
Deut 15:5 unto the v of the LORD thy God
Deut 18:16 again the v of the LORD my God
Deut 21:18 will not obey the v of his father
Deut 21:18 or the v of his mother, and that,
Deut 21:20 he will not obey our v
Deut 26:7 our fathers, the LORD heard our v
Deut 26:14 to the v of the LORD my God
Deut 26:17 and to hearken unto his v
Deut 27:10 obey the v of the LORD thy God
Deut 27:14 the men of Israel with a loud v
Deut 28:1 unto the v of the LORD thy God
Deut 28:2 unto the v of the LORD thy God
Deut 28:15 unto the v of the LORD thy God
Deut 28:45 unto the v of the LORD thy God
Deut 28:62 obey the v of the LORD thy God
Deut 30:2 shalt obey his v according to all
Deut 30:8 obey the v of the LORD, and do all
Deut 30:10 unto the v of the LORD thy God
Deut 30:20 and that thou mayest obey his v
Deut 33:7 the v of Judah, and bring him unto

Josh 5:6 they obeyed not the *v* of the LORD
Josh 6:10 nor make any noise with your *v*
Josh 10:14 hearkened unto the *v* of a man
Josh 22:2 have obeyed my *v* in all that I
Josh 24:24 we serve, and his *v* will we obey
Judg 2:2 but ye have not obeyed my *v*
Judg 2:4 that the people lifted up their *v*
Judg 2:20 and have not hearkened unto my *v*
Judg 6:10 but ye have not obeyed my *v*
Judg 9:7 mount Gerizim, and lifted up his *v*
Judg 13:9 God hearkened to the *v* of Manoah
Judg 18:3 they knew the *v* of the young man
Judg 18:25 Let not thy *v* be heard among us,
Judg 20:13 would not hearken to the *v* of
Ruth 1:9 and they lifted up their *v*
Ruth 1:14 And they lifted up their *v*
1Sa 1:13 moved, but her *v* was not heard
1Sa 2:25 not unto the *v* of their father
1Sa 8:7 Hearken unto the *v* of the people
1Sa 8:9 therefore hearken unto their *v*
1Sa 8:19 refused to obey the *v* of Samuel
1Sa 8:22 to Samuel, Hearken unto their *v*
1Sa 12:1 I have hearkened unto your *v* in
1Sa 12:14 LORD, and serve him, and obey his *v*
1Sa 12:15 will not obey the *v* of the LORD
1Sa 15:1 the *v* of the words of the LORD
1Sa 15:19 thou not obey the *v* of the LORD
1Sa 15:20 I have obeyed the *v* of the LORD
1Sa 15:22 as in obeying the *v* of the LORD
1Sa 15:24 the people, and obeyed their *v*
1Sa 19:6 hearkened unto the *v* of Jonathan
1Sa 24:16 that Saul said, Is this thy *v*
1Sa 24:16 And Saul lifted up his *v*, and wept
1Sa 25:35 see, I have hearkened to thy *v*
1Sa 26:17 And Saul knew David's *v*
1Sa 26:17 and said, Is this thy *v*
1Sa 26:17 And David said, It is my *v*
1Sa 28:12 Samuel, she cried with a loud *v*
1Sa 28:18 obeyedst not the *v* of the LORD
1Sa 28:21 thine handmaid hath obeyed thy *v*
1Sa 28:22 also unto the *v* of thine handmaid
1Sa 28:23 and he hearkened unto their *v*
1Sa 30:4 were with him lifted up their *v*
2Sa 3:32 and the king lifted up his *v*
2Sa 12:18 he would not hearken unto our *v*
2Sa 13:14 he would not hearken unto her *v*
2Sa 13:36 sons came, and lifted up their *v*
2Sa 15:23 the country wept with a loud *v*
2Sa 19:4 and the king cried with a loud *v*
2Sa 19:35 any more the *v* of singing men
2Sa 22:7 he did hear my *v* out of his
2Sa 22:14 and the most High uttered his *v*
1Kin 8:55 of Israel with a loud *v*, saying,
1Kin 17:22 And the LORD heard the *v* of Elijah
1Kin 18:26 But there was no *v*, nor any that
1Kin 18:29 that there was neither *v*
1Kin 19:12 and after the fire a still small *v*
1Kin 19:13 behold, there came a *v* unto him
1Kin 20:25 And he hearkened unto their *v*
1Kin 20:36 hast not obeyed the *v* of the LORD
2Kin 4:31 but there was neither *v*, nor
2Kin 7:10 no man there, neither *v* of man
2Kin 10:6 and if ye will hearken unto my *v*
2Kin 18:12 not the *v* of the LORD their God
2Kin 18:28 cried with a loud *v* in the Jews'
2Kin 19:22 whom hast thou exalted thy *v*
1Chr 15:16 by lifting up the *v* with joy
2Chr 5:13 up their *v* with the trumpets
2Chr 15:14 sware unto the LORD with a loud *v*
2Chr 20:19 of Israel with a loud *v* on high
2Chr 30:27 their *v* was heard, and their
2Chr 32:18 Then they cried with a loud *v* in
Ezr 3:12 their eyes, wept with a loud *v*
Ezr 10:12 answered and said with a loud *v*
Neh 9:4 cried with a loud *v* unto the LORD
Job 2:12 him not, they lifted up their *v*
Job 3:7 let no joyful *v* come therein
Job 3:18 hear not the *v* of the oppressor
Job 4:10 the *v* of the fierce lion, and the
Job 4:16 there was silence, and I heard a *v*
Job 9:16 that he had hearkened unto my *v*
Job 30:31 into the *v* of them that weep
Job 33:8 I have heard the *v* of thy words
Job 34:16 hearken to the *v* of my words
Job 37:2 attentively the noise of his *v*
Job 37:4 After it a *v* roareth
Job 37:4 with the *v* of his excellency
Job 37:4 not stay them when his *v* is heard
Job 37:5 marvellously with his *v*
Job 38:34 thou lift up thy *v* to the clouds
Job 40:9 thou thunder with a *v* like him
Ps 3:4 I cried unto the LORD with my *v*
Ps 5:2 Hearken unto the *v* of my cry
Ps 5:3 My *v* shalt thou hear in the
Ps 6:8 hath heard the *v* of my weeping
Ps 18:6 he heard my *v* out of his temple,
Ps 18:13 and the Highest gave his *v*
Ps 19:3 where their *v* is not heard
Ps 26:7 with the *v* of thanksgiving
Ps 27:7 O LORD, when I cry with my *v*
Ps 28:2 Hear the *v* of my supplications,
Ps 28:6 heard the *v* of my supplications
Ps 29:3 The *v* of the LORD is upon the
Ps 29:4 The *v* of the LORD is powerful
Ps 29:4 the *v* of the LORD is full of
Ps 29:5 The *v* of the LORD breaketh the
Ps 29:7 The *v* of the LORD divideth the
Ps 29:8 The *v* of the LORD shaketh the
Ps 29:9 The *v* of the LORD maketh the
Ps 31:22 the *v* of my supplications when I
Ps 42:4 house of God, with the *v* of joy
Ps 44:16 For the *v* of him that reproacheth
Ps 46:6 he uttered his *v*, the earth
Ps 47:1 unto God with the *v* of triumph
Ps 55:3 Because of the *v* of the enemy
Ps 55:17 and he shall hear my *v*
Ps 58:5 not hearken to the *v* of charmers
Ps 64:1 Hear my *v*, O God, in my prayer
Ps 66:8 make the *v* of his praise to be
Ps 66:19 attended to the *v* of my prayer
Ps 68:33 out his *v*, and that a mighty *v*
Ps 74:23 Forget not the *v* of thine enemies
Ps 77:1 I cried unto God with my *v*
Ps 77:1 even unto God with my *v*
Ps 77:18 The *v* of thy thunder was in the
Ps 81:11 people would not hearken to my *v*
Ps 86:6 and attend to the *v* of my
Ps 93:3 the floods have lifted up their *v*
Ps 95:7 To day if ye will hear his *v*
Ps 98:5 the harp, and the *v* of a psalm
Ps 102:5 By reason of the *v* of my groaning
Ps 103:20 hearkening unto the *v* of his word
Ps 104:7 at the *v* of thy thunder they
Ps 106:25 not unto the *v* of the LORD
Ps 116:1 LORD, because he hath heard my *v*
Ps 118:15 The *v* of rejoicing and salvation
Ps 119:149 Hear my *v* according unto thy
Ps 130:2 Lord, hear my *v*
Ps 130:2 to the *v* of my supplications
Ps 140:6 hear the *v* of my supplications, O
Ps 141:1 give ear unto my *v*, when I cry
Ps 142:1 I cried unto the LORD with my *v*
Ps 142:1 with my *v* unto the LORD did I
Prov 1:20 she uttereth her *v* in the streets
Prov 2:3 and liftest up thy *v* for
Prov 5:13 not obeyed the *v* of my teachers
Prov 8:1 and understanding put forth her *v*
Prov 8:4 my *v* is to the sons of man
Prov 27:14 blesseth his friend with a loud *v*
Eccl 5:3 a fool's *v* is known by multitude
Eccl 5:6 should God be angry at thy *v*
Eccl 10:20 bird of the air shall carry the *v*
Eccl 12:4 rise up at the *v* of the bird
Song 2:8 The *v* of my beloved
Song 2:12 the *v* of the turtle is heard in
Song 2:14 countenance, let me hear thy *v*
Song 2:14 for sweet is thy *v*, and thy
Song 5:2 it is the *v* of my beloved that
Song 8:13 the companions hearken to thy *v*
Is 6:4 moved at the *v* of him that cried
Is 6:8 Also I heard the *v* of the Lord
Is 10:30 Lift up thy *v*, O daughter of
Is 13:2 mountain, exalt the *v* unto them
Is 15:4 their *v* shall be heard even unto
Is 24:14 They shall lift up their *v*
Is 28:23 Give ye ear, and hear my *v*
Is 29:4 thy *v* shall be, as of one that
Is 30:19 unto thee at the *v* of thy cry
Is 30:30 cause his glorious *v* to be heard
Is 30:31 For through the *v* of the LORD
Is 31:4 he will not be afraid of their *v*
Is 32:9 hear my *v*, ye careless daughters
Is 36:13 cried with a loud *v* in the Jews'
Is 37:23 whom hast thou exalted thy *v*
Is 40:3 The *v* of him that crieth in the
Is 40:6 The *v* said, Cry
Is 40:9 lift up thy *v* with strength
Is 42:2 nor cause his *v* to be heard in
Is 42:11 cities thereof lift up their *v*
Is 48:20 with a *v* of singing declare ye,
Is 50:10 that obeyeth the *v* of his servant
Is 51:3 thanksgiving, and the *v* of melody
Is 52:8 Thy watchmen shall lift up the *v*
Is 52:8 with the *v* together shall they
Is 58:1 lift up thy *v* like a trumpet, and
Is 58:4 to make your *v* to be heard on
Is 65:19 the *v* of weeping shall be no more
Is 65:19 heard in her, nor the *v* of crying
Is 66:6 A *v* of noise from the city
Is 66:6 a *v* from the temple
Is 66:6 a *v* of the LORD that rendereth
Jer 3:13 tree, and ye have not obeyed my *v*
Jer 3:21 A *v* was heard upon the high
Jer 3:25 obeyed the *v* of the LORD our God
Jer 4:15 For a *v* declareth from Dan, and
Jer 4:16 give out their *v* against the
Jer 4:31 For I have heard a *v* as of a
Jer 4:31 the *v* of the daughter of Zion,
Jer 6:23 their *v* roareth like the sea
Jer 7:23 I them, saying, Obey my *v*
Jer 7:28 not the *v* of the LORD their God
Jer 7:34 the *v* of mirth
Jer 7:34 the *v* of gladness
Jer 7:34 the *v* of the bridegroom
Jer 7:34 and the *v* of the bride
Jer 8:19 Behold the *v* of the cry of the
Jer 9:10 can men hear the *v* of the cattle
Jer 9:13 them, and have not obeyed my *v*
Jer 9:19 For a *v* of wailing is heard out
Jer 10:13 When he uttereth his *v*, there is
Jer 11:4 iron furnace, saying, Obey my *v*
Jer 11:7 and protesting, saying, Obey my *v*
Jer 16:9 the *v* of mirth
Jer 16:9 the *v* of gladness
Jer 16:9 the *v* of the bridegroom
Jer 16:9 and the *v* of the bride
Jer 18:10 my sight, that it obey not my *v*
Jer 18:19 hearken to the *v* of them that
Jer 22:20 and lift up thy *v* in Bashan
Jer 22:21 that thou obeyedst not my *v*
Jer 25:10 take from them the *v* of mirth
Jer 25:10 the *v* of gladness
Jer 25:10 the *v* of the bridegroom
Jer 25:10 the *v* of the bride
Jer 25:30 utter his *v* from his holy
Jer 25:36 A *v* of the cry of the shepherds,
Jer 26:13 obey the *v* of the LORD your God
Jer 30:5 We have heard a *v* of trembling
Jer 30:19 the *v* of them that make merry
Jer 31:15 A *v* was heard in Ramah,
Jer 31:16 Refrain thy *v* from weeping, and
Jer 32:23 but they obeyed not thy *v*
Jer 33:11 The *v* of joy
Jer 33:11 the *v* of gladness
Jer 33:11 the *v* of the bridegroom
Jer 33:11 the *v* of the bride
Jer 33:11 the *v* of them that shall say,
Jer 35:8 Thus have we obeyed the *v* of
Jer 38:20 the *v* of the LORD, which I speak
Jer 40:3 LORD, and have not obeyed his *v*
Jer 42:6 we will obey the *v* of the LORD
Jer 42:6 when we obey the *v* of the LORD
Jer 42:13 neither obey the *v* of the LORD
Jer 42:21 obeyed the *v* of the LORD your God
Jer 43:4 obeyed not the *v* of the LORD
Jer 43:7 they obeyed not the *v* of the LORD
Jer 44:23 have not obeyed the *v* of the LORD
Jer 46:22 The *v* thereof shall go like a
Jer 48:3 A *v* of crying shall be from
Jer 48:34 Jahaz, have they uttered their *v*
Jer 50:28 The *v* of them that flee and escape
Jer 50:42 their *v* shall roar like the sea,
Jer 51:16 When he uttereth his *v*, there is
Jer 51:55 destroyed out of her the great *v*
Jer 51:55 a noise of their *v* is uttered
Lam 3:56 Thou hast heard my *v*
Eze 1:24 as the *v* of the Almighty, the
Eze 1:24 the *v* of speech, as the noise of
Eze 1:25 there was a *v* from the firmament
Eze 1:28 I heard a *v* of one that spake
Eze 3:12 behind me a *v* of a great rushing
Eze 8:18 cry in mine ears with a loud *v*
Eze 9:1 also in mine ears with a loud *v*
Eze 10:5 as the *v* of the Almighty God when
Eze 11:13 my face, and cried with a loud *v*
Eze 19:9 that his *v* should no more be
Eze 21:22 to lift up the *v* with shouting
Eze 23:42 a *v* of a multitude being at ease
Eze 27:30 shall cause their *v* to be heard
Eze 33:32 of one that hath a pleasant *v*

Eze 43:2 his *v* was like a noise of many
Dan 4:31 mouth, there fell a *v* from heaven
Dan 6:20 with a lamentable *v* unto Daniel
Dan 7:11 *v* of the great words which the
Dan 8:16 I heard a man's *v* between the
Dan 9:10 obeyed the *v* of the LORD our God
Dan 9:11 that they might not obey thy *v*
Dan 9:14 for we obeyed not his *v*
Dan 10:6 the *v* of his words like the
Dan 10:6 words like the *v* of a multitude
Dan 10:9 Yet heard I the *v* of his words
Dan 10:9 when I heard the *v* of his words
Joel 2:11 shall utter his *v* before his army
Joel 3:16 utter his *v* from Jerusalem
Amos 1:2 utter his *v* from Jerusalem
Jonah 2:2 cried I, and thou heardest my *v*
Jonah 2:9 thee with the *v* of thanksgiving
Mic 6:1 and let the hills hear thy *v*
Mic 6:9 The LORD's *v* crieth unto the city
Nah 2:7 lead her as with the *v* of doves
Nah 2:13 the *v* of thy messengers shall no
Hab 3:10 the deep uttered his *v*, and lifted
Hab 3:16 my lips quivered at the *v*
Zeph 1:14 even the *v* of the day of the LORD
Zeph 2:14 their *v* shall sing in the windows
Zeph 3:2 She obeyed not the *v*
Hag 1:12 obeyed the *v* of the LORD their
Zec 6:15 obey the *v* of the LORD your God
Zec 11:3 There is a *v* of the howling of
Zec 11:3 a *v* of the roaring of young lions
Mt 2:18 In Rama was there a *v* heard
Mt 3:3 The *v* of one crying in the
Mt 3:17 lo a *v* from heaven, saying, This
Mt 12:19 any man hear his *v* in the streets
Mt 17:5 behold a *v* out of the cloud,
Mt 27:46 hour Jesus cried with a loud *v*
Mt 27:50 he had cried again with a loud *v*
Mk 1:3 The *v* of one crying in the
Mk 1:11 And there came a *v* from heaven
Mk 1:26 torn him, and cried with a loud *v*
Mk 5:7 And cried with a loud *v*, and said,
Mk 9:7 a *v* came out of the cloud, saying
Mk 15:34 hour Jesus cried with a loud *v*
Mk 15:37 And Jesus cried with a loud *v*
Lk 1:42 And she spake out with a loud *v*
Lk 1:44 For, lo, as soon as the *v* of thy
Lk 3:4 The *v* of one crying in the
Lk 3:22 a *v* came from heaven, which said,
Lk 4:33 devil, and cried out with a loud *v*
Lk 8:28 before him, and with a loud *v* said
Lk 9:35 there came a *v* out of the cloud,
Lk 9:36 And when the *v* was past, Jesus was
Lk 11:27 of the company lifted up her *v*
Lk 17:15 with a loud *v* glorified God,
Lk 19:37 praise God with a loud *v* for all
Lk 23:46 Jesus had cried with a loud *v*
Jn 1:23 I am the *v* of one crying in the
Jn 3:29 because of the bridegroom's *v*
Jn 5:25 hear the *v* of the Son of God
Jn 5:28 in the graves shall hear his *v*
Jn 5:37 neither heard his *v* at any time
Jn 10:3 and the sheep hear his *v*
Jn 10:4 for they know his *v*
Jn 10:5 they know not the *v* of strangers
Jn 10:16 bring, and they shall hear my *v*
Jn 10:27 My sheep hear my *v*, and I know
Jn 11:43 spoken, he cried with a loud *v*
Jn 12:28 Then came there a *v* from heaven
Jn 12:30 This *v* came not because of me,
Jn 18:37 that is of the truth heareth my *v*
Acts 2:14 with the eleven, lifted up his *v*
Acts 4:24 they lifted up their *v* to God
Acts 7:31 the *v* of the Lord came unto him,
Acts 7:57 Then they cried out with a loud *v*
Acts 7:60 down, and cried with a loud *v*
Acts 8:7 spirits, crying with loud *v*
Acts 9:4 heard a *v* saying unto him, Saul,
Acts 9:7 him stood speechless, hearing a *v*
Acts 10:13 And there came a *v* to him, Rise,
Acts 10:15 the *v* spake unto him again the
Acts 11:7 I heard a *v* saying unto me, Arise
Acts 11:9 But the *v* answered me again from
Acts 12:14 And when she knew Peter's *v*
Acts 12:22 saying, It is the *v* of a god
Acts 14:10 Said with a loud *v*, Stand upright
Acts 16:28 But Paul cried with a loud *v*
Acts 19:34 all with one *v* about the space of
Acts 22:7 heard a *v* saying unto me, Saul,
Acts 22:9 but they heard not the *v* of him
Acts 22:14 shouldest hear the *v* of his mouth
Acts 24:21 Except it be for this one *v*
Acts 26:10 death, I gave my *v* against them
Acts 26:14 I heard a *v* speaking unto me, and
Acts 26:24 Festus said with a loud *v*
1Cor 14:11 I know not the meaning of the *v*
1Cor 14:19 that by my *v* I might teach others
Gal 4:20 with you now, and to change my *v*
1Th 4:16 with the *v* of the archangel, and
Heb 3:7 To day if ye will hear his *v*
Heb 3:15 To day if ye will hear his *v*
Heb 4:7 To day if ye will hear his *v*
Heb 12:19 of a trumpet, and the *v* of words
Heb 12:19 which *v* they that heard intreated
Heb 12:26 Whose *v* then shook the earth
2Pet 1:17 when there came such a *v* to him
2Pet 1:18 this *v* which came from heaven we
2Pet 2:16 man's *v* forbad the madness of the
Rev 1:10 day, and heard behind me a great *v*
Rev 1:12 to see the *v* that spake with me
Rev 1:15 his *v* as the sound of many waters
Rev 3:20 if any man hear my *v*, and open the
Rev 4:1 the first *v* which I heard was as
Rev 5:2 angel proclaiming with a loud *v*
Rev 5:11 I heard the *v* of many angels
Rev 5:12 Saying with a loud *v*, Worthy is
Rev 6:6 I heard a *v* in the midst of the
Rev 6:7 I heard the *v* of the fourth beast
Rev 6:10 And they cried with a loud *v*
Rev 7:2 with a loud *v* to the four angels
Rev 7:10 And cried with a loud *v*, saying,
Rev 8:13 of heaven, saying with a loud *v*
Rev 9:13 I heard a *v* from the four horns
Rev 10:3 And cried with a loud *v*, as when a
Rev 10:4 I heard a *v* from heaven saying
Rev 10:7 of the *v* of the seventh angel
Rev 10:8 the *v* which I heard from heaven
Rev 11:12 they heard a great *v* from heaven
Rev 12:10 I heard a loud *v* saying in heaven
Rev 14:2 I heard a *v* from heaven
Rev 14:2 as the *v* of many waters
Rev 14:2 as the *v* of a great thunder
Rev 14:2 I heard the *v* of harpers harping
Rev 14:7 Saying with a loud *v*, Fear God,
Rev 14:9 them, saying with a loud *v*
Rev 14:13 I heard a *v* from heaven saying
Rev 14:15 crying with a loud *v* to him that
Rev 16:1 I heard a great *v* out of the
Rev 16:17 there came a great *v* out of the
Rev 18:2 he cried mightily with a strong *v*
Rev 18:4 And I heard another *v* from heaven
Rev 18:22 the *v* of harpers, and musicians,
Rev 18:23 the *v* of the bridegroom and of the
Rev 19:1 great *v* of much people in heaven
Rev 19:5 a *v* came out of the throne,
Rev 19:6 were the *v* of a great multitude
Rev 19:6 as the *v* of many waters
Rev 19:6 as the *v* of mighty thunderings,
Rev 19:17 and he cried with a loud *v*
Rev 21:3 I heard a great *v* out of heaven

**VOICES**
Judg 21:2 before God, and lifted up their *v*
1Sa 11:4 all the people lifted up their *v*
Lk 17:13 And they lifted up their *v*
Lk 23:23 And they were instant with loud *v*
Lk 23:23 the *v* of them and of the chief
Acts 13:27 nor yet the *v* of the prophets
Acts 14:11 had done, they lifted up their *v*
Acts 22:22 word, and then lifted up their *v*
1Cor 14:10 so many kinds of *v* in the world
Rev 4:5 lightnings and thunderings and *v*
Rev 8:5 and there were *v*, and thunderings,
Rev 8:13 *v* of the trumpet of the three
Rev 10:3 seven thunders uttered their *v*
Rev 10:4 thunders had uttered their *v*
Rev 11:15 and there were great *v* in heaven
Rev 11:19 and there were lightnings, and *v*
Rev 16:18 And there were *v*, and thunders, and

**VOID**
Gen 1:2 the earth was without form, and *v*
Num 30:12 them *v* on the day he heard them
Num 30:12 her husband hath made them *v*
Num 30:13 it, or her husband may make it *v*
Num 30:15 *v* after that he hath heard them
Deut 32:28 they are a nation *v* of counsel
1Kin 22:10 in a *v* place in the entrance of
2Chr 18:9 they sat in a *v* place at the
Ps 89:39 Thou hast made *v* the covenant of
Ps 119:126 for they have made *v* thy law
Prov 7:7 a young man *v* of understanding,
Prov 10:13 of him that is *v* of understanding
Prov 11:12 He that is *v* of wisdom despiseth
Prov 12:11 persons is *v* of understanding
Prov 17:18 A man *v* of understanding striketh
Prov 24:30 of the man *v* of understanding
Is 55:11 it shall not return unto me *v*
Jer 4:23 and, lo, it was without form, and *v*
Jer 19:7 I will make *v* the counsel of
Nah 2:10 She is empty, and *v*, and waste
Acts 24:16 *v* of offence toward God, and
Rom 3:31 Do we then make *v* the law through
Rom 4:14 the law be heirs, faith is made *v*
1Cor 9:15 any man should make my glorying *v*

**VOLUME**
Ps 40:7 in the *v* of the book it is
Heb 10:7 I come (in the *v* of the book it

**VOLUNTARILY**
Eze 46:12 peace offerings *v* unto the LORD

**VOLUNTARY**
Lev 1:3 his own *v* will at the door of the
Lev 7:16 or a *v* offering, it shall be
Eze 46:12 a *v* burnt offering or peace
Col 2:18 of your reward in a *v* humility

**VOMIT**
Job 20:15 and he shall *v* them up again
Prov 23:8 thou hast eaten shalt thou *v* up
Prov 25:16 thou be filled therewith, and *v* it
Prov 26:11 As a dog returneth to his *v*
Is 19:14 a drunken man staggereth in his *v*
Is 28:8 For all tables are full of *v*
Jer 48:26 Moab also shall wallow in his *v*
2Pet 2:22 dog is turned to his own *v* again

**VOMITED**
Jonah 2:10 it *v* out Jonah upon the dry land

**VOMITETH**
Lev 18:25 the land itself *v* out her

**VOPHSI** *(vof'-si) A spy sent to the Promised Land.*
Num 13:14 of Naphtali, Nahbi the son of V

**VOW**
Gen 28:20 And Jacob vowed a *v*, saying, If
Gen 31:13 and where thou vowedst a *v* unto me
Lev 7:16 sacrifice of his offering be a *v*
Lev 22:21 unto the LORD to accomplish his *v*
Lev 22:23 but for a *v* it shall not be
Lev 27:2 a man shall make a singular *v*
Num 6:2 separate themselves to *v*
Num 6:2 a *v* of a Nazarite, to
Num 6:5 All the days of the *v* of his
Num 6:21 according to the *v* which he vowed
Num 15:3 or a sacrifice in performing a *v*
Num 15:8 for a sacrifice in performing a *v*
Num 21:2 And Israel vowed a *v* unto the LORD
Num 30:2 If a man *v* a
Num 30:2 a *v* unto the LORD
Num 30:3 If a woman also *v* a
Num 30:3 a *v* unto the LORD
Num 30:4 And her father hear her *v*, and her
Num 30:8 shall make her *v* which she vowed
Num 30:9 But every *v* of a widow, and of her
Num 30:13 Every *v*, and every binding oath to
Deut 12:11 vows which ye *v* unto the LORD
Deut 23:18 of the LORD thy God for any *v*
Deut 23:21 When thou shalt *v* a
Deut 23:21 a *v* unto the LORD thy God
Deut 23:22 But if thou shalt forbear to *v*
Judg 11:30 Jephthah vowed a *v* unto the LORD
Judg 11:39 to his *v* which he had vowed
1Sa 1:11 And she vowed a *v*, and said, O LORD
1Sa 1:21 the yearly sacrifice, and his *v*
2Sa 15:7 pray thee, let me go and pay my *v*
2Sa 15:8 For thy servant vowed a *v* while I
Ps 65:1 thee shall the *v* be performed
Ps 76:11 *V*, and pay unto the LORD your God
Eccl 5:4 When thou vowest a *v* unto God
Eccl 5:5 is it that thou shouldest not *v*
Eccl 5:5 than that thou shouldest *v*
Is 19:21 oblation; yea, they shall *v*
Is 19:21 a *v* unto the LORD
Acts 18:18 for he had a *v*
Acts 21:23 four men which have a *v* on them

**VOWED**
Gen 28:20 And Jacob *v* a vow, saying, If God

Lev 27:8 that *v* shall the priest value him
Num 6:21 law of the Nazarite who hath *v*
Num 6:21 according to the vow which he *v*
Num 21:2 Israel *v* a vow unto the LORD, and
Num 30:6 had at all an husband, when she *v*
Num 30:8 he shall make her vow which she *v*
Num 30:10 if she *v* in her husband's house,
Deut 23:23 thou hast *v* unto the LORD thy God
Judg 11:30 Jephthah *v* a vow unto the LORD,
Judg 11:39 to his vow which he had *v*
1Sa 1:11 she *v* a vow, and said, O LORD of
2Sa 15:7 which I have *v* unto the LORD, in
2Sa 15:8 For thy servant *v* a vow while I
Ps 132:2 *v* unto the mighty God of Jacob
Eccl 5:4 pay that which thou hast *v*
Jer 44:25 perform our vows that we have *v*
Jonah 2:9 I will pay that that I have *v*

**VOWEDST**
Gen 31:13 where thou *v* a vow unto me

**VOWEST**
Deut 12:17 nor any of thy vows which thou *v*
Eccl 5:4 When thou *v* a vow unto God, defer

**VOWETH**
Mal 1:14 hath in his flock a male, and *v*

**VOWS**
Lev 22:18 offer his oblation for all his *v*
Lev 23:38 your gifts, and beside all your *v*
Num 29:39 in your set feasts, beside your *v*
Num 30:4 then all her *v* shall stand
Num 30:5 not any of her *v*, or of her bonds
Num 30:7 then her *v* shall stand, and her
Num 30:11 then all her *v* shall stand
Num 30:12 out of her lips concerning her *v*
Num 30:14 then he establisheth all her *v*
Deut 12:6 offerings of your hand, and your *v*
Deut 12:11 all your choice *v* which ye vow
Deut 12:17 nor any of thy *v* which thou
Deut 12:26 things which thou hast, and thy *v*
Job 22:27 thee, and thou shalt pay thy *v*
Ps 22:25 I will pay my *v* before them that
Ps 50:14 pay thy *v* unto the most High
Ps 56:12 Thy *v* are upon me, O God
Ps 61:5 For thou, O God, hast heard my *v*
Ps 61:8 that I may daily perform my *v*
Ps 66:13 I will pay thee my *v*,
Ps 116:14 I will pay my *v* unto the LORD now
Ps 116:18 I will pay my *v* unto the LORD now
Prov 7:14 this day have I payed my *v*
Prov 20:25 holy, and after *v* to make enquiry
Prov 31:2 and what, the son of my *v*
Jer 44:25 perform our *v* that we have vowed
Jer 44:25 ye will surely accomplish your *v*
Jer 44:25 and surely perform your *v*
Jonah 1:16 unto the LORD, and made *v*
Nah 1:15 thy solemn feasts, perform thy *v*

**VOYAGE**
Acts 27:10 that this *v* will be with hurt

**VULTURE**
Lev 11:14 And the *v*, and the kite after his
Deut 14:13 kite, and the *v* after his kind,

**VULTURE'S**
Job 28:7 which the *v* eye hath not seen

**VULTURES**
Is 34:15 there shall the *v* also be

# W

**WAFER**
Ex 29:23 one *w* out of the basket of the
Lev 8:26 a cake of oiled bread, and one *w*
Num 6:19 the basket, and one unleavened *w*

**WAFERS**
Ex 16:31 of it was like *w* made with honey
Ex 29:2 *w* unleavened anointed with oil
Lev 2:4 or unleavened *w* anointed with oil
Lev 7:12 unleavened *w* anointed with oil,
Num 6:15 *w* of unleavened bread anointed

**WAG**
Jer 18:16 be astonished, and *w* his head
Lam 2:15 *w* their head at the daughter of
Zeph 2:15 by her shall hiss, and *w* his hand

**WAGES**
Gen 29:15 tell me, what shall thy *w* be
Gen 30:28 And he said, Appoint me thy *w*
Gen 31:7 me, and changed my *w* ten times
Gen 31:8 thus, The speckled shall be thy *w*
Gen 31:41 thou hast changed my *w* ten times
Ex 2:9 for me, and I will give thee thy *w*
Lev 19:13 the *w* of him that is hired shall
Jer 22:13 his neighbour's service without *w*
Eze 29:18 yet had he no *w*, nor his army,
Eze 29:19 and it shall be the *w* for his army
Hag 1:6 he that earneth *w* earneth *w*
Mal 3:5 oppress the hireling in his *w*
Lk 3:14 and be content with your *w*
Jn 4:36 And he that reapeth receiveth *w*
Rom 6:23 For the *w* of sin is death
2Cor 11:8 taking *w* of them, to do you
2Pet 2:15 son of Bosor, who loved the *w* of

**WAGGING**
Mt 27:39 by reviled him, *w* their heads,
Mk 15:29 *w* their heads, and saying, Ah,

**WAGON**
Num 7:3 a *w* for two of the princes, and

**WAGONS**
Gen 45:19 take you *w* out of the land of
Gen 45:21 and Joseph gave them *w*, according
Gen 45:27 when he saw the *w* which Joseph
Gen 46:5 in the *w* which Pharaoh had sent
Num 7:3 before the LORD, six covered *w*
Num 7:6 And Moses took the *w* and the oxen,
Num 7:7 Two *w* and four oxen he gave unto
Num 7:8 And four *w* and eight oxen he gave
Eze 23:24 against thee with chariots, *w*

**WAIL**
Eze 32:18 *w* for the multitude of Egypt, and
Mic 1:8 Therefore I will *w* and howl, I
Rev 1:7 the earth shall *w* because of him

**WAILED**
Mk 5:38 and them that wept and *w* greatly

**WAILING**
Est 4:3 and fasting, and weeping, and *w*
Jer 9:10 will I take up a weeping and *w*
Jer 9:18 make haste, and take up a *w* for us
Jer 9:19 For a voice of *w* is heard out of
Jer 9:20 mouth, and teach your daughters *w*
Eze 7:11 neither shall there be *w* for them
Eze 27:31 bitterness of heart and bitter *w*
Eze 27:32 in their *w* they shall take up a
Amos 5:16 *W* shall be in all streets
Amos 5:16 are skilful of lamentation to *w*
Amos 5:17 And in all vineyards shall be *w*
Mic 1:8 I will make a *w* like the dragons,
Mt 13:42 there shall be *w* and gnashing of
Mt 13:50 there shall be *w* and gnashing of
Rev 18:15 fear of her torment, weeping and *w*
Rev 18:19 heads, and cried, weeping and *w*

**WAIT**
Ex 21:13 And if a man lie not in *w*, but God
Num 3:10 they shall *w* on their priest's
Num 8:24 in to *w* upon the service of the
Num 35:20 or hurl at him by laying of *w*
Num 35:22 him any thing without laying of *w*
Deut 19:11 lie in *w* for him, and rise up
Josh 8:4 ye shall lie in *w* against the
Josh 8:13 their liers in *w* on the west of
Judg 9:25 in *w* for him in the top of the
Judg 9:32 thee, and lie in *w* in the field
Judg 9:34 they laid *w* against Shechem in
Judg 9:35 were with him, from lying in *w*
Judg 9:43 laid *w* in the field, and looked,
Judg 16:2 laid *w* for him all night in the
Judg 16:9 Now there were men lying in *w*
Judg 16:12 there were liers in *w* abiding in
Judg 20:29 set liers in *w* round about Gibeah
Judg 20:33 the liers in *w* of Israel came
Judg 20:36 in *w* which they had set beside
Judg 20:37 And the liers in *w* hasted, and
Judg 20:37 the liers in *w* drew themselves
Judg 20:38 men of Israel and the liers in *w*
Judg 21:20 lie in *w* in the vineyards
1Sa 15:2 how he laid *w* for him in the way,
1Sa 15:5 Amalek, and laid *w* in the valley
1Sa 22:8 servant against me, to lie in *w*
1Sa 22:13 rise against me, to lie in *w*
2Kin 6:33 what should I *w* for the LORD any
1Chr 23:28 Because their office was to *w* on
2Chr 5:11 and did not then *w* by course
2Chr 13:10 the Levites *w* upon their business
Ezr 8:31 and of such as lay in *w* by the way
Job 14:14 of my appointed time will I *w*
Job 17:13 If I *w*, the grave is mine house
Job 31:9 or if I have laid *w* at my
Job 38:40 abide in the covert to lie in *w*
Ps 10:9 He lieth in *w* secretly as a lion
Ps 10:9 he lieth in *w* to catch the poor
Ps 25:3 let none that *w* on thee be
Ps 25:5 on thee do I *w* all the day
Ps 25:21 for I *w* on thee
Ps 27:14 *W* on the LORD
Ps 27:14 *w*, I say, on the LORD
Ps 37:7 the LORD, and *w* patiently for him
Ps 37:9 but those that *w* upon the LORD
Ps 37:34 *W* on the LORD, and keep his way,
Ps 39:7 And now, Lord, what *w* I for
Ps 52:9 and I will *w* on thy name
Ps 56:6 my steps, when they *w* for my soul
Ps 59:3 lo, they lie in *w* for my soul
Ps 59:9 his strength will I *w* upon thee
Ps 62:5 My soul, *w* thou only upon God
Ps 69:3 eyes fail while I *w* for my God
Ps 69:6 Let not them that *w* on thee
Ps 71:10 they that lay *w* for my soul take
Ps 104:27 These *w* all upon thee
Ps 123:2 so our eyes *w* upon the LORD our
Ps 130:5 *w* for the LORD, my soul doth *w*
Ps 145:15 The eyes of all *w* upon thee
Prov 1:11 with us, let us lay *w* for blood
Prov 1:18 they lay *w* for their own blood
Prov 7:12 lieth in *w* at every corner
Prov 12:6 wicked are to lie in *w* for blood
Prov 20:22 but *w* on the LORD, and he shall
Prov 23:28 She also lieth in *w* as for a prey
Prov 24:15 Lay not *w*, O wicked man, against
Is 8:17 I will *w* upon the LORD, that
Is 30:18 And therefore will the LORD *w*
Is 30:18 are all they that *w* for him
Is 40:31 But they that *w* upon the LORD
Is 42:4 and the isles shall *w* for his law
Is 49:23 not be ashamed that *w* for me
Is 51:5 the isles shall *w* upon me
Is 59:9 we *w* for light, but behold
Is 60:9 Surely the isles shall *w* for me
Jer 5:26 they lay *w*, as he that setteth
Jer 9:8 but in heart he layeth his *w*
Jer 14:22 therefore we will *w* upon thee
Lam 3:10 was unto me as a bear lying in *w*
Lam 3:25 is good unto them that *w* for him
Lam 3:26 quietly *w* for the salvation of
Lam 4:19 they laid *w* for us in the
Hos 6:9 as troops of robbers *w* for a man
Hos 7:6 an oven, whiles they lie in *w*
Hos 12:6 and *w* on thy God continually
Mic 7:2 they all lie in *w* for blood
Mic 7:7 I will *w* for the God of my
Hab 2:3 though it tarry, *w* for it
Zeph 3:8 Therefore *w* ye upon me, saith the
Mk 3:9 that a small ship should *w* on him
Lk 11:54 Laying *w* for him, and seeking to
Lk 12:36 unto men that *w* for their lord
Acts 1:4 but *w* for the promise of the
Acts 20:3 And when the Jews laid *w* for him
Acts 20:19 me by the lying in *w* of the Jews
Acts 23:16 son heard of their lying in *w*
Acts 23:21 for there lie in *w* for him of
Acts 23:30 that the Jews laid *w* for the man
Acts 25:3 laying *w* in the way to kill him
Rom 8:25 then do we with patience *w* for it
Rom 12:7 let us *w* on our ministering
1Cor 9:13 they which *w* at the altar are
Gal 5:5 For we through the Spirit *w* for

Eph 4:14 whereby they lie in *w* to deceive
1Th 1:10 to *w* for his Son from heaven,

## WAITED

Gen 49:18 I have *w* for thy salvation, O
1Kin 20:38 *w* for the king by the way, and
2Kin 5:2 and she *w* on Naaman's wife
1Chr 6:32 then they *w* on their office
1Chr 6:33 they that *w* with their children
1Chr 9:18 Who hitherto *w* in the king's gate
2Chr 7:6 the priests *w* on their offices
2Chr 17:19 These *w* on the king, beside those
2Chr 35:15 the porters *w* at every gate
Neh 12:44 priests and for the Levites that *w*
Job 6:19 the companies of Sheba *w* for them
Job 15:22 and he is *w* for of the sword
Job 29:21 Unto me men gave ear, and *w*
Job 29:23 they *w* for me as for the rain
Job 30:26 when I *w* for light, there came
Job 32:4 Now Elihu had *w* till Job had
Job 32:11 Behold, I *w* for your words
Job 32:16 When I had *w*, (for they spake not
Ps 40:1 I *w* patiently for the LORD
Ps 106:13 they *w* not for his counsel
Ps 119:95 The wicked have *w* for me to
Is 25:9 we have *w* for him, and he will
Is 25:9 we have *w* for him, we will be
Is 26:8 O LORD, have we *w* for thee
Is 33:2 we have *w* for thee
Eze 19:5 Now when she saw that she had *w*
Mic 1:12 of Maroth *w* carefully for good
Zec 11:11 *w* upon me knew that it was the
Mk 15:43 which also *w* for the kingdom of
Lk 1:21 the people *w* for Zacharias, and
Lk 23:51 who also himself *w* for the
Acts 10:7 of them that *w* on him continually
Acts 10:24 And Cornelius *w* for them, and had
Acts 17:16 Now while Paul *w* for them at
1Pet 3:20 of God *w* in the days of Noah

## WAITETH

Job 24:15 the adulterer *w* for the twilight
Ps 33:20 Our soul *w* for the LORD
Ps 62:1 Truly my soul *w* upon God
Ps 65:1 Praise *w* for thee, O God in Sion
Ps 130:6 My soul *w* for the Lord more than
Prov 27:18 so he that *w* on his master shall
Is 64:4 prepared for him that *w* for him
Dan 12:12 Blessed is he that *w*, and cometh
Mic 5:7 nor *w* for the sons of men
Rom 8:19 expectation of the creature *w* for
Jas 5:7 the husbandman *w* for the precious

## WAITING

Num 8:25 cease *w* upon the service thereof
Prov 8:34 *w* at the posts of my doors
Lk 2:25 *w* for the consolation of Israel
Lk 8:40 for they were all *w* for him
Jn 5:3 *w* for the moving of the water
Rom 8:23 *w* for the adoption, to wit, the
1Cor 1:7 *w* for the coming of our Lord
2Th 3:5 and into the patient *w* for Christ

## WAKE

Jer 51:39 sleep a perpetual sleep, and not *w*
Jer 51:57 sleep a perpetual sleep, and not *w*
Joel 3:9 *w* up the mighty men, let all the
1Th 5:10 us, that, whether we *w* or sleep

## WAKED

Zec 4:1 *w* me, as a man that is wakened

## WAKENED

Joel 3:12 Let the heathen be *w*, and come up
Zec 4:1 a man that is *w* out of his sleep

## WAKENETH

Is 50:4 he *w* morning by morning
Is 50:4 he *w* mine ear to hear as the

## WAKETH

Ps 127:1 city, the watchman *w* but in vain
Song 5:2 I sleep, but my heart *w*

## WAKING

Ps 77:4 Thou holdest mine eyes *w*

## WALK

Gen 13:17 *w* through the land in the length
Gen 17:1 *w* before me, and be thou perfect
Gen 24:40 me, The LORD, before whom I *w*
Gen 48:15 my fathers Abraham and Isaac did *w*
Ex 16:4 whether they will *w* in my law
Ex 18:20 them the way wherein they must *w*
Ex 21:19 *w* abroad upon his staff, then
Lev 18:3 neither shall ye *w* in their
Lev 18:4 mine ordinances, to *w* therein
Lev 20:23 ye shall not *w* in the manners of
Lev 26:3 If ye *w* in my statutes, and keep
Lev 26:12 I will *w* among you, and will be
Lev 26:21 if ye *w* contrary unto me, and will
Lev 26:23 but will *w* contrary unto me
Lev 26:24 Then will I also *w* contrary unto
Lev 26:27 unto me, but *w* contrary unto me
Lev 26:28 Then I will *w* contrary unto you
Deut 5:33 Ye shall *w* in all the ways which
Deut 8:6 to *w* in his ways, and to fear him
Deut 8:19 *w* after other gods, and serve them
Deut 10:12 to *w* in all his ways, and to love
Deut 11:22 to *w* in all his ways, and to
Deut 13:4 Ye shall *w* after the LORD your
Deut 13:5 thy God commanded thee to *w* in
Deut 19:9 thy God, and to *w* ever in his ways
Deut 26:17 to *w* in his ways, and to keep his
Deut 28:9 LORD thy God, and *w* in his ways
Deut 29:19 though I *w* in the imagination of
Deut 30:16 to *w* in his ways, and to keep his
Josh 18:8 *w* through the land, and describe
Josh 22:5 to *w* in all his ways, and to keep
Judg 2:22 the way of the LORD to *w* therein
Judg 5:10 sit in judgment, and *w* by the way
1Sa 2:30 should *w* before me for ever
1Sa 2:35 he shall *w* before mine anointed
1Sa 8:5 thy sons *w* not in thy ways
1Kin 2:3 to *w* in his ways, to keep his
1Kin 2:4 to *w* before me in truth with all
1Kin 3:14 And if thou wilt *w* in my ways
1Kin 3:14 as thy father David did *w*
1Kin 6:12 if thou wilt *w* in my statutes, and
1Kin 6:12 all my commandments to *w* in them
1Kin 8:23 that *w* before thee with all their
1Kin 8:25 that they *w* before me as thou
1Kin 8:36 good way wherein they should *w*
1Kin 8:58 to *w* in all his ways, and to keep
1Kin 8:61 to *w* in his statutes, and to keep
1Kin 9:4 And if thou wilt *w* before me
1Kin 11:38 wilt *w* in my ways, and do that is
1Kin 16:31 been a light thing for him to *w*
2Kin 10:31 But Jehu took no heed to *w* in the
2Kin 23:3 to *w* after the LORD, and to keep
2Chr 6:14 that *w* before thee with all their
2Chr 6:16 heed to their way to *w* in my law
2Chr 6:27 good way, wherein they should *w*
2Chr 6:31 to *w* in thy ways, so long as they
2Chr 7:17 thee, if thou wilt *w* before me
2Chr 34:31 to *w* after the LORD, and to keep
Neh 5:9 ought ye not to *w* in the fear of
Neh 10:29 to *w* in God's law, which was
Ps 12:8 The wicked *w* on every side, when
Ps 23:4 though I *w* through the valley of
Ps 26:11 I will *w* in mine integrity
Ps 48:12 *W* about Zion, and go round about
Ps 56:13 that I may *w* before God in the
Ps 78:10 God, and refused to *w* in his law
Ps 82:5 they *w* on in darkness
Ps 84:11 from them that *w* uprightly
Ps 86:11 I will *w* in thy truth
Ps 89:15 they shall *w*, O LORD, in the
Ps 89:30 my law, and *w* not in my judgments
Ps 101:2 I will *w* within my house with a
Ps 115:7 feet have they, but they *w* not
Ps 116:9 I will *w* before the LORD in the
Ps 119:1 who *w* in the law of the LORD
Ps 119:3 they *w* in his ways
Ps 119:45 And I will *w* at liberty
Ps 138:7 Though I *w* in the midst of
Ps 143:8 know the way wherein I should *w*
Prov 1:15 *w* not thou in the way with them
Prov 2:7 buckler to them that *w* uprightly
Prov 2:13 to *w* in the ways of darkness
Prov 2:20 That thou mayest *w* in the way of
Prov 3:23 Then shalt thou *w* in thy way
Eccl 4:15 the living which *w* under the sun
Eccl 6:8 that knoweth to *w* before the
Eccl 11:9 *w* in the ways of thine heart, and
Is 2:3 ways, and we will *w* in his paths
Is 2:5 let us *w* in the light of the LORD
Is 3:16 *w* with stretched forth necks and
Is 8:11 not *w* in the way of this people
Is 30:2 That *w* to go down into Egypt, and
Is 30:21 *w* ye in it, when ye turn to the
Is 35:9 but the redeemed shall *w* there
Is 40:31 and they shall *w*, and not faint
Is 42:5 and spirit to them that *w* therein
Is 42:24 for they would not *w* in his ways
Is 50:11 *w* in the light of your fire, and
Is 59:9 brightness, but we *w* in darkness
Jer 3:17 neither shall they *w* any more
Jer 3:18 shall *w* with the house of Israel
Jer 6:16 *w* therein, and ye shall find rest
Jer 6:16 they said, We will not *w* therein
Jer 6:25 into the field, nor *w* by the way
Jer 7:6 neither *w* after other gods to
Jer 7:9 *w* after other gods whom ye know
Jer 7:23 *w* ye in all the ways that I have
Jer 9:4 neighbour will *w* with slanders
Jer 13:10 which *w* in the imagination of
Jer 13:10 *w* after other gods, to serve them
Jer 16:12 behold, ye *w* every one after the
Jer 18:12 but we will *w* after our own
Jer 18:15 to *w* in paths, in a way not cast
Jer 23:14 commit adultery, and *w* in lies
Jer 26:4 to *w* in my law, which I have set
Jer 31:9 I will cause them to *w* by the
Jer 42:3 shew us the way wherein we may *w*
Lam 5:18 is desolate, the foxes *w* upon it
Eze 11:20 That they may *w* in my statutes,
Eze 20:18 *W* ye not in the statutes of your
Eze 20:19 *w* in my statutes, and keep my
Eze 33:15 *w* in the statutes of life,
Eze 36:12 I will cause men to *w* upon you
Eze 36:27 cause you to *w* in my statutes, and
Eze 37:24 they shall also *w* in my judgments
Eze 42:4 before the chambers was a *w* of
Dan 4:37 those that *w* in pride he is able
Dan 9:10 to *w* in his laws, which he set
Hos 11:10 They shall *w* after the LORD
Hos 14:9 and the just shall *w* in them
Joel 2:8 they shall *w* every one in his
Amos 3:3 Can two *w* together, except they
Mic 4:2 ways, and we will *w* in his paths
Mic 4:5 For all people will *w* every one
Mic 4:5 we will *w* in the name of the LORD
Mic 6:8 and to *w* humbly with thy God
Mic 6:16 Ahab, and ye *w* in their counsels
Nah 2:5 they shall stumble in their *w*
Hab 3:15 Thou didst *w* through the sea with
Hab 3:19 he will make me to *w* upon mine
Zeph 1:17 that they shall *w* like blind men
Zec 1:10 whom the LORD hath sent to *w* to
Zec 3:7 If thou wilt *w* in my ways
Zec 3:7 to *w* among these that stand by
Zec 6:7 sought to go that they might *w* to
Zec 6:7 *w* to and fro through the earth
Zec 10:12 and they shall *w* up and down in his
Mt 9:5 or to say, Arise, and *w*
Mt 11:5 their sight, and the lame *w*
Mt 15:31 maimed to be whole, the lame to *w*
Mk 2:9 Arise, and take up thy bed, and *w*
Mk 7:5 Why *w* not thy disciples according
Lk 5:23 or to say, Rise up and *w*
Lk 7:22 that the blind see, the lame *w*
Lk 11:44 the men that *w* over them are not
Lk 13:33 Nevertheless I must *w* to day
Lk 20:46 which desire to *w* in long robes
Lk 24:17 ye have one to another, as ye *w*
Jn 5:8 him, Rise, take up thy bed, and *w*
Jn 5:11 unto me, Take up thy bed, and *w*
Jn 5:12 unto thee, Take up thy bed, and *w*
Jn 7:1 for he would not *w* in Jewry
Jn 8:12 me shall not *w* in darkness
Jn 11:9 If any man *w* in the day, he
Jn 11:10 But if a man *w* in the night
Jn 12:35 *W* while ye have the light, lest
Acts 3:6 Christ of Nazareth rise up and *w*
Acts 3:12 we had made this man to *w*
Acts 14:16 nations to *w* in their own ways
Acts 21:21 neither to *w* after the customs
Rom 4:12 but who also *w* in the steps of
Rom 6:4 also should *w* in newness of life
Rom 8:1 who *w* not after the flesh, but
Rom 8:4 who *w* not after the flesh, but
Rom 13:13 Let us *w* honestly, as in the day
1Cor 3:3 are ye not carnal, and *w* as men
1Cor 7:17 called every one, so let him *w*
2Cor 5:7 (For we *w* by faith, not by sight
2Cor 6:16 will dwell in them, and *w* in them
2Cor 10:3 For though we *w* in the flesh
Gal 5:16 *W* in the Spirit, and ye shall not
Gal 5:25 let us also *w* in the Spirit
Gal 6:16 as many as *w* according to this
Eph 2:10 ordained that we should *w* in them
Eph 4:1 beseech you that ye *w* worthy of
Eph 4:17 *w* not as other Gentiles *w*
Eph 5:2 *w* in love, as Christ also hath
Eph 5:8 *w* as children of light

Eph 5:15 See then that ye *w* circumspectly
Phil 3:16 let us *w* by the same rule, let us
Phil 3:17 mark them which *w* so as ye have
Phil 3:18 (For many *w*, of whom I have told
Col 1:10 That ye might *w* worthy of the
Col 2:6 Jesus the Lord, so *w* ye in him
Col 4:5 *W* in wisdom toward them that are
1Th 2:12 That ye would *w* worthy of God
1Th 4:1 received of us how ye ought to *w*
1Th 4:12 That ye may *w* honestly toward
2Th 3:11 some which *w* among you disorderly
2Pet 2:10 But chiefly them that *w* after the
1Jn 1:6 *w* in darkness, we lie, and do not
1Jn 1:7 But if we *w* in the light, as he
1Jn 2:6 in him ought himself also so to *w*
2Jn 6 that we *w* after his commandments
2Jn 6 the beginning, ye should *w* in it
3Jn 4 hear that my children *w* in truth
Jude 18 who should *w* after their own
Rev 3:4 they shall *w* with me in white
Rev 9:20 neither can see, nor hear, nor *w*
Rev 16:15 his garments, lest he *w* naked
Rev 21:24 saved shall *w* in the light of it

## WALKED

Gen 5:22 Enoch *w* with God after he begat
Gen 5:24 And Enoch *w* with God
Gen 6:9 generations, and Noah *w* with God
Ex 2:5 her maidens *w* along by the
Ex 14:29 But the children of Israel *w* upon
Lev 26:40 also they have *w* contrary unto me
Lev 26:41 that I also have *w* contrary unto
Josh 5:6 For the children of Israel *w*
Judg 2:17 the way which their fathers *w* in
Judg 5:6 the travellers *w* through byways
Judg 11:16 *w* through the wilderness unto the
1Sa 8:3 his sons *w* not in his ways, but
1Sa 12:2 I have *w* before you from my
2Sa 2:29 his men *w* all that night through
2Sa 7:6 but have *w* in a tent and in a
2Sa 7:7 all the places wherein I have *w*
2Sa 11:2 *w* upon the roof of the king's
1Kin 3:6 according as he *w* before thee in
1Kin 8:25 me as thou hast *w* before me
1Kin 9:4 before me, as David thy father *w*
1Kin 11:33 have not *w* in my ways, to do that
1Kin 15:3 he *w* in all the sins of his
1Kin 15:26 *w* in the way of his father, and in
1Kin 15:34 *w* in the way of Jeroboam, and in
1Kin 16:2 thou hast *w* in the way of
1Kin 16:26 For he *w* in all the way of
1Kin 22:43 he *w* in all the ways of Asa his
1Kin 22:52 *w* in the way of his father, and in
2Kin 4:35 and *w* in the house to and fro
2Kin 8:18 he *w* in the way of the kings of
2Kin 8:27 he *w* in the way of the house of
2Kin 13:6 made Israel sin, but *w* therein
2Kin 13:11 but he *w* therein
2Kin 16:3 But he *w* in the way of the kings
2Kin 17:8 *w* in the statutes of the heathen,
2Kin 17:19 but *w* in the statutes of Israel
2Kin 17:22 For the children of Israel *w* in
2Kin 20:3 how I have *w* before thee in truth
2Kin 21:21 he *w* in all the way that his
2Kin 21:21 all the way that his father *w* in
2Kin 21:22 *w* not in the way of the LORD
2Kin 22:2 *w* in all the way of David his
1Chr 17:6 I have *w* with all Israel, spake I
1Chr 17:8 thee whithersoever thou hast *w*
2Chr 6:16 my law, as thou hast *w* before me
2Chr 7:17 before me, as David thy father *w*
2Chr 11:17 years they *w* in the way of David
2Chr 17:3 because he *w* in the first ways of
2Chr 17:4 *w* in his commandments, and not
2Chr 20:32 he *w* in the way of Asa his father
2Chr 21:6 he *w* in the way of the kings of
2Chr 21:12 Because thou hast not *w* in the
2Chr 21:13 But hast *w* in the way of the
2Chr 22:3 He also *w* in the ways of the
2Chr 22:5 He *w* also after their counsel, and
2Chr 28:2 For he *w* in the ways of the kings
2Chr 34:2 *w* in the ways of David his father
Est 2:11 Mordecai *w* every day before the
Job 29:3 by his light I *w* through darkness
Job 31:5 If I have *w* with vanity, or if my
Job 31:7 mine heart *w* after mine eyes, and
Job 38:16 or hast thou *w* in the search of
Ps 26:1 for I have *w* in mine integrity
Ps 26:3 and I have *w* in thy truth
Ps 55:14 *w* unto the house of God in
Ps 81:12 they *w* in their own counsels
Ps 81:13 me, and Israel had *w* in my ways
Ps 142:3 In the way wherein I *w* have they
Is 9:2 The people that *w* in darkness
Is 20:3 as my servant Isaiah hath *w* naked
Is 38:3 how I have *w* before thee in truth
Jer 2:5 have *w* after vanity, and are
Jer 2:8 *w* after things that do not profit
Jer 7:24 but *w* in the counsels and in the
Jer 8:2 served, and after whom they have *w*
Jer 9:13 my voice, neither *w* therein
Jer 9:14 But have *w* after the imagination
Jer 11:8 their ear, but *w* every one in the
Jer 16:11 have *w* after other gods, and have
Jer 32:23 thy voice, neither *w* in thy law
Jer 44:10 nor *w* in my law, nor in my
Jer 44:23 nor *w* in his law, nor in his
Eze 5:6 statutes, they have not *w* in them
Eze 5:7 have not *w* in my statutes,
Eze 11:12 for ye have not *w* in my statutes
Eze 16:47 hast thou not *w* after their ways
Eze 18:9 Hath *w* in my statutes, and hath
Eze 18:17 judgments, hath *w* in my statutes
Eze 20:13 they *w* not in my statutes, and
Eze 20:16 *w* not in my statutes, but
Eze 20:21 they *w* not in my statutes,
Eze 23:31 Thou hast *w* in the way of thy
Eze 28:14 thou hast *w* up and down in the
Dan 4:29 At the end of twelve months he *w*
Hos 5:11 because he willingly *w* after the
Amos 2:4 the which their fathers have *w*
Nah 2:11 the lion, even the old lion, *w*
Zec 1:11 trees, and said, We have *w* to
Zec 6:7 So they *w* to and fro through the
Mal 2:6 he *w* with me in peace and equity,
Mal 3:14 that we have *w* mournfully before
Mt 14:29 he *w* on the water, to go to Jesus
Mk 1:16 Now as he *w* by the sea of Galilee
Mk 5:42 the damsel arose, and *w*
Mk 16:12 form unto two of them, as they *w*
Jn 1:36 And looking upon Jesus as he *w*
Jn 5:9 whole, and took up his bed, and *w*
Jn 6:66 went back, and *w* no more with him
Jn 7:1 these things Jesus *w* in Galilee
Jn 10:23 And Jesus *w* in the temple in
Jn 11:54 Jesus therefore *w* no more openly
Acts 3:8 And he leaping up stood, and *w*
Acts 14:8 mother's womb, who never had *w*
Acts 14:10 And he leaped and *w*
2Cor 10:2 as if we *w* according to the flesh
2Cor 12:18 *w* we not in the same spirit
2Cor 12:18 *w* we not in the same steps
Gal 2:14 But when I saw that they *w* not
Eph 2:2 Wherein in time past ye *w*
Col 3:7 In the which ye also *w* some time
1Pet 4:3 when we *w* in lasciviousness,
1Jn 2:6 also so to walk, even as he *w*

## WALKEDST

Jn 21:18 and *w* whither thou wouldest

## WALKEST

Deut 6:7 when thou *w* by the way, and when
Deut 11:19 when thou *w* by the way, when thou
1Kin 2:42 *w* abroad any whither, that thou
Is 43:2 when thou *w* through the fire,
Acts 21:24 that thou thyself also *w* orderly
Rom 14:15 now *w* thou not charitably
3Jn 3 thee, even as thou *w* in the truth

## WALKETH

Gen 24:65 What man is this that *w* in the
Deut 23:14 For the LORD thy God *w* in the
1Sa 12:2 behold, the king *w* before you
Job 18:8 own feet, and he *w* upon a snare
Job 22:14 he *w* in the circuit of heaven
Job 34:8 of iniquity, and *w* with wicked men
Ps 1:1 Blessed is the man that *w* not in
Ps 15:2 He that *w* uprightly, and worketh
Ps 39:6 Surely every man *w* in a vain shew
Ps 73:9 their tongue *w* through the earth
Ps 91:6 the pestilence that *w* in darkness
Ps 101:6 he that *w* in a perfect way, he
Ps 104:3 who *w* upon the wings of the wind
Ps 128:1 that *w* in his ways
Prov 6:12 man, *w* with a froward mouth
Prov 10:9 that *w* uprightly *w* surely
Prov 13:20 He that *w* with wise men shall be
Prov 14:2 He that *w* in his uprightness
Prov 15:21 man of understanding *w* uprightly
Prov 19:1 the poor that *w* in his integrity
Prov 20:7 The just man *w* in his integrity
Prov 28:6 poor that *w* in his uprightness
Prov 28:18 Whoso *w* uprightly shall be saved
Prov 28:26 but whoso *w* wisely, he shall be
Eccl 2:14 but the fool *w* in darkness
Eccl 10:3 he that is a fool *w* by the way
Is 33:15 He that *w* righteously, and
Is 50:10 that *w* in darkness, and hath no
Is 65:2 which *w* in a way that was not
Jer 10:23 in man that *w* to direct his steps
Jer 23:17 *w* after the imagination of his
Eze 11:21 heart *w* after the heart of their
Mic 2:7 do good to him that *w* uprightly
Mt 12:43 he *w* through dry places, seeking
Lk 11:24 he *w* through dry places, seeking
Jn 12:35 for he that *w* in darkness knoweth
2Th 3:6 every brother that *w* disorderly
1Pet 5:8 *w* about, seeking whom he may
1Jn 2:11 *w* in darkness, and knoweth not
Rev 2:1 who *w* in the midst of the seven

## WALKING

Gen 3:8 *w* in the garden in the cool of
Deut 2:7 he knoweth thy *w* through this
1Kin 3:3 *w* in the statutes of David his
1Kin 16:19 in *w* in the way of Jeroboam, and
Job 1:7 and fro in the earth, and from *w* up
Job 2:2 and fro in the earth, and from *w* up
Job 31:26 or the moon *w* in brightness
Eccl 10:7 princes *w* as servants upon the
Is 3:16 forth necks and wanton eyes, *w*
Is 20:2 And he did so, *w* naked and barefoot
Is 57:2 each one *w* in his uprightness
Jer 6:28 revolters, *w* with slanders
Dan 3:25 *w* in the midst of the fire, and
Mic 2:11 If a man *w* in the spirit and
Mt 4:18 *w* by the sea of Galilee, saw two
Mt 14:25 went unto them, *w* on the sea
Mt 14:26 disciples saw him *w* on the sea
Mk 6:48 *w* upon the sea, and would have
Mk 6:49 when they saw him *w* upon the sea
Mk 8:24 and said, I see men as trees, *w*
Mk 11:27 as he was *w* in the temple, there
Lk 1:6 *w* in all the commandments and
Jn 6:19 they see Jesus *w* on the sea
Acts 3:8 with them into the temple, *w*
Acts 3:9 And all the people saw him *w*
Acts 9:31 *w* in the fear of the Lord, and in
2Cor 4:2 not *w* in craftiness, nor handling
2Pet 3:3 *w* after their own lusts,
2Jn 4 found of thy children *w* in truth
Jude 16 *w* after their own lusts

## WALL

Gen 49:6 selfwill they digged down a *w*
Gen 49:22 whose branches run over the *w*
Ex 14:22 the waters were a *w* unto them on
Ex 14:29 the waters were a *w* unto them on
Lev 14:37 in sight are lower than the *w*
Lev 25:31 no *w* round about them shall be
Num 22:24 a *w* being on this side, and a *w*
Num 22:25 she thrust herself unto the *w*
Num 22:25 Balaam's foot against the *w*
Num 35:4 reach from the *w* of the city
Josh 2:15 for her house was upon the town *w*
Josh 2:15 and she dwelt upon the *w*
Josh 6:5 the *w* of the city shall fall down
Josh 6:20 that the *w* fell down flat, so
1Sa 18:11 smite David even to the *w* with it
1Sa 19:10 even to the *w* with the javelin
1Sa 19:10 he smote the javelin into the *w*
1Sa 20:25 times, even upon a seat by the *w*
1Sa 25:16 They were a *w* unto us both by
1Sa 25:22 any that pisseth against the *w*
1Sa 25:34 any that pisseth against the *w*
1Sa 31:10 his body to the *w* of Beth-shan
1Sa 31:12 his sons from the *w* of Beth-shan
2Sa 11:20 that they would shoot from the *w*
2Sa 11:21 a millstone upon him from the *w*
2Sa 11:21 why went ye nigh the *w*
2Sa 11:24 from off the *w* upon thy servants
2Sa 18:24 the roof over the gate unto the *w*
2Sa 20:15 were with Joab battered the *w*
2Sa 20:21 be thrown to thee over the *w*
2Sa 22:30 by my God have I leaped over a *w*
1Kin 3:1 the *w* of Jerusalem round about
1Kin 4:33 that springeth out of the *w*
1Kin 6:5 against the *w* of the house he
1Kin 6:6 for without in the *w* of the house
1Kin 6:27 wing of the one touched the one *w*
1Kin 6:27 other cherub touched the other *w*
1Kin 6:31 posts were a fifth part of the *w*

1Kin 6:33 tree, a fourth part of the *w*
1Kin 9:15 the *w* of Jerusalem, and Hazor, and
1Kin 14:10 him that pisseth against the *w*
1Kin 16:11 not one that pisseth against a *w*
1Kin 20:30 there a *w* fell upon twenty and
1Kin 21:21 him that pisseth against the *w*
1Kin 21:23 eat Jezebel by the *w* of Jezreel
2Kin 3:27 for a burnt offering upon the *w*
2Kin 4:10 chamber, I pray thee, on the *w*
2Kin 6:26 Israel was passing by upon the *w*
2Kin 6:30 and he passed by upon the *w*
2Kin 9:8 him that pisseth against the *w*
2Kin 9:33 her blood was sprinkled on the *w*
2Kin 14:13 brake down the *w* of Jerusalem
2Kin 18:26 of the people that are on the *w*
2Kin 18:27 me to the men which sit on the *w*
2Kin 20:2 Then he turned his face to the *w*
2Chr 3:11 reaching to the *w* of the house
2Chr 3:12 reaching to the *w* of the house
2Chr 25:23 brake down the *w* of Jerusalem
2Chr 26:6 and brake down the *w* of Gath
2Chr 26:6 the *w* of Jabneh, and the
2Chr 26:6 the *w* of Ashdod, and built cities
2Chr 26:9 gate, and at the turning of the *w*
2Chr 27:3 on the *w* of Ophel he built much
2Chr 32:5 up all the *w* that was broken
2Chr 32:5 the towers, and another *w* without
2Chr 32:18 of Jerusalem that were on the *w*
2Chr 33:14 a *w* without the city of David
2Chr 36:19 and brake down the *w* of Jerusalem
Ezr 5:3 this house, and to make up this *w*
Ezr 9:9 and to give us a *w* in Judah
Neh 1:3 the *w* of Jerusalem also is broken
Neh 2:8 for the *w* of the city, and for the
Neh 2:15 by the brook, and viewed the *w*
Neh 2:17 us build up the *w* of Jerusalem
Neh 3:8 Jerusalem unto the broad *w*
Neh 3:13 on the *w* unto the dung gate
Neh 3:15 the *w* of the pool of Siloah by
Neh 3:19 armoury at the turning of the *w*
Neh 3:20 from the turning of the *w* unto
Neh 3:24 Azariah unto the turning of the *w*
Neh 3:25 over against the turning of the *w*
Neh 3:27 out, even unto the *w* of Ophel
Neh 4:1 heard that we builded the *w*
Neh 4:3 even break down their stone *w*
Neh 4:6 So built we the *w*
Neh 4:6 all the *w* was joined together
Neh 4:10 we are not able to build the *w*
Neh 4:13 in the lower places behind the *w*
Neh 4:15 we returned all of us to the *w*
Neh 4:17 They which builded on the *w*
Neh 4:19 and we are separated upon the *w*
Neh 5:16 I continued in the work of this *w*
Neh 6:1 heard that I had builded the *w*
Neh 6:6 which cause thou buildest the *w*
Neh 6:15 So the *w* was finished in the
Neh 7:1 when the *w* was built, and I had
Neh 12:27 at the dedication of the *w* of
Neh 12:30 people, and the gates, and the *w*
Neh 12:31 the princes of Judah upon the *w*
Neh 12:31 upon the *w* toward the dung gate
Neh 12:37 David, at the going up of the *w*
Neh 12:38 the half of the people upon the *w*
Neh 12:38 furnaces even unto the broad *w*
Neh 13:21 them, Why lodge ye about the *w*
Ps 18:29 by my God have I leaped over a *w*
Ps 62:3 as a bowing *w* shall ye be
Prov 18:11 as an high *w* in his own conceit
Prov 24:31 the stone *w* thereof was broken
Song 2:9 behold, he standeth behind our *w*
Song 8:9 If she be a *w*, we will build upon
Song 8:10 I am a *w*, and my breasts like
Is 2:15 tower, and upon every fenced *w*
Is 5:5 and break down the *w* thereof
Is 22:10 ye broken down to fortify the *w*
Is 25:4 ones is as a storm against the *w*
Is 30:13 to fall, swelling out in a high *w*
Is 36:11 of the people that are on the *w*
Is 36:12 me to the men that sit upon the *w*
Is 38:2 turned his face toward the *w*
Is 59:10 We grope for the *w* like the blind
Jer 15:20 this people a fenced brasen *w*
Jer 49:27 a fire in the *w* of Damascus
Jer 51:44 the *w* of Babylon shall fall
Lam 2:8 the *w* of the daughter of Zion
Lam 2:8 the rampart and the *w* to lament
Lam 2:18 O *w* of the daughter of Zion, let
Eze 4:3 set it for a *w* of iron between
Eze 8:7 I looked, behold a hole in the *w*
Eze 8:8 me, Son of man, dig now in the *w*
Eze 8:8 and when I had digged in the *w*
Eze 8:10 pourtrayed upon the *w* round about
Eze 12:5 thou through the *w* in their sight
Eze 12:7 through the *w* with mine hand
Eze 12:12 the *w* to carry out thereby
Eze 13:10 and one built up a *w*, and, lo,
Eze 13:12 when the *w* is fallen, shall it
Eze 13:14 the *w* that ye have daubed with
Eze 13:15 I accomplish my wrath upon the *w*
Eze 13:15 The *w* is no more, neither they
Eze 23:14 she saw men pourtrayed upon the *w*
Eze 38:20 every *w* shall fall to the ground
Eze 40:5 behold a *w* on the outside of the
Eze 41:5 he measured the *w* of the house
Eze 41:6 they entered into the *w* which was
Eze 41:6 not hold in the *w* of the house
Eze 41:9 The thickness of the *w*, which was
Eze 41:12 the *w* of the building was five
Eze 41:17 by all the *w* round about within
Eze 41:20 made, and on the *w* of the temple
Eze 42:7 the *w* that was without over
Eze 42:10 *w* of the court toward the east
Eze 42:12 before the *w* toward the east
Eze 42:20 it had a *w* round about, five
Eze 43:8 the *w* between me and them, they
Dan 5:5 of the *w* of the king's palace
Dan 9:25 shall be built again, and the *w*
Hos 2:6 thy way with thorns, and make a *w*
Joel 2:7 shall climb the *w* like men of war
Joel 2:9 they shall run upon the *w*
Amos 1:7 will send a fire on the *w* of Gaza
Amos 1:10 send a fire on the *w* of Tyrus
Amos 1:14 kindle a fire in the *w* of Rabbah
Amos 5:19 and leaned his hand on the *w*
Amos 7:7 upon a *w* made by a plumbline
Nah 2:5 shall make haste to the *w* thereof
Nah 3:8 sea, and her *w* was from the sea
Hab 2:11 the stone shall cry out of the *w*
Zec 2:5 will be unto her a *w* of fire
Acts 9:25 let him down by the *w* in a basket
Acts 23:3 shall smite thee, thou whited *w*
2Cor 11:33 a basket was I let down by the *w*
Eph 2:14 middle *w* of partition between us
Rev 21:12 And had a *w* great and high, and had
Rev 21:14 the *w* of the city had twelve
Rev 21:15 gates thereof, and the *w* thereof
Rev 21:17 And he measured the *w* thereof
Rev 21:18 of the *w* of it was of jasper
Rev 21:19 the foundations of the *w* of the

**WALLED**
Lev 25:29 sell a dwelling house in a *w* city
Lev 25:30 *w* city shall be established for
Num 13:28 in the land, and the cities are *w*
Deut 1:28 are great and *w* up to heaven

**WALLOW**
Jer 6:26 sackcloth, and *w* thyself in ashes
Jer 25:34 *w* yourselves in the ashes, ye
Jer 48:26 Moab also shall *w* in his vomit
Eze 27:30 they shall *w* themselves in the

**WALLOWED**
2Sa 20:12 Amasa *w* in blood in the midst of
Mk 9:20 fell on the ground, and *w* foaming

**WALLOWING**
2Pet 2:22 was washed to her *w* in the mire

**WALLS**
Lev 14:37 if the plague be in the *w* of the
Lev 14:39 be spread in the *w* of the house
Deut 3:5 cities were fenced with high *w*
Deut 28:52 fenced *w* come down, wherein thou
1Kin 4:13 threescore great cities with *w*
1Kin 6:5 against the *w* of the house round
1Kin 6:6 be fastened in the *w* of the house
1Kin 6:15 he built the *w* of the house
1Kin 6:15 house, and the *w* of the cieling
1Kin 6:16 the *w* with boards of cedar
1Kin 6:29 he carved all the *w* of the house
2Kin 25:4 the way of the gate between two *w*
2Kin 25:10 brake down the *w* of Jerusalem
1Chr 29:4 to overlay the *w* of the houses
2Chr 3:7 the *w* thereof, and the doors
2Chr 3:7 and graved cherubims on the *w*
2Chr 8:5 the nether, fenced cities, with *w*
2Chr 14:7 cities, and make about them *w*
Ezr 4:12 and have set up the *w* thereof
Ezr 4:13 the *w* set up again, then will
Ezr 4:16 the *w* thereof set up, by this
Ezr 5:8 and timber is laid in the *w*
Ezr 5:9 this house, and to make up these *w*
Neh 2:13 viewed the *w* of Jerusalem, which
Neh 4:7 heard that the *w* of Jerusalem
Job 24:11 Which make oil within their *w*
Ps 51:18 build thou the *w* of Jerusalem
Ps 55:10 go about it upon the *w* thereof
Ps 122:7 Peace be within thy *w*, and
Prov 25:28 that is broken down, and without *w*
Song 5:7 the keepers of the *w* took away my
Is 22:5 of vision, breaking down the *w*
Is 22:11 also a ditch between the two *w*
Is 25:12 fort of thy *w* shall he bring down
Is 26:1 salvation will God appoint for *w*
Is 49:16 thy *w* are continually before me
Is 56:5 mine house and within my *w* a place
Is 60:10 of strangers shall build up thy *w*
Is 60:18 thou shalt call thy *w* Salvation
Is 62:6 I have set watchmen upon thy *w*
Jer 1:15 against all the *w* thereof round
Jer 1:18 brasen *w* against the whole land,
Jer 5:10 Go ye up upon her *w*, and destroy
Jer 21:4 which besiege you without the *w*
Jer 39:4 by the gate betwixt the two *w*
Jer 39:8 and brake down the *w* of Jerusalem
Jer 50:15 are fallen, her *w* are thrown down
Jer 51:12 standard upon the *w* of Babylon
Jer 51:58 The broad *w* of Babylon shall be
Jer 52:7 way of the gate between the two *w*
Jer 52:14 brake down all the *w* of Jerusalem
Lam 2:7 of the enemy the *w* of her palaces
Eze 26:4 they shall destroy the *w* of Tyrus
Eze 26:9 set engines of war against thy *w*
Eze 26:10 thy *w* shall shake at the noise of
Eze 26:12 and they shall break down thy *w*
Eze 27:11 army were upon thy *w* round about
Eze 27:11 shields upon thy *w* round about
Eze 33:30 are talking against thee by the *w*
Eze 38:11 all of them dwelling without *w*
Eze 41:13 the building, with the *w* thereof
Eze 41:22 the *w* thereof, were of wood
Eze 41:25 like as were made upon the *w*
Mic 7:11 day that thy *w* are to be built
Zec 2:4 *w* for the multitude of men
Heb 11:30 By faith the *w* of Jericho fell

**WANDER**
Gen 20:13 when God caused me to *w* from my
Num 14:33 your children shall *w* in the
Num 32:13 he made them *w* in the wilderness
Deut 27:18 the blind to *w* out of the way
Job 12:24 causeth them to *w* in a wilderness
Job 38:41 unto God, they *w* for lack of meat
Ps 55:7 Lo, then would I *w* far off
Ps 59:15 Let them *w* up and down for meat,
Ps 107:40 and causeth them to *w* in the
Ps 119:10 O let me not *w* from thy
Is 47:15 they shall *w* every one to his
Jer 14:10 people, Thus have they loved to *w*
Jer 48:12 that shall cause him to *w*
Amos 8:12 they shall *w* from sea to sea, and

**WANDERED**
Gen 21:14 *w* in the wilderness of Beer-sheba
Josh 14:10 of Israel *w* in the wilderness
Ps 107:4 They *w* in the wilderness in a
Is 16:8 they *w* through the wilderness
Lam 4:14 They have *w* as blind men in the
Lam 4:15 when they fled away and *w*, they
Eze 34:6 My sheep *w* through all the
Amos 4:8 or three cities *w* unto one city
Heb 11:37 they *w* about in sheepskins and
Heb 11:38 they *w* in deserts, and in

**WANDERERS**
Jer 48:12 LORD, that I will send unto him *w*
Hos 9:17 they shall be *w* among the nations

**WANDEREST**
Jer 2:20 and under every green tree thou *w*

**WANDERETH**
Job 15:23 He *w* abroad for bread, saying,
Prov 21:16 The man that *w* out of the way of
Prov 27:8 As a bird that *w* from her nest
Prov 27:8 so is a man that *w* from his place
Is 16:3 bewray not him that *w*
Jer 49:5 none shall gather up him that *w*

**WANDERING**
Gen 37:15 and, behold, he was *w* in the field
Prov 26:2 As the bird by *w*, as the swallow
Eccl 6:9 the eyes than the *w* of the desire
Is 16:2 as a *w* bird cast out of the nest,

1Ti 5:13 *w* about from house to house
Jude 13 *w* stars, to whom is reserved the

**WANDERINGS**
Ps 56:8 Thou tellest my *w*

**WANT**
Deut 28:48 nakedness, and in *w* of all things
Deut 28:57 for she shall eat them for *w* of
Judg 18:10 a place where there is no *w* of
Judg 19:19 there is no *w* of any thing
Job 24:8 the rock for *w* of a shelter
Job 30:3 For *w* and famine they were
Job 31:19 seen any perish for *w* of clothing
Ps 23:1 I shall not *w*
Ps 34:9 for there is no *w* to them that
Ps 34:10 LORD shall not *w* any good thing
Prov 6:11 and thy *w* as an armed man
Prov 10:21 but fools die for *w* of wisdom
Prov 13:23 is destroyed for *w* of judgment
Prov 13:25 the belly of the wicked shall *w*
Prov 14:28 but in the *w* of people is the
Prov 21:5 every one that is hasty only to *w*
Prov 22:16 the rich, shall surely come to *w*
Prov 24:34 and thy *w* as an armed man
Is 34:16 shall fail, none shall *w* her mate
Jer 33:17 David shall never *w* a man to sit
Jer 33:18 shall the priests the Levites *w* a
Jer 35:19 the son of Rechab shall not *w* a
Lam 4:9 stricken through for *w* of the
Eze 4:17 That they may *w* bread and water,
Amos 4:6 *w* of bread in all your places
Mk 12:44 but she of her *w* did cast in all
Lk 15:14 and he began to be in *w*
2Cor 8:14 may be a supply for their *w*
2Cor 8:14 also may be a supply for your *w*
2Cor 9:12 supplieth the *w* of the saints
Phil 4:11 Not that I speak in respect of *w*

**WANTED**
Jer 44:18 we have *w* all things, and have
Jn 2:3 And when they *w* wine, the mother
2Cor 11:9 when I was present with you, and *w*

**WANTETH**
Deut 15:8 for his need, in that which he *w*
Prov 9:4 as for him that *w* understanding
Prov 9:16 as for him that *w* understanding
Prov 10:19 of words there *w* not sin
Prov 28:16 The prince that *w* understanding
Eccl 6:2 so that he *w* nothing for his soul
Song 7:2 round goblet, which *w* not liquor

**WANTING**
2Kin 10:19 let none be *w*
2Kin 10:19 whosoever shall be *w*, he shall
Prov 19:7 with words, yet they are *w* to him
Eccl 1:15 that which is *w* cannot be
Dan 5:27 in the balances, and art found *w*
Titus 1:5 in order the things that are *w*
Titus 3:13 that nothing be *w* unto them
Jas 1:4 be perfect and entire, *w* nothing

**WANTON**
Is 3:16 *w* eyes, walking and mincing as
1Ti 5:11 begun to wax *w* against Christ
Jas 5:5 pleasure on the earth, and been *w*

**WANTONNESS**
Rom 13:13 not in chambering and *w*, not in
2Pet 2:18 of the flesh, through much *w*

**WANTS**
Judg 19:20 let all thy *w* lie upon me
Phil 2:25 and he that ministered to my *w*

**WAR**
Gen 14:2 That these made *w* with Bera king
Ex 1:10 when there falleth out any *w*
Ex 13:17 the people repent when they see *w*
Ex 15:3 The LORD is a man of *w*
Ex 17:16 sworn that the LORD will have *w*
Ex 32:17 There is a noise of *w* in the camp
Num 1:3 able to go forth to *w* in Israel
Num 1:20 that were able to go forth to *w*
Num 1:22 that were able to go forth to *w*
Num 1:24 that were able to go forth to *w*
Num 1:26 that were able to go forth to *w*
Num 1:28 that were able to go forth to *w*
Num 1:30 that were able to go forth to *w*
Num 1:32 that were able to go forth to *w*
Num 1:34 that were able to go forth to *w*
Num 1:36 that were able to go forth to *w*
Num 1:38 that were able to go forth to *w*
Num 1:40 that were able to go forth to *w*
Num 1:42 that were able to go forth to *w*
Num 1:45 able to go forth to *w* in Israel
Num 10:9 if ye go to *w* in your land
Num 26:2 are able to go to *w* in Israel
Num 31:3 Arm some of yourselves unto the *w*
Num 31:4 of Israel, shall ye send to the *w*
Num 31:5 twelve thousand armed for *w*
Num 31:6 And Moses sent them to the *w*
Num 31:6 of Eleazar the priest, to the *w*
Num 31:21 men of *w* which went to the battle
Num 31:27 them that took the *w* upon them
Num 31:28 men of *w* which went out to battle
Num 31:32 which the men of *w* had caught
Num 31:36 of them that went out to *w*
Num 31:49 of *w* which are under our charge
Num 31:53 (For the men of *w* had taken spoil
Num 32:6 Shall your brethren go to *w*
Num 32:20 go armed before the LORD to *w*
Num 32:27 pass over, every man armed for *w*
Deut 1:41 on every man his weapons of *w*
Deut 2:14 the generation of the men of *w*
Deut 2:16 all the men of *w* were consumed
Deut 3:18 all that are meet for the *w*
Deut 4:34 by signs, and by wonders, and by *w*
Deut 20:12 but will make *w* against thee
Deut 20:19 in making *w* against it to take it
Deut 20:20 the city that maketh *w* with thee
Deut 21:10 forth to *w* against thine enemies
Deut 24:5 wife, he shall not go out to *w*
Josh 4:13 for *w* passed over before the LORD
Josh 5:4 were males, even all the men of *w*
Josh 5:6 all the people that were men of *w*
Josh 6:3 compass the city, all ye men of *w*
Josh 8:1 all the people of *w* with thee
Josh 8:3 arose, and all the people of *w*
Josh 8:11 people of *w* that were with him
Josh 10:5 Gibeon, and made *w* against it
Josh 10:7 and all the people of *w* with him
Josh 10:24 the men of *w* which went with him
Josh 11:7 and all the people of *w* with him
Josh 11:18 Joshua made *w* a long time with
Josh 11:23 And the land rested from *w*
Josh 14:11 even so is my strength now, for *w*
Josh 14:15 And the land had rest from *w*
Josh 17:1 because he was a man of *w*
Josh 22:12 to go up to *w* against them
Judg 3:2 might know, to teach them *w*
Judg 3:10 judged Israel, and went out to *w*
Judg 5:8 then was *w* in the gates
Judg 11:4 of Ammon made *w* against Israel
Judg 11:5 of Ammon made *w* against Israel
Judg 11:27 doest me wrong to *w* against me
Judg 18:11 men appointed with weapons of *w*
Judg 18:16 appointed with their weapons of *w*
Judg 18:17 were appointed with weapons of *w*
Judg 20:17 all these were men of *w*
Judg 21:22 not to each man his wife in the *w*
1Sa 8:12 and to make his instruments of *w*
1Sa 14:52 there was sore *w* against the
1Sa 16:18 mighty valiant man, and a man of *w*
1Sa 17:33 he a man of *w* from his youth
1Sa 18:5 and Saul set him over the men of *w*
1Sa 19:8 And there was *w* again
1Sa 23:8 all the people together to *w*
1Sa 28:15 the Philistines make *w* against me
2Sa 1:27 and the weapons of *w* perished
2Sa 3:1 Now there was long *w* between the
2Sa 3:6 while there was *w* between the
2Sa 11:7 did, and how the *w* prospered
2Sa 11:18 all the things concerning the *w*
2Sa 11:19 matters of the *w* unto the king
2Sa 17:8 and thy father is a man of *w*
2Sa 21:15 had yet *w* again with Israel
2Sa 22:35 He teacheth my hands to *w*
1Kin 2:5 and shed the blood of *w* in peace
1Kin 2:5 put the blood of *w* upon his
1Kin 9:22 but they were men of *w*, and his
1Kin 14:30 there was *w* between Rehoboam and
1Kin 15:6 there was *w* between Rehoboam and
1Kin 15:7 there was *w* between Abijam and
1Kin 15:16 there was *w* between Asa and Baasha
1Kin 15:32 there was *w* between Asa and Baasha
1Kin 20:18 or whether they be come out for *w*
1Kin 22:1 years without *w* between Syria
2Kin 8:28 Joram the son of Ahab to the *w*
2Kin 13:25 hand of Jehoahaz his father by *w*
2Kin 14:7 ten thousand, and took Selah by *w*
2Kin 16:5 Israel came up to Jerusalem to *w*
2Kin 18:20 counsel and strength for the *w*
2Kin 24:16 all that were strong and apt for *w*
2Kin 25:4 all the men of *w* fled by night by
2Kin 25:19 that was set over the men of *w*
1Chr 5:10 they made *w* with the Hagarites
1Chr 5:18 shoot with bow, and skilful in *w*
1Chr 5:18 that went out to the *w*
1Chr 5:19 they made *w* with the Hagarites,
1Chr 5:22 slain, because the *w* was of God
1Chr 7:4 were bands of soldiers for *w*
1Chr 7:11 soldiers, fit to go out for *w*
1Chr 7:40 of them that were apt to the *w*
1Chr 12:1 the mighty men, helpers of the *w*
1Chr 12:8 men of *w* fit for the battle, that
1Chr 12:23 that were ready armed to the *w*
1Chr 12:24 hundred, ready armed to the *w*
1Chr 12:25 mighty men of valour for the *w*
1Chr 12:33 went forth to battle, expert in *w*
1Chr 12:33 with all instruments of *w*
1Chr 12:35 of the Danites expert in *w* twenty
1Chr 12:36 went forth to battle, expert in *w*
1Chr 12:37 instruments of *w* for the battle
1Chr 12:38 All these men of *w*, that could
1Chr 18:10 (for Hadarezer had *w* with Tou
1Chr 20:4 that there arose *w* at Gezer with
1Chr 20:5 there was *w* again with the
1Chr 20:6 And yet again there was *w* at Gath
1Chr 28:3 because thou hast been a man of *w*
2Chr 6:34 If thy people go out to *w* against
2Chr 8:9 but they were men of *w*, and chief
2Chr 13:2 there was *w* between Abijah and
2Chr 13:3 with an army of valiant men of *w*
2Chr 14:6 he had no *w* in those years
2Chr 15:19 there was no more *w* unto the five
2Chr 17:10 made no *w* against Jehoshaphat
2Chr 17:13 and the men of *w*, mighty men of
2Chr 17:18 thousand ready prepared for the *w*
2Chr 18:3 and we will be with thee in the *w*
2Chr 22:5 son of Ahab king of Israel to *w*
2Chr 25:5 choice men, able to go forth to *w*
2Chr 26:11 men, that went out to *w* by bands
2Chr 26:13 that made *w* with mighty power, to
2Chr 28:12 against them that came from the *w*
2Chr 32:6 set captains of *w* over the people
2Chr 33:14 put captains of *w* in all the
2Chr 35:21 the house wherewith I have *w*
Job 5:20 in *w* from the power of the sword
Job 10:17 changes and *w* are against me
Job 38:23 against the day of battle and *w*
Ps 18:34 He teacheth my hands to *w*
Ps 27:3 though *w* should rise against me,
Ps 55:21 butter, but *w* was in his heart
Ps 68:30 thou the people that delight in *w*
Ps 120:7 but when I speak, they are for *w*
Ps 140:2 are they gathered together for *w*
Ps 144:1 which teacheth my hands to *w*
Prov 20:18 and with good advice make *w*
Prov 24:6 counsel thou shalt make thy *w*
Eccl 3:8 a time of *w*, and a time of peace
Eccl 8:8 there is no discharge in that *w*
Eccl 9:18 is better than weapons of *w*
Song 3:8 hold swords, being expert in *w*
Is 2:4 shall they learn *w* any more
Is 3:2 The mighty man, and the man of *w*
Is 3:25 the sword, and thy mighty in the *w*
Is 7:1 toward Jerusalem to *w* against it
Is 21:15 and from the grievousness of *w*
Is 36:5 I have counsel and strength for *w*
Is 37:9 is come forth to make *w* with thee
Is 41:12 they that *w* against thee shall be
Is 42:13 stir up jealousy like a man of *w*
Jer 4:19 of the trumpet, the alarm of *w*
Jer 6:4 Prepare ye *w* against her
Jer 6:23 array as men for *w* against thee
Jer 21:2 of Babylon maketh *w* against us
Jer 21:4 of *w* that are in your hands
Jer 28:8 and against great kingdoms, of *w*
Jer 38:4 the hands of the men of *w* that
Jer 39:4 saw them, and all the men of *w*
Jer 41:3 were found there, and the men of *w*
Jer 41:16 of Ahikam, even mighty men of *w*
Jer 42:14 of Egypt, where we shall see no *w*
Jer 48:14 mighty and strong men for the *w*
Jer 49:2 of *w* to be heard in Rabbah of the
Jer 49:26 all the men of *w* shall be cut off
Jer 50:30 all her men of *w* shall be cut off
Jer 51:20 art my battle ax and weapons of *w*
Jer 51:32 the men of *w* are affrighted
Jer 52:7 up, and all the men of *w* fled
Jer 52:25 had the charge of the men of *w*
Eze 17:17 company make for him in the *w*
Eze 26:9 engines of *w* against thy walls
Eze 27:10 were in thine army, thy men of *w*

### WASHED
Gen 43:24 them water, and they *w* their feet
Gen 43:31 he *w* his face, and went out, and
Gen 49:11 he *w* his garments in wine, and his
Ex 19:14 and they *w* their clothes
Ex 40:31 his sons *w* their hands and their
Ex 40:32 came near unto the altar, they *w*
Lev 8:6 and his sons, and *w* them with water
Lev 8:21 he *w* the inwards and the legs in
Lev 13:55 on the plague, after that it is *w*
Lev 13:58 it shall be *w* the second time
Lev 15:17 shall be *w* with water, and be
Num 8:21 purified, and they *w* their clothes
Judg 19:21 they *w* their feet, and did eat and
2Sa 12:20 David arose from the earth, and *w*
2Sa 19:24 nor *w* his clothes, from the day
1Kin 22:38 one *w* the chariot in the pool of
1Kin 22:38 and they *w* his armour
2Chr 4:6 the burnt offering they *w* in them
Job 29:6 When I *w* my steps with butter, and
Ps 73:13 vain, and *w* my hands in innocency
Prov 30:12 eyes, and yet is not *w* from their
Song 5:3 I have *w* my feet
Song 5:12 *w* with milk, and fitly set
Is 4:4 When the Lord shall have *w* away
Eze 16:4 neither wast thou *w* in water to
Eze 16:9 Then *w* I thee with water
Eze 16:9 I throughly *w* away thy blood from
Eze 40:38 where they *w* the burnt offering
Mt 27:24 *w* his hands before the multitude,
Lk 7:44 but she hath *w* my feet with tears
Lk 11:38 he had not first *w* before dinner
Jn 9:7 He went his way therefore, and *w*
Jn 9:11 and I went and *w*, and I received
Jn 9:15 put clay upon mine eyes, and I *w*
Jn 13:10 He that is *w* needeth not save to
Jn 13:12 So after he had *w* their feet
Jn 13:14 Lord and Master, have *w* your feet
Acts 9:37 whom when they had *w*, they laid
Acts 16:33 of the night, and *w* their stripes
1Cor 6:11 but ye are *w*, but ye are
1Ti 5:10 if she have *w* the saints' feet,
Heb 10:22 our bodies *w* with pure water
2Pet 2:22 the sow that was *w* to her
Rev 1:5 *w* us from our sins in his own
Rev 7:14 have *w* their robes, and made them

### WASHEST
Job 14:19 thou *w* away the things which grow

### WASHING
Lev 13:56 somewhat dark after the *w* of it
2Sa 11:2 the roof he saw a woman *w* herself
Neh 4:23 that every one put them off for *w*
Song 4:2 shorn, which came up from the *w*
Song 6:6 of sheep which go up from the *w*
Mk 7:4 as the *w* of cups, and pots, brasen
Mk 7:8 of men, as the *w* of pots and cups
Lk 5:2 out of them, and were *w* their nets
Eph 5:26 cleanse it with the *w* of water by
Titus 3:5 by the *w* of regeneration, and

### WASHINGS
Heb 9:10 in meats and drinks, and divers *w*

### WASHPOT
Ps 60:8 Moab is my *w*
Ps 108:9 Moab is my *w*

### WAST
Gen 3:11 Who told thee that thou *w* naked
Gen 3:19 for out of it *w* thou taken
Gen 33:10 of God, and thou *w* pleased with me
Gen 40:13 manner when thou *w* his butler
Deut 5:15 remember that thou *w* a servant in
Deut 15:15 thou shalt remember that thou *w* a
Deut 16:12 that thou *w* a bondman in Egypt
Deut 23:7 because thou *w* a stranger in his
Deut 24:18 that thou *w* a bondman in Egypt
Deut 24:22 thou shalt remember that thou *w* a
Deut 25:18 behind thee, when thou *w* faint
Deut 28:60 of Egypt, which thou *w* afraid of
Ruth 3:2 with whose maidens thou *w*
1Sa 15:17 When thou *w* little in thine own
1Sa 15:17 *w* thou not made the head of the
2Sa 1:14 How *w* thou not afraid to stretch
2Sa 1:25 thou *w* slain in thine high places
2Sa 5:2 thou *w* he that leddest out and
1Chr 11:2 thou *w* he that leddest out and
Job 15:7 or *w* thou made before the hills
Job 38:4 Where *w* thou when I laid the
Job 38:21 thou it, because thou *w* then born
Ps 99:8 thou *w* a God that forgavest them,
Ps 114:5 Jordan, that thou *w* driven back
Is 12:1 though thou *w* angry with me,
Is 14:3 wherein thou *w* made to serve
Is 33:1 spoilest, and thou *w* not spoiled
Is 43:4 Since thou *w* precious in my sight
Is 48:8 *w* called a transgressor from the
Is 54:6 of youth, when thou *w* refused
Is 57:10 therefore thou *w* not grieved
Jer 2:36 as thou *w* ashamed of Assyria
Jer 50:24 O Babylon, and thou *w* not aware
Eze 16:4 in the day thou *w* born thy navel
Eze 16:4 neither *w* thou washed in water to
Eze 16:4 thou *w* not salted at all, nor
Eze 16:5 but thou *w* cast out in the open
Eze 16:5 in the day that thou *w* born
Eze 16:6 thee when thou *w* in thy blood
Eze 16:6 thee when thou *w* in thy blood
Eze 16:7 is grown, whereas thou *w* naked
Eze 16:13 Thus *w* thou decked with gold and
Eze 16:13 thou *w* exceeding beautiful, and
Eze 16:22 of thy youth, when thou *w* naked
Eze 16:22 bare, and *w* polluted in thy blood
Eze 16:28 because thou *w* unsatiable
Eze 16:29 yet thou *w* not satisfied herewith
Eze 16:47 thou *w* corrupted more than they
Eze 21:30 in the place where thou *w* created
Eze 24:13 thou *w* not purged, thou shalt not
Eze 26:17 that *w* inhabited of seafaring men
Eze 26:17 which *w* strong in the sea, she and
Eze 27:25 thou *w* replenished, and made very
Eze 28:13 in the day that thou *w* created
Eze 28:14 thou *w* upon the holy mountain of
Eze 28:15 Thou *w* perfect in thy ways from
Eze 28:15 from the day that thou *w* created
Obad 11 even thou *w* as one of them
Mt 26:69 Thou also *w* with Jesus of Galilee
Mk 14:67 thou also *w* with Jesus of
Jn 1:48 when thou *w* under the fig tree, I
Jn 9:34 Thou *w* altogether born in sins,
Jn 21:18 say unto thee, When thou *w* young
Rev 5:9 for thou *w* slain, and hast
Rev 11:17 God Almighty, which art, and *w*
Rev 16:5 O Lord, which art, and *w*, and

### WASTE
Lev 26:31 And I will make your cities *w*
Lev 26:33 be desolate, and your cities *w*
Num 21:30 have laid them *w* even unto Nophah
Deut 32:10 in the *w* howling wilderness
1Kin 17:14 The barrel of meal shall not *w*
2Kin 19:25 lay *w* fenced cities into ruinous
1Chr 17:9 of wickedness *w* them any more
Neh 2:3 my fathers' sepulchres, lieth *w*
Neh 2:17 we are in, how Jerusalem lieth *w*
Job 30:3 in former time desolate and *w*
Job 38:27 satisfy the desolate and *w* ground
Ps 79:7 laid *w* his dwelling place
Ps 80:13 boar out of the wood doth *w* it
Is 5:6 And I will lay it *w*
Is 5:17 the *w* places of the fat ones
Is 15:1 in the night Ar of Moab is laid *w*
Is 15:1 the night Kir of Moab is laid *w*
Is 23:1 for it is laid *w*, so that there
Is 23:14 for your strength is laid *w*
Is 24:1 the earth empty, and maketh it *w*
Is 33:8 The highways lie *w*, the wayfaring
Is 34:10 to generation it shall lie *w*
Is 37:18 have laid *w* all the nations
Is 37:26 *w* defenced cities into ruinous
Is 42:15 I will make *w* mountains and hills,
Is 49:17 they that made thee *w* shall go
Is 49:19 For thy *w* and thy desolate places,
Is 51:3 he will comfort all her *w* places
Is 52:9 ye *w* places of Jerusalem
Is 58:12 thee shall build the old *w* places
Is 61:4 and they shall repair the *w* cities
Is 64:11 our pleasant things are laid *w*
Jer 2:15 yelled, and they made his land *w*
Jer 4:7 and thy cities shall be laid *w*
Jer 27:17 should this city be laid *w*
Jer 46:19 for Noph shall be *w* and desolate
Jer 49:13 a desolation, a reproach, a *w*
Jer 50:21 *w* and utterly destroy after them,
Eze 5:14 Moreover I will make thee *w*
Eze 6:6 the cities shall be laid *w*
Eze 6:6 that your altars may be laid *w*
Eze 12:20 are inhabited shall be laid *w*
Eze 19:7 and he laid *w* their cities
Eze 26:2 be replenished, now she is laid *w*
Eze 29:9 of Egypt shall be desolate and *w*
Eze 29:10 make the land of Egypt utterly *w*
Eze 29:12 *w* shall be desolate forty years
Eze 30:12 and I will make the land *w*
Eze 35:4 I will lay thy cities *w*, and thou
Eze 36:35 and the *w* and desolate and ruined
Eze 36:38 so shall the *w* cities be filled
Eze 38:8 Israel, which have been always *w*
Joel 1:7 He hath laid my vine *w*, and barked
Amos 7:9 of Israel shall be laid *w*
Amos 9:14 and they shall build the *w* cities
Mic 5:6 they shall *w* the land of Assyria
Nah 2:10 She is empty, and void, and *w*
Nah 3:7 thee, and say, Nineveh is laid *w*
Zeph 3:6 I made their streets *w*, that none
Hag 1:4 houses, and this house lie *w*
Hag 1:9 Because of mine house that is *w*
Mal 1:3 his heritage *w* for the dragons of
Mt 26:8 saying, To what purpose is this *w*
Mk 14:4 Why was this *w* of the ointment

### WASTED
Num 14:33 carcases be *w* in the wilderness
Num 24:22 the Kenite shall be *w*, until
Deut 2:14 of the men of war were *w* out from
1Kin 17:16 And the barrel of meal *w* not
1Chr 20:1 *w* the country of the children of
Ps 137:3 they that *w* us required of us
Is 6:11 cities be *w* without inhabitant
Is 19:5 the sea, and the river shall be *w*
Is 60:12 those nations shall be utterly *w*
Jer 44:6 and they are *w* and desolate, as at
Eze 30:7 midst of the cities that are *w*
Joel 1:10 The field is *w*, the land mourneth
Joel 1:10 for the corn is *w*
Lk 15:13 there *w* his substance with
Lk 16:1 unto him that he had *w* his goods
Gal 1:13 the church of God, and *w* it

### WASTENESS
Zeph 1:15 trouble and distress, a day of *w*

### WASTER
Prov 18:9 brother to him that is a great *w*
Is 54:16 I have created the *w* to destroy

### WASTES
Is 61:4 And they shall build the old *w*
Jer 49:13 thereof shall be perpetual *w*
Eze 33:24 they that inhabit those *w* of the
Eze 33:27 in the *w* shall fall by the sword
Eze 36:4 to the valleys, to the desolate *w*
Eze 36:10 and the *w* shall be builded
Eze 36:33 cities, and the *w* shall be builded

### WASTETH
Job 14:10 But man dieth, and *w* away
Ps 91:6 the destruction that *w* at noonday
Prov 19:26 He that *w* his father, and chaseth

### WASTING
Is 59:7 *w* and destruction are in their
Is 60:18 *w* nor destruction within thy

### WATCH
Gen 31:49 The LORD *w* between me and thee,
Ex 14:24 that in the morning *w* the LORD
Judg 7:19 in the beginning of the middle *w*
Judg 7:19 and they had but newly set the *w*
1Sa 11:11 of the host in the morning *w*
1Sa 19:11 to *w* him, and to slay him in the
2Sa 13:34 kept the *w* lifted up his eyes
2Kin 11:5 of the *w* of the king's house
2Kin 11:6 shall ye keep the *w* of the house
2Kin 11:7 even they shall keep the *w* of the
2Chr 20:24 the *w* tower in the wilderness
2Chr 23:6 shall keep the *w* of the LORD
Ezr 8:29 *W* ye, and keep them, until ye
Neh 4:9 set a *w* against them day and night
Neh 7:3 of Jerusalem, every one in his *w*
Job 7:12 that thou settest a *w* over me
Job 14:16 dost thou not *w* over my sin
Ps 90:4 is past, and as a *w* in the night
Ps 102:7 I *w*, and am as a sparrow alone
Ps 130:6 than they that *w* for the morning
Ps 130:6 than they that *w* for the morning
Ps 141:3 Set a *w*, O LORD, before my mouth
Is 21:5 *w* in the watchtower, eat, drink
Is 29:20 all that *w* for iniquity are cut
Jer 5:6 a leopard shall *w* over their
Jer 31:28 so will I *w* over them, to build,
Jer 44:27 I will *w* over them for evil, and
Jer 51:12 of Babylon, make the *w* strong
Nah 2:1 *w* the way, make thy loins strong,
Hab 2:1 I will stand upon my *w*, and set me

Hab 2:1 will *w* to see what he will say
Mt 14:25 in the fourth *w* of the night
Mt 24:42 *W* therefore
Mt 24:43 in what *w* the thief would come
Mt 25:13 *W* therefore, for ye know neither
Mt 26:38 tarry ye here, and *w* with me
Mt 26:40 could ye not *w* with me one hour
Mt 26:41 *W* and pray, that ye enter not into
Mt 27:65 said unto them, Ye have a *w*
Mt 27:66 sealing the stone, and setting a *w*
Mt 28:11 some of the *w* came into the city,
Mk 6:48 about the fourth *w* of the night
Mk 13:33 Take ye heed, *w* and pray
Mk 13:34 and commanded the porter to *w*
Mk 13:35 *W* ye therefore
Mk 13:37 I say unto you I say unto all, *W*
Mk 14:34 tarry ye here, and *w*
Mk 14:37 couldest not thou *w* one hour
Mk 14:38 *W* ye and pray, lest ye enter into
Lk 2:8 keeping *w* over their flock by
Lk 12:38 if he shall come in the second *w*
Lk 12:38 or come in the third *w*
Lk 21:36 *W* ye therefore, and pray always,
Acts 20:31 Therefore *w*, and remember, that by
1Cor 16:13 *W* ye, stand fast in the faith,
Col 4:2 *w* in the same with thanksgiving
1Th 5:6 but let us *w* and be sober
2Ti 4:5 But *w* thou in all things, endure
Heb 13:17 for they *w* for your souls, as
1Pet 4:7 therefore sober, and *w* unto prayer
Rev 3:3 If therefore thou shalt not *w*

**WATCHED**
Ps 59:*t* they *w* the house to kill him
Jer 20:10 All my familiars *w* for my halting
Jer 31:28 that like as I have *w* over them
Lam 4:17 in our watching we have *w* for a
Dan 9:14 hath the LORD *w* upon the evil
Mt 24:43 thief would come, he would have *w*
Mt 27:36 And sitting down they *w* him there
Mk 3:2 And they *w* him, whether he would
Lk 6:7 And the scribes and Pharisees *w* him
Lk 12:39 thief would come, he would have *w*
Lk 14:1 the sabbath day, that they *w* him
Lk 20:20 And they *w* him, and sent forth
Acts 9:24 they *w* the gates day and night to

**WATCHER**
Dan 4:13 head upon my bed, and, behold, a *w*
Dan 4:23 And whereas the king saw a *w*

**WATCHERS**
Jer 4:16 that *w* come from a far country,
Dan 4:17 matter is by the decree of the *w*

**WATCHES**
Neh 7:3 appoint *w* of the inhabitants of
Neh 12:9 were over against them in the *w*
Ps 63:6 meditate on thee in the night *w*
Ps 119:148 Mine eyes prevent the night *w*
Lam 2:19 in the beginning of the *w* pour

**WATCHETH**
Ps 37:32 The wicked *w* the righteous, and
Eze 7:6 it *w* for thee
Rev 16:15 Blessed is he that *w*, and keepeth

**WATCHFUL**
Rev 3:2 Be *w*, and strengthen the things

**WATCHING**
1Sa 4:13 sat upon a seat by the wayside *w*
Prov 8:34 *w* daily at my gates, waiting at
Lam 4:17 in our *w* we have watched for a
Mt 27:54 *w* Jesus, saw the earthquake, and
Lk 12:37 lord when he cometh shall find *w*
Eph 6:18 *w* thereunto with all perseverance

**WATCHINGS**
2Cor 6:5 in tumults, in labours, in *w*
2Cor 11:27 in *w* often, in hunger and thirst,

**WATCHMAN**
2Sa 18:24 the *w* went up to the roof over
2Sa 18:25 the *w* cried, and told the king
2Sa 18:26 the *w* saw another man running
2Sa 18:26 the *w* called unto the porter, and
2Sa 18:27 the *w* said, Me thinketh the
2Kin 9:17 there stood a *w* on the tower in
2Kin 9:18 the *w* told, saying, The messenger
2Kin 9:20 the *w* told, saying, He came even
Ps 127:1 city, the *w* waketh but in vain
Is 21:6 Lord said unto me, Go, set a *w*
Is 21:11 He calleth to me out of Seir, *W*
Is 21:11 *W*, what of the night
Is 21:12 The *w* said, The morning cometh,
Eze 3:17 I have made thee a *w* unto the
Eze 33:2 coasts, and set him for their *w*
Eze 33:6 But if the *w* see the sword come,
Eze 33:7 I have set thee a *w* unto the
Hos 9:8 The *w* of Ephraim was with my God

**WATCHMAN'S**
Eze 33:6 will I require at the *w* hand

**WATCHMEN**
1Sa 14:16 the *w* of Saul in Gibeah of
2Kin 17:9 tower of the *w* to the fenced city
2Kin 18:8 tower of the *w* to the fenced city
Song 3:3 The *w* that go about the city
Song 5:7 The *w* that went about the city
Is 52:8 Thy *w* shall lift up the voice
Is 56:10 His *w* are blind
Is 62:6 I have set *w* upon thy walls, O
Jer 6:17 Also I set *w* over you, saying,
Jer 31:6 that the *w* upon the mount Ephraim
Jer 51:12 the watch strong, set up the *w*
Mic 7:4 the day of thy *w* and thy

**WATCHTOWER**
Is 21:5 Prepare the table, watch in the *w*
Is 21:8 upon the *w* in the daytime

**WATER**
Gen 2:10 went out of Eden to *w* the garden
Gen 16:7 a fountain of *w* in the wilderness
Gen 18:4 Let a little *w*, I pray you, be
Gen 21:14 and took bread, and a bottle of *w*
Gen 21:15 the *w* was spent in the bottle, and
Gen 21:19 her eyes, and she saw a well of *w*
Gen 21:19 went, and filled the bottle with *w*
Gen 21:25 Abimelech because of a well of *w*
Gen 24:11 of *w* at the time of the evening
Gen 24:11 time that women go out to draw *w*
Gen 24:13 I stand here by the well of *w*
Gen 24:13 of the city come out to draw *w*
Gen 24:17 drink a little *w* of thy pitcher
Gen 24:19 I will draw *w* for thy camels also
Gen 24:20 ran again unto the well to draw *w*
Gen 24:32 *w* to wash his feet, and the men's
Gen 24:43 Behold, I stand by the well of *w*
Gen 24:43 the virgin cometh forth to draw *w*
Gen 24:43 a little *w* of thy pitcher to
Gen 24:45 down unto the well, and drew *w*
Gen 26:18 Isaac digged again the wells of *w*
Gen 26:19 found there a well of springing *w*
Gen 26:20 herdmen, saying, The *w* is ours
Gen 26:32 and said unto him, We have found *w*
Gen 29:7 *w* ye the sheep, and go and feed
Gen 29:8 then we *w* the sheep
Gen 37:24 was empty, there was no *w* in it
Gen 43:24 Joseph's house, and gave them *w*
Gen 49:4 Unstable as *w*, thou shalt not
Ex 2:10 Because I drew him out of the *w*
Ex 2:16 and they came and drew *w*, and filled
Ex 2:16 troughs to *w* their father's flock
Ex 2:19 also drew *w* enough for us, and
Ex 4:9 shalt take of the *w* of the river
Ex 4:9 the *w* which thou takest out of
Ex 7:15 lo, he goeth out unto the *w*
Ex 7:18 to drink of the *w* of the river
Ex 7:19 and upon all their pools of *w*
Ex 7:21 not drink of the *w* of the river
Ex 7:24 about the river for *w* to drink
Ex 7:24 not drink of the *w* of the river
Ex 8:20 lo, he cometh forth to the *w*
Ex 12:9 it raw, nor sodden at all with *w*
Ex 15:22 in the wilderness, and found no *w*
Ex 15:27 where were twelve wells of *w*
Ex 17:1 there was no *w* for the people to
Ex 17:2 Give us *w* that we may drink
Ex 17:3 the people thirsted there for *w*
Ex 17:6 and there shall come *w* out of it
Ex 20:4 that is in the *w* under the earth
Ex 23:25 shall bless thy bread, and thy *w*
Ex 29:4 and shalt wash them with *w*
Ex 30:18 and thou shalt put *w* therein
Ex 30:20 they shall wash with *w*, that
Ex 32:20 powder, and strawed it upon the *w*
Ex 34:28 neither eat bread, nor drink *w*
Ex 40:7 the altar, and shalt put *w* therein
Ex 40:12 congregation, and wash them with *w*
Ex 40:30 put *w* there, to wash withal
Lev 1:9 and his legs shall he wash in *w*
Lev 1:13 the inwards and the legs with *w*
Lev 6:28 be both scoured, and rinsed in *w*
Lev 8:6 his sons, and washed them with *w*
Lev 8:21 the inwards and the legs in *w*
Lev 11:32 is done, it must be put into *w*
Lev 11:34 that on which such *w* cometh shall
Lev 11:36 pit, wherein there is plenty of *w*
Lev 11:38 But if any *w* be put upon the seed
Lev 14:5 an earthen vessel over running *w*
Lev 14:6 was killed over the running *w*
Lev 14:8 his hair, and wash himself in *w*
Lev 14:9 also he shall wash his flesh in *w*
Lev 14:50 an earthen vessel over running *w*
Lev 14:51 slain bird, and in the running *w*
Lev 14:52 the bird, and with the running *w*
Lev 15:5 clothes, and bathe himself in *w*
Lev 15:6 clothes, and bathe himself in *w*
Lev 15:7 clothes, and bathe himself in *w*
Lev 15:8 clothes, and bathe himself in *w*
Lev 15:10 clothes, and bathe himself in *w*
Lev 15:11 and hath not rinsed his hands in *w*
Lev 15:11 clothes, and bathe himself in *w*
Lev 15:12 of wood shall be rinsed in *w*
Lev 15:13 and bathe his flesh in running *w*
Lev 15:16 he shall wash all his flesh in *w*
Lev 15:17 shall be washed with *w*, and be
Lev 15:18 shall both bathe themselves in *w*
Lev 15:21 clothes, and bathe himself in *w*
Lev 15:22 clothes, and bathe himself in *w*
Lev 15:27 clothes, and bathe himself in *w*
Lev 16:4 shall he wash his flesh in *w*
Lev 16:24 flesh with *w* in the holy place
Lev 16:26 clothes, and bathe his flesh in *w*
Lev 16:28 clothes, and bathe his flesh in *w*
Lev 17:15 clothes, and bathe himself in *w*
Lev 22:6 unless he wash his flesh with *w*
Num 5:17 take holy *w* in an earthen vessel
Num 5:17 shall take, and put it into the *w*
Num 5:18 bitter *w* that causeth the curse
Num 5:19 bitter *w* that causeth the curse
Num 5:22 this *w* that causeth the curse
Num 5:23 blot them out with the bitter *w*
Num 5:24 bitter *w* that causeth the curse
Num 5:24 the *w* that causeth the curse
Num 5:26 cause the woman to drink the *w*
Num 5:27 he hath made her to drink the *w*
Num 5:27 that the *w* that causeth the curse
Num 8:7 Sprinkle *w* of purifying upon them
Num 19:7 and he shall bathe his flesh in *w*
Num 19:8 her shall wash his clothes in *w*
Num 19:8 and bathe his flesh in *w*
Num 19:9 of Israel for a *w* of separation
Num 19:13 because the *w* of separation was
Num 19:17 running *w* shall be put thereto in
Num 19:18 take hyssop, and dip it in the *w*
Num 19:19 clothes, and bathe himself in *w*
Num 19:20 the *w* of separation hath not been
Num 19:21 that he that sprinkleth the *w* of
Num 19:21 he that toucheth the *w* of
Num 20:2 And there was no *w* for the
Num 20:5 neither is there any *w* to drink
Num 20:8 and it shall give forth his *w*
Num 20:8 forth to them *w* out of the rock
Num 20:10 we fetch you *w* out of this rock
Num 20:11 the *w* came out abundantly, and the
Num 20:13 This is the *w* of Meribah
Num 20:17 we drink of the *w* of the wells
Num 20:19 if I and my cattle drink of thy *w*
Num 20:24 my word at the *w* of Meribah
Num 21:5 no bread, neither is there any *w*
Num 21:16 together, and I will give them *w*
Num 24:7 He shall pour the *w* out of his
Num 27:14 me at the *w* before their eyes
Num 27:14 that is the *w* of Meribah in
Num 31:23 purified with the *w* of separation
Num 31:23 ye shall make go through the *w*
Num 33:9 Elim were twelve fountains of *w*
Num 33:14 where was no *w* for the people to
Deut 2:6 also buy *w* of them for money
Deut 2:28 give me *w* for money, that I may
Deut 8:7 good land, a land of brooks of *w*
Deut 8:15 and drought, where there was no *w*
Deut 8:15 who brought thee forth *w* out of
Deut 9:9 neither did eat bread nor drink *w*
Deut 9:18 neither eat bread, nor drink *w*
Deut 11:4 how he made the *w* of the Red sea
Deut 11:11 drinketh *w* of the rain of heaven
Deut 12:16 shall pour it upon the earth as *w*
Deut 12:24 shalt pour it upon the earth as *w*
Deut 15:23 pour it upon the ground as *w*
Deut 23:4 with *w* in the way, when ye came
Deut 23:11 on, he shall wash himself with *w*
Deut 29:11 thy wood unto the drawer of thy *w*
Josh 2:10 up the *w* of the Red sea for you

Josh 3:8 to the brink of the *w* of Jordan
Josh 3:15 were dipped in the brim of the *w*
Josh 7:5 the people melted, and became as *w*
Josh 9:21 drawers of *w* unto all the
Josh 9:23 drawers of *w* for the house of my
Josh 9:27 drawers of *w* for the congregation
Josh 15:9 the fountain of the *w* of Nephtoah
Josh 15:19 give me also springs of *w*
Josh 16:1 unto the *w* of Jericho on the east
Judg 1:15 give me also springs of *w*
Judg 4:19 I pray thee, a little *w* to drink
Judg 5:4 the clouds also dropped *w*
Judg 5:11 in the places of drawing *w*
Judg 5:25 He asked *w*, and she gave him milk
Judg 6:38 of the fleece, a bowl full of *w*
Judg 7:4 bring them down unto the *w*
Judg 7:5 down the people unto the *w*
Judg 7:5 lappeth of the *w* with his tongue
Judg 7:6 down upon their knees to drink *w*
Judg 15:19 the jaw, and there came *w* thereout
1Sa 7:6 together to Mizpeh, and drew *w*
1Sa 9:11 young maidens going out to draw *w*
1Sa 25:11 I then take my bread, and my *w*
1Sa 26:11 at his bolster, and the cruse of *w*
1Sa 26:12 the cruse of *w* from Saul's
1Sa 26:16 the cruse of *w* that was at his
1Sa 30:11 and they made him drink *w*
1Sa 30:12 eaten no bread, nor drunk any *w*
2Sa 14:14 are as *w* spilt on the ground,
2Sa 17:20 They be gone over the brook of *w*
2Sa 17:21 Arise, and pass quickly over the *w*
2Sa 21:10 the beginning of harvest until *w*
2Sa 23:15 the *w* of the well of Beth-lehem
2Sa 23:16 drew *w* out of the well of
1Kin 13:8 bread nor drink *w* in this place
1Kin 13:9 saying, Eat no bread, nor drink *w*
1Kin 13:16 drink *w* with thee in this place
1Kin 13:17 eat no bread nor drink *w* there
1Kin 13:18 that he may eat bread and drink *w*
1Kin 13:19 bread in his house, and drank *w*
1Kin 13:22 drunk *w* in the place, of the
1Kin 13:22 thee, Eat no bread, and drink no *w*
1Kin 14:15 as a reed is shaken in the *w*
1Kin 17:10 a little *w* in a vessel, that I
1Kin 18:4 cave, and fed them with bread and *w*
1Kin 18:5 the land, unto all fountains of *w*
1Kin 18:13 cave, and fed them with bread and *w*
1Kin 18:33 and said, Fill four barrels with *w*
1Kin 18:35 the *w* ran round about the altar
1Kin 18:35 he filled the trench also with *w*
1Kin 18:38 licked up the *w* that was in the
1Kin 19:6 and a cruse of *w* at his head
1Kin 22:27 with *w* of affliction, until I
2Kin 2:19 but the *w* is naught, and the
2Kin 3:9 and there was no *w* for the host
2Kin 3:11 which poured *w* on the hands of
2Kin 3:17 valley shall be filled with *w*
2Kin 3:19 good tree, and stop all wells of *w*
2Kin 3:20 there came *w* by the way of Edom,
2Kin 3:20 and the country was filled with *w*
2Kin 3:22 and the sun shone upon the *w*
2Kin 3:22 the Moabites saw the *w* on the
2Kin 3:25 they stopped all the wells of *w*
2Kin 6:5 beam, the ax head fell into the *w*
2Kin 6:22 *w* before them, that they may eat
2Kin 8:15 a thick cloth, and dipped it in *w*
2Kin 20:20 brought *w* into the city, are they
1Chr 11:17 the *w* of the well of Beth-lehem
1Chr 11:18 drew *w* out of the well of
2Chr 18:26 with *w* of affliction, until I
2Chr 32:4 of Assyria come, and find much *w*
Ezr 10:6 he did eat no bread, nor drink *w*
Neh 3:26 the *w* gate toward the east
Neh 8:1 street that was before the *w* gate
Neh 8:3 the *w* gate from the morning until
Neh 8:16 and in the street of the *w* gate
Neh 9:15 broughtest forth *w* for them out
Neh 9:20 gavest them *w* for their thirst
Neh 12:37 even unto the *w* gate eastward
Neh 13:2 of Israel with bread and with *w*
Job 8:11 can the flag grow without *w*
Job 9:30 If I wash myself with snow *w*
Job 14:9 the scent of *w* it will bud
Job 15:16 which drinketh iniquity like *w*
Job 22:7 Thou hast not given *w* to the
Job 34:7 who drinketh up scorning like *w*
Job 36:27 he maketh small the drops of *w*
Ps 1:3 a tree planted by the rivers of *w*
Ps 6:6 I *w* my couch with my tears
Ps 22:14 I am poured out like *w*, and all my
Ps 42:1 hart panteth after the *w* brooks
Ps 63:1 and thirsty land, where no *w* is
Ps 65:9 river of God, which is full of *w*
Ps 66:12 we went through fire and through *w*
Ps 72:6 as showers that *w* the earth
Ps 77:17 The clouds poured out *w*
Ps 79:3 shed like *w* round about Jerusalem
Ps 88:17 came round about me daily like *w*
Ps 107:35 the wilderness into a standing *w*
Ps 109:18 it come into his bowels like *w*
Ps 114:8 turned the rock into a standing *w*
Prov 8:24 no fountains abounding with *w*
Prov 17:14 is as when one letteth out *w*
Prov 20:5 the heart of man is like deep *w*
Prov 21:1 of the LORD, as the rivers of *w*
Prov 25:21 be thirsty, give him *w* to drink
Prov 27:19 As in *w* face answereth to face,
Prov 30:16 earth that is not filled with *w*
Eccl 2:6 I made me pools of *w*
Eccl 2:6 to *w* therewith the wood that
Is 1:22 dross, thy wine mixed with *w*
Is 1:30 and as a garden that hath no *w*
Is 3:1 of bread, and the whole stay of *w*
Is 12:3 with joy shall ye draw *w* out of
Is 14:23 for the bittern, and pools of *w*
Is 16:9 I will *w* thee with my tears, O
Is 21:14 brought *w* to him that was thirsty
Is 22:11 walls for the *w* of the old pool
Is 27:3 I will *w* it every moment
Is 30:14 or to take *w* withal out of the
Is 30:20 the *w* of affliction, yet shall
Is 32:2 as rivers of *w* in a dry place, as
Is 35:7 and the thirsty land springs of *w*
Is 37:25 I have digged, and drunk *w*
Is 41:17 When the poor and needy seek *w*
Is 41:18 make the wilderness a pool of *w*
Is 41:18 and the dry land springs of *w*
Is 44:3 For I will pour *w* upon him that
Is 44:4 as willows by the *w* courses
Is 44:12 he drinketh no *w*, and is faint
Is 49:10 springs of *w* shall he guide them
Is 50:2 stinketh, because there is no *w*
Is 58:11 garden, and like a spring of *w*
Is 63:12 arm, dividing the *w* before them
Jer 2:13 cisterns, that can hold no *w*
Jer 8:14 given us *w* of gall to drink,
Jer 9:15 give them *w* of gall to drink
Jer 13:1 thy loins, and put it not in *w*
Jer 14:3 came to the pits, and found no *w*
Jer 23:15 and make them drink the *w* of gall
Jer 38:6 And in the dungeon there was no *w*
Lam 1:16 eye, mine eye runneth down with *w*
Lam 2:19 pour out thine heart like *w*
Lam 3:48 of *w* for the destruction of the
Lam 5:4 We have drunken our *w* for money
Eze 4:11 shalt drink also *w* by measure
Eze 4:16 and they shall drink *w* by measure
Eze 4:17 That they may want bread and *w*
Eze 7:17 and all knees shall be weak as *w*
Eze 12:18 drink thy *w* with trembling and
Eze 12:19 drink their *w* with astonishment,
Eze 16:4 thou washed in *w* to supple thee
Eze 16:9 Then washed I thee with *w*
Eze 17:7 that he might *w* it by the furrows
Eze 21:7 and all knees shall be weak as *w*
Eze 24:3 set it on, and also pour *w* into it
Eze 26:12 and thy dust in the midst of the *w*
Eze 31:14 in their height, all that drink *w*
Eze 31:16 best of Lebanon, all that drink *w*
Eze 32:6 I will also *w* with thy blood the
Eze 36:25 will I sprinkle clean *w* upon you
Dan 1:12 us pulse to eat, and *w* to drink
Hos 2:5 that give me my bread and my *w*
Hos 5:10 out my wrath upon them like *w*
Hos 10:7 is cut off as the foam upon the *w*
Joel 3:18 shall *w* the valley of Shittim
Amos 4:8 unto one city, to drink *w*
Amos 8:11 of bread, nor a thirst for *w*
Jonah 3:7 let them not feed, nor drink *w*
Nah 2:8 is of old like a pool of *w*
Hab 3:10 overflowing of the *w* passed by
Zec 9:11 out of the pit wherein is no *w*
Mt 3:11 you with *w* unto repentance
Mt 3:16 went up straightway out of the *w*
Mt 10:42 *w* only in the name of a disciple
Mt 14:28 bid me come unto thee on the *w*
Mt 14:29 of the ship, he walked on the *w*
Mt 17:15 into the fire, and oft into the *w*
Mt 27:24 a tumult was made, he took *w*
Mk 1:8 I indeed have baptized you with *w*
Mk 1:10 coming up out of the *w*, he saw
Mk 9:41 a cup of *w* to drink in my name
Mk 14:13 you a man bearing a pitcher of *w*
Lk 3:16 all, I indeed baptize you with *w*
Lk 7:44 thou gavest me no *w* for my feet
Lk 8:23 and they were filled with *w*
Lk 8:24 the wind and the raging of the *w*
Lk 8:25 he commandeth even the winds and *w*
Lk 16:24 dip the tip of his finger in *w*
Lk 22:10 meet you, bearing a pitcher of *w*
Jn 1:26 them, saying, I baptize with *w*
Jn 1:31 am I come baptizing with *w*
Jn 1:33 he that sent me to baptize with *w*
Jn 2:7 them, Fill the waterpots with *w*
Jn 2:9 tasted the *w* that was made wine
Jn 2:9 servants which drew the *w* knew
Jn 3:5 thee, Except a man be born of *w*
Jn 3:23 because there was much *w* there
Jn 4:7 a woman of Samaria to draw *w*
Jn 4:10 he would have given thee living *w*
Jn 4:11 then hast thou that living *w*
Jn 4:13 of this *w* shall thirst again
Jn 4:14 the *w* that I shall give him shall
Jn 4:14 but the *w* that I shall give him
Jn 4:14 *w* springing up into everlasting
Jn 4:15 unto him, Sir, give me this *w*
Jn 4:46 Galilee, where he made the *w* wine
Jn 5:3 waiting for the moving of the *w*
Jn 5:4 into the pool, and troubled the *w*
Jn 5:4 after the troubling of the *w*
Jn 5:7 when the *w* is troubled, to put me
Jn 7:38 shall flow rivers of living *w*
Jn 13:5 that he poureth *w* into a bason
Jn 19:34 came there out blood and *w*
Acts 1:5 For John truly baptized with *w*
Acts 8:36 way, they came unto a certain *w*
Acts 8:36 the eunuch said, See, here is *w*
Acts 8:38 and they went down both into the *w*
Acts 8:39 they were come up out of the *w*
Acts 10:47 Can any man forbid *w*, that these
Acts 11:16 said, John indeed baptized with *w*
Eph 5:26 with the washing of *w* by the word
1Ti 5:23 Drink no longer *w*, but use a
Heb 9:19 of calves and of goats, with *w*
Heb 10:22 and our bodies washed with pure *w*
Jas 3:11 forth at the same place sweet *w*
Jas 3:12 can no fountain both yield salt *w*
1Pet 3:20 is, eight souls were saved by *w*
2Pet 2:17 These are wells without *w*
2Pet 3:5 out of the *w* and in the *w*
2Pet 3:6 then was, being overflowed with *w*
1Jn 5:6 This is he that came by *w*
1Jn 5:6 not by *w* only, but by *w*
1Jn 5:8 in earth, the spirit, and the *w*
Jude 12 clouds they are without *w*
Rev 12:15 *w* as a flood after the woman
Rev 16:12 the *w* thereof was dried up, that
Rev 21:6 fountain of the *w* of life freely
Rev 22:1 me a pure river of *w* of life
Rev 22:17 let him take the *w* of life freely

## WATERCOURSE

2Chr 32:30 also stopped the upper *w* of Gihon
Job 38:25 Who hath divided a *w* for the

## WATERED

Gen 2:6 *w* the whole face of the ground
Gen 13:10 that it was well *w* every where
Gen 29:2 of that well they *w* the flocks
Gen 29:3 *w* the sheep, and put the stone
Gen 29:10 *w* the flock of Laban his mother's
Ex 2:17 and helped them, and *w* their flock
Ex 2:19 enough for us, and *w* the flock
Prov 11:25 watereth shall be *w* also himself
Is 58:11 and thou shalt be like a *w* garden
Jer 31:12 their soul shall be as a *w* garden
1Cor 3:6 I have planted, Apollos *w*

## WATEREDST

Deut 11:10 *w* it with thy foot, as a garden

## WATEREST

Ps 65:9 Thou visitest the earth, and *w* it
Ps 65:10 Thou *w* the ridges thereof

## WATERETH

Ps 104:13 He *w* the hills from his chambers
Prov 11:25 he that *w* shall be watered also
Is 55:10 but *w* the earth, and maketh it
1Cor 3:7 any thing, neither he that *w*
1Cor 3:8 planteth and he that *w* are one

## WATERFLOOD

Ps 69:15 Let not the *w* overflow me

### WATERING
Gen 30:38 flocks in the gutters in the *w*
Job 37:11 Also by *w* he wearieth the thick
Lk 13:15 the stall, and lead him away to *w*

### WATERPOT
Jn 4:28 The woman then left her *w*

### WATERPOTS
Jn 2:6 were set there six *w* of stone
Jn 2:7 unto them, Fill the *w* with water

### WATERS
Gen 1:2 God moved upon the face of the *w*
Gen 1:6 a firmament in the midst of the *w*
Gen 1:6 it divide the *w* from the *w*
Gen 1:7 divided the *w* which were under
Gen 1:7 under the firmament from the *w*
Gen 1:9 Let the *w* under the heaven be
Gen 1:10 together of the *w* called he Seas
Gen 1:20 Let the *w* bring forth abundantly
Gen 1:21 which the *w* brought forth
Gen 1:22 fill the *w* in the seas, and let
Gen 6:17 bring a flood of *w* upon the earth
Gen 7:6 the flood of *w* was upon the earth
Gen 7:7 because of the *w* of the flood
Gen 7:10 that the *w* of the flood were upon
Gen 7:17 the *w* increased, and bare up the
Gen 7:18 And the *w* prevailed, and were
Gen 7:18 ark went upon the face of the *w*
Gen 7:19 the *w* prevailed exceedingly upon
Gen 7:20 cubits upward did the *w* prevail
Gen 7:24 the *w* prevailed upon the earth an
Gen 8:1 over the earth, and the *w* asswaged
Gen 8:3 the *w* returned from off the earth
Gen 8:3 and fifty days the *w* were abated
Gen 8:5 the *w* decreased continually until
Gen 8:7 until the *w* were dried up from
Gen 8:8 to see if the *w* were abated from
Gen 8:9 for the *w* were on the face of the
Gen 8:11 so Noah knew that the *w* were
Gen 8:13 the *w* were dried up from off the
Gen 9:11 off any more by the *w* of a flood
Gen 9:15 the *w* shall no more become a
Ex 7:17 upon the *w* which are in the river
Ex 7:19 thine hand upon the *w* of Egypt
Ex 7:20 smote the *w* that were in the
Ex 7:20 all the *w* that were in the river
Ex 8:6 out his hand over the *w* of Egypt
Ex 14:21 dry land, and the *w* were divided
Ex 14:22 the *w* were a wall unto them on
Ex 14:26 that the *w* may come again upon
Ex 14:28 the *w* returned, and covered the
Ex 14:29 the *w* were a wall unto them on
Ex 15:8 the *w* were gathered together
Ex 15:10 they sank as lead in the mighty *w*
Ex 15:19 again the *w* of the sea upon them
Ex 15:23 could not drink of the *w* of Marah
Ex 15:25 which when he had cast into the *w*
Ex 15:25 the *w* were made sweet
Ex 15:27 and they encamped there by the *w*
Lev 11:9 ye eat of all that are in the *w*
Lev 11:9 hath fins and scales in the *w*
Lev 11:10 rivers, of all that move in the *w*
Lev 11:10 living thing which is in the *w*
Lev 11:12 hath no fins nor scales in the *w*
Lev 11:46 creature that moveth in the *w*
Num 21:22 not drink of the *w* of the well
Num 24:6 and as cedar trees beside the *w*
Num 24:7 and his seed shall be in many *w*
Deut 4:18 is in the *w* beneath the earth
Deut 5:8 is in the *w* beneath the earth
Deut 10:7 to Jotbath, a land of rivers of *w*
Deut 14:9 eat of all that are in the *w*
Deut 32:51 Israel at the *w* of Meribah-kadesh
Deut 33:8 didst strive at the *w* of Meribah
Josh 3:13 shall rest in the *w* of Jordan
Josh 3:13 that the *w* of Jordan shall be cut
Josh 3:13 the *w* that come down from above
Josh 3:16 That the *w* which came down from
Josh 4:7 That the *w* of Jordan were cut off
Josh 4:7 the *w* of Jordan were cut off
Josh 4:18 that the *w* of Jordan returned
Josh 4:23 the *w* of Jordan from before you
Josh 5:1 the *w* of Jordan from before the
Josh 11:5 together at the *w* of Merom
Josh 11:7 them by the *w* of Merom suddenly
Josh 15:7 passed toward the *w* of En-shemesh
Josh 18:15 out to the well of *w* of Nephtoah
Judg 5:19 in Taanach by the *w* of Megiddo
Judg 7:24 before them the *w* unto Beth-barah
Judg 7:24 took the *w* unto Beth-barah and
2Sa 5:20 before me, as the breach of *w*
2Sa 12:27 and have taken the city of *w*
2Sa 22:12 pavilions round about him, dark *w*
2Sa 22:17 he drew me out of many *w*
2Kin 2:8 it together, and smote the *w*
2Kin 2:14 fell from him, and smote the *w*
2Kin 2:14 and when he also had smitten the *w*
2Kin 2:21 forth unto the spring of the *w*
2Kin 2:21 the LORD, I have healed these *w*
2Kin 2:22 So the *w* were healed unto this
2Kin 5:12 better than all the *w* of Israel
2Kin 18:31 ye every one the *w* of his cistern
2Kin 19:24 I have digged and drunk strange *w*
1Chr 14:11 hand like the breaking forth of *w*
2Chr 32:3 his mighty men to stop the *w* of
Neh 9:11 as a stone into the mighty *w*
Job 3:24 are poured out like the *w*
Job 5:10 sendeth *w* upon the fields
Job 11:16 remember it as *w* that pass away
Job 12:15 Behold, he withholdeth the *w*
Job 14:11 As the *w* fail from the sea, and
Job 14:19 The *w* wear the stones
Job 22:11 and abundance of *w* cover thee
Job 24:18 He is swift as the *w*
Job 24:19 and heat consume the snow *w*
Job 26:5 are formed from under the *w*
Job 26:8 He bindeth up the *w* in his thick
Job 26:10 hath compassed the *w* with bounds
Job 27:20 Terrors take hold on him as *w*
Job 28:4 even the *w* forgotten of the foot
Job 28:25 and he weigheth the *w* by measure
Job 29:19 My root was spread out by the *w*
Job 30:14 me as a wide breaking in of *w*
Job 37:10 breadth of the *w* is straitened
Job 38:25 for the overflowing of *w*, or a
Job 38:30 The *w* are hid as with a stone, and
Job 38:34 abundance of *w* may cover thee
Ps 18:11 round about him were dark *w*
Ps 18:15 Then the channels of *w* were seen
Ps 18:16 took me, he drew me out of many *w*
Ps 23:2 he leadeth me beside the still *w*
Ps 29:3 voice of the LORD is upon the *w*
Ps 29:3 the LORD is upon many *w*
Ps 32:6 *w* they shall not come nigh unto
Ps 33:7 He gathereth the *w* of the sea
Ps 46:3 Though the *w* thereof roar and be
Ps 58:7 away as *w* which run continually
Ps 69:1 for the *w* are come in unto my
Ps 69:2 I am come into deep *w*, where the
Ps 69:14 hate me, and out of the deep *w*
Ps 73:10 *w* of a full cup are wrung out to
Ps 74:13 the heads of the dragons in the *w*
Ps 77:16 The *w* saw thee, O God, the *w*
Ps 77:19 sea, and thy path in the great *w*
Ps 78:13 he made the *w* to stand as an heap
Ps 78:16 caused *w* to run down like rivers
Ps 78:20 that the *w* gushed out, and the
Ps 81:7 I proved thee at the *w* of Meribah
Ps 93:4 mightier than the noise of many *w*
Ps 104:3 beams of his chambers in the *w*
Ps 104:6 the *w* stood above the mountains
Ps 105:29 He turned their *w* into blood
Ps 105:41 the rock, and the *w* gushed out
Ps 106:11 the *w* covered their enemies
Ps 106:32 him also at the *w* of strife
Ps 107:23 that do business in great *w*
Ps 114:8 the flint into a fountain of *w*
Ps 119:136 Rivers of *w* run down mine eyes,
Ps 124:4 Then the *w* had overwhelmed us,
Ps 124:5 Then the proud *w* had gone over
Ps 136:6 out the earth above the *w*
Ps 144:7 me, and deliver me out of great *w*
Ps 147:18 his wind to blow, and the *w* flow
Ps 148:4 ye *w* that be above the heavens
Prov 5:15 Drink *w* out of thine own cistern,
Prov 5:15 running *w* out of thine own well
Prov 5:16 rivers of *w* in the streets
Prov 8:29 that the *w* should not pass his
Prov 9:17 Stolen *w* are sweet, and bread
Prov 18:4 of a man's mouth are as deep *w*
Prov 25:25 As cold *w* to a thirsty soul, so
Prov 30:4 who hath bound the *w* in a garment
Eccl 11:1 Cast thy bread upon the *w*
Song 4:15 of gardens, a well of living *w*
Song 5:12 eyes of doves by the rivers of *w*
Song 8:7 Many *w* cannot quench love,
Is 8:6 the *w* of Shiloah that go softly
Is 8:7 up upon them the *w* of the river
Is 11:9 the LORD, as the *w* cover the sea
Is 15:6 For the *w* of Nimrim shall be
Is 15:9 For the *w* of Dimon shall be full
Is 17:12 like the rushing of mighty *w*
Is 17:13 rush like the rushing of many *w*
Is 18:2 vessels of bulrushes upon the *w*
Is 19:5 the *w* shall fail from the sea, and
Is 19:8 nets upon the *w* shall languish
Is 22:9 together the *w* of the lower pool
Is 23:3 by great *w* the seed of Sihor, the
Is 28:2 a flood of mighty *w* overflowing
Is 28:17 the *w* shall overflow the hiding
Is 30:25 streams of *w* in the day of the
Is 32:20 are ye that sow beside all *w*
Is 33:16 his *w* shall be sure
Is 35:6 the wilderness shall *w* break out
Is 36:16 one the *w* of his own cistern
Is 40:12 Who hath measured the *w* in the
Is 43:2 When thou passest through the *w*
Is 43:16 sea, and a path in the mighty *w*
Is 43:20 because I give *w* in the
Is 48:1 come forth out of the *w* of Judah
Is 48:21 he caused the *w* to flow out of
Is 48:21 rock also, and the *w* gushed out
Is 51:10 the sea, the *w* of the great deep
Is 54:9 this is as the *w* of Noah unto me
Is 54:9 for as I have sworn that the *w* of
Is 55:1 that thirsteth, come ye to the *w*
Is 57:20 whose *w* cast up mire and dirt
Is 58:11 spring of water, whose *w* fail not
Is 64:2 the fire causeth the *w* to boil
Jer 2:13 me the fountain of living *w*
Jer 2:18 of Egypt, to drink the *w* of Sihor
Jer 2:18 to drink the *w* of the river
Jer 6:7 As a fountain casteth out her *w*
Jer 9:1 Oh that my head were *w*, and mine
Jer 9:18 and our eyelids gush out with *w*
Jer 10:13 a multitude of *w* in the heavens
Jer 14:3 sent their little ones to the *w*
Jer 15:18 me as a liar, and as *w* that fail
Jer 17:8 be as a tree planted by the *w*
Jer 17:13 LORD, the fountain of living *w*
Jer 18:14 or shall the cold flowing *w* that
Jer 31:9 the rivers of *w* in a straight way
Jer 41:12 by the great *w* that are in Gibeon
Jer 46:7 whose *w* are moved as the rivers
Jer 46:8 his *w* are moved like the rivers
Jer 47:2 *w* rise up out of the north, and
Jer 48:34 for the *w* also of Nimrim shall be
Jer 50:38 A drought is upon her *w*
Jer 51:13 O thou that dwellest upon many *w*
Jer 51:16 a multitude of *w* in the heavens
Jer 51:55 her waves do roar like great *w*
Lam 3:54 *W* flowed over mine head
Eze 1:24 wings, like the noise of great *w*
Eze 17:5 he placed it by great *w*, and set
Eze 17:8 planted in a good soil by great *w*
Eze 19:10 in thy blood, planted by the *w*
Eze 19:10 of branches by reason of many *w*
Eze 26:19 thee, and great *w* shall cover thee
Eze 27:26 have brought thee into great *w*
Eze 27:34 depths of the *w* thy merchandise
Eze 31:4 The *w* made him great, the deep
Eze 31:5 because of the multitude of *w*
Eze 31:7 for his root was by great *w*
Eze 31:14 the *w* exalt themselves for their
Eze 31:15 and the great *w* were stayed
Eze 32:2 and troubledst the *w* with thy feet
Eze 32:13 thereof from beside the great *w*
Eze 32:14 Then will I make their *w* deep
Eze 34:18 and to have drunk of the deep *w*
Eze 43:2 voice was like a noise of many *w*
Eze 47:1 *w* issued out from under the
Eze 47:1 the *w* came down from under from
Eze 47:2 there ran out *w* on the right side
Eze 47:3 and he brought me through the *w*
Eze 47:3 the *w* were to the ancles
Eze 47:4 and brought me through the *w*
Eze 47:4 the *w* were to the knees
Eze 47:4 the *w* were to the loins
Eze 47:5 for the *w* were risen
Eze 47:5 *w* to swim in, a river that could
Eze 47:8 These *w* issue out toward the east
Eze 47:8 the sea, the *w* shall be healed
Eze 47:9 because these *w* shall come
Eze 47:12 because their *w* they issued
Eze 47:19 even to the *w* of strife in Kadesh
Eze 48:28 unto the *w* of strife in Kadesh
Dan 12:6 which was upon the *w* of the river
Dan 12:7 which was upon the *w* of the river
Joel 1:20 for the rivers of *w* are dried up
Joel 3:18 rivers of Judah shall flow with *w*

Amos 5:8 that calleth for the *w* of the sea
Amos 5:24 But let judgment run down as *w*
Amos 9:6 that calleth for the *w* of the sea
Jonah 2:5 The *w* compassed me about, even to
Mic 1:4 as the *w* that are poured down a
Nah 3:8 that had the *w* round about it,
Nah 3:14 Draw thee *w* for the siege,
Hab 2:14 the LORD, as the *w* cover the sea
Hab 3:15 through the heap of great *w*
Zec 14:8 that living *w* shall go out from
Mt 8:32 the sea, and perished in the *w*
Mk 9:22 him into the fire, and into the *w*
2Cor 11:26 journeyings often, in perils of *w*
Rev 1:15 his voice as the sound of many *w*
Rev 7:17 them unto living fountains of *w*
Rev 8:10 and upon the fountains of *w*
Rev 8:11 part of the *w* became wormwood
Rev 8:11 and many men died of the *w*
Rev 11:6 have power over *w* to turn them to
Rev 14:2 heaven, as the voice of many *w*
Rev 14:7 and the sea, and the fountains of *w*
Rev 16:4 upon the rivers and fountains of *w*
Rev 16:5 And I heard the angel of the *w* say
Rev 17:1 whore that sitteth upon many *w*
Rev 17:15 The *w* which thou sawest, where
Rev 19:6 and as the voice of many *w*

## WATERSPOUTS
Ps 42:7 unto deep at the noise of thy *w*

## WATERSPRINGS
Ps 107:33 and the *w* into dry ground
Ps 107:35 water, and dry ground into *w*

## WAVE
Ex 29:24 shalt *w* them for a
Ex 29:24 them for a *w* offering
Ex 29:26 and *w* it for a
Ex 29:26 it for a *w* offering before
Ex 29:27 the breast of the *w* offering
Lev 7:30 for a *w* offering before the LORD
Lev 7:34 For the *w* breast and the heave
Lev 8:27 waved them for a *w* offering
Lev 8:29 waved it for a *w* offering before
Lev 9:21 for a *w* offering before the LORD
Lev 10:14 the *w* breast and heave shoulder
Lev 10:15 the *w* breast shall they bring
Lev 10:15 to *w* it for a *w* offering
Lev 14:12 *w* them for a
Lev 14:12 them for a *w* offering before
Lev 14:24 the priest shall *w* them for a
Lev 14:24 for a *w* offering before the LORD
Lev 23:11 he shall *w* the sheaf before the
Lev 23:11 the sabbath the priest shall *w* it
Lev 23:12 ye *w* the sheaf an he lamb without
Lev 23:15 the sheaf of the *w* offering
Lev 23:17 two *w* loaves of two tenth deals
Lev 23:20 the priest shall *w* them with the
Lev 23:20 for a *w* offering before the LORD
Num 5:25 shall *w* the offering before the
Num 6:20 the priest shall *w* them for a
Num 6:20 for a *w* offering before the LORD
Num 6:20 for the priest, with the *w* breast
Num 18:11 with all the *w* offerings of the
Num 18:18 shall be thine, as the *w* breast
Jas 1:6 For he that wavereth is like a *w*

## WAVED
Ex 29:27 of the heave offering, which is *w*
Lev 7:30 that the breast may be *w* for a
Lev 8:27 *w* them for a wave offering before
Lev 8:29 *w* it for a wave offering before
Lev 9:21 the right shoulder Aaron *w* for a
Lev 14:21 for a trespass offering to be *w*

## WAVERETH
Jas 1:6 For he that *w* is like a wave of

## WAVERING
Heb 10:23 profession of our faith without *w*
Jas 1:6 let him ask in faith, nothing *w*

## WAVES
2Sa 22:5 When the *w* of death compassed me,
Job 9:8 and treadeth upon the *w* of the sea
Job 38:11 here shall thy proud *w* be stayed
Ps 42:7 all thy *w* and thy billows are gone
Ps 65:7 of the seas, the noise of their *w*
Ps 88:7 hast afflicted me with all thy *w*
Ps 89:9 when the *w* thereof arise, thou
Ps 93:3 the floods lift up their *w*
Ps 93:4 yea, than the mighty *w* of the sea
Ps 107:25 which lifteth up the *w* thereof
Ps 107:29 so that the *w* thereof are still
Is 48:18 righteousness as the *w* of the sea
Is 51:15 divided the sea, whose *w* roared
Jer 5:22 though the *w* thereof toss
Jer 31:35 the sea when the *w* thereof roar
Jer 51:42 the multitude of the *w* thereof
Jer 51:55 when her *w* do roar like great
Eze 26:3 the sea causeth his *w* to come up
Jonah 2:3 billows and thy *w* passed over me
Zec 10:11 and shall smite the *w* in the sea
Mt 8:24 the ship was covered with the *w*
Mt 14:24 midst of the sea, tossed with *w*
Mk 4:37 the *w* beat into the ship, so that
Lk 21:25 the sea and the *w* roaring
Acts 27:41 broken with the violence of the *w*
Jude 13 Raging *w* of the sea, foaming out

## WAX
Ex 22:24 And my wrath shall *w* hot, and I
Ex 32:10 my wrath may *w* hot against them
Ex 32:11 why doth thy wrath *w* hot against
Ex 32:22 not the anger of my lord *w* hot
Lev 25:47 or stranger *w* rich by thee
Lev 25:47 that dwelleth by him *w* poor
1Sa 3:2 place, and his eyes began to *w* dim
Job 6:17 What time they *w* warm, they
Job 14:8 root thereof *w* old in the earth
Ps 22:14 my heart is like *w*
Ps 68:2 as *w* melteth before the fire, so
Ps 97:5 The hills melted like *w* at the
Ps 102:26 all of them shall *w* old like a
Is 17:4 fatness of his flesh shall *w* lean
Is 29:22 neither shall his face now *w* pale
Is 50:9 they all shall *w* old as a garment
Is 51:6 the earth shall *w* old like a
Jer 6:24 our hands *w* feeble
Mic 1:4 as *w* before the fire, and as the
Mt 24:12 the love of many shall *w* cold
Lk 12:33 yourselves bags which *w* not old
1Ti 5:11 begun to *w* wanton against Christ
2Ti 3:13 men and seducers shall *w* worse
Heb 1:11 they all shall *w* old as doth a

## WAXED
Gen 18:12 After I am *w* old shall I have
Gen 26:13 And the man *w* great, and went
Gen 41:56 the famine *w* sore in the land of
Ex 1:7 multiplied, and *w* exceeding mighty
Ex 1:20 multiplied, and *w* very mighty
Ex 16:21 and when the sun *w* hot, it melted
Ex 19:19 *w* louder and louder, Moses spake,
Ex 32:19 and Moses' anger *w* hot, and he cast
Num 11:23 Moses, Is the LORD's hand *w* short
Deut 8:4 Thy raiment *w* not old upon thee,
Deut 32:15 But Jeshurun *w* fat, and kicked
Josh 23:1 round about, that Joshua *w* old
1Sa 2:5 hath many children is *w* feeble
2Sa 3:1 but David *w* stronger and stronger,
2Sa 3:1 and the house of Saul *w* weaker
2Sa 21:15 and David *w* faint
2Kin 4:34 and the flesh of the child *w* warm
1Chr 11:9 So David *w* greater and greater
2Chr 13:21 But Abijah *w* mighty, and married
2Chr 17:12 Jehoshaphat *w* great exceedingly
2Chr 24:15 But Jehoiada *w* old, and was full
Neh 9:21 their clothes *w* not old, and their
Est 9:4 for this man Mordecai *w* greater
Ps 32:3 my bones *w* old through my roaring
Jer 49:24 Damascus is *w* feeble, and turneth
Jer 50:43 of them, and his hands *w* feeble
Dan 8:8 the he goat *w* very great
Dan 8:9 which *w* exceeding great, toward
Dan 8:10 it *w* great, even to the host of
Mt 13:15 this people's heart is *w* gross
Lk 1:80 *w* strong in spirit, and was in the
Lk 2:40 *w* strong in spirit, filled with
Lk 13:19 and it grew, and *w* a great tree
Acts 13:46 Then Paul and Barnabas *w* bold
Acts 28:27 heart of this people is *w* gross
Heb 11:34 *w* valiant in fight, turned to
Rev 18:3 *w* rich through the abundance of

## WAXEN
Gen 19:13 because the cry of them is *w*
Lev 25:25 If thy brother be *w* poor, and hath
Lev 25:35 And if thy brother be *w* poor
Lev 25:39 that dwelleth by thee be *w* poor
Deut 29:5 clothes are not *w* old upon you
Deut 29:5 thy shoe is not *w* old upon thy
Deut 31:20 and filled themselves, and *w* fat
Deut 32:15 thou art *w* fat, thou art grown
Josh 17:13 children of Israel were *w* strong
Jer 5:27 they are become great, and *w* rich
Jer 5:28 They are *w* fat, they shine
Eze 16:7 *w* great, and thou art come to

## WAXETH
Ps 6:7 it *w* old because of all mine
Heb 8:13 *w* old is ready to vanish away

## WAXING
Phil 1:14 *w* confident by my bonds, are much

## WAY
Gen 3:24 sword which turned every *w*
Gen 3:24 to keep the *w* of the tree of life
Gen 6:12 corrupted his *w* upon the earth
Gen 12:19 thy wife, take her, and go thy *w*
Gen 14:11 their victuals, and went their *w*
Gen 16:7 by the fountain in the *w* to Shur
Gen 18:16 with them to bring them on the *w*
Gen 18:19 they shall keep the *w* of the LORD
Gen 18:33 And the LORD went his *w*, as soon
Gen 21:16 over against him a good *w* off
Gen 24:27 I being in the *w*, the LORD led me
Gen 24:40 angel with thee, and prosper thy *w*
Gen 24:42 thou do prosper my *w* which I go
Gen 24:48 *w* to take my master's brother's
Gen 24:56 the LORD hath prospered my *w*
Gen 24:61 took Rebekah, and went his *w*
Gen 24:62 Isaac came from the *w* of the well
Gen 25:34 drink, and rose up, and went his *w*
Gen 28:20 will keep me in this *w* that I go
Gen 32:1 And Jacob went on his *w*, and the
Gen 33:16 that day on his *w* unto Seir
Gen 35:3 was with me in the *w* which I went
Gen 35:16 but a little *w* to come to Ephrath
Gen 35:19 and was buried in the *w* to Ephrath
Gen 38:14 which is by the *w* to Timnath
Gen 38:16 And he turned unto her by the *w*
Gen 38:21 that was openly by the *w* side
Gen 42:25 to give them provision for the *w*
Gen 42:38 him by the *w* in the which ye go
Gen 45:21 and gave them provision for the *w*
Gen 45:23 and meat for his father by the *w*
Gen 45:24 See that ye fall not out by the *w*
Gen 48:7 me in the land of Canaan in the *w*
Gen 48:7 a little *w* to come unto Ephrath
Gen 48:7 her there in the *w* of Ephrath
Gen 49:17 Dan shall be a serpent by the *w*
Ex 2:12 And he looked this *w* and that *w*,
Ex 4:24 came to pass by the *w* in the inn
Ex 5:20 and Aaron, who stood in the *w*
Ex 13:17 God led them not through the *w* of
Ex 13:18 through the *w* of the wilderness
Ex 13:21 of a cloud, to lead them the *w*
Ex 18:8 that had come upon them by the *w*
Ex 18:20 shalt shew them the *w* wherein
Ex 18:27 he went his *w* into his own land
Ex 23:20 thee, to keep thee in the *w*
Ex 32:8 of the *w* which I commanded them
Ex 33:3 lest I consume thee in the *w*
Ex 33:13 in thy sight, shew me now thy *w*
Num 13:17 them, Get you up this *w* southward
Num 14:25 by the *w* of the Red sea
Num 20:17 we will go by the king's high *w*
Num 20:19 him, We will go by the high *w*
Num 21:1 Israel came by the *w* of the spies
Num 21:4 mount Hor by the *w* of the Red sea
Num 21:4 much discouraged because of the *w*
Num 21:22 go along by the king's high *w*
Num 21:33 and went up by the *w* of Bashan
Num 22:22 *w* for an adversary against him
Num 22:23 of the LORD standing in the *w*
Num 22:23 the ass turned aside out of the *w*
Num 22:23 the ass, to turn her into the *w*
Num 22:26 where was no *w* to turn either to
Num 22:31 of the LORD standing in the *w*
Num 22:32 because thy *w* is perverse before
Num 22:34 thou stoodest in the *w* against me
Num 24:25 and Balak also went his *w*
Deut 1:2 Horeb by the *w* of mount Seir unto
Deut 1:19 which ye saw by the *w* of the
Deut 1:22 again by what *w* we must go up
Deut 1:31 in all the *w* that ye went, until
Deut 1:33 Who went in the *w* before you
Deut 1:33 shew you by what *w* ye should go
Deut 1:40 by the *w* of the Red sea
Deut 2:1 by the *w* of the Red sea, as the
Deut 2:8 through the *w* of the plain from
Deut 2:8 passed by the *w* of the wilderness
Deut 2:27 I will go along by the high *w*
Deut 3:1 and went up the *w* to Bashan
Deut 6:7 and when thou walkest by the *w*
Deut 8:2 thou shalt remember all the *w*

| | |
|---|---|
| Deut 9:12 | of the *w* which I commanded them |
| Deut 9:16 | *w* which the LORD had commanded |
| Deut 11:19 | and when thou walkest by the *w* |
| Deut 11:28 | but turn aside out of the *w* which |
| Deut 11:30 | by the *w* where the sun goeth down |
| Deut 13:5 | of the *w* which the LORD thy God |
| Deut 14:24 | if the *w* be too long for thee, so |
| Deut 17:16 | henceforth return no more that *w* |
| Deut 19:3 | Thou shalt prepare thee a *w* |
| Deut 19:6 | him, because the *w* is long |
| Deut 22:4 | ass or his ox fall down by the *w* |
| Deut 22:6 | before thee in the *w* in any tree |
| Deut 23:4 | with bread and with water in the *w* |
| Deut 24:9 | thy God did unto Miriam by the *w* |
| Deut 25:17 | Amalek did unto thee by the *w* |
| Deut 25:18 | How he met thee by the *w*, and |
| Deut 27:18 | the blind to wander out of the *w* |
| Deut 28:7 | shall come out against thee one *w* |
| Deut 28:25 | shalt go out one *w* against them |
| Deut 28:68 | by the *w* whereof I spake unto |
| Deut 31:29 | turn aside from the *w* which I |
| Josh 1:8 | thou shalt make thy *w* prosperous |
| Josh 2:7 | the *w* to Jordan unto the fords |
| Josh 2:16 | and afterward may ye go your *w* |
| Josh 2:22 | sought them throughout all the *w* |
| Josh 3:4 | know the *w* by which ye must go |
| Josh 3:4 | have not passed this *w* heretofore |
| Josh 5:4 | died in the wilderness by the *w* |
| Josh 5:5 | born in the wilderness by the *w* |
| Josh 5:7 | had not circumcised them by the *w* |
| Josh 8:15 | fled by the *w* of the wilderness |
| Josh 8:20 | power to flee this *w* or that *w* |
| Josh 10:10 | chased them along the *w* that |
| Josh 12:3 | the east, the *w* to Beth-jeshimoth |
| Josh 23:14 | I am going the *w* of all the earth |
| Josh 24:17 | us in all the *w* wherein we went |
| Judg 2:17 | *w* which their fathers walked in |
| Judg 2:19 | doings, nor from their stubborn *w* |
| Judg 2:22 | whether they will keep the *w* of |
| Judg 5:10 | sit in judgment, and walk by the *w* |
| Judg 8:11 | Gideon went up by the *w* of them |
| Judg 9:25 | that came along that *w* by them |
| Judg 18:5 | that we may know whether our *w* |
| Judg 18:6 | the LORD is your *w* wherein ye go |
| Judg 18:22 | when they were a good *w* from the |
| Judg 18:26 | the children of Dan went their *w* |
| Judg 19:5 | of bread, and afterward go your *w* |
| Judg 19:9 | to morrow get you early on your *w* |
| Judg 19:14 | And they passed on and went their *w* |
| Judg 19:27 | house, and went out to go his *w* |
| Judg 20:42 | unto the *w* of the wilderness |
| Ruth 1:7 | they went on the *w* to return unto |
| Ruth 1:12 | again, my daughters, go your *w* |
| 1Sa 1:18 | So the woman went her *w*, and did |
| 1Sa 6:9 | up by the *w* of his own coast to |
| 1Sa 6:12 | *w* to the *w* of Beth-shemesh |
| 1Sa 9:6 | shew us our *w* that we should go |
| 1Sa 9:8 | the man of God, to tell us our *w* |
| 1Sa 12:23 | teach you the good and the right *w* |
| 1Sa 13:17 | unto the *w* that leadeth to Ophrah |
| 1Sa 13:18 | turned the *w* to Beth-horon |
| 1Sa 13:18 | *w* of the border that looketh to |
| 1Sa 15:2 | how he laid wait for him in the *w* |
| 1Sa 15:20 | have gone the *w* which the LORD |
| 1Sa 17:52 | fell down by the *w* to Shaaraim |
| 1Sa 20:22 | go thy *w* |
| 1Sa 24:3 | came to the sheepcotes by the *w* |
| 1Sa 24:7 | out of the cave, and went on his *w* |
| 1Sa 25:12 | David's young men turned their *w* |
| 1Sa 26:3 | is before Jeshimon, by the *w* |
| 1Sa 26:25 | So David went on his *w*, and Saul |
| 1Sa 28:22 | when thou goest on thy *w* |
| 1Sa 30:2 | them away, and went on their *w* |
| 2Sa 2:24 | the *w* of the wilderness of Gibeon |
| 2Sa 13:30 | to pass, while they were in the *w* |
| 2Sa 13:34 | the *w* of the hill side behind him |
| 2Sa 15:2 | and stood beside the *w* of the gate |
| 2Sa 15:23 | toward the *w* of the wilderness |
| 2Sa 16:13 | as David and his men went by the *w* |
| 2Sa 18:23 | Ahimaaz ran by the *w* of the plain |
| 2Sa 19:36 | *w* over Jordan with the king |
| 2Sa 22:31 | As for God, his *w* is perfect |
| 2Sa 22:33 | and he maketh my *w* perfect |
| 1Kin 1:49 | rose up, and went every man his *w* |
| 1Kin 2:2 | I go the *w* of all the earth |
| 1Kin 2:4 | thy children take heed to their *w* |
| 1Kin 8:25 | thy children take heed to their *w* |
| 1Kin 8:32 | to bring his *w* upon his head |
| 1Kin 8:36 | good *w* wherein they should walk |
| 1Kin 11:29 | the Shilonite found him in the *w* |
| 1Kin 13:9 | by the same *w* that thou camest |
| 1Kin 13:10 | So he went another *w*, and returned |
| 1Kin 13:10 | returned not by the *w* that he |
| 1Kin 13:12 | said unto them, What *w* went he |
| 1Kin 13:12 | seen what *w* the man of God went |
| 1Kin 13:17 | to go by the *w* that thou camest |
| 1Kin 13:24 | was gone, a lion met him by the *w* |
| 1Kin 13:24 | and his carcase was cast in the *w* |
| 1Kin 13:25 | and saw the carcase cast in the *w* |
| 1Kin 13:26 | him back from the *w* heard thereof |
| 1Kin 13:28 | found his carcase cast in the *w* |
| 1Kin 13:33 | returned not from his evil *w* |
| 1Kin 15:26 | and walked in the *w* of his father |
| 1Kin 15:34 | and walked in the *w* of Jeroboam |
| 1Kin 16:2 | hast walked in the *w* of Jeroboam |
| 1Kin 16:19 | in walking in the *w* of Jeroboam |
| 1Kin 16:26 | For he walked in all the *w* of |
| 1Kin 18:6 | Ahab went one *w* by himself |
| 1Kin 18:6 | Obadiah went another *w* by himself |
| 1Kin 18:7 | And as Obadiah was in the *w* |
| 1Kin 19:15 | return on thy *w* to the wilderness |
| 1Kin 20:38 | and waited for the king by the *w* |
| 1Kin 22:24 | Which *w* went the Spirit of the |
| 1Kin 22:52 | and walked in the *w* of his father |
| 1Kin 22:52 | in the *w* of his mother, and in the |
| 1Kin 22:52 | in the *w* of Jeroboam the son of |
| 2Kin 2:23 | and as he was going up by the *w* |
| 2Kin 3:8 | he said, Which *w* shall we go up |
| 2Kin 3:8 | The *w* through the wilderness of |
| 2Kin 3:20 | there came water by the *w* of Edom |
| 2Kin 4:29 | staff in thine hand, and go thy *w* |
| 2Kin 5:19 | he departed from him a little *w* |
| 2Kin 6:19 | said unto them, This is not the *w* |
| 2Kin 7:15 | all the *w* was full of garments and |
| 2Kin 8:18 | he walked in the *w* of the kings |
| 2Kin 8:27 | he walked in the *w* of the house |
| 2Kin 9:27 | he fled by the *w* of the garden |
| 2Kin 10:12 | at the shearing house in the *w* |
| 2Kin 11:16 | she went by the *w* by the which |
| 2Kin 11:19 | came by the *w* of the gate of the |
| 2Kin 16:3 | But he walked in the *w* of the |
| 2Kin 19:28 | by the *w* by which thou camest |
| 2Kin 19:33 | By the *w* that he came, by the |
| 2Kin 21:21 | he walked in all the *w* that his |
| 2Kin 21:22 | walked not in the *w* of the LORD |
| 2Kin 22:2 | walked in all the *w* of David his |
| 2Kin 25:4 | *w* of the gate between two walls |
| 2Kin 25:4 | king went the *w* toward the plain |
| 2Chr 6:16 | heed to their *w* to walk in my law |
| 2Chr 6:23 | his *w* upon his own head |
| 2Chr 6:27 | thou hast taught them the good *w* |
| 2Chr 6:34 | the *w* that thou shalt send them |
| 2Chr 11:17 | they walked in the *w* of David |
| 2Chr 18:23 | Which *w* went the Spirit of the |
| 2Chr 20:32 | he walked in the *w* of Asa his |
| 2Chr 21:6 | he walked in the *w* of the kings |
| 2Chr 21:13 | in the *w* of the kings of Israel |
| Ezr 8:21 | to seek of him a right *w* for us |
| Ezr 8:22 | us against the enemy in the *w* |
| Ezr 8:31 | of such as lay in wait by the *w* |
| Neh 8:10 | Then he said unto them, Go your *w* |
| Neh 8:12 | the people went their *w* to eat |
| Neh 9:12 | in the *w* wherein they should go |
| Neh 9:19 | by day, to lead them in the *w* |
| Neh 9:19 | the *w* wherein they should go |
| Est 4:17 | So Mordecai went his *w*, and did |
| Job 3:23 | given to a man whose *w* is hid |
| Job 6:18 | paths of their *w* are turned aside |
| Job 8:19 | Behold, this is the joy of his *w* |
| Job 12:24 | a wilderness where there is no *w* |
| Job 16:22 | then I shall go the *w* whence I |
| Job 17:9 | also shall hold on his *w*, and he |
| Job 18:10 | and a trap for him in the *w* |
| Job 19:8 | fenced up my *w* that I cannot pass |
| Job 19:12 | and raise up their *w* against me |
| Job 21:29 | not asked them that go by the *w* |
| Job 21:31 | shall declare his *w* to his face |
| Job 22:15 | Hast thou marked the old *w* which |
| Job 23:10 | But he knoweth the *w* that I take |
| Job 23:11 | his *w* have I kept, and not |
| Job 24:4 | They turn the needy out of the *w* |
| Job 24:18 | not the *w* of the vineyards |
| Job 24:24 | taken out of the *w* as all other |
| Job 28:23 | God understandeth the *w* thereof |
| Job 28:26 | a *w* for the lightning of the |
| Job 29:25 | I chose out their *w*, and sat chief |
| Job 31:7 | my step hath turned out of the *w* |
| Job 36:23 | Who hath enjoined him his *w* |
| Job 38:19 | Where is the *w* where light |
| Job 38:24 | By what *w* is the light parted, |
| Job 38:25 | or a *w* for the lightning of |
| Ps 1:1 | nor standeth in the *w* of sinners |
| Ps 1:6 | knoweth the *w* of the righteous |
| Ps 1:6 | but the *w* of the ungodly shall |
| Ps 2:12 | be angry, and ye perish from the *w* |
| Ps 5:8 | make thy *w* straight before my |
| Ps 18:30 | As for God, his *w* is perfect |
| Ps 18:32 | strength, and maketh my *w* perfect |
| Ps 25:8 | will he teach sinners in the *w* |
| Ps 25:9 | and the meek will he teach his *w* |
| Ps 25:12 | in the *w* that he shall choose |
| Ps 27:11 | Teach me thy *w*, O LORD, and lead |
| Ps 32:8 | teach thee in the *w* which thou |
| Ps 35:3 | stop the *w* against them that |
| Ps 35:6 | Let their *w* be dark and slippery |
| Ps 36:4 | himself in a *w* that is not good |
| Ps 37:5 | Commit thy *w* unto the LORD |
| Ps 37:7 | of him who prospereth in his *w* |
| Ps 37:23 | and he delighteth in his *w* |
| Ps 37:34 | Wait on the LORD, and keep his *w* |
| Ps 44:18 | our steps declined from thy *w* |
| Ps 49:13 | This their *w* is their folly |
| Ps 67:2 | That thy *w* may be known upon |
| Ps 77:13 | Thy *w*, O God, is in the sanctuary |
| Ps 77:19 | Thy *w* is in the sea, and thy path |
| Ps 78:50 | He made a *w* to his anger |
| Ps 80:12 | which pass by the *w* do pluck her |
| Ps 85:13 | set us in the *w* of his steps |
| Ps 86:11 | Teach me thy *w*, O LORD |
| Ps 89:41 | All that pass by the *w* spoil him |
| Ps 101:2 | myself wisely in a perfect *w* |
| Ps 101:6 | he that walketh in a perfect *w* |
| Ps 102:23 | He weakened my strength in the *w* |
| Ps 107:4 | in the wilderness in a solitary *w* |
| Ps 107:7 | he led them forth by the right *w* |
| Ps 107:40 | wilderness, where there is no *w* |
| Ps 110:7 | shall drink of the brook in the *w* |
| Ps 119:1 | are the undefiled in the *w* |
| Ps 119:9 | shall a young man cleanse his *w* |
| Ps 119:14 | in the *w* of thy testimonies |
| Ps 119:27 | understand the *w* of thy precepts |
| Ps 119:29 | Remove from me the *w* of lying |
| Ps 119:30 | I have chosen the *w* of truth |
| Ps 119:32 | I will run the *w* of thy |
| Ps 119:33 | me, O LORD, the *w* of thy statutes |
| Ps 119:37 | and quicken thou me in thy *w* |
| Ps 119:101 | my feet from every evil *w* |
| Ps 119:104 | therefore I hate every false *w* |
| Ps 119:128 | and I hate every false *w* |
| Ps 139:24 | if there be any wicked *w* in me |
| Ps 139:24 | and lead me in the *w* everlasting |
| Ps 142:3 | In the *w* wherein I walked have |
| Ps 143:8 | cause me to know the *w* wherein I |
| Ps 146:9 | but the *w* of the wicked he |
| Prov 1:15 | walk not thou in the *w* with them |
| Prov 1:31 | eat of the fruit of their own *w* |
| Prov 2:8 | and preserveth the *w* of his saints |
| Prov 2:12 | thee from the *w* of the evil man |
| Prov 2:20 | mayest walk in the *w* of good men |
| Prov 3:23 | shalt thou walk in thy *w* safely |
| Prov 4:11 | taught thee in the *w* of wisdom |
| Prov 4:14 | and go not in the *w* of evil men |
| Prov 4:19 | The *w* of the wicked is as |
| Prov 5:8 | Remove thy *w* far from her, and |
| Prov 6:23 | of instruction are the *w* of life |
| Prov 7:8 | he went the *w* to her house, |
| Prov 7:27 | Her house is the *w* to hell |
| Prov 8:2 | by the *w* in the places of the |
| Prov 8:13 | and arrogancy, and the evil *w* |
| Prov 8:20 | I lead in the *w* of righteousness, |
| Prov 8:22 | me in the beginning of his *w* |
| Prov 9:6 | go in the *w* of understanding |
| Prov 10:17 | He is in the *w* of life that |
| Prov 10:29 | The *w* of the LORD is strength to |
| Prov 11:5 | of the perfect shall direct his *w* |
| Prov 11:20 | in their *w* are his delight |
| Prov 12:15 | The *w* of a fool is right in his |
| Prov 12:26 | but the *w* of the wicked seduceth |
| Prov 12:28 | In the *w* of righteousness is life |
| Prov 13:6 | him that is upright in the *w* |
| Prov 13:15 | but the *w* of transgressors is |
| Prov 14:8 | prudent is to understand his *w* |
| Prov 14:12 | There is a *w* which seemeth right |
| Prov 15:9 | The *w* of the wicked is an |
| Prov 15:10 | unto him that forsaketh the *w* |
| Prov 15:19 | The *w* of the slothful man is as |
| Prov 15:19 | but the *w* of the righteous is |
| Prov 15:24 | The *w* of life is above to the |
| Prov 16:9 | A man's heart deviseth his *w* |
| Prov 16:17 | keepeth his *w* preserveth his soul |

Prov 16:25 There is a *w* that seemeth right
Prov 16:29 him into the *w* that is not good
Prov 16:31 found in the *w* of righteousness
Prov 19:3 of man perverteth his *w*
Prov 20:14 but when he is gone his *w*
Prov 20:24 a man then understand his own *w*
Prov 21:2 Every *w* of a man is right in his
Prov 21:8 The *w* of man is froward and
Prov 21:16 *w* of understanding shall remain
Prov 21:29 the upright, he directeth his *w*
Prov 22:5 are in the *w* of the froward
Prov 22:6 up a child in the *w* he should go
Prov 23:19 and guide thine heart in the *w*
Prov 26:13 saith, There is a lion in the *w*
Prov 28:10 to go astray in an evil *w*
Prov 29:27 he that is upright in the *w* is
Prov 30:19 The *w* of an eagle in the air
Prov 30:19 the *w* of a serpent upon a rock
Prov 30:19 the *w* of a ship in the midst of
Prov 30:19 the *w* of a man with a maid
Prov 30:20 Such is the *w* of an adulterous
Eccl 9:7 Go thy *w*, eat thy bread with joy,
Eccl 10:3 that is a fool walketh by the *w*
Eccl 11:5 not what is the *w* of the spirit
Eccl 12:5 high, and fears shall be in the *w*
Song 1:8 go thy *w* forth by the footsteps
Is 3:12 destroy the *w* of thy paths
Is 8:11 not walk in the *w* of this people
Is 9:1 afflict her by the *w* of the sea
Is 15:5 for in the *w* of Horonaim they
Is 26:7 The *w* of the just is uprightness
Is 26:8 in the *w* of thy judgments, O LORD
Is 28:7 strong drink are out of the *w*
Is 28:7 they are out of the *w* through
Is 30:11 Get you out of the *w*, turn aside
Is 30:21 thee, saying, This is the *w*
Is 35:8 an highway shall be there, and a *w*
Is 35:8 shall be called The *w* of holiness
Is 37:29 by the *w* by which thou camest
Is 37:34 By the *w* that he came, by the
Is 40:3 Prepare ye the *w* of the LORD
Is 40:14 to him the *w* of understanding
Is 40:27 My *w* is hid from the LORD, and my
Is 41:3 even by the *w* that he had not
Is 42:16 blind by a *w* that they knew not
Is 43:16 LORD, which maketh a *w* in the sea
Is 43:19 even make a *w* in the wilderness
Is 48:15 and he shall make his *w* prosperous
Is 48:17 by the *w* that thou shouldest go
Is 49:11 I will make all my mountains a *w*
Is 51:10 made the depths of the sea a *w*
Is 53:6 turned every one to his own *w*
Is 55:7 Let the wicked forsake his *w*
Is 56:11 they all look to their own *w*
Is 57:10 wearied in the greatness of thy *w*
Is 57:14 ye up, cast ye up, prepare the *w*
Is 57:14 out of the *w* of my people
Is 57:17 frowardly in the *w* of his heart
Is 59:8 The *w* of peace they know not
Is 62:10 prepare ye the *w* of the people
Is 65:2 walketh in a *w* that was not good
Jer 2:17 God, when he led thee by the *w*
Jer 2:18 hast thou to do in the *w* of Egypt
Jer 2:18 thou to do in the *w* of Assyria
Jer 2:23 see thy *w* in the valley, know
Jer 2:33 trimmest thou thy *w* to seek love
Jer 2:36 about so much to change thy *w*
Jer 3:21 for they have perverted their *w*
Jer 4:7 of the Gentiles is on his *w*
Jer 4:18 Thy *w* and thy doings have procured
Jer 5:4 they know not the *w* of the LORD
Jer 5:5 they have known the *w* of the LORD
Jer 6:16 old paths, where is the good *w*
Jer 6:25 into the field, nor walk by the *w*
Jer 6:27 thou mayest know and try their *w*
Jer 10:2 Learn not the *w* of the heathen,
Jer 10:23 I know that the *w* of man is not
Jer 12:1 Wherefore doth the *w* of the
Jer 18:11 ye now every one from his evil *w*
Jer 18:15 walk in paths, in a *w* not cast up
Jer 21:8 *w* of life, and the *w* of death
Jer 23:12 Wherefore their *w* shall be unto
Jer 23:22 turned them from their evil *w*
Jer 25:5 now every one from his evil *w*
Jer 25:35 shepherds shall have no *w* to flee
Jer 26:3 and turn every man from his evil *w*
Jer 28:11 the prophet Jeremiah went his *w*
Jer 31:9 rivers of waters in a straight *w*
Jer 31:21 even the *w* which thou wentest
Jer 32:39 give them one heart, and one *w*
Jer 35:15 ye now every man from his evil *w*
Jer 36:3 return every man from his evil *w*
Jer 36:7 return every one from his evil *w*
Jer 39:4 by the *w* of the king's garden, by
Jer 39:4 and he went out the *w* of the plain
Jer 42:3 shew us the *w* wherein we may walk
Jer 48:19 of Aroer, stand by the *w*, and espy
Jer 50:5 They shall ask the *w* to Zion with
Jer 52:7 the *w* of the gate between the two
Jer 52:7 they went by the *w* of the plain
Eze 3:18 warn the wicked from his wicked *w*
Eze 3:19 wickedness, nor from his wicked *w*
Eze 7:27 I will do unto them after their *w*
Eze 8:5 eyes now the *w* toward the north
Eze 8:5 mine eyes the *w* toward the north
Eze 9:2 from the *w* of the higher gate
Eze 9:10 their *w* upon their head
Eze 11:21 their *w* upon their own heads
Eze 13:22 not return from his wicked *w*
Eze 14:22 unto you, and ye shall see their *w*
Eze 16:25 high place at every head of the *w*
Eze 16:27 which are ashamed of thy lewd *w*
Eze 16:31 place in the head of every *w*
Eze 16:43 recompense thy *w* upon thine head
Eze 18:25 The *w* of the Lord is not equal
Eze 18:25 Is not my *w* equal
Eze 18:29 The *w* of the Lord is not equal
Eze 21:16 Go thee one *w* or other, either on
Eze 21:19 at the head of the *w* to the city
Eze 21:20 Appoint a *w*, that the sword may
Eze 21:21 stood at the parting of the *w*
Eze 22:31 their own *w* have I recompensed
Eze 23:13 that they took both one *w*
Eze 23:31 walked in the *w* of thy sister
Eze 33:8 to warn the wicked from his *w*
Eze 33:9 wicked of his *w* to turn from it
Eze 33:9 if he do not turn from his *w*
Eze 33:11 that the wicked turn from his *w*
Eze 33:17 The *w* of the Lord is not equal
Eze 33:17 as for them, their *w* is not equal
Eze 33:20 The *w* of the Lord is not equal
Eze 36:17 they defiled it by their own *w*
Eze 36:17 their *w* was before me as the
Eze 36:19 according to their *w* and according
Eze 42:1 court, the *w* toward the north
Eze 42:4 breadth inward, a *w* of one cubit
Eze 42:11 the *w* before them was like the
Eze 42:12 was a door in the head of the *w*
Eze 42:12 even the *w* directly before the
Eze 43:2 came from the *w* of the east
Eze 43:4 *w* of the gate whose prospect is
Eze 44:1 the *w* of the gate of the outward
Eze 44:3 he shall enter by the *w* of the
Eze 44:3 shall go out by the *w* of the same
Eze 44:4 Then brought he me the *w* of the
Eze 46:2 the *w* of the porch of that gate
Eze 46:8 he shall go in by the *w* of the
Eze 46:8 shall go forth by the *w* thereof
Eze 46:9 he that entereth in by the *w* of
Eze 46:9 go out by the *w* of the south gate
Eze 46:9 he that entereth by the *w* of the
Eze 46:9 forth by the *w* of the north gate
Eze 46:9 he shall not return by the *w* of
Eze 47:2 of the *w* of the gate northward
Eze 47:2 led me about the *w* without unto
Eze 47:2 by the *w* that looketh eastward
Eze 47:15 the *w* of Hethlon, as men go to
Eze 48:1 to the coast of the *w* of Hethlon
Dan 12:9 And he said, Go thy *w*, Daniel
Dan 12:13 But go thou thy *w* till the end be
Hos 2:6 I will hedge up thy *w* with thorns
Hos 6:9 murder in the *w* by consent
Hos 10:13 because thou didst trust in thy *w*
Hos 13:7 by the *w* will I observe them
Amos 2:7 and turn aside the *w* of the meek
Jonah 3:8 turn every one from his evil *w*
Jonah 3:10 they turned from their evil *w*
Nah 1:3 LORD hath his *w* in the whirlwind
Nah 2:1 keep the munition, watch the *w*
Zec 10:2 they went their *w* as a flock
Mal 2:8 But ye are departed out of the *w*
Mal 3:1 he shall prepare the *w* before me
Mt 2:12 into their own country another *w*
Mt 3:3 Prepare ye the *w* of the Lord
Mt 4:15 by the *w* of the sea, beyond
Mt 5:24 before the altar, and go thy *w*
Mt 5:25 whiles thou art in the *w* with him
Mt 7:13 is the gate, and broad is the *w*
Mt 7:14 is the gate, and narrow is the *w*
Mt 8:4 but go thy *w*, shew thyself to the
Mt 8:13 said unto the centurion, Go thy *w*
Mt 8:28 that no man might pass by that *w*
Mt 8:30 there was a good *w* off from them
Mt 10:5 Go not into the *w* of the Gentiles
Mt 11:10 shall prepare thy *w* before thee
Mt 13:4 some seeds fell by the *w* side
Mt 13:19 which received seed by the *w* side
Mt 13:25 among the wheat, and went his *w*
Mt 15:32 fasting, lest they faint in the *w*
Mt 20:4 And they went their *w*
Mt 20:14 Take that thine is, and go thy *w*
Mt 20:17 twelve disciples apart in the *w*
Mt 20:30 blind men sitting by the *w* side
Mt 21:8 spread their garments in the *w*
Mt 21:8 trees, and strawed them in the *w*
Mt 21:19 when he saw a fig tree in the *w*
Mt 21:32 you in the *w* of righteousness
Mt 22:16 teachest the *w* of God in truth,
Mt 22:22 and left him, and went their *w*
Mt 27:65 go your *w*, make it as sure as ye
Mk 1:2 shall prepare thy *w* before thee
Mk 1:3 Prepare ye the *w* of the Lord
Mk 1:44 but go thy *w*, shew thyself to the
Mk 2:11 go thy *w* into thine house
Mk 4:4 he sowed, some fell by the *w* side
Mk 4:15 And these are they by the *w* side
Mk 7:29 her, For this saying go thy *w*
Mk 8:3 houses, they will faint by the *w*
Mk 8:27 by the *w* he asked his disciples,
Mk 9:33 among yourselves by the *w*
Mk 9:34 for by the *w* they had disputed
Mk 10:17 when he was gone forth into the *w*
Mk 10:21 go thy *w*, sell whatsoever thou
Mk 10:32 they were in the *w* going up to
Mk 10:52 And Jesus said unto him, Go thy *w*
Mk 10:52 sight, and followed Jesus in the *w*
Mk 11:2 Go your *w* into the village over
Mk 11:4 And they went their *w*, and found
Mk 11:8 spread their garments in the *w*
Mk 11:8 trees, and strawed them in the *w*
Mk 12:12 and they left him, and went their *w*
Mk 12:14 teachest the *w* of God in truth
Mk 16:7 But go your *w*, tell his disciples
Lk 1:79 our feet into the *w* of peace
Lk 3:4 Prepare ye the *w* of the Lord
Lk 4:30 the midst of them went his *w*
Lk 5:19 they could not find by what *w*
Lk 7:22 said unto them, Go your *w*
Lk 7:27 shall prepare thy *w* before thee
Lk 8:5 he sowed, some fell by the *w* side
Lk 8:12 Those by the *w* side are they that
Lk 8:39 And he went his *w*, and published
Lk 9:57 pass, that, as they went in the *w*
Lk 10:4 and salute no man by the *w*
Lk 10:31 came down a certain priest that *w*
Lk 12:58 magistrate, as thou art in the *w*
Lk 14:32 the other is yet a great *w* off
Lk 15:20 But when he was yet a great *w* off
Lk 17:19 he said unto him, Arise, go thy *w*
Lk 18:35 man sat by the *w* side begging
Lk 19:4 for he was to pass that *w*
Lk 19:32 they that were sent went their *w*
Lk 19:36 spread their clothes in the *w*
Lk 20:21 but teachest the *w* of God truly
Lk 22:4 And he went his *w*, and communed
Lk 24:32 while he talked with us by the *w*
Lk 24:35 what things were done in the *w*
Jn 1:23 Make straight the *w* of the Lord
Jn 4:28 went her *w* into the city, and
Jn 4:50 Jesus saith unto him, Go thy *w*
Jn 4:50 spoken unto him, and he went his *w*
Jn 8:21 Jesus again unto them, I go my *w*
Jn 9:7 He went his *w* therefore, and
Jn 10:1 but climbeth up some other *w*
Jn 11:28 she had so said, she went her *w*
Jn 14:4 I go ye know, and the *w* ye know
Jn 14:5 and how can we know the *w*
Jn 14:6 Jesus saith unto him, I am the *w*
Jn 16:5 But now I go my *w* to him that
Jn 18:8 ye seek me, let these go their *w*
Acts 8:26 go toward the south unto the *w*
Acts 8:36 And as they went on their *w*
Acts 8:39 and he went on his *w* rejoicing
Acts 9:2 that if he found any of this *w*
Acts 9:15 the Lord said unto him, Go thy *w*
Acts 9:17 And Ananias went his *w*, and entered
Acts 9:17 unto thee in the *w* as thou camest
Acts 9:27 how he had seen the Lord in the *w*
Acts 15:3 brought on their *w* by the church
Acts 16:17 shew unto us the *w* of salvation

Acts 18:25 instructed in the *w* of the Lord
Acts 18:26 him the *w* of God more perfectly
Acts 19:9 of that *w* before the multitude
Acts 19:23 arose no small stir about that *w*
Acts 21:5 days, we departed and went our *w*
Acts 21:5 and they all brought us on our *w*
Acts 22:4 persecuted this *w* unto the death
Acts 24:14 that after the *w* which they call
Acts 24:22 more perfect knowledge of that *w*
Acts 24:25 answered, Go thy *w* for this time
Acts 25:3 laying wait in the *w* to kill him
Acts 26:13 I saw in the *w* a light from
Rom 3:2 Much every *w*: chiefly
Rom 3:12 They are all gone out of the *w*
Rom 3:17 the *w* of peace have they not
Rom 14:13 to fall in his brother's *w*
Rom 15:24 on my *w* thitherward by you
1Cor 10:13 also make a *w* to escape, that ye
1Cor 12:31 I unto you a more excellent *w*
1Cor 16:7 I will not see you now by the *w*
2Cor 1:16 be brought on my *w* toward Judaea
Phil 1:18 notwithstanding, every *w*, whether
Col 2:14 to us, and took it out of the *w*
1Th 3:11 Christ, direct our *w* unto you
2Th 2:7 until he be taken out of the *w*
Heb 5:2 and on them that are out of the *w*
Heb 9:8 that the *w* into the holiest of
Heb 10:20 By a new and living *w*, which he
Heb 12:13 is lame be turned out of the *w*
Jas 1:24 beholdeth himself, and goeth his *w*
Jas 2:25 and had sent them out another *w*
Jas 5:20 *w* shall save a soul from death
2Pet 2:2 by reason of whom the *w* of truth
2Pet 2:15 Which have forsaken the right *w*
2Pet 2:15 following the *w* of Balaam the son
2Pet 2:21 have known the *w* of righteousness
2Pet 3:1 pure minds by *w* of remembrance
Jude 11 they have gone in the *w* of Cain
Rev 16:12 that the *w* of the kings of the

### WAYFARING

Judg 19:17 he saw a *w* man in the street of
2Sa 12:4 to dress for the *w* man that was
Is 33:8 lie waste, the *w* man ceaseth
Is 35:8 the *w* men, though fools, shall
Jer 9:2 a lodging place of *w* men
Jer 14:8 as a *w* man that turneth aside to

### WAYMARKS

Jer 31:21 Set thee up *w*, make thee high

### WAYS

Gen 19:2 rise up early, and go on your *w*
Lev 20:4 *w* hide their eyes from the man
Lev 26:22 your high *w* shall be desolate
Num 30:15 But if he shall any *w* make them
Deut 5:33 Ye shall walk in all the *w* which
Deut 8:6 LORD thy God, to walk in his *w*
Deut 10:12 thy God, to walk in all his *w*
Deut 11:22 your God, to walk in all his *w*
Deut 19:9 thy God, and to walk ever in his *w*
Deut 26:17 be thy God, and to walk in his *w*
Deut 28:7 way, and flee before thee seven *w*
Deut 28:9 LORD thy God, and walk in his *w*
Deut 28:25 them, and flee seven *w* before them
Deut 28:29 thou shalt not prosper in thy *w*
Deut 30:16 LORD thy God, to walk in his *w*
Deut 32:4 for all his *w* are judgment
Josh 22:5 your God, and to walk in all his *w*
1Sa 8:3 And his sons walked not in his *w*
1Sa 8:5 and thy sons walk not in thy *w*
1Sa 18:14 himself wisely in all his *w*
2Sa 22:22 For I have kept the *w* of the LORD
1Kin 2:3 LORD thy God, to walk in his *w*
1Kin 3:14 And if thou wilt walk in my *w*
1Kin 8:39 to every man according to his *w*
1Kin 8:58 unto him, to walk in all his *w*
1Kin 11:33 Ammon, and have not walked in my *w*
1Kin 11:38 thee, and wilt walk in my *w*
1Kin 22:43 in all the *w* of Asa his father
2Kin 17:13 saying, Turn ye from your evil *w*
2Chr 6:30 man according unto all his *w*
2Chr 6:31 may fear thee, to walk in thy *w*
2Chr 7:14 face, and turn from their wicked *w*
2Chr 13:22 of the acts of Abijah, and his *w*
2Chr 17:3 the first *w* of his father David
2Chr 17:6 lifted up in the *w* of the LORD
2Chr 21:12 the *w* of Jehoshaphat thy father
2Chr 21:12 nor in the *w* of Asa king of Judah
2Chr 22:3 in the *w* of the house of Ahab
2Chr 27:6 his *w* before the LORD his God
2Chr 27:7 Jotham, and all his wars, and his *w*
2Chr 28:2 For he walked in the *w* of the
2Chr 28:26 rest of his acts and of all his *w*
2Chr 32:13 the nations of those lands any *w*
2Chr 34:2 walked in the *w* of David his
Job 4:6 hope, and the uprightness of thy *w*
Job 13:15 maintain mine own *w* before him
Job 21:14 desire not the knowledge of thy *w*
Job 22:3 that thou makest thy *w* perfect
Job 22:28 the light shall shine upon thy *w*
Job 24:13 they know not the *w* thereof
Job 24:23 yet his eyes are upon their *w*
Job 26:14 Lo, these are parts of his *w*
Job 30:12 me the *w* of their destruction
Job 31:4 Doth not he see my *w*, and count
Job 34:11 man to find according to his *w*
Job 34:21 his eyes are upon the *w* of man
Job 34:27 would not consider any of his *w*
Job 40:19 He is the chief of the *w* of God
Ps 10:5 His *w* are always grievous
Ps 18:21 For I have kept the *w* of the LORD
Ps 25:4 Shew me thy *w*, O LORD
Ps 39:1 I said, I will take heed to my *w*
Ps 51:13 will I teach transgressors thy *w*
Ps 81:13 me, and Israel had walked in my *w*
Ps 84:5 in whose heart are the *w* of them
Ps 91:11 thee, to keep thee in all thy *w*
Ps 95:10 and they have not known my *w*
Ps 103:7 He made known his *w* unto Moses
Ps 119:3 they walk in his *w*
Ps 119:5 O that my *w* were directed to keep
Ps 119:15 and have respect unto thy *w*
Ps 119:26 I have declared my *w*, and thou
Ps 119:59 I thought on my *w*, and turned my
Ps 119:168 for all my *w* are before thee
Ps 125:5 turn aside unto their crooked *w*
Ps 128:1 that walketh in his *w*
Ps 138:5 shall sing in the *w* of the LORD
Ps 139:3 and art acquainted with all my *w*
Ps 145:17 LORD is righteous in all his *w*
Prov 1:19 So are the *w* of every one that is
Prov 2:13 to walk in the *w* of darkness
Prov 2:15 Whose *w* are crooked, and they
Prov 3:6 In all thy *w* acknowledge him, and
Prov 3:17 Her *w* are *w* of pleasantness,
Prov 3:31 and choose none of his *w*
Prov 4:26 let all thy *w* be established
Prov 5:6 her *w* are moveable, that thou
Prov 5:21 For the *w* of man are before the
Prov 6:6 consider her *w*, and be wise
Prov 7:25 not thine heart decline to her *w*
Prov 8:32 blessed are they that keep my *w*
Prov 9:15 who go right on their *w*
Prov 10:9 perverteth his *w* shall be known
Prov 14:2 perverse in his *w* despiseth him
Prov 14:12 end thereof are the *w* of death
Prov 14:14 shall be filled with his own *w*
Prov 16:2 All the *w* of a man are clean in
Prov 16:7 When a man's *w* please the LORD,
Prov 16:25 end thereof are the *w* of death
Prov 17:23 to pervert the *w* of judgment
Prov 19:16 he that despiseth his *w* shall die
Prov 22:25 Lest thou learn his *w*, and get a
Prov 23:26 and let thine eyes observe my *w*
Prov 28:6 than he that is perverse in his *w*
Prov 28:18 in his *w* shall fall at once
Prov 31:3 women, nor thy *w* to that which
Prov 31:27 well to the *w* of her household
Eccl 11:9 walk in the *w* of thine heart, and
Song 3:2 in the broad *w* I will seek him
Is 2:3 and he will teach us of his *w*
Is 42:24 for they would not walk in his *w*
Is 45:13 and I will direct all his *w*
Is 49:9 They shall feed in the *w*, and
Is 55:8 neither are your *w* my *w*
Is 55:9 so are my *w* higher than your *w*
Is 57:18 I have seen his *w*, and will heal
Is 58:2 me daily, and delight to know my *w*
Is 58:13 honour him, not doing thine own *w*
Is 63:17 thou made us to err from thy *w*
Is 64:5 those that remember thee in thy *w*
Is 66:3 Yea, they have chosen their own *w*
Jer 2:23 swift dromedary traversing her *w*
Jer 2:33 also taught the wicked ones thy *w*
Jer 3:2 In the *w* hast thou sat for them,
Jer 3:13 hast scattered thy *w* to the
Jer 6:16 saith the LORD, Stand ye in the *w*
Jer 7:3 the God of Israel, Amend your *w*
Jer 7:5 For if ye throughly amend your *w*
Jer 7:23 walk ye in all the *w* that I have
Jer 12:16 learn the *w* of my people, to
Jer 15:7 they return not from their *w*
Jer 16:17 mine eyes are upon all their *w*
Jer 17:10 give every man according to his *w*
Jer 18:11 from his evil way, and make your *w*
Jer 18:15 in their *w* from the ancient paths
Jer 23:12 as slippery *w* in the darkness
Jer 26:13 Therefore now amend your *w*
Jer 32:19 upon all the *w* of the sons of men
Jer 32:19 give every one according to his *w*
Lam 1:4 The *w* of Zion do mourn, because
Lam 3:9 inclosed my *w* with hewn stone
Lam 3:11 He hath turned aside my *w*
Lam 3:40 Let us search and try our *w*
Eze 7:3 judge thee according to thy *w*
Eze 7:4 I will recompense thy *w* upon thee
Eze 7:8 judge thee according to thy *w*
Eze 7:9 thee according to thy *w* and thine
Eze 14:23 comfort you, when ye see their *w*
Eze 16:47 thou not walked after their *w*
Eze 16:47 more than they in all thy *w*
Eze 16:61 Then thou shalt remember thy *w*
Eze 18:23 that he should return from his *w*
Eze 18:25 are not your *w* unequal
Eze 18:29 of Israel, are not my *w* equal
Eze 18:29 are not your *w* unequal
Eze 18:30 every one according to his *w*
Eze 20:43 And there shall ye remember your *w*
Eze 20:44 not according to your wicked *w*
Eze 21:19 son of man, appoint thee two *w*
Eze 21:21 the way, at the head of the two *w*
Eze 24:14 according to thy *w*, and according
Eze 28:15 Thou wast perfect in thy *w* from
Eze 33:11 turn ye, turn ye from your evil *w*
Eze 33:20 judge you every one after his *w*
Eze 36:31 shall ye remember your own evil *w*
Eze 36:32 and confounded for your own *w*
Dan 4:37 are truth, and his *w* judgment
Dan 5:23 breath is, and whose are all thy *w*
Hos 4:9 and I will punish them for their *w*
Hos 9:8 a snare of a fowler in all his *w*
Hos 12:2 punish Jacob according to his *w*
Hos 14:9 for the *w* of the LORD are right,
Joel 2:7 shall march every one on his *w*
Mic 4:2 and he will teach us of his *w*
Nah 2:4 against another in the broad *w*
Hab 3:6 his *w* are everlasting
Hag 1:5 Consider your *w*
Hag 1:7 Consider your *w*
Zec 1:4 Turn ye now from your evil *w*
Zec 1:6 to do unto us, according to our *w*
Zec 3:7 If thou wilt walk in my *w*
Mal 2:9 as ye have not kept my *w*, but
Mt 8:33 went their *w* into the city, and
Mt 22:5 made light of it, and went their *w*
Mk 11:4 in a place where two *w* met
Lk 1:76 face of the Lord to prepare his *w*
Lk 3:5 the rough *w* shall be made smooth
Lk 10:3 Go your *w*
Lk 10:10 go your *w* out into the streets of
Jn 11:46 went their *w* to the Pharisees
Acts 2:28 made known to me the *w* of life
Acts 13:10 pervert the right *w* of the Lord
Acts 14:16 nations to walk in their own *w*
Rom 3:16 and misery are in their *w*
Rom 11:33 and his *w* past finding out
1Cor 4:17 of my *w* which be in Christ
Heb 3:10 and they have not known my *w*
Jas 1:8 man is unstable in all his *w*
Jas 1:11 the rich man fade away in his *w*
2Pet 2:2 shall follow their pernicious *w*
Rev 15:3 just and true are thy *w*, thou King
Rev 16:1 to the seven angels, Go your *w*

### WAYSIDE

1Sa 4:13 sat upon a seat by the *w* watching
Ps 140:5 they have spread a net by the *w*

### WEAK

Num 13:18 whether they be strong or *w*
Judg 16:7 never dried, then shall I be *w*
Judg 16:11 were occupied, then shall I be *w*
Judg 16:17 go from me, and I shall become *w*
2Sa 3:39 And I am this day *w*, though
2Sa 17:2 *w* handed, and will make him afraid
2Chr 15:7 and let not your hands be *w*
Job 4:3 hast strengthened the *w* hands
Ps 6:2 for I am *w*
Ps 109:24 My knees are *w* through fasting
Is 14:10 Art thou also become *w* as we
Is 35:3 Strengthen ye the *w* hands
Eze 7:17 and all knees shall be *w* as water

Eze 16:30 How *w* is thine heart, saith the
Eze 21:7 and all knees shall be *w* as water
Joel 3:10 let the *w* say, I am strong
Mt 26:41 is willing, but the flesh is *w*
Mk 14:38 is ready, but the flesh is *w*
Acts 20:35 ye ought to support the *w*
Rom 4:19 And being not *w* in faith, he
Rom 8:3 in that it was *w* through the
Rom 14:1 Him that is *w* in the faith
Rom 14:2 another, who is *w*, eateth herbs
Rom 14:21 or is offended, or is made *w*
Rom 15:1 to bear the infirmities of the *w*
1Cor 1:27 God hath chosen the *w* things of
1Cor 4:10 we are *w*, but ye are strong
1Cor 8:7 conscience being *w* is defiled
1Cor 8:9 stumblingblock to them that are *w*
1Cor 8:10 is *w* be emboldened to eat those
1Cor 8:11 shall the *w* brother perish
1Cor 8:12 and wound their *w* conscience
1Cor 9:22 To the *w* became I as *w*
1Cor 9:22 as *w*, that I might gain the *w*
1Cor 11:30 For this cause many are *w*
2Cor 10:10 but his bodily presence is *w*
2Cor 11:21 reproach, as though we had been *w*
2Cor 11:29 Who is *w*, and I am not *w*
2Cor 12:10 for when I am *w*, then am I strong
2Cor 13:3 in me, which to you-ward is not *w*
2Cor 13:4 For we also are *w* in him, but we
2Cor 13:9 For we are glad, when we are *w*
Gal 4:9 God, how turn ye again to the *w*
1Th 5:14 the feebleminded, support the *w*

### WEAKEN
Is 14:12 ground, which didst *w* the nations

### WEAKENED
Ezr 4:4 land *w* the hands of the people of
Neh 6:9 hands shall be *w* from the work
Ps 102:23 He *w* my strength in the way

### WEAKENETH
Job 12:21 *w* the strength of the mighty
Jer 38:4 for thus he *w* the hands of the

### WEAKER
2Sa 3:1 house of Saul waxed *w* and *w*
1Pet 3:7 the wife, as unto the *w* vessel

### WEAKNESS
1Cor 1:25 the *w* of God is stronger than men
1Cor 2:3 And I was with you in *w*, and in
1Cor 15:43 it is sown in *w*
2Cor 12:9 my strength is made perfect in *w*
2Cor 13:4 though he was crucified through *w*
Heb 7:18 going before for the *w* and
Heb 11:34 out of *w* were made strong, waxed

### WEALTH
Gen 34:29 And all their *w*, and all their
Deut 8:17 mine hand hath gotten me this *w*
Deut 8:18 that giveth thee power to get *w*
Ruth 2:1 her husband's, a mighty man of *w*
1Sa 2:32 in all the *w* which God shall give
2Kin 15:20 even of all the mighty men of *w*
2Chr 1:11 and thou hast not asked riches, *w*
2Chr 1:12 and I will give thee riches, and *w*
Ezr 9:12 their peace or their *w* for ever
Est 10:3 seeking the *w* of his people, and
Job 21:13 They spend their days in *w*
Job 31:25 I rejoiced because my *w* was great
Ps 44:12 not increase thy *w* by their price
Ps 49:6 They that trust in their *w*
Ps 49:10 and leave their *w* to others
Ps 112:3 *W* and riches shall be in his house
Prov 5:10 strangers be filled with thy *w*
Prov 10:15 The rich man's *w* is his strong
Prov 13:11 *W* gotten by vanity shall be
Prov 13:22 the *w* of the sinner is laid up
Prov 18:11 The rich man's *w* is his strong
Prov 19:4 *W* maketh many friends
Eccl 5:19 whom God hath given riches and *w*
Eccl 6:2 to whom God hath given riches, *w*
Zec 14:14 the *w* of all the heathen round
Acts 19:25 that by this craft we have our *w*
1Cor 10:24 own, but every man another's *w*

### WEALTHY
Ps 66:12 broughtest us out into a *w* place
Jer 49:31 get you up unto the *w* nation

### WEANED
Gen 21:8 And the child grew, and was *w*
Gen 21:8 the same day that Isaac was *w*
1Sa 1:22 not go up until the child be *w*
1Sa 1:23 tarry until thou have *w* him
1Sa 1:23 gave her son suck until she *w* him
1Sa 1:24 And when she had *w* him, she took
1Kin 11:20 whom Tahpenes *w* in Pharaoh's
Ps 131:2 a child that is *w* of his mother
Ps 131:2 my soul is even as a *w* child
Is 11:8 the *w* child shall put his hand on
Is 28:9 them that are *w* from the milk
Hos 1:8 Now when she had *w* Lo-ruhamah

### WEAPON
Num 35:18 smite him with an hand *w* of wood
Deut 23:13 shalt have a paddle upon thy *w*
2Chr 23:10 man having his *w* in his hand
Neh 4:17 and with the other hand held a *w*
Job 20:24 He shall flee from the iron *w*
Is 54:17 No *w* that is formed against thee
Eze 9:1 with his destroying *w* in his hand
Eze 9:2 man a slaughter *w* in his hand

### WEAPONS
Gen 27:3 take, I pray thee, thy *w*, thy
Deut 1:41 girded on every man his *w* of war
Judg 18:11 men appointed with *w* of war
Judg 18:16 men appointed with their *w* of war
Judg 18:17 that were appointed with *w* of war
1Sa 21:8 brought my sword nor my *w* with me
2Sa 1:27 fallen, and the *w* of war perished
2Kin 11:8 every man with his *w* in his hand
2Kin 11:11 every man with his *w* in his hand
2Chr 23:7 every man with his *w* in his hand
Eccl 9:18 Wisdom is better than *w* of war
Is 13:5 the *w* of his indignation, to
Jer 21:4 I will turn back the *w* of war
Jer 22:7 thee, every one with his *w*
Jer 50:25 forth the *w* of his indignation
Jer 51:20 Thou art my battle ax and *w* of war
Eze 32:27 down to hell with their *w* of war
Eze 39:9 shall set on fire and burn the *w*
Eze 39:10 they shall burn the *w* with fire
Jn 18:3 with lanterns and torches and *w*
2Cor 10:4 (For the *w* of our warfare are not

### WEAR
Ex 18:18 Thou wilt surely *w* away, both
Deut 22:5 The woman shall not *w* that which
Deut 22:11 Thou shalt not *w* a garment of
1Sa 2:28 incense, to *w* an ephod before me
1Sa 22:18 persons that did *w* a linen ephod
Est 6:8 brought which the king useth to *w*
Job 14:19 The waters *w* the stones
Is 4:1 own bread, and *w* our own apparel
Dan 7:25 shall *w* out the saints of the
Zec 13:4 neither shall they *w* a rough
Mt 11:8 they that *w* soft clothing are in
Lk 9:12 And when the day began to *w* away

### WEARETH
Jas 2:3 to him that *w* the gay clothing

### WEARIED
Gen 19:11 so that they *w* themselves to find
Is 43:23 offering, nor *w* thee with incense
Is 43:24 thou hast *w* me with thine
Is 47:13 Thou art *w* in the multitude of
Is 57:10 Thou art *w* in the greatness of
Jer 4:31 for my soul is *w* because of
Jer 12:5 the footmen, and they have *w* thee
Jer 12:5 thou trustedst, they *w* thee
Eze 24:12 She hath *w* herself with lies, and
Mic 6:3 and wherein have I *w* thee
Mal 2:17 Ye have *w* the LORD with your
Mal 2:17 Yet ye say, Wherein have we *w* him
Jn 4:6 being *w* with his journey, sat
Heb 12:3 against himself, lest ye be *w*

### WEARIETH
Job 37:11 by watering he *w* the thick cloud
Eccl 10:15 the foolish *w* every one of them

### WEARINESS
Eccl 12:12 and much study is a *w* of the flesh
Mal 1:13 said also, Behold, what a *w* is it
2Cor 11:27 In *w* and painfulness, in watchings

### WEARING
1Sa 14:3 priest in Shiloh, *w* an ephod
Jn 19:5 *w* the crown of thorns, and the
1Pet 3:3 of *w* of gold, or of putting on of

### WEARISOME
Job 7:3 *w* nights are appointed to me

### WEARY
Gen 27:46 I am *w* of my life because of the
Deut 25:18 thee, when thou wast faint and *w*
Judg 4:21 for he was fast asleep and *w*
Judg 8:15 bread unto thy men that are *w*
2Sa 16:14 people that were with him, came *w*
2Sa 17:2 will come upon him while he is *w*
2Sa 17:29 said, The people is hungry, and *w*
2Sa 23:10 Philistines until his hand was *w*
Job 3:17 and there the *w* be at rest
Job 10:1 My soul is *w* of my life
Job 16:7 But now he hath made me *w*
Job 22:7 not given water to the *w* to drink
Ps 6:6 I am *w* with my groaning
Ps 68:9 thine inheritance, when it was *w*
Ps 69:3 I am *w* of my crying
Prov 3:11 neither be *w* of his correction
Prov 25:17 lest he be *w* of thee, and so hate
Is 1:14 I am *w* to bear them
Is 5:27 None shall be *w* nor stumble among
Is 7:13 it a small thing for you to *w* men
Is 7:13 but will ye *w* my God also
Is 16:12 that Moab is *w* on the high place
Is 28:12 ye may cause the *w* to rest
Is 32:2 of a great rock in a *w* land
Is 40:28 earth, fainteth not, neither is *w*
Is 40:30 the youths shall faint and be *w*
Is 40:31 they shall run, and not be *w*
Is 43:22 but thou hast been *w* of me
Is 46:1 they are a burden to the *w* beast
Is 50:4 a word in season to him that is *w*
Jer 2:24 seek her will not *w* themselves
Jer 6:11 I am *w* with holding in
Jer 9:5 *w* themselves to commit iniquity
Jer 15:6 I am *w* with repenting
Jer 20:9 I was *w* with forbearing, and I
Jer 31:25 For I have satiated the *w* soul
Jer 51:58 in the fire, and they shall be *w*
Jer 51:64 and they shall be *w*
Hab 2:13 the people shall *w* themselves for
Lk 18:5 by her continual coming she *w* me
Gal 6:9 And let us not be *w* in well doing
2Th 3:13 brethren, be not *w* in well doing

### WEASEL
Lev 11:29 the *w*, and the mouse, and the

### WEATHER
Job 37:22 Fair *w* cometh out of the north
Prov 25:20 taketh away a garment in cold *w*
Mt 16:2 ye say, It will be fair *w*
Mt 16:3 morning, It will be foul *w* to day

### WEAVE
Is 19:9 flax, and they that *w* networks
Is 59:5 eggs, and *w* the spider's web

### WEAVER
Ex 35:35 and in fine linen, and of the *w*
Is 38:12 I have cut off like a *w* my life

### WEAVER'S
1Sa 17:7 of his spear was like a *w* beam
2Sa 21:19 of whose spear was like a *w* beam
1Chr 11:23 hand was a spear like a *w* beam
1Chr 20:5 spear staff was like a *w* beam
Job 7:6 days are swifter than a *w* shuttle

### WEAVEST
Judg 16:13 If thou *w* the seven locks of my

### WEB
Judg 16:13 seven locks of my head with the *w*
Judg 16:14 pin of the beam, and with the *w*
Job 8:14 whose trust shall be a spider's *w*
Is 59:5 eggs, and weave the spider's *w*

### WEBS
Is 59:6 Their *w* shall not become garments

### WEDDING
Mt 22:3 them that were bidden to the *w*
Mt 22:8 The *w* is ready, but they which
Mt 22:10 the *w* was furnished with guests
Mt 22:11 man which had not on a *w* garment
Mt 22:12 in hither not having a *w* garment
Lk 12:36 when he will return from the *w*
Lk 14:8 thou art bidden of any man to a *w*

### WEDGE
Josh 7:21 a *w* of gold of fifty shekels
Josh 7:24 the *w* of gold, and his sons, and
Is 13:12 a man than the golden *w* of Ophir

### WEDLOCK
Eze 16:38 judge thee, as women that break *w*

### WEEDS
Jonah 2:5 the *w* were wrapped about my head

### WEEK
Gen 29:27 Fulfil her *w*, and we will give
Gen 29:28 Jacob did so, and fulfilled her *w*

Dan 9:27 the covenant with many for one *w*
Dan 9:27 in the midst of the *w* he shall
Mt 28:1 toward the first day of the *w*
Mk 16:2 morning the first day of the *w*
Mk 16:9 early the first day of the *w*
Lk 18:12 I fast twice in the *w*, I give
Lk 24:1 Now upon the first day of the *w*
Jn 20:1 The first day of the *w* cometh
Jn 20:19 being the first day of the *w*
Acts 20:7 And upon the first day of the *w*
1Cor 16:2 Upon the first day of the *w* let

### WEEKS
Ex 34:22 thou shalt observe the feast of *w*
Lev 12:5 then she shall be unclean two *w*
Num 28:26 the LORD, after your *w* be out
Deut 16:9 Seven *w* shalt thou number unto
Deut 16:9 seven *w* from such time as thou
Deut 16:10 of *w* unto the LORD thy God with a
Deut 16:16 bread, and in the feast of *w*
2Chr 8:13 bread, and in the feast of *w*
Jer 5:24 us the appointed *w* of the harvest
Dan 9:24 Seventy *w* are determined upon thy
Dan 9:25 the Prince shall be seven *w*
Dan 9:25 and threescore and two *w*
Dan 9:26 two *w* shall Messiah be cut off,
Dan 10:2 Daniel was mourning three full *w*
Dan 10:3 till three whole *w* were fulfilled

### WEEP
Gen 23:2 mourn for Sarah, and to *w* for her
Gen 43:30 and he sought where to *w*
Num 11:10 *w* throughout their families
Num 11:13 for they *w* unto me, saying, Give
1Sa 11:5 aileth the people that they *w*
1Sa 30:4 until they had no more power to *w*
2Sa 1:24 *w* over Saul, who clothed you in
2Sa 12:21 *w* for the child, while it was
2Chr 34:27 rend thy clothes, and *w* before me
Neh 8:9 mourn not, nor *w*
Job 27:15 and his widows shall not *w*
Job 30:25 Did not I *w* for him that was in
Job 30:31 into the voice of them that *w*
Eccl 3:4 A time to *w*, and a time to laugh
Is 15:2 to Dibon, the high places, to *w*
Is 22:4 I will *w* bitterly, labour not to
Is 30:19 thou shalt *w* no more
Is 33:7 of peace shall *w* bitterly
Jer 9:1 of tears, that I might *w* day
Jer 13:17 my soul shall *w* in secret places
Jer 13:17 and mine eye shall *w* sore, and run
Jer 22:10 *W* ye not for the dead, neither
Jer 22:10 but *w* sore for him that goeth
Jer 48:32 I will *w* for thee with the
Lam 1:16 For these things I *w*
Eze 24:16 neither shalt thou mourn nor *w*
Eze 24:23 ye shall not mourn nor *w*
Eze 27:31 they shall *w* for thee with
Joel 1:5 Awake, ye drunkards, and *w*
Joel 2:17 *w* between the porch and the altar,
Mic 1:10 it not at Gath, *w* ye not at all
Zec 7:3 Should I *w* in the fifth month,
Mk 5:39 them, Why make ye this ado, and *w*
Lk 6:21 Blessed are ye that *w* now
Lk 6:25 for ye shall mourn and *w*
Lk 7:13 on her, and said unto her, *W* not
Lk 8:52 but he said, *W* not
Lk 23:28 *w* not for me, but *w* for
Jn 11:31 goeth unto the grave to *w* there
Jn 16:20 I say unto you, That ye shall *w*
Acts 21:13 Paul answered, What mean ye to *w*
Rom 12:15 rejoice, and *w* with them that *w*
1Cor 7:30 And they that *w*, as though they
Jas 4:9 Be afflicted, and mourn, and *w*
Jas 5:1 Go to now, ye rich men, *w*
Rev 5:5 the elders saith unto me, *W* not
Rev 18:11 merchants of the earth shall *w*

### WEEPEST
1Sa 1:8 to her, Hannah, why *w* thou
Jn 20:13 say unto her, Woman, why *w* thou
Jn 20:15 saith unto her, Woman, why *w* thou

### WEEPETH
2Sa 19:1 was told Joab, Behold, the king *w*
2Kin 8:12 And Hazael said, Why *w* my lord
Ps 126:6 He that goeth forth and *w*, bearing
Lam 1:2 She *w* sore in the night, and her

### WEEPING
Num 25:6 who were *w* before the door of the
Deut 34:8 so the days of *w* and mourning for
2Sa 3:16 her along *w* behind her to Bahurim
2Sa 15:30 they went up, *w* as they went up
Ezr 3:13 the noise of the *w* of the people
Ezr 10:1 and when he had confessed, *w*
Est 4:3 among the Jews, and fasting, and *w*
Job 16:16 My face is foul with *w*, and on my
Ps 6:8 LORD hath heard the voice of my *w*
Ps 30:5 *w* may endure for a night, but joy
Ps 102:9 bread, and mingled my drink with *w*
Is 15:3 one shall howl, *w* abundantly
Is 15:5 Luhith with *w* shall they go it up
Is 16:9 I will bewail with the *w* of Jazer
Is 22:12 the Lord GOD of hosts call to *w*
Is 65:19 the voice of *w* shall be no more
Jer 3:21 was heard upon the high places, *w*
Jer 9:10 the mountains will I take up a *w*
Jer 31:9 They shall come with *w*, and with
Jer 31:15 Ramah, lamentation, and bitter *w*
Jer 31:15 Rahel *w* for her children refused
Jer 31:16 Refrain thy voice from *w*, and
Jer 41:6 meet them, *w* all along as he went
Jer 48:5 of Luhith continual *w* shall go up
Jer 48:32 weep for thee with the *w* of Jazer
Jer 50:4 of Judah together, going and *w*
Eze 8:14 there sat women *w* for Tammuz
Joel 2:12 heart, and with fasting, and with *w*
Mal 2:13 of the LORD with tears, with *w*
Mt 2:18 a voice heard, lamentation, and *w*
Mt 2:18 Rachel *w* for her children, and
Mt 8:12 there shall be *w* and gnashing of
Mt 22:13 there shall be *w* and gnashing of
Mt 24:51 there shall be *w* and gnashing of
Mt 25:30 there shall be *w* and gnashing of
Lk 7:38 And stood at his feet behind him *w*
Lk 13:28 There shall be *w* and gnashing of
Jn 11:33 When Jesus therefore saw her *w*
Jn 11:33 the Jews also *w* which came with
Jn 20:11 stood without at the sepulchre *w*
Acts 9:39 and all the widows stood by him *w*
Phil 3:18 you often, and now tell you even *w*
Rev 18:15 for the fear of her torment, *w*
Rev 18:19 dust on their heads, and cried, *w*

### WEIGH
1Chr 20:2 found it to *w* a talent of gold,
Ezr 8:29 until ye *w* them before the chief
Ps 58:2 ye *w* the violence of your hands
Is 26:7 dost *w* the path of the just
Is 46:6 *w* silver in the balance, and hire
Eze 5:1 then take thee balances to *w*

### WEIGHED
Gen 23:16 Abraham *w* to Ephron the silver,
Num 7:85 the silver vessels *w* two thousand
1Sa 2:3 and by him actions are *w*
1Sa 17:7 his spear's head *w* six hundred
2Sa 14:26 he *w* the hair of his head at two
2Sa 21:16 the weight of whose spear *w* three
Ezr 8:25 *w* unto them the silver, and the
Ezr 8:26 I even *w* unto their hand six
Ezr 8:33 the vessels *w* in the house of our
Job 6:2 O that my grief were throughly *w*
Job 28:15 silver be *w* for the price thereof
Job 31:6 Let me be *w* in an even balance,
Is 40:12 *w* the mountains in scales, and the
Jer 32:9 *w* him the money, even seventeen
Jer 32:10 *w* him the money in the balances
Dan 5:27 Thou art *w* in the balances, and
Zec 11:12 So they *w* for my price thirty

### WEIGHETH
Job 28:25 he *w* the waters by measure
Prov 16:2 but the LORD *w* the spirits

### WEIGHING
Num 7:85 charger of silver *w* an hundred
Num 7:86 *w* ten shekels apiece, after the

### WEIGHT
Gen 24:22 golden earring of half a shekel *w*
Gen 24:22 hands of ten shekels *w* of gold
Gen 43:21 of his sack, our money in full *w*
Ex 30:34 of each shall there be a like *w*
Lev 19:35 in judgment, in meteyard, in *w*
Lev 26:26 deliver you your bread again by *w*
Num 7:13 the *w* thereof was an hundred and
Num 7:19 the *w* whereof was an hundred and
Num 7:25 the *w* whereof was an hundred and
Num 7:31 charger of the *w* of an hundred
Num 7:37 the *w* whereof was an hundred and
Num 7:43 charger of the *w* of an hundred
Num 7:49 the *w* whereof was an hundred and
Num 7:55 charger of the *w* of an hundred
Num 7:61 the *w* whereof was an hundred and
Num 7:67 the *w* whereof was an hundred and
Num 7:73 the *w* whereof was an hundred and
Num 7:79 the *w* whereof was an hundred and
Deut 25:15 shalt have a perfect and just *w*
Josh 7:21 wedge of gold of fifty shekels *w*
Judg 8:26 the *w* of the golden earrings that
1Sa 17:5 the *w* of the coat was five
2Sa 12:30 the *w* whereof was a talent of
2Sa 14:26 shekels after the king's *w*
2Sa 21:16 the *w* of whose spear weighed
2Sa 21:16 hundred shekels of brass in *w*
1Kin 7:47 neither was the *w* of the brass
1Kin 10:14 Now the *w* of gold that came to
2Kin 25:16 all these vessels was without *w*
1Chr 21:25 six hundred shekels of gold by *w*
1Chr 22:3 and brass in abundance without *w*
1Chr 22:14 and of brass and iron without *w*
1Chr 28:14 of gold by *w* for things of gold
1Chr 28:14 all instruments of silver by *w*
1Chr 28:15 Even the *w* for the candlesticks
1Chr 28:15 by *w* for every candlestick, and
1Chr 28:15 the candlesticks of silver by *w*
1Chr 28:16 by *w* he gave gold for the tables
1Chr 28:17 he gave gold by *w* for every bason
1Chr 28:17 likewise silver by *w* for every
1Chr 28:18 of incense refined gold by *w*
2Chr 3:9 the *w* of the nails was fifty
2Chr 4:18 for the *w* of the brass could not
2Chr 9:13 Now the *w* of gold that came to
Ezr 8:30 the Levites the *w* of the silver
Ezr 8:34 By number and by *w* of every one
Ezr 8:34 all the *w* was written at that
Job 28:25 To make the *w* for the winds
Prov 11:1 but a just *w* is his delight
Prov 16:11 A just *w* and balance are the
Jer 52:20 all these vessels was without *w*
Eze 4:10 thou shalt eat shall be by *w*
Eze 4:16 and they shall eat bread by *w*
Zec 5:8 he cast the *w* of lead upon the
Jn 19:39 aloes, about an hundred pound *w*
2Cor 4:17 exceeding and eternal *w* of glory
Heb 12:1 let us lay aside every *w*
Rev 16:21 stone about the *w* of a talent

### WEIGHTIER
Mt 23:23 have omitted the *w* matters of the

### WEIGHTS
Lev 19:36 Just balances, just *w*, a just
Deut 25:13 not have in thy bag divers *w*
Prov 16:11 all the *w* of the bag are his work
Prov 20:10 Divers *w*, and divers measures,
Prov 20:23 Divers *w* are an abomination unto
Mic 6:11 and with the bag of deceitful *w*

### WEIGHTY
Prov 27:3 A stone is heavy, and the sand *w*
2Cor 10:10 For his letters, say they, are *w*

### WELFARE
Gen 43:27 And he asked them of their *w*
Ex 18:7 they asked each other of their *w*
1Chr 18:10 king David, to enquire of his *w*
Neh 2:10 the *w* of the children of Israel
Job 30:15 my *w* passeth away as a cloud
Ps 69:22 should have been for their *w*
Jer 38:4 seeketh not the *w* of this people

### WELLBELOVED
Song 1:13 A bundle of myrrh is my *w* unto me
Is 5:1 Now will I sing to my *w* a song of
Is 5:1 My *w* hath a vineyard in a very
Mk 12:6 yet therefore one son, his *w*
Rom 16:5 Salute my *w* Epaenetus, who is the
3Jn 1 The elder unto the *w* Gaius

### WELLFAVOURED
Nah 3:4 of the whoredoms of the *w* harlot

### WELLPLEASING
Phil 4:18 a sacrifice acceptable, *w* to God
Heb 13:21 you that which is *w* in his sight

### WELL'S
Gen 29:2 great stone was upon the *w* mouth
Gen 29:3 rolled the stone from the *w* mouth
Gen 29:3 upon the *w* mouth in his place
Gen 29:8 roll the stone from the *w* mouth
Gen 29:10 rolled the stone from the *w* mouth
2Sa 17:19 a covering over the *w* mouth

### WELLS
Gen 26:15 For all the *w* which his father's
Gen 26:18 Isaac digged again the *w* of water
Ex 15:27 where were twelve *w* of water
Num 20:17 we drink of the water of the *w*

Deut 6:11 *w* digged, which thou diggedst not
2Kin 3:19 good tree, and stop all *w* of water
2Kin 3:25 they stopped all the *w* of water
2Chr 26:10 in the desert, and digged many *w*
Neh 9:25 goods, *w* digged, vineyards, and
Is 12:3 water out of the *w* of salvation
2Pet 2:17 These are *w* without water, clouds

### WELLSPRING
Prov 16:22 Understanding is a *w* of life unto
Prov 18:4 the *w* of wisdom as a flowing

### WEN
Lev 22:22 broken, or maimed, or having a *w*

### WENCH
2Sa 17:17 and a *w* went and told them

### WEPT
Gen 21:16 him, and lift up her voice, and *w*
Gen 27:38 And Esau lifted up his voice, and *w*
Gen 29:11 and lifted up his voice, and *w*
Gen 33:4 and they *w*
Gen 37:35 Thus his father *w* for him
Gen 42:24 himself about from them, and *w*
Gen 43:30 into his chamber, and *w* there
Gen 45:2 And he *w* aloud
Gen 45:14 his brother Benjamin's neck, and *w*
Gen 45:14 and Benjamin *w* upon his neck
Gen 45:15 all his brethren, and *w* upon them
Gen 46:29 *w* on his neck a good while
Gen 50:1 *w* upon him, and kissed him
Gen 50:17 Joseph *w* when they spake unto him
Ex 2:6 and, behold, the babe *w*
Num 11:4 children of Israel also *w* again
Num 11:18 for ye have *w* in the ears of the
Num 11:20 have *w* before him, saying, Why
Num 14:1 and the people *w* that night
Deut 1:45 ye returned and *w* before the LORD
Deut 34:8 the children of Israel *w* for
Judg 2:4 lifted up their voice, and *w*
Judg 14:16 And Samson's wife *w* before him
Judg 14:17 she *w* before him the seven days,
Judg 20:23 *w* before the LORD until even, and
Judg 20:26 came unto the house of God, and *w*
Judg 21:2 lifted up their voices, and *w* sore
Ruth 1:9 they lifted up their voice, and *w*
Ruth 1:14 lifted up their voice, and *w* again
1Sa 1:7 therefore she *w*, and did not eat
1Sa 1:10 prayed unto the LORD, and *w* sore
1Sa 11:4 lifted up their voices, and *w*
1Sa 20:41 *w* one with another, until David
1Sa 24:16 And Saul lifted up his voice, and *w*
1Sa 30:4 him lifted up their voice and *w*
2Sa 1:12 And they mourned, and *w*, and fasted
2Sa 3:32 voice, and *w* at the grave of Abner
2Sa 3:32 and all the people *w*
2Sa 3:34 all the people *w* again over him
2Sa 12:22 was yet alive, I fasted and *w*
2Sa 13:36 and lifted up their voice and *w*
2Sa 13:36 and all his servants *w* very sore
2Sa 15:23 all the country *w* with a loud
2Sa 15:30 *w* as he went up, and had his head
2Sa 18:33 the chamber over the gate, and *w*
2Kin 8:11 and the man of God *w*
2Kin 13:14 *w* over his face, and said, O my
2Kin 20:3 And Hezekiah *w* sore
2Kin 22:19 rent thy clothes, and *w* before me
Ezr 3:12 their eyes, *w* with a loud voice
Ezr 10:1 for the people *w* very sore
Neh 1:4 these words, that I sat down and *w*
Neh 8:9 For all the people *w*, when they
Job 2:12 they lifted up their voice, and *w*
Ps 69:10 When I *w*, and chastened my soul
Ps 137:1 there we sat down, yea, we *w*
Is 38:3 And Hezekiah *w* sore
Hos 12:4 he *w*, and made supplication unto
Mt 26:75 And he went out, and *w* bitterly
Mk 5:38 seeth the tumult, and them that *w*
Mk 14:72 And when he thought thereon, he *w*
Mk 16:10 with him, as they mourned and *w*
Lk 7:32 mourned to you, and ye have not *w*
Lk 8:52 And all *w*, and bewailed her
Lk 19:41 he beheld the city, and *w* over it,
Lk 22:62 And Peter went out, and *w* bitterly
Jn 11:35 Jesus *w*
Jn 20:11 and as she *w*, she stooped down, and
Acts 20:37 And they all *w* sore, and fell on
1Cor 7:30 that weep, as though they *w* not
Rev 5:4 I *w* much, because no man was

### WEST
Gen 12:8 his tent, having Beth-el on the *w*
Gen 28:14 thou shalt spread abroad to the *w*
Ex 10:19 turned a mighty strong *w* wind
Ex 27:12 *w* side shall be hangings of fifty
Ex 38:12 for the *w* side were hangings of
Num 2:18 On the *w* side shall be the
Num 34:6 this shall be your *w* border
Num 35:5 on the *w* side two thousand cubits
Deut 33:23 of the LORD, possess thou the *w*
Josh 8:9 and Ai, on the *w* side of Ai
Josh 8:12 on the *w* side of the city
Josh 8:13 in wait on the *w* of the city
Josh 11:2 and in the borders of Dor on the *w*
Josh 11:3 Canaanite on the east and on the *w*
Josh 12:7 on this side Jordan on the *w*
Josh 15:12 the *w* border was to the great sea
Josh 18:14 this was the *w* quarter
Josh 18:15 and the border went out on the *w*
Josh 19:34 reacheth to Asher on the *w* side
1Kin 7:25 and three looking toward the *w*
1Chr 9:24 the porters, toward the east, *w*
1Chr 12:15 toward the east, and toward the *w*
2Chr 4:4 and three looking toward the *w*
2Chr 32:30 the *w* side of the city of David
2Chr 33:14 on the *w* side of Gihon, in the
Ps 75:6 from the east, nor from the *w*
Ps 103:12 As far as the east is from the *w*
Ps 107:3 from the east, and from the *w*
Is 11:14 of the Philistines toward the *w*
Is 43:5 east, and gather thee from the *w*
Is 45:6 rising of the sun, and from the *w*
Is 49:12 from the north and from the *w*
Is 59:19 the name of the LORD from the *w*
Eze 41:12 the *w* was seventy cubits broad
Eze 42:19 He turned about to the *w* side
Eze 45:7 from the *w* side westward, and from
Eze 45:7 from the *w* border unto the east
Eze 47:20 The *w* side also shall be the
Eze 47:20 This is the *w* side
Eze 48:1 for these are his sides east and *w*
Eze 48:2 the east side unto the *w* side
Eze 48:3 east side even unto the *w* side
Eze 48:4 the east side unto the *w* side
Eze 48:5 the east side unto the *w* side
Eze 48:6 east side even unto the *w* side
Eze 48:7 the east side unto the *w* side
Eze 48:8 the east side unto the *w* side
Eze 48:8 the east side unto the *w* side
Eze 48:10 toward the *w* ten thousand in
Eze 48:16 the *w* side four thousand and five
Eze 48:17 toward the *w* two hundred and fifty
Eze 48:21 thousand toward the *w* border
Eze 48:23 the east side unto the *w* side
Eze 48:24 the east side unto the *w* side
Eze 48:25 the east side unto the *w* side
Eze 48:26 the east side unto the *w* side
Eze 48:27 the east side unto the *w* side
Eze 48:34 At the *w* side four thousand and
Dan 8:5 an he goat came from the *w* on the
Hos 11:10 children shall tremble from the *w*
Zec 8:7 country, and from the *w* country
Zec 14:4 toward the east and toward the *w*
Mt 8:11 shall come from the east and *w*
Mt 24:27 east, and shineth even unto the *w*
Lk 12:54 ye see a cloud rise out of the *w*
Lk 13:29 come from the east, and from the *w*
Acts 27:12 and lieth toward the south *w*
Acts 27:12 and north *w*
Rev 21:13 and on the *w* three gates

### WESTERN
Num 34:6 And as for the *w* border, ye shall

### WESTWARD
Gen 13:14 and southward, and eastward, and *w*
Ex 26:22 *w* thou shalt make six boards
Ex 26:27 tabernacle, for the two sides *w*
Ex 36:27 tabernacle *w* he made six boards
Ex 36:32 of the tabernacle for the sides *w*
Num 3:23 pitch behind the tabernacle *w*
Deut 3:27 Pisgah, and lift up thine eyes *w*
Josh 5:1 were on the side of Jordan *w*
Josh 15:8 before the valley of Hinnom *w*
Josh 15:10 from Baalah *w* unto mount Seir
Josh 16:3 goeth down *w* to the coast of
Josh 16:8 Tappuah *w* unto the river Kanah
Josh 18:12 went up through the mountains *w*
Josh 19:26 and reacheth to Carmel *w*, and to
Josh 19:34 coast turneth *w* to Aznoth-tabor
Josh 22:7 brethren on this side Jordan *w*
Josh 23:4 off, even unto the great sea *w*
1Chr 7:28 *w* Gezer, with the towns thereof
1Chr 26:16 and Hosah the lot came forth *w*
1Chr 26:18 At Parbar *w*, four at the causeway
1Chr 26:30 of Israel on this side Jordan *w*
Eze 45:7 of the city, from the west side *w*
Eze 46:19 was a place on the two sides *w*
Eze 48:18 eastward, and ten thousand *w*
Eze 48:21 *w* over against the five and twenty
Dan 8:4 I saw the ram pushing *w*, and

### WET
Job 24:8 They are *w* with the showers of
Dan 4:15 let it be *w* with the dew of
Dan 4:23 let it be *w* with the dew of
Dan 4:25 they shall *w* thee with the dew of
Dan 4:33 his body was *w* with the dew of
Dan 5:21 his body was *w* with the dew of

### WHALE
Job 7:12 Am I a sea, or a *w*, that thou
Eze 32:2 and thou art as a *w* in the seas

### WHALE'S
Mt 12:40 and three nights in the *w* belly

### WHALES
Gen 1:21 And God created great *w*, and every

### WHEAT
Gen 30:14 went in the days of *w* harvest
Ex 9:32 But the *w* and the rie were not
Ex 34:22 of the firstfruits of *w* harvest
Num 18:12 the best of the wine, and of the *w*
Deut 8:8 A land of *w*, and barley, and vines,
Deut 32:14 with the fat of kidneys of *w*
Judg 6:11 threshed *w* by the winepress
Judg 15:1 after, in the time of *w* harvest
Ruth 2:23 of barley harvest and of *w* harvest
1Sa 6:13 their *w* harvest in the valley
1Sa 12:17 Is it not *w* harvest to day
2Sa 4:6 though they would have fetched *w*
2Sa 17:28 basons, and earthen vessels, and *w*
1Kin 5:11 of *w* for food to his household
1Chr 21:20 Now Ornan was threshing *w*
1Chr 21:23 the *w* for the meat offering
2Chr 2:10 thousand measures of beaten *w*
2Chr 2:15 Now therefore the *w*, and the
2Chr 27:5 and ten thousand measures of *w*
Ezr 6:9 offerings of the God of heaven, *w*
Ezr 7:22 and to an hundred measures of *w*
Job 31:40 Let thistles grow instead of *w*
Ps 81:16 also with the finest of the *w*
Ps 147:14 thee with the finest of the *w*
Prov 27:22 in a mortar among *w* with a pestle
Song 7:2 heap of *w* set about with lilies
Is 28:25 and cast in the principal *w*
Jer 12:13 They have sown *w*, but shall reap
Jer 23:28 What is the chaff to the *w*
Jer 31:12 the goodness of the LORD, for *w*
Jer 41:8 have treasures in the field, of *w*
Eze 4:9 Take thou also unto thee *w*
Eze 27:17 traded in thy market *w* of Minnith
Eze 45:13 part of an ephah of an homer of *w*
Joel 1:11 O ye vinedressers, for the *w*
Joel 2:24 And the floors shall be full of *w*
Amos 5:11 and ye take from him burdens of *w*
Amos 8:5 sabbath, that we may set forth *w*
Amos 8:6 yea, and sell the refuse of the *w*
Mt 3:12 gather his *w* into the garner
Mt 13:25 came and sowed tares among the *w*
Mt 13:29 ye root up also the *w* with them
Mt 13:30 but gather the *w* into my barn
Lk 3:17 will gather the *w* into his garner
Lk 16:7 he said, An hundred measures of *w*
Lk 22:31 you, that he may sift you as *w*
Jn 12:24 Except a corn of *w* fall into the
Acts 27:38 and cast out the *w* into the sea
1Cor 15:37 bare grain, it may chance of *w*
Rev 6:6 say, A measure of *w* for a penny
Rev 18:13 wine, and oil, and fine flour, and *w*

### WHEATEN
Ex 29:2 of *w* flour shalt thou make them

### WHEEL
1Kin 7:32 and the height of a *w* was a cubit
1Kin 7:33 was like the work of a chariot *w*
Ps 83:13 O my God, make them like a *w*
Prov 20:26 and bringeth the *w* over them
Eccl 12:6 or the *w* broken at the cistern
Is 28:27 neither is a cart *w* turned about
Is 28:28 break it with the *w* of his cart
Eze 1:15 behold one *w* upon the earth by

Eze 1:16 were a *w* in the middle of a *w*
Eze 10:9 one *w* by one cherub, and another
Eze 10:9 another *w* by another cherub
Eze 10:10 as if a *w* had been in the midst
Eze 10:10 had been in the midst of a *w*
Eze 10:13 unto them in my hearing, O *w*

**WHEELS**
Ex 14:25 And took off their chariot *w*
Judg 5:28 Why tarry the *w* of his chariots
1Kin 7:30 And every base had four brasen *w*
1Kin 7:32 And under the borders were four *w*
1Kin 7:32 the axletrees of the *w* were
1Kin 7:33 the work of the *w* was like the
Is 5:28 and their *w* like a whirlwind
Jer 18:3 he wrought a work on the *w*
Jer 47:3 and at the rumbling of his *w*
Eze 1:16 The appearance of the *w* and their
Eze 1:19 went, the *w* went by them
Eze 1:19 the earth, the *w* were lifted up
Eze 1:20 the *w* were lifted up over against
Eze 1:20 the living creature was in the *w*
Eze 1:21 the *w* were lifted up over against
Eze 1:21 the living creature was in the *w*
Eze 3:13 the noise of the *w* over against
Eze 10:2 and said, Go in between the *w*
Eze 10:6 Take fire from between the *w*
Eze 10:6 he went in, and stood beside the *w*
Eze 10:9 looked, behold the four *w* by the
Eze 10:9 the appearance of the *w* was as
Eze 10:12 hands, and their wings, and the *w*
Eze 10:12 even the *w* that they four had
Eze 10:13 As for the *w*, it was cried unto
Eze 10:16 went, the *w* went by them
Eze 10:16 the same *w* also turned not from
Eze 10:19 the *w* also were beside them, and
Eze 11:22 their wings, and the *w* beside them
Eze 23:24 thee with chariots, wagons, and *w*
Eze 26:10 of the horsemen, and of the *w*
Dan 7:9 flame, and his *w* as burning fire
Nah 3:2 noise of the rattling of the *w*

**WHELP**
Gen 49:9 Judah is a lion's *w*
Deut 33:22 of Dan he said, Dan is a lion's *w*
Nah 2:11 old lion, walked, and the lion's *w*

**WHELPS**
2Sa 17:8 bear robbed of her *w* in the field
Job 4:11 the stout lion's *w* are scattered
Job 28:8 The lion's *w* have not trodden it,
Prov 17:12 a bear robbed of her *w* meet a man
Jer 51:38 they shall yell as lions' *w*
Eze 19:2 nourished her *w* among young lions
Eze 19:3 And she brought up one of her *w*
Eze 19:5 then she took another of her *w*
Hos 13:8 a bear that is bereaved of her *w*
Nah 2:12 tear in pieces enough for his *w*

**WHET**
Deut 32:41 If I *w* my glittering sword, and
Ps 7:12 he turn not, he will *w* his sword
Ps 64:3 Who *w* their tongue like a sword,
Eccl 10:10 be blunt, and he do not *w* the edge

**WHIP**
Prov 26:3 A *w* for the horse, a bridle for
Nah 3:2 The noise of a *w*, and the noise of

**WHIPS**
1Kin 12:11 father hath chastised you with *w*
1Kin 12:14 father also chastised you with *w*
2Chr 10:11 my father chastised you with *w*
2Chr 10:14 my father chastised you with *w*

**WHIRLETH**
Eccl 1:6 it *w* about continually, and the

**WHIRLWIND**
2Kin 2:1 take up Elijah into heaven by a *w*
2Kin 2:11 Elijah went up by a *w* into heaven
Job 37:9 Out of the south cometh the *w*
Job 38:1 LORD answered Job out of the *w*
Job 40:6 the LORD unto Job out of the *w*
Ps 58:9 shall take them away as with a *w*
Prov 1:27 and your destruction cometh as a *w*
Prov 10:25 As the *w* passeth, so is the
Is 5:28 flint, and their wheels like a *w*
Is 17:13 like a rolling thing before the *w*
Is 40:24 the *w* shall take them away as
Is 41:16 away, and the *w* shall scatter them
Is 66:15 and with his chariots like a *w*
Jer 4:13 and his chariots shall be as a *w*
Jer 23:19 a *w* of the LORD is gone forth in
Jer 23:19 forth in fury, even a grievous *w*
Jer 25:32 a great *w* shall be raised up from
Jer 30:23 the *w* of the LORD goeth forth
Jer 30:23 forth with fury, a continuing *w*
Eze 1:4 a *w* came out of the north, a
Dan 11:40 shall come against him like a *w*
Hos 8:7 wind, and they shall reap the *w*
Hos 13:3 with the *w* out of the floor
Amos 1:14 a tempest in the day of the *w*
Nah 1:3 the LORD hath his way in the *w*
Hab 3:14 came out as a *w* to scatter me
Zec 7:14 But I scattered them with a *w*

**WHIRLWINDS**
Is 21:1 As *w* in the south pass through
Zec 9:14 and shall go with *w* of the south

**WHISPER**
Ps 41:7 All that hate me *w* together
Is 29:4 speech shall *w* out of the dust

**WHISPERED**
2Sa 12:19 David saw that his servants *w*

**WHISPERER**
Prov 16:28 a *w* separateth chief friends

**WHISPERERS**
Rom 1:29 deceit, malignity; *w*,

**WHISPERINGS**
2Cor 12:20 wraths, strifes, backbitings, *w*

**WHIT**
Deut 13:16 and all the spoil thereof every *w*
1Sa 3:18 And Samuel told him every *w*
Jn 7:23 every *w* whole on the sabbath day
Jn 13:10 his feet, but is clean every *w*
2Cor 11:5 not a *w* behind the very chiefest

**WHITE**
Gen 30:35 every one that had some *w* in it
Gen 30:37 pilled *w* strakes in them
Gen 30:37 made the *w* appear which was in
Gen 40:16 I had three *w* baskets on my head
Gen 49:12 wine, and his teeth *w* with milk
Ex 16:31 and it was like coriander seed, *w*
Lev 13:3 hair in the plague is turned *w*
Lev 13:4 If the bright spot be *w* in the
Lev 13:4 the hair thereof be not turned *w*
Lev 13:10 if the rising be *w* in the skin
Lev 13:10 and it have turned the hair *w*
Lev 13:13 it is all turned *w*
Lev 13:16 turn again, and be changed unto *w*
Lev 13:17 if the plague be turned into *w*
Lev 13:19 of the boil there be a *w* rising
Lev 13:19 or a bright spot, *w*
Lev 13:20 and the hair thereof be turned *w*
Lev 13:21 there be no *w* hairs therein, and
Lev 13:24 that burneth have a *w* bright spot
Lev 13:24 somewhat reddish, or *w*
Lev 13:25 in the bright spot be turned *w*
Lev 13:26 there be no *w* hair in the bright
Lev 13:38 bright spots, even *w* bright spots
Lev 13:39 skin of their flesh be darkish *w*
Lev 13:42 bald forehead, a *w* reddish sore
Lev 13:43 be *w* reddish in his bald head
Num 12:10 Miriam became leprous, *w* as snow
Judg 5:10 Speak, ye that ride on *w* asses
2Kin 5:27 his presence a leper as *w* as snow
2Chr 5:12 being arrayed in *w* linen
Est 1:6 Where were *w*, green, and blue,
Est 1:6 a pavement of red, and blue, and *w*
Est 8:15 in royal apparel of blue and *w*
Job 6:6 any taste in the *w* of an egg
Ps 68:14 it was *w* as snow in Salmon
Eccl 9:8 Let thy garments be always *w*
Song 5:10 My beloved is *w* and ruddy, the
Is 1:18 they shall be as *w* as snow
Eze 27:18 in the wine of Helbon, and *w* wool
Dan 7:9 sit, whose garment was *w* as snow
Dan 11:35 and to purge, and to make them *w*
Dan 12:10 Many shall be purified, and made *w*
Joel 1:7 the branches thereof are made *w*
Zec 1:8 there red horses, speckled, and *w*
Zec 6:3 And in the third chariot *w* horses
Zec 6:6 the *w* go forth after them
Mt 5:36 not make one hair *w* or black
Mt 17:2 and his raiment was *w* as the light
Mt 28:3 and his raiment *w* as snow
Mk 9:3 shining, exceeding *w* as snow
Mk 9:3 as no fuller on earth can *w* them
Mk 16:5 side, clothed in a long *w* garment
Lk 9:29 was altered, and his raiment was *w*
Jn 4:35 for they are *w* already to harvest
Jn 20:12 And seeth two angels in *w* sitting
Acts 1:10 men stood by them in *w* apparel
Rev 1:14 *w* like wool, as *w* as snow
Rev 2:17 manna, and will give him a *w* stone
Rev 3:4 and they shall walk with me in *w*
Rev 3:5 shall be clothed in *w* raiment
Rev 3:18 *w* raiment, that thou mayest be
Rev 4:4 sitting, clothed in *w* raiment
Rev 6:2 And I saw, and behold a *w* horse
Rev 6:11 *w* robes were given unto every one
Rev 7:9 the Lamb, clothed with *w* robes
Rev 7:13 which are arrayed in *w* robes
Rev 7:14 made them *w* in the blood of the
Rev 14:14 And I looked, and behold a *w* cloud
Rev 15:6 *w* linen, and having their breasts
Rev 19:8 arrayed in fine linen, clean and *w*
Rev 19:11 opened, and behold a *w* horse
Rev 19:14 heaven followed him upon *w* horses
Rev 19:14 clothed in fine linen, *w*
Rev 20:11 And I saw a great *w* throne

**WHITED**
Mt 23:27 for ye are like unto *w* sepulchres
Acts 23:3 God shall smite thee, thou *w* wall

**WHITER**
Ps 51:7 me, and I shall be *w* than snow
Lam 4:7 than snow, they were *w* than milk

**WHOLE**
Gen 2:6 watered the *w* face of the ground
Gen 2:11 compasseth the *w* land of Havilah
Gen 2:13 compasseth the *w* land of Ethiopia
Gen 7:19 that were under the *w* heaven
Gen 8:9 were on the face of the *w* earth
Gen 9:19 and of them was the *w* earth
Gen 11:1 the *w* earth was of one language,
Gen 11:4 upon the face of the *w* earth
Gen 13:9 Is not the *w* land before thee
Gen 47:28 so the *w* age of Jacob was an
Ex 10:15 covered the face of the *w* earth
Ex 12:6 and the *w* assembly of the
Ex 16:2 the *w* congregation of the
Ex 16:3 to kill this *w* assembly with
Ex 16:10 as Aaron spake unto the *w*
Ex 19:18 the *w* mount quaked greatly
Ex 29:18 burn the *w* ram upon the altar
Lev 3:9 the *w* rump, it shall he take off
Lev 4:12 Even the *w* bullock shall he carry
Lev 4:13 if the *w* congregation of Israel
Lev 7:14 he shall offer one out of the *w*
Lev 8:21 Moses burnt the *w* ram upon the
Lev 10:6 the *w* house of Israel, bewail the
Lev 25:29 within a *w* year after it is sold
Num 3:7 the charge of the *w* congregation
Num 8:9 thou shalt gather the *w* assembly
Num 10:2 of a *w* piece shalt thou make them
Num 11:20 But even a *w* month, until it come
Num 11:21 that they may eat a *w* month
Num 14:2 the *w* congregation said unto them
Num 14:29 you, according to your *w* number
Num 20:1 even the *w* congregation, into the
Num 20:22 Israel, even the *w* congregation,
Deut 2:25 that are under the *w* heaven
Deut 4:19 all nations under the *w* heaven
Deut 27:6 of the LORD thy God of *w* stones
Deut 29:23 that the *w* land thereof is
Deut 33:10 *w* burnt sacrifice upon thine
Josh 5:8 in the camp, till they were *w*
Josh 8:31 of Moses, an altar of *w* stones
Josh 10:13 not to go down about a *w* day
Josh 11:23 So Joshua took the *w* land
Josh 18:1 the *w* congregation of the
Josh 22:12 the *w* congregation of the
Josh 22:16 Thus saith the *w* congregation of
Josh 22:18 with the *w* congregation of Israel
Judg 19:2 and was there four *w* months
Judg 21:13 the *w* congregation sent some to
2Sa 1:9 because my life is yet *w* in me
2Sa 3:19 good to the *w* house of Benjamin
2Sa 6:19 even among the *w* multitude of
2Sa 14:7 the *w* family is risen against
1Kin 6:22 the *w* house he overlaid with gold
1Kin 6:22 also the *w* altar that was by the
1Kin 11:34 the *w* kingdom out of his hand
2Kin 9:8 For the *w* house of Ahab shall
2Chr 6:3 blessed the *w* congregation of
2Chr 15:15 and sought him with their *w* desire
2Chr 16:9 to and fro throughout the *w* earth
2Chr 26:12 The *w* number of the chief of the
2Chr 30:23 the *w* assembly took counsel to
2Chr 33:8 them, according to the *w* law
Ezr 2:64 The *w* congregation together was

Neh 7:66 The *w* congregation together was
Est 3:6 the *w* kingdom of Ahasuerus
Job 5:18 he woundeth, and his hands make *w*
Job 28:24 and seeth under the *w* heaven
Job 34:13 Or who hath disposed the *w* world
Job 37:3 directeth it under the *w* heaven
Job 41:11 is under the *w* heaven is mine
Ps 9:1 thee, O LORD, with my *w* heart
Ps 48:2 situation, the joy of the *w* earth
Ps 51:19 offering and *w* burnt offering
Ps 72:19 let the *w* earth be filled with
Ps 97:5 of the LORD of the *w* earth
Ps 105:16 he brake the *w* staff of bread
Ps 111:1 praise the LORD with my *w* heart
Ps 119:2 and that seek him with the *w* heart
Ps 119:10 With my *w* heart have I sought
Ps 119:34 shall observe it with my *w* heart
Ps 119:58 thy favour with my *w* heart
Ps 119:69 keep thy precepts with my *w* heart
Ps 119:145 I cried with my *w* heart
Ps 138:1 will praise thee with my *w* heart
Prov 1:12 and *w*, as those that go down into
Prov 16:33 but the *w* disposing thereof is of
Prov 26:26 shewed before the *w* congregation
Eccl 12:13 the conclusion of the *w* matter
Eccl 12:13 for this is the *w* duty of man
Is 1:5 the *w* head is sick
Is 1:5 and the *w* heart faint
Is 3:1 the *w* stay of bread
Is 3:1 and the *w* stay of water
Is 6:3 the *w* earth is full of his glory
Is 10:12 his *w* work upon mount Zion
Is 13:5 to destroy the *w* land
Is 14:7 The *w* earth is at rest, and is
Is 14:26 that is purposed upon the *w* earth
Is 14:29 *w* Palestina, because the rod of
Is 14:31 *w* Palestina, art dissolved
Is 21:8 and I am set in my ward *w* nights
Is 28:22 even determined upon the *w* earth
Is 54:5 The God of the *w* earth shall he
Jer 1:18 brasen walls against the *w* land
Jer 3:10 turned unto me with her *w* heart
Jer 4:20 for the *w* land is spoiled
Jer 4:27 The *w* land shall be desolate
Jer 4:29 The *w* city shall flee for the
Jer 7:15 even the *w* seed of Ephraim
Jer 8:16 the *w* land trembled at the sound
Jer 12:11 the *w* land is made desolate,
Jer 13:11 unto me the *w* house of Israel
Jer 13:11 the *w* house of Judah, saith the
Jer 15:10 man of contention to the *w* earth
Jer 19:11 that cannot be made *w* again
Jer 24:7 return unto me with their *w* heart
Jer 25:11 this *w* land shall be a desolation
Jer 31:40 the *w* valley of the dead bodies,
Jer 32:41 my *w* heart and with my *w* soul
Jer 35:3 the *w* house of the Rechabites
Jer 37:10 the *w* army of the Chaldeans that
Jer 45:4 I will pluck up, even this *w* land
Jer 50:23 of the *w* earth cut in asunder
Jer 51:41 praise of the *w* earth surprised
Jer 51:47 her *w* land shall be confounded,
Lam 2:15 of beauty, The joy of the *w* earth
Eze 5:10 the *w* remnant of thee will I
Eze 7:13 touching the *w* multitude thereof
Eze 10:12 And their *w* body, and their backs,
Eze 15:5 Behold, when it was *w*, it was
Eze 32:4 beasts of the *w* earth with thee
Eze 35:14 When the *w* earth rejoiceth, I
Eze 37:11 bones are the *w* house of Israel
Eze 39:25 mercy upon the *w* house of Israel
Eze 43:11 they may keep the *w* form thereof
Eze 43:12 the top of the mountain the *w*
Eze 45:6 be for the *w* house of Israel
Dan 2:35 mountain, and filled the *w* earth
Dan 2:48 over the *w* province of Babylon
Dan 6:1 should be over the *w* kingdom
Dan 6:3 to set him over the *w* realm
Dan 7:23 and shall devour the *w* earth
Dan 7:27 of the kingdom under the *w* heaven
Dan 8:5 west on the face of the *w* earth
Dan 9:12 for under the *w* heaven hath not
Dan 10:3 till three *w* weeks were fulfilled
Dan 11:17 the strength of his *w* kingdom
Amos 1:6 away captive the *w* captivity
Amos 1:9 up the *w* captivity to Edom
Amos 3:1 against the *w* family which I
Mic 4:13 unto the Lord of the *w* earth
Zeph 1:18 but the *w* land shall be devoured
Zec 4:10 run to and fro through the *w* earth
Zec 4:14 stand by the Lord of the *w* earth
Zec 5:3 over the face of the *w* earth
Mal 3:9 robbed me, even this *w* nation
Mt 5:29 not that thy *w* body should be
Mt 5:30 not that thy *w* body should be
Mt 6:22 thy *w* body shall be full of light
Mt 6:23 thy *w* body shall be full of
Mt 8:32 the *w* herd of swine ran violently
Mt 8:34 the *w* city came out to meet Jesus
Mt 9:12 They that be *w* need not a
Mt 9:21 touch his garment, I shall be *w*
Mt 9:22 thy faith hath made thee *w*
Mt 9:22 woman was made *w* from that hour
Mt 12:13 and it was restored *w*, like as the
Mt 13:2 the *w* multitude stood on the
Mt 13:33 of meal, till the *w* was leavened
Mt 14:36 as touched were made perfectly *w*
Mt 15:28 was made *w* from that very hour
Mt 15:31 dumb to speak, the maimed to be *w*
Mt 16:26 if he shall gain the *w* world
Mt 26:13 shall be preached in the *w* world
Mt 27:27 unto him the *w* band of soldiers
Mk 2:17 They that are *w* have no need of
Mk 3:5 hand was restored *w* as the other
Mk 4:1 the *w* multitude was by the sea on
Mk 5:28 but his clothes, I shall be *w*
Mk 5:34 thy faith hath made thee *w*
Mk 5:34 in peace, and be *w* of thy plague
Mk 6:55 ran through that *w* region round
Mk 6:56 many as touched him were made *w*
Mk 8:36 man, if he shall gain the *w* world
Mk 10:52 thy faith hath made thee *w*
Mk 12:33 more than all *w* burnt offerings
Mk 14:9 preached throughout the *w* world
Mk 15:1 the *w* council, and bound Jesus, and
Mk 15:16 and they call together the *w* band
Mk 15:33 the *w* land until the ninth hour
Lk 1:10 the *w* multitude of the people
Lk 5:31 They that are *w* need not a
Lk 6:10 hand was restored *w* as the other
Lk 6:19 the *w* multitude sought to touch
Lk 7:10 found the servant *w* that had been
Lk 8:37 Then the *w* multitude of the
Lk 8:39 published throughout the *w* city
Lk 8:48 thy faith hath made thee *w*
Lk 8:50 only, and she shall be made *w*
Lk 9:25 if he gain the *w* world, and lose
Lk 11:34 thy *w* body also is full of light
Lk 11:36 If thy *w* body therefore be full
Lk 11:36 the *w* shall be full of light, as
Lk 13:21 of meal, till the *w* was leavened
Lk 17:19 thy faith hath made thee *w*
Lk 19:37 the *w* multitude of the disciples
Lk 21:35 dwell on the face of the *w* earth
Lk 23:1 the *w* multitude of them arose, and
Jn 4:53 himself believed, and his *w* house
Jn 5:4 *w* of whatsoever disease he had
Jn 5:6 unto him, Wilt thou be made *w*
Jn 5:9 immediately the man was made *w*
Jn 5:11 answered them, He that made me *w*
Jn 5:14 unto him, Behold, thou art made *w*
Jn 5:15 was Jesus, which had made him *w*
Jn 7:23 every whit *w* on the sabbath day
Jn 11:50 that the *w* nation perish not
Acts 4:9 man, by what means he is made *w*
Acts 4:10 this man stand here before you *w*
Acts 6:5 saying pleased the *w* multitude
Acts 9:34 Jesus Christ maketh thee *w*
Acts 11:26 that a *w* year they assembled
Acts 13:44 sabbath day came almost the *w*
Acts 15:22 and elders, with the *w* church
Acts 19:29 the *w* city was filled with
Acts 28:30 Paul dwelt two *w* years in his own
Rom 1:8 spoken of throughout the *w* world
Rom 8:22 know that the *w* creation groaneth
Rom 16:23 mine host, and of the *w* church
1Cor 5:6 leaven leaveneth the *w* lump
1Cor 12:17 If the *w* body were an eye, where
1Cor 12:17 If the *w* were hearing, where were
1Cor 14:23 If therefore the *w* church be come
Gal 5:3 he is a debtor to do the *w* law
Gal 5:9 leaven leaveneth the *w* lump
Eph 3:15 Of whom the *w* family in heaven and
Eph 4:16 From whom the *w* body fitly joined
Eph 6:11 Put on the *w* armour of God, that
Eph 6:13 take unto you the *w* armour of God
1Th 5:23 and I pray God your *w* spirit
Titus 1:11 be stopped, who subvert *w* houses
Jas 2:10 whosoever shall keep the *w* law
Jas 3:2 and able also to bridle the *w* body
Jas 3:3 and we turn about their *w* body
Jas 3:6 that it defileth the *w* body
1Jn 2:2 also for the sins of the *w* world
1Jn 5:19 the *w* world lieth in wickedness
Rev 12:9 which deceiveth the *w* world
Rev 16:14 of the earth and of the *w* world

## WHOLESOME

Prov 15:4 A *w* tongue is a tree of life
1Ti 6:3 and consent not to *w* words

## WHOLLY

Lev 6:22 it shall be *w* burnt
Lev 6:23 for the priest shall be *w* burnt
Lev 19:9 thou shalt not *w* reap the corners
Num 3:9 they are *w* given unto him out of
Num 4:6 spread over it a cloth *w* of blue
Num 8:16 For they are *w* given unto me from
Num 32:11 they have not *w* followed me
Num 32:12 for they have *w* followed the LORD
Deut 1:36 because he hath *w* followed the
Josh 14:8 but I *w* followed the LORD my God
Josh 14:9 because thou hast *w* followed the
Josh 14:14 because that he *w* followed the
Judg 17:3 I had *w* dedicated the silver unto
1Sa 7:9 a burnt offering *w* unto the LORD
1Chr 28:21 will be *w* at thy commandment
Job 21:23 being *w* at ease and quiet
Is 22:1 that thou art *w* gone up to the
Jer 2:21 thee a noble vine, *w* a right seed
Jer 6:6 she is *w* oppression in the midst
Jer 13:19 it shall be *w* carried away
Jer 42:15 If ye *w* set your faces to enter
Jer 46:28 I not leave thee *w* unpunished
Jer 50:13 but it shall be *w* desolate
Eze 11:15 and all the house of Israel *w*
Amos 8:8 and it shall rise up *w* as a flood
Amos 9:5 it shall rise up *w* like a flood
Acts 17:16 saw the city *w* given to idolatry
1Th 5:23 very God of peace sanctify you *w*
1Ti 4:15 give thyself *w* to them

## WHORE

Lev 19:29 daughter, to cause her to be a *w*
Lev 21:7 shall not take a wife that is a *w*
Lev 21:9 profane herself by playing the *w*
Deut 22:21 to play the *w* in her father's
Deut 23:17 There shall be no *w* of the
Deut 23:18 shalt not bring the hire of a *w*
Judg 19:2 played the *w* against him, and went
Prov 23:27 For a *w* is a deep ditch
Is 57:3 seed of the adulterer and the *w*
Eze 16:28 Thou hast played the *w* also with
Rev 17:1 *w* that sitteth upon many waters
Rev 17:15 thou sawest, where the *w* sitteth
Rev 17:16 the beast, these shall hate the *w*
Rev 19:2 for he hath judged the great *w*

## WHOREDOM

Gen 38:24 behold, she is with child by *w*
Lev 19:29 lest the land fall to *w*, and the
Lev 20:5 to commit *w* with Molech, from
Num 25:1 *w* with the daughters of Moab
Jer 3:9 through the lightness of her *w*
Jer 13:27 neighings, the lewdness of thy *w*
Eze 16:17 men, and didst commit *w* with them
Eze 16:33 unto thee on every side for thy *w*
Eze 20:30 and commit ye *w* after their
Eze 23:8 and poured their *w* upon her
Eze 23:17 and they defiled her with their *w*
Eze 23:27 thy *w* brought from the land of
Eze 43:7 they, nor their kings, by their *w*
Eze 43:9 Now let them put away their *w*
Hos 1:2 the land hath committed great *w*
Hos 4:10 they shall commit *w*, and shall not
Hos 4:11 *W* and wine and new wine take away
Hos 4:13 your daughters shall commit *w*
Hos 4:14 your daughters when they commit *w*
Hos 4:18 they have committed *w* continually
Hos 5:3 now, O Ephraim, thou committest *w*
Hos 6:10 there is the *w* of Ephraim

## WHOREDOMS

Num 14:33 forty years, and bear your *w*
2Kin 9:22 so long as the *w* of thy mother
2Chr 21:13 like to the *w* of the house of
Jer 3:2 hast polluted the land with thy *w*
Eze 16:20 Is this of thy *w* a small matter
Eze 16:22 thy *w* thou hast not remembered
Eze 16:25 passed by, and multiplied thy *w*
Eze 16:26 and hast increased thy *w*, to
Eze 16:34 in thee from other women in thy *w*
Eze 16:34 none followeth thee to commit *w*

Eze 16:36 through thy *w* with thy lovers
Eze 23:3 And they committed *w* in Egypt
Eze 23:3 they committed *w* in their youth
Eze 23:7 she committed her *w* with them
Eze 23:8 left she her *w* brought from Egypt
Eze 23:11 in her *w* more than her sister in
Eze 23:11 more than her sister in her *w*
Eze 23:14 And that she increased her *w*
Eze 23:18 So she discovered her *w*, and
Eze 23:19 Yet she multiplied her *w*, in
Eze 23:29 of thy *w* shall be discovered
Eze 23:29 both thy lewdness and thy *w*
Eze 23:35 thou also thy lewdness and thy *w*
Eze 23:43 Will they now commit *w* with her
Hos 1:2 Go, take unto thee a wife of *w*
Hos 1:2 and children of *w*
Hos 2:2 put away her *w* out of her sight
Hos 2:4 for they be the children of *w*
Hos 4:12 for the spirit of *w* hath caused
Hos 5:4 for the spirit of *w* is in the
Nah 3:4 the *w* of the wellfavoured harlot
Nah 3:4 selleth nations through her *w*

## WHOREMONGER
Eph 5:5 For this ye know, that no *w*

## WHOREMONGERS
1Ti 1:10 For *w*, for them that defile
Heb 13:4 but *w* and adulterers God will
Rev 21:8 abominable, and murderers, and *w*
Rev 22:15 are dogs, and sorcerers, and *w*

## WHORE'S
Jer 3:3 and thou hadst a *w* forehead

## WHORES
Eze 16:33 They give gifts to all *w*
Hos 4:14 themselves are separated with *w*

## WHORING
Ex 34:15 they go a *w* after their gods, and
Ex 34:16 daughters go a *w* after their gods
Ex 34:16 thy sons go a *w* after their gods
Lev 17:7 after whom they have gone a *w*
Lev 20:5 off, and all that go a *w* after him
Lev 20:6 to go a *w* after them, I will even
Num 15:39 after which ye use to go a *w*
Deut 31:16 go a *w* after the gods of the
Judg 2:17 but they went a *w* after other
Judg 8:27 Israel went thither a *w* after it
Judg 8:33 went a *w* after Baalim, and made
1Chr 5:25 went a *w* after the gods of the
2Chr 21:13 of Jerusalem to go a *w*, like to
Ps 73:27 all them that go a *w* from thee
Ps 106:39 works, and went a *w* with their own
Eze 6:9 which go a *w* after their idols
Eze 23:30 hast gone a *w* after the heathen
Hos 4:12 they have gone a *w* from under
Hos 9:1 thou hast gone a *w* from thy God

## WHORISH
Prov 6:26 For by means of a *w* woman a man
Eze 6:9 I am broken with their *w* heart
Eze 16:30 the work of an imperious *w* woman

## WICKED
Gen 13:13 But the men of Sodom were *w*
Gen 18:23 destroy the righteous with the *w*
Gen 18:25 to slay the righteous with the *w*
Gen 18:25 the righteous should be as the *w*
Gen 38:7 was *w* in the sight of the LORD
Ex 9:27 and I and my people are *w*
Ex 23:1 put not thine hand with the *w* to
Ex 23:7 for I will not justify the *w*
Lev 20:17 it is a *w* thing
Num 16:26 from the tents of these *w* men
Deut 15:9 be not a thought in thy *w* heart
Deut 17:5 which have committed that *w* thing
Deut 23:9 then keep thee from every *w* thing
Deut 25:1 the righteous, and condemn the *w*
Deut 25:2 if the *w* man be worthy to be
1Sa 2:9 the *w* shall be silent in darkness
1Sa 24:13 Wickedness proceedeth from the *w*
1Sa 30:22 Then answered all the *w* men
2Sa 3:34 as a man falleth before *w* men
2Sa 4:11 when *w* men have slain a righteous
1Kin 8:32 thy servants, condemning the *w*
2Kin 17:11 wrought *w* things to provoke the
2Chr 6:23 thy servants, by requiting the *w*
2Chr 7:14 face, and turn from their *w* ways
2Chr 24:7 that *w* woman, had broken up the
Neh 9:35 turned they from their *w* works
Est 7:6 and enemy is this *w* Haman
Est 9:25 by letters that his *w* device
Job 3:17 There the *w* cease from troubling
Job 8:22 of the *w* shall come to nought
Job 9:22 destroyeth the perfect and the *w*
Job 9:24 is given into the hand of the *w*
Job 9:29 If I be *w*, why then labour I in
Job 10:3 shine upon the counsel of the *w*
Job 10:7 Thou knowest that I am not *w*
Job 10:15 If I be *w*, woe unto me
Job 11:20 But the eyes of the *w* shall fail
Job 15:20 The *w* man travaileth with pain
Job 16:11 me over into the hands of the *w*
Job 18:5 light of the *w* shall be put out
Job 18:21 such are the dwellings of the *w*
Job 20:5 the triumphing of the *w* is short
Job 20:22 every hand of the *w* shall come
Job 20:29 the portion of a *w* man from God
Job 21:7 Wherefore do the *w* live, become
Job 21:16 counsel of the *w* is far from me
Job 21:17 is the candle of the *w* put out
Job 21:28 are the dwelling places of the *w*
Job 21:30 That the *w* is reserved to the day
Job 22:15 old way which *w* men have trodden
Job 22:18 counsel of the *w* is far from me
Job 24:6 they gather the vintage of the *w*
Job 27:7 Let mine enemy be as the *w*
Job 27:13 the portion of a *w* man with God
Job 29:17 And I brake the jaws of the *w*
Job 31:3 Is not destruction to the *w*
Job 34:8 iniquity, and walketh with *w* men
Job 34:18 fit to say to a king, Thou art *w*
Job 34:26 He striketh them as *w* men in the
Job 34:36 because of his answers for *w* men
Job 36:6 preserveth not the life of the *w*
Job 36:17 fulfilled the judgment of the *w*
Job 38:13 that the *w* might be shaken out of
Job 38:15 from the *w* their light is
Job 40:12 tread down the *w* in their place
Ps 7:9 of the *w* come to an end
Ps 7:11 God is angry with the *w* every day
Ps 9:5 thou hast destroyed the *w*
Ps 9:16 the *w* is snared in the work of
Ps 9:17 The *w* shall be turned into hell,
Ps 10:2 The *w* in his pride doth persecute
Ps 10:3 For the *w* boasteth of his heart's
Ps 10:4 The *w*, through the pride of his
Ps 10:13 Wherefore doth the *w* contemn God
Ps 10:15 Break thou the arm of the *w*
Ps 11:2 the *w* bend their bow, they make
Ps 11:5 but the *w* and him that loveth
Ps 11:6 Upon the *w* he shall rain snares,
Ps 12:8 The *w* walk on every side, when
Ps 17:9 From the *w* that oppress me, from
Ps 17:13 deliver my soul from the *w*
Ps 22:16 of the *w* have inclosed me
Ps 26:5 and will not sit with the *w*
Ps 27:2 When the *w*, even mine enemies and
Ps 28:3 Draw me not away with the *w*
Ps 31:17 let the *w* be ashamed, and let them
Ps 32:10 Many sorrows shall be to the *w*
Ps 34:21 Evil shall slay the *w*
Ps 36:1 of the *w* saith within my heart
Ps 36:11 not the hand of the *w* remove me
Ps 37:7 who bringeth *w* devices to pass
Ps 37:10 while, and the *w* shall not be
Ps 37:12 The *w* plotteth against the just,
Ps 37:14 The *w* have drawn out the sword,
Ps 37:16 better than the riches of many *w*
Ps 37:17 the arms of the *w* shall be broken
Ps 37:20 But the *w* shall perish, and the
Ps 37:21 The *w* borroweth, and payeth not
Ps 37:28 seed of the *w* shall be cut off
Ps 37:32 The *w* watcheth the righteous, and
Ps 37:34 when the *w* are cut off, thou
Ps 37:35 I have seen the *w* in great power
Ps 37:38 the end of the *w* shall be cut off
Ps 37:40 he shall deliver them from the *w*
Ps 39:1 bridle, while the *w* is before me
Ps 50:16 But unto the *w* God saith, What
Ps 55:3 of the oppression of the *w*
Ps 58:3 The *w* are estranged from the womb
Ps 58:10 his feet in the blood of the *w*
Ps 59:5 merciful to any *w* transgressors
Ps 64:2 from the secret counsel of the *w*
Ps 68:2 so let the *w* perish at the
Ps 71:4 my God, out of the hand of the *w*
Ps 73:3 I saw the prosperity of the *w*
Ps 74:19 unto the multitude of the *w*
Ps 75:4 and to the *w*, Lift not up the horn
Ps 75:8 all the *w* of the earth shall
Ps 75:10 of the *w* also will I cut off
Ps 82:2 and accept the persons of the *w*
Ps 82:4 rid them out of the hand of the *w*
Ps 91:8 behold and see the reward of the *w*
Ps 92:7 When the *w* spring as the grass,
Ps 92:11 of the *w* that rise up against me
Ps 94:3 LORD, how long shall the *w*
Ps 94:3 how long shall the *w* triumph
Ps 94:13 until the pit be digged for the *w*
Ps 97:10 them out of the hand of the *w*
Ps 101:3 I will set no *w* thing before mine
Ps 101:4 I will not know a *w* person
Ps 101:8 destroy all the *w* of the land
Ps 101:8 that I may cut off all *w* doers
Ps 104:35 earth, and let the *w* be no more
Ps 106:18 the flame burned up the *w*
Ps 109:2 For the mouth of the *w* and the
Ps 109:6 Set thou a *w* man over him
Ps 112:10 The *w* shall see it, and be grieved
Ps 112:10 the desire of the *w* shall perish
Ps 119:53 of the *w* that forsake thy law
Ps 119:61 The bands of the *w* have robbed me
Ps 119:95 The *w* have waited for me to
Ps 119:110 The *w* have laid a snare for me
Ps 119:119 all the *w* of the earth like dross
Ps 119:155 Salvation is far from the *w*
Ps 125:3 For the rod of the *w* shall not
Ps 129:4 cut asunder the cords of the *w*
Ps 139:19 Surely thou wilt slay the *w*
Ps 139:24 see if there be any *w* way in me
Ps 140:4 O LORD, from the hands of the *w*
Ps 140:8 not, O LORD, the desires of the *w*
Ps 140:8 further not his *w* device
Ps 141:4 to practise *w* works with men that
Ps 141:10 Let the *w* fall into their own
Ps 145:20 but all the *w* will he destroy
Ps 146:9 but the way of the *w* he turneth
Ps 147:6 he casteth the *w* down to the
Prov 2:14 in the frowardness of the *w*
Prov 2:22 But the *w* shall be cut off from
Prov 3:25 of the desolation of the *w*
Prov 3:33 the LORD is in the house of the *w*
Prov 4:14 Enter not into the path of the *w*
Prov 4:19 The way of the *w* is as darkness
Prov 5:22 shall take the *w* himself, and he
Prov 6:12 a *w* man, walketh with a froward
Prov 6:18 that deviseth *w* imaginations
Prov 9:7 he that rebuketh a *w* man getteth
Prov 10:3 away the substance of the *w*
Prov 10:6 covereth the mouth of the *w*
Prov 10:7 but the name of the *w* shall rot
Prov 10:11 covereth the mouth of the *w*
Prov 10:16 the fruit of the *w* to sin
Prov 10:20 heart of the *w* is little worth
Prov 10:24 The fear of the *w*, it shall come
Prov 10:25 passeth, so is the *w* no more
Prov 10:27 years of the *w* shall be shortened
Prov 10:28 expectation of the *w* shall perish
Prov 10:30 but the *w* shall not inhabit the
Prov 10:32 of the *w* speaketh frowardness
Prov 11:5 but the *w* shall fall by his own
Prov 11:7 When a *w* man dieth, his
Prov 11:8 the *w* cometh in his stead
Prov 11:10 and when the *w* perish, there is
Prov 11:11 overthrown by the mouth of the *w*
Prov 11:18 The *w* worketh a deceitful work
Prov 11:21 the *w* shall not be unpunished
Prov 11:23 the expectation of the *w* is wrath
Prov 11:31 much more the *w* and the sinner
Prov 12:2 but a man of *w* devices will he
Prov 12:5 the counsels of the *w* are deceit
Prov 12:6 The words of the *w* are to lie in
Prov 12:7 The *w* are overthrown, and are not
Prov 12:10 tender mercies of the *w* are cruel
Prov 12:12 The *w* desireth the net of evil
Prov 12:13 The *w* is snared by the
Prov 12:21 but the *w* shall be filled with
Prov 12:26 the way of the *w* seduceth them
Prov 13:5 but a *w* man is loathsome, and
Prov 13:9 lamp of the *w* shall be put out
Prov 13:17 A *w* messenger falleth into
Prov 13:25 but the belly of the *w* shall want
Prov 14:11 The house of the *w* shall be
Prov 14:17 a man of *w* devices is hated
Prov 14:19 the *w* at the gates of the
Prov 14:32 The *w* is driven away in his
Prov 15:6 the revenues of the *w* is trouble
Prov 15:8 The sacrifice of the *w* is an
Prov 15:9 The way of the *w* is an
Prov 15:26 The thoughts of the *w* are an
Prov 15:28 but the mouth of the *w* poureth

Prov 15:29 The LORD is far from the *w*
Prov 16:4 even the *w* for the day of evil
Prov 17:4 A *w* doer giveth heed to false
Prov 17:15 He that justifieth the *w*, and he
Prov 17:23 A *w* man taketh a gift out of the
Prov 18:3 When the *w* cometh, then cometh
Prov 18:5 to accept the person of the *w*
Prov 19:28 the mouth of the *w* devoureth
Prov 20:26 A wise king scattereth the *w*
Prov 21:4 heart, and the plowing of the *w*
Prov 21:7 of the *w* shall destroy them
Prov 21:10 The soul of the *w* desireth evil
Prov 21:12 considereth the house of the *w*
Prov 21:12 the *w* for their wickedness
Prov 21:18 The *w* shall be a ransom for the
Prov 21:27 sacrifice of the *w* is abomination
Prov 21:27 when he bringeth it with a *w* mind
Prov 21:29 A *w* man hardeneth his face
Prov 24:15 O *w* man, against the dwelling of
Prov 24:16 but the *w* shall fall into
Prov 24:19 neither be thou envious at the *w*
Prov 24:20 candle of the *w* shall be put out
Prov 24:24 He that saith unto the *w*, Thou
Prov 25:5 Take away the *w* from before the
Prov 25:26 the *w* is as a troubled fountain
Prov 26:23 a *w* heart are like a potsherd
Prov 28:1 The *w* flee when no man pursueth
Prov 28:4 that forsake the law praise the *w*
Prov 28:12 but when the *w* rise, a man is
Prov 28:15 so is a *w* ruler over the poor
Prov 28:28 When the *w* rise, men hide
Prov 29:2 but when the *w* beareth rule
Prov 29:7 but the *w* regardeth not to know
Prov 29:12 to lies, all his servants are *w*
Prov 29:16 When the *w* are multiplied,
Prov 29:27 the way is abomination to the *w*
Eccl 3:17 judge the righteous and the *w*
Eccl 7:15 there is a *w* man that prolongeth
Eccl 7:17 Be not over much *w*, neither be
Eccl 8:10 And so I saw the *w* buried, who had
Eccl 8:13 it shall not be well with the *w*
Eccl 8:14 according to the work of the *w*
Eccl 8:14 again, there be *w* men, to whom it
Eccl 9:2 to the righteous, and to the *w*
Is 3:11 Woe unto the *w*
Is 5:23 Which justify the *w* for reward
Is 11:4 of his lips shall he slay the *w*
Is 13:11 evil, and the *w* for their iniquity
Is 14:5 hath broken the staff of the *w*
Is 26:10 Let favour be shewed to the *w*
Is 32:7 he deviseth *w* devices to destroy
Is 48:22 peace, saith the LORD, unto the *w*
Is 53:9 And he made his grave with the *w*
Is 55:7 Let the *w* forsake his way, and the
Is 57:20 But the *w* are like the troubled
Is 57:21 no peace, saith my God, to the *w*
Jer 2:33 also taught the *w* ones thy ways
Jer 5:26 among my people are found *w* men
Jer 5:28 they overpass the deeds of the *w*
Jer 6:29 for the *w* are not plucked away
Jer 12:1 doth the way of the *w* prosper
Jer 15:21 thee out of the hand of the *w*
Jer 17:9 all things, and desperately *w*
Jer 23:19 grievously upon the head of the *w*
Jer 25:31 give them that are *w* to the sword
Jer 30:23 with pain upon the head of the *w*
Eze 3:18 When I say unto the *w*, Thou shalt
Eze 3:18 to warn the *w* from his *w* way
Eze 3:18 the same *w* man shall die in his
Eze 3:19 Yet if thou warn the *w*, and he
Eze 3:19 wickedness, nor from his *w* way
Eze 7:21 to the *w* of the earth for a spoil
Eze 8:9 behold the *w* abominations that
Eze 11:2 give *w* counsel in this city
Eze 13:22 strengthened the hands of the *w*
Eze 13:22 should not return from his *w* way
Eze 18:20 of the *w* shall be upon him
Eze 18:21 But if the *w* will turn from all
Eze 18:23 at all that the *w* should die
Eze 18:24 abominations that the *w* man doeth
Eze 18:27 when the *w* man turneth away from
Eze 20:44 not according to your *w* ways
Eze 21:3 from thee the righteous and the *w*
Eze 21:4 from thee the righteous and the *w*
Eze 21:25 profane *w* prince of Israel, whose
Eze 21:29 of them that are slain, of the *w*
Eze 30:12 the land into the hand of the *w*
Eze 33:8 When I say unto the *w*
Eze 33:8 O *w* man, thou shalt surely die
Eze 33:8 speak to warn the *w* from his way
Eze 33:8 that *w* man shall die in his
Eze 33:9 if thou warn the *w* of his way to
Eze 33:11 no pleasure in the death of the *w*
Eze 33:11 but that the *w* turn from his way
Eze 33:12 as for the wickedness of the *w*
Eze 33:14 Again, when I say unto the *w*
Eze 33:15 If the *w* restore the pledge, give
Eze 33:19 But if the *w* turn from his
Dan 12:10 but the *w* shall do wickedly
Dan 12:10 none of the *w* shall understand
Mic 6:10 wickedness in the house of the *w*
Mic 6:11 them pure with the *w* balances
Nah 1:3 and will not at all acquit the *w*
Nah 1:11 against the LORD, a *w* counsellor
Nah 1:15 for the *w* shall no more pass
Hab 1:4 for the *w* doth compass about the
Hab 1:13 holdest thy tongue when the *w*
Hab 3:13 head out of the house of the *w*
Zeph 1:3 and the stumblingblocks with the *w*
Mal 3:18 between the righteous and the *w*
Mal 4:3 And ye shall tread down the *w*
Mt 12:45 other spirits more *w* than himself
Mt 12:45 it be also unto this *w* generation
Mt 13:19 it not, then cometh the *w* one
Mt 13:38 are the children of the *w* one
Mt 13:49 sever the *w* from among the just,
Mt 16:4 A *w* and adulterous generation
Mt 18:32 O thou *w* servant, I forgave thee
Mt 21:41 miserably destroy those *w* men
Mt 25:26 answered and said unto him, Thou *w*
Lk 11:26 other spirits more *w* than himself
Lk 19:22 will I judge thee, thou *w* servant
Acts 2:23 by *w* hands have crucified and
Acts 18:14 a matter of wrong or *w* lewdness
1Cor 5:13 among yourselves that *w* person
Eph 6:16 all the fiery darts of the *w*
Col 1:21 enemies in your mind by *w* works
2Th 2:8 And then shall that *W* be revealed
2Th 3:2 from unreasonable and *w* men
2Pet 2:7 the filthy conversation of the *w*
2Pet 3:17 led away with the error of the *w*
1Jn 2:13 ye have overcome the *w* one
1Jn 2:14 and ye have overcome the *w* one
1Jn 3:12 as Cain, who was of that *w* one
1Jn 5:18 that *w* one toucheth him not

## WICKEDLY

Gen 19:7 I pray you, brethren, do not so *w*
Deut 9:18 in doing *w* in the sight of the
Judg 19:23 nay, I pray you, do not so *w*
1Sa 12:25 But if ye shall still do *w*
2Sa 22:22 have not *w* departed from my God
2Sa 24:17 I have sinned, and I have done *w*
2Kin 21:11 hath done *w* above all that the
2Chr 6:37 have done amiss, and have dealt *w*
2Chr 20:35 king of Israel, who did very *w*
2Chr 22:3 mother was his counsellor to do *w*
Neh 9:33 done right, but we have done *w*
Job 13:7 Will ye speak *w* for God
Job 34:12 Yea, surely God will not do *w*
Ps 18:21 have not *w* departed from my God
Ps 73:8 speak *w* concerning oppression
Ps 74:3 hath done *w* in the sanctuary
Ps 106:6 iniquity, we have done *w*
Ps 139:20 For they speak against thee *w*
Dan 9:5 iniquity, and have done *w*, and have
Dan 9:15 we have sinned, we have done *w*
Dan 11:32 such as do *w* against the covenant
Dan 12:10 but the wicked shall do *w*
Mal 4:1 the proud, yea, and all that do *w*

## WICKEDNESS

Gen 6:5 God saw that the *w* of man was
Gen 39:9 how then can I do this great *w*
Lev 18:17 it is *w*
Lev 19:29 and the land become full of *w*
Lev 20:14 a wife and her mother, it is *w*
Lev 20:14 that there be no *w* among you
Deut 9:4 but for the *w* of these nations
Deut 9:5 but for the *w* of these nations
Deut 9:27 of this people, nor to their *w*
Deut 13:11 any such *w* as this is among you
Deut 17:2 that hath wrought *w* in the sight
Deut 28:20 because of the *w* of thy doings
Judg 9:56 God rendered the *w* of Abimelech
Judg 20:3 Israel, Tell us, how was this *w*
Judg 20:12 What *w* is this that is done among
1Sa 12:17 and see that your *w* is great
1Sa 12:20 ye have done all this *w*
1Sa 24:13 *W* proceedeth from the wicked
1Sa 25:39 the *w* of Nabal upon his own head
2Sa 3:39 doer of evil according to his *w*
2Sa 7:10 of *w* afflict them any more
1Kin 1:52 but if *w* shall be found in him,
1Kin 2:44 Thou knowest all the *w* which
1Kin 2:44 return thy *w* upon thine own head
1Kin 8:47 perversely, we have committed *w*
1Kin 21:25 work *w* in the sight of the LORD
2Kin 21:6 he wrought much *w* in the sight of
1Chr 17:9 children of *w* waste them any more
Job 4:8 they that plow iniquity, and sow *w*
Job 11:11 he seeth *w* also
Job 11:14 away, and let not *w* dwell in thy
Job 20:12 Though *w* be sweet in his mouth,
Job 22:5 Is not thy *w* great
Job 24:20 *w* shall be broken as a tree
Job 27:4 My lips shall not speak *w*
Job 34:10 it from God, that he should do *w*
Job 35:8 Thy *w* may hurt a man as thou art
Ps 5:4 not a God that hath pleasure in *w*
Ps 5:9 their inward part is very *w*
Ps 7:9 Oh let the *w* of the wicked come
Ps 10:15 seek out his *w* till thou find
Ps 28:4 according to the *w* of their
Ps 45:7 lovest righteousness, and hatest *w*
Ps 52:7 and strengthened himself in his *w*
Ps 55:11 *W* is in the midst thereof
Ps 55:15 for *w* is in their dwellings, and
Ps 58:2 Yea, in heart ye work *w*
Ps 84:10 than to dwell in the tents of *w*
Ps 89:22 nor the son of *w* afflict him
Ps 94:23 shall cut them off in their own *w*
Ps 107:34 for the *w* of them that dwell
Prov 4:17 For they eat the bread of *w*
Prov 8:7 *w* is an abomination to my lips
Prov 10:2 Treasures of *w* profit nothing
Prov 11:5 wicked shall fall by his own *w*
Prov 12:3 man shall not be established by *w*
Prov 13:6 but *w* overthroweth the sinner
Prov 14:32 wicked is driven away in his *w*
Prov 16:12 abomination to kings to commit *w*
Prov 21:12 the wicked for their *w*
Prov 26:26 his *w* shall be shewed before the
Prov 30:20 mouth, and saith, I have done no *w*
Eccl 3:16 of judgment, that *w* was there
Eccl 7:15 that prolongeth his life in his *w*
Eccl 7:25 things, and to know the *w* of folly
Eccl 8:8 neither shall *w* deliver those
Is 9:18 For *w* burneth as the fire
Is 47:10 For thou hast trusted in thy *w*
Is 58:4 and to smite with the fist of *w*
Is 58:6 to loose the bands of *w*, to undo
Jer 1:16 against them touching all their *w*
Jer 2:19 Thine own *w* shall correct thee,
Jer 3:2 with thy whoredoms and with thy *w*
Jer 4:14 wash thine heart from *w*, that
Jer 4:18 this is thy *w*, because it is
Jer 6:7 waters, so she casteth out her *w*
Jer 7:12 it for the *w* of my people Israel
Jer 8:6 no man repented him of his *w*
Jer 12:4 for the *w* of them that dwell
Jer 14:16 for I will pour their *w* upon them
Jer 14:20 We acknowledge, O LORD, our *w*
Jer 22:22 and confounded for all thy *w*
Jer 23:11 in my house have I found their *w*
Jer 23:14 that none doth return from his *w*
Jer 33:5 for all whose *w* I have hid my
Jer 44:3 Because of their *w* which they
Jer 44:5 their ear to turn from their *w*
Jer 44:9 forgotten the *w* of your fathers
Jer 44:9 the *w* of the kings of Judah, and
Jer 44:9 the *w* of their wives, and your own
Jer 44:9 of their wives, and your own *w*
Jer 44:9 the *w* of your wives, which they
Lam 1:22 Let all their *w* come before thee
Eze 3:19 wicked, and he turn not from his *w*
Eze 5:6 into *w* more than the nations
Eze 7:11 is risen up into a rod of *w*
Eze 16:23 it came to pass after all thy *w*
Eze 16:57 Before thy *w* was discovered, as
Eze 18:20 the *w* of the wicked shall be upon
Eze 18:27 from his *w* that he hath committed
Eze 31:11 I have driven him out for his *w*
Eze 33:12 as for the *w* of the wicked, he
Eze 33:12 day that he turneth from his *w*
Eze 33:19 But if the wicked turn from his *w*
Hos 7:1 discovered, and the *w* of Samaria
Hos 7:2 that I remember all their *w*
Hos 7:3 make the king glad with their *w*
Hos 9:15 All their *w* is in Gilgal
Hos 9:15 for the *w* of their doings I will

Hos 10:13 Ye have plowed *w*, ye have reaped
Hos 10:15 unto you because of your great *w*
Joel 3:13 for their *w* is great
Jonah 1:2 for their *w* is come up before me
Mic 6:10 of *w* in the house of the wicked
Nah 3:19 hath not thy *w* passed continually
Zec 5:8 And he said, This is *w*
Mal 1:4 shall call them, The border of *w*
Mal 3:15 yea, they that work *w* are set up
Mt 22:18 But Jesus perceived their *w*
Mk 7:22 Thefts, covetousness, *w*, deceit,
Lk 11:39 part is full of ravening and *w*
Acts 8:22 Repent therefore of this thy *w*
Acts 25:5 man, if there be any *w* in him
Rom 1:29 unrighteousness, fornication, *w*
1Cor 5:8 with the leaven of malice and *w*
Eph 6:12 spiritual *w* in high places
1Jn 5:19 and the whole world lieth in *w*

## WIDE

Deut 15:8 shalt open thine hand *w* unto him
Deut 15:11 thine hand *w* unto thy brother
1Chr 4:40 and good, and the land was *w*
Job 29:23 mouth *w* as for the latter rain
Job 30:14 me as a *w* breaking in of waters
Ps 35:21 opened their mouth *w* against me
Ps 81:10 open thy mouth *w*, and I will fill
Ps 104:25 *w* sea, wherein are things
Prov 13:3 but he that openeth *w* his lips
Prov 21:9 a brawling woman and in a *w* house
Prov 25:24 a brawling woman and in a *w* house
Is 57:4 against whom make ye a *w* mouth
Jer 22:14 saith, I will build me a *w* house
Nah 3:13 be set *w* open unto thine enemies
Mt 7:13 for *w* is the gate, and broad is

## WIDENESS

Eze 41:10 *w* of twenty cubits round about

## WIDOW

Gen 38:11 Remain a *w* at thy father's house,
Ex 22:22 Ye shall not afflict any *w*
Lev 21:14 A *w*, or a divorced woman, or
Lev 22:13 if the priest's daughter be a *w*
Num 30:9 But every vow of a *w*, and of her
Deut 10:18 judgment of the fatherless and *w*
Deut 14:29 and the fatherless, and the *w*
Deut 16:11 and the fatherless, and the *w*
Deut 16:14 and the fatherless, and the *w*
Deut 24:19 for the fatherless, and for the *w*
Deut 24:20 for the fatherless, and for the *w*
Deut 24:21 for the fatherless, and for the *w*
Deut 26:12 the fatherless, and the *w*
Deut 26:13 to the fatherless, and to the *w*
Deut 27:19 of the stranger, fatherless, and *w*
2Sa 14:5 answered, I am indeed a *w* woman
1Kin 11:26 a *w* woman, even he lifted up his
1Kin 17:9 I have commanded a *w* woman there
1Kin 17:10 the *w* woman was there gathering
1Kin 17:20 upon the *w* with whom I sojourn
Job 24:21 and doeth not good to the *w*
Job 31:16 caused the eyes of the *w* to fail
Ps 94:6 They slay the *w* and the stranger,
Ps 109:9 be fatherless, and his wife a *w*
Ps 146:9 he relieveth the fatherless and *w*
Prov 15:25 establish the border of the *w*
Is 1:17 the fatherless, plead for the *w*
Is 1:23 the cause of the *w* come unto them
Is 47:8 I shall not sit as a *w*, neither
Jer 7:6 the fatherless, and the *w*
Jer 22:3 the fatherless, nor the *w*
Lam 1:1 how is she become as a *w*
Eze 22:7 vexed the fatherless and the *w*
Eze 44:22 they take for their wives a *w*
Eze 44:22 or a *w* that had a priest before
Zec 7:10 And oppress not the *w*, nor the
Mal 3:5 the hireling in his wages, the *w*
Mk 12:42 And there came a certain poor *w*
Mk 12:43 That this poor *w* hath cast more
Lk 2:37 she was a *w* of about fourscore and
Lk 4:26 Sidon, unto a woman that was a *w*
Lk 7:12 son of his mother, and she was a *w*
Lk 18:3 there was a *w* in that city
Lk 18:5 Yet because this *w* troubleth me
Lk 21:2 he saw also a certain poor *w*
Lk 21:3 that this poor *w* hath cast in
1Ti 5:4 But if any *w* have children or
1Ti 5:5 Now she that is a *w* indeed
1Ti 5:9 Let not a *w* be taken into the
Rev 18:7 heart, I sit a queen, and am no *w*

## WIDOWHOOD

Gen 38:19 and put on the garments of her *w*
2Sa 20:3 day of their death, living in *w*
Is 47:9 day, the loss of children, and *w*
Is 54:4 the reproach of thy *w* any more

## WIDOW'S

Gen 38:14 she put her *w* garments off from
Deut 24:17 nor take a *w* raiment to pledge
1Kin 7:14 He was a *w* son of the tribe of
Job 24:3 they take the *w* ox for a pledge
Job 29:13 I caused the *w* heart to sing for

## WIDOWS

Ex 22:24 and your wives shall be *w*, and your
Job 22:9 Thou hast sent *w* away empty
Job 27:15 and his *w* shall not weep
Ps 68:5 fatherless, and a judge of the *w*
Ps 78:64 their *w* made no lamentation
Is 9:17 mercy on their fatherless and *w*
Is 10:2 that *w* may be their prey, and that
Jer 15:8 Their *w* are increased to me above
Jer 18:21 of their children, and be *w*
Jer 49:11 and let thy *w* trust in me
Lam 5:3 fatherless, our mothers are as *w*
Eze 22:25 her many *w* in the midst thereof
Lk 4:25 many *w* were in Israel in the days
Acts 6:1 because their *w* were neglected in
Acts 9:39 all the *w* stood by him weeping,
Acts 9:41 he had called the saints and *w*
1Cor 7:8 therefore to the unmarried and *w*
1Ti 5:3 Honour *w* that are *w* indeed
1Ti 5:11 But the younger *w* refuse
1Ti 5:16 or woman that believeth have *w*
1Ti 5:16 relieve them that are *w* indeed
Jas 1:27 *w* in their affliction, and to keep

## WIDOWS'

Mt 23:14 for ye devour *w* houses, and for a
Mk 12:40 Which devour *w* houses, and for a
Lk 20:47 Which devour *w* houses, and for a

## WIFE

Gen 2:24 and shall cleave unto his *w*
Gen 2:25 were both naked, the man and his *w*
Gen 3:8 his *w* hid themselves from the
Gen 3:17 hearkened unto the voice of thy *w*
Gen 3:21 to his *w* did the LORD God make
Gen 4:1 And Adam knew Eve his *w*
Gen 4:17 And Cain knew his *w*
Gen 4:25 And Adam knew his *w* again
Gen 6:18 ark, thou, and thy sons, and thy *w*
Gen 7:7 went in, and his sons, and his *w*
Gen 7:13 the sons of Noah, and Noah's *w*
Gen 8:16 forth of the ark, thou, and thy *w*
Gen 8:18 went forth, and his sons, and his *w*
Gen 11:29 the name of Abram's *w* was Sarai
Gen 11:29 and the name of Nahor's *w*, Milcah,
Gen 11:31 in law, his son Abram's *w*
Gen 12:5 And Abram took Sarai his *w*
Gen 12:11 that he said unto Sarai his *w*
Gen 12:12 they shall say, This is his *w*
Gen 12:17 because of Sarai Abram's *w*
Gen 12:18 not tell me that she was thy *w*
Gen 12:19 I might have taken her to me to *w*
Gen 12:19 now therefore behold thy *w*
Gen 12:20 and they sent him away, and his *w*
Gen 13:1 up out of Egypt, he, and his *w*
Gen 16:1 Now Sarai Abram's *w* bare him no
Gen 16:3 Sarai Abram's *w* took Hagar her
Gen 16:3 to her husband Abram to be his *w*
Gen 17:15 unto Abraham, As for Sarai thy *w*
Gen 17:19 Sarah thy *w* shall bear thee a son
Gen 18:9 unto him, Where is Sarah thy *w*
Gen 18:10 Sarah thy *w* shall have a son
Gen 19:15 Lot, saying, Arise, take thy *w*
Gen 19:16 hand, and upon the hand of his *w*
Gen 19:26 But his *w* looked back from behind
Gen 20:2 And Abraham said of Sarah his *w*
Gen 20:3 for she is a man's *w*
Gen 20:7 therefore restore the man his *w*
Gen 20:12 and she became my *w*
Gen 20:14 and restored him Sarah his *w*
Gen 20:17 and God healed Abimelech, and his *w*
Gen 20:18 because of Sarah Abraham's *w*
Gen 21:21 his mother took him a *w* out of
Gen 23:19 Abraham buried Sarah his *w* in the
Gen 24:3 that thou shalt not take a *w* unto
Gen 24:4 take a *w* unto my son Isaac
Gen 24:7 thou shalt take a *w* unto my son
Gen 24:15 the *w* of Nahor, Abraham's brother
Gen 24:36 Sarah my master's *w* bare a son to
Gen 24:37 Thou shalt not take a *w* to my son
Gen 24:38 kindred, and take a *w* unto my son
Gen 24:40 thou shalt take a *w* for my son of
Gen 24:51 let her be thy master's son's *w*
Gen 24:67 took Rebekah, and she became his *w*
Gen 25:1 Then again Abraham took a *w*
Gen 25:10 Abraham buried, and Sarah his *w*
Gen 25:20 old when he took Rebekah to *w*
Gen 25:21 intreated the LORD for his *w*
Gen 25:21 him, and Rebekah his *w* conceived
Gen 26:7 of the place asked him of his *w*
Gen 26:7 for he feared to say, She is my *w*
Gen 26:8 was sporting with Rebekah his *w*
Gen 26:9 Behold, of a surety she is thy *w*
Gen 26:10 lightly have lien with thy *w*
Gen 26:11 *w* shall surely be put to death
Gen 26:34 to *w* Judith the daughter of Beeri
Gen 27:46 if Jacob take a *w* of the
Gen 28:1 Thou shalt not take a *w* of the
Gen 28:2 take thee a *w* from thence of the
Gen 28:6 to take him a *w* from thence
Gen 28:6 Thou shalt not take a *w* of the
Gen 28:9 sister of Nebajoth, to be his *w*
Gen 29:21 said unto Laban, Give me my *w*
Gen 29:28 him Rachel his daughter to *w* also
Gen 30:4 gave him Bilhah her handmaid to *w*
Gen 30:9 her maid, and gave her Jacob to *w*
Gen 34:4 saying, Get me this damsel to *w*
Gen 34:8 I pray you give her him to *w*
Gen 34:12 but give me the damsel to *w*
Gen 36:10 the son of Adah the *w* of Esau
Gen 36:10 son of Bashemath the *w* of Esau
Gen 36:12 were the sons of Adah Esau's *w*
Gen 36:13 the sons of Bashemath Esau's *w*
Gen 36:14 the daughter of Zibeon, Esau's *w*
Gen 36:17 the sons of Bashemath Esau's *w*
Gen 36:18 the sons of Aholibamah Esau's *w*
Gen 36:18 the daughter of Anah, Esau's *w*
Gen 38:6 Judah took a *w* for Er his
Gen 38:8 Onan, Go in unto thy brother's *w*
Gen 38:9 he went in unto his brother's *w*
Gen 38:12 daughter of Shuah Judah's *w* died
Gen 38:14 she was not given unto him to *w*
Gen 39:7 that his master's *w* cast her eyes
Gen 39:8 and said unto his master's *w*
Gen 39:9 but thee, because thou art his *w*
Gen 39:19 master heard the words of his *w*
Gen 41:45 he gave him to *w* Asenath the
Gen 44:27 Ye know that my *w* bare me two
Gen 46:19 The sons of Rachel Jacob's *w*
Gen 49:31 buried Abraham and Sarah his *w*
Gen 49:31 buried Isaac and Rebekah his *w*
Ex 2:1 took to *w* a daughter of Levi
Ex 4:20 And Moses took his *w* and his sons,
Ex 6:20 Jochebed his father's sister to *w*
Ex 6:23 sister of Naashon, to *w*
Ex 6:25 of the daughters of Putiel to *w*
Ex 18:2 in law, took Zipporah, Moses' *w*
Ex 18:5 his *w* unto Moses into the
Ex 18:6 am come unto thee, and thy *w*
Ex 20:17 shalt not covet thy neighbour's *w*
Ex 21:3 then his *w* shall go out with him
Ex 21:4 If his master have given him a *w*
Ex 21:4 the *w* and her children shall be
Ex 21:5 say, I love my master, my *w*
Ex 21:10 If he take him another *w*
Ex 22:16 surely endow her to be his *w*
Lev 18:8 father's *w* shalt thou not uncover
Lev 18:14 thou shalt not approach to his *w*
Lev 18:15 she is thy son's *w*
Lev 18:16 the nakedness of thy brother's *w*
Lev 18:18 shalt thou take a *w* to her sister
Lev 18:20 carnally with thy neighbour's *w*
Lev 20:10 adultery with another man's *w*
Lev 20:10 adultery with his neighbour's *w*
Lev 20:11 *w* hath uncovered his father's
Lev 20:14 And if a man take a *w* and her
Lev 20:20 man shall lie with his uncle's *w*
Lev 20:21 a man shall take his brother's *w*
Lev 21:7 not take a *w* that is a whore
Lev 21:13 And he shall take a *w* in her
Lev 21:14 a virgin of his own people to *w*
Num 5:12 them, If any man's *w* go aside
Num 5:14 him, and he be jealous of his *w*
Num 5:14 him, and he be jealous of his *w*
Num 5:15 man bring his *w* unto the priest
Num 5:29 when a *w* goeth aside to another
Num 5:30 him, and he be jealous over his *w*
Num 26:59 name of Amram's *w* was Jochebed
Num 30:16 Moses, between a man and his *w*

Num 36:8 shall be *w* unto one of the family
Deut 5:21 thou desire thy neighbour's *w*
Deut 13:6 or the *w* of thy bosom, or thy
Deut 20:7 is there that hath betrothed a *w*
Deut 21:11 thou wouldest have her to thy *w*
Deut 21:13 husband, and she shall be thy *w*
Deut 22:13 If any man take a *w*, and go in
Deut 22:16 my daughter unto this man to *w*
Deut 22:19 and she shall be his *w*
Deut 22:24 he hath humbled his neighbour's *w*
Deut 22:29 of silver, and she shall be his *w*
Deut 22:30 man shall not take his father's *w*
Deut 24:1 When a man hath taken a *w*
Deut 24:2 she may go and be another man's *w*
Deut 24:3 die, which took her to be his *w*
Deut 24:4 not take her again to be his *w*
Deut 24:5 When a man hath taken a new *w*
Deut 24:5 shall cheer up his *w* which he
Deut 25:5 the *w* of the dead shall not marry
Deut 25:5 unto her, and take her to him to *w*
Deut 25:7 like not to take his brother's *w*
Deut 25:7 then let his brother's *w* go up to
Deut 25:9 Then shall his brother's *w* come
Deut 25:11 the *w* of the one draweth near for
Deut 27:20 he that lieth with his father's *w*
Deut 28:30 Thou shalt betroth a *w*, and
Deut 28:54 toward the *w* of his bosom, and
Josh 15:16 I give Achsah my daughter to *w*
Josh 15:17 gave him Achsah his daughter to *w*
Judg 1:12 I give Achsah my daughter to *w*
Judg 1:13 gave him Achsah his daughter to *w*
Judg 4:4 the *w* of Lapidoth, she judged
Judg 4:17 of Jael the *w* of Heber the Kenite
Judg 4:21 Then Jael Heber's *w* took a nail
Judg 5:24 Jael the *w* of Heber the Kenite be
Judg 11:2 And Gilead's *w* bare him sons
Judg 13:2 his *w* was barren, and bare not
Judg 13:11 Manoah arose, and went after his *w*
Judg 13:19 and Manoah and his *w* looked on
Judg 13:20 his *w* looked on it, and fell on
Judg 13:21 more appear to Manoah and to his *w*
Judg 13:22 And Manoah said unto his *w*
Judg 13:23 But his *w* said unto him, If the
Judg 14:2 now therefore get her for me to *w*
Judg 14:3 to take a *w* of the uncircumcised
Judg 14:15 that they said unto Samson's *w*
Judg 14:16 Samson's *w* wept before him, and
Judg 14:20 But Samson's *w* was given to his
Judg 15:1 Samson visited his *w* with a kid
Judg 15:1 go in to my *w* into the chamber
Judg 15:6 because he had taken his *w*
Judg 21:1 his daughter unto Benjamin to *w*
Judg 21:18 be he that giveth a *w* to Benjamin
Judg 21:21 catch you every man his *w* of the
Judg 21:22 not to each man his *w* in the war
Ruth 1:1 the country of Moab, he, and his *w*
Ruth 1:2 and the name of his *w* Naomi
Ruth 4:5 the *w* of the dead, to raise up
Ruth 4:10 the *w* of Mahlon, have I purchased
Ruth 4:10 have I purchased to be my *w*
Ruth 4:13 Boaz took Ruth, and she was his *w*
1Sa 1:4 he gave to Peninnah his *w*
1Sa 1:19 and Elkanah knew Hannah his *w*
1Sa 2:20 And Eli blessed Elkanah and his *w*
1Sa 4:19 his daughter in law, Phinehas' *w*
1Sa 14:50 the name of Saul's *w* was Ahinoam
1Sa 18:17 Merab, her will I give thee to *w*
1Sa 18:19 unto Adriel the Meholathite to *w*
1Sa 18:27 gave him Michal his daughter to *w*
1Sa 19:11 and Michal David's *w* told him
1Sa 25:3 and the name of his *w* Abigail
1Sa 25:14 young men told Abigail, Nabal's *w*
1Sa 25:37 his *w* had told him these things,
1Sa 25:39 Abigail, to take her to him to *w*
1Sa 25:40 thee, to take thee to him to *w*
1Sa 25:42 of David, and became his *w*
1Sa 25:44 Michal his daughter, David's *w*
1Sa 27:3 the Carmelitess, Nabal's *w*
1Sa 30:5 Abigail the *w* of Nabal the
1Sa 30:22 save to every man his *w* and his
2Sa 2:2 Abigail Nabal's *w* the Carmelite
2Sa 3:3 of Abigail the *w* of Nabal the
2Sa 3:5 Ithream, by Eglah David's *w*
2Sa 3:14 saying, Deliver me my *w* Michal
2Sa 11:3 the *w* of Uriah the Hittite
2Sa 11:11 and to drink, and to lie with my *w*
2Sa 11:26 when the *w* of Uriah heard that
2Sa 11:27 to his house, and she became his *w*
2Sa 12:9 hast taken his *w* to be thy *w*
2Sa 12:10 hast taken the *w* of Uriah the
2Sa 12:10 of Uriah the Hittite to be thy *w*
2Sa 12:15 that Uriah's *w* bare unto David
2Sa 12:24 David comforted Bath-sheba his *w*
1Kin 2:17 me Abishag the Shunammite to *w*
1Kin 2:21 to Adonijah thy brother to *w*
1Kin 4:11 the daughter of Solomon to *w*
1Kin 4:15 the daughter of Solomon to *w*
1Kin 7:8 daughter, whom he had taken to *w*
1Kin 9:16 unto his daughter, Solomon's *w*
1Kin 11:19 so that he gave him to *w* the
1Kin 11:19 the sister of his own *w*
1Kin 14:2 And Jeroboam said to his *w*
1Kin 14:2 not known to be the *w* of Jeroboam
1Kin 14:4 And Jeroboam's *w* did so, and arose,
1Kin 14:5 the *w* of Jeroboam cometh to ask a
1Kin 14:6 said, Come in, thou *w* of Jeroboam
1Kin 14:17 And Jeroboam's *w* arose, and
1Kin 16:31 that he took to *w* Jezebel the
1Kin 21:5 But Jezebel his *w* came to him
1Kin 21:7 Jezebel his *w* said unto him, Dost
1Kin 21:25 whom Jezebel his *w* stirred up
2Kin 5:2 and she waited on Naaman's *w*
2Kin 8:18 the daughter of Ahab was his *w*
2Kin 14:9 Give thy daughter to my son to *w*
2Kin 22:14 the *w* of Shallum the son of
1Chr 2:18 begat children of Azubah his *w*
1Chr 2:24 then Abiah Hezron's *w* bare him
1Chr 2:26 Jerahmeel had also another *w*
1Chr 2:29 the name of the *w* of Abishur was
1Chr 2:35 to Jarha his servant to *w*
1Chr 3:3 the sixth, Ithream by Eglah his *w*
1Chr 4:18 his *w* Jehudijah bare Jered the
1Chr 4:19 the sons of his *w* Hodiah the
1Chr 7:15 Machir took to *w* the sister of
1Chr 7:16 Maachah the *w* of Machir bare a
1Chr 7:23 And when he went in to his *w*
1Chr 8:9 And he begat of Hodesh his *w*
2Chr 8:11 My *w* shall not dwell in the house
2Chr 11:18 of Jerimoth the son of David to *w*
2Chr 21:6 he had the daughter of Ahab to *w*
2Chr 22:11 the *w* of Jehoiada the priest,
2Chr 25:18 Give thy daughter to my son to *w*
2Chr 34:22 the *w* of Shallum the son of
Ezr 2:61 which took a *w* of the daughters
Neh 7:63 of Barzillai the Gileadite to *w*
Est 5:10 for his friends, and Zeresh his *w*
Est 5:14 Then said Zeresh his *w* and all his
Est 6:13 And Haman told Zeresh his *w*
Est 6:13 wise men and Zeresh his *w* unto him
Job 2:9 Then said his *w* unto him, Dost
Job 19:17 My breath is strange to my *w*
Job 31:10 Then let my *w* grind unto another,
Ps 109:9 be fatherless, and his *w* a widow
Ps 128:3 Thy *w* shall be as a fruitful vine
Prov 5:18 rejoice with the *w* of thy youth
Prov 6:29 goeth in to his neighbour's *w*
Prov 18:22 Whoso findeth a *w* findeth a good
Prov 19:13 the contentions of a *w* are a
Prov 19:14 a prudent *w* is from the LORD
Eccl 9:9 Live joyfully with the *w* whom
Is 54:1 the children of the married *w*
Is 54:6 a *w* of youth, when thou wast
Jer 3:1 They say, If a man put away his *w*
Jer 3:20 Surely as a *w* treacherously
Jer 5:8 neighed after his neighbour's *w*
Jer 6:11 husband with the *w* shall be taken
Jer 16:2 Thou shalt not take thee a *w*
Eze 16:32 But as a *w* that committeth
Eze 18:6 hath defiled his neighbour's *w*
Eze 18:11 and defiled his neighbour's *w*
Eze 18:15 not defiled his neighbour's *w*
Eze 22:11 with his neighbour's *w*
Eze 24:18 and at even my *w* died
Eze 33:26 every one his neighbour's *w*
Hos 1:2 take unto thee a *w* of whoredoms
Hos 2:2 for she is not my *w*, neither am I
Hos 12:12 Syria, and Israel served for a *w*
Hos 12:12 and for a *w* he kept sheep
Amos 7:17 Thy *w* shall be an harlot in the
Mal 2:14 the *w* of thy youth, against whom
Mal 2:14 and the *w* of thy covenant
Mal 2:15 against the *w* of his youth
Mt 1:6 her that had been the *w* of Urias
Mt 1:20 not to take unto thee Mary thy *w*
Mt 1:24 him, and took unto him his *w*
Mt 5:31 Whosoever shall put away his *w*
Mt 5:32 whosoever shall put away his *w*
Mt 14:3 sake, his brother Philip's *w*
Mt 18:25 him to be sold, and his *w*, and
Mt 19:3 to put away his *w* for every cause
Mt 19:5 mother, and shall cleave to his *w*
Mt 19:9 Whosoever shall put away his *w*
Mt 19:10 case of the man be so with his *w*
Mt 19:29 or father, or mother, or *w*
Mt 22:24 his brother shall marry his *w*
Mt 22:25 first, when he had married a *w*
Mt 22:25 left his *w* unto his brother
Mt 22:28 whose *w* shall she be of the seven
Mt 27:19 his *w* sent unto him, saying, Have
Mk 6:17 sake, his brother Philip's *w*
Mk 6:18 for thee to have thy brother's *w*
Mk 10:2 for a man to put away his *w*
Mk 10:7 and mother, and cleave to his *w*
Mk 10:11 Whosoever shall put away his *w*
Mk 10:29 or father, or mother, or *w*
Mk 12:19 leave his *w* behind him, and leave
Mk 12:19 his brother should take his *w*
Mk 12:20 and the first took a *w*, and dying
Mk 12:23 whose *w* shall she be of them
Mk 12:23 for the seven had her to *w*
Lk 1:5 his *w* was of the daughters of
Lk 1:13 thy *w* Elisabeth shall bear thee a
Lk 1:18 my *w* well stricken in years
Lk 1:24 days his *w* Elisabeth conceived
Lk 2:5 be taxed with Mary his espoused *w*
Lk 3:19 Herodias his brother Philip's *w*
Lk 8:3 Joanna the *w* of Chuza Herod's
Lk 14:20 another said, I have married a *w*
Lk 14:26 not his father, and mother, and *w*
Lk 16:18 Whosoever putteth away his *w*
Lk 17:32 Remember Lot's *w*
Lk 18:29 or parents, or brethren, or *w*
Lk 20:28 any man's brother die, having a *w*
Lk 20:28 his brother should take his *w*
Lk 20:29 and the first took a *w*, and died
Lk 20:30 And the second took her to *w*
Lk 20:33 whose *w* of them is she
Lk 20:33 for seven had her to *w*
Jn 19:25 Mary the *w* of Cleophas, and Mary
Acts 5:1 Ananias, with Sapphira his *w*
Acts 5:2 his *w* also being privy to it, and
Acts 5:7 of three hours after, when his *w*
Acts 18:2 from Italy, with his *w* Priscilla
Acts 24:24 Felix came with his *w* Drusilla
1Cor 5:1 one should have his father's *w*
1Cor 7:2 let every man have his own *w*
1Cor 7:3 render unto the *w* due benevolence
1Cor 7:3 also the *w* unto the husband
1Cor 7:4 The *w* hath not power of her own
1Cor 7:4 power of his own body, but the *w*
1Cor 7:10 Let not the *w* depart from her
1Cor 7:11 not the husband put away his *w*
1Cor 7:12 hath a *w* that believeth not
1Cor 7:14 husband is sanctified by the *w*
1Cor 7:14 the unbelieving *w* is sanctified
1Cor 7:16 For what knowest thou, O *w*
1Cor 7:16 whether thou shalt save thy *w*
1Cor 7:27 Art thou bound unto a *w*
1Cor 7:27 Art thou loosed from a *w*
1Cor 7:27 seek not a *w*
1Cor 7:33 world, how he may please his *w*
1Cor 7:34 is difference also between a *w*
1Cor 7:39 The *w* is bound by the law as long
1Cor 9:5 power to lead about a sister, a *w*
Eph 5:23 the husband is the head of the *w*
Eph 5:28 that loveth his *w* loveth himself
Eph 5:31 and shall be joined unto his *w*
Eph 5:33 so love his *w* even as himself
Eph 5:33 the *w* see that she reverence her
1Ti 3:2 blameless, the husband of one *w*
1Ti 3:12 deacons be the husbands of one *w*
1Ti 5:9 old, having been the *w* of one man
Titus 1:6 blameless, the husband of one *w*
1Pet 3:7 giving honour unto the *w*
Rev 19:7 his *w* hath made herself ready
Rev 21:9 shew thee the bride, the Lamb's *w*

## WIFE'S

Gen 3:20 And Adam called his *w* name Eve
Gen 20:11 they will slay me for my *w* sake
Gen 36:39 his *w* name was Mehetabel, the
Lev 18:11 of thy father's *w* daughter
Judg 11:2 his *w* sons grew up, and they
1Chr 1:50 his *w* name was Mehetabel, the
1Chr 8:29 whose *w* name was Maachah
1Chr 9:35 Jehiel, whose *w* name was Maachah
Mt 8:14 he saw his *w* mother laid, and sick
Mk 1:30 But Simon's *w* mother lay sick of
Lk 4:38 Simon's *w* mother was taken with a

## WILD

| | |
|---|---|
| Gen 16:12 | And he will be a *w* man |
| Lev 26:22 | will also send *w* beasts among you |
| Deut 14:5 | the *w* goat, and the pygarg |
| Deut 14:5 | the pygarg, and the *w* ox |
| 1Sa 17:46 | to the *w* beasts of the earth |
| 1Sa 24:2 | men upon the rocks of the *w* goats |
| 2Sa 2:18 | was as light of foot as a *w* roe |
| 2Kin 4:39 | gather herbs, and found a *w* vine |
| 2Kin 4:39 | gathered thereof *w* gourds his lap |
| 2Kin 14:9 | there passed by a *w* beast that |
| 2Chr 25:18 | there passed by a *w* beast that |
| Job 6:5 | Doth the *w* ass bray when he hath |
| Job 11:12 | man be born like a *w* ass's colt |
| Job 24:5 | as *w* asses in the desert, go they |
| Job 39:1 | *w* goats of the rock bring forth |
| Job 39:5 | Who hath sent out the *w* ass free |
| Job 39:5 | loosed the bands of the *w* ass |
| Job 39:15 | or that the *w* beast may break |
| Ps 50:11 | the *w* beasts of the field are |
| Ps 80:13 | the *w* beast of the field doth |
| Ps 104:11 | the *w* asses quench their thirst |
| Ps 104:18 | are a refuge for the *w* goats |
| Is 5:2 | and it brought forth *w* grapes |
| Is 5:4 | grapes, brought it forth *w* grapes |
| Is 13:21 | But *w* beasts of the desert shall |
| Is 13:22 | the *w* beasts of the islands shall |
| Is 32:14 | dens for ever, a joy of *w* asses |
| Is 34:14 | The *w* beasts of the desert shall |
| Is 34:14 | with the *w* beasts of the island |
| Is 51:20 | the streets, as a *w* bull in a net |
| Jer 2:24 | A *w* ass used to the wilderness, |
| Jer 14:6 | the *w* asses did stand in the high |
| Jer 50:39 | Therefore the *w* beasts of the |
| Jer 50:39 | the *w* beasts of the islands shall |
| Dan 5:21 | his dwelling was with the *w* asses |
| Hos 8:9 | Assyria, a *w* ass alone by himself |
| Hos 13:8 | the *w* beast shall tear them |
| Mt 3:4 | his meat was locusts and *w* honey |
| Mk 1:6 | and he did eat locusts and *w* honey |
| Mk 1:13 | and was with the *w* beasts |
| Acts 10:12 | *w* beasts, and creeping things, and |
| Acts 11:6 | *w* beasts, and creeping things, and |
| Rom 11:17 | being a *w* olive tree, wert |
| Rom 11:24 | olive tree which is *w* by nature |

## WILDERNESS

| | |
|---|---|
| Gen 14:6 | unto El-paran, which is by the *w* |
| Gen 16:7 | by a fountain of water in the *w* |
| Gen 21:14 | wandered in the *w* of Beer-sheba |
| Gen 21:20 | and he grew, and dwelt in the *w* |
| Gen 21:21 | And he dwelt in the *w* of Paran |
| Gen 36:24 | that found the mules in the *w* |
| Gen 37:22 | into this pit that is in the *w* |
| Ex 3:18 | three days' journey into the *w* |
| Ex 4:27 | Go into the *w* to meet Moses |
| Ex 5:1 | may hold a feast unto me in the *w* |
| Ex 7:16 | that they may serve me in the *w* |
| Ex 8:27 | go three days' journey into the *w* |
| Ex 8:28 | to the LORD your God in the *w* |
| Ex 13:18 | the way of the *w* of the Red sea |
| Ex 13:20 | in Etham, in the edge of the *w* |
| Ex 14:3 | the land, the *w* hath shut them in |
| Ex 14:11 | taken us away to die in the *w* |
| Ex 14:12 | than that we should die in the *w* |
| Ex 15:22 | they went out into the *w* of Shur |
| Ex 15:22 | and they went three days in the *w* |
| Ex 16:1 | of Israel came unto the *w* of Sin |
| Ex 16:2 | against Moses and Aaron in the *w* |
| Ex 16:3 | have brought us forth into this *w* |
| Ex 16:10 | that they looked toward the *w* |
| Ex 16:14 | upon the face of the *w* there lay |
| Ex 16:32 | wherewith I have fed you in the *w* |
| Ex 17:1 | journeyed from the *w* of Sin |
| Ex 18:5 | and his wife unto Moses into the *w* |
| Ex 19:1 | day came they into the *w* of Sinai |
| Ex 19:2 | of Sinai, and had pitched in the *w* |
| Lev 7:38 | unto the LORD, in the *w* of Sinai |
| Lev 16:10 | him go for a scapegoat into the *w* |
| Lev 16:21 | the hand of a fit man into the *w* |
| Lev 16:22 | he shall let go the goat in the *w* |
| Num 1:1 | unto Moses in the *w* of Sinai |
| Num 1:19 | numbered them in the *w* of Sinai |
| Num 3:4 | in the *w* of Sinai, and they had no |
| Num 3:14 | unto Moses in the *w* of Sinai |
| Num 9:1 | unto Moses in the *w* of Sinai |
| Num 9:5 | month at even in the *w* of Sinai |
| Num 10:12 | journeys out of the *w* of Sinai |
| Num 10:12 | cloud rested in the *w* of Paran |
| Num 10:31 | how we are to encamp in the *w* |
| Num 12:16 | and pitched in the *w* of Paran |
| Num 13:3 | sent them from the *w* of Paran |
| Num 13:21 | land from the *w* of Zin unto Rehob |
| Num 13:26 | of Israel, unto the *w* of Paran |
| Num 14:2 | would God we had died in this *w* |
| Num 14:16 | he hath slain them in the *w* |
| Num 14:22 | which I did in Egypt and in the *w* |
| Num 14:25 | get you into the *w* by the way of |
| Num 14:29 | carcases shall fall in this *w* |
| Num 14:32 | they shall fall in this *w* |
| Num 14:33 | shall wander in the *w* forty years |
| Num 14:33 | your carcases be wasted in the *w* |
| Num 14:35 | in this *w* they shall be consumed, |
| Num 15:32 | children of Israel were in the *w* |
| Num 16:13 | and honey, to kill us in the *w* |
| Num 20:4 | of the LORD into this *w*, that we |
| Num 21:5 | up out of Egypt to die in the *w* |
| Num 21:11 | in the *w* which is before Moab, |
| Num 21:13 | which is in the *w* that cometh out |
| Num 21:18 | from the *w* they went to Mattanah |
| Num 21:23 | out against Israel into the *w* |
| Num 24:1 | but he set his face toward the *w* |
| Num 26:64 | of Israel in the *w* of Sinai |
| Num 26:65 | They shall surely die in the *w* |
| Num 27:3 | Our father died in the *w*, and he |
| Num 27:14 | Meribah in Kadesh in the *w* of Zin |
| Num 32:13 | them wander in the *w* forty years |
| Num 32:15 | yet again leave them in the *w* |
| Num 33:6 | which is in the edge of the *w* |
| Num 33:8 | the midst of the sea into the *w* |
| Num 33:8 | days' journey in the *w* of Etham |
| Num 33:11 | sea, and encamped in the *w* of Sin |
| Num 33:12 | their journey out of the *w* of Sin |
| Num 33:15 | and pitched in the *w* of Sinai |
| Num 33:36 | and pitched in the *w* of Zin |
| Num 34:3 | *w* of Zin along by the coast of |
| Deut 1:1 | on this side Jordan in the *w* |
| Deut 1:19 | all that great and terrible *w* |
| Deut 1:31 | And in the *w*, where thou hast seen |
| Deut 1:40 | the *w* by the way of the Red sea |
| Deut 2:1 | the *w* by the way of the Red sea |
| Deut 2:7 | thy walking through this great *w* |
| Deut 2:8 | by the way of the *w* of Moab |
| Deut 2:26 | I sent messengers out of the *w* of |
| Deut 4:43 | Namely, Bezer in the *w*, in the |
| Deut 8:2 | thee these forty years in the *w* |
| Deut 8:15 | through that great and terrible *w* |
| Deut 8:16 | Who fed thee in the *w* with manna |
| Deut 9:7 | LORD thy God to wrath in the *w* |
| Deut 9:28 | them out to slay them in the *w* |
| Deut 11:5 | And what he did unto you in the *w* |
| Deut 11:24 | from the *w* and Lebanon, from the |
| Deut 29:5 | have led you forty years in the *w* |
| Deut 32:10 | land, and in the waste howling *w* |
| Deut 32:51 | Meribah-kadesh, in the *w* of Zin |
| Josh 1:4 | From the *w* and this Lebanon even |
| Josh 5:4 | of war, died in the *w* by the way |
| Josh 5:5 | people that were born in the *w* by |
| Josh 5:6 | walked forty years in the *w* |
| Josh 8:15 | them, and fled by the way of the *w* |
| Josh 8:20 | the people that fled to the *w* |
| Josh 8:24 | in the *w* wherein they chased them |
| Josh 12:8 | and in the springs, and in the *w* |
| Josh 14:10 | of Israel wandered in the *w* |
| Josh 15:1 | the *w* of Zin southward was the |
| Josh 15:61 | In the *w*, Beth-arabah, Middin, and |
| Josh 16:1 | to the *w* that goeth up from |
| Josh 18:12 | were at the *w* of Beth-aven |
| Josh 20:8 | they assigned Bezer in the *w* upon |
| Josh 24:7 | ye dwelt in the *w* a long season |
| Judg 1:16 | of Judah into the *w* of Judah |
| Judg 8:7 | flesh with the thorns of the *w* |
| Judg 8:16 | of the city, and thorns of the *w* |
| Judg 11:16 | through the *w* unto the Red sea |
| Judg 11:18 | they went along through the *w* |
| Judg 11:22 | from the *w* even unto Jordan |
| Judg 20:42 | of Israel unto the way of the *w* |
| Judg 20:45 | fled toward the *w* unto the rock |
| Judg 20:47 | fled to the *w* unto the rock |
| 1Sa 4:8 | with all the plagues in the *w* |
| 1Sa 13:18 | the valley of Zeboim toward the *w* |
| 1Sa 17:28 | left those few sheep in the *w* |
| 1Sa 23:14 | abode in the *w* in strong holds |
| 1Sa 23:14 | in a mountain in the *w* of Ziph |
| 1Sa 23:15 | David was in the *w* of Ziph in a |
| 1Sa 23:24 | and his men were in the *w* of Maon |
| 1Sa 23:25 | a rock, and abode in the *w* of Maon |
| 1Sa 23:25 | after David in the *w* of Maon |
| 1Sa 24:1 | David is in the *w* of En-gedi |
| 1Sa 25:1 | and went down to the *w* of Paran |
| 1Sa 25:4 | David heard in the *w* that Nabal |
| 1Sa 25:14 | out of the *w* to salute our master |
| 1Sa 25:21 | that this fellow hath in the *w* |
| 1Sa 26:2 | and went down to the *w* of Ziph |
| 1Sa 26:2 | to seek David in the *w* of Ziph |
| 1Sa 26:3 | But David abode in the *w*, and he |
| 1Sa 26:3 | Saul came after him into the *w* |
| 2Sa 2:24 | by the way of the *w* of Gibeon |
| 2Sa 15:23 | over, toward the way of the *w* |
| 2Sa 15:28 | will tarry in the plain of the *w* |
| 2Sa 16:2 | as be faint in the *w* may drink |
| 2Sa 17:16 | this night in the plains of the *w* |
| 2Sa 17:29 | and weary, and thirsty, in the *w* |
| 1Kin 2:34 | buried in his own house in the *w* |
| 1Kin 9:18 | And Baalath, and Tadmor in the *w* |
| 1Kin 19:4 | went a day's journey into the *w* |
| 1Kin 19:15 | on thy way to the *w* of Damascus |
| 2Kin 3:8 | The way through the *w* of Edom |
| 1Chr 5:9 | of the *w* from the river Euphrates |
| 1Chr 6:78 | Bezer in the *w* with her suburbs, |
| 1Chr 12:8 | the hold to the *w* men of might |
| 1Chr 21:29 | LORD, which Moses made in the *w* |
| 2Chr 1:3 | of the LORD had made in the *w* |
| 2Chr 8:4 | And he built Tadmor in the *w* |
| 2Chr 20:16 | the brook, before the *w* of Jeruel |
| 2Chr 20:20 | and went forth into the *w* of Tekoa |
| 2Chr 20:24 | toward the watch tower in the *w* |
| 2Chr 24:9 | of God laid upon Israel in the *w* |
| Neh 9:19 | forsookest them not in the *w* |
| Neh 9:21 | didst thou sustain them in the *w* |
| Job 1:19 | came a great wind from the *w* |
| Job 12:24 | in a *w* where there is no way |
| Job 24:5 | the *w* yieldeth food for them and |
| Job 30:3 | fleeing into the *w* in former time |
| Job 38:26 | on the *w*, wherein there is no man |
| Job 39:6 | Whose house I have made the *w* |
| Ps 29:8 | voice of the LORD shaketh the *w* |
| Ps 29:8 | the LORD shaketh the *w* of Kadesh |
| Ps 55:7 | far off, and remain in the *w* |
| Ps 63:t | when he was in the *w* of Judah |
| Ps 65:12 | drop upon the pastures of the *w* |
| Ps 68:7 | thou didst march through the *w* |
| Ps 72:9 | in the *w* shall bow before him |
| Ps 74:14 | to the people inhabiting the *w* |
| Ps 78:15 | He clave the rocks in the *w* |
| Ps 78:17 | provoking the most High in the *w* |
| Ps 78:19 | Can God furnish a table in the *w* |
| Ps 78:40 | oft did they provoke him in the *w* |
| Ps 78:52 | guided them in the *w* like a flock |
| Ps 95:8 | in the day of temptation in the *w* |
| Ps 102:6 | I am like a pelican of the *w* |
| Ps 106:9 | the depths, as through the *w* |
| Ps 106:14 | But lusted exceedingly in the *w* |
| Ps 106:26 | them, to overthrow them in the *w* |
| Ps 107:4 | in the *w* in a solitary way |
| Ps 107:33 | He turneth rivers into a *w* |
| Ps 107:35 | He turneth the *w* into a standing |
| Ps 107:40 | causeth them to wander in the *w* |
| Ps 136:16 | led his people through the *w* |
| Prov 21:19 | It is better to dwell in the *w* |
| Song 3:6 | of the *w* like pillars of smoke |
| Song 8:5 | is this that cometh up from the *w* |
| Is 14:17 | That made the world as a *w* |
| Is 16:1 | of the land from Sela to the *w* |
| Is 16:8 | they wandered through the *w* |
| Is 23:13 | it for them that dwell in the *w* |
| Is 27:10 | forsaken, and left like a *w* |
| Is 32:15 | the *w* be a fruitful field, and the |
| Is 32:16 | judgment shall dwell in the *w* |
| Is 33:9 | Sharon is like a *w* |
| Is 35:1 | The *w* and the solitary place shall |
| Is 35:6 | for in the *w* shall waters break |
| Is 40:3 | voice of him that crieth in the *w* |
| Is 41:18 | I will make the *w* a pool of water |
| Is 41:19 | I will plant in the *w* the cedar |
| Is 42:11 | Let the *w* and the cities thereof |
| Is 43:19 | I will even make a way in the *w* |
| Is 43:20 | because I give waters in the *w* |
| Is 50:2 | up the sea, I make the rivers a *w* |
| Is 51:3 | and he will make her *w* like Eden |
| Is 63:13 | the deep, as an horse in the *w* |
| Is 64:10 | are a *w*, Zion is a *w* |
| Jer 2:2 | thou wentest after me in the *w* |
| Jer 2:6 | Egypt, that led us through the *w* |
| Jer 2:24 | A wild ass used to the *w*, that |
| Jer 2:31 | Have I been a *w* unto Israel |
| Jer 3:2 | for them, as the Arabian in the *w* |
| Jer 4:11 | the *w* toward the daughter of my |
| Jer 4:26 | lo, the fruitful place was a *w* |
| Jer 9:2 | Oh that I had in the *w* a lodging |

Jer 9:10 of the *w* a lamentation, because
Jer 9:12 and is burned up like a *w*, that
Jer 9:26 corners, that dwell in the *w*
Jer 12:10 my pleasant portion a desolate *w*
Jer 12:12 all high places through the *w*
Jer 13:24 passeth away by the wind of the *w*
Jer 17:6 the parched places in the *w*
Jer 22:6 yet surely I will make thee a *w*
Jer 23:10 places of the *w* are dried up
Jer 31:2 of the sword found grace in the *w*
Jer 48:6 and be like the heath in the *w*
Jer 50:12 of the nations shall be a *w*
Jer 51:43 a desolation, a dry land, and a *w*
Lam 4:3 like the ostriches in the *w*
Lam 4:19 they laid wait for us in the *w*
Lam 5:9 because of the sword of the *w*
Eze 6:14 than the *w* toward Diblath
Eze 19:13 And now she is planted in the *w*
Eze 20:10 Egypt, and brought them into the *w*
Eze 20:13 rebelled against me in the *w*
Eze 20:13 out my fury upon them in the *w*
Eze 20:15 up my hand unto them in the *w*
Eze 20:17 I make an end of them in the *w*
Eze 20:18 said unto their children in the *w*
Eze 20:21 my anger against them in the *w*
Eze 20:23 mine hand unto them also in the *w*
Eze 20:35 you into the *w* of the people
Eze 20:36 in the *w* of the land of Egypt
Eze 23:42 were brought Sabeans from the *w*
Eze 29:5 will leave thee thrown into the *w*
Eze 34:25 they shall dwell safely in the *w*
Hos 2:3 she was born, and make her as a *w*
Hos 2:14 her, and bring her into the *w*
Hos 9:10 found Israel like grapes in the *w*
Hos 13:5 I did know thee in the *w*, in the
Hos 13:15 the LORD shall come up from the *w*
Joel 1:19 devoured the pastures of the *w*
Joel 1:20 devoured the pastures of the *w*
Joel 2:3 them, and behind them a desolate *w*
Joel 2:22 the pastures of the *w* do spring
Joel 3:19 and Edom shall be a desolate *w*
Amos 2:10 led you forty years through the *w*
Amos 5:25 and offerings in the *w* forty years
Amos 6:14 of Hemath unto the river of the *w*
Zeph 2:13 a desolation, and dry like a *w*
Mal 1:3 waste for the dragons of the *w*
Mt 3:1 preaching in the *w* of Judaea
Mt 3:3 The voice of one crying in the *w*
Mt 4:1 the *w* to be tempted of the devil
Mt 11:7 went ye out into the *w* to see
Mt 15:33 we have so much bread in the *w*
Mk 1:3 The voice of one crying in the *w*
Mk 1:4 John did baptize in the *w*
Mk 1:12 the spirit driveth him into the *w*
Mk 1:13 he was there in the *w* forty days
Mk 8:4 men with bread here in the *w*
Lk 3:2 the son of Zacharias in the *w*
Lk 3:4 The voice of one crying in the *w*
Lk 4:1 was led by the Spirit into the *w*
Lk 5:16 And he withdrew himself into the *w*
Lk 7:24 went ye out into the *w* for to see
Lk 8:29 driven of the devil into the *w*
Lk 15:4 leave the ninety and nine in the *w*
Jn 1:23 the voice of one crying in the *w*
Jn 3:14 lifted up the serpent in the *w*
Jn 6:49 fathers did eat manna in the *w*
Jn 11:54 unto a country near to the *w*
Acts 7:30 there appeared to him in the *w* of
Acts 7:36 Red sea, and in the *w* forty years
Acts 7:38 *w* with the angel which spake to
Acts 7:42 the space of forty years in the *w*
Acts 7:44 tabernacle of witness in the *w*
Acts 13:18 he their manners in the *w*
Acts 21:38 leddest out into the *w* four
1Cor 10:5 for they were overthrown in the *w*
2Cor 11:26 in the city, in perils in the *w*
Heb 3:8 in the day of temptation in the *w*
Heb 3:17 whose carcases fell in the *w*
Rev 12:6 And the woman fled into the *w*
Rev 12:14 that she might fly into the *w*
Rev 17:3 me away in the spirit into the *w*

## WILES
Num 25:18 For they vex you with their *w*
Eph 6:11 stand against the *w* of the devil

## WILFULLY
Heb 10:26 For if we sin *w* after that we

## WILILY
Josh 9:4 They did work *w*, and went and made

## WILLOW
Eze 17:5 waters, and set it as a *w* tree

## WILLOWS
Lev 23:40 of thick trees, and *w* of the brook
Job 40:22 the *w* of the brook compass him
Ps 137:2 upon the *w* in the midst thereof
Is 15:7 carry away to the brook of the *w*
Is 44:4 as *w* by the water courses

## WIMPLES
Is 3:22 apparel, and the mantles, and the *w*

## WIN
2Chr 32:1 thought to *w* them for himself
Phil 3:8 but dung, that I may *w* Christ

## WIND
Gen 8:1 God made a *w* to pass over the
Gen 41:6 the east *w* sprung up after them
Gen 41:23 thin, and blasted with the east *w*
Gen 41:27 ears blasted with the east *w*
Ex 10:13 the LORD brought an east *w* upon
Ex 10:13 the east *w* brought the locusts
Ex 10:19 turned a mighty strong west *w*
Ex 14:21 by a strong east *w* all that night
Ex 15:10 Thou didst blow with thy *w*
Num 11:31 went forth a *w* from the LORD
2Sa 22:11 was seen upon the wings of the *w*
1Kin 18:45 heaven was black with clouds and *w*
1Kin 19:11 strong *w* rent the mountains, and
1Kin 19:11 but the LORD was not in the *w*
1Kin 19:11 after the *w* an earthquake
2Kin 3:17 the LORD, Ye shall not see *w*
Job 1:19 there came a great *w* from the
Job 6:26 that is desperate, which are as *w*
Job 7:7 O remember that my life is *w*
Job 8:2 of thy mouth be like a strong *w*
Job 15:2 and fill his belly with the east *w*
Job 21:18 They are as stubble before the *w*
Job 27:21 The east *w* carrieth him away, and
Job 30:15 they pursue my soul as the *w*
Job 30:22 Thou liftest me up to the *w*
Job 37:17 quieteth the earth by the south *w*
Job 37:21 but the *w* passeth, and cleanseth
Job 38:24 the east *w* upon the earth
Ps 1:4 chaff which the *w* driveth away
Ps 18:10 did fly upon the wings of the *w*
Ps 18:42 small as the dust before the *w*
Ps 35:5 Let them be as chaff before the *w*
Ps 48:7 ships of Tarshish with an east *w*
Ps 78:26 He caused an east *w* to blow in
Ps 78:26 power he brought in the south *w*
Ps 78:39 a *w* that passeth away, and cometh
Ps 83:13 as the stubble before the *w*
Ps 103:16 For the *w* passeth over it, and it
Ps 104:3 walketh upon the wings of the *w*
Ps 107:25 and raiseth the stormy *w*, which
Ps 135:7 he bringeth the *w* out of his
Ps 147:18 he causeth his *w* to blow, and the
Ps 148:8 stormy *w* fulfilling his word
Prov 11:29 his own house shall inherit the *w*
Prov 25:14 is like clouds and *w* without rain
Prov 25:23 The north *w* driveth away rain
Prov 27:16 Whosoever hideth her hideth the *w*
Prov 30:4 hath gathered the *w* in his fists
Eccl 1:6 The *w* goeth toward the south, and
Eccl 1:6 the *w* returneth again according
Eccl 5:16 he that hath laboured for the *w*
Eccl 11:4 observeth the *w* shall not sow
Song 4:16 Awake, O north *w*
Is 7:2 of the wood are moved with the *w*
Is 11:15 with his mighty *w* shall he shake
Is 17:13 of the mountains before the *w*
Is 26:18 have as it were brought forth *w*
Is 27:8 he stayeth his rough *w* in the day
Is 27:8 the day of the east *w*
Is 32:2 be as an hiding place from the *w*
Is 41:16 the *w* shall carry them away, and
Is 41:29 their molten images are *w*
Is 57:13 but the *w* shall carry them all
Is 64:6 and our iniquities, like the *w*
Jer 2:24 snuffeth up the *w* at her pleasure
Jer 4:11 A dry *w* of the high places in the
Jer 4:12 Even a full *w* from those places
Jer 5:13 And the prophets shall become *w*
Jer 10:13 bringeth forth the *w* out of his
Jer 13:24 away by the *w* of the wilderness
Jer 14:6 snuffed up the *w* like dragons
Jer 18:17 with an east *w* before the enemy
Jer 22:22 The *w* shall eat up all thy
Jer 51:1 up against me, a destroying *w*
Jer 51:16 bringeth forth the *w* out of his
Eze 5:2 part thou shalt scatter in the *w*
Eze 12:14 I will scatter toward every *w* all
Eze 13:11 and a stormy *w* shall rend it
Eze 13:13 it with a stormy *w* in my fury
Eze 17:10 when the east *w* toucheth it
Eze 19:12 the east *w* dried up her fruit
Eze 27:26 the east *w* hath broken thee in
Eze 37:9 he unto me, Prophesy unto the *w*
Eze 37:9 son of man, and say to the *w*
Dan 2:35 the *w* carried them away, that no
Hos 4:19 The *w* hath bound her up in her
Hos 8:7 For they have sown the *w*, and they
Hos 12:1 Ephraim feedeth on *w*
Hos 12:1 and followeth after the east *w*
Hos 13:15 an east *w* shall come
Hos 13:15 the *w* of the LORD shall come up
Amos 4:13 the mountains, and createth the *w*
Jonah 1:4 sent out a great *w* into the sea
Jonah 4:8 God prepared a vehement east *w*
Hab 1:9 faces shall sup up as the east *w*
Zec 5:9 and the *w* was in their wings
Mt 11:7 A reed shaken with the *w*
Mt 14:24 for the *w* was contrary
Mt 14:30 But when he saw the *w* boisterous
Mt 14:32 come into the ship, the *w* ceased
Mk 4:37 And there arose a great storm of *w*
Mk 4:39 And he arose, and rebuked the *w*
Mk 4:39 the *w* ceased, and there was a
Mk 4:41 of man is this, that even the *w*
Mk 6:48 for the *w* was contrary unto them
Mk 6:51 and the *w* ceased
Lk 7:24 A reed shaken with the *w*
Lk 8:23 down a storm of *w* on the lake
Lk 8:24 Then he arose, and rebuked the *w*
Lk 12:55 And when ye see the south *w* blow
Jn 3:8 The *w* bloweth where it listeth,
Jn 6:18 by reason of a great *w* that blew
Acts 2:2 heaven as of a rushing mighty *w*
Acts 27:7 the *w* not suffering us, we sailed
Acts 27:13 And when the south *w* blew softly
Acts 27:14 arose against it a tempestuous *w*
Acts 27:15 and could not bear up into the *w*
Acts 27:40 hoised up the mainsail to the *w*
Acts 28:13 and after one day the south *w* blew
Eph 4:14 about with every *w* of doctrine
Jas 1:6 wave of the sea driven with the *w*
Rev 6:13 when she is shaken of a mighty *w*
Rev 7:1 that the *w* should not blow on the

## WINDING
1Kin 6:8 they went up with *w* stairs into
Eze 41:7 a *w* about still upward to the
Eze 41:7 for the *w* about of the house went

## WINDOW
Gen 6:16 A *w* shalt thou make to the ark,
Gen 8:6 that Noah opened the *w* of the ark
Gen 26:8 the Philistines looked out at a *w*
Josh 2:15 them down by a cord through the *w*
Josh 2:18 line of scarlet thread in the *w*
Josh 2:21 bound the scarlet line in the *w*
Judg 5:28 of Sisera looked out at a *w*
1Sa 19:12 Michal let David down through a *w*
2Sa 6:16 daughter looked through a *w*
2Kin 9:30 her head, and looked out at a *w*
2Kin 9:32 And he lifted up his face to the *w*
2Kin 13:17 And he said, Open the *w* eastward
1Chr 15:29 out at a *w* saw king David dancing
Prov 7:6 For at the *w* of my house I looked
Acts 20:9 there sat in a *w* a certain young
2Cor 11:33 through a *w* in a basket was I let

## WINDOWS
Gen 7:11 the *w* of heaven were opened
Gen 8:2 the *w* of heaven were stopped, and
1Kin 6:4 house he made *w* of narrow lights
1Kin 7:4 there were *w* in three rows, and
1Kin 7:5 and posts were square, with the *w*
2Kin 7:2 the LORD would make *w* in heaven
2Kin 7:19 the LORD should make *w* in heaven
Eccl 12:3 look out of the *w* be darkened
Song 2:9 wall, he looketh forth at the *w*
Is 24:18 for the *w* from on high are open,
Is 54:12 And I will make thy *w* of agates
Is 60:8 cloud, and as the doves to their *w*
Jer 9:21 For death is come up into our *w*
Jer 22:14 chambers, and cutteth him out *w*
Eze 40:16 there were narrow *w* to the little
Eze 40:16 *w* were round about inward
Eze 40:22 And their *w*, and their arches, and
Eze 40:25 And there were *w* in it and in the

Eze 40:25 thereof round about, like those *w*
Eze 40:29 and there were *w* in it and in the
Eze 40:33 and there were *w* therein and in the
Eze 40:36 and the *w* to it round about
Eze 41:16 The door posts, and the narrow *w*
Eze 41:16 and from the ground up to the *w*
Eze 41:16 and the *w* were covered
Eze 41:26 And there were narrow *w* and palm
Dan 6:10 his *w* being open in his chamber
Joel 2:9 enter in at the *w* like a thief
Zeph 2:14 their voice shall sing in the *w*
Mal 3:10 will not open you the *w* of heaven

**WINDS**

Job 28:25 To make the weight for the *w*
Jer 49:32 I will scatter into all *w* them
Jer 49:36 four *w* from the four quarters of
Jer 49:36 scatter them toward all those *w*
Eze 5:10 will I scatter into all the *w*
Eze 5:12 a third part into all the *w*
Eze 17:21 shall be scattered toward all *w*
Eze 37:9 Come from the four *w*, O breath,
Dan 7:2 the four *w* of the heaven strove
Dan 8:8 ones toward the four *w* of heaven
Dan 11:4 toward the four *w* of heaven
Zec 2:6 as the four *w* of the heaven
Mt 7:25 the *w* blew, and beat upon that
Mt 7:27 the *w* blew, and beat upon that
Mt 8:26 Then he arose, and rebuked the *w*
Mt 8:27 of man is this, that even the *w*
Mt 24:31 his elect from the four *w*
Mk 13:27 his elect from the four *w*
Lk 8:25 for he commandeth even the *w*
Acts 27:4 because the *w* were contrary
Jas 3:4 great, and are driven of fierce *w*
Jude 12 without water, carried about of *w*
Rev 7:1 holding the four *w* of the earth

**WINDY**

Ps 55:8 hasten my escape from the *w* storm

**WINE**

Gen 9:21 And he drank of the *w*, and was
Gen 9:24 Noah awoke from his *w*, and knew
Gen 14:18 of Salem brought forth bread and *w*
Gen 19:32 let us make our father drink *w*
Gen 19:33 their father drink *w* that night
Gen 19:34 make him drink *w* this night also
Gen 19:35 father drink *w* that night also
Gen 27:25 and he brought him *w*, and he drank
Gen 27:28 the earth, and plenty of corn and *w*
Gen 27:37 corn and *w* have I sustained him
Gen 49:11 he washed his garments in *w*
Gen 49:12 His eyes shall be red with *w*
Ex 29:40 an hin of *w* for a drink offering
Lev 10:9 Do not drink *w* nor strong drink,
Lev 23:13 offering thereof shall be of *w*
Num 6:3 He shall separate himself from *w*
Num 6:3 and shall drink no vinegar of *w*
Num 6:20 that the Nazarite may drink *w*
Num 15:5 the fourth part of an hin of *w*
Num 15:7 the third part of an hin of *w*
Num 15:10 a drink offering half an hin of *w*
Num 18:12 the oil, and all the best of the *w*
Num 28:7 shalt thou cause the strong *w* to
Num 28:14 half an hin of *w* unto a bullock
Deut 7:13 of thy land, thy corn, and thy *w*
Deut 11:14 gather in thy corn, and thy *w*
Deut 12:17 tithe of thy corn, or of thy *w*
Deut 14:23 the tithe of thy corn, of thy *w*
Deut 14:26 for oxen, or for sheep, or for *w*
Deut 16:13 gathered in thy corn and thy *w*
Deut 18:4 also of thy corn, of thy *w*
Deut 28:39 but shalt neither drink of the *w*
Deut 28:51 not leave thee either corn, *w*
Deut 29:6 have ye drunk *w* or strong drink
Deut 32:33 Their *w* is the poison of dragons,
Deut 32:38 drank the *w* of their drink
Deut 33:28 shall be upon a land of corn and *w*
Josh 9:4 *w* bottles, old, and rent, and bound
Josh 9:13 And these bottles of *w*, which we
Judg 9:13 unto them, Should I leave my *w*
Judg 13:4 drink not *w* nor strong drink, and
Judg 13:7 now drink no *w* nor strong drink,
Judg 13:14 let her drink *w* or strong drink
Judg 19:19 *w* also for me, and for thy
1Sa 1:14 put away thy *w* from thee
1Sa 1:15 neither *w* nor strong drink
1Sa 1:24 ephah of flour, and a bottle of *w*
1Sa 10:3 and another carrying a bottle of *w*
1Sa 16:20 with bread, and a bottle of *w*
1Sa 25:18 loaves, and two bottles of *w*
1Sa 25:37 when the *w* was gone out of Nabal,
2Sa 6:19 piece of flesh, and a flagon of *w*
2Sa 13:28 Amnon's heart is merry with *w*
2Sa 16:1 summer fruits, and a bottle of *w*
2Sa 16:2 and the *w*, that such as be faint
2Kin 18:32 own land, a land of corn and *w*
1Chr 9:29 and the fine flour, and the *w*
1Chr 12:40 figs, and bunches of raisins, and *w*
1Chr 16:3 piece of flesh, and a flagon of *w*
1Chr 27:27 of the vineyards for the *w*
2Chr 2:10 and twenty thousand baths of *w*
2Chr 2:15 and the barley, the oil, and the *w*
2Chr 11:11 store of victual, and of oil and *w*
2Chr 31:5 the firstfruits of corn, *w*
2Chr 32:28 for the increase of corn, and *w*
Ezr 6:9 the God of heaven, wheat, salt, *w*
Ezr 7:22 and to an hundred baths of *w*
Neh 2:1 the king, that *w* was before him
Neh 2:1 and I took up the *w*, and gave it
Neh 5:11 the money, and of the corn, the *w*
Neh 5:15 and had taken of them bread and *w*
Neh 5:18 ten days store of all sorts of *w*
Neh 10:37 of all manner of trees, of *w*
Neh 10:39 of the corn, of the new *w*
Neh 13:5 the tithes of the corn, the new *w*
Neh 13:12 tithe of the corn and the new *w*
Neh 13:15 as also *w*, grapes, and figs, and
Est 1:7 royal *w* in abundance, according
Est 1:10 of the king was merry with *w*
Est 5:6 unto Esther at the banquet of *w*
Est 7:2 second day at the banquet of *w*
Est 7:7 of *w* in his wrath went into the
Est 7:8 the place of the banquet of *w*
Job 1:13 drinking *w* in their eldest
Job 1:18 drinking *w* in their eldest
Job 32:19 my belly is as *w* which hath no
Ps 4:7 their corn and their *w* increased
Ps 60:3 us to drink the *w* of astonishment
Ps 75:8 there is a cup, and the *w* is red
Ps 78:65 man that shouteth by reason of *w*
Ps 104:15 *w* that maketh glad the heart of
Prov 3:10 shall burst out with new *w*
Prov 4:17 and drink the *w* of violence
Prov 9:2 she hath mingled her *w*
Prov 9:5 drink of the *w* which I have
Prov 20:1 *W* is a mocker, strong drink is
Prov 21:17 he that loveth *w* and oil shall not
Prov 23:30 They that tarry long at the *w*
Prov 23:30 they that go to seek mixed *w*
Prov 23:31 thou upon the *w* when it is red
Prov 31:4 it is not for kings to drink *w*
Prov 31:6 *w* unto those that be of heavy
Eccl 2:3 mine heart to give myself unto *w*
Eccl 9:7 drink thy *w* with a merry heart
Eccl 10:19 for laughter, and *w* maketh merry
Song 1:2 for thy love is better than *w*
Song 1:4 remember thy love more than *w*
Song 4:10 much better is thy love than *w*
Song 5:1 I have drunk my *w* with my milk
Song 7:9 like the best *w* for my beloved
Song 8:2 cause thee to drink of spiced *w*
Is 1:22 dross, thy *w* mixed with water
Is 5:11 until night, till *w* inflame them
Is 5:12 viol, the tabret, and pipe, and *w*
Is 5:22 them that are mighty to drink *w*
Is 16:10 tread out no *w* in their presses
Is 22:13 eating flesh, and drinking *w*
Is 24:7 The new *w* mourneth, the vine
Is 24:9 shall not drink *w* with a song
Is 24:11 is a crying for *w* in the streets
Is 27:2 ye unto her, A vineyard of red *w*
Is 28:1 of them that are overcome with *w*
Is 28:7 they also have erred through *w*
Is 28:7 drink, they are swallowed up of *w*
Is 29:9 they are drunken, but not with *w*
Is 36:17 own land, a land of corn and *w*
Is 49:26 their own blood, as with sweet *w*
Is 51:21 and drunken, but not with *w*
Is 55:1 yea, come, buy *w* and milk without
Is 56:12 Come ye, say they, I will fetch *w*
Is 62:8 stranger shall not drink thy *w*
Is 65:8 As the new *w* is found in the
Jer 13:12 bottle shall be filled with *w*
Jer 13:12 bottle shall be filled with *w*
Jer 23:9 like a man whom *w* hath overcome
Jer 25:15 Take the *w* cup of this fury at my
Jer 31:12 of the LORD, for wheat, and for *w*
Jer 35:2 chambers, and give them *w* to drink
Jer 35:5 of the Rechabites pots full of *w*
Jer 35:5 and I said unto them, Drink ye *w*
Jer 35:6 But they said, We will drink no *w*
Jer 35:6 us, saying, Ye shall drink no *w*
Jer 35:8 to drink no *w* all our days, we,
Jer 35:14 commanded his sons not to drink *w*
Jer 40:10 but ye, gather ye *w*, and summer
Jer 40:12 unto Mizpah, and gathered *w*
Jer 48:33 I have caused *w* to fail from the
Jer 51:7 the nations have drunken of her *w*
Lam 2:12 their mothers, Where is corn and *w*
Eze 27:18 in the *w* of Helbon, and white wool
Eze 44:21 Neither shall any priest drink *w*
Dan 1:5 meat, and of the *w* which he drank
Dan 1:8 nor with the *w* which he drank
Dan 1:16 the *w* that they should drink
Dan 5:1 drank *w* before the thousand
Dan 5:2 whiles he tasted the *w*,
Dan 5:4 They drank *w*, and praised the gods
Dan 5:23 concubines, have drunk *w* in them
Dan 10:3 came flesh nor *w* in my mouth
Hos 2:8 know that I gave her corn, and *w*
Hos 2:9 my *w* in the season thereof, and
Hos 2:22 shall hear the corn, and the *w*
Hos 3:1 other gods, and love flagons of *w*
Hos 4:11 Whoredom and *w* and new
Hos 4:11 new *w* take away the heart
Hos 7:5 made him sick with bottles of *w*
Hos 7:14 assemble themselves for corn and *w*
Hos 9:2 the new *w* shall fail in her
Hos 9:4 They shall not offer *w* offerings
Hos 14:7 shall be as the *w* of Lebanon
Joel 1:5 and howl, all ye drinkers of *w*
Joel 1:5 because of the new *w*
Joel 1:10 the new *w* is dried up, the oil
Joel 2:19 I will send you corn, and *w*
Joel 2:24 and the fats shall overflow with *w*
Joel 3:3 an harlot, and sold a girl for *w*
Joel 3:18 mountains shall drop down new *w*
Amos 2:8 they drink the *w* of the condemned
Amos 2:12 ye gave the Nazarites *w* to drink
Amos 5:11 but ye shall not drink *w* of them
Amos 6:6 That drink *w* in bowls, and anoint
Amos 9:13 the mountains shall drop sweet *w*
Amos 9:14 vineyards, and drink the *w* thereof
Mic 2:11 I will prophesy unto thee of *w*
Mic 6:15 with oil; and sweet *w*
Mic 6:15 but shalt not drink *w*
Hab 2:5 because he transgresseth by *w*
Zeph 1:13 but not drink the *w* thereof
Hag 1:11 upon the corn, and upon the new *w*
Hag 2:12 do touch bread, or pottage, or *w*
Zec 9:15 and make a noise as through *w*
Zec 9:17 men cheerful, and new *w* the maids
Zec 10:7 heart shall rejoice as through *w*
Mt 9:17 do men put new *w* into old bottles
Mt 9:17 the *w* runneth out, and the bottles
Mt 9:17 they put new *w* into new bottles
Mk 2:22 putteth new *w* into old bottles
Mk 2:22 else the new *w* doth burst the
Mk 2:22 the *w* is spilled, and the bottles
Mk 2:22 but new *w* must be put into new
Mk 15:23 him to drink *w* mingled with myrrh
Lk 1:15 drink neither *w* nor strong drink
Lk 5:37 putteth new *w* into old bottles
Lk 5:37 else the new *w* will burst the
Lk 5:38 But new *w* must be put into new
Lk 5:39 old *w* straightway desireth new
Lk 7:33 eating bread nor drinking *w*
Lk 10:34 his wounds, pouring in oil and *w*
Jn 2:3 And when they wanted *w*, the mother
Jn 2:3 saith unto him, They have no *w*
Jn 2:9 tasted the water that was made *w*
Jn 2:10 beginning doth set forth good *w*
Jn 2:10 hast kept the good *w* until now
Jn 4:46 where he made the water *w*
Acts 2:13 said, These men are full of new *w*
Rom 14:21 to eat flesh, nor to drink *w*
Eph 5:18 And be not drunk with *w*, wherein
1Ti 3:3 Not given to *w*, no striker, not
1Ti 3:8 not given to much *w*, not greedy
1Ti 5:23 but use a little *w* for thy
Titus 1:7 not soon angry, not given to *w*
Titus 2:3 accusers, not given to much *w*
1Pet 4:3 lusts, excess of *w*, revellings,
Rev 6:6 thou hurt not the oil and the *w*
Rev 14:8 made all nations drink of the *w*
Rev 14:10 of the *w* of the wrath of God
Rev 16:19 *w* of the fierceness of his wrath
Rev 17:2 with the *w* of her fornication
Rev 18:3 all nations have drunk of the *w*
Rev 18:13 ointments, and frankincense, and *w*

### WINEBIBBER
Mt 11:19 Behold a man gluttonous, and a *w*
Lk 7:34 Behold a gluttonous man, and a *w*

### WINEBIBBERS
Prov 23:20 Be not among *w*

### WINEFAT
Is 63:2 like him that treadeth in the *w*
Mk 12:1 it, and digged a place for the *w*

### WINEPRESS
Num 18:27 and as the fulness of the *w*
Num 18:30 and as the increase of the *w*
Deut 15:14 out of thy floor, and out of thy *w*
Judg 6:11 Gideon threshed wheat by the *w*
Judg 7:25 Zeeb they slew at the *w* of Zeeb
2Kin 6:27 of the barnfloor, or out of the *w*
Is 5:2 of it, and also made a *w* therein
Is 63:3 I have trodden the *w* alone
Lam 1:15 the daughter of Judah, as in a *w*
Hos 9:2 the *w* shall not feed them, and the
Mt 21:33 round about, and digged a *w* in it
Rev 14:19 the great *w* of the wrath of God
Rev 14:20 the *w* was trodden without the
Rev 14:20 city, and blood came out of the *w*
Rev 19:15 and he treadeth the *w* of the

### WINEPRESSES
Neh 13:15 some treading *w* on the sabbath
Job 24:11 their walls, and tread their *w*
Jer 48:33 caused wine to fail from the *w*
Zec 14:10 of Hananeel unto the king's *w*

### WINES
Is 25:6 a feast of *w* on the lees, of fat
Is 25:6 of *w* on the lees well refined

### WING
1Kin 6:24 was the one *w* of the cherub
1Kin 6:24 cubits the other *w* of the cherub
1Kin 6:24 the uttermost part of the one *w*
1Kin 6:27 so that the *w* of the one touched
1Kin 6:27 the *w* of the other cherub touched
2Chr 3:11 one *w* of the one cherub was five
2Chr 3:11 the other *w* was likewise five
2Chr 3:11 reaching to the *w* of the other
2Chr 3:12 one *w* of the other cherub was
2Chr 3:12 the other *w* was five cubits also,
2Chr 3:12 joining to the *w* of the other
Is 10:14 there was none that moved the *w*
Eze 17:23 shall dwell all fowl of every *w*

### WINGED
Gen 1:21 every *w* fowl after his kind
Deut 4:17 the likeness of any *w* fowl that

### WINGS
Ex 19:4 and how I bare you on eagles' *w*
Ex 25:20 stretch forth their *w* on high
Ex 25:20 the mercy seat with their *w*
Ex 37:9 spread out their *w* on high
Ex 37:9 covered with their *w* over the
Lev 1:17 cleave it with the *w* thereof
Deut 32:11 her young, spreadeth abroad her *w*
Deut 32:11 them, beareth them on her *w*
Ruth 2:12 under whose *w* thou art come to
2Sa 22:11 was seen upon the *w* of the wind
1Kin 6:27 forth the *w* of the cherubims
1Kin 6:27 their *w* touched one another in
1Kin 8:6 even under the *w* of the cherubims
1Kin 8:7 spread forth their two *w* over the
1Chr 28:18 that spread out their *w*, and
2Chr 3:11 the *w* of the cherubims were
2Chr 3:13 The *w* of these cherubims spread
2Chr 5:7 even under the *w* of the cherubims
2Chr 5:8 their *w* over the place of the ark
Job 39:13 the goodly *w* unto the peacocks
Job 39:13 or *w* and feathers unto the ostrich
Job 39:26 stretch her *w* toward the south
Ps 17:8 hide me under the shadow of thy *w*
Ps 18:10 he did fly upon the *w* of the wind
Ps 36:7 trust under the shadow of thy *w*
Ps 55:6 said, Oh that I had *w* like a dove
Ps 57:1 in the shadow of thy *w* will I
Ps 61:4 will trust in the covert of thy *w*
Ps 63:7 shadow of thy *w* will I rejoice
Ps 68:13 yet shall ye be as the *w* of a
Ps 91:4 under his *w* shalt thou trust
Ps 104:3 walketh upon the *w* of the wind
Ps 139:9 If I take the *w* of the morning,
Prov 23:5 certainly make themselves *w*
Eccl 10:20 that which hath *w* shall tell the
Is 6:2 each one had six *w*
Is 8:8 the stretching out of his *w* shall
Is 18:1 Woe to the land shadowing with *w*
Is 40:31 shall mount up with *w* as eagles
Jer 48:9 Give *w* unto Moab, that it may
Jer 48:40 and shall spread his *w* over Moab
Jer 49:22 and spread his *w* over Bozrah
Eze 1:6 faces, and every one had four *w*
Eze 1:8 under their *w* on their four sides
Eze 1:8 four had their faces and their *w*
Eze 1:9 Their *w* were joined one to
Eze 1:11 their *w* were stretched upward
Eze 1:11 two *w* of every one were joined
Eze 1:23 firmament were their *w* straight
Eze 1:24 I heard the noise of their *w*
Eze 1:24 they stood, they let down their *w*
Eze 1:25 stood, and had let down their *w*
Eze 3:13 *w* of the living creatures that
Eze 10:5 *w* was heard even to the outer
Eze 10:8 of a man's hand under their *w*
Eze 10:12 backs, and their hands, and their *w*
Eze 10:16 *w* to mount up from the earth
Eze 10:19 the cherubims lifted up their *w*
Eze 10:21 faces apiece, and every one four *w*
Eze 10:21 hands of a man was under their *w*
Eze 11:22 did the cherubims lift up their *w*
Eze 17:3 A great eagle with great *w*
Eze 17:7 another great eagle with great *w*
Dan 7:4 was like a lion, and had eagle's *w*
Dan 7:4 I beheld till the *w* thereof were
Dan 7:6 the back of it four *w* of a fowl
Hos 4:19 wind hath bound her up in her *w*
Zec 5:9 women, and the wind was in their *w*
Zec 5:9 had *w* like the *w* of a stork
Mal 4:2 arise with healing in his *w*
Mt 23:37 her chickens under her *w*, and ye
Lk 13:34 doth gather her brood under her *w*
Rev 4:8 had each of them six *w* about him
Rev 9:9 the sound of their *w* was as the
Rev 12:14 were given two *w* of a great eagle

### WINK
Job 15:12 and what do thy eyes *w* at,
Ps 35:19 neither let them *w* with the eye

### WINKED
Acts 17:30 times of this ignorance God *w* at

### WINKETH
Prov 6:13 He *w* with his eyes, he speaketh
Prov 10:10 He that *w* with the eye causeth

### WINNETH
Prov 11:30 and he that *w* souls is wise

### WINNOWED
Is 30:24 which hath been *w* with the shovel

### WINNOWETH
Ruth 3:2 he *w* barley to night in the

### WINTER
Gen 8:22 and cold and heat, and summer and *w*
Ps 74:17 thou hast made summer and *w*
Song 2:11 the *w* is past, the rain is over
Is 18:6 of the earth shall *w* upon them
Amos 3:15 I will smite the *w* house with the
Zec 14:8 in summer and in *w* shall it be
Mt 24:20 that your flight be not in the *w*
Mk 13:18 that your flight be not in the *w*
Jn 10:22 of the dedication, and it was *w*
Acts 27:12 haven was not commodious to *w* in
Acts 27:12 attain to Phenice, and there to *w*
1Cor 16:6 *w* with you, that ye may bring me
2Ti 4:21 Do thy diligence to come before *w*
Titus 3:12 for I have determined there to *w*

### WINTERED
Acts 28:11 which had *w* in the isle, whose

### WINTERHOUSE
Jer 36:22 sat in the *w* in the ninth month

### WIPE
2Kin 21:13 I will *w* Jerusalem as a man
Neh 13:14 *w* not out my good deeds that I
Is 25:8 the Lord GOD will *w* away tears
Lk 7:38 did *w* them with the hairs of her
Lk 10:11 on us, we do *w* off against you
Jn 13:5 feet, and to *w* them with the towel
Rev 7:17 God shall *w* away all tears from
Rev 21:4 God shall *w* away all tears from

### WIPED
Prov 6:33 his reproach shall not be *w* away
Lk 7:44 *w* them with the hairs of her head
Jn 11:2 *w* his feet with her hair, whose
Jn 12:3 and *w* his feet with her hair

### WIPETH
2Kin 21:13 wipe Jerusalem as a man *w* a dish
Prov 30:20 *w* her mouth, and saith, I have

### WIPING
2Kin 21:13 *w* it, and turning it upside down

### WIRES
Ex 39:3 thin plates, and cut it into *w*

### WISDOM
Ex 28:3 have filled with the spirit of *w*
Ex 31:3 him with the spirit of God, in *w*
Ex 31:6 are wise hearted I have put *w*
Ex 35:26 them up in *w* spun goats' hair
Ex 35:31 him with the spirit of God, in *w*
Ex 35:35 hath he filled with *w* of heart
Ex 36:1 man, in whom the LORD put *w*
Ex 36:2 in whose heart the LORD had put *w*
Deut 4:6 for this is your *w* and your
Deut 34:9 Nun was full of the spirit of *w*
2Sa 14:20 according to the *w* of an angel of
2Sa 20:22 went unto all the people in her *w*
1Kin 2:6 Do therefore according to thy *w*
1Kin 3:28 saw that the *w* of God was in him
1Kin 4:29 And God gave Solomon *w* and
1Kin 4:30 Solomon's *w* excelled the *w*
1Kin 4:30 country, and all the *w* of Egypt
1Kin 4:34 people to hear the *w* of Solomon
1Kin 4:34 earth, which had heard of his *w*
1Kin 5:12 And the LORD gave Solomon *w*
1Kin 7:14 and he was filled with *w*, and
1Kin 10:4 of Sheba had seen all Solomon's *w*
1Kin 10:6 own land of thy acts and of thy *w*
1Kin 10:7 thy *w* and prosperity exceedeth the
1Kin 10:8 before thee, and that hear thy *w*
1Kin 10:23 of the earth for riches and for *w*
1Kin 10:24 sought to Solomon, to hear his *w*
1Kin 11:41 and all that he did, and his *w*
1Chr 22:12 Only the LORD give thee *w*
2Chr 1:10 Give me now *w* and knowledge, that
2Chr 1:11 but hast asked *w* and knowledge for
2Chr 1:12 *W* and knowledge is granted unto
2Chr 9:3 Sheba had seen the *w* of Solomon
2Chr 9:5 land of thine acts, and of thy *w*
2Chr 9:6 of thy *w* was not told me
2Chr 9:7 before thee, and hear thy *w*
2Chr 9:22 kings of the earth in riches and *w*
2Chr 9:23 of Solomon, to hear his *w*
Ezr 7:25 after the *w* of thy God, that is
Job 4:21 they die, even without *w*
Job 6:13 is *w* driven quite from me
Job 11:6 would shew thee the secrets of *w*
Job 12:2 people, and *w* shall die with you
Job 12:12 With the ancient is *w*
Job 12:13 With him is *w* and strength, he
Job 12:16 With him is strength and *w*
Job 13:5 and it should be your *w*
Job 15:8 dost thou restrain *w* to thyself
Job 26:3 thou counseled him that hath no *w*
Job 28:12 But where shall *w* be found
Job 28:18 the price of *w* is above rubies
Job 28:20 Whence then cometh *w*
Job 28:28 the fear of the LORD, that is *w*
Job 32:7 multitude of years should teach *w*
Job 32:13 should say, We have found out *w*
Job 33:33 peace, and I shall teach thee *w*
Job 34:35 and his words were without *w*
Job 36:5 he is mighty in strength and *w*
Job 38:36 Who hath put *w* in the inward
Job 38:37 Who can number the clouds in *w*
Job 39:17 God hath deprived her of *w*
Job 39:26 Doth the hawk fly by thy *w*
Ps 37:30 mouth of the righteous speaketh *w*
Ps 49:3 My mouth shall speak of *w*
Ps 51:6 part thou shalt make me to know *w*
Ps 90:12 we may apply our hearts unto *w*
Ps 104:24 In *w* hast thou made them all
Ps 105:22 and teach his senators *w*
Ps 111:10 of the LORD is the beginning of *w*
Ps 136:5 To him that by *w* made the heavens
Prov 1:2 To know *w* and instruction
Prov 1:3 To receive the instruction of *w*
Prov 1:7 but fools despise *w* and
Prov 1:20 *W* crieth without
Prov 2:2 thou incline thine ear unto *w*
Prov 2:6 For the LORD giveth *w*
Prov 2:7 up sound *w* for the righteous
Prov 2:10 When *w* entereth into thine heart,
Prov 3:13 Happy is the man that findeth *w*
Prov 3:19 The LORD by *w* hath founded the
Prov 3:21 keep sound *w* and discretion

Prov 4:5 Get *w*, get understanding
Prov 4:7 *W* is the principal thing
Prov 4:7 therefore get *w*
Prov 4:11 have taught thee in the way of *w*
Prov 5:1 My son, attend unto my *w*, and bow
Prov 7:4 Say unto *w*, Thou art my sister
Prov 8:1 Doth not *w* cry
Prov 8:5 O ye simple, understand *w*
Prov 8:11 For *w* is better than rubies
Prov 8:12 I *w* dwell with prudence, and find
Prov 8:14 Counsel is mine, and sound *w*
Prov 9:1 *W* hath builded her house, she
Prov 9:10 of the LORD is the beginning of *w*
Prov 10:13 hath understanding *w* is found
Prov 10:21 but fools die for want of *w*
Prov 10:23 but a man of understanding hath *w*
Prov 10:31 of the just bringeth forth *w*
Prov 11:2 but with the lowly is *w*
Prov 11:12 He that is void of *w* despiseth
Prov 12:8 be commended according to his *w*
Prov 13:10 but with the well advised is *w*
Prov 14:6 A scorner seeketh *w*, and findeth
Prov 14:8 The *w* of the prudent is to
Prov 14:33 *W* resteth in the heart of him
Prov 15:21 joy to him that is destitute of *w*
Prov 15:33 the LORD is the instruction of *w*
Prov 16:16 better is it to get *w* than gold
Prov 17:16 in the hand of a fool to get *w*
Prov 17:24 *W* is before him that hath
Prov 18:1 and intermeddleth with all *w*
Prov 18:4 the wellspring of *w* as a flowing
Prov 19:8 He that getteth *w* loveth his own
Prov 21:30 There is no *w* nor understanding
Prov 23:4 cease from thine own *w*
Prov 23:9 will despise the *w* of thy words
Prov 23:23 also *w*, and instruction, and
Prov 24:3 Through *w* is an house builded
Prov 24:7 *W* is too high for a fool
Prov 24:14 knowledge of *w* be unto thy soul
Prov 29:3 Whoso loveth *w* rejoiceth his
Prov 29:15 The rod and reproof give *w*
Prov 30:3 I neither learned *w*, nor have the
Prov 31:26 She openeth her mouth with *w*
Eccl 1:13 search out by *w* concerning all
Eccl 1:16 have gotten more *w* than all they
Eccl 1:16 heart had great experience of *w*
Eccl 1:17 And I gave my heart to know *w*
Eccl 1:18 For in much *w* is much grief
Eccl 2:3 yet acquainting mine heart with *w*
Eccl 2:9 also my *w* remained with me
Eccl 2:12 And I turned myself to behold *w*
Eccl 2:13 Then I saw that *w* excelleth folly
Eccl 2:21 is a man whose labour is in *w*
Eccl 2:26 a man that is good in his sight *w*
Eccl 7:11 *W* is good with an inheritance
Eccl 7:12 For *w* is a defence, and money is a
Eccl 7:12 that *w* giveth life to them that
Eccl 7:19 *W* strengtheneth the wise more
Eccl 7:23 All this have I proved by *w*
Eccl 7:25 and to search, and to seek out *w*
Eccl 8:1 a man's *w* maketh his face to
Eccl 8:16 I applied mine heart to know *w*
Eccl 9:10 nor device, nor knowledge, nor *w*
Eccl 9:13 This *w* have I seen also under the
Eccl 9:15 he by his *w* delivered the city
Eccl 9:16 *W* is better than strength
Eccl 9:16 the poor man's *w* is despised
Eccl 9:18 *W* is better than weapons of war
Eccl 10:1 him that is in reputation for *w*
Eccl 10:3 his *w* faileth him, and he saith to
Eccl 10:10 but *w* is profitable to direct
Is 10:13 hand I have done it, and by my *w*
Is 11:2 rest upon him, the spirit of *w*
Is 29:14 for the *w* of their wise men shall
Is 33:6 And *w* and knowledge shall be the
Is 47:10 Thy *w* and thy knowledge, it hath
Jer 8:9 and what *w* is in them
Jer 9:23 not the wise man glory in his *w*
Jer 10:12 established the world by his *w*
Jer 49:7 Is *w* no more in Teman
Jer 49:7 is their *w* vanished
Jer 51:15 established the world by his *w*
Eze 28:4 With thy *w* and with thine
Eze 28:5 By thy great *w* and by thy traffick
Eze 28:7 against the beauty of thy *w*
Eze 28:12 sealest up the sum, full of *w*
Eze 28:17 thou hast corrupted thy *w* by
Dan 1:4 favoured, and skilful in all *w*
Dan 1:17 and skill in all learning and *w*
Dan 1:20 And in all matters of *w* and
Dan 2:14 *w* to Arioch the captain of the
Dan 2:20 for *w* and might are his
Dan 2:21 he giveth *w* unto the wise, and
Dan 2:23 my fathers, who hast given me *w*
Dan 2:30 any *w* that I have more than any
Dan 5:11 light and understanding and *w*
Dan 5:11 like the *w* of the gods, was found
Dan 5:14 excellent *w* is found in thee
Mic 6:9 the man of *w* shall see thy name
Mt 11:19 But *w* is justified of her
Mt 12:42 earth to hear the *w* of Solomon
Mt 13:54 said, Whence hath this man this *w*
Mk 6:2 what *w* is this which is given
Lk 1:17 disobedient to the *w* of the just
Lk 2:40 strong in spirit, filled with *w*
Lk 2:52 And Jesus increased in *w* and
Lk 7:35 But *w* is justified of all her
Lk 11:31 earth to hear the *w* of Solomon
Lk 11:49 Therefore also said the *w* of God
Lk 21:15 For I will give you a mouth and *w*
Acts 6:3 full of the Holy Ghost and *w*
Acts 6:10 were not able to resist the *w*
Acts 7:10 *w* in the sight of Pharaoh king of
Acts 7:22 in all the *w* of the Egyptians
Rom 11:33 depth of the riches both of the *w*
1Cor 1:17 not with *w* of words, lest the
1Cor 1:19 I will destroy the *w* of the wise
1Cor 1:20 made foolish the *w* of this world
1Cor 1:21 For after that in the *w* of God
1Cor 1:21 God the world by *w* knew not God
1Cor 1:22 sign, and the Greeks seek after *w*
1Cor 1:24 the power of God, and the *w* of God
1Cor 1:30 who of God is made unto us *w*
1Cor 2:1 with excellency of speech or of *w*
1Cor 2:4 with enticing words of man's *w*
1Cor 2:5 should not stand in the *w* of men
1Cor 2:6 Howbeit we speak *w* among them
1Cor 2:6 yet not the *w* of this world, nor
1Cor 2:7 But we speak the *w* of God in a
1Cor 2:7 in a mystery, even the hidden *w*
1Cor 2:13 the words which man's *w* teacheth
1Cor 3:19 For the *w* of this world is
1Cor 12:8 given by the Spirit the word of *w*
2Cor 1:12 sincerity, not with fleshly *w*
Eph 1:8 hath abounded toward us in all *w*
Eph 1:17 may give unto you the spirit of *w*
Eph 3:10 the church the manifold *w* of God
Col 1:9 knowledge of his will in all *w*
Col 1:28 and teaching every man in all *w*
Col 2:3 are hid all the treasures of *w*
Col 2:23 a shew of *w* in will worship
Col 3:16 dwell in you richly in all *w*
Col 4:5 Walk in *w* toward them that are
Jas 1:5 If any of you lack *w*, let him ask
Jas 3:13 his works with meekness of *w*
Jas 3:15 This *w* descendeth not from above,
Jas 3:17 But the *w* that is from above is
2Pet 3:15 Paul also according to the *w*
Rev 5:12 to receive power, and riches, and *w*
Rev 7:12 Blessing, and glory, and *w*, and
Rev 13:18 Here is *w*
Rev 17:9 And here is the mind which hath *w*

## WISE

Gen 3:6 tree to be desired to make one *w*
Gen 41:8 Egypt, and all the *w* men thereof
Gen 41:33 look out a man discreet and *w*
Gen 41:39 none so discreet and *w* as thou art
Ex 7:11 Pharaoh also called the *w* men
Ex 22:23 If thou afflict them in any *w*
Ex 23:8 for the gift blindeth the *w*
Ex 28:3 speak unto all that are *w* hearted
Ex 31:6 are *w* hearted I have put wisdom
Ex 35:10 every *w* hearted among you shall
Ex 35:25 all the women that were *w* hearted
Ex 36:1 every *w* hearted man, in whom the
Ex 36:2 every *w* hearted man, in whose
Ex 36:4 And all the *w* men, that wrought
Ex 36:8 every *w* hearted man among them
Lev 7:24 but ye shall in no *w* eat of it
Lev 19:17 thou shalt in any *w* rebuke thy
Lev 27:19 the field will in any *w* redeem it
Num 6:23 On this *w* ye shall bless the
Deut 1:13 Take you *w* men, and understanding,
Deut 1:15 *w* men, and known, and made them
Deut 4:6 Surely this great nation is a *w*
Deut 16:19 gift doth blind the eyes of the *w*
Deut 17:15 Thou shalt in any *w* set him king
Deut 21:23 shalt in any *w* bury him that day
Deut 22:7 shalt in any *w* let the dam go
Deut 32:29 O that they were *w*, that they
Josh 6:18 in any *w* keep yourselves from the
Josh 23:12 Else if ye do in any *w* go back
Judg 5:29 Her *w* ladies answered her, yea,
1Sa 6:3 but in any *w* return him a
2Sa 14:2 and fetched thence a *w* woman
2Sa 14:20 and my lord is *w*, according to the
2Sa 20:16 Then cried a *w* woman out of the
1Kin 2:9 for thou art a *w* man, and knowest
1Kin 3:12 lo, I have given thee a *w*
1Kin 3:26 living child, and in no *w* slay it
1Kin 3:27 living child, and in no *w* slay it
1Kin 5:7 a *w* son over this great people
1Kin 11:22 howbeit let me go in any *w*
1Chr 26:14 a *w* counsellor, they cast lots
1Chr 27:32 counsellor, a *w* man, and a scribe
2Chr 2:12 given to David the king a *w* son
Est 1:13 Then the king said to the *w* men
Est 6:13 Then said his *w* men and Zeresh his
Job 5:13 He taketh the *w* in their own
Job 9:4 He is *w* in heart, and mighty in
Job 11:12 For vain man would be *w*, though
Job 15:2 Should a *w* man utter vain
Job 15:18 Which *w* men have told from their
Job 17:10 I cannot find one *w* man among you
Job 22:2 as he that is *w* may be profitable
Job 32:9 Great men are not always *w*
Job 34:2 Hear my words, O ye *w* men
Job 34:34 let a *w* man hearken unto me
Job 37:24 not any that are *w* of heart
Ps 2:10 Be *w* now therefore, O ye kings
Ps 19:7 LORD is sure, making *w* the simple
Ps 36:3 he hath left off to be *w*, and to
Ps 37:8 not thyself in any *w* to do evil
Ps 49:10 For he seeth that *w* men die
Ps 94:8 and ye fools, when will ye be *w*
Ps 107:43 Whoso is *w*, and will observe these
Prov 1:5 A *w* man will hear, and will
Prov 1:5 shall attain unto *w* counsels
Prov 1:6 the words of the *w*, and their dark
Prov 3:7 Be not *w* in thine own eyes
Prov 3:35 The *w* shall inherit glory
Prov 6:6 consider her ways, and be *w*
Prov 8:33 Hear instruction, and be *w*
Prov 9:8 rebuke a *w* man, and he will love
Prov 9:9 Give instruction to a *w* man
Prov 9:12 If thou be *w*, thou shalt
Prov 9:12 thou shalt be *w* for thyself
Prov 10:1 A *w* son maketh a glad father
Prov 10:5 gathereth in summer is a *w* son
Prov 10:8 The *w* in heart will receive
Prov 10:14 *W* men lay up knowledge
Prov 10:19 he that refraineth his lips is *w*
Prov 11:29 be servant to the *w* of heart
Prov 11:30 and he that winneth souls is *w*
Prov 12:15 that hearkeneth unto counsel is *w*
Prov 12:18 but the tongue of the *w* is health
Prov 13:1 A *w* son heareth his father's
Prov 13:14 The law of the *w* is a fountain of
Prov 13:20 walketh with *w* men shall
Prov 13:20 men shall be *w*
Prov 14:1 Every *w* woman buildeth her house
Prov 14:3 lips of the *w* shall preserve them
Prov 14:16 A *w* man feareth, and departeth
Prov 14:24 crown of the *w* is their riches
Prov 14:35 favour is toward a *w* servant
Prov 15:2 The tongue of the *w* useth
Prov 15:7 The lips of the *w* disperse
Prov 15:12 neither will he go unto the *w*
Prov 15:20 A *w* son maketh a glad father
Prov 15:24 The way of life is above to the *w*
Prov 15:31 of life abideth among the *w*
Prov 16:14 but a *w* man will pacify it
Prov 16:21 The *w* in heart shall be called
Prov 16:23 The heart of the *w* teacheth his
Prov 17:2 A *w* servant shall have rule over
Prov 17:10 a *w* man than an hundred stripes
Prov 17:28 holdeth his peace, is counted *w*
Prov 18:15 and the ear of the *w* seeketh
Prov 19:20 mayest be *w* in thy latter end
Prov 20:1 is deceived thereby is not *w*
Prov 20:26 A *w* king scattereth the wicked,
Prov 21:11 is punished, the simple is made *w*
Prov 21:11 when the *w* is instructed, he
Prov 21:20 and oil in the dwelling of the *w*
Prov 21:22 A *w* man scaleth the city of the
Prov 22:17 ear, and hear the words of the *w*
Prov 23:15 My son, if thine heart be *w*
Prov 23:19 Hear thou, my son, and be *w*
Prov 23:24 he that begetteth a *w* child shall

Prov 24:5 A *w* man is strong
Prov 24:6 For by *w* counsel thou shalt make
Prov 24:23 These things also belong to the *w*
Prov 25:12 so is a *w* reprover upon an
Prov 26:5 lest he be *w* in his own conceit
Prov 26:12 Seest thou a man *w* in his own
Prov 27:11 My son, be *w*, and make my heart
Prov 28:7 Whoso keepeth the law is a *w* son
Prov 28:11 The rich man is *w* in his own
Prov 29:8 but *w* men turn away wrath
Prov 29:9 If a *w* man contendeth with a
Prov 29:11 but a *w* man keepeth it in till
Prov 30:24 earth, but they are exceeding *w*
Eccl 2:14 The *w* man's eyes are in his head
Eccl 2:15 and why was I then more *w*
Eccl 2:16 *w* more than of the fool for ever
Eccl 2:16 And how dieth the *w* man
Eccl 2:19 he shall be a *w* man or a fool
Eccl 2:19 shewed myself *w* under the sun
Eccl 4:13 a *w* child than an old and foolish
Eccl 6:8 For what hath the *w* more than the
Eccl 7:4 The heart of the *w* is in the
Eccl 7:5 to hear the rebuke of the *w*
Eccl 7:7 oppression maketh a *w* man mad
Eccl 7:16 neither make thyself over *w*
Eccl 7:19 Wisdom strengtheneth the *w* more
Eccl 7:23 I said, I will be *w*
Eccl 8:1 Who is as the *w* man
Eccl 8:5 a *w* man's heart discerneth both
Eccl 8:17 though a *w* man think to know it,
Eccl 9:1 that the righteous, and the *w*
Eccl 9:11 neither yet bread to the *w*
Eccl 9:15 was found in it a poor *w* man
Eccl 9:17 The words of *w* men are heard in
Eccl 10:2 A *w* man's heart is at his right
Eccl 10:12 The words of a *w* man's mouth are
Eccl 12:9 because the preacher was *w*
Eccl 12:11 The words of the *w* are as goads
Is 5:21 them that are *w* in their own eyes
Is 19:11 the counsel of the *w* counsellors
Is 19:11 Pharaoh, I am the son of the *w*
Is 19:12 where are thy *w* men
Is 29:14 of their *w* men shall perish
Is 31:2 Yet he also is *w*, and will bring
Is 44:25 that turneth *w* men backward
Jer 4:22 they are *w* to do evil, but to do
Jer 8:8 How do ye say, We are *w*, and the
Jer 8:9 The *w* men are ashamed, they are
Jer 9:12 Who is the *w* man, that may
Jer 9:23 Let not the *w* man glory in his
Jer 10:7 all the *w* men of the nations
Jer 18:18 priest, nor counsel from the *w*
Jer 50:35 her princes, and upon her *w* men
Jer 51:57 drunk her princes, and her *w* men
Eze 27:8 thy *w* men, O Tyrus, that were in
Eze 27:9 the *w* men thereof were in thee
Dan 2:12 destroy all the *w* men of Babylon
Dan 2:13 that the *w* men should be slain
Dan 2:14 to slay the *w* men of Babylon
Dan 2:18 the rest of the *w* men of Babylon
Dan 2:21 he giveth wisdom unto the *w*
Dan 2:24 to destroy the *w* men of Babylon
Dan 2:24 Destroy not the *w* men of Babylon
Dan 2:27 hath demanded cannot the *w* men
Dan 2:48 over all the *w* men of Babylon
Dan 4:6 the *w* men of Babylon before me
Dan 4:18 forasmuch as all the *w* men of my
Dan 5:7 said to the *w* men of Babylon,
Dan 5:8 Then came in all the king's *w* men
Dan 5:15 And now the *w* men, the astrologers
Dan 12:3 they that be *w* shall shine as the
Dan 12:10 but the *w* shall understand
Hos 14:9 Who is *w*, and he shall understand
Obad 8 destroy the *w* men out of Edom
Zec 9:2 and Zidon, though it be very *w*
Mt 1:18 of Jesus Christ was on this *w*
Mt 2:1 there came *w* men from the east to
Mt 2:7 he had privily called the *w* men
Mt 2:16 that he was mocked of the *w* men
Mt 2:16 diligently enquired of the *w* men
Mt 5:18 shall in no *w* pass from the law
Mt 7:24 I will liken him unto a *w* man
Mt 10:16 be ye therefore *w* as serpents
Mt 10:42 he shall in no *w* lose his reward
Mt 11:25 hast hid these things from the *w*
Mt 21:24 I in like *w* will tell you by what
Mt 23:34 prophets, and *w* men, and scribes
Mt 24:45 *w* servant, whom his lord hath
Mt 25:2 And five of them were *w*, and five
Mt 25:4 But the *w* took oil in their
Mt 25:8 And the foolish said unto the *w*
Mt 25:9 But the *w* answered, saying, Not
Mk 14:31 I will not deny thee in any *w*
Lk 10:21 hast hid these things from the *w*
Lk 12:42 *w* steward, whom his lord shall
Lk 13:11 could in no *w* lift up herself
Lk 18:17 child shall in no *w* enter therein
Jn 6:37 to me I will in no *w* cast out
Jn 21:1 on this *w* shewed he himself
Acts 7:6 And God spake on this *w*, That his
Acts 13:34 to corruption, he said on this *w*
Acts 13:41 which ye shall in no *w* believe
Rom 1:14 both to the *w*, and to the unwise
Rom 1:22 Professing themselves to be *w*
Rom 3:9 No, in no *w*:
Rom 10:6 is of faith speaketh on this *w*
Rom 11:25 lest ye should be *w* in your own
Rom 12:16 Be not *w* in your own conceits
Rom 16:19 you *w* unto that which is good
Rom 16:27 To God only *w*, be glory through
1Cor 1:19 will destroy the wisdom of the *w*
1Cor 1:20 Where is the *w*
1Cor 1:26 how that not many *w* men after the
1Cor 1:27 of the world to confound the *w*
1Cor 3:10 as a *w* masterbuilder, I have laid
1Cor 3:18 you seemeth to be *w* in this world
1Cor 3:18 become a fool, that he may be *w*
1Cor 3:19 He taketh the *w* in their own
1Cor 3:20 knoweth the thoughts of the *w*
1Cor 4:10 sake, but ye are *w* in Christ
1Cor 6:5 there is not a *w* man among you
1Cor 10:15 I speak as to *w* men
2Cor 10:12 among themselves, are not *w*
2Cor 11:19 seeing ye yourselves are *w*
Eph 5:15 not as fools, but as *w*,
1Ti 1:17 invisible, the only *w* God
2Ti 3:15 which are able to make thee *w*
Heb 4:4 of the seventh day on this *w*
Jas 3:13 Who is a *w* man and endued with
Jude 25 To the only *w* God our Saviour, be
Rev 21:27 there shall in no *w* enter into it

## WISELY

Ex 1:10 Come on, let us deal *w* with them
1Sa 18:5 sent him, and behaved himself *w*
1Sa 18:14 behaved himself *w* in all his ways
1Sa 18:15 that he behaved himself very *w*
1Sa 18:30 *w* than all the servants of Saul
2Chr 11:23 And he dealt *w*, and dispersed of
Ps 58:5 of charmers, charming never so *w*
Ps 64:9 for they shall *w* consider of his
Ps 101:2 behave myself *w* in a perfect way
Prov 16:20 a matter *w* shall find good
Prov 21:12 The righteous man *w* considereth
Prov 28:26 but whoso walketh *w*, he shall be
Eccl 7:10 not enquire *w* concerning this
Lk 16:8 steward, because he had done *w*

## WISER

1Kin 4:31 For he was *w* than all men
Job 35:11 maketh us *w* than the fowls of
Ps 119:98 hast made me *w* than mine enemies
Prov 9:9 a wise man, and he will be yet *w*
Prov 26:16 The sluggard is *w* in his own
Eze 28:3 Behold, thou art *w* than Daniel
Lk 16:8 *w* than the children of light
1Cor 1:25 foolishness of God is *w* than men

## WISH

Job 33:6 according to thy *w* in God's stead
Ps 40:14 and put to shame that *w* me evil
Ps 73:7 they have more than heart could *w*
Rom 9:3 For I could *w* that myself were
2Cor 13:9 and this also we *w*, even your
3Jn 2 I *w* above all things that thou

## WISHED

Jonah 4:8 *w* in himself to die, and said, It
Acts 27:29 of the stern, and *w* for the day

## WISHING

Job 31:30 to sin by *w* a curse to his soul

## WIST

Ex 16:15 for they *w* not what it was
Ex 34:29 that Moses *w* not that the skin of
Lev 5:17 though he *w* it not, yet is he
Lev 5:18 *w* it not, and it shall be forgiven
Josh 2:4 but I *w* not whence they were
Josh 8:14 but he *w* not that there were
Judg 16:20 he *w* not that the LORD was
Mk 9:6 For he *w* not what to say
Mk 14:40 neither *w* they what to answer
Lk 2:49 *w* ye not that I must be about my
Jn 5:13 that was healed *w* not who it was
Acts 12:9 *w* not that it was true which was
Acts 23:5 I *w* not, brethren, that he was

## WIT

Gen 24:21 to *w* whether the LORD had made
Ex 2:4 to *w* what would be done to him
Josh 17:1 to *w*, for Machir the firstborn of
1Kin 2:32 David not knowing thereof, to *w*
1Kin 7:50 for the doors of the house, to *w*
1Kin 13:23 he saddled for him the ass, to *w*
2Kin 10:29 not from after them, to *w*
1Chr 7:2 of their father's house, to *w*
1Chr 27:1 Israel after their number, to *w*
2Chr 4:12 To *w*, the two pillars, and the
2Chr 25:7 the LORD is not with Israel, to *w*
2Chr 25:10 Then Amaziah separated them, to *w*
2Chr 31:3 for the burnt offerings, to *w*
Neh 11:3 possession in their cities, to *w*
Est 2:12 purifications accomplished, to *w*
Jer 25:18 To *w*, Jerusalem, and the cities of
Jer 34:9 serve himself of them, to *w*
Eze 13:16 To *w*, the prophets of Israel
Rom 8:23 waiting for the adoption, to *w*
2Cor 5:19 To *w*, that God was in Christ,
2Cor 8:1 we do you to *w* of the grace of

## WITCH

Ex 22:18 Thou shalt not suffer a *w* to live
Deut 18:10 of times, or an enchanter, or a *w*

## WITCHCRAFT

1Sa 15:23 For rebellion is as the sin of *w*
2Chr 33:6 and used enchantments, and used *w*
Gal 5:20 Idolatry, *w*, hatred, variance,

## WITCHCRAFTS

2Kin 9:22 Jezebel and her *w* are so many
Mic 5:12 I will cut off *w* out of thine
Nah 3:4 harlot, the mistress of *w*
Nah 3:4 and families through her *w*

## WITHDRAW

1Sa 14:19 unto the priest, *W* thine hand
Job 9:13 If God will not *w* his anger
Job 13:21 *W* thine hand far from me
Job 33:17 That he may *w* man from his
Prov 25:17 *W* thy foot from thy neighbour's
Eccl 7:18 also from this *w* not thine hand
Is 60:20 neither shall thy moon *w* itself
Joel 2:10 the stars shall *w* their shining
Joel 3:15 the stars shall *w* their shining
2Th 3:6 that ye *w* yourselves from every
1Ti 6:5 from such *w* thyself

## WITHDRAWEST

Ps 74:11 Why *w* thou thy hand, even thy

## WITHDRAWETH

Job 36:7 He *w* not his eyes from the

## WITHDRAWN

Deut 13:13 have *w* the inhabitants of their
Song 5:6 but my beloved had *w* himself
Lam 2:8 he hath not *w* his hand from
Eze 18:8 that hath *w* his hand from
Hos 5:6 he hath *w* himself from them
Lk 22:41 he was *w* from them about a

## WITHDREW

Neh 9:29 *w* the shoulder, and hardened their
Eze 20:22 Nevertheless I *w* mine hand
Mt 12:15 knew it, he *w* himself from thence
Mk 3:7 But Jesus *w* himself with his
Lk 5:16 he *w* himself into the wilderness,
Gal 2:12 but when they were come, he *w*

## WITHER

Ps 1:3 his leaf also shall not *w*
Ps 37:2 the grass, and *w* as the green herb
Is 19:6 the reeds and flags shall *w*
Is 19:7 thing sown by the brooks, shall *w*
Is 40:24 blow upon them, and they shall *w*
Jer 12:4 and the herbs of every field *w*
Eze 17:9 off the fruit thereof, that it *w*
Eze 17:9 it shall *w* in all the leaves of
Eze 17:10 shall it not utterly *w*, when the
Eze 17:10 it shall *w* in the furrows where
Amos 1:2 and the top of Carmel shall *w*

## WITHERED

Gen 41:23 And, behold, seven ears, *w*
Ps 102:4 heart is smitten, and *w* like grass
Ps 102:11 and I am *w* like grass
Is 15:6 for the hay is *w* away, the grass
Is 27:11 When the boughs thereof are *w*
Lam 4:8 it is *w*, it is become like a

Eze 19:12 her strong rods were broken and *w*
Joel 1:12 all the trees of the field, are *w*
Joel 1:12 because joy is *w* away from the
Joel 1:17 for the corn is *w*
Amos 4:7 piece whereupon it rained not *w*
Jonah 4:7 and it smote the gourd that it *w*
Mt 12:10 was a man which had his hand *w*
Mt 13:6 they had no root, they *w* away
Mt 21:19 And presently the fig tree *w* away
Mt 21:20 How soon is the fig tree *w* away
Mk 3:1 a man there which had a *w* hand
Mk 3:3 unto the man which had the *w* hand
Mk 4:6 because it had no root, it *w* away
Mk 11:21 which thou cursedst is *w* away
Lk 6:6 was a man whose right hand was *w*
Lk 6:8 to the man which had the *w* hand
Lk 8:6 it *w* away, because it lacked
Jn 5:3 impotent folk, of blind, halt, *w*
Jn 15:6 cast forth as a branch, and is *w*

## WITHERETH
Job 8:12 it *w* before any other herb
Ps 90:6 the evening it is cut down, and *w*
Ps 129:6 which *w* afore it groweth up
Is 40:7 The grass *w*, the flower fadeth
Is 40:8 The grass *w*, the flower fadeth
Jas 1:11 but it *w* the grass, and the flower
1Pet 1:24 The grass *w*, and the flower
Jude 12 trees whose fruit *w*, without

## WITHHELD
Gen 20:6 for I also *w* thee from sinning
Gen 22:12 seeing thou hast not *w* thy son
Gen 22:16 this thing, and hast not *w* thy son
Gen 30:2 who hath *w* from thee the fruit of
Job 31:16 If I have *w* the poor from their
Eccl 2:10 I *w* not my heart from any joy

## WITHHELDEST
Neh 9:20 *w* not thy manna from their mouth,

## WITHHOLD
Gen 23:6 none of us shall *w* from thee his
2Sa 13:13 for he will not *w* me from thee
Job 4:2 but who can *w* himself from
Ps 40:11 *W* not thou thy tender mercies
Ps 84:11 no good thing will he *w* from them
Prov 3:27 *W* not good from them to whom it
Prov 23:13 *W* not correction from the child
Eccl 11:6 in the evening *w* not thine hand
Jer 2:25 *W* thy foot from being unshod, and

## WITHHOLDEN
1Sa 25:26 seeing the LORD hath *w* thee from
Job 22:7 thou hast *w* bread from the hungry
Job 38:15 from the wicked their light is *w*
Job 42:2 no thought can be *w* from thee
Ps 21:2 hast not *w* the request of his
Jer 3:3 Therefore the showers have been *w*
Jer 5:25 your sins have *w* good things from
Eze 18:16 hath not *w* the pledge, neither
Joel 1:13 the drink offering is *w* from the
Amos 4:7 also I have *w* the rain from you,

## WITHHOLDETH
Job 12:15 he *w* the waters, and they dry up
Prov 11:24 there is that *w* more than is meet
Prov 11:26 He that *w* corn, the people shall
2Th 2:6 now ye know what *w* that he might

## WITHS
Judg 16:7 green *w* that were never dried
Judg 16:8 green *w* which had not been dried
Judg 16:9 And he brake the *w*, as a thread of

## WITHSTAND
Num 22:32 behold, I went out to *w* thee
2Chr 13:7 and could not *w* them
2Chr 13:8 now ye think to *w* the kingdom of
2Chr 20:6 so that none is able to *w* thee
Est 9:2 and no man could *w* them
Eccl 4:12 against him, two shall *w* him
Dan 11:15 the arms of the south shall not *w*
Dan 11:15 shall there be any strength to *w*
Acts 11:17 what was I, that I could *w* God
Eph 6:13 may be able to *w* in the evil day

## WITHSTOOD
2Chr 26:18 they *w* Uzziah the king, and said
Dan 10:13 of the kingdom of Persia *w* me one
Acts 13:8 name by interpretation) *w* them
Gal 2:11 I *w* him to the face, because he
2Ti 3:8 Now as Jannes and Jambres *w* Moses
2Ti 4:15 for he hath greatly *w* our words

## WITNESS
Gen 21:30 that they may be a *w* unto me
Gen 31:44 and let it be for a *w* between me
Gen 31:48 said, This heap is a *w* between me
Gen 31:50 God is *w* betwixt me and thee
Gen 31:52 This heap be *w*
Gen 31:52 and this pillar be *w*
Ex 20:16 false *w* against thy neighbour
Ex 22:13 then let him bring it for *w*
Ex 23:1 the wicked to be an unrighteous *w*
Lev 5:1 the voice of swearing, and is a *w*
Num 5:13 and there be no *w* against her
Num 17:7 the LORD in the tabernacle of *w*
Num 17:8 went into the tabernacle of *w*
Num 18:2 before the tabernacle of *w*
Num 35:30 but one *w* shall not testify
Deut 4:26 earth to *w* against you this day,
Deut 5:20 false *w* against thy neighbour
Deut 17:6 but at the mouth of one *w* he
Deut 19:15 One *w* shall not rise up against a
Deut 19:16 If a false *w* rise up against any
Deut 19:18 if the *w* be a false *w*
Deut 31:19 that this song may be a *w* for me
Deut 31:21 shall testify against them as a *w*
Deut 31:26 may be there for a *w* against thee
Josh 22:27 But that it may be a *w* between us
Josh 22:28 but it is a *w* between us and you
Josh 22:34 for it shall be a *w* between us
Josh 24:27 this stone shall be a *w* unto us
Josh 24:27 shall be therefore a *w* unto you
Judg 11:10 The LORD be *w* between us
1Sa 12:3 *w* against me before the LORD, and
1Sa 12:5 them, The LORD is *w* against you
1Sa 12:5 and his anointed is *w* this day
1Sa 12:5 And they answered, He is *w*
1Kin 21:10 to bear *w* against him, saying,
2Chr 24:6 Israel, for the tabernacle of *w*
Job 16:8 wrinkles, which is a *w* against me
Job 16:8 up in me beareth *w* to my face
Job 16:19 my *w* is in heaven, and my record
Job 29:11 the eye saw me, it gave *w* to me
Ps 89:37 and as a faithful *w* in heaven
Prov 6:19 A false *w* that speaketh lies, and
Prov 12:17 but a false *w* deceit
Prov 14:5 A faithful *w* will not lie
Prov 14:5 but a false *w* will utter lies
Prov 14:25 A true *w* delivereth souls
Prov 14:25 but a deceitful *w* speaketh lies
Prov 19:5 A false *w* shall not be unpunished
Prov 19:9 A false *w* shall not be unpunished
Prov 19:28 An ungodly *w* scorneth judgment
Prov 21:28 A false *w* shall perish
Prov 24:28 Be not a *w* against thy neighbour
Prov 25:18 A man that beareth false *w*
Is 3:9 countenance doth *w* against them
Is 19:20 for a *w* unto the LORD of hosts in
Is 55:4 given him for a *w* to the people
Jer 29:23 even I know, and am a *w*, saith the
Jer 42:5 faithful *w* between us, if we do
Lam 2:13 thing shall I take to *w* for thee
Mic 1:2 let the Lord GOD be *w* against you
Mal 2:14 the LORD hath been *w* between thee
Mal 3:5 I will be a swift *w* against the
Mt 15:19 fornications, thefts, false *w*
Mt 19:18 Thou shalt not bear false *w*
Mt 24:14 world for a *w* unto all nations
Mt 26:59 sought false *w* against Jesus, to
Mt 26:62 is it which these *w* against thee
Mt 27:13 many things they *w* against thee
Mk 10:19 Do not steal, Do not bear false *w*
Mk 14:55 all the council sought for *w*
Mk 14:56 For many bare false *w* against him
Mk 14:56 but their *w* agreed not together
Mk 14:57 bare false *w* against him, saying,
Mk 14:59 so did their *w* agree together
Mk 14:60 is it which these *w* against thee
Mk 15:4 many things they *w* against thee
Lk 4:22 And all bare him *w*, and wondered at
Lk 11:48 Truly ye bear *w* that ye allow the
Lk 18:20 Do not steal, Do not bear false *w*
Lk 22:71 said, What need we any further *w*
Jn 1:7 The same came for a *w*
Jn 1:7 to bear *w* of the Light, that all
Jn 1:8 was sent to bear *w* of that Light
Jn 1:15 John bare *w* of him, and cried,
Jn 3:11 and ye receive not our *w*
Jn 3:26 Jordan, to whom thou barest *w*
Jn 3:28 Ye yourselves bear me *w*, that I
Jn 5:31 If I bear *w* of myself
Jn 5:31 of myself, my *w* is not true
Jn 5:32 is another that beareth *w* of me
Jn 5:32 I know that the *w* which he
Jn 5:33 John, and he bare *w* unto the truth
Jn 5:36 have greater *w* than that of John
Jn 5:36 bear *w* of me, that the Father
Jn 5:37 hath sent me, hath borne *w* of me
Jn 8:18 I am one that bear *w* of myself
Jn 8:18 that sent me beareth *w* of me
Jn 10:25 Father's name, they bear *w* of me
Jn 15:27 And ye also shall bear *w*, because
Jn 18:23 spoken evil, bear *w* of the evil
Jn 18:37 I should bear *w* unto the truth
Acts 1:22 a *w* with us of his resurrection
Acts 4:33 great power gave the apostles *w*
Acts 7:44 tabernacle of *w* in the wilderness
Acts 10:43 To him give all the prophets *w*
Acts 14:17 he left not himself without *w*
Acts 15:8 knoweth the hearts, bare them *w*
Acts 22:5 the high priest doth bear me *w*
Acts 22:15 For thou shalt be his *w* unto all
Acts 23:11 so must thou bear *w* also at Rome
Acts 26:16 a *w* both of these things which
Rom 1:9 For God is my *w*, whom I serve
Rom 2:15 their conscience also bearing *w*
Rom 8:16 itself beareth *w* with our spirit
Rom 9:1 bearing me *w* in the Holy Ghost
Rom 13:9 Thou shalt not bear false *w*
1Th 2:5 God is *w*
Titus 1:13 This *w* is true
Heb 2:4 God also bearing them *w*, both
Heb 10:15 the Holy Ghost also is a *w* to us
Heb 11:4 by which he obtained *w* that he
Jas 5:3 of them shall be a *w* against you
1Pet 5:1 a *w* of the sufferings of Christ,
1Jn 1:2 and we have seen it, and bear *w*
1Jn 5:6 it is the Spirit that beareth *w*
1Jn 5:8 are three that bear *w* in earth
1Jn 5:9 If we receive the *w* of men
1Jn 5:9 the *w* of God is greater
1Jn 5:9 for this is the *w* of God which he
1Jn 5:10 Son of God hath the *w* in himself
3Jn 6 Which have borne *w* of thy charity
Rev 1:5 Christ, who is the faithful *w*
Rev 3:14 the Amen, the faithful and true *w*
Rev 20:4 were beheaded for the *w* of Jesus

## WITNESSED
1Kin 21:13 the men of Belial *w* against him
Rom 3:21 being *w* by the law and the
1Ti 6:13 Pilate *w* a good confession
Heb 7:8 of whom it is *w* that he liveth

## WITNESSES
Num 35:30 be put to death by the mouth of *w*
Deut 17:6 of two *w*, or three *w*
Deut 17:7 The hands of the *w* shall be first
Deut 19:15 at the mouth of two *w*
Deut 19:15 or at the mouth of three *w*
Josh 24:22 Ye are *w* against yourselves that
Josh 24:22 And they said, We are *w*
Ruth 4:9 Ye are *w* this day, that I have
Ruth 4:10 ye are *w* this day
Ruth 4:11 and the elders, said, We are *w*
Job 10:17 Thou renewest thy *w* against me
Ps 27:12 for false *w* are risen up against
Ps 35:11 False *w* did rise up
Is 8:2 took unto me faithful *w* to record
Is 43:9 let them bring forth their *w*
Is 43:10 Ye are my *w*, saith the LORD, and
Is 43:12 therefore ye are my *w*, saith the
Is 44:8 ye are even my *w*
Is 44:9 and they are their own *w*
Jer 32:10 evidence, and sealed it, and took *w*
Jer 32:12 in the presence of the *w* that
Jer 32:25 the field for money, and take *w*
Jer 32:44 take *w* in the land of Benjamin,
Mt 18:16 in the mouth of two or three *w*
Mt 23:31 Wherefore ye be *w* unto yourselves
Mt 26:60 yea, though many false *w* came
Mt 26:60 At the last came two false *w*
Mt 26:65 what further need have we of *w*
Mk 14:63 saith, What need we any further *w*
Lk 24:48 And ye are *w* of these things
Acts 1:8 ye shall be *w* unto me both in
Acts 2:32 raised up, whereof we all are *w*
Acts 3:15 whereof we are *w*
Acts 5:32 we are his *w* of these things
Acts 6:13 And set up false *w*, which said,
Acts 7:58 the *w* laid down their clothes at
Acts 10:39 we are *w* of all things which he
Acts 10:41 but unto *w* chosen before of God,

Acts 13:31 who are his *w* unto the people
1Cor 15:15 and we are found false *w* of God
2Cor 13:1 In the mouth of two or three *w*
1Th 2:10 Ye are *w*, and God also, how holily
1Ti 5:19 but before two or three *w*
1Ti 6:12 a good profession before many *w*
2Ti 2:2 hast heard of me among many *w*
Heb 10:28 mercy under two or three *w*
Heb 12:1 about with so great a cloud of *w*
Rev 11:3 I will give power unto my two *w*

## WITNESSETH
Jn 5:32 witness which he *w* of me is true
Acts 20:23 the Holy Ghost *w* in every city

## WITNESSING
Acts 26:22 *w* both to small and great, saying

## WIT'S
Ps 107:27 man, and are at their *w* end

## WITTINGLY
Gen 48:14 head, guiding his hands *w*

## WITTY
Prov 8:12 out knowledge of *w* inventions

## WIVES
Gen 4:19 And Lamech took unto him two *w*
Gen 4:23 And Lamech said unto his *w*
Gen 4:23 ye *w* of Lamech, hearken unto my
Gen 6:2 they took them *w* of all which
Gen 6:18 wife, and thy sons' *w* with thee
Gen 7:7 his wife, and his sons' *w* with him
Gen 7:13 the three *w* of his sons with them
Gen 8:16 sons, and thy sons' *w* with thee
Gen 8:18 his wife, and his sons' *w* with him
Gen 11:29 And Abram and Nahor took them *w*
Gen 28:9 took unto the *w* which he had
Gen 30:26 Give me my *w* and my children, for
Gen 31:17 set his sons and his *w* upon camels
Gen 31:50 take other *w* beside my daughters
Gen 32:22 up that night, and took his two *w*
Gen 34:21 take their daughters to us for *w*
Gen 34:29 their *w* took they captive, and
Gen 36:2 Esau took his *w* of the daughters
Gen 36:6 And Esau took his *w*, and his sons,
Gen 37:2 sons of Zilpah, his father's *w*
Gen 45:19 your little ones, and for your *w*
Gen 46:5 and their little ones, and their *w*
Gen 46:26 loins, besides Jacob's sons' *w*
Ex 19:15 come not at your *w*
Ex 22:24 your *w* shall be widows, and your
Ex 32:2 which are in the ears of your *w*
Num 14:3 to fall by the sword, that our *w*
Num 16:27 door of their tents, and their *w*
Num 32:26 Our little ones, our *w*, our
Deut 3:19 But your *w*, and your little ones,
Deut 17:17 shall he multiply *w* to himself
Deut 21:15 If a man have two *w*, one beloved,
Deut 29:11 Your little ones, your *w*, and thy
Josh 1:14 Your *w*, your little ones, and your
Judg 3:6 their daughters to be their *w*
Judg 8:30 for he had many *w*
Judg 21:7 How shall we do for *w* for them
Judg 21:7 give them of our daughters to *w*
Judg 21:14 they gave them *w* which they had
Judg 21:16 How shall we do for *w* for them
Judg 21:18 not give them *w* of our daughters
Judg 21:23 Benjamin did so, and took them *w*
Ruth 1:4 they took them *w* of the women of
1Sa 1:2 And he had two *w*
1Sa 25:43 they were also both of them his *w*
1Sa 27:3 even David with his two *w*
1Sa 30:3 and their *w*, and their sons, and
1Sa 30:5 David's two *w* were taken captives
1Sa 30:18 and David rescued his two *w*
2Sa 2:2 up thither, and his two *w* also
2Sa 5:13 *w* out of Jerusalem, after he was
2Sa 12:8 thy master's *w* into thy bosom, and
2Sa 12:11 I will take thy *w* before thine
2Sa 12:11 he shall lie with thy *w* in the
2Sa 19:5 daughters, and the lives of thy *w*
1Kin 11:3 And he had seven hundred *w*
1Kin 11:3 his *w* turned away his heart
1Kin 11:4 that his *w* turned away his heart
1Kin 11:8 did he for all his strange *w*
1Kin 20:3 thy *w* also and thy children, even
1Kin 20:5 thy silver, and thy gold, and thy *w*
1Kin 20:7 for he sent unto me for my *w*
2Kin 4:1 the *w* of the sons of the prophets
2Kin 24:15 king's mother, and the king's *w*
1Chr 4:5 the father of Tekoa had two *w*
1Chr 7:4 for they had many *w* and sons
1Chr 8:8 Hushim and Baara were his *w*
1Chr 14:3 And David took more *w* at Jerusalem
2Chr 11:21 of Absalom above all his *w*
2Chr 11:21 (for he took eighteen *w*, and
2Chr 11:23 And he desired many *w*
2Chr 13:21 mighty, and married fourteen *w*
2Chr 20:13 with their little ones, their *w*
2Chr 21:14 people, and thy children, and thy *w*
2Chr 21:17 house, and his sons also, and his *w*
2Chr 24:3 And Jehoiada took for him two *w*
2Chr 29:9 our *w* are in captivity for this
2Chr 31:18 of all their little ones, their *w*
Ezr 10:2 have taken strange *w* of the
Ezr 10:3 our God to put away all the *w*
Ezr 10:10 and have taken strange *w*, to
Ezr 10:11 the land, and from the strange *w*
Ezr 10:14 them which have taken strange *w*
Ezr 10:17 *w* by the first day of the first
Ezr 10:18 found that had taken strange *w*
Ezr 10:19 that they would put away their *w*
Ezr 10:44 All these had taken strange *w*
Ezr 10:44 some of them had *w* by whom they
Neh 4:14 sons, and your daughters, your *w*
Neh 5:1 of their *w* against their brethren
Neh 10:28 unto the law of God, their *w*
Neh 12:43 the *w* also and the children
Neh 13:23 Jews that had married *w* of Ashdod
Neh 13:27 our God in marrying strange *w*
Est 1:20 all the *w* shall give to their
Is 13:16 be spoiled, and their *w* ravished
Jer 6:12 with their fields and *w* together
Jer 8:10 will I give their *w* unto others
Jer 14:16 none to bury them, them, their *w*
Jer 18:21 let their *w* be bereaved of their
Jer 29:6 Take ye *w*, and beget sons and
Jer 29:6 take *w* for your sons, and give
Jer 29:23 adultery with their neighbours' *w*
Jer 35:8 no wine all our days, we, our *w*
Jer 38:23 So they shall bring out all thy *w*
Jer 44:9 and the wickedness of their *w*
Jer 44:9 and the wickedness of your *w*
Jer 44:15 *w* had burned incense unto other
Jer 44:25 your *w* have both spoken with your
Eze 44:22 they take for their *w* a widow
Dan 5:2 the king, and his princes, his *w*
Dan 5:3 the king, and his princes, his *w*
Dan 5:23 and thou, and thy lords, thy *w*
Dan 6:24 them, their children, and their *w*
Zec 12:12 of David apart, and their *w* apart
Zec 12:12 of Nathan apart, and their *w* apart
Zec 12:13 of Levi apart, and their *w* apart
Zec 12:13 of Shimei apart, and their *w* apart
Zec 12:14 family apart, and their *w* apart
Mt 19:8 suffered you to put away your *w*
Lk 17:27 eat, they drank, they married *w*
Acts 21:5 all brought us on our way, with *w*
1Cor 7:29 that both they that have *w* be as
Eph 5:22 *W*, submit yourselves unto your
Eph 5:24 so let the *w* be to their own
Eph 5:25 Husbands, love your *w*, even as
Eph 5:28 love their *w* as their own bodies
Col 3:18 *W*, submit yourselves unto your
Col 3:19 Husbands, love your *w*, and be not
1Ti 3:11 Even so must their *w* be grave
1Pet 3:1 Likewise, ye *w*, be in subjection
1Pet 3:1 won by the conversation of the *w*

## WIVES'
1Ti 4:7 old *w* fables, and exercise thyself

## WIZARD
Lev 20:27 a familiar spirit, or that is a *w*
Deut 18:11 with familiar spirits, or a *w*

## WIZARDS
Lev 19:31 spirits, neither seek after *w*
Lev 20:6 have familiar spirits, and after *w*
1Sa 28:3 had familiar spirits, and the *w*
1Sa 28:9 have familiar spirits, and the *w*
2Kin 21:6 dealt with familiar spirits and *w*
2Kin 23:24 with familiar spirits, and the *w*
2Chr 33:6 with a familiar spirit, and with *w*
Is 8:19 unto *w* that peep, and that mutter
Is 19:3 familiar spirits, and to the *w*

## WOE
Num 21:29 *W* to thee, Moab
1Sa 4:7 And they said, *W* unto us
1Sa 4:8 *W* unto us
Job 10:15 If I be wicked, *w* unto me
Ps 120:5 *W* is me, that I sojourn in Mesech
Prov 23:29 Who hath *w*
Eccl 4:10 but *w* to him that is alone when
Eccl 10:16 *W* to thee, O land, when thy king
Is 3:9 *W* unto their soul
Is 3:11 *W* unto the wicked
Is 5:8 *W* unto them that join house to
Is 5:11 *W* unto them that rise up early in
Is 5:18 *W* unto them that draw iniquity
Is 5:20 *W* unto them that call evil good,
Is 5:21 *W* unto them that are wise in
Is 5:22 *W* unto them that are mighty to
Is 6:5 Then said I, *W* is me
Is 10:1 *W* unto them that decree
Is 17:12 *W* to the multitude of many people
Is 18:1 *W* to the land shadowing with
Is 24:16 leanness, my leanness, *w* unto me
Is 28:1 *W* to the crown of pride, to the
Is 29:1 *W* to Ariel, to Ariel, the city
Is 29:15 *W* unto them that seek deep to
Is 30:1 *W* to the rebellious children,
Is 31:1 *W* to them that go down to Egypt
Is 33:1 *W* to thee that spoilest, and thou
Is 45:9 *W* unto him that striveth with his
Is 45:10 *W* unto him that saith unto his
Jer 4:13 *W* unto us
Jer 4:31 her hands, saying, *W* is me now
Jer 6:4 *W* unto us
Jer 10:19 *W* is me for my hurt
Jer 13:27 *W* unto thee, O Jerusalem
Jer 15:10 *W* is me, my mother, that thou
Jer 22:13 *W* unto him that buildeth his
Jer 23:1 *W* be unto the pastors that
Jer 45:3 Thou didst say, *W* is me now
Jer 48:1 *W* unto Nebo
Jer 48:46 *W* be unto thee, O Moab
Jer 50:27 *w* unto them
Lam 5:16 *w* unto us, that we have sinned
Eze 2:10 lamentations, and mourning, and *w*
Eze 13:3 *W* unto the foolish prophets, that
Eze 13:18 *W* to the women that sew pillows
Eze 16:23 *w*, *w* unto thee
Eze 24:6 *W* to the bloody city, to the pot
Eze 24:9 *W* to the bloody city
Eze 30:2 Howl ye, *W* worth the day
Eze 34:2 *W* be to the shepherds of Israel
Hos 7:13 *W* unto them
Hos 9:12 *w* also to them when I depart from
Amos 5:18 *W* unto you that desire the day of
Amos 6:1 *W* to them that are at ease in
Mic 2:1 *W* to them that devise iniquity,
Mic 7:1 *W* is me
Nah 3:1 *W* to the bloody city
Hab 2:6 *W* to him that increaseth that
Hab 2:9 *W* to him that coveteth an evil
Hab 2:12 *W* to him that buildeth a town
Hab 2:15 *W* unto him that giveth his
Hab 2:19 *W* unto him that saith to the wood
Zeph 2:5 *W* unto the inhabitants of the sea
Zeph 3:1 *W* to her that is filthy and
Zec 11:17 *W* to the idol shepherd that
Mt 11:21 *W* unto thee, Chorazin
Mt 11:21 *w* unto thee, Bethsaida
Mt 18:7 *W* unto the world because of
Mt 18:7 but *w* to that man by whom the
Mt 23:13 But *w* unto you, scribes and
Mt 23:14 *W* unto you, scribes and Pharisees,
Mt 23:15 *W* unto you, scribes and Pharisees,
Mt 23:16 *W* unto you, ye blind guides,
Mt 23:23 *W* unto you, scribes and Pharisees,
Mt 23:25 *W* unto you, scribes and Pharisees,
Mt 23:27 *W* unto you, scribes and Pharisees,
Mt 23:29 *W* unto you, scribes and Pharisees,
Mt 24:19 *w* unto them that are with child,
Mt 26:24 but *w* unto that man by whom the
Mk 13:17 But *w* to them that are with child
Mk 14:21 but *w* to that man by whom the Son
Lk 6:24 But *w* unto you that are rich
Lk 6:25 *W* unto you that are full
Lk 6:25 *W* unto you that laugh now
Lk 6:26 *W* unto you, when all men shall
Lk 10:13 *W* unto thee, Chorazin
Lk 10:13 *w* unto thee, Bethsaida
Lk 11:42 But *w* unto you, Pharisees
Lk 11:43 *W* unto you, Pharisees
Lk 11:44 *W* unto you, scribes and Pharisees,
Lk 11:46 *W* unto you also, ye lawyers
Lk 11:47 *W* unto you! for ye build the
Lk 11:52 *W* unto you, lawyers
Lk 17:1 but *w* unto him, through whom they
Lk 21:23 But *w* unto them that are with
Lk 22:22 but *w* unto that man by whom he is

1Cor 9:16 *w* is unto me, if I preach not the
Jude 11 *W* unto them
Rev 8:13 saying with a loud voice, *W*, *w*
Rev 8:13 with a loud voice, *W*, *w*, *w*
Rev 9:12 One *w* is past
Rev 11:14 The second *w* is past
Rev 11:14 the third *w* cometh quickly
Rev 12:12 *W* to the inhabiters of the earth

## WOEFUL
Jer 17:16 neither have I desired the *w* day

## WOES
Rev 9:12 there come two *w* more hereafter

## WOLF
Gen 49:27 Benjamin shall ravin as a *w*
Is 11:6 The *w* also shall dwell with the
Is 65:25 The *w* and the lamb shall feed
Jer 5:6 a *w* of the evenings shall spoil
Jn 10:12 sheep are not, seeth the *w* coming
Jn 10:12 and the *w* catcheth them, and

## WOLVES
Eze 22:27 are like *w* ravening the prey
Hab 1:8 more fierce than the evening *w*
Zeph 3:3 her judges are evening *w*
Mt 7:15 but inwardly they are ravening *w*
Mt 10:16 forth as sheep in the midst of *w*
Lk 10:3 I send you forth as lambs among *w*
Acts 20:29 grievous *w* enter in among you

## WOMAN
Gen 2:22 had taken from man, made he a *w*
Gen 2:23 she shall be called *W*, because
Gen 3:1 And he said unto the *w*, Yea, hath
Gen 3:2 the *w* said unto the serpent, We
Gen 3:4 And the serpent said unto the *w*
Gen 3:6 when the *w* saw that the tree was
Gen 3:12 The *w* whom thou gavest to be with
Gen 3:13 And the LORD God said unto the *w*
Gen 3:13 the *w* said, The serpent beguiled
Gen 3:15 put enmity between thee and the *w*
Gen 3:16 Unto the *w* he said, I will
Gen 12:11 thou art a fair *w* to look upon
Gen 12:14 the *w* that she was very fair
Gen 12:15 the *w* was taken into Pharaoh's
Gen 20:3 for the *w* which thou hast taken
Gen 24:5 Peradventure the *w* will not be
Gen 24:8 if the *w* will not be willing to
Gen 24:39 Peradventure the *w* will not
Gen 24:44 let the same be the *w* whom the
Gen 46:10 Shaul the son of a Canaanitish *w*
Ex 2:2 the *w* conceived, and bare a son
Ex 2:9 the *w* took the child, and nursed
Ex 3:22 But every *w* shall borrow of her
Ex 6:15 Shaul the son of a Canaanitish *w*
Ex 11:2 every *w* of her neighbour, jewels
Ex 21:22 hurt a *w* with child, so that her
Ex 21:28 If an ox gore a man or a *w*
Ex 21:29 that he hath killed a man or a *w*
Ex 35:29 unto the LORD, every man and *w*
Ex 36:6 Let neither man nor *w* make any
Lev 12:2 If a *w* have conceived seed, and
Lev 13:29 If a man or *w* have a plague upon
Lev 13:38 If a man also or a *w* have in the
Lev 15:18 The *w* also with whom man shall
Lev 15:19 if a *w* have an issue, and her
Lev 15:25 if a *w* have an issue of her blood
Lev 15:33 an issue, of the man, and of the *w*
Lev 18:17 not uncover the nakedness of a *w*
Lev 18:19 unto a *w* to uncover her nakedness
Lev 18:23 neither shall any *w* stand before
Lev 19:20 whosoever lieth carnally with a *w*
Lev 20:13 mankind, as he lieth with a *w*
Lev 20:16 if a *w* approach unto any beast,
Lev 20:16 thereto, thou shalt kill the *w*
Lev 20:18 lie with a *w* having her sickness
Lev 20:27 A man also or *w* that hath a
Lev 21:7 a *w* put away from her husband
Lev 21:14 A widow, or a divorced *w*, or
Lev 24:10 And the son of an Israelitish *w*
Lev 24:10 and this son of the Israelitish *w*
Num 5:6 When a man or *w* shall commit any
Num 5:18 shall set the *w* before the LORD
Num 5:19 her by an oath, and say unto the *w*
Num 5:21 the *w* with an oath of cursing
Num 5:21 the priest shall say unto the *w*
Num 5:22 the *w* shall say, Amen, amen
Num 5:24 he shall cause the *w* to drink the
Num 5:26 cause the *w* to drink the water
Num 5:27 the *w* shall be a curse among her
Num 5:28 if the *w* be not defiled, but be
Num 5:30 shall set the *w* before the LORD,
Num 5:31 this *w* shall bear her iniquity
Num 6:2 When either man or *w* shall
Num 12:1 Ethiopian *w* whom he had married
Num 12:1 for he had married an Ethiopian *w*
Num 25:6 *w* in the sight of Moses, and in
Num 25:8 and the *w* through her belly
Num 25:14 was slain with the Midianitish *w*
Num 25:15 *w* that was slain was Cozbi
Num 30:3 If a *w* also vow a vow unto the
Num 31:17 kill every *w* that hath known man
Deut 15:12 an Hebrew man, or an Hebrew *w*
Deut 17:2 thy God giveth thee, man or *w*
Deut 17:5 bring forth that man or that *w*
Deut 17:5 gates, even that man or that *w*
Deut 21:11 among the captives a beautiful *w*
Deut 22:5 The *w* shall not wear that which
Deut 22:14 upon her, and say, I took this *w*
Deut 22:22 with a *w* married to an husband
Deut 22:22 that lay with the *w*, and the *w*
Deut 28:56 delicate *w* among you, which would
Deut 29:18 should be among you man, or *w*
Josh 2:4 the *w* took the two men, and hid
Josh 6:21 was in the city, both man and *w*
Josh 6:22 house, and bring out thence the *w*
Judg 4:9 sell Sisera into the hand of a *w*
Judg 9:53 a certain *w* cast a piece of a
Judg 9:54 men say not of me, A *w* slew him
Judg 11:2 thou art the son of a strange *w*
Judg 13:3 of the LORD appeared unto the *w*
Judg 13:6 Then the *w* came and told her
Judg 13:9 the *w* as she sat in the field
Judg 13:10 the *w* made haste, and ran, and
Judg 13:11 the man that spakest unto the *w*
Judg 13:13 I said unto the *w* let her beware
Judg 13:24 the *w* bare a son, and called his
Judg 14:1 saw a *w* in Timnath of the
Judg 14:2 I have seen a *w* in Timnath of the
Judg 14:3 Is there never a *w* among the
Judg 14:7 went down, and talked with the *w*
Judg 14:10 his father went down unto the *w*
Judg 16:4 that he loved a *w* in the valley
Judg 19:26 Then came the *w* in the dawning of
Judg 19:27 the *w* his concubine was fallen
Judg 20:4 husband of the *w* that was slain
Judg 21:11 every *w* that hath lain by man
Ruth 1:5 the *w* was left of her two sons and
Ruth 3:8 and, behold, a *w* lay at his feet
Ruth 3:11 know that thou art a virtuous *w*
Ruth 3:14 that a *w* came into the floor
Ruth 4:11 The LORD make the *w* that is come
Ruth 4:12 shall give thee of this young *w*
1Sa 1:15 I am a *w* of a sorrowful spirit
1Sa 1:18 So the *w* went her way, and did eat
1Sa 1:23 So the *w* abode, and gave her son
1Sa 1:26 I am the *w* that stood by thee
1Sa 2:20 *w* for the loan which is lent to
1Sa 15:3 but slay both man and *w*, infant and
1Sa 20:30 son of the perverse rebellious *w*
1Sa 25:3 she was a *w* of good understanding
1Sa 27:9 and left neither man nor *w* alive
1Sa 27:11 saved neither man nor *w* alive
1Sa 28:7 Seek me a *w* that hath a familiar
1Sa 28:7 there is a *w* that hath a familiar
1Sa 28:8 and they came to the *w* by night
1Sa 28:9 the *w* said unto him, Behold, thou
1Sa 28:11 Then said the *w*, Whom shall I
1Sa 28:12 when the *w* saw Samuel, she cried
1Sa 28:12 the *w* spake to Saul, saying, Why
1Sa 28:13 the *w* said unto Saul, I saw gods
1Sa 28:21 the *w* came unto Saul, and saw that
1Sa 28:23 his servants, together with the *w*
1Sa 28:24 the *w* had a fat calf in the house
2Sa 3:8 with a fault concerning this *w*
2Sa 11:2 roof he saw a *w* washing herself
2Sa 11:2 the *w* was very beautiful to look
2Sa 11:3 sent and enquired after the *w*
2Sa 11:5 the *w* conceived, and sent and told
2Sa 11:21 did not a *w* cast a piece of a
2Sa 13:17 said, Put now this *w* out from me
2Sa 14:2 and fetched thence a wise *w*
2Sa 14:2 but be as a *w* that had a long
2Sa 14:4 when the *w* of Tekoah spake to the
2Sa 14:5 answered, I am indeed a widow *w*
2Sa 14:8 And the king said unto the *w*
2Sa 14:9 the *w* of Tekoah said unto the
2Sa 14:12 Then the *w* said, Let thine
2Sa 14:13 the *w* said, Wherefore then hast
2Sa 14:18 king answered and said unto the *w*
2Sa 14:18 the *w* said, Let my lord the king
2Sa 14:19 the *w* answered and said, As thy
2Sa 14:27 she was a *w* of a fair countenance
2Sa 17:19 the *w* took and spread a covering
2Sa 17:20 came to the *w* to the house
2Sa 17:20 the *w* said unto them, They be
2Sa 20:16 cried a wise *w* out of the city
2Sa 20:17 the *w* said, Art thou Joab
2Sa 20:21 the *w* said unto Joab, Behold, his
2Sa 20:22 Then the *w* went unto all the
1Kin 3:17 And the one *w* said, O my lord, I
1Kin 3:17 this *w* dwell in one house
1Kin 3:18 that this *w* was delivered also
1Kin 3:22 And the other *w* said, Nay
1Kin 3:26 Then spake the *w* whose the living
1Kin 11:26 name was Zeruah, a widow *w*
1Kin 14:5 feign herself to be another *w*
1Kin 17:9 a widow *w* there to sustain thee
1Kin 17:10 the widow *w* was there gathering
1Kin 17:17 things, that the son of the *w*
1Kin 17:24 the *w* said to Elijah, Now by this
2Kin 4:1 Now there cried a certain *w* of
2Kin 4:8 to Shunem, where was a great *w*
2Kin 4:17 the *w* conceived, and bare a son at
2Kin 6:26 wall, there cried a *w* unto him
2Kin 6:28 This *w* said unto me, Give thy son
2Kin 6:30 the king heard the words of the *w*
2Kin 8:1 Then spake Elisha unto the *w*
2Kin 8:2 the *w* arose, and did after the
2Kin 8:3 that the *w* returned out of the
2Kin 8:5 body to life, that, behold, the *w*
2Kin 8:5 My lord, O king, this is the *w*
2Kin 8:6 And when the king asked the *w*
2Kin 9:34 said, Go, see now this cursed *w*
1Chr 16:3 one of Israel, both man and *w*
2Chr 2:14 The son of a *w* of the daughters
2Chr 15:13 small or great, whether man or *w*
2Chr 24:7 sons of Athaliah, that wicked *w*
Est 4:11 that whosoever, whether man or *w*
Job 14:1 is born of a *w* is of few days
Job 15:14 and he which is born of a *w*
Job 25:4 he be clean that is born of a *w*
Job 31:9 heart have been deceived by a *w*
Ps 48:6 and pain, as of a *w* in travail
Ps 58:8 like the untimely birth of a *w*
Ps 113:9 maketh the barren *w* to keep house
Prov 2:16 deliver thee from the strange *w*
Prov 5:3 a strange *w* drop as an honeycomb
Prov 5:20 son, be ravished with a strange *w*
Prov 6:24 To keep thee from the evil *w*
Prov 6:24 of the tongue of a strange *w*
Prov 6:26 For by means of a whorish *w* a man
Prov 6:32 with a *w* lacketh understanding
Prov 7:5 may keep thee from the strange *w*
Prov 7:10 there met him a *w* with the attire
Prov 9:13 A foolish *w* is clamorous
Prov 11:16 A gracious *w* retaineth honour
Prov 11:22 so is a fair *w* which is without
Prov 12:4 A virtuous *w* is a crown to her
Prov 14:1 Every wise *w* buildeth her house
Prov 20:16 a pledge of him for a strange *w*
Prov 21:9 housetop, than with a brawling *w*
Prov 21:19 with a contentious and an angry *w*
Prov 23:27 a strange *w* is a narrow pit
Prov 25:24 housetop, than with a brawling *w*
Prov 27:13 a pledge of him for a strange *w*
Prov 27:15 day and a contentious *w* are alike
Prov 30:20 is the way of an adulterous *w*
Prov 30:23 For an odious *w* when she is
Prov 31:10 Who can find a virtuous *w*
Prov 31:30 but a *w* that feareth the LORD,
Eccl 7:26 find more bitter than death the *w*
Eccl 7:28 but a *w* among all those have I
Is 13:8 be in pain as a *w* that travaileth
Is 21:3 the pangs of a *w* that travaileth
Is 26:17 Like as a *w* with child, that
Is 42:14 will I cry like a travailing *w*
Is 45:10 or to the *w*, What hast thou
Is 49:15 Can a *w* forget her sucking child,
Is 54:6 hath called thee as a *w* forsaken
Jer 4:31 a voice as of a *w* in travail
Jer 6:2 of Zion to a comely and delicate *w*
Jer 6:24 us, and pain, as of a *w* in travail
Jer 13:21 take thee, as a *w* in travail
Jer 22:23 the pain as of a *w* in travail
Jer 30:6 as a *w* in travail, and all faces
Jer 31:8 the *w* with child and her that
Jer 31:22 earth, A *w* shall compass a man
Jer 44:7 to cut off from you man and *w*
Jer 48:41 as the heart of a *w* in her pangs
Jer 49:22 as the heart of a *w* in her pangs

## WOMANKIND



## WOMAN'S



## WOMB



## WOMBS



## WOMEN

Neh 7:67 and five singing men and singing *w*
Neh 8:2 the congregation both of men and *w*
Neh 8:3 midday, before the men and the *w*
Neh 13:26 him did outlandish *w* cause to sin
Est 1:9 the *w* in the royal house which
Est 1:17 shall come abroad unto all *w*
Est 2:3 the palace, to the house of the *w*
Est 2:3 chamberlain, keeper of the *w*
Est 2:8 custody of Hegai, keeper of the *w*
Est 2:9 best place of the house of the *w*
Est 2:12 according to the manner of the *w*
Est 2:12 things for the purifying of the *w*
Est 2:13 of the *w* unto the king's house
Est 2:14 into the second house of the *w*
Est 2:15 chamberlain, the keeper of the *w*
Est 2:17 king loved Esther above all the *w*
Est 3:13 and old, little children and *w*
Est 8:11 them, both little ones and *w*
Job 2:10 as one of the foolish *w* speaketh
Job 42:15 in all the land were no *w* found
Ps 45:9 were among thy honourable *w*
Prov 22:14 mouth of strange *w* is a deep pit
Prov 23:33 Thine eyes shall behold strange *w*
Prov 31:3 Give not thy strength unto *w*
Eccl 2:8 *w* singers, and the delights of the
Song 1:8 know not, O thou fairest among *w*
Song 5:9 beloved, O thou fairest among *w*
Song 6:1 gone, O thou fairest among *w*
Is 3:12 oppressors, and *w* rule over them
Is 4:1 in that day seven *w* shall take
Is 19:16 day shall Egypt be like unto *w*
Is 27:11 the *w* come, and set them on fire
Is 32:9 Rise up, ye *w* that are at ease
Is 32:10 ye be troubled, ye careless *w*
Is 32:11 Tremble, ye *w* that are at ease
Jer 7:18 the *w* knead their dough, to make
Jer 9:17 ye, and call for the mourning *w*
Jer 9:17 and send for cunning *w*, that they
Jer 9:20 hear the word of the LORD, O ye *w*
Jer 38:22 all the *w* that are left in the
Jer 38:22 those *w* shall say, Thy friends
Jer 40:7 had committed unto him men, and *w*
Jer 41:16 even mighty men of war, and the *w*
Jer 43:6 Even men, and *w*, and children, and
Jer 44:15 all the *w* that stood by, a great
Jer 44:20 people, to the men, and to the *w*
Jer 44:24 all the people, and to all the *w*
Jer 50:37 and they shall become as *w*
Jer 51:30 they became as *w*
Lam 2:20 Shall the *w* eat their fruit, and
Lam 4:10 The hands of the pitiful *w* have
Lam 5:11 They ravished the *w* in Zion
Eze 8:14 there sat *w* weeping for Tammuz
Eze 9:6 maids, and little children, and *w*
Eze 13:18 Woe to the *w* that sew pillows to
Eze 16:34 from other *w* in thy whoredoms
Eze 16:38 as *w* that break wedlock and shed
Eze 16:41 upon thee in the sight of many *w*
Eze 23:2 Son of man, there were two *w*
Eze 23:10 and she became famous among *w*
Eze 23:44 and unto Aholibah, the lewd *w*
Eze 23:45 the manner of *w* that shed blood
Eze 23:48 that all *w* may be taught not to
Dan 11:17 shall give him the daughter of *w*
Dan 11:37 his fathers, nor the desire of *w*
Hos 13:16 their *w* with child shall be
Amos 1:13 up the *w* with child of Gilead
Mic 2:9 The *w* of my people have ye cast
Nah 3:13 people in the midst of thee are *w*
Zec 5:9 and, behold, there came out two *w*
Zec 8:4 old *w* dwell in the streets of
Zec 14:2 houses rifled, and the *w* ravished
Mt 11:11 Among them that are born of *w*
Mt 14:21 about five thousand men, beside *w*
Mt 15:38 were four thousand men, beside *w*
Mt 24:41 Two *w* shall be grinding at the
Mt 27:55 many *w* were there beholding afar
Mt 28:5 angel answered and said unto the *w*
Mk 15:40 There were also *w* looking on afar
Mk 15:41 many other *w* which came up with
Lk 1:28 blessed art thou among *w*
Lk 1:42 and said, Blessed art thou among *w*
Lk 7:28 Among those that are born of *w*
Lk 8:2 And certain *w*, which had been
Lk 17:35 Two *w* shall be grinding together
Lk 23:27 great company of people, and of *w*
Lk 23:49 the *w* that followed him from
Lk 23:55 the *w* also, which came with him
Lk 24:10 other *w* that were with them,
Lk 24:22 certain *w* also of our company
Lk 24:24 it even so as the *w* had said
Acts 1:14 and supplication, with the *w*
Acts 5:14 Lord, multitudes both of men and *w*
Acts 8:3 *w* committed them to prison
Acts 8:12 they were baptized, both men and *w*
Acts 9:2 way, whether they were men or *w*
Acts 13:50 up the devout and honourable *w*
Acts 16:13 spake unto the *w* which resorted
Acts 17:4 and of the chief *w* not a few
Acts 17:12 of honourable *w* which were Greeks
Acts 22:4 into prisons both men and *w*
Rom 1:26 for even their *w* did change the
1Cor 14:34 Let your *w* keep silence in the
1Cor 14:35 for it is a shame for *w* to speak
Phil 4:3 help those *w* which laboured with
1Ti 2:9 that *w* adorn themselves in modest
1Ti 2:10 But (which becometh *w* professing
1Ti 5:2 The elder *w* as mothers
1Ti 5:14 that the younger *w* marry, bear
2Ti 3:6 captive silly *w* laden with sins
Titus 2:3 The aged *w* likewise, that they be
Titus 2:4 may teach the young *w* to be sober
Heb 11:35 *W* received their dead raised to
1Pet 3:5 in the old time the holy *w* also
Rev 9:8 And they had hair as the hair of *w*
Rev 14:4 which were not defiled with *w*

**WOMEN'S**

Est 2:11 before the court of the *w* house

**WOMENSERVANTS**

Gen 20:14 and oxen, and menservants, and *w*
Gen 32:5 flocks, and menservants, and *w*
Gen 32:22 took his two wives, and his two *w*

**WON**

1Chr 26:27 Out of the spoils *w* in battles
Prov 18:19 harder to be *w* than a strong city
1Pet 3:1 be *w* by the conversation of the

**WONDER**

Deut 13:1 and giveth thee a sign or a *w*
Deut 13:2 And the sign or the *w* come to pass
Deut 28:46 upon thee for a sign and for a *w*
2Chr 32:31 the *w* that was done in the land
Ps 71:7 I am as a *w* unto many
Is 20:3 *w* upon Egypt and upon Ethiopia
Is 29:9 Stay yourselves, and *w*
Is 29:14 even a marvellous work and a *w*
Jer 4:9 and the prophets shall *w*
Hab 1:5 and regard, and *w* marvellously
Acts 3:10 and they were filled with *w*
Acts 13:41 Behold, ye despisers, and *w*
Rev 12:1 appeared a great *w* in heaven
Rev 12:3 appeared another *w* in heaven
Rev 17:8 that dwell on the earth shall *w*

**WONDERED**

Is 59:16 *w* that there was no intercessor
Is 63:5 I *w* that there was none to uphold
Zec 3:8 for they are men *w* at
Mt 15:31 Insomuch that the multitude *w*
Mk 6:51 themselves beyond measure, and *w*
Lk 2:18 all they that heard it *w* at those
Lk 4:22 *w* at the gracious words which
Lk 8:25 And they being afraid *w*, saying
Lk 9:43 But while they *w* every one at all
Lk 11:14 and the people *w*
Lk 24:41 yet believed not for joy, and *w*
Acts 7:31 Moses saw it, he *w* at the sight
Acts 8:13 he continued with Philip, and *w*
Rev 13:3 all the world *w* after the beast
Rev 17:6 I *w* with great admiration

**WONDERFUL**

Deut 28:59 the LORD will make thy plagues *w*
2Sa 1:26 thy love to me was *w*, passing the
2Chr 2:9 about to build shall be *w* great
Job 42:3 things too *w* for me, which I knew
Ps 40:5 are thy *w* works which thou hast
Ps 78:4 his *w* works that he hath done
Ps 107:8 for his *w* works to the children
Ps 107:15 for his *w* works to the children
Ps 107:21 for his *w* works to the children
Ps 107:31 for his *w* works to the children
Ps 111:4 He hath made his *w* works to be
Ps 119:129 Thy testimonies are *w*
Ps 139:6 Such knowledge is too *w* for me
Prov 30:18 things which are too *w* for me
Is 9:6 and his name shall be called *W*
Is 25:1 for thou hast done *w* things
Is 28:29 which is *w* in counsel, and
Jer 5:30 A *w* and horrible thing is
Mt 7:22 and in thy name done many *w* works
Mt 21:15 scribes saw the *w* things that he
Acts 2:11 in our tongues the *w* works of God

**WONDERFULLY**

1Sa 6:6 when he had wrought *w* among them
Ps 139:14 for I am fearfully and *w* made
Lam 1:9 therefore she came down *w*
Dan 8:24 and he shall destroy *w*, and shall

**WONDERING**

Gen 24:21 the man *w* at her held his peace,
Lk 24:12 *w* in himself at that which was
Acts 3:11 is called Solomon's, greatly *w*

**WONDEROUSLY**

Judg 13:19 and the angel did *w*

**WONDERS**

Ex 3:20 smite Egypt with all my *w* which I
Ex 4:21 do all those *w* before Pharaoh
Ex 7:3 my *w* in the land of Egypt
Ex 11:9 that my *w* may be multiplied in
Ex 11:10 did all these *w* before Pharaoh
Ex 15:11 fearful in praises, doing *w*
Deut 4:34 by temptations, by signs, and by *w*
Deut 6:22 And the LORD shewed signs and *w*
Deut 7:19 eyes saw, and the signs, and the *w*
Deut 26:8 and with signs, and with *w*
Deut 34:11 In all the signs and the *w*
Josh 3:5 the LORD will do *w* among you
1Chr 16:12 works that he hath done, his *w*
Neh 9:10 *w* upon Pharaoh, and on all his
Neh 9:17 thy *w* that thou didst among them
Job 9:10 yea, and *w* without number
Ps 77:11 I will remember thy *w* of old
Ps 77:14 Thou art the God that doest *w*
Ps 78:11 his *w* that he had shewed them
Ps 78:43 his *w* in the field of Zoan
Ps 88:10 Wilt thou shew *w* to the dead
Ps 88:12 Shall thy *w* be known in the dark
Ps 89:5 And the heavens shall praise thy *w*
Ps 96:3 heathen, his *w* among all people
Ps 105:5 his *w*, and the judgments of his
Ps 105:27 them, and *w* in the land of Ham
Ps 106:7 understood not thy *w* in Egypt
Ps 107:24 of the LORD, and his *w* in the deep
Ps 135:9 *w* into the midst of thee, O Egypt
Ps 136:4 To him who alone doeth great *w*
Is 8:18 for *w* in Israel from the LORD of
Jer 32:20 *w* in the land of Egypt, even unto
Jer 32:21 of Egypt with signs, and with *w*
Dan 4:2 *w* that the high God hath wrought
Dan 4:3 and how mighty are his *w*
Dan 6:27 *w* in heaven and in earth, who hath
Dan 12:6 shall it be to the end of these *w*
Joel 2:30 I will shew *w* in the heavens and
Mt 24:24 and shall shew great signs and *w*
Mk 13:22 rise, and shall shew signs and *w*
Jn 4:48 him, Except ye see signs and *w*
Acts 2:19 I will shew *w* in heaven above, and
Acts 2:22 of God among you by miracles and *w*
Acts 2:43 and many *w* and signs were done by
Acts 4:30 *w* may be done by the name of thy
Acts 5:12 *w* wrought among the people
Acts 6:8 of faith and power, did great *w*
Acts 7:36 out, after that he had shewed *w*
Acts 14:3 *w* to be done by their hands
Acts 15:12 *w* God had wrought among the
Rom 15:19 Through mighty signs and *w*
2Cor 12:12 in all patience, in signs, and *w*
2Th 2:9 all power and signs and lying *w*
Heb 2:4 witness, both with signs and *w*
Rev 13:13 And he doeth great *w*, so that he

**WONDROUS**

1Chr 16:9 him, talk ye of all his *w* works
Job 37:14 and consider the *w* works of God
Job 37:16 the *w* works of him which is
Ps 26:7 and tell of all thy *w* works
Ps 71:17 have I declared thy *w* works
Ps 72:18 Israel, who only doeth *w* things
Ps 75:1 name is near thy *w* works declare
Ps 78:32 and believed not for his *w* works
Ps 86:10 thou art great, and doest *w* things
Ps 105:2 talk ye of all his *w* works
Ps 106:22 *W* works in the land of Ham, and
Ps 119:18 that I may behold *w* things out of
Ps 119:27 so shall I talk of thy *w* works
Ps 145:5 of thy majesty, and of thy *w* works
Jer 21:2 us according to all his *w* works

**WONDROUSLY**

Joel 2:26 God, that hath dealt *w* with you

## WONT

Ex 21:29 But if the ox were *w* to push with
Num 22:30 was I ever *w* to do so unto thee
1Sa 30:31 and his men were *w* to haunt
2Sa 20:18 They were *w* to speak in old time,
Dan 3:19 more than it was *w* to be heated
Mt 27:15 *w* to release unto the people a
Mk 10:1 and, as he was *w*, he taught them
Lk 22:39 came out, and went, as he was *w*
Acts 16:13 where prayer was *w* to be made

## WOOD

Gen 6:14 Make thee an ark of gopher *w*
Gen 22:3 clave the *w* for the burnt
Gen 22:6 Abraham took the *w* of the burnt
Gen 22:7 he said, Behold the fire and the *w*
Gen 22:9 there, and laid the *w* in order
Gen 22:9 laid him on the altar upon the *w*
Ex 7:19 of Egypt, both in vessels of *w*
Ex 25:5 and badgers' skins, and shittim *w*
Ex 25:10 shall make an ark of shittim *w*
Ex 25:13 shalt make staves of shittim *w*
Ex 25:23 also make a table of shittim *w*
Ex 25:28 make the staves of shittim *w*
Ex 26:15 of shittim *w* standing up
Ex 26:26 thou shalt make bars of shittim *w*
Ex 26:32 of shittim *w* overlaid with gold
Ex 26:37 hanging five pillars of shittim *w*
Ex 27:1 shalt make an altar of shittim *w*
Ex 27:6 the altar, staves of shittim *w*
Ex 30:1 of shittim *w* shalt thou make it
Ex 30:5 make the staves of shittim *w*
Ex 35:7 and badgers' skins, and shittim *w*
Ex 35:24 *w* for any work of the service
Ex 35:33 to set them, and in carving of *w*
Ex 36:20 for the tabernacle of shittim *w*
Ex 36:31 And he made bars of shittim *w*
Ex 36:36 four pillars of shittim *w*
Ex 37:1 made the ark of shittim *w*
Ex 37:4 And he made staves of shittim *w*
Ex 37:10 And he made the table of shittim *w*
Ex 37:15 he made the staves of shittim *w*
Ex 37:25 the incense altar of shittim *w*
Ex 37:28 he made the staves of shittim *w*
Ex 38:1 of burnt offering of shittim *w*
Ex 38:6 he made the staves of shittim *w*
Lev 1:7 lay the *w* in order upon the fire
Lev 1:8 in order upon the *w* that is on
Lev 1:12 *w* that is on the fire which is
Lev 1:17 upon the *w* that is upon the fire
Lev 3:5 which is upon the *w* that is on
Lev 4:12 and burn him on the *w* with fire
Lev 6:12 shall burn *w* on it every morning
Lev 11:32 whether it be any vessel of *w*
Lev 14:4 birds alive and clean, and cedar *w*
Lev 14:6 he shall take it, and the cedar *w*
Lev 14:49 the house two birds, and cedar *w*
Lev 14:51 And he shall take the cedar *w*
Lev 14:52 living bird, and with the cedar *w*
Lev 15:12 every vessel of *w* shall be rinsed
Num 13:20 lean, whether there be *w* therein
Num 19:6 And the priest shall take cedar *w*
Num 31:20 hair, and all things made of *w*
Num 35:18 him with an hand weapon of *w*
Deut 4:28 gods, the work of men's hands, *w*
Deut 10:1 mount, and make thee an ark of *w*
Deut 10:3 And I made an ark of shittim *w*
Deut 19:5 As when a man goeth into the *w*
Deut 19:5 his neighbour to hew *w*
Deut 28:36 shalt thou serve other gods, *w*
Deut 28:64 thy fathers have known, even *w*
Deut 29:11 from the hewer of thy *w* unto the
Deut 29:17 abominations, and their idols, *w*
Josh 9:21 but let them be hewers of *w*
Josh 9:23 being bondmen, and hewers of *w*
Josh 9:27 made them that day hewers of *w*
Josh 17:15 then get thee up to the *w* country
Josh 17:18 for it is a *w*, and thou shalt cut
Judg 6:26 a burnt sacrifice with the *w* of
1Sa 6:14 and they clave the *w* of the cart
1Sa 14:25 all they of the land came to a *w*
1Sa 14:26 the people were come into the *w*
1Sa 23:15 in the wilderness of Ziph in a *w*
1Sa 23:16 and went to David into the *w*
1Sa 23:18 and David abode in the *w*, and
1Sa 23:19 with us in strong holds in the *w*
2Sa 6:5 of instruments made of fir *w*
2Sa 18:6 battle was in the *w* of Ephraim
2Sa 18:8 the *w* devoured more people that
2Sa 18:17 him into a great pit in the *w*
2Sa 24:22 instruments of the oxen for *w*
1Kin 6:15 covered them on the inside with *w*
1Kin 18:23 cut it in pieces, and lay it on *w*
1Kin 18:23 the other bullock, and lay it on *w*
1Kin 18:33 And he put the *w* in order, and cut
1Kin 18:33 in pieces, and laid him on the *w*
1Kin 18:33 the burnt sacrifice, and on the *w*
1Kin 18:38 the burnt sacrifice, and the *w*
2Kin 2:24 forth two she bears out of the *w*
2Kin 6:4 came to Jordan, they cut down *w*
2Kin 19:18 but the work of men's hands, *w*
1Chr 16:33 Then shall the trees of the *w*
1Chr 21:23 the threshing instruments for *w*
1Chr 22:4 brought much cedar *w* to David
1Chr 29:2 of iron, and *w* for things of *w*
2Chr 2:16 we will cut *w* out of Lebanon, as
Neh 8:4 scribe stood upon a pulpit of *w*
Neh 10:34 for the *w* offering, to bring it
Neh 13:31 for the *w* offering, at times
Job 41:27 as straw, and brass as rotten *w*
Ps 80:13 boar out of the *w* doth waste it
Ps 83:14 As the fire burneth a *w*, and as
Ps 96:12 all the trees of the *w* rejoice
Ps 132:6 found it in the fields of the *w*
Ps 141:7 cleaveth *w* upon the earth
Prov 26:20 Where no *w* is, there the fire
Prov 26:21 to burning coals, and *w* to fire
Eccl 2:6 to water therewith the *w* that
Eccl 10:9 he that cleaveth *w* shall be
Song 2:3 tree among the trees of the *w*
Song 3:9 a chariot of the *w* of Lebanon
Is 7:2 as the trees of the *w* are moved
Is 10:15 up itself, as if it were no *w*
Is 30:33 pile thereof is fire and much *w*
Is 37:19 but the work of men's hands, *w*
Is 45:20 up the *w* of their graven image
Is 60:17 for *w* brass, and for stones iron
Jer 5:14 thy mouth fire, and this people *w*
Jer 7:18 The children gather *w*, and the
Jer 28:13 Thou hast broken the yokes of *w*
Jer 46:22 her with axes, as hewers of *w*
Lam 5:4 our *w* is sold unto us
Lam 5:13 and the children fell under the *w*
Eze 15:3 Shall *w* be taken thereof to do
Eze 20:32 of the countries, to serve *w*
Eze 24:10 Heap on *w*, kindle the fire,
Eze 39:10 shall take no *w* out of the field
Eze 41:16 door, cieled with *w* round about
Eze 41:22 The altar of *w* was three cubits
Eze 41:22 and the walls thereof, were of *w*
Dan 5:4 silver, of brass, of iron, of *w*
Dan 5:23 and gold, of brass, iron, *w*
Mic 7:14 which dwell solitarily in the *w*
Hab 2:19 Woe unto him that saith to the *w*
Hag 1:8 Go up to the mountain, and bring *w*
Zec 12:6 an hearth of fire among the *w*
1Cor 3:12 gold, silver, precious stones, *w*
2Ti 2:20 gold and of silver, but also of *w*
Rev 9:20 and brass, and stone, and of *w*
Rev 18:12 silk, and scarlet, and all thyine *w*
Rev 18:12 manner vessels of most precious *w*

## WOODS

Eze 34:25 the wilderness, and sleep in the *w*

## WOOF

Lev 13:48 Whether it be in the warp, or *w*
Lev 13:49 either in the warp, or in the *w*
Lev 13:51 either in the warp, or in the *w*
Lev 13:52 that garment, whether warp or *w*
Lev 13:53 either in the warp, or in the *w*
Lev 13:56 out of the warp, or out of the *w*
Lev 13:57 either in the warp, or in the *w*
Lev 13:58 And the garment, either warp, or *w*
Lev 13:59 linen, either in the warp, or *w*

## WOOL

Judg 6:37 put a fleece of *w* in the floor
2Kin 3:4 hundred thousand rams, with the *w*
Ps 147:16 He giveth snow like *w*
Prov 31:13 She seeketh *w*, and flax, and
Is 1:18 like crimson, they shall be as *w*
Is 51:8 and the worm shall eat them like *w*
Eze 27:18 in the wine of Helbon, and white *w*
Eze 34:3 fat, and ye clothe you with the *w*
Eze 44:17 no *w* shall come upon them, whiles
Dan 7:9 hair of his head like the pure *w*
Hos 2:5 me my bread and my water, my *w*
Hos 2:9 thereof, and will recover my *w*
Heb 9:19 goats, with water, and scarlet *w*
Rev 1:14 and his hairs were white like *w*

## WOOLLEN

Lev 13:47 is in, whether it be a *w* garment
Lev 13:48 of linen, or of *w*
Lev 13:52 in *w* or in linen, or any thing of
Lev 13:59 in a garment of *w* or linen
Lev 19:19 of linen and *w* come upon thee
Deut 22:11 garment of divers sorts, as of *w*

## WORD

Gen 15:1 After these things the *w* of the
Gen 15:4 the *w* of the LORD came unto him,
Gen 30:34 it might be according to thy *w*
Gen 37:14 and bring me *w* again
Gen 41:40 according unto thy *w* shall all my
Gen 44:2 to the *w* that Joseph had spoken
Gen 44:18 speak a *w* in my lord's ears, and
Ex 8:10 he said, Be it according to thy *w*
Ex 8:13 did according to the *w* of Moses
Ex 8:31 did according to the *w* of Moses
Ex 9:20 He that feared the *w* of the LORD
Ex 9:21 he that regarded not the *w* of the
Ex 12:35 did according to the *w* of Moses
Ex 14:12 Is not this the *w* that we did
Ex 32:28 did according to the *w* of Moses
Lev 10:7 did according to the *w* of Moses
Num 3:16 according to the *w* of the LORD
Num 3:51 according to the *w* of the LORD
Num 4:45 the *w* of the LORD by the hand of
Num 11:23 thou shalt see now whether my *w*
Num 13:26 and brought back *w* unto them
Num 14:20 have pardoned according to thy *w*
Num 15:31 hath despised the *w* of the LORD
Num 20:24 my *w* at the water of Meribah
Num 22:8 and I will bring you *w* again
Num 22:18 beyond the *w* of the LORD my God
Num 22:20 but yet the *w* which I shall say
Num 22:35 but only the *w* that I shalt speak
Num 22:38 the *w* that God putteth in my
Num 23:5 the LORD put a *w* in Balaam's
Num 23:16 put a *w* in his mouth, and said, Go
Num 27:21 at his *w* shall they go out
Num 27:21 at his *w* they shall come in, both
Num 30:2 he shall not break his *w*, he
Num 36:5 according to the *w* of the LORD
Deut 1:22 bring us *w* again by what way we
Deut 1:25 unto us, and brought us *w* again
Deut 4:2 unto the *w* which I command you
Deut 5:5 to shew you the *w* of the LORD
Deut 8:3 but by every *w* that proceedeth
Deut 9:5 that he may perform the *w* which
Deut 18:20 presume to speak a *w* in my name
Deut 18:21 How shall we know the *w* which the
Deut 21:5 and by their *w* shall every
Deut 30:14 But the *w* is very nigh unto thee,
Deut 33:9 for they have observed thy *w*
Deut 34:5 according to the *w* of the LORD
Josh 1:13 Remember the *w* which Moses the
Josh 6:10 neither shall any *w* proceed out
Josh 8:27 according unto the *w* of the LORD
Josh 8:35 There was not a *w* of all that
Josh 14:7 I brought him *w* again as it was
Josh 14:10 the LORD spake this *w* unto Moses
Josh 19:50 According to the *w* of the LORD
Josh 22:9 according to the *w* of the LORD by
Josh 22:32 Israel, and brought them *w* again
1Sa 1:23 only the LORD establish his *w*
1Sa 3:1 the *w* of the LORD was precious in
1Sa 3:7 neither was the *w* of the LORD yet
1Sa 3:21 in Shiloh by the *w* of the LORD
1Sa 4:1 the *w* of Samuel came to all
1Sa 9:27 that I may shew thee the *w* of God
1Sa 15:10 Then came the *w* of the LORD unto
1Sa 15:23 hast rejected the *w* of the LORD
1Sa 15:26 hast rejected the *w* of the LORD
2Sa 3:11 could not answer Abner a *w* again
2Sa 7:4 that the *w* of the LORD came unto
2Sa 7:7 I a *w* with any of the tribes of
2Sa 7:25 the *w* that thou hast spoken
2Sa 14:12 speak one *w* unto my lord the king
2Sa 14:17 The *w* of my lord the king shall
2Sa 15:28 until there come *w* from you to
2Sa 19:10 not a *w* of bringing the king back
2Sa 19:14 they sent this *w* unto the king
2Sa 22:31 the *w* of the LORD is tried
2Sa 23:2 by me, and his *w* was in my tongue
2Sa 24:4 king's *w* prevailed against Joab
2Sa 24:11 the *w* of the LORD came unto the
1Kin 2:4 *w* which he spake concerning me
1Kin 2:23 this *w* against his own life
1Kin 2:27 he might fulfil the *w* of the LORD

1Kin 2:30 Benaiah brought the king *w* again
1Kin 2:42 The *w* that I have heard is good
1Kin 6:11 the *w* of the LORD came to Solomon
1Kin 6:12 will I perform my *w* with thee
1Kin 8:20 performed his *w* that he spake
1Kin 8:26 now, O God of Israel, let thy *w*
1Kin 8:56 one *w* of all his good promise
1Kin 12:22 But the *w* of God came unto
1Kin 12:24 therefore to the *w* of the LORD
1Kin 12:24 according to the *w* of the LORD
1Kin 13:1 by the *w* of the LORD unto Beth-el
1Kin 13:2 the altar in the *w* of the LORD
1Kin 13:5 had given by the *w* of the LORD
1Kin 13:9 charged me by the *w* of the LORD
1Kin 13:17 said to me by the *w* of the LORD
1Kin 13:18 unto me by the *w* of the LORD
1Kin 13:20 that the *w* of the LORD came unto
1Kin 13:26 unto the *w* of the LORD
1Kin 13:26 according to the *w* of the LORD
1Kin 13:32 saying which he cried by the *w* of
1Kin 14:18 according to the *w* of the LORD
1Kin 16:1 Then the *w* of the LORD came to
1Kin 16:7 the *w* of the LORD against Baasha
1Kin 16:12 according to the *w* of the LORD
1Kin 16:34 according to the *w* of the LORD
1Kin 17:1 years, but according to my *w*
1Kin 17:2 the *w* of the LORD came unto him,
1Kin 17:5 according unto the *w* of the LORD
1Kin 17:8 the *w* of the LORD came unto him,
1Kin 17:16 according to the *w* of the LORD
1Kin 17:24 that the *w* of the LORD in thy
1Kin 18:1 that the *w* of the LORD came to
1Kin 18:21 the people answered him not a *w*
1Kin 18:31 unto whom the *w* of the LORD came,
1Kin 18:36 done all these things at thy *w*
1Kin 19:9 the *w* of the LORD came to him, and
1Kin 20:9 departed, and brought him *w* again
1Kin 20:35 neighbour in the *w* of the LORD
1Kin 21:4 displeased because of the *w* which
1Kin 21:17 the *w* of the LORD came to Elijah
1Kin 21:28 the *w* of the LORD came to Elijah
1Kin 22:5 at the *w* of the LORD to day
1Kin 22:13 let thy *w*, I pray thee
1Kin 22:13 be like the *w* of one of them, and
1Kin 22:19 thou therefore the *w* of the LORD
1Kin 22:38 according unto the *w* of the LORD
2Kin 1:16 God in Israel to enquire of his *w*
2Kin 1:17 So he died according to the *w* of
2Kin 3:12 The *w* of the LORD is with him
2Kin 4:44 according to the *w* of the LORD
2Kin 6:18 according to the *w* of Elisha
2Kin 7:1 said, Hear ye the *w* of the LORD
2Kin 7:16 according to the *w* of the LORD
2Kin 9:26 according to the *w* of the LORD
2Kin 9:36 said, This is the *w* of the LORD
2Kin 10:10 nothing of the *w* of the LORD
2Kin 14:25 according to the *w* of the LORD
2Kin 15:12 This was the *w* of the LORD which
2Kin 18:28 Hear the *w* of the great king, the
2Kin 18:36 peace, and answered him not a *w*
2Kin 19:21 This is the *w* that the LORD hath
2Kin 20:4 that the *w* of the LORD came to
2Kin 20:16 Hezekiah, Hear the *w* of the LORD
2Kin 20:19 Good is the *w* of the LORD which
2Kin 22:9 king, and brought the king *w* again
2Kin 22:20 And they brought the king *w* again
2Kin 23:16 according to the *w* of the LORD
2Kin 24:2 according to the *w* of the LORD
1Chr 10:13 even against the *w* of the LORD
1Chr 11:3 according to the *w* of the LORD by
1Chr 11:10 according to the *w* of the LORD
1Chr 12:23 according to the *w* of the LORD
1Chr 15:15 according to the *w* of the LORD
1Chr 16:15 the *w* which he commanded to a
1Chr 17:3 that the *w* of God came to Nathan,
1Chr 17:6 spake I a *w* to any of the judges
1Chr 21:4 king's *w* prevailed against Joab
1Chr 21:6 for the king's *w* was abominable
1Chr 21:12 therefore advise thyself what *w* I
1Chr 22:8 But the *w* of the LORD came to me,
2Chr 6:10 his *w* that he hath spoken
2Chr 6:17 let thy *w* be verified, which thou
2Chr 10:15 that the LORD might perform his *w*
2Chr 11:2 But the *w* of the LORD came to
2Chr 12:7 the *w* of the LORD came to
2Chr 18:4 at the *w* of the LORD to day
2Chr 18:12 let thy *w* therefore, I pray thee,
2Chr 18:18 Therefore hear the *w* of the LORD
2Chr 30:12 the princes, by the *w* of the LORD
2Chr 34:16 and brought the king *w* back again
2Chr 34:21 have not kept the *w* of the LORD
2Chr 34:28 So they brought the king *w* again
2Chr 35:6 the *w* of the LORD by the hand of
2Chr 36:21 To fulfil the *w* of the LORD by
2Chr 36:22 that the *w* of the LORD spoken by
Ezr 1:1 that the *w* of the LORD by the
Ezr 6:11 that whosoever shall alter this *w*
Ezr 10:5 should do according to this *w*
Neh 1:8 the *w* that thou commandedst thy
Est 1:21 did according to the *w* of Memucan
Est 7:8 As the *w* went out of the king's
Job 2:13 and none spake a *w* unto him
Ps 17:4 by the *w* of thy lips I have kept
Ps 18:30 the *w* of the LORD is tried
Ps 33:4 For the *w* of the LORD is right
Ps 33:6 By the *w* of the LORD were the
Ps 56:4 In God I will praise his *w*
Ps 56:10 In God will I praise his *w*
Ps 56:10 in the LORD will I praise his *w*
Ps 68:11 The Lord gave the *w*
Ps 103:20 unto the voice of his *w*
Ps 105:8 the *w* which he commanded to a
Ps 105:19 Until the time that his *w* came
Ps 105:19 the *w* of the LORD tried him
Ps 105:28 they rebelled not against his *w*
Ps 106:24 land, they believed not his *w*
Ps 107:20 He sent his *w*, and healed them, and
Ps 119:9 heed thereto according to thy *w*
Ps 119:11 Thy *w* have I hid in mine heart,
Ps 119:16 I will not forget thy *w*
Ps 119:17 that I may live, and keep thy *w*
Ps 119:25 thou me according to thy *w*
Ps 119:28 thou me according unto thy *w*
Ps 119:38 Stablish thy *w* unto thy servant,
Ps 119:41 thy salvation, according to thy *w*
Ps 119:42 for I trust in thy *w*
Ps 119:43 take not the *w* of truth utterly
Ps 119:49 Remember the *w* unto thy servant,
Ps 119:50 for thy *w* hath quickened me
Ps 119:58 unto me according to thy *w*
Ps 119:65 O LORD, according unto thy *w*
Ps 119:67 but now have I kept thy *w*
Ps 119:74 because I have hoped in thy *w*
Ps 119:76 to thy *w* unto thy servant
Ps 119:81 but I hope in thy *w*
Ps 119:82 Mine eyes fail for thy *w*, saying,
Ps 119:89 thy *w* is settled in heaven
Ps 119:101 evil way, that I might keep thy *w*
Ps 119:105 Thy *w* is a lamp unto my feet, and
Ps 119:107 me, O LORD, according unto thy *w*
Ps 119:114 I hope in thy *w*
Ps 119:116 Uphold me according unto thy *w*
Ps 119:123 for the *w* of thy righteousness
Ps 119:133 Order my steps in thy *w*
Ps 119:140 Thy *w* is very pure
Ps 119:147 I hoped in thy *w*
Ps 119:148 that I might meditate in thy *w*
Ps 119:154 quicken me according to thy *w*
Ps 119:158 because they kept not thy *w*
Ps 119:160 Thy *w* is true from the beginning
Ps 119:161 my heart standeth in awe of thy *w*
Ps 119:162 I rejoice at thy *w*, as one that
Ps 119:169 understanding according to thy *w*
Ps 119:170 deliver me according to thy *w*
Ps 119:172 My tongue shall speak of thy *w*
Ps 130:5 doth wait, and in his *w* do I hope
Ps 138:2 thy *w* above all thy name
Ps 139:4 For there is not a *w* in my tongue
Ps 147:15 his *w* runneth very swiftly
Ps 147:18 He sendeth out his *w*, and melteth
Ps 147:19 He sheweth his *w* unto Jacob
Ps 148:8 stormy wind fulfilling his *w*
Prov 12:25 but a good *w* maketh it glad
Prov 13:13 the *w* shall be destroyed
Prov 14:15 The simple believeth every *w*
Prov 15:23 a *w* spoken in due season, how
Prov 25:11 A *w* fitly spoken is like apples
Prov 30:5 Every *w* of God is pure
Eccl 8:4 Where the *w* of a king is, there
Is 1:10 Hear the *w* of the LORD, ye rulers
Is 2:1 The *w* that Isaiah the son of Amoz
Is 2:3 the *w* of the LORD from Jerusalem
Is 5:24 despised the *w* of the Holy One of
Is 8:10 speak the *w*, and it shall not
Is 8:20 speak not according to this *w*
Is 9:8 The Lord sent a *w* into Jacob
Is 16:13 This is the *w* that the LORD hath
Is 24:3 for the LORD hath spoken this *w*
Is 28:13 But the *w* of the LORD was unto
Is 28:14 Wherefore hear the *w* of the LORD
Is 29:21 make a man an offender for a *w*
Is 30:12 Israel, Because ye despise this *w*
Is 30:21 ears shall hear a *w* behind thee
Is 36:21 peace, and answered him not a *w*
Is 37:22 This is the *w* which the LORD hath
Is 38:4 Then came the *w* of the LORD to
Is 39:5 Hear the *w* of the LORD of hosts
Is 39:8 Good is the *w* of the LORD which
Is 40:8 but the *w* of our God shall stand
Is 41:28 I asked of them, could answer a *w*
Is 44:26 confirmeth the *w* of his servant
Is 45:23 the *w* is gone out of my mouth in
Is 50:4 I should know how to speak a *w* in
Is 55:11 So shall my *w* be that goeth forth
Is 66:2 spirit, and trembleth at my *w*
Is 66:5 Hear the *w* of the LORD
Is 66:5 ye that tremble at his *w*
Jer 1:2 To whom the *w* of the LORD came in
Jer 1:4 Then the *w* of the LORD came unto
Jer 1:11 Moreover the *w* of the LORD came
Jer 1:12 I will hasten my *w* to perform it
Jer 1:13 the *w* of the LORD came unto me
Jer 2:1 Moreover the *w* of the LORD came
Jer 2:4 Hear ye the *w* of the LORD
Jer 2:31 see ye the *w* of the LORD
Jer 5:13 wind, and the *w* is not in them
Jer 5:14 of hosts, Because ye speak this *w*
Jer 6:10 the *w* of the LORD is unto them a
Jer 7:1 The *w* that came to Jeremiah from
Jer 7:2 house, and proclaim there this *w*
Jer 7:2 Hear the *w* of the LORD, all ye of
Jer 8:9 have rejected the *w* of the LORD
Jer 9:20 Yet hear the *w* of the LORD
Jer 9:20 ear receive the *w* of his mouth
Jer 10:1 Hear ye the *w* which the LORD
Jer 11:1 The *w* that came to Jeremiah from
Jer 13:2 according to the *w* of the LORD
Jer 13:3 the *w* of the LORD came unto me
Jer 13:8 Then the *w* of the LORD came unto
Jer 13:12 thou shalt speak unto them this *w*
Jer 14:1 The *w* of the LORD that came to
Jer 14:17 thou shalt say this *w* unto them
Jer 15:16 thy *w* was unto me the joy and
Jer 16:1 The *w* of the LORD came also unto
Jer 17:15 me, Where is the *w* of the LORD
Jer 17:20 them, Hear ye the *w* of the LORD
Jer 18:1 The *w* which came to Jeremiah from
Jer 18:5 Then the *w* of the LORD came to me
Jer 18:18 nor the *w* from the prophet
Jer 19:3 And say, Hear ye the *w* of the LORD
Jer 20:8 because the *w* of the LORD was
Jer 20:9 But his *w* was in mine heart as a
Jer 21:1 The *w* which came unto Jeremiah
Jer 21:11 say, Hear ye the *w* of the LORD
Jer 22:1 of Judah, and speak there this *w*
Jer 22:2 Hear the *w* of the LORD, O king of
Jer 22:29 earth, hear the *w* of the LORD
Jer 23:18 and hath perceived and heard his *w*
Jer 23:18 who hath marked his *w*, and heard
Jer 23:28 and he that hath my *w*
Jer 23:28 let him speak my *w* faithfully
Jer 23:29 Is not my *w* like as a fire
Jer 23:36 for every man's *w* shall be his
Jer 23:38 Because ye say this *w*, The burden
Jer 24:4 Again the *w* of the LORD came unto
Jer 25:1 The *w* that came to Jeremiah
Jer 25:3 the *w* of the LORD hath come unto
Jer 26:1 Judah came this *w* from the LORD
Jer 26:2 diminish not a *w*
Jer 27:1 *w* unto Jeremiah from the LORD
Jer 27:18 if the *w* of the LORD be with them
Jer 28:7 this *w* that I speak in thine ears
Jer 28:9 when the *w* of the prophet shall
Jer 28:12 Then the *w* of the LORD came unto
Jer 29:10 and perform my good *w* toward you
Jer 29:20 ye therefore the *w* of the LORD
Jer 29:30 Then came the *w* of the LORD unto
Jer 30:1 The *w* that came to Jeremiah from
Jer 31:10 Hear the *w* of the LORD, O ye
Jer 32:1 The *w* that came to Jeremiah from
Jer 32:6 The *w* of the LORD came unto me,
Jer 32:8 according to the *w* of the LORD
Jer 32:8 that this was the *w* of the LORD
Jer 32:26 Then came the *w* of the LORD unto
Jer 33:1 Moreover the *w* of the LORD came
Jer 33:19 the *w* of the LORD came unto
Jer 33:23 Moreover the *w* of the LORD came
Jer 34:1 The *w* which came unto Jeremiah
Jer 34:4 Yet hear the *w* of the LORD
Jer 34:5 for I have pronounced the *w*

| | |
|---|---|
| Jer 34:8 | This is the *w* that came unto |
| Jer 34:12 | Therefore the *w* of the LORD came |
| Jer 35:1 | The *w* which came unto Jeremiah |
| Jer 35:12 | Then came the *w* of the LORD unto |
| Jer 36:1 | that this *w* came unto Jeremiah |
| Jer 36:27 | Then the *w* of the LORD came to |
| Jer 37:6 | Then came the *w* of the LORD unto |
| Jer 37:17 | Is there any *w* from the LORD |
| Jer 38:21 | this is the *w* that the LORD hath |
| Jer 39:15 | Now the *w* of the LORD came unto |
| Jer 40:1 | The *w* that came to Jeremiah from |
| Jer 42:7 | that the *w* of the LORD came unto |
| Jer 42:15 | therefore hear the *w* of the LORD |
| Jer 43:8 | Then came the *w* of the LORD unto |
| Jer 44:1 | The *w* that came to Jeremiah |
| Jer 44:16 | As for the *w* that thou hast |
| Jer 44:24 | Hear the *w* of the LORD, all Judah |
| Jer 44:26 | hear ye the *w* of the LORD |
| Jer 45:1 | The *w* that Jeremiah the prophet |
| Jer 46:1 | The *w* of the LORD which came to |
| Jer 46:13 | The *w* that the LORD spake to |
| Jer 47:1 | The *w* of the LORD that came to |
| Jer 49:34 | The *w* of the LORD that came to |
| Jer 50:1 | The *w* that the LORD spake against |
| Jer 51:59 | The *w* which Jeremiah the prophet |
| Lam 2:17 | he hath fulfilled his *w* that he |
| Eze 1:3 | The *w* of the LORD came expressly |
| Eze 3:16 | that the *w* of the LORD came unto |
| Eze 3:17 | therefore hear the *w* at my mouth |
| Eze 6:1 | the *w* of the LORD came unto me, |
| Eze 6:3 | hear the *w* of the Lord GOD |
| Eze 7:1 | Moreover the *w* of the LORD came |
| Eze 11:14 | Again the *w* of the LORD came unto |
| Eze 12:1 | The *w* of the LORD also came unto |
| Eze 12:8 | came the *w* of the LORD unto me |
| Eze 12:17 | Moreover the *w* of the LORD came |
| Eze 12:21 | the *w* of the LORD came unto me, |
| Eze 12:25 | the *w* that I shall speak shall |
| Eze 12:25 | house, will I say the *w*, and will |
| Eze 12:26 | Again the *w* of the LORD came to |
| Eze 12:28 | but the *w* which I have spoken |
| Eze 13:1 | the *w* of the LORD came unto me, |
| Eze 13:2 | hearts, Hear ye the *w* of the LORD |
| Eze 13:6 | that they would confirm the *w* |
| Eze 14:2 | the *w* of the LORD came unto me, |
| Eze 14:12 | The *w* of the LORD came again to |
| Eze 15:1 | the *w* of the LORD came unto me, |
| Eze 16:1 | Again the *w* of the LORD came unto |
| Eze 16:35 | O harlot, hear the *w* of the LORD |
| Eze 17:1 | the *w* of the LORD came unto me, |
| Eze 17:11 | Moreover the *w* of the LORD came |
| Eze 18:1 | The *w* of the LORD came unto me |
| Eze 20:2 | Then came the *w* of the LORD unto |
| Eze 20:45 | Moreover the *w* of the LORD came |
| Eze 20:46 | drop thy *w* toward the south, and |
| Eze 20:47 | the south, Hear the *w* of the LORD |
| Eze 21:1 | the *w* of the LORD came unto me, |
| Eze 21:2 | drop thy *w* toward the holy places |
| Eze 21:8 | Again the *w* of the LORD came unto |
| Eze 21:18 | The *w* of the LORD came unto me |
| Eze 22:1 | Moreover the *w* of the LORD came |
| Eze 22:17 | the *w* of the LORD came unto me, |
| Eze 22:23 | the *w* of the LORD came unto me, |
| Eze 23:1 | The *w* of the LORD came again unto |
| Eze 24:1 | the *w* of the LORD came unto me, |
| Eze 24:15 | Also the *w* of the LORD came unto |
| Eze 24:20 | The *w* of the LORD came unto me, |
| Eze 25:1 | The *w* of the LORD came again unto |
| Eze 25:3 | Hear the *w* of the Lord GOD |
| Eze 26:1 | that the *w* of the LORD came unto |
| Eze 27:1 | The *w* of the LORD came again unto |
| Eze 28:1 | The *w* of the LORD came again unto |
| Eze 28:11 | Moreover the *w* of the LORD came |
| Eze 28:20 | Again the *w* of the LORD came unto |
| Eze 29:1 | the *w* of the LORD came unto me, |
| Eze 29:17 | the *w* of the LORD came unto me, |
| Eze 30:1 | The *w* of the LORD came again unto |
| Eze 30:20 | that the *w* of the LORD came unto |
| Eze 31:1 | that the *w* of the LORD came unto |
| Eze 32:1 | that the *w* of the LORD came unto |
| Eze 32:17 | that the *w* of the LORD came unto |
| Eze 33:1 | Again the *w* of the LORD came unto |
| Eze 33:7 | thou shalt hear the *w* at my mouth |
| Eze 33:23 | Then the *w* of the LORD came unto |
| Eze 33:30 | hear what is the *w* that cometh |
| Eze 34:1 | the *w* of the Lord came unto me, |
| Eze 34:7 | shepherds, hear the *w* of the LORD |
| Eze 34:9 | shepherds, hear the *w* of the LORD |
| Eze 35:1 | Moreover the *w* of the LORD came |
| Eze 36:1 | of Israel, hear the *w* of the LORD |
| Eze 36:4 | hear the *w* of the Lord GOD |
| Eze 36:16 | Moreover the *w* of the LORD came |
| Eze 37:4 | dry bones, hear the *w* of the LORD |
| Eze 37:15 | The *w* of the LORD came again unto |
| Eze 38:1 | the *w* of the LORD came unto me, |
| Dan 3:28 | him, and have changed the king's *w* |
| Dan 4:17 | demand by the *w* of the holy ones |
| Dan 4:31 | While the *w* was in the king's |
| Dan 9:2 | whereof the *w* of the LORD came to |
| Dan 10:11 | when he had spoken this *w* unto me |
| Hos 1:1 | The *w* of the LORD that came unto |
| Hos 1:2 | of the *w* of the LORD by Hosea |
| Hos 4:1 | Hear the *w* of the LORD, ye |
| Joel 1:1 | The *w* of the LORD that came to |
| Joel 2:11 | he is strong that executeth his *w* |
| Amos 3:1 | Hear this *w* that the LORD hath |
| Amos 4:1 | Hear this *w*, ye kine of Bashan, |
| Amos 5:1 | Hear ye this *w* which I take up |
| Amos 7:16 | hear thou the *w* of the LORD |
| Amos 7:16 | drop not thy *w* against the house |
| Amos 8:12 | and fro to seek the *w* of the LORD |
| Jonah 1:1 | Now the *w* of the LORD came unto |
| Jonah 3:1 | the *w* of the LORD came unto Jonah |
| Jonah 3:3 | according to the *w* of the LORD |
| Jonah 3:6 | For *w* came unto the king of |
| Mic 1:1 | The *w* of the LORD that came to |
| Mic 4:2 | the *w* of the LORD from Jerusalem |
| Hab 3:9 | oaths of the tribes, even thy *w* |
| Zeph 1:1 | The *w* of the LORD which came unto |
| Zeph 2:5 | the *w* of the LORD is against you |
| Hag 1:1 | came the *w* of the LORD by Haggai |
| Hag 1:3 | Then came the *w* of the LORD by |
| Hag 2:1 | came the *w* of the LORD by the |
| Hag 2:5 | According to the *w* that I |
| Hag 2:10 | came the *w* of the LORD by Haggai |
| Hag 2:20 | again the *w* of the LORD came unto |
| Zec 1:1 | came the *w* of the LORD unto |
| Zec 1:7 | came the *w* of the LORD unto |
| Zec 4:6 | This is the *w* of the LORD unto |
| Zec 4:8 | Moreover the *w* of the LORD came |
| Zec 6:9 | the *w* of the LORD came unto me, |
| Zec 7:1 | that the *w* of the LORD came unto |
| Zec 7:4 | Then came the *w* of the LORD of |
| Zec 7:8 | the *w* of the LORD came unto |
| Zec 8:1 | Again the *w* of the LORD of hosts |
| Zec 8:18 | the *w* of the LORD of hosts came |
| Zec 9:1 | The burden of the *w* of the LORD |
| Zec 11:11 | that it was the *w* of the LORD |
| Zec 12:1 | The burden of the *w* of the LORD |
| Mal 1:1 | The burden of the *w* of the LORD |
| Mt 2:8 | have found him, bring me *w* again |
| Mt 2:13 | thou there until I bring thee *w* |
| Mt 4:4 | but by every *w* that proceedeth |
| Mt 8:8 | but speak the *w* only, and my |
| Mt 8:16 | cast out the spirits with his *w* |
| Mt 12:32 | whosoever speaketh a *w* against |
| Mt 12:36 | That every idle *w* that men shall |
| Mt 13:19 | one heareth the *w* of the kingdom |
| Mt 13:20 | the same is he that heareth the *w* |
| Mt 13:21 | ariseth because of the *w*, by and |
| Mt 13:22 | thorns is he that heareth the *w* |
| Mt 13:22 | of riches, choke the *w*, and he |
| Mt 13:23 | ground is he that heareth the *w* |
| Mt 15:23 | But he answered her not a *w* |
| Mt 18:16 | every *w* may be established |
| Mt 22:46 | no man was able to answer him a *w* |
| Mt 26:75 | Peter remembered the *w* of Jesus |
| Mt 27:14 | And he answered him to never a *w* |
| Mt 28:8 | did run to bring his disciples *w* |
| Mk 2:2 | and he preached the *w* unto them |
| Mk 4:14 | The sower soweth the *w* |
| Mk 4:15 | the way side, where the *w* is sown |
| Mk 4:15 | taketh away the *w* that was sown |
| Mk 4:16 | who, when they have heard the *w* |
| Mk 4:18 | such as hear the *w*, |
| Mk 4:19 | things entering in, choke the *w* |
| Mk 4:20 | such as hear the *w*, and receive it |
| Mk 4:33 | parables spake he the *w* unto them |
| Mk 5:36 | Jesus heard the *w* that was spoken |
| Mk 7:13 | Making the *w* of God of none |
| Mk 14:72 | the *w* that Jesus said unto him |
| Mk 16:20 | confirming the *w* with signs |
| Lk 1:2 | and ministers of the *w* |
| Lk 1:38 | be it unto me according to thy *w* |
| Lk 2:29 | in peace, according to thy *w* |
| Lk 3:2 | the *w* of God came unto John the |
| Lk 4:4 | alone, but by every *w* of God |
| Lk 4:32 | for his *w* was with power |
| Lk 4:36 | saying, What a *w* is this |
| Lk 5:1 | upon him to hear the *w* of God |
| Lk 5:5 | nevertheless at thy *w* I will let |
| Lk 7:7 | but say in a *w*, and my servant |
| Lk 8:11 | The seed is the *w* of God |
| Lk 8:12 | taketh away the *w* out of their |
| Lk 8:13 | they hear, receive the *w* with joy |
| Lk 8:15 | and good heart, having heard the *w* |
| Lk 8:21 | are these which hear the *w* of God |
| Lk 10:39 | at Jesus' feet, and heard his *w* |
| Lk 11:28 | are they that hear the *w* of God |
| Lk 12:10 | speak a *w* against the Son of man |
| Lk 22:61 | remembered the *w* of the Lord |
| Lk 24:19 | *w* before God and all the people |
| Jn 1:1 | In the beginning was the *W* |
| Jn 1:1 | the *W* was with God |
| Jn 1:1 | and the *W* was God |
| Jn 1:14 | the *W* was made flesh, and dwelt |
| Jn 2:22 | the *w* which Jesus had said |
| Jn 4:41 | believed because of his own *w* |
| Jn 4:50 | the man believed the *w* that Jesus |
| Jn 5:24 | unto you, He that heareth my *w* |
| Jn 5:38 | ye have not his *w* abiding in you |
| Jn 8:31 | on him, If ye continue in my *w* |
| Jn 8:37 | because my *w* hath no place in you |
| Jn 8:43 | even because ye cannot hear my *w* |
| Jn 10:35 | gods, unto whom the *w* of God came |
| Jn 12:48 | the *w* that I have spoken, the |
| Jn 14:24 | the *w* which ye hear is not mine, |
| Jn 15:3 | *w* which I have spoken unto you |
| Jn 15:20 | Remember the *w* that I said unto |
| Jn 15:25 | that the *w* might be fulfilled |
| Jn 17:6 | and they have kept thy *w* |
| Jn 17:14 | I have given them thy *w* |
| Jn 17:17 | thy *w* is truth |
| Jn 17:20 | believe on me through their *w* |
| Acts 2:41 | received his *w* were baptized |
| Acts 4:4 | them which heard the *w* believed |
| Acts 4:29 | all boldness they may speak thy *w* |
| Acts 4:31 | they spake the *w* of God with |
| Acts 6:2 | that we should leave the *w* of God |
| Acts 6:4 | and to the ministry of the *w* |
| Acts 6:7 | And the *w* of God increased |
| Acts 8:4 | went every where preaching the *w* |
| Acts 8:14 | Samaria had received the *w* of God |
| Acts 8:25 | and preached the *w* of the Lord |
| Acts 10:36 | The *w* which God sent unto the |
| Acts 10:37 | That *w*, I say, ye know, which was |
| Acts 10:44 | on all them which heard the *w* |
| Acts 11:1 | had also received the *w* of God |
| Acts 11:16 | remembered I the *w* of the Lord |
| Acts 11:19 | preaching the *w* to none but unto |
| Acts 12:24 | But the *w* of God grew and |
| Acts 13:5 | they preached the *w* of God in the |
| Acts 13:7 | and desired to hear the *w* of God |
| Acts 13:15 | if ye have any *w* of exhortation |
| Acts 13:26 | to you is the *w* of this salvation |
| Acts 13:44 | together to hear the *w* of God |
| Acts 13:46 | It was necessary that the *w* of |
| Acts 13:48 | and glorified the *w* of the Lord |
| Acts 13:49 | the *w* of the Lord was published |
| Acts 14:3 | testimony unto the *w* of his grace |
| Acts 14:25 | they had preached the *w* in Perga |
| Acts 15:7 | should hear the *w* of the gospel |
| Acts 15:35 | and preaching the *w* of the Lord |
| Acts 15:36 | have preached the *w* of the Lord |
| Acts 16:6 | Ghost to preach the *w* in Asia |
| Acts 16:32 | spake unto him the *w* of the Lord |
| Acts 17:11 | in that they received the *w* with |
| Acts 17:13 | had knowledge that the *w* of God |
| Acts 18:11 | teaching the *w* of God among them |
| Acts 19:10 | heard the *w* of the Lord Jesus |
| Acts 19:20 | So mightily grew the *w* of God |
| Acts 20:32 | to the *w* of his grace, which is |
| Acts 22:22 | gave him audience unto this *w* |
| Acts 28:25 | after that Paul had spoken one *w* |
| Rom 9:6 | Not as though the *w* of God hath |
| Rom 9:9 | For this is the *w* of promise |
| Rom 10:8 | The *w* is nigh thee, even in thy |
| Rom 10:8 | the *w* of faith, which we preach |
| Rom 10:17 | and hearing by the *w* of God |
| Rom 15:18 | make the Gentiles obedient, by *w* |
| 1Cor 4:20 | the kingdom of God is not in *w* |
| 1Cor 12:8 | by the Spirit the *w* of wisdom |
| 1Cor 12:8 | to another the *w* of knowledge by |
| 1Cor 14:36 | came the *w* of God out from you |
| 2Cor 1:18 | our *w* toward you was not yea and |
| 2Cor 2:17 | many, which corrupt the *w* of God |
| 2Cor 4:2 | nor handling the *w* of God |
| 2Cor 5:19 | unto us the *w* of reconciliation |
| 2Cor 6:7 | By the *w* of truth, by the power |
| 2Cor 10:11 | such as we are in *w* by letters |

2Cor 13:1 shall every *w* be established
Gal 5:14 all the law is fulfilled in one *w*
Gal 6:6 the *w* communicate unto him that
Eph 1:13 that ye heard the *w* of truth
Eph 5:26 the washing of water by the *w*
Eph 6:17 the Spirit, which is the *w* of God
Phil 1:14 bold to speak the *w* without fear
Phil 2:16 Holding forth the *w* of life
Col 1:5 the *w* of the truth of the gospel
Col 1:25 for you, to fulfil the *w* of God
Col 3:16 Let the *w* of Christ dwell in you
Col 3:17 And whatsoever ye do in *w* or deed
1Th 1:5 came not unto you in *w* only
1Th 1:6 received the *w* in much affliction
1Th 1:8 out the *w* of the Lord not only in
1Th 2:13 when ye received the *w* of God
1Th 2:13 received it not as the *w* of men
1Th 2:13 the *w* of God, which effectually
1Th 4:15 say unto you by the *w* of the Lord
2Th 2:2 neither by spirit, nor by *w*
2Th 2:15 ye have been taught, whether by *w*
2Th 2:17 and stablish you in every good *w*
2Th 3:1 that the *w* of the Lord may have
2Th 3:14 obey not our *w* by this epistle
1Ti 4:5 it is sanctified by the *w* of God
1Ti 4:12 an example of the believers, in *w*
1Ti 5:17 they who labour in the *w* and
2Ti 2:9 but the *w* of God is not bound
2Ti 2:15 rightly dividing the *w* of truth
2Ti 2:17 their *w* will eat as doth a canker
2Ti 4:2 Preach the *w*
Titus 1:3 his *w* through preaching, which is
Titus 1:9 faithful *w* as he hath been taught
Titus 2:5 that the *w* of God be not
Heb 1:3 all things by the *w* of his power
Heb 2:2 For if the *w* spoken by angels was
Heb 4:2 but the *w* preached did not profit
Heb 4:12 For the *w* of God is quick, and
Heb 5:13 in the *w* of righteousness
Heb 6:5 And have tasted the good *w* of God
Heb 7:28 but the *w* of the oath, which was
Heb 11:3 were framed by the *w* of God
Heb 12:19 *w* should not be spoken to them
Heb 12:27 And this *w*, Yet once more,
Heb 13:7 have spoken unto you the *w* of God
Heb 13:22 suffer the *w* of exhortation
Jas 1:18 begat he us with the *w* of truth
Jas 1:21 with meekness the engrafted *w*
Jas 1:22 But be ye doers of the *w*, and not
Jas 1:23 For if any be a hearer of the *w*
Jas 3:2 If any man offend not in *w*
1Pet 1:23 of incorruptible, by the *w* of God
1Pet 1:25 But the *w* of the Lord endureth
1Pet 1:25 this is the *w* which by the gospel
1Pet 2:2 desire the sincere milk of the *w*
1Pet 2:8 to them which stumble at the *w*
1Pet 3:1 that, if any obey not the *w*
1Pet 3:1 they also may without the *w* be
2Pet 1:19 also a more sure *w* of prophecy
2Pet 3:5 that by the *w* of God the heavens
2Pet 3:7 by the same *w* are kept in store,
1Jn 1:1 have handled, of the *W* of life
1Jn 1:10 him a liar, and his *w* is not in us
1Jn 2:5 But whoso keepeth his *w*, in him
1Jn 2:7 The old commandment is the *w*
1Jn 2:14 the *w* of God abideth in you, and
1Jn 3:18 children, let us not love in *w*
1Jn 5:7 in heaven, the Father, the *W*
Rev 1:2 Who bare record of the *w* of God
Rev 1:9 called Patmos, for the *w* of God
Rev 3:8 strength, and hast kept my *w*
Rev 3:10 hast kept the *w* of my patience
Rev 6:9 that were slain for the *w* of God
Rev 12:11 by the *w* of their testimony
Rev 19:13 his name is called The *W* of God
Rev 20:4 of Jesus, and for the *w* of God

**WORD'S**

2Sa 7:21 For thy *w* sake, and according to
Mk 4:17 ariseth for the *w* sake,

**WORDS**

Gen 24:30 when he heard the *w* of Rebekah
Gen 24:52 Abraham's servant heard their *w*
Gen 27:34 Esau heard the *w* of his father
Gen 27:42 these *w* of Esau her elder son
Gen 31:1 he heard the *w* of Laban's sons,
Gen 34:18 their *w* pleased Hamor, and Shechem
Gen 37:8 more for his dreams, and for his *w*
Gen 39:17 unto him according to these *w*
Gen 39:19 master heard the *w* of his wife
Gen 42:16 that your *w* may be proved,
Gen 42:20 so shall your *w* be verified
Gen 43:7 according to the tenor of these *w*
Gen 44:6 he spake unto them these same *w*
Gen 44:7 Wherefore saith my lord these *w*
Gen 44:10 let it be according unto your *w*
Gen 44:24 we told him the *w* of my lord
Gen 45:27 they told him all the *w* of Joseph
Gen 49:21 he giveth goodly *w*
Ex 4:15 unto him, and put *w* in his mouth
Ex 4:28 Moses told Aaron all the *w* of the
Ex 4:30 Aaron spake all the *w* which the
Ex 5:9 and let them not regard vain *w*
Ex 19:6 These are the *w* which thou shalt
Ex 19:7 *w* which the LORD commanded him
Ex 19:8 Moses returned the *w* of the
Ex 19:9 Moses told the *w* of the people
Ex 20:1 And God spake all these *w*, saying,
Ex 23:8 perverteth the *w* of the righteous
Ex 24:3 the people all the *w* of the LORD
Ex 24:3 All the *w* which the LORD hath
Ex 24:4 Moses wrote all the *w* of the LORD
Ex 24:8 with you concerning all these *w*
Ex 34:1 write upon these tables the *w*
Ex 34:27 unto Moses, Write thou these *w*
Ex 34:27 *w* I have made a covenant with
Ex 34:28 the tables the *w* of the covenant
Ex 35:1 These are the *w* which the LORD
Num 11:24 told the people the *w* of the LORD
Num 12:6 And he said, Hear now my *w*
Num 16:31 an end of speaking all these *w*
Num 22:7 and spake unto him the *w* of Balak
Num 24:4 said, which heard the *w* of God
Num 24:16 said, which heard the *w* of God
Deut 1:1 These be the *w* which Moses spake
Deut 1:34 LORD heard the voice of your *w*
Deut 2:26 king of Heshbon with *w* of peace
Deut 4:10 and I will make them hear my *w*
Deut 4:12 ye heard the voice of the *w*
Deut 4:36 thou heardest his *w* out of the
Deut 5:22 These *w* the LORD spake unto all
Deut 5:28 LORD heard the voice of your *w*
Deut 5:28 the voice of the *w* of this people
Deut 6:6 And these *w*, which I command thee
Deut 9:10 written according to all the *w*
Deut 10:2 *w* that were in the first tables
Deut 11:18 lay up these my *w* in your heart
Deut 12:28 hear all these *w* which I command
Deut 13:3 unto the *w* of that prophet
Deut 16:19 pervert the *w* of the righteous
Deut 17:19 to keep all the *w* of this law
Deut 18:18 will put my *w* in his mouth
Deut 18:19 will not hearken unto my *w* which
Deut 27:3 upon them all the *w* of this law
Deut 27:8 the *w* of this law very plainly
Deut 27:26 all the *w* of this law to do them
Deut 28:14 not go aside from any of the *w*
Deut 28:58 wilt not observe to do all the *w*
Deut 29:1 These are the *w* of the covenant,
Deut 29:9 therefore the *w* of this covenant
Deut 29:19 he heareth the *w* of this curse
Deut 29:29 we may do all the *w* of this law
Deut 31:1 spake these *w* unto all Israel
Deut 31:12 to do all the *w* of this law
Deut 31:24 the *w* of this law in a book
Deut 31:28 I may speak these *w* in their ears
Deut 31:30 of Israel the *w* of this song
Deut 32:1 hear, O earth, the *w* of my mouth
Deut 32:44 spake all the *w* of this song in
Deut 32:45 all these *w* to all Israel
Deut 32:46 Set your hearts unto all the *w*
Deut 32:46 to do, all the *w* of this law
Deut 33:3 every one shall receive of thy *w*
Josh 1:18 will not hearken unto thy *w* in
Josh 2:21 she said, According unto your *w*
Josh 3:9 hear the *w* of the LORD your God
Josh 8:34 he read all the *w* of the law
Josh 22:30 heard the *w* that the children of
Josh 24:26 Joshua wrote these *w* in the book
Josh 24:27 for it hath heard all the *w* of
Judg 2:4 angel of the LORD spake these *w*
Judg 9:3 the men of Shechem all these *w*
Judg 9:30 the *w* of Gaal the son of Ebed
Judg 11:10 we do not so according to thy *w*
Judg 11:11 Jephthah uttered all his *w* before
Judg 11:28 *w* of Jephthah which he sent him
Judg 13:12 Now let thy *w* come to pass
Judg 16:16 she pressed him daily with her *w*
1Sa 3:19 none of his *w* fall to the ground
1Sa 8:10 Samuel told all the *w* of the LORD
1Sa 8:21 heard all the *w* of the people
1Sa 15:1 the voice of the *w* of the LORD
1Sa 15:24 commandment of the LORD, and thy *w*
1Sa 17:11 heard those *w* of the Philistine
1Sa 17:23 and spake according to the same *w*
1Sa 17:31 when the *w* were heard which David
1Sa 18:23 those *w* in the ears of David
1Sa 18:26 his servants told David these *w*
1Sa 21:12 laid up these *w* in his heart
1Sa 24:7 stayed his servants with these *w*
1Sa 24:9 Wherefore hearest thou men's *w*
1Sa 24:16 end of speaking these *w* unto Saul
1Sa 25:9 all those *w* in the name of David
1Sa 25:24 hear the *w* of thine handmaid
1Sa 26:19 king hear the *w* of his servant
1Sa 28:20 because of the *w* of Samuel
1Sa 28:21 have hearkened unto thy *w* which
2Sa 3:8 wroth for the *w* of Ish-bosheth
2Sa 7:17 According to all these *w*, and
2Sa 7:28 thy *w* be true, and thou hast
2Sa 14:3 So Joab put the *w* in her mouth
2Sa 14:19 he put all these *w* in the mouth
2Sa 19:43 the *w* of the men of Judah were
2Sa 19:43 than the *w* of the men of Israel
2Sa 20:17 Hear the *w* of thine handmaid
2Sa 22:1 unto the LORD the *w* of this song
2Sa 23:1 Now these be the last *w* of David
1Kin 1:14 in after thee, and confirm thy *w*
1Kin 3:12 I have done according to thy *w*
1Kin 5:7 when Hiram heard the *w* of Solomon
1Kin 8:59 And let these my *w*, wherewith I
1Kin 10:7 Howbeit I believed not the *w*
1Kin 12:7 them, and speak good *w* to them
1Kin 13:11 the *w* which he had spoken unto
1Kin 21:27 to pass, when Ahab heard those *w*
1Kin 22:13 the *w* of the prophets declare
2Kin 1:7 to meet you, and told you these *w*
2Kin 6:12 the *w* that thou speakest in thy
2Kin 6:30 the king heard the *w* of the woman
2Kin 18:20 sayest, (but they are but vain *w*
2Kin 18:27 and to thee, to speak these *w*
2Kin 18:37 told him the *w* of Rab-shakeh
2Kin 19:4 will hear all the *w* of Rab-shakeh
2Kin 19:4 will reprove the *w* which the LORD
2Kin 19:6 Be not afraid of the *w* which thou
2Kin 19:16 hear the *w* of Sennacherib, which
2Kin 22:11 the *w* of the book of the law
2Kin 22:13 concerning the *w* of this book
2Kin 22:13 hearkened unto the *w* of this book
2Kin 22:16 even all the *w* of the book which
2Kin 22:18 As touching the *w* which thou hast
2Kin 23:2 the *w* of the book of the covenant
2Kin 23:3 to perform the *w* of this covenant
2Kin 23:16 who proclaimed these *w*
2Kin 23:24 that he might perform the *w* of
1Chr 17:15 According to all these *w*, and
1Chr 23:27 For by the last *w* of David the
1Chr 25:5 the king's seer in the *w* of God
2Chr 9:6 Howbeit I believed not their *w*
2Chr 10:7 them, and speak good *w* to them
2Chr 11:4 And they obeyed the *w* of the LORD
2Chr 15:8 And when Asa heard these *w*
2Chr 18:12 the *w* of the prophets declare
2Chr 29:15 by the *w* of the LORD, to cleanse
2Chr 29:30 unto the LORD with the *w* of David
2Chr 32:8 the *w* of Hezekiah king of Judah
2Chr 33:18 the *w* of the seers that spake to
2Chr 34:19 king had heard the *w* of the law
2Chr 34:21 concerning the *w* of the book that
2Chr 34:26 the *w* which thou hast heard
2Chr 34:27 heardest his *w* against this place
2Chr 34:30 the *w* of the book of the covenant
2Chr 34:31 to perform the *w* of the covenant
2Chr 35:22 hearkened not unto the *w* of Necho
2Chr 36:16 of God, and despised his *w*
Ezr 7:11 even a scribe of the *w* of the
Ezr 9:4 at the *w* of the God of Israel
Neh 1:1 The *w* of Nehemiah the son of
Neh 1:4 to pass, when I heard these *w*
Neh 2:18 as also the king's *w* that he had
Neh 5:6 when I heard their cry and these *w*
Neh 6:6 their king, according to these *w*
Neh 6:7 to the king according to these *w*
Neh 6:19 before me, and uttered my *w* to him
Neh 8:9 when they heard the *w* of the law
Neh 8:12 *w* that were declared unto them
Neh 8:13 to understand the *w* of the law
Neh 9:8 his seed, and hast performed thy *w*
Est 4:9 and told Esther the *w* of Mordecai

Est 4:12 they told to Mordecai Esther's *w*
Est 9:26 for all the *w* of this letter
Est 9:30 with *w* of peace and truth,
Job 4:4 Thy *w* have upholden him that was
Job 6:3 therefore my *w* are swallowed up
Job 6:10 concealed the *w* of the Holy One
Job 6:25 How forcible are right *w*
Job 6:26 Do ye imagine to reprove *w*
Job 8:2 how long shall the *w* of thy mouth
Job 8:10 utter *w* out of their heart
Job 9:14 choose out my *w* to reason with
Job 11:2 the multitude of *w* be answered
Job 12:11 Doth not the ear try *w*
Job 15:13 lettest such *w* go out of thy
Job 16:3 Shall vain *w* have an end
Job 16:4 I could heap up *w* against you
Job 18:2 it be ere ye make an end of *w*
Job 19:2 and break me in pieces with *w*
Job 19:23 Oh that my *w* were now written
Job 22:22 lay up his *w* in thine heart
Job 23:5 I would know the *w* which he would
Job 23:12 I have esteemed the *w* of his
Job 26:4 To whom hast thou uttered *w*
Job 29:22 After my *w* they spake not again
Job 31:40 The *w* of Job are ended
Job 32:11 Behold, I waited for your *w*
Job 32:12 Job, or that answered his *w*
Job 32:14 not directed his *w* against me
Job 33:1 speeches, and hearken to all my *w*
Job 33:3 My *w* shall be of the uprightness
Job 33:5 set thy *w* in order before me,
Job 33:8 I have heard the voice of thy *w*
Job 34:2 Hear my *w*, O ye wise men
Job 34:3 For the ear trieth *w*, as the
Job 34:16 hearken to the voice of my *w*
Job 34:35 his *w* were without wisdom
Job 34:37 and multiplieth his *w* against God
Job 35:16 he multiplieth *w* without
Job 36:4 For truly my *w* shall not be false
Job 38:2 counsel by *w* without knowledge
Job 41:3 will he speak soft *w* unto thee
Job 42:7 LORD had spoken these *w* unto Job
Ps 5:1 Give ear to my *w*, O LORD
Ps 7:*t* concerning the *w* of Cush the
Ps 12:6 The *w* of the LORD
Ps 12:6 the LORD are pure *w*
Ps 17:4 Concerning the *w* of men, by the
Ps 18:*t* who spake unto the LORD the *w* of
Ps 19:4 their *w* to the end of the world
Ps 19:14 Let the *w* of my mouth, and the
Ps 22:1 me, and from the *w* of my roaring
Ps 36:3 The *w* of his mouth are iniquity
Ps 50:17 and castest my *w* behind thee
Ps 52:4 Thou lovest all devouring *w*
Ps 54:2 give ear to the *w* of my mouth
Ps 55:21 The *w* of his mouth were smoother
Ps 55:21 his *w* were softer than oil, yet
Ps 56:5 Every day they wrest my *w*
Ps 59:12 the *w* of their lips let them even
Ps 64:3 shoot their arrows, even bitter *w*
Ps 78:1 your ears to the *w* of my mouth
Ps 106:12 Then believed they his *w*
Ps 107:11 rebelled against the *w* of God
Ps 109:3 me about also with *w* of hatred
Ps 119:57 have said that I would keep thy *w*
Ps 119:103 How sweet are thy *w* unto my taste
Ps 119:130 entrance of thy *w* giveth light
Ps 119:139 mine enemies have forgotten thy *w*
Ps 138:4 when they hear the *w* of thy mouth
Ps 141:6 places, they shall hear my *w*
Prov 1:2 to perceive the *w* of
Prov 1:6 the *w* of the wise, and their dark
Prov 1:21 in the city she uttereth her *w*
Prov 1:23 I will make known my *w* unto you
Prov 2:1 My son, if thou wilt receive my *w*
Prov 2:16 which flattereth with her *w*
Prov 4:4 me, Let thine heart retain my *w*
Prov 4:5 decline from the *w* of my mouth
Prov 4:20 My son, attend to my *w*
Prov 5:7 depart not from the *w* of my mouth
Prov 6:2 snared with the *w* of thy mouth
Prov 6:2 art taken with the *w* of thy mouth
Prov 7:1 My son, keep my *w*, and lay up my
Prov 7:5 which flattereth with her *w*
Prov 7:24 and attend to the *w* of my mouth
Prov 8:8 All the *w* of my mouth are in
Prov 10:19 In the multitude of *w* there
Prov 12:6 The *w* of the wicked are to lie in
Prov 15:1 but grievous *w* stir up anger
Prov 15:26 but the *w* of the pure are
Prov 15:26 the pure are pleasant *w*
Prov 16:24 Pleasant *w* are as an honeycomb,
Prov 17:27 that hath knowledge spareth his *w*
Prov 18:4 The *w* of a man's mouth are as
Prov 18:8 The *w* of a talebearer are as
Prov 19:7 he pursueth them with *w*, yet they
Prov 19:27 to err from the *w* of knowledge
Prov 22:12 the *w* of the transgressor
Prov 22:17 hear the *w* of the wise, and apply
Prov 22:21 the certainty of the *w* of truth
Prov 22:21 that thou mightest answer the *w*
Prov 23:8 vomit up, and lose thy sweet *w*
Prov 23:9 will despise the wisdom of thy *w*
Prov 23:12 thine ears to the *w* of knowledge
Prov 26:22 The *w* of a talebearer are as
Prov 29:19 will not be corrected by *w*
Prov 29:20 thou a man that is hasty in his *w*
Prov 30:1 The *w* of Agur the son of Jakeh,
Prov 30:6 Add thou not unto his *w*, lest he
Prov 31:1 The *w* of king Lemuel, the
Eccl 1:1 The *w* of the Preacher, the son of
Eccl 5:2 therefore let thy *w* be few
Eccl 5:3 voice is known by multitude of *w*
Eccl 5:7 many *w* there are also divers
Eccl 7:21 heed unto all *w* that are spoken
Eccl 9:16 despised, and his *w* are not heard
Eccl 9:17 The *w* of wise men are heard in
Eccl 10:12 The *w* of a wise man's mouth are
Eccl 10:13 The beginning of the *w* of his
Eccl 10:14 A fool also is full of *w*
Eccl 12:10 sought to find out acceptable *w*
Eccl 12:10 was upright, even *w* of truth
Eccl 12:11 The *w* of the wise are as goads,
Is 29:11 as the *w* of a book that is sealed
Is 29:18 the deaf hear the *w* of the book
Is 31:2 evil, and will not call back his *w*
Is 32:7 to destroy the poor with lying *w*
Is 36:5 are but vain *w*) I have counsel
Is 36:12 and to thee to speak these *w*
Is 36:13 Hear ye the *w* of the great king,
Is 36:22 and told him the *w* of Rabshakeh
Is 37:4 God will hear the *w* of Rabshakeh
Is 37:4 will reprove the *w* which the LORD
Is 37:6 of the *w* that thou hast heard
Is 37:17 hear all the *w* of Sennacherib,
Is 41:26 there is none that heareth your *w*
Is 51:16 And I have put my *w* in thy mouth
Is 58:13 nor speaking thine own *w*
Is 59:13 from the heart *w* of falsehood
Is 59:21 my *w* which I have put in thy
Jer 1:1 The *w* of Jeremiah the son of
Jer 1:9 I have put my *w* in thy mouth
Jer 3:12 proclaim these *w* toward the north
Jer 5:14 I will make my *w* in thy mouth
Jer 6:19 they have not hearkened unto my *w*
Jer 7:4 Trust ye not in lying *w*, saying,
Jer 7:8 Behold, ye trust in lying *w*
Jer 7:27 shalt speak all these *w* unto them
Jer 11:2 Hear ye the *w* of this covenant,
Jer 11:3 not the *w* of this covenant
Jer 11:6 Proclaim all these *w* in the
Jer 11:6 Hear ye the *w* of this covenant,
Jer 11:8 them all the *w* of this covenant
Jer 11:10 which refused to hear my *w*
Jer 12:6 they speak fair *w* unto thee
Jer 13:10 people, which refuse to hear my *w*
Jer 15:16 Thy *w* were found, and I did eat
Jer 16:10 shew this people all these *w*
Jer 18:2 I will cause thee to hear my *w*
Jer 18:18 us not give heed to any of his *w*
Jer 19:2 proclaim there the *w* that I shall
Jer 19:15 that they might not hear my *w*
Jer 22:5 But if ye will not hear these *w*
Jer 23:9 because of the *w* of his holiness
Jer 23:16 Hearken not unto the *w* of the
Jer 23:22 had caused my people to hear my *w*
Jer 23:30 that steal my *w* every one from
Jer 23:36 perverted the *w* of the living God
Jer 25:8 Because ye have not heard my *w*
Jer 25:13 bring upon that land all my *w*
Jer 25:30 thou against them all these *w*
Jer 26:2 all the *w* that I command thee to
Jer 26:5 To hearken to the *w* of my
Jer 26:7 these *w* in the house of the LORD
Jer 26:12 city all the *w* that ye have heard
Jer 26:15 to speak all these *w* in your ears
Jer 26:20 to all the *w* of Jeremiah
Jer 26:21 and all the princes, heard his *w*
Jer 27:12 of Judah according to all these *w*
Jer 27:14 Therefore hearken not unto the *w*
Jer 27:16 Hearken not to the *w* of your
Jer 28:6 the LORD perform thy *w* which thou
Jer 29:1 Now these are the *w* of the letter
Jer 29:19 they have not hearkened to my *w*
Jer 29:23 and have spoken lying *w* in my name
Jer 30:2 Write thee all the *w* that I have
Jer 30:4 these are the *w* that the LORD
Jer 34:6 the prophet spake all these *w*
Jer 34:18 which have not performed the *w* of
Jer 35:13 instruction to hearken to my *w*
Jer 35:14 The *w* of Jonadab the son of
Jer 36:2 write therein all the *w* that I
Jer 36:4 of Jeremiah all the *w* of the LORD
Jer 36:6 the *w* of the LORD in the ears of
Jer 36:8 reading in the book the *w* of the
Jer 36:10 read Baruch in the book the *w* of
Jer 36:11 of the book all the *w* of the LORD
Jer 36:13 them all the *w* that he had heard
Jer 36:16 when they had heard all the *w*
Jer 36:16 tell the king of all these *w*
Jer 36:17 write all these *w* at his mouth
Jer 36:18 these *w* unto me with his mouth
Jer 36:20 told all the *w* in the ears of the
Jer 36:24 servants that heard all these *w*
Jer 36:27 the *w* which Baruch wrote at the
Jer 36:28 write in it all the former *w* that
Jer 36:32 the *w* of the book which Jehoiakim
Jer 36:32 besides unto them many like *w*
Jer 37:2 hearken unto the *w* of the LORD
Jer 38:1 heard the *w* that Jeremiah had
Jer 38:4 in speaking such *w* unto them
Jer 38:24 Let no man know of these *w*
Jer 38:27 *w* that the king had commanded
Jer 39:16 I will bring my *w* upon this city
Jer 42:4 LORD your God according to your *w*
Jer 43:1 all the *w* of the LORD their God
Jer 43:1 him to them, even all these *w*
Jer 44:28 shall know whose *w* shall stand
Jer 44:29 that ye may know that my *w* shall
Jer 45:1 these *w* in a book at the mouth of
Jer 51:60 even all these *w* that are written
Jer 51:61 see, and shalt read all these *w*
Jer 51:64 Thus far are the *w* of Jeremiah
Eze 2:6 neither be afraid of their *w*
Eze 2:6 be not afraid of their *w*, nor be
Eze 2:7 thou shalt speak my *w* unto them
Eze 3:4 and speak with my *w* unto them
Eze 3:6 whose *w* thou canst not understand
Eze 3:10 all my *w* that I shall speak unto
Eze 12:28 of my *w* be prolonged any more
Eze 33:31 as my people, and they hear thy *w*
Eze 33:32 for they hear thy *w*, but they do
Eze 35:13 have multiplied your *w* against me
Dan 2:9 corrupt *w* to speak before me,
Dan 5:10 by reason of the *w* of the king
Dan 6:14 the king, when he heard these *w*
Dan 7:11 the great *w* which the horn spake
Dan 7:25 he shall speak great *w* against
Dan 9:12 And he hath confirmed his *w*
Dan 10:6 the voice of his *w* like the voice
Dan 10:9 Yet heard I the voice of his *w*
Dan 10:9 when I heard the voice of his *w*
Dan 10:11 understand the *w* that I speak
Dan 10:12 thy *w* were heard
Dan 10:12 and I am come for thy *w*
Dan 10:15 when he had spoken such *w* unto me
Dan 12:4 But thou, O Daniel, shut up the *w*
Dan 12:9 for the *w* are closed up and sealed
Hos 6:5 slain them by the *w* of my mouth
Hos 10:4 They have spoken *w*, swearing
Hos 14:2 Take with you *w*, and turn to the
Amos 1:1 The *w* of Amos, who was among the
Amos 7:10 is not able to bear all his *w*
Amos 8:11 but of hearing the *w* of the LORD
Mic 2:7 do not my *w* do good to him that
Hag 1:12 the *w* of Haggai the prophet, as
Zec 1:6 But my *w* and my statutes, which I
Zec 1:13 that talked with me with good *w*
Zec 1:13 and comfortable *w*
Zec 7:7 Should ye not hear the *w* which
Zec 7:12 the *w* which the LORD of hosts
Zec 8:9 *w* by the mouth of the prophets
Mal 2:17 have wearied the LORD with your *w*
Mal 3:13 Your *w* have been stout against me
Mt 10:14 not receive you, nor hear your *w*
Mt 12:37 For by thy *w* thou shalt be
Mt 12:37 by thy *w* thou shalt be condemned
Mt 22:22 When they had heard these *w*
Mt 24:35 but my *w* shall not pass away
Mt 26:44 the third time, saying the same *w*

**WORK**

**WORKER**



**WORKERS**

Phil 3:2 Beware of dogs, beware of evil *w*
Col 4:11 fellow *w* unto the kingdom of God

## WORKETH

Job 33:29 all these things *w* God oftentimes
Ps 15:2 *w* righteousness, and speaketh the
Ps 101:7 He that *w* deceit shall not dwell
Prov 11:18 The wicked *w* a deceitful work
Prov 26:28 and a flattering mouth *w* ruin
Prov 31:13 *w* willingly with her hands
Eccl 3:9 What profit hath he that *w* in
Is 44:12 the tongs both *w* in the coals
Is 44:12 *w* it with the strength of his
Is 64:5 *w* righteousness, those that
Dan 6:27 he *w* signs and wonders in heaven
Jn 5:17 them, My Father *w* hitherto
Acts 10:35 *w* righteousness, is accepted with
Rom 2:10 peace, to every man that *w* good
Rom 4:4 Now to him that *w* is the reward
Rom 4:5 But to him that *w* not, but
Rom 4:15 Because the law *w* wrath
Rom 5:3 that tribulation *w* patience
Rom 13:10 Love *w* no ill to his neighbour
1Cor 12:6 the same God which *w* all in all
1Cor 12:11 But all these *w* that one and the
1Cor 16:10 for he *w* the work of the Lord, as
2Cor 4:12 So then death *w* in us, but life
2Cor 4:17 *w* for us a far more exceeding and
2Cor 7:10 For godly sorrow *w* repentance to
2Cor 7:10 the sorrow of the world *w* death
Gal 3:5 *w* miracles among you, doeth he it
Gal 5:6 but faith which *w* by love
Eph 1:11 to the purpose of him who *w* all
Eph 2:2 the spirit that now *w* in the
Eph 3:20 to the power that *w* in us
Phil 2:13 God which *w* in you both to will
Col 1:29 working, which *w* in me mightily
1Th 2:13 which effectually *w* also in you
Jas 1:3 trying of your faith *w* patience
Jas 1:20 For the wrath of man *w* not the
Rev 21:27 neither whatsoever *w* abomination

## WORKFELLOW

Rom 16:21 Timotheus my *w*, and Lucius, and

## WORKING

Ps 52:2 like a sharp rasor, *w* deceitfully
Ps 74:12 *w* salvation in the midst of the
Is 28:29 in counsel, and excellent in *w*
Eze 46:1 east shall be shut the six *w* days
Mk 16:20 where, the Lord *w* with them, and
Rom 1:27 men with men *w* that which is
Rom 7:13 *w* death in me by that which is
1Cor 4:12 And labour, *w* with our own hands
1Cor 9:6 have not we power to forbear *w*
1Cor 12:10 To another the *w* of miracles
Eph 1:19 according to the *w* of his mighty
Eph 3:7 by the effectual *w* of his power
Eph 4:16 according to the effectual *w* in
Eph 4:28 *w* with his hands the thing which
Phil 3:21 according to the *w* whereby he is
Col 1:29 striving according to his *w*
2Th 2:9 the *w* of Satan with all power
2Th 3:11 *w* not at all, but are busybodies
Heb 13:21 his will, *w* in you that which is
Rev 16:14 *w* miracles, which go forth unto

## WORKMAN

Ex 35:35 the engraver, and of the cunning *w*
Ex 38:23 Dan, an engraver, and a cunning *w*
Song 7:1 work of the hands of a cunning *w*
Is 40:19 The *w* melteth a graven image, and
Is 40:20 *w* to prepare a graven image
Jer 10:3 the work of the hands of the *w*
Jer 10:9 from Uphaz, the work of the *w*
Hos 8:6 the *w* made it
Mt 10:10 for the *w* is worthy of his meat
2Ti 2:15 a *w* that needeth not to be

## WORKMANSHIP

Ex 31:3 knowledge, and in all manner of *w*
Ex 31:5 to work in all manner of *w*
Ex 35:31 knowledge, and in all manner of *w*
2Kin 16:10 according to all the *w* thereof
1Chr 28:21 of *w* every willing skilful man
Eze 28:13 the *w* of thy tabrets and of thy
Eph 2:10 For we are his *w*, created in

## WORKMEN

2Kin 12:14 But they gave that to the *w*
2Kin 12:15 the money to be bestowed on *w*
1Chr 22:15 Moreover there are *w* with thee in
1Chr 25:1 the number of the *w* according to
2Chr 24:13 So the *w* wrought, and the work
2Chr 34:10 *w* that had the oversight of the
2Chr 34:10 they gave it to the *w* that
2Chr 34:17 and to the hand of the *w*
Ezr 3:9 to set forward the *w* in the house
Is 44:11 and the *w*, they are of men
Acts 19:25 with the *w* of like occupation

## WORKMEN'S

Judg 5:26 and her right hand to the *w* hammer

## WORK'S

1Th 5:13 highly in love for their *w* sake

## WORKS

Ex 5:4 let the people from their *w*
Ex 5:13 them, saying, Fulfil your *w*
Ex 23:24 serve them, nor do after their *w*
Ex 31:4 To devise cunning *w*, to work in
Ex 35:32 And to devise curious *w*, to work
Num 16:28 hath sent me to do all these *w*
Deut 2:7 thee in all the *w* of thy hand
Deut 3:24 that can do according to thy *w*
Deut 15:10 God shall bless thee in all thy *w*
Deut 16:15 in all the *w* of thine hands,
Josh 24:31 had known all the *w* of the LORD
Judg 2:7 seen all the great *w* of the LORD
Judg 2:10 nor yet the *w* which he had done
1Sa 8:8 According to all the *w* which they
1Sa 19:4 because his *w* have been to
1Kin 7:14 and cunning to work all *w* in brass
1Kin 13:11 told him all the *w* that the man
2Kin 22:17 with all the *w* of their hands
1Chr 16:9 talk ye of all his wondrous *w*
1Chr 16:12 marvellous *w* that he hath done
1Chr 16:24 his marvellous *w* among all
1Chr 28:19 even all the *w* of this pattern
2Chr 20:37 the LORD hath broken thy *w*
2Chr 32:30 Hezekiah prospered in all his *w*
2Chr 34:25 with all the *w* of their hands
Neh 6:14 according to these their *w*
Neh 9:35 turned they from their wicked *w*
Job 34:25 Therefore he knoweth their *w*
Job 37:14 and consider the wondrous *w* of God
Job 37:16 the wondrous *w* of him which is
Ps 8:6 dominion over the *w* of thy hands
Ps 9:1 shew forth all thy marvellous *w*
Ps 14:1 they have done abominable *w*
Ps 26:7 and tell of all thy wondrous *w*
Ps 28:5 they regard not the *w* of the LORD
Ps 33:4 all his *w* are done in truth
Ps 33:15 he considereth all their *w*
Ps 40:5 are thy wonderful *w* which thou
Ps 46:8 behold the *w* of the LORD, what
Ps 66:3 How terrible art thou in thy *w*
Ps 66:5 Come and see the *w* of God
Ps 71:17 have I declared thy wondrous *w*
Ps 73:28 GOD, that I may declare all thy *w*
Ps 75:1 is near thy wondrous *w* declare
Ps 77:11 I will remember the *w* of the LORD
Ps 78:4 his wonderful *w* that he hath done
Ps 78:7 God, and not forget the *w* of God
Ps 78:11 And forgat his *w*, and his wonders
Ps 78:32 believed not for his wondrous *w*
Ps 86:8 there any *w* like unto thy *w*
Ps 92:4 triumph in the *w* of thy hands
Ps 92:5 O LORD, how great are thy *w*
Ps 103:22 all his *w* in all places of his
Ps 104:13 satisfied with the fruit of thy *w*
Ps 104:24 O LORD, how manifold are thy *w*
Ps 104:31 the LORD shall rejoice in his *w*
Ps 105:2 talk ye of all his wondrous *w*
Ps 105:5 marvellous *w* that he hath done
Ps 106:13 They soon forgat his *w*
Ps 106:22 Wondrous *w* in the land of Ham, and
Ps 106:35 the heathen, and learned their *w*
Ps 106:39 they defiled with their own *w*
Ps 107:8 for his wonderful *w* to the
Ps 107:15 for his wonderful *w* to the
Ps 107:21 for his wonderful *w* to the
Ps 107:22 declare his *w* with rejoicing
Ps 107:24 These see the *w* of the LORD
Ps 107:31 for his wonderful *w* to the
Ps 111:2 The *w* of the LORD are great,
Ps 111:4 his wonderful *w* to be remembered
Ps 111:6 his people the power of his *w*
Ps 111:7 The *w* of his hands are verity and
Ps 118:17 and declare the *w* of the LORD
Ps 119:27 so shall I talk of thy wondrous *w*
Ps 138:8 forsake not the *w* of thine own
Ps 139:14 marvellous are thy *w*
Ps 141:4 to practise wicked *w* with men
Ps 143:5 I meditate on all thy *w*
Ps 145:4 shall praise thy *w* to another
Ps 145:5 thy majesty, and of thy wondrous *w*
Ps 145:9 tender mercies are over all his *w*
Ps 145:10 All thy *w* shall praise thee, O
Ps 145:17 his ways, and holy in all his *w*
Prov 7:16 of tapestry, with carved *w*
Prov 8:22 of his way, before his *w* of old
Prov 16:3 Commit thy *w* unto the LORD, and
Prov 24:12 to every man according to his *w*
Prov 31:31 let her own *w* praise her in the
Eccl 1:14 I have seen all the *w* that are
Eccl 2:4 I made me great *w*
Eccl 2:11 Then I looked on all the *w* that
Eccl 3:22 a man should rejoice in his own *w*
Eccl 9:1 and the wise, and their *w*, are in
Eccl 9:7 for God now accepteth thy *w*
Eccl 11:5 not the *w* of God who maketh all
Is 26:12 also hast wrought all our *w* in us
Is 29:15 their *w* are in the dark, and they
Is 41:29 their *w* are nothing
Is 57:12 thy righteousness, and thy *w*
Is 59:6 cover themselves with their *w*
Is 59:6 their *w* are *w* of iniquity
Is 66:18 For I know their *w* and their
Jer 1:16 worshipped the *w* of their own
Jer 7:13 because ye have done all these *w*
Jer 21:2 according to all his wondrous *w*
Jer 25:6 to anger with the *w* of your hands
Jer 25:7 provoke me to anger with the *w* of
Jer 25:14 according to the *w* of their own
Jer 44:8 wrath with the *w* of your hands
Jer 48:7 thou hast trusted in thy *w*
Eze 6:6 down, and your *w* may be abolished
Dan 4:37 of heaven, all whose *w* are truth
Dan 9:14 in all his *w* which he doeth
Amos 8:7 will never forget any of their *w*
Jonah 3:10 And God saw their *w*, that they
Mic 6:16 all the *w* of the house of Ahab,
Mt 5:16 that they may see your good *w*
Mt 7:22 in thy name done many wonderful *w*
Mt 11:2 in the prison the *w* of Christ
Mt 11:20 most of his mighty *w* were done
Mt 11:21 for if the mighty *w*, which were
Mt 11:23 for if the mighty *w*, which have
Mt 13:54 this wisdom, and these mighty *w*
Mt 13:58 he did not many mighty *w* there
Mt 14:2 therefore mighty *w* do shew forth
Mt 16:27 every man according to his *w*
Mt 23:3 but do not ye after their *w*
Mt 23:5 But all their *w* they do for to be
Mk 6:2 that even such mighty *w* are
Mk 6:14 therefore mighty *w* do shew forth
Lk 10:13 for if the mighty *w* had been done
Lk 19:37 the mighty *w* that they had seen
Jn 5:20 shew him greater *w* than these
Jn 5:36 for the *w* which the Father hath
Jn 5:36 the same *w* that I do, bear
Jn 6:28 that we might work the *w* of God
Jn 7:3 may see the *w* that thou doest
Jn 7:7 that the *w* thereof are evil
Jn 8:39 ye would do the *w* of Abraham
Jn 9:3 but that the *w* of God should be
Jn 9:4 I must work the *w* of him that
Jn 10:25 the *w* that I do in my Father's
Jn 10:32 Many good *w* have I shewed you
Jn 10:32 which of those *w* do ye stone me
Jn 10:37 If I do not the *w* of my Father
Jn 10:38 ye believe not me, believe the *w*
Jn 14:10 dwelleth in me, he doeth the *w*
Jn 14:12 the *w* that I do shall he do also
Jn 14:12 greater *w* than these shall he do
Jn 15:24 the *w* which none other man did
Acts 2:11 tongues the wonderful *w* of God
Acts 7:41 rejoiced in the *w* of their own
Acts 9:36 this woman was full of good *w*
Acts 15:18 Known unto God are all his *w* from
Acts 26:20 God, and do *w* meet for repentance
Rom 3:27 what law? of *w*?
Rom 4:2 if Abraham were justified by *w*
Rom 4:6 imputeth righteousness without *w*
Rom 9:11 to election might stand, not of *w*
Rom 9:32 as it were by the *w* of the law
Rom 11:6 by grace, then is it no more of *w*
Rom 11:6 But if it be of *w*, then is it no
Rom 13:3 rulers are not a terror to good *w*
Rom 13:12 cast off the *w* of darkness
2Cor 11:15 end shall be according to their *w*
Gal 2:16 not justified by the *w* of the law
Gal 2:16 and not by the *w* of the law
Gal 2:16 for by the *w* of the law shall no

Gal 3:2 ye the Spirit by the *w* of the law
Gal 3:5 doeth he it by the *w* of the law
Gal 3:10 For as many as are of the *w* of
Gal 5:19 Now the *w* of the flesh are
Eph 2:9 Not of *w*, lest any man should
Eph 2:10 in Christ Jesus unto good *w*
Eph 5:11 with the unfruitful *w* of darkness
Col 1:21 enemies in your mind by wicked *w*
1Ti 2:10 professing godliness) with good *w*
1Ti 5:10 Well reported of for good *w*
1Ti 5:25 Likewise also the good *w* of some
1Ti 6:18 good, that they be rich in good *w*
2Ti 1:9 calling, not according to our *w*
2Ti 3:17 furnished unto all good *w*
2Ti 4:14 reward him according to his *w*
Titus 1:16 but in *w* they deny him, being
Titus 2:7 thyself a pattern of good *w*
Titus 2:14 people, zealous of good *w*
Titus 3:5 Not by *w* of righteousness which
Titus 3:8 be careful to maintain good *w*
Titus 3:14 good *w* for necessary uses
Heb 1:10 heavens are the *w* of thine hands
Heb 2:7 set him over the *w* of thy hands
Heb 3:9 me, and saw my *w* forty years
Heb 4:3 although the *w* were finished from
Heb 4:4 the seventh day from all his *w*
Heb 4:10 also hath ceased from his own *w*
Heb 6:1 of repentance from dead *w*
Heb 9:14 dead *w* to serve the living God
Heb 10:24 to provoke unto love and to good *w*
Jas 2:14 say he hath faith, and have not *w*
Jas 2:17 Even so faith, if it hath not *w*
Jas 2:18 say, Thou hast faith, and I have *w*
Jas 2:18 shew me thy faith without thy *w*
Jas 2:18 I will shew thee my faith by my *w*
Jas 2:20 man, that faith without *w* is dead
Jas 2:21 Abraham our father justified by *w*
Jas 2:22 thou how faith wrought with his *w*
Jas 2:22 by *w* was faith made perfect
Jas 2:24 how that by *w* a man is justified
Jas 2:25 Rahab the harlot justified by *w*
Jas 2:26 so faith without *w* is dead also
Jas 3:13 his *w* with meekness of wisdom
1Pet 2:12 they may by your good *w*, which
2Pet 3:10 the *w* that are therein shall be
1Jn 3:8 might destroy the *w* of the devil
1Jn 3:12 Because his own *w* were evil
Rev 2:2 I know thy *w*, and thy labour, and
Rev 2:5 and repent, and do the first *w*
Rev 2:9 I know thy *w*, and tribulation, and
Rev 2:13 I know thy *w*, and where thou
Rev 2:19 I know thy *w*, and charity, and
Rev 2:19 faith, and thy patience, and thy *w*
Rev 2:23 one of you according to your *w*
Rev 2:26 keepeth my *w* unto the end, to him
Rev 3:1 I know thy *w*, that thou hast a
Rev 3:2 found thy *w* perfect before God
Rev 3:8 I know thy *w*
Rev 3:15 I know thy *w*, that thou art
Rev 9:20 not of the *w* of their hands
Rev 14:13 and their *w* do follow them
Rev 15:3 Great and marvellous are thy *w*
Rev 18:6 her double according to her *w*
Rev 20:12 the books, according to their *w*
Rev 20:13 every man according to their *w*

## WORKS'

Jn 14:11 believe me for the very *w* sake

## WORLD

1Sa 2:8 and he hath set the *w* upon them
2Sa 22:16 of the *w* were discovered, at the
1Chr 16:30 the *w* also shall be stable, that
Job 18:18 darkness, and chased out of the *w*
Job 34:13 Or who hath disposed the whole *w*
Job 37:12 the face of the *w* in the earth
Ps 9:8 judge the *w* in righteousness
Ps 17:14 hand, O LORD, from men of the *w*
Ps 18:15 the foundations of the *w* were
Ps 19:4 their words to the end of the *w*
Ps 22:27 the ends of the *w* shall remember
Ps 24:1 the *w*, and they that dwell therein
Ps 33:8 of the *w* stand in awe of him
Ps 49:1 ear, all ye inhabitants of the *w*
Ps 50:12 for the *w* is mine, and the fulness
Ps 73:12 the ungodly, who prosper in the *w*
Ps 77:18 the lightnings lightened the *w*
Ps 89:11 as for the *w* and the fulness
Ps 90:2 hadst formed the earth and the *w*
Ps 93:1 the *w* also is stablished, that it
Ps 96:10 the *w* also shall be established
Ps 96:13 judge the *w* with righteousness
Ps 97:4 His lightnings enlightened the *w*
Ps 98:7 the *w*, and they that dwell therein
Ps 98:9 shall he judge the *w*, and the
Prov 8:26 highest part of the dust of the *w*
Eccl 3:11 he hath set the *w* in their heart
Is 13:11 will punish the *w* for their evil
Is 14:17 That made the *w* as a wilderness,
Is 14:21 the face of the *w* with cities
Is 18:3 All ye inhabitants of the *w*
Is 23:17 the *w* upon the face of the earth
Is 24:4 the *w* languisheth and fadeth away,
Is 26:9 the inhabitants of the *w* will
Is 26:18 the inhabitants of the *w* fallen
Is 27:6 fill the face of the *w* with fruit
Is 34:1 the *w*, and all things that come
Is 38:11 with the inhabitants of the *w*
Is 45:17 nor confounded *w* without end
Is 62:11 proclaimed unto the end of the *w*
Is 64:4 of the *w* men have not heard
Jer 10:12 established the *w* by his wisdom
Jer 25:26 and all the kingdoms of the *w*
Jer 51:15 established the *w* by his wisdom
Lam 4:12 and all the inhabitants of the *w*
Nah 1:5 at his presence, yea, the *w*
Mt 4:8 him all the kingdoms of the *w*
Mt 5:14 Ye are the light of the *w*
Mt 12:32 forgiven him, neither in this *w*
Mt 12:32 neither in the *w* to come
Mt 13:22 and the care of this *w*, and the
Mt 13:35 from the foundation of the *w*
Mt 13:38 The field is the *w*
Mt 13:39 the harvest is the end of the *w*
Mt 13:40 shall it be in the end of this *w*
Mt 13:49 shall it be at the end of the *w*
Mt 16:26 if he shall gain the whole *w*
Mt 18:7 Woe unto the *w* because of
Mt 24:3 coming, and of the end of the *w*
Mt 24:14 shall be preached in all the *w*
Mt 24:21 beginning of the *w* to this time
Mt 25:34 you from the foundation of the *w*
Mt 26:13 shall be preached in the whole *w*
Mt 28:20 alway, even unto the end of the *w*
Mk 4:19 And the cares of this *w*, and the
Mk 8:36 man, if he shall gain the whole *w*
Mk 10:30 in the *w* to come eternal life
Mk 14:9 preached throughout the whole *w*
Mk 16:15 unto them, Go ye into all the *w*
Lk 1:70 which have been since the *w* began
Lk 2:1 that all the *w* should be taxed
Lk 4:5 of the *w* in a moment of time
Lk 9:25 if he gain the whole *w*, and lose
Lk 11:50 shed from the foundation of the *w*
Lk 12:30 the nations of the *w* seek after
Lk 16:8 for the children of this *w* are in
Lk 18:30 in the *w* to come life everlasting
Lk 20:34 The children of this *w* marry
Lk 20:35 accounted worthy to obtain that *w*
Jn 1:9 every man that cometh into the *w*
Jn 1:10 He was in the *w*
Jn 1:10 the *w* was made by him, and the
Jn 1:10 by him, and the *w* knew him not
Jn 1:29 taketh away the sin of the *w*
Jn 3:16 For God so loved the *w*, that he
Jn 3:17 into the *w* to condemn the *w*
Jn 3:17 but that the *w* through him might
Jn 3:19 that light is come into the *w*
Jn 4:42 the Christ, the Saviour of the *w*
Jn 6:14 that should come into the *w*
Jn 6:33 heaven, and giveth life unto the *w*
Jn 6:51 I will give for the life of the *w*
Jn 7:4 things, shew thyself to the *w*
Jn 7:7 The *w* cannot hate you
Jn 8:12 saying, I am the light of the *w*
Jn 8:23 ye are of this *w*
Jn 8:23 I am not of this *w*
Jn 8:26 I speak to the *w* those things
Jn 9:5 As long as I am in the *w*
Jn 9:5 I am the light of the *w*
Jn 9:32 Since the *w* began was it not
Jn 9:39 judgment I am come into this *w*
Jn 10:36 sanctified, and sent into the *w*
Jn 11:9 he seeth the light of this *w*
Jn 11:27 God, which should come into the *w*
Jn 12:19 behold, the *w* is gone after him
Jn 12:25 *w* shall keep it unto life eternal
Jn 12:31 Now is the judgment of this *w*
Jn 12:31 the prince of this *w* be cast out
Jn 12:46 I am come a light into the *w*
Jn 12:47 for I came not to judge the *w*
Jn 12:47 but to save the *w*
Jn 13:1 out of this *w* unto the Father
Jn 13:1 loved his own which were in the *w*
Jn 14:17 whom the *w* cannot receive,
Jn 14:19 while, and the *w* seeth me no more
Jn 14:22 unto us, and not unto the *w*
Jn 14:27 not as the *w* giveth, give I unto
Jn 14:30 for the prince of this *w* cometh
Jn 14:31 But that the *w* may know that I
Jn 15:18 If the *w* hate you, ye know that
Jn 15:19 If ye were of the *w*
Jn 15:19 the *w* would love his own
Jn 15:19 but because ye are not of the *w*
Jn 15:19 I have chosen you out of the *w*
Jn 15:19 therefore the *w* hateth you
Jn 16:8 he will reprove the *w* of sin
Jn 16:11 the prince of this *w* is judged
Jn 16:20 lament, but the *w* shall rejoice
Jn 16:21 joy that a man is born into the *w*
Jn 16:28 the Father, and am come into the *w*
Jn 16:28 again, I leave the *w*, and go to
Jn 16:33 In the *w* ye shall have
Jn 16:33 I have overcome the *w*
Jn 17:5 I had with thee before the *w* was
Jn 17:6 which thou gavest me out of the *w*
Jn 17:9 I pray not for the *w*, but for
Jn 17:11 And now I am no more in the *w*
Jn 17:11 but these are in the *w*
Jn 17:12 While I was with them in the *w*
Jn 17:13 and these things I speak in the *w*
Jn 17:14 the *w* hath hated them
Jn 17:14 because they are not of the *w*
Jn 17:14 even as I am not of the *w*
Jn 17:15 shouldest take them out of the *w*
Jn 17:16 They are not of the *w*
Jn 17:16 even as I am not of the *w*
Jn 17:18 As thou hast sent me into the *w*
Jn 17:18 have I also sent them into the *w*
Jn 17:21 that the *w* may believe that thou
Jn 17:23 that the *w* may know that thou
Jn 17:24 me before the foundation of the *w*
Jn 17:25 the *w* hath not known thee
Jn 18:20 him, I spake openly to the *w*
Jn 18:36 My kingdom is not of this *w*
Jn 18:36 if my kingdom were of this *w*
Jn 18:37 for this cause came I into the *w*
Jn 21:25 I suppose that even the *w* itself
Acts 3:21 holy prophets since the *w* began
Acts 11:28 great dearth throughout all the *w*
Acts 15:18 works from the beginning of the *w*
Acts 17:6 These that have turned the *w*
Acts 17:24 God that made the *w* and all things
Acts 17:31 *w* in righteousness by that man
Acts 19:27 all Asia and the *w* worshippeth
Acts 24:5 all the Jews throughout the *w*
Rom 1:8 spoken of throughout the whole *w*
Rom 1:20 of the *w* are clearly seen
Rom 3:6 then how shall God judge the *w*
Rom 3:19 all the *w* may become guilty
Rom 4:13 he should be the heir of the *w*
Rom 5:12 by one man sin entered into the *w*
Rom 5:13 until the law sin was in the *w*
Rom 10:18 words unto the ends of the *w*
Rom 11:12 of them be the riches of the *w*
Rom 11:15 them be the reconciling of the *w*
Rom 12:2 And be not conformed to this *w*
Rom 16:25 was kept secret since the *w* began
1Cor 1:20 where is the disputer of this *w*
1Cor 1:20 made foolish the wisdom of this *w*
1Cor 1:21 God the *w* by wisdom knew not God
1Cor 1:27 of the *w* to confound the wise
1Cor 1:27 *w* to confound the things which
1Cor 1:28 And base things of the *w*, and
1Cor 2:6 yet not the wisdom of this *w*
1Cor 2:6 nor of the princes of this *w*
1Cor 2:7 before the *w* unto our glory
1Cor 2:8 of the princes of this *w* knew
1Cor 2:12 received, not the spirit of the *w*
1Cor 3:18 you seemeth to be wise in this *w*
1Cor 3:19 For the wisdom of this *w* is
1Cor 3:22 or Apollos, or Cephas, or the *w*
1Cor 4:9 are made a spectacle unto the *w*
1Cor 4:13 we are made as the filth of the *w*
1Cor 5:10 with the fornicators of this *w*
1Cor 5:10 must ye needs go out of the *w*
1Cor 6:2 that the saints shall judge the *w*
1Cor 6:2 if the *w* shall be judged by you,
1Cor 7:31 And they that use this *w*, as not
1Cor 7:31 fashion of this *w* passeth away
1Cor 7:33 for the things that are of the *w*

1Cor 7:34 careth for the things of the *w*
1Cor 8:4 that an idol is nothing in the *w*
1Cor 8:13 eat no flesh while the *w* standeth
1Cor 10:11 whom the ends of the *w* are come
1Cor 11:32 not be condemned with the *w*
1Cor 14:10 so many kinds of voices in the *w*
2Cor 1:12 had our conversation in the *w*
2Cor 4:4 In whom the god of this *w* hath
2Cor 5:19 reconciling the *w* unto himself
2Cor 7:10 the sorrow of the *w* worketh death
Gal 1:4 us from this present evil *w*
Gal 4:3 under the elements of the *w*
Gal 6:14 by whom the *w* is crucified unto
Gal 6:14 unto me, and I unto the *w*
Eph 1:4 before the foundation of the *w*
Eph 1:21 that is named, not only in this *w*
Eph 2:2 according to the course of this *w*
Eph 2:12 no hope, and without God in the *w*
Eph 3:9 of the *w* hath been hid in God
Eph 3:21 all ages, *w* without end
Eph 6:12 rulers of the darkness of this *w*
Phil 2:15 whom ye shine as lights in the *w*
Col 1:6 unto you, as it is in all the *w*
Col 2:8 men, after the rudiments of the *w*
Col 2:20 from the rudiments of the *w*
Col 2:20 why, as though living in the *w*
1Ti 1:15 came into the *w* to save sinners
1Ti 3:16 Gentiles, believed on in the *w*
1Ti 6:7 we brought nothing into this *w*
1Ti 6:17 them that are rich in this *w*
2Ti 1:9 Christ Jesus before the *w* began
2Ti 4:10 me, having loved this present *w*
Titus 1:2 lie, promised before the *w* began
Titus 2:12 and godly, in this present *w*
Heb 1:6 in the firstbegotten into the *w*
Heb 2:5 put in subjection the *w* to come
Heb 4:3 from the foundation of the *w*
Heb 6:5 and the powers of the *w* to come
Heb 9:26 since the foundation of the *w*
Heb 9:26 *w* hath he appeared to put away
Heb 10:5 when he cometh into the *w*
Heb 11:7 by the which he condemned the *w*
Heb 11:38 (Of whom the *w* was not worthy
Jas 1:27 keep himself unspotted from the *w*
Jas 2:5 the poor of this *w* rich in faith
Jas 3:6 tongue is a fire, a *w* of iniquity
Jas 4:4 of the *w* is enmity with God
Jas 4:4 of the *w* is the enemy of God
1Pet 1:20 before the foundation of the *w*
1Pet 5:9 your brethren that are in the *w*
2Pet 1:4 that is in the *w* through lust
2Pet 2:5 And spared not the old *w*, but
2Pet 2:5 flood upon the *w* of the ungodly
2Pet 2:20 *w* through the knowledge of the
2Pet 3:6 Whereby the *w* that then was,
1Jn 2:2 also for the sins of the whole *w*
1Jn 2:15 Love not the *w*, neither the
1Jn 2:15 the things that are in the *w*
1Jn 2:15 If any man love the *w*, the love
1Jn 2:16 For all that is in the *w*, the
1Jn 2:16 of the Father, but is of the *w*
1Jn 2:17 the *w* passeth away, and the lust
1Jn 3:1 therefore the *w* knoweth us not,
1Jn 3:13 my brethren, if the *w* hate you
1Jn 4:1 prophets are gone out into the *w*
1Jn 4:3 even now already is it in the *w*
1Jn 4:4 in you, than he that is in the *w*
1Jn 4:5 They are of the *w*
1Jn 4:5 therefore speak they of the *w*
1Jn 4:5 and the *w* heareth them
1Jn 4:9 his only begotten Son into the *w*
1Jn 4:14 Son to be the Saviour of the *w*
1Jn 4:17 as he is, so are we in this *w*
1Jn 5:4 is born of God overcometh the *w*
1Jn 5:4 the victory that overcometh the *w*
1Jn 5:5 Who is he that overcometh the *w*
1Jn 5:19 the whole *w* lieth in wickedness
2Jn 7 deceivers are entered into the *w*
Rev 3:10 which shall come upon all the *w*
Rev 11:15 The kingdoms of this *w* are become
Rev 12:9 which deceiveth the whole *w*
Rev 13:3 all the *w* wondered after the
Rev 13:8 from the foundation of the *w*
Rev 16:14 of the earth and of the whole *w*
Rev 17:8 life from the foundation of the *w*

## WORLDLY

Titus 2:12 *w* lusts, we should live soberly,
Heb 9:1 divine service, and a *w* sanctuary

## WORLD'S

1Jn 3:17 But whoso hath this *w* good

## WORLDS

Heb 1:2 by whom also he made the *w*
Heb 11:3 faith we understand that the *w*

## WORM

Ex 16:24 neither was there any *w* therein
Job 17:14 to the *w*, Thou art my mother, and
Job 24:20 the *w* shall feed sweetly on him
Job 25:6 How much less man, that is a *w*
Job 25:6 and the son of man, which is a *w*
Ps 22:6 But I am a *w*, and no man
Is 14:11 the *w* is spread under thee, and
Is 41:14 thou *w* Jacob, and ye men of Israel
Is 51:8 the *w* shall eat them like wool
Is 66:24 for their *w* shall not die,
Jonah 4:7 But God prepared a *w* when the
Mk 9:44 Where their *w* dieth not, and the
Mk 9:46 Where their *w* dieth not, and the
Mk 9:48 Where their *w* dieth not, and the

## WORMS

Ex 16:20 until the morning, and it bred *w*
Deut 28:39 for the *w* shall eat them
Job 7:5 My flesh is clothed with *w*
Job 19:26 after my skin *w* destroy this body
Job 21:26 dust, and the *w* shall cover them
Is 14:11 under thee, and the *w* cover thee
Mic 7:17 their holes like *w* of the earth
Acts 12:23 and he was eaten of *w*, and gave up

## WORMWOOD

Deut 29:18 you a root that beareth gall and *w*
Prov 5:4 But her end is bitter as *w*
Jer 9:15 them, even this people, with *w*
Jer 23:15 Behold, I will feed them with *w*
Lam 3:15 he hath made me drunken with *w*
Lam 3:19 affliction and my misery, the *w*
Amos 5:7 Ye who turn judgment to *w*
Rev 8:11 the name of the star is called *W*
Rev 8:11 third part of the waters became *w*

## WORSHIP

Gen 22:5 I and the lad will go yonder and *w*
Ex 24:1 and *w* ye afar off
Ex 34:14 For thou shalt *w* no other god
Deut 4:19 shouldest be driven to *w* them
Deut 8:19 *w* them, I testify against you
Deut 11:16 and serve other gods, and *w* them
Deut 26:10 *w* before the LORD thy God
Deut 30:17 *w* other gods, and serve them
Josh 5:14 his face to the earth, and did *w*
1Sa 1:3 up out of his city yearly to *w*
1Sa 15:25 with me, that I may *w* the LORD
1Sa 15:30 that I may *w* the LORD thy God
1Kin 9:6 go and serve other gods, and *w* them
1Kin 12:30 people went to *w* before the one
2Kin 5:18 the house of Rimmon to *w* there
2Kin 17:36 shall ye fear, and him shall ye *w*
2Kin 18:22 Ye shall *w* before this altar in
1Chr 16:29 *w* the LORD in the beauty of
2Chr 7:19 go and serve other gods, and *w* them
2Chr 32:12 Ye shall *w* before one altar, and
Ps 5:7 in thy fear will I *w* toward thy
Ps 22:27 the nations shall *w* before thee
Ps 22:29 be fat upon earth shall eat and *w*
Ps 29:2 *w* the LORD in the beauty of
Ps 45:11 and *w* thou him
Ps 66:4 All the earth shall *w* thee
Ps 81:9 shalt thou *w* any strange god
Ps 86:9 come and *w* before thee, O Lord
Ps 95:6 O come, let us *w* and bow down
Ps 96:9 O *w* the LORD in the beauty of
Ps 97:7 *w* him, all ye gods
Ps 99:5 our God, and *w* at his footstool
Ps 99:9 our God, and *w* at his holy hill
Ps 132:7 we will *w* at his footstool
Ps 138:2 I will *w* toward thy holy temple,
Is 2:8 they *w* the work of their own
Is 2:20 made each one for himself to *w*
Is 27:13 shall *w* the LORD in the holy
Is 36:7 Ye shall *w* before this altar
Is 46:6 they fall down, yea, they *w*
Is 49:7 and arise, princes also shall *w*
Is 66:23 all flesh come to *w* before me
Jer 7:2 in at these gates to *w* the LORD
Jer 13:10 to *w* them, shall even be as this
Jer 25:6 to *w* them, and provoke me not to
Jer 26:2 which come to *w* in the LORD's
Jer 44:19 did we make her cakes to *w* her
Eze 46:2 he shall *w* at the threshold of
Eze 46:3 the people of the land shall *w* at
Eze 46:9 *w* shall go out by the way of the
Dan 3:5 down and *w* the golden image that
Dan 3:10 fall down and *w* the golden image
Dan 3:12 nor *w* the golden image which thou
Dan 3:14 nor *w* the golden image which I
Dan 3:15 *w* the image which I have made
Dan 3:15 but if ye *w* not, ye shall be cast
Dan 3:18 nor *w* the golden image which thou
Dan 3:28 might not serve nor *w* any god
Mic 5:13 thou shalt no more *w* the work of
Zeph 1:5 them that *w* the host of heaven
Zeph 1:5 and them that *w* and that swear by
Zeph 2:11 and men shall *w* him, every one
Zec 14:16 from year to year to *w* the King
Zec 14:17 unto Jerusalem to *w* the King
Mt 2:2 in the east, and are come to *w* him
Mt 2:8 that I may come and *w* him also
Mt 4:9 if thou wilt fall down and *w* me
Mt 4:10 Thou shalt *w* the Lord thy God, and
Mt 15:9 But in vain they do *w* me,
Mk 7:7 Howbeit in vain do they *w* me
Lk 4:7 If thou therefore wilt *w* me
Lk 4:8 Thou shalt *w* the Lord thy God, and
Lk 14:10 then shalt thou have *w* in the
Jn 4:20 is the place where men ought to *w*
Jn 4:21 yet at Jerusalem, *w* the Father
Jn 4:22 Ye *w* ye know not what
Jn 4:22 we know what we *w*
Jn 4:23 shall *w* the Father in spirit
Jn 4:23 the Father seeketh such to *w* him
Jn 4:24 they that *w* him must
Jn 4:24 must *w* him in spirit
Jn 12:20 that came up to *w* at the feast
Acts 7:42 gave them up to *w* the host of
Acts 7:43 figures which ye made to *w* them
Acts 8:27 and had come to Jerusalem for to *w*
Acts 17:23 Whom therefore ye ignorantly *w*
Acts 18:13 men to *w* God contrary to the law
Acts 24:11 I went up to Jerusalem for to *w*
Acts 24:14 so *w* I the God of my fathers,
1Cor 14:25 down on his face he will *w* God
Phil 3:3 which *w* God in the spirit, and
Col 2:23 indeed a shew of wisdom in will *w*
Heb 1:6 let all the angels of God *w* him
Rev 3:9 *w* before thy feet, and to know
Rev 4:10 *w* him that liveth for ever and
Rev 9:20 that they should not *w* devils
Rev 11:1 the altar, and them that *w* therein
Rev 13:8 dwell upon the earth shall *w* him
Rev 13:12 therein to *w* the first beast
Rev 13:15 *w* the image of the beast should
Rev 14:7 *w* him that made heaven, and earth,
Rev 14:9 voice, If any man *w* the beast
Rev 14:11 who *w* the beast and his image, and
Rev 15:4 shall come and *w* before thee
Rev 19:10 And I fell at his feet to *w* him
Rev 19:10 *w* God
Rev 22:8 I fell down to *w* before the feet
Rev 22:9 *w* God

## WORSHIPPED

Gen 24:26 down his head, and *w* the LORD
Gen 24:48 *w* the LORD, and blessed the LORD
Gen 24:52 he *w* the LORD, bowing himself to
Ex 4:31 then they bowed their heads and *w*
Ex 12:27 And the people bowed the head and *w*
Ex 32:8 them a molten calf, and have *w* it
Ex 33:10 and all the people rose up and *w*
Ex 34:8 his head toward the earth, and *w*
Deut 17:3 *w* them, either the sun, or moon,
Deut 29:26 *w* them, gods whom they knew not,
Judg 7:15 interpretation thereof, that he *w*
1Sa 1:19 *w* before the LORD, and returned,
1Sa 1:28 And he *w* the LORD there
1Sa 15:31 and Saul *w* the LORD
2Sa 12:20 into the house of the LORD, and *w*
2Sa 15:32 top of the mount, where he *w* God
1Kin 9:9 upon other gods, and have *w* them
1Kin 11:33 have *w* Ashtoreth the goddess of
1Kin 16:31 and went and served Baal, and *w* him
1Kin 22:53 *w* him, and provoked to anger the
2Kin 17:16 *w* all the host of heaven, and
2Kin 21:3 *w* all the host of heaven, and
2Kin 21:21 that his father served, and *w* them
1Chr 29:20 heads, and *w* the LORD, and the king
2Chr 7:3 ground upon the pavement, and *w*
2Chr 7:22 gods, and *w* them, and served them
2Chr 29:28 And all the congregation *w*
2Chr 29:29 with him bowed themselves, and *w*

2Chr 29:30 and they bowed their heads and *w*
2Chr 33:3 *w* all the host of heaven, and
Neh 8:6 *w* the LORD with their faces to
Neh 9:3 and *w* the LORD their God
Job 1:20 fell down upon the ground, and *w*
Ps 106:19 in Horeb, and *w* the molten image
Jer 1:16 *w* the works of their own hands
Jer 8:2 have sought, and whom they have *w*
Jer 16:11 have served them, and have *w* them
Jer 22:9 *w* other gods, and served them
Eze 8:16 they *w* the sun toward the east
Dan 2:46 *w* Daniel, and commanded that they
Dan 3:7 down and *w* the golden image that
Mt 2:11 mother, and fell down, and *w* him
Mt 8:2 *w* him, saying, Lord, if thou wilt
Mt 9:18 *w* him, saying, My daughter is
Mt 14:33 *w* him, saying, Of a truth thou
Mt 15:25 *w* him, saying, Lord, help me
Mt 18:26 *w* him, saying, Lord, have
Mt 28:9 and held him by the feet, and *w* him
Mt 28:17 And when they saw him, they *w* him
Mk 5:6 Jesus afar off, he ran and *w* him,
Mk 15:19 him, and bowing their knees *w* him
Lk 24:52 And they *w* him, and returned to
Jn 4:20 Our fathers *w* in this mountain
Jn 9:38 And he *w* him
Acts 10:25 fell down at his feet, and *w* him
Acts 16:14 the city of Thyatira, which *w* God
Acts 17:25 Neither is *w* with men's hands, as
Acts 18:7 named Justus, one that *w* God
Rom 1:25 the truth of God into a lie, and *w*
2Th 2:4 that is called God, or that is *w*
Heb 11:21 and *w*, leaning upon the top of his
Rev 5:14 *w* him that liveth for ever and
Rev 7:11 throne on their faces, and *w* God,
Rev 11:16 fell upon their faces, and *w* God,
Rev 13:4 they *w* the dragon which gave
Rev 13:4 they *w* the beast, saying, Who is
Rev 16:2 and upon them which *w* his image
Rev 19:4 *w* God that sat on the throne,
Rev 19:20 beast, and them that *w* his image
Rev 20:4 God, and which had not *w* the beast

## WORSHIPPER

Jn 9:31 but if any man be a *w* of God
Acts 19:35 is a *w* of the great goddess Diana

## WORSHIPPERS

2Kin 10:19 he might destroy the *w* of Baal
2Kin 10:21 all the *w* of Baal came, so that
2Kin 10:22 vestments for all the *w* of Baal
2Kin 10:23 Baal, and said unto the *w* of Baal
2Kin 10:23 the LORD, but the *w* of Baal only
Jn 4:23 when the true *w* shall worship the
Heb 10:2 because that the *w* once purged

## WORSHIPPETH

Neh 9:6 and the host of heaven *w* thee
Is 44:15 yea, he maketh a god, and *w* it
Is 44:17 *w* it, and prayeth unto it, and
Dan 3:6 *w* shall the same hour be cast
Dan 3:11 And whoso falleth not down and *w*
Acts 19:27 whom all Asia and the world *w*

## WORSHIPPING

2Kin 19:37 as he was *w* in the house of
2Chr 20:18 fell before the LORD, *w* the LORD
Is 37:38 as he was *w* in the house of
Mt 20:20 *w* him, and desiring a certain
Col 2:18 *w* of angels, intruding into those

## WORTH

Gen 23:9 it is *w* he shall give it me for a
Gen 23:15 the land is *w* four hundred
Lev 27:23 unto him the *w* of thy estimation
Deut 15:18 for he hath been *w* a double hired
2Sa 18:3 but now thou art *w* ten thousand
1Kin 21:2 give thee the *w* of it in money
Job 24:25 liar, and make my speech nothing *w*
Prov 10:20 heart of the wicked is little *w*
Eze 30:2 Howl ye, Woe *w* the day

## WORTHIES

Nah 2:5 He shall recount his *w*

## WORTHILY

Ruth 4:11 do thou *w* in Ephratah, and be

## WORTHY

Gen 32:10 I am not *w* of the least of all
Deut 17:6 shall he that is *w* of death be
Deut 19:6 whereas he was not *w* of death
Deut 21:22 have committed a sin *w* of death
Deut 22:26 in the damsel no sin *w* of death
Deut 25:2 the wicked man be *w* to be beaten
1Sa 1:5 unto Hannah he gave a *w* portion
1Sa 26:16 the LORD liveth, ye are *w* to die
2Sa 22:4 the LORD, who is *w* to be praised
1Kin 1:52 If he will shew himself a *w* man
1Kin 2:26 for thou art *w* of death
Ps 18:3 the LORD, who is *w* to be praised
Jer 26:11 saying, This man is *w* to die
Jer 26:16 This man is not *w* to die
Mt 3:11 I, whose shoes I am not *w* to bear
Mt 8:8 I am not *w* that thou shouldest
Mt 10:10 for the workman is *w* of his meat
Mt 10:11 enter, enquire who in it is *w*
Mt 10:13 And if the house be *w*, let your
Mt 10:13 but if it be not *w*, let your
Mt 10:37 more than me is not *w* of me
Mt 10:37 more than me is not *w* of me
Mt 10:38 after me, is not *w* of me
Mt 22:8 they which were bidden were not *w*
Mk 1:7 shoes I am not *w* to stoop down
Lk 3:8 therefore fruits *w* of repentance
Lk 3:16 whose shoes I am not *w* to unloose
Lk 7:4 That he was *w* for whom he should
Lk 7:6 for I am not *w* that thou
Lk 7:7 I myself *w* to come unto thee
Lk 10:7 for the labourer is *w* of his hire
Lk 12:48 and did commit things *w* of stripes
Lk 15:19 am no more *w* to be called thy son
Lk 15:21 am no more *w* to be called thy son
Lk 20:35 accounted *w* to obtain that world
Lk 21:36 that ye may be accounted *w* to
Lk 23:15 nothing *w* of death is done unto
Jn 1:27 latchet I am not *w* to unloose
Acts 5:41 that they were counted *w* to
Acts 13:25 of his feet I am not *w* to loose
Acts 23:29 his charge *w* of death or of bonds
Acts 24:2 that very *w* deeds are done unto
Acts 25:11 committed any thing *w* of death
Acts 25:25 had committed nothing *w* of death
Acts 26:31 nothing *w* of death or of bonds
Rom 1:32 commit such things are *w* of death
Rom 8:18 of this present time are not *w* to
Eph 4:1 beseech you that ye walk *w* of the
Col 1:10 That ye might walk *w* of the Lord
1Th 2:12 That ye would walk *w* of God
2Th 1:5 counted *w* of the kingdom of God
2Th 1:11 would count you *w* of this calling
1Ti 1:15 *w* of all acceptation, that Christ
1Ti 4:9 saying and *w* of all acceptation
1Ti 5:17 be counted *w* of double honour
1Ti 5:18 The labourer is *w* of his reward
1Ti 6:1 their own masters *w* of all honour
Heb 3:3 *w* of more glory than Moses
Heb 10:29 suppose ye, shall he be thought *w*
Heb 11:38 (Of whom the world was not *w*
Jas 2:7 Do not they blaspheme that *w* name
Rev 3:4 for they are *w*
Rev 4:11 Thou art *w*, O Lord, to receive
Rev 5:2 Who is *w* to open the book, and to
Rev 5:4 no man was found *w* to open
Rev 5:9 Thou art *w* to take the book, and
Rev 5:12 *W* is the Lamb that was slain to
Rev 16:6 for they are *w*

## WOT

Gen 21:26 I *w* not who hath done this thing
Gen 44:15 *w* ye not that such a man as I can
Ex 32:1 we *w* not what is become of him
Ex 32:23 we *w* not what is become of him
Num 22:6 for I *w* that he whom thou
Josh 2:5 whither the men went I *w* not
Acts 3:17 I *w* that through ignorance ye did
Acts 7:40 we *w* not what is become of him
Rom 11:2 *W* ye not what the scripture saith
Phil 1:22 yet what I shall choose I *w* not

## WOTTETH

Gen 39:8 my master *w* not what is with me

## WOUND

Ex 21:25 *w* for *w*, stripe for stripe
Deut 32:39 I *w*, and I heal
1Kin 22:35 the blood ran out of the *w* into
Job 34:6 my *w* is incurable without
Ps 68:21 But God shall *w* the head of his
Ps 110:6 he shall *w* the heads over many
Prov 6:33 A *w* and dishonour shall he get
Prov 20:30 The blueness of a *w* cleanseth
Is 30:26 and healeth the stroke of their *w*
Jer 10:19 my *w* is grievous
Jer 15:18 my *w* incurable, which refuseth to
Jer 30:12 incurable, and thy *w* is grievous
Jer 30:14 thee with the *w* of an enemy
Hos 5:13 his sickness, and Judah saw his *w*
Hos 5:13 heal you, nor cure you of your *w*
Obad 7 bread have laid a *w* under thee
Mic 1:9 For her *w* is incurable
Nah 3:19 thy *w* is grievous
Jn 19:40 *w* it in linen clothes with the
Acts 5:6 *w* him up, and carried him out, and
1Cor 8:12 *w* their weak conscience, ye sin
Rev 13:3 and his deadly *w* was healed
Rev 13:12 beast, whose deadly *w* was healed
Rev 13:14 beast, which had the *w* by a sword

## WOUNDED

Deut 23:1 He that is *w* in the stones, or
Judg 9:40 many were overthrown and *w*
1Sa 17:52 the *w* of the Philistines fell
1Sa 31:3 he was sore *w* of the archers
2Sa 22:39 *w* them, that they could not arise
1Kin 20:37 him, so that in smiting he *w* him
1Kin 22:34 for I am *w*
2Kin 8:28 and the Syrians *w* Joram
1Chr 10:3 him, and he was *w* of the archers
2Chr 18:33 for I am *w*
2Chr 35:23 for I am sore *w*
Job 24:12 and the soul of the *w* crieth out
Ps 18:38 I have *w* them that they were not
Ps 64:7 suddenly shall they be *w*
Ps 69:26 grief of those whom thou hast *w*
Ps 109:22 needy, and my heart is *w* within me
Prov 7:26 For she hath cast down many *w*
Prov 18:14 but a *w* spirit who can bear
Song 5:7 me, they smote me, they *w* me
Is 51:9 hath cut Rahab, and *w* the dragon
Is 53:5 But he was *w* for our
Jer 30:14 for I have *w* thee with the wound
Jer 37:10 remained but *w* men among them
Jer 51:52 all her land the *w* shall groan
Lam 2:12 when they swooned as the *w* in the
Eze 26:15 sound of thy fall, when the *w* cry
Eze 28:23 the *w* shall be judged in the
Eze 30:24 the groanings of a deadly *w* man
Joel 2:8 the sword, they shall not be *w*
Zec 13:6 Those with which I was *w* in the
Mk 12:4 *w* him in the head, and sent him
Lk 10:30 *w* him, and departed, leaving him
Lk 20:12 they *w* him also, and cast him out
Acts 19:16 fled out of that house naked and *w*
Rev 13:3 his heads as it were *w* to death

## WOUNDEDST

Hab 3:13 thou *w* the head out of the house

## WOUNDETH

Job 5:18 he *w*, and his hands make whole

## WOUNDING

Gen 4:23 for I have slain a man to my *w*

## WOUNDS

2Kin 8:29 to be healed in Jezreel of the *w*
2Kin 9:15 to be healed in Jezreel of the *w*
2Chr 22:6 in Jezreel because of the *w* which
Job 9:17 and multiplieth my *w* without cause
Ps 38:5 My *w* stink and are corrupt because
Ps 147:3 in heart, and bindeth up their *w*
Prov 18:8 words of a talebearer are as *w*
Prov 23:29 who hath *w* without cause
Prov 26:22 words of a talebearer are as *w*
Prov 27:6 Faithful are the *w* of a friend
Is 1:6 but *w*, and bruises, and putrifying
Jer 6:7 me continually is grief and *w*
Jer 30:17 and I will heal thee of thy *w*
Zec 13:6 What are these *w* in thine hands
Lk 10:34 And went to him, and bound up his *w*

## WOVE

2Kin 23:7 where the women *w* hangings for

## WOVEN

Ex 28:32 it shall have a binding of *w* work
Ex 39:22 the robe of the ephod of *w* work
Ex 39:27 of fine linen of *w* work for Aaron
Jn 19:23 *w* from the top throughout

## WRAP

Is 28:20 than that he can *w* himself in it
Mic 7:3 so they *w* it up

## WRAPPED

Gen 38:14 *w* herself, and sat in an open
1Sa 21:9 it is here *w* in a cloth behind
1Kin 19:13 that he *w* his face in his mantle,
2Kin 2:8 *w* it together, and smote the
Job 8:17 His roots are *w* about the heap,
Job 40:17 of his stones are *w* together
Eze 21:15 it is *w* up for the slaughter

Jonah 2:5 the weeds were *w* about my head
Mt 27:59 he *w* it in a clean linen cloth,
Mk 15:46 *w* him in the linen, and laid him
Lk 2:7 *w* him in swaddling clothes, and
Lk 2:12 the babe *w* in swaddling clothes
Lk 23:53 *w* it in linen, and laid it in a
Jn 20:7 but *w* together in a place by

## WRATH

Gen 39:19 that his *w* was kindled
Gen 49:7 and their *w*, for it was cruel
Ex 15:7 thou sentest forth thy *w*, which
Ex 22:24 my *w* shall wax hot, and I will
Ex 32:10 that my *w* may wax hot against
Ex 32:11 why doth thy *w* wax hot against
Ex 32:12 Turn from thy fierce *w*, and repent
Lev 10:6 lest *w* come upon all the people
Num 1:53 that there be no *w* upon the
Num 11:33 the *w* of the LORD was kindled
Num 16:46 for there is *w* gone out from the
Num 18:5 that there be no *w* any more upon
Num 25:11 hath turned my *w* away from the
Deut 9:7 thy God to *w* in the wilderness
Deut 9:8 Horeb ye provoked the LORD to *w*
Deut 9:22 ye provoked the LORD to *w*
Deut 11:17 then the LORD's *w* be kindled
Deut 29:23 in his anger, and in his *w*
Deut 29:28 of their land in anger, and in *w*
Deut 32:27 that I feared the *w* of the enemy
Josh 9:20 lest *w* be upon us, because of the
Josh 22:20 *w* fell on all the congregation of
1Sa 28:18 his fierce *w* upon Amalek,
2Sa 11:20 if so be that the king's *w* arise
2Kin 22:13 for great is the *w* of the LORD
2Kin 22:17 therefore my *w* shall be kindled
2Kin 23:26 the fierceness of his great *w*
1Chr 27:24 because there fell *w* for it
2Chr 12:7 my *w* shall not be poured out upon
2Chr 12:12 the *w* of the LORD turned from him
2Chr 19:2 therefore is *w* upon thee from
2Chr 19:10 so *w* come upon you, and upon your
2Chr 24:18 *w* came upon Judah and Jerusalem
2Chr 28:11 for the fierce *w* of the LORD is
2Chr 28:13 there is fierce *w* against Israel
2Chr 29:8 Wherefore the *w* of the LORD was
2Chr 29:10 that his fierce *w* may turn away
2Chr 30:8 of his *w* may turn away from you
2Chr 32:25 therefore there was *w* upon him
2Chr 32:26 so that the *w* of the LORD came
2Chr 34:21 for great is the *w* of the LORD
2Chr 34:25 therefore my *w* shall be poured
2Chr 36:16 until the *w* of the LORD arose
Ezr 5:12 provoked the God of heaven unto *w*
Ezr 7:23 for why should there be *w* against
Ezr 8:22 his *w* is against all them that
Ezr 10:14 until the fierce *w* of our God for
Neh 13:18 yet ye bring more *w* upon Israel
Est 1:18 arise too much contempt and *w*
Est 2:1 when the *w* of king Ahasuerus was
Est 3:5 then was Haman full of *w*
Est 7:7 his *w* went into the palace garden
Est 7:10 Then was the king's *w* pacified
Job 5:2 For *w* killeth the foolish man, and
Job 14:13 me secret, until thy *w* be past
Job 16:9 He teareth me in his *w*, who
Job 19:11 also kindled his *w* against me
Job 19:29 for *w* bringeth the punishments of
Job 20:23 cast the fury of his *w* upon him
Job 20:28 flow away in the day of his *w*
Job 21:20 drink of the *w* of the Almighty
Job 21:30 be brought forth to the day of *w*
Job 32:2 Then was kindled the *w* of Elihu
Job 32:2 against Job was his *w* kindled
Job 32:3 three friends was his *w* kindled
Job 32:5 three men, then his *w* was kindled
Job 36:13 the hypocrites in heart heap up *w*
Job 36:18 Because there is *w*, beware lest
Job 40:11 Cast abroad the rage of thy *w*
Job 42:7 My *w* is kindled against thee, and
Ps 2:5 shall he speak unto them in his *w*
Ps 2:12 when his *w* is kindled but a
Ps 21:9 shall swallow them up in his *w*
Ps 37:8 Cease from anger, and forsake *w*
Ps 38:1 O LORD, rebuke me not in thy *w*
Ps 55:3 upon me, and in *w* they hate me
Ps 58:9 both living, and in his *w*
Ps 59:13 Consume them in *w*, consume them,
Ps 76:10 Surely the *w* of man shall praise
Ps 76:10 the remainder of *w* shalt thou
Ps 78:31 The *w* of God came upon them, and
Ps 78:38 and did not stir up all his *w*
Ps 78:49 the fierceness of his anger, *w*
Ps 79:6 Pour out thy *w* upon the heathen
Ps 85:3 Thou hast taken away all thy *w*
Ps 88:7 Thy *w* lieth hard upon me, and thou
Ps 88:16 Thy fierce *w* goeth over me
Ps 89:46 shall thy *w* burn like fire
Ps 90:7 and by thy *w* are we troubled
Ps 90:9 our days are passed away in thy *w*
Ps 90:11 to thy fear, so is thy *w*
Ps 95:11 Unto whom I sware in my *w* that
Ps 102:10 of thine indignation and thy *w*
Ps 106:23 in the breach, to turn away his *w*
Ps 106:40 Therefore was the *w* of the LORD
Ps 110:5 through kings in the day of his *w*
Ps 124:3 when their *w* was kindled against
Ps 138:7 against the *w* of mine enemies
Prov 11:4 Riches profit not in the day of *w*
Prov 11:23 expectation of the wicked is *w*
Prov 12:16 A fool's *w* is presently known
Prov 14:29 He that is slow to *w* is of great
Prov 14:35 but his *w* is against him that
Prov 15:1 A soft answer turneth away *w*
Prov 16:14 The *w* of a king is as messengers
Prov 19:12 The king's *w* is as the roaring of
Prov 19:19 A man of great *w* shall suffer
Prov 21:14 and a reward in the bosom strong *w*
Prov 21:24 his name, who dealeth in proud *w*
Prov 24:18 and he turn away his *w* from him
Prov 27:3 but a fool's *w* is heavier than
Prov 27:4 *W* is cruel, and anger is
Prov 29:8 but wise men turn away *w*
Prov 30:33 so the forcing of *w* bringeth
Eccl 5:17 sorrow and *w* with his sickness
Is 9:19 Through the *w* of the LORD of
Is 10:6 of my *w* will I give him a charge
Is 13:9 LORD cometh, cruel both with *w*
Is 13:13 in the *w* of the LORD of hosts, and
Is 14:6 in *w* with a continual stroke
Is 16:6 and his pride, and his *w*
Is 54:8 In a little *w* I hid my face from
Is 60:10 for in my *w* I smote thee, but in
Jer 7:29 forsaken the generation of his *w*
Jer 10:10 at his *w* the earth shall tremble,
Jer 18:20 and to turn away thy *w* from them
Jer 21:5 anger, and in fury, and in great *w*
Jer 32:37 and in my fury, and in great *w*
Jer 44:8 In that ye provoke me unto *w* with
Jer 48:30 I know his *w*, saith the LORD
Jer 50:13 Because of the *w* of the LORD it
Lam 2:2 in his *w* the strong holds of the
Lam 3:1 affliction by the rod of his *w*
Eze 7:12 for *w* is upon all the multitude
Eze 7:14 for my *w* is upon all the
Eze 7:19 in the day of the *w* of the LORD
Eze 13:15 I accomplish my *w* upon the wall
Eze 21:31 against thee in the fire of my *w*
Eze 22:21 blow upon you in the fire of my *w*
Eze 22:31 them with the fire of my *w*
Eze 38:19 in the fire of my *w* have I spoken
Hos 5:10 out my *w* upon them like water
Hos 13:11 anger, and took him away in my *w*
Amos 1:11 and he kept his *w* for ever
Nah 1:2 he reserveth *w* for his enemies
Hab 3:2 in *w* remember mercy
Hab 3:8 was thy *w* against the sea, that
Zeph 1:15 That day is a day of *w*, a day of
Zeph 1:18 them in the day of the LORD's *w*
Zec 7:12 a great *w* from the LORD of hosts
Zec 8:14 your fathers provoked me to *w*
Mt 3:7 you to flee from the *w* to come
Lk 3:7 you to flee from the *w* to come
Lk 4:28 these things, were filled with *w*
Lk 21:23 the land, and *w* upon this people
Jn 3:36 but the *w* of God abideth on him
Acts 19:28 sayings, they were full of *w*
Rom 1:18 For the *w* of God is revealed from
Rom 2:5 *w* against the day of *w*
Rom 2:5 *w* against the day of *w*
Rom 2:8 unrighteousness, indignation and *w*
Rom 4:15 Because the law worketh *w*
Rom 5:9 shall be saved from *w* through him
Rom 9:22 if God, willing to shew his *w*
Rom 9:22 of *w* fitted to destruction
Rom 12:19 but rather give place unto *w*
Rom 13:4 a revenger to execute *w* upon him
Rom 13:5 needs be subject, not only for *w*
Gal 5:20 hatred, variance, emulations, *w*
Eph 2:3 were by nature the children of *w*
Eph 4:26 not the sun go down upon your *w*
Eph 4:31 Let all bitterness, and *w*, and
Eph 5:6 of these things cometh the *w* of
Eph 6:4 provoke not your children to *w*
Col 3:6 For which things' sake the *w* of
Col 3:8 anger, *w*, malice, blasphemy,
1Th 1:10 delivered us from the *w* to come
1Th 2:16 for the *w* is come upon them to
1Th 5:9 God hath not appointed us to *w*
1Ti 2:8 lifting up holy hands, without *w*
Heb 3:11 So I sware in my *w*, They shall
Heb 4:3 he said, As I have sworn in my *w*
Heb 11:27 not fearing the *w* of the king
Jas 1:19 to hear, slow to speak, slow to *w*
Jas 1:20 For the *w* of man worketh not the
Rev 6:16 throne, and from the *w* of the Lamb
Rev 6:17 the great day of his *w* is come
Rev 11:18 thy *w* is come, and the time of the
Rev 12:12 down unto you, having great *w*
Rev 14:8 wine of the *w* of her fornication
Rev 14:10 drink of the wine of the *w* of God
Rev 14:19 great winepress of the *w* of God
Rev 15:1 in them is filled up the *w* of God
Rev 15:7 golden vials full of the *w* of God
Rev 16:1 of the *w* of God upon the earth
Rev 16:19 wine of the fierceness of his *w*
Rev 18:3 wine of the *w* of her fornication
Rev 19:15 fierceness and *w* of Almighty God

## WRATHFUL

Ps 69:24 let thy *w* anger take hold of them
Prov 15:18 A *w* man stirreth up strife

## WRATHS

2Cor 12:20 there be debates, envyings, *w*

## WREATH

2Chr 4:13 rows of pomegranates on each *w*

## WREATHED

Lam 1:14 they are *w*, and come up upon my

## WREATHEN

Ex 28:14 of *w* work shalt thou make them,
Ex 28:14 fasten the *w* chains to the ouches
Ex 28:22 the ends of *w* work of pure gold
Ex 28:24 thou shalt put the two *w* chains
Ex 28:25 the other two ends of the two *w*
Ex 39:15 the ends, of *w* work of pure gold
Ex 39:17 they put the two *w* chains of gold
Ex 39:18 the two ends of the two *w* chains
2Kin 25:17 the *w* work, and pomegranates upon
2Kin 25:17 had the second pillar with *w* work

## WREATHS

1Kin 7:17 work, and *w* of chain work, for the
2Chr 4:12 the two *w* to cover the two
2Chr 4:13 hundred pomegranates on the two *w*

## WREST

Ex 23:2 decline after many to *w* judgment
Ex 23:6 Thou shalt not *w* the judgment of
Deut 16:19 Thou shalt not *w* judgment
Ps 56:5 Every day they *w* my words
2Pet 3:16 that are unlearned and unstable *w*

## WRESTLE

Eph 6:12 For we *w* not against flesh and

## WRESTLED

Gen 30:8 have I *w* with my sister, and I
Gen 32:24 there *w* a man with him until the
Gen 32:25 out of joint, as he *w* with him

## WRESTLINGS

Gen 30:8 With great *w* have I wrestled with

## WRETCHED

Rom 7:24 O *w* man that I am
Rev 3:17 and knowest not that thou art *w*

## WRETCHEDNESS

Num 11:15 and let me not see my *w*

## WRING

Lev 1:15 *w* off his head, and burn it on the
Lev 5:8 *w* off his head from his neck, but
Ps 75:8 of the earth shall *w* them out

## WRINGED

Judg 6:38 *w* the dew out of the fleece, a

## WRINGING

Prov 30:33 the *w* of the nose bringeth forth

## WRINKLE

Eph 5:27 church, not having spot, or *w*

## WRINKLES

Job 16:8 And thou hast filled me with *w*

**WRITE**

Ex 17:14 *W* this for a memorial in a book,
Ex 34:1 I will *w* upon these tables the
Ex 34:27 unto Moses, *W* thou these words
Num 5:23 the priest shall *w* these curses
Num 17:2 *w* thou every man's name upon his
Num 17:3 thou shalt *w* Aaron's name upon
Deut 6:9 thou shalt *w* them upon the posts
Deut 10:2 I will *w* on the tables the words
Deut 11:20 thou shalt *w* them upon the door
Deut 17:18 that he shall *w* him a copy of
Deut 24:1 then let him *w* her a bill of
Deut 24:3 *w* her a bill of divorcement, and
Deut 27:3 thou shalt *w* upon them all the
Deut 27:8 thou shalt *w* upon the stones all
Deut 31:19 Now therefore *w* ye this song for
2Chr 26:22 the prophet, the son of Amoz, *w*
Ezr 5:10 that we might *w* the names of the
Neh 9:38 we make a sure covenant, and *w* it
Est 8:8 *W* ye also for the Jews, as it
Prov 3:3 *w* them upon the table of thine
Prov 7:3 *w* them upon the table of thine
Is 8:1 roll, and *w* in it with a man's pen
Is 10:1 that *w* grievousness which they
Is 10:19 be few, that a child may *w* them
Is 30:8 *w* it before them in a table, and
Jer 22:30 *W* ye this man childless, a man
Jer 30:2 *W* thee all the words that I have
Jer 31:33 parts, and *w* it in their hearts
Jer 36:2 *w* therein all the words that I
Jer 36:17 How didst thou *w* all these words
Jer 36:28 *w* in it all the former words that
Eze 24:2 *w* thee the name of the day, even
Eze 37:16 *w* upon it, For Judah, and for the
Eze 37:16 *w* upon it, For Joseph, the stick
Eze 43:11 *w* it in their sight, that they
Hab 2:2 *W* the vision, and make it plain
Mk 10:4 Moses suffered to *w* a bill of
Lk 1:3 to *w* unto thee in order, most
Lk 16:6 and sit down quickly, and *w* fifty
Lk 16:7 Take thy bill, and *w* fourscore
Jn 1:45 the law, and the prophets, did *w*
Jn 19:21 *W* not, The King of the Jews
Acts 15:20 But that we *w* unto them, that
Acts 25:26 certain thing to *w* unto my lord
Acts 25:26 had, I might have somewhat to *w*
1Cor 4:14 I *w* not these things to shame you
1Cor 14:37 that the things that I *w* unto you
2Cor 1:13 For we *w* none other things unto
2Cor 2:9 For to this end also did I *w*
2Cor 9:1 is superfluous for me to *w* to you
2Cor 13:2 being absent now I *w* to them
2Cor 13:10 Therefore I *w* these things being
Gal 1:20 Now the things which I *w* unto you
Phil 3:1 To *w* the same things to you, to
1Th 4:9 ye need not that I *w* unto you
1Th 5:1 ye have no need that I *w* unto you
2Th 3:17 so I *w*
1Ti 3:14 These things *w* I unto thee
Heb 8:10 mind, and *w* them in their hearts
Heb 10:16 and in their minds will I *w* them
2Pet 3:1 beloved, I now *w* unto you
1Jn 1:4 And these things *w* we unto you
1Jn 2:1 these things *w* I unto you
1Jn 2:7 I *w* no new commandment unto you,
1Jn 2:8 a new commandment I *w* unto you
1Jn 2:12 I *w* unto you, little children,
1Jn 2:13 I *w* unto you, fathers, because ye
1Jn 2:13 I *w* unto you, young men, because
1Jn 2:13 I *w* unto you, little children,
2Jn 12 Having many things to *w* unto you
2Jn 12 I would not *w* with paper
3Jn 13 I had many things to *w*, but I
3Jn 13 not with ink and pen *w* unto thee
Jude 3 to *w* unto you of the common
Jude 3 was needful for me to *w* unto you
Rev 1:11 *w* in a book, and send it unto the
Rev 1:19 *W* the things which thou hast seen
Rev 2:1 angel of the church of Ephesus *w*
Rev 2:8 angel of the church in Smyrna *w*
Rev 2:12 angel of the church in Pergamos *w*
Rev 2:18 angel of the church in Thyatira *w*
Rev 3:1 angel of the church in Sardis *w*
Rev 3:7 of the church in Philadelphia *w*
Rev 3:12 I will *w* upon him the name of my
Rev 3:12 I will *w* upon him my new name
Rev 3:14 of the church of the Laodiceans *w*
Rev 10:4 their voices, I was about to *w*
Rev 10:4 thunders uttered, and *w* them not
Rev 14:13 from heaven saying unto me, *W*
Rev 19:9 And he saith unto me, *W*, Blessed
Rev 21:5 And he said unto me, *W*

**WRITER**

Judg 5:14 they that handle the pen of the *w*
Ps 45:1 my tongue is the pen of a ready *w*

**WRITER'S**

Eze 9:2 with a *w* inkhorn by his side
Eze 9:3 which had the *w* inkhorn by his

**WRITEST**

Job 13:26 For thou *w* bitter things against
Eze 37:20 the sticks whereon thou *w* shall

**WRITETH**

Ps 87:6 when he *w* up the people, that

**WRITING**

Ex 32:16 the *w* was the *w* of God,
Ex 39:30 pure gold, and wrote upon it a *w*
Deut 10:4 tables, according to the first *w*
Deut 31:24 when Moses had made an end of *w*
1Chr 28:19 in *w* by his hand upon me, even
2Chr 2:11 the king of Tyre answered in *w*
2Chr 21:12 there came a *w* to him from Elijah
2Chr 35:4 according to the *w* of David king
2Chr 35:4 according to the *w* of Solomon his
2Chr 36:22 his kingdom, and put it also in *w*
Ezr 1:1 his kingdom, and put it also in *w*
Ezr 4:7 the *w* of the letter was written
Est 1:22 according to the *w* thereof
Est 3:12 according to the *w* thereof
Est 3:14 The copy of the *w* for a
Est 4:8 he gave him the copy of the *w* of
Est 8:8 for the *w* which is written in the
Est 8:9 according to the *w* thereof
Est 8:9 to the Jews according to their *w*
Est 8:13 The copy of the *w* for a
Est 9:27 two days according to their *w*
Is 38:9 The *w* of Hezekiah king of Judah,
Eze 13:9 in the *w* of the house of Israel
Dan 5:7 Whosoever shall read this *w*
Dan 5:8 but they could not read the *w*
Dan 5:15 me, that they should read this *w*
Dan 5:16 now if thou canst read the *w*
Dan 5:17 I will read the *w* unto the king
Dan 5:24 and this *w* was written
Dan 5:25 this is the *w* that was written,
Dan 6:8 the decree, and sign the *w*
Dan 6:9 king Darius signed the *w* and the
Dan 6:10 Daniel knew that the *w* was signed
Mt 5:31 him give her a *w* of divorcement
Mt 19:7 to give a *w* of divorcement
Lk 1:63 And he asked for a *w* table
Jn 19:19 the *w* was, JESUS OF NAZARETH

**WRITINGS**

Jn 5:47 But if ye believe not his *w*

**WRITTEN**

Ex 24:12 and commandments which I have *w*
Ex 31:18 stone, *w* with the finger of God
Ex 32:15 the tables were *w* on both their
Ex 32:15 side and on the other were they *w*
Ex 32:32 out of thy book which thou hast *w*
Num 11:26 and they were of them that were *w*
Deut 9:10 of stone *w* with the finger of God
Deut 9:10 on them was *w* according to all
Deut 28:58 this law that are *w* in this book
Deut 28:61 which is not *w* in the book of
Deut 29:20 all the curses that are *w* in this
Deut 29:21 are *w* in this book of the law
Deut 29:27 curses that are *w* in this book
Deut 30:10 his statutes which are *w* in this
Josh 1:8 to all that is *w* therein
Josh 8:31 as it is *w* in the book of the law
Josh 8:34 that is *w* in the book of the law
Josh 10:13 Is not this *w* in the book of
Josh 23:6 to do all that is *w* in the book
2Sa 1:18 it is *w* in the book of Jasher
1Kin 2:3 as it is *w* in the law of Moses,
1Kin 11:41 are they not *w* in the book of the
1Kin 14:19 they are *w* in the book of the
1Kin 14:29 are they not *w* in the book of the
1Kin 15:7 are they not *w* in the book of the
1Kin 15:23 are they not *w* in the book of the
1Kin 15:31 are they not *w* in the book of the
1Kin 16:5 are they not *w* in the book of the
1Kin 16:14 are they not *w* in the book of the
1Kin 16:20 are they not *w* in the book of the
1Kin 16:27 are they not *w* in the book of the
1Kin 21:11 as it was *w* in the letters which
1Kin 22:39 are they not *w* in the book of the
1Kin 22:45 are they not *w* in the book of the
2Kin 1:18 are they not *w* in the book of the
2Kin 8:23 are they not *w* in the book of the
2Kin 10:34 are they not *w* in the book of the
2Kin 12:19 are they not *w* in the book of the
2Kin 13:8 are they not *w* in the book of the
2Kin 13:12 are they not *w* in the book of the
2Kin 14:6 according unto that which is *w* in
2Kin 14:15 are they not *w* in the book of the
2Kin 14:18 are they not *w* in the book of the
2Kin 14:28 are they not *w* in the book of the
2Kin 15:6 are they not *w* in the book of the
2Kin 15:11 they are *w* in the book of the
2Kin 15:15 they are *w* in the book of the
2Kin 15:21 are they not *w* in the book of the
2Kin 15:26 they are *w* in the book of the
2Kin 15:31 they are *w* in the book of the
2Kin 15:36 are they not *w* in the book of the
2Kin 16:19 are they not *w* in the book of the
2Kin 20:20 are they not *w* in the book of the
2Kin 21:17 are they not *w* in the book of the
2Kin 21:25 are they are not *w* in the book of
2Kin 22:13 all that which is *w* concerning us
2Kin 23:3 covenant that were *w* in this book
2Kin 23:21 as it is *w* in the book of this
2Kin 23:24 *w* in the book that Hilkiah the
2Kin 23:28 are they not *w* in the book of the
2Kin 24:5 are they not *w* in the book of the
1Chr 4:41 these *w* by name came in the days
1Chr 9:1 they were *w* in the book of the
1Chr 16:40 that is *w* in the law of the LORD
1Chr 29:29 they are *w* in the book of Samuel
2Chr 9:29 are they not *w* in the book of
2Chr 12:15 are they not *w* in the book of
2Chr 13:22 are *w* in the story of the prophet
2Chr 16:11 they are *w* in the book of the
2Chr 20:34 they are *w* in the book of Jehu
2Chr 23:18 as it is *w* in the law of Moses,
2Chr 24:27 they are *w* in the story of the
2Chr 25:4 but did as it is *w* in the law in
2Chr 25:26 are they not *w* in the book of the
2Chr 27:7 they are *w* in the book of the
2Chr 28:26 they are *w* in the book of the
2Chr 30:5 time in such sort as it was *w*
2Chr 30:18 passover otherwise than it was *w*
2Chr 31:3 as it is *w* in the law of the LORD
2Chr 32:32 they are *w* in the vision of
2Chr 33:18 they are *w* in the book of the
2Chr 33:19 they are *w* among the sayings of
2Chr 34:21 after all that is *w* in this book
2Chr 34:24 are *w* in the book which they have
2Chr 34:31 covenant which are *w* in this book
2Chr 35:12 as it is *w* in the book of Moses
2Chr 35:25 they are *w* in the lamentations
2Chr 35:26 was *w* in the law of the LORD
2Chr 35:27 they are *w* in the book of the
2Chr 36:8 they are *w* in the book of the
Ezr 3:2 as it is *w* in the law of Moses
Ezr 3:4 feast of tabernacles, as it is *w*
Ezr 4:7 letter was *w* in the Syrian tongue
Ezr 5:7 unto him, wherein was *w* thus
Ezr 6:2 and therein was a record thus *w*
Ezr 6:18 as it is *w* in the book of Moses
Ezr 8:34 all the weight was *w* at that time
Neh 6:6 Wherein was *w*, It is reported
Neh 7:5 at the first, and found *w* therein,
Neh 8:14 they found *w* in the law which the
Neh 8:15 trees, to make booths, as it is *w*
Neh 10:34 our God, as it is *w* in the law
Neh 10:36 as it is *w* in the law, and the
Neh 12:23 were *w* in the book of the
Neh 13:1 and therein was found *w*, that the
Est 1:19 let it be *w* among the laws of the
Est 2:23 it was *w* in the book of the
Est 3:9 let it be *w* that they may be
Est 3:12 there was *w* according to all that
Est 3:12 name of king Ahasuerus was it *w*
Est 6:2 And it was found *w*, that Mordecai
Est 8:5 let it be *w* to reverse the
Est 8:8 which is *w* in the king's name
Est 8:9 it was *w* according to all that
Est 9:23 and as Mordecai had *w* unto them
Est 9:32 and it was *w* in the book
Est 10:2 are they not *w* in the book of the
Job 19:23 Oh that my words were now *w*
Job 31:35 that mine adversary had *w* a book
Ps 40:7 volume of the book it is *w* of me
Ps 69:28 not be *w* with the righteous
Ps 102:18 This shall be *w* for the
Ps 139:16 in thy book all my members were *w*

Ps 149:9 execute upon them the judgment *w*
Prov 22:20 Have not I *w* to thee excellent
Eccl 12:10 and that which was *w* was upright
Is 4:3 even every one that is *w* among
Is 65:6 Behold, it is *w* before me
Jer 17:1 of Judah is *w* with a pen of iron
Jer 17:13 from me shall be *w* in the earth
Jer 25:13 even all that is *w* in this book
Jer 36:6 which thou hast *w* from my mouth
Jer 36:29 saying, Why hast thou *w* therein
Jer 45:1 when he had *w* these words in a
Jer 51:60 words that are *w* against Babylon
Eze 2:10 and it was *w* within and without
Eze 2:10 there was *w* therein lamentations,
Eze 13:9 neither shall they be *w* in the
Dan 5:24 and this writing was *w*
Dan 5:25 And this is the writing that was *w*
Dan 9:11 the oath that is *w* in the law of
Dan 9:13 As it is *w* in the law of Moses,
Dan 12:1 that shall be found *w* in the book
Hos 8:12 I have *w* to him the great things
Mal 3:16 a book of remembrance was *w*
Mt 2:5 for thus it is *w* by the prophet
Mt 4:4 But he answered and said, It is *w*
Mt 4:6 for it is *w*, He shall give his
Mt 4:7 said unto him, It is *w* again
Mt 4:10 for it is *w*, Thou shalt worship
Mt 11:10 For this is he, of whom it is *w*
Mt 21:13 And said unto them, It is *w*
Mt 26:24 of man goeth as it is *w* of him
Mt 26:31 for it is *w*, I will smite the
Mt 27:37 up over his head his accusation *w*
Mk 1:2 As it is *w* in the prophets,
Mk 7:6 of you hypocrites, as it is *w*
Mk 9:12 how it is *w* of the Son of man,
Mk 9:13 they listed, as it is *w* of him
Mk 11:17 saying unto them, Is it not *w*
Mk 14:21 indeed goeth, as it is *w* of him
Mk 14:27 for it is *w*, I will smite the
Mk 15:26 of his accusation was *w* over
Lk 2:23 (As it is *w* in the law of the
Lk 3:4 As it is *w* in the book of the
Lk 4:4 answered him, saying, It is *w*
Lk 4:8 for it is *w*, Thou shalt worship
Lk 4:10 For it is *w*, He shall give his
Lk 4:17 he found the place where it was *w*
Lk 7:27 This is he, of whom it is *w*
Lk 10:20 your names are *w* in heaven
Lk 10:26 unto him, What is *w* in the law
Lk 18:31 all things that are *w* by the
Lk 19:46 Saying unto them, It is *w*
Lk 20:17 said, What is this then that is *w*
Lk 21:22 which are *w* may be fulfilled
Lk 22:37 that this that is *w* must yet be
Lk 23:38 a superscription also was *w* over
Lk 24:44 which were *w* in the law of Moses,
Lk 24:46 And said unto them, Thus it is *w*
Jn 2:17 remembered that it was *w*, The
Jn 6:31 as it is *w*, He gave them bread
Jn 6:45 It is *w* in the prophets, And they
Jn 8:17 It is also *w* in your law, that
Jn 10:34 Is it not *w* in your law, I said,
Jn 12:14 as it is *w*,
Jn 12:16 that these things were *w* of him
Jn 15:25 fulfilled that is *w* in their law
Jn 19:20 it was *w* in Hebrew, and Greek, and
Jn 19:22 What I have *w* I have *w*
Jn 20:30 which are not *w* in this book
Jn 20:31 But these are *w*, that ye might
Jn 21:25 if they should be *w* every one
Jn 21:25 the books that should be *w*
Acts 1:20 For it is *w* in the book of Psalms
Acts 7:42 as it is *w* in the book of the
Acts 13:29 fulfilled all that was *w* of him
Acts 13:33 as it is also *w* in the second
Acts 15:15 as it is *w*,
Acts 21:25 Gentiles which believe, we have *w*
Acts 23:5 for it is *w*, Thou shalt not speak
Acts 24:14 all things which are *w* in the law
Rom 1:17 as it is *w*, The just shall live
Rom 2:15 work of the law *w* in their hearts
Rom 2:24 Gentiles through you, as it is *w*
Rom 3:4 as it is *w*, That thou mightest be
Rom 3:10 As it is *w*, There is none
Rom 4:17 (As it is *w*, I have made thee a
Rom 4:23 Now it was not *w* for his sake
Rom 8:36 As it is *w*, For thy sake we are
Rom 9:13 As it is *w*, Jacob have I loved,
Rom 9:33 As it is *w*, Behold, I lay in Sion
Rom 10:15 as it is *w*, How beautiful are the
Rom 11:8 (According as it is *w*, God hath
Rom 11:26 as it is *w*, There shall come out
Rom 12:19 for it is *w*, Vengeance is mine
Rom 14:11 For it is *w*, As I live, saith the
Rom 15:3 but, as it is *w*, The reproaches
Rom 15:4 For whatsoever things were *w*
Rom 15:4 aforetime were *w* for our learning
Rom 15:9 as it is *w*, For this cause I will
Rom 15:15 I have *w* the more boldly unto you
Rom 15:21 But as it is *w*, To whom he was
Rom *s* *W* to the Romans from Corinthus,
1Cor 1:19 For it is *w*, I will destroy the
1Cor 1:31 That, according as it is *w*
1Cor 2:9 But as it is *w*, Eye hath not seen
1Cor 3:19 For it is *w*, He taketh the wise
1Cor 4:6 of men above that which is *w*
1Cor 5:11 But now I have *w* unto you not to
1Cor 9:9 For it is *w* in the law of Moses,
1Cor 9:10 our sakes, no doubt, this is *w*
1Cor 9:15 neither have I *w* these things
1Cor 10:7 as it is *w*, The people sat down
1Cor 10:11 they are *w* for our admonition,
1Cor 14:21 In the law it is *w*, With men of
1Cor 15:45 And so it is *w*, The first man Adam
1Cor 15:54 to pass the saying that is *w*
1Cor *s* was *w* from Philippi by Stephanus
2Cor 3:2 are our epistle *w* in our hearts
2Cor 3:3 *w* not with ink, but with the
2Cor 3:7 if the ministration of death, *w*
2Cor 4:13 of faith, according as it is *w*
2Cor 8:15 As it is *w*, He that had gathered
2Cor 9:9 (As it is *w*, He hath dispersed
2Cor *s* Corinthians was *w* from Philippi
Gal 3:10 for it is *w*, Cursed is every one
Gal 3:10 not in all things which are *w* in
Gal 3:13 for it is *w*, Cursed is every one
Gal 4:22 For it is *w*, that Abraham had two
Gal 4:27 For it is *w*, Rejoice, thou barren
Gal 6:11 *w* unto you with mine own hand
Gal *s* Unto the Galatians *w* from Rome
Eph *s* *W* from Rome unto the Ephesians by
Phil *s* It was *w* to the Philippians from
Col *s* *W* from Rome to the Colossians by
1Th *s* Thessalonians was *w* from Athens
2Th *s* Thessalonians was *w* from Athens
1Ti *s* The first to Timothy was *w* from
2Ti *s* was *w* from Rome, when Paul was
Titus *s* It was *w* to Titus, ordained the
Philem 19 I Paul have *w* it with mine own
Philem *s* *W* from Rome to Philemon, by
Heb 10:7 volume of the book it is *w* of me
Heb 12:23 firstborn, which are *w* in heaven
Heb 13:22 for I have *w* a letter unto you in
Heb *s* *W* to the Hebrews from Italy by
1Pet 1:16 Because it is *w*, Be ye holy
1Pet 5:12 I have *w* briefly, exhorting, and
2Pet 3:15 given unto him hath *w* unto you
1Jn 2:14 I have *w* unto you, fathers,
1Jn 2:14 I have *w* unto you, young men,
1Jn 2:21 I have not *w* unto you because ye
1Jn 2:26 These things have I *w* unto you
1Jn 5:13 These things have I *w* unto you
Rev 1:3 those things which are *w* therein
Rev 2:17 and in the stone a new name *w*
Rev 5:1 sat on the throne a book *w* within
Rev 13:8 whose names are not *w* in the book
Rev 14:1 name *w* in their foreheads
Rev 17:5 And upon her forehead was a name *w*
Rev 17:8 whose names were not *w* in the
Rev 19:12 and he had a name *w*, that no man
Rev 19:16 vesture and on his thigh a name *w*
Rev 20:12 things which were *w* in the books
Rev 20:15 whosoever was not found *w* in the
Rev 21:12 names *w* thereon, which are the
Rev 21:27 but they which are *w* in the
Rev 22:18 plagues that are *w* in this book
Rev 22:19 things which are *w* in this book

### WRONG

Gen 16:5 unto Abram, My *w* be upon thee
Ex 2:13 and he said to him that did the *w*
Deut 19:16 against him that which is *w*
Judg 11:27 thou doest me *w* to war against me
1Chr 12:17 there is no *w* in mine hands
1Chr 16:21 He suffered no man to do them *w*
Est 1:16 hath not done *w* to the king only
Job 19:7 Behold, I cry out of *w*, but I am
Ps 105:14 He suffered no man to do them *w*
Jer 22:3 and do no *w*, do no violence to the
Jer 22:13 and his chambers by *w*
Lam 3:59 O LORD, thou hast seen my *w*
Hab 1:4 therefore *w* judgment proceedeth
Mt 20:13 and said, Friend, I do thee no *w*
Acts 7:24 And seeing one of them suffer *w*
Acts 7:26 why do ye *w* one to another
Acts 7:27 his neighbour *w* thrust him away
Acts 18:14 a matter of *w* or wicked lewdness
Acts 25:10 to the Jews have I done no *w*
1Cor 6:7 Why do ye not rather take *w*
1Cor 6:8 Nay, ye do *w*, and defraud, and that
2Cor 7:12 for his cause that had done the *w*
2Cor 7:12 nor for his cause that suffered *w*
2Cor 12:13 forgive me this *w*
Col 3:25 But he that doeth *w* shall receive
Col 3:25 for the *w* which he hath done

### WRONGED

2Cor 7:2 we have *w* no man, we have
Philem 18 If he hath *w* thee, or oweth thee

### WRONGETH

Prov 8:36 sinneth against me *w* his own soul

### WRONGFULLY

Job 21:27 which ye *w* imagine against me
Ps 35:19 mine enemies *w* rejoice over me
Ps 38:19 that hate me *w* are multiplied
Ps 69:4 destroy me, being mine enemies *w*
Ps 119:86 they persecute me *w*
Eze 22:29 have oppressed the stranger *w*
1Pet 2:19 God endure grief, suffering *w*

### WROTE

Ex 24:4 Moses *w* all the words of the LORD
Ex 34:28 he *w* upon the tables the words of
Ex 39:30 *w* upon it a writing, like to the
Num 33:2 And Moses *w* their goings out
Deut 4:13 he *w* them upon two tables of
Deut 5:22 he *w* them in two tables of stone,
Deut 10:4 he *w* on the tables, according to
Deut 31:9 Moses *w* this law, and delivered it
Deut 31:22 Moses therefore *w* this song the
Josh 8:32 he *w* there upon the stones a copy
Josh 8:32 which he *w* in the presence of the
Josh 24:26 Joshua *w* these words in the book
1Sa 10:25 *w* it in a book, and laid it up
2Sa 11:14 that David *w* a letter to Joab, and
2Sa 11:15 he *w* in the letter, saying, Set
1Kin 21:8 So she *w* letters in Ahab's name,
1Kin 21:9 she *w* in the letters, saying,
2Kin 10:1 Jehu *w* letters, and sent to
2Kin 10:6 Then he *w* a letter the second
2Kin 17:37 commandment, which he *w* for you
1Chr 24:6 *w* them before the king, and the
2Chr 30:1 *w* letters also to Ephraim and
2Chr 32:17 He *w* also letters to rail on the
Ezr 4:6 *w* they unto him an accusation
Ezr 4:7 the days of Artaxerxes *w* Bishlam
Ezr 4:8 Shimshai the scribe *w* a letter
Ezr 4:9 Then *w* Rehum the chancellor, and
Est 8:5 which he *w* to destroy the Jews
Est 8:10 he *w* in the king Ahasuerus' name,
Est 9:20 Mordecai *w* these things, and sent
Est 9:29 *w* with all authority, to confirm
Jer 36:4 Baruch *w* from the mouth of
Jer 36:18 I *w* them with ink in the book
Jer 36:27 the words which Baruch *w* at the
Jer 36:32 who *w* therein from the mouth of
Jer 51:60 So Jeremiah *w* in a book all the
Dan 5:5 *w* over against the candlestick
Dan 5:5 saw the part of the hand that *w*
Dan 6:25 king Darius *w* unto all people
Dan 7:1 then he *w* the dream, and told the
Mk 10:5 your heart he *w* you this precept
Mk 12:19 Moses *w* unto us, If a man's
Lk 1:63 asked for a writing table, and *w*
Lk 20:28 Moses *w* unto us, If any man's
Jn 5:46 for he *w* of me
Jn 8:6 with his finger *w* on the ground
Jn 8:8 stooped down, and *w* on the ground
Jn 19:19 Pilate *w* a title, and put it on
Jn 21:24 these things, and *w* these things
Acts 15:23 they *w* letters by them after this
Acts 18:27 pass into Achaia, the brethren *w*
Acts 23:25 he *w* a letter after this manner
Rom 16:22 who *w* this epistle, salute you in
1Cor 5:9 I *w* unto you in an epistle not to
1Cor 7:1 the things whereof ye *w* unto me
2Cor 2:3 I *w* this same unto you, lest,

2Cor 2:4 anguish of heart I *w* unto you
2Cor 7:12 Wherefore, though I *w* unto you
Eph 3:3 (as I *w* afore in few words,
Philem 21 in thy obedience I *w* unto thee
2Jn 5 lady, not as though I *w* a new
3Jn 9 I *w* unto the church

**WROTH**
Gen 4:5 And Cain was very *w*, and his
Gen 4:6 said unto Cain, Why art thou *w*
Gen 31:36 And Jacob was *w*, and chode with
Gen 34:7 were grieved, and they were very *w*
Gen 40:2 Pharaoh was *w* against two of his
Gen 41:10 Pharaoh was *w* with his servants,
Ex 16:20 and Moses was *w* with them
Num 16:15 And Moses was very *w*, and said unto
Num 16:22 wilt thou be *w* with all the
Num 31:14 Moses was *w* with the officers of
Deut 1:34 the voice of your words, and was *w*
Deut 3:26 But the LORD was *w* with me for
Deut 9:19 wherewith the LORD was *w* against
Josh 22:18 that to morrow he will be *w* with
1Sa 18:8 And Saul was very *w*, and the saying
1Sa 20:7 but if he be very *w*, then be sure
1Sa 29:4 the Philistines were *w* with him
2Sa 3:8 Then was Abner very *w* for the
2Sa 13:21 all these things, he was very *w*
2Sa 22:8 moved and shook, because he was *w*
2Kin 5:11 But Naaman was *w*, and went away,
2Kin 13:19 And the man of God was *w* with him
2Chr 16:10 Then Asa was *w* with the seer, and
2Chr 26:19 Then Uzziah was *w*, and had a
2Chr 26:19 while he was *w* with the priests,
2Chr 28:9 of your fathers was *w* with Judah
Neh 4:1 we builded the wall, he was *w*
Neh 4:7 be stopped, then they were very *w*
Est 1:12 therefore was the king very *w*
Est 2:21 those which kept the door, were *w*
Ps 18:7 and were shaken, because he was *w*
Ps 78:21 the LORD heard this, and was *w*
Ps 78:59 When God heard this, he was *w*
Ps 78:62 was *w* with his inheritance
Ps 89:38 thou hast been *w* with thine
Is 28:21 he shall be *w* as in the valley of
Is 47:6 I was *w* with my people, I have
Is 54:9 that I would not be *w* with thee
Is 57:16 ever, neither will I be always *w*
Is 57:17 of his covetousness was I *w*
Is 57:17 I hid me, and was *w*, and he went on
Is 64:5 behold, thou art *w*
Is 64:9 Be not *w* very sore, O LORD,
Jer 37:15 the princes were *w* with Jeremiah
Lam 5:22 thou art very *w* against us
Mt 2:16 of the wise men, was exceeding *w*
Mt 18:34 And his lord was *w*, and delivered
Mt 22:7 the king heard thereof, he was *w*
Rev 12:17 the dragon was *w* with the woman

**WROUGHT**
Gen 34:7 because he had *w* folly in Israel
Ex 10:2 what things I have *w* in Egypt
Ex 26:36 twined linen, *w* with needlework
Ex 27:16 twined linen, *w* with needlework
Ex 36:1 Then *w* Bezaleel and Aholiab, and
Ex 36:4 that *w* all the work of the
Ex 36:8 hearted man among them that *w* the
Ex 39:6 they *w* onyx stones inclosed in
Lev 20:12 they have *w* confusion
Num 23:23 and of Israel, What hath God *w*
Num 31:51 gold of them, even all *w* jewels
Deut 13:14 such abomination is *w* among you
Deut 17:2 that hath *w* wickedness in the
Deut 17:4 such abomination is *w* in Israel
Deut 21:3 which hath not been *w* with
Deut 22:21 she hath *w* folly in Israel
Deut 31:18 the evils which they shall have *w*
Josh 7:15 because he hath *w* folly in Israel
Judg 20:10 folly that they have *w* in Israel
Ruth 2:19 mother in law with whom she had *w*
Ruth 2:19 name with whom I *w* to day is Boaz
1Sa 6:6 when he had *w* wonderfully among
1Sa 11:13 LORD hath *w* salvation in Israel
1Sa 14:45 who hath *w* this great salvation
1Sa 14:45 for he hath *w* with God this day
1Sa 19:5 the LORD *w* a great salvation for
2Sa 18:13 Otherwise I should have *w*
2Sa 23:10 the LORD *w* a great victory that
2Sa 23:12 the LORD *w* a great victory
1Kin 5:16 the people that *w* in the work
1Kin 7:14 king Solomon, and *w* all his work
1Kin 7:26 the brim thereof was *w* like the
1Kin 9:23 the people that *w* in the work
1Kin 16:20 Zimri, and his treason that he *w*
1Kin 16:25 But Omri *w* evil in the eyes of
2Kin 3:2 he *w* evil in the sight of the
2Kin 12:11 that *w* upon the house of the LORD
2Kin 17:11 *w* wicked things to provoke the
2Kin 21:6 he *w* much wickedness in the sight
1Chr 4:21 house of them that *w* fine linen
1Chr 22:2 he set masons to hew *w* stones to
2Chr 3:14 linen, and *w* cherubims thereon
2Chr 21:6 he *w* that which was evil in the
2Chr 24:12 the LORD, and also such as *w* iron
2Chr 24:13 So the workmen *w*, and the work was
2Chr 31:20 *w* that which was good and right and
2Chr 33:6 he *w* much evil in the sight of
2Chr 34:10 that *w* in the house of the LORD
2Chr 34:13 that *w* the work in any manner of
Neh 4:16 half of my servants *w* in the work
Neh 4:17 one of his hands *w* in the work
Neh 6:16 that this work was *w* of our God
Neh 9:18 and had *w* great provocations
Neh 9:26 they *w* great provocations
Job 12:9 the hand of the LORD hath *w* this
Job 36:23 who can say, Thou hast *w* iniquity
Ps 31:19 which thou hast *w* for them that
Ps 45:13 her clothing is of *w* gold
Ps 68:28 that which thou hast *w* for us
Ps 78:43 How he had *w* his signs in Egypt,
Ps 139:15 curiously *w* in the lowest parts
Eccl 2:11 all the works that my hands had *w*
Eccl 2:17 because the work that is *w* under
Is 26:12 for thou also hast *w* all our
Is 26:18 we have not *w* any deliverance in
Is 41:4 Who hath *w* and done it, calling
Jer 11:15 seeing she hath *w* lewdness with
Jer 18:3 he *w* a work on the wheels
Eze 20:9 But I *w* for my name's sake, that
Eze 20:14 But I *w* for my name's sake, that
Eze 20:22 *w* for my name's sake, that it
Eze 20:44 when I have *w* with you for my
Eze 29:20 against it, because they *w* for me
Dan 4:2 the high God hath *w* toward me
Jonah 1:11 for the sea *w*, and was tempestuous
Jonah 1:13 for the sea *w*, and was tempestuous
Zeph 2:3 which have *w* his judgment
Mt 20:12 These last have *w* but one hour
Mt 26:10 for she hath *w* a good work upon
Mk 6:2 mighty works are *w* by his hands
Mk 14:6 she hath *w* a good work on me
Jn 3:21 manifest, that they are *w* in God
Acts 5:12 wonders *w* among the people
Acts 15:12 wonders God had *w* among the
Acts 18:3 craft, he abode with them, and *w*
Acts 19:11 God *w* special miracles by the
Acts 21:19 what things God had *w* among the
Rom 7:8 *w* in me all manner of
Rom 15:18 which Christ hath not *w* by me
2Cor 5:5 Now he that hath *w* us for the
2Cor 7:11 what carefulness it *w* in you
2Cor 12:12 were *w* among you in all patience
Gal 2:8 (For he that *w* effectually in
Eph 1:20 Which he *w* in Christ, when he
2Th 3:8 but *w* with labour and travail
Heb 11:33 *w* righteousness, obtained
Jas 2:22 thou how faith *w* with his works
1Pet 4:3 have *w* the will of the Gentiles
2Jn 8 not those things which we have *w*
Rev 19:20 that *w* miracles before him

**WROUGHTEST**
Ruth 2:19 and where *w* thou

**WRUNG**
Lev 1:15 the blood thereof shall be *w* out
Lev 5:9 *w* out at the bottom of the altar
Ps 73:10 of a full cup are *w* out to them
Is 51:17 cup of trembling, and *w* them out

# Y

**YARN**
1Kin 10:28 brought out of Egypt, and linen *y*
1Kin 10:28 received the linen *y* at a price
2Chr 1:16 brought out of Egypt, and linen *y*
2Chr 1:16 received the linen *y* at a price

**YEAR**
Gen 7:11 six hundredth *y* of Noah's life
Gen 8:13 in the six hundredth and first *y*
Gen 14:4 in the thirteenth *y* they rebelled
Gen 14:5 fourteenth *y* came Chedorlaomer
Gen 17:21 at this set time in the next *y*
Gen 26:12 in the same *y* an hundredfold
Gen 47:17 for all their cattle for that *y*
Gen 47:18 When that *y* was ended, they came
Gen 47:18 they came unto him the second *y*
Ex 12:2 the first month of the *y* to you
Ex 12:5 blemish, a male of the first *y*
Ex 13:10 in his season from *y* to *y*
Ex 13:10 in his season from *y* to *y*
Ex 23:11 But the seventh *y* thou shalt let
Ex 23:14 keep a feast unto me in the *y*
Ex 23:16 which is in the end of the *y*
Ex 23:17 Three times in the *y* all thy
Ex 23:29 out from before thee in one *y*
Ex 29:38 first *y* day by day continually
Ex 30:10 in a *y* with the blood of the sin
Ex 30:10 once in the *y* shall he make
Ex 34:23 Thrice in the *y* shall all your
Ex 34:24 the LORD thy God thrice in the *y*
Ex 40:17 the first month in the second *y*
Lev 9:3 and a lamb, both of the first *y*
Lev 12:6 the first *y* for a burnt offering
Lev 14:10 of the first *y* without blemish
Lev 16:34 for all their sins once a *y*
Lev 19:24 But in the fourth *y* all the fruit
Lev 19:25 in the fifth *y* shall ye eat of
Lev 23:12 without blemish of the first *y*
Lev 23:18 without blemish of the first *y*
Lev 23:19 two lambs of the first *y* for a
Lev 23:41 unto the LORD seven days in the *y*
Lev 25:4 But in the seventh *y* shall be a
Lev 25:5 for it is a *y* of rest unto the
Lev 25:10 And ye shall hallow the fiftieth *y*
Lev 25:11 shall that fiftieth *y* be unto you
Lev 25:13 In the *y* of this jubile ye shall
Lev 25:20 What shall we eat the seventh *y*
Lev 25:21 blessing upon you in the sixth *y*
Lev 25:22 And ye shall sow the eighth *y*
Lev 25:22 of old fruit until the ninth *y*
Lev 25:28 bought it until the *y* of jubile
Lev 25:29 within a whole *y* after it is sold
Lev 25:29 within a full *y* may he redeem it
Lev 25:30 within the space of a full *y*
Lev 25:33 shall go out in the *y* of jubile
Lev 25:40 serve thee unto the *y* of jubile
Lev 25:50 *y* that he was sold to him unto
Lev 25:50 sold to him unto the *y* of jubile
Lev 25:52 few years unto the *y* of jubile
Lev 25:54 shall go out in the *y* of jubile
Lev 27:17 his field from the *y* of jubile
Lev 27:18 even unto the *y* of the jubile
Lev 27:23 even unto the *y* of the jubile
Lev 27:24 In the *y* of the jubile the field
Num 1:1 in the second *y* after they were
Num 6:12 first *y* for a trespass offering
Num 6:14 one he lamb of the first *y*
Num 6:14 first *y* without blemish for a sin
Num 7:15 one ram, one lamb of the first *y*
Num 7:17 goats, five lambs of the first *y*
Num 7:21 one ram, one lamb of the first *y*
Num 7:23 goats, five lambs of the first *y*
Num 7:27 one ram, one lamb of the first *y*
Num 7:29 goats, five lambs of the first *y*
Num 7:33 one ram, one lamb of the first *y*
Num 7:35 goats, five lambs of the first *y*

| | |
|---|---|
| Num 7:39 | one ram, one lamb of the first y |
| Num 7:41 | goats, five lambs of the first y |
| Num 7:45 | one ram, one lamb of the first y |
| Num 7:47 | goats, five lambs of the first y |
| Num 7:51 | one ram, one lamb of the first y |
| Num 7:53 | goats, five lambs of the first y |
| Num 7:57 | one ram, one lamb of the first y |
| Num 7:59 | goats, five lambs of the first y |
| Num 7:63 | one ram, one lamb of the first y |
| Num 7:65 | goats, five lambs of the first y |
| Num 7:69 | one ram, one lamb of the first y |
| Num 7:71 | goats, five lambs of the first y |
| Num 7:75 | one ram, one lamb of the first y |
| Num 7:77 | goats, five lambs of the first y |
| Num 7:81 | one ram, one lamb of the first y |
| Num 7:83 | goats, five lambs of the first y |
| Num 7:87 | the lambs of the first y twelve |
| Num 7:88 | the lambs of the first y sixty |
| Num 9:1 | the first month of the second y |
| Num 9:22 | were two days, or a month, or a y |
| Num 10:11 | the second month, in the second y |
| Num 14:34 | even forty days, each day for a y |
| Num 15:27 | of the first y for a sin offering |
| Num 28:3 | two lambs of the first y without |
| Num 28:9 | lambs of the first y without spot |
| Num 28:11 | lambs of the first y without spot |
| Num 28:14 | throughout the months of the y |
| Num 28:19 | and seven lambs of the first y |
| Num 28:27 | ram, seven lambs of the first y |
| Num 29:2 | of the first y without blemish |
| Num 29:8 | and seven lambs of the first y |
| Num 29:13 | and fourteen lambs of the first y |
| Num 29:17 | lambs of the first y without spot |
| Num 29:20 | of the first y without blemish |
| Num 29:23 | of the first y without blemish |
| Num 29:26 | lambs of the first y without spot |
| Num 29:29 | of the first y without blemish |
| Num 29:32 | of the first y without blemish |
| Num 29:36 | of the first y without blemish |
| Num 33:38 | in the fortieth y after the |
| Deut 1:3 | it came to pass in the fortieth y |
| Deut 11:12 | from the beginning of the y even |
| Deut 11:12 | y even unto the end of the y |
| Deut 14:22 | field bringeth forth y by y |
| Deut 14:22 | field bringeth forth y by y |
| Deut 14:28 | of thine increase the same y |
| Deut 15:9 | heart, saying, The seventh y |
| Deut 15:9 | the y of release, is at hand |
| Deut 15:12 | then in the seventh y thou shalt |
| Deut 15:20 | y by y in the place which the |
| Deut 15:20 | by y in the place which the LORD |
| Deut 16:16 | Three times in a y shall all thy |
| Deut 24:5 | he shall be free at home one y |
| Deut 26:12 | of thine increase the third y |
| Deut 26:12 | which is the y of tithing |
| Deut 31:10 | the solemnity of the y of release |
| Josh 5:12 | of the land of Canaan that y |
| Judg 10:8 | that y they vexed and oppressed |
| Judg 11:40 | the Gileadite four days in a y |
| Judg 17:10 | ten shekels of silver by the y |
| 1Sa 1:7 | And as he did so y by y |
| 1Sa 2:19 | brought it to him from y to y |
| 1Sa 7:16 | he went from y to y in circuit |
| 1Sa 13:1 | Saul reigned one y |
| 1Sa 27:7 | of the Philistines was a full y |
| 2Sa 11:1 | after the y was expired, at the |
| 2Sa 21:1 | David three years, y after y |
| 1Kin 4:7 | his month in a y made provision |
| 1Kin 5:11 | gave Solomon to Hiram y by y |
| 1Kin 6:1 | eightieth y after the children of |
| 1Kin 6:1 | in the fourth y of Solomon's |
| 1Kin 6:37 | In the fourth y was the |
| 1Kin 6:38 | And in the eleventh y, in the |
| 1Kin 9:25 | three times in a y did Solomon |
| 1Kin 10:14 | one y was six hundred threescore |
| 1Kin 10:25 | and mules, a rate y by y |
| 1Kin 14:25 | in the fifth y of king Rehoboam |
| 1Kin 15:1 | Now in the eighteenth y of king |
| 1Kin 15:9 | in the twentieth y of Jeroboam |
| 1Kin 15:25 | the second y of Asa king of Judah |
| 1Kin 15:28 | Even in the third y of Asa king |
| 1Kin 15:33 | In the third y of Asa king of |
| 1Kin 16:8 | sixth y of Asa king of Judah |
| 1Kin 16:10 | seventh y of Asa king of Judah, |
| 1Kin 16:15 | seventh y of Asa king of Judah |
| 1Kin 16:23 | first y of Asa king of Judah |
| 1Kin 16:29 | eighth y of Asa king of Judah |
| 1Kin 18:1 | came to Elijah in the third y |
| 1Kin 20:22 | for at the return of the y the |
| 1Kin 20:26 | to pass at the return of the y |
| 1Kin 22:2 | And it came to pass in the third y |
| 1Kin 22:41 | fourth y of Ahab king of Israel |
| 1Kin 22:51 | in Samaria the seventeenth y of |
| 2Kin 1:17 | second y of Jehoram the son of |
| 2Kin 3:1 | in Samaria the eighteenth y of |
| 2Kin 8:16 | in the fifth y of Joram the son |
| 2Kin 8:25 | In the twelfth y of Joram the son |
| 2Kin 8:26 | and he reigned one y in Jerusalem |
| 2Kin 9:29 | in the eleventh y of Joram the |
| 2Kin 11:4 | the seventh y Jehoiada sent and |
| 2Kin 12:1 | In the seventh y of Jehu Jehoash |
| 2Kin 12:6 | twentieth y of king Jehoash the |
| 2Kin 13:1 | twentieth y of Joash the son of |
| 2Kin 13:10 | seventh y of Joash king of Judah |
| 2Kin 13:20 | land at the coming in of the y |
| 2Kin 14:1 | In the second y of Joash son of |
| 2Kin 14:23 | In the fifteenth y of Amaziah the |
| 2Kin 15:1 | seventh y of Jeroboam king of |
| 2Kin 15:8 | eighth y of Azariah king of Judah |
| 2Kin 15:13 | thirtieth y of Uzziah king of |
| 2Kin 15:17 | thirtieth y of Azariah king of |
| 2Kin 15:23 | In the fiftieth y of Azariah king |
| 2Kin 15:27 | fiftieth y of Azariah king of |
| 2Kin 15:30 | in the twentieth y of Jotham the |
| 2Kin 15:32 | In the second y of Pekah the son |
| 2Kin 16:1 | In the seventeenth y of Pekah the |
| 2Kin 17:1 | In the twelfth y of Ahaz king of |
| 2Kin 17:4 | Assyria, as he had done y by y |
| 2Kin 17:6 | In the ninth y of Hoshea the king |
| 2Kin 18:1 | it came to pass in the third y of |
| 2Kin 18:9 | in the fourth y of king Hezekiah |
| 2Kin 18:9 | which was the seventh y of Hoshea |
| 2Kin 18:10 | even in the sixth y of Hezekiah |
| 2Kin 18:10 | that is the ninth y of Hoshea |
| 2Kin 18:13 | fourteenth y of king Hezekiah did |
| 2Kin 19:29 | Ye shall eat this y such things |
| 2Kin 19:29 | in the second y that which |
| 2Kin 19:29 | and in the third y sow ye, and reap |
| 2Kin 22:3 | the eighteenth y of king Josiah |
| 2Kin 23:23 | the eighteenth y of king Josiah |
| 2Kin 24:12 | him in the eighth y of his reign |
| 2Kin 25:1 | pass in the ninth y of his reign |
| 2Kin 25:2 | the eleventh y of king Zedekiah |
| 2Kin 25:8 | which is the nineteenth y of king |
| 2Kin 25:27 | thirtieth y of the captivity of |
| 2Kin 25:27 | king of Babylon in the y that he |
| 1Chr 20:1 | that after the y was expired |
| 1Chr 26:31 | In the fortieth y of the reign of |
| 1Chr 27:1 | all the months of the y, of every |
| 2Chr 3:2 | in the fourth y of his reign |
| 2Chr 8:13 | feasts, three times in the y |
| 2Chr 9:13 | Solomon in one y was six hundred |
| 2Chr 9:24 | and mules, a rate y by y |
| 2Chr 12:2 | that in the fifth y of king |
| 2Chr 13:1 | Now in the eighteenth y of king |
| 2Chr 15:10 | in the fifteenth y of the reign |
| 2Chr 15:19 | thirtieth y of the reign of Asa |
| 2Chr 16:1 | thirtieth y of the reign of Asa |
| 2Chr 16:12 | ninth y of his reign was diseased |
| 2Chr 16:13 | one and fortieth y of his reign |
| 2Chr 17:7 | Also in the third y of his reign |
| 2Chr 22:2 | and he reigned one y in Jerusalem |
| 2Chr 23:1 | in the seventh y Jehoiada |
| 2Chr 24:5 | house of your God from y to y |
| 2Chr 24:23 | came to pass at the end of the y |
| 2Chr 27:5 | of Ammon gave him the same y an |
| 2Chr 27:5 | pay unto him, both the second y |
| 2Chr 29:3 | He in the first y of his reign |
| 2Chr 34:3 | For in the eighth y of his reign |
| 2Chr 34:3 | in the twelfth y he began to |
| 2Chr 34:8 | in the eighteenth y of his reign |
| 2Chr 35:19 | In the eighteenth y of the reign |
| 2Chr 36:10 | when the y was expired, king |
| 2Chr 36:22 | Now in the first y of Cyrus king |
| Ezr 1:1 | Now in the first y of Cyrus king |
| Ezr 3:8 | Now in the second y of their |
| Ezr 4:24 | So it ceased unto the second y of |
| Ezr 5:13 | But in the first y of Cyrus the |
| Ezr 6:3 | In the first y of Cyrus the king |
| Ezr 6:15 | which was in the sixth y of the |
| Ezr 7:7 | in the seventh y of Artaxerxes |
| Ezr 7:8 | was in the seventh y of the king |
| Neh 1:1 | month Chisleu, in the twentieth y |
| Neh 2:1 | in the twentieth y of Artaxerxes |
| Neh 5:14 | the twentieth y even unto the two |
| Neh 5:14 | thirtieth y of Artaxerxes the |
| Neh 10:31 | that we would leave the seventh y |
| Neh 10:34 | at times appointed y by y |
| Neh 10:34 | at times appointed y by y |
| Neh 10:35 | all fruit of all trees, y by y |
| Neh 13:6 | thirtieth y of Artaxerxes king of |
| Est 1:3 | In the third y of his reign |
| Est 2:16 | in the seventh y of his reign |
| Est 3:7 | Nisan, in the twelfth y of king |
| Est 9:27 | to their appointed time every y |
| Job 3:6 | be joined unto the days of the y |
| Ps 65:11 | crownest the y with thy goodness |
| Is 6:1 | In the y that king Uzziah died I |
| Is 14:28 | In the y that king Ahaz died was |
| Is 20:1 | In the y that Tartan came unto |
| Is 21:16 | the Lord said unto me, Within a y |
| Is 29:1 | add ye y to y |
| Is 34:8 | the y of recompences for the |
| Is 36:1 | the fourteenth y of king Hezekiah |
| Is 37:30 | Ye shall eat this y such as |
| Is 37:30 | the second y that which springeth |
| Is 37:30 | and in the third y sow ye, and reap |
| Is 61:2 | the acceptable y of the LORD |
| Is 63:4 | the y of my redeemed is come |
| Jer 1:2 | in the thirteenth y of his reign |
| Jer 1:3 | unto the end of the eleventh y of |
| Jer 11:23 | even the y of their visitation |
| Jer 17:8 | be careful in the y of drought |
| Jer 23:12 | even the y of their visitation, |
| Jer 25:1 | people of Judah in the fourth y |
| Jer 25:1 | of Judah, that was the first y of |
| Jer 25:3 | From the thirteenth y of Josiah |
| Jer 25:3 | that is the three and twentieth y |
| Jer 28:1 | And it came to pass the same y |
| Jer 28:1 | king of Judah, in the fourth y |
| Jer 28:16 | this y thou shalt die, because |
| Jer 28:17 | the same y in the seventh month |
| Jer 32:1 | tenth y of Zedekiah king of Judah |
| Jer 32:1 | eighteenth y of Nebuchadrezzar |
| Jer 36:1 | it came to pass in the fourth y |
| Jer 36:9 | it came to pass in the fifth y of |
| Jer 39:1 | In the ninth y of Zedekiah king |
| Jer 39:2 | And in the eleventh y of Zedekiah |
| Jer 45:1 | in the fourth y of Jehoiakim the |
| Jer 46:2 | y of Jehoiakim the son of Josiah |
| Jer 48:44 | the y of their visitation, saith |
| Jer 51:46 | a rumour shall both come one y |
| Jer 51:46 | in another y shall come a rumour |
| Jer 51:59 | in the fourth y of his reign |
| Jer 52:4 | pass in the ninth y of his reign |
| Jer 52:5 | the eleventh y of king Zedekiah |
| Jer 52:12 | which was the nineteenth y of |
| Jer 52:28 | in the seventh y three thousand |
| Jer 52:29 | In the eighteenth y of |
| Jer 52:30 | twentieth y of Nebuchadrezzar |
| Jer 52:31 | thirtieth y of the captivity of |
| Jer 52:31 | king of Babylon in the first y of |
| Eze 1:1 | came to pass in the thirtieth y |
| Eze 1:2 | which was the fifth y of king |
| Eze 4:6 | appointed thee each day for a y |
| Eze 8:1 | And it came to pass in the sixth y |
| Eze 20:1 | it came to pass in the seventh y |
| Eze 24:1 | Again in the ninth y, in the |
| Eze 26:1 | it came to pass in the eleventh y |
| Eze 29:1 | In the tenth y, in the tenth |
| Eze 29:17 | pass in the seven and twentieth y |
| Eze 30:20 | it came to pass in the eleventh y |
| Eze 31:1 | it came to pass in the eleventh y |
| Eze 32:1 | it came to pass in the twelfth y |
| Eze 32:17 | to pass also in the twelfth y |
| Eze 33:21 | in the twelfth y of our captivity |
| Eze 40:1 | twentieth y of our captivity, in |
| Eze 40:1 | in the beginning of the y |
| Eze 40:1 | in the fourteenth y after that |
| Eze 46:13 | of the first y without blemish |
| Eze 46:17 | shall be his to the y of liberty |
| Dan 1:1 | In the third y of the reign of |
| Dan 1:21 | unto the first y of king Cyrus |
| Dan 2:1 | in the second y of the reign of |
| Dan 7:1 | In the first y of Belshazzar king |
| Dan 8:1 | In the third y of the reign of |
| Dan 9:1 | In the first y of Darius the son |
| Dan 9:2 | In the first y of his reign I |
| Dan 10:1 | In the third y of Cyrus king of |
| Dan 11:1 | in the first y of Darius the Mede |
| Mic 6:6 | offerings, with calves of a y old |
| Hag 1:1 | In the second y of Darius the |
| Hag 1:15 | in the second y of Darius the |
| Hag 2:10 | month, in the second y of Darius |
| Zec 1:1 | month, in the second y of Darius |
| Zec 1:7 | Sebat, in the second y of Darius |
| Zec 7:1 | in the fourth y of king Darius |
| Zec 14:16 | y to y to worship the King |
| Lk 2:41 | y at the feast of the passover |
| Lk 3:1 | Now in the fifteenth y of the |

Lk 4:19 the acceptable y of the Lord
Lk 13:8 Lord, let it alone this y also
Jn 11:49 being the high priest that same y
Jn 11:51 but being high priest that y
Jn 18:13 was the high priest that same y
Acts 11:26 that a whole y they assembled
Acts 18:11 And he continued there a y
2Cor 8:10 but also to be forward a y ago
2Cor 9:2 that Achaia was ready a y ago
Heb 9:7 high priest alone once every y
Heb 9:25 every y with blood of others
Heb 10:1 y by y continually make the
Heb 10:1 which they offered y by y
Heb 10:3 again made of sins every y
Jas 4:13 a city, and continue there a y
Rev 9:15 and a day, and a month, and a y

## YEARLY

Lev 25:53 as a y hired servant shall he be
Judg 11:40 went y to lament the daughter of
Judg 21:19 y in a place which is on the
1Sa 1:3 up out of his city y to worship
1Sa 1:21 unto the LORD the y sacrifice
1Sa 2:19 husband to offer the y sacrifice
1Sa 20:6 for there is a y sacrifice there
Neh 10:32 to charge ourselves y with the
Est 9:21 the fifteenth day of the same, y

## YEARN

Gen 43:30 his bowels did y upon his brother

## YEARNED

1Kin 3:26 for her bowels y upon her son

## YEAR'S

Ex 34:22 feast of ingathering at the y end
2Sa 14:26 (for it was at every y end that

## YEARS

Gen 1:14 and for seasons, and for days, and y
Gen 5:3 Adam lived an hundred and thirty y
Gen 5:4 Seth were eight hundred y
Gen 5:5 were nine hundred and thirty y
Gen 5:6 Seth lived an hundred and five y
Gen 5:7 Enos eight hundred and seven y
Gen 5:8 were nine hundred and twelve y
Gen 5:9 And Enos lived ninety y, and begat
Gen 5:10 Cainan eight hundred and fifteen y
Gen 5:11 Enos were nine hundred and five y
Gen 5:12 And Cainan lived seventy y
Gen 5:13 eight hundred and forty y, and
Gen 5:14 Cainan were nine hundred and ten y
Gen 5:15 Mahalaleel lived sixty and five y
Gen 5:16 Jared eight hundred and thirty y
Gen 5:17 eight hundred ninety and five y
Gen 5:18 lived an hundred sixty and two y
Gen 5:19 he begat Enoch eight hundred y
Gen 5:20 were nine hundred sixty and two y
Gen 5:21 And Enoch lived sixty and five y
Gen 5:22 begat Methuselah three hundred y
Gen 5:23 three hundred sixty and five y
Gen 5:25 an hundred eighty and seven y
Gen 5:26 seven hundred eighty and two y
Gen 5:27 were nine hundred sixty and nine y
Gen 5:28 lived an hundred eighty and two y
Gen 5:30 five hundred ninety and five y
Gen 5:31 seven hundred seventy and seven y
Gen 5:32 And Noah was five hundred y old
Gen 6:3 shall be an hundred and twenty y
Gen 7:6 Noah was six hundred y old when
Gen 9:28 flood three hundred and fifty y
Gen 9:29 Noah were nine hundred and fifty y
Gen 11:10 Shem was an hundred y old
Gen 11:10 Arphaxad two y after the flood
Gen 11:11 he begat Arphaxad five hundred y
Gen 11:12 Arphaxad lived five and thirty y
Gen 11:13 Salah four hundred and three y
Gen 11:14 And Salah lived thirty y, and begat
Gen 11:15 Eber four hundred and three y
Gen 11:16 And Eber lived four and thirty y
Gen 11:17 Peleg four hundred and thirty y
Gen 11:18 And Peleg lived thirty y, and begat
Gen 11:19 begat Reu two hundred and nine y
Gen 11:20 And Reu lived two and thirty y
Gen 11:21 Serug two hundred and seven y
Gen 11:22 And Serug lived thirty y, and begat
Gen 11:23 he begat Nahor two hundred y
Gen 11:24 And Nahor lived nine and twenty y
Gen 11:25 Terah an hundred and nineteen y
Gen 11:26 And Terah lived seventy y, and
Gen 11:32 Terah were two hundred and five y
Gen 12:4 five y old when he departed out
Gen 14:4 Twelve y they served Chedorlaomer
Gen 15:9 Take me an heifer of three y old
Gen 15:9 old, and a she goat of three y old
Gen 15:9 old, and a ram of three y old
Gen 15:13 shall afflict them four hundred y
Gen 16:3 dwelt ten y in the land of Canaan
Gen 16:16 Abram was fourscore and six y old
Gen 17:1 And when Abram was ninety y old
Gen 17:17 unto him that is an hundred y old
Gen 17:17 shall Sarah, that is ninety y old
Gen 17:24 And Abraham was ninety y old
Gen 17:25 his son was thirteen y old
Gen 21:5 And Abraham was an hundred y old
Gen 23:1 hundred and seven and twenty y old
Gen 23:1 these were the y of the life of
Gen 25:7 these are the days of the y of
Gen 25:7 hundred threescore and fifteen y
Gen 25:8 old age, an old man, and full of y
Gen 25:17 these are the y of the life of
Gen 25:17 an hundred and thirty and seven y
Gen 25:20 Isaac was forty y old when he
Gen 25:26 Isaac was threescore y old when
Gen 26:34 Esau was forty y old when he took
Gen 29:18 I will serve thee seven y for
Gen 29:20 Jacob served seven y for Rachel
Gen 29:27 serve with me yet seven other y
Gen 29:30 served with him yet seven other y
Gen 31:38 This twenty y have I been with
Gen 31:41 have I been twenty y in thy house
Gen 31:41 fourteen y for thy two daughters
Gen 31:41 and six y for thy cattle
Gen 35:28 were an hundred and fourscore y
Gen 37:2 Joseph, being seventeen y old
Gen 41:1 to pass at the end of two full y
Gen 41:26 The seven good kine are seven y
Gen 41:26 the seven good ears are seven y
Gen 41:27 came up after them are seven y
Gen 41:27 wind shall be seven y of famine
Gen 41:29 there come seven y of great
Gen 41:30 after them seven y of famine
Gen 41:34 of Egypt in the seven plenteous y
Gen 41:35 food of those good y that come
Gen 41:36 against the seven y of famine
Gen 41:46 Joseph was thirty y old when he
Gen 41:47 in the seven plenteous y the
Gen 41:48 up all the food of the seven y
Gen 41:50 sons before the y of famine came
Gen 41:53 the seven y of plenteousness,
Gen 41:54 the seven y of dearth began to
Gen 45:6 For these two y hath the famine
Gen 45:6 and yet there are five y, in the
Gen 45:11 yet there are five y of famine
Gen 47:9 Pharaoh, The days of the y of my
Gen 47:9 are an hundred and thirty y
Gen 47:9 the days of the y of my life been
Gen 47:9 y of the life of my fathers in
Gen 47:28 in the land of Egypt seventeen y
Gen 47:28 was an hundred forty and seven y
Gen 50:22 Joseph lived an hundred and ten y
Gen 50:26 being an hundred and ten y old
Ex 6:16 the y of the life of Levi were an
Ex 6:16 were an hundred thirty and seven y
Ex 6:18 the y of the life of Kohath were
Ex 6:18 were an hundred thirty and three y
Ex 6:20 the y of the life of Amram were
Ex 6:20 an hundred and thirty and seven y
Ex 7:7 And Moses was fourscore y old
Ex 7:7 and Aaron fourscore and three y old
Ex 12:40 was four hundred and thirty y
Ex 12:41 of the four hundred and thirty y
Ex 16:35 of Israel did eat manna forty y
Ex 21:2 servant, six y he shall serve
Ex 23:10 six y thou shalt sow thy land, and
Ex 30:14 are numbered, from twenty y old
Ex 38:26 to be numbered, from twenty y old
Lev 19:23 three y shall it be as
Lev 25:3 Six y thou shalt sow thy field,
Lev 25:3 six y thou shalt prune thy
Lev 25:8 seven sabbaths of y unto thee
Lev 25:8 unto thee, seven times seven y
Lev 25:8 of y shall be unto thee forty
Lev 25:8 be unto thee forty and nine y
Lev 25:15 According to the number of y
Lev 25:15 of y of the fruits he shall sell
Lev 25:16 y thou shalt increase the price
Lev 25:16 according to the fewness of y
Lev 25:16 according to the number of the y
Lev 25:21 bring forth fruit for three y
Lev 25:27 count the y of the sale thereof
Lev 25:50 be according unto the number of y
Lev 25:51 If there be yet many y behind
Lev 25:52 but few y unto the year of jubile
Lev 25:52 according unto his y shall he
Lev 25:54 if he be not redeemed in these y
Lev 27:3 be of the male from twenty y old
Lev 27:3 even unto sixty y old
Lev 27:5 if it be from five y old even
Lev 27:5 y old even unto twenty y old
Lev 27:6 a month old even unto five y old
Lev 27:7 And if it be from sixty y old
Lev 27:18 according to the y that remain
Num 1:3 From twenty y old and upward, all
Num 1:18 of the names, from twenty y old
Num 1:20 every male from twenty y old
Num 1:22 every male from twenty y old
Num 1:24 of the names, from twenty y old
Num 1:26 of the names, from twenty y old
Num 1:28 of the names, from twenty y old
Num 1:30 of the names, from twenty y old
Num 1:32 of the names, from twenty y old
Num 1:34 of the names, from twenty y old
Num 1:36 of the names, from twenty y old
Num 1:38 of the names, from twenty y old
Num 1:40 of the names, from twenty y old
Num 1:42 of the names, from twenty y old
Num 1:45 their fathers, from twenty y old
Num 4:3 From thirty y old and upward even
Num 4:3 and upward even until fifty y old
Num 4:23 From thirty y old and upward until
Num 4:23 upward until fifty y old shalt
Num 4:30 From thirty y old and upward even
Num 4:30 upward even unto fifty y old
Num 4:35 From thirty y old and upward even
Num 4:35 and upward even unto fifty y old
Num 4:39 From thirty y old and upward even
Num 4:39 and upward even unto fifty y old
Num 4:43 From thirty y old and upward even
Num 4:43 and upward even unto fifty y old
Num 4:47 From thirty y old and upward even
Num 4:47 and upward even unto fifty y old
Num 8:24 from twenty and five y old
Num 8:25 from the age of fifty y they
Num 13:22 seven y before Zoan in Egypt
Num 14:29 whole number, from twenty y old
Num 14:33 wander in the wilderness forty y
Num 14:34 your iniquities, even forty y
Num 26:2 of Israel, from twenty y old
Num 26:4 of the people, from twenty y old
Num 32:11 out of Egypt, from twenty y old
Num 32:13 wander in the wilderness forty y
Num 33:39 three y old when he died in mount
Deut 2:7 these forty y the LORD thy God
Deut 2:14 Zered, was thirty and eight y
Deut 8:2 these forty y in the wilderness
Deut 8:4 did thy foot swell, these forty y
Deut 14:28 At the end of three y thou shalt
Deut 15:1 seven y thou shalt make a release
Deut 15:12 unto thee, and serve thee six y
Deut 15:18 to thee, in serving thee six y
Deut 29:5 led you forty y in the wilderness
Deut 31:2 hundred and twenty y old this day
Deut 31:10 At the end of every seven y
Deut 32:7 of old, consider the y of many
Deut 34:7 twenty y old when he died
Josh 5:6 walked forty y in the wilderness
Josh 13:1 Joshua was old and stricken in y
Josh 13:1 Thou art old and stricken in y
Josh 14:7 Forty y old was I when Moses the
Josh 14:10 as he said, these forty and five y
Josh 14:10 this day fourscore and five y old
Josh 24:29 being an hundred and ten y old
Judg 2:8 being an hundred and ten y old
Judg 3:8 served Chushan-rishathaim eight y
Judg 3:11 And the land had rest forty y
Judg 3:14 Eglon the king of Moab eighteen y
Judg 3:30 And the land had rest fourscore y
Judg 4:3 twenty y he mightily oppressed
Judg 5:31 And the land had rest forty y
Judg 6:1 into the hand of Midian seven y
Judg 6:25 the second bullock of seven y old
Judg 8:28 forty y in the days of Gideon
Judg 9:22 had reigned three y over Israel
Judg 10:2 judged Israel twenty and three y
Judg 10:3 and judged Israel twenty and two y
Judg 10:8 eighteen y, all the children of
Judg 11:26 coasts of Arnon, three hundred y
Judg 12:7 And Jephthah judged Israel six y
Judg 12:9 And he judged Israel seven y
Judg 12:11 and he judged Israel ten y
Judg 12:14 and he judged Israel eight y
Judg 13:1 hand of the Philistines forty y

Judg 15:20 days of the Philistines twenty y
Judg 16:31 And he judged Israel twenty y
Ruth 1:4 and they dwelled there about ten y
1Sa 4:15 Now Eli was ninety and eight y old
1Sa 4:18 And he had judged Israel forty y
1Sa 7:2 for it was twenty y
1Sa 13:1 he had reigned two y over Israel
1Sa 29:3 with me these days, or these y
2Sa 2:10 Saul's son was forty y old when
2Sa 2:10 over Israel, and reigned two y
2Sa 2:11 the house of Judah was seven y
2Sa 4:4 He was five y old when the
2Sa 5:4 David was thirty y old when he
2Sa 5:4 to reign, and he reigned forty y
2Sa 5:5 he reigned over Judah seven y
2Sa 5:5 three y over all Israel and Judah
2Sa 13:23 it came to pass after two full y
2Sa 13:38 to Geshur, and was there three y
2Sa 14:28 dwelt two full y in Jerusalem
2Sa 15:7 And it came to pass after forty y
2Sa 19:32 aged man, even fourscore y old
2Sa 19:35 I am this day fourscore y old
2Sa 21:1 in the days of David three y
2Sa 24:13 Shall seven y of famine come unto
1Kin 1:1 David was old and stricken in y
1Kin 2:11 reigned over Israel were forty y
1Kin 2:11 seven y reigned he in Hebron, and
1Kin 2:11 three y reigned he in Jerusalem
1Kin 2:39 to pass at the end of three y
1Kin 6:38 So was he seven y in building it
1Kin 7:1 building his own house thirteen y
1Kin 9:10 to pass at the end of twenty y
1Kin 10:22 once in three y came the navy of
1Kin 11:42 over all Israel was forty y
1Kin 14:20 reigned were two and twenty y
1Kin 14:21 one y old when he began to reign,
1Kin 14:21 reigned seventeen y in Jerusalem
1Kin 15:2 Three y reigned he in Jerusalem
1Kin 15:10 one y reigned he in Jerusalem
1Kin 15:25 and reigned over Israel two y
1Kin 15:33 in Tirzah, twenty and four y
1Kin 16:8 over Israel in Tirzah, two y
1Kin 16:23 to reign over Israel, twelve y
1Kin 16:23 six y reigned he in Tirzah
1Kin 16:29 Israel in Samaria twenty and two y
1Kin 17:1 shall not be dew nor rain these y
1Kin 22:1 they continued three y without
1Kin 22:42 five y old when he began to reign
1Kin 22:42 twenty and five y in Jerusalem
1Kin 22:51 and reigned two y over Israel
2Kin 3:1 of Judah, and reigned twelve y
2Kin 8:1 also come upon the land seven y
2Kin 8:2 land of the Philistines seven y
2Kin 8:17 two y old was he when he began to
2Kin 8:17 he reigned eight y in Jerusalem
2Kin 8:26 twenty y old was Ahaziah when he
2Kin 10:36 in Samaria was twenty and eight y
2Kin 11:3 in the house of the LORD six y
2Kin 11:21 Seven y old was Jehoash when he
2Kin 12:1 forty y reigned he in Jerusalem
2Kin 13:1 Samaria, and reigned seventeen y
2Kin 13:10 in Samaria, and reigned sixteen y
2Kin 14:2 five y old when he began to reign
2Kin 14:2 twenty and nine y in Jerusalem
2Kin 14:17 Jehoahaz king of Israel fifteen y
2Kin 14:21 Azariah, which was sixteen y old
2Kin 14:23 and reigned forty and one y
2Kin 15:2 Sixteen y old was he when he
2Kin 15:2 two and fifty y in Jerusalem
2Kin 15:17 and reigned ten y in Samaria
2Kin 15:23 in Samaria, and reigned two y
2Kin 15:27 in Samaria, and reigned twenty y
2Kin 15:33 twenty y old was he when he began
2Kin 15:33 he reigned sixteen y in Jerusalem
2Kin 16:2 Twenty y old was Ahaz when he
2Kin 16:2 and reigned sixteen y in Jerusalem
2Kin 17:1 in Samaria over Israel nine y
2Kin 17:5 Samaria, and besieged it three y
2Kin 18:2 five y old was he when he began
2Kin 18:2 twenty and nine y in Jerusalem
2Kin 18:10 the end of three y they took it
2Kin 20:6 will add unto thy days fifteen y
2Kin 21:1 Manasseh was twelve y old when he
2Kin 21:1 fifty and five y in Jerusalem
2Kin 21:19 two y old when he began to reign,
2Kin 21:19 and he reigned two y in Jerusalem
2Kin 22:1 Josiah was eight y old when he
2Kin 22:1 thirty and one y in Jerusalem
2Kin 23:31 three y old when he began to
2Kin 23:36 five y old when he began to reign
2Kin 23:36 he reigned eleven y in Jerusalem
2Kin 24:1 became his servant three y
2Kin 24:8 Jehoiachin was eighteen y old
2Kin 24:18 one y old when he began to reign,
2Kin 24:18 he reigned eleven y in Jerusalem
1Chr 2:21 when he was threescore y old
1Chr 3:4 and there he reigned seven y
1Chr 3:4 he reigned thirty and three y
1Chr 23:3 numbered from the age of thirty y
1Chr 23:24 LORD, from the age of twenty y
1Chr 23:27 were numbered from twenty y old
1Chr 27:23 number of them from twenty y old
1Chr 29:27 reigned over Israel was forty y
1Chr 29:27 seven y reigned he in Hebron, and
1Chr 29:27 three y reigned he in Jerusalem
2Chr 8:1 to pass at the end of twenty y
2Chr 9:21 every three y once came the ships
2Chr 9:30 Jerusalem over all Israel forty y
2Chr 11:17 son of Solomon strong, three y
2Chr 11:17 for three y they walked in the
2Chr 12:13 forty y old when he began to
2Chr 12:13 reigned seventeen y in Jerusalem
2Chr 13:2 He reigned three y in Jerusalem
2Chr 14:1 his days the land was quiet ten y
2Chr 14:6 rest, and he had no war in those y
2Chr 18:2 after certain y he went down to
2Chr 20:31 five y old when he began to reign
2Chr 20:31 twenty and five y in Jerusalem
2Chr 21:5 two y old when he began to reign,
2Chr 21:5 he reigned eight y in Jerusalem
2Chr 21:19 of time, after the end of two y
2Chr 21:20 two y old was he when he began to
2Chr 21:20 he reigned in Jerusalem eight y
2Chr 22:2 two y old was Ahaziah when he
2Chr 22:12 hid in the house of God six y
2Chr 24:1 Joash was seven y old when he
2Chr 24:1 he reigned forty y in Jerusalem
2Chr 24:15 thirty y old was he when he died
2Chr 25:1 five y old when he began to reign
2Chr 25:1 twenty and nine y in Jerusalem
2Chr 25:5 numbered them from twenty y old
2Chr 25:25 Jehoahaz king of Israel fifteen y
2Chr 26:1 Uzziah, who was sixteen y old
2Chr 26:3 Sixteen y old was Uzziah when he
2Chr 26:3 fifty and two y in Jerusalem
2Chr 27:1 five y old when he began to reign
2Chr 27:1 he reigned sixteen y in Jerusalem
2Chr 27:8 twenty y old when he began to
2Chr 27:8 and reigned sixteen y in Jerusalem
2Chr 28:1 Ahaz was twenty y old when he
2Chr 28:1 he reigned sixteen y in Jerusalem
2Chr 29:1 when he was five and twenty y old
2Chr 29:1 nine and twenty y in Jerusalem
2Chr 31:16 of males, from three y old
2Chr 31:17 and the Levites from twenty y old
2Chr 33:1 Manasseh was twelve y old when he
2Chr 33:1 fifty and five y in Jerusalem
2Chr 33:21 twenty y old when he began to
2Chr 33:21 reigned two y in Jerusalem
2Chr 34:1 Josiah was eight y old when he
2Chr 34:1 in Jerusalem one and thirty y
2Chr 36:2 three y old when he began to
2Chr 36:5 five y old when he began to reign
2Chr 36:5 he reigned eleven y in Jerusalem
2Chr 36:9 Jehoiachin was eight y old when
2Chr 36:11 twenty y old when he began to
2Chr 36:11 and reigned eleven y in Jerusalem
2Chr 36:21 to fulfil threescore and ten y
Ezr 3:8 the Levites, from twenty y old
Ezr 5:11 that was builded these many y ago
Neh 5:14 the king, that is, twelve y
Neh 9:21 forty y didst thou sustain them
Neh 9:30 Yet many y didst thou forbear
Job 10:5 are thy y as man's days,
Job 15:20 the number of y is hidden to the
Job 16:22 When a few y are come, then I
Job 32:7 multitude of y should teach
Job 36:11 and their y in pleasures
Job 36:26 number of his y be searched out
Job 42:16 lived Job an hundred and forty y
Ps 31:10 with grief, and my y with sighing
Ps 61:6 his y as many generations
Ps 77:5 of old, the y of ancient times
Ps 77:10 but I will remember the y of the
Ps 78:33 in vanity, and their y in trouble
Ps 90:4 For a thousand y in thy sight are
Ps 90:9 we spend our y as a tale that is
Ps 90:10 of our y are threescore y
Ps 90:10 of strength they be fourscore y
Ps 90:15 the y wherein we have seen evil
Ps 95:10 Forty y long was I grieved with
Ps 102:24 thy y are throughout all
Ps 102:27 same, and thy y shall have no end
Prov 4:10 the y of thy life shall be many
Prov 5:9 others, and thy y unto the cruel
Prov 9:11 the y of thy life shall be
Prov 10:27 but the y of the wicked shall be
Eccl 6:3 hundred children, and live many y
Eccl 6:3 so that the days of his y be many
Eccl 6:6 he live a thousand y twice told
Eccl 11:8 But if a man live many y, and
Eccl 12:1 nor the y draw nigh, when thou
Is 7:8 five y shall Ephraim be broken,
Is 15:5 Zoar, an heifer of three y old
Is 16:14 spoken, saying, Within three y
Is 16:14 as the y of an hireling, and the
Is 20:3 and barefoot three y for a sign
Is 21:16 according to the y of an hireling
Is 23:15 Tyre shall be forgotten seventy y
Is 23:15 after the end of seventy y shall
Is 23:17 pass after the end of seventy y
Is 32:10 y shall ye be troubled, ye
Is 38:5 will add unto thy days fifteen y
Is 38:10 deprived of the residue of my y
Is 38:15 I shall go softly all my y in the
Is 65:20 child shall die an hundred y old
Is 65:20 hundred y old shall be accursed
Jer 25:11 the king of Babylon seventy y
Jer 25:12 when seventy y are accomplished,
Jer 28:3 Within two full y will I bring
Jer 28:11 within the space of two full y
Jer 29:10 the LORD, That after seventy y be
Jer 34:14 At the end of seven y let ye go
Jer 34:14 and when he hath served thee six y
Jer 48:34 as an heifer of three y old
Jer 52:1 twenty y old when he began to
Jer 52:1 he reigned eleven y in Jerusalem
Eze 4:5 upon thee the y of their iniquity
Eze 22:4 near, and art come even unto thy y
Eze 29:11 shall it be inhabited forty y
Eze 29:12 waste shall be desolate forty y
Eze 29:13 At the end of forty y will I
Eze 38:8 in the latter y thou shalt come
Eze 38:17 prophesied in those days many y
Eze 39:9 shall burn them with fire seven y
Dan 1:5 so nourishing them three y
Dan 5:31 about threescore and two y old
Dan 9:2 by books the number of the y
Dan 9:2 he would accomplish seventy y in
Dan 11:6 in the end of y they shall join
Dan 11:8 he shall continue more y than the
Dan 11:13 after certain y with a great army
Joel 2:2 even to the y of many generations
Joel 2:25 I will restore to you the y that
Amos 1:1 two y before the earthquake
Amos 2:10 led you forty y through the
Amos 4:4 and your tithes after three y
Amos 5:25 in the wilderness forty y
Hab 3:2 thy work in the midst of the y
Hab 3:2 in the midst of the y make known
Zec 1:12 these threescore and ten y
Zec 7:3 as I have done these so many y
Zec 7:5 month, even those seventy y
Mal 3:4 days of old, and as in former y
Mt 2:16 coasts thereof, from two y old
Mt 9:20 with an issue of blood twelve y
Mk 5:25 had an issue of blood twelve y
Mk 5:42 she was of the age of twelve y
Lk 1:7 both were now well stricken in y
Lk 1:18 and my wife well stricken in y
Lk 2:36 seven y from her virginity
Lk 2:37 of about fourscore and four y
Lk 2:42 And when he was twelve y old
Lk 3:23 began to be about thirty y of age
Lk 4:25 the heaven was shut up three y
Lk 8:42 daughter, about twelve y of age
Lk 8:43 having an issue of blood twelve y
Lk 12:19 much goods laid up for many y
Lk 13:7 these three y I come seeking
Lk 13:11 a spirit of infirmity eighteen y
Lk 13:16 hath bound, lo, these eighteen y
Lk 15:29 these many y do I serve thee,
Jn 2:20 six y was this temple in building
Jn 5:5 an infirmity thirty and eight y
Jn 8:57 him, Thou art not yet fifty y old
Acts 4:22 For the man was above forty y old
Acts 7:6 entreat them evil four hundred y
Acts 7:23 And when he was full forty y old
Acts 7:30 when forty y were expired, there
Acts 7:36 sea, and in the wilderness forty y

Acts 7:42 of forty y in the wilderness
Acts 9:33 which had kept his bed eight y
Acts 13:18 about the time of forty y
Acts 13:20 space of four hundred and fifty y
Acts 13:21 Benjamin, by the space of forty y
Acts 19:10 continued by the space of two y
Acts 20:31 that by the space of three y I
Acts 24:10 many y a judge unto this nation
Acts 24:17 Now after many y I came to bring
Acts 24:27 But after two y Porcius Festus
Acts 28:30 Paul dwelt two whole y in his own
Rom 4:19 he was about an hundred y old
Rom 15:23 these many y to come unto you
2Cor 12:2 in Christ above fourteen y ago
Gal 1:18 Then after three y I went up to
Gal 2:1 Then fourteen y after I went up
Gal 3:17 four hundred and thirty y after
Gal 4:10 days, and months, and times, and y
1Ti 5:9 the number under threescore y old
Heb 1:12 the same, and thy y shall not fail
Heb 3:9 me, and saw my works forty y
Heb 3:17 with whom was he grieved forty y
Heb 11:24 Moses, when he was come to y
Jas 5:17 the earth by the space of three y
2Pet 3:8 is with the Lord as a thousand y
2Pet 3:8 and a thousand y as one day
Rev 20:2 Satan, and bound him a thousand y
Rev 20:3 till the thousand y should be
Rev 20:4 reigned with Christ a thousand y
Rev 20:5 the thousand y were finished
Rev 20:6 shall reign with him a thousand y
Rev 20:7 when the thousand y are expired

## YEARS'
2Kin 8:3 came to pass at the seven y end
1Chr 21:12 Either three y famine

## YELL
Jer 51:38 they shall y as lions' whelps

## YELLED
Jer 2:15 lions roared upon him, and y

## YELLOW
Lev 13:30 and there be in it a y thin hair
Lev 13:32 not, and there be in it no y hair
Lev 13:36 priest shall not seek for y hair
Ps 68:13 and her feathers with y gold

## YESTERDAY
Ex 5:14 your task in making brick both y
1Sa 20:27 son of Jesse to meat, neither y
2Sa 15:20 Whereas thou camest but y
2Kin 9:26 Surely I have seen y the blood of
Job 8:9 (For we are but of y, and know
Ps 90:4 are but as y when it is past
Jn 4:52 Y at the seventh hour the fever
Acts 7:28 as thou diddest the Egyptian y
Heb 13:8 Jesus Christ the same y, and to

## YESTERNIGHT
Gen 19:34 Behold, I lay y with my father
Gen 31:29 of your father spake unto me y
Gen 31:42 of my hands, and rebuked thee y

## YIELD
Gen 4:12 y unto thee her strength
Gen 49:20 he shall y royal dainties
Lev 19:25 that it may y unto you the
Lev 25:19 And the land shall y her fruit
Lev 26:4 and the land shall y her increase
Lev 26:4 of the field shall y their fruit
Lev 26:20 land shall not y her increase
Lev 26:20 trees of the land y their fruits
Deut 11:17 and that the land y not her fruit
2Chr 30:8 but y yourselves unto the LORD,
Ps 67:6 shall the earth y her increase
Ps 85:12 and our land shall y her increase
Ps 107:37 which may y fruits of increase
Prov 7:21 fair speech she caused him to y
Is 5:10 of vineyard shall y one bath
Is 5:10 seed of an homer shall y an ephah
Eze 34:27 of the field shall y her fruit
Eze 34:27 and the earth shall y her increase
Eze 36:8 y your fruit to my people of
Hos 8:7 the bud shall y no meal
Hos 8:7 if so be it y, the strangers
Joel 2:22 the vine do y their strength
Hab 3:17 and the fields shall y no meat
Mk 4:8 did y fruit that sprang up and
Acts 23:21 But do not thou y unto them
Rom 6:13 Neither y ye your members as
Rom 6:13 but y yourselves unto God, as
Rom 6:16 that to whom ye y yourselves
Rom 6:19 even so now y your members
Jas 3:12 can no fountain both y salt water

## YIELDED
Gen 49:33 y up the ghost, and was gathered
Num 17:8 and bloomed blossoms, and y almonds
Dan 3:28 y their bodies, that they might
Mt 27:50 with a loud voice, y up the ghost
Mk 4:7 and choked it, and it y no fruit
Acts 5:10 at his feet, and y up the ghost
Rom 6:19 for as ye have y your members
Rev 22:2 and y her fruit every month

## YIELDETH
Neh 9:37 it y much increase unto the kings
Job 24:5 the wilderness y food for them
Prov 12:12 the root of the righteous y fruit
Heb 12:11 it y the peaceable fruit of

## YIELDING
Gen 1:11 forth grass, the herb y seed
Gen 1:11 the fruit tree y fruit after his
Gen 1:12 herb y seed after his kind, and
Gen 1:12 his kind, and the tree y fruit
Gen 1:29 is the fruit of a tree y seed
Eccl 10:4 for y pacifieth great offences
Jer 17:8 neither shall cease from y fruit

## YOKE
Gen 27:40 break his y from off thy neck
Lev 26:13 I have broken the bands of your y
Num 19:2 and upon which never came y
Deut 21:3 and which hath not drawn in the y
Deut 28:48 he shall put a y of iron upon thy
1Sa 6:7 on which there hath come no y
1Sa 11:7 And he took a y of oxen, and hewed
1Sa 14:14 which a y of oxen might plow
1Kin 12:4 Thy father made our y grievous
1Kin 12:4 his heavy y which he put upon us,
1Kin 12:9 Make the y which thy father did
1Kin 12:10 Thy father made our y heavy
1Kin 12:11 heavy y, I will add to your y
1Kin 12:14 My father made your y heavy
1Kin 12:14 and I will add to your y
1Kin 19:19 with twelve y of oxen before him
1Kin 19:21 took a y of oxen, and slew them,
2Chr 10:4 Thy father made our y grievous
2Chr 10:4 his heavy y that he put upon us,
2Chr 10:9 Ease somewhat the y that thy
2Chr 10:10 Thy father made our y heavy
2Chr 10:11 my father put a heavy y upon you
2Chr 10:11 you, I will put more to your y
2Chr 10:14 My father made your y heavy
Job 1:3 camels, and five hundred y of oxen
Job 42:12 camels, and a thousand y of oxen
Is 9:4 hast broken the y of his burden
Is 10:27 his y from off thy neck, and the
Is 10:27 the y shall be destroyed because
Is 14:25 then shall his y depart from off
Is 47:6 hast thou very heavily laid thy y
Is 58:6 go free, and that ye break every y
Is 58:9 away from the midst of thee the y
Jer 2:20 of old time I have broken thy y
Jer 5:5 have altogether broken the y
Jer 27:8 the y of the king of Babylon
Jer 27:11 the y of the king of Babylon
Jer 27:12 the y of the king of Babylon
Jer 28:2 I have broken the y of the king
Jer 28:4 for I will break the y of the
Jer 28:10 Hananiah the prophet took the y
Jer 28:11 Even so will I break the y of
Jer 28:12 the y from off the neck of the
Jer 28:14 I have put a y of iron upon the
Jer 30:8 break his y from off thy neck
Jer 31:18 a bullock unaccustomed to the y
Jer 51:23 the husbandman and his y of oxen
Lam 1:14 The y of my transgressions is
Lam 3:27 that he bear the y in his youth
Eze 34:27 have broken the bands of their y
Hos 11:4 that take off the y on their jaws
Nah 1:13 will I break his y from off thee
Mt 11:29 Take my y upon you, and learn of
Mt 11:30 For my y is easy, and my burden is
Lk 14:19 I have bought five y of oxen
Acts 15:10 to put a y upon the neck of the
Gal 5:1 again with the y of bondage
1Ti 6:1 y count their own masters worthy

## YOKED
2Cor 6:14 Be ye not unequally y together

## YOKEFELLOW
Phil 4:3 And I intreat thee also, true y

## YOKES
Jer 27:2 Make thee bonds and y, and put them
Jer 28:13 Thou hast broken the y of wood
Jer 28:13 shalt make for them y of iron
Eze 30:18 shall break there the y of Egypt

## YONDER
Gen 22:5 and I and the lad will go y
Num 16:37 and scatter thou the fire y
Num 23:15 offering, while I meet the LORD y
Num 32:19 with them on y side Jordan
2Kin 4:25 Behold, y is that Shunammite
Mt 17:20 mountain, Remove hence to y place
Mt 26:36 Sit ye here, while I go and pray y

## YOUNG
Gen 4:23 wounding, and a y man to my hurt
Gen 14:24 that which the y men have eaten
Gen 15:9 and a turtledove, and a y pigeon
Gen 18:7 and good, and gave it unto a y man
Gen 19:4 the house round, both old and y
Gen 22:3 and took two of his y men with him
Gen 22:5 And Abraham said unto his y men
Gen 22:19 Abraham returned unto his y men
Gen 31:38 she goats have not cast their y
Gen 33:13 and herds with y are with me
Gen 34:19 the y man deferred not to do the
Gen 41:12 there was there with us a y man
Ex 10:9 Moses said, We will go with our y
Ex 23:26 There shall nothing cast their y
Ex 24:5 he sent y men of the children of
Ex 29:1 Take one y bullock, and two rams
Ex 33:11 a y man, departed not out of the
Lev 1:14 of turtledoves, or of y pigeons
Lev 4:3 a y bullock without blemish unto
Lev 4:14 offer a y bullock for the sin
Lev 5:7 or two y pigeons, unto the LORD
Lev 5:11 or two y pigeons, then he that
Lev 9:2 Take thee a y calf for a sin
Lev 12:6 a y pigeon, or a turtledove, for
Lev 12:8 two turtles, or two y pigeons
Lev 14:22 or two y pigeons, such as he is
Lev 14:30 turtledoves, or of the y pigeons
Lev 15:14 or two y pigeons, and come before
Lev 15:29 or two y pigeons, and bring them
Lev 16:3 with a y bullock for a sin
Lev 22:28 kill it and her y both in one day
Lev 23:18 one y bullock, and two rams
Num 6:10 or two y pigeons, to the priest,
Num 7:15 One y bullock, one ram, one lamb
Num 7:21 One y bullock, one ram, one lamb
Num 7:27 One y bullock, one ram, one lamb
Num 7:33 One y bullock, one ram, one lamb
Num 7:39 One y bullock, one ram, one lamb
Num 7:45 One y bullock, one ram, one lamb
Num 7:51 One y bullock, one ram, one lamb
Num 7:57 One y bullock, one ram, one lamb
Num 7:63 One y bullock, one ram, one lamb
Num 7:69 One y bullock, one ram, one lamb
Num 7:75 One y bullock, one ram, one lamb
Num 7:81 One y bullock, one ram, one lamb
Num 8:8 Then let them take a y bullock
Num 8:8 another y bullock shalt thou take
Num 11:27 And there ran a y man, and told
Num 11:28 of Moses, one of his y men
Num 15:24 y bullock for a burnt offering
Num 23:24 and lift up himself as a y lion
Num 28:11 y bullocks, and one ram, seven
Num 28:19 two y bullocks, and one ram, and
Num 28:27 two y bullocks, one ram, seven
Num 29:2 one y bullock, one ram, and seven
Num 29:8 one y bullock, one ram, and seven
Num 29:13 thirteen y bullocks, two rams, and
Num 29:17 ye shall offer twelve y bullocks
Deut 22:6 ground, whether they be y ones
Deut 22:6 and the dam sitting upon the y
Deut 22:6 shalt not take the dam with the y
Deut 22:7 the dam go, and take the y to thee
Deut 28:50 the old, nor shew favour to the y
Deut 28:57 toward her y one that cometh out
Deut 32:11 her nest, fluttereth over her y
Deut 32:25 shall destroy both the y man
Josh 6:21 in the city, both man and woman, y
Josh 6:23 the y men that were spies went in
Judg 6:25 him, Take thy father's y bullock
Judg 8:14 caught a y man of the men of
Judg 9:54 unto the y man his armourbearer
Judg 9:54 his y man thrust him through, and
Judg 14:5 a y lion roared against him
Judg 14:10 for so used the y men to do
Judg 17:7 And there was a y man out of

Judg 17:11 the y man was unto him as one of
Judg 17:12 the y man became his priest, and
Judg 18:3 the voice of the y man the Levite
Judg 18:15 the house of the y man the Levite
Judg 19:19 for the y man which is with thy
Judg 21:12 four hundred y virgins, that had
Ruth 2:9 have I not charged the y men that
Ruth 2:9 that which the y men have drawn
Ruth 2:15 glean, Boaz commanded his y men
Ruth 2:21 Thou shalt keep fast by my y men
Ruth 3:10 as thou followedst not y men
Ruth 4:12 shall give thee of this y woman
1Sa 1:24 and the child was y
1Sa 2:17 Wherefore the sin of the y men
1Sa 8:16 and your goodliest y men, and your
1Sa 9:2 name was Saul, a choice y man
1Sa 9:11 they found y maidens going out to
1Sa 14:1 the y man that bare his armour
1Sa 14:6 Jonathan said to the y man that
1Sa 17:58 Whose son art thou, thou y man
1Sa 20:22 But if I say thus unto the y man
1Sa 21:4 if the y men have kept themselves
1Sa 21:5 the vessels of the y men are holy
1Sa 25:5 And David sent out ten y men
1Sa 25:5 men, and David said unto the y men
1Sa 25:8 Ask thy y men, and they will shew
1Sa 25:8 Wherefore let the y men find
1Sa 25:9 And when David's y men came
1Sa 25:12 So David's y men turned their way
1Sa 25:14 But one of the y men told Abigail
1Sa 25:25 saw not the y men of my lord
1Sa 25:27 the y men that follow my lord
1Sa 26:22 and let one of the y men come over
1Sa 30:13 I am a y man of Egypt, servant to
1Sa 30:17 of them, save four hundred y men
2Sa 1:5 said unto the y man that told him
2Sa 1:6 the y man that told him said, As
2Sa 1:13 said unto the y man that told him
2Sa 1:15 And David called one of the y men
2Sa 2:14 Let the y men now arise, and play
2Sa 2:21 lay thee hold on one of the y men
2Sa 4:12 And David commanded his y men
2Sa 9:12 And Mephibosheth had a y son
2Sa 13:32 all the y men the king's sons
2Sa 13:34 the y man that kept the watch
2Sa 14:21 bring the y man Absalom again
2Sa 16:2 summer fruit for the y men to eat
2Sa 18:5 gently for my sake with the y man
2Sa 18:12 that none touch the y man Absalom
2Sa 18:15 ten y men that bare Joab's armour
2Sa 18:29 Is the y man Absalom safe
2Sa 18:32 Is the y man Absalom safe
2Sa 18:32 do thee hurt, be as that y man is
1Kin 1:2 for my lord the king a y virgin
1Kin 11:28 Solomon seeing the y man that he
1Kin 12:8 consulted with the y men that
1Kin 12:10 the y men that were grown up with
1Kin 12:14 after the counsel of the y men
1Kin 20:14 Even by the y men of the princes
1Kin 20:15 Then he numbered the y men of the
1Kin 20:17 the y men of the princes of the
1Kin 20:19 So these y men of the princes of
2Kin 4:22 me, I pray thee, one of the y men
2Kin 5:22 to me from mount Ephraim two y
2Kin 6:17 LORD opened the eyes of the y man
2Kin 8:12 their y men wilt thou slay with
2Kin 9:4 So the y man, even the y man
2Kin 9:4 even the y man the prophet, went
1Chr 12:28 a y man mighty of valour, and of
1Chr 22:5 David said, Solomon my son is y
1Chr 29:1 alone God hath chosen, is yet y
2Chr 10:8 took counsel with the y men that
2Chr 10:10 the y men that were brought up
2Chr 10:14 after the advice of the y men
2Chr 13:7 of Solomon, when Rehoboam was y
2Chr 13:9 himself with a y bullock and seven
2Chr 34:3 of his reign, while he was yet y
2Chr 36:17 who slew their y men with the
2Chr 36:17 compassion upon y man or maiden
Ezr 6:9 both y bullocks, and rams, and
Est 2:2 Let there be fair y virgins
Est 2:3 gather together all the fair y
Est 3:13 cause to perish, all Jews, both y
Est 8:10 mules, camels, and y dromedaries
Job 1:19 house, and it fell upon the y men
Job 4:10 lion, and the teeth of the y lions
Job 19:18 Yea, y children despised me
Job 29:8 The y men saw me, and hid
Job 32:6 Buzite answered and said, I am y
Job 38:39 fill the appetite of the y lions
Job 38:41 when his y ones cry unto God,
Job 39:3 they bring forth their y ones
Job 39:4 Their y ones are in good liking,
Job 39:16 is hardened against her y ones
Job 39:30 Her y ones also suck up blood
Ps 17:12 as it were a y lion lurking in
Ps 29:6 and Sirion like a y unicorn
Ps 34:10 The y lions do lack, and suffer
Ps 37:25 I have been y, and now am old
Ps 58:6 the great teeth of the y lions
Ps 78:63 The fire consumed their y men
Ps 78:71 y he brought him to feed Jacob
Ps 84:3 herself, where she may lay her y
Ps 91:13 the y lion and the dragon shalt
Ps 104:21 The y lions roar after their prey
Ps 119:9 shall a y man cleanse his way
Ps 147:9 to the y ravens which cry
Ps 148:12 Both y men, and maidens
Prov 1:4 to the y man knowledge and
Prov 7:7 a y man void of understanding,
Prov 20:29 The glory of y men is their
Prov 30:17 the y eagles shall eat it
Eccl 11:9 Rejoice, O y man, in thy youth
Song 2:9 beloved is like a roe or a y hart
Song 2:17 be thou like a roe or a y hart
Song 4:5 like two y roes that are twins
Song 7:3 like two y roes that are twins
Song 8:14 to a y hart upon the mountains of
Is 5:29 they shall roar like y lions
Is 7:21 that a man shall nourish a y cow
Is 9:17 shall have no joy in their y men
Is 11:6 the y lion and the fatling
Is 11:7 their y ones shall lie down
Is 13:18 shall dash the y men to pieces
Is 20:4 and the Ethiopians captives, y
Is 23:4 neither do I nourish up y men
Is 30:6 anguish, from whence come the y
Is 30:6 upon the shoulders of y asses
Is 30:24 the y asses that ear the ground
Is 31:4 the y lion roaring on his prey,
Is 31:8 his y men shall be discomfited
Is 40:11 gently lead those that are with y
Is 40:30 the y men shall utterly fall
Is 62:5 For as a y man marrieth a virgin,
Jer 2:15 The y lions roared upon him, and
Jer 6:11 the assembly of y men together
Jer 9:21 the y men from the streets
Jer 11:22 the y men shall die by the sword
Jer 15:8 of the y men a spoiler at noonday
Jer 18:21 let their y men be slain by the
Jer 31:12 for the y of the flock and of the
Jer 31:13 rejoice in the dance, both y men
Jer 48:15 his chosen y men are gone down to
Jer 49:26 Therefore her y men shall fall in
Jer 50:30 Therefore shall her y men fall in
Jer 51:3 and spare ye not her y men
Jer 51:22 will I break in pieces old and y
Jer 51:22 will I break in pieces the y man
Lam 1:15 against me to crush my y men
Lam 1:18 my y men are gone into captivity
Lam 2:19 for the life of thy y children
Lam 2:21 The y and the old lie on the
Lam 2:21 my y men are fallen by the sword
Lam 4:3 they give suck to their y ones
Lam 4:4 the y children ask bread, and no
Lam 5:13 They took the y men to grind
Lam 5:14 the y men from their musick
Eze 9:6 Slay utterly old and y, both maids
Eze 17:4 off the top of his y twigs
Eze 17:22 top of his y twigs a tender one
Eze 19:2 her whelps among y lions
Eze 19:3 it became a y lion, and it learned
Eze 19:5 her whelps, and made him a y lion
Eze 19:6 the lions, he became a y lion
Eze 23:6 all of them desirable y men
Eze 23:12 all of them desirable y men
Eze 23:23 all of them desirable y men
Eze 30:17 The y men of Aven and of Pi-beseth
Eze 31:6 of the field bring forth their y
Eze 32:2 Thou art like a y lion of the
Eze 38:13 with all the y lions thereof,
Eze 41:19 the face of a y lion toward the
Eze 43:19 a y bullock for a sin offering
Eze 43:23 thou shalt offer a y bullock
Eze 43:25 shall also prepare a y bullock
Eze 45:18 thou shalt take a y bullock
Eze 46:6 be a y bullock without blemish
Hos 5:14 as a y lion to the house of Judah
Joel 2:28 your y men shall see visions
Amos 2:11 of your y men for Nazarites
Amos 3:4 will a y lion cry out of his den,
Amos 4:10 your y men have I slain with the
Amos 8:13 virgins and y men faint for thirst
Mic 5:8 as a y lion among the flocks of
Nah 2:11 the feeding place of the y lions
Nah 2:13 sword shall devour thy y lions
Nah 3:10 her y children also were dashed
Zec 2:4 him, Run, speak to this y man
Zec 9:17 shall make the y men cheerful
Zec 11:3 a voice of the roaring of y lions
Zec 11:16 off, neither shall seek the y one
Mt 2:8 search diligently for the y child
Mt 2:9 stood over where the y child was
Mt 2:11 they saw the y child with Mary
Mt 2:13 Arise, and take the y child
Mt 2:13 seek the y child to destroy him
Mt 2:14 he arose, he took the y child
Mt 2:20 Arise, and take the y child
Mt 2:20 which sought the y child's life
Mt 2:21 And he arose, and took the y child
Mt 19:20 The y man saith unto him, All
Mt 19:22 But when the y man heard that
Mk 7:25 whose y daughter had an unclean
Mk 10:13 they brought y children to him,
Mk 14:51 followed him a certain y man
Mk 14:51 the y men laid hold on him
Mk 16:5 they saw a y man sitting on the
Lk 2:24 of turtledoves, or two y pigeons
Lk 7:14 Y man, I say unto thee, Arise
Jn 12:14 Jesus, when he had found a y ass
Jn 21:18 I say unto thee, When thou wast y
Acts 2:17 your y men shall see visions, and
Acts 5:6 the y men arose, wound him up, and
Acts 5:10 the y men came in, and found her
Acts 7:19 they cast out their y children
Acts 7:58 their clothes at a y man's feet
Acts 20:9 a certain y man named Eutychus
Acts 20:12 And they brought the y man alive
Acts 23:17 Bring this y man unto the chief
Acts 23:18 me to bring this y man unto thee
Acts 23:22 captain then let the y man depart
Titus 2:4 may teach the y women to be sober
Titus 2:6 Y men likewise exhort to be sober
1Jn 2:13 y men, because ye have overcome
1Jn 2:14 y men, because ye are strong, and

## YOUNGER

Gen 9:24 knew what his y son had done unto
Gen 19:31 And the firstborn said unto the y
Gen 19:34 the firstborn said unto the y
Gen 19:35 the y arose, and lay with him
Gen 19:38 And the y, she also bare a son, and
Gen 25:23 and the elder shall serve the y
Gen 27:15 and put them upon Jacob her y son
Gen 27:42 sent and called Jacob her y son
Gen 29:16 and the name of the y was Rachel
Gen 29:18 years for Rachel thy y daughter
Gen 29:26 country, to give the y before the
Gen 43:29 and said, Is this your y brother
Gen 48:14 Ephraim's head, who was the y
Gen 48:19 but truly his y brother shall be
Judg 1:13 son of Kenaz, Caleb's y brother
Judg 3:9 son of Kenaz, Caleb's y brother
Judg 15:2 is not her y sister fairer than
1Sa 14:49 and the name of the y Michal
1Chr 24:31 over against their y brethren
Job 30:1 But now they that are y than I
Eze 16:46 thy y sister, that dwelleth at
Eze 16:61 thy sisters, thine elder and thy y
Lk 15:12 the y of them said to his father,
Lk 15:13 not many days after the y son
Lk 22:26 among you, let him be as the y
Rom 9:12 her, The elder shall serve the y
1Ti 5:1 and the y men as brethren
1Ti 5:2 the y as sisters, with all purity
1Ti 5:11 But the y widows refuse
1Ti 5:14 therefore that the y women marry
1Pet 5:5 Likewise, ye y, submit yourselves

## YOUNGEST

Gen 42:13 the y is this day with our father
Gen 42:15 except your y brother come hither
Gen 42:20 But bring your y brother unto me
Gen 42:32 the y is this day with our father
Gen 42:34 bring your y brother unto me
Gen 43:33 the y according to his youth
Gen 44:2 cup, in the sack's mouth of the y
Gen 44:12 at the eldest, and left at the y
Gen 44:23 Except your y brother come down
Gen 44:26 if our y brother be with us, then
Gen 44:26 except our y brother be with us

Josh 6:26 in his y son shall he set up the
Judg 9:5 the y son of Jerubbaal was left
1Sa 16:11 said, There remaineth yet the y
1Sa 17:14 And David was the y
1Kin 16:34 gates thereof in his y son Segub
2Chr 21:17 save Jehoahaz, the y of his sons
2Chr 22:1 his y son king in his stead

**YOUTH**
Gen 8:21 of man's heart is evil from his y
Gen 43:33 the youngest according to his y
Gen 46:34 cattle from our y even until now
Lev 22:13 her father's house, as in her y
Num 30:3 in her father's house in her y
Num 30:16 being yet in her y in her
Judg 8:20 But the y drew not his sword
Judg 8:20 he feared, because he was yet a y
1Sa 17:33 for thou art but a y, and he a man
1Sa 17:33 and he a man of war from his y
1Sa 17:42 for he was but a y, and ruddy, and
1Sa 17:55 host, Abner, whose son is this y
2Sa 19:7 befell thee from thy y until now
1Kin 18:12 servant fear the LORD from my y
Job 13:26 to possess the iniquities of my y
Job 20:11 are full of the sin of his y
Job 29:4 As I was in the days of my y
Job 30:12 Upon my right hand rise the y
Job 31:18 (For from my y he was brought up
Job 33:25 shall return to the days of his y
Job 36:14 They die in y, and their life is
Ps 25:7 Remember not the sins of my y
Ps 71:5 thou art my trust from my y
Ps 71:17 thou hast taught me from my y
Ps 88:15 and ready to die from my y up
Ps 89:45 The days of his y hast thou
Ps 103:5 so that thy y is renewed like the
Ps 110:3 thou hast the dew of thy y
Ps 127:4 so are children of the y
Ps 129:1 have they afflicted me from my y
Ps 129:2 have they afflicted me from my y
Ps 144:12 be as plants grown up in their y
Prov 2:17 forsaketh the guide of her y
Prov 5:18 and rejoice with the wife of thy y
Eccl 11:9 Rejoice, O young man, in thy y
Eccl 11:9 cheer thee in the days of thy y
Eccl 11:10 for childhood and y are vanity
Eccl 12:1 thy Creator in the days of thy y
Is 47:12 thou hast laboured from thy y
Is 47:15 even thy merchants, from thy y
Is 54:4 shalt forget the shame of thy y
Is 54:6 grieved in spirit, and a wife of y
Jer 2:2 thee, the kindness of thy y
Jer 3:4 thou art the guide of my y
Jer 3:24 labour of our fathers from our y
Jer 3:25 from our y even unto this day, and
Jer 22:21 hath been thy manner from thy y
Jer 31:19 I did bear the reproach of my y
Jer 32:30 done evil before me from their y
Jer 48:11 Moab hath been at ease from his y
Lam 3:27 that he bear the yoke in his y
Eze 4:14 for from my y up even till now
Eze 16:22 not remembered the days of thy y
Eze 16:43 not remembered the days of thy y
Eze 16:60 with thee in the days of thy y
Eze 23:3 committed whoredoms in their y
Eze 23:8 for in her y they lay with her,
Eze 23:19 to remembrance the days of her y
Eze 23:21 remembrance the lewdness of thy y
Eze 23:21 Egyptians for the paps of thy y
Hos 2:15 there, as in the days of her y
Joel 1:8 for the husband of her y
Zec 13:5 me to keep cattle from my y
Mal 2:14 between thee and the wife of thy y
Mal 2:15 against the wife of his y
Mt 19:20 things have I kept from my y up
Mk 10:20 these have I observed from my y
Lk 18:21 these have I kept from my y up
Acts 26:4 My manner of life from my y
1Ti 4:12 Let no man despise thy y

**YOUTHFUL**
2Ti 2:22 Flee also y lusts

**YOUTHS**
Prov 7:7 ones, I discerned among the y
Is 40:30 Even the y shall faint and be

**YOU-WARD**
2Cor 1:12 world, and more abundantly to y
2Cor 13:3 which to y is not weak, but is
Eph 3:2 of God which is given me to y

# Z

**ZAANAIM** *(za-an-a'-im)* See ZAANANNIM. *A plain in Naphtali.*
Judg 4:11 his tent unto the plain of Z

**ZAANAN** *(za'-an-an)* See ZENAN. *A city of Judah.*
Mic 1:11 the inhabitant of Z came not

**ZAANANNIM** *(za-an-an'-nim) Same as Zaanaim.*
Josh 19:33 was from Heleph, from Allon to Z

**ZAAVAN** *(za'-av-an)* See ZAVAN. *A son of Ezer.*
Gen 36:27 Bilhan, and Z, and Akan

**ZABAD** *(za'-bad)* See JOSABAD, JOZACHAR.
*1. A son of Nathan.*
1Chr 2:36 begat Nathan, and Nathan begat Z
1Chr 2:37 Z begat Ephlal, and Ephlal begat
*2. Son of Tahath.*
1Chr 7:21 Z his son, and Shuthelah his son,
*3. A "mighty man" of David.*
1Chr 11:41 the Hittite, Z the son of Ahlai,
*4. A son of Shimeath.*
2Chr 24:26 Z the son of Shimeath an
*5. A son of Zatta.*
Ezr 10:27 Mattaniah, and Jeremoth, and Z
*6. A son of Hasham.*
Ezr 10:33 Mattenai, Mattathah, Z, Eliphelet
*7. A son of Nebo.*
Ezr 10:43 Jeiel, Mattithiah, Z, Zebina,

**ZABBAI** *(zab'-bahee)* See ZACCAI.
*1. Married a foreigner in exile.*
Ezr 10:28 Jehohanan, Hananiah, Z, and Athlai
*2. Father of Baruch.*
Neh 3:20 After him Baruch the son of Z

**ZABBUD** *(zab'-bud)* See ZACCUR. *An exile with Ezra.*
Ezr 8:14 Uthai, and Z, and with them seventy

**ZABDI** *(zab'-di)* See ZACCHUR, ZICHRI.
*1. Father of Carmi.*
Josh 7:1 the son of Carmi, the son of Z
Josh 7:17 and Z was taken
Josh 7:18 the son of Carmi, the son of Z
*2. Son of Shimhi.*
1Chr 8:19 And Jakim, and Zichri, and Z
*3. A storekeeper in David's court.*
1Chr 27:27 wine cellars was Z the Shiphmite
*4. A Levite.*
Neh 11:17 the son of Micha, the son of Z

**ZABDIEL** *(zab'-de-el)*
*1. Father of Jashobeam.*
1Chr 27:2 month was Jashobeam the son of Z
*2. An overseer of priests.*
Neh 11:14 and their overseer was Z, the son

**ZABUD** *(za'-bud) A family of exiles.*
1Kin 4:5 Z the son of Nathan was principal

**ZABULON** *(zab'-u-lon)* See ZEBULUN. *Greek form of Zebulon.*
Mt 4:13 sea coast, in the borders of Z
Mt 4:15 The land of Z, and the land of
Rev 7:8 Of the tribe of Z were sealed

**ZACCAI** *(zac'-cahee)* See ZABBAI. *A family of exiles.*
Ezr 2:9 The children of Z, seven hundred
Neh 7:14 The children of Z, seven hundred

**ZACCHAEUS** *(zak-ke'-us) A tax collector visited by Jesus.*
Lk 19:2 behold, there was a man named Z
Lk 19:5 and saw him, and said unto him, Z
Lk 19:8 Z stood, and said unto the Lord

**ZACCHUR** *(zac'-cur)* See ZACCUR. *Father of Shimei.*
1Chr 4:26 Z his son, Shimei his son

**ZACCUR** *(zac'-cur)* See ZABBUD, ZABDI, ZACCHUR, ZICHRI.
*1. Father of Shammua.*
Num 13:4 of Reuben, Shammua the son of Z
*2. A sanctuary servant.*
1Chr 24:27 Beno, and Shoham, and Z, and Ibri
*3. A son of Asaph.*
1Chr 25:2 Z, and Joseph, and Nethaniah, and
1Chr 25:10 The third to Z, he, his sons, and
Neh 12:35 the son of Michaiah, the son of Z
*4. A rebuilder of Jerusalem's wall.*
Neh 3:2 to them builded Z the son of Imri
*5. A Levite who renewed the covenant.*
Neh 10:12 Z, Sherebiah, Shebaniah,
*6. Father of Hanan.*
Neh 13:13 to them was Hanan the son of Z

**ZACHARIAH** *(zak-a-ri'-ah)* See ZECHARIAH.
*1. A king of Israel.*
2Kin 14:29 Z his son reigned in his stead
2Kin 15:8 of Azariah king of Judah did Z
2Kin 15:11 And the rest of the acts of Z
*2. Father of Abi.*
2Kin 18:2 also was Abi, the daughter of Z

**ZACHARIAS** *(zak'-a-ri'-as)* See ZECHARIAH.
*1. Son of Barachias.*
Mt 23:35 the blood of Z son of Barachias
Lk 11:51 blood of Abel unto the blood of Z
*2. Father of John the Baptist.*
Lk 1:5 Judaea, a certain priest named Z
Lk 1:12 when Z saw him, he was troubled,
Lk 1:13 angel said unto him, Fear not, Z
Lk 1:18 Z said unto the angel, Whereby
Lk 1:21 And the people waited for Z
Lk 1:40 And entered into the house of Z
Lk 1:59 and they called him Z, after the
Lk 1:67 his father Z was filled with the
Lk 3:2 the son of Z in the wilderness

**ZACHER** *(za'-kur)* See ZECHARIAH. *Father of Gibeon.*
1Chr 8:31 And Gedor, and Ahio, and Z

**ZADOK** *(za'-dok)* See ZADOK'S.
*1. A priest in David's time.*
2Sa 8:17 Z the son of Ahitub, and Ahimelech
2Sa 15:24 lo Z also, and all the Levites
2Sa 15:25 And the king said unto Z, Carry
2Sa 15:27 king said also unto Z the priest
2Sa 15:29 Z therefore and Abiathar carried
2Sa 15:35 hast thou not there with thee Z
2Sa 15:35 house, thou shalt tell it to Z
2Sa 17:15 Then said Hushai unto Z and to
2Sa 18:19 Then said Ahimaaz the son of Z
2Sa 18:22 the son of Z yet again to Joab
2Sa 18:27 running of Ahimaaz the son of Z
2Sa 19:11 And king David sent to Z and to
2Sa 20:25 and Z and Abiathar were the priests
1Kin 1:8 But Z the priest, and Benaiah the
1Kin 1:26 Z the priest, and Benaiah the son
1Kin 1:32 Call me Z the priest, and Nathan
1Kin 1:34 let Z the priest and Nathan the
1Kin 1:38 So Z the priest, and Nathan the
1Kin 1:39 Z the priest took an horn of oil
1Kin 1:44 hath sent with him Z the priest
1Kin 1:45 Z the priest and Nathan the
1Kin 2:35 Z the priest did the king put in
1Kin 4:2 Azariah the son of Z the priest
1Kin 4:4 and Z and Abiathar were the priests
1Chr 6:8 And Ahitub begat Z
1Chr 6:8 and Z begat Ahimaaz
1Chr 6:53 Z his son, Ahimaaz his son
1Chr 15:11 And David called for Z and Abiathar
1Chr 16:39 Z the priest, and his brethren the
1Chr 18:16 Z the son of Ahitub, and Abimelech
1Chr 24:3 both Z of the sons of Eleazar, and

1Chr 24:6 Z the priest, and Ahimelech the
1Chr 24:31 presence of David the king, and Z
1Chr 27:17 of the Aaronites, Z
1Chr 29:22 chief governor, and Z to be priest
2Chr 31:10 of the house of Z answered him
Ezr 7:2 The son of Shallum, the son of Z
Eze 40:46 these are the sons of Z among the
Eze 43:19 Levites that be of the seed of Z
Eze 44:15 the Levites, the sons of Z
Eze 48:11 are sanctified of the sons of Z
*2. Father of Jerusha.*
2Kin 15:33 was Jerusha, the daughter of Z
2Chr 27:1 was Jerushah, the daughter of Z
*3. Son of Ahitub.*
1Chr 6:12 And Ahitub begat Z, and Zadok begat
1Chr 6:12 begat Zadok, and Z begat Shallum,
1Chr 9:11 son of Meshullam, the son of Z
*4. A warrior in David's army.*
1Chr 12:28 And Z, a young man mighty of
*5. The son of Baana.*
Neh 3:4 them repaired Z the son of Baana
*6. A priest who rebuilt the wall.*
Neh 3:29 After them repaired Z the son of
*7. A renewer of the covenant.*
Neh 10:21 Meshezabeel, Z, Jaddua,
*8. A son of Meraioth.*
Neh 11:11 son of Meshullam, the son of Z
*9. A Temple servant.*
Neh 13:13 Z the scribe, and of the Levites,

**ZADOK'S** *(za'-doks) Refers to Zadok 1.*
2Sa 15:36 their two sons, Ahimaaz Z son

**ZAHAM** *(za'-ham) A son of Rehoboam.*
2Chr 11:19 Jeush, and Shamariah, and Z

**ZAIR** *(za'-ur) A city in Edom.*
2Kin 8:21 So Joram went over to Z, and all

**ZALAPH** *(za'-laf) Father of Hanun.*
Neh 3:30 and Hanun the sixth son of Z

**ZALMON** *(zal'-mon)* See ILAI, SALMON.
*1. A hill in Ephraim.*
Judg 9:48 Abimelech gat him up to mount Z
*2. A "mighty man" of David.*
2Sa 23:28 Z the Ahohite, Maharai the

**ZALMONAH** *(zal'-mo-nah) An Israelite encampment in the wilderness.*
Num 33:41 from mount Hor, and pitched in Z
Num 33:42 And they departed from Z, and

**ZALMUNNA** *(zal-mun'-nah) A Midianite king.*
Judg 8:5 and I am pursuing after Zebah and Z
Judg 8:6 Z now in thine hand, that we
Judg 8:7 Z into mine hand, then I will
Judg 8:10 Z were in Karkor, and their hosts
Judg 8:12 Z fled, he pursued after them, and
Judg 8:12 two kings of Midian, Zebah and Z
Judg 8:15 and said, Behold Zebah and Z
Judg 8:15 Z now in thine hand, that we
Judg 8:18 Then said he unto Zebah and Z
Judg 8:21 Z said, Rise thou, and fall upon
Judg 8:21 Gideon arose, and slew Zebah and Z
Ps 83:11 their princes as Zebah, and as Z

**ZAMZUMMIMS** *(zam-zum'-mims)* See ZUZIMS. *A tribe in Canaan.*
Deut 2:20 and the Ammonites call them Z

**ZANOAH** *(za-no'-ah)*
*1. A city on the plain of Judah.*
Josh 15:34 And Z, and En-gannim, Tappuah, and
Neh 3:13 Hanun, and the inhabitants of Z
Neh 11:30 Z, Adullam, and in their villages,
*2. A city in the hills of Judah.*
Josh 15:56 And Jezreel, and Jokdeam, and Z
*3. A descendant of Caleb.*
1Chr 4:18 and Jekuthiel the father of Z

**ZAPHNATH-PAANEAH** *(zaf'-nath-pa-a-ne'-ah) Name given to Joseph by Pharaoh.*
Gen 41:45 And Pharaoh called Joseph's name Z

**ZAPHON** *(za'-fon) A city in Gad.*
Josh 13:27 and Beth-nimrah, and Succoth, and Z

**ZARA** *(za'-rah)* See ZARAH, ZERAH. *Greek form of Zarah; an ancestor of Jesus.*
Mt 1:3 Judas begat Phares and Z of Thamar

**ZARAH** *(za'-rah)* See ZARA, ZERAH. *A son of Judah.*
Gen 38:30 and his name was called Z
Gen 46:12 Onan, and Shelah, and Pharez, and Z

**ZAREAH** *(za'-re-ah)* See ZAREATHITES, ZORAH. *A city in Judah.*
Neh 11:29 And at En-rimmon, and at Z, and at

**ZAREATHITES** *(za'-re-ath-ites)* See ZORATHITES. *Descendants of Shobal.*
1Chr 2:53 of them came the Z, and the

**ZARED** *(za'-red)* See ZERED. *A brook near the Dead Sea.*
Num 21:12 and pitched in the valley of Z

**ZAREPHATH** *(zar'-e-fath)* See SAREPTA. *A city in Phoenicia.*
1Kin 17:9 Arise, get thee to Z, which
1Kin 17:10 So he arose and went to Z
Obad 20 of the Canaanites, even unto Z

**ZARETAN** *(zar'-e-tan)* See ZARTANAH, ZEREDATHAH. *A city in Ephraim.*
Josh 3:16 the city Adam, that is beside Z

**ZARETH-SHAHAR** *(za'-reth-sha'-har) A city in Reuben.*
Josh 13:19 Z in the mount of the valley,

**ZARHITES** *(zar'-hites)*
*1. Descendants of Zerah, the Simeonite.*
Num 26:13 Of Zerah, the family of the Z
Josh 7:17 and he took the family of the Z
Josh 7:17 the family of the Z man by man
1Chr 27:11 Sibbecai the Hushathite, of the Z
1Chr 27:13 the Netophathite, of the Z
*2. Descendants of Zerah, son of Judah.*
Num 26:20 of Zerah, the family of the Z

**ZARTANAH** *(zar'-ta-nah)* See ZARETAN, ZARTHAN. *Same as Zaretan.*
1Kin 4:12 which is by Z beneath Jezreel,

**ZARTHAN** *(zar'-than)* See ZARETAN, ZARTANAH. *Same as Zaretan.*
1Kin 7:46 clay ground between Succoth and Z

**ZATTHU** *(zath'-u)* See ZATTU. *A renewer of the covenant.*
Neh 10:14 Parosh, Pahath-moab, Elam, Z

**ZATTU** *(zat'-tu)* See ZATTHU. *A family of exiles.*
Ezr 2:8 The children of Z, nine hundred
Ezr 10:27 And of the sons of Z
Neh 7:13 The children of Z, eight hundred

**ZAVAN** *(za'-van)* See ZAAVAN. *Son of Ezer.*
1Chr 1:42 Bilhan, and Z, and Jakan

**ZAZA** *(za'-zah) A son of Jonathan.*
1Chr 2:33 Peleth, and Z

**ZEAL**
2Sa 21:2 his *z* to the children of Israel
2Kin 10:16 with me, and see my *z* for the LORD
2Kin 19:31 the *z* of the LORD of hosts shall
Ps 69:9 For the *z* of thine house hath
Ps 119:139 My *z* hath consumed me, because
Is 9:7 The *z* of the LORD of hosts will
Is 37:32 the *z* of the LORD of hosts shall
Is 59:17 and was clad with *z* as a cloke
Is 63:15 where is thy *z* and thy strength,
Eze 5:13 I the LORD have spoken it in my *z*
Jn 2:17 The *z* of thine house hath eaten
Rom 10:2 record that they have a *z* of God
2Cor 7:11 what vehement desire, yea, what *z*
2Cor 9:2 your *z* hath provoked very many
Phil 3:6 Concerning *z*, persecuting the
Col 4:13 that he hath a great *z* for you

**ZEALOUS**
Num 25:11 while he was *z* for my sake among
Num 25:13 because he was *z* for his God
Acts 21:20 and they are all *z* of the law
Acts 22:3 was *z* toward God, as ye all are
1Cor 14:12 as ye are *z* of spiritual gifts
Gal 1:14 being more exceedingly *z* of the
Titus 2:14 peculiar people, *z* of good works
Rev 3:19 be *z* therefore, and repent

**ZEALOUSLY**
Gal 4:17 They *z* affect you, but not well
Gal 4:18 But it is good to be *z* affected

**ZEBADIAH** *(zeb-ad-i'-ah)*
*1. Grandson of Elpael.*
1Chr 8:15 And Z, and Arad, and Ader,
*2. A son of Elpael.*
1Chr 8:17 And Z, and Meshullam, and Hezeki
*3. A warrior in David's army.*
1Chr 12:7 And Joelah, and Z, the sons of
*4. A Levite gatekeeper.*
1Chr 26:2 Z the third, Jathniel the fourth,
*5. A son of Asahel.*
1Chr 27:7 of Joab, and Z his son after him
*6. A messenger for King Jehoshaphat.*
2Chr 17:8 even Shemaiah, and Nethaniah, and Z
*7. Son of Ishmael.*
2Chr 19:11 Z the son of Ishmael, the ruler
*8. A family of exiles.*
Ezr 8:8 Z the son of Michael, and with him
*9. Married a foreigner in exile.*
Ezr 10:20 Hanani, and Z

**ZEBAH** *(ze'-bah) A king of Midian.*
Judg 8:5 faint, and I am pursuing after Z
Judg 8:6 Succoth said, Are the hands of Z
Judg 8:7 when the LORD hath delivered Z
Judg 8:10 Now Z and Zalmunna were in Karkor,
Judg 8:12 And when Z and Zalmunna fled, he
Judg 8:12 took the two kings of Midian, Z
Judg 8:15 men of Succoth, and said, Behold Z
Judg 8:15 me, saying, Are the hands of Z
Judg 8:18 Then said he unto Z and Zalmunna,
Judg 8:21 Then Z and Zalmunna said, Rise
Judg 8:21 And Gideon arose, and slew Z
Ps 83:11 yea, all their princes as Z

**ZEBAIM** *(ze-ba'-im) Residence of some exiles in Babylonia.*
Ezr 2:57 the children of Pochereth of Z
Neh 7:59 the children of Pochereth of Z

**ZEBEDEE** *(zeb'-e-dee)* See ZEBEDEE'S. *Father of James and John.*
Mt 4:21 two brethren, James the son of Z
Mt 4:21 in a ship with Z their father
Mt 10:2 James the son of Z, and John his
Mt 26:37 him Peter and the two sons of Z
Mk 1:19 thence, he saw James the son of Z
Mk 1:20 they left their father Z in the
Mk 3:17 And James the son of Z, and John
Mk 10:35 And James and John, the sons of Z
Lk 5:10 James, and John, the sons of Z
Jn 21:2 Cana in Galilee, and the sons of Z

**ZEBEDEE'S** *(zeb'-e-dees)*
Mt 20:20 of Z children with her sons
Mt 27:56 and the mother of Z children

**ZEBINA** *(ze-bi'-nah) Married a foreigner in exile.*
Ezr 10:43 Jeiel, Mattithiah, Zabad, Z

**ZEBOIIM** *(ze-boy'-im)* See ZEBOIM. *City destroyed with Sodom and Gomorrah.*
Gen 14:2 of Admah, and Shemeber king of Z
Gen 14:8 king of Admah, and the king of Z

**ZEBOIM** *(ze-bo'-im)* See ZEBOIIM.
*1. Same as Zeboiim.*
Gen 10:19 and Gomorrah, and Admah, and Z
Deut 29:23 Sodom, and Gomorrah, Admah, and Z
Hos 11:8 how shall I set thee as Z
*2. A city in Benjamin.*
1Sa 13:18 valley of Z toward the wilderness
Neh 11:34 Hadid, Z, Neballat,

**ZEBUDAH** *(ze-bu'-dah) Mother of King Jehoshaphat.*
2Kin 23:36 And his mother's name was Z

**ZEBUL** *(ze'-bul) A ruler of Shechem.*
Judg 9:28 and Z his officer
Judg 9:30 when Z the ruler of the city
Judg 9:36 Gaal saw the people, he said to Z
Judg 9:36 Z said unto him, Thou seest the
Judg 9:38 Then said Z unto him, Where is
Judg 9:41 Z thrust out Gaal and his brethren

**ZEBULONITE** *(zeb'-u-lon-ite)* See ZEBULONITES. *A descendant of Zebulun 1.*
Judg 12:11 And after him Elon, a Z, judged
Judg 12:12 And Elon the Z died, and was buried

**ZEBULUN** *(zeb'-u-lun)* See ZABULON, ZEBULONITE, ZEBULONITES.
*1. A son of Jacob.*
Gen 30:20 and she called his name Z
Gen 35:23 Levi, and Judah, and Issachar, and Z
Gen 46:14 And the sons of Z
Gen 49:13 Z shall dwell at the haven of the
Ex 1:3 Issachar, Z, and Benjamin,
1Chr 2:1 Levi, and Judah, Issachar, and Z
*2. Descendants of Zebulun.*
Num 1:9 Of Z; Eliab the
Num 1:30 Of the children of Z, by their

Num 1:31 of them, even of the tribe of Z
Num 2:7 Then the tribe of Z
Num 2:7 be captain of the children of Z
Num 7:24 prince of the children of Z
Num 10:16 of Z was Eliab the son of Helon
Num 13:10 Of the tribe of Z, Gaddiel the
Num 26:26 Of the sons of Z after their
Num 34:25 of the tribe of the children of Z
Deut 27:13 Reuben, Gad, and Asher, and Z
Deut 33:18 And of Zebulun he said, Rejoice, Z
Josh 19:10 of Z according to their families
Josh 19:16 of Z according to their families
Josh 19:27 to Beth-dagon, and reacheth to Z
Josh 19:34 reacheth to Z on the south side,
Josh 21:7 of Gad, and out of the tribe of Z
Josh 21:34 Levites, out of the tribe of Z
Judg 1:30 Neither did Z drive out the
Judg 4:6 Naphtali and of the children of Z
Judg 4:10 And Barak called Z and Naphtali to
Judg 5:14 out of Z they that handle the pen
Judg 5:18 Z and Naphtali were a people that
Judg 6:35 messengers unto Asher, and unto Z
Judg 12:12 in Aijalon in the country of Z
1Chr 6:63 of Gad, and out of the tribe of Z
1Chr 6:77 were given out of the tribe of Z
1Chr 12:33 Of Z, such as went forth to
1Chr 12:40 them, even unto Issachar and Z
1Chr 27:19 Of Z, Ishmaiah the son of Obadiah
2Chr 30:10 Ephraim and Manasseh even unto Z
2Chr 30:11 of Z humbled themselves, and came
2Chr 30:18 and Manasseh, Issachar, and Z
Ps 68:27 their council, the princes of Z
Is 9:1 lightly afflicted the land of Z
Eze 48:26 unto the west side, Z a portion
Eze 48:27 And by the border of Z, from the
Eze 48:33 gate of Issachar, one gate of Z

**ZEBULUNITES** *(zeb'-u-lun-ites) Descendants of Zebulun.*
Num 26:27 Z according to those that were

**ZECHARIAH** *(zek-a-ri'-ah)* See ZACCUR, ZACHARIAH, ZACHARIAS, ZACHER.
*1. A chief Reubenite.*
1Chr 5:7 were the chief, Jeiel, and Z
*2. A Levite gatekeeper.*
1Chr 9:21 Z the son of Meshelemiah was
1Chr 26:2 Z the firstborn, Jediael the
1Chr 26:14 Then for Z his son, a wise
2Chr 29:1 was Abijah, the daughter of Z
*3. A Benjamite.*
1Chr 9:37 And Gedor, and Ahio, and Z, and
*4. A Levite musician.*
1Chr 15:18 brethren of the second degree, Z
1Chr 15:20 And Z, and Aziel, and Shemiramoth,
1Chr 16:5 Asaph the chief, and next to him Z
*5. A Tabernacle priest.*
1Chr 15:24 and Nethaneel, and Amasai, and Z
*6. A son of Isshiah.*
1Chr 24:25 sons of Isshiah; Z
*7. Son of Hosah.*
1Chr 26:11 Tebaliah the third, Z the fourth
*8. A chief of Manasseh.*
1Chr 27:21 in Gilead, Iddo the son of Z
*9. A messenger of King Jehoshaphat.*
2Chr 17:7 Ben-hail, and to Obadiah, and to Z
*10. Father of Jehaziel.*
2Chr 20:14 Then upon Jahaziel the son of Z
*11. A son of Jehoshaphat.*
2Chr 21:2 Azariah, and Jehiel, and Z
*12. Son of Jehoida.*
2Chr 24:20 the Spirit of God came upon Z the
*13. A prophet in King Uzziah's time.*
2Chr 26:5 And he sought God in the days of Z
*14. A Levite who cleansed the Temple.*
2Chr 29:13 Z, and Mattaniah
*15. An overseer of the Temple repairs.*
2Chr 34:12 and Z and Meshullam, of the sons of
*16. A prince of Judah.*
2Chr 35:8 Hilkiah and Z and Jehiel, rulers of
*17. A prophet in Judah.*
Ezr 5:1 Z the son of Iddo, prophesied
Ezr 6:14 the prophet and Z the son of Iddo
Zec 1:1 came the word of the LORD unto Z
Zec 1:7 came the word of the LORD unto Z
Zec 7:1 Z in the fourth day of the ninth
Zec 7:8 the word of the LORD came unto Z
*18. A son of Pharosh.*
Ezr 8:3 sons of Pharosh; Z
*19. A son of Bebai.*
Ezr 8:11 Z the son of Bebai, and with him
Ezr 8:16 Elnathan, and for Nathan, and for Z
*20. Married a foreigner in exile.*
Ezr 10:26 Mattaniah, Z, and Jehiel, and Abdi,
*21. A prince who aided Ezra.*
Neh 8:4 and Hashum, and Hashbadana, Z
*22. A descendant of Pharez.*
Neh 11:4 the son of Uzziah, the son of Z
*23. A son of Shiloni.*
Neh 11:5 the son of Joiarib, the son of Z
*24. Father of a resettler in Jerusalem.*
Neh 11:12 the son of Amzi, the son of Z
*25. A priest in Joiakim's time.*
Neh 12:16 Of Iddo, Z
*26. A priest who dedicated the wall.*
Neh 12:35 Z the son of Jonathan, the son of
Neh 12:41 Miniamin, Michaiah, Elioenai, Z
*27. Son of Jeber.*
Is 8:2 and Z the son of Jeberechiah

**ZEDAD** *(ze'-dad) A place near Hamath.*
Num 34:8 forth of the border shall be to Z
Eze 47:15 way of Hethlon, as men go to Z

**ZEDEKIAH** *(zed-e-ki'-ah)* See MATTANIAH, ZEDEKIAH'S, ZIDKIJAH.
*1. A false prophet.*
1Kin 22:11 Z the son of Chenaanah made him
1Kin 22:24 But Z the son of Chenaanah went
2Chr 18:10 Z the son of Chenaanah had made
2Chr 18:23 Then Z the son of Chenaanah came
*2. Name given to Mattaniah by Nebuchadnezzar.*
2Kin 24:17 stead, and changed his name to Z
2Kin 24:18 Z was twenty and one years old
2Kin 24:20 that Z rebelled against the king
2Kin 25:2 unto the eleventh year of king Z
2Kin 25:7 the sons of Z before his eyes
2Kin 25:7 eyes, and put out the eyes of Z
1Chr 3:15 the second Jehoiakim, the third Z
2Chr 36:10 made Z his brother king over
2Chr 36:11 Z was one and twenty years old
Jer 1:3 Z the son of Josiah king of Judah
Jer 21:1 when king Z sent unto him Pashur
Jer 21:3 unto them, Thus shall ye say to Z
Jer 21:7 I will deliver Z king of Judah
Jer 24:8 So will I give Z the king of
Jer 27:3 to Jerusalem unto Z king of Judah
Jer 27:12 I spake also to Z king of Judah
Jer 28:1 of the reign of Z king of Judah
Jer 29:3 (whom Z king of Judah sent unto
Jer 32:1 the tenth year of Z king of Judah
Jer 32:3 For Z king of Judah had shut him
Jer 32:4 Z king of Judah shall not escape
Jer 32:5 And he shall lead Z to Babylon
Jer 34:2 speak to Z king of Judah, and tell
Jer 34:4 of the LORD, O Z king of Judah
Jer 34:6 unto Z king of Judah in Jerusalem
Jer 34:8 after that the king Z had made a
Jer 34:21 Z king of Judah and his princes
Jer 37:1 king Z the son of Josiah reigned
Jer 37:3 Z the king sent Jehucal the son
Jer 37:17 Then Z the king sent, and took him
Jer 37:18 Jeremiah said unto king Z
Jer 37:21 Then Z the king commanded that
Jer 38:5 Then Z the king said, Behold, he
Jer 38:14 Then Z the king sent, and took
Jer 38:15 Then Jeremiah said unto Z
Jer 38:16 So Z the king sware secretly unto
Jer 38:17 Then said Jeremiah unto Z
Jer 38:19 Z the king said unto Jeremiah, I
Jer 38:24 Then said Z unto Jeremiah, Let no
Jer 39:1 the ninth year of Z king of Judah
Jer 39:2 And in the eleventh year of Z
Jer 39:4 that when Z the king of Judah saw
Jer 39:5 overtook Z in the plains of
Jer 39:6 of Z in Riblah before his eyes
Jer 44:30 as I gave Z king of Judah into
Jer 49:34 of the reign of Z king of Judah
Jer 51:59 when he went with Z the king of
Jer 52:1 Z was one and twenty years old
Jer 52:3 that Z rebelled against the king
Jer 52:5 unto the eleventh year of king Z
Jer 52:8 overtook Z in the plains of
Jer 52:10 the sons of Z before his eyes
Jer 52:11 Then he put out the eyes of Z
*3. Grandson of Jehoiakim.*
1Chr 3:16 Jeconiah his son, Z his son
*4. A false prophet denounced by Jeremiah.*
Jer 29:21 of Z the son of Maaseiah, which
Jer 29:22 saying, The LORD make thee like Z
*5. A prince of Judah.*
Jer 36:12 Z the son of Hananiah, and all the

**ZEDEKIAH'S** *(zed-e-ki'-ahs) Refers to Zedekiah 2.*
Jer 39:7 Moreover he put out Z eyes

**ZEEB** *(ze'-eb) A Midianite prince.*
Judg 7:25 of the Midianites, Oreb and Z
Judg 7:25 Z they slew at the winepress of
Judg 7:25 they slew at the winepress of Z
Judg 7:25 Z to Gideon on the other side
Judg 8:3 the princes of Midian, Oreb and Z
Ps 83:11 their nobles like Oreb, and like Z

**ZELAH** *(ze'-lah) A city in Benjamin.*
Josh 18:28 And Z, Eleph, and Jebusi, which is
2Sa 21:14 in the country of Benjamin in Z

**ZELEK** *(ze'-lek) A "mighty man" of David.*
2Sa 23:37 Z the Ammonite, Nahari the
1Chr 11:39 Z the Ammonite, Naharai the

**ZELOPHEHAD** *(ze-lo'-fe-had) Son of Hepher.*
Num 26:33 Z the son of Hepher had no sons,
Num 26:33 of the daughters of Z were Mahlah
Num 27:1 Then came the daughters of Z
Num 27:7 The daughters of Z speak right
Num 36:2 Z our brother unto his daughters
Num 36:6 concerning the daughters of Z
Num 36:10 Moses, so did the daughters of Z
Num 36:11 and Noah, the daughters of Z
Josh 17:3 But Z, the son of Hepher, the son
1Chr 7:15 and the name of the second was Z
1Chr 7:15 and Z had daughters

**ZELOTES** *(ze-lo-teze)* See CANAANITE, SIMON. *Surname of Simon, disciple of Jesus.*
Lk 6:15 of Alphaeus, and Simon called Z
Acts 1:13 the son of Alphaeus, and Simon Z

**ZELZAH** *(zel'-zah) A city in Benjamin.*
1Sa 10:2 in the border of Benjamin at Z

**ZEMARAIM** *(zem-a-ra'-im)* See ZEMARITE.
*1. A city in Benjamin.*
Josh 18:22 And Beth-arabah, and Z, and Beth-el,
*2. A mountain in Ephraim.*
2Chr 13:4 And Abijah stood up upon mount Z

**ZEMARITE** *A descendant of Canaan.*
Gen 10:18 And the Arvadite, and the Z
1Chr 1:16 And the Arvadite, and the Z

**ZEMIRA** *(ze-mi'-rah) A son of Becher.*
1Chr 7:8 Z, and Joash, and Eliezer, and

**ZENAN** *(ze'-nan)* See ZAANAN. *A city in Judah.*
Josh 15:37 Z, and Hadashah, and Migdal-gad,

**ZENAS** *(ze'-nas) A Christian lawyer.*
Titus 3:13 Bring Z the lawyer and Apollos on

**ZEPHANIAH** *(zef-a-ni'-ah)*
*1. A priest in exile.*
2Kin 25:18 Z the second priest, and the three
Jer 21:1 Z the son of Maaseiah the priest,
Jer 29:25 to Z the son of Maaseiah the
Jer 29:29 Z the priest read this letter in
Jer 37:3 Z the son of Maaseiah the priest
Jer 52:24 Z the second priest, and the three
*2. An ancestor of Samuel.*
1Chr 6:36 the son of Azariah, the son of Z
*3. A prophet.*
Zeph 1:1 came unto Z the son of Cushi
*4. Son of Josiah the priest.*
Zec 6:10 the house of Josiah the son of Z
Zec 6:14 Jedaiah, and to Hen the son of Z

**ZEPHATH** *(ze'-fath)* See HORMAH. *A city in Simeon.*
Judg 1:17 the Canaanites that inhabited Z

**ZEPHATHAH** *(zef'-a-thah) A valley in Judah.*
2Chr 14:10 in the valley of Z at Mareshah

**ZEPHI** *(ze'-fi)* See ZEPHO. *Son of Eliphaz.*
1Chr 1:36 Teman, and Omar, Z, and Gatam,

**ZEPHO** *(ze'-fo)* See ZEPHI. *Same as Zephi.*
Gen 36:11 of Eliphaz were Teman, Omar, Z
Gen 36:15 duke Teman, duke Omar, duke Z

**ZEPHON** *(ze'-fon)* See ZEPHONITES, ZIPHION. *A son of Gad.*
Num 26:15 of Z, the family of the

**ZEPHONITES** *(zef'-on-ites) Descendants of Zephon.*
Num 26:15 of Zephon, the family of the Z

**ZER** *(zur) A city in Naphtali.*
Josh 19:35 the fenced cities are Ziddim, Z

**ZERAH** *(ze'-rah)* See EZRAHITE, ZARAH, ZARHITES, ZOHAR.
*1. A son of Reuel.*
Gen 36:13 and Z, Shammah, and Mizzah
Gen 36:17 duke Nahath, duke Z, duke Shammah
1Chr 1:37 Nahath, Z, Shammah, and Mizzah
*2. Father of Jobab.*
Gen 36:33 Jobab the son of Z of Bozrah
1Chr 1:44 Jobab the son of Z of Bozrah
*3. Son of Judah.*
Num 26:20 of Z, the family of the Zarhites
Josh 7:1 the son of Zabdi, the son of Z
Josh 7:18 the son of Zabdi, the son of Z
Josh 7:24 with him, took Achan the son of Z
Josh 22:20 son of Z commit a trespass in the
1Chr 2:4 in law bare him Pharez and Z
1Chr 2:6 And the sons of Z
1Chr 9:6 And of the sons of Z
Neh 11:24 children of Z the son of Judah
*4. A son of Simeon.*
Num 26:13 Of Z, the family of the Zarhites
1Chr 4:24 were, Nemuel, and Jamin, Jarib, Z
*5. Son of Iddo.*
1Chr 6:21 Z his son, Jeaterai his son
*6. Father of Ethni.*
1Chr 6:41 The son of Ethni, the son of Z
*7. An Ethiopian king.*
2Chr 14:9 there came out against them Z the

**ZERAHIAH** *(zer-a-hi'-ah)*
*1. An ancestor of Ezra.*
1Chr 6:6 And Uzzi begat Z, and Z
1Chr 6:6 Z, and Z begat Meraioth,
1Chr 6:51 his son, Uzzi his son, Z his son,
Ezr 7:4 The son of Z, the son of Uzzi,
*2. Father of Elihoenai.*
Ezr 8:4 Elihoenai the son of Z, and with

**ZERED** *(ze'-red)* See ZARED. *Same as Zared.*
Deut 2:13 I, and get you over the brook Z
Deut 2:13 And we went over the brook Z
Deut 2:14 we were come over the brook Z

**ZEREDA** *(zer'-e-dah) A city north of Mt. Ephraim.*
1Kin 11:26 son of Nebat, an Ephrathite of Z

**ZEREDATHAH** *(ze-red'-a-thah)* See ZARTHAN, ZERERATH. *A city in Manasseh.*
2Chr 4:17 clay ground between Succoth and Z

**ZERERATH** *(zer'-e-rath)* See ZARTHAN, ZEREDATHAH. *A district in Manasseh.*
Judg 7:22 host fled to Beth-shittah in Z

**ZERESH** *(ze'-resh) Wife of Haman.*
Est 5:10 for his friends, and Z his wife
Est 5:14 Then said Z his wife and all his
Est 6:13 And Haman told Z his wife and all
Est 6:13 Z his wife unto him, If Mordecai

**ZERETH** *(ze'-reth) A descendant of Judah.*
1Chr 4:7 And the sons of Helah were, Z

**ZERI** *(ze'-ri)* See IZRI. *Son of Jeduthun.*
1Chr 25:3 Gedaliah, and Z, and Jeshaiah,

**ZEROR** *(ze'-ror) Ancestor of King Saul.*
1Sa 9:1 the son of Abiel, the son of Z

**ZERUAH** *(ze-ru'-ah) Mother of Jeroboam I.*
1Kin 11:26 whose mother's name was Z

**ZERUBBABEL** *(ze-rub'-ba-bel)* See SHESHBAZZAR, ZOROBABEL. *A leader of a group of exiles.*
1Chr 3:19 And the sons of Pedaiah were, Z
1Chr 3:19 and the sons of Z
Ezr 2:2 Which came with Z
Ezr 3:2 Z the son of Shealtiel, and his
Ezr 3:8 began Z the son of Shealtiel, and
Ezr 4:2 Then they came to Z, and to the
Ezr 4:3 But Z, and Jeshua, and the rest of
Ezr 5:2 Then rose up Z the son of
Neh 7:7 Who came with Z, Jeshua, Nehemiah
Neh 12:1 up with Z the son of Shealtiel
Neh 12:47 And all Israel in the days of Z
Hag 1:1 unto Z the son of Shealtiel
Hag 1:12 Then Z the son of Shealtiel, and
Hag 1:14 spirit of Z the son of Shealtiel
Hag 2:2 Speak now to Z the son of
Hag 2:4 Yet now be strong, O Z, saith the
Hag 2:21 Speak to Z, governor of Judah,
Hag 2:23 of hosts, will I take thee, O Z
Zec 4:6 is the word of the LORD unto Z
Zec 4:7 before Z thou shalt become a
Zec 4:9 The hands of Z have laid the
Zec 4:10 in the hand of Z with those seven

**ZERUIAH** *(ze-ru-i'-ah) Sister of David.*
1Sa 26:6 and to Abishai the son of Z
2Sa 2:13 And Joab the son of Z, and the
2Sa 2:18 there were three sons of Z there
2Sa 3:39 the sons of Z be too hard for me
2Sa 8:16 Joab the son of Z was over the
2Sa 14:1 Now Joab the son of Z perceived
2Sa 16:9 the son of Z unto the king
2Sa 16:10 I to do with you, ye sons of Z
2Sa 17:25 sister to Z Joab's mother
2Sa 18:2 the hand of Abishai the son of Z
2Sa 19:21 But Abishai the son of Z answered
2Sa 19:22 I to do with you, ye sons of Z
2Sa 21:17 the son of Z succoured him
2Sa 23:18 the brother of Joab, the son of Z
2Sa 23:37 armourbearer to Joab the son of Z
1Kin 1:7 conferred with Joab the son of Z
1Kin 2:5 what Joab the son of Z did to me
1Kin 2:22 priest, and for Joab the son of Z
1Chr 2:16 Whose sisters were Z, and Abigail
1Chr 2:16 And the sons of Z
1Chr 11:6 Joab the son of Z went first up
1Chr 11:39 armourbearer of Joab the son of Z
1Chr 18:12 Abishai the son Z slew of the
1Chr 18:15 Joab the son of Z was over the
1Chr 26:28 son of Ner, and Joab the son of Z
1Chr 27:24 Joab the son of Z began to number

**ZETHAM** *(ze'-tham) A descendant of Laadan.*
1Chr 23:8 the chief was Jehiel, and Z
1Chr 26:22 Z, and Joel his brother, which

**ZETHAN** *(ze'-than) A son of Bilhan.*
1Chr 7:10 and Ehud, and Chenaanah, and Z

**ZETHAR** *(ze'-thar) A servant of King Ahasuerus.*
Est 1:10 Harbona, Bigtha, and Abagtha, Z

**ZIA** *(zi'-ah) A Gadite in Bashan.*
1Chr 5:13 Sheba, and Jorai, and Jachan, and Z

**ZIBA** *(zi'-bah) A servant of King Saul.*
2Sa 9:2 Saul a servant whose name was Z
2Sa 9:2 king said unto him, Art thou Z
2Sa 9:3 Z said unto the king, Jonathan
2Sa 9:4 Z said unto the king, Behold, he
2Sa 9:9 Then the king called to Z
2Sa 9:10 Now Z had fifteen sons and twenty
2Sa 9:11 Then said Z unto the king,
2Sa 9:12 all that dwelt in the house of Z
2Sa 16:1 Z the servant of Mephibosheth met
2Sa 16:2 And the king said unto Z, What
2Sa 16:2 Z said, The asses be for the
2Sa 16:3 Z said unto the king, Behold, he
2Sa 16:4 Then said the king to Z, Behold,
2Sa 16:4 Z said, I humbly beseech thee
2Sa 19:17 Z the servant of the house of
2Sa 19:29 said, Thou and Z divide the land

**ZIBEON** *(zib'-e-un)*
*1. Grandfather of Adah.*
Gen 36:2 Anah the daughter of Z the Hivite
Gen 36:14 of Anah the daughter of Z
*2. A son of Seir.*
Gen 36:20 Lotan, and Shobal, and Z, and Anah,
Gen 36:24 And these are the children of Z
Gen 36:24 he fed the asses of Z his father
Gen 36:29 duke Lotan, duke Shobal, duke Z
1Chr 1:38 Lotan, and Shobal, and Z, and Anah,
1Chr 1:40 And the sons of Z

**ZIBIA** *(zib'-e-ah) Son of Hodesh.*
1Chr 8:9 of Hodesh his wife, Jobab, and Z

**ZIBIAH** *(zib'-e-ah) Mother of King Jehoash.*
2Kin 12:1 mother's name was Z of Beer-sheba
2Chr 24:1 name also was Z of Beer-sheba

**ZICHRI** *(zik'-ri)* See ZITHRI.
*1. A son of Izhar.*
Ex 6:21 Korah, and Nepheg, and Z
*2. A Benjamite.*
1Chr 8:19 And Jakim, and Z, and Zabdi,
*3. Son of Shishak.*
1Chr 8:23 And Abdon, and Z, and Hanan,
*4. Son of Jeroham.*
1Chr 8:27 And Jaresiah, and Eliah, and Z
*5. Son of Asaph.*
1Chr 9:15 the son of Micah, the son of Z
*6. Descendant of Eliezer.*
1Chr 26:25 Z his son, and Shelomith his son
*7. Father of Eliezer.*
1Chr 27:16 was Eliezer the son of Z
*8. Father of Amasiah.*
2Chr 17:16 next him was Amasiah the son of Z
*9. Father of Elishaphat.*
2Chr 23:1 and Elishaphat the son of Z
*10. A "mighty man" of Ephraim.*
2Chr 28:7 And Z, a mighty man of Ephraim,
*11. Father of Joel.*
Neh 11:9 Joel the son of Z was their
*12. A priest with Zerubbabel.*
Neh 12:17 Of Abijah, Z

**ZIDDIM** *(zid'-dim) A city in Naphtali.*
Josh 19:35 And the fenced cities are Z

**ZIDKIJAH** *(zid-ki'-jah)* See ZEDEKIAH. *A clan leader who renewed the covenant.*
Neh 10:1 the son of Hachaliah, and Z

**ZIDON** *(zi'-don)*
*1. A city in Asher.*
Gen 49:13 and his border shall be unto Z
Josh 11:8 them, and chased them unto great Z
Josh 19:28 and Kanah, even unto great Z
Judg 1:31 Accho, nor the inhabitants of Z
Judg 10:6 gods of Syria, and the gods of Z
Judg 18:28 because it was far from Z
2Sa 24:6 came to Dan-jaan, and about to Z
1Kin 17:9 Zarephath, which belongeth to Z
Ezr 3:7 and drink, and oil, unto them of Z
Is 23:2 thou whom the merchants of Z
Is 23:4 Be thou ashamed, O Z
Is 23:12 oppressed virgin, daughter of Z
Jer 25:22 of Tyrus, and all the kings of Z
Jer 27:3 of Tyrus, and to the king of Z
Jer 47:4 Z every helper that remaineth
Eze 27:8 The inhabitants of Z and Arvad
Eze 28:21 of man, set thy face against Z
Eze 28:22 Behold, I am against thee, O Z
Joel 3:4 ye to do with me, O Tyre, and Z
Zec 9:2 Tyrus, and Z, though it be very
*2. A son of Canaan.*
1Chr 1:13 Canaan begat Z his firstborn, and

**ZIDONIANS** *(zi-do'-ne-uns)* See SIDONIANS. *Inhabitants of Zidon.*
Judg 10:12 The Z also, and the Amalekites, and
Judg 18:7 after the manner of the Z
Judg 18:7 and they were far from the Z
1Kin 11:1 Moabites, Ammonites, Edomites, Z
1Kin 11:5 Ashtoreth the goddess of the Z
1Kin 11:33 Ashtoreth the goddess of the Z
1Kin 16:31 daughter of Ethbaal king of the Z
2Kin 23:13 the abomination of the Z, and for
1Chr 22:4 for the Z and they of Tyre brought
Eze 32:30 north, all of them, and all the Z

**ZIF** *(zif) Second month of the Hebrew year.*
1Kin 6:1 reign over Israel, in the month Z
1Kin 6:37 of the LORD laid, in the month Z

**ZIHA** *(zi'-hah)*
*1. A family of exiles.*
Ezr 2:43 the children of Z, the children
Neh 7:46 the children of Z, the children
*2. An overseer of Temple servants.*
Neh 11:21 and Z and Gispa were over the

**ZIKLAG** *(zik'-lag) A city in Judah.*
Josh 15:31 And Z, and Madmannah, and
Josh 19:5 And Z, and Beth-marcaboth, and
1Sa 27:6 Then Achish gave him Z that day
1Sa 27:6 wherefore Z pertaineth unto the
1Sa 30:1 were come to Z on the third day
1Sa 30:1 south, and Z, and smitten Z
1Sa 30:14 and we burned Z with fire
1Sa 30:26 And when David came to Z, he sent
2Sa 1:1 and David had abode two days in Z
2Sa 4:10 hold of him, and slew him in Z
1Chr 4:30 at Bethuel, and at Hormah, and at Z

1Chr 12:1 are they that came to David to Z
1Chr 12:20 As he went to Z, there fell to
Neh 11:28 And at Z, and at Mekonah, and in the

**ZILLAH** *(zil'-lah) A wife of Lamech.*
Gen 4:19 Adah, and the name of the other Z
Gen 4:22 And Z, she also bare Tubal-cain,
Gen 4:23 said unto his wives, Adah and Z

**ZILPAH** *(zil'-pah) Handmaid of Leah.*
Gen 29:24 Leah Z his maid for an handmaid
Gen 30:9 left bearing, she took Z her maid
Gen 30:10 Z Leah's maid bare Jacob a son
Gen 30:12 Z Leah's maid bare Jacob a second
Gen 35:26 And the sons of Z, Leah's handmaid
Gen 37:2 of Bilhah, and with the sons of Z
Gen 46:18 These are the sons of Z, whom

**ZILTHAI** *(zil'-thahee)*
*1. Son of Shimhi.*
1Chr 8:20 And Elienai, and Z, and Eliel,
*2. A warrior in David's army.*
1Chr 12:20 and Jozabad, and Elihu, and Z

**ZIMMAH** *(zim'-mah)*
*1. A son of Jahath.*
1Chr 6:20 son, Jahath his son, Z his son,
*2. A Gershonite.*
1Chr 6:42 The son of Ethan, the son of Z
*3. Father of Joah.*
2Chr 29:12 Joah the son of Z, and Eden the

**ZIMRAN** *(zim'-ran) A son of Abraham.*
Gen 25:2 And she bare him Z, and Jokshan, and
1Chr 1:32 she bare Z, and Jokshan, and Medan,

**ZIMRI** *(zim'-ri)*
*1. A Simeonite.*
Num 25:14 with the Midianitish woman, was Z
*2. A king of Israel.*
1Kin 16:9 And his servant Z, captain of half
1Kin 16:10 Z went in and smote him, and killed
1Kin 16:12 Thus did Z destroy all the house
1Kin 16:15 did Z reign seven days in Tirzah
1Kin 16:16 Z hath conspired, and hath also
1Kin 16:18 when Z saw that the city was
1Kin 16:20 Now the rest of the acts of Z
2Kin 9:31 Had Z peace, who slew his master
*3. A son of Zerah.*
1Chr 2:6 Z, and Ethan, and Heman, and Calcol,
*4. Son of Jehoadah.*
1Chr 8:36 begat Alemeth, and Azmaveth, and Z
1Chr 8:36 and Z begat Moza,
1Chr 9:42 begat Alemeth, and Azmaveth, and Z
1Chr 9:42 and Z begat Moza
*5. An unspecified place.*
Jer 25:25 And all the kings of Z, and all the

**ZIN** *(zin) A wilderness south of Judah.*
Num 13:21 the wilderness of Z unto Rehob
Num 20:1 desert of Z in the first month
Num 27:14 my commandment in the desert of Z
Num 27:14 in Kadesh in the wilderness of Z
Num 33:36 and pitched in the wilderness of Z
Num 34:3 of Z along by the coast of Edom
Num 34:4 of Akrabbim, and pass on to Z
Deut 32:51 in the wilderness of Z
Josh 15:1 of Edom the wilderness of Z
Josh 15:3 and passed along to Z, and

**ZINA** *(zi'-nah) A son of Shimei.*
1Chr 23:10 sons of Shimei were, Jahath, Z

**ZION** *(zi'-un)* See SION, ZION'S. *A term for Jerusalem.*
2Sa 5:7 David took the strong hold of Z
1Kin 8:1 of the city of David, which is Z
2Kin 19:21 daughter of Z hath despised thee
2Kin 19:31 they that escape out of mount Z
1Chr 11:5 David took the castle of Z
2Chr 5:2 of the city of David, which is Z
Ps 2:6 my king upon my holy hill of Z
Ps 9:11 to the LORD, which dwelleth in Z
Ps 9:14 in the gates of the daughter of Z
Ps 14:7 of Israel were come out of Z
Ps 20:2 and strengthen thee out of Z
Ps 48:2 of the whole earth, is mount Z
Ps 48:11 Let mount Z rejoice, let the
Ps 48:12 Walk about Z, and go round about
Ps 50:2 Out of Z, the perfection of
Ps 51:18 good in thy good pleasure unto Z
Ps 53:6 of Israel were come out of Z
Ps 69:35 For God will save Z, and will
Ps 74:2 this mount Z, wherein thou hast
Ps 76:2 and his dwelling place in Z
Ps 78:68 the mount Z which he loved
Ps 84:7 of them in Z appeareth before God
Ps 87:2 The LORD loveth the gates of Z
Ps 87:5 of Z it shall be said, This and
Ps 97:8 Z heard, and was glad
Ps 99:2 The LORD is great in Z
Ps 102:13 shalt arise, and have mercy upon Z
Ps 102:16 When the LORD shall build up Z
Ps 102:21 declare the name of the LORD in Z
Ps 110:2 the rod of thy strength out of Z
Ps 125:1 in the LORD shall be as mount Z
Ps 126:1 turned again the captivity of Z
Ps 128:5 LORD shall bless thee out of Z
Ps 129:5 and turned back that hate Z
Ps 132:13 For the LORD hath chosen Z
Ps 133:3 descended upon the mountains of Z
Ps 134:3 and earth bless thee out of Z
Ps 135:21 Blessed be the LORD out of Z
Ps 137:1 we wept, when we remembered Z
Ps 137:3 Sing us one of the songs of Z
Ps 146:10 reign for ever, even thy God, O Z
Ps 147:12 praise thy God, O Z
Ps 149:2 let the children of Z be joyful
Song 3:11 Go forth, O ye daughters of Z
Is 1:8 the daughter of Z is left as a
Is 1:27 Z shall be redeemed with judgment
Is 2:3 for out of Z shall go forth the
Is 3:16 the daughters of Z are haughty
Is 3:17 of the head of the daughters of Z
Is 4:3 pass, that he that is left in Z
Is 4:4 the filth of the daughters of Z
Is 4:5 every dwelling place of mount Z
Is 8:18 hosts, which dwelleth in mount Z
Is 10:12 his whole work upon mount Z
Is 10:24 O my people that dwellest in Z
Is 10:32 the mount of the daughter of Z
Is 12:6 and shout, thou inhabitant of Z
Is 14:32 That the LORD hath founded Z
Is 16:1 the mount of the daughter of Z
Is 18:7 of the LORD of hosts, the mount Z
Is 24:23 of hosts shall reign in mount Z
Is 28:16 I lay in Z for a foundation a
Is 29:8 be, that fight against mount Z
Is 30:19 shall dwell in Z at Jerusalem
Is 31:4 come down to fight for mount Z
Is 31:9 the LORD, whose fire is in Z
Is 33:5 he hath filled Z with judgment
Is 33:14 The sinners in Z are afraid
Is 33:20 Look upon Z, the city of our
Is 34:8 for the controversy of Z
Is 35:10 and come to Z with songs and
Is 37:22 The virgin, the daughter of Z
Is 37:32 they that escape out of mount Z
Is 40:9 O Z, that bringest good tidings,
Is 41:27 The first shall say to Z, Behold,
Is 46:13 in Z for Israel my glory
Is 49:14 But Z said, The LORD hath
Is 51:3 For the LORD shall comfort Z
Is 51:11 and come with singing unto Z
Is 51:16 of the earth, and say unto Z
Is 52:1 put on thy strength, O Z
Is 52:2 thy neck, O captive daughter of Z
Is 52:7 that saith unto Z, Thy God
Is 52:8 when the LORD shall bring again Z
Is 59:20 And the Redeemer shall come to Z
Is 60:14 The Z of the Holy One of Israel
Is 61:3 appoint unto them that mourn in Z
Is 62:11 Say ye to the daughter of Z
Is 64:10 Z is a wilderness, Jerusalem a
Is 66:8 for as soon as Z travailed
Jer 3:14 family, and I will bring you to Z
Jer 4:6 Set up the standard toward Z
Jer 4:31 the voice of the daughter of Z
Jer 6:2 the daughter of Z to a comely
Jer 6:23 war against thee, O daughter of Z
Jer 8:19 Is not the LORD in Z
Jer 9:19 of wailing is heard out of Z
Jer 14:19 hath thy soul lothed Z
Jer 26:18 Z shall be plowed like a field,
Jer 30:17 an Outcast, saying, This is Z
Jer 31:6 let us go up to Z unto the LORD
Jer 31:12 come and sing in the height of Z
Jer 50:5 They shall ask the way to Z with
Jer 50:28 to declare in Z the vengeance of
Jer 51:10 let us declare in Z the work of
Jer 51:24 they have done in Z in your sight
Jer 51:35 shall the inhabitant of Z say
Lam 1:4 The ways of Z do mourn, because
Lam 1:6 from the daughter of Z all her
Lam 1:17 Z spreadeth forth her hands, and
Lam 2:1 of Z with a cloud in his anger
Lam 2:4 tabernacle of the daughter of Z
Lam 2:6 and sabbaths to be forgotten in Z
Lam 2:8 the wall of the daughter of Z
Lam 2:10 daughter of Z sit upon the ground
Lam 2:13 thee, O virgin daughter of Z
Lam 2:18 Lord, O wall of the daughter of Z
Lam 4:2 The precious sons of Z,
Lam 4:11 and hath kindled a fire in Z
Lam 4:22 is accomplished, O daughter of Z
Lam 5:11 They ravished the women in Z
Lam 5:18 Because of the mountain of Z
Joel 2:1 Blow ye the trumpet in Z, and
Joel 2:15 Blow the trumpet in Z, sanctify a
Joel 2:23 Be glad then, ye children of Z
Joel 2:32 for in mount Z and in Jerusalem
Joel 3:16 The LORD also shall roar out of Z
Joel 3:17 the LORD your God dwelling in Z
Joel 3:21 for the LORD dwelleth in Z
Amos 1:2 said, The LORD will roar from Z
Amos 6:1 Woe to them that are at ease in Z
Obad 17 But upon mount Z shall be
Obad 21 Z to judge the mount of Esau
Mic 1:13 of the sin to the daughter of Z
Mic 3:10 They build up Z with blood
Mic 3:12 Therefore shall Z for your sake
Mic 4:2 for the law shall go forth of Z
Mic 4:7 them in mount Z from henceforth
Mic 4:8 strong hold of the daughter of Z
Mic 4:10 to bring forth, O daughter of Z
Mic 4:11 and let our eye look upon Z
Mic 4:13 Arise and thresh, O daughter of Z
Zeph 3:14 Sing, O daughter of Z
Zeph 3:16 and to Z, Let not thine hands be
Zec 1:14 for Z with a great jealousy
Zec 1:17 and the LORD shall yet comfort Z
Zec 2:7 Deliver thyself, O Z, that
Zec 2:10 Sing and rejoice, O daughter of Z
Zec 8:2 I was jealous for Z with great
Zec 8:3 I am returned unto Z, and will
Zec 9:9 Rejoice greatly, O daughter of Z
Zec 9:13 and raised up thy sons, O Z

**ZION'S** *(zi'-uns)*
Is 62:1 For Z sake will I not hold my

**ZIOR** *(zi'-or) A city in Judah.*
Josh 15:54 which is Hebron, and Z

**ZIPH** *(zif)* See ZIPHITES.
*1. A city in southeast Judah.*
Josh 15:24 Z, and Telem, and Bealoth,
1Sa 23:14 a mountain in the wilderness of Z
1Sa 23:15 in the wilderness of Z in a wood
1Sa 23:24 arose, and went to Z before Saul
1Sa 26:2 went down to the wilderness of Z
1Sa 26:2 seek David in the wilderness of Z
2Chr 11:8 And Gath, and Mareshah, and Z
*2. A city in Judah near Carmel.*
Josh 15:55 Maon, Carmel, and Z, and Juttah,
*3. A descendant of Caleb.*
1Chr 2:42 which was the father of Z
*4. A son of Jehalaleel.*
1Chr 4:16 Z, and Ziphah, Tiria, and Asareel

**ZIPHAH** *(zi'-fah) A son of Jehalaleel.*
1Chr 4:16 Ziph, and Z, Tiria, and Asareel

**ZIPHIMS** *(zif'-ims)* See ZIPHITES. *Same as Ziphites.*
Ps 54:*t* A Psalm of David, when the Z came

**ZIPHION** *(zif'-e-on)* See ZEPHON. *A son of Gad.*
Gen 46:16 Z, and Haggi, Shuni, and Ezbon, Eri

**ZIPHITES** *(zif'-ites)* See ZIPHIMS. *Inhabitants of Ziph.*
1Sa 23:19 Then came up the Z to Saul to
1Sa 26:1 the Z came unto Saul to Gibeah,

**ZIPHRON** *(zif'-ron) A place in northern Palestine.*
Num 34:9 And the border shall go on to Z

**ZIPPOR** *(zip'-por) Father of Balak.*
Num 22:2 Balak the son of Z saw all that
Num 22:4 Balak the son of Z was king of
Num 22:10 said unto God, Balak the son of Z
Num 22:16 Thus saith Balak the son of Z
Num 23:18 hearken unto me, thou son of Z
Josh 24:9 Then Balak the son of Z, king of
Judg 11:25 better than Balak the son of Z

**ZIPPORAH** *(zip-po'-rah) Wife of Moses.*
Ex 2:21 and he gave Moses Z his daughter
Ex 4:25 Then Z took a sharp stone, and cut
Ex 18:2 Moses' father in law, took Z

**ZITHRI** *(zith'-ri)* See ZICHRI. *A son of Uzziel.*
Ex 6:22 Mishael, and Elzaphan, and Z

**ZIZ** *(ziz) A place in Judah.*
2Chr 20:16 they come up by the cliff of Z

**ZIZA** *(zi'-zah)* See ZIZAH.
*1. Son of Ziphi.*
1Chr 4:37 Z the son of Shiphi, the son of
*2. A son of Rehoboam.*
2Chr 11:20 bare him Abijah, and Attai, and Z

**ZIZAH** *(zi'-zah)* See ZINA, ZIZA. *Son of Shimei.*
1Chr 23:11 was the chief, and Z the second

**ZOAN** *(zo'-an) An Egyptian city.*
Num 13:22 seven years before Z in Egypt
Ps 78:12 land of Egypt, in the field of Z
Ps 78:43 and his wonders in the field of Z
Is 19:11 Surely the princes of Z are fools
Is 19:13 The princes of Z are become fools
Is 30:4 For his princes were at Z
Eze 30:14 desolate, and will set fire in Z

**ZOAR** *(zo'-ar) A Canaanite city.*
Gen 13:10 of Egypt, as thou comest unto Z
Gen 14:2 and the king of Bela, which is Z
Gen 14:8 the king of Bela (the same is Z
Gen 19:22 the name of the city was called Z
Gen 19:23 the earth when Lot entered into Z
Gen 19:30 And Lot went up out of Z, and dwelt
Gen 19:30 for he feared to dwell in Z
Deut 34:3 the city of palm trees, unto Z
Is 15:5 his fugitives shall flee unto Z
Jer 48:34 from Z even unto Horonaim, as an

**ZOBA** *(zo'-bah)* See ZOBAH. *A district in northern Syria.*
2Sa 10:6 Beth-rehob, and the Syrians of Z
2Sa 10:8 and the Syrians of Z, and of Rehob,

**ZOBAH** *(zo'-bah)* See ZOBA. *Same as Zoba.*
1Sa 14:47 Edom, and against the kings of Z
2Sa 8:3 the son of Rehob, king of Z
2Sa 8:5 to succour Hadadezer king of Z
2Sa 8:12 son of Rehob, king of Z
2Sa 23:36 Igal the son of Nathan of Z
1Kin 11:23 from his lord Hadadezer king of Z
1Kin 11:24 a band, when David slew them of Z
1Chr 18:3 Hadarezer king of Z unto Hamath
1Chr 18:5 came to help Hadarezer king of Z
1Chr 18:9 the host of Hadarezer king of Z
1Chr 19:6 out of Syria-maachah, and out of Z

**ZOBEBAH** *(zo-be'-bah) A daughter of Coz.*
1Chr 4:8 And Coz begat Anub, and Z, and the

**ZOHAR** *(zo'-har)* See ZERAH, ZEROR.
*1. Father of Ephron.*
Gen 23:8 for me to Ephron the son of Z
Gen 25:9 Ephron the son of Z the Hittite
*2. Son of Simeon.*
Gen 46:10 Jamin, and Ohad, and Jachin, and Z
Ex 6:15 Jamin, and Ohad, and Jachin, and Z

**ZOHELETH** *(zo'-he-leth) A stone near En-rogel.*
1Kin 1:9 and fat cattle by the stone of Z

**ZOHETH** *(zo'heth) Son of Ishi.*
1Chr 4:20 And the sons of Ishi were, Z

**ZOPHAH** *(zo'-fah) Son of Helem.*
1Chr 7:35 Z, and Imna, and Shelesh, and Amal
1Chr 7:36 The sons of Z

**ZOPHAI** *(zo'-fahee)* See ZUPH. *Brother of Samuel.*
1Chr 6:26 Z his son, and Nahath his son,

**ZOPHAR** *(zo'-far)*
Job 2:11 the Shuhite, and Z the Naamathite
Job 11:1 Then answered Z the Naamathite,
Job 20:1 Then answered Z the Naamathite,
Job 42:9 Z the Naamathite went, and did

**ZOPHIM** *(zo'-fim) A peak on Mt. Pisgah.*
Num 23:14 brought him into the field of Z

**ZORAH** *(zo'-rah)* See ZAREAH, ZORATHITES, ZOREAH, ZORITES. *A city in Judah.*
Josh 19:41 coast of their inheritance was Z
Judg 13:2 And there was a certain man of Z
Judg 13:25 in the camp of Dan between Z
Judg 16:31 him up, and buried him between Z
Judg 18:2 coasts, men of valour, from Z
Judg 18:8 came unto their brethren to Z
Judg 18:11 family of the Danites, out of Z
2Chr 11:10 And Z, and Aijalon, and Hebron,

**ZORATHITES** *(zo'-rath-ites) Descendants of Shobal.*
1Chr 4:2 These are the families of the Z

**ZOREAH** *(zo'-re-ah) Same as Zorah.*
Josh 15:33 And in the valley, Eshtaol, and Z

**ZORITES** *(zo'-rites)* See ZAREATHITES, ZORATHITES. *Descendants of Salma.*
1Chr 2:54 half of the Manahethites, the Z

**ZOROBABEL** *(zo-rob'-a-bel)* See ZERUBBABEL. *Father of Abiud; ancestor of Jesus.*
Mt 1:12 and Salathiel begat Z
Mt 1:13 And Z begat Abiud
Lk 3:27 of Rhesa, which was the son of Z

**ZUAR** *(zu'-ar) Father of Nethaneel.*
Num 1:8 Nethaneel the son of Z
Num 2:5 Nethaneel the son of Z shall be
Num 7:18 second day Nethaneel the son of Z
Num 7:23 of Nethaneel the son of Z
Num 10:15 was Nethaneel the son of Z

**ZUPH** *(zuf)*
*1. An ancestor of Samuel.*
1Sa 1:1 the son of Tohu, the son of Z
1Chr 6:35 The son of Z, the son of Elkanah,
*2. A district in Jerusalem.*
1Sa 9:5 they were come to the land of Z

**ZUR** *(zur)*
*1. Father of Cozbi.*
Num 25:15 was Cozbi, the daughter of Z
Num 31:8 namely, Evi, and Rekem, and Z
Josh 13:21 of Midian, Evi, and Rekem, and Z
*2. Son of Jeiel.*
1Chr 8:30 And his firstborn son Abdon, and Z
1Chr 9:36 his firstborn son Abdon, then Z

**ZURIEL** *(zu'-re-el) Son of Abihail.*
Num 3:35 Merari was Z the son of Abihail

**ZURISHADDAI** *(zu-re-shad'-da-i) Father of Shelumiel.*
Num 1:6 Shelumiel the son of Z
Num 2:12 shall be Shelumiel the son of Z
Num 7:36 fifth day Shelumiel the son of Z
Num 7:41 of Shelumiel the son of Z
Num 10:19 Simeon was Shelumiel the son of Z

**ZUZIMS** *(zu'-zims)* See ZAMZUMMIMS. *A tribe in the land of Ham.*
Gen 14:5 the Z in Ham, and the Emims in